Institut français ... rench public opinion

All **entries** (words, abbreviations appear in alphabetical order and a Abbreviations are followed by the

oo

egan, begun> **I.** *vt*

nettre à

English phrasal verbs come directly after the base verb and are signalled by u.

. (*domicile*) *a.* INFOR change address; ~ **de** ... **ique** e-mail address

Arabic superscripts indicate identically spelt words with different meanings (**homographs**).

pl **1.** (*dextérité*) skill

ıkeɪt] *vt form* quitter

The International Phonetic Alphabet is used for all phonetic transcriptions, including American pronunciations.

Angle brackets are used to show **irregular plural forms**, **numbers** referring to the French conjugation tables in the appendix or **forms of English irregular verbs and adjectives**.

<-ier, -iest> ...

-tʀis] *m, f* **1.** THEAT,

French feminine forms are shown unless they are identical to the masculine form. French nouns are followed by their gender.

l **1.** (*speech*) babillage ia *m* **2.** (*sound*) mur-

Roman numerals are used for the **grammatical divisions** of a word, and Arabic numerals for **sense divisions**.

adj (*cardinal*) four **à** ~ to bound up the **endre l'escalier** ~ **à** tairs four at a time; eat like a wolf; **boire** a fish ...

The **swung dash** represents the entry word in examples and idioms. The ► sign introduces **a block of set expressions, idioms and proverbs**. Key words are underlined as a guide.

Various kinds of **meaning indicators** are used to guide users to the required translation:

, -iest> **1.** ZOOL écail-tré(e)

- **areas of specialization**

1. (*personne, cœur*) sé: *chaussures, vête-*

- **definitions** or **synonyms,** typical **subjects** or **objects** of verbs, typical **nouns** used with adjectives, etc.

ɑ̃] *m Belgique* (*avant-* d *Brit,* center-forward

- **Regional vocabulary and variants** are shown both as headword and translations

- **Language registers**

verte *small sticker for converters* ... s (*anise-flavoured alco-*

When a word or expression has no direct translation, there is an explanation or a cultural equivalent (≈). Where a translation may be unclear, it is followed by an explanation in brackets.

tting shop *n Brit* ≈

brun(e), marron *inv;* e ...

s. a. invites the reader to consult a **model entry** for further information.

DICTIONNAIRE

Cambridge Klett Compact

Français – Anglais
English – French

PUBLISHED BY THE PRESS SYNDICATE OF THE UNIVERSITY OF CAMBRIDGE
The Pitt Building, Trumpington Street, Cambridge, United Kingdom

CAMBRIDGE UNIVERSITY PRESS
The Edinburgh Building, Cambridge CB2 2RU, UK
40 West 20th Street, New York NY10011-4211, USA
477 Williamstown Road, Port Melbourne, VIC 3207, Australia
Ruiz de Alarcón 13, 28014 Madrid, Spain
Dock House, The Waterfront, Cape Town 8001, South Africa

http://www.cambridge.org

First published 2002

Printed in Germany at Clausen und Bosse, Leck

Typeface: Univers Black, Weidemann

A catalogue record for this book is available from the British Library

Library of Congress Cataloguing in Publication data applied for

ISBN 0521 803004 hardback

ISBN 0521 752965 hardback + CD-ROM

Editorial Management: Sylvie Cloeren

Contributors: Richard Alderman, Nathalie Avedissian, Isabelle Bailey, Alexander Burden, Dr. Dora Carpenter, Edwin Carpenter, Anne Choffrut, Hazel Curties, Héléna Denny, Rachel Gachod-Schinko, Jean Goldscheider, Magali Guenette, Anthony Healy, Kay Hollingsworth, Nathalie Karanfilovic, Anne-Laure Le Merre, Annick Lieutaud , Matthew C. Maxwell, Dr. Michèle Moncharmont, Josh Ord-Hume, Anne-Lucie Robert Colson, Anne Rommeru, Catherine Roux, Béatrice Simon, Anja Tauchmann, Catherine Vieutemps

Typesetting: Dörr und Schiller GmbH, Stuttgart
Data processing: Andreas Lang, conTEXT AG für Information und Kommunikation, Zürich

Table des matières

Contents

Introduction

Le *Dictionnaire Cambridge Klett Compact* est un tout nouveau dictionnaire bilingue pour les Francophones qui apprennent l'anglais et pour les Anglophones qui apprennent le français. Il a été rédigé et édité par un grand nombre de personnes de langue maternelle, ce qui en fait un outil moderne pour la compréhension des langues.

Il recouvre l'anglais britannique et américain, ce qui en fait un guide fiable de l'anglais comme langue internationale. Il contient aussi un grand nombre de mots nouveaux qui sont apparus en anglais et en français au cours des dernières années, en particulier dans les domaines de l'informatique, Internet et divertissements.

Le dictionnaire aide aussi dans des domaines difficiles pour ceux qui apprennent les langues. Par exemple, on trouvera des informations complètes sur les verbes irréguliers des deux langues et il y a un chapitre spécial ‚faux amis' qui sont souvent déroutants.

Nous espérons que vous apprécierez ce livre et que vous aurez grand plaisir à apprendre votre nouvelle langue.

Vous pouvez acheter ce livre avec ou sans CD-ROM et vous pouvez trouver plus ample information sur notre site à l'adresse suivante:

dictionary.cambridge.org

Introduction

The *Dictionnaire Cambridge Klett Compact* is a completely new bilingual dictionary for French-speaking learners of English and English-speaking learners of French. It has been written and edited by a large team of native speakers of both languages so that it provides an up-to-date and comprehensive language tool.

It covers British English and American English, so that it provides a reliable guide to English as an international language. It also includes many new words that have come into English and French in the last few years, especially in areas such as computing, the Internet and entertainment.

The dictionary provides extra help with many areas that learners find difficult. For example, there is full information about the irregular verb patterns of the two languages and there is a special section on the ‚false friends' that can be confusing for learners.

We hope that you enjoy using this book and that you enjoy learning your new language.

You can buy this book with or without a CD-ROM and you can find out more information on our website at:

dictionary.cambridge.org

Signes utilisés pour la transcription phonétique

[ø]	**Eu**rope
[a]	b**a**c
[ɑ]	cl**a**sse
[ɛ]	c**ai**sse
[ɑ̃]	ch**an**son
[b]	**b**eau
[d]	**d**u
[e]	**é**tat
[ə]	m**e**nace
[ɛ̃]	af**in**
[f]	**f**eu
[g]	**g**ant
[ˊ]	**h**éros (h aspiré)
[i]	d**i**plôme
[j]	**y**acht
[ʒ]	**j**our
[k]	**c**œur
[l]	**l**oup
[m]	**m**arché
[n]	**n**ature
[ɲ]	di**gn**e
[ŋ]	campi**ng**
[o]	**au**to
[ɔ]	**o**btenir
[œ]	c**œ**ur
[ɔ̃]	b**on**b**on**
[œ̃]	auc**un**
[p]	**p**age
[ʀ]	**r**ègle
[s]	**s**el
[ʃ]	**ch**ef
[t]	**t**imbre
[u]	c**ou**p
[v]	**v**apeur
[w]	Ku**w**ait
[y]	nat**u**re
[ɥ]	h**u**ile
[z]	**z**èbre

Phonetic Symbols

[ɑː]	pl**a**nt, f**a**rm, f**a**ther
[aɪ]	l**i**fe
[aʊ]	h**ou**se
[æ]	m**a**n, s**a**d
[b]	**b**een, **b**lind
[d]	**d**o, ha**d**
[ð]	**th**is, fa**th**er
[e]	g**e**t, b**e**d
[eɪ]	n**a**me, l**a**me
[ə]	**a**go, bett**er**
[ɜː]	b**i**rd, h**er**
[eə]	th**ere**, c**are**
[ʌ]	b**u**t, s**o**n
[f]	**f**ather, wol**f**
[g]	**g**o, be**g**
[ŋ]	lo**ng**, si**ng**
[h]	**h**ouse
[ɪ]	**i**t, w**i**sh
[iː]	b**ee**, m**e**, b**ea**t, bel**ie**f
[ɪə]	h**ere**
[j]	**y**outh
[k]	**k**eep, mil**k**
[l]	**l**amp, oi**l**, i**ll**
[m]	**m**an, a**m**
[n]	**n**o, ma**nn**er
[ɒ]	n**o**t, l**o**ng
[ɔː]	l**aw**, **a**ll
[ɔɪ]	b**oy**, **oi**l
[p]	**p**a**p**er, ha**pp**y
[r]	**r**ed, d**r**y
[s]	**s**tand, **s**and, ye**s**
[ʃ]	**sh**ip, sta**ti**on
[t]	**t**ell, fa**t**
[tʃ]	**ch**ur**ch**, ca**tch**
[ʊ]	p**u**sh, l**oo**k
[uː]	y**ou**, d**o**
[ʊə]	p**oor**, s**ure**
[v]	**v**oice, li**v**e

	[w]	**w**ater, **w**e, **wh**ich
	[z]	**z**eal, the**s**e, ga**z**e
	[ʒ]	plea**s**ure
	[dʒ]	**j**am, ob**j**ect
	[θ]	**th**ank, dea**th**

A

A, a [ɑ] *m inv* A, a; ~ **comme Anatole** a for Andrew *Brit,* a for Apple *Am*

a [a] *indic prés de* **avoir**

a [a] *m* INFOR **a commercial** at-sign

à [a] <à + le = au, à la, à + les = aux> *prep* **1.** (*introduit un complément de temps*) at; **à 8 heures/Noël** at 8 o'clock/Christmas; **à quelle heure?** what time?, when?; **le cinq juin au matin** on the morning of the fifth of June **2.** (*indique une époque*) in; **au printemps** in (the) spring; **aux premiers beaux jours** with the first days of fine weather; **nous te reverrons à Pâques** we shall see you again at Easter **3.** (*indique une date ultérieure*) **on se verra aux prochaines vacances** we shall see each other next holidays; **à mon retour** when I get back **4.** (*pour prendre rendez-vous*) **à demain!** see you tomorrow! **5.** (*jusque*) until; **je serai absent de lundi à jeudi** I shall be away from Monday to Thursday **6.** (*pour indiquer une direction*) to; **aller à l'école/au Japon/aux États-Unis** to go to school/to Japan/to the United States; **s'asseoir à son bureau** to sit down at one's desk **7.** (*indique le lieu où l'on est*) **être à la piscine/poste** to be at the swimming pool/the post office; **habiter à Paris/aux États-Unis** to live in Paris/in the United States; **habiter au troisième étage** to live on the third floor; **être assis à son bureau** to be at one's desk; **au coin de la rue** at the corner of the street; **à cinq minutes/trois kilomètres d'ici** five minutes/three kilometres from here; **à la télévision/la page 36/l'épaule** on television/page 36/the shoulder; **avoir mal à la tête** to have a headache; **avoir les larmes aux yeux** to have tears in one's eyes **8.** (*indique le nombre de personnes*) **nous travaillons à 2/3/12 sur ce projet** there are 2/3/12 of us working on this project; **on peut tenir à 50 dans cette salle** this room can hold 50 people **9.** (*par*) **à l'heure** by the hour; **à la journée** on a daily basis; **7 litres aux 100** (**kilomètres**) 7 litres per 100 (kilometres); **vendre/acheter au poids/à la douzaine** to sell/buy by weight/by the dozen **10.** (*cause*) **à sa démarche, on voit qu'il a mal** you can tell from the way he walks that he is in pain; **à cette nouvelle, j'ai sursauté** I was startled when I heard this news **11.** (*conséquence*) to; **à ma plus grande surprise** to my utter surprise **12.** (*d'après*) **à la demande de qn** at sb's request **13.** (*indique une appartenance*) **c'est à moi/lui** it's mine/his; **un ami à eux** a friend of theirs; **avoir une maison à soi** to have a house of one's own **14.** (*indique le moyen*) **coudre qc à la machine** to sew sth by machine; **cuisiner au beurre** to cook with butter; **à la loupe** through a magnifying glass; **au microscope** under the microscope; **boire à la bouteille** to drink from the bottle **15.** (*introduit un superlatif*) **elle est au plus mal** she is very ill; **venir au plus tôt** to come as soon as possible **16.** (*au point de*) **s'ennuyer à mourir** to be bored to death; **c'est à rendre fou** it's enough to drive you mad; **c'est à mourir de rire** it's a scream **17.** (*complément indirect*) **donner qc à qn** to give sth to sb, give sb sth; **jouer aux cartes** to play cards; **penser à qn/qc** to think about [*o* of] sth/sb; **parler à qn** to speak to sb; **téléphoner à qn** to (tele)phone sb; **participer à qc** to take part in sth **18.** (*locution verbale*) **elle prend plaisir à cuisiner** she enjoys cooking; **il se met à pleuvoir** it's beginning to rain; **c'est facile à faire** it's easy to do; **rien à faire!** it's no good!; **maison à vendre** house for sale

abaissant(e) [abɛsɑ̃, ɑ̃t] *adj* degrading

abaissement [abɛsmɑ̃] *m* **1.** (*action de faire descendre, action de diminuer: d'une vitre, d'un niveau, des prix, d'un taux*) lowering **2.** (*baisse: des températures*) fall **3.** (*humiliation*) humbling

abaisser [abese] <1> **I.** *vt* **1.** (*faire descendre, diminuer: rideau, température, prix, âge de la retraite*) to lower **2.** (*avilir*) to humble **3.** GASTR ~ **qc** to roll sth out **II.** *vpr* **s'**~ **1.** (*descendre: vitre, rideau*) to be lowered **2.** (*s'humilier*) to humble oneself

abandon [abɑ̃dɔ̃] *m* **1.** (*désertion, délaissement*) abandonment **2.** (*fait de renoncer à: des études, d'une piste, des recherches*) giving up **3.** (*renonciation: du pouvoir*) giving up; (*de ses biens*) surrender **4.** SPORT withdrawal

abandonné(e) [abɑ̃dɔne] *adj* abandoned; (*chat*) stray

abandonner [abɑ̃dɔne] <1> **I.** *vt* **1.** (*déserter, quitter*) to abandon **2.** (*laisser derrière soi: déchets*) to leave behind **3.** (*renoncer à: hypothèse, méthode*) to discard; (*pouvoir, fonction*) to relinquish; (*piste, biens, fortune, combat, études*) to give up **4.** (*laisser*) ~ **qn à son sort** to abandon sb to their fate **II.** *vi* to give up; **j'abandonne!** I give up! **III.** *vpr* **1.** (*se détendre*) **s'**~ to let oneself go **2.** (*se relâcher*) **elle s'abandonna dans les bras de sa mère** she fell into her mother's arms **3.** (*se laisser aller à*) **s'**~ **aux larmes** to start weeping helplessly; **s'**~ **au désespoir** to give way to despair

abasourdir [abazuʀdiʀ] <8> *vt* **1.** (*stupéfier*) to stun **2.** (*assourdir*) to deafen

abat-jour [abaʒuʀ] *m inv* lampshade

abats [aba] *mpl* (*de porc, mouton*) offal *no pl;* (*de volaille*) giblets

abattage [abataʒ] *m* **1.** (*d'un mur, d'une maison*) knocking down; (*d'un arbre*) felling **2.** (*d'un animal de boucherie*) slaughtering ►**avoir de l'**~ *inf* to have go

abattant [abatɑ̃] *m* leaf; ~ **d'un W-C** toilet lid

abattement [abatmɑ̃] *m* **1.** (*lassitude*) exhaustion **2.** (*découragement*) despondency

3. (*rabais*) reduction **4.** FIN allowance

abat(t)is [abati] *m Québec* (*terrain déboisé, qui n'est pas encore essouché*) area of felled trees

abattoir [abatwaʀ] *m* abattoir

abattre [abatʀ] *irr* **I.** *vt* **1.** (*faire tomber*) ~ **qc** (*mur, maison, quille*) to knock sth down; (*cloison*) to break sth down; (*arbre*) to fell sth; (*forêt*) to chop sth down; (*avion*) to shoot sth down **2.** (*tuer: animal de boucherie*) to slaughter; ~ **un animal blessé** to put down an injured animal; ~ **du gibier** to shoot down game **3.** (*assassiner*) to kill **4.** (*affaiblir*) ~ **qn** (*fièvre, maladie*) to lay sb low **5.** (*décourager: souci*) to demoralize; (*tâche, travail*) to drain **6.** (*travailler vite et beaucoup*) ~ **de la besogne** to get through a lot of work **7.** (*rabattre*) ~ **qc** (*vent, tornade*) to blow sth down ►~ **son jeu** to put one's cards on the table **II.** *vpr* **s'~ 1.** (*tomber*) to fall down; **s'~ sur le sol** to collapse on the ground **2.** (*tomber brutalement: pluie*) to come pouring down; (*grêle*) to pelt down **3.** (*fondre sur*) **s'~ sur sa proie** (*aigle*) to swoop down on its prey; **s'~ sur un champ de blé** (*criquets*) to engulf a field of wheat **4.** *fig* **des injures s'abattirent sur lui** insults rained down on him; **le malheur s'abattit sur lui** bad luck got him in its grip

abattu(e) [abaty] **I.** *part passé de* **abattre** **II.** *adj* **1.** (*physiquement*) exhausted **2.** (*moralement*) despondent

abbaye [abei] *f* abbey; **l'~ de Westminster** Westminster Abbey

abbé [abe] *m* **1.** (*prêtre*) priest **2.** (*supérieur d'une abbaye*) abbot

abbesse [abɛs] *f* abbess

ABC [ɑbesɛ] *m inv* **1.** (*livre*) ABC book **2.** (*début*) **c'est l'~ du métier** these are the basics of the job

abcès [apsɛ] *m* abscess

abdication [abdikasjɔ̃] *f* abdication

abdiquer [abdike] <1> *vi* **1.** (*démissionner: roi, souverain*) to abdicate **2.** (*renoncer*) to give up

abdomen [abdɔmɛn] *m* abdomen

abdominal(e) [abdɔminal, o] <-aux> *adj* abdominal

abdominaux [abdɔmino] *mpl* **1.** ANAT abdominal muscles **2.** SPORT **faire des ~** (*en redressant le torse*) to do sit-ups

abeille [abɛj] *f* bee

aberrant(e) [abeʀɑ̃, ɑ̃t] *adj* deviant; (*idée*) preposterous; (*prix*) ridiculous

aberration [abeʀasjɔ̃] *f* aberration

abêtir [abetiʀ] <8> **I.** *vt* **1.** (*rendre bête*) ~ **qc** to make sb stupid **2.** (*abrutir*) to stupefy **II.** *vpr* **s'~** to become stupid

abêtissant(e) [abetisɑ̃, ɑ̃t] *adj* stupefying

abîme [abim] *m* **1.** *soutenu* (*gouffre*) abyss **2.** (*divergence*) chasm

abîmé(e) [abime] *adj* (*endommagé*) damaged

abîmer [abime] <1> **I.** *vt* (*détériorer*) to ruin **II.** *vpr* **1.** (*se gâter*) **s'~** to spoil; (*fruits, légumes*) to go bad **2.** (*détériorer*) **s'~ les yeux/la santé** to ruin one's eyes/health

abject(e) [abʒɛkt] *adj* contemptible; (*goût*) appalling; **avoir un comportement ~ envers qn** to behave abominably towards sb

abjection [abʒɛksjɔ̃] *f* total humiliation

abjurer [abʒyʀe] <1> *vt, vi* to recant

ablation [ablasjɔ̃] *f* (*d'une tumeur*) removal; (*d'un membre*) ablation

abnégation [abnegasjɔ̃] *f* self-denial; **esprit d'~** selflessness

aboiement [abwamɑ̃] *m* bark; **les ~s d'un chien** a dog's barking

abois [abwa] *mpl* **être aux ~** to be in dire straits; (*animal*) to be at bay

abolir [abɔliʀ] <8> *vt* (*esclavage, loi*) to abolish

abolition [abɔlisjɔ̃] *f* abolition

abominable [abɔminabl] *adj* **1.** (*horrible*) appalling; (*action*) heinous **2.** (*très mauvais, insupportable*) abominable

abominablement [abɔminabləmɑ̃] *adv* **1.** + *vb* (*très mal*) abominably **2.** (*très*) terribly

abomination [abɔminasjɔ̃] *f* **1.** (*dégoût*) loathing **2.** (*acte particulièrement répugnant*) abomination

abondamment [abɔ̃damɑ̃] *adv* (*servir*) plentifully; (*fleurir*) abundantly

abondance [abɔ̃dɑ̃s] *f* **1.** (*profusion*) abundance; **en ~** in abundance **2.** (*richesse*) wealth

abondant(e) [abɔ̃dɑ̃, ɑ̃t] *adj* (*nourriture*) copious; (*réserves*) plentiful; **des pluies ~es** heavy rainful

abonder [abɔ̃de] <1> *vi* **1.** (*exister en grande quantité*) to be plentiful **2.** (*avoir en quantité*) ~ **en qc** to be full of sth **3.** (*être de même avis*) ~ **dans le sens de qn** to agree wholeheartedly with sb

abonné(e) [abɔne] **I.** *adj* (*qui a un abonnement*) **être ~ à un journal** to subscribe to a newspaper; **être ~ au téléphone** to be on the phone *inf* **II.** *m(f)* (*théâtre*) season-ticket holder; (*d'un journal, service*) subscriber

abonnement [abɔnmɑ̃] *m* (*au bus*) season ticket; ~ **téléphonique** telephone (line) rental; ~ **hebdomadaire/mensuel** weekly/monthly subscription; **prendre un ~ à un journal** to take out a subscription to a newspaper; **carte d'~ au théâtre** season ticket for the theatre

abonner [abɔne] <1> **I.** *vpr* **s'~ à un journal** to subscribe to a newspaper; **s'~ au théâtre** to buy a season ticket for the theatre; **s'~ à un club** to join a club **II.** *vt* ~ **qn au théâtre** to buy sb a season ticket for the theatre; ~ **qn à un journal** to buy sb a subscription to a newspaper

abord [abɔʀ] *m* **1.** (*alentours*) **les ~s d'une ville** the area around a town **2.** (*attitude*) **être d'un ~ facile/difficile** to be approachable/unapproachable; **il est d'un ~ chaleureux** he makes you feel welcome; **il est d'un** ~ **rude** he's a prickly character ▸**au premier** ~ (*dès la première rencontre*) initially; (*à première vue*) at first sight; (**tout**) **d'**~ (*temporel*) at first; (*avant tout*) first of all; **d'**~ *inf* **d'**~ **tu n'avais qu'à demander!** for a start all you had to do was ask!

abordable [abɔʀdabl] *adj* (*bon marché*) affordable

aborder [abɔʀde] <1> **I.** *vt* **1.** (*accoster, évoquer*) to tackle **2.** (*appréhender, amorcer: vie, auteur, texte, épreuve, virage*) to approach **3.** NAUT ~ **un navire** to collide with a ship **II.** *vi* NAUT to land **III.** *vpr* **s'**~ **1.** (*se rencontrer: personnes*) to meet up **2.** NAUT to collide

aborigène [abɔʀiʒɛn] *adj* aboriginal

Aborigène [abɔʀiʒɛn] *mf* Aborigine

abortif, **-ive** [abɔʀtif, -iv] *adj* abortive; **risque** ~ risk of abortion

aboutir [abutiʀ] <8> *vi* **1.** (*réussir*) to succeed *inf;* (*projet*) to be a success; **ne pas** ~ not to come off **2.** (*conduire à*) ~ **à/dans qc** (*rue*) to lead to/into sth **3.** (*se terminer par*) ~ **à qc** (*démarche*) to lead to sth

aboutissement [abutismɑ̃] *m* outcome

aboyer [abwaje] <6> *vi* (*chien*) to bark

abracadabrant(**e**) [abʀakadabʀɑ̃, ɑ̃t] *adj* **1.** (*extravagant*) fantastic **2.** (*invraisemblable*) preposterous

abrasif, **-ive** [abʀɑzif, -iv] *adj* abrasive; **avoir des propriétés abrasives** to be abrasive

abrégé [abʀeʒe] *m* **1.** (*texte réduit*) summary; **mot en** ~ abbreviated form of a word **2.** (*ouvrage*) handbook

abréger [abʀeʒe] <2aé 5> *vt* ~ **qc** (*souffrances, rencontre*) to cut sth short; (*mot, texte*) to abbreviate sth

abreuver [abʀœve] <1> **I.** *vt* **1.** (*donner à boire: animal*) to water **2.** (*couvrir de*) ~ **qn de compliments** to shower sb with compliments **II.** *vpr* **1.** (*boire*) **s'**~ (*animal*) to drink **2.** (*se nourrir*) **s'**~ **de romans** to devour novels

abreuvoir [abʀœvwaʀ] *m* **1.** (*lieu*) watering place **2.** (*auge dans l'étable, le poulailler*) (drinking) trough **3.** (*dans une cage*) drinking bowl

abréviation [abʀevjasjɔ̃] *f* abbreviation

abri [abʀi] *m* **1.** (*protection naturelle*) shelter; **être à l'**~ **des gelées/intempéries** to be sheltered from frost/bad weather; **être à l'**~ **des balles** to be shielded against bullets; **se mettre à l'**~ **du vent** to shelter from the wind; **mettre qc à l'**~ to put sth under cover **2.** (*souterrain*) (underground) shelter **3.** (*lieu aménagé*) shelter; ~ **de jardin** garden shed; **être à l'**~ (*personne*) to be under cover; **mettre des papiers à l'**~ to put papers in a safe place ▸**être à l'**~ **du besoin** to be protected from hardship

abribus® [abʀibys] *m* bus shelter

abricot [abʀiko] *m, adj inv* (*couleur*) apricot

abricotier [abʀikɔtje] *m* apricot tree

abrité(**e**) [abʀite] *adj* sheltered

abriter [abʀite] <1> **I.** *vt* **1.** (*protéger*) to shelter **2.** (*héberger*) to harbour **II.** *vpr* **1.** (*se protéger*) **s'**~ to take shelter; **s'**~ **du feu/des balles** to take cover from the gunfire/the bullets **2.** (*se protéger des intempéries*) **s'**~ to take shelter

abrupt [abʀypt] *m* steep slope

abrupt(**e**) [abʀypt] *adj* **1.** (*raide: pente*) steep **2.** (*brutal: ton*) abrupt

abruti(**e**) [abʀyti] **I.** *adj* **1.** *inf* (*idiot*) idiotic **2.** *fig* **être** ~ **par l'alcool** to be stupefied with drink **II.** *m(f) inf* idiot

abrutir [abʀytiʀ] <8> **I.** *vt* to exhaust; ~ **qn de travail** to exhaust sb with work **II.** *vpr* **1.** (*s'étourdir*) **s'**~ **de qc** to exhaust oneself with sth **2.** (*s'abêtir*) to stupefy oneself

abrutissant(**e**) [abʀytisɑ̃, ɑ̃t] *adj* (*travail*) mind-numbing; (*musique*) deafening; **ce bruit est** ~ this noise drives you silly

abrutissement [abʀytismɑ̃] *m* **1.** (*extrême fatigue*) exhaustion; **travailler jusqu'à l'**~ to work till one drops **2.** (*abêtissement*) mindless state

ABS [ɑbeɛs] *m abr de* **Anti Blockier System** ABS

abscisse [apsis] *f* abscissa

absence [apsɑ̃s] *f* **1.** (*opp: présence*) absence; **en l'**~ **de qn** in the absence of sb; **les** ~**s de cet élève sont rares** this pupil is rarely absent **2.** (*manque*) lack; **en l'**~ **de preuves** in the absence of proof **3.** (*inattention*) **elle a des** ~**s par moments** at times she's absent-minded

absent(**e**) [apsɑ̃, ɑ̃t] **I.** *adj* **1.** (*opp: présent*) absent; **les élèves** ~**s** absentees; **être** ~ **à une réunion/au cours** to be absent from a meeting/class; **être** ~ **du bureau** to be out of the office **2.** (*qui manque*) **être** ~ **de qc** to be absent from sth; **il était** ~ **de la réunion** he was not at the meeting **3.** (*distrait: air, regard*) vacant **II.** *m(f)* absentee

absentéisme [apsɑ̃teism] *m* absenteeism; (*d'un élève*) truancy

absenter [apsɑ̃te] <1> *vpr* **s'**~ (*ne pas venir*) not to attend; (*être absent*) to be absent; (*partir*) to leave; **je ne me suis absenté que deux minutes** I was only away for two minutes

absolu [apsɔly] *m* PHILOS **l'**~ the Absolute ▸**dans l'**~ in absolute terms

absolu(**e**) [apsɔly] *adj* **1.** (*total: silence*) utter; (*confiance*) absolute; (*amour*) perfect **2.** (*sans concession: jugement*) uncompromising **3.** POL, LING absolute

absolument [apsɔlymɑ̃] *adv* **1.** (*à tout prix*) without fail **2.** (*totalement*) entirely; ~ **pas/rien** absolutely not/nothing ▸~**!** absolutely!; **vous êtes sûr? –** ~**!** are you sure? positive!; **mais** ~**!** of course!

absorbant(**e**) [apsɔʀbɑ̃, ɑ̃t] *adj* **1.** (*hydrophile: tissu*) absorbent **2.** (*prenant: travail*) absorbing

absorber [apsɔʀbe] <1> I. *vt* 1. (*consommer*) to consume; (*médicament*) to take 2. (*s'imbiber*) to absorb 3. (*faire disparaître*) **cette voiture a absorbé toutes mes économies** this car's soaked up all my savings 4. ECON ~ **un concurrent** to take over a competitor 5. (*accaparer: travail*) to occupy; **cette idée absorbait mon esprit** my mind was completely taken up with this idea; **être absorbé par une lecture** to be engrossed in reading II. *vpr* **s'~ dans son travail** to be engrossed in one's work

absorption [apsɔʀpsjɔ̃] *f* 1. (*action de manger, de boire*) swallowing 2. (*action d'avaler un médicament*) taking 3. (*pénétration*) absorption; **masser jusqu'à ~ complète par la peau** massage well into the skin 4. ECON takeover

abstenir [apstəniʀ] <9> *vpr* 1. (*éviter*) **s'~ de faire qc** to refrain from doing sth; **s'~ de vin/de tabac** to avoid wine/tobacco 2. POL (*ne pas voter*) **s'~** to abstain

abstention [apstɑ̃sjɔ̃] *f* abstention

abstentionniste [apstɑ̃sjɔnist] I. *adj* (*électorat*) non-voting II. *mf* non-voter

abstinence [apstinɑ̃s] *f* abstinence

abstraction [apstʀaksjɔ̃] *f* 1. (*action d'abstraire*) abstraction; **faire ~ de qc** to disregard sth 2. (*idée*) abstraction

abstraire [apstʀɛʀ] *vt irr* 1. (*schématiser*) to abstract 2. (*isoler par la pensée*) to isolate

abstrait [apstʀɛ] *m* 1. (*abstraction*) abstract ideas *pl* 2. ART abstract art 3. (*peintre*) abstract artist

abstrait(e) [apstʀɛ, ɛt] *adj* abstract

absurde [apsyʀd] I. *adj* absurd II. *m* PHILOS, LIT **l'~** the absurd

absurdité [apsyʀdite] *f* absurdity

abus [aby] *m* 1. (*consommation excessive, usage abusif*) abuse; **lutter contre l'~ d'alcool/de tabac** to fight against alcohol/tobacco abuse 2. (*injustice*) injustice 3. JUR ~ **de biens sociaux** misuse of corporate assets; ~ **de pouvoir** abuse of power

abuser [abyze] <1> I. *vi* 1. (*consommer avec excès*) to overindulge; ~ **de l'alcool/du tabac** to drink/smoke too much 2. (*profiter de qn*) to go too far 3. (*exploiter*) ~ **de la crédulité de qn** to take advantage of sb's credulity II. *vpr* (*se tromper*) **si je ne m'abuse** if I'm not mistaken

abusif, -ive [abyzif, -iv] *adj* 1. (*exagéré*) excessive; **consommation abusive d'alcool** alcohol abuse 2. (*incorrect*) **usage ~ d'un mot** misuse of a word 3. (*injuste: licenciement*) wrongful

acacia [akasja] *m* acacia

académicien(ne) [akademisjɛ̃, jɛn] *m(f)* 1. (*membre d'une académie*) academician 2. (*membre de l'Académie française*) *member of the French Academy*

académie [akademi] *f* 1. (*société savante*) academy 2. (*école*) ~ **de danse** dance academy 3. ECOLE, UNIV ≈ local (education) authority

Académie [akademi] *f* academy; **l'~ française** the French Academy

> The **Académie française** acts as a formal authority on the French language. The 40 life members debate questions of acceptability and award prizes for work in French literature.

académique [akademik] *adj* 1. (*d'une société savante, conventionnel*) *a.* ECOLE, UNIV academic 2. (*de l'Académie française*) of the French Academy 3. *Belgique, Québec, Suisse* (*universitaire*) **année ~** academic [*o* university] year

Acadie [akadi] *f* **l'~** Acadia

acadien [akadjɛ̃] *m* Acadian; *v. a.* **français**

acadien(ne) [akadjɛ̃, ɛn] *adj* Acadian

Acadien(ne) [akadjɛ̃, ɛn] *m(f)* Acadian

acajou [akaʒu] *m, adj inv* mahogany

acariâtre [akaʀjɑtʀ] *adj* cantankerous

acarien [akaʀjɛ̃] *m* dust mite; ZOOL acarid

accablant(e) [akablɑ̃, ɑ̃t] *adj* 1. (*psychiquement pénible: chaleur*) oppressive; (*douleur*) excruciating; (*travail*) exhausting 2. (*psychologiquement pénible: nouvelle*) devastating 3. (*accusateur: témoignage, preuve, reproche*) damning

accablement [akabləmɑ̃] *m* 1. (*abattement physique*) exhaustion 2. (*abattement moral*) dejection

accabler [akable] <1> *vt* 1. (*abattre: douleur, dettes, travail*) to overwhelm; (*nouvelle*) to devastate 2. (*imposer*) ~ **qn de reproches** to heap reproaches on sb; ~ **le peuple d'impôts** to overburden the people with taxes 3. (*confondre: témoignage*) to damn

accalmie [akalmi] *f* 1. METEO (*de la pluie, du vent*) lull 2. *fig* (*dans un combat*) lull; (*dans les affaires, les transactions*) slack period

accaparant(e) [akapaʀɑ̃, ɑ̃t] *adj* demanding

accaparer [akapaʀe] <1> *vt* 1. (*monopoliser*) to monopolize; (*poste-clé, attention*) to grab 2. (*occuper complètement*) ~ **qn** (*travail*) to leave sb with no time for anything else

accéder [aksede] <5> *vt* 1. (*parvenir*) **on accède à la cuisine par la salle à manger** you get to the kitchen through the dining room 2. (*atteindre*) ~ **à un poste** to obtain a post; ~ **en finale** to get through to the finals 3. (*consentir: souhait, prière, requête*) to grant

accélérateur [akseleʀatœʀ] *m* accelerator; **donner un coup d'~** to accelerate; **appuyer sur l'~** to step on the accelerator; **lâcher l'~** to come off the accelerator

accélération [akseleʀasjɔ̃] *f* acceleration

accélérer [akseleʀe] <5> I. *vt, vi* to accelerate; **vas-y, accélère!** come on, get a move on! *inf* II. *vpr* **s'~** (*pouls*) to quicken; **les travaux s'accélèrent** the pace of the work is speeding up

accent [aksɑ̃] *m* **1.** (*signe sur les voyelles*) accent; **e ~ aigu/grave/circonflexe** e acute/grave/circumflex **2.** (*manière de prononcer*) accent **3.** (*accentuation*) stress **4.** (*intonation expressive*) tone ▶ **~ de sincérité** note of sincerity; **mettre l'~ sur qc** to stress sth

accentuation [aksɑ̃tɥasjɔ̃] *f* **1.** (*augmentation: du chômage*) rise; (*des symptômes*) worsening **2.** LING accentuation **3.** (*insistance*) emphasis

accentué(e) [aksɑ̃tɥe] *adj* **1.** LING (*voyelle*) stressed **2.** (*prononcé: traits*) marked

accentuer [aksɑ̃tɥe] <1> **I.** *vt* **1.** (*tracer un accent*) **~ une lettre** to put an accent on a letter **2.** (*prononcer un accent*) to stress **3.** (*intensifier: effet, action*) to intensify; (*force, ressemblance, risque, efforts*) to increase **II.** *vpr* **s'~** to become more pronounced; **le froid s'accentue** it is becoming noticeably colder; **le chômage s'accentue** unemployment is rising

acceptable [aksɛptabl] *adj* acceptable; (*repas*) decent; (*prix*) reasonable

acceptation [aksɛptasjɔ̃] *f* acceptance

accepter [aksɛpte] <1> *vt* **1.** (*prendre, se soumettre à*) to accept **2.** (*être d'accord*) **~ qc** to agree to sth; **~ de** *+infin* to agree to *+infin* **3.** (*tolérer*) **~ qn** to put up with sb **4.** (*relever: défi*) to accept

accès [aksɛ] *m* **1.** (*entrée*) access; **~ interdit** no entry **2.** (*action d'accéder à une position*) **~ à un club** admission to a club **3.** (*crise: de fièvre*) bout; **~ d'humeur** fit of (bad) temper **4.** INFOR access; **~ à l'Internet** Internet access

accessible [aksesibl] *adj* **1.** (*compréhensible, où l'on peut accéder*) accessible; **musée ~ au public** museum open to the public; **une théorie ~ à tous** a theory which can be understood by everybody **2.** (*abordable: prix*) affordable; **une voiture qui n'est pas ~ à tous** a car which not everybody can afford

accession [aksesjɔ̃] *f* accession; **son ~ au poste de directeur** his rise to the position of director; **~ à la propriété** home-buying

accessoire [akseswaʀ] **I.** *adj* incidental **II.** *m* **1.** (*pièce complémentaire*) accessory **2.** PHILOS **l'~** the unessential **3.** THEAT, CINE **les ~s** props

accessoirement [akseswaʀmɑ̃] *adv* secondarily; **il est ~ acteur** he is also an actor; **le bureau sert ~ de chambre d'amis** the office can also be used as a guest room

accessoiriste [akseswaʀist] *mf* THEAT, CINE property master *m*, property mistress *f*

accident [aksidɑ̃] *m* accident; **~ du travail** industrial injury *Brit*, industrial accident *Am*; **~ de parcours** mishap

accidenté(e) [aksidɑ̃te] **I.** *adj* **1.** (*inégal: terrain*) uneven; (*région*) undulating **2.** (*qui a eu un accident*) injured; (*voiture*) damaged **II.** *m(f)* casualty; **~ de la circulation** road accident victim

accidentel(le) [aksidɑ̃tɛl] *adj* **1.** (*dû à un accident*) accidental **2.** (*dû au hasard*) fortuitous

accidentellement [aksidɑ̃tɛlmɑ̃] *adv* **1.** (*dans un accident*) **mourir ~** to die accidentally **2.** (*par hasard*) by accident

acclamation [aklamasjɔ̃] *f* cheering *no pl;* **les ~s du public** the cheers of the audience

acclamer [aklame] <1> *vt* to cheer

acclimatation [aklimatasjɔ̃] *f* acclimatization

acclimater [aklimate] <1> **I.** *vt* **~ un animal dans un zoo** to acclimatize an animal to a zoo *Brit,* to acclimate an animal to a zoo *Am* **II.** *vpr* **1.** (*s'adapter*) **s'~** to adapt **2.** (*s'habituer*) **s'~ à une maison** to adapt [*o* get used to] to a house

accolade¹ [akɔlad] *f* embrace; **donner l'~ à qn** to embrace sb

accolade² [akɔlad] *f* TYP brace; **entre ~s** bracketed together

accommodant(e) [akɔmɔdɑ̃, ɑ̃t] *adj* (*camarade, patron, directeur*) accommodating

accommodation [akɔmɔdasjɔ̃] *f* **1.** (*adaptation*) adaptation **2.** PHYS focusing

accommoder [akɔmɔde] <1> **I.** *vt* **1.** (*adapter*) to adapt **2.** GASTR to prepare; **~ des restes** to use up left-overs **II.** *vpr* **1.** (*s'arranger*) **s'~ avec qn** to come to an agreement with sb **2.** (*se contenter de*) **s'~ de qc** to make do with sth **3.** (*supporter*) **s'~ de qc** to put up with sth

accompagnateur, **-trice** [akɔ̃paɲatœʀ, -tʀis] *m, f* **1.** (*guide*) guide **2.** MUS accompanist **3.** ECOLE leader

accompagnement [akɔ̃paɲmɑ̃] *m a.* MUS, GASTR accompaniment

accompagner [akɔ̃paɲe] <1> **I.** *vt* **1.** (*aller avec, être joint à*) *a.* MUS to accompany; **du vin accompagne le plat** GASTR the dish is accompanied by wine **2.** (*survenir en même temps*) **~ qc** to go (together) with sth; **la terreur qui accompagne la guerre** the terror which comes with war **II.** *vpr* **1.** MUS **s'~ à la guitare** to accompany oneself on the guitar **2.** (*aller avec*) **s'~ de qc** to come with sth; **une défaite s'accompagne toujours d'humiliation** defeat always brings humiliation with it

accompli [akɔ̃pli] *m* LING **l'~** the perfective

accompli(e) [akɔ̃pli] *adj* **1.** (*parfait*) accomplished **2.** (*révolu*) **elle a trente ans ~s** she's in her thirty-first year

accomplir [akɔ̃pliʀ] <8> **I.** *vt* **1.** (*s'acquitter de*) **~ qc** (*travail, tâche, devoir*) to carry sth out; (*promesse*) to fulfil sth *Brit,* to fulfill sth *Am* **2.** (*exécuter, réaliser: ordre, miracle*) to perform **II.** *vpr* **1.** (*s'épanouir*) **elle s'accomplit dans son travail** she finds fulfilment in her work **2.** (*se produire*) **s'~** (*prophétie, vœux*) to come true; (*miracle*) to take place

accomplissement [akɔ̃plismɑ̃] *m* **1.** (*réalisation: d'un travail, d'une tâche*) accomplishment; (*d'un projet*) completion; (*d'un miracle*) working; (*d'une prédiction, de rêves*) fulfilment *Brit,* fulfillment *Am* **2.** (*épanouissement*) fulfilment *Brit,* fulfillment *Am*

accord [akɔʀ] *m* **1.** (*consentement, convention*) agreement; **faire qc d'un commun** ~ to do sth by mutual agreement; **donner son** ~ **à qn** to give one's agreement to sb; ~ **à l'amiable** informal agreement **2.** (*bonne intelligence*) harmony **3.** MUS (*association de plusieurs sons*) chord; (*réglage*) tuning **4.** LING **faute d'**~ mistake in agreement ►**il vivent en parfait** ~ they live in perfect harmony; **être d'**~ to agree; **être d'**~ **avec qn sur qc** to agree with sb about sth; **être en** ~ **avec soi-même** to be in harmony with oneself; **se mettre** [*o* **tomber**] **d'**~ **avec qn** to come to an agreement with sb; (**c'est**) **d'**~! OK! *inf*

accordéon [akɔʀdeɔ̃] *m* accordion

accordéoniste [akɔʀdeɔnist] *mf* accordionist

accorder [akɔʀde] <1> **I.** *vt* **1.** (*donner: crédit, délai, permission, faveur*) to grant; (*confiance*) to give; **voulez-vous m'**~ **cette danse?** may I have this dance? **2.** (*attribuer*) ~ **de la valeur à qc** to value sth; ~ **de l'importance à qc** to attach importance to sth **3.** MUS to tune **4.** LING ~ **l'adjectif avec le nom** to make the adjective agree with the noun **II.** *vpr* **1.** (*se mettre d'accord*) **s'**~ **avec qn sur une solution** to agree on a solution with sb **2.** (*s'entendre*) **s'**~ **avec qn** to get on with sb **3.** (*s'octroyer*) **s'**~ **une journée de congé** to allow oneself a day off **4.** LING **s'**~ **avec qc** (*verbe, adjectif*) to agree with sth

accoster [akɔste] <1> **I.** *vi* NAUT to dock **II.** *vt* **1.** (*aborder*) to accost **2.** NAUT (*quai*) to come alongside

accotement [akɔtmɑ̃] *m* **1.** (*d'une route*) verge *Brit,* shoulder *Am;* ~**s non stabilisés** soft verge **2.** CHEMDFER shoulder

accouchement [akuʃmɑ̃] *m* **1.** MED birth **2.** (*élaboration difficile*) gestation

accoucher [akuʃe] <1> **I.** *vi* **1.** MED to give birth; ~ **d'une fille** to give birth to [*o* have] a girl **2.** *inf* (*parler*) **allez, accouche!** come on, spit it out! **II.** *vt* (*aider une femme à mettre* (*un enfant*) *au monde*) **c'est cette sage-femme qui l'a accouchée** this is the midwife who delivered her baby

accoucheur, **-euse** [akuʃœʀ, -øz] *m, f* obstetrician

accouder [akude] <1> *vpr* **s'**~ **à qc** to lean on sth; **elle était accoudée au comptoir** she had her elbows on the counter

accoudoir [akudwaʀ] *m* armrest

accouplement [akupləmɑ̃] *m* **1.** *a. péj* ZOOL mating **2.** (*fait d'accoupler*) linking; ELEC connecting

accoupler [akuple] <1> **I.** *vpr* **1.** ZOOL **s'**~ to couple **2.** *péj* **s'**~ (*personnes*) to mate **II.** *vt* **1.** ZOOL to mate **2.** (*mettre par deux: chevaux*) to yoke **3.** TECH (*générateurs, locomotives*) to couple; ELEC to connect (up)

accourir [akuʀiʀ] *vi irr avoir o être* (*personne*) to rush *fig,* to come running

accoutrement [akutʀəmɑ̃] *m* outfit

accoutrer [akutʀe] <1> **I.** *vpr* **s'**~ to get oneself up; **s'**~ **bizarrement/d'une drôle de façon** to have a weird/funny get-up **II.** *vt* ~ **qn** to rig sb out

accoutumance [akutymɑ̃s] *f* **1.** (*adaptation*) familiarization **2.** (*besoin*) addiction

accoutumé(**e**) [akutyme] *adj* usual

accoutumer [akutyme] <1> **I.** *vt* (*habituer*) ~ **son mari à qc/à faire qc** to get one's husband used to sth/doing sth **II.** *vpr* **s'**~ **à qc/à faire qc** to get used to sth/doing sth

accréditer [akʀedite] <1> *vt* **1.** (*rendre crédible*) ~ **qc** to lend weight to sth **2.** (*conférer une autorité: ambassadeur, médiateur*) to accredit

accro [akʀo] *abr de* **accroché** **I.** *adj inf* **1.** (*dépendant d'une drogue*) hooked **2.** (*passionné*) ~ **de jazz** mad about jazz **II.** *mf inf* **1.** (*drogué*) addict **2.** (*passionné*) fanatic

accroc [akʀo] *m* **1.** (*déchirure*) tear; **faire un** ~ **à sa chemise** to tear one's shirt **2.** (*incident*) hitch **3.** (*infraction*) **un** ~ **à un contrat** a breach of a contract

accrochage [akʀɔʃaʒ] *m* **1.** (*action d'accrocher: d'un tableau*) hanging; (*d'un wagon*) coupling **2.** (*collision*) crash **3.** (*altercation*) quarrel **4.** MIL skirmish

accrocher [akʀɔʃe] <1> **I.** *vt* **1.** (*suspendre*) to hang **2.** (*déchirer*) to snag **3.** (*entrer en collision*) to hit; **j'ai accroché son rétroviseur extérieur en le dépassant** I caught his wing mirror as I was overtaking him *Brit,* I caught his sideview mirror as I was passing him *Am* **4.** (*attirer: regards*) to catch **5.** (*aborder*) to grab **6.** (*intéresser*) ~ **qn** (*film*) to grab sb's attention *inf* **II.** *vpr* **1.** (*se retenir*) **s'**~ **à qc** to cling to sth **2.** (*se faire un accroc*) **s'**~ **à qc** to get caught on sth **3.** (*persévérer*) **s'**~ to stick at it; **il faut s'**~ **pour le suivre** you have to hang on in there to keep up with him **4.** *inf* (*mettre ses espoirs dans*) **s'**~ **à qc** to cling to sth **5.** *inf* (*se disputer*) **s'**~ **avec qn** to clash with sb **III.** *vi* **1.** *inf* (*bien établir le contact*) to click; **il n'accroche pas en maths** maths is just not his subject **2.** (*plaire*) to catch on

accrocheur, **-euse** [akʀɔʃœʀ, -øz] *adj* (*slogan*) catchy; (*film*) crowd-pulling

accroissement [akʀwasmɑ̃] *m* (*du chômage*) rise; (*du chiffre d'affaires*) increase; ~ **de la population** population growth

accroître [akʀwɑtʀ] *irr* **I.** *vt* to increase; (*patrimoine*) to add to; (*pouvoir, chances*) to increase **II.** *vpr* **s'**~ to grow

accroupir [akʀupiʀ] <8> *vpr* **s'**~ to squat (down); **en position accroupie** in a squatting position

accru(**e**) [akʀy] *adj* enhanced

accueil [akœj] *m* **1.** (*fait de recevoir*) welcome; **faire bon/mauvais** ~ **à qn** to give sb a warm/cold welcome **2.** (*lieu*) reception

accueillant(**e**) [akœjɑ̃, ɑ̃t] *adj* (*hôte*) hospitable; (*sourire*) warm; (*maison*) welcoming

accueillir [akœjiʀ] *vt irr* **1.** (*recevoir*) to welcome **2.** (*héberger*) ~ **qn** (*hôte*) to accommodate sb **3.** (*réagir à: nouvelle*) to greet; (*projet, idée*) to receive; **la proposition a été mal accueillie** the proposal was poorly received

acculer [akyle] <1> *vt* **1.** (*coincer*) to corner **2.** (*contraindre*) ~ **qn à la faillite/au suicide** to drive sb to bankrupcy/suicide; ~ **qn aux aveux** to force a confession out of sb

accumulateur [akymylatœʀ] *m* **1.** (*pile rechargeable*) storage battery **2.** INFOR accumulator

accumulation [akymylasjɔ̃] *f* accumulation; (*de marchandises*) stockpiling; (*de preuves*) mass; (*d'énergie*) storage

accumuler [akymyle] <1> **I.** *vt* to accumulate; (*énergie*) to store; (*preuves, erreurs*) to amass; (*marchandises*) to stockpile **II.** *vpr* **s'**~ to accumulate; (*dettes, vaisselle, déchets*) to pile up

accusateur, -trice [akyzatœʀ, -tʀis] **I.** *adj* (*regard*) accusing; (*document*) incriminating **II.** *m, f* accuser

accusatif [akyzatif] *m* LING accusative

accusation [akyzasjɔ̃] *f* **1.** (*reproche*) accusation **2.** JUR charge; **porter une** ~ **contre qn** to make an accusation against sb

accusé [akyze] *m* ~ **de réception** acknowledgement of receipt

accusé(e) [akyze] **I.** *m(f)* JUR defendant **II.** *adj* (*visage, traits*) pronounced

accuser [akyze] <1> **I.** *vt* **1.** (*déclarer coupable*) to accuse; ~ **qn d'un vol** to accuse sb of theft; (*police*) to charge sb with theft **2.** (*souligner*) to highlight **3.** (*montrer*) **il accuse la fatigue des jours passés** he's showing the strain of the last few days **II.** *vpr* **s'**~ **de qc 1.** (*se déclarer coupable*) to confess to sth **2.** (*se rendre responsable*) to take the blame for sth

ace [ɛs] *m* SPORT ace

acerbe [asɛʀb] *adj* (*ton, paroles*) acerbic; (*critique, écrits*) cutting

acéré(e) [aseʀe] *adj* sharp

achalandé(e) [aʃalɑ̃de] *adj* **être bien** ~ (*magasin*) to be well-stocked

acharné(e) [aʃaʀne] *adj* (*travailleur*) hard; (*joueur*) tenacious; (*combat*) fierce; **être** ~ **à faire qc** to be intent on doing sth

acharnement [aʃaʀnəmɑ̃] *m* (*d'un combattant*) relentlessness; (*d'un joueur*) tenacity; **votre** ~ **au travail** your unrelenting work

acharner [aʃaʀne] <1> *vpr* **1.** (*persévérer*) **s'**~ **sur un projet** to work away at a project; **je m'acharne à lui faire comprendre** I'm trying desperately to make him understand **2.** (*ne pas lâcher prise*) **s'**~ **sur une victime** to hound a victim **3.** (*poursuivre*) **le sort s'acharne contre elle** she is dogged by fate **4.** (*tourmenter*) **les médias s'acharnent sur elle** she's being hounded by the media

achat [aʃa] *m* **1.** (*action*) buying **2.** (*chose achetée*) purchase; **faire des ~s** to shop

acheminement [aʃ(ə)minmɑ̃] *m* (*des voyageurs, des réfugiés, troupes*) transportation; (*du courrier*) delivery; (*des marchandises*) transport

acheminer [aʃ(ə)mine] <1> **I.** *vt* **1.** (*transporter: courrier*) to deliver; (*réfugiés, voyageurs, marchandises*) to transport **2.** (*conduire*) ~ **un convoi vers une destination** to route a convoy to a destination **II.** *vpr* **1.** (*aller en direction de*) **s'**~ **vers le bois** to head for the wood **2.** *fig* **s'**~ **vers une conclusion** to move towards a conclusion

acheter [aʃ(ə)te] <4> **I.** *vt* to buy; ~ **qc à qn** to buy sth from sb **II.** *vpr* **s'**~ **qc** to buy oneself sth

acheteur, -euse [aʃtœʀ, -øz] *m, f* **1.** (*client*) buyer; JUR purchaser **2.** (*de profession*) buyer ►**être** ~ to be in the market

achevé(e) [aʃəve] *adj* (*terminé*) finished

achèvement [aʃɛvmɑ̃] *m* (*d'un immeuble, de travaux*) completion; (*d'une discussion*) conclusion

achever [aʃ(ə)ve] <4> **I.** *vt* **1.** (*accomplir: discours*) to end; (*œuvre, bouteille*) to finish; ~ **un livre** to reach the end of a book; ~ **de faire qc** to finish doing sth **2.** (*tuer*) ~ **qn** to finish sb off **3.** (*épuiser*) **cette journée m'a achevé!** today nearly finished me off! **II.** *vpr* (*se terminer*) **s'**~ (*vie, journée*) to draw to an end

acide [asid] **I.** *adj* **1.** (*aigre: fruit, saveur*) sour; (*remarque*) cutting **2.** CHIM (*solution*) acidic **II.** *m* CHIM acid

acidité [asidite] *f* **1.** (*aigreur: d'un fruit*) sourness; (*d'une critique, remarque*) sharpness **2.** CHIM acidity

acidulé(e) [asidyle] *adj* sour

acier [asje] *m* **1.** (*métal*) steel **2.** (*industrie*) **l'**~ the steel industry

aciérie [asjeʀi] *f* steelworks

acné [akne] *f* acne

acolyte [akɔlit] *m péj* associate

acompte [akɔ̃t] *m* **1.** (*engagement d'achat*) deposit **2.** (*avance*) advance **3.** *inf* (*avant-goût*) foretaste; **un petit** ~ **sur l'été** a foretaste of summer

acoquiner [akɔkine] <1> *vpr péj* **s'**~ **avec qn** to get together with sb

Açores [asɔʀ] *fpl* **les** ~ the Azores

à-côté [akote] <à-côtés> *m* **1.** (*détail*) side issue **2.** (*gain occasionnel*) extra

à-coup [aku] <à-coups> *m* **1.** (*saccade: d'un moteur*) sputter; **par à-coups** in fits and starts **2.** ECON upheaval

acoustique [akustik] **I.** *adj* acoustic; **isolation** ~ soundproofing **II.** *f sans pl* acoustics + *vb sing*

acquéreur [akeʀœʀ] *m* buyer; **se porter** ~ **de qc** to state one's intention to buy sth

acquérir [akeʀiʀ] *irr* **I.** *vt* **1.** (*devenir propriétaire*) to acquire **2.** (*obtenir: compétence*) to acquire; (*faveur*) to win; (*habileté, expérience,* *importance*) to gain **II.** *vpr* (*s'obtenir*) **les connaissances s'acquièrent peu à peu** knowledge comes gradually

acquiescer [akjese] <2> *vi* **1.** (*approuver*) to approve **2.** (*consentir*) ~ **à une requête** to accede to a request

acquis [aki] *mpl* **1.** (*savoir*) experience **2.** (*avantages sociaux*) **les ~ sociaux** social benefits

acquis(e) [aki, iz] **I.** *part passé de* **acquérir** **II.** *adj* **1.** (*obtenu: fortune, habitude, richesse, expérience*) acquired; (*droit, avantages*) established **2.** (*reconnu*) accepted; **tenir qc pour ~** to take sth for granted

acquisition [akizisjɔ̃] *f* acquisition; **faire l'~ de qc** to acquire sth

acquit [aki] *m* receipt ▸**par ~ de conscience** to set one's mind at rest; **pour ~** received

acquittement [akitmɑ̃] *m* **1.** JUR (*d'un accusé*) acquittal **2.** (*règlement: d'une dette*) paying off; (*d'une facture, taxe*) payment **3.** (*exécution: d'une promesse*) fulfilment *Brit,* fulfillment *Am;* (*d'une tâche, mission*) carrying out; (*d'une fonction*) performance

acquitter [akite] <1> **I.** *vt* **1.** (*déclarer non coupable: accusé*) to acquit **2.** (*payer*) to pay; (*dette*) to settle **3.** (*signer: livraison*) to receipt **II.** *vpr* **s'~ d'une dette** to pay off a debt; **s'~ de ses responsabiltés** to discharge one's responsibilities; **s'~ d'une fonction** to perform a function

âcre [ɑkʀ] *adj* **1.** (*irritant: fumée, odeur, saveur*) acrid **2.** *fig* (*remarque*) caustic

âcreté [ɑkʀəte] *f* (*de la fumée*) acridness; (*d'un parfum, d'une saveur, odeur*) pungency

acridiens [akʀidjɛ̃] *mpl* Acrididae

acrobate [akʀɔbat] *mf* acrobat

acrobatie [akʀɔbasi] *f* **1.** (*discipline*) acrobatics + *vb sing* **2.** (*tour*) acrobatic feat; **~ aérienne** acrobatics *pl* **3.** *pl, fig* **j'ai fait des ~s pour le finir** I bent over backwards to get it done

acrobatique [akʀɔbatik] *adj* acrobatic

acronyme [akʀɔnim] *m* acronym

acrylique [akʀilik] CHIM **I.** *adj* acrylic **II.** *m* acrylic

acte [akt] *m* **1.** (*action*) act; **faire ~ de candidature à qc** to apply for sth; **faire ~ de présence** to put in a token appearance; **passer à l'~** to act; **traduire qc en ~s** to put sth into practice **2.** JUR (*manifestation de volonté*) act; (*document*) certificate; (*contrat*) deed; **~ d'accusation** (bill of) indictment; **~ de l'état civil** *certificate delivered by the Registrar of births deaths and marriages;* **~ de mariage/naissance/décès** marriage/birth/death certificate; **~ de succession** attestation of inheritance; **~ de vente** bill of sale; **prendre ~ de qc** to note sth; (*écrire*) to take note of sth; (*prendre connaissance de*) to bear sth in mind **3.** THEAT act

Acte [akt] *m* **l'~ Unique Européen** the Single European Act

acteur, -trice [aktœʀ, -tʀis] *m, f* **1.** THEAT, CINE actor, actress *m, f* **2.** (*participant*) **les ~s d'un événement** those involved in an event; **les ~s de la vie politique** the parties involved in political life

actif [aktif] *m* **1.** FIN **l'~** assets **2.** LING active voice; **à l'~** in the active (voice)

actif, -ive [aktif, -iv] **I.** *adj* **1.** (*dynamique, productif*) *a.* ELEC, LING active; **vie active** working life; (*mouvementée*) active life **2.** FIN (*marché*) buoyant **3.** ECON (*population*) working **4.** (*efficace*) active; (*poison*) potent **5.** MIL **l'armée active** the regular army **II.** *m, f* (*travailleur*) working person

action [aksjɔ̃] *f* **1.** (*acte*) action; **il n'est pas responsable de ses ~s** he's not responsible for his actions; **faire une bonne ~** to do a good deed **2.** *sans pl* (*fait d'agir, démarche*) action; **passer à l'~** to take action **3.** (*effet*) effect; **l'~ de qc sur qc** the effect of sth on sth; (*intervention: du gouvernement*) action; **le mur s'est détérioré sous l'~ du gel** the frost has damaged the wall **4.** (*péripéties, intrigue*) action; **ce film manque d'~** there's not enough action in this film **5.** (*mesure ponctuelle*) **~ revendicative** industrial action; **~ syndicale** trade union action **6.** JUR lawsuit; **~ judiridique** legal action; **entraver l'~ de la justice** to obstruct justice; **intenter une ~ contre qn** to take legal action against sb **7.** FIN share

actionnaire [aksjɔnɛʀ] *mf* shareholder

actionnement [aksjɔnmɑ̃] *m* activation

actionner [aksjɔne] <1> *vt* **1.** (*mettre en mouvement: levier*) to move; (*moteur*) to start **2.** JUR (*personne*) to sue

activation [aktivasjɔ̃] *f* **1.** (*accélération: de travaux*) speeding up **2.** PHYS, CHIM activation

activement [aktivmɑ̃] *adv* actively

activer [aktive] <1> **I.** *vt* **1.** (*accélérer: circulation sanguine, processus, travaux*) **~qc** to speed sth up; (*feu*) to stoke **2.** CHIM, INFOR to activate **II.** *vi inf* to get a move on **III.** *vpr* **s'~** **1.** (*s'affairer*) to be very busy **2.** *inf* (*se dépêcher*) to hurry up

activiste [aktivist] **I.** *adj* militant **II.** *mf* activist

activité [aktivite] *f* **1.** *sans pl* (*fait d'être actif*) activity; (*d'une personne*) energy; **entrer en ~** (*volcan*) to become active; **un homme d'une ~ débordante** a man who is bursting with energy **2.** (*occupation*) activity; **pratiquer une ~ sportive** to take part in a sport **3.** (*profession*) employment; **exercer une ~ commerciale** to be engaged in business; **reprendre ses ~s** (*personne*) to go back to work; (*entreprise*) to start doing business again; **avoir plusieurs ~s** to have several jobs **4.** *sans pl* (*ensemble d'actes*) activity; **relancer l'~ économique** to give a boost to the economy

actrice [aktʀis] *f v.* **acteur**

actualisation [aktɥalizasjɔ̃] *f* **1.** (*proces-

sus) updating **2.** (*résultat*) update

actualiser [aktɥalize] <1> *vt* (*mettre à jour*) to update

actualité [aktɥalite] *f* **1.** *sans pl* (*modernité: d'un sujet*) topicality; **être d'~** to be very topical **2.** *sans pl* (*événements*) current events; **l'~ politique/quotidienne** political/daily events *pl;* **l'~ sociale** current social issues; **l'~ sportive** the sports news **3.** *pl* TV, RADIO the news + *vb sing;* CINE newsreel + *vb sing*

actuel(le) [aktɥɛl] *adj* **1.** (*présent*) current; **le monde ~** the world today **2.** (*d'actualité*) topical

actuellement [aktɥɛlmɑ̃] *adv* at present

acuponcteur, -trice [akypɔ̃ktœʀ, -tʀis] *m, f* acupuncturist

acuponcture [akypɔ̃ktyʀ] *f* acupuncture

acupuncteur, -trice [akypɔ̃ktœʀ, -tʀis] *m, f v.* **acuponcteur**

acupuncture [akypɔ̃ktyʀ] *f v.* **acuponcture**

adaptateur [adaptatœʀ] *m* TECH adapter

adaptation [adaptasjɔ̃] *f* **1.** *sans pl* (*action de s'adapter*) adaptation **2.** CINE, THEAT adaptation

adapter [adapte] <1> **I.** *vt* **1.** (*poser: embout*) to fix **2.** (*accorder*) *a.* CINE, THEAT to adapt **II.** *vpr* **1.** (*s'habituer à*) **s'~ à qn/qc** to adapt to sb/sth **2.** (*s'ajuster à*) **s'~ à qc** (*clé*) to fit sth

addition [adisjɔ̃] *f* **1.** (*somme*) addition; (*de problèmes*) sum **2.** (*facture*) bill *Brit,* check *Am* **3.** (*ajout*) addition

additionner [adisjɔne] <1> **I.** *vt* **1.** (*faire l'addition de*) **~ qc** to add sth up **2.** (*ajouter*) **~ qc à qc** to add sth to sth **II.** *vpr* **s'~** (*erreurs, problèmes*) to accumulate; (*chiffres*) to add up

adepte [adɛpt] *mf* (*d'une secte*) follower; (*d'un sport*) fan

adéquat(e) [adekwa, at] *adj* appropriate; (*tenue*) suitable

adhérence [adeʀɑ̃s] *f* adhesion; (*d'un pneu, d'une semelle*) grip; **~ des pneus au sol** roadholding

adhérent(e) [adeʀɑ̃, ɑ̃t] **I.** *adj* adherent; **une matière ~e à la peau** a substance which sticks to the skin **II.** *m(f)* member

adhérer [adeʀe] <5> *vi* **1.** (*coller*) **~ à qc** to stick to sth; **~ à la route** to grip the road **2.** (*approuver*) **~ à un point de vue** to share a view **3.** (*reconnaître*) **~ à un idéal** to subscribe to an ideal **4.** (*devenir membre de*) **~ à un parti** to join a party

adhésif [adezif] *m* (*substance*) adhesive

adhésif, -ive [adezif, -iv] *adj* adhesive; **pansement ~** sticking plaster *Brit,* Band-Aid® *Am*

adhésion [adezjɔ̃] *f* **1.** (*approbation*) **~ à qc** support for sth **2.** (*inscription*) **~ à l'Union européenne** joining the European Union **3.** (*fait d'être membre*) membership

ad hoc [adɔk] *adj inv* (*adéquat*) suitable

adieu [adjø] <x> **I.** *m* (*prise de congé*) farewell *soutenu;* **dire ~ à qn** to say goodbye to sb; **faire ses ~x à qn** to bid farewell to sb **II.** *interj* goodbye; **~, les beaux jours** farewell summer; **tu peux dire ~ à ta carrière** you can kiss your career goodbye

adjacent(e) [adʒasɑ̃, ɑ̃t] *adj* (*maison, pays*) adjoining; (*rue*) adjacent; **être ~ à qc** to be adjacent to sth

adjectif [adʒɛktif] *m* adjective; **~ épithète** attributive adjective

adjectival(e) [adʒɛktival, o] <-aux> *adj* adjectival

adjectivé(e) [adʒɛktive] *adj* used as an adjective

adjoindre [adʒwɛ̃dʀ] *irr* **I.** *vt* **1.** (*ajouter*) **~ qc à une chose** to attach sth to a thing **2.** (*associer*) **~ une personne à qn** to appoint a person to assist sb **II.** *vpr* **s'~ un collaborateur** to appoint an assistant

adjoint(e) [adʒwɛ̃, wɛ̃t] **I.** *adj* assistant **II.** *m(f)* assistant; **~ au maire** deputy mayor

adjudant [adʒydɑ̃] *m* MIL ≈ sergeant major *Brit,* ≈ master sergeant *Am*

adjudication [adʒydikasjɔ̃] *f* **1.** (*vente aux enchères*) auction sale **2.** (*appel d'offres*) invitation to tender **3.** (*attribution: d'un contrat*) award

adjuger [adʒyʒe] <2a> **I.** *vt* **1.** (*attribuer aux enchères*) to auction; **~ un tableau à qn** to knock a painting down to sb; **une fois, deux fois, trois fois, adjugé!** going once, going twice, three times, gone! **2.** (*décerner, confier à*) **~ une prime à qn** to award sb a bonus; **~ un marché à une entreprise** to award a market to a company **II.** *vpr* **1.** (*obtenir*) **s'~ une grosse part du marché** to grab a large market share **2.** (*s'approprier*) **s'~ qc** to take sth for oneself

admettre [admɛtʀ] *vt irr* **1.** (*laisser entrer*) to admit **2.** (*recevoir*) **~ qn à sa table** to invite sb to eat with one **3.** (*accueillir, accepter: excuse*) to accept; **j'admets que tu as raison** I accept that you may be right **4.** ECOLE, UNIV (*à un concours*) to pass; **être admis quatrième à un examen** to come fourth in an exam **5.** (*reconnaître*) to admit to; **~ un crime** to admit to a crime; **il est admis que ...** it is an accepted fact that ... **6.** (*supposer*) to assume; **admettons que** +*subj* let's suppose that; **en admettant que** +*subj* supposing **7.** (*permettre*) to allow; **ce livre admet plusieurs interprétations** this book can be interpreted in several ways

administrateur [administʀatœʀ] *m* **~ de site** webmaster

administrateur, -trice [administʀatœʀ, -tʀis] *m, f* **1.** (*gestionnaire: d'organisme, établissement public, de théâtre*) administrator **2.** (*légal*) **~ judiciaire** receiver **3.** (*membre d'un conseil d'administration*) director

administratif, -ive [administʀatif, -iv] *adj* **1.** (*bâtiment, autorités*) administrative **2.** (*officiel*) **langue adminstrative** official language

administration [administRasjɔ̃] *f* **1.** *sans pl* (*gestion: d'une entreprise*) management; ~ **d'un pays** government of a country **2.** (*secteur du service public*) department; ~ **des Douanes** ≈ Customs and Excise *Brit,* ≈ Customs Service *Am;* ~ **des impôts** ≈ Inland Revenue *Brit,* ≈ Internal Revenue Service *Am;* ~ **pénitentiaire** prison authorities *pl* **3.** *sans pl* (*action de donner: d'un médicament*) administering

Administration [administRasjɔ̃] *f sans pl* **l'**~ ≈ the Civil Service

administrativement [administRativmɑ̃] *adv* administratively

administrer [administRe] <1> *vt* **1.** (*gérer: entreprise, projet*) to manage; (*pays*) to govern **2.** (*donner*) ~ **un remède à qn** to administer a remedy to sb

admirable [admiRabl] *adj* admirable

admirablement [admiRabləmɑ̃] *adv* wonderfully; (*travailler*) admirably; (*cuisiné*) superbly

admirateur, **-trice** [admiRatœR, -tRis] *m, f* admirer

admiratif, **-ive** [admiRatif, -iv] *adj* admiring

admiration [admiRasjɔ̃] *f sans pl* admiration; **regarder qc avec** ~ to look admiringly at sth; **être en** ~ **devant qc/qn** to be lost in admiration for sth/sb

admirer [admiRe] <1> *vt* **1.** (*apprécier*) to admire **2.** *iron, soutenu* (*s'étonner de*) to marvel at

admissible [admisibl] **I.** *adj* **1.** (*tolérable, concevable*) acceptable **2.** (*accepté: à un examen*) eligible (*for the next stage, usually an oral exam*) **II.** *mf* eligible candidate

admission [admisjɔ̃] *f* **1.** *sans pl* (*accès*) ~ **dans un club/à l'Union européenne** admission to a club/the European Union; ~ **dans une discothèque** entry to a discotheque **2.** ECOLE, UNIV admission; ~ **à un examen** eligibility for the next stage of an exam **3.** AUTO induction; (*d'un gaz, de la vapeur*) intake

ADN [ɑdeɛn] *m abr de* **acide désoxyribonucléique** DNA

ado [ado] *mf inf abr de* **adolescent**

adolescence [adɔlesɑ̃s] *f* adolescence

adolescent(**e**) [adɔlesɑ̃, ɑ̃t] *adj, m(f)* adolescent

adonner [adɔne] <1> *vpr* **s'**~ **à qc** to devote oneself to sth; **s'**~ **à un vice/à la boisson/au jeu** to indulge in a vice/in drink/in gambling

adopter [adɔpte] <1> *vt* **1.** (*prendre comme son enfant*) to adopt **2.** (*s'approprier: point de vue*) to take; (*cause*) to take up; ~ **la coiffure de Marilyn Monroe** to style one's hair like Marilyn Monroe **3.** POL (*motion, loi*) to pass

adoptif, **-ive** [adɔptif, -iv] *adj* (*enfant*) adopted; (*parents*) adoptive

adoption [adɔpsjɔ̃] *f* **1.** adoption; **d'**~ adopted **2.** (*approbation*) approval; (*d'une loi*) passing

adorable [adɔRabl] *adj* **1.** (*joli: enfant*) adorable; (*endroit, objet*) beautiful **2.** (*gentil: enfant*) delightful; (*personne*) charming; (*sourire*) lovely; **tu es** ~**!** you're so kind!

adorateur, **-trice** [adɔRatœR, -tRis] *m, f* (*d'une divinité*) worshipper; (*d'une femme*) admirer

adoration [adɔRasjɔ̃] *f sans pl a.* REL adoration; **être en** ~ **devant qn** to worship sb

adorer [adɔRe] <1> *vt* (*aimer*) *a.* REL to adore; ~ **faire qc** to love doing sth

adosser [adose] <1> **I.** *vt* ~ **qc contre un mur** to put sth against a wall; ~ **une échelle contre le mur** to lean a ladder against a wall; **être adossé au mur** (*meuble*) to be right up against the wall; (*personne*) to be leaning against the wall **II.** *vpr* **s'**~ **à qc** (*personne*) to lean with one's back against sth; (*bâtiment*) to be built against sth

adoucir [adusiR] <8> **I.** *vt* (*linge, eau, peau*) to soften; (*voix*) to moderate; (*contraste*) to tone down; (*chagrin, peine, épreuve*) to ease; (*personne*) to mellow; (*boisson*) to sweeten; ~ **la dureté de qc** to soften sth; ~ **la saveur de qc** to make sth taste milder **II.** *vpr* **s'**~ (*personne, saveur*) to mellow; (*voix, couleur, peau*) to soften; (*pente*) to become more gentle; **la température s'est adoucie** the weather has got milder

adoucissant [adusisɑ̃] *m* softener; (*pour le linge*) fabric softener

adoucissement [adusismɑ̃] *m* (*d'une saveur, acidité*) sweetening; (*de la peau, voix, de l'eau, d'une consonne*) softening; (*des couleurs, d'un contraste*) toning down; (*d'une surface, des aspérités*) smoothing; (*d'une peine*) easing; (*du linge*) conditioning

adoucisseur [adusisœR] *m* ~ (**d'eau**) water softener

adresse[1] [adRɛs] *f* **1.** (*domicile*) *a.* INFOR address; **changer d'**~ to change address; ~ **de messagerie,** ~ **électronique** e-mail address **2.** (*discours*) speech

adresse[2] [adRɛs] *f sans pl* **1.** (*dextérité*) skill **2.** (*tact*) tact

adresser [adRese] <1> **I.** *vt* **1.** (*envoyer*) to address; (*lettre, colis*) to send **2.** (*émettre*) ~ **un compliment à qn** to pay sb a compliment; ~ **la parole à qn** to speak to sb **3.** (*diriger*) ~ **qn à un spécialiste** to refer sb to a specialist **II.** *vpr* **s'**~ **à qn** to speak to sb; **adressez-vous à l'office de tourisme** ask at the tourist office

Adriatique [adRijatik] *f* **l'**~ the Adriatic

adroit(**e**) [adRwa, wat] *adj* **1.** (*habile*) dexterous; ~ **de ses mains** good with one's hands **2.** (*subtil*) shrewd

adroitement [adRwatmɑ̃] *adv* skilfully *Brit,* skillfully *Am*

adulte [adylt] **I.** *adj* **1.** (*opp: jeune: personne*) adult; (*animal*) full-grown **2.** (*digne d'une personne* ~*: attitude*) mature **II.** *mf* adult; **réservé aux** ~**s** for adults only

adultère [adyltɛR] **I.** *adj* adulterous; **femme** ~ adulteress **II.** *m* adultery

advenir [advəniʀ] <9> **I.** *vi* to happen **II.** *vi impers* **1.** (*arriver*) **quoi qu'il advienne** come what may **2.** (*devenir, résulter de*) **que va-t-il ~ de moi?** what will become of me?

adverbe [advɛʀb] *m* adverb

adverbial(e) [advɛʀbjal, jo] <-aux> *adj* adverbial

adversaire [advɛʀsɛʀ] *mf* opponent

adverse [advɛʀs] *adj* **1.** (*forces, équipe*) opposing; (*parti, camp*) opposite **2.** JUR **la partie ~** the other side

adversité [advɛʀsite] *f soutenu sans pl* (*détresse*) adversity

aération [aeʀasjɔ̃] *f sans pl* **1.** (*action d'aérer: d'une pièce*) airing **2.** (*circulation d'air*) ventilation

aéré(e) [aeʀe] *adj* **1.** (*ventilé: pièce*) well-ventilated **2.** (*clair*) well-spaced

aérer [aeʀe] <5> **I.** *vt* **1.** (*ventiler: pièce, literie*) to air; (*terre*) to aerate **2.** (*alléger*) to lighten **II.** *vpr* **s'~** to get some fresh air

aérien(ne) [aeʀjɛ̃, jɛn] *adj* **1.** AVIAT **transport ~** air transport; **ligne ~ne** airline; **compagnie ~ne** airline company **2.** (*en l'air: câble*) overhead; **métro ~** *elevated section of the underground*

aérobic [aeʀɔbik] *f* aerobics + *vb sing*

aéro-club <aéro-clubs>, **aéroclub** [aeʀoklœb] *m* flying club

aérodrome [aeʀodʀom] *m* aerodrome

aérodynamique [aeʀodinamik] **I.** *adj* (*véhicule, ligne*) streamlined **II.** *f* aerodynamics + *vb sing*

aérodynamisme [aeʀodinamism] *m* aerodynamics *pl*

aérogare [aeʀogaʀ] *f* (air) terminal

aéroglisseur [aeʀoglisœʀ] *m* hovercraft

aéronautique [aeʀonotik] **I.** *adj* aeronautical; **secteur/industrie ~** aeronautics sector/industry **II.** *f sans pl* aeronautics + *vb sing*

aéronaval(e) [aeʀonaval] <s> *adj* (*forces, bataille*) air and sea

Aéronavale [aeʀonaval] *f* **l'~** naval aviation, ≈ the Fleet Air Arm *Brit*

aéronef [aeʀonɛf] *m* aircraft

aéroplane [aeʀoplan] *m* aeroplane *Brit,* airplane *Am*

aéroport [aeʀopɔʀ] *m* airport

aéroporté(e) [aeʀopɔʀte] *adj* airborne

Aéropostale [aeʀopɔstal] *f* **l'~** *the* (*French*) *airmail service* (*between 1927 and 1933*)

aérosol [aeʀosɔl] *m* **1.** aerosol **2.** (*pulvérisateur*) **déodorant en ~** deodorant spray

aérospatial(e) [aeʀospasjal, jo] <-aux> *adj* aerospace

aérospatiale [aeʀospasjal] *f* (*industrie*) aerospace industry

affable [afabl] *adj* affable

affaiblir [afebliʀ] <8> **I.** *vt* **1.** *a.* POL, MIL to weaken **2.** (*diminuer l'intensité: sentiments*) to dull; (*bruit*) to muffle **II.** *vpr* **s'~** to weaken; (*personne, sens d'un mot*) to become weaker; (*vent*) to die down; (*autorité, pouvoir, économie*) to be weakened; **l'euro s'est affaibli face au dollar** the euro has weakened against the dollar

affaiblissement [afeblismɑ̃] *m* weakening; (*d'un bruit*) fading; (*de quantité*) reduction

affaire [afɛʀ] *f* **1.** (*préoccupation*) business; **ce n'est pas mon/ton ~** it's none of your/my business; **faire son ~ de qc** to take a matter in hand **2.** *sans pl* (*problème*) matter; **embarquer qn dans une ~** to get sb mixed up in a business; **se tirer d'~** to manage; **tirer qn d'~** to sort sb out **3.** (*scandale*) affair; **sale ~** nasty business; **étouffer une ~** to hush up a scandal; **tremper dans une ~ sordide** to be involved in a sordid affair; **l'~ des pots-de-vin** the bribery scandal **4.** JUR case; **classer/plaider une ~** to close/to plead a case **5.** (*transaction*) transaction **6.** *sans pl* (*entreprise*) concern **7.** *pl* (*commerce*) **être dans les ~s** to be in business; **parler ~s** to talk business; **repas/relations d'~s** business meal/relations **8.** *pl* POL affairs; **~ d'État** affair of state; **faire une ~ d'État de qc** *iron* to make a song and dance about sth **9.** *pl* (*effets personnels*) **prendre toutes ses ~s** to take all one's belongings ►**la <u>belle</u> ~!** big deal!; **c'est une ~ <u>classée</u>!** the matter is closed!; **<u>avoir</u> ~ à qn/qc** to be dealing with sb/sth; **<u>en</u> voilà une ~!** *inf* what a business!; **<u>hors</u> d'~** to be in the clear

Affaire [afɛʀ] *f* **les ~s étrangères** Foreign affairs; (*ministère*) ≈ Foreign Office *Brit,* ≈ Department of State *Am*

affairé(e) [afeʀe] *adj* busy

affairer [afeʀe] <1> *vpr* **s'~ auprès** [*o* **autour**] **de qn/à faire qc** to bustle about sb/doing sth

affaissement [afɛsmɑ̃] *m* subsidence

affaisser [afese] <1> *vpr* **s'~** **1.** (*baisser de niveau*) to subside; (*poutre*) to sag; (*tête*) to droop **2.** (*s'écrouler: personne*) to collapse

affaler [afale] <1> *vpr* **s'~ sur le sol** to collapse on the ground; **être affalé dans un fauteuil** to be slumped in an armchair

affamé(e) [afame] *adj* starving

affectation [afɛktasjɔ̃] *f* **1.** *sans pl* (*mise à disposition*) **l'~ d'une somme à qc** the allocation of a sum of money to sth **2.** (*nomination*) ADMIN appointment; MIL posting; **l'~ de qn dans une région/un pays** (*en parlant d'un fonctionnaire*) the appointment of sb to a region/country **3.** (*manque de naturel*) affectation

affecté(e) [afɛkte] *adj* **1.** (*feint: sentiment*) feigned **2.** (*maniéré: personne, style, comportement*) affected

affecter [afɛkte] <1> *vt* **1.** (*feindre: sentiment, attitude*) to feign **2.** (*nommer*) **~ qn à un poste** to appoint sb to a post; **~ qn dans une région** to post sb to a region **3.** (*émouvoir*) to move **4.** (*concerner: épidémie, événement*) to affect **5.** (*mettre à disposition*) ~

une somme à qc to allocate a sum to sth; ~ **un bâtiment à qc** to assign a building to sth

affectif, **-ive** [afɛktif, -iv] *adj* **1.** emotional **2.** PSYCH affective

affection [afɛksjɔ̃] *f* **1.** (*tendresse*) *a.* PSYCH affection; **prendre qn en** ~ to become fond of sb **2.** MED ailment

affectionner [afɛksjɔne] <1> *vt* (*préférer*) ~ **qc** to be fond of sth

affectivité [afɛktivite] *f sans pl* feelings *pl*

affectueusement [afɛktɥøzmɑ̃] *adv* affectionately; **bien** ~ with fond regards

affectueux, **-euse** [afɛktɥø, -øz] *adj* affectionate

affermir [afɛʀmiʀ] <8> **I.** *vt* **1.** (*consolider*) to consolidate; (*paix*) to reinforce; (*pouvoir*) to strengthen; ~ **qn dans son opinion/sa résolution** to reinforce sb's opinion/resolve **2.** (*rendre plus ferme: chairs*) to strengthen; (*muscles, peau*) to tone **II.** *vpr* **s'**~ (*santé*) to improve; (*autorité*) to strengthen

affichage [afiʃaʒ] *m* **1.** *sans pl* (*action de poser des affiches*) posting; ~ **électoral/publicitaire** sticking up election/advertising posters **2.** INFOR display; ~ **à cristaux liquides** liquid crystal display

affiche [afiʃ] *f* **1.** (*feuille imprimée*) *a.* ADMIN notice **2.** (*avis officiel*) public notice **3.** (*poster*) poster; ~ **électorale** election poster **4.** *sans pl* (*programme théâtral*) bill; **tenir l'**~ to run; **être à l'**~ to be on

afficher [afiʃe] <1> **I.** *vt* **1.** (*placarder*) ~ **qc** to stick up sth; (*résultat d'un examen*) to post sth up **2.** (*montrer publiquement*) *a.* CINE to show **3.** THEAT ~ **complet** to be sold out **4.** INFOR, TECH to display; **être affiché sur l'écran** to be displayed on the screen **II.** *vi* **défense d'**~ no billposting **III.** *vpr* (*s'exhiber*) **s'**~ (*quelque chose*) to be displayed; (*personne*) to flaunt oneself; **il s'affiche avec elle** he parades around with her

affilée [afile] **d'**~ (*sans interruption*) at a stretch; (*l'un après l'autre*) one after the other

affiliation [afiljasjɔ̃] *f* affiliation

affilié(e) [afilje] **I.** *adj* **être** ~ **à un syndicat** to belong to a union **II.** *m(f)* member

affilier [afilje] <1a> **I.** *vt* ~ **qn à une association** to affiliate sb to an association **II.** *vpr* **s'**~ **à un club/un syndicat** to join a club/union; **s'**~ **à la Sécurité sociale** to affiliate with the social security system

affiner [afine] <1> **I.** *vt* **1.** (*purifier, rendre plus fin: métal, verre, style*) to refine; (*odorat, ouïe*) to sharpen **2.** (*achever la maturation: fromage*) to mature **II.** *vpr* **s'**~ (*style, goût*) to refine; (*odorat, ouïe*) to sharpen

affinité [afinite] *f* affinity

affirmatif [afiʀmatif] *interj inf a.* TEL affirmative

affirmatif, **-ive** [afiʀmatif, -iv] *adj* (*opp: négatif*) *a.* LING affirmative; (*ton*) assertive; **être** ~ to be positive

affirmation [afiʀmasjɔ̃] *f* **1.** (*déclaration, opp: négation*) affirmation **2.** *sans pl* (*manifestation*) *a.* LING assertion; ~ **d'une amitié** confirmation of a friendship

affirmative [afiʀmativ] *f sans pl* **répondre par l'**~ to reply in the affirmative

affirmativement [afiʀmativmɑ̃] *adv* affirmatively

affirmer [afiʀme] <1> **I.** *vt* **1.** (*soutenir*) to maintain; ~ **sur l'honneur que** to give one's word that **2.** (*manifester: originalité, autorité, position*) to assert **3.** *soutenu* (*proclamer*) to affirm **II.** *vpr* **s'**~ **comme sculpteur** to establish oneself as a sculptor; **son autorité s'affirme** she is establishing her authority

affleurer [aflœʀe] <1> *vi* to show; (*récif, roche*) to show on the surface; (*filon, couche*) to outcrop; (*sentiment*) to rise to the surface

affliction [afliksjɔ̃] *f* affliction

affligeant(e) [afliʒɑ̃, ʒɑ̃t] *adj* **1.** (*désespérant*) distressing **2.** (*lamentable*) pathetic

affluence [aflyɑ̃s] *f sans pl* affluence; (*de visiteurs*) crowd

affluent [aflyɑ̃] *m* tributary

affluer [aflye] <1> *vi* **1.** (*arriver en grand nombre: foule*) to flock; **des lettres affluaient sur le bureau** letters were pouring onto the desk **2.** (*couler en abondance: sang*) to rush **3.** (*apparaître en abondance: argent*) to flow

afflux [afly] *m sans pl* (*arrivée massive: de clients*) influx; (*de fluide*) inrush; ~ **de visiteurs** flood; ~ **de capitaux** capital inflow

affolant(e) [afɔlɑ̃, ɑ̃t] *adj* **1.** (*effrayant*) frightening **2.** *inf* (*incroyable*) alarming

affolé(e) [afɔle] *adj* (*paniqué: personne, foule, animal*) panic-stricken; **être** ~ (*boussole*) wildly fluctuating

affolement [afɔlmɑ̃] *m sans pl* panic; **pas d'**~**!** nobody panic!

affoler [afɔle] <1> **I.** *vt* **1.** (*effrayer*) ~ **qn** (*nouvelle*) to throw sb into turmoil **2.** (*inquiéter*) ~ **qn** to throw sb into a panic **II.** *vpr* **s'**~ to panic

affranchir [afʀɑ̃ʃiʀ] <8> *vt* **1.** (*avec des timbres*) to stamp; (*machine*) to frank **2.** HIST (*esclave*) to set free

affranchissement [afʀɑ̃ʃismɑ̃] *m* **1.** (*mettre des timbres*) stamping **2.** (*frais de port*) postage; **tarifs d'**~ postal rates **3.** (*libération: d'un pays*) liberation; (*d'un esclave*) freeing

affréter [afʀete] <5> *vt* **1.** AVIAT, NAUT to charter **2.** AUTO to hire

affreusement [afʀøzmɑ̃] *adv* **1.** (*horriblement*) horribly; (*en retard*) dreadfully **2.** (*extrêmement*) terribly; (*vexé*) awfully

affreux, **-euse** [afʀø, -øz] *adj* **1.** (*laid*) hideous **2.** (*horrible: cauchemar*) horrible; (*mort*) terrible **3.** (*désagréable*) awful; (*temps*) dreadful

affriolant(e) [afʀijɔlɑ̃, ɑ̃t] *adj* **1.** (*excitant: vêtement*) sexy **2.** *souvent nég* (*attirant*) exciting

affront [afʀɔ̃] *m soutenu* affront

affrontement [afʀɔ̃tmɑ̃] *m* **1.** MIL, POL confrontation **2.** (*conflit*) conflict

affronter [afʀɔ̃te] <1> **I.** *vt* **1.** (*combattre*) *a.* SPORT to face **2.** (*faire face à: situation difficile, hiver*) to confront **II.** *vpr* **s'~** to confront one another

affublé(e) [afyble] *adj* (*accoutré*) dressed up ▶**être ~ d'un nom ridicule** to be lumbered with a stupid name

affût [afy] *m* **être à l'~ de qc** to be on the look-out for sth

affûter [afyte] <1> *vt* to grind; (*crayon*) to sharpen

afghan [afgɑ̃] *m* Afghan; *v. a.* **français**

afghan(e) [afgɑ̃, aːn] *adj* Afghan

Afghan(e) [afgɑ̃, aːn] *m(f)* Afghan

Afghanistan [afganistɑ̃] *m* **l'~** Afghanistan

afin [afɛ̃] *prep* (in order) to; **~ de gagner la course** (so as) to win the race; **~ qu'on puisse vous prévenir** so that we can let you know

AFNOR [afnɔʀ] *f abr de* **Association française de normalisation** *French industrial standards association*

a fortiori [afɔʀsjɔʀi] *adv soutenu* all the more so

AFP [ɑɛfpe] *f abr de* **Agence France-Presse** *French press agency*

africain(e) [afʀikɛ̃, ɛn] **I.** *adj* African **II.** *m(f)* African

africanisation [afʀikanizasjɔ̃] *f* africanization

Afrikan(d)er [afʀikanɛʀ, afʀikɑ̃dɛʀ] *m, f* Afrikaner

afrikans [afʀikɑ̃s] *m* Afrikaans; *v. a.* **français**

Afrique [afʀik] *f* **l'~** Africa; **l'~ du Nord/Sud** North/South Africa; **l'~ noire** Black Africa

afro-américain(e) [afʀoameʀikɛ̃, ɛn] <afro-américains> *adj* African-American

Afro-américain(e) [afʀoameʀikɛ̃, ɛn] <afro-Américains> *m(f)* African-American

agaçant(e) [agasɑ̃, ɑ̃t] *adj* irritating

agacé(e) [agase] *adj* irritated

agacement [agasmɑ̃] *m* irritation; **un soupir d'~** a sigh of irritation; **éprouver une sorte d'~** to feel rather annoyed; **provoquer l'~ de qn** to irritate sb

agacer [agase] <2> *vt* **1.** (*énerver*) to irritate **2.** (*taquiner*) to tease

agate [agat] *f* agate

agave [agav] *m* agave

âge [ɑʒ] *m* **1.** (*temps de vie*) age; **arriver à l'~ adulte** to reach adulthood; **avoir l'~ de** +*infin* to be old enough to +*infin;* **faire plus vieux que son ~** to look older than one's age; **elle a passé l'~ de voyager** she is too old to travel; **prendre de l'~** to get older; **à l'~ de 8 ans** at the age of eight; **quel ~ as-tu/a-t-il?** how old are you/is he? **2.** (*ère*) age ▶**le troisième ~** (*la vieillesse*) old age; (*les personnes*) senior citizens; **~ de la retraite** retirement age

âgé(e) [ɑʒe] *adj* old; **les personnes ~es** the elderly; **être ~ de 10 ans** to be 10 years old; **avoir un fils ~ de 10 ans** to have a 10-year-old son

agence [aʒɑ̃s] *f* **1.** (*bureau*) agency; **~ de presse/de publicité/de voyages/de mannequins** news/advertising/travel/modelling agency **2.** (*représentation commerciale*) sales office **3.** (*succersale*) branch

Agence [aʒɑ̃s] *f* **l'~ nationale pour l'emploi** *national employment agency*

agencer [aʒɑ̃se] <2> **I.** *vt* **1.** (*ordonner: éléments*) to arrange **2.** (*structurer, combiner: phrase, mots*) to put together; (*roman*) to structure; (*couleurs*) to harmonize **3.** (*aménager: local*) to lay out; **être bien agencé** to be well laid-out **4.** (*équiper: cuisine*) to equip **II.** *vpr* **s'~** (*pièces d'un puzzle*) to fit together; **s'~ en phrases** (*mots*) to come together in sentences

agenda [aʒɛ̃da] *m* **1.** diary; **~ de bureau** desk diary **2.** INFOR **~ électronique** organizer **3.** POL agenda

agenouiller [aʒ(ə)nuje] <1> *vpr* **1.** (*poser les genoux sur*) **s'~** to kneel down; **être agenouillé sur qc** to be kneeling on sth **2.** *fig* **s'~ devant le pouvoir** to bow to authority

agent [aʒɑ̃] *m* **1.** (*policier*) police officer, policeman, policewoman *m, f;* **~ de la circulation** ≈ traffic officer **2.** ECON, POL, CHIM, ART agent; **~ commercial** sales representative; **~ immobilier/d'assurances** estate/insurance agent; **~ technique** technician; **~ artistique** theatrical agent **3.** (*employé*) employee; **~ administratif** official

agent(e) [aʒɑ̃, ɑ̃t] *m(f)* (*espion*) agent

agglo [aglo] *m abr de* **aggloméré**

agglomération [aglɔmeʀasjɔ̃] *f* **1.** (*zone urbaine*) urban area; **l'~ bordelaise** Bordeaux and its suburbs **2.** (*ville et banlieue*) town **3.** (*assemblage: de matériaux*) conglomeration

aggloméré [aglɔmeʀe] *m inf* CONSTR conglomerate; (*bois*) chipboard; (*briquette*) briquette

agglomérer [aglɔmeʀe] <5> **I.** *vt* **1.** (*amonceler: neige, sable*) to pile up **2.** TECH (*bois, charbon*) to compress; **bois aggloméré** chipboard **II.** *vpr* **1.** (*s'amonceler: neige, terre*) to pile up **2.** TECH to agglomerate

agglutiner [aglytine] <1> **I.** *vt* **1.** (*agglomérer*) to agglutinate; (*matériaux*) to stick together **2.** (*rassembler*) **des gens sont agglutinés dans la rue** people have congregated in the street **II.** *vpr* **1.** (*s'agglomérer*) **s'~** (*globules, molécules*) to agglutinate **2.** (*se rassembler*) **s'~ devant une vitrine** to huddle together in front of a window

aggravant(e) [agʀavɑ̃, ɑ̃t] *adj* aggravating

aggravation [agʀavasjɔ̃] *f* (*d'une crise, d'une situation*) worsening; (*du chômage*) increase

aggraver [agʀave] <1> **I.** *vt* **1.** (*faire empirer: situation, crise*) to aggravate; (*risque,* *chômage*) to increase **2.** (*renforcer: peine*) to increase; ~ **une maladie** to make an illness worse **II.** *vpr* **s'~** (*pollution, chômage*) to increase; (*conditions sociales, difficultés*) to get worse

agile [aʒil] *adj* agile

agilité [aʒilite] *f sans pl* **1.** (*aisance*) agility **2.** *fig* ~ **d'esprit** mental agility

agios [aʒio] *mpl* charges

agir [aʒiʀ] <8> **I.** *vi* **1.** (*faire, être actif*) to act; ~ **bien** to do the right thing **2.** (*exercer une influence*) ~ **sur qc** to act on sth; ~ **sur qn** to bring pressure to bear on sb **3.** (*opérer: médicament, poison*) to take effect **II.** *vpr impers* **1.** (*il est question de*) **il s'agit de qn/qc** it concerns sb/sth; **de quoi s'agit-il?** what is it about? **2.** (*il faut*) **il s'agit de faire qc** sth must be done

agissements [aʒismɑ̃] *mpl péj* **1.** (*machinations*) machinations **2.** (*menées*) intrigues

agitateur, **-trice** [aʒitatœʀ, -tʀis] *m, f* POL agitator

agitation [aʒitasjɔ̃] *f* **1.** (*animation*) activity **2.** (*excitation*) excitement **3.** (*troubles*) agitation **4.** (*malaise social*) unrest

agité(e) [aʒite] *adj* **1.** (*animé de mouvements: mer*) rough **2.** (*nerveux*) agitated **3.** (*excité*) excited **4.** (*troublé: situation*) hectic; (*époque*) turbulent

agiter [aʒite] <1> **I.** *vt* **1.** (*secouer: bouteille*) to shake; (*drapeau, mouchoir, main*) to wave **2.** (*inquiéter*) to upset; **cette idée l'agite beaucoup** this thought is troubling her a lot **II.** *vpr* **s'~** **1.** (*bouger*) to move about **2.** (*s'exciter*) to fidget **3.** (*s'énerver*) to get worked up **4.** (*s'affairer*) to hurry; **arrête de t'~ comme ça!** don't be in such a hurry!

agneau, **agnelle** [aɲo, aɲɛl] <x> *m, f* lamb

agonie [agɔni] *f* death throes *pl*

agonir [agɔniʀ] <8> *vt* ~ **qn d'injures** to heap abuse on sb

agonisant(e) [agɔnizɑ̃, ɑ̃t] *adj* **1.** dying **2.** *fig* (*régime*) in its death throes

agoniser [agɔnize] <1> *vi* to be dying

agrafe [agʀaf] *f* **1.** COUT hook **2.** (*pour papiers*) staple **3.** MED clamp

agrafer [agʀafe] <1> *vt* **1.** (*attacher: feuilles*) to staple (together) **2.** (*fermer: jupe*) to fasten

agrafeuse [agʀaføz] *f* stapler

agraire [agʀɛʀ] *adj* (*politique*) agrarian; (*réforme*) land

agrandir [agʀɑ̃diʀ] <8> **I.** *vt* **1.** (*rendre plus grand*) to enlarge **2.** (*rendre plus large*) to widen **3.** (*développer: entreprise*) to expand **4.** PHOT to enlarge **II.** *vpr* **s'~** **1.** (*se creuser, s'élargir*) to get bigger; (*passage*) to get wider; (*écart*) to widen **2.** (*se développer: entreprise, ville*) to expand **3.** (*devenir plus nombreux: famille*) to grow **4.** *inf* (*se loger plus spacieusement*) to get more space for oneself

agrandissement [agʀɑ̃dismɑ̃] *m* **1.** (*extension: d'une maison*) extension; (*d'une entreprise*) expansion **2.** PHOT enlargement

agréable [agʀeabl] **I.** *adj* **1.** (*gentil: personne*) pleasant; **il est ~ à vivre** he is nice to be with **2.** (*qui plaît, agrée*) nice **II.** *m* **l'~ dans ce poste, c'est les longues vacances** the nice thing about this job is the long holidays

agréablement [agʀeabləmɑ̃] *adv* pleasantly

agréé(e) [agʀee] *adj* JUR (*expert*) registered; **fournisseur** ~ authorized dealer

agréer [agʀee] <1> *vt soutenu* (*remerciements*) to accept; **veuillez ~, Madame/Monsieur, mes salutations distinguées** yours faithfully

agrèg [agʀɛg] *f inf,* **agrégation** [agʀegasjɔ̃] *f* UNIV *prestigious competitive examination for teachers in France*

agrégé(e) [agʀeʒe] **I.** *adj* UNIV **être** ~ to be a teacher with the aggrégation **II.** *m(f)* (*au lycée*) *person who has passed the aggrégation*

agrément [agʀemɑ̃] *m* **1.** (*approbation*) approval **2.** (*plaisir*) pleasure; **jardin d'~** ornamental garden; **voyage d'~** pleasure trip **3.** (*attrait*) charm; (*de la vie*) pleasure; **dépourvu de tout ~** utterly charmless

agrémenter [agʀemɑ̃te] <1> *vt* (*pièce*) to decorate

agrès [agʀɛ] *mpl* SPORT apparatus; **les exercices aux ~** apparatus work

agresser [agʀese] <1> *vt* **1.** (*attaquer, insulter*) to attack; **se faire ~** to be assaulted **2.** (*irriter*) **agressé par la vie urbaine** stressed by city life **3.** (*menacer*) **elle se sent agressée par son mari** she feels her husband is hostile towards her **4.** (*avoir un effet nocif sur*) to damage

agresseur [agʀɛsœʀ] **I.** *m* **1.** (*personne*) assailant **2.** (*État*) aggressor **II.** *app* **État/pays** ~ aggressor

agressif, **-ive** [agʀesif, -iv] *adj* (*personne, comportement*) aggressive; (*pays*) hostile

agression [agʀesjɔ̃] *f* **1.** (*attaque, coups*) attack; **être victime d'une ~** to be attacked; (*être volé*) to be mugged **2.** (*nuisance*) ~ **sonore** noise disturbance **3.** MIL **acte d'~** act of aggression

agressivement [agʀesivmɑ̃] *adv* aggressively

agressivité [agʀesivite] *f* aggression

agricole [agʀikɔl] *adj* agricultural; (*produit*) farm; (*peuple*) farming; **ouvrier ~** farm hand

agriculteur, **-trice** [agʀikyltœʀ, -tʀis] *m, f* farmer

agriculture [agʀikyltyʀ] *f* farming

agripper [agʀipe] <1> **I.** *vt* to grab **II.** *vpr* **s'~ à qn/qc** to cling on to sb/sth

agroalimentaire [agʀoalimɑ̃tɛʀ] **I.** *adj* food-processing; **recherche ~** food research **II.** *m* **l'~** the food-processing industry

agronome [agʀɔnɔm] *adj* **ingénieur ~** agronomist

agronomie [agʀɔnɔmi] *f* agronomics + *vb*

sing

agrotourisme [agʀoturism] *m* agrotourism

agrume [agʀym] *m* citrus fruit

aguerrir [ageʀiʀ] <8> **I.** *vt* **1.** (*endurcir*) ~ **qn au** [*o* **contre le**] **froid** to harden sb against the cold **2.** (*habituer à la guerre*) ~ **qn** (*troupes, soldats*) to toughen sb up **II.** *vpr* **s'~ au** [*o* **contre le**] **froid** to harden oneself against the cold

aguets [agɛ] **être aux** ~ to be on the lookout

aguichant(e) [agiʃɑ̃, ɑ̃t] *adj* alluring

ah [ˊɑ] **I.** *interj* **1.** (*de joie, sympathie, déception, d'admiration*) **~!** oh! **2.** *iron* **~ ~, tu l'as écrit toi-même?** so you wrote it yourself, did you? **3.** (*rire*) **~! ~!** ha! ha! ▶ **~ bon** oh well; **~ bon?** really?; **~ non** oh no; **~ non alors!** certainly not!; **~ oui** oh yes; **~ oui, je vois ...** oh, I see... **II.** *m* **1.** (*d'admiration*) gasp **2.** (*de soulagement*) sigh

ahuri(e) [ayʀi] **I.** *adj* **1.** (*stupéfait*) stunned **2.** (*stupide*) stupefied **II.** *m(f)* *péj, inf* halfwit

ahurissant(e) [ayʀisɑ̃, ɑ̃t] *adj* stupefying; (*personne*) incredible; (*chiffre*) staggering

ai [e] *indic prés de* **avoir**

aide [ɛd] **I.** *f* **1.** (*assistance*) help; **~ médicale** health care; **à l'~!** help!; **appeler qn à l'~** to call on sb's help; **apporter son ~ à qn** to help sb **2.** *fig* **à l'~ d'un couteau** with a knife; **enlever la roue à l'~ d'une clef en croix** remove the wheel using a wheel brace **3.** (*secours financier*) aid; **~ sociale** benefits *pl Brit*, ≈ welfare *Am* **II.** *mf* (*assistant*) assistant; **~ familiale** mother's help; **~ de cuisine** kitchen hand

aide-mémoire [ɛdmemwaʀ] *m inv* **1.** ECOLE notes *pl* **2.** (*feuille*) aide-mémoire *form*

aide-ménagère [ɛdmenaʒɛʀ] <aides-ménagères> *f* home help

aider [ede] <1> **I.** *vt* **1.** (*seconder*) to help **2.** (*donner de l'argent*) to aid **3.** (*prêter assistance*) to assist **II.** *vi* **1.** (*être utile: personne, conseil*) to be useful **2.** (*contribuer*) **~ à qc** to help towards sth; **la campagne publicitaire a aidé au succès du film** the advertising campaign contributed to the film's success; **le temps aidant** with time **III.** *vpr* **1.** (*utiliser*) **s'~ de qc** to use sth **2.** (*s'entraider*) **s'~** to help each other

aide-soignant(e) [ɛdswaɲɑ̃t] <aides-soignants> *m(f)* nursing auxiliary *Brit*, nurse's aide *Am*

aie [ɛ] *subj prés de* **avoir**

aïe [aj] *interj* **1.** (*douleur*) **~!** ouch! **2.** (*de surprise*) **~, les voilà!** oh no, here they come! **3.** (*d'ennui*) **~ ~ ~, qu'est-ce qu'on va devenir?** oh dear, what's going to happen to us?

aïeul(e) [ajœl] *m(f)* grandfather *m*, grandmother *f*

aigle [ɛgl] **I.** *mf* ZOOL eagle **II.** *f* MIL eagle

Aiglon [ɛglɔ̃] *m* HIST **l'~** Napoleon II

aiglon(ne) [ɛglɔ̃, ɔn] *m(f)* eaglet

aigre [ɛgʀ] *adj* **1.** (*acide: odeur, lait*) sour **2.** (*criard et perçant: son*) shrill **3.** (*acerbe: critique, ton*) sharp **4.** (*vif: froid, vent*) bitter

aigre-doux, -douce [ɛgʀədu, -dus] <aigres-doux> *adj* sweet and sour

aigrelet(te) [ɛgʀəlɛ, ɛt] *adj* **1.** (*un peu acide*) sourish **2.** (*aigu et fluet*) shrill

aigreur [ɛgʀœʀ] *f* **1.** (*acidité*) sourness **2.** (*saveur aigre*) acidity **3.** (*animosité: d'une remarque*) sharpness **4.** MED **avoir des ~s d'estomac** to have heartburn

aigri(e) [egʀi] *adj* embittered

aigrir [egʀiʀ] <8> **I.** *vt* **~ le caractère de qn** to sour sb's personality **II.** *vpr* **s'~ 1.** (*devenir acide: lait, vin*) to turn sour **2.** (*devenir amer: personne*) to become embittered

aigu(ë) [egy] **I.** *adj* **1.** (*pointu*) sharp; (*pointe*) pointed **2.** (*coupant*) cutting **3.** (*strident: voix, note*) high-pitched **4.** (*vif: intelligence, perception*) keen **5.** (*violent, pénétrant: douleur*) acute; **avoir un sens ~ de qc** to have a keen sense of sth **6.** (*à son paroxysme: crise*) severe **II.** *mpl* **les ~s** the high notes

aiguillage [egɥijaʒ] *m* **1.** CHEMDFER (*dispositif*) points *pl Brit*, switch *Am* **2.** CHEMDFER (*manœuvre*) shunting **3.** (*orientation*) **il y a une erreur d'~** there has been some confusion

aiguille [egɥij] *f* **1.** COUT, MED (*d'une seringue, de l'acupuncteur*) needle; **~ à coudre/tricoter** sewing/knitting needle **2.** (*petite tige pointue: d'une montre*) hand; (*d'une balance*) pointer; **~ de pin** pine needle **3.** GEO peak **4.** ARCHIT (*d'une église*) spire **5.** CHEMDFER (*aiguillage*) point *Brit*, switch *Am*

aiguiller [egɥije] <1> *vt* **1.** CHEMDFER to shunt **2.** (*orienter*) **mal ~ qn** to misguide sb; **~ qn vers/sur qc** to steer sb towards/onto sth

aiguilleur [egɥijœʀ] *m* **~ du ciel** air-traffic controller

aiguillon [egɥijɔ̃] *m* (*d'une abeille, guêpe*) sting

aiguiser [egize] <1> *vt* **1.** (*affiler: outil, couteau, intelligence*) to sharpen **2.** (*stimuler: appétit*) to whet; (*curiosité, désir*) to rouse; (*ouïe, toucher*) to stimulate

aïkido [aikido] *m* aikido

ail [aj] *m* garlic

aile [ɛl] *f* **1.** ANAT, AUTO, AVIAT, ARCHIT wing; (*d'un moulin*) sail **2.** MIL flank ▶ **voler de ses propres ~s** to stand on one's own two feet

ailé(e) [ele] *adj* winged

aileron [ɛlʀɔ̃] *m* **1.** ANAT, GASTR, NAUT (*de l'oiseau*) wing tip; (*du requin*) fin **2.** AVIAT (*d'un avion, aéronef*) aileron **3.** AUTO aerofoil

ailette [ɛlɛt] *f* **1.** (*empennage: d'un missile*) fin; (*d'une fléchette*) flight **2.** (*aube: d'une turbine, d'un ventilateur*) blade

ailier [elje] *m* winger; **~ droit** right winger

aille [aj] *subj prés de* **aller**

ailleurs [ajœʀ] *adv* (*autre part*) elsewhere; **regarder ~** to look somewhere else; **nulle part ~** nowhere else; **partout ~** everywhere else ▶ **il est ~!** he's miles away!; **va voir ~ si**

j'y suis! *inf* get lost!; **d'~ ...** moreover ...; **par ~** (*sinon*) otherwise; (*en outre*) moreover

ailloli [ajɔli] *m* aioli

aimable [ɛmabl] *adj* **1.** (*attentionné*) kind; **trop ~!** *iron* how very kind of you! **2.** (*agréable, souriant*) pleasant

aimablement [ɛmabləmɑ̃] *adv* **1.** (*avec politesse*) politely **2.** (*avec cordialité*) kindly

aimant [ɛmɑ̃] *m* magnet

aimanté(e) [ɛmɑ̃te] *adj* magnetic

aimanter [ɛmɑ̃te] <1> *vt* to magnetize

aimer [eme] <1> **I.** *vt* **1.** (*éprouver de l'amour*) to love; **je t'aime** I love you **2.** (*éprouver de l'affection*) **~ qc** to be fond of sth **3.** (*apprécier, prendre plaisir à, trouver bon: nourriture, boisson, nature*) to like; **je n'aime pas tellement ce vin** I'm not so keen on this wine **4.** (*désirer, souhaiter*) **j'aimerais** +*infin* I would like to +*infin* **5.** (*préférer*) **~ mieux le football que le tennis** to prefer football to tennis; **j'aimerais mieux du fromage** I'd prefer some cheese; **ah bon! j'aime autant cela!** ah! it's just as well!; **j'aime autant m'en aller** I'd rather leave; **j'aimerais mieux que tu viennes** I'd rather you came **II.** *vpr* **1.** (*d'amour*) **s'~** to love each other **2.** (*d'amitié*) **s'~** to like each other **3.** (*se plaire*) **s'~ dans une robe** to think one looks good in a dress **4.** (*faire l'amour*) **s'~** to make love

aine [ɛn] *f* ANAT groin

aîné(e) [ene] **I.** *adj* **1.** (*plus âgé de deux*) elder **2.** (*plus âgé de plusieurs*) eldest **II.** *m(f)* **1.** (*plus âgé de deux*) **l'~** the elder boy; **l'~e** the elder girl **2.** (*plus âgé parmi plusieurs*) **l'~** the eldest boy; **l'~e** the eldest girl; **elle est mon ~e de 3 ans** she is three years older than me **III.** *mpl Québec* **les ~s** (*le troisième âge*) senior citizens

ainsi [ɛ̃si] *adv* **1.** (*de cette manière*) this [*o* that] way; **c'est mieux ~** it's better this [*o* that] way; **et ~ de suite** and so on (and so forth); **pour ~ dire** (*presque*) virtually; (*si l'on peut le dire*) so to speak **2.** REL **~ soit-il!** amen; *fig* so be it! **3.** (*par exemple*) for instance ▶**~ donc vous avez perdu votre poste** so you have lost your job

air¹ [ɛʀ] *m* **1.** *sans pl* (*gaz*) air; **~ conditionné** air-conditioning; **en plein ~** (*concert*) open-air; (*piscine*) outdoor **2.** *sans pl* (*brise dans une pièce*) air **3.** *pl* (*ciel*) **voler dans les ~s** to fly through the skies **4.** (*haut*) **les mains en l'~!** hands up! **5.** (*atmosphère, ambiance*) **l'~ dans l'entreprise est irrespirable** the atmosphere in the company is unbearable; **avoir besoin de changer d'~** to need a change of scene ▶**être libre comme l'~** to be as free as air; **des paroles en l'~** idle words

air² [ɛʀ] *m* **1.** (*apparence*) air; **avoir l'~ distingué/d'une reine** to look distinguished/like a queen; **avoir l'~ (d'être) triste** to look sad; **le gâteau a l'~ délicieux** the cake looks delicious; **cette proposition m'a l'~ idiote** that suggestion seems stupid to me; **elle m'a l'~ d'être assez intelligente** she strikes me as being fairly intelligent; **il a l'~ de faire froid** it looks cold; **il est très fortuné sans en avoir l'~** he might not look it but he's very wealthy **2.** (*ressemblance*) **elle a un faux ~ de ma femme** she looks a little like my wife; **un faux ~ de modestie** an air of false modesty **3.** (*expression*) look; **d'un ~ décidé** in a resolute manner ▶**prendre de grands ~s** to put on airs; **de quoi aurais-je l'~?** I'd look a fool!

air³ [ɛʀ] *m* **1.** (*mélodie*) tune **2.** (*aria*) aria **3.** *péj* (*discours*) **jouer toujours le même ~** to come out with the same old story every time

airbag® [ɛʀbag] *m* air-bag

airbus® [ɛʀbys] *m* Airbus®

aire [ɛʀ] *f* **1.** (*emplacement*) *a.* MAT area; **~ de repos** rest area **2.** (*domaine*) **~ d'influence** sphere of influence **3.** (*nid*) eyrie *Brit,* aerie *Am*

airelle [ɛʀɛl] *f* **1.** (*à baies noires*) blueberry **2.** (*à baies rouges*) cranberry

aisance [ɛzɑ̃s] *f* **1.** (*richesse*) affluence; **ils vivent dans l'~** they are well-off **2.** (*facilité, naturel*) ease

aise [ɛz] *f* **se sentir à l'~** to feel at ease; **se mettre à l'~** (*s'installer confortablement*) to make oneself at home; (*enlever sa veste*) to make oneself comfortable ▶**prends tes ~s, surtout!** *iron* do make yourself comfortable!

aisé(e) [eze] *adj* **1.** *soutenu* (*facile*) easy **2.** (*fortuné*) wealthy **3.** (*naturel: style*) flowing

aisément [ezemɑ̃] *adv* (*sans peine*) easily

aisselle [ɛsɛl] *f* armpit

Aix-la-Chapelle [ɛkslaʃapɛl] Aachen

ajaccien(ne) [aʒaksjɛ̃, ɛn] *adj* from Ajaccio; (*accent, région*) Ajaccio; (*vie, restaurants*) in Ajaccio

Ajaccien(ne) [aʒaksjɛ̃, ɛn] *m(f)* person from Ajaccio; **les ~** (*à Ajaccio*) people in Ajaccio; (*ailleurs*) people from Ajaccio

ajonc [aʒɔ̃] *m* gorse bush

ajourner [aʒuʀne] <1> *vt* **1.** (*reporter*) to postpone; (*paiement*) to delay; (*débat, procès, séance, réunion*) to adjourn **2.** (*renvoyer: candidat, conscrit*) to refer

ajout [aʒu] *m* addition

ajouter [aʒute] <1> **I.** *vt* (*mettre en plus, additionner, dire en plus*) to add; **~ 3 à 4** to add 3 and 4 (together); **sans ~ un mot** without saying another word; **je n'ai rien à ~** I have nothing (further) to add; **ajoute deux assiettes!** lay two extra plates! **II.** *vpr* **s'~ à qc** to add to sth

ajusté(e) [aʒyste] *adj* (*vêtement*) tailored

ajustement [aʒystəmɑ̃] *m* **1.** (*retouche: d'un texte*) editing + *vb sing;* (*d'une jupe*) adjustment **2.** TECH fit **3.** ECON realignment; **~ des prix** price adjustment

ajuster [aʒyste] <1> **I.** *vt* **1.** (*régler: vêtement*) to alter; (*ceinture de sécurité*) to adjust **2.** (*adapter*) **~ une soupape à qc** to fit a valve on to sth **3.** (*viser*) **~ un sanglier** to take aim at a wild boar **II.** *vpr* **1.** (*s'emboîter*) **s'~ sur qc** to fit on to sth **2.** (*s'adapter*) **s'~** to be adjustable

alaise *v.* **alèse**

alambic [alɑ̃bik] *m* still

alangui(e) [alɑ̃gi] *adj* (*langoureux*) **des regards ~s** languid looks

alarmant(e) [alaʀmɑ̃, ɑ̃t] *adj* alarming

alarme [alaʀm] *f* **1.** (*signal, dispositif*) alarm; **donner** [*o* **sonner**] **l'~** to raise the alarm; **c'est une fausse ~** it's a false alarm **2.** (*trouble, agitation*) anxiety; **à la première ~** at the first sign of danger

alarmer [alaʀme] <1> **I.** *vt* (*personne*) to alarm; (*bruit*) to startle **II.** *vpr* **s'~ de qc** to become alarmed about sth

alarmiste [alaʀmist] *adj* alarmist

albanais [albanɛ] *m* Albanian; *v. a.* **français**

albanais(e) [albanɛ, ɛz] *adj* Albanian

Albanais(e) [albanɛ, ɛz] *m(f)* Albanian

Albanie [albani] *f* **l'~** Albania

albâtre [albɑtʀ] *m* (*matière*) alabaster; **d'** [*o* **en**] **~** alabaster

albatros [albatʀos] *m* albatross

albinos [albinos] *mf* albino

album [albɔm] *m* album; (*volume illustré*) illustrated book

alchimie [alʃimi] *f* alchemy

alchimiste [alʃimist] *mf* alchemist

alcool [alkɔl] *m* **1.** CHIM alcohol; **~ à 90°** ≈ surgical spirit; **~ à brûler** methylated spirits **2.** (*spiritueux*) spirit; **tenir l'~** to be able to hold one's drink

alcoolémie [alkɔlemi] *f* **taux d'~** (blood) alcohol level

alcoolique [alkɔlik] *adj, mf* alcoholic

alcoolisé(e) [alkɔlize] *adj* alcoholic

Alcootest® [alkɔtɛst] *m* **1.** (*appareil*) Breathalyser® **2.** (*test*) breath test; **faire subir une épreuve d'~ à qn** to breathalyse sb

aléas [alea] *mpl* hazard; **les ~ du métier** the risks of the job

aléatoire [aleatwaʀ] *adj* **1.** (*incertain*) uncertain; (*événement*) unpredictable; (*entreprise*) risky **2.** MAT, INFOR random **3.** JUR (*contrat*) aleatory

alémanique [alemanik] **I.** *adj* Alemannic; **la Suisse ~** German-speaking Switzerland **II.** *m* Alemannic; *v. a.* **français**

alentours [alɑ̃tuʀ] *mpl* **1.** (*abords*) surroundings; **les ~ de la ville** the area around the town; **dans les ~** in the vicinity **2.** *fig* **aux ~ de minuit** around midnight; **aux ~ de 500 gens** about 500 people

alerte [alɛʀt] **I.** *adj* alert; (*style*) lively; (*démarche*) brisk **II.** *f* **1.** (*alarme*) alert; **~ à la bombe** bomb scare; **donner l'~** to raise the alarm; **être en** (**état d'**)**~** to be on the alert **2.** (*signes inquiétants*) warning signs *pl*

alerter [alɛʀte] <1> *vt* **1.** (*donner l'alarme*) to alert **2.** (*informer*) to notify **3.** (*prévenir*) to warn

alèse [alɛz] *f* drawsheet

alevin [alvɛ̃] *m* young fish

alexandrin [alɛksɑ̃dʀɛ̃] *m* alexandrine

algèbre [alʒɛbʀ] *f* algebra

algébrique [alʒebʀik] *adj* algebraic

Alger [alʒe] Algiers

Algérie [alʒeʀi] *f* **l'~** Algeria

algérien [alʒeʀjɛ̃] *m* Algerian; *v. a.* **français**

algérien(ne) [alʒeʀjɛ̃, jɛn] *adj* Algerian

Algérien(ne) [alʒeʀjɛ̃, jɛn] *m(f)* Algerian

algérois(e) [alʒeʀwa, waz] *adj* of Algiers; *v. a.* **ajaccien**

Algérois(e) [alʒeʀwa, waz] *m(f)* person from Algiers; *v. a.* **Ajaccien**

algue [alg] *f* **les ~s** algae; (*sur la plage*) seaweed + *vb sing*

alias [aljas] *adv* alias

alibi [alibi] *m* **1.** JUR alibi **2.** (*prétexte*) excuse

aliénation [aljenasjɔ̃] *f* **1.** PHILOS alienation **2.** (*perte*) loss **3.** JUR transfer of property **4.** MED **~ mentale** insanity

aliéné(e) [aljene] *m(f)* insane person

aligné(e) [aliɲe] *adj* lined up

alignement [aliɲ(ə)mɑ̃] *m* **1.** (*action d'aligner, rangée*) alignment **2.** ARCHIT building line **3.** (*mise en conformité*) alignment; **~ monétaire** monetary alignment

aligner [aliɲe] <1> **I.** *vt* **1.** (*mettre en ligne*) **~ des soldats** to line up soldiers; **~ des chiffres** to align figures **2.** *péj* (*énoncer mécaniquement*) **~ des mots** to string words together **3.** (*rendre conforme*) **~ une monnaie sur qc** to bring a currency into alignment with sth; **~ une politique sur qc** to bring a policy into line with sth **II.** *vpr* **1.** (*se mettre en ligne*) **s'~** to line up; (*soldats*) to fall into line **2.** (*être en ligne*) to be in a line **3.** (*se conformer*) **s'~ sur qn/qc** to fall into line with sb/sth **4.** POL **s'~ sur qn/qc** to align oneself with sb/sth

aliment [alimɑ̃] *m* **1.** (*pour une personne*) food; **des ~s** food + *vb sing* **2.** (*pour un animal d'élevage*) feed

alimentaire [alimɑ̃tɛʀ] *adj* **industrie ~** food industry; **régime ~** diet

alimentation [alimɑ̃tasjɔ̃] *f* **1.** (*action: d'une personne, d'un animal*) feeding **2.** (*produits pour une personne, un animal*) diet **3.** (*commerce*) food retailing; **magasin d'~** grocery **4.** (*industrie*) food industry; **~ animale** animal nutrition **5.** (*approvisionnement*) **l'~ d'une usine en charbon** the supply of coal to a factory **6.** INFOR **~ papier** paper feed

alimenter [alimɑ̃te] <1> **I.** *vt* **1.** (*nourrir: personne, animal*) to feed **2.** (*approvisionner*) **~ une ville en eau** to supply water to a town; **~ un compte** to pay money into an account **3.** (*entretenir*) **~ la conversation** (*personne*) to keep the conversation going; (*événement*) to fuel conversation **II.** *vpr* **s'~** **1.** (*bébé*) to feed oneself **2.** (*manger*) to eat

alinéa [alinea] *m* **1.** (*au début d'un paragraphe*) indent **2.** (*paragraphe*) paragraph

aliter [alite] <1> *vt* to confine to bed; **être**

alité to be bedridden

allaitement [alɛtmɑ̃] *m* ~ **maternel** (*d'un bébé*) breast-feeding; (*d'un animal*) suckling; ~ **au biberon** bottle-feeding

allaiter [alete] <1> *vt* **1.** (*pour un bébé*) to breast-feed **2.** (*pour un animal*) to suckle

alléchant(e) [aleʃɑ̃, ɑ̃t] *adj* (*odeur, plat*) mouth-watering; (*proposition, promesse*) tempting

allécher [aleʃe] <5> *vt* **1.** (*mettre en appétit*) ~ **qn** to give sb an appetite **2.** (*tenter en faisant miroiter qc: personne*) to entice

allée [ale] *f* **1.** (*chemin dans une forêt, un jardin*) path **2.** (*rue*) road **3.** (*passage*) ~ **centrale** aisle **4.** *Suisse* (*couloir d'entrée d'un immeuble*) hall ►~**s et venues** comings and goings

allégé(e) [aleʒe] *adj* low-fat; **produits ~s** low-calorie products

allégement, allègement [alɛʒmɑ̃] *m* (*des charges*) reduction; ~ **fiscal** tax relief + *vb sing*

alléger [aleʒe] <2aé 5> *vt* **1.** (*rendre moins lourd*) to lighten **2.** (*réduire: impôts, dettes*) to reduce; (*programmes scolaires*) to cut down

allègre [a(l)lɛɡʀ] *adj* cheerful; (*musique, démarche*) lively

allégresse [a(l)legʀɛs] *f* joy

Allemagne [almaɲ] *f* **l'~** Germany; **l'~ de l'Est/de l'Ouest** HIST East/West Germany; **la République fédérale d'~** the Federal Republic of Germany; **la réunification des deux ~s** the reunification of Germany

allemand [almɑ̃] *m* German; *v. a.* **français**

allemand(e) [almɑ̃, ɑ̃d] *adj* German

Allemand(e) [almɑ̃, ɑ̃d] *m(f)* German

aller[1] [ale] *irr* **I.** *vi être* **1.** (*se déplacer à pied*) to go; **on a sonné; peux-tu y ~?** there is someone at the door; can you go?; **y ~ en courant/en nageant** to run/swim there; **~ et venir** (*de long en large*) to pace up and down; (*entre deux destinations*) to come and go; **pour ~ à l'hôtel de ville?** how do I get to the town hall? **2.** (*se déplacer à cheval*) to ride; (*se déplacer à vélo*) to cycle **3.** (*pour faire quelque chose*) ~ **à la boulangerie** to go to the bakery; ~ **se coucher/se promener** to go to bed/for a walk; ~ **voir qn** to go and see sb; **je vais voir ce qui se passe** I'm going to see what's going on; ~ **chercher les enfants à l'école** to go and pick up the children from school **4.** (*rouler*) to drive **5.** (*voler*) **j'irai en avion** I'll fly **6.** (*être acheminé*) ~ **à Paris** to go to Paris **7.** (*mener*) **cette rue va vers la plage** this road leads to the beach **8.** (*s'étendre, atteindre*) ~ **de ... à ...** (*étendue*) to stretch from... to...; ~ **jusqu'à la mer** to reach the sea; **mon congé maternité va jusqu'à la fin de l'année** my maternity leave runs until the end of the year **9.** (*avoir sa place quelque part*) ~ **à la cave** to belong in the cellar **10.** (*être conçu pour*) **ce plat ne va pas au micro-ondes** this dish is not suitable for the microwave **11.** (*oser*) ~ **jusqu'à** +*infin* to go so far as to +*infin* **12.** (*progresser*) ~ **vite** (*personne, chose*) to go fast; (*nouvelles*) to travel fast **13.** (*se porter*) **il va bien/mal/mieux** he's well/not well/better; **comment ça va/vas-tu/allez-vous?** how are you?; **comment va la santé?** *inf* how are you keeping?; **ça va pas(, la tête)!** *inf* are you mad! **14.** (*fonctionner, évoluer*) **ça va les études ?** how are your studies?; **tout va bien/mal** everything's going well/wrong; **quelque chose ne va pas** something's wrong **15.** (*connaître bientôt*) ~ **au-devant de difficultés** to let oneself in for problems **16.** (*prévenir*) ~ **au-devant des désirs de qn** to anticipate sb's wishes **17.** (*pour donner un âge approximatif*) **il va sur la quarantaine** he's approaching forty **18.** (*convenir à qn*) **ça va** that's fine; **ça ira** (*suffire*) that'll do; (*faire l'affaire*) that'll be fine; **ça peut** ~ it's not too bad; ~ **à qn** to suit sb; **ça (te) va?** is that all right with you?; **ça me va!** that's fine by me! **19.** (*être seyant*) ~ **bien à qn** to suit sb; **cette robe vous va mal** this dress doesn't suit you **20.** (*être coordonné, assorti*) ~ **avec qc** to go with sth; ~ **ensemble** to go together; ~ **bien avec qc** to go well with sth **21.** (*convenir, être adapté à*) **cet outil va en toute circonstance** this tool can be used in all situations **22.** (*se dérouler*) **les choses vont très vite** things are moving very quickly; **plus ça va, plus j'aime le théâtre** I love the theatre more and more **23.** (*pour commencer, démarrer*) **on y va?** (*pour initier un départ*) shall we go?; (*pour initier un commencement*) shall we make a start? **24.** *impers* (*être en jeu*) **il y va de notre vie** our lives are at stake **25.** (*ne rien faire*) **se laisser** ~ (*se négliger*) to let oneself go; (*abandonner, se décontracter*) to let go **26.** (*être*) **il en va de même pour toi** the same applies to you ►**cela/il va sans dire que qn a bien fait qc** needless to say sb has done sth; **cela va de soi** it goes without saying; **ça va (comme ça)!** *inf* OK; **où allons-nous?** what's the world coming to! **II.** *aux être* **1.** (*pour exprimer le futur proche*) ~ +*infin* to be going to +*infin* **2.** (*pour exprimer la crainte*) **et s'il allait tout raconter?** what if he told everything?; **ne va pas croire/imaginer que qn a fait qc** don't go believing/thinking that sb has done sth **III.** *vpr être* **s'en ~ 1.** (*partir à pied*) to go away; (*en voiture, à vélo, en bateau, en avion*) to drive/cycle/sail away/fly away; **s'en ~ en vacances/à l'étranger** to go on holiday/abroad **2.** (*disparaître: années*) to pass; (*forces*) to fail; (*cicatrice, tache, fatigue*) to fade (away) **IV.** *interj* **1.** (*invitation à agir*) **vas-y/allons-y/allez-y!** (*en route!*) let's go!; (*au travail!, pour encourager*) come on!; **vas-y/allez-y!, allons!** go on!; **allons debout!** come on, on your feet!; **allez, presse-toi un peu!** come on, hurry up!; **allez, allez, circulez!** come on, move along now!; **allez,**

au revoir! right, bye then!; **allons/allez donc!** *iron, inf* (*c'est évident!*) oh come on!; (*vraiment?*) no, really? **2.** (*voyons!*) **un peu de calme, allons!** come on, let's have a bit of quiet! **3.** (*pour exprimer la résignation, la conciliation*) **je le sais bien, va!** I know!; **allez, allez, ça ne sera rien!** come on, it won't be anything serious!; **va/allez savoir!** who knows! **4.** (*non!?*) **allez!** *inf* you're joking! **5.** (*d'accord!*) **alors, va pour le ciné!** the cinema it is then!

aller² [ale] *m* **1.** (*trajet*) outward journey; **après deux ~s et retours** after two return trips; **à l'~ on est passé par Amsterdam** on the flight out we went via Amsterdam; **à l'~ on a pris une autoroute à péage** on the way there we took a toll motorway *Brit,* on the way there we took a turnpike *Am* **2.** (*billet*) ~ (**simple**) single ticket *Brit,* one-way ticket *Am;* **un ~ pour Grenoble, s'il vous plaît** a single for Grenoble, please *Brit,* a one-way ticket to Grenoble, please *Am;* ~ **retour** return ticket **3.** *inf* (*gifle*) **un ~ et retour** a slap

allergie [alɛʀʒi] *f* allergy

allergique [alɛʀʒik] *adj* MED allergic; **être ~ aux pollens/au travail** to be allergic to pollen/to work

alliage [aljaʒ] *m* alloy

alliance [aljɑ̃s] *f* **1.** (*engagement mutuel*) alliance; REL covenant; **faire ~** to enter into an alliance **2.** (*union*) **~ entre deux personnes** marriage between two people; **par ~** by marriage; **être (des) parents par ~** to be related by marriage **3.** (*combinaison*) combination **4.** (*anneau*) wedding ring

allié(e) [alje] **I.** *adj* **1.** POL allied **2.** JUR **être ~ à qn** to be related to sb by marriage **II.** *m(f)* **1.** POL ally **2.** (*ami*) supporter

allier [alje] <1> **I.** *vt* **1.** (*associer*) **~ la grâce à la force** to combine grace and power **2.** CHIM **~ l'or à l'argent** to alloy gold with silver **3.** (*par un mariage: familles*) to unite **II.** *vpr* **1.** POL **s'~** to become allies **2.** POL (*conclure une alliance avec*) **s'~ à un pays** to form an alliance with a country **3.** (*s'associer*) **la grâce s'allie à la force** grace combines with power

Alliés [alje] *mpl* HIST **les ~** the Allies

alligator [aligatɔʀ] *m* alligator

allô [alo] *interj* hello

allocation [alɔkasjɔ̃] *f* (*somme*) allowance; **~ chômage/logement** unemployment/housing benefit; **~ vieillesse** old-age pension; **~s familiales** child benefit

allocution [alɔkysjɔ̃] *f* speech

allongement [alɔ̃ʒmɑ̃] *m* (*d'un muscle*) stretching; (*des métaux*) elongation; (*d'une voyelle*) lengthening; (*d'un réseau de transport*) extension

allonger [alɔ̃ʒe] <2a> **I.** *vi* (*devenir plus long*) **les jours allongent à partir du 21 décembre** the days start to get longer on December 21 **II.** *vt* **1.** (*rendre plus long*) to lengthen **2.** (*étendre: bras*) to stretch out; **s'~ le cou** to stretch one's neck **3.** (*coucher: blessé*) to lay down; **être allongé** to be lying down **4.** (*diluer: sauce*) to thin **III.** *vpr* **s'~** **1.** (*devenir plus long: personne*) to grow taller; (*ombres*) to lengthen **2.** (*se prolonger: jours*) to get longer; (*durée moyenne de la vie*) to increase **3.** (*s'éterniser: discours*) to drag on **4.** (*s'étendre: route*) to stretch out **5.** (*se coucher*) to lie down

allouer [alwe] <1> *vt* (*attribuer*) to allocate

allumage [alymaʒ] *m* **1.** lighting **2.** AUTO ignition

allume-cigare [alymsigaʀ] <allume-cigares> *m* cigar lighter **allume-gaz** [alymgaz] *m inv* gas lighter

allumer [alyme] <1> **I.** *vt* **1.** (*faire brûler, mettre en marche, faire de la lumière: feu, cigarette, four, poêle*) to light; **être allumé** (*feu, cigarette*) to be lit **2.** (*faire de la lumière: lampe, projecteur*) to switch on; **~ le couloir** to turn the light on in the corridor; **la cuisine est allumée** the light is on in the kitchen **II.** *vpr* **s'~** **1.** (*s'enflammer: bûche, bois, papier*) to catch fire; (*briquet*) to light **2.** (*devenir lumineux*) **sa fenêtre vient de s'~** a light has just come on at her window; **ses yeux se sont allumés** his eyes lit up **3.** (*se mettre en marche automatiquement*) **s'~** (*appareil*) to turn itself on **4.** (*être mis en marche*) **s'~** (*moteur*) to start **5.** (*prendre naissance*) **s'~** (*sentiment*) to be aroused

allumette [alymɛt] *f* match; **gratter une ~** to strike a match

allumeuse [alymøz] *f péj, inf* tease

allure [alyʀ] *f* **1.** *sans pl* (*vitesse*) speed; **à toute ~** at full speed **2.** *sans pl* (*apparence*) look; **avoir de l'~** to have style; **avoir une drôle d'~** to look odd **3.** *pl* (*airs*) ways; **avoir des ~ d'enfant** to behave like a child

allusion [a(l)lyzjɔ̃] *f* (*sous-entendu*) allusion; **faire ~ à qn/qc** to allude to sb/sth

alluvions [a(l)lyvjɔ̃] *fpl* alluvial deposits

almanach [almana] *m* almanac

alors [alɔʀ] **I.** *adv* **1.** (*à ce moment-là*) then; **jusqu'~** until then **2.** (*par conséquent*) so; **ma voiture était en panne, ~ j'ai pris l'autobus** my car had broken down, so I took the bus **3.** (*dans ce cas*) so; **~, je comprends!** in that case I understand!; **~, qu'est-ce qu'on fait?** so what are we going to do? **4.** *inf* (*impatience, indignation*) **~, tu viens?** so are you coming or not? ►**ça ~!** my goodness!; **et ~?** (*suspense*) and then what happened?; (*perplexité*) so what?; **~ là, je ne sais pas!** well I really don't know about that!; **non, mais ~!** honestly! **II.** *conj* **~ que ...** +*indic* **1.** (*pendant que*) **il s'est mis à pleuvoir ~ que nous étions encore en train de manger** it started to rain while we were still eating **2.** (*tandis que*) **il part en Espagne ~ que je reste à Paris** he's going to Spain while I stay in Paris **3.** (*bien que*) **elle a allumé une cigarette ~ que c'était interdit de fumer** she lit a cigarette even though smoking was forbidden

alouette [alwɛt] *f* lark

alourdir [aluʀdiʀ] <8> **I.** *vt* **1.** (*rendre plus lourd*) ~ **qc** to weigh sth down; **alourdi par la pluie** heavy with rain **2.** (*augmenter: impôts, charges*) to increase **II.** *vpr* **s'**~ (*paupières*) to droop; (*démarche*) to slow down; (*taille*) to get thicker

alpage [alpaʒ] *m* mountain pasture

Alpes [alp] *fpl* **les** ~ the Alps

alphabet [alfabɛ] *m* alphabet

alphabétique [alfabetik] *adj* alphabetical; **par ordre** ~ in alphabetical order

alphabétisation [alfabetizasjɔ̃] *f* elimination of illiteracy

alphabétiser [alfabetize] <1> *vt* (*personne*) ~ **qn** to teach sb to read and write

alpin(e) [alpɛ̃, in] *adj* **1.** GEO alpine **2.** (*relatif à la montagne: plante*) mountain; (*chalet*) alpine **3.** (*relatif à l'alpinisme: club*) mountaineering

alpinisme [alpinism] *m* mountaineering

alpiniste [alpinist] *mf* mountaineer

Alsace [alzas] *f* **l'**~ Alsace

alsacien [alzasjɛ̃] *m* Alsatian; *v. a.* **français**

alsacien(ne) [alzasjɛ̃, jɛn] *adj* Alsatian

Alsacien(ne) [alzasjɛ̃, jɛn] *m(f)* Alsatian

altercation [altɛʀkasjɔ̃] *f* dispute

altérer [alteʀe] <5> **I.** *vt* **1.** (*détériorer*) to spoil; (*couleur*) to alter; (*qualité*) to lower; (*caractère, métal*) to affect **2.** (*décomposer: visage, traits*) to distort; (*voix*) to strain **3.** (*falsifier*) to distort **II.** *vpr* **s'**~ **1.** (*se détériorer: qualité*) to deteriorate; (*aliment*) to go off; (*vin*) to become spoiled; (*relations*) to break down; (*couleur, matière*) to change; (*sentiment*) to deteriorate; (*caractère*) to change for the worse **2.** (*se décomposer: visage, traits*) to be distorted; (*voix*) to be broken

alternance [altɛʀnɑ̃s] *f* **1.** (*succession*) alternation; **faire qc en** ~ **avec qn** to take turns doing sth **2.** POL change-over

alternateur [altɛʀnatœʀ] *m* alternator

alternatif, **-ive** [altɛʀnatif, -iv] *adj* **1.** TECH **mouvement** ~ alternating movement **2.** ELEC **courant** ~ alternating current **3.** (*qui offre un choix: solution*) alternative

alternative [altɛʀnativ] *f* alternative

alternativement [altɛʀnativmɑ̃] *adv* alternately

alterner [altɛʀne] <1> **I.** *vi* to alternate **II.** *vt* **1.** to alternate **2.** AGR ~ **les cultures** to rotate crops

Altesse [altɛs] *f* **Son** ~ **Royale** (*prince*) His Royal Highness; (*princesse*) Her Royal Highness; **votre** ~ *form* your Highness

altier, **-ière** [altje, jɛʀ] *adj* haughty

altiste [altist] *mf* violist

altitude [altityd] *f* **1.** GEO altitude; **village d'**~ mountain village; **l'**~ **de ce mont est de 400 m** this mountain is 400m high; **avoir une faible** ~ (*ville*) to be low-lying; **en** ~ (*en montagne*) high up; METEO at high altitude **2.** AVIAT **vol à basse** ~ low-level flying; **voler à basse/haute** ~ to fly at low/high altitude; **prendre de l'**~ to climb

alto [alto] **I.** *m* **1.** (*instrument*) viola **2.** (*musicien*) violist **II.** *f* (*voix, partie*) alto **III.** *app inv* alto

altruiste [altʀɥist] **I.** *adj* altruistic **II.** *mf* altruist

alu *inf*, **aluminium** [alyminjɔm] *m* aluminium *Brit*, aluminum *Am*

alunir [alyniʀ] <8> *vi* to land (on the moon)

alunissage [alynisaʒ] *m* moon landing

AM [ɑɛm] *abr de* **ante meridiem** a.m.

amabilité [amabilite] *f* **1.** (*gentillesse*) kindness; **ayez l'**~ **de m'apporter un café** be so kind as to bring me a coffee **2.** *pl* (*politesses*) polite remarks

amadouer [amadwe] <1> *vt* **1.** (*gagner à ses fins*) to coax; ~ **qn pour qu'il fasse qc** (*subj*) to coax sb into doing sth; **ne pas être facile à** ~ to not be easily won round **2.** (*apaiser*) to soothe **3.** (*apprivoiser*) to tame

amaigrir [amegʀiʀ] <8> **I.** *vt* ~ **qc** to make sth thinner; **ses soucis l'ont beaucoup amaigri** his worries have left him a lot thinner **II.** *vpr* **s'**~ to lose weight

amaigrissant(e) [amegʀisɑ̃, ɑ̃t] *adj* slimming

amaigrissement [amegʀismɑ̃] *m* (*d'une personne*) weight loss; (*du visage*) thinness

amalgame [amalgam] *m* **1.** (*alliage de métaux, matière obturatrice*) *a.* MED amalgam **2.** (*mélange: de matériaux*) mixture; **un** ~ **d'idées** a hotchpotch of ideas

amande [amɑ̃d] *f* **1.** (*fruit*) almond; **en** ~ almond-shaped **2.** (*graine*) kernel

amandier [amɑ̃dje] *m* almond tree

amanite [amanit] *f* Amanita; ~ **phalloïde** death cap; ~ **tue-mouche(s)** fly agaric

amant [amɑ̃] *m* lover; **les** ~**s** lovers

amarre [amaʀ] *f* mooring line; **larguez les** ~**s!** slip the moorings!

amas [amɑ] *m* (*de pierres*) heap; (*de papiers*) pile; (*de souvenirs*) mass

amasser [amɑse] <1> **I.** *vt* (*objets, fortune*) to amass; (*preuves, données*) to gather together **II.** *vi* **1.** (*thésauriser*) to hoard money **2.** (*accumuler*) to accumulate **III.** *vpr* **s'**~ (*personnes*) to gather; (*problèmes*) to accumulate

amateur, **-trice** [amatœʀ, -tʀis] **I.** *m, f* **1.** (*opp: professionnel*) amateur; **en** ~ as an amateur **2.** *sans art* (*connaisseur*) ~ **d'art** art lover; **être** ~ **de bons vins** to be a connoisseur of fine wines; **être** ~ **de films** to be a keen film-goer; **je m'intéresse au cinéma en** ~ I have an amateur interest in the cinema **3.** *péj* (*dilettante*) **je ne le fais qu'en** ~ I only do it as a mere amateur **4.** (*acheteur*) **je ne suis pas** ~ *inf* I don't really go in for that sort of thing **II.** *adj pas de forme féminine* amateur

amateurisme [amatœʀism] *m* **1.** SPORT amateurism **2.** *péj* (*en art, dans le travail*) amateurishness

amazone [amazon] *f* **1.**(*cavalière*) horsewoman; **monter en** ~ to ride side-saddle **2.**(*guerrière*) Amazon

Amazone [amazon] *f* Amazon

ambassade [ɑ̃basad] *f* (*institution, bâtiment*) embassy; **l'~ de France** the French embassy

ambassadeur, -drice [ɑ̃basadœʀ, -dʀis] *m, f* (*diplomate, représentant*) ambassador

ambiance [ɑ̃bjɑ̃s] *f* **1.**(*climat*) atmosphere; **d'~** (*lumière*) subdued; (*musique*) mood **2.**(*gaieté*) **la musique met de l'~** music livens things up

ambiant(e) [ɑ̃bjɑ̃, jɑ̃t] *adj* (*température*) ambient; (*idées, influences*) prevailing

ambigu(ë) [ɑ̃bigy] *adj* ambiguous

ambiguïté [ɑ̃bigɥite] *f* ambiguity; **sans ~** (*comportement*) unambiguous; (*parler*) unambiguously

ambitieux, -euse [ɑ̃bisjø, -jøz] **I.** *adj* ambitious **II.** *m, f* man , woman *m, f* with ambition

ambition [ɑ̃bisjɔ̃] *f* **1.**(*désir de réussite*) ambition **2.**(*prétention*) aspiration

ambitionner [ɑ̃bisjɔne] <1> *vt* **1.**(*convoiter: poste, prix, titre*) to strive after; (*couronne*) to seek **2.**(*souhaiter*) ~ **de** +*infin* to have an ambition to +*infin*

ambivalent(e) [ɑ̃bivalɑ̃, ɑ̃t] *adj* ambivalent

ambre [ɑ̃bʀ] *m* **1.**(*résine*) ~ (**jaune**) amber; **avoir une couleur d'~** to be amber coloured *Brit,* to be amber colored *Am* **2.**(*substance parfumée*) ~ **gris** ambergris

ambré(e) [ɑ̃bʀe] *adj* **1.**(*jaune, doré*) amber **2.**(*parfumé*) amber-scented

ambulance [ɑ̃bylɑ̃s] *f* ambulance

ambulancier, -ière [ɑ̃bylɑ̃sje, -jɛʀ] *m, f* **1.**(*conducteur*) ambulance driver **2.**(*infirmier*) ambulance man, woman *m, f*

ambulant(e) [ɑ̃bylɑ̃, ɑ̃t] *adj* (*marchand, cirque*) travelling; (*musicien*) strolling

âme [ɑm] *f* **1.** *a.* REL soul; **mettre toute son ~ à faire qc** to put one's heart and soul into sth **2.**(*personne*) **il n'y a pas ~ qui vive** there isn't a living soul **3.**(*qualité morale*) soul **4.** PSYCH (*esprit, conscience*) soul; **chercher l'~ sœur** to look for one's soul mate ►**vendre son ~ au diable** to sell one's soul to the devil; **être violoniste dans l'~** to be a born violinist

amélioration [ameljɔʀasjɔ̃] *f* **1.** *pl* (*travaux*) **apporter des ~s à une maison** to carry out improvements on a house **2.**(*progrès*) improvement; (*de la conjonture*) upturn **3.** METEO improvement

améliorer [ameljɔʀe] <1> **I.** *vt* (*rendre meilleur*) *a.* ARCHIT (*conditions de travail, vie*) to improve; (*qualité, production, budget*) to increase **II.** *vpr* **s'~** to improve; (*temps*) to get better; **tu ne t'améliores pas!** *iron* you don't change, do you!

amen [amɛn] *interj* amen

aménagement [amenaʒmɑ̃] *m* **1.**(*équipement*) fitting out **2.** ARCHIT (*modification*) conversion; (*installation*) setting up; (*construction*) construction **3.**(*création: d'un quartier, d'une usine*) construction; (*d'un jardin*) laying out **4.**(*adaptation*) improvement **5.**(*réorganisation*) ~ **du temps de travail** (*réforme*) restructuring of working hours; (*gestion*) flexible time management **6.** ADMIN development; ~ **du territoire** town and country planning **7.** POL (*d'un texte de loi, décret*) redrafting

aménager [amenaʒe] <2a> *vt* **1.**(*équiper: pièce*) to arrange; (*étagère, placard*) to build **2.**(*modifier par des travaux*) ~ **un grenier en atelier** to convert a loft into a studio **3.**(*créer: parc, quartier*) to lay out **4.**(*adapter: finances, horaire*) to arrange **5.** ADMIN (*ville*) to develop **6.** POL (*texte de loi, décret*) to redraft

amende [amɑ̃d] *f* (*p-v*) parking ticket; (*à payer*) fine ►**mettre qn à l'~** to penalize sb

amener [am(ə)ne] <4> **I.** *vt* **1.** *inf* (*apporter, mener*) to bring; ~ **qn chez qn** to bring sb to sb's house; **qu'est-ce qui t'amène ici?** what brings you here? **2.**(*acheminer: gaz, liquide*) to transport **3.**(*provoquer*) to bring about **4.**(*entraîner*) **son métier l'amène à voyager** his job involves travelling **5.**(*introduire: thème, citation, plaisanterie*) to introduce **6.**(*diriger*) ~ **la conversation sur un sujet** to lead the conversation on to a subject **7.**(*convaincre*) ~ **qn à** +*infin* to lead sb to +*infin* **8.**(*inciter*) **il m'a amené à démissionner** he talked me into resigning **II.** *vpr inf* (*se rappliquer*) **s'~** to show up; **amène-toi!** come on!

amenuiser [amənɥize] <1> **I.** *vt* **1.**(*amincir*) to thin down **2.**(*réduire: chances, espoir*) to fade **II.** *vpr* **s'~** (*espoir, forces, valeur*) to dwindle; (*ressources*) to run low; (*temps*) to run out

amer, -ère [amɛʀ] *adj* bitter

amèrement [amɛʀmɑ̃] *adv* bitterly

américain [ameʀikɛ̃] *m* American (English); *v. a.* **français**

américain(e) [ameʀikɛ̃, ɛn] *adj* American

Américain(e) [ameʀikɛ̃, ɛn] *m(f)* American

américanisation [ameʀikanizasjɔ̃] *f* Americanization

américaniser [ameʀikanize] <1> **I.** *vt* to americanize **II.** *vpr* **s'~** to become americanized

américanisme [ameʀikanism] *m* **1.**(*emprunt*) americanism **2.**(*études*) American studies *pl*

amérindien(ne) [ameʀɛ̃djɛ̃, ɛn] *adj* Amerindian

Amérindien(ne) [ameʀɛ̃djɛ̃, ɛn] *m(f)* Amerindian

Amérique [ameʀik] *f* **l'~** America; **l'~ centrale/latine/du Nord/du Sud** Central/Latin/North/South America

amerrir [ameʀiʀ] <8> *vi* to land (in the sea)

amerrissage [ameʀisaʒ] *m* sea landing

amertume [amɛʀtym] *f* bitterness

améthyste [ametist] *f, app inv* amethyst

ameublement [amœbləmɑ̃] *m* **1.**(*meubles*) furniture **2.**(*action de meubler*) furnishing

ameuter [amøte] <1> *vt* **1.** (*alerter*) to bring out; **tais-toi, tu vas ~ toute la rue** shut up, you'll have the whole street out **2.** (*soulever*) **~ la foule contre qn/qc** to stir up the crowd against sb/sth

ami(**e**) [ami] **I.** *m(f)* **1.** (*opp: ennemi*) friend; **~ des bêtes** animal lover; **mon cher ~** my dear friend; **mes chers ~s!** ladies and gentlemen!; **se faire des ~s** to make friends **2.** (*amant*) boyfriend; **petite ~e** girlfriend **II.** *adj* (*regard, parole*) friendly; **pays ~** friendly country; **être très ~ avec qn** to be very good friends with sb

amiable [amjabl] *adj* (*décision, constat*) amicable; **s'arranger à l'~** to reach an amicable settlement

amiante [amjɑ̃t] *m* asbestos

amical(**e**) [amikal, o] <-aux> *adj a.* SPORT friendly

amicale [amikal] *f* (*association*) club

amicalement [amikalmɑ̃] *adv* **1.** in a friendly manner; (*recevoir*) warmly **2.** (*formule de fin de lettre*) **bien ~** yours ever

amidon [amidɔ̃] *m* starch

amiénois(**e**) [amjenwa, waz] *adj* of Amiens; *v. a.* **ajaccien**

Amiénois(**e**) [amjenwa, waz] *m(f)* person from Amiens; *v. a.* **Ajaccien**

amincir [amɛ̃siʀ] <8> **I.** *vt* **~ qn/qc** to make sb/sth look thinner **II.** *vi inf* to lose weight **III.** *vpr* **s'~** (*personne*) to get slimmer; (*tissu, couche*) to get thinner

amiral [amiʀal, o] <-aux> *m* admiral

amitié [amitje] *f* **1.** *a.* POL friendship; **se lier d'~ avec qn** to strike up a friendship with sb; **avoir de l'~ pour qn** to be fond of sb **2.** *pl* (*formule de fin de lettre*) **~s, Bernadette** kind regards, Bernadette; **faire toutes ses ~s à qn** to send one's best wishes to sb

ammoniac, -iaque [amɔnjak] *adj* ammoniac

ammoniaque [amɔnjak] *f* (*liquide*) ammonia

amnésie [amnezi] *f* amnesia

amnésique [amnezik] **I.** *adj* amnesic **II.** *mf* amnesiac

amnistie [amnisti] *f* amnesty

amnistier [amnistje] <1> *vt* to amnesty

amocher [amɔʃe] <1> **I.** *vt inf* **1.** (*abîmer*) to ruin; (*voiture*) to bash up **2.** *inf* (*blesser*) **~ qn** to mess sb up **II.** *vpr inf* (*se blesser*) to get oneself bashed up

amoindrir [amwɛ̃dʀiʀ] <8> **I.** *vt* (*autorité*) to weaken; (*importance*) to dwindle **II.** *vpr* **s'~** (*facultés*) to slip away; (*forces, fortune*) to dwindle

amollir [amɔliʀ] <8> **I.** *vt* **1.** (*rendre mou*) to soften **2.** (*rendre moins énergique*) **~ qn** to turn sb soft **II.** *vpr* **s'~ 1.** (*devenir mou*) to go soft **2.** (*faiblir: personne*) to go soft; (*énergie*) to weaken; **ses jambes s'amollissent** his legs are weakening

amonceler [amɔ̃s(ə)le] <3> **I.** *vt* **1.** (*entasser*) to pile up **2.** (*accumuler: richesses*) to amass; (*documents, preuves*) to accumulate **II.** *vpr* **s'~** (*neige*) to drift; (*courrier*) to pile up; (*nuages*) to bank up; (*preuves, demandes*) to accumulate

amoncellement [amɔ̃sɛlmɑ̃] *m* heap; (*de lettres*) pile

amont [amɔ̃] *m* (*partie supérieure: d'un cours d'eau*) upstream water; **aller vers l'~** to go upstream ▸**en ~ de Valence** upriver from Valence; **industrie en ~** upstream industry

amoral(**e**) [amɔʀal, o] <-aux> *adj* amoral

amorce [amɔʀs] *f* **1.** (*d'une cartouche*) primer; (*d'un obus, d'une mine*) priming; (*d'un pistolet d'enfant*) cap; **pistolet à ~s** cap gun **2.** (*appât*) bait **3.** (*début: d'une route, voie ferrée*) initial section; (*d'une pellicule*) leader; **faire l'~ d'un trou** to start a hole **4.** (*phase initiale: d'une négociation, idée, d'un projet*) start; (*d'une réforme*) beginnings *pl* **5.** INFOR bootstrap

amorcer [amɔʀse] <2> **I.** *vt* **1.** (*garnir d'une amorce: explosif*) to arm **2.** (*pour la pêche*) to bait **3.** (*mettre en état de fonctionner: syphon*) to prime **4.** (*commencer à percer: trou*) to start **5.** (*ébaucher un mouvement*) **~ un virage** to take a bend **6.** (*engager: conversation*) to start up; (*réforme*) to initiate **7.** INFOR to boot **II.** *vpr* **s'~** (*dialogue*) to begin; (*projet*) to get under way

amorphe [amɔʀf] *adj* **1.** (*sans énergie*) lifeless **2.** (*sans réaction: personne, foule*) passive

amortir [amɔʀtiʀ] <8> *vt* **1.** (*affaiblir: choc, chute*) to cushion; (*bruit, douleur*) to deaden **2.** (*rembourser*) to redeem; (*dette, emprunt*) to pay off **3.** (*rentabiliser: coût*) to recoup

amortisseur [amɔʀtisœʀ] *m* AUTO shock absorber

amour [amuʀ] **I.** *m* **1.** (*sentiment*) love; **l'~ maternel** mother love **2.** (*acte*) love-making; **pendant l'~** while making love; **faire l'~** to make love **3.** (*personne*) love **4.** (*attachement, altruisme, goût pour*) **~ de la justice/du prochain** love of justice/one's neighbour; **~ de la nature/du sport** love of nature/sport **5.** (*terme d'affection*) **mon ~** my darling; **va me chercher le journal, tu seras un ~** *inf* be a dear and fetch me the newspaper ▸**pour l'~ de Dieu!** for heaven's sake!; **vivre d'~ et d'eau fraîche** to live on love alone **II.** *mpl f si poétique* loves; **comment vont tes ~s?** how's your love-life? ▸**à tes/vos ~s!** *iron* cheers!

amouracher [amuʀaʃe] <1> *vpr péj* **s'~ de qn** to become infatuated with sb

amoureusement [amuʀøzmɑ̃] *adv* (*avec amour, soin*) lovingly

amoureux, -euse [amuʀø, -øz] **I.** *adj* (*personne, regard*) loving; **la vie amoureuse de qn** sb's love life; **être/tomber ~ de qn** to be/fall in love with sb **II.** *m, f* **1.** (*soupirant*) sweetheart; (*sentiment plus profond*) lover; **manger en ~** to eat alone together

A

2. (*passionné*) ~ **de la musique/de la nature** music/nature lover

amour-propre [amuʀpʀɔpʀ] <amours-propres> *m* self-esteem; **on a quand même son** ~ one has one's pride

amovible [amɔvibl] *adj* detachable; (*disque*) removable

ampère [ɑ̃pɛʀ] *m* ampere

amphibie [ɑ̃fibi] **I.** *adj* amphibious **II.** *m* amphibian

amphithéâtre [ɑ̃fiteɑtʀ] *m* **1.** ARCHIT amphitheatre **2.** UNIV lecture hall **3.** THEAT (upper) gallery

amphore [x] *f* amphora

ample [ɑ̃pl] *adj* **1.** (*large*) loose **2.** (*d'une grande amplitude: mouvement*) sweeping; (*voix*) sonorous **3.** (*abondant: provisions*) plentiful **4.** (*opp: restreint: projet, sujet*) vast; **de plus ~s informations** further information

amplement [ɑ̃pləmɑ̃] *adv* fully; **être ~ suffisant** to be more than enough

ampleur [ɑ̃plœʀ] *f* **1.** (*largeur: d'un vêtement*) looseness; (*d'une voix*) sonorousness **2.** (*étendue: d'un récit*) opulence; (*d'un sujet*) scope; (*d'une catastrophe*) extent; **prendre de l'~** (*épidémie*) to spread; (*manifestation*) to grow considerably

ampli *inf*, **amplificateur** [ɑ̃plifikatœʀ] *m* amplifier

amplifier [ɑ̃plifje] <1> **I.** *vt* **1.** (*augmenter*) to increase; (*image*) to enlarge **2.** (*développer: échanges, coopération, idée*) to develop **3.** (*exagérer*) ~ **qc** to build sth up **II.** *vpr* **s'~** (*bruit*) to grow; (*échange, mouvement, tendance*) to increase; (*scandale*) to intensify; (*idée*) to develop

amplitude [ɑ̃plityd] *f* **1.** (*écart de deux valeurs*) range **2.** (*ampleur*) extent

ampoule [ɑ̃pul] *f* **1.** ELEC bulb **2.** (*cloque*) blister

amputation [ɑ̃pytasjɔ̃] *f* **1.** ANAT amputation **2.** (*diminution: d'un texte, du territoire national*) truncation; ~ **d'un budget** cutback in a budget

amputer [ɑ̃pyte] <1> *vt* **1.** ANAT to amputate; **être amputé d'un bras** to have one's arm amputated **2.** *fig* (*texte, budget*) ~ **qc** to hack sth down

amulette [amylɛt] *f* amulet

amusant(e) [amyzɑ̃, ɑ̃t] *adj* **1.** (*divertissant: jeu, travail, vacances*) fun **2.** (*drôle, curieux*) funny

amuse-gueule [amyzgœl] <amuse-gueule(s)> *m inf* appetizer; (*petit sandwich*) snack

amusement [amyzmɑ̃] *m* **1.** (*divertissement*) entertainment **2.** (*jeu*) game

amuser [amyze] <1> **I.** *vt* **1.** (*divertir*) to entertain **2.** (*faire rire*) ~ **qn** to make sb laugh; **tu m'amuses** you're making me laugh; **cela ne l'amuse pas d'être pris pour un imbécile** he doesn't enjoy being taken for a fool **3.** (*détourner l'attention*) to divert **II.** *vpr* **s'~** **1.** (*jouer*) to play; **l'enfant s'amuse avec ses lacets** the child's fiddling with his laces **2.** (*se divertir*) **bien s'~** to have a very good time; (*à une soirée*) to enjoy oneself; **amuse-toi/amusez-vous bien!** have fun!; **qn s'est amusé à casser la portière** sb's gone and broken the door **3.** (*batifoler*) to frolic **4.** (*traîner*) to dawdle

amusette [amyzɛt] *f Belgique, fam* (*personne frivole*) fun-lover

amuseur, -euse [amyzœʀ, -øz] *m, f* **1.** entertainer **2.** *péj* clown

amygdale [amidal] *f* tonsil

an [ɑ̃] *m* year; **avoir cinq ~s** to be five (years old); **homme de cinquante ~s** a fifty-year-old (man); **fêter ses vingt ~s** to celebrate one's twentieth birthday; **l'~ dernier/prochain** last/next year; **tous les ~s** every year; **par ~** per year; **en l'~ 200 avant Jésus-Christ** in (the year) 200 BC; **le nouvel ~, le premier de l'~** New Year's day

anachronique [anakʀɔnik] *adj* anachronistic

anachronisme [anakʀɔnism] *m* anachronism

anaconda [anakɔ̃da] *m* anaconda

anagramme [anagʀam] *f* anagram

anal(e) [anal, o] <-aux> *adj* anal

analgésique [analʒezik] *adj, m* analgesic

anallergique [analɛʀʒik] *adj* hypoallergenic

analogie [analɔʒi] *f* analogy; **par ~** by analogy

analphabète [analfabɛt] *adj, mf* illiterate

analyse [analiz] *f* **1.** (*opp: synthèse*) *a.* MAT analysis; **faire l'~ de qc** to analyse sth **2.** MED ~ **de sang** blood test

analyser [analize] <1> *vt* **1.** LING (*mot*) to parse **2.** MAT, MED, PSYCH to analyse; **se faire ~** to undergo analysis

analyste [analist] *mf* **1.** (*technicien*) analyst **2.** PSYCH (psycho)analyst

analytique [analitik] *adj* analytical

ananas [anana(s)] *m* pineapple

anarchie [anaʀʃi] *f* anarchy

anarchique [anaʀʃik] *adj* anarchic

anarchiste [anaʀʃist] *adj, mf* anarchist

anatomie [anatɔmi] *f a. inf* (*science*) anatomy

anatomique [anatɔmik] *adj* anatomic

ANC [ɑɛnse] *m abr de* **African National Congress** ANC

ancestral(e) [ɑ̃sɛstʀal, o] <-aux> *adj* ancestral

ancêtre [ɑ̃sɛtʀ] **I.** *mf* **1.** (*aïeul, à l'origine d'une famille*) ancestor **2.** (*précurseur: d'un genre artistique*) forerunner **3.** *inf* (*vieillard*) oldster **II.** *mpl* HIST forebears

anchois [ɑ̃ʃwa] *m* anchovy

ancien [ɑ̃sjɛ̃] *m* **1.** (*objets*) antiques *pl* **2.** *pl* HIST Ancients

ancien(ne) [ɑ̃sjɛ̃, jɛn] **I.** *adj* **1.** (*vieux: bâtiment, coutume*) old; (*objet d'art*) antique; (*livre*) antiquarian **2.** *antéposé* (*ex-*) old

3. (*antique: culture, peuple*) ancient 4. (*qui a de l'ancienneté*) **être ~ dans le métier** to have been doing a job for a long time II. *m(f)* 1. (*personne*) **les ~s** the elderly; SOCIOL the elders 2. (*collaborateur*) **être un ~ dans l'entreprise** to have been in a company a long time

anciennement [ɑ̃sjɛnmɑ̃] *adv* 1. (*autrefois*) formerly 2. (*dans les temps anciens*) in ancient times

ancienneté [ɑ̃sjɛnte] *f* 1. (*dans la fonction publique/une entreprise*) length of service 2. (*avantages acquis*) seniority

ancre [ɑ̃kʀ] *f* anchor ►**jeter l'~** to drop anchor; *fig* to put down roots

andorran(e) [ɑ̃dɔʀɑ̃, aːn] *adj* Andorran

Andorran(e) [ɑ̃dɔʀɑ̃, aːn] *m(f)* Andorran

Andorre [ɑ̃dɔʀ] *f* **l'~** Andorra

andouille [ɑ̃duj] *f* 1. GASTR andouille (sausage) 2. *inf* (*imbécile*) **une triple ~** a total idiot; **faire l'~** to act [*o* play] the fool

andouillette [ɑ̃dujɛt] *f* andouillette (sausage)

androgyne [ɑ̃dʀɔʒin] I. *adj* BIO androgynous II. *mf* BIO androgyne

âne [ɑn] *m* 1. ZOOL donkey; *v. a.* **ânesse** 2. (*imbécile*) **quel ~!** what a fool! ►**être têtu comme un ~** to be as stubborn as a mule

anéantir [aneɑ̃tiʀ] <8> I. *vt* 1. (*détruire: ennemi*) to annihilate; (*armée, ville, effort*) to wipe out; (*espoir*) to dash 2. (*déprimer, accabler*) to overwhelm; (*mauvaise nouvelle*) to crush II. *vpr* **s'~** to disappear; (*volonté*) to be broken

anéantissement [aneɑ̃tismɑ̃] *m* 1. (*disparition*) annihilation 2. (*fatigue*) (state of) exhaustion; (*abattement*) (state of) dejection

anecdote [anɛkdɔt] *f* anecdote

anémie [anemi] *f* 1. MED anaemia 2. (*crise*) slump

anémier [anemje] <1a> *vt* to weaken

anémique [anemik] *adj* anaemic *Brit,* anemic *Am*

anémone [anemɔn] *f* anemone

ânerie [ɑnʀi] *f* 1. (*caractère stupide*) stupidity 2. (*parole*) silly remark 3. (*acte*) stupid mistake

ânesse [ɑnɛs] *f* she-ass; *v. a.* **âne**

anesthésie [anɛstezi] *f* 1. MED (*état*) anaesthesia *Brit,* anesthesia *Am;* (*drogue*) anaesthetic *Brit,* anesthetic *Am* 2. (*manque de sensibilité*) insensibility

anesthésier [anɛstezje] <1> *vt* to anaesthetise *Brit,* to anesthetize *Am*

anesthésiste [anɛstezist] *mf* anaesthetist *Brit,* anesthesiologist *Am*

ange [ɑ̃ʒ] *m* angel ►**~ gardien** guardian angel; (*garde du corps*) bodyguard

angine [ɑ̃ʒin] *f* sore throat; **avoir une ~** to have a sore throat

anglais [ɑ̃glɛ] *m* English; *v. a.* **français**

anglais(e) [ɑ̃glɛ, ɛz] *adj* English ►**filer à l'~e** to take French leave

Anglais(e) [ɑ̃glɛ, ɛz] *m(f)* 1. (*personne d'Angleterre*) Englishman, Englishwoman *m, f;* **les ~** the English 2. *Québec* (*anglophone*) English-speaker

angle [ɑ̃gl] *m* 1. (*coin*) corner 2. MAT, PHOT angle; **grand-~** wide-angle; **~ mort** blind spot 3. (*point de vue*) angle

Angleterre [ɑ̃glətɛʀ] *f* **l'~** England

anglicisme [ɑ̃glisism] *m* (*emprunt*) anglicism

angliciste [ɑ̃glisist] *mf* English specialist

anglo-américain [ɑ̃gloameʀikɛ̃] *m* American English; *v. a.* **français**

anglo-canadien(ne) [ɑ̃glokanadjɛ̃, jɛn] <anglo-canadiens> *adj* English-speaking Canadian

Anglo-Canadien(ne) [ɑ̃glokanadjɛ̃, jɛn] <Anglo-Canadiens> *m(f)* English-speaking Canadian

anglo-normand [ɑ̃glonɔʀmɑ̃] *m* Anglo-Norman; *v. a.* **français**

anglo-normand(e) [ɑ̃glonɔʀmɑ̃, ɑ̃d] <anglo-normands> *adj* Anglo-Norman

Anglo-normand(e) [ɑ̃glonɔʀmɑ̃, ɑ̃d] <Anglo-normands> *adj* **îles Anglo-normandes** Channel Islands

anglophile [ɑ̃glɔfil] *adj, mf* anglophile

anglophone [ɑ̃glɔfɔn] I. *adj* English-speaking; **être ~** to be an English-speaker II. *mf* English-speaker

anglo-saxon(ne) [ɑ̃glosaksɔ̃, ɔn] <anglo-saxons> *adj* Anglo-Saxon

Anglo-Saxon(ne) [ɑ̃glosaksɔ̃, ɔn] <Anglo-Saxons> *m(f)* Anglo-Saxon

angoissant(e) [ɑ̃gwasɑ̃, ɑ̃t] *adj* agonizing; (*moment, jour*) harrowing

angoisse [ɑ̃gwas] *f* 1. (*peur, malaise*) anxiety 2. (*douleur*) agony 3. PHILOS angst

angoissé(e) [ɑ̃gwase] I. *adj* anxious II. *m(f)* worrier

angoisser [ɑ̃gwase] <1> *vt* (*inquiéter*) to worry; (*situation, nouvelle, silence*) to distress

angora [ɑ̃gɔʀa] I. *adj* **laine ~** angora wool II. *m* (*chat, lapin, laine*) angora

anguille [ɑ̃gij] *f* eel

anguleux, -euse [ɑ̃gylø, -øz] *adj* (*menton, visage*) angular; (*coude*) bony

anicroche [anikʀɔʃ] *f* hitch

animal [animal, o] <-aux> *m* 1. (*bête*) animal; **~ domestique/sauvage** domestic/wild animal 2. (*personne stupide*) imbecile 3. (*personne brutale*) brute

animal(e) [animal, o] <-aux> *adj* 1. ZOOL, BIO (*matières, fonctions*) animal 2. (*rapporté à l'homme: instinct*) animal; (*comportement, confiance*) instinctive 3. *péj* (*bestial*) brutish

animalier, -ière [animalje, -jɛʀ] I. *m, f* 1. (*peintre*) animal painter 2. (*sculpteur*) animal sculptor II. *adj* animal

animateur, -trice [animatœʀ, -tʀis] *m, f* 1. (*spécialiste de l'animation: d'un groupe*) leader; (*d'un club de vacances*) activity leader *Brit,* camp counselor *Am;* (*d'un club de sport*) coach; (*d'une fête*) entertainer **2.** (*présentateur: d'un débat, jeu*) host; RADIO, TV presenter **3.** (*personne dynamique: d'un projet*) organizer **4.** CINE animator

animation [animasjɔ̃] *f* **1.** (*grande activité: d'un bureau*) activity; (*d'un quartier*) life **2.** (*vivacité: d'une discussion*) liveliness; **mettre de l'~** to liven things up **3.** (*excitation*) excitement **4.** (*conduite de groupe*) leadership **5.** CINE animation

animé(e) [anime] *adj* (*discussion*) animated; (*rue*) busy; (*personne*) lively; **dessin ~** cartoon; **devenir très ~** to liven up

animer [anime] <1> **I.** *vt* **1.** (*mener: débat, groupe, entreprise*) to lead; (*émission*) to present **2.** (*mouvoir*) to drive **3.** (*égayer*) **~ qc** to liven sth up **4.** (*ressusciter*) to revive **II.** *vpr* **s'~** (*yeux*) to light up; (*conversation, rue*) to liven up; (*statue*) to come to life

animosité [animozite] *f* animosity

anis [anis] *m* **1.** BOT anise **2.** GASTR aniseed

anisette [anizɛt] *f* anisette

ankylosé(e) [ɑ̃kiloze] *adj* (*bras*) numb; (*personne*) stiff

annales [anal] *fpl* annals

anneau [ano] <x> *m* **1.** (*cercle, bague*) *a.* ASTR ring **2.** (*maillon*) link **3.** ZOOL (*d'un ver*) segment **4.** *pl* SPORT race track

année [ane] *f* **1.** (*durée*) year; **~ civile/bissextile** calendar/leap year; **au cours des dernières ~s** over the last years; **bien des ~s après** many years later; **dans les ~s à venir** in the years to come; **pour de longues ~s** for many years; **tout au long de l'~** the whole year round; **~ scolaire** school year; **~ universitaire** academic [*o* university] year **2.** (*âge*) year **3.** (*date*) year; **l'~ prochaine/dernière/passée** next/last year; **~ de naissance** year of birth; **en début/en fin d'~** at the beginning/end of the year; **d'une ~ à l'autre** from one year to another; **les ~s trente** the (nineteen) thirties; **1985, c'est une bonne ~ pour le Bordeaux** 1985 was a vintage year for Bordeaux; **bonne ~, bonne santé!** health and happiness in the New Year!; **souhaiter la bonne ~ à qn** to wish sb a happy New Year ►**les ~s folles** the Roaring Twenties

année-lumière [anelymjɛʀ] <années-lumière> *f* light year

annexion [anɛksjɔ̃] *f* (*d'un pays, territoire*) annexation

annihiler [aniile] <1> *vt* (*efforts, espoir*) to wreck; (*vie*) to ruin; (*volonté*) to destroy; **le chagrin l'a complètement annihilé** he was devastated by grief

anniversaire [anivɛʀsɛʀ] **I.** *adj* (*jour, cérémonie*) anniversary; **le jour ~ de leurs 50 ans de mariage** on their 50th wedding anniversary; **la cérémonie ~ de l'armistice** the ceremony of the anniversary of the armistice **II.** *m* (*d'une personne*) birthday; (*d'un événement*) anniversary; **bon ~!** Happy Birthday!; (*à un couple*) Happy Anniversary!

annonce [anɔ̃s] *f* **1.** (*avis: d'un événement imminent*) announcement **2.** (*information officielle*) **~ de qc** notice of sth; (*transmise par les médias*) announcement of sth **3.** (*petite ~*) classified advertisements; **les petites ~s** classified ads; **passer une ~ dans un journal** to place an ad in the paper **4.** (*présage*) sign; (*indice*) indication **5.** JEUX declaration

annoncer [anɔ̃se] <2> **I.** *vt* **1.** (*communiquer: fait, décision*) to announce **2.** (*prédire*) to predict **3.** (*être le signe de: printemps*) to be the harbinger of; (*signal*) to give **4.** JEUX to declare **II.** *vpr* **1.** (*arriver*) **s'~** to approach; (*été*) to be on the way **2.** (*se présenter*) **bien/mal s'~** to seem promising/unpromising; **ça s'annonce bien** things look promising

annonceur, -euse [anɔ̃sœʀ, -søz] *m, f* **1.** (*speaker*) announcer **2.** PRESSE (*a. qui passe une petite annonce*) advertiser **3.** (*bénéficiaire d'une publicité, sponsor*) advertiser

annotation [anɔtasjɔ̃] *f* annotation

annoter [anɔte] <1> *vt* to annotate

annuaire [anɥɛʀ] *m* directory; **~ téléphonique** [*o* **des téléphones**] telephone directory

annuel(le) [anɥɛl] *adj* **1.** (*périodique*) annual **2.** (*qui dure un an*) year-long

annuellement [anɥɛlmɑ̃] *adv* annually

annulaire [anylɛʀ] **I.** *m* ring finger **II.** *adj* ring-shaped

annulation [anylasjɔ̃] *f* **1.** (*suppression: d'une commande, d'un rendez-vous*) cancellation **2.** JUR (*d'un examen, contrat*) cancellation; (*d'un jugement*) overturning

annuler [anyle] <1> **I.** *vt* **1.** (*supprimer*) *a.* INFOR to cancel **2.** JUR (*jugement*) to overturn; (*mariage*) to annul **II.** *vpr* **s'~** to cancel each other out

anoblir [anɔbliʀ] <8> *vt* to ennoble

anodin(e) [anɔdɛ̃, in] *adj* (*personne*) insignificant; (*critique, détail, propos, remède*) trivial; (*blessure*) superficial

anomalie [anɔmali] *f* **1.** (*caractère inhabituel*) *a.* LING, BIO anomaly **2.** (*singularité*) peculiarity **3.** (*caractère déviant*) irregularity **4.** TECH fault

ânon [ɑnɔ̃] *m* (ass's) foal

anonymat [anɔnima] *m* anonymity; **rester dans l'~** to remain anonymous

anonyme [anɔnim] *adj* anonymous

anorak [anɔʀak] *m* anorak

anorexie [anɔʀɛksi] *f* (*refus de s'alimenter*) anorexia; **~ mentale** anorexia nervosa

anorexique [anɔʀɛksik] *adj, mf* anorexic

anormal(e) [anɔʀmal, o] <-aux> **I.** *adj* **1.** (*inhabituel*) unusual **2.** (*non conforme à la règle*) abnormal; (*comportement*) perverse **3.** (*injuste*) unfair **II.** *m(f)* **1.** (*déséquilibré*) unbalanced person **2.** (*enfant arriéré*) handicapped child

anormalement [anɔʀmalmɑ̃] *adv* abnormally

ANPE [ɑɛnpeø] *f abr de* **Agence nationale**

pour l'emploi 1. (*organisme national*) National Employment Agency (*government agency managing employment legislation and job searches*) 2. (*agence locale*) ≈ Jobcentre *Brit*, employment office *Am*

anse [ɑ̃s] *f* 1. (*d'un panier*) handle 2. (*petite baie*) cove

antagonisme [ɑ̃tagɔnism] *m* antagonism

antalgique [ɑ̃talʒik] *adj, m* analgesic

antan [ɑ̃tɑ̃] *soutenu* **d'**~ of yesteryear

antarctique [ɑ̃taʀktik] *adj* antarctic; **le cercle polaire/la péninsule** ~ the Antarctic Circle/Peninsula

Antarctique [ɑ̃taʀktik] *m* **l'**~ the Antarctic

antécédent [ɑ̃tesedɑ̃] *m* 1. LING, PHILOS antecedent 2. *pl* MED (medical) history + *vb sing* 3. *pl* (*actes du passé: d'une personne*) past record + *vb sing*; (*d'une affaire*) antecedents

antécédent(e) [ɑ̃tesedɑ̃, ɑ̃t] *adj* ~ **à qc** preceding sth

antémémoire [ɑ̃tememwa:ʀ] *f* INFOR cache memory

antenne [ɑ̃tɛn] *f* 1. (*pour capter*) aerial 2. RADIO, TV **une heure d'**~ an hour of airtime; **à l'**~ on the air; **rendre l'**~ **à qn** to hand back to sb 3. ZOOL antenna 4. MIL (*poste avancé*) outpost

antérieur(e) [ɑ̃teʀjœʀ] *adj* 1. (*précédent*) previous; **être** ~ **à qc** to be prior to sth 2. ANAT **patte** ~**e** forefoot; **membre** ~ forelimb 3. LING anterior

antérieurement [ɑ̃teʀjœʀmɑ̃] *adv* earlier; ~ **à qc** prior to sth

antériorité [ɑ̃teʀjɔʀite] *f* 1. (*dans le temps*) precedence 2. LING anteriority

anthologie [ɑ̃tɔlɔʒi] *f* anthology

anthropologie [ɑ̃tʀɔpɔlɔʒi] *f* anthropology

anthropologue [ɑ̃tʀɔpɔlɔg] *mf* anthropologist

anthropophage [ɑ̃tʀɔpɔfaʒ] I. *adj* cannibal; **être** ~ to be a cannibal II. *mf* cannibal

antialcoolique [ɑ̃tialkɔlik] *adj* **campagne** ~ campaign against alcoholism

antibiotique [ɑ̃tibjɔtik] *adj, m* antibiotic

antibrouillard [ɑ̃tibʀujaʀ] I. *adj* fog II. *m* fog lamp *Brit*, fog light *Am*

anticipation [ɑ̃tisipasjɔ̃] *f* 1. (*prévision*) anticipation 2. LIT, CINE science fiction 3. FIN ~ **de paiement** advance payment; **par** ~ in advance

anticipé(e) [ɑ̃tisipe] *adj* early; **retraite** ~**e** early retirement; **avec mes remerciements** ~**s, je vous prie de croire, …** thanking you in advance, yours sincerely, …

anticiper [ɑ̃tisipe] <1> I. *vi* 1. (*devancer les faits*) to look too far ahead 2. (*se représenter à l'avance*) to think ahead; (*prévoir*) to plan II. *vt* 1. (*prévoir: avenir, événement*) to predict 2. FIN, SPORT to anticipate

anticlérical(e) [ɑ̃tikleʀikal, o] <-aux> *adj, m(f)* anticlerical

anticonformiste [ɑ̃tikɔ̃fɔʀmist] *adj, mf* nonconformist

anticonstitutionnel(le) [ɑ̃tikɔ̃stitysjɔnɛl] *adj* anticonstitutional

anticorps [ɑ̃tikɔʀ] *m* antibody

anticyclone [ɑ̃tisiklon] *m* METEO anticyclone

antidépresseur [ɑ̃tidepʀesœʀ] *adj, m* antidepressant

antidote [ɑ̃tidɔt] *m* MED antidote

antidouleur [ɑ̃tidulœʀ] *adj inv* painkilling

antigel [ɑ̃tiʒɛl] *m* antifreeze

antigouvernemental(e) [ɑ̃tiguvɛʀnəmɑ̃tal, o] <-aux> *adj* antigovernmental

Antigua-et-Barbuda [ɑ̃tigwa e baʀbyda] Antigua and Barbuda

antiguais(e) [ɑ̃tigɛ, ɛz] *adj* Antiguan

Antiguais(e) [ɑ̃tigɛ, ɛz] *m(f)* Antiguan

antihéros [ɑ̃tieʀo] *m* anti-hero

anti-inflammatoire [ɑ̃tiɛ̃flamatwaʀ] <anti-inflammatoires> *adj* anti-inflammatory

antillais(e) [ɑ̃tijɛ, jɛz] *adj* West Indian

Antillais(e) [ɑ̃tijɛ, ɛz] *m(f)* West Indian

Antilles [ɑ̃tij] *fpl* **les** ~ the West Indies

antilope [ɑ̃tilɔp] *f* antelope

antimilitariste [ɑ̃timilitaʀist] I. *adj* antimilitaristic II. *mf* antimilitarist

antimite [ɑ̃timit] I. *adj* mothproof II. *m* moth repellant

antiparasite [ɑ̃tipaʀazit] I. *adj* anti-interference II. *m* suppressor

antipathie [ɑ̃tipati] *f* antipathy; ~ **pour qn/qc** dislike of sb/sth

antipathique [ɑ̃tipatik] *adj* unpleasant; (*comportement*) anti-social

antipelliculaire [ɑ̃tipelikylɛʀ] *adj* anti-dandruff

antipodes [ɑ̃tipɔd] *mpl* 1. GEO antipodes 2. *fig* **être aux** ~ **de qc** to be the total opposite of sth

antipoison [ɑ̃tipwazɔ̃] *adj inv* **centre** ~ poison treatment centre *Brit*, poison control center *Am*

antiquaire [ɑ̃tikɛʀ] *mf* antique dealer

antique [ɑ̃tik] *adj* antique; (*lieu*) ancient

antiquité [ɑ̃tikite] I. *f sans pl* (*période très reculée*) ancient times *pl* II. *fpl* 1. (*œuvres d'art antiques*) antiquities 2. (*objets, meubles anciens*) antiques

Antiquité [ɑ̃tikite] *f sans pl* HIST **l'**~ antiquity

antiraciste [ɑ̃tiʀasist] *adj* antiracist

antirides [ɑ̃tiʀid] *adj* anti-wrinkle

antirouille [ɑ̃tiʀuj] I. *adj inv* anti-rust II. *m* anti-rust compound

antisèche [ɑ̃tisɛʃ] *f inf* crib *Brit*, cheat sheet *Am*

antisémite [ɑ̃tisemit] I. *adj* anti-Semitic II. *mf* anti-Semite

antisémitisme [ɑ̃tisemitism] *m* anti-Semitism

antiseptique [ɑ̃tisɛptik] I. *adj* antiseptic II. *m* antiseptic

antitabac [ɑ̃titaba] *adj inv* anti-smoking

antiterroriste [ɑ̃titeʀɔʀist] *adj* antiterrorist
antitétanique [ɑ̃titetanik] *adj* tetanus
anti-virus [ɑ̃tiviʀys] *inv* **I.** *adj* INFOR anti-virus; **utilitaire** ~ anti-virus programme **II.** *m* INFOR virus checker
antivol [ɑ̃tivɔl] **I.** *adj inv* anti-theft **II.** *m* (*d'une voiture*) steering wheel lock; (*d'un vélo*) bicycle lock
antonyme [ɑ̃tɔnim] *m* LING antonym
antre [ɑ̃tʀ] *m* **1.**(*d'un animal*) lair **2.***fig* (*d'une personne, d'un écrivain*) den; (*d'un sorcier*) cave ►**l'**~ **du lion** the lion's den
anus [anys] *m* anus
Anvers [ɑ̃vɛʀ] Antwerp
anversois(**e**) [ɑ̃vɛʀswa, waz] *adj* of Antwerp; *v. a.* **ajaccien**
Anversois(**e**) [ɑ̃vɛʀswa, waz] *m(f)* person from Antwerp; *v. a.* **Ajaccien**
anxiété [ɑ̃ksjete] *f* **1.** MED, PSYCH anxiety **2.**(*trait de caractère*) worry
anxieusement [ɑ̃ksjøzmɑ̃] *adv* anxiously
anxieux, **-euse** [ɑ̃ksjø, -jøz] **I.** *adj* worried; (*attente*) anxious **II.** *m, f* worrier
AOC [ɑose] *abr de* **appellation d'origine contrôlée** (*regional quality control label for wine, cheese, etc.*)
aorte [aɔʀt] *f* aorta
août [u(t)] *m* **1.** August; ~ **est un mois d'été** August is a summer month **2.**(*pour indiquer la date, un laps de temps*) **en** ~ in August; **début/fin** ~ at the beginning/end of August; **pendant tout le mois d'**~ for the whole of August; **le 15** ~**, c'est l'Assomption** the Assumption is on August 15th
aoûtien(**ne**) [ausjɛ̃, jɛn] *m(f)* August holiday maker *Brit,* August vacationer *Am*
apaisant(**e**) [apɛzɑ̃, ɑ̃t] *adj* **1.**(*qui calme*) calming **2.**(*qui ramène la paix*) conciliatory
apaiser [apeze] <1> **I.** *vt* to calm; (*douleur*) to soothe; (*faim, désir*) to satisfy; (*soif*) to slake; (*protestations*) to quell; (*colère*) to pacify; (*scrupules, craintes*) to allay; (*dieux*) to appease **II.** *vpr* **s'**~ (*personne*) to calm down; (*douleur*) to die down; (*colère, tempête*) to abate
aparté [apaʀte] *m* (*entretien*) private conversation; THEAT aside; **en** ~ in an aside
apartheid [apaʀtɛd] *m* apartheid
apathique [apatik] *adj* apathetic
apatride [apatʀid] *mf* stateless person
apercevoir [apɛʀsəvwaʀ] <12> **I.** *vt* **1.**(*entrevoir*) to see **2.**(*remarquer*) to notice **3.**(*distinguer*) to distinguish; (*percevoir*) to perceive **4.**(*prevoir*) to see **II.** *vpr* **1.**(*se voir*) **s'**~ to notice each other **2.**(*se rendre compte*) **s'**~ **d'une erreur/des manigances de qn** to notice an error/sb's scheming; **s'**~ **de la présence de qn** to notice that sb is there; **sans s'en** ~ without noticing
aperçu [apɛʀsy] *m* **1.**(*idée générale*) overview **2.** INFOR preview
apéritif [apeʀitif] *m* aperitif

> In France, people are not invited over for tea, but for an **apéritif**. The adults usually drink Pastis, Whisky, Martini or punch and the children have soft drinks such as cordials or syrup (mint, strawberry, grenadine etc.). Guests understand that they are not invited to dinner.

apéro [apeʀo] *m inf abr de* **apéritif**
apesanteur [apəzɑ̃tœʀ] *f* weightlessness
à-peu-près [apøpʀɛ] *m inv* (*approximation*) approximation; **c'est de l'**~ it's approximate
apeuré(**e**) [apœʀe] *adj* frightened
aphasique [afazik] **I.** *adj* aphasic **II.** *mf* aphasic
aphone [afɔn, afon] *adj* voiceless
aphte [aft] *m* MED (mouth) ulcer
API [ɑpei] *f abr de* **Association** (**ou alphabet**) **phonétique international**(**e**) IPA
à-pic [apik] <à-pics> *m* cliff
apiculteur, **-trice** [apikyltœʀ, -tʀis] *m, f* beekeeper
apitoiement [apitwamɑ̃] *m* ~ **sur qn** pity for sb; ~ **sur soi-même** self-pity
apitoyer [apitwaje] <6> *vpr* **s'**~ **sur qn/qc** to feel sorry for sb/sth
aplanir [aplaniʀ] <8> **I.** *vt* **1.**(*niveler*) to level **2.**(*faire disparaître: obstacles, difficultés*) to smooth away **II.** *vpr* **s'**~ to level out
aplati(**e**) [aplati] *adj* flat
aplatir [aplatiʀ] <8> **I.** *vt* to flatten; ~ **qc** (*voute*) to flatten sth down; (*pli*) to smooth sth out **II.** *vpr* **1.**(*se plaquer*) **s'**~ **sur la table** to lie flat on the table; **s'**~ **contre le mur** to flatten oneself against the wall **2.**(*devenir plat*) **s'**~ to become flatter **3.**(*être rendu plat*) **s'**~ to be flattened **4.**(*s'écraser*) **s'**~ **contre qc** to smash into sth
aplomb [aplɔ̃] *m* **1.**(*équilibre*) balance; (*verticalité*) perpendicularity; **à l'**~ at the base; **d'**~ steady **2.**(*assurance*) composure **3.**(*effronterie*) nerve; **avoir de l'**~ to have (a) nerve **4.**(*équilibre physique/moral*) **être d'**~ to be balanced; **remettre qn d'**~ to put sb back on their feet
apnée [apne] *f* **1.** MED apnoea *Brit,* apnea *Am* **2.** SPORT diving without oxygen
apocalypse [apɔkalips] *f* (*désastre*) apocalypse
Apocalypse [apɔkalips] *f* REL **l'**~ the Apocalypse
apocalyptique [apɔkaliptik] *adj* apocalyptic
apogée [apɔʒe] *m* summit
apolitique [apɔlitik] *adj* apolitical
apollon [apɔlɔ̃] *m* (*bel homme*) adonis
Apollon [apɔlɔ̃] *m* MYTH Apollo
apologie [apɔlɔʒi] *f* (*justification*) apologia
a posteriori [a pɔsteʀjɔʀi] *adv, adj* after the event
apostrophe [apɔstʀɔf] *f* **1.**(*signe*) apostrophe **2.**(*interpellation*) insult

A

apostropher [apɔstʀɔfe] <1> *vt* ~ **qn** to shout at sb

apothéose [apɔteoz] *f* **1.**(*consécration*) apotheosis **2.**(*sommet*) summit **3.**(*partie finale*) grand finale

apôtre [apotʀ] *m* **1.** REL, HIST apostle **2.**(*propagateur d'une idée*) advocate

Appalaches [apalaʃ(ə)] *mpl* **les** (**monts**) ~ the Appalachian Mountains

apparaître [apaʀɛtʀ] *vi irr être* **1.**(*se montrer*) to appear **2.**(*surgir: fièvre*) to break out; (*difficulté, idée, vérité*) to arise; (*obstacle*) to loom **3.**(*se révéler*) ~ **à qn** (*vérité*) to reveal itself to sb; **laisser qc** ~ to let sth reveal itself **4.**(*sembler*) ~ **grand à qn** to appear big to sb **5.**(*se présenter*) ~ **comme qc à qn** to appear to sb to be sth

appareil [apaʀɛj] *m* **1.**(*machine, instrument*) device; (*radio, télévision*) set; ~ **téléphonique** telephone; **à l'**~ on the telephone; **qui est à l'~?** who is speaking?; ~ **photo**(**graphique**) camera; ~**s ménagers** household appliances; ~ **de mesure** measuring device **2.**(*prothèse*) appliance; (*dentaire*) brace; (*dentier*) denture; ~ **auditif** hearing aid **3.**(*avion*) aircraft **4.** ANAT system **5.** POL machinery **6.** *pl* SPORT apparatus

appareiller [apaʀeje] <1> **I.** *vi* to get under way **II.** *vt* **1.** NAUT to fit out **2.**(*assortir*) to match

apparemment [apaʀamɑ̃] *adv* apparently; (*vraisemblablement*) probably

apparence [apaʀɑ̃s] *f* **1.**(*aspect*) appearance **2.**(*ce qui semble être*) outward appearance ►**sauver les** ~**s** to save face

apparent(**e**) [apaʀɑ̃, ɑ̃t] *adj* **1.**(*visible*) apparent; **être** ~ to be apparent **2.**(*évident, manifeste*) obvious **3.**(*supposé, trompeur*) apparent

apparenté(**e**) [apaʀɑ̃te] *adj* **1.**(*ressemblant*) ~ **à qc** resembling sth **2.**(*parent*) ~ **à qn/qc** related to sb/sth

apparenter [apaʀɑ̃te] <1> *vpr* **s'**~ **à qc** **1.**(*ressembler*) to be similar to sth **2.**(*se lier par mariage*) to marry into sth

apparition [apaʀisjɔ̃] *f* **1.**(*action de paraître: d'une personne*) appearance **2.** *sans pl* (*fait de devenir visible*) appearance **3.**(*manifestation: d'un être surnaturel*) apparition **4.**(*fantôme*) apparition

appart *inf,* **appartement** [apaʀtəmɑ̃] *m* **1.**(*habitation*) flat *Brit,* apartment *Am* **2.**(*dans un hôtel*) suite

appartenance [apaʀtənɑ̃s] *f* **1.**(*dépendance*) **mon** ~ **à un parti** my membership of a party; **mon** ~ **à une famille** my belonging to a family **2.** MAT ~ **à qc** membership of sth

appartenir [apaʀtəniʀ] <9> **I.** *vi* **1.**(*être la propriété de*) ~ **à qn** to belong to sb **2.**(*faire partie de*) *a.* MAT ~ **à qc** to be a member of sth **II.** *vi impers* **il appartient à qn de** +*infin* it is up to sb to +*infin*

appât [apɑ] *m* bait; **l'**~ **du gain** the lure of gain

appâter [apɑte] <1> *vt* **1.**(*à la chasse et à la pêche: poisson, oiseau, gibier*) to lure **2.**(*allécher*) to entice

appauvrir [apovʀiʀ] <8> **I.** *vt* (*personne, pays*) to impoverish; (*intelligence*) to dull **II.** *vpr* **s'**~ to become impoverished; (*intelligence*) to dim

appauvrissement [apovʀismɑ̃] *m* impoverishment

appel [apɛl] *m* **1.**(*cri, signal*) *a.* INFOR call; **service d'**~**s** dial-up service **2.**(*demande*) appeal; **faire** ~ **à qn/qc** to call on sb/sth; **faire** ~ **à son courage/ses souvenirs** to draw on one's courage/memories **3.**(*exhortation*) ~ **à qc** call to sth; **lancer un** ~ **à qn** to make an appeal to sb **4.**(*vérification de présence*) register; MIL roll-call; **faire l'**~ to call the register; MIL to do roll-call **5.** TEL ~ **téléphonique** telephone call **6.** SPORT take-off ►**faire** ~ to appeal; **sans** ~ without appeal; ~ **d'offres** invitation to tender

appelé(**e**) [aple] *m(f)* MIL conscript

appeler [aple] **I.** *vt* **1.**(*interpeller, nommer*) to call **2.**(*faire venir*) to summon; **faire** ~ **qn** to send for sb **3.**(*téléphoner à*) to call **4.**(*réclamer*) ~ **toute l'attention de qn** (*situation, conduite*) to call for sb's undivided attention; **les affaires/le devoir m'appelle**(**nt**) business/duty calls **5.**(*désigner*) ~ **qn à une charge/un poste/une fonction** to appoint sb to a duty/a job/a function **6.**(*se référer à*) **en** ~ **à qc** to appeal to sth **7.** INFOR ~ **qc** to call up sth **II.** *vi* (*héler, téléphoner*) to call **III.** *vpr* **1.**(*porter comme nom*) **s'**~ to be called; **comment t'appelles-tu/s'appelle cette plante?** what's your/this plant's name?; **je m'appelle** my name is **2.**(*être équivalent à*) **cela s'appelle faire qc** *inf* that's what you call doing sth

appellation [apelasjɔ̃, apɛllasjɔ̃] *f* appellation; ~ **d'origine** label of origin

appendice [apɛ̃dis] *m* appendix

appendicite [apɛ̃disit] *f* MED appendicitis

appentis [apɑ̃ti] *m* lean-to

appesantir [apəzɑ̃tiʀ] <8> **I.** *vt* to weigh down; (*ralentir*) to slow down **II.** *vpr* **s'**~ (*devenir lourd: tête*) to become heavier; (*esprit*) to become duller; (*geste, pas*) to slow down

appétissant(**e**) [apetisɑ̃, ɑ̃t] *adj* **1.**(*alléchant*) appetizing **2.** *inf* (*attirant*) attractive

appétit [apeti] *m* **1.**(*faim*) appetite; **avoir de l'~/bon** ~ to have an/a good appetite; **donner de/couper l'**~ **à qn** to give sb an/to ruin sb's appetite; **bon ~!** enjoy your meal! **2.** *fig* ~ **de richesses/vengeance** thirst for riches/revenge

applaudimètre [aplodimɛtʀ] *m* applause meter, clapometer *Brit*

applaudir [aplodiʀ] <8> *vi, vt* to applaud

applaudissements [aplodismɑ̃] *mpl* applause + *vb sing*

application [aplikasjɔ̃] *f* **1.**(*pose, utilisation*) *a.* INFOR application; **lancer une ~** to start a programme **2.**(*mise en pratique: d'une idée*) putting into practice; (*d'une décision, mesure*) implementation; **mettre qc en ~** to put sth into practice

appliqué(e) [aplike] *adj* **1.**(*attentif et studieux*) conscientious **2.**(*soigné*) careful **3.**(*mis en pratique*) applied **4.**(*assené*) **bien ~** firm

appliquer [aplike] <1> **I.** *vt* **1.**(*poser*) **~ de la peinture sur qc** to paint sth; **~ une échelle contre le mur** to lean a ladder against the wall **2.**(*mettre en pratique*) to implement; (*remède*) to administer; (*mode d'emploi, règlement*) to follow **II.** *vpr* **1.**(*se poser*) **s'~ sur qc** to be applied to sth **2.**(*correspondre à*) **s'~ à qn/qc** to apply to sb/sth **3.**(*s'efforcer*) **s'~ à faire qc** to apply oneself to doing sth

appoint [apwɛ̃] *m* (*complément*) extra contribution; (*aide*) extra help; **d'~** extra ►**avoir l'~** to have the right change; **faire l'~ à qn** to give the right change to sb

appointements [apwɛ̃tmɑ̃] *mpl* salary

appontement [apɔ̃tmɑ̃] *m* landing stage

apport [apɔʀ] *m* **1.**(*contribution*) **l'~ de qn/qc à qc** the contribution of sb/sth to sth **2.**(*source*) **~ de vitamines/chaleur** supply of vitamins/heat **3.** FIN financial contribution

apporter [apɔʀte] <1> *vt* **1.**(*porter*) to bring **2.**(*fournir*) **~ une preuve à qc** to supply proof for sth; **~ sa contribution/son concours à qc** to contribute to/support sth **3.**(*procurer*) to supply; (*consolation, soulagement*) to give; (*ennuis*) to bring **4.**(*produire*) **~ une modification/un changement à qc** to make a modification/change to sth **5.**(*mettre*) **~ du soin/beaucoup de précaution à qc** to exercise care/great caution in doing sth **6.**(*profiter à*) **~ beaucoup à qn/qc** to give a lot to sb/sth

apposer [apoze] <1> *vt* (*appliquer*) **~ un timbre sur qc** to stick a stamp on sth; **~ une signature sur qc** to append a signature to sth

apposition [apozisjɔ̃] *f* **1.** LING apposition **2.**(*application*) fixing; (*d'un timbre*) sticking; **~ d'une signature sur un document** signing of a document

appréciable [apʀesjabl] *adj* appreciable; (*changement*) noticeable

appréciation [apʀesjasjɔ̃] *f* **1.** *sans pl* (*évaluation: d'une distance*) estimation; (*d'une situation*) appraisal; (*d'un objet de valeur*) valuation **2.**(*commentaire*) evaluation **3.**(*jugement*) assessment

apprécier [apʀesje] <1> **I.** *vt* **1.**(*évaluer: distance, vitesse*) to estimate; (*objet, valeur*) to value; (*importance*) to assess **2.**(*aimer*) to like **II.** *vi inf* **il n'a pas apprécié!** he didn't take kindly to that!; **je vous laisse ~** I will leave you to judge **III.** *vpr* **s'~** (*monnaie*) to appreciate

appréhender [apʀeɑ̃de] <1> *vt* **1.**(*redouter*) **~ de faire qc** to dread doing sth **2.**(*arrêter*) to apprehend

appréhension [apʀeɑ̃sjɔ̃] *f* apprehension

apprenant(e) [apʀənɑ̃, ɑ̃t] *m(f)* learner

apprendre [apʀɑ̃dʀ] <13> **I.** *vt* **1.**(*être informé de*) **~ qc** to hear sth; (*événement*) to learn of sth **2.**(*annoncer*) **~ une chose à qn** to announce sth to sb **3.**(*étudier: leçon, langue, métier, technique*) to learn **4.**(*devenir capable de*) **~ à +infin** to learn to +*infin* **5.**(*enseigner*) **~ qc à qn** to teach sth to sb **II.** *vi* to learn **III.** *vpr* **s'~ facilement** (*langue*) to be easy to learn

apprenti(e) [apʀɑ̃ti] *m(f)* **1.**(*élève*) apprentice; **elle est ~e couturière** she is an apprentice dressmaker **2.**(*débutant*) novice

apprentissage [apʀɑ̃tisaʒ] *m* (*formation*) training; **être en ~ chez qn** to be an apprentice to sb; **il fait son ~ de menuisier** he is doing his apprenticeship as a carpenter

apprêter [apʀete] <1> **I.** *vt* TECH to finish **II.** *vpr* **s'~ à +infin** (*se préparer*) to get ready to +*infin;* (*être sur le point de*) to be just about to +*infin*

apprivoisé(e) [apʀivwaze] *adj* (*animal*) tame

apprivoiser [apʀivwaze] <1> *vt* to tame

approbateur, -trice [apʀɔbatœʀ, -tʀis] *adj* approving

approbation [apʀɔbasjɔ̃] *f* **1.**(*accord*) approval **2.**(*jugement favorable*) approbation; (*du public*) approval

approchant(e) [apʀɔʃɑ̃, ɑ̃t] *adj* similar

approche [apʀɔʃ] *f* **1.**(*arrivée, manière d'aborder un sujet*) approach; **à l'~ de la ville** near the town; **mon ~ du problème** my approach to the problem **2.**(*proximité*) **l'~ d'un événement/danger** the approaching event/danger; **à l'~ du printemps** at the onset of spring **3.** *pl* (*parages*) surrounding area + *vb sing*

approcher [apʀɔʃe] <1> **I.** *vi* (*personne*) to approach; (*moment, date, saison, orage*) to draw near; (*nuit*) to close in; (*jour*) to draw on **II.** *vt* **1.**(*mettre plus près*) **~ une chose de qn/qc** to move a thing closer to sb/sth; **elle approcha son visage du sien** she brought her face close to his **2.**(*venir plus près*) to approach; **ne m'approche pas!** don't come near me! **III.** *vpr* **s'~ de qn/qc** to approach sb/sth

approfondi(e) [apʀɔfɔ̃di] *adj* deep; (*connaissance*) thorough

approfondir [apʀɔfɔ̃diʀ] <8> *vt* **1.**(*creuser*) to deepen **2.**(*étudier: connaissances*) to deepen; **~ une question** to go deeper into a question

appropriation [apʀɔpʀijasjɔ̃] *f Belgique* (*nettoyage*) cleaning

approprié(e) [apʀɔpʀije] *adj* **~ à qc** suitable for sth; (*réponse, style*) appropriate for sth

approprier¹ [apʀɔpʀije] <1> **I.** *vt* **~ qc à qc** to adapt sth to sth **II.** *vpr* **s'~ un bien** to appropriate property; **s'~ un droit** to assume a right

approprier² [apʀɔpʀije] <1> *vt Belgique* (*nettoyer*) to clean

approuver [apʀuve] <1> *vt* **1.** (*agréer*) to approve; **~ que qn fasse qc** (*subj*) to approve of sb doing sth **2.** JUR (*contrat*) to ratify; (*projet de loi*) to pass; (*nomination, procès-verbal*) to approve

approvisionné(e) [apʀɔvizjɔne] *adj* **1.** (*achalandé*) **bien/mal ~** well/poorly stocked **2.** FIN **compte ~** account in credit

approvisionnement [apʀɔvizjɔnmɑ̃] *m* **1.** (*ravitaillement*) **~ en qc** supplying of sth **2.** (*réserve*) **~ en qc** supplies of sth

approvisionner [apʀɔvizjɔne] <1> **I.** *vt* **~ une ville en qc** to supply a town with sth; **~ un magasin en qc** to stock a shop with sth; **~ un compte en qc** to pay sth into an account **II.** *vpr* **s'~ en qc** to stock up with sth

approximatif, -ive [apʀɔksimatif, iv] *adj* approximate; (*valeur*) rough; (*terme*) imprecise

approximation [apʀɔksimasjɔ̃] *f* estimate; MAT approximation

approximativement [apʀɔksimativmɑ̃] *adv* approximately

appui [apɥi] *m* **1.** (*support*) support **2.** (*aide*) help **3.** ARCHIT **~ de fenêtre** windowsill **4.** (*justification*) **à l'~ de qc** in support of sth

appuie-tête [apɥitɛt] <appuie-tête(s)> *m* headrest

appuyer [apɥije] <6> **I.** *vi* **1.** (*presser*) **~ sur qc** to press on sth **2.** (*insister sur*) **~ sur qc** (*prononciation*) to stress sth; (*argumentation*) to emphasize sth **II.** *vt* **1.** (*poser*) **~ qc contre/sur qc** to lean sth against/on sth **2.** (*presser*) **~ sa main/son pied sur qc** to press on sth with one's hand/foot **3.** (*soutenir*) to support **III.** *vpr* **1.** (*prendre appui*) **s'~ contre/sur qn/qc** to lean against/on sb/sth **2.** (*compter sur*) **s'~ sur qn/qc** to rely on sb/sth **3.** (*se fonder sur*) **s'~ sur qc** (*preuves*) to be based on sth

âpre [ɑpʀ] *adj* **1.** (*qui racle la gorge*) rough **2.** (*désagréablement rude: froid*) bitter; (*vent, voix, hiver, ton*) harsh **3.** (*dur: discussion, critique, lutte, concurrence, détermination, résolution*) fierce; (*vie*) hard

après [apʀɛ] **I.** *prep* **1.** (*plus loin/tard que*) after; **bien/peu ~ qc** a long/short time after sth; **~ avoir fait qc** after doing sth **2.** (*derrière*) after; **courir ~ l'autobus** to run after the bus; **~ toi/vous!** after you! **3.** *inf* (*contre*) **être furieux ~ qn** to be furious with sb; **en avoir ~ qn** to have it in for sb **4.** (*chaque*) **semaine ~ semaine, jour ~ jour** week after week, day after day; **page ~ page** page after page **5.** (*selon*) **d'~ qn/qc** according to sb/sth; **d'~ moi** in my opinion **II.** *adv* **1.** (*plus tard/loin, ensuite/derrière*) later; (*par la suite*) after; **aussitôt ~** straight afterwards; **longtemps/peu ~** a long time/slightly after **2.** (*dans un classement*) behind **3.** (*qui suit*) **d'~** following ►**et ~?** *inf* and then?; **~ tout** after all **III.** *conj* **~ que qn a** [*o* **ait**] **fait qc** after sb did sth

après-demain [apʀɛdmɛ̃] *adv* the day after tomorrow

après-guerre [apʀɛɡɛʀ] <après-guerres> *m* **l'~** (*période*) the post-war years *pl;* (*situation*) the post-war situation

après-midi [apʀɛmidi] **I.** *m o f inv* afternoon; **cet(te) ~** this afternoon; **(dans) l'~** in the afternoon; **4 heures de l'~** 4 o'clock in the afternoon **II.** *adv* **mardi/demain ~** Tuesday/tomorrow afternoon; **tous les lundis ~** every Monday afternoon

après-mur [apʀɛmyʀ] *m* post-communist era

après-rasage [apʀɛʀɑzaʒ] **I.** *m inv* after-shave **II.** *adj inv* (*lotion*) after-shave

après-ski [apʀɛski] *m inv* après-ski

après-vente [apʀɛvɑ̃t] *adj inv* **service ~** after sales service

a priori [apʀijɔʀi] **I.** *adv* **1.** (*au premier abord*) at first sight **2.** (*en principe*) in theory **II.** *m inv* preconception **III.** *adj inv* a priori

à-propos [apʀɔpo] *m* **esprit d'~** (*en parlant*) aptness; (*en agissant*) presence of mind; **avec ~** (*au bon moment*) aptly

apte [apt] *adj* **1.** (*capable*) able **2.** MIL **être ~ au service** to be fit for duty

aptitude [aptityd] *f* aptitude

aquarelle [akwaʀɛl] *f* watercolour *Brit,* watercolor *Am*

aquarium [akwaʀjɔm] *m* aquarium

aquatique [akwatik] *adj* aquatic

aqueduc [akdyk] *m* aqueduct

aquitain(e) [akitɛ̃, ɛn] *adj* of Aquitaine

Aquitain(e) [akitɛ̃, ɛn] *m(f)* person from Aquitaine

Aquitaine [akitɛn] *f* **l'~** Aquitaine

arabe [aʀab] **I.** *adj* Arab; **les Émirats ~s (unis)** the (United) Arab Emirates **II.** *m* Arabic; *v. a.* **français**

Arabe [aʀab] *mf* Arab

arabesque [aʀabɛsk] *f* arabesque

Arabie [aʀabi] *f* **l'~ (Saoudite)** (Saudi) Arabia

arable [aʀabl] *adj* (*terre*) arable

arachide [aʀaʃid] *f* **1.** (*plante*) groundnut **2.** *Québec* (*cacaouète*) **des ~s salées** salted peanuts

araignée [aʀeɲe] *f* spider

arbalète [aʀbalɛt] *f* crossbow

arbitrage [aʀbitʀaʒ] *m* **1.** (*fonction*) refereeing; (*au tennis, cricket*) umpiring **2.** (*juridiction, médiation*) arbitration; FIN arbitrage **3.** (*sentence*) arbitrament

arbitraire [aʀbitʀɛʀ] **I.** *adj* arbitrary **II.** *m* arbitrariness

arbitrairement [aʀbitʀɛʀmɑ̃] *adv* arbitrarily

arbitre [aʀbitʀ] *mf* **1.** SPORT referee; (*au tennis, cricket*) umpire **2.** (*conciliateur*) arbitrator

arbitrer [aʀbitʀe] <1> *vt* **1.** (*servir de conciliateur*) to arbitrate **2.** SPORT to referee; (*tennis, cricket*) to umpire

arboré(e) [aʀbɔʀe] *adj Belgique* (*planté d'arbres*) **jardin ~** tree garden

A

arborer [aʀbɔʀe] <1> *vt* **1.** (*hisser: drapeau*) to fly; (*bannière, pancarte*) to bear **2.** (*montrer*) to sport; (*air, sourire*) to wear **3.** PRESSE (*gros titre, manchette*) to carry

arborescence [aʀbɔʀesɑ̃s] *f* INFOR directory structure

arboriculteur, **-trice** [aʀbɔʀikyltœʀ, tʀis] *m, f* arboriculturist

arboriculture [aʀbɔʀikyltyʀ] *f* arboriculture

arbre [aʀbʀ] *m* **1.** BOT tree **2.** TECH shaft

arbrisseau [aʀbʀiso] <x> *m* shrub

arbuste [aʀbyst] *m* bush

arc [aʀk] *m* **1.** (*arme*) bow **2.** MAT arc; ~ **de cercle** arc of a circle **3.** ARCHIT arch; ~ **de triomphe** triumphal arch

ARC [aʀk] *f abr de* **Association pour le développement de la recherche sur le cancer** *French cancer research association*

arcade [aʀkad] *f* **1.** ARCHIT archway **2.** ANAT ~ **sourcilière** arch of the eyebrows

arc-boutant [aʀkbutɑ̃] <arcs-boutants> *m* ARCHIT flying buttress

arc-bouter [aʀkbute] <1> *vpr* **s'~ contre** [*o* **à**] **qc/sur qc** to brace oneself against sth

arc-en-ciel [aʀkɑ̃sjɛl] <arcs-en-ciel> *m* rainbow

archaïque [aʀkaik] *adj* archaic

archaïsme [aʀkaism] *m* archaism

arche [aʀʃ] *f* **1.** (*forme*) arch **2.** REL ~ **de Noé** Noah's Ark

archelle [aʀʃɛl] *f Belgique* (*étagère de salle à manger, munie de crochets pour ustensiles à anses*) dresser

archéologie [aʀkeɔlɔʒi] *f* archaeology

archéologique [aʀkeɔlɔʒik] *adj* archaeological

archéologue [aʀkeɔlɔg] *mf* archaeologist

archer, **-ère** [aʀʃe, -ɛʀ] *m, f* archer

archet [aʀʃɛ] *m* bow

archétype [aʀketip] *m* archetype

archevêque [aʀʃəvɛk] *m* archbishop

archiconnu(**e**) [aʀʃikɔny] *adj* very well-known

archifaux, **-fausse** [aʀʃifo, -fos] *adj* completely false

archipel [aʀʃipɛl] *m* archipelago

architecte [aʀʃitɛkt] *mf* architect

architectural(**e**) [aʀʃitɛktyʀal, o] <-aux> *adj* architectural

architecture [aʀʃitɛktyʀ] *f* **1.** ARCHIT, INFOR architecture; (*style*) design **2.** (*structure: d'un texte*) structure

archive [aʀʃiv] *f* INFOR archive; **une ~ zip** a zip archive

archiver [aʀʃive] <1> *vt* to archive

archives [aʀʃiv] *fpl* **1.** (*documents publics*) archives **2.** (*documents personnels*) records

Archives [aʀʃiv] *fpl* **les ~ nationales** the National Archives

arctique [aʀktik] *adj* arctic; **le cercle polaire/l'océan ~** the Arctic Circle/Ocean

Arctique [aʀktik] *m* **l'~** the Arctic

ardemment [aʀdamɑ̃] *adv* ardently

ardennais(**e**) [aʀɛnɛ, ɛz] *adj* of the Ardennnes

Ardennais(**e**) [aʀɛnɛ, ɛz] *m(f)* person from the Ardennes

ardent(**e**) [aʀdɑ̃, ɑ̃t] *adj* **1.** (*brûlant*) burning **2.** (*violent: désir, passion*) burning; (*amour, lutte, haine*) passionate; (*vœu, imagination*) fervent **3.** (*bouillant: partisan*) ardent; (*nature, jeunesse, tempérament*) passionate; (*amant*) fervent

ardeur [aʀdœʀ] *f* **1.** (*chaleur*) ardour *Brit,* ardor *Am* **2.** (*force vive*) keenness; (*de la foi, conviction*) fervour; (*de la jeunesse, d'une passion*) ardour *Brit,* ardor *Am* **3.** (*zèle*) zeal; ~ **à qc** zeal for sth

ardoise [aʀdwaz] **I.** *f sans pl* slate **II.** *adj inv* (*couleur*) slate grey

ardoisier [aʀdwazje] *m Belgique* (*couvreur*) tiler

ardu(**e**) [aʀdy] *adj* **1.** (*problème, question*) difficult; (*épreuve*) arduous; (*travail*) laborious **2.** (*chemin*) steep

are [aʀ] *m* are, one hundred square metres *Brit,* one hundred square meters *Am*

arène [aʀɛn] *f* **1.** (*piste*) arena **2.** *pl* (*lieu de corrida*) ring; (*amphithéâtre romain*) arena **3.** GEO sand

arête [aʀɛt] *f* **1.** ZOOL (*d'un poisson*) (fish)bone **2.** (*bord saillant*) edge; (*du nez*) bridge

argent [aʀʒɑ̃] **I.** *m* **1.** FIN money; ~ **de poche** pocket money; **payer en ~ comptant** to pay cash **2.** (*métal*) silver **II.** *adj inv* (*couleur*) silver

argenté(**e**) [aʀʒɑ̃te] *adj* **1.** (*ton*) silvery; (*couleur, reflets, cheveux*) silver **2.** (*recouvert d'argent*) silver-plated

argenterie [aʀʒɑ̃tʀi] *f sans pl* **1.** (*vaisselle*) silverware **2.** (*couverts*) silver

argentin(**e**) [aʀʒɑ̃tɛ̃, in] *adj* Argentinian *Brit,* Argentinean *Am*

Argentin(**e**) [aʀʒɑ̃tɛ̃, in] *m(f)* Argentinian *Brit,* Argentinean *Am*

Argentine [aʀʒɑ̃tin] *f* **l'~** Argentina

argile [aʀʒil] *f* clay

argileux, **-euse** [aʀʒilø, -øz] *adj* clayey

argot [aʀgo] *m* **1.** *sans pl* (*langue verte*) slang **2.** (*langage particulier*) jargon

argotique [aʀgɔtik] *adj* slangy

argument [aʀgymɑ̃] *m* (*raisonnement, preuve*) argument

argumentaire [aʀgymɑ̃tɛʀ] *m* sales brief

argumentation [aʀgymɑ̃tasjɔ̃] *f* argumentation

argumenter [aʀgymɑ̃te] <1> *vi* ~ **contre qn/qc** to argue with sb/sth

Argus [aʀgys] *m* ≈ Black Book *Brit,* ≈ (Kelley®) *Blue Book Am*

aride [aʀid] *adj* dry

aridité [aʀidite] *f sans pl* dryness

aristocrate [aʀistɔkʀat] *mf* aristocrat

aristocratie [aʀistɔkʀasi] *f* aristocracy

aristocratique [aʀistɔkʀatik] *adj* aristocratic

arithmétique [aritmetik] **I.** *f* arithmetic **II.** *adj* arithmetical

armada [armada] *f* armada

armagnac [armaɲak] *m* armagnac

armateur [armatœr] *m* ship owner

armature [armatyr] *f* (*charpente*) armature; (*d'une tente, d'un abat-jour, parapluie*) frame; (*d'un soutien-gorge*) underwiring

arme [arm] *f* **1.** (*instrument*) weapon **2.** (*corps de l'armée*) branch (of the armed services)

armé(e) [arme] *adj* armed

armée [arme] *f* **1.** (*institution, troupes*) **l'~** the armed services *pl;* ~ **de terre** the Army; **être à l'~** to be in the army; ~ **de libération** liberation army; ~ **du Salut** Salvation Army **2.** (*foule*) crowd

armement [arməmɑ̃] *m* **1.** *sans pl* (*action: d'un pays, d'une armée, d'un soldat*) arming; (*d'un navire*) fitting out; (*d'un fusil*) cocking; (*d'un appareil photo*) winding-on **2.** (*armes: d'un soldat, d'une troupe*) weapons *pl;* (*d'un pays, avion, bateau*) arms *pl*

Arménie [armeni] *f* **l'~** Armenia

arménien [armenjɛ̃] *m* Armenian; *v. a.* **français**

arménien(ne) [armenjɛ̃, jɛn] *adj* Armenian

Arménien(ne) [armenjɛ̃, jɛn] *m(f)* Armenian

armer [arme] <1> **I.** *vt* **1.** (*munir d'armes: soldat, pays*) to arm **2.** (*équiper: soldat*) to equip; (*bateau*) to fit out **3.** (*aguerrir*) ~ **qn contre qc** to arm sb against sth **4.** (*charger: fusil*) to cock; ~ **un appareil photo** to wind on (the film in a camera) **5.** (*renforcer: béton*) to reinforce **II.** *vpr* **1.** (*se munir d'armes*) **s'~ contre qn/qc** (*soldat, pays, peuple*) to arm oneself against sb/sth **2.** (*se munir de*) **s'~ de patience** to call upon all one's patience

armistice [armistis] *m* armistice

Armistice [armistis] *m* **l'~** the Armistice

> The **Armistice** is a national holiday in France on November 11, held in remembrance of the ceasefire at the end of the First World War and the signature of the Treaty of Versailles on that day in 1918. Flowers are laid and candles are lit at memorials. There is a perpetual flame at the grave of the unknown soldier beneath the Arc de Triomphe in Paris.

armoire [armwar] *f* cupboard

armoiries [armwari] *fpl* coat of arms + *vb sing*

armure [armyr] *f* **1.** MIL armour *Brit,* armor *Am* **2.** *fig* defence *Brit,* defense *Am*

armurerie [armyrri] *f* (*commerce*) gun shop

armurier [armyrje] *m* **1.** (*marchand, fabricant*) gunsmith **2.** HIST, MIL armourer *Brit,* armorer *Am*

ARN [aɛrɛn] *m abr de* **acide ribonucléique** RNA

arnaque [arnak] *f inf* con

arnaquer [arnake] <1> *vt inf* (*escroquer*) to con

arnaqueur, -euse [arnakœr, -øz] *m, f inf* swindler

arobas [arɔba(z)] *m* INFOR at-sign

aromate [arɔmat] *m* **les ~s** herbs and spices

aromatique [arɔmatik] *adj* aromatic

aromatisé(e) [arɔmatize] *adj* ~ **à la fraise/au chocolat** strawberry/chocolate flavoured *Brit,* strawberry/chocolate flavored *Am*

aromatiser [arɔmatize] <1> *vt* (*aliment*) to flavour *Brit,* to flavor *Am;* (*savon*) to perfume

arôme, arome [arom] *m* **1.** (*odeur: du café*) aroma; (*d'un vin*) nose **2.** (*additif alimentaire*) flavour *Brit,* flavor *Am*

arpent [arpɑ̃] *m* **1. se disputer pour quelques ~s de terre** to argue over a few acres of land **2.** *Québec* arpent *(linear measure of 58.47 metres, 191.8 feet, or a surface measure of 34.2 ares, 36,802 square feet, or just under an acre)*

arpenter [arpɑ̃te] <1> *vt* **1.** (*parcourir: pièce*) to pace (up and down) **2.** (*mesurer*) to measure

arpenteur [arpɑ̃tœr] *m* surveyor

arqué(e) [arke] *adj* (*sourcils*) arched; (*dos*) curved; **avoir les jambes ~es** to be bow-legged

arrachage [araʃaʒ] *m* lifting; (*des mauvaises herbes*) weeding; (*d'un arbre*) uprooting; (*des légumes*) lifting; (*d'un clou*) removal; (*d'une dent*) extraction

arrachement [araʃmɑ̃] *m* (*déchirement*) wrench

arrache-pied [araʃpje] *adv* **d'~** (*lutter, travailler*) relentlessly

arracher [araʃe] <1> **I.** *vt* **1.** (*extraire: herbes*) to pull up; (*arbre*) to uproot; (*légumes*) to dig up; (*clou, poil, page*) to pull out; (*dent*) to extract **2.** (*déchirer: affiche*) to rip down; ~ **un bras à qn** (*personne*) to rip sb's arm off; (*chien*) to bite sb's arm off **3.** (*prendre*) ~ **qn à qn** to rescue sb from sb; ~ **qn/qc des mains de qn** to grab sb/sth from sb's hands; ~ **qn de l'emprise de qn** to wrench sb from sb's domination **4.** (*obtenir*) ~ **de l'argent à qn** to extract money from sb; ~ **une larme à qn** to make sb cry **5.** (*soustraire*) ~ **qn à son travail** to drag sb away from their work; ~ **qn à la mort** to snatch sb from death **II.** *vpr* **1.** (*se déchirer*) **s'~ les cheveux** to tear one's hair out **2.** (*se disputer*) **s'~ qn/qc** to fight over sb/sth **3.** *inf* (*partir*) **s'~** to tear oneself away

arracheur [araʃœr] **mentir comme un ~ de dents** to lie through one's teeth

arrangeant(e) [arɑ̃ʒɑ̃, ʒɑ̃t] *adj* accommodating; (*dans une négociation*) obliging

arrangement [arɑ̃ʒmɑ̃] *m* arrangement; (*d'une coiffure*) fixing

arranger [aʀɑ̃ʒe] <2a> **I.** *vt* **1.** (*disposer*) to arrange; (*coiffure*) to fix; (*vêtement*) to straighten **2.** (*organiser: voyage, réunion, affaires, rencontre*) to arrange **3.** (*régler*) to sort out **4.** (*contenter*) to suit; **si ça vous arrange** if it's convenient for you; **ça l'arrange que qn fasse qc** (*subj*) it suits him for sb to do sth **5.** (*réparer*) to mend **6.** *inf* (*malmener*) to fix **II.** *vpr* **1.** (*se mettre d'accord*) **s'~ avec qn pour** +*infin* to arrange with sb to +*infin* **2.** (*s'améliorer*) **s'~** (*problème*) to be sorted out; (*situation, état de santé*) to improve **3.** (*se débrouiller*) **s'~ pour que qn fasse qc** (*subj*) to see to it that sb does sth **4.** (*ajuster sa toilette*) **s'~** to tidy oneself up; **s'~ les cheveux/le maquillage** to fix up one's hair/make-up

arrestation [aʀɛstasjɔ̃] *f* arrest

arrêt [aʀɛ] *m* **1.** (*interruption: d'une machine, d'un moteur, véhicule, de la production*) stopping; (*d'une centrale, d'un réacteur*) shutdown; (*des négociations, hostilités, essais*) cessation; **~ cardiaque** cardiac arrest; **sans ~** (*sans interruption*) non-stop; (*fréquemment*) continually **2.** (*halte, station: d'un train, automobiliste*) stop; **dix minutes d'~ à Nancy** a ten-minute stop at Nancy; **le train est sans ~ de Paris à Lyon** the train is non-stop from Paris to Lyons; **être à l'~** (*véhicule, chauffeur*) to be stationary; **rester** [*o* **tomber**] **en ~** to stop short; **~ d'autobus** bus stop **3.** JUR (*jugement*) ruling **4.** MIL (*sanction*) **mettre qn aux ~s** to put sb under arrest ►**~ de jeu** stoppage; **~ de maladie** (*congé*) sick leave; (*certificat*) doctor's certificate; **être en ~ de maladie** to be on sick leave; **prescrire un ~ de maladie de 15 jours à qn** to prescribe 2 weeks sick leave for sb; **~ de travail** (*grève*) stoppage; (*congé*) leave; (*certificat*) doctor's certificate; **être en ~ de travail** to be on sick leave

arrêté [aʀete] *m* order; **~ d'expulsion** (*d'un étranger*) deportation order; (*d'un locataire*) eviction order

arrêté(e) [aʀete] *adj* (*décision*) firm; (*idée*) fixed

arrêter [aʀete] <1> **I.** *vi* **1.** (*stopper*) to stop; **~ de faire qc** to stop doing sth; **arrête, je ne te crois pas!** stop it, I don't believe you! **2.** (*s'interrompre*) **~ de parler** to stop talking **II.** *vt* **1.** (*stopper, interrompre*) to stop; (*télé, machine*) to switch off **2. au voleur, arrêtez-le!** stop thief! **3.** (*terminer*) to end **4.** (*bloquer*) to block **5.** (*abandonner*) to give up **6.** (*faire prisonnier*) to arrest **7.** (*fixer: détails, date*) to fix **III.** *vpr* **1.** (*s'immobiliser, s'interrompre*) **s'~** to stop; **s'~ de faire qc** to stop doing sth **2.** (*séjourner*) to stop off **3.** (*cesser*) **s'~** to cease; (*épidémie*) to end; (*pluie, inflation, travail, hémorragie*) to stop; **s'~ de fumer** to stop smoking

arrêt-maladie [aʀɛmaladi] <arrêts-maladie> *m* (*congé*) sick leave; (*certificat*) doctor's certificate; **être en ~** to be on sick leave

arrhes [aʀ] *fpl* deposit; **verser des ~** to pay a deposit

arrière [aʀjɛʀ] **I.** *m* **1.** *sans pl* (*queue: d'un train*) rear; (*d'un bateau*) stern; (*d'une voiture, avion*) back; **à l'~ de la voiture** in the back of the car **2.** (*pour une indication spatiale, temporelle*) **être en ~ de qn/qc** to be behind sb/sth; **se pencher/aller en ~** to lean/go backwards; **regarder en ~** (*derrière soi*) to look behind one [*o* back]; (*vers le passé*) to look back; **rester en ~** to stay behind **3.** SPORT full-back; **jouer ~ centre/droit** to play centre back/right back *Brit,* to play center back/right back *Am* **4.** MIL **l'~** the rear **II.** *adj inv* **roue/siège ~** back wheel/seat

arriéré(e) [aʀjeʀe] **I.** *adj* **1.** (*demeuré: personne*) backward **2.** (*en retard: région*) underdeveloped **II.** *m(f)* PSYCH backward person

arrière-boutique [aʀjɛʀbutik] <arrière-boutiques> *f* back of the shop **arrière-cour** [aʀjɛʀkuʀ] <arrière-cours> *f* backyard **arrière-garde** [aʀjɛʀgaʀd] <arrière-gardes> *f* rearguard **arrière-goût** [aʀjɛʀgu] <arrière-goûts> *m* aftertaste **arrière-grand-mère** [aʀjɛʀgʀɑ̃mɛʀ] <arrière-grands-mères> *f* great-grandmother **arrière-grand-père** [aʀjɛʀgʀɑ̃pɛʀ] <arrière-grands-pères> *m* great-grandfather **arrière-grands-parents** [aʀjɛʀgʀɑ̃paʀɑ̃] *mpl* great-grandparents **arrière-pays** [aʀjɛʀpei] *m inv* hinterland **arrière-pensée** [aʀjɛʀpɑ̃se] <arrière-pensées> *f* ulterior motive **arrière-petite-fille** [aʀjɛʀpətitfij] <arrière-petites-filles> *f* great-granddaughter **arrière-petit-fils** [aʀjɛʀpətifis] <arrière-petits-fils> *m* great-grandson **arrière-petits-enfants** [aʀjɛʀpətizɑ̃fɑ̃] *mpl* great-grandchildren **arrière-plan** [aʀjɛʀplɑ̃] <arrière-plans> *m a. fig* background; **être à l'~** to be in the background; **passer à l'~** to move into the background; **être relégué à l'~** to be pushed into the background **arrière-saison** [aʀjɛʀsɛzɔ̃] <arrière-saisons> *f* late autumn **arrière-train** [aʀjɛʀtʀɛ̃] <arrière-trains> *m* **1.** ZOOL hindquarters **2.** (*fesses*) rump

arrivage [aʀivaʒ] *m* **1.** (*arrivée: de marchandises*) delivery **2.** (*marchandises*) consignment

arrivant(e) [aʀivɑ̃, ɑ̃t] *m(f)* newcomer

arrivée [aʀive] *f* **1.** (*action, halle d'~*) arrival **2.** (*endroit: d'une course*) finish **3.** TECH (*robinet*) inlet

arriver [aʀive] <1> **I.** *vi être* **1.** (*venir*) to arrive; **comment arrive-t-on chez eux?** how do we get to their place? **2.** (*approcher*) to come; (*nuit*) to close in **3.** (*terminer une compétition*) **~ (le) premier** to come in first; **~ avant/après qn, ~ devant/derrière qn** to come in in front of/behind sb **4.** (*aller jusque*) **~ aux mollets** (*robe*) to come down to one's calves; ~ **jusqu'à la maison** (*conduite, câble*) to reach the house; **il m'arrive à l'épaule** he comes up to my shoulder; ~ **jusqu'aux oreilles de qn** (*bruit, nouvelle*) to reach sb's ears **5.** (*atteindre*) ~ **au terme de son existence** to reach the end of one's life **6.** (*réussir*) ~ **à** +*infin* to manage to +*infin* **7.** (*réussir socialement*) **être arrivé** to have arrived **8.** (*survenir*) **qu'est-ce qui est arrivé?** what's happened? **9.** (*aboutir*) **en** ~ **à faire qc** to end up doing sth **II.** *vi impers être* **1.** (*survenir*) **qu'est-ce qu'il t'est arrivé?** what's happened to you? **2.** (*se produire de temps en temps*) **il m'arrive de faire qc** sometimes I do sth

arriviste [aʀivist] *mf* arriviste

arrogance [aʀɔgɑ̃s] *f* arrogance

arrogant(e) [aʀɔgɑ̃, ɑ̃t] *adj* arrogant

arrondir [aʀɔ̃diʀ] <8> **I.** *vt* **1.** (*rendre rond*) ~ **qc** to round sth off **2.** (*accroître: fortune*) to increase **3.** (*simplifier*) ~ **qc à qc** (*en augmentant*) to round sth up to sth; (*en diminuant*) to round sth down to sth **II.** *vpr* **s'**~ **1.** (*grossir*) to fill out **2.** (*devenir moins anguleux: relief*) to soften; (*paysage*) to become more undulating **3.** (*augmenter: fortune*) to swell

arrondissement [aʀɔ̃dismɑ̃] *m* district (*administrative division of major French cities*)

arrosage [aʀozaʒ] *m* **1.** (*au jet*) spraying **2.** (*à l'arrosoir*) watering

arroser [aʀoze] <1> *vt* **1.** (*à l'arrosoir, couler à travers*) to water **2.** (*au jet, avec un produit*) to spray **3.** (*mouiller: pluie*) to drench **4.** GASTR (*rôti*) to baste; (*gâteau*) to soak **5.** *inf* (*fêter*) to celebrate **6.** (*accompagner d'alcool*) **ça a été un repas bien arrosé** there was plenty of wine with the meal

arroseur [aʀozœʀ] *m* (*appareil*) sprinkler

arrosoir [aʀozwaʀ] *m* watering can

arsenal [aʀsənal, o] <-aux> *m* arsenal

arsenic [aʀsənik] *m* arsenic

art [aʀ] *m* **1.** ART art; **les** ~**s décoratifs** decorative arts; ~ **de vivre** art of living **2.** *sans pl* (*style*) art; **l'**~ **nouveau** art nouveau **3.** *sans pl* (*technique, talent*) skill; **avoir l'**~ **du compromis** to have a knack for compromise **4.** *Québec* (*lettre*) **faculté des** ~**s** arts faculty ►**le** septième ~ the cinema

ARTE [aʀte] *f abr de* **Association relative à la télévision européenne** *Franco-German cultural television channel*

artère [aʀtɛʀ] *f* **1.** ANAT artery **2.** (*voie de communication en ville*) main thoroughfare **3.** (*voie de communication dans un pays*) trunk road

artériel(le) [aʀteʀjɛl] *adj* arterial

arthrose [aʀtʀoz] *f* MED osteoarthritis

artichaut [aʀtiʃo] *m* artichoke

article [aʀtikl] *m* **1.** (*marchandise*) item **2.** (*écrit*) *a.* JUR, LING article; ~ **de journal** newspaper article; ~ **défini/indéfini/partitif** definite/indefinite/partitive article **3.** INFOR ~ **de forum** news item

articulaire [aʀtikylɛʀ] *adj* articular

articulation [aʀtikylasjɔ̃] *f* **1.** ANAT, TECH joint **2.** (*enchaînement*) linking phrase **3.** (*combinaison*) joining **4.** (*prononciation*) articulation

articulé(e) [aʀtikyle] *adj* **1.** (*opp: rigide: poupée*) jointed; (*bus*) articulated **2.** (*opp: inarticulé: langage*) articulate

articuler [aʀtikyle] <1> **I.** *vt* (*prononcer: son*) to articulate; (*mot, phrase*) to pronounce; **bien/mal** ~ **qc** to pronounce sth properly/wrongly **II.** *vpr* **1.** ANAT, TECH **s'**~ **sur qc** to articulate on sth; **s'**~ **à qc** (*os*) to articulate with sth **2.** (*s'organiser*) **bien s'**~ (*parties d'un texte*) to flow well

artifice [aʀtifis] *m* **1.** (*moyen ingénieux*) device **2.** *souvent pl* (*tromperie*) trick

artificiel(le) [aʀtifisjɛl] *adj* **1.** (*fabriqué*) artificial; (*parfum*) synthetic **2.** (*factice*) forgery; (*sourire, style, raisonnement*) false; (*enthousiasme, gaieté*) forced

artificiellement [aʀtifisjɛlmɑ̃] *adv* artificially

artificier [aʀtifisje] *m* **1.** (*fabricant, organisateur*) pyrotechnist **2.** (*spécialiste du désamorçage*) bomb disposal expert

artillerie [aʀtijʀi] *f* artillery

artisan(e) [aʀtizɑ̃, an] *m(f)* craftsman *m*, craftswoman *f*; ~ **boulanger** traditional baker

artisanal(e) [aʀtizanal, o] <-aux> *adj* traditional; (*produit*) home-made

artisanat [aʀtizana] *m* **1.** (*métier*) craft industry **2.** (*les artisans*) craftspeople

artiste [aʀtist] **I.** *mf* artist; (*personne non-conformiste*) bohemian **II.** *adj* **milieu** ~ artistic scene

artistique [aʀtistik] *adj* artistic

arum [aʀɔm] *m* arum lily *Brit*, calla lily *Am*

aryen(ne) [aʀjɛ̃, jɛn] *adj* Aryan

Aryen(ne) [aʀjɛ̃, jɛn] *m(f)* Aryan

as[1] [a] *indic prés de* **avoir**

as[2] [ɑs] *m* (*champion*) *a.* JEUX ace; ~ **de cœur** ace of hearts; ~ **du volant** driving ace; **l'**~ **des** ~ the best of the best

ascendance [asɑ̃dɑ̃s] *f sans pl* **1.** (*origine*) ancestry **2.** ASTR ascent **3.** METEO rising

ascendant [asɑ̃dɑ̃] *m* **1.** *sans pl* (*influence*) ~ **sur qn/qc** influence over sb/sth; **avoir/exercer de l'**~ **sur qn** to have/exert influence over sb; **subir l'**~ **de qn** to be under sb's influence **2.** *sans pl* ASTR ascendant **3.** *pl* JUR (*parents*) ascendants

ascendant(e) [asɑ̃dɑ̃, ɑ̃t] *adj* (*air chaud*) rising; (*mélodie*) ascending; (*vent*) upward; **mouvement** ~ upward movement; (*du soleil*) rising; (*d'un oiseau/avion*) soaring; **tendance** ~**e de l'activité économique** upswing in economic activity

ascenseur [asɑ̃sœʀ] *m* lift *Brit*, elevator *Am*

ascension [asɑ̃sjɔ̃] *f* ascent; (*d'une monnaie*) rise; ~ **sociale** rise in social status; **faire l'**~ **d'une montagne** to climb a mountain

Ascension [asɑ̃sjɔ̃] *f sans pl* REL **l'~** the Ascension
ascète [asɛt] *mf* ascetic; **mener une vie d'~** to lead the life of an ascetic
ascétique [asetik] *adj* ascetic
aseptisé(e) [asɛptize] *adj a. fig* sterilized; (*chambre, plaie*) disinfected
aseptiser [asɛptize] <1> *vt* (*instrument, pansement*) to sterilize; (*chambre, plaie*) to disinfect
asexué(e) [asɛksɥe] *adj* **1.** asexual **2.** *fig* sexless
asiatique [azjatik] *adj* Asian
Asiatique [azjatik] *mf* Asian
Asie [azi] *f* **l'~** Asia; **l'~ centrale** Central Asia; **l'~ Mineure** Asia Minor
asile [azil] *m* **1.** REL, JUR, POL asylum; **offrir un ~ à qn** to offer asylum to sb **2.** (*refuge*) refuge
asocial(e) [asɔsjal, jo] <-aux> **I.** *adj* antisocial **II.** *m(f)* (social) misfit
aspect [aspɛ] *m* **1.** *sans pl* (*apparence*) appearance **2.** (*trait de caractère*) side **3.** (*point de vue*) aspect
asperge [aspɛʀʒ] *f* **1.** (*légume*) asparagus + *vb sing* **2.** *inf* (*personne*) beanpole
asperger [aspɛʀʒe] <2a> **I.** *vt* **~ qn/qc d'eau** to spray sb/sth with water **II.** *vpr* **s'~ de parfum/d'eau** to spray oneself with perfume/water; **s'~ le visage d'eau** to splash one's face with water
aspérité [aspeʀite] *f* **1.** *gén pl* bumps **2.** (*rugosité*) roughness
asphalte [asfalt] *m* asphalt
asphyxiant(e) [asfiksjɑ̃, jɑ̃t] *adj* **1.** (*air*) suffocating; (*fumée*) asphyxiating; (*chaleur*) stifling **2.** *fig* (*ambiance*) stifling
asphyxie [asfiksi] *f sans pl* **1.** (*suffocation*) asphyxiation; **mourir par ~** to die of suffocation **2.** *fig* smothering
asphyxier [asfiksje] <1> **I.** *vt* to suffocate; (*gaz*) to asphyxiate **II.** *vpr* (*ne plus pouvoir respirer*) **s'~** to suffocate
aspic [aspik] *m* **1.** GASTR aspic; **~ de volaille** chicken in aspic **2.** ZOOL asp
aspirateur [aspiʀatœʀ] *m* vacuum cleaner; **passer l'~** [*o* **un coup d'~**] to vacuum
aspiration [aspiʀasjɔ̃] *f* **1.** *sans pl* (*inspiration*) inhalation **2.** TECH drawing up; (*d'un liquide, de poussières*) sucking up **3.** (*avec la bouche*) sucking up **4.** LING, MED aspiration **5.** *sans pl* (*élan*) ambition; **~ à la liberté** longing for freedom **6.** *pl* (*désirs*) aspirations
aspiré(e) [aspiʀe] *adj* LING aspirated
aspirée [aspiʀe] *f* LING aspirate
aspirer [aspiʀe] <1> **I.** *vt* **1.** (*inspirer*) to breathe in; **~ à pleins poumons** to take a deep breath **2.** (*inhaler: air, gaz, odeur*) to inhale **3.** (*avec la bouche*) to suck in **4.** LING to aspirate **5.** TECH to suck up **II.** *vi* **1.** (*désirer*) **~ à qc** to aspire to sth **2.** (*chercher à obtenir*) **~ à qc** to long for sth
aspirine [aspiʀin] *f* aspirin
assagir [asaʒiʀ] <8> **I.** *vt* (*passions*) to calm, **~ qn,** to calm sb down **II.** *vpr* **s'~** (*personne*) to settle down; (*passion*) to calm down
assaillant(e) [asajɑ̃, jɑ̃t] *m(f)* assailant
assaillir [asajiʀ] *vt irr* **1.** (*attaquer*) to attack **2.** (*se ruer sur*) **~ qn de questions** to bombard sb with questions **3.** (*tourmenter*) to torment
assainir [aseniʀ] <8> *vt* ARCHIT, FIN to stabilize
assainissement [asenismɑ̃] *m* cleaning up; (*d'un marécage*) draining; (*de l'eau, de l'air*) decontamination; (*d'une monnaie, situation, du climat social*) stabilization
assaisonnement [asɛzɔnmɑ̃] *m sans pl* (*action, ingrédient*) seasoning; (*d'une salade*) dressing
assaisonner [asɛzɔne] <1> *vt* **1.** (*épicer*) to season; **~ la salade** to dress a salad; **être trop assaisonné** to be over-seasoned **2.** (*relever*) **~ qc** to spice sth up **3.** (*agrémenter*) **~ qc de qc** to embellish sth with sth
assassin [asasɛ̃] *m* murderer; POL assassin
assassin(e) [asasɛ̃, in] *adj* **1.** (*séducteur: regard*) provocative **2.** (*qui tue: main*) deadly; (*regard*) murderous
assassinat [asasina] *m* murder; POL assassination
assassiner [asasine] <1> *vt* to murder; POL to assassinate
assaut [aso] *m* **1.** MIL **~ d'une forteresse** assault on a fortress; **aller à l'~ de qc** to launch an attack on sth; **à l'~!** charge! **2.** *fig* assault **3.** (*ruée*) stampede
assèchement [asɛʃmɑ̃] *m* emptying; (*d'un canal*) draining
assécher [aseʃe] <5> *vt* **1.** (*mettre à sec*) to dry **2.** (*vider*) to drain
ASSEDIC [asedik] *fpl abr de* **Association pour l'emploi dans l'industrie et le commerce** **1.** (*organisme*) *organization managing unemployment benefits* **2.** (*régime d'assurance*) ≈ national insurance **3.** (*cotisation*) ≈ national insurance contribution **4.** (*indemnités*) benefits; **toucher les ~** to receive unemployment benefit
assemblage [asɑ̃blaʒ] *m* **1.** AUTO, CINE (*action*) assembly; COUT sewing together; (*d'une charpente, de pièces de bois*) joining; (*de feuilles*) binding **2.** (*résultat: de couleurs, formes*) collection; (*de charpente*) structure
assemblée [asɑ̃ble] *f* (*réunion*) meeting; POL assembly
Assemblée [asɑ̃ble] *f* POL **l'~ nationale** the (French) National Assembly; **l'~ fédérale** *Suisse* the (Swiss) Federal Assembly

The **Assemblée nationale** is the lower chamber of the French Parliament, elected normally every five years. It has 490 members. The Belgian lower house is called "la Chambre des Représentants" and is elected every four years.

assembler [asɑ̃ble] <1> **I.** *vt* **1.** (*monter: pièces*) to assemble **2.** (*réunir: couleurs*) to put together; (*vêtement, pièces d'étoffe*) to sew together; (*feuilles volantes*) to gather **3.** (*recueillir: pièces*) to assemble; (*idées, données*) to gather **II.** *vpr* **s'~** to gather

assembleur [asɑ̃blœʀ] *m* INFOR assembler

assener <4> *vt,* **asséner** [asene] <5> *vt* (*coup, gifle*) to deliver; (*vérité*) to point out; (*réplique*) to fling back

assentiment [asɑ̃timɑ̃] *m* assent; **en signe d'~** in assent; **l'~ de qn à qc** sb's consent to sth

asseoir [aswaʀ] *irr* **I.** *vt* to sit; **faire ~ qn** to make sb sit down; **être/rester assis** to remain seated; **assis!** sit! **II.** *vpr* **s'~** to sit; **asseyez-vous!** sit down!

assermenté(e) [asɛʀmɑ̃te] *adj* on oath; **être ~** to be under oath

assertion [asɛʀsjɔ̃] *f* assertion

asservir [asɛʀviʀ] <8> *vt* to overcome; (*peuple, presse*) to enslave

assez [ase] *adv* **1.** (*suffisamment*) enough; **il y a ~ de place** there is enough room; **être ~ riche** to be rich enough; **~ parlé!** enough talking! **2.** (*plutôt*) rather; **aimer ~ les films de Bergman** to quite like Bergman's films **3.** (*quantité suffisante*) **c'est ~** it's enough [*o* sufficient] **4.** (*de préférence, dans l'ensemble*) **être ~ content de soi** to be quite pleased with oneself **5.** ECOLE **~ bien** satisfactory **6.** (*exprimant la lassitude*) **~!** enough!; **c'(en) est ~!** that's (quite) enough!; **en voilà ~!** that will do!; **en avoir plus qu'~ de qn/qc** to have more than enough of sb/sth; **j'en ai ~ de toi/de tes bêtises!** I've had enough of you/your stupidity!

assidu(e) [asidy] *adj* **1.** (*régulier: présence, travail, soins*) regular; (*élève, employé, lecteur*) assiduous **2.** (*empressé: amoureux*) assiduous

assiduité [asidɥite] *f sans pl* (*d'un élève, d'un employé*) regularity; **son ~ dans le travail** his careful work; **son ~ au travail** his regular attendance at work

assiéger [asjeʒe] <2a, 5> *vt* **1.** MIL (*place, population*) to lay siege to; (*armée*) to besiege **2.** (*prendre d'assaut: guichet*) to besiege; (*personne, hôtel*) to mob

assiette [asjɛt] *f* **1.** GASTR plate; **~ plate** plate; **~ creuse** bowl; **~ à dessert** dessert plate; **~ à soupe** [*o* **profonde**] *Belgique* soup bowl; **~ de crudités** plate of salad vegetables; **~ de soupe** bowl of soup **2.** (*base de calcul*) base for mortgage calculations

assignation [asiɲasjɔ̃] *f* assignation

assigner [asiɲe] <1> *vt* **1.** (*attribuer*) to assign **2.** (*fixer*) to fix; **~ une cause à qc** to give a reason for sth **3.** JUR **~ qn à résidence** to put sb under house arrest; **~ qn en justice** to issue a writ against sb; **~ un témoin à comparaître** to subpoena a witness

assimilation [asimilasjɔ̃] *f* **1.** (*comparaison*) **~ à qc** comparison with sth **2.** (*amalgame*) **~ de qc à qc,** equating of sth and sth **3.** BIO assimilation; BOT photosynthesis **4.** *fig* (*de connaissances*) assimilation **5.** (*intégration*) **~ à qc** integration into sth

assimiler [asimile] <1> **I.** *vt* **1.** (*confondre*) **~ qn/qc à qn/qc** to equate sb/sth with sb/sth **2.** BIO to assimilate; BOT to photosynthesize **3.** (*apprendre: connaissances*) to take in **4.** (*intégrer*) to integrate **II.** *vi* to assimilate **III.** *vpr* **1.** (*s'identifier*) **s'~ à qn** to identify with sb **2.** (*s'apprendre*) to be taken in **3.** (*s'intégrer*) **s'~ à qc** to integrate into sth

assis(e) [asi, iz] **I.** *part passé de* **asseoir** **II.** *adj* **1.** (*position*) sitting **2.** (*affermi*) **être bien ~** to be well established

assise [asiz] *f* **1.** ARCHIT (*rangée*) course **2.** *souvent pl* (*fondement*) foundation **3.** *pl* GEO strata

assises [asiz] *fpl* **1.** JUR (*cour*) assizes; **être envoyé aux ~** to be sent to the assizes **2.** (*réunion*) meeting; (*d'un parti politique*) conference; **tenir ses ~** to hold its conference

assistanat [asistana] *m* UNIV, ECOLE assistantship

assistance [asistɑ̃s] *f* **1.** (*public*) audience **2.** (*secours*) assistance; **demander ~ à qn** to ask sb for help; **prêter ~ à qn** to help sb **3.** (*dons*) **prêter ~ à qn** to give aid to sb; (*mécène*) to sponsor sb **4.** (*aide organisée*) **~ médicale** medical care; **~ technique** technical support **5.** (*type d'assurance*) national insurance

assistant [asistɑ̃] *m* INFOR **~ personnel de communication** personal digital assistant; **~ pages web** web page wizard

assistant(e) [asistɑ̃, ɑ̃t] *m(f)* **1.** (*aide*) assistant; MED medical assistant; **~ social** social worker **2.** (*public*) **les ~s** those present

assisté(e) [asiste] **I.** *adj* **1.** SOCIOL (*enfant*) in care; (*famille*) on benefit *Brit,* on welfare *Am* **2.** AUTO **direction ~e** power-assisted steering **3.** INFOR **dessin/traduction ~(e) par ordinateur** computer-aided design/translation **II.** *m(f)* person on benefit

assister [asiste] <1> **I.** *vi* **1.** (*être présent*) **~ à qc** to be present at sth **2.** (*regarder*) **~ à qc** to watch sth **3.** (*être témoin de*) **~ à qc** to be a witness to sth **4.** (*participer*) **~ à qc** to take part in sth **II.** *vt* **1.** (*aider*) **~ qn dans qc** to help sb with sth **2.** (*en chirurgie*) **~ qn dans qc** to assist sb with sth **3.** (*être aux côtés de*) to comfort **4.** JUR (*curateur*) to aid

associatif, -ive [asɔsjatif, -iv] *adj* **1.** PSYCH, MAT associative **2.** (*relatif à une association*) **vie associative** community life

association [asɔsjasjɔ̃] *f* association; **en ~ avec un ami** in partnership with a friend; **~ économique/sportive** economic/sporting association; **~ de qc à qc** association of sth with sth

associé(e) [asɔsje] **I.** *m(f)* associate **II.** *adj* (*gérant*) associate

associer [asɔsje] <1> **I.** *vt* **1.** (*faire participer*) ~ **qn à sa joie** to share one's joy with sb; ~ **qn à un travail** to involve sb in a job; ~ **les travailleurs aux bénéfices** to give the workers a share of the profits **2.** (*unir, lier: choses, personnes*) to associate; (*couleurs*) to combine **II.** *vpr* **1.** (*s'allier*) **s'~ à** [*o* **avec**] **qn** to join with sb **2.** (*s'adjoindre*) **s'~ un collaborateur** to take sb on as a partner **3.** (*s'accorder*) **s'~** (*choses*) to go together **4.** (*participer à*) **s'~ à la joie de qn** to share in sb else's happiness; **s'~ au projet de qn** to involve oneself in sb's project

assoiffé(e) [aswafe] *adj* **1.** (*qui a soif*) parched **2.** (*avide*) ~ **de lectures** avid reader; ~ **de vengeance** hungry for revenge

assombri(e) [asɔ̃bʀi] *adj* **1.** (*obscurci*) darkened **2.** (*triste, grave: regard*) sad; (*futur, avenir*) gloomy; (*jours*) dark

assombrir [asɔ̃bʀiʀ] <8> **I.** *vt* **1.** (*obscurcir*) to darken **2.** (*rembrunir, peser sur: personne*) to sadden; (*situation*) to cast a shadow over **II.** *vpr* **s'~** to darken; (*horizon, visage*) to cloud over; (*personne*) to grow sad; (*situation*) to become gloomy

assommer [asɔme] <1> **I.** *vt* **1.** (*étourdir*) to knock out; (*animal*) to stun **2.** (*abasourdir*) **cette nouvelle m'a assommé** this news knocked me out **3.** (*abrutir*) **le soleil m'a assommé** the sun drained me **4.** *inf* (*ennuyer*) ~ **qn** to bore sb to death **II.** *vpr* **s'~** **1.** (*se cogner*) to knock oneself out **2.** *inf* (*se battre*) to lay into each other

Assomption [asɔ̃psjɔ̃] *f* **l'~** the Assumption

> **L'Assomption**, 15 August, is both a religious and a national holiday in France. For many people it marks the end of the summer holidays and road congestion is common.

assorti(e) [asɔʀti] *adj* (*couleurs, vêtements*) matching; **être ~ aux rideaux** to match the curtains; **des personnes/choses sont bien/mal ~es** people/things are well/badly matched

assortiment [asɔʀtimɑ̃] *m* **1.** (*mélange*) selection; ~ **de charcuterie/gâteaux** selection of cold meats/cakes **2.** (*arrangement*) ~ **de couleurs** colour arrangement

assortir [asɔʀtiʀ] <8> **I.** *vt* **1.** (*harmoniser: couleurs, fleurs*) to match; ~ **les rideaux au tapis** to match the curtains with the carpets **2.** (*réunir: personnes*) to mix **3.** (*accompagner*) ~ **son exposé d'anecdotes** to sprinkle one's presentation with anecdotes **II.** *vpr* **s'~** to match

assoupi(e) [asupi] *adj* **1.** (*somnolent*) sleepy **2.** (*affaibli: passion*) calmed; (*douleur*) dulled

assoupir [asupiʀ] <8> **I.** *vt* **1.** (*endormir*) ~ **qn** to make sb drowsy **2.** (*affaiblir: sens, sensualité, douleur, haine*) to dull **II.** *vpr* **s'~** to fall asleep

assoupissement [asupismɑ̃] *m* drowsiness

assouplir [asupliʀ] <8> **I.** *vt* **1.** (*rendre plus souple: cheveux, linge*) to soften; ~ **le cuir** to make leather supple; ~ **les muscles** to exercise the muscles **2.** (*rendre moins rigoureux: règlement*) to relax **II.** *vpr* **s'~** **1.** (*devenir plus souple: chaussures*) to soften; (*cuir*) to become supple; (*personne*) to become more flexible **2.** (*devenir moins rigide*) to relax

assouplissant [asuplisɑ̃] *m* fabric softener

assourdir [asuʀdiʀ] <8> **I.** *vt* **1.** (*abasourdir*) to deafen **2.** (*rendre moins sonore: bruit, pas*) to muffle **II.** *vpr* **s'~** (*bruit*) to be muffled

assourdissant(e) [asuʀdisɑ̃, ɑ̃t] *adj* deafening

assouvir [asuviʀ] <8> **I.** *vt* (*faim, vengeance, passion*) to appease; (*curiosité, gourmandise, instinct, désir*) to satisfy **II.** *vpr* **s'~** (*faim*) to be appeased; (*passion, curiosité*) to be satisfied

assujetti(e) [asyʒeti] **I.** *adj* (*soumis*) **être ~ à l'impôt** to be liable for tax; **être ~ à qn** to be subjected to sb **II.** *m(f)* ADMIN **1.** (*à l'impôt*) person liable (for tax) **2.** (*à la sécurité sociale*) person liable (for contibutions)

assujettir [asyʒetiʀ] <8> **I.** *vt* **1.** (*astreindre*) ~ **qn à l'impôt** to make sb liable to tax; **son métier l'assujettit à une présence constante** his job requires that he's there constantly **2.** (*fixer: porte, volet*) to secure; (*poutre*) to make fast **II.** *vpr soutenu* **1.** (*se plier*) **s'~ à des règles** to submit to rules; **s'~ à un régime alimentaire** to follow a diet **2.** (*conquérir*) **s'~ un peuple** to conquer a nation

assumer [asyme] <1> **I.** *vt* **1.** (*exercer, supporter: risque, responsabilité*) to take on; (*tâche, fonction*) to undertake; (*poste*) to take up; (*douleur*) to accept **2.** (*accepter: condition*) to accept; (*instincts*) to trust **II.** *vpr* **1.** (*s'accepter*) **s'~** to accept onself **2.** (*se supporter*) **une amputation s'assume difficilement** an amputation is difficult to come to terms with **III.** *vi inf* to accept one's situation

assurance [asyʀɑ̃s] *f* **1.** *sans pl* (*aplomb*) self-confidence; **avec ~** with confidence **2.** (*garantie*) insurance **3.** (*contrat*) insurance policy **4.** (*société*) insurance company **5.** SPORT belaying

assuré(e) [asyʀe] **I.** *adj* **1.** (*opp: hésitant: démarche*) confident; (*regard*) knowing **2.** (*garanti*) guaranteed **II.** *m(f)* insured party

assurément [asyʀemɑ̃] *adv soutenu* certainly

assurer [asyʀe] <1> **I.** *vt* **1.** (*affirmer, garantir, par un contrat d'assurance*) to insure **2.** (*se charger de*) ~ **qc** (*protection*) to deal with sth **3.** (*rendre sûr: avenir, fortune*) to insure **4.** (*accorder*) ~ **une retraite à qn** to provide a pension for sb **5.** SPORT to belay **II.** *vpr* **1.** (*contracter une assurance*) **s'~ à la compagnie X contre qc** to insure against sth with company X **2.** (*vérifier*) **s'~ de qc** to make sure of sth **3.** (*gagner*) **s'~ l'appui de qn** to win sb's support **II.** *vi inf* to cope

assureur [asyʀœʀ] *m* insurer

astérisque [asteʀisk] *m* asterisk

astéroïde [asteʀɔid] *m* asteroid

asthmatique [asmatik] *adj, mf* asthmatic

asthme [asm] *m* asthma

asticot [astiko] *m inf* (*ver*) maggot

asticoter [astikɔte] <1> *vt inf* ~ **qn** to get at sb

astigmate [astigmat] *adj, mf* astigmatic

astiquer [astike] <1> *vt* to polish; (*meubles, pomme*) to shine

astrakan [astʀakɑ̃] *m* astrakhan

astral(e) [astʀal, o] <-aux> *adj* **signe ~** sign of the zodiac

astre [astʀ] *m* star

astreignant(e) [astʀɛɲɑ̃, ɑ̃t] *adj* exacting; (*horaire, règle*) demanding

astreindre [astʀɛ̃dʀ] *irr* **I.** *vt* ~ **qn à un travail** to oblige sb to do a job; ~ **qn à un régime sévère** (*médecin*) to put sb on a strict diet; ~ **qn à** +*infin* to oblige sb to +*infin* **II.** *vpr* **s'~ à qc/à** +*infin* to compel oneself to sth/to +*infin*

astreinte [astʀɛ̃t] *f* **1.** (*contrainte*) constraint **2.** JUR penalty

astrologie [astʀɔlɔʒi] *f* astrology

astrologique [astʀɔlɔʒik] *adj* astrological

astrologue [astʀɔlɔg] *mf* astrologer

astronaute [astʀonot] *mf* astronaut

astronautique [astʀonotik] *f* astronautics + *vb sing*

astronef [astʀonɛf] *m* spaceship

astronome [astʀɔnɔm] *mf* astronomer

astronomie [astʀɔnɔmi] *f* astronomy

astronomique [astʀɔnɔmik] *adj* **1.** ASTR astronomic **2.** (*faramineux: nombre, prix*) astronomical

astuce [astys] *f* **1.** *sans pl* (*qualité*) astuteness **2.** *souvent pl* (*truc*) trick **3.** *gén pl, inf* (*plaisanterie*) joke

astucieusement [astysjøzmɑ̃] *adv* (*éviter, défendre*) shrewdly; (*répondre*) cleverly

astucieux, -euse [astysjø, -jøz] *adj* clever

asymétrie [asimetʀi] *f* asymmetry

asymétrique [asimetʀik] *adj* asymmetrical

atchoum [atʃum] *interj* atishoo

atelier [atəlje] *m* **1.** (*lieu de travail*) workshop; (*d'un artiste*) studio **2.** ECON (*d'une usine*) factory floor; ~ **de fabrication** workshop; ~ **de montage** assembly shop **3.** (*ensemble des ouvriers*) workshop **4.** (*groupe de réflexion*) workshop

athée [ate] **I.** *adj* atheistic **II.** *mf* atheist

athénée [atene] *m* **1.** *Belgique, Suisse* (*établissement destiné à des lectures, des leçons publiques*) institute **2.** *Belgique* (*collège, lycée*) secondary school

Athènes [atɛn] Athens

athénien(ne) [atenjɛ̃, jɛn] *adj* Athenian

Athénien(ne) [atenjɛ̃, jɛn] *m(f)* Athenian

athlète [atlɛt] *mf* athlete

athlétique [atletik] *adj* athletic

athlétisme [atletism] *m* athletics + *vb sing Brit*, track and field *Am*

atlantique [atlɑ̃tik] *adj* Atlantic; **côte ~** Atlantic coast

Atlantique [atlɑ̃tik] *m* **l'~** the Atlantic

atlas [atlɑs] *m* GEO, ANAT atlas

atmosphère [atmɔsfɛʀ] *f* atmosphere

atmosphérique [atmɔsfeʀik] *adj* atmospheric

atoll [atɔl] *m* atoll

atome [atom] *m* PHYS atom

atomique [atɔmik] *adj* atomic

atomiseur [atɔmizœʀ] *m* spray

atours [atuʀ] *mpl* **dans ses plus beaux ~** *iron* in all her finery

atout [atu] *m* **1.** asset; JEUX trump card **2.** (*qualité*) asset

âtre [ɑtʀ] *m* hearth

atroce [atʀɔs] *adj* **1.** (*horrible: crime, image*) appalling; (*vengeance, peur*) terrible **2.** *inf* (*affreux: musique, film*) appalling; (*temps, repas*) terrible; (*personne*) awful

atrocement [atʀɔsmɑ̃] *adv* **1.** (*horriblement: faire mal, souffrir*) horribly **2.** *inf* (*affreusement*) atrociously

atrocité [atʀɔsite] *f* **1.** (*cruauté*) atrocity **2.** *pl* (*action*) atrocities **3.** (*calomnie*) **dire des ~s** to say wicked things

atrophie [atʀɔfi] *f* MED atrophy

atrophié(e) [atʀɔfje] *adj* atrophied

atrophier [atʀɔfje] <1> **I.** *vpr* (*diminuer*) **s'~** to waste away **II.** *vt* (*faire dépérir: muscle*) to atrophy

attabler [atable] <1> **I.** *vpr* **s'~** to sit down at the table **II.** *vi* **être attablés autour d'une bouteille de vin** to be sitting down at the table drinking wine

attachant(e) [ataʃɑ̃, ɑ̃t] *adj* (*personne, personnalité, film, roman, région*) captivating; (*enfant, animal*) endearing

attache [ataʃ] *f* **1.** (*lien*) link **2.** (*pour attacher des animaux*) lead **3.** (*pour attacher des plantes, des arbres*) tie **4.** (*pour attacher un cadre*) clip **5.** *gén pl* (*relations*) tie **6.** BOT tendril **7.** ANAT joint

attaché(e) [ataʃe] **I.** *adj* **1.** (*lié par l'affection, l'habitude*) **être ~ à qn/qc** to be attached to sb/sth **2.** (*ligoté*) **être ~ à qn/qc** to be tied to sb/sth **3.** (*associé*) **être ~ à qc** (*avantage, rétribution*) to be linked to sth; (*bonheur*) to depend on sth **II.** *m(f)* attaché; ~ **d'ambassade/de presse** embassy/press attaché

attaché-case [ataʃekɛz] <attachés-cases> *m* attaché case

attachement [ataʃmɑ̃] *m* (*affection*) *a.* INFOR attachment

attacher [ataʃe] <1> **I.** *vt* **1.** (*fixer*) ~ **qc à qc** to fasten sth to sth **2.** (*fixer avec une corde, ficelle*) ~ **qn/qc sur qc** to tie sb/sth to sth **3.** (*fixer avec des clous*) ~ **qn sur qc** to nail sb to sth **4.** (*mettre ensemble*) to attach; (*feuilles de papier*) to staple; ~ **les mains à qn** to tie sb's hands **5.** (*fermer: lacets, tablier*) to tie;

(*montre, collier*) to fasten; ~ **sa ceinture de sécurité** to put on one's safety belt **6.** (*faire tenir*) ~ **ses cheveux avec un élastique** to tie back one's hair with a hair elastic; ~ **un paquet avec de la ficelle/du ruban adhésif** to do up a package with string/adhesive tape **7.** (*maintenir*) **des pinces à linge attachent les dessins à la ficelle** the drawings are held on the string with clothes pegs *Brit*, the drawings are held on the string with clothespins *Am* **8.** (*lier affectivement*) ~ **qn à qn/qc** to tie sb to sb/sth **9.** (*enchaîner*) ~ **qn à qn/qc** to bind sb to sb/sth **10.** (*attribuer*) ~ **de l'importance à qc** to attach importance to sth; ~ **de la valeur à qc** to value sth; **quel sens attaches-tu à ce mot?** what meaning do you give to this word? **II.** *vi inf* (*aliment, gâteau*) to stick **III.** *vpr* **1.** (*mettre sa ceinture de sécurité*) **s'~** to belt up **2.** (*être attaché*) **s'~ à qc** to become attached to sth **3.** (*s'encorder*) **s'~ à une corde** to tie oneself on to a rope **4.** (*se fermer*) **s'~ avec/par qc** to fasten with sth **5.** (*se lier d'affection*) **s'~ à qn/qc** to become attached to sb/sth

attaquant(**e**) [atakɑ̃, ɑ̃t] *m(f)* attacker

attaque [atak] *f* **1.** (*acte de violence*) *a.* MIL, MED, SPORT attack **2.** (*critique acerbe*) ~ **contre qn/qc** attack on sb/sth **3.** MUS attack

attaquer [atake] <1> **I.** *vt* **1.** (*assaillir*) *a.* SPORT to attack **2.** (*pour voler: personne*) to mug **3.** (*critiquer*) ~ **qn sur qc** to attack sb about sth **4.** JUR (*jugement, testament*) to contest; ~ **une loi** to challenge a law; ~ **qn en justice** to bring an action against sb **5.** (*ronger: organe, fer*) to attack; (*falaise*) to erode **6.** (*commencer*) to begin; (*sujet*) to launch into; (*travail*) to start **7.** MUS ~ **un morceau** to launch into a piece **8.** *inf* (*commencer à manger*) ~ **un plat** to dig into a meal **9.** (*chercher à surmonter: difficulté*) to tackle; ~ **le mal à sa racine** to tackle evil at the roots **II.** *vpr* **1.** (*affronter*) **s'~ à qn/qc** to attack sb/sth **2.** (*chercher à résoudre*) **s'~ à une difficulté** to tackle a problem **3.** (*commencer*) **s'~ à qc** to launch into sth

attardé(**e**) [ataʀde] **I.** *adj* **1.** (*en retard*) late **2.** PSYCH retarded **II.** *m(f) péj* retard

attarder [ataʀde] <1> **I.** *vt* to make late **II.** *vpr* **s'~** to linger

atteindre [atɛ̃dʀ] *vt irr* **1.** (*toucher, parvenir à, joindre par téléphone*) to reach **2.** (*rattraper*) ~ **qn/qc** to catch up with sb/sth **3.** (*avoir un effet nuisible sur*) **la gelée a atteint les plantes** the frost has got at the plants **4.** (*blesser moralement*) to wound **5.** (*troubler intellectuellement*) to impair **6.** (*émouvoir*) to affect; **ça ne m'atteint pas!** that doesn't affect me!

atteint(**e**) [atɛ̃, ɛ̃t] *adj* **1.** (*malade*) **être très ~** (*personne*) to be very ill; (*organe*) to be badly affected; **le malade ~ du cancer** the patient suffering from cancer **2.** *inf* (*fou*) mad

atteinte [atɛ̃t] *f* **1.** (*dommage causé*) ~ **à un droit** infringement of a right; **c'est une ~ à ma réputation** it is an attack on my reputation; ~ **à la sûreté de l'État** breach of national security **2.** *pl* (*effet pénible*) **~s de l'âge/du froid** effects of age/of the cold **3.** (*portée*) **réputation hors d'~** reputation beyond reproach; **se mettre hors d'~** to put oneself out of danger

attelage [at(ə)laʒ] *m* **1.** (*dispositif: de chevaux*) harness; (*d'un véhicule de chemin de fer*) coupling **2.** (*action: d'un cheval*) harnessing; (*d'un bœuf*) hitching up; (*d'un wagon*) coupling

atteler [at(ə)le] <3> **I.** *vt* (*attacher: voiture, animal*) to hitch up **II.** *vpr* **s'~ à un travail** to get down to work

attelle [atɛl] *f* hame; MED splint

attendre [atɑ̃dʀ] <14> **I.** *vt* **1.** (*patienter*) ~ **qn/qc** to wait for sb/sth **2.** (*ne rien faire avant de*) ~ **qn/qc pour faire qc** to wait for sb/sth before doing sth **3.** (*compter sur*) to expect; **n'~ que ça** to expect just that; **en attendant mieux** until something better comes along **4.** (*être préparé*) ~ **qn** (*voiture, surprise*) to be waiting for sb; (*sort, déception*) to lay in wait for sb **5.** *inf* (*se montrer impatient avec*) ~ **après qn** to wait for ever for sb **6.** *inf* (*avoir besoin de*) ~ **après qc** to be waiting on sth **7.** (*jusqu'à*) **mais en attendant** but in the meantime; **en attendant que qn fasse qc** (*subj*) while waiting for sb to do sth **8.** (*toujours est-il*) **en attendant** all the same **II.** *vi* **1.** (*patienter*) to wait; **faire ~ qn** to make sb wait; **tu peux toujours ~!** you're in for a long wait! **2.** (*retarder*) **sans ~ plus longtemps** without waiting any longer **3.** (*interjection*) **attends!** (*pour interrompre, pour réfléchir*) wait!; (*pour menacer*) just you wait! **III.** *vpr* **s'~ à qc** to expect sth; (*en cas de chose désagréable*) to dread sth; **comme il fallait s'y ~** as you might have expected

attendri(**e**) [atɑ̃dʀi] *adj* tender

attendrir [atɑ̃dʀiʀ] <8> **I.** *vt* **1.** (*émouvoir*) to move **2.** (*apitoyer: cœur*) to melt; ~ **qn** to move sb to pity **3.** GASTR to tenderize **II.** *vpr* **1.** (*s'émouvoir*) **se laisser ~** to be moved; (*changer d'avis*) to relent **2.** (*s'apitoyer*) **s'~ sur qn** to feel sorry for sb; **s'~ sur soi-même** to feel sorry for oneself

attendrissant(**e**) [atɑ̃dʀisɑ̃, ɑ̃t] *adj* moving

attendrissement [atɑ̃dʀismɑ̃] *m* emotion

attendu(**e**) [atɑ̃dy] **I.** *part passé de* **attendre** **II.** *adj* (*espéré*) expected

attentat [atɑ̃ta] *m* ~ **contre qn** assassination attempt on sb; ~ **contre qc** attack on sth

attente [atɑ̃t] *f* **1.** (*expectative*) **l'~ de qn/qc** the wait for sb/sth; **salle d'~** waiting room **2.** (*espoir*) **contre toute ~** against all expectation; **dans l'~ de qc** in the hope of sth

attenter [atɑ̃te] <1> *vi* ~ **à ses jours** to attempt suicide; ~ **à la vie de qn** to make an attempt on sb's life

attentif, **-ive** [atɑ̃tif, -iv] *adj* **1.** (*vigilant, pré-*

venant) attentive **2.** (*veillant soigneusement*) **être ~ aux différences** to pay attention to the differences
attention [atɑ̃sjɔ̃] *f* **1.** (*concentration, intérêt*) attention; **avec ~** attentively; **à l'~ de qn** for the attention of sb; **prêter ~ à qn/qc** to pay attention to sb/sth **2.** *souvent pl* (*prévenance*) attention *no pl* **3.** (*soin*) **faire ~ à qn/qc** to be careful with sb/sth; **fais ~!** be careful! **4.** (*avertissement*) **~!** watch out!; **~ à la marche!** mind [*o* watch] the step!; **mais ~! vous en êtes responsable**(**s**)! but be careful! you're responsible for it!; **alors là, ~ (les yeux)**! *inf* watch out!
attentionné(**e**) [atɑ̃sjɔne] *adj* **~ envers qn** considerate towards sb
attentivement [atɑ̃tivmɑ̃] *adv* attentively
atténuant(**e**) [atenɥɑ̃, ɑ̃t] *adj* **circonstance ~e** mitigating circumstance
atténuer [atenɥe] <1> **I.** *vt* (*douleur*) to relieve; (*bruit, amertume*) to lessen; (*passion*) to soothe; (*couleur*) to soften; (*faute*) to mitigate **II.** *vpr* **s'~** to subside; (*bruit, douleur*) to die down; (*amertume*) to ease; (*secousse sismique*) to die away
atterrant(**e**) [atɛʀɑ̃, ɑ̃t] *adj* appalling
atterré(**e**) [ateʀe] *adj* appalled
atterrer [ateʀe] <1> *vt* to dismay
atterrir [ateʀiʀ] <8> *vi* **1.** AVIAT, NAUT (*avion*) to land; (*bateau*) to dock **2.** *inf* (*se retrouver*) to end up
atterrissage [ateʀisaʒ] *m* landing; **~ en catastrophe** crash landing
attestation [atɛstasjɔ̃] *f* certificate; **~ d'assurance** insurance certificate
attesté(**e**) [atɛste] *adj* **fait ~** proven fact
attester [atɛste] <1> *vt* **1.** (*certifier*) **~ qc/que qn a fait qc** to attest that sb/sth has done sth **2.** (*certifier par écrit*) **~ qc/que qn a fait qc** to certify that sb/sth has done sth **3.** (*être la preuve*) **~ qc/que qn a fait qc** to prove that sb/sth has done sth
attifer [atife] <1> **I.** *vt inf* **~ qn** to get sb up **II.** *vpr inf* **s'~** to get oneself up
attirail [atiʀaj] *m inf* gear
attirance [atiʀɑ̃s] *f* attraction; **éprouver une certaine/de l'~ pour qn** to feel a certain/an attraction to sb
attirant(**e**) [atiʀɑ̃, ɑ̃t] *adj* (*personne, physionomie*) attractive; (*proposition, publicité*) appealing
attirer [atiʀe] <1> **I.** *vt* **1.** (*tirer à soi, retenir*) *a.* PHYS **~ le regard/l'attention** to make people look/pay attention **2.** (*faire venir: personne*) to attract; (*animal*) to lure **3.** (*allécher*) to entice **4.** (*intéresser: projet, pays*) to draw **5.** (*procurer*) **~ des ennuis à qn** to cause sb problems **6.** (*susciter*) **~ sur soi la colère de toute la ville** to bring down the anger of the whole town on oneself **II.** *vpr* **1.** (*se plaire*) **s'~** to attract each other; PHYS to attract **2.** (*obtenir, susciter*) **s'~ qn** to win sb over; **s'~ de nombreux ennemis/amis** to make many enemies/friends
attitré(**e**) [atitʀe] *adj* (*promoteur*) accredited
attitude [atityd] *f* **1.** (*du corps*) bearing **2.** (*disposition*) attitude **3.** *souvent pl* (*affectation*) façade
attouchement [atuʃmɑ̃] *m* **1.** (*toucher*) touch **2.** (*caresse légère*) stroke **3.** *souvent pl* (*caresse sexuelle*) fondling + *vb sing*
attractif, -ive [atʀaktif, -iv] *adj* (*séduisant*) attractive
attraction [atʀaksjɔ̃] *f* (*séduction, divertissement*) *a.* PHYS, LING attraction
attrait [atʀɛ] *m* appeal
attrape [atʀap] *f* trick
attrape-nigaud [atʀapnigo] <attrape-nigauds> *m* con
attraper [atʀape] <1> **I.** *vt* **1.** (*capturer, saisir*) **~ qn/un animal par qc** to catch sb/an animal with sth **2.** (*saisir, atteindre, avoir*) to catch; **~ qn à faire qc** to catch sb doing sth; **~ le bus/une maladie** to catch the bus/a disease; **attrape!** catch! **3.** (*tromper*) **~ qn** to catch sb out; **être bien attrapé** to be caught out **4.** (*comprendre: bribes, paroles*) to catch **5.** (*savoir reproduire: comportement, style, accent*) to pick up **6.** (*recevoir: punition, amende*) to get **II.** *vpr* **s'~ 1.** (*se transmettre: maladie contagieuse*) to get caught **2.** (*s'assimiler*) **l'accent anglais, ça ne s'attrape qu'en Angleterre!** you can only pick up the English accent in England!
attrayant(**e**) [atʀɛjɑ̃, jɑ̃t] *adj* (*paysage, personne*) attractive
attribuer [atʀibɥe] <1> **I.** *vt* **1.** (*donner*) **~ un prix/une bourse d'études à qn** to award a prize/a study grant to sb **2.** (*considérer comme propre à*) **~ un mérite à qn** to give sb credit; **~ de l'importance à qc** to attach importance to sth **II.** *vpr* **1.** (*s'approprier*) **s'~ qc** to give oneself sth **2.** (*s'adjuger, revendiquer*) **s'~ qc** to claim sth
attribut [atʀiby] **I.** *m* **1.** (*propriété, symbole*) attribute **2.** LING **~ du sujet** noun complement **II.** *adj* LING (*adjectif*) predicative
attribution [atʀibysjɔ̃] *f* **1.** (*action*) awarding; (*d'une indemnité*) allocation **2.** *pl* (*compétences*) attributions
attristant(**e**) [atʀistɑ̃] *adj* **1.** (*désolant, pénible, triste*) saddening **2.** (*déplorable*) deplorable
attrister [atʀiste] <1> **I.** *vt* to sadden **II.** *vpr* **s'~ devant qc** to be saddened by sth
attroupement [atʀupmɑ̃] *m* gathering
attrouper [atʀupe] <1> *vpr* **s'~ sur la place** to gather in the square
au [o] = **à + le** *v.* **à**
aubaine [obɛn] *f* **1.** (*avantage*) godsend; **profiter de l'~** [*o* **la bonne ~**] to make the most of an opportunity; **tu parles d'une ~!** *iron* talk about good news!; **quelle ~!** what a godsend! **2.** *Québec* (*solde*) sale
aube [ob] *f* (*point du jour*) dawn; **à l'~** at dawn

A

aubépine [obepin] *f* hawthorn
auberge [obɛʀʒ] *f* inn; ~ **de jeunesse** youth hostel ▸**on n'est pas sorti de l'~!** we are not out of the woods yet!
aubergine [obɛʀʒin] **I.** *f* (*légume*) aubergine *Brit,* eggplant *Am* **II.** *adj inv* (*couleur*) aubergine *Brit,* eggplant *Am*
aubergiste [obɛʀʒist] *mf* innkeeper; (*d'une auberge de jeunesse*) warden
aubette [obɛt] *f Belgique* (*kiosque à journaux, abribus®*) shelter
aucun(e) [okœ̃, yn] **I.** *adj antéposé* **1.** (*nul*) ~ **... ne ..., ne ...** ~ **...** no; **n'avoir ~e preuve** to have no proof; **en ~e façon** in no way; **sans faire ~ bruit** without making any noise **2.** (*dans une question*) any **II.** *pron* ~ **ne ..., ne ...** ~ not ... any; **n'aimer ~ de ces romans** to not like any of these books
aucunement [okynmɑ̃] *adv* in no way; **n'avoir ~ envie de partir** to feel not at all like leaving; **êtes-vous d'accord? – ~!** do you agree? – Not at all!
audace [odas] *f* **1.** (*témérité*) daring; **avoir de l'~** to be daring **2.** (*effronterie*) audacity
audacieux, -euse [odasjø, -jøz] **I.** *adj* **1.** (*hardi*) daring **2.** (*effronté*) audacious **3.** (*risqué, osé: projet*) risky; (*mode*) daring **II.** *m, f* brave person
au-dedans [odədɑ̃] **I.** *adv* inside **II.** *prep* ~ **de qc** inside sth
au-dehors [odəɔʀ] **I.** *adv* outside **II.** *prep* ~ **de qc** outside sth
au-delà [od(ə)la] **I.** *adv* beyond **II.** *prep* beyond sth **III.** *m* beyond
au-dessous [od(ə)su] **I.** *adv* underneath **II.** *prep* **1.** (*plus bas*) ~ **de qn/qc** under sb/sth **2.** (*au sud de, inférieur à*) below
au-dessus [od(ə)sy] **I.** *adv* **1.** (*plus haut*) above **2.** (*mieux*) **il n'y a rien** ~ there's nothing better **II.** *prep* ~ **de qn/qc** above sb/sth
au-devant [od(ə)vɑ̃] *prep* **aller ~ des désirs de qn** to anticipate sb's wishes
audible [odibl] *adj* (*qu'on peut entendre*) audible
audience [odjɑ̃s] *f* **1.** (*entretien*) audience; **tenir** ~ to have an audience **2.** JUR hearing; **tenir** ~ to have a hearing **3.** (*indice d'écoute*) audience
audimat [odimat] *m* **l'~** the ratings *pl* (*monitoring device used for television ratings*)
audiovisuel [odjovisɥɛl] *m* (*procédés*) audio-visual methods *pl*
audiovisuel(le) [odjovisɥɛl] *adj* audio-visual
auditeur, -trice [oditœʀ, -tʀis] *m, f* **1.** (*de médias*) listener; (*d'une télévision*) viewer **2.** ECON (*métier*) auditor **3.** UNIV ~ **libre** unregistered student, auditor *Am* **4.** POL ~ **au Conseil d'État** *official at the Council of State*
auditif, -ive [oditif, -iv] *adj* (*mémoire*) auditive; **appareil** ~ hearing aid
audition [odisjɔ̃] *f* **1.** (*sens, écoute*) *a.* JUR hearing; **test d'~** hearing test **2.** THEAT, CINE audition
auditionner [odisjɔne] <1> *vi, vt* to audition
auditoire [oditwaʀ] *m* **1.** (*assistance*) audience **2.** *Belgique, Suisse* (*amphithéâtre, salle de cours d'une université*) lecture hall
auditorium [oditɔʀjɔm] *m* auditorium
augmentation [ɔgmɑ̃tasjɔ̃] *f* ~ **du chômage/de l'inflation** rise in unemployment/inflation; ~ **d'une production** growth in production
augmenter [ɔgmɑ̃te] <1> **I.** *vt* **1.** (*accroître*) to increase **2.** (*accroître le salaire*) ~ **qn de 1000 euros** to give sb a 1000 euros raise **II.** *vi* **1.** (*s'accroître*) to increase; (*salaire*) to go up; (*douleur*) to get worse **2.** (*devenir plus cher: impôts, prix, loyer*) to rise; (*marchandise, vie*) to become more expensive
augure¹ [ogyʀ] *m* **être de bon/mauvais** ~ to augur well/badly
augure² [ogyʀ] *m* **1.** HIST augur **2.** (*devin*) soothsayer; **consulter les ~s** to consult the oracle
aujourd'hui [oʒuʀdɥi] *adv* **1.** (*opp: hier, demain*) today; **quel jour sommes-nous ~?** what day is it today?; **à compter/dater/partir d'~** as of today; **dès** ~ from today; **il y a ~ huit jours/un an que qn a fait qc** eight days/a year ago today sb did sth **2.** (*actuellement*) today; **au jour d'~** *inf* as of now ▸**c'est pour ~ ou pour demain?** *inf* is it going to happen before midnight?
aula [ola] *f Suisse* (*amphithéâtre*) lecture hall; (*grande salle*) hall
aulne [o(l)n] *m* alder
aumône [omon] *f* (*don*) alms *pl*
aumônier [omonje] *m* ~ **d'un lycée/d'une prison/d'un hôpital** college/prison/hospital chaplain
auparavant [opaʀavɑ̃] *adv* before
auprès de [opʀɛ də] *prep* **1.** (*tout près, à côté de*) **être ~ qn** to be near sb; **viens t'asseoir ~ moi** come and sit down next to me **2.** (*en comparaison de*) ~ **qn/qc** compared to sb/sth **3.** (*aux yeux de*) in the opinion of **4.** ADMIN to; **conseiller auprès du Président** advisor to the President
auquel [okɛl] = **à + lequel** *v.* **lequel**
aura [ɔʀa] *f* aura
aurai [ɔʀɛ] *fut de* **avoir**
auréole [ɔʀeɔl] *f* **1.** (*tache*) ring **2.** (*halo: d'un astre*) aureole **3.** (*cercle doré: d'un saint*) halo
auriculaire [ɔʀikylɛʀ] *m* little finger
aurifère [ɔʀifɛʀ] *adj* gold-bearing
aurore [ɔʀɔʀ] *f* **1.** (*aube*) daybreak; (*heure du jour*) dawn **2.** ASTR ~ **australe/boréale/polaire** southern/northern/polar lights *pl*
auscultation [ɔskyltasjɔ̃] *f* auscultation
ausculter [ɔskylte] <1> *vt* to auscultate
auspices [ɔspis] *mpl* **1.** (*augure*) **sous de**

bons/de mauvais ~ under favourable/unfavourable auspices *Brit,* under favorable/unfavorable auspices *Am* **2.** (*appui*) **sous les ~ de qn/de la municipalité** under the patronage of sb/the town

aussi [osi] **I.** *adv* **1.** (*élément de comparaison*) **elle est ~ grande que moi** she is as tall as me; **il est ~ grand qu'il est bête** he is as tall as he is stupid **2.** (*également*) too; **c'est ~ mon avis** that's my opinion too; **bon appétit! – merci, vous ~!** enjoy your meal! – thank you, and you too!; **ça peut tout ~ bien être faux!** that could just as well be false! **3.** (*en plus*) also; **non seulement ..., mais ~** not only ..., but also **4.** *inf* (*non plus*) **moi ~, je ne suis pas d'accord** me too, I don't agree **5.** (*bien que*) **~ riche soit-il** however rich he may be **6.** (*autant* (*que*)) **Paul ~ bien que son frère** Paul as much as his brother **7.** (*d'ailleurs*) **mais ~ ...?** and ...? **II.** *conj* **~** (**bien**) so

aussitôt [osito] **I.** *adv* **1.** (*tout de suite*) right away; **~ après** straight after **2.** (*sitôt*) immediately; **~ dit, ~ fait** no sooner said than done **II.** *conj* **~ que qn a fait qc** as soon as sb has done sth

austère [ostɛʀ] *adj* austere

austérité [osteʀite] *f* austerity

austral(**e**) [ɔstʀal] <s> *adj* (*hémisphère*) southern; **pôle ~** south pole

Australie [ostʀali] *f* **l'~** Australia

Australie-Méridionale *f* **l'~** South Australia

australien [ostʀaljɛ̃] *m* Australian; *v. a.* **français**

australien(**ne**) [ostʀaljɛ̃, jɛn] *adj* Australian

Australien(**ne**) [ɔstʀaljɛ̃, jɛn] *m(f)* Australian

Australie-Occidentale *f* **l'~** Western Australia

autant [otɑ̃] *adv* **1.** (*tant*) as much; **comment peut-il dormir ~?** how can he sleep that much?; **~ d'argent** as much money **2.** (*relation d'égalité*) **~ que** as much as; **en faire ~** to do as much; **d'~** accordingly; **il n'y a pas ~ de neige que l'année dernière** there is not as much snow as last year **3.** (*cela revient à*) you might as well **4.** (*sans exception*) **ces personnes sont ~ de chômeurs** these people are all unemployed; **tous ~ que vous êtes** each and every one of you **5.** (*pour comparer*) **~ j'aime la mer, ~ je déteste la montagne** I dislike the mountains as much as I like the sea **6.** (*dans la mesure où*) (**pour**) **~ que qn fasse qc** (*subj*) as much as sb does sth **7.** (*encore plus/moins* (*pour la raison que*)) **d'~ moins ... que qn a fait qc** even less so ... since sb has done sth; **d'~** (**plus**) **que qn a fait qc** even more so given that sb has done sth; **d'~ mieux/moins/plus** that much better/less/more ►**pour ~** for all that; **il va mieux; il n'est pas remis pour ~** he is better; however he's not cured; **~ pour moi!** *inf* sorry, my mistake!

autarcie [otaʀsi] *f* autarky

autel [otɛl] *m* altar ►**conduire/suivre qn à l'~** *soutenu* to lead/follow sb to the altar

auteur [otœʀ] *m* **1.** (*créateur*) author **2.** (*responsable*) author; (*d'un attentat*) perpetrator **3.** (*compositeur*) composer

auteur, -trice [otœʀ, -tʀis] *m, f* (*écrivain*) author

auteur-compositeur [otœʀkɔ̃pozitœʀ] <auteurs-compositeurs> *m* composer-songwriter

authenticité [otɑ̃tisite] *f* **1.** (*véracité: d'un document, d'une œuvre*) authenticity **2.** (*sincérité: d'une interprétation*) faithfulness

authentifier [otɑ̃tifje] <1> *vt* (*document, signature, tableau*) to authenticate

authentique [otɑ̃tik] *adj* **1.** (*véritable*) authentic **2.** (*sincère: personne*) sincere; (*émotion*) genuine

autiste [otist] **I.** *adj* autistic **II.** *mf* autisic person

auto [oto] *f abr de* **automobile** car; **~ tamponneuse** bumper car, dodgem *Brit*

autobiographie [otobjɔgʀafi] *f* autobiography

autobiographique [otobjɔgʀafik] *adj* autobiographical

autobus [otobys] *m* bus; **~ scolaire** *Québec* (*car de ramassage scolaire*) school bus

autocar [otokaʀ] *m* coach

autocassable [otokasabl] *adj* break-open

autochenille [otoʃnij] *f* half-track

autochtone [otokton] **I.** *adj* native; (*indigène*) indigenous **II.** *mf* native

autocollant [otokɔlɑ̃] *m* sticker

autocollant(**e**) [otokɔlɑ̃, ɑ̃t] *adj* self-adhesive

autocrate [otokʀat] *mf* autocrat ►**en ~** (*se comporter, régner*) autocratically

autocuiseur [otokɥizœʀ] *m* pressure cooker

autodafé [otodafe] *m* HIST auto-da-fé

autodéfense [otodefɑ̃s] *f* self-defence *Brit,* self-defense *Am;* (*prévention*) self-protection

autodérision [otodeʀizjɔ̃] *f* self-ridicule

autodétermination [otodetɛʀminasjɔ̃] *f* self-determination

autodétruire [otodetʀɥiʀ] *vpr irr* **s'~** (*machine, cassette, personne*) to self-destruct

autodidacte [otodidakt] **I.** *adj* self-taught **II.** *mf* autodidact

autodiscipline [otodisiplin] *f* self-discipline

autoécole, auto-école [otoekɔl] <auto-écoles> *f* driving school

autofocus [otofɔkys] *adj, m* auto-focus

autogestion [otoʒɛstjɔ̃] *f* self-management

autographe [otogʀaf] *m* autograph

automate [otomat] *m* automaton

automatique [otomatik] **I.** *adj* automatic **II.** *m* **1.** TEL direct dialling *Brit,* direct dialing *Am* **2.** (*pistolet*) automatic **III.** *f* AUTO automatic

automatiquement [otomatikmɑ̃] *adv* automatically

automatisation [otomatizasjɔ̃] *f* automation

automatiser [otomatize] <1> *vt* to automate

automatisme [otomatism] *m* automatism

automitrailleuse [otomitʀɑjøz] *f* armoured car *Brit*, armored car *Am*

automnal(e) [otɔnal, o] <-aux> *adj* autumnal

automne [otɔn] *m* autumn, fall *Am;* **cet ~** this autumn; **en ~** in autumn; **l'~, ...** in autumn, ...; **l'~ dernier** last autumn

automobile [otomɔbil] **I.** *adj* **1.** TECH **voiture/véhicule ~** motor car/vehicle **2.** (*relatif à la voiture*) car; **sport ~** motor racing **II.** *f* **1.** (*voiture, industrie*) car, automobile *Am* **2.** (*sport*) driving

automobiliste [otomɔbilist] *mf* motorist

autonome [otonom] *adj* **1.** (*indépendant*) autonomous; **gestion ~** managerial autonomy; **travailleur ~** *Québec* (*freelance*) freelance **2.** (*responsable: vie*) autonomous; (*personne, existence*) self-sufficient **3.** INFOR off-line; **poste ~** stand-alone

autonomie [otonomi] *f* autonomy; (*d'une personne*) independence; **~ administrative** administrative autonomy; **~ financière** (*d'une administration*) financial autonomy; (*d'une entreprise*) self-management

autonomiste [otonomist] *adj, mf* separatist

autoportrait [otopɔʀtʀɛ] *m* self-portrait

autopropulsé(e) [otopʀɔpylse] *adj* self-propelled

autopsie [otɔpsi] *f* MED autopsy

autoradio [otoʀadjo] *m* car radio

autorail [otoʀaj] *m* railcar

autoreverse [otoʀivœʀs] *adj inv* autoreverse

autorisation [otoʀizasjɔ̃] *f* **1.** (*permission*) permission **2.** JUR authorization **3.** (*permis*) permit; **~ de sortie du territoire** exit permit

autorisé(e) [otoʀize] *adj* authorized; (*tournure*) official

autoriser [otoʀize] <1> *vt* **1.** (*permettre, habiliter*) to authorize; **~ qn à** +*infin* to authorize sb to +*infin* **2.** (*rendre licite: stationnement*) to permit; (*manifestation, sortie*) to authorize **3.** (*donner lieu à: abus, excès*) to permit; (*espoir*) to allow (for)

autoritaire [otoʀitɛʀ] *adj* authoritarian

autorité [otoʀite] *f* **1.** (*pouvoir*) authority; **agir avec ~** to act with authority; **faire preuve d'~** to show one's authority; **avoir de l'~ sur qn** to have authority over sb **2.** (*capacité de se faire obéir, personne influente, organisme*) authority **3.** (*influence, considération*) influence; **jouir d'une grande ~** to enjoy great influence; **faire ~** (*ouvrage*) to be accepted as authoritative; (*personne*) to be accepted as an authority

autoroute [otoʀut] *f* **1.** AUTO motorway *Brit*, highway *Am;* **~ à péage** toll motorway *Brit*, turnpike *Am;* **~ du Soleil** *motorway between Paris and Marseilles* **2.** INFOR **~s de l'information** information [super]highway

autoroutier, -ière [otoʀutje, -jɛʀ] *adj* motorway *Brit*, highway *Am*

autostop, auto-stop [otostɔp] *m sans pl* hitch-hiking *Brit*, hitchhiking *Am;* **faire de l'~** to hitch-hike *Brit*, to hitchhike *Am;* **prendre qn en ~** to pick up a hitch-hiker *Brit*, to pick up a hitchhiker *Am*

autostoppeur, -euse, auto-stoppeur, -euse [otostɔpœʀ, -øz] <auto-stoppeurs> *m, f* hitch-hiker *Brit*, hitchhiker *Am*

autour [otuʀ] **I.** *adv* around **II.** *prep* **1.** (*entourant, environ*) **~ de qn/des 1000 euros** around sb/1000 euros; **~ des 15 heures** around 3 pm **2.** (*à proximité de*) **~ de qn/qc** around sb/sth

autre [otʀ] **I.** *adj antéposé* **1.** (*différent*) other; **~ chose** something else; **d'une ~ manière** in another way **2.** (*supplémentaire*) other; **il nous faut une ~ chaise** we need another chair **3.** (*second des deux*) **l'~ ...** the other ... ▶**nous ~s ..., vous ~s ...** US/WE ..., YOU ...; **sans ~** *Suisse* (*bien entendu*) of course **II.** *pron indéf* **1.** other; **un ~/une ~ (que)** someone other (than); **quelqu'un d'~** someone else; **qui d'~?** who else? **2.** (*chose différente, supplémentaire*) other; **d'~s** others; **quelques ~s** some others; **quelque chose d'~** something else; **rien d'~** nothing else; **quoi d'~?** what else? **3.** (*personne supplémentaire*) another **4.** (*opp: l'un*) **l'un l'~/l'une l'~/les uns les ~s** one another ▶**entre ~s** among others; **une ~!** same again!

autrefois [otʀəfwɑ] *adv* in the past

autrement [otʀəmɑ̃] *adv* **1.** (*différemment*) differently; **tout ~** altogether differently; **je ne pouvais pas faire ~** I couldn't do otherwise [*o* anything else] **2.** (*sinon, sans quoi, à part cela*) otherwise ▶**~ dit** in other words

Autriche [otʀiʃ] *f* **l'~** Austria

autrichien(ne) [otʀiʃjɛ̃, jɛn] *adj* Austrian

Autrichien(ne) [otʀiʃjɛ̃, jɛn] *m(f)* Austrian

autruche [otʀyʃ] *f* ostrich

autrui [otʀɥi] *pron inv* someone else; (*les autres*) others; **pour le compte d'~** for a third party

auvent [ovɑ̃] *m* canopy; **toit en ~** canopy roof

auvergnat(e) [ovɛʀɲa, at] *adj* of the Auvergne

Auvergnat(e) [ɔvɛʀɲa, at] *m(f)* person from the Auvergne

aux [o] = **à + les** *v.* **à**

auxiliaire [ɔksiljɛʀ] **I.** *adj* **1.** (*annexe, troupe, verbe, moteur, armée, service*) auxiliary **2.** (*non titulaire*) auxiliary; **personnel ~** auxiliary staff; (*temporaire*) temporary staff **II.** *mf* auxiliary **III.** *m* LING auxiliary; **~ de mode** modal auxiliary

avachi(e) [avaʃi] *adj* **1.** (*amorphe: personne*)

out of shape; (*attitude, air*) sloppy **2.** (*déformé: chaussures*) misshapen; (*sac, vêtement*) baggy

avachir [avaʃiʀ] <8> *vpr* **1.** (*s'affaisser*) **s'~** (*silhouette, muscles, traits*) to become flabby; (*chaussures*) to get misshapen **2.** *inf* (*devenir amorphe*) to become shapeless

avais [avɛ] *imparf de* **avoir**

aval [aval] *m* **1.** (*partie inférieure: d'un cours d'eau*) downstream water; **en ~** downstream **2.** (*soutien*) authorization

avalanche [avalɑ̃ʃ] *f* **1.** (*masse de neige*) avalanche **2.** (*accumulation*) **~ d'injures** shower of insults; **~ de dossiers** avalanche of files

avaler [avale] <1> *vt* **1.** (*absorber, manger, encaisser*) to swallow **2.** *fig* (*roman, livre*) to devour; (*kilomètre, route*) to eat up; **~ qn** (*personne*) to eat sb alive **3.** (*croire*) **on peut lui faire ~ n'importe quoi** you can make him believe anything

avance [avɑ̃s] *f* **1.** (*progression*) advance **2.** (*opp: retard*) **être en ~** (*personne, train*) to be early; **arriver en ~ de cinq minutes** to arrive five minutes early; **être en ~ dans son programme** to be running ahead of schedule **3.** (*précocité*) **être en ~ pour son âge** to be advanced for one's age; **être en ~ sur qn** to be ahead of sb **4.** (*distance*) **avoir de l'~ sur qn/qc** to be ahead of sth/sb **5.** (*somme sur un achat*) advance payment; (*somme sur le salaire*) advance; **faire une ~ sur le loyer** to pay some advance rent **6.** *pl* (*approche amoureuse*) **faire des ~s à qn** to make advances on sb ►**à l'~**, **d'~** in advance; **il n'y a pas d'~ à faire qc** *Belgique* (*cela n'avance à rien de*) doing sth doesn't get you anywhere

avancé(e) [avɑ̃se] *adj* **1.** (*en avant dans l'espace*) ahead **2.** (*en avance dans le temps*) advanced; (*végétation*) early; (*idées, opinions*) progressive; **être ~ dans son travail** to be ahead in one's work ►**ne pas être plus ~** to not have got any further

avancée [avɑ̃se] *f* **1.** (*saillie*) overhang **2.** (*progrès: de la science*) advance

avancement [avɑ̃smɑ̃] *m* **1.** (*progrès: des travaux, des négociations, des sciences, des technologies*) progress **2.** (*promotion*) promotion; **avoir de l'~** to be promoted

avancer [avɑ̃se] <2> **I.** *vt* **1.** (*opp: retarder*) **~ qc** (*rendez-vous, départ*) to bring sth forward; (*montre*) to put sth forward; **~ la date du départ d'un jour** to move the departure date forward by one day **2.** (*pousser en avant*) **~ qc** (*chaise, table*) to move sth forward; (*voiture*) to drive sth forward; **~ de huit cases** JEUX move forward eight squares **3.** (*affirmer*) to suggest; (*idée, thèse*) to put forward **4.** (*faire progresser: travail*) to speed up **5.** (*payer par avance: argent*) to pay in advance **6.** (*prêter: argent*) to lend ►**ça t'avance/nous avance à quoi?** where does that get you/us?; **ça ne t'avance/nous avance à rien!** that doesn't get you/us anywhere! **II.** *vi* **1.** (*approcher: armée*) to advance; (*personne, conducteur, voiture*) to move forward; **avance vers moi!** come towards me! **2.** (*être en avance*) **~ de 5 minutes** (*montre*) to be 5 minutes fast **3.** (*former une avancée, une saillie: rocher, balcon*) to overhang **4.** (*progresser: personne, travail*) to progress; (*nuit*) to close in; (*jour*) to draw on; **à mesure que l'on avance en âge** as one gets older **III.** *vpr* **1.** **s'~** (*pour sortir d'un rang, en s'approchant*) to move forward; (*pour continuer sa route*) to advance; **s'~ vers qn/qc** to move towards sb/sth **2.** (*prendre de l'avance*) **s'~ dans son travail** to progress in one's work **3.** (*se risquer, anticiper*) **s'~ trop** to take too big a risk; **là, tu t'avances trop!** you're going too far there!

avant [avɑ̃] **I.** *prep* **1.** (*temporel*) before; **bien/peu ~ qc** well/shortly before sth; **~ de faire qc** before doing sth **2.** (*devant*) in front of; **en ~ de qn/qc** in front of sb/sth ►**~ tout** above all **II.** *adv* **1.** (*devant*) in front; **passer ~** to go in front; **en ~** in front **2.** *après compl* (*plus tôt*) before; **plus/trop ~** earlier/too early; **le jour/l'année d'~** the day/year before ►**en ~ (marche)!** forward (march)! **III.** *conj* **~ que qn ne fasse qc** (*subj*) before sb does sth **IV.** *m* **1.** (*partie antérieure*) front; **à/vers l'~** at/to the front; **à l'~ du bateau** in the bow of the boat **2.** SPORT (*joueur*) forward ►**jouer à l'~** SPORT to play as a forward **V.** *adj inv* (*opp: arrière*) front; **traction ~** front-wheel drive; **le clignotant ~ droit** the front right indicator *Brit,* the front right blinker *Am*

avantage [avɑ̃taʒ] *m* **1.** (*intérêt*) advantage; **à son ~** to his advantage; **être à son ~** to be at one's best; **tirer ~ de** to benefit from sth; **tourner à l'~ de qn** to turn out to sb's advantage; **qc présente l'~ de faire qc** sth has the advantage of doing sth **2.** *souvent pl* (*gain*) benefit; **~ en nature** fringe benefits **3.** (*supériorité*) *a.* SPORT advantage; **avoir l'~ sur qn** to have the advantage over sb; **avoir l'~** to have the advantage **4.** *soutenu* (*plaisir*) privilege

avantager [avɑ̃taʒe] <2a> *vt* **1.** (*favoriser*) **~ qn par rapport à qn/au détriment de qn** to favour sb over sb/to the detriment of sb **2.** (*mettre en valeur*) to flatter

avantageusement [avɑ̃taʒøzmɑ̃] *adv* favourably *Brit,* favorably *Am;* (*vendre*) at a good price; **il remplace ~ qn/qc** he makes a highly satisfactory replacement for sb/sth

avantageux, -euse [avɑ̃taʒø, -ʒøz] *adj* **1.** (*intéressant: investissement*) profitable; (*rendement*) attractive **2.** (*favorable: portrait*) flattering; (*termes*) favourable *Brit,* favorable *Am;* (*opinion, idée*) worthwhile

avant-bras [avɑ̃bʀa] <avant-bras> *m* forearm **avant-centre** [avɑ̃sɑ̃tʀ] <avants-centres> *m* centre-forward *Brit,* center-forward *Am* **avant-dernier, -ière** [avɑ̃dɛʀnje, -jɛʀ] <avant-derniers> *adj, m, f* penultimate **avant-garde** [avɑ̃gaʀd] <avant-gardes> *f* ART, LIT avant-garde

A

avant-goût [avɑ̃gu] <avant-goûts> *m* ~ **de qc** foretaste of sth **avant-hier** [avɑ̃tjɛʀ] *adv* the day before yesterday **avant-midi** [avɑ̃midi] *m o f, masc en Belgique et fém au Québec, inv* (*matinée*) morning **avant-poste** [avɑ̃pɔst] <avant-postes> *m* outpost **avant-première** [avɑ̃pʀəmjɛʀ] <avant-premières> *f* preview **avant-propos** [avɑ̃pʀɔpo] <avant-propos> *m* foreword **avant-veille** [avɑ̃vɛj] <avant-veilles> *f* two days before; **l'~ de qc** two days before sth

avare [avaʀ] **I.** *adj* miserly; **être ~ de qc** to be sparing with sth; **être ~ de paroles** to be a person of few words **II.** *mf* miser

avarice [avaʀis] *f* avarice

avarie [avaʀi] *f* damage *no pl*

avarié(e) [avaʀje] *adj* **1.** (*en panne: bateau*) damaged **2.** (*pourri: nourriture*) rotten

avec [avɛk] **I.** *prep* **1.** (*ainsi que, contre, au moyen de, grâce à, envers*) with; **être gentil/poli ~ qn** to be kind/polite towards sb **2.** (*à cause de*) because of; **~ la pluie, les routes sont glissantes** the roads are slippery because of [*o* with] the rain **3.** (*en ce qui concerne*) **~ moi, vous pouvez avoir confiance** with me, you've got nothing to worry about; **~ ces gens on n'est jamais sûr de rien** with these people, you can never be sure **4.** (*d'après*) **~ ma sœur, il faudrait ...** according to my sister, we should ... ▶**et ~ ça ...** *inf* on top of that; **~ tout ça** *inf* with all that; **et ~ cela (Madame/Monsieur)?** anything else (Sir/Madam)? **II.** *adv inf* **tu viens ~?** *Belgique* are you coming along? ▶**il faut faire ~** *prov* you've got to make the best of a bad job *prov*

avenant(e) [av(ə)nɑ̃, ɑ̃t] *adj* pleasant

avènement [avɛnmɑ̃] *m* **1.** (*d'un roi*) accession; (*d'un régime*) advent **2.** (*percée, instauration: d'une politique, idée*) birth; (*d'une époque, ère*) dawn **3.** REL (*du Messie*) Advent

avenir [av(ə)niʀ] *m* future; **à l'~** in future; **d'~** of the future; **dans un proche ~** in the near future; **avoir un bel ~ devant soi** to have good prospects

aventure [avɑ̃tyʀ] *f* **1.** (*histoire*) adventure; **il m'est arrivé une ~** something happened to me; **j'ai eu une drôle d'~/une fâcheuse ~** I had a funny/unfortunate experience; **chercher (l')~** to seek adventure **2.** (*liaison*) affair ▶**dire la bonne ~ à qn** to tell sb's fortune; **à l'~** aimlessly; **partir à l'~** to go in search of adventure

aventurer [avɑ̃tyʀe] <1> **I.** *vt* (*argent, réputation*) to risk **II.** *vpr* **s'~ sur la route** to venture on to the road; **s'~ dans une affaire risquée** to get involved in a risky business; **s'~ sur un terrain glissant** *fig* to skate on thin ice

aventureusement [avɑ̃tyʀøzmɑ̃] *adv* adventurously

aventureux, -euse [avɑ̃tyʀø, -øz] *adj* **1.** (*audacieux*) adventurous **2.** (*risqué: entreprise, projet*) risky

aventurier, -ière [avɑ̃tyʀje, -jɛʀ] *m, f* adventurer

avenue [av(ə)ny] *f* avenue

avérer [aveʀe] <5> *vpr* **s'~ exact/faux** to turn out to be true/false

averse [avɛʀs] *f a. fig* shower; **~ de grêle** hail storm

aversion [avɛʀsjɔ̃] *f* aversion

averti(e) [avɛʀti] *adj* well-informed

avertir [avɛʀtiʀ] <8> *vt* **1.** (*informer*) to inform **2.** (*mettre en garde*) to warn

avertissement [avɛʀtismɑ̃] *m* **1.** (*mise en garde, signal*) warning **2.** SPORT (*sanction*) caution

avertisseur [avɛʀtisœʀ] *m* alarm

aveu [avø] <x> *m* confession; **faire l'~ de qc à qn** to confess sth to sb; **arracher des ~x à qn** to bully a confession out of sb; **faire des ~x complets** to make a full confession; **passer aux ~x** to make a confession

aveuglant(e) [avœglɑ̃, ɑ̃t] *adj* **1.** (*éblouissant: lumière, soleil*) dazzling; **être ~** (*lumière*) to be blinding **2.** (*évident*) blindingly obvious

aveugle [avœgl] **I.** *adj* blind; **être ~ d'un œil/des deux yeux** to be blind in one eye/both eyes **II.** *mf* blind person ▶**en ~** blind

aveuglement [avœgləmɑ̃] *m* blindness

aveuglément [avœglemɑ̃] *adv* blindly

aveugler [avœgle] <1> *vt* **1.** (*éblouir*) to dazzle **2.** (*priver de discernement*) to blind

aveuglette [avœglɛt] **à l'~** (*à tâtons*) cautiously; (*au hasard*) blindly; **aller à l'~** to grope one's way along; **prendre une décision à l'~** to take a decision in the dark

avez [ave] *indic prés de* **avoir**

aviateur, -trice [avjatœʀ, -tʀis] *m, f* aviator

aviation [avjasjɔ̃] *f* **1.** aviation; (*sport*) flying; **compagnie d'~** aviation company; **~ civile/militaire** civil/military aviation **2.** MIL air force

aviculture [avikyltyʀ] *f* **1.** (*élevage de volailles*) poultry farming **2.** (*élevage d'oiseaux*) bird breeding

avide [avid] *adj* (*personne, regard, yeux, curiosité*) avid; (*lèvres*) greedy; **~ d'argent/de pouvoir** greedy for money/power; **~ de connaissances** eager for knowledge; **~ de vengeance** hungry for revenge; **être ~ d'apprendre** to be keen to learn

avidement [avidmɑ̃] *adv* **1.** (*avec une avidité physique*) greedily **2.** (*avec une avidité intellectuelle*) avidly

avidité [avidite] *f* (*désir physique, cupidité*) greed; (*enthousiasme*) eagerness; **~ de qc** greed for sth; **~ de savoir** [*o* **connaissances**] thirst for knowledge; **~ de lectures** eagerness for reading; **avec ~** greedily

avilir [aviliʀ] <8> **I.** *vt* to degrade **II.** *vpr* **s'~** to degrade oneself

avion [avjɔ̃] *m* plane, aeroplane *Brit,* airplane *Am;* **~ commercial/militaire** commercial/military plane; **~ sanitaire/supersonique** ambulance/supersonic plane; **~ à hélice/à réaction** propeller/jet plane; **~ de chasse**

fighter plane; ~ **de combat/de tourisme** fighter/tourist plane; ~ **de ligne** airliner; ~ **de transport** transport aircraft; **aller/voyager en** ~ to go/travel by plane; **il est malade en** ~ he gets air-sick; **par** ~ (*sur les lettres*) airmail

avion-cargo [avjɔ̃kaʀgo] <avions-cargos> *m* cargo plane

avionnerie [avjɔnʀi] *f Québec* (*usine de constructions aéronautiques*) aeronautics factory

aviron [aviʀɔ̃] *m* **1.** (*rame*) oar **2.** (*sport*) rowing; **course d'**~ boat race; **faire de l'**~ to row

avis [avi] *m* **1.** (*opinion*) opinion; **dire son ~ sur qc** to give one's opinion on sth; **être d'~ de faire qc** to think that sth should be done; **je suis d'~ qu'il vienne** I think he should come; **être de l'~ de qn** to share sb's opinion; **à mon/son humble** ~ in my/his humble opinion; **de l'~ de tous** in everyone's opinion **2.** (*notification*) notice; ~ **au lecteur** foreword; ~ **à la population** (*titre d'une affiche*) notice; (*au haut-parleur*) announcement; ~ **de décès/mariage** announcement of death/marriage; ~ **de recherche** (*écrit*) wanted notice; (*radiodiffusé/télédiffusé*) missing persons notice; **sauf** ~ **contraire** unless otherwise indicated ►~ **aux amateurs!** any takers?

avisé(e) [avize] *adj* sensible; **être bien/mal ~ de** +*infin* to be well-advised/ill-advised to +*infin*

aviser [avize] <1> **I.** *vt* to advise; ~ **qn de qc** to inform sb of sth **II.** *vpr* **s'~ de** +*infin* to dare to +*infin*; **ne t'avise pas de tout dépenser!** don't you dare go spending everything! **III.** *vi* to see; **nous aviserons plus tard** we will see later

avocat [avɔka] *m* avocado

avocat(e) [avɔka, at] *m(f)* (*profession*) lawyer; (*notaire*) solicitor *Brit,* attorney *Am;* ~ **général/de la défense** counsel for the prosecution/for the defence *Brit,* counsel for the prosecution/for the defense *Am;* ~ **de la partie civile** counsel for the plaintiff ►~ **marron** crooked lawyer *inf*

avoine [avwan] *f* oats *pl*

avoir [avwaʀ] *irr* **I.** *vt* **1.** (*devoir, recevoir, assister à*) *a.* MED to have; **ne pas ~ à** +*infin* to not have to +*infin;* **tu n'as pas à t'occuper de ça** you don't have to take care of that **2.** (*obtenir, attraper: train*) to catch; (*examen*) to pass; (*logement, aide, renseignement*) to get; **pouvez-vous m'~ ce livre?** could you get me this book?; **j'ai eu des vertiges** I felt dizzy **3.** (*porter sur ou avec soi: canne, pipe*) to have; (*chapeau, vêtement*) to wear **4.** (*être doté de*) **quel âge as-tu?** how old are you?; ~ **15 ans** to be 15 years old; ~ **2 mètres de haut/large** to be 2 metres tall/wide *Brit,* to be 2 meters tall/wide *Am* **5.** (*éprouver*) ~ **faim/soif/peur** to be hungry/thirsty/afraid **6.** *inf* (*rouler*) **vous m'avez bien eu!** you had me there! ►**en ~ après qn** *inf* to have it in for sb; **en ~ jusque-là de qc** *inf* to have had it up to there with sth; **j'en ai pour deux minutes** I'll be two minutes; **vous en avez pour 100 euros** it'll be around 100 euros; **j'ai!** JEUX, SPORT mine!; **on les aura!** we'll get them!; **qu'est-ce qu'il/elle a?** what's the matter with him/her? **II.** *aux* **il n'a rien dit** he didn't say anything; **il n'a toujours rien dit** he still hasn't said anything; **elle a couru/marché deux heures** (*hier*) she ran/walked for two hours; (*vient de*) she has run/walked for two hours; **l'Italie a été battue par le Brésil** Italy was beaten by Brazil **III.** *vt impers* **1.** (*exister*) **il y a du beurre sur la table** there's butter on the table; **il y a des verres dans le placard** there are glasses in the cupboard; **il y a des jours où ...** there are days when ...; **il y a champagne et champagne** there's champagne and then there's champagne; **il n'y a pas que l'argent dans la vie** there's more to life than money; **qu'y a-t-il?** [*o* **qu'est-ce qu'il y a?**] **– il y a que j'ai faim!** what's the matter? – I'm hungry, that's what!; **il n'y a pas à discuter** there's no two ways about it; **il n'y a qu'à partir plus tôt** we'll just have to leave earlier; **il n'y a que toi pour faire cela!** only you would do that! **2.** (*temporel*) **il y a 3 jours/4 ans** 3 days/4 years ago ►**il n'y a plus rien à faire** there's nothing else can be done; **il n'y en a que pour lui/elle** he/she gets all the attention; **il n'y a pas de quoi!** don't mention it! **IV.** *m* **1.** (*crédit*) credit **2.** (*bon d'achat*) credit note

avoisinant(e) [avwazinɑ̃, ɑ̃t] *adj* neighbouring *Brit,* neighboring *Am;* (*rue*) nearby

avoisiner [avwazine] <1> *vt a. fig* to border

avons [avɔ̃] *indic prés de* **avoir**

avortement [avɔʀtəmɑ̃] *m* abortion; (*spontané*) miscarriage

avorter [avɔʀte] <1> **I.** *vi* **1.** (*de façon volontaire*) to abort; (*de façon spontanée*) to miscarry; **se faire** ~ to have an abortion **2.** (*échouer*) to fail; **faire ~ qc** to wreck sth **II.** *vt* to fail

avorton [avɔʀtɔ̃] *m péj* freak; **espèce d'~!** little runt!

avouable [avwabl] *adj* respectable

avoué(e) [avwe] *adj* avowed

avouer [avwe] <1> **I.** *vt* to admit; ~ **faire qc** to admit to doing sth; **je dois vous ~ que** I must confess to you that **II.** *vi* **1.** (*confesser*) to confess **2.** (*admettre*) to admit **III.** *vpr* **s'~ coupable** to confess one's guilt; **s'~ vaincu** to admit defeat

avril [avʀil] *m* April ►**poisson d'**~ April Fool; **poisson d'~!** April Fool!; *v. a.* **août**

axe [aks] *m* **1.** *a.* MAT axis; ~ **de symétrie** line of symmetry; **dans l'~ de qc** in line with sth **2.** (*tige, pièce: d'une roue, pédale*) axle **3.** (*ligne directrice: d'un discours, d'une politique*) theme **4.** (*voie de circulation*) main road; ~ **ferroviaire/routier** main line/thoroughfare; **grand** ~ trunk road *Brit,* main highway *Am*

axer [akse] <1> *vt* ~ **qc sur qc** to centre sth around sth else *Brit,* to center sth around sth else *Am*

ayant [ɛjɑ̃] *part prés de* **avoir**

Azerbaïdjan [azɛʀbaidʒɑ̃] *m* **l'**~ Azerbaijan

azerbaïdjanais(e) [azɛʀbaidʒanɛ, ɛz] *adj* Azerbaijani

Azerbaïdjanais(e) [azɛʀbaidʒanɛ, ɛz] *m(f)* Azerbaijani

azote [azɔt] *m* nitrogen

aztèque [astɛk] *adj* Aztec

Aztèque [astɛk] *mf* Aztec

azur [azyʀ] *m* **ciel d'**~ azure sky

B

B, b [be] *m inv* B, b; ~ **comme Berthe** (*on telephone*) b for Benjamin *Brit,* b for Baker *Am*

BA [bea] *f abr de* **bonne action** good deed

babiller [babije] <1> *vi* (*bébé, enfant*) to babble

babines [babin] *fpl* (*d'un animal*) chops

babiole [babjɔl] *f* bauble; *fig* trifle

bâbord [bɑbɔʀ] *m* port

babouin [babwɛ̃] *m* ZOOL baboon

baby-foot® [babifut] *m inv* table football, foosball *Am*

Babylone [babilɔn] Babylon

baby-sitter [babisitœʀ] <baby-sitters> *mf* baby-sitter **baby-sitting** [bebisitiŋ, babisitiŋ] *m sans pl* baby-sitting; **faire du** ~ to baby-sit

bac[1] [bak] *m* **1.** (*récipient*) tank; (*cuvette*) basin; (*d'un évier*) sink; (*d'un réfrigérateur*) tray **2.** (*bateau*) ferry

bac[2] [bak] *m inf abr de* **baccalauréat** baccalaureate

baccalauréat [bakalɔʀea] *m* **1.** (*examen à la fin de la terminale*) baccalaureate (*secondary school examinations*) **2.** *Québec* (*études universitaires de premier cycle, ≈ DEUG en France*) associate degree *Am*

> The **baccalauréat** is the final exam for secondary school students, and the entrance requirement for university. The state sets the content and timing of this exam for the whole country. In Belgium, there is no exam of this type. Students receive a diploma, the CESS (Certificat d'Enseignement Secondaire Supérieur).

bâche [bɑʃ] *f* tarpaulin

bachelier, -ière [baʃəlje, -jɛʀ] *m, f: person with the baccalaureat*

bâcher [bɑʃe] <1> *vt* to cover (*with a tarpaulin*)

bachoter [baʃɔte] <1> *vi* to cram, to swot *Brit*

bacille [basil] *m* bacillus

background [bakgʀaund] *m* background

bâcler [bɑkle] <1> *vt inf* (*devoir, travail*) to bodge

bactéricide [bakteʀisid] **I.** *adj* bactericidal **II.** *m* bactericide

bactérie [bakteʀi] *f* bacterium

bactériologique [bakteʀjɔlɔʒik] *adj* bacteriological

badaud(e) [bado, od] *m(f)* onlooker, gawper *pej*

badge [badʒ] *m* badge

badigeon [badiʒɔ̃] *m* colourwash *Brit,* whitewash *Am*

badigeonner [badiʒɔne] <1> *vt* **1.** (*mettre du badigeon*) to colourwash *Brit,* to whitewash *Am* **2.** MED to paint

badiner [badine] <1> *vi* to banter

BAFA [bafa] *m abr de* **brevet d'aptitude aux fonctions d'animateur** *certificate for activity leaders in holiday camps*

baffe [baf] *f inf* slap; **donner une** ~ **à qn** to clout sb

baffle [bafl] *m* speaker

bafouer [bafwe] <1> *vt* (*sentiment*) to ridicule; (*règlement*) to defy

bafouiller [bafuje] <1> *vt, vi inf* to stammer

bâfrer [bɑfʀe] <1> **I.** *vt inf* to wolf down **II.** *vi inf* (*être glouton*) to fill one's face

bagage [bagaʒ] *m* **1.** *pl* luggage + *vb sing Brit,* baggage + *vb sing Am* **2.** (*connaissances*) baggage + *vb sing;* (*pour assumer une tâche*) qualifications

bagarre [bagaʀ] *f* **1.** (*pugilat*) fighting **2.** (*lutte*) fight **3.** (*compétition*) battle

bagarrer [bagaʀe] <1> **I.** *vi inf* to fight **II.** *vpr inf* **1.** (*se battre*) **se** ~ **avec qn** to fight with sb **2.** (*se quereller*) **se** ~ **avec qn** to argue with sb **3.** (*s'opposer*) **se** ~ **contre qn/qc** to struggle against sb/sth

bagarreur, -euse [bagaʀœʀ, -øz] **I.** *adj inf* **être** ~ to get into fights; (*combatif*) to be a fighter **II.** *m, f inf* **1.** (*querelleur*) brawler **2.** (*battant*) fighter

bagatelle [bagatɛl] *f* **1.** (*somme*) trifling sum **2.** (*vétille*) trifle

bagnard [baɲaʀ] *m* convict

bagne [baɲ] *m* **quel** ~**!** it's slavery!

bagnole [baɲɔl] *f inf* car

bagou(t) [bagu] *m* **avoir du** ~ to have the gift of the gab; **quel** ~**!** he can't half talk!

bague [bag] *f a.* TECH ring

baguette [bagɛt] *f* **1.** (*pain*) baguette **2.** (*bâton*) stick; (*d'un tambour*) drumstick; (*d'un chef d'orchestre*) baton **3.** (*couvert chinois*) chopstick **4.** TECH beading

bah [ba] *interj* so what!

Bahamas [baamaːs] *fpl* **les** ~ the Bahamas

bahamien(ne) [baamjɛ̃, ɛn] *adj* Bahamian

Bahamien(ne) [baamjɛ̃, ɛn] *m(f)* Bahamian

bahut [bay] *m* **1.** (*buffet*) sideboard **2.** (*coffre*) chest **3.** *inf* (*lycée*) school **4.** *inf*

B

(*camion*) truck

baie [bɛ] *f* **1.** GEO bay **2.** (*fenêtre*) ~ **vitrée** bay window **3.** BOT berry

baignade [bɛɲad] *f* **1.** (*action*) swim; (*activité*) swimming **2.** (*lieu*) swimming place

baigner [beɲe] <1> **I.** *vt* to bathe **II.** *vi* ~ **dans qc** to be swimming in sth **III.** *vpr* **se** ~ to have a bath; (*dans une piscine*) to go swimming

baigneur [bɛɲœʀ] *m* (*poupée*) baby doll

baignoire [bɛɲwaʀ] *f* **1.** (*pour se baigner*) bath *Brit,* bathtub *Am* **2.** THEAT stalls box

bail [baj, bo] <-aux> *m* (*contrat: d'un local commercial*) lease

bâillement [bɑjmɑ̃] *m* yawn

bâiller [bɑje] <1> *vi* **1.** (*action: personne*) to yawn **2.** (*être entrouvert: porte*) to be ajar; (*col*) to gape

bâillon [bɑjɔ̃] *m* gag

bâillonner [bɑjɔne] <1> *vt* **1.** (*action*) to gag **2.** *fig* (*opposition, presse*) to stifle

bain [bɛ̃] *m* **1.** (*action*) bath **2.** (*eau*) bath(water) **3.** (*baignoire*) bath *Brit,* bathtub *Am* **4.** (*bassin*) **grand/petit** ~ big/little pool **5.** (*exposition volontaire au soleil*) **prendre un** ~ **de soleil** to sunbathe

bain-marie [bɛ̃maʀi] <bains-marie> *m* double boiler, bain-marie; **faire cuire au** ~ to cook in a double boiler

baïonnette [bajɔnɛt] *f* bayonet

baise [bɛz] *f Belgique* (*bise*) kiss

baisemain [bɛzmɛ̃] *m: the action of kissing sb's hand*

baiser[1] [beze] *m* **1.** (*bise*) kiss **2.** (*en formule*) **bons ~s** (with) love

baiser[2] <1> **I.** [beze] *vt* **1.** *soutenu* to kiss **2.** *inf* (*coucher avec*) to screw **3.** *inf* (*tromper*) to have **II.** *vi inf* to screw

baisse [bɛs] *f* **1.** (*le fait de baisser*) lowering; (*de pouvoir, d'influence*) decline; (*de popularité*) decrease; (*de pression*) drop **2.** FIN fall ► ~ **de** tension ELEC drop in voltage; MED drop in pressure

baisser [bese] <1> **I.** *vt* **1.** (*faire descendre: store, rideau*) to lower; (*vitre de voiture*) to wind down; (*col*) to turn down **2.** (*fixer plus bas, réviser à la baisse*) to lower **3.** (*orienter vers le bas: tête*) to bow; (*yeux*) to lower **4.** (*rendre moins fort: son*) to turn down; (*voix*) to lower **II.** *vi* **1.** (*diminuer de niveau, d'intensité: forces, mémoire, vue*) to fail; (*vent, niveau, rivière*) to go down; (*baromètre*) to fall; (*température*) to drop **2.** ECON, FIN to drop; (*prix*) to fall **3.** (*s'affaiblir: personne*) to weaken **III.** *vpr* **se** ~ to stoop; (*pour esquiver*) to duck

Bakou [baku] Baku

bal [bal] <s> *m* **1.** (*réunion populaire*) dance; (*réunion d'apparat*) ball **2.** (*lieu*) dance hall

balade [balad] *f inf* **1.** (*promenade à pied*) walk; (*promenade en voiture*) drive **2.** (*excursion*) jaunt

balader [balade] <1> **I.** *vt inf* ~ **qn** to take sb for a walk **II.** *vpr* **se** ~ *inf* (*se promener à pied*) to go for a walk; (*se promener en voiture*) to go for a drive

baladeur [baladœʀ] *m* Walkman®

balafre [balɑfʀ] *f* **1.** (*blessure*) gash **2.** (*cicatrice*) scar

balai [balɛ] *m* **1.** (*ustensile*) broom **2.** ELEC (*d'une dynamo*) brush **3.** AUTO ~ **d'essuie-glace** windscreen wiper blade *Brit,* windshield wiper blade *Am*

balai-brosse [balɛbʀɔs] <balais-brosses> *m* scrubbing brush

balan [balɑ̃] *m Suisse* **je suis sur le** ~ (*j'hésite entre diverses solutions*) I can't make my mind up; (*je suis incertain d'un résultat*) I'm on tenterhooks

balance [balɑ̃s] *f* **1.** (*instrument*) scales *pl* **2.** POL, ECON balance

Balance [balɑ̃s] *f* Libra; **être** (**du signe de la**) ~ to be a Libran

balancé(e) [balɑ̃se] *adj* **1.** (*équilibré*) balanced **2.** *inf* (*bien bâti*) **bien** ~ to have a great figure

balancelle [balɑ̃sɛl] *f* swing seat

balancement [balɑ̃smɑ̃] *m* **1.** rocking; (*d'un pendule*) swinging; (*des hanches*) swaying **2.** (*rythme: d'une phrase*) balance

balancer [balɑ̃se] <2> **I.** *vt* **1.** (*ballotter: personne*) to swing; ~ **les bras/ses jambes** to swing one's arms/legs **2.** (*tenir en agitant: sac, encensoire, lustre*) to swing; (*branche, bateau*) to rock **3.** *inf* (*envoyer: objet*) to throw **4.** *inf* (*se débarrasser: objet*) to chuck; (*employé*) to sack **II.** *vpr* **se** ~ **1.** (*bouger: bateau*) to rock; (*branches*) to sway **2.** (*sur une balançoire*) to swing **III.** *vi* **1.** *inf* (*avoir du rythme*) **ça balance!** it's swinging! **2.** *Suisse* (*être incertain, pencher d'un côté puis de l'autre*) to be in two minds

balancier [balɑ̃sje] *m* (*d'une horloge*) pendulum; (*d'un funambule*) balancing pole

balançoire [balɑ̃swaʀ] *f* swing

balayage [balɛjaʒ] *m* **1.** (*action*) sweeping **2.** INFOR scanning

balayer [baleje] <7> *vt* **1.** (*ramasser*) to sweep up **2.** (*nettoyer*) to sweep **3.** (*passer sur*) ~ **qc** (*faisceau lumineux*) to sweep over sth; (*vent*) to sweep across sth **4.** INFOR to scan **5.** (*chasser: doute*) to sweep away; (*obstacle, objection, argument*) to brush aside; **le vent balaie les feuilles** the wind's blowing the leaves around

balayette [balɛjɛt] *f* brush (*for a dustpan*), whiskbroom *Am*

balayeur, -euse [balɛjœʀ, -jøz] *m, f* roadsweeper

balayeuse [balɛjøz] *f* roadsweeping machine *Brit,* streetsweeping machine *Am*

balayures [balejyʀ] *fpl* sweepings

balbutiement [balbysimɑ̃] *m* **1.** (*action*) stammering; (*d'un bébé*) babbling **2.** *pl* (*débuts*) beginnings

balbutier [balbysje] <1> **I.** *vi* (*bredouiller*)

to stammer; (*bébé*) to babble **II.** *vt* (*bredouiller: excuses*) to stammer out; ~ **des mots** (*bébé*) to babble words

balcon [balkɔ̃] *m* **1.** (*balustrade*) balcony **2.** THEAT circle

baldaquin [baldakɛ̃] *m* **lit à** ~ four-poster (bed)

Bâle [bɑl] Basel

Baléares [baleaʀ] *fpl* **les** ~ the Balearics; **les Îles** ~ the Balearic Islands

baleine [balɛn] *f* **1.** ZOOL whale **2.** (*renfort*) ~ **de corset** corset bone

baleinier [balenje] *m* whaler

balèze [balɛz] **I.** *adj inf* **1.** (*musclé*) brawny; **être drôlement** ~ to be all muscle **2.** (*doué*) terrific; **être** ~ **en maths** to be brilliant at maths **II.** *m inf* hulk

balisage [balizaʒ] *m* **1.** (*action*) marking out; (*d'une piste d'atterrissage*) beaconing **2.** (*signaux: d'une cheminé, piste de ski*) markers *pl*; (*d'une route*) signs *pl*

balise [baliz] *f* **1.** AVIAT, NAUT beacon **2.** (*de sentier*) waymark **3.** INFOR tag

baliser [balize] <1> *vt* **1.** (*signaliser*) ~ **qc** *a.* AVIAT, NAUT to mark sth out; (*sentier*) to waymark sth **2.** INFOR (*texte*) to highlight

balistique [balistik] **I.** *adj* ballistic **II.** *f* ballistics + *vb sing*

baliverne [balivɛʀn] *f* nonsense *no pl*

balkanique [balkanik] *adj* Balkan

Balkans [balkɑ̃] *mpl* **les** ~ the Balkans

ballade [balad] *f* ballad

ballant(e) [balɑ̃, ɑ̃t] *adj* (*jambes*) dangling; (*bras*) loose; **rester les bras** ~**s** *fig* to stand there inanely

ballast [balast] *m* ballast

balle [bal] *f* **1.** JEUX, SPORT ball; **jouer à la** ~ to play ball **2.** (*projectile*) bullet **3.** (*ballot*) bale **4.** *pl, inf* (*francs*) **100** ~**s** 100 francs

ballerine [balʀin] *f* **1.** (*danseuse*) ballerina **2.** (*chaussure*) ballet shoe

ballet [balɛ] *m* ballet

ballon [balɔ̃] *m* **1.** JEUX, SPORT ball; **jouer au** ~ to play ball **2.** (*baudruche, aérostat*) balloon **3.** GEO round-topped mountain **4.** (*appareil de production d'eau chaude*) ~ **d'eau chaude** hot water tank **5.** (*test*) ~ **d'essai** feeler **6.** MED ~ **d'oxygène** oxygen bottle **7.** (*verre*) (balloon) glass; (*contenu*) glass **8.** *Suisse* (*dans un restaurant, verre d'une contenance d'un décilitre*) wineglass (*holding ten centilitres*)

ballonné(e) [balɔne] *adj* **se sentir** ~ to feel bloated

ballonnements [balɔnmɑ̃] *mpl* bloated feeling

ballot [balo] *m* **1.** (*paquet*) package; (*de livres*) bundle **2.** *inf* (*imbécile*) idiot

ballottage [balɔtaʒ] *m* **être en** ~ to be in a runoff (*after a first round of voting*)

ballotter [balɔte] <1> **I.** *vi* to be tossed around **II.** *vt* **être balloté par la voiture** to be tossed around in the car

ball-trap [baltʀap] <ball-traps> *m* **1.** (*sport*) clay-pigeon shooting **2.** (*lieu*) shooting ground

balluchon [balyʃɔ̃] *m* bundle

bal-musette [balmyzɛt] <bals-musettes> *m* dance (*with an accordeon band*)

balnéaire [balneɛʀ] *adj* **station** ~ seaside resort

bâlois(e) [balwa, waz] *adj* of Basel; *v. a.* **ajaccien**

Bâlois(e) [balwa, waz] *m(f)* person from Basel; *v. a.* **Ajaccien**

balourd [baluʀ] *m* **1.** (*maladroit*) clumsy person **2.** TECH unbalance

balourd(e) [baluʀ, uʀd] *adj* clumsy

balourdise [baluʀdiz] *f* **1.** (*caractère*) clumsiness **2.** (*acte ou propos*) blunder

balte [balt] *adj* **les États** ~**s** the Baltic States

Balte [balt] *mf* Balt

Baltique [baltik] *f* **la** (**mer**) ~ the Baltic (Sea)

baluchon [balyʃɔ̃] *m v.* **balluchon**

balustrade [balystʀad] *f* balustrade

bambin(e) [bɑ̃bɛ̃] *m(f)* infant

bambou [bɑ̃bu] *m* bamboo

ban [bɑ̃] *m* **1.** *pl* (*publication: de mariage*) banns **2.** *inf* (*applaudissements*) cheer ▶**mettre à** ~ *Suisse* (*interdire, par décision judiciaire, l'accès de*) to close

banal(e) [banal] <s> *adj* banal; (*idée, affaire*) conventional; (*propos*) commonplace; (*personne, choses*) ordinary

banalement [banalmɑ̃] *adv* in a very ordinary way

banalisation [banalizasjɔ̃] *f* trivialization

banaliser [banalize] <1> *vt* ~ **qc** to make sth commonplace

banalité [banalite] *f* **1.** (*platitude*) triteness; (*de la vie*) ordinariness; (*d'un propos*) banality **2.** (*propos*) platitude

banane [banan] *f* **1.** (*fruit*) banana **2.** (*pochette*) bum-bag *Brit*, fanny pack *Am*

bananeraie [bananʀɛ] *f* banana plantation

bananier [bananje] *m* **1.** (*plante*) banana tree **2.** (*bateau*) banana boat

banc [bɑ̃] *m* **1.** (*meuble*) bench **2.** GEO layer **3.** (*colonie: de poissons*) shoal *Brit*, school *Am*; ~ **d'huîtres** oyster bed **4.** TECH ~ **de menuisier** carpenter's workbench **5.** (*amas*) ~ **de sable** sandbank **6.** *Québec* ~ **de neige** (*congère*) snowdrift **7.** JUR ~ **des accusés** dock

bancaire [bɑ̃kɛʀ] *adj* bank

bancal(e) [bɑ̃kal] <s> *adj* **1.** (*instable: meuble*) rickety; (*personne*) lame **2.** *fig* (*raisonnement*) lame

bandage [bɑ̃daʒ] *m* **1.** (*bande*) bandage **2.** (*action*) bandaging

bande[1] [bɑ̃d] *f* **1.** (*long morceau étroit: de métal*) strip; (*d'un magnétophone*) tape; CINE film **2.** MED bandage ▶~ **dessinée** cartoon

bande[2] [bɑ̃d] *f* **1.** (*groupe: de personnes*) bunch; (*de loups, chiens*) pack; (*d'oiseaux*) flock **2.** (*groupe constitué*) gang; ~ **d'amis** band of friends

bande-annonce [bɑ̃danɔ̃s] <bandes-annonces> *f* trailer

bandeau [bɑ̃do] <x> *m* **1.** (*dans les cheveux*) coiled hairstyle **2.** (*serre-tête*) headband **3.** (*sur les yeux*) blindfold

bander [bɑ̃de] <1> **I.** *vt* **1.** (*panser*) to bandage **2.** (*tendre*) to tense **II.** *vi inf* to have a hard-on

banderole [bɑ̃dʀɔl] *f* **1.** (*petite bannière*) streamer **2.** (*bande avec inscription*) banner

bande-son [bɑ̃dsɔ̃] <bandes-son> *f* soundtrack

bande-vidéo [bɑ̃dvideo] <bandes-vidéo> *f* videotape

bandit [bɑ̃di] *m* **1.** (*malfaiteur*) bandit **2.** (*personne malhonnête*) crook

banditisme [bɑ̃ditism] *m* crime

bandoulière [bɑ̃duljɛʀ] *f* shoulder strap

bang [bɑ̃g] **I.** *interj* bang **II.** *m inv* bang

bangladais(**e**) [bɑ̃gladɛ, ɛz] *adj* Bangladeshi

Bangladais(**e**) [bɑ̃gladɛ, ɛz] *m(f)* Bangladeshi

Bangladesh [bɑ̃gladɛʃ] *m* Bangladesh

banjo [bɑ̃dʒo] *m* banjo

banlieue [bɑ̃ljø] *f* (*d'une ville*) suburb; **la ~** the suburbs; **train de ~** suburban [*o* commuter] train

banlieusard(**e**) [bɑ̃ljøzaʀ, aʀd] *m(f)* suburbanite

banni(**e**) [bani] **I.** *adj* (*personne*) exiled **II.** *m(f)* **1.** (*exilé*) exile **2.** (*exclu*) outcast

bannière [banjɛʀ] *f* streamer; REL banner

bannir [baniʀ] <8> *vt* **1.** (*mettre au ban*) **~ qn d'un pays** to banish sb from a country **2.** (*supprimer*) to ban; **~ qc de qc** to ban sth from sth

bannissement [banismɑ̃] *m* banishment

banque [bɑ̃k] *f* FIN, INFOR bank; **la Banque de France** the Bank of France; **~ de données** databank, database; **administrateur de ~ de données** database administrator; **~ d'informations génétiques** DNA bank

Banque centrale *f* Central Bank; **~ nationale indépendante** Independent National Central Bank; **~ européenne** European Central Bank

Banque européenne d'investissement *f* European Investment Bank

banquer [bɑ̃ke] <1> *vi fam* to fork out

banqueroute [bɑ̃kʀut] *f* bankruptcy; **faire ~** to go bankrupt

banquet [bɑ̃kɛ] *m* banquet

banquette [bɑ̃kɛt] *f* **1.** (*siège*) seat; **~ avant/arrière** AUTO front/back seat **2.** ARCHIT window seat **3.** (*chemin*) path; (*d'une voie*) verge

banquier, **-ière** [bɑ̃kje, -jɛʀ] *m, f* FIN, JEUX banker

banquise [bɑ̃kiz] *f* ice floe

baobab [baɔbab] *m* BOT baobab

baptême [batɛm] *m* baptism

baptiser [batize] <1> *vt* **1.** (*appeler*) **~ qn Pierre** to christen sb Pierre **2.** (*surnommer*) **~ qn "l'Asperge"** to call sb "beanpole"

baptismal(**e**) [batismal, o] <-aux> *adj* baptismal

baptistère [batistɛʀ] *m* baptistery

baquet [bakɛ] *m* tub

bar[1] [baʀ] *m* bar

> **Bars** in France are small, simple cafes, in which coffee or an aperitif can be drunk at the bar or sitting at a table. They open very early to serve a basic breakfast.

bar[2] [baʀ] *m* ZOOL bass

bar[3] [baʀ] *m* PHYS bar

baragouin [baʀagwɛ̃] *m inf* gibberish

baragouiner [baʀagwine] <1> **I.** *vt inf* (*parler mal*) **~ une langue** to speak a language badly **II.** *vi inf* to gabble

baraque [baʀak] *f* **1.** (*cabane*) hut; (*pour les outils de jardinage*) (tool) shed **2.** *inf* (*maison*) pad; (*maison délabrée*) shack

baraqué(**e**) [baʀake] *adj inf* hefty

baraquement [baʀakmɑ̃] *m* camp

baratin [baʀatɛ̃] *m inf* smooth talk; (*pour vendre*) (sales) patter

baratiner [baʀatine] <1> **I.** *vt inf* **1.** (*bonimenter*) **~ qn** to give sb the patter **2.** (*essayer de persuader*) to sweet-talk **3.** (*draguer*) **~ qn** to chat sb up **II.** *vi inf* to chatter

Barbade [baʀbad(ə)] *f* **la ~** Barbados

barbadien(**ne**) [baʀbadjɛ̃, ɛn] *adj* Barbadian

Barbadien(**ne**) [baʀbadjɛ̃, ɛn] *m(f)* Barbadian

barbant(**e**) [baʀbɑ̃, ɑ̃t] *adj inf* boring

barbaque [baʀbak] *f fam* tough meat

barbare [baʀbaʀ] **I.** *adj* **1.** (*cruel*) barbaric **2.** (*grossier*) barbarous **II.** *m* barbarian

barbarie [baʀbaʀi] *f* **1.** (*opp: civilisation*) barbarism **2.** (*cruauté*) barbarity

barbe [baʀb] *f* **1.** (*poils*) *a.* ZOOL beard; (*d'un chat*) whiskers *pl* **2.** BOT **~ de capucin** wild chicory **3.** GASTR **~ à papa** candy floss *Brit,* cotton candy *Am* **4.** *pl* TECH jagged edge

barbeau [baʀbo] <x> *m* **1.** ZOOL barbel **2.** BOT cornflower

barbecue [baʀbəkju] *m* barbecue; **faire un ~** to have a barbecue

barbelé(**e**) [baʀbəle] **I.** *adj* **fil de fer ~** barbed wire **II.** *m* barbed wire *no pl*

barber [baʀbe] <1> **I.** *vt inf* **~ qn** to bore sb stiff **II.** *vpr inf* **se ~** to get bored stiff

Barberousse [baʀbəʀus(ə)] *m* Barbarossa

barbiche [baʀbiʃ] *f* goatee

barbier [baʀbje] *m Québec* (*coiffeur pour hommes*) barber

barbiturique [baʀbityʀik] *m* BIO barbiturate

barboter [baʀbɔte] <1> **I.** *vi* **~ dans qc** to be mixed up in sth **II.** *vt inf* to pinch

barbouillage [baʀbujaʒ] *m* **1.** (*peinture*) daub **2.** (*écriture*) scrawl

barbouillé(**e**) [baʀbuje] *adj* **être ~** to have an upset stomach

barbouiller [baʀbuje] <1> I. *vt* 1. (*enduire*) ~ **qn/qc de qc** to smear sb/sth with sth 2. (*peindre*) ~ **qc** to daub paint on sth; (*mur*) to daub sth 3. *péj* (*écrire*) ~ **qc** (*papier, page*) to scribble over sth II. *vpr* **se** ~ **le visage de confiture** to smear one's face with jam

barbu [baʀby] *m* bearded man

barbu(e) [baʀby] *adj* bearded

barbue [baʀby] *f* ZOOL brill

barde[1] [baʀd] *f* bard

barde[2] [baʀd] *m* bard

barder [baʀde] <1> I. *vt* 1. GASTR to bard 2. (*garnir*) ~ **qn de décorations** to cover sb with medals II. *vi inf* **ça barde** the sparks are flying

barème [baʀɛm] *m* scale; (*tableau*) table; ECOLE marking scale *Brit*, grading scale *Am*

baril [baʀil] *m* barrel

barillet [baʀijɛ] *m* (*d'une montre*) barrel; (*d'un revolver*) cylinder

bariolé(e) [baʀjɔle] *adj* multicoloured *Brit*, multicolored *Am*

barioler [baʀjɔle] <1> *vt* to splash with colours

barjo [baʀʒo] *adj inv, inf* crazy

barman [baʀman, -mɛn] <s *o* -men> *m* barman, bartender *Am*

baromètre [baʀɔmɛtʀ] *m* barometer

baron(ne) [baʀɔ̃, ɔn] *m(f)* baron, baroness *m, f*

baroque [baʀɔk] I. *adj* 1. ARCHIT, MUS baroque 2. (*bizarre*) weird II. *m* Baroque

baroudeur [baʀudœʀ] *m inf* fighter

barque [baʀk] *f* boat ►**bien mener sa** ~ to do well for oneself

barquette [baʀkɛt] *f* 1. (*tartelette*) tartlet 2. (*récipient: de fraises*) punnet

barrage [baʀaʒ] *m* 1. (*barrière*) barrier 2. ELEC dam

barre [baʀ] *f* 1. (*pièce*) bar; ~ **de chocolat** strip of chocolate; (*tablette*) bar of chocolate 2. JUR (*au tribunal*) ~ **des témoins** witness box *Brit*, witness stand *Am* 3. (*trait*) slash 4. SPORT (*pour la danse*) barre; (*en athlétisme*) bar 5. MUS ~ **de mesure** bar line 6. NAUT helm 7. INFOR ~ **de défilement** scroll bar; ~ **de menu** menu toolbar; ~ **d'espacement** spacebar; ~ **des tâches** task bar; ~ **de titre** title bar

barré [baʀe] *m* MUS **exécuter un** ~ to strike a bar chord

barré(e) [baʀe] *adj* (*rue*) blocked; (*porte*) barred

barreau [baʀo] <x> *m* 1. JUR bar 2. (*tube, barre: d'une échelle*) rung; (*d'une grille*) bar

barrer [baʀe] <1> I. *vt* 1. (*bloquer: route*) to block; (*porte*) to bar; ~ **le chemin** (*personne*) to stand in the way; (*voiture*) to block the road 2. (*biffer*) ~ **qc** to cross sth out 3. NAUT to steer 4. *Québec* (*fermer à clé*) to lock II. *vi* to steer III. *vpr inf* **se** ~ to take off

barrette [baʀɛt] *f* 1. (*pince*) hair slide *Brit*, barrette *Am* 2. (*bijou*) brooch 3. (*décoration*) bar

barreur, -euse [baʀœʀ, -øz] *m, f* helmsman, helmswoman *m, f*

barricade [baʀikad] *f* barricade

barricader [baʀikade] <1> I. *vt* (*porte, rue*) to barricade II. *vpr* 1. (*derrière une barricade*) **se** ~ to barricade oneself 2. (*s'enfermer*) **se** ~ **dans sa chambre** to lock oneself in one's room

barrière [baʀjɛʀ] *f* 1. (*fermeture*) gate; CHEMDFER (level crossing) gate, (grade crossing) gate *Am* 2. (*clôture*) fence 3. (*séparation*) *a.* SPORT barrier; ~ **de roesti(s)** *Suisse: imaginary border between French- and German-speaking Switzerland*

barrique [baʀik] *f* barrel

barrir [baʀiʀ] <8> *vi* (*éléphant*) to trumpet

barrissement [baʀismɑ̃] *m* trumpeting

bar-tabac [baʀtaba] <bars-tabac> *m: cafe selling tobacco*

baryton [baʀitɔ̃] *m* baritone

bas[1] [bɑ] *m* (*partie inférieure*) bottom; (*d'une maison*) downstairs

bas[2] [bɑ] *m* stocking

bas(se) [bɑ, bɑs] I. *adj* 1. (*de peu de/à faible hauteur*) low; (*stature*) short 2. (*peu intense*) mild 3. (*dans la hiérarchie sociale*) lowly II. *adv* 1. (*à faible hauteur*) low 2. (*au-dessous*) **loger en** ~ to live downstairs 3. (*ci-dessous*) **voir plus** ~ see below 4. (*au pied de*) **en** ~ **de la colline** at the bottom of the hill 5. (*opp: aigu*) low 6. (*doucement*) softly; **parler** ~ **tout bas** to speak in a low voice

basalte [bazalt] *m* GEO basalt

basané(e) [bazane] *adj* 1. (*bronzé*) suntanned 2. (*de couleur*) swarthy

bas-côté [bɑkote] <bas-côtés> *m* 1. (*bord: d'une route, autoroute*) shoulder 2. ARCHIT (*d'une église*) side aisle

bascule [baskyl] *f* 1. (*balançoire*) seesaw 2. (*balance*) scale

basculer [baskyle] <1> I. *vi* 1. (*tomber*) to fall over 2. *fig* ~ **dans qc** to topple over into sth II. *vt* 1. (*faire pivoter*) ~ **qc** to tip sth over 2. (*faire tomber*) ~ **qc dans qc** to topple sth into sth 3. ELEC to switch

base [bɑz] *f* 1. (*pied*) *a.* LING base 2. (*principe, composant principal*) basis 3. (*connaissances élémentaires*) **la** ~, **les** ~**s** the basics 4. MIL, MAT, CHIM, INFOR base; ~ **de données** database; ~ **de registres** system registry

baser [bɑze] <1> I. *vt* 1. (*fonder*) ~ **qc sur qc** to base sth on sth 2. MIL **être basé à Strasbourg** to be based in Strasburg II. *vpr* **se** ~ **sur qc** to base oneself on sth

bas-fond [bɑfɔ̃] <bas-fonds> *m* 1. (*endroit*) shoal 2. *pl* (*d'une ville*) slums; (*d'une société*) dregs

basilic [bazilik] *m* basil

basilique [bazilik] *f* basilica

basique [bazik] *adj* CHIM basic

basket [baskɛt] *f souvent pl* (*chaussure*) tennis shoe

basket [baskɛt], **basket-ball** *m* basketball

basketteur, **-euse** [basketœʀ, -øz] *m, f* basketball player

basque¹ [bask] **I.** *adj* Basque; **Pays** ~ Basque Country **II.** *m* Basque; *v. a.* **français**

basque² [bask] *f* basque

Basque [bask] *mf* Basque

bas-relief [baʀəljɛf] <bas-reliefs> *m* bas-relief

basse [bas] *f* bass

basse-cour [baskuʀ] <basses-cours> *f* **1.** (*lieu*) farmyard **2.** (*animaux*) poultry

bassement [basmɑ̃] *adv* (*d'une manière indigne*) basely

bassesse [basɛs] *f* servility; (*d'un sentiment*) meanness

bassin [basɛ̃] *m* **1.** (*récipient*) bowl **2.** (*pièce d'eau: d'une fontaine, piscine*) pool; (*d'un jardin*) pond **3.** (*dans un port*) dock **4.** GEO basin **5.** ANAT pelvis

bassine [basin] *f* bowl

bassiner [basine] <1> *vt* **1.** (*humecter: plante*) to moisten **2.** (*chauffer*) to warm **3.** *inf* (*ennuyer*) ~ **qn** to bore sb rigid

bassiste [basist] *mf* bass player

basson [basɔ̃] *m* **1.** (*instrument*) bassoon **2.** (*musicien*) bassoonist

baster [baste] <1> *vi Suisse* (*céder, s'incliner*) ~ **devant qn** to give way to sb

bastille [bastij] *f* (*château-fort*) fortress

Bastille [bastij] *f* **la** ~ the Bastille

bastingage [bastɛ̃gaʒ] *m* ship's rail

bastion [bastjɔ̃] *m* **1.** (*fortification*) stronghold **2.** (*haut lieu*) bastion

baston [bastɔ̃] *m o f inf* **il va y avoir du** ~ there's going to be trouble

bas-ventre [bavɑ̃tʀ] <bas-ventres> *m* stomach

bataille [bataj] *f* **1.** (*pendant une guerre*) battle **2.** (*épreuve de force*) struggle **3.** (*bagarre*) fight **4.** (*jeu*) ≈ beggar-my-neighbour *Brit*, ≈ war *Am*

batailler [bataje] <1> *vi* **1.** (*se battre*) ~ **pour qc** to fight for sth **2.** (*argumenter*) to argue **3.** *inf* (*faire des efforts*) to battle

batailleur, **-euse** [batajœʀ, -jøz] **I.** *adj* **être** ~ to be a fighter **II.** *m, f* fighter

bataillon [batajɔ̃] *m* **1.** MIL batallion **2.** (*grand nombre*) army

bâtard(**e**) [bataʀ, aʀd] **I.** *adj* **1.** (*illégitime: enfant*) illegitimate; (*chien*) mongrel **2.** (*de fantaisie*) **pain** ~ country loaf (*of white bread*) **II.** *m(f)* **1.** (*enfant*) bastard **2.** (*chien*) mongrel, mutt *Am*

bateau [bato] <x> **I.** *adj inf* trite **II.** *m* (*embarcation*) boat

bateau-citerne [batositɛʀn] <bateaux-citernes> *m* tanker **bateau-mouche** [batomuʃ] <bateaux-mouches> *m: sightseeing boat on the River Seine in Paris* **bateau-pilote** [batopilɔt] <bateaux-pilotes> *m* pilot boat

batelier, **-ière** [batəlje, -jɛʀ] *m, f* boatman *m*, boatwoman *f*

bâti [bati] *m* **1.** COUT tacking **2.** TECH frame

bâti(**e**) [bati] *adj* **être bien** ~ to be well-built

batifoler [batifɔle] <1> *vi inf* to lark about

bâtiment [batimɑ̃] *m* **1.** (*édifice*) building **2.** ECON building [*o* construction] industry **3.** NAUT ship

bâtir [batiʀ] <8> *vt* **1.** (*construire*) to build **2.** (*fonder*) ~ **une théorie sur qc** to build a theory on sth **3.** COUT to tack

bâtisse [batis] *f* building

bâtisseur, **-euse** [batisœʀ, -øz] *m, f* builder

bâton [batɔ̃] *m* **1.** (*canne, stick*) stick **2.** (*trait vertical*) vertical line

bâtonnet [batɔnɛ] *m* short stick; (*pour examiner la gorge*) tongue depressor

batracien [batʀasjɛ̃] *m* ZOOL batrachian

battage [bataʒ] *m* (*publicité*) hype *no pl*

battant [batɑ̃] *m* **1.** (*pièce métallique: d'une cloche*) clapper **2.** (*panneau mobile: d'une fenêtre*) opener; (*d'une porte*) door (*right or left part of a double door*)

battant(**e**) [batɑ̃, ɑ̃t] **I.** *adj* (*personne*) **être** ~ to be a fighter **II.** *m(f)* fighter

battement [batmɑ̃] *m* **1.** (*bruit*) banging; (*de la pluie*) beating **2.** (*mouvement*) ~ **des cils** flutter of one's eyelashes **3.** (*rythme: du pouls, cœur*) beating *no pl* **4.** (*intervalle de temps*) break

batterie [batʀi] *f* **1.** (*groupe*) *a.* AUTO, MIL battery **2.** MUS percussion **3.** (*ensemble d'ustensiles*) ~ **de cuisine** kitchen utensils *pl*

batteur [batœʀ] *m* **1.** (*mixeur*) whisk **2.** MUS drummer

battre [batʀ] *irr* **I.** *vt* **1.** (*frapper, vaincre*) to hit **2.** (*travailler en tapant: blé*) to thresh; (*fer, tapis, matelas*) to beat **3.** (*mélanger, mixer: blanc d'œuf, œuf entier*) to beat; (*crème*) to whip **4.** (*frapper*) **faire** ~ **les volets** (*vent, tempête*) to make the shutters bang **5.** (*parcourir en cherchant: campagne, région*) to scour **6.** MUS (*mesure, tambour*) to beat **II.** *vi* **1.** (*cogner*) to bang; (*porte, volet*) to slam **2.** (*frapper*) ~ **contre qc** to knock against sth; (*pluie*) to beat against sth **3.** (*agiter*) ~ **des ailes** to flap one's wings; ~ **des cils** to flutter one's eyelashes; ~ **des mains** to clap one's hands **III.** *vpr* **1.** (*se bagarrer*) **se** ~ **contre qn** to fight sb **2.** (*se disputer*) **se** ~ **avec qn pour qc** to fight with sb over sth **3.** (*militer*) **se** ~ **pour qc** to fight for sth **4.** (*avoir des difficultés*) **se** ~ **avec un problème** to struggle with a problem

battu(**e**) [baty] **I.** *part passé de* **battre** **II.** *adj* (*vaincu*) beaten

battue [baty] *f* (*à la chasse*) beat

batture [batyʀ] *f Québec* (*estran*) strand

baud [bo] *m* INFOR baud [rate]

baudruche [bodʀyʃ] *f* **ballon de** ~ (toy) balloon

bauge [boʒ] *f* wallow; (*taudis*) hovel

baume [bom] *m* balm

baux [bo] *v.* **bail**

bauxite [boksit] *f* bauxite

bavard(**e**) [bavaʀ, aʀd] **I.** *adj* **1.** (*loquace*) talkative **2.** (*indiscret*) gossipy **II.** *m(f)* **1.** (*qui parle beaucoup*) chatterbox *inf* **2.** (*indiscret*) gossip

bavardage [bavaʀdaʒ] *m* **1.** (*papotage*) chatting *no pl* **2.** (*propos vides*) twaddle *no pl* **3.** (*commérages*) gossip *no pl*

bavarder [bavaʀde] <1> *vi* **1.** (*papoter*) ~ **avec qn** to chat with sb **2.** (*divulguer un secret*) to blab *inf*

bavarois [bavaʀwa] *m* **1.** (*dialecte*) Bavarian; *v. a.* **français** **2.** GASTR ≈ mousse

bavarois(e) [bavaʀwa, waz] *adj* Bavarian

bavasser [bavase] <1> *vi péj, inf* to natter

bave [bav] *f* **1.** (*salive*) drool; (*d'un animal enragé*) foam **2.** (*liquide gluant: des gastéropodes*) slime

baver [bave] <1> *vi* **1.** (*saliver*) to drool; (*escargot, limace*) to leave a trail **2.** (*couler: stylo, porte-plume*) to leak **3.** (*médire*) ~ **sur qn/qc** to malign sb/sth **4.** (*être ahuri de*) **en ~ d'envie** to drool over sth

bavette [bavɛt] *f* **1.** (*bavoir: a. d'un vêtement*) bib **2.** (*viande*) *cut of steak taken from just below the sirloin*

baveux, -euse [bavø, -øz] *adj* **1.** (*qui bave: personne*) dribbly; (*animal*) drooling; (*escargot, limace*) slimy **2.** GASTR **omelette baveuse** runny omelette

bavoir [bavwaʀ] *m* bib

bavure [bavyʀ] *f* **1.** (*tache*) smudge **2.** (*erreur*) blunder

bazar [bazaʀ] *m* **1.** (*magasin*) general store **2.** (*souk*) bazaar **3.** *inf* (*désordre*) mess; (*amas d'objets hétéroclites*) junk

bazarder [bazaʀde] <1> *vt inf* ~ **qc** to get rid of sth; (*vendre*) to sell sth off

bazooka [bazuka] *m* bazooka

BCBG [besebeʒe] *adj abr de* **bon chic bon genre** *well-off French upper-middle class*

BCE [beseø] *f abr de* **Banque centrale européenne** ECB

BCG [beseʒe] *m abr de* **bacille de Calmette et Guérin** BCG

BD [bede] *f abr de* **bande dessinée** comic strip; (*livre*) comic book

béant(e) [beɑ̃, ɑ̃t] *adj* (*yeux*) wide open; (*blessure, gouffre, trou*) gaping

béat(e) [bea, at] *adj* **1.** (*heureux*) blissful **2.** (*content de soi*) smug **3.** (*niais*) beatific

béatification [beatifikasjɔ̃] *f* beatification

béatifier [beatifje] <1> *vt* to beatify

béatitude [beatityd] *f* beatitude

beau [bo] <x> *m* **1.** (*beauté*) **le ~** the beautiful **2.** METEO **le temps se met au ~** the weather's turning fine ►**être au ~ fixe** (*baromètre*) to be set fair; (*temps*) to be settled

beau, belle [bo, bɛl] <*devant un nom masculin commençant par une voyelle ou un h muet* **bel**, x> *adj antéposé* **1.** (*opp: laid*) beautiful; (*homme*) handsome **2.** (*qui plaît à l'esprit*) fine; **c'est du ~ travail** that's nice work **3.** (*agréable*) fine; (*voyage*) lovely; **la mer est belle** the sea is calm **4.** (*intensif*) excellent **5.** (*sacré*) terrible ►**il a ~ faire qc** although he does sth; **il fait ~** the weather's good; **se faire ~(belle)** to get dressed up; (*se maquiller*) to put on one's make-up; **de plus belle** even more

beaucoup [boku] *adv* **1.** (*en grande quantité*) **boire ~** to drink a lot **2.** (*intensément*) **ce film m'a ~ plu** I liked this film very much **3.** (*fréquemment*) **aller ~ au cinéma** to go to the cinema often [*o* a lot] **4.** (*plein de*) ~ **de neige** a lot of snow **5.** (*de nombreux*) ~ **de voitures** many cars **6.** (~ *de personnes*) ~ **pensent la même chose** many (people) think the same (thing) **7.** (~ *de choses*) **il y a encore ~ à faire** there is still much to be done **8.** *avec un comparatif* ~ **plus rapide/petit** much faster/smaller **9.** *avec un adverbe* **c'est ~ trop** it's much too much

beauf [bof] *m inf* **1.** (*beau-frère*) brother-in-law **2.** (*pauvre type*) *narrow-minded Frenchman*

beau-fils [bofis] <beaux-fils> *m* **1.** (*gendre*) son-in-law **2.** (*fils du conjoint*) stepson **beau-frère** [bofʀɛʀ] <beaux-frères> *m* brother-in-law

beaujolais [boʒɔlɛ] *m* (*vin*) Beaujolais

beau-père [bopɛʀ] <beaux-pères> *m* **1.** (*père du conjoint*) father-in-law **2.** (*conjoint de la mère*) stepfather

beauté [bote] *f* (*a. personne*) beauty

beaux-arts [bozaʀ] *mpl* **les ~** the fine arts

beaux-enfants [bozɑ̃fɑ̃] *mpl* stepchildren

beaux-parents [bopaʀɑ̃] *mpl* in-laws

bébé [bebe] *m* baby

bébé-éprouvette [bebeepʀuvɛt] <bébés-éprouvettes> *m* test-tube baby

bec [bɛk] *m* **1.** (*chez un oiseau*) beak **2.** *inf* (*bouche*) mouth **3.** (*extrémité pointue: d'une plume*) nib; (*d'une clarinette, flûte*) mouthpiece **4.** *Belgique, Québec, Suisse, Nord, inf* **donner un ~** (*faire un bisou*) to kiss

bécane [bekan] *f inf* **1.** (*moto*) bike **2.** (*machine, ordinateur*) machine

bécarre [bekaʀ] *m* MUS natural

bécasse [bekas] *f* **1.** (*oiseau*) woodcock **2.** *inf* (*sotte*) ninny

bécasseau [bekaso] <x> *m* (*oiseau*) sandpiper

bécassine [bekasin] *f* **1.** (*oiseau*) snipe **2.** *inf* (*fille*) ninny

béchamel [beʃamɛl] *f* béchamel (sauce)

bêche [bɛʃ] *f* spade

bêcher [beʃe] <1> **I.** *vt* AGR to dig **II.** *vi* **1.** AGR to dig **2.** *inf* (*être fier*) to swank

bécoter [bekɔte] <1> **I.** *vt inf* to kiss **II.** *vpr inf* **se ~** to smooch

becquée [beke] *f* **donner la ~ à qn** to spoon-feed sb

becquerel [bɛkʀɛl] *m* becquerel

becqueter [bɛkte] <3> *vt* ~ **une branche** (*oiseau*) to peck (at) a branch

becter [bɛkte] <1> *vt inf* to eat

bedaine [bədɛn] *f inf* paunch; (*d'un enfant*)

tummy

bédé [bede] *f inf* comic strip; (*livre*) comic book

bedeau [bədo] <x> *m* verger *Brit*

bedonnant(e) [bədɔnɑ̃, ɑ̃t] *adj inf* portly

bédouin(e) [bedwɛ̃, in] *m(f)* Bedouin

bée [be] *adj v.* **bouche**

beefsteak [biftɛk] *v.* **bifteck**

beffroi [befʀwa] *m* (*a. d'une église*) belfry

bégaiement [begɛmɑ̃] *m* stammering

bégayant(e) [begɛjɑ̃, ɑ̃t] *adj* stammering

bégayer [begeje] <7> **I.** *vi* to stammer **II.** *vt* to stammer (out)

bégonia [begɔnja] *m* begonia

bègue [bɛg] **I.** *adj* stammering **II.** *mf* stammerer

béguine [begin] *f Belgique* (*religieuse soumise à la vie conventuelle sans avoir prononcé de vœux*) Beguine

beige [bɛʒ] *adj, m* beige

beigne[1] [bɛɲ] *f inf* slap; **donner une ~ à qn** to clout sb

beigne[2] [bɛ̞gn̩] *m Québec* (*beignet*) **~ au chocolat** chocolate doughnut

beignet [bɛɲɛ] *m* fritter; **pâte à ~s** fritter batter; **~s aux pommes** apple fritters

bel [bɛl] *v.* **beau**

bel canto [bɛlkɑ̃to] *m* bel canto

bêler [bele] <1> *vi* to bleat

belette [bəlɛt] *f* ZOOL weasel

belge [bɛlʒ] *adj* Belgian

Belge [bɛlʒ] *mf* Belgian

belgicisme [bɛlʒisism] *m* belgicism

Belgique [bɛlʒik] *f* **la ~** Belgium

Belgrade [bɛlgʀad] Belgrade

bélier [belje] *m* **1.** ZOOL ram **2.** MIL battering ram

Bélier [belje] *m* Aries; *v. a.* **Balance**

Belize [beli:z] *m* **le ~** Belize

belizien(ne) [beli:zjɛ̃, ɛn] *adj* Belizean

Belizien(ne) [beli:zjɛ̃, ɛn] *m(f)* Belizean

belle [bɛl] **I.** *adj v.* **beau II.** *f* **1.** SPORT decider **2.** (*conquête*) beauty; (*petite amie*) girlfriend ►**la Belle au bois dormant** Sleeping Beauty

belle-fille [bɛlfij] <belles-filles> *f* **1.** (*bru*) daughter-in-law **2.** (*fille du conjoint*) stepdaughter **belle-mère** [bɛlmɛʀ] <belles-mères> *f* **1.** (*mère du conjoint*) mother-in-law **2.** (*conjointe du père*) stepmother **belle-sœur** [bɛlsœʀ] <belles-sœurs> *f* sister-in-law

belliciste [belisist] **I.** *adj* bellicose **II.** *mf* warmonger

belligérant(e) [beliʒeʀɑ̃, ɑ̃t] **I.** *adj* belligerent **II.** *mpl* belligerents

belliqueux, -euse [belikø, -øz] *adj* **1.** (*guerrier*) warlike; (*discours*) aggressive **2.** (*querelleur*) quarrelsome; (*tempérament*) aggressive; (*personne*) bellicose

belon [bəlɔ̃] *f* Belon oyster

belote [bəlɔt] *f: popular card game*

belvédère [bɛlvedɛʀ] *m* **1.** (*édifice*) belvedere **2.** (*point de vue*) panoramic viewpoint

bémol [bemɔl] *m* MUS flat

bénédictin(e) [benediktɛ̃, in] **I.** *adj* Benedictine **II.** *m(f)* Benedictine

Bénédictine [benediktin] *f* (*liqueur*) **la ~** Benedictine

bénédiction [benediksjɔ̃] *f* **1.** (*grâce*) grace **2.** (*action: d'un(e) fidèle, d'une cloche, d'un navire*) blessing; **~ nuptiale** nuptial blessing

bénéfice [benefis] *m* **1.** COM profit **2.** (*avantage*) benefit

bénéficiaire [benefisjɛʀ] **I.** *mf* **1.** beneficiary **2.** *Suisse* (*d'une retraite*) pensioner **II.** *adj* (*entreprise, opération*) profit-making

bénéficier [benefisje] <1> *vi* **~ de qc** (*avoir*) to have sth; (*avoir comme avantage*) to benefit from sth

bénéfique [benefik] *adj* beneficial

Benelux [benelyks] *m* **le ~** the Benelux countries

benêt [bənɛ] *m* simpleton

bénévolat [benevɔla] *m* volunteering; (*activité*) voluntary work

bénévole [benevɔl] **I.** *adj* **1.** (*volontaire*) voluntary **2.** (*gratuit*) unpaid; (*fonction*) voluntary **II.** *mf* volunteer; (*dans une fonction*) voluntary worker

bénévolement [benevɔlmɑ̃] *adv* voluntarily; (*gratuitement*) free

bengali [bɛ̃gali] *m* (*oiseau*) waxbill

Bengladesh [bɑ̃gladɛʃ] *v.* **Bangladesh**

béni(e) [beni] *adj soutenu* blessed

bénin, -igne [benɛ̃, -iɲ] *adj* harmless; (*tumeur*) benign; (*punition*) mild

Bénin [benɛ̃] *m* **le ~** Benin

béninois(e) [beninwa, az] *adj* Beninese

Béninois(e) [beninwa, az] *m(f)* Beninese

bénir [beniʀ] <8> *vt a.* REL to bless

bénit(e) [beni, it] *adj* blessed; (*eau*) holy

bénitier [benitje] *m* font

benjamin(e) [bɛ̃ʒamɛ̃, in] *m(f)* youngest child

benne [bɛn] *f* **1.** TECH (*de charbon, minerai*) tub **2.** (*container*) skip; (*d'un camion*) dumper **3.** (*cabine: d'un téléphérique*) cable car

benzine [bɛ̃zin] *f* benzine

BEP [beøpe] *m abr de* **brevet d'études professionelles** *vocational school certificate*

BEPC [beøpese] *m abr de* **brevet d'études du premier cycle** *general exams taken at age 16*

béqueter [bekte] <3> *v.* **becqueter**

béquille [bekij] *f* **1.** (*canne*) crutch **2.** (*support: d'une moto, d'un vélo*) stand

berbère [bɛʀbɛʀ] *adj, m* Berber; *v. a.* **français**

Berbère [bɛʀbɛʀ] *mf* Berber

bercail [bɛʀkaj] *m* **rentrer** [*o* **revenir**] **au ~** to return to the fold

berçant(e) [bɛʀsɑ̃, ɑ̃t] *adj Québec* **chaise ~e** (*rocking-chair*) rocking chair

berçante [bɛʀsɑ̃t] *f Québec* (*rocking-chair*) rocking chair

berce [bɛʀs] *f Belgique* (*berceau d'enfant*) cradle

berceau [bɛʀso] <x> *m* **1.** (*couffin*) cradle **2.** (*lieu d'origine: d'une idée, technique, personne*) birthplace **3.** ARCHIT barrel vault **4.** BOT bower

bercement [bɛʀsəmɑ̃] *m* rocking

bercer [bɛʀse] <2> **I.** *vt* (*personne, canot, navire*) to rock **II.** *vpr* **se ~ d'illusions sur le compte de qn/qc** to harbour illusions about sb/sth

berceuse [bɛʀsøz] *f* **1.** (*chanson*) lullaby **2.** (*fauteuil*) rocking chair

béret [beʀɛ] *m* **~ basque** beret

bergamote [bɛʀgamɔt] *f* BOT bergamot

berge [bɛʀʒ] *f* **1.** (*rive*) bank **2.** *plé, inf* (*années*) years; **avoir bien 50 ~s** to be well past 50

berger [bɛʀʒe] *m* (*chien*) sheepdog; **~ allemand** German shepherd

berger, **-ère** [bɛʀʒe, -ɛʀ] *m, f* shepherd, shepherdess *m, f*

bergère [bɛʀʒɛʀ] *f* (*fauteuil*) wing chair

bergerie [bɛʀʒəʀi] *f* sheepfold

bergeronnette [bɛʀʒəʀɔnɛt] *f* wagtail

berk [bɛʀk] *interj* yuck

Berlin [bɛʀlɛ̃] Berlin

berline [bɛʀlin] *f* **1.** AUTO saloon car *Brit*, sedan *Am* **2.** MIN truck

berlingot [bɛʀlɛ̃go] *m* **1.** (*bonbon*) *boiled sweet* **2.** (*emballage*) carton

berlue [bɛʀly] *f inf* **dis donc, j'ai la ~** goodness, I must be seeing things; **si je n'ai pas la ~** if I'm not seeing things

bermuda [bɛʀmyda] *m* (pair of) bermuda shorts

Bermudes [bɛʀmyd(ə)] *fpl* **les ~** Bermuda

Berne [bɛʀn] Bern

berner [bɛʀne] <1> *vt* to fool

bernois(**e**) [bɛʀnwa, waz] *adj* of Bern; *v. a.* **ajaccien**

Bernois(**e**) [bɛʀnwa, waz] *m(f)* person from Bern; *v. a.* **Ajaccien**

berzingue [bɛʀzɛ̃g] *inf* **à toute ~** flat out

besace [bəzas] *f* beggar's bag

besogne [bəzɔɲ] *f* work

besogneux, **-euse** [bəzɔɲø, -øz] *adj* **1.** (*nécessiteux*) needy **2.** (*affecté à de petits travaux*) hard-working

besoin [bəzwɛ̃] *m* **1.** (*nécessité*) **le ~ de sommeil de qn** sb's need for sleep **2.** *pl* (*nécessités*) **les ~s financiers de qn** sb's financial requirements **3.** (*nécessité d'uriner*) **~ naturel** call of nature ►**avoir ~ de qc** to need sth; **au ~** if necessary; **dans le ~** in need

bestial(**e**) [bɛstjal, jo] <-aux> *adj* beastly; (*instinct, avidité*) animal

bestialité [bɛstjalite] *f* bestiality

bestiaux [bɛstjo] *mpl* livestock

bestiole [bɛstjɔl] *f inf* (*insecte*) creature; (*petit animal*) beastie

best-seller [bɛstsɛlœʀ] <best-sellers> *m* bestseller

bêta [beta] *app* INFOR **version ~ d'un programme** beta version of a program

bétail [betaj] *m sans pl* livestock

bétaillère [betajɛʀ] *f* cattle truck

bête [bɛt] **I.** *f* **1.** (*animal*) animal **2.** (*insecte*) bug **3.** (*qui a du talent*) star **II.** *adj* (*personne, histoire, question*) stupid ►**c'est tout ~** it's so simple

bêtement [bɛtmɑ̃] *adv* **1.** stupidly **2.** (*malencontreusement*) foolishly ►**tout ~** quite simply

bêtifier [betifje] <1> *vi* **~ avec qn** to talk babytalk to sb

bêtise [betiz] *f* **1.** (*manque d'intelligence*) stupidity **2.** (*parole*) nonsense *no pl* **3. faire une ~** to do something silly; **arrête tes ~s** stop being silly

béton [betɔ̃] *m* concrete

bétonner [betɔne] <1> **I.** *vt* to concrete **II.** *vi* SPORT to stonewall

bétonnière [betɔnjɛʀ] *f* **1.** (*machine*) cement mixer **2.** (*camion*) cement lorry [*o* truck *Am*]

bette [bɛt] *f* Chinese cabbage

betterave [bɛtʀav] *f* beetroot *Brit*, beet *Am*

beuglement [bøgləmɑ̃] *m* **1.** (*meuglement: de la vache, du veau*) moo; (*du taureau, bœuf*) bellow **2.** *fig* (*de la radio, télé*) blare

beugler [bøgle] <1> *vi* **1.** (*meugler: vache, veau*) to moo; (*taureau, bœuf*) to bellow **2.** *fig* (*radio, télé*) to blare (out)

beur(**e**) [bœʀ] *m(f) inf: person born in France of North African parents*

beurk [bœʀk] *interj v.* **berk**

beurre [bœʀ] *m* butter

beurré(**e**) [bœʀe] *adj inf* tanked-up

beurrer [bœʀe] <1> *vt* to butter

beurrier [bœʀje] *m* butter dish

beurrier, **-ière** [bœʀje, -jɛʀ] *adj* butter

beuverie [bœvʀi] *f* (drinking) binge

bévue [bevy] *f* blunder

biais [bjɛ] *m* device; (*échappatoire*) way; **par le ~ de** through ►**de ~** indirectly

biaiser [bjeze] <1> *vi* to equivocate

bibelot [biblo] *m* trinket

biberon [bibʀɔ̃] *m* (baby's) bottle

bible [bibl] *f* bible

biblio [biblijo] *f inf abr de* **bibliothèque**

bibliobus [biblijobys] *m* mobile library

bibliographie [biblijɔgʀafi] *f* bibliography

bibliographique [biblijɔgʀafik] *adj* bibliographical

bibliophile [biblijɔfil] *mf* book lover

bibliothécaire [biblijɔtekɛʀ] *mf* librarian

bibliothèque [biblijɔtɛk] *f* **1.** (*salle, collection*) library; **~ publique/~-en-ligne** public/on-line library **2.** (*étagère*) bookshelf; (*armoire*) bookcase

biblique [biblik] *adj* biblical

bicarbonate [bikaʀbɔnat] *m* bicarbonate

bicentenaire [bisɑ̃tnɛʀ] *m* bicentenary

biceps [bisɛps] *m* biceps

biche [biʃ] *f* doe

bichonner [biʃɔne] <1> **I.** *vt* **~ qn** to dress sb up; (*prendre bien soin de*) to pamper sb

II. *vpr* **se** ~ to dress up

bicolore [bikɔlɔʀ] *adj* bicoloured *Brit,* bicolored *Am*

bicoque [bikɔk] *f péj, inf* (*maison*) shack

bicorne [bikɔʀn] *m* cocked hat

bicross [bikʀɔs] *m* **1.** (*bicyclette*) BMX bike **2.** (*sport*) stunt biking

bicyclette [bisiklɛt] *f* bicycle; **faire de la ~** to go cycling

bide [bid] *m inf* **1.** (*ventre*) belly **2.** (*échec*) flop; **faire un ~ complet** to be a total flop

bidet [bidɛ] *m* **1.** (*cuvette*) bidet **2.** *inf* (*cheval*) nag

bidon [bidɔ̃] **I.** *m* **1.** (*récipient*) can; (*de lait*) milk-churn **2.** (*gourde*) flask **3.** MIL water bottle **4.** *inf* (*ventre*) belly **II.** *adj inv, inf* (*attentat, attaque*) phoney

bidonner [bidɔne] <1> *vpr inf* **se ~** to split one's sides (laughing)

bidonville [bidɔ̃vil] *m* slum; (*du tiers-monde*) shantytown

bidule [bidyl] *m inf* contraption

bielle [bjɛl] *f* (*de voiture*) track rod; (*de locomotive*) connecting rod

bielorusse [bjelɔʀys(ə)] **I.** *adj* Belorussian **II.** *m* Belorussian; *v. a.* **français**

Bielorusse [bjelɔʀys(ə)] *mf* Belorussian

Bielorussie [bjelɔʀysi] *f* **la ~** Belarus

bien [bjɛ̃] **I.** *adv* **1.** (*beaucoup*) **~ des gens** many people; **il a ~ du mal à** *+infin* he finds it very hard to *+infin* **2.** (*très*) very **3.** (*au moins*) at least **4.** (*plus*) **c'est ~ mieux** it's much better; **~ assez** more than enough **5.** (*de manière satisfaisante*) well; **tu ferais ~ de me le dire** you should tell me **6.** (*comme il se doit: agir, se conduire, se tenir*) well; (*s'asseoir*) properly **7.** (*vraiment: avoir l'intention*) really; (*rire, boire*) a lot; (*imaginer, voir*) clearly; **aimer ~ qn/qc** to really like sb/sth; **je veux ~, merci!** I would really like that, thank you!; **je veux ~ t'aider** I'm happy to help you; **j'y compte ~!** I'm counting on it!; **j'avais ~ l'intention de venir** I (really) did intend to come **8.** (*à la rigueur*) **il a ~ voulu nous recevoir** he was kind enough to see us; **je vous prie de ~ vouloir faire qc** I should be grateful if you could do sth; **j'espère ~!** I should hope so! **9.** (*pourtant*) however **10.** (*en effet*) **il faut ~ s'occuper** you have to keep busy(, don't you?) **11.** (*aussi*) **tu l'as ~ fait, toi!** YOU did it, didn't you! **12.** (*effectivement*) really **13.** (*sans le moindre doute*) definitely **14.** (*typiquement*) **c'est ~ toi** that's just like you **15.** (*probablement*) probably; (*sûrement*) surely ►**aller** ~ to be fine; **comment allez-vous? – ~ merci** how are you? – fine, thank you; **ou** ~ or; **~ plus** much more; **~ que tu sois trop jeune** although you are too young; **tant ~ que mal** after a fashion **II.** *adj inv* **1.** (*satisfaisant*) **être ~** to be good **2.** (*en forme*) **être ~** to be fit; **se sentir ~** to feel good **3.** (*à l'aise*) **être ~** to be OK; **être ~ avec qn** to be well-in with sb **4.** (*joli*) pretty; (*homme*) good-looking **5.** (*sympathique, qui présente bien*) nice **6.** (*comme il faut*) fine **III.** *m* **1.** (*capital physique ou moral*) good; **le ~ général** the general good; **le ~ et le mal** good and evil **2.** (*capital matériel*) *a.* JUR possessions; **avoir du ~** to have property **3.** ECON **~s de consommation** consumer goods

Bien-aimé [bjɛ̃neme] *m* beloved; **Louis XV, dit le ~** Louis XV, known as the beloved **bien-aimé(e)** [bjɛ̃neme] <bien-aimés> *adj* beloved **bien-être** [bjɛ̃nɛtʀ] *m sans pl* **1.** well-being; **une sensation de ~** a feeling of well-being **2.** (*confort*) comfort

bienfaisance [bjɛ̃fəzɑ̃s] *f* charity

bienfaisant(e) [bjɛ̃fəzɑ̃, ɑ̃t] *adj* (*personne*) kindly; (*climat, pluie*) beneficial

bienfait [bjɛ̃fɛ] *m* **1.** (*action généreuse*) kindness; (*du ciel, des dieux*) godsend **2.** *pl* (*effet: de la science, civilisation, d'un traitement, de la paix*) benefits

bienfaiteur, -trice [bjɛ̃fɛtœʀ, -tʀis] *m, f* **1.** (*sauveur*) saviour *Brit,* savior *Am* **2.** (*mécène*) benefactor

bienheureux, -euse [bjɛ̃nœʀø, -øz] **I.** *adj* REL (*personne*) blessed **II.** *m, f* blessed one

bienséance [bjɛ̃seɑ̃s] *f* decorum *no pl*

bientôt [bjɛ̃to] *adv* **1.** (*prochainement*) soon; **à ~!** see you soon! **2.** (*rapidement*) quickly

bienveillance [bjɛ̃vɛjɑ̃s] *f* kindness

bienveillant(e) [bjɛ̃vɛjɑ̃, jɑ̃t] *adj* kindly; (*comportement*) kind; **se montrer ~ envers qn** to be kind to sb

bienvenu(e) [bjɛ̃v(ə)ny] **I.** *adj* welcome **II.** *m(f)* **être le/la ~(e) pour qn/qc** to be very welcome to sb/sth

bienvenue [bjɛ̃v(ə)ny] **I.** *f* **souhaiter la ~ à qn** to welcome sb **II.** *interj Québec, inf* **~!** (*de rien! je vous en prie!*) you're welcome!

bière[1] [bjɛʀ] *f* beer; **~ blonde** lager; **~ brune** dark ale; **~ (à la) pression** draught [*o* draft *Am*] beer

bière[2] [bjɛʀ] *f* coffin *Brit,* casket *Am*

biffer [bife] <1> *vt* **~ qc** to cross sth out

bifocal(e) [bifɔkal, o] <-aux> *adj* bifocal

bifteck [biftɛk] *m* steak

bifurcation [bifyʀkasjɔ̃] *f* **1.** (*embranchement*) fork **2.** BOT, ANAT branching

bifurquer [bifyʀke] <1> *vi* **1.** (*se diviser*) to divide **2.** (*changer de direction*) to turn off

bigame [bigam] *adj* bigamous

bigamie [bigami] *f* bigamy

bigarré(e) [bigaʀe] *adj* (*tissu*) multicoloured *Brit,* multicolored *Am;* (*foule*) motley; (*langue*) colourful *Brit,* colorful *Am;* (*société*) diverse

bigorneau [bigɔʀno] <x> *m* ZOOL winkle

bigot(e) [bigo, ɔt] **I.** *adj* sanctimonious **II.** *m(f)* relgious zealot

bigoudi [bigudi] *m* curler

bihebdomadaire [biɛbdɔmadɛʀ] *adj* **être ~** (*journal, revue*) bi-weekly

bijou [biʒu] <x> *m* **1.** (*joyau*) jewel; **des ~x** jewellery *Brit,* jewelry *Am* **2.** (*chef-d'œuvre*) gem

bijouterie [biʒutʀi] *f* **1.** (*boutique*) jeweller's [*o* jeweler's *Am*] shop **2.** (*art*) jewellery-making **3.** (*commerce*) jewellery trade **4.** (*objets*) jewellery

bijoutier, -ière [biʒutje, -jɛʀ] *m, f* jeweller *Brit,* jeweler *Am*

bilan [bilɑ̃] *m* **1.** FIN balance sheet **2.** (*résultat*) final result; (*d'un accident*) final toll; **faire un ~ de qc** to assess sth **3.** MED checkup **4.** COM, ECON **déposer le ~** to file for bankruptcy

bilatéral(e) [bilateʀal, o] <-aux> *adj* (*des deux côtés*) *a.* MED, JUR, POL bilateral; (*stationnement*) on both sides

bile [bil] *f* **1.** ANAT bile **2.** (*amertume*) bitterness ▶**se faire de la ~** to worry

biliaire [biljɛʀ] *adj* biliary; **calculs ~s** gallstones

bilingue [bilɛ̃g] **I.** *adj* bilingual **II.** *mf* bilingual person

bilinguisme [bilɛ̃gɥism] *m* bilingualism

billard [bijaʀ] *m* **1.** (*jeu*) billiards + *vb sing,* pool *Am* **2.** (*lieu*) billiard room, pool hall *Am* **3.** (*table*) billiard [*o* pool *Am*] table

bille¹ [bij] *f* **1.** (*petite boule*) marble **2.** (*au billard*) billiard [*o* pool *Am*] ball **3.** TECH **crayon** [*o* **stylo**] **à ~** ball-point pen; **roulement à ~s** ball bearings *pl*

bille² [bij] *f inf* face

billet [bijɛ] *m* **1.** (*entrée, titre de transport*) ticket; **~ aller/aller-retour** single/return ticket **2.** (*numéro*) ticket **3.** (*argent*) (bank)note *Brit,* bill *Am* **4.** FIN **~ à ordre** promissory note **5.** (*message*) note

billetterie [bijɛtʀi] *f* **1.** (*caisse*) ticket office **2.** (*distributeur de billets*) **~ automatique** cash dispenser *Brit,* ATM

bimensuel(le) [bimɑ̃sɥɛl] *adj* (*journal, revue*) twice-monthly

bimestriel(le) [bimɛstʀijɛl] *adj* **être ~** (*journal, revue*) bimonthly

bimoteur [bimɔtœʀ] **I.** *adj inv* (*avion, bateau*) twin-engined **II.** *m* (*avion*) twin-engined plane

binaire [binɛʀ] *adj, m* binary; **des données ~s** binary data

biner [bine] <1> *vt* to hoe

binette [binɛt] *f* **1.** hoe **2.** *inf* (*visage*) mug; **t'en fais une sacrée ~** you should see your face

bingo [biŋgo] *m* bingo

biniou [binju] *m* bagpipes *pl*

biocarburant [bjokaʀbyʀɑ̃] *m* biofuel

biochimie [bjoʃimi] *f* biochemistry

biochimiste [bjoʃimist] *mf* biochemist

biodégradable [bjodegʀadabl] *adj* ECOL biodegradable

biodégrader [bjodegʀade] *vpr* ECOL **se ~** to biodegrade

biodiversité [bjodivɛʀsite] *f* ECOL biodiversity

bioénergétique [bjoenɛʀʒetik] *f* PHYS bioenergetics + *vb sing*

bioénergie [bjoenɛʀʒi] *f* PSYCH bioenergy

bioéthique [bjoetik] *f* bioethics + *vb sing*

biographie [bjɔgʀafi] *f* biography

biographique [bjɔgʀafik] *adj* biographical

bioindustrie [bjɔɛ̃dystʀi] *f* bio-industry

biologie [bjɔlɔʒi] *f* biology

biologique [bjɔlɔʒik] *adj* (*conditions, agriculture*) biological; **aliments ~s** organic food + *vb sing*

biologiste [bjɔlɔʒist] *mf* biologist

biomasse [bjomas] *f* biomass

biopsie [bjɔpsi] *f* biopsy

biorythme [bjɔʀitm] *m* biorhythm

biosphère [bjosfɛʀ] *f* biosphere

biosynthèse [bjosɛ̃tɛz] *f* biosynthesis

biotechnique [bjotɛknik] *f* biotechnics + *vb sing*

biotechnologie [bjotɛknɔlɔʒi] *f* biotechnology

biotope [bjɔtɔp] *m* biotope

bip [bip] *m* **1.** (*son*) beep; **~ sonore** tone **2.** *inf* (*appareil*) pager

biparti(e) [bipaʀti] *adj,* **bipartite** [bipaʀtit] *adj* bipartite

bipartition [bipaʀtisjɔ̃] *f* bipartition

bipède [bipɛd] **I.** *adj* biped **II.** *m* biped; *iron* (*homme*) man

biphasé(e) [bifaze] *adj* diphase

biplace [biplas] *adj, m* two-seater

biplan [biplɑ̃] *m* biplane

bique [bik] *f inf* nanny goat ▶**vieille ~** *péj* old hag

biréacteur [biʀeaktœʀ] *m* twin-engined jet

Birmanie [biʀmani] *f* **la ~** Burma

bis [bis] **I.** *adv* **1. n° 12 ~** n° 12 a **2.** MUS repeat ▶**~!** encore! **II.** *m* encore

bis(e) [bi, biz] *adj* grey-brown *Brit,* gray-brown *Am;* **pain ~** brown bread

bisaïeul(e) [bizajœl] *m(f)* great-grandfather, great-grandmother *m, f*

bisannuel(le) [bizanɥɛl] *adj* biennial

biscornu(e) [biskɔʀny] *adj* (*forme*) irregular; (*idée, esprit*) weird

biscoteau [biskɔto] <x> *m inf* biceps

biscotte [biskɔt] *f* melba toast

biscuit [biskɥi] *m* **1.** (*gâteau sec*) biscuit *Brit,* cookie *Am* **2.** (*pâtisserie*) sponge **3.** (*céramique*) biscuit

bise¹ [biz] *f* (*vent du Nord*) north wind

bise² [biz] *f inf* kiss; **se faire la ~** to kiss each another on the cheek; **grosses ~s!** love and kisses!

biseau [bizo] <x> *m* bevel

biseauter [bizote] <1> *vt* **1.** TECH to bevel **2.** JEUX to mark

bisexualité [bisɛksɥalite] *f* bisexuality

bisexuel(le) [bisɛksɥɛl] *adj* bisexual

bison [bizɔ̃] *m* American buffalo; (*d'Europe*) bison

> **Bison futé** is an information system for drivers, warning of traffic blackspots and jams. This information is available on the radio or on notice boards at motorway services.

bisontin(e) [bizɔ̃tɛ̃, in] *adj* of Besançon; *v. a.* **ajaccien**

Bisontin(e) [bizɔ̃tɛ̃, in] *m(f)* person from Besançon; *v. a.* **Ajaccien**

bisou [bizu] *m inf* kiss

bissectrice [bisɛktʀis] *f* MAT bisector

bisser [bise] <1> *vt* (*vers, chanson*) to repeat; ~ **un musicien** to encore a musician

bissextile [bisɛkstil] *adj* **année** ~ leap year

bistouri [bistuʀi] *m* lancet

bistre [bistʀ] *adj inv* bistre

bistro(t) [bistʀo] *m inf* bistro

bit [bit] *m* INFOR *abr de* **BInary digiT, chiffre binaire** bit

bite [bit] *f inf* cock

bitume [bitym] *m* **1.** (*asphalte*) asphalt **2.** *inf* (*trottoir*) pavement

bitumer [bityme] <1> *vt* to asphalt

bivouac [bivwak] *m* bivouac

bivouaquer [bivwake] <1> *vi* to bivouac

bizarre [bizaʀ] **I.** *adj* strange **II.** *m* **le ~, c'est que** the strange part of it is that

bizarrement [bizaʀmɑ̃] *adv* strangely

bizarrerie [bizaʀʀi] *f* (*d'une personne*) weird ways *pl;* (*d'une idée, initiative*) strangeness

bizarroïde [bizaʀɔid] *adj inf* weird

bizness [biznɛs] *m* business

blablabla [blablabla] *m inf* blather

black-out [blakaut] *m inv, a. fig* blackout

blafard(e) [blafaʀ, aʀd] *adj* pale

blague [blag] *f inf* **1.** (*histoire drôle*) joke **2.** (*farce*) trick **3.** (*tabatière*) tobacco pouch ▸<u>**sans**</u> **~!** you're kidding!

blaguer [blage] <1> *vi* to be kidding

blagueur, -euse [blagœʀ, -øz] **I.** *adj* (*sourire, air*) teasing; **être ~** to be a joker **II.** *m, f* joker

blaireau [blɛʀo] <x> *m* **1.** ZOOL badger **2.** (*pour la barbe*) shaving brush

blâmable [blɑmabl] *adj* blameworthy

blâme [blɑm] *m* **1.** (*désapprobation*) blame **2.** (*sanction*) reprimand

blâmer [blɑme] <1> *vt* **1.** (*désapprouver*) to disapprove **2.** (*condamner moralement*) to blame **3.** (*sanctionner*) to reprimand

blanc [blɑ̃] **I.** *m* **1.** (*couleur, vin, linge*) white; **se marier en ~** to have a white wedding **2.** TYP, INFOR space **3.** (*espace vide dans une traduction, un devoir*) blank **4.** (*espace vide sur une cassette*) space **5.** (*fard ~*) white powder **6.** GASTR ~ **d'œuf** egg white; ~ **de poulet** white meat (*of chicken*) **7.** BOT (*maladie*) powdery mildew **II.** *adv* **laver plus ~** to wash whiter

blanc(he) [blɑ̃, blɑ̃ʃ] *adj* **1.** (*de couleur blanche*) white **2.** (*non écrit: bulletin de vote, feuille*) blank **3.** (*propre: draps*) clean **4.** (*pâle, non bronzé: personne, peau*) white **5.** (*innocent*) pure **6.** (*fictif: mariage*) unconsummated; (*examen*) mock

Blanc(he) [blɑ̃, blɑ̃ʃ] *m(f)* White

blanchâtre [blɑ̃ʃɑtʀ] *adj* whitish

blanche [blɑ̃ʃ] **I.** *adj v.* **blanc II.** *f* **1.** MUS minim *Brit,* half-note *Am* **2.** (*boule de billard*) white (ball)

blancheur [blɑ̃ʃœʀ] *f* whiteness; (*du visage, teint*) paleness

blanchiment [blɑ̃ʃimɑ̃] *m* (*d'un mur, d'une façade*) whitewashing; ~ **de l'argent** money laundering

blanchir [blɑ̃ʃiʀ] <8> **I.** *vt* **1.** (*rendre blanc*) to whiten; (*mur*) to whitewash; (*linge, draps, cheveux*) to bleach **2.** (*nettoyer: linge*) to launder **3.** (*disculper*) ~ **qn** to exonerate sb **4.** (*légaliser: argent*) to launder **5.** GASTR (*légumes*) to blanch **II.** *vi* to turn white; ~ **sous l'effet de la lumière/au lavage** to go white in the light/the wash **III.** *vpr* **se ~** to exonerate oneself

blanchisserie [blɑ̃ʃisʀi] *f* laundry

blanquette [blɑ̃kɛt] *f* **1.** blanquette **2.** (*vin*) ~ **de Limoux** *sparkling white wine*

blasé(e) [blɑze] **I.** *adj* blasé **II.** *m(f)* blasé individual

blason [blɑzɔ̃] *m* coat of arms

blasphématoire [blasfematwaʀ] *adj* blasphemous

blasphème [blasfɛm] *m* blasphemy

blasphémer [blasfeme] <5> *vt, vi* to blaspheme

blatte [blat] *f* beetle; (*cafard*) cockroach

blazer [blazɛʀ, blazœʀ] *m* blazer

blé [ble] *m* **1.** (*plante*) wheat **2.** (*grain*) grain **3.** *inf* (*argent*) dough

bled [blɛd] *m péj, inf* (godforsaken) hole

blême [blɛm] *adj* (*visage*) sallow; (*lumière*) pale

blêmir [blemiʀ] <8> *vi* (*personne*) to turn pale; (*horizon*) to grow pale

blennorragie [blenɔʀaʒi] *f* MED gonorrhoea *Brit,* gonorrhea *Am*

blessant(e) [blesɑ̃, ɑ̃t] *adj* hurtful

blessé(e) [blese] **I.** *adj* **1.** MED injured; (*soldat*) wounded **2.** (*offensé*) hurt **II.** *m(f) a.* MIL casualty; **les ~s** the injured

blesser [blese] <1> **I.** *vt* **1.** MED to injure; MIL to wound **2.** (*meurtrir*) ~ **les pieds** (*chaussures*) to hurt one's feet **3.** (*offenser*) to hurt; (*oreille, vue*) to offend **II.** *vpr* **se ~** to hurt oneself; (*sérieusement*) to injure oneself

blessure [blesyʀ] *f* **1.** (*lésion, plaie*) *a.* MIL wound **2.** *soutenu* (*offense*) offence *Brit,* offense *Am*

blet(te) [blɛ, blɛt] *adj* (*poire, nèfle*) overripe

blette [blɛt] *f* Swiss chard *Brit,* Chinese cabbage *Am*

bleu [blø] *m* **1.** (*couleur*) blue; ~ **ciel** sky-blue; ~ **clair/foncé** light/dark blue **2.** (*marque*) bruise **3.** (*vêtement*) (pair of) overalls **4.** (*fromage*) blue cheese **5.** CHIM ~ **de méthylène** methylene blue **6.** *pl* SPORT **les ~s** the blues (*the French national football team, which wears blue*)

bleu(e) [blø] *adj* **1.** (*de couleur bleue*) blue **2.** GASTR (*steak*) very rare

bleuâtre [bløɑtʀ] *adj* bluish
bleue [blø] *f* **la grande** ~ the open sea
bleuet [bløɛ] *m* **1.** (*fleur*) cornflower **2.** (*fruit*) blueberry
bleuir [bløiʀ] <8> **I.** *vt* **j'ai les mains/les lèvres toutes bleuies par le froid** my hands/lips are blue with cold **II.** *vi* (*a. visage*) to turn blue
bleuté(e) [bløte] *adj* bluish; **des verres ~s** blue-tinted glasses
blindé [blɛ̃de] *m* armoured [*o* armored *Am*] vehicle
blindé(e) [blɛ̃de] *adj* **1.** (*renforcé: porte*) reinforced; (*voiture*) armoured *Brit,* armored *Am* **2.** *inf* (*endurci*) **être ~ contre qc** to be immune to sth
blinder [blɛ̃de] <1> *vt* **1.** (*renforcer: porte*) to reinforce; (*véhicule*) to armour *Brit,* armor *Am* **2.** *inf* (*endurcir*) **~ qn contre qc** to make sb immune to sth
bloc [blɔk] *m* **1.** (*masse de matière*) block **2.** (*cahier, carnet*) pad **3.** (*ensemble, pâté de maisons, immeuble*) block **4.** (*union*) group; **~ monétaire** monetary bloc ►**en** ~ as a whole
blocage [blɔkaʒ] *m* **1.** (*action: des roues, freins*) locking; (*d'une pièce mobile, porte, d'un boulon*) jamming; (*d'un écrou, d'une vis*) overtightening; (*avec une cale*) wedging **2.** ECON (*des prix, salaires, commandes, d'un crédit*) freezing **3.** PSYCH block
bloc-cuisine [blɔkkɥizin] <blocs-cuisines> *m* kitchen unit **bloc-cylindres** [blɔksilɛ̃dʀ] <blocs-cylindre> *m* cylinder block **bloc-évier** [blɔkevje] <blocs-éviers> *m* sink unit
bloc-moteur [blɔkmɔtœʀ] <blocs-moteurs> *m* TECH, AUTO engine block **bloc-notes** [blɔknɔt] <blocs-notes> *m* notepad
blocus [blɔkys] *m* blockade
blond [blɔ̃] *m* (*couleur*) blond; **~ cendré/foncé** ash/dark blond
blond(e) [blɔ̃, blɔ̃d] **I.** *adj* blond; (*tabac, cigarettes*) mild; (*bière*) lager **II.** *m(f)* (*personne*) blond; (*femme*) blonde
blonde [blɔ̃d] *f* **1.** (*bière*) lager **2.** (*cigarette*) mild cigarette **3.** *Québec* (*maîtresse, fiancée*) **la ~ d'un homme** a man's girlfriend
blondir [blɔ̃diʀ] <8> *vi* (*cheveux*) to become fairer
bloquer [blɔke] <1> **I.** *vt* **1.** (*immobiliser*) to jam; (*passage, route, porte*) to block; (*vis, écrou*) to overtighten; (*pièce mobile, boulon*) to tighten; **être bloqué dans l'ascenseur** to be trapped in the lift [*o* elevator *Am*] **2.** ECON (*a. négociations*) to freeze **3.** (*regrouper: jours de congé*) to group together; (*paragraphes*) to combine **4.** SPORT (*balle*) to block **5.** *Belgique, fam* (*bûcher, potasser*) to cram [*o* slog away] **6.** *Québec* (*coller, échouer*) to fail **II.** *vpr* **se ~** **1.** (*s'immobiliser*) to jam; (*roues, freins*) to lock **2.** PSYCH to freeze **3.** INFOR **se ~** (*programme*) to seize up **III.** *vi* **1.** *inf* PSYCH **~ qc** to block sth (out) **2.** INFOR (*programme*) to block
blottir [blɔtiʀ] <8> *vpr* **se ~ contre qn** to snuggle up against sb; **se ~ dans un coin** to huddle in a corner
blouse [bluz] *f* **1.** (*tablier*) overall **2.** (*corsage*) blouse
blouson [bluzɔ̃] *m* jacket ►**~ noir** hell's angel
blues [blus] *m inv* **1.** (*musique*) blues **2.** (*cafard*) **avoir un coup de ~** to have the blues
bluff [blœf] *m* bluff
bluffer [blœfe] <1> *vt, vi* to bluff
boa [bɔa] *m* boa
bob [bɔb] *m* SPORT bobsleigh
bobard [bɔbaʀ] *m inf* fib
bobine [bɔbin] *f* **1.** (*cylindre*) reel; (*de fil*) reel *Brit,* bobbin *Am* **2.** ELEC **~ d'allumage** coil **3.** *inf* (*mine*) face
bobiner [bɔbine] <1> *vt* **~ qc sur qc** to wind sth on sth
bobo [bobo] *m enfantin, inf* injury; **se faire ~** to get hurt
bobonne [bɔbɔn] *f péj, inf sans dét* (*épouse*) **venir avec ~** to come with one's better half
bobsleigh [bɔbslɛg] *m v.* **bob**
bocage [bɔkaʒ] *m* bocage (*land crossed with trees*)
bocal [bɔkal, o] <-aux> *m* jar
bock [bɔk] *m* **1.** (*verre d'1/8 litre*) beer glass **2.** (*contenu*) beer
body [bɔdi] *m* body, leotard
bœuf [bœf, bø] **I.** *m* **1.** ZOOL ox **2.** (*opp: taureau, vache*) bullock **3.** (*viande*) beef **II.** *adj Suisse, fam* (*bête*) **c'est ~** that's silly
bof [bɔf] *interj* pfff (*expressing a lack of interest or enthusiasm*)
bogue [bɔg] *m o f* INFOR bug; **le ~ de l'an 2000** the millennium bug
bohème [bɔɛm] **I.** *adj* bohemian **II.** *mf* bohemian **III.** *f* Bohemia
Bohême [bɔɛm] *f* **la ~** Bohemia
bohémien(ne) [bɔemjɛ̃, jɛn] *m(f)* Bohemian
boille [bɔj] *f Suisse* (*récipient servant notamment au transport du lait*) milk churn
boire [bwaʀ] *irr* **I.** *vt* **1.** (*avaler un liquide*) to drink; **~ à la bouteille** to drink from the bottle **2.** (*s'imprégner de*) to absorb **II.** *vi* to drink; **~ à la santé de qn** to drink (to) sb's health **III.** *vpr* **se ~ à l'apéritif** to be drunk as an aperitif
bois [bwɑ] **I.** *m* **1.** (*forêt*) wood **2.** (*matériau*) **wood** (*en planches, sur pied*) timber **3.** (*gravure*) woodcut ►**toucher du ~** to knock on wood **II.** *mpl* **1.** MUS woodwind **2.** (*cornes: des cervidés*) antlers
boisé(e) [bwɑze] *adj* wooded
boiser [bwɑze] <1> *vt* **~ qc** (*région*) to plant sth with trees
boiserie [bwɑzʀi] *f* woodwork *no pl*
boisson [bwasɔ̃] *f* **1.** (*liquide buvable*) drink **2.** (*alcoolisme*) drinking

boîte [bwat] *f* **1.** (*récipient*) box; ~ **à outils/en plastique** tool/plastic box; ~ **à lunch** *Québec* (*gamelle*) lunch box; ~ **à** [*o* **aux**] **lettres** letter box, mailbox *Am;* ~ **postale** post office box **2.** (*conserve*) tin *Brit,* can; ~ **de conserves** tin [*o* can] (of food); **en** ~ tinned *Brit,* canned *Am* **3.** *inf* (*discothèque*) club; ~ **de nuit** nightclub **4.** *inf* (*entreprise*) company **5.** MED ~ **crânienne** cranium **6.** AVIAT ~ **noire** black box **7.** AUTO ~ **de vitesses** gearbox **8.** INFOR ~ **aux lettres** [**électronique**] [electronic] mailbox; **relever sa** ~ **aux lettres** [**électronique**] to collect one's email; ~ **de dialogue** dialogue box; ~ **de réception** inbox

boiter [bwate] <1> *vi* **1.** (*clopiner*) to limp **2.** *fig* (*raisonnement, comparaison*) to fall down

boiteux, **-euse** [bwatø, -øz] *adj* **1.** (*bancal: meuble*) wobbly; (*personne*) lame **2.** *fig* (*explication, raisonnement*) lame; (*paix*) shaky

boîtier [bwatje] *m* **1.** (*boîte*) box; (*pour des instruments, cassettes*) case **2.** ELEC ~ **de mixage** mixing table; ~ **de télécommande** remote control

boitiller [bwatije] <1> *vi* to hobble

boiton [bwatɔ̃] *m Suisse* (*porcherie*) pigsty

bol [bɔl] *m* **1.** (*récipient*) bowl **2.** *inf* (*chance*) luck; **avoir du** ~ to be lucky **3.** *Québec* (*cuvette*) ~ **de toilette** toilet bowl ►**en avoir ras le** ~ *inf* to be fed up

boléro [bɔleʀo] *m* (*gilet*) bolero

bolet [bɔlɛ] *m* BOT boletus

bolide [bɔlid] *m* sports car

Bolivie [bɔlivi] *f* **la** ~ Bolivia

bolivien(**ne**) [bɔlivjɛ̃, ɛn] *adj* Bolivian

Bolivien(**ne**) [bɔlivjɛ̃, ɛn] *m(f)* Bolivian

bombance [bɔ̃bɑ̃s] *f inf* **faire** ~ to feast

bombardement [bɔ̃baʀdəmɑ̃] *m* **1.** MIL bombing; ~ **aérien** aerial bombardment **2.** PHYS bombardment

bombarder [bɔ̃baʀde] <1> *vt* **1.** MIL to bomb; ~ **qn de tomates** to pelt sb with tomatoes **2.** PHYS ~ **qc de qc** to bombard sth with sth **3.** *inf* (*nommer à un poste*) ~ **qn directeur** to thrust sb into the role of director

bombe [bɔ̃b] *f* **1.** MIL bomb; ~ **atomique** atomic bomb; ~ **lacrymogène** teargas grenade **2.** (*atomiseur*) spray **3.** (*casquette*) riding hat **4.** GASTR ~ **glacée** (iced) bombe

bombé(**e**) [bɔ̃be] *adj* rounded

bomber [bɔ̃be] <1> **I.** *vt* **1.** (*gonfler: poitrine, torse*) to stick out **2.** *inf* (*peindre*) ~ **qc sur qc** to spray-paint sth **3.** (*passer un insecticide*) to spray **II.** *vi* (*bois, planche*) to warp; (*mur*) to camber

bon [bɔ̃] **I.** *m* **1.** (*coupon d'échange*) voucher *Brit,* coupon *Am;* ~ **de caisse** cash voucher **2.** FIN ~ **du Trésor** Treasury bill **3.** (*ce qui est* ~) good part **4.** (*personne*) good person ►**avoir du** ~ to have one's merits **II.** *adv* **sentir** ~ to smell good ►**il fait** ~ the weather's nice

bon(**ne**) [bɔ̃, bɔn] <meilleur> *adj antéposé* **1.** (*opp: mauvais*) good; **être** ~ **en latin/maths** to be good at latin/maths [*o* math *Am*] **2.** (*adéquat, correct*) right; (*remède, conseil a.*) good; **tous les moyens sont ~s** anything goes **3.** (*valable: billet, ticket*) valid **4.** (*agréable*) good; (*soirée, surprise, moment, vacances, week-end*) nice; (*eau*) good **5.** (*délicieux*) good; (*comestible*) OK **6.** (*intensif de quantité, de qualité*) good **7.** (*être fait pour*) **c'est** ~ **à savoir** that's worth knowing **8.** (*être destiné à*) **être** ~ **pour qc** to be in for sth ►**c'est** ~ (*a bon goût, fait du bien*) it's good; (*ça ira comme ça*) that's fine; (*tant pis*) that'll have to do; **n'être** ~ **à rien** to be good for nothing; **à quoi** ~**?** what's the use?; **pour de** ~**?** for good?

bonbon [bɔ̃bɔ̃] *m* **1.** (*friandise*) sweet *Brit,* candy *Am;* ~ **acidulé** acid drop; ~ **à la menthe** mint *Brit,* mint candy *Am* **2.** *Belgique* (*biscuit*) biscuit

bonbonne [bɔ̃bɔn] *f* demijohn

bonbonnière [bɔ̃bɔnjɛʀ] *f* sweet box *Brit,* candy box *Am*

bond [bɔ̃] *m* **1.** (*action: d'une personne, d'un animal*) leap; SPORT jump; (*d'une balle*) bounce **2.** ECON ~ **en avant** leap forward **3.** (*rebond*) **faire plusieurs ~s** to bounce several times

bonde [bɔ̃d] *f* **1.** (*ouverture: du tonneau*) bunghole; (*de l'évier, de la baignoire*) plughole **2.** (*bouchon: du tonneau*) stopper; (*de l'évier, de la baignoire*) plug

bondé(**e**) [bɔ̃de] *adj* jam-packed

bondelle [bɔ̃dɛl] *f Suisse* (*poisson du genre corégone*) whitefish

bondir [bɔ̃diʀ] <8> *vi* **1.** (*sauter*) to jump; ~ **hors du lit** to jump out of bed; ~ **à la porte** to leap to the door **2.** (*sursauter*) to jump; ~ **de joie** to jump with joy; **faire** ~ **qn** to make sb jump

bonheur [bɔnœʀ] *m* **1.** (*état*) happiness **2.** (*chance*) luck; **le** ~ **de vivre** the good fortune to be alive; **porter** ~ **à qn** to bring sb (good) luck ►**ne pas connaître son** ~ not to know one's luck; **par** ~ luckily

bonhomie [bɔnɔmi] *f* good-naturedness

bonhomme [bɔnɔm, bɔ̃zɔm] <bonshommes> *m* **1.** *inf* (*homme*) man; (*plutôt négatif*) guy; ~ **de neige** snowman **2.** (*petit garçon*) **petit** ~ little fellow **3.** (*dessin*) stick figure

boni [bɔni] *m* profit

bonification [bɔnifikasjɔ̃] *f* **1.** (*amélioration: d'un vin*) maturation **2.** (*bonus*) bonus **3.** SPORT advantage

bonifier [bɔnifje] <1> **I.** *vt* (*terres*) to improve **II.** *vpr* **se** ~ to improve; (*vin*) to mature

boniment [bɔnimɑ̃] *m* **1.** (*baratin: d'un vendeur, camelot*) sales talk *no pl* **2.** (*mensonges*) tall tale

bonjour [bɔ̃ʒuʀ] **I.** *interj* **1.** (*salutation*)

hello; **dire ~ à qn** to say hello to sb **2.** *Québec* (*bonne journée*) have a nice day **II.** *m* **donner bien le ~ à qn de la part de qn** to pass on sb's regards to sb

> **bonjour** is used for both good morning and good afternoon, Morning. In the evening, use "bonsoir" and "bonne nuit" at the end of the day.

bonne [bɔn] *f* maid; ~ **d'enfants** nanny; *v. a.* **bon**
bonnement [bɔnmɑ̃] *adv* **tout ~** quite simply
bonnet [bɔnɛ] *m* **1.** (*coiffure*) hat; (*du nourrisson, du bébé*) bonnet; ~ **de bain** swimming cap, shower cap *Am* **2.** (*poche: du soutien-gorge*) cup
bonneterie [bɔnɛtʀi, bɔn(ə)tʀi] *f* **1.** (*articles*) hosiery **2.** (*commerce*) hosiery trade **3.** (*magasin*) hosier's shop
bonsoir [bɔ̃swaʀ] *interj* (*en arrivant*) good evening; (*en partant*) good night
bonté [bɔ̃te] *f* kindness; **avec ~** kindly
bonus [bɔnys] *m* bonus
bonze [bɔ̃z] *m* **1.** bonze **2.** *péj, inf* (*personnage en vue*) bigwig
boom [bum] *m* boom
boomerang [bumʀɑ̃g] *m* boomerang; **effet de ~** boomerang effect; **faire ~** to boomerang
booter [bute] <1> *vi* INFOR to boot up
bord [bɔʀ] *m* side; (*d'une table*) edge; (*d'un trottoir*) kerb *Brit,* curb *Am;* (*d'un lac, d'une rivière*) bank; (*de la mer*) shore; (*d'un chapeau*) brim; **au ~ de (la) mer** by the sea ▶**passer par-dessus ~** to go overboard; **virer de ~** to tack; **à ~** on board; **au ~ du lac** by the lake
bordeaux [bɔʀdo] **I.** *m* Bordeaux (wine) **II.** *adj inv* burgundy
bordée [bɔʀde] *f* **1.** broadside **2.** *fig, inf* ~ **d'injures** volley of insults; ~ **d'applaudissements** wave of applause
bordel [bɔʀdɛl] **I.** *m* **1.** *vulg* (*maison close*) brothel **2.** *inf* (*désordre*) chaos **II.** *interj inf* bloody hell *Brit,* goddammit *Am*
bordelais(**e**) [bɔʀdəlɛ, ɛz] *adj* of Bordeaux; *v. a.* **ajaccien**
Bordelais(**e**) [bɔʀdəlɛ, ɛz] *m(f)* person from Bordeaux; *v. a.* **Ajaccien**
bordélique [bɔʀdelik] *adj inf* **c'est ~** (*mal organisé*) it's chaos; (*mal rangé*) it's a tip
border [bɔʀde] <1> *vt* **1.** (*longer*) **la route est bordée d'arbres** trees run alongside the road; **la place est bordée d'arbres** the square is surrounded by trees **2.** COUT ~ **un mouchoir de dentelle** to edge a handkerchief with lace **3.** (*couvrir*) ~ **qn** to tuck sb up; ~ **un lit** to tuck the covers in **4.** NAUT ~ **une voile** to pull on a sail
bordereau [bɔʀdəʀo] <x> *m* **1.** (*formulaire*) note; ~ **d'achat** receipt; ~ **de livraison** delivery slip **2.** (*liste*) list **3.** (*facture*) invoice
bordier [bɔʀdje] *m Suisse* (*riverain*) (local) resident
bordure [bɔʀdyʀ] *f* **1.** (*bord*) side; (*d'un quai*) edge; (*du trottoir*) kerb *Brit,* curb *Am;* (*empiècement*) surround **2.** (*rangée*) line
boréal(**e**) [bɔʀeal, o] <s *o* -aux> *adj* northern
borgne [bɔʀɲ] *adj* **1.** (*éborgné: personne*) blind in one eye **2.** ARCHIT (*fenêtre*) blind **3.** (*mal famé: hôtel, rue*) dodgy
borne [bɔʀn] *f* **1.** (*pierre*) marker; ~ **kilométrique** kilometre [*o* kilometer *Am*] marker **2.** (*protection*) bollard **3.** *pl* (*limite*) limits; **dépasser les ~s** (*personne*) to go too far; (*ignorance, bêtise*) to know no bounds **4.** *inf* (*distance de 1 km*) kilometre *Brit,* kilometer *Am* **5.** ELEC terminal
borné(**e**) [bɔʀne] *adj* limited; (*personne*) narrow-minded; (*vue*) short-sighted
borner [bɔʀne] <1> **I.** *vt* **1.** (*limiter: terrain*) to mark out **2.** *fig* ~ **son ambition à qc** to limit one's ambitions to sth **II.** *vpr* **se ~ à qc** (*se limiter à*) to limit oneself to sth; (*se contenter de*) to content oneself with sth
bosniaque [bɔsnjak(ə)] *adj* Bosnian
Bosniaque [bɔsnjak(ə)] *mf* Bosnian
Bosnie-Herzégovine [bɔsni ɛʀzegɔvin(ə)] *f* **la ~** Bosnia-Herzegovina
bosnien(**ne**) [bɔsnjɛ̃, ɛn] *adj* Bosnian
Bosnien(**ne**) [bɔsnjɛ̃, ɛn] *m(f)* Bosnian
bosquet [bɔskɛ] *m* copse
bosse [bɔs] *f* **1.** (*déformation*) bump **2.** (*protubérance, difformité*) hump **3.** (*don*) **avoir la ~ de la musique** *inf* to have a gift for music
bosser [bɔse] <1> **I.** *vi inf* to work; (*travailler dur*) to slave; (*bûcher*) to swot **II.** *vt inf* (*matière*) to cram (for)
bosseur, **-euse** [bɔsœʀ, -øz] *m, f inf* hard worker
bossu(**e**) [bɔsy] **I.** *adj* hunchbacked; (*voûté*) hunched **II.** *m(f)* hunchback
botanique [bɔtanik] **I.** *adj* botanical **II.** *f* botany
botaniste [bɔtanist] *mf* botanist
Botswana [bɔtswana] *m* **le ~** Botswana
Botswanais [bɔtswanɛ] *mpl* **les ~** Batswana
botswanais(**e**) [bɔtswanɛ, ɛz] *adj* Motswana
Botswanais(**e**) [bɔtswanɛ, ɛz] *m(f)* Motswana
botte [bɔt] *f* **1.** (*chaussure*) boot **2.** (*paquet: de légumes, fleurs*) bunch; (*de foin, paille*) (*en gerbe*) sheaf; (*au carré*) bale **3.** (*en escrime*) thrust
botté(**e**) [bɔte] *adj* **être ~** to be wearing boots
botter [bɔte] <1> *vt* ~ **le derrière/les fesses à qn** to give sb a kick in the rear
bottillon [bɔtijɔ̃] *m* ankle boot
bottin® [bɔtɛ̃] *m* directory
bottine [bɔtin] *f* bootee
bouc [buk] *m* **1.** ZOOL billy goat **2.** (*barbe*) goatee ▶~ **émissaire** scapegoat

B

boucan [bukɑ̃] *m inf* racket

bouche [buʃ] *f* (*ouverture*) *a.* ANAT, ZOOL, GEO mouth; **parler la ~ pleine** to speak with one's mouth full; **les ~s du Rhône** the mouth of the River Rhone; **~ de métro** metro [*o* subway *Am*] entrance ►**~ bée** open mouthed; **être une fine ~** to be a gourmet

bouché(e) [buʃe] *adj* **1.** METEO (*temps*) cloudy; (*ciel*) overcast **2.** (*sans avenir*) hopeless **3.** *inf* (*idiot: personne*) stupid

bouche-à-bouche [buʃabuʃ] *m sans pl* mouth-to-mouth; **faire du ~ à qn** to give sb the kiss of life

bouchée [buʃe] *f* **1.** (*petit morceau*) morsel **2.** (*ce qui est dans la bouche*) mouthful ►**pour une ~ de pain** for a song

boucher [buʃe] <1> **I.** *vt* (*bouteille*) to cork; (*trou, toilettes, évier*) to block, to fill in; (*fente*) to fill; **~ les trous de la route** to fill in the holes in the road; **avoir le nez bouché** to have a stuffed-up nose **II.** *vpr* **se ~** (*évier*) to get blocked; **se ~ le nez** to hold one's nose; **se ~ les oreilles** to plug one's ears; **se ~ les yeux** *fig* to cover one's eyes

boucher, -ère [buʃe, -ɛʀ] *m, f a. péj* butcher

bouchère [buʃɛʀ] *f* (*femme du boucher*) butcher's wife

boucherie [buʃʀi] *f* **1.** (*magasin*) butcher's (shop) **2.** (*métier*) butchery **3.** (*massacre*) slaughter ►**faire ~** *Suisse, Québec* (*tuer le cochon*) to slaughter the pig

boucherie-charcuterie [buʃʀiʃaʀkytʀi] <boucheries-charcuteries> *f* butcher's shop and delicatessen

bouche-trou [buʃtʀu] <bouche-trous> *m* **1.** (*personne*) stopgap **2.** TV filler

bouchon [buʃɔ̃] *m* **1.** (*pour boucher: d'une bouteille*) stopper; (*de liège*) cork; (*d'une carafe, d'un évier*) plug; (*d'un bidon, tube, radiateur, réservoir*) cap; **sentir le ~** (*vin*) to be corked **2.** (*à la pêche*) float **3.** (*embouteillage*) tailback

bouchonné(e) [buʃɔne] *adj* **un vin ~** a corked wine

boucle [bukl] *f* **1.** (*objet en forme d'anneau: de soulier, ceinture, d'un harnais*) buckle; **~ d'oreille** earring **2.** (*qui s'enroule*) **~ de cheveux** curl **3.** (*forme géométrique*) *a.* INFOR, AVIAT loop **4.** SPORT (*en voiture, à pied*) lap

bouclé(e) [bukle] *adj* (*cheveux, poils*) curly

boucler [bukle] <1> **I.** *vt* **1.** (*attacher*) to buckle; **~ la ceinture de sécurité** to put on one's safety belt **2.** *inf* (*fermer: magasin, porte, bagages*) to close **3.** (*terminer*) **~ qc** (*affaire, recherches, travail*) to wrap sth up **4.** (*équilibrer: budget*) to balance **5.** POL, MIL (*encercler*) to surround; (*quartier*) to seal off **6.** *inf* (*enfermer*) **~ qn** to shut sb up **7.** (*friser, onduler*) **~ ses cheveux** to curl one's hair **II.** *vi* **1.** (*friser*) **ses cheveux bouclent naturellement** her hair is naturally curly **2.** INFOR to loop **III.** *vpr* **1.** (*se faire des boucles*) **se ~** to curl **2.** (*s'enfermer*) **se ~ dans sa chambre** to shut oneself in one's room

bouclier [buklije] *m* (*protection*) *a.* MIL shield

Bouddha [buda] *m* Buddha

bouddhisme [budism] *m* Buddhism

bouddhiste [budist] *adj, mf* Buddhist

bouder [bude] <1> **I.** *vi* to sulk **II.** *vt* **1.** (*montrer du mécontentement à qn*) to ignore **2.** (*ne plus rechercher qc*) **~ un produit** to keep away from a product

bouderie [budʀi] *f* sulking *no pl*

boudeur, -euse [budœʀ, -øz] **I.** *adj* sulky **II.** *m, f* sulker

boudin [budɛ̃] *m* **1.** (*charcuterie*) pudding; **~ noir/blanc** black/white pudding **2.** *inf* (*fille grosse et disgrâcieuse*) dumpling **3.** *Belgique, Nord* (*traversin*) bolster

boudiné(e) [budine] *adj* **1.** (*en forme de boudin: doigt*) podgy **2.** (*serré dans un vêtement étriqué*) **se sentir ~ dans qc** to feel like a sack of potatoes in sth

boue [bu] *f* mud

bouée [bwe] *f* **1.** (*balise*) buoy **2.** (*protection gonflable*) rubber ring; **~ de sauvetage** life belt; *fig* lifeline

boueux, -euse [bwø, -øz] *adj* (*chaussures, chemin, eau*) muddy

bouffant(e) [bufɑ̃, ɑ̃t] *adj* **des manches ~es** puffed sleeves; **pantalon ~** baggy trousers

bouffe [buf] *f inf* grub

bouffée [bufe] *f* **1.** (*souffle*) **tirer des ~s de sa pipe** to puff on one's pipe; **~ d'air frais/chaud** puff of cold/warm air **2.** (*odeur*) whiff **3.** (*haleine*) **des ~s d'ail** wafts of garlic **4.** (*poussée*) **~ de chaleur** hot flush [*o* flash *Am*]; **~ de fièvre** flush of fever

bouffer [bufe] <1> **I.** *vi* **1.** *inf* (*manger*) to eat **2.** (*se gonfler*) to puff up **II.** *vt inf* **1.** (*manger*) to eat **2.** (*consommer: essence, huile*) to swallow; (*kilomètres*) to eat up

bouffi(e) [bufi] *adj* **1.** (*gonflé: visage*) bloated; (*yeux*) puffy; (*mains*) swollen **2.** *péj* **être ~ d'orgueil** to be puffed up with pride

bouffon(ne) [bufɔ̃, ɔn] **I.** *adj* farcical **II.** *m(f)* clown

bouffonnerie [bufɔnʀi] *f* antics; (*d'une scène, pièce*) drollery

bouge [buʒ] *m* **1.** (*bar mal famé*) dive **2.** (*taudis*) dump

bougeoir [buʒwaʀ] *m* candle-stick

bougeotte [buʒɔt] *f inf* **avoir la ~** to have the fidgets

bouger [buʒe] <2a> **I.** *vi* **1.** (*remuer*) to move **2.** POL (*protester*) to kick up a fuss **3.** *inf* (*changer, s'altérer*) to change; (*couleur*) to fade; (*tissu*) to shrink; **ne pas ~** (*prix, taux*) to stay the same **4.** (*se déplacer, voyager*) to move around; **je ne bouge pas d'ici!** I'm staying right here! **II.** *vt* to move **III.** *vpr inf* **se ~** **1.** (*se remuer*) to move **2.** (*faire un effort*) to put oneself out

bougie [buʒi] *f* **1.** (*chandelle*) candle **2.** AUTO spark plug

bougon(**ne**) [bugɔ̃, ɔn] I. *adj* grumpy II. *m(f)* grouch

bougonner [bugɔne] <1> *vi* ~ **contre qn/qc** to grumble about sb/sth

bougre, **-esse** [bugʀ, -ɛs] *m, f inf* bugger

bouillabaisse [bujabɛs] *f* GASTR bouillabaise (*Provençale soup with fish cooked in water or white wine, seasoned with garlic, saffron and olive oil*)

bouillant(**e**) [bujɑ̃, jɑ̃t] *adj* **1.** (*qui bout, très chaud*) boiling **2.** (*fougueux*) fiery

bouille [buj] *f inf* face

bouillie [buji] *f* baby food

bouillir [bujiʀ] *irr* I. *vi* **1.** (*être en ébullition*) to be boiling **2.** (*porter à ébullition*) to boil **3.** (*laver à l'eau bouillante, stériliser*) to boil (wash) **4.** (*s'emporter*) ~ **de colère/de rage** to be seething with anger/rage II. *vt* (*lait, eau, viande, légumes*) to boil; (*linge*) to boil(-wash)

bouilloire [bujwaʀ] *f* kettle

bouillon [bujɔ̃] *m* **1.** (*soupe*) stock **2.** (*bouillonnement*) bubble **3.** BIO ~ **de culture** culture medium; *fig* breeding ground

bouillon-cube [bujɔ̃kyb] <bouillon-cubes> *m* stock cube

bouillonnement [bujɔnmɑ̃] *m a. fig* bubbling; (*des idées*) ferment

bouillonner [bujɔne] <1> *vi* **1.** (*produire des bouillons*) to bubble **2.** (*être énervé*) ~ **de rage/colère** to be seething with rage/anger **3.** (*être imaginatif*) ~ **d'idées** to be bubbling with ideas

bouillotte [bujɔt] *f* hot-water bottle

boulanger, **-ère** [bulɑ̃ʒe, -ɛʀ] *m, f* baker

boulangère [bulɑ̃ʒɛʀ] *f* (*femme d'un boulanger*) baker's wife

boulangerie [bulɑ̃ʒʀi] *f* **1.** (*magasin, métier*) bakery **2.** (*usine*) ~ **industrielle** industrial bakery

boulangerie-pâtisserie [bulɑ̃ʒʀipatisʀi] <boulangeries-pâtisseries> *f* bakery and pastry shop

boulanger-pâtissier [bulɑ̃ʒepatisje] <boulangers-pâtissiers> *m* baker-pastry-cook

boule [bul] *f* **1.** (*sphère*) ball **2.** (*objet de forme ronde*) ~ **de glace** scoop of ice-cream; ~ **de neige** snowball; ~ **de laine** ball of wool; ~ **de coton** cottonwool ball *Brit,* cotton ball *Am;* ~ **à thé** tea infuser **3.** *plé, inf* (*testicules*) balls **4.** *pl* JEUX **jeu de ~s** game of bowls; **jouer aux ~s** to play bowls **5.** *inf* (*tête*) **avoir la ~ à zéro** to be empty-headed; **perdre la ~** (*devenir fou*) to go mad; (*s'affoler*) to lose one's head **6.** INFOR ~ **de commande** trackball **7.** *Belgique* (*bonbon*) sweet

bouleau [bulo] <x> *m* BOT (silver) birch

bouledogue [buldɔg] *m* ZOOL bulldog

boulet [bulɛ] *m* **1.** (*boule de métal pour charger les canons*) cannonball **2.** (*boule de métal attachée aux pieds des condamnés*) ball **3.** (*fardeau*) ball and chain **4.** (*charbon*) lump

boulette [bulɛt] *f* **1.** (*petite boule*) pellet **2.** GASTR meatball

boulevard [bulvaʀ] *m* boulevard

bouleversant(**e**) [bulvɛʀsɑ̃, ɑ̃t] *adj* (*spectacle, récit*) distressing; (*acteur, rôle*) moving

bouleversement [bulvɛʀsəmɑ̃] *m* distress; (*dans la vie d'une personne*) upheaval

bouleverser [bulvɛʀse] <1> *vt* **1.** (*causer une émotion violente: personne*) to shake **2.** (*apporter des changements brutaux*) ~ **qc** (*carrière, vie*) to turn sth upside down; (*emploi du temps, programme*) to disrupt sth **3.** (*mettre sens dessus dessous*) ~ **une maison/pièce** to turn a house/room upside down

boulimie [bulimi] *f* **1.** MED bulimia **2.** (*désir intense*) **avoir une ~ de voyage** to be a compulsive traveller

boulimique [bulimik] I. *adj* **1.** (*vorace*) bulimic **2.** (*insatiable*) compulsive II. *mf* bulimic

bouliste [bulist] *mf* bowls player

boulodrome [bulodʀom] *m* bowling pitch

boulon [bulɔ̃] *m* bolt

boulonner [bulɔne] <1> I. *vt* to bolt down II. *vi inf* (*travailler*) to slave

boulot [bulo] *m inf* **1.** (*travail*) work **2.** (*emploi*) job

boulotter [bulɔte] <1> *vt, vi fam* to eat; **qu'est-ce qu'il boulotte!** he can really stuff it down!

boum[1] [bum] I. *interj* bang II. *m* (*bruit sonore*) boom

boum[2] [bum] *f inf* party

bouquet [bukɛ] *m* **1.** (*botte: de fleurs*) bunch; (*chez le fleuriste*) bouquet; (*de persil, thym*) bunch **2.** (*gerbe finale: d'un feu d'artifice*) grand finale (*of a firework display*) **3.** (*parfum: d'un vin*) bouquet **4.** (*grosse crevette*) prawn

bouquetin [buktɛ̃] *m* ZOOL ibex

bouquin [bukɛ̃] *m inf* book

bouquiner [bukine] <1> *vi inf* to read

bouquiniste [bukinist] *mf* secondhand bookseller (*especially one with a stall on the banks of the Seine in Paris*)

bourbeux, **-euse** [buʀbø, -øz] *adj* muddy

bourbier [buʀbje] *m* mess

bourbon [buʀbɔ̃] *m* bourbon

bourde [buʀd] *f inf* (*bévue*) blunder

bourdon [buʀdɔ̃] *m* **1.** ZOOL bumble-bee **2.** MUS drone; (*d'un orgue*) bourdon

bourdonnement [buʀdɔnmɑ̃] *m* (*d'un insecte*) buzzing; (*d'un moteur*) humming; (*des voix*) buzz

bourdonner [buʀdɔne] <1> *vi* (*moteur, hélice*) to hum; (*insecte*) to buzz

bourg [buʀ] *m* village

bourgeois(**e**) [buʀʒwa, waz] I. *adj* **1.** (*relatif à la bourgeoisie*) bourgeois; **classe ~e** middle-class **2.** *péj* (*étroitement conservateur*) bourgeois II. *m(f)* **1.** (*qui appartient à la bourgeoisie*) *a. péj* bourgeois **2.** HIST burgess **3.** *Suisse* (*personne possédant la bourgeoisie*) burgess

bourgeoisie [buʀʒwazi] *f* **1.** (*classe*

sociale) bourgeoisie, middle-classes *pl* **2.** HIST burgesses *pl* **3.** *Suisse* (*droit de cité que possède toute personne dans sa commune d'origine*) right of residence

bourgeon [buʀʒɔ̃] *m* bud

bourgeonner [buʀʒɔne] <1> *vi* **1.** BOT (*arbre*) to bud **2.** *fig* to come out in spots

bourgmestre [buʀgmɛstʀ] *m Belgique* (*maire*) burgomaster

bourgogne [buʀgɔɲ] *m* Burgundy (*wine*)

Bourgogne [buʀgɔɲ] *f* **la** ~ Burgundy

bourguignon(**ne**) [buʀgiɲɔ̃, ɔn] *adj* **1.** (*de Bourgogne*) Burgundian **2.** GASTR **bœuf** ~ bœuf bourguignon (*beef cooked in red wine*)

Bourguignon(**ne**) [buʀgiɲɔ̃, ɔn] *m(f)* Burgundian

bourlinguer [buʀlɛ̃ge] <1> *vi fig, inf* to get around

bourrade [buʀad] *f* shove

bourrage [buʀaʒ] *m* **1.** (*l'action de bourrer qc: d'un coussin, matelas*) stuffing; (*d'une pipe*) filling **2.** *fig, inf* ~ **de crâne** (*endoctrinement*) brainwashing; (*gavage intellectuel*) cramming **3.** INFOR ~ **de papier** paper jam

bourrasque [buʀask] *f* **1.** METEO (*de vent*) gust; (*de neige*) flurry **2.** *fig* (*d'injures, de mots, paroles*) flurry

bourratif, **-ive** [buʀatif, -iv] *adj inf* (*aliment*) filling

bourre [buʀ] *f* **1.** (*matière de remplissage*) stuffing; (*d'une arme, cartouche*) wadding **2.** (*duvet des bourgeons*) down

bourré(**e**) [buʀe] *adj* **1.** (*plein à craquer*) jam-packed; (*portefeuille*) full; **être** ~ **de fautes/préjugés** to be full of mistakes/prejudices **2.** (*trop plein*) **une valise** ~**e** a bursting suitcase **3.** *inf* (*ivre*) plastered

bourreau [buʀo] <x> *m* **1.** (*exécuteur*) executioner **2.** (*tortionnaire*) torturer; ~ **d'enfants** child-batterer; ~ **des cœurs** *iron* lady-killer; ~ **de travail** workaholic

bourrelet [buʀlɛ] *m* **1.** (*pour isoler*) draught excluder *Brit,* weather strip *Am* **2.** ANAT (*de chair, graisse*) spare tyre [*o* tire *Am*] *inf*

bourrer [buʀe] <1> **I.** *vt* **1.** (*remplir*) to stuff; (*pipe*) to fill **2.** (*gaver*) ~ **qn de nourriture** to stuff sb with food **II.** *vpr* **se** ~ **de qc** to stuff oneself with sth

bourriche [buʀiʃ] *f* **1.** (*panier*) hamper **2.** (*contenu*) **manger une** ~ **d'huitres** to eat a hamper of oysters

bourrique [buʀik] *f inf* ass ►**faire tourner qn en** ~ to drive sb up the wall

bourru(**e**) [buʀy] *adj* (*peu aimable*) surly

bourse[1] [buʀs] *f* **1.** (*porte-monnaie*) purse **2.** (*allocation*) ~ **d'études** study grant **3.** *pl* ANAT scrotum

bourse[2] [buʀs] *f* FIN **la Bourse** (*lieu*) the Stock Exchange; (*ensemble des cours*) the stock market; **jouer à la Bourse** to play the stock market

boursier, **-ière**[1] [buʀsje, -jɛʀ] **I.** *adj* **étudiant** ~/**étudiante boursière** grant-holder **II.** *m, f* grant-holder

boursier, **-ière**[2] [buʀsje, -jɛʀ] **I.** *adj* (*relatif à la Bourse*) Stock Exchange [*o* Market *Am*] **II.** *m, f* (*professionnel de la Bourse*) stock market operator

boursouflé(**e**) [buʀsufle] *adj* **1.** (*gonflé*) swollen **2.** (*emphatique: style, discours*) bombastic

boursoufler [buʀsufle] <1> *vt* to puff up

boursouflure [buʀsuflyʀ] *f* (*de la peau, du visage*) puffiness; (*d'une surface, peinture*) blistering

bouscueil [buskœj] *m Québec* (*mouvement des glaces sous l'action du vent, de la marée ou du courant*) ice movement

bousculade [buskylad] *f* **1.** (*remous de foule*) crush **2.** (*précipitation*) rush

bousculer [buskyle] <1> **I.** *vt* **1.** (*heurter: personne*) to shove; ~ **qc** (*livres, chaises*) to knock sth over **2.** (*mettre sens dessus dessous*) ~ **qc** to turn sth upside down **3.** (*modifier brutalement*) ~ **qc** (*conception, traditions*) to turn sth upside down; (*projet*) to turn sth around **4.** (*exercer une pression sur qn*) to pressure **II.** *vpr* **se** ~ **1.** (*se pousser mutuellement*) to jostle each other **2.** (*être en confusion: sentiments*) to be confused

bouse [buz] *f* cow pat *Brit,* cow dung *no pl*

bousiller [buzije] <1> *vt inf* **1.** (*mettre hors d'usage*) to ruin **2.** (*mal faire: travail*) to bungle

boussole [busɔl] *f* compass

bout [bu] *m* **1.** (*extrémité: du doigt, nez*) tip; (*d'un objet*) end; **de** ~ **en** ~ from start to finish; ~ **à** ~ end to end; **jusqu'au** ~ to the end **2.** (*limite*) end; **tout au** ~ at the very end **3.** (*morceau*) bit; ~ **d'essai** CINE screen test **4.** (*terme*) end; **au** ~ **d'un moment/d'une année** after a moment/year ►**savoir qc sur le** ~ **des doigts** to have sth at one's fingertips; **tenir le bon** ~ to be over the worst; **joindre les deux** ~**s** to make (both) ends meet; **à** ~ **de bras** at arm's length; **à tout** ~ **de champ** all the time; **être à** ~ **de forces/nerfs** to be exhausted/at the end of one's tether; **être à** ~ **de souffle** to be out of breath; **mettre qn à** ~ to push sb to the limit; **venir à** ~ **de qn** to get the better of sb; **venir à** ~ **de qc** to finish sth off; **au** ~ **du compte** at the end of the day

boutade [butad] *f* wisecrack

boute-en-train [butɑ̃tʀɛ̃] *m inv* party animal; **le** ~ **de qc** the life and soul of sth

boutefas [butfa] *m Suisse* (*saucisson de porc enveloppé dans le gros boyau de l'animal*) *type of pork sausage*

bouteille [butɛj] *f* ~ **consignée/non consignée** returnable/non-returnable bottle; **boire à la** ~ to drink from the bottle; **une bonne** ~ a good bottle

boutique [butik] *f* **1.** (*magasin*) shop **2.** (*magasin de prêt-à-porter*) boutique **3.** *inf* (*entreprise*) outfit

bouton [butɔ̃] *m* **1.** COUT (*de vêtement*) button **2.** (*commande d'un mécanisme: de la radio, télé, sonnette*) button; (*de porte*) door-knob; (*d'un interrupteur*) switch **3.** MED ~ **de fièvre** coldsore; ~ **d'acné** spot **4.** BOT bud **5.** INFOR button; ~ **Démarrer** Start button; ~ **droit/gauche de la souris** right/left mouse button

bouton-d'or [butɔ̃dɔʀ] <boutons-d'or> *m* BOT buttercup

boutonné(e) [butɔne] *adj* buttoned

boutonner [butɔne] <1> **I.** *vt* to button (up) **II.** *vi* to button **III.** *vpr* **se** ~ (*vêtement*) to button (up); (*personne*) to button oneself up

boutonneux, -euse [butɔnø, -øz] *adj* spotty

boutonnière [butɔnjɛʀ] *f* buttonhole

bouton-poussoir [butɔ̃puswaʀ] <boutons-poussoirs> *m* (push) button **bouton-pression** [butɔ̃pʀesjɔ̃] <boutons-pression> *m* press stud *Brit,* snap fastener *Am*

bouture [butyʀ] *f* cutting

bouvreuil [buvʀœj] *m* bullfinch

bovidés [bɔvide] *mpl* bovines

bovin(e) [bɔvɛ̃, in] **I.** *adj* (*qui concerne le bœuf*) bovine **II.** *mpl* cattle

bowling [buliŋ] *m* **1.** (*jeu*) (tenpin) bowling **2.** (*lieu*) bowling alley

box [bɔks] <es> *m* **1.** (*dans une écurie*) loose-box; (*dans un garage*) lock-up garage **2.** JUR ~ **des accusés** dock

boxe [bɔks] *f* boxing

boxer [bɔkse] <1> **I.** *vi* to box; ~ **contre qn** to box sb **II.** *vt inf* ~ **qn** to punch sb

boxeur, -euse [bɔksœʀ, -øz] *m, f* boxer

box-office [bɔksɔfis] <box-offices> *m* box office

boxon [bɔksɔ̃] *m inf* whorehouse

boyau [bwajo] <x> *m* **1.** *pl* ANAT guts **2.** (*chambre à air*) inner tube **3.** (*corde: d'une raquette, d'un violon*) (cat)gut

boycott [bɔjkɔt] *m,* **boycottage** [bɔjkɔtaʒ] *m* boycott

boycotter [bɔjkɔte] <1> *vt* to boycott

boy-scout [bɔjskut] <boys-scouts> *m* boy scout

BP [bepe] *abr de* **boîte postale**

brabançon(ne) [bʀabɑ̃sɔ̃, ɔn] *adj* of Brabant

Brabançon(ne) [bʀabɑ̃sɔ̃, ɔn] *m(f)* person from Brabant

Brabant [bʀabɑ̃] *m* **le** ~ Brabant

bracelet [bʀaslɛ] *m* bracelet; (*rigide*) bangle

bracelet-montre [bʀaslɛmɔ̃tʀ] <bracelets-montres> *m* wristwatch

braconner [bʀakɔne] <1> *vi* (*à la chasse, à la pêche*) to poach

braconnier, -ière [bʀakɔnje, -ijɛʀ] *m, f* (*à la chasse, à la pêche*) poacher

brader [bʀade] <1> *vt* **1.** COM ~ **qc** to sell sth cheaply **2.** (*se débarrasser de*) to sell sth off

braderie [bʀadʀi] *f* flea market

braguette [bʀagɛt] *f* (trouser) fly

braillard(e) [bʀajaʀ, -jaʀd] **I.** *adj inf* (*bébé, enfant*) bawling; (*ivrogne, foule*) screaming **II.** *m(f) inf* bawler

braille [bʀaj] *m* Braille

braillement [bʀajmɑ̃] *m* screaming *no pl*

brailler [bʀaje] <1> **I.** *vi* to bawl **II.** *vt* ~ **qc** to bawl sth out

braire [bʀɛʀ] *vt irr* **1.** (*âne*) to bray **2.** *inf* (*brailler*) to bawl **3.** *inf* (*suer*) **faire** ~ **qn** to drive sb mad

braise [bʀɛz] *f* embers *pl*

braisé(e) [bʀeze] *adj* braised

braiser [bʀeze] <1> *vt* to braise

brame [bʀam] *m,* **bramement** [bʀammɑ̃] *m* bell

bramer [bʀame] <1> *vi* **1.** ZOOL (*cerf, daim*) to bell **2.** (*se plaindre*) to wail

brancard [bʀɑ̃kaʀ] *m* **1.** (*civière*) stretcher **2.** (*bras d'une civière, d'une brouette*) pole **3.** (*pour attacher un cheval*) shaft

brancardier, -ière [bʀɑ̃kaʀdje, -jɛʀ] *m, f* stretcher bearer

branchages [bʀɑ̃ʃaʒ] *mpl* branches

branche [bʀɑ̃ʃ] *f* **1.** (*famille, domaine*) *a.* BOT branch **2.** (*tige: d'une paire de lunettes*) arm; (*d'un chandelier*) branch; (*de ciseaux*) blade; (*d'un compas*) leg

branché(e) [bʀɑ̃ʃe] *adj inf* cool; **être** ~ **cinéma/moto** (*adorer*) to be a cinema/bike fan; (*s'y connaître*) to be a cinema/bike buff

branchement [bʀɑ̃ʃmɑ̃] *m* **1.** (*action*) connecting **2.** (*circuit*) connection **3.** INFOR ~ **Internet** Internet access

brancher [bʀɑ̃ʃe] <1> **I.** *vt* **1.** (*raccorder*) ~ **le téléphone sur le réseau** to connect the telephone (to the network) **2.** (*orienter*) ~ **la conversation sur un autre sujet** to change the conversation to another subject **II.** *vpr* **se** ~ **sur qc** to tune into sth

branchies [bʀɑ̃ʃi] *fpl* gills

brandir [bʀɑ̃diʀ] <8> *vt* (*arme*) to brandish; (*drapeau*) to wave

branlant(e) [bʀɑ̃lɑ̃, ɑ̃t] *adj* shaky

branle-bas [bʀɑ̃lba] *m inv, fig* commotion

branler [bʀɑ̃le] <1> **I.** *vi* to wobble **II.** *vpr vulg* **se** ~ to wank *Brit,* to jerk off *Am*

branleur, -euse [bʀɑ̃lœʀ, -øz] *m, f inf* **1.** idiot **2.** (*paresseux*) lazy bugger

brante [bʀɑ̃t] *f Suisse* (*récipient en bois servant à transporter la vendange à dos d'homme*) grape basket

braquage [bʀakaʒ] *m* **1.** (*des roues*) lock **2.** *inf* (*attaque*) stickup

braquer [bʀake] <1> **I.** *vt* **1.** AUTO ~ **le volant à droite** to swing the (steering) wheel to the right **2.** (*diriger*) ~ **le regard sur qn** to look at sb; ~ **une arme sur qn** to aim a weapon at sb **3.** *inf* (*attaquer: banque, magasin*) to rob **4.** (*provoquer l'hostilité*) ~ **un collègue contre le chef/projet** to turn a colleague against the boss/project **II.** *vi* ~ **bien/mal** (*voiture*) to have a good/bad lock **III.** *vpr* **se** ~ to dig one's heels in

braquet [bʀakɛ] *m* SPORT gear ratio; **changer**

de ~ to change gears
braqueur, **-euse** [bʀakœʀ, -øz] *m, f* armed robber
bras [bʀa] *m* **1.** (*membre*) arm; **se donner le** ~ to link arms; ~ **dessus** ~ **dessous** arm in arm **2.** (*main-d'œuvre*) worker **3.** TECH (*d'un levier, électrophone*) arm; (*d'un fauteuil*) arm(rest); (*d'un brancard*) shaft **4.** GEO inlet; ~ **de mer** sound ▸**rester les** ~ **ballants** to stand there inanely; **baisser les** ~ to throw in the towel
brasero [bʀazeʀo] *m* brazier
brasier [bʀɑzje] *m a. fig* blaze
bras-le-corps [bʀaləkɔʀ] **prendre un enfant à** ~ to take a child around the waist; **prendre un problème à** ~ to face up to a problem
brassard [bʀasaʀ] *m* armband
brasse [bʀas] *f* breast-stroke; ~ **papillon** butterfly
brassée [bʀase] *f* armful
brasser [bʀase] <1> *vt* **1.** (*mélanger*) to mix; (*pâte*) to knead **2.** *fig* ~ **de l'argent/des affaires** to be in the money/in big business **3.** (*fabriquer: bière*) to brew
brasserie [bʀasʀi] *f* **1.** (*restaurant*) brasserie **2.** (*industrie*) brewing industry **3.** (*entreprise*) brewery

> A **brasserie** has a large dining room typical of the nineteenth century and serves traditional food, often with beer rather than wine. Many have a high reputation for their food.

brasseur [bʀasœʀ] *m* brewer
brassière [bʀasjɛʀ] *f* **1.** (*sous-vêtement*) vest *Brit*, undershirt *Am* (*for a baby*) **2.** (*chandail*) jumper *Brit*, sweater *Am* **3.** *Québec, inf* (*soutien-gorge*) bra **4.** NAUT ~ **de sauvetage** life-jacket *Brit*, life vest *Am*
bravade [bʀavad] *f* bravado; **par** ~ out of bravado
brave [bʀav] *adj* **1.** (*courageux*) brave **2.** *antéposé* (*honnête*) decent **3.** (*naïf*) naive
bravement [bʀavmɑ̃] *adv* **1.** (*avec bravoure*) bravely **2.** (*résolument*) boldly
braver [bʀave] <1> *vt* **1.** (*défier*) ~ **un adversaire** to stand up to an opponent; ~ **le danger/la mort** to defy danger/death **2.** (*ne pas respecter: convenances, loi*) to flout
bravo [bʀavo] **I.** *interj* bravo! **II.** *m* cheer
bravoure [bʀavuʀ] *f* bravery
break [bʀɛk] *m* **1.** AUTO estate car *Brit*, station wagon *Am* **2.** (*pause*) *a.* SPORT break
brebis [bʀəbi] *f* ewe ▸~ **galeuse** black sheep
brèche [bʀɛʃ] *f* (*dans une clôture, une haie, un mur*) gap; (*dans une coque*) hole; (*sur une lame*) notch; MIL (*sur le front*) breach
bredouillage [bʀədujaʒ] *m* mumbling
bredouille [bʀəduj] *adj* (*sans rien, sans succès*) empty-handed
bredouillement [bʀədujmɑ̃] *m* mumbling
bredouiller [bʀəduje] <1> **I.** *vi* to stammer; (*parler confusément*) to mumble **II.** *vt* ~ **qc** to stammer sth out
bref, **brève** [bʀɛf, bʀɛv] **I.** *adj* brief; (*concis*) short; **soyez** ~! get on with it!; **d'un ton** ~ sharply **II.** *adv* **en** ~ in short; **enfin** ~ in short
breloque [bʀəlɔk] *f* charm
Brésil [bʀezil] *m* **le** ~ Brazil
brésilien(ne) [bʀeziljɛ̃, -jɛn] *adj* Brazilian
Brésilien(ne) [bʀeziljɛ̃, -jɛn] *m(f)* Brazilian
Bretagne [bʀətaɲ] *f* **la** ~ Brittany
bretelle [bʀətɛl] *f* **1.** COUT (*de soutien-gorge*) strap; (*de sac*) (shoulder) strap **2.** *pl* (*de pantalon*) braces *Brit*, suspenders *Am* **3.** (*bifurcation d'autoroute*) slip road *Brit*, on/off ramp *Am*; ~ **d'accès/de raccordement** access road; ~ **de contournement** bypass
breton [bʀətɔ̃] *m* Breton; *v. a.* **français**
breton(ne) [bʀətɔ̃, ɔn] *adj* Breton
Breton(ne) [bʀətɔ̃, -ɔn] *m(f)* Breton
bretzel [bʀɛtzɛl] *m* pretzel
breuvage [bʀœvaʒ] *m* **1.** (*boisson d'une composition spéciale*) brew; *péj* potion **2.** *Québec* (*boisson non alcoolisée*) beverage
brève [bʀɛv] *adj v.* **bref**
brevet [bʀəvɛ] *m* **1.** (*diplôme*) diploma **2.** (*certificat*) certificate; ~ **d'invention** patent; ~ **de pilot** pilot's licence *Brit*, license *Am*
breveté(e) [bʀəv(ə)te] *adj* **1.** (*pourvu d'un brevet: invention*) patented **2.** (*diplômé: ingénieur, interprète*) qualified
breveter [bʀəv(ə)te] <3> *vt* to patent; **faire** ~ **qc** to take out a patent for sth
bréviaire [bʀevjɛʀ] *m* breviary
bribe [bʀib] *f souvent pl, fig* (*de conversation*) fragment; (*d'une langue*) bits; (*d'une fortune, d'un héritage*) remnants
bric-à-brac [bʀikabʀak] *m inv* odds and ends; (*d'un antiquaire*) bric-a-brac
bricelet [bʀislɛ] *m Suisse* (*gaufre très mince et croustillante*) wafer
bricolage [bʀikɔlaʒ] *m* **1.** (*travail d'amateur*) handiwork, DIY *Brit* **2.** (*mauvais travail*) makeshift job
bricole [bʀikɔl] *f* **1.** (*objet de peu de valeur*) trifle; **des** ~**s** odds and ends **2.** (*petit événement*) spot of bother
bricoler [bʀikɔle] <1> **I.** *vi* **1.** (*effectuer des petits travaux*) to do odd jobs; **savoir** ~ to be a handyman **2.** *péj* (*faire du mauvais travail*) to do a botched job **3.** (*ne pas avoir de travail fixe*) to drift in and out of work **II.** *vt* **1.** (*construire, installer*) ~ **qc** to fix sth up **2.** (*réparer tant bien que mal*) to fix
bricoleur, **-euse** [bʀikɔlœʀ, -øz] **I.** *adj* do-it-yourself **II.** *m, f* handyman, handywoman *m, f*
bride [bʀid] *f* **1.** (*pièce de harnais*) bridle **2.** (*lien: d'un bonnet, d'une cape*) string; TECH strap
bridé(e) [bʀide] *adj* **des yeux** ~**s** slanting eyes
brider [bʀide] <1> *vt* **1.** (*mettre la bride: cheval*) to bridle **2.** (*réprimer*) to restrain;

(*passion, enthousiasme*) to curb; ~ **qn** to hold sb in check **3.** TECH (*tuyau*) to flange

bridge [bʀidʒ] *m* JEUX, MED bridge

brie [bʀi] *m* brie (*large round soft cheese*)

briefing [bʀifiŋ] *m* briefing

brièvement [bʀijɛvmɑ̃] *adv* **1.** (*de manière succincte*) concisely **2.** (*pour peu de temps*) briefly

brièveté [bʀijɛvte] *f* **1.** (*courte longueur*) briefness **2.** (*courte durée*) brevity

brigade [bʀigad] *f* **1.** MIL brigade; ~ **anti-drogue** drug squad; ~ **des stupéfiants** drug squad **2.** (*équipe*) ~ **du matin** early team **3.** POL **les ~s rouges** the red brigades

brigadier [bʀigadje] *m* (*de gendarmerie*) sergeant; (*d'artillerie, de cavalerie*) corporal

brigand [bʀigɑ̃] *m péj* crook

briguer [bʀige] <1> *vt* (*solliciter: emploi*) to seek

brillamment [bʀijamɑ̃] *adv* brilliantly

brillance [bʀijɑ̃s] *f* brilliance

brillant [bʀijɑ̃] *m* **1.** (*diamant*) brilliant **2.** (*aspect brillant*) **le** ~ (*d'un objet*) sparkle; (*d'un propos, du langage*) brilliance

brillant(e) [bʀijɑ̃, jɑ̃t] *adj* **1.** (*étincelant: meubles, yeux, cheveux*) shining; (*couleurs*) brilliant; (*plan d'eau*) sparkling **2.** (*qui a de l'allure*) brilliant; (*victoire*) dazzling

brillantine [bʀijɑ̃tin] *f* brilliantine

briller [bʀije] <1> *vi* **1.** (*rayonner: soleil, étoile, visage, chaussures, cheveux, yeux*) to shine; (*diamant*) to sparkle; (*éclair*) to flash **2.** (*se mettre en valeur*) ~ **par qc** to shine by sth **3.** (*vanter*) **faire** ~ **un voyage à qn** to paint a glowing picture of a trip to sb

brimade [bʀimad] *f* bullying *no pl*

brimer [bʀime] <1> *vt* (*faire subir des vexations*) to bully; (*désavantager*) to frustrate

brin [bʀɛ̃] *m* **1.** (*mince tige*) blade; ~ **de paille** wisp of straw; ~ **de muguet** sprig of lily of the valley **2.** (*filament*) ~ **de laine** scrap of wool **3.** (*petite quantité*) **un** ~ **d'espoir** a glimmer of hope

brindille [bʀɛ̃dij] *f* twig

bringue[1] [bʀɛ̃g] *f péj, inf* (*gigue*) **grande** ~ beanpole

bringue[2] [bʀɛ̃g] *f* **1.** *inf* (*fête*) binge **2.** *Suisse* (*querelle*) row

brio [bʀijo] *m* brio

brioche [bʀijɔʃ] *f* brioche

brioché(e) [bʀijɔʃe] *adj* (*pâte, pain*) brioche

brique[1] [bʀik] **I.** *f* **1.** (*matériau*) brick; **maison de** ~ brick house **2.** (*matière ayant cette forme*) ~ **de savon/tourbe** block of soap/peat **3.** *inf* (*francs*) one million old francs ►**mettre en ~s** *Suisse* (*casser en nombreux morceaux*) to smash; **pas une** ~ **de qc** *Suisse* (*pas du tout de*) not a ounce of sth **II.** *app inv* (*couleur*) brick red

brique®[2] [bʀik] *f* (*emballage*) carton

briquet [bʀikɛ] *m* (cigarette) lighter

briqueterie [bʀik(ə)tʀi, bʀikɛtʀi] *f* brick-yard

bris [bʀi] *m* break-in

brisant [bʀizɑ̃] *m* **1.** (*rocher*) reef **2.** (*écume*) breaker

brise [bʀiz] *f* breeze

brise-glace [bʀizglas] *m inv* icebreaker **brise-jet** [bʀizʒɛ] *m inv* swirl **brise-lames** [bʀizlam] *m inv* breakwater **brise-mottes** [bʀizmɔt] *m inv* harrow

briser [bʀize] <1> **I.** *vt* **1.** (*casser*) to break **2.** (*mater: révolte*) to quell; (*grève, blocus*) to break **3.** (*anéantir: espoir, illusions*) to shatter; (*amitié*) to break up; (*forces, volonté, silence*) to break **4.** (*fatiguer: voyage*) to exhaust **5.** (*interrompre: conversation*) to interrupt; (*monotonie, ennui, silence*) to break ►~ **le cœur à qn** to break sb's heart; **être brisé** *Québec* (*être en panne*) to be broken **II.** *vpr* **1.** (*se casser*) **se** ~ (*vitre, porcelaine*) to break; **mon cœur se brise** my heart is breaking **2.** (*échouer*) **se** ~ **contre/sur qc** (*résistance, assauts*) to break down against/on sth; (*vagues*) to break against/on sth

brise-tout [bʀiztu] *m inv* butterfingers

briseur, -euse [bʀizœʀ, -øz] *m, f* ~ **de grève** strikebreaker

britannique [bʀitanik] *adj* British

Britannique [bʀitanik] **I.** *mf* British person **II.** *adj* **les Îles ~s** the Britisn Isles

broc [bʀo] *m* pitcher

brocante [bʀɔkɑ̃t] *f* **1.** (*boutique*) second-hand shop [*o* store *Am*] **2.** (*foire*) flea market

brocanteur, -euse [bʀɔkɑ̃tœʀ, -øz] *m, f* secondhand dealer

broche [bʀɔʃ] *f* **1.** (*bijou*) brooch **2.** GASTR skewer **3.** MED pin

brochet [bʀɔʃɛ] *m* pike

brochette [bʀɔʃɛt] *f* **1.** GASTR skewer **2.** *iron* (*groupe de personnes*) bunch **3.** (*petite broche*) ~ **de décorations** row of medals

brochure [bʀɔʃyʀ] *f* brochure

brocoli [bʀɔkɔli] *m* broccoli

brodequin [bʀɔd(ə)kɛ̃] *m* laced boot

broder [bʀɔde] <1> **I.** *vt* (*étoffe, motif*) to embroider **II.** *vi* **1.** COUT to embroider **2.** (*affabuler*) to add embellishments

broderie [bʀɔdʀi] *f* embroidery

brome [bʀom] *m* CHIM bromine

bromure [bʀɔmyʀ] *m* CHIM bromide

broncher [bʀɔ̃ʃe] <1> *vi* to react; **sans** ~ without turning a hair

bronches [bʀɔ̃ʃ] *fpl* ANAT bronchial tubes

bronchite [bʀɔ̃ʃit] *f* MED bronchitis *no pl*

brontosaure [bʀɔ̃tɔsɔʀ] *m* brontosaurus

bronzage [bʀɔ̃zaʒ] *m* tan

bronze [bʀɔ̃z] *m* bronze

bronzé(e) [bʀɔ̃ze] *adj* tanned

bronzer [bʀɔ̃ze] <1> **I.** *vt* ART, TECH to bronze **II.** *vi* to tan **III.** *vpr* to sunbathe

bronzette [bʀɔ̃zɛt] *f inf* **faire** ~ to do a bit of sunbathing

brosse [bʀɔs] *f* **1.** (*ustensile, pinceau*) brush; ~ **à cheveux** hairbrush; ~ **à dents** toothbrush **2.** (*coupe de cheveux*) crew-cut

brosser [bʀɔse] <1> **I.** *vt* **1.** (*épousseter*) to brush **2.** (*esquisser: situation, portrait*) to paint **3.** *Belgique, fam* (*sécher*) ~ **un cours** to skip a lesson **II.** *vpr* **se** ~ to brush one's clothes; **se** ~ **les cheveux/les dents** to brush one's hair/teeth

brouette [bʀuɛt] *f* wheelbarrow

brouhaha [bʀuaa] *m* hubbub

brouillage [bʀujaʒ] *m* jamming; ~ **sonore/visuel** sound/picture interference

brouillard [bʀujaʀ] *m* **1.** (*épais*) fog **2.** (*léger*) mist **3.** (*créé par la pollution*) smog

brouille [bʀuj] *f* quarrel

brouillé(e) [bʀuje] *adj* **1.** (*fâché*) **être** ~ **avec qn** to be on bad terms with sb **2.** *inf* (*nul*) **être** ~ **avec les chiffres** to be hopeless with figures **3.** (*atteint*) **avoir le teint** ~ to have a muddy complexion; **avoir les idées ~es** to have muddled ideas

brouiller [bʀuje] <1> **I.** *vt* **1.** (*rendre trouble*) to muddle **2.** (*embrouiller*) ~ **les idées** [*o* **l'esprit**] **à qn** to confuse sb **3.** (*mettre en désordre: dossiers, papiers*) to jumble **4.** (*rendre inintelligible: émission, émetteur, combinaison d'un coffre*) to scramble **5.** (*fâcher*) **des querelles d'héritage ont brouillé les deux frères** arguments over their inheritance have set the two brothers at odds ►~ **les cartes** [*o* **les pistes**] to confuse the issue **II.** *vpr* **1.** (*se fâcher*) **se** ~ **avec qn** to fall out with sb **2.** (*se troubler*) **ma vue se brouille** my sight is getting cloudy; **mes idées se brouillent** I'm getting muddled **3.** (*se couvrir*) **se** ~ (*ciel*) to cloud over

brouillon [bʀujɔ̃] *m* rough copy; (*pour une lettre, un discours*) (rough) draft

brouillon(ne) [bʀujɔ̃, jɔn] *adj* **1.** (*désordonné: élève*) careless **2.** (*peu clair*) muddled

broussaille [bʀusɑj] *f* undergrowth

broussailleux, -euse [bʀusɑjø, -jøz] *adj* bushy; (*jardin*) overgrown

brousse [bʀus] *f* **1.** (*contrée tropicale*) brush **2.** *inf* (*région isolée*) back of beyond

brouter [bʀute] <1> **I.** *vt* ~ **de l'herbe** to graze grass; (*cervidés*) to browse grass **II.** *vi* to graze; (*cervidés*) to browse

broutille [bʀutij] *f fig* trifle

broyer [bʀwaje] <6> *vt* (*écraser, détruire: aliments, ordures*) to crush; (*céréales*) to grind

broyeur [bʀwajœʀ] *m* crusher

broyeur, -euse [bʀwajœʀ, -jøz] *adj* (*insecte, mandibules*) crushing

brugeois(e) [bʀyʒwa, waz] *adj* of Bruges; *v. a.* **ajaccien**

Brugeois(e) [bʀyʒwa, waz] *m(f)* person from Bruges; *v. a.* **Ajaccien**

Bruges [bʀyʒ] Bruges

brugnon [bʀyɲɔ̃] *m* nectarine

bruine [bʀɥin] *f* drizzle

bruiner [bʀɥine] <1> *vi impers* **il bruine** it is drizzling

bruire [bʀɥiʀ] *vi irr, défec* (*vent, feuilles, papier, tissu*) to rustle; (*ruisseau*) to murmur; (*insectes*) to buzz

bruissement [bʀɥismɑ̃] *m* (*des feuilles, du vent, du tissu, papier*) rustling; (*d'un ruisseau*) murmur; (*des insectes*) humming

bruit [bʀɥi] *m* **1.** (*son*) noise; (*de vaisselle*) clatter; (*de ferraille*) rattle **2.** (*vacarme*) racket **3.** (*rumeur*) rumour *Brit,* rumor *Am;* **le** ~ **court que** there's a rumour [*o* rumor *Am*] going around that ►**faire du** ~ to cause a sensation

bruitage [bʀɥitaʒ] *m* sound effects; ~ **des films** film sound effects

brûlant(e) [bʀylɑ̃, ɑ̃t] *adj* **1.** (*très chaud*) burning; (*liquide*) boiling **2.** (*passionné*) passionate; (*regard*) fiery **3.** (*délicat: sujet, question*) burning

brûlé [bʀyle] *m* **1.** (*résultat*) **ça sent le** ~ there's a smell of burning **2.** (*blessé*) **grand** ~ victim with third degree burns

brûlé(e) [bʀyle] *adj* (*a. plat*) burnt

brûle-gueule [bʀylgœl] *m inv* short pipe

brûle-parfum [bʀylpaʀfœ̃] *m inv* perfume burner **brûle-pourpoint** [bʀylpuʀpwɛ̃] *m* **à** ~ point-blank

brûler [bʀyle] <1> **I.** *vi* **1.** (*se consumer*) *a.* GASTR to burn **2.** (*être très chaud*) to be burning **3.** (*être irrité: bouche, gorge, yeux*) to burn **4.** (*être dévoré*) ~ **de soif** to be dying of thirst; ~ **de** +*infin* to be longing to +*infin* **5.** (*être proche du but*) **tu brûles!** you're getting hot! **II.** *vt* **1.** (*détruire par le feu: forêt*) to burn; ~ **une maison** to burn down a house **2.** (*pour chauffer, éclairer: bois, charbon, allumette*) to burn **3.** (*endommager*) ~ **un tissu** (*bougie, cigarette, fer à repasser*) to burn some material; ~ **les bourgeons** (*gel*) to damage buds **4.** (*irriter*) **le sable me brûle les pieds** the sand is burning my feet **5.** (*ne pas respecter: stop, signal*) to run; (*étape*) to skip; ~ **un feu rouge** to run a red light **6.** (*consommer*) *a.* GASTR to burn **III.** *vpr* **se** ~ to burn oneself; **se** ~ **les doigts** to burn one's fingers

brûleur [bʀylœʀ] *m* burner

brûlot [bʀylo] *m Québec* (*moustique*) mosquito

brûlure [bʀylyʀ] *f* **1.** (*blessure, plaie, tache*) burn **2.** (*irritation*) **~s d'estomac** heartburn

brume [bʀym] *f* **1.** (*brouillard*) mist **2.** *pl, fig* **les ~s de l'alcool** the alcoholic haze

brumeux, -euse [bʀymø, -øz] *adj* **1.** METEO misty **2.** (*confus*) hazy

brumisateur® [bʀymizatœʀ] *m* spray

brun [bʀœ̃] *m* (*couleur*) brown

brun(e) [bʀœ̃, bʀyn] **I.** *adj* **1.** (*opp: blond: cheveux, peau, tabac*) dark; **bière ~e** dark ale; **cheveux** ~ **clair/foncé** light/dark brown hair; **être** ~ to have dark hair **2.** (*bronzé*) tanned **II.** *m(f)* man with dark hair, brunette *f*

brunante [bʀynɑ̃t] *f Québec* (*tombée de la nuit*) nightfall

brunâtre [bʀynɑtʀ] *adj* brownish

brune [bʀyn] **I.** *adj v.* **brun II.** *f* **1.** (*cigarette*) cigarette made from dark tobacco **2.** (*bière*) dark ale

Brunei [bʀynej] *m* **le ~** Brunei

brunéien(ne) [bʀynejɛ̃, ɛn] *adj* Bruneian

Brunéien(ne) [bʀynejɛ̃, ɛn] *m(f)* Bruneian

brunir [bʀyniʀ] <8> **I.** *vi* to tan; (*cheveux*) to go darker **II.** *vt* to tan; (*boiserie*) to polish

brunnante [bʀynɑ̃t] *f Québec* (*crépuscule*) dusk

brun-roux [bʀœʀu] *adj inv* reddish brown; *v. a.* **bleu**

brushing® [bʀœʃiŋ] *m* blow-dry

brusque [bʀysk] *adj* **1.**(*soudain*) abrupt **2.**(*sec: personne, ton, manières*) blunt; (*geste*) abrupt

brusquement [bʀyskəmɑ̃] *adv* abruptly

brusquer [bʀyske] <1> *vt* to rush

brusquerie [bʀyskəʀi] *f* abruptness

brut(e) [bʀyt] *adj* **1.**(*naturel*) raw; (*champagne*) extra dry; (*diamant*) uncut; (*toile*) unbleached **2.** *fig* (*fait*) raw; (*idée*) basic **3.** ECON gross

brutal(e) [bʀytal, o] <-aux> *adj* **1.**(*violent*) brutal; (*manières*) rough; (*instinct*) savage **2.**(*qui choque: langage, réponse*) blunt; (*franchise, réalisme, vérité*) stark **3.**(*soudain: choc, mort*) sudden; (*coup, décision*) brutal

brutalement [bʀytalmɑ̃] *adv* **1.**(*violemment*) violently **2.**(*sans ménagement*) brutally **3.**(*soudainement*) suddenly

brutaliser [bʀytalize] <1> *vt* to bully

brutalité [bʀytalite] *f* **1.** *sans pl* (*violence*) violence; (*de paroles, d'un jeu*) brutality **2.** *pl* (*actes violents*) **être victime de ~s** to be a victim of brutality **3.** *sans pl* (*soudaineté*) suddenness

brute [bʀyt] *f* **1.**(*violent*) brute **2.**(*rustre*) lout

Bruxelles [bʀy(k)sɛl] Brussels

bruxellois(e) [bʀysɛlwa, waz] *adj* of Brussels; *v. a.* **ajaccien**

Bruxellois(e) [bʀysɛlwa, waz] *m(f)* person from Brussels; *v. a.* **Ajaccien**

bruyamment [bʀyjamɑ̃, bʀɥijamɑ̃] *adv* **1.**(*avec bruit*) noisily **2.**(*avec insistance*) strongly

bruyant(e) [bʀyjɑ̃, bʀɥijɑ̃, jɑ̃t] *adj* (*a. réunion, foule*) noisy

bruyère [bʀyjɛʀ, bʀɥijɛʀ] *f* heather

BTS [beteɛs] *m abr de* **brevet de technicien supérieur** *vocational examination taken at age 18*

bu(e) [by] *part passé de* **boire**

buanderie [bɥɑ̃dʀi] *f* **1.**(*dans une maison*) laundry (room) **2.** *Québec* (*blanchisserie*) laundry

buandier, -ière [bɥɑ̃dje, jɛʀ] *m, f Québec* (*blanchisseur*) launderer

Bucarest [bykaʀɛst] Bucharest

buccal(e) [bykal, o] <-aux> *adj* oral

buccodentaire [bykodɑ̃tɛʀ] *adj* (*hygiène*) oral

bûche [byʃ] *f* **1.**(*bois*) log **2.** GASTR **~ de Noël** Yule log

bûcher¹ [byʃe] *m* **1.**(*amas de bois*) **le ~** the stake **2.**(*local*) woodshed

bûcher² [byʃe] <1> **I.** *vi inf* to cram **II.** *vt inf* **~ qc** to cram for sth

bûcheron(ne) [byʃʀɔ̃, ɔn] *m(f)* lumberjack

bûcheur, -euse [byʃœʀ, -øz] **I.** *adj inf* hard-working **II.** *m, f inf* slogger

Buckingham [bykiŋgam] **le palais de ~** Buckingham Palace

bucolique [bykɔlik] *adj* (*existence*) bucolic; (*paysage*) pastoral

Budapest [bydapɛst] Budapest

budget [bydʒɛ] *m* FIN budget; **le ~ de l'Etat** State budget

budgétaire [bydʒetɛʀ] *adj* budgetary

budgéter [bydʒete] <5> *vt* **~ qc** to budget for sth

budgétiser [bydʒetize] <1> *vt* **~ qc** to budget for sth

buée [bɥe] *f* **se couvrir de ~** to mist up

buffet [byfɛ] *m* **1.** GASTR buffet **2.**(*meuble*) **~ de cuisine** kitchen dresser; **~ de la gare** (*lieu de restauration*) station buffet

buffle [byfl] *m* buffalo

bug [bœg] *m* INFOR bug

building [b(y)ildiŋ] *m* building

buis [bɥi] *m* BOT box

buisson [bɥisɔ̃] *m* bush

buissonnière [bɥisɔnjɛʀ] *adj* **faire l'école ~** to play truant

bulbe [bylb] *m* **1.** BOT, ANAT bulb; **~ pileux** hair bulb; **~ rachidien** medulla **2.** ARCHIT onion dome

bulgare [bylgaʀ] **I.** *adj* Bulgarian **II.** *m* Bulgarian; *v. a.* **français**

Bulgare [bylgaʀ] *mf* Bulgarian

Bulgarie [bylgaʀi] *f* **la ~** Bulgaria

bulldozer [byldɔzɛʀ, buldozœʀ] *m* bulldozer

bulle [byl] *f* **1.** PHYS, MED bubble **2.**(*dans une bande dessinée*) speech bubble

bulletin [byltɛ̃] *m* **1.**(*communiqué, journal, rubrique*) bulletin; **~ d'information** news bulletin **2.** POL **~ de vote** ballot paper **3.** ECOLE **~ scolaire** school report *Brit,* report card *Am* **4.**(*certificat*) certificate; **~ de paye** payslip *Brit,* paycheck stub *Am*

bulletin-réponse [byltɛ̃ʀepɔ̃s] <bulletins-réponses> *m* reply coupon

bungalow [bœ̃galo] *m* bungalow

buraliste [byʀalist] *mf* tobacconist

bureau [byʀo] <x> *m* **1.**(*meuble*) desk **2.**(*pièce, lieu de travail*) office **3.**(*service*) centre *Brit,* center *Am;* **~ de renseignements** information centre [*o* center *Am*]; **~ des objets trouvés** lost property office *Brit,* lost and found (office) *Am* **4.**(*comité*) **~ exécutif** executive committee **5.**(*établissement réservé au public*) **~ de change** bureau de change; **~ de poste** post office; **~ de tabac** tobacconist's *Brit,* tobacco shop *Am;* **~ de vote** polling station **6.** INFOR **ordinateur de ~** desktop

bureaucrate [byʀokʀat] *mf* bureaucrat

bureaucratie [byʀokʀasi] *f* bureaucracy
bureaucratique [byʀokʀatik] *adj* bureaucratic
bureautique® [byʀotik] *f* office automation
burette [byʀɛt] *f* **1.** TECH oil can **2.** CHIM burette **3.** REL cruet
burin [byʀɛ̃] *m* **1.** (*outil*) graver **2.** (*gravure*) engraving **3.** (*ciseau*) chisel
buriné(e) [byʀine] *adj* (*visage*) lined; (*traits*) furrowed
burkinabé(e) [buʀkinabe] *adj* Burkinabe
Burkinabé(e) [buʀkinabe] *m(f)* Burkinabe
Burkina Faso [buʀkinafaso] *m* **le** ~ Burkina Faso
burlesque [byʀlɛsk] **I.** *adj* **1.** THEAT, CINE burlesque **2.** (*extravagant*) ludicrous **II.** *m* CINE burlesque
burnous [byʀnu(s)] *m* burnous
burundais(e) [buʀundɛ, ɛz] *adj* Burundi
Burundais(e) [buʀundɛ, ɛz] *m(f)* Burundian
Burundi [buʀundi] *m* **le** ~ Burundi
bus¹ [bys] *m abr de* **autobus** bus
bus² [bys] *m* INFOR ~ **de données** data bus
bus³ [by] *passé simple de* **boire**
busard [byzaʀ] *m* harrier
buse¹ [byz] *f* (*oiseau*) buzzard
buse² [byz] *f* TECH duct
busqué(e) [byske] *adj* (*nez*) hooked
buste [byst] *m* **1.** (*torse*) chest **2.** (*poitrine de femme, sculpture*) bust
bustier [bystje] *m* **1.** (*sous-vêtement*) longline bra **2.** (*vêtement*) bustier
but [by(t)] *m* **1.** (*destination*) *a.* SPORT goal **2.** (*objectif*) aim
butane [bytan] *m* butane
buté(e) [byte] *adj* stubborn
butée [byte] *f* TECH stop
buter [byte] <1> **I.** *vi* **1.** (*heurter*) ~ **contre qc** to stumble over sth **2.** (*faire face à une difficulté*) ~ **contre qc** to come up against sth **II.** *vt* **1.** (*énerver*) ~ **qn** to set sb against one **2.** *inf* (*tuer*) ~ **qn** to knock sb off **III.** *vpr* **se** ~ **sur qc** to come up against sth
buteur [bytœʀ] *m* SPORT striker
butin [bytɛ̃] *m* spoils; (*d'une fouille*) haul
butiner [bytine] <1> *vi* to gather
butoir [bytwaʀ] *m* **1.** CHEMDFER buffer **2.** TECH stop
butte [byt] *f* hill; **la butte Montmartre** *the hill on which Montmartre stands*
buvable [byvabl] *adj* (*potable*) drinkable; **ne pas être** ~ to be undrinkable
buvais [byvɛ] *imparf de* **boire**
buvant [byvɑ̃] *part prés de* **boire**
buvard [byvaʀ] *m* blotter
buvette [byvɛt] *f* **1.** (*local*) cafe; (*en plein air*) refreshment stand **2.** (*thermale*) *stand where natural spring water is drunk*
buveur, -euse [byvœʀ, -øz] *m, f* **1.** (*alcoolique*) drinker **2.** (*consommateur: d'un restaurant*) customer
buvez [byve], **buvons** [byvɔ̃] *indic prés et impératif de* **boire**
byte [bajt] *m* INFOR byte
byzantin(e) [bizɑ̃tɛ̃, in] *adj* Byzantine

C

C, c [se] *m inv* C; **c cédille** c cedilla; ~ **comme Célestin** c as in Charlie; (*on telephone*) c for Charlie
c' <devant a ç'> *pron dém v.* **ce**
ça [sa] *pron dém* **1.** *inf* (*pour désigner ou renforcer*) that; **qu'est-ce que c'est que ~?** what's that?; **ah ~ non!** definitely not!; ~ **est Belgique** (*c'est*) it's; *v. a.* **cela** **2.** *inf* (*répétitif*) **les haricots? si, j'aime** ~ beans? yes, I do like them; **le fer,** ~ **rouille** iron simply rusts **3.** *péj* (*personne*) **et** ~ **vote!** and people like that vote! ►~ **par exemple!**, ~ **alors!** (my) goodness!; **c'est toujours** ~ that's something at least; **c'est** ~ that's right; **c'est comme** ~ that's how it is; ~ **va?** how are things?; **je l'ai dit comme** ~ I was just talking; **pas de ~!** that's out of the question!; **pour** ~ **oui** you can say that again; *v. a.* **cela**
çà [sa] ~ **et là** here and there
caban [kabɑ̃] *m* car coat
cabane [kaban] *f* **1.** (*abri*) hut; *péj* shack **2.** *inf* (*prison*) clink **3.** *Québec* (*bâtiment construit à l'intérieur d'une propriété agricole dans une forêt d'érables, destiné à la fabrication du sucre et du sirop d'érable*) maple syrup shed **4.** *Suisse* (*refuge de haute montagne*) (mountain) refuge
cabanon [kabanɔ̃] *m* shed
cabaret [kabaʀɛ] *m* **1.** (*boîte de nuit*) night club **2.** *Québec* (*plateau*) tray
cabas [kabɑ] *m* shopping bag
cabestan [kabɛstɑ̃] *m* capstan
cabillaud [kabijo] *m* cod
cabine [kabin] *f* **1.** (*poste de commande: d'un camion*) cab; (*d'un avion, véhicule spatial*) cockpit; ~ **spatiale** space capsule **2.** (*petit local*) cabin; ~ **téléphonique** (tele)phone box *Brit,* (tele)phone booth *Am;* ~ **d'essayage** fitting room
cabinet [kabinɛ] *m* **1.** *pl* (*toilettes*) toilet; **être aux ~s** to be in the toilet **2.** (*bureau: d'un médecin*) surgery *Brit,* office *Am;* (*d'un avocat*) chambers *pl* **3.** POL cabinet **4.** (*endroit isolé*) ~ **particulier** private dining room; ~ **de toilette** bathroom; ~ **de travail** study
câble [kɑbl] *m* **1.** (*corde*) cable; **poser un** ~ to lay a cable; ~ **métallique** wire cable; ~ **du téléphone** telephone line **2.** TV cable television
câblé(e) [kɑble] *adj* cabled; **être** ~ *inf* to have cable
câbler [kɑble] <1> *vt* **1.** (*transmettre*) to cable **2.** TV to link up to the cable network
câblodistribution [kɑblɔdistʀibysjɔ̃] *f*

cable broadcasting

cabossé(e) [kabɔse] *adj* bashed-in

cabosser [kabɔse] <1> *vt* to dent

caboteur [kabɔtœʀ] *m* coaster

cabotin(e) [kabɔtɛ̃, in] **I.** *adj inf* theatrical **II.** *m(f) inf* **1.** show-off **2.** THEAT, CINE ham (actor)

cabrer [kabʀe] *vpr* **se ~** (*cheval*) to rear up

cabri [kabʀi] *m* kid; **sauter comme un ~** to gambol like a lamb

cabriole [kabʀijɔl] *f* capering; (*d'un danseur*) cabriole; (*d'un cheval*) capriole

cabriolet [kabʀijɔlɛ] *m* AUTO convertible

CAC [kak] *m abr de* **Compagnie des agents de change l'indice: ~ 40** CAC index (*Paris stock exchange index*)

caca [kaka] *m enfantin, inf* **faire ~** to do a pooh *Brit,* to go number two *Am* ►**~ d'oie** greenish-yellow

cacahouète, cacahuète [kakawɛt] *f* peanut

cacao [kakao] *m* cocoa

cacatoès [kakatɔɛs] *m* cockatoo

cachalot [kaʃalo] *m* sperm whale

cache [kaʃ] *m* **1.** PHOT, CINE mask; **mettre un ~ sur qc** to cover up sth **2.** INFOR memory

cache-cache [kaʃkaʃ] *m inv* hide-and-seek **cache-col** [kaʃkɔl] *m inv* scarf

cachemire [kaʃmiʀ] **I.** *m* cashmere **II.** *app* **motif ~** paisley pattern

cache-nez [kaʃne] *m inv* scarf **cache-pot** [kaʃpo] <cache-pots> *m* flowerpot holder **cache-prise** [kaʃpʀiz] <cache-prise(s)> *m* socket cover

cacher¹ [kaʃe] <1> **I.** *vt* to hide; **~ qc à qn** to hide [*o* conceal *Am*] sth from sb **II.** *vpr* **1.** (*se dissimuler*) **se ~** to hide; **va te ~!** get out of my sight! **2.** (*être introuvable*) **mais où se cache le directeur?** where's the director hiding? **3.** (*tenir secret*) **ne pas se ~ de qc** to make no secret of sth

cacher² [kaʃɛʀ] *adj v.* **casher**

cache-sexe [kaʃsɛks] <cache-sexe(s)> *m* G-string

cachet [kaʃɛ] *m* **1.** MED tablet **2.** (*tampon*) stamp **3.** (*rétribution*) fee ►**avoir du ~** to have style

cacheter [kaʃte] <3> *vt* to seal

cachette [kaʃɛt] *f* hiding-place ►**en ~** on the sly; **en ~ de qn** unknown to sb; (*en cas d'action répréhensible*) behind sb's back

cachot [kaʃo] *m* (*cellule*) dungeon

cachotterie [kaʃɔtʀi] *f gén pl* secretiveness; **faire des ~s à qn** to be secretive about sth to sb

cachottier, -ière [kaʃɔtje, -jɛʀ] **I.** *adj* secretive **II.** *m, f* secretive person

cachou [kaʃu] *m* cachou

cacophonie [kakɔfɔni] *f* cacophony

cactus [kaktys] *m* cactus

c.-à-d. *abr de* **c'est-à-dire** i.e.

cadastre [kadastʀ] *m* **1.** (*registre*) land register **2.** (*service*) land registry

cadavérique [kadaveʀik] *adj* (*teint*) deathly; **rigidité ~** rigor mortis; **être d'une pâleur ~** to be deathly pale

cadavre [kadɑvʀ] *m* (*d'une personne*) corpse; (*d'un animal*) carcass ►**être un ~ ambulant** *inf* to be a walking skeleton

caddie [kadi] *m* SPORT caddie

cadeau [kado] <x> *m* present; **faire ~ de qc à qn** to give sth as a present to sb; **en ~** as a present

cadenas [kadnɑ] *m* padlock

cadenassé(e) [kadnase] *adj* padlocked

cadence [kadɑ̃s] *f* **1.** (*rythme*) rhythm; **marquer la ~** to beat time; **en ~** in time **2.** (*vitesse*) rate

cadencé(e) [kadɑ̃se] *adj* rhythmical; **au pas ~** in quick time

cadet(te) [kadɛ, ɛt] **I.** *adj* **1.** (*le plus jeune*) youngest **2.** (*plus jeune que qn*) younger **II.** *m(f)* **1.** (*dernier-né*) youngest child; **le ~ des garçons** the youngest boy **2.** (*plus jeune que qn*) younger child; **c'est ma ~te** that's my younger sister; **elle est ma ~te de trois mois** she's three months younger than me **3.** SPORT *15–17 year old sportsperson* **4.** MIL, HIST cadet ►**c'est le ~ de mes soucis** it's the least of my worries

cadrage [kɑdʀaʒ] *m* centring *Brit,* centering *Am*

cadran [kadʀɑ̃] *m* **1.** (*affichage*) dial; (*d'un baromètre*) face; **~ solaire** sundial **2.** *Québec, inf* (*réveil*) alarm (clock)

cadre [kɑdʀ] **I.** *m* **1.** (*encadrement*) *a.* INFOR frame; **mettre un tableau dans un ~** to frame a picture **2.** (*environnement*) surroundings *pl;* **dans un ~ de verdure** in a country setting **3.** (*limites*) scope; **cela entre bien dans le ~ de qc** that's well within the scope of sth; **dans le ~ de qc** within the context of sth **II.** *mf* executive; **~ moyen/supérieur** middle ranking/senior executive

cadré(e) [kadʀe] *adj* **photo bien/mal ~e** properly/badly composed picture

cadrer [kɑdʀe] <1> **I.** *vi* **~ avec qc** to tally with sth **II.** *vt* to centre *Brit,* to center *Am*

cadreur [kɑdʀœʀ] *m* cameraman

caduc, caduque [kadyk] *adj* **1.** (*périmé*) obsolete **2.** BOT deciduous

caennais(e) [kanɛ, ɛz] *adj* of Caen; *v. a.* **ajaccien**

Caennais(e) [kanɛ, ɛz] *m(f)* person from Caen; *v. a.* **Ajaccien**

CAF [kaf] *f abr de* **caisse d'allocations familiales** family allowance centre

cafard [kafaʀ] *m* **1.** (*insecte*) cockroach **2.** (*spleen*) depression; **avoir le ~** to be down in the dumps; **donner le ~ à qn** to get sb down

cafardeux, -euse [kafaʀdø, -øz] *adj* gloomy

café [kafe] *m* **1.** (*boisson*) coffee; **~ crème/serré** white/strong coffee; **~ liégeois** coffee ice cream; **~ au lait** café au lait **2.** (*établisse-*

ment) café; ~ **avec terrasse** street café; ~ **électronique** Internet café **3.** (*plante*) coffee bush; ~ **en grains** coffee beans **4.** (*moment du repas*) **au** ~ at the end of the meal **5.** *Suisse* (*dîner*) **un** ~ **complet** dinner

> If you ask for a **café** in France, you will be served an expresso. Adding a little milk will change the expresso into "une noisette". If you want a large cup of coffee with milk, you must ask for a "café crème". Milk is always added to coffee before it is served and is never served separately.

café-concert [kafekɔ̃sɛʀ] <cafés-concerts> *m: cabaret during which drinks are served*

caféine [kafein] *f* caffeine

café-restaurant [kafeʀɛstɔʀɑ̃] <cafés-restaurants> *m: café serving light meals*
café-tabac [kafetaba] <cafés-tabacs> *m: café and tobacconist's in one*

cafétéria [kafeteʀja] *f* cafeteria

café-théâtre [kafeteɑtʀ] <cafés-théâtres> *m: little theatre in which drinks are served*

cafetière [kaftjɛʀ] *f* coffee pot; ~ **électrique** coffee machine

cafouiller [kafuje] <1> *vi inf* **1.** (*agir avec confusion*) to fumble **2.** (*s'embrouiller: discussion, organisation*) to get into a muddle; ~ **dans qc** (*personne*) to get mixed up in sth **3.** (*mal foncionner: moteur*) to misfire; (*appareil*) to go on the blink

cage [kaʒ] *f* **1.** (*pour enfermer*) cage; ~ **à lapin** (rabbit) hutch; *péj, inf* (*H.L.M.*) high-rise flat *Brit,* apartment in the projects *Am* **2.** SPORT goal **3.** ANAT ~ **thoracique** rib cage **4.** TECH ~ **d'ascenseur** lift shaft *Brit,* elevator shaft *Am;* ~ **d'escalier** stairwell

cageot [kaʒo] *m* **1.** (*emballage*) crate **2.** *inf* (*fille*) dog

cagette [kaʒɛt] *f* crate

cagibi [kaʒibi] *m* junk room

cagne [kaɲ] *f v.* **khâgne**

cagnotte [kaɲɔt] *f* **1.** (*caisse*) kitty **2.** *inf* (*économies*) nest egg

cagoule [kagul] *f* **1.** (*couvre-chef*) balaclava **2.** (*masque*) mask **3.** (*capuchon*) hood

cahier [kaje] *m* **1.** ECOLE notebook; ~ **de brouillon** roughbook *Brit,* scratchpad *Am;* ~ **d'exercices** workbook; ~ **de textes** homework notebook **2.** TYP section **3.** *pl* (*publication*) journal

cahin-caha [kaɛ̃kaa] *adv inf* to hobble along; **se déplacer** ~ to hobble around

cahot [kao] *m* jolt

cahoter [kaɔte] <1> *vt, vi* to jolt; **être cahoté de ville en ville** to be shunt around from town to town

cahoteux, -euse [kaɔtø, -øz] *adj* **chemin** ~ bumpy road

cahute [kayt] *f* shack

caïd [kaid] *m* **1.** *inf* (*meneur*) boss **2.** *inf* (*ponte*) big shot

caille [kaj] *f* (*oiseau*) quail

cailler [kaje] <1> **I.** *vi* **1.** (*coaguler: lait*) to curdle; (*sang*) to coagulate **2.** *inf* (*avoir froid*) to be freezing **II.** *vt* to curdle **III.** *vpr* **se** ~ **1.** (*se coaguler: lait*) to curdle; (*sang*) to coagulate **2.** *inf* (*avoir froid: personne*) to be freezing

caillot [kajo] *m* (blood) clot

caillou [kaju] <x> *m* (*pierre*) pebble

caillouteux, -euse [kajutø, -øz] *adj* (*route*) stony; (*plage*) pebbly

caïman [kaimɑ̃] *m* ZOOL cayman

Caïman [kaimɑ̃] *fpl* **les îles** ~ Cayman Islands

Caire [kɛʀ] *m* **le** ~ Cairo

caisse [kɛs] *f* **1.** (*boîte*) box **2.** FIN (*dans un magasin*) cash desk; (*dans un supermarché*) checkout; (*dans une banque*) cashier's desk; ~ **enregistreuse** cash register; ~ **noire** slush fund; **faire la** [*o* **sa**] ~ to cash up; **tenir la** ~ to be the cashier; **passer à la** ~ to go to the cashier; ~ **d'épargne** savings bank **3.** (*organisme de gestion*) fund; ~ **d'assurance maladie** medical insurance company **4.** (*boîtier: d'une horloge*) casing; (*d'un tambour*) soundbox; (*d'une voiture*) bodywork; **grosse** ~ big drum **5.** *inf* (*voiture*) car ▶**avoir une** ~ *Suisse* (*être ivre*) to be tanked up; **prendre une** ~ *Suisse* (*s'ennivrer*) to get tanked up; **à fond la** ~ *inf* at full tilt

caissette [kɛsɛt] *f* (small) box

caissier, -ière [kesje, -jɛʀ] *m, f* cashier

cajoler [kaʒɔle] <1> *vt* (*câliner*) to cuddle; ~ **qn pour obtenir qc** to coax sth out of sb

cajolerie [kaʒɔlʀi] *f gén pl* tender words

cajoleur, -euse [kaʒɔlœʀ, -øz] *adj* loving; (*voix*) wheedling

cajou [kaʒu] *m* cashew

cake [kɛk] *m* fruit cake

calaisien(ne) [kalɛzjɛ̃, ɛn] *adj* of Calais; *v. a.* **ajaccien**

Calaisien(ne) [kalɛzjɛ̃, ɛn] *m(f)* person from Calais; *v. a.* **Ajaccien**

calamar [kalamaʀ] *m* squid

calamité [kalamite] *f* calamity

calanque [kalɑ̃k] *f* rocky inlet

calcaire [kalkɛʀ] **I.** *adj* chalky; (*roche, relief*) limestone **II.** *m* GEO limestone

calciné(e) [kalsine] *adj* charred

calcium [kalsjɔm] *m* calcium

calcul[1] [kalkyl] *m* **1.** (*opération*) calculation; **faire le** ~ **de** to calculate; **faire une erreur de** ~ [*o* **un mauvais** ~] to miscalculate; ~ **mental** mental arithmetic **2.** (*arithmétique*) ~ **algébrique** algebra; ~ **différentiel/intégral** differential/integral calculus **3.** *pl* (*estimation*) calculations; **faire rentrer qc dans ses ~s** to take sth into account

calcul[2] [kalkyl] *m* MED stone

calculatrice [kalkylatʀis] *f* calculator; ~ **de poche** pocket calculator

calculer [kalkyle] <1> **I.** *vi* **1.** MAT ~ **men-**

talement to calculate in one's head 2. (*compter ses sous*) to economize; ~ **au plus juste** to calculate down to the last penny II. *vt* 1. (*déterminer par le calcul*) to calculate 2. (*évaluer, prévoir: risque*) to gauge; (*chances*) to weigh up; **tout bien calculé** all things considered 3. (*étudier: attitude*) to study; (*geste*) to calculate

calculette [kalkylɛt] *f* pocket calculator

cale[1] [kal] *f* NAUT hold; **être/mettre en ~ sèche** to be in/put into dry dock; ~ **de chargement** slipway

cale[2] [kal] *f* (*coin*) wedge

calé(e) [kale] *adj inf* (*fort*) knowledgeable; **être ~ en qc** to be an ace at sth

calèche [kalɛʃ] *f* barouche

caleçon [kalsɔ̃] *m* 1. (*pour homme*) boxer shorts *pl;* ~ **de bain** swimming trunks *pl;* **des ~s longs** long johns *pl* 2. (*pour femme*) leggings *pl*

calédonien(ne) [kaledɔnjɛ̃, ɛn] *adj* Caledonian

Calédonien(ne) [kaledɔnjɛ̃, ɛn] *m(f)* Caledonian

calembour [kalɑ̃buʀ] *m* pun; **faire un ~** to pun

calendrier [kalɑ̃dʀije] *m* 1. (*almanach*) calendar 2. (*programme*) schedule; ~ **des examens** exam timetable

cale-pied [kalpje] <cale-pieds> *m* toe clip

calepin [kalpɛ̃] *m* 1. notebook 2. *Belgique* (*cartable porté à la main*) briefcase; (*sur le dos*) satchel

caler [kale] <1> I. *vi* 1. AUTO to stall 2. *inf* (*être rassasié*) to be filled up II. *vt* 1. (*fixer avec une cale*) to wedge; (*roue*) to chock 2. (*rendre stable*) ~ **un malade** to prop up a patient 3. AUTO to stall III. *vpr* **se ~ dans un fauteuil** to settle into an armchair

calfeutrer [kalføtʀe] <1> I. *vt* to stop up II. *vpr* **se ~** to shut oneself away; (*rester au chaud*) to make oneself cosy

calibre [kalibʀ] *m a. fig* calibre *Brit,* caliber *Am;* (*des fruits, œufs*) grade; **un fusil de gros ~** a large-bore rifle

calice [kalis] *m* 1. ANAT, BOT calyx 2. REL chalice ►**boire le ~ jusqu'à la <u>lie</u>** to drink the cup down to the last drop

calife [kalif] *m* caliph

Californie [kalifɔʀni] *f* **la ~** California

californien(ne) [kalifɔʀnjɛ̃, ɛn] *adj* Californian

califourchon [kalifuʀʃɔ̃] **à ~** astride; **monter à ~** to ride astride

câlin(e) [kɑlɛ̃, in] I. *adj* 1. (*qui aime les caresses*) cuddly 2. (*caressant*) tender II. *m* cuddle; **faire un ~ à qn** *inf* to give sb a cuddle

câliner [kɑline] <1> *vt* ~ **qn** to cuddle sb

calleux, -euse [kalø, -øz] *adj* (*peau*) calloused

call-girl [kolgœʀl] <call-girls> *f* call girl

calligraphie [ka(l)ligʀafi] *f* calligraphy

calmant(e) [kalmɑ̃, ɑ̃t] I. *adj* 1. (*tranquilisant*) tranquillizing *Brit,* tranquilizing; **tisane ~e** soothing herbal tea 2. (*antidouleur*) painkilling II. *m* 1. (*tranquilisant*) tranquillizer *Brit,* tranquilizer *Am* 2. (*antidouleur*) painkiller

calmar [kalmaʀ] *m v.* **calamar**

calme [kalm] I. *adj* calm; (*lieu*) quiet II. *m* 1. (*sérénité*) calmness; **rester ~** to remain calm; **du ~!** calm down! 2. (*tranquillité*) quietness; **du ~!** quiet! 3. METEO calm ►**le ~ avant la <u>tempête</u>** the calm before the storm; ~ **<u>plat</u>** dead calm; ECON lull; *fig* dead quiet

calmement [kalməmɑ̃] *adv* calmly

calmer [kalme] <1> I. *vt* 1. (*apaiser: personne, esprits*) to calm (down); (*discussion*) to tone down 2. (*soulager: douleur*) to soothe; (*colère, nerfs*) to calm; (*fièvre*) to bring down; (*impatience*) to curb; ~ **la faim de qn** to take the edge off sb's hunger II. *vpr* **se ~** to calm down; (*discussion*) to quiet down; (*tempête*) to die down; (*crainte*) to subside

calmos [kalmos] *interj inf* cool it!

calomnie [kalɔmni] *f* calumny

calomnier [kalɔmnje] <1a> *vt* to slander

calomnieux, -euse [kalɔmnjø, -jøz] *adj* slanderous

calorie [kalɔʀi] *f* calorie

calorifique [kalɔʀifik] *adj* calorific

calorique [kalɔʀik] *adj* high-calorie

calot [kalo] *m* 1. (*coiffure*) forage cap 2. (*bille*) alley

calotte [kalɔt] *f* 1. *inf* (*gifle*) slap 2. ANAT ~ **crânienne** top of the skull 3. GEO ~ **glaciaire** icecap

calque [kalk] *m* 1. (*copie*) tracing 2. (*papier*) tracing paper

calumet [kalymɛ] *m* peace pipe; **fumer le ~ de la paix avec qn** to make (one's) peace with sb

calva [kalva] *m inf,* **calvados** [kalvados] *m* calvados

calvaire [kalvɛʀ] *m* 1. (*épreuve*) ordeal 2. (*croix*) wayside cross 3. (*peinture*) Calvary

calvinisme [kalvinism] *m* Calvinism

calvitie [kalvisi] *f* 1. (*tonsure*) bald patch 2. (*phénomène*) baldness

camaïeu [kamajø] <x> *m* monochrome

camarade [kamaʀad] *mf* 1. (*collègue*) colleague; ~ **d'études** fellow student 2. POL comrade

camaraderie [kamaʀadʀi] *f* companionship

Camargue [kamaʀg] *f* **la ~** the Camargue

Cambodge [kɑ̃bɔdʒ] *m* **le ~** Cambodia

cambodgien(ne) [kɑ̃bɔdʒɛ̃, ɛn] *adj* Cambodian

Cambodgien(ne) [kɑ̃bɔdʒɛ̃, ɛn] *m(f)* Cambodian

cambouis [kɑ̃bwi] *m* dirty grease

cambré(e) [kɑ̃bʀe] *adj* **être très ~** (*personne*) to have a very arched back

cambriolage [kɑ̃bʀijɔlaʒ] *m* burglary

cambrioler [kɑ̃bʀijɔle] <1> *vt* ~ **qc** to burgle *Brit,* to burglarize *Am;* **qn se fait ~** sb is

burgled
cambrioleur, -euse [kɑ̃bʀijɔlœʀ, -øz] *m, f* burglar
cambrousse [kɑ̃bʀus] *f inf* country; **en pleine** ~ in the middle of nowhere; **débarquer de sa** ~ to arrive from the sticks
came [kam] *f inf* (*drogue*) junk
camé(e) [kame] *m(f) inf* junkie
caméléon [kameleɔ̃] *m* chameleon
camélia [kamelja] *m* camellia
camelot [kamlo] *m* pedlar
camelote [kamlɔt] *f inf* junk
camembert [kamɑ̃bɛʀ] *m* **1.** (*fromage*) Camembert **2.** ECON pie chart
camer [kame] <1> *vpr inf* **se** ~ to be on drugs
caméra [kameʀa] *f* camera
caméraman <s *o* -men> [kameʀaman, -mɛn] *m* cameraman
Cameroun [kamʀun] *m* **le** ~ Cameroon
camerounais(e) [kamʀunɛ, ɛz] *adj* Cameroonian
Camerounais(e) [kamʀunɛ, ɛz] *m(f)* Cameroonian
caméscope [kameskɔp] *m* camcorder
camion [kamjɔ̃] *m* lorry *Brit,* truck *Am*
camion-citerne [kamjɔ̃sitɛʀn] <camions-citernes> *m* tanker
camionnette [kamjɔnɛt] *f* van, pick-up
camionneur [kamjɔnœʀ] *m* lorry driver *Brit,* truck driver *Am*
camomille [kamɔmij] *f* **1.** (*fleur*) camomile **2.** (*tisane*) camomile tea
camouflage [kamuflaʒ] *m* MIL **1.** (*résultat*) camouflage **2.** (*action*) camouflaging
camoufler [kamufle] <1> *vt* **1.** MIL to camouflage **2.** (*tenir secret*) to conceal
camp [kɑ̃] *m* **1.** camp; **lever le** ~ to strike camp; *fig* to leave; ~ **de concentration** concentration camp **2.** *Québec* (*chalet, villa*) ~ (**d'été**) villa ►**ficher** [*o* **foutre**] **le** ~ *inf* to take off, to clear off *Brit;* **fiche-moi le** ~**!** *inf* beat it!
campagnard(e) [kɑ̃paɲaʀ, aʀd] **I.** *adj* (*vie*) country; (*manières*) rustic **II.** *m(f)* countryman, countrywoman *m, f*
campagne [kɑ̃paɲ] *f* **1.** (*opp: ville*) country; **à la** ~ in the country; **en pleine** ~ in the countryside **2.** (*paysage*) countryside; **en rase** ~ in the open countryside **3.** *a.* MIL campaign; ~ **électorale/publicitaire** election/advertising campaign
campagnol [kɑ̃paɲɔl] *m* vole
campanule [kɑ̃panyl] *f* campanula
campement [kɑ̃pmɑ̃] *m* **1.** (*résultat*) camp **2.** (*action*) camping
camper [kɑ̃pe] <1> **I.** *vi* to camp **II.** *vpr* **se** ~ **devant qn/qc** to plant oneself firmly in front of sb/sth
campeur, -euse [kɑ̃pœʀ, -øz] *m, f* camper
camping [kɑ̃piŋ] *m* **1.** (*action de camper*) camping; **faire du** ~ to go camping **2.** (*lieu*) (**terrain de**) ~ campsite *Brit,* campground *Am*
camping-car [kɑ̃piŋkaʀ] <camping-cars> *m* Dormobile® *Brit,* motorhome *Am*
camping-gaz® [kɑ̃piŋgɑz] *m inv* camping stove
campus [kɑ̃pys] *m* campus
canada [kanada] *f Québec* (*variété de pomme de reinette*) canada (*type of russet*)
Canada [kanada] *m* **le** ~ Canada
Canadair® [kanadɛʀ] *m* fire-fighting aircraft
canadien(ne) [kanadjɛ̃, jɛn] *adj* Canadian
Canadien(ne) [kanadjɛ̃, jɛn] *m(f)* Canadian
canadienne [kanadjɛn] *f* **1.** (*veste*) *sheepskin-lined jacket* **2.** (*tente*) ridge tent
canaille [kanɑj] **I.** *adj* (*air, manière*) coarse **II.** *f a. iron* rascal
canal [kanal, o] <-aux> *m* **1.** canal **2.** *Québec* (*chaîne*) ~ **de télévision** television channel
canalisation [kanalizasjɔ̃] *f* **1.** (*réseau*) mains *pl* **2.** (*tuyau*) pipe
canaliser [kanalize] <1> *vt* **1.** (*rendre navigable*) to canalize **2.** (*centraliser: énergie, foule*) to channel
canapé [kanape] *m* **1.** (*meuble*) sofa; ~ **convertible** sofa bed **2.** GASTR canapé
canapé-lit [kanapeli] <canapés-lits> *m* sofa bed
canard [kanaʀ] *m* **1.** (*oiseau*) duck **2.** (*opp: cane*) drake **3.** *inf* (*journal*) rag **4.** MUS **faire un** ~ to play a false note
canari [kanaʀi] **I.** *adj inv* **jaune** ~ canary yellow **II.** *m* canary
canasson [kanasɔ̃] *m péj* nag
cancan [kɑ̃kɑ̃] *m* **1.** *pl* (*racontars*) gossip **2.** (*danse*) **french** ~ cancan
cancer [kɑ̃sɛʀ] *m* cancer; ~ **généralisé** *cancer which has metastasized;* **avoir un** ~ **du sang/du sein** to have leukaemia/breast cancer
Cancer [kɑ̃sɛʀ] *m* Cancer; *v. a.* **Balance**
cancéreux, -euse [kɑ̃seʀø, -øz] **I.** *adj* cancerous **II.** *m, f: person with cancer*
cancérigène [kɑ̃seʀiʒɛn] *adj,* **cancérogène** [kɑ̃seʀɔʒɛn] *adj* carcinogenic
cancérologue [kɑ̃seʀɔlɔg] *mf* oncologist
cancre [kɑ̃kʀ] *m inf* dunce
candélabre [kɑ̃delɑbʀ] *m* candelabra
candeur [kɑ̃dœʀ] *f* naivety
candi [kɑ̃di] *adj v.* **sucre**
candidat(e) [kɑ̃dida, at] *m(f)* **1.** (*à un examen, un jeu, aux élections*) candidate **2.** (*à un poste*) applicant; **être** ~ **à un poste** to be an applicant for a job
candidature [kɑ̃didatyʀ] *f* **1.** (*aux élections*) candidature *Brit,* candidacy *Am;* **poser sa** ~ **aux élections** to stand in an election **2.** (*à un poste, un jeu*) application; ~ **spontanée** unsolicited application; **poser sa** ~ **à un poste** to apply for a job
candide [kɑ̃did] *adj* **1.** (*ingénu*) ingenuous **2.** *péj* (*crédule*) gullible
cane [kan] *f* (*opp: mâle*) (female) duck
caneton [kantɔ̃] *m* duckling
canette [kanɛt] *f* **1.** (*bouteille*) small bottle

2. (*bobine*) spool

canevas [kanva] *m* 1. (*toile*) canvas 2. (*esquisse*) framework

caniche [kaniʃ] *m* poodle

caniculaire [kanikylɛʀ] *adj* (*chaleur*) scorching

canicule [kanikyl] *f* 1. (*période*) dog days 2. (*chaleur*) scorching heat

canidés [kanide] *mpl* dog family + *vb sing*

canif [kanif] *m* penknife

canin(e) [kanɛ̃, in] *adj* **races ~es** dog species

canine [kanin] *f* canine

caniveau [kanivo] <x> *m* gutter

cannabis [kanabis] *m* cannabis

canne [kan] *f* 1. (*bâton*) (walking) stick 2. (*tige*) **~ à sucre** sugar cane 3. (*gaule*) **~ à pêche** fishing rod

cannelle [kanɛl] *f* cinnamon

canner [kane] <1> *vt Québec, inf* (*mettre en boîtes de conserve*) to can

cannibale [kanibal] I. *adj* cannibal; **toast ~** *Belgique* (*steak tartare*) steak tartare II. *mf* cannibal

canoë [kanɔe] *m* 1. (*embarcation*) canoe 2. (*sport*) canoeing

canoë-kayak [kanɔekajak] <canoës-kayaks> *m* canoeing; **faire du ~** to go canoeing

canon [kanɔ̃] I. *adj inv, inf* **super ~** fantastic II. *m* 1. (*arme*) gun; HIST cannon 2. (*tube: d'un fusil*) barrel 3. (*machine*) **~ à neige** snow cannon

canoniser [kanɔnize] <1> *vt* to canonize

canonnade [kanɔnad] *f* canonnade; (*bruit*) gunfire

canot [kano] *m* 1. (small) boat; **~ pneumatique/à moteur/de sauvetage** rubber dingy/motor boat/lifeboat 2. *Québec* (*canoë*) canoe

canotage [kanɔtaʒ] *m* boating; **faire du ~** to go boating

canoter [kanɔte] <1> *vi* 1. to go boating 2. *Québec* (*faire du canot*) to go canoeing

cantal [kantal] <s> *m* cantal (*hard full-flavoured cheese*)

cantate [kɑ̃tat] *f* cantata

cantatrice [kɑ̃tatʀis] *f* opera singer

cantine [kɑ̃tin] *f* canteen

cantique [kɑ̃tik] *m* hymn

canton [kɑ̃tɔ̃] *m* 1. (*en France*) ≈ district 2. (*en Suisse*) canton

cantonade [kɑ̃tɔnad] *f* **crier qc à la ~** to call out (for all to hear)

cantonais(e) [kɑ̃tɔnɛ, ɛz] *adj* **riz ~** fried rice

cantonal(e) [kɑ̃tɔnal, o] <-aux> I. *adj* 1. (*en France*) **élections ~es** ≈ district elections 2. (*en Suisse*) cantonal II. *fpl* by-election

cantonnement [kɑ̃tɔnmɑ̃] *m* 1. (*action*) billeting 2. (*campement*) billet

cantonner [kɑ̃tɔne] <1> I. *vt* (*reléguer*) **~ qn dans qc** to confine sb to sth II. *vpr* 1. (*s'isoler*) **se ~ chez soi** to stay cooped up at home; **se ~ dans le silence** to remain silent 2. (*se limiter*) **se ~ dans qc** to confine oneself to sth

cantonnier [kɑ̃tɔnje] *m* roadworker, roadmender *Brit*

canular [kanylaʀ] *m inf* hoax

canyon [kanjɔn] *m* canyon

CAO [seao] *abr de* **conception assistée par ordinateur** CAD

caoutchouc [kautʃu] *m* 1. (*matière*) rubber 2. (*élastique*) rubber band 3. (*plante*) rubber plant

caoutchouteux, -euse [kautʃutø, -øz] *adj* rubbery

cap [kap] *m* 1. (*pointe de terre*) cape 2. (*direction*) course; **mettre le ~ sur qc** to head for sth

Cap [kap] *m* **Le ~** Cape Town; **~ canaveral** Cape Canaveral

CAP [seape] *m abr de* **certificat d'aptitude professionnelle** *vocational training certificate*

capable [kapabl] *adj* capable

capacité [kapasite] *f* 1. (*contenance, puissance*) *a.* INFOR capacity 2. (*faculté*) ability; **posséder une grande ~ de travail** to be very hard-working 3. ECOLE **~ en droit** *basic legal qualification*

cape [kap] *f* (*vêtement*) cape ►**rire sous ~** to laugh up one's sleeve

CAPES [kapɛs] *m abr de* **certificat d'aptitude au professorat de l'enseignement secondaire** *secondary school teaching certificate*

> The **CAPES** is a state exam. Teachers with a CAPES can teach in a secondary school ("collège"). They are continuously assessed and must teach 18 hours a week. The test follows a year as a student teacher.

CAPET [kapɛt] *m abr de* **certificat d'aptitude au professorat de l'enseignement technique** *secondary school teacher certificate*

capillaire [kapilɛʀ] I. *adj* 1. (*pour les cheveux*) **lotion ~** hair lotion 2. ANAT **vaisseau ~** capillary vessel II. *m* ANAT capillary

capitaine [kapitɛn] *m* 1. MIL, NAUT, SPORT captain; **"mon ~"** yes sir; **~ des pompiers** fire chief 2. AVIAT flight lieutenant *Brit*, flight captain *Am*

capital [kapital, o] <-aux> *m* 1. (*somme d'argent*) capital; **société anonyme au ~ de 25 millions d'euros** limited company with a capital of 25 million euros 2. *pl* FIN capital 3. (*richesse*) **~ artistique/intellectuel** artistic/intellectual wealth

capital(e) [kapital, o] <-aux> *adj* fundamental; **attacher une importance ~e à qc** to consider sth to be of utmost importance

capitale [kapital] *f* 1. (*ville*) capital (city) 2. (*lettre*) capital; **en ~s d'imprimerie** in block capitals

capitalisme [kapitalism] *m* capitalism
capitaliste [kapitalist] **I.** *adj* capitalist(ic) **II.** *mf* capitalist; **gros ~** major capitalist
capiteux, **-euse** [kapitø, -øz] *adj* (*parfum, vin*) heady; (*beauté, femme, regard*) sensuous
capitonné(e) [kapitɔne] *adj* **fauteuil ~** padded armchair
capitulation [kapitylasjɔ̃] *f a.* MIL capitulation
capituler [kapityle] <1> *vi* to capitulate
caporal [kapɔʀal, o] <-aux> *m* corporal
caporal-chef [kapɔʀalʃɛf] <caporaux-chefs> *m* lance corporal *Brit,* private first class *Am*
capot [kapo] *m* AUTO bonnet *Brit,* hood *Am*
capote [kapɔt] *f* **1.** AUTO (*d'une voiture*) top **2.** (*manteau*) greatcoat **3.** *inf* (*préservatif*) **~ (anglaise)** rubber, French letter *Brit*
capoter [kapɔte] <1> *vi inf* **1.** (*se retourner: auto, avion*) to overturn **2.** (*échouer: projet, entreprise*) to come to grief; **faire ~ qc** to scupper sth, to ruin sth
câpre [kɑpʀ] *f* caper
caprice [kapʀis] *m* **1.** (*fantaisie*) whim; **passer à qn tous ses ~s** to indulge sb's every whim **2.** (*amourette*) passing fancy **3.** *pl* (*changement*) vagaries **4.** (*exigence d'un enfant*) **faire un ~** to throw a tantrum
capricieux, **-euse** [kapʀisjø, -jøz] *adj* **1.** (*instable: personne*) capricious **2.** (*irrégulier: chose*) unreliable; (*temps*) unpredictable
Capricorne [kapʀikɔʀn] *m* Capricorn; *v. a.* **Balance**
capsule [kapsyl] *f* **1.** (*bouchon: d'une bouteille*) cap **2.** (*médicament*) capsule **3.** AVIAT **~ spatiale** space capsule
capter [kapte] <1> *vt* **1.** (*canaliser: source*) to harness; (*énergie*) to capture **2.** (*recevoir: émission, message*) to get **3.** (*chercher à obtenir*) **~ l'attention de qn** to catch sb's attention
captif, **-ive** [kaptif, -iv] **I.** *adj* captive **II.** *m, f* captive
captivant(e) [kaptivɑ̃, ɑ̃t] *adj* captivating
captiver [kaptive] <1> *vt* to captivate
captivité [kaptivite] *f* captivity
capture [kaptyʀ] *f* **1.** (*action*) capture **2.** (*proie*) catch
capturer [kaptyʀe] <1> *vt* to capture
capuche [kapyʃ] *f* hood
capuchon [kapyʃɔ̃] *m* **1.** (*capuche*) hood **2.** (*bouchon*) cap
capucine [kapysin] *f* **1.** BOT nasturtium **2.** REL Capuchin nun
caquet [kakɛ] *m* gossip ►**rabattre** [*o* **rabaisser**] **le ~ à qn** *inf* to take sb down a peg or two
caqueter [kakte] <3> *vi* (*poule*) to cluck; (*personne*) to gossip
car[1] [kaʀ] *m* coach *Brit,* bus *Am;* **~ de ramassage scolaire** school bus
car[2] [kaʀ] *conj* because, for
carabine [kaʀabin] *f* rifle; **~ à air comprimé** air rifle
caracoler [kaʀakɔle] <1> *vi* **1.** (*cheval*) to prance; (*cavalier*) to caracole **2.** (*s'agiter: enfants*) to dance around **3.** (*être largement en tête*) **~ en tête de la course** to be way out in front
caractère [kaʀaktɛʀ] *m* **1.** (*tempérament, nature*) nature; **avoir un ~ de cochon** *inf* to have a foul temper; **ce n'est pas dans son ~ de** +*infin* it's not like him/her to +*infin;* **présenter tous les ~s de qc** to show all the signs of sth **2.** (*fermeté, personne, symbole*) character; **avoir beaucoup de ~** to have lots of character; **~s d'imprimerie** block capitals; **en ~s gras/italiques** in bold type/italics **3.** (*cachet*) **sans ~** characterless
caractériel(le) [kaʀakteʀjɛl] **I.** *adj* (*personne*) emotionally disturbed; **des troubles ~s** emotional problems **II.** *m(f)* disturbed person [*o* child]
caractériser [kaʀakteʀize] <1> **I.** *vt* **1.** (*être typique de qn*) to be characteristic of sb; **avec la franchise qui le caractérise** with his characteristic frankness **2.** (*définir*) to characterize **II.** *vpr* **se ~ par qc** to be characterized by sth
caractéristique [kaʀakteʀistik] **I.** *adj* **être ~ de qn/qc** to be characteristic of sb/sth **II.** *f* characteristic; **~s techniques** design features
carafe [kaʀaf] *f* carafe
Caraïbes [kaʀaib] *fpl* **les ~** the Caribbean
carambolage [kaʀɑ̃bɔlaʒ] *m* pile-up
caramel [kaʀamɛl] *m* **1.** (*bonbon*) toffee **2.** (*substance*) caramel
caramélisé(e) [kaʀamelize] *adj* caramelized
caraméliser [kaʀamelize] <1> **I.** *vt* **1.** (*recouvrir*) to coat with caramel **2.** (*cuire: sucre*) to caramelize **II.** *vi, vpr* to caramelize
carapace [kaʀapas] *f* **1.** (*d'un crabe, d'une tortue*) shell **2.** (*couche: de boue*) crust; (*de glace*) sheath **3.** (*protection morale*) shield
caravane [kaʀavan] *f* caravan *Brit,* trailer *Am*
caravelle [kaʀavɛl] *f* caravel
carbonate [kaʀbɔnat] *m* carbonate
carbone [kaʀbɔn] *m* **1.** (*substance*) carbon **2.** (*papier*) carbon paper *no pl* **3.** (*copie*) carbon (copy)
carbonique [kaʀbɔnik] *adj* **gaz ~** carbon dioxide
carbonisé(e) [kaʀbɔnize] *adj* charred; **mourir ~** to be burned to death
carburant [kaʀbyʀɑ̃] *m* fuel
carburateur [kaʀbyʀatœʀ] *m* carburettor *Brit,* carburetor *Am*
carcan [kaʀkɑ̃] *m* **1.** HIST (*collier*) iron collar **2.** (*contrainte*) yoke
carcasse [kaʀkas] *f* **1.** (*squelette*) carcass **2.** *inf* (*corps*) **ma vieille ~** my (poor) old bones **3.** (*charpente: d'un bateau*) skeleton; (*d'un édifice*) frame
carcéral(e) [kaʀseʀal, o] <-aux> *adj* prison
cardiaque [kaʀdjak] **I.** *adj* **malaise ~** heart

trouble **II.** *mf: person suffering from a heart condition*

cardigan [kaʀdigɑ̃] *m* cardigan

cardinal [kaʀdinal, o] <-aux> *m* cardinal

cardinal(e) [kaʀdinal, o] <-aux> *adj* MAT cardinal

cardiologie [kaʀdjɔlɔʒi] *f* cardiology

cardiologue [kaʀdjɔlɔg] *mf* cardiologist

cardiovasculaire [kaʀdjovaskylɛʀ] *adj* cardiovascular

carême [kaʀɛm] *m* **1.** (*jeûne*) fast **2.** (*période*) Lent

carence [kaʀɑ̃s] *f* **1.** MED deficiency; ~ **alimentaire** nutritional deficiency; ~ **en fer/en protéines** iron/protein deficiency **2.** PSYCH ~ **affective** emotional deprivation **3.** (*impuissance: du pouvoir*) failing

caressant(e) [kaʀesɑ̃, ɑ̃t] *adj* (*personne*) affectionate; (*voix*) tender

caresse [kaʀɛs] *f* caress; **faire des ~s à qn/un animal** to caress sb/to pet an animal

caresser [kaʀese] <1> *vt* **1.** (*effleurer*) to caress **2.** *fig* ~ **une idée** to toy with an idea

cargaison [kaʀgɛzɔ̃] *f* **1.** (*chargement*) cargo **2.** *inf* (*grande quantité*) **des ~s d'histoires drôles** loads of funny stories

cargo [kaʀgo] *m* freighter

caribou [kaʀibu] *m* caribou

caricatural(e) [kaʀikatyʀal, o] <-aux> *adj* grotesque; (*exagéré*) caricatured

caricature [kaʀikatyʀ] *f* caricature; **faire la ~ de qn/qc** to caricature sb/sth

caricaturer [kaʀikatyʀe] <1> *vt* to caricature

caricaturiste [kaʀikatyʀist] *mf* caricaturist

carie [kaʀi] *f* MED caries; **avoir une** ~ to have a cavity

carié(e) [kaʀje] *adj* decayed; **avoir une dent ~e** to have a bad tooth

carillon [kaʀijɔ̃] *m* **1.** (*d'une église*) bells *pl* **2.** (*sonnerie: d'une horloge*) chimes *pl;* (*d'une porte d'entrée*) ring; ~ **électrique** electric chimes *pl* **3.** (*horloge*) chiming clock **4.** (*air*) chimes *pl*

carillonner [kaʀijɔne] <1> **I.** *vi* **1.** (*résonner: cloche*) to ring; (*horloge*) to chime **2.** (*sonner*) ~ **à la porte** to ring at the door **II.** *vt* ~ **toutes les heures/tous les quarts** (*horloge*) to chime on the hour/the quarter(hour)

caritatif, -ive [kaʀitatif, -iv] *adj* charitable

carlingue [kaʀlɛ̃g] *f* AVIAT cabin

carmin [kaʀmɛ̃] **I.** *adj inv* carmine **II.** *m* **1.** (*colorant*) cochineal **2.** (*couleur*) carmine

carnage [kaʀnaʒ] *m a. fig* carnage

carnassier, -ière [kaʀnasje, -jɛʀ] **I.** *adj* carnivorous **II.** *m* carnivore

carnaval [kaʀnaval] <s> *m* carnival

carnet [kaʀnɛ] *m* **1.** (*calepin*) notebook; ~ **d'adresses** address book; ~ **de notes** report card; ~ **d'épargne** *Suisse* (*livret*) savings book; ~ **de santé** health record **2.** (*paquet*) ~ **de timbres** book of stamps; ~ **de chèques** cheque book *Brit,* checkbook *Am*

carnivore [kaʀnivɔʀ] **I.** *adj* carnivorous **II.** *m* carnivore

carnotset [kaʀnɔtsɛ] *m Suisse* (*local, souvent aménagé dans une cave, pour manger et boire entre amis*) cellar room for entertaining friends

Caroline-du-Nord [kaʀɔlin(ə)dynɔːʀ] *f* **la** ~ North Carolina

Caroline-du-Sud [kaʀɔlin(ə)dysyd] *f* **la** ~ South Carolina

carolingien(ne) [kaʀɔlɛ̃ʒjɛ̃, jɛn] *adj* Carolingian

carotide [kaʀɔtid] *f* carotid

carotte [kaʀɔt] **I.** *f* carrot; ~ **rouge** *Suisse* (*betterave*) beetroot **II.** *adj inv* **avoir les cheveux** ~ to have carroty hair

carotter [kaʀɔte] <1> *vt inf* (*objet, argent*) to pinch; ~ **qn de deux euros/de deux jours de vacances** to cheat sb out of two euros/two days' holiday

carpe [kaʀp] *f* carp ►**muet(te) comme une** ~ as silent as a post

carquois [kaʀkwa] *m* quiver

carré(e) [kaʀe] **I.** *adj* **1.** (*rectangulaire*) square **2.** (*robuste*) ~ **d'épaules** broad-shouldered **3.** MAT **mètre/kilomètre** ~ square metre/kilometre *Brit,* square meter/kilometer *Am* **II.** *m* **1.** MAT square; **élever un nombre au** ~ to square a number; **quatre/six au** ~ four/six squared **2.** JEUX **un** ~ **d'as** four aces **3.** (*parcelle*) ~ **de terre** plot of land

carreau [kaʀo] <x> *m* **1.** (*vitre*) window(pane); **faire les ~x** to clean the windows **2.** (*carrelage*) tiled floor **3.** (*motif*) **tissu à grands ~x** large-checked fabric; **papier à petits ~x** small-squared paper **4.** JEUX diamond; **as de** ~ ace of diamonds ►**se tenir à** ~ to watch one's step

carrefour [kaʀfuʀ] *m a. fig* crossroads; **Strasbourg,** ~ **de l'Europe** Strasbourg, the crossroads of Europe

carrelage [kaʀlaʒ] *m* **1.** (*action*) tiling **2.** (*revêtement*) tiles *pl*

carrelé(e) [kaʀle] *adj* tiled

carreler [kaʀle] <3> *vt* to tile

carrelet [kaʀlɛ] *m* plaice

carreleur, -euse [kaʀlœʀ, -øz] *m, f* tiler

carrément [kaʀemɑ̃] *adv inf* **1.** (*franchement*) straight out; **y aller** ~ to go straight ahead **2.** (*complètement*) completely

carrière¹ [kaʀjɛʀ] *f* career; **faire** ~ to make a career

carrière² [kaʀjɛʀ] *f* ~ **de pierres** stone quarry; ~ **de sable** sandpit

carriériste [kaʀjeʀist] *mf péj* careerist

carriole [kaʀjɔl] *f* **1.** (*petite charrette*) cart **2.** *Québec* (*voiture d'hiver hippomobile, montée sur patins*) horse-drawn sleigh

carrossable [kaʀɔsabl] *adj* suitable for traffic

carrosse [kaʀɔs] *m* (horse-drawn) coach

carrosserie [kaʀɔsʀi] *f* **1.** AUTO bodywork

2. (*métier*) coachbuilding

carrure [kaʀyʀ] *f* 1. (*largeur du dos*) breadth across the shoulders; **être trop étroit/large de** ~ (*veste*) to be too tight/too loose across the shoulders 2. (*envergure*) stature

cartable [kaʀtabl] *m* 1. ECOLE schoolbag 2. *Québec* (*classeur à anneaux*) ring binder

carte [kaʀt] *f* 1. GEO map; ~ **au 1/25 000** map on a scale of 1: 25,000; ~ **routière** road map; ~ **en relief** relief map 2. JEUX ~ **à jouer** playing card; **jouer aux ~s** to play cards; **tirer les ~s à qn** to read sb's cards 3. (*dans le domaine postal*) ~ **postale** postcard 4. GASTR menu 5. (*bristol*) ~ **de visite** visiting card 6. (*moyen de paiement*) ~ **à mémoire/à puce** smart card; ~ **bancaire/de crédit** bank/credit card; ~ **de téléphone** phonecard 7. (*document*) ~ **d'électeur** polling card *Brit,* voter registration card *Am;* ~ **d'étudiant** student (ID) card; ~ (**nationale**) **d'identité** ID card; ~ **de sécurité sociale** ≈ national insurance card; ~ **de séjour** residence permit; ~ **grise** car registration book *Brit,* car registration papers *Am* 8. INFOR ~ **enfichable/réseau/son/vidéo/d'extension** plug-in/network/sound/video/expansion card; ~ **graphique/mère** graphics card/motherboard ▶**jouer ~s sur table** to put one's cards on the table; **jouer sa dernière** ~ to play one's last card; **brouiller les ~s** to confuse the issue; **donner** [*o* **laisser**] ~ **blanche à qn** to give sb a free hand

carte-réponse [kaʀtʀepɔ̃s] <cartes-réponses> *f* reply card

cartésien(**ne**) [kaʀtezjɛ̃, jɛn] *adj* 1. PHILOS Cartesian 2. (*rationnel*) rational

carte-vue [kaʀtvy] <cartes-vues> *f Belgique* (*carte représentant une vue*) picture postcard

cartilage [kaʀtilaʒ] *m* cartilage; ~ **articulaire** joint cartilage

cartilagineux, **-euse** [kaʀtilaʒinø, -øz] *adj* (*viande*) gristly; (*poisson, tissu*) cartilaginous

cartomancien(**ne**) [kaʀtɔmɑ̃sjɛ̃, jɛn] *m(f)* fortune teller

carton [kaʀtɔ̃] *m* 1. (*matière*) cardboard 2. (*emballage*) (cardboard) box; **un** ~ **de lait** a carton of milk 3. (*classeur*) ~ **à dessin** portfolio ▶~ **jaune/rouge** yellow/red card; **faire un** ~ *inf* (*avoir du succès*) to be a smash (hit); **taper le** ~ *inf* to play cards

cartonné(**e**) [kaʀtɔne] *adj* bound; **livre** ~ hardback

carton-pâte [kaʀtɔ̃pɑt] *m* pasteboard

cartouche [kaʀtuʃ] *f* 1. (*munition: d'un fusil*) cartridge; ~ **à blanc** blank cartridge 2. (*emballage*) ~ **de cigarettes** carton of cigarettes 3. (*recharge*) ~ **d'encre** ink cartridge; ~ **de données** data cartridge

cas [kɑ] *m* 1. *a.* MED, JUR, LING case; ~ **d'urgence** emergency; ~ **limite** borderline case; **c'est bien le** ~ it is the case; **dans ce** ~ in that case; **dans le** ~ **contraire** otherwise; **dans le** ~ **présent** in this particular case; **dans tous les** ~ in any case; **en aucun** ~ on no account 2. (*hypothèse*) **au ~/dans le ~/pour le ~ où qn ferait qc** in case sb does sth; **en** ~ **de qc** in case of sth; **en** ~ **de besoin** if necessary; **en** ~ **de pluie** in case it rains

casanier, **-ière** [kazanje, -jɛʀ] *adj* (*personne, vie*) stay-at-home, homebody *Am;* **personne casanière** stay-at-home; **prendre des habitudes casanières** to stop wanting to go out

casaque [kazak] *f* silks *pl* ▶**tourner** ~ *inf* to do a U-turn

cascade [kaskad] *f* 1. (*chute d'eau*) waterfall 2. *fig* ~ **d'applaudissements** storm of applause; ~ **de rires** burst of laughter 3. CINE stunt

cascadeur, **-euse** [kaskadœʀ, -øz] *m, f* CINE stuntman, stuntwoman *m, f*

case [kɑz] *f* 1. (*carré: d'un formulaire*) box; (*d'un damier*) square; **avancer de huit ~s** to move forward eight squares; ~ **départ** start; *fig* square one 2. (*casier*) compartment 3. (*hutte*) hut 4. *Suisse, Québec* (*boîte*) ~ **postale** post office box ▶**il lui manque une** ~ *inf* he has a screw loose

caser [kɑze] <1> I. *vt* 1. (*loger*) to put up 2. (*marier*) to marry off II. *vpr* **se** ~ 1. (*se loger*) to find a place to stay 2. (*se marier*) to get married

caserne [kazɛʀn] *f* barracks *pl*

cash [kaʃ] *adv inf* cash

casher [kaʃɛʀ] *adj inv* kosher

casier [kɑzje] *m* 1. (*case*) compartment; ~ **à bouteilles** bottle rack 2. JUR ~ **judiciaire** police record; **avoir un** ~ **judiciaire vierge** to have a clean police record 3. (*à la pêche*) pot

casino [kazino] *m* casino

casque [kask] *m* 1. (*protection*) helmet; (*d'un motocycliste*) crash helmet 2. (*séchoir*) hair dryer 3. MUS headphones *pl* ▶~ **bleu** blue helmet (*member of the U.N. peacekeeping force*)

casqué(**e**) [kaske] *adj* in a helmet

casquer [kaske] <1> *vi inf* to cough up

casquette [kaskɛt] *f* cap

cassant(**e**) [kɑsɑ̃, ɑ̃t] *adj* 1. (*fragile: substance*) brittle 2. (*sec: ton*) curt

cassation [kɑsasjɔ̃] *f* 1. JUR cassation; **prononcer la** ~ **de qc** to declare sth invalid 2. MIL reduction to the ranks

casse [kɑs] I. *f* 1. (*dégât*) damage; **payer la** ~ to pay for breakage 2. (*bagarre*) **il va y avoir de la** ~ *inf* things are going to get rough 3. (*commerce du ferrailleur*) scrap yard II. *m inf* break-in; **faire un** ~ to do a break-in

cassé(**e**) [kɑse] *adj* (*vieillard*) bent; (*voix*) hoarse

casse-cou [kɑsku] *m inv, inf* daredevil

casse-croûte [kɑskʀut] *m inv* 1. (*collation*) snack 2. *Québec* (*café, restaurant où l'on sert des repas rapides*) snack bar

casse-gueule [kɑsgœl] *inv* I. *adj inf* reckless II. *m inf* **c'est un vrai ~!** (*endroit glissant*) it's really treacherous!; (*entreprise périlleuse*) it's a dicey business! **casse-noix** [kɑsnwa] *m inv* nutcracker **casse-pieds** [kɑspje] *inv* **I.** *adj inf* **1.** (*importun*) annoying; **ce que tu peux être ~, bon sang!** what a pain in the neck you can be, damn it! **2.** (*ennuyeux*) boring **II.** *mf inf* pain in the neck

casser [kɑse] <1> **I.** *vt* **1.** (*briser: objet*) to break; (*branche*) to snap; (*noix*) to crack **2.** (*troubler: ambiance*) to disturb; **~ le moral à qn** *inf* to break sb's spirit **3.** ECON (*croissance*) to stop; **~ les prix** to slash prices **4.** POL, SOCIOL (*grève*) to break **5.** JUR (*jugement*) to quash; (*mariage*) to annul **6.** MIL to demote ►**~ les pieds à qn** *inf* to annoy sb; **à tout ~** *inf* (*au maximum*) at the most; (*extraordinaire*) fantastic; **ça ne casse rien** *inf* it's nothing to get worked up about **II.** *vi* (*objet*) to break; (*branche, fil*) to snap **III.** *vpr* **1.** (*se rompre*) **se ~** to break; (*branche*) to snap; **se ~ en mille morceaux** to break into a thousand pieces **2.** (*être fragile*) **se ~** to be fragile **3.** (*se briser*) **se ~ un bras** to break one's arm; **se ~ une dent** to break off a tooth **4.** *inf* (*se fatiguer*) **ne pas se ~** not to strain oneself; **se ~ la tête** to rack one's brain **5.** *inf* (*s'en aller*) to split, to clear off *Brit*

casserole [kasʀɔl] *f* saucepan

casse-tête [kɑstɛt] *m inv* **1.** (*problème*) headache; **~ chinois** brainteaser **2.** *Québec* (*puzzle*) puzzle

cassette [kasɛt] *f* cassette; **~ vidéo** video (cassette)

cassettothèque [kasɛtɔtɛk] *f* cassette library

casseur, **-euse** [kɑsœʀ, -øz] *m, f* **1.** (*ferrailleur*) scrap merchant **2.** (*au cours d'une manifestation*) rioter

cassis [kasis] *m* (*fruit*) blackcurrant

cassoulet [kasulɛ] *m* cassoulet (*meat and bean stew*)

cassure [kɑsyʀ] *f* **1.** (*brisure*) break **2.** (*rupture: d'une amitié*) rupture

castagne [kastaɲ] *f inf* fighting

castagnettes [kastaɲɛt] *fpl* castanets

caste [kast] *f* caste

castor [kastɔʀ] *m* beaver

castrateur, **-trice** [kastʀatœʀ, -tʀis] *adj* castrating

castration [kastʀasjɔ̃] *f* castration

castrer [kastʀe] <1> *vt* to castrate

cataclysme [kataklism] *m a. fig* cataclysm

catacombes [katakɔ̃b] *fpl* catacombs

catalogne [katalɔɲ] *f Québec* (*étoffe dont la trame est faite de bandes de tissus généralement multicolores*) *brightly coloured rug or blanket*

catalogue [katalɔg] *m* catalogue

cataloguer [katalɔge] <1> *vt* **1.** (*classer*) to catalogue *Brit,* to catalog *Am* **2.** *péj* to label

catalyser [katalize] <1> *vt a. fig* to catalyse *Brit,* to catalyze *Am*

catamaran [katamaʀɑ̃] *m* catamaran

cataplasme [kataplasm] *m* MED poultice

catapulte [katapylt] *f* catapult

cataracte[1] [kataʀakt] *f* (*d'une rivière*) waterfall ►**il tombe des ~s** it's pouring down

cataracte[2] [kataʀakt] *f* MED cataract

catastrophe [katastʀɔf] *f* catastrophe; **~ ferroviaire** rail disaster; **faire qc en ~** to do sth in a mad rush; **atterrir en ~** to make a forced landing

catastrophique [katastʀɔfik] *adj* catastrophic

catch [katʃ] *m* wrestling; **faire du ~** to wrestle

catcheur, **-euse** [katʃœʀ, -øz] *m, f* wrestler

catéchisme [kateʃism] *m* **1.** (*enseignement, livre*) catechism **2.** (*dogme*) dogma

catégorie [kategɔʀi] *f* **1.** (*groupe*) category; **~ socioprofessionnelle** social and occupational group; **~ d'âge** age group **2.** SPORT class **3.** (*qualité*) **de 1ère ~** (*produit alimentaire*) top-grade food product; (*hôtel*) first class hotel

catégorique [kategɔʀik] *adj* categoric(al); **être ~ sur qc** to be adamant about sth

catégoriquement [kategɔʀikmɑ̃] *adv* categorically

catelle [katɛl] *f Suisse* (*carreau de faïence vernissée*) ceramic tile

cathédrale [katedʀal] *f* cathedral

catholicisme [katɔlisism] *m* catholicism; **se convertir au ~** to convert to catholicism

catholique [katɔlik] **I.** *adj* **1.** REL (Roman) Catholic **2.** *fig, inf* **ne pas être (très) ~** to be (rather) shady **II.** *mf* (Roman) Catholic

catimini [katimini] **en ~** on the sly; **partir en ~** to steal away

cauchemar [koʃmaʀ] *m a. fig* nightmare; **faire un ~** to have a nightmare

cauchemardesque [koʃmaʀdɛsk] *adj* nightmarish; **vision ~** nightmare; **devenir ~** to turn into a nightmare

causant(e) [kozɑ̃, ɑ̃t] *adj* talkative

cause [koz] **I.** *f* **1.** (*raison, ensemble d'intérêts*) cause; **fermé pour ~ de maladie** closed because of illness; **et pour ~!** and with good reason!; **pour la bonne ~** for a good cause **2.** JUR lawsuit; **plaider une ~** to plead a case ►**en tout état de ~** in any case; **mettre qc en ~** to call sth into question; **mettre qn en ~** to implicate sb **II.** *prep* **à ~ de** because of

causer[1] [koze] <1> *vt* (*provoquer*) to cause; **~ de la joie à qn** to give pleasure to sb

causer[2] [koze] <1> *vt, vi* **1.** (*parler*) to talk; (*sans façon*) to chat; **assez causé!** *inf* enough said!; **je te/vous cause!** *inf* I'm talking to you!; **cause toujours!** *inf* keep talking! **2.** *inf* (*médire*) **faire ~** to be the talk of the town

causse [kos] *m* causse (*limestone plateau*)

Causses [kos] *mpl* **les ~** *limestone plateau south of the Massif Central*

caustique [kostik] *adj* caustic

caution [kosjɔ̃] *f* **1.** FIN guarantee; **se porter ~ pour qn** to stand guarantor for sb **2.** JUR bail; **être libéré sous ~** to be released on bail

3. (*appui*) support; **apporter sa ~ à qn/qc** to back sb/sth

cautionner [kosjɔne] <1> *vt* 1. JUR to stand guarantee for 2. (*approuver*) to support

cavalcade [kavalkad] *f* 1. (*défilé*) procession 2. (*course tumultueuse*) stampede

cavaler [kavale] <1> *vi inf* (*courir*) to run

cavalerie [kavalʀi] *f* MIL cavalry

cavaleur, -euse [kavalœʀ, -øz] *m, f inf* 1. (*homme*) womanizer 2. (*femme*) man-chaser

cavalier, -ière [kavalje, -jɛʀ] I. *adj* 1. *péj* (*impertinent*) offhand 2. (*réservé aux cavaliers*) **piste cavalière** bridle path II. *m, f* 1. SPORT horseman, horsewoman *m, f* 2. (*au bal*) partner III. *m* 1. MIL cavalryman 2. JEUX knight 3. (*titre de politesse*) gentleman

cavalièrement [kavaljɛʀmɑ̃] *adv* off-handedly; (*agir*) in a cavalier fashion

cave [kav] *f* 1. (*local souterrain, provision de vins*) cellar; ~ **voûtée** vault 2. *pl* (*propriété*) ~**s viticoles** wine cellars 3. (*cabaret*) club ►**de la ~ au grenier** in every nook and cranny

caveau [kavo] <x> *m* (*tombeau*) vault

caverne [kavɛʀn] *f* cavern

caverneux, -euse [kavɛʀnø, -øz] *adj* 1. cavernous 2. (*grave: voix*) hollow 3. MED (*poumon, rein*) cavernous

caviar [kavjaʀ] *m* GASTR caviar

caviste [kavist] *mf* wine merchant

cavité [kavite] *f* cavity

CB [sibi] *f abr de* **Citizens' band** CB radio

CCP [sesepe] *m abr de* **compte chèques postal** post office (bank) account

CD [sede] *m abr de* **Compact Disc** CD

CDD [sesede] *m abr de* **contrat à durée déterminée** *limited employment contract*

CDI [sedei] *m* 1. *abr de* **contrat à durée indéterminée** permanent employment contract 2. *abr de* **centre de documentation et d'information** *learning resources centre* 3. *abr de* **centre des impôts** tax centre

CD-I [sedei] *m abr de* **Compact Disc Interactive** CD-I

CD-R [sedeɛʀ] *m inv abr de* **Compact Disc Recordable** CD-R

CD-ROM [sedeʀɔm] *m abr de* **Compact Disc Read Only Memory** CD-ROM; **introduire un ~ dans le lecteur de CD-ROM** to insert a CD-ROM in the CD-ROM drive

CD-RW *m inv abr de* **Compact Disc Rewritable Unit** CD-RW

CDV [sedeve] *m abr de* **Compact Disc Video** VCD

ce^1 [sə] <*devant en et formes de "être" commençant par une voyelle* c', *devant a* ç'> *pron dém* 1. (*pour désigner*) **c'est un beau garçon** he's a handsome boy; ~ **sont de bons souvenirs** they're happy memories; **c'est beau, la vie** life is beautiful; **c'est moi/lui/nous** it's me/him/us; **à qui est ce livre? – c'est à lui** whose book is this? – it's his 2. (*dans une question*) **qui est-ce?, c'est qui?** *inf* (*sur un homme*) who is he?; (*sur une femme*) who is she?; (*sur plusieurs personnes*) who are they?; (*au téléphone*) who is speaking?; **qui est-ce qui/que** who/whom; **qu'est-ce** (**que c'est**)?, **c'est quoi?** *inf* what is it?; **qu'est-ce qui/que** what; **c'est qui** [*o* **qui c'est**] **ce Monsieur?** *inf* who is this man?; **est-ce vous?, c'est vous?** *inf* is it you? 3. (*pour insister*) **c'est plus tard qu'elle y songea** she didn't think about it until later; **c'est maintenant qu'on en a besoin** right now is when we need it; **c'est en tombant que l'objet a explosé** the thing exploded when it fell; **c'est vous qui le dites!** that's what you say!; **c'est un scandale de voir cela** it's scandalous to see that; **c'est à elle de** +*infin* (*c'est à son tour*) it's her turn to +*infin;* (*c'est son rôle*) she has to +*infin;* **c'est à vous de prendre cette décision** you have to make this decision 4. (*pour expliquer*) **c'est que ...** you see ...; (*dans une réponse*) actually ...; (*pour préciser la raison*) it's because ... 5. (*devant une relative*) **voilà tout ~ que je sais** that's all I know; **dis-moi ~ dont tu as besoin** tell me what you need; ~ **à quoi je ne m'attendais pas** what I wasn't expecting; ~ **à quoi j'ai pensé** what I thought; ~ **que c'est idiot!** how stupid it is!; ~ **que** [*o* **qu'est-ce que**] **ce paysage est beau!** how beautiful this landscape is!; **qu'est-ce qu'on s'amuse!** *inf* what a good time we're having!; ~ **qu'il parle bien** *inf* how well he speaks ►**et ~** and that; **à ~ qu'on dit, qn a fait qc** it is said that sb has done sth; **sur ~** whereupon; **sur ~, je vous dis au revoir** so now I'll just say goodbye

ce^2 [sə] *adj dém* 1. (*pour désigner*) this; *v. a.* **cette** 2. (*intensif, péjoratif*) **comment peut-il raconter ~ mensonge!** how can he tell such a lie! 3. (*avec étonnement*) what (a); ~ **toupet!** what a cheek! 4. (*en opposition*) ~ **livre-ci ... ~ livre-là** this book ... that book 5. (*temporel*) ~ **jour-là** that day; ~ **mois-ci** this month

CE [seø] *f* 1. HIST *abr de* **Communauté européenne** EC 2. *abr de* **comité d'entreprise** employees' council

CE1 [seøœ̃] *m abr de* **cours élémentaire première année** *second year of primary school*

CE2 [seødø] *m abr de* **cours élémentaire deuxième année** *third year of primary school*

ceci [səsi] *pron dém* this; ~ **explique cela** one thing explains another; **il a ~ d'agréable qu'il est gai** what is pleasant about him is that he is cheerful; **à ~ près qu'il ment** except that he's lying; *v. a.* **cela**

cécité [sesite] *f* blindness

céder [sede] <5> I. *vt* 1. (*abandonner au profit de qn*) ~ **qc à qn** to let sb have sth; ~ **son tour à qn** to let sb go first 2. (*vendre*) to sell II. *vi* 1. (*renoncer*) to give up 2. (*capituler*) to give in; (*troupes*) to withdraw 3. (*succomber*) ~ **à qc** to give way to sth; ~ **à la ten-**

tation to yield to temptation **4.** (*se rompre*) to give (way)

CEDEX [sedɛks] *m abr de* **courrier d'entreprise à distribution exceptionnelle** *postal code for official use*

cédille [sedij] *f* cedilla

cèdre [sɛdʀ] *m* cedar

CEE [seəə] *f abr de* **Communauté économique européenne** HIST EEC

CEI [seøi] *f abr de* **Communauté des États indépendants** HIST CIS

ceindre [sɛ̃dʀ] *vt irr* **1.** (*entourer*) ~ **une ville de murailles** to surround a town with walls; ~ **ses épaules d'un châle** to put a shawl around one's shoulders **2.** (*revêtir: écharpe*) to put on

ceint(e) [sə, ɛ̃t] *part passé de* **ceindre**

ceinture [sɛ̃tyʀ] *f* **1.** *a.* AUTO, AVIAT, SPORT belt; **attacher sa ~ de sécurité** to fasten one's seatbelt; **il est ~ noire** he is a black belt **2.** (*partie d'un vêtement*) waistband **3.** (*zone environnante*) ~ **de barbelés/collines** strip of barbed wire/range of hills **4.** (*route périphérique*) ring road *Brit,* beltway *Am*

ceinturer [sɛ̃tyʀe] <1> *vt* **1.** (*prendre à la taille: personne*) to seize round the waist; (*pour l'arrêter*) to tackle round the waist **2.** (*entourer: ville, champ*) to encircle

ceinturon [sɛ̃tyʀɔ̃] *m* MIL belt

cela [s(ə)la] *pron dém* **1.** (*pour désigner*) that; ~ **te plaît?** do you like that?; **après ~** after that; **je ne pense qu'à ~** that's all I'm thinking about **2.** (*pour renforcer*) **qui/quand/où ~?** who/when/where is/was that?; **comment ~?** what do you mean?; ~ **fait dix jours que j'attends** I've been waiting for ten days ►**c'est ~ même** exactly; **si ce n'est que ~** if that's all it is; **et avec ~?** anything else?; **sans ~** otherwise; *v. a.* **ça, ceci**

célébration [selebʀasjɔ̃] *f* celebration; ~ **du mariage** marriage ceremony

célèbre [selɛbʀ] *adj* famous; ~ **dans le monde entier** world famous; **se rendre ~ par qc** to become famous for sth

célébrer [selebʀe] <5> *vt* **1.** (*fêter*) to celebrate **2.** (*vanter: exploit*) to praise **3.** REL ~ **un service religieux** to hold a church service

célébrité [selebʀite] *f* fame; **qn est une ~** sb is a celebrity

céleri [sɛlʀi] *m* celery

céleri-rave [sɛlʀiʀav] <céleris-raves> *m* celeriac

célérité [seleʀite] *f* speed; **avec ~** swiftly

céleste [selɛst] *adj* **1.** (*relatif au ciel*) celestial **2.** (*divin: béatitude*) celestial; (*colère*) divine **3.** (*merveilleux*) heavenly

célibat [seliba] *m* single status; (*d'un prêtre*) celibacy

célibataire [selibatɛʀ] **I.** *adj* single **II.** *mf* single person

celle, celui [sɛl] <s> *pron dém* **1.** + *prép* ~ **de Paul est plus jolie** Paul's is more beautiful **2.** + *pron rel* ~ **que tu as achetée est moins chère** the one that you bought is cheaper **3.** + *adj/part passé/part prés/inf* (*en opposition*) the one; **cette marchandise est meilleure que ~ que vous vendez** these goods are better than the ones that you sell

celle-ci, celui-ci [sɛlsi] <celles-ci> *pron dém* **1.** (*en désignant: chose*) this one; (*personne*) she **2.** (*référence à un antécédent*) the latter; **il écrit à sa sœur – ~ ne répond pas** he writes to his sister but she doesn't answer **3.** (*en opposition*) ~ **est moins chère que celle-là** this one is cheaper than that one; (*avec un geste*) this one here; *v. a.* **celle-là**

celle-là, celui-là [sɛlla] <celles-là> *pron dém* **1.** (*en désignant: chose*) that one; (*personne*) she **2.** (*référence à un antécédent*) **ah! je la retiens ~ alors!** *inf* I'll remember her all right!; **elle est bien bonne ~!** that's a good one! **3.** (*en opposition*) *v.* **celle-ci**

celles, ceux [sɛl] *pl pron dém* **1.** + *prép* those; ~ **d'entre vous** those of you **2.** + *pron rel* ~ **qui ont fini peuvent sortir** those who have finished may leave **3.** + *adj/part passé/part prés/inf* those; *v. a.* **celle**

celles-ci, ceux-ci [sɛlsi] *pl pron dém* **1.** (*pour distinguer*) these (ones) **2.** (*référence à un antécédent*) the latter; *v. a.* **celle-ci 3.** (*en opposition*) ~ **sont moins chères que celles-là** these are cheaper than those; (*avec un geste*) these here; *v. a.* **celles-là**

celles-là, ceux-là [sɛlla] *pl pron dém* **1.** (*en désignant*) those (ones) **2.** (*référence à un antécédent*) **ah! je les retiens ~ alors!** *inf* I'll remember them all right! **3.** (*en opposition*) *v.* **celles-ci**

cellier [selje] *m* storeroom (*for food and wine*)

cellophane® [selɔfan] *f* cellophane®

cellulaire [selylɛʀ] **I.** *adj* **1.** BIO **division ~** cell division **2.** (*relatif à la prison*) **régime ~** solitary confinement; **fourgon ~** prison van **II.** *m Québec* (*téléphone portable*) mobile (phone) *Brit,* cellphone *Am*

cellule [selyl] *f* cell

cellulite [selylit] *f* MED cellulite

cellulose [selyloz] *f* cellulose

celte [sɛlt] *adj* Celtic

Celte [sɛlt] *m, f* Celt

celtique [sɛltik] **I.** *adj* Celtic **II.** *m* Celtic; *v. a.* **français**

celui, celle [səlɥi] <ceux> *pron dém* the one; *v. a.* **celle**

celui-ci, celle-ci [səlɥisi] <ceux-ci> *pron dém* (*chose*) this one; (*personne*) he; *v. a.* **celle-ci, celui-là**

celui-là, celle-là [səlɥila] <ceux-là> *pron dém* **1.** (*en désignant: chose*) that one; (*personne*) he **2.** (*avec un geste*) ~ **est meilleur** that one is better **3.** (*référence à un antécédent*) *v.* **celle-là 4.** (*en opposition*) *v.* **celui-ci, celle-ci**

cendre [sɑ̃dʀ] *f* ash

cendré(e) [sɑ̃dʀe] *adj* **des cheveux gris ~**

ash grey hair *Brit,* ash gray hair *Am*
cendrée [sɑ̃dʀe] *f* SPORT cinder track
cendrier [sɑ̃dʀije] *m* (*d'un fumeur*) ashtray
Cendrillon [sɑ̃dʀijɔ̃] *f* Cinderella
cenellier [sənelje] *m Québec* (*aubépine*) hawthorn
censé(e) [sɑ̃se] *adj* **1.** (*présumé en train de faire qc*) **être ~** +*infin* to be supposed to +*infin* **2.** (*présumé capable de faire qc*) **je suis ~ connaître la réponse** I'm supposed to know the answer **3.** (*présumé devoir faire qc*) **je te le dis, mais tu n'es pas ~ le savoir** I'm telling you it, but you're not supposed to know it
censeur [sɑ̃sœʀ] *m* **1.** CINE, PRESSE censor **2.** ECOLE *person responsible for discipline in a school*
censure [sɑ̃syʀ] *f* **1.** CINE, PRESSE censorship **2.** POL censure; **déposer une motion de ~** to put forward censure motion
censurer [sɑ̃syʀe] <1> *vt* CINE, PRESSE to censor
cent[1] [sɑ̃] **I.** *adj* a [*o* one] hundred; **cinq ~s euros** five hundred euros; **~ un** a [*o* one] hundred and one ►**avoir ~ <u>fois</u> raison** to be absolutely right; <u>**pour**</u> **~** per cent *Brit,* percent *Am;* **~ pour ~** a [*o* one] hundred per cent **II.** *m inv* hundred; *v. a.* **cinq, cinquante**
cent[2] [sɛnt] *m* FIN cent
centaine [sɑ̃tɛn] *f* **1.** (*environ cent*) **une ~ de personnes** about a hundred people; **des ~s de personnes** hundreds of people; **plusieurs ~s de manifestants** several hundred demonstrators; **par ~s** in hundreds **2.** (*cent unités*) hundred
centaure [sɑ̃tɔʀ] *m* centaur
centenaire [sɑ̃tnɛʀ] **I.** *adj* hundred-year-old; **être ~** to be a hundred years old **II.** *mf* centenarian **III.** *m* centenary *Brit,* centennial *Am*
centésimal(e) [sɑ̃tezimal, o] <-aux> *adj* centesimal
centième [sɑ̃tjɛm] **I.** *adj antéposé* hundredth **II.** *mf* **le/la ~** the hundredth **III.** *m* (*fraction*) fraction **IV.** *f* THEAT hundredth performance; *v. a.* **cinquième**
centigramme [sɑ̃tigʀam] *m* centigramme
centilitre [sɑ̃tilitʀ] *m* centilitre *Brit,* centiliter *Am*
centime [sɑ̃tim] *m* centime; **une pièce de 50 ~s** a 50 centime coin ►**ne pas avoir un ~ sur <u>soi</u>** not to have a penny
centimètre [sɑ̃timɛtʀ] *m* **1.** (*unité*) centimetre *Brit,* centimeter *Am* **2.** (*ruban*) tape measure
centrafricain(e) [sɑ̃tʀafʀikɛ̃, ɛn] *adj* Central African; **la République ~e** Central African Republic
Centrafricain(e) [sɑ̃tʀafʀikɛ̃, ɛn] *m(f)* Central African
central [sɑ̃tʀal, o] <-aux> *m* TEL (telephone) exchange
central(e) [sɑ̃tʀal, o] <-aux> *adj* (*situé au centre, important*) central; **partie ~e** main part; **le personnage ~** the main character
centrale [sɑ̃tʀal] *f* **1.** ELEC power station **2.** POL **~ syndicale** confederation of trade unions **3.** COM head office **4.** (*prison*) prison
Centrale [sɑ̃tʀal] *f* ECOLE *college for training engineers*
centralisation [sɑ̃tʀalizasjɔ̃] *f* centralization
centraliser [sɑ̃tʀalize] <1> *vt* to centralize
centre [sɑ̃tʀ] *m* **1.** (*milieu, organisme*) centre *Brit,* center *Am;* **~ ferroviaire** railway junction; **~ aéré** childrens outdoor activity centre; **~ commercial/culturel** shopping/arts centre; **~ hospitalier régional** regional hospital complex; **~ universitaire** university; **~ d'achats** *Québec* (*~ commercial*) shopping centre *Brit,* shopping center *Am;* **~ équestre** riding school; **~ de détention pour jeunes** juvenile detention centre **2.** SPORT (*terrain*) midfield; (*joueur*) midfield player; (*passe*) centre pass *Brit,* center pass *Am*
Centre [sɑ̃tʀ] *m* **le ~** Central France
centre-avant [sɑ̃tʀavɑ̃] *m Belgique* (*avant-centre*) centre forward *Brit,* center-forward *Am*
centrer [sɑ̃tʀe] <1> *vt* to centre *Brit,* to center *Am;* **~ son discours sur un sujet** to centre one's speech around a subject
centre(-)ville [sɑ̃tʀəvil] <centres-villes> *m* town centre *Brit,* town center *Am*
centrifuge [sɑ̃tʀifyʒ] *adj* centrifugal
centuple [sɑ̃typl] **I.** *adj* a hundred times as large; **mille est un nombre ~ de dix** a thousand is a hundred times ten **II.** *m a. fig* hundredfold; **rendre une dette à qn au ~** to repay a debt a hundred times over
cep [sɛp] *m* vine stock
cépage [sepaʒ] *m* varietal
cèpe [sɛp] *m* cep
cependant [s(ə)pɑ̃dɑ̃] *adv* however
céramique [seʀamik] **I.** *adj* ceramic **II.** *f* **1.** (*objet*) ceramic **2.** (*art*) ceramics *pl* **3.** MED **~ dentaire** dental ceramics *pl*
cerceau [sɛʀso] <x> *m* hoop
cercle [sɛʀkl] *m* **1.** (*forme géométrique, groupe*) circle **2.** (*groupe sportif*) club **3.** MIL **~ des officiers** officers' mess
cerclé(e) [sɛʀkle] *adj* ringed
cercueil [sɛʀkœj] *m* coffin, casket *Am*
céréale [seʀeal] *f: cereal*
cérébral(e) [seʀebʀal, o] <-aux> **I.** *adj* **1.** ANAT cerebral **2.** (*intellectuel*) intellectual **II.** *m(f)* **être un pur ~** to be a purely cerebral type
cérémonial [seʀemɔnjal] <s> *m* ceremonial
cérémonie [seʀemɔni] *f* ceremony
cérémonieux, -euse [seʀemɔnjø, -jøz] *adj* ceremonious; (*salut, ton, accueil*) formal; **prendre des airs ~** to behave formally
cerf [sɛʀ] *m* ZOOL stag
cerfeuil [sɛʀfœj] *m* chervil
cerf-volant [sɛʀvɔlɑ̃] <cerfs-volants> *m*

1. (*jouet*) kite; **faire voler un** ~ to fly a kite 2. ZOOL stag beetle

cerise [s(ə)ʀiz] I. *f* cherry II. *adj inv* (**rouge**) ~ cherry(-red)

cerisier [s(ə)ʀizje] *m* 1. (*arbre*) cherry (tree) 2. (*bois*) cherry (wood)

cerne [sɛʀn] *m* 1. ANAT ring 2. BOT (*d'un arbre*) tree ring

cerné(e) [sɛʀne] *adj* **avoir les yeux ~s** to have rings under one's eyes

cerneau [sɛʀno] <x> *m* (*noix verte*) unripe walnut

cerner [sɛʀne] <1> *vt* 1. *a. fig* (*entourer d'un trait*) to outline 2. (*encercler: ennemi*) to surround 3. (*évaluer: problème*) to define; (*difficulté*) to assess; ~ **qn** *inf* to make sb out

certain(e) [sɛʀtɛ̃, ɛn] I. *adj* certain; **être sûr et** ~ to be absolutely certain II. *adj indéf* 1. *pl antéposé* (*quelques*) some 2. (*bien déterminé*) **un ~ endroit** a certain place III. *pron pl* some; **~s d'entre vous** some of you; **aux yeux de ~s** in some people's eyes

certainement [sɛʀtɛnmɑ̃] *adv* 1. (*selon toute apparence*) most probably 2. (*sans aucun doute*) certainly

certes [sɛʀt] *adv* (*pour exprimer une réserve*) **c'est le plus doué, ~! mais ...** he's the most talented, admittedly, but ...; **il n'est ~ pas doué** he's certainly not talented

certificat [sɛʀtifika] *m* 1. (*attestation*) certificate; ~ **de scolarité** proof of attendance; **délivrer un ~ à qn** to issue a certificate to sb 2. (*diplôme*) diploma

certifier [sɛʀtifje] <1> *vt* 1. (*assurer*) to assure 2. JUR to certify; **cette copie est certifiée conforme à l'original** this is a certified copy of the original

certitude [sɛʀtityd] *f* certainly

cérumen [seʀymɛn] *m* ear wax

cerveau [sɛʀvo] <x> *m* 1. *a.* ANAT brain 2. (*esprit*) mind 3. (*organisateur*) brains *pl*

cervelle [sɛʀvɛl] *f* 1. *inf* (*esprit*) brain; **ne rien avoir dans la** ~ to be brainless 2. GASTR brains *pl*

cervical(e) [sɛʀvikal, o] <-aux> *adj* ANAT **les vertèbres ~es** the cervical vertebra

cervicales [sɛʀvikal] *fpl* ANAT **les** ~ the cervical vertebra

ces [se] *adj dém pl* 1. (*pour désigner*) these; *v. a.* **cette** 2. *inf* (*intensif, péjoratif*) **il a de ~ idées!** he has some funny ideas; **comment peut-il raconter ~ mensonges** how can he tell such lies 3. (*avec étonnement*) ~ **mensonges!** what lies! 4. (*en opposition*) ~ **gens-ci ...** ~ **gens-là** these people ... those people 5. (*temporel*) ~ **nuits-ci** these last few nights; **dans ~ années-là** during those years

CES [seøɛs] *m* 1. ECOLE *abr de* **collège d'enseignement secondaire** secondary school *Brit,* junior high school *Am* 2. (*emploi*) *abr de* **contrat emploi-solidarité** *part-time community work contracts for the unemployed*

César [seza:ʀ] *m* HIST **Jules** ~ Julius Caesar

césarienne [sezaʀjɛn] *f* MED Caesarean (section)

cesse [sɛs] **n'avoir (pas) de ~ que** not to rest until; **sans** ~ (*sans interruption*) constantly; (*de manière répétitive*) always

cesser [sese] <1> I. *vt* to stop; **cessez ces cris!** stop shouting!; **faire ~ qc** to put an end to sth; ~ **de fumer** to stop smoking II. *vi* to stop; (*conflit*) to come to an end; (*fièvre*) to pass

cessez-le-feu [sesel(e)fø] *m inv* cease-fire

cession [sesjɔ̃] *f* transfer; (*vente*) sale

c'est-à-dire [sɛtadiʀ] *conj* 1. (*à savoir*) that is (to say) 2. (*justification*) ~ **que ...** which means that ... 3. (*rectification*) ~ **que ...** well, actually ...

cet [sɛt] *adj dém v.* **ce**

CET [seøte] *m abr de* **collège d'enseignement technique** ≈ technical school

cétacé [setase] *m* ZOOL cetacean

cette [sɛt] *adj dém* 1. (*pour désigner*) this; **en ~ dernière semaine de l'avent** in this last week in Advent; **alors, ~ grippe, comment ça va?** well then, how's your flu? 2. (*intensif, péjoratif*) **comment peut-il raconter ~ histoire!** how can he tell such a story! 3. (*avec étonnement*) what (a); ~ **chance!** what luck! 4. (*en opposition*) ~ **version-ci ...** ~ **version-là** this version ... that version 5. (*temporel*) ~ **nuit** (*la nuit dernière*) last night; (*la nuit qui vient*) tonight; ~ **semaine** this week; ~ **semaine-là** that week

ceux, celles [sø] *pl pron dém* those; *v. a.* **celles**

ceux-ci, celles-ci [søsi] *pl pron dém* 1. (*pour distinguer*) these (ones) 2. (*référence à un antécédent*) the latter; *v. a.* **celle-ci** 3. (*en opposition*) *v.* **ceux-là, celles-ci**

ceux-là, celles-là [søla] *pl pron dém* 1. (*en désignant*) those 2. (*référence à un antécédent*) *v.* **celle-là** 3. (*en opposition*) those; *v. a.* **ceux-ci, celles-ci**

Cévennes [sevɛn] *fpl* **les** ~ the Cévennes

Ceylan [sɛlɑ̃] *f* HIST Ceylon

cf, Cf [kɔ̃fɛʀ] *abr de* **confer** cf

CFA [seɛfɑ] *adj abr de* **communauté financière africaine: franc** ~ CFA franc

CFC [seɛfse] *m abr de* **chlorofluorocarbone** CFC

CFDT [seɛfdete] *f abr de* **Confédération française démocratique du travail** *French trade union*

CGT [seʒete] *f abr de* **Confédération générale du travail** *French trade union*

ch [ʃəvo] *abr de* **cheval-vapeur** hp

chacal [ʃakal] <s> *m* ZOOL jackal

chacun(e) [ʃakœ̃, ʃakyn] *pron* 1. (*chose ou personne dans un ensemble défini*) each (one); **~/~e de nous** each (one) of us; ~ **à sa façon** each in his own way; ~ **(à) son tour** each in turn 2. (*de deux personnes*) ~ **des deux** both of them 3. (*toute personne*) everyone ►~ **ses goûts** *prov* every man to his own

C

taste
chagrin [ʃagʀɛ̃] *m* (*peine*) grief
chagriner [ʃagʀine] <1> *vt* ~ **qn** (*causer de la peine*) to grieve sb; (*contrarier*) to bother sb
chah [ʃa] *m v.* **schah**
chahut [ʃay] *m* uproar; (*bruit*) racket; **faire du** ~ to make a racket
chahuté(e) [ʃayte] *adj* (*professeur*) with no class control
chahuter [ʃayte] <1> **I.** *vi* (*élèves*) to create a rumpus; (*enfants*) to romp around; (*faire du bruit*) to make a racket **II.** *vt* **1.** (*bousculer par plaisir*) ~ **qn** to jostle sb **2.** (*troubler par du chahut*) ~ **un professeur** to rag a teacher
chahuteur, -euse [ʃaytœʀ, -øz] **I.** *adj* rowdy **II.** *m, f* (*élève indiscipliné*) rowdy
chaîne [ʃɛn] *f* **1.** (*bijou, dispositif métallique, suite d'éléments*) chain; **réaction en** ~ chain reaction **2.** *pl* AUTO ~ **à neige** snow chains **3.** ECON assembly line **4.** RADIO, TV (*émetteur*) channel; (*programme*) programme *Brit,* program *Am;* ~ **câblée** cable channel; **sur la 3e** ~ on the third programme **5.** (*appareil stéréo*) ~ **haute-fidélité** [*o* **hi-fi**] [*o* **stéréo**] hi-fi system **6.** COM (*groupement*) ~ **de magasins** chain of stores
chaînette [ʃɛnɛt] *f* (*petite chaîne*) chain
chaînon [ʃɛnɔ̃] *m* **1.** *a. fig* (*maillon d'une chaîne*) link; ~ **du raisonnement** link in the logic **2.** (*chaîne de montagnes secondaires*) secondary chain
chair [ʃɛʀ] **I.** *f* **1.** (*viande, pulpe*) flesh; ~ **à pâté** [*o* **saucisse**] mincemeat **2.** *a.* REL, LIT (*corps opposé à esprit*) flesh ▸**avoir la** ~ **de poule** to have goose pimples **II.** *adj inv* **couleur** ~ flesh-coloured *Brit,* flesh-colored *Am*
chaire [ʃɛʀ] *f* **1.** (*tribune*) rostrum; (*du prêtre*) pulpit **2.** UNIV chair
chaise [ʃɛz] *f* chair
chaland [ʃalɑ̃] *m* (*péniche*) barge
châle [ʃɑl] *m* shawl
chalet [ʃalɛ] *m* **1.** (*maison de bois en montagne*) chalet **2.** *Québec* (*maison de campagne située près d'un lac ou d'une rivière*) chalet (*near water*)
chaleur [ʃalœʀ] *f* **1.** (*température élevée*) warmth; (*très élevée*) *a.* PHYS heat; **vague de** ~ heatwave; **il fait une** ~ **accablante** the heat is oppressive **2.** *fig* heat; (*d'un accueil*) warmth; **discuter avec** ~ to discuss heatedly
chaleureusement [ʃalœʀøzmɑ̃] *adv* warmly
chaleureux, -euse [ʃalœʀø, -øz] *adj* warm; (*soirée*) pleasant
chalonnais(e) [ʃalɔne, ɛz] *adj* of Chalon-sur-Saône; *v. a.* **ajaccien**
Chalonnais(e) [ʃalɔne, ɛz] *m(f)* person from Chalon-sur-Saône; *v. a.* **Ajaccien**
chaloupe [ʃalup] *f* **1.** (*canot*) launch **2.** *Québec* (*petit bateau à rames*) small boat
chalumeau [ʃalymo] <x> *m* (*pour souder*) welding torch; (*pour découper*) cutting torch
chalut [ʃaly] *m* (*pour la pêche*) trawl; **se pêcher au** ~ (*poissons, crevettes*) to be trawled
chalutier [ʃalytje] *m* **1.** (*bateau*) trawler **2.** (*pêcheur*) trawlerman
chamailler [ʃamaje] <1> *vpr inf* **se** ~ to squabble
chamarré(e) [ʃamaʀe] *adj* bedecked; ~ **de décorations** covered in decorations; ~ **de citations** larded with quotations
chambardement [ʃɑ̃baʀdəmɑ̃] *m inf* upheaval; (*des valeurs, des idées*) jettisoning
chambranle [ʃɑ̃bʀɑ̃l] *m* (*d'une porte, fenêtre*) frame; (*d'une cheminée*) (*au-dessus*) mantelshelf; (*autour*) mantelpiece
chambre [ʃɑ̃bʀ] *f* **1.** (*pièce où l'on couche*) bedroom; ~ **individuelle/double** single/double room; ~ **d'amis** guest room; **faire** ~ **à part** to sleep in separate rooms **2.** (*pièce spéciale*) ~ **forte** strongroom; ~ **froide** cold (storage) room **3.** POL house **4.** JUR division **5.** COM ~ **syndicale** employers' federation; ~ **de commerce et d'industrie** chamber of commerce **6.** (*tuyau*) ~ **à air** inner tube
chambrer [ʃɑ̃bʀe] <1> *vt* **1.** (*tempérer*) to bring to room temperature **2.** *inf* (*se moquer de*) to tease
chameau [ʃamo] <x> *m* **1.** ZOOL camel **2.** *inf* (*femme*) beast **3.** *inf* (*homme*) heel
chamelier [ʃaməlje] *m* camel driver
chamelle [ʃamɛl] *f* (she-)camel
chamois [ʃamwa] **I.** *m* **1.** ZOOL chamois **2.** (*cuir*) **peau de** ~ chamois leather **II.** *adj inv* fawn
champ [ʃɑ̃] *m* **1.** *a.* AGR, PHYS, MIL field; ~ **de Mars** *garden in front of the Eiffel Tower in Paris, formerly used for military parades* **2.** *pl* (*campagne*) country(side); **vie des ~s** country life; **couper à travers ~s** to cut across the fields; **vivre en pleins ~s** to live out in the open country; **fleurs des ~s** wild flowers ▸**laisser du** ~ **libre à qn** to leave sb room to manoeuvre; **laisser le** ~ **libre à qn** to give sb a free hand; **sur le** ~ at once
champagne [ʃɑ̃paɲ] *m* champagne
champenois(e) [ʃɑ̃pənwa, waz] *adj* of Champagne
Champenois(e) [ʃɑ̃pənwa, waz] *m(f)* person from Champagne
champêtre [ʃɑ̃pɛtʀ] *adj* **fête** ~ village fête; **vie** ~ country life
champignon [ʃɑ̃piɲɔ̃] *m* **1.** BOT, GASTR mushroom **2.** *a.* MED fungus **3.** *inf* (*accélérateur*) accelerator
champion(ne) [ʃɑ̃pjɔ̃, -jɔn] **I.** *adj inf* **être** ~ to be great **II.** *m(f)* (*vainqueur*) *a. fig* champion; ~ **du monde de boxe** boxing champion of the world
championnat [ʃɑ̃pjɔna] *m* championship
chance [ʃɑ̃s] *f* **1.** (*bonne fortune, hasard*) (good) luck; **coup de** ~ stroke of luck; **avoir de la** ~ to be lucky; **avoir de la** ~ **de** +*infin* to be lucky enough to +*infin;* **porter** ~ **à qn** to bring sb (good) luck; **la** ~ **a tourné** his/her

luck has changed; **par** ~ luckily; **bonne ~!** good luck!; **pas de ~!** *inf* hard luck!; **quelle ~!** what a stroke of (good) luck! **2.** (*probabilité, possibilité de succès*) chance; **tenter sa** ~ to try one's luck; **mettre toutes les ~s de son côté** to take no chances; **rater une** ~ to miss an opportunity

chancelant(e) [ʃɑ̃slɑ̃, ɑ̃t] *adj* (*objet*) unsteady; (*pas, démarche*) tottering; (*autorité, foi*) wavering; (*stabilité, paix, économie, santé*) faltering; **marcher d'un pas** ~ to totter along; (*ivrogne*) to stagger along

chanceler [ʃɑ̃s(ə)le] <3> *vi* **1.** (*tituber*) to totter; (*ivrogne*) to stagger; **faire** ~ **qc** to make sth rock **2.** (*faiblir: décision, autorité, santé*) to falter; (*courage*) to waver

chancelier [ʃɑ̃səlje] *m* HIST chancellor

Chancelier [ʃɑ̃səlje] *m* (*ministre*) Chancellor; ~ **de l'Échiquier** Chancellor of the Exchequer

chancellerie [ʃɑ̃sɛlʀi] *f* **1.** (*administration*) chancellery **2.** (*ministère de la Justice en France*) French Ministry of Justice

chanceux, -euse [ʃɑ̃sø, -øz] *adj* **être** ~ to be lucky

chandail [ʃɑ̃daj] *m* pullover

Chandeleur [ʃɑ̃d(ə)lœʀ] *f* REL **la** ~ Candlemas

> The 2nd of February is the **chandeleur**, an originally Christian feast day on which crêpes are eaten with family and friends. While cooking the crêpes, a coin is held in one hand and the crêpe is tossed with the other. Those who successfully land the crêpe in the pan will have a prosperous year.

chandelier [ʃɑ̃dəlje] *m* candelabra; (*bougeoir*) candlestick

chandelle [ʃɑ̃dɛl] *f* **1.** (*bougie*) candle; **dîner aux ~s** candlelit dinner **2.** SPORT **faire la** ~ to do a shoulder stand; **faire une** ~ (*au tennis*) to hit a lob; (*au football*) to loft the ball **3.** AVIAT **monter en** ~ to climb vertically ▶**devoir une fière ~ à qn** to be greatly indebted to sb; **voir trente-six ~s** to see stars; **tenir la ~ à qn** *iron* to play gooseberry *Brit*, to be a third wheel *Am*

change [ʃɑ̃ʒ] *m* **1.** (*échange d'une monnaie*) (foreign) exchange; **bureau de** ~ bureau de change **2.** (*taux du change*) exchange rate

changeant(e) [ʃɑ̃ʒɑ̃, ɑ̃t] *adj* changeable; (*couleur, reflets, aspect, forme*) changeing; **être d'humeur ~e** to have constant mood changes

changement [ʃɑ̃ʒmɑ̃] *m* **1.** (*modification*) change; ~ **en bien/mal** change for the better/worst; ~ **de temps** change in the weather; **il n'y a aucun** ~ there's been no change **2.** CHEMDFER **il n'y a aucun** ~ you don't have to change; **vous avez un ~ à Francfort** you have to change at Frankfurt **3.** TECH ~ **de vitesse** (*dispositif*) gears *pl;* (*mouvement*) change of gear(s)

changer [ʃɑ̃ʒe] <2a> **I.** *vt* **1.** (*modifier, remplacer*) to change **2.** (*déplacer*) ~ **qc de place** to move sth to a different place; ~ **qn de poste** to move sb to a different job **3.** (*échanger*) ~ **pour** [*o* **contre**] **qc** to exchange for sth **4.** FIN (*convertir*) ~ **contre qc** to change for sth **5.** (*divertir*) ~ **qn de qc** to be a change for sb from sth; **cela m'a changé les idées** that took my mind off things ▶**pour (pas)** ~ *inf* as usual **II.** *vi* **1.** (*se transformer, substituer*) to change; ~ **de forme** to change shape; ~ **de voiture/chemise** to change one's car/shirt **2.** (*déménager*) ~ **de ville** to move to another town **3.** AUTO ~ **de vitesse** to change gears **4.** (*faire un échange*) ~ **de place avec qn** to change (places) with sb **5.** CHEMDFER ~ **à Paris** to change at Paris; ~ **de train** to change trains **6.** (*pour exprimer le franchissement*) ~ **de trottoir** to cross over to the other side of the road; ~ **de file** [*o* **voie**] to change lanes **III.** *vpr* **se** ~ to get changed

chanson [ʃɑ̃sɔ̃] *f* **1.** MUS song; ~ **à la mode,** ~ **populaire** pop song **2.** *inf* (*rengaine*) old story ▶**ça, c'est une autre ~!** that's another story!; **c'est toujours la même ~!** *inf* it's always the same old story!; **connaître la** ~ *inf* to have heard it all before

chansonnier [ʃɑ̃sɔnje] *m* nightclub satirist

chant [ʃɑ̃] *m* **1.** (*action de chanter, musique vocale*) singing; **apprendre le** ~ to learn singing **2.** (*chanson*) song; ~ **populaire** popular song; ~ **de Noël** (Christmas) carol **3.** (*bruits harmonieux: du coq*) crow(ing); (*du grillon*) chirp(ing); (*des oiseaux*) singing

chantage [ʃɑ̃taʒ] *m* blackmail; **faire du ~ à qn** to blackmail sb; **elle lui fait du ~ au suicide** she is blackmailing him by threatening to kill herself

chanter [ʃɑ̃te] <1> **I.** *vi* **1.** (*produire des sons*) to sing; (*coq*) to crow; (*poule*) to cackle; (*insecte*) to chirp **2.** (*menacer*) **faire ~ qn** to blackmail sb ▶**si ça te/vous chante** *inf* if you feel like it **II.** *vt* **1.** (*interpréter*) to sing **2.** (*célébrer*) ~ **les mérites de qn** to sing of sb's merits **3.** (*raconter*) **qu'est-ce que tu me/nous chantes là?** what are you telling me/us?

chanterelle [ʃɑ̃tʀɛl] *f* (*champignon*) chanterelle

chanteur, -euse [ʃɑ̃tœʀ, -øz] **I.** *adj* **oiseau** ~ songbird **II.** *m, f* singer

chantier [ʃɑ̃tje] *m* **1.** (*lieu*) building [*o* construction *Am*] site; (*travaux*) building work; ~ **interdit au public** no entry to the public; **être en** ~ (*immeuble*) to be under construction **2.** *inf* (*désordre*) mess; **quel ~!** what a mess! **3.** *Québec* (*exploitation forestière*) lumber camp ▶**avoir qc en** ~ to be working on sth; **être en** ~ (*roman*) to be in the process of being written

chantilly [ʃɑ̃tiji] *f* chantilly cream

chantonner [ʃɑ̃tɔne] <1> *vt, vi* to hum

chanvre [ʃɑ̃vʀ] *m* hemp

chaos [kao] *m* chaos

chaotique [kaɔtik] *adj* chaotic

chaparder [ʃapaʀde] <1> *vt, vi inf* to pinch

chapeau [ʃapo] <x> *m* (*couvre-chef*) hat; ~ **haut-de-forme** top hat; ~ **melon** bowler hat *Brit,* derby hat *Am;* ~ **de sécurité** *Québec* (*casque*) safety helmet ►~**!** *inf* well done!; **démarrer sur les ~x de roues** *inf* to shoot off at top speed; *fig* to get off to a good start

chapelet [ʃaplɛ] *m* **1.** REL rosary; **dire** [*o* **égrener**] **son** ~ to say the rosary **2.** (*série: d'injures, de saucisses, d'îles*) string; (*bombes*) stick ►**dévider** [*o* **défiler**] **son** ~ to get everything off one's chest

chapelier, **-ière** [ʃapəlje, -jɛʀ] *m, f* **1.** (*pour hommes*) hatter **2.** (*pour femmes*) milliner

chapelle [ʃapɛl] *f* chapel; ~ **ardente** (*dans une église*) chapel of rest; (*dans un lieu profane*) temporary morgue

chapelure [ʃaplyʀ] *f* breadcrumbs *pl*

chapiteau [ʃapito] <x> *m* **1.** (*tente de cirque, le cirque*) big top **2.** (*tente pour une manifestation*) marquee **3.** ARCHIT (*couronnement*) capital

chapitre [ʃapitʀ] *m* chapter

chapon [ʃapɔ̃] *m* capon

chaque [ʃak] *adj inv* **1.** (*qui est pris séparément*) each, every **2.** *inf* (*chacun*) each; **un peu de** ~ a little of everything **3.** (*tous/toutes les*) every

char [ʃaʀ] *m* **1.** MIL tank **2.** (*voiture décorée*) float ►**arrête ton** ~**!** *inf* come off it!

charabia [ʃaʀabja] *m inf* gobbledegook

charade [ʃaʀad] *f* charade

charbon [ʃaʀbɔ̃] *m* **1.** (*combustible*) coal; ~ **de bois** charcoal **2.** MED anthrax **3.** (*fusain*) charcoal ►**aller au** ~**!** *inf* to go to work

charbonnier, **-ière** [ʃaʀbɔnje, -jɛʀ] **I.** *adj* coal; **industries charbonnières et sidérurgiques** coal and steel industries **II.** *m, f* coal merchant ►~ **est maître dans sa maison** [*o* **chez soi**] *prov* a man's home is his castle

charcuter [ʃaʀkyte] <1> *vt péj, inf* **1.** (*découper: viande*) to mangle **2.** *fig* (*personne*) to hack about; (*texte*) to carve up

charcuterie [ʃaʀkytʀi] *f* **1.** (*boutique*) pork butcher's (shop) **2.** (*spécialité*) cooked pork meats *pl*

charcutier, **-ière** [ʃaʀkytje, -jɛʀ] *m, f* pork butcher

chardon [ʃaʀdɔ̃] *m* thistle

chardonneret [ʃaʀdɔnʀɛ] *m* goldfinch

charentaise [ʃaʀɑ̃tɛz] *f* slipper

charge [ʃaʀʒ] *f* **1.** (*fardeau*) burden; (*d'un camion*) load; ~ **utile** payload; ~ **maximale** maximum load **2.** (*responsabilité*) responsibility; **avoir la** ~ **de faire qc** to be responsible for doing sth; **avoir la** ~ **de qn/qc** to be responsible for sb/sth; **être à** (**la**) ~ **de qn** (*personne*) to be dependent on sb; **personnes à** ~ dependents; **qn prend un enfant en** ~ sb takes charge of a child; **prendre qc en** ~ to take care of sth; **à** ~ **pour qn de** +*infin* it's up to sb to +*infin* **3.** (*fonction*) office; **occuper une** ~ to hold an office **4.** *souvent pl* (*obligations financières*) expenses *pl* **5.** JUR, MIL charge

chargé(**e**) [ʃaʀʒe] **I.** *adj* **1.** (*qui porte une charge*) ~ **de qc** loaded with sth; **voyageur très** ~ traveller laden down with luggage *Brit,* traveler laden down with luggage *Am* **2.** (*plein: programme, journée*) full **3.** (*responsable*) ~ **de qn/qc** to be in charge of sb/sth **4.** (*garni: fusil*) loaded; (*batterie*) charged; **mon appareil photo n'est pas** ~ my camera isn't loaded **5.** (*lourd: conscience*) troubled **6.** MED (*estomac*) overloaded; (*langue*) furred **7.** (*rempli*) **le ciel restera** ~ the sky will remain overcast **8.** (*exagéré: style*) intricate **9.** (*riche*) **être** ~ **de qc** to be rich in sth; ~ **de sens** significant **II.** *m(f)* ~ **de cours** ≈ junior lecturer

chargement [ʃaʀʒəmɑ̃] *m* **1.** (*action*) *a.* INFOR loading **2.** (*marchandises*) load **3.** (*fret*) freight

charger [ʃaʀʒe] <2a> **I.** *vt* **1.** (*faire porter une charge: marchandise*) to load; ~ **qn/qc de qc** to load sb/sth up with sth; ~ **sur/dans qc** to load onto/into sth **2.** (*attribuer une mission à*) ~ **qn de qc** to make sb responsible for sth; **être chargé de qc** to be in charge of sth; **il m'a chargé de vous saluer** he asked me to give you his regards **3.** (*accuser*) ~ **qn de qc** to charge sb with sth **4.** (*attaquer*) to charge (at) **5.** TECH (*arme*) to load; (*batterie*) to charge; ~ **un appareil photo** to load a camera **6.** INFOR to load **II.** *vi* (*attaquer*) to charge **III.** *vpr* **1.** (*s'occuper de*) **se** ~ **de qn/qc** to take care of sb/sth; **se** ~ **de** +*infin* to undertake to +*infin* **2.** (*s'alourdir*) **se** ~ to weigh oneself down

chargeur [ʃaʀʒœʀ] *m* **1.** (*docker*) loader **2.** TECH (*d'une arme à feu*) cartridge clip; (*d'une pile, batterie*) charger **3.** PHOT magazine

chariot [ʃaʀjo] *m* **1.** (*plate-forme tractée*) wagon **2.** (*petit engin de transport*) truck; ~ **élévateur** fork-lift truck **3.** (*caddy à bagages*) luggage trolley *Brit,* luggage cart *Am* **4.** COM shopping trolley *Brit,* shopping cart *Am* **5.** GASTR trolley *Brit,* cart *Am*

charisme [kaʀism] *m* charisma

charitable [ʃaʀitabl] *adj* charitable

charité [ʃaʀite] *f* **1.** (*amour du prochain, action*) charity; **demander la** ~ to ask for charity; **vivre de la** ~ **publique** to live on welfare **2.** (*bonté*) **avoir la** ~ **de** +*infin* to be kind enough to +*infin*

charivari [ʃaʀivaʀi] *m* hullabaloo

charlatan [ʃaʀlatɑ̃] *m* **1.** (*escroc*) con man **2.** (*mauvais médecin*) quack (doctor)

Charles [ʃaʀlə] *m* ~ **le Téméraire** Charles the Bold

Charles-Quint [ʃaʀləkɛ̃] *m* Charles the Fifth (of Spain)

charlot [ʃaʀlo] *m inf* clown

Charlot [ʃaʀlo] *m* Charlie Chaplin

charlotte [ʃaʀlɔt] *f* **1.** GASTR charlotte **2.** (*bonnet de plastique*) mobcap

charmant(e) [ʃaʀmɑ̃, ɑ̃t] *adj a. iron* **1.** (*agréable*) charming **2.** (*ravissant*) delightful

charme [ʃaʀm] *m* **1.** (*attrait: d'une personne, d'un lieu*) charm; **faire du ~ à qn** to use one's charms on sb **2.** *souvent pl* (*beauté*) charms *pl* **3.** (*envoûtement*) spell

charmé(e) [ʃaʀme] *adj* **être ~ de qc** to be delighted by sth

charmer [ʃaʀme] <1> *vt* **1.** (*enchanter*) to charm **2.** (*envoûter*) to enchant

charmeur, -euse [ʃaʀmœʀ, -øz] **I.** *adj* (*sourire*) winning; (*air*) charming **II.** *m, f* **1.** (*séducteur*) charmer **2.** (*magicien*) **~ de serpents** snake charmer

charnel(le) [ʃaʀnɛl] *adj* **1.** (*corporel*) physical **2.** (*sexuel*) carnal

charnier [ʃaʀnje] *m* mass grave

charnière [ʃaʀnjɛʀ] **I.** *f* **1.** (*gond*) hinge **2.** (*point de jonction*) **être à la ~ de deux époques** to be at the turning point between two eras **II.** *adj* **1.** (*de transition*) transitional **2.** (*décisif*) **rôle ~** pivotal role

charnu(e) [ʃaʀny] *adj* fleshy

charognard [ʃaʀɔɲaʀ] *m* **1.** (*animal*) carrion eater **2.** *a. fig* vulture

charogne [ʃaʀɔɲ] *f* **1.** (*cadavre: d'un animal*) decaying carcass; (*d'une personne*) decaying corpse **2.** *péj, inf* bastard

charpente [ʃaʀpɑ̃t] *f* **1.** (*bâti*) frame(work); **~ du toit** roof structure **2.** (*carrure: d'une personne*) build

charpentier [ʃaʀpɑ̃tje] *m* carpenter

charpie [ʃaʀpi] *f* **1. faire de la ~ avec qc** to tear sth to shreds **2.** (*battre*) **faire de la ~ avec qn** to make mincemeat of sb

charretier [ʃaʀtje] *m* carter ▸**jurer comme un ~** to swear like a trooper

charrette¹ [ʃaʀɛt] *f* cart

charrette² [ʃaʀɛt] *f Suisse* (*coquin, canaille*) so-and-so

charrier [ʃaʀje] <1> **I.** *vt* **1.** (*transporter*) **~ qc** to cart (along) sth; (*rivière*) to carry (along) sth **2.** *inf* to kid on *Brit,* to put on *Am* **II.** *vi inf* to go too far; (**il ne**) **faut pas ~!** *inf* that's going too far!

charrue [ʃaʀy] *f* plough *Brit,* plow *Am* ▸**mettre la ~ avant** [*o* **devant**] **les bœufs** to put the cart before the horse

charte [ʃaʀt] *f* charter

charter [ʃaʀtɛʀ] **I.** *m* **1.** (*vol*) charter flight **2.** (*avion*) chartered plane **II.** *app inv* charter

chasse¹ [ʃas] *f* **1.** (*action*) hunting; **~ au trésor** treasure hunt; **la ~ est ouverte/fermée** it's the open/close season *Brit,* it's open/closed season *Am;* **aller à la ~** to go hunting; **faire la ~ à un criminel** to hunt down a criminal; **faire la ~ aux souris** to chase mice **2.** (*poursuite*) **~ aux sorcières** witch hunt; **prendre qn/qc en ~** to give chase to sb/sth **3.** (*lieu*) hunting ground; **~ gardée** private hunting ground **4.** AVIAT **la ~** fighter planes *pl;* **pilote de ~** fighter pilot ▸**qui va à la ~ perd sa place** *prov* if you leave your place you will lose it

chasse² [ʃas] *f inf* (*chasse d'eau*) (toilet) flush; **tirer la ~** to flush the toilet

chassé-croisé [ʃasekʀwaze] <chassés-croisés> *m* comings and goings; (*des estivants*) heavy traffic in both directions

chasse-neige [ʃasnɛʒ] *m inv* **1.** (*véhicule*) snowplough *Brit,* snowplow *Am* **2.** (*en ski*) **descendre en ~** to snowplough down *Brit,* to snowplow down *Am*

chasser [ʃase] <1> **I.** *vi* **1.** (*aller à la chasse*) to go hunting **2.** (*déraper*) to skid **II.** *vt* **1.** (*aller à la chasse*) to hunt **2.** (*faire partir*) **~ qn/qc de qc** to drive sb/sth out [*o* away] from sth **3.** *fig* (*idées noires*) to dispel

chasseur [ʃasœʀ] *m* **1.** MIL chasseur **2.** (*avion*) fighter **3.** (*groom*) bellboy **4.** *fig* **~ de têtes** headhunter

chasseur, -euse [ʃasœʀ, -øz] *m, f* hunter

châssis [ʃɑsi] *m* **1.** TECH, AUTO chassis **2.** (*cadre: d'une fenêtre, une toile*) frame

chaste [ʃast] *adj* chaste

chasteté [ʃastəte] *f* chastity

chat¹ [ʃa] *m* (*animal*) cat; (*mâle*) tomcat; **~ de gouttière** (*espèce banale*) ordinary cat; *v. a.* **chatte** ▸**~ échaudé craint l'eau froide** *prov* once bitten, twice shy; **avoir un ~ dans la gorge** to have a frog in one's throat; **quand le ~ n'est pas là, les souris dansent** *prov* when the cat's away the mice will play; **il n'y a pas un ~ dans la rue** there's not a soul in the street

chat² [tʃat] *m* INFOR chat

châtaigne [ʃɑtɛɲ] *f* **1.** (*fruit*) (sweet) chestnut **2.** *fig, inf* **je lui ai flanqué une de ces ~s!** I gave him a clout!

châtaignier [ʃɑteɲe] *m* **1.** (*arbre*) (sweet) chestnut tree **2.** (*bois*) chestnut

châtain [ʃɑtɛ̃] *adj pas de forme féminine* chestnut brown; **être ~ clair** to have light brown hair

château [ʃɑto] <x> *m* **1.** (*palais*) palace **2.** (*forteresse*) **~ fort** castle **3.** (*belle maison*) manor (house) **4.** (*fig*) **~ d'eau** water tower; **~ de cartes** house of cards; **~ de sable** sand castle

châtelain(e) [ʃɑt(ə)lɛ̃, ɛn] *m(f)* **1.** HIST lord **2.** (*seigneur d'un château fortifié*) lord of the manor **3.** (*propriétaire d'un manoir*) owner of the manor

chat-huant [ʃayɑ̃] <chats-huants> *m* tawny owl

châtier [ʃɑtje] <1> *vt* **1.** *soutenu* (*punir*) to chastize **2.** REL **~ son corps** [*o* **sa chair**] to mortify one's flesh **3.** (*soigner: style, langage*) to refine

châtiment [ʃɑtimɑ̃] *m* punishment

chatoiement [ʃatwamɑ̃] *m* shimmering; (*d'un diamant*) sparkle

chaton [ʃatɔ̃] *m* **1.** (*jeune chat*) kitten **2.** BOT catkin

chatouiller [ʃatuje] <1> *vt* **1.** (*faire des cha-*

C

touilles) to tickle; **elle lui chatouille le bras** she is tickling his arm **2.** (*flatter*) to flatter; (*curiosité*) to tickle; **ça chatouille le palais** that titillates your palate

chatouilles [ʃatuj] *fpl* tickling; **faire des ~ à qn** to tickle sb

chatouilleux, -euse [ʃatujø, -jøz] *adj* **1.** (*sensible aux chatouilles*) ticklish **2.** (*susceptible*) touchy

chatoyant(e) [ʃatwajɑ̃, ɑ̃t] *adj* shimmering; (*pierre précieuse*) sparkling

chatoyer [ʃatwaje] <6> *vi* to shimmer; (*bijou*) to sparkle

châtrer [ʃɑtʀe] <1> *vt* to castrate

chatte [ʃat] *f* (female) cat; *v. a.* **chat**

chatter [tʃate] <1> *vi* INFOR to chat

chaud [ʃo] *m* (*chaleur*) warmth; (*chaleur extrême*) heat; **il fait ~** it's warm [*o* hot]; **tenir ~ à qn** to keep sb warm; **crever de ~** *inf* to be sweltering; **garder** [*o* **tenir**] **qc au ~** to keep sth warm [*o* hot]; **il/elle a assez/trop ~** he/she is warm enough/too warm ▸**ne faire ni ~ ni froid à qn** to make no difference to sb; **il/elle a eu ~** *inf* he/she had a narrow escape **II.** *adv* **reportage à ~** on-the-spot report; **faire qc à ~** to do sth immediately

chaud(e) [ʃo, ʃod] *adj* (*opp: froid*) warm; (*très chaud*) hot; **repas ~** hot meal; **vin ~** mulled wine; **chocolat ~** hot chocolate **2.** *antéposé* (*intense: discussion*) heated; **avec les plus ~es recommandations** with the warmest recommendations; **l'alerte a été ~e** it was a close thing **3.** (*chaleureux: couleur, ton*) warm **4.** *inf* (*sensuel*) hot

chaudement [ʃodmɑ̃] *adv* **1.** (*contre le froid*) warmly **2.** (*vivement: féliciter*) warmly; (*recommander*) heartily

chaudière [ʃodjɛʀ] *f* boiler

chaudron [ʃodʀɔ̃] *m* cauldron

chauffage [ʃofaʒ] *m* **1.** (*installation*) heating **2.** (*appareil*) heater

chauffant(e) [ʃofɑ̃, ɑ̃t] *adj* heating; (*brosse*) heated

chauffard [ʃofaʀ] *m* reckless driver

chauffe-eau [ʃofo] *m inv* water heater; (*à accumulation*) immersion heater **chauffe-plat** [ʃofpla] <chauffe-plats> *m* plate-warmer

chauffer [ʃofe] <1> **I.** *vi* **1.** (*être sur le feu*) to be warming up; (*très chaud*) to be heating up **2.** (*devenir chaud*) to warm up; (*très chaud*) to heat up **3.** (*devenir trop chaud: moteur*) to overheat ▸**ça va ~** *inf* there's going to be trouble **II.** *vt* **1.** (*rendre plus chaud: personne*) to warm [*o* to heat] up; (*pièce, maison*) to heat; (*eau*) to heat (up); **faire ~** to warm [*o* to heat *Am*] (up); **faire ~ le four** to heat (up) the oven **2.** TECH to heat; **~ à blanc** to make white-hot **3.** (*mettre dans l'ambiance*) to warm up **III.** *vpr* **se ~ au soleil** to warm oneself in the sun; **se ~ au gaz/charbon** to use gas/coal for heating

chauffeur [ʃofœʀ] *m* **1.** (*conducteur*) driver; **~ routier** long-distance lorry driver *Brit,* long-distance truck driver *Am;* **~ de taxi** taxi driver **2.** (*personnel*) chauffeur ▸**~ du dimanche** *inf* Sunday driver

chauffeuse [ʃoføz] *f* low fireside chair

chaume [ʃom] *m* **1.** (*partie des tiges*) stubble **2.** (*toiture*) thatch

chaumière [ʃomjɛʀ] *f* (*à toit de chaume*) thatched cottage

chaussée [ʃose] *f* road(way) ▸**"~ déformée"** "uneven road surface"; **~ glissante** slippery surface

chausse-pied [ʃospje] <chausse-pieds> *m* shoehorn

chausser [ʃose] <1> **I.** *vt* **1.** (*mettre: chaussures*) to put on; (*skis*) to clip on; **être chaussé de bottes** to be wearing boots **2.** (*aller*) **bien/mal ~** (*chaussure*) well/poorly shod **II.** *vi* **~ du 38/42** to take a size 38/42 *Brit,* to wear size 38/42; **du combien chaussez-vous?** what size do you take? **III.** *vpr* **se ~** to put one's shoes on; **se ~ chez qn** to buy one's shoes at sb's

chaussette [ʃosɛt] *f* **1.** (*soquette*) sock **2.** (*mi-bas*) knee sock

chausson [ʃosɔ̃] *m* **1.** (*chaussure*) slipper; **des ~s pour bébés** bootees; **~ de danse** ballet shoe **2.** GASTR **~ aux pommes** apple turnover

chaussure [ʃosyʀ] *f* **1.** (*soulier*) shoe; **~s à talons** high-heeled shoes; **~s à crampons** (*d'athlète*) spikes **2.** (*industrie*) shoe industry **3.** (*commerce*) shoe trade ▸**trouver ~ à son pied** to find a suitable match

chauve [ʃov] **I.** *adj* chauve **II.** *m* bald(-headed) man

chauve-souris [ʃovsuʀi] <chauves-souris> *f* bat

chauvin(e) [ʃovɛ̃, in] **I.** *adj* chauvinistic **II.** *m(f)* chauvinist

chauvinisme [ʃovinism] *m* chauvinism

chaux [ʃo] *f* lime

chavirer [ʃaviʀe] <1> **I.** *vi* **1.** (*se retourner*) to capsize; **faire ~ un bateau** to capsize a boat **2.** (*s'émouvoir*) **~ de bonheur** to reel in delight **II.** *vt* **1.** (*renverser*) to capsize **2.** (*bouleverser*) **être tout chaviré** to be overwhelmed

chef [ʃɛf] *m* **1.** (*responsable*) boss; (*d'une tribu*) chief(tain); **rédacteur/ingénieur en ~** chief editor/engineer; **~ d'État** head of state; **~ d'entreprise** company head; **~ d'orchestre** conductor; **jouer au petit ~** *inf* to throw one's weight around **2.** (*meneur*) leader **3.** *inf* (*champion*) ace; **se débrouiller comme un ~** to do magnificently well **4.** MIL (*sergent-~*) sergeant; **oui ~!** yes, Sarge! **5.** (*cuisinier*) chef

chef-d'œuvre [ʃɛdœvʀ] <chefs-d'œuvre> *m* masterpiece

chef-lieu [ʃɛfljø] <chefs-lieux> *m* administrative centre *Brit,* administrative center *Am*

cheik [ʃɛk] *m* sheikh

chemin [ʃ(ə)mɛ̃] *m* **1.** way; **demander son ~ à qn** to ask sb the way; **prendre le ~ de la gare** to head for the station; **rebrousser ~** to turn back; **~ faisant, en ~** on the way; **se tromper de ~** to go the wrong way; **un bon bout de ~** a good way; **faire tout le ~ à pied/bicyclette/en voiture** to walk/cycle/drive all the way; **le ~ de la réussite** the road to success; **en prendre/ne pas en prendre le ~** to be going the right/wrong way about it; **ça en prend/n'en prend pas le ~** it looks/it doesn't look likely **2.** INFOR path ▶**tous les ~s mènent à Rome** *prov* all roads lead to Rome; **le droit ~** the straight and narrow (way); **ne pas y aller par quatre ~s** not to beat about the bush

chemin de fer [ʃ(ə)mɛ̃dəfɛʀ] <chemins de fer> *m* railway *Brit,* railroad *Am*

cheminée [ʃ(ə)mine] *f* **1.** (*à l'extérieur*) chimney (stack); (*de locomotive*) funnel **2.** (*dans une pièce*) fireplace **3.** (*encadrement*) mantelpiece **4.** (*conduit*) chimney

cheminer [ʃ(ə)mine] <1> *vi* **1.** (*aller*) to walk (along) **2.** *fig* (*pensée*) to progress

cheminot [ʃ(ə)mino] *m* railway worker

chemise [ʃ(ə)miz] *f* **1.** (*vêtement*) shirt; **~ de nuit** (*de femme*) nightgown; (*d'homme*) nightshirt **2.** (*dossier*) folder ▶**y laisser jusqu'à sa dernière ~** to ruin oneself; **qn se fiche de qc comme de sa première ~** *inf* sb doesn't give two hoots about sth *Brit,* sb doesn't give a hoot about sth *Am*

chemisette [ʃ(ə)mizɛt] *f* short-sleeved blouse

chemisier [ʃ(ə)mizje] *m* blouse

chenal [ʃənal, o] <-aux> *m* (*passage*) channel

chenapan [ʃ(ə)napɑ̃] *m* rascal

chêne [ʃɛn] *m* **1.** (*arbre*) oak (tree) **2.** (*bois*) oak

chêne-liège [ʃɛnljɛʒ] <chênes-lièges> *m* cork oak

chenet [ʃ(ə)nɛ] *m* andiron

chenil [ʃ(ə)nil] *m* **1.** (*abri pour les chiens*) kennels *pl* **2.** *Suisse* (*désordre, objets sans valeur*) junk

chenille [ʃ(ə)nij] *f* caterpillar

cheptel [ʃɛptɛl] *m* livestock; **~ bovin/ovin/porcin** cattle/sheep/pigs

chèque [ʃɛk] *m* **1.** (*pièce bancaire*) cheque *Brit,* check *Am;* **~ sans provision** bad cheque; **~ bancaire** cheque; **~ postal** ≈ giro cheque *Brit;* **faire un ~ de 100 euros à qn** to write out a cheque for 100 euros to sb **2.** (*bon*) voucher

chèque-restaurant [ʃɛkʀɛstɔʀɑ̃] <chèques-restaurant> *m* luncheon voucher *Brit,* meal ticket *Am*

chèque-vacances [ʃɛkvakɑ̃s] <chèques-vacances> *m: voucher, partly paid for by employers, entitling employees to holiday at reduced price*

chéquier [ʃekje] *m* cheque-book *Brit,* checkbook *Am*

cher, **chère** [ʃɛʀ] **I.** *adj* **1.** (*coûteux*) expensive, dear **2.** (*aimé*) dear; **c'est mon plus ~ désir** it's my greatest desire **3.** *antéposé* (*estimé*) dear; **~ Monsieur** dear Sir; **chère Madame** dear Madame; **~s tous** dear all **II.** *m, f appellatif* **mon ~/ma chère** my dear **III.** *adv* **1.** (*opp: bon marché*) a lot (of money); **acheter qc trop ~** to pay too much for sth; **avoir pour pas ~** *inf* to get cheap; **coûter/valoir ~** to cost/to be worth a lot; **revenir ~ à qn** to be expensive for sb **2.** *fig* **coûter ~ à qn** to cost sb dearly; **payer ~ qc** to pay dearly for sth; **payer** [*o* **donner**] **~ pour connaître la clef de l'énigme** to give a lot to know the key to the riddle

chercher [ʃɛʀʃe] <1> **I.** *vt* **1.** (*rechercher: personne, objet, compromis*) to look for; **~ qn des yeux** to look around for sb **2.** (*ramener, rapporter*) **aller/venir ~ qn/qc** to go/to come and get sb/sth; **envoyer un enfant ~ qn/qc** to send a child for sb/sth ▶**~ qn** *inf* to be looking for an argument with sb; **tu l'as (bien) cherché!** you've been asking for it!; **qu'est-ce que tu vas ~ (là)!** what are you thinking of! **II.** *vi* **1.** (*s'efforcer de*) **~ à** *+infin* to try to *+infin;* **~ à ce que qn fasse qc** (*subj*) to try to make sb do sth **2.** (*fouiller*) **~ dans qc** to look in sth **3.** (*réfléchir*) to think ▶**ça peut aller ~ loin!** *inf* that can cost a lot!

chercheur, **-euse** [ʃɛʀʃœʀ, -øz] *m, f* **1.** (*savant*) researcher **2.** (*aventurier*) **~ d'or** gold digger

chère [ʃɛʀ] *f soutenu* fare ▶**faire bonne ~** to eat well

chèrement [ʃɛʀmɑ̃] *adv* (*payer, vendre*) dearly

chéri(e) [ʃeʀi] **I.** *adj* beloved **II.** *m(f)* **1.** (*personne aimée*) darling **2.** *péj* (*favori*) **le ~/la ~e de qn** sb's darling

chérir [ʃeʀiʀ] <8> *vt* (*aimer*) to cherish

chérot [ʃeʀo] *adj inf* **c'est** [*o* **ça fait** (**un peu**)] **~** it's on the pricey side

cherry <s *o* -ries> [ʃeʀi] *m* cherry brandy

chérubin [ʃeʀybɛ̃] *m* cherub

chétif, **-ive** [ʃetif, -iv] *adj* (*arbre*) stunted; (*personne*) puny

cheval [ʃ(ə)val, o] <-aux> **I.** *m* **1.** ZOOL horse **2.** SPORT **faire du ~** to go (horse) riding *Brit,* to go horseback riding *Am;* **monter à ~** to ride a horse; **promenade à ~** (horse) ride **3.** AUTO, FIN **~ fiscal** *horsepower, used to determine automobile tax;* **elle fait combien de chevaux votre voiture?** what horsepower is your car? **4.** JEUX knight **5.** (*figure*) **chevaux de bois** merry-go-round; **~ à bascule** rocking horse **II.** *adv* **être à ~ sur la chaise** to be sitting astride the chair; **être à ~ sur les principes** to be a stickler for principles; **le paiement de la facture est à ~ sur deux mois** the payment of the bill is spread over two months

chevaleresque [ʃ(ə)valʀɛsk] *adj* chivalrous; (*littérature*) of chivalry; (*honneur*) knightly

C

chevalerie [ʃ(ə)valʀi] *f* chivalry
chevalet [ʃ(ə)valɛ] *m* (*de peintre*) easel; (*d'un violon*) bridge
chevalier [ʃ(ə)valje] *m* knight
chevalière [ʃ(ə)valjɛʀ] *f* signet ring
chevalin(**e**) [ʃ(ə)valɛ̃, in] *adj* **sourire** ~ horsey smile
cheval-vapeur [ʃ(ə)valvapœʀ] <chevaux-vapeur> *m* horsepower
chevauchée [ʃ(ə)voʃe] *f* (*promenade*) ride
chevaucher [ʃ(ə)voʃe] <1> **I.** *vt* ~ **qc** to sit astride sth **II.** *vpr* **se** ~ to overlap **III.** *vi* to ride
chevelu(**e**) [ʃəvly] **I.** *adj* hairy **II.** *m(f) péj: person with a bushy mane of hair*
chevelure [ʃəvlyʀ] *f* **1.** (*cheveux*) hair **2.** (*traînée lumineuse: d'une comète*) tail
chevet [ʃ(ə)vɛ] *m* bedhead; **table de** ~ bedside table; **être au** ~ **de qn** to be at sb's bedside
cheveu [ʃ(ə)vø] <x> *m* hair; **avoir les ~x courts/longs** to have short/long hair; **n'avoir plus un** ~ **sur la tête** not to have a single hair (left) on one's head ▸**avoir un** ~ **sur la langue** to have a lisp; **comme un** ~ **sur la soupe** at a very awkward moment; **couper les ~x en quatre** to split hairs; **c'était à un** ~ **près, il s'en est fallu d'un** ~ it was a (very) close thing; **être tiré par les ~x** to be far-fetched
cheville [ʃ(ə)vij] *f* **1.** ANAT ankle **2.** (*tige pour assembler*) peg **3.** (*tige pour boucher*) dowel ▸**ne pas arriver à la** ~ **de qn** not to be able to hold a candle to sb
chèvre [ʃɛvʀ] **I.** *f* **1.** (*animal*) goat **2.** (*femelle*) nanny goat **II.** *m* (*fromage*) goat's cheese
chevreau [ʃəvʀo] <x> *m* kid
chèvrefeuille [ʃɛvʀəfœj] *m* honeysuckle
chevreuil [ʃəvʀœj] *m* **1.** (*animal*) roe deer **2.** (*mâle*) roebuck **3.** GASTR venison **4.** *Québec* (*cerf de Virginie*) deer
chevrier, **-ière** [ʃəvʀije, -jɛʀ] *m, f* goatherd
chevron [ʃəvʀɔ̃] *m* **1.** (*poutre*) rafter **2.** (*galon, ornement*) *a.* MIL chevron
chevronné(**e**) [ʃəvʀɔne] *adj* experienced
chevrotant(**e**) [ʃəvʀɔtɑ̃, ɑ̃t] *adj* quavering
chevrotine [ʃəvʀɔtin] *f* buckshot
chewing-gum [ʃwiŋgɔm] <chewing-gums> *m* chewing gum
chez [ʃe] *prep* **1.** (*au logis de qn*) ~ **qn** at sb's place; ~ **soi** at home; **je vais/rentre** ~ **moi** I'm going home; **je viens** ~ **toi** I'll come to your place; **passer** ~ **qn** to stop by sb's place; **aller** ~ **le coiffeur** to go to the hairdresser's; **faites comme** ~ **vous!** make yourself at home!; **à côté** [*o* **près**] **de** ~ **moi** near my place **2.** (*dans le pays de qn*) **ils rentrent** ~ **eux, en Italie** they're going back home to Italy; **une coutume bien de** ~ **nous** *inf* a good old local custom **3.** (*dans la personne*) ~ **les Durand** at the Durand's; ~ **Corneille** in Corneille; **c'est une habitude** ~ **lui** it's a habit with him
chez-moi [ʃemwa] *m inv,* **chez-soi** [ʃeswa] *m inv* (own) home
chialer [ʃjale] <1> *vi inf* to blubber
chiant(**e**) [ʃjɑ̃, ʃjɑ̃t] *adj inf* bloody [*o* damn *Am*] annoying
chic [ʃik] **I.** *m sans pl* chic ▸**avoir le** ~ **pour faire qc** to have the knack of doing sth **II.** *adj inv* **1.** (*élégant*) chic; (*allure*) stylish **2.** (*sélect*) smart **3.** *inf* (*gentil*) ~ **type** nice guy; **ce n'est pas très** ~ **de sa part** it's not very nice of him/her ▸**bon** ~ **bon genre** *iron* chic and conservative; **quartier bon** ~ **bon genre** posh neighbourhood *Brit,* posh neighborhood *Am* **III.** *interj inf* ~ (**alors**)! great!
chicane [ʃikan] *f* **1.** (*morceau de route*) chicane **2.** (*querelle*) squabble
chicaner [ʃikane] <1> **I.** *vi* ~ **sur qc** to squabble about sth **II.** *vt* **1.** (*chercher querelle à*) ~ **qn sur qc** to quibble with sb over sth **2.** *Québec* (*ennuyer, tracasser*) to bother **III.** *vpr inf* **se** ~ to squabble
chiche [ʃiʃ] **I.** *adj* **1.** (*avare de*) **être** ~ **d'explications** to be sparing with explanations **2.** (*pas grand-chose*) **c'est un peu** ~ it's rather meagre *Brit,* it's rather meager *Am* **3.** (*capable*) **t'es pas** ~ **de faire ça!** *inf* you couldn't do that! **II.** *interj inf* ~ **que je le fais!** (*capable*) I bet you I can do it!; ~**!** (*pari accepté*) you're on
chichement [ʃiʃmɑ̃] *adv* **vivre** ~ to eke out a livelihood
chichis [ʃiʃi] *mpl inf* **faire des** ~ to make a fuss; **pas tant de** ~**!** no more fuss, please!
chicon [ʃikɔ̃] *m Belgique* (*endive*) chicory *Brit,* endive *Am*
chicorée [ʃikɔʀe] *f* **1.** (*plante*) endive *Brit,* chicory *Am* **2.** (*café*) chicory coffee
chié(**e**) [ʃje] *adj inf* **1.** (*super*) bloody great *Brit,* bitchin *Am* **2.** (*incroyable*) **être** ~ to be bloody [*o* damned *Am*] impossible
chien [ʃjɛ̃] **I.** *m* **1.** (*animal*) dog; ~ **bâtard** mongrel; ~ **de race** pedigree dog; (**attention**) ~ **méchant!** beware of the dog!; *v. a.* **chienne** **2.** (*pièce coudée: d'un fusil*) hammer ▸**s'entendre** [*o* **vivre**] **comme** ~ **et chat** to fight like cat and dog; **entre** ~ **et loup** in the twilight; **vie de** ~ dog's life; **temps de** ~ foul weather; **métier de** ~ rotten job; **avoir un caractère de** ~ to have a foul temper; **il a un mal de** ~ **pour finir son travail** he has great difficulty in finishing his work **II.** *adj inv* (*avare*) mean; **ne pas être** ~ **avec qn** to be quite generous towards sb
chiendent [ʃjɛ̃dɑ̃] *m* couch grass
chienne [ʃjɛn] *f* bitch; *v. a.* **chien** ▸~ **de vie** dog's life
chier [ʃje] <1a> *vt, vi vulg* to shit ▸**y a pas à** ~**!** there's no two ways about it!; **faire** ~ **qn** to get up sb's nose; **fais pas** ~**!** piss off!; **se faire** ~ to be bored out of one's skull; **ça va** ~ (**des bulles**)! the shit'll hit the fan!
chiffon [ʃifɔ̃] *m* **1.** (*tissu*) rag **2.** (*document sans valeur*) **ce devoir est un vrai** ~ this homework is an awful mess **3.** (*vêtement de femme*) **parler** [*o* **causer**] **~s** *inf* to talk

(about) clothes

chiffonné(e) [ʃifɔne] *adj* **1.** (*froissé*) crumpled **2.** *fig* **avoir la mine ~e** to look worn-out

chiffonner [ʃifɔne] <1> **I.** *vt* **1.** (*froisser*) to crumple **2.** (*chagriner*) to bother **II.** *vpr* **se ~** to crumple

chiffonnier, -ière [ʃifɔnje, -jɛʀ] *m, f* **se disputer comme des ~s** to quarrel like fishwives

chiffre [ʃifʀ] *m* **1.** (*caractère*) figure; **~ romain** roman numeral; **un numéro à trois ~s** a three-figure number **2.** (*montant*) total; **~ d'affaires** turnover *Brit,* sales *Am* **3.** (*nombre: des naissances*) number **4.** (*statistiques*) **les ~s** the figures; **en ~s ronds** in round figures; **les ~s du chômage** the unemployment statistics **5.** (*code: d'un coffre-fort*) combination; (*d'un message*) code

chiffré(e) [ʃifʀe] *adj* **message ~** coded message

chiffrer [ʃifʀe] <1> **I.** *vt* **1.** (*numéroter*) to number **2.** (*évaluer*) to assess **3.** (*coder*) to encode **II.** *vi inf* **ça chiffre** it all adds up **III.** *vpr* **se ~ à qc** to amount to sth

chignole [ʃiɲɔl] *f* **1.** (*perceuse*) hand drill **2.** *péj, inf* (*voiture*) jalopy, (old) banger *Brit*

chignon [ʃiɲɔ̃] *m* bun

chiite [ʃiit] *adj* Shiite

Chiite [ʃiit] *mf* Shiite

Chili [ʃili] *m* **le ~** Chile

chilien(ne) [ʃiljɛ̃, jɛn] *adj* Chilean

Chilien(ne) [ʃiljɛ̃, jɛn] *m(f)* Chilean

chimère [ʃimɛːʀ(ə)] *f* (*utopie*) wild dream

chimérique [ʃimeʀik] *adj* (*imagination, projet*) fanciful; **c'est un esprit ~** his head's in the clouds

chimie [ʃimi] *f* chemistry

chimio [ʃimjo] *f inf,* **chimiothérapie** [ʃimjoteʀapi] *f* chemotherapy

chimique [ʃimik] *adj* chemical

chimiste [ʃimist] *mf* chemist

chimpanzé [ʃɛ̃pɑ̃ze] *m* chimpanzee

chinchilla [ʃɛ̃ʃila] *m* chinchilla

Chine [ʃin] *f* **la ~** China

chiné(e) [ʃine] *adj* chiné

Chinetoque [ʃintɔk] *mf péj, inf* Chink

chinois(e) [ʃinwa, waz] **I.** *adj* Chinese **II.** *m* **1.** (*langue*) Chinese; *v. a.* **français 2.** GASTR (conical) strainer ►**pour moi c'est du ~** it's all Greek to me

Chinois(e) [ʃinwa, waz] *m(f)* Chinese *no art*

chinoiser [ʃinwaze] <1> *vi* to split hairs

chinoiserie [ʃinwazʀi] *f* **1.** (*bibelot*) **des ~s** chinoiserie **2.** *pl* (*complication*) unnecessary complications

chiot [ʃjo] *m* pup(py)

chiottes [ʃjɔt] *fpl inf* bog *Brit,* john *Am*

chiper [ʃipe] <1> *vt inf* to pinch

chipie [ʃipi] *f* **1.** (*mégère*) dragon; **vieille ~** old battleaxe *Brit,* old battleax *Am* **2.** (*petite fille*) little minx

chipoter [ʃipɔte] <1> *vi* **1.** (*ergoter*) **~ sur qc** to quibble about sth **2.** (*marchander*) **~ sur le prix** to haggle over the price

chips [ʃips] *f gén pl* crisps *Brit,* chips *Am*

chique [ʃik] *f* **1.** (*tabac*) plug **2.** *Belgique* (*bonbon*) sweet

chiqué [ʃike] *m inf* **1.** (*affectation*) airs *pl;* **faire du ~** [*o* **tout au ~**] to put on airs **2.** (*bluff*) sham; **c'est du ~** it's a put-on

chiquenaude [ʃiknod] *f* **1.** (*pichenette*) flick **2.** (*petite impulsion*) push

chiquer [ʃike] <1> *vi* to chew tobacco

chiromancie [kiʀɔmɑ̃si] *f* palmistry

chiropracteur [kiʀɔpʀaktœʀ] *m,* **chiropraticien(ne)** [kiʀɔpʀatisjɛ̃, jɛn] *m(f)* chiropractor

chirurgical(e) [ʃiʀyʀʒikal, o] <-aux> *adj* surgical

chirurgie [ʃiʀyʀʒi] *f* surgery; **~ esthétique** plastic surgery

chirurgien(ne) [ʃiʀyʀʒjɛ̃, jɛn] *m(f)* surgeon; **~ dentiste** dental surgeon

chlinguer [ʃlɛ̃ge] <1> *vi v.* **schlinguer**

chlore [klɔʀ] *m* chlorine

chloroforme [klɔʀɔfɔʀm] *m* chloroform

chlorophylle [klɔʀɔfil] *f* chlorophyll

chlorure [klɔʀyʀ] *m* **~ de sodium** sodium chloride

chnoque [ʃnɔk] *m inf v.* **schnock**

choc [ʃɔk] *m* **1.** (*émotion brutale*) shock; **être en état de ~** to be in a state of shock **2.** *fig* (*des idées*) clash; **~ culturel** culture shock **3.** (*coup*) shock; **ce matériau ne résiste pas aux ~s** this material is not shock-resistant **4.** (*heurt*) impact **5.** (*collision*) crash ►**traitement de ~** shock treatment

chochotte [ʃɔʃɔt] **I.** *adj inf* (*snob*) **être ~** to be affected **II.** *f inf* **faire la** [*o* **sa**] **~** to make a fuss (about nothing)

chocolat [ʃɔkɔla] **I.** *m* chocolate; **barre de ~** chocolate bar; **œuf en ~** chocolate egg; **~ en poudre** drinking chocolate; **~ liégeois** chocolate ice cream (*with whipped cream*) **II.** *adj inv* (*couleur*) chocolate(-coloured)

chocolaté(e) [ʃɔkɔlate] *adj* **crème ~e** chocolate cream

chocolatier, -ière [ʃɔkɔlatje, -jɛʀ] **I.** *adj* **industrie chocolatière** chocolate industry **II.** *m, f* **1.** (*producteur*) chocolate maker **2.** (*commerçant*) chocolate seller

chœur [kœʀ] *m* **1.** (*chanteurs*) choir **2.** (*groupe*) chorus

choir [ʃwaʀ] *vi irr, inf* **laisser ~ qn** to let sb down

choisi(e) [ʃwazi] *adj* **1.** (*sélectionné: morceau*) selected **2.** (*élégant: langage*) refined

choisir [ʃwaziʀ] <8> **I.** *vi* to choose **II.** *vt* to choose **III.** *vpr* **se ~ qn/qc** to choose sb/sth

choix [ʃwa] *m* **1.** (*action de choisir: d'un ami, cadeau*) choice; **à ton/leur ~** as you/they wish; **un dessert au ~** a choice of dessert; **laisser le ~ à qn** to let sb decide **2.** (*décision*) **c'est un ~ à faire** it's a choice which has to be made; **arrêter** [*o* **fixer**] [*o* **porter**] **son ~ sur qc** to decide on sth **3.** (*variété*) selection

4. (*qualité*) **de ~** choice; **de premier/second ~** top grade/grade two

choléra [kɔleʀa] *m* cholera

cholestérol [kɔlɛsteʀɔl] *m* cholesterol

chômage [ʃomaʒ] *m* unemployment; **être au ~** to be unemployed; **s'inscrire au ~** to apply for unemployment benefits; **toucher le ~** *inf* to get unemployment benefits

chômé(e) [ʃome] *adj* **jour ~** public holiday

chômer [ʃome] <1> *vi* **1.** (*être sans travail*) to be unemployed **2.** (*ne pas travailler*) to be idle

chômeur, -euse [ʃomœʀ, -øz] *m, f* unemployed person

chope [ʃɔp] *f* **1.** (*verre*) beer mug **2.** (*contenu*) pint

choper [ʃɔpe] <1> *vt inf* (*attraper: grippe*) to catch

chopine [ʃɔpin] *f Québec* (*mesure de capacité pour les liquides valant une demi-pinte* (*0.568l*)) half-pint

choquant(e) [ʃɔkɑ̃, ɑ̃t] *adj* shocking

choquer [ʃɔke] <1> **I.** *vt* **1.** (*scandaliser*) to shock **2.** (*offusquer: pudeur*) to offend (against); **~ le bon goût** to offend against good taste **3.** (*commotionner*) **~ qn** to shake (up) sb **II.** *vpr* **se ~ facilement** to be easily shocked; **je ne me choque plus de rien** I'm not shocked at anything any more

choral [kɔʀal] <s> *m* chorale

choral(e) [kɔʀal] <-aux *o* s> *adj* choral

chorale [kɔʀal] *f* choral society

chorégraphe [kɔʀegʀaf] *mf* choreographer

chorégraphie [kɔʀegʀafi] *f* choreography

choriste [kɔʀist] *mf* (*d'église*) choir member; (*d'opéra*) member of the chorus

chose [ʃoz] **I.** *f* **1.** (*objet*) thing; **appeler les ~s par leur nom** to call a spade a spade; **ne pas faire les ~s à moitié** not to do things by halves; **chaque ~ en son temps** everything in its own time; **les meilleures ~s ont une fin** all good things come to an end; **c'est la moindre des ~s** it's the least I could do **2.** (*ensemble d'événements, de circonstances*) **les ~s** things; **comment les ~s se sont-elles passées?** how did it happen?; **voyons où en sont les ~s!** let's see how things stand!; **les ~s étant ce qu'elles sont** things being as they are; **au point où en sont les ~s** at the point we've got to; **les ~s se gâtent** things are taking a turn for the worst **3.** (*ce dont il s'agit*) matter; **comment a-t-il pris la ~?** how did he take it?; **encore une ~** something else; **c'est ~ faite** it's done; **mettre les ~s au point** to clear things up; **c'est tout autre ~** that's quite different **4.** (*paroles*) **j'ai deux/plusieurs ~s à vous dire** I've (got) several things to tell you; **vous lui direz bien des ~s de ma part** please give him/her my (best) regards; **parler de ~s et d'autres** to talk about one thing and another; **passer à autre ~** to talk about something else ▸**voilà <u>autre</u> ~!** *inf* that's something else; **faire <u>bien</u> les ~s** to do things properly; **pas <u>grand</u>-~** nothing much; **avant <u>toute</u> ~** above all (else); **~ <u>promise</u>, ~ due** *prov* a promise is a promise; **être <u>porté</u> sur la ~** to have a one-track mind; **la ~ <u>publique</u>** the state; **à <u>peu</u> de ~s près** more or less **II.** *adj inv, inf* **avoir l'air tout ~** to look quite confused; **être/se sentir tout ~** to be/feel not quite oneself

Chose [ʃoz] *m inf* **monsieur ~** Mr. what's-his-name

chou [ʃu] <x> *m* **1.** (*légume*) cabbage; **~ de Bruxelles** Brussels sprout **2.** GASTR **~ à la crème** cream puff ▸**faire ~ <u>blanc</u>** to draw a blank; **<u>rentrer</u> dans le ~ à qn** to beat sb up

chouan [ʃwɑ̃] *m: French royalist counter-revolutionary*

chouchou [ʃuʃu] *m* (*élastique*) scrunchy

chouchou(te) [ʃuʃu, ut] *m(f) inf* pet; **~ de qn** sb's darling

chouchouter [ʃuʃute] <1> *vt inf* (*enfant*) to pamper

choucroute [ʃukʀut] *f* sauerkraut; **~ garnie** *sauerkraut with meat* ▸**<u>pédaler</u> dans la ~** *inf* to be at a (complete) loss

chouette [ʃwɛt] **I.** *adj inf* great **II.** *f* (*oiseau*) owl

chou-fleur [ʃuflœʀ] <choux-fleurs> *m* cauliflower

chou-rave [ʃuʀav] <choux-raves> *m* kohlrabi

choyer [ʃwaje] <6> *vt* **~ qn** to pamper sb

chrétien(ne) [kʀetjɛ̃, jɛn] **I.** *adj* Christian **II.** *m(f)* Christian

chrétienté [kʀetjɛ̃te] *f* Christendom

christ [kʀist] *m* (*crucifix*) crucifix

christianisme [kʀistjanism] *m* Christianity

Christophe [kʀistɔf(ə)] *m* HIST **~ Colomb** Christopher Columbus

chrome [kʀom] *m* (*métal*) chromium

chromé(e) [kʀome] *adj* chromium-plated

chromosome [kʀomozom] *m* chromosome

chronique [kʀɔnik] **I.** *adj* chronic **II.** *f* **1.** LIT chronicle **2.** TV, RADIO programme; **~ littéraire** literary feature section ▸**<u>défrayer</u> la ~** to be the talk of the town

chroniqueur, -euse [kʀɔnikœʀ, -øz] *m, f* **1.** LIT chronicler **2.** TV, RADIO, PRESSE **~ littéraire** book reviewer; **~ financier/sportif** financial/sports editor

chrono [kʀɔno] *m inf abr de* **chronomètre** stopwatch; **faire un bon ~** to do a good time

chronologie [kʀɔnɔlɔʒi] *f* chronology

chronologique [kʀɔnɔlɔʒik] *adj* chronological

chronomètre [kʀɔnɔmɛtʀ] *m* SPORT stopwatch

chronométrer [kʀɔnɔmetʀe] <5> *vt* to time

chrysanthème [kʀizɑ̃tɛm] *m* chrysanthemum

ch'timi, chtimi [ʃtimi] *adj inv, inf* northern

chu(e) [ʃy] *part passé de* **choir**

CHU [seaʃy] *m abr de* **centre hospitalier**

universitaire ≈ university hospital

chuchotement [ʃyʃɔtmɑ̃] *m* whispering

chuchoter [ʃyʃɔte] <1> *vt, vi* to whisper

chus [ʃy] *passé simple de* **choir**

chut [ʃyt] *interj* shh

chute [ʃyt] *f* **1.** (*action: d'une personne, des feuilles*) fall; ~ **des cheveux** hair loss; **faire une** ~ **de 5 m** to fall 5 m; **en** ~ **libre** in free fall **2.** (*effondrement: d'un gouvernement, du dollar*) fall **3.** GEO ~ **d'eau** waterfall; **les ~s du Niagara** Niagara Falls **4.** METEO ~ **de neige** snowfall **5.** (*baisse rapide*) ~ **de pression/température** drop in pressure/temperature **6.** (*déchets: de tissu, papier*) offcut **7.** (*pente*) slope **8.** (*fin: d'une histoire*) punchline; ~ **du rideau** end of the performance

chuter [ʃyte] <1> *vi* **1.** *inf* (*tomber*) to fall **2.** *inf* (*échouer: candidat*) to fail **3.** (*baisser*) to fall

Chypre [ʃipʀ] *f* (**l'île de**) ~ (the island of) Cyprus

chypriote [ʃipʀɔt] *adj* Cypriot

Chypriote [ʃipʀɔt] *mf* Cypriot

ci [si] *adv* **comme** ~ **comme ça** *inf* so-so; ~ **et ça** this and that; **à cette heure-**~ (*à une heure precise*) at this time; *v. a.* **ceci, celui**

CIA [seiɑ] *f abr de* **Central Intelligence Agency** CIA

ci-après [siapʀɛ] *adv* below

cibiste [sibist] *mf* CB enthusiast

cible [sibl] **I.** *f* **1.** SPORT target; **atteindre la** ~ to hit the target **2.** COM, CINE, TV target group **3.** *fig* **servir de** ~ **aux quolibets** to be the butt of sb's gibes **II.** *adj* **langue** ~ target language

cibler [sible] <1> *vt* to target

ciboulette [sibulɛt] *f* **1.** BOT chive **2.** GASTR chives *pl*

cicatrice [sikatʀis] *f* scar

cicatrisation [sikatʀizasjɔ̃] *f* scarring; **la** ~ **de cette égratignure sera rapide** the scratch will soon scar over

cicatriser [sikatʀize] <1> **I.** *vt a. fig* to heal **II.** *vi, vpr* to heal (up)

ci-contre [sikɔ̃tʀ] *adv* opposite

ci-dessous [sid(ə)su] *adv* below

ci-dessus [sid(ə)sy] *adv* above

cidre [sidʀ] *m* cider

Cie *abr de* **compagnie** Co.

ciel <cieux *o* s> [sjɛl, sjø] *m* **1.** <s> (*firmament*) sky **2.** REL heaven; **grâce au** ~ thank heavens ▸**au nom du** ~**!** for heaven's sake; **remuer** ~ **et terre** to move heaven and earth; **à** ~ **ouvert** (*théâtre*) open-air; **aide-toi, le** ~ **t'aidera** *prov* God helps those who help themselves; **tomber du** ~ **à qn** to be a godsend to sb

cierge [sjɛʀʒ] *m* (*chandelle*) candle ▸**se tenir droit comme un** ~ to stand bolt upright

cieux [sjø] *pl de* **ciel**

cigale [sigal] *f* cicada

cigare [sigaʀ] *m* **1.** cigar **2.** *Belgique* (*remontrance*) rocket ▸**ne rien avoir dans le** ~ *inf* to have sawdust between one's ears

cigarette [sigaʀɛt] *f* cigarette

ci-gît [siʒi] here lies

cigogne [sigɔɲ] *f* stork

ci-inclus [siɛ̃kly] enclosed

ci-joint [siʒwɛ̃] enclosed

cil [sil] *m* eyelash

cime [sim] *f* (*d'un arbre*) top; (*d'une montagne*) summit

ciment [simɑ̃] *m* cement

cimenter [simɑ̃te] <1> *vt a. fig* to cement

cimetière [simtjɛʀ] *m* cemetary

ciné [sine] *m inf abr de* **cinéma**

cinéaste [sineast] *m* film director

ciné-club [sineklœb] <ciné-clubs> *m* film club

cinéma [sinema] *m* (*art, salle*) cinema; ~ **muet** silent films, silent movies *pl Am;* ~ **parlant** talking films *pl;* **faire du** ~ to be in films ▸**arrête ton** ~ *inf* cut out the play-acting; **faire tout un** ~ *inf* to imagine things

Cinémascope® [sinemaskɔp] *m* Cinemascope®

cinémathèque [sinematɛk] *f* (*archives*) film archive(s)

cinématographique [sinematɔgʀafik] *adj* film, movie *Am*

ciné-parc, **cinéparc** [sinepaʀk] <ciné-parcs> *m Québec* (*cinéma de plein air*) drive-in (cinema)

cinéphile [sinefil] *mf* movie fan

cinglant(**e**) [sɛ̃glɑ̃, ɑ̃t] *adj* **1.** (*pluie*) driving; (*bise*) biting **2.** (*réflexion, remarque, phrase*) cutting; (*reproche, affrontement*) scathing; (*leçon*) bitter

cinglé(**e**) [sɛ̃gle] **I.** *adj inf* crazy **II.** *m(f) inf* **quel** ~ what a loony!

cingler [sɛ̃gle] <1> *vt* **1.** (*frapper: grêle*) ~ **le visage à qn** to sting sb's face **2.** (*fouetter*) to lash

cinoche [sinɔʃ] *m inf* pictures *Brit,* movies *Am*

cinq [sɛ̃k, *devant une consonne* sɛ̃] **I.** *adj* **1.** five; **en** ~ **exemplaires** in quintuplicate; **dans** ~ **jours** in five days' time; **faire qc un jour sur** ~ to do sth once every five days; **un Français/foyer sur** ~ one in five Frenchmen/households; **vendre qc par** ~ to sell sth in fives; **rentrer** ~ **par** ~ to come in [*o* to go in] five at a time; **ils sont venus à** ~ five of them came **2.** (*dans l'indication de l'âge, la durée*) **avoir** ~ **ans** to be five (years old); **à** ~ **ans** at the age of five; **période de** ~ **ans** five-year period **3.** (*dans l'indication de l'heure*) **il est** ~ **heures** it's five o'clock; **il est dix heures** ~**/moins** ~ it's five past ten/five to ten; **toutes les** ~ **heures** every five hours **4.** (*dans l'indication de la date*) **le** ~ **mars** the fifth of March, March the fifth; **arriver le** ~ **mars** to arrive (on) March the fifth; **arriver le** ~ to arrive on the fifth; **nous sommes** [*o* **on est**] **le** ~ **mars** it's the fifth of March; **le vendredi** ~ **mars** on Friday, the fifth of March; **Aix, le** ~ **mars** Aix, March the fifth; **tous les** ~ **du mois**

on the fifth of each month **5.** (*dans l'indication de l'ordre*) **arriver ~ ou sixième** to finish fifth or sixth **6.** (*dans les noms de personnages*) **Charles V** Charles V, Charles the Fifth ►**c'était moins ~!** *inf* it was a near thing!; **en ~ sec** in no time **II.** *m inv* **1.** five; **deux et trois font ~** two and three are five *Brit,* two and three make five *Am;* **compter de ~ en ~** to count in fives **2.** (*numéro*) five; **habiter (au) 5, rue de l'église** to live at 5 Church Street **3.** (*bus*) **le ~** the (number) five **4.** JEUX **le ~ de cœur** the five of hearts **5.** ECOLE **avoir ~ sur dix** ≈ to have a grade of D ►**~ sur ~** perfectly **III.** *f* (*table/chambre/... numéro ~*) five **IV.** *adv* fifthly

cinquantaine [sɛ̃kɑ̃tɛn] *f* **1.** (*environ cinquante*) **une ~ de personnes/pages** about fifty people/pages **2.** (*âge approximatif*) **avoir la ~** [*o* **une ~ d'années**] to be about fifty (years old); **approcher de la ~** to be getting on for fifty; **avoir (largement) dépassé la ~** to be (well) over fifty (years old)

cinquante [sɛ̃kɑ̃t] **I.** *adj* **1.** fifty; **à ~ (à l'heure)** [*o* **(kilomètres à l'heure)**] at fifty miles an hour **2.** (*dans l'indication des époques*) **les années ~** the fifties ►**je ne répéterai pas ~ fois la même chose!** I won't repeat the same thing a thousand times! **II.** *m inv* **1.** (*cardinal*) fifty **2.** (*taille de confection*) **faire du ~** (*homme*) to take a size forty *Brit,* to wear a size forty *Am;* (*femme*) to take a size twenty *Brit,* to wear a size sixteen *Am; v. a.* **cinq**

cinquantenaire [sɛ̃kɑ̃tnɛʀ] *m* fiftieth anniversary

cinquantième [sɛ̃kɑ̃tjɛm] **I.** *adj antéposé* fiftieth **II.** *mf* **le/la ~** the fiftieth **III.** *m* (*fraction*) fiftieth; *v. a.* **cinquième**

cinquième [sɛ̃kjɛm] **I.** *adj antéposé* fifth; **la ~ page avant la fin** the fifth last page; **arriver ~/obtenir la ~ place** to finish fifth/to get fifth place; **le ~ centenaire** the fifth anniversary **II.** *mf* **le/la ~** the fifth; **être le/la ~ de la classe** to be fifth in the class **III.** *m* **1.** (*fraction*) fifth; **les trois ~s du gâteau** three fifths of the cake **2.** (*étage*) fifth; **habiter au ~** to live on the fifth floor **3.** (*arrondissement*) **habiter dans le ~** to live in the fifth arrondissement **4.** (*dans une charade*) fifth syllable **IV.** *f* **1.** (*vitesse*) fifth gear; **passer en ~** to change into fifth gear **2.** ECOLE second year (*of secondary school*)

cinquièmement [sɛ̃kjɛmmɑ̃] *adv* fifthly

cintre [sɛ̃tʀ] *m* **1.** (*portemanteau*) (coat) hanger **2.** ARCHIT curve; **plein ~** round arch

cintré(e) [sɛ̃tʀe] *adj* **1.** (*chemise*) waisted **2.** ARCHIT (*porte, fenêtre*) arched; (*galerie*) vaulted

CIO [seio] *m* **1.** *abr de* **Comité international olympique** IOC **2.** *abr de* **centre d'information et d'orientation** information centre

cirage [siʀaʒ] *m* **1.** (*produit*) (shoe) polish **2.** (*action*) polishing ►**être dans le ~** *inf* (*être inconscient*) to be half-conscious; (*ne rien comprendre*) to be all at sea

circoncis(e) [siʀkɔ̃si, iz] *adj* circumcized

circoncision [siʀkɔ̃sizjɔ̃] *f* circumcision

circonférence [siʀkɔ̃feʀɑ̃s] *f* circumference

circonscription [siʀkɔ̃skʀipsjɔ̃] *f* **1.** ADMIN district **2.** POL constituency *Brit,* district *Am* **3.** TEL **~ tarifaire** tarif zone

circonscrire [siʀkɔ̃skʀiʀ] *vt irr* **1.** (*délimiter*) to delimit **2.** (*borner*) **~ les recherches à un secteur** to limit the search to one area **3.** (*empêcher l'extension de: incendie*) to contain **4.** (*cerner: sujet*) to define

circonspect(e) [siʀkɔ̃spɛ(kt), ɛkt] *adj* cautious; **d'un œil ~** circumspectly

circonstance [siʀkɔ̃stɑ̃s] *f* **1.** *souvent pl* (*conditions*) circumstance; **en toutes ~s** in any case; **~s indépendantes de notre volonté** unforseen circumstances **2.** (*occasion*) occasion; **air de ~** apt expression

circonstancié(e) [siʀkɔ̃stɑ̃sje] *adj* detailed

circonstanciel(le) [siʀkɔ̃stɑ̃sjɛl] *adj* LING **subordonnée ~le** Adverbial clause; **complément ~ de temps/lieu/manière** adverbial phrase of time/place/manner

circonvenir [siʀkɔ̃vniʀ] *vt irr* to circumvent; **s'efforcer** [*o* **tenter**] **de ~ qn** to attempt to get around sb

circuit [siʀkɥi] *m* **1.** (*itinéraire touristique*) tour **2.** (*parcours*) roundabout route **3.** SPORT, ELEC circuit **4.** (*jeu*) **~ électrique** electric track **5.** ECON **~ de distribution** distribution network

circulaire [siʀkylɛʀ] **I.** *adj* circular **II.** *f* circular

circulation [siʀkylasjɔ̃] *f* **1.** (*trafic*) traffic; **~ interdite** (*aux piétons*) closed to pedestrians; (*aux voitures*) closed to traffic; **faire la ~** (*policier*) to be on traffic duty; **la ~ est difficile** traffic conditions are bad **2.** ECON, MED circulation; **mettre en ~** to put into circulation; **retirer de la ~** to withdraw from circulation

circulatoire [siʀkylatwaʀ] *adj* **appareil ~** circulation; **assistance ~** assisted circulation

circuler [siʀkyle] <1> *vi* **1.** (*aller et venir*) to get around; **~ en voiture** to travel (around) by car; **circulez!** move along! **2.** (*passer de main en main, couler*) to circulate **3.** (*se renouveler*) **l'air circule dans la pièce** the air circulates in the room **4.** (*se répandre: nouvelle*) to circulate; **faire ~ qc** to circulate sth

cire [siʀ] *f* wax

ciré [siʀe] *m* oilskin

cirer [siʀe] <1> *vt* to polish ►**j'en ai rien à ~, moi, de toutes tes histoires!** *inf* I don't give a damn about all that!

cireur, **-euse** [siʀœʀ, -øz] *m, f* **~ de chaussures** shoe-shine boy

cireux, **-euse** [siʀø, -øz] *adj* waxy

cirque [siʀk] *m* circus

cirrhose [siʀoz] *f* cirrhosis
cisaille [sizɑj] *f* ~ **de jardinier** gardening shears
cisailler [sizɑje] <1> *vt* **1.** (*couper*) to cut **2.** (*élaguer*) to prune
ciseau [sizo] <x> *m* **1.** *pl* (*instrument*) (pair of) scissors *pl* **2.** (*outil*) chisel
ciselé(e) [sizle] *adj* chiselled *Brit*, chiseled *Am*
ciseler [sizle] <4> *vt* to chisel
citadelle [sitadɛl] *f* citadel
citadin(e) [sitadɛ̃, in] **I.** *adj* **la vie ~e** city [*o* town] life **II.** *m(f)* city dweller
citation [sitasjɔ̃] *f* **1.** (*extrait*) quotation **2.** JUR ~ **d'un accusé** summons *pl + sing vb;* ~ **d'un temoin** subpoena **3.** MIL ~ **à l'ordre du jour** mention in dispatches
cité [site] *f* **1.** (*ville moyenne*) town **2.** (*grande ville*) *a.* HIST city; **la ~ de Westminster** Westminster City **3.** (*immeubles*) housing estate; ~ **universitaire** student halls *pl* of residence
cité-dortoir [sitedɔʀtwaʀ] <cités-dortoirs> *f* dormitory town
citer [site] <1> *vt* **1.** (*rapporter*) to quote **2.** (*énumérer*) to name **3.** (*reconnaître les mérites*) to commend; ~ **en exemple** to hold up as an example **4.** JUR (*accusé*) to summon; (*témoin*) to subpoena
citerne [sitɛʀn] *f* **1.** (*réservoir*) tank **2.** (*pour l'eau de pluie*) water tank
citoyen(ne) [sitwajɛ̃, jɛn] *m(f)* citizen; ~ **d'honneur** freeman
citron [sitʀɔ̃] **I.** *m* **1.** (*fruit*) lemon; ~ **pressé** *fresh lemon juice* **2.** *inf* (*tête*) nut **II.** *adj inv* (**jaune**) ~ lemon yellow
citronnade [sitʀɔnad] *f* lemonade
citronnelle [sitʀɔnɛl] *f* BOT citronella
citronnier [sitʀɔnje] *m* **1.** (*arbre*) lemon tree **2.** (*bois*) lemon wood
citrouille [sitʀuj] *f* BOT pumpkin ►**ne rien avoir dans la ~** *inf* to be brainless
civet [sivɛ] *m: stew*
civière [sivjɛʀ] *f* stretcher
civil(e) [sivil] **I.** *adj* **1.** (*relatif au citoyen*) *a.* JUR civil; **année ~e** calendar year; **guerre ~e** civil war; **procédure ~e** civil proceedings *pl;* **responsabilité ~e** personal liability; **se porter partie ~e** to take civil action **2.** (*opp: religieux*) **mariage ~** civil wedding **II.** *m* **1.** (*personne*) civilian **2.** (*vie ~e*) **dans le ~** in civilian life
civilement [sivilmɑ̃] *adv* **1.** JUR in the civil court(s) **2.** (*opp: religieusement*) in a registry [*o* register] office
civilisation [sivilizasjɔ̃] *f* civilization
civilisé(e) [sivilize] *adj* civilized
civiliser [sivilize] <1> **I.** *vt* to civilize **II.** *vpr inf* **se ~** to become civilized
civique [sivik] *adj* civic; **instruction ~** civics *pl + sing vb*
civisme [sivism] *m* public-spiritedness
clac [klak] *interj* (*d'une porte*) slam
clafoutis [klafuti] *m: sweet dish made of cherries baked in pancake batter*
clair(e) [klɛʀ] **I.** *adj* **1.** (*lumineux*) light; (*flamme, pièce*) bright **2.** (*opp: foncé*) light **3.** (*peu consistant*) thin **4.** (*intelligible, transparent, évident*) clear; **avoir les idées ~es** to think clearly ►**ne pas être ~** *inf* (*être saoul*) to be tipsy; (*être suspect*) to be a bit dubious; (*être fou*) to be rather crazy **II.** *adv* **1.** clearly; **tu ne vois pas ~** you can't see well **2.** *fig* **voir ~ dans qc** to get to the bottom of sth; **parler ~ et net** to speak quite openly **III.** *m* (*clarté*) ~ **de lune** moonlight ►**le plus ~ de son/mon temps** most of my/his time; **tirer qc au ~** to clarify sth; **en ~** (*dire sans ambiguïté*) to put it clearly; **émission en ~** unscrambled programme
claire [klɛʀ] *f* **1.** (*bassin*) oyster bed **2.** (*huître*) *oyster from an oyster bed*
clairement [klɛʀmɑ̃] *adv* clearly
claire-voie [klɛʀvwa] <claires-voies> *f* **1.** (*clôture*) lattice **2.** ARCHIT clerestory **3.** (*avec des espaces*) **volet/barrière à ~** openwork shutter/fence
clairière [klɛʀjɛʀ] *f* clearing
clair-obscur [klɛʀɔpskyʀ] <clairs-obscurs> *m* **1.** ART chiaroscuro **2.** (*lumière tamisée*) twilight
clairon [klɛʀɔ̃] *m* **1.** (*instrument*) bugle **2.** (*personne*) bugler
claironner [klɛʀɔne] <1> **I.** *vt iron* to shout from the rooftops **II.** *vi* to play the bugle
clairsemé(e) [klɛʀsəme] *adj* **1.** (*dispersé*) scattered **2.** (*peu dense*) thin
clairvoyance [klɛʀvwajɑ̃s] *f* perceptiveness
clairvoyant(e) [klɛʀvwajɑ̃, jɑ̃t] *adj* clear-sighted; (*esprit*) perceptive
clamer [klɑme] <1> *vt* to shout; (*innocence*) to proclaim
clameur [klɑmœʀ] *f* clamour *Brit*, clamor *Am*
clamser [klamse] <1> *vi inf* to kick the bucket
clan [klɑ̃] *m a.* HIST clan
clandestin(e) [klɑ̃dɛstɛ̃, in] **I.** *adj* clandestine; **passager ~** stowaway; **mouvement ~** underground movement **II.** *m(f)* (*immigrant*) illegal immigrant
clandestinement [klɑ̃dɛstinmɑ̃] *adv* in secret
clandestinité [klɑ̃dɛstinite] *f* **1.** (*fait de ne pas être déclaré*) secrecy **2.** (*vie cachée*) **entrer dans la ~** to go underground
clapet [klapɛ] *m* **1.** TECH valve **2.** *inf* (*bouche*) trap
clapier [klapje] *m* **1.** (*cage*) rabbit hutch **2.** *péj* (*logement*) hole
clapoter [klapɔte] <1> *vi* to lap
claquage [klakaʒ] *m* MED **1.** (*action*) pulling of a muscle **2.** (*résultat*) pulled muscle
claque[1] [klak] *f* **1.** (*tape sur la joue*) slap **2.** THEAT claque **3.** *Québec* (*protection de chaussure, en caoutchouc*) tip ►**j'en ai/il en a sa ~** *inf* I'm/he's fed up (to the back teeth);

C

prendre une de ces ~s *inf* to take a beating
claque² [klak] *m* opera hat
claqué(e) [klake] *adj inf* worn out
claquement [klakmɑ̃] *m* (*d'un volet, d'une porte*) banging; (*d'un drapeau*) flapping; (*d'un coup de feu, du fouet*) crack; (*des talons*) clicking; (*des doigts*) snap; (*de la langue*) click; (*des dents*) chatter
claquer [klake] <1> **I.** *vt* **1.** (*jeter violemment*) to slam **2.** *inf* (*dépenser*) to blow **3.** *inf* (*fatiguer*) to wear out **II.** *vi* **1.** (*produire un bruit sec: drapeau*) to flap; (*porte, volet*) to bang; (*fouet*) to crack; **il claque ~ des dents** his teeth are chattering; **~ des mains** to clap (one's hands) **2.** *inf* (*mourir*) to kick the bucket **3.** *inf* (*se casser: élastique*) to snap; (*verre*) to shatter **III.** *vpr* **1.** *inf* MED **se ~ un muscle** to pull a muscle **2.** *inf* (*se fatiguer*) **se ~** to wear oneself out
claquettes [klakɛt] *fpl* (*danse*) tap dancing; **faire des ~** to tap-dance
clarifier [klaʀifje] <1> **I.** *vt a. fig* to clarify **II.** *vpr* **se ~** (*fait*) to become clarified
clarinette [klaʀinɛt] *f* MUS clarinet
clarté [klaʀte] *f* **1.** (*lumière: d'une bougie*) light; (*d'une étoile, du ciel*) brightness **2.** (*transparence: d'eau*) clearness **3.** (*opp: confusion*) clarity; **s'exprimer avec ~** to express oneself clearly
classe [klɑs] *f* **1.** (*groupe*) class; **~s moyennes** middle classes; **~ ouvrière/dirigeante** working/ruling class; **~ d'âge** age group **2.** (*rang*) **de grande/première ~** first class; **billet de première/deuxième ~** first/second class ticket **3.** *inf* (*élégance*) **être ~** to be classy; **c'est ~!** that's chic! **4.** ECOLE class; (*salle*) classroom; **en ~** in class; **~ de cinquième/seconde** second/fifth year (*of secondary school*); **~ terminale** final year; **passer dans la ~ supérieure** to go up a year; **faire (la) ~** to teach; **être en ~, avoir ~** to be teaching; **aller en ~** to go to school; **demain, il n'y a pas ~** there's no school tommorrow; **~ préparatoire** preparatory class (*for entry to the grandes écoles*) **5.** (*séjour*) **~ verte** *school (field) trip to the country* **6.** MIL annual levy; **faire ses ~s** to do one's elementary training; *fig* to make a beginning
classé(e) [klɑse] *adj* **1.** (*protégé: bâtiment*) listed **2.** (*réglé: affaire*) closed **3.** (*de valeur*) classified
classement [klɑsmɑ̃] *m* **1.** (*rangement*) filing **2.** (*classification: d'un élève*) grading; (*d'un joueur*) ranking; (*d'un hôtel*) rating **3.** (*place sur une liste*) classification
classer [klɑse] <1> **I.** *vt* **1.** (*ordonner*) to classify **2.** (*répartir*) to class **3.** (*ranger selon la performance*) to rank **4.** (*régler*) to close **5.** (*mettre dans le patrimoine national: monument*) to list **6.** *péj* (*juger définitivement*) to size up **II.** *vpr* (*obtenir un certain rang*) **se ~ premier** to rank first
classeur [klɑsœʀ] *m* **1.** (*dossier*) file **2.** INFOR folder
classicisme [klasisism] *m* ART classicism
classification [klasifikasjɔ̃] *f* classification; **~ périodique des éléments** periodic table of elements
classifier [klasifje] <1> *vt* to classify
classique [klasik] **I.** *adj* **1.** ART, ECOLE classical; **filière ~** classics stream *Brit,* classical studies track *Am* **2.** (*habituel*) classic; (*produit*) standard; **c'est (le coup) ~!** *inf* that's typical! **II.** *m* **1.** (*auteur, œuvre*) classic **2.** (*musique*) classical music
clause [kloz] *f* clause
claustrophobe [klostʀɔfɔb] **I.** *adj* claustrophobic **II.** *mf: person suffering from claustrophobia*
claustrophobie [klostʀɔfɔbi] *f* claustrophobia
clavecin [klavsɛ̃] *m* MUS harpsicord
clavicule [klavikyl] *f* ANAT collarbone
clavier [klavje] *m* keyboard
claviste [klavist] *mf* keyboarder
clé [kle] *f* **1.** (*instrument*) key; **~ de contact** ignition key; **fermer à ~** to lock **2.** (*moyen d'accéder à*) **la ~ du succès** the key to success **3.** (*outil*) wrench, spanner *Brit;* **~ anglaise** adjustable spanner **4.** MUS (*signe*) key; (*pièce*) peg; **~ de sol** G clef **5.** SPORT lock
clean [klin] *adj inf* **1.** (*propre*) bare **2.** (*bien*) OK **3.** (*opp: speedé*) clean
clébard [klebaʀ] *m,* **clebs** [klɛps] *m inf* mutt
clef [kle] *f v.* **clé**
clémence [klemɑ̃s] *f* clemency
clément(e) [klemɑ̃, ɑ̃t] *adj* clement; (*temps*) mild
clémentine [klemɑ̃tin] *f* clementine
clenche [klɑ̃ʃ] *f Belgique* (*poignée de porte*) (door) handle
Cléopâtre [kleɔpɑːtʀ(ə)] *f* Cleopatra
cleptomane [klɛptɔman] *mf* kleptomaniac
clerc [klɛʀ] *m* **1.** JUR (*de notaire*) clerk **2.** REL cleric
clergé [klɛʀʒe] *m* clergy
clérical(e) [kleʀikal, o] <-aux> **I.** *adj* clerical **II.** *m(f)* clerical
clermontois(e) [klɛʀmɔ̃twa, waz] *adj* of Clermont-Ferrand; *v. a.* **ajaccien**
Clermontois(e) [klɛʀmɔ̃twa, waz] *m(f)* person from Clermont-Ferrand; *v. a.* **Ajaccien**
clic [klik] **I.** *interj* click **II.** *m* **~ sur la souris** mouse click
cliché [kliʃe] *m* **1.** (*banalité*) cliché **2.** (*photo*) shot
client(e) [klijɑ̃, jɑ̃t] *m(f)* **1.** (*acheteur*) customer **2.** (*bénéficiaire d'un service: d'un restaurant*) diner; (*d'un avocat*) client; (*d'un médecin*) patient **3.** ECON buyer
clientèle [klijɑ̃tɛl] *f* (*d'un magasin, restaurant*) clientele; (*d'un avocat*) clients *pl;* (*d'un médecin*) patients *pl*
cligner [kliɲe] <1> **I.** *vt* **1.** (*fermer à moitié*) to screw up **2.** (*ciller*) **~ des yeux** to blink; ~

de l'œil to wink **II.** *vi* to blink

clignotant [kliɲɔtɑ̃] *m* AUTO indicator *Brit,* blinker *Am;* **mettre le/son ~** to indicate

clignotant(e) [kliɲɔtɑ̃, ɑ̃t] *adj* blinking

clignoter [kliɲɔte] <1> *vi* **1.** (*ciller*) **ses yeux** [*o* **paupières**] **clignotaient** he/she was blinking **2.** (*éclairer*) to go on and off

clignoteur [kliɲɔtœʀ] *m Belgique* (*clignotant*) indicator, blinker *Am*

clim [klim] *f abr de* **climatisation** aircon *Brit,* air *Am*

climat [klima] *m a.* METEO climate

climatique [klimatik] *adj* **1.** (*concernant le climat*) climatic **2.** (*d'un climat sain*) **station ~** health resort

climatisation [klimatizasjɔ̃] *f* air conditioning

climatisé(e) [klimatize] *adj* **voiture ~e** air-conditioned car; **air ~** air-conditioning

climatiser [klimatize] <1> *vt* to air-condition

climatiseur [klimatizœʀ] *m* air conditioner

clin d'œil <clins d'œil *o* clins d'yeux> [klɛ̃dœj] *m* wink; **faire un ~ à qn** to wink at sb ▶**en un ~** in a flash

clinique [klinik] **I.** *adj* clinical **II.** *f* clinic

clinquant(e) [klɛ̃kɑ̃, ɑ̃t] *adj* flashy

clip [klip] *m* **1.** TV video **2.** (*bijou*) clip

clique [klik] *f péj, inf* clique ▶**prendre ses ~s et ses claques** *inf* to pack up and go

cliquer [klike] <1> *vi* INFOR to click; **~ sur un symbole avec la souris** to click on an icon with the mouse; **~ deux fois de suite sur l'icône** double-click on the icon

cliqueter [klik(ə)te] <3> *vi* (*monnaie, clés*) to jangle; (*verre*) to clink

cliquetis [klik(ə)ti] *m* (*de la monnaie, clés*) jangling; (*de verres*) clinking

clitoris [klitɔʀis] *m* clitoris

clochard(e) [klɔʃaʀ, aʀd] *m(f)* tramp

cloche[1] [klɔʃ] *f* bell

cloche[2] [klɔʃ] **I.** *adj inf* **1.** (*maladroit*) clumsy **2.** (*stupide*) stupid **II.** *f inf* **1.** (*maladroit*) clumsy thing **2.** (*idiot*) dope **3.** (*clochards*) tramps *pl*

cloche-pied [klɔʃpje] **à ~** hopping

clocher[1] [klɔʃe] *m* (church) tower

clocher[2] [klɔʃe] <1> *vi inf* to be not right

clochette [klɔʃɛt] *f* little bell

clodo [klodo] *m inf abr de* **clochard**

cloison [klwazɔ̃] *f* partition

cloisonner [klwazɔne] <1> *vt* (*pièce*) to partition; (*tiroir*) to divide; (*activités*) to compartmentalize

cloître [klwatʀ] *m* cloister

cloîtrer [klwatʀe] <1> **I.** *vt fig* to shut away **II.** *vpr* **se ~ dans sa maison** to shut oneself away at home

clone [klon] *m* BIO, INFOR clone

clope [klɔp] *m o f inf* **1.** (*cigarette*) smoke, fag *Brit* **2.** (*mégot*) butt

clopin-clopant [klɔpɛ̃klɔpɑ̃] *adv inf* **aller ~** to hobble along

cloque [klɔk] *f* blister

cloquer [klɔke] <1> *vi* to blister

clore [klɔʀ] *vt irr* **1.** (*terminer*) to conclude; **~ un discours** (*conclusion, remerciements*) to bring a speech to a close **2.** (*entourer: terrain, propriété*) to enclose **3.** FIN (*compte*) to close

clos [klo] *m* (*vignoble*) garden

clos(e) [klo, kloz] **I.** *part passé de* **clore II.** *adj* **1.** (*fermé*) close; **trouver porte ~e** to find nobody at home **2.** (*achevé*) closed

clôture [klotyʀ] *f* **1.** (*enceinte*) fence; (*d'arbustes, en ciment*) wall **2.** (*fin: d'un festival*) close; (*d'un débat*) conclusion; (*d'un compte*) closure **3.** INFOR **~ de session** logoff

clôturer [klotyʀe] <1> *vt* **1.** (*entourer*) to enclose **2.** (*finir*) to conclude

clou [klu] *m* **1.** (*pointe*) nail **2.** (*attraction*) highlight **3.** *pl, inf* (*passage*) crossing + *vb sing* **4.** GASTR **~ de girofle** clove ▶**ne pas valoir un ~** *inf* to be not worth a thing; **des ~s!** *inf* no way!

cloué(e) [klue] *adj* **~ sur place** fixed to the spot

clouer [klue] <1> *vt* **1.** (*fixer*) to nail; (*planches, caisse*) to nail down; **~ le tableau sur le mur** to nail the picture to the wall **2.** *inf* (*immobiliser*) **~ qn au lit** to keep sb stuck in bed

clouté(e) [klute] *adj* (*chaussures, pneus*) studded

clown [klun] *m* clown

clownerie [klunʀi] *f* clowning *no pl;* **faire des ~s** to clown around

club [klœb] *m* club; **~ de théâtre/de volley** drama/volleyball club; **~ d'écriture** creative writing group

CM1 [seɛmœ̃] *m abr de* **cours moyen première année** ≈ year 2

CM2 [seɛmdø] *m abr de* **cours moyen deuxième année** ≈ year 3

C.N.R.S. [seɛnɛʀɛs] *m abr de* **Centre national de la recherche scientifique** ≈ SRC *Brit,* ≈ NSF *Am* (*state body sponsoring research*)

coaguler [kɔagyle] <1> *vt, vi, vpr* (**se**) **~** to coagulate

coaliser [kɔalize] *vpr* **se ~** to form an alliance

coalition [kɔalisjɔ̃] *f* coalition

coassement [kɔasmɑ̃] *m* croaking

coasser [kɔase] <1> *vi* to croak

coauteur [kootœʀ] *m* **1.** LIT co-author **2.** JUR accomplice

cobaye [kɔbaj] *m* guinea pig

cobra [kɔbʀa] *m* cobra

coca(-cola)® [kɔka(kɔla)] *m* Coca Cola®

cocaïne [kɔkain] *f* cocaine

cocarde [kɔkaʀd] *f* rosette

cocasse [kɔkas] *adj inf* comical

coccinelle [kɔksinɛl] *f* **1.** ZOOL ladybird *Brit,* ladybug *Am* **2.** AUTO Beetle®

coccyx [kɔksis] *m* ANAT coccyx

coche [kɔʃ] *m* **rater le ~** *inf* to miss the boat

cocher[1] [kɔʃe] <1> *vt* to check off, to tick off

Brit

cocher[2] [kɔʃe] *m* coachman

cochère [kɔʃɛʀ] *adj v.* **porte**

cochon [kɔʃɔ̃] *m* **1.**(*animal*) pig **2.** GASTR pork **3.**(*cobaye*) ~ **d'Inde** guinea pig

cochon(ne) [kɔʃɔ̃, ɔn] **I.** *adj inf* **1.**(*sale*) dirty **2.**(*obscène*) smutty **II.** *m(f) péj, inf* **1.**(*personne sale*) pig **2.**(*vicieux*) swine; **vieux** ~ dirty old man

cochonnailles [kɔʃɔnaj] *fpl inf* pork meats

cochonner [kɔʃɔne] <1> *vt inf* **1.**(*bâcler*) to botch **2.**(*salir*) to muck up

cochonnerie [kɔʃɔnʀi] *f inf* **1.**(*nourriture*) muck *no pl* **2.**(*toc*) junk *no pl* **3.** *souvent pl, inf* (*obscénités*) smut *no pl* **4.** *pl* (*saletés*) mess; **ne fais pas de ~s sur la table** don't make a mess on the table

cochonnet [kɔʃɔnɛ] *m* **1.** ZOOL piglet **2.**(*aux boules*) jack

cocker [kɔkɛʀ] *m* cocker spaniel

cockpit [kɔkpit] *m* cockpit

cocktail [kɔktɛl] *m* **1.**(*boisson, mélange*) cocktail; ~ **de bienvenue** welcome cocktail; ~ **Molotov** Molotov cocktail **2.**(*réunion*) cocktail party

coco [koko] *m* **1.**(*terme affectueux*) **mon (petit)** ~ little man **2.** *péj* (*type*) individual

cocon [kɔkɔ̃] *m* cocoon

cocorico [kɔkɔʀiko] *m* cock-a-doodle-doo

cocotier [kɔkɔtje] *m* coconut palm

cocotte [kɔkɔt] *f* **1.**(*marmite*) casserole dish **2.** *enfantin* (*poule*) hen; ~ **en papier** paper bird **3.** *inf* (*terme affectueux*) **ma** ~ darling

cocotte-minute® [kɔkɔtminyt] <cocottes-minute> *f* pressure cooker

cocu(e) [kɔky] **I.** *adj inf* deceived; **faire qn** ~ to be unfaithful to sb **II.** *m(f) inf* deceived husband, wife *m, f*

code [kɔd] *m* **1.**(*chiffrage*) code; ~ **postal** postcode **2.**(*permis*) theory (test) **3.**(*feux*) dipped headlights; **mettre ses ~s, se mettre en ~(s)** to dip one's headlights **4.** JUR civil code; ~ **de la route** highway code

codé(e) [kɔde] *adj* **message** ~ coded message

code-barre [kɔdbaʀ] <codes-barres> *m* barcode

codécision [kodesizjɔ̃] *f* joint decision

coder [kɔde] <1> *vt* to encode

codifier [kɔdifje] <1> *vt* to codify

coédition [koedisjɔ̃] *f* co-edition

coefficient [kɔefisjɑ̃] *m* **1.** MAT, PHYS coefficient **2.**(*facteur*) ~ **d'erreur** margin of error; ~ **annuel** *Suisse* tax threshold

coentreprise [koɑ̃tʀəpʀiz] *f* joint-venture

coéquipier, -ière [koekipje, -jɛʀ] *m, f* team-mate *Brit,* teammate *Am*

cœur [kœʀ] *m* heart; **en plein ~ de l'hiver** in the depths of winter ▶**avoir le ~ sur la main** to be open-handed; **avoir un ~ d'or/de pierre** to have a heart of gold/stone; **faire qc de bon ~** to do sth willingly; **avoir le ~ gros** to feel very sad; **avoir mal au ~** to feel sick; **si le ~ lui/vous en dit** *inf* if you feel like it; **fendre le ~** to break one's heart; **prendre qc à ~** to take sth to heart; **soulever le ~** to turn one's stomach; **tenir à ~** to mean a lot to one; **apprendre/connaître/réciter par ~** to learn/know/recite sth by heart; **sans ~** heartless

coexister [kɔegziste] <1> *vi* to coexist

coffre [kɔfʀ] *m* **1.**(*meuble*) chest; ~ **à jouets/outils** toy/tool box **2.** AUTO boot **3.**(*coffre-fort*) safe

coffre-fort [kɔfʀəfɔʀ] <coffres-forts> *m* safe

coffrer [kɔfʀe] <1> *vt inf* to put away

coffret [kɔfʀɛ] *m* case; ~ **à bijoux** jewel box

COGEMA [kɔʒema] *f abr de* **Compagnie générale des matières nucléaires** *French nuclear material company*

cognac [kɔɲak] *m* cognac

cogner [kɔɲe] <1> **I.** *vt* (*heurter*) to bang into **II.** *vi* **1.**(*taper*) ~ **à/sur/contre qc** to bang at/on/against sth **2.**(*heurter*) ~ **contre qc** (*volet, caillou*) to bang against sth **3.** *inf* (*chauffer: soleil*) to beat down **III.** *vpr* **se ~ la tête contre qc** to bang one's head against sth

cohabitation [koabitasjɔ̃] *f* cohabitation

cohabiter [koabite] <1> *vi* to cohabit

cohérence [koeʀɑ̃s] *f* consistency

cohérent(e) [koeʀɑ̃, ɑ̃t] *adj* (*ensemble*) coherent; (*conduite, texte*) consistent

cohésion [koezjɔ̃] *f* (*solidarité*) cohesion

cohue [kɔy] *f* **1.**(*foule*) crowd **2.**(*bousculade*) crush

coiffe [kwaf] *f* headdress

coiffé(e) [kwafe] *adj* **1.**(*peigné*) **être** ~ to have done one's hair **2.**(*chapeauté*) **être ~ de qc** to be crowned with sth

coiffer [kwafe] <1> **I.** *vt* **1.**(*peigner*) ~ **qn** to do sb's hair **2.**(*mettre un chapeau*) to put a hat on **3.**(*dépasser*) to pip at the post *Brit,* to nose out *Am* **II.** *vpr* **1.**(*se peigner*) **se** ~ to do one's hair **2.**(*mettre un chapeau*) **se ~ de qc** to put sth on (one's head)

coiffeur, -euse [kwafœʀ, -øz] *m, f* hairdresser

coiffeuse [kwaføz] *f* dressing table

coiffure [kwafyʀ] *f* **1.**(*façon d'être peigné*) hairstyle **2.**(*chapeau*) hat **3.**(*métier*) hairdressing

coin [kwɛ̃] *m* **1.**(*angle*) corner; **mettre au** ~ to put in the corner; **au ~ de la rue** at the corner of the street; **regard en** ~ sidelong glance; **sourire en** ~ half-smile **2.**(*petit espace*) spot; **un ~ à l'ombre** a spot in the shade; ~ **cuisine/repas** kitchen/dining area ▶**aux quatre ~s du monde** all over the world; **ça t'en/vous en bouche un ~!** *inf* that gives you something to think about!

coincé(e) [kwɛ̃se] *adj inf* hung-up

coincer [kwɛ̃se] <2> **I.** *vt* **1.**(*caler*) ~ **entre deux chaises** to wedge between two chairs **2.**(*immobiliser*) ~ **qc** (*personne*) to jam sth; (*grain de sable, panne*) to jam sth up

3. (*acculer*) ~ **qn contre un mur** to pin sb against a wall **4.** *inf* (*attraper*) to grab **5.** *inf* (*coller*) to catch out **II.** *vi* (*poser problème*) to get sticky **III.** *vpr* **se** ~ **le doigt** to pinch one's finger

coïncidence [kɔɛ̃sidɑ̃s] *f* coincidence

coïncider [kɔɛ̃side] <1> *vi* **1.** (*être concomitant*) to coincide **2.** (*correspondre*) to match up

coing [kwɛ̃] *m* quince

coin-repas [kwɛ̃ʀəpa] <coins-repas> *m* dining area

coït [kɔit] *m* coitus

col [kɔl] *m* **1.** COUT (*d'un vêtement*) collar; ~ **roulé** polo neck **2.** GEO pass **3.** (*goulot*) neck **4.** ANAT (*du fémur*) neck; ~ **de l'utérus** cervix

coléoptère [kɔleɔptɛʀ] *m* beetle

colère [kɔlɛʀ] *f* **1.** (*irritation*) anger **2.** (*accès d'irritation*) fit of rage; **être/se mettre en** ~ **contre qn** to be/get angry with sb; **piquer une** ~ *inf* to fly into a rage; **en** ~ angry

coléreux, **-euse** [kɔleʀø, -øz], **colérique** [kɔleʀik] *adj* quick-tempered

colibri [kɔlibʀi] *m* hummingbird

colimaçon [kɔlimasɔ̃] *m* snail

colin [kɔlɛ̃] *m* coley, coalfish

colin-maillard [kɔlɛ̃majaʀ] *m sans pl* **jouer à** ~ blind man's buff

colique [kɔlik] *f* **1.** (*diarrhée*) diarrhoea *Brit*, diarrhea *Am* **2.** *gén pl* (*douleurs*) stomach ache

colis [kɔli] *m* parcel

collabo *inf*, **collaborateur**, **-trice** [ko(l)labɔʀatœʀ, -tʀis] *m, f* **1.** (*membre du personnel*) staff member **2.** (*intervenant occasionnel*) associate **3.** (*pendant une guerre*) collaborator

collaboration [ko(l)labɔʀasjɔ̃] *f* **1.** (*coopération, pendant une guerre*) collaboration; **en** ~ **avec** in collaboration with **2.** (*contribution*) contribution; **apporter sa** ~ **à qc** to make one's contribution to sth

collaborer [ko(l)labɔʀe] <1> *vi* **1.** (*coopérer*) to collaborate; ~ **à qc** to work on sth **2.** (*pendant une guerre*) to collaborate

collage [kɔlaʒ] *m* **1.** (*action: d'une étiquette, du bois*) sticking on; (*de papier peint*) pasting; (*d'une affiche*) posting; (*de pièces*) sticking together **2.** ART, MUS collage **3.** (*clarification: du vin*) fining

collant [kɔlɑ̃] *m* **1.** (*bas*) tights *pl* **2.** (*body pour la gymnastique*) body(suit) **3.** (*body pour la danse, l'acrobatie*) leotard

collant(e) [kɔlɑ̃, ɑ̃t] *adj* **1.** (*moulant*) clinging **2.** (*poisseux*) sticky **3.** *inf* (*importun: enfant*) clingy; **il est vraiment** ~ (*visiteur*) he just won't let go of you

collation [kɔlasjɔ̃] *f* light meal

colle [kɔl] *f* **1.** (*matière*) glue; ~ **universelle** all-purpose glue **2.** (*masse*) sticky mass **3.** (*punition*) detention; **avoir une** ~ to have detention

collecte [kɔlɛkt] *f* (*quête*) collection

collecter [kɔlɛkte] <1> *vt* (*dons*) to collect

collectif, **-ive** [kɔlɛktif, -iv] *adj* **1.** (*commun*) common; (*travail*) collective; **équipements** ~**s** shared facilities **2.** LING collective

collection [kɔlɛksjɔ̃] *f* collection; ~ **de timbres** stamp collection; **toute la** ~ **des œuvres de X** the complete collection of X's works; **faire la** ~ **de qc** to collect sth

collectionner [kɔlɛksjɔne] <1> *vt* to collect

collectionneur, **-euse** [kɔlɛksjɔnœʀ, -øz] *m, f* collector

collectivement [kɔlɛktivmɑ̃] *adv* **1.** (*dans la totalité*) **s'adresser** ~ **au personnel** to speak to the staff as a body **2.** (*ensemble: démissionner, protester*) collectively

collectivité [kɔlɛktivite] *f* **1.** (*société*) community **2.** JUR organization; ~**s locales** local authorities **3.** (*communauté*) group

collège [kɔlɛʒ] *m* ECOLE school; **aller au** ~ to go to school

> At the end of primary school, students aged 11 to 16 years go to **collège**. It is a comprehensive school in which students go through four classes ("sixième", "cinquième", "quatrième" und "troisième"). They finish school with a "Brevet des collèges".

Collège [kɔlɛʒ] *m* ~ **de France** Collège de France (*institute in Paris where prominent academics give public lectures*)

collégien(ne) [kɔleʒjɛ̃, jɛn] *m(f)* (*élève*) pupil

collègue [kɔ(l)lɛg] *mf* colleague

coller [kɔle] <1> **I.** *vt* **1.** (*fixer*) to stick; (*enveloppe*) to stick down; (*pièces*) to stick together; (*timbre, étiquette*) to stick on; (*affiche, papier peint*) to stick up **2.** (*presser*) ~ **à qc** to stick sth on sth **3.** *inf* (*donner*) ~ **un devoir à qn** to give sb some homework; ~ **une baffe à qn** to slap sb **4.** *inf* (*embarrasser par une question*) to catch out **5.** *inf* (*suivre*) to tail **6.** *inf* (*planter*) to stick **7.** *inf* (*rester*) **être collé quelque part** to be stuck somewhere **II.** *vi* **1.** (*adhérer*) to stick; **qc qui colle** sth sticky **2.** (*mouler*) to cling **3.** *inf* (*suivre*) ~ **à qc** to hang on to sth **4.** (*s'adapter*) ~ **à la route** to grip the road; ~ **au sujet** to stick (close) to the subject **5.** *inf* (*bien marcher*) **ça colle** things are OK; **entre eux, ça ne colle pas** they're not getting along **III.** *vpr* **1.** (*s'accrocher*) **se** ~ **à qn** to cling to sb **2.** (*se presser*) **se** ~ **à** [*o* **contre**] **qc** to snuggle up to sb

collet [kɔlɛ] *m* **1.** (*piège*) snare **2.** GASTR neck ►**être** ~ **monté** to be straitlaced; **prendre** [*o* **saisir**] **au** ~ to grab sb by the neck

colleur, **-euse** [kɔlœʀ, -øz] *m, f* ~ **d'affiches** bill poster

collier [kɔlje] *m* **1.** (*bijou*) necklace; (*rigide*) chain **2.** (*courroie: d'un chien, cheval*) collar **3.** (*barbe*) beard (*without moustache*)

collimateur [kɔlimatœʀ] *m* **avoir qn dans**

le ~ to have one's sights on sb
colline [kɔlin] *f* hill
collision [kɔlizjɔ̃] *f* collision
collocation [kɔlɔkasjɔ̃] *f Belgique* (*internement, emprisonnement*) imprisonment
colloque [kɔ(l)lɔk] *m* conference
colmater [kɔlmate] <1> *vt* (*fuite*) to stop; (*fissure*) to fill; (*brèche*) to close
colo [kɔlɔ] *f inf abr de* **colonie de vacances**
colocataire [kolɔkatɛʀ] *mf* co-tenant
colombage [kɔlɔ̃baʒ] *m* half-timbering; **maison à** ~ half-timbered house
colombe [kɔlɔ̃b] *f* dove
Colombie [kɔlɔ̃bi] *f* **la** ~ Colombia
Colombie-Britannique [kɔlɔ̃bibʀitanik] *f* **la** ~ British-Colombia
colombien(ne) [kɔlɔ̃bjɛ̃, ɛn] *adj* Colombian
Colombien(ne) [kɔlɔ̃bjɛ̃, ɛn] *m(f)* Colombian
colon [kɔlɔ̃] *m* **1.** (*opp: indigène*) colonist **2.** (*enfant*) child (*at a colonie de vacance*) **3.** (*pionnier*) settler
colonel [kɔlɔnɛl] *m* colonel
colonial(e) [kɔlɔnjal, jo] <-aux> *adj* colonial
colonialisme [kɔlɔnjalism] *m* colonialism
colonie [kɔlɔni] *f* **1.** (*territoire, communauté*) colony **2.** (*centre*) ~ **de vacances** summer camp
colonisation [kɔlɔnizasjɔ̃] *f* colonization
coloniser [kɔlɔnize] <1> *vt* to colonize
colonne [kɔlɔn] *f* **1.** ARCHIT, MIL, PRESSE column; **cinq ~s à la une** all over the front page **2.** ANAT ~ **vertébrale** spinal column
colorant [kɔlɔʀɑ̃] *m* colouring *Brit,* coloring *Am*
colorant(e) [kɔlɔʀɑ̃, ɑ̃t] *adj* colouring *Brit,* coloring *Brit;* **shampooing** ~ hair dye
coloration [kɔlɔʀasjɔ̃] *f* **1.** (*processus*) colouring *Brit,* coloring *Am* **2.** (*teinte*) tint; **prendre une** ~ **rouge** to go red **3.** (*nuance*) colour *Brit,* color *Am*
coloré(e) [kɔlɔʀe] *adj* **1.** (*en couleurs*) coloured *Brit,* colored *Am* **2.** *fig* (*style, description*) colourful *Brit,* colorful *Am*
colorer [kɔlɔʀe] <1> **I.** *vt* to colour *Brit,* to color *Am* **II.** *vpr* **se** ~ (*visage*) to go red
coloriage [kɔlɔʀjaʒ] *m* **1.** (*action*) colouring *Brit,* coloring *Am;* **faire du** ~ (*enfant*) to do some colouring in; ART to colour **2.** (*résultat*) colouring *Brit,* coloring *Am;* ART coloured drawing
colorier [kɔlɔʀje] <1> *vt* **1.** (*jeu*) to colour in *Brit,* to color in *Am* **2.** ART to colour *Brit,* to color *Am*
coloris [kɔlɔʀi] *m* **1.** (*teinte*) shade **2.** (*couleur*) colour *Brit,* color *Am*
colossal(e) [kɔlɔsal, o] <-aux> *adj* colossal
colosse [kɔlɔs] *m* **1.** (*géant*) colossus **2.** *fig* giant
colporter [kɔlpɔʀte] <1> *vt* **1.** (*vendre*) to peddle **2.** *péj* (*répandre*) to hawk
colporteur, -euse [kɔlpɔʀtœʀ, -øz] *m, f* pedlar
colza [kɔlza] *m* rape
coma [kɔma] *m* coma; **être dans le** ~ to be in a coma
combat [kɔ̃ba] *m* combat
combatif, -ive [kɔ̃batif, -iv] *adj* combative
combattant(e) [kɔ̃batɑ̃, ɑ̃t] *m(f)* combatant; **ancien** ~ veteran
combattre [kɔ̃batʀ] *irr* **I.** *vt, vi* to fight **II.** *vpr* **se** ~ to fight each other
combi [kɔ̃bi] *f inf abr de* **combinaison de ski**
combien [kɔ̃bjɛ̃] **I.** *adv* **1.** (*concernant la quantité*) how much; ~ **de temps** how long; **depuis** ~ **de temps** for how long; ~ **coûte cela?** how much does that cost?; **ça fait ~?** *inf* how much is that?; **je vous dois ~?** what do I owe you? **2.** (*concernant le nombre*) how many; ~ **de personnes/kilomètres** how many people/kilometres; ~ **de fois** how often **II.** *m inf* **1.** (*en parlant de la date*) **nous sommes le ~?** what's the date today? **2.** (*en parlant d'un intervalle*) **le bus passe tous les ~?** how often does the bus come by? **III.** *mf* **c'est le/la ~?** how many does he/she make it?
combinaison [kɔ̃binɛzɔ̃] *f* **1.** (*assemblage*) *a.* CHIM combination **2.** (*chiffres*) code **3.** (*mot*) password **4.** (*sous-vêtement*) slip **5.** (*vêtement*) suit; ~ **de plongée/ski** diving/ski suit **6.** (*stratagème*) scheme; **avoir/trouver une** ~ to have/find a way
combine [kɔ̃bin] *f inf* scheme; **connaître la** ~ to know the way ▸**être dans la** ~ to be on on the business
combiné [kɔ̃bine] *m* **1.** TEL handset **2.** (*épreuve*) ~ **alpin/nordique** alpine/northern combined competition
combiner [kɔ̃bine] <1> **I.** *vt* **1.** (*réunir*) *a.* CHIM ~ **qc avec qc** to combine sth with sth **2.** (*organiser: plan*) to think up; (*mauvais coup*) to cook up **II.** *vpr* **1.** (*s'assembler*) *a.* CHIM **se** ~ **avec qc** to combine with sth **2.** (*s'arranger*) **bien/mal se** ~ to work out all right/all wrong
comble¹ [kɔ̃bl] *m* **1.** (*summum: de la bêtise*) height; **c'est le** [*o* **un**] **~!** that beats everything! **2.** *souvent pl* (*grenier*) eaves
comble² [kɔ̃bl] *adj* packed
comblé(e) [kɔ̃ble] *adj* **je suis** ~ I'm so pleased; **être une personne ~e** to be a contented person
combler [kɔ̃ble] <1> *vt* **1.** (*boucher*) to fill in **2.** (*rattraper: déficit*) to make up for; (*lacune*) to fill; ~ **un retard** to catch up **3.** (*satisfaire: personne, vœu*) to satisfy **4.** (*couvrir, remplir de*) ~ **qn de cadeaux** to shower sb with gifts; ~ **qn de joie** to fill sb with joy
combustible [kɔ̃bystibl] **I.** *adj* combustible **II.** *m* fuel
combustion [kɔ̃bystjɔ̃] *f* combustion
comédie [kɔmedi] *f* **1.** (*pièce*) play; ~ **musi-**

cale musical (comedy) **2.** (*film*) comedy **3.** (*simulation*) performance

comédien(ne) [kɔmedjɛ̃, jɛn] **I.** *m(f)* **1.** (*acteur*) actor **2.** (*hypocrite*) phoney **II.** *adj* **être un peu** ~ to put it on

comestible [kɔmɛstibl] *adj* edible

comète [kɔmɛt] *f* comet

comique [kɔmik] **I.** *adj* **1.** (*amusant*) funny **2.** THEAT, CINE, LIT comic **II.** *m* **1.** (*auteur*) comic author **2.** (*interprète*) comic actor **3.** (*genre*) comedy

comité [kɔmite] *m* (*réunion*) committee; ~ **directeur** steering committee; ~ **d'entreprise** ≈ works council (*dealing with welfare and cultural matters*)

Comité des régions *m* Regional Commission

Comité économique et social *m* Economic and Social Commission (*dealing with regional matters*)

commandant(e) [kɔmɑ̃dɑ̃, ɑ̃t] *m(f)* **1.** MIL (*chef*) commander; (*grade*) major; (*dans l'armée de l'air*) squadron leader *Brit*, major *Am;* ~ **en chef** commander-in-chief **2.** AVIAT, NAUT captain

commande [kɔmɑ̃d] *f* **1.** (*achat, marchandise*) order; **passer une** ~ to place an order **2.** TECH ~ **à distance** remote control **3.** INFOR command; **message d'attente de** ~ command prompt ►**prendre** **les** ~**s** to take control; **sourire de** ~ forced smile; **vendre/pleurer sur** ~ to sell/cry to order

commandement [kɔmɑ̃dmɑ̃] *m* **1.** (*direction*) control **2.** (*état-major*) **le haut** ~ the High Command **3.** (*ordre*) command **4.** REL commandment

commander [kɔmɑ̃de] <1> **I.** *vt* **1.** (*passer commande*) ~ **qc à qn** to order sth from sb **2.** (*exercer son autorité*) to command **3.** (*ordonner*) ~ **qc à qn** to command sth from sb **4.** (*diriger*) to direct **5.** (*faire fonctionner*) to control **II.** *vi* **1.** (*passer commande*) to order **2.** (*exercer son autorité*) to command **III.** *vpr* **1.** (*être actionné*) **se** ~ **de l'extérieur** to be controlled from outside **2.** (*se contrôler*) **ne pas se** ~ (*sentiments*) to be beyond one's control

commando [kɔmɑ̃do] *m* commando

comme [kɔm] **I.** *conj* **1.** (*au moment où, étant donné que*) as **2.** (*de même que*) (just) like; **hier** ~ **aujourd'hui** yesterday just like today **3.** (*exprimant une comparaison*) **il était** ~ **mort** it was as if he was dead; **grand/petit** ~ **ça** this big/small; ~ **si** as if **4.** (*en tant que*) as; **apprécier qn** ~ **collègue** to think of sb as a colleague; ~ **plat principal** as the main course **5.** (*tel que*) like; **je n'ai jamais vu un film** ~ **celui-ci** I've never seen a film like this **6.** (*quel genre de*) in the way of; **qu'est-ce que tu fais** ~ **sport?** what sport(s) do you play? ►**...** ~ **tout** *inf* **il est mignon** ~ **tout!** he's so sweet!; **rusé/fort** ~ **pas un** *inf* not half crafty/strong **II.** *adv* **1.** (*exclamatif*) ~ **c'est gentil!** isn't that kind! **2.** (*manière*) how; **savoir** ~ to know the way; ~ **ça** like that; **c'est** ~ **ça** that's the way it is; **il n'est pas** ~ **ça** he's not like that ►~ **ci** ~ **ça** so-so; ~ **quoi** (*disant que*) to the effect that; (*ce qui prouve*) which goes to show

commémoratif, -ive [kɔmemɔʀatif, -iv] *adj* commemorative

commémoration [kɔmemɔʀasjɔ̃] *f* commemoration; **en** ~ **de qc** in commemoration of sth

commémorer [kɔmemɔʀe] <1> *vt* to commemorate

commencé(e) [kɔmɑ̃se] *adj* begun

commencement [kɔmɑ̃smɑ̃] *m* beginning ►**il y a un** ~ **à tout** you have to begin somewhere

commencer [kɔmɑ̃se] <2> **I.** *vt* to begin **II.** *vi* **1.** (*débuter: événement*) to begin **2.** (*faire en premier*) ~ **par qc/par faire qc** to begin with sth/by doing sth ►**ça commence bien** *iron* that's a good start; **ça commence à bien faire** things are going too far; **pour** ~ to start with

comment [kɔmɑ̃] *adv* **1.** (*de quelle façon*) how; ~ **ça va?** how are things?; **et toi,** ~ **tu t'appelles?** and what's your name?; ~ **est-ce que ça s'appelle en français?** what's the word for that in French? **2.** (*invitation à répéter*) ~**?** what? ►(**mais**) ~ **donc!** of course!; ~ **cela?** how come?; **et** ~**!** and how!

commentaire [kɔmɑ̃tɛʀ] *m* **1.** RADIO, TV commentary **2.** (*explication*) ~ **composé** textual commentary **3.** *péj* (*remarque*) comment; **sans** ~**!** no comment!; **pas de** ~**s!** none of your remarks, thank you!

commentateur, -trice [kɔmɑ̃tatœʀ, -tʀis] *m, f* commentator

commenter [kɔmɑ̃te] <1> *vt* (*événement*) to comment on; (*texte*) to give an intepretation of

commérage [kɔmeʀaʒ] *m souvent pl* gossip *no pl*

commerçant(e) [kɔmɛʀsɑ̃, ɑ̃t] **I.** *adj* **1.** (*avec des magasins: rue*) shopping **2.** (*habile*) **être** ~ to have business sense **II.** *m(f)* (*personne*) shopkeeper; ~ **en gros** wholesaler

commerce [kɔmɛʀs] *m* **1.** (*activité*) business; **faire du** ~ to be in business; **dans le** ~ in business; **école de** ~ business school; **chambre de** ~ chamber of commerce; **employé de** ~ shop assistant; ~ **électronique** e-commerce **2.** (*magasin*) shop, store *Am;* **tenir un** ~ to have a shop; ~ **de détail** retailing; ~ **en gros** wholesaling

commercial(e) [kɔmɛʀsjal, jo] <-aux> **I.** *adj* **1.** COM commercial; **centre** ~ shopping centre *Brit*, shopping center *Am* **2.** *péj* (*film*) commercial; (*sourire*) mercenary **II.** *m(f)* sales rep(resentative)

commercialiser [kɔmɛʀsjalize] <1> *vt* **1.** (*vendre*) to market **2.** (*lancer*) to put on the

market
commère [kɔmɛʀ] *f péj* gossip
commettre [kɔmɛtʀ] *vt irr* (*délit, attentat*) to commit; (*faute*) to make
commis [kɔmi] *m* assistant; **grands ~ de l'État** senior civil servant
commissaire [kɔmisɛʀ] *m* **1.** (*policier*) superintendant; **madame le ~** ma'am; **monsieur le ~** sir **2.** (*membre d'une commission*) commissioner
commissaire-priseur [kɔmisɛʀpʀizœʀ] <commissaires-priseurs> *m* auctioneer
commissariat [kɔmisaʀja] *m* police station
commission [kɔmisjɔ̃] *f* **1.** ADMIN, COM commission; **~ d'examen** exam board; **la ~ prélevée par la banque** the commission levied by the bank **2.** (*message*) message; **faire une ~ à qn** to give sb a message **3.** (*mission*) commission **4.** *pl* (*courses*) shopping; **faire les ~s** to do the shopping
Commission européenne *f* European Commission
commissures [kɔmisyʀ] *fpl* **les ~ des lèvres** the corner of the mouth
commode[1] [kɔmɔd] *adj* **1.** (*pratique*) practical **2.** *souvent négatif* (*facile*) convenient; **ce serait trop ~!** that'd be too easy! **3.** (*d'un caractère facile*) **ses parents n'ont pas l'air ~** her parents don't look easy to get on with
commode[2] [kɔmɔd] *f* commode
commodément [kɔmɔdemɑ̃] *adv* **1.** (*confortablement*) comfortably **2.** (*aisément*) easily
commodité [kɔmɔdite] *f* **1.** (*agrément*) comfort **2.** (*simplification*) convenience; **pour plus de ~** for the sake of convenience **3.** *pl* (*éléments de confort*) conveniences
commotion [komosjɔ̃] *f* shock; **~ cérébrale** concussion
commun [kɔmœ̃] *m* **le ~ des mortels** ordinary mortals *pl;* **hors du ~** out of the ordinary; **en ~** in common; **faire qc en ~** to do sth together
commun(e) [kɔmœ̃, yn] *adj* **1.** (*comparable, général, courant, trivial*) common; **n'avoir rien de ~ avec qn/qc** to have nothing in common with sb/sth **2.** (*collectif*) communal
communal(e) [kɔmynal, o] <-aux> *adj* **1.** (*fonds*) communal; (*du village*) village; (*de la ville*) town **2.** *Belgique* **conseil ~** (*conseil municipal*) town council; **maison ~e** (*mairie*) town hall
communautaire [kɔmynotɛʀ] *adj* **1.** (*commun*) common **2.** (*de l'UE*) Community; **la politique ~** community policy
communauté [kɔmynote] *f* **1.** (*groupe*) *a.* REL community **2.** (*identité*) sharing
Communauté économique européenne *f* European Economic Community
Communauté européenne *f* European Community
commune [kɔmyn] *f* commune
communément [kɔmynemɑ̃] *adv* commonly; **on dit ~ que …** it is often said that …
communiant(e) [kɔmynjɑ̃, jɑ̃t] *m(f)* communicant
communicant(e) [kɔmynikɑ̃, ɑ̃t] *adj* (*pièces, salles*) adjoining; (*vases*) communicating
communicatif, -ive [kɔmynikatif, -iv] *adj* **1.** (*contagieux*) transmissible **2.** (*expansif*) communicative
communication [kɔmynikasjɔ̃] *f* **1.** (*transmission*) communication **2.** TEL (*jonction*) connection; (*conversation*) call; **être en ~ avec qn** to be on the phone with sb; **prendre une ~** to take a call **3.** (*message*) message **4.** (*relation*) public relations **5.** (*liaison*) **moyen de ~** means of communication
communier [kɔmynje] <1> *vi* REL to go to communion
communion [kɔmynjɔ̃] *f* communion
communiqué [kɔmynike] *m* communiqué; **~ de presse** press release
communiquer [kɔmynike] <1> **I.** *vt* **1.** (*faire connaître*) **~ une demande à qn** to convey a request to sb **2.** (*transmettre*) **~ un dossier à qn** to pass a file on to sb **II.** *vi* **~ avec qn** to communicate with sb
communisme [kɔmynism] *m* communism
communiste [kɔmynist] **I.** *adj* communist **II.** *mf* communist
Comores [kɔmɔʀ] *fpl* **les ~** Comoros
comorien(ne) [kɔmɔʀjɛ̃, ɛn] *adj* Comoran
Comorien(ne) [kɔmɔʀjɛ̃, ɛn] *m(f)* Comoran
compact [kɔ̃pakt] *m* CD
compact(e) [kɔ̃pakt] *adj* **1.** (*dense*) dense **2.** (*petit*) compact
compagne [kɔ̃paɲ] *f* partner
compagnie [kɔ̃paɲi] *f* company ►**fausser ~ à qn** to give sb the slip; **tenir ~ à qn** to keep sb company; **en ~ de qn** in sb's company
compagnon [kɔ̃paɲɔ̃] *m* **1.** (*concubin*) partner **2.** (*ouvrier*) journeyman
comparable [kɔ̃paʀabl] *adj* comparable
comparaison [kɔ̃paʀɛzɔ̃] *f* comparison; **en ~ de/par ~ à** [*o* **avec**] in comparison with; **sans ~** far and away
comparaître [kɔ̃paʀɛtʀ] *vi irr* **~ devant qn** to appear before sb
comparatif [kɔ̃paʀatif] *m* comparative
comparatif, -ive [kɔ̃paʀatif, -iv] *adj* comparative
comparativement [kɔ̃paʀativmɑ̃] *adv* comparatively; **~ à** in comparision with
comparer [kɔ̃paʀe] <1> **I.** *vt, vi* to compare **II.** *vpr* **se ~ à qn** to compare oneself to sb
compartiment [kɔ̃paʀtimɑ̃] *m* compartment
compas [kɔ̃pɑ] *m* compass ►**avoir le ~ dans l'œil** to have an eye for measurements
compassion [kɔ̃pasjɔ̃] *f soutenu* compassion
compatibilité [kɔ̃patibilite] *f* compatibility
compatible [kɔ̃patibl] *adj* compatible
compatir [kɔ̃patiʀ] <8> *vi soutenu* to sympathize

compatriote [kɔ̃patʀijɔt] *mf* compatriot

compensation [kɔ̃pɑ̃sasjɔ̃] *f* **1.** (*dédommagement*) compensation **2.** (*équilibre*) balance **3.** FIN (*d'une dette*) offsetting ►**en** ~ in compensation

compenser [kɔ̃pɑ̃se] <1> **I.** *vt* **1.** (*équilibrer*) ~ **qc par qc** to offset sth with sth **2.** (*dédommager*) **pour** ~ to compensate **3.** (*remercier*) **pour** ~ to make up **II.** *vpr* **se** ~ to cancel out

compétence [kɔ̃petɑ̃s] *f* **1.** (*capacité*) competence; **avec** ~ competently **2.** (*responsabilité*) domain; **cela ne relève pas de ma** ~ that is outside my responsibility

compétent(**e**) [kɔ̃petɑ̃, ɑ̃t] *adj* competent; **être** ~ **en qc** to be competent at sth

compétitif, **-ive** [kɔ̃petitif, -iv] *adj* competitive

compétition [kɔ̃petisjɔ̃] *f* competition

compilateur [kɔ̃pilatœʀ] *m* INFOR compiler

compilation [kɔ̃pilasjɔ̃] *f* compilation

compiler [kɔ̃pile] <1> *vt* INFOR to compile

complainte [kɔ̃plɛ̃t] *f* lament

complaire [kɔ̃plɛʀ] *vpr irr* **se** ~ **à faire qc** to enjoy doing sth; **se** ~ **dans son malheur** to wallow in one's misery

complaisance [kɔ̃plɛzɑ̃s] *f* **1.** *soutenu* (*obligeance*) kindness; **par** ~ out of politeness **2.** *péj* (*indulgence*) indulgence **3.** (*autosatisfaction*) smugness

complaisant(**e**) [kɔ̃plɛzɑ̃, ɑ̃t] *adj* **1.** (*obligeant*) obliging; **vous n'êtes pas très** ~ you're not very helpful **2.** (*indulgent*) kindly **3.** (*satisfait*) self-satisfied

complément [kɔ̃plemɑ̃] *m* **1.** (*ce qui s'ajoute*) **un** ~ **d'information** further information **2.** LING complement; ~ **du verbe** verb complement; ~ **circonstanciel de temps/lieu** adverbial phrase of time/place; ~ **d'attribution** indirect object; ~ **du nom** noun phrase; ~ **d'objet direct** direct object

complémentaire [kɔ̃plemɑ̃tɛʀ] *adj* complementary; (*renseignement*) additional

complet, **-ète** [kɔ̃plɛ, -ɛt] *adj* **1.** complete; (*pain*) wholemeal *Brit,* whole-wheat *Am* **2.** (*achevé*) utter **3.** (*plein: autobus, hôtel, parking*) full; **afficher** ~ to play to full houses ►**l'école/les joueurs au** (**grand**) ~ every one in the school/of the players

complètement [kɔ̃plɛtmɑ̃] *adv* competely

compléter [kɔ̃plete] <5> **I.** *vt* to complete **II.** *vpr* **se** ~ to complement each other

complexe [kɔ̃plɛks] **I.** *adj* complex **II.** *m* complex; **sans** (**aucun**) ~ without any inhibition

complexé(**e**) [kɔ̃plɛkse] *adj inf* **1.** PSYCH neurotic **2.** (*coincé*) hung-up

complexer [kɔ̃plɛkse] <1> *vt* to give a complex

complexité [kɔ̃plɛksite] *f* complexity

complication [kɔ̃plikasjɔ̃] *f* complication

complice [kɔ̃plis] **I.** *adj* **1.** (*acolyte*) **être** ~ **d'un vol** to be party to a theft **2.** (*de connivence*) knowing **II.** *mf* accomplice

complicité [kɔ̃plisite] *f* **1.** (*participation*) complicity; ~ **de vol** JUR aiding and abetting a theft **2.** (*connivence*) complicity

compliment [kɔ̃plimɑ̃] *m* **1.** (*éloge*) compliment **2.** (*félicitations*) congratulations; **tous mes ~s!** my congratulations!

complimenter [kɔ̃plimɑ̃te] <1> *vt* **1.** (*congratuler*) ~ **qn pour qc** to congratulate sb on sth **2.** (*faire l'éloge*) ~ **qn pour** [*o* **sur**] **qc** to compliment sb on sth

compliqué(**e**) [kɔ̃plike] *adj* complicated; **c'est pas** ~ *inf* it's easy enough

compliquer [kɔ̃plike] <1> **I.** *vt* to complicate **II.** *vpr* **1.** (*devenir plus compliqué*) **se** ~ (*choses, situation*) to get complicated; **la maladie se complique** complications have set in; **ça se complique** *inf* things are getting complicated **2.** (*rendre plus compliqué*) **se** ~ **la vie** to make life complicated for oneself

complot [kɔ̃plo] *m* conspiracy

comploter [kɔ̃plɔte] <1> **I.** *vt* to conspire; **qu'est-ce que vous complotez?** what are you plotting? **II.** *vi* ~ **contre qn** to conspire against sb

comportement [kɔ̃pɔʀtəmɑ̃] *m* behaviour *no pl Brit,* behavior *no pl Am;* **avoir un** ~ **étrange** to behave strangely

comporter [kɔ̃pɔʀte] <1> **I.** *vt* **1.** (*être constitué de*) to consist of **2.** (*inclure*) to have **II.** *vpr* **se** ~ **1.** (*se conduire*) to behave **2.** (*réagir*) to respond

composant [kɔ̃pozɑ̃] *m* **1.** CHIM constituent **2.** ELEC component

composant(**e**) [kɔ̃pozɑ̃, ɑ̃t] *adj* component

composante [kɔ̃pozɑ̃t] *f* component

composé [kɔ̃poze] *m* compound

composé(**e**) [kɔ̃poze] *adj* compound

composer [kɔ̃poze] <1> **I.** *vt* **1.** (*constituer*) to form; (*équipe*) to select **2.** (*créer: plat*) to devise; (*musique*) to compose; (*texte*) to write **3.** (*former*) to make up **II.** *vi* MUS to compose **III.** *vpr* **se** ~ **de qc** to be composed of sth

compositeur, **-trice** [kɔ̃pozitœʀ, -tʀis] *m, f* composer

composition [kɔ̃pozisjɔ̃] *f* **1.** (*organisation*) make-up **2.** ART, LIT, MUS (*d'une musique*) composition; (*d'un texte*) writing **3.** (*œuvre, structure*) composition; **une œuvre de ma/ta/sa** ~ a work composed by me/you/her

composter [kɔ̃pɔste] <1> *vt* to datestamp

> When travelling by train in France, you must **composter** your ticket at a small pillar in front of the platform or in the main station before getting on the train. There is no conductor, so it is up to each individual to ensure he has a valid, stamped ticket.

compote [kɔ̃pɔt] *f* compote

compréhensible [kɔ̃pʀeɑ̃sibl] *adj* comprehensible

C

compréhensif, -ive [kɔ̃pReɑ̃sif, -iv] *adj* understanding

compréhension [kɔ̃pReɑ̃sjɔ̃] *f* **1.** (*clarté*) intelligibility **2.** (*tolérance*) understanding **3.** (*intelligence*) comprehension

comprendre [kɔ̃pRɑ̃dR] <13> **I.** *vt* **1.** (*saisir, concevoir, s'apercevoir de*) to understand; **faire ~ qc à qn** (*expliquer*) to get sb to understand sth; (*dire indirectement*) to give sb to understand sth; **ne ~ rien à rien** *inf* to understand absolutely nothing **2.** (*comporter*) to comprise **3.** (*inclure*) to include **II.** *vi* to understand; **il ne faut pas chercher à ~** it's no use trying to understand; **se faire ~** (*par un étranger*) to make oneself understood; (*dire carrément*) to make oneself clear **III.** *vpr* **se ~** **1.** (*être compréhensible*) to be comprehensible **2.** (*communiquer*) to understand each other **3.** (*s'accorder: personnes*) to reach an understanding

compresse [kɔ̃pRɛs] *f* compress

compressible [kɔ̃pResibl] *adj* **1.** PHYS compressible **2.** FIN **nos dépenses ne sont pas ~s** our spending is impossible to reduce

compression [kɔ̃pResjɔ̃] *f* **1.** PHYS, INFOR compression; **routine de ~** packing routine **2.** (*réduction*) reduction; **~ de personnel** staff cut; **~s budgétaires** budget cuts

comprimé [kɔ̃pRime] *m* tablet

comprimé(e) [kɔ̃pRime] *adj* **1.** (*serré*) **je suis ~ dans ce pantalon** these trousers are tight on me **2.** PHYS **air ~** compressed air

comprimer [kɔ̃pRime] <1> *vt* **1.** (*presser*) *a.* INFOR to compress **2.** (*serrer*) **la ceinture lui comprime le ventre** the belt is too tight around his waist **3.** (*réduire*) to cut

compris(e) [kɔ̃pRi, iz] **I.** *part passé de* **comprendre II.** *adj* **1.** (*inclus*) included; **T.V.A. ~e** including VAT; **(la) T.V.A. non ~e** VAT not included **2.** (*situé*) **être ~ entre cinq et sept pourcent** to be between five and seven per cent; **période ~e entre 1920 et 1930** period from 1920 to 1930

compromettant(e) [kɔ̃pRɔmetɑ̃, ɑ̃t] *adj* compromising

compromettre [kɔ̃pRɔmɛtR] *irr* **I.** *vt* **1.** (*impliquer*) to compromise **2.** (*menacer*) to put at risk **II.** *vpr* **se ~ avec qn/dans qc** to compromise oneself with sb/in sth

compromis [kɔ̃pRɔmi] *m* compromise

comptabiliser [kɔ̃tabilize] <1> *vt* FIN to list

comptabilité [kɔ̃tabilite] *f* **1.** (*discipline*) accountancy **2.** (*comptes, service*) accounts *pl*

comptable [kɔ̃tabl] *mf* accountant

comptant [kɔ̃tɑ̃] **I.** *m sans pl* cash **II.** *adv* (*payer*) (in) cash

compte [kɔ̃t] *m* **1.** *sans pl* (*calcul*) calculation; (*des points*) scoring; **~ à rebours** countdown **2.** *sans pl* (*résultat*) total; **avez-vous le bon ~ de chaises?** (*suffisamment*) have you got enough chairs?; (*le même nombre*) have you got all the chairs?; **le ~ est bon** (*en payant*) that's right; (*rien ne manque*) everything's there; **le ~ y est** *inf* it's all there; **cela fait un ~ rond** that makes a round figure **3.** (*note*) bill; **faire le ~** to reckon up **4.** (*écritures comptables*) account; **faire/tenir les ~s** to do/to keep the accounts **5.** (*~ en banque*) bank account; **~ chèque** cheque account *Brit,* checking account *Am;* **~ chèque postal** ≈ Girobank account *Brit;* **~ courant/(d')épargne** current/savings acount; **ouvrir/fermer un ~** to open/close an account ▶**les bons ~s font les bons amis** *prov* pay your debts and keep your friends; **au bout du ~** at the end of the day; **en fin de ~** when all is said and done; **être loin du ~** to be a long way out; **tout ~ fait** all things considered; **son ~ est bon!** *inf* his goose is cooked!; **s'en tirer à bon ~** to get off lightly; **mettre qc sur le ~ de qn/qc** to put sth down to sb/sth; **rendre ~ de qc à qn** (*pour se justifier*) to justify sth to sb; (*avertir*) to report sth to sb; **se rendre ~ de qc** to realize sth; **tu te rends ~!** (*imagine*) just think!; **tenir ~ de qc** to take account of sth; **à ce ~-là** looking at it like that; **demander** [*o* **réclamer**] **des ~s à qn** to call sb to account; **à son ~** (*travailler*) for oneself; **pour le ~ de qn/qc** for sb/sth

compte-gouttes [kɔ̃tgut] *m inv* dropper ▶**au ~** bit by bit

compter [kɔ̃te] <1> **I.** *vt* **1.** (*chiffrer, ajouter*) to count; **dix personnes sans ~ les enfants** ten people not counting the children **2.** (*totaliser*) to count up **3.** (*facturer*) **~ 100 euros à qn pour le dépannage** to charge sb for 100 euros for the repair **4.** (*prévoir*) **~ 200 g/20 euros par personne** to allow 200 grams/20 euros per head **5.** (*prendre en compte*) to allow for **6.** (*ranger parmi*) **~ qn/qc parmi** [*o* **au nombre de**] **...** to place sb/sth among ... **7.** (*comporter*) to have; **la ville compte 10000 habitants** the town has 10000 inhabitants **8.** (*avoir l'intention de*) **~** *+infin* to intend to *+infin;* (*espérer*) to expect to *+infin* **II.** *vi* **1.** (*énumérer, calculer*) to count; **~ sur ses doigts** to count on one's fingers; **~ large** to be generous (in one's calcutions) **2.** (*être économe*) **dépenser sans ~** to spend without thinking of the cost **3.** (*tenir compte de*) **~ avec qn/qc** to reckon with sb/sth **4.** (*s'appuyer*) **~ sur qn/qc** to count on sb/sth; **tu peux ~ (là-)dessus!** you can count on it!; **n'y comptez pas avant mardi!** don't count on it before Tuesday! **5.** (*avoir de l'importance*) to count; **~ pour qn** to mean a lot to sb; **ce qui compte, c'est d'être en bonne santé** being in good health, that's what counts **III.** *vpr* (*s'inclure*) **se ~** to include oneself

compte rendu [kɔ̃tRɑ̃dy] *m* account; TV, RADIO report

compteur [kɔ̃tœR] *m* **1.** AUTO mileometer *Brit,* odometer *Am* **2.** (*enregistreur: électricité*) meter; **relever le ~** to read the meter

comptine [kɔ̃tin] *f* rhyme

comptoir [kɔ̃twaR] *m* counter

comte [kɔ̃t] *m* count
comté [kɔ̃te] *m* county
comtesse [kɔ̃tɛs] *f* countess
comtois(e) [kɔ̃twa, waz] *adj* of Franche-Comté
Comtois(e) [kɔ̃twa, waz] *m(f)* person from Franche-Comté
con(ne) [kɔ̃, kɔn] **I.** *adj parfois inv, inf* stupid **II.** *m(f) inf* fool; **pauvre** [*o* **sale**] *péj* **~!** you great prick! *vulg;* **pauvre** [*o* **sale**] *péj* **~ne** stupid cow!; **faire le ~** to fool around; **oh! le ~/la ~ne!** what a prick/stupid cow!
conard [kɔnaʀ] *m inf v.* **connard**
conasse [kɔnas] *f inf v.* **connasse**
concasser [kɔ̃kɑse] <1> *vt* (*roche*) to crush; (*épices, grain*) to grind
concave [kɔ̃kav] *adj* concave
concentration [kɔ̃sɑ̃tʀasjɔ̃] *f* concentration
concentré [kɔ̃sɑ̃tʀe] *m* GASTR concentrate; **~ de tomate** tomato purée
concentré(e) [kɔ̃sɑ̃tʀe] *adj* **1.** (*condensé*) concentrated; (*lait*) condensed **2.** (*attentif*) **être ~** to be concentrating
concentrer [kɔ̃sɑ̃tʀe] <1> **I.** *vt* (*rassembler*) to concentrate **II.** *vpr* **se ~ sur qn/qc** to concentrate on sb/sth
concentrique [kɔ̃sɑ̃tʀik] *adj* concentric
concept [kɔ̃sɛpt] *m* concept
conception [kɔ̃sɛpsjɔ̃] *f* **1.** *sans pl* (*idée*) *a.* BIO conception **2.** *sans pl* (*élaboration*) design; **~ assistée par ordinateur** computer-aided design ►**Immaculée Conception** Immaculate Conception
concernant [kɔ̃sɛʀnɑ̃] *prep* (*quant à*) concerning
concerner [kɔ̃sɛʀne] <1> *vt* to concern; **en** [*o* **pour**] **ce qui concerne qn/qc** as far as sb/sth is concerned
concert [kɔ̃sɛʀ] *m* concert ►**~ de sifflets/d'exclamations** chorus of whistles/cheers; **agir de ~ avec qn** to act jointly with sb; **décider qc de ~ avec qn** to come to a joint decision with sb
concertation [kɔ̃sɛʀtasjɔ̃] *f* consultation
concerter [kɔ̃sɛʀte] <1> *vpr* **se ~ sur qc** to consult about sth
concertiste [kɔ̃sɛʀtist] *mf* concert performer
concerto [kɔ̃sɛʀto] *m* concerto
concession [kɔ̃sesjɔ̃] *f* **1.** (*compromis, terrain*) *a.* ADMIN concession **2.** COM dealership
concessionnaire [kɔ̃sesjɔnɛʀ] *mf* COM dealer
concevable [kɔ̃s(ə)vabl] *adj* conceivable
concevoir [kɔ̃s(ə)vwaʀ] <12> **I.** *vt* **1.** *soutenu* (*engendrer*) to conceive **2.** (*se représenter*) to imagine; (*solution*) to think of; **~ qc comme qc** to think of sth as sth **3.** (*élaborer*) to design **4.** (*comprendre*) **on conçoit sa déception** you can understand her disppointment **II.** *vpr* **1.** (*se comprendre*) **cela se conçoit facilement** that is easily understandable **2.** *soutenu* (*être imaginé*) **se ~** to be thought of
concierge [kɔ̃sjɛʀʒ] *mf* concierge
conciergerie [kɔ̃sjɛʀʒəʀi] *f Québec* (*grand immeuble d'habitation généralement en location*) block of flats *Brit,* apartment building *Am*
concile [kɔ̃sil] *m* council
conciliabule [kɔ̃siljabyl] *m* **tenir** [*o* **faire**] **des ~s avec qn** to be in a huddle with sb
conciliant(e) [kɔ̃siljɑ̃, jɑ̃t] *adj* conciliatory
conciliation [kɔ̃siljasjɔ̃] *f* **1.** (*médiation*) conciliation; **tentative de ~** attempt at conciliation; **par esprit de ~** in a spirit of conciliation **2.** JUR arbitration; **être cité en ~** to be called before the arbitrators
concilier [kɔ̃silje] <1> **I.** *vt* (*harmoniser*) to reconcile **II.** *vpr* **se ~ l'amitié de qn** to win sb's friendship
concis(e) [kɔ̃si, iz] *adj* concise; **soyez ~** be brief
concision [kɔ̃sizjɔ̃] *f sans pl* concision
concitoyen(ne) [kɔ̃sitwajɛ̃, jɛn] *m(f)* fellow citizen
conclave [kɔ̃klav] *m* conclave
concluant(e) [kɔ̃klyɑ̃, ɑ̃t] *adj* conclusive
conclure [kɔ̃klyʀ] *irr* **I.** *vt* **1.** (*signer: marché, pacte*) to sign; (*accord*) to reach **2.** (*terminer: discours*) to conclude; (*repas*) to finish (off) **3.** (*déduire*) **~ qc de qc** to conclude sth from sth **II.** *vi* (*terminer*) **~ par qc** to conclude with sth; **pour ~** in conclusion **III.** *vpr* **se ~ par qc** to end with sth
conclusion [kɔ̃klyzjɔ̃] *f* **1.** (*signature: d'un accord*) signing; (*d'un mariage*) conclusion **2.** (*fin, déduction*) conclusion; **en ~** in conclusion; **~, ...** the upshot is, ...; **(en) arriver à la ~ que ...** to reach the conclusion that ...
concombre [kɔ̃kɔ̃bʀ] *m* cucumber
concordance [kɔ̃kɔʀdɑ̃s] *f* **1.** (*accord*) agreement **2.** LING **~ des temps** sequence of tenses
concorde [kɔ̃kɔʀd] *f sans pl, soutenu* harmony; **vivre dans la ~** to live in harmony
concorder [kɔ̃kɔʀde] <1> *vi* to agree
concourir [kɔ̃kuʀiʀ] *vi irr* **1.** *soutenu* (*contribuer*) **~ à qc** to work towards sth **2.** (*être en compétition*) **~ à qc** to compete in sth
concours [kɔ̃kuʀ] *m* **1.** (*compétition, jeu*) *a.* SPORT competition **2.** ECOLE, UNIV (*pour une école*) entrance examination; (*pour un prix*) prize competition **3.** (*aide*) support; **prêter son ~ à qc** to lend sth one's support **4.** (*coïncidence: de circonstances*) combination
concret [kɔ̃kʀɛ] *m sans pl* concrete
concret, -ète [kɔ̃kʀɛ, -ɛt] *adj* concrete
concrètement [kɔ̃kʀɛtmɑ̃] *adv* in concrete terms
concrétisation [kɔ̃kʀetizasjɔ̃] *f* materialization
concrétiser [kɔ̃kʀetize] <1> **I.** *vt* **1.** (*réaliser: rêve, projet*) to realize **2.** (*matérialiser*) to bring to fruition **II.** *vpr* **se ~** to be realized

conçu(e) [kɔ̃sy] *part passé de* **concevoir**
concubin(e) [kɔ̃kybɛ̃, in] *m(f)* partner
concubinage [kɔ̃kybinaʒ] *m* cohabitation
concurrence [kɔ̃kyʀɑ̃s] *f sans pl* **1.** (*compétition*) *a.* COM competition; ~ **déloyale** unfair competition; **défiant toute** ~ (*prix*) unbeatable; **être en** ~ to be in competition **2.** (*les concurrents*) **la** ~ the competition
concurrencer [kɔ̃kyʀɑ̃se] <2> *vt* to be in competion with
concurrent(e) [kɔ̃kyʀɑ̃, ɑ̃t] **I.** *adj* competing **II.** *m(f)* competitior
concurrentiel(le) [kɔ̃kyʀɑ̃sjɛl] *adj* competitive
condamnable [kɔ̃danabl] *adj* reprehensible
condamnation [kɔ̃danasjɔ̃] *f* **1.** *sans pl* JUR (*action*) conviction; (*peine*) sentence; ~ **avec sursis** suspended sentence **2.** (*réprobation*) condemnation **3.** (*fermeture*) closing; **la** ~ **des portes se fait automatiquement** the doors close automatically
condamné(e) [kɔ̃dane] *m(f)* (convicted) prisoner; ~ **à mort** prisoner sentenced to death
condamner [kɔ̃dane] <1> *vt* **1.** JUR (*déclarer coupable*) to convict; ~ **qn à 10 ans de prison** to sentence sb to ten years in prison **2.** (*obliger*) ~ **qn à** +*infin* to condemn sb to +*infin* **3.** (*fermer avec des pierres*) to wall up; (*avec du bois*) to board up; (*rue*) to seal off; (*à clé*) to lock
condensation [kɔ̃dɑ̃sasjɔ̃] *f sans pl* condensation
condenser [kɔ̃dɑ̃se] *vt, vpr* (**se**) ~ to condense
condiment [kɔ̃dimɑ̃] *m* condiment; *fig* spice
condition [kɔ̃disjɔ̃] *f* condition; ~ **sine qua non** prerequisite; **les ~s d'admission à qc** the conditions for admission to sth; **à ~ de faire qc/que** +*subj* on conditon you do sth/that; **sans ~(s)** (*offre*) unconditional; (*se rendre*) unconditionally; **~s de livraison** delivery conditions; **se mettre en ~ pour qc** SPORT, PSYCH to get oneself into condition for sth; **~s de travail/vie** working/living conditions; **dans ces ~s** in that case; **des gens de toutes les ~s** people of all conditions
conditionné(e) [kɔ̃disjɔne] *adj* **1.** (*climatisé*) **air** ~ air conditioning **2.** (*automatique*) **réflexe** ~ conditioned reflex
conditionnel [kɔ̃disjɔnɛl] *m* conditional; ~ **présent** present conditional
conditionnel(le) [kɔ̃disjɔnɛl] *adj* conditional
conditionnelle [kɔ̃disjɔnɛl] *f* conditional clause
condoléances [kɔ̃dɔleɑ̃s] *fpl form* condolences; (**toutes**) **mes ~!** my deepest sympathy!
condor [kɔ̃dɔʀ] *m* condor
conducteur, -trice [kɔ̃dyktœʀ, -tʀis] **I.** *adj* PHYS conducting **II.** *m, f* driver
conduire [kɔ̃dɥiʀ] *irr* **I.** *vi* **1.** (*piloter*) to drive **2.** (*aboutir*) ~ **à la catastrophe** to lead to disaster **II.** *vt* **1.** (*guider, diriger*) to lead **2.** (*en voiture*) ~ **qn en ville** to take sb into town **3.** (*mener*) ~ **qn à** +*infin* to lead sb to +*infin;* **où cela va-t-il nous ~?** where is this going to take us? **III.** *vpr* **1.** (*se comporter*) **se** ~ to behave **2.** AUTO **se ~ facilement** to drive nicely
conduit [kɔ̃dɥi] *m* pipe; ANAT duct
conduite [kɔ̃dɥit] *f* **1.** *sans pl* AUTO ~ **à droite/à gauche** right-/left-hand drive **2.** (*façon de conduire*) driving; **leçon de** ~ driving lesson; ~ **accompagnée** driving with an instructor **3.** *sans pl* (*responsabilité*) management **4.** (*comportement*) conduct **5.** (*tuyau*) pipe
cône [kon] *m* cone; **en** (**forme de**) ~ conical
confection [kɔ̃fɛksjɔ̃] *f* **1.** GASTR preparation **2.** *sans pl* (*prêt-à-porter*) ready-to-wear
confectionner [kɔ̃fɛksjɔne] <1> *vt* **1.** GASTR to prepare **2.** (*fabriquer*) to make
confédération [kɔ̃fedeʀasjɔ̃] *f* **1.** POL confederation **2.** (*syndicat, groupement*) union
Confédération [kɔ̃fedeʀasjɔ̃] *f* **la ~ helvétique** the Swiss Confederation
confédéré(e) [kɔ̃fedeʀe] *adj* (*états*) Confederate
Confédéré(e) [kɔ̃fedeʀe] *m(f)* **1.** *Suisse* (*membre de la Confédération helvétique*) *member of the Swiss Confederation* **2.** *pl* (*pendant la guerre de Sécession en Amérique*) **les ~s** the Confederates
conférence [kɔ̃feʀɑ̃s] *f* **1.** (*exposé*) lecture; **tenir une ~ sur qc** to give a lecture on sth **2.** (*réunion*) *a.* POL conference; ~ **au sommet** summit conference; ~ **de presse** press conference; ~ **de rédaction** editorial meeting
conférencier, -ière [kɔ̃feʀɑ̃sje, -jɛʀ] *m, f* lecturer
confesser [kɔ̃fese] <1> **I.** *vi* to go to confession **II.** *vt* (*péché, erreur*) to confess; ~ **qn** to hear sb's confession **III.** *vpr* **se ~ à qn** to confess to sb; **aller se** ~ to go to confession
confesseur [kɔ̃fesœʀ] *m* confessor
confession [kɔ̃fesjɔ̃] *f* **1.** (*sacrement, aveu*) confession; **entendre qn en** ~ to hear sb's confession **2.** (*religion*) denomination
confessionnal [kɔ̃fesjɔnal, o] <-aux> *m* confessionnal
confetti [kɔ̃feti] *m* confetti
confiance [kɔ̃fjɑ̃s] *f sans pl* confidence; **personne de** ~ confidant; **inspirer ~ à qn** to inspire confidence in sb; **perdre/reprendre** ~ (**en soi**) to lose/get back one's self-confidence
confiant(e) [kɔ̃fjɑ̃, jɑ̃t] *adj* **1.** (*sans méfiance*) trusting; ~ **en** [*o* **dans**] **qn/qc** trusting in sb/sth **2.** (*sûr de soi*) confident
confidence [kɔ̃fidɑ̃s] *f* confidence; **être dans la** ~ to be in on a secret; **mettre qn dans la** ~ to let sb into one's confidence
confidentiel(le) [kɔ̃fidɑ̃sjɛl] *adj* **1.** (*secret*) confidential **2.** (*restreint: tirage*) limited
confier [kɔ̃fje] <1> **I.** *vt* **1.** (*dévoiler*) to confide **2.** (*remettre*) ~ **une mission à qn** to

entrust sb with a mission **II.** *vpr* (*se confesser*) **se ~ à qn** to confide in sb
confiné(e) [kɔ̃fine] *adj* **1.** (*reclus: être, rester*) shut up **2.** (*lourd: atmosphère*) enclosed; (*air*) stale
confins [kɔ̃fɛ̃] *mpl* **aux ~ de qc et de qc** on the borders of sth and sth; **aux ~ de la science** at the borders of science
confirmation [kɔ̃firmasjɔ̃] *f* confirmation
confirmé(e) [kɔ̃firme] *adj* confirmed
confirmer [kɔ̃firme] <1> **I.** *vt* to confirm **II.** *vpr* (*être exact*) **se ~** to prove correct
confiserie [kɔ̃fizri] *f* (*sucrerie*) sweet
confisquer [kɔ̃fiske] <1> *vt* to confiscate
confit [kɔ̃fi] *m* **~ d'oie** goose conserve
confit(e) [kɔ̃fi, it] *adj* (*fruits*) candied; (*condiments*) pickled
confiture [kɔ̃fityr] *f* jam; **~ de fraises** strawberry jam
conflictuel(le) [kɔ̃fliktɥɛl] *adj* (*pulsions, intérêts*) conflicting; (*rapports*) of conflict; **situation ~le** conflict
conflit [kɔ̃fli] *m* conflict; **~s sociaux** social conflict
confluent [kɔ̃flyɑ̃] *m* confluent
confondre [kɔ̃fɔ̃dr] <14> **I.** *vi* to make a mistake **II.** *vt* (*mêler*) to confuse; **j'ai dû vous ~ avec une autre** I must have confused you with somebody else **III.** *vpr* **1.** (*se mêler*) **se ~ dans l'esprit de qn** to get mixed up in sb's mind **2.** (*prodiguer*) **se ~ en remerciements** to be profuse in one's thanks
conforme [kɔ̃fɔrm] *adj* **1.** (*correspondant*) **être ~ à qc** (*normes*) to comply with sth; **copie certifiée ~** certified copy **2.** (*en accord avec*) **être ~ à qc** to be in accordance with sth **3.** (*conformiste*) conventional
conformément [kɔ̃fɔrmemɑ̃] *adv* **~ aux termes de votre courrier du ...** *form* as set out in your letter of ...
conformer [kɔ̃fɔrme] <1> **I.** *vt soutenu* **~ qc à qc** to match sth to sth **II.** *vpr* **se ~ à qc** to match sth
conformisme [kɔ̃fɔrmism] *m* conformity
conformiste [kɔ̃fɔrmist] *adj, mf* conformist
conformité [kɔ̃fɔrmite] *f* conformity; **en ~ avec l'original** in accordance with the original; **être en ~ avec les normes en vigueur** to comply with current standards
confort [kɔ̃fɔr] *m* **1.** *sans pl* (*luxe*) comfort **2.** (*commodité*) **offrir un grand ~ d'utilisation** to be designed for easy use **3.** *sans pl* (*bien-être*) well-being; **aimer son ~** to like to feel at ease
confortable [kɔ̃fɔrtabl] *adj* comfortable
confortablement [kɔ̃fɔrtabləmɑ̃] *adv* **1.** (*commodément*) comfortably **2.** (*largement*) **vivre ~** to live in comfort
conforter [kɔ̃fɔrte] <1> *vt* **~ qn dans son opinion** to back sb's view up
confrère [kɔ̃frɛr] *m* colleague
confrontation [kɔ̃frɔ̃tasjɔ̃] *f* confrontation
confronter [kɔ̃frɔ̃te] <1> **I.** *vt* **1.** JUR to confront **2.** (*mettre en face de*) to compare **II.** *vpr* **se ~ à qc** to be confronted with sth
confus(e) [kɔ̃fy, yz] *adj* **1.** (*indistinct*) vague **2.** (*embrouillé*) confused **3.** (*embarrassé*) ashamed; **je suis ~!** (*de reconnaissance*) I'm overwhelmed!
confusion [kɔ̃fyzjɔ̃] *f* **1.** *sans pl* (*embarras*) embarrassment **2.** (*erreur*) confusion; **il y a ~!** there's some mistake!; **prêter à ~** to lead to confusion **3.** *sans pl* (*agitation*) confusion; (*désordre*) chaos; **jeter** [*o* **mettre**] **la ~** to create confusion
congé [kɔ̃ʒe] *m* **1.** (*vacances*) holiday *Brit,* vacation *Am;* **~s payés** paid holiday; **avoir 2 jours de ~** to have two days off; **être en ~ de maladie** to be on sick leave; **~ (de) maternité** maternity leave **2.** (*licenciement*) **donner son ~ à qn** to dismiss sb **3.** (*salutation*) **prendre ~ de qn/qc** to take (one's) leave of sb/sth
congédier [kɔ̃ʒedje] <1> *vt* (*employé*) to dismiss; (*visiteur*) to send away
congélateur [kɔ̃ʒelatœr] *m* freezer
congelé(e) [kɔ̃ʒle] *adj* frozen
congeler [kɔ̃ʒ(ə)le] <4> *vt, vpr* (**se**) **~** to freeze
congère [kɔ̃ʒɛr] *m* snowdrift
congestion [kɔ̃ʒɛstjɔ̃] *f* MED congestion; **~ cérébrale** stroke
congestionné(e) [kɔ̃ʒɛstjɔne] *adj* **visage ~** flushed face
conglomérat [kɔ̃glɔmera] *m* conglomerate
Congo [kɔ̃gɔ] *m* **le ~** the Congo; **République démocratique du ~** Democratic Republic of Congo
congolais(e) [kɔ̃gɔlɛ, ɛz] *adj* Congolese
Congolais(e) [kɔ̃gɔlɛ, ɛz] *m(f)* Congolese
congratuler [kɔ̃gratyle] <1> *vt soutenu* to congratulate
congre [kɔ̃gr] *m* conger eel
congrès [kɔ̃grɛ] *m* congress
congressiste [kɔ̃gresist] *mf* conference attender
conifère [kɔnifɛr] *m* conifer
conique [kɔnik] *adj* conical
conjecture [kɔ̃ʒɛktyr] *f* conjecture
conjoint(e) [kɔ̃ʒwɛ̃, wɛ̃t] *m(f) form* spouse
conjointement [kɔ̃ʒwɛ̃tmɑ̃] *adv* together
conjonction [kɔ̃ʒɔ̃ksjɔ̃] *f* conjunction; **~ de coordination/subordination** coordinating/subordinating conjunction
conjoncture [kɔ̃ʒɔ̃ktyr] *f* **1.** *sans pl* (*situation*) situation **2.** *sans pl* ECON economic situation; **basse/haute ~** downturn/upswing in the economy
conjugaison [kɔ̃ʒygɛzɔ̃] *f* conjugation
conjugal(e) [kɔ̃ʒygal, o] <-aux> *adj* conjugal
conjuguer [kɔ̃ʒyge] <1> **I.** *vt* **1.** LING to conjugate **2.** (*unir*) to combine **II.** *vpr* LING **se ~** to conjugate
conjuration [kɔ̃ʒyrasjɔ̃] *f* **1.** (*complot*) conspiracy **2.** (*exorcisme*) conjuration
conjurer [kɔ̃ʒyre] <1> **I.** *vt* **1.** (*éviter: échec,*

crise, sort) to ward off **2.** (*supplier*) to plead with; **je vous en conjure!** I beg you! **II.** *vpr* **se ~** to conspire

connaissance [kɔnɛsɑ̃s] *f* **1.** *sans pl* (*fait de connaître*) knowledge; **il est porté à la ~ du public que ...** the public are advised that ...; **prendre ~ de qc** to learn of sth; **à ma ~** to my knowledge; **en ~ de cause** knowingly **2.** *pl* (*choses apprises*) knowledge; **avoir une bonne ~ des langues** to have a good command of languages; **approfondir ses ~s** to deepen one's knowledge **3.** (*personne*) acquaintance; **faire la ~ de qn** to make sb's acquaintance; **je suis enchanté de faire votre ~** I'm delighted to make your acquaintance **4.** (*lucidité*) consciousness; **perdre ~** to faint; MED to lose consciousness; **sans ~** unconscious

connaisseur, **-euse** [kɔnɛsœʀ, -øz] **I.** *adj* knowledgeable **II.** *m, f* ART, GASTR connoisseur; **être très ~ en la matière** to be an expert on the subject

connaître [kɔnɛtʀ] *irr* **I.** *vt* **1.** (*savoir*) know; **on connaît les meurtriers?** do we know the murderers?; **vous connaissez la nouvelle?** have you heard the news?; **comme je te connais, ...** knowing you the way I do, ...; **ça me connaît!** *inf* I know all about that!; **on connaît la musique** we've heard all this before; **~ qc comme le fond de sa poche** to know sth inside out **2.** (*comprendre*) **~ son métier** to know one's job; **~ le français** to know French; **ne rien ~ à qc** to know nothing about sth **3.** (*rencontrer*) to get to know; **faire ~ qn à qn** to introduce sb to sb **4.** (*éprouver*) to have; **~ un succès fou** to be a huge success; **ne ~ aucune exception** to have no exceptions **II.** *vpr* **1.** (*se fréquenter*) **se ~ depuis longtemps** to have known each other a long time **2.** (*être capable de se juger*) **se ~** to know oneself; **tel que je me connais** knowing how I am **3.** (*être spécialiste*) **s'y ~** to be an expert; **s'y ~ en ordinateurs** to know all about computers

connard [kɔnaʀ] *m inf* stupid fool

connasse [kɔnas] *f inf* stupid cow

connecter [kɔnɛkte] <1> **I.** *vt* to connect; **~ des ordinateurs en réseau** to network computers; **connecté** on-line; **non connecté** offline **II.** *vpr* **se ~ au réseau** to get onto the network; **se ~ à Internet** to get on the Internet

connecteur [kɔnɛktœʀ] *m* INFOR connector

connerie [kɔnʀi] *f* **1.** *sans pl, inf* (*stupidité*) stupidity **2.** *inf* (*acte*) idiocy; **tout ça, c'est des ~s!** that all a load of crap!

connexion [kɔnɛksjɔ̃] *f a.* INFOR connection; **obtenir une ~ à Internet** to connect to the Internet

connivence [kɔnivɑ̃s] *f* connivence; **un sourire de ~** a conniving smile; **être de ~ avec qn** to be in connivance with sb; **agir de ~ avec qn** to connive with sb

connotation [kɔnɔtasjɔ̃] *f* connotation

connoter [kɔnɔte] <1> *vt* to connote; **~ une valeur poétique** (*mot*) to have a poetic connotation

connu(**e**) [kɔny] **I.** *part passé de* **connaître** **II.** *adj* known

conquérant(**e**) [kɔ̃keʀɑ̃, ɑ̃t] **I.** *adj* (*esprit*) dominating; (*air*) swaggering **II.** *m(f)* conqueror

conquérir [kɔ̃keʀiʀ] *vt irr* to conquer; (*cœur, personne*) to win

conquête [kɔ̃kɛt] *f* conquest; **partir à la ~ de qc** to set out to conquer sth

conquis(**e**) [kɔ̃ki, iz] *part passé de* **conquérir**

consacré(**e**) [kɔ̃sakʀe] *adj* **1.** REL (*église*) consecrated **2.** (*habituel*) established **3.** (*célèbre*) recognized

consacrer [kɔ̃sakʀe] <1> **I.** *vt* **1.** (*donner*) to devote **2.** REL to consecrate **II.** *vpr* **se ~ à qn/qc** to devote oneself to sth

consciemment [kɔ̃sjamɑ̃] *adj* consciously

conscience [kɔ̃sjɑ̃s] *f* **1.** *sans pl* PSYCH consciousness; **avoir/prendre ~ de qc** to be/become conscious of sth; **perdre/reprendre ~** to lose/regain consciousness **2.** *sans pl* (*connaissance*) **la ~ de qc** the knowledge of sth **3.** *sans pl* (*sens moral*) conscience; **avoir la ~ en paix** to have a quiet conscience; **donner bonne ~ à qn** to put sb's conscience at ease; **donner mauvaise ~ à qn** to upset sb's conscience

consciencieusement [kɔ̃sjɑ̃sjøzmɑ̃] *adv* conscientiously

consciencieux, **-euse** [kɔ̃sjɑ̃sjø, -jøz] *adj* conscientious

conscient(**e**) [kɔ̃sjɑ̃, jɑ̃t] *adj* **1.** (*informé*) aware **2.** (*lucide*) conscious

conscrit [kɔ̃skʀi] *m* conscript

consécration [kɔ̃sekʀasjɔ̃] *f sans pl* (*confirmation*) crowning (point)

consécutif, **-ive** [kɔ̃sekytif, -iv] *adj* **1.** (*à la file*) consecutive; **être ~ à qc** to follow on from sth **2.** (*résultant de*) **~ à qc** following sth

conseil [kɔ̃sɛj] *m* **1.** (*recommandation*) piece of advice; **donner des ~s à qn** to give sb advice; **demander ~ à qn** to ask sb for advice; **faire qc sur le ~ de qn** to do sth on sb's advice **2.** (*personne*) adviser **3.** (*assemblée*) council; **~ municipal** town council; **~ de classe** staff meeting (*to discuss a particular class*); **~ des jeunes** youth council; **~ de discipline** disciplinary board; **passer en ~ de guerre** to be court-martialled *Brit*, to be court-martialed *Am*; **~ de l'Europe** Council of Europe; **~ européen** European Council

Conseil [kɔ̃sɛj] *m* **1.** **~ de sécurité** Security Council; **~ des ministres** Council of Ministers; **~ d'État** Council of State; **~ de l'Union européenne** European Council **2.** *Suisse* **~ exécutif** Executive Council; **~ fédéral** Federal Council; **~ national** National Council

conseiller [kɔ̃seje] <1> **I.** *vt* **1.** (*recommander: vin*) to recommend; **~ la prudence à**

qn to advice sb to be careful **2.** (*inciter*) ~ **à qn de** +*infin* to advise sb to +*infin* **3.** (*guider*) ~ **qn dans qc** to advise sb on sth **II.** *vt impers* **il est conseillé à qn de** +*infin* sb is advised to +*infin*

conseiller, -ère [kɔ̃seje, -ɛʀ] *m, f* **1.** (*qui donne des conseils*) adviser **2.** (*expert*) ~ **en entreprise** business consultant **3.** ADMIN, POL councillor; ~ **municipal** town councillor; ~ **fédéral** *Suisse* federal councillor **4.** ECOLE ~ **d'orientation** careers adviser

consensus [kɔ̃sɛ̃sys] *m* consensus; **recueillir un large** ~ to gain widespread backing

consentant(e) [kɔ̃sɑ̃tɑ̃, ɑ̃t] *adj* **être** ~ to consent

consentement [kɔ̃sɑ̃tmɑ̃] *m* consent

consentir [kɔ̃sɑ̃tiʀ] <10> **I.** *vi* (*accepter*) ~ **à qc** to consent to sth; ~ **à ce que qn fasse qc** (*subj*) to consent to sb doing sth **II.** *vt* (*accorder*) to grant

conséquence [kɔ̃sekɑ̃s] *f* consequence; **avoir qc pour** [*o* **comme**] ~ to result in sth; **tirer les ~s de qc** to draw conclusions from sth; **sans** ~ of no consequence; **accident sans** ~ an unimportant accident; **en** ~ (*donc*) consequently; (*conformément à cela*) accordingly; **en** ~ **de qc** as a consequence of sth

conséquent(e) [kɔ̃sekɑ̃, ɑ̃t] *adj* **1.** (*cohérent*) consistent; **par** ~ in consequence **2.** *inf* (*considérable*) sizeable

conservateur, -trice [kɔ̃sɛʀvatœʀ, -tʀis] **I.** *adj* **1.** POL conservative **2.** GASTR **agent** ~ preservative **II.** *m, f* **1.** (*directeur: d'un musée*) curator **2.** POL conservative **III.** *m* preservative

conservation [kɔ̃sɛʀvasjɔ̃] *f* (*action: d'un aliment*) preserving; (*d'un monument*) conservation; (*garde: d'un aliment*) keeping; (*des archives*) conservation

conservatoire [kɔ̃sɛʀvatwaʀ] *m* **1.** MUS conservatoire *Brit,* conservatory *Am* **2.** THEAT academy

conserve [kɔ̃sɛʀv] *f* tin; **des petits pois en** ~ tinned peas *Brit,* canned peas *Am;* **mettre qc en** ~ (*industriellement*) to can; (*à la maison*) to preserve

conservé(e) [kɔ̃sɛʀve] *adj inf* well-preserved

conserver [kɔ̃sɛʀve] <1> **I.** *vt* **1.** (*garder: papiers, aliments*) to keep; (*monument*) to maintain **2.** GASTR to preserve **3.** (*ne pas perdre*) to keep; ~ **son calme** to stay calm **II.** *vi inf* **qc/ça conserve** sth/that keeps you young **III.** *vpr* **se** ~ (*aliment*) to keep

considérable [kɔ̃sideʀabl] *adj* considerable; (*travail*) sizeable

considérablement [kɔ̃sideʀabləmɑ̃] *adv* considerably

considération [kɔ̃sideʀasjɔ̃] *f* **1.** *pl* (*raisonnement*) consideration **2.** (*estime*) respect **3.** (*attention*) **digne de** ~ worthy of consideration; **en** ~ **de qc** in consideration of sth; **prendre qn/qc en** ~ to take sb/sth into consideration

considérer [kɔ̃sideʀe] <5> **I.** *vt* **1.** (*étudier*) to consider; **tout bien considéré** all things considered; **considérant que** considering (that) **2.** (*estimer*) **être considéré** to be respected **3.** (*contempler*) to stare at **4.** (*penser*) ~ **que ...** to think that ... **5.** (*tenir pour*) ~ **qn comme un traître** to considerer sb a traitor **II.** *vpr* (*se tenir pour*) **se** ~ **comme le responsable** to consider oneself responsible

consigne [kɔ̃siɲ] *f* **1.** *sans pl* left luggage *Brit,* baggage check *Am;* ~ **automatique** left luggage locker *Brit,* baggage locker *Am* **2.** *sans pl* COM deposit **3.** (*instructions*) orders *pl*

consigné(e) [kɔ̃siɲe] *adj* returnable

consigner [kɔ̃siɲe] <1> *vt* **1.** (*mettre à la consigne*) ~ **ses bagages** to leave one's bags in the left luggage *Brit,* to leave one's bags at the baggage check *Am* **2.** (*facturer*) **la bouteille est consignée** there is a deposit on the bottle **3.** (*enregistrer*) to record

consistance [kɔ̃sistɑ̃s] *f* **1.** consistency; **prendre** ~ (*pâte*) to form a dough; (*liquide*) to thicken **2.** *fig* **nouvelle sans** ~ baseless piece of news

consistant(e) [kɔ̃sistɑ̃, ɑ̃t] *adj* **1.** (*épais*) thick **2.** *inf* (*substantiel*) substantial **3.** (*fondé*) well-founded

consister [kɔ̃siste] <1> *vi* ~ **en qc** to consist of sth; ~ **à faire qc** to consist in doing sth

consœur [kɔ̃sœʀ] *f* colleague; *v. a.* **confrère**

consolant(e) [kɔ̃sɔlɑ̃, ɑ̃t] *adj* consoling

consolation [kɔ̃sɔlasjɔ̃] *f* consolation

console [kɔ̃sɔl] *f* **1.** (*meuble*) console (table) **2.** TECH console; ~ **de mixage** mixing console

consoler [kɔ̃sɔle] <1> **I.** *vt* to console **II.** *vpr* **se** ~ to console each other

consolider [kɔ̃sɔlide] <1> **I.** *vt* **1.** (*rendre solide*) to strengthen; (*mur, table*) to brace **2.** *fig a.* FIN (*position*) to consolidate **II.** *vpr* **se** ~ **1.** (*affermir: position*) to be consolidated **2.** MED to set

consommateur, -trice [kɔ̃sɔmatœʀ, -tʀis] *m, f* consumer

consommation [kɔ̃sɔmasjɔ̃] *f* **1.** *sans pl* (*usage*) *a.* ECON ~ **de qc** consumption of sth; **impropre à la** ~ unfit for consumption **2.** (*boisson*) drink

consommé [kɔ̃sɔme] *m* consommé

consommer [kɔ̃sɔme] <1> **I.** *vi* **1.** (*boire*) to drink **2.** (*acheter*) to consume **II.** *vt* **1.** GASTR (*plat*) to eat; (*vin*) to drink **2.** (*user*) to consume **III.** *vpr* **se** ~ **chaud** to be eaten hot; (*boisson*) to be drunk hot; **à** ~ **avant le ...** use by ...

consonne [kɔ̃sɔn] *f* consonant

conspirateur, -trice [kɔ̃spiʀatœʀ, -tʀis] *m, f* conspirator

conspiration [kɔ̃spiʀasjɔ̃] *f* ~ **contre qn/qc** conspiracy against sb/sth

conspirer [kɔ̃spiʀe] <1> *vi* to conspire

constamment [kɔ̃stamɑ̃] *adv* constantly

constance [kɔ̃stɑ̃s] *f* constancy

constant(e) [kɔ̃stɑ̃, ɑ̃t] *adj* constant

constante [kɔ̃stɑ̃t] *f* constant

constat [kɔ̃sta] *m* report; ~ **à l'amiable** joint accident report

constatation [kɔ̃statasjɔ̃] *f* observation; **arriver à la ~ que ...** to reach the conclusion that ...

constater [kɔ̃state] <1> *vt* to observe

constellation [kɔ̃stelasjɔ̃] *f* ASTR constellation

consternant(e) [kɔ̃stɛʀnɑ̃, ɑ̃t] *adj* dismaying

consternation [kɔ̃stɛʀnasjɔ̃] *f* consternation

consterné(e) [kɔ̃stɛʀne] *adj* dismayed

consterner [kɔ̃stɛʀne] <1> *vt* to dismay

constipation [kɔ̃stipasjɔ̃] *f* constipation

constipé(e) [kɔ̃stipe] *adj* **1.** MED constipated **2.** *inf* (*guindé*) stiff

constituant(e) [kɔ̃stitɥɑ̃, ɑ̃t] *adj* constituent

constituante [kɔ̃stitɥɑ̃t] *f Québec* (*université ou institut de recherches faisant partie de l'université du Québec*) constituent institution

constitué(e) [kɔ̃stitɥe] *adj* **1.** (*composé*) **être ~ de qc** to be made up of **2.** (*conformé*) **bien ~** well-built

constituer [kɔ̃stitɥe] <1> **I.** *vt* **1.** (*composer*) to make up **2.** (*former: gouvernement*) to form; (*dossier*) to build up; (*société*) to set up **3.** (*représenter*) to constitute **II.** *vpr* **1.** JUR (*s'instituer*) **se ~ témoin** to come forward as a witness **2.** (*accumuler*) **se ~** to build up

constitution [kɔ̃stitysjɔ̃] *f* **1.** POL constitution **2.** *sans pl* (*élaboration: d'un groupe*) formation; (*d'une bibliothèque*) creation; (*d'un dossier*) putting together **3.** *sans pl* (*composition*) make-up

Constitution [kɔ̃stitysjɔ̃] *f* **la ~** the Constitution

constitutionnel(le) [kɔ̃stitysjɔnɛl] *adj* constitutional

constructeur [kɔ̃stʀyktœʀ] *m* builder

constructible [kɔ̃stʀyktibl] *adj* **terrain ~** building land *no pl*

constructif, -ive [kɔ̃stʀyktif, -iv] *adj* constructive

construction [kɔ̃stʀyksjɔ̃] *f* **1.** *sans pl* (*action*) building; **la ~ de l'Europe** *fig* the building of Europe **2.** (*secteur*) construction; **être en ~** to be under construction **3.** (*édifice*) building **4.** ECON **~ mécanique** machine manufacturing

construire [kɔ̃stʀɥiʀ] *irr* **I.** *vt* **1.** (*bâtir*) to build **2.** (*fabriquer*) to make **3.** (*élaborer*) to construct **II.** *vpr* LING **se ~ avec l'indicatif** to take the indicative

consul [kɔ̃syl] *m* consul

consulat [kɔ̃syla] *m* consulate

consultant(e) [kɔ̃syltɑ̃, ɑ̃t] **I.** *adj* consultant **II.** *m(f)* consultant

consultation [kɔ̃syltasjɔ̃] *f* **1.** *sans pl* (*examen: d'un ouvrage*) consulting; (*d'un agenda, d'un horaire*) checking **2.** (*séance*) consultation **3.** POL **~ de l'opinion** vote **4.** *Suisse* (*prise de position*) consultation

consulte [kɔ̃sylt] *f Suisse* (*ancienne assemblée administrative*) former administrative assembly

consulter [kɔ̃sylte] <1> **I.** *vi* to consult **II.** *vt* **1.** (*demander avis*) to consult **2.** (*regarder: montre, agenda, ouvrage*) to check **3.** POL **~ l'opinion** to ballot public opinion **III.** *vpr* **se ~** to confer

consumer [kɔ̃syme] <1> **I.** *vt* (*brûler*) to consume **II.** *vpr* **se ~** to waste away; (*cigarette*) to burn away

contact [kɔ̃takt] *m* **1.** *sans pl* (*toucher*) contact; **au ~ de l'air** in contact with air; **des choses entrent/sont en ~** things come into/are in contact **2.** (*rapport*) contact; **au ~ de qn** through contact with sb; **entrer en** [*o* **prendre**] **~ avec qn/qc** to get in contact with sb/sth; **rester en ~ avec qn/qc** to stay in contact with sb/sth **3.** ELEC, AUTO connection; **faux** [*o* **mauvais**] **~** bad connection; **couper/mettre le ~** to turn the engine off/on

contacter [kɔ̃takte] <1> *vt* to contact

contagieux, -euse [kɔ̃taʒjø, -jøz] *adj* contagious

contagion [kɔ̃taʒjɔ̃] *f* contagion

container [kɔ̃tɛnɛʀ] *m* container

contaminer [kɔ̃tamine] <1> *vt* (*personne, virus*) to infect; (*milieu*) to contaminate

conte [kɔ̃t] *m* tale; **~ des 1001 nuits** tale of the 1001 nights

contemplation [kɔ̃tɑ̃plasjɔ̃] *f sans pl* contemplation; **rester en ~ devant qc** to contemplate sth

contempler [kɔ̃tɑ̃ple] <1> **I.** *vt* to contemplate **II.** *vpr* **se ~** to gaze at oneself

contemporain(e) [kɔ̃tɑ̃pɔʀɛ̃, ɛn] **I.** *adj* contemporary; **être ~ de qn** to be sb's contemporary; **être ~ de qc** to be contemporary with sth **II.** *m(f)* contemporary

contenance [kɔ̃t(ə)nɑ̃s] *f* **1.** (*capacité*) capacity **2.** (*attitude*) attitude

contenant [kɔ̃t(ə)nɑ̃] *m* container

conteneur [kɔ̃t(ə)nœʀ] *m* container

contenir [kɔ̃t(ə)niʀ] <9> **I.** *vt* **1.** (*renfermer*) to contain **2.** (*maîtriser: foule*) to restrain; **~ un rire** to hold in one's laughter **II.** *vpr* **se ~** to contain oneself

content(e) [kɔ̃tɑ̃, ɑ̃t] *adj* **1.** (*heureux*) **~ de qc** happy about sth; **être ~ pour qn** to be glad for sb; **être ~ que** +*subj* to be glad that **2.** (*satisfait*) **~ de qn/qc** pleased with sb/sth; **être ~ de soi** to be pleased with oneself

contentement [kɔ̃tɑ̃tmɑ̃] *m sans pl* satisfaction

contenter [kɔ̃tɑ̃te] <1> **I.** *vt* (*personne*) to please; (*besoin*) to satisfy; **on ne peut pas toujours ~ tout le monde!** you can't please everybody all the time! **II.** *vpr* **se ~ de qc** to satisfy oneself with sth

contenu [kɔ̃t(ə)ny] *m* content

contenu(e) [kɔ̃t(ə)ny] *adj* restrained
contestable [kɔ̃tɛstabl] *adj* questionable
contestataire [kɔ̃tɛstatɛʀ] I. *adj* **être** ~ to call things into question; (*mouvement*) to protest II. *mf* protester
contestation [kɔ̃tɛstasjɔ̃] *f* protest; **faire de la** ~ to call things into question
contester [kɔ̃tɛste] <1> I. *vi* to call things into question II. *vt* (*discuter*) to dispute; **je ne conteste pas que** +*subj* I don't dispute that; **être contesté** to be questioned
conteur, -euse [kɔ̃tœʀ, tøz] *m, f* storyteller
contexte [kɔ̃tɛkst] *m* 1. LING context 2. (*situation*) background; **le** ~ **familial** the family beackground; **dans le** ~ **actuel** in the present circumstances
contigu(ë) [kɔ̃tigy] *adj* ~ **à un territoire/édifice** adjoining a territory/building
continent [kɔ̃tinɑ̃] *m* 1. GEO continent 2. (*opp: île*) mainland
continental(e) [kɔ̃tinɑ̃tal, o] <-aux> *adj* continental
contingent [kɔ̃tɛ̃ʒɑ̃] *m* 1. MIL contingent 2. (*part*) share 3. COM quota; ~ **à l'importation** import quota 4. *fig* **tout un** ~ **de touristes** a whole troop of tourists
continu [kɔ̃tiny] *m sans pl* **en** ~ continuously
continu(e) [kɔ̃tiny] *adj* (*ligne*) unbroken; (*effort, bruit*) continuous
continuation [kɔ̃tinɥasjɔ̃] *f* continuation; **bonne ~!** good luck for the rest of it!
continuel(le) [kɔ̃tinɥɛl] *adj* 1. (*fréquent*) constant 2. (*ininterrompu*) continual
continuellement [kɔ̃tinɥɛlmɑ̃] *adv* 1. (*fréquemment*) constantly 2. (*sans s'arrêter*) continually
continuer [kɔ̃tinɥe] <1> I. *vi* 1. (*se poursuivre*) to continue; (*bruit, pluie*) to go on; **tout a continué comme avant** everything continued as before 2. (*poursuivre*) to carry on; (*à pied*) to walk on; (*en voiture*) to drive on; ~ **à lire** to carry on reading 3. (*persister*) ~ **à croire que ...** to continue to believe that ...; ~ **à faire qc** to continue doing sth; **si tu continues, je vais me fâcher!** if you carry on, I'll get angry! II. *vt* 1. (*poursuivre*) to continue; (*politique*) to pursue 2. (*prolonger*) to extend
continuité [kɔ̃tinɥite] *f* continuity
contorsion [kɔ̃tɔʀsjɔ̃] *f* contortion
contour [kɔ̃tuʀ] *m* outline; (*appréciation esthétique*) *a.* GEO contour
contourner [kɔ̃tuʀne] <1> *vt* 1. (*faire le tour*) ~ **qc** (*route, voiture*) to bypass sth; (*personne*) to go round sth 2. (*éluder*) to get round
contraceptif [kɔ̃tʀasɛptif] *m* contraceptive
contraceptif, -ive [kɔ̃tʀasɛptif, -iv] *adj* contraceptive
contraception [kɔ̃tʀasɛpsjɔ̃] *f* contraception
contracté(e) [kɔ̃tʀakte] *adj* 1. (*tendu*) tense 2. LING contracted
contracter [kɔ̃tʀakte] <1> I. *vt* ANAT **le froid contracte qc** cold makes sth contract II. *vpr* **se** ~ to contract; (*visage*) to tense
contractuel(le) [kɔ̃tʀaktɥɛl] I. *adj* (*obligation*) contractual; (*employé*) contract II. *m(f)* 1. (*agent d'un service public*) contract worker (*in public service*) 2. (*auxiliaire de police*) traffic warden *Brit,* traffic policeman *Am*
contradiction [kɔ̃tʀadiksjɔ̃] *f sans pl* contradiction; **être en** ~ **avec qn** to be in disagreement with sb; **être en** ~ **avec qc** to be inconsistent with sth
contradictoire [kɔ̃tʀadiktwaʀ] *adj* (*incompatible*) contradictory; (*influences*) conflicting
contraignant(e) [kɔ̃tʀɛɲɑ̃, ɑ̃t] *adj* restricting
contraindre [kɔ̃tʀɛ̃dʀ] *irr* I. *vt* ~ **qn à l'économie/à l'action** to force sb to be economical/to act II. *vpr* **se** ~ **à l'économie/à l'action** to force oneself to be economical/to act
contraint(e) [kɔ̃tʀɛ̃, ɛ̃t] *adj* forced
contrainte [kɔ̃tʀɛ̃t] *f* constraint; **être soumis à des ~s** to be subject to certain constraints; **sous la** ~ under pressure
contraire [kɔ̃tʀɛʀ] I. *adj* 1. (*opposé*) opposite; (*preuve*) opposing; (*opinions*) conflicting 2. (*incompatible*) ~ **à l'usage** contrary to general practice; ~ **aux intérêts de** against the interests of; ~ **à la loi** against the law 3. (*défavorable*) contrary II. *m* contrary; **bien** [*o* **tout**] **au** ~ on the contrary
contrairement [kɔ̃tʀɛʀmɑ̃] *adv* ~ **à qn/qc** contrary to sb/sth; ~ **à ce que je croyais** contrary to what I thought
contrariant(e) [kɔ̃tʀaʀjɑ̃, jɑ̃t] *adj* 1. (*opp: docile*) annoying 2. (*fâcheux*) upsetting
contrarié(e) [kɔ̃tʀaʀje] *adj* 1. (*ennuyé*) **être** ~ to be annoyed; **avoir l'air** ~ to look annoyed 2. (*forcé*) **gaucher** ~ frustrated left-hander
contrarier [kɔ̃tʀaʀje] <1> *vt* 1. (*fâcher*) to annoy 2. (*gêner: projets*) to thwart
contrariété [kɔ̃tʀaʀjete] *f sans pl* annoyance
contraste [kɔ̃tʀast] *m* contrast; **par** ~ by contrast
contraster [kɔ̃tʀaste] <1> *vi* ~ **avec qc** to contrast with sth
contrat [kɔ̃tʀa] *m* contract; ~ **à durée déterminée/indéterminée** fixed-term/open; **passer/conclure un** ~ **avec qn** to sign/agree a contract with sb; ~ **de location** rental agreement; ~ **de travail** work contract
contravention [kɔ̃tʀavɑ̃sjɔ̃] *f* 1. (*infraction*) ~ **à qc** infringement of sth; **être en** ~ to be in breach of the law 2. (*procès-verbal*) parking ticket 3. (*amende*) fine
contre [kɔ̃tʀ] I. *prep* 1. (*opposition, contact*) against; **venir tout** ~ **qn** to come right up against sb; **serrés les uns** ~ **les autres** squashed up against each other; **danser joue** ~ **joue** to dance cheek to cheek; **avoir qc** ~

qn/qc to have sth against sb/sth; **être furieux** ~ **qn** to be furious with sb; ~ **toute attente** contrary to expectation **2.** (*échange*) for; **échanger un sac** ~ **une montre** to exhange a bag for a watch **3.** (*proportion*) **ils se battaient à dix** ~ **un** they were fighting ten against one; **le projet de loi a été adopté à 32 voix** ~ **24** the bill was passed by 32 votes to 24 **II.** *adv* (*opposition*) **être/voter** ~ to be/vote against (it); **je n'ai rien** ~ I've no objection; **par** ~ on the other hand **III.** *m* SPORT counter

contre-allée [kɔ̃tʀale] <contre-allées> *f* side path **contre-attaquer** [kɔ̃tʀatake] <1> *vi* to counterattack

contrebalancer [kɔ̃tʀəbalɑ̃se] <2> **I.** *vt* **1.** (*équilibrer*) to counterbalance **2.** (*compenser*) to offset **II.** *vpr inf* **je m'en contrebalance** I couldn't care less

contrebande [kɔ̃tʀəbɑ̃d] *f* **1.** (*activité*) smuggling; **faire de la** ~ to smuggle **2.** (*marchandise*) contraband

contrebandier, **-ière** [kɔ̃tʀəbɑ̃dje, -jɛʀ] *m, f* smuggler

contrebas [kɔ̃tʀəba] *adv* **en** ~ **de qc** below sth

contrebasse [kɔ̃tʀəbɑs] *f* double bass

contrecarrer [kɔ̃tʀəkaʀe] <1> *vt* to thwart

contrecœur [kɔ̃tʀəkœʀ] *adv* **à** ~ reluctantly

contrecoup [kɔ̃tʀəku] *m* repercussion; **par** ~ as an aftereffect

contre-courant [kɔ̃tʀəkuʀɑ̃] <contre-courants> *m* countercurrent; **à** ~ against the current

contredanse [kɔ̃tʀədɑ̃s] *f inf* **1.** (*procès-verbal*) parking ticket **2.** (*amende*) fine

contredire [kɔ̃tʀədiʀ] *irr* **I.** *vt* to contradict **II.** *vpr* **se** ~ to contradict oneself

contrefaçon [kɔ̃tʀəfasɔ̃] *f* **1.** (*action*) forging **2.** (*chose*) forgery

contrefaire [kɔ̃tʀəfɛʀ] *vt irr* **1.** (*imiter*) to forge **2.** (*déguiser*) to imitate

contrefait(**e**) [kɔ̃tʀəfɛ, ɛt] *adj* **1.** (*imité*) counterfeit **2.** (*difforme*) deformed

contrefort [kɔ̃tʀəfɔʀ] *m* **1.** ARCHIT buttress **2.** GEO spur; (*des Alpes*) foothill

contre-indiqué(**e**) [kɔ̃tʀɛ̃dike] *adj* **1.** MED **être** ~ to be counterindicated **2.** (*déconseillé*) inadvisable **contre-interrogatoire** [kɔ̃tʀɛ̃tɛʀɔgatwaʀ] *m* cross-examination **contre-jour** [kɔ̃tʀəʒuʀ] *m* back light; **à** ~ into the light

contremaître, **-esse** [kɔ̃tʀəmɛtʀ, -ɛs] *m, f* foreman, forewoman *m, f*

contre-offensive [kɔ̃tʀɔfɑ̃siv] *f* counteroffensive

contrepartie [kɔ̃tʀəpaʀti] *f* compensation ►**en** ~ in compensation; (*par contre*) on the other hand

contre-performance [kɔ̃tʀəpɛʀfɔʀmɑ̃s] *f* poor performance **contre-pied** [kɔ̃tʀəpje] *m sans pl* **1.** (*contraire*) opposite **2.** SPORT **prendre qn à** ~ to catch sb off-balance

contre-plaqué [kɔ̃tʀəplake] *m sans pl* plywood

contrepoids [kɔ̃tʀəpwa] *m* counterweight; (*d'une horloge*) balance weight; **faire** ~ to act as a counterbalance; **servir de** [*o* **apporter un**] ~ **à qc** to counterbalance sth

contrepoison [kɔ̃tʀəpwazɔ̃] *m* antidote

contre-proposition [kɔ̃tʀəpʀɔpozisjɔ̃] *f* counterproposal

contrer [kɔ̃tʀe] <1> **I.** *vi* JEUX to counter **II.** *vt* to block

contresens [kɔ̃tʀəsɑ̃s] *m* misinterpretation; (*dans une traduction*) mistranslation

contretemps [kɔ̃tʀətɑ̃] *m* mishap; **à** ~ at the wrong moment; MUS off the beat

contrevenant(**e**) [kɔ̃tʀəv(ə)nɑ̃, ɑ̃t] *m(f)* offender

contrevenir [kɔ̃tʀəv(ə)niʀ] <9> *vi* ~ **à qc** to contravene sth

contribuable [kɔ̃tʀibɥabl] *mf* taxpayer

contribuer [kɔ̃tʀibɥe] <1> *vi* ~ **à qc** to contribue to sth

contribution [kɔ̃tʀibysjɔ̃] *f* **1.** (*participation*) ~ **à qc** contribution to sth; **mettre qn à** ~ **pour qc** to make use of sb for sth **2.** *pl* (*impôts*) council tax *Brit,* local tax *Am* **3.** *pl* (*service*) tax office **4.** INFOR news item

contrôle [kɔ̃tʀol] *m* **1.** (*vérification: des passeports*) control; (*douane*) check; **passer un** ~ to go through a check; ~ **d'identité** identity check; ~ **technique** *motor vehicle safety inspection,* ≈ MOT *Brit* **2.** *sans pl* (*surveillance*) monitoring; **exercer un** ~ **sur qc** to monitor sth **3.** ECOLE test; ~ **de géographie** georaphy test; ~ **continu** UNIV continuous assessment **4.** (*maîtrise*) **garder/perdre le** ~ **de qc** to keep/lose control of sth

> The **contrôle technique** must be done every two years. It is a test to ensure the ability of every vehicle to travel on the roads and the safety of its gas emissions. When all necessary repairs have been made, a small sticker must be put on the windscreen. Without this sticker, the vehicle must be kept off the roads.

contrôler [kɔ̃tʀole] <1> **I.** *vt* **1.** (*vérifier: liste, affirmation*) to check; (*comptes*) to audit **2.** (*surveiller: opération*) to supervise; (*prix*) to monitor **3.** (*maîtriser*) to control; ~ **la situation** to be in control of the situation **II.** *vpr* **se** ~ to control oneself

contrôleur [kɔ̃tʀolœʀ] *m* INFOR controller

contrôleur, **-euse** [kɔ̃tʀolœʀ, -øz] *m, f* **1.** (*dans le train*) inspector **2.** FIN auditor

contrordre [kɔ̃tʀɔʀdʀ] *m* counterorder

controverse [kɔ̃tʀɔvɛʀs] *f* controversy; **prêter à** ~ to cause controversy

controversé(**e**) [kɔ̃tʀɔvɛʀse] *adj* controversial

contusion [kɔ̃tyzjɔ̃] *f* contusion

convaincant(**e**) [kɔ̃vɛ̃kɑ̃, ɑ̃t] *adj* convincing

convaincre [kɔ̃vɛ̃kʀ] *irr* **I.** *vt* **1.** (*persuader*)

~ **qn de qc** (*par des arguments*) to convince sb of sth; ~ **qn de** +*infin* to persuade sb to +*infin* **2.** (*prouver la culpabilité*) ~ **qn de trahison/crime** to convict sb of treason/of a crime **II.** *vpr* **se** ~ **de qc** to convince sb of sth

convaincu(e) [kɔ̃vɛ̃ky] **I.** *part passé de* **convaincre** **II.** *adj* **être** ~ **de qc** to be convinced of sth

convalescence [kɔ̃valesɑ̃s] *f* convalescence

convalescent(e) [kɔ̃valesɑ̃, ɑ̃t] **I.** *adj* convalescent **II.** *m(f)* convalescent

convenable [kɔ̃vnabl] *adj* **1.** (*adéquat*) suitable; (*distance*) reasonable **2.** (*correct*) appropriate; **il n'est pas** ~ **de** +*infin* it is inappropriate to +*infin* **3.** (*acceptable: salaire, vin*) decent

convenablement [kɔ̃vnabləmɑ̃] *adv* **1.** (*de manière adéquate: habillé, être équipé*) suitably **2.** (*décemment: se tenir, s'exprimer, s'habiller*) properly **3.** (*de manière acceptable*) reasonably

convenance [kɔ̃vnɑ̃s] *f* **1.** *pl* (*bon usage*) suitability; **respecter les ~s** to respect the proprieties **2.** (*agrément*) **trouver qc à sa** ~ to find sth to one's liking

convenir¹ [kɔ̃vniʀ] <9> **I.** *vi* **1.** (*aller*) ~ **à qn** (*climat, nourriture*) to suit sb **2.** (*être approprié*) ~ **à qc** to suit sth; **c'est tout à fait l'homme qui convient** he's absolutely the right man; **trouver les mots qui conviennent** to find the right words **II.** *vi impers* **il convient de** +*infin* it is advisable to +*infin;* **comme il convient** as is right

convenir² [kɔ̃vniʀ] <9> **I.** *vi* **1.** (*s'entendre*) ~ **de qc** to agree on sth **2.** (*reconnaître*) ~ **de qc** to admit sth **II.** *vt impers* **il est convenu que** +*subj* it is agreed that; **comme convenu** as agreed **III.** *vt* (*reconnaître*) ~ **que ...** to agree that ...

convention [kɔ̃vɑ̃sjɔ̃] *f* **1.** (*accord*) agreement **2.** (*règle*) convention; **de** ~ conventional; **sourire de** ~ standard smile; **par** ~ as a convention

conventionné(e) [kɔ̃vɑ̃sjɔne] *adj* (*établissement, médecin*) recognized (*by French Social Security*)

conventionnel(le) [kɔ̃vɑ̃sjɔnɛl] *adj* conventional

convenu(e) [kɔ̃vny] **I.** *part passé de* **convenir** **II.** *adj* agreed; **c'était une chose ~e!** we had agreed on it!

convergence [kɔ̃vɛʀʒɑ̃s] *f* convergence

converger [kɔ̃vɛʀʒe] <2a> *vi* (*intérêts, efforts*) to converge; **les regards convergent sur/vers qn/qc** all eyes turned to/towards sb/sth

conversation [kɔ̃vɛʀsasjɔ̃] *f* **1.** (*discussion*) conversation; ~ **téléphonique** telephone conversation; **être en grande** ~ **avec qn** to be deep in conversation with sb; **faire la** ~ **à qn** to make conversation with sb; **détourner la** [*o* **changer de**] ~ to change the subject **2.** (*manière de discuter*) **avoir de la** ~ *inf* to be a good conversationalist

converser [kɔ̃vɛʀse] <1> *vi soutenu* ~ **avec qn** to converse with sb; **ils/elles conversent** they are in conversation

conversion [kɔ̃vɛʀsjɔ̃] *f* ~ **de qc en qc** conversion of sth into sth

converti(e) [kɔ̃vɛʀti] **I.** *adj* converted **II.** *m(f)* convert ►**prêcher un** ~ to preach to the converted

convertir [kɔ̃vɛʀtiʀ] <8> **I.** *vt* to convert **II.** *vpr* (*adopter*) **se** ~ **au catholicisme** to convert to catholicism

convexe [kɔ̃vɛks] *adj* convex

conviction [kɔ̃viksjɔ̃] *f* conviction; **avoir la** ~ **de qc** to be convinced of sth; **manquer de** ~ to lack conviction

convier [kɔ̃vje] <1> *vt soutenu* **1.** (*inviter*) ~ **qn à un repas** to invite sb to a meal **2.** (*inciter*) ~ **qn à donner son avis** to call on sb to give their opinion

convive [kɔ̃viv] *mf gén pl* guest

convivial(e) [kɔ̃vivjal, jo] <-aux> *adj* **1.** (*sociable*) convivial **2.** INFOR user-friendly

convocation [kɔ̃vɔkasjɔ̃] *f* **1.** (*avant une réunion*) convening; (*d'une personne*) invitation **2.** JUR summons; **se rendre à une** ~ to answer a summons **3.** ECOLE notification (*of examinees*) **4.** MIL call-up

convoi [kɔ̃vwa] *m* **1.** (*véhicules*) convoy **2.** (*personnes*) column **3.** CHEMDFER train; ~ **de marchandises** goods train **4.** (*cortège funèbre*) funeral cortège

convoiter [kɔ̃vwate] <1> *vt* to long for; *péj* to covet

convoitise [kɔ̃vwatiz] *f* lust

convoquer [kɔ̃vɔke] <1> *vt* **1.** (*faire venir*) to invite; (*assemblée*) to convene; **être convoqué pour l'examen** to be notified of an examination date **2.** MIL to call up **3.** JUR to summons

convulsif, -ive [kɔ̃vylsif, -iv] *adj* convulsive; **rire** ~/**sanglots ~s** convulsions of laughter/sobbing; **des mouvements ~s secouent qn/qc** sb/sth is shaken with convulsions

convulsion [kɔ̃vylsjɔ̃] *f gén pl* **1.** (*crise*) **~s sociales** social upheaval + *vb sing* **2.** MED convulsion

cool [kul] *adj inv, inf* cool; **super** ~ really cool

coopérant(e) [kɔɔpeʀɑ̃, ɑ̃t] **I.** *m(f)* aid worker; MIL *young person doing community work, often abroad, as national service* **II.** *adj* (*coopératif*) cooperative

coopératif, -ive [kɔ(ɔ)peʀatif, -iv] *adj* cooperative

coopération [kɔɔpeʀasjɔ̃] *f* **1.** (*collaboration*) ~ **de qn à un projet** sb's cooperation on a project; **apporter sa** ~ **à un projet** to cooperate on a project **2.** POL overseas development **3.** *sans pl* MIL *community work, often done abroad, as national service*

cooperative [kɔ(ɔ)peʀativ] *f* cooperative

coopérer [kɔɔpeʀe] <5> *vi* (*collaborer*) ~ **à**

qc to cooperate on sth

coordinateur, **-trice** [kɔɔʀdinatœʀ, -tʀis] *m, f v.* **coordonnateur**

coordination [kɔɔʀdinasjɔ̃] *f sans pl* coordination

coordonnateur, **-trice** [kɔɔʀdɔnatœʀ, -tʀis] **I.** *adj* coordinating **II.** *m, f* coordinator; **être ~ de qc** to coordinate sth

coordonné(e) [kɔɔʀdɔne] *adj* coordinated

coordonnées [kɔɔʀdɔne] *fpl* **1.** *inf* (*renseignements*) **les ~ de qn** sb's details; **laissez-moi vos ~** give me your details **2.** MAT coordinates

coordonner [kɔɔʀdɔne] <1> *vt* (*harmoniser*) to coordinate

coordonnés [kɔɔʀdɔne] *mpl* coordinates

copain, **copine** [kɔpɛ̃, kɔpin] *m, f inf* friend; **avec sa bande de ~s** with all his friends; **être très ~/copine avec qn** to be very close to sb; **petit ~/petite copine** boyfriend/girlfriend

copeau [kɔpo] <x> *m* chip

Copenhague [kɔpɛnag] Copenhagen

copie [kɔpi] *f* **1.** (*double, produit*) *a.* PRESSE copy; **~ certifiée conforme** certified copy **2.** INFOR **~ de sécurité** [*o* **de sauvegarde**] backup (copy) **3.** (*feuille double*) sheet **4.** (*devoir*) paper; **rendre sa ~/(une) ~ blanche** to hand in one's paper/a blank paper

copier [kɔpje] <1> **I.** *vt* **1.** (*transcrire*) **~ qc dans un livre** to copy sth from a book; **tu me copieras cent fois: ...** you are to write out a hundred lines: ... **2.** (*photocopier*) to (photo)copy **3.** (*imiter, plagier*) to copy **II.** *vi* ECOLE **~ sur qn** to copy off sb

copieur [kɔpjœʀ] *m* (*appareil*) copier

copieur, **-euse** [kɔpjœʀ, -jøz] *m, f* ECOLE copycat

copieusement [kɔpjøzmɑ̃] *adv* **1.** (*abondamment*) copiously **2.** (*beaucoup*) thoroughly

copieux, **-euse** [kɔpjø, -jøz] *adj* copious

copilote [kopilɔt] *mf* **1.** AVIAT copilot **2.** AUTO navigator

copine [kɔpin] *f v.* **copain**

copiner [kɔpine] <1> *vi inf* **~ avec qn/avec tout le monde** to be pals with sb/everybody

coproduction [kopʀɔdyksjɔ̃] *f* coproduction

copropriétaire [kopʀɔpʀijetɛʀ] *mf* joint owner

copuler [kɔpyle] <1> *vi* to copulate

copyright [kɔpiʀajt] *m inv* copyright

coq [kɔk] *m* **1.** (*mâle*) cock **2.** GASTR **~ au vin** coq au vin **3.** SPORT **poids ~** bantamweight ▸**passer** [*o* **sauter**] **du ~ à l'âne** to jump from one subject to another

coquard, **coquart** [kɔkaʀ] *m inf* black eye

coque [kɔk] *f* **1.** TECH (*d'un navire*) hull; (*d'une voiture*) body **2.** ZOOL cockle

coqueleux [kɔklø] *m Belgique* (*éleveur de coqs de combat*) cock breeder

coquelicot [kɔkliko] *m* poppy ▸**être rouge comme un ~** to be as red as a poppy

coqueluche [kɔklyʃ] *f* MED whooping cough

coquet(te) [kɔkɛ, ɛt] *adj* **1.** (*élégant*) **être ~** to be smart **2.** (*charmant*) charming **3.** *inf* (*important*) tidy

coquetier [kɔktje] *m* egg cup

coquetterie [kɔkɛtʀi] *f* **1.** (*souci d'élégance*) smartness **2.** (*désir de plaire*) charm

coquillage [kɔkijaʒ] *m* shell

coquille [kɔkij] *f* **1.** ZOOL shell; **~ Saint-Jacques** scallop shell; GASTR scallop **2.** TYP misprint **3.** GASTR (*récipient*) shell **4.** ART shell motif

coquin(e) [kɔkɛ̃, in] **I.** *adj* **1.** (*espiègle*) mischievous **2.** (*grivois*) naughty **II.** *m(f)* rascal

cor[1] [kɔʀ] *m* MUS horn ▸**réclamer qn/qc à ~ et à cri** to clamour for sb/sth *Brit,* to clamor for sb/sth *Am*

cor[2] [kɔʀ] *m* MED corn

corail [kɔʀaj, o] <-aux> **I.** *m* coral **II.** *app inv* coral

corail® [kɔʀaj] *adj inv* CHEMDFER **train ~** ≈ express train

Coran [kɔʀɑ̃] *m* **le ~** the Coran

coranique [kɔʀanik] *adj* coranic

corbeau [kɔʀbo] <x> *m* **1.** (*oiseau*) crow **2.** *inf* (*dénonciateur*) poison pen letter writer

corbeille [kɔʀbɛj] *f* (*panier*) basket; **~ à papier/à pain** wastepaper/bread basket

corbillard [kɔʀbijaʀ] *m* hearse

cordage [kɔʀdaʒ] *m* **1.** (*corde*) rope **2.** NAUT rigging **3.** SPORT stringing

corde [kɔʀd] *f* **1.** (*lien, câble*) rope; (*plus fine*) cord; **~ à linge** washing line; **~ à sauter** skipping rope **2.** (*d'un instrument, d'une raquette*) string; **les (instruments à) cordes** the strings; **~ lisse** climbing rope; **grimper** [*o* **monter**] **à la ~** to go up the climbing rope **3.** *sans pl* (*bord de piste*) rail **4.** ANAT **~s vocales** vocal cords ▸**avoir plus d'une ~** [*o* **plusieurs ~s**] **à son arc** to have more than one string to one's bow; **il pleut** [*o* **tombe**] **des ~s** it's raining cats and dogs, it's bucketing down *Brit*

cordée [kɔʀde] *f* roped party

cordelette [kɔʀdəlɛt] *f* cord

cordial(e) [kɔʀdjal, jo] <-aux> *adj* cordial

cordialement [kɔʀdjalmɑ̃] *adv* cordially

cordialité [kɔʀdjalite] *f sans pl* cordiality

cordillère [kɔʀdijɛʀ] *f* mountain range; **~ des Andes** the Andes

cordon [kɔʀdɔ̃] *m* **1.** (*petite corde*) cord; (*d'un tablier*) string **2.** (*décoration*) sash **3.** GEO **~ littoral** offshore bar **4.** ANAT **~ ombilical** umbilical cord

cordon-bleu [kɔʀdɔ̃blø] <cordons-bleus> *m inf* cordon bleu cook

cordonnier, **-ière** [kɔʀdɔnje, -jɛʀ] *m, f* **1.** (*réparateur*) shoe mender **2.** (*fabricant*) shoemaker

Corée [kɔʀe] *f* **la ~** Korea; **la ~ du Nord/du Sud** North/South Korea

coréen [kɔʀeɛ̃] *m* Korean; *v. a.* **français**

coréen(ne) [kɔʀeɛ̃, ɛn] *adj* Korean

Coréen(ne) [kɔʀeɛ̃, ɛn] *m(f)* Korean

coriace [kɔʀjas] *adj* tough; (*personne*) hard-headed
coriandre [kɔʀjɑ̃dʀ] *f* coriander
cormoran [kɔʀmɔʀɑ̃] *m* cormorant
corne [kɔʀn] *f* **1.** ZOOL horn; **les ~s** (*d'un cerf*) the antlers **2.** (*pli*) dog-ear **3.** *sans pl* (*callosité*) calluses *pl* ▶**avoir des ~s** *inf* to have an unfaithful wife
cornée [kɔʀne] *f* ANAT cornea
corneille [kɔʀnɛj] *f* crow
cornélien(ne) [kɔʀneljɛ̃, jɛn] *adj* **1.** (*dramatique: situation*) where love conflicts with duty; (*personnage*) with a heroic sense of duty **2.** LIT **la tragédie ~ne** Cornelian tragedy
cornemuse [kɔʀnəmyz] *f* MUS bagpipes *pl*
corner[1] [kɔʀne] <1> *vt* **~ une page** to dog-ear a page; **être tout corné** to be completely dog-eared
corner[2] [kɔʀnɛʀ] *m* SPORT corner
cornet [kɔʀnɛ] *m* **1.** GASTR cone; **un ~ de glace** an ice cream cone **2.** *Suisse* (*sachet, poche* (*en papier, en plastique*)) bag
corniaud [kɔʀnjo] **I.** *adj inf* mongrel **II.** *m* **1.** (*chien*) mongrel **2.** *inf* (*imbécile*) nitwit
corniche [kɔʀniʃ] *f* **1.** ARCHIT cornice **2.** (*escarpement*) ledge **3.** (*route*) corniche
cornichon [kɔʀniʃɔ̃] *m* **1.** GASTR gherkin **2.** *inf* (*personne*) nitwit
Cornouailles [kɔʀnwɑj] *f* **la ~** Cornwall
cornu(e) [kɔʀny] *adj* horned; **être ~** to have horns
corolle [kɔʀɔl] *f* corolla
coron [kɔʀɔ̃] *m* mining village
coronaire [kɔʀɔnɛʀ] *adj* ANAT coronary
corporatif, -ive [kɔʀpɔʀatif, -iv] *adj* corporate
corporation [kɔʀpɔʀasjɔ̃] *f* **1.** (*association*) corporate body **2.** HIST guild
corporatisme [kɔʀpɔʀatism] *m* **1.** *péj* (*intérêts particuliers*) professional self-interest **2.** (*doctrine*) corporatism
corporel(le) [kɔʀpɔʀɛl] *adj* **1.** (*physique*) bodily; (*soins*) personal **2.** JUR **biens ~s** corporeal property
corps [kɔʀ] *m* **1.** ANAT, CHIM body; **trembler de tout son ~** to shiver all over; **~ et âme** body and soul; **~ à corps** man to man; **jusqu'au milieu du ~** halfway down the body **2.** (*groupe*) **~ diplomatique** diplomatic corps; **réunion du ~ enseignant** teachers' meeting; **~ médical** medical profession; **~ de métier** building trade; (*des artisans*) builders; **~ d'armée** army corps; **chef de ~** corps commander **3.** ASTR **~ céleste** celestial body ▶**avoir du ~** (*vin*) to have body; **prendre ~** to take shape
corpulence [kɔʀpylɑ̃s] *f* build; **de ~ moyenne** of medium build; **être de forte ~** to be corpulent
corpulent(e) [kɔʀpylɑ̃, ɑ̃t] *adj* corpulent
correct(e) [kɔʀɛkt] *adj* **1.** (*exact*) correct; **c'est ~** *Québec* (*ça va bien*) everything's OK **2.** (*convenable*) decent; **être ~ avec qn** to be decent with sb **3.** *inf* (*acceptable*) OK
correctement [kɔʀɛktəmɑ̃] *adv* correctly; (*se conduire, s'habiller*) properly; **gagner ~ sa vie** to earn a decent living
correcteur [kɔʀɛktœʀ] *m* corrector; **~ liquide** correction fluid; **~ orthographique** INFOR spell-checker
correcteur, -trice [kɔʀɛktœʀ, -tʀis] **I.** *adj* (*ruban*) correction; (*mesure*) corrective **II.** *m, f* ECOLE examiner; TYP proofreader
correction [kɔʀɛksjɔ̃] *f* **1.** (*action*) correction; ECOLE to mark sth; **faire la ~ de qc** to correct sth **2.** (*châtiment*) beating; **recevoir une bonne ~** to get a good beating **3.** (*justesse*) accuracy **4.** (*bienséance*) good manners; **avec ~** to behave correctly; **être d'une parfaite ~** to have perfect manners
correctionnel(le) [kɔʀɛksjɔnɛl] *adj* correctional; (*tribunal*) criminal
correctionnelle [kɔʀɛksjɔnɛl] *f inf* **passer en ~** to appear in court
corrélation [kɔʀelasjɔ̃] *f* correlation; **être en ~ avec qc** to correlate to sth; **mettre deux choses en ~** to correlate two things
corres [kɔʀɛs] *mf inf abr de* **correspondant**
correspondance [kɔʀɛspɔ̃dɑ̃s] *f* **1.** (*échange de lettres*) *a.* COM correspondence **2.** (*en voyage*) connection; **nous avons une ~ à Stuttgart** we have to make a connection at Stuttgart
correspondant(e) [kɔʀɛspɔ̃dɑ̃, ɑ̃t] **I.** *adj* corresponding **II.** *m(f)* **1.** (*contact*) correspondent; (*d'un jeune*) pen-friend *Brit*, pen-pal *Am* **2.** (*au téléphone*) **votre ~** the person you are calling **3.** COM associate **4.** CINE, TV correspondent; **~ de guerre** war correspondent
correspondre [kɔʀɛspɔ̃dʀ] <14> **I.** *vi* **1.** (*être en contact*) **~ avec qn** to write to sb; **~ par fax/courrier électronique** to send messages by fax/e-mail **2.** (*en voyage*) **~ avec qc** to connect with sth **3.** (*aller avec*) **~ à qc** to correspond to sth; **ci-joint un chèque correspondant à la facture** herewith a cheque for the amount of the bill **4.** (*s'accorder avec*) **sa version des faits ne correspond pas à la réalité** his version of the facts does not match up with reality **5.** (*être typique*) **~ à qn** to be very like sb **6.** (*être l'équivalent de*) **ce mot correspond exactement au terme anglais** this word corresponds exactly to the English term **II.** *vpr* **se ~** to correspond
corrida [kɔʀida] *f* bullfight
corridor [kɔʀidɔʀ] *m* corridor
corrigé [kɔʀiʒe] *m* ECOLE model answer
corriger [kɔʀiʒe] <2a> **I.** *vt* **1.** (*relever les fautes*) to mark **2.** (*supprimer les fautes*) to correct **3.** (*rectifier: théorie*) to correct; (*prévisions*) to adjust; (*mauvaise habitude*) to break; **~ à la hausse/à la baisse** to adjust upwards/downwards **4.** (*punir*) to beat; **se faire ~ par qn** to get a beating from sb **II.** *vpr* (*devenir raisonnable*) **se ~** to mend one's ways

corrompre [kɔʀɔ̃pʀ] *vt irr* (*acheter*) to bribe
corrompu(e) [kɔʀɔ̃py] **I.** *part passé de* **corrompre** **II.** *adj* **1.** (*malhonnête*) corrupt **2.** (*perverti*) depraved
corrosif, -ive [kɔʀozif, -iv] *adj* corrosive
corrosion [kɔʀozjɔ̃] *f* corrosion
corruptible [kɔʀyptibl] *adj* venal
corruption [kɔʀypsjɔ̃] *f* **1.** (*délit*) bribery **2.** *sans pl* (*moral*) corruption
corsage [kɔʀsaʒ] *m* blouse; (*d'une robe*) bodice
corsaire [kɔʀsɛʀ] *m* **1.** (*marin*) pirate **2.** (*navire*) privateer **3.** (*pantalon*) breeches *pl*
corse [kɔʀs] **I.** *adj* Corsican **II.** *m* Corsican; *v. a.* **français**
Corse [kɔʀs] **I.** *f* **la ~** Corsica **II.** *mf* Corsican
corsé(e) [kɔʀse] *adj* **1.** (*épicé*) spicy; (*vin*) full-bodied; (*café*) strong-flavoured *Brit,* strong-flavored *Am* **2.** (*scabreux*) spicy **3.** (*excessif*) steep **4.** (*compliqué*) tough
corser [kɔʀse] <1> **I.** *vt* **~ qc** (*mets, récit*) to spice sth up; (*situation*) to liven sth up **II.** *vpr* **se ~** (*situation*) to get lively
corset [kɔʀsɛ] *m* corset
cortège [kɔʀtɛʒ] *m* procession; **~ nuptial** bridal procession; **~ funèbre** funeral cortege
cortex [kɔʀtɛks] *m* ANAT cortex
cortisone [kɔʀtizɔn] *f* cortisone
corvée [kɔʀve] *f* **1.** (*obligation pénible*) chore; **être de ~ de vaisselle** to be on dish-washing duty; **quelle ~!** what a pain! **2.** MIL fatigue **3.** HIST corvée **4.** *Suisse, Québec* (*travail non payé, fait de plein gré*) *voluntary community work*
cosaque [kɔzak] *m* cossack
cosigner [kosiɲe] <1> *vt* **~ qc** to sign sth jointly
cosinus [kɔsinys] *m* MAT cosine
cosmétique [kɔsmetik] *adj* cosmetic; **les soins ~s** cosmetic care
cosmique [kɔsmik] *adj* cosmic; (*fusée*) space
cosmonaute [kɔsmɔnot] *mf* cosmonaut
cosmopolite [kɔsmɔpɔlit] *adj* cosmopolitan
cosmos [kɔsmos] *m* cosmos
cossard(e) [kɔsaʀ, aʀd] **I.** *adj fam* lazy **II.** *m(f) fam* lazy so-and-so
cosse [kɔs] *f* **1.** BOT pod **2.** ELEC cable terminal
cossu(e) [kɔsy] *adj* (*personne*) affluent; (*villa, intérieur*) affluent-looking
costard [kɔstaʀ] *m inf* suit
costaud(e) [kɔsto, od] **I.** *adj inf* **1.** (*fort*) tough **2.** (*solide*) sturdy **II.** *m* **c'est du ~!** *inf* it's good strong stuff!
costume [kɔstym] *m* **1.** (*complet*) suit; **~ sur mesure** custom-tailored suit **2.** (*tenue: d'époque, de théâtre, d'un pays*) costume
costumé(e) [kɔstyme] *adj* **bal ~** costume ball
costumer [kɔstyme] <1> *vpr* **se ~ en clown** to dress up as a clown
costumier, -ière [kɔstymje, -jɛʀ] *m, f* **1.** (*loueur*) costumier **2.** (*fabricant*) costume maker **3.** THEAT, CINE wardrobe master, mistress *m, f*
cotation [kɔtasjɔ̃] *f* FIN quotation
cote [kɔt] *f* **1.** FIN share price **2.** (*popularité*) popularity; **avoir la ~ avec** [*o* **auprès de**] **qn** *inf* to be popular with sb **3.** SPORT (*d'un cheval*) odds
côte [kot] *f* **1.** (*littoral*) coast; **la ~ atlantique** the Atlantic coast **2.** (*pente, colline*) hill; **démarrer en ~** to do a hill start; **les ~s du Rhône** the Rhône hills **3.** ANAT rib **4.** GASTR chop; **~ de bœuf** beef rib ▶**~ à ~** side by side
côté [kote] **I.** *m* **1.** (*partie latérale*) side; **des deux ~s de qc** from both sides of sth; **sauter de l'autre ~ du ruisseau** to jump across the stream; **du ~ de ...** from the ... side **2.** (*aspect*) side; **par certains ~s** in some ways **3.** (*direction*) way; **~ cour** on the courtyard side; THEAT stage left; **de quel ~ allez-vous?** which way are you going?; **du ~ de la mer** by the sea; **du ~ opposé** on the opposite side **4.** (*parti*) side; **du ~ de qn** on sb's side; **mettre qn de son ~** to get sb's backing; **aux ~s de qn** at sb's side; **de mon ~** for my part; **du ~ paternel** [*o* **du père**] on the father's side ▶**d'un ~ ..., de l'autre** (**~**) [*o* **d'un autre ~**] on the one hand ..., on the other; **de ce ~** *inf* in that respect; **mettre de l'argent de ~** to put some money by; **laisser qn/qc de ~** to leave sb/sth aside **II.** *adv* **1.** (*à proximité*) **chambre à ~** next room **2.** (*en comparaison*) **à ~** in comparison **3.** (*en plus*) **à ~** on the side **4.** (*voisin*) **les gens (d')à ~** the people next door; **nos voisins (d')à ~** our next-door neighbours *Brit,* our next-door neighbors *Am;* **la maison d'à ~** the house next door ▶**passer à ~ de qc** to miss sth **III.** *prep* **1.** (*à proximité de*) **à ~ de qn/qc** next to sb/sth; **à ~ de Paris** near Paris; **juste** [*o* **tout**] **à ~ de qc** just by sth **2.** (*en comparaison de*) **à ~ de qn/qc** next to sb/sth **3.** (*hors de*) **répondre à ~ de la question** to miss the point of the question; (*intentionnellement*) to avoid the question; **être à ~ du sujet** to be off the subject
coté(e) [kɔte] *adj* reputed
coteau [kɔto] <x> *m* **1.** (*versant*) hill **2.** (*vignoble*) vineyard
Côte d'Azur [kotdazyʀ] *f* **la ~** the Côte d'Azur, the Riviera
Côte d'Ivoire [kotdivwaʀ] *f* **la ~** the Ivory Coast, the Côte d'Ivoire
côtelé(e) [kot(ə)le] *adj* ribbed
côtelette [kotlɛt] *f* GASTR cutlet
coter [kɔte] <1> *vt* **1.** FIN to list **2.** (*apprécier*) **être coté** to be listed; **la voiture est cotée à l'Argus** the car is listed in the Black Book *Brit,* the car is listed in the (Kelley®) *Blue Book Am* **3.** SPORT **être coté à 5 contre 1** to have odds of 5 to 1
côtier, -ière [kotje, -jɛʀ] *adj* coastal
cotillons [kɔtijɔ̃] *mpl* petticoat + *vb sing*
cotisant(e) [kɔtizɑ̃, ɑ̃t] *m(f)* contributor; (*d'un club*) member

cotisation [kɔtizasjɔ̃] *f* subscription; ~ **ouvrière/patronale** worker/employer contributions
cotiser [kɔtize] <1> **I.** *vi* ~ **à qc** to contribute to sth **II.** *vpr* **se** ~ **pour** +*infin* to club together to +*infin*
coton [kɔtɔ̃] *m* **1.** (*matière, fil*) cotton **2.** (*ouate*) cotton wool; **du** ~ (some) cotton wool ►**avoir les jambes en** ~ my legs feel like jelly
cotonnade [kɔtɔnad] *f* cotton (fabric)
cotonneux, **-euse** [kɔtɔnø, -øz] *adj* (*qui ressemble à du coton*) **des nuages** ~ cotton-wool clouds
coton-tige® [kɔtɔ̃tiʒ] <cotons-tiges> *m* cotton bud, Q-tip®
côtoyer [kotwaje] <6> **I.** *vt soutenu* **1.** (*fréquenter*) to frequent; **être amené à** ~ **beaucoup de gens** to be called on to mix with many people **2.** (*longer*) to run alongside **II.** *vpr soutenu* **se** ~ **1.** (*se fréquenter*) to mix **2.** (*se toucher*) to meet
cotte [kɔt] *f* ~ **de mailles** coat of mail
cou [ku] *m* neck; **je fais ... cm de tour de** ~ I take a ... cm collar ►**se casser** [*o* **se rompre**] **le** ~ (*dans un accident*) to break one's neck; (*échouer*) to come a cropper
couac [kwak] *m* false note
couchage [kuʃaʒ] *m* bed; **matériel de** ~ bedding
couchant [kuʃɑ̃] **I.** *adj* setting; **au soleil** ~ at sunset **II.** *m* sunset
couche [kuʃ] *f* **1.** (*épaisseur*) *a.* GEO, METEO layer; **passer deux** ~**s de peinture sur qc** to put two coats of paint on sth **2.** SOCIOL level **3.** (*lange*) nappy *Brit,* diaper *Am;* ~ **jetable** disposable nappy **4.** *pl* MED confinement; **en** ~**s** in childbirth; **faire une fausse** ~ to have a miscarriage
couché(**e**) [kuʃe] *adj* **1.** (*étendu*) lying down **2.** (*au lit*) **être déjà** ~ to be already in bed; **rester** ~ to stay in bed
couche-culotte [kuʃkylɔt] <couches-culottes> *f* disposable nappy *Brit,* disposable diaper *Am*
coucher [kuʃe] <1> **I.** *vi* **1.** (*dormir*) to sleep; ~ **à l'hôtel** to spend the night at a hotel **2.** *inf* (*avoir des relations sexuelles*) ~ **avec qn** to sleep with sb **II.** *vt* **1.** (*mettre au lit*) to put to bed **2.** (*offrir un lit*) **on peut vous** ~ **si vous voulez** we can put you up if you like **3.** (*étendre*) to lay down; (*bouteille*) to lay on its side; (*blés*) to flatten **III.** *vpr* **1.** (*aller au lit*) **se** ~ to go to bed; **envoyer qn se** ~ to send sb to bed **2.** (*s'allonger*) **se** ~ to lie down **3.** (*se courber sur*) **se** ~ **sur qc** to lean over sth **4.** (*disparaître*) **le soleil se couche** the sun is setting **IV.** *m* **1.** (*fait d'aller au lit*) going to bed; **le** ~ **d'un enfant** putting a child to bed; **c'est l'heure du** ~ it's bedtime **2.** (*crépuscule*) setting; **au** ~ **du soleil** at sunset
couchette [kuʃɛt] *f* couchette; **compartiment** (**à**) ~**s** couchette compartment
couci-couça [kusikusa] *adv inf* so-so
coucou [kuku] **I.** *m* **1.** (*oiseau*) cuckoo **2.** (*pendule*) cuckoo clock **3.** *péj* (*vieil avion*) crate **4.** BOT cowslip **II.** *interj* peekabo
coude [kud] *m* **1.** ANAT elbow **2.** (*courbure*) bend ►**jouer des** ~**s** to jostle; **lever le** ~ *inf* to be a boozer; **se serrer les** ~**s** to stick together; ~ **à** ~ shoulder to shoulder
coudé(**e**) [kude] *adj* bent; (*paille*) bendy; **être** ~ to have a bend
cou-de-pied [kudpje] <cous-de-pied> *m* instep
coudoyer [kudwaje] <6> *vt* **1.** (*frôler*) to brush against **2.** (*côtoyer*) ~ **qn** to rub shoulders with sb; ~ **qc** to stand side by side with
coudre [kudʀ] *irr* **I.** *vi* to sew **II.** *vt* **1.** (*assembler*) to sew together **2.** (*fixer*) ~ **un bouton à qc** to sew a button on sth; ~ **une pièce sur qc** to patch sth
couenne [kwan] *f a. Suisse* (*croûte du fromage*) rind
couette [kwɛt] *f* **1.** (*édredon*) duvet **2.** *gén pl* (*coiffure*) bunches
couffin [kufɛ̃] *m* basket
couille [kuj] *f* **1.** *gén pl, vulg* (*testicule*) ball **2.** *inf* (*ennui*) cock-up ►~ **molle** *inf* wimp; **casser les** ~**s à qn** *inf* to get on sb's nerves
couillon(**ne**) [kujɔ̃, jɔn] *m(f) inf* berk
couillonner [kujɔne] <1> *vt inf* to con
couiner [kwine] <1> *vi* (*lièvre, porc*) to squeal; (*rat*) to squeak; (*personne*) to whine; (*porte*) to creak
coulant(**e**) [kulɑ̃, ɑ̃t] *adj* **1.** *inf* (*indulgent*) easy-going **2.** (*fluide: pâte, fromage*) runny **3.** (*léger: style*) free-flowing
coulée [kule] *f* ~ **de lave** lava flow
couler [kule] <1> **I.** *vi* **1.** (*s'écouler*) to flow; (*faiblement*) to ooze; (*fortement*) to pour **2.** (*préparer*) **faire** ~ **un bain à qn** to run a bath for sb **3.** (*fuir*) to leak **4.** (*goutter*) to drip; (*œil*) to run **5.** (*sombrer*) to sink **II.** *vt* **1.** (*verser*) ~ **du plomb dans un moule** to cast lead in a mould *Brit,* to cast lead in a mold *Am* **2.** (*sombrer, faire échouer*) to sink **III.** *vpr* **se** ~ **dans qc** to slip into sth
couleur [kulœʀ] **I.** *f* **1.** (*teinte, peinture*) *a.* POL colour *Brit,* color *Am;* **changer de** ~ to change colour; **prendre des** ~**s** to get one's colour back **2.** (*linge*) coloured *Brit,* colored *Am* ►**passer par toutes les** ~**s de l'arc-en-ciel** to go through all the colours of the rainbow; **c'est un personnage haut en** ~ he's a colourful character **II.** *adj sans pl* ~ **rose** rose-coloured *Brit,* rose-colored *Am*
couleuvre [kulœvʀ] *f* grass snake
coulis [kuli] *m* GASTR (*de crustacés*) bisque; (*de légumes, fruits*) coulis
coulissant(**e**) [kulisɑ̃, ɑ̃t] *adj* sliding
coulisse [kulis] *f* **1.** *souvent pl* THEAT wings; **dans les** ~**s** [*o* **la** ~], **en** ~ (*lieu*) in the wings, behind the scenes; (*direction*) offstage **2.** (*rainure: d'un tiroir*) runner

coulisser [kulise] <1> *vi* ~ **sur qc** to slide along sth

couloir [kulwaʀ] *m* **1.** (*corridor*) *a.* CHEMDFER corridor **2.** AVIAT aisle **3.** SPORT lane **4.** GEO gully **5.** ~ **aérien** air corridor; ~ **d'autobus** bus lane

coup [ku] *m* **1.** (*agression*) blow; **donner un ~ à qn** to hit sb; **être noir de ~s** to be black and blue; ~ **de bâton** blow with a stick; ~ **de poing/de pied** punch/kick; ~ **de couteau** stab; **d'un ~ de dent** with a bite **2.** (*bruit*) knock; **frapper trois ~s** to knock three times; ~ **de sifflet** blast of the whistle **3.** (*heurt*) knock **4.** (*décharge*) shot; ~ **de feu** shot; **revolver à six ~s** six-shooter **5.** (*choc moral*) blow; **être un ~ pour qn** to be a blow to sb; **porter un ~ à qn** to deal sb a blow; **c'est un ~ rude pour elle** it's a hard knock for her **6.** (*action rapide*) **d'un ~ de crayon** with a pencil stroke; **passer un ~ d'éponge sur qc** to sponge sth down; **se donner un ~ de peigne** to give one's hair a quick comb; **donner un ~ de fer à qc** to give sth a quick iron; **donner un ~ de frein** to brake; ~ **de fil** [*o* **téléphone**] phone call **7.** SPORT shot; **le ~ droit** forehand stroke; ~ **franc** (*au foot*) free kick; (*au basket*) free throw; **donner le ~ d'envoi à qc** to kick sth off **8.** JEUX go **9.** (*manifestation brusque*) ~ **de tonnerre** roll of thunder; ~ **de vent** gust of wind; ~ **de foudre** lightning flash; (*pour qn*) love at first sight; ~ **de soleil** sunstroke **10.** (*accès*) **avoir un ~ de cafard** to be down in the dumps **11.** (*action*) ~ **d'État** coup d'état; ~ **de maître** masterstroke; **être sur un ~** to be on to sth; **calculer son ~** to plan one's move **12.** (*action désagréable*) **ça c'est un ~ des enfants** the kids were up to something here; ~ **de vache** *inf* dirty trick; **il nous fait le ~ (à) chaque fois** he pulls the same trick on us every time; **faire/mijoter un mauvais ~** to play/plan a dirty trick **13.** (*quantité bue*) drink; **boire un ~** *inf* to have a drink **14.** (*événement*) ~ **de chance** [*o* **veine**] bit of luck ►**avoir un ~ dans l'<u>aile</u>** to be a bit merry; **avoir un (véritable) ~ de <u>cœur</u> pour qc** to fall for sth; **prendre un ~ de <u>froid</u>** to catch a chill; **sur le ~ de trois/quatre <u>heures</u>** on the stroke of three/four; **avoir le ~ de <u>main</u>** to have the knack; **donner un ~ de <u>main</u> à qn** to give sb a hand; **jeter** [*o* **lancer**] **un ~ d'<u>œil</u> à qn** to glance at sb; **jeter un ~ d'<u>œil</u> sur le feu** to keep an eye on the fire; **avoir un ~ de <u>pompe</u>** [*o* **barre**] *inf* to suddenly feel tired; ~ **de <u>tête</u>** impulse; **passer en ~ de <u>vent</u>** to rush past; **prendre un ~ de <u>vieux</u>** *inf* to age suddenly; **<u>tenir</u> le ~** *inf* (*personne*) to cope; (*objet, voiture*) to stand the strain; **ça <u>vaut</u> le ~ de faire qc** it's worth doing sth; **du <u>même</u> ~** at the same time; **du <u>premier</u> ~** at the first go; **d'un <u>seul</u> ~** in one go; **tout <u>à</u> ~** suddenly; **<u>après</u> ~** afterwards; **<u>du</u> ~** *inf* as a result; **tout <u>d'un</u> ~** suddenly; **<u>sur</u> le ~** (*aussitôt*) instantly; (*au début*) straightaway; **à <u>tous</u> les ~s** every time; (*à tout propos*) all the time

coupable [kupabl] **I.** *adj* **1.** (*fautif*) **plaider (non)** ~ to plead (not) guilty **2.** (*condamnable*) guilty **II.** *mf* **1.** (*responsable*) guilty party **2.** (*malfaiteur*) culprit

coupant(e) [kupɑ̃, ɑ̃t] *adj* sharp

coupe [kup] *f* **1.** (*verre*) glass **2.** (*récipient*) dish **3.** SPORT cup; **la ~ du monde de football** the World Cup

coupé [kupe] *m* AUTO coupé

coupé(e) [kupe] *adj* **1.** cut; (*bois*) sawn; ~ **en tranches** sliced **2.** (*divisé: mot*) divided; **être ~ en deux/trois** to be broken down into two/three **3.** COUT **bien/mal** ~ well/badly cut **4.** (*barré: col, route, chemin*) cut off; (*encombré*) blocked **5.** TEL (*communication*) cut off; (*ligne*) down **6.** (*dilué: vin*) diluted

coupe-faim [kupfɛ̃] <coupe-faim(s)> *m* snack **coupe-feu** [kupfø] <coupe-feu(x)> **I.** *m* firebreak; (*mur*) fireguard **II.** *app inv* **porte** ~ fire door **coupe-gorge** [kupgɔʀʒ] <coupe-gorge(s)> *m* death trap **coupe-ongle** [kupɔ̃gl] <coupe-ongles> *m* nail clippers **coupe-papier** [kuppapje] *m inv* paper knife, paper cutter

couper [kupe] <1> **I.** *vi* **1.** (*être tranchant*) to cut; **attention, ça coupe!** careful, it's sharp! **2.** (*prendre un raccourci*) to take a short cut **3.** TEL **ne coupez pas!** hold the line! **4.** CINE **coupez!** cut! **5.** JEUX to cut **6.** (*être mordant*) to bite **7.** *inf* (*échapper à*) ~ **à une corvée** to get out of doing a chore, to skive off a chore *Brit* **II.** *vt* **1.** (*trancher*) to cut; (*tête, branche*) to cut off; (*volaille*) to cut up; (*arbre*) to cut down; ~ **les cheveux à qn** to cut sb's hair **2.** (*isoler*) to cut off **3.** (*raccourcir: texte*) to cut **4.** (*interrompre: ligne téléphonique*) to cut; (*communication*) to cut off; ~ **l'eau/l'électricité à qn** to cut off sb's water/electricity **5.** (*mettre un terme: relations*) to end; (*fièvre*) to bring down; ~ **sa faim** to take the edge of one's hunger; ~ **les ponts avec qn** to cut oneself off from sb **6.** (*bloquer: route*) to cut off; ~ **les vivres à qn** to cut off sb's allowance; ~ **la respiration à qn** to wind sb **7.** (*diluer*) to dilute **8.** (*mordre*) **le froid me coupe le visage** my face is stinging with the cold **9.** JEUX to cut **10.** (*scinder: mot, paragraphe*) to break ►**ça me/te <u>la</u> coupe!** *inf* that shuts me/you up! **III.** *vpr* **1.** (*se blesser*) **se** ~ to cut oneself; **se ~ la main** to cut one's hand **2.** (*trancher*) **se ~ les ongles** to cut one's nails; **se ~ du pain** to cut (oneself) some bread **3.** (*se contredire*) **se** ~ to contradict oneself **4.** (*être coupé*) **bien se** ~ to give oneself a nasty cut ►**se ~ en <u>quatre</u> pour qn** to bend over backwards for sb

couperose [kupʀoz] *f* blotches *pl* (*on the face*)

couperosé(e) [kupʀoze] *adj* (*visage, nez*) red and blotchy

coupe-vent [kupvɑ̃] <coupe-vent(s)> *m* **1.** (*vêtement*) windcheater *Brit,* Windbreaker® *Am* **2.** (*abri*) windbreak

couple [kupl] **I.** *m* couple **II.** *f Québec, inf* **une ~ de qc** (*quelques*) a couple of sth

couplet [kuplɛ] *m* couplet

coupole [kupɔl] *f* dome

coupon [kupɔ̃] *m* **1.** COUT roll **2.** (*bon*) voucher **3.** FIN coupon

coupon-réponse [kupɔ̃Repɔ̃s] <coupons-réponse> *m* reply coupon

coupure [kupyR] *f* **1.** (*blessure*) cut **2.** PRESSE **~ de journal** [*o* **de presse**] press clipping **3.** LIT, CINE cut **4.** (*interruption*) **~ d'électricité** (*involontaire*) power failure; (*volontaire*) power cut **5.** (*billet*) **petites ~s** small notes *Brit,* small bills *Am* **6.** (*changement*) **une ~ dans la vie de qn** a big break in sb's life

couque [kuk] *f Belgique* (*pain d'épice*) gingerbread

cour [kuR] *f* **1.** (*espace clos: d'un bâtiment*) courtyard; **~ de l'école** playground **2.** (*courtisans*) court **3.** (*cercle de personnes: d'un puissant*) courtiers *pl* **4.** JUR **~ d'appel** court of appeals; **~ d'assises** ≈ Crown Court *Brit;* **~ de cassation** court of cassation **5.** *Belgique* (*toilettes*) toilet ►**faire la ~ à qn** to court sb

Cour [kuR] *f* **la ~ suprême** the Supreme Court

courage [kuRaʒ] *m* **1.** (*bravoure*) courage; **perdre ~** to lose heart; (**du**) **~!** courage!; **bon ~!** best of luck! **2.** (*ardeur*) spirit; **avec ~** with a will ►**prendre son ~ à deux mains** to muster all one's courage

courageusement [kuRaʒøzmɑ̃] *adv* courageously

courageux, -euse [kuRaʒø, -ʒøz] *adj* **1.** (*opp: lâche*) courageous **2.** (*travailleur*) willing ►**~, mais pas téméraire!** brave, but not stupid!

couramment [kuRamɑ̃] *adv* **1.** (*aisément: parler*) fluently **2.** (*souvent*) commonly

courant [kuRɑ̃] *m* **1.** (*cours d'eau, d'air*) *a.* ELEC current; **descendre/remonter le ~** to go with/against the current; **~ d'air** air current; (*gênant*) draught *Brit,* draft *Am;* **il y a un ~ d'air** there's a draught **2.** (*mouvement*) movement; **un ~ de pensée** a school of thought **3.** (*cours*) **dans le ~ de la journée** during the day ►**être au ~ de qc** to be aware of sth; **mettre** [*o* **tenir**] **qn au ~ de qc** to keep sb up to date on sth

courant(**e**) [kuRɑ̃, ɑ̃t] *adj* **1.** (*habituel*) usual; (*dépenses, procédé, langue*) everyday **2.** (*standard*) **modèle ~** standard model **3.** (*en cours: année, affaires, prix*) current; **le 3 ~** the third instant

courbatu(**e**) [kuRbaty] *adj* aching; **j'ai les membres ~s** my limbs are aching

courbature [kuRbatyR] *f souvent pl* ache

courbaturé(**e**) [kuRbatyRe] *adj* **être ~** to be aching

courbe [kuRb] **I.** *adj* curved; (*ligne, trajectoire, surface*) curving **II.** *f* GEO, FIN curve; (*d'une route, d'un fleuve*) bend; (*des reins*) line

courbé(**e**) [kuRbe] *adj* bowed down

courber [kuRbe] <1> **I.** *vi* **~ sous qc** (*personne, bois*) to bend under sth **II.** *vt* **1.** (*plier*) to bend **2.** (*pencher*) **~ le dos** to stoop; **~ les épaules** to hunch one's shoulders; **~ la tête devant qn** to give in to sb **III.** *vpr* **se ~** **1.** (*se baisser*) to bend down; (*à cause de l'âge*) to be bent; (*pour saluer*) to bow **2.** (*ployer*) to bend

courbette [kuRbɛt] *f* **faire des ~s à** [*o* **devant**] **qn** to kowtow to sb

courbure [kuRbyR] *f* (*des sourcils, du nez*) line; (*d'une ligne, surface*) curve

coureur [kuRœR] *m Québec* **~ des bois** (*chasseur et trappeur*) trapper

coureur, -euse [kuRœR, -øz] *m, f* **1.** SPORT (*athlète, cheval*) runner; (*voiture, cycliste*) entrants **2.** (*~ de jupons*) womanizer

courge [kuRʒ] *f* marrow

courgette [kuRʒɛt] *f* courgette

courir [kuRiR] *irr* **I.** *vi* **1.** (*se mouvoir, se dépêcher*) *a.* SPORT to run; (*plus vite*) to dash; **~ partout** to run all over the place; **~ faire qc** to run and do sth; **~ chercher le médecin** to run and get the doctor; **bon, j'y cours** OK, I'm off **2.** (*se répandre*) to go round; **faire ~ le bruit que qn est mort** to spread the rumour that sb's dead **3.** (*se diriger vers*) **~ à la faillite** to be heading for bankruptcy ►**laisse ~!** *inf* forget it!; **tu peux toujours ~!** you can whistle for it; **rien ne sert de ~, il faut partir à point!** *prov* more haste, less speed *prov;* **faire qc en courant** to do sth in a rush **II.** *vt* **1.** (*participer à une course*) to run (in) **2.** (*parcourir: campagne, monde, mers*) to roam; (*magasins*) to do **3.** (*fréquenter*) **~ les bars** to spend one's life in bars; **~ les filles** to chase women

couronne [kuRɔn] *f* **1.** BOT, MED, FIN, POL crown **2.** (*pain*) ring

couronné [kuRɔne] *adj* crowned

couronnement [kuRɔnmɑ̃] *m* coronation

couronner [kuRɔne] <1> *vt* **1.** (*coiffer d'une couronne, décorer, consacrer*) to crown; **couronné de succès** crowned with success **2.** (*récompenser*) to award a prize to

courrier [kuRje] *m* **1.** (*lettres*) mail, post *Brit;* **faire son ~** to go through one's post **2.** PRESSE (*nom*) **le ~ ...** ≈ the Mail ...; **le ~ économique** (*rubrique*) the economy page; **le ~ du cœur** problem page; **le ~ des lecteurs** readers' letters **3.** (*personne*) courier **4.** INFOR **~ électronique** electronic mail; **~ "arrivée"/"départ"** incoming/outgoing mail

courroie [kuRwa] *f* belt

cours [kuR] *m* **1.** (*déroulement*) course; **au ~ de qc** in the course of sth; **le mois en ~** the current month **2.** (*leçon*) lesson; UNIV lecture; **~ magistral** lecture; **~ particuliers** [*o* **privé**] private lessons; **faire ~ de qc à qn** to teach sb sth; **suivre un ~** [*o* **des ~**] to do a course; **~ de maths** *inf* maths lessons *Brit,* math lessons *Am* **3.** (*école*) school **4.** FIN (*d'une monnaie*) rate;

C

(*de produits*) price; **avoir** ~ to be legal tender **5.** (*courant*) ~ **d'eau** stream; (*rivière*) river; **suivre son** ~ to follow its course

course [kuʀs] *f* **1.** (*action de courir*) running; **au pas de** ~ at a run; **c'est la** ~**!** *inf* it's a mad rush! **2.** (*épreuve*) race; **vélo de** ~ racing bike; **faire la** ~ **avec qn** to race (with) sb; ~ **contre la montre** *a. fig* race agains the clock; ~ **à pied** race; ~ **de vitesse** speed trial; ~ **en sac** sack race **3.** JEUX **les** ~**s** the races; **jouer** [*o* **parier**] **aux** ~**s** to bet on the races **4.** (*déplacement*) journey; ~ **en taxi** taxi journey **5.** (*commission*) **les** ~**s** the shopping; **faire les** [*o* **ses**] ~**s** to do the shopping; **faire une** ~ (*règler qc*) to go and do sth; (*faire un achat*) to go and buy sth **6.** (*ruée*) **la** ~ **aux armements** the arms race **7.** *Suisse* (*excursion, voyage organisé*) excursion

coursier, -ière [kuʀsje, -jɛʀ] *m, f* (motorcycle) courier

court [kuʀ] *m* ~ **de tennis** tennis court

court(e) [kuʀ, kuʀt] **I.** *adj* (*opp: long*) short; **c'est un peu** ~**!** it's a bit short! **II.** *adv* **1.** (*opp: long*) short; **s'habiller** ~ to wear short dresses **2.** (*concis*) **faire** ~ to be brief; **tout** ~ simply ►**être à** ~ **de qc** to be short of sth

courtage [kuʀtaʒ] *m* **1.** (*profession*) brokerage **2.** (*commission*) commission

court-bouillon [kuʀbujɔ̃] <courts-bouillons> *m* stock **court-circuit** [kuʀsiʀkɥi] <courts-circuits> *m* short-circuit

courtier, -ière [kuʀtje, -jɛʀ] *m, f* broker

courtisan [kuʀtizɑ̃] *m* courtier

courtiser [kuʀtize] <1> *vt* to court

court-métrage [kuʀmetʀaʒ] <courts-métrages> *m* CINE short film

courtois(e) [kuʀtwa, waz] *adj* courteous

courtoisie [kuʀtwazi] *f* courtesy

couru(e) [kuʀy] **I.** *part passé de* **courir II.** *adj* **ce bar est** ~ **du tout Paris** everyone in Paris goes to this bar ►**c'est** ~ **d'avance** it's a foregone conclusion

couscous [kuskus] *m* couscous

couscoussier [kuskusje] *m* couscous steamer

cousin(e) [kuzɛ̃, in] *m(f)* cousin; ~**s germains** first cousin

coussin [kusɛ̃] *m* **1.** (*objet moelleux, rembourré*) cushion; ~ **d'air** air cushion **2.** *Belgique* (*oreiller*) pillow

cousu(e) [kuzy] **I.** *part passé de* **coudre II.** *adj* sewn; ~ **main** handsewn ►**c'est** ~ **de fil blanc** it sticks out a mile

coût [ku] *m* cost

coûtant [kutɑ̃] *adj* **prix** ~ cost price

couteau [kuto] <x> *m* **1.** (*ustensile*) knife; ~ **de cuisine/suisse** kitchen/Swiss Army knife **2.** (*coquillage*) razor shell ►**mettre le** ~ **sous** [*o* **sur**] **la gorge de qn** to put a knife to sb's throat; **remuer** [*o* **retourner**] **le** ~ **dans la plaie** to twist the knife in the wound

coutelas [kutla] *m* cook's knife

coutellerie [kutɛlʀi] *f* **1.** (*industrie*) cutlery industry **2.** (*produits*) cutlery

coûter [kute] <1> *vt* to cost; **ça m'a coûté 10 euros** it cost me 10 euros; **ça coûte cher** it's expensive; **ça coûte combien?** how much does it cost? ►**ça va me** ~ **cher de** +*infin* it will be painful for me to +*infin*

coûteux, -euse [kutø, -øz] *adj* expensive

coutume [kutym] *f* custom; **avoir** ~ **de** +*infin* to be accustomed to +*infin*

coutumier, -ière [kutymje, -jɛʀ] *adj* **1.** (*habituel*) accustomed; **être** ~ **à qn** to be sb's custom **2.** JUR **droit** ~ customary law

couture [kutyʀ] *f* **1.** (*action, ouvrage*) sewing **2.** (*profession*) dressmaking; **la haute** ~ haute couture; **une maison de** ~ a fashion house **3.** (*suite de points*) seam ►**se faire battre à plate(s)** ~**(s)** to be thrashed; **examiner** [*o* **inspecter**] **qn/qc sous toutes les** ~**s** to examine sb/sth minutely

couturier [kutyʀje] *m* (**grand**) ~ (fashion) designer

couturière [kutyʀjɛʀ] *f* (*à son compte*) dressmaker

couvée [kuve] *f* **1.** (*œufs*) clutch **2.** (*poussins*) brood

couvent [kuvɑ̃] *m* convent

couver [kuve] <1> **I.** *vi* (*feu*) to smoulder *Brit*, to smolder *Am;* (*émeute*) to be brewing **II.** *vt* **1.** ZOOL to sit on **2.** (*materner*) to cocoon; ~ **qn des yeux** [*o* **du regard**] to look lovingly at sb **3.** (*porter*) to be coming down with **4.** (*nourrir*) to plot

couvercle [kuvɛʀkl] *m* lid

couvert [kuvɛʀ] *m* **1.** (*ustensiles*) cutlery *no pl;* **mettre le** ~ to lay the cutlery **2.** (*place*) place setting; **je mets combien de** ~**s?** how many places do I lay? **3.** (*prétexte*) **sous le** ~ **de qc** hiding behind sth

couvert(e) [kuvɛʀ, ɛʀt] **I.** *part passé de* **couvrir II.** *adj* **1.** (*habillé*) **être trop** ~ to be wearing too much **2.** (*protégé*) **être** ~ to be covered **3.** (*assuré*) **être** ~ **par une assurance** to be covered by insurance **4.** (*opp: en plein air*) indoor **5.** METEO (*ciel, temps*) overcast **6.** (*recouvert*) ~ **de feuilles/poussière** covered in leaves/dust **7.** (*plein de*) **être** ~ **de sang** to be covered in blood **8.** (*caché*) **s'exprimer à mots** ~**s** to speak guardedly

couverture [kuvɛʀtyʀ] *f* **1.** (*tissu: d'un lit*) blanket **2.** (*toiture*) ~ **de tuiles** tiled roof **3.** (*page*) cover; **faire la** ~ **d'un magazine** to be on the cover of a magazine **4.** PRESSE (*d'un événement*) coverage **5.** ADMIN, FIN cover **6.** (*prétexte*) front

couveuse [kuvøz] *f* **1.** (*poule*) sitter **2.** (*incubateur*) ~ **artificielle** incubator

couvrant(e) [kuvʀɑ̃, ɑ̃t] *adj* (*couleur, peinture*) with good coverage; **pouvoir** ~ coverage

couvre-feu [kuvʀəfø] <couvre-feux> *m* curfew **couvre-lit** [kuvʀəli] <couvre-lits> *m* bedspread

couvreur, -euse [kuvʀœʀ, -øz] *m, f* roofer

couvrir [kuvʀiʀ] <11> **I.** *vt* **1.** (*mettre sur*) to cover; (*récipient*) to put the lid on; (*livre*) to back; ~ **un toit** (**de tuiles**) to tile a roof **2.** (*recouvrir*) ~ **qc** (*couverture, toile*) to cover sth up; **qc couvre qn** sb is covered in sth; ~ **de qc** to cover in sth **3.** (*habiller*) to dress **4.** (*cacher: visage*) to cover up; (*son*) to drown **5.** (*protéger, garantir, parcourir, relater*) to cover **6.** (*combler*) ~ **qn de baisers/cadeaux** to shower sb with kisses/gifts; ~ **qn de reproches** to heap reproach on sb **II.** *vpr* **1. se** ~ (*s'habiller*) to dress; (*mettre un chapeau*) to put one's hat on; **couvre-toi, il fait froid!** cover up warmly, it's cold! **2.** (*se protéger*) **se** ~ to cover opeself **3.** METEO **le ciel se couvre** (**de nuages**) the sky is becoming overcast **4.** (*se remplir de*) **se** ~ **de bourgeons** to burst out in buds; **se** ~ **de taches** to get stains all over oneself

cover-girl [kɔvœʀgœʀl] <cover-girls> *f* cover girl

covoiturage [kovwatyʀaʒ] *m* car sharing, car pooling *Am*

cow-boy [kobɔj, kaobɔj] <cow-boys> *m* cowboy

coyote [kɔjɔt] *m* coyote

CP [sepe] *m abr de* **cours préparatoire** ≈ year one

CQFD [cekyɛkde] *abr de* **ce qu'il fallait démontrer** QED

crabe [kʀɑb] *m* crab

crac [kʀak] *interj* crack

crachat [kʀaʃa] *m* spit

craché(**e**) [kʀaʃe] *adj* **c'est lui tout** ~ *inf* (*très ressemblant*) he's the spitting image of him; (*typique de qn*) it's him all over

cracher [kʀaʃe] <1> **I.** *vi* **1.** (*expectorer*) to spit **2.** (*baver*) to blot ▶**ne pas** ~ **sur qn/qc** *inf* not to turn one's nose up at sb/sth **II.** *vt* **1.** (*rejeter*) to spit **2.** (*émettre: fumée, lave*) to spit out

cracheur [kʀaʃœʀ] *m* ~ **de feu** fire-eater

crachin [kʀaʃɛ̃] *m* drizzle

crade [kʀɑd] *adj inf,* **cradingue** [kʀadɛ̃g] *adj inf,* **crado** [kʀɑdo] *adj inf* filthy

craie [kʀɛ] *f* chalk

craindre [kʀɛ̃dʀ] *irr* **I.** *vt* **1.** (*redouter*) to be afraid of **2.** (*pressentir*) to fear **3.** (*être sensible à*) ~ **la chaleur** to dislike the heat **II.** *vi* ~ **pour qn/qc** to fear for sb/sth; **il n'y a rien à** ~ there's nothing to be afraid of; **ça ne craint rien** it can take anything ▶**ça craint!** *inf* that's a bit off!

crainte [kʀɛ̃t] *f* **1.** (*peur*) ~ **de qn/qc** fear of sb/sth; **soyez sans** ~(**s**)! never fear!; **de** [*o* **dans la**] [*o* **par**] ~ **de qc** for fear of sth **2.** (*pressentiment*) worry; **avoir des ~s au sujet de qn/qc** to be worried about sb/sth

craintif, -ive [kʀɛ̃tif, -iv] *adj* timid

cramé [kʀame] *m inf* **sentir le** ~ to smell of burning

cramer [kʀame] <1> *vi inf* (*maison, meuble*) to go up in smoke; (*aliment, câble*) to burn

cramique [kʀamik] *m Belgique* (*pain au lait et au beurre, garni de raisins de Corinthe*) fruit bread

cramoisi(**e**) [kʀamwazi] *adj* crimson; **devenir** ~ to turn puce

crampe [kʀɑ̃p] *f* cramp

crampon [kʀɑ̃pɔ̃] *m* SPORT crampon; (*de foot*) stud

cramponner [kʀɑ̃pɔne] <1> **I.** *vt inf* to pester **II.** *vpr* **1.** (*se tenir*) **se** ~ **à qn/qc** to cling on to sb/sth **2.** *fig* **se** ~ **à la vie** to cling on to life

cran[1] [kʀɑ̃] *m* **1.** (*entaille: d'une arme*) notch; **hausser/baisser qc d'un** ~ to raise/lower sth a notch **2.** (*trou*) hole **3.** (*coiffure*) wave

cran[2] [kʀɑ̃] *m inf* **avoir du** ~ to have guts

crâne [kʀɑn] *m* skull ▶**ne rien avoir dans le** ~ to be a total numskull; **bourrer le** ~ **à qn** *inf* to sell sb a line; **se bourrer le** ~ **avec qc** to stuff sb's head with sth

crâner [kʀɑne] <1> *vi inf* to show off

crâneur, -euse [kʀɑnœʀ, -øz] **I.** *adj* **être** ~ to be a show-off **II.** *m, f* show-off

crânien(**ne**) [kʀɑnjɛ̃, jɛn] *adj* cranial

crapaud [kʀapo] *m* toad

crapule [kʀapyl] *f* villain

crapuleux, -euse [kʀapylø, -øz] *adj* villainous; (*vie*) dissolute

craquant(**e**) [kʀakɑ̃, ɑ̃t] *adj inf* gorgeous

craquelé(**e**) [kʀakle] *adj* cracked

craqueler [kʀakle] <3> **I.** *vt* to crackle **II.** *vpr* **se** ~ to craze

craquelure [kʀaklyʀ] *f* cracks *pl*

craquement [kʀakmɑ̃] *m* (*d'un arbre, plancher, de la banquise*) creaking *no pl;* (*du bois qui brûle*) crackling *pl;* (*de chaussures*) squeaking *pl;* (*des feuilles mortes, de la neige*) crackle *pl*

craquer [kʀake] <1> **I.** *vi* **1.** (*faire un bruit: bonbon*) to be crunchy; (*chaussures, bois, parquet*) to squeak; (*feuilles mortes, neige*) to crunch; (*disque*) to crackle; **faire** ~ **une allumette** to strike a match; **faire** ~ **ses doigts** to crack one's knuckles **2.** (*céder: branche*) to snap; (*glace*) to crack; (*se déchirer: vêtement*) to tear; (*aux coutures*) to come apart **3.** (*s'effondrer: personne*) to crack up; (*nerfs*) to crack **4.** (*s'attendrir*) ~ **pour qc** to go for sth ▶**plein à** ~ full to bursting **II.** *vt* (*allumette*) to strike

crash [kʀaʃ] <(e)s> *m* crash

crasse [kʀas] *f* (*saleté*) filth

crasseux, -euse [kʀasø, -øz] *adj* filthy

cratère [kʀatɛʀ] *m* cratère

cravache [kʀavaʃ] *f* riding crop

cravacher [kʀavaʃe] <1> **I.** *vt* (*animal*) to use the whip on **II.** *vi* **1.** (*à cheval*) to use the whip **2.** *inf* (*travailler dur*) to get a move on

cravate [kʀavat] *f* tie

crawl [kʀol] *m* crawl

crawler [kʀole] <1> *vi* **dos crawlé** backstroke

crayeux, -euse [kʀɛjø, -jøz] *adj* chalky

crayon [kʀɛjɔ̃] *m* pencil; ~ **feutre** felt-tip; ~ **optique** light pen; ~ **de couleur** coloured pencil *Brit*, colored pencil *Am;* ~ **pour les yeux** eye pencil

crayonner [kʀɛjɔne] <1> *vt* to sketch (in pencil)

créancier, **-ière** [kʀeɑ̃sje, -jɛʀ] *m, f* FIN creditor

Créateur [kʀeatœʀ] *m* REL **le** ~ the Creator

créateur, **-trice** [kʀeatœʀ, -tʀis] **I.** *adj* creative **II.** *m, f* ART designer

créatif, **-ive** [kʀeatif, -iv] *adj* creative

création [kʀeasjɔ̃] *f* creation; ~ **d'emploi** job creation; ~ **d'entreprise** company set-up

Création [kʀeasjɔ̃] *f* REL **la** ~ the Creation

créativité [kʀeativite] *f* creativity

créature [kʀeatyʀ] *f* creature

crécelle [kʀesɛl] *f* rattle

crèche [kʀɛʃ] *f* **1.** REL crib **2.** (*pouponnière*) creche

crécher [kʀeʃe] <5> *vi inf* to live; **tu peux** ~ **chez moi cette nuit** you can crash out at my place tonight

crédibilité [kʀedibilite] *f* credibility

crédible [kʀedibl] *adj* credible

crédit [kʀedi] *m* **1.** (*paiement échelonné*) credit; **acheter/vendre à** ~ to buy/sell on credit **2.** (*prêt*) loan; **accorder un** ~ **à qn** to give sb a loan **3.** (*banque*) bank **4.** (*opp: débit*) credit; **la somme est portée** [*o* **mise**] **au** ~ **de votre compte** the amount has been credited to your account **5.** *pl* POL funds **6.** (*confiance*) **jouir d'un grand** ~ **auprès de qn** to be high in sb's esteem

créditer [kʀedite] <1> *vt* ~ **un compte de 100 euros** to credit 100 euros to an account

créditeur, **-trice** [kʀeditœʀ, -tʀis] **I.** *adj* **compte** ~ account in credit **II.** *m, f* creditor

crédule [kʀedyl] *adj* credulous

crédulité [kʀedylite] *f* credulity

créer [kʀee] <1> **I.** *vt* **1.** (*emploi, œuvre, problèmes*) to create; (*entreprise*) to set up **2.** THEAT ~ **une pièce** to put on the first performance of a play **II.** *vi* to create **III.** *vpr* **se** ~ **des besoins/problèmes** to create needs/problems for oneself

crémaillère [kʀemajɛʀ] *f* **pendre la** ~ to have a housewarming (party)

crémation [kʀemasjɔ̃] *f* cremation

crématoire [kʀematwaʀ] *adj* **four** ~ crematorium

crématorium, **crematorium** [kʀematɔʀjɔm] *m* crematorium

crème [kʀɛm] **I.** *adj inv* cream **II.** *f* **1.** (*produit laitier, entremets, de soins*) cream; ~ **chantilly** whipped cream; ~ **fraîche** crème fraîche; ~ **glacée** ice cream; ~ **à raser** shaving cream **2.** (*liqueur*) ~ **de cassis** blackcurrant liqueur **3.** (*le meilleur*) **la** ~ **de ...** the best of ...; **c'est la** ~ **des hommes** he's a wonderful man **III.** *m* white coffee

crémerie [kʀɛmʀi] *f* dairy ►**changer de** ~ to look elsewhere

crémeux, **-euse** [kʀemø, -øz] *adj* creamy

crémier, **-ière** [kʀemje, -jɛʀ] *m, f* dairyman, dairywoman *m, f*

créneau [kʀeno] <x> *m* **1.** AUTO parking space; **faire un** ~ to parallel park **2.** COM opening

créole [kʀeɔl] **I.** *adj* Creole **II.** *m* Creole; *v. a.* **français**

Créole [kʀeɔl] *mf* Creole

crêpe [kʀɛp] *f* GASTR crêpe

crêper [kʀepe] <1> **I.** *vt* (*cheveux*) to backcomb **II.** *vpr* **se** ~ **les cheveux** to backcomb one's hair ►**se** ~ **le chignon** to have a go at each other

crêperie [kʀɛpʀi] *f* crêpe restaurant

crépi [kʀepi] *m* roughcast

crêpière [kʀepjɛʀ] *f* **1.** (*plaque*) pancake griddle **2.** (*poêle*) pancake pan

crépir [kʀepiʀ] <8> *vt* to roughcast

crépitement [kʀepitmɑ̃] *m* (*de la pluie, de l'eau*) patter; (*du feu*) crackle; (*d'une arme*) rattle; (*d'une radio*) crackling

crépiter [kʀepite] <1> *vi* (*feu*) to crackle; (*arme*) to rattle

crépu(e) [kʀepy] *adj* frizzy

crépuscule [kʀepyskyl] *m* twilight

cresson [kʀesɔ̃, kʀəsɔ̃] *m* watercress

crête [kʀɛt] *f* **1.** ZOOL crest; (*de coq*) comb **2.** (*sommet: d'une montagne, d'un toit*) ridge; (*d'une vague*) crest

Crète [kʀɛt] *f* **la** ~ Crete

crétin(e) [kʀetɛ̃, in] **I.** *adj inf* cretinous **II.** *m(f) inf* cretin

creuser [kʀøze] <1> **I.** *vt* **1.** (*excaver*) to dig; (*sillon*) to plough *Brit*, to plow *Am* **2.** (*évider: tombe*) to dig; (*pomme, falaise*) to hollow out; ~ **le sable** to dig in the sand ►~ **l'estomac** to work up an appetite **II.** *vi* to dig **III.** *vpr* **se** ~ to grow hollow; (*roche*) to be hollowed out ►**se** ~ **la tête** to rack one's brains

creuset [kʀøzɛ] *m* CHIM, IND crucible

creux [kʀø] *m* **1.** (*cavité*) cavity; (*dans un terrain, de la main*) hollow; (*d'une vague*) trough **2.** ANAT **le** ~ **des reins** the small of the back; **le** ~ **de l'aisselle** tha armpit **3.** (*manque d'activité*) slack period **4.** *inf* (*faim*) **avoir un** ~ to be a bit hungry, to feel peckish *Brit*

creux, **-euse** [kʀø, -øz] *adj* **1.** (*vide*) hollow; (*ventre, tête*) empty **2.** (*vain: paroles*) empty **3.** (*concave*) hollow **4.** (*rentré: visage*) gaunt; **avoir les yeux** ~ to be hollow-eyed **5.** (*sans activité*) slack; **les heures creuses** off-peak hours

crevaison [kʀəvɛzɔ̃] *f* puncture

crevant(e) [kʀəvɑ̃, ɑ̃t] *adj inf* exhausting

crevasse [kʀəvas] *f* **1.** (*fissure*) crevice **2.** (*gerçure*) crack

crevasser [kʀəvase] <1> **I.** *vt* to crack **II.** *vpr* **se** ~ (*peau*) to get chapped

crève [kʀɛv] *f inf* cold; **avoir/attraper la** ~ to have/catch a cold

crevé(e) [kʀəve] *adj inf* (*fatigué*) dead

crever [kʀəve] <4> **I.** *vi* **1.** (*éclater: ballon,* *sac*) to burst **2.** AUTO to have a puncture **3.** (*être plein de*) ~ **de jalousie** to be dying of jealousy **4.** *inf* (*souffrir*) ~ **de froid** to be freezing; ~ **de faim** to be starving; ~ **d'envie de qc** to be dying for sth; **une chaleur à** ~ boiling heat **II.** *vt* **1.** (*percer: abcès, ballon, pneu*) to burst **2.** *inf* (*exténuer*) to kill **III.** *vpr inf* **se** ~ to kill; **se** ~ **à faire qc** to kill oneself doing sth

crevette [kʀəvɛt] *f* prawn

cri [kʀi] *m* **pousser un** ~ to cry out ►**le dernier** ~ *inf* the latest thing

criant(e) [kʀijɑ̃, jɑ̃t] *adj* **1.** (*révoltant: injustice*) screaming **2.** (*manifeste: preuve*) striking

criard(e) [kʀijaʀ, jaʀd] *adj* **1.** (*braillard: personne*) squealing; (*voix*) piercing **2.** (*tapageur*) loud

crible [kʀibl] *m* screen; (*manuel*) riddle ►**passer qc au** ~ to go through sth with a fine-tooth comb

criblé(e) [kʀible] *adj* **1.** (*percé*) ~ **de balles** riddled with bullets **2.** (*couvert de*) ~ **de boutons** covered in spots; ~ **de dettes** up to one's neck in debt

cribler [kʀible] <1> *vt* (*percer*) ~ **qn de balles** to shoot sb full of holes; ~ **qc de trous** to riddle sth with holes

cric [kʀik] *m* jack

cricket [kʀikɛt] *m* cricket

cri-cri, **cricri** [kʀikʀi] *m* **1.** (*cri du grillon*) chirp **2.** (*grillon*) cricket

criée [kʀije] *f* **vente à la** ~ sale by auction

crier [kʀije] <1> **I.** *vi* **1.** (*hurler*) to cry (out); (*bébé*) to scream; ~ **de peur** to scream with fear **2.** *inf* (*se fâcher*) ~ **contre/après qn** to yell at sb **3.** (*émettre des sons: mouette*) to cry; (*oiseau*) to call; (*cochon*) to squeal; (*oie*) to honk; (*souris*) to squeak **4.** (*dénoncer*) ~ **au scandale** to describe the situation as a scandal **II.** *vt* **1.** (*à voix forte*) ~ **qc à qn** to yell sth to sb **2.** (*proclamer*) ~ **son innocence** to protest one's innocence ►**sans** ~ **gare** without warning

crime [kʀim] *m* **1.** (*meurtre*) *a.* JUR crime; **heure du** ~ time of death **2.** (*faute morale*) **c'est un** ~**!** it's criminal!

criminalité [kʀiminalite] *f sans pl* criminality

criminel(le) [kʀiminɛl] **I.** *adj* criminal **II.** *m(f)* **1.** (*assassin*) murderer **2.** (*coupable*) criminal

crin [kʀɛ̃] *m* **1.** (*poil*) hair **2.** *sans pl* (*matière*) horsehair

crinière [kʀinjɛʀ] *f* mane

crique [kʀik] *f* creek

criquet [kʀikɛ] *m* grasshopper; (*dévastateur*) locust

crise [kʀiz] *f* **1.** MED attack; ~ **cardiaque** heart attack; ~ **d'appendicite** appendicitis attack; **faire une** ~ **de nerfs** to have an attack of nerves **2.** ECON, POL, FIN crisis ►**faire sa** ~ *inf* to have a tantrum; **piquer une** ~ (**de colère**) *inf* to fly into a temper

crispé(e) [kʀispe] *adj* tense; (*poing*) clenched

crisper [kʀispe] <1> **I.** *vt* **1.** (*contracter*) to tense; **l'effort crispe ses muscles** his muscles were tensed with the effort; **la douleur lui crispait le visage** his face was tense with pain **2.** (*agacer*) ~ **qn** to get on sb's nerves **II.** *vpr* **se** ~ **1.** (*se contracter*) to tense **2.** (*se serrer: main*) to tighten; (*poing*) to clench

crisser [kʀise] <1> *vi* (*pneus, freins*) to squeal; (*gravier, pas*) to crunch

cristal [kʀistal, o] <-aux> *m* **1.** (*en minéralogie, verre*) crystal **2.** *pl* (*cristallisation*) crystals

cristallin [kʀistalɛ̃] *m* (*de l'œil*) crystalline lens

cristallin(e) [kʀistalɛ̃, in] *adj* **1.** (*voix, son*) crystal; (*eau*) crystal-clear **2.** MIN crystalline

cristallisé [kʀistalize] *adj* crystalized; **du sucre** ~ sugar crystals

cristalliser [kʀistalize] <1> *vi, vt, vpr* CHIM (**se**) ~ to crystallize

critère [kʀitɛʀ] *m* criterion

critiquable [kʀitikabl] *adj* open to criticism

critique [kʀitik] **I.** *adj* critical **II.** *f* (*reproche*) criticism; (*revue*) review; **faire la** ~ **d'un livre/film** to review a book/film; **la** ~ **a bien accueilli son livre** her book was well received by the critics **III.** *mf* critic

critiquer [kʀitike] <1> *vt* **1.** (*condamner*) to criticize **2.** (*juger*) to review

croassement [kʀɔasmɑ̃] *m* croak

croasser [kʀɔase] <1> *vi* to croak

croate [kʀɔat] **I.** *adj* Croatian **II.** *m* Croatian; *v. a.* **français**

Croate [kʀɔat] *mf* Croat

Croatie [kʀɔasi] *f* **la** ~ Croatia

croc [kʀo] *m* fang; **le chien montre les** ~**s** the dog bares its teeth

croc-en-jambe [kʀɔkɑ̃ʒɑ̃b] <crocs-en-jambe> *m* **faire un** ~ **à qn** to trip sb up

croche [kʀɔʃ] *f* MUS quaver; **double** ~ semiquaver; **triple** ~ demisemiquaver; **quadruple** ~ hemidemisemiquaver

croche-pied [kʀɔʃpje] <croche-pieds> *m* **faire un** ~ **à qn** to trip sb up

crocher [kʀɔʃe] <1> *vt Suisse* (*attacher solidement*) ~ **qc** to do sth up tight

crochet [kʀɔʃɛ] *m* **1.** (*pour accrocher*) *a.* SPORT hook **2.** (*aiguille*) crochet hook **3.** *pl* TYP square brackets **4.** *pl* (*dent*) fangs **5.** (*détour*) **faire un** ~ (*route*) to bend; (*personne*) to make a detour ►**vivre aux** ~**s de qn** to sponge off sb

crocheter [kʀɔʃte] <4> *vt* (*ouvrir: serrure*) to pick; ~ **une porte** to pick the lock on a door

crochu(e) [kʀɔʃy] *adj* (*bec, doigts*) claw-like; **avoir le nez** ~ to have a hook nose

croco *inf*, **crocodile** [kʀɔkɔdil] *m* (*cuir*) crocodile

crocus [kʀɔkys] *m* crocus

croire [kʀwaʀ] *irr* **I.** *vt* **1.** (*tenir pour vrai*) to believe; **faire** ~ **qc à qn** to make sb think sth **2.** (*avoir confiance en*) to believe **3.** (*s'i-

maginer) to think **4.** (*supposer*) **c'est à ~ qu'il va pleuvoir** you'd think it was going to rain; **il faut ~ que le patron a raison** it seems the boss is right; **il croit que je suis bête?** does he think I'm stupid? **5.** (*estimer*) ~ **qn capable** to think sb capable; **on l'a crue morte** we thought she was dead ▸**il n'en croyait pas ~ ses oreilles/yeux** he couldn't believe his ears/eyes; **tu ne croyais pas ~ si bien dire** you didn't know how right you were **II.** *vi* ~ **en qn/qc** to believe in sb/sth ▸**je vous prie de ~ à l'expression de ma considération distinguée, veuillez ~ à mes sentiments les meilleurs** *form* ≈ Yours sincerely **III.** *vpr* **se ~ intelligent** to think oneself clever; **se ~ tout permis** to think one can get away with anything; **qu'est-ce qu'il se croit, celui-là?** who does he think he is(, anyway)?

croisade [kʀwazad] *f* HIST crusade

croisé(e) [kʀwaze] *adj* **les bras ~s** with one's arms crossed ▸**rester les bras ~s** to sit and do nothing; **mots ~s** crossword

croisée [kʀwaze] *f* (*fenêtre*) casement ▸**à la ~ des chemins** at the parting of the ways

croisement [kʀwazmɑ̃] *m* **1.** *sans pl* AUTO **feux de ~** dipped headlights *Brit,* low beams *Am* **2.** (*intersection*) crossroads **3.** (*mélange*) cross

croiser [kʀwaze] <1> **I.** *vt* **1.** (*mettre en croix: bras*) to fold; (*jambes, mains*) to cross **2.** (*couper: route, regard*) to cross; (*véhicule*) to pass **3.** (*passer à côté de qn*) ~ **qn** to meet sb; ~ **qc** (*regard*) to fall on sth; **son regard a croisé le mien** our eyes crossed **4.** BIO, ZOOL to cross **II.** *vpr* **se ~ 1.** (*passer l'un à côté de l'autre: personnes, regards*) to meet **2.** (*se couper*) to cross

croiseur [kʀwazœʀ] *m* cruiser

croisière [kʀwazjɛʀ] *f* cruise

croissance [kʀwasɑ̃s] *f sans pl* growth

croissant [kʀwasɑ̃] *m* **1.** GASTR croissant **2.** *sans pl* (*forme*) ~ **de lune** crescent **3.** REL crescent

croissant(e) [kʀwasɑ̃, ɑ̃t] *adj* growing

croissanterie [kʀwasɑ̃tʀi] *f* croissant bakery

croître [kʀwatʀ] *vi irr* **1.** (*grandir*) to grow **2.** (*augmenter: choses, colère*) to increase; (*chômage*) to go up

croix [kʀwa] *f* cross; **faire un signe de ~** to make the sign of the cross; **mettre une ~ dans la case qui convient** to put a cross in the appropriate box; ~ **de la Légion d'honneur** Cross of the Legion of Honour *Brit,* Cross of the Legion of Honor *Am* ▸**faire une ~ sur qc** *inf* to kiss sth goodbye

Croix-Rouge [kʀwaʀuʒ] *f* **la ~** the Red Cross

croquant(e) [kʀɔkɑ̃, ɑ̃t] *adj* crisp; (*biscuit*) crunchy

croque-madame [kʀɔkmadam] *m inv* *toasted ham and cheese sandwich with an egg* **croque-monsieur** [kʀɔkməsjø] *m inv* *toasted ham and cheese sandwich* **croque-mort** [kʀɔkmɔʀ] <croque-morts> *m inf* undertaker *Brit,* mortician *Am*

croquer [kʀɔke] <1> **I.** *vt* **1.** (*manger*) to munch **2.** *inf* (*dépenser*) ~ **son argent** to fritter one's money away **3.** (*dessiner*) to sketch ▸**être à ~** to be gorgeous **II.** *vi* **1.** (*être croustillant: salade*) to be crisp; (*bonbons*) to be crunchy **2.** (*mordre*) ~ **dans une pomme** to bite into an apple

croquet [kʀɔkɛ] *m* SPORT croquet

croquette [kʀɔkɛt] *f* croquette; ~ **de poisson** fish croquette

croquis [kʀɔki] *m* sketch

cross [kʀɔs] *m* **1.** (*course à pied*) cross-country race **2.** (*sport*) cross-country running **3.** (*course de moto*) motocross

crosse [kʀɔs] *f* **1.** (*manche: d'un fusil*) butt; (*d'un revolver*) grip **2.** REL crosier **3.** SPORT stick

crotale [kʀɔtal] *m* rattlesnake

crotte [kʀɔt] *f* **1.** (*excrément: de chien*) turd; (*de cheval, lapin*) droppings *pl;* (*de nez*) bogey *Brit,* booger *Am* **2.** GASTR ~ **en chocolat** chocolate drop

crotté(e) [kʀɔte] *adj* covered in mud

crottin [kʀɔtɛ̃] *m* **1.** (*excrément*) droppings *pl* **2.** (*fromage*) *round goat's milk cheese*

crouler [kʀule] <1> *vi* **1.** (*s'écrouler*) to collapse **2.** *fig* ~ **sous les fruits** (*arbre*) to be weighed down with fruit; ~ **sous le travail** to be going under with work; ~ **sous les applaudissements** to ring with applause **3.** (*s'effondrer*) to fall in

croupe [kʀup] *f* rump ▸**monter en ~** to ride pillion

croupier, -ière [kʀupje, -jɛʀ] *m, f* croupier

croupion [kʀupjɔ̃] *m* GASTR parson's nose *Brit,* pope's nose *Am*

croupir [kʀupiʀ] <8> *vi* **1.** (*se corrompre: eau*) to stagnate; (*détritus*) to rot **2.** (*végéter*) ~ **en prison** to rot away in jail

CROUS [kʀus] *m abr de* **Centre régional des œuvres universitaires et scolaires** *student welfare office*

croustillant(e) [kʀustijɑ̃, jɑ̃t] *adj* **1.** (*pain*) crusty; (*biscuit*) crunchy **2.** (*grivois*) tasty

croustille [kʀustij] *f Québec* crisps *pl*

croustiller [kʀustije] <1> *vi* (*pain*) to be crusty; (*biscuit*) to be crunchy

croûte [kʀut] *f* **1.** *sans pl* (*couche externe: de pain, fromage*) crust **2.** GASTR pastry; **pâté en ~** pâté en croûte, *pâté surrounded by crust and served in slices* **3.** *sans pl* (*couche*) layer; MED scab **4.** (*sédiment*) scale **5.** GEO ~ **terrestre** earth's crust ▸**casser la ~** *inf* to have something to eat; **gagner sa ~** *inf* to earn a living

croûton [kʀutɔ̃] *m* **1.** (*extrémité*) crust **2.** (*pain frit*) crouton ▸**vieux ~** *inf* old fogy

croyable [kʀwajabl] *adj* **c'est à peine ~** you can hardly believe it

croyance [kʀwajɑ̃s] *f* **1.** *sans pl* (*le fait de croire*) **la ~ dans/en qc** belief in sth **2.** (*ce que l'on croit*) ~ **religieuse** religious belief

croyant [kʀwajɑ̃] *part prés de* **croire**

croyant(e) [kʀwajɑ̃, jɑ̃t] I. *adj* believing II. *m(f)* believer

CRS [seɛʀɛs] *m abr de* **compagnie républicaine de sécurité** security police; (*policier*) security policeman; **les** ~ the security police

cru [kʀy] *m* 1. (*terroir*) vineyard 2. (*vin*) **un grand** ~ a great vintage; **un des grands ~s de Bourgogne** of of the great crus of Burgundy 3. (*invention*) **c'est de mon propre** ~ it's my own invention

cru(e) [kʀy] I. *part passé de* **croire** II. *adj* 1. (*opp: cuit: aliments*) raw 2. (*vif*) harsh 3. (*direct*) blunt

crû(e) [kʀy] *part passé de* **croître**

cruauté [kʀyote] *f sans pl* cruelty

cruche [kʀyʃ] *f* 1. (*récipient*) jug 2. *inf* (*sot*) dumb

crucial(e) [kʀysjal, jo] <-aux> *adj* crucial

crucifier [kʀysifje] <1> *vt* to crucify

crucifix [kʀysifi] *m* crucifix

crucifixion [kʀysifiksjɔ̃] *f* crucifixion

cruciforme [kʀysifɔʀm] *adj* 1. ARCHIT cruciform 2. TECH **tournevis** ~ Phillips® screwdriver

cruciverbiste [kʀysivɛʀbist] *mf* crossword puzzler

crudités [kʀydite] *fpl* GASTR raw vegetables; **assiette de** ~ mixed vegetable salad

crue [kʀy] *f* 1. (*montée*) rise in the water level 2. (*inondation*) flood

cruel(le) [kʀyɛl] *adj* 1. (*méchant*) cruel 2. (*douloureux: sort*) cruel; (*épreuve*) harsh

cruellement [kʀyɛlmɑ̃] *adv* (*méchamment*) cruelly

crûment [kʀymɑ̃] *adv* 1. (*directement*) bluntly; (*grossièrement*) crudely 2. (*avec une lumière crue: éclairer*) harshly

crus [kʀy] *passé simple de* **croire**

crûs [kʀy] *passé simple de* **croître**

crustacé [kʀystase] *m* 1. crustacean 2. GASTR ~**s** seafood

cryptage [kʀiptaʒ] *m* INFOR (*système*) cipher; (*procédure*) encryption

crypte [kʀipt] *f* crypt

crypter [kʀipte] <1> *vt* to encrypt

CSG [seɛsʒe] *f abr de* **contribution sociale généralisée** *social security contribution benefitting the under-privileged*

Cuba [kyba] (**l'île de**) ~ Cuba

cubain(e) [kybɛ̃, ɛn] *adj* Cuban

Cubain(e) [kybɛ̃, ɛn] *m(f)* Cuban

cube [kyb] *m* 1. (*mesure volumétrique*) **mètre** ~ cubic metre *Brit,* cubic meter *Am* 2. (*jouet*) block 3. MAT cube; **élever des chiffres au** ~ to cube numbers

cubique [kybik] *adj* 1. (*en forme de cube*) cubic 2. MAT **racine** ~ cube root

cubisme [kybism] *m* ART cubism

cucu(l) [kyky] *adj inv, inf* silly

cueillette [kœjɛt] *f sans pl* 1. (*action*) picking 2. (*récolte*) harvest

cueillir [kœjiʀ] *vt irr* 1. (*ramasser*) to pick 2. *inf* (*arrêter*) to nick 3. *inf* (*prendre au passage*) to snatch

cui-cui [kɥikɥi] *interj, m inv, inf* tweet-tweet

cuiller, cuillère [kɥijɛʀ] *f* 1. (*ustensile*) spoon; ~ **à café**, ~ **à thé** *Québec* teaspoon; ~ **à soupe**, ~ **à table** *Québec* tablespoon 2. (*contenu: d'huile*) spoonful ►**ne pas y aller avec le dos de la** ~ not to go in for half-measures; **être à ramasser à la petite** ~ *inf* to be half-dead

cuillerée, cuillérée [kɥijeʀe] *f* ~ **à café** teaspoonful; ~ **à soupe** tablespoonful

cuir [kɥiʀ] *m sans pl* leather ►~ **chevelu** scalp

cuirasse [kɥiʀas] *f* 1. MIL armour *Brit,* armor *Am* 2. HIST breastplate ►**le défaut de la** ~ the chink in the armour *Brit,* the chink in the armor *Am*

cuirassé [kɥiʀase] *m* battleship

cuirassé(e) [kɥiʀase] *adj* 1. (*revêtu d'une cuirasse*) wearing a breastplate; (*navire*) armoured *Brit,* armored *Am* 2. (*endurci*) **être ~ contre qc** to be hardened to sth

cuirassier [kɥiʀasje] *m* MIL **le 1er/2ème** ~ the 1st/2nd armoured [*o* armored *Am*] cavalry

cuire [kɥiʀ] *irr* I. *vt* 1. GASTR to cook; (*à la vapeur*) to steam; (*à l'étouffée*) to braise; (*au four: viande*) to roast; (*pain, gâteau*) to bake; (*à la poêle*) to fry; **faire ~ qc au bain-marie** to cook sth in a bain-marie; **faire ~ qc au four** to cook sth in the oven 2. TECH to fire ►**être dur à** ~ to be a hard nut to crack II. *vi* 1. GASTR (*viande, légumes*) to cook; (*pain, gâteau*) to bake 2. *inf* (*avoir très chaud*) to roast 3. (*brûler*) to burn

cuisant(e) [kɥizɑ̃, ɑ̃t] *adj* (*déception*) bitter

cuisine [kɥizin] *f* 1. (*pièce*) kitchen 2. (*art culinaire*) cookery; (*nourriture*) cooking; **livre de** ~ cookery book *Brit,* cookbook *Am;* **recette de** ~ recipe; **aimer la bonne** ~ to love good cooking; **faire la** ~ to cook

cuisiné(e) [kɥizine] *adj* **plat** ~ ready meal

cuisiner [kɥizine] <1> I. *vi* (*faire la cuisine*) to cook II. *vt* 1. (*préparer des plats*) to cook 2. *inf* (*interroger*) to grill

cuisinier, -ière [kɥizinje, -jɛʀ] *m, f* cook

cuisinière [kɥizinjɛʀ] *f* cooker

cuissardes [kɥisaʀd] *fpl* (*de pêcheur*) waders; (*de femme*) thigh boots

cuisse [kɥis] *f* 1. ANAT thigh 2. GASTR leg

cuissettes [kɥisɛt] *fpl Suisse* (*culottes courtes de sport sans poche ni braguette*) cycling shorts

cuisson [kɥisɔ̃] *m* 1. *sans pl* GASTR cooking; **et la ~: bien cuit, à point, saignant?** how would you like it cooked? Well done, medium, rare? 2. (*durée*) cooking time 3. *sans pl* TECH firing

cuistot [kɥisto] *m inf* cook

cuit(e) [kɥi, kɥit] I. *part passé de* **cuire** II. *adj* 1. GASTR cooked; **ne pas être assez** ~ to be undercooked; **être trop** ~ to be overcooked; **une baguette bien ~e** a well-baked baguette

2. TECH fired; **terre ~e** terracotta ►**c'est** ~ *inf* so much for that!; **c'est du tout** ~ *inf* it's as good as done; **être** ~ *inf* to be done for
cuite [kɥit] *f inf* **tenir une sacrée** ~ to be legless; **prendre une** ~ to get plastered
cuiter [kɥite] <1> *vpr inf* **se** ~ to get plastered
cuivre [kɥivʀ] *m* **1.** (*métal et ustensiles*) copper **2.** *pl* MUS **les ~s** the brass
cuivré(e) [kɥivʀe] *adj* **1.** (*rougeâtre*) coppery **2.** (*sonore*) sonorous
cul [ky] *m sans pl, inf* arse *Brit,* ass *Am* ►**s'entendre comme** ~ **et chemise** *inf* to be as thick as thieves; **coûter la peau du** ~ *inf* to cost an arm and a leg; **boire** ~ **sec** *inf* to down one's drink in one gulp
culasse [kylas] *f* **1.** AUTO (*d'un moteur*) cylinder head **2.** (*partie du canon: d'un fusil*) breech
culbute [kylbyt] *f* **1.** (*galipette*) **faire une** ~ to turn a somersault **2.** (*chute*) **faire des ~s dans l'escalier** to topple down the stairs
culbuter [kylbyte] <1> **I.** *vi* (*tomber*) to tumble **II.** *vt* (*faire tomber*) to knock over
cul-de-jatte [kydʒat] <culs-de-jatte> *mf* legless person **cul-de-sac** [kydsak] <culs-de-sac> *m* cul-de-sac
culinaire [kylinɛʀ] *adj* **art** ~ art of cooking
culminant(e) [kylminɑ̃, ɑ̃t] *adj* **1.** (*point d'une montagne*) highest **2.** *fig* **point** ~ **de qc** the peak of sth
culot [kylo] *m* **1.** (*fond: d'une ampoule, d'un obus*) base **2.** *inf* (*assurance*) nerve; **avoir du** ~ to have nerve; **avoir un sacré** ~ to have a lot of nerve; **avoir le** ~ **de** +*infin* to have the nerve to +*infin*
culotte [kylɔt] *f* **1.** (*slip*) knickers *Brit,* panties *pl Am* **2.** (*short*) shorts *pl* **3.** SPORT trousers; **~(s) de golf** plus fours *pl;* **~(s) de cheval** riding breeches; *fig* fat thighs
culotté(e) [kylɔte] *adj inf* **1.** (*effronté*) cheeky *Brit,* sassy *Am* **2.** (*audacieux*) daring
culpabiliser [kylpabilize] <1> **I.** *vt* to make feel guilty **II.** *vi* to feel guilty **III.** *vpr* **se** ~ to make oneself feel guilty
culpabilité [kylpabilite] *f sans pl* guilt
culte [kylt] *m* **1.** *sans pl* (*vénération*) cult **2.** *sans pl* (*cérémonie chrétienne*) worship; (*païenne*) cult; (*religion*) religion **3.** (*office protestant*) service **4.** *fig* **vouer un** ~ **à qn** to worship sb; **avoir le** ~ **de l'argent** to worship money; ~ **de la personnalité** cult of personality
cul-terreux [kyteʀø] <culs-terreux> *m péj* yokel, hick *Am*
cultivable [kyltivabl] *adj* arable
cultivateur, -trice [kyltivatœʀ, -tʀis] *m, f* farmer
cultivé(e) [kyltive] *adj* cultivated
cultiver [kyltive] <1> **I.** *vt* **1.** AGR (*terres*) to farm; (*blé, fruits*) to grow; **des terrains cultivés** farmland; **des plantes cultivées** cultivated plants **2.** (*exercer: mémoire*) to exercise; (*don*) to cultivate; ~ **son esprit** to improve one's mind **3.** (*entretenir: relation*) to cultivate; (*langue*) to keep up **II.** *vpr* **se** ~ **en faisant qc** to improve oneself doing sth
culture [kyltyʀ] *f* **1.** *sans pl* (*agriculture*) farming; ~ **de la vigne** wine growing **2.** *pl* (*terres cultivées*) fields **3.** BIO culture **4.** *sans pl* (*savoir*) learning; (*connaissances spécialisées*) culture; ~ **générale** general knowledge **5.** (*civilisation*) culture **6.** SPORT ~ **physique** exercises
Culture [kyltyʀ] *f* **ministre de la** ~ Minister of Culture
culturel(le) [kyltyʀɛl] *adj* cultural
culturisme [kyltyʀism] *m sans pl* bodybuilding
cumin [kymɛ̃] *m* cumin
cumul [kymyl] *m sans pl* ~ **de mandats** holding of several offices
cumuler [kymyle] <1> *vt* (*accumuler*) to accumulate; ~ **des mandats** to hold several offices concurrently
cupidité [kypidite] *f sans pl, soutenu* greed; **la** ~ **de son regard** his greedy look
curatif, -ive [kyʀatif, -iv] *adj* curative
cure [kyʀ] *f* treatment; ~ **de désintoxication** detoxification course; ~ **thermale** spa cure
curé [kyʀe] *m* priest; ~ **de campagne** country priest
cure-dent [kyʀdɑ̃] <cure-dents> *m* toothpick
curer [kyʀe] <1> **I.** *vt* to clean out **II.** *vpr* **se** ~ **les ongles** to clean one's nails
curieusement [kyʀjøzmɑ̃] *adv* curiously
curieux, -euse [kyʀjø, -jøz] **I.** *adj* **1.** (*indiscret, étrange*) curious; **ce qui est ~, c'est que ..., chose curieuse, ...** the odd thing is, ... **2.** (*intéressé*) **être** ~ **de qc** to be keen on sth; **être** ~ **de faire qc** to be keen on doing sth; **être** ~ **d'apprendre qc** to be keen to learn sth; **être** ~ **de savoir** to be interested in knowing **II.** *m, f* **1.** *sans pl* (*indiscret*) inquisitive person; **c'est un** ~ he's so inquisitive **2.** *mpl* (*badauds*) onlookers; **se protéger des** ~ to avoid the eyes of onlookers
curiosité [kyʀjozite] *f* curiosity
curiste [kyʀist] *mf* patient having spa treatment
curriculum (vitae) [kyʀikylɔm(vite)] *m inv* curriculum vitae
curry [kyʀi] *m sans pl* curry
curseur [kyʀsœʀ] *m* cursor
cursus [kyʀsys] *m* UNIV (degree) course
cutané(e) [kytane] *adj* **affection/maladie ~e** skin infection/disease
cuti [kyti] *f inf abr de* **cutiréaction** ►**virer sa** ~ *inf* to make a complete turn round [*o* turnaround *Am*]
cutiréaction [kytiʀeaksjɔ̃] *f* skin test (*for tuberculosis*)
cutter [kœtœʀ, kytɛʀ] *m* cutter
cuve [kyv] *f* **1.** (*pour vin*) vat; ~ **à vin** wine vat **2.** (*pour pétrole, eau*) tank

cuvée [kyve] *f* vintage

cuver [kyve] <1> **I.** *vi* to ferment **II.** *vt* ~ **son vin** *inf* to sleep it off

cuvette [kyvɛt] *f* **1.** (*récipient*) bowl **2.** (*partie creuse: d'un évier*) basin **3.** GEO basin

CV **1.** *abr de* **cheval fiscal** **2.** *abr de* **curriculum vitae**

cyanure [sjanyʀ] *m* cyanide

cyberboutique [sibɛʀbutik] *f* cybershop

cybercafé [sibɛʀkafe] *m* cybercafé

cyberespace [sibɛʀɛspas] *m* cyberspace

cybernaute [sibɛʀnot] *mf* INFOR cybernaut

cybernétique [sibɛʀnetik] *f* cybernetics

cybersexe [sibɛʀsɛks] *m* INFOR cybersex

cyclable [siklabl] *adj v.* **piste**

cyclamen [siklamɛn] *m* cyclamen

cycle [sikl] *m* **1.** BIO, MED, ASTR, ECON cycle **2.** ECOLE **premier** ~ years 7 to 10 *Brit,* middle school *Am;* **deuxième** ~ years 11 to 13 *Brit,* high school *Am;* ~ **d'orientation** transitional cycle (*leading to the choice of candidate's baccalauréat*) **3.** UNIV **premier** ~ first two years (*leading to DEUG or equivalent*)*;* **deuxième** ~ final year (*leading to the licence*)*;* **troisième** ~ postgraduate study

cyclique [siklik] *adj* cyclic

cyclisme [siklism] *m sans pl* cycling

cycliste [siklist] **I.** *adj* **course** ~ cycle race; **coureur** ~ racing cyclist **II.** *mf* cyclist **III.** *m* cycle shorts *pl*

cyclocross, **cyclo-cross** [siklokʀɔs] *m* cyclocross

cyclomoteur [siklomɔtœʀ] *m* scooter

cyclomotoriste [siklomɔtɔʀist] *mf* scooter rider

cyclone [siklon] *m* **1.** (*tempête*) hurricane **2.** METEO cyclone

cyclope [siklɔp] *m* cyclops

cyclotourisme [siklotuʀism] *m sans pl* bicycle touring, cycling holidays *pl*

cygne [siɲ] *m* swan

cylindre [silɛ̃dʀ] *m* cylinder; **une quatre/six** ~**s** *inf* a four/six cylinder (engine)

cylindrée [silɛ̃dʀe] *f* **1.** *sans pl* (*volume*) capacity **2.** (*voiture*) **petite** ~ small engine; **une grosse** ~ (*moto*) high-powered bike

cylindrique [silɛ̃dʀik] *adj* cylindrical

cymbale [sɛ̃bal] *f sans pl* MUS cymbal

cynique [sinik] **I.** *adj* **1.** (*brutal*) cynical **2.** PHILOS cynic **II.** *mf a.* PHILOS cynic

cynisme [sinism] *m a.* PHILOS cynicism; **avec** ~ cynically

cyprès [sipʀɛ] *m* cypress

cypriote [sipʀijɔt] *adj* Cypriot

Cypriote [sipʀijɔt] *mf* Cypriot

D

D

D, d [de] *m inv* D, d; ~ **comme Désiré** d as in David *Brit,* d as in Dog *Am;* (*on telephone*) d for David *Brit,* d for Dog *Am*

d' *v.* **de**

d'abord [dabɔʀ] *v.* **abord**

d'accord [dakɔʀ] *v.* **accord**

dactylo [daktilo] **I.** *mf* typist **II.** *f abr de* **dactylographie: apprendre la** ~ to learn to type; **cours de** ~ typing lessons

dactylographe [daktilɔgʀaf] *m Québec* (*machine à écrire*) typewriter

dactylographié(**e**) [daktilɔgʀafje] *adj* typewritten

dactylographier [daktilɔgʀafje] <1> *vt* (*lettre, texte*) to type; **un C.V. dactylographié** a typewritten CV

dada¹ [dada] *m* **1.** *enfantin* (*cheval*) horsey **2.** *inf* (*marotte, manie*) hobbyhorse; **avoir un** ~ to have a bee in one's bonnet

dada² [dada] *adj inv* ART, LIT Dada; **le mouvement** ~ Dadaism

dadais [dadɛ] *m* **grand** ~ great lump

dague [dag] *f* **1.** (*poignard*) dagger **2.** (*bois, défense: d'un cerf*) spike; (*d'un sanglier*) tusk

dahlia [dalja] *m* dahlia

daigner [deɲe] <1> *vt* ~ +*infin* to deign to +*infin*

daim [dɛ̃] *m* **1.** ZOOL deer; (*mâle*) buck **2.** (*cuir*) suede

Dakota-du-Nord [dakɔtadynɔːʀ] *m* **le** ~ North Dakota

Dakota-du-Sud [dakɔtadysyd] *m* **le** ~ South Dakota

dallage [dalaʒ] *m* paving; ~ **de marbre** marble pavement

dalle [dal] *f* (*plaque*) slab ►**avoir la** ~ *inf* to be ravenous; **que** ~**!** *inf* absolutely nothing, not a thing, zilch *Am;* **je**(**n'**)**y comprenais que** ~ *inf* I couldn't understand a damn thing; **on** (**n'**)**y voyait que** ~ *inf* we couldn't see a (damn) thing

dallé(**e**) [dale] *adj* paved

dam [dɑ̃, dam] *m* **au grand** ~ **de qn** *soutenu* to the detriment of sb

Damas [damɑːs] Damascus

dame [dam] **I.** *f* **1.** (*femme*) lady; **grande** ~ great lady; **la première** ~ **de France** the First Lady of France **2.** *pl* (*jeu*) draughts *Brit,* checkers *Am* **3.** JEUX queen; ~ **de trèfle** queen of clubs **II.** *interj inf* ~**!** my word!

damer [dame] <1> *vt* **1.** (*tasser: terre*) to ram down; (*neige*) to pack down; ~ **une piste de ski** to piste down a ski slope *Brit,* to tread down a ski slope *Am* **2.** JEUX (*aux échecs*) to queen; (*aux dames*) to crown ►~ **le pion à qn** to thwart sb

damier [damje] *m* **1.** JEUX draughtsboard *Brit,* checkerboard *Am* **2.** (*dessin*) check; **une nappe à** ~**, blanche et rouge** a red and white checkered tablecloth

damnation [danasjɔ̃] *f sans pl* damnation

damné(e) [dane] **I.** *adj antéposé, inf* damned **II.** *m(f)* damned man, woman *m, f;* **les ~s** the damned

dandiner [dɑ̃dine] <1> *vpr* **se ~** to waddle

Danemark [danmaʀk] *m* **le ~** Denmark

danger [dɑ̃ʒe] *m* danger; **les ~s de la route** road hazards; **pas de ~!** no way!; **attention ~!** danger!; **~ de mort!** risk of death!; **courir un ~** to run a risk; **mettre qc en ~** to put sth in danger ▶**un** (**vrai**) **~** <u>**public**</u> *inf* a public menace

dangereusement [dɑ̃ʒʀøzmɑ̃] *adv* dangerously

dangereux, -euse [dɑ̃ʒʀø, -øz] *adj* dangerous; **zone dangereuse** danger zone

danois [danwa] *m* Danish; *v. a.* **français**

danois(e) [danwa, waz] *adj* Danish

Danois(e) [danwa, waz] *m(f)* Dane

dans [dɑ̃] *prep* **1.** (*à l'intérieur de*) in; **jouer ~ la cour** to play in the playground **2.** (*à travers*) through; (*dedans*) in; **regarder ~ une longue vue** to look through a telescope; **regarder ~ un miroir** to look in a mirror; **rentrer ~ un arbre** to run into a tree **3.** (*contenant*) **boire ~ un verre** to drink from a glass **4.** (*futur, dans un délai de, état, manière, cause*) in; **~ une heure** in an hour; **~ combien de temps?** when?; **~ les délais** on schedule; **~ ces conditions** in that case; **travailler ~ les ordinateurs** to work in computers **5.** (*dans le courant de*) during **6.** (*environ*) around; **peser ~ les 60 kilos** to weigh around 60 kilos

dansant(e) [dɑ̃sɑ̃, ɑ̃t] *adj* (*mélodie*) skipping; (*rythme, reflet, lueur*) dancing; **soirée ~e** dance

danse [dɑ̃s] *f* dance ▶<u>**mener**</u> **la ~** to run the show

danser [dɑ̃se] <1> *vt, vi* to dance

danseur, -euse [dɑ̃sœʀ, -øz] *m, f* dancer; **~ étoile** principal (dancer), prima ballerina *m, f*

Danube [danyb] *m* **le ~** the Danube

dard [daʀ] *m* (*organe*) sting

dare-dare [daʀdaʀ] *adv inf* at the double *Brit,* on the double *Am*

darwinisme [daʀwinism] *m* Darwinism

DASS [das] *f abr de* **Direction d'action sanitaire et sociale** ≈ Social Services (*State organization dealing with child welfare*)

date [dat] *f* date; **~ limite d'envoi** last posting date; **à quelle ~?** on what date?; **amitié de longue ~** long-standing friendship; **en ~ du 10 mai** dated 10 May; **les grandes ~s de l'Histoire** the great dates in History

dater [date] <1> **I.** *vt* to date; **être daté du ...** to be dated ... **II.** *vi* **1.** (*remonter à*) **~ du XIVème siècle** (*objet, maison*) to date from the fourteenth century; **~ du mois dernier** (*changement, rencontre*) to date back to last month; **cette décision date de quelques minutes** this decision was made a few minutes ago; **à ~ d'aujourd'hui** (as) from today; **~ dans la vie de qn** to be a big event is sb's life **2.** (*être démodé*) to date ▶**ne pas ~ d'**<u>**hier**</u> to go back a long way

datif [datif] *m* dative

datte [dat] *f* date

dattier [datje] *m* date palm

dauphin [dofɛ̃] *m* ZOOL dolphin

dauphinois(e) [dofinwa, waz] *adj* from the Dauphiné; **gratin ~** gratin dauphinois (*potato slices baked in egg and milk, topped with grilled cheese*)

daurade [dɔʀad] *f* ZOOL sea bream

davantage [davɑ̃taʒ] *adv* **1.** (*plus: gagner, travailler, manger*) more; (**bien**) **~ de ...** a lot more of ... **2.** (*plus longtemps*) any longer

DCA [desea] *f abr de* **défense contre avions** anti-aircraft defence *Brit,* anti-aircraft defense *Am*

de[1] [də, dy, de] <d', de la, du, des> *prep* **1.** (*point de départ*) from; **~ ... à ...** from ... to ... **2.** (*origine*) from; **venir ~ Paris/d'Angleterre** to be from Paris/England; **le vin d'Italie** Italian wine; **tu es d'où?** where are you from?; **le train ~ Paris** (*provenance*) the train from Paris; (*destination*) the train to Paris **3.** (*appartenance, partie*) of; **la femme d'Antoine** Antoine's wife; **la majorité des Français** the majority of French people **4.** (*matière*) **~ bois/verre** wooden/glass **5.** (*spécificité*) **roue ~ secours** spare tyre *Brit,* spare tire *Am* **6.** (*contenu*) **un sac ~ pommes de terre** a bag of potatos; **combien ~ kilos?** how many kilos?; **un billet ~ cent euros** a hundred euros note; **une jeune fille ~ 20 ans** a twenty-year old girl; **avancer/reculer ~ 3 pas** to move 3 steps forward/back; **gagner 30 euros ~ l'heure** to earn 30 euros an hour **7.** (*qualification*) **cet idiot ~ Durand** that idiot Durand; **chienne ~ vie!** life's a bitch! **8.** (*qualité*) **ce film est d'un ennui/d'un triste!** this film is so boring/so sad **9.** (*particule nobiliaire*) de; **le général ~ Gaulle** General de Gaulle **10.** (*agent, temporel*) by; **~ quoi ...?** by what?; **~ qui?** who by?; **~ nuit** by night; **ne rien faire ~ la journée** to do nothing all day; **~ temps en temps** from time to time; **~ loin en loin** every now and then **11.** (*manière*) **~ mémoire** from memory **12.** (*moyen*) with; **faire signe ~ la main** to wave **13.** (*introduction d'un complément*) **c'est à toi ~ jouer** it's up to you now; **j'évite ~ sortir de la maison** I avoid leaving the house

de[2] [də, dy, de] <d', de la, du, des> *art partitif, parfois non traduit* **du vin/~ la bière/des gâteaux** (some) wine/beer/cakes; **il ne boit pas ~ vin/d'eau** he doesn't drink wine/water

dé[1] [de] *m* **1.** (*jeu*) die; **jeter les ~s** to throw the dice; **jouer aux ~s** to play dice **2.** (*cube*) **couper qc en ~s** to dice sth ▶**les ~s sont** <u>**jetés**</u> the die is cast

dé[2] [de] *m* **~ à coudre** thimble

DEA [deøa] *m abr de* **diplôme d'études**

approfondies *diploma taken before PhD*

dealer [dilœʀ] *m inf* dealer

déambuler [deɑ̃byle] <1> *vi* to stroll

débâcle [debɑkl] *f* **1.** (*déroute*) debacle; ~ **électorale** electoral debacle **2.** (*fonte des glaces*) the break-up (of the ice)

déballage [debalaʒ] *m* **1.** (*opp: emballage: d'un paquet*) unpacking **2.** (*étalage: de marchandises, d'objets*) display **3.** *inf* (*désordre*) jumble **4.** *péj, inf* (*divulgations*) outpouring

déballer [debale] <1> *vt* **1.** (*sortir*) to unpack **2.** *inf* (*raconter: secrets*) come out with; **il voulait ~ sa science** he wanted to pour out his wisdom

débandade [debɑ̃dad] *f a.* MIL rout; **ça a été la ~ générale** there was general panic

débander [debɑ̃de] <1> **I.** *vt* **1.** MED **~ le bras à qn** to unbandage sb's arm **2.** (*enlever le bandeau*) **~ les yeux à qn** to take the blindfold off sb **II.** *vi inf* to go soft

débarbouiller [debaʀbuje] <1> **I.** *vt* **~ qn** to clean sb up (quickly) **II.** *vpr* **se ~** to clean oneself up (quickly)

débarbouillette [debaʀbujɛt] *f Québec* (*gant de toilette*) facecloth *Brit,* washcloth *Am*

débarcadère [debaʀkadɛʀ] *m* landing stage

débardeur [debaʀdœʀ] *m* **1.** (*pull sans bras*) slipover **2.** (*t-shirt sans bras*) tank top **3.** (*ouvrier*) docker

débarquement [debaʀkəmɑ̃] *m* **1.** (*opp: embarquement: des marchandises*) unloading; (*des voyageurs*) landing **2.** (*descente: des troupes*) landing

débarquer [debaʀke] <1> **I.** *vt* NAUT (*marchandises*) to unload; (*passagers*) to land **II.** *vi* **1.** (*opp: embarquer: passager*) to land; NAUT to disembark; (*troupes*) to land **2.** *inf* (*arriver*) **~ chez qn** to turn up at sb's place **3.** *inf* (*ne pas être au courant*) to have no idea what's going on

débarras [debaʀɑ] *m* junk room ►**bon ~!** good riddance!

débarrasser [debaʀɑse] <1> **I.** *vt* (*pièce, grenier*) to clear out; (*table*) to clear; **~ qn de son manteau** to take sb's coat **II.** *vpr* **1.** (*ôter*) **se ~ de son manteau** to take off one's coat **2.** (*donner ou vendre*) **se ~ de vieux livres** to get rid of old books **3.** (*liquider*) **se ~ d'une affaire** to finish a matter **4.** (*éloigner*) **se ~ de qn** to get rid of sb

débat [deba] *m* **1.** (*discussion*) discussion **2.** (*discussion entre deux candidats*) debate **3.** JUR proceedings, hearing

débatteur [debatœʀ] *m* debater

débattre [debatʀ] *irr* **I.** *vt* to discuss; (*de façon formelle*) to debate ►**à ~** negotiable; **prix à ~** price negotiable **II.** *vi* **~ de qc** to discuss sth **III.** *vpr* **se ~** to struggle; **se ~ contre qn** to struggle with sb

débauche [deboʃ] *f* **1.** (*vice*) debauchery **2.** (*abondance, excès*) abundance

débauché(**e**) [deboʃe] *m(f)* debauchee

débaucher [deboʃe] <1> **I.** *vt* **1.** (*détourner d'un travail*) to lure away **2.** (*licencier*) to lay off **II.** *vpr* **se ~** to take to a life of debauchery

débile [debil] **I.** *adj* **1.** *inf* (*stupide*) crazy **2.** (*atteint de débilité*) feeble-minded **3.** (*frêle: corps*) feeble; (*enfant*) sickly; (*santé*) poor **II.** *mf* **1.** MED person with a weak constitution; **~ mental** feeble-minded person **2.** *péj, inf* (*imbécile*) cretin

débilité [debilite] *f* **1.** MED (*de l'esprit*) feebleness; (*du corps*) weakness **2.** *inf* (*stupidité*) idiocy

débiner [debine] <1> **I.** *vt inf* (*dénigrer*) **~ qn** to run sb down; **~ son collègue auprès du patron** to run down [*o* rubbish] a colleague in front of the boss **II.** *vpr inf* **se ~** to clear off

débit [debi] *m* **1.** COM turnover; **avoir du ~** to have a good turnover **2.** (*écoulement: d'un tuyau, d'une rivière*) rate of flow **3.** (*élocution*) delivery **4.** FIN debit; **le ~ et le crédit** debit and credit

débiter [debite] <1> *vt* **1.** FIN **~ un compte de 100 euros** to debit 100 euros from an account **2.** (*vendre*) to sell **3.** *péj* (*dire: discours, poème*) to spew out; (*banalités, sottises*) to come out with **4.** (*produire*) to produce **5.** (*écouler*) **le robinet/le tuyau débite une grande quantité d'eau** the tap/pipe has a high flow (rate) **6.** (*découper: tissu, viande*) to cut up; (*bois*) to saw up

débiteur, **-trice** [debitœʀ, -tʀis] **I.** *m, f* debtor; **être le ~ de qn** to be in debt to sb **II.** *adj* (*compte*) in debit; **un solde ~** a debit balance

déblais [deblɛ] *mpl* rubble *no pl*

déblatérer [deblateʀe] <5> *vi inf* **~ contre** [*o* **sur**] **qn/qc** to sound off about sb/sth

déblayer [debleje] <7> *vt* (*débarrasser*) to clear

déblocage [deblɔkaʒ] *m* **1.** TECH (*d'un frein, mécanisme*) releasing **2.** ECON (*du crédit, des prix*) relaxation **3.** (*issue: de la situation, d'une crise*) easing

débloquer [deblɔke] <1> **I.** *vt* **1.** TECH (*frein*) to release; (*écrou, vis*) to loosen; (*serrure, porte*) to unjam **2.** ECON (*crédit, marchandise*) to release **3.** (*trouver une issue à: crise*) to ease **II.** *vi inf* to be crazy **III.** *vpr* TECH **se ~** (*vis*) to loosen; (*serrure, porte*) to unjam

déboires [debwaʀ] *mpl* **1.** (*déceptions*) disappointments **2.** (*épreuves*) trials **3.** (*revers*) setbacks

déboisement [debwazmɑ̃] *m* deforestation

déboiser [debwaze] <1> *vt* to deforest; **région déboisée** deforested area

déboîter [debwate] <1> **I.** *vt* **1.** MED **sa chute lui a déboîté une épaule** he dislocated a shoulder when he fell **2.** (*démonter: porte*) to take off its hinges; (*tuyaux*) to disconnect **II.** *vpr* **se ~ une épaule** to dislocate a shoulder **III.** *vi* AUTO to pull out

débordant(**e**) [debɔʀdɑ̃, ɑ̃t] *adj* (*activité*) frenzied; (*enthousiasme, imagination, joie*) unbridled

débordé(**e**) [debɔʀde] *adj* **1.** (*submergé*)

overwhelmed; **être** ~ **d'occupations** to be overwhelmed with things to do **2.** (*détaché du bord: drap*) untucked; (*lit*) unmade

débordement [debɔRdəmɑ̃] *m* **1.** (*inondation: d'un liquide, d'une rivière*) overflowing **2.** (*flot, explosion*) ~ **de paroles** flood of words **3.** *gén pl* (*désordres*) uncontrolled behaviour *Brit,* uncontrolled behavior *Am* **4.** *pl* (*excès*) excess

déborder [debɔRde] <1> **I.** *vi* **1.** (*sortir: liquide, récipient*) to overflow; (*lac, rivière*) to burst its banks **2.** (*être plein de*) ~ **de joie** to be overflowing with joy **3.** (*dépasser les limites*) ~ **sur le terrain voisin** to grow out onto the neighbouring land *Brit,* to grow out onto the neighboring land *Am* **II.** *vt* **1.** (*dépasser*) ~ **les autres** to stand out from the others **2.** (*aller au-delà de*) **il déborda le temps imparti** he overran (his time) **3.** MIL, POL, SPORT **se laisser** ~ to be outflanked **4.** (*être dépassé*) **être débordé par qn/qc** to be overwhelmed by sb/sth **5.** (*tirer les draps*) ~ **un drap/une couverture** to pull a sheet/blanket out

débouché [debuʃe] *m* **1.** (*marché*) outlet **2.** *pl* (*perspectives*) prospects **3.** (*issue*) opening; (*d'une rue*) end

déboucher [debuʃe] <1> **I.** *vt* **1.** (*désobstruer: nez, lavabo*) to unclog **2.** (*ouvrir*) to open; (*bouteille*) to uncork; (*tube*) to take the top off **II.** *vpr* **se** ~ (*tuyau, lavabo, nez*) to unclog **III.** *vi* **1.** (*sortir: piéton*) to step out; (*véhicule*) to move out **2.** (*sortir à grande vitesse: véhicule*) to hurtle out **3.** (*aboutir*) ~ **dans/sur une rue** (*personne, voie*) to come out into/onto a road **4.** (*aboutir à*) ~ **sur qc** to lead onto sth

déboucler [debukle] <1> *vt* (*ceinture*) to undo

débouler [debule] <1> *vi fig, inf* (*faire irruption*) ~ **chez qn** to burst in on sb

débourser [debuRse] <1> *vt* to pay (out)

déboussolé(e) [debusɔle] *adj* **être** ~ to be totally lost

déboussoler [debusɔle] <1> *vt inf* ~ **qn** to disorientate sb

debout [d(ə)bu] *adj, adv inv* **1.** (*en position verticale: personne*) standing (up); **manger/voyager** ~ to stand while eating/travelling *Brit,* to stand while eating/traveling *Am;* **être** ~ to be standing up; **se mettre** ~ to get up; **poser qc** ~ to stand sth up (straight); **il tient** ~ **tout seul** (*personne*) he can stand up on his own; (*chose*) it stands up by itself **2.** (*levé*) **être/rester** ~ to be/stay up **3.** (*opp: malade, fatigué*) **je ne tiens plus** ~ I'm ready to drop **4.** (*en bon état*) **tenir encore** ~ (*construction, institution*) to be still standing ►**dormir** ~ **elle dort** ~ she's dead on her feet; **des histoires à dormir** ~ cock-and-bull stories; **tenir** ~ (*théorie, histoire*) to hold water

déboutonner [debutɔne] <1> **I.** *vt* (*chemise, gilet*) to unbutton; (*bouton*) to undo **II.** *vpr* **se** ~ (*personne*) to undo one's buttons; (*vêtement*) to come undone

débraillé(e) [debRɑje] *adj* (*personne, tenue, allure*) scruffy; (*manières*) slovenly

débrancher [debRɑ̃ʃe] <1> *vt* to unplug

débrayage [debRɛjaʒ] *m* **1.** AUTO letting the clutch out **2.** (*grève*) stoppage

débrayer [debReje] <7> *vi* **1.** AUTO to release the clutch **2.** (*faire grève*) to stop work

débridé(e) [debRide] *adj* unbridled

débris [debRi] *m* **1.** *gén pl* (*fragment*) bits; (*d'une explosion*) debris **2.** *pl* (*restes*) remains

débrouillard(e) [debRujaR, jaRd] **I.** *adj inf* resourceful; **être** ~ to know how to handle things **II.** *m(f) inf* shrewd operator

débrouillardise [debRujaRdiz] *f* resourcefulness

débrouiller [debRuje] <1> **I.** *vt* **1.** (*démêler: écheveau, fil*) to unravel **2.** (*élucider: affaire*) to sort out **3.** *inf* (*former*) ~ **qn** to show sb the basics **II.** *vpr inf* **se** ~ (*s'en sortir*) to manage; (*réussir*) to sort things out; **est-ce que tu te débrouilles?** are you managing all right?; **se** ~ **pour** +*infin* to fix it to +*infin*

débroussailler [debRusɑje] <1> *vt* **1.** (*défricher: terrain*) to clear **2.** (*éclaircir*) ~ **une affaire/un texte** to do the groundwork on a deal/a text

débusquer [debyske] <1> *vt* (*animal*) to drive out; (*personne*) to flush out

début [deby] *m* **1.** (*commencement*) beginning; **au** ~ **de qc** at the beginning of sth; **du** ~ **à la fin** from beginning to end **2.** *pl* (*tentatives, apparitions*) **les** ~**s de qn dans/à qc** sb's early days in sth; **il va faire ses** ~**s dans qc** he is going to make his debut in sth

débutant(e) [debytɑ̃, ɑ̃t] **I.** *adj* (*joueur, footballeur*) novice; **un pianiste** ~ a pianist making his debut **II.** *m(f)* **1.** (*élève, ouvrier*) beginner; SPORT novice **2.** (*acteur*) actor making his debut

débuter [debyte] <1> *vi, vt* to start; **elle va** ~ **au théâtre** she is going to make her debut on stage

deça [dəsa] **être en** ~ **de la vérité** to be short of the truth

déca [deka] *m inf abr de* **décaféiné** decaf

décacheter [dekaʃte] <3> *vt* (*lettre*) to open; (*document scellé*) to break open

décade [dekad] *f* **1.** (*dix jours*) ten-day period **2.** (*décennie*) decade

décadence [dekadɑ̃s] *f* **1.** (*état*) decadence **2.** (*déclin*) decline; **tomber en** ~ to go into decline

décadent(e) [dekadɑ̃, ɑ̃t] *adj* (*art, civilisation*) decadent

décaféiné [dekafeine] *m* decaffeinated

décalage [dekalaʒ] *m* **1.** (*action: d'un horaire*) pushing back **2.** (*écart temporel*) time difference; (*entre événements*) time lag; (*après un vol*) jet lag **3.** (*écart spatial*) staggering; **il y a un** ~ **entre ces deux maisons** one of the houses is set back from the other **4.** (*dif-

férence) discrepancy

décalcification [dekalsifikasjɔ̃] *f* MED decalcification

décalcomanie [dekalkɔmani] *f* transfer

décalé(e) [dekale] *adj* **1.** (*non aligné*) **la maison est ~e** the house is set back/forward **2.** (*bancal*) wobbly **3.** (*inattendu: humour, ton*) off-key **4.** (*déphasé*) **être ~** (*dans le temps*) out of sync; (*dans une société*) out of step

décaler [dekale] <1> **I.** *vt* **1.** (*avancer/retarder*) **~ qc d'un jour** to bring sth forward/put sth back a day **2.** (*déplacer: meuble, appareil*) to move forward/back; (*titre, paragraphe*) to shift **II.** *vpr* **se ~ en arrière/vers la droite** to move back/to the right

décalquer [dekalke] <1> *vt* **1.** (*copier*) **~ qc sur qc** to trace sth on to sth **2.** (*reporter*) **~ qc sur qc** to transfer sth on to sth

décamper [dekɑ̃pe] <1> *vi inf* to clear off

décanter [dekɑ̃te] <1> **I.** *vt* (*liquide, vin*) to allow to settle **II.** *vi* (*liquide, vin*) to settle **III.** *vpr* **se ~** (*liquide*) to settle; (*idées, réflexions*) to get clearer; (*choses, situation*) to settle down

décapant [dekapɑ̃] *m* **1.** (*pour métal*) abrasive **2.** (*pour peinture*) stripper

décapant(e) [dekapɑ̃, ɑ̃t] *adj* **1.** (*abrasif: produit*) stripping; (*pouvoir*) abrasive **2.** (*sans complaisance: article, humour*) caustic

décaper [dekape] <1> *vt* (*métal*) to clean; (*bois, meuble*) to strip

décapiter [dekapite] <1> *vt* **1.** (*étêter: condamné*) to behead; (*fleur*) to take the head off **2.** *fig* (*parti, réseau*) to leave without a leader

décapotable [dekapɔtabl] **I.** *adj* convertible **II.** *f* convertible

décapsuler [dekapsyle] <1> *vt* (*bouteille*) to take the top off

décapsuleur [dekapsylœʀ] *m* bottle opener

décarcasser [dekaʀkase] <1> *vpr inf* **se ~ pour** +*infin* to kill oneself to +*infin*

décathlon [dekatlɔ̃] *m* decathlon

décauser [dekoze] <1> *vt Belgique* (*dire du mal de*) to be nasty about

décédé(e) [desede] *adj* deceased

décéder [desede] <5> *vi être form* to pass away

déceler [des(ə)le] <4> *vt* **1.** (*découvrir*) to detect; (*cause, raison, intrigue*) to discover; (*sentiment, fatigue*) to discern **2.** (*être l'indice de*) to reveal

décembre [desɑ̃bʀ] *m* December; *v. a.* **août**

décemment [desamɑ̃] *adv* **1.** (*s'exprimer, se comporter*) properly; (*s'habiller*) decently **2.** (*assez bien*) reasonably

décence [desɑ̃s] *f* decency; **choquer la ~** to offend against decency

décennal(e) [desenal, o] <-aux> *adj* **1.** (*de dix ans: contrat, garantie*) ten-year **2.** (*qui revient tous les dix ans: exposition, fête, prix*) ten-yearly

décennie [deseni] *f* decade

décent(e) [desɑ̃, ɑ̃t] *adj* decent

décentralisation [desɑ̃tʀalizasjɔ̃] *f* decentralization

décentraliser [desɑ̃tʀalize] <1> **I.** *vt* to decentralize **II.** *vpr* **se ~** to be decentralized

décentrer [desɑ̃tʀe] <1> **I.** *vt* to move off-centre *Brit,* to move off-center *Am* **II.** *vpr* **se ~** to shift off-centre *Brit,* to shift off-center *Am*

déception [desɛpsjɔ̃] *f* disappointment

décerner [desɛʀne] <1> *vt* to award

décès [desɛ] *m form* (*mort*) death

décevant(e) [des(ə)vɑ̃, ɑ̃t] *adj* disappointing; **se montrer/se révéler ~** to prove disappointing

décevoir [des(ə)vwaʀ] <12> *vt* to disappoint; **ça m'a déçu** it was a disappointment to me

déchaîné(e) [deʃene] *adj* (*passions, vent, mer*) raging; (*instincts*) unbridled; (*foule, enfant*) wild; **être ~ contre qn/qc** to be furious with sb

déchaînement [deʃɛnmɑ̃] *m* (*de la tempête, mer*) raging; (*de la haine, violence, des passions*) unleashing; (*attaque*) outburst

déchaîner [deʃene] <1> **I.** *vt* (*passions*) to unleash; (*enthousiasme, conflit, indignation*) to arouse **II.** *vpr* **se ~** to get into a rage; **se ~ contre qn/qc** to get in a rage against sb/sth

déchanter [deʃɑ̃te] <1> *vi inf* **il va ~** he will lose his illusions

décharge [deʃaʀʒ] *f* **1.** (*dépôt*) dump **2.** (*salve: de carabine*) shot; (*de plombs*) volley **3.** ELEC, JUR discharge; **recevoir une ~** to get a shock **4.** MED **~ d'adrénaline** rush of adrenalin

déchargé(e) [deʃaʀʒe] *adj* **arme ~e** empty gun

déchargement [deʃaʀʒəmɑ̃] *m* unloading

décharger [deʃaʀʒe] <2a> **I.** *vt* **1.** (*débarrasser de sa charge: voiture*) to unload **2.** (*enlever, débarquer: passagers*) to land **3.** (*libérer*) **~ qn d'un travail** to relieve sb of a job **4.** (*soulager*) to vent; **il veut ~ sa colère sur toi** he wants to vent his anger on you **5.** (*tirer*) **il allait ~ son révolver sur elle** he was going to fire (his revolver) on her **6.** ELEC, JUR to discharge **II.** *vpr* **1.** (*se libérer*) **se ~ du travail sur qn** to pass off work onto sb **2.** ELEC (*batterie*) **se ~** to go flat **III.** *vi inf* (*éjaculer*) to come

décharné(e) [deʃaʀne] *adj* emaciated

déchausser [deʃose] <1> **I.** *vt* (*skis*) to take off; **~ qn** to take sb's shoes off **II.** *vpr* **se ~ 1.** (*enlever ses chaussures*) **se ~** to take one's shoes off **2.** MED (*dent*) to come loose

dèche [dɛʃ] *f inf* utter poverty; **c'est la ~ complète** I'm flat broke

déchéance [deʃeɑ̃s] *f* **1.** (*déclin*) degeneration; (*d'une civilisation*) decline **2.** JUR (*d'un souverain*) deposition; **~ de l'autorité paternelle** loss of parental rights

déchet [deʃɛ] *m pl* (*ordures*) rubbish *Brit,* garbage *Am;* (*restes*) scraps; **~s biodégrad-**

ables/nucléaires/toxiques biodegradable/nuclear/toxic waste

déchetterie [deʃɛtʀi] *f* waste collection centre *Brit,* waste collection center *Am*

déchiffrer [deʃifʀe] <1> **I.** *vt* **1.** (*décrypter: message, code, hiéroglyphes*) to decipher **2.** MUS ~ **un morceau** to sight-read a piece **3.** (*déceler: intentions*) to work out; (*sentiments*) to make out **II.** *vi* MUS to sight-read

déchiqueté(e) [deʃikte] *adj* (*feuille*) jagged-edged; (*côte, sommet*) jagged

déchiqueter [deʃikte] <3> *vt* to tear to pieces; **mon chien a déchiqueté le steak en un clin d'œil** my dog tore into the steak in no time

déchirant(e) [deʃiʀɑ̃, ɑ̃t] *adj* heartrending

déchiré(e) [deʃiʀe] *adj* torn

déchirement [deʃiʀmɑ̃] *m* **1.** (*déchirure: d'un muscle, d'un tissu*) tearing **2.** (*souffrance*) heartache **3.** (*divisions*) splits

déchirer [deʃiʀe] <1> **I.** *vt* **1.** (*déchirer*) to tear; ~ **qc en morceaux** to tear sth up **2.** (*couper: enveloppe*) to tear (open) **3.** (*troubler: silence*) to tear through **4.** (*faire souffrir*) ~ **qn** to tear sb apart **5.** (*diviser: parti, pays*) to split **II.** *vpr* **1.** (*rompre*) **se** ~ (*sac*) to tear (open); (*vêtement*) to get torn; (*nuage*) to break up; (*cœur*) to break **2.** MED **se** ~ **un muscle** to tear a muscle **3.** (*se quereller*) **se** ~ to tear each other apart

déchirure [deʃiʀyʀ] *f* **1.** (*accroc: d'un vêtement*) tear **2.** MED ~ **ligamentaire/musculaire** torn ligament/muscle **3.** (*trouée: du ciel*) break

déchoir [deʃwaʀ] *vi irr* (*personne*) to demean oneself; ~ **de qc** to forfeit sth

déchu(e) [deʃy] *adj* **1.** (*souverain*) dethroned **2.** JUR **être** ~ **d'un droit** to forfeit a right **3.** REL fallen

déci [desi] *m Suisse* (*décilitre de vin*) decilitre (*of wine*) *Brit,* deciliter (*of wine*) *Am*

décibel [desibɛl] *m* decibel

décidé(e) [deside] *adj* (*air, personne*) decisive; **c'est ~, ...** it's (all) settled; **je suis ~ à partir** my mind's made up, I'm leaving

décidément [desidemɑ̃] *adv* **1.** (*après répétition d'une expérience désagréable*) well! **2.** (*après hésitation ou réflexion*) **oui, ~, c'est bien lui le meilleur!** yes, he's the best, definitely!

décider [deside] <1> **I.** *vt* **1.** (*prendre une décision*) to decide on; ~ **de** +*infin* to decide to +*infin* **2.** (*persuader*) ~ **qn à** +*infin* to convince sb to +*infin* **II.** *vi* ~ **de qc** to determine sth **III.** *vpr* **1.** (*être fixé*) **se** ~ (*chose, événement*) to be decided **2.** (*prendre une décision*) **se** ~ to decide; **se ~ à** +*infin* to make a decision to +*infin* **3.** METEO **va-t-il enfin se ~ à neiger?** will it end up snowing after all?

décigramme [desigʀam] *m* decigram

décilitre [desilitʀ] *m* decilitre *Brit,* deciliter *Am*

décimal(e) [desimal, o] <-aux> *adj* decimal; **le système ~** the decimal system; **3,14 est un nombre ~** 3.14 is a decimal number

décimer [desime] <1> *vt* to decimate

décimètre [desimɛtʀ] *m* **1.** (*mesure*) decimetre *Brit,* decimeter *Am* **2.** (*règle*) **double ~** ruler

décisif, -ive [desizif, -iv] *adj* (*moment, bataille*) critical; (*argument, preuve, ton*) decisive; (*intervention, rôle*) crucial

décision [desizjɔ̃] *f* **1.** (*choix*) decision; **prendre une ~** to make a decision **2.** (*fermeté*) decisiveness; **avoir l'esprit de ~** to be decisive

déclamation [deklamasjɔ̃] *f* declamation; *péj* ranting

déclamatoire [deklamatwaʀ] *adj* (*ton, style*) declamatory

déclamer [deklame] <1> *vt* (*poème, vers*) to declaim

déclaration [deklaʀasjɔ̃] *f* **1.** (*discours, témoignage*) statement **2.** (*propos*) declaration; ~ **des droits de l'homme et du citoyen** Declaration of the Rights of Man and of the Citizen **3.** (*aveu d'amour*) ~ **d'amour** declaration of love **4.** ADMIN (*enregistrement: d'un décès, changement de domicile*) registration **5.** (*formulaire*) ~ **d'accident** accident report; ~ **de sinistre** insurance claim

déclaré(e) [deklaʀe] *adj* (*socialiste, athée*) avowed; (*ennemi*) sworn

déclarer [deklaʀe] <1> **I.** *vt* **1.** (*annoncer*) ~ **que ...** to say that ...; **il va lui ~ son amour** he is going to declare his love to her; ~ **qn coupable** to find sb guilty; ~ **la guerre** to declare war **2.** (*enregistrer: employé, marchandise*) to declare; (*décès, naissance*) to register; (**vous n'avez**) **rien à ~?, vous avez quelque chose à ~?** (have you) anything to declare? **II.** *vpr* **1.** (*se manifester*) **se** ~ (*incendie, orage*) to break out; (*fièvre, maladie*) to set in **2.** (*se prononcer*) **se ~ pour/contre qn/qc** to declare oneself for/against sb/sth **3.** (*se dire*) **se ~ l'auteur du crime** to admit to having committed the crime **4.** (*faire une déclaration d'amour*) **se ~ à qn** to declare oneself to sb

déclassé(e) [deklase] *adj* **1.** (*pas dans l'ordre*) out of order **2.** (*dans une catégorie plus basse*) downgraded

déclenchement [deklɑ̃ʃmɑ̃] *m* (*d'un mécanisme*) activation; (*d'un conflit*) setting off; (*d'une offensive*) launch

déclencher [deklɑ̃ʃe] <1> **I.** *vt* **1.** TECH (*ressort*) to release; (*mécanisme*) to activate **2.** (*provoquer: conflit, réaction*) to set off; (*offensive*) to launch **II.** *vpr* **se** ~ (*mécanisme*) to be set off; (*attaque, grève*) to be launched

déclencheur [deklɑ̃ʃœʀ] *m* release; PHOT shutter release; ~ **à retardement** timed release

déclic [deklik] *m* **1.** (*mécanisme*) release mecanism **2.** (*bruit*) click ►**c'est/ça a été le ~** something went click (in my mind)

déclin [deklɛ̃] *m* (*des forces physiques et mentales*) decline; (*de la popularité*) falling off; (*du jour*) closing; (*du soleil*) setting

déclinaison [deklinɛzɔ̃] *f* **1.** LING declension **2.** ASTR declination

décliner [dekline] <1> **I.** *vt* **1.** (*refuser*) *a.* LING to decline **2.** (*dire*) to state **II.** *vi* **1.** (*baisser: jour*) to draw to a close; (*forces, prestige*) to decline **2.** ASTR to set **III.** *vpr* **se ~** LING to decline

décocher [dekɔʃe] <1> *vt* **~ une remarque/une réponse à qn** to fire off a comment/an answer at sb; **~ un regard/une œillade** to flash a look/a wink at sb

décoder [dekɔde] <1> *vt* (*message*) to decode

décodeur [dekɔdœʀ] *m* decoder

décoiffer [dekwafe] <1> **I.** *vt* **~ qn** to spoil sb's hair; **elle est toute décoiffée** her hair is in a mess **II.** *vi* **ça décoiffe** *inf* it makes you sit up

décoincer [dekwɛ̃se] <2> *vt* **1.** (*dégager: pied, doigt, tiroir, pièce*) to get loose; (*porte*) to unjam **2.** *inf* (*détendre*) **~ qn** to make sb less uptight

décolérer [dekɔleʀe] <5> *vi* **ne pas ~** to be constantly angry; **il ne décolère pas contre elle** he's still furious with her

décollage [dekɔlaʒ] *m* **1.** (*envol*) *a.* ECON take-off; **~ économique** economic lift-off **2.** (*décollement: d'un papier peint, timbre-poste*) removal

décoller [dekɔle] <1> **I.** *vt* (*timbre*) to unstick **II.** *vi* **1.** AVIAT, ECON to take off; **nous décollons à 13 h** take-off is at one o'clock *Brit,* takeoff is at one o'clock *Am* **2.** *inf* (*partir, sortir*) **ne pas ~ du lit** not to shift from bed; **ne pas ~ de devant la télé** to be glued to the TV; **ne pas ~ de chez qn** to refuse to clear out of sb's place **3.** *inf* (*maigrir*) to slim down **III.** *vpr* **se ~** (*timbre*) to peel off; (*carrelage*) to come off; (*rétine*) to become detached

décolleté [dekɔlte] *m* décolleté; **~ plongeant** plunging neckline

décolleté(e) [dekɔlte] *adj* **1.** (*échancré: vêtement*) low-cut **2.** (*dénudé: personne*) décolleté

décolonisation [dekɔlɔnizasjɔ̃] *f a. fig* decolonization

décoloniser [dekɔlɔnize] <1> *vt* (*pays, habitants*) to decolonize

décolorant [dekɔlɔʀɑ̃] *m* bleaching agent

décolorant(e) [dekɔlɔʀɑ̃, ɑ̃t] *adj* (*action, pouvoir*) bleaching; **produit ~** bleaching agent; **shampooing ~** peroxide shampoo

décoloration [dekɔlɔʀasjɔ̃] *f* decolorization; (*des cheveux*) bleaching; (*des rideaux, de la tapisserie, d'une matière*) fading

décoloré(e) [dekɔlɔʀe] *adj* (*cheveux, poils*) bleached; (*couleur*) washed-out; (*papier, affiches*) faded; (*lèvres*) pale

décolorer [dekɔlɔʀe] <1> **I.** *vt* **~ des tissus/vêtements avec qc** to take the colour out of cloth/clothes with sth *Brit,* to take the color out of cloth/clothes with sth *Am;* **~ des cheveux avec qc** to bleach hair with sth **II.** *vpr* **1.** (*perdre sa couleur*) **se ~** (*cheveux*) to lose their colour *Brit,* to lose its color *Am;* (*étoffe*) to fade **2.** (*enlever la couleur*) **se ~ les cheveux** to bleach one's hair

décombres [dekɔ̃bʀ] *mpl* rubble; *fig* ruins

décommander [dekɔmɑ̃de] <1> **I.** *vt* (*rendez-vous, réunion*) to call off; (*marchandise*) to cancel; **~ qn** to put sb off **II.** *vpr* **se ~** to cancel

décomplexé(e) [dekɔ̃plɛkse] *adj inf* laid-back

décomplexer [dekɔ̃plɛkse] <1> *vt inf* **~ qn** to make sb feel more laid-back

décomposé(e) [dekɔ̃poze] *adj* **1.** (*putréfié: substance organique*) rotting; (*cadavre*) decomposed **2.** (*altéré: visage, traits*) distorted

décomposer [dekɔ̃poze] <1> **I.** *vt* **1.** (*détailler, diviser*) *a.* CHIM, MAT, LING to break down; **~ un élément en ses composants** to break an element down into its components **2.** PHYS to resolve **3.** MAT to factorize **4.** LING to parse **5.** (*analyser: idée, problème, savoir*) to analyse *Brit,* to analyze *Am* **6.** (*altérer: substance*) to rot; (*morale*) to shake; (*visage, trait*) to unsettle **II.** *vpr* **1.** (*se diviser, se détailler*) **se ~ en qc** CHIM to break down into sth; PHYS, MAT to resolve into sth; MAT to factorize into sth; LING to be analysable as *Brit,* to be analyzable as *Am* **2.** (*pouvoir s'analyser*) **se ~ en qc** (*problème, idée, savoir*) to break down into sth **3.** (*s'altérer*) **se ~** (*substance organique*) to rot; (*cadavre*) to decompose; (*visage, traits*) to collapse; (*société*) to break down

décomposition [dekɔ̃pozisjɔ̃] *f* **1.** (*détail, chute*) *a.* CHIM breakdown **2.** PHYS, MAT resolution **3.** (*analyse: d'un problème, d'une difficulté*) analysis **4.** (*putréfaction: d'une substance organique*) rotting; (*d'un cadavre*) decomposition **5.** (*altération*) **la ~ de son visage** the crumpling of his/her face

décompresser [dekɔ̃pʀese] <1> *vi inf* to relax

décompression [dekɔ̃pʀesjɔ̃] *f* **1.** (*dilatation*) *a.* INFOR decompression; **soupape de ~** decompression valve **2.** *inf* (*détente*) relaxation

décomprimer [dekɔ̃pʀime] <1> *vt* TECH (*air*) to decompress

décompte [dekɔ̃t] *m* **1.** (*compte: des bulletins de vote*) counting; (*des points*) reckoning; **faire le ~ de qc** to reckon sth (up) **2.** (*facture*) statement **3.** (*déduction*) deduction

déconcentration [dekɔ̃sɑ̃tʀasjɔ̃] *f* ADMIN decentralization

déconcentré(e) [dekɔ̃sɑ̃tʀe] *adj* decentralized

déconcentrer [dekɔ̃sɑ̃tʀe] <1> **I.** *vt* **1.** ADMIN, ECON to decentralize **2.** (*dévier l'attention de qn*) **~ qn** to disturb sb's concentration; **cela m'a déconcentré de mon tra-**

vail that made my attention wander from my work **II.** *vpr* **se** ~ to lose one's concentration

déconcertant(e) [dekɔ̃sɛʀtɑ̃, ɑ̃t] *adj* disconcerting

déconcerter [dekɔ̃sɛʀte] <1> *vt* to disconcert

déconfit(e) [dekɔ̃fi, it] *adj* downcast

déconfiture [dekɔ̃fityʀ] *f* **1.** *inf* (*faillite*) collapse; **être en (pleine)** ~ (*entreprise, personne*) to be falling apart **2.** *inf* (*chute: d'un parti politique, de l'État, des valeurs morales*) collapse; (*d'une armée*) rout; **tourner à la** ~ (*projet*) to go awry **3.** JUR bankruptcy

décongeler [dekɔ̃ʒ(ə)le] <4> *vt, vi* to defrost

déconnecter [dekɔnɛkte] <1> **I.** *vt* **1.** ELEC, INFOR to disconnect **2.** (*séparer*) ~ **qn/qc du monde environnant** to cut sb/sth off from the world around them/it **II.** *vi inf* to take a break **III.** *vpr* **se** ~ **de son travail** get away from one's work

déconner [dekɔne] <1> *vi inf* **1.** (*dire des bêtises*) to talk (a load of) nonsense **2.** (*faire des bêtises*) to fool around **3.** (*être détraqué*) ~ **complètement** to be completely haywire; **déconne pas!** stop fooling around! ►**faut pas** ~**!** come off it!

déconseillé(e) [dekɔ̃seje] *adj* unadvisable

déconseiller [dekɔ̃seje] <1> *vt, vi* to advise; ~ **à un collègue de faire qc** to advise a friend against doing sth

déconsidérer [dekɔ̃sideʀe] <5> **I.** *vt* to discredit; **être complètement déconsidéré auprès de qn** to have completely lost sb's consideration **II.** *vpr* **se** ~ **auprès de qn** to completely lose sb's respect; **se** ~ **aux yeux de qn** to completely discredit oneself in sb's eyes

décontamination [dekɔ̃taminasjɔ̃] *f* decontamination

décontaminer [dekɔ̃tamine] <1> *vt* (*lieu, personne, rivière*) to decontaminate; INFOR (*disquettes*) to repair

décontenancer [dekɔ̃t(ə)nɑ̃se] <2> **I.** *vt* to put out of countenance **II.** *vpr* **se** ~ to lose one's composure

décontracté(e) [dekɔ̃tʀakte] **I.** *adj* **1.** (*détendu: partie du corps, personne*) relaxed **2.** *inf* (*sûr de soi*) laid-back; *péj* cocksure **3.** *inf* (*non guindé: atmosphère, situation, style, ton*) relaxed; (*tenue*) casual **II.** *adv inf* (*s'habiller*) casually; (*conduire*) in a relaxed way

décontracter [dekɔ̃tʀakte] <1> **I.** *vt* to relax **II.** *vpr* **se** ~ to relax

décontraction [dekɔ̃tʀaksjɔ̃] *f* **1.** (*détente: du corps, d'une personne*) relaxation **2.** (*désinvolture*) casualness; *péj* (rather) casual manner

décor [dekɔʀ] *m* **1.** (*agencement, art de la décoration*) decoration **2.** THEAT scenery; CINE set **3.** (*cadre*) scenery; (*arrière-plan*) setting; **dans un** ~ **de verdure** surrounded by greenery; **un** ~ **de hautes montagnes/de rocailles** in mountain/rocky scenery **4.** (*style*) decor; ~ **Empire/Louis XV** Empire/Louis XV decor ►**changer de** ~ THEAT to change the scenery; **envoyer qn dans le** ~ *inf* to push sb off the road; **planter le** ~ to set up the scenery

décorateur, -trice [dekɔʀatœʀ, -tʀis] *m, f* **1.** (*designer*) decorator; ~ **d'intérieurs** interior decorator **2.** CINE, THEAT designer

décoratif, -ive [dekɔʀatif, -iv] *adj* decorative; **motifs** ~**s** ornamental motifs

décoration [dekɔʀasjɔ̃] *f* **1.** (*fait de décorer, résultat, distinction*) decoration; ~**s de Noël** Christmas decorations **2.** (*art*) decorative art

décoré(e) [dekɔʀe] *adj* **1.** (*orné: lieu, plat*) decorated; (*vitrines*) dressed **2.** (*médaillé: personne*) decorated; (*sur ses habits*) wearing a decoration

décorer [dekɔʀe] <1> *vt* to decorate; ~ **une vitrine de qc** to dress a window with sth; ~ **qn d'une médaille** to decorate sb with a medal

décortiquer [dekɔʀtike] <1> *vt* **1.** (*enlever l'enveloppe: arbre, tige*) to take the bark off; (*noix, noisettes, graines*) to shell **2.** (*détailler: texte*) to dissect; (*affaire*) to examine from every angle

découcher [dekuʃe] <1> *vi* to spend the entire night out

découdre [dekudʀ] *irr* **I.** *vt* (*boutons*) to unsew; (*ourlet, doublure*) to unpick ►**être décidé** [*o* **prêt**] **à en** ~ **avec qn** to be ready to have it out with sb **II.** *vpr* **se** ~ to come unsewn

découler [dekule] <1> *vi* ~ **de qc** to ensue from sth; ~ **d'un droit** to follow from a right; **il découle de qc …** it follows from sth …; **il en découle qu'il a tort** it follows that he is wrong

découpage [dekupaʒ] *m* **1.** (*fait de trancher avec un couteau: d'un gâteau*) cutting (up); (*d'une viande*) (*par le boucher*) cutting up; (*pour servir*) carving; (*d'une volaille*) jointing **2.** (*fait de couper suivant un contour, tracé*) cutout **3.** ADMIN, POL division; ~ **électoral** drawing of electoral boundaries **4.** CINE (*d'un film*) division into scenes

découpe [dekup] *f* **1.** COUT inset **2.** TECH cutting up; (*avec une scie*) sawing up

découpé(e) [dekupe] *adj* (*côte, sommet, relief*) jagged; (*feuille*) jagged(-edged)

découper [dekupe] <1> **I.** *vt* **1.** (*trancher: gâteau*) to cut (up); (*volaille*) joint; (*tranche de saucisson*) to slice; ~ **la viande** (*boucher*) to cut the meat; (*serveur*) to carve the meat **2.** (*couper suivant un contour, tracé: tissu, moquette*) to cut out; ~ **un article dans qc** to cut out an article from sth **II.** *vpr* (*se profiler*) **se** ~ **dans/sur qc** to stand out against sth

découragé(e) [dekuʀaʒe] *adj* discouraged

décourageant(e) [dekuʀaʒɑ̃, ʒɑ̃t] *adj* discouraging; (*nouvelle, résultats, travail*) disheartening; **vous êtes** ~ you're so disheartening

découragement [dekuʀaʒmɑ̃] *m* discouragement

décourager [dekuʀaʒe] <2a> **I.** *vt* **1.** (*démoraliser, empêcher de faire*) to discourage **2.** (*dissuader*) ~ **qn de la création d'une entreprise** to put sb off starting up a business **II.** *vpr* **se** ~ to get discouraged

décousu [dekuzy] *m sans pl* disjointed/rambling nature

décousu(e) [dekuzy] *adj* **1.** COUT unsewn **2.** (*dépourvu de logique: conversation, récit, devoir*) disjointed; (*idées*) incoherent; (*style*) rambling

découvert [dekuvɛʀ] *m* **1.** FIN deficit; (*d'un compte*) overdraft; ~ **autorisé** authorized overdraft (facility); **je suis à** ~ I'm overdrawn **2.** MIL (*terrain*) exposed terrain ►**à** ~ FIN in deficit; (*compte*) overdrawn; (*ouvertement*) openly; MIL exposed

découvert(e) [dekuvɛʀ, ɛʀt] *adj* **1.** (*nu*) bare **2.** (*dégagé: lieu, zone*) open

découverte [dekuvɛʀt] *f* discovery; **faire la** ~ **de qc** to discover sth; **être à la** ~ **de qc** to be in search of sth; **partir à la** ~ to set out on a journey of discovery ►**c'est pas une** ~**!** *inf* tell me something I don't know!

découvrir [dekuvʀiʀ] <11> **I.** *vt* **1.** (*trouver, deviner, percer, déceler*) to discover; ~ **du pétrole** to strike oil; ~ **que qc est vrai** to find out that sth is true **2.** (*enlever la couverture, mettre à jour*) to uncover **3.** (*ouvrir*) ~ **une casserole** to take the lid off a saucepan **4.** (*enlever ce qui couvre*) to take the cover off; (*statue*) to unveil **5.** (*apercevoir: panorama*) to get a view of; (*personne*) to see **6.** (*laisser voir: jambes, épaules, ciel*) to reveal; (*racines, terre*) to uncover **7.** (*révéler*) ~ **un secret à son ami** to share a secret with a friend **II.** *vpr* **1.** (*enlever sa couverture*) **se** ~ (*au lit*) to push back the bedclothes; (*enlever son vêtement*) to remove one's clothing; (*enlever son chapeau*) to take one's hat off **2.** (*s'exposer aux attaques*) **se** ~ (*armée*) to expose itself; (*boxeur, escrimeur*) to leave oneself open **3.** (*se confier*) **se** ~ **à qn** to confide in sb; (*abattre son jeu*) to show one's hand **4.** (*apprendre*) **se** ~ **lui-même** to discover oneself; **se** ~ **des dons/un goût pour qc** to discover a gift/a taste for sth **5.** (*apparaître*) **se** ~ (*panorama, paysage*) to come into view; (*secret*) to come into the open; (*vérité*) to become known **6.** (*s'éclaircir*) **le ciel se découvre** the sky is clearing

décrasser [dekʀase] <1> **I.** *vt* **1.** (*nettoyer*) to clean; (*planchers, faitouts*) to scrub down **2.** (*laver: personne, mains, visage*) to wash; *fig* (*poumons*) to clean out **3.** (*dégrossir*) ~ **qn** to give sb a few tips; (*rendre moins ignorant*) to smarten sb up **II.** *vpr* **se** ~ **1.** (*se laver*) to have a wash **2.** *fig* to smarten up

décret [dekʀɛ] *m* POL decree; ~ **sur qc** decree on sth

décréter [dekʀete] <5> **I.** *vt* **1.** POL to decree; (*mesures*) to order; (*état d'urgence*) to declare **2.** *fig* ~ **que qc doit se faire** to decree that sth must be done **II.** *vpr* **qc/ça ne se décrète pas** sth/that can't be legislated (for)

décrié(e) [dekʀije] *adj* decried

décrire [dekʀiʀ] *vt irr* to describe

décrocher [dekʀɔʃe] <1> **I.** *vt* **1.** (*dépendre: linge, rideaux, tableau*) to take down; (*wagon*) to uncouple; (*laisse, sangle, volets*) to undo; ~ **le téléphone** (*pour répondre*) to pick up the phone; (*pour ne pas être dérangé*) to take the phone off the hook **2.** *inf* (*obtenir: prix*) to win; ~ **un poste** to get (oneself) a job **3.** SPORT (*concurrents, peloton*) to pull away from, to leave behind **II.** *vpr* **se** ~ (*personne, poisson*) to get off the hook; (*vêtement, tableau*) to come down **III.** *vi* **1.** (*au téléphone*) answer; **tu peux** ~**?** Can you get it? **2.** *inf* (*décompresser*) to take a break; (*se désintéresser*) to give up; (*arrêter le travail*) to call a halt; (*abandonner une activité, course*) to drop out; ~ **de qc** (*politique, cinéma*) to give up on sth; (*temporairement*) to break off from sth **3.** (*ne plus écouter*) to switch off **4.** (*se détacher: armée, troupes*) to pull back **5.** AVIAT (*avion*) to stall **6.** RADIO (*émetteur*) to break off

décroiser [dekʀwɑze] <1> *vt* (*jambes*) to uncross; (*bras*) to unfold; (*fils*) to untwist

décroissant(e) [dekʀwasɑ̃, ɑ̃t] *adj* (*intensité, vitesse*) decreasing; (*bruit*) fading; **à vitesse** ~**e** losing speed

décroître [dekʀwɑtʀ] *vi irr avoir o être* to decrease; (*jours*) to draw in; (*vitesse*) to go down

décrue [dekʀy] *f* (*des eaux*) fall

déçu(e) [desy] **I.** *part passé de* **décevoir** **II.** *adj* disappointed **III.** *m(f) souvent pl* **les** ~**s** the disillusioned

déculpabiliser [dekylpabilize] <1> *vt* (*action, situation*) to take the guilt out of; ~ **qn** to rid sb of guilt

décupler [dekyple] <1> *vi, vt* **1.** (*prix, quantité, valeur*) to increase tenfold **2.** *fig* (*forces, colère, vitalité*) to increase dramatically; **ses forces ont décuplé** she's grown ten times stronger

dédaignable [dedɛɲabl] *adj* **ce n'est pas** ~ it's not to be sniffed at

dédaigner [dedeɲe] <1> *vt* to despise; ~ **de** +*infin* not to deign to +*infin;* **ce n'est pas à** ~ it's not to be sniffed at; **ne pas** ~ **qc/de faire qc** not to be averse to sth/doing sth

dédaigneux, **-euse** [dedɛɲø, -øz] *adj* contemptuous ►**faire le/la** ~**(-euse)** to turn one's nose up

dédain [dedɛ̃] *m* contempt; **avec** ~ with contempt; ~ **de** [*o* **envers**] **qn/qc** contempt for sb/sth; **avoir du** ~ **pour qn/qc** to feel contempt for sb/sth; **manifester du** ~ **pour qn/qc** to show contempt for sb/sth

dédale [dedal(ə)] *m* **1.** (*de rues, chemins*) maze **2.** *fig* ~ **de pensées** tortuous thought process; ~ **de contradictions** maze of contra-

D

dictions

dedans [d(ə)dɑ̃] I. *adv* + *verbe de mouvement* in; + *verbe d'état* inside; **de** ~ from inside; **en** ~ (on the) inside; *fig* (deep) inside; **en ~ de lui-même, il réprouve cet acte** deep inside (himself) he condemns what was done ▸**mettre en plein** ~ to muddle up; **mettre qn** ~ *inf* to put sb inside; **rentrer** (**en plein**) ~ *inf* (*heurter en voiture*) to crash right into sb; (*heurter à pied*) to barge right into sb; **je vais lui rentrer** ~ *inf* I'm going to lay into him; **ils se sont rentrés** ~ they laid into each other II. *m sans pl* inside

dédicace [dedikas] *f* 1. (*sur une photo, un livre*) dedication; (*sur un monument*) inscription 2. (*consécration: d'une église, d'un temple*) dedication

dédicacer [dedikase] <2> *vt* ~ **un roman à qn** to dedicate a novel to sb

dédier [dedje] <1> *vt* ~ **une œuvre à qn** to dedicate a work to sb; ~ **sa vie à la recherche** to dedicate one's life to research

dédire [dediʀ] *vpr irr, soutenu* 1. (*contredire*) **se** ~ to go back on one's word 2. (*renier*) **se ~ de qc** to go back on sth

dédommagement [dedɔmaʒmɑ̃] *m* compensation

dédommager [dedɔmaʒe] <2a> I. *vt* ~ **une victime de qc** to compensate a victim for sth II. *vpr* **se ~ de qc** to make it up to oneself for sth

dédoublement [dedubləmɑ̃] *m* 1. (*d'une classe, d'un fil*) dividing into two; (*d'une autoroute*) building extra lanes; **le ~ des trains** laying on extra trains 2. PSYCH ~ **de la personnalité** dual personality

dédramatiser [dedʀamatize] <1> *vt* to take some of the drama out of

déductible [dedyktibl] *adj* FIN **être ~ des impôts** to be (tax-)deductible

déductif, **-ive** [dedyktif, -iv] *adj* deductive; **avoir un esprit** ~ to have a gift for deduction

déduction [dedyksjɔ̃] *f* deduction; ~ **d'impôt** tax deduction; **moins la ~ de 10%** less 10% deduction; **entrer en ~ de qc** to be deductible from sth

déduire [dedɥiʀ] *irr* I. *vt* 1. (*retrancher: acompte, frais*) to deduct 2. (*conclure*) to deduce; ~ **de qc qu'il a réussi** to conclude from sth that he's succeeded II. *vpr* **se ~ de qc** to be deductible from sth

déesse [deɛs] *f* goddess

défaillance [defajɑ̃s] *f* 1. (*faiblesse: d'une personne*) (*physique*) faint spell; (*morale*) weakness; (*intellectuelle*) lapse of memory 2. (*dysfonctionnement: d'un moteur, système*) failure; (*d'une loi*) deficiency 3. JUR (*d'un témoin*) failure to appear; (*d'un contractant*) default ▸**avoir une** ~ (*s'évanouir*) to faint; (*s'assoupir*) to feel faint; (*perdre la mémoire*) to have a lapse of memory; (*céder*) to have a moment of weakness; **tomber en** ~ to feel faint

défaillant(**e**) [defajɑ̃, jɑ̃t] *adj* 1. (*insuffisant: mémoire, volonté*) weak; (*forces, santé*) failing 2. (*affaibli: personne*) weak; (*voix*) faltering; (*main*) unsteady 3. (*absent: témoin*) defaulting; (*candidat*) failing to appear

défaillir [defajiʀ] *vi irr* (*capacités, forces, qualités, mémoire*) to fail; (*personne, courage*) to falter; ~ **de joie/de faim/d'angoisse** to be faint with joy/hunger/anxiety; **le cœur défaillant d'angoisse** her heart faint with anxiety; **sans** ~ without flinching

défaire [defɛʀ] *irr* I. *vt* 1. (*détacher*) to undo 2. (*enlever ce qui est fait*) to undo; (*ourlet, rangs d'un tricot*) to unpick; (*construction*) to take down; ~ **le lit** (*pour changer de drap*) to strip the bed; (*pour se coucher*) to pull back the bedclothes; (*mettre en désordre*) to mess up the bed 3. (*mettre en désordre*) to spoil 4. (*déballer*) to unpack 5. (*rompre: contrat*) to break; (*plan, projet*) to finish off; (*mariage*) to break up 6. (*battre: armée*) to defeat 7. (*débarrasser*) ~ **qn d'une habitude** to rid sb of a habit II. *vpr* 1. (*se détacher*) **se** ~ (*paquet, ourlet, bouton, lacets*) to come undone; (*coiffure*) to get messed up 2. *fig* **se** ~ (*amitié, relation*) to come to an end 3. (*se séparer*) **se ~ de qn/qc** to get rid of sb/sth

défait(**e**) [defɛ, defɛt] I. *part passé de* **défaire** II. *adj* (*mine, visage, air*) weary

défaite [defɛt] *f* defeat

défaitiste [defetist] I. *adj* defeatist II. *mf* defeatist; **esprit** ~ defeatist attitude

défaut [defo] *m* 1. (*travers*) fault 2. (*imperfection physique*) blemish; (*d'une matière*) flaw 3. (*faiblesse, inconvénient*) problem 4. (*manque*) ~ **de preuves** insufficient evidence ▸**y a comme un** ~ *inf* there's something wrong here; **être en** ~ to be at fault; **faire** ~ to be lacking; **mettre qn en** ~ to put sb in the wrong; **à** ~ failing that; **par** ~ by default

défavorable [defavɔʀabl] *adj* 1. (*difficile: conditions, temps*) unfavourable *Brit*, unfavorable *Am* 2. (*opp: en faveur de*) **être ~ à un projet** to be against a project 3. (*qui ne convient pas*) **le climat lui est** ~ the climate doesn't suit her; **le climat est ~ à l'agriculture** the climate isn't suitable for agricuture

défavorablement [defavoʀabləmɑ̃] *adv* unfavourably *Brit*, unfavorably *Am*

défavorisé(**e**) [defavɔʀize] *adj* underprivileged

défavoriser [defavɔʀize] <1> *vt* ~ **Jean par rapport à Paul** to favour Paul over Jean *Brit*, to favor Paul over Jean *Am*

défection [defɛksjɔ̃] *f* (*d'un partisan, ami, membre d'un parti*) defection; (*d'un invité, candidat*) failure to appear; **faire** ~ to defect

défectueux, **-euse** [defɛktɥø, -øz] *adj* (*qui présente des défauts: appareil, prononciation*) faulty; (*organisation*) inadequate

défendre[1] [defɑ̃dʀ] <14> I. *vt* to defend; ~ **un acteur contre qn/qc** to defend an actor against sb/sth; ~ **une cause** to stand up for a cause **II.** *vpr* **1.** (*se protéger*) **se ~ contre un agresseur** to defend oneself against an attacker **2.** (*se préserver*) **se ~ de la chaleur** to protect oneself from the heat **3.** (*se débrouiller*) **se ~ en qc** to get by in sth **4.** (*résister aux assauts de l'âge*) **se ~** to do all right **5.** *inf* (*être défendable*) **se ~** (*idée, projet*) to have something to be said for it

défendre[2] [defɑ̃dʀ] <1> **I.** *vt* (*interdire*) to forbid; ~ **à qn de** *+infin* to forbid sb to *+infin* **II.** *vpr* **1.** (*s'interdire*) **se ~ tout plaisir** to refuse all pleasures **2.** (*se retenir*) **ne pouvoir se ~ de qc** to be unable to resist sth

défendu(e) [defɑ̃dy] **I.** *part passé de* **défendre II.** *adj* forbidden

défense[1] [defɑ̃s] *f* **1.** (*fait de défendre*) defence *Brit,* defense *Am;* ~ **civile** (*en cas d'attaque aérienne, de guerre atomique*) civil defence; (*organisation non-violente*) civil disobedience; **légitime ~** self-defence; **appel de préparation à la ~** *call-up for young people for a short civil defence course, intended to replace military service;* **prendre la ~ de qn/qc** to defend sb/sth; **sans ~** defenceless; **la meilleure ~, c'est l'attaque** the best defence is attack **2.** PSYCH **l'instinct/les réflexes de ~** self-defence instinct/reflex *Brit,* self-defense instinct/reflex *Am* **3.** SPORT defence *Brit,* defense *Am;* **être bon en ~** to be strong defensively

défense[2] [defɑ̃s] *f* (*interdiction*) prohibition; ~ **de fumer** no smoking; ~ **de se pencher au-dehors** do not lean out

défense[3] [defɑ̃s] *f* ZOOL tusk

Défense [defɑ̃s] *f* POL **le ministre de la ~** the Minister of Defence *Brit,* the Minister of Defense *Am;* **la ~ nationale** national defence *Brit,* national defense *Am*

défenseur [defɑ̃sœʀ] *m* defender; JUR defence counsel *Brit,* defense attorney *Am;* ~ **des droits de l'Homme/de l'environnement** human rights/environmental activist

défensif, -ive [defɑ̃sif, -iv] *adj* defensive

défensive [defɑ̃siv] *f* **être sur la ~** to be on the defensive

déféquer [defeke] <5> *vi form* to defecate

déférence [defeʀɑ̃s] *f* deference; **avec ~** with deference; **par ~ pour** [*o* **à l'égard de**] **qn** in deference to sb

déferlement [defɛʀləmɑ̃] *m* (*des vagues*) breaking; (*de la mer*) surging; ~ **d'enthousiasme** surge of enthusiasm

déferler [defɛʀle] <1> *vi* (*vagues*) to break; (*mer*) to surge; **la foule déferle dans la rue** the crowd surges into the street

défi [defi] *m* (*provocation, challenge*) challenge; ~ **à la science** challenge to science; **mettre qn au ~ de prouver le contraire** to defy sb to prove the contrary

défiance [defjɑ̃s] *f* mistrust; **mettre qn en ~** to arouse sb's mistrust; **avec/sans ~** with some/without any mistrust

déficience [defisjɑ̃s] *f* **1.** (*faiblesse*) deficiency; **une ~ rénale** renal insufficiency **2.** (*manque*) ~ **en magnésium/calcium** magnesium/calcium deficiency

déficient(e) [defisjɑ̃, jɑ̃t] **I.** *adj* (*intelligence, forces, personne*) feeble; (*raisonnement*) weak; **un enfant ~** (*intellectuellement*) a mentally handicapped child; (*physiquement*) a physically disabled child **II.** *m(f)* ~ **mental** mentally handicapped person

déficit [defisit] *m* **1.** FIN deficit; ~ **de la balance des paiements** balance of payments deficit; **combler le ~** to make up the deficit; **être en ~** to be in deficit **2.** (*perte*) *a.* MED ~ **de qc** deficiency in sth; ~ **hormonal/en fer** hormone/iron deficiency; ~ **immunitaire** immunodeficiency

déficitaire [defisitɛʀ] *adj* (*budget, entreprise*) in deficit; (*année, récolte*) poor

défier [defje] <1> **I.** *vt* **1.** (*provoquer*) ~ **qn aux échecs** to challenge sb at chess **2.** (*parier, braver*) **je te défie de faire ça** I dare you to do it **3.** (*soutenir l'épreuve de*) ~ **la raison/le bon sens** to defy reason/common sense; **des prix défiant toute concurrence** prices that can't be beaten **II.** *vpr* **se ~ de qn/qc** to distrust sb/sth

défigurer [defigyʀe] <1> *vt* **1.** (*abîmer le visage de qn*) to disfigure; (*rendre moins beau*) to spoil **2.** (*enlaidir: monument*) to deface; (*paysage*) to spoil **3.** (*travestir: faits, vérité*) to distort; (*article, texte*) to mar

défilé [defile] *m* **1.** (*cortège de manifestants*) march; (*cortège de fête*) parade; ~ **de mode** fashion show **2.** (*succession*) ~ **d'images/de souvenirs** stream of images/memories **3.** (*gorge*) pass

défiler [defile] <1> **I.** *vi* **1.** (*marcher en colonne, file: soldats, armée, manifestants*) to march; (*pour une cérémonie*) to parade; (*cortège*) to file past; (*mannequins*) to parade past **2.** (*se succéder: clients, visiteurs*) to come and go one after the other; (*voitures, rames*) to come by in a constant stream; (*souvenirs, images*) to keep coming in succession; (*jours*) to come and go endlessly **3.** (*passer en continu: bande, film*) to unreel; (*texte*) to scroll; (*paysage*) to pass by **4.** INFOR **faire ~ qc vers le haut/bas** to scroll sth up/down **II.** *vpr inf* (*se dérober*) **se ~** to wriggle out of; (*s'éclipser*) to slip away

défini(e) [defini] *adj* **1.** (*déterminé: chose*) precise; **mot bien/mal ~** well-/ill-defined word; **douleur bien/mal ~e** definite/vague pain **2.** LING (*article*) definite

définir [definiʀ] <8> **I.** *vt* to define **II.** *vpr* **se ~ comme qn** to define oneself as sb

définitif [definitif] *m inf* **c'est du ~** this is for good

définitif, -ive [definitif, -iv] *adj* **1.** (*opp: provisoire*) definitive; (*refus, décision, victoire*) final **2.** (*sans appel: argument*) conclusive; (*jugement*) final ►**en définitive** when all

D

is said and done
définition [definisjɔ̃] *f* definition; **par** ~ by definition
définitivement [definitivmɑ̃] *adv* definitely; (*s'installer, quitter*) for good
déflagration [deflagʀasjɔ̃] *f* explosion
déflation [deflasjɔ̃] *f* deflation
défoncé(e) [defɔ̃se] *adj* **1.** (*détérioré*) battered; (*canapé, sommier, matelas*) broken-down **2.** (*déformé: route, chaussée*) pot-holed **3.** *inf* (*sous l'effet de la drogue*) **être** ~ to be high
défoncer [defɔ̃se] <2> **I.** *vt* **1.** (*casser en enfonçant: porte, vitre*) to smash in **2.** (*enlever le fond*) to knock the bottom out of **3.** (*détériorer*) **les chars défoncent la route** the tanks are ruining the road surface **4.** *inf* (*droguer*) ~ **qn** (*drogue*) to get sb high; *fig* to give sb a high **II.** *vpr* **se** ~ **1.** (*se détériorer: sol*) to get broken up **2.** *inf* (*se droguer*) to get high **3.** *inf* (*se donner du mal*) to knock oneself out
déforcer [defɔʀse] <1> *vt Belgique* ~ **qn** (*enlever à qn ses forces morales, déprimer*) to get sb down
déforestation [defɔʀɛstasjɔ̃] *f* deforestation
déformant(e) [defɔʀmɑ̃, ɑ̃t] *adj* **miroir** ~ distorting mirror
déformation [defɔʀmasjɔ̃] *f* **1.** (*altération*) putting out of shape; (*qui plie*) bending (out of shape); (*qui tord*) twisting (out of shape); (*qui comprime*) crushing; (*d'un nom*) corruption; (*de pensées, faits*) deformation; (*d'un caractère*) warping **2.** MED malformation ►~ **professionnelle** occupational obsession
déformer [defɔʀme] <1> **I.** *vt* **1.** (*altérer*) to put out of shape; (*en pliant*) to bend (out of shape); (*en tordant*) to twist (out of shape); (*en comprimant*) to crush (out of shape); (*jambes, doigts*) to deform; (*chaussures*) to spoil the shape of; (*bouche*) to twist **2.** (*fausser: faits, pensées, voix*) to distort; (*goût*) to pervert **II.** *vpr* **se** ~ (*chaussures, vêtements*) to lose their shape; (*étagère*) to get twisted
défouler [defule] <1> **I.** *vpr* **se** ~ to let off steam **II.** *vt* **1.** (*libérer son agressivité*) ~ **son ressentiment sur qn/une voiture** to take out one's resentment on sb/a car **2.** (*décontracter*) **la course me défoule** running helps me to relax
défraîchi(e) [defʀeʃi] *adj* (*couleur, tissu, vêtement, charmes, fruits*) faded; (*usé*) worn; (*légumes*) old; (*article*) shop-soiled
défranchi(e) [defʀɑ̃ʃi] *adj Belgique* (*qui a perdu son assurance, est intimidé*) shaken
défrayer [defʀeje] <7> *vt* **1.** (*rembourser*) ~ **qn du trajet** to pay sb's travel expenses **2.** (*être le sujet de conversation*) ~ **la chronique** to be the subject of everyone's conversations
défrichage [defʀiʃaʒ] *m*, **défrichement** [defʀiʃmɑ̃] *m* **1.** (*d'une forêt, d'un terrain*) clearing **2.** (*préparatifs*) groundwork
défricher [defʀiʃe] <1> *vt* **1.** (*forêt, terrain*) to clear **2.** (*traiter, préparer*) ~ **qc** to do the groundwork on sth; (*domaine scientifique*) to make the first steps toward sth; ~ **le terrain** to clear the ground
défriser [defʀize] <1> *vt* **1.** *inf* (*gêner*) to bug **2.** (*enlever la frisure*) ~ **qn** to straighten sb's hair
défroisser [defʀwase] <1> *vt* (*vêtement, feuille de papier*) to smooth out
défroqué [defʀɔke] *m* unfrocked
dégagé(e) [degaʒe] *adj* **1.** (*opp: encombré: ciel, vue, route*) clear; (*sommet*) clearly visible **2.** (*découvert*) **elle avait le front** ~ her hair was gathered back from her forehead; **il avait la nuque** ~ his hair was cut short in the back **3.** (*décontracté: allure, air, ton, manière*) casual
dégagement [degaʒmɑ̃] *m* **1.** (*fait de déterrer: d'une poterie, d'un objet*) unearthing; (*fait de décoincer: d'un boulon, membre*) loosening; (*d'une personne*) freeing **2.** (*déblaiement: d'une route, rue*) clearing **3.** (*émanation*) ~ **de gaz/de chaleur** gas/heat given off **4.** (*passage: d'un appartement, lotissement*) passageway
dégager [degaʒe] <2a> **I.** *vt* **1.** (*libérer: objet enfoui*) to unearth; (*objet couvert*) to uncover; (*objet coincé*) to loosen; ~ **des personnes ensevelies de qc** to free people buried under sth **2.** (*désobstruer: bronches, nez, rue, couloir*) to free; **dégagez la piste!** *inf* out of the way! **3.** (*faire apparaître: cou, épaules*) to bare **4.** (*soustraire à une obligation*) ~ **sa responsabilité** to deny responsibility **5.** *inf* (*enlever*) ~ **des jouets de la table** to clear toys off the table **6.** (*produire: odeur, parfum, gaz, fumée*) to give off **7.** SPORT to clear **8.** ECON, FIN (*crédits*) to free; (*profits, bénéfices*) to produce **9.** (*extraire*) ~ **une idée de qc** to bring out an idea from sth **10.** (*mettre en valeur*) **cette robe dégage bien sa taille** this dress shows off her waist **II.** *vpr* **1.** (*se libérer*) **se** ~ (*passage, voie d'accès*) to be cleared; (*voie respiratoire*) to clear; **le ciel se dégage** the sky is clearing **2.** *fig* **se** ~ **de ses obligations** to free oneself from one's obligations; **se** ~ *inf* (*trouver du temps libre*) to find some time **3.** (*émaner*) **se** ~ **de qc** (*fumée, odeur*) to come from sth; (*gaz, vapeur*) to be given off by sth **4.** (*ressortir*) **se** ~ **de qc** (*idée, vérité*) to emerge from sth; (*impression, mystère*) to be created by sth **III.** *vi inf* **1.** (*sentir mauvais*) to reek **2.** (*déguerpir*) to clear off; (*s'écarter*) to get out of the way; **dégage de là!** out the way!
dégaine [degɛn] *f péj, inf* **quelle** ~**!** just look at that!; **il a une** ~ **de noceur** he looks like someone who lives it up
dégainer [degene] <1> *vt, vi* to draw
dégarni(e) [degaʀni] *adj* **front** ~ receding hairline
dégarnir [degaʀniʀ] <8> **I.** *vpr* **1.** (*se vider*)

se ~ (*lieu*) to empty **2.** (*perdre ses cheveux*) **il se dégarnit** he's getting thin on top; **son front se dégarnit/ses tempes se dégarnissent** he's starting to go bald **3.** (*devenir moins touffu*) **se** ~ (*bois*) to thin out; (*arbre*) to lose its leaves **II.** *vt* (*vider: vitrine, boîte de chocolats*) to empty; (*table*) to clear; ~ **un sapin de Noël** to take down the decorations from a Christmas tree; ~ **une ville** MIL to withdraw one's troops from a town

dégât [degɑ] *m* damage *sans pl;* ~**s matériels** structural damage ►**il y a du** ~! *inf* there's been a lot of damage!; **il va y avoir du** ~! there's going to be mayhem!; **faire des** ~**s** to wreak havoc; **limiter les** ~**s** to avoid the worst; **bonjour les** ~**s!** there's trouble ahead!

dégel [deʒɛl] *m* **1.** (*fonte des glaces*) *a.* POL thaw; **c'est le** ~ the thaw has come **2.** ECON revival **3.** FIN unfreezing

dégeler [deʒ(ə)le] <4> **I.** *vt* **1.** (*faire fondre*) to thaw **2.** (*réchauffer détendre*) to thaw out **3.** (*débloquer: crédits, dossier*) to unfreeze **II.** *vi* **1.** (*fondre*) to thaw **2.** *impers* **il dégèle** it's thawing out **III.** *vpr* **1.** (*être moins réservé*) **se** ~ to warm up **2.** (*se réchauffer*) **se** ~ **les pieds/mains** to warm one's feet/hands

dégénéré(e) [deʒeneʀe] **I.** *adj* degenerate **II.** *m(f)* degenerate

dégénérer [deʒeneʀe] <5> *vi* **1.** (*perdre ses qualités, se changer en*) to degenerate; **son refroidissement a dégénéré en bronchite** his cold got worse and turned into bronchitis **2.** (*se dégrader*) to deteriorate; **à chaque fois, ça dégénère!** it gets worse each time!

dégivrer [deʒivʀe] <1> *vt* (*réfrigérateur*) to defrost; (*vitres, avion*) to de-ice

déglingué(e) [deglɛ̃ge] *adj inf* falling to bits

dégonflé(e) [degɔ̃fle] **I.** *adj* **1.** (*pneu*) flat; (*ballon*) deflated **2.** *inf* (**ne**) **pas être** ~ not to chicken out **II.** *m(f) inf* chicken

dégonfler [degɔ̃fle] <1> **I.** *vt* **1.** (*décompresser: enflure*) to bring down; (*ballon, pneu*) to let the air out of **2.** (*diminuer: prix, budget*) to slim down **3.** (*minimiser: importance*) to play down **II.** *vpr* **se** ~ **1.** (*se décompresser: ballon, pneu*) to deflate; (*enflure*) to go down **2.** *inf* (*avoir peur*) to chicken out; (*reculer*) to back down **III.** *vi* (*enflure*) to go down

dégouliner [deguline] <1> *vi* (*liquide, confiture*) (*goutte à goutte*) to drip; (*en filet*) to trickle

dégourdi(e) [deguʀdi] **I.** *adj* smart **II.** *m(f)* smart kid; **tu es une belle** ~**e!** *iron* that was clever!

dégourdir [deguʀdiʀ] <8> **I.** *vt* (*affranchir*) to wake up **II.** *vpr* **1.** (*se donner de l'exercice*) **se** ~ to warm up; **se** ~ **les jambes** to stretch one's legs **2.** (*perdre sa gaucherie*) **se** ~ (*jeune homme, jeune fille*) to learn about life

dégoût [degu] *m* **1.** (*écœurement*) disgust; ~ **du fromage** distaste for cheese; **avec** ~ with disgust **2.** (*aversion*) **son** ~ **pour qn/qc** the disgust he felt for sb/sth **3.** (*lassitude*) weariness; **il a un** ~ **de lui-même** he's weary of himself

dégoûtant(e) [degutɑ̃, ɑ̃t] **I.** *adj* disgusting; **c'est** ~ **de** +*infin* it is disgusting to +*infin* **II.** *m(f) inf* **1.** (*personne sale*) filthy person **2.** (*vicieux*) revolting person

dégoûté(e) [degute] **I.** *adj* (*écœuré: personne, mine*) disgusted; **je suis** ~ (*scandalisé*) I'm disgusted; (*lassé*) I'm sick and tired of it all; **être** ~ **de la vie/de vivre** to be sick of life/of living ►**n'être pas** ~ not to be put off **II.** *m(f)* **il va faire le** ~ he is going to turn up his nose; (*jouer le difficile*) he is going to be hard to please

dégoûter [degute] <1> **I.** *vt* **1.** (*répugner physiquement*) to disgust **2.** (*ôter l'envie de*) ~ **qn** to put sb off; ~ **qn du sport** to put sb off with sport **II.** *vpr* **se** ~ **de qn/qc** to get sick of sb/sth

dégradant(e) [degʀadɑ̃, ɑ̃t] *adj* degrading

dégradation [degʀadasjɔ̃] *f* **1.** (*dégâts*) damage; (*de l'environnement*) damaging; **causer des** ~**s à qc** to cause damage to sth **2.** (*détérioration*) deterioration **3.** (*avilissement*) *a.* MIL degradation

dégradé [degʀade] *m* **1.** (*camaïeu: de couleurs*) gradation **2.** (*coupe de cheveux*) layered cut

dégrader [degʀade] <1> **I.** *vt* **1.** (*détériorer: édifice, route*) to damage; (*situation, climat social*) to worsen; ~ **l'environnement** to harm the environment **2.** (*faire un dégradé*) to layer **3.** MIL to degrade **II.** *vpr* **se** ~ **1.** (*s'avilir*) to degrade oneself **2.** (*se détériorer: édifice*) to deteriorate; (*situation, climat social, temps*) to worsen

dégrafer [degʀafe] <1> *vt, vpr* (**se**) ~ to unfasten; **elle se dégrafe comme ça** it unfastens like that

dégrafeur [degʀafœʀ] *m* staple remover

dégraissage [degʀɛsaʒ] *m* **1.** (*d'un bouillon, d'une sauce*) skimming (the fat off); (*d'une viande*) removing the fat; (*de la laine, d'un métal*) degreasing **2.** *inf* ECON downsizing

dégraissant [degʀɛsɑ̃] *m* **1.** (*solvant*) grease remover **2.** (*détachant*) spot remover

dégraissant(e) [degʀɛsɑ̃, ɑ̃t] *adj* grease-removing

dégraisser [degʀese] <1> *vt* **1.** (*nettoyer: métal, laine*) to degrease **2.** (*enlever la graisse: cheveux*) to make less greasy; ~ **un bouillon** to skim the grease off **3.** *inf* ECON (*effectifs, entreprise*) to slim down

degré [dəgʀe] *m* **1.** (*intensité*) *a.* MED degree; (*de l'échelle de Richter*) point; **jusqu'à un certain** ~ up to a point; **généreux au dernier/plus haut** ~ generous in the extreme; **équation du premier** ~ equation of the first degree **2.** (*dans la hiérarchie*) level **3.** ECOLE **l'enseignement du premier/second** ~ primary/secondary education **4.** MAT, GEO, MUS degree; **20** ~**s Celsius** 20 degrees Celsius; **à 5**

~**s de latitude nord** at 5 degrees north; ~ **en alcool** alcohol content ▶~ **zéro** (**d'une civilisation/culture**) starting point (of a civilization/culture); **à ce** ~ **de bêtise, ...** at that level of stupidity, ...; **par** ~(**s**) by degrees

dégressif, -ive [degʀesif, -iv] *adj* progressively lower; **tarif** ~ sliding scale

dégriffé(**e**) [degʀife] *adj* without the designer label

dégringolade [degʀɛ̃gɔlad] *f inf* (*d'une monnaie, des titres*) collapse

dégringoler [degʀɛ̃gɔle] <1> **I.** *vi inf* **1.** (*s'effondrer: actions, monnaie*) collapse; (*notes*) to plummet **2.** (*tomber*) ~ **de qc** to tumble down from somewhere **II.** *vt inf* (*escalier*) to hurtle down

dégriser [degʀize] <1> **I.** *vt* **1.** (*désenivrer*) to sober up **2.** (*désillusionner*) to bring back down to earth **II.** *vpr* **se** ~ to come back down to earth

dégrossir [degʀosiʀ] <8> *vt* to trim; (*pierre*) to rough-hew; ~ **un problème** to get to work on a problem; ~ **le travail** to do the groundwork ▶**mal dégrossi**(**e**) churlish

déguenillé(**e**) [deg(ə)nije] *adj* ragged

déguerpir [degɛʀpiʀ] <8> *vi* to clear off; **déguerpissez d'ici tout de suite!** clear out of here right now!; **faire** ~ **qn** to drive sb away

dégueu [degœ] *adj inv, inf,* **dégueulasse** [degœlas] *adj inf* **1.** (*sale: mains, pantalon, personne*) filthy **2.** (*dégoûtant: personne, comportement*) sickening **3.** (*mauvais: temps, aliment*) foul

dégueulasser [degœlase] <1> **I.** *vt inf* to make a big mess of; **ils ont tout dégueulassé** they've made a filthy mess everywhere **II.** *vpr inf* **se** ~ to soil oneself

dégueuler [degœle] <1> **I.** *vi vulg* **1.** to puke **2.** (*débiner*) ~ **sur qn/qc** to run sb/sth down **II.** *vt vulg* to spew

déguisé(**e**) [degize] *adj* **1.** (*pour tromper*) disguised; **cette écriture/voix** ~ this disguised voice/handwriting; **une dévaluation** ~**e** a devaluation in disguise **2.** (*costumé*) dressed up; (*pour le carneval*) in fancy dress

déguisement [degizmɑ̃] *m* **1.** (*travestissement*) disguise **2.** (*costume*) fancy dress *no pl*

déguiser [degize] <1> **I.** *vt* **1.** (*costumer*) ~ **un enfant en pirate** to dress up a child as a pirate **2.** (*contrefaire: voix, écriture, vérité*) to disguise **II.** *vpr* **se** ~ **en qc** (*pour tromper*) to disguise oneself as sth; (*pour s'amuser*) to dress up as sth

dégustation [degystasjɔ̃] *f* (*de fruits de mer, fromage*) sampling; (*de vin, café*) tasting

déguster [degyste] <1> **I.** *vt* **1.** (*goûter*) to taste **2.** (*savourer*) to savour *Brit,* to savor *Am* **II.** *vi* **1.** (*savourer*) to savour *Brit,* to savor *Am* **2.** *inf* (*subir des coups*) to get done over; (*subir des douleurs*) to go through hell; (*subir des réprimandes*) to get bawled out

déhancher [deɑ̃ʃe] <1> *vpr* **se** ~ to wriggle one's hips

dehors [dəɔʀ] **I.** *adv* **1.** (*à l'extérieur*) outside; (*en plein air*) outdoors **2.** (*pas chez soi*) out ▶**ficher qn/qc** ~ *inf* to kick sb out; **mettre qn** ~ to throw sb out; **passer par** ~ to go round the outside; **au** ~ outside; **de** ~ from outside; **se pencher en** ~ to lean out; **rester en** ~ to stay outside; **en** ~ **de** (*à l'extérieur de*) outside; (*mis à part*) apart from; **être en** ~ **du sujet** to be (right) off the subject; ~**!** out! **II.** *m* **1.** (*extérieur*) **les bruits du** ~ the noises from outside **2.** *gén pl* (*apparences: d'une personne*) (outward) appearances

déhoussable [deusabl] *adj* with removable covers

déjà [deʒa] **I.** *adv* **1.** (*dès maintenant*) already; **il était** ~ **parti** he had already gone **2.** (*auparavant*) before; **à cette époque** ~ even at this time; **tu as** ~ **vu le film?** have you (ever) seen the film?; **j'ai** ~ **vu le film** I've seen the film (before) **3.** (*intensif*) as it is; **il est** ~ **assez paresseux!** he's lazy enough as it is!; **c'est** ~ **quelque chose!** well that's something! **4.** (*à la fin d'une question*) **comment vous appelez-vous** ~**?** what's your name again? **II.** *conj inf* ~ **qu'elle a fait ça** well at least she's done that

déjeté(**e**) [deʒ(ə)te] *adj Belgique, inf* (*en désordre*) untidy

déjeuner [deʒœne] <1> **I.** *vi* **1.** (*à midi*) to have lunch; **inviter qn à** ~ to invite sb to lunch **2.** (*le matin*) to have breakfast **II.** *m* (*repas de midi*) lunch; **au** ~ at lunch(time)

déjouer [deʒwe] <1> *vt* (*plan*) to foil; ~ **la surveillance** to elude surveillance

délabré(**e**) [delɑbʀe] *adj* (*maison, mur, façade*) delapidated; **sa santé** ~ his wretched state of health

délabrement [delɑbʀəmɑ̃] *m* (*d'une maison, d'un mur*) delapidated state; (*de la santé*) poor state

délabrer [delɑbʀe] <1> **I.** *vt* (*santé*) to ruin **II.** *vpr* **1.** (*se dégrader*) **se** ~ (*maison, mur*) to become delapidated; (*santé*) to ruin; (*affaires*) to fall apart **2.** (*se ruiner*) **se** ~ **qc** to ruin; **elle va se** ~ **la santé** she's going to ruin her health

délacer [delase] <2> *vt* to undo

délai [delɛ] *m* **1.** (*temps accordé*) time limit; (*date butoir*) deadline; **au dernier** ~ at the latest; **disposer d'un** ~ **de sept jours** to have seven days **2.** (*sursis*) more time; (*pour un contrat*) extension ▶**à bref** ~ at short notice; **dans les plus brefs** ~**s** as soon as possible; **dans les** ~**s** on time; **dans un** ~ **de** within; **sans** ~ without delay

délaissé(**e**) [delese] *adj* **1.** (*abandonné*) abandoned **2.** (*négligé: aspect*) neglected

délaisser [delese] <1> *vt* **1.** (*négliger*) to neglect **2.** (*abandonner: enfant*) to abandon; (*activité*) to give up

délassant(**e**) [delasɑ̃, ɑ̃t] *adj* refreshing

délassement [delasmɑ̃] *m* relaxation; **avoir besoin de** ~ to need relaxation; **la lecture est pour moi un** ~ reading is a form of relaxation for me

délasser [delɑse] <1> *vt, vi, vpr* (**se**) ~ to relax

délateur, **-trice** [delatœʀ, -tʀis] *m, f* informer

délation [delasjɔ̃] *f* informing; **inciter qn à la** ~ to encourage sb to inform

délavé(**e**) [delave] *adj* **1.**(*pâle: couleur*) faded; (*yeux*) watery; **ses yeux d'un bleu** ~ his watery blue eyes **2.**(*éclairci par des lavages: couleur, tissu, jeans*) faded **3.**(*détrempé: terre*) waterlogged

délaver [delave] <1> **I.** *vt* **1.**(*diluer: peinture, couleur*) to water down **2.**(*éclaircir: jean*) to fade; (*inscription*) to wash away **II.** *vpr* **se** ~ (*peinture*) to fade; (*inscription*) to be washed away

délayer [deleje] <7> *vt* **1.**(*diluer*) ~ **la farine/le plâtre dans de l'eau** to mix the flour/plaster with water **2.** *fig* to water down

délectation [delɛktasjɔ̃] *f* enjoyment; (*plus intense*) delight

délecter [delɛkte] <1> *vpr* **se** ~ **à/de qc** to delight in sth

délégation [delegasjɔ̃] *f* **1.**(*groupe, agence d'État*) delegation **2.**(*mandat*) proxy; **en vertu d'une** ~, **par** ~ by authority given him/her **3.** COM ~ **commerciale** (*filiale*) bureau; (*représentants*) trade delegation

délégué(**e**) [delege] **I.** *adj* delegated; **les membres** ~**s** the delegates **II.** *m(f)* (*d'une association, d'un parti*) delegate

déléguer [delege] <5> **I.** *vt* **1.** ~ **qn à un congrès/une négociation** to assign sb to attend a congress/handle negotiations; **il nous avait délégué le sous-chef** he had assigned his second-in-command to us **2.**(*transmettre*) ~ **sa responsabilité à qn** to delegate one's responsibility to sb **II.** *vi* to delegate

délestage [delɛstaʒ] *m* **1.** ELEC power cut **2.** AUTO diversion; **itinéraire de** ~ relief route

délester [delɛste] <1> **I.** *vt* **1.** ELEC ~ **qc** to cut off power from sth **2.** AUTO ~ **une route** to relieve congestion on a road **3.** AVIAT to unballast **4.** *iron* (*voler*) ~ **qn de son argent** to relieve sb of their money **II.** *vpr inf* **se** ~ **de qc** to unburden oneself of sth

délibération [delibeʀasjɔ̃] *f* **1.**(*débat: de l'assemblée*) debate; **les** ~**s du jury** UNIV the jury deliberations **2.**(*décision*) resolution **3.**(*réflexion*) deliberation; **après mûre** ~/ **mille** ~**s** after due consideration

délibéré(**e**) [delibeʀe] *adj* (*intention, volonté*) deliberate; **de manière** ~**e** deliberately; **c'était** ~ it was deliberate

délibérément [delibeʀemɑ̃] *adv* deliberately

délibérer [delibeʀe] <5> *vi* **1.**(*débattre*) ~ **sur qc** to deliberate on sth **2.**(*décider*) ~ **sur** [*o* **de**] **qc** to resolve on sth **3.**(*réfléchir*) ~ **sur qc** to consider sth

délicat(**e**) [delika, at] *adj* **1.**(*fin, fragile*) delicate; **il a une santé** ~**e** he is fragile **2.**(*léger*) **d'un geste** ~ delicately **3.**(*difficile*) **c'est une question/situation** ~**e** it's a delicate matter/situation; **il est** ~ **de faire ça** doing that is rather awkward **4.**(*raffiné, sensible: personne, esprit, odorat, oreilles*) refined; (*palais*) discerning **5.**(*plein de tact: personne, geste*) thoughtful; **utiliser des procédés bien peu** ~**s** to go about things without much tact

délicatement [delikatmɑ̃] *adv* **1.**(*finement, avec tact*) delicately **2.**(*avec douceur*) gently

délicatesse [delikatɛs] *f* **1.**(*finesse, difficulté: d'un objet, travail*) delicacy **2.**(*douceur*) gentleness **3.**(*raffinement*) refinement **4.**(*tact*) consideration; **manque de** ~ tactlessness

délice [delis] **I.** *m* (*jouissance*) delight; **ton dessert est un** ~ your dessert is delicious **II.** *fpl* delights; **faire les** ~**s de qn** to be sb's delight

délicieusement [delisjøzmɑ̃] *adv* deliciously; ~ **bon** (*plat*) delicious; **jouer** ~ **du piano** to play the piano delightfully

délicieux, **-euse** [delisjø, -jøz] *adj* **1.**(*exquis: mets*) delicious; (*sensation, sentiment*) delightful **2.**(*charmant: personne*) delightful

délier [delje] <1a> **I.** *vt* **1.**(*détacher*) to untie **2.**(*dégager*) ~ **qn d'une promesse** to release sb from a promise **II.** *vpr* **1.**(*se détacher*) **se** ~ (*prisonnier*) to untie oneself; (*paquet, corde*) to come undone **2.**(*se désengager*) **se** ~ **d'une promesse** to release oneself from a promise; **se** ~ **d'une obligation** to free oneself from an obligation

délimitation [delimitasjɔ̃] *f* delimitation; ~ **des frontières** defining of borders

délimiter [delimite] <1> *vt* **1.**(*borner*) ~ **qc** to mark sth out **2.** *fig* (*responsabilités, sujet*) to define

délinquance [delɛ̃kɑ̃s] *f* crime, criminality; **grande/petite** ~ serious/petty crime; ~ **juvénile** juvenile delinquency

délinquant(**e**) [delɛ̃kɑ̃, ɑ̃t] **I.** *adj* delinquent; **enfance/jeunesse** ~**e** child/young offenders **II.** *m(f)* delinquent; ~ **primaire** first offender

délirant(**e**) [deliʀɑ̃, ɑ̃t] *adj* (*histoire, idée*) hilarious; (*enthousiasme, joie*) frenzied

délire [deliʀ] *m* **1.**(*divagation*) delirium; **crise de** ~ fit of delirium **2.**(*exaltation*) frenzy; **une foule en** ~ a frenzied crowd ►**c'est le** ~ **total!** *inf* it's complete madness!

délirer [deliʀe] <1> *vi* **1.** MED to be delirious **2.**(*être exalté*) ~ **de joie/d'enthousiasme** to be wild with joy/enthusiasm **3.**(*dérailler*) to be out of one's mind **4.**(*dire des bêtises*) to talk rubbish

délit [deli] *m* crime; ~ **informatique** computer crime; ~ **mineur** petty offence *Brit,* petty offense *Am;* **prendre qn en flagrant** ~ **de qc** to catch sb red-handed doing sth

délivrance [delivʀɑ̃s] *f* **1.**(*soulagement, li-*

bération) relief **2.** ADMIN issue **3.** MED delivery

délivrer [delivʀe] <1> **I.** *vt* **1.** (*libérer*) ~ **l'otage de qc** to free the hostage from sth **2.** *a. fig* (*débarrasser*) ~ **qn d'un raseur** to deliver sb from a bore **3.** ADMIN (*certificat, passeport*) to issue **II.** *vpr* **se** ~ **de ses liens** to free oneself from one's bonds

délocaliser [delɔkalize] <1> *vt* to relocate

déloger [delɔʒe] <2a> **I.** *vt* to get out; (*locataire, habitant*) to evict; (*animal*) to start **II.** *vi Belgique* (*découcher*) to spend the (entire) night out

déloyal(e) [delwajal, jo] <-aux> *adj* unfair

delta [dɛlta] *m* delta; **le** ~ **du Nil** the Nile delta

deltaplane® [dɛltaplan] *m* **1.** (*appareil*) hang-glider **2.** (*sport*) hang-gliding; **faire du** ~ to go hang-gliding

déluge [delyʒ] *m* **1.** (*averse*) downpour **2.** *fig* ~ **de compliments** shower of compliments; **recevoir un** ~ **de protestations** to be inundated with protests

déluré(e) [delyʀe] *adj* **1.** (*enfant, air*) sharp **2.** *péj* (*fille*) brazen

démagnétisé(e) [demaɲetize] *adj* demagnetized

démago [demago] *adj inf abr de* **démagogue**

démagogie [demagɔʒi] *f* demagogy; **faire de la** ~ to go in for crowd-pleasing

démagogique [demagɔʒik] *adj* crowd-pleasing

démagogue [demagɔg] **I.** *mf* demagogue **II.** *adj* crowd-pleasing; **être** ~ to be a crowd-pleaser

demain [d(ə)mɛ̃] *adv* tomorrow; ~ **soir** tomorrow night; ~ **en huit** a week from tomorrow; **le temps pour** ~ tomorrow's weather; **à** ~**!** see you tomorrow!

demande [d(ə)mɑ̃d] *f* **1.** (*souhait, prière*) request; ~ **en mariage** proposal; ~ **de rançon de 500.000 euros** ransom demand for 500.000 euros **2.** ADMIN request; ~ **d'emploi** job application; **faire une** ~ to make a request **3.** PSYCH ~ **de qc** need for sth **4.** ECON ~ **en qc** demand for sth **5.** JUR **faire une** ~ **en dommages-intérêts** to claim for damages **6.** (*formulaire*) claim form ►**à la** ~ on request; ADMIN on demand; **à la** ~ **de qn** (*souhait*) at sb's request; **sur (simple)** ~ by request

demandé(e) [d(ə)mɑ̃de] *adj* **être** ~ to be in demand

demander [d(ə)mɑ̃de] <1> **I.** *vt* **1.** (*solliciter*) ~ **conseil** to ask advice; ~ **un renseignement à qn** to ask sb for information; ~ **pardon à qn** to apologize to sb **2.** (*appeler: médecin, plombier*) to call (for) **3.** (*vouloir parler à*) ~ **un employé/poste** to ask for an employee/sb's extension **4.** (*s'enquérir de*) ~ **à qn** to ask sb; ~ **le chemin/l'heure à qn** to ask sb the way/the time **5.** (*nécessiter: soin, eau, travail*) to require; **ce projet m'a demandé beaucoup d'efforts** I had to put in a lot of effort into this project **6.** (*exiger*) ~ **de l'obéissance à qn** to demand obedience from sb; ~ **la liberté** to demand freedom; **en** ~ **beaucoup/trop à qn** to ask a lot/too much of sb **7.** (*rechercher*) ~ **du personnel qualifié** to look for qualified staff **8.** (*exiger un prix*) ~ **un prix pour qc** to ask a price for sth ►**ne pas** ~ **mieux que de** +*infin* to be more than happy to +*infin;* **elle ne demande qu'à faire ça** that's all she wants to do **II.** *vi* ~ **à qn si** to ask sb if; ~ **après qn** *inf* to ask about sb ►**il n'y a qu'à** ~ you only have to ask; **je demande à voir** that I must see **III.** *vpr* **se** ~ **ce que/comment** to wonder what/how ►**c'est à se** ~ **si** *inf* it makes you wonder if

demandeur, -euse [d(ə)mɑ̃dœʀ, -øz] *m, f* **1.** TEL caller **2.** (*requérant*) claimant; ~ **d'emploi/d'asile** job/asylum seeker; **le nombre de** ~**s d'emploi** the number of those seeking work ►**être** ~ **de qc** to be ready to buy sth

démangeaison [demɑ̃ʒɛzɔ̃] *f gén pl* **1.** (*irritation*) itch; **il a des** ~**s** he's got an itch **2.** *fig, inf* (*désir*) **ça me donne des** ~**s de le faire** I've got an itch to do it

démanger [demɑ̃ʒe] <2a> **I.** *vt* to itch; **ça me démange dans le dos** my back is itching **II.** *vi* (*avoir envie*) **la main me démange** I could just hit him; **ça me/le démange de le faire** *inf* I'm/he's (just) itching to do it

démanteler [demɑ̃t(ə)le] <4> *vt* to dismantle

démantibulé(e) [demɑ̃tibyle] *adj inf* falling to bits

démaquillant [demakijɑ̃] *m* make-up remover

démaquillant(e) [demakijɑ̃, jɑ̃t] *adj* cleansing; **lait** ~ cleansing lotion

démaquiller [demakije] <1> **I.** *vt* ~ **qn** to take sb's make-up off **II.** *vpr* **se** ~ **le visage** to take one's face make-up off

démarcation [demaʀkasjɔ̃] *f a. fig* demarcation; **ligne de** ~ boundary (line); MIL demarcation line

démarche [demaʀʃ] *f* **1.** (*allure*) walk **2.** (*cheminement: d'une argumentation*) approach; (*d'une personne*) (line of) approach **3.** (*intervention*) step; **faire des** ~**s** to take steps; **faire des** ~**s auprès de qn** to approach sb

démarcher [demaʀʃe] <1> *vt* to canvass; ~ **les gens par téléphone** POL to canvass people by phone; (*pour vendre*) to sell by telephone

démarqué(e) [demaʀke] *adj* **1.** (*dégriffé*) without its designer label **2.** (*soldé*) marked down

démarquer [demaʀke] <1> **I.** *vt* **1.** (*dégriffer*) to sell as a brand-name second **2.** (*solder*) to mark down **II.** *vpr* **1.** SPORT **se** ~ to get rid of one's marker **2.** (*prendre ses distances*) **se** ~ **de qn/qc** to distinguish oneself from sb/sth

démarrage [demaʀaʒ] *m* **1.** (*mise en marche*) start-up **2.** (*départ*) moving off

3. SPORT burst of speed **4.** (*lancement*) launch **5.** INFOR ~ **à chaud/à froid** warm/cold boot ▸**au** ~ upon starting the engine; *fig* at the start

démarrer [demaʀe] <1> **I.** *vi* **1.** (*mettre en marche*) to start up; **je n'ai pas réussi à** ~ I couldn't get it started **2.** (*se mettre en marche: voiture*) to move off; (*machine*) to start up; **faire** ~ **qc** to start sth up **3.** (*partir*) to leave **4.** (*débuter: campagne, exposition*) to launch; (*conversation*) to start up; (*industrie, économie*) to take off; ~ **bien/mal en maths** to get off to a good/poor start in maths *Brit,* to get off to a good/poor start in math *Am* **5.** SPORT to pull away **6.** INFOR ~ **un logiciel** [*o* **un programme**] to start a programme **II.** *vt* **1.** (*mettre en marche*) to start up **2.** *inf* (*lancer*) to start up; (*mouvement*) to launch; (*processus*) to get under way **3.** *inf* (*commencer*) ~ **le travail/les peintures** to get the work/the painting started **4.** INFOR ~ **un logiciel** to boot up software

démarreur [demaʀœʀ] *m* starter

démasquer [demaske] <1> **I.** *vt* (*voleur, traître, espion*) to unmask; (*plan, fraude, trahison*) to expose **II.** *vpr* **se** ~ to drop one's mask

démâter [demɑte] <1> *vi* to be dismasted

démêlé [demele] *m* trouble

démêler [demele] <1> *vt* **1.** (*défaire: fil, cheveux*) to untangle **2.** (*éclaircir: affaire*) to sort out; (*intentions, plans*) to penetrate

démêloir [demɛlwaʀ] *m* wide-toothed comb

démembrer [demɑ̃bʀe] <1> *vt* (*pays, propriété*) to carve up

déménagement [demenaʒmɑ̃] *m* **1.** (*changement de domicile, départ d'un logement*) move **2.** (*fait de quitter le logement, déplacement de meubles*) removal **3.** (*fait de vider une pièce*) emptying

déménager [demenaʒe] <2a> **I.** *vi* **1.** (*changer de domicile, quitter un logement*) to move; ~ **à Paris/rue de ...** to move to Paris/ ... Street **2.** *inf* (*partir*) **faire** ~ **qn** to kick sb out **3.** *inf* (*déraisonner*) **il déménage** he's off his rocker **II.** *vt* **1.** (*transporter ailleurs: meubles*) to move; (*pour débarrasser: meubles, objet*) to clear out **2.** (*vider: maison, pièce*) to clear (out)

déménageur [demenaʒœʀ] *m* **1.** (*débardeur*) removal man *Brit,* mover *Am* **2.** (*entrepreneur*) (furniture) remover

démence [demɑ̃s] *f* dementia; ~ **sénile** senile dementia; **crise/état de** ~ fit/state of dementia ▸**c'est de la** ~**!** it's sheer madness!

démener [dem(ə)ne] <4> *vpr* **1.** (*se débattre*) **se** ~ to struggle **2.** (*faire des efforts*) **se** ~ **pour** +*infin* to put in a lot of effort to +*infin*

dément(e) [demɑ̃, ɑ̃t] **I.** *adj* **1.** (*aliéné*) demented **2.** *inf* (*insensé, super*) brilliant **II.** *m(f)* person with dementia

démenti [demɑ̃ti] *m* denial; **opposer un** ~ **à qc** to deny sth formally

démentir [demɑ̃tiʀ] <10> **I.** *vt* **1.** (*contredire*) ~ **qn** to deny sb's claim **2.** (*nier*) to deny; ~ **faire qc** to deny doing sth **3.** (*infirmer*) to contradict **II.** *vi* to issue a denial **III.** *vpr* **une amitié qui ne se dément pas** a friendship which never fails; **un succès qui ne se dément pas** an ongoing success

démerdard(e) [demɛʀdaʀ, aʀd] *adj inf* **être** ~ to know how to sort things out

démerder [demɛʀde] <1> *vpr inf* **se** ~ to manage; **démerdez-vous!** sort it out yourself!

démesure [deməzyʀ] *f* excessiveness; **faire dans la** ~ to tend to the excessive

démesuré(e) [deməzyʀe] *adj* enormous; (*importance, proportions*) excessive; (*orgueil*) immoderate; **des bras/pieds** ~**s** incredibly long arms/big feet

démesurément [deməzyʀemɑ̃] *adv* (*grand, long*) immoderately; (*exagérer*) wildly

démettre [demɛtʀ] *irr* **I.** *vt* **1.** (*luxer: bras, poignet*) to wrench; (*épaule*) to dislocate **2.** (*révoquer*) ~ **qn de ses fonctions/de son poste** to relieve sb of their duties/post **II.** *vpr* **1.** (*se luxer*) **se** ~ **le bras** to wrench one's arm; **se** ~ **l'épaule** to dislocate one's shoulder **2.** (*renoncer à*) **se** ~ **de qc** to resign from sth

demeure [d(ə)mœʀ] *f* home ▸**conduire qn (jusqu')à sa dernière** ~ to carry sb to their last resting place

demeuré(e) [dəmœʀe] **I.** *adj* half-witted **II.** *m(f)* half-wit; **le** ~ **du village** the village idiot

demeurer [dəmœʀe] <1> *vi* **1.** *avoir* (*habiter*) to reside; **demeurant à** residing at **2.** *avoir* (*subsister*) to remain **3.** *être* (*rester*) to remain; ~ **ministre/une énigme** to remain a minister/a mystery **4.** *impers* **il demeure que c'est arrivé** it still happened

demi [d(ə)mi] *m* **1.** (*fraction*) **un** ~ a half; **trois** ~**s** three halves **2.** (*bière*) glass of beer

demi(e) [d(ə)mi] **I.** *m(f)* (*moitié*) half **II.** *adj* **une heure et** ~**e** an hour and a half; **avoir quatre ans et** ~ to be four and a half; **être à** ~ **satisfait** to be only half-satisfied; **un verre/une bouteille à** ~ **plein(e)** a half-full glass/bottle; **être à** ~ **plein** to be half-full; **n'être qu'à** ~ **rassuré** not to be completely reassured; **il ouvrit à** ~ **les yeux** he half-opened his eyes; **ne pas faire les choses à** ~ not do things by halves

demiard [dəmjaʀ] *m Québec* (*mesure de capacité pour les liquides, valant la moitié d'une chopine ou le quart d'une pinte* (*soit 0,284 litre*)) quarter-pint

demi-bouteille [d(ə)mibutɛj] <demi-bouteilles> *f* half-bottle **demi-cercle** [d(ə)misɛʀkl] <demi-cercles> *m* semi-circle; **en** ~ in a semi-circle **demi-dieu** [d(ə)midjø] <demi-dieux> *m* demigod **demi-douzaine** [d(ə)miduzɛn] <demi-douzaines> *f* half a dozen

demie [d(ə)mi] *f* (*heure*) **neuf heures et** ~ half past nine; **sonner les heures et les** ~**s** to sound the hour and the half hour; **partir à la** ~

to leave at half past; **il est la** ~ (**passée**) it's gone half past

demi-finale [d(ə)mifinal] <demi-finales> *f* semi-final **demi-finaliste** [d(ə)mifinalist] <demi-finalistes> *mf* semi-finalist **demi-frère** [d(ə)mifʀɛʀ] <demi-frères> *m* half-brother **demi-heure** [d(ə)mijœʀ] <demi-heures> *f* half-hour **demi-journée** [d(ə)miʒuʀne] <demi-journées> *f* half-day

démilitariser [demilitaʀize] <1> *vt* to demilitarize

demi-litre [d(ə)militʀ] <demi-litres> *m* **1.** (*contenu*) half a litre *Brit,* half a liter *Am* **2.** (*contenant*) half-litre *Brit,* half-liter *Am* **demi-mesure** [d(ə)mim(ə)zyʀ] <demi-mesures> *f* half-measure **demi-mot** [dəmimo] **à** ~ without having to say everything

déminer [demine] <1> *vt* ~ **qc** to clear sth of mines

demi-pension [d(ə)mipɑ̃sjɔ̃] <demi-pensions> *f* **1.** (*hôtel*) *hotel providing half board for guests;* **en** ~ on half board **2.** ECOLE half board **demi-pensionnaire** [d(ə)mipɑ̃sjɔnɛʀ] <demi-pensionnaires> *mf* half boarder

démis(**e**) [demi, iz] **I.** *part passé de* **démettre II.** *adj* dislocated

demi-saison [d(ə)misɛzɔ̃] <demi-saisons> *f* (*printemps*) spring; (*automne*) autumn; **vêtements de** ~ clothes for mild weather **demi-sel** [d(ə)misɛl] **I.** *adj inv* GASTR slightly salted **II.** *m* cream cheese **demi-siècle** [dəmisjɛkl] <demi-siècles> *m* half-century **demi-sœur** [d(ə)misœʀ] <demi-sœurs> *f* half-sister

démission [demisjɔ̃] *f* **1.** (*action*) resignation **2.** (*renoncement*) abdication (of responsibility)

démissionner [demisjɔne] <1> *vi* (*se démettre*) ~ **de sa fonction** to give up one's duties; ~ **de son poste** to resign from one's position

demi-tarif [d(ə)mitaʀif] <demi-tarifs> *m* half-price; **à** ~ half-price **demi-ton** [d(ə)mitɔ̃] <demi-tons> *m* semitone, half step *Am;* ~ **chromatique**/**diatonique** chromatic/diatonic semitone **demi-tour** [d(ə)mituʀ] <demi-tours> *m* (*d'une personne*) about-turn *Brit,* about-face *Am;* (*de manivelle*) half-turn; **faire** ~ (*à pied, en voiture*) to make a U-turn; MIL to about face

démobilisation [demɔbilizasjɔ̃] *f* **1.** MIL demobilization **2.** POL creation of voter apathy

démobiliser [demɔbilize] <1> **I.** *vt* **1.** MIL to demobilize **2.** POL ~ **qn** to create apathy in sb **II.** *vpr* **se** ~ to demobilize

démocrate [demɔkʀat] **I.** *adj* democratic **II.** *mf* democrat

démocratie [demɔkʀasi] *f* democracy

démocratique [demɔkʀatik] *adj* democratic

démocratiquement [demɔkʀatikmɑ̃] *adv* democratically

démocratiser [demɔkʀatize] <1> **I.** *vt* to make more democratic; (*sport*) to popularize; ~ **un pays** to bring democracy to a country **II.** *vpr* **se** ~ to become more democratic; (*sport*) to be popularized

démodé(**e**) [demɔde] *adj* old-fashioned; (*procédé, théorie*) outdated

démoder [demɔde] <1> *vpr* **se** ~ to go out of fashion

démographie [demɔgʀafi] *f* **1.** (*science*) demography **2.** (*évolution de la population*) population growth

démographique [demɔgʀafik] *adj* (*données, étude*) demographic; **croissance** ~ population growth

demoiselle [d(ə)mwazɛl] *f* (*jeune fille*) young lady; (*femme non mariée*) single lady; **c'est une vraie** ~ **maintenant!** she's a real little lady now!; ~ **d'honneur** bridesmaid

démolir [demɔliʀ] <8> **I.** *vt* **1.** (*détruire*) to demolish; (*mur*) to knock down **2.** *inf* (*frapper*) to beat the living daylights out of **3.** *inf* (*critiquer*) to tear to shreds **4.** *inf* (*saper le moral: événement, nouvelle*) to shatter **5.** *inf* (*endommager: santé*) to ruin; (*estomac*) to tear up **II.** *vpr inf* **se** ~ **l'estomac**/**la santé** to do terrible things to one's stomach/health

démolisseur, **-euse** [demɔlisœʀ, -øz] *m, f* **1.** (*ouvrier*) demolition worker **2.** (*destructeur*) wrecker; **c'est un** ~ **d'idées** he knocks back all your ideas; **c'est une démolisseuse de ménages** she's a home wrecker

démolition [demɔlisjɔ̃] *f* **1.** (*opp: construction: d'une maison, d'un mur*) demolition; **l'immeuble est en** ~ the building's being demolished **2.** *fig* destruction

démon [demɔ̃] *m* demon; (*enfant*) devil

démoniaque [demɔnjak] *adj* diabolical

démonstrateur, **-trice** [demɔ̃stʀatœʀ, -tʀis] *m, f* demonstrator

démonstratif [demɔ̃stʀatif] *m* demonstrative

démonstratif, **-ive** [demɔ̃stʀatif, -iv] *adj* **1.** (*grimace, mimique*) expressive; (*personne*) demonstrative; **peu** ~ undemonstrative **2.** LING (*pronom*) demonstrative

démonstration [demɔ̃stʀasjɔ̃] *f* **1.** (*preuve, argumentation*) *a.* MAT demonstration; **faire la** ~ **d'un produit** to demonstrate a product; **voiture de** ~ demo car **2.** *gén pl* (*manifestation*) ~**s de joie** show of joy

démontable [demɔ̃tabl] *adj* **les meubles sont** ~**s** the furniture can be taken apart

démontage [demɔ̃taʒ] *m* dismantling; (*d'une tente*) taking down

démonté(**e**) [demɔ̃te] *adj* (*mer*) raging

démonter [demɔ̃te] <1> **I.** *vt* **1.** (*défaire: meuble*) to take apart; (*appareil*) to dismantle; (*auvent, tente*) to take down; (*pneu, porte*) to take off **2.** (*déconcerter*) to take aback **II.** *vpr* **se** ~ **1.** (*être démontable*) **l'appareil se**

démonte the machine can be dismantled; **le bureau se démonte facilement** the desk is easy to take apart; (*accidentellement*) the desk keeps falling apart **2.** (*se troubler*) to be taken aback; **sans se** ~ without turning a hair

démontrer [demɔ̃tʀe] <1> **I.** *vt* to demonstrate **II.** *vpr* **cela se démontre** that can be demonstrated

démoralisant(e) [demɔʀalizɑ̃, ɑ̃t] *adj* demoralizing

démoraliser [demɔʀalize] <1> **I.** *vt* to demoralize **II.** *vi* to be demoralizing **III.** *vpr* **se** ~ to become demoralized

démordre [demɔʀdʀ] <14> *vi* **ne pas** ~ **de qc** to stick to sth; **il n'en démord pas** he won't budge

démotivant(e) [demɔtivɑ̃, ɑ̃t] *adj* demotivating, discouraging

démotivation [demɔtivasjɔ̃] *f* loss of motivation

démotiver [demɔtive] <1> **I.** *vt* to cause to lose motivation **II.** *vpr* **se** ~ to become demotivated *Brit,* to become unmotivated *Am*

démouler [demule] <1> *vt* ~ **qc** to turn sth out

démuni(e) [demyni] *adj* **1.** (*pauvre*) destitute **2.** (*impuissant*) ~ **devant qn/qc** powerless in the face of sb/sth **3.** (*privé de*) **être** ~ **de qc** to be without sth; ~ **d'intérêt** devoid of interest; ~ **de protection** unprotected

démunir [demyniʀ] <8> **I.** *vt* (*priver*) ~ **qn de l'argent** to deprive sb of money **II.** *vpr* (*se défaire*) **se** ~ **de qc** to part with sth; (*se priver*) to give sth up

démystifier [demistifje] <1a> *vt* **1.** (*détromper*) to disabuse **2.** (*démythifier*) to demystify

dénaturé(e) [denatyʀe] *adj* unnatural

dénaturer [denatyʀe] <1> *vt* **1.** (*altérer: goût, saveur*) to spoil **2.** (*déformer: paroles, propos*) to distort; (*faits, vérité*) to misrepresent

déneigement [denɛʒmɑ̃] *m* snow clearing; **le** ~ **d'une route** clearing the snow from a road

déneiger [deneʒe] <2a> *vt* ~ **une route** to clear the snow from a road

dénicher [deniʃe] <1> *vt* (*bistrot, objet rare*) to discover; (*personne*) to track down

dénigrement [denigʀəmɑ̃] *m* denigration; **l'esprit de** ~ disparaging attitude

dénigrer [denigʀe] <1> *vt* to denigrate

dénivellation [denivelasjɔ̃] *f* **1.** (*inégalité*) dip **2.** (*différence de niveau*) difference in height

dénombrer [denɔ̃bʀe] <1> *vt* to count

dénominateur [denɔminatœʀ] *m* MAT denominator; ~ **commun** *a. fig* common denominator

dénomination [denɔminasjɔ̃] *f* denomination

dénommé(e) [denɔme] *adj antéposé* **un/une** ~ **Durand** a certain Durand; **le/la** ~ **Durand** the (afore)said Durand

dénommer [denɔme] <1> *vt* to call

dénoncer [denɔ̃se] <2> **I.** *vt* **1.** (*trahir: criminel, complice*) to denounce; ~ **un opposant politique à qn** to give a political opponent away to sb; ~ **qn à la police** to give sb away to the police **2.** (*s'élever contre: abus, injustice*) to denounce **II.** *vpr* **se** ~ **à la police** to turn oneself in to the police

dénonciateur, -trice [denɔ̃sjatœʀ, -tʀis] *m, f* **1.** (*délateur: d'une personne*) informant **2.** (*accusateur: d'une injustice*) denouncer

dénonciation [denɔ̃sjasjɔ̃] *f* **1.** (*délation*) denunciation; (*dans une dictature*) informing; **sur** ~ on the claims of an informant **2.** (*accusation*) denunciation

dénoter [denɔte] <1> *vt a.* LING to denote

dénouement [denumɑ̃] *m* (*d'une intrigue*) dénouement; (*de l'enquête*) outcome

dénouer [denwe] <1> **I.** *vt* (*ficelle, lacets, nœud*) to untie; (*intrigue, affaire*) to clear up **II.** *vpr* **se** ~ to conclude

dénoyauter [denwajote] <1> *vt* to stone

denrée [dɑ̃ʀe] *f* commodity; ~**s alimentaires** foodstuffs ►~ **rare** rare commodity

dense [dɑ̃s] *adj* **1.** *a.* PHYS dense **2.** (*condensé: œuvre, film*) condensed; (*style*) compact

densité [dɑ̃site] *f* density

dent [dɑ̃] *f* **1.** ANAT (*de l'homme, animal*) tooth; ~ **creuse/gâtée** hollow/bad tooth; ~ **de devant/de lait** front/milk tooth *Brit,* front/baby tooth *Am;* **faire ses** ~**s** to teethe; **se laver les** ~**s** to brush one's teeth; **brosse à** ~**s** toothbrush **2.** *fig* (*d'une fourchette*) tine; (*d'un peigne, engrenage*) tooth **3.** (*sommet de montagne*) peak ►**en** ~**s de scie** serrated; *fig* with ups and downs; **armé(e) jusqu'aux** ~**s** armed to the teeth; **avoir les** ~**s longues** to have one's sights on great things; (*être avide*) to be grasping; **avoir une** ~ **contre qn** to hold a grudge against sb; **grincer des** ~**s** to grind one's teeth; **être sur les** ~**s** to be on the go; **se faire les** ~**s** to cut one's teeth, to teethe; **n'avoir rien à se mettre sous la** ~ to have nothing to eat

dentaire [dɑ̃tɛʀ] *adj* dental

denté(e) [dɑ̃te] *adj* toothed; **roue** ~**e** cogwheel

dentelé(e) [dɑ̃t(ə)le] *adj* jagged

dentelle [dɑ̃tɛl] *f* lace

dentier [dɑ̃tje] *m* denture

dentifrice [dɑ̃tifʀis] *m* toothpaste

dentiste [dɑ̃tist] *mf* dentist

dentition [dɑ̃tisjɔ̃] *f* teeth *pl*

dénudé(e) [denyde] *adj* bare

dénuder [denyde] <1> **I.** *vt* **1.** (*dévêtir*) to bare **2.** (*laisser voir: dos, bras*) to show (off) **3.** ELEC (*câble*) to strip **II.** *vpr* **se** ~ (*personne*) to take one's clothes off; (*arbre*) to go bare; **son crâne commence à se** ~ he is beginning to go bald

dénué(e) [denɥe] *adj* **être** ~ **d'intérêt** to be devoid of interest

D

dénuement [denymɑ̃] *m* destitution; **vivre dans le ~ le plus complet** to be in a state of utter destitution
déodorant [deɔdɔʀɑ̃] *m* deodorant; **~ en aérosol** spray deodorant
déodorant(e) [deɔdɔʀɑ̃, ɑ̃t] *adj* deodorant
dépannage [depanaʒ] *m* **1.** (*réparation: d'une machine, voiture*) fixing; **service de ~** breakdown service **2.** (*solution provisoire*) stopgap; **à titre de ~** as a stopgap
dépanner [depane] <1> *vt* **1.** (*réparer: machine, voiture*) to fix; **~ qn** to help out sb who's broken down; (*remorquer*) to give sb a tow **2.** *inf* (*aider*) **~ qn** to help sb out
dépanneur [depanœʀ] *m Québec* (*épicerie qui reste ouverte au-delà des heures d'ouverture des autres commerces*) late-night store
dépanneur, **-euse** [depanœʀ, -øz] *m, f* (emergency) mechanic
dépanneuse [depanøz] *f* breakdown van *Brit,* tow truck *Am*
dépaqueter [depakte] <3> *vt* to unwrap
dépareillé(e) [depaʀeje] *adj* (*incomplet: service de verres, collection*) incomplete; (*isolé, pas assorti: gant, tasse, chaise*) odd
déparer [depaʀe] <1> **I.** *vt* (*paysage, collection*) to mar; (*visage*) to disfigure **II.** *vi* **ne pas ~ à côté de/avec/dans qc** not to be out of place next to/with/in sth
départ [depaʀ] *m* **1.** (*action de partir*) departure; **après leur ~** after they left; **mon ~ en vacances n'est pas encore fixé** I haven't made up my mind when I'm going off on holiday *Brit,* I haven't made up my mind when to take a vacation *Am;* **les grands ~s en vacances** the great wave of holiday departures (*at the beginning of July and August*); **tableau des ~s et des arrivées** departures and arrivals board **2.** SPORT start; **~ en flèche** flying start; **donner le ~** to give the starting signal **3.** (*lieu*) **quai de ~ des grandes lignes** the main line departure platform **4.** (*d'un poste*) leaving; **~ à la retraite** retirement; **après mon ~ du gouvernement** after I left the government **5.** (*début, origine*) start; **mon idée de ~** my original idea; **point de ~** starting point; **au/dès le ~** at/from the outset ►**prendre un bon/mauvais ~** to get off to a good/bad start; **prendre un nouveau ~ (dans la vie)** to make a fresh start (in life); **car/avion au ~ de Paris** coach/plane leaving from Paris; **être sur le ~** to be on the point of leaving
départager [depaʀtaʒe] <2a> **I.** *vt* **~ les candidats** to decide between candidates; **~ les bons et les mauvais** to sort out the good from the bad **II.** *vpr* **les concurrents peuvent se ~** a decision can be made over the contenders
département [depaʀtəmɑ̃] *m* **1.** ADMIN département (*one of the main administrative divisions of France*); **~ d'outre-mer** overseas département **2.** (*secteur*) *a.* UNIV department **3.** *Suisse* (*subdivision du pouvoir exécutif, fédéral ou cantonal*) department (*administrative division in Switzerland*) **4.** *Québec* **~ d'État** (*ministère des Affaires étrangères*) Foreign Office *Brit,* State Department *Am*

> In France a **département** is an administrative unit of the state with some authority, e.g. social and medical matters. In Switzerland, a département is a unit of state administration which deals with specific areas, e.g. foreign problems, police departments or financial matters.

départemental(e) [depaʀtəmɑ̃tal, o] <-aux> *adj* departmental; **route ~e** secondary road
dépassé(e) [depɑse] *adj* **1.** (*démodé*) outdated **2.** (*désorienté*) **je suis ~ par tout ça** I'm out of my depth in all this
dépasser [depɑse] <1> **I.** *vt* **1.** (*doubler*) to overtake *Brit,* to pass *Am* **2.** (*aller plus loin que*) to go past **3.** (*outrepasser: limite*) to go beyond **4.** (*aller plus loin en quantité: dose*) to exceed; **~ qn de dix centimètres** to be ten centimetres taller than sb; **~ trois heures** (*réunion*) to go on after three o'clock; **cela dépasse mes moyens** it's beyond my means **5.** (*surpasser*) to outdo; **~ l'attente de qn** to exceed sb's expectations ►**ça me/le dépasse!** it's beyond me! **II.** *vi* **1.** (*doubler*) to overtake *Brit,* to pass *Am;* **défense de ~!** no overtaking! *Brit,* no passing! *Am* **2.** (*être trop haut, trop long: bâtiment, tour*) to tower above; (*vêtement*) to show; **~ de qc** (*vêtement*) to show under sth **III.** *vpr* **se ~** to surpass oneself
dépassionner [depasjɔne] <1> *vt* **~ une dispute** to take the heat out of an argument
dépatouiller [depatuje] <1> *vpr inf* **se ~** to get out of a jam
dépaysant(e) [depeizɑ̃, ɑ̃t] *adj* **séjour ~** a trip that takes you away from everything
dépaysé(e) [depeize] *adj* **être ~** to be out of one's natural environment
dépaysement [depeizmɑ̃] *m* **1.** (*désorientation*) disorientation **2.** (*changement*) change of surroundings **3.** (*changement salutaire*) change of scenery
dépayser [depeize] <1> *vt* **1.** (*désorienter*) to disorientate **2.** (*changer les idées*) **~ qn** to give sb a change of scenery
dépecer [depəse] <2> *vt* **1. ~ sa proie/son livre** to tear one's prey/book apart **2.** (*démembrer: territoire*) to dismember
dépêche [depɛʃ] *f* dispatch
dépêcher [depeʃe] <1> **I.** *vpr* **se ~** to hurry (up); **se ~ de faire qc** to hurry up and do sth **II.** *vt form* **~ qn auprès de qn** to dispatch sb to sb
dépeigner [depeɲe] <1> *vt* **~ qn** to ruffle sb's hair
dépeindre [depɛ̃dʀ] *vt irr* to depict
dépenaillé(e) [dep(ə)naje] *adj* (*personne*)

scruffy; (*vêtement*) ragged

dépendance [depɑ̃dɑ̃s] *f* (*assujettissement*) dependency; (*d'un drogué*) addiction; ~ **à l'égard de qn/qc** dependency on sb/sth

dépendant(e) [depɑ̃dɑ̃, ɑ̃t] *adj* dependent; **être ~ de la drogue** to be addicted to drugs

dépendre [depɑ̃dʀ] <14> **I.** *vi* **1.** (*être sous la dépendance de*) ~ **de qn/qc** to be dependent on sb/sth **2.** (*faire partie de*) ~ **de qc** (*terrain*) to belong to sth **3.** (*relever de*) ~ **de qn/qc** to be answerable to sb/sth **4.** (*être conditionné par*) ~ **de qc/qn** to depend on sb/sth; **ça dépend** *inf* that depends; **ça dépend d'elle** it's up to her; **ça dépend du temps** it depends on the weather **II.** *vt* (*décrocher*) to take down

dépens [depɑ̃] **aux ~ de qn** at sb's expense

dépense [depɑ̃s] *f* **1.** (*frais*) expense; **c'est une grosse ~** it's a lot of money (to spend); **~s publiques/de l'État** public/state spending; **~ en électricité** electricity spending; **engager des ~s** to make financial commitments; **faire face à des ~s** to meet financial commitments; **se lancer dans de grosses ~s** to lay out a lot of money **2.** (*usage*) expenditure; **~ nerveuse** expenditure of nervous energy; **~ physique** physical exercise ►**ne pas regarder à la ~** to spare no expense

dépenser [depɑ̃se] <1> **I.** *vt* **1.** (*débourser*) to spend **2.** (*consommer: électricité, énergie*) to consume **3.** (*user*) **il voudrait ~ son temps à dessiner** he'd like to spend his time drawing **II.** *vpr* **se ~** to expend energy; (*enfant*) to use up their energy ►**elle se dépense sans compter** (**pour son travail**) (*s'engager*) she gives her work everything she's got

dépensier, -ière [depɑ̃sje, -jɛʀ] **I.** *adj* extravagant **II.** *m, f* spendthrift

déperdition [depɛʀdisjɔ̃] *f* **~ de chaleur/d'énergie** heat/energy loss; **~ de forces** (*chez un malade*) loss of strength

dépérir [depeʀiʀ] <8> *vi* **1.** (*personne, animal*) to fade away; (*plante*) to wither; **la pollution fait ~ les arbres** pollution is withering the trees **2.** (*péricliter*) to decline

dépêtrer [depetʀe] <1> *vpr* **se ~ de qc** to extricate oneself from sth

dépeuplement [depœpləmɑ̃] *m* depopulation

dépeupler [depœple] <1> **I.** *vt* (*pays, région*) to depopulate **II.** *vpr* **se ~** to be depopulated

dépilatoire [depilatwaʀ] *adj* hair remover

dépistage [depistaʒ] *m* (*d'un malfaiteur*) tracking down; (*d'une maladie*) detection; **~ précoce** early detection; **~ du cancer** cancer screening; **test de ~ du Sida** AIDS test

dépister [depiste] <1> *vt* (*rechercher: personne, animal*) to track down; (*maladie*) to detect

dépit [depi] *m* pique; **~ amoureux** heartache; **de** [*o* **par**] **~** out of spite; **éprouver du ~** to feel piqued; **crever de ~** to be sick with spite; **ravaler son ~** to choke back one's dismay; **causer du ~ à qn** to greatly upset sb ►**en ~ du bon sens** against all common sense; **agir en ~ du bon sens** to fly in the face of common sense; **en ~ de qc** in spite of sth; **en ~ de tout et de tous** in spite of everyone and everything; **en ~ de sa jeunesse/de la pluie** in spite of her youth/the rain

dépité(e) [depite] *adj* piqued

déplacé(e) [deplase] *adj* **1.** (*inopportun: intervention, présence*) inappropriate **2.** (*inconvenant: geste, propos*) uncalled for

déplacement [deplasmɑ̃] *m* **1.** (*changement de place: d'un objet*) moving; (*d'un os*) dislocation **2.** (*voyage*) trip; **être en ~** to be on a trip **3.** (*mouvement*) movement **4.** (*mutation*) transfer ►**cela vaut le ~** it's worth going (out of your way) to see

déplacer [deplase] <2> **I.** *vt* **1.** (*changer de place: objet, meuble*) to move **2.** MED (*articulation*) to dislocate; **~ une vertèbre à qn** to cause sb to slip a disc **3.** (*muter: fonctionnaire*) to transfer **4.** (*réinstaller*) *a.* TECH to displace **5.** (*éluder*) **~ une question** to change the point of a question **II.** *vpr* **1.** (*être en mouvement, se décaler*) **se ~** to move; **se ~ en chaise roulante** to get around in a wheelchair **2.** (*voyager*) **se ~ en avion/voiture** to travel by plane/car, fly/drive **3.** MED **se ~ une articulation** to dislocate a joint

déplaire [deplɛʀ] *irr* **I.** *vi* (*ne pas plaire*) **~ à qn** to displease sb; (*irriter*) to annoy sb ►**n'en déplaise à qn** *iron* with all due respect to sb **II.** *vpr* **se ~ en ville/dans un emploi** not to be happy in town/with a job

déplaisant(e) [deplɛzɑ̃, ɑ̃t] *adj* unpleasant

dépliant [deplijɑ̃] *m* leaflet; **~ touristique** travel brochure

déplier [deplije] <1> **I.** *vt* (*drap, vêtement, plan, journal*) to unfold; (*sur une table*) to spread out; (*jambes*) to stretch out **II.** *vpr* **se ~** to fold out; **ce canapé peut se ~** you can fold the sofa out

déploiement [deplwamɑ̃] *m* **1.** (*action de déployer: d'une aile*) spreading; (*d'un drapeau*) unfurling **2.** (*étalage: de richesses*) display **3.** (*dépense*) **~ d'énergie** exertion

déplorable [deplɔʀabl] *adj* (*effet, fin, oubli*) regrettable; (*comportement, personne, situation, résultats*) appalling; **être dans un état ~** (*enfant*) to be in a terrible state

déplorer [deplɔʀe] <1> *vt* **1.** (*regretter*) to deplore; **~ ne pas pouvoir faire qc** to regret that one cannot do sth **2.** (*enregistrer*) **on déplore des victimes** there have been a number of victims **3.** (*être affligé de: malheur, mort*) to mourn

déployer [deplwaje] <7> **I.** *vt* **1.** (*déplier: ailes, carte*) to spread out; (*voile, drapeau*) to unfurl **2.** (*mettre en œuvre: énergie, ingéniosité, courage*) to display **3.** (*étaler: charmes, richesses*) to show off **II.** *vpr* **1.** (*se déplier*) **se ~** (*ailes, tissu*) to be spread out; (*voile, dra-

peau) to be unfurled **2.** (*se disperser: soldats, troupes*) to be deployed; (*cortège*) to spread out

déplumé(e) [deplyme] *adj* (*oiseau*) plucked; *inf* (*arbre, crâne, personne*) thin on top

dépoli(e) [depɔli] *adj* (*verre*) frosted

dépolluer [depɔlɥe] <1> *vt* (*lieu*) to decontaminate; (*rivière, mer*) to clean up

dépollution [depɔlysjɔ̃] *f* decontamination; (*d'une rivière, de la mer*) cleaning up

dépopulation [depɔpylasjɔ̃] *f* depopulation

déportation [depɔʀtasjɔ̃] *f* HIST deportation; **en ~** in the (concentration) camps

déporté(e) [depɔʀte] *m(f)* deportee

déporter [depɔʀte] <1> **I.** *vt* **1.** (*exiler, bannir*) to deport **2.** HIST (*interner*) to send to a concentration camp **3.** (*faire dévier: voiture, vélo*) to push off course **II.** *vpr* AUTO **se ~** to swerve

déposer [depoze] <1> **I.** *vt* **1.** (*poser*) to place **2.** (*se débarrasser*) to put down **3.** (*conduire, livrer: personne*) to drop off; (*ordures*) to dump **4.** (*décanter*) **~ de la boue/du sable** to deposit mud/sand **5.** (*confier: bagages, lettre, carte de visite*) to leave **6.** FIN (*argent, chèque, valeur*) to deposit; **~ 100 euros sur son compte** to put 100 euros into one's account **7.** (*faire enregistrer: brevet, rapport*) to file; (*marque*) to register; (*projet de loi*) to table *Brit,* to bring up for discussion *Am;* (*réclamation, plainte*) to lodge **8.** (*démonter: appareil*) to take down; (*moteur*) to strip down **9.** (*abdiquer: couronne*) to abdicate; **~ le pouvoir** to renounce power **10.** (*destituer*) to depose **II.** *vi* **1.** (*témoigner*) to give evidence **2.** (*laisser un dépôt: vin, eau*) to settle **III.** *vpr* **se ~** (*lie, poussière*) to settle

dépositaire [depozitɛʀ] *m* **1.** (*détenteur*) despository; (*d'un secret*) guardian; **~ de l'autorité de l'État** state official *Brit,* public official *Am* **2.** (*concessionnaire*) agent; **~ de journaux** newsagent

déposition [depozisjɔ̃] *f* **1.** (*témoignage*) statement; **faire/recueillir/signer une ~** to make/take/sign a statement **2.** (*destitution: d'un souverain*) deposition

déposséder [depɔsede] <5> *vt* (*personne*) to dispossess

dépossession [depɔsesjɔ̃] *f* dispossession

dépôt [depo] *m* **1.** (*présentation: d'un projet de loi*) introduction **2.** (*enregistrement: d'une plainte*) lodging; (*d'une marque déposée*) registration; (*d'un brevet*) filing **3.** FIN (*d'un chèque, d'argent, de titres*) depositing; (*somme déposé*) deposit; **~ de bilan** bankruptcy petition **4.** (*fait de confier*) **nous recommandons le ~ de vos articles de valeur/manteaux à la réception** we recommend you leave valuables/coats at reception; **laisser qc en ~ chez qn** to leave sth with sb for safekeeping **5.** (*fait de poser: d'une gerbe*) laying **6.** (*sédiment*) deposit **7.** (*entrepôt: d'autobus*) depot; **~ d'ordures** dump

dépotoir [depɔtwaʀ] *m* (*dépôt d'ordures*) tip *Brit,* dump *Am;* **c'est un véritable ~** *inf* this place is a real tip

dépouille [depuj] *f* **1.** (*peau: d'un animal à fourrure*) skin; (*d'un serpent*) slough **2.** *form* (*corps*) **~ mortelle** *form* (mortal) remains **3.** *pl* spoils; (*héritage*) personal effects

dépouillé(e) [depuje] *adj* **1.** (*sobre: décor*) bare; (*style, texte*) unadorned **2.** (*exempt*) **être ~ de qc** devoid of sth

dépouillement [depujmɑ̃] *m* (*examen*) **~ du scrutin** counting the votes; **~ du courrier** going through the mail

dépouiller [depuje] <1> **I.** *vt* **1.** (*ouvrir*) **~ le scrutin** to count the votes; **~ le courrier** to go through the mail **2.** (*dévaliser*) to rob; **~ qn de ses biens** to strip sb of their possessions **3.** (*déshabiller*) **~ qn de ses vêtements** to strip sb of their clothes **II.** *vpr* **1.** (*se déshabiller*) **se ~ de ses vêtements** to take off one's clothes **2.** (*faire don*) **se ~ de sa fortune** to give up one's fortune

dépourvu(e) [depuʀvy] *adj* **1.** (*privé*) **être ~** to have nothing; **être ~ de bon sens** to have no common sense **2.** (*ne pas être équipé*) **être ~ de chauffage** to be without heating ►<u>prendre</u> **qn au ~** to take sb unawares

dépoussiérer [depusjeʀe] <5> *vt* **1.** (*nettoyer*) to dust **2.** (*rajeunir*) to blow the dust off

dépravé(e) [depʀave] **I.** *adj* depraved **II.** *m(f)* pervert

déprécier [depʀesje] <1a> **I.** *vt* **1.** (*faire perdre de la valeur: monnaie, valeur*) to depreciate; **~ une marchandise** to bring down the price of a commodity **2.** (*minimiser*) to belittle **II.** *vpr* **se ~ 1.** (*se dévaluer: bien, marchandise*) to fall in price; (*monnaie, valeur*) to fall in value **2.** (*se dénigrer*) to belittle oneself

déprédation [depʀedasjɔ̃] *f gén pl* (*dégâts*) damage *no pl;* (*pillage*) plunder *no pl;* (*malversation*) misappropriation; **commettre** [*o* **se livrer à**] **des ~s** to embezzle

dépressif, -ive [depʀesif, -iv] **I.** *adj* depressive **II.** *m, f* depressive

dépression [depʀesjɔ̃] *f* **1.** (*découragement*) *a.* PSYCH, METEO depression; **faire une ~ nerveuse** to have a nervous breakdown **2.** ECON slump

déprimant(e) [depʀimɑ̃, ɑ̃t] *adj* (*démoralisant*) depressing

déprime [depʀim] *f inf* depression; **être en pleine ~** to be completely down

déprimé(e) [depʀime] *adj* (*personne*) depressed

déprimer [depʀime] <1> **I.** *vt* (*démoraliser*) to depress **II.** *vi inf* to be depressed

déprogrammer [depʀɔgʀame] <1> *vt* **1.** CINE, TV (*émission, spectacle*) to take off **2.** INFOR (*robot*) to deprogram

dépuceler [depys(ə)le] <3> *vt inf* to deflower

depuis [dəpɥi] I. *prep* 1. (*à partir d'un moment*) since; (*à partir d'un lieu*) from; ~ **quelle date?** since when?; ~ **Paris, ...** from Paris; **toutes les tailles** ~ **le 36** all sizes from 36 up; ~ **mon plus jeune âge** since my childhood; ~ **le début jusqu'à la fin** from the beginning to the end; ~ **que qn a fait qc** ever since sb did sth 2. (*durée*) for; ~ **longtemps/plusieurs kilomètres** for a long time/a few kilometres; **je la connais** ~ **peu** I've (only) known her a short while; ~ **cela** since then II. *adv* since

député(e) [depyte] *m(f)* deputy

der [dɛʀ] *mf inf abr de* **dernier, dernière boire le** ~ to drink one last one ►**la** ~ des ~**s** the very last; **les combattants en 1914 croyaient que ce serait la** ~ the men who fought in 1914 thought it would be the war to end all wars

déraciner [deʀasine] <1> *vt* 1. (*arracher: arbre, peuple*) to uproot 2. (*éliminer: préjugé*) to root out; ~ **une habitude** to get rid of a habit

déraillement [deʀɑjmɑ̃] *m* (*d'un train*) derailing

dérailler [deʀɑje] <1> *vi* 1. (*sortir des rails: train*) to be derailed; **faire** ~ **un train** to derail a train 2. *inf* (*déraisonner*) to talk rubbish; **il déraille complètement** he's out of his head 3. (*mal fonctionner: machine, appareil*) to play up

dérailleur [deʀɑjœʀ] *m* derailleur

déraisonnable [deʀɛzɔnabl] *adj* unreasonably

déraisonner [deʀɛzɔne] <1> *vi* to talk nonsense

dérangé(e) [deʀɑ̃ʒe] *adj* 1. *inf* (*fou*) off their head 2. MED **être** ~ to have an upset stomach; **avoir l'intestin** ~ to have bowel trouble 3. (*désordonné*) in a mess

dérangement [deʀɑ̃ʒmɑ̃] *m* 1. (*gêne*) trouble *no pl;* ~ **intestinal** bowel trouble; **excusez-moi du** ~**!** sorry for the trouble!; **causer du** ~ **à qn** to cause sb trouble 2. (*incident technique*) **être en** ~ (*ligne, téléphone*) to be out of order

déranger [deʀɑ̃ʒe] <2a> I. *vt* 1. (*gêner*) to disturb; **je peux te** ~ **pour un service?** can I bother you for a favour? *Brit,* can I bother you for favor? *Am* 2. (*mettre en désordre*) to untidy; (*objets, affaires, coiffure*) to mess up 3. (*perturber: projets*) to spoil; **ce repas m'a dérangé l'estomac** that meal upset my stomach II. *vi* 1. (*arriver mal à propos*) to be a nuisance 2. (*mettre mal à l'aise*) to upset people III. *vpr* 1. (*se déplacer*) **se** ~ to go/come out; **je me suis dérangé pour rien** it was a waste of time going 2. (*interrompre ses occupations*) **se** ~ **pour qn** to go to trouble for sb; **ne vous dérangez pas pour moi!** don't put yourself out for me!

dérapage [deʀapaʒ] *m* 1. AUTO skid; ~ **contrôlé** controlled skid 2. (*acte imprévu, impair*) slip; ~ (**verbal**) slip of the tongue 3. (*dérive*) **il y a un** ~ **des prix** prices are getting out of control

déraper [deʀape] <1> *vi* 1. (*glisser: personne, semelles*) to slip; (*voiture*) to skid 2. (*dévier: personne, conversation*) to veer off; ~ **vers la politique** (*roman, discussion*) to veer off on to politics 3. ECON (*prix, politique économique*) to get out of control

déréglé(e) [deʀegle] *adj* 1. (*dérangé: estomac*) upset; (*pouls, appétit*) unsettled; **le mécanisme est** ~ the mechanism isn't working properly; **le temps est** ~ the weather's unsettled 2. (*désordonné: habitudes*) unsettled; (*vie, existence*) disordered; (*mœurs*) dissolute

déréglementer [deʀɛgləmɑ̃te] <1> *vt* to deregulate

dérégler [deʀegle] <5> I. *vt* 1. (*déranger: mécanisme*) to disturb; (*climat, appétit*) to unsettle; **ça a déréglé la machine** it made the machine go wrong; **ça a déréglé mon estomac** it upset my stomach 2. (*pervertir: mœurs*) to corrupt II. *vpr* 1. (*mal fonctionner*) **se** ~ (*machine*) to go wrong; (*climat, estomac*) to become unsettled 2. (*se pervertir: mœurs*) to be corrupted

dérider [deʀide] <1> I. *vt* ~ **qn** to cheer sb up II. *vpr* **se** ~ to cheer up; (*visage*) to brighten up; **ne jamais se** ~ (*personne*) to never have a smile on one's face

dérision [deʀizjɔ̃] *f* mockery; **tourner qn/qc en** ~ to mock sb/sth; **geste de** ~ derisive gesture; **par** ~ derisively

dérisoire [deʀizwaʀ] *adj* derisory; **à un prix** ~ (*vendre*) at a ridiculous price

dérivatif [deʀivatif] *m* distraction; ~ **à qc** distraction from sth; **cela ferait un** ~ **à tes soucis** that'll take your mind off your problems

dérivation [deʀivasjɔ̃] *f* (*d'un cours d'eau, d'une route*) diversion

dérive [deʀiv] *f* 1. (*déviation: d'un avion, bateau*) drift; ~ **des continents** continental drift; **être à la** ~ (*bateau*) to be adrift 2. AVIAT fin; NAUT centreboard *Brit,* centerboard *Am* 3. FIN (*d'une monnaie, de l'économie*) slump; **la** ~ **de leur politique** the way their policy has slipped out of control ►**partir à la** ~ to drift; (*projets*) to go awry; **à la** ~ going downhill

dérivé [deʀive] *m* CHIM, LING derivative; (*produit*) by-product

dérivé(e) [deʀive] *adj* **être** ~ **de qc** (*race*) to come from sth; (*style, œuvre d'art/littéraire*) to derive from sth

dériver [deʀive] <1> I. *vt* (*détourner*) to divert II. *vi* 1. LING ~ **de qc** to derive from sth 2. (*s'écarter: barque*) to drift

dériveur [deʀivœʀ] *m* 1. (*voile*) storm sail 2. (*petit voilier*) sailing boat (*with a centreboard*)

dermatologie [dɛʀmatɔlɔʒi] *f* dermatology

D

dermatologue [dɛʀmatɔlɔg] *mf* dermatologist

dernier [dɛʀnje] *m Belgique* **le ~ de tout** (*la fin de tout*) the last straw

dernier, -ière [dɛʀnje, -jɛʀ] **I.** *adj* **1.** *antéposé* (*ultime*) last; **avant le 15 mai, ~ délai** by 15 May at the latest; **être ~ en classe** to be bottom of the class; **examiner qc dans les ~s détails** to examine sth in the finest detail **2.** *antéposé* (*le plus récent: œuvre, mode, nouvelle, édition*) latest; **ces ~s temps** just recently; **ces ~s jours** these last few days; **aux dernières nouvelles, il ...** the last we heard was that he ...; **le ~ cri** the latest thing **3.** *postposé* (*antérieur: an, mois, semaine, siècle*) last; **l'an ~ à cette époque** this time last year **II.** *m, f* **le/la ~(-ière)** the last; **son petit ~** his/her youngest; **c'est le ~ de mes soucis** that's the last of my worries; **habiter au ~** to live on the top floor; **ils ont été tués jusqu'au ~** every last one of them was killed; **être le ~ des imbéciles** to be a complete idiot; **en ~** lastly ►**rira bien qui rira le ~** *prov* he who laughs last laughs longest

dernière [dɛʀnjɛʀ] *f* **1.** (*représentation*) **la ~** the last night **2.** *inf* (*histoire, nouvelle*) **la ~** the latest

dernièrement [dɛʀnjɛʀmɑ̃] *adv* lately

dernier-né, dernière-née [dɛʀnjene, dɛʀnjɛʀne] <derniers-nés> *m, f* last-born; **la dernière-née des voitures Renault** Renault's latest model

dérobée [deʀɔbe] **à la ~** *soutenu* furtively

dérober [deʀɔbe] <1> *vt* (*voler*) to steal

dérogation [deʀɔgasjɔ̃] *f* **1.** (*exception*) exemption; **par ~** by way of exemption; **obtenir une ~** to obtain an exemption; **admettre quelques ~s** (*règlement*) to allow a few exceptions **2.** (*violation*) breach; **être une ~ à la loi** to be a breach of the law

dérougir [deʀuʒiʀ] <8> *vi Québec* **ça ne dérougit pas!** (*l'activité ne diminue pas*) there's no let-up!

dérouillée [deʀuje] *f inf* belting; **prendre** [*o* **recevoir**] **une ~** to get slapped about

dérouiller [deʀuje] <1> **I.** *vt* (*ôter la rouille*) to remove the rust from **II.** *vi inf* (*recevoir une correction*) to catch it; (*souffrir*) to be put through it **III.** *vpr* **se ~ les muscles** to loosen up

déroulement [deʀulmɑ̃] *m* **1.** (*processus: d'une cérémonie*) course; (*suite des faits: d'un crime*) stages; **pendant le ~ du film** while the film was being shown **2.** (*fait de dérouler*) unwinding

dérouler [deʀule] <1> **I.** *vt* (*dévider: tuyau, rouleau*) to unroll; (*store*) to wind down **II.** *vpr* **1.** (*s'écouler*) **se ~** (*vie, manifestation, crime, événement, cérémonie, concert*) to take place; **pendant que l'action/le film se déroulait** as the action/film progressed; **tout s'est déroulé comme prévu** everything went off as planned **2.** (*se dévider*) **se ~** (*bobine, cassette*) to unwind

déroutant(e) [deʀutɑ̃, ɑ̃t] *adj* disconcerting; **c'est vraiment quelqu'un de ~** he's so disconcerting

déroute [deʀut] *f* rout; (*effondrement*) collapse

dérouter [deʀute] <1> *vt* **1.** (*écarter de sa route*) to reroute **2.** (*déconcerter*) to take aback

derrick [deʀik] *m* derrick

derrière [dɛʀjɛʀ] **I.** *prep* behind; **être ~ qn** (*dans un classement*) to be behind sb; (*soutenir qn*) to be (right) behind sb; **faire qc ~ qn** *fig* to do sth behind sb's back; **laisser qn/qc ~ soi** to leave sb behind; **par ~** at the back; **par ~ qc** at the back of sth; **passez par ~!** go round the back! **II.** *adv* behind; **de ~** from behind; **là ~** over at the back **III.** *m* **1.** (*partie arrière: d'une maison*) back; **la porte de ~** the back door **2.** *inf* (*postérieur: d'un animal*) rump; (*d'une personne*) backside ►**botter le ~ à qn** to smack sb's backside

des¹ [de] **I.** *art déf pl contracté* **les pages ~ livres** (*ces livres*) the pages of the books; (*livres en général*) the pages of books; *v. a.* **de II.** *art partitif, parfois non traduit* **je mange ~ épinards** I eat spinach

des² [de, də] <*devant adjectif* de> *art indéf pl, parfois non traduit* **j'ai acheté ~ pommes et de beaux citrons** I bought (some) apples and some lovely lemons

dès [dɛ] *prep* (*à partir de*) as from; **~ lors** (*à partir de ce moment-là*) from then on; (*par conséquent*) in which case; **~ maintenant** from now on; **~ qu'elle a fait ça** once she'd done that; **~ le matin ...** as soon as morning comes/came; **~ l'époque romaine ...** from Roman times onwards; **~ mon retour je ferai ...** as soon as I get back I shall do ...; **~ Valence** after Valence; **~ le premier verre** after the first glass

désabusé(e) [dezabyze] *adj* disenchanted; **prendre un air ~** to look disenchanted; **~ de qc** disillusioned with sth

désaccord [dezakɔʀ] *m* **1.** (*mésentente*) discord **2.** (*divergence, désapprobation*) disagreement; **~ d'idées** difference of opinion; **être en ~ avec qn/qc sur qc** to be in disagreement with sb/sth over sth **3.** (*contradiction*) discrepancy

désaccordé(e) [dezakɔʀde] *adj* out of tune

désaccorder [dezakɔʀde] <1> **I.** *vt* to put out of tune **II.** *vpr* **se ~** to go out of tune

désaffecté(e) [dezafɛkte] *adj* (*église, école, usine*) disused

désagréable [dezagʀeabl] *adj* unpleasant

désagréablement [dezagʀeabləmɑ̃] *adv* unpleasantly; (*répondre*) in an unpleasant way

désagrégation [dezagʀegasjɔ̃] *f* **1.** (*désintégration: d'une roche*) weathering; CHIM disintegration **2.** (*décomposition: d'une nation, d'un empire, d'une équipe*) break-up

désagréger [dezagʀeʒe] <2a, 5> **I.** *vt*

1. (*désintégrer*) to disintegrate 2. (*décomposer: groupe, parti*) to break up II. *vpr* **se ~** (*corps chimique, roche*) to disintegrate; (*foule*) to break up

désagrément [dezagʀemɑ̃] *m* inconvenience; **attirer** [*o* **causer**] **du ~ à qn** to cause sb trouble; **cette voiture m'a valu bien des ~s** this car's given me a lot of trouble

désalper [dezalpe] <1> *vi Suisse* (*descendre de l'alpage à la fin de l'estivage*) to come down from the mountains

désaltérant(e) [dezalteʀɑ̃, ɑ̃t] *adj* thirst-quenching; **le thé est une boisson ~e** tea quenches your thirst

désaltérer [dezalteʀe] <5> I. *vt* **~ qn** to quench the thirst of sb II. *vpr* **se ~** to quench one's thirst

désamiantage [dezamjɑ̃taʒ] *m* asbestos removal

désamorcer [dezamɔʀse] <2> I. *vt* 1. (*interrompre le fonctionnement de: arme*) to unprime; (*bombe*) to defuse; (*pompe, siphon*) to drain 2. (*neutraliser: situation, crise*) to defuse; (*danger*) to avert II. *vpr* **se ~** (*pompe, siphon*) to drain

désappointé(e) [dezapwɛ̃te] *adj* disappointed; **être ~ de qc** to be disappointed with sth

désappointement [dezapwɛ̃tmɑ̃] *m* disappointment

désapprobateur, -trice [dezapʀɔbatœʀ, -tʀis] *adj* disapproving

désapprobation [dezapʀɔbasjɔ̃] *f* disapproval; **~ muette** [*o* **silencieuse**] silent disapproval; **la ~ de sa mère** his mother's disapproval; **des murmures de ~** murmurs of disapproval; **manifester sa ~** to show one's disapproval

désapprouver [dezapʀuve] <1> I. *vt* **~ qn/qc** to disapprove of sb/sth II. *vi* to disapprove

désarçonner [dezaʀsɔne] <1> *vt* 1. (*jeter à bas*) to unseat 2. (*désemparer: candidat, orateur*) to throw

désarmant(e) [dezaʀmɑ̃, ɑ̃t] *adj* disarming

désarmement [dezaʀməmɑ̃] *m* (*d'une personne, population*) disarmament; (*d'un navire*) laying up

désarmer [dezaʀme] <1> I. *vt* 1. (*dépouiller de ses armes*) to disarm 2. (*déséquiper*) **~ un navire** to lay up a ship 3. (*décharger: arme*) to unload; (*mettre le cran de sûreté*) to put the safety catch on 4. (*désemparer: personne*) to disarm II. *vi* 1. (*gouvernement, pays*) to disarm 2. (*s'adoucir*) **ne pas ~ contre qn** (*ennemi, haine, vengeance*) to be unrelenting towards sb; (*douleurs*) not to let up on sb 3. (*ne pas lâcher prise*) **ne pas ~** to not give an inch

désarroi [dezaʀwa] *m* 1. (*trouble*) confusion 2. (*désespoir*) helplessness; **être en grand** [*o* **plein**] **~** to feel uttlerly helpless; **plonger qn dans le plus profond ~** (*matériellement*) to leave sb utterly helpless; (*moralement*) to leave sb utterly dismayed

désastre [dezastʀ] *m* disaster

désastreux, -euse [dezastʀø, -øz] *adj* 1. (*catastrophique*) disastrous 2. (*nul*) terrible; **c'était ~** it was a disaster

désavantage [dezavɑ̃taʒ] *m* disadvantage; (*physique*) handicap; **à son/leur ~** not to his/their advantage; (*changer*) so as to put him/them at a disadvantage; **c'est à son ~** it's against him; **tourner au ~ de qn** to put sb at a disadvantage

désavantager [dezavɑ̃taʒe] <2a> *vt* **~ qn** to put sb at a disadvantage

désavantageux, -euse [dezavɑ̃taʒø, -jøz] *adj* disadvantageous

désaveu [dezavø] <x> *m* 1. (*rétractation*) retraction; (*reniement*) disowning 2. (*condamnation: d'un comportement, d'une personne*) disavowal; (*réprobation*) repudiation; **infliger un ~ cinglant à qn** to inflict a stinging rebuke on sb

désavouer [dezavwe] <1> *vt* 1. (*refuser comme sien: ouvrage, collaborateur*) to disown; (*paternité*) to deny; (*signature, paroles, enfant*) to repudiate 2. (*rétracter: opinion, propos*) to retract 3. (*désapprouver: personne, conduite de qn, loi*) to disown

desceller [desele] <1> I. *vt* 1. (*enlever le sceau*) **~ une lettre** to break the seal on a letter 2. (*détacher*) to free II. *vpr* **se ~** (*pavé, pierre*) to come free

descendance [desɑ̃dɑ̃s] *f* 1. (*postérité*) descendants *pl* 2. (*origine*) descent

descendant(e) [desɑ̃dɑ̃, ɑ̃t] I. *adj* (*chemin*) going down; (*gamme*) descending II. *m(f)* descendant

descendre [desɑ̃dʀ] <14> I. *vi être* 1. (*aller du haut vers le bas: vu d'en haut/d'en bas: avion*) to go/come down; (*oiseau*) to fly down; (*parachutiste*) to float down; **~ à la cave/par l'escalier** to go down to the cellar/by the stairs; **~ par l'ascenseur** to go down in the lift *Brit*, to go down in the elevator *Am*; **~ en voiture/en avion** to drive/fly down; **~ dans la plaine** (*rivière, route*) to go down into the plain 2. (*quitter, sortir*) **~ du bateau/du train** to get off the boat/the train; **~ de la voiture** to get out of the car; **~ du cheval** to get off a horse; **fais ~ le chat de la table** get the cat down from the table 3. (*aller, se rendre*) **~ en ville** to go into town 4. (*faire irruption*) **~ dans un bar** (*police, voyous*) to burst into a pub 5. (*loger*) **~ à l'hôtel/chez qn** to stay at a hotel/at a friend's place 6. (*être issu de*) **~ de qn** to descend from sb; **~ d'une famille pauvre** to be from a poor family 7. (*aller en pente*) **~ en pente douce** (*route, chemin*) to go down; (*vignoble, terrain*) to slope downwards 8. (*baisser: marée*) to go out; (*niveau de l'eau, prix, taux*) to go down; (*baromètre, thermomètre*) to fall 9. (*atteindre*) *a.* MUS **~ à/jusqu'à** (*robe, cheveux, puits*) to go down to/

D

as far as ►~ **dans la rue** to take to the streets; **ça fait** ~ *inf* that helps it down **II.** *vt avoir* **1.** (*se déplacer à pied: vu d'en haut: escalier, colline*) to go down; (*vu d'en bas*) to come down **2.** (*se déplacer en véhicule: vu d'en haut/d'en bas: rue, route*) to drive down **3.** (*porter en bas: vu d'en haut*) to take down; (*vu d'en bas*) to bring down; ~ **qc à la cave** to take sth down to the cellar **4.** (*baisser: stores, rideaux*) to lower; (*tableau, étagère*) to take down **5.** *inf* (*déposer*) ~ **qn à l'école** to drop sb at school **6.** *inf* (*abattre: avion*) to shoot down; (*personne*) to do in **7.** *inf* (*critiquer: film, auteur*) to slam **8.** *inf* (*boire, manger*) to down **9.** MUS ~ **la gamme** (*chanteur, joueur*) to go down the scale ►~ **en flammes** *inf* to shoot down in flames

descente [desɑ̃t] *f* **1.** (*opp: montée: d'une pente*) way down; (*à pied*) walk down; (*en voiture*) drive down; (*en escalade*) climb down; (*à ski*) ski down; (*d'un fleuve*) sail down **2.** AVIAT descent **3.** (*arrivée*) **à la** ~ **d'avion/de bateau** as the passengers disembarked; **accueillir qn à la** ~ **de l'avion/du train** to meet sb off the plane/train **4.** (*action de descendre au fond de*) ~ **dans qc** descent into sth **5.** (*attaque brusque*) **une** ~ **de police** a police raid; **faire une** ~ **dans un bar** *inf* to hit a bar **6.** (*pente*) downward slope; **dans la** ~**/les** ~**s** going downhill **7.** (*action de porter en bas, déposer: vu d'en haut*) taking down; (*vu d'en bas*) bringing down; **la** ~ **des bagages de la voiture** getting the luggage out of the car ►~ **aux enfers** descent into Hell; **avoir une bonne** ~ *inf* to be a big drinker

descriptif [dɛskʀiptif] *m* specifications *pl*

descriptif, -ive [dɛskʀiptif, -iv] *adj* descriptive; **musique** ~ programme music *Brit,* program music *Am*

description [dɛskʀipsjɔ̃] *f* description; (*d'un événement*) account

désemparé(e) [dezɑ̃paʀe] *adj* (*personne*) distraught

désemplir [dezɑ̃pliʀ] <8> *vi* **ne pas** ~ to be always full

désenchanté(e) [dezɑ̃ʃɑ̃te] *adj* disenchanted

désenfler [dezɑ̃fle] <1> **I.** *vt* ~ **qc** to bring down the swelling in sth **II.** *vi, vpr* (**se**) ~ to go down; **son genou (se) désenfle** (the swelling in) his knee is going down

désengager [dezɑ̃gaʒe] <2a> *vpr* **se** ~ to pull out

déséquilibre [dezekilibʀ] *m* **1.** (*instabilité, inégalité: des forces, valeurs*) imbalance; (*d'une construction, personne*) instability; ~ **entre l'offre et la demande** imbalance between supply and demand; **être en** ~ (*personne, objet*) to be off balance **2.** PSYCH ~ **mental** mental instability

déséquilibré(e) [dezekilibʀe] **I.** *adj* (*personne*) off balance; PSYCH unstable; (*balance*) badly adjusted; (*quantités*) unbalanced **II.** *m(f)* (*personne*) unbalanced person

déséquilibrer [dezekilibʀe] <1> *vt* (*personne*) to throw off balance; *fig* to unbalance; (*objet*) to make unsteady; (*budget*) to unbalance

désert [dezɛʀ] *m* **1.** GEO desert **2.** (*lieu dépeuplé*) wilderness ►**prêcher dans le** ~ to cry out in the wilderness

désert(e) [dezɛʀ, ɛʀt] *adj* **1.** (*sans habitant: pays, région, maison*) deserted; (*île*) desert **2.** (*peu fréquenté: plage, rue*) deserted

déserter [dezɛʀte] <1> **I.** *vt* **1.** (*quitter: lieu, son poste*) to abandon **2.** (*abandonner, renier: cause, syndicat, parti*) to desert; (*réunions*) to forsake **II.** *vi* MIL to desert

déserteur [dezɛʀtœʀ] **I.** *m* MIL deserter **II.** *adj* deserting

désertion [dezɛʀsjɔ̃] *f* **1.** MIL desertion; ~ **devant qn** desertion in the face of sb **2.** (*fait de quitter*) ~ **de qc par qn** the abandonment of sth by sb; **la** ~ **des campagnes par les populations** people abandoning the countryside **3.** (*défection*) ~ **du parti** desertion from the party

désertique [dezɛʀtik] *adj* (*climat, plante, région*) desert

désespérant(e) [dezɛspeʀɑ̃, ɑ̃t] *adj* (*décourageant*) **être** ~ (*notes, comportement*) to be hopeless

désespéré(e) [dezɛspeʀe] **I.** *adj* (*personne*) desperate; (*cas, situation*) (*critique*) desperate; (*sans espoir*) hopeless **II.** *m(f)* person in despair

désespérément [dezɛspeʀemɑ̃] *adv* desperately

désespérer [dezɛspeʀe] <5> **I.** *vi* to despair; ~ **de qc** to despair of sth; **c'est à** ~ it would drive you to despair **II.** *vt* **1.** (*affliger*) ~ **qn** to drive sb to despair **2.** (*décourager*) ~ **qn** to make sb despair **III.** *vpr* **se** ~ to despair

désespoir [dezɛspwaʀ] *m* despair; **faire le** ~ **de qn** to drive sb to despair ►**en** ~ **de cause** in desperation

déshabillé [dezabije] *m* (*vêtement*) revealing

déshabillé(e) [dezabije] *adj* undressed; (*scène, séquence*) (in the) nude

déshabiller [dezabije] <1> **I.** *vt* (*personne*) to undress **II.** *vpr* **se** ~ **1.** (*se dévêtir*) to get undressed **2.** (*se mettre à l'aise*) **je vais me** ~ I'm going to take my things off

déshabituer [dezabitɥe] <1> **I.** *vt* ~ **qn de qc** to get sb out of the habit of doing sth **II.** *vpr* **se** ~ **de qc** (*exprès*) to rid oneself of a habit; (*sans essayer*) to lose the habit of doing sth

déshérité(e) [dezeʀite] **I.** *adj* **1.** (*privé d'héritage*) disinherited **2.** (*désavantagé*) underprivileged **II.** *mpl* **les** ~**s** the underprivileged

déshériter [dezeʀite] <1> *vt* **1.** JUR to disinherit **2.** (*priver d'avantages*) to deprive

déshonneur [dezɔnœʀ] *m* dishonour *Brit,* dishonor *Am;* **il n'y a pas de** ~ **à faire cela**

there's no shame in doing that; **c'est le ~ de la famille** he is the black sheep of the family
déshonorant(e) [dezɔnɔʀɑ̃, ɑ̃t] *adj* shameful
déshonorer [dezɔnɔʀe] <1> **I.** *vt* **1.** (*porter atteinte à l'honneur de*) to dishonour *Brit,* to dishonor *Am* **2.** (*défigurer: monument, paysage*) to disfigure **II.** *vpr* **se ~** to bring shame on oneself
déshydraté(e) [dezidʀate] *adj* **1.** (*sans eau: légumes*) dried **2.** *inf* (*assoiffé*) **être ~** to be parched
déshydrater [dezidʀate] <1> *vpr* **se ~** to dehydrate
désignation [deziɲasjɔ̃] *f* **1.** (*appellation*) name **2.** (*nomination*) nomination **3.** (*indication*) naming
designer [dizajnœʀ, dezajnœʀ] *mf* designer
désigner [deziɲe] <1> *vt* **1.** (*montrer, indiquer*) to indicate; **~ qn/qc du doigt** to point at sb/sth **2.** (*signaler*) **~ qn à l'attention de qn** to bring sb to sb's attention **3.** (*choisir*) **~ qn comme qc** to designate sb as sth **4.** (*qualifier*) **être tout désigné pour qc** to be ideal for sth **5.** (*dénommer*) **~ qn par son nom** to refer to sb by their name; **~ qc sous qc** to refer to sth as sth
désillusion [dezi(l)lyzjɔ̃] *f* disillusionment
désinence [dezinɑ̃s] *f* inflection
désinfectant [dezɛ̃fɛktɑ̃] *m* disinfectant
désinfectant(e) [dezɛ̃fɛktɑ̃, ɑ̃t] *adj* disinfectant
désinfecter [dezɛ̃fɛkte] <1> *vt* to disinfect
désinfection [dezɛ̃fɛksjɔ̃] *f* disinfection
désinformation [dezɛ̃fɔʀmasjɔ̃] *f* disinformation
désintégration [dezɛ̃tegʀasjɔ̃] *f a.* GEO, PHYS disintegration
désintégrer [dezɛ̃tegʀe] <5> **I.** *vt* **1.** GEO, PHYS to disintegrate **2.** *fig* (*famille, parti*) to split up **II.** *vpr* **se ~ 1.** (*se désagréger*) to split up **2.** GEO, PHYS to disintegrate
désintéressé(e) [dezɛ̃teʀese] *adj* disinterested
désintéressement [dezɛ̃teʀɛsmɑ̃] *m* **1.** disinterest; **avec ~** disinterestedly **2.** (*dédommagement*) buying out
désintéresser [dezɛ̃teʀese] <1> **I.** *vt* (*dédommager: créancier*) to pay off; (*partenaire*) to buy out **II.** *vpr* **se ~ de qn/qc** to take no interest in sb/sth; (*perdre intérêt*) to lose interest in sb/sth
désintérêt [dezɛ̃teʀɛ] *m* lack of interest; **son ~ pour qc** his lack of interest in sth
désintoxication [dezɛ̃tɔksikasjɔ̃] *f* MED detoxification
désintoxiquer [dezɛ̃tɔksike] <1> **I.** *vt* **1.** MED (*drogué, alcoolique*) to detoxify; **se faire ~** to get detoxified **2.** (*purifier l'organisme: citadin, fumeur*) to clean out the system of **II.** *vpr* **se ~ 1.** MED (*alcoolique, toxicomane*) to get detoxified **2.** (*s'oxygéner*) to clean out the system
désinvolte [dezɛ̃vɔlt] *adj* **1.** (*décontracté: mouvement, attitude, style*) casual **2.** (*sans-gêne: air, attitude, réponse*) offhanded
désinvolture [dezɛ̃vɔltyʀ] *f* **1.** (*aisance*) casualness **2.** (*sans-gêne*) offhandedness; **avec ~** (*répondre*) offhandedly
désir [deziʀ] *m* **1.** (*souhait*) **~ de qc** wish for sth; **vos ~s sont des ordres** *iron* your wish is my command **2.** (*appétit sexuel*) desire
désirable [deziʀabl] *adj* desirable
désirer [deziʀe] <1> *vt* **1.** (*souhaiter*) to want; **je désire/désirerais un café** I want/would like a coffee **2.** (*convoiter*) to desire ►**se faire ~** to be desirable; **laisser à ~** to leave much to be desired
désireux, -euse [deziʀø, -øz] *adj* **être ~ de qc** avid for sth; **être ~ de** +*infin* anxious to +*infin*
désister [deziste] <1> *vpr* **se ~ en faveur de qn** to stand down in favour of sb *Brit,* to stand down in favor of sb *Am*
désobéir [dezɔbeiʀ] <8> *vi* **~ à qn/un ordre** to disobey sb/an order; **~ à la loi** to break the law
désobéissance [dezɔbeisɑ̃s] *f* disobedience *no pl;* **~ à qn/un ordre** disobeying sb/an order; **~ à une loi** breaking the law
désobéissant(e) [dezɔbeisɑ̃, ɑ̃t] *adj* disobedient
désodorisant [dezɔdɔʀizɑ̃] *m* deodorizer
désodorisant(e) [dezɔdɔʀizɑ̃, ɑ̃t] *adj* deodorizing
désœuvré(e) [dezœvʀe] *adj* idle
désœuvrement [dezœvʀəmɑ̃] *m* idleness; **faire qc par ~** to do sth for want of better
désolant(e) [dezɔlɑ̃, ɑ̃t] *adj* (*spectacle,*) woeful; (*temps, nouvelle*) appalling; **il est ~ qu'elle le fasse** (*subj*) it's dreadful that she should do it
désolation [dezɔlasjɔ̃] *f* distress; **plonger qn dans la ~** to plunge sb into deep distress
désolé(e) [dezɔle] *adj* **1.** (*éploré*) disconsolate **2.** (*navré*) sorry; **je suis vraiment ~** I am truly sorry **3.** (*désert et triste: lieu, paysage*) desolate
désoler [dezɔle] <1> **I.** *vt* **1.** (*affliger*) to sadden; **ça me désole de te dire qu'elle l'a fait** I'm so sorry to tell you she did it **2.** (*contrarier*) to upset **II.** *vpr* (*être navré*) **se ~** to be sorry; **se ~ de qc/faire qc** to be sorry for sth/for doing sth
désolidariser [desɔlidaʀize] <1> *vpr* **se ~ de qn** to dissociate oneself from sb
désopilant(e) [dezɔpilɑ̃, ɑ̃t] *adj* hilarious
désordonné(e) [dezɔʀdɔne] *adj* **1.** (*qui manque d'ordre*) untidy **2.** (*qui manque d'organisation: esprit, personne*) disorganized **3.** (*incontrôlé: gestes, mouvements*) uncoordinated; (*élans*) wild; (*fuite, combat*) disorderly
désordre [dezɔʀdʀ] *m* **1.** *sans pl* (*absence d'ordre: d'une personne, d'un lieu*) untidiness; **le Tiercé dans le ~** *a bet on the top three finishing horses in a race in any order*

2. (*confusion: de l'esprit, des idées*) lack of organization 3. (*absence de discipline*) disorder; **semer le** ~ to create disorder 4. *gén pl* POL riots

désorganisation [dezɔʀganizasjɔ̃] *f* disorganization

désorganiser [dezɔʀganize] <1> *vt* (*service, projets*) to disrupt; **être désorganisé** (*service, administration*) to be disorganized

désorienté(**e**) [dezɔʀjɑ̃te] *adj* disorientated

désorienter [dezɔʀjɑ̃te] <1> *vt* 1. (*égarer: personne*) to disorientate; (*avion*) to throw off course 2. (*déconcerter*) to confuse

désormais [dezɔʀmɛ] *adv* 1. (*au passé*) from then on 2. (*au présent*) from now on

désosser [dezɔse] <1> *vt* 1. GASTR (*viande*) to bone; **dinde désossée** boned turkey 2. (*démonter: véhicule, machine*) to take to pieces

despote [dɛspɔt] I. *m* 1. POL despot; ~ **éclairé** enlightened despot 2. (*personne tyrannique*) tyrant II. *adj* despotic

despotique [dɛspɔtik] *adj a.* POL despotic

desquels, **desquelles** [dekɛl] *pron v.* **lequel**

DESS [deøɛsɛs] *m abr de* **diplôme d'études supérieures spécialisées** *postgraduate diploma specializing in one subject*

dessaisir [desezir] <8> *vpr* **se** ~ **d'un objet** to part with an object; **se** ~ **d'une affaire** JUR to give up a case

dessaler [desale] <1> I. *vt* (*poisson*) to soak; ~ **qc** to remove the salt from sth II. *vpr* **se** ~ to wake up III. *vi* NAUT to capsize

dessaouler [desule] <1> *vi v.* **dessoûler**

desséché(**e**) [deseʃe] *adj* **lèvres ~es** dry lips; **légumes ~s** withered vegetables

dessèchement [desɛʃmɑ̃] *m* (*de la peau, du sol*) drying (out)

dessécher [deseʃe] <1> I. *vt* 1. (*rendre sec: terre, peau, bouche*) to dry (out); (*végétation, plantes*) to wither; (*fruits*) to dry up; **mes lèvres sont desséchées** my lips are dry 2. (*rendre maigre: personne, corps*) to wither 3. (*rendre insensible: personne*) to harden II. *vpr* **se** ~ 1. (*devenir sec: bouche, lèvres*) to get parched; (*terre, peau*) to dry up; (*végétation*) to wither 2. (*maigrir*) to shrivel 3. (*devenir insensible*) to grow hardened

desserré(**e**) [deseʀe] *adj* (*vis, nœud, lacet, ceinture*) loosened; (*frein*) off; (*col*) undone

desserrer [deseʀe] <1> I. *vt* 1. (*dévisser*) to unscrew 2. (*relâcher: étau, cravate, ceinture*) to loosen; (*frein à main*) to let off 3. (*écarter: poing*) to unclench II. *vpr* **se** ~ (*vis, étau, nœud*) to work loose; (*frein à main*) to come off; (*personnes, rangs*) to break up

dessert [desɛʀ] *m* GASTR (*mets, moment*) pudding *Brit,* dessert *Am;* **au** ~ at the dessert course

desserte [desɛʀt] *f* 1. (*meuble*) sideboard 2. (TRANSPORT) SERVICE service; **la desserte du village se fait par autocar** there is a bus service to the village

desservir [desɛʀviʀ] *vt irr* 1. (*débarrasser: table*) to clear 2. (*nuire à*) to do a disservice to 3. (*s'arrêter*) **le train dessert cette gare/ce village** the train stops at this station/this village; **être desservi par bus** to have a bus service

dessin [desɛ̃] *m* 1. (*image*) drawing; ~(**s**) **animé**(**s**) cartoon 2. (*activité*) drawing 3. (*motif*) design 4. (*ligne: du visage*) line; (*des veines*) pattern ►**il faut te/vous faire un ~?** *inf* do I have to spell it all out for you?

dessinateur, **-trice** [desinatœʀ, -tʀis] *m, f* 1. ART draughtsman *Brit,* draftsman *Am* 2. ECON designer

dessiner [desine] <1> I. *vi* to draw; ~ **au crayon** to draw in pencil II. *vt* 1. ART to draw 2. TECH (*plan d'une maison*) to draw (up); (*meuble, véhicule,jardin*) to design 3. (*souligner: contours, formes*) to show off 4. (*former: courbe, virages*) to form

dessoûler [desule] <1> I. *vi* to sober up; **ne pas** ~ to never be sober II. *vt inf* ~ **qn** to sober sb up

dessous [d(ə)su] I. *adv* 1. (*sous: passer, regarder, être* (*placé*)) underneath 2. *fig* **agir** (**par**) **en** ~ to act deceitfully II. *prep* 1. (*sous*) **en** ~ **de qc** under; **le voisin d'en** ~ *inf* the neighbour downstairs *Brit,* the neighbor downstairs *Am;* **habiter en ~ de chez qn** to live on the floor below sb 2. (*plus bas que*) **en ~ de qc** under sth; **être en ~ de tout** (*person*) not to be up to anything; (*travail, comportement*) to be nowhere near good enough III. *m* 1. (*face inférieure, de ce qui est plus bas: d'une assiette, langue*) underside; (*d'une étoffe*) wrong side; (*des pieds, chaussures*) sole; **l'étage du** ~ the next floor down; **le voisin du** ~ the neighbour downstairs *Brit,* the neighbor downstairs *Am* 2. *pl* (*sous-vêtements*) underwear *no pl* 3. *pl* (*aspects secrets: d'une affaire, de la politique*) underside

dessous-de-bouteille [d(ə)sud(ə)butɛj] *m inv* coaster **dessous-de-plat** [d(ə)sud(ə)pla] *m inv* table mat (*to go under hot dishes*) **dessous-de-table** [d(ə)sud(ə)tabl] *m inv* bribe

dessus [d(ə)sy] I. *adv* (*sur qn/qc*) on top; (*là-haut*) above; (*marcher, appuyer*) on it; (*voler*) over it; **mettre qc** ~ to put sth on top; **voici une chaise, mets-toi** ~ here's a chair, sit on it; **elle lui a tapé/tiré** ~ she hit/shot him II. *prep* **enlever qc de ~ qc** to take sth off (the top of) sth III. *m* (*partie supérieure, ce qui est au-dessus: de la tête, du pied*) top; (*de la main*) back; **le voisin du** ~ the upstairs neighbour *Brit,* the upstairs neighbor *Am;* **l'étage du** ~ the next floor up ►**<u>avoir</u> le** ~ to have the upper hand; **il va <u>prendre</u>/<u>reprendre</u> le** ~ he's going to to get/get back on top; (*après une maladie*) he's going to get back on his feet

dessus-de-lit [d(ə)syd(ə)li] *m inv* bed-

spread
déstabilisation [destabilizasjɔ̃] *f* destabilization
déstabiliser [destabilize] <1> *vt* to destabilize
destin [dɛstɛ̃] *m* fate
destinataire [dɛstinatɛʀ] *mf* addressee; (*d'un mandat*) payee
destination [dɛstinasjɔ̃] *f* **1.**(*lieu*) destination; **le train/les voyageurs à ~ de Paris** the train/passengers for Paris **2.**(*utilisation prévue, vocation*) purpose
destinée [dɛstine] *f* **1.**(*fatalité*) fate **2.**(*destin particulier: d'une personne, d'un peuple, d'une œuvre*) destiny ▸**être promis à de hautes ~s** to be destined for great things
destiner [dɛstine] <1> **I.** *vt* **1.**(*réserver à, attribuer*) ~ **un poste à qn** to mean sb to have a job; **être destiné à qn** (*fortune, emploi, ballon*) to be (meant) for; (*livre, remarque, allusion*) to be aimed at **2.**(*prévoir un usage*) ~ **un local à qc** to intend that a place should be used for sth **3.**(*vouer*) **elle le destine à être avocat/son successeur** she intends him to be a lawyer/her successor **II.** *vpr* **se ~ à la politique** to intend to go into politics; **elle se destine à le faire** she's setting her sights on doing it
destituer [dɛstitɥe] <1> *vt* (*ministre, fonctionnaire*) to remove from office; (*souverain*) to depose; (*officier*) to break; ~ **qn de ses fonctions** to relieve sb of their duties
destitution [dɛstitysjɔ̃] *f* dismissal
destructeur, **-trice** [dɛstʀyktœʀ, -tʀis] **I.** *adj* destructive **II.** *m, f* (*personne*) destroyer
destructif, **-ive** [dɛstʀyktif, -iv] *adj* destructive
destruction [dɛstʀyksjɔ̃] *f* **1.**(*action, dégât*) destruction **2.**(*extermination*) extermination **3.**(*altération: des tissus organiques*) destruction
désuet, **-ète** [dezɥɛ, -ɛt] *adj* (*coutume, vêtement*) old-fashioned; (*expression*) dated; (*mode, aspect*) outdated
désuétude [dezɥetyd] *f* **tomber en ~** (*coutume, expression*) to fall into disuse; (*loi*) to fall into abeyance
désunion [dezynjɔ̃] *f* (*d'un parti, d'une famille*) disunity
désunir [dezyniʀ] <8> *vt* (*couple, famille*) to divide; (*équipe*) to split up
détachable [detaʃabl] *adj* (*amovible: partie, capuche*) removable; (*feuilles*) tear-out
détachant [detaʃɑ̃] *m* stain remover
détaché(**e**) [detaʃe] *adj* **1.**(*indifférent: air*) detached; **d'un œil ~/d'un ton ~** with detachment; **avoir l'air ~** to look detached **2.** ADMIN (*fonctionnaire*) on secondment
détachement [detaʃmɑ̃] *m* **1.**(*indifférence*) detachment; **avec ~/un certain ~** with detachment/a certain detachment **2.** MIL detachment **3.** ADMIN secondment; **être en ~** to be on secondment
détacher[1] [detaʃe] <1> **I.** *vt* **1.**(*délier, libérer: prisonnier*) to unchain; (*chien*) to let loose; (*en enlevant un lien*) to let off the leash **2.**(*défaire: cheveux, nœud*) to untie; (*lacet, ceinture*) to undo **3.**(*arracher, retirer: timbre*) to tear off; (*feuille, pétale*) to pull off **4.** ADMIN ~ **qn à Paris/en province** to send sb to Paris/to the provinces on secondment **5.**(*ne pas lier: lettres, notes*) to keep separate **6.**(*détourner*) **être détaché de qn** to have broken off with sb; **être détaché de qc** to have broken away from sth **II.** *vpr* **1.**(*se libérer*) **se ~** to untie oneself **2.**(*se séparer*) **se ~ de qc** (*bateau, satellite*) to detach itself from sth; (*par accident*) to come away from sth **3.**(*se défaire*) **se ~** (*chaîne*) to come away; (*lacet*) to come undone **4.**(*prendre ses distances*) **se ~ de qn** to break off with sb; **se ~ de qc** to break away from sth
détacher[2] [detaʃe] <1> *vt* ~ **qc** to remove a stain from sth
détail [detaj] <s> *m* **1.**(*particularité, élément d'un ensemble*) detail; **dans les moindres ~s** down to the last detail **2.** *sans pl* (*énumération: des dépenses, d'un compte*) breakdown **3.** *sans pl* COM **commerce de ~** retail business; **vente au ~** retail sale **4.**(*accessoire*) detail; **à un ~ près** except for one small detail
détaillant(**e**) [detajɑ̃, jɑ̃t] *m(f)* retailer
détaillé(**e**) [detaje] *adj* detailed
détailler [detaje] <1> *vt* **1.** COM (*articles*) to sell separately; (*marchandise*) to (sell) retail **2.**(*couper en morceaux: tissu*) to sell lengths of **3.**(*faire le détail de: plan, raisons*) to set out in detail; (*histoire*) to tell in detail **4.**(*énumérer: défauts, points*) to list
détaler [detale] <1> *vi inf* to clear off; (*fuir*) to make a run for it
détartrer [detaʀtʀe] <1> *vt* (*chaudière, conduit*) to descale; ~ **les dents de qn** to clean sb's teeth
détaxer [detakse] <1> *vt* FIN ~ **qc** (*exonérer*) to lift the duty from sth; (*réduire*) to lower the duty on sth; **être détaxé** to be duty free
détecter [detɛkte] <1> *vt* to detect
détection [detɛksjɔ̃] *f* detection
détective [detɛktiv] *mf* detective
déteindre [detɛ̃dʀ] *irr* **I.** *vi* **1.** to run; ~ **au lavage** to run in the wash; ~ **au soleil** to fade in the sun; ~ **sur qc** to run into sth **2.**(*influencer*) ~ **sur qn/qc** to rub off on sb/sth **II.** *vt* (*soleil*) to fade; ~ **qc à qc** to bleach sth with sth
dételer [det(ə)le] <3> *vt* (*bœuf*) to unyoke; (*charrette, cheval, wagon*) to unhitch
détendre [detɑ̃dʀ] <14> **I.** *vt* (*relâcher: arc, ressort, corde*) to slacken; (*personne, muscle, atmosphère*) to relax; (*situation*) to ease **II.** *vpr* **se ~** (*se relâcher: ressort*) to be released; (*arc*) to unbend; (*corde*) to slacken; (*muscle, personne, atmosphère*) to relax;

D

(*situation*) to ease

détendu(e) [detɑ̃dy] *adj* relaxed; (*relâché: corde*) slack; (*ressort*) untensed

détenir [det(ə)niʀ] <9> *vt* **1.** (*posséder: objet, pouvoir, preuve, majorité, secret*) to have; (*objets volés, document*) to have (in one's possession); (*poste, position*) to occupy; (*record, titre*) to hold **2.** (*retenir prisonnier*) to detain

détente [detɑ̃t] *f* **1.** (*relâchement: d'un ressort*) release; (*d'une corde*) slackening **2.** (*délassement*) relaxation ►**être dur à la** ~ *inf* to be slow on the uptake

détenteur, **-trice** [detɑ̃tœʀ, -tʀis] *m, f* (*d'un objet, d'un document*) possessor; (*d'un compte, d'un brevet*) holder; ~ **du titre/du record** title/record holder; **le** ~ **du pouvoir** the one in power

détention [detɑ̃sjɔ̃] *f* **1.** (*possession: d'un document, d'une somme, d'un secret, d'armes*) possession **2.** (*incarcération*) detention; ~ **provisoire** temporary custody

détenu(e) [det(ə)ny] *m(f)* prisoner

détergent [detɛʀʒɑ̃] *m* detergent

détergent(e) [detɛʀʒɑ̃, ʒɑ̃t] *adj* detergent

détérioration [deteʀjɔʀasjɔ̃] *f* (*d'un appareil, de marchandises*) deterioration; (*des conditions de vie, des relations*) worsening

détériorer [deteʀjɔʀe] <1> **I.** *vt* **1.** (*endommager: appareil, marchandise*) to damage **2.** (*nuire à: climat social, relations*) to worsen; (*santé*) to deteriorate **II.** *vpr* **se** ~ **1.** (*s'abîmer: appareil, marchandise*) to be damaged **2.** (*se dégrader: temps, conditions, santé*) to worsen; (*pouvoir d'achat*) to go down

déterminant(e) [detɛʀminɑ̃, ɑ̃t] *adj* (*action, rôle, événement*) decisive; (*argument, raison*) deciding

détermination [detɛʀminasjɔ̃] *f* **1.** (*fixation: d'une grandeur, de l'heure, du lieu, de la cause*) determining **2.** (*décision*) resolution **3.** (*fermeté*) *a.* PHILOS determination

déterminé(e) [detɛʀmine] *adj* **1.** (*précis: idée, lieu, but*) specific **2.** (*défini: moment, heure, quantité*) precise **3.** (*décidé: personne, air*) determined

déterminer [detɛʀmine] <1> **I.** *vt* **1.** (*définir, préciser: sens, inconnue, distance*) to determine; (*adresse, coupable, cause*) to discover **2.** (*convenir de: date, lieu*) to set; (*détails*) to settle **3.** (*décider*) ~ **qn à qc/à faire qc** to decide sb on sth **4.** (*motiver, entraîner: retards, crise, phénomène, révolte*) to bring about **II.** *vpr* (*se décider*) **se** ~ **à** +*infin* to determine to +*infin*

déterminisme [detɛʀminism] *m* determinism

déterrer [deteʀe] <1> *vt* **1.** (*exhumer: arbre, trésor, personne*) to dig up; (*mine, obus*) to dig out **2.** (*dénicher: vieux manuscrit, loi*) to unearth

détestable [detɛstabl] *adj* (*personne, comportement, procédé, habitude*) loathsome; (*humeur, temps*) foul

détester [detɛste] <1> **I.** *vt* to hate; ~ **que qn fasse qc** (*subj*) to hate sb doing sth **II.** *vpr* **se** ~ to hate oneself; **elles se détestent** they hate each other

détonateur [detɔnatœʀ] *m* **1.** (*dispositif*) detonator **2.** *fig* trigger

détonation [detɔnasjɔ̃] *f* (*d'une arme à feu*) shot; (*d'une bombe, d'un obus*) explosion; (*d'un canon*) boom

détour [detuʀ] *m* **1.** (*sinuosité*) bend; **au** ~ **du chemin** at the bend in the path **2.** (*trajet plus long*) detour; **le château vaut le** ~ the château is worth going out of your way to see **3.** (*biais*) roundabout phrases; **parler sans** ~ to speak plainly ►**au** ~ **d'une conversation** in the course of a conversation

détourné(e) [detuʀne] *adj* **1.** (*faisant un détour: sentier*) winding **2.** (*indirect: reproche, allusion*) indirect

détournement [detuʀnəmɑ̃] *m* **1.** (*déviation*) diversion; ~ **d'avion** hijacking **2.** (*vol*) misappropriation; (*de fonds*) misappropriation; ~ **de mineur** corruption of a minor

détourner [detuʀne] <1> **I.** *vt* **1.** (*changer la direction de: rivière, circulation*) to divert; (*par la contrainte: avion*) to hijack; (*coup*) to ward off; (*tir*) to push away **2.** (*tourner d'un autre côté: tête, visage*) to turn away; ~ **son regard** to look away **3.** (*dévier: colère, fléau*) to avert; (*texte*) to twist; ~ **qn de sa route** to take sb away from their path **4.** (*distraire*) ~ **qn de qc** to take sb's mind off sth **5.** (*dissuader*) ~ **qn de qc** to dissuade sb from doing sth **6.** (*soustraire: somme, fonds*) to misappropriate **II.** *vpr* **1.** (*tourner la tête*) **se** ~ to look away **2.** (*se détacher*) **se** ~ **de qn/qc** to turn away from sb/sth **3.** (*s'égarer*) **se** ~ **de sa route** to wander from one's route; (*prendre une autre route*) to take a detour

détracteur, **-trice** [detʀaktœʀ, -tʀis] *m, f* detractor

détraqué(e) [detʀake] **I.** *adj* **1.** (*déréglé: appareil, mécanisme*) broken down **2.** (*dérangé: estomac*) upset; **avoir la santé** ~ to be in poor health **3.** *inf* (*dérangé*) cracked **II.** *m(f) inf* weirdo

détraquer [detʀake] <1> **I.** *vt* **1.** (*abîmer: appareil*) to upset the workings of **2.** *inf* (*déranger: santé*) to weaken; (*estomac, nerfs*) to upset; (*personne*) to unhinge **II.** *vpr* **se** ~ **1.** (*être abîmé: montre*) to go wrong **2.** (*être dérangé: estomac*) to be upset **3.** METEO (*temps*) (*se gâter*) to turn bad; (*se dérégler*) to become unsettled **4.** *inf* (*rendre malade*) **se** ~ **l'estomac** to do damage to one's stomach

détrempé(e) [detʀɑ̃pe] *adj* (*sol, chemin*) waterlogged

détremper [detʀɑ̃pe] <1> *vt* (*papier peint*) to soak; ~ **des couleurs/du mortier** to mix colours/mortar with water *Brit,* to mix colors/mortar with water *Am*

détresse [detʀɛs] *f* (*sentiment, situation*)

distress

détriment [detʀimɑ̃] **au ~ de qn** to the detriment of sth

détritus [detʀity(s)] *mpl* rubbish *Brit,* garbage *Am;* **tas de ~** pile of rubbish; **~ ménagers** household waste

détroit [detʀwa] *m* strait; **~ de Gibraltar** straits of Gibraltar

détromper [detʀɔ̃pe] <1> **I.** *vt* **~ qn** to set sb stright **II.** *vpr* **détrompe-toi/détrompez-vous!** think again!

détrôner [detʀone] <1> *vt* **1.** (*destituer: souverain*) to dethrone **2.** (*supplanter: rival, chanteur*) to oust

détrousser [detʀuse] <1> *vt iron* to rob

détruire [detʀɥiʀ] *irr* **I.** *vt* **1.** (*démolir*) to destroy; (*clôture, mur*) to knock down **2.** (*anéantir: armes, population*) to wipe out; (*déchets, machine*) to destroy **3.** (*ruiner, anéantir: personne, illusions*) to shatter; (*santé, réputation*) to ruin; (*plans, espoirs*) to wreck; (*capitalisme, dictature*) to destroy **II.** *vi* to destroy **III.** *vpr* **se ~** (*effets contraires, mesures*) to cancel each other out; **il pourrait se ~** he could end his own life

dette [dɛt] *f a. fig* debt; **avoir une ~ envers qn** to be indebted to sb

DEUG [dœg] *m abr de* **diplôme d'études universitaires générales** *diploma taken after the first two years at university*

deuil [dœj] *m* **1.** (*affliction*) grief **2.** (*décès*) bereavement **3.** (*signes, durée du deuil*) mourning; **porter/quitter le ~** to be in/come out of mourning

deux [dø] **I.** *adj* **1.** two; **tous les ~** both of them; **à ~** together **2.** (*quelques*) **j'habite à ~ pas d'ici** I live just down the road from here; **il ne faut que ~ minutes pour aller à la gare** the station is only two minutes away; **j'ai ~ mots à vous dire!** I've got something to say to you! **II.** *m inv* **1.** (*cardinal*) two **2.** (*aviron à deux rameurs*) **un ~ avec/sans barreur** a coxed/coxless two ►**jamais ~ sans trois** *prov* if it happens twice it'll happen a third time; (*un malheur n'arrive jamais seul*) it never rains but it pours; **c'est clair comme ~ et ~ font quatre** it's as simple as ABC; (**il n'**) **y en a pas ~ comme lui/elle** *inf* he's/she's one of a kind; **à nous ~!** here we go!; **en moins de ~** *inf* in two secs; **entre les ~** between the two; *v. a.* **cinq**

deuxième [døzjɛm] **I.** *adj antéposé* second; **vingt-~** twenty-second **II.** *mf* **le/la ~** the second **III.** *f* (*vitesse*) second (gear); *v. a.* **cinquième**

deuxièmement [døzjɛmmɑ̃] *adv* secondly

deux-pièces [døpjɛs] *m inv* **1.** (*appartement*) two-room flat *Brit,* two-room apartment *Am* **2.** (*maillot de bain, vêtement féminin*) two-piece **deux-points** [døpwɛ̃] *mpl inv* LING colon **deux-roues** [døʀu] *m inv* two-wheeled vehicle, *bicycle or motorbike*

deuzio [døzjo] *adv* secondly

dévaler [devale] <1> **I.** *vi* (*personne, voiture, camion*) to race down from sth; (*rocher*) to hurtle down from sth; (*lave*) to pour down from sth **II.** *vt* **~ qc** (*personne*) to race down sth; (*en glissant*) to slither down sth; (*voiture, avalanche*) to hurtle down sth; (*lave*) to pour down sth

dévaliser [devalize] <1> *vt* **1.** (*voler*) to rob **2.** *inf* (*vider: réfrigérateur, magasin*) to raid

dévaloir [devalwaʀ] *m Suisse* **1.** (*glissoir à bois utilisant la pente dans une forêt*) timber slide **2.** (*vide-ordures*) rubbish chute *Brit,* garbage chute *Am*

dévalorisant(e) [devalɔʀizɑ̃, -ɑ̃t] *adj* humiliating

dévaloriser [devalɔʀize] <1> **I.** *vt* **1.** (*dévaluer*) to devalue; (*pouvoir d'achat*) to fall **2.** (*déprécier: mérite, talent, personne*) to depreciate; **être dévalorisé** (*métier*) to be undervalued **II.** *vpr* **se ~ 1.** (*se déprécier: monnaie, marchandise*) to lose value **2.** (*se dénigrer: personne*) to undervalue oneself

dévaluation [devalɥasjɔ̃] *f* FIN devaluation

dévaluer [devalɥe] <1> **I.** *vt* FIN to devalue **II.** *vpr* **se ~ 1.** FIN to be devalued **2.** (*se dévaloriser*) to undervalue oneself

devancer [d(ə)vɑ̃se] <2> *vt* **1.** (*distancer*) **~ qn de cinq secondes/mètres** to be five seconds/metres ahead of sb *Brit,* to be five seconds/meters ahead of sb *Am* **2.** (*être le premier: rival, concurrent*) to lead **3.** (*précéder*) **~ qn** to go on ahead of sb; **~ qn au feu** to get to the light before sb **4.** (*aller au devant de: personne, question*) to anticipate **5.** (*anticiper*) **~ un paiement** to make a payment before the due date

devancier, **-ière** [d(ə)vɑ̃sje, -jɛʀ] *m, f* predecessor

devant [d(ə)vɑ̃] **I.** *prep* **1.** (*en face de: être, se trouver, rester*) in front of; (*avec mouvement: aller, passer*) past **2.** (*en avant de*) in front of; (*à une certaine distance*) ahead of; **aller droit ~ soi** to go straight ahead **3.** (*face à, en présence de*) **~ qn** (*s'exprimer*) to; (*pleurer*) in front of; **~ le danger** in the face of danger; **~ la gravité de la situation** faced with the gravity of the situation; **mener/l'emporter ~ Nantes 2 à 0** to lead/beat Nantes two nil ►**avoir du temps ~ soi** to have have some time ahead of oneself **II.** *adv* **1.** (*en face*) in front; **mets-toi ~** stand in front; **en passant ~, regarde si le magasin est ouvert!** when you pass by, see if the shop's open! **2.** (*en avant*) in front; (*avec mouvement*) forward; **passer qc ~** to pass sth forward; **être loin ~** to be way out in front; **s'asseoir ~** to sit at the front **III.** *m* (*partie avant: d'un vêtement, d'une maison*) front; (*d'un bateau*) prow; (*d'un objet*) front (part) ►**être sur le ~ de la scène** to be in the limelight; **prendre les ~s** to take the initiative

devanture [d(ə)vɑ̃tyʀ] *f* **1.** (*façade*) frontage **2.** (*étalage*) display; **en ~** in the window

dévastateur, **-trice** [devastatœʀ, -tʀis] *adj* devastating

dévaster [devaste] <1> *vt* **1.** (*détruire: pays, terres, récoltes*) to devastate **2.** *fig* (*âme*) to ravage

déveine [devɛn] *f inf* bad luck

développé(**e**) [dev(ə)lɔpe] *adj* developed; (*odorat*) acute; (*vue*) keen

développement [devlɔpmɑ̃] *m* **1.** BIO (*croissance*) development; (*multiplication: de bactéries, d'une espèce*) growth **2.** ECON (*de l'industrie, d'une affaire, de la production*) growth; **être en plein ~** to be growing rapidly; **pays en voie de ~** developing country **3.** (*extension: des relations, des connaissances*) growth; (*d'une maladie*) development; (*d'une épidemie, d'une crise*) spread **4.** (*évolution: de l'intelligence*) development; (*d'une civilisation*) growth; **~ de l'esprit** development of the mind **5.** *pl* (*conséquences: d'une action, d'un incident*) consequences **6.** (*exposition détaillée*) *a.* ECOLE, MUS development **7.** PHOT developing

développer [dev(ə)lɔpe] <1> **I.** *vt* **1.** (*faire progresser, croître, mette au point*) *a.* MUS, MED to develop **2.** (*exposer en détail: thème, pensée, plan*) to elaborate on; (*chapitre*) to develop **3.** MAT (*fonction*) to develop; (*calcul*) to carry out **4.** PHOT **faire ~ une pellicule** to have film developed **II.** *vpr* **se ~** **1.** *a.* ECON, TECH to develop; (*personnalité*) to evolve; (*plante, tumeur*) to grow **2.** (*s'intensifier: échanges, haine, relations*) to grow **3.** (*se propager*) to develop; (*usage*) to grow up

devenir [dəv(ə)niʀ] <9> **I.** *vi être* **~ riche/ingénieur** to become rich/an engineer; **qu'est-ce que tu deviens?** *inf* what are you up to?; **qu'est-ce qu'elle est devenue?** what's happened to her?; **il devient une star** he's turning into a star **II.** *m soutenu* **1.** (*évolution*) evolution **2.** (*avenir*) future

dévergondé(**e**) [devɛʀgɔ̃de] **I.** *adj* (*personne*) brazen; (*vie, allure*) shameless **II.** *m(f)* loose liver

déverser [devɛʀse] <1> **I.** *vt* **1.** (*verser: liquide*) to pour **2.** (*décharger: sable, ordures*) to dump; (*bombes*) to shower **II.** *vpr* **se ~ dans une rivière** to pour into a river

dévêtir [devetiʀ] *vt, vpr irr* (**se**) ~ to undress

dévêtu(**e**) [devety] **I.** *part passé de* **dévêtir** **II.** *adj soutenu* unclad

déviant(**e**) [devjɑ̃, jɑ̃t] *adj* deviant

déviation [devjasjɔ̃] *f* **1.** (*action/résultat: de la circulation*) diversion; (*d'un projectile, d'une aiguille aimantée*) deviation; (*d'un rayon lumineux*) deflection **2.** (*chemin*) diversion **3.** (*déformation: de la colonne vertébrale*) curvature **4.** (*attitude différente*) deviation

dévier [devje] <1> **I.** *vi* (*véhicule*) to swerve; (*bateau*) to go off course; (*aiguille magnétique*) to deviate **II.** *vt* (*circulation*) to divert; (*coup, balle, rayon lumineux*) to deflect; (*conversation*) to steer away

devin, **-ineresse** [dəvɛ̃, in(ə)ʀɛs] *m, f* soothsayer

deviner [d(ə)vine] <1> **I.** *vt* **1.** (*trouver: réponse, secret, énigme*) to guess **2.** (*pressentir: sens, pensée*) to guess; (*menace, danger*) to see **3.** (*entrevoir*) to make out **II.** *vpr* **1.** (*se trouver*) **la réponse se devine facilement** the answer is easy to guess **2.** (*transparaître*) **se ~** (*tendance, goût*) to be apparent

devinette [d(ə)vinɛt] *f* riddle; **je te pose une ~** I've got a riddle for you

devis [d(ə)vi] *m* estimate

dévisager [devizaʒe] <2a> *vt* to stare at

devise [d(ə)viz] *f* **1.** (*formule, règle de conduite*) motto **2.** (*monnaie*) currency

dévisser [devise] <1> **I.** *vi* SPORT to fall **II.** *vt* (*écrou, couvercle, tube*) to unscrew; (*roue*) to unbolt **III.** *vpr* **se ~** **1.** (*pouvoir être enlevé/ouvert*) to screw off **2.** (*se desserrer*) to come loose

dévoilement [devwalmɑ̃] *m* (*d'une statue*) unveiling; (*d'un secret*) revealing

dévoiler [devwale] <1> **I.** *vt* **1.** (*découvrir: statue, plaque*) to unveil; (*charmes, rondeurs*) to reveal **2.** (*révéler*) to reveal; (*scandale, perfidie*) to bring to light **II.** *vpr* **se ~** **1.** (*apparaître: mystère, fourberie*) to be revealed **2.** (*révéler sa vraie nature*) **va-t-il se ~?** is he going to drop his mask?

devoir [d(ə)vwaʀ] *irr* **I.** *vt* (*argent*) to owe; **~ une partie à qn** to owe sb a game **II.** *aux* **1.** (*nécessité*) ~ +*infin* to have to +*infin;* **tu ne dois pas mentir** you mustn't lie **2.** (*obligation exprimée par autrui*) **tu aurais dû rentrer** you should have gone home **3.** (*fatalité*) **cela devait arriver un jour** that was bound to happen one day **4.** (*prévision*) **normalement, il doit arriver ce soir** if all goes well, he should arrive tonight **5.** (*hypothèse*) **il doit se faire tard, non?** it must be getting late, mustn't it? **III.** *vpr* **se ~ de** +*infin* to owe it to oneself to +*infin;* **comme il se doit** (*comme c'est l'usage*) as is right and proper; (*comme prévu*) as intended **IV.** *m* **1.** (*obligation morale*) duty; **par ~** out of duty **2.** ECOLE test; (*~ surveillé*) in-class test; **~ sur table** written test; **faire un ~ de math** to do a maths exercise *Brit*, to do a math exercise *Am* **3.** *pl* (*~s à la maison*) homework ►<u>**manquer**</u> **à son ~** to fail in one's duty

dévorer [devɔʀe] <1> **I.** *vi* (*personne*) to have a voracious appetite **II.** *vt* **1.** *a. fig* (*avaler*) to devour **2.** (*regarder*) **~ des yeux** to look voraciously at **3.** (*tourmenter*) **~ qn** (*tâche*) to eat up sb's time; (*remords, peur, soif*) to eat away at sb

dévot(**e**) [devo, ɔt] **I.** *adj* **1.** (*pieux*) devoted **2.** *péj* (*bigot*) sanctimonious **II.** *m(f) péj* pharisee

dévotion [devosjɔ̃] *f* **1.** (*piété*) devoutness **2.** (*culte*) **~ à Saint François/Marie** devotion to Saint Francis/to Mary; **faire ses ~s** to make

one's devotions **3.** (*vénération*) devotion; **être à la ~ de qn** to be devoted to sb
dévoué(e) [devwe] *adj* devoted
dévouement [devumɑ̃] *m* devotion
dévouer [devwe] <1> *vpr* **se ~** to make a sacrifice; **se ~ à qn/qc** to devote oneself to sb/sth
dévoyé(e) [devwaje] **I.** *adj* delinquent **II.** *m(f)* delinquent
dextérité [dɛksteʀite] *f* **1.** (*adresse*) skill; (*des doigts*) dexterity **2.** (*adresse d'esprit*) wit
diabète [djabɛt] *m* diabetes
diabétique [djabetik] **I.** *adj* diabetic **II.** *mf* diabetic
diable [djɑbl] *m* **1.** (*démon, person*) devil **2.** (*chariot*) trolley **3.** (*marmite*) pot ►**avoir le ~ au corps** to be the very devil; **tirer le ~ par la queue** to live from hand to mouth; **allez au ~!** get lost!; **au ~ qc!** to hell with sth!; **signer un pacte avec le ~** to make a pact with the devil; **se faire l'avocat du ~** to play devil's advocate
diablement [djɑbləmɑ̃] *adv inf* devilishly
diablotin [djablɔtɛ̃] *m* imp
diabolique [djabɔlik] *adj* **1.** (*venant du diable*) diabolic **2.** (*très méchant*) diabolical
diaboliser [djabɔlize] <1> *vt soutenu* to demonize
diabolo [djabɔlo] *m* **1.** (*jouet*) diabolo **2.** (*boisson*) **~ menthe** *mint cordial with lemonade*
diadème [djadɛm] *m* **1.** (*bijou*) tiara **2.** HIST diadem
diagnostic [djagnɔstik] *m a. fig* MED diagnosis
diagnostiquer [djagnɔstike] <1> *vt a. fig* MED to diagnose
diagonale [djagɔnal] *f* diagonal line
dialecte [djalɛkt] *m* dialect
dialogue [djalɔg] *m* dialogue; (*en tête-à-tête*) conversation
dialoguer [djalɔge] <1> **I.** *vi* **1.** (*converser*) **~ avec qn** to talk with sb **2.** (*négocier*) **~ avec qn** to have a dialogue with sb **3.** INFOR **~ avec qc** to interact with sth **II.** *vt* to turn into dialogue
dialoguiste [djalɔgist] *mf* dialogue writer
diam [djam] *m inf,* **diamant** [djamɑ̃] *m* diamond
diamantaire [djamɑ̃tɛʀ] *mf* **1.** (*tailleur*) diamond cutter **2.** (*commerçant*) diamond dealer
diamétralement [djametʀalmɑ̃] *adv* diametrically
diamètre [djamɛtʀ] *m* diameter
diapason [djapazɔ̃] *m* **1.** (*instrument*) tuning fork **2.** (*sifflet*) pitchpipe **3.** (*note*) standard pitch **4.** (*registre*) range
diaphragme [djafʀagm] *m a.* ANAT diaphragm
diapositive [djapozitiv] *f* slide; **séance de ~s** slide show; **passer des ~s** to show slides
diarrhée [djaʀe] *f* diarrhoea *Brit,* diarrhea *Am*
diatribe [djatʀib] *f* **~ contre qn/qc** diatribe against sb/sth
dicastère [dikastɛʀ] *m Suisse* (*subdivision d'une administration communale*) *local government division in Switzerland*
dictateur, -trice [diktatœʀ, -tʀis] *m, f* dictator
dictatorial(e) [diktatɔʀjal, jo] <-aux> *adj* dictatorial
dictature [diktatyʀ] *f* **1.** POL dictatorship **2.** (*autoritarisme*) tyranny
dictée [dikte] *f a.* ECOLE dictation
dicter [dikte] <1> *vt* **1.** (*faire écrire*) to dictate **2.** (*imposer*) **~ ses volontés** (*personne*) to dictate one's will; (*circonstance, événement*) to impose its own terms
diction [diksjɔ̃] *f* diction; **prendre des cours de ~** to have lessons in diction
dictionnaire [diksjɔnɛʀ] *m* dictionary
dicton [diktɔ̃] *m* saying
didacticiel [didaktisjɛl] *m* INFOR courseware
didactique [didaktik] *adj* didactic
dièse [djɛz] *m* sharp
diesel [djezɛl] *m* diesel
diète [djɛt] *f* diet; **mettre qn/être à la ~** to put sb/to be on a diet
diététicien(ne) [djetetisjɛ̃, jɛn] *m(f)* dietician
diététique [djetetik] **I.** *adj* healthy; **aliments ~s** health foods **II.** *f* dietetics
diététiste [djetetist] *mf Québec* (*diététicien(ne)*) dietician
dieu [djø] <x> *m* (*divinité*) god
Dieu [djø] *m sans pl* **~ le père** God the Father; **le bon ~** *inf* God ►**ni ~, ni maître** no God no master; **~ merci!** thank God!; **bon ~ de bon ~!** *inf* good lord!; **~ soit loué!** praise be!; **~ sait** God knows; **oh, mon ~!** oh my God!
diffamation [difamasjɔ̃] *f* defamation
diffamatoire [difamatwaʀ] *adj* defamatory
diffamer [difame] <1> *vt* to slander; (*par écrit*) to libel
différé [difeʀe] *m* TV recorded programme *Brit,* recorded program *Am;* **match retransmis en ~** recorded match
différemment [difeʀamɑ̃] *adv* differently
différence [difeʀɑ̃s] *f* difference; **à la ~ de qn/qc** unlike sb/sth; **une ~ de 20 euros** a twenty-euro difference
différencier [difeʀɑ̃sje] <1> **I.** *vt* to differentiate **II.** *vpr* **1.** (*se distinguer*) **se ~ de qn par qc** to be unlike sb in sth **2.** BIO **se ~** to differentiate
différend [difeʀɑ̃] *m* dispute
différent(e) [difeʀɑ̃, ɑ̃t] *adj* different; **~ de** different from
différer [difeʀe] <5> **I.** *vi* **1.** (*être différent*) to differ **2.** (*avoir une opinion différente*) **~ sur qc** to differ over sth **II.** *vt* to postpone; (*échéance, paiement*) to defer
difficile [difisil] *adj* **1.** (*ardu*) difficult; **un morceau ~ d'exécution** a hard piece to play;

il lui est ~ de le faire it's hard for him to do it **2.** (*incommode: sentier, escalade*) hard; **~ d'accès** hard to get to **3.** (*qui donne du souci: moment*) difficult **4.** (*contrariant, exigeant: personne, caractère*) difficult; **~ à vivre** hard to live with ►**faire le/la ~** to be difficult; **être ~ sur la nourriture** to be finicky about food

difficilement [difisilmɑ̃] *adv* **1.** (*péniblement*) with difficulty **2.** (*à peine*) barely; **~ analysable** hard to analyse *Brit,* hard to analyze *Am*

difficulté [difikylte] *f* difficulty; **de ~ croissante** of increasing difficulty; **être/se retrouver en ~** to be/to find oneself in difficulty; **mettre en ~** to put in a difficult situation; **se heurter à des ~s** to come up against problems

difforme [difɔʀm] *adj* (*membre, bête*) deformed; (*arbre*) twisted

diffus(e) [dify, yz] *adj* **1.** (*disséminé: douleur*) diffuse; (*lumière, chaleur*) diffused **2.** (*sans netteté*) vague; (*sentiments, souvenirs*) dim **3.** (*verbeux: écrivain, style*) nebulous

diffuser [difyze] <1> **I.** *vt* **1.** (*répandre: lumière, bruit*) to give out; (*idée*) to spread **2.** (*retransmettre*) to broadcast **3.** (*commercialiser*) to distribute **4.** (*distribuer: tract, photo*) to distribute; (*pétition, document*) to circulate **II.** *vpr* **se ~** (*bruit, chaleur, odeur*) to emanate

diffuseur, **-euse** [difyzœʀ, -øz] *m, f* COM distributor

diffusion [difyzjɔ̃] *f* **1.** (*propagation: de la chaleur, lumière*) diffusion **2.** (*d'un concert,d'une émission*) broadcasting **3.** (*commercialisation, distribution*) distribution **4.** (*action de se diffuser: d'un poison, gaz*) spreading

digérer [diʒeʀe] <5> **I.** *vi* to digest; **bien/mal ~** to digest well/poorly **II.** *vt* **1.** (*assimiler*) *a.* ANAT to digest **2.** *inf* (*accepter: affront*) to stomach **III.** *vpr* **bien/mal se ~** be easy/hard to digest

digeste [diʒɛst] *adj* digestible

digestif [diʒɛstif] *m* (after dinner) liqueur

digestif, **-ive** [diʒɛstif, -iv] *adj* digestive

digestion [diʒɛstjɔ̃] *f* digestion

digicode [diʒikɔd] *m* coded entry system

digital(e) [diʒital, o] <-aux> *adj* digital

digitale [diʒital] *f* digitalis

digne [diɲ] *adj* (*qui mérite*) **~ de ce nom** worthy of the name

dignement [diɲ(ə)mɑ̃] *adv* **1.** (*noblement*) with dignity **2.** (*comme il faut*) fittingly

dignitaire [diɲitɛʀ] *mf* dignitary

dignité [diɲite] *f* **1.** (*noblesse, titre*) dignity **2.** (*amour-propre*) (sense of) dignity

digression [digʀesjɔ̃] *f* digression; **se perdre dans des ~s** to get lost in one's digressions

digue [dig] *f* **1.** dyke **2.** (*rempart*) sea wall

dijonnais(e) [diʒɔnɛ, ɛz] *adj* of Dijon; *v. a.* ajaccien

Dijonnais(e) [diʒɔnɛ, ɛz] *m(f)* person from Dijon; *v. a.* **Ajaccien**

dilapider [dilapide] <1> *vt* to waste; (*fortune, patrimoine*) to squander

dilatation [dilatasjɔ̃] *f a.* PHYS dilation

dilater [dilate] <1> **I.** *vt* **1.** (*augmenter le volume de*) to expand **2.** (*agrandir un conduit, orifice*) to dilate; (*narines*) to flare **II.** *vpr* **se ~** (*métal, corps*) to expand; (*pupille, cœur, poumons*) to dilate; (*narines*) to flare

dilemme [dilɛm] *m* dilemma; **être devant un ~** to be faced with a dilemma

dilettante [dilетɑ̃t] **I.** *adj* dilettantish **II.** *mf a. péj* dilettante

diligence [diliʒɑ̃s] *f* (*voiture*) stagecoach

diluer [dilɥe] <1> **I.** *vt* **1.** (*étendre, délayer*) **~ avec de l'eau/dans de l'eau** to dilute with water/in water **2.** (*affaiblir*) **~ qc** to water sth down **II.** *vpr* **se ~ 1.** (*se délayer*) to be diluted **2.** *fig* (*identité, personnalité*) to be lost

dilution [dilysjɔ̃] *f* (*action, substance: de la peinture*) dilution; (*du sucre*) dissolving

dimanche [dimɑ̃ʃ] *m* **1.** (*veille de lundi*) Sunday; **~ de l'Avent/de Pâques/des Rameaux** Advent/Easter/Palm Sunday; **~, on part en vacances** on Sunday we're going off on holiday *Brit,* on Sunday we're going on vacation *Am;* **le ~** on Sunday(s); **tous les ~s** every Sunday; **ce ~** this Sunday; **ce ~-là, ...** that Sunday, ...; **~ matin** on Sunday morning; **le ~ matin** on Sunday morning(s); **~ dans la nuit** during Sunday night **2.** (*jour férié*) **promenade du ~** Sunday walk; **il faut mettre les habits du ~** you must put on your Sunday best

dîme [dim] *f* HIST tithe

dimension [dimɑ̃sjɔ̃] *f* **1.** (*taille*) size **2.** *pl* (*mesures*) measurements; (*géométriques*) dimensions; **prendre les ~s de la table** to measure the table **3.** (*importance*) proportions; **prendre la ~ de qn/qc** to get the measure of sb/sth; **à la ~ de qc** corresponding to sth **4.** (*aspect*) dimension

diminué(e) [diminɥe] *adj* **il est très ~ physiquement** he is in very poor shape; **il est très ~ mentalement** his mind is impaired

diminuer [diminɥe] <1> **I.** *vi* to diminish; (*bruit, vent, lumière, niveau de l'eau, fièvre*) to go down; (*nombre, forces*) to dwindle; (*brouillard*) to clear; (*jours*) to shorten; **faire ~** to reduce; **~ de cinq euros** to go down by five euros; **~ de longueur/de largeur/d'épaisseur** to become shorter/narrower/thinner **II.** *vt* **1.** (*réduire*) to reduce; (*impôts, prix*) to lower; (*durée, rideau*) to shorten; (*gaz, chauffage*) to turn down; **~ qn** to cut sb's pay; **faire ~ un nombre de qc** to reduce the number of sth **2.** (*affaiblir: autorité, mérite, joie, souffrance*) to diminish; (*violence*) to reduce; (*forces*) to decrease **3.** (*discréditer*) to depreciate **III.** *vpr* **se ~** (*se rabaisser*) to depreciate oneself

diminutif [diminytif] *m* diminutive

diminutif, **-ive** [diminytif, -iv] *adj* diminutive

diminution [diminysjɔ̃] *f* **1.** (*baisse, affaiblissement: de l'appétit, de la chaleur*) loss; (*des forces, des chances*) dwindling; (*de la circulation, du nombre*) decrease; (*de l'autorité*) lessening; (*des impôts, prix*) reduction; (*de la température, de la fièvre*) fall; **en ~** (*nombre, température*) falling **2.** (*réduction: de la consommation, des prix, impôts, salaires*) reduction; (*d'une durée*) shortening

dinde [dɛ̃d] *f* turkey

dindon [dɛ̃dɔ̃] *m a.* GASTR turkey (cock) ►**être le ~ de la farce** to be the one that gets fooled

dindonneau [dɛ̃dɔno] <x> *m* (turkey) poult

dîner [dine] <1> **I.** *vi* **1.** to have dinner **2.** *Belgique, Québec* (*prendre le repas de midi*) to have lunch **II.** *m* **1.** dinner; **au ~** at dinner **2.** *Belgique, Québec* (*repas de midi, déjeuner*) lunch

> The French eat mostly hot and fairly rich meals at **dîner**. There is rarely just a main course and often cheese is served afterwards. Bread is always served with dinner, but without butter.

dînette [dinɛt] *f* **1.** (*jouet*) tea set **2.** (*petit repas*) bite to eat; **faire la ~** to have a bite to eat

dingue [dɛ̃g] **I.** *adj inf* crazy; **~ de qn/qc** crazy about sb/sth **II.** *mf inf* **1.** (*fou*) loony **2.** (*fan*) **~ du foot** football fanatic

dinosaure [dinɔzɔʀ] *m a. fig* dinosaur

diocèse [djɔsɛz] *m* diocese

diphtérie [difteʀi] *f* diphtheria

diphtongue [diftɔ̃g] *f* diphthong

diplodocus [diplɔdɔkys] *m* diplodocus

diplomate [diplɔmat] **I.** *adj* diplomatic **II.** *mf* diplomat

diplomatie [diplɔmasi] *f* **1.** (*relations extérieures, carrière, habileté*) diplomacy **2.** (*personnel*) diplomatic corps

diplomatique [diplɔmatik] *adj* diplomatic

diplôme [diplom] *m* diploma; **~ de fin d'études** graduation diploma; **~ d'ingénieur/d'infirmière** engineering/nursing diploma; **préparer un ~ d'agronomie/d'agronome** to be getting a degree in agronomics

diplômé(e) [diplome] **I.** *adj* qualified; **très ~** highly qualified **II.** *m(f)* **~ d'une université** graduate of a university

dire [diʀ] *irr* **I.** *vt* **1.** (*exprimer, prétendre, traduire*) to say; (*peur*) to put into words; **dis voir** hey, ...; **dis donc, ...** listen, ...; **~ que non/oui** to say yes/no; **~ du bien/mal de qn/qc** to say nice/bad things about sb/sth; **qu'est-ce que tu dis de ça?** what do you say to that?; **c'est vous qui le dites!** *inf* you said it!; **que ~?** what can you say?; **..., comment ~, ...,** how can I put it, ...; **entre nous soit dit, ...** between ourselves, ...; **dis, comment tu t'appelles, toi?** hey, what's your name?; **quoi qu'on (en) dise** whatever they say; **entendre ~ qc** to hear sb say **2.** (*ordonner*) **~ à qn de venir** to tell sb to come **3.** (*plaire*) **cela me dit** I'd like that; **cela ne me dit rien** I'm not in the mood for that **4.** (*croire, penser*) **je veux ~ qu'elle l'a fait** I mean that she's done it; **on dirait que...** anyone would think ...; **qui aurait dit cela!/qu'elle le ferait** who would have thought that!/that she'd do it **5.** (*reconnaître*) **il faut ~ qu'elle a raison** it must be said that she's right **6.** (*réciter: chapelet, messe, prière*) to say; (*poème*) to recite **7.** (*signifier*) **vouloir ~** to mean; **ce qui veut ~ (que)** which means (that) **8.** (*évoquer*) to tell; **quelque chose me dit qu'elle va le faire** something tells me she's going to do it **9.** JEUX to call ►**disons** let's say; **je ne te/vous le fais pas ~!** you're telling me!; **ce qui est dit est dit** what's said can't be unsaid; **eh ben dis/dites donc!** *inf* well then! **II.** *vpr* **1.** (*penser*) **se ~ que qn a fait qc** to think that sb's done sth **2.** (*se prétendre*) **se ~ médecin/malade** to claim to be a doctor/ill **3.** (*l'un(e) à l'autre*) **se ~ qc** to tell each other sth **4.** (*s'employer*) **ça se dit/ne se dit pas en français** you say that/don't say that in French **5.** (*être traduit: nom*) to be called; **ça se dit ... en français** the French for that is ...; **comment se dit ... en français?** how do you say ... in French? **6.** (*se croire*) **on se dirait au paradis** you'd think you were in paradise **III.** *m gén pl* claims; (*d'un témoin*) statement; **au ~/selon les ~s de qn** according to sb

direct [diʀɛkt] *m* **1.** TV **le ~** live TV; **en ~** live **2.** CHEMDFER non-stop train **3.** SPORT straight punch

direct(e) [diʀɛkt] *adj* direct; **des propos très ~s** some straight talking

directement [diʀɛktəmɑ̃] *adv* **1.** (*tout droit*) straight **2.** (*sans transition ou intermédiaire*) directly

directeur, **-trice** [diʀɛktœʀ, -tʀis] **I.** *adj* (*idée, ligne*) main; (*principe*) guiding; (*rôle*) leading; (*roue*) front **II.** *m, f* director; (*d'une école primaire*) head

direction [diʀɛksjɔ̃] *f* **1.** (*orientation*) direction; **prendre la ~ de Nancy** to head towards Nancy **2.** (*action*) management; (*d'un groupe, pays*) running; **avoir/prendre la ~ de qc** to be in/take charge of sth **3.** (*fonction, bureau*) management; **changer de ~** to come under new management **4.** AUTO steering

directive [diʀɛktiv] *f gén pl* directives

directorial(e) [diʀɛktɔʀjal, jo] <-aux> *adj* **salaire/bureau ~** director's salary/office

directrice [diʀɛktʀis] *v.* **directeur**

dirigeable [diʀiʒabl] *m* airship, blimp

dirigeant(e) [diʀiʒɑ̃, ʒɑ̃t] **I.** *adj* (*parti*) ruling; (*fonction, pouvoir, rôle*) executive **II.** *m(f)* leader; **les ~s** (*dans une entreprise*) the management; (*dans un parti*) the leadership; (*dans*

D

un pays) the executive

diriger [diʀiʒe] <2a> **I.** *vi* to lead **II.** *vt* **1.** (*gouverner: administration, journal, entreprise*) to run; (*syndicat, personnes*) to lead; (*musicien, orchestre*) to conduct; (*mouvement, manœuvre, instincts*) to direct **2.** (*être le moteur de*) ~ **le cours de la vie de qn** to direct the course of sb's life **3.** (*piloter: voiture*) to drive; (*avion*) to fly; (*bateau*) to steer **4.** (*faire aller*) ~ **qn vers la gare** to direct sb to the station; ~ **un bateau sur Marseille** to steer a boat towards Marseille **5.** (*orienter*) ~ **une arme contre qn/qc** to aim a gun at sb/sth **III.** *vpr* **1.** (*aller*) **se** ~ **vers qn/qc** to head towards sb/sth; **se** ~ **vers Marseille** (*avion, bateau*) to head towards Marseille **2.** (*s'orienter*) **se** ~ **vers le nord** (*aiguille*) to point north **3.** ECOLE, UNIV **se** ~ **vers la médecine** to head towards a career in medicine

dis [di] *indic prés et passé simple de* **dire**

discernement [disɛʀnəmɑ̃] *m* discernment; **agir avec beaucoup de ~/sans aucun ~** to show good judgment/no sense of judgment

discerner [disɛʀne] <1> *vt* **1.** (*percevoir*) to make out **2.** (*saisir*) to perceive; (*mobile*) to see **3.** (*différencier*) ~ **qc de qc** to distinguish sth from sth

disciple [disipl] *m* disciple

disciplinaire [disiplinɛʀ] *adj* disciplinary

discipline [disiplin] *f* discipline

discipliné(e) [disipline] *adj* disciplined; **peu** ~ undisciplined

disco [disko] **I.** *m* disco **II.** *adj inv* disco

discontinu(e) [diskɔ̃tiny] *adj* (*ligne*) broken; (*effort*) intermittent

discordant(e) [diskɔʀdɑ̃, ɑ̃t] *adj* (*incompatible*) discordant; (*opinions, caractères*) conflicting; (*couleurs*) clashing; (*sons*) discordant; (*cri*) harsh

discothèque [diskɔtɛk] *f* **1.** (*boîte de nuit*) discotheque **2.** (*collection*) record library **3.** (*meuble*) disc rack **4.** (*organisme de prêt*) record library

discourir [diskuʀiʀ] *vi irr* ~ **sur** [*o* **de**] **qc** to hold forth on sth

discours [diskuʀ] *m* **1.** (*allocution*) speech; ~ **télévisé** televised address **2.** (*propos*) **si on écoute leur** ~ if you listen to what they say; **leur** ~ **sur l'immigration** the way they talk about immigration **3.** (*bavardage*) talk; **beaux** ~ *péj* fine words

discourtois(e) [diskuʀtwa, waz] *adj soutenu* discourteous

discréditer [diskʀedite] <1> **I.** *vt* ~ **qn/qc auprès de qn** to discredit sb/sth with sb **II.** *vpr* **se** ~ **auprès de qn** to lose one's credibility with sb

discret [diskʀɛ, -ɛt] *adj* **1.** (*réservé, sobre*) discreet **2.** (*retiré*) secluded

discrètement [diskʀɛtmɑ̃] *adv* discreetly; (*s'habiller*) quietly; **je lui ai parlé** ~ I had a discreet word with him

discrétion [diskʀesjɔ̃] *f* **1.** (*réserve, silence*) discretion; ~ **assurée** confidentiality guaranteed **2.** (*sobriété*) discreetness; (*d'une toilette, d'un maquillage*) simplicity; (*des décors*) unobtrusiveness; **s'habiller avec** ~ to dress quietly

discrimination [diskʀiminasjɔ̃] *f* (*ségrégation*) discrimination; **sans** ~ indiscriminately

discriminatoire [diskʀiminatwaʀ] *adj* discriminatory

disculper [diskylpe] <1> **I.** *vt* ~ **qn de qc** to find sb not guilty of sth **II.** *vpr* **se** ~ to clear oneself

discussion [diskysjɔ̃] *f* **1.** (*conversation, débat*) discussion; ~ **sur qc** discussion about sth; **être en** ~ to be under discussion **2.** POL ~ **du budget** budget debate **3.** (*querelle*) argument

discutable [diskytabl] *adj* (*théories*) debatable; (*goût*) questionable

discutailler [diskytaje] <1> *vi péj* to argue (over nothing)

discuté(e) [diskyte] *adj* controversial

discuter [diskyte] <1> **I.** *vt* **1.** (*débattre*) to discuss **2.** (*contester: ordre, autorité*) to question; ~ **le prix** to argue over the price **II.** *vi* **1.** (*bavarder*) ~ **de qc avec qn** to talk to sb about sth; ~ **d'un problème** to discuss a problem **2.** (*négocier*) ~ **avec qn** to discuss with sb **3.** (*contester*) **on ne discute pas!** no arguments! **III.** *vpr* **se** ~ to be a subject for discussion; **ça se discute** that's debatable

disent [diz] *indic et subj prés de* **dire**

disette [dizɛt] *f* famine; ~ **de qc** dearth of sth

disgracieux, -euse [disgʀasjø, -jøz] *adj* (*démarche, proportions*) ungainly; (*gestes*) inelegant

disjoindre [disʒwɛ̃dʀ] *irr* **I.** *vt* **1.** (*disloquer*) ~ **qc** to take sth apart **2.** (*isoler*) ~ **qc de qc** to separate sth from sth **II.** *vpr* **se** ~ to come apart

disjoint(e) [disʒwɛ̃, wɛ̃t] *adj* (*planche*) loose; (*questions, aspects*) discrete

disjoncter [disʒɔ̃kte] <1> **I.** *vi inf* **1.** ELEC **ça a disjoncté!** a fuse has blown! **2.** (*débloquer*) to be off one's head **II.** *vt* ELEC to blow

disjoncteur [disʒɔ̃ktœʀ] *m* circuit breaker

disloquer [dislɔke] <1> **I.** *vt* **1.** (*démolir*) to smash; (*parti, famille, domaine*) to break up; (*empire*) to dismantle **2.** (*disperser: manifestation*) to break up **II.** *vpr* **1.** (*se défaire*) **se** ~ (*meuble, voiture, jouet*) to fall to pieces; (*empire*) to dismantle; (*famille, manifestation, assemblage, parti, société*) to break up **2.** MED **se** ~ **qc** to dislocate sth

disons [dizɔ̃] *indic prés et impératif de* **dire**

disparaître [dispaʀɛtʀ] *vi irr avoir* **1.** (*ne plus être là*) to disappear **2.** (*passer, s'effacer: trace, tache*) to disappear; (*douleur, espoir, crainte, soucis*) to vanish (away); (*colère*) to evaporate; **faire** ~ **les traces** to cover up the traces **3.** (*ne plus exister: obstacle*) to disappear; (*s'éteindre: culture, espèce, mode, dia-

lecte, coutume) to die out; (*mourir: personne*) to pass away; (*dans un naufrage*) to be lost; **faire ~ qn** to make sb disappear

disparate [disparat] *adj* (*couleurs, garde-robe, mobilier*) ill-assorted; (*œuvre, société*) disparate

disparité [disparite] *f* (*d'une œuvre, des opinions*) disparity; (*des couleurs*) mismatch; **~s régionales** regional disparities; **~ d'âge** disparity of age

disparition [disparisjɔ̃] *f* **1.**(*opp: apparition*) disappearance; (*d'une coutume, d'une culture*) passing; (*du soleil*) (*le soir*) setting; (*par mauvais temps*) disappearance **2.**(*mort*) death

disparu(e) [dispary] **I.** *part passé de* **disparaître II.** *adj* **être porté ~** to be reported missing **III.** *m(f)* **1.**(*défunt*) deceased **2.**(*porté manquant*) missing person

dispensaire [dispɑ̃sɛʀ] *m: clinic*

dispense [dispɑ̃s] *f* exemption; **~ de qc** exemption from sth

dispenser [dispɑ̃se] <1> **I.** *vt* **1.**(*exempter*) **~ qn de qc** to exempt sb from sth; **se faire ~ de qc** to be exempted from sth **2.**(*distribuer*) **~ qc à qn** to give sth to sb; **~ des soins à un malade** to care for a sick person; **~ des encouragements à qn** to give sb encouragement **II.** *vpr* **se ~ de qc** (*tâche*) to excuse oneself from sth; (*commentaire*) to refrain from sth; **je me dispenserais bien de la voir** I could do without seeing her

disperser [dispɛʀse] <1> **I.** *vt* **1.**(*éparpiller: papiers, cendres*) to scatter; (*troupes*) to disperse **2.**(*répartir*) to spread out **II.** *vpr* **se ~ 1.**(*partir dans tous les sens*) to scatter **2.**(*se déconcentrer*) **elle se disperse** she takes on more than she can handle

dispersion [dispɛʀsjɔ̃] *f* (*des graines, cendres*) scattering; (*d'un attroupement*) dispersal; (*de l'esprit*) overstretching

disponibilité [dispɔnibilite] *f sans pl* availability

disponible [dispɔnibl] *adj* available; **je suis ~ demain** I'm free tomorrow

dispos(e) [dispo, dispoz] *adj v.* **frais**

disposé(e) [dispoze] *adj* **être bien/mal ~** to be in a good/bad mood; **être ~ à** +*infin* to be inclined to +*infin*

disposer [dispoze] <1> **I.** *vt* **1.**(*arranger, placer: fleurs*) to arrange; (*objets*) to lay out; (*joueurs, soldats*) to position **2.**(*engager*) **~ qn à** +*infin* to incline sb to +*infin* **II.** *vi* **1.**(*avoir à sa disposition*) **~ de qc** to have sth; **vous disposez d'une voiture** you have a car at your disposal; **nous disposons de dix hommes** we have ten men available **2.** *soutenu* (*aliéner*) **~ de qc** to dispose of sth **III.** *vpr* **se ~ à** +*infin* to be preparing to +*infin*

dispositif [dispozitif] *m* **1.**(*mécanisme*) device **2.**(*ensemble de mesures*) measures *pl;* **un ~ policier** a police presence

disposition [dispozisjɔ̃] *f* **1.** *sans pl* (*agencement*) arrangement; (*d'un article, texte*) structure **2.**(*clause*) provision ►**il veut avoir une voiture à sa ~** he wants to have a car at his disposal; **prendre des ~s pour qc** to make arrangements for sth

disproportion [dispʀɔpɔʀsjɔ̃] *f* lack of proportion

disproportionné(e) [dispʀɔpɔʀsjɔne] *adj* (*corps*) disproportionate; (*réactions*) exaggerated

dispute [dispyt] *f* quarrel; (*entre adversaires*) dispute

disputer [dispyte] <1> **I.** *vt* **1.** *inf* (*gronder*) **~ qn** to tell sb off **2.**(*contester*) **~ qc à qn** to fight with sb over sth **3.** SPORT (*match*) to fight; **être très disputé** to be a close match **II.** *vpr* **1.**(*se quereller*) **se ~ avec qn** to quarrel with sb **2.**(*lutter pour*) **se ~ qc** to fight for sth **3.** SPORT **se ~** (*match*) to be held

disquaire [diskɛʀ] *m* record dealer

disqualification [diskalifikasjɔ̃] *f* disqualification

disqualifier [diskalifje] <1> **I.** *vt* to disqualify **II.** *vpr* **se ~** to be disqualified

disque [disk] *m* **1.**(*objet rond*) disc **2.** MUS record; **~ compact** compact disc; **mettre un ~** to put a record on **3.** SPORT discus **4.** INFOR **~ dur** hard disk; **~ optique compact** optical compact disc; **~ numérique polyvalent** Digital Versatile Disk ►**change de ~!** *inf* give us a break!

disquette [diskɛt] *f* floppy disk; **~ double face, haute densité** double-sided, high density disk; **une ~ double densité** a double density disk; **une ~ formatée pour lecteurs de 1,44 Mo.** a formatted 1.44MB floppy disk; **~ de démarrage** start-up disk; **~ d'installation** installation disk

dissection [disɛksjɔ̃] *f* dissection

dissemblable [disɑ̃blabl] *adj* dissimilar

disséminer [disemine] <1> **I.** *vt* (*graines*) to scatter; (*idées*) to disseminate **II.** *vpr* **se ~ 1.**(*se disperser*) to be scattered **2.**(*se répandre*) to spread out

dissension [disɑ̃sjɔ̃] *f* disagreement

disséquer [diseke] <5> *vt* to dissect

dissertation [disɛʀtasjɔ̃] *f* **1.** ECOLE essay **2.** UNIV dissertation

dissident(e) [disidɑ̃, ɑ̃t] **I.** *adj* dissident **II.** *m(f)* dissident

dissimulation [disimylasjɔ̃] *f* **1.** *sans pl* (*duplicité*) dissimulation **2.**(*action de cacher*) concealment

dissimulé(e) [disimyle] *adj* secretive

dissimuler [disimyle] <1> **I.** *vt* **1.**(*cacher*) *a.* FIN to conceal **2.**(*taire*) **~ qc à qn** to hide sth from sb **II.** *vi* **elle sait ~** she can put on a good act **III.** *vpr* **se ~** to conceal oneself; **se ~ que qn a fait qc** to hide from oneself the fact that sb has done sth

dissipation [disipasjɔ̃] *f* (*morale*) dissipation; (*du patrimoine*) waste; (*de la brume*) lifting

dissipé(e) [disipe] *adj* undisciplined
dissiper [disipe] <1> **I.** *vt* **1.** (*faire disparaître*) to dissipate **2.** (*lever: soupçons, doutes*) to dissipate; (*illusions*) to scatter; (*malentendu*) to clear up **3.** (*dilapider*) to squander **4.** ECOLE to distract **II.** *vpr* **se ~** (*brume*) to lift; (*doutes, craintes, soupçons, inquiétude*) to vanish; ECOLE to be distracted
dissocier [disɔsje] <1> *vt* (*envisager séparément*) ~ **qc de qc** to dissociate sth from sth
dissolution [disɔlysjɔ̃] *f* **1.** (*action*) dissolution **2.** (*liquide*) solution
dissolvant [disɔlvɑ̃] *m* solvent; (*pour les ongles*) varnish [*o* nail polish] remover
dissolvant(e) [disɔlvɑ̃, ɑ̃t] *adj* solvent
dissoudre [disudʀ] *irr* **I.** *vt* to dissolve **II.** *vpr* **se ~** to be dissolved
dissous, -oute [disu, -ut] **I.** *part passé de* **dissoudre II.** *adj* dissolved
dissuader [disɥade] <1> *vt* ~ **qn de qc** to dissuade sb from sth
dissuasif, -ive [disɥazif, -iv] *adj* dissuasive
dissuasion [disɥazjɔ̃] *f* dissuasion
dissymétrique [disimetʀik] *adj* dissymetrical
distance [distɑ̃s] *f* **1.** (*éloignement*) *a.* MAT, SPORT distance; **la ~ entre Nancy et Paris/de la terre à la lune** the distance between Nancy and Paris/from the earth to the moon; **à quelle ~ est Aix?** how far (away) is Aix?; **à une ~ de 500 m** 500 metres away *Brit,* 500 meters away *Am* **2.** (*écart*) gap ►**prendre ses ~s à l'égard de qn** to distance oneself from sb; **tenir qn à ~** to keep sb at a distance; **à ~** (*dans l'espace: communiquer, juger, voir*) at a distance; (*dans le temps: juger*) in hindsight; **commande/commandé à ~** remote control/-controlled; **à 5 ans de ~** five years on
distancer [distɑ̃se] <2> *vt* **1.** SPORT to outdistance **2.** (*surpasser*) to outdo
distant(e) [distɑ̃, ɑ̃t] *adj* **1.** (*réservé: personne, attitude*) distant **2.** (*éloigné*) separated; **ces deux événements sont ~s de plusieurs années** these two events happened several years apart
distendre [distɑ̃dʀ] <14> **I.** *vt* (*peau*) to stretch; (*liens*) to loosen; **être distendu** (*ressort, élastique*) to be stretched; (*courroie*) to be loose; (*ligament*) to be strained **II.** *vpr* **se ~** (*peau, élastique*) to get stretched; (*ligament*) to be strained; (*liens*) to get loose
distillation [distilasjɔ̃] *f* distillation
distiller [distile] <1> *vt* to distil
distillerie [distilʀi] *f* distillery
distinct(e) [distɛ̃, ɛ̃kt] *adj* distinct
distinctement [distɛ̃ktəmɑ̃] *adv* distinctly
distinctif, -ive [distɛ̃ktif, -iv] *adj* distinctive; **signe ~** distinguising mark
distinction [distɛ̃ksjɔ̃] *f* distinction; **être d'une grande ~** to be highly distinguished
distingué(e) [distɛ̃ge] *adj* (*élégant, éminent*) distinguished; **ça fait très ~** that's very elegant
distinguer [distɛ̃ge] <1> **I.** *vt* **1.** (*percevoir, différencier*) to distinguish **2.** (*caractériser*) **sa grande taille le distingue** he is distinguished by his height **3.** (*honorer*) to honour *Brit,* to honor *Am* **II.** *vi* (*faire la différence*) ~ **entre qn et qn/entre qc et qc** to distinguish sb from sb else/sth from sth else **III.** *vpr* **1.** (*différer*) **se ~ de qn/qc par qc** to be distinguished from sb/sth by sth **2.** (*s'illustrer*) **se ~ par qc** to distinguish oneself by sth
distraction [distʀaksjɔ̃] *f* **1.** *sans pl* (*inattention*) lack of concentration **2.** (*étourderie*) absent-mindedness **3.** *sans pl* (*dérivatif*) distraction **4.** *gén pl* (*passe-temps*) pastime
distraire [distʀɛʀ] *irr* **I.** *vt* **1.** (*délasser*) to amuse **2.** (*déranger*) ~ **qn de qc** to distract sb from sth **II.** *vpr* **se ~** to enjoy oneself
distrait(e) [distʀɛ, ɛt] **I.** *part passé de* **distraire II.** *adj* absent-minded
distraitement [distʀɛtmɑ̃] *adv* absent-mindedly; **écouter qn ~** to only half listen to sb
distrayant(e) [distʀɛjɑ̃, jɑ̃t] *adj* entertaining
distribuer [distʀibɥe] <1> *vt* **1.** (*donner*) *a.* FIN, COM to distribute; (*cartes*) to deal; ~ **des coups/gifles** to go round hitting/slapping people; ~ **le courrier** to deliver the mail; ~ **de l'électricité à qn/qc** to supply electricity to sb/sth **2.** (*arranger, répartir: éléments, mots*) to arrange; (*joueurs de foot*) to position
distributeur [distʀibytœʀ] *m* (slot) machine; ~ **de billets/boissons** cash/drink machine
distributeur, -trice [distʀibytœʀ, -tʀis] *m, f* **1.** (*personne*) ~ **de prospectus** sb who distributes fliers **2.** COM, CINE distributor; (*entreprise*) dealer; (*diffuseur*) distributor; ~ **agréé/exclusif** official/exclusive dealer
distribution [distʀibysjɔ̃] *f* **1.** (*répartition*) distribution; (*du courrier*) delivery; (*des cartes*) dealing **2.** FIN (*des dividendes*) distribution; (*des actions*) issue; ~ **des prix** prize-giving **3.** COM supply; **la ~ d'eau** the supply of water **4.** CINE, THEAT cast **5.** (*arrangement: des éléments, mots*) arrangement; (*des pièces, de l'appartement*) layout; (*des joueurs*) positioning
district [distʀikt] *m* district
dit [di] *indic prés de* **dire**
dit(e) [di, dit] **I.** *part passé de* **dire II.** *adj* (*touristique, socialiste*) so-called; ~ **le Sage/le Bègue** known as the Wise/the Stammerer
dites [dit] *indic prés de* **dire**
diurne [djyʀn] *adj* diurnal
diva [diva] *f* diva
divagation [divagasjɔ̃] *f gén pl* rambling
divaguer [divage] <1> *vi* **1.** (*délirer: malade*) to be delirious **2.** *inf* (*déraisonner*) to talk nonsense
divan [divɑ̃] *m* couch, sofa
divergence [divɛʀʒɑ̃s] *f* divergence
divergent(e) [divɛʀʒɑ̃, ʒɑ̃t] *adj* divergent

diverger [divɛʀʒe] <2a> *vi* to diverge
divers(e) [divɛʀ, ɛʀs] **I.** *adj* **1.** (*différent, varié*) various **2.** (*inégal, contradictoire: mouvements, intérêts*) diverse **3.** *toujours au pl* (*plusieurs*) various; **à ~es reprises** on several occasions **II.** *mpl* sundries
diversification [divɛʀsifikasjɔ̃] *f* diversification
diversifier [divɛʀsifje] <1> *vt* to diversify
diversion [divɛʀsjɔ̃] *f* MIL diversion
diversité [divɛʀsite] *f* diversity
divertir [divɛʀtiʀ] <8> **I.** *vt* **1.** (*délasser*) to amuse **2.** (*changer les idées de qn*) ~ **qn** to take sb's mind off things **II.** *vpr* **se** ~ to enjoy oneself
divertissant(e) [divɛʀtisɑ̃, ɑ̃t] *adj* entertaining; **il trouve ~ de les regarder** he enjoys watching them
divertissement [divɛʀtismɑ̃] *m* **1.** *sans pl* (*action*) amusement; (*passe-temps*) pastime **2.** MUS divertissement
divin(e) [divɛ̃, in] *adj* **1.** REL divine **2.** (*exceptionnel*) heavenly
divination [divinasjɔ̃] *f* divination
divinement [divinmɑ̃] *adv* (*chanter*) divinely; **il fait ~ beau** it's a heavenly day; **elle est ~ belle** she's exquisitely beautiful
divinité [divinite] *f* **1.** *sans pl* (*caractère divin*) divinity **2.** (*dieu*) deity
diviser [divize] <1> **I.** *vt* (*fractionner, désunir*) *a.* MAT ~ **qc en qc** to divide sth into sth; **divisé par** divided by ►~ **pour régner** *prov* divide and rule **II.** *vpr* **1.** (*se séparer*) **se ~ en qc** (*cellule, route*) to divide into sth; (*parti*) to split into sth **2.** (*être divisible*) **se** ~ (*nombre*) to divide; (*ouvrage*) to divide (up)
diviseur [divizœʀ] *m* divisor
divisible [divizibl] *adj* ~ **par qc** divisible by sth
division [divizjɔ̃] *f* **1.** division; ~ **en qc** division into sth **2.** *Québec* (*service intermédiaire entre la direction et la section d'une entreprise*) division (*of a company*)
divorce [divɔʀs] *m* divorce; ~ **avec qn** divorce from sb
divorcé(e) [divɔʀse] **I.** *adj* ~ **de qn** divorced from sb **II.** *m(f)* divorcee
divorcer [divɔʀse] <2> *vi* ~ **de qn** to divorce sb
divulgation [divylgasjɔ̃] *f* disclosure
divulguer [divylge] <1> *vt* to disclose; ~ **un secret à qn** to tell sb a secret
dix [dis, *devant une voyelle* diz, *devant une consonne* di] **I.** *adj* ten ►**répéter/recommencer ~ fois la même chose** to say/do the same thing over and over again **II.** *m inv* ten; *v. a.* **cinq**
dix-huit [dizɥit, *devant une consonne* dizɥi] **I.** *adj* eighteen **II.** *m inv* eighteen; *v. a.* **cinq**
dix-huitième [dizɥitjɛm] <dix-huitièmes> **I.** *adj antéposé* eighteenth **II.** *mf* **le/la** ~ the eighteenth **III.** *m* (*fraction*) eighteenth; *v. a.* **cinquième**
dixième [dizjɛm] **I.** *adj antéposé* tenth **II.** *mf* **le/la** ~ the tenth **III.** *m* (*fraction*) tenth; **les neuf ~s des gens** nine out of ten people; *v. a.* **cinquième**
dix-neuf [diznœf] **I.** *adj* nineteen **II.** *m inv* nineteen; *v. a.* **cinq**
dix-neuvième [diznœvjɛm] <dix-neuvièmes> **I.** *adj antéposé* nineteenth **II.** *mf* **le/la** ~ the nineteenth **III.** *m* (*fraction*) nineteenth; *v. a.* **cinquième**
dix-sept [dissɛt] **I.** *adj* seventeen **II.** *m inv* seventeen; *v. a.* **cinq**
dix-septième [dissɛtjɛm] <dix-septièmes> **I.** *adj antéposé* seventeenth **II.** *mf* **le/la** ~ the seventeenth **III.** *m* (*fraction*) seventeenth; *v. a.* **cinquième**
dizaine [dizɛn] *f* **1.** (*environ dix*) **une ~ de personnes/pages** ten people/pages or so; **quelques/plusieurs ~s de personnes** a couple/a few dozen people **2.** (*âge approximatif*) **avoir une ~ d'années** to be around ten; **elle approche de la ~** she's nearing ten; **avoir (largement) dépassé la ~** to be well over ten
DJ [didʒe] *m abr de* **disc-jockey** DJ
Djibouti [dʒibuti] Djibouti
djiboutien(ne) [dʒibutjɛ̃, jɛn] *adj* Djiboutian
Djiboutien(ne) [dʒibutjɛ̃, jɛn] *m(f)* Djiboutian
DM [dœtʃmaʀk] *abr de* **Deutsche Mark** DM
do [do] *m inv* C; ~ **dièse/bémol** C sharp/flat
doc [dɔk] *f inf abr de* **documentation**
DOC [dɔk] *m abr de* **disque optique compact** compact laser disk
docile [dɔsil] *adj* docile
docilité [dɔsilite] *f* docility; **ce poney est d'une grande ~** this pony is very docile; **avec ~** obediently
docker [dɔkɛʀ] *m* docker
docks [dɔks] *mpl* warehouses
docteur [dɔktœʀ] *m* doctor

> In France, people who have a doctorate are not addressed as doctor. They are simply called Monsieur or Madame x. The title is only used in correspondance by the sender (e.g. "Monsieur le **docteur**").

doctorat [dɔktɔʀa] *m* doctorate; **un ~ en** a doctorate in; ~ **d'État** doctorate, *similar to a Ph.D.*
doctrine [dɔktʀin] *f* doctrine
document [dɔkymɑ̃] *m* **1.** document **2.** (*preuve*) piece of evidence
documentaire [dɔkymɑ̃tɛʀ] **I.** *adj* documentary **II.** *m* documentary
documentaliste [dɔkymɑ̃talist] *mf* ECOLE librarian
documentation [dɔkymɑ̃tasjɔ̃] *f* documentation
documenter [dɔkymɑ̃te] <1> **I.** *vt* ~ **qn sur qn/qc** to provide sb with full information

on sb/sth **II.** *vpr* **se ~ sur qn/qc** to inform oneself fully on sb/sth

dodo [dodo] *m enfantin, inf* **faire ~** (*s'endormir*) to go to beddy-byes *Brit,* to go night-night *Am;* (*dormir*) to be in dreamland

dodu(e) [dɔdy] *adj inf* chubby; (*poule*) plump

dogme [dɔgm] *m* dogma

doigt [dwa] *m* ANAT (*de la main, d'un gant*) finger; **lever le ~** to lift a finger ▸**être à deux ~s de la mort** to be at death's door; **il l'a fait les ~s dans le nez** *inf* he did it with his hands behind his back; **je suis à un ~ de le faire** I'm this close to doing it; **filer entre les ~s de qn** to slip between sb's fingers; **tu as mis le ~ sur quelque chose** you've put your finger on something

doigté [dwate] *m* **1.** MUS fingering **2.** (*savoir-faire*) adroitness

dois [dwa] *indic prés de* **devoir**

doit [dwa] **I.** *indic prés de* **devoir II.** *m* debit

doivent [dwav] *indic et subj prés de* **devoir**

doléances [dɔleɑ̃s] *fpl* grievances; **faire ses ~ à qn au sujet de qc** to express one's grievances about sth

dollar [dɔlaʀ] *m* dollar; **~ canadien** Canadian dollar

dolmen [dɔlmɛn] *m* dolmen

DOM [dɔm] *m abr de* **département d'outre-mer** French overseas département

> The **DOM** are the French overseas départements. They include French Guiana, Reunion Island, Martinique and Guadeloupe. These colonies are treated today as French economic zones and are responsible, like all départements, for matters specific to their areas.

domaine [dɔmɛn] *m* **1.** (*terre*) estate **2.** (*sphère*) field **3.** INFOR domain

Domaine [dɔmɛn] *m* ADMIN **le ~** state property

domanial(e) [dɔmanjal, jo] <-aux> *adj* **biens domaniaux** state land *Brit,* public land *Am*

dôme [dom] *m* dome

domestique [dɔmɛstik] **I.** *adj* **1.** (*ménager: vie, affaires, ennuis*) domestic; **animal ~** pet **2.** ECON (*marché*) domestic **II.** *mf* servant

domestiquer [dɔmɛstike] <1> *vt* (*énergie solaire, vent, marées*) to harness

domicile [dɔmisil] *m* **1.** (*demeure*) home **2.** ADMIN residence ▸**à ~** at home; **recevoir qc à ~** to receive sth at one's home; **travail/visite à ~** home working/visit

domicilié(e) [dɔmisilje] *adj* living

domicilier [dɔmisilje] <1> *vt form* **être domicilié à Paris** to reside in Paris

dominant(e) [dɔminɑ̃, ɑ̃t] *adj* (*position, nation*) dominant; (*opinion, vent*) prevailing

dominante [dɔminɑ̃t] *f* (*caractéristique*) dominant characteristic

dominateur, -trice [dɔminatœʀ, -tʀis] *adj* dominating

domination [dɔminasjɔ̃] *f* (*suprématie*) domination

dominer [dɔmine] <1> **I.** *vt* **1.** (*être le maître de*) to dominate **2.** (*contrôler: larmes, chagrin*) to suppress; (*sujet*) to be master of **3.** (*surpasser*) to outclass **4.** (*surplomber*) to look out over **5.** (*être plus fort que*) **~ le tumulte** (*orateur, voix*) to make oneself heard above the row; **~ qn** (*passion du jeu*) to have a hold on sb **II.** *vi* **1.** (*prédominer, commander*) *a.* SPORT to dominate **2.** (*commander sur les mers*) to rule **III.** *vpr* **se ~** to take hold of oneself

dominicain(e) [dɔminikɛ̃, ɛn] *adj* Dominican; **la République ~e** Dominican Republic

Dominicain(e) [dɔminikɛ̃, ɛn] *m(f)* Dominican

dominicais(e) [dɔminikɛ, ɛz] *adj* Dominican

Dominicais(e) [dɔminikɛ, ɛz] *m(f)* Dominican

dominical(e) [dɔminikal, o] <-aux> *adj* **repos ~** Sunday rest

dominiquais(e) *v.* **dominicais**

Dominiquais(e) *v.* **Dominicais**

Dominique *f* GEO Dominica

domino [dɔmino] *m* (*pièce*) domino; *pl* (*jeu*) dominoes; **jouer aux ~s** to play dominoes

dommage [dɔmaʒ] *m* **1.** (*préjudice*) harm *sans pl;* **~s corporels** physical harm; **~s matériels** material damage; **~ et intérêts** damages **2.** *pl* (*dégâts*) damage *no pl* ▸**c'est bien ~!** it's a real pity!; **quel ~!** what a pity!

dompter [dɔ̃(p)te] <1> *vt* (*cheval, fauve*) to tame; (*rebelles, imagination, passions, peur*) to subdue

dompteur, -euse [dɔ̃(p)tœʀ, -øz] *m, f* tamer

DOM-TOM [dɔmtɔm] *mpl abr de* **départements et territoires d'outre-mer** French overseas départements and territories

don [dɔ̃] *m* (*action, cadeau, aptitude*) gift; (*charitable*) donation; **~ d'organe** organ donation; **faire un ~ à qn** to give sb a gift; **avoir le ~ de faire qc** to have the gift for doing sth

donateur, -trice [dɔnatœʀ, -tʀis] *m, f* donor

donation [dɔnasjɔ̃] *f* donation

donc [dɔ̃k] *conj* so; **si ~ je ne suis pas là à 20 heures** so if I'm not here at eight o'clock; **vas-y ~!** get on with it then!

donjon [dɔ̃ʒɔ̃] *m* keep

don Juan [dɔ̃ʒyɑ̃] <dons Juans> *m* Don Juan

donnant [dɔnɑ̃] **avec lui, c'est ~ ~** you have to give to get something back with him

donné(e) [dɔne] *adj* (*déterminé*) given ▸**étant ~ qc** given that; **c'est ~** *inf* it's practically free

donnée [dɔne] *f gén pl* **1.** (*élément d'appréciation*) given **2.** ECOLE **~s du problème** details of the problem **3.** *pl* INFOR, ADMIN data

donner [dɔne] <1> **I.** *vt* **1.** (*remettre*) ~ **qc à qn** to give sth to sb, to give sb sth **2.** (*communiquer*) ~ **de ses nouvelles** to say how one is getting on; ~ **le bonjour à qn** to say hello to sb **3.** (*causer*) **ça donne faim/soif** it makes you hungry/thirsty; **ça lui donne chaud** it makes him hot; **elle/ça lui donne envie de partir** she/it makes him want to leave **4.** (*conférer*) **cette couleur te donne un air sévère** that colour makes you look severe *Brit,* that color makes you look severe *Am* **5.** (*attribuer*) ~ **de l'importance à qn/qc** to give importance to sb/sth **6.** (*produire*) ~ **des fruits** to produce fruit; ~ **des résultats** (*recherches*) to give results **7.** (*faire passer pour*) ~ **qc pour certain** to say sth is a certainty; ~ **qn perdant** to say sb is going to lose **II.** *vi* (*s'ouvrir sur*) ~ **sur qc** (*pièce, fenêtre*) to look (out) onto sth; (*porte*) to open out to sth **III.** *vpr* **1.** (*se dévouer*) **se** ~ **à qn/qc** to devote oneself to sb/sth **2.** (*faire l'amour*) **se** ~ **à qn** to give oneself to sb

donneur, -euse [dɔnœʀ, -øz] *m, f a.* MED donor; ~ **de sang** blood donor

don Quichotte [dɔ̃kiʃɔt] *m inv* **être un** ~ to be something of a Don Quixote

dont [dɔ̃] *pron rel* **1.** *compl d'un subst* **cet acteur,** ~ **le dernier film** that actor, whose latest film **2.** *compl d'un verbe* **la femme** ~ **vous me parlez** the woman you are telling me about **3.** (*partie d'un tout*) including; **cet accident a fait six victimes,** ~ **deux enfants** there were six victims of the accident, two of them children

dopage [dɔpaʒ] *m* drug use

dopé(e) [dɔpe] *adj* drugged

doper [dɔpe] <1> **I.** *vt* **1.** (*stimuler*) to stimulate **2.** SPORT to give drugs to **II.** *vpr* **se** ~ to use drugs

dorade [dɔʀad] *f v.* **daurade**

doré [dɔʀe] *m Québec* (*poisson d'eau douce à chair estimée*) yellow pike

doré(e) [dɔʀe] *adj* **1.** (*avec de l'or*) gilded **2.** (*de couleur ressemblant à de l'or, agréable*) golden; **prison ~e** gilded cage

dorénavant [dɔʀenavɑ̃] *adv* henceforth

dorer [dɔʀe] <1> **I.** *vt* **1.** (*recouvrir d'or, colorer*) to gild **2.** GASTR (*gâteau*) to brown **II.** *vi* GASTR to brown **III.** *vpr* **se faire** ~ **au soleil** to sunbathe

dorloter [dɔʀlɔte] <1> *vt* to pamper

dormant [dɔʀmɑ̃] *m* (*d'une fenêtre, porte*) frame

dormant(e) [dɔʀmɑ̃, ɑ̃t] *adj* **eau ~e** stagnant water

dormeur, -euse [dɔʀmœʀ, -øz] *m, f* sleeper; **gros** ~ heavy sleeper

dormir [dɔʀmiʀ] *vi irr* **1.** (*sommeiller*) to sleep **2.** (*être négligé: capitaux, affaire*) to lie dormant **3.** (*être calme, sans bruit: maison, nature*) to be asleep ►**ça ne l'empêche pas de** ~ *inf* it doesn't keep him awake at nights

dorsal(e) [dɔʀsal, o] <-aux> *adj* dorsal; **les muscles dorsaux** the back muscles

dortoir [dɔʀtwaʀ] *m* dormitory

dorure [dɔʀyʀ] *f* **1.** (*or*) gilt **2.** (*art, effet*) gilding

doryphore [dɔʀifɔʀ] *m* Colorado beetle

dos [do] *m* (*d'une personne, d'un objet*) back ►**elle n'y vas pas avec le** ~ **de la cuillère** *inf* she doesn't pull her punches; **en avoir plein le** ~ *inf* to be fed up; **n'avoir rien à se mettre sur le** ~ to have nothing to wear; **être sur le** ~ **de qn** *inf* to be on sb's back; **faire qc dans le** ~ **de qn** to do sth behind sb's back; **faire qc sur le** ~ **de qn** to do sth at sb's expense

dosage [dozaʒ] *m* MED dosage; *fig* mixture

dose [doz] *f* **1.** BIO dose **2.** GASTR part; **trois ~s de farine pour une** ~ **de sucre** three parts flour to one part sugar ►**une bonne** ~ **de courage** a good helping of courage; **par petites ~s** in small doses

doser [doze] <1> *vt* **1.** BIO (*médicament*) to measure a dose of; (*ingrédients*) to measure out; (*cocktail*) to mix in the right proportions **2.** (*mesurer*) to use just the right amount of

dossard [dosaʀ] *m* SPORT number

dossier [dosje] *m* **1.** (*appui pour le dos*) back **2.** (*classeur*) *a.* ADMIN file; ~ **de candidature** application

dot [dɔt] *f* dowry; **apporter qc en** ~ **à qn** to bring sth to sb in one's dowry

doté(e) [dɔte] *adj* **être** ~ **de qc** (*machine*) to have sth; (*personne*) to be endowed with sth

doter [dɔte] <1> **I.** *vt* **1.** ~ **une fille** to give a girl a dowry **2.** (*attribuer*) ~ **de qc** to provide with sth; (*concours*) to endow with sth **II.** *vpr* **se** ~ **de qc** (*pays, groupe*) to acquire sth

douane [dwan] *f* **1.** (*administration, poste*) customs *pl;* **être saisi en** ~ to be seized by customs **2.** (*droit*) (customs) duty

douanier, -ière [dwanje, -jɛʀ] **I.** *adj* customs **II.** *m, f* customs officer

doublage [dublaʒ] *m* **1.** CINE (*en langue étrangère*) dubbing; (*pour les cascades*) doubling **2.** COUT lining

double [dubl] **I.** *adj* double; ~ **personnalité** dual personality **II.** *adv* (*voir*) double; **compter** ~ to count twice the number/amount **III.** *m* **1.** (*quantité*) twice the amount; **il a mis le** ~ **de temps** he took twice the time **2.** (*copie, exemplaire identique*) copy; (*personne*) double; **un** ~ **de clé** a spare key; **je l'ai en** ~ I've got another one; **j'ai tout en** ~ I've got two of everything **3.** SPORT doubles *pl*

doublé(e) [duble] *adj* **1.** COUT (*vêtement*) lined **2.** CINE (*en langue étrangère*) dubbed

double-cliquer [dublklike] *vi* INFOR ~ **sur le bouton gauche de la souris** to double-click on the left mouse button

doublement [dubləmɑ̃] **I.** *adv* doubly **II.** *m* **1.** doubling; (*élargissement: d'une voie, route*) widening **2.** ECOLE repeating a year

doubler [duble] <1> **I.** *vt* **1.** (*multiplier par deux*) to double **2.** (*mettre en double: papier*) to fold (in two); (*fil*) to double **3.** (*garnir inté-

rieurement) to line **4.** *Belgique* (*redoubler*) ~ **une classe** to repeat a year **5.** CINE (*en langue étrangère*) to dub; (*pour les cascades*) to double **6.** THEAT ~ **qn** to stand in for **7.** (*dépasser: véhicule*) to overtake *Brit,* to pass *Am;* **se faire** ~ to be overtaken **8.** *inf* (*tromper*) to take in **II.** *vi* (*être multiplié par deux: nombre, prix*) to double **III.** *vpr* **se** ~ **de qc** to be coupled with sth

doublure [dublyʀ] *f* **1.** COUT (*d'un vêtement*) lining **2.** CINE stand-in **3.** THEAT understudy

douce [dus] *v.* **doux**

douceâtre [dusɑtʀ] *adj* sickly

doucement [dusmɑ̃] *adv* **1.** (*avec précaution*) carefully **2.** (*sans bruit*) quietly **3.** (*avec délicatesse, graduellement*) gently **4.** (*faiblement*) softly **5.** (*médiocrement*) not so well

doucettement [dusɛtmɑ̃] *adv inf* **tout** ~ ever so slowly

douceur [dusœʀ] *f* **1.** (*sensation: d'une étoffe, musique, de la lumière*) softness; (*d'un fruit*) sweetness; (*de la température*) mildness; **se passer en** ~ to go off smoothly **2.** (*sentiment: d'un caractère, de la vie*) sweetness **3.** *gén pl* (*friandises*) sweets; (*plat sucré*) puddings *Brit,* desserts *Am* **4.** *pl* (*amabilités*) sweet words

douche [duʃ] *f* shower ►**c'est la** ~ **écossaise** you don't know what's coming next

doucher [duʃe] <1> **I.** *vt* **1.** (*tremper*) to shower **2.** (*décevoir: enthousiasme*) to drown **II.** *vpr* **se** ~ to have a shower

doudoune [dudun] *f* anorak

doué(e) [dwe] *adj* gifted; **être** ~ **de ses mains** to be good with one's hands

douille [duj] *f* **1.** TECH casing; (*d'une cartouche*) case **2.** ELEC socket

douillet(te) [dujɛ, jɛt] *adj* **1.** (*sensible*) (over)sensitive **2.** (*pleurnicheur*) susceptible **3.** (*confortable: logis, nid, lit*) cosy

douleur [dulœʀ] *f* **1.** (*physique*) pain; **de** ~ of pain **2.** (*moral*) sorrow; **avoir la** ~ **de** +*infin* to be deeply sorry to +*infin*

douloureuse [duluʀøz] *f inf* bill

douloureux, -euse [duluʀø, -øz] *adj* (*qui fait mal, qui fait de la peine*) painful; **regard** ~ pained look

doute [dut] *m* doubt; **ne laisser aucun** ~ **sur qc** to leave no doubt about sth ►**mettre qc en** ~ to put sth in doubt; **sans** ~ no doubt

douter [dute] <1> **I.** *vi* **1.** (*être incertain*) ~ **de qc** to doubt sth; ~ **que qn ait fait qc** to doubt that sb did sth **2.** (*se méfier*) ~ **de qn/qc** to have doubts about sb/sth ►**à n'en pas** ~ undoubtedly; **ne** ~ **de rien** *iron* to have no idea **II.** *vpr* (*pressentir*) **se** ~ **de qc** to suspect sth; **je m'en doute** I expect so

douteux, -euse [dutø, -øz] *adj* **1.** (*incertain*) doubtful **2.** *péj* (*goût, mœurs*) dubious; (*vêtement*) none too clean

Douvres [duːvʀ(ə)] Dover

doux [du] **I.** *adv* **ça va tout** ~ *inf* things are OK **II.** *m* (*temps*) the mild weather

doux, douce [du, dus] *adj* **1.** (*au toucher, à l'oreille, à la vue*) soft **2.** (*au goût: fruit, saveur, vin*) sweet; (*piment, moutarde, tabac*) mild; **les drogues douces** soft drugs **3.** (*à l'odorat: odeur, parfum*) sweet **4.** (*clément: climat, temps*) mild **5.** (*gentil, patient: personne*) kind **6.** (*modéré: peine*) mild; (*croissance*) gradual; (*fiscalité*) moderate; (*gestes, pente*) gentle; **à feu** ~ on moderate heat **7.** (*agréable: vie, souvenir, visage*) sweet ►**se la couler douce** *inf* to have it easy; **en douce** *inf* on the quiet

douzaine [duzɛn] *f* **1.** (*douze*) dozen; **à la** ~ by the dozen **2.** (*environ douze*) **une** ~ **de personnes/choses** twelve or so people/things

douze [duz] **I.** *adj inv* twelve **II.** *m inv* twelve; *v. a.* **cinq**

douzième [duzjɛm] **I.** *adj antéposé* twelfth **II.** *mf* **le/la** ~ the twelfth **III.** *m* twelfth; *v. a.* **cinquième**

downloader [doʊnlode] *vt* INFOR to download

doyen(ne) [dwajɛ̃, jɛn] *m(f)* **1.** (*aîné*) doyen **2.** UNIV dean

drache [dʳaʃ] *f Belgique* (*pluie battante, averse*) downpour

draconien(ne) [dʀakɔnjɛ̃, jɛn] *adj* draconian

dragée [dʀaʒe] *f* sugared almond

dragon [dʀagɔ̃] *m* dragon

dragonne [dʀagɔn] *f* (wrist)strap

drag-queen [dʀagkwin] <drag-queens> *f* drag queen

drague [dʀag] *f* **1.** (*filet*) dragnet **2.** (*appareil*) dredger **3.** *inf* (*racolage*) pulling *Brit,* hitting on people *Am*

draguer [dʀage] <1> **I.** *vt* **1.** (*pêcher*) to use a dragnet to fish for **2.** (*dégager: chenal, sable*) to dredge; (*mines*) to sweep **3.** *inf* (*racoler*) to try to pull *Brit,* to hit on sb *Am* **II.** *vi inf* (*racoler*) to be on the pull *Brit,* to try to pick up people *Am*

dragueur [dʀagœʀ] *m* dredger; ~ **de mines** minesweeper

drain [dʀɛ̃] *m* MED drain

drainage [dʀɛnaʒ] *m* **1.** MED, AGR drainage **2.** (*de capitaux*) tapping

drainer [dʀene] <1> *vt* **1.** MED, AGR to drain **2.** (*rassembler: capitaux*) to tap; ~ **la clientèle/la main-d'œuvre** to drain off customers/workers

drakkar [dʀakaʀ] *m* drakkar

dramatique [dʀamatik] *adj* dramatic; **genre** ~ drama

dramatiquement [dʀamatikmɑ̃] *adv* dramatically

dramatiser [dʀamatize] <1> **I.** *vt* to dramatize **II.** *vi* to overdramatize

drame [dʀam] *m a. fig* (*pièce*) drama; **tourner au** ~ to take a tragic turn

drap [dʀa] *m* **1.** (*linge: de lit*) sheet **2.** *Belgique* (*serviette*) towel; ~ **de maison** (*tor-*

chon) tea towel *Brit,* dishtowel *Am* ►**être dans de beaux** ~**s** *inf* to be in a fine mess

drapeau [dRapo] <x> *m* flag

draper [dRape] <1> **I.** *vt* (*envelopper, plisser*) ~ **qc/qn de qc** to drape sb/sth in sth **II.** *vpr* **se** ~ **dans une cape** to drape oneself in a cloak

draperie [dRapRi] *f* **1.** (*tenture*) *a.* COM drapery **2.** (*fabrique*) cloth factory

drap-housse [dRa] <draps-housses> *m* fitted sheet

drave [dRav] *f Québec* (*flottage du bois*) rafting

draver [dRave] <1> *vi Québec* (*diriger le flottage du bois*) to drive

draveur [dRavœR] *m Québec* (*ouvrier travaillant au flottage du bois*) driver

dressage [dResaʒ] *m* **1.** (*domptage: d'un animal*) taming; (*pour un concours hippique*) dressage **2.** (*montage*) putting up

dresser [dRese] <1> **I.** *vt* **1.** (*établir: bilan, liste, carte, procuration*) to draw up; ~ **un procès-verbal à qn** to give sb a ticket **2.** (*ériger: barrière, monument*) to raise; (*échafaudage, tente*) to put up **3.** (*lever: buste*) to draw up; (*menton, tête*) to lift up; (*oreilles*) to prick up **4.** (*disposer: plat*) to lay out; (*piège*) to set; (*autel*) to raise **5.** (*dompter: animal*) to tame; (*chien*) to train; *péj* (*enfant, soldat*) to break in **6.** (*mettre en opposition*) ~ **qn contre qn/qc** to set sb against sb/sth **II.** *vpr* **1.** (*se mettre droit*) **se** ~ to draw oneself up **2.** (*s'élever*) **se** ~ (*bâtiment, statue*) to rise **3.** (*s'insurger*) **se** ~ **contre qn/qc** to rise against sb/sth

dresseur, -euse [dResœR, -øz] *m, f* trainer

drève [dRɛv] *f Nord, Belgique* (*allée carossable bordée d'arbres*) (tree-lined) drive

dribbler [dRible] <1> **I.** *vi* to dribble **II.** *vt* ~ **qn** to dribble past sb

dring [dRiŋ] *interj* (*bruit d'une sonnette*) ding

dringuelle [dRɛ̃gɛl] *f Belgique* (*pourboire*) tip

drogue [dRɔg] *f a. fig* drug

drogué(e) [dRɔge] *m(f)* (drug) addict

droguer [dRɔge] <1> **I.** *vt* to drug **II.** *vpr* **se** ~ to take drugs

droguerie [dRɔgRi] *f* hardware shop

droguiste [dRɔgist] *mf* ironmonger, hardware merchant

droit [dRwa] **I.** *adv* straight ►**aller** ~ **à la catastrophe** to be going downhill fast; **marcher** ~ to toe the line; **tout** ~ straight ahead **II.** *m* **1.** (*prérogative*) right; **de quel** ~ **l'a-t-il fait?** what right had he to do it?; **avoir** ~ **à qc** to be entitled to sth; **avoir le** ~ **de** +*infin* to be entitled to +*infin* **2.** JUR (*règles*) law; **faire son** ~ to study law; ~ **civil/public** civil/public law **3.** *pl* (*taxe*) tax **4.** SPORT straight

droit(e) [dRwa, dRwat] *adj* **1.** (*opp: gauche*) right **2.** (*non courbe, non penché: chemin, ligne, nez*) straight; **angle** ~ right angle; **être** ~ to be straight **3.** (*honnête, loyal: personne*) upright; **le** ~ **chemin** the straight and narrow

droite [dRwat] *f* **1.** MAT straight line **2.** (*côté droit*) *a.* POL right; **un parti de** ~ a right-wing party; **à** ~ on the right; **tourner à** ~ to turn right; **de** ~ right(-hand); **par la** ~ by the right; **serrez à** ~**!** keep right!

droitier, -ière [dRwatje, -jɛR] **I.** *m, f* (*personne*) right-handed person **II.** *adj inf* POL right-wing

droiture [dRwatyR] *f* **1.** (*franchise*) honesty **2.** (*honnêteté*) uprightness

drôle [dRol] *adj* funny; **ça n'a vraiment rien de** ~**!** there's nothing funny about that!; **ça me fait tout** ~ it makes me feel all funny

drôlement [dRolmɑ̃] *adv* **1.** (*bizarrement*) in a funny way **2.** *inf* (*rudement*) really

drôlerie [dRolRi] *f* **1.** (*blague*) funny remark **2.** (*caractère*) funny character; **être d'une grande** ~ to be very funny

dromadaire [dRɔmadɛR] *m* dromedary

dru(e) [dRy] *adj* (*barbe, herbe*) thick

druide [dRɥid] *m* druid

du [dy] = **de + le** *v.* **de**

dû [dy] <dus> *m* due; **réclamer son** ~ to claim one's due

dû, due [dy] <dus> **I.** *part passé de* **devoir II.** *adj* **1.** (*que l'on doit*) owed **2.** (*imputable*) **être** ~ **à qc** to be due to sth **3.** (*mérité*) **être** ~ **à qn** to be sb's due

dubitatif, -ive [dybitatif, -iv] *adj* doubtful

Dublin [dyblɛ̃] Dublin

Dublinois(e) [dyblinwa, waz] *m(f)* Dubliner

duc [dyk] *m* duke

ducasse [dykas] *f Nord, Belgique* (*fête patronale ou publique, kermesse*) fête

duché [dyʃe] *m* duchy

duchesse [dyʃɛs] *f* duchess

duel [dɥɛl] *m a. fig* duel

duffel-coat [dœfœlkot] <duffel-coats> *m* duffle coat

dulcinée [dylsine] *f iron* lady-love

dûment [dymɑ̃] *adv* duly

dune [dyn] *f* dune

duo [dɥo, dyo] *m* MUS duet

dupe [dyp] *adj* **être** ~ **de qc** to be fooled by sth

duper [dype] <1> *vt* to fool

duperie [dypRi] *f* deception

duplex [dyplɛks] *m* **1.** ARCHIT **appartement en** ~ maisonette *Brit,* duplex *Am* **2.** CINE, TV link-up

duplicata [dyplikata] *m* duplicate

duplicité [dyplisite] *f* duplicity

duquel, de laquelle [dykɛl] <desquel(le)s> = **de + lequel** *v.* **lequel**

dur(e) [dyR] **I.** *adj* **1.** (*ferme*) hard; (*porte, serrure*) stiff; (*viande*) tough; (*sommeil*) heavy **2.** (*difficile, pénible: travail, obligation, vie, climat*) hard; ~, ~**!** that's rough! **3.** (*sévère: regard, critique*) harsh **II.** *adv* (*travailler*) hard; **taper** ~ (*soleil*) to beat down **III.** *m(f)* **1.** (*personne inflexible*) hard man, woman *m, f* **2.** *inf* (*personne sans peur*) hard case **3.** TECH **mai-**

son en ~ traditionally built house ▸**un** ~ **à cuire** *inf* a hard case; **jouer les ~s** *inf* to act hard

durable [dyʀabl] *adj* (*chose, construction*) durable; (*souvenir, effet, influence*) lasting

durablement [dyʀabləmɑ̃] *adv* lastingly

durant [dyʀɑ̃] *prep* **1.** (*au cours de*) during; ~ **l'hiver** during the winter **2.** (*tout au long de*) **travailler sa vie** ~ to work all one's life

durcir [dyʀsiʀ] <8> **I.** *vt* to harden; (*acier*) to temper **II.** *vi* (*aliment, pâte*) to harden; (*colle, peinture*) to set **III.** *vpr* **se** ~ to harden; (*colle*) to set

durcissement [dyʀsismɑ̃] *m* hardening; (*du ciment, de la colle*) setting

durée [dyʀe] *f* **1.** duration; **pendant la** ~ **des travaux** for the duration of the work; **la** ~ **de chaque classe** the length of each class; **les chômeurs de longue** ~ the long-term unemployed **2.** (*permanence*) durability

durement [dyʀmɑ̃] *adv* **1.** (*rudement*) sorely **2.** (*sans bonté: parler, répondre*) harshly **3.** (*cruellement*) brutally

durer [dyʀe] <1> *vi* **1.** + *compl de temps* (*avoir une certaine durée, se prolonger*) to last **2.** (*se conserver: personne*) to endure; (*matériel, vêtement*) to last ▸**faire** ~ **les choses** to spin things out; **ça ne peut plus** ~ this can't go on; **pourvu que ça dure!** let's hope it lasts!

dureté [dyʀte] *f* **1.** (*fermeté*) hardness **2.** (*rigueur*) harshness

durillon [dyʀijɔ̃] *m* callus

dus [dy] *passé simple de* **devoir**

DUT [deyte] *m abr de* **diplôme universitaire de technologie** *technical diploma taken after the baccalauréat and before university*

duvet [dyvɛ] *m* **1.** (*plumes, poils*) down **2.** (*sac de couchage*) sleeping bag

duveté(e) [dyvte] *adj* downy

DVD [devede] *m inv* INFOR *abr de* **Digital Versatile Disk** DVD

dynamique [dinamik] **I.** *adj* dynamic **II.** *f* dynamic

dynamiser [dinamize] <1> *vt* to inject dynamism into

dynamisme [dinamism] *m* dynamism

dynamitage [dinamitaʒ] *m* **1.** dynamiting **2.** *fig* demolition

dynamite [dinamit] *f* dynamite

dynamiter [dinamite] <1> *vt* to dynamite

dynamo [dinamo] *f* dynamo

dynastie [dinasti] *f* dynasty

dysenterie [disɑ̃tʀi] *f* MED dysentery

dyslexique [dislɛksik] *adj, mf* dyslexic

E

E, e [ø] *m inv* E, e; ~ **comme Eugène** e as in Edward; (*on telephone*) e for Edward

eau [o] <x> *f* water; ~ **du robinet/de table** tap/table water; ~ **minérale/de source** mineral/spring water; ~ **de toilette** toilet water; **fermer/ouvrir l'**~ to turn the water off/on; **au bord de l'**~ at the water's edge ▸**être clair comme de l'**~ **de roche** to be crystal clear

> In France, wine or still water is drunk with meals and a **carafe d'eau**, a jug of water is often on the table. In restaurants, this is most often tap water.

eau-de-vie [od(ə)vi] <eaux-de-vie> *f* brandy

ébahi(e) [ebai] *adj* astounded

ébahir [ebaiʀ] <8> *vt* to astonish; **être ébahi de qc** to be astonished at sth

ébats [eba] *mpl* (*des animaux, enfants*) frolicking; **prendre ses** ~ to frolic ▸~ **amoureux** lovemaking

ébattre [ebatʀ] *vpr irr* **s'**~ to frolic

ébauche [eboʃ] *f* (*d'une œuvre*) outline; (*d'un tableau*) sketch; (*d'un sourire*) flicker

ébaucher [eboʃe] <1> **I.** *vt* (*œuvre, projet, peinture*) to sketch out; (*statue*) to rough out; ~ **un sourire** to smile vaguely; ~ **un geste** to start to make a gesture **II.** *vpr* **s'**~ (*idée, projet*) to take shape; **une réconciliation s'ébauchait** there were the beginnings of a reconciliation

ébène [ebɛn] *f* ebony; **noir comme l'**~, **d'un noir d'**~ as black as night

ébéniste [ebenist] *mf* cabinet maker

ébénisterie [ebenist(ə)ʀi] *f* cabinetmaking; **du bois d'**~ cabinet wood

éberlué(e) [ebɛʀlɥe] *adj inf* dumbfounded

éblouir [ebluiʀ] <8> *vt* to dazzle

éblouissant(e) [ebluisɑ̃, ɑ̃t] *adj* **1.** (*aveuglant*) dazzling **2.** (*merveilleux: forme*) stunning

éblouissement [ebluismɑ̃] *m* **1.** (*trouble de la vue*) dazzle **2.** (*émerveillement*) bedazzlement **3.** MED (*étourdissement*) dizzy spell

éborgner [ebɔʀɲe] <1> *vt* ~ **qn** to blind sb in one eye

éboueur [ebuœʀ] *m* dustman *Brit*, garbage man *Am*

ébouillanter [ebujɑ̃te] <1> *vpr* **s'**~ **qc** to scald sth

éboulement [ebulmɑ̃] *m* **1.** landslip **2.** (*amas*) fallen rocks

ébouler [ebule] <1> *vpr* **s'**~ to collapse

éboulis [ebuli] *m* fallen rocks

ébouriffant(e) [ebuʀifɑ̃, ɑ̃t] *adj inf* (*nouvelle*) staggering

ébouriffé(e) [ebuʀife] *adj* dishevelled

ébrancher [ebʀɑ̃ʃe] <1> *vt* ~ **un arbre** to lop branches off a tree

ébranlement [ebʀɑ̃lmɑ̃] *m* **1.** *a. fig* (*secousse*) shock **2.** (*départ: du train*) moving off

ébranler [ebʀɑ̃le] <1> **I.** *vt* to shake **II.** *vpr* **s'~** (*convoi*) to set off; (*train*) to move off

ébréché(e) [ebʀeʃe] *adj* chipped

ébriété [ebʀijete] *f form* drunkenness

ébrouer [ebʀue] <1> *vpr* **s'~** (*cheval*) to snort; (*chien*) to shake itself

ébruiter [ebʀɥite] <1> *vt, vpr* (**s'**)**~** to spread

ébullition [ebylisjɔ̃] *f* (*d'un liquide*) boiling; **porter à ~** to bring to a boil ►**quartier en ~** district in turmoil; **esprit en ~** mind teeming with ideas

écaille [ekaj] *f* **1.** ZOOL scale **2.** (*petite particule*) **se détacher par ~s** (*peinture*) to flake off **3.** (*matière*) tortoiseshell; **une paire de lunettes à monture d'~** a pair of tortoiseshell spectacles

écailler [ekaje] <1> **I.** *vt* (*poisson*) to scale; (*huîtres*) to open **II.** *vpr* **s'~** to flake off

écarquiller [ekaʀkije] <1> *vt* **~ les yeux devant qc** to stare wide-eyed at sth

écart [ekaʀ] *m* **1.** (*distance*) gap **2.** (*différence: de prix, cours*) difference **3.** (*contradiction*) discrepancy **4.** (*mouvement brusque*) **faire un ~** (*personne*) to move out of the way ►**faire le grand ~** to do the splits; **mettre qn à l'~** to keep sb out of the way; **vivre à l'~** to live in isolation

écarté(e) [ekaʀte] *adj* **1.** (*isolé: lieu*) out of the way **2.** (*distant: bras*) spread out; (*dents*) spaced; (*jambes*) wide apart

écartement [ekaʀtəmɑ̃] *m* spread; (*des rails*) gauge; **l'~ des essieux** the wheelbase

écarter [ekaʀte] <1> **I.** *vt* **1.** (*séparer: objets*) to move apart; (*rideaux*) to pull open; (*bras*) to open; (*doigts, jambes*) to spread out **2.** (*exclure: plan*) to rule out; (*objection*) to overrule; (*idée*) to brush aside; (*danger*) to remove; **~ qn de qc** to exclude sb from sth **3.** (*éloigner*) **~ qn de qc** to move sb away from sth; *fig* to keep sb away from sth **4.** *Québec* (*perdre*) to mislay **II.** *vpr* **1.** (*se séparer*) **s'~** (*foule*) to move aside **2.** (*s'éloigner*) **s'~ de qc** to move out of the way of sth; **s'~ du sujet** to wander off the subject; **écarte-toi/écartez-vous (de là)!** get out of the way! **3.** *Québec* (*s'égarer*) to get lost

ecchymose [ekimoz] *f* bruise

ecclésiastique [eklezjastik] **I.** *adj* ecclesiastical; (*vie*) religious **II.** *m* clergyman

écervelé(e) [esɛʀvəle] **I.** *adj* scatterbrained **II.** *m(f)* scatterbrain

échafaud [eʃafo] *m* scaffold; **finir sur l'~** to die on the scaffold

échafaudage [eʃafodaʒ] *m* **1.** (*construction*) scaffolding **2.** (*empilement*) pile

échafauder [eʃafode] <1> **I.** *vt* (*projets*) to lay; (*système, théorie, hypothèse*) to construct **II.** *vi* CONSTR to put up scaffolding

échalas [eʃalɑ] *m* **1.** (*pieu*) stake **2.** *inf* (*personne*) beanpole; **un grand ~** a great lanky thing

échalote [eʃalɔt] *f* shallot

échancré(e) [eʃɑ̃kʀe] *adj* (*robe*) with a low neckline

échancrure [eʃɑ̃kʀyʀ] *f* (*d'une robe*) low neckline

échange [eʃɑ̃ʒ] *m* **1.** (*action d'échanger*) **~ de qc contre qc** exchanging sth for sth; **~ standard** factory replacement; **faire un ~ avec qn** to exchange with sb; **en ~ de qc** in exchange for sth **2.** *gén pl* ECON trade **3.** ECOLE **~s scolaires** school exchanges ►**~ de coups** altercation; **vifs ~s** lively exchanges

échanger [eʃɑ̃ʒe] <2a> *vt* (*adresses, idées, anneaux*) to exchange; (*timbres*) to swap; (*marchandises*) to trade; **~ qc avec qn contre qc** to trade sb sth for sth; **~ des sourires/des regards** to smile/look at each other

échangeur [eʃɑ̃ʒœʀ] *m* interchange

échantillon [eʃɑ̃tijɔ̃] *m* sample

échappatoire [eʃapatwaʀ] *f* **1.** (*subterfuge*) loophole **2.** (*issue*) way out

échappement [eʃapmɑ̃] *m* **1.** (*gaz*) exhaust; **~ de gaz** gas escape; **~ libre** cutout **2.** (*mécanisme régulateur d'horlogerie*) escapement

échapper [eʃape] <1> **I.** *vi* **1.** (*s'enfuir*) **~ à qn** to escape from sb; **~ à un danger** to escape (a) danger; **faire ~ qn** to help sb escape **2.** (*se soustraire à*) **~ à qc** to avoid sth; **~ au contrôle** to avoid the checkpoint; **~ à la mort** to escape death **3.** (*être oublié*) **son nom m'échappe** his/her name escapes me **4.** (*ne pas être remarqué*) **~ à** [*o* **à l'attention de**] **qn** to escape sb's attention; **laisser ~ une faute** to miss a mistake **5.** (*ne pas être compris*) **le problème lui échappe** he doesn't grasp the problem **6.** (*glisser des mains*) **le plateau lui est échappé (des mains)** the tray slipped from her hands; **laisser ~ qc** to drop sth **7.** (*dire par inadvertance*) **~ à qn** (*gros mot, paroles*) to slip out; **un cri/soupir lui a échappé** she let out a cry/a sigh **II.** *vpr* **1.** (*s'évader*) **s'~ de qc** to escape from sth **2.** (*s'esquiver*) **s'~ de qc** to get away from sth **3.** (*sortir*) **s'~ de qc** (*fumée, cri*) to come from sth; (*gaz*) to escape from sth; (*flammes*) to rise from sth **III.** *vt Québec* (*laisser tomber involontairement*) to drop

écharde [eʃaʀd] *f* splinter

écharpe [eʃaʀp] *f* **1.** (*vêtement*) scarf **2.** (*étoffe servant d'insigne: du maire*) sash **3.** (*bandage*) sling

écharper [eʃaʀpe] <1> *vt* **~ qc** to tear sth to pieces; **se faire ~ par la foule** to get torn apart by the crowd; **se faire ~ par les critiques** to get panned by the critics

échasse [eʃɑs] *f* stilt

échassier [eʃɑsje] *m* wading bird

échauder [eʃode] <1> *vt* **1.** (*ébouillanter: théière*) to warm; (*tomates*) to put in hot water; (*volaille*) to scald **2.** *fig* **se faire ~** to get one's fingers burnt ►**chat échaudé craint**

E

l'eau froide *prov* once bitten twice shy *prov*

échauffement [eʃofmɑ̃] *m* **1.** (*fait de devenir chaud: de l'atmosphère, du sol*) warming **2.** SPORT warm-up

échauffer [eʃofe] <1> *vpr* **s'~** **1.** SPORT to warm up **2.** (*s'énerver*) to get heated

échauffourée [eʃofuʀe] *f* **1.** (*bagarre*) clash; **être pris dans une ~** to get caught up in a clash **2.** MIL skirmish

échéance [eʃeɑ̃s] *f* **1.** (*date limite*) **date d'~** (*pour une dette*) due date; (*d'un bon*) maturity date; (*pour un travail*) deadline; **arriver** [*o* **venir**] **à ~ le 15 du mois** to be due on the fifteenth of the month **2.** (*délai*) time; FIN term **3.** (*règlement*) payment due ▶**à brève** [*o* **courte**] **~** before very long; FIN short-term

échéant(e) [eʃeɑ̃, ɑ̃t] *adj* (*annuité, traite*) due

échec¹ [eʃɛk] *m* failure ▶**aller à** [*o* **courir au devant de**] **l'~** to be heading for failure

échec² [eʃɛk] *m pl* (*jeu*) chess + *vb sing;* **jeu d'~s** game of chess; **jouer aux ~s** to play chess ▶(**être**) **~ et mat** to be checkmate

échelle [eʃɛl] *f* **1.** (*escabeau, hiérarchie*) ladder **2.** (*proportion, rapport, graduation*) scale; **à l'~ de 1:100 000** at a scale of 1:100 000; **à l'~ de l'enfant** at a child's level; **à l'~ nationale/communale** [*o* **de la nation/commune**] on a national/local level; **~ des températures** temperature scale ▶**être en haut** [*o* **au sommet**]/**en bas de l'~** to be at the top/bottom of the ladder; **être parvenu au sommet de l'~** (**sociale**) to have reached the top; **sur une grande ~** on a large scale

échelon [eʃlɔ̃] *m* **1.** (*barreau*) rung **2.** ADMIN (*de la hiérarchie*) grade; **passer par tous les ~s administratifs** to climb all the rungs of the administrative ladder; **être au premier/dernier ~** to be on the bottom/top grade; **descendre d'un ~ dans la hiérarchie** to go down a grade in the hierarchy; **gravir** [*o* **grimper**] **un ~** to go up a grade

échelonner [eʃ(ə)lɔne] <1> **I.** *vt* **1.** (*étaler: paiements*) to spread out **2.** (*graduer: difficultés*) to graduate; **~ les salaires** to set up a salary scale **3.** (*disposer à intervalles réguliers*) to space out **II.** *vpr* **s'~ sur deux ans** to be spread out over two years

échevelé(e) [eʃəv(ə)le] *adj* **1.** (*décoiffé: personne*) dishevelled **2.** (*effréné*) frenzied

échevin [eʃ(ə)vɛ̃] *m* **1.** *Belgique* (*Magistrat adjoint au bourgmestre*) deputy mayor **2.** *Québec* (*conseiller municipal*) town councillor

échevinal(e) [eʃ(ə)vinal, o] <-aux> *adj Belgique* **collège ~** (*collège communal*) town school

échine [eʃin] *f* **1.** (*colonne vertébrale*) spine; **~ dorsale** spinal column **2.** GASTR chine ▶**avoir l'~ souple** to be spineless; **courber** [*o* **plier**] **l'~ devant qn/qc** to kowtow to sb

échiner [eʃine] <1> *vpr* **s'~ à qc/à faire qc** to kill oneself on sth/doing sth

échiquier [eʃikje] *m* chess board ▶**sur l'~ européen** on the European stage

écho [eko] *m* **1.** (*réflexion sonore: d'une montagne*) echo; **ça fait** (**de l'**) **~** there's an echo **2.** (*rubrique*) gossip column **3.** (*effet*) reaction; (*dans la presse*) coverage; **rester sans ~** to get no response ▶**avoir eu des ~s de qc** to hear things about sth

échographie [ekɔgʀafi] *f* (ultrasound) scan; **passer une ~** to have a scan

échoir [eʃwaʀ] *vi irr être* **1.** (*être dû: dettes*) to fall due; (*délai*) to expire; **à terme échu** at the end of the rental period; **~ tous les 1ers du mois** to be due on the first of each month **2.** (*revenir*) **~ à qn** to fall to sb; **~ en partage à qn** to be left to sb; **il échoit à cet élève de** +*infin* it is for this pupil to +*infin*

échoppe [eʃɔp] *f* shop

échouer [eʃwe] <1> **I.** *vi* to fail; **~ à l'examen** to fail the exam **II.** *vt* **faire ~ qc** to wreck sth; **faire ~ un complot** to foil a conspiracy

éclabousser [eklabuse] <1> *vt* to splash

éclaboussure [eklabusyʀ] *f* **1.** (*giclement*) splash; **recevoir des ~s** to get splashed; **~ de sang/vin** blood/wine stain **2.** (*contrecoup: d'un scandale*) stain; **sa réputation a reçu quelques ~s** his reputation has been besmirched

éclair [eklɛʀ] **I.** *m* **1.** METEO ligtning flash; **des ~s** lightning; **~ de chaleur** summer lightning **2.** PHOT flash **3.** GASTR éclair **4.** (*bref moment*) **~ de bon sens** flash of genius; **~ de lucidité** lucid moment; **dans un ~ de colère** in a fit of anger ▶**en un ~** in a flash **II.** *app inv* **visite ~** flying visit

éclairage [eklɛʀaʒ] *m* lighting ▶**sous cet ~** in this light; **apparaître sous un tout autre ~** to appear in a completely different light

éclairagiste [eklɛʀaʒist] *mf* CINE, THEAT lighting engineer

éclairant(e) [eklɛʀɑ̃, ɑ̃t] *adj* **gaz ~** lighting gas; **fusée ~e** flare; **pouvoir ~** power

éclaircie [eklɛʀsi] *f* METEO sunny spell

éclaircir [eklɛʀsiʀ] <8> **I.** *vt* **1.** (*rendre clair*) to lighten **2.** (*élucider: situation*) to clarify; (*meurtre, énigme*) to solve; (*affaire*) to clear up **II.** *vpr* **1.** (*se dégager*) **s'~** (*temps*) to brighten up **2.** (*rendre plus distinct*) **s'~ la gorge** [*o* **la voix**] to clear one's throat **3.** (*devenir compréhensible*) **s'~** (*idée*) to become clear; (*mystère*) to be cleared up

éclaircissement [eklɛʀsismɑ̃] *m* (*d'une situation, d'un point de vue*) clarification; (*d'un mystère*) explanation; (*d'un malentendu*) clearing up; (*des soupçons*) lifting

éclairé(e) [ekleʀe] *adj* (*averti*) enlightened; **agir en esprit ~** to behave in an enlightened way

éclairer [ekleʀe] <1> **I.** *vt* **1.** (*fournir de la lumière*) to light (up); **~ qn** to light the way for sb **2.** (*laisser passer la lumière*) **~ une pièce** to give light to a room **3.** (*expliquer: texte*) to clarify; **~ une situation** to throw light on a situation **4.** (*instruire*) ~ **un collègue sur qn/qc** to enlighten a colleague about sb/sth **II.** *vi* to give light **III.** *vpr* **1.** (*se fournir de la lumière*) **s'~ à l'électricité/au gaz** to have electric/gas lighting **2.** (*devenir lumineux*) **s'~** (*visage*) to light up **3.** (*se clarifier*) **s'~** (*situation*) to become clear

éclaireur, **-euse** [eklɛʀœʀ, -øz] *app* **avion** ~ reconnaissance plane

éclat [ekla] *m* **1.** (*fragment*) splinter **2.** (*bruit*) ~ **de joie** joyful outburst; **partir d'un ~ de rire** to burst out laughing **3.** (*scandale*) fuss **4.** (*luminosité: d'un métal*) shine; (*d'un astre*) brightness; (*d'une couleur*) brilliance; (*d'un diamant*) sparkle ►**rire aux ~s** to laugh out loud; **voler** [*o* **partir**] **en ~s** to be smashed

éclatant(e) [eklatɑ̃, ɑ̃t] *adj* **1.** (*radieux: beauté, santé*) radiant **2.** (*remarquable: exemple*) shining; (*succès*) brilliant; (*victoire*) resounding; (*revanche*) spectacular

éclatement [eklatmɑ̃] *m* **1.** (*explosion*) explosion **2.** (*crevaison*) bursting **3.** *fig* (*d'un parti*) splitting

éclater [eklate] <1> **I.** *vi* **1.** (*exploser: bombe*) to explode **2.** (*déborder, crever: tête, pneu*) to burst; ~ **de santé** to be glowing with health **3.** (*se fragmenter: structure*) to break up; (*verre*) to shatter **4.** (*commencer: orage*) to break out **5.** (*survenir brusquement: nouvelle*) to break; **le scandale a éclaté** the scandal erupted **6.** (*retentir: cris*) to go up; (*coup de feu, détonation*) to ring out; ~ **de rire** to burst out laughing; **des rires ont éclaté** there were roars of laughter **7.** (*se manifester*) ~ **dans les yeux/sur le visage de qn** (*bonne foi, mauvaise foi*) to show in sb's eyes/on sb's face; ~ **en pleurs** to burst out crying; **faire ~ le scandale** to set off the scandal; **laisser ~ sa colère** to explode with anger **8.** (*s'emporter*) to explode; **faire ~ qn** to make sb explode; ~ **de colère/rage** to explode with anger/fury; ~ **en menaces** to come out with threats **II.** *vpr inf* (*se défouler*) **s'~** to have a great time; **s'~ à faire** [*o* **en faisant**] **qc** to get one's kicks doing sth

éclectique [eklɛktik] *adj* eclectic

éclipse [eklips] *f* eclipse; ~ **de lune/soleil** lunar/solar eclipse; ~ **partielle/totale** partial/total eclipse ►**phare à ~s** lighthouse with an intermittent beam; **avoir une mémoire à ~s** to have a memory that comes and goes

éclipser [eklipse] <1> **I.** *vt* **1.** ASTR to eclipse **2.** (*surpasser*) to outshine; ~ **qn par qc** to outshine sb in sth; **se faire ~ par qn** to be overshadowed by sb **II.** *vpr* **s'~** to slip away

éclopé(e) [eklɔpe] **I.** *adj* **1.** (*boiteux*) lame; **depuis l'accident il est ~** since the accident he's had a limp **2.** (*blessé: dans un accident*) injured; (*à la guerre*) wounded; **être ~** to be wounded **II.** *m(f)* (*boiteux*) person with a limp; (*blessé*) injured person; (*à la guerre*) wounded person

éclore [eklɔʀ] *vi irr être* **1.** (*s'ouvrir: bourgeon, fleur*) to open; (*œuf*) to hatch; **les œufs sont éclos** the eggs have hatched **2.** (*naître: poussin*) to hatch (out); (*amour*) to blossom; (*projet, vocation, talent*) to emerge; (*jour*) to break

éclosion [eklozjɔ̃] *f* (*d'une couvée*) hatching; (*d'un bourgeon*) opening; (*d'une fleur*) blooming; (*du jour*) break; (*d'un sentiment*) blossoming; (*d'un talent*) emergence

écluse [eklyz] *f* lock

éclusier, **-ière** [eklyzje, -jɛʀ] *m, f* lock keeper

éco [eko] *adj inf abr de* **économique**

écobilan [ekɔbilɑ̃] *m* environmental assessment

écœurant(e) [ekœʀɑ̃, ɑ̃t] *adj* **1.** (*trop sucré*) cloying **2.** (*trop gras*) heavy **3.** (*physiquement*) revolting **4.** (*moralement*) disgusting **5.** (*décourageant: facilité, injustice*) sickening ►**en ~** *Québec* (*très, beaucoup*) fantastically

écœurement [ekœʀmɑ̃] *m* **1.** (*nausée*) nausea **2.** (*dégoût*) disgust **3.** (*découragement*) **ressentir un immense ~** to feel thoroughly sick

écœurer [ekœʀe] <1> **I.** *vi* (*dégoûter*) to be sickening **II.** *vt* **1.** (*dégoûter*) ~ **qn** to make sb feel sick **2.** (*indigner*) to revolt **3.** (*décourager: injustice, déception*) to sicken

éco-industrie [ekɔɛ̃dystʀi] *f* eco-industry

écolage [ekɔlaʒ] *m Suisse* (*frais de scolarité* (*plutôt dans une école privée*)) school fees

école [ekɔl] *f* school; ~ **cantonale** *Suisse* local school; ~ **commerciale/hôtelière** business/hotel management school; ~ **laïque** state education *Brit,* public education *Am* (*excluding religious instruction and worship*); ~ **pour adultes** adult education college; ~ **du soir** night school; ~ **de la vie** school of life; ~ **primaire** [*o* **élémentaire**]/**secondaire** primary/secondary school; ~ **professionnelle** vocational college; ~ **publique** state school *Brit,* public school *Am;* **aller à l'~** to go to school; **renvoyer qn de l'~** to expel sb from school; **retirer qn de l'~** to take sb out of school; **manquer l'~** to miss school; **sécher l'~** *inf* to bunk off school *Brit,* to ditch school *Am;* **entrer à l'~** to start school; **mettre qn à l'~** to send sb to school; **l'~ impressioniste/réaliste** ART, LIT the Impressionist/realist school

> Children in France go to **école primaire** from the age of six years and spend five years there. They start in class CP, progress on to CE1 and CE2 and finish with CM1 and CM2. At 11 years old, children go to "collège".

écolier, **-ière** [ekɔlje, -jɛʀ] *m, f* schoolboy, schoolgirl *m, f*

écolo [ekɔlo] **I.** *m, f inf abr de* **écologiste** Green **II.** *adj inf abr de* **écologique**

écologie [ekɔlɔʒi] *f* ecology; **les partisans de l'~** environmentalists

écologique [ekɔlɔʒik] *adj* (*catastrophe, solution*) ecological; (*société*) environmentally friendly

écologiste [ekɔlɔʒist] **I.** *m, f* **1.** (*ami de la nature, spécialiste de l'écologie*) ecologist **2.** POL environmentalist **II.** *adj* (*pratique*) environmentally friendly; (*politique, mouvement, groupe*) environmental; (*parti*) green; **être ~** to be green

écologue [ekɔlɔg] *mf* ecologist

écomusée [ekɔmyse] *m* museum of man and the environment

éconduire [ekɔ̃dɥiʀ] *vt irr, soutenu* **1.** (*renvoyer*) to dismiss **2.** (*repousser*) to reject

économe [ekɔnɔm] *adj* **être ~** to be thrifty

économie [ekɔnɔmi] *f* **1.** (*vie économique*) economy; **~ de libre entreprise** free enterprise economy; **~ de marché** market economy; **~ de troc** barter economy **2.** (*science*) economics **3.** (*gain*) saving **4.** *pl* (*épargne*) savings ►**il n'y a pas de petites ~s** every penny counts

économique [ekɔnɔmik] *adj* **1.** (*bon marché*) economical; **classe ~** economy (class) **2.** (*qui a rapport à l'économie*) economic

économiser [ekɔnɔmize] <1> **I.** *vi* (*mettre de l'argent de côté*) to save; (*dépenser moins*) to economize; **~ sur qc** to cut down on sth **II.** *vt* to save; **~ de l'essence** to save petrol *Brit,* to save gas *Am*

économiseur [ekɔnɔmizœʀ] *m* INFOR **~ d'écran** screen saver

économiste [ekɔnɔmist] *mf* economist

écoper [ekɔpe] <1> **I.** *vt* **1.** NAUT **~ l'eau** to bail out water **2.** *inf* (*subir: coup*) to cop; **~ dix ans** to go down for ten years **II.** *vi* **1.** NAUT to bale out **2.** *inf* (*être puni*) to take the rap

écorce [ekɔʀs] *f* **1.** BIO (*d'un arbre*) bark; (*d'un fruit*) rind **2.** ANAT **~ cérébrale** cerebral cortex **3.** GEO **~ terrestre** earth's crust

écorché(e) [ekɔʀʃe] *m(f)* **être un ~ vif** to be hypersensitive

écorcher [ekɔʀʃe] <1> **I.** *vt* **1.** (*égratigner*) **être écorché** (*genou*) to be grazed; (*visage*) to be scratched **2.** (*faire mal*) **~ les oreilles** to grate on one's ears **3.** (*déformer: nom*) to mispronounce; (*vérité*) to distort; **~ le français** to speak awful French **II.** *vpr* (*s'égratigner*) **s'~** to get scratched; **s'~ le visage** to get one's face scratched

écorchure [ekɔʀʃyʀ] *f* scratch

écossais [ekɔsɛ] *m* **1.** (*gaélique*) Gaelic **2.** (*du sud*) Scots; *v. a.* **français**

écossais(e) [ekɔsɛ, ɛz] *adj* Scottish; **jupe ~e** kilt; **tissu ~** tartan

Écossais(e) [ekɔsɛ, ɛz] *m(f)* Scot; **un ~** a Scotsman; **une ~e** a Scotswoman

Écosse [ekɔs] *f* **l'~** Scotland

écosser [ekɔse] <1> *vt* to shell

écotourisme [ekɔtuʀism] *m* ecotourism

écotype [ekɔtip] *m* ecotype

écoulement [ekulmɑ̃] *m* **1.** (*évacuation: d'un liquide*) outflow **2.** (*mouvement: du temps*) passing **3.** COM (*des stocks*) movement; (*des produits*) sale

écouler [ekule] <1> **I.** *vt* **1.** COM (*marchandises*) to sell **2.** (*mettre en circulation: faux billets*) to circulate **II.** *vpr* **s'~** **1.** (*s'épancher: liquide*) to flow; **s'~ dans/de qc** to flow into/out of sth **2.** (*passer: temps*) to pass **3.** (*disparaître: fonds*) to get spent **4.** (*se vendre: marchandises*) to be sold

écourter [ekuʀte] <1> *vt* **1.** (*raccourcir*) to shorten **2.** (*abréger: séjour, attente*) to cut short **3.** (*tronquer*) **être écourté** (*citation*) to be curtailed

écoute [ekut] *f* **1.** RADIO, TV **avoir une grande ~** to have a big audience **2.** (*surveillance*) **~s téléphoniques** phone tapping ►**être à l'~ de qn** to be listening to sb; **être à l'~ d'une radio** to be tuned in to a radio; **rester à l'~** (*à la radio*) to stay tuned; (*au téléphone*) to hold the line

écouter [ekute] <1> **I.** *vt* **1.** (*prêter l'oreille*) **~ qn/qc** to listen to sb/sth; **~ qn chanter** to listen to sb singing; **faire ~ un disque à qn** to play sb a record **2.** (*tenir compte de*) **~ qn/qc** to take notice of sb/sth; **qn/qc est écouté** sb/sth is influential; **se faire ~ de qn** to make oneself heard by sb **3.** (*obéir*) **~ qn** to listen to sb **II.** *vi* to listen ►**écoute/écoutez (voir)!** listen to this! **III.** *vpr* (*s'observer avec complaisance*) **trop s'~** to take a bit too much care of oneself; **aimer s'~ parler** to love the sound of one's own voice

écouteur [ekutœʀ] *m* **1.** (*récepteur: du téléphone*) handset **2.** *pl* (*casque*) earphones *pl*

écoutille [ekutij] *f* MIL, NAUT hatch

écrabouiller [ekʀabuje] <1> **I.** *vt inf* to squash; **se faire ~ par qn** to get run over by sb **II.** *vpr inf* **s'~ par terre** to get smashed on the floor

écran [ekʀɑ̃] *m* **1.** (*protection*) shield; **~ total** total sunblock **2.** TV, CINE, INFOR screen; **à l'~** TV on TV; CINE on the screen; **sur les ~s** TV on TV; CINE at the cinema; **~ de projection** projector screen; **~ 15 pouces** 15-inch screen; **~ partagé/tactile** split/touch screen; **~ à cristaux liquides** liquid crystal display

écrasant(e) [ekʀɑzɑ̃, ɑ̃t] *adj* (*accablant: poids*) unbearable; (*nombre*) overwhelming; (*défaite*) crushing

écrasé(e) [ekʀɑze] *adj* **au nez ~** pug-nosed

écrasement [ekʀɑzmɑ̃] *m* crushing

écraser [ekʀɑze] <1> **I.** *vt* **1.** (*broyer*) to crush; (*légumes*) to mash; (*cigarette*) to stub out; **être écrasé par la foule** to be crushed by the crowd **2.** (*appuyer fortement sur*) **~ la pédale d'accélérateur** to step hard on the accelerator **3.** (*tuer*) **~ qn/qc** (*conducteur*) to run sb/sth over; (*avalanche*) to crush sb/sth **4.** (*accabler*) **~ qn** (*douleur*) to weigh sb down; (*impôt*) to overburden sb **5.** (*dominer*) **~ qn en math** to outshine sb in maths *Brit,* to outshine sb in math *Am;* **~ qn par son savoir** to put sb down with one's knowledge

6. (*vaincre: rébellion, ennemi, équipe*) to crush **II.** *vi inf* (*ne pas insister*) to shut up **III.** *vpr* **1.** (*heurter de plein fouet*) **s'~ au** [*o* **sur le**] **sol/contre un arbre** to crash into the ground/a tree **2.** (*se crasher*) **s'~** to crash **3.** (*se serrer*) **s'~ dans qc** to be crushed in sth; **s'~ contre le mur/sur le sol** to be crushed up against the wall/on the ground **4.** *inf* (*se taire*) **s'~ devant qn** to shut up in front of sb **5.** (*ne pas protester*) to keep one's mouth shut

écrevisse [ekʀəvis] *f* crayfish

écrier [ekʀije] <1> *vpr* **s'~** to cry out

écrin [ekʀɛ̃] *m* case; (*pour un bijou*) casket; **~ à alliances** ring box; **~ à couverts** cutlery case

écrire [ekʀiʀ] *irr* **I.** *vt* **1.** (*tracer, inscrire, rédiger*) **~ qc dans/sur qc** to write sth in/on sth; **les devoirs sont écrits au tableau** the homework is written (up) on the board **2.** (*orthographier*) **comment écrit-on ce mot?** how do you spell that word? **II.** *vi* (*tracer, rédiger*) to write; **~ à la main/machine/au stylo** to write by hand/on a typewriter/in pen; **~ à qn** to write to sb ▸**il est écrit que cela arrivera** it is fated that that will happen **III.** *vpr* **s'~** to be spelt; **ce mot s'écrit avec y** that word is written with a y

écrit [ekʀi] *m* **1.** (*document*) written document **2.** (*ouvrage*) text **3.** (*épreuve, examen*) written paper; **l'~** the (written) exam ▸**par ~** in writing

écriteau [ekʀito] <x> *m* sign

écriture [ekʀityʀ] *f* **1.** (*façon d'écrire*) handwriting **2.** (*alphabet, style*) writing; **~ chiffrée** coded writing

Écriture [ekʀityʀ] *f* REL **l'~ sainte, les Saintes ~s** the Holy Scriptures

écrivain [ekʀivɛ̃] *m* writer

écrou [ekʀu] *m* nut

écrouer [ekʀue] <1> *vt* to imprison

écroulement [ekʀulmɑ̃] *m* collapse

écrouler [ekʀule] <1> *vpr* **s'~** **1.** (*tomber: maison*) to collapse; (*arbre, rocher*) to fall down **2.** (*baisser brutalement: cours de la bourse*) to collapse **3.** (*prendre fin brutalement: empire, projet, gouvernement, théorie*) to collapse; (*fortune*) to vanish **4.** (*s'affaler*) to collapse; **s'~ dans un fauteuil** to collapse in an armchair

ECU [eky] *m abr de* **European Currency Unit** ecu

écueil [ekœj] *m* (*difficulté*) pitfall; (*dans la mer*) reef

écuelle [ekɥɛl] *f* bowl

éculé(e) [ekyle] *adj* **1.** (*usé: chaussures*) down-at-heel **2.** (*connu: terme, plaisanterie*) tired

écumer [ekyme] <1> **I.** *vt* **1.** (*enlever l'écume*) to skim **2.** (*piller: région*) to plunder; **~ les côtes/mers** to scour the coast/seas **II.** *vi* **1.** (*se couvrir d'écume*) to foam **2.** (*baver*) to foam at the mouth **3.** (*suer*) to lather **4.** (*être furieux*) **~ de colère** [*o* **rage**] to foam at the mouth

écumoire [ekymwaʀ] *f* skimmer

écureuil [ekyʀœj] *m* squirrel ▸**être agile/vif(vive) comme un ~** to be as nimble as a goat

écurie [ekyʀi] *f* stable

écuyer, -ère [ekɥije, ɛʀ] *m, f* **1.** HIST (*gentilhomme, titre à la cour*) equerry **2.** (*cavalier*) horseman **3.** (*professeur d'équitation*) riding master **4.** (*au cirque*) rider

eczéma [ɛgzema] *m* eczema

édam [edam] *m* (*fromage*) Edam cheese

edelweiss [edɛlvɛs, edɛlvajs] *m* edelweiss

édenté(e) [edɑ̃te] *adj* toothless

EDF [ødeɛf] *f abr de* **Électricité de France** *French electricity company*

édifiant(e) [edifjɑ̃, jɑ̃t] *adj* edifying

édification [edifikasjɔ̃] *f* **1.** (*construction*) building **2.** (*création: d'une théorie*) construction; (*de la paix*) forging **3.** (*instruction*) edification

édifice [edifis] *m* **1.** (*bâtiment*) building **2.** (*ensemble organisé*) edifice; **~ social d'un État** social structure of a state

édifier [edifje] <1> *vt* **1.** (*bâtir: temple, palais*) to build **2.** (*créer: empire*) to build; (*théorie*) to build up; (*paix*) to forge **3.** (*instruire: personne*) to edify ▸**te voilà édifié maintenant!** *iron* so now you know!

Édimbourg [edɛ̃buːʀ] Edinburgh

édit [edi] *m* HIST, POL edict

éditer [edite] <1> *vt* to publish

éditeur [editœʀ] *m* INFOR editor; **~ de textes** text editor

éditeur, -trice [editœʀ, -tʀis] **I.** *adj* **maison éditrice** publishing house; **la maison éditrice Klett** Klett Publishers **II.** *m, f* publisher

édition [edisjɔ̃] *f* **1.** (*publication: d'un disque*) issue; (*d'un livre*) publication **2.** (*livre*) edition; **~ revue et corrigée** completely revised edition **3.** (*métier*) **l'~** publishing **4.** (*établissement*) **les ~s** publishers *pl* **5.** PRESSE (*tirage*) edition **6.** INFOR editing

éditique [editik] *m* INFOR desktop publishing

éditorial [editɔʀjal, jo] <-aux> *m* editorial

édredon [edʀədɔ̃] *m* eiderdown

éducateur, -trice [edykatœʀ, -tʀis] **I.** *adj* (*fonction*) educative; **personne éducatrice** educator **II.** *m, f* educator

éducatif, -ive [edykatif, -tiv] *adj* (*jeu*) educative; (*méthode*) educational; (*système*) education

éducation [edykasjɔ̃] *f* **1.** (*pédagogie*) education; **l'Éducation nationale** State education system; POL Department of Education **2.** (*bonnes manières*) (good) manners; **être sans ~** to be ill-mannered ▸**donner une ~ à qn** to bring sb up

éduquer [edyke] <1> *vt* (*former*) to educate

efface [efas] *f Québec* (*gomme*) rubber *Brit*, eraser *Am*

effacé(e) [efase] *adj* **1.** (*estompé: couleur*) faded **2.** (*discret: rôle, personne*) self-effacing;

E

(*manière*) retiring
effacement [efasmɑ̃] *m* **1.** (*l'oubli: d'une inscription*) effacement **2.** (*suppression d'information: d'un support magnétique*) erasure **3.** (*disparition: des craintes*) dispelling; (*d'une faute*) blotting out; (*avec une gomme*) rubbing out **4.** (*retrait: d'une personne*) **l'~ de qn devant** [*o* **au profit de**] **qn** sb's giving way to sb ►**vivre dans l'~** to live a self-effacing life
effacer [efase] <2> **I.** *vt* **1.** (*faire disparaître: trace*) to erase; (*tache*) to remove; (*avec du correcteur*) to paint out *Brit,* to white out *Am;* **~ qc avec une gomme** to erase sth **2.** (*supprimer une information: tableau noir*) to clean; (*disquette*) to wipe; (*texte sur écran*) to delete **3.** (*faire oublier*) to erase; (*crainte*) to dispel; (*faute*) to wipe away; **~ qc de sa mémoire** to erase sth from one's memory **II.** *vpr* **s'~ 1.** (*s'estomper: crainte*) to be dispelled **2.** (*se laisser enlever: tache*) to go **3.** (*se faire petit*) to be unobtrusive; **s'~ devant qn** to give way to sb
effaceur [efasœʀ] *m* eraser pen
effarant(e) [efaʀɑ̃, ɑ̃t] *adj* frightening
effaré(e) [efaʀe] *adj* (*personne*) frightened; **avoir l'air ~** to look frightened; **être ~ par qc** to be scared by sth
effarement [efaʀmɑ̃] *m* alarm; **dans l'~ général** amid the general alarm
effaroucher [efaʀuʃe] <1> **I.** *vt* **1.** (*mettre en fuite*) **~ un animal** to scare an animal away **2.** (*faire peur*) to scare **3.** (*choquer*) to upset **II.** *vpr* **1.** (*prendre la fuite*) **s'~** to shy **2.** (*se troubler*) **s'~ de qc** to be upset by sth
effectif [efɛktif] *m* (*d'une armée, d'un parti*) strength; (*d'une entreprise*) staff; **vérifier l'~ de la classe** to check the number of children in the class
effectif, -ive [efɛktif, -iv] *adj* (*aide*) real; (*pouvoir*) effective; (*travail*) actual; **être ~ à partir du 1er janvier** to take effect from 1 January
effectivement [efɛktivmɑ̃] *adv* **1.** (*concrètement: aider, travailler*) effectively **2.** (*réellement*) actually; **il est ~ parti** he has indeed left
effectuer [efɛktɥe] <1> **I.** *vt* (*faire: investissement*) to make; (*parcours*) to do; (*réforme*) to carry out **II.** *vpr* **s'~** (*mouvement, paiement*) to be made; (*parcours*) to be done; (*transaction*) to be carried out
efféminé(e) [efemine] *adj* effeminate
effervescence [efɛʀvesɑ̃s] *f* **1.** (*bouillonnement*) effervescence **2.** (*agitation*) agitation
effervescent(e) [efɛʀvesɑ̃, ɑ̃t] *adj* **1.** (*pétillant: liquide*) effervescent; **comprimé ~** effervescent tablet **2.** (*tumultueux*) turbulent
effet [efɛ] *m* **1.** (*résultat*) effect; **~ boule de neige** snowball effect; **~ secondaire** side effect; **être l'~ du hasard** to be pure chance; **avoir** [*o* **faire**] **l'~ d'une bombe** to be a bombshell; **sous l'~ de qc** under the influence of sth; **agir sous l'~ de la colère** to act while in the grip of anger **2.** (*impression*) impression; **faire ~ sur qn** to make an impression on sb **3.** (*phénomène*) effect; **~s spéciaux** special effects; **~ de serre** greenhouse effect ►**~ bœuf** a hell of an effect; **en ~** indeed; (*pour justifier ses propos*) as a matter of fact; (*pour confirmer le propos d'un tiers*) that's right
effeuiller [efœje] <1> **I.** *vt* **~ un arbre** to strip (the leaves off) a tree; **~ une fleur** to pull the petals off a flower **II.** *vpr* **s'~** (*arbre*) to shed its leaves
efficace [efikas] *adj* effective; (*personne*) efficient
efficacement [efikasmɑ̃] *adv* effectively
efficacité [efikasite] *f* (*d'une méthode*) effectiveness; (*d'une personne, machine*) efficiency
effigie [efiʒi] *f* effigy ►**à l'~ de qn une pièce de monnaie à l'~ de la reine** a coin bearing the effigy of the queen
effilé(e) [efile] *adj* **1.** slender **2.** GASTR (*amandes*) flaked; (*volaille*) drawn
effilocher [efilɔʃe] <1> *vt, vpr* **(s')~** to fray
efflanqué(e) [eflɑ̃ke] *adj* raw-boned
effleurer [eflœʀe] <1> *vt* **1.** (*toucher*) to brush against; (*aborder: sujet*) to touch on **2.** (*passer par la tête*) **~ qn** to occur to sb
effluve [eflyv] *m souvent pl* **1.** (*parfum*) fragrance **2.** (*mauvaise odeur*) stink; **les ~s des caniveaux** the stink of the gutter
effondré(e) [efɔ̃dʀe] *adj* (*personne*) prostrate
effondrement [efɔ̃dʀəmɑ̃] *m* **1.** (*écroulement*) collapse **2.** (*fin brutale: d'une civilisation, d'un projet*) collapse; (*des prix*) slump; (*d'une fortune*) melting away
effondrer [efɔ̃dʀe] <1> *vpr* **s'~ 1.** (*s'écrouler: pont*) to collapse; (*plancher, sol*) to cave in **2.** (*être anéanti: empire, civilisation, preuve, argumentation*) to collapse; (*projet*) to fall through; (*fortune*) to melt away **3.** (*baisser brutalement: cours de la bourse*) to slump **4.** (*craquer: personne*) to break down **5.** INFOR (*ordinateur*) to crash
efforcer [efɔʀse] <2> *vpr* **s'~ de** +*infin* to endeavour to +*infin Brit,* to endeavor to +*infin Am*
effort [efɔʀ] *m* effort; **faire un ~ d'attention** to make an effort to concentrate ►**n'épargner aucun ~ pour** +*infin* to spare no effort to +*infin;* **faire un ~ sur soi-même pour** +*infin* to force onseself to +*infin*
effraction [efʀaksjɔ̃] *f* **1.** (*cambriolage*) break-in **2.** (*accusation*) breaking and entering
effraie [efʀɛ] *f* barn owl
effrayant(e) [efʀɛjɑ̃, ɑ̃t] *adj* **1.** (*qui fait peur*) frightening; (*silence*) dreadful **2.** *inf* (*extrême: prix*) terrifying
effrayer [efʀeje] <7> **I.** *vt* (*faire très peur à*) to terrify; **il est effrayé à l'idée de partir** he's terrified at the idea of leaving **II.** *vpr* (*craindre*) **s'~ de qc** to be scared of sth
effréné(e) [efʀene] *adj* wild

effriter [efʀite] <1> **I.** *vt* ~ **qc** to make sth crumble **II.** *vpr* **s'~** (*roche*) to crumble; (*cours de la bourse*) to collapse; (*majorité*) to tumble

effronté(e) [efʀɔ̃te] **I.** *adj* impudent **II.** *m(f)* impudent individual

effrontément [efʀɔ̃temɑ̃] *adv* shamelessly

effronterie [efʀɔ̃tʀi] *f* impudence; **avec ~** impudently

effroyable [efʀwajabl] *adj* **1.** (*épouvantable*) appalling **2.** *inf* (*incroyable*) dreadful

effusion [efyzjɔ̃] *f* outpouring; **~ de sang** bloodshed *no pl*

égal(e) [egal, o] <-aux> **I.** *adj* **1.** (*de même valeur*) equal; **de prix ~** at the same price; **nous sommes tous égaux devant la loi** we are all equal before the law; **la partie est très ~e** it's a fair match **2.** (*sans variation*) **être d'humeur ~e** to be even-tempered ►**être/rester ~ à soi-même** to be/stay the same as ever **II.** *m(f)* **la femme est l'~e de l'homme** woman is man's equal; **considérer qn comme son ~** to consider sb as one's equal ►**il n'a pas son ~ pour faire qc** he has no equal for doing sth; **négocier** [*o* **traiter**] **d'~ à ~** to negotiate on equal terms; **sans ~** without equal

égalable [egalabl] *adj* **être difficilement ~** to be hard to equal

également [egalmɑ̃] *adv* **1.** (*pareillement*) equally **2.** (*aussi*) also

égaler [egale] <1> *vt* **1.** MAT **deux plus deux égale(nt) quatre** two and two make four **2.** (*être pareil*) to equal; **~ qn/qc en beauté** to be the equal of sb/sth in beauty; **~ qn en grosseur** to be as fat as sb

égalisation [egalizasjɔ̃] *f* **1.** (*nivellement*) levelling (out) **2.** SPORT equalizing

égaliser [egalize] <1> **I.** *vt* to equal (out); (*revenus*) to level (out); (*cheveux*) to trim **II.** *vi* to equalize **III.** *vpr* **s'~** to level (out)

égalitaire [egalitɛʀ] *adj* egalitarian

égalitarisme [egalitaʀism] *m* egalitarianism

égalité [egalite] *f* **1.** (*absence de différences*) equality; (*des adversaires*) even match; **~ des forces/chances/droits** equal strength/opportunities/rights **2.** (*absence de variations*) **~ d'humeur** even temper **3.** MAT equality ►**être à ~** (*match*) to be drawn; (*joueurs*) to be level

égard [egaʀ] *m pl* consideration ►**à cet ~** in this respect; **avoir des ~s pour qn, être plein d'~s pour qn** to show sb great consideration; **à l'~ de qn** towards sb; **par ~ pour qn/qc** out of consideration for sb/sth

égaré(e) [egaʀe] *adj* **1.** (*perdu*) lost **2.** (*troublé*) distraught

égarement [egaʀmɑ̃] *m* **1.** (*trouble mental*) distraction **2.** *pl* (*conduite*) lapses; **revenir de ses ~s** to mend one's ways

égarer [egaʀe] <1> **I.** *vt* **1.** (*induire en erreur*) to mislead **2.** (*perdre*) to mislay **3.** (*faire perdre la raison*) **~ qn** to make sb distraught **II.** *vpr* **1.** (*se perdre*) **s'~** to get lost; **s'~ du droit chemin** to wander from the straight and narrow; **la lettre s'est égarée** the letter went astray **2.** (*divaguer*) **s'~** to wander; **s'~ dans les détails** to get bogged down in details

égayer [egeje] <7> **I.** *vt* **~ qn/qc** to brighten sb/sth up **II.** *vpr* **s'~** to brighten up

églantine [eglɑ̃tin] *f* dog rose

églefin [egləfɛ̃] *m* haddock

église [egliz] *f* **1.** (*édifice*) church; **se marier à l'~** to get married in church **2.** (*communauté*) **l'Église protestante/catholique** the Protestant/Catholic Church

égocentrique [egosɑ̃tʀik] **I.** *adj* self-centred **II.** *mf* self-centred individual

égoïsme [egɔism] *m* selfishness

égoïste [egɔist] **I.** *adj* selfish **II.** *mf* selfish person

égorger [egɔʀʒe] <2a> **I.** *vt* **1.** (*couper la gorge*) **~ qn/un animal avec qc** to cut sb's/an animal's throat **2.** *inf* (*ruiner*) to bleed white **II.** *vpr* **s'~** to cut each other's throats

égosiller [egozije] <1> *vpr* **s'~** **1.** (*crier*) to shout oneself hoarse **2.** (*chanter: personne*) to sing at the top of one's voice *Brit,* to sing at the top of one's lungs *Am;* (*oiseau*) to warble

égout [egu] *m* sewer; **bouche d'~** manhole; **eaux d'~** waste water

égoutier [egutje] *m* sewer worker

égoutter [egute] <1> **I.** *vt* (**faire**) **~ qc** to drain sth **II.** *vpr* **s'~** (*feuilles, linge*) to drip; (*vaisselle*) to drain

égouttoir [egutwaʀ] *m* **~ à vaisselle** dish drainer

égratigner [egʀatiɲe] <1> **I.** *vt* to scratch **II.** *vpr* **s'~ le genou/la jambe** to scratch one's knee/one's leg

égratignure [egʀatiɲyʀ] *f* scratch

égrener [egʀəne] <4> **I.** *vt* **1.** (*dégarnir de ses grains: cosse, épi*) to shell; (*coton*) to gin; **~ une grappe/du raisin** to take the grapes off **2.** (*dévider*) **~ son chapelet** to tell one's beads **3.** (*sonner*) **l'horloge égrenait les heures** the clock chimed the passing hours **II.** *vpr* **s'~** **1.** (*perdre ses grains: blé*) to fall from the stalk; (*raisin*) to fall off the bunch **2.** (*se présenter un à un*) **les échoppes de Noël s'égrènent le long de la rue** there was a string of Christmas stalls along the road; **les voitures s'égrenaient sur l'autoroute** cars strung themselves along the motorway

égrillard(e) [egʀijaʀ, aʀd] *adj* ribald

Égypte [eʒipt] *f* **l'~** Egypt

égyptien [eʒipsjɛ̃] *m* Egyptian Arabic; **l'~ moderne** modern Egyptian; *v. a.* **français**

égyptien(ne) [eʒipsjɛ̃, jɛn] *adj* Egyptian

Égyptien(ne) [eʒipsjɛ̃, jɛn] *m(f)* Egyptian

eh [e, ɛ] *interj* hey; **~ oui!** yes!; **~ bien ça par exemple!** well now!; **~ bien!** *inf* well well!; **eh bien, …** well, …

éhonté(e) [eɔ̃te] *adj* shameless

éjaculation [eʒakylasjɔ̃] *f* ejaculation; **~ précoce** premature ejaculation

E

éjaculer [eʒakyle] <1> *vi* to ejaculate

éjectable [eʒɛktabl] *adj* **siège** ~ ejector seat

éjecter [eʒɛkte] <1> *vt* **1.**(*rejeter: machine*) to eject **2.** *inf*(*expulser*) to kick out

élaboration [elabɔʀasjɔ̃] *f* (*composition: d'un plan*) working out

élaborer [elabɔʀe] <1> **I.** *vt* (*composer: plan*) to work out **II.** *vpr* **s'~** to develop

élaguer [elage] <1> *vt* **1.**(*couper: arbre*) to prune **2.**(*retrancher*) ~ **un article** to pare down an article

élan [elɑ̃] *m* **1.**(*mouvement*) **prendre son ~** to get up speed; (*en courant*) to take a run up; **prendre de l'~** to gather momentum **2.**(*accès: de tendresse*) surge; (*d'enthousiasme*) burst ►**~ vital** life force

élancé(e) [elɑ̃se] *adj* slender

élancement [elɑ̃smɑ̃] *m* shooting [*o* sharp] pain

élancer[1] [elɑ̃se] <2> *vi* **ma jambe m'élance** I have shooting pains in my leg

élancer[2] [elɑ̃se] <2> *vpr* **1.**(*se précipiter*) **s'~ vers qn/qc** to rush up to sb/sth; **s'~ à la poursuite de qn** to rush after sb **2.**(*prendre son élan*) **s'~** to take a run-up; **s'~ dans les airs** to soar into the air

élargir [elaʀʒiʀ] <8> **I.** *vt* **1.**(*rendre plus large*) to widen **2.** COUT (*jupe*) to let out **3.**(*développer: horizon, débat*) to broaden **II.** *vpr* **s'~** (*fleuve*) to widen; (*chaussures*) to give; (*horizon*) to broaden (out) **III.** *vi* (*pull*) to go baggy

élargissement [elaʀʒismɑ̃] *m* **1.**(*action: d'une route, de chaussures*) widening; (*d'une jupe*) letting out; (*d'un débat*) broadening out; (*d'une majorité, de l'Union européenne*) enlargement; (*d'un détenu*) release **2.**(*fait de s'élargir: d'un canal, d'une route*) widening; (*de l'Union européenne*) enlargement

élasticité [elastisite] *f* elasticity

élastique [elastik] **I.** *adj* elastic; (*pas*) springy; (*loi*) flexible **II.** *m a.* COUT elastic; (*bracelet*) rubber band

Elbe [elb(ə)] **l'île d'~** Elba

elbot [ɛlbo] *m Belgique* (*flétan*) halibut

électeur, **-trice** [elɛktœʀ, -tʀis] *m, f* voter ►**grands ~s** *electoral college electing members of French Senate,* Electoral College *Am*

élection [elɛksjɔ̃] *f* **1.** election; **~s européennes/législatives** European/general elections **2.**(*choix*) **patrie/pays d'~** adopted homeland/country

électoral(e) [elɛktɔʀal, -o] <-aux> *adj* electoral

électorat [elɛktɔʀa] *m* electorate

électricien(ne) [elɛktʀisjɛ̃, jɛn] *m(f)* electrician

électricité [elɛktʀisite] *f* electricity; **se chauffer à l'~** to have electric heating; **allumer/éteindre l'~** *inf* to turn the electricity on/off ►**il y a de l'~ dans l'air** the atmosphere was electric

électrifier [elɛktʀifje] <1a> *vt* to electrify

électrique [elɛktʀik] *adj* (*cuisinière, moteur*) electric; **centrale ~** power station

électriser [elɛktʀize] <1> *vt* to electrify

électrocardiogramme [elɛktʀokaʀdjɔgʀam] *m* electrocardiogram

électrocuter [elɛktʀɔkyte] <1> **I.** *vt* **être électrocuté** to be electrocuted **II.** *vpr* **s'~ avec qc** to get electrocuted with sth

électrocution [elɛktʀɔkysjɔ̃] *f* electrocution; **condamner qn par ~** to sentence sb to the electric chair

électro-encéphalogramme [elɛktʀoɑ̃sefalɔgʀam] <électro-encéphalogrammes> *m* electrencephalogram

électroménager [elɛktʀomenaʒe] **I.** *adj* **appareil ~** (household) electrical **II.** *m* **1.**(*appareils*) household appliances *pl* **2.**(*commerce*) household appliances *pl*

électron [elɛktʀɔ̃] *m* electron

électronicien(ne) [elɛktʀɔnisjɛ̃, jɛn] *m(f)* electronics engineer

électronique [elɛktʀɔnik] **I.** *adj* electronic **II.** *f* electronics + *vb sing*

électrophone [elɛktʀɔfɔn] *m* record player

élégamment [elegamɑ̃] *adv* (*s'habiller*) stylishly

élégance [elegɑ̃s] *f sans pl* elegance; **perdre avec ~** to be a good loser

élégant(e) [elegɑ̃, ɑ̃t] *adj* elegant

élégie [eleʒi] *f* elegy

élément [elemɑ̃] **I.** *m* **1.**(*composant, donnée, groupe*) *a.* CHIM element; **très bons ~s** very good people **2.**(*mobilier*) unit ►**être dans son ~** to be in one's element **II.** *mpl* elements; **~s de composition** Elementary Composition; **des ~s de français** basic French

élémentaire [elemɑ̃tɛʀ] *adj* elementary ►**~, mon cher Watson!** *inf* elementary, my dear Watson!; **c'est ~!** *inf* (*c'est évident*) it's elementary!; (*c'est bien le moins qu'on puisse faire*) it's the least one can do!

éléphant [elefɑ̃] *m* elephant; **~ mâle/femelle** bull/cow elephant ►**comme un ~ dans un magasin de porcelaine** *inf* like a bull in a china shop

élevage [el(ə)vaʒ] *m* **1.**(*action*) breeding **2.**(*ensemble d'animaux*) animals *pl* **3.**(*exploitation*) farm

élévateur [elevatœʀ] *m* ANAT, CONSTR elevator

élévation [elevasjɔ̃] *f* **1.**(*accession*) elevation; **~ de qn à une dignité** sb's elevation to an honour **2.**(*hausse*) rise; **~ de la température** rise in temperature **3.**(*noblesse*) nobility; **~ d'esprit** loftiness of spirit **4.** MAT **~ au carré** squaring **5.** REL elevation

élève [elɛv] *mf* pupil

élevé(e)[1] [el(ə)ve] *adj* **1.**(*haut*) high **2.**(*noble: conversation, style*) elevated; (*opinion*) high; **être de condition ~e** to be high-born

élevé(e)[2] [el(ə)ve] **I.** *adj* (*éduqué*) **bien/mal**

~ well/badly brought up **II.** *m(f)* **mal** ~ rude individual

élever¹ [el(ə)ve] <4> **I.** *vt* **1.** (*ériger: monument, mur*) to erect **2.** (*porter vers le haut*) to raise up **3.** (*porter plus haut: niveau, ton, voix*) to raise **4.** (*promouvoir*) ~ **qn au rang de ...** to elevate sb to the rank of ... **5.** (*susciter: critique, doute*) to express; (*objection*) to raise **6.** MAT ~ **un nombre au carré** to square a number **II.** *vpr* **1.** (*être construit*) **s'**~ (*mur, édifice*) to go up **2.** (*se dresser*) **s'**~ **à 10/100 mètres** (*plateau*) to rise to 10/100 metres **3.** (*se faire entendre*) **s'**~ to rise up **4.** (*surgir*) **s'**~ (*discussion, doutes*) to arise **5.** (*se chiffrer*) **s'**~ **à 1000 euros** to come to 1000 euros **6.** (*mépriser*) **s'**~ **au-dessus des injures** to rise above the insults **7.** (*socialement*) **s'**~ **par son seul travail** to make one's way through one's own work **8.** (*s'opposer à*) **s'**~ **contre qc** to protest against sth

élever² [el(ə)ve] <4> *vt* **1.** (*prendre soin de: personne*) to bring up, to raise **2.** (*éduquer*) to educate **3.** (*faire l'élevage de: vaches*) to breed; (*volaille*) to farm

éleveur, **-euse** [el(ə)vœʀ, -øz] *m, f* breeder

elfe [ɛlf] *m* elf

élider [to elide] <1> **I.** *vt* (*voyelle*) to elide **II.** *vpr* **s'**~ (*voyelle*) to be elided

éligible [eliʒibl] *adj* eligible

élimé(**e**) [elime] *adj* ~ **à qc** worn at sth

élimination [eliminasjɔ̃] *f* removal; (*d'un adversaire, d'une tache, d'un joueur*) elimination; (*des cafards, d'une espèce*) eradication ▶**procéder par** ~ to work by a process of elimination

éliminatoire [eliminatwaʀ] **I.** *adj* **1.** ECOLE, UNIV (*note, faute*) failing; **épreuve** ~ eliminatory exam **2.** SPORT preliminary **II.** *f souvent pl* preliminary (heat)

éliminer [elimine] <1> **I.** *vt* **1.** (*supprimer*) to eliminate; (*tartre*) to remove; (*pièces défectueuses*) to get rid of; **il a été éliminé à l'oral** he was eliminated after the oral (exam) **2.** (*tuer*) to liquidate **3.** SPORT ~ **qn de la course** to eliminate sb from the race; (*pour dopage*) to disqualify sb from the race **4.** ECON (*déchets*) to dispose of **II.** *vpr* **s'**~ **facilement** (*tache*) to be easy to remove

élire [eliʀ] *vt irr* to elect; **il a été élu président** he was elected president

élision [elizjɔ̃] *f* elision

élite [elit] *f* elite

élitiste [elitist] *adj* **école** ~ elistist school

élixir [eliksiʀ] *m* elixir; ~ **de longue vie** elixir of life

elle [ɛl] *pron pers* **1.** (*personne*) she; (*chose*) it; ~ **est grande** (*femme*) she's tall; (*objet*) it's big; **lui est là, mais pas** ~ he's there, but she isn't **2.** *interrog, non traduit* **Sophie a-t-**~ **ses clés?** has Sophie got her keys?; *v. a.* **il** **3.** (*répétitif*) **regarde la lune comme** ~ **est ronde** look how big the moon is; **la vache,** ~ **fait meuh** cows go moo; *v. a.* **il** **4.** *inf* (*pour renforcer*) **la mer,** ~ **aussi, est polluée** the sea, too, is polluted; ~**, elle n'a pas ouvert la bouche** SHE didn't open her mouth; **c'est** ~ **qui l'a dit** it was she who said so; **il veut l'aider,** ~**?** he wants to help HER? **5.** *avec une préposition* **avec/sans** ~ with/without her; **à** ~ **seule** on her own; **la maison est à** ~ the house is hers; **c'est à** ~ **de décider** it's up to her to decide; **c'est à** ~**!** it's hers! **6.** *dans une comparaison* her; **il est comme** ~ he is like her; **plus fort qu'**~ stronger than her **7.** (*soi*) herself; **elle ne pense qu'à** ~ she only thinks about herself; *v. a.* **lui**

elle-même [ɛlmɛm] *pron pers* (*elle en personne*) herself; (*chose*) itself; *v. a.* **lui-même**

elles [ɛl] *pron pers* **1.** (*fém pl*) they; ~ **sont grandes** (*personnes*) they're tall; (*choses*) they're big; **eux sont là, mais pas** ~ they're here, but they aren't **2.** *interrog, non traduit* **les filles, sont-**~ **venues?** have the girls come? **3.** (*répétitif*) **regarde les fleurs comme** ~ **sont belles** look how lovely the flowers are; *v. a.* **il** **4.** *inf* (*pour renforcer*) ~**, elles n'ont pas ouvert la bouche** THEY didn't open their mouths; **c'est** ~ **qui l'ont dit** it was they who said so; **il veut les aider,** ~**?** he wants to help THEM? **5.** *avec une préposition* **avec/sans** ~ with/without them; **à** ~ **seules** by themselves **6.** *dans une comparaison* them; **ils sont comme** ~ they're like them **7.** (*soi*) themselves; *v. a.* **elle**

elles-mêmes [ɛlmɛm] *pron pers* (*elles en personne*) themselves; *v. a.* **moi-même, nous-même**

ellipse [elips] *f* **1.** LING ellipsis **2.** GEOM ellipse

elliptique [eliptik] *adj* elliptical

élocution [elɔkysjɔ̃] *f* diction; **avoir une** ~ **lente/rapide** to speak slowly/quickly; **avoir une grande facilité d'**~ to speak with ease; **défaut d'**~ speech impediment; **professeur d'**~ elocution teacher

éloge [elɔʒ] *m* (*louange*) praise; **faire l'**~ **de qn** to praise sb (to the skies)

élogieux, **-euse** [elɔʒjø, -jøz] *adj* (*paroles*) complimentary

éloigné(**e**) [elwaɲe] *adj* **1.** (*dans l'espace*) ~ **de qc** a long way from sth; ~ **de 10 km** ten kilometres away *Brit,* ten kilometers away *Am;* **se tenir** ~ **de qc** to keep away from sth **2.** (*isolé*) remote **3.** (*dans le temps, la parenté*) distant **4.** (*différent*) ~ **de qc** far (removed) from sth

éloignement [elwaɲmɑ̃] *m* **1.** (*distance*) **l'**~ distance **2.** (*séparation d'avec*) **l'**~ **de qn** removal of sb **3.** (*fait de se tenir à l'écart*) ~ **de qc** keeping away from sth

éloigner [elwaɲe] <1> **I.** *vt* **1.** (*mettre à distance: objet*) to move away; (*personne*) to take away **2.** (*détourner*) ~ **qn du sujet** to take sb away from the subject; ~ **qn de la vie politique** to take sb away from politics **3.** (*dans le temps*) **chaque jour qui passe nous éloigne de notre jeunesse** every passing day takes us further away from our youth **4.**(*écarter: soupçons*) to dispel; (*danger*) to ward off **5.**(*détacher*) ~ **qn de qn** to estrange sb from sb **II.** *vpr* **1.**(*devenir de plus en plus lointain*) **s'~** (*nuages*) to go away; (*bruit*) to fade into the distance; (*vent, tempête*) to pass over **2.**(*aller ailleurs*) **s'~** to move away **3.**(*aller plus loin*) **ne t'éloigne pas trop, s'il te plaît!** don't go too far away, please! **4.**(*dans le temps*) **s'~ de qc** to get further away from sth **5.**(*s'estomper*) **s'~** (*souvenir*) to fade; (*danger*) to pass **6.**(*s'écarter de*) **s'~ du sujet** to wander off the subject **7.**(*prendre ses distances par rapport à*) **s'~ de qn/qc** to grow away from sb/sth

éloquence [elɔkɑ̃s] *f* eloquence; **parler avec ~** to speak eloquently

éloquent(e) [elɔkɑ̃, ɑ̃t] *adj* eloquent

élu(e) [ely] **I.** *part passé de* **élire II.** *adj* elected **III.** *m(f)* **1.** POL elected representative **2.** REL **les ~s** the elect

élucider [elyside] <1> *vt* to elucidate

éluder [elyde] <1> *vt* to elude

Élysée [elize] *m* **l'~** the Élysée (Palace) (*the official residence of the French President*)

élytre [elitʀ] *m* elytron

émacié(e) [emasje] *adj* emaciated

email, E-mail, e-mail [imel] *m* e-mail

émail [emaj, emo] <-aux> *m* **a.** ANAT enamel; **~ dentaire** dental enamel; **en ~** enamelled; **baignoire en ~** enamel bath

émaillé(e) [emaje] *adj* **1.**(*revêtu d'émail*) enamelled **2.** *iron* (*parsemé*) **~ de citations/fautes** peppered with quaotations/mistakes

émancipation [emɑ̃sipasjɔ̃] *f* emancipation

émancipé(e) [emɑ̃sipe] *adj* emancipated

émanciper [emɑ̃sipe] <1> *vpr* **s'~** to become emancipated

émaner [emane] <1> *vi* **~ de qn/qc** (*autorité, charme, odeur, lumière, chaleur*) to emanate from sb/sth; (*ordre, demande*) to come from sb/sth

émasculer [emaskyle] <1> *vt* (*animal*) to castrate; (*homme*) to emasculate

emballage [ɑ̃balaʒ] *m* **1.**(*en papier*) wrapping **2.**(*conditionnement*) packaging

emballant(e) [ɑ̃balɑ̃, ɑ̃t] *adj inf* (*enthousiasmant*) exciting

emballer [ɑ̃bale] <1> **I.** *vt* **1.**(*empaqueter avec du papier*) to wrap; (*empaqueter dans un conditionnement rigide*) to package **2.** *inf* (*enthousiasmer*) **être emballé par qc** to be turned on by sth **3.** AUTO (*moteur*) to race **4.** *inf* (*séduire*) to pull **II.** *vpr* **1.** *inf* (*s'enthousiasmer*) **s'~ pour qc** to get turned on by sth **2.** *inf* (*s'emporter*) **s'~** to get worked up **3.**(*partir à une allure excessive*) **s'~** (*animal*) to bolt; (*moteur*) to race

embarcadère [ɑ̃baʀkadɛʀ] *m* landing stage

embarcation [ɑ̃baʀkasjɔ̃] *f* boat, craft

embardée [ɑ̃baʀde] *f* **1.** AUTO swerve **2.** NAUT yaw

embargo [ɑ̃baʀgo] *m* embargo; **mettre l'~ sur qc** to put an embargo on sth; **lever l'~ sur qc** to lift the embargo on sth; **~ sur la nouvelle** embargo on the news

embarquement [ɑ̃baʀkəmɑ̃] *m* **1.**(*chargement: des marchandises*) loading **2.** NAUT embarcation **3.** AVIAT **~ immédiat, porte 5!** immediate boarding, gate 5!

embarquer [ɑ̃baʀke] <1> **I.** *vi* **1. ~ dans l'avion** to board the plane **2.** *Québec* (*monter*) **~ dans l'autobus/dans une voiture** to get on the bus/into a car **II.** *vt* **1.**(*prendre à bord d'un bateau*) to embark; (*marchandises*) to load **2.**(*à bord d'un véhicule: passagers*) to take on board; (*animaux*) to load **3.**(*voler*) to pinch **4.** *inf* (*arrêter: voleur*) to cart off ►**elle est mal embarquée** *inf* she's made a bad start **III.** *vpr* **1.**(*monter à bord d'un bateau*) **s'~** to board **2.**(*s'engager*) **s'~ dans qc** to get involved in sth

embarras [ɑ̃baʀa] *m* **1.**(*gêne*) embarrassment **2.**(*tracas*) trouble ►**n'avoir que l'~ du choix** to be spoilt for choice; **mettre** [*o* **plonger**] **qn dans l'~** (*le mettre mal à l'aise*) to embarrass sb; (*l'enfermer dans un dilemme*) to put sb in a difficult position

embarrassant(e) [ɑ̃baʀasɑ̃, ɑ̃t] *adj* **1.**(*délicat*) awkward **2.**(*ennuyeux: situation*) uncomfortable **3.**(*encombrant*) cumbersome

embarrassé(e) [ɑ̃baʀase] *adj* **1.**(*gêné: personne*) self-conscious; (*air, sourire*) embarrassed **2.**(*encombré*) **~ de qc** (*personne*) burdened with sth; (*couloir*) cluttered with sth

embarrasser [ɑ̃baʀase] <1> **I.** *vt* **1.**(*déconcerter*) **~ qn** to put sb in an awkward position **2.**(*tracasser*) to bother **3.**(*gêner dans ses mouvements*) to hamper **4.**(*encombrer: couloir*) to clutter **II.** *vpr* **1.**(*s'encombrer*) **s'~ de qn/qc** to burden oneself with sb/sth **2.**(*se soucier*) **s'~ de qc** to trouble oneself with sth

embauche [ɑ̃boʃ] *f* **1.**(*recrutement*) hiring **2.**(*travail*) vacancy; **offre d'~** job offer

embaucher [ɑ̃boʃe] <1> **I.** *vt* ECON **~ qn** to take sb on, to hire sb *Am* **II.** *vi* to take on workers, to hire workers *Am*

embauchoir [ɑ̃boʃwaʀ] *m* shoetree

embaumer [ɑ̃bome] <1> **I.** *vi* (*fleur, fruit*) to be scented **II.** *vt* **1.**(*parfumer: maison, jardin*) **~ qc** to fill sth with a lovely smell; **la lavande embaume le linge** lavender gives a lovely smell to linen **2.**(*sentir bon*) **~ le lilas** to smell of lilac **3.**(*cadavre*) to embalm

embellir [ɑ̃beliʀ] <8> **I.** *vi* to grow more attractive **II.** *vt* (*personne*) to make more attractive; (*maison, ville*) to beautify; (*réalité*) to embellish

embellissement [ɑ̃belismɑ̃] *m* **1.** *sans pl* (*action d'embellir: d'un lieu, édifice*) improvement **2.**(*élément qui embellit*) embellishment

embêtant [ɑ̃bɛtɑ̃] *m inf* **l'~, c'est qu'il est sourd** the trouble is he's deaf

embêtant(e) [ɑ̃bɛtɑ̃, ɑ̃t] *adj inf* **1.**(*agaçant: personne*) annoying **2.**(*fâcheux*) awkward

embêtement [ɑ̃bɛtmɑ̃] *m inf* problem
embêter [ɑ̃bete] <1> **I.** *vt inf* **1.** (*importuner, contrarier*) to bother; **je suis embêté, je n'ai plus de lait** I've got a problem, I've no more milk **2.** (*casser les pieds*) to pester **II.** *vpr inf* **1.** (*s'ennuyer*) **s'~** to be bored **2.** (*se démener*) **s'~ à faire qc** to go to the trouble of doing sth ►**ne pas s'~** (*n'être pas à plaindre*) to be all right; (*en profiter*) to be doing all right
emblée [ɑ̃ble] *adv* **d'~** right away
emblème [ɑ̃blɛm] *m* **1.** (*insigne*) symbol **2.** (*symbole*) emblem
embobiner [ɑ̃bɔbine] <1> *vt inf* **~ qn** to take sb in
emboîter [ɑ̃bwate] <1> **I.** *vt* to fit together **II.** *vpr* **des choses s'emboîtent les unes dans les autres** things fit into each other
embolie [ɑ̃bɔli] *f* embolism; **~ pulmonaire** pulmonary embolism
embonpoint [ɑ̃bɔ̃pwɛ̃] *m* stoutness
embouché(e) [ɑ̃buʃe] *adj* **être mal ~** to be foul-mouthed
embouchure [ɑ̃buʃyʀ] *f* **1.** GEO mouth **2.** MUS embouchure **3.** (*mors*) mouthpiece
embourber [ɑ̃buʀbe] <1> **I.** *vt* **~ qc** to get sth stuck **II.** *vpr* **1.** (*s'enliser*) **s'~** to get stuck **2.** (*s'empêtrer*) **s'~ dans qc** to get bogged down in sth **3.** (*s'enfoncer*) **s'~ dans qc** to sink into sth
embourgeoiser [ɑ̃buʀʒwaze] <1> *vpr* **s'~** to become middle class
embout [ɑ̃bu] *m* **1.** (*d'une chaussure*) toe-cap; (*d'un parapluie*) tip; (*d'une échelle, d'un trépied*) cap **2.** (*pour la bouche*) mouthpiece **3.** (*embout de gonflage*) air inlet
embouteillage [ɑ̃butɛjaʒ] *m* AUTO traffic jam
embouteiller [ɑ̃buteje] <1> *vt* jammed; **être embouteillé** (*rue, passage*) blocked; (*lignes téléphoniques*) overloaded
emboutir [ɑ̃butiʀ] <8> *vt* AUTO to bang into
embranchement [ɑ̃bʀɑ̃ʃmɑ̃] *m* **1.** (*point de jonction*) junction **2.** (*ramification*) fork
embrassades [ɑ̃bʀasad] *fpl* hugs and kisses
embrasser [ɑ̃bʀase] <1> **I.** *vt* **1.** (*donner un baiser*) to kiss; **va l'~!** give him a kiss! **2.** (*saluer*) **je t'/vous embrasse** (with) love **3.** (*prendre dans les bras*) to embrace **II.** *vpr* **s'~ 1.** (*donner un baiser*) to kiss (each other) **2.** (*prendre dans ses bras*) to embrace
embrasure [ɑ̃bʀɑzyʀ] *f* frame
embrayage [ɑ̃bʀɛjaʒ] *m* clutch; **voiture à ~ automatique** automatic (car)
embrayer [ɑ̃bʀeje] <7> *vi* **1.** AUTO (*conducteur*) to put into gear **2.** (*commencer à parler*) **~ sur qn/qc** to launch onto sb/sth
embrigader [ɑ̃bʀigade] <1> *vt péj* **1.** (*endoctriner*) to brainwash **2.** (*enrôler*) **~ qn dans qc** to press-gang sb into sth
embringuer [ɑ̃bʀɛ̃ge] <1> *vt inf* **être embringué dans qc** to be dragged into sth; **se laisser ~ dans qc** to get oneself mixed up in sth
embrocher [ɑ̃bʀɔʃe] <1> *vt* (*viande*) to spit
embrouillamini [ɑ̃bʀujamini] *m inf* muddle
embrouille [ɑ̃bʀuj] *f* funny business *no pl*
embrouillé(e) [ɑ̃bʀuje] *adj* muddled
embrouiller [ɑ̃bʀuje] <1> **I.** *vt* **1.** (*rendre confus: chose*) to tangle **2.** (*faire perdre le fil: personne*) to muddle **II.** *vpr* **s'~** to get muddled; **s'~ dans un récit/des explications** to get muddled with a story/explanations
embroussaillé(e) [ɑ̃bʀusaje] *adj* (*terrain*) overgrown; (*sourcils*) bushy
embruns [ɑ̃bʀœ̃] *mpl* spray
embryon [ɑ̃bʀijɔ̃] *m* **1.** BIO embryo **2.** (*germe: d'une idée*) beginnings; **à l'état d'~** at an embryonic stage
embûches [ɑ̃byʃ] *fpl* pitfall; **sujet plein d'~** tricky exam question
embuer [ɑ̃bɥe] <1> *vt* **~ qc** to mist sth up
embuscade [ɑ̃byskad] *f* **dresser** [*o* **tendre**] **une ~ à qn** to set an ambush for sb; **être** [*o* **se tenir**] **en ~** to lie in ambush; **mettre** [*o* **placer**] **des personnes en ~** to set an ambush for sb
embusquer [ɑ̃byske] <1> *vpr* **s'~** to lie in ambush
éméché(e) [emeʃe] *adj inf* tipsy
émeraude [emʀod] **I.** *adj inv* emerald (green) **II.** *f* emerald
émergence [emɛʀʒɑ̃s] *f* emergence
émerger [emɛʀʒe] <2a> *vi* **1.** (*sortir*) **~ de qc** (*plongeur*) to come up from sth; (*soleil*) to come out from sth **2.** (*être apparent*) to stand out **3.** *inf* (*se réveiller*) to emerge **4.** (*sortir du stress*) to get one's head above water
émerveillement [emɛʀvɛjmɑ̃] *m* wonder
émerveiller [emɛʀveje] <1> **I.** *vt* **~ qn** to make sb marvel **II.** *vpr* **s'~ de** [*o* **devant**] **qc** to marvel at sth
émetteur [emetœʀ] *m* CINE, TV transmitter; LING speaker
émetteur, -trice [emetœʀ, -tʀis] **I.** *adj* **1.** CINE, TV **poste ~** transmitter; **station émettrice** transmitting station **2.** FIN issuing **II.** *m, f* FIN (*d'un chèque*) drawer
émetteur-récepteur [emetœʀʀesɛptœʀ] <émetteurs-récepteurs> *m* transmitter-receiver
émettre [emɛtʀ] *irr* **I.** *vi* CINE, TV to broadcast **II.** *vt* **1.** (*produire: son, lumière*) to give out; (*odeur*) to give off; (*radiations*) to emit **2.** (*formuler: opinion*) to express; (*hypothèse*) to put forward **3.** FIN to issue; (*chèque*) to write
émeute [emøt] *f* riot
émietter [emjete] <1> *vt, vpr* **s'~** to crumble
émigrant(e) [emigʀɑ̃, ɑ̃t] *m(f)* emigrant
émigration [emigʀasjɔ̃] *f* emigration
émigré(e) [emigʀe] *m(f)* emigrant
émigrer [emigʀe] <1> *vi* to emigrate
émincer [emɛ̃se] <2> *vt* to slice thinly
éminence [eminɑ̃s] *f* **1.** GEO (*hauteur*) hill **2.** (*titre*) **Son/Votre Éminence** His/Your eminence ►**~ grise** éminence grise

éminent(e) [eminɑ̃, ɑ̃t] *adj* eminent
émir [emiʀ] *m* emir
émirati(e) [emiʀati] *adj* Emirian
émissaire [emisɛʀ] *m* emissary
émission [emisjɔ̃] *f* **1.** CINE, TV programme *Brit,* program *Am;* ~ **radiophonique/télévisée** radio/television programme; ~ **en différé** recorded programme; ~ **en direct** live programme **2.** PHYS emission **3.** FIN issuing; (*d'un chèque*) writing **4.** (*à la poste: d'un timbre-poste*) issue
emmagasiner [ɑ̃magazine] <1> *vt* **1.** (*entreposer*) to store **2.** (*accumuler: chaleur*) to store; (*objets*) to accumulate
emmailloter [ɑ̃majɔte] <1> *vt* (*envelopper dans un bandage*) ~ **qn/qc dans qc** to bundle sb/sth up in sth; ~ **un bébé dans des langes** to swaddle a baby
emmancher [ɑ̃mɑ̃ʃe] <1> **I.** *vt* **1.** (*outil, couteau*) ~ **qc** to fit a handle on to sth **2.** *inf* (*commencer*) **être mal emmanché** (*négociation*) to be off to a bad start **II.** *vpr inf* **mal s'**~ (*négociation*) to get off to a bad start
emmanchure [ɑ̃mɑ̃ʃyʀ] *f* armhole
emmêler [ɑ̃mele] <1> **I.** *vt* (*enchevêtrer*) to tangle **II.** *vpr* **1.** (*s'enchevêtrer*) **s'**~ to get tangled **2.** (*s'embrouiller*) **s'**~ **dans un récit** to muddle up a story; **s'**~ **dans des explications** to get muddled up explaining
emménagement [ɑ̃menaʒmɑ̃] *m* **après l'**~ after moving in
emménager [ɑ̃menaʒe] <2a> *vi* ~ **dans un appartement** to move into a flat *Brit,* to move into an apartment *Am*
emmener [ɑ̃m(ə)ne] <4> *vt* **1.** (*conduire*) ~ **qn au cinéma** to take sb to the cinema *Brit,* to take sb to the movies *Am* **2.** *inf* (*prendre avec soi, emporter*) to take **3.** (*comme prisonnier*) to take away **4.** (*comme otage*) to take (off)
emmerdant(e) [ɑ̃mɛʀdɑ̃, ɑ̃t] *adj inf* **être** ~ **1.** (*agaçant*) to be a pain in the arse *Brit,* to be a pain in the ass *Am* **2.** (*fâcheux*) to be a bloody nuisance *Brit,* to be a damned nuisance *Am* **3.** (*ennuyeux*) to be a bloody bore *Brit,* to be a damned bore *Am*
emmerde [ɑ̃mɛʀd] *f inf* hassle
emmerdement [ɑ̃mɛʀdəmɑ̃] *m inf* pain; **quel ~, cette voiture!** this car's a pain!
emmerder [ɑ̃mɛʀde] <1> **I.** *vt inf* **1.** (*énerver*) ~ **qn** to get on sb's nerves **2.** (*contrarier: problème*) to bug; **être emmerdé par ...** to be in a bloody mess with ... **3.** (*barber*) ~ **qn** to bore sb to death ►**(eh bien, moi) je vous/t'emmerde!** screw you! **II.** *vpr inf* **1.** (*s'ennuyer*) **s'**~ to be bored to death **2.** (*se démener*) **s'**~ **à faire qc** to go to all the bloody trouble of doing sth ►**il/elle ne s'emmerde pas!** it's all right for him/her!
emmerdeur, -euse [ɑ̃mɛʀdœʀ, -øz] *m, f inf* pain in the arse *Brit,* pain in the ass *Am*
emmitoufler [ɑ̃mitufle] <1> **I.** *vt* **être emmitouflé dans qc** to be all wrapped up in sth **II.** *vpr* **s'**~ **dans qc** to wrap oneself up in sth
emmurer [ɑ̃myʀe] <1> *vt* **1.** (*enfermer*) ~ **qc** to wall sth up **2.** (*bloquer*) to imprison
emoticon [emotikɔn] *m* INFOR emoticon
émotif, -ive [emɔtif, -iv] *adj* (*personne*) emotional; **choc** ~ psychological shock
émotion [emosjɔ̃] *f* **1.** (*surprise, chagrin*) shock; **causer une vive** ~ **à qn** to give sb quite a stir; **donner des ~s à qn** *inf* to give sb a scare, to give sb a fright *Brit* **2.** (*joie*) joy **3.** (*sentiment*) emotion ►**~s fortes** strong sensations
émotionnel(le) [emosjɔnɛl] *adj* (*choc*) psychological; (*réaction*) emotional
émotivité [emotivite] *f* emotionalism
émousser [emuse] <1> **I.** *vt* **être émoussé** to be blunt **II.** *vpr* **s'**~ (*couteau, pointe*) to go blunt; (*sentiment, désir*) to fade
émoustiller [emustije] <1> *vt* to titillate
émouvant(e) [emuvɑ̃, ɑ̃t] *adj* moving
émouvoir [emuvwaʀ] *irr* **I.** *vt* **1.** (*bouleverser*) to move; ~ **qn (jusqu')aux larmes** to move sb to tears **2.** (*changer de sentiment*) **se laisser** ~ **par qn/qc** to be moved by sb/sth **II.** *vpr* **s'**~ **de qc** to be moved by sb/sth
empaillé(e) [ɑ̃paje] *adj* **1.** (*rempli de paille: animal*) stuffed; (*siège*) straw-bottomed **2.** *inf* (*empoté*) **avoir l'air** ~ to look like a stuffed dummy
empaqueter [ɑ̃pak(ə)te] <3> *vt* to pack
emparer [ɑ̃paʀe] <1> *vpr* **1.** (*saisir*) **s'**~ **de qc** (*pour le tenir*) to take hold of sth; (*pour l'emporter*) to grab sth; **s'**~ **d'une information** to get hold of some news **2.** (*conquérir*) **s'**~ **d'un territoire** to seize a territory; **s'**~ **du pouvoir** to seize power; **s'**~ **d'un marché** to take over a market **3.** (*envahir*) **s'**~ **de qn** to take hold of sb
empattement [ɑ̃patmɑ̃] *m* **1.** AUTO wheelbase **2.** CONSTR footing **3.** TYP serif
empêché(e) [ɑ̃peʃe] *adj* **être** ~ (*retenu*) to be detained
empêchement [ɑ̃pɛʃmɑ̃] *m* **j'ai eu un** ~ sth had come up
empêcher [ɑ̃peʃe] <1> **I.** *vt* (*faire obstacle à, ne pas permettre*) to prevent; ~ **que qn fasse qc** (*subj*), ~ **qn de faire qc** to prevent sb from doing sth ►**n'empêche** *inf* all the same; **(il) n'empêche que c'est arrivé** it happened all the same **II.** *vpr* **je ne peux pas m'**~ **de le faire** I can't stop myself from doing it
empereur [ɑ̃pʀœʀ] *m* emperor; *v. a.* **impératrice**
empester [ɑ̃pɛste] <1> **I.** *vi* to stink **II.** *vt* **1.** (*empuantir*) to stink out **2.** (*répandre une mauvaise odeur de*) ~ **qc** to stink of sth
empêtrer [ɑ̃petʀe] <1> *vpr* **s'**~ **dans qc** to get tangled up in sth
emphase [ɑ̃faz] *f* **1.** (*force expressive*) emphasis **2.** (*grandiloquence*) pomposity
emphatique [ɑ̃fatik] *adj* **1.** (*enflé, grandiloquent*) pompous **2.** LING emphatic

empierrer [ɑ̃pjeʀe] <1> *vt* to metal

empiéter [ɑ̃pjete] <5> *vi* **1.**(*usurper, déborder dans l'espace*) ~ **sur qc** to encroach on sth **2.**(*déborder dans le temps*) to overlap

empiffrer [ɑ̃pifʀe] <1> *vpr inf* **s'~ de qc** to stuff oneself with sth

empiler [ɑ̃pile] <1> *vt, vpr* (**s'**)~ to pile up

empire [ɑ̃piʀ] *m* POL empire; **le premier/second Empire** the First/Second Empire; **le Saint Empire romain germanique** the Holy Roman Empire; **Empire britannique** British Empire ►**avoir de l'~ sur soi-même** to have control over oneself; **pas pour un ~** not for the world; **sous l'~ de la colère/terreur** in the grip of anger/terror

empirer [ɑ̃piʀe] <1> *vi* to worsen

empirique [ɑ̃piʀik] *adj* empirical; **procéder par une méthode ~** to proceed empirically

emplacement [ɑ̃plasmɑ̃] *m* **1.**(*endroit*) site **2.**(*place*) position; (*d'un tombeau*) site **3.**(*dans un parking*) space **4.**(*sur un camping*) site

emplettes [ɑ̃plɛt] *fpl* **faire des ~** to do some shopping

emploi [ɑ̃plwa] *m* **1.**(*poste*) job; **un ~ d'informaticienne** a job as a computer expert; **~ à mi-temps/à temps partiel/à plein temps** half-time/part-time/full-time job **2.** ECON **l'~** employment; **être sans ~** to be unemployed **3.**(*utilisation*) *a.* LING use; **j'en ai l'~** I have a use for it; **être d'un ~ facile/délicat** to be easy/tricky to use; **ce mot a différents ~s** the word is used in different ways ►**~ du temps** schedule; ECOLE timetable; **faire double ~** to be spare

employé(**e**) [ɑ̃plwaje] *m(f)* employee; **~ de banque/de bureau** bank/office worker; **~ de commerce** sales assistant *Brit,* sales clerk *Am;* **~ de magasin** shop worker; **~ de maison** domestic help; **~ des chemins de fer/des postes** railway/postal worker; **l'~ du gaz** the man from the gas

employer [ɑ̃plwaje] <6> **I.** *vt* **1.**(*faire travailler*) to employ **2.**(*utiliser*) *a.* LING to use; **~ du temps à qc** to spend time on sth **II.** *vpr* **1.** LING **s'~** to be used **2.**(*se consacrer*) **s'~ à faire qc** to apply oneself to doing sth

employeur, -euse [ɑ̃plwajœʀ, -jøz] *m, f* employer

empocher [ɑ̃pɔʃe] <1> *vt* (*argent*) to pocket

empoignade [ɑ̃pwaɲad] *f* (*bagarre*) brawl

empoigner [ɑ̃pwaɲe] <1> **I.** *vt* (*personne*) to grab **II.** *vpr* **s'~** to exchange blows

empoisonnant(**e**) [ɑ̃pwazɔnɑ̃, ɑ̃t] *adj inf* **1.**(*insupportable*) **être ~** to be a pain **2.**(*assommant*) dreary

empoisonnement [ɑ̃pwazɔnmɑ̃] *m* **1.**(*intoxication*) food poisoning; **~ dû à des champignons** food poisoning caused by mushrooms **2.** *sans pl* (*crime*) poisoning **3.**(*meurtre*) poisoning **4.** *gén pl, inf* (*tracas*) nuisance

empoisonner [ɑ̃pwazɔne] <1> **I.** *vt* **1.**(*intoxiquer*) to poison; **être mort empoisonné** to die of poisoning **2.**(*contenir du poison*) **être empoisonné** to be poisoned **3.**(*être venimeux*) **être empoisonné** (*propos*) to be venomous **4.**(*gâter*) **elle m'empoisonne la vie** she makes my life miserable **5.**(*empuantir*) **~ l'air** to make a stench **6.** *inf* (*embêter*) **~ qn avec qc** to drive sb mad [*o* crazy] with sth **II.** *vpr* **1.**(*s'intoxiquer*) **s'~ avec qc** to poison oneself with sth **2.** *inf* (*s'ennuyer*) **qu'est-ce qu'on s'empoisonne ici!** what a drag this is! **3.** *inf* (*se démener*) **s'~ à faire qc** to go to the trouble of doing sth

emporté(**e**) [ɑ̃pɔʀte] *adj* quick-tempered

emporter [ɑ̃pɔʀte] <1> **I.** *vt* **1.**(*prendre avec soi*) to take away; **tous les plats à ~** take-away on all dishes *Brit,* take-out on all dishes *Am* **2.**(*enlever*) to take away; (*blessé*) to carry away; **une pneumonie l'a emportée** she died of pneumonia **3.**(*transporter*) **~ qn vers qc** to take sb off to sth **4.**(*entraîner, arracher*) **~ qc** (*vent*) to carry sth off; **~ qn** (*enthousiasme, récit, rêve*) to carry sb away ►**l'~ sur qn** to beat sb; **l'~ sur qc** to prevail over; **les inconvénients l'emportent sur les avantages** the disadvantages outweigh the advantages **II.** *vpr* **s'~ contre qn/qc** to get angry with sb/sth

empoté(**e**) [ɑ̃pɔte] **I.** *adj inf* **1.**(*maladroit*) clumsy; **un garçon ~ de ses mains** a clumsy boy **2.**(*lent*) dopey **II.** *m(f) inf* **1.** clumsy oaf **2.**(*traînard*) dope

empreint(**e**) [ɑ̃pʀɛ̃, ɛ̃t] *adj* **~ de bonté, amour** full of goodness/love

empreinte [ɑ̃pʀɛ̃t] *f* **1.**(*trace*) prints; **des ~s** (**de pas**) footprints; (*d'un animal*) tracks; **~s digitales** fingerprints **2.**(*marque durable*) mark; **marquer qn/qc de son ~** to leave one's mark on sb/sth

empressé(**e**) [ɑ̃pʀese] *adj* attentive

empressement [ɑ̃pʀɛsmɑ̃] *m* attentiveness

empresser [ɑ̃pʀese] <1> *vpr* **1.**(*se hâter de*) **s'~ de** +*infin* to hasten to +*infin* **2.**(*faire preuve de zèle*) **s'~ auprès de qn** to make a fuss over sb

emprise [ɑ̃pʀiz] *f* hold; **avoir de l'~ sur qn** to have a hold over sb; **agir sous l'~ de la colère/jalousie** to act while in the grip of anger/jealousy

emprisonnement [ɑ̃pʀizɔnmɑ̃] *m* imprisonment

emprisonner [ɑ̃pʀizɔne] <1> *vt* **1.**(*incarcérer*) to imprison **2.**(*enfermer*) **~ qn/un animal dans qc** to shut sb/an animal up in sth **3.**(*serrer fermement*) to hold; (*main, bras*) to grip **4.**(*enlever toute liberté*) **~ qn/qc par qc** to trap sb/sth in sth

emprunt [ɑ̃pʀœ̃] *m* **1.**(*somme, objet*) loan; **fiche d'~** borrowing card **2.**(*emprunt public*) borrowing; **~ d'État** state borrowing; **souscrire à un ~** to take out a loan

emprunté(**e**) [ɑ̃pʀœ̃te] *adj* **1.**(*mal à l'aise*) self-conscious **2.**(*faux*) false

E

emprunter [ɑ̃pʀœ̃te] <1> I. *vi* FIN to borrow II. *vt* 1. (*se faire prêter, imiter*) to borrow 2. (*prendre: passage souterrain, autoroute*) to take

emprunteur, **-euse** [ɑ̃pʀœ̃tœʀ, -øz] *m, f* borrower

ému(e) [emy] *adj* moved; ~ **jusqu'aux larmes** moved to tears

émulation [emylasjɔ̃] *f a.* INFOR emulation; **esprit d'**~ spirit of rivalry

émuler [emyle] <1> *vt* INFOR to emulate

émulsion [emylsjɔ̃] *f* emulsion

en [ɑ̃] I. *prep* 1. (*lieu*) in; ~ **mer** at sea; **être** ~ **pleine mer** to be out at sea; ~ **bateau** in a boat; **être** ~ **5ème** to be in year 8 *Brit,* to be in the seventh grade *Am;* **elle se disait** ~ **elle-même que c'était possible** deep down she thought it was possible; **elle aime** ~ **lui sa gentillesse** what she likes about him is his kindness 2. (*direction*) to; **passer** ~ **seconde** to move into second 3. (*date, moment*) in; ~ **semaine** during the week; ~ **ce dimanche de la Pentecôte** on this day of Pentecost; **de jour** ~ **jour** from day to day; **samedi** ~ **huit** a week from Saturday 4. (*manière d'être, de faire*) **être** ~ **bonne/mauvaise santé** to be in good/bad health; **être/se mettre** ~ **colère** to be/get angry; **être** ~ **réunion/déplacement** to be in a meeting/on a trip; **être parti** ~ **voyage** to be away on a trip; ~ **deuil** in mourning; **des cerisiers** ~ **fleurs** cherry trees in blossom; **une voiture** ~ **panne** a car that has broken down; **écouter** ~ **silence** to listen in silence; **peindre qc** ~ **blanc** to paint sth white 5. (*transformation: changer, convertir*) into; (*se déguiser*) as 6. (*en tant que*) as; **il l'a traité** ~ **ami** he treated him as a friend 7. *gérondif* (*simultanéité*) ~ **sortant** on one's way out 8. *gérondif* (*condition*) by; ~ **travaillant beaucoup, tu réussiras** by working hard you'll succeed 9. *gérondif* (*concession*) while; **il lui souriait tout** ~ **la maudissant intérieurement** he smiled at her while cursing her from within 10. *gérondif* (*manière*) ~ **chantant/courant** singing/running 11. (*état, forme*) in; **du café** ~ **grains/**~ **poudre** coffee beans/instant coffee; **deux boîtes** ~ **plus/**~ **trop** two cans extra/too many 12. (*fait de*) **c'est** ~ **laine/bois** it's wool/wood 13. (*moyen de transport*) by; ~ **train/voiture** by train/car 14. (*partage, division*) in; **je coupe le gâteau** ~ **six** I'm cutting the cake in(to) six 15. (*pour indiquer le domaine*) in; ~ **économie** in economics 16. *après certains verbes* **croire** ~ **qn** to believe in sb; **avoir confiance** ~ **qn** to have confidence in sb; **espérer** ~ **des temps meilleurs** to hope for better times to come; **parler** ~ **son nom** to speak in sb's name ▸**s'**~ **aller** to go away; ~ **arrière** behind; ~ **plus, ...** moreover, ...; ~ **plus** besides; ~ **plus de ...** besides ... II. *pron* 1. *non traduit* (*pour des indéfinis, des quantités*) **as-tu un stylo? – oui, j'**~ **ai un/non, je n'**~ **ai pas** have you got a pen? – yes, I have/no I haven't; **il** ~ **sait quelque chose** he knows something about it 2. *tenant lieu de subst* **j'**~ **connais qui feraient mieux de ...** some people would do well to ... 3. (*de là*) **j'**~ **viens** I've just been there 4. (*de cela*) **on** ~ **parle** people are talking about it; **j'**~ **ai besoin** I need it; **je m'**~ **souviens** I remember that; **j'**~ **suis fier/sûr** I'm proud/sure of it; **j'**~ **conclus que ...** I conclude from this that ... 5. (*à cause de cela*) **elle** ~ **est malade** it has made her ill; **j'**~ **suis malheureux** I'm unhappy about it 6. *annonce ou reprend un subst* **j'**~ **vends, des livres** Now I sell some books!; **vous** ~ **avez, de la chance!** you're lucky all right! 7. *avec valeur de possessif* **ne jette pas cette rose, je voudrais** ~ **garder les pétales** don't throw that rose away, I want its petals

ENA [ena] *f abr de* **École nationale d'administration** *French college training senior civil servants*

énarque [enaʀk] *mf inf: graduate of the Ecole Normale d'Administration*

encablure [ɑ̃kablyʀ] *f* cable's length, *195 metre;* **à deux/quelques** ~**s de qc** not far/not too far from sth

encadré [ɑ̃kadʀe] *m* box

encadrement [ɑ̃kadʀəmɑ̃] *m* 1. (*cadre*) frame 2. (*prise en charge*) training

encadrer [ɑ̃kadʀe] <1> *vt* 1. (*mettre dans un cadre*) to frame 2. (*entourer*) to put a border around; (*annonce, éditorial*) to (put in a) box; (*visage*) to frame; (*cible*) to draw a circle around 3. (*s'occuper de*) to supervise; (*diriger*) to lead 4. MIL to straddle 5. *inf* (*dans un carambolage*) ~ **qc** to smash into sth ▸**je ne peux pas les** ~ *inf* I can't stand them

encaissé(e) [ɑ̃kese] *adj* GEO steep-sided

encaisser [ɑ̃kese] <1> I. *vi* 1. (*toucher de l'argent*) to get one's money 2. *inf* (*savoir prendre des coups*) to take it II. *vt* 1. (*percevoir*) to receive; (*chèque*) to cash 2. *inf* (*recevoir, supporter*) to take; **c'est dur à** ~ it's hard to take ▸**je ne peux pas les** ~ *inf* I can't stand them

encanailler [ɑ̃kanaje] <1> *vpr iron* **s'**~ to mix with the riff-raff

en-cas [ɑ̃ka] *m inv* snack

encastrable [ɑ̃kastʀabl] *adj* built-in

encastrer [ɑ̃kastʀe] <1> I. *vt* ~ **qc dans/sous qc** to build sth in/under sth II. *vpr* **s'**~ **dans/sous qc** to be fitted in/under sth; (*automobile*) to jam under sth

encaustique [ɑ̃kostik] *f* wax

encaustiquer [ɑ̃kostike] <1> *vt* to wax

encavage [ɑ̃kavaʒ] *m Suisse* (*action de mettre en cave des aliments*) *taking food down to the cellar*

enceinte[1] [ɑ̃sɛ̃t] *adj* **être** ~ **de qn** to be pregnant by sb; **être** ~ **de son troisième enfant** to be pregnant with one's third child; **être** ~ **de trois mois** to be three months pregnant

enceinte² [ɑ̃sɛ̃t] *f* **1.** (*fortification, rempart*) (surrounding) wall **2.** (*espace clos*) enclosure; (*d'une foire, d'un parc naturel*) area; **dans l'~ de la ville/du tribunal** within the town/the courtroom **3.** (*haut-parleur*) speaker; **~s acoustiques** speakers
encens [ɑ̃sɑ̃] *m* incense
encenser [ɑ̃sɑ̃se] <1> *vt* **1.** (*répandre de l'encens*) to incense **2.** (*louer*) to laud
encensoir [ɑ̃sɑ̃swaʀ] *m* thurible
encerclement [ɑ̃sɛʀkləmɑ̃] *m* encirclement
encercler [ɑ̃sɛʀkle] <1> *vt* **1.** (*entourer, être disposé autour de*) to surround; **des curieux encerclaient le blessé** onlookers were standing around the injured man **2.** (*cerner*) to encircle
enchaînement [ɑ̃ʃɛnmɑ̃] *m* **1.** (*succession, structure logique*) sequence **2.** (*transition*) **~ entre qc et qc** progression from one thing to another
enchaîner [ɑ̃ʃene] <1> **I.** *vt* **1.** (*attacher avec une chaîne*) **~ des personnes l'une à l'autre** to chain people to each other **2.** (*mettre bout à bout: idées*) to link up **II.** *vpr* **1.** (*s'attacher avec une chaîne*) **des personnes s'enchaînent à qc/l'une à l'autre** people chain themselves to sth/to each other **2.** (*se succéder*) **s'~** to connect **III.** *vi* (*continuer*) **~ sur qc** to carry on and talk about sth
enchanté(**e**) [ɑ̃ʃɑ̃te] *adj* **1.** (*ravi*) **être ~ de qc** to be delighted with sth; **être ~ que qn ait fait qc** to be delighted that sb has done sth **2.** (*magique*) enchanted; **la Flûte ~e de Mozart** Mozart's Magic Flute ▶**~!** delighted!; **~ de faire votre connaissance** delighted to meet you
enchantement [ɑ̃ʃɑ̃tmɑ̃] *m* **1.** (*ravissement*) delight; **être un ~** to be delightful; **être dans l'~** to be transported **2.** (*sortilège*) enchantment; **briser** [*o* **rompre**] **l'~** to break the spell; **par ~** by magic; **comme par ~** as if by magic
enchanter [ɑ̃ʃɑ̃te] <1> *vt* **1.** (*ravir*) to delight **2.** (*ensorceler*) to enchant
enchanteur, **-eresse** [ɑ̃ʃɑ̃tœʀ, (ə)ʀɛs] **I.** *adj* enchanting **II.** *m, f* wizard *m*, enchantress *f*
enchère [ɑ̃ʃɛʀ] *f gén pl* (*offre d'achat*) bid; **les ~s sont ouvertes** the bidding is open; **acheter aux ~s** to buy at auction; **mettre aux ~s** to (sell at) auction; **faire monter les ~s** to raise the bidding; *fig* to raise the stakes
enchérir [ɑ̃ʃeʀiʀ] <8> *vi* **~ sur qn/qc** to bid more than sb/sth; **~ de 1000 euros sur l'offre précédente** to offer 1000 euros more than the last bidder
enchevêtré(**e**) [ɑ̃ʃ(ə)vetʀe] *adj* (*fils*) tangled; (*pensées*) muddled; (*phrases, intrigue*) involved
enchevêtrement [ɑ̃ʃ(ə)vɛtʀəmɑ̃] *m* (*de branches, liens*) tangle; (*de pensées, phrases, d'une intrigue*) muddle; (*de ruelles*) maze
enchevêtrer [ɑ̃ʃ(ə)vetʀe] <1> *vpr* **s'~** (*branches*) to grow in a tangle; (*fils*) to get tangled; (*pensées*) to get muddled
enclave [ɑ̃klav] *f* enclave
enclencher [ɑ̃klɑ̃ʃe] <1> **I.** *vt* **1.** TECH (*vitesse*) to engage **2.** (*engager*) to set in motion **II.** *vpr* **s'~** to engage
enclin(**e**) [ɑ̃klɛ̃, in] *adj* **être ~ à qc/faire qc** to be inclined to sth/to do sth
enclore [ɑ̃klɔʀ] *vt irr, soutenu* (*entourer: haie, mur, enceinte*) to enclose; **~ son terrain d'une haie** to enclose one's land with a hedge
enclos [ɑ̃klo] *m* **1.** (*espace*) enclosure; (*pour le bétail*) pen; (*pour des chevaux*) paddock **2.** (*clôture*) wall
enclume [ɑ̃klym] *f* anvil ▶**être entre l'~ et le marteau** to be between the devil and the deep blue sea
encoche [ɑ̃kɔʃ] *f* notch; **~s d'un dictionnaire** thumb index of a dictionary; (*d'une flèche*) nock
encoignure [ɑ̃kwaɲyʀ] *f* **1.** (*angle*) corner **2.** (*meuble*) corner cupboard
encoller [ɑ̃kɔle] <1> *vt* to paste
encolure [ɑ̃kɔlyʀ] *f* **1.** (*cou: d'un animal, d'une personne*) neck; **forte ~** thick neck; **l'emporter d'une ~** (*cheval*) to win by a neck **2.** (*col: d'une robe*) neck(line) **3.** (*tour de cou*) collar size
encombrant(**e**) [ɑ̃kɔ̃bʀɑ̃, ɑ̃t] *adj* **1.** (*embarrassant*) cumbersome **2.** (*importun*) burdensome **3.** *iron* (*compromettant: personne, passé*) troublesome
encombre [ɑ̃kɔ̃bʀ] **sans ~** without incident
encombré(**e**) [ɑ̃kɔ̃bʀe] *adj* **1.** (*embouteillé: route*) congested **2.** (*trop plein: pièce, table*) cluttered **3.** (*surchargé: lignes téléphoniques*) busy
encombrement [ɑ̃kɔ̃bʀəmɑ̃] *m* **1.** (*sans passage possible: d'une rue*) congestion; (*des lignes téléphoniques*) overloading **2.** (*embouteillage*) traffic jam
encombrer [ɑ̃kɔ̃bʀe] <1> **I.** *vt* **1.** (*bloquer: passage*) to obstruct **2.** (*s'amonceler sur*) to clutter up **3.** (*surcharger*) to overload **II.** *vpr* (*s'embarrasser de*) **ne pas s'~ de qn/qc** not to burden oneself with sb/sth
encontre [ɑ̃kɔ̃tʀ] **aller à l'~ de qc** to run counter to sth
encorder [ɑ̃kɔʀde] <1> *vpr* **s'~** to rope oneself up; **des personnes s'encordent** people rope themselves together
encore [ɑ̃kɔʀ] **I.** *adv* **1.** (*continuation*) still; **le chômage augmente ~** unemployment is still rising; **en être ~ à qc** to still be at the stage of sth; **hier/ce matin ~** just yesterday/this morning **2.** (*répétition*) again; **je peux essayer ~ une fois?** can I try again?; **voulez-vous ~ une tasse de thé?** would you like another cup of tea?; **c'est ~ de ma faute** it's my fault again; **c'est ~ moi!** it's me again! **3.** + *nég* **pas ~/~ pas** not yet; **elle n'est ~ jamais partie** she has still never gone away **4.** + *comp*

E

~ **mieux/moins/plus** even better/less/more; **il aime ~ mieux qc** he likes sth even more **5.** (*renforcement*) **non seulement ..., mais ~** not only ..., but besides; ~ **et toujours** as always; **mais ~?** and then what? **6.** (*objection*) ~ **faut-il le savoir!** you've got to know that though! **7.** (*restriction*) ~ **heureux qu'elle l'ait fait** thank goodness she did it; **..., et ~!** ..., and even then!; **si ~ on avait son adresse!** if we only had her address ►**quoi** ~**?** (*qu'est-ce qu'il y a?*) what now?; (*pour ajouter qc*) what else?; **et puis quoi ~!** whatever next! **II.** *conj* **il acceptera, ~ que, avec lui, on ne sait jamais** *inf* he'll agree, although you never know with him

encornet [ãkɔʀnɛ] *m* squid

encourageant(e) [ãkuʀaʒã, ãt] *adj* encouraging; **voilà qui est ~!** *iron* that's encouraging!

encouragement [ãkuʀaʒmã] *m* **1.** encouragement **2.** ECOLE praise

encourager [ãkuʀaʒe] <2a> *vt* to encourage; ~ **qn d'un regard** to give sb an encouraging look; ~ **un joueur en criant** to cheer a player on

encourir [ãkuʀiʀ] *vt irr* **1.** ~ **un châtiment/une amende** to incur a punishment/a fine; ~ **une peine** to incur a penalty **2.** *soutenu* ~ **une punition/des reproches** to bring a punishment/reproach on oneself; ~ **une responsabilité** to incur a responsibility

encouru(e) [ãkuʀy] *part passé de* **encourir**

encrasser [ãkʀase] <1> **I.** *vt* to soil; (*suie, fumée*) to soot up; (*calcaire*) to scale up **II.** *vpr* **s'~** to get dirty; (*chaudière*) to get scaled up; (*cheminée*) to clog up with soot

encre [ãkʀ] *f* (*pour écrire*) ink; ~ **sympathique** invisible ink; **à l'~** in ink; ~ **de Chine** Indian ink; ~ **d'imprimerie** printer's ink; ~ **en poudre** toner ►**il a fait couler de l'~** to cause a lot of ink to flow

encrier [ãkʀije] *m* inkwell

encroûter [ãkʀute] <1> **I.** *vt* **1.** (*couvrir d'une croûte*) to encrust **2.** (*abêtir*) ~ **qn** to get sb into rut; **rien ne nous encroûte plus que la paresse** there's nothing like laziness for getting you into a rut **II.** *vpr* **1.** TECH **s'~** (*chaudière*) to fur up **2.** (*s'abêtir*) **s'~** to get into a rut; **s'~ dans ses habitudes** to get set in one's ways; **ils se sont encroûtés dans leur confort** their comfortable lifestyle's got them into a rut

enculé [ãkyle] *m vulg* stupid bastard

enculer [ãkyle] <1> *vt vulg* to bugger; **se faire ~** to be buggered

encyclopédie [ãsiklɔpedi] *f* encyclopedia

encyclopédique [ãsiklɔpedik] *adj* encyclopedic

endémique [ãdemik] *adj a.* MED endemic; **être à l'état ~** to be endemic

endetté(e) [ãdete] *adj* ~ **de 2000 euros** 2000 euros in debt

endettement [ãdɛtmã] *m* indebtedness; ~ **public** national debt

endetter [ãdete] <1> **I.** *vt* ~ **qn** to get sb into debt **II.** *vpr* **s'~** to get into debt; **s'~ de 2000 euros auprès de qn** to borrow 2000 euros from sb

endeuiller [ãdœje] <1> *vt* (*personne, famille, pays*) to plunge into mourning; (*épreuve sportive, manifestation*) to cast a shadow over

endiablé(e) [ãdjɑble] *adj* (*danse, rythme*) frenzied; (*vitalité*) boisterous

endiguer [ãdige] <1> *vt* **1.** to dyke **2.** *fig* (*violence, inflation, chômage*) to check; (*foule, invasion*) to hold back

endimanché(e) [ãdimãʃe] *adj* in one's Sunday best

endimancher [ãdimãʃe] <1> *vpr* **s'~** to put on one's Sunday best

endive [ãdiv] *f* endive, chicory *no pl*

endoctriner [ãdɔktʀine] <1> *vt* to indoctrinate

endolori(e) [ãdɔlɔʀi] *adj* painful; (*personne*) in pain; **j'ai le bras/dos ~** my arm/back is aching

endommager [ãdɔmaʒe] <2a> *vt* to damage

endormant(e) [ãdɔʀmã, ãt] *adj* dreary

endormi(e) [ãdɔʀmi] **I.** *adj* **1.** (*opp: éveillé*) asleep; (*passion*) dormant **2.** (*engourdi*) **j'ai la main/jambe ~e** my hand/leg has gone to sleep **3.** *inf* (*apathique: personne, esprit*) sluggish; (*regard*) sleepy **II.** *m(f) inf* sluggard

endormir [ãdɔʀmiʀ] *irr* **I.** *vt* **1.** (*faire dormir, ennuyer*) ~ **qn** to put sb to sleep **2.** (*anesthésier*) ~ **qn** to put sb under **3.** (*faire disparaître: douleur*) to deaden; (*soupçons*) to lull; (*vigilance*) to dupe **4.** (*tromper*) ~ **qn avec qc** to use sth to make sb drop their guard **II.** *vpr* **s'~ 1.** (*s'assoupir*) to fall asleep **2.** (*devenir très calme: ville*) to go to sleep **3.** (*s'atténuer: sensation*) to die down; (*faculté, sens*) to go to sleep

endossement [ãdosmã] *m* endorsement

endosser [ãdose] <1> *vt* (*responsabilité*) to take on; ~ **les conséquences** to take responsibility for the consequences; **faire ~ qc à qn** to pass the responsibility for sth on to sb else

endroit¹ [ãdʀwa] *m* place; **un bon ~ pour** *+infin* a good place to *+infin;* **à plusieurs ~s** in several places; **par ~s** in places; **un ~ peu sûr** an unsafe place ►~ **sensible** a sensitive spot

endroit² [ãdʀwa] *m* (*opp: envers, tapis: d'un vêtement*) right side; **être à l'~** (*vêtement*) to be the right way out; (*feuille*) to be the right way up; **tricoter qc à l'~** to knit sth

enduire [ãdɥiʀ] *irr* **I.** *vt* ~ **de qc** to coat with sth; ~ **le papier peint de colle** to paste the wallpaper **II.** *vpr* **s'~ de qc** to cover oneself with sth; **s'~ de crème** to smother oneself with cream

enduit [ãdɥi] *m* coating

endurance [ãdyʀãs] *f* endurance

endurant(e) [ãdyʀã, ãt] *adj* tough

endurci(e) [ãdyʀsi] *adj* **1.** (*insensible: cœur,*

criminel) hardened; (*personne*) hard-hearted **2.** (*invétéré: célibataire*) confirmed; (*fumeur*) hardened; (*joueur*) seasoned **3.** (*résistant*) ~ **au froid/aux privations** inured to cold/privation

endurcir [ɑ̃dyʀsiʀ] <8> **I.** *vt* **1.** (*physiquement*) ~ **qn à qc** to inure sb to sth **2.** (*moralement*) to harden **II.** *vpr* **1.** (*physiquement*) **s'~ à qc** to inure oneself to sth **2.** (*moralement*) **s'~** to harden one's heart; **s'~ contre qn/qc** to harden one's heart against sb/sth

endurer [ɑ̃dyʀe] <1> *vt* (*insulte*) to bear; (*privations*) to endure

énergétique [enɛʀʒetik] *adj* **1.** ECON **les besoins ~s** energy needs **2.** ANAT **valeur ~** energy value; **aliment ~** energy-giving food

énergie [enɛʀʒi] *f* energy; (*d'un style*) vigour *Brit,* vigor *Am;* **avec ~** vigorously; **plein d'~** vigorous; **avoir de l'~ à revendre** to be bursting with energy; **forme d'~** energy source

énergique [enɛʀʒik] *adj* energetic

énergiquement [enɛʀʒikmɑ̃] *adv* energetically

énergumène [enɛʀgymɛn] *m inf* fanatic

énervant(e) [enɛʀvɑ̃, ɑ̃t] *adj* irritating; (*travail, attente*) annoying

énervé(e) [enɛʀve] *adj* **1.** (*agacé*) irritated **2.** (*excité*) restless **3.** (*nerveux*) edgy

énervement [enɛʀvəmɑ̃] *m* **1.** (*agacement*) irritation **2.** (*surexcitation*) restlessness **3.** (*nervosité*) edginess

énerver [enɛʀve] <1> **I.** *vt* **1.** (*agacer*) to irritate **2.** (*exciter*) to make restless **II.** *vpr* **s'~ après qn/qc** to get annoyed at sb/sth; **ne nous énervons pas!** let's stay calm!

enfance [ɑ̃fɑ̃s] *f* **1.** (*période*) childhood; **petite ~** infancy; **première ~** early childhood; **dès la petite ~** from his infancy **2.** *sans pl* (*les enfants*) children ►**(re)tomber en ~** to fall into one's second childhood

enfant [ɑ̃fɑ̃] *mf* **1.** (*garçon, fille*) child; **~ trouvé** foundling; **faire un ~** to have a child; **~ unique** only child **2.** *pl* (*descendants*) children **3.** (*par rapport à l'origine*) **c'est un ~ de la ville** he's a son of the city ►**~ de <u>chœur</u>** (*qui chante*) choirboy; (*à la messe*) altar boy; **ne pas être un ~ de chœur** *fig* to be no angel; **~ du premier/deuxième <u>lit</u>** child by one's first/second marriage; **être <u>bon</u> ~** good-natured; (*public*) friendly; **~ <u>gâté</u>/<u>pourri</u>** spoilt child; **~ <u>prodige</u>** prodigy; **l'~ <u>prodigue</u>** the prodigal son; **il n'y <u>a</u> plus d'~s!** children are so grown-up these days!; **les ~s s'<u>amusent</u>!** kids will have their fun!; **ne <u>fais</u>/<u>faites</u> pas l'~!** don't be childish!

enfantillage [ɑ̃fɑ̃tijaʒ] *m* childish nonsense *no pl*

enfantin(e) [ɑ̃fɑ̃tɛ̃, in] *adj* **1.** (*relatif à l'enfant: rires*) childish; **chanson ~e** children's song **2.** (*simple*) childishly simple

enfer [ɑ̃fɛʀ] *m* **1.** (*situation*) *a.* REL hell; **c'est l'~** it's hell on earth **2.** *pl* HIST underworld ►**<u>d'</u>~** brilliant; **avoir un look d'~** *inf* to look fabulous; **bruit d'~** hell of a commotion

enfermer [ɑ̃fɛʀme] <1> **I.** *vt* **1.** (*mettre dans un lieu fermé: enfant, prisonnier*) to lock up; (*animal*) to pen up; **~ de l'argent** to lock some money away **2.** (*maintenir*) **~ qn/qc dans le rôle de ...** to confine sb/sth in the role of ...; **être enfermé dans ses contradictions** to be trapped in one's own contradictions **3.** (*entourer*) to enclose ►**il est <u>bon</u> à ~** he should be locked up; **être enfermé <u>dehors</u>** *inf* to be locked out; **être/rester enfermé <u>chez</u> soi** to be/stay shut away at home **II.** *vpr* **1.** (*s'isoler*) **s'~ dans qc** to shut oneself away in sth **2.** (*se cantonner*) **s'~ dans une attitude/une position** to stick rigidly to an attitude/a position; **s'~ dans le silence** to retreat into silence

enferrer [ɑ̃feʀe] <1> *vpr* **s'~ dans des mensonges** to ensnare oneself in one's own lies

enfiévrer [ɑ̃fjevʀe] <5> **I.** *vt* (*exalter*) **~ qn** to stir sb up **II.** *vpr* **s'~ pour qc** to get wildly excited about sth

enfilade [ɑ̃filad] *f* (*de couloirs, portes*) succession; **~ de pièces** string of rooms; **phrases en ~** a long string of phrases ►**<u>prendre</u> des personnes/qc en ~** (*tireurs*) to rake; **tir <u>d'</u>~** raking

enfiler [ɑ̃file] <1> **I.** *vt* **1.** (*traverser par un fil: aiguille, perles*) to thread **2.** (*passer: pullover*) to pull on **II.** *vpr* **1.** *inf* (*s'envoyer*) **s'~ une boisson** to knock back a drink **2.** *inf* (*se taper*) **s'~ tout le travail** to be stuck with all the work, to be lumbered with all the work *Brit*

enfin [ɑ̃fɛ̃] *adv* **1.** (*fin d'une attente*) at last **2.** (*fin d'une énumération*) finally **3.** (*pour corriger ou préciser*) anyway; **elle est jolie, ~, à mon sens** she's nice-looking, I think so anyway **4.** (*marquant la gêne*) well; **tu as fait ce travail? – ben oui ... ~ non** have you done the job? – er yes ..., well, no **5.** (*bref*) after all **6.** (*pour clore la discussion*) **~, ...** anyway, ... **7.** (*tout de même*) really; **comment, tu ne sais pas la réponse! ~, c'est facile!** what, you don't know the answer! really, it's easy! **8.** (*marque l'irritation*) come on; **~, à quoi tu penses?** come on, what are you thinking about? ►**~ <u>bref</u>** not to waste words; **~ <u>passons</u>** anyway, let's move on; **~ <u>voilà</u>, je n'en sais pas plus** so there you are, I don't know any more than that; **ce n'est certes pas beaucoup, <u>mais</u> ~, c'est toujours ça** it's not much, but it's something anyway

enflammé(e) [ɑ̃flame] *adj* **1.** (*passionné: paroles*) impassioned; (*nature*) hot-blooded **2.** MED inflamed

enflammer [ɑ̃flame] <1> **I.** *vt* **1.** (*mettre le feu à*) to set on fire **2.** (*exalter*) to set alight; (*imagination*) to fire **II.** *vpr* **1.** (*prendre feu*) **s'~** to catch fire **2.** (*s'animer: personne*) to come alive

enflé(e) [ɑ̃fle] *adj* MED swollen

enfler [ɑ̃fle] <1> **I.** *vt* (*faire augmenter:*

E

rivière) to swell; (*voix*) to raise; ~ **les doigts** to make the finger's swell up **II.** *vi, vpr* (**s'**)~ to swell up; **à cause de la cortisone, son corps a tendance à** ~ with the cortisone, his body tends to swell up

enflure [ɑ̃flyʀ] *f* **1.** MED swelling **2.** (*forme emphatique: du style*) pompousness **3.** *inf* (*enflé*) dummy

enfoiré [ɑ̃fwaʀe] *m vulg* dirty bastard, (great) cunt *Brit*

enfoncé(**e**) [ɑ̃fɔ̃se] *adj* (*yeux*) sunken

enfoncement [ɑ̃fɔ̃smɑ̃] *m* (*niche, creux: d'une pièce*) indentation; (*d'une falaise*) recess

enfoncer [ɑ̃fɔ̃se] <2> **I.** *vt* **1.** (*planter: clou*) to knock in; (*punaise*) to press in; (*couteau*) to push in; (*coude*) to dig in **2.** (*mettre*) ~ **ses mains dans qc** to put one's hands down into sth; ~ **son chapeau sur ses yeux** to push one's hat down over one's eyes **3.** (*briser en poussant: porte*) to break down **4.** (*aggraver la situation de*) ~ **qn dans la dépendance** to push sb further into dependence **5.** *inf* (*laisser se perdre*) to crush; (*candidat*) to destroy **II.** *vi* ~ **dans qc** to sink into sth **III.** *vpr* **1.** (*aller vers le fond*) **s'**~ **dans la neige/les sables mouvants** to sink into the snow/the quicksand; **s'**~ **dans un liquide** to sink down in a liquid **2.** (*se creuser*) **s'**~ (*mur, maison*) to subside; (*sol, matelas*) to sink **3.** (*se planter*) **s'**~ **une aiguille dans le bras** to stick a needle into one's arm **4.** (*pénétrer*) **s'**~ **dans qc** (*vis*) to work its way into sth **5.** (*s'engager*) **s'**~ **dans l'obscurité** to plunge into the darkness **6.** (*s'installer au fond*) **s'**~ **dans un fauteuil** to sink into an armchair **7.** *inf* (*se perdre*) **s'**~ to get oneself into more trouble

enfoui(**e**) [ɑ̃fwi] **I.** *part passé de* **enfouir** **II.** *adj* **1.** (*recouvert*) ~ **dans/sous qc** buried in/under sth **2.** (*caché: village*) tucked away

enfouir [ɑ̃fwiʀ] <8> **I.** *vt* (*mettre en terre, cacher*) to bury **II.** *vpr* **1.** (*se blottir*) **s'**~ **sous ses couvertures** to snuggle down under the covers **2.** (*se réfugier*) **s'**~ **dans un trou/terrier** to dive into a hole/burrow

enfourcher [ɑ̃fuʀʃe] <1> *vt* (*cheval, vélo*) to mount; (*chaise*) to sit down astride

enfourner [ɑ̃fuʀne] <1> *vt* **1.** (*mettre au four*) to put in the oven **2.** *inf* (*ingurgiter*) to put away

enfreindre [ɑ̃fʀɛ̃dʀ] *vt irr* to infringe

enfuir [ɑ̃fɥiʀ] *vpr irr* (*fuir*) **s'**~ to run away

enfumé(**e**) [ɑ̃fyme] *adj* smoky

enfumer [ɑ̃fyme] <1> *vt* **1.** (*emplir de fumée: pièce*) to fill with smoke **2.** (*incommoder par la fumée*) ~ **qn** to smoke sb out

engagé(**e**) [ɑ̃gaʒe] **I.** *adj* ~ **dans qc** committed to sth **II.** *m(f)* **1.** MIL volunteer **2.** SPORT entrants

engageant(**e**) [ɑ̃gaʒɑ̃, ɑ̃t] *adj* (*aspect, avenir*) inviting; (*paroles*) winning; (*mine*) appealing; (*sourire*) engaging

engagement [ɑ̃gaʒmɑ̃] *m* **1.** (*promesse, dépense*) a. POL commitment **2.** (*embauche*) taking on **3.** (*bataille*) engagement **4.** THEAT, CINE contract **5.** SPORT (*coup d'envoi*) kickoff; (*inscription*) entry ►**sans** ~ **de votre part** with no obligation

engager [ɑ̃gaʒe] <2a> **I.** *vt* **1.** (*mettre en jeu: parole*) to give; (*honneur, vie*) to put at stake; (*responsabilité*) to accept **2.** (*lier*) to commit **3.** (*embaucher: représentant*) to take on, to hire *Am;* (*comédien*) to engage **4.** (*commencer: débat*) to open; ~ **la bataille** to give battle **5.** (*faire prendre une direction à*) **être mal engagé** to be badly positioned **II.** *vpr* **1.** (*promettre*) **s'**~ **à** +*infin* to undertake to +*infin;* **s'**~ **vis-à-vis de la Constitution** to make a constitutional commitment; **s'**~ **sur une question** to take up a position on an issue **2.** (*louer ses services*) **être prêt à s'**~ **comme n'importe quoi** to be ready to take on any job; **s'**~ MIL to volunteer; **s'**~ **dans la marine** to join the navy **3.** (*pénétrer*) **s'**~ **dans une rue** to enter a street **4.** (*se lancer*) **s'**~ **dans qc** to get involved in sth **5.** (*prendre position*) **s'**~ **dans la lutte contre qc** to get involved in the struggle against sth **6.** (*commencer*) **s'**~ (*processus, négociation*) to get under way

engelure [ɑ̃ʒlyʀ] *f* chilblain

engendrer [ɑ̃ʒɑ̃dʀe] <1> *vt* **1.** (*donner naissance à*) to father **2.** (*avoir pour effet*) to create; GEOM (*sphère, cylindre*) to generate

engin [ɑ̃ʒɛ̃] *m* **1.** *inf* (*machin*) thingumajig **2.** TECH machine **3.** MIL weaponry; (*de guerre*) engine; ~ **atomique** atomic device; ~ **spatial** spacecraft **4.** *inf* (*objet encombrant*) contraption **5.** (*véhicule*) heavy vehicle

englober [ɑ̃glɔbe] <1> *vt* to encompass

engloutir [ɑ̃glutiʀ] <8> **I.** *vi* to devour **II.** *vt* **1.** (*dévorer*) to wolf down **2.** (*dilapider: personne*) to run through; (*entreprise*) to swallow up; ~ **sa fortune dans qc** to sink one's fortune into sth **3.** (*faire disparaître: inondation, vagues, brume*) to swallow up; (*éruption*) to engulf **III.** *vpr* **s'être englouti dans la mer** to be swallowed up by the sea

engoncer [ɑ̃gɔ̃se] <2> *vt* (*vêtement*) to restrict; **il a l'air engoncé dans cette veste** (*personne*) that jacket looks too tight on him; **son cou est engoncé là-dedans** it's strangling his neck

engorger [ɑ̃gɔʀʒe] <2a> **I.** *vt* (*conduit, tuyau*) to block; (*route*) to congest; (*marché*) to glut; MED to engorge **II.** *vpr* **s'**~ (*tuyau*) to get blocked; (*bronches*) to get congested

engouement [ɑ̃gumɑ̃] *m* infatuation

engouffrer [ɑ̃gufʀe] <1> **I.** *vt* **1.** (*entraîner: tempête*) to engulf **2.** *inf* (*dévorer*) to wolf down **3.** (*dilapider*) ~ **de l'argent dans qc** to sink money into sth **II.** *vpr* **elles s'engouffrèrent dans le couloir** they plunged into the corridor

engourdi(**e**) [ɑ̃guʀdi] *adj* (*doigts*) numb; (*esprit*) sluggish

engourdir [ɑ̃guʀdiʀ] <8> **I.** *vt* **1.** (*ankyloser:

doigts, mains) to numb **2.** *(affaiblir: personne)* to make drowsy; *(volonté, esprit)* to numb **II.** *vpr* **s'~ 1.** *(s'ankyloser)* to go numb; *(bras)* to go to sleep **2.** *(s'affaiblir: personne)* to become drowsy; *(esprit, facultés, sentiment)* to be numbed

engourdissement [ɑ̃guʀdismɑ̃] *m* **1.** *(ankylose)* numbness **2.** *(torpeur)* drowsiness

engrais [ɑ̃gʀɛ] *m* fertilizer

engraisser [ɑ̃gʀese] <1> **I.** *vt* **1.** *(rendre plus gras)* to fatten **2.** *(fertiliser)* to fertilize **II.** *vi* to fatten up **III.** *vpr* **s'~ de qc** to grow fat on sth

engrenage [ɑ̃gʀənaʒ] *m* gears *pl;* **~ de la violence** the (downward) spiral of violence ►**être pris dans un/l'~** to be caught in a downward spiral

engrosser [ɑ̃gʀose] <1> *vt vulg* **~ qn** to make [*o* get] sb pregnant; **se faire ~ par qn** to get pregnant by sb

engueulade [ɑ̃gœlad] *f inf* *(blâme)* bawling out; *(dispute)* row, bawl; **avoir une ~ avec qn** to have a shouting match with sb

engueuler [ɑ̃gœle] <1> **I.** *vt inf* to bawl out **II.** *vpr inf* **1.** *(se crier dessus)* **s'~** to have a shouting match **2.** *(se disputer)* **s'~ avec qn** to have a row

enhardir [ɑ̃aʀdiʀ] <8> **I.** *vt* **~ qn** to give sb courage; **~ qn à** *+infin* to give sb the courage to *+infin* **II.** *vpr* **s'~** to get up one's courage; **s'~ à poser une question/sortir seul** to get [*o* screw] up one's courage to ask a question/go out on one's own

énième [ɛnjɛm] *adj* **le/la ~** the umpteenth; **pour la ~ fois** for the umpteenth time

énigmatique [enigmatik] *adj* enigmatic

énigme [enigm] *f* riddle

enivrant(e) [ɑ̃nivʀɑ̃, ɑ̃t] *adj* intoxicating; *(parfum)* heady

enivrer [ɑ̃nivʀe] <1> *vpr* **1.** *(se soûler)* **s'~** to get drunk **2.** *fig* **s'~ de qc** to be intoxicated by sth

enjambée [ɑ̃ʒɑ̃be] *f* stride

enjamber [ɑ̃ʒɑ̃be] <1> *vt* *(franchir: mur)* to straddle; **~ un fossé** to stride over a ditch

enjeu [ɑ̃ʒø] <x> *m* **1.** *(argent)* stake **2.** *fig* **être l'~ de qc** to be at stake in sth

enjôler [ɑ̃ʒole] <1> *vt* **~ qn par** [*o* **avec**] **qc** to cajole sb with sth

enjôleur, -euse [ɑ̃ʒolœʀ, -øz] **I.** *adj* wheedling **II.** *m, f* wheedler

enjoliver [ɑ̃ʒɔlive] <1> *vt* **1.** *(orner)* to adorn **2.** *(broder: texte)* to embroider

enjoliveur [ɑ̃ʒɔlivœʀ] *m* hubcap

enjoué(e) [ɑ̃ʒwe] *adj* cheerful; **être d'un caractère ~** to be a cheerful type

enlacer [ɑ̃lase] <2> **I.** *vt* to embrace **II.** *vpr* **1.** *(s'étreindre)* **s'~** to embrace **2.** *(entourer)* **s'~ autour de qc** to twine around sth

enlaidir [ɑ̃lediʀ] <8> **I.** *vi* *(devenir laid)* to become ugly **II.** *vt* *(rendre laid: personne)* to make ugly; *(paysage)* to disfigure

enlèvement [ɑ̃lɛvmɑ̃] *m* abduction

enlever [ɑ̃lve] <4> **I.** *vt* **1.** *(déplacer de par-dessus)* to take off; *(débarrasser)* to take away; **~ les draps d'un lit** to take the sheets off a bed; **enlève tes mains de tes poches!** take your hands out of your pockets! **2.** *(faire disparaître: tache)* to remove; *(mot)* to cut out **3.** *(ôter)* **~ l'envie/le goût à qn de** *+infin* to put sb off wanting to *+infin;* **~ la garde des enfants à qn** to take sb's children away from them **4.** *(retirer: chapeau, montre, vêtement)* to take off **5.** *(kidnapper)* to abduct **II.** *vpr* **s'~ 1.** *(disparaître: tache)* to go **2.** *(se détacher)* to come off **3.** *inf* *(se pousser)* **enlève-toi de là!** clear off!

enliser [ɑ̃lize] <1> *vpr* **s'~ 1.** *(s'enfoncer)* to sink **2.** *(stagner)* to get bogged down

enluminure [ɑ̃lyminyʀ] *f* illumination

enneigé(e) [ɑ̃neʒe] *adj* snow-covered; *(village, voiture)* snowed in

enneigement [ɑ̃nɛʒmɑ̃] *m* snowfall; **les conditions d'~** snow conditions

ennemi(e) [en(ə)mi] **I.** *adj* enemy; *(frères)* rival **II.** *m(f)* enemy; **~ public numéro un** public enemy number one; **~ héréditaire/juré** traditional/sworn enemy ►**passer à l'~** to go over to the enemy

ennoblir [ɑ̃nɔbliʀ] <8> *vt* to ennoble

ennui [ɑ̃nɥi] *m* **1.** *(désœuvrement)* boredom; **tromper son ~** to stave off boredom **2.** *(lassitude)* ennui **3.** *souvent pl* *(problème)* trouble ►**l'~, c'est que ...** the problem is that ...

ennuyant(e) [ɑ̃nɥijɑ̃, ɑ̃t] *adj* *Québec* *(ennuyeux(-euse))* boring

ennuyé(e) [ɑ̃nɥije] *adj* bothered; **être bien ~** to feel really awkward; *(avoir un problème)* to be in a real mess; **être ~ de qc** to feel very bad about sth; **il est ~ de devoir le faire** it bothers him to have to do it; **je suis ~ qu'elle le fasse** *(subj)* I'm bothered by her doing it

ennuyer [ɑ̃nɥije] <6> **I.** *vt* **1.** *(lasser)* to bore **2.** *(être peu attrayant)* **~ qn** to be a nuisance to sb **3.** *(être gênant)* **ça m'ennuie de devoir le faire** I bothers me to have to do it **4.** *(irriter)* **~ qn avec qc** to trouble sb with sth **5.** *(déplaire)* to annoy **II.** *vpr* **s'~** to be bored

ennuyeux, -euse [ɑ̃nɥijø, -jøz] *adj* **1.** *(lassant)* boring; **~ à mourir** deadly boring **2.** *(contrariant)* bothersome

énoncé [enɔ̃se] *m* **1.** wording; **l'~ du jugement** the reading of the verdict **2.** LING utterance

énoncer [enɔ̃se] <2> **I.** *vt* *(exposer)* to express; *(faits, vérité)* to set out **II.** *vpr* **s'~ clairement** to be clearly expressed

enorgueillir [ɑ̃nɔʀgœjiʀ] <8> *vpr* **s'~ de qc/de faire qc** to be proud of sth/doing sth

énorme [enɔʀm] *adj* **1.** *(très gros)* enormous **2.** *(incroyable)* tremendous

énormément [enɔʀmemɑ̃] *adv* *(difficile, riche)* tremendously; *(aimer, boire)* an awful lot; **~ d'argent/de gens** an awful lot of money/people

E

énormité [enɔʀmite] *f* **1.** (*propos extravagant*) enormity **2.** (*ineptie*) outrageous comment **3.** (*grosse faute*) blunder

enquête [ɑ̃kɛt] *f* **1.** (*étude*) ~ **sur qc** survey on sth **2.** (*sondage d'opinions*) survey **3.** ADMIN, JUR inquiry; **ouvrir une** ~ to open an inquiry

enquêter [ɑ̃kete] <1> *vi* **1.** (*s'informer*) *a.* ADMIN, JUR ~ **sur qn/qc** to investigate sb/sth; **la police va** ~ **sur qc** the police are going to investigate sth **2.** (*faire une enquête, un sondage*) *a.* COM, SOCIOL ~ **sur qc** to conduct a survey on sth

enquêteur, **-euse** [ɑ̃kɛtœʀ, -øz] *m, f* (*policier*) investigating officer

enquiquinant(**e**) [ɑ̃kikinɑ̃, ɑ̃t] *adj inf* **être** ~ to be a pain

enquiquiner [ɑ̃kikine] <1> **I.** *vt inf* (*importuner*) ~ **qn avec qc** to pester sb with sth **II.** *vpr inf* **1.** (*s'ennuyer*) **s'**~ to be bored **2.** (*se donner du mal*) **s'**~ **avec qc/à** +*infin* to put oneself out over sth/to +*infin*

enquiquineur, **-euse** [ɑ̃kikinœʀ, -øz] *m, f inf* pain

enragé(**e**) [ɑ̃ʀaʒe] **I.** *adj* **1.** (*atteint de la rage*) rabid **2.** (*passionné: chasseur, joueur*) fanatical **3.** (*furieux*) livid **II.** *m(f)* fanatic; **c'est un** ~ **du jeu/de la lecture** he's addicted to gambling/reading; **c'est une** ~**e de la voiture/du football** she's a car/football fanatic

enrager [ɑ̃ʀaʒe] <2a> *vi* to be livid

enrayer [ɑ̃ʀeje] <7> **I.** *vt* **1.** (*juguler: chômage, hausse des prix, épidémie, maladie*) to check **2.** (*stopper*) to stop **II.** *vpr* **s'**~ to jam

enregistrement [ɑ̃ʀ(ə)ʒistʀəmɑ̃] *m* **1.** CINE, TV recording **2.** INFOR (*action*) logging; (*document*) record **3.** AUTO registration

enregistrer [ɑ̃ʀ(ə)ʒistʀe] <1> **I.** *vt* **1.** CINE, TV to record; ~ **sur cassette** to record on a cassette **2.** (*mémoriser*) to register **3.** (*noter par écrit: déclaration*) to register; (*commande*) to take; ~ **qc dans qc** to record sth in sth **4.** AUTO to register; **faire** ~ **ses bagages** to check in one's luggage **5.** (*constater: phénomène*) to show; ~ **une évolution rapide** to show rapid growth **6.** INFOR to save; ~ **sous ...** to save as ... **II.** *vi* CINE, TV, INFOR to record

enrhumer [ɑ̃ʀyme] <1> **I.** *vt* **être enrhumé** to have a cold **II.** *vpr* **s'**~ to catch a cold

enrichi(**e**) [ɑ̃ʀiʃi] *adj* **personne** ~**e** nouveau riche

enrichir [ɑ̃ʀiʃiʀ] <8> **I.** *vt* to enrich **II.** *vpr* **s'**~ **de qc** **1.** (*devenir riche*) to get rich with sth **2.** (*s'améliorer, augmenter*) to be enriched with sth

enrichissant(**e**) [ɑ̃ʀiʃisɑ̃, ɑ̃t] *adj* enriching

enrichissement [ɑ̃ʀiʃismɑ̃] *m* enrichment

enrobé(**e**) [ɑ̃ʀɔbe] *adj inf* plump

enrôler [ɑ̃ʀole] <1> **I.** *vt* **1.** (*recruter*) ~ **qn dans qc** to recruit sb into sth **2.** MIL to enlist **II.** *vpr* **s'**~ **dans qc** to join sth

enroué(**e**) [ɑ̃ʀwe] *adj* hoarse

enrouler [ɑ̃ʀule] <1> **I.** *vt* (*câble*) to coil **II.** *vpr* **s'**~ **autour de/sur qc** to wind around/on sth; **s'**~ **sur soi-même** (*chat*) to curl up

ensabler [ɑ̃sɑble] <1> *vpr* (*s'échouer*) **s'**~ to get stuck in the sand

ensanglanté(**e**) [ɑ̃sɑ̃glɑ̃te] *adj* bloody; (*vêtement*) bloodstained

ensanglanter [ɑ̃sɑ̃glɑ̃te] <1> *vt* to bloody; (*vêtement*) to stain with blood

enseignant(**e**) [ɑ̃sɛɲɑ̃, ɑ̃t] **I.** *adj* **le corps** ~ teachers *pl;* **dans le milieu** ~ among teachers **II.** *m(f)* teacher

enseigne [ɑ̃sɛɲ] *f* sign

enseignement [ɑ̃sɛɲ(ə)mɑ̃] *m* **1.** (*activité, profession*) teaching; **l'**~ **des langues vivantes** modern language teaching **2.** (*institution*) education; ~ **laïque** non-religious education; ~ **obligatoire** compulsory education; ~ **public** state education *Brit,* public education *Am;* ~ **secondaire/supérieur/technique/universitaire** secondary/higher/technical/university education **3.** (*leçon*) lesson; **tirer un** ~ **de qc** to learn a lesson from sth

enseigner [ɑ̃seɲe] <1> *vt* to teach

ensemble [ɑ̃sɑ̃bl] **I.** *adv* together; **tous** ~ all together ►<u>**aller**</u> **bien/mal** ~ to go well/badly together; **aller** ~ to match **II.** *m* **1.** (*totalité*) **l'**~ **du personnel/des questions** all the staff/questions **2.** (*unité*) whole **3.** (*groupement*) ~ **de lois** set of laws; ~ **de bâtiments/d'habitations** building/housing scheme **4.** MUS ensemble **5.** MAT set **6.** (*vêtement*) outfit **7.** (*groupe d'habitations*) **grand** ~ estate ►**impression/vue** <u>**d'**</u>~ overall impression/view; **l'électorat** <u>**dans**</u> **son** ~**/les spectateurs dans leur** ~ the electorate/viewers as a whole; <u>**dans**</u> **l'**~ on the whole

ensemencer [ɑ̃s(ə)mɑ̃se] <2> *vt* (*terre*) to sew; (*étang, rivière*) to stock; (*bouillon de culture*) to culture

ensevelir [ɑ̃səvliʀ] <8> *vt* (*recouvrir*) ~ **qn/qc sous qc** to bury sb/sth under sth

ensoleillé(**e**) [ɑ̃sɔleje] *adj* sunny

ensommeillé(**e**) [ɑ̃sɔmeje] *adj* (*personne*) drowsy; (*paysage, ville*) sleepy

ensorceler [ɑ̃sɔʀsəle] <3> *vt* **1.** (*envoûter*) to enchant **2.** (*fasciner*) to bewitch

ensorcellement [ɑ̃sɔʀsɛlmɑ̃] *m* enchantment

ensuite [ɑ̃sɥit] *adv* **1.** (*par la suite*) afterwards **2.** (*derrière en suivant*) then; **d'accord, mais** ~**?** OK, but then what? **3.** (*en plus*) what is more

ensuivre [ɑ̃sɥivʀ] *vpr irr, défec* **s'**~ to ensue; **la crise qui s'ensuivit** the ensuing crisis

entaille [ɑ̃taj] *f* **1.** (*encoche*) notch **2.** (*coupure*) gash

entailler [ɑ̃taje] <1> **I.** *vt* **1.** (*faire une entaille*) to notch **2.** (*blesser*) ~ **la joue à qn** to gash sb's cheek **II.** *vpr* **s'**~ **la joue avec qc** to gash one's cheek on sth

entame [ɑ̃tam] *f* **1.** (*de jambon*) first slice; (*de pain*) crust **2.** JEUX **faire une** ~ **à carreau** to lead on diamonds; **faire une mauvaise** ~ to open badly

entamer [ãtame] <1> *vt* **1.** (*prendre le début de: bouteille*) to open; (*fromage*) to start (on) **2.** (*attaquer*) ~ **qc** to cut into sth **3.** (*amorcer*) to start; (*négociations*) to open; (*poursuites*) to institute

entartrer [ãtaʀtʀe] <1> **I.** *vt* to scale up; ~ **une chaudière** to scale [*o* fur] a boiler; ~ **les dents** to cover the teeth in plaque **II.** *vpr* **s'~** (*chaudière, conduite*) to scale up; **lave-toi les dents, sinon elles s'entartreront** brush your teeth or they'll get covered in plaque

entassement [ãtasmã] *m* **1.** (*action: d'objets*) piling up **2.** (*pile*) pile **3.** (*encombrement*) crowding

entasser [ãtase] <1> **I.** *vt* **1.** (*amonceler*) to pile up; (*argent*) to amass **2.** (*serrer*) to cram **II.** *vpr* **1.** (*s'amonceler*) **s'~** to pile up **2.** (*se serrer*) **s'~ dans une pièce** to cram into a room

entendre [ãtãdʀ] <14> **I.** *vi* to hear; **se faire** ~ to make oneself heard **II.** *vt* **1.** (*percevoir*) to hear; ~ **qn parler/la pluie tomber** to hear sb talking/the rain falling; **je l'ai entendu dire** I've heard it said **2.** (*écouter*) ~ **qn/qc** to listen to sb/sth **3.** (*comprendre*) to understand; **ne pas ~ la plaisanterie** not to get the joke; **laisser ~ que ...** (*faire savoir*) to make it known that ...; (*faire croire*) to give the impression that ...; **qu'est-ce que vous entendez par là?** what do you mean by that? **4.** (*vouloir*) ~ *+infin* to intend to *+infin;* **faites comme vous l'entendez!** do as you see fit! ►**tu entendras/vous entendrez** __parler__ **de moi** you're going to hear from me!; ~ __**parler**__ **de qn/qc** to hear of sb/sth; **à qui** __**veut**__ **l'~** to anyone who'll listen; **je ne** __**veux**__ **rien ~!** I'm not listening!; __**à**__ ~ **les gens** to hear people talk; **je l'entends d'**__**ici**__ I can hear him from here; __**qu'est-ce**__ **que j'entends?** what's this I hear? **III.** *vpr* **1.** (*avoir de bons rapports*) **s'~ avec qn** to get along with sb **2.** (*se mettre d'accord*) **s'~ sur qc** to agree on sth; **s'~ pour** *+infin* to agree to *+infin* **3.** (*s'y connaître*) **s'y ~ en qc** to know about sth **4.** (*être audible*) **le bruit s'entend** the noise can be heard ►**on ne s'entend plus** __**parler**__ you can't hear yourself speak; **entendons-nous** __**bien**__**!** let's get this straight!

entendu(e) [ãtãdy] **I.** *part passé de* **entendre II.** *adj* **1.** (*convenu*) agreed; **il est (bien)** ~ **qu'il vient aussi** it's agreed that he's coming too **2.** (*complice: regard*) knowing ►__**bien**__ ~ of course; **comme de** __**bien**__ ~ as you'd expect

entente [ãtãt] *f* **1.** (*amitié*) friendship **2.** (*fait de s'accorder*) understanding **3.** (*accord*) *a.* ECON agreement; **arriver** [*o* **parvenir**] **à une** ~ to come to an agreement **4.** POL entente

entériner [ãteʀine] <1> *vt* **1.** (*approuver*) to adopt **2.** JUR, POL to ratify

enterrement [ãtɛʀmã] *m* burial

enterrer [ãteʀe] <1> **I.** *vt* **1.** to bury; ~ **un scandale** to hush up a scandal **2.** (*renoncer à*) to put (sth) behind one ►**il** __**nous**__ **enterrera tous** *iron* he'll outlast us all **II.** *vpr* **s'~ à la campagne** to hide oneself away in the country

en-tête [ãtɛt] <en-têtes> *f* (*d'un journal*) headline; (*d'un papier à lettres*) letterhead

entêté(e) [ãtete] **I.** *adj* (*personne*) obstinate **II.** *m(f)* stubborn individual

entêtement [ãtɛtmã] *m* stubbornness

entêter [ãtete] <1> *vpr* **s'~ dans qc/à faire qc** to persist in sth/in doing sth

enthousiasmant(e) [ãtuzjasmã, ãt] *adj* (*perspective, idée*) exciting; (*spectacle*) thrilling; **la situation n'est pas ~e** the situation's none too cheerful

enthousiasme [ãtuzjasm] *m* enthusiasm

enthousiasmer [ãtuzjasme] <1> **I.** *vt* ~ **qn** to fill sb with enthusiasm **II.** *vpr* **s'~ pour qn/qc** to get enthusiastic about sb/sth

enthousiaste [ãtuzjast] **I.** *adj* enthusiastic **II.** *mf* enthusiast

entier [ãtje] *m* whole number ►**la nation** __**dans**__ **son** ~ the nation as a whole; **le livre/l'orchestre** __**en**__ ~ the whole book/orchestra

entier, -ière [ãtje, -jɛʀ] *adj* **1.** (*dans sa totalité*) whole; **dans le monde** ~ in the whole world **2.** (*absolu*) complete; **ma confiance en lui est entière** I have complete confidence in him **3.** (*intact: personne*) safe and sound; (*objet, collection*) intact **4.** (*non réglé*) **la question reste entière** the question is still unsolved **5.** (*sans concession: personne*) strong-minded; **être** ~ **dans ses opinions** to have very strong opinions ►__**être**__ **tout ~ à qc** to be completely wrapped up in sth; __**tout**__ ~ entire

entièrement [ãtjɛʀmã] *adv* entirely

entièreté [ãtjɛʀte] *f Belgique* (*totalité, intégrité*) totality

entomologie [ãtɔmɔlɔʒi] *f* entomology

entonner [ãtɔne] <1> *vt* to start singing; ~ **les louanges** [*o* **l'éloge**] **de qn/qc** to sing sb's/sth's praises

entonnoir [ãtɔnwaʀ] *m* funnel; **en** ~ funnel-shaped

entorse [ãtɔʀs] *f* sprain ►__**faire**__ **une ~ à la vérité/au règlement** to stretch the truth/the rules

entortiller [ãtɔʀtije] <1> **I.** *vt* **1.** (*enrouler*) ~ **qc autour de qc** to twine sth around sth **2.** (*enjôler*) to cajole **II.** *vpr* **1.** (*s'enrouler*) **s'~ autour de qc** to twine around sth **2.** (*s'envelopper*) **s'~ dans qc** to wrap oneself up in sth **3.** (*s'embrouiller*) **s'~ dans qc** to get in a muddle over sth

entourage [ãtuʀaʒ] *m* entourage

entouré(e) [ãtuʀe] *adj* **1.** (*admiré*) **être** ~ to be the centre of attention *Brit,* to be the center of attention *Am* **2.** (*aidé*) **être** ~ to have friends rallying around **3.** (*accompagné*) **être bien/mal** ~ to keep good/bad company

entourer [ãtuʀe] <1> **I.** *vt* **1.** (*être autour*) to surround **2.** (*mettre autour*) ~ **un mot** to

E

circle a word; ~ **un jardin d'une clôture** to fence off a garden **3.** (*soutenir*) ~ **qn** to rally around sb; ~ **qn de soins** to give sb every attention **4.** *fig* ~ **qc de mystère** to surround sth in mystery **II.** *vpr* **s'~ de bons amis** to surround oneself with good friends; **s'~ de précautions** to take every precaution; **s'~ de garanties** to insist on guarantees

entourloupe [ɑ̃tuʀlup] *f inf*, **entourloupette** [ɑ̃tuʀlupɛt] *f inf* lousy trick; **faire une ~ à qn** to play a lousy trick on sb

entracte [ɑ̃tʀakt] *m* THEAT, CINE interval

entraide [ɑ̃tʀɛd] *f* mutual support

entraider [ɑ̃tʀede] <1> *vpr* **s'~** to help each other

entrailles [ɑ̃tʀɑj] *fpl* **1.** (*viscères*) entrails **2.** (*profondeurs: de la terre*) bowels

entrain [ɑ̃tʀɛ̃] *m* spirit

entraînant(e) [ɑ̃tʀɛnɑ̃, ɑ̃t] *adj* lively

entraînement [ɑ̃tʀɛnmɑ̃] *m* **1.** (*pratique*) practice; **c'est une question d'~** it's a matter of practice **2.** SPORT training

entraîner [ɑ̃tʀene] <1> **I.** *vt* **1.** (*emporter*) ~ **qc** to carry sth along **2.** (*emmener*) ~ **qn** to take sb off; ~ **qn vers la sortie** to take sb off towards the exit **3.** (*inciter*) ~ **qn à** [*o* **dans**] **qc** to drag sb into sth; ~ **qn à faire qc** to push sb into doing sth **4.** (*causer*) ~ **qc** to lead to sth **5.** (*stimuler*) ~ **qn** (*éloquence, musique*) to carry sb along **6.** SPORT (*exercer: joueur*) to train **II.** *vpr* **s'~ à** [*o* **pour**] **qc/à faire qc** to practice sth/doing sth

entraîneur, **-euse** [ɑ̃tʀɛnœʀ, -øz] *m, f* SPORT trainer

entraîneuse [ɑ̃tʀɛnøz] *f* hostess

entrave [ɑ̃tʀav] *f* **1.** (*obstacle*) hindrance; ~ **à la circulation** hindrance to traffic; ~ **au commerce/au progrès** obstacle to trade/progress **2.** *gén pl* (*lien*) fetters ►**être une ~ à qc** to be a hindrance [*o* obstacle] to sth; **sans ~s** unfettered

entraver [ɑ̃tʀave] <1> *vt* **1.** (*gêner*) ~ **qn/qc dans qc** to hinder [*o* be a hindrance to] sb/sth in sth; ~ **la réalisation d'un projet** to hinder the realization of a project **2.** (*mettre des entraves à*) to fetter

entre [ɑ̃tʀ] *prep* **1.** between **2.** (*parmi des personnes*) among; **je le reconnaîtrais ~ tous** I'd recognize him anywhere; **la plupart d'~ eux/elles** the majority of them; ~ **autres** among others; ~ **nous** between ourselves; ~ **hommes** among men **3.** (*à travers*) through; **passer ~ les mailles du filet** to slip through the net **4.** (*dans*) into; **remettre son sort ~ les mains de son médecin** to put one's fate into his doctor's hands **5.** (*indiquant une relation*) **ils se sont disputés ~ eux** they had an argument

entrebâillement [ɑ̃tʀəbɑjmɑ̃] *m* **par l'~ de la porte** through the half-open door

entrebâiller [ɑ̃tʀəbɑje] <1> *vt* to half-open; **être entrebâillé** to be half-open

entrechoquer [ɑ̃tʀəʃɔke] <1> **I.** *vt* to bang together **II.** *vpr* **s'~** to bang together; (*verres*) to clink; (*dents*) to chatter; (*épées*) to clash

entrecôte [ɑ̃tʀəkot] *f* rib steak

entrecoupé(e) [ɑ̃tʀəkupe] *adj* (*voix*) broken; ~ **de qc** interrupted by sth; **faire un voyage ~ de haltes** to keep making stops on a journey

entrecroiser [ɑ̃tʀəkʀwaze] <1> **I.** *vt* to intertwine **II.** *vpr* **s'~** (*routes*) to intersect

entrée [ɑ̃tʀe] *f* **1.** (*arrivée: d'une personne*) coming in; (*d'un acteur*) entrance; (*d'un train*) arrival; **à l'~ de qn** when sb comes in; **faire une ~ triomphale** to make a triumphant entry **2.** (*accès*) entrance; **à l'~ de qc** at the entrance to sth; ~ **de service** service entrance **3.** (*droit d'entrer*) entry; ~ **interdite** no entry; ~ **interdite à tout véhicule** no vehicle access **4.** (*vestibule: d'un appartement, d'une maison*) hall; (*d'un hôtel, immeuble*) entrance hall **5.** (*billet*) ticket; ~ **non payante** free ticket **6.** (*somme perçue*) receipt **7.** (*adhésion*) **son ~ dans le parti** his joining the party **8.** (*admission*) ~ **dans un club** admission **9.** (*commencement*) ~ **en action** coming into play; ~ **en fonction** taking up one's post; ~ **en matière** introduction; ~ **en vigueur** coming into force **10.** GASTR first course; **en** [*o* **comme**] ~ as a first course **11.** TYP (*d'un dictionnaire*) headword **12.** INFOR input **13.** ECON **l'~ en scène de l'euro** the arrival of the euro

entrefaites [ɑ̃tʀəfɛt] *fpl* **sur ces ~** at that moment

entrefilet [ɑ̃tʀəfilɛ] *m* paragraph

entrelacer [ɑ̃tʀəlase] <2> **I.** *vt* to intertwine **II.** *vpr* **s'~** to intertwine; **s'~ autour de qc** to twine around sth

entrelardé(e) [ɑ̃tʀəlaʀde] *adj* streaked with fat

entremêler [ɑ̃tʀəmele] <1> **I.** *vt fig* ~ **qc de qc** to intermingle sth and sth **II.** *vpr* **s'~** (*doigts*) to intertwine; (*lèvres*) to intermingle; **s'~ à** [*o* **avec**] **qc** to mingle with sth

entremets [ɑ̃tʀəmɛ] *m* dessert

entremise [ɑ̃tʀəmiz] *f* intervention; **grâce à l'~ de qn** thanks to sb's intervention; **par l'~ de qn** through sb's intervention

entrepont [ɑ̃tʀəpɔ̃] *m* steerage

entreposer [ɑ̃tʀəpoze] <1> *vt* (*meubles*) to put into store; ~ **qc en douane** to put in a bonded warehouse; **marchandises entreposées** warehoused goods

entrepôt [ɑ̃tʀəpo] *m* warehouse

entreprenant(e) [ɑ̃tʀəpʀənɑ̃, ɑ̃t] *adj* **1.** (*dynamique*) enterprising **2.** (*galant*) forward

entreprendre [ɑ̃tʀəpʀɑ̃dʀ] <13> *vt* (*commencer*) ~ **une étude/une carrière** to embark on a study/a career

entrepreneur, **-euse** [ɑ̃tʀəpʀənœʀ, -øz] *m, f* **1.** (*créateur d'entreprise*) entrepreneur; **petit ~** small businessman, businesswoman *m, f* **2.** TECH contractor

entreprise [ɑ̃tʀəpʀiz] *f* **1.** (*firme*) business; ~ **familiale/individuelle** family/one-man business; **petites et moyennes ~s** small and medium-sized businesses; ~ **privée/publique** private/state enterprise; ~ **de construction/transports** building/transport firm *Brit,* construction/transportation firm *Am* **2.** (*opération*) undertaking

entrer [ɑ̃tʀe] <1> **I.** *vi être* **1.** (*pénétrer*) to enter; (*vu de l'intérieur*) to come in; (*vu de l'extérieur*) to go in; **défense d'~!** no entry!; **faire/laisser ~ qn** to show/let sb in; **faire/laisser ~ un animal** to get/let an animal in **2.** (*pénétrer dans un lieu*) ~ **dans qc** to enter sth; (*vu de l'intérieur*) to come into sth; (*vu de l'extérieur*) to go into sth; ~ **en gare** to enter the station **3.** (*aborder*) ~ **dans les détails** to go into detail; ~ **dans le vif du sujet** to get to the heart of the matter **4.** *inf* (*heurter*) ~ **dans qc** to slam into sth **5.** (*s'engager dans*) ~ **dans un club/un parti/la police** to join a club/a party/the police; ~ **dans la vie active** to embark on working life **6.** (*être admis*) ~ **à l'hôpital** to go into the hospital; ~ **à l'école/en sixième** to start school/year seven *Brit,* to start school/sixth grade *Am;* ~ **en apprentissage/à l'université** to start an apprenticeship/university; **faire ~ qn dans un club/une entreprise** to get sb into a club/a business **7.** (*s'enfoncer*) **la clé n'entre pas dans le trou de la serrure** the key won't go into the lock **8.** (*s'associer à*) ~ **dans la discussion** to join the discussion **9.** (*faire partie de*) ~ **dans la composition d'un produit** to be an ingredient of a product **10.** (*comme verbe-support*) ~ **en application** to come into force; ~ **en contact avec qn** to make contact with sb; ~ **en collision avec qn/qc** to collide with sb/sth; ~ **en guerre** to go to war; ~ **en scène** to enter; ~ **en ligne de compte** to be taken into consideration; ~ **en fonction** to take up office ►**je ne fais qu'~ et** sortir I'm just popping in (and out) **II.** *vt avoir* **1.** (*faire pénétrer*) ~ **qc dans qc** to bring/take sth into sth; ~ **l'armoire par la fenêtre** to get the wardrobe in through the window **2.** INFOR to enter

entresol [ɑ̃tʀəsɔl] *m* mezzanine

entre-temps [ɑ̃tʀətɑ̃] *adv* meanwhile

entretenir [ɑ̃tʀət(ə)niʀ] <9> **I.** *vt* **1.** (*maintenir en bon état: machine, voiture*) to maintain; (*beauté, vêtement*) to look after **2.** (*faire vivre*) to support; (*maîtresse*) to keep; **se faire ~ par qn** to be kept by sb **3.** (*faire durer: correspondance*) to carry on; (*espoir, illusions*) to foster; (*souvenirs*) to keep alive; ~ **des relations** to keep up a relationship; ~ **un feu** to keep a fire burning; ~ **sa forme** to keep in shape; **cela entretient le doute** that still leaves doubts **4.** (*parler à*) ~ **qn de qn/qc** to converse with sb about sb/sth **II.** *vpr* **1.** (*converser*) **s'~ avec qn de qn/qc** to speak with sb about sb/sth **2.** (*se conserver en bon état*) **s'~** (*personne*) to keep in shape; **la moquette/le bois s'entretient facilement** the carpet/the wood is easy to maintain

entretenu(e) [ɑ̃tʀət(ə)ny] **I.** *part passé de* **entretenir II.** *adj* **1.** (*tenu en bon état*) well maintained; (*maison*) well kept **2.** (*pris en charge*) **c'est une femme ~e/un homme ~** she's/he's a kept woman/man

entretien [ɑ̃tʀətjɛ̃] *m* **1.** (*maintien en bon état: de la peau, d'un vêtement*) care; (*d'une maison*) upkeep; (*d'une machine*) maintenance; **sans ~** maintenance free **2.** (*discussion en privé*) discussion; (*pour un emploi*) interview

entretuer [ɑ̃tʀətɥe] <1> *vpr* **s'~** to kill each other

entrevoir [ɑ̃tʀəvwaʀ] *vt irr* **1.** (*voir indistinctement*) ~ **qc** to make sth out; (*voir brièvement*) to catch a glimpse of sth **2.** (*pressentir*) to foresee

entrevue [ɑ̃tʀəvy] *f* interview

entrouvert(e) [ɑ̃tʀuvɛʀ, ɛʀt] *adj* half-open

entrouvrir [ɑ̃tʀuvʀiʀ] <11> *vt, vpr* **(s')~** to half-open

énumération [enymeʀasjɔ̃] *f* enumeration; **faire une ~ de qc** to list sth

énumérer [enymeʀe] <5> *vt* to list

envahir [ɑ̃vaiʀ] <8> *vt* **1.** MIL (*pays*) to invade **2.** (*se répandre, infester*) ~ **les rues** to swarm into the streets; ~ **le terrain de football** to invade the pitch *Brit,* to invade the playing field *Am;* ~ **un lieu** (*insectes, mauvaises herbes*) to invade a place; (*eau*) to flood a place; ~ **le marché** (*nouveau produit*) to flood the market **3.** (*gagner*) **le doute/la terreur envahit qn** sb is seized by doubt/terror **4.** (*importuner*) to intrude on

envahissant(e) [ɑ̃vaisɑ̃, ɑ̃t] *adj* (*importun: personne*) intrusive

envahissement [ɑ̃vaismɑ̃] *m* MIL *a. fig* invasion

envahisseur, -euse [ɑ̃vaisœʀ, -øz] *m, f* invader

envaser [ɑ̃vaze] <1> *vpr* **s'~** (*baie, port, rivière*) to silt up; (*personne, bateau, voiture*) to get stuck in the mud; (*s'enfoncer*) to sink into the mud

enveloppe [ɑ̃vlɔp] *f* **1.** (*pour le courrier*) envelope; ~ **autocollante** [*o* **autoadhésive**] self-sealing envelope; **être/mettre sous ~** to be/put in an envelope **2.** (*protection*) covering **3.** (*budget*) budget; **une ~ de 14 millions** a 14 million budget; ~ **budgétaire** budget allocation

enveloppé(e) [ɑ̃vlɔpe] *adj* tubby

envelopper [ɑ̃vlɔpe] <1> **I.** *vt* (*verre*) to wrap up; ~ **un bébé dans une couverture** to wrap a baby up in a blanket **II.** *vpr* **s'~ dans son manteau** to wrap oneself up in one's coat

envenimé(e) [ɑ̃v(ə)nime] *adj* **1.** (*blessure*) infected **2.** *fig* (*propos*) poisonous

envenimer [ɑ̃v(ə)nime] <1> **I.** *vt* (*aggraver*) to inflame **II.** *vpr* (*se détériorer*) **s'~**

(*situation, conflit*) to aggravate
envergure [ɑ̃vɛʀgyʀ] *f* **1.** (*dimension: d'un avion, oiseau*) wingspan; (*d'un bateau, d'une voile*) breadth; **4,20 m d'~** 4.2 metres broad **2.** (*valeur, ampleur*) scale; (*d'une personne*) calibre; **de grande ~** high calibre; (*action*) large-scale; **avoir de l'~** (*personne*) to have calibre; (*chose*) to be sizeable; **prendre de l'~** (*personne*) to shape up; (*société*) to expand; (*scandale, dispute*) to become more serious; (*grève*) to escalate
envers [ɑ̃vɛʀ] **I.** *prep* **~ qn/qc** towards sb/sth; **avoir une dette ~ qn** (*financière*) to be in debt to sb; (*morale*) to be indebted to sb; **son mépris ~ qn/qc** her contempt for sb/sth **II.** *m* (*d'une feuille de papier*) other side; (*d'une étoffe, d'un vêtement*) wrong side; (*d'une assiette, feuille d'arbre*) underside ►**l'~ du décor** the other side of the coin; **à l'~** (*dans le mauvais sens*) the wrong way; (*à rebours*) the wrong way around; (*de bas en haut*) the wrong way up; (*à reculons*) backwards; (*en désordre*) upside down; **tout marche à l'~** everything's upside down
enviable [ɑ̃vjabl] *adj* enviable
envie [ɑ̃vi] *f* **1.** (*désir, besoin*) desire; **ses ~s de voyage** her wish to travel; **avoir ~ de cacahuètes** to feel like some peanuts; **avoir ~ de faire qc** to feel like doing sth; **avoir ~ de faire pipi/d'aller au W.-C.** *inf* to want to go pee/go to the loo *Brit*, to want to go pee/to the bathroom *Am*; **brûler d'~ de** *+infin form* to be longing to *+infin*; **mourir d'~ de** *+infin* to be dying to *+infin*; **l'~ lui prend** [*o* **vient**] **d'aller à la piscine** he feels like going to the swimming pool; **ça me donne ~ de partir en vacances** it makes me want to go off on holiday *Brit*, it makes me want to take a vacation *Am*; **avec tes histoires tu me donnes ~ de rire** you and your problems make me feel like laughing; **l'~ lui en est passée** [*o* **lui a passé**] he didn't feel like it any more **2.** (*convoitise, jalousie, péché capital*) envy ►**faire ~ à qn** (*personne, réussite*) to make sb envious; (*nourriture*) to tempt sb; **ça fait ~** it's very tempting; (*met en appétit*) it's very appealing
envier [ɑ̃vje] <1> *vt* **~ qn pour sa richesse/d'être riche** to envy sb for their wealth/for being rich; **je ne t'envie pas pour ton succès** I don't envy (you) for your success ►**qn/qc n'a rien à ~ à qn/à qc** there's nothing to choose between sb/sth and sb/sth
envieux, **-euse** [ɑ̃vjø, -jøz] **I.** *adj* **~ de qn/qc** envious of sb/sth **II.** *m, f* envious person; **tu n'es qu'une envieuse** you're just envious
environ [ɑ̃viʀɔ̃] **I.** *adv* around **II.** *mpl* (*d'une ville*) surroundings; **Reims et ses ~s** Reims and the surrounding area; **dans les ~s du château** in the area around the castle; **aux ~s de Pâques** around Easter; **aux ~s de 100 euros** in the neighbourhood of 100 euros *Brit*, in the neighborhood of 100 euros *Am*
environnant(e) [ɑ̃viʀɔnɑ̃, ɑ̃t] *adj* surrounding; **le milieu ~** the background
environnement [ɑ̃viʀɔnmɑ̃] *m* **1.** (*milieu écologique*) environment **2.** (*environs*) surroundings **3.** (*milieu social*) background
environner [ɑ̃viʀɔne] <1> **I.** *vt* to surround **II.** *vpr* **s'~ de qn/qc** to surround oneself with sb/sth
envisageable [ɑ̃vizaʒabl] *adj* conceivable
envisager [ɑ̃vizaʒe] <2a> *vt* **1.** (*considérer: question, situation*) to consider; (*avenir, mort*) to contemplate **2.** (*projeter*) **~ un voyage pour qn** to envisage a journey for sb; **~ de faire qc** to envisage doing sth **3.** (*prévoir: orage, visite*) to foresee; **~ que qn vienne** to foresee sb coming
envoi [ɑ̃vwa] *m* **1.** (*expédition: d'un paquet, d'une lettre*) sending; (*d'une marchandise, commande, de vivres*) dispatch **2.** (*colis*) package; (*courrier*) letter; **~ contre remboursement** cash on delivery; **~ recommandé** registered post
envol [ɑ̃vɔl] *m* (*d'un oiseau*) taking flight; **prendre son ~** (*oiseau*) to take flight
envolée [ɑ̃vɔle] *f* **1.** (*envol*) *a. fig* flight **2.** (*hausse: de la monnaie, valeur*) sudden rise; **l'~ de la bourse** soaring stock market prices
envoler [ɑ̃vɔle] <1> *vpr* **s'~ 1.** (*quitter le sol*) to fly away; (*avion*) to take off; **s'~ dans le ciel** (*ballon*) to fly off into the sky **2.** (*augmenter: monnaie, prix*) to soar **3.** (*disparaître: peur, paroles*) to vanish; (*temps*) to fly
envoûtant(e) [ɑ̃vutɑ̃, ɑ̃t] *adj* (*beauté, musique, regard*) bewitching; (*atmosphère*) spellbinding
envoûtement [ɑ̃vutmɑ̃] *m* spell
envoûter [ɑ̃vute] <1> *vt* to bewitch
envoyé(e) [ɑ̃vwaje] *m(f)* **1.** PRESSE correspondent; **~ spécial** special correspondent **2.** POL, REL envoy
envoyer [ɑ̃vwaje] *irr* **I.** *vt* **1.** (*expédier*) to send; (*démission*) to put in **2.** (*lancer: ballon*) to throw; (*avec le pied*) to kick; (*balle de tennis*) to serve; (*coup de pied, gifle, signal*) to give; **~ un baiser à qn** to blow sb a kiss ►**~ balader qn** *inf* to send sb packing; **~ valdinguer qn/qc contre le mur** *inf* to send sb/sth crashing into the wall; **~ tout promener** *inf* to throw everything up **II.** *vpr* (*se transmettre*) **s'~ des vœux** to send each other greetings; **s'~ des baisers** to blow each other kisses
envoyeur, **-euse** [ɑ̃vwajœʀ, -jøz] *m, f* v. **retour**
éolien(ne) [eɔljɛ̃, jɛn] *adj* **énergie ~ne** wind power
éolienne [eɔljɛn] *f* (*machine*) windmill
épagneul(e) [epaɲœl] *m(f)* spaniel
épais(se) [epɛ, ɛs] **I.** *adj* thick; **être ~ de 4 cm** to be 4 centimetres thick *Brit*, to be 4 centimeters thick *Am* **II.** *adv* **il n'y en a pas ~** *inf* there's not much of it
épaisseur [epɛsœʀ] *f* (*dimension*) thickness; (*de la neige*) depth; (*d'une couche, cou-

verture) layer; **avoir une ~ de 7 cm** [*o* **7 cm d'~**] to be 7 cm thick

épaissir [epesiʀ] <8> **I.** *vi* (*liquide*) to thicken **II.** *vpr* **s'~** (*devenir plus consistant: liquide, air*) to thicken; (*forêt, brouillard*) to get thicker

épanchement [epɑ̃ʃmɑ̃] *m* outpouring

épancher [epɑ̃ʃe] <1> **I.** *vt form* (*cœur*) to opem; (*sentiment, secret*) to pour out **II.** *vpr* **1.** MED **s'~ de qc** (*bile, sang*) to pour out sth **2.** *form* (*se confier*) **s'~** to pour out one's feelings; **s'~ auprès de qn** to pour out one's feelings to sb

épandage [epɑ̃daʒ] *m* (*du fumier, d'un engrais*) spreading; **en période d'~** at manuring time

épanoui(**e**) [epanwi] *adj* **1.** (*ouvert: fleur*) in bloom **2.** (*radieux: sourire, visage*) radiant **3.** (*développé harmonieusement: corps*) glowing with health **4.** (*équilibré: caractère, personne*) fulfilled

épanouir [epanwiʀ] <8> *vpr* **s'~ 1.** (*s'ouvrir: fleur*) to bloom **2.** (*devenir joyeux: visage*) to light up **3.** (*trouver le bonheur, prendre des formes*) to blossom **4.** (*se développer: personne, compétence*) to develop; **s'~ dans un travail** to be fulfilled in a job

épanouissement [epanwismɑ̃] *m* (*d'une fleur*) blooming; *fig* blossoming

épargnant(**e**) [epaʀɲɑ̃, ɑ̃t] *m(f)* saver

épargne [epaʀɲ] *f* **1.** (*action*) saving **2.** (*sommes*) savings *pl*

épargne-logement [epaʀɲlɔʒmɑ̃] *f sans pl* **plan d'~** home savings plan

épargner [epaʀɲe] <1> **I.** *vt* **1.** (*par économie*) to save **2.** (*compter, ménager: forces*) to conserve; (*peine*) to spare; **ne rien ~ pour** +*infin* to spare nothing to +*infin* **3.** (*éviter*) **~ un discours à qn** to spare sb a speech; **cela m'a été épargné** I was spared that **4.** (*laisser vivre*) to spare **II.** *vpr* **s'~ qc** to spare oneself sth

éparpillement [epaʀpijmɑ̃] *m* **1.** (*dissémination*) scattering **2.** (*dispersion: des efforts, idées*) dissipation

éparpiller [epaʀpije] <1> **I.** *vt* **1.** (*disséminer: personnes*) to disperse; (*miettes*) to scatter **2.** (*disperser inefficacement: forces, talent*) to dissipate; **~ ses efforts/son attention** to fail to focus one's efforts/one's attention **II.** *vpr* **s'~ 1.** (*se disséminer: foule*) to scatter; (*maisons*) to be scattered **2.** (*se disperser: personne*) to fail to focus oneself

épars(**e**) [epaʀ, aʀs] *adj* (*maisons, ruines*) scattered; (*en désordre: vêtements, jouets, cheveux*) untidy

épatant(**e**) [epatɑ̃, ɑ̃t] *adj inf* splendid

épaté(**e**) [epate] *adj inf* staggering

épater [epate] <1> *vt inf* (*stupéfier*) to amaze; **ça t'épate, hein?** amazing, isn't it?

épaule [epol] *f* ANAT shoulder; **hausser les ~s** to shrug one's shoulders

épauler [epole] <1> **I.** *vt* **1.** (*aider*) **~ qn** to help sb (out) **2.** (*appuyer: arme*) to raise (to one's shoulder) **II.** *vi* to raise one's gun (to one's shoulder) **III.** *vpr* **1.** (*s'entraider*) **s'~** to help each other out **2.** (*s'appuyer*) **s'~ contre qn/qc** to lean against sb/sth

épave [epav] *f* **1.** (*débris*) wreckage **2.** (*véhicule, personne*) wreck

épée [epe] *f* sword

épéiste [epeist] *mf* swordsman *m*, swordswoman *f*

épeler [ep(ə)le] <3> *vt, vi* to spell

épépiner [epepine] <1> *vt* to seed

éperdu(**e**) [epɛʀdy] *adj* **1.** (*affolé, fou: personne*) distraught; (*gestes, regard*) wild; **être ~ de douleur/reconnaissance** to be overcome with sorrow/gratitude **2.** (*fort: besoin, désir*) intense; (*amour*) passionate **3.** (*très rapide: fuite*) headlong; (*rythme*) frantic

éperdument [epɛʀdymɑ̃] *adv* **1.** *form* (*follement*) wildly; (*chercher*) frantically **2.** (*totalement*) **il s'en moque ~** he couldn't care less

éperlan [epɛʀlɑ̃] *m* smelt

éperon [ep(ə)ʀɔ̃] *m* **1.** *a.* GEO spur; **donner des ~s à un cheval** to spur on a horse **2.** NAUT cutwater

éperonner [ep(ə)ʀɔne] <1> *vt* **1. ~ un cheval/un candidat** to spur on a horse/a candidate **2.** NAUT to ram

épervier [epɛʀvje] *m* **1.** ZOOL sparrowhawk **2.** (*filet de pêche*) cast net

éphèbe [efɛb] *m iron* Adonis

éphémère [efemɛʀ] *adj* (*bonheur*) short-lived; (*beauté*) transient; (*instant, vie*) fleeting

éphéméride [efemeʀid] *f* (*calendrier*) tear-off calender

épi [epi] *m* **1.** (*de maïs, de blé*) ear **2.** (*mèche*) tuft ►**en ~** at an angle (to the kerb); **le stationnement en ~** angle parking

épice [epis] *f* spice

épicé(**e**) [epise] *adj* **1.** GASTR spicy **2.** (*grivois: histoire*) juicy

épicéa [episea] *m* spruce

épicer [epise] <2> *vt* **1.** (*assaisonner*) to spice **2.** (*corser*) **~ une histoire de qc** to spice up a story with sth

épicerie [episʀi] *f* (*magasin*) grocery *Brit*, grocery store *Am*; **la petite ~ du coin** the little grocery on the corner *Brit*, the corner store *Am*; **~ fine** delicatessen

épicier, -ière [episje, -jɛʀ] *m, f* **1.** (*tenant d'épicerie*) grocer **2.** *péj* shopkeeper

épidémie [epidemi] *f* epidemic

épidémique [epidemik] *adj* (*maladie*) epidemic

épiderme [epidɛʀm] *m* skin ►**avoir l'~ sensible** [*o* **chatouilleux**] *inf* to be thin-skinned

épier [epje] <1> **I.** *vt* **~ qn** to spy on sb; **~ un bruit** to listen out for a sound; **le chat épie la souris** the cat is keeping an eye on the mouse **II.** *vpr* **s'~** to watch each other closely

épieu [epjø] <x> *m* (*à la chasse*) spear; MIL pike

épilation [epilasjɔ̃] *f* hair removal; (*des sourcils*) plucking; **l'~ de la lèvre/des**

jambes removal of lip/leg hair; (*avec de la cire*) lip/leg waxing

épilepsie [epilɛpsi] *f* epilepsy

épileptique [epilɛptik] **I.** *adj* epileptic **II.** *mf* **être** ~ to be (an) epileptic

épiler [epile] <1> **I.** *vt* ~ **les jambes** to remove leg hair; (~ *les sourcils*) to pluck one's eyebrows; ~ **le menton/visage à qn** to remove hair on the chin/face **II.** *vpr* **s'**~ **les jambes** to remove the hair on one's legs; (*avec de la cire*) to wax one's legs

épilogue [epilɔg] *m* **1.** (*conclusion*) ending; **connaître un** ~ **heureux/triste** to have a happy/sad ending **2.** LIT epilogue

épiloguer [epilɔge] <1> *vi* ~ **sur qc** to go on (and on) about sth

épinard [epinaʀ] *m* spinach *no pl*

épine [epin] *f* thorn ►**enlever à qn une belle** ~ **du pied** to get sb out of a jam

épinette [epinɛt] *f Québec* (*épicéa*) spruce

épineux, **-euse** [epinø, -øz] *adj* **1.** (*piquant: arbuste, buisson*) thorny; (*animal, cactus*) spiny **2.** (*délicat: question, situation*) thorny

épingle [epɛ̃gl] *f* pin; ~ **à cheveux** hairpin; ~ **à nourrice** safety pin ►**tirer son** ~ **du jeu** (*s'en sortir*) to get out in time; (*réussir*) to do nicely for oneself; **être tiré à quatre** ~**s** to be dressed to the nines

épingler [epɛ̃gle] <1> *vt* **1.** (*accrocher avec des épingles*) ~ **des photos au mur** to pin photos to the wall **2.** *inf* (*attraper*) to nick

épique [epik] *adj* epic

épiscopal(**e**) [episkɔpal, o] <-aux> *adj* episcopal

épisode [epizɔd] *m* episode; **roman/film à** ~**s** serialized novel/film ►**par** ~**s** episodically

épisodique [epizɔdik] *adj* occasional

épisodiquement [epizɔdikmɑ̃] *adv* occasionally

épistolaire [epistɔlɛʀ] *adj* (*roman, littérature*) epistolary

épitaphe [epitaf] *f* epitaph

épithète [epitɛt] *f* **1.** LING attribute; **adjectif** ~ attributive adjective **2.** (*qualificatif*) epithet **3.** (*sobriquet*) nickname

éploré(**e**) [eplɔʀe] *adj* tearful

épluchage [eplyʃaʒ] *m* **1.** (*des fruits, légumes, crevettes*) peeling; (*de la salade*) removing the outer leaves; (*des radis, haricots verts*) topping and tailing **2.** *fig* (*des comptes, dossiers, textes*) dissection

éplucher [eplyʃe] <1> *vt* **1.** (*nettoyer: fruits, légumes, crevettes*) to peel; ~ **une salade** to remove the outer layer off a (head of) lettuce **2.** *fig* (*comptes*) to dissect

épluchette [eplyʃɛt] *f Québec* (*réunion*) meeting

épluchure [eplyʃyʀ] *f souvent pl* peelings; **une** ~ a scrap of peelings

éponge [epɔ̃ʒ] *f* sponge ►**jeter l'**~ to throw in the towel; **passer l'**~ **sur qc** to forget about sth; **passons l'**~**!** let's let bygones be bygones!

éponger [epɔ̃ʒe] <2a> **I.** *vt* (*table*) to wipe down; (*sol*) to mop; (*liquide*) to mop up **II.** *vpr* **s'**~ **le front** to mop one's brow

épopée [epɔpe] *f* **1.** LIT epic **2.** (*aventures*) saga

époque [epɔk] *f* (*moment*) time; (*ère*) age; **l'**~ **glaciaire/moderne** the ice/modern age; **l'**~ **révolutionnaire** the age of revolution; **la Belle Époque** the Belle Époque; **à l'**~ [*o* **à cette** ~] in those days; **à l'**~ **de qn** in sb's day; **à l'**~ **de qc** at the time of sth; **à cette** ~ **de l'année** at this time of year ►**vivre avec son** ~ to be of one's time; **d'**~ period

époumoner [epumɔne] <1> *vpr* **s'**~ **à faire qc** (*hurler*) to yell; (*se fatiguer en parlant*) to talk oneself hoarse

épouser [epuze] <1> *vt* **1.** (*se marier avec*) to marry **2.** (*partager: idées, cause*) to espouse; (*intérêts*) to take up **3.** (*s'adapter à*) ~ **les formes du corps** (*robe*) to cling to the body

épousseter [epuste] <3> *vt* to dust

époustouflant(**e**) [epustuflɑ̃, ɑ̃t] *adj inf* staggering

époustoufler [epustufle] <1> *vt inf* to stagger

épouvantable [epuvɑ̃tabl] *adj* terrible; (*temps*) appalling

épouvantail [epuvɑ̃taj] <s> *m* scarecrow

épouvante [epuvɑ̃t] *f* horror; **film d'**~ horror film

épouvanter [epuvɑ̃te] <1> **I.** *vt* **1.** (*horrifier*) to terrify **2.** (*inquiéter*) to frighten; **il est épouvanté de faire qc** he's frightened of doing sth **II.** *vpr* **1.** (*prendre peur*) **s'**~ to be terrified **2.** (*redouter*) **il s'épouvante de qc** sth frightens him

époux, **-ouse** [epu, -uz] *m, f form* spouse; **les** ~ the bride and groom; **Mme Dumas, épouse Meier** Mme Dumas, married name Meier

épreuve [epʀœv] *f* **1.** (*test*) test; **mettre qn/qc à l'**~**/à rude** ~ to put sb/sth to the test/to a tough test **2.** ECOLE (*examen*) examination **3.** SPORT event **4.** (*moment difficile, malheur*) trial; **dure** ~ severe trial ►~ **de force** showdown; **résister à l'**~ **du temps** to stand the test of time; **résister à l'**~ **du vent** to stand up to the wind; **être à l'**~ **du feu/de l'eau** to be fireproof/waterproof; **à l'**~ **des balles** bulletproof; **à l'**~ **des des bombes** bomb-proof; **à toute** ~ (*nerfs, santé*) rock-solid; (*courage*) indomitable; (*patience, optimisme*) unfailing; (*énergie*) unflagging

épris(**e**) [epʀi, iz] *adj* ~ **de qn/d'une idée** in love with sb/an idea; ~ **de justice/liberté** passionate about justice/freedom; **être** ~ **de son métier/sa voiture** to have a passion for one's job/one's car

éprouvant(**e**) [epʀuvɑ̃, ɑ̃t] *adj* trying; (*climat, chaleur*) testing

éprouvé(**e**) [epʀuve] *adj* **1.** (*ébranlé: personne, région*) stricken; **être très** ~**e** to be hard-hit **2.** (*confirmé*) tried and tested

éprouver [epʀuve] <1> *vt* **1.** (*ressentir: besoin, sentiment*) to feel **2.** (*subir: malheur, désagréments*) to suffer **3.** (*tester*) to put to the test **4.** (*ébranler physiquement, moralement*) to distress **5.** (*ébranler matériellement*) to strike

éprouvette [epʀuvɛt] *f* test tube

EPS [øpeɛs] *f abr de* **éducation physique et sportive** P.E.

épuisant(e) [epɥizɑ̃, ɑ̃t] *adj* exhausting

épuisé(e) [epɥize] *adj* **1.** (*éreinté*) tired-out; **être ~ de fatigue** to be exhausted **2.** (*tari: filon, réserves, gisement*) exhausted **3.** (*totalement vendu: édition, livre*) out of print

épuisement [epɥizmɑ̃] *m* **1.** (*fatigue, tarissement*) exhaustion **2.** (*vente totale*) **jusqu'à ~ du stock** while stocks last

épuiser [epɥize] <1> **I.** *vt* **1.** (*fatiguer*) **~ qn** to tire sb out **2.** (*tarir, venir à bout de: économies, réserves, sujet*) to exhaust **3.** (*vendre totalement*) **~ un article** to run out of an article; **les stocks sont épuisés** the stocks have run out **II.** *vpr* **1.** (*se tarir*) **s'~** (*réserves*) to run out; (*sol*) to be worked out; (*source*) to dry up; (*forces*) to be exhausted **2.** (*se fatiguer*) **s'~ à faire qc/sur qc** to tire oneself out doing sth/over sth

épuisette [epɥizɛt] *f* landing net; (*d'enfant*) shrimp net

épuration [epyʀasjɔ̃] *f* **1.** CHIM purification **2.** POL purge

épurer [epyʀe] <1> *vt* **1.** (*purifier*) to purify **2.** (*rendre meilleur: style*) to refine; (*personne*) to reform; (*langue*) to purify **3.** POL to purge

équateur [ekwatœʀ] *m* equator

Équateur [ekwatœʀ] *m* **l'~** Ecuador

équation [ekwasjɔ̃] *f* equation; **~ du premier/second degré** first-/second-degree equation

équatorial(e) [ekwatɔʀjal, jo] <-aux> *adj* equatorial

équatorien(ne) [ekwatɔʀjɛ̃, ɛn] *adj* Ecuadorian

Équatorien(ne) [ekwatɔʀjɛ̃, ɛn] *m(f)* Ecuadorian

équerre [ekɛʀ] *f* set square

équestre [ekɛstʀ] *adj* (*exercice*) riding; (*randonnée*) horseback; (*statue*) equestrian

équidistant(e) [ekɥidistɑ̃, ɑ̃t] *adj* equidistant

équilatéral(e) [ekɥilateʀal, o] <-aux> *adj* **1.** (*triangle*) equilateral **2.** *inf* **ça m'est ~** I couldn't care less

équilibre [ekilibʀ] *m* **1.** *a.* POL, ECON balance; **en ~** balanced; **être en ~ sur le bord de la table** to be balanced on the edge of the table; **mettre qc en ~** to balance sth; **rompre l'~ entre deux choses** to disturb the balance of two things **2.** PSYCH equilibrium; **faire preuve d'~** to show balance

équilibré(e) [ekilibʀe] *adj* **1.** (*en équilibre*) balanced **2.** (*stable: personne, esprit*) stable

équilibrer [ekilibʀe] <1> **I.** *vt* **1.** (*mettre en équilibre*) to balance; **bien ~ ses repas** to eat well-balanced meals **2.** (*stabiliser*) to bring into balance **3.** (*contrebalancer*) to counterbalance **II.** *vpr* **s'~** to balance out

équilibriste [ekilibʀist] *mf* acrobat; (*funambule*) tightrope walker; **à force de faire l'~** [*o* **jouer les ~s**], **...** with all these acrobatics ...; **~ de la haute finance** a financial high wire artist

équinoxe [ekinɔks] *m* equinox

équipage [ekipaʒ] *m* (*d'un avion, bateau*) crew

équipe [ekip] *f a.* SPORT team; **faire ~ avec qn** to team up with sb; **l'~ de jour/nuit/du matin/soir** (*à l'usine*) the day/night/morning/evening shift; **en ~** in a team

équipée [ekipe] *f* **1.** (*aventure*) escapade **2.** (*longue promenade*) hike **3.** (*virée*) jaunt

équipement [ekipmɑ̃] *m* **1.** (*action: d'un hôtel, hôpital*) fitting; **l'~ industriel de la région** the industrial plant in a region; **plan d'~ de la région** regional industrial development plan **2.** (*matériel*) equipment; (*d'une voiture*) fittings **3.** *souvent pl* (*installations*) facilities

Équipement [ekipmɑ̃] *m* ADMIN **l'~** (**du territoire**) planning and works department

équiper [ekipe] <1> *vpr* **s'~ en qc** to equip oneself with sth

équipier, -ière [ekipje, -jɛʀ] *m, f* team member; NAUT crew member

équitable [ekitabl] *adj* fair

équitablement [ekitabləmɑ̃] *adv* fairly

équitation [ekitasjɔ̃] *f* horseriding *Brit*, horseback riding *Am;* **faire de l'~** to go horseriding

équité [ekite] *f* (*d'un jugement, d'une loi*) fairness; **en toute ~** in all fairness

équivalence [ekivalɑ̃s] *f* **1.** (*valeur égale*) equivalence **2.** UNIV *recognition of a foreign degree;* **elle a obtenu une ~ pour son diplôme** her diploma has been recognized

équivalent [ekivalɑ̃] *m* equivalent; **accepter serait l'~ de céder** agreeing would be tantamount to giving in; **sans ~** without an exact equivalent

équivalent(e) [ekivalɑ̃, ɑ̃t] *adj* equivalent; **elle gagne un salaire ~ au mien** she earns the same salary as I do

équivaloir [ekivalwaʀ] *vi irr* **~ à qc** to be equivalent to sth

équivoque [ekivɔk] **I.** *adj* **1.** (*ambigu: expression, terme*) ambiguous; (*attitude*) equivocal **2.** (*louche: personne, relation, passé*) dubious; (*regard*) questionable **II.** *f* (*ambiguïté*) ambiguity; (*malentendu*) misunderstanding; (*incertitude*) doubt; **sans ~** unambiguous; **pour éviter l'~** to avoid any misunderstanding; **rester dans l'~** to remain in a state of uncertainty

érable [eʀabl] *m* maple

érablière [eʀablijɛʀ] *f Québec* (*plantation*

E

d'érables à sucre) maple plantation

éradication [eʀadikasjɔ̃] *f* eradication

érafler [eʀɑfle] <1> **I.** *vt* to graze **II.** *vpr* **s'~ le genou** to scrape one's knee

éraflure [eʀɑflyʀ] *f* scratch

éraillé(e) [eʀɑje] *adj* **1.** (*voix*) hoarse **2.** (*usé*) threadbare

ère [ɛʀ] *f* **1.** era; **~ industrielle** industrial age; **avant notre ~** B.C. **2.** GEO period; **~ tertiaire/quaternaire** Tertiary/Quaternary (period)

érection [eʀɛksjɔ̃] *f* (*d'un pénis*) erection

éreintant(e) [eʀɛ̃tɑ̃, ɑ̃t] *adj* backbreaking

éreinter [eʀɛ̃te] <1> **I.** *vt* **1.** (*épuiser*) to exhaust **2.** (*critiquer*) to slate **II.** *vpr* **s'~ à faire qc** to kill oneself doing sth

érémiste [eʀemist] *mf: claimant receiving the RMI*

Erevan [eʀevan] Yerevan

ergot [ɛʀgo] *m* **1.** (*d'un coq*) spur; (*d'un chien*) dewclaw **2.** (*du seigle*) ergot **3.** TECH (*d'un engrenage*) lug; **les petits ~s de fixation** the little fixing lugs ▸**monter sur ses ~s** to get on one's high horse

ergoter [ɛʀgɔte] <1> *vi* **~ sur qc** to quibble about sth

ériger [eʀiʒe] <2a> **I.** *vt form* **1.** (*dresser, élever: monument*) to erect **2.** (*élever au rang de*) **~ qn en martyr** to make sb into a martyr; **~ qc en règle générale** to make into a general rule **II.** *vpr form* **s'~ en juge** to set oneself up as a judge

ermitage [ɛʀmitaʒ] *m* hermitage

ermite [ɛʀmit] *m* hermit

érogène [eʀɔʒɛn] *adj* (*zone*) erogenous

érosion [eʀɔzjɔ̃] *f* **1.** GEO erosion **2.** (*affaiblissement*) weakening; **~ du pouvoir d'achat** erosion of purchasing power; **~ monétaire** erosion of the value of money; **l'~ du parti est spectaculaire** the drop in support for the party is dramatic

érotique [eʀɔtik] *adj* erotic

érotisme [eʀɔtism] *m* eroticism

errant(e) [eʀɑ̃, ɑ̃t] *adj* (*personne, regard, vie*) wandering; (*animal*) stray

erratum [eʀatɔm, eʀata] <errata> *m* erratum

errements [ɛʀmɑ̃] *mpl form* errant ways

errer [eʀe] <1> *vi* to wander

erreur [eʀœʀ] *f* error, mistake; **~ d'ordinateur/de système** computer/system error; **~ de jugement** error of judgment; **raccrochez! c'est une ~ (de numéro)** hang up! it's a wrong number; **~ judiciaire** miscarriage of justice; **~ médicale** medical error; **il y a ~/n'y a pas d'~** there's some mistake/no mistake; **j'ai commis une ~** I've made a mistake; **excusez-moi; c'est une ~ de ma part** I'm sorry, it's my mistake; **être dans l'~** to be wrong; **faire ~** to be mistaken; **induire qn en ~** to mislead sb; **par ~** by mistake; **sauf ~ de ma part** unless I'm mistaken ▸**~ de jeunesse** error of youth; **il y a ~ sur la personne** it's a case of mistaken identity; **l'~ est humaine** *prov* to err is human

erroné(e) [eʀɔne] *adj* wrong

ersatz [ɛʀsats] *m inv* substitute; **~ de café/savon** coffee/soap substitute

érudit(e) [eʀydi, it] **I.** *adj* (*ouvrage, étude*) erudite; (*personne*) learned; **~ en archéologie** learned in archeology **II.** *m(f)* scholar; **des querelles d'~s** scholarly quarrels

érudition [eʀydisjɔ̃] *f* erudition; **des ouvrages d'~** erudite works; **~ en histoire** historical learning

éruption [eʀypsjɔ̃] *f* **1.** MED outbreak; **~ dentaire** teething *no pl* **2.** GEO eruption; **en ~** (*volcan*) erupting

es [ɛ] *indic prés de* **être**

esbroufe [ɛsbʀuf] *f inf* bluff; **un joli coup d'~** a fine bluff; **faire de l'~** to bluff; **y aller à l'~** to bluff one's way through; **arracher un marché à l'~** to bluff one's way into a deal; **tu ne nous la feras pas à l'~** we're calling your bluff

escabeau [ɛskabo] <x> *m* **1.** (*échelle*) steps *pl* **2.** (*tabouret*) stool

escadre [ɛskadʀ] *f* squadron

escadrille [ɛskadʀij] *f* (*de bombardement, chasse*) squadron

escadron [ɛskadʀɔ̃] *m* (*de cavalerie*) squadron; (*de chasseurs, gendarmerie, police*) company

escalade [ɛskalad] *f* **1.** (*ascension*) climb; **faire l'~ d'une montagne** to climb a mountain **2.** (*sport*) climbing; **faire de l'~** to go climbing **3.** (*surenchère*) escalation

escalader [ɛskalade] <1> *vt* **1.** (*monter: montagne*) to climb **2.** (*franchir*) **~ un mur** to scale a wall

escalator [ɛskalatɔʀ] *m* escalator

escale [ɛskal] *f* **1.** NAUT port of call **2.** AVIAT (*arrêt*) stop; **~ technique** refuelling stop; **le vol s'effectue sans ~** it is a non-stop flight; (*lieu*); **une ~ à Tokyo** a stopover at Tokyo

escalier [ɛskalje] *m sing o pl* stairs *pl;* **~ roulant** escalator; **~ de service** back stairs; **être dans l'~** to be on the stairs; **tomber dans les ~s** to fall down the stairs

escalope [ɛskalɔp] *f* escalope

escamotable [ɛskamɔtabl] *adj* (*antenne, train d'atterrissage*) retractable; (*clavier, meuble, machine à coudre*) folding; **lit ~** foldaway bed

escamoter [ɛskamɔte] <1> **I.** *vt* **1.** (*rentrer: antenne, train d'atterrissage*) to retract **2.** (*faire disparaître*) to vanish **3.** (*dérober*) to pinch **4.** (*éluder: incident, problème*) to slide over; (*mot, note de musique*) to skip; (*une difficulté*) to evade **II.** *vpr* **s'~** (*train d'atterrissage*) to retract; (*lit*) to fold away

escampette [ɛskɑ̃pɛt] *f v.* **poudre**

escapade [ɛskapad] *f* escapade; **faire une ~** (*faire une fugue*) to run off; (*faire une infidélité*) to have a fling; (*sécher*) to bunk off

escargot [ɛskaʀgo] *m* **1.** ZOOL, GASTR snail; **~ de Bourgogne** Burgundy snail **2.** (*personne,*

véhicule) slowcoach *Brit,* slowpoke *Am;* **rouler comme un** ~ to drive at a snail's pace
escarmouche [ɛskaʀmuʃ] *f a.* MIL skirmish
escarpé(e) [ɛskaʀpe] *adj* steep
escarpement [ɛskaʀpəmɑ̃] *m* (*déclivité: d'une côte, montagne*) steepness; (*versant raide*) steep slope
escarpin [ɛskaʀpɛ̃] *m* court shoe
escient [esjɑ̃] *m* **à bon/mauvais** ~ wisely/ill-advisedly; (*au bon/mauvais moment*) appropriately/inappropriately
esclaffer [ɛsklafe] <1> *vpr* **s'**~ to burst out laughing
esclandre [ɛsklɑ̃dʀ] *m* scene
esclavage [ɛsklavaʒ] *m a. fig* slavery; **l'**~ **de l'alcool/la drogue** enslavement to alcohol/drugs; **la mode est un véritable** ~ fashion is a slavemaster; **tomber en** ~ to be enslaved; **réduire qn en** ~ to enslave sb
esclavagiste [ɛsklavaʒist] **I.** *adj* (*théorie, personne*) proslavery; **société** ~ slave society; **être** ~ to beleive in slavery **II.** *mf* (*trafiquant*) slaver; (*propriétaire*) slave-owner
esclave [ɛsklav] **I.** *adj* enslaved; ~ **de qn/qc** enslaved to sb/sth **II.** *mf* slave
escogriffe [ɛskɔgʀif] *m inf* beanpole; **grand** ~ great beanpole
escompte [ɛskɔ̃t] *m* COM, FIN discount
escompter [ɛskɔ̃te] <1> *vt* **1.** (*espérer*) ~ **qc/que qn va faire qc** to count on sth/on sb doing sth; **ne pas** ~ **qc/que qn fasse qc** (*subj*) not to count on sth/on sb doing sth; ~ + *infin* to expect to + *infin* **2.** FIN to discount
escorte [ɛskɔʀt] *f* escort
escorter [ɛskɔʀte] <1> *vt* to escort
escouade [ɛskwad] *f* (*groupe*) gang; MIL squad; **par** ~**s** in gangs
escrime [ɛskʀim] *f* fencing; **faire de l'**~ to fence
escrimer [ɛskʀime] <1> *vpr* **s'**~ **sur qc** to struggle with sth; **s'**~ **à** + *infin* to struggle to + *infin*
escroc [ɛskʀo] *m* swindler
escroquer [ɛskʀɔke] <1> *vt* ~ **une signature à qn** to wheedle a signature out of sb; ~ **qn de mille euros** to swindle sb out of a thousand euros; **se faire** ~ **par qn de 500 euros** to be swindled out of 500 euros
escroquerie [ɛskʀɔkʀi] *f* fraud
ésotérique [ezɔteʀik] *adj* esoteric
espace [ɛspas] **I.** *m* space; **avoir assez d'**~ **pour danser** to have enough room to dance; ~ **publicitaire** advertising space; ~ **aérien** air space; **dans l'**~ **d'un été/moment** in (the space of) a summer/a moment **II.** *f* TYP, INFOR space
espacement [ɛspasmɑ̃] *m* **1.** (*distance*) space; TYP (*des lignes, mots*) spacing; ~ **entre ta maison et la mienne** the gap between your house and mine **2.** (*action d'espacer*) **l'**~ **de mes visites** the time between my visits
espacer [ɛspase] <2> **I.** *vt* (*séparer*) to space out; **il espace ses visites** he's making less frequent visits **II.** *vpr* (*devenir plus rare*) **s'**~ to become less frequent
espadon [ɛspadɔ̃] *m* ZOOL swordfish
espadrille [ɛspadʀij] *f* **1.** espadrille **2.** *Québec* (*basket*) plimsoll *Brit,* sneaker *Am;* ~**s de tennis** tennis shoes
Espagne [ɛspaɲ] *f* **l'**~ Spain
espagnol [ɛspaɲɔl] *m* Spanish; *v. a.* **français**
espagnol(e) [ɛspaɲɔl] *adj* Spanish
Espagnol(e) [ɛspaɲɔl] *m(f)* Spaniard
espagnolette [ɛspaɲɔlɛt] *f* catch (*bar mechanism on windows in France*)*;* **fermer la fenêtre à l'**~ to leave the window oen he catch
espalier [ɛspalje] *m* **1.** BOT espalier; **être en** ~ to be espaliered **2.** SPORT wall bars *pl*
espèce [ɛspɛs] *f* **1.** BIO (*catégorie*) species; ~ **animale** species of animal; ~ **canine** dog species; **l'**~ (**humaine**) the human race **2.** *souvent péj* (*sorte*) sort; **c'est un(e)** ~ **de pot de chambre** it's a sort of chamber pot [*o* bedpan]; ~ **d'imbécile!** *inf* you damn idiot!; **de ton** ~ like you; **de cette/de la pire** ~ *inf* of that/the worst sort **3.** *pl* (*argent liquide*) cash *no pl;* **régler** [*o* **payer**] **en** ~**s** to pay cash
espérance [ɛspeʀɑ̃s] *f* **1.** (*espoir*) hope; (*attente*) expectation; **donner de grandes** ~**s** to show great promise; **fonder de grandes** ~**s sur qn/qc** to have high expectations of sb/sth; **répondre à toutes les** ~**s** to live up to expectations; **contre toute** ~ against all expectations; **dans l'**~ **de faire qc/que qn fasse qc** (*subj*) in the hope of doing sth/that sb may do sth **2.** (*durée*) ~ **de vie** life expectancy
espéranto [ɛspeʀɑ̃to] *m* Esperanto; *v. a.* **français**
espérer [ɛspeʀe] <5> **I.** *vt* **1.** (*souhaiter*) to hope; **je l'espère bien** I hope so; **nous espérons vous revoir bientôt** we hope to see you again soon; **j'espère n'avoir rien oublié** I hope I haven't forgotten anything **2.** (*compter sur*) ~ **qc** to hope for sth; **on ne l'espère plus** we've given up hoping he'll come; **espères-tu qu'il te vienne en aide?** are you hoping he'll help you out? **II.** *vi* to hope; **espérons!** let's just hope!; ~ **en l'avenir** to have faith in the future
espiègle [ɛspjɛgl] *adj* (*enfant, sourire*) roguish
espièglerie [ɛspjɛgləʀi] *f* mischievousness
espion(ne) [ɛspjɔ̃, jɔn] **I.** *m(f)* spy; **arrête de jouer les** ~**s!** stop spying on people! **II.** *app* spy
espionnage [ɛspjɔnaʒ] *m* espionage; **les services d'**~ the intelligence services; **film/roman d'**~ spy film/novel
espionner [ɛspjɔne] <1> *vt* ~ **qn** to spy on sb; ~ **une conversation** to eavesdrop on a conversation
esplanade [ɛsplanad] *f* esplanade
espoir [ɛspwaʀ] *m* hope; **sans** ~ hopeless; **conserver l'**~ to keep hoping; **ne pas perdre** ~ not to lose hope; **enlever tout** ~ **à qn** to

take away all hope from sb; **avoir le ferme ~ d'y parvenir** to have every hope of succeeding; **fonder** [*o* **placer**] **de grands ~s sur** [*o* **en**] **qn/qc** to have high hopes of sb/sth; **tu as encore l'~ qu'il réussisse?** do you still hope he'll succeed?; **je garde l'~ qu'il viendra** I go on hoping he will come; **dans l'~ de faire qc** in the hope of doing sth; **les ~s de la boxe française** the (bright) hopes of French boxing ►**l'~ fait vivre** *prov* one must live in hope

esprit [ɛspʀi] *m* **1.** (*pensée*) mind; **avoir l'~ étroit/large** to be narrow-/broad-minded **2.** (*tête*) **avoir qn/qc à l'~** to have sb/sth on one's mind; **une idée me traverse l'~** an idea has crossed my mind; **une idée/un mot me vient à l'~** an idea/word has come into my head; **dans mon/son ~** (*souvenir*) as I/she remembers it; (*opinion*) in my/her mind; **elle a l'~ libre** her mind is free; **avoir l'~ ailleurs** to be miles away; **faible** [*o* **simple**] **d'~** feeble-minded **3.** (*humour*) wit; **plein d'~** witty; **faire de l'~** to try to be witty **4.** (*personne*) **~ fort** [*o* **libre**] rationalist; **faire** [*o* **jouer**] **l'~ fort** to be clever; **grand/petit ~** great/small mind; **~ retors** devious mind **5.** (*caractère*) **avoir bon/mauvais ~** to be helpful/unhelpful **6.** (*intention, prédisposition, être spirituel*) spirit; **il a l'~ à qc** his mind is on sth; **dans cet ~** in this spirit; **avoir l'~ de compétition/de contradiction** to be competitive/argumentative; **avoir l'~ de famille** to be a family person; **avoir l'~ d'observation** to be observant; **avoir l'~ d'organisation** to be an organizer; **~ de sacrifice** sense of (self-)sacrifice; **avoir l'~ d'entreprise** to be enterprising ►**les grands ~s se rencontrent** *inf* great minds think alike; **faire du mauvais ~** to make trouble; **avoir l'~ mal tourné** to have a dirty mind; **reprendre ses ~s** to get a grip on oneself; **rester jeune d'~** to stay young at heart

esquimau [ɛskimo] *m* (*langue*) Eskimo; *v. a.* **français**

esquimau® [ɛskimo] <x> *m* GASTR choc ice *Brit,* Eskimo Pie *Am*

esquimau(de) [ɛskimo, od] <x> *adj* Eskimo; **le peuple ~** the Eskimo people

Esquimau(de) [ɛskimo, od] *m(f)* Eskimo

esquinté(e) [ɛskɛ̃te] *adj inf* ruined

esquinter [ɛskɛ̃te] <1> **I.** *vt inf* **1.** (*abîmer: chose*) to wreck; (*voiture*) to smash up; **~ qn** to beat sb up **2.** (*épuiser: santé*) to wreck **II.** *vpr inf* **s'~** (*personne*) to kill oneself; **s'~ les yeux** to ruin one's eyes; **s'~ à faire qc** to kill oneself doing sth

esquisse [ɛskis] *f* **1.** ART, ECON sketch; **dessiner une ~ de qc** to do a sketch of sth **2.** (*amorce: d'un sourire, regret*) hint **3.** (*présentation rapide*) outline

esquisser [ɛskise] <1> **I.** *vt* **1.** ART to sketch **2.** (*amorcer*) **~ un sourire** to give a hint of a smile; **ne pas ~ un geste pour aider qn** not to lift a hand to help sb **3.** (*présenter rapidement*) to outline **II.** *vpr* **s'~** (*silhouette, solution*) to begin to emerge; **s'~ sur le visage de qn** (*sourire*) to flicker across sb's face

esquiver [ɛskive] <1> **I.** *vt* (*éviter*) to dodge **II.** *vpr* **s'~** to slip away

essai [esɛ] *m* **1.** *gén pl* (*test*) test; (*d'un appareil, médicament*) trial; **faire l'~ de qc** to try sth out; **être à l'~** to undergo testing; **mettre qn à l'~** to put sb to the test **2.** (*tentative*) attempt; **ne pas en être à son premier ~** to have made many previous attempts **3.** SPORT try; (*en sport automobile*) trial **4.** LIT essay ►**marquer/transformer un ~** SPORT to score/convert a try

essaim [esɛ̃] *m* swarm; **un ~ d'abeilles/de moustiques** a swarm of bees/mosquitos; **un ~ d'enfants** a horde of children

essayage [esɛjaʒ] *m* (*sur mesures*) fitting; (*prêt-à-porter*) trying on; **cabine/salon d'~** changing room

essayer [eseje] <7> **I.** *vt* **1.** (*tester: chaussures, vêtement*) to try on; (*nourriture, médicament, méthode*) to try out; (*boucher, coiffeur*) to try **2.** (*tenter*) to try **II.** *vi* to try; **~ de** +*infin* to try to +*infin;* **ça ne coûte rien d'~** it costs nothing to try **III.** *vpr* **s'~ à une chose/activité** to try one's hand at sth/an activity

essayiste [esejist] *mf* essayist

essence [esɑ̃s] *f* **1.** (*carburant*) petrol *Brit,* gas *Am;* **prendre de l'~** to get some petrol; **tondeuse/tronçonneuse à ~** petrol mower/saw **2.** (*nature profonde*) essence; **l'~ du livre** the essence of the book; **par ~** essentially

essentiel [esɑ̃sjɛl] *m* **1.** (*le plus important*) **l'~** the main thing; **emporter l'~** to take the bare essentials; **pour l'~** essentially; **tu es en bonne santé? c'est l'~** you're in good health? that's what's most important; **l'~ est que vous me répondiez** the important thing is that you answer me; **aller à l'~** to go straight to the point **2.** (*la plus grande partie*) **l'~ de qc** the best part of sth; **il passe l'~ du temps à se plaindre** he spends most of his time complaining

essentiel(le) [esɑ̃sjɛl] *adj a.* PHILOS essential; **être ~ à** [*o* **pour**] **qc/pour faire qc** to be essential for sth/for doing sth; **~ à la vie** essential to life

essentiellement [esɑ̃sjɛlmɑ̃] *adv* essentially

essieu [esjø] <x> *m* AUTO, TECH axle; **rupture d'~** broken axle; **~ arrière/avant** rear/front axle

essor [esɔʀ] *m* (*développement*) rise; (*d'un art, d'une civilisation*) high point; **être en plein ~** to be thriving; (*ville*) to be booming; **connaître un nouvel ~** (*cinéma*) to take on a new life ►**prendre son ~** (*industrie, secteur, entreprise*) to take off; (*oiseau*) to soar

essorage [esɔʀaʒ] *m* (*à la machine*) spinning; (*à la main*) wringings; **plusieurs ~s successifs** a series of spins

essorer [esɔʀe] <1> *vt, vi* (*à la main*) to wring; (*à la machine*) to spin-dry

essoufflement [esufləmɑ̃] *m* breathlessness; (*dégradation: de la bourse, des affaires*) run-down state; **être dans un tel état d'~ que** to be so breathless that

essouffler [esufle] <1> **I.** *vt* ~ **qn** to leave sb out of breath; **être complètement essoufflé** to be completely out of breath **II.** *vpr* **s'~ à faire qc** to get out of breath doing sth; *fig* to wear oneself out doing sth

essuie-glace [esɥiglas] <essuie-glaces> *m* windscreen wiper *Brit,* windshield wiper *Am* **essuie-mains** [esɥimɛ̃] *m inv* hand towel **essuie-tout** [esɥitu] *m inv* kitchen paper *Brit,* paper towel *Am*

essuyer [esɥije] <6> **I.** *vt* **1.** (*sécher*) to dry; (*larmes*) to wipe away **2.** (*éponger: surface*) to mop; (*de l'eau par terre*) to mop up **3.** (*nettoyer: meubles*) to clean; (*chaussures*) to wipe **4.** (*subir: échec, perte*) to suffer; ~ **des reproches/des coups** to be blamed/beaten; ~ **un refus** to meet with a refusal **II.** *vpr* **1.** (*se sécher*) **s'~** to dry oneself **2.** (*se nettoyer*) **s'~ les pieds** to wipe one's feet

est[1] [ɛ] *indic prés de* **être**

est[2] [ɛst] **I.** *m sans pl* east; **l'~/l'Est** the east/East; **l'autoroute de l'Est** the eastern motorway *Brit,* the eastern highway *Am;* **les régions de l'~** eastern regions; **les gens de l'Est** people from the East; **l'Europe de l'~** Eastern Europe; **les pays de l'Est** the eastern countries; **le bloc de l'Est** the Eastern Bloc; **le conflit entre l'Est et l'Ouest** the East/West conflict; **à l'~** (*vers le point cardinal*) eastwards; (*dans/vers la région*) to the east; **à l'~ de qc** east of sth; **dans l'~ de** in the east of; **vers l'~** (*direction*) eastwards; (*position*) towards the east; **d'~ en ouest** from east to west **II.** *adj inv* east

estafilade [ɛstafilad] *f* gash; **se faire une ~ en se rasant** to cut oneself shaving

est-allemand(e) [ɛstalmɑ̃, ɑ̃d] *adj* East German

estaminet [ɛstaminɛ] *m Nord, Belgique* (*petit café populaire, bistrot*) café

estampe [ɛstɑ̃p] *f* (*image*) engraving; (*sur métal*) etching; (*sur bois*) woodcut; (*sur pierre*) lithograph

est-ce que [ɛskə] *adv ne se traduit pas* **où ~ tu vas?** where are you going?

esthète [ɛstɛt] *mf* aesthete

esthétique [ɛstetik] **I.** *adj* aesthetic; **n'avoir aucun sens ~** to have no sense of the aesthetic **II.** *f* **1.** (*beauté*) aesthetic **2.** (*théorie*) aesthetics + *vb sing* ▶ ~ <u>**industrielle**</u> industrial design

estimable [ɛstimabl] *adj* **1.** (*digne d'estime: personne*) estimable; (*travail*) respectable **2.** (*assez bon, honnête: résultats*) respectable **3.** (*évaluable*) calculable

estimatif, -ive [ɛstimatif, -iv] *adj* (*bilan, coûts*) estimated; **devis ~** estimate

estimation [ɛstimasjɔ̃] *f* assessment

estime [ɛstim] *f* esteem; **digne d'~** worthy of esteem; **l'~ de soi-même** self-esteem; **avoir l'~ de qn** to be held in esteem by sb; **avoir de l'~ pour qn** to esteem sb

estimer [ɛstime] <1> **I.** *vt* **1.** (*évaluer*) to estimate **2.** (*considérer*) ~ **qc inutile** to consider sth unnecessary; ~ **avoir le droit de donner son avis** to consider oneself entitled to express one's opinion; **je n'estime pas qu'elle ait réussi** (*subj*) I don't consider her to have succeeded **3.** (*respecter*) ~ **qn pour ses qualités humaines** to esteem sb for their human qualities; **savoir ~ un service à sa juste valeur** to recognize the true value of a favour *Brit,* to recognize the true value of a favor *Am* **II.** *vpr* **s'~ trahi** to consider oneself betrayed; **s'~ heureux d'avoir été sélectionné** to consider oneself lucky to have been selected

estival(e) [ɛstival, o] <-aux> *adj* (*mode, période*) summer

estivant(e) [ɛstivɑ̃, ɑ̃t] *m(f)* holidaymaker

estomac [ɛstɔma] *m* stomach; **avoir mal à l'~** to have stomach ache ▶**il a l'~ dans les <u>talons</u>** he is starving; <u>**caler**</u> **l'~ à qn** to fill sb up; <u>**creuser**</u> **l'~ à qn** to make sb hungry; **avoir l'~** <u>**noué**</u> to have a knot in one's stomach; <u>**peser**</u> [*o* <u>**rester**</u> *inf*] **sur l'~ à qn** to weigh on sb's stomach

estomper [ɛstɔ̃pe] <1> **I.** *vt* (*contours, dessin, souvenirs*) to blur; (*rides*) to hide; (*affaiblir: chagrin, sentiment*) to dull; ~ **les défauts sur une photo** to blur away the defects of a photo **II.** *vpr* **s'~** (*rivages, montagnes, mémoire, souvenirs, image*) to become blurred; (*tristesse, colère*) to fade

Estonie [ɛstɔni] *f* **l'~** Estonia

estonien [ɛstɔnjɛ̃] *m* Estonian; *v. a.* **français**

estonien(ne) [ɛstɔnjɛ̃, jɛn] *adj* Estonian

Estonien(ne) [ɛstɔnjɛ̃, jɛn] *m(f)* Estonian

estrade [ɛstʀad] *f* platform

estragon [ɛstʀagɔ̃] *m* tarragon

estropié(e) [ɛstʀɔpje] **I.** *adj* crippled **II.** *m(f)* cripple

estropier [ɛstʀɔpje] <1a> **I.** *vt* to cripple; (*langue, nom*) to mangle **II.** *vpr* **s'~** to be crippled

estuaire [ɛstɥɛʀ] *m* estuary

esturgeon [ɛstyʀʒɔ̃] *m* sturgeon

et [e] *conj* and; **à quatre heures ~ demie** at half past four; ~ **son mari ~ son amant ...** both her husband and her lover ...; ~ **le public d'applaudir** *soutenu* whereupon the audience burst into applause; ~ **alors!** so what!

ETA [øtea] *f abr de* **Euzkadi ta Azkatasuna** ETA

étable [etabl] *f* cowshed

établi(e) [etabli] *adj* **1.** (*en place: ordre*) established; (*pouvoir*) ruling; **c'est un usage bien ~** it's a well established practice **2.** (*sûr: vérité, fait*) established **3.** *Suisse* (*installé*) settled

établir [etabliʀ] <8> **I.** *vt* **1.** (*édifier*) to set up **2.** (*fixer: liste, emploi du temps*) to draw up; (*prix*) to set **3.** (*rédiger: facture, chèque*) to make out; (*constat*) to draw up **4.** (*faire: comparaison*) to draw; (*rapport*) to draw up **5.** (*déterminer: circonstances, identité*) to establish **6.** SPORT (*record*) to set **II.** *vpr* **s'**~ **1.** (*s'installer*) to settle **2.** (*professionnellement*) to set up (in business); **s'**~ **à son compte** to set up (in business) on one's own **3.** (*s'instaurer: usage*) to become customary; (*relations*) to develop; (*régime*) to become established; **le silence s'établit/s'établit de nouveau** silence fell/was restored **4.** (*se rendre indépendant*) to settle (down); **tous mes enfants se sont établis** all my children are settled

établissement [etablismɑ̃] *m* **1.** (*institution*) setting up; **les** ~**s Dupond** Dupond Ltd; ~ **scolaire** school; ~ **d'enseignement** educational establishment; ~ **d'enseignement secondaire** secondary school **2.** (*hôtel*) establishment

étage [etaʒ] *m* (*d'une maison*) floor; **immeuble à** [*o* **de**] **trois/quatre** ~**s** three/four storey building *Brit,* three/four story building *Am;* **à l'**~ upstairs

étager [etaʒe] <2a> **I.** *vt* (*objets*) to arrange in tiers **II.** *vpr* **s'**~ (*objets*) to be arranged in tiers; (*vignes, jardins*) to be tiered; (*maisons*) to stand in tiers

étagère [etaʒɛʀ] *f* **1.** (*tablette*) shelf **2.** (*meuble*) shelves *pl*

étai [etɛ] *m* prop

étain [etɛ̃] *m* pewter

étais [etɛ] *imparf de* **être**

étal [etal] <s> *m* stall; (*d'une boucherie*) block

étalage [etalaʒ] *m* **1.** COM (*action*) window dressing **2.** (*devanture*) display; (*tréteaux*) stall **3.** (*déploiement*) show; **faire** ~ **de qc** to put on a show [*o* display] of sth

étalagiste [etalaʒist] *mf* window dresser

étalement [etalmɑ̃] *m* **1.** (*action d'étaler: de papiers*) spreading **2.** (*échelonnement: d'une opération, d'un paiement*) spreading; (*des horaires*) staggering

étaler [etale] <1> **I.** *vt* **1.** (*éparpiller*) to strew **2.** (*déployer: carte, journal*) to spread out; (*tapis*) to unroll **3.** (*exposer pour la vente*) to set out **4.** (*étendre: peinture, gravier*) to spread **5.** (*dans le temps*) to spread out **6.** (*exhiber: connaissances*) to parade; (*luxe*) to flaunt **7.** *inf* (*échouer*) **se faire** ~ **à un examen** to flunk an exam **II.** *vpr* **1.** (*s'étendre*) **bien/mal s'**~ (*beurre*) to spread with ease/difficulty; (*peinture*) to go on with ease/difficulty **2.** (*dans l'espace*) **s'**~ (*plaine, ville*) to spread out **3.** (*s'afficher*) **s'**~ (*inscription, nom*) to be written **4.** (*s'exhiber*) **s'**~ (*luxe*) to flaunt itself **5.** (*se vautrer*) **s'**~ to sprawl **6.** *inf* (*tomber*) **s'**~ to go sprawling **7.** (*dans le temps*) **s'**~ **dans le temps** to be spread out over time

étalon [etalɔ̃] *m* (*cheval*) stallion

étalon-or [etalɔ̃ɔʀ] *m sans pl* gold standard

étamine [etamin] *f* **1.** BOT stamen **2.** (*tissu*) muslin

étanche [etɑ̃ʃ] *adj* (*montre*) waterproof; (*compartiment*) watertight

étanchéité [etɑ̃ʃeite] *f* **vérifier l'**~ **de qc** to check that sth is waterproof

étang [etɑ̃] *m* pond

étant [etɑ̃] *part prés de* **être**

étape [etap] *f* **1.** (*trajet, période*) stage; ~ **de la vie** stage in life; **d'**~ **en** ~ step by step; **faire qc par** ~**s** to do sth in steps; **il ne faut pas brûler les** ~**s!** one mustn't take short cuts! **2.** (*lieu d'arrêt, de repos*) stopping point; **faire** ~ to stop off

état [eta] *m* **1.** (*manière d'être*) state; ~ **d'urgence** state of emergency; **dans l'**~ **actuel des choses** as things are (at present); ~ **mental/physique** physical/mental condition; **être en** ~ (*stylo*) to work; (*machine, appareil*) to be in working order; (*appartement, maison*) to be in good condition; **être en** ~ **de marche** (*voiture, bicyclette*) to be in working condition; (*appareil, machine*) to be in working order; **être en** ~ **de** +*infin* to be in a fit state to +*infin* **2.** (*liste: des recettes, dépenses*) statement ►**en tout** ~ **de** <u>**cause**</u> in any event; ~ **d'**<u>**esprit**</u> state of mind; ~ <u>**civil**</u> civil status; (*service*) ≈ Registry Office; **ne pas être dans son** ~ <u>**normal**</u> not to be one's usual self; **être dans un** ~ <u>**second**</u> (*drogué*) to be on a high; <u>**avoir**</u> **des** ~**s d'âme** to be in the grip of anxiety; <u>**être**</u> **dans tous ses** ~**s** to be (all) worked up; <u>**être**</u> **en** ~ **de choc** MED to be in a state of shock

État [eta] *m* POL state; ~ **de droit** legitimate state; ~**s membres de l'UE** member states of the EU

étatiser [etatize] <1> *vt* to bring under state control

état-major [etamaʒɔʀ] <états-majors> *m* **1.** MIL (*personnes*) staff; (*bureaux*) staff headquarters **2.** POL (*d'un ministre*) advisers; (*d'un parti*) leadership; ECON (*d'une entreprise*) management

États-Unis [etazyni] *mpl* **les** ~ **d'Amérique** the United States of America

étau [eto] <x> *m* vice ►**être** <u>**pris**</u> (**comme**) **dans un** ~ to have one's head in a noose

étayer [eteje] <7> *vt* **1.** (*soutenir*) to shore up **2.** (*fonder*) ~ **son argument/raisonnement sur qc** to support one's argument/reasoning with sth; **une suite d'affirmations que rien n'étaie** a series of totally unsupported claims

etc [ɛtseteʀa] *abr de* **et cætera, et cetera** etc.

été[1] [ete] *m* summer; **l'**~ **indien** *Québec* (*bref retour du beau temps en octobre*) indian summer; *v. a.* **automne**

été[2] [ete] *part passé de* **être**

éteindre [etɛ̃dʀ] *irr* **I.** *vt* **1.** (*lumière, radio, chauffage*) to turn off; (*bougie*) to blow out; (*feu, cigarette*) to put out **2.** (*éteindre la* *lumière de*) ~ **la pièce/l'escalier** to turn the light off in the room/the stairs **II.** *vi* to put the light out **III.** *vpr* **s'~** (*cesser de brûler*) to go out

éteint(e) [etɛ̃, ɛ̃t] **I.** *part passé de* **éteindre II.** *adj* (*bougie, cigarette*) extinguished; (*volcan*) extinct

étendard [etɑ̃daʀ] *m* standard ▶**brandir** [*o* **lever**] **l'~ de la révolte** *soutenu* to raise the standard of revolt

étendre [etɑ̃dʀ] <14> **I.** *vt* **1.** (*coucher*) to lay out **2.** (*poser à plat: tapis*) to unroll; ~ **une couverture sur qn** to pull a blanket over sb **3.** (*faire sécher*) to hang out **4.** (*déployer: bras, jambes*) to stretch; (*ailes*) to spread **5.** *inf* (*faire tomber*) to floor **6.** *inf* (*coller à un examen*) to fail; **se faire ~** to get failed **II.** *vpr* **1.** (*se reposer*) **s'~** to lie down **2.** (*s'allonger*) to stretch oneself out **3.** (*s'appesantir*) **s'~ sur qc** to expand on sth **4.** (*occuper*) **s'~** to stretch out **5.** (*augmenter*) **s'~** (*épidémie, incendie, tache*) to spread; (*ville, pouvoir, connaissances, cercle*) to grow **6.** (*s'appliquer*) **s'~ à qn/qc** to apply to sb/sth

étendu(e) [etɑ̃dy] **I.** *part passé de* **étendre II.** *adj* **1.** (*déployé: corps, jambes*) outstretched; (*ailes*) outspread **2.** (*vaste: plaine, vue*) wide; (*ville*) sprawling **3.** (*considérable: connaissances, vocabulaire*) extensive; (*pouvoir*) wide-ranging; (*signification*) broad

étendue [etɑ̃dy] *f* **1.** (*dimension: d'un pays*) area **2.** (*espace*) expanse **3.** (*ampleur: d'une catastrophe*) scale; **l'~ des connaissances de qn** the extent of sb's knowledge

éternel(le) [etɛʀnɛl] *adj* **1.** (*qui dure longtemps*) eternal; (*regrets*) endless; (*recommencement*) constant **2.** *antéposé* (*inévitable*) inevitable **3.** *antéposé, péj* (*sempiternel*) perpetual

éternellement [etɛʀnɛlmɑ̃] *adv* eternally; (*depuis toujours*) always; (*sans arrêt*) constantly

éterniser [etɛʀnize] <1> **I.** *vt* (*faire traîner*) ~ **qc** to drag sth out **II.** *vpr* **s'~ 1.** (*traîner*) to drag on **2.** *inf* (*s'attarder*) to take for ever; **s'~ sur un sujet** to dwell endlessly on a subject

éternité [etɛʀnite] *f* eternity

éternuement [etɛʀnymɑ̃] *m gén pl* sneeze; **des ~s** sneezing + *vb sing*

éternuer [etɛʀnɥe] <1> *vi* to sneeze

êtes [ɛt] *indic prés de* **être**

éther [etɛʀ] *m* ether

Éthiopie [etjɔpi] *f* **l'~** Ethiopia

éthiopien [etjɔpjɛ̃] *m* Ethiopian; *v. a.* **français**

éthiopien(ne) [etjɔpjɛ̃, jɛn] *adj* Ethiopian

Éthiopien(ne) [etjɔpjɛ̃, jɛn] *m(f)* Ethiopian

éthique [etik] **I.** *adj* ethical **II.** *f* ethics *pl*

ethniciser [ɛtnisize] <1> *vt* ~ **qc** to give an ethnic dimension to sth

ethnie [ɛtni] *f* ethnic group

ethnique [ɛtnik] *adj* ethnic

ethnologie [ɛtnɔlɔʒi] *f* ethnology

étincelant(e) [etɛ̃s(ə)lɑ̃, ɑ̃t] *adj* **1.** (*scintillant*) sparkling **2.** (*éclatant: couleurs*) brilliant **3.** (*brillant: regard*) shining; (*yeux*) (*de joie*) gleaming; (*de haine*) flashing

étinceler [etɛ̃s(ə)le] <3> *vi* **1.** (*à la lumière: diamant*) to sparkle; (*or, couteau, lame*) to gleam; (*étoile*) to twinkle **2.** (*de propreté: vitre*) to gleam **3.** (*lancer comme des étincelles: yeux*) (*de joie*) to gleam; (*de haine*) to flash

étincelle [etɛ̃sɛl] *f* **1.** (*parcelle incandescente*) spark **2.** (*lueur*) **des ~s s'allument dans ses yeux** fire flashed in her eyes **3.** (*un petit peu de*) **une ~ de génie/d'intelligence** a spark of genius/intelligence ▶**cela fera des ~s** *inf* sparks will fly; **faire des ~s** *inf* to shine

étioler [etjɔle] <1> **I.** *vt* (*plantes*) to blanch; (*personne*) to weaken **II.** *vpr* **s'~** (*plante*) to wither; (*personne*) to fade away; (*esprit*) to stagnate

étiqueter [etikte] <3> *vt* to label

étiquette [etikɛt] *f* **1.** (*marque*) *a.* INFOR label; ~ **de réseau** netiquette **2.** (*adhésif*) sticker; (*de prix*) ticket **3.** (*protocole*) **l'~** etiquette

étirer [etiʀe] <1> *vpr* **s'~ 1.** (*s'allonger*) to stretch out **2.** (*se distendre: textile*) to stretch

étoffe [etɔf] *f* material

étoffer [etɔfe] <1> **I.** *vt* LIT (*récit, personnage*) to flesh out; (*devoir*) to fill out **II.** *vpr* **s'~** (*devenir plus fort: adolescent, sportif*) to fill out; (*devenir plus gros*) to broaden out

étoile [etwal] *f* star; ~ **filante/du berger** shooting/evening star; **en ~** star-shaped; **restaurant cinq ~s** five-star restaurant ▶**coucher** [*o* **dormir**] **à la belle ~** to sleep under the stars; **avoir foi** [*o* **être confiant**] **en son ~** to follow one's star

étoilé(e) [etwale] *adj* (*nuit*) starry

étonnamment [etɔnamɑ̃] *adv antéposé* (*bien, petit*) surprisingly

étonnant [etɔnɑ̃, ɑ̃t] *m* **l'~ est qu'elle reste** the amazing thing is that she's staying

étonnant(e) [etɔnɑ̃, ɑ̃t] *adj* **1.** (*surprenant*) amazing; **c'est ~, ...** it's amazing, ...; **ce n'est pas ~** it's no surprise **2.** (*remarquable: personne, ouvrage*) astonishing

étonné(e) [etɔne] *adj* astonished

étonnement [etɔnmɑ̃] *m* astonishment

étonner [etɔne] <1> **I.** *vt* to astonish **II.** *vpr* **s'~ de qc** to be surprised at sth; **s'~ que qn fasse qc** (*subj*) to be surprised at sb doing sth

étouffant(e) [etufɑ̃, ɑ̃t] *adj* stifling

étouffé(e) [etufe] *adj* (*bruit, son*) muffled; (*rires*) stifled

étouffée [etufe] *f* **cuire à l'~** to steam; (*viande*) to braise

étouffement [etufmɑ̃] *m* **1.** *sans pl* (*mort*) suffocation **2.** (*gêne*) **crise d'~** attack of breathlessness; **cette sensation d'~** this feeling of suffocation; **mourir d'~/être mort par ~** to die/have died of suffoation; **provoquer des ~s** to bring on attacks of breathlessness **3.** *sans pl* (*répression: d'une révolte*) stifling;

(*d'un scandale*) cover-up

étouffer [etufe] <1> I. *vt* 1. (*priver d'air*) to stifle; (*tuer*) to suffocate; **cette chaleur m'étouffe** I'm stifled by this heat; **la fureur étouffe qn** sb is overcome with anger 2. (*arrêter: feu*) to smother 3. (*atténuer: bruit*) to muffle 4. (*dissimuler: bâillement*) to stifle; (*sanglot*) to strangle; (*scandale*) to hush up 5. (*faire taire: rumeur, opposition*) to stifle 6. (*réprimer: révolte*) to put down; ~ **un complot dans l'œuf** to nip a plot in the bud ►**ce n'est pas la politesse qui l'étouffe** *inf* he doesn't care much about politeness II. *vi* to suffocate; **on étouffe ici!** it's suffocating in here! III. *vpr* **s'~** to choke

étourderie [etuʀdəʀi] *f* 1. *sans pl* (*caractère*) absent-mindedness 2. (*acte*) careless mistake

étourdi(e) [etuʀdi] I. *adj* scatterbrained II. *m(f)* scatterbrain

étourdir [etuʀdiʀ] <8> I. *vt* 1. (*assommer*) to stun; **ce choc à la tête l'a étourdi** he was dazed by that blow to the head 2. (*abrutir*) ~ **qn** (*bruit*) to deafen sb; (*mouvement*) to make sb dizzy; (*paroles*) to daze sb 3. (*enivrer*) ~ **qn** (*parfum, vin*) to go to sb's head II. *vpr* **s'~** to make oneself numb

étourdissant(e) [etuʀdisɑ̃, ɑ̃t] *adj* (*bruit*) deafening; (*succès, personne*) stunning; (*rythme*) dizzying

étourdissement [etuʀdismɑ̃] *m* dizzy spell; **l'odeur lui cause des ~s** the smell makes him feel dizzy

étourneau [etuʀno] <x> *m* starling

étrange [etʀɑ̃ʒ] *adj* strange

étrangement [etʀɑ̃ʒmɑ̃] *adv* 1. (*de façon étrange*) strangely 2. (*beaucoup, très*) surprisingly

étranger [etʀɑ̃ʒe] *m* **l'~** foreign countries; **séjourner à l'~** to live abroad

étranger, -ère [etʀɑ̃ʒe, -ɛʀ] I. *adj* 1. (*d'un autre pays*) foreign 2. (*d'un autre groupe*) outside; **être ~ à la famille** not to belong to the family 3. (*non familier: usage, notion*) unfamiliar 4. (*extérieur*) **être ~ au sujet** to be irrelevant to the subject; **être ~ à une affaire/un complot** to have nothing to do with an affair/a plot II. *m, f* 1. (*d'un autre pays*) foreigner 2. (*d'une autre région*) outsider

étrangeté [etʀɑ̃ʒte] *f sans pl* (*originalité*) strangeness

étranglé(e) [etʀɑ̃gle] *adj* (*voix, son*) strained

étranglement [etʀɑ̃gləmɑ̃] *m* 1. (*strangulation*) strangling; **la victime est morte par ~** the victim died by strangulation [*o* was strangled] 2. (*resserrement: d'un tuyau*) constriction; (*d'une vallée*) neck; ~ **d'une rue** bottleneck 3. (*de la voix*) strained tone

étrangler [etʀɑ̃gle] <1> I. *vt* 1. (*tuer*) to strangle; ~ **un animal** to wring an animal's neck 2. (*serrer le cou*) ~ **qn** (*cravate*) to choke sb 3. (*empêcher qn de parler*) **l'émotion/la fureur l'étranglait** she was choking with emotion/fury II. *vpr* **s'~ avec qc** 1. (*mourir*) to strangle oneself with sth 2. (*en mangeant*) to choke on sth

étrangleur, -euse [etʀɑ̃glœʀ, -øz] *m, f* strangler

étrave [etʀav] *f* stem

être [ɛtʀ] *irr* I. *vi* 1. (*pour qualifier, indiquer le lieu*) to be; ~ **professeur/infirmière** to be a teacher/a nurse; **le stylo est là, sur le bureau** the pen's over there on the desk 2. (*pour indiquer la date, la période*) **quel jour sommes-nous?** what day is it?; **on est le 2 mai/mercredi** it's May 2/Wednesday 3. (*appartenir*) ~ **à qn** to belong to sb 4. (*travailler*) ~ **dans l'enseignement/le textile** to be in teaching/textiles 5. (*pour indiquer l'activité en cours*) ~ **toujours à faire qc** to be always doing sth 6. (*pour exprimer une étape d'une évolution*) **où en es-tu de tes maths?** how are you doing in maths? *Brit*, how are you doing in math? *Am;* **en ~ à faire qc** to have got as far as doing sth; (*en arriver à*) to have got to the point of doing sth; **j'en suis à me demander si ...** I'm beginning to wonder if ... 7. (*être absorbé par, attentif à*) ~ **tout à son travail** to be completely taken up with one's work; **ne pas ~ à ce qu'on fait** not to have one's mind on what one's doing 8. (*pour exprimer l'obligation*) **qc est à faire** sth must be done; **ce livre est à lire absolument** this book is a must (read) 9. (*provenir*) ~ **de qn** (*enfant*) to be sb's; (*œuvre*) to be by sb; ~ **d'une région/famille** to be from a region/family 10. (*être vêtu/chaussé de*) ~ **en costume/pantoufles** to be in a suit/slippers; ~ **tout en rouge** to be all in red 11. *au passé* (*aller*) **avoir été faire/acheter qc** to have gone to do/buy sth 12. (*exister*) to be; **la voiture la plus économique qui soit** the most economical car around ►**je suis <u>à</u> toi/vous tout de suite** I'll be with you right away; **je n'y suis <u>pour</u> rien** it's nothing to do with me; **ça <u>y</u> est** (*c'est fini*) that's it; (*je comprends*) I see; (*je te l'avais dit*) there you are; (*pour calmer qn*) there, there; **ça y est, voilà qu'il pleut!** there you are, it's raining; **ça y est?** OK?; **c'est vrai, n'est-ce <u>pas</u>?** it's true, isn't it? II. *vi impers* **il est impossible/étonnant que qn ait fait qc** (*subj*) it's impossible/surprising that sb did sth; **il est dix heures/midi/minuit** it's ten o'clock/noon/midnight III. *aux* 1. (*comme auxiliaire du passé actif*) ~ **venu** to have come; **s'~ rencontrés** to have met 2. (*comme auxiliaire du passif*) **le sol est lavé chaque jour** the floor is washed every day IV. *m* being

étreindre [etʀɛ̃dʀ] *irr* I. *vt* 1. (*ami*) to embrace; (*adversaire*) to seize 2. (*s'emparer de*) ~ **qn** (*angoisse, douleur*) to take hold of sb 3. (*serrer*) ~ **le cœur à qn** to break sb's heart II. *vpr* **s'~** (*amis*) to embrace; (*lutteurs*) to take hold of each other

étreinte [etʀɛ̃t] *f* (*d'un ami*) embrace; (*d'un

adversaire, serpent) grip; (*d'un bras, d'une main*) clasp; **desserrer son ~ autour de qn/qc** (*ennemi, armée*) to loosen one's grip on sb/sth; **resserrer son ~ autour de qn/qc** to tighten one's grip on sb/sth

étrenner [etRene] <1> *vt* (*vêtement*) to wear for the first time; (*appareil*) to try [*o* use] for the first time

étrennes [etRɛn] *fpl* **1.** first use **2.** (*à un enfant*) present (*at New Year*); **recevoir qc pour ses ~** to get sth for New Year

étrier [etRije] *m* stirrup; **vider les ~s** (*tomber de cheval*) to fall off

étriller [etRije] <1> *vt* (*cheval*) to curry

étriqué(e) [etRike] *adj* **1.** (*vêtement*) tight **2.** (*mentalité*) narrow; (*esprit*) mean

étroit(e) [etRwa, wat] *adj* **1.** (*opp: large: rue*) narrow; (*chaussures*) tight; **il est à l'~ dans cette veste** that jacket is rather tight on him; **vivre à l'~** to live on a tight budget; **être logé à l'~** to live in cramped conditions **2.** (*opp: lâche, relâché: lien, surveillance*) tight

étroitement [etRwatmɑ̃] *adv* **1.** (*serré*) tight(ly); (*être logé*) in cramped conditions **2.** (*lié, surveiller*) closely; (*uni*) tightly

étroitesse [etRwatɛs] *f* **1. l'~ de sa jupe la gênait** her tight dress was bothering her; **l'~ du chemin est telle ...** the road is so narrow that ...; **être surpris par l'~ du logement** to be surprised at how cramped the accommodation is **2.** *péj* (*des vues, pensées*) narrowness

étude [etyd] **I.** *f* **1.** (*apprentissage*) study *no pl* **2.** (*recherches, ouvrage: de la nature, d'un dossier, projet*) study; **l'~ d'une question** studying a question; **~ de marché** market research *no pl;* **~ sur qc** study on sth **3.** (*bureau: d'un notaire*) office **4.** ECOLE (*moment*) prep **II.** *fpl* study; **~s primaires/secondaires/supérieures** primary/secondary/higher education; **faire des ~s** to go to university *Brit,* to go to college *Am;* **faire des ~s de médecine** to study medicine

> In France, studies are not separated by semester, but by year. Study courses can be taken by those who lag behind. In this way, students have generally finished their **études** by 26 or 27 years old.

étudiant(e) [etydjɑ̃, jɑ̃t] **I.** *adj* student **II.** *m(f)* student

étudié(e) [etydje] *adj* **1.** (*soigné*) **jeu d'un acteur très ~** very studied acting **2.** (*avantageux*) **conditions très ~es** highly competitive terms; **prix très ~** highly competitive price **3.** (*recherché*) **robe très ~e** skilfully designed dress **4.** (*affecté: gestes, politesse*) studied

étudier [etydje] <1> **I.** *vt, vi* to study **II.** *vpr* **s'~ 1.** (*s'analyser*) to analyse oneself **2.** (*s'observer mutuellement*) to study each other

étui [etɥi] *m* case; **~ à cigarettes/lunettes** cigarette/spectacle case; **~ à violon** violin case; **~ de parapluie** umbrella cover

étuve [etyv] *f* **1.** (*à désinfection*) sterilizer **2.** (*fournaise*) oven; **quelle ~ ici!** it's boiling in here!

étuvée [etyve] *f v.* **étouffée**

étymologie [etimɔlɔʒi] *f* etymology

étymologique [etimɔlɔʒik] *adj* etymological

eu(e) [y] *part passé de* **avoir**

eucalyptus [økaliptys] *m* eucalyptus

eucharistie [økaRisti] *f* **l'~** the eucharist

euh [ø] *interj* er

eunuque [ønyk] *m* eunuch

euphémisme [øfemism] *m* euphemism

euphorie [øfɔRi] *f* euphoria

euphorique [øfɔRik] *adj* euphoric

EUR *m abr de* **euro** EUR

eurasien(ne) [øRazjɛ̃, jɛn] *adj* Eurasian

Eurasien(ne) [øRazjɛ̃, jɛn] *m(f)* Eurasian

euro [øRo] *m* euro

euro centime *m* euro-cent

eurochèque [øRoʃɛk] *m* Eurocheque

eurodevise [øRod(ə)viz] *f* eurocurrency

Europe [øRɔp] *f* **l'~** Europe; **l'~ centrale/de l'Est/l'Ouest** Central/Eastern/Western Europe; **l'~ des Quinze** the fifteen; **faire l'~** to build Europe

européanisation [øRɔpeanizasjɔ̃] *f* Europeanization

européaniser [øRɔpeanize] <1> **I.** *vt* to Europeanize **II.** *vpr* **s'~** to be Europeanized

européen(ne) [øRɔpeɛ̃, ɛn] **I.** *adj* **1.** GEO **le continent ~** the European continent; **les fleuves ~s** the rivers of Europe **2.** POL, ECON European; **l'Union ~ne** the European Union **II.** *fpl* (*les élections ~nes*) the European elections

Européen(ne) [øRɔpeɛ̃, ɛn] *m(f)* European

eurosceptique [øRosɛptik] *adj, mf* eurosceptic

eurosignal [øRosiɲal] *m* pager

eus [y] *passé simple de* **avoir**

euthanasie [øtanazi] *f* euthanasia; **pratiquer l'~** to practise euthanasia

eux [ø] *pron pers, pl masc ou mixte* **1.** *inf* (*pour renforcer*) **~, ils n'ont pas ouvert la bouche** THEY didn't open their mouths; **c'est ~ qui l'ont dit** THEY said it; **il veut les aider, ~?** he wants to help THEM? **2.** *avec une préposition* **avec/sans ~** with/without them; **à ~ seuls** by themselves; **la maison est à ~** the house is theirs; **c'est à ~ de décider** it's up to them to decide; **c'est à ~!** it's theirs! **3.** *dans une comparaison* them; **elles sont comme ~** they're like them; **plus fort qu'~** stronger than them **4.** (*soi*) them; *v. a.* **lui**

eux-mêmes [ømɛm] *pron pers* (*eux en personne*) themselves; *v. a.* **moi-même, nous-même**

évacuation [evakɥasjɔ̃] *f* **1.** (*opération organisée: des habitants, blessés*) evacuation; (*d'une salle de tribunal*) clearing **2.** (*écoulement*) draining; **système d'~** drainage system; **l'~ des eaux usées se fait ...** waste

E

water is drained off ... **3.** *Suisse* (*action de vider*) ~ **des ordures** waste disposal

évacuer [evakɥe] <1> *vt* **1.** *a.* MIL (*ville, habitants, blessés*) to evacuate **2.** (*vider: eaux usées*) to drain away

évadé(e) [evade] *m(f)* escapee

évader [evade] <1> *vpr* **1.** (*s'échapper*) **s'~ d'une prison** to escape from prison **2.** (*fuir*) **s'~ du réel** to escape reality

évaluateur, -trice [evalɥatœʀ, -tʀis] *m, f Québec* (*personne qui évalue notamment les biens immobiliers*) appraiser

évaluation [evalɥasjɔ̃] *f* **1.** (*estimation approximative: des coûts, risques, chances*) assessment; (*d'une fortune*) valuation **2.** (*par expertise: des dégâts*) appraisal; ~ **des connaissances** ECOLE assessment of attainment *Brit,* aptitude test *Am*

évaluer [evalɥe] <1> *vt* (*poids, distance*) to estimate; (*chances*) to assess

évangéliser [evɑ̃ʒelize] <1> *vt* (*peuple, pays*) to evangelize

évangile [evɑ̃ʒil] *m* (*texte, livre*) gospel

évanoui(e) [evanwi] *adj* **1.** (*sans conscience: personne*) unconscious; **tomber** ~ to faint **2.** (*disparu: bonheur, rêve*) vanished

évanouir [evanwiʀ] <8> *vpr* **1.** (*perdre connaissance*) **s'~ de qc** to faint with sth **2.** (*disparaître*) **s'~** (*image, fantôme*) to vanish; (*illusions, espoirs*) to fade away

évanouissement [evanwismɑ̃] *m* **1.** (*syncope*) faint; **avoir un** ~ to faint **2.** (*disparition*) disappearance; (*d'une illusion, d'un rêve*) vanishing

évaporation [evapɔʀasjɔ̃] *f* evaporation

évaporé(e) [evapɔʀe] *adj* scatterbrained

évaporer [evapɔʀe] <1> *vpr* **s'~** (*eau, parfum*) to evaporate

évasé(e) [evɑze] *adj* (*jupe, manche*) flared; **être ~ à la base** (*colonne*) splayed at the base

évasif, -ive [evazif, -iv] *adj* evasive

évasion [evazjɔ̃] *f* escape

évasivement [evazivmɑ̃] *adv* evasively

Ève [ɛːv(ə)] *f* Eve ►**ne connaître qn ni d'~ ni d'Adam** to not know sb from Adam

évêché [eveʃe] *m* **1.** (*territoire*) diocese **2.** (*palais*) bishop's palace

éveil [evɛj] *m* **1.** (*état éveillé*) **tenir qn en ~** to keep sb on the alert **2.** (*réveil*) ~ **des sens/d'un sentiment chez qn** the awakening of the senses/of a feeling in sb

éveillé(e) [eveje] *adj* **1.** (*en état de veille*) awake **2.** (*alerte*) alert; **esprit** ~ lively mind

éveiller [eveje] <1> **I.** *vt* **1.** (*faire naître: attention*) to attract; (*désir, soupçons*) to arouse **2.** (*développer: intelligence*) to stimulate **II.** *vpr* **1.** (*naître*) **s'~ chez** [*o* **en**] **qn** (*amour*) to awaken in sb; (*soupçon*) to be aroused in sb's mind **2.** (*éprouver pour la première fois*) **s'~ à l'amour** (*personne*) to awaken to love **3.** (*se mettre à fonctionner*) **s'~** (*esprit*) to come to life

événement, évènement [evɛnmɑ̃] *m* event; **les ~s de mai 1968** the events of May 1968 ►**créer l'~** to be the major event; **elle est dépassée par les ~s** she's been overtaken by the events

éventail [evɑ̃taj] <s> *m* **1.** fan; **en** ~ fan-shaped; **disposés en** ~ fanned out **2.** (*choix*) range

éventaire [evɑ̃tɛʀ] *m* **1.** (*plateau*) tray **2.** (*étalage*) stall

éventé(e) [evɑ̃te] *adj* (*exposé au vent: terrasse*) windy; (*altéré par l'air: parfum*) stale; (*vin*) musty; (*découvert: secret*) open

éventer [evɑ̃te] <1> **I.** *vt* **1.** ~ **qn** to fan sb **2.** (*découvrir: complot*) to lay bare; (*secret*) to lay open **II.** *vpr* **s'~** **1.** (*personne*) to fan oneself **2.** (*vin*) to go musty; (*parfum*) to go stale

éventrer [evɑ̃tʀe] <1> *vt* **1.** (*tuer*) to disembowel **2.** (*ouvrir: sac, matelas*) to rip open; (*porte*) to smash open

éventualité [evɑ̃tɥalite] *f* **1.** (*caractère*) **dans l'~ d'une guerre** in the event of a war **2.** (*possibilité*) possibility

éventuel(le) [evɑ̃tɥɛl] *adj* possible

éventuellement [evɑ̃tɥɛlmɑ̃] *adv* possibly

évêque [evɛk] *m* bishop

évertuer [evɛʀtɥe] <1> *vpr* **s'~ à** +*infin* to endeavour to +*infin*

évidemment [evidamɑ̃] *adv* **1.** (*en tête de phrase, en réponse*) of course **2.** (*comme on peut le voir*) obviously

évidence [evidɑ̃s] *f* **1.** *sans pl* (*caractère*) obviousness; **de toute** [*o* **à l'**] ~ obviously **2.** (*fait*) obvious fact; **c'est une** ~ it's obvious; **se rendre à l'~** to accept the obvious; **refuser de se rendre à l'~** to ignore the obvious **3.** (*vue*) **être bien en** ~ (*objet*) to be there for all to see; **se mettre en** ~ to push oneself foreward

évident(e) [evidɑ̃, ɑ̃t] *adj* obvious; (*signe*) clear; (*bonne volonté*) evident; **il est ~ que qn a fait qc** it's obvious sb did sth ►**c'est pas ~!** *inf* it's not a simple matter!

évider [evide] <1> *vt* to scoop out

évier [evje] *m* sink

évincer [evɛ̃se] <2> *vt* JUR to evict; (*personne*) to oust

évitable [evitabl] *adj* avoidable

éviter [evite] <1> **I.** *vt* **1.** (*se soustraire à, fuir: erreur, endroit, regard, conflit*) to avoid; ~ **de faire qc** to avoid doing sth; ~ **que qn** (**ne**) **fasse qc** (*subj*) to prevent sb from doing sth; **évite de passer par Lyon** avoid going via Lyon; **il m'évite** he's avoiding me **2.** (*se dérober à: sort, corvée*) to evade; ~ **de faire qc** to get out of doing sth; **pour ~ d'aller en prison** to avoid going to prison; **pour ~ d'avoir à éplucher les légumes** to get out of peeling the vegetables **3.** (*épargner*) ~ **qc à qn** to spare sb sth **II.** *vpr* **1.** (*essayer de ne pas se rencontrer*) **s'~** to avoid each other **2.** (*ne pas avoir*) **s'~ des soucis/tracas** to avoid worries/trouble

évocateur, -trice [evɔkatœʀ, -tʀis] *adj*

(*style*) evocative; (*titre d'un roman*) suggestive; **pouvoir** ~ power of suggestion; **être** ~ **de qc** to be suggestive of sth

évocation [evɔkasjɔ̃] *f* (*de souvenirs*) evocation; (*de faits, d'un passé*) recalling

évolué(e) [evɔlɥe] *adj* (*pays, société*) advanced; (*idées, personne*) progressive

évoluer [evɔlɥe] <1> *vi* **1.** (*changer: chose, monde*) to change; (*sciences*) to evolve, to advance; (*goûts, situation*) to develop **2.** (*se transformer: personne, maladie*) to develop; ~ **vers qc** to develop into sth; **ce séjour l'a fait** ~ this stay has helped his personal development

évolutif, -ive [evɔlytif, -iv] *adj* (*maladie*) progressive

évolution [evɔlysjɔ̃] *f* **1.** (*développement: d'une personne, maladie, d'un phénomène*) development; (*des goûts, comportements*) change; (*des sciences*) advance; **l'**~ **des techniques** technical progress **2.** BIO evolution; **théorie de l'**~ theory of evolution

évolutionnisme [evɔlysjɔnism] *m* evolutionism

évoquer [evɔke] <1> *vt* **1.** (*rappeler à la mémoire: fait, enfance, souvenirs*) to recall; ~ **qn** to call sb to mind **2.** (*décrire*) to conjure up **3.** (*faire allusion à: problème, sujet*) to bring up **4.** (*faire penser à*) **ce mot n'évoque rien pour moi** the word doesn't bring anything to mind

ex [ɛks] *mf inf* ex

ex, ex. [ɛks] *abr de* **exemple** e.g.

exacerber [ɛgzasɛʀbe] <1> *vt* (*jalousie, passion*) to heighten; (*haine, dépit*) to deepen; (*douleur*) to exacerbate

exact(e) [ɛgzakt] *adj* **1.** (*précis: description, valeur, mots*) exact **2.** (*correct: calculs, réponse*) right; **c'est** ~ **qu'elle l'a fait** it is true that she did it **3.** (*ponctuel: personne*) punctual

exactement [ɛgzaktəmɑ̃] *adv* exactly; **c'est** ~ **ce que j'ai dit** that's exactly what I said

exactions [ɛgzaksjɔ̃] *fpl* (*violences*) acts of violence

exactitude [ɛgzaktityd] *f* **1.** (*précision*) accuracy; **avec** ~ accurately **2.** (*ponctualité*) punctuality; **arriver avec** ~ to arrive right on time; **être d'une parfaite** ~ to be absolutely punctual

ex æquo [ɛgzeko] **I.** *adj inv* **être premier** ~ **en qc** to be joint first in sth *Brit*, to be tied for first in sth *Am* **II.** *adv* (*classer*) equal; **arriver en troisième place** ~ to finish in joint third place *Brit*, to finish tied for third place *Am*; **premiers/premier prix** ~ joint first/first prizewinners **III.** *mpl* joint winners, co-winners

exagération [ɛgzaʒeʀasjɔ̃] *f* exaggeration

exagéré(e) [ɛgzaʒeʀe] *adj* exaggerated; (*prix*) inflated; **être un peu** ~ (*plaisanterie*) to be a bit much

exagérément [ɛgzaʒeʀemɑ̃] *adv* excessively

exagérer [ɛgzaʒeʀe] <5> **I.** *vt* to exaggerate; **il ne faut rien** ~, **n'exagérons rien** let's not exaggerate **II.** *vi* **1.** (*amplifier en parlant*) to exaggerate **2.** (*abuser*) to go too far

exaltant(e) [ɛgzaltɑ̃, ɑ̃t] *adj* exciting; **ce n'est pas** ~ it's no big thrill; **pour qu'un travail soit** ~ for a job to be rewarding

exaltation [ɛgzaltasjɔ̃] *f* **1.** (*excitation*) excitement; ~**s intellectuelles et mystiques** mental and mystical exaltation **2.** (*éloge*) glorification

exalté(e) [ɛgzalte] **I.** *adj* excited; (*personne*) elated; (*imagination*) fevered; **il parlait sur un ton un peu** ~ he was speaking rather excitedly **II.** *m(f) péj* hothead

exalter [ɛgzalte] <1> **I.** *vt* **1.** *soutenu* (*célébrer*) to glorify **2.** (*faire vibrer: esprit, imagination*) to arouse; (*foule, jeunesse*) to fire **II.** *vpr* **s'**~ (*personne*) to get excited; (*imagination*) to be fired; **les passions politiques s'exaltent** political passions are aroused

examen [ɛgzamɛ̃] *m* **1.** examination; ~ **d'entrée/de passage** entrance/end-of-year exam *Brit*, entrance/final exam *Am* **2.** JUR **mise en** ~ charging

examinateur, -trice [ɛgzaminatœʀ, -tʀis] *m, f* examiner

examiner [ɛgzamine] <1> **I.** *vt* to examine; (*maison*) to look over **II.** *vpr* **s'**~ **dans un miroir** to examine oneself in a mirror

exaspérant(e) [ɛgzaspeʀɑ̃, ɑ̃t] *adj* exasperating; **être d'une lenteur** ~**e** to be exasperatingly slow; **c'est** ~**!** it's (so) exasperating!; **il est** ~ **avec sa manie de ...** he's so exasperating the way he ...

exaspération [ɛgzaspeʀasjɔ̃] *f* exasperation; **d'**~, **elle se mit à sangloter** she began to sob with exasperation

exaspérer [ɛgzaspeʀe] <5> *vt* ~ **qn avec qc** to exasperate sb with sth; **ton père est exaspéré** your father's exasperated

exaucer [ɛgzose] <2> *vt* **1.** (*écouter: Dieu*) to hear **2.** (*réaliser: désir, souhait*) to grant

excavateur, -trice [ɛkskavatœʀ, tʀis] *m, f* digger

excavation [ɛkskavasjɔ̃] *f* (*cavité*) excavation; (*causée par une bombe*) crater; ~ **naturelle** hollow; **creuser des** ~**s** (*archéologues*) to dig

excédent [ɛksedɑ̃] *m* surplus; ~ **de bagages** excess baggage

excédentaire [ɛksedɑ̃tɛʀ] *adj* surplus; (*balance commerciale*) in surplus; **production** ~ production surplus to requirements

excéder [ɛksede] <5> *vt* **1.** (*dépasser: poids, durée, moyens, forces*) to exceed; **ne pas** ~ **3000 euros** not to exceed 3000 euros; **le stationnement ne doit pas** ~ **15 minutes** parking 15 minutes maximum **2.** (*exaspérer*) ~ **qn avec** [*o* **par**] **qc** to exasperate sb with sth; **être excédé** (*être à bout*) to be worn out; (*être

énervé) to be infuriated
excellence [ɛkselɑ̃s] *f* excellence; **l'~ de son goût** her excellent taste ▶**par** ~ par excellence
excellent(e) [ɛkselɑ̃, ɑ̃t] *adj* excellent
exceller [ɛksele] <1> *vi* ~ **en musique/dans son domaine/aux échecs** to excel in music/in one's field/at chess; ~ **à cuisiner/écrire** to be an excellent cook/writer
excentricité [ɛksɑ̃tʀisite] *f sans pl* eccentricity; **l'~ de son comportement/caractère** his eccentric behaviour/character *Brit,* his eccentric behavior/character *Am*
excentrique [ɛksɑ̃tʀik] **I.** *adj* eccentric **II.** *mf* eccentric
excepté [ɛksɛpte] *prep* except; ~ **que/si qn fait qc** except that/if sb does sth; **avoir tout prévu,** ~ **ce cas** to have foreseen everyhing but this situation
excepter [ɛksɛpte] <1> *vt* ~ **qn de qc** to except sth from sth; **tous les devoirs, sans en** ~ **un seul, sont mauvais** all the assignments, with no exceptions, are bad
exception [ɛksɛpsjɔ̃] *f* exception; **régime d'~** special treatment; **faire** ~ **à la règle** to be an exception to the rule; **à l'~ de qn/qc** with the exception of sb/sth; **sauf** ~ allowing for exceptions
exceptionnel(le) [ɛksɛpsjɔnɛl] *adj* **1.**(*extraordinaire: personne*) exceptional; (*occasion*) unique; **cela n'a rien d'~** there's nothing remarkable about that **2.**(*occasionnel: prime, congé, mesure*) special; **à titre** ~ exceptionally
exceptionnellement [ɛksɛpsjɔnɛlmɑ̃] *adv* exceptionally
excès [ɛksɛ] *m* **1.**(*surplus*) ~ **de vitesse** speeding; ~ **de zèle** overzealousness **2.** *pl* (*abus, violences*) excesses ▶**tomber dans l'~ inverse** to go to the opposite extreme; **pousser qc à l'~** to take sth to extremes; **manger/dépenser avec/sans** ~ to eat/spend to excess/in moderation
excessif, -ive [ɛksesif, -iv] *adj* **1.** excessive **2.**(*immodéré: tempérament*) extreme; **être** ~ **dans son jugement** to go to extremes in one's judgments
excessivement [ɛksesivmɑ̃] *adv* excessively; (*manger*) to excess; **être** ~ **cher** to be inordinately expensive
excipient [ɛksipjɑ̃] *m* MED excipient
exciser [ɛksize] <1> *vt* to excise
excision [ɛksizjɔ̃] *f* MED excision
excitant(e) [ɛksitɑ̃, ɑ̃t] *adj* **1.** exciting **2.**(*stimulant: café*) stimulating
excitation [ɛksitasjɔ̃] *f* excitement
excité(e) [ɛksite] **I.** *adj* excited **II.** *m(f)* hothead
exciter [ɛksite] <1> **I.** *vt* **1.**(*provoquer: désir, curiosité*) to arouse **2.**(*aviver: imagination*) to excite; (*douleur*) to increase **3.**(*passionner*) ~ **qn** (*idée, travail*) to excite sb; (*sensation*) to give sb a thrill **4.**(*mettre en colère*) ~ **qn** (*personne*) to irritate sb; (*alcool, chaleur*) to make sb irritable **5.**(*troubler sexuellement*) to arouse **II.** *vpr* **s'~ sur qc 1.**(*s'énerver*) to get worked up about sth **2.** *inf* (*s'acharner*) to go hard at sth
exclamatif, -ive [ɛksklamatif, -iv] *adj* **phrase exclamative** exclamatory phrase
exclamation [ɛksklamasjɔ̃] *f* exclamation; ~ **de douleur/de joie** cry of pain/joy; **point d'~** exclamation mark
exclamer [ɛksklame] <1> *vpr* **s'~ de joie** to shout for joy; **s'~ de douleur** to scream in pain; **s'~ sur qc** to gasp in admiration
exclu(e) [ɛkskly] **I.** *part passé de* **exclure** **II.** *adj* **1.**(*impossible*) **il n'est pas** ~ **que** +*subj* it is not impossible that **2.**(*non compris*) **mardi** ~ Tuesday excepted **III.** *m(f)* **les ~s** the excluded
exclure [ɛksklyʀ] *irr* **I.** *vt* **1.**(*sortir*) ~ **qn d'un parti/d'une école** to expel sb from a party/a school; ~ **qn d'une équipe** to bar sb from a team *Brit,* to kick sb off a team *Am;* ~ **qn d'une salle** to throw sb out of a room **2.**(*écarter: possibilité, hypothèse*) to rule out; (*élément*) to ignore **II.** *vpr* **s'~** to be mutually exclusive
exclusif, -ive [ɛksklyzif, -iv] *adj* exclusive
exclusion [ɛksklyzjɔ̃] *f* exclusion; (*du lycée*) expulsion
exclusivement [ɛksklyzivmɑ̃] *adv* **1.**(*seulement, uniquement*) exclusively **2.**(*exclu*) exclusive
exclusivité [ɛksklyzivite] *f* exclusive rights *pl;* **une** ~ **XY** an XY exclusive, a scoop ▶**en** ~ exclusively
excommunier [ɛkskɔmynje] <1a> *vt* to excommunicate
excroissance [ɛkskʀwasɑ̃s] *f* excrescence
excursion [ɛkskyʀsjɔ̃] *f* excursion
excusable [ɛkskyzabl] *adj* excusable
excuse [ɛkskyz] *f* **1.**(*raison, prétexte*) excuse; **la belle ~!** that's a fine excuse! **2.** *pl* (*regret*) **faire des ~s** to apologize; **mille ~s!** I'm so sorry!
excuser [ɛkskyze] <1> **I.** *vt* **1.**(*pardonner: faute, retard*) to forgive; **excuse-moi/excusez-moi!** forgive me! **2.**(*défendre: personne, conduite*) to excuse ▶**vous êtes tout excusé** don't apologize **II.** *vpr* **s'~ de qc** to apologize for sth ▶**je m'excuse de vous déranger** forgive me for bothering you
exécrable [ɛgzekʀabl] *adj* appalling; (*nourriture*) foul; (*film, poème*) ghastly
exécrer [ɛgzekʀe] <1> *vt* to abhor
exécutant(e) [ɛgzekytɑ̃, ɑ̃t] *m(f)* **1.**(*agent*) subordinate; **être un simple** ~ to just carry out orders **2.** MUS performer
exécuter [ɛgzekyte] <1> *vt* **1.**(*effectuer: projet*) to carry out; (*travail*) to do; ~ **les dernières volontés de qn** to grant sb's last wishes **2.** INFOR (*fichier*) to run **3.**(*tuer*) to execute
exécutif [ɛgzekytif] *m* executive
exécutif, -ive [ɛgzekytif, -iv] *adj* **comité** ~

executive committee; **pouvoir** ~ executive power

exécution [ɛgzekysjɔ̃] *f* **1.** (*d'un travail*) doing; (*d'un projet*) carrying out; (*d'un programme*) implementation; (*d'une commande*) fulfilment *Brit*, fulfillment *Am*; **mettre une loi à** ~ to enforce a law; **mettre une menace à** ~ to carry out a threat **2.** JUR (*d'un jugement*) enforcement **3.** (*mise à mort*) execution

exemplaire [ɛgzɑ̃plɛʀ] **I.** *adj* exemplary **II.** *m* **1.** (*copie: d'un livre*) copy; **en deux ~s** in duplicate **2.** (*spécimen*) specimen

exemplatif, **-ive** [ɛgzɑ̃platif, -iv] *adj Belgique* (*relatif à l'exemple*) exemplificative

exemple [ɛgzɑ̃pl] *m* (*modèle, illustration*) example; **citer qn/qc en** ~ to give sb/sth as an example; **donner l'**~ to show an example; **prendre** ~ **sur qn** to follow sb's example; **par** ~ for example ►(**ça/tiens**) **par** ~! *inf* (*indignation*) well, really!; (*surprise*) well, how about that!

exempt(**e**) [ɛgzɑ̃(pt), ɑ̃(p)t] *adj* **1.** (*dispensé: personne*) exempt; **être** ~ **du service militaire** to be exempt from military service; ~ **de taxes/d'affranchissement** tax/postage free **2.** (*dépourvu*) free; ~ **de danger, défaut** free from danger/defect; ~ **d'erreur** error-free

exempter [ɛgzɑ̃(p)te] <1> *vt* **1.** (*personne*) to exempt; (*décharger*) to discharge; **être exempté d'impôts/de T.V.A.** (*revenu, marchandise*) to be tax-free/VAT-free **2.** (*préserver*) ~ **qn de la paresse** to keep sb from becoming lazy

exercer [ɛgzɛʀse] <2> **I.** *vt* **1.** (*pratiquer: fonction*) to fulfil *Brit*, to fulfill *Am*; ~ **le métier de professeur/d'infirmière** to work as a teacher/nurse **2.** (*mettre en usage: pouvoir, droit*) to exercise; (*talent*) to use; (*pression, autorité*) to exert **3.** (*entraîner: oreille, goût, mémoire*) to train; (*jugement*) to exercise; ~ **les élèves à lire à voix basse** to give pupils lessons in reading quietly **II.** *vi* to practise *Brit*, to practice *Am* **III.** *vpr* **1.** (*s'entraîner*) **s'**~ to practise *Brit*, to practice *Am*; SPORT to train; **s'**~ **à la trompette** to practise the trumpet **2.** (*se manifester*) **s'**~ **dans un domaine** (*habileté, influence*) to be put to use in a field

exercice [ɛgzɛʀsis] *m* **1.** ECOLE, MUS, SPORT exercise; ~ **à trous** fill-in-the-gap exercise *Brit*, fill-in-the blank exercise *Am*; **faire des ~s au piano** to do piano exercises **2.** *sans pl* (*activité physique*) exercise; **faire** [*o* **prendre**] **de l'**~ to exercise **3.** (*pratique: d'un droit, du pouvoir*) exercise; (*de la médecine*) practice; **l'**~ **d'un métier** doing a job; **dans l'**~ **de ses fonctions** in the exercise of one's duties ►**en** ~ practising *Brit*, practicing *Am*; POL in office

ex-femme [ɛksfam] <ex-femmes> *f* **mon** ~ my ex-wife

exhaler [ɛgzale] <1> **I.** *vt* **1.** (*répandre*) ~ **qc** to give off sth **2.** (*laisser échapper: soupir*) to heave; ~ **le dernier soupir** to breathe one's last **II.** *vpr* **s'**~ **de qc** (*gémissement*) to came from; (*parfum*) to emanate from

exhaustif, **-ive** [ɛgzostif, -iv] *adj* exhaustive

exhiber [ɛgzibe] <1> **I.** *vt* **1.** (*montrer*) to show; (*document, preuve*) to produce; (*animal*) to exhibit **2.** (*étaler*) ~ **qc** to show sth off **II.** *vpr* **s'**~ to put oneself on display

exhibition [ɛgzibisjɔ̃] *f* display; (*d'un animal*) exhibiting ►**faire** ~ **de ses sentiments** to make a show of one's feelings

exhibitionniste [ɛgzibisjɔnist] **I.** *mf* exhibitionist **II.** *adj* exhibitionistic

exhortation [ɛgzɔʀtasjɔ̃] *f* exhortation

exhumer [ɛgzyme] <1> *vt* (*corps*) to exhume; (*ruines, document*) to dig out

exigeant(**e**) [ɛgziʒɑ̃, ʒɑ̃t] *adj* demanding; **être** ~ **à l'égard de qn** to demand a lot of sb

exigence [ɛgziʒɑ̃s] *f* **1.** (*caractère*) demanding attitude **2.** *pl* (*prétentions*) demands **3.** *pl* (*impératifs*) **~s de la mode** (fashion) dictates

exiger [ɛgziʒe] <2a> *vt* **1.** (*réclamer*) to demand; ~ **que** +*subj* to demand that **2.** (*nécessiter: personne, animal, plante*) to require; (*travail, circonstances*) to demand

exigu(**ë**) [ɛgzigy] *adj* (*logement*) cramped

exil [ɛgzil] *m* exile; **condamner qn à l'**~ to exile sb

exilé(**e**) [ɛgzile] **I.** *adj* exiled **II.** *m(f)* exile

exiler [ɛgzile] <1> **I.** *vt* to exile **II.** *vpr* **s'**~ to go into exile; **s'**~ **de France** to exile oneself from France; **s'**~ **en France** to go off to France in exile

existant(**e**) [ɛgzistɑ̃, ɑ̃t] *adj* existing

existence [ɛgzistɑ̃s] *f* existence; **pendant sa courte** ~ during his short life

exister [ɛgziste] <1> *vi* to exist

ex-mari [ɛksmaʀi] <ex-maris> *m* **mon** ~ my ex-husband

exode [ɛgzɔd] *m* exodus; ~ **rural** rural exodus

exonération [ɛgzɔneʀasjɔ̃] *f* FIN ~ **d'impôts** [*o* **fiscale**] tax exemption

exorbitant(**e**) [ɛgzɔʀbitɑ̃, ɑ̃t] *adj* (*prétentions*) inordinate; (*prix*) exorbitant

exorciser [ɛgzɔʀsize] <1> *vt* to exorcise

exotique [ɛgzɔtik] *adj* exotic

exotisme [ɛgzɔtism] *m* exoticism; **l'**~ **déplace les foules** people will come miles for the exotic

expansif, **-ive** [ɛkspɑ̃sif, -iv] *adj* expansive; **être d'un naturel** ~ to have an expansive nature

expansion [ɛkspɑ̃sjɔ̃] *f* ECON expansion; ~ **démographique** population growth; **être en pleine** ~ to be booming; **secteur en pleine** ~ boom sector

expatrié(**e**) [ɛkspatʀije] *m(f)* expatriate; (*expulsé*) exile

expatrier [ɛkspatʀije] <1> **I.** *vt* (*personne*) to expatriate **II.** *vpr* **s'**~ to leave one's own country

expédient [ɛkspedjɑ̃] *m* expedient; (*échappatoire*) way out; **ne plus savoir à quels ~s recourir** not to know which way to turn

E

▸**vivre d'~s** to live by one's wits

expédier [ɛkspedje] <1> *vt* (*envoyer*) to send; ~ **qc par bateau** to send sth by sea

expéditeur, **-trice** [ɛkspeditœʀ, -tʀis] **I.** *m, f* sender **II.** *adj* **bureau** ~ forwarding office

expéditif, **-ive** [ɛkspeditif, -iv] *adj* **1.** (*rapide: solution, méthode*) expeditious; **justice expéditive** rough justice **2.** (*trop rapide*) hasty

expédition [ɛkspedisjɔ̃] *f* **1.** (*envoi*) dispatching; (*par la poste*) sending **2.** (*mission*) expedition **3.** (*exécution: des affaires courantes*) dispatching

expérience [ɛkspeʀjɑ̃s] *f* **1.** *sans pl* (*pratique*) experience; **par** ~ from experience; **avoir l'~ des hommes** to know the ways of men **2.** (*événement*) experience; ~ **amoureuse** love affair **3.** (*essai*) experiment; **~s sur les animaux** animal experiments

expérimental(**e**) [ɛkspeʀimɑ̃tal, o] <-aux> *adj* experimental; **au stade** ~ at the experimental stage; **à titre** ~ as an experiment

expérimenté(**e**) [ɛkspeʀimɑ̃te] *adj* experienced

expérimenter [ɛkspeʀimɑ̃te] <1> *vt* ~ **un médicament sur qn/un animal** to test a drug on sb/an animal

expert(**e**) [ɛkspɛʀ, ɛʀt] **I.** *adj* (*cuisinière*) expert; (*médecin*) specialist; (*technicien*) trained; **être** ~ **en** [*o* **dans**] **qc** to be an expert in sth **II.** *m(f)* **1.** (*spécialiste*) expert **2.** JUR (*pour évaluer un objet, des dommages*) assessor

expert-comptable, **experte-comptable** [ɛkspɛʀkɔ̃tabl] <experts-comptables> *m, f* accountant

expertise [ɛkspɛʀtiz] *f* **1.** (*estimation de la valeur*) valuation **2.** (*examen*) appraisal

expertiser [ɛkspɛʀtize] <1> *vt* **1.** (*étudier l'authenticité*) to appraise **2.** (*estimer*) to assess

expier [ɛkspje] <1a> *vt* ~ **qc** to atone for sth; ~ **une faute par qc** to atone for a fault by sth

expiration [ɛkspiʀasjɔ̃] *f* **1.** ANAT exhalation **2.** (*fin: d'un délai, mandat*) expiry

expirer [ɛkspiʀe] <1> **I.** *vt* to exhale **II.** *vi* (*s'achever: mandat, délai*) to expire

explicable [ɛksplikabl] *adj* explainable

explicatif, **-ive** [ɛksplikatif, -iv] *adj* explanatory

explication [ɛksplikasjɔ̃] *f* **1.** (*indication, raison*) explanation **2.** (*commentaire, annotation*) commentary; ~ **de texte** critical analysis **3.** (*discussion*) discussion **4.** *pl* (*mode d'emploi*) instructions

explicite [ɛksplisit] *adj* explicit

explicitement [ɛksplisitmɑ̃] *adv* explicitly

expliquer [ɛksplike] <1> **I.** *vt* **1.** (*faire connaître*) to explain; ~ **à qn pourquoi/comment qn a fait qc** to explain to sb why/how sb did sth; **cela explique son départ** that accounts for his departure **2.** (*faire comprendre: fonctionnement*) to explain; (*texte*) to comment on ▸**je t'explique pas!** *inf* need I explain? **II.** *vpr* **1.** (*se faire comprendre*) **s'~** to explain **2.** (*justifier*) **s'~ sur son choix** to explain one's choice **3.** (*rendre des comptes à*) **s'~ devant le tribunal/la police** to explain to the court/the police; **s'~ devant son père** to explain oneself to one's father **4.** (*avoir une discussion*) **s'~ avec son fils sur qc** to have it out with one's son about sth **5.** (*comprendre*) **s'~ qc** to explain sth **6.** (*être compréhensible*) **s'~** to become clear; **son départ s'explique par qc** sth accounts for his departure

exploit [ɛksplwa] *m* **1.** (*prouesse*) feat **2.** *iron* exploit

exploitant(**e**) [ɛksplwatɑ̃, ɑ̃t] *m(f)* ~ **agricole** farmer; **petit** ~ small farmer

exploitation [ɛksplwatasjɔ̃] *f* **1.** (*action: d'une ferme, mine*) working; (*de ressources naturelles*) exploitation **2.** (*entreprise*) concern; ~ **agricole** farm **3.** (*utilisation: d'une situation, idée*) exploitation; (*de données*) utilization **4.** (*abus*) exploitation

exploiter [ɛksplwate] <1> *vt* **1.** (*faire valoir: terre, mine*) to work; (*ressources*) to exploit **2.** (*utiliser: situation*) to exploit; ~ **une idée/les résultats** to make use of an idea/the results **3.** (*abuser*) to exploit

exploiteur, **-euse** [ɛksplwatœʀ, -øz] *m, f* exploiter; **être un ~ de la misère humaine** to exploit human misery

explorateur [ɛksplɔʀatœʀ] *m* INFOR browser; ~ **de réseau** network explorer

explorateur, **-trice** [ɛksplɔʀatœʀ, -tʀis] *m, f* explorer

exploration [ɛksplɔʀasjɔ̃] *f a.* INFOR exploration

explorer [ɛksplɔʀe] <1> *vt* to explore

exploser [ɛksploze] <1> *vi* to explode; **laisser sa colère** ~ to blow up

explosif [ɛksplozif] *m* explosive

explosif, **-ive** [ɛksplozif, -iv] *adj* explosive; **obus** ~ exploding shell; **consonne explosive** plosive consonant

explosion [ɛksplozjɔ̃] *f* **1.** (*éclatement: d'une bombe*) explosion **2.** (*manifestation soudaine*) ~ **de joie/colère** outburst of joy/anger; ~ **démographique** population explosion

exportable [ɛkspɔʀtabl] *adj* exportable

exportateur [ɛkspɔʀtatœʀ] *m* (*pays*) exporting

exportateur, **-trice** [ɛkspɔʀtatœʀ, -tʀis] **I.** *adj* exporting **II.** *m, f* (*personne*) exporter

exportation [ɛkspɔʀtasjɔ̃] *f* **1.** (*action*) export(ing) **2.** *pl* (*biens*) exports **3.** INFOR export

exporter [ɛkspɔʀte] <1> *vt a.* INFOR to export; ~ **des fichiers sur qc** to export files to sth

exposé [ɛkspoze] *m* **1.** (*discours*) talk; **faire un ~ sur qc** to give a talk on sth **2.** (*description*) account

exposer [ɛkspoze] <1> **I.** *vt* **1.** (*montrer: ta-

bleau) to exhibit; (*marchandise*) to display **2.** (*décrire*) ~ **qc** to set sth out **3.** (*mettre en péril: vie, honneur*) to risk; ~ **qn au ridicule** to lay sb open to ridicule **4.** (*disposer*) ~ **qc au soleil** to expose sth to the sun; ~ **un film à la lumière** to expose film to light; **une pièce bien exposée** a well-lit room **II.** *vpr* **s'**~ **à qc** to expose oneself to sth

exposition [ɛkspozisjɔ̃] *f* **1.** (*étalage: de marchandise*) display **2.** (*présentation, foire*) *a.* ART exhibition **3.** (*orientation*) ~ **au sud** southern exposure **4.** (*action de soumettre à qc*) *a.* PHOT exposure

exprès [ɛkspʀɛ] *adv* **1.** (*intentionnellement*) on purpose **2.** (*spécialement*) (**tout**) ~ specially

express [ɛkspʀɛs] **I.** *adj* **café** ~ espresso coffee; **train** ~ fast train **II.** *m* **1.** (*café*) espresso **2.** (*train*) fast train

expressément [ɛkspʀesemɑ̃] *adv* expressly

expressif, -ive [ɛkspʀesif, -iv] *adj* expressive

expression [ɛkspʀesjɔ̃] *f* expression; **mode d'**~ means of expression; ~ **familière/figée** colloquial/set expression ►**veuillez** agréer **l'**~ **de mes sentiments distingués** yours faithfully, yours truly *Am*

expressionnisme [ɛkspʀesjɔnism] *m* expressionnism

expressionniste [ɛkspʀesjɔnist] **I.** *adj* expressionnist **II.** *mf* expressionnist

exprimer [ɛkspʀime] <1> **I.** *vt* **1.** (*faire connaître*) to express **2.** (*indiquer*) ~ **qc** (*signe*) to indicate sth; ~ **qc en mètres/euros** to express sth in metres/euros *Brit,* to express sth in meters/euros *Am* **II.** *vpr* **1.** (*parler*) to expres oneself; **s'**~ **en français** to speak in French; **ne pas s'**~ to say nothing; **s'**~ **par gestes** to use gestures to express oneself **2.** (*se manifester*) **s'**~ **dans qc** (*volonté*) to be expressed in sth; **s'**~ **sur un visage** to show on a face

exproprier [ɛkspʀɔpʀije] <1a> *vt* to expropriate

expulser [ɛkspylse] <1> *vt* (*élève, étranger*) to expel; (*joueur*) to send off *Brit,* to eject *Am;* ~ **un locataire de son appartement** to evict a tenant from his apartment

expulsion [ɛkspylsjɔ̃] *f* (*d'un élève, étranger*) expulsion; (*d'un locataire*) eviction; (*d'un joueur*) sending off *Brit,* ejection *Am*

exquis(e) [ɛkski, iz] *adj* (*goût, manières, plat, parfum*) exquisite; (*personne, journée*) delightful; **être d'une politesse** ~**e** to be exquisitely polite

extase [ɛkstɑz] *f* ecstasy; **être en** ~ **devant qn/qc** to be in raptures over sb/sth

extasier [ɛkstɑzje] *vpr* **s'**~ **devant** [*o* **sur**] **qn/qc** to go into raptures over sb/sth

extensible [ɛkstɑ̃sibl] *adj* extending

extension [ɛkstɑ̃sjɔ̃] *f* **1.** (*allongement: d'un ressort*) stretching; (*d'un bras*) extension **2.** (*accroissement: d'une ville*) growth; (*d'un incendie, d'une épidémie*) spreading **3.** INFOR ~ **de mémoire** memory expansion ►**prendre de l'**~ (*incendie, épidémie, grève*) to spread; (*affaires*) to expand; par ~ by extension

exténuant(e) [ɛkstenɥɑ̃, ɑ̃t] *adj* extenuating

exténuer [ɛkstenɥe] <1> **I.** *vt* to exhaust **II.** *vpr* **s'**~ **à faire qc** to exhaust oneself doing sth; **s'**~ **en efforts inutiles** to exhaust oneself in wasted effort

extérieur [ɛksteʀjœʀ] *m* **1.** (*monde extérieur*) outside world **2.** (*dehors*) outside; **aller à l'**~ to go outside; **à l'**~ **de la ville** outside the town; **de l'**~ from outside

extérieur(e) [ɛksteʀjœʀ] *adj* **1.** (*décor*) exterior; (*bruit*) from outside; (*activité*) outside **2.** (*objectif: réalité*) external **3.** (*visible*) outward **4.** POL, COM **politique** ~**e** foreign policy **5.** *Québec* (*étranger(-ère)*) **ministère des affaires** ~**es** Foreign affairs ministry

extérieurement [ɛksteʀjœʀmɑ̃] *adv* **1.** (*à l'extérieur*) externally **2.** (*en apparence*) outwardly

extérioriser [ɛksteʀjɔʀize] <1> **I.** *vt* (*sentiment*) to express; PSYCH to externalize **II.** *vpr* **s'**~ (*personne*) to express oneself; (*colère, joie*) to be (outwardly) expressed

extermination [ɛkstɛʀminasjɔ̃] *f* extermination

exterminer [ɛkstɛʀmine] <1> *vt* exterminate

externat [ɛkstɛʀna] *m* ECOLE day school

externe [ɛkstɛʀn] **I.** *adj* (*surface*) outer **II.** *mf* ECOLE day pupil

extincteur [ɛkstɛ̃ktœʀ] *m* extinguisher

extinction [ɛkstɛ̃ksjɔ̃] *f* **1.** (*action: d'un incendie*) extinction; (*des lumières*) turning out; ~ **des feux à huit heures** lights out at eight o'clock **2.** (*disparition*) extinction **3.** *fig* ~ **de voix** loss of voice

extirper [ɛkstiʀpe] <1> *vt* **1.** (*mauvaises herbes*) to dig out; (*tumeur*) to remove **2.** *fig* (*préjugé*) to eradicate; ~ **qn de son lit** *inf* to drag sb out of bed

extorquer [ɛkstɔʀke] <1> *vt* to extort

extorsion [ɛkstɔʀsjɔ̃] *f* extortion

extra [ɛkstʀa] **I.** *adj inv* **1.** (*qualité*) super **2.** *inf* (*formidable*) great **II.** *m* (*gâterie*) **un** ~ treat

extraction [ɛkstʀaksjɔ̃] *f* **1.** MIN (*du pétrole/charbon*) extraction; (*du marbre*) quarrying **2.** (*d'une dent, d'une balle*) extraction **3.** (*origine*) être **de haute/basse** ~ to be of noble/humble origin

extradition [ɛkstʀadisjɔ̃] *f* extradition

extrafin(e) [ɛkstʀafɛ̃, fin] *adj* extra fine

extraire [ɛkstʀɛʀ] *vt irr* **1.** (*sortir: charbon, pétrole, dent*) to extract; (*marbre*) to quarry; **passage extrait d'un livre** passage from a book **2.** (*séparer*) to extract

extrait [ɛkstʀɛ] *m* extract; ~ **de compte** bank statement; ~ **de naissance** birth certificate

extralucide [ɛkstʀalysid] **I.** *adj* **voyante** ~ clairvoyant **II.** *mf* clairvoyant

extraordinaire [ɛkstʀaɔʀdinɛʀ] *adj* **1.** (*opp: ordinaire: réunion, budget*) extraordinary; (*dépenses*) exceptional **2.** (*insolite: nouvelle, histoire*) extraordinary **3.** (*exceptionnel*) remarkable

extrapoler [ɛkstʀapɔle] <1> *vi a.* MAT extrapolate

extraterrestre [ɛkstʀateʀɛstʀ] *mf* alien

extravagance [ɛkstʀavagɑ̃s] *f* **1.** (*caractère*) eccentricity **2.** (*action*) extravagance **3.** (*idée*) extravagant idea

extravagant(e) [ɛkstʀavagɑ̃, ɑ̃t] **I.** *adj* extravagant **II.** *m(f)* eccentric

extrême [ɛkstʀɛm] **I.** *adj* **1.** (*au bout d'un espace*) farthest; (*au bout d'une durée*) latest; **date ~** last date **2.** (*excessif*) extreme; **d'~ droite/gauche** far right/left **II.** *m* **1.** (*dernière limite*) extreme **2.** *pl* (*opposé*) *a.* MAT extremes **3.** POL **l'~ gauche/droite** the far right/left ▸**pousser qc à l'~** to take sth to extremes

extrêmement [ɛkstʀɛmmɑ̃] *adv* extremely; (*jaloux*) insanely

extrême-onction [ɛkstʀɛmɔ̃ksjɔ̃] <extrêmes-onctions> *f* extreme unction

Extrême-Orient [ɛkstʀɛmɔʀjɑ̃] *m* **l'~** the Far East

extrémiste [ɛkstʀemist] **I.** *adj* POL extremist **II.** *mf* POL extremist

extrémité [ɛkstʀemite] *f* **1.** (*bout*) end; **~ de la forêt/d'une ville** edge of the forest/town; **à l'~ de la rue** at the (far) end of the street **2.** *pl* (*mains, pieds*) extremities

exubérance [ɛgzybeʀɑ̃s] *f* exuberance

exubérant(e) [ɛgzybeʀɑ̃, ɑ̃t] *adj* exuberant

exulter [ɛgzylte] <1> *vi* to exult

exutoire [ɛgzytwaʀ] *m* **~ à qc** outlet for sth

eye-liner [ajlajnœʀ] <eye-liners> *m* eyeliner

eye-shadow [ajʃɛdo] <eye-shadows> *m* eye shadow

F

F, f [ɛf] *m inv* F, f; **~ comme François** f as in Frederick *Brit,* f as in Fox *Am;* (*on telephone*) f for Frederick *Brit,* f for Fox *Am*

F 1. *abr de* **franc** F **2.** *abr de* **fluor** F **3.** (*appartement*) **F2/F3** two/three room flat *Brit,* two/three room apartment *Am,* one/two bedroom flat

fa [fa] *m inv* **1.** MUS F **2.** (*solfège*) fa; *v. a.* **do**

fable [fɑbl] *f* LIT fable

fabricant(e) [fabʀikɑ̃, ɑ̃t] *m(f)* manufacturer

fabricateur, -trice [fabʀikatœʀ, -tʀis] *m, f péj* fabricator

fabrication [fabʀikasjɔ̃] *f* manufacturing; (*artisanale*) making; **défaut/secret de ~** manufacturing defect/secret ▸**de ma/sa ~** of my own making

fabrique [fabʀik] *f* factory

fabriquer [fabʀike] <1> **I.** *vt* **1.** (*produire*) to manufacture **2.** *inf* (*faire*) **mais qu'est-ce que tu fabriques?** what on earth are you up to?; (*avec impatience*) what do you think you're doing? **3.** (*inventer*) to fabricate **II.** *vpr* **1.** (*se produire*) to be mass-produced; **ce modèle se fabrique en série** this is a mass-production model **2.** (*se construire*) **se ~ une table avec qc** to make a table out of sth **3.** (*s'inventer*) **se ~ une histoire** to think up a story

fabulateur, -trice [fabylatœʀ, -tʀis] *m, f* storyteller

fabulation [fabylasjɔ̃] *f* storytelling *no pl;* PSYCH fantasizing

fabuler [fabyle] <1> *vi* to tell stories; PSYCH to fantasize

fabuleusement [fabyløzmɑ̃] *adv* fabulously

fabuleux, -euse [fabylø, -øz] *adj* **1.** *inf* (*fantastique*) fabulous **2.** *inf* (*incroyable*) incredible **3.** LIT mythical; (*animal*) fabulous; **récit ~** myth

fac [fak] *f inf abr de* **faculté** university

façade [fasad] *f* **1.** (*devant: d'un édifice*) façade; (*d'un magasin*) front **2.** (*région côtière*) coast **3.** (*apparence trompeuse*) façade

face [fas] *f* **1.** (*visage, côté, aspect*) face; **changer la ~ du monde** to change the face of the earth **2.** (*côté d'une monnaie, disquette, d'un disque*) *a.* MAT, MIN side; **pile ou ~?** heads or tails? **3.** (*indiquant une orientation*) **photographier de ~** to take a photo of sb from the front; **attaquer de ~** to attack from the front; **aborder de ~** to tackle sb on; **être en ~ de qn/qc** to be opposite sb/sth; **le voisin d'en ~** the neighbour opposite *Brit,* the neighbor opposite *Am;* **regarder qc bien en ~** to look sth in the face ▸**être/se trouver ~ à ~ avec qn** to be face to face with sb; **être/se trouver ~ à ~ avec qc** to be right opposite sth; *fig* to be faced with; **faire ~** to confront the situation; **regarder la mort en ~** to stare death in the face; **~ à cette crise ...** faced with this crisis ...; **il faut voir les choses en ~** you have to face the facts

face-à-face [fasafas] *m inv* encounter

facétie [fasesi] *f* joke

facétieux, -euse [fasesjø, -jøz] **I.** *adj* facetious **II.** *m, f* joker

facette [fasɛt] *f* facet

fâché(e) [fɑʃe] *adj* **1.** (*en colère*) angry **2.** (*navré*) **il est ~ de tout ceci** he's sorry about all this **3.** (*en mauvais termes*) **être ~ avec qn** to be at odds with sb; **être ~ avec qc** *inf* to be fed up with sth

fâcher [fɑʃe] <1> **I.** *vt* (*irriter*) to annoy **II.** *vpr* **1.** (*se mettre en colère*) **se ~ contre qn** to get angry with sb **2.** (*se brouiller*) **se ~ avec**

qn to fall out with sb
fâcherie [faʃʀi] *f* quarrelling *no pl*
fâcheusement [faʃøzmɑ̃] *adv* regrettably; **être ~ semblable à qn** to bear an unfortunate resemblance to sb
fâcheux, -euse [faʃø, -øz] *adj* **1.** (*regrettable: idée*) regrettable; (*contretemps*) unfortunate; **il est ~ que qn fasse qc** (*subj*) it's unfortunate that sb should do sth **2.** (*déplaisant: nouvelle*) unpleasant
facial(e) [fasjal, jo] <-aux> *adj* facial
faciès [fasjɛs] *m* (*mine*) features *pl;* **avoir le ~ de quelqu'un qui ...** to have the face of somebody who ...
facile [fasil] **I.** *adj* **1.** (*simple*) easy; **avoir le contact ~** to be easy to get along with; **c'est plus ~ de** +*infin* it's easier to +*infin;* **c'est ~ comme bonjour** [*o* **tout**] it's as easy as falling off a log **2.** *péj* (*sans recherche: plaisanterie*) facile; **c'est un peu ~!** that's a bit cheap **3.** (*conciliant*) easy-going **II.** *adv inf* **1.** (*sans difficulté*) easy; **faire qc ~** to do sth no problem **2.** (*au moins*) easily
facilement [fasilmɑ̃] *adv* easily
facilité [fasilite] *f* **1.** (*opp: difficulté*) ease; **~ d'emploi** ease of use; **être d'une grande ~** to be very easy; **pour plus de ~, ...** for greater simplicity ... **2.** (*aptitude*) gift; **~ de caractère** easy-going character; **avoir des ~s** to be gifted; **avoir une grande ~ à s'exprimer** to express oneself with great ease **3.** *sans pl, péj* facility; **céder à la ~** to take the easy option **4.** *pl* (*occasion*) opportunities **5.** (*possibilité*) chance
faciliter [fasilite] <1> *vt* to facilitate
façon [fasɔ̃] *f* **1.** (*manière*) **~ de faire qc** way of doing sth; **de** [*o* **d'une**] **~ très impolie** very impolitely; **de** [*o* **d'une**] **~ plus rapide que d'habitude** more quickly than usual **2.** *pl* (*comportement*) manners; **avoir des ~s de ...** to behave like ...; **faire des ~s** to put on airs; (*faire le difficile*) to make a fuss **3.** (*travail*) tailoring, making up *Brit;* **travailler à ~** to make up customers' material **4.** (*forme*) cut **5.** + *subst* (*imitation*) **un sac ~ croco** a crocodile-look bag ►**avoir bonne/mauvaise ~** *Suisse* (*présenter bien ou mal, faire bonne ou mauvaise impression*) to look attractive/unattractive; **en aucune ~** not at all; **d'une ~ générale** in a general way; **de toute ~, ...** anyway, ...; **de toutes les ~s** at any rate; **dire à qn sa ~ de penser** to give sb a piece of one's mind; (**c'est une**) **~ de parler** in a manner of speaking; **faire un jeu à la ~ de qn** to play a game sb's way; **à ma ~** in my own way; **faire qc de ~ à ce que** +*subj* to do sth so that; **de ma/ta/sa ~** of mine/yours/hers; (*gâteau*) the way I/you/she makes it; **repas sans ~** simple meal; **personne sans ~** an easy-going person; **non merci, sans ~** no thanks, all the same
façonner [fasɔne] <1> **I.** *vt* **1.** (*travailler*) to shape; (*pierre*) to work **2.** (*faire*) to make; (*statuette de bois*) to carve **3.** (*usiner*) to shape; **~ qc dans un bloc de marbre** to sculpt sth out of a block of marble **II.** *vpr* **se ~** **1.** (*se travailler: bois, métal*) to be worked **2.** (*se fabriquer*) to be made
fac-similé [faksimile] <fac-similés> *m* (*reproduction*) facsimile
facteur [faktœʀ] *m* factor; **être un ~ de dépression** to be a cause of depression
facteur, -trice [faktœʀ, -tʀis] *m, f* **1.** (*livreur de courrier*) postman, postwoman *m, f,* mailman *Am* **2.** (*fabricant*) **~ d'orgues** organ builder
factice [faktis] *adj* **1.** (*faux*) artificial; (*livres, bouteilles*) dummy **2.** (*affecté: voix*) artificial; (*sourire*) feigned; (*gaieté*) sham
faction [faksjɔ̃] *f* **1.** (*groupe*) faction **2.** (*garde*) **être de/en ~** to be on guard **3.** (*surveillance*) **être/rester en ~** to be/stay on watch
factrice [faktʀis] *f v.* **facteur**
factuel(le) [faktɥɛl] *adj* factual
facturation [faktyʀasjɔ̃] *f* **1.** (*action*) invoicing **2.** (*service*) invoice office
facture¹ [faktyʀ] *f* COM bill ►**la ~ du chômage** the cost of unemployment; **qui va payer la ~?** who's going to pay (the bill)?
facture² [faktyʀ] *f* **1.** ART (*d'un tableau, poème*) technique; (*d'une pièce de théâtre*) construction **2.** (*fabrication*) **~ d'orgue** organ builders
facturer [faktyʀe] <1> *vt* **1.** (*établir une facture*) **~ une réparation à qn** to invoice sb for a repair **2.** (*faire payer*) **~ une réparation à qn** to put a repair on sb's bill
facturette [faktyʀɛt] *f* credit card slip
facultatif, -ive [fakyltatif, -iv] *adj* optional
faculté¹ [fakylte] *f* UNIV (*université*) university; (*département*) faculty; **~ de droit** law faculty
faculté² [fakylte] *f* **1.** (*disposition*) faculty **2.** (*possibilité*) **la ~ de faire qc** the facility of doing sth; (*droit*) the right to do sth
fada [fada] **I.** *adj inf* cracked **II.** *m, f inf* nut
fadaise [fadɛz] *f gén pl* **1.** (*balivernes*) nonsense **2.** (*propos*) drivel
fadasse [fadas] *adj inf* bland; (*couleur*) wishy-washy
fade [fad] *adj* **1.** (*sans saveur: plat, goût*) bland; **c'est ~** it's tasteless **2.** (*sans éclat: ton*) dull; **d'un blond ~** a dull blond colour *Brit,* a dull blond color *Am* **3.** (*sans intérêt: personne, propos*) dreary; (*traits*) bland **4.** *Belgique* (*lourd*) **il fait ~** it's muggy
fadeur [fadœʀ] *f* **1.** (*manque de saveur*) blandness **2.** (*manque d'éclat*) dullness **3.** *fig* (*d'un roman*) dreariness
fagot [fago] *m* bundle of firewood ►**de derrière les ~s** rather special
fagoté(e) [fagɔte] *adj inf* **être mal ~** to be dressed like nothing on earth
fagoter [fagɔte] <1> *vt péj* to dress up
faiblard(e) [fɛblaʀ, aʀd] *adj péj, inf* (*argument*) pathetic; (*élève*) feeble; (*enfant*)

F

weakly

faible [fɛbl] I. *adj* **1.** (*sans force, défense*) weak; **être ~ de constitution/du cœur** to have a weak constitution/heart; **sa vue est ~** he has poor eyesight **2.** (*influençable, sans volonté*) **être ~ de caractère** to have a weak character **3.** (*trop indulgent*) **être ~ avec qn** to be soft on sb **4.** *antéposé* (*restreint: espoir*) faint; (*protestation, résistance*) feeble; **à une ~ majorité** by a narrow majority; **à ~ altitude** at low altitude; **avoir de ~s chances de s'en tirer** to have a slim chance of pulling through; **être de ~ rendement** (*terre*) to give a poor yield **5.** (*peu perceptible*) faint **6.** (*médiocre: élève*) weak; (*devoir*) poor; **le terme est ~** that's putting it mildly **7.** ECON **économiquement ~** with a low income **8.** (*bête*) **~ d'esprit** feeble-minded **II.** *m, f* **1.** weak person **2.** (*personne sans volonté*) weakling **3.** ECON **les économiquement ~s** low-income groups **III.** *m sans pl* (*défaut*) weak point; **avoir un ~ pour qn** to have a soft spot for sb; **avoir un ~ pour qc** to have a fondness for sth

faiblement [fɛbləmɑ̃] *adv* **1.** (*mollement*) weakly **2.** (*légèrement*) slightly; **bière ~ alcoolisée** low-alcohol beer

faiblesse [fɛblɛs] *f* **1.** (*manque de force, grande indulgence, insuffisance*) weakness; **sa ~ de constitution** her weak constitution; **~ pour** [*o* **à l'égard de**] **qn/qc** weakness towards sb/sth; **par ~** out of weakness; **la ~ du revenu des agriculteurs** the low income of farmers **2.** (*manque d'intensité*) **la ~ du bruit** the faintness of the noise; **la ~ de sa vue** his/her weak eyesight **3.** (*médiocrité: d'un élève*) weakness; (*d'un devoir*) feebleness; **~ d'esprit** feeble-mindedness **4.** *souvent pl* (*défaillance*) dizzy spell **5.** (*syncope*) fainting fit

faiblir [febliʀ] <8> *vi* (*personne, pouls, résistance*) to weaken; (*cœur, force*) to fail; (*espoir, lumière*) to fade; (*ardeur*) to wane; (*revenu, rendement*) to fall; (*chances, écart*) to lessen; (*vent*) to drop

faïence [fajɑ̃s] *f* earthenware *no pl*

faïencerie [fajɑ̃sʀi] *f* **1.** (*industrie*) pottery **2.** (*fabrique*) earthenware factory **3.** (*vaisselle*) earthenware

faille¹ [faj] *subj prés de* **falloir**

faille² [faj] *f* **1.** GEO fault **2.** (*crevasse*) rift **3.** (*défaut*) flaw; **il y a une ~ dans leur amitié** there is something amiss in their friendship; **volonté sans ~** iron will; **détermination sans ~** utter determination

faillible [fajibl] *adj* fallible

faillir [fajiʀ] *vi irr* **1.** (*manquer*) **il a failli acheter ce livre** he almost bought that book **2.** (*manquer à*) **~ à son devoir** to fail in one's duty; **~ à sa parole** to fail to keep one's word; **~ à la tradition** to go against tradition **3.** (*faire défaut*) **ma mémoire n'a pas failli** my memory did not fail me

faillite [fajit] *f* **1.** COM, JUR bankruptcy; **faire ~** to go bankrupt **2.** (*échec*) failure; **c'est la ~ de mes espérances** this is the end of my hopes

faim [fɛ̃] *f* **1.** hunger; **avoir ~** to be hungry; **avoir une ~ de loup** to be starving; **donner ~ à qn** to make sb hungry; **ne pas manger à sa ~** to not have enough to eat **2.** (*famine*) famine **3.** (*désir ardent*) **avoir ~ de qc** to hunger for sth ►**laisser qn sur sa ~** to leave sb wanting more; **rester sur sa ~** (*après un repas*) to still feel hungry; (*ne pas être satisfait*) to be left wanting more

faîne, **faine** [fɛn] *f* beechnut

fainéant(e) [fɛneɑ̃, ɑ̃t] **I.** *adj* idle **II.** *m(f)* idler

fainéanter [fɛneɑ̃te] <1> *vi* to idle

fainéantise [fɛneɑ̃tiz] *f* idleness

faire [fɛʀ] *irr* **I.** *vt* **1.** (*fabriquer: objet, vêtement, produit, gâteau*) to make; (*maison, nid*) to build; **le bébé fait ses dents** the baby's teething; **~ le repas** to do the meal **2.** (*mettre au monde*) **~ un enfant/des petits** to have a child/young **3.** (*évacuer*) **~ ses besoins** to do one's business **4.** (*être l'auteur de: faute, offre, discours, loi, prévisions*) to make; (*livre, chèque*) to write; (*conférence, cadeau*) to give; **~ une visite à qn** to pay sb a visit; **~ une promesse à qn** to make sb a promise; **~ la guerre contre qn** to make war against sb; **~ la paix** to make peace; **~ l'amour à qn** to make love to sb; **~ une farce à qn** to play a trick on sb; **~ la bise à qn** to kiss sb on the cheek; **~ du bruit** to make noise; *fig* to cause a sensation; **~ l'école buissonnière** to bunk off school *Brit,* to play hooky *Am;* **~ étape** to stop off; **~ grève** to strike; **~ signe à qn** to motion to sb; (*de s'approcher*) to beckon sb; **~ sa toilette** to wash **5.** (*avoir une activité: travail, métier, service militaire*) to do; **je n'ai rien à ~** I've nothing to do; **qu'est-ce qu'ils peuvent bien ~?** what on earth can they be doing?; **~ une bonne action** to do a good deed; **~ du théâtre** (*acteur de cinéma*) to act in the theatre; (*étudiants*) to do some acting; (*comme carrière*) to go on the stage; **~ du violon/du piano/du jazz** to play the violin/the piano/jazz; **~ de la politique** to be involved in politics; **~ du sport** to do sport; **~ de l'escalade/de la voile** to go rock climbing/sailing; **~ du tennis** to play tennis; **~ du vélo/canoë** to go cycling/canoeing; **~ du cheval** to go horse-riding *Brit,* to go horseback riding *Am;* **~ du patin à roulettes** to roller-skate; **~ du skate/ski** to go skateboarding/skiing; **~ un petit jogging** to go for a little jog; **~ du camping** to go camping; **~ de la couture/du tricot** to sew/knit; **~ des photos** to take photos; **~ du cinéma** to be in films; **ne ~ que bavarder** to do nothing but talk; **que faites-vous dans la vie?** what do you do in life? **6.** (*étudier*) **~ des études** to go to university; **~ son droit/de la recherche** to do law/research; **~ du français** to do French; **il veut ~ médecin** he wants to be a doctor **7.** (*pré-

parer) ~ **un café à qn** to make sb a coffee; ~ **ses bagages** to pack (one's bags); ~ **la cuisine** to cook **8.** (*nettoyer, ranger: argenterie, chaussures, chambre*) to clean; (*lit*) to make; ~ **le ménage** (*nettoyer*) to do the cleaning; (*mettre de l'ordre*) to tidy up; ~ **la vaisselle** to do the dishes **9.** (*accomplir: mouvement*) to make; ~ **une promenade** to go for a walk; ~ **un tournoi** to take part in a tournament; ~ **un shampoing à qn** to give sb a shampoo; ~ **un pansement à qn** to put a bandage on sb; ~ **le plein (d'essence**) to fill up; ~ **un bon score** to get a high score; ~ **un numéro de téléphone** to dial a number; ~ **les courses** to do the shopping; ~ **la manche** *inf* to beg, to panhandle *Am;* ~ **le portrait de qn** to do sb's portrait; ~ **bon voyage** to have a good journey **10.** *inf* MED ~ **de la fièvre** to have a fever **11.** (*parcourir: distance, trajet, pays, magasins*) to do; ~ **des zigzags/du stop** to zigzag/hitch-hike **12.** (*offrir à la vente: produit*) to do; (**pour**) **combien faites-vous ce fauteuil?** what will let me have this for?; **ils/elles font combien?** how much are they going for? **13.** (*cultiver*) to grow **14.** (*feindre, agir comme*) ~ **le pitre** [*o* **le clown**] to clown around; ~ **l'idiot** [*o* **l'imbécile**] (*faire mine de ne pas comprendre*) to act stupid; (*vouloir amuser, se conduire stupidement*) to fool around; ~ **l'enfant** to act childishly; ~ **le Père Noël** to play Father Christmas *Brit,* to play Santa Claus *Am;* **il a fait comme s'il ne me voyait pas** he pretended not to see me **15.** (*donner une qualité, transformer*) ~ **qn son héritier** to make sb one's heir; **il a fait de lui une star** he made him a star; **je vous fais juge** you be the judge **16.** (*causer*) ~ **plaisir à qn** (*personne*) to please sb; ~ **le bonheur de qn** to make sb happy; ~ **du bien à qn** to do sb good; ~ **du mal à qn** to harm sb; **ça ne fait rien** it doesn't matter; ~ **honte à qn** to shame sb; **l'accident a fait de nombreuses victimes** there were many victims in the accident; **qu'est-ce que ça peut bien te ~?** what's it got to do with you? **17.** (*servir de*) **la cuisine fait salle à manger** the kitchen serves as a dining room; **cet hôtel fait aussi restaurant** the hotel is [*o* has] a restaurant too **18.** (*laisser quelque part*) **qu'ai-je bien pu ~ de mes lunettes?** what can I have done with my glasses? **19.** (*donner comme résultat*) to make; **deux et deux font quatre** two and two make [*o* are] four **20.** (*habituer*) ~ **qn à qc** to get sb used to sth **21.** (*devenir*) **il fera un excellent avocat** he'll make an excellent lawyer; **cette branche fera une belle canne** this branch will do very well as a walking stick **22.** (*dire*) **il a fait "non" en hochant la tête** he shook his head no; ~ **comprendre qc à qn** to explain sth to sb **23.** (*avoir pour conséquence*) ~ **que qn a été sauvé** to mean that sb was saved **24.** (*être la cause de*) ~ **chavirer un bateau** to make a boat capsize; **la pluie fait pousser l'herbe** the rain makes the grass grow **25.** (*aider à*) ~ **faire pipi à un enfant** to help a child with doing a wee **26.** (*inviter à*) ~ **venir un médecin** to call a doctor; **dois-je le ~ monter?** shall I show him up?; ~ **entrer/sortir le chien** to let the dog in/put the dog out; ~ **voir qc à qn** to show sb sth **27.** (*charger de*) ~ **réparer/changer qc par qn** to get [*o* have] sth repaired/changed by sb; ~ **faire qc à qn** to get sb to do sth **28.** (*forcer, inciter à*) ~ **ouvrir qc** to have sth opened; ~ **payer qn** to make sb pay **29.** (*pour remplacer un verbe déjà énoncé*) **elle le fait/l'a fait** she is doing so/has done so **II.** *vi* **1.** (*agir*) ~ **vite** to be quick; ~ **attention à qc** to be careful about sth; ~ **de son mieux** to do one's best; **tu peux mieux ~** you can do better; **il a bien fait de ne rien dire** he did the right thing by keeping quiet; **tu fais bien de me le rappeler** it's a good thing you reminded me; **tu ferais mieux/bien de te taire** you should keep quiet; ~ **comme si de rien n'était** as if there was nothing the matter **2.** (*dire*) to say; **"sans doute", fit-il** "no doubt", he said **3.** *inf* (*durer*) **ce manteau me fera encore un hiver** this coat will do [*o* last] me another year; **ce disque fait une heure d'écoute** this disc has one hour's playing time **4.** (*paraître, rendre*) ~ **vieux/paysan** to look old/like a peasant; **ce tableau ferait mieux dans l'entrée** this picture would look better in the hall; ~ **bon/mauvais effet** to look good/bad; ~ **désordre** (*pièce*) to look untidy **5.** (*mesurer, peser*) ~ **1,2 m de long/de large/de haut** to be 1.2 metres long/wide/high *Brit,* to be 1.2 meters long/wide/high *Am;* ~ **trois kilos** to be [*o* weigh] three kilos; ~ **40 cm de tour de cou** to measure 40 cm around the neck, to have a size 16 collar; ~ **70 litres** to be [*o* contain] 70 litres *Brit,* to be [*o* contain] 70 liters *Am;* ~ **60 W** to be 60 watts; ~ **8 euros** to come to 8 euros; **ça fait peu** that's not much **6.** (*être incontinent*) ~ **dans la culotte** to mess one's pants ►**l'homme à tout** ~ the odd job man; ~ **partie de qc** to be part of sth; ~ **la queue** *inf* to queue up *Brit,* to line up *Am;* ~ **la une** *inf* to make the front page; ~ **manger qn** to help sb eat; **ne ~ que passer** to be just passing; **il fait bon vivre** life is sweet; **faites comme chez vous!** *iron* make yourself at home!; **ne pas s'en ~** *inf* not to worry; **se ~ mal** to hurt oneself; **je (n')en ai rien à ~** *inf* (*ne m'y intéresse pas*) it's nothing to do with me; (*m'en fous*) I couldn't care less; **rien n'y fait** it can't be helped; **ça ne se fait pas** that's (just) not done; **tant qu'à ~, allons-y** let's go, we might as well **III.** *vi impers* **1.** METEO **il fait chaud/froid/jour/nuit** it's hot/cold/light/dark; **il fait beau/mauvais** the weather's fine/awful; **il fait (du) soleil** the sun's shining; **il fait du brouillard** it's foggy; **il fait dix degrés** it's ten degrees **2.** (*temps écoulé*) **cela fait bien huit ans** it's a good eight years ago now; **cela fait deux ans**

F

que nous ne nous sommes pas vus we haven't seen each other for two years **3.** (*pour indiquer l'âge*) **ça me fait 40 ans** *inf* I'll be 40 **IV.** *vpr* **1. se ~ une robe** to make oneself a dress; **se ~ 6000 euros par mois** *inf* to earn 6000 euros a month; **se ~ une idée exacte de qc** to get a clear idea of sth; **se ~ des illusions** to have illusions; **se ~ une opinion personnelle** to form one's own opinion; **se ~ une raison de qc** to resign oneself to sth; **se ~ des amis** to make friends **2.** (*action réciproque*) **se ~ des caresses** to stroke each other; **se ~ des politesses** to exchange courtesies **3.** *inf* (*se taper*) **il faut se le ~ celui-là!** he's a real pain; **je me le/la suis fait(e)** I've had him/her; **je vais me le ~ celui-là!** I'm going to do him over! **4.** (*se former*) **se ~** (*fromage, vin*) to mature; **se ~ tout seul** (*homme politique*) to make it on one's own **5.** (*devenir*) **se ~ vieux** to get on in years; **se ~ beau** to make oneself up; **se ~ rare** to be a stranger; **se ~ curé** to be a priest **6.** (*s'habituer à*) **se ~ à la discipline** to get used to discipline **7.** (*être à la mode*) **se ~** (*activité, look, vêtement*) to be popular; **ça se fait beaucoup de ~ qc** doing sth is very popular **8.** (*arriver, se produire*) **se ~** to happen; (*film*) to get made; **mais finalement ça ne s'est pas fait** but in the end it never happened **9.** *impers* **comment ça se fait?** how come?; **il se fait tard** it's getting on [*o* late] **10.** (*agir en vue de*) **se ~ maigrir** to get (oneself) slim; **se ~ vomir** to make oneself sick; **je te conseille de te ~ oublier** I'd advise you to make yourself scarce **11.** (*sens passif*) **se ~ opérer** to have an operation; **il s'est fait retirer son permis** he lost his licence *Brit,* he lost his license *Am;* **il s'est fait voler son permis** he had his licence stolen ▶**ne <u>pas</u> s'en ~** *inf* (*ne pas s'inquiéter*) not to worry; (*ne pas se gêner*) not to bother oneself; **t'en fais <u>pas</u>!** *inf* never mind

faire-part [fɛʀpaʀ] *m inv* announcement; (*pour inviter*) invitation

fair-play [fɛʀplɛ] *inv* **I.** *m* fair play **II.** *adj* fair

faisabilité [fəzabilite] *f* feasibility

faisable [fəzabl] *adj* (*en principe*) feasible; (*en pratique*) possible; **c'est ~ aujourd'hui?** can it be done today?

faisan(e) [fəzɑ̃, an] *m(f)* pheasant

faisandé(e) [fəzɑ̃de] *adj* gamey

faisceau [fɛso] <x> *m* **1.** (*rayon*) beam **2.** (*fagot*) bundle **3.** (*ensemble*) **~ de faits** set of facts

faiseur, -euse [fəzœʀ, -øz] *m, f péj* **1.** (*auteur*) **~ de belles phrases** phrase-maker; **~ de bons mots** wit **2.** (*vantard*) bragger

faisselle [fɛsɛl] *f* **1.** (*passoire*) cheese strainer **2.** (*fromage blanc*) *soft cheese made in a faisselle*

fait [fɛ] *m* **1.** fact **2.** (*événement*) event; (*phénomène*) phenomenon; **les ~s se sont passés à minuit** the incident occurred at midnight **3.** JUR **les ~s** (*action criminelle, délit*) crime; (*éléments constitutifs*) acts amounting to a crime; (*état des choses*) evidence; **~s de guerre** acts of war **4.** (*conséquence*) **être le ~ de qc** to be the result of sth; **c'est le ~ du hasard si** it's pure chance if **5.** RADIO, PRESSE **~ divers** PRESSE news story; (*événement*) incident; **~s divers** (*rubrique*) news in brief ▶**prendre ~ et <u>cause</u> pour qn** to side with sb; **les ~s et <u>gestes</u> de qn** sb's every action; **être <u>sûr</u> de son ~** to be sure of one's facts; **<u>aller</u> (droit) au ~** to get straight to the point; **<u>être</u> le ~ de qn** to be sb's doing; **<u>mettre</u> qn au ~ de qc** to inform sb about sth; **<u>prendre</u> qn sur le ~** to catch sb red-handed; **en <u>venir</u> au ~** to get to the point; **<u>au</u> ~** by the way; **tout <u>à</u> ~** quite; (*comme réponse*) absolutely; **être <u>de</u> ~ que** to be true [*o* a fact] that; **gouvernement <u>de</u> ~** de facto government; **<u>de</u> ce ~** thereby; **<u>du</u> ~ de qc** by the very fact of sth; **<u>du</u> ~ que qn fait toujours qc** as sb always does sth; **<u>en</u> ~** actually; **<u>en</u> ~ de qc** (*en matière de*) by way of sth; (*en guise de*) in the way of sth

fait(e) [fɛ, fɛt] **I.** *part passé de* **faire II.** *adj* **1.** (*propre à*) **être ~ pour qc** to be made for sth; **être ~ pour faire qc** (*être approprié à*) to be designed for doing sth; (*être destiné à*) to be meant for doing sth; **c'est ~ pour** *inf* that's what it's for **2.** (*constitué*) **avoir la jambe bien ~e** to have good legs; **c'est une femme bien ~e** she's a good-looking woman **3.** (*arrangé: ongles*) varnished; (*yeux*) made up **4.** (*mûr: fromage*) ready **5.** *inf* (*pris*) **être ~** to be done for **6.** (*tout prêt*) **des plats tout ~s** ready-to-eat dishes; **expression toute ~e** set expression ▶**c'est <u>bien</u> ~ pour toi/lui** serves you/him right; **c'est <u>toujours</u> ça de ~** that's one thing done; **<u>vite</u> ~ bien ~** quickly and efficiently; **c'en <u>est</u> ~ de notre vie calme** so much for our quiet life; **c'<u>est</u> comme si c'était ~** consider it done

faîte [fɛt] *m* (*de l'arbre*) top; (*d'une montagne*) summit; **~ du toit** rooftop

faitout, fait-tout [fɛtu] *m inv* stewpot

fakir [fakiʀ] *m* fakir

falaise [falɛz] *f* **1.** (*paroi*) cliff face **2.** (*côte, rocher*) cliff

falbalas [falbala] *mpl* **1.** *péj* (*colifichets*) frills **2.** (*grandes toilettes*) finery

falloir [falwaʀ] *irr* **I.** *vi impers* **1.** (*besoin*) **il faut qn/qc pour** *+infin* sb/sth is needed to *+infin;* **il me faudra du temps** I'll need time **2.** (*devoir*) **il faut faire qc** sth must be done; **que faut-il faire?** what must be done?; (*moi/toi/il*) what must I/you/he do?; **il a bien fallu!** it had to be done!; **il me/te faut faire qc** I/you must [*o* have (got) to] do sth; **il faut que** *+subj* sb has got to *+infin* **3.** (*être probablement*) **il faut être fou pour parler ainsi** you have to be mad to talk like that **4.** (*se produire fatalement*) **j'ai fait ce qu'il fallait** I did what I had to [*o* what had to be done]; **il fallait que ça arrive** that (just) had to happen **5.** (*faire absolument*) **il fallait me le dire** you should have told me; **il faut l'avoir vu** you have to have seen it; **il ne faut surtout pas lui en parler** you really must not talk about it to him ►**il faut te/vous dire que c'est l'usage** you have to tell yourself that's the way things are; (**il**) **faut se le/la faire** [*o* **farcir**] *inf* he's/she's a real pain; **il le faut** it has to be done; **comme il faut** properly; **une vieille dame très comme il faut** a very proper old lady; **il ne fallait pas!** you shouldn't have! **II.** *vpr impers* (*manquer*) **il s'en faut de qc, nous avons failli nous rencontrer, il s'en est fallu de peu** we almost met, it was very close; **il s'en faut de beaucoup** not by a long way; **il s'en est fallu d'un cheveu que je me fasse écraser** (*subj*) I was this close to being run over

falot(e) [falo, ɔt] *adj* (*personne*) insipid; (*lueur*) pale

falsification [falsifikasjɔ̃] *f* (*d'un document, d'une monnaie, signature*) forgery; (*de la vérité*) altering; (*d'une marchandise*) adulteration

falsifier [falsifje] <1> *vt* (*document, signature*) to falsify; (*monnaie*) to forge; (*vérité, histoire*) to alter

falzar [falzaʀ] *m inf* trousers *pl Brit,* pants *pl Am*

famé(e) [fame] *adj* **mal** ~ of ill-repute

famélique [famelik] *adj* starved-looking

fameusement [famøzmɑ̃] *adv inf* (*très*) really

fameux, -euse [famø, -øz] *adj* **1.** (*excellent: mets, vin*) superb; (*idée, travail*) excellent; **ce n'est pas** ~ *inf* it's not too good **2.** *antéposé, souvent iron* (*énorme: problème, erreur*) terrible; (*raclée*) terrific **3.** (*célèbre*) famous

familial(e) [familjal, jo] <-aux> *adj* family

familiariser [familjaʀize] <1> **I.** *vt* ~ **qn avec qc** to familiarize sb with sth **II.** *vpr* **se** ~ **avec une méthode** to familiarize oneself with a method; **se** ~ **avec une ville/une langue** to get to know a town/a language; **se** ~ **avec qn** to become acquainted with sb

familiarité [familjaʀite] *f* **1.** (*bonhomie, amitié, comportement*) familiarity **2.** (*habitude de*) ~ **avec qc** knowledge of sth **3.** *pl, péj* (*paroles*) overfamiliar remarks

familier [familje] *m* regular; ~ **de la maison** regular visitor to the house

familier, -ière [familje, -jɛʀ] *adj* **1.** familiar; ~ **à qn, cette technique m'est familière** I'm familiar with this technique **2.** (*routinier: comportement, tâche*) usual; **le mensonge lui est devenu** ~ lying has become second nature to him **3.** (*simple, bonhomme: conduite, entretien*) informal; (*personne*) casual **4.** (*non recherché: expression, style*) informal **5.** *péj* (*cavalier*) ~ **avec qn** offhand with sb **6.** (*domestique*) **des animaux ~s** pets

familièrement [familjɛʀmɑ̃] *adv* **1.** (*en langage courant*) in (ordinary) conversation **2.** (*simplement: s'exprimer*) informally **3.** (*amicalement*) in a familiar way **4.** *péj* (*cavalièrement*) offhandedly

famille [famij] *f* **1.** family; ~ **d'accueil** host family; ~ **proche** close family; **en** ~ with the family; **nous sommes en** ~ we're a family here **2.** *Belgique, Suisse* **attendre de la** ~ (*être enceinte*) to be in the family way **3.** *Suisse* **grande** ~ (*famille nombreuse*) large family

famine [famin] *f* famine ►**crier** ~ to cry famine; (*estomac*) to complain loudly

fan [fan] *mf* fan

fana [fana] *abr de* **fanatique I.** *adj inf* **être** ~ **de qn/qc** to be mad about sb/sth **II.** *mf inf* fanatic; ~ **d'ordinateur** computer freak, computer geek *Am*

fanal [fanal, o] <-aux> *m* **1.** (*lanterne*) lantern **2.** (*signal: d'une locomotive*) headlight; (*d'un navire*) lantern

fanatique [fanatik] **I.** *adj* fanatical **II.** *mf* fanatic; ~ **de football** football fanatic

fanatiser [fanatize] <1> *vt* to fanaticize

fanatisme [fanatism] *m* fanaticism; **avec** ~ fanatically

fané(e) [fane] *adj* (*fleur*) wilted; (*couleur, étoffe, beauté*) faded

faner [fane] <1> **I.** *vpr* **se** ~ (*fleur*) to wilt; (*couleur*) to fade **II.** *vt* **1.** (*ternir: couleur, étoffe, beauté*) to fade **2.** (*flétrir*) ~ **une plante** to make a plant wilt **3.** (*retourner: foin*) to toss **III.** *vi* to make hay

fanes [fan] *fpl* (*de carottes*) top; (*de radis*) leaves *pl*

fanfare [fɑ̃faʀ] *f* **1.** (*orchestre*) band **2.** (*air*) fanfare ►**annoncer qc en** ~ to trumpet sth; **arriver en** ~ to arrive in a blaze of glory

fanfaron(ne) [fɑ̃faʀɔ̃, ɔn] **I.** *adj* (*personne*) boastful; (*air, attitude*) swaggering **II.** *m(f)* braggart; **faire le** ~ to crow

fanfaronnade [fɑ̃faʀɔnad] *f* swaggering *no pl*

fanfaronner [fɑ̃faʀɔne] <1> *vi* to brag

fanfreluche [fɑ̃fʀəlyʃ] *f gén pl, souvent péj* frills

fanion [fanjɔ̃] *m* **1.** (*petit drapeau servant d'emblème*) pennant **2.** (*sur un terrain de sport*) flag

fantaisie [fɑ̃tezi] *f* **1.** (*caprice*) whim; **à** [*o* **selon**] **sa** ~ as the fancy takes him **2.** (*extravagance*) extravagance **3.** (*délire, idée*) fantasy **4.** (*imagination, originalité*) imagination; **être plein de** ~ (*personne*) to have great imagination; (*décoration, histoire*) to show great imagination; **être dépourvu de** ~ to lack imagination; **sa vie manque de** ~ there's no fantasy in her life **5.** (*qui sort de la norme, original*) **bijoux/bouton** ~ novelty jewellery/button *Brit,* novelty jewelry/button *Am* ►**s'offrir** [*o* **se payer**] **une petite** ~ to give oneself a treat

fantaisiste [fɑ̃tezist] **I.** *adj* **1.** (*peu sérieux: explication, hypothèse*) fanciful **2.** (*peu fiable*) unreliable **3.** (*anticonformiste*) eccentric

F

4. (*bizarre*) odd **II.** *mf* **1.** (*personne peu sérieuse*) joker **2.** (*anticonformiste*) eccentric

fantasmagorique [fɑ̃tasmagɔʀik] *adj* magical

fantasme [fɑ̃tasm] *m* fantasy; **vivre dans ses ~s** to live in a fantasy world

fantasmer [fɑ̃tasme] <1> *vi* to fantasize

fantasque [fɑ̃task] *adj* fanciful; (*bizarre*) odd; (*excentrique*) eccentric

fantassin [fɑ̃tasɛ̃] *m* foot soldier

fantastique [fɑ̃tastik] **I.** *adj* fantastic; (*atmosphère*) uncanny; (*événement, rêve*) from the realms of fantasy **II.** *m* **le ~** the fantastic

fantoche [fɑ̃tɔʃ] *m* puppet

fantôme [fɑ̃tom] **I.** *m* **1.** (*spectre*) ghost **2.** (*illusion, souvenir*) phantom; **les ~s du passé** the ghosts of the past **II.** *app* (*sans réalité: administration, cabinet*) shadow; (*société*) bogus ►**train** ~ ghost train; **le "Vaisseau ~"** the "Flying Dutchman"

faon [fɑ̃] *m* fawn

FAQ [ɛfaky] *f* INFOR *abr de* **foire aux questions** FAQ

far [faʀ] *m* ~ **breton** far (*Breton tart with prunes*)

faramineux, **-euse** [faʀaminø, -øz] *adj inf* amazing

farandole [faʀɑ̃dɔl] *f* (*danse*) farandole

farce¹ [faʀs] *f* **1.** (*tour*) trick **2.** (*plaisanterie*) joke **3.** (*chose peu sérieuse*) *a.* THEAT farce **4.** (*objet*) **~s et attrapes** tricks

farce² [faʀs] *f* GASTR stuffing

farceur, **-euse** [faʀsœʀ, -øz] **I.** *m, f* practical joker **II.** *adj* **être ~** to be a practical joker

farci(e) [faʀsi] *adj* GASTR stuffed

farcir [faʀsiʀ] <8> **I.** *vt* **1.** GASTR ~ **qc de qc** to stuff sth with sth **2.** *péj* (*bourrer*) ~ **qc de qc** to stuff sth full of sth **II.** *vpr péj, inf* **1.** (*supporter*) **se ~ qn/qc** to put up with sb/sth; **il faut se le ~!** it's a pain in the neck **2.** (*se payer*) **se ~ la vaisselle** to do the dishes

fard [faʀ] *m* makeup; ~ **à joues** blusher; ~ **à paupières** eyeshadow ►**piquer un** ~ *inf* to go red; **sans** ~ plain; **dire qc sans** ~ to say sth plainly

farde [faʀd] *f Belgique* (*chemise, dossier; liasse de copies*) file

fardé(e) [faʀde] *adj* made-up

fardeau [faʀdo] <x> *m* burden; ~ **des impôts** tax burden; **plier sous le ~ de qc** to bend under the burden of sth

farder [faʀde] <1> **I.** *vt* to make up **II.** *vpr* **se ~** to make up

fardoches [faʀdɔʃ] *fpl Québec* (*broussailles*) undergrowth

farfelu(e) [faʀfəly] **I.** *adj inf* crazy **II.** *m(f) inf* crank

farfouiller [faʀfuje] <1> *vi inf* ~ **dans qc** to rummage about

farine [faʀin] *f* flour

fariner [faʀine] <1> *vt* (*poisson*) to coat with flour; (*plaque de four*) to flour

farineux [faʀinø] *m* floury

farineux, **-euse** [faʀinø, -øz] *adj* **1.** (*couvert de farine*) floury **2.** (*abîmé, sec: pomme, pomme de terre*) starchy; (*fromage*) chalky

farniente [faʀnjɛnte, faʀnjɑ̃t] *m* lazing around

farouche [faʀuʃ] *adj* **1.** (*timide*) shy **2.** (*peu sociable*) unsociable; (*air*) standoffish; **ne pas être ~** (*animal*) to be quite tame; **elle n'est pas ~** she doesn't fend off the men **3.** (*violent, hostile: air, regard*) fierce **4.** (*opiniâtre: volonté, résistance*) ferocious; (*énergie*) frenzied

farouchement [faʀuʃmɑ̃] *adv* fiercely; **être ~ hostile à qc** to be fiercely hostile to sth

fart [faʀt] *m* wax

farter [faʀte] <1> *vt* to wax

Far West [faʀwɛst] *m* **le ~** the Far West

fascicule [fasikyl] *m* **1.** (*livret*) part; **être publié par ~s** (*roman*) to be published in instalments *Brit,* to be published in installments *Am;* (*ouvrage de vulgarisation*) to be published in parts **2.** (~ *d'information*) information booklet

fascinant(e) [fasinɑ̃, ɑ̃t] *adj* fascinating

fascination [fasinasjɔ̃] *f* fascination

fasciner [fasine] <1> *vt* **1.** (*hypnotiser*) to fascinate **2.** (*séduire*) to beguile; **se laisser ~ par de belles promesses** to be beguiled by fancy promises

fascisme [faʃism, fasism] *m* fascism

fasciste [faʃist, fasist] **I.** *adj* fascist(ic) **II.** *mf* fascist

fasse [fas] *subj prés de* **faire**

faste¹ [fast] *m* splendour *Brit,* splendor *Am*

faste² [fast] *adj* **1.** (*favorable*) lucky **2.** (*couronné de succès*) good; **jour ~** lucky day

fast-food, **fastfood** [fastfud] <fast-foods> *m* fast food place

fastidieux, **-euse** [fastidjø, -jøz] *adj* tedious

fastoche [fastɔʃ] *adj inf* dead easy

fastueux, **-euse** [fastɥø, -øz] *adj* (*cadre, décor*) sumptuous; (*fête*) magnificent; (*vie*) luxurious

fatal(e) [fatal] *adj* **1.** (*malheureux, irrésistible*) fatal; **être ~ à qn** to be fatal for sb; **porter un coup ~ à qn/qc** to deal sb/sth a fatal blow **2.** (*inévitable*) inevitable; **il est ~ que qn fasse qc** (*subj*) sb is bound to do sth **3.** (*marqué par le destin: moment, jour, air, regard*) fateful

fatalement [fatalmɑ̃] *adv* (*blessé*) fatally

fataliste [fatalist] **I.** *adj* fatalistic **II.** *mf* fatalist

fatalité [fatalite] *f* **1.** (*destin hostile*) fate **2.** (*inévitabilité*) inevitability; **ce n'est pas une ~** it is by no means inevitable

fatidique [fatidik] *adj* fateful

fatigant(e) [fatigɑ̃, ɑ̃t] *adj* **1.** (*épuisant: études, travail*) tiring; **être ~ pour les nerfs** to be a strain on the nerves **2.** (*assommant: personne*) tiresome

fatigue [fatig] *f* **1.** (*diminution des forces: d'une personne*) tiredness *no pl;* (*des yeux*) strain **2.** (*état d'épuisement*) exhaustion *no pl;*

se remettre des ~s de la journée to recover after an exhausting day 3. (*usure: d'un mécanisme, moteur*) wear

fatigué(e) [fatige] *adj* 1. (*personne, cœur*) tired; (*foie*) upset 2. (*usé: chaussures, vêtement*) worn-out 3. (*excédé*) **être ~ de qn/qc** to be tired of sb/sth

fatiguer [fatige] <1> I. *vt* 1. (*causer de la fatigue*) **~ qn** (*travail, marche*) to tire sb (out); (*personne*) to overwork sb 2. (*déranger*) **~ le foie/l'organisme** to put a strain on one's liver/body 3. (*excéder*) **~ qn** to get on sb's nerves 4. (*ennuyer*) **~ qn** to wear sb out II. *vi* 1. (*peiner: machine, moteur*) to labour *Brit,* to labor *Am;* (*cœur*) to get tired 2. (*s'user: pièce, joint*) to get worn; (*poutre*) to show the strain 3. *inf* (*en avoir assez*) to be fed up III. *vpr* 1. (*peiner*) **se ~** (*personne, cœur*) to get tired 2. (*se lasser*) **se ~ de qc** to tire of sth; **se ~ à faire qc** to tire of doing sth 3. (*s'évertuer*) **se ~ à faire qc** to wear oneself out doing sth

fatma [fatma] *f: North African woman*

fatras [fatʀɑ] *m* clutter; (*choses sans valeurs, inutiles*) junk; **un ~ d'idées** a load of muddled ideas

fatuité [fatɥite] *f* smugness

faubourg [fobuʀ] *m* suburb

fauche [foʃ] *f sans pl, inf* thieving; **il y a beaucoup de ~** a lot of thieving goes on

fauché(e) [foʃe] *adj inf* **être ~** to be broke; **être trop ~ pour** *+infin* to be too broke to *+infin*

faucher [foʃe] <1> *vt* 1. (*couper*) to reap 2. (*abattre*) **~ qn** (*véhicule*) to mow sb down; (*mort*) to cut sb down 3. *inf* (*voler*) **~ qc à qn** to pinch sth off sb

faucheuse [foʃøz] *f* reaper

faucille [fosij] *f* sickle

faucon [fokɔ̃] *m* 1. (*oiseau*) falcon 2. POL hawk

faudra [fodʀa] *fut de* **falloir**

faufiler [fofile] <1> *vpr* **se ~ dans un passage étroit** to slip through a narrrow passage; **se ~ parmi la foule** to slip through the crowd; **se ~ dans une réunion** to sneak into a meeting

faune[1] [fon] *f* 1. ZOOL fauna 2. *péj* (*personnes*) crowd

faune[2] [fon] *m* HIST faun

faussaire [fosɛʀ] *mf* forger

fausse [fos] *adj v.* **faux**

faussé(e) [fose] *adj* distorted; (*porte*) warped

fausser [fose] <1> *vt* 1. (*altérer*) to distort; (*intentionnellement*) to falsify 2. (*déformer: bois*) to warp; (*mécanisme*) to damage

fausseté [foste] *f* 1. falsity 2. (*hypocrisie: d'une personne*) deceit; (*d'un sentiment*) falseness

faut [fo] *indic prés de* **falloir**

faute [fot] *f* 1. (*erreur*) mistake 2. (*mauvaise action*) misdeed 3. (*manquement à des lois, règles*) offence *Brit,* offense *Am;* **~ de goût** lapse of taste; **commettre une ~** to do something wrong; **commettre une ~ envers qc** to wrong sb; **faire un sans ~** to get everything right; **sans ~** without fail 4. (*responsabilité*) **faire retomber** [*o* **rejeter**] **la ~ sur qn** to put the blame on sb; **c'est (de) la ~ de qn** it's sb's fault; **c'est (de) la ~ de qc** sth is to blame; **c'est (de) ma ~** it's my fault; **alors à qui la ~?** so who's to blame?, who's fault is it? 5. SPORT fault; (*agression*) foul 6. JUR **~ pénale** criminal offence *Brit,* criminal offense *Am* 7. (*par manque de*) **~ de temps** for lack of time; **~ de preuves** through lack of evidence; **~ de mieux** for lack of anything better ►**être en ~** to be at fault; **prendre qn en ~** to catch sb out; **~ de quoi** failing which

fauteuil [fotœj] *m* 1. (*siège*) armchair; **~ roulant** wheelchair; **~ à bascule** rocking chair 2. (*place dans une assemblée*) seat; **~ de maire** mayor's seat

fauteur [fotœʀ] *m* **~ de désordre/troubles** troublemaker

fautif, -ive [fotif, -iv] I. *adj* 1. (*coupable*) at fault; **être ~** to be in the wrong 2. (*avec des fautes: texte*) faulty; (*citation, calcul*) inaccurate; (*mémoire*) defective II. *m, f* guilty party

fauve [fov] I. *adj* 1. (*couleur*) fawn 2. (*sauvage*) wild; **odeur ~** musky II. *m* 1. (*couleur*) fawn 2. (*animal*) big cat

fauvette [fovɛt] *f* warbler

faux [fo] I. *f* (*outil*) scythe II. *m* 1. false; **discerner le vrai du ~** to tell truth from falsehood 2. (*falsification, imitation*) forgery III. *adv* (*chanter*) out of tune

faux, fausse [fo, fos] *adj* 1. *antéposé* (*imité: marbre, perle, meuble*) imitation; (*papiers, signature, tableau*) forged; (*monnaie*) counterfeit 2. *antéposé* (*postiche: barbe, dents, nom*) false 3. *antéposé* (*simulé: dévotion, humilité*) feigned; (*modestie, pudeur*) false 4. *antéposé* (*mensonger: promesse, réponse, serment*) false 5. *antéposé* (*pseudo: col*) detachable; (*fenêtre, porte, plafond*) false 6. *postposé* (*fourbe: air, caractère, personne*) deceitful; (*attitude*) dishonest 7. *antéposé* (*imposteur: ami, prophète*) false 8. (*erroné: raisonnement, résultat, numéro*) wrong; (*affirmation, thermomètre*) inaccurate; **votre instrument est ~** your instrument is out of tune 9. *antéposé* (*non fondé: espoir, principe*) false; (*crainte, soupçon*) groundless 10. *postposé* (*ambigu: atmosphère, situation*) awkward 11. *antéposé* (*maladroit*) **une fausse manœuvre** a clumsy move; (*au volant*) a steering error; **faire fausse route** to go the wrong way; **faire un ~ pas** (*en marchant*) to stumble 12. MUS (*note*) wrong

faux-filet [fofilɛ] <faux-filets> *m* sirloin **faux-fuyant** [fofɥijɑ̃] <faux-fuyants> *m* dodge; (*prétexte*) excuse; **chercher un ~** to try to evade the issue **faux-monnayeur** [fomɔnɛjœʀ] <faux-monnayeurs> *m* counterfeiter **faux-sens** [fosɑ̃s] *m inv* mistranslation

faveur [favœʀ] *f* **1.** (*bienveillance, bienfait*) favour *Brit*, favor *Am* **2.** (*considération*) **être en ~ auprès de qn** to be in favour with sb *Brit*, to be in favor with sb *Am*; **gagner la ~ du public** to win public approval; **voter en ~ de qn** to vote for sth; **se déclarer** [*o* **se prononcer**] **en ~ de qn/qc** to come out in favour of sth; **en ma/ta ~** in my/your favour ►**de ~** preferential; **en ~ de qc** (*en raison de*) in consideration of sth; (*pour aider*) in aid of; (*testament*) in favour of *Brit*, in favor of *Am*

favorable [favɔʀabl] *adj* favourable *Brit*, favorable *Am*; **jouir d'un préjugé ~** to be viewed favourably; **donner un avis ~** to give a positive response; **être ~ à qn/qc** to feel favourable to sb/sth; (*circonstances, suffrages, opinion*) to favour sb/sth; **être ~ à ce que qn fasse qc** (*subj*) to be in favour of sb doing sth

favorablement [favɔʀabləmɑ̃] *adv* favourably *Brit*, favorably *Am*

favori(**te**) [favɔʀi, it] **I.** *adj* favourite *Brit*, favorite *Am* **II.** *m(f)* *a.* SPORT favourite *Brit*, favorite *Am*

favoris [favɔʀi] *mpl* side whiskers

favorisé(**e**) [favɔʀize] *adj* privileged

favoriser [favɔʀize] <1> *vt* **1.** to favour *Brit*, to favor *Am*; **les familles les plus favorisées** the most fortunate families **2.** (*aider*) to further

favorite [favɔʀit] *adj v.* **favori**

favoritisme [favɔʀitism] *m* POL, ECON favoritism

fax [faks] *m abr de* **téléfax** fax

faxer [fakse] <1> *vt* to fax

fayot [fajo] *m inf* (*haricot*) bean

FB *m abr de* **franc belge** *v.* **franc**

FBI [ɛfbiaj] *m abr de* **Federal Bureau of Investigation** FBI

FC [ɛfse] *m abr de* **football club** F.C.

fébrile [febʀil] *adj* feverish

fébrilité [febʀilite] *f* **1.** (*activité débordante*) fevered activity **2.** (*excitation*) fevered state; **faire qc avec ~** to do sth feverishly

fécal(**e**) [fekal, o] <-aux> *adj* faecal *Brit*, fecal *Am*; **les matières ~es** the faeces *Brit*, the feces *Am*

fécond(**e**) [fekɔ̃, ɔ̃d] *adj* **1.** (*productif: esprit*) fertile; (*idée, conversation, sujet*) fruitful; (*écrivain, siècle*) prolific **2.** (*prolifique*) rich; **~ en surprises** full of surprises; **~ en événements** eventful

fécondation [fekɔ̃dasjɔ̃] *f* fertilization; (*des fleurs*) pollination

féconder [fekɔ̃de] <1> *vt* to fertilize; (*fleur*) to pollinate

fécondité [fekɔ̃dite] *f* fertility

fécule [fekyl] *f* starch; GASTR corn starch; **être riche en ~** to be rich in starch

féculent [fekylɑ̃] *m* starchy food

fédéral(**e**) [fedeʀal, o] <-aux> *adj* federal

fédéralisme [fedeʀalism] *m* federalism

fédéraliste [fedeʀalist] **I.** *adj* federalist **II.** *mf* federalist

fédérateur, **-trice** [fedeʀatœʀ, -tʀis] *adj* (*thème*) federative; (*rôle*) unifying

fédération [fedeʀasjɔ̃] *f* federation

fédéré(**e**) [fedeʀe] *adj* federate; (*au sein d'une association*) member

fédérer [fedeʀe] <5> *vt* to federate

fée [fe] *f* fairy

feeling [filiŋ] *m* feeling

féerie [fe(e)ʀi] *f* **1.** (*ravissement*) enchantment **2.** THEAT, CINE extravaganza

féerique [fe(e)ʀik] *adj* magical; **l'Orient ~** the magic of the Orient; **le monde** [*o* **l'univers**] **~ de l'enfance** the fairytale [*o* magical] world of childhood

feignant(**e**) [fɛɲɑ̃, ɑ̃t] *v.* **fainéant**

feindre [fɛ̃dʀ] *vt irr* (*colère, innocence, joie, tristesse*) to feign; (*prétexter: maladie*) to sham; **~ l'indifférence** to feign indifference; **~ de ne rien** [*o* **pas**] **comprendre** to pretend not to understand; **~ d'être malade** to pretend to be ill

feint(**e**) [fɛ̃, fɛ̃t] **I.** *part passé de* **feindre** **II.** *adj* feigned; (*maladie*) sham

feinte [fɛ̃t] *f* **1.** (*ruse*) pretence *Brit*, pretense *Am* **2.** SPORT dummy

feinter [fɛ̃te] <1> *vt* **1.** SPORT to dummy **2.** *inf* (*rouler*) to take in

fêlé(**e**) [fele] *adj* **1.** (*fendu*) cracked **2.** *inf* (*dérangé*) **avoir le cerveau ~** to be not right in the head; **tu es complètement ~!** you're off your head!

fêler [fele] <1> **I.** *vt* **son opération à la gorge a fêlé sa voix** his throat operation left him with a cracked voice **II.** *vpr* **se ~** to crack; **se ~ qc** to get a crack in sth

félicitations [felisitasjɔ̃] *fpl* congratulations; **avec les ~ du jury** with the commendation of the examiners; **recevoir les ~ de qn à l'occasion de qc** to be congratulated by sb on sth

féliciter [felisite] <1> **I.** *vt* **~ qn de** [*o* **pour**] **qc** to congratulate sb on sth; **~ qn de faire qc** to congratulate sb on doing sth **II.** *vpr* **se ~ de qc** to feel pleased (with oneself) about sth

félin [felɛ̃] *m* cat

félin(**e**) [felɛ̃, in] *adj* (*race*) of cats; (*démarche, grâce*) feline

fellation [felasjɔ̃, fɛllasjɔ̃] *f* fellatio

fêlure [felyʀ] *f* crack

femelle [fəmɛl] **I.** *adj* (*animal, organe*) female; **léopard ~** leopardess **II.** *f* female

féminin [feminɛ̃] *m* LING feminine

féminin(**e**) [feminɛ̃, in] *adj* **1.** (*opp: masculin: population, sexe*) female **2.** (*avec un aspect féminin*) *a.* LING feminine **3.** (*de femmes: voix*) woman's; (*vêtements, mode, revendications, football*) women's; (*condition*) female

féminisation [feminizasjɔ̃] *f* **~ de l'enseignement** (*action*) the growing number of women teachers; (*résultat*) the predominance of women in teaching

féminiser [feminize] <1> **I.** *vt* (*homme*) to make effeminate; (*femme*) to make more feminine; ~ **une profession** to bring more women into a profession **II.** *vpr* **se** ~ **1.** (*se faire femme*) to become effeminate **2.** (*comporter de plus en plus de femmes: parti politique*) to be taken over by women

féminisme [feminism] *m* feminism

féministe [feminist] **I.** *adj* feminist; **mouvement** ~ women's movement **II.** *mf* feminist

féminité [feminite] *f* femininity

femme [fam] *f* **1.** (*opp: homme*) woman; **vêtements de** [*o* **pour**] ~**s** women's clothes; **t'as vu la bonne** ~ **là-bas!** *inf* have you seen that woman over there? **2.** (*épouse*) wife; **une** ~ **accomplie** a complete woman; **ma/ta bonne** ~ *péj, inf* my/your old woman **3.** (*adulte*) (grown) woman **4.** (*profession*) **une** ~ **ingénieur/médecin** a female engineer/doctor; ~ **politique** (woman) politician; ~ **d'État** stateswoman; ~ **au foyer** housewife; ~ **de chambre** chambermaid; ~ **de ménage** cleaning lady; ~ **de service** (*pour le nettoyage*) cleaner; (*à la cantine*) dinner lady; ~ **d'intérieur** housewife

femme-enfant [famɑ̃fɑ̃] <femmes-enfants> *f* woman that is still a child

femmelette [famlɛt] *f péj* **1.** (*homme*) weakling **2.** (*femme*) frail female

fémur [femyʀ] *m* femur, thighbone

FEN [fɛn] *f abr de* **Fédération de l'Éducation nationale** *one of the teaching unions in France*

fenaison [fənɛzɔ̃] *f* haymaking

fendillé(**e**) [fɑ̃dije] *adj* crazed

fendiller [fɑ̃dije] <1> *vpr* **se** ~ to craze

fendre [fɑ̃dʀ] <14> **I.** *vt* **1.** (*couper en deux: bois*) to split **2.** (*fissurer: glace*) to crack open; (*pierre, rochers*) to split **II.** *vpr* **1.** (*se fissurer*) **se** ~ to crack **2.** (*se blesser*) **se** ~ **la lèvre** to cut one's lip open

fendu(**e**) [fɑ̃dy] *adj* **1.** (*ouvert: crâne*) cracked; (*lèvre*) cut **2.** (*fissuré*) cracked **3.** (*avec une fente d'aisance: jupe, veste*) slashed

fenêtre [f(ə)nɛtʀ] *f* window

fennec [fenɛk] *m* ZOOL fennec

fenouil [fənuj] *m* fennel

fente [fɑ̃t] *f* **1.** (*fissure: d'un mur, rocher*) crack **2.** (*interstice*) slit; (*pour une lame, lettre*) slot; (*dans une veste*) vent

féodal [feɔdal] <-aux> *m* HIST feudal lord

féodal(**e**) [feɔdal, o] <-aux> *adj* feudal

féodalité [feɔdalite] *f* HIST feudalism

fer [fɛʀ] *m* **1.** (*métal, sels de* ~) iron; **en** ~ [*o* **de**] iron **2.** (*pièce métallique: d'une lance, flèche*) head; ~ **à cheval** horseshoe; **en** ~ **à cheval** in a horseshoe **3.** (*appareil*) ~ **à friser** curling tongs; ~ **à repasser** iron ►**tomber les quatre** ~**s en l'air** *inf* to fall flat on one's back; **le** ~ **de lance d'une organisation** the spearhead of an organization; **battre le** ~ **tant qu'il est chaud** to strike while the iron is hot; **santé de** ~ robust health

ferai [f(ə)ʀɛ] *fut de* **faire**

fer-blanc [fɛʀblɑ̃] <fers-blancs> *m* tin (plate)

férié(**e**) [feʀje] *adj* **jour** ~ public holiday

fermage [fɛʀmaʒ] *m* tenant farming

ferme[1] [fɛʀm] **I.** *adj* **1.** (*consistant, résolu*) firm **2.** (*assuré: écriture, voix, main*) firm; (*pas*) steady **3.** (*définitif: achat, commande, prix*) firm; (*cours, marché*) steady **II.** *adv* **1.** (*beaucoup: boire, travailler*) hard; **s'ennuyer** ~ to be bored out of one's mind **2.** (*avec ardeur: discuter*) passionately; (*pour acheter*) hard **3.** (*définitivement: acheter, vendre*) firm; **commander** ~ to place a firm order **4.** (*avec opiniâtreté*) **tenir** ~ to hold firm

ferme[2] [fɛʀm] *f* **1.** (*bâtiment*) farmhouse **2.** (*exploitation*) farm

ferme[3] [fɛʀm] **la** ~**!** *inf* shut up!

fermé(**e**) [fɛʀme] *adj* **1.** (*opp: ouvert: magasin, porte*) closed; (*à clé*) locked; (*vêtement*) done up; (*robinet*) turned off; (*mer*) enclosed **2.** (*privé: milieu, monde*) closed; (*club, cercle*) exclusive **3.** (*peu communicatif: personne*) uncommunicative; (*air, visage*) impassive **4.** (*insensible à*) **être** ~ **à qc** to be untouched by sth

fermement [fɛʀməmɑ̃] *adv* firmly

ferment [fɛʀmɑ̃] *m* BIO ferment; ~**s lactiques** lactic fermenting agents

fermentation [fɛʀmɑ̃tasjɔ̃] *f* BIO fermentation

fermenté(**e**) [fɛʀmɑ̃te] *adj* fermented

fermenter [fɛʀmɑ̃te] <1> *vi* (*jus*) to ferment; (*pâte*) to leaven

fermer [fɛʀme] <1> **I.** *vi* **1.** (*être, rester fermé*) to close **2.** (*pouvoir être fermé*) **bien/mal** ~ (*vêtement*) to do up/not do up properly; (*boîte, porte*) to close/not close properly **II.** *vt* **1.** (*opp: ouvrir: porte, yeux, école, passage, compte*) to close; (*rideau*) to draw; ~ **la main/le poing** to close one's hand/fist; ~ **une maison à clé** to lock up a house; **fermez la parenthèse!** close brackets! *Brit,* close the parentheses! *Am* **2.** (*boutonner*) to button up **3.** (*cacheter: enveloppe*) to seal **4.** (*arrêter: robinet, appareil*) to turn off **5.** (*rendre inaccessible*) **cette carrière m'est fermée** this career is closed to me; ~ **son cœur à la détresse des autres** to close one's heart to the troubles of others **III.** *vpr* **1.** (*se refermer*) **se** ~ (*porte, yeux*) to close; (*plaie*) to close up **2.** (*passif*) **se** ~ (*boîte, appareil*) to close; **se** ~ **par devant** (*robe*) to do up at the front **3.** (*refuser l'accès à*) **se** ~ (*personne*) to close up; **se** ~ **à qn/qc** (*pays*) to close its borders to sb/sth

fermeté [fɛʀməte] *f* **1.** (*solidité, autorité*) firmness; ~ **du jugement** firm judgment; **parler/affirmer avec** ~ to speak/declare firmly **2.** (*courage*) steadfastness **3.** (*concision: d'un style*) sureness **4.** FIN (*d'un cours, marché, d'une monnaie*) stability

fermette [fɛʀmɛt] *f* small farm

fermeture [fɛʀmətyʀ] *f* **1.** (*dispositif: d'un sac, vêtement*) fastening; **avec** ~ **à clé** lock-

F

able; ~ **automatique** automatic closing **2.** (*action: d'une porte, d'un magasin, guichet*) closing; (*d'une école, frontière, entreprise*) closure; **après la ~ des bureaux/du magasin** after office/shop hours

fermier, **-ière** [fɛʀmje, -jɛʀ] **I.** *adj* (*de ferme: beurre*) dairy; (*poulet, canard*) free range **II.** *m, f* farmer

fermoir [fɛʀmwaʀ] *m* clasp

féroce [feʀɔs] *adj* **1.** (*sauvage: animal*) ferocious **2.** (*impitoyable: personne*) ferocious; (*critique, satire*) savage; (*air, regard*) fierce **3.** (*irrésistible: appétit*) voracious; (*envie*) raging

férocement [feʀɔsmɑ̃] *adv* fiercely

férocité [feʀɔsite] *f* **1.** (*sauvagerie: d'un animal*) ferocity **2.** (*barbarie: d'un dictateur*) savagery **3.** (*violence: d'un combat*) savagery; (*d'un regard*) fierceness **4.** (*ironie méchante: d'une critique, attaque*) savagery; **se moquer avec ~ de qn** to mock sb savagely

ferraille [fɛʀɑj] *f* **1.** (*vieux métaux*) scrap (iron); **être bon à mettre à la ~** to be fit for the scrapyard; **mettre une voiture à la ~** to scrap a car **2.** *inf* (*monnaie*) small change

ferrailleur, **-euse** [fɛʀɑjœʀ, -jøz] *m, f* scrap merchant

ferré(e) [feʀe] *adj* (*cheval*) shod; (*bâton, soulier*) steel-tipped

ferrer [feʀe] <1> *vt* (*cheval*) to shoe; ~ **qc** (*souliers, canne*) to fit a tip to sth

ferreux, **-euse** [fɛʀø, -øz] *adj* ferrous

ferronnerie [fɛʀɔnʀi] *f* (*objets*) ironwork; **en ~** iron; ~ **d'art** wrought iron work

ferroviaire [fɛʀɔvjɛʀ] *adj* railway

ferrure [feʀyʀ] *f* (*d'un meuble, d'une porte*) hinge; (*fers d'un cheval*) shoes

ferry [feʀi] <ferries> *m abr de* **ferry-boat**, **car-ferry**, **train-ferry**

ferry-boat [feʀibot] <ferry-boats> *m* ferry (boat)

fertile [fɛʀtil] *adj* fertile; ~ **en aventures** (*roman, vie*) full of adventures

fertilisant [fɛʀtilizɑ̃] *m* (*engrais*) fertilizer

fertilisant(e) [fɛʀtilizɑ̃, ɑ̃t] *adj* fertilizing

fertilisation [fɛʀtilizasjɔ̃] *f* fertilization

fertiliser [fɛʀtilize] <1> *vt* to fertilize

fertilité [fɛʀtilite] *f* **1.** (*richesse: d'une région, terre*) fertility **2.** (*créativité*) ~ **d'esprit/d'imagination** fertile mind/imagination

fervent(e) [fɛʀvɑ̃, ɑ̃t] **I.** *adj* fervent **II.** *m(f)* ~ **de football** football enthusiast; ~ **de musique** musical devotee

ferveur [fɛʀvœʀ] *f* fervour *Brit*, fervor *Brit*; **remercier qn avec ~** to thank sb ardently

fesse [fɛs] *f* buttock; **tes ~s** your bum *Brit*, your butt *Am* ►**avoir qn aux ~s** *inf* to have sb on one's tail; **serrer les ~s** *inf* to be scared out of one's wits, to have the wind up *Brit*

fessée [fese] *f* **donner une ~ à qn** to smack sb's bottom

fessier [fesje] **I.** *adj* (*muscle*) gluteal **II.** *m* iron, *inf* rear end

festin [fɛstɛ̃] *m* feast

festival [fɛstival] <s> *m* festival; **le ~ de Cannes** the Cannes film festival

festivalier, **-ière** [fɛstivalje, -jɛʀ] *m, f* festival-goer

festivités [fɛstivite] *fpl* festivities

festoyer [fɛstwaje] <6> *vi* to feast

fêtard(e) [fɛtaʀ, aʀd] *m(f) inf* party-goer

fête [fɛt] *f* **1.** (*religieuse*) feast; (*civile*) holiday **2.** (*jour férié*) ~ **des Mères/Pères** Mother's/Father's Day; ~ **du travail** (*en Europe*) May Day; (*aux Etats-Unis*) Labor Day **3.** (*jour du prénom*) name day **4.** *pl* (*congé*) holidays **5.** (*kermesse*) ~ **foraine** fair; ~ **de la bière à Munich** Munich beer festival **6.** (*réception*) party; **un jour de ~** holiday ►**elle n'est pas à la ~** *inf* she's being put through it; **faire ~ à qn** to give sb a big welcome; **ambiance/air/atmosphère de ~** (*solennel*) feast day feeling/air/atmosphere; (*gai*) festive feeling/air/atmosphere; **village en ~** village in a party mood; **le collège en ~** the school fete

> The **fêtes** generally fall between Christmas and New Year's, although the public holidays in this period are 25th December and 1st January.

Fête-Dieu [fɛtdjø] <Fêtes-Dieu> *f* **la ~** Corpus Christi

fêter [fete] <1> *vt* **1.** (*célébrer*) to celebrate **2.** (*faire fête à*) ~ **qn** to put on a celebration for sb

fétiche [fetiʃ] **I.** *m* **1.** (*amulette*) fetish **2.** (*mascotte*) mascot **II.** *app* (*film*) cult; **objet ~** lucky charm

fétichisme [fetiʃism] *m* fetishism

fétichiste [fetiʃist] **I.** *adj* fetishistic **II.** *mf* fetishist

fétide [fetid] *adj* fetid

fétu [fety] *m* ~ **de paille** wisp of straw

feu [fø] <x> *m* **1.** (*source de chaleur, incendie*) fire; ~ **de camp** camp fire; **mettre le ~ à qc** to set sth on fire **2.** *souvent pl* (*lumière*) **les ~x des projecteurs** the spotlight; **être sous le ~ des projecteurs** to be in the spotlight **3.** *souvent pl* AVIAT, AUTO, NAUT lights **4.** AUTO ~ **tricolore/de signalisation** traffic lights; **passer au ~ rouge** to go through on red, to run a red light *Am*; **le ~ est (au) rouge** the light is red **5.** (*brûleur d'un réchaud à gaz*) burner; **à ~ doux/vif** on low/high heat **6.** *soutenu* (*ardeur*) heat; **dans le ~ de l'action** in the heat of action **7.** (*spectacle*) ~ **d'artifice** fireworks *pl* ►**ne pas faire long ~** not to last long; **laisser mijoter qn à petit ~** to prolong the agony for sb; ~ **vert** (*permission*) green light; **y'a pas le ~!** *inf*, **y'a pas le ~ au lac!** *Suisse* there's no rush!; **être (pris) entre deux ~x** to be caught in the crossfire; **péter le ~** to be full of life; **n'y voir que du ~** to be completely taken in; **tempérament de ~** fiery

temperament
feuillage [fœjaʒ] *m* **1.** (*ensemble de feuilles*) foliage **2.** (*rameaux coupés*) greenery
feuille [fœj] *f* **1.** BOT (*d'un arbre, d'une fleur, salade*) leaf **2.** (*plaque mince: d'aluminium, or*) leaf; (*de carton, contreplaqué*) sheet **3.** (*page*) ~ **de papier** sheet of paper **4.** (*formulaire*) ~ **de maladie/soins** *form issued by doctor for claiming medical expenses;* ~ **de paie** pay slip *Brit,* paystub *Am;* ~ **d'impôt** (*déclaration d'impôt*) tax return; (*avis d'imposition*) tax demand **5.** INFOR sheet; ~ **de styles** style sheet **6.** (*journal*) ~ **de chou** *péj* rag ►**trembler comme une** ~ to shake like a leaf
feuillet [fœjɛ] *m* page
feuilleté [fœjte] *m* GASTR puff pastry
feuilleté(e) [fœjte] *adj* **1.** (*triplex*) **verre** ~ laminated glass **2.** GASTR **pâte ~e** puff pastry
feuilleter [fœjte] <3> *vt* **1.** (*tourner les pages*) ~ **un livre** to leaf through a book **2.** (*parcourir*) ~ **un livre** to glance through a book
feuilleton [fœjtɔ̃] *m* **1.** PRESSE serial **2.** TV ~ **télévisé** soap (opera) **3.** (*événement à rebondissements*) saga
feuillu [fœjy] *m* broad-leaved tree
feuillu(e) [fœjy] *adj* **1.** (*chargé de feuilles*) leafy **2.** (*opp: résineux*) broad-leaved
feuillure [fœjyʀ] *f* rebate
feutre [føtʀ] *m* **1.** (*étoffe*) felt **2.** (*stylo*) felt-tip (pen) **3.** (*chapeau*) felt hat
feutré(e) [føtʀe] *adj* **1.** (*fait de feutre*) felt **2.** (*discret: bruit, pas*) muffled; **marcher à pas ~s** to pad along
feutrer [føtʀe] <1> *vi, vpr* (**se**) ~ to felt
feutrine [føtʀin] *f* felt
fève [fɛv] *f* **1.** broad bean **2.** *Québec* (*haricot*) bean
février [fevʀije] *m* February; *v. a.* **août**
FF [ɛfɛf] **I.** *m abr de* **franc français** *v.* **franc II.** *f* SPORT *abr de* **Fédération française** French Federation
FFI [ɛfɛfi] *fpl* HIST *abr de* **Forces françaises de l'intérieur** *French Resistance fighters during the Second World War*
fiabilité [fjabilite] *f* (*d'un appareil de mesure*) accuracy; (*d'un mécanisme, d'une personne*) reliability
fiable [fjabl] *adj* (*appareil de mesure*) accurate; (*mécanisme, personne*) reliable
fiacre [fjakʀ] *m* (hackney) carriage
fiançailles [fjɑ̃sɑj] *fpl* engagement
fiancé(e) [fjɑ̃se] **I.** *adj* engaged **II.** *m(f)* fiancé *m,* fiancée *f*
fiancer [fjɑ̃se] <2> **I.** *vt* ~ **qn avec** [*o* **à**] **qn** to betroth sb to sb **II.** *vpr* **se** ~ **avec** [*o* **à**] **qn** to get engaged to sb
fiasco [fjasko] *m* fiasco; **être un** ~ to be a fiasco; (*pièce*) to be a flop
fibre [fibʀ] *f* **1.** (*substance filamenteuse: d'un bois, muscle, d'une plante, viande*) fibre *Brit,* fiber *Am* **2.** (*sensibilité*) **avoir la** ~ **sensible** to be a sensitive soul
fibreux, -euse [fibʀø, -øz] *adj* fibrous
fibrome [fibʀom] *m* MED fibroid
ficelé(e) [fis(ə)le] *adj inf* **être mal** ~ *inf* (*personne, intrigue, travail*) to be a mess; **être bien** ~ (*intrigue, travail*) to be a clever job
ficeler [fis(ə)le] <3> *vt* to tie up
ficelle [fisɛl] *f* **1.** (*corde*) string **2.** (*pain*) ficelle (*stick of French bread*) ►**connaître toutes les ~s du métier** to know the tricks of the trade; **tirer les ~s** to pull the strings
fiche [fiʃ] *f* **1.** (*piquet*) pin **2.** (*carte*) card **3.** (*feuille, formulaire*) form; ~ **de paie** pay slip *Brit,* paystub *Am;* ~ **d'état civil** attestation of civil status; ~ **technique** specifications *pl* **4.** *Suisse* (*dossier*) file
fiche-horaire [fiʃɔʀɛʀ] <fiches-horaires> *f* pocket timetable
ficher¹ [fiʃe] <1> **I.** *vt part passé: fichu, inf* **1.** (*faire*) to do; **ne rien** ~ to do not a damn thing, to do damn all *Brit* **2.** (*donner: claque, coup*) to give; **en** ~ **une à qn** to lay one on sb **3.** (*mettre*) ~ **qc par terre** to send sth flying; ~ **qn dehors/à la porte** to kick sb out; ~ **qn en colère** [*o* **en rogne**] to get sb mad **4.** (*se désintéresser*) **j'en ai rien à fiche!** I couldn't care less! ►~ **un coup à qn** to belt sb; **je t'en fiche!** chance would be a fine thing! **II.** *vpr part passé: fichu, inf* **1.** (*se mettre*) **fiche-toi ça dans le crâne!** get that into your (thick) head! **2.** (*se flanquer*) **se** ~ **un coup de marteau** to hit oneself with a hammer **3.** (*se moquer*) **se** ~ **de qn** to pull sb's leg **4.** (*se désintéresser*) **elle se fiche de toi/tout ça** she couldn't care less about you/all that
ficher² [fiʃe] <1> **I.** *vt* (*inscrire*) ~ **qn/qc** to put sb/sth on file **II.** *vpr* **se** ~ **dans qc** (*arête*) to get stuck in sth; (*flèche, pieu, piquet*) to stick in sth
fichier [fiʃje] *m a.* INFOR file
fichier-texte [fiʃjetɛkst] *m* INFOR text file
fichu [fiʃy] *m* (head)scarf
fichu(e) [fiʃy] **I.** *part passé de* **ficher II.** *adj inf* **1.** *antéposé* (*sale: caractère, métier, temps*) lousy **2.** *antéposé* (*sacré: habitude, idée*) damn; **un** ~ **problème** one hell of a problem **3.** (*en mauvais état*) **être** ~ (*vêtement, appareil*) to have had it; **la voiture est ~e** the car's a write-off *Brit,* the car's totaled *Am* **4.** (*gâché*) **être** ~ (*vacances, soirée*) to be completely ruined, to be a write-off *Brit* **5.** (*perdu, condamné*) **être** ~ (*personne*) to be done for **6.** (*capable*) **être/n'être pas** ~ **de faire qc** to be perfectly capable of doing/not up to doing sth ►**être bien/mal** ~ (*bien bâti*) to have a good/lousy body; (*habillé*) to look good/a mess; **elle est bien ~e** she's a looker; **il est mal** ~ (*malade*) he's in a bad way
fictif, -ive [fiktif, -iv] *adj* **1.** (*imaginaire: personnage, récit*) imaginary **2.** (*faux: adresse, nom*) false; (*concurrence*) artificial; (*vente, contrat*) bogus
fiction [fiksjɔ̃] *f* **1.** (*imagination*) imagination

F

2. (*fait imaginé*) invention; **film de ~** film that tells a story 3. (*œuvre d'imagination*) work of fiction
ficus [fikys] *m* ficus
fidèle [fidɛl] I. *adj* 1. (*constant*) faithful 2. (*qui ne trahit pas qc*) **être ~ à une habitude** to stick to a habit; **être ~ à une promesse** to be true to one's promise 3. (*exact: récit, reproduction, traduction*) faithful; (*souvenir, historien, narrateur*) accurate 4. (*fiable: mémoire*) reliable; (*montre*) accurate II. *mf* (*personne: d'un homme politique*) follower; (*d'un magasin*) regular (customer) III. *mpl* REL faithful
fidèlement [fidɛlmɑ̃] *adv* 1. (*loyalement: servir, obéir*) faithfully 2. (*régulièrement: suivre une émission*) regularly 3. (*d'après l'original: reproduire, traduire*) faithfully; (*décrire*) accurately
fidéliser [fidelize] <1> *vt* **~ ses clients** to establish customer loyalty
fidélité [fidelite] *f* 1. (*dévouement*) **~ à** [*o* **envers**] **qn** faithfulness to sb; (*dans le couple*) fidelity to sb 2. (*attachement*) **~ à une habitude** adherence to a habit 3. (*exactitude: d'une copie, traduction, d'un portrait*) fidelity
Fidji [fidʒi] *fpl* **les** (**îles**) **~** Fiji
fidjien(**ne**) [fidʒiɛ̃, ɛn] *adj* Fijian
Fidjien(**ne**) [fidʒiɛ̃, ɛn] *m(f)* Fijian
fief [fjɛf] *m* 1. POL (*d'un parti*) stronghold 2. HIST fief
fiel [fjɛl] *m* gall
fiente [fjɑ̃t] *f* droppings *pl*
fier [fje] <1> *vpr* **se ~ à qn** to put one's trust in sb; **se ~ à des promesses** to rely on promises
fier, **fière** [fjɛʀ] I. *adj* **~ de qn/qc** proud of sb/sth II. *m, f* **faire le ~ avec qn** (*crâner*) to act big in front of sb; (*être méprisant*) to lord it over sb
fier-à-bras [fjɛʀabʀɑ] <fiers-à-bras> *m* braggart
fièrement [fjɛʀmɑ̃] *adv* proudly
fierté [fjɛʀte] *f* pride; **tirer une ~ de qc** to take pride in sth
fiesta [fjɛsta] *f inf* party
fièvre [fjɛvʀ] *f* 1. MED fever 2. (*vive agitation*) excitement 3. (*désir ardent*) burning desire
fiévreusement [fjevʀøzmɑ̃] *adv* feverishly
fiévreux, **-euse** [fjevʀø, -øz] *adj* feverish
FIFA [fifa] *f abr de* **Fédération internationale de football association** FIFA
fifre [fifʀ] *m* fife
figé(**e**) [fiʒe] *adj* fixed; (*attitude*) rigid
figer [fiʒe] <2a> I. *vt* 1. (*durcir: graisse, sauce*) to congeal 2. (*horrifier*) **~ qn** (*surprise, terreur*) to root sb to the spot II. *vpr* 1. (*durcir*) **se ~** (*graisse, huile, sauce*) to congeal; (*sang*) to clot; (*visage*) to harden; (*sourire*) to set 2. (*s'immobiliser*) **se ~ dans une de refus** to adopt a rigid attitude of refusal
fignoler [fiɲɔle] <1> I. *vi inf* to polish things up II. *vt inf* to polish up
figue [fig] *f* fig
figuier [figje] *m* fig tree
figurant(**e**) [figyʀɑ̃, ɑ̃t] *m(f)* 1. CINE extra 2. THEAT walk-on 3. (*potiche*) puppet
figuratif, **-ive** [figyʀatif, -iv] *adj* figurative
figuration [figyʀasjɔ̃] *f* 1. CINE being an extra 2. THEAT doing walk-ons 3. (*représentation*) representation ►**faire de la ~** CINE to work as an extra; THEAT to do walk-ons; (*en politique*) to be a bit player
figure [figyʀ] *f* 1. (*visage, mine*) face 2. (*personnage*) *a.* MAT figure 3. (*image*) illustration; **livre orné de ~s** illustrated book 4. SPORT figure; **~s imposées** compulsory figures; **~s libres** freestyle ►**faire bonne/mauvaise ~** (*se montrer sous un bon/mauvais jour*) to make a good/bad impression; (*s'en sortir bien/mal*) to do all right/badly; **casser la ~ à qn** *inf* to smash sb's face in; **se casser la ~** *inf* to have a nasty fall; (*projet*) to fail miserably; **faire ~ de favori** to look like the favourite *Brit*, to look like the favorite *Am*; **prendre ~** to take shape
figuré(**e**) [figyʀe] *adj* 1. (*opp: concret: sens*) figurative 2. (*riche en figures: langage*) full of imagery
figurer [figyʀe] <1> I. *vi* 1. THEAT to have a walk-on part 2. CINE to be an extra 3. SPORT, POL **ne faire que ~** to play a minor role; (*dans un classement*) to be an also-ran 4. (*être mentionné*) to appear II. *vt* (*représenter*) to represent III. *vpr* **se ~ qn/qc** to imagine sb/sth; **je l'aime, figure-toi!** I love her, if you can believe that!
figurine [figyʀin] *f* figurine
fil [fil] *m* 1. (*pour coudre*) thread; (*pour tricoter*) yarn; (*de haricot*) string; **~ de fer** wire; **~ de fer barbelé** barbed wire; **maigre comme un ~** thin as a rake 2. (*câble: d'un téléphone, d'une lampe*) wire 3. (*conducteur électrique*) line 4. (*corde à linge*) washing line 5. *pl* (*ficelles*) **les ~ d'une affaire** the ins and outs of a business 6. (*enchaînement*) **suivre le ~ de la conversation** to follow the thread of the conversation ►**de ~ en aiguille** one thing leading to another; **il n'a pas inventé le ~ à couper le beurre** *inf* he's no genius; **c'est cousu de ~ blanc** it's staring you in the face; **donner du ~ à retordre à qn** to be a headache for sb; **au ~ de l'eau** [*o* **du courant**] with the current; **au ~ des ans** over the years
filament [filamɑ̃] *m* 1. ELEC filament 2. (*fil: d'une bave, glu*) thread
filandreux, **-euse** [filɑ̃dʀø, -øz] *adj* 1. (*rempli de filandres: viande*) stringy 2. (*long: discours*) long-winded
filant(**e**) [filɑ̃, ɑ̃t] *adj v.* **étoile**
filasse [filas] *adj inv, péj* **cheveux d'un blond ~** dull blond hair
filature [filatyʀ] *f* 1. (*usine*) mill 2. (*action*) spinning 3. (*surveillance*) tailing; **prendre qn en ~** to tail sb
file [fil] *f* 1. (*colonne*) line; (*d'attente*) queue; **se mettre à** [*o* **prendre**] **la ~** to get into line

2. (*voie de circulation*) lane; **prendre** [*o* **se mettre dans**] **la ~ de droite** to get into the right lane ►**en ~ indienne** in indian file; **à la ~** one after the other

filer [file] <1> **I.** *vi* **1.** (*s'abîmer: maille, collant*) to run **2.** (*s'écouler lentement: essence*) to run; (*sable, sirop*) to trickle **3.** (*aller vite: personne, voiture, temps*) to fly by; (*étoile*) to shoot down; (*argent*) to disappear **4.** *inf* (*partir vite: personne pressée*) to dash (off); (*voleur*) to make off; **~ à l'anglaise** to take French leave; **laisser ~ qn** to let sb get away; **laisser ~ une chance** to let an opportunity slip away; **il faut que je file** I must dash **II.** *vt* **1.** (*tisser*) to spin **2.** (*surveiller*) to tail **3.** *inf* (*donner*) **~ de l'argent à qn** to slip sb some money; **~ une claque à qn** to slap sb; **~ une maladie à qn** to give sb an illness

filet [filɛ] *m* **1.** (*réseau de maille*) net **2.** GASTR fillet **3.** (*petite quantité*) **~ d'huile/de sang/d'eau** trickle of oil/blood/water; **~ d'air** gasp of air

fileur, -euse [filœʀ, -øz] *m, f* spinner

filial(e) [filjal, jo] <-aux> *adj* (*amour, piété*) filial

filiale [filjal] *f* subsidiary company

filiation [filjasjɔ̃] *f* **1.** (*descendance*) filiation **2.** (*relation: des idées, mots*) relation

filière [filjɛʀ] *f* **1.** (*suite de formalités*) channel **2.** UNIV course option **3.** (*réseau: de la drogue, du trafic*) network

filiforme [filifɔʀm] *adj* (*jambes, personne*) spindly; (*antennes*) filiform

filigrane [filigʀan] *m* (*d'un billet de banque, timbre*) watermark ►**lire en ~** to read between the lines; **apparaître en ~** to be apparent beneath the surface

fille [fij] *f* **1.** (*opp: garçon*) girl **2.** (*opp: fils*) daughter **3.** (*prostituée*) whore ►**être bien la ~ de son père** to be one's father's daughter

fillette [fijɛt] *f* little girl

filleul(e) [fijœl] *m(f)* godson, goddaughter *m, f*

film [film] *m* **1.** (*pellicule, couche*) film **2.** (*œuvre*) movie; **~ vidéo** video film; **~ d'action** action movie

filmer [filme] <1> *vt, vi* to film

filmographie [filmɔgʀafi] *f* filmography

filon [filɔ̃] *m* **1.** (*en minéralogie*) vein **2.** *inf* (*travail*) cushy number

filou [filu] *m inf* **1.** (*personne malhonnête*) rogue **2.** (*enfant, chien espiègle*) rascal

filouter [filute] <1> *vt inf* (*objet*) to pinch; (*personne*) to swindle

filouterie [filutʀi] *f* **1.** (*action de filou*) thieving **2.** JUR fraud

fils [fis] *m* (*opp: fille*) son; **Dupont ~** Dupont junior; **Alexandre Dumas ~** Alexandre Dumas fils [*o* the son] ►**de père en ~** from father to son; **être bien le ~ de son père** to be one's father's son

filtre [filtʀ] *m* filter

filtrer [filtʀe] <1> **I.** *vi* to filter through **II.** *vt* **1.** (*pénétrer: liquide, lumière, son*) to filter **2.** (*contrôler: informations*) to screen

fin [fɛ̃] *f* **1.** (*issue, mort*) end; **~ de série** oddment; **~ de siècle** end of line; **la ~ du monde** the end of the world; **mettre ~ à qc** to put an end to sth; **mettre ~ à ses jours** to end one's own life; **à la ~** at the end; **sans ~** endless **2.** (*but*) **~ en soi** end in itself; **arriver** [*o* **parvenir**] **à ses ~s** to achieve one's ends **3.** *Québec* **~ de semaine** (*week-end*) weekend ►**en ~ de compte** at the end of the day; **c'est la ~ des haricots** *inf* (*tout est perdu*) the game's up; (*c'est le bouquet*) that's the last straw; **arrondir ses ~s de mois** to make a bit extra; **la ~ justifie les moyens** *prov* the end justifies the means; **à toutes ~s utiles** for information

fin(e) [fɛ̃, fin] **I.** *adj* **1.** (*opp: épais*) fine; (*couche, étoffe, tranche*) thin **2.** (*gracieux: traits, visage*) delicate; (*jambes, taille*) slender **3.** (*recherché: mets, vin*) choice **4.** (*de qualité supérieure: mets, vin, lingerie*) fine **5.** (*subtil: personne, remarque*) astute; (*humour, nuance*) witty; (*esprit, observation*) sharp **6.** *antéposé* (*très habile: cuisinier, tireur*) expert; **~ connaisseur** connoisseur; **~ gourmet** gourmet **7.** *Québec* (*aimable, gentil*) kind ►**le ~ du ~** the last word **II.** *adv* **1.** (*complètement: soûl*) blind; (*prêt*) absolutely **2.** (*finement: écrire*) small

final(e) [final, o] <s *o* -aux> *adj* (*qui vient à la fin: consonne, résultat*) final; (*discours, accord*) closing; **point ~** full stop *Brit,* period *Am*

finale¹ [final] *m* MUS finale

finale² [final] *f* **1.** SPORT final **2.** (*syllabe*) final syllable **3.** (*voyelle*) final vowel

finalement [finalmɑ̃] *adv* **1.** (*pour finir*) finally **2.** (*en définitive*) in the end

finaliste [finalist] **I.** *adj* (*joueur*) in the final **II.** *mf* finalist

finalité [finalite] *f* **1.** PHILOS finality **2.** (*but*) end

finance [finɑ̃s] *f* **1.** *pl* (*ressources pécuniaires: d'une personne, d'un pays*) finances **2.** (*ministère*) **les Finances** Ministry of Finance; **Monsieur X est aux Finances** Mr X is at Finance ►**moyennant ~** for a consideration

financement [finɑ̃smɑ̃] *m* financing

financer [finɑ̃se] <2> **I.** *vi iron* to cough up **II.** *vt* to finance

financier [finɑ̃sje] *m* financier

financier, -ière [finɑ̃sje, -jɛʀ] *adj* (*problèmes, crise, politique, soucis*) financial; **établissement ~** finance house

financièrement [finɑ̃sjɛʀmɑ̃] *adv* financially

finasser [finase] <1> *vi* to scheme; **~ avec qn** to try one's tricks on sb

finasserie [finasʀi] *f* scheming *no pl*

finaud(e) [fino, od] **I.** *adj* crafty **II.** *m(f)* crafty so-and-so

fine [fin] *f* brandy (*distilled from any fruit*)

F

finement [finmɑ̃] *adv* **1.** (*délicatement: brodé, ciselé*) delicately **2.** (*astucieusement: manœuvrer, agir*) astutely; (*faire remarquer, observer*) shrewdly

finesse [finɛs] *f* **1.** (*minceur: des cheveux, d'une pointe de stylo*) fineness; (*d'une tranche*) thinness **2.** (*délicatesse: d'un visage*) delicacy; (*des mains, de la taille*) slenderness **3.** (*raffinement: d'une broderie, porcelaine*) delicacy; (*d'un aliment*) refinement **4.** (*sensibilité: d'un goût*) keenness; (*d'une ouïe, de l'odorat*) acuteness **5.** (*subtilité: d'une personne*) shrewdness; (*d'une allusion*) subtlety; **sa ~ d'esprit** his shrewd mind **6.** *pl* (*difficultés: d'une langue, d'un art*) subtleties

fini [fini] *m* **1.** (*perfection: d'un produit*) finish; **ça manque de ~** it lacks finish **2.** MAT, PHILOS **le ~** the finite

fini(e) [fini] *adj* **1.** (*terminé*) **être ~** to be finished; (*jour, spectacle*) to be over; **~s les bavardages** enough chatter; **tout est ~ entre nous** it's all over between us; **tu es ~!** you're finished! **2.** (*opp: infini*) finite **3.** *péj* (*complet: menteur, voleur*) accomplished **4.** (*cousu*) **bien/mal ~** well/badly finished

finir [finiʀ] <8> **I.** *vi* **1.** (*s'arrêter: rue, propriété*) to end; (*vacances, spectacle, contrat*) to (come to an) end; **tout ça n'en finit pas** all that takes for ever **2.** (*terminer*) to finish; **avoir fini** to have [*o* be] finished; **laissez-moi ~ (de parler)!** let me finish!; **je finirai par le plus important ...** I shall conclude with the most important thing ...; **en ~ avec qc** to get sth over with; **en avoir fini avec une affaire** to have settled a matter **3.** SPORT **~ à la quatrième place** to finish fourth **4.** (*en venir à*) **~ par faire qc** (*choix final*) to end up doing sth; (*après des retards*) to finally do sth; **tu finis par m'ennuyer avec ...** you're starting to get on my nerves with **5.** (*se retrouver*) **~ en prison** to end up in prison; **~ dans un accident de voiture** to die in a car accident **II.** *vt* **1.** (*arriver au bout de*) *a.* SPORT to finish; **~ de manger/de s'habiller** to finish eating/getting dressed; **~ le mois** to get to the end of the month; **~ une course à la quatrième place** to finish fourth in a race **2.** (*consommer, utiliser jusqu'au bout: plat, assiette, bouteille*) to finish (off); (*vêtement*) to wear out **3.** (*passer la fin de*) **~ ses jours à la campagne** to end one's days in the country **4.** (*cesser: dispute*) to stop; **~ de se plaindre** to stop complaining; **on n'a pas fini de parler d'elle** we haven't heard the last of her **5.** (*être le dernier élément de*) to complete **6.** (*fignoler*) **~ un ouvrage** to finish off a job

finish [finiʃ] *m inv* SPORT finish; **match au ~** match fought to the finish

finition [finisjɔ̃] *f* **1.** (*action: d'un meuble, d'une œuvre d'art*) finishing **2.** (*résultat*) finish **3.** *gén pl* TECH finishing touches

finlandais(e) [fɛ̃lɑ̃dɛ, ɛz] *adj* Finnish

Finlandais(e) [fɛ̃lɑ̃dɛ, ɛz] *m(f)* Finn

Finlande [fɛ̃lɑ̃d] *f* **la ~** Finland

finnois [finwa] *m* Finnish; *v. a.* **français**

finnois(e) [finwa, waz] *adj* Finnish

Finnois(e) [finwa, waz] *m(f)* Finn

fiole [fjɔl] *f* **1.** phial, vial **2.** *inf* mug

fiord [fjɔʀd] *m* fjord

fioriture [fjɔʀityʀ] *f* flourish; **sans ~s** plain (and unadorned)

fioul [fjul] *m v.* **fuel**

firent [fiʀ] *passé simple de* **faire**

firmament [fiʀmamɑ̃] *m* firmament

firme [fiʀm] *f* firm

fis [fi] *passé simple de* **faire**

fisc [fisk] *m* **le ~** the taxman

fiscal(e) [fiskal, o] <-aux> *adj* fiscal

fiscalité [fiskalite] *f* tax regime

fission [fisjɔ̃] *f* fission

fissure [fisyʀ] *f* crack

fissurer [fisyʀe] <1> **I.** *vt* (*éclair*) to fork **II.** *vpr* **se ~** to crack

fiston [fistɔ̃] *m inf* kid

fistule [fistyl] *f* fistula

fit [fi] *passé simple de* **faire**

fîtes [fit] *passé simple de* **faire**

FIV [fiv] *f abr de* **fécondation in vitro** IVF

fixateur [fiksatœʀ] *m* PHOT fixer

fixation [fiksasjɔ̃] *f* **1.** (*pose*) settling **2.** (*détermination*) fixing **3.** (*obsession*) fixation; **faire une ~ sur qn/qc** to have a fixation on sb/sth; **tourner à la ~** to become a fixation **4.** (*dispositif*) fastening; **~ de sécurité** safety fastening

fixe [fiks] **I.** *adj* fixed; **idée ~** idée fixe **II.** *m* basic (salary) **III.** *interj* **~!** attention!

fixé(e) [fikse] *adj* **1.** PSYCH (*personne*) fixated **2.** (*renseigné*) **être ~ sur le compte de qn** to have sb sized up, to have sb sussed *Brit* **3.** (*décidé*) **ne pas encore être ~** to have not yet decided

fixement [fiksəmɑ̃] *adv* **regarder qn/qc ~** to give sb/sth a fixed stare

fixer [fikse] <1> **I.** *vt* **1.** (*attacher, conserver, arranger*) *a.* CHIM, PHOT to fix **2.** (*retenir: population*) to settle **3.** (*regarder*) **~ qn/qc** to look hard at sb/sth; **~ son regard sur qn/qc** to fix one's gaze on sb/sth **4.** (*arrêter*) **~ son attention sur qc** to focus one's attention on sth **5.** (*définir: règle, conditions, limites*) to set **6.** (*renseigner*) **~ un collègue sur une date** to inform a colleague of a date **II.** *vpr* **1.** (*s'accrocher*) **se ~ au mur** to hang on the wall **2.** (*se déposer*) **se ~** to be deposited **3.** (*s'établir*) **se ~ à Paris** to settle in Paris **4.** (*se poser*) **se ~ sur qn/qc** (*attention*) to settle on sb/sth; (*choix*) to fall on sb/sth; **il s'est fixé sur le moins cher** he settled [*o* decided] on the cheapest **5.** (*se définir*) **se ~ un but** to set oneself a target

fixité [fiksite] *f* fixedness

fjord [fjɔʀd] *m v.* **fiord**

flac [flak] *interj* splash

flacon [flakɔ̃] *m* bottle; (*de parfum*) perfume bottle

flagada [flagada] *adj inv, inf* **être** ~ to be washed-out

flagellation [flaʒelasjɔ̃, flaʒɛllasjɔ̃] *f* flagellation

flageller [flaʒele] <1> **I.** *vt* to flog **II.** *vpr* **se** ~ to scourge oneself

flageoler [flaʒɔle] <1> *vi* to shake; (*jambes*) to tremble

flagrant(e) [flagʀɑ̃, ɑ̃t] *adj* blatant; (*injustice*) flagrant

flair [flɛʀ] *m* (*du chien*) (sense of) smell ▸**avoir du** ~ (*odorat*) to have a good nose; (*idées*) to have a sixth sense; **manquer de** ~ to have no nose for things

flairer [fleʀe] <1> *vt* **1.** (*renifler*) to sniff **2.** (*sentir: animal*) to scent **3.** (*pressentir: animal, personne*) to sense

flamand [flamɑ̃] *m* Flemish; *v. a.* **français**

flamand(e) [flamɑ̃, ɑ̃d] *adj* Flemish

Flamand(e) [flamɑ̃, ɑ̃d] *m(f)* Fleming

flamant [flamɑ̃] *m* flamingo

flambé(e) [flɑ̃be] *adj* **1.** GASTR flambé **2.** *inf* (*fichu*) **être** ~ (*personne*) done for; (*affaire*) down the drain

flambeau [flɑ̃bo] <x> *m* torch

flambée [flɑ̃be] *f* **1.** (*feu*) blaze **2.** (*brusque accès, montée: de violence*) flare-up; (*du dollar*) upward surge; (*de terrorisme*) outbreak; ~ **de colère** angry outburst

flamber [flɑ̃be] <1> **I.** *vi* to blaze; (*maison*) to burn down **II.** *vt* **1.** (*cheveux, volaille*) to singe **2.** GASTR to flambé

flamboyant [flɑ̃bwajɑ̃] *m* BOT flame tree

flamboyant(e) [flɑ̃bwajɑ̃, jɑ̃t] *adj* **1.** (*étincellant: feu, soleil*) blazing; (*couleur*) flaming; (*chrome*) gleaming; (*source de lumière*) flashing **2.** ART flamboyant

flamboyer [flɑ̃bwaje] <6> *vi* (*soleil*) to blaze; (*couleur*) to flame; (*source de lumière*) to flash; (*chrome*) to gleam

flamenco [flamɛnko] **I.** *m* flamenco **II.** *adj* flamenco

flamme [flam] *f* **1.** flame **2.** *pl* (*brasier*) flames; **être en ~s** to be ablaze **3.** (*éclat: des yeux*) fire **4.** (*pavillon*) pennant **5.** (*tampon de la poste*) slogan **6.** (*ampoule*) candle (bulb) ▸**descendre qn/qc en ~s** to shoot sb down in flames; **ça va péter des ~s** *inf* things are going to turn nasty

flammé(e) [flame] *adj* flambé

flammèche [flamɛʃ] *f* (flying) spark

flan [flɑ̃] *m* egg custard

flanc [flɑ̃] *m* **1.** (*partie latérale: du corps, d'un navire, d'une montagne*) side; (*d'un cheval*) flank **2.** MIL flank ▸**être sur le** ~ *inf* (*malade*) to be laid up; (*fatigué*) to be worn-out; **mettre qn sur le** ~ *inf* to take it out of sb; **tirer au** ~ *inf* to skive

flancher [flɑ̃ʃe] <1> *vi inf* (*personne*) to waver; (*son cœur/sa mémoire a flanché*) his heart/his memory let him down

Flandre [flɑ̃dʀ] *f* **la ~/les ~s** Flanders; **la ~ orientale/occidentale** Eastern/Western Flanders

flanelle [flanɛl] *f* flannel

flâner [flɑne] <1> *vi* **1.** (*se promener*) to stroll **2.** (*musarder*) to hang around

flânerie [flɑnʀi] *f* **1.** (*promenade*) stroll **2.** (*musardise*) idling; (*au lit*) lying around

flaneur, -euse [flanœʀ, -øz] **I.** *adj* idle **II.** *m, f* (*promeneur*) stroller; (*oisif*) idler

flanqué(e) [flɑ̃ke] *adj* **1. être ~ d'une maison** to have a house adjoining **2.** *péj* (*personne*) **être ~ de qn** to have sb hanging on

flanquer [flɑ̃ke] <1> **I.** *vt inf* **1.** (*envoyer*) ~ **des objets à la figure de qn** to fling things in sb's face **2.** (*mettre*) ~ **qn à la porte/dehors** to kick sb out; ~ **qn au pensionnat** to stick sb in a boarding school **3.** (*donner*) ~ **une gifle à qn** to clout sb; ~ **la frousse à qn** to put the wind up [*o* frighten] sb **II.** *vpr inf* **1.** (*s'envoyer*) **se ~ des objets à la figure** to fling things at each other **2.** (*se mettre*) **se ~ dans une situation délicate** to get oneself into an awkward situation **3.** (*tomber*) **se ~ par terre** to hit the deck

flapi(e) [flapi] *adj inf* worn out

flaque [flak] *f* puddle; (*de sang*) pool

flash [flaʃ] <es> *m* **1.** PHOT, CINE flash **2.** RADIO, TV ~ **info** [*o* **d'information**] newsflash

flash-back [flaʃbak] *m inv* flashback

flasher [flaʃe] <1> *vi inf* ~ **sur qn/qc** to go wild about sb/sth

flasque [flask] **I.** *adj* flabby **II.** *f* flask **III.** *m* flange; (*de mécanique*) cheek

flatter [flate] <1> **I.** *vt* **1.** (*louer*) ~ **qn/la vanité de qn** to flatter sb/sb's vanity; **être flatté de qc** to be flattered about sth **2.** (*caresser: animal*) to stroke **3.** (*être agréable à*) ~ **le palais** to appeal to the palate **II.** *vpr* **1.** (*se féliciter*) **se ~ de qc** to pride oneself on sth **2.** (*aimer à croire*) **se ~ de faire qc** to like to think one can do sth

flatterie [flatʀi] *f* flattery

flatteur, -euse [flatœʀ, -øz] **I.** *adj* flattering **II.** *m, f* flatterer

fléau [fleo] <x> *m* **1.** (*calamité*) scourge **2.** (*partie d'une balance*) beam **3.** AGR flail

fléchage [fleʃaʒ] *m* (*résultat*) signposting

flèche¹ [flɛʃ] *f* **1.** (*arme, signe d'orientation*) arrow **2.** (*critique acerbe*) jibe **3.** (*sur une église*) spire **4.** (*bras mobile: d'une charrue*) beam; (*d'une grue*) boom; (*d'un cargo*) pole **5.** PHYS (*d'une trajectoire*) highest point ▸**c'est une sacrée ~!** he's no mean archer!; **monter en** ~ (*prix*) to soar; (*dans sa carrière*) to have a meteoric rise

flèche² [flɛʃ] *f* **~s de lard** flitch of bacon

fléché(e) [fleʃe] *adj* signposted (with arrows)

flécher [fleʃe] <5> *vt* to signpost

fléchette [fleʃɛt] *f* **1.** (*petite flèche*) dart **2.** *pl* (*jeu*) darts

fléchir [fleʃiʀ] <8> **I.** *vt* **1.** (*plier: bras, genoux*) to bend **2.** (*faire céder: personne*) to sway **II.** *vi* **1.** (*se plier*) to bend **2.** (*diminuer*) to fall; (*exigences, sévérité*) to be tempered;

(*volonté*) to weaken; (*prix, cours*) to slip **3.** (*céder*) to yield

fléchissement [fleʃismɑ̃] *m* **1.** (*flexion: du bras, de la jambe*) bending; (*d'une poutre, planche*) sagging **2.** (*diminution: de la production, natalité*) falling off; (*des prix*) fall **3.** (*renoncement: de la volonté*) yielding

flegmatique [flɛgmatik] **I.** *adj* phlegmatic **II.** *mf* phlegmatic person

flegme [flɛgm] *m* composure

flemmard(**e**) [flemaʀ, aʀd] **I.** *adj inf* lazy **II.** *m(f) inf* lazy so-and-so

flemme [flɛm] *f inf* laziness; **j'ai la ~ de faire la vaisselle** I can't be bothered doing the dishes

flétri(**e**) [fletʀi] *adj* (*plante*) withered; (*fleur*) wilted

flétrir [fletʀiʀ] <8> **I.** *vt* **1.** (*faner: fleur*) to wilt **2.** (*rider: visage*) to wither **3.** HIST to brand **II.** *vpr* **se ~ 1.** (*se faner: plante*) to wither; (*fleur*) to wilt **2.** (*se rider: visage*) to wither

flétrissement [fletʀismɑ̃] *m* BOT withering

fleur [flœʀ] *f* **1.** flower; (*d'un cerisier, pommier*) blossom *no pl;* **en ~**(**s**) in flower; **chapeau à ~s** flowery hat; **tissu/papier à ~s** flowered fabric/paper **2.** (*partie du cuir*) grain side **3.** *gén pl* BIO (*de vin*) flowers; **~ de sel** *layer of crystallized salt* **4.** (*compliment*) **jeter des ~s à qn** *inf* to lavish praise on sb **5.** *sans pl, soutenu* (*ce qu'il y a de meilleur*) **la** (**fine**) **~ de la ville** the town's high society ▶**à** [*o* **dans**] **la ~ de l'âge** in one's prime; **partir la ~ au fusil** to go off whistling on one's way to war; **être belle/fraîche comme une ~** to be as pretty/as fresh as a rose; **~ bleue** sentimental; **à ~ d'eau** at the surface of the water; **avoir une sensibilité à ~ de peau** to be highly susceptible; **arriver** [*o* **s'amener**] **comme une ~** *inf* to breeze in; **faire qc comme une ~** *inf* to do sth without breaking sweat

fleuret [flœʀɛ] *m* foil

fleurette [flœʀɛt] **conter ~ à une femme** *iron* to whisper sweet nothings to a woman

fleuri(**e**) [flœʀi] *adj* **1.** (*en fleurs*) in bloom **2.** (*couvert, garni de fleurs*) decorated with flowers **3.** (*avec des motifs floraux*) flowered **4.** (*coloré: teint*) florid **5.** (*qui sent les fleurs*) flower-scented **6.** (*orné: style*) flowery

fleurir [flœʀiʀ] <8> **I.** *vi* **1.** (*mettre des fleurs*) to flower **2.** (*s'épanouir: amitié*) to blossom **3.** *iron* (*se couvrir de poils*) to sprout hair **II.** *vt* (*orner, décorer: table, tombe*) to put flowers on; **~ sa boutonnière d'un œillet** to put a carnation in one's buttonhole

fleuriste [flœʀist] *mf* florist

fleuron [flœʀɔ̃] *m* **1.** ART (*d'une couronne*) floweret **2.** BOT floret ▶**être le** (**plus beau**) **~ d'une collection** to be the jewel of a collection

fleuve [flœv] *m* **1.** (*rivière*) river **2.** (*flot*) **~ de lave/de boue** torrent of lava/mud; **~ de paroles** torrent of words; **~ de larmes** flood of tears

flexibilité [flɛksibilite] *f* flexibility

flexible [flɛksibl] **I.** *adj* **1.** (*souple: tige en bois*) pliable; (*en plastique, métal*) flexible **2.** (*adaptable*) flexible; *péj* pliable **II.** *m* hose

flexion [flɛksjɔ̃] *f* **1.** (*mouvement corporel*) bending; **~ du genou** flexing of the knee **2.** LING inflection **3.** PHYS flexion

flibustier [flibystje] *m* freebooter

flic [flik] *m inf* cop

flicaille [flikɑj] *f péj, inf* **la ~** the law

flic flac (**floc**) [flikflak(flɔk)] splish splash

flingue [flɛ̃g] *m inf* gun, shooter

flinguer [flɛ̃ge] <1> **I.** *vt inf* **1.** (*tuer*) to waste **2.** (*critiquer*) to shoot to pieces **II.** *vpr inf* **se ~** to put a bullet in oneself

flipper[1] [flipœʀ] *m* pinball machine

flipper[2] [flipe] <1> *vi* **1.** *inf* (*être angoissé*) to be on a downer **2.** *inf* (*être excité*) to be high

flirt [flœʀt] *m* **1.** (*amourette*) flirtation **2.** (*petite histoire d'amour*) quick romance **3.** (*personne*) flirt

flirter [flœʀte] <1> *vi* to flirt

FLN [ɛfɛlɛn] *m abr de* **Front de libération nationale** National Liberation Front

FLNC [ɛfɛlɛnse] *m abr de* **Front de libération nationale de la Corse** Corsican liberation front

floc [flɔk] **faire ~** (**~**) (*caillou qui tombe dans l'eau*) to go plop; (*bottes qui ont pris l'eau*) to squelch

flocon [flɔkɔ̃] *m* **1.** (*petite masse peu dense: de neige*) flake **2.** (*petite touffe: de coton, bourre*) tuft **3.** GASTR flake; **~s de maïs** cornflakes

floconneux, -euse [flɔkɔnø, øz] *adj* fluffy

flonflons [flɔ̃flɔ̃] *mpl inf* oompahs

flopée [flɔpe] *f inf* **une ~ de gamins/touristes** a crowd of kids/tourists

floraison [flɔʀɛzɔ̃] *f* **1.** (*fait de fleurir*) flowering; **avoir plusieurs ~s** to flower several times **2.** (*fleurs*) blooms *pl* **3.** (*époque*) heyday **4.** (*épanouissement*) blossoming; (*de talents*) flowering

floral(**e**) [flɔʀal, o] <-aux> *adj* floral; **exposition ~e** flower show

floralies [flɔʀali] *fpl* flower show

flore [flɔʀ] *f* flora

Floride [flɔʀid(ə)] *f* **la ~** Florida; **le soleil de ~** the Florida sun

florifère [flɔʀifɛʀ] *adj* flowering

florilège [flɔʀilɛʒ] *m* anthology

florin [flɔʀɛ̃] *m* florin

florissait [flɔʀisɛ] *imparf de* **fleurir**

florissant(**e**) [flɔʀisɑ̃, ɑ̃t] *adj* **1.** (*prospère*) flourishing **2.** (*resplendissant: santé, teint*) blooming

flot [flo] *m* **1.** (*vague*) wave **2.** *soutenu* (*quantité importante: d'images, de souvenirs, larmes*) flood; (*de personnes, sang*) stream; (*de paroles*) torrent; **un ~ de joie** overflowing joy; **couler à ~s** to flow freely; **entrer à ~s** (*lumière*) to flood in **3.** *sans pl* (*marée mon-*

tante) rising tide ►**un ~ de** __sang__ **lui monta au visage** blood rushed to his face; **être** __**à**__ **~** *(bateau)* to be afloat; *(personne) (avoir suffisamment d'argent)* to be doing all right; *(être à jour dans son travail)* to be keeping one's head above water; **se maintenir/se remettre** __**à**__ **~** to stay/get back afloat; **mettre qc** __**à**__ **~** to launch sth; **remettre qc** __**à**__ **~** to get sth back on an even keel

flottant(e) [flɔtɑ̃, ɑ̃t] *adj* **1.** *a.* FIN floating **2.** *(dans l'air: foulard, drapeaux)* streaming; *(crinière, chevelure)* flowing; **brume ~e** drifting mist **3.** *(instable)* irresolute

flotte[1] [flɔt] *f* fleet

flotte[2] [flɔt] *f inf* **1.** *(eau)* water **2.** *(pluie)* rain

flottement [flɔtmɑ̃] *m* **1.** *(ondulation: d'un drapeau)* fluttering **2.** *(hésitation)* undecidedness

flotter [flɔte] <1> **I.** *vi* **1.** *(être porté sur un liquide)* to float **2.** *(être en suspension dans l'air: brouillard)* to drift; *(parfum)* to float **3.** *(onduler)* to flutter **4.** *(être ample)* **sa jupe flotte autour d'elle** her skirt flaps around her **5.** *(hésiter)* to waver **II.** *vi impers, inf (pleuvoir)* to pour down **III.** *vt (bois)* to float

flotteur [flɔtœʀ] *m* TECH float

flou [flu] **I.** *m* **1.** *(opp: netteté)* vagueness **2.** CINE, PHOT blur; **~ artistique** soft focus **3.** *(non ajustement: d'une coiffure, d'une mode)* looseness **4.** *(imprécision: d'une pensée)* haziness; *(d'une argumentation)* wooliness **II.** *adv* in a blur

flou(e) [flu] *adj* **1.** blurred; *(photo)* out of focus **2.** *(non ajusté: vêtement, coiffure)* loose **3.** *(imprécis: idée, pensée)* hazy; *(relation, rôle)* vague

fluctuation [flyktɥasjɔ̃] *f* fluctuation; *(de l'opinion)* swing

fluctuer [flyktɥe] <1> *vi* to fluctuate

fluet(te) [flyɛ, ɛt] *adj* **1.** *(frêle)* slender **2.** *(peu sonore: voix)* reedy

fluide [flyid, flɥid] **I.** *adj* **1.** *(qui s'écoule facilement)* fluid **2.** *(ample: style, vêtement)* flowing **3.** *(difficile à saisir: pensée)* elusive **II.** *m* **1.** CHIM fluid; **mécanique des ~s** fluid mechanics **2.** *(force occulte)* aura; **avoir un ~ magnétique** to have strange powers

fluidifier [flɥidifje] <1> *vt* to fluidify

fluidité [flɥidite] *f* **1.** *(liquidité: du sang)* fluidity **2.** AUTO **~ du trafic** free-flowing traffic **3.** ECON *(d'un marché)* flexibility **4.** *fig (d'un style)* flow; *(d'une pensée)* elusiveness

fluo [flyɔ] *adj sans pl abr de* **fluorescent**

fluor [flyɔʀ] *m* fluorine

fluoré(e) [flyɔʀe] *adj (eau)* fluoridated; *(dentifrice)* fluoride

fluorescence [flyɔʀesɑ̃s] *f* fluorescence

fluorescent(e) [flyɔʀesɑ̃, ɑ̃t] *adj* fluorescent

flûte [flyt] **I.** *f* **1.** *(instrument)* flute **2.** *(pain)* French stick **3.** *(verre)* flute (glass) **II.** *interj inf* sugar

flûté(e) [flyte] *adj (voix)* piping

flûtiste [flytist] *mf* flautist *Brit,* flutist *Am*

fluvial(e) [flyvjal, jo] <-aux> *adj* GEO fluvial; *(port, transport)* river

flux [fly] *m* **1.** *(marée)* ebb [*o* incoming] tide; **le ~ et le reflux** the ebb and flow **2.** MED, PHYS, ECON flow

fluxion [flyksjɔ̃] *f* **~ des gencives** gumboil; **~ de poitrine** pneumonia

FM [ɛfɛm] *f abr de* **Frequency Modulation** FM

FMI [ɛfɛmi] *m abr de* **Fonds monétaire international** IMF

FN [ɛfɛn] *m abr de* **Front national** National Front *(French political party)*

FO [ɛfo] *f abr de* **Force ouvrière** *French trade union*

foc [fɔk] *m* jib; **grand/petit ~** outer/inner jib

focal(e) [fɔkal, o] <-aux> *adj (distance, plan)* focal

focale [fɔkal] *f* focal distance

focaliser [fɔkalize] <1> **I.** *vt* to focus **II.** *vpr* **1.** PHYS **se ~** to be focussed **2.** *(se concentrer)* **se ~ sur qn/qc** to focus on sb/sth

foehn [føn] *m Suisse (sèche-cheveux)* hair drier

fœtal(e) [fetal, o] <-aux> *adj* foetal *Brit,* fetal *Am*

fœtus [fetys] *m* foetus *Brit,* fetus *Am*

fofolle [fɔfɔl] *adj v.* **foufou**

foi [fwa] *f* **1.** *(croyance)* **~ en qn** faith in sb; **avoir la ~** to have faith; **il n'y a que la ~ qui sauve** *iron* such touching faith **2.** *(confiance)* **avoir ~ en qn/qc** *soutenu* to have faith [*o* confidence] in sb/sth; **avoir ~ en l'avenir** to have faith in the future; **accorder** [*o* **ajouter**] [*o* **prêter**] **~ à qn/qc** to believe sb/sth ►**la ~ du** __**charbonnier**__ simple faith; **sous la ~ du** __**serment**__ under oath; **être de** __**bonne**__**/**__**mauvaise**__ **~** to be in good/bad faith; __**avoir**__ **la ~** to beleive in oneself; __**faire**__ **~** to be valid; __**ma**__ **~** well; __**ma**__ **~ oui/non** why yes/no; **c'est** __**ma**__ **~ vrai** it's true enough

foie [fwa] *m* **1.** ANAT liver; **avoir mal au ~** to have an upset stomach **2.** GASTR **~ gras** foie gras ►__**avoir**__ **les ~s** *inf* to be scared stiff

foin [fwɛ̃] *m sans pl* hay *no pl* ►**être** __**bête**__ **à manger du ~** *inf* to be as thick as two short planks; __**faire**__ **du ~** [*o* **un de ces ~s**] [*o* **un ~ de tous les diables**] *inf (du bruit)* to make a terrible commotion; *(un scandale)* to make a terrible fuss

foire [fwaʀ] *f* **1.** *(marchée, exposition, fête)* fair; **~ du Trône** *annual funfair held outside Paris* **2.** *inf (endroit bruyant)* madhouse **3.** INFOR **~ aux questions** frequently asked questions [file] ►__**faire**__ **la ~** *inf* to live it up

foirer [fwaʀe] <1> *vi* **1.** *inf (rater)* to come to grief **2.** *inf (être défectueux: écrou, vis)* to slip; *(obus, fusée)* to misfire

foireux, -euse [fwaʀø, -øz] **I.** *adj inf* **1.** *(qui a peur)* chicken-hearted **2.** *(mauvais)* lousy **II.** *m, f inf* chicken

fois [fwa] *f* **1.** *(fréquence)* time; **une ~** once; *Belgique (donc)* then; **une ~ par an** [*o* **l'an**] once a year; **deux** ~ twice; **d'autres/les autres** ~ other times; (**à**) **chaque** ~ each time; **payer en plusieurs** ~ to pay in several instalments; **il était une** ~ **...** once upon a time; **pour une** ~ for once; **trente-six** ~ a hundred times **2.** *dans un comparatif* **deux** ~ **plus/moins vieux que qn/qc** twice as old/young than sb/sth; **cinq** ~ **plus élevé que** five times higher than; **cinq** ~ **plus d'argent/de personnes** five times more money/people **3.** (*comme multiplicateur*) **9** ~ **3 font 27** 9 times 3 is 27; **une** ~ **et demie plus grand** one and a half times bigger ►**s'y prendre** [*o* **reprendre**] **à deux** ~ to have two goes; **plutôt deux** ~ **qu'une** not just the once; **neuf** ~ **sur dix** nine times out of ten; **trois** ~ **rien** absolutely nothing; **pour trois** ~ **rien** for next to nothing; **un seul enfant/bateau à la** ~ just one child/boat at a time; **tout à la** ~ at one and the same time; **des** ~ *inf* sometimes; **des** ~ **qu'il viendrait!** *inf* in case he comes!; **non mais des** ~**!** *inf* really now!; **une** ~**, deux** ~**, trois** ~ (*dans une vente aux enchères*) going once, going twice, sold; (*pour menacer*) I'm telling you one, two, that's it; **une** ~ (**qu'il fut**) **parti, ...** once he'd gone, ...

foison [fwazɔ̃] **à** ~ in plenty

foisonner [fwazɔne] <1> *vi* to abound

fol [fɔl] *adj v.* **fou**

folâtre [fɔlɑtʀ] *adj* playful

folâtrer [fɔlɑtʀe] <1> *vi* to play about

foldingue [fɔldɛ̃g] *inf* **I.** *adj* batty **II.** *mf* nutcase

folichon(**ne**) [fɔliʃɔ̃, ɔn] *adj inf* **ne pas être** ~ not to be a lot of fun

folie [fɔli] *f* **1.** (*démence, déraison*) madness **2.** (*passion*) ~ **de qc** mad passion for sth; **avoir la** ~ **de qc** to be mad about sth; **aimer qn/qc à la** ~ to love sb/sth madly **3.** (*conduite/paroles*) foolish deed/word; ~ **des grandeurs** delusions of grandeur; **faire une** ~**/des** ~**s** (*faire une dépense excessive*) to go mad; (*se conduire mal*) to do wild things **4.** HIST folly

folié(**e**) [fɔlje] *adj* foliate

folio [fɔljo] *m* TYP folio

foliole [fɔljɔl] *f* leaflet

folklo [fɔlklo] *adj inv, inf abr de* **folklorique**

folklore [fɔlklɔʀ] *m* **1.** (*traditions populaire*) folklore **2.** *péj* (*cinéma*) nonsense

folklorique [fɔlklɔʀik] *adj* **1.** (*relatif au folklore*) folk **2.** *péj, inf* (*farfelu*) weird

folle [fɔl] **I.** *adj v.* **fou II.** *f péj, inf* (*homosexuel*) queen

follement [fɔlmɑ̃] *adv* wildly; (*amoureux*) madly; (*comique*) uproariously

foncé(**e**) [fɔ̃se] *adj* dark

foncer [fɔ̃se] <2> **I.** *vt* **1.** (*rendre plus foncé*) to darken **2.** (*creuser*) to dig; (*puits*) to sink **3.** GASTR to line **II.** *vi* **1.** *inf* (*aller très vite en courant*) ~ **sur qn/qc** to rush at sb/sth; (*en voiture*) to charge at sb/sth **2.** *inf* (*aller très vite en agissant très vite*) to show drive **3.** (*devenir plus foncé*) to go darker

fonceur, **-euse** [fɔ̃sœʀ, -øz] *m, f* **1.** *inf* (*personne dynamique*) dynamic individual **2.** (*audacieux*) go-getter

foncier, **-ière** [fɔ̃sje, -jɛʀ] *adj* **1.** land; (*revenus*) from land **2.** (*fondamental: défaut, erreur, problème*) fundamental; (*qualité, gentillesse*) innate

foncièrement [fɔ̃sjɛʀmɑ̃] *adv* fundamentally

fonction [fɔ̃ksjɔ̃] *f* **1.** *a.* BIO, CHIM, LING, MAT, TECH, INFOR function; **elle a pour** ~ **de** +*infin* her function is to +*infin;* **faire** ~ **de qc** to act as sth; **faire** ~ **de qn** to do instead of sth **2.** (*activité professionnelle*) post **3.** (*charge*) duty; **logement de** ~ (*d'un fonctionnaire*) official accommodation; (*d'un employé*) company accommodation ►**la** ~ **publique** public service (*state sector employment*)**; être** ~ **de qc** to depend on sth; **en** ~ **de qc** in accordance with sth; **en** ~ **du temps** depending on the weather

fonctionnaire [fɔ̃ksjɔnɛʀ] *mf* state employee; (*dans l'administration*) civil servant

fonctionnalité [fɔ̃ksjɔnalite] *f* **1.** *sans pl* practicality **2.** *gén pl* INFOR functionality

fonctionnariser [fɔ̃ksjɔnaʀize] <1> *vt* **1.** (*assimiler aux fonctionnaires: entreprise, personne*) to bring into the state sector **2.** (*bureaucratiser: service, Etat*) to bureaucratize

fonctionnel(**le**) [fɔ̃ksjɔnɛl] *adj* functionnal

fonctionnement [fɔ̃ksjɔnmɑ̃] *m* working

fonctionner [fɔ̃ksjɔne] <1> *vi* to work; (*organe, administration*) to function ►~ **à la bière** *inf* to run on beer

fond [fɔ̃] *m* **1.** (*partie inférieure*) bottom; **les** ~**s sous-marins** the sea bed; **au** ~ **du sac** at the bottom of the bag **2.** TECH, ARCHIT base **3.** (*partie la plus éloignée: d'une pièce, d'un couloir*) far end; (*d'une armoire*) back; **au** ~ **du jardin** at the bottom of the garden; **au** (**fin**) ~ **du monde** at the end of the world; **au** ~ **de la cour** at the far end of the playground; **au** ~ **de la scène** at the back of the stage; **examiner le** ~ **de la gorge** to examine the back of the throat **4.** (*partie intime*) **au** ~ **du cœur/de l'âme** deep in one's heart/soul; **avoir un bon** ~ to be a good person deep down; **regarder qn au** ~ **des yeux** to look deep into sb's eyes; **du** ~ **du cœur** from the bottom of one's heart **5.** (*degré le plus bas*) ~ **de la misère** dire poverty; **être au** ~ **de l'abîme** to be in the depths of despair **6.** (*ce qui est essentiel: des choses, d'un problème*) heart; **expliquez le** ~ **de votre pensée** explain what you think deep down; **aller au** ~ **des choses** to get to the heart of the matter **7.** (*opp: forme*) content **8.** (*dans une bouteille, un verre*) **vider les** ~**s** to empty what's left; **il reste un** ~ there's a drop left **9.** (*hauteur d'eau*) depth **10.** (*pièce rapportée*) patch **11.** (*arrière-plan*) background **12.** GASTR base; ~ **de tarte** tart base **13.** SPORT (*résistance*) staying power; (*course*) long-distance race; **ski de** ~ cross-country skiing **14.** (*base*) ~ **de teint** foundation ►**le** ~ **de l'air est frais** there's a chill in the air; **user ses ~s de culotte sur les bancs de l'école** to sit on the hard school bench; **connaître qc comme le ~ de sa poche** to know sth like tha back of one's hand; **faire** [*o* **vider**] **les ~s de tiroir** *inf* to scrape around; **avoir un ~ de qc** to have a degree of sth; **il y a un grand ~ de vérité dans tout ça** there's a large element of truth in all that; **à** ~ thoroughly; (*respirer*) deeply; (*connaître*) in depth; **à ~ la caisse** *inf* at full tilt; **être à ~ de cale** *inf* to be stony broke *Brit,* to be stone broke *Am;* **à ~ de train** at full tilt; **au** [*o* **dans le**] **~, ...** *inf* when it comes down to it; **de** ~ background; **article de** ~ feature article; **de ~ en comble** from top to bottom; **sur le** ~ essentially

fondamental(e) [fɔ̃damɑ̃tal, o] <-aux> *adj* **1.** basic; (*élément, propriété, loi*) fundamental **2.** (*essentiel*) vital **3.** (*en science: recherche*) basic **4.** MUS fundamental **5.** LING **l'anglais** ~ basic English

fondamentale [fɔ̃damɑ̃tal] *f* fundamental

fondamentalement [fɔ̃damɑ̃talmɑ̃] *adv* fundamentally

fondamentaliste [fɔ̃damɑ̃talist] **I.** *adj* fundamentalist **II.** *mf* fundamentalist

fondant [fɔ̃dɑ̃, ɑ̃t] *m* **1.** TECH flux **2.** GASTR ~ **au chocolat** chocolate fondant

fondant(e) [fɔ̃dɑ̃, ɑ̃t] *adj* **1.** (*qui fond: glace, neige*) melting **2.** (*mûr: poire*) that melts in the mouth **3.** (*tendre*) tender

fondateur, -trice [fɔ̃datœʀ, -tʀis] *m, f* founder

fondation [fɔ̃dasjɔ̃] *f* **1.** (*fait de fonder, institution*) foundation **2.** (*création par don ou legs*) establishment **3.** *pl* ARCHIT (*d'un bâtiment*) foundations

fondé(e) [fɔ̃de] **I.** *adj* **être bien** ~ (*crainte, critique, confiance*) to be fully justified; (*opinion*) to be well-founded; (*pressentiment*) to be well-grounded; **être ~ à faire qc** to have grounds for doing sth **II.** *m(f)* ~ **de pouvoir** proxy

fondement [fɔ̃dmɑ̃] *m* **1.** *pl* foundations **2.** (*motif, raison*) grounds; **ne reposer sur aucun** ~ to have no foundation **3.** PHILOS fundament

fonder [fɔ̃de] <1> **I.** *vt* **1.** to found **2.** (*financer: prix*) to found; (*dispensaire, institution*) to set up **3.** (*faire reposer*) ~ **une décision sur qc** to base a decision on sth **II.** *vpr* **se ~ sur qc** (*personne*) to base oneself on; (*attitude, raisonnement*) to be based on

fonderie [fɔ̃dʀi] *f* **1.** (*usine*) foundry **2.** (*fabrication*) founding

fondeur [fɔ̃dœʀ] *m* smelter

fondeur, -euse [fɔ̃dœʀ, -øz] *m, f* (*au ski*) cross-country skier

fondre [fɔ̃dʀ] <14> **I.** *vi* **1.** to melt **2.** (*se dissoudre*) ~ **dans un liquide/sous la langue** to dissolve in a liquid/under the tongue **3.** (*s'attendrir*) ~ **de pitié** to melt with pity; ~ **en larmes** to break into tears **4.** *inf* (*maigrir*) ~ **de 10 kilos** to shed 10 kilos **5.** (*diminuer rapidement: argent, muscles*) to vanish; (*diminuer partiellement*) to dwindle; ~ **devant qc** (*sentiment*) to vanish **6.** (*dissiper*) **faire ~ sa colère** to melt away one's anger **7.** (*se précipiter*) ~ **sur qn/qc** (*oiseau, ennemi*) to bear down on sb/sth; ~ **sur qn** *fig* to descend on sb **II.** *vt* **1.** to melt; (*bijoux, argenterie*) to melt down **2.** (*fabriquer*) to cast **3.** (*fusionner*) ~ **qc dans qc** to combine sth into sth **4.** (*incorporer*) ~ **qc dans qc** to merge sth with sth **III.** *vpr* **1.** (*former un tout avec*) **se ~ dans qc** to merge into sth **2.** (*disparaître*) **se ~ dans le brouillard** to vanish into the mist; (*appel*) to be lost in the mist

fonds [fɔ̃] *m* **1.** (*commerce*) business **2.** (*terrain*) land **3.** (*organisme, capital*) fund; ~ **de grève** strike fund; ~ **publics** [*o* **d'État**] public funds; ~ **de roulement** working capital; **gérer les** ~ to manage the money; **prêter qc à ~ perdu** to lend sth without security; **rentrer dans ses** ~ *inf* to recoup one's costs **4.** (*ressources*) assets *pl;* (*d'une langue*) resources *pl* **5.** (*œuvres: d'une bibliothèque*) collection **6.** (*qualités physiques ou intellectuelles*) resources

fondu [fɔ̃dy] *m* CINE ~ **enchaîné** fade-in fade-out

fondu(e) [fɔ̃dy] **I.** *part passé de* **fondre II.** *adj* (*couleurs, tons*) blending; (*fromage*) melted; **neige ~e** melted snow; (*au sol*) slush

fondue [fɔ̃dy] *f* fondue; ~ **savoyarde** fondue savoyarde (*hot cheese sauce into which bread is dipped*)

font [fɔ̃] *indic prés de* **faire**

fontaine [fɔ̃tɛn] *f* **1.** (*construction*) fountain **2.** (*source*) spring **3.** GASTR (*creux dans la farine*) well ►**pleurer comme une** ~ *iron* to cry like a baby

fonte [fɔ̃t] *f* **1.** (*fusion: d'un métal*) smelting **2.** (*fabrication*) founding **3.** (*métal*) cast iron

fonts [fɔ̃] *mpl* ~ **baptismaux** baptismal font

foot(ball) [fut(bol)] *m sans pl* football *Brit,* soccer *Am*

footballeur, -euse [futbolœʀ, -øz] *m, f* footballer *Brit,* soccer player *Am*

footing [futiŋ] *m* jogging *no pl;* **faire du/son** ~ to go/be jogging

forage [fɔʀaʒ] *m* drilling

forain(e) [fɔʀɛ̃, ɛn] **I.** *adj* (*attraction, baraque*) fairground; **marchand** ~ stallholder *Brit,* carny *Am;* **fête ~e** funfair *Brit,* carnival *Am* **II.** *m(f)* stallholder *Brit,* carny *Am*

forban [fɔʀbɑ̃] *m* **1.** (*pirate*) freebooter **2.** *inf* (*escroc*) crook

forçat [fɔʀsa] *m* **1.** (*condamné aux travaux forcés*) convict **2.** (*condamné aux galères*) galley slave ►~ **du travail** wage slave; **travailler comme un** ~ to work like a slave

F

force [fɔʀs] *f* **1.** ANAT strength **2.** PHYS force **3.** (*courage*) strength; ~ **d'âme** fortitude **4.** (*niveau intellectuel*) intellect **5.** (*pouvoir*) force; ~ **de dissuasion** deterrent; ~ **publique** police; **employer la** ~ to use force; **l'union fait la** ~ unity is strength **6.** *gén pl* (*ensemble de personnes*) force; ~ **électorale** electoral strength **7.** MIL ~ **de frappe** strike force; ~**s d'intervention** task force; ~**s d'occupation** occupying forces; ~**s de l'ordre** police; ~(**s**) **armée**(**s**)/**militaire**(**s**) armed forces **8.** (*autorité: de l'habitude, de la loi*) force; (*d'un argument, préjugé*) power; **avoir** [*o* **faire**]/ **prendre** ~ **de loi** to have/acquire force of law; **avoir** ~ **exécutoire** to be legally enforceable; **par la** ~ **des choses** in the way of things **9.** (*degré d'intensité: d'un choc, coup, tremblement de terre, du vent*) force; (*d'une carte, passion, d'un désir, sentiment*) strength; (*de l'égoïsme, de la haine*) intensity; ~ **du son**/ **bruit** loudness of the sound/noise; **frapper avec** ~ to strike with force; **un vent de** ~ **7** a force 7 wind **10.** TECH (*d'un câble, mur, d'une barre*) strength **11.** (*puissance, efficacité: d'un moteur*) power; (*d'un médicament, poison*) strength **12.** (*vigueur: d'un style, terme*) strength; **dans toute la** ~ **du terme** in the strongest sense of the word **13.** *sans pl* (*électricité*) three-phase current ►**être dans la** ~ **de l'<u>âge</u>** to be in the prime of life; **avoir une** ~ **de <u>cheval</u>** *inf* to be as strong as a horse; **c'est une** ~ **de la <u>nature</u>** she's a force of nature; **<u>être</u> de** ~ **à faire qc** to be up to doing sth; **<u>à</u>** ~, **tu vas**/ **il va le renverser** you'll/he'll end up knocking it over; **à** ~ **de pleurer** by dint of crying; **faire qc <u>avec</u>** ~ to do sth with force; **faire qc <u>de</u>** ~ to do sth by force; **faire qc <u>par</u>** ~ to do sth through force

forcé(**e**) [fɔʀse] **I.** *part passé de* **forcer** **II.** *adj* **1.** (*imposé: atterrissage, mariage*) forced; (*bain*) unintended; (*travaux* ~*s*) forced labour *Brit,* forced labor *Am* **2.** (*artificiel: attitude*) affected; (*rire, sourire*) forced; (*amabilité, gaieté*) false **3.** *inf* (*inévitable: conséquence, suite*) inevitable **4.** LIT, ART (*style, trait*) unnatural; (*comparaison, effet*) strained ►**<u>c'était</u>** ~**!** *inf* bound to happen!

forcément [fɔʀsemɑ̃] *adv* inevitably; **pas** ~ not necessarily; ~**!** of course!

forcené(**e**) [fɔʀsəne] **I.** *adj* **1.** (*très violent*) frenzied **2.** (*démesuré*) wild; (*partisan*) fanatical **II.** *m(f)* maniac; **être un** ~ **du vélo** *inf* to be a cycling freak; **être un** ~ **du boulot** *inf* to be a workaholic

forcer [fɔʀse] <2> **I.** *vt* **1.** (*obliger*) ~ **qn à** +*infin* to force sb to +*infin* **2.** (*tordre: sens*) to distort **3.** (*enfoncer: porte, serrure*) to force; (*coffre*) to force open; (*barrage*) to force one's way through; ~ **l'entrée de qc** to force one's way into sth **4.** (*susciter: admiration, estime, sympathie, confiance*) to compel; (*attention*) to demand; (*respect*) to command **5.** (*vouloir obtenir plus de qc: cheval*) to override; ~ **le moteur** to put a strain on the engine **6.** (*vouloir infléchir: conscience, destin, succès*) to force; (*consentement*) to exact **7.** (*intensifier: voix*) to strain; ~ **le pas** to force the pace **8.** (*exagérer: dépense, note*) to push up **II.** *vi* **1.** to force **2.** (*agir avec force*) ~ **sur qc** to put force on sth **3.** *inf* (*abuser*) ~ **sur les pâtisseries** to overdo the pastries **4.** (*supporter un effort excessif: moteur*) to labour *Brit,* to labor *Am* **III.** *vpr* **se** ~ **à** +*infin* to force oneself to +*infin;* **elle ne se force pas pour le faire** doing it comes naturally to her

forcing [fɔʀsiŋ] *m sans pl* **1.** SPORT pressure **2.** *inf* (*déploiement d'énergie*) sprint; **faire le** ~ **pour obtenir qc** *inf* to pile on pressure to get sth; **faire qc au** ~ to do sth under pressure

forcir [fɔʀsiʀ] <8> *vi* **1.** (*devenir plus fort*) to get stronger **2.** (*grossir*) to fill out

forer [fɔʀe] <1> *vt* **1.** (*former en creusant: trou, puits*) to dig **2.** (*faire un trou dans: roche*) to drill through

forestier, **-ière** [fɔʀɛstje, -jɛʀ] **I.** *adj* forest **II.** *m, f* forester

foret [fɔʀɛ] *m* drill

forêt [fɔʀɛ] *f* **1.** (*bois*) forest **2.** (*grande quantité*) mass

forêt-noire [fɔʀɛnwaʀ] <forêts-noires> *f* (*gâteau*) Black Forest gateau *Brit,* Black Forest cake *Am* **Forêt-Noire** [fɔʀɛnwaʀ] *f* GEO **la** ~ the Black Forest

forfait [fɔʀfɛ] *m* **1.** (*prix fixé*) all-in price **2.** FIN estimated tax **3.** SPORT ~ **de neige** skipass ►**<u>déclarer</u>** ~ to scratch

forfaitaire [fɔʀfɛtɛʀ] *adj* (*indemnité*) lump; (*montant, prix*) all-in

forge [fɔʀʒ] *f* **1.** (*fourneau*) forge **2.** *pl* (*usine*) ironworks

forger [fɔʀʒe] <2a> **I.** *vt* **1.** (*façonner*) to forge **2.** (*inventer: excuse, prétexte*) to think up **II.** *vpr* **1.** (*se fabriquer*) **se** ~ **une réputation** to forge oneself a reputation; **se** ~ **un idéal** to create an ideal for oneself **2.** (*s'inventer*) **se** ~ **un prétexte** to dream up an excuse

forgeron [fɔʀʒəʀɔ̃] *m* blacksmith

for intérieur [fɔʀɛ̃teʀjœʀ] **dans mon/ton** ~ deep down inside

formaliser [fɔʀmalize] <1> **I.** *vpr* **se** ~ **de qc** to take offence at sth *Brit,* to take offense at sth *Am* **II.** *vt* to formalize

formalisme [fɔʀmalism] *m péj* formality

formalité [fɔʀmalite] *f* formality; **sans autre** ~ without further ado

format [fɔʀma] *m* format

formatage [fɔʀmataʒ] *m* INFOR formatting

formater [fɔʀmate] <1> *vt* INFOR to format

formateur, **-trice** [fɔʀmatœʀ, -tʀis] **I.** *adj* training; (*expérience, influence*) formative **II.** *m, f* trainer

formation [fɔʀmasjɔ̃] *f* **1.** LING, GEO, BOT, SPORT formation **2.** MAT (*d'un cercle, cylindre*) describing **3.** (*action de se former: du monde, des dunes, d'une couche*) formation; (*du capi-

talisme, d'un embryon, os, système nerveux) development **4.** (*apprentissage professionnel*) training *no pl;* ~ **professionnelle** vocational training; ~ **continue** [*o* **permanente**] ongoing education **5.** (*éducation morale et intellectuelle*) upbringing; (*du caractère, goût*) forming **6.** (*groupe de personnes*) *a.* MIL, SPORT formation; (*dans le domaine politique*) grouping **7.** (*puberté*) puberty

forme [fɔʀm] *f* **1.** (*aspect extérieur: en deux dimensions*) shape; (*en trois dimensions*) form; **en** ~ **de croix/de cœur** cross-/heart-shaped; **sous la** ~ **de qn/qc** in the shape of sb/sth; **sous toutes ses** ~**s** in all its forms **2.** (*silhouette*) shape **3.** *pl* (*galbe du corps*) figure **4.** (*variante, condition physique, intellectuelle*) *a.* ART, LIT, MUS, LING, JUR form **5.** *pl* (*bienséance*) conventions ►**sans autre** ~ **de procès** without further ado; **en bonne** (**et due**) ~ in due form; (**y**) **mettre les** ~**s** to show tact; **prendre** ~ (*projet*) to take shape; **faire qc dans les** ~**s** to do sth in the proper manner

formé(**e**) [fɔʀme] *adj* **1.** (*développé: plante*) mature **2.** *inf* (*adulte*) **adolescente** ~**e** physically adult adolescent **3.** (*correct*) **mot/phrase bien/mal** ~(**e**) well/wrongly formed word/sentence

formel(**le**) [fɔʀmɛl] *adj* **1.** (*explicite: déclaration, engagement*) definite; (*refus, ordre*) clear; (*preuve*) positive; **être** ~ **sur qc** to be categorical about sth **2.** ART, LIT, LING, PHILOS formal **3.** (*de pure forme*) outward

formellement [fɔʀmɛlmɑ̃] *adv* **1.** (*expressément*) categorically **2.** (*concernant la forme*) formally

former [fɔʀme] <1> **I.** *vt* **1.** (*façonner, constituer, produire*) to form **2.** (*créer, organiser: association, parti, coalition*) to form; (*complot*) to organize **3.** (*assembler des éléments: équipes, collection*) to build; (*cortège, armée*) to form **4.** (*concevoir: idée, pensée*) to have; ~ **le projet/dessein de** +*infin* to plan/intend to +*infin;* **nous formons des vœux pour votre réussite** we wish you success **5.** (*instruire: personne*) to train; (*caractère*) to form; ~ **qn** (*voyage, épreuve*) to form sb's character **6.** (*prendre l'aspect, la forme de: cercle*) to describe; (*boucle*) to form **II.** *vpr* **1.** (*naître*) **se** ~ (*images*) to form **2.** (*se disposer*) **se** ~ **en colonne** to draw up in a column **3.** (*s'instruire*) **se** ~ to educate oneself

formica® [fɔʀmika] *m* formica®

formidable [fɔʀmidabl] *adj* **1.** *inf* (*très bien: film, type*) terrific **2.** (*hors du commun: volonté*) remarkable; (*dépense, détonation*) tremendous; **c'est** ~**!** it's incredible!

formidablement [fɔʀmidabləmɑ̃] *adv* incredibly

formol [fɔʀmɔl] *m* formalin

formulaire [fɔʀmylɛʀ] *m* **1.** (*papier*) form **2.** (*recueil de formules*) formulary

formulation [fɔʀmylasjɔ̃] *f* formulation

formule [fɔʀmyl] *f* **1.** (*en science, chimie*) formula **2.** (*paroles rituelles*) phrase; ~ **de politesse** letter ending **3.** (*choix, possibilité*) option; ~ **à 10 euros** 10 euros menu **4.** (*façon de faire*) method **5.** AUTO, SPORT ~ **I** Formula 1

formuler [fɔʀmyle] <1> *vt* **1.** (*exprimer: pensée*) to formulate; (*demande, requête*) to make **2.** (*mettre en formule*) to formulate

fornication [fɔʀnikasjɔ̃] *f* fornication

forniquer [fɔʀnike] <1> *vi* ~ **avec qn** to fornicate with sb

forsythia [fɔʀsisja] *m* forsythia

fort [fɔʀ] **I.** *adv* **1.** (*intensément: frapper*) hard; (*parler, crier*) loudly; (*sentir*) powerfully; **son cœur battait très** ~ his heart was beating very fast; **le vent souffle** ~ the wind's blowing hard; **respirez** ~**!** breathe in deeply! **2.** (*beaucoup*) **avoir** ~ **à faire** to have much to do; **ça me déplaît** ~ I am not pleased about this; **j'en doute** ~ I very much doubt it **3.** *antéposé* (*très: intéressant, mécontent*) very **4.** *inf* (*bien*) **toi, ça ne va pas** ~ you're in a bad way ►~ **bien!** very well!; **se faire** ~ **de faire qc** to be confident one can do sth; **y aller un peu/trop** ~ *inf* you're going a bit/rather too far **II.** *m* **1.** (*forteresse*) fort **2.** (*spécialité*) **la cuisine, ce n'est pas mon** ~ cooking is not my forte **3.** (*milieu, cœur*) **au plus** ~ **de l'été** at the height of summer; **au plus** ~ **de la bataille** in the thick of battle

fort(**e**) [fɔʀ, fɔʀt] **I.** *adj* **1.** (*robuste, puissant*) strong; ~ **de sa supériorité** having the strength her superiority gave her; ~ **de leur appui** with the strength coming from their support **2.** (*de grande intensité: averse, mer*) heavy; (*lumière, rythme, goût*) strong; (*battement*) loud; (*chaleur*) intense **3.** (*pour les sensations/sentiments*) strong; (*colère, dégoût, douleur, émotion*) deep; (*rhume*) heavy; (*désir, ferveur*) intense; (*fièvre*) high **4.** MUS, LING (*temps*) strong **5.** (*important qualitativement: œuvre, phrase, geste politique*) powerful; (*présomption*) strong; **exprimer son opinion en termes très** ~**s** to express one's opinion forcefully; **dire qc haut et** ~ to say sth out loud **6.** (*important quantitativement: somme, baisse, hausse*) large; (*différence*) great; (*mortalité, consommation de gaz*) high; **il y a de** ~**es chances pour qu'elle le fasse** (*subj*) there's a strong chance she'll do it; **faire payer le prix** ~ to pay full price **7.** (*doué*) good; **être très** ~ **sur un sujet** to be well up in a subject; **ne pas être très** ~ **en cuisine** not to be good at cooking; **être très** ~ **pour critiquer** *iron* to be very good at criticizing **8.** (*excessif: plaisanterie*) off; (*terme*) strong; **cette histoire est un peu** ~**e** this business is a bit much **9.** (*gros: chevilles, jambes*) thick; (*personne*) stout; (*poitrine*) large; **être un peu** ~ **des hanches** to be a bit big round the hips **10.** *postposé* (*courageux*) brave; (*âme*) brave ►**c'est plus** ~ **que moi** I can't help it; **le** [*o* **ce qu'il y a de**] **plus** ~**, c'est que** *iron* the best of it is that; **c'est trop** [*o* **un peu**] ~**!** it's a

F

bit much!; **elle est ~e, celle-là!** *inf* that's a good one! **II.** *m(f)* (*personne*) strong person ►**~ en thème** *inf* swot *Brit*

fortement [fɔʀtəmɑ̃] *adv* **1.**(*vigoureusement*) strongly; (*secouer*) hard; **s'exprimer ~** to express oneself forcefully **2.**(*vivement*) **insister ~ sur qc** to insist strongly on sth; **je suis ~ attiré par cela** I'm strongly attracted by that **3.**(*beaucoup*) very much; **il est ~ question de qc** there is a lot of talk about sth

forteresse [fɔʀtəʀɛs] *f* fortress

fortiche [fɔʀtiʃ] *adj inf* **1.**(*calé*) **être ~ en math** to be a hotshot at maths *Brit,* to be a hotshot in math *Am* **2.**(*malin*) **c'est pas ~ d'avoir fait cela** that was not a clever thing to do

fortifiant [fɔʀtifjɑ̃] *m* (*remède*) tonic

fortifiant(e) [fɔʀtifjɑ̃, jɑ̃t] *adj* (*remède*) fortifying; **nourriture ~e** nourishing food

fortification [fɔʀtifikasjɔ̃] *f* fortification

fortifier [fɔʀtifje] <1> **I.** *vt* **1.**(*rendre vigoureux*) *a.* MIL to fortify **2.**(*affermir: volonté, amitié*) to strengthen; **~ qn dans sa conviction** to strengthen sb in their conviction **II.** *vi* (*tonifier*) to fortify **III.** *vpr* **se ~ 1.**(*devenir fort: santé, personne*) to grow stronger **2.**(*s'affermir: amitié, croyance*) to be strengthened **3.** MIL to be fortified

fortin [fɔʀtɛ̃] *m* small fort

fortuit(e) [fɔʀtɥi, it] *adj* fortuitous; (*remarque*) chance; **cas ~** fortuitous case

fortuitement [fɔʀtɥitmɑ̃] *adv* fortuitously

fortune [fɔʀtyn] *f* **1.**(*richesse*) wealth; **avoir de la ~** to be rich; **faire ~** to make a fortune **2.** *inf* (*grosse somme*) fortune **3.**(*magnat*) **les grandes ~s** large private fortunes **4.**(*chance*) luck; **la bonne ~** good luck ►**faire contre mauvaise ~ bon cœur** to smile in the face of adversity; **de ~** makeshift

fortuné(e) [fɔʀtyne] *adj* (*riche*) wealthy

forum [fɔʀɔm] *m* **1.** forum **2.** INFOR newsgroup; **~ de discussion sur Internet** chat room

fosse [fos] *f* **1.**(*cavité*) *a.* MUS pit **2.** GEO trench **3.**(*tombe, charnier*) grave **4.** ANAT **~s nasales** nasal fossae

fossé [fose] *m* **1.**(*tranchée*) ditch **2.**(*écart*) gap; **~ des générations** generation gap; **un ~ culturel sépare ces deux peuples** the two peoples are divided by a culture gap

fossette [fosɛt] *f* dimple

fossile [fosil] **I.** *adj* **1.** GEO fossil(ized) **2.** *péj, inf* (*démodé*) fossilized **II.** *m inf* GEO *a. fig* fossil

fossilifère [fosilifɛʀ] *adj* fossiliferous

fossilisation [fosilizasjɔ̃] *f* fossilization

fossiliser [fosilize] <1> **I.** *vt* GEO (*rendre fossile*) to fossilize **II.** *vpr* **se ~ 1.** GEO (*devenir fossile*) to fossilize **2.** *fig, inf* (*personne*) to become a fossil; (*idée*) to become fossilized

fossoyeur [foswajœʀ] *m* gravedigger

fou, folle [fu, fɔl] <*devant un nom masculin commençant par une voyelle ou un h muet* fol> **I.** *adj* **1.**(*dément*) mad; **devenir ~ furieux/folle furieuse** to go raving mad **2.**(*dérangé*) **être ~ à lier** to be raving mad; **ne pas être ~** *inf* not to be mad; **devenir ~** to go mad; **c'est à devenir ~, il y a de quoi devenir ~** it would drive you mad; **il me rendra ~** he'll be the death of me; **ils sont ~s, ces Romains!** *iron* these guys are nuts! **3.**(*idiot*) **il est/serait ~ de faire ça** he's/he'd be mad to do that; **il faut être ~ pour faire cela** only a madman would do that **4.**(*insensé: idée, projet, tentative*) crazy; (*imagination, jeunesse, désir, rires*) wild; (*joie*) insane; (*regard*) crazed; **folle audace** audacious folly; **c'est l'amour ~** they're head over heels (in love); **faire des dépenses folles** to spend an incredible amount of money; **passer une folle nuit** to have a wild night; **avoir le ~ rire** to have (a fit of) the giggles [*o* laugh attack]; **les rumeurs les plus folles** the wildest rumours *Brit,* the wildest rumors *Am* **5.**(*éperdu*) **être ~ de chagrin** to be mad with grief; **être ~ de désir** to be wild with desire; **être ~ de colère** to be blazing with anger **6.**(*amoureux*) **être ~ de qn** to be wild about sb; **être ~ de jazz** to be mad on [*o* about] jazz **7.**(*énorme, incroyable: courage, énergie, mal*) unbelievable; **un argent ~** an unbelievable amount of money; **il y avait un monde ~** the place was packed **8.**(*exubérant*) **être tout ~** to be beside oneself with excitement; **devenir tout ~** to get madly excited **9.**(*en désordre, incontrôlé: cheveux, mèche*) untidy; **un camion/cheval ~** a runaway lorry/horse *Brit,* a runaway truck/horse *Am* **II.** *m, f* **1.**(*dément*) madman, madwoman *m, f* **2.**(*écervelé*) **jeune ~** young fool; **vieux ~** crazy old fool; **crier/travailler comme un ~** to yell/work like mad **3.**(*personne exubérante*) **faire le ~** (*faire, dire des bêtises*) to talk like an idiot; (*se défouler*) to act the fool; **arrête de faire le ~!** stop playing the fool! **4.** JEUX bishop **5.**(*bouffon*) jester ►**s'amuser comme un petit ~** *inf* to have a whale of a time

foudre¹ [fudʀ] *f* **1.** METEO lightning *no pl* **2.** *pl, soutenu* (*condamnation, reproche: d'une personne*) wrath *no pl* ►**c'est le coup de ~** it's love at first sight; **avoir le coup de ~ pour qc** to fall in love with sth

foudre² [fudʀ] *m* **~ de guerre** war leader; **~ d'éloquence** great orator

foudre³ [fudʀ] *m* (*tonneau*) tun

foudroyant(e) [fudʀwajɑ̃, jɑ̃t] *adj* **1.**(*soudain: mort*) instant; (*succès*) overnight; (*vitesse, progrès, attaque*) lightning; (*nouvelle*) devastating **2.**(*mortel: maladie, poison*) devastating **3.**(*réprobateur*) **jeter un regard ~ sur qn** to look daggers at sb

foudroyer [fudʀwaje] <6> *vt* **1.**(*frapper par la foudre*) **être foudroyé** to be struck by lightning **2.**(*électrocuter*) **être foudroyé** to be electrocuted **3.**(*tuer*) to strike down; **la maladie l'a foudroyé** illness struck him down **4.**(*abattre, rendre stupéfait*) **~ qn** (*malheur*) to devastate sb; (*surprise*) to knock sb flat

fouet [fwɛ] *m* **1.** (*verge*) whip **2.** GASTR whisk **3.** (*châtiment*) **donner le ~ à qn** to whip sb ▸**de plein ~** head-on

fouetter [fwete] <1> **I.** *vt* **1.** (*frapper: personne, animal*) to whip; **la pluie fouette les vitres** the rain is lashing the windows; **le vent me fouette au visage** the wind is whipping my face **2.** GASTR (*blanc d'œufs*) to whisk; (*crème*) to whip **3.** (*stimuler: amour-propre, orgueil*) to sting; (*désir*) to whip up; (*imagination*) to stir; **~ le sang** to warm up the blood **II.** *vi* (*frapper*) **la pluie fouette contre les vitres** the rain is lashing the windows

foufou, **fofolle** [fufu, fɔfɔl] *adj inf* **être un peu ~** (*personne*) to be a bit scatterbrained; (*chien*) to be a bit excited

fougère [fuʒɛʀ] *f* BOT fern

fougue [fug] *f* ardour *Brit*, ardor *Am*

fougueux, **-euse** [fugø, -øz] *adj* (*réponse, intervention, attaque, cheval*) spirited; (*tempérament, personne, orateur, discours*) fiery

fouille [fuj] *f* **1.** (*inspection*) search; **~ corporelle** body search **2.** *pl* (*en archéologie*) dig **3.** (*excavation*) excavation

fouillé(e) [fuje] *adj* (*commentaire, étude*) detailed; (*travail*) painstaking

fouille-merde [fujmɛʀd] <fouille-merdes> *mf inf* muckraker

fouiller [fuje] <1> **I.** *vt* **1.** (*inspecter: lieu, poches*) to search; (*horizon*) to scan; (*dossier*) to examine; **~ un problème** to go into a problem; **~ la vie de qn** to delve into sb's life; **~ l'obscurité des yeux** to peer into the darkness; **il fouilla la pièce des yeux** [*o* **du regard**] his eyes scoured the room **2.** (*creuser*) **~ qc** (*animal*) to dig sth; (*archéologue*) to excavate sth **II.** *vi* **1.** (*inspecter*) **~ dans qc** to look through sth; **~ dans ses souvenirs** to dig among one's memories **2.** (*creuser*) to dig **III.** *vpr* **se ~** to go through one's pockets

fouillis [fuji] *m* muddle; **~ de lianes** a mass of tangled creepers; **le texte fait vraiment ~** the text is a real muddle

fouine [fwin] *f* ZOOL stone marten ▸**c'est une vraie ~** he's a real busybody

fouiner [fwine] <1> *vi inf* to snoop around; **il est sans cesse à ~ partout** he's always nosing around all over the place

fouineur, **-euse** [fwinœʀ, -øz] *m, f* busybody

foulard [fulaʀ] *m* **1.** (*fichu*) (head)scarf **2.** (*écharpe*) scarf **3.** (*tissu*) foulard

foule [ful] *f* **1.** (*multitude de personnes*) crowd; **il y a/n'y a pas ~** there are loads of/not a lot of people; **ce n'était pas la grande ~ aux guichets** people weren't thronging the box office **2.** (*grand nombre*) **une ~ de gens/questions** masses of people/questions **3.** (*peuple*) **la ~** the mob

foulée [fule] *f* SPORT stride; **à grandes/petites ~s** taking big/small strides; **allonger la ~** to take bigger strides; **rester dans la ~ de qn** to stay on sb's heels ▸**dans la ~ de qc** in the wake of sth; **je lui ai téléphoné dans la ~** I rang [*o* phoned] him while I was at it

fouler [fule] <1> **I.** *vt* (*écraser: raisin*) to tread; TECH (*cuir, peau*) to tan **II.** *vpr* **1.** (*se tordre*) **se ~ la cheville** to sprain one's ankle **2.** *iron, inf* (*se fatiguer*) **se ~** to kill oneself

foulure [fulyʀ] *f* MED sprain

four [fuʀ] *m* **1.** GASTR oven; **~ (à) micro-ondes** microwave (oven); **ce plat ne va pas au ~** this dish isn't ovenproof **2.** TECH furnace; (*pour la poterie*) kiln; **~ électrique** electric furnace **3.** *inf* (*échec*) flop ▸**il fait noir comme dans un ~** it's as dark as night

fourbe [fuʀb] *adj* deceitful; (*gentillesse*) guileful

fourberie [fuʀbəʀi] *f* guile

fourbi [fuʀbi] *m inf* **1.** (*attirail*) kit **2.** (*truc*) whatsit

fourbir [fuʀbiʀ] <8> *vt* **1.** (*astiquer*) to polish **2.** (*préparer soigneusement*) **~ ses arguments** to prepare ones arguments

fourbu(e) [fuʀby] *adj* all-in

fourche [fuʀʃ] *f* **1.** (*outil, de bicyclette, branchement*) fork **2.** COUT (*d'un pantalon*) crotch **3.** *Belgique* (*temps libre d'une ou deux heures dans un horaire de cours*) break

fourcher [fuʀʃe] <1> *vi* (*cheveux*) to split; **(c'est) ma langue (qui) a fourché** it was a slip of the tongue

fourchette [fuʀʃɛt] *f* **1.** GASTR fork **2.** (*marge*) range; **se situer dans une ~ de 41 à 47 %** to lie in the 41 to 47 % range ▸**être une solide ~** to be a good eater

fourchu(e) [fuʀʃy] *adj* (*branche*) forked; **cheveux ~s** split ends

fourgon [fuʀgɔ̃] *m* **1.** CHEMDFER coach; **~ à bagages** luggage van **2.** (*voiture*) van; MIL wagon; **~ de police** police van; **~ blindé** armoured car *Brit,* armored car *Am;* **~ funéraire** hearse

fourgonnette [fuʀgɔnɛt] *f* van

fourgon-pompe [fuʀgɔ̃pɔ̃p] <fourgons-pompes> *m* fire engine

fourguer [fuʀge] <1> *vt inf* **1.** (*vendre*) **~ qc à qn** to flog sth to sb **2.** (*refiler*) **~ qc à qn** to land sb with sb

fourme [fuʀm] *f* fourme (*type of soft cheese from the centre of France*)

fourmi [fuʀmi] *f* **1.** ZOOL ant **2.** (*symbole d'activité*) busy bee ▸**avoir des ~s dans les jambes** to have pins and needles in one's legs

fourmilier [fuʀmilje] *m* ZOOL anteater

fourmilière [fuʀmiljɛʀ] *f* **1.** ZOOL anthill **2.** (*foule grouillante*) hive of activity

fourmillement [fuʀmijmɑ̃] *m* **1.** (*agitation*) swarming **2.** (*foisonnement*) teeming **3.** (*picotement*) tingling; **j'ai des ~s dans les bras** I've got pins and needles in my arms

fourmiller [fuʀmije] <1> *vi* **1.** (*abonder*) **les moustiques/fautes fourmillent** it's swarming with mosquitoes/mistakes; **la forêt fourmille de champignons** the forest is teeming with mushrooms; **elle fourmille de projets** she has dozens of plans on the go **2.** (*picoter*) **j'ai les pieds qui (me) fourmillent** I've got pins and needles in my feet

fournaise [fuʀnɛz] *f* **1.** (*foyer ardent*) blaze **2.** (*lieu surchauffé*) **c'est une ~ ici** it's like an oven in here **3.** (*lieu de combat*) battleground **4.** *Québec* (*appareil de chauffage central*) boiler

fourneau [fuʀno] <x> *m* **1.** (*cuisinière*) stove; **~ à charbon** coal-burning stove **2.** (*chaufferie*) furnace; **haut ~** blast furnace

fournée [fuʀne] *f* **~ de pains** batch of loaves; **~ de touristes** bunch of tourists; **par ~s** in bunches

fourni(e) [fuʀni] *adj* **1.** (*épais: chevelure, cheveux*) lush; (*barbe, sourcils*) bushy **2.** (*approvisionné*) stocked; **être bien ~** (*magasin*) to be well-stocked; (*table*) to be groaning; **sa garde-robe est bien ~e** she has a well-stocked wardrobe

fournil [fuʀni] *m* bakery

fournir [fuʀniʀ] <8> **I.** *vt* **1.** (*approvisionner*) **~ un client/un commerce en qc** to supply a customer/a business with sth **2.** (*procurer*) **~ qc à des réfugiés** to provide refugees with sth; **~ un logement/travail à qn** to find sb a place to live/a job; **~ un prétexte à qn** to give sb an excuse; **~ un renseignement à qn** to provide sb with some information; **~ l'occasion à qn** to provide sb with the opportunity; **~ le vivre et le couvert à qn** to provide money and food for sb; **~ des précisions** to give details **3.** (*présenter: alibi, preuve*) to provide; (*autorisation*) to give; (*pièce d'identité*) to produce **4.** (*produire*) to produce; **la centrale fournit de l'énergie** the power station produces energy; **les abeilles fournissent du miel** bees produce honey; **~ un gros effort** to put in a lot of effort; **ce vignoble fournit un vin renommé** this vineyard produces a famous wine **II.** *vi* (*subvenir à*) **le magasin n'arrivait plus à ~** the shop couldn't cope **III.** *vpr* **se ~ en charbon chez qn** to get one's coal from sb

fournisseur [fuʀnisœʀ] *m* INFOR provider; **~ d'accès Internet** Internet service provider; **~ de services en ligne** on-line service provider

fournisseur, -euse [fuʀnisœʀ, -øz] **I.** *m, f* supplier **II.** *adj* **les pays ~s de l'Espagne** countries supplying Spain

fourniture [fuʀnityʀ] *f* **1.** (*livraison*) supply; **~ de documents** supply of documents **2.** *pl* (*accessoires*) supplies

fourrage [fuʀaʒ] *m* fodder

fourrager, -ère [fuʀaʒe, -ɛʀ] *adj* fodder

fourré [fuʀe] *m* thicket

fourré(e) [fuʀe] *adj* **1.** (*doublé de fourrure: gants, manteau*) fur-lined **2.** GASTR (*bonbons, gâteau*) filled

fourre [fuʀ] *f Suisse* (*taie d'oreiller, édredon*) eiderdown

fourreau [fuʀo] <x> *m* **1.** (*gaine: d'une épée*) sheath; (*d'un parapluie*) cover **2.** (*robe moulante*) sheath

fourrer [fuʀe] <1> **I.** *vt* **1.** *inf* (*mettre*) **~ qc dans qc** to put sth in sth; **qui a bien pu lui ~ cette idée dans la tête?** who could have put that idea in his head? **2.** (*garnir*) **~ qc avec du lapin** to trim sth with rabbit fur **3.** GASTR **~ qc au chocolat** to put a chocolate filling in sth **II.** *vpr inf* (*se mettre*) **se ~ sous les couvertures** to dive under the bedclothes [*o* covers]; **se ~ les doigts dans le nez** to pick one's nose; **être tout le temps fourré au café** to be always down at the café; **quelle idée s'est-il fourré dans la tête?** what's this idea he's got into his head? ▶**ne plus <u>savoir</u> où se ~** not to know where to put oneself; **s'en ~ <u>jusque-là</u>** to stuff oneself

fourre-tout [fuʀtu] *m inv* **1.** *péj* (*local*) junk room **2.** (*sac*) holdall *Brit*, carryall *Am*

fourreur, -euse [fuʀœʀ, -øz] *m, f* furrier

fourrière [fuʀjɛʀ] *f* (*pour voitures, animaux*) pound; **tu vas retrouver ta voiture à la ~!** you're going to find your car's been towed away!

fourrure [fuʀyʀ] *f* fur

fourvoyer [fuʀvwaje] <> *vpr soutenu* **se ~** to make a (serious) mistake

foutaise [futɛz] *f inf* **1.** (*chose sans valeur*) bit of rubbish **2.** (*futilité*) bull *no pl;* **quelle ~!** what a load of bull!

foutoir [futwaʀ] *m péj, vulg* tip

foutre [futʀ] <14> **I.** *vt inf* **1.** (*faire*) **ne rien ~** to do not a damn thing, to do damn all; **qu'est-ce que tu fous?** what are you up to? **2.** (*donner*) **~ une baffe à qn** to clout sb; **fous-moi la paix!** get lost!, bugger off! *Brit;* **ce temps de cochon me fout le cafard** this lousy weather gives me the creeps **3.** (*mettre*) **~ qc dans sa poche** to shove sth in one's pocket; **~ qc par terre** (*par accident*) to send sth flying; (*exprès*) to sling sth on the ground; **son arrivée a tout foutu par terre** it loused everything up when he arrived ▶**je n'en <u>ai</u> rien à ~!** I couldn't give a damn!; **~ <u>bas</u>** *Suisse* (*jeter* (*avec violence*)) to chuck away; **~ qn <u>dedans</u>** to mix sb up; **ça la fout <u>mal</u>** it doesn't look good; **qu'est-ce que ça <u>peut</u> me/te ~?** what the hell's that got to do with me/you?; **je t'<u>en</u> fous!** no chance!; **je t'<u>en</u> foutrais des ordinateurs!** don't you talk to me about computers! **II.** *vpr inf* **1.** (*se mettre*) **se ~ un coup de marteau sur les doigts** to hit one's fingers with a hammer; **foutez-vous par terre!** hit the deck!; **fous-toi ça dans le crâne!** get that into your thick head! **2.** (*se moquer*) **se ~ de qn** to mock sb, to take the mickey out of sb *Brit;* **il se fout de notre gueule!** he's taking us for damn idiots! **3.** (*se désintéresser*) **se ~ de qn/qc** not to give a damn about sb/sth; **ton beau-frère, je m'en fous** I couldn't give a damn for your brother-in-law; **il se fout que tu aies fait ça** he couldn't give a damn about you doing that ▶**<u>va</u> te faire ~!** (*va te faire voir*) go screw yourself!; (*rien à faire*) no way!; **se ~** **dedans** to screw up; **s'en ~ jusque-là** to stuff oneself

foutrement [futʀəmɑ̃] *adv inf* goddamn, bloody *Brit*

foutu(e) [futy] **I.** *part passé de* **foutre II.** *adj inf* **1.** (*perdu: chose*) bust; **être ~** (*chose*) to be bust; (*personne*) to have had it; (*malade*) to be a goner **2.** *antéposé* (*maudit*) damned, bloody *Brit* **3.** (*vêtu*) **comment es-tu encore ~ ce matin?** what on earth are you wearing this morning? **4.** (*capable*) **être/ne pas être ~ de faire qc** to be capable of/not up to doing sth ►**être bien/mal ~** (*personne*) to have a good/lousy body; (*travail, appareil*) to be a good/lousy job; **être mal ~** to feel lousy; **~ pour ~** the mess things are in

fox-trot [fɔkstʀɔt] *m inv* foxtrot

foyer [fwaje] *m* **1.** (*famille*) family; (*maison*) home; **~ paternel** paternal home; **les jeunes ~s** young families; **fonder un ~** to start a family; **retrouver un ~** to find a new home **2.** (*résidence*) hostel; **~ d'urgence** emergency hostel **3.** (*salle de réunion*) hall **4.** THEAT foyer **5.** (*âtre*) hearth **6.** (*cheminée*) fireplace **7.** (*centre: d'une civilisation*) centre *Brit,* center *Am;* **~ lumineux** light source; **le ~ de la crise/de l'épidémie** the epicentre of the crisis/the epidemic *Brit,* the epicenter of the crisis/the epidemic *Am;* **ce quartier est un ~ de voyous** this district is a magnet for layabouts **8.** (*incendie*) heart **9.** (*chambre de combustion*) firebox **10.** (*en optique*) a. MAT, PHYS focus ►**renvoyer un soldat dans ses ~s** to demobilize a soldier

frac [fʀak] *m* tailcoat

fracas [fʀaka] *m* (*bruit de choses qui se heurtent*) crash; (*bruit sourd*) roar; **~ du tonnerre** crash of thunder; **~ de la ville** roar of the city; **à grand ~** making a great stir

fracasser [fʀakase] <1> *vt, vpr* (**se**) **~** to smash

fraction [fʀaksjɔ̃] *f* **1.** MAT, REL fraction **2.** (*partie d'un tout: d'un groupe, d'une somme*) part; **une ~ de seconde** a fraction of a second

fractionnaire [fʀaksjɔnɛʀ] *adj* fractional

fractionnel(le) [fʀaksjɔnɛl] *adj* divisive

fractionnement [fʀaksjɔnmɑ̃] *m* CHIM fractionation; (*d'un patrimoine, paiement*) division

fractionner [fʀaksjɔne] <1> **I.** *vt* **1.** (*diviser*) to divide up **2.** (*partager*) to share out; **~ le/un paiement** to divide up the/a payment **3.** CHIM to fractionate **II.** *vpr* **se ~ en plusieurs groupes** to divide up into (several) groups

fractionniste [fʀaksjɔnist] **I.** *adj* wrecking **II.** *mf* wrecker

fracture [fʀaktyʀ] *f* **1.** MED fracture; **se faire une ~ du poignet** to fracture one's wrist **2.** *fig* **~ sociale** social breakdown

fracturer [fʀaktyʀe] <1> **I.** *vt* **1.** (*briser: porte, voiture*) to break open **2.** MED to fracture **II.** *vpr* MED **se ~ le bras** to fracture one's arm

fragile [fʀaʒil] *adj* **1.** (*cassant*) fragile **2.** (*délicat, faible: personne, santé, organisme*) delicate; (*estomac, cœur*) weak; **être ~ du cœur/des poumons** to have a weak heart/chest **3.** (*précaire: paix, bonheur, gloire*) fragile; (*argument, preuve, hypothèse*) flimsy; (*équilibre, économie*) shaky **4.** (*peu solide: bâtiment*) flimsy

fragilisé(e) [fʀaʒilize] *adj* (*santé*) weakened

fragiliser [fʀaʒilize] <1> *vt* to weaken; (*au niveau psychologique*) to destabilize

fragilité [fʀaʒilite] *f* **1.** (*facilité à se casser*) fragility **2.** (*faiblesse*) weakness; **être d'une grande ~ morale** to be weak psychologically **3.** (*précarité: des arguments, d'une hypothèse, d'une preuve*) flimsiness; (*d'un équilibre, d'une économie*) instability; (*de la paix*) fragility

fragment [fʀagmɑ̃] *m* **1.** (*débris*) bit **2.** (*extrait d'une œuvre*) extract **3.** (*œuvre incomplète*) fragment **4.** (*partie: d'une vie*) episode

fragmentaire [fʀagmɑ̃tɛʀ] *adj* (*connaissance, exposé*) sketchy; (*effort, travail*) patchy

fragmentation [fʀagmɑ̃tasjɔ̃] *f* BIO, GEO fragmentation; (*d'un pays*) breaking up; (*d'un problème*) breaking down

fragmenter [fʀagmɑ̃te] <1> **I.** *vt* **~ qc en qc** to split sth up into sth; **~ son travail** to break up one's work **II.** *vpr* **se ~** to fragment

fraîche [fʀɛʃ] **I.** *adj v.* **frais II.** *f* **à la ~** (*le matin*) in the cool of the early morning; (*le soir*) in the cool of the evening

fraîchement [fʀɛʃmɑ̃] *adv* (*récemment: cueilli, labouré*) freshly; (*arrivé*) newly

fraîcheur [fʀɛʃœʀ] *f* **1.** (*sensation agréable*) coolness; (*sensation désagréable*) chilliness; **chercher la ~** to look for somewhere cool **2.** (*froideur: d'un accueil*) coolness **3.** (*éclat: d'une fleur, couleur, d'un teint*) freshness; (*d'une robe*) crispness; (*d'un livre*) originality **4.** (*bonne forme*) vitality; (*d'une équipe*) freshness **5.** (*qualité d'une production récente: d'un produit alimentaire*) freshness **6.** (*pureté, vivacité: d'un sentiment*) freshness; (*d'une idée*) originality

fraîchir [fʀeʃiʀ] <8> *vi* (*air, temps*) to turn cool; (*eau*) to cool; (*vent*) to freshen

frais[1] [fʀɛ] *mpl* **1.** costs; (*pour services professionels*) fees; **~ de scolarité** tuition fees; **faux ~** overheads; **tous ~ compris** all inclusive **2.** COM, ECON **~ d'entretien** upkeep; (*pour nettoyage, réparations*) maintenance costs; **~ généraux** overheads; **~ de gestion/de main d'œuvre** management/labour costs *Brit,* management/labor costs *Am* **3.** JUR **~ de justice** (legal) costs; **~ de garde** (*garde d'enfants*) childcare costs; (*dépôt*) storage costs ►**faire les ~ de la conversation** to have everyone talking about one; **aux ~ de la princesse** *iron* all expenses paid; (*aux dépens de l'entreprise*) on the company; (*aux dépens de l'Etat*) at public expense; **à grands** ~ at great expense; (*avec beaucoup de peine*) with great difficulty; **à moindre** ~ cheaper; (*avec peu de mal*) more easily; **arrêter les** ~ *inf* to stop messing around; (*cesser de se donner du mal*) to stop putting oneself out; **en être pour ses** ~ to be out of pocket; **faire des** ~ to spend money; **faire les** ~ **de qc** to spend a lot on sth; **à peu de** ~ cheaply; (*avec peu de mal*) without much effort; **s'en tirer à peu de** ~ to get off lightly

frais² [fʀɛ] *m* (*fraîcheur*) cool; **mettre une bouteille de vin au** ~ to chill a bottle of wine; **à conserver** [*o* **garder**] **au** ~ keep cool; **être au** ~ (*personne*) to be in the cooler; (*chose*) to be on ice ►**mettre qn au** ~ *inf* to put sb inside

frais, fraîche [fʀɛ, fʀɛʃ] *adj* **1.** (*légèrement froid: endroit, eau, vent*) cool; **servir qc très** ~ to serve sth chilled **2.** (*opp: avarié, sec, en conserve*) fresh; (*œuf*) new-laid **3.** (*peu cordial*) cool **4.** (*agréable: fleur, teint, couleur, parfum*) fresh; (*son, voix*) bright **5.** (*en forme: personne*) lively; (*reposé, sain*) refreshed; **être** ~ **et dispos** to be fresh as a daisy **6.** (*récent: peinture*) wet; (*blessure, souvenir*) fresh; **l'encre est encore fraîche** the ink is not yet dry; **une nouvelle toute fraîche** a piece of fresh news; **des nouvelles fraîches** some fresh news **7.** *iron, inf* (*dans une sale situation*) **eh bien, nous voilà** ~**!** well, we're in a fine mess! **8.** (*pur: âme, joie*) pure; (*sentiment*) untainted

fraise [fʀɛz] **I.** *f* **1.** (*fruit*) strawberry; **confiture de** ~**(s)** strawberry jam; **à la** ~ strawberry **2.** (*collerette*) ruff **3.** (*chez le dentiste*) drill **4.** *inf* (*figure*) mug; **ramener sa** ~ *inf* to horn in, to shove one's oar in *Brit* **II.** *adj inv* strawberry

fraisier [fʀezje] *m* strawberry plant

framboise [fʀɑ̃bwaz] *f* **1.** (*fruit*) raspberry **2.** (*eau-de-vie*) raspberry liqueur

framboisier [fʀɑ̃bwazje] *m* raspberry bush

franc [fʀɑ̃] *m* (*monnaie*) franc; ~ **français/suisse/belge** French/Swiss/Belgian franc; **ancien/nouveau** ~ [*o* ~ **lourd**] old/new franc

franc(he) [fʀɑ̃, ɑ̃ʃ] *adj* **1.** (*loyal, sincère: personne, contact*) straightforward; (*rire, gaieté*) open; (*regard*) candid; **pour être** ~ to be frank; **être** ~ **avec qn** to be frank with sb **2.** (*net: couleur*) strong; (*hostilité*) open; (*situation*) clear-cut; **un oui** ~ **et massif** a clear and overwhelming yes; **aimer les situations franches** to like clear situations **3.** *antéposé* (*véritable*) utter; (*succès*) complete **4.** (*libre*) free; **port** ~ free port

franc, franque [fʀɑ̃, fʀɑ̃k] *adj* Frankish; **la langue franque** the Frankish language; **les rois** ~**s** the Frankish kings

Franc, Franque [fʀɑ̃, fʀɑ̃k] *m, f* Frank

français [fʀɑ̃sɛ] *m* **1. le** ~ French; **le** ~ **familier/standard** everyday/standard French; **parler (le)**~ to speak French; **écrire en** ~ to write in French; **traduire en** ~ to translate into French **2.** THEAT **le Français** the Comédie française ►**en bon** ~ *iron* in language anyone could understand; **tu ne comprends pas/vous ne comprenez pas le** ~**?** *inf* don't you understand plain English?; **je parle (le)** ~ **pourtant** I'm not speaking Chinese, am I?

français(e) [fʀɑ̃sɛ, ɛz] *adj* French

Français(e) [fʀɑ̃sɛ, ɛz] *m(f)* Frenchman, Frenchwoman *m, f*; **les** ~ the French

française [fʀɑ̃sɛz] *f* **à la** ~ in the French style

franc-comtois(e) [fʀɑ̃kɔ̃twa, waz] *adj v.* **comtois**

Franc-Comtois(e) [fʀɑ̃kɔ̃twa, waz] *m(f) v.* **Comtois**

France [fʀɑ̃s] *f* **la** ~ France ►**de** ~ **et de Navarre** *iron* in the whole damn country; **être assez/très vieille** ~ (*dans ses attitudes*) to be very prim and proper; (*dans ses vêtements*) to have an old-fashioned elegance

franchement [fʀɑ̃ʃmɑ̃] *adv* **1.** (*sincèrement*) frankly **2.** (*sans hésiter*) **entrer** ~ **dans le sujet** to get straight to the point **3.** (*clairement*) plainly **4.** (*vraiment*) really ►~**!** really!; (*refus indigné*) come off it!

franchir [fʀɑ̃ʃiʀ] <8> *vt* **1.** (*passer par-dessus*) ~ **un fossé** to step over a ditch; ~ **un obstacle** to clear an obstacle; ~ **un ruisseau** (*personne, animal, pont*) to cross a stream; (*d'un bond*) to jump across a stream; ~ **la voie** to cross the line; ~ **des pas décisifs** to take decisive steps **2.** (*aller au-delà*) to cross; (*barrage*) to get past; (*seuil*) to step across; (*limite*) to go beyond; ~ **la ligne d'arrivée** to cross the finishing line; **ta renommée a franchi les frontières** your fame goes before you **3.** (*surmonter: examen, épreuve*) to get through; (*difficulté*) to get over; **la réforme a franchi le premier obstacle** the reform has cleared the first hurdle **4.** (*parcourir, traverser: col*) to go across; **sa gloire a franchi les siècles** her glory has lasted down the centuries; **une étape importante vient d'être franchie** an important stage has been achieved

franchise [fʀɑ̃ʃiz] *f* **1.** (*sincérité: d'une personne*) frankness; (*d'un regard*) openness; **en toute** ~ in all honesty **2.** (*des assurances*) excess **3.** (*exonération*) allowance; ~ **de bagages** baggage allowance; **en** ~ duty-free **4.** (*montant*) tax allowance **5.** COM franchise

franchisé(e) [fʀɑ̃ʃize] **I.** *m(f)* COM franchisee **II.** *adj* COM franchised; **magasin** ~ franchise

franchissable [fʀɑ̃ʃisabl] *adj* (*obstacle*) clearable; **la limite est** ~ the limit can be exceeded; **la rivière est** ~ the river can be crossed

franchissement [fʀɑ̃ʃismɑ̃] *m* **1.** (*saut: de la barre*) clearing **2.** (*traversée: d'une frontière, rivière*) crossing

franchouillard(e) [fʀɑ̃ʃujaʀ, jaʀd] *adj péj* narrow-mindedly French

francilien(ne) [fʀɑ̃siljɛ̃, ɛn] *adj* of the Ile-de-

France

Francilien(ne) [fʀɑ̃siljɛ̃, ɛn] *m(f)* person from the Ile-de-France

franciscain(e) [fʀɑ̃siskɛ̃, ɛn] **I.** *adj* Franciscan **II.** *m(f)* Franciscan

franciser [fʀɑ̃size] <1> *vt* ~ **un mot** to turn into a French word

franc-maçon(ne) [fʀɑ̃masɔ̃, ɔn] <francs-maçons> *m(f)* Freemason

franc-maçonnerie [fʀɑ̃masɔnʀi] <franc-maçonneries> *f* **1.** (*société secrète*) Freemasonry **2.** (*camaraderie*) freemasonry

franco [fʀɑ̃ko] *adv* **1.** COM postage paid **2.** *inf* (*carrément*) **y aller** ~ to get right on with it

franco-allemand(e) [fʀɑ̃koalmɑ̃, ɑ̃d] <franco-allemands> *adj* Franco-German

francophile [fʀɑ̃kɔfil] **I.** *adj* francophile **II.** *mf* francophile

francophobe [fʀɑ̃kɔfɔb] **I.** *adj* francophobic **II.** *mf* francophobe

francophone [fʀɑ̃kɔfɔn] **I.** *adj* (*pays, région*) francophone; (*personne*) French-speaking; **être** ~ to be a French-speaker **II.** *mf* French-speaker

francophonie [fʀɑ̃kɔfɔni] *f* **la** ~ the French-speaking world

> **Francophonie** is the whole of the French-speaking world. This includes countries in Africa, America, Asia and Europe. There are regular summits between these francophone countries, where duties and the spread of the French language are discussed.

franc-parler [fʀɑ̃paʀle] <francs-parlers> *m* forthrightness; **avoir son** ~ to be outspoken

franc-tireur [fʀɑ̃tiʀœʀ] <francs-tireurs> *m* **1.** MIL irregular **2.** *fig* maverick; **en** ~ off one's own bat

frange [fʀɑ̃ʒ] *f* fringe

frangin(e) [fʀɑ̃ʒɛ̃, ʒin] *m(f)* *inf* brother

frangipane [fʀɑ̃ʒipan] *f* frangipane

franglais [fʀɑ̃glɛ] *m* Franglais

franque [fʀɑ̃k] *adj v.* **franc**

franquette [fʀɑ̃kɛt] **à la bonne** ~ *inf* simply

franquisme [fʀɑ̃kism] *m* Francoism

franquiste [fʀɑ̃kist] **I.** *adj* pro-Franco; **l'Espagne** ~ Franco's Spain **II.** *mf* Franco supporter

frappant(e) [fʀapɑ̃, ɑ̃t] *adj* striking

frappe [fʀap] *f* **1.** TECH (*d'une monnaie*) minting **2.** (*façon de frapper: d'une dactylo, pianiste*) touch; (*d'un boxeur*) punch; (*d'un footballeur*) kick **3.** (*exemplaire dactylographié*) typescript; **être à la** ~ to be being typed

frappé(e) [fʀape] *adj* **1.** (*saisi*) ~ **de stupeur** thunderstruck; ~ **de panique** panic-stricken **2.** (*refroidi*) chilled; **café** ~ iced coffee **3.** *inf* (*fou*) screwy

frapper [fʀape] <1> **I.** *vt* **1.** (*heurter, cogner*) ~ **qn au visage** to hit sb in the face; **la pierre l'a frappé à la tête** the stone hit him on the head; **la pluie frappe les vitres** the rain is lashing the windows **2.** (*avec un couteau*) to stab **3.** (*saisir*) ~ **qn d'horreur** to fill sb with horror; ~ **qn de stupeur** to leave sb thunderstruck **4.** (*affliger*) ~ **qn** (*maladie, malheur*) to strike sb; (*mesure, impôt*) to affect sb; (*sanction*) to hit sb; **cette nouvelle tragique l'a beaucoup frappée** this tragic news hit him hard; **être frappé d'amnésie** to be affected by amnesia **5.** (*étonner*) to strike; (*imagination*) to fire; **être frappé de la ressemblance** to be struck by the resemblance **6.** TECH (*médaille*) to strike; (*monnaie*) to mint **7.** (*glacer: champagne*) to chill; (*café*) to ice **II.** *vi* **1.** (*donner des coups*) to knock; ~ **à la porte** to knock at the door **2.** (*taper*) ~ **dans ses mains** to clap one's hands; ~ **du poing sur la table** to hit the table with one's fist **III.** *vpr* (*se donner des coups*) **se** ~ **le front** to slap one's forehead; **se** ~ **la poitrine** to beat one's breast

frasil [fʀazi(l)] *m Québec* (*cristaux ou fragments de glace entraînés par le courant et flottant à la surface d'un cours d'eau; pellicule formée par la glace qui commence à prendre*) frazil

frasque [fʀask] *f* **1.** (*bêtise*) prank; ~**s de jeunesse** youthful mischief **2.** (*dans un couple*) escapade

fraternel(le) [fʀatɛʀnɛl] *adj* **1.** (*de frère: amour*) brotherly **2.** (*de sœur: amour*) sisterly **3.** (*affectueux*) fraternal

fraternellement [fʀatɛʀnɛlmɑ̃] *adv iron* fraternally; **s'aimer** ~ to love each other like brothers

fraternisation [fʀatɛʀnizasjɔ̃] *f* fraternization

fraterniser [fʀatɛʀnize] <1> *vi* **1.** to fraternize **2.** (*sympathiser*) to get along

fraternité [fʀatɛʀnite] *f* brotherhood; **la** ~ **humaine** the brotherhood of man; ~ **d'armes** the brotherhood of arms; ~ **d'esprit** kinship of spirit

fratricide [fʀatʀisid] **I.** *adj* fratricidal **II.** *m* (*meurtre*) fratricide **III.** *mf* (*personne*) fratricide

fraude [fʀod] *f* **1.** fraud; ~ **douanière** customs fraud; ~ **fiscale** tax evaison; ~ **sur les vins** adulteration of wine **2.** (*aux examens*) cheating ▶**en** ~ (*illégalement*) fraudulently; (*en secret*) on the quiet, in secret; **fumer en** ~ to smoke on the quiet; **passer des marchandises à la frontière en** ~ to smuggle in goods

frauder [fʀode] <1> **I.** *vt* (*tromper*) to defraud; ~ **le fisc** [*o* **les impôts**] to cheat the taxman; ~ **la douane** to defraud customs **II.** *vi* (*tricher*) ~ **à un examen** to cheat at an exam; ~ **sur le poids des denrées** to give short weight

fraudeur, -euse [fʀodœʀ, -øz] *m, f* **1.** (*escroc*) crook **2.** (*à la frontière*) smuggler **3.** (*aux examens*) cheat(er)

frauduleusement [fʀodyløzmɑ̃] *adv* fraudulently

frauduleux, -euse [fʀodylø, -øz] *adj* (*concurrence, moyen, dossier, trafic*) fraudulent;

(*banquier*) dishonest

frayer [fʀeje] <7> I. *vt* (*ouvrir*) ~ **à qn un passage dans la foule** to clear a way through the crowd for sb; ~ **la voie au progrès** to make way for progress II. *vi* 1. ZOOL (*se reproduire*) to spawn 2. (*fréquenter*) ~ **avec qn** to associate with sb III. *vpr* **se** ~ **un passage/une voie/un chemin** to get through; *fig* to make one's way

frayeur [fʀɛjœʀ] *f* fright

freak [fʀik] *m* bum

fredaine [fʀədɛn] *f* prank; **des ~s de jeunesse** youthful mischief

fredonner [fʀədɔne] <1> *vt* to hum

free-lance [fʀilɑ̃s] <free-lances> I. *mf* freelance(r); **travailler en** ~ to work freelance II. *adj inv* (*journaliste, styliste*) freelance

freesia [fʀezja] *m* freesia

freezer [fʀizœʀ] *m* freezer

frégate [fʀegat] *f* (*bateau*) frigate

frein [fʀɛ̃] *m* 1. (*dispositif*) brake 2. (*entrave, limite*) **être/mettre un** ~ **à qc** to be/put a curb on sth; **sans** ~ unchecked ►**ronger son** ~ to champ at the bit

freinage [fʀɛnaʒ] *m* 1. (*action*) braking 2. (*ralentissement: de la hausse des prix*) curbing

freiner [fʀene] <1> I. *vi* to brake II. *vt* 1. (*ralentir, entraver*) to slow down 2. (*modérer: personne, ambitions*) to curb; (*hausse des prix, offre*) to check; (*production*) to slow down; ~ **le succès de qn** to put a damper on sb's success III. *vpr inf* (*se modérer*) **se** ~ to restrain oneself

frelaté(e) [fʀəlate] *adj* (*alcool, vin*) adulterated

frelater [fʀəlate] <1> *vt* to adulterate

frêle [fʀɛl] *adj* (*personne, corps, espoirs, tige*) frail; (*bateau*) fragile; (*silhouette*) slim

frelon [fʀəlɔ̃] *m* ZOOL hornet

freluquet [fʀəlykɛ] *m* whippersnapper

frémir [fʀemiʀ] <8> *vi* 1. *soutenu* (*frissonner*) ~ **d'impatience/de colère** to seethe with impatience/anger; ~ **d'horreur** to shudder with horror; ~ **tout entier** to shiver all over; **faire** ~ **qn** (*récit, criminel*) to make sb shudder 2. (*s'agiter légèrement: feuillage*) to tremble; (*ailes*) to quiver 3. (*être sur le point de bouillir: eau*) to shiver

frémissant(e) [fʀemisɑ̃, ɑ̃t] *adj* (*voix*) trembling; (*eau*) simmering; **être** ~ **de colère/désir** to be seething with anger/desire

frémissement [fʀemismɑ̃] *m* 1. *soutenu* (*frisson d'émotion: des lèvres*) tremble; (*du corps, d'une personne*) shiver; ~ **d'horreur** shudder; ~ **de fièvre** feverish tremble 2. (*mouvement léger: d'une corde, des ailes*) vibration; (*de l'eau*) ripple; (*du feuillage*) trembling 3. (*murmure: des feuilles*) rustling 4. ECON, POL slight upturn

french cancan [fʀɛnʃkɑ̃kɑ̃] <french cancans> *m* cancan

frêne [fʀɛn] *m* BOT ash

frénésie [fʀenezi] *f* frenzy; ~ **de consommation** frenzied consumption; **avec** ~ wildly

frénétique [fʀenetik] *adj* 1. (*passionné: sentiment, personne, passion*) frenzied; (*enthousiasme*) wild 2. (*au rythme déchaîné: agitation, danse*) frenetic; (*applaudissements*) wild; (*personne*) frenzied

frénétiquement [fʀenetikmɑ̃] *adv* wildly

fréon® [fʀeɔ̃] *m* Freon®

fréquemment [fʀekamɑ̃] *adv* frequently

fréquence [fʀekɑ̃s] *f* 1. frequency 2. INFOR ~ **de rafraîchissement d'image** screen refresh rate

fréquent(e) [fʀekɑ̃, ɑ̃t] *adj* frequent

fréquentable [fʀekɑ̃tabl] *adj* (*lieu*) where one can safely go; (*personne*) that you can safely be seen with; **une rue peu** ~ not the sort of street to hang around in; **un type peu** ~ not a nice sort of guy

fréquentation [fʀekɑ̃tasjɔ̃] *f* 1. (*action*) ~ **d'une personne** seeing a person; **la** ~ **de l'exposition est satisfaisante** attendance at the exhibition is satisfactory 2. *gén pl* (*relation*) acquaintance; **avoir de bonnes/mauvaises ~s** to keep good/bad company; **il choisit ses ~s** he's careful about the people he sees

fréquenté(e) [fʀekɑ̃te] *adj* (*établissement, lieu, rue*) busy; (*promenade*) popular; **ce lieu est bien** ~ (*qualitatif*) the people who come here are nice; (*quantitatif*) this is a popular place

fréquenter [fʀekɑ̃te] <1> I. *vt* 1. (*aller fréquemment dans: bars, théâtres*) to frequent; ~ **l'école** to go to school; ~ **la maison de qn** to be a regular visitor to sb's house 2. (*avoir des relations avec*) to see II. *vpr* 1. (*par amitié*) **se** ~ to see each other 2. (*par amour*) **se** ~ to be courting

frère [fʀɛʀ] *m* 1. (*opp: sœur*) *a.* REL brother; ~ **siamois** Siamese twin brother; **partager en ~s** to share like brothers; **ressembler à qn comme un** ~ to bear a close resemblance to sb; **se ressembler comme des ~s jumeaux** to be like two peas in a pod; **être élevé chez les ~s** to be educated by the Brothers 2. *inf* (*objet*) twin

frérot [fʀeʀo] *m inf* kid brother

frésia [fʀezja] *m v.* **freesia**

fresque [fʀɛsk] *f* (*peinture*) fresco

fret [fʀɛ(t)] *m* NAUT, AVIAT 1. (*prix*) freight charge 2. (*chargement*) freight

fréteur [fʀetœʀ] *m* (*armateur*) owner

frétillant(e) [fʀetijɑ̃, jɑ̃t] *adj* 1. (*remuant: poisson*) wriggling; (*queue*) wagging 2. *fig* **être** ~ **d'impatience** to quiver with impatience; **être** ~ **de joie** to be quivering with joy

frétiller [fʀetije] <1> *vi* 1. (*remuer: poisson*) to wriggle; **le chien frétille de la queue** the dog was wagging its tail 2. *fig* ~ **d'impatience** to quiver with impatience; ~ **de joie** to be quivering with joy

fretin [fʀətɛ̃] *m* fry ►**menu** ~ *péj* small fry

freudien(ne) [fʀødjɛ̃, jɛn] **I.** *adj* Freudian **II.** *m(f)* Freudian

friable [fʀijabl] *adj* (*pâte*) crumbly; (*roche, sol*) friable

friand [fʀijɑ̃] *m* **1.** (*pâté*) ≈ meat pie **2.** (*gâteau*) almond cake

friand(e) [fʀijɑ̃, jɑ̃d] *adj* ~ **de chocolat/nouveautés** fond of chocolate/novelty

friandise [fʀijɑ̃diz] *f* sweet(s); **donne-moi une ~!** give me a sweet!

fribourgeois(e) [fʀibuʀʒwa, waz] *adj* of Fribourg; *v. a.* **ajaccien**

Fribourgeois(e) [fʀibuʀʒwa, waz] *m(f)* person from Fribourg; *v. a.* **Ajaccien**

fric [fʀik] *m inf* (*argent*) dough

fricassée [fʀikase] *f* fricassee

fric-frac [fʀikfʀak] *m inv, inf* break-in

friche [fʀiʃ] *f* AGR fallow; **être en ~** to lie fallow

fricoter [fʀikɔte] <1> **I.** *vt péj* to cook up **II.** *vi iron, inf* ~ **avec qn** to hang around with sb

friction [fʀiksjɔ̃] *f* **1.** (*frottement*) massage; ~ **de cheveux** scalp massage; **se faire faire une ~** to have one's scalp massaged **2.** PHYS friction **3.** *gén pl* (*désaccord*) friction *no pl*

frictionner [fʀiksjɔne] <1> **I.** *vt* to rub down ▶**je vais lui ~ les oreilles!** *inf* I'm going to fetch him one! **II.** *vpr* **se ~** to rub oneself down

frigidaire® [fʀiʒidɛʀ] *m* fridge

frigide [fʀiʒid] *adj* frigid

frigidité [fʀiʒidite] *f* frigidity

frigo [fʀigo] *m inf abr de* **frigidaire**

frigorifier [fʀigɔʀifje] <1> *vt* **1.** *inf* (*avoir très froid*) **être frigorifié** to be frozen stiff **2.** (*congeler*) to freeze

frigorifique [fʀigɔʀifik] *adj* refrigerated; (*machine*) refrigerating

frileusement [fʀiløzmɑ̃] *adv* **1.** (*en raison du froid*) to keep out the cold **2.** (*craintivement*) timidly

frileux, -euse [fʀilø, -øz] *adj* **1.** (*sensible au froid: personne*) that feels the cold **2.** (*craintif*) timid

frilosité [fʀilozite] *f* **1.** (*sensibilité au froid*) susceptibility to the cold **2.** (*manque d'audace*) **la ~ des marchés** the nervousness of the markets

frime [fʀim] *f inf* **1.** (*bluff*) put-on **2.** (*vantardise*) show; **c'est pour la ~** it's just showing off

frimer [fʀime] <1> *vi inf* **1.** (*fanfaronner*) to show off **2.** (*se vanter*) to make oneself look big

frimeur, -euse [fʀimœʀ, -øz] *m, f inf* show-off

frimousse [fʀimus] *f inf* **1.** (*visage*) sweet little face **2.** INFOR smiley

fringale [fʀɛ̃gal] *f* **1.** *inf* (*faim*) **avoir la ~** to be hungry; **j'ai été pris d'une vraie ~** I suddenly felt ravenous **2.** (*envie*) ~ **de lectures** craving to read; **avoir une ~ de bandes dessinées** to have a craving for comic books

fringant(e) [fʀɛ̃gɑ̃, ɑ̃t] *adj* (*personne*) dashing; (*personne âgée*) spry; (*cheval*) frisky

fringué(e) [fʀɛ̃ge] *adj inf* dressed up; **être bien ~** to be smartly dressed; **c'est un mec ~ comme un ministre** the guy dresses like someone in the government

fringuer [fʀɛ̃ge] <1> *vt, vpr inf* (**se**) ~ to dress (oneself) up

fringues [fʀɛ̃g] *fpl inf* clothes

fripe [fʀip] *f gén pl* **1.** (*vieux vêtements*) old clothes **2.** (*vêtements d'occasion*) second-hand clothes

fripé(e) [fʀipe] *adj* crumpled

friper [fʀipe] <1> **I.** *vt* to crease **II.** *vpr* **se ~** to get creased

friperie [fʀipʀi] *f* **1.** *péj* (*vieux habits*) second-hand clothes **2.** (*commerce*) second-hand clothes trade

fripier, -ière [fʀipje, -jɛʀ] *m, f* second-hand clothes dealer

fripon(ne) [fʀipɔ̃, ɔn] **I.** *adj inf* (*air, visage*) mischievous; **il a le regard ~** [*o* **les yeux ~s**] he's got a twinkle in his eye **II.** *m(f) inf* (*malin*) rogue; **petit ~!** little vilain!

fripouille [fʀipuj] *f inf* rascal

friqué(e) [fʀike] *adj inf* loaded

frire [fʀiʀ] *vt, vi irr* to fry

frisbee® [fʀizbi] *m* Frisbee®

frise [fʀiz] *f* ARCHIT frieze

frisé(e) [fʀize] *adj* (*cheveux*) curly; (*fille*) curly-haired; **être ~ comme un mouton** to have frizzy hair

frisée [fʀize] *f* (*salade*) curly endive

friser [fʀize] <1> **I.** *vt* **1.** (*mettre en boucles: cheveux, moustache*) to curl; ~ (**les cheveux à**) **qn** to put curls in sb's hair **2.** (*frôler*) ~ **la mort/l'accident** to narrowly miss death/an accident; ~ **le ridicule** (*situation, remarque*) to border on the ridiculous; **tu frises le ridicule** you're beginning to look ridiculous; ~ **la soixantaine** to be pushing sixty; ~ **les 10%** to be getting on for 10% **II.** *vi* (*cheveux*) to curl; **qn frise** (*naturellement*) sb is curly; (*à l'humidité*) sb goes frizzy **III.** *vpr* (*se faire des boucles*) **se faire ~** to have one's hair curled

frisette [fʀizɛt] *f* **1.** (*bouclette*) curl **2.** (*planche*) panel

frisotté(e) [fʀizɔte] *adj* **cheveux ~** frizzy hair

frisotter [fʀizɔte] <1> *vi* (*cheveux*) to go curly; **elle frisotte** her hair goes curly

frisquet(te) [fʀiskɛ, ɛt] *adj inf* nippy

frisson [fʀisɔ̃] *m* shiver; ~ **de dégoût** shudder of disgust; **avoir des ~s** to shiver ▶**le grand ~** a big thrill; **donner le grand ~ à qn** to make the earth move for sb; **j'en ai le ~** it gives me the shivers

frissonnant(e) [fʀisɔnɑ̃, ɑ̃t] *adj* shivering; **être ~ de fièvre** to be shivering with fever

frissonner [fʀisɔne] <1> *vi* (*avoir des frissons*) ~ **de désir/plaisir** to tremble with desire/pleasure; ~ **de froid/peur** to shiver with cold/fear; **il frissonne d'horreur** he is shuddering with horror

frisure [fRizyR] *f* curls *pl;* ~ **légère** loose curls

frit(e) [fRi, fRit] **I.** *part passé de* **frire II.** *adj inf* (*fichu*) damn

frite [fRit] *f* **des ~s** chips *Brit,* french fries *Am;* **cornet de ~s** bag of chips ►**avoir la** ~ to be in (top) form

friterie [fRitRi] *f* **1.** (*baraque à frites*) chip stand *Brit,* french fry stand *Am* **2.** (*atelier de friture*) frying shop

friteuse [fRitøz] *f* GASTR deep fryer

friture [fRityR] *f* **1.** (*aliments*) fried food **2.** *Belgique* (*baraque à frites*) chip stand *Brit,* french fry stand *Am* **3.** (*graisse*) fat **4.** (*action*) frying **5.** RADIO, TEL interference

frivole [fRivɔl] *adj* (*personne, spectacle*) frivolous; (*discours*) shallow; (*occupation, lecture*) trivial

frivolité [fRivɔlite] *f* (*d'une personne*) frivolousness; (*d'une conversation, d'une occupation*) triviality; (*d'un discours*) shallowness

froc [fRɔk] *m inf* (*pantalon*) trousers *pl Brit,* pants *pl Am* ►**baisser son** ~ **devant qn** *inf* to back down from sb, to drop one's trousers in front of sb; **faire dans son** ~ *inf* to wet onself

froid [fRwa] **I.** *m* **1.** (*température*) cold; **il fait** ~ it's cold; **avoir** ~ to be cold; **j'ai** ~ **aux pieds** my feet are cold; **attraper** [*o* **prendre**] (**un coup de**) ~ to catch (a) cold; **mourir de** ~ to die of the cold; (*avoir très froid*) to be freezing **2.** (*brouille*) **être en** ~ **avec qn** to be on bad terms with sb; **jeter un** ~ (*personne*) to cast gloom (all around); (*intervention, remarque*) to cause a chill ►**il fait un** ~ **de canard** [*o* **loup**] *inf* it's freezing out; **j'en ai** ~ **dans le dos** it makes my blood run cold; **ne pas avoir** ~ **aux yeux** (*être dynamique*) to have drive; (*avoir du courage*) to have spirit **II.** *adv* **à** ~ TECH cold; (*sans préparation*) (from) cold; (*sans émotion*) cold-bloodedly; (*avec insensibilité*) coolly; **démarrage à** ~ cold start

froid(e) [fRwa, fRwad] *adj* cold; **laisser qn** ~ to leave sb cold; **prendre un air** ~ to look cold; **rester** ~ **comme le marbre** to remain as cold as ice

froidement [fRwadmɑ̃] *adv* **1.** (*sans chaleur*) coldly; (*accueillir, recevoir*) coolly **2.** (*avec sang-froid: raisonner*) with a cool head; (*réagir*) coolly **3.** (*avec insensibilité*) coolly

froideur [fRwadœR] *f* (*d'un comportement*) coldness; (*d'un accueil, d'une réaction*) coolness; **accueillir qc avec** ~ to give sth a cool reception

froissable [fRwasabl] *adj* **être** ~ to crease easily

froissé(e) [fRwase] *adj* **1.** (*fripé: tissu*) crumpled **2.** (*meurtri: muscle*) strained

froissement [fRwasmɑ̃] *m* **1.** (*bruit*) rustle **2.** (*claquage*) ~ **d'un muscle** strain(ing) **3.** (*blessure*) bad feeling

froisser [fRwase] <1> **I.** *vt* **1.** (*chiffonner: tôles, papier*) to crumple; (*tissu*) to crease **2.** (*blesser: personne, orgueil*) to hurt **II.** *vpr* **1.** (*se chiffonner*) **se** ~ (*tissu*) to crease; (*papier*) to get crumpled **2.** (*se claquer*) **se** ~ **un muscle** to strain a muscle **3.** (*se vexer*) **se** ~ to get offended; **être froissé** to be offended

frôlement [fRolmɑ̃] *m* **1.** (*contact léger*) touch **2.** (*frémissement*) swish

frôler [fRole] <1> **I.** *vt* **1.** (*effleurer*) to brush against **2.** (*passer très près*) to graze; ~ **le ridicule** (*remarque, situation*) to border on the ridiculous; **tu frôles le ridicule** you're beginning to look ridiculous; **le thermomètre frôle les 20°** it's around 20° **3.** (*éviter de justesse*) ~ **la mort** to narrowly escape death **II.** *vpr* **se** ~ (*avec contact*) to brush against each other; (*sans contact*) to pass by each other

fromage [fRɔmaʒ] *m* cheese; ~ **blanc** fromage frais ►**faire un** ~ **de qc** *inf* to make a big fuss about sth

fromager, -ère [fRɔmaʒe, -ɛR] **I.** *adj* (*industrie, production*) cheese; **association fromagère** cheese-makers' association **II.** *m, f* cheese dealer, cheesemonger *Brit*

fromagerie [fRɔmaʒRi] *f* **1.** (*industrie*) cheese-making industry **2.** (*lieu de fabrication*) dairy

froment [fRɔmɑ̃] *m* wheat

fronce [fRɔ̃s] *f* gather; **jupe à ~s** gathered skirt

froncement [fRɔ̃smɑ̃] *m* (*du nez*) wrinkling; ~ **des sourcils** frown

froncer [fRɔ̃se] <2> *vt* **1.** COUT to gather **2.** (*plisser: nez*) to wrinkle; ~ **les sourcils** to frown

fronces [fRɔ̃s] *fpl* gathers; **à** ~ gathered

frondaison [fRɔ̃dɛzɔ̃] *f* BOT **1.** (*apparition des feuilles*) foliation **2.** (*feuillage*) foliage

fronde¹ [fRɔ̃d] *f* catapult *Brit,* slingshot *Am*

fronde² [fRɔ̃d] *f* **1.** (*insurrection*) revolt **2.** HIST **la Fronde** the Fronde (*civil war during the beginning of the reign of Louis XIV*)

fronde³ [fRɔ̃d] *f* BOT frond

frondeur, -euse [fRɔ̃dœR, -øz] *adj* rebellious

front [fRɔ̃] *m* **1.** ANAT forehead **2.** (*façade*) façade; (*d'une montagne*) face; ~ **de mer** seafront **3.** MIL, METEO, POL front; **Front populaire** Popular Front (*leftwing government coalition elected in 1936*) ►**faire** ~ **commun/offrir un** ~ **commun contre qn/qc** to close ranks; **marcher le** ~ **haut** to walk with one's head held high; **baisser le** ~ to bow one's head; **relever le** ~ to lift one's head high; **de** ~ (*côte à côte*) side by side; **attaquer un problème de** ~ to tackle a problem head on; **se heurter de** ~ to collide head on

frontal [fRɔ̃tal, o] <-aux> *m* MED frontal bone

frontal(e) [fRɔ̃tal, o] <-aux> *adj* **1.** MED frontal **2.** (*de face: attaque, collision*) head-on

frontalier, **-ière** [fʀɔ̃talje, -jɛʀ] **I.** *adj* border **II.** *m, f* border dweller
frontière [fʀɔ̃tjɛʀ] **I.** *f* border; **à la ~ du rêve et de la réalité** on the borders between dream and reality **II.** *app inv* border
fronton [fʀɔ̃tɔ̃] *m* pediment
frotte-manche [fʀɔtmɑ̃ʃ] <frotte-manches> *m Belgique, inf* (*lèche-botte*) bootlicker
frottement [fʀɔtmɑ̃] *m* **1.** (*bruit*) rubbing (noise) **2.** (*contact*) rubbing; **des traces de ~ sur le plancher** signs of wear on the floor; **étoffe usée par les ~s** fabric that has been worn thin **3.** PHYS friction **4.** *pl* (*frictions*) friction
frotter [fʀɔte] <1> **I.** *vi* **~ contre qc** to rub against sth; (*porte*) to scrape against sth **II.** *vt* **1.** (*astiquer: chaussures, meubles*) to polish **2.** (*nettoyer*) to rub; (*avec une brosse*) to scrub; **~ ses semelles sur le paillasson** to wipe one's soles on the doormat **3.** (*cirer: parquet*) to polish **4.** (*frictionner pour laver*) to scrub; (*frictionner pour sécher*) to rub down; (*frictionner pour réchauffer*) to rub **5.** (*gratter: allumette*) to strike; **~ qc contre/sur qc** to rub sth against/on sth; **~ qc à la toile émeri** to polish sth with emery cloth **6.** (*enduire*) **~ qc d'ail** to rub sth with garlic **III.** *vpr* **1.** (*se laver*) **se ~** to give oneself a scrub **2.** (*se sécher*) **se ~** to rub oneself down **3.** (*se nettoyer*) **se ~ les ongles** to scrub one's nails **4.** (*se gratter*) **se ~ les yeux/le nez** to rub one's eyes/nose; **se ~ contre les jambes de qn** to rub against sb's legs; **se ~ contre un arbre** to scratch oneself/itself against a tree **5.** (*entrer en conflit*) **se ~ à qn** to cross sb
frottis [fʀɔti] *m* smear (test) *Brit,* Pap smear *Am*
froufrou [fʀufʀu] *m* **1.** (*bruit*) rustling **2.** *pl* (*dentelles*) frills **3.** (*dessous*) frillies
froussard(**e**) [fʀusaʀ, aʀd] **I.** *adj inf* chicken **II.** *m(f) inf* chicken
frousse [fʀus] *f inf* fright; **avoir la ~** to be scared out of one's wits
fructifier [fʀyktifje] <1> *vi* **1.** (*produire: arbre, idée*) to bear; (*terre*) to yield; **~ tardivement** to give a late crop **2.** (*rapporter: capital*) to yield a profit; **faire ~ qc** to make sth yield a profit
fructueux, **-euse** [fʀyktɥø, -øz] *adj* (*collaboration*) fruitful; (*lecture*) rewarding; (*recherches, efforts, essai, travaux*) productive; (*opération financière, commerce*) profitable
frugal(**e**) [fʀygal, o] <-aux> *adj* frugal
frugalité [fʀygalite] *f* frugalness
fruit [fʀɥi] *m* **1.** *pl* fruit; **tu veux un ~?** do you want some fruit?; **jus de ~(s)** fruit juice; **~s rouges/confits** summer/glacé fruit **2.** (*crustacés*) **~s de mer** seafood **3.** (*résultat: de l'expérience, de la réflexion, d'un effort*) fruits; (*d'une union, de l'amour*) fruit; **être le ~ du hasard** to come about by chance; **le ~ d'une imagination délirante** the child of a fevered imagination; **porter ses ~s** to bear fruit ►**~ défendu** forbidden fruit
fruité(**e**) [fʀɥite] *adj* fruity
fruitier, **-ière**[1] [fʀɥitje, -jɛʀ] **I.** *adj* (*arbre*) fruit **II.** *m, f* fruit merchant, fruiterer *Brit*
fruitier, **-ière**[2] [fʀɥitje, -jɛʀ] *m Suisse* **1.** (*coopération de fabrication des fromages*) cheesemaking cooperative **2.** (*personne qui fabrique des fromages*) cheesemaker
frusques [fʀysk] *fpl inf* stuff *no pl*
fruste [fʀyst] *adj* (*personne*) rough-mannered; (*manières*) rough
frustrant(**e**) [fʀystʀɑ̃, ɑ̃t] *adj* frustrating
frustration [fʀystʀasjɔ̃] *f* frustration
frustré(**e**) [fʀystʀe] **I.** *adj* frustrated **II.** *m(f) inf* frustrated individual
frustrer [fʀystʀe] <1> *vt* **1.** *a.* PSYCH to frustrate **2.** (*priver*) **~ qn de qc** to deprive sb of sth
FS [ɛfɛs] *m abr de* **franc suisse** SF
fuchsia [fyʃja, fyksja] **I.** *m a.* BOT fuchsia **II.** *adj inv* fuchsia
fuel [fjul] *m* **1.** (*combustible*) **~ domestique** heating oil; **se chauffer au ~** to have oil heating **2.** (*carburant*) diesel
fugace [fygas] *adj* transient; (*beauté*) fleeting
fugitif, **-ive** [fyʒitif,-iv] **I.** *adj* **1.** (*en fuite*) runaway **2.** (*éphémère*) fleeting **II.** *m, f* (*de sa famille*) runaway; (*de la justice*) fugitive
fugitivement [fyʒitivmɑ̃] *adv* fleetingly
fugue [fyg] *f* **1.** (*fuite*) **un mineur en ~** a runaway minor; **faire une ~/des ~s** to run away **2.** MUS fugue
fuguer [fyge] <1> *vi inf* to run away
fugueur, **-euse** [fygœʀ,-øz] **I.** *m, f* runaway **II.** *adj* **enfant ~** young runaway
fuir [fɥiʀ] *irr* **I.** *vi* **1.** (*s'enfuir*) **~ d'un pays** to flee a country **2.** (*détaler*) **~ devant qn/qc** to run away from sb/sth; **faire ~ qn** to make sb run away **3.** (*se dérober*) **~ devant qc** to run away from sth **4.** (*ne pas être étanche*) to leak **5.** (*s'échapper: liquide*) to leak (out); (*gaz*) to escape **II.** *vt* (*éviter: danger*) to evade; **~ ses responsabilités** to try to escape one's responsibilities; **~ la présence de qn** to keep away from sb
fuite [fɥit] *f* **1.** flight; **prendre la ~** to take flight; (*chauffeur accidenté*) to drive away; **prisonnier en ~** escaped prisoner; **être en ~** (*accusé*) to be on the run **2.** (*dérobade*) **~ devant qc** to run away from sth; **chercher la ~ dans qc** to find escape in sth **3.** (*trou*) **avoir une ~** to have a leak **4.** (*perte*) leak; **il y a une ~ d'eau quelque part** water's leaking out somewhere; **il y a une ~ de gaz quelque part** there's a gas escape somewhere; **il y a une ~** there's a leak **5.** (*indiscrétion: d'une information*) leak; **l'auteur de la ~** the leaker; **en raison de ~s répétées** owing to constant leaks
fulgurant(**e**) [fylgyʀɑ̃, ɑ̃t] *adj* **1.** (*rapide: vitesse, réplique*) lightning; (*progrès*) staggering **2.** (*violent: douleur*) shooting **3.** (*éblouis-*

F

sant: lueur) dazzling; (*regard*) blazing

fulminant(**e**) [fylminɑ̃, ɑ̃t] *adj* **1.** (*furieux*) enraged; ~ **de colère** [*o* **de rage**] in a blind rage **2.** (*menaçant: regard*) blazing; (*lettre*) furious

fulminer [fylmine] <1> *vi* ~ **contre qn/qc** to fulminate against sb/sth

fumant(**e**) [fymɑ̃, ɑ̃t] *adj* **1.** (*qui dégage de la fumée*) smoking **2.** (*qui dégage de la vapeur*) steaming **3.** *inf* (*sensationnel*) dazzling

fumasse [fymas] *adj inf* (*furieux*) livid

fumé(**e**) [fyme] *adj* smoked; (*verres de lunettes*) smoke-tinted

fume-cigarette [fymsigaʀɛt] <fume-cigarettes> *m* cigarette-holder

fumée [fyme] *f* **1.** smoke; (*polluante*) fumes; ~**s industrielles/d'échappement** industrial/exhaust fumes; **la** ~ **ne vous gêne pas?** does the smoke bother you?; **avaler la** ~ to inhale (the smoke) **2.** (*vapeur légère*) steam **3.** (*vapeur épaisse*) fumes *pl*

fumer [fyme] <1> **I.** *vi* **1.** (*aspirer de la fumée de tabac, dégager de la fumée*) to smoke **2.** (*dégager de la vapeur*) to steam; (*acide*) to give off fumes **II.** *vt* to smoke

fumet [fymɛ] *m* **1.** (*odeur*) aroma **2.** (*bouquet: d'un vin*) bouquet

fumeur, **-euse** [fymœʀ, -øz] **I.** *m, f* smoker **II.** *app* AUTO **zone** ~/**non-**~ smoking/no-smoking area

> In principle, smoking is forbidden in France in all open places, e.g. underground stations, train stations and public buildings. Pubs are obliged to create a **zone non-fumeur**.

fumeux, **-euse** [fymø, -øz] *adj* (*théorie, explication, idées*) woolly

fumier [fymje] *m* **1.** (*engrais naturel*) manure **2.** *inf* (*salaud*) bastard

fumigation [fymigasjɔ̃] *f a.* MED fumigation; **faire des** ~**s** to fumigate

fumigène [fymiʒɛn] *adj* **grenade/bombe** ~ smoke grenade/bomb; **engin/appareil** ~ smoke generator

fumiste [fymist] **I.** *adj péj, inf* lazy **II.** *mf* **1.** *péj, inf* joker **2.** (*ouvrier*) chimney sweep

fumisterie [fymistəʀi] *f inf* **1.** (*mystification*) moonshine **2.** (*farce*) joke

fumoir [fymwaʀ] *m* smoking room

fun [fɔn] *m Québec* (*amusement*) entertainment

funambule [fynɑ̃byl] *mf* tightrope walker

funboard [fœnbɔʀd] *m* **1.** (*planche à voile*) funboard **2.** (*sport*) funboarding

funèbre [fynɛbʀ] *adj* **1.** (*funéraire*) funeral; **veillée** ~ wake **2.** (*lugubre: silence*) funereal; (*idées, mine*) gloomy

funérailles [fyneʀaj] *fpl* funeral; ~ **nationales** state funeral

funéraire [fyneʀɛʀ] *adj* (*monument*) funerary; **dalle** ~ tombstone; **salon** ~ *Québec* (*entreprise de pompes funèbres*) funeral parlour *Brit,* funeral parlor *Am*

funérarium [fyneʀaʀjɔm] *m* funeral parlour *Brit,* funeral parlor *Am*

funeste [fynɛst] *adj* **1.** (*fatal: coup*) fatal; (*jour*) fateful; (*suites*) tragic; **être** ~ **à qn/qc** to have dire consequences for sb/sth **2.** (*de mort: pressentiment, vision*) deathly; **de** ~**s pressentiments** a premonition of death **3.** (*triste: récit*) sad

funiculaire [fynikylɛʀ] *m* funicular

funk [fœnk] *adj inv* funky; **musique** ~ funk(y music)

fur [fyʀ] **au** ~ **et à mesure** as one goes along; **passe-moi les photos au** ~ **et à mesure** pass me the photos over as you look at them; **au** ~ **et à mesure qu'on approche/progresse dans notre travail** as we gradually get nearer/our work gradually progresses

furax [fyʀaks] *adj inf* (*furieux*) livid

furet [fyʀɛ] *m* ferret

fureter [fyʀ(ə)te] <4> *vi* to ferret around

fureteur [fyʀ(ə)tœʀ] *m Québec* INFOR browser

fureteur, **-euse** [fyʀ(ə)tœʀ, -øz] **I.** *m, f* pry **II.** *adj* (*regard*) prying

fureur [fyʀœʀ] *f* **1.** rage; **mettre qn en** ~ to infuriate sb; **être en** ~ **contre qn** to be furious at sb; **des accès de** ~ **incontrôlables** uncontrollable rages; **avec** ~ furiously **2.** (*violence*) fury ▸**faire** ~ to be (all) the rage; **la** ~ **de vivre** lust for life

furibond(**e**) [fyʀibɔ̃, ɔ̃d] *adj* (*regard, ton*) enraged; (*personne*) livid

furie [fyʀi] *f* **1.** (*violence*) fury; **mer en** ~ raging sea; **personne/animal en** ~ enraged person/animal; **être en** ~ to be in a rage; **mettre qn en** ~ to infuriate sb **2.** *péj* (*femme déchaînée*) fury

furieusement [fyʀjøzmɑ̃] *adv* **1.** (*avec violence*) furiously **2.** *iron* (*extrêmement*) wildly

furieux, **-euse** [fyʀjø, -jøz] *adj* **1.** (*en colère, violent*) furious **2.** *iron* (*extrême: envie*) overwhelming; (*appétit*) furious

furoncle [fyʀɔ̃kl] *m* boil

furtif, **-ive** [fyʀtif, -iv] *adj* furtive

furtivement [fyʀtivmɑ̃] *adv* furtively

fus [fy] *passé simple de* **être**

fusain [fyzɛ̃] *m* **1.** (*dessin*) charcoal drawing **2.** (*crayon*) charcoal pencil **3.** BOT spindle tree

fuseau [fyzo] <x> *m* **1.** (*instrument*) spindle **2.** (*pantalon*) ski-pants *pl* **3.** GEO ~ **horaire** time zone

fusée [fyze] *f* rocket

fuselage [fyz(ə)laʒ] *m* fuselage

fuselé(**e**) [fyz(ə)le] *adj* tapering

fuser [fyze] <1> *vi* (*liquide, vapeur*) to spurt out; (*étincelles*) to fly (up); (*lumière*) to shine out; (*rires, cris*) to go up; (*coups de feu*) to ring out; **les questions fusent** questions are coming thick and fast; **le pétrole fuse** the oil is gushing out

fusible [fyzibl] *m* fuse

fusil [fyzi] *m* **1.** (*à chevrotines*) shotgun; (*à

balles) rifle; ~ **sous-marin** speargun **2.** (*aiguisoir*) steel ▶**changer son ~ d'épaule** (*changer de méthode/d'opinion*) to have a change of heart; (*retourner sa veste*) to switch sides; **être un bon ~** to be a good shot

fusilier [fyzilje] *m* ~ **marin** marine

fusillade [fyzijad] *f* **1.** (*coups de feu*) gunfire *no pl* **2.** (*exécution*) shooting

fusiller [fyzije] <1> *vt* to shoot

fusil-mitrailleur [fyzimitʀajœʀ] <fusils-mitrailleurs> *m* machine gun

fusion [fyzjɔ̃] *f* **1.** (*fonte: des atomes*) fusion; (*d'un métal*) melting; (*de la glace*) thawing; **en ~** molten **2.** ECON, POL merger **3.** (*union: de cœurs, corps, d'esprits*) union **4.** INFOR (*de fichiers*) mergeing; **obtenir la ~ de deux fichiers** to merge two files

fusionner [fyzjɔne] <1> *vi, vt a.* INFOR to merge

fût [fy] *m* cask

futaie [fytɛ] *f* forest

futal [fytal] *m inf* (*pantalon*) trousers *Brit,* pants *Am*

futé(e) [fyte] **I.** *adj* smart **II.** *m(f)* **petit ~** clever so-and-so

fute-fute [fytfyt] *adj* **ne pas être très ~** not to have a lot up top

futile [fytil] *adj* **1.** (*inutile, creux: choses, occupation*) pointless; (*conversation, propos*) empty; (*prétexte, raison*) trivial; **il était ~ de faire ça** it was pointless to do that **2.** (*frivole: personne, esprit*) trivial

futilité [fytilite] *f* **1.** *sans pl* (*inutilité, insignifiance: d'une occupation*) pointlessness; (*d'une conversation, d'un propos, d'une vie*) emptiness **2.** *sans pl* (*frivolité: d'une personne, d'un esprit*) triviality; (*d'un raisonnement*) vacuity **3.** *pl* (*bagatelles*) trivialities

futur [fytyʀ] *m* future

futur(e) [fytyʀ] **I.** *adj* future; **une ~e maman** a mother-to-be **II.** *m(f) inf* (*fiancé*) fiancé, fiancée *m, f*

futuriste [fytyʀist] *adj* futuristic

futurologie [fytyʀɔlɔʒi] *f* futurology

futurologue [fytyʀɔlɔg] *mf* futurologist

fuyais [fɥijɛ] *imparf de* **fuir**

fuyant [fɥijɑ̃] *part prés de* **fuir**

fuyant(e) [fɥijɑ̃, ɑ̃t] *adj* **1.** (*évasif: attitude*) evasive; (*regard*) shifty; **être ~** (*personne*) to be hard to grasp; **prendre un air ~** to look evasive **2.** (*incurvé: menton, front*) receding

fuyard(e) [fɥijaʀ, aʀd] *m(f)* **1.** (*fugitif*) runaway **2.** (*déserteur*) deserter

fuyez [fɥije], **fuyons** [fɥijɔ̃] *indic prés et impératif de* **fuir**

G

G, g [ʒe] *m inv* G, g; ~ **comme Gaston** g as in George; (*on telephone*) g for George

gabarit [gabaʀi] *m* **1.** (*dimension*) size **2.** *inf* (*stature*) build

gabegie [gabʒi] *f* chaos; **c'est la vraie ~ ici** it is a real mess here

Gabon [gabɔ̃] *m* **le ~** Gabon

gabonais(e) [gabɔnɛ, ɛz] *adj* Gabonese

Gabonais(e) [gabɔnɛ, ɛz] *m(f)* Gabonese

gâché(e) [gɑʃe] *adj* **vie ~e** wasted life; **encore un jour de ~!** another wasted day!

gâcher [gɑʃe] <1> *vt* (*plaisir, vacances*) to ruin; (*vie*) to fritter away; (*temps, argent*) to waste

gâchette [gɑʃɛt] *f* (*d'une arme*) trigger; **appuyer sur la ~** to pull the trigger ▶**avoir la ~ facile** to be trigger-happy

gâchis [gɑʃi] *m* **1.** (*gaspillage*) waste **2.** (*mauvais résultat*) mess

gadget [gadʒɛt] *m* **1.** (*bidule*) whatsit **2.** (*innovation*) gadget

gadoue [gadu] *f* mud

gaffe[1] [gaf] *f inf* blunder; **faire une ~** to put one's foot in it

gaffe[2] [gaf] *f inf* **faire ~** to be careful

gaffer [gafe] <1> *vi inf* to blunder; (*en parole*) to put one's foot in it

gaffeur, -euse [gafœʀ, -øz] **I.** *adj inf* blundering **II.** *m, f inf* idiot

gag [gag] *m* gag

gaga [gaga] **I.** *adj inf* **1.** (*gâteux*) gaga **2.** (*fou*) **être ~ de qn** to be crazy about sb **II.** *m inf* **vieux ~** old fool

gage [gaʒ] *m* **1.** (*garantie*) guarantee; (*témoignage*) proof **2.** (*dépôt*) security; **mettre qc en ~** to pawn sth **3.** JEUX forfeit **4.** *pl* (*salaire*) wages

gageure [gaʒyʀ] *f* **réussir la ~** to pull off the challenge

gagnant(e) [gaɲɑ̃, ɑ̃t] **I.** *adj* winning ▶**donner un animal ~** to be the favourite *Brit,* to be the favorite *Am;* **partir ~** to start out favourite **II.** *m(f)* winner

gagne-pain [gaɲpɛ̃] *m inv* meal ticket

gagne-petit [gaɲpəti] *mf inv, péj* **être un ~** to scratch a living

gagner [gaɲe] <1> **I.** *vi* **1.** (*vaincre*) ~ **à qc** to win at sth; **on a gagné!** we won! **2.** (*trouver un avantage*) **est-ce que j'y gagne?** what do I get out of this? **3.** (*avoir une meilleure position*) ~ **à être connu** to improve on acquaintance; **y ~ en clarté** to become clearer **II.** *vt* **1.** (*s'assurer: argent, récompense*) to earn; (*prix*) to win **2.** (*remporter: lot, argent*) to win **3.** (*économiser: place, temps*) to save **4.** (*obtenir comme résultat: réputation*) to gain **5.** (*conquérir: ami, confiance*) to win over **6.** (*atteindre: lieu*) to reach **7.** (*avancer*) ~ **qc** (*incendie, épidémie*) to overtake sth **8.** (*envahir*) ~ **qn** (*maladie*) to spread to sb; (*fatigue,*

G

peur) to overcome sb; **le froid la gagnait** the cold was overcoming her; **l'envie me gagne de tout laisser tomber** I feel like dropping everything; **être gagné par le sommeil/un sentiment** to be overcome by sleep/a feeling; **se laisser ~ par le découragement** to let oneself be discouraged ►**c'est toujours ça de gagné** that's always something; **c'est gagné!** *iron* everything will be just fine!
gagneur, **-euse** [gaɲœʀ, -øz] *m, f* winner
gai(e) [ge, gɛ] *adj* cheerful; (*personne*) happy; (*événement*) cheerful; (*ambiance*) lively; (*vêtement, pièce, couleur*) bright ►**c'est ~!** *iron* that's great!; **ça va être ~!** it's going be a load of fun!
gaiement [gemɑ̃, gɛmɑ̃] *adv* cheerfully ►**allons-y ~!** *iron* come on then!
gaieté [gete] *f* gaiety; (*d'une personne*) cheerfulness ►**ne pas faire qc de ~ de cœur** to do sth with great reluctance
gaillard [gajaʀ] *m* **1.** (*costaud*) hefty lad **2.** *inf* (*lascar*) guy; **mon ~!** chum!
gaillard(e) [gajaʀ, aʀd] *adj* (*personne*) lively
gaîment [gemɑ̃, gɛmɑ̃] *adv v.* **gaiement**
gain [gɛ̃] *m* **1.** (*profit*) profit; **tirer un ~ d'une expérience** to benefit from an experience **2.** (*économie*) saving ►**donner ~ de cause à qn** to declare sb (to be) right; JUR to decide in sb's favour *Brit*, to decide in sb's favor *Am*; **obtenir ~ de cause** to be proved right; JUR to win one's case; **être âpre au ~** to be greedy
gaine [gɛn] *f* **1.** (*ceinture*) girdle **2.** (*étui*) sheath; (*d'un pistolet*) holster; **~ de câble/d'aération** cable/ventilation shaft
gaîté [gete] *f v.* **gaieté**
gala [gala] *m* gala; **~ de bienfaisance** charity gala
galant(e) [galɑ̃, ɑ̃t] *adj* **1.** (*courtois*) gallant **2.** (*d'amour*) **rendez-vous ~** romantic engagement
galanterie [galɑ̃tʀi] *f* gallantry
galantine [galɑ̃tin] *f* galantine
galaxie [galaksi] *f* galaxy
galbe [galb] *m* curve
galbé(e) [galbe] *adj* (*objet*) curved; (*jambe*) shapely
gale [gal] *f* **1.** (*chez les hommes*) scabies **2.** (*chez les animaux*) mange ►**être mauvais comme la ~** to be a nasty piece of work; **ne pas avoir la ~** to not have the plague
galéjade [galeʒad] *f* tall story
galéjer [galeʒe] <5> *vi* to tell tall stories
galère [galɛʀ] *f* **1.** *inf* (*corvée*) mess; **quelle ~!** what a drag! **2.** HIST galley ►**et vogue la ~!** and come what may!
galérer [galeʀe] <5> *vi inf* **1.** (*chercher*) to struggle **2.** (*travailler dur*) to slog away
galerie [galʀi] *f* **1.** (*souterrain*) tunnel; (*d'une mine*) level; **~ d'aération** ventilation shaft **2.** **~ marchande** shopping centre *Brit*, shopping mall *Am* **3.** (*balcon*) circle **4.** ART gallery; **~ de peinture** art gallery **5.** AUTO roof rack ►**amuser la ~** to clown around; **épater la ~** to show off
galérien [galeʀjɛ̃] *m* galley slave
galet [galɛ] *m* pebble
galette [galɛt] *f* (*crêpe*) (savoury) pancake
galeux, **-euse** [galø, -øz] *adj* (*mur*) flaking
Galilée [galile] *m* Galileo
galimatias [galimatja] *m* (*écrit*) twaddle; (*propos*) gibberish
galion [galjɔ̃] *m* galleon
galipette [galipɛt] *f inf* somersault
gallicisme [ga(l)lisism] *m* gallicism
gallois *m* Welsh; *v. a.* **français**
gallois(e) [galwa, az] *adj* Welsh
Gallois(e) [galwa, az] *m(f)* Welshman, Welshwoman *m, f*
gallo-romain(e) [ga(l)loʀɔmɛ̃, ɛn] <gallo-romains> *adj* Gallo-Roman
galoche [galɔʃ] *f* clog
galon [galɔ̃] *m* **1.** *pl* MIL stripes **2.** COUT braid **3.** *Québec* (*ruban gradué en pieds, en pouces et en lignes*) tape measure ►**prendre du ~** to get promoted
galop [galo] *m* gallop; **au ~** at a gallop; **se mettre au ~** (*cheval*) to break into a gallop; **partir au ~** to gallop off ►**arriver au (triple) ~** to arrive at top speed
galopade [galɔpad] *f* **1.** (*course précipitée*) dash **2.** (*chevauchée*) gallop **3.** SPORT hand gallop
galoper [galɔpe] <1> *vi* to gallop
galopin [galɔpɛ̃] *m inf* (*gamin des rues*) urchin
galvaniser [galvanize] <1> *vt* to galvanize
galvaudé(e) [galvode] *adj* trite
galvauder [galvode] <1> *vt* (*réputation, nom*) to tarnish; (*talent*) to prostitute
gambade [gɑ̃bad] *f souvent pl* leap; **faire des ~s** to leap about
gambader [gɑ̃bade] <1> *vi* to leap; (*animal*) to gambol
gambas [gɑ̃bas] *fpl* gambas
gamberger [gɑ̃bɛʀʒe] <2a> *vi inf* to rack one's brains
gambette [gɑ̃bɛt] *f inf* leg
Gambie [gɑ̃bi] *f* **la ~** Gambia
gambien(ne) [gɑ̃bjɛ̃, ɛn] *adj* Gambian
Gambien(ne) [gɑ̃bjɛ̃, ɛn] *m(f)* Gambian
gamelle [gamɛl] *f* (*d'un campeur*) billy-can; (*d'un soldat*) mess tin; (*d'un ouvrier*) lunch box; (*d'un chien*) bowl ►**prendre une ~** *inf* to fall flat on one's face
gamin(e) [gamɛ̃, in] **I.** *adj* childish; (*air*) playful **II.** *m(f) inf* kid
gaminerie [gaminʀi] *f* playfulness *no pl*
gamme [gam] *f* range; MUS scale
Gand [gɑ̃] Ghent
gang [gɑ̃g] *m* gang
ganglion [gɑ̃glijɔ̃] *m* ganglion
gangrène [gɑ̃gʀɛn] *f* **1.** (*infection de plaie*) gangrene **2.** *fig* corruption
gangster [gɑ̃gstɛʀ] *m* gangster
gangstérisme [gɑ̃gsteʀism] *m* gangster-

ism; **c'est du ~!** it's daylight robbery!

gangue [gɑ̃g] *f* (*d'un minerai*) gangue; **une ~ de terre/boue** a crust of earth/mud

gant [gɑ̃] *m* **a.** INFOR glove; **~ de toilette** facecloth *Brit,* washcloth *Am;* **~ de données** dataglove ▸**aller à qn comme un ~** (*vêtement*) to fit sb like a glove; **le rôle lui va comme un ~** the role might have been written for her; **prendre des ~s avec qn** to handle sb with kid gloves; **retourner qn comme un ~** to wind sb round one's little finger

ganté(e) [gɑ̃te] *adj* (*main*) gloved; (*personne*) wearing gloves; **être ~** to be wearing gloves

gantois(e) [gɑ̃twa, waz] *adj* of Ghent; *v. a.* **ajaccien**

Gantois(e) [gɑ̃twa, waz] *m(f)* person from Ghent; *v. a.* **Ajaccien**

garage [gaʀaʒ] *m* garage; **~ à vélos** bicycle shed

garagiste [gaʀaʒist] *mf* **1.** (*qui tient un garage*) garage owner; **chez le ~** at the garage **2.** (*mécanicien*) mechanic

garant(e) [gaʀɑ̃, ɑ̃t] *m(f)* guarantor; **se porter ~ de qc** to guarantee sth; JUR to be responsible for sth; **ça, je m'en porte ~!** I guarantee that!

garantie [gaʀɑ̃ti] *f* **1.** (*bulletin de ~*) guarantee (card); **qc est encore sous ~** sth is still under guarantee **2.** (*gage, caution*) security; (*de paiement*) guarantee **3.** (*sûreté*) **sans ~** without guarantee **4.** (*assurance*) **~ contre les risques** risk insurance **5.** (*certitude*) **pouvez-vous me donner votre ~ que …** can you assure me that … **6.** (*précaution*) **prendre des ~s** to take precautions

garantir [gaʀɑ̃tiʀ] <8> *vt* **1.** (*répondre de, par contrat*) **~ qc à qn** to guarantee sth to sb; **être garanti un an** to be guaranteed (for) one year **2.** (*assurer*) to assure **3.** *iron* **je te garantis que …** I guarantee that …

garce [gaʀs] *f péj, inf* bitch

garçon [gaʀsɔ̃] *m* **1.** (*enfant*) boy **2.** (*jeune homme*) young man; **être beau ~** to be good-looking; **~ d'honneur** best man **3.** (*fils*) son **4.** (*serveur*) waiter **5.** (*employé subalterne*) **~ coiffeur/boucher** hairdresser's/butcher's assistant ▸**c'est un véritable ~ manqué** she is a real tomboy; **mauvais ~** bad boy; **vieux ~** bachelor

garçonnet [gaʀsɔnɛ] *m soutenu* little boy

garde[1] [gaʀd] *f* **1.** *sans pl* (*surveillance*) **avoir la ~ de qn** to be in charge of looking after sb; **à la ~ de qn** in sb's care; **confier qn à la ~ de qn** to put sb in sb's care **2.** JUR (*d'enfants*) custody; **~ à vue** police custody; **il est laissé à la ~ de la mère** his mother has been given custody **3.** (*veille*) guard duty **4.** (*permanence le week-end*) weekend duty; (*permanence de nuit*) night duty; **infirmière de ~** duty nurse; **être de ~** (*médecin, pharmacie*) to be on duty **5.** (*patrouille*) patrol; **la relève de la ~** the changing of the guard; **~ républicaine** Republican Guard ▸**la vieille ~** the old guard; **être sur ses ~s** to be on one's guard; **mettre qn en ~ contre qn/qc** to warn sb about sb/sth; **monter la ~** to be on guard; (*soldat*) to mount guard; **prendre ~ à qn/qc** to take care of sb/sth; (*se méfier*) to watch out for sb/sth; **sans y prendre ~** without realizing it; **en ~!** on guard!

garde[2] [gaʀd] *m* **1.** (*surveillant: d'une propriété*) guard; **~ champêtre** rural policeman; **~ forestier** forest warden [*o* ranger]; **~ du corps** bodyguard **2.** (*sentinelle*) guard; (*soldat*) guardsman

garde-à-vous [gaʀdavu] *m inv* **~!** attention!; **être au ~** to be at [*o* standing to] attention; **se mettre au ~** to stand to attention

garde-barrière [gaʀd(ə)baʀjɛʀ] <gardes-barrières> *mf* level-crossing keeper *Brit,* grade crossing keeper *Am* **garde-boue** [gaʀdəbu] *m inv* mudguard *Brit,* fender *Am* **garde-chasse** [gaʀdəʃas] <gardes-chasse(s)> *mf* gamekeeper **garde-côte** [gaʀdəkot] <garde-côtes> *m* coastguard **garde des Sceaux** [gaʀdeso] *mf: French Minister of Justice* **garde-fou** [gaʀdəfu] <garde-fous> *m* railing **garde-malade** [gaʀd(ə)malad] <gardes-malades> *mf* home nurse **garde-manger** [gaʀd(ə)mɑ̃ʒe] *m inv* meat safe *Brit,* cooler *Am* **garde-meuble** [gaʀdəmœbl] <garde-meubles> *m* furniture store **garde-pêche** [gaʀdəpɛʃ] <gardes-pêche> *mf* water bailiff *Brit,* fish and game warden *Am*

garder [gaʀde] <1> **I.** *vt* **1.** (*surveiller*) to watch; (*maison, enfant, animal*) to look after; (*personne âgée*) to care for; **donner qc à ~ à qn** to give sth to sb to look after **2.** (*stocker*) to keep; (*marchandises*) to stock; **~ sous clé** to lock away **3.** (*ne pas perdre*) to keep; (*espoir, défaut, manie*) to still have; **~ les séquelles de qc** to be scarred by sth **4.** (*réserver*) to reserve; (*place*) to save **5.** (*tenir, ne pas dévoiler*) to keep **6.** (*retenir*) to detain **7.** (*conserver sur soi*) **~ qc** to keep sth on **8.** (*ne pas quitter: lit, chambre*) to stay in **II.** *vpr* **1.** (*se conserver*) **se ~** (*aliment*) to keep; **ça se garde au frais** it must be kept in the fridge **2.** (*s'abstenir*) **se ~ de** +*infin* to be careful not to +*infin*

garderie [gaʀdəʀi] *f* (day) nursery

garde-robe [gaʀdəʀɔb] <garde-robes> *f* wardrobe

gardien(ne) [gaʀdjɛ̃, jɛn] **I.** *m(f)* **1.** (*surveillant*) warden; (*d'un immeuble*) caretaker *Brit,* building manager *Am;* (*d'un entrepôt*) guard; (*d'un zoo, cimetière*) keeper; **~ de musée** museum attendant; **~ de prison** prison warder *Brit,* corrections officer *Am;* **~ de nuit** night watchman; **~ne d'enfants** nanny, child minder *Brit* **2.** (*défenseur*) protector; **~ de l'ordre public** guardian of public order; **~ de la paix** policeman **II.** *adj Belgique* (*mater-*

nelle) **école ~ne** nursery
gardiennage [gaʀdjenaʒ] *m* **1.**(*d'immeuble*) caretaking **2.**(*de locaux*) guarding; **société de** ~ security company
gardon [gaʀdɔ̃] *m* **frais comme un** ~ fresh as a daisy
gare[1] [gaʀ] *f* station; ~ **centrale** central station; ~ **routière** coach station *Brit,* bus station *Am;* ~ **de marchandises** cargo terminal; ~ **de triage** marshalling yard *Brit,* marshaling yard *Am;* **entrer en** ~ to approach the platform
gare[2] [gaʀ] *interj* ~ **à toi!** watch it! ▶**sans crier** ~ without warning
garenne [gaʀɛn] *f* (*bois*) warren; *v. a.* **lapin**
garer [gaʀe] <1> **I.** *vt* to park; **il est garé à 100 m** he is parked 100 m away **II.** *vpr* **se** ~ **1.**(*parquer*) to park **2.**(*se ranger*) to pull over
gargantuesque [gaʀgɑ̃tɥɛsk] *adj* gigantic
gargariser [gaʀgaʀize] <1> *vpr* **1.**(*se rincer*) **se** ~ to gargle **2.** *péj, inf*(*savourer*) **se** ~ **de qc** to delight in sth
gargarisme [gaʀgaʀizm] *m* gargle
gargote [gaʀgɔt] *f péj* greasy spoon
gargouille [gaʀguj] *f* gargoyle
gargouillement [gaʀgujmɑ̃] *m* gurgling
gargouiller [gaʀguje] <1> *vi* to gurgle; (*estomac*) to rumble
garnement [gaʀnəmɑ̃] *m* rascal
garni(e) [gaʀni] *adj* **1.** GASTR garnished **2.**(*rempli*) **portefeuille bien** ~ fat wallet
garnir [gaʀniʀ] <8> *vt* **1.**(*orner*) to garnish **2.**(*équiper*) ~ **qc de qc** to equip sth with sth **3.**(*renforcer*) to reinforce **4.**(*remplir*) **être garni de qc** to be filled with sth
garnison [gaʀnizɔ̃] *f* garrison; **être en** ~ **à Strasbourg** to be garrisoned in Strasbourg
garniture [gaʀnityʀ] *f* **1.**(*ornement*) trimming **2.** GASTR vegetables **3.**(*renfort*) covering **4.** AUTO lining; ~ **de frein** brake lining
garrigue [gaʀig] *f* scrubland; (*dans le Midi*) garrigue (*heathland in Provence*)
garrot [gaʀo] *m* **1.** MED tourniquet **2.**(*partie du corps: d'un cheval*) withers
gars [gɑ] *m inf* lad; **salut les ~!** hi guys!
gas-oil, **gasoil** [gazwal] *m* diesel oil
gaspillage [gaspijaʒ] *m* waste
gaspiller [gaspije] <1> *vt* (*fortune*) to squander; (*eau, temps, talent*) to waste
gastéropodes [gasteʀɔpɔd] *mpl* gastropods
gastrique [gastʀik] *adj* **troubles ~s** stomach problems
gastroentérite [gastʀoɑ̃teʀit] *f* gastroenteritis
gastronome [gastʀɔnɔm] *mf* gourmet
gastronomie [gastʀɔnɔmi] *f* gastronomy
gastronomique [gastʀɔnɔmik] *adj* (*restaurant*) gourmet; (*guide*) food
gâté(e) [gɑte] *adj* **1.**(*capricieux*) **enfant** ~ spoilt child **2.**(*carié*) **dent ~e** bad tooth **3.**(*pourri*) **fruits ~s** fruit that's gone bad
gâteau [gɑto] <x> **I.** *m* cake; ~ **sec** biscuit *Brit,* cookie *Am;* ~ **de riz** rice pudding; ~ **au chocolat/à la crème** chocolate/cream cake; **faire un** ~ to make a cake ▶**c'est pas du ~!** *inf* it is not easy! **II.** *app inv, inf*(*maman, papa*) indulgent; **grand-mère** ~ doting grandmother
gâter [gɑte] <1> **I.** *vt* (*combler: personne*) to spoil ▶**nous sommes gâtés** just our luck; **cela ne gâte rien** that's no bad thing **II.** *vpr* **se** ~ (*viande*) to go off; (*fruits*) to spoil; (*choses, temps*) to turn bad; (*situation, ambiance*) to go sour
gâterie [gɑtʀi] *f* (*friandise*) treat; **apporter des ~s à qn** to bring sb some treats; **faire une ~ à qn** to give sb a treat
gâteux, **-euse** [gɑtø, -øz] **I.** *adj* **1.** *péj* (*sénile*) senile **2.**(*fou de*) besotted **II.** *m, f péj* senile old fool
GATT [gat] *m abr de* **General Agreement on Tariffs and Trade** GATT
gauche [goʃ] **I.** *adj* **1.**(*opp: droit*) left **2.**(*maladroit*) uneasy; (*geste*) jerky **II.** *m* **un crochet du** ~ a left hook **III.** *f* **1.** left; **à** ~ on the left; **à la** ~ **de qn** on sb's left; **sur la** ~ **de qc** on the left of sth; **tiroir de** ~ left drawer; **de** ~ **à droite** from left to right **2.** POL **la** ~ the Left; **idées/partis de** ~ left-wing ideas/parties
gauchement [goʃmɑ̃] *adv* clumsily
gaucher, **-ère** [goʃe, -ɛʀ] **I.** *adj* left-handed **II.** *m, f* left-hander, southpaw
gaucherie [goʃʀi] *f* awkwardness
gauchiste [goʃist] *mf* leftist
gaufre [gofʀ] *f* waffle
gaufrette [gofʀɛt] *f* wafer
gaufrier [gofʀije] *m* waffle iron
Gaule [gol] *f* **la** ~ Gaul
gaullisme [golism] *m* Gaullism
gaulliste [golist] *mf* Gaullist
gaulois(e) [golwa, waz] *adj* Gallic
Gaulois(e) [golwa, waz] *m(f)* Gaul
gauloiserie [golwazʀi] *f* **1.**(*propos*) ribald remark **2.**(*caractère*) bawdiness
gaver [gave] <1> **I.** *vt* **1.**(*engraisser: oie*) to force-feed **2.**(*bourrer*) ~ **qn de qc** to cram sb with sth **II.** *vpr* **se** ~ **de qc** to gorge oneself on sth
gavroche [gavʀɔʃ] *m* street urchin
gay [gɛ] **I.** *adj inv* gay **II.** *m* gay
gaz [gɑz] *m* **1.**(*vapeur invisible*) gas; ~ **lacrymogène** teargas; ~ **de combat** poison gas; ~ **d'échappement** exhaust fumes *pl;* ~ **de pétrole liquéfié** liquid petroleum gas **2.** *pl* (*flatulence*) wind; **avoir des** ~ to have wind
gaze [gɑz] *f* gauze
gazelle [gazɛl] *f* gazelle
gazer [gɑze] <1> *vt* to gas
gazeux, **-euse** [gɑzø, -øz] *adj* **1.**(*relatif au gaz*) gaseous **2.**(*qui contient du gaz*) sparkling
gazinière [gɑzinjɛʀ] *f* gas cooker
gazoduc [gɑzodyk] *m* gas pipeline
gazole [gazɔl] *m* diesel oil
gazon [gɑzɔ̃] *m* lawn
gazonné(e) [gazɔne] *adj* lawn-covered
gazouillement [gazujmɑ̃] *m* (*d'un bébé*)

gurgling; (*d'un oiseau*) chirping

gazouiller [gazuje] <1> *vi* (*bébé*) to gurgle; (*oiseau*) to chirp

gazouillis [gazuji] *m v.* **gazouillement**

GDF [ʒedeɛf] *abr de* **Gaz de France** *French national gas company*

geai [ʒɛ] *m* jay

géant(e) [ʒeɑ̃, -ɑ̃t] **I.** *adj* giant **II.** *m(f)* giant

geignard(e) [ʒɛɲaʀ, aʀd] **I.** *adj péj, inf* moaning; (*enfant*) whiny, whingeing *Brit* **II.** *m(f) péj, inf* moaner

geindre [ʒɛ̃dʀ] *vi irr* **1.** (*gémir*) to moan; ~ **de douleur** to moan with pain **2.** *péj, inf* (*pleurnicher*) to whine

geisha [gɛʃa, gɛjʃa] *f* geisha

gel [ʒɛl] *m* **1.** METEO ice **2.** (*blocage*) freeze; ~ **des salaires** salary freeze **3.** (*crème*) gel

gélatine [ʒelatin] *f* gelatine

gélatineux, -euse [ʒelatinø, -øz] *adj* gelatinous

gelée [ʒ(ə)le] *f* **1.** METEO frost **2.** GASTR jelly

geler [ʒ(ə)le] <4> **I.** *vt* to freeze; (*bourgeons*) to nip; **ce vent me gèle** this wind is freezing me **II.** *vi* **1.** METEO to freeze; (*rivière*) to freeze over; (*fleurs*) to be nipped; **la récolte a gelé** the harvest was ruined by frost **2.** (*avoir froid*) to be cold; **on gèle ici!** we're freezing in here!; **gelé** frozen **3.** *impers* **il gèle** it is freezing

gélule [ʒelyl] *f* capsule

Gémeaux [ʒemo] *mpl* Gemini; *v. a.* **Balance**

gémir [ʒemiʀ] <8> *vi* to moan; ~ **sur son sort** to bemoan one's fate

gémissant(e) [ʒemisɑ̃, ɑ̃t] *adj* **dire qc d'une voix ~e** to say sth with a moan

gémissement [ʒemismɑ̃] *m* moaning *no pl*

gênant(e) [ʒɛnɑ̃, ɑ̃t] *adj* irritating; (*question, situation*) embarassing

gencive [ʒɑ̃siv] *f* gum

gendarme [ʒɑ̃daʀm] *m* **1.** (*policier*) police officer; ~ **mobile** riot police officer **2.** *inf* (*personne autoritaire*) bossyboots *Brit* ►**jouer au(x) ~(s) et au(x) voleur(s)** to play cops and robbers

gendarmer [ʒɑ̃daʀme] <1> *vpr* **se ~ contre qn** to get angry with sb

gendarmerie [ʒɑ̃daʀməʀi] *f* **1.** (*corps militaire*) police force **2.** (*bâtiment*) police station

> The **gendarmerie** is a unit of the army with the function of a police force. There is a gendarmerie in every town.

gendre [ʒɑ̃dʀ] *m* son-in-law

gène [ʒɛn] *m* gene

gêne [ʒɛn] *f* **1.** (*malaise*) discomfort **2.** (*ennui*) **devenir une ~ pour qn** to become a problem for sb **3.** (*trouble*) trouble ►**être dans la ~** to have problems; **être sans ~** to be thoughtless

généalogie [ʒenealɔʒi] *f* genealogy; (*d'une personne*) ancestry

généalogique [ʒenealɔʒik] *adj* genealogical; **arbre ~** family tree

gêner [ʒene] <1> **I.** *vt* **1.** (*déranger*) to bother **2.** (*entraver: piétons*) to disrupt; **être gêné dans ses mouvements** to be restricted in one's movements **3.** (*mettre mal à l'aise*) to cause to feel ill at ease; **être gêné** to feel ill at ease; **ça gêne qn de faire qc/que qn fasse qc** (*subj*) sb feels uneasy about doing sth/sb doing sth; **ça me gêne de vous dire ça** I feel uneasy about telling you that **II.** *vpr* **1. se ~ pour** +*infin* to put oneself out to +*infin;* **ne pas se ~ pour dire qc** to say sth straight out; **ne vous gênez pas pour moi!** don't mind me!; **vas-y! ne te gêne pas!** *iron, inf* go right ahead! **2.** *Suisse* (*être intimidé, avoir honte*) **se ~** to feel awkward

général [ʒeneʀal, o] <-aux> *m* general; ~ **en chef** general-in-command; **oui mon ~!** yes, sir!

général(e) [ʒeneʀal, o] <-aux> *adj* **1.** (*commun, collectif*) general; **le conseil ~** departmental council; **en règle ~e** generally (speaking) **2.** (*vague*) vague **3.** (*qui embrasse l'ensemble*) **directeur ~** director general; **procureur ~** public prosecutor; **quartier ~** headquarters **4.** (*total*) **atteint de paralysie ~e** affected by overall paralysis ►**en ~** in general; **d'une façon ~e** generally; (*dans l'ensemble*) as a whole

générale [ʒeneʀal] *f* THEAT dress rehersal

généralement [ʒeneʀalmɑ̃] *adv* **1.** (*habituellement*) usually **2.** (*opp: en détail*) generally

généralisation [ʒeneʀalizasjɔ̃] *f* (*d'un conflit*) spread; (*d'une mesure*) generalization

généraliser [ʒeneʀalize] <1> **I.** *vt* **1.** (*rendre général*) to make general **2.** (*répandre: méthode, mesure*) to generalize **II.** *vpr* **se ~** (*procédé*) to become widespread; **le cancer s'est généralisé** the cancer has spread

généraliste [ʒeneʀalist] *adj* **médecin ~** general practitioner

généralité [ʒeneʀalite] *f gén pl* (*idées générales*) general points; *péj* generalities

générateur, -trice [ʒeneʀatœʀ, -tʀis] **I.** *adj* **~ de qc** generative of sth; **être ~ de richesse** to be wealth-creating **II.** *m, f* generator

génération [ʒeneʀasjɔ̃] *f* generation

générer [ʒeneʀe] <5> *vt* **1.** (*produire*) to produce **2.** INFOR to generate

généreusement [ʒeneʀøzmɑ̃] *adv* generously

généreux, -euse [ʒeneʀø, -øz] *adj* **1.** (*libéral*) generous **2.** (*riche: terre*) rich; (*vin*) generous **3.** *iron* (*plantureux: formes, poitrine*) ample; (*décolleté*) generous

générique [ʒeneʀik] **I.** *m* credits *pl* **II.** *adj* generic

générosité [ʒeneʀozite] *f* **1.** (*libéralité*) generosity **2.** (*magnanimité*) magnanimity **3.** *pl* (*cadeau*) kindnesses

genèse [ʒənɛz] *f* (*production*) genesis

Genèse [ʒənɛz] *f* REL **la ~** Genesis

genêt [ʒənɛ] *m* broom
généticien(**ne**) [ʒenetisjɛ̃, jɛn] *m(f)* geneticist
génétique [ʒenetik] **I.** *adj* genetic **II.** *f* genetics
gêneur, **-euse** [ʒɛnœʀ, -øz] *m, f* intruder
Genève [ʒ(ə)nɛv] Geneva
genevois [ʒənvwa] *m* Genevan; *v. a.* **français**
genevois(**e**) [ʒən(ə)vwa, -waz] *adj* Genevan
Genevois(**e**) [ʒən(ə)vwa, -waz] *m(f)* Genevan
génial(**e**) [ʒenjal, jo] <-aux> *adj* **1.** (*ingénieux*) inspired **2.** *inf* (*formidable*) great
génialement [ʒenjalmɑ̃] *adv* brilliantly
génie [ʒeni] *m* **1.** (*esprit*) genius; **avoir du ~** to have genius; **de ~** brilliant **2.** (*don*) **avoir le ~ de dire qc** to have the gift for saying sth **3.** HIST genie **4.** MIL Engineers *pl* **5.** (*art*) **~ civil/génétique** civil/genetic engineering
genièvre [ʒənjɛvʀ] *m* juniper
génique [ʒenik] *adj* gene
génisse [ʒenis] *f* heifer
génital(**e**) [ʒenital, o] <-aux> *adj* genital
génitif [ʒenitif] *m* genitive
génocide [ʒenɔsid] *m* genocide
génoise [ʒenwaz] *f* (*gâteau*) sponge cake
génothèque [ʒenɔtɛk] *f* (*banque de génotypes*) gene bank
genou [ʒ(ə)nu] <x> *m* knee; **sur les ~x de qn** on sb's knees; **à ~x** kneeling ►**être sur les ~x** *inf* to be ready to drop; **faire du ~ à qn** to play footsie with sb
genouillère [ʒənujɛʀ] *f* kneeler; MED knee support
genre [ʒɑ̃ʀ] *m* **1.** (*sorte*) type **2.** (*allure*) appearance **3.** ART genre; **~ dramatique/comique** dramatic/comic style **4.** (*espèce*) **~ humain** mankind **5.** LING gender ►**c'est pas le ~ de la maison** *iron, inf* that's not the way we do things here; **ça fait mauvais ~** that looks bad; **unique en son ~** one of a kind; **se donner un ~** to put on airs; **ce n'est pas mon ~** it is not my style; **ce n'est pas son ~** it is not like him/her; **de ce/du même ~** of this type/of the same type; **des trucs de ce ~** things like this; **en tout ~** [*o* **tous ~s**] of every kind
gens [ʒɑ̃] *mpl, fpl* people; **petites ~** people of modest means; **~ d'armes** men-at-arms; **~ de cœur** kind-hearted people; **~ de lettres** writers; **~ de maison** domestic servants; **~ du monde** society people
gent [ʒɑ̃(t)] *f iron* **la ~ féminine** the fairer sex
gentiane [ʒɑ̃sjan] *f* gentian
gentil(**le**) [ʒɑ̃ti, ij] *adj* **1.** (*aimable*) kind; **~ avec qn** kind to sb **2.** (*joli*) pretty **3.** (*sage*) good **4.** *iron* (*coquet*) **~le somme** tidy sum ►**c'est (bien) ~, mais …** *inf* that's all very well, but …
gentilhomme [ʒɑ̃tijɔm, ʒɑ̃tizɔm] <gentilshommes> *m* gentleman
gentillesse [ʒɑ̃tijɛs] *f* **1.** (*qualité*) kindness; **avoir la ~ de** *+infin* to be kind enough to *+infin* **2.** (*action, parole*) favour *Brit,* favor *Am*
gentiment [ʒɑ̃timɑ̃] *adv* **1.** (*aimablement*) kindly **2.** (*sagement*) clearly
gentleman [dʒɛntləman, ʒɑ̃tləman, -mɛn] <s *o* -men> *m* gentleman
géo [ʒeo] *f inf abr de* **géographie**
géode [ʒeɔd] *f* geode
géographe [ʒeɔgʀaf] *mf* georapher
géographie [ʒeɔgʀafi] *f* georaphy
géographique [ʒeɔgʀafik] *adj* georaphical
géologie [ʒeɔlɔʒi] *f* geology
géologique [ʒeɔlɔʒik] *adj* geological
géologue [ʒeɔlɔg] *mf* geologist
géomètre [ʒeɔmɛtʀ] *mf* surveyor
géométrie [ʒeɔmetʀi] *f* geometry; **~ dans l'espace** solid geometry
géométrique [ʒeɔmetʀik] *adj* geometric
géophysicien(**ne**) [ʒeofizisjɛ̃, jɛn] *m(f)* geophysicist
géopolitique [ʒeopɔlitik] *f* geopolitics + *vb sing*
Géorgie [ʒeɔʀʒi] *f* **la ~ (du Sud)** (South) Georgia
géothermique [ʒeotɛʀmik] *adj* geothermal
gérance [ʒeʀɑ̃s] *f* (*gestion*) management; **mettre/prendre qc en ~** to put sth under management/take over the management of sth
géranium [ʒeʀanjɔm] *m* geranium
gérant(**e**) [ʒeʀɑ̃, ɑ̃t] *m(f)* manager
gerbe [ʒɛʀb] *f* (*de blé*) sheaf; (*de fleurs, d'eau, d'écume*) spray; **déposer une ~ sur une tombe** to place a spray of flowers on a grave
gercé(**e**) [ʒɛʀse] *adj* chapped
gercer [ʒɛʀse] <2> *vi* to crack
gerçure [ʒɛʀsyʀ] *f* **avoir des ~s aux mains** to have chapped hands
gérer [ʒeʀe] <5> *vt* **1.** (*diriger*) to manage **2.** (*coordonner: crise*) to handle; (*temps libre*) to manage
gériatrie [ʒeʀjatʀi] *f* geriatrics + *vb sing*
Germain(**e**) [ʒɛʀmɛ̃, ɛn] *m(f)* German
germanique [ʒɛʀmanik] *adj* Germanic
germanisme [ʒɛʀmanism] *m* germanism
germaniste [ʒɛʀmanist] *mf* German scholar
germanophile [ʒɛʀmanɔfil] *adj* germanophile
germanophobe [ʒɛʀmanɔfɔb] *adj* germanophobe
germanophone [ʒɛʀmanɔfɔn] **I.** *adj* German-speaking; **être ~** to be a German-speaker **II.** *mf* German-speaker
germe [ʒɛʀm] *m* **1.** (*semence*) seed; **en ~** in embryo **2.** MED germ
germer [ʒɛʀme] <1> *vi* to sprout; (*idée, sentiment*) to form
germination [ʒɛʀminasjɔ̃] *f a.* BOT germination
gérondif [ʒeʀɔ̃dif] *m* gerund
gérontologie [ʒeʀɔ̃tɔlɔʒi] *f* gerontology
gésier [ʒezje] *m* gizzard; **salade de ~s** salad

with chicken gizzards

gestation [ʒɛstasjɔ̃] *f* **1.** (*grossesse*) gestation **2.** (*genèse*) preparation; **être en** ~ to be in gestation

geste [ʒɛst] *m* **1.** (*mouvement*) gesture; ~ **de la main** wave of the hand **2.** (*action*) act; ~ **d'amour** gesture of love ►**joindre le** ~ **à la parole** to match one's actions to one's words; **faire un** ~ to make a gesture; **il n'a pas fait un** ~ **pour m'aider** he didn't lift a finger to help me

gesticuler [ʒɛstikyle] <1> *vi* to gesticulate

gestion [ʒɛstjɔ̃] *f* management; ~ **d'entreprise** business management

gestionnaire [ʒɛstjɔnɛʀ] **I.** *mf* management **II.** *m* INFOR ~ **d'imprimante** printer driver; ~ **de fichiers** file manager

gestuel(le) [ʒɛstɥɛl] *adj* gestural

geyser [ʒɛzɛʀ] *m* (*source*) geyser

Ghana [gana] *m* **le** ~ Ghana

ghanéen(ne) [ganeɛ̃, ɛn] *adj* Ghanaian

Ghanéen(ne) [ganeɛ̃, ɛn] *m(f)* Ghanaian

ghetto [geto] *m* ghetto

gibet [ʒibɛ] *m* gibbet

gibier [ʒibje] *m* **1.** (*animaux de chasse*) game; **gros** ~ large game **2.** *fig* ~ **de potence** gallows bird

giboulée [ʒibule] *f* sudden shower

giclée [ʒikle] *f* (*d'encre*) squirt; (*de vapeur*) spurt

gicler [ʒikle] <1> **I.** *vi* (*eau*) to squirt; (*boue*) to spurt **II.** *vt Suisse* (*asperger, éclabousser*) to splash

gicleur [ʒiklœʀ] *m* jet

gifle [ʒifl] *f* slap

gifler [ʒifle] <1> *vt* **1.** (*battre*) to slap **2.** (*fouetter*) **la pluie me giflait la figure** the rain lashed my face

gigantesque [ʒigɑ̃tɛsk] *adj* gigantic

giga-octet [ʒigaɔktɛ] <giga-octets> *m* gigabyte

GIGN [ʒeiʒeɛn] *m abr de* **Groupe d'intervention de la gendarmerie nationale** *special arm of the French police force*

gigolo [ʒigɔlo] *m péj* gigolo

gigot [ʒigo] *m* leg

gigoter [ʒigɔte] <1> *vi inf* to wriggle about

gilet [ʒilɛ] *m* **1.** (*vêtement sans manches*) waistcoat *Brit,* vest *Am;* ~ **de sauvetage** life jacket; ~ **pare-balles** bullet-proof jacket *Brit,* bullet-proof vest *Am* **2.** (*lainage*) cardigan

gin [dʒin] *m* gin

gingembre [ʒɛ̃ʒɑ̃bʀ] *m* ginger

gingivite [ʒɛ̃ʒivit] *f* gingivitis

girafe [ʒiʀaf] *f* giraffe

giratoire [ʒiʀatwaʀ] *adj* **sens** ~ roundabout

girl [gœʀl] *f* show girl

girofle [ʒiʀɔfl] *m v.* **clou**

giroflée [ʒiʀɔfle] *f* wallflower

girolle [ʒiʀɔl] *f* chanterelle

giron [ʒiʀɔ̃] *m* lap ►**pleurer dans le** ~ **de qn** *inf* to cry on sb's shoulder

girouette [ʒiʀwɛt] *f* **1.** (*plaque placée au sommet d'un édifice*) weather vane **2.** *inf* (*personne*) waverer

gisant [ʒizɑ̃] *m* ART recumbent figure (*on a tomb*)

gisement [ʒizmɑ̃] *m* deposit

gitan(e) [ʒitɑ̃, an] *m(f)* gypsy

gîte [ʒit] *m* shelter; ~ **rural** self-catering cottage *Brit;* ~ **d'étape** lodge

givrant(e) [ʒivʀɑ̃, ɑ̃t] *adj* freezing

givre [ʒivʀ] *m* frost

givré(e) [ʒivʀe] *adj* **1.** (*couvert de givre*) covered in frost; (*fenêtre*) frosted **2.** *inf* (*fou*) **être** ~ to be mad [*o* crazy]

glabre [glɑbʀ] *adj* clean-shaven

glace [glas] *f* **1.** (*eau congelée*) ice; **pont de** ~ *Québec* (*chemin de glace formé dans un cours d'eau, l'hiver, et utilisé pour passer en voiture d'une rive à l'autre*) ice bridge **2.** GASTR ice-cream; ~ **à la fraise/au chocolat** strawberry/chocolate ice-cream **3.** (*miroir*) mirror **4.** (*vitre*) plate glass ►**rompre la** ~ to break the ice

glacé(e) [glase] *adj* **1.** (*très froid*) freezing; (*personne*) frozen **2.** GASTR (*fruit, marrons*) glacé; (*gâteau*) iced; **café/chocolat** ~ iced coffee/chocolate; **servir** ~ to serve ice-cold **3.** (*recouvert d'un apprêt brillant*) **papier** ~ gloss paper **4.** (*inamical: accueil, regard*) icy

glacer [glase] <2> **I.** *vt* **1.** (*refroidir*) to ice **2.** (*impressionner*) to chill **II.** *vpr* **se** ~ to freeze

glaciaire [glasjɛʀ] *adj* ice

glacial(e) [glasjal, jo] <s *o* -aux> *adj* **1.** (*très froid*) freezing **2.** (*inamical*) icy

glaciation [glasjasjɔ̃] *f* glaciation

glacier [glasje] *m* **1.** GEO glacier **2.** (*métier*) ice-cream maker

glacière [glasjɛʀ] *f* **1.** (*coffre*) cool-box *Brit,* cooler *Am* **2.** *inf* (*lieu*) fridge

glaçon [glasɔ̃] *m* **1.** (*petit cube*) ice cube **2.** *inf* (*personne*) cold fish **3.** *pl* (*pieds, mains*) blocks of ice

gladiateur [gladjatœʀ] *m* gladiator

glaïeul [glajœl] *m* gladiolus

glaise [glɛz] *f* clay

glaive [glɛv] *m* two-edged sword

gland [glɑ̃] *m* acorn

glande [glɑ̃d] *f* gland

glander [glɑ̃de] <1> *vi inf* to mess about *Brit,* to screw around *Am*

glandeur, -euse [glɑ̃dœʀ, -øz] *m, f inf* layabout

glaner [glane] <1> *vt* to glean

glapir [glapiʀ] <8> *vi* to yap

glapissement [glapismɑ̃] *m* (*du renard*) bark; (*du chiot*) yap; (*du lapin, d'une personne*) squeal

glas [glɑ] *m* **1.** (*tintement*) toll; **sonner le** ~ to toll the bell **2.** *fig* **sonner le** ~ **de qc** to sound the knell of sth

Glasgow [glasgo] Glasgow; **habitant de** ~ Glaswegian

glauque [glok] *adj* **1.** (*verdâtre*) blue-green

G

2. (*lugubre*) dreary
glissade [glisad] *f* **1.** (*action de glisser par jeu*) slide **2.** (*dérapage accidentel*) slip; **attention aux ~s!** be careful not to slip!
glissant(e) [glisɑ̃, ɑ̃t] *adj* **1.** (*qui glisse*) slippery; **chaussée ~e!** slippery surface! **2.** (*dangereux*) dangerous
glisse [glis] *f* **1.** (*aptitude à glisser*) glide **2.** *Suisse* (*traîneau, luge*) sled
glissement [glismɑ̃] *m* ~ **de terrain** landslide
glisser [glise] <1> **I.** *vi* **1.** (*être glissant*) to be slippery **2.** (*se déplacer*) ~ **sur l'eau/sur la neige** to glide over the water/snow; ~ **dans l'eau** to slip into the water; **faire** ~ **qc sur la glace** to make sth slide across the ice **3.** (*tomber*) ~ (**le long**) **de qc** to slip along sth; **se laisser** ~ to slide **4.** (*déraper*) to skid; ~ **sur le verglas** to slip on the black ice; (*véhicule*) to skid on the black ice **5.** (*échapper de*) **ça m'a glissé des mains** it slipped out of my hands **6.** (*ne faire qu'une impression faible*) ~ **sur qn** (*critique, remarque*) to wash over sb **II.** *vt* to slide; (*regard*) to sneak; ~ **qc à qn** to slip sth to sb; (*dire*) to mention sth to sb **III.** *vpr* **1.** (*pénétrer*) **se** ~ **dans la maison** to slip into the house **2.** (*s'insinuer*) **se** ~ **dans qc** to creep into sth
glissière [glisjɛʀ] *f* ~ **de sécurité** crash barrier
global(e) [glɔbal, o] <-aux> *adj* global; (*somme*) total
globalement [glɔbalmɑ̃] *adv* globally
globalité [glɔbalite] *f* global nature
globe [glɔb] *m* globe; ~ **oculaire** eyeball
globe-trotter [glɔbtʀɔtœʀ, -tʀɔtɛʀ] <globe-trotters> *mf* globetrotter
globule [glɔbyl] *m* globule
globuleux, -euse [glɔbylø, -øz] *adj* (*yeux*) protruding
gloire [glwaʀ] *f* **1.** (*célébrité*) fame **2.** (*mérite*) distinction **3.** (*personne*) celebrity ►**à la** ~ **de qn/qc** in praise of sb/sth; **pour la** ~ for the sake of glory
glorieux, -euse [glɔʀjø, -jøz] *adj* glorious
glorification [glɔʀifikasjɔ̃] *f* glorification
glorifier [glɔʀifje] <1> **I.** *vt* to glorify **II.** *vpr* **se** ~ **de qc** to glory in sth
gloriole [glɔʀjɔl] *f* misplaced vanity
glossaire [glɔsɛʀ] *m* glossary
glotte [glɔt] *f* glottis
glouglou [gluglu] *m inf* **faire** ~ to gurgle
gloussement [glusmɑ̃] *m* **1.** (*cri*) cluck **2.** *inf* (*rire*) chuckle
glousser [gluse] <1> *vi* **1.** (*pousser des gloussements: poule*) to cluck **2.** *inf* (*rire: personne*) to chuckle
glouton(ne) [glutɔ̃, ɔn] **I.** *adj* greedy **II.** *m(f)* glutton
gloutonnerie [glutɔnʀi] *f* gluttony
glu [gly] *f* **1.** (*colle*) birdlime **2.** *inf* (*personne*) leech
gluant(e) [glyɑ̃, ɑ̃t] *adj* sticky
glucide [glysid] *m* carbohydrate
glucose [glykoz] *m* glucose
gluten [glytɛn] *m* gluten
glycémie [glisemi] *f* glycaemia *Brit,* glycemia *Am*
glycine [glisin] *f* wisteria
GMT [ʒeɛmte] *abr de* **Greenwich Mean Time** GMT
gnangnan [ɲɑ̃ɲɑ̃] *adj inv, inf* **être** ~ (*personne*) to be a wimp; (*musique, histoire*) to be soppy
gnôle [ɲol] *f inf* hooch
gnon [ɲɔ̃] *m inf* bash
go [go] **tout de** ~ *inf* without hesitating
Go *abr de* **giga-octet** GB
GO [ʒeo] *fpl abr de* **grandes ondes** LW
gobelet [gɔblɛ] *m* beaker
gober [gɔbe] <1> *vt* **1.** (*avaler en aspirant: huître, œuf*) to swallow whole **2.** *inf* (*croire*) to swallow
goberger [gɔbɛʀʒe] <2a> *vpr inf* **se** ~ **1.** (*faire bonne chère*) to live it up **2.** (*se prélasser*) to laze around
godasse [gɔdas] *f inf* shoe
godemiché [gɔdmiˌschˌe] *m* dildo
godet [gɔdɛ] *m* **1.** (*gobelet*) beaker **2.** (*pour la peinture*) pot **3.** *inf* (*verre*) jar; **tu viens boire un ~?** are you coming for a drink?, are you coming for a jar? *Brit* **4.** TECH (*d'une pelleteuse mécanique*) bucket; **excavateur à ~s** digger **5.** COUT gore; **une jupe à ~s** a gored dress
godiche [gɔdiʃ] *adj inf* lumpish
godille [gɔdij] *f* scull ►**à la** ~ crummy
godiller [gɔdije] <1> *vi* **1.** NAUT to scull **2.** (*en ski*) to wedeln
goéland [gɔelɑ̃] *m* seagull
goélette [gɔelɛt] *f* schooner
goémon [gɔemɔ̃] *m* wrack
gogo [gogo] **à** ~ *inf* plenty of
goguenard(e) [gɔg(ə)naʀ, aʀd] *adj* mocking
goinfre [gwɛ̃fʀ] **I.** *adj* piggish **II.** *mf péj* greedy pig
goinfrer [gwɛ̃fʀe] <1> *vpr péj, inf* **se** ~ **de qc** to pig out on sth
goinfrerie [gwɛ̃fʀəʀi] *f péj* piggery
goitre [gwatʀ] *m* goitre *Brit,* goiter *Am*
golf [gɔlf] *m* golf; (*terrain*) golf course
golfe [gɔlf] *m* gulf
Golfe de Gascogne *m* **le** ~ Bay of Biscay
Golfe du Lion *m* **le** ~ Gulf of Lions
golfeur, -euse [gɔlfœʀ, -øz] *m, f* golfer
gominer [gɔmine] <1> *vpr* **se** ~ to put on hair gel
gomme [gɔm] *f* **1.** (*bloc de caoutchouc*) rubber *Brit,* eraser *Am* **2.** (*substance*) gum ►**mettre la** ~ *inf* to put one's foot hard down *Brit,* to floor it *Am*
gommé(e) [gɔme] *adj* gummed
gommer [gɔme] <1> *vt* to rub out; (*de sa mémoire*) to erase
gommette [gɔmɛt] *f* sticker

gond [gɔ̃] *m* hinge ▶**sortir de ses ~s** to fly off the handle
gondole [gɔ̃dɔl] *f* gondola
gondoler [gɔ̃dɔle] <1> *vi* to crinkle; (*planche*) to warp
gondolier, **-ière** [gɔ̃dɔlje, -jɛʀ] *m, f* gondolier
gonflable [gɔ̃flabl] *adj* inflatable
gonflage [gɔ̃flaʒ] *m* (*des pneus*) inflation; (*d'un ballon*) blowing up
gonflé(e) [gɔ̃fle] *adj* **1.** (*rempli*) swollen; (*yeux, visage*) puffy **2.** *inf* (*culotté*) cheeky
gonflement [gɔ̃fləmɑ̃] *m* **1.** (*d'un pneu*) inflation; (*d'un ballon*) blowing up; (*d'une plaie, d'un organe, du visage*) swelling; **provoquer un ~ du visage** to cause facial swelling **2.** (*augmentation: des effectifs*) expansion; (*de l'épargne*) build-up; **~ du crédit** pumping up credit **3.** (*surestimation: d'une facture, note de frais*) inflation; (*d'un incident*) exaggeration
gonfler [gɔ̃fle] <1> **I.** *vt* (*pneus*) to inflate; (*ballon*) to blow up; (*voiles*) to fill; **~ les poumons** to fill one's lungs **II.** *vi* to swell; (*pâte*) to rise **III.** *vpr* **se ~** (*poitrine*) to expand; (*voiles*) to fill
gonfleur [gɔ̃flœʀ] *m* (air) pump
gong [gɔ̃(g)] *m* gong; **coup de ~** bang on the gong
gonzesse [gɔ̃zɛs] *f péj, inf* chick, bird *Brit*
goret [gɔʀɛ] *m* **1.** (*porcelet*) piglet **2.** (*enfant sale*) dirty little pig
gorge [gɔʀʒ] *f* **1.** (*partie du cou*) throat **2.** GEO gorge ▶**faire des ~s chaudes de qc** *inf* to scorn sth; **à ~ déployée** at the top of one's voice; **avoir la ~ nouée** [*o* **serrée**] to have a lump in one's throat; **prendre qn à la ~** (*fumée*) to get in sb's throat; (*odeur*) to get in sb's nose; (*émouvoir*) to give sb a lump in his/her throat; (*financièrement*) to put a gun to sb's head; **rester à qn en travers de la ~** to stick in sb's throat
gorgé(e) [gɔʀʒe] *adj* **fruits ~s de soleil** sun-kissed fruit; **terre ~e d'eau** earth saturated with water
gorgée [gɔʀʒe] *f* mouthful
gorger [gɔʀʒe] <2a> *vpr soutenu* (*se gaver*) **se ~ de qc** to gorge oneself on sth
gorille [gɔʀij] *m* gorilla
gosette [gozɛt] *f Belgique* (*chausson aux fruits*) turnover
gosier [gozje] *m* throat
gosse [gɔs] *mf inf* kid; **sale ~** brat ▶**être beau ~** to be good-looking
gothique [gɔtik] **I.** *adj* Gothic **II.** *m* Gothic
gouache [gwaʃ] *f* gouache, poster paint
gouailleur, **-euse** [gwajœʀ, -øz] *adj inf* cheeky
gouda [guda] *m* gouda
goudron [gudʀɔ̃] *m* tar
goudronné(e) [gudʀɔne] *adj* tarred
goudronner [gudʀɔne] <1> *vt* to tar
goudronneuse [gudʀɔnøz] *f* tar spreader
gouffre [gufʀ] *m* **1.** (*abîme*) abyss **2.** (*chose ruineuse*) bottomless pit
gouine [gwin] *f péj, inf* dyke
goujat [guʒa] *m* boor
goujon [guʒɔ̃] *m* gudgeon ▶**taquiner le ~** *inf* to do some fishing
goulache [gulaʃ] *m o f* goulash
goulafre [gulafʀ] *m Belgique, Nord* (*goinfre, glouton*) guzzler
goulet [gulɛ] *m* **~ d'étranglement** bottleneck
goulot [gulo] *m* **1.** (*col d'une bouteille*) neck; **boire au ~** to drink from the bottle **2.** (*goulet*) **~ d'étranglement** bottleneck
goulu(e) [guly] *adj* greedy
goulûment [gulymɑ̃] *adv* greedily
goupiller [gupije] <1> **I.** *vt inf* to fix; **bien ~ son coup** to fix things nicely for oneself **II.** *vpr inf* **bien/mal se ~** to come off/not come off
goupillon [gupijɔ̃] *m* **1.** REL aspergillum **2.** (*brosse*) bottle brush
gourd(e) [guʀ, guʀd] *adj* numb
gourde [guʀd] *f* **1.** (*bouteille*) flask **2.** *inf* (*personne*) clot
gourdin [guʀdɛ̃] *m* club
gourer [guʀe] *vpr inf* **se ~ de qc** to get sth wrong
gourmand(e) [guʀmɑ̃, ɑ̃d] **I.** *adj* **être ~** to be greedy; **être ~ de sucreries** to have a sweet tooth **II.** *m(f)* gourmand; (*de sucreries*) a person with a sweet tooth
gourmandise [guʀmɑ̃diz] *f* fondness for good food; (*défaut*) greediness; **manger par/avec ~** to eat for the pleasure of eating
gourmet [guʀmɛ] *m* gourmet
gourmette [guʀmɛt] *f* chain bracelet
gourou [guʀu] *m* guru
gousse [gus] *f* **~ de vanille** vanilla pod; **~ d'ail** garlic clove
goût [gu] *m* **1.** *sans pl* (*sens, saveur, jugement*) taste; **être sans ~** to be tasteless; **avoir un ~ de qc** to taste of sth; **avoir bon ~** (*plat*) to taste good; (*personne*) to have good taste; **être de mauvais ~** to be in bad taste; **trouver qn/qc à son ~** to find sb/sth to one's taste; **une femme de ~** a woman of taste; **avec ~** tastefully **2.** *sans pl* (*envie*) inclination; **par ~** from inclination; **~ de vivre** enjoyment of life; **~ d'écrire** passion for writing; **prendre ~ à qc** to get a taste for sth; **reprendre ~ à qc** to start to enjoy sth again; **ne plus avoir ~ à rien** to not want to do anything **3.** *sans pl* (*penchant*) **~ pour les maths** gift for maths *Brit*, gift for math *Am;* **~ pour la boisson** taste for drink; **~ du risque** liking for risk **4.** *pl* (*préférences*) taste; **avoir des ~s de luxe** to have expensive taste **5.** (*avis*) **à mon ~** in my opinion ▶**être au ~ du jour** to be in fashion; **tous les ~s sont dans la nature** *prov* it take all sorts to make a world; **chacun ses ~s** *prov* to each his own
goûter [gute] <1> **I.** *vi* **1.** (*prendre le goûter: enfant*) to have an afternoon snack

2. (*essayer*) ~ **à qc** to try sth **3.** (*toucher*) ~ **aux plaisirs de la vie** to sample life's pleasures **4.** *Belgique, Québec* (*plaire par le goût*) to be tasty **II.** *vt* **1.** (*essayer*) to try **2.** (*savourer*) to savour *Brit,* to savor *Am* **3.** *Belgique, Québec* (*avoir le goût de*) ~ **qc** to taste of sth **III.** *m* afternoon snack

> When primary school children come home at 4.30 p.m., they have a **goûter**, or a small snack. Usually, it consists of fruit juice or hot chocolate and a cake or pastry.

goutte [gut] *f* drop; ~ **à** ~ drop by drop; **avoir la** ~ **au nez** *inf* to have a runny nose ▶**c'est la** ~ **d'eau qui fait déborder le vase** *prov* it's the straw that breaks the camel's back; **c'est une** ~ **d'eau dans la mer** it's a drop in the ocean; **se ressembler comme deux** ~**s d'eau** to be like two peas in a pod; **passer entre les** ~**s** to come out unscathed
goutte-à-goutte [gutagut] *m inv* drip
gouttelette [gutlɛt] *f* tiny drop
goutter [gute] <1> *vi* to drip; (*canalisation*) to leak; **le toit/le plafond goutte** the roof/ceiling is leaking
gouttière [gutjɛʀ] *f* gutter
gouvernable [guvɛʀnabl] *adj* governable
gouvernail [guvɛʀnaj] *m* **1.** (*barre*) helm **2.** *fig* **tenir le** ~ to be at the helm
gouvernante [guvɛʀnɑ̃t] *f* **1.** (*bonne*) housekeeper **2.** (*préceptrice*) governess
gouvernants [guvɛʀnɑ̃] *mpl* rulers
gouverne [guvɛʀn] *f* **pour ta** ~ for your guidance
gouvernement [guvɛʀnəmɑ̃] *m* government; **entrer/être au** ~ to join/be in the government
gouvernemental(e) [guvɛʀnəmɑ̃tal, o] <-aux> *adj* (*journal*) pro-government; (*parti, politique*) governing
gouverner [guvɛʀne] <1> **I.** *vi* to govern **II.** *vt* **1.** (*diriger*) to govern **2.** (*maîtriser*) to control
gouverneur [guvɛʀnœʀ] *m* governor
goyave [gɔjav] *f* guava
GPL [ʒepeɛl] *m abr de* **gaz de pétrole liquéfié** L.P.G.
GR [ʒeɛʀ] *m abr de* (**sentier de**) **grande randonnée** *main hiking route*
grabat [gʀaba] *m* pallet
grabataire [gʀabatɛʀ] **I.** *adj* bedridden **II.** *mf* invalid (*bedridden*)
grabuge [gʀabyʒ] *m inf* **faire du** ~ to create havoc; **il y a du** ~ there is chaos
grâce [gʀɑs] *f* **1.** *sans pl* (*charme*) grace; **avoir de la** ~ to be graceful; **avec** ~ gracefully; (*parler*) charmingly **2.** *sans pl* (*faveur*) favour *Brit,* favor *Am;* **trouver** ~ **aux yeux de qn** to find favour with sb **3.** *sans pl* (*clémence*) mercy; **crier/demander** ~ to cry/beg for mercy **4.** JUR pardon ▶**à la** ~ **de Dieu** it's in God's hands; **faire qc de bonne/mauvaise** ~ to do sth with good/bad grace; **faire** ~ **à qn de qc** to spare sb sth; ~ **à qn/qc** thanks to sb/sth

> Whenever a new President of the Republic is elected, he announces a short period of **grâce** and often shortens the prison sentences of youths or gives an "amnistie" on traffic fines given on a particular day.

gracier [gʀasje] <1> *vt* to pardon
gracieusement [gʀasjøzmɑ̃] *adv* **1.** (*charmant*) charmingly **2.** (*gratuitement*) free of charge
gracieux, -euse [gʀasjø, -jøz] *adj* **1.** (*charmant*) charming **2.** (*aimable*) kindly **3.** (*gratuit*) free of charge
gradation [gʀadasjɔ̃] *f* gradation
grade [gʀad] *m* grade; UNIV status; (*de capitaine*) rank; **monter en** ~ to be promoted ▶**en prendre pour son** ~ *inf* to be hauled over the coals
gradé(e) [gʀade] *m(f)* officer
gradins [gʀadɛ̃] *mpl* terraces
graduation [gʀadɥasjɔ̃] *f* gradation
gradué(e) [gʀadɥe] *adj* **1.** graduated; **verre** ~ measuring jug **2.** (*progressif*) graded
graduel(le) [gʀadɥɛl] *adj* gradual
graduellement [gʀadɥɛlmɑ̃] *adv* gradually
graduer [gʀadɥe] <1> *vt* **1.** (*augmenter graduellement*) to increase in difficulty; **les difficultés sont graduées** there are graded levels of difficulty **2.** (*diviser en degrés*) to graduate
graffiti [gʀafiti] <(s)> *m* graffiti
graillon [gʀɑjɔ̃] *m* **1.** bit of burnt fat; **sentir le** ~ to smell of frying **2.** *inf* (*crachat*) gob
grain [gʀɛ̃] *m* **1.** *sing o pl* (*petite chose arrondie*) spot; ~ **de beauté** beauty spot **2.** (*graine*) grain; (*d'une grenade*) seed; ~ **de café** coffee bean; ~ **de poivre** peppercorn; ~ **de moutarde** mustard seed; ~ **de cassis** blackcurrant; ~ **de raisin** grape **3.** (*particule*) speck; ~ **de poussière** speck of dust **4.** (*texture*) texture; (*d'un cuir*) grain **5.** *sans pl* (*petite quantité*) touch **6.** METEO heavy shower ▶~ **de sable** grain of sand; **mettre son** ~ **de sel** *inf* to stick one's oar in; **veiller au** ~ to keep an eye out for trouble
graine [gʀɛn] *f* seed ▶**c'est de la de voyou** he has the makings of a hooligan; **être de la mauvaise** ~ to be a bad lot; **casser la** ~ *inf* to have a bite to eat; **monter en** ~ (*plante*) to run to seed; *inf* (*enfant*) to shoot up; **en prendre de la** ~ *inf* to take a leaf out of his/her book
grainetier, -ière [gʀɛntje, -jɛʀ] *m, f* seed merchant
graisse [gʀɛs] *f* **1.** (*matière grasse*) fat **2.** (*lubrifiant*) grease
graisser [gʀese] <1> *vt* to grease
graisseux, -euse [gʀɛsø, -øz] *adj* greasy; (*cahier, nappe*) grease-stained
graminées [gʀamine] *fpl* grasses

grammaire [gʀa(m)mɛʀ] *f* grammar
grammatical(**e**) [gʀamatikal, o] <-aux> *adj* (*analyse*) grammatical; (*exercice*) grammar
grammaticalement [gʀamatikalmɑ̃] *adv* grammatically
gramme [gʀam] *m* gram ►**ne pas avoir un ~ de bon sens** [*o* **de jugeote**] *inf* not to have an ounce of common sense
grand(**e**) [gʀɑ̃, ɑ̃d] **I.** *adj* **1.** (*dont la taille dépasse la moyenne*) big; (*arbre*) tall; (*jambe, avenue*) long; (*format, entreprise*) large; **~ magasin** department store **2.** (*extrême, fameux*) great; (*buveur, fumeur*) heavy; (*travailleur*) hard; (*collectionneur*) great; **être un ~ malade/invalide** to be seriously ill/disabled; **être un ~ brûlé/blessé** to be badly burned/injured; **faire un ~ froid** to be very cold **3.** (*intense*) great; (*bruit, cri*) loud; (*vent*) strong; (*coup*) hard; (*soupir*) heavy; **avoir ~ besoin de** to be badly in need of **4.** (*respectable: dame, monsieur*) great; **~es écoles** *France's prestigious graduate level schools* **5.** (*généreux: sentiment*) noble **6.** (*exagéré: mots*) big; (*gestes*) sweeping; **faire de ~es phrases** to make high-flown speeches; **prendre de ~s airs** to take on airs **II.** *adv* **ouvrir tout ~ qc** to open sth wide; **voir ~** to things on a large scale **III.** *m(f)* **1.** (*personne/objet grands*) big person/thing **2.** (*personne importante*) **un ~ du football** a football legend

> The **grandes écoles** are prestigious higher education establishments with a tough selection process following a two-year university or preparatory course (classes préparatoires). They include the Ecole Polytechnique and l'Ecole Centrale, which train engineers, or l'Ecole des Hautes Etudes commerciales (HEC) which teaches management and economics. Graduates usually achieve high positions in business or goverment.

grand-angle [gʀɑ̃tɑ̃gl] <grands-angles> *m* wide-angle lens **grand-chose** [gʀɑ̃ʃoz] **pas ~** not much **grand-duc** [gʀɑ̃dyk] <grands-ducs> *m* grand duke **grand-ducal**(**e**) [gʀɑ̃dykal, o] <-aux> *adj Belgique* (*du grand-duché de Luxembourg, luxembourgeois*) grand-ducal **grand-duché** [gʀɑ̃dyʃe] <grands-duchés> *m* grand duchy
Grande-Bretagne [gʀɑ̃dbʀətaɲ] *f* **la ~** Great Britain
grandement [gʀɑ̃dmɑ̃] *adv* greatly; (*avoir raison*) absolutely
grandeur [gʀɑ̃dœʀ] *f* **1.** (*dimension*) size; **être de la ~ de qc** to be the size of sth; **de quelle ~ est ...?** how big is ...?; **de même ~** of the same size; **~ nature** life-size **2.** (*puissance*) greatness **3.** (*générosité*) generosity; **~ d'âme** big-heartedness
grandiloquence [gʀɑ̃dilɔkɑ̃s] *f* bombast
grandiloquent(**e**) [gʀɑ̃dilɔkɑ̃, ɑ̃t] *adj* bombastic
grandiose [gʀɑ̃djoz] *adj* imposing
grandir [gʀɑ̃diʀ] <8> **I.** *vi* **1.** (*devenir plus grand*) to grow; **~ de dix centimètres** to grow ten centimetres *Brit*, to grow ten centimeters *Am* **2.** (*devenir plus mûr*) to grow up **3.** (*augmenter*) to increase; (*foule*) to get bigger; **l'obscurité grandit** the darkness grew deeper **4.** *fig* **~ en sagesse** to become wiser; **sortir grandi de qc** to come out of sth a better person **II.** *vt* **1.** (*rendre plus grand: personne*) to make taller; (*chose*) to make bigger **2.** (*ennoblir*) **qc grandit qn** sth make sb a better person **III.** *vpr* **1.** (*se rendre plus grand*) **se ~** to get bigger **2.** (*s'élever*) **se ~ par qc** to grow up through sth
grand-mère [gʀɑ̃mɛʀ] <grand(s)-mères> *f* grandmother **grand-oncle** [gʀɑ̃tɔ̃kl] <grands-oncles> *m* great-uncle **grand-peine** [gʀɑ̃pɛn] **avoir ~ à faire qc** to have great difficulty in doing sth; **à ~** with great difficulty **grand-père** [gʀɑ̃pɛʀ] <grands-pères> *m* grandfather **grand-rue** [gʀɑ̃ʀy] <grand-rues> *f* high street *Brit*, main street *Am* **grands-parents** [gʀɑ̃paʀɑ̃] *mpl* grandparents **grand-tante** [gʀɑ̃tɑ̃t] <grands-tantes> *f* great-aunt
grange [gʀɑ̃ʒ] *f* barn
granit(**e**) [gʀanit] *m* granite
granitique [gʀanitik] *adj* granite
granulé [gʀanyle] *m* granule
granulé(**e**) [gʀanyle] *adj* granular
granuleux, **-euse** [gʀanylø, -øz] *adj* granular; (*cuir*) textured; (*peau, roche*) grainy
graphie [gʀafi] *f* written form
graphique [gʀafik] **I.** *adj* graphic **II.** *m* graph
graphisme [gʀafism] *m* **1.** (*écriture*) handwriting **2.** (*aspect d'une lettre*) script **3.** ART graphics; (*d'un artiste*) drawing style
graphiste [gʀafist] *mf* graphic designer
graphite [gʀafit] *m* graphite
graphologie [gʀafɔlɔʒi] *f sans pl* graphology
graphologue [gʀafɔlɔg] *mf* graphologist
grappe [gʀap] *f* cluster; **~ de raisin** bunch of grapes
grappiller [gʀapije] <1> *vt* **1.** (*cueillir: fruits, fleurs*) to pick **2.** (*prendre au hasard: nouvelles, idées*) to pick up; (*argent*) to get together
grappin [gʀapɛ̃] *m* **mettre le ~ sur qn** *inf* to grab sb
gras [gʀɑ] **I.** *m* **1.** GASTR fat **2.** (*graisse*) grease **3.** (*partie charnue: de la jambe*) fleshy part **II.** *adv* coarsely
gras(**se**) [gʀɑ, gʀɑs] *adj* **1.** (*formé de graisse*) fatty; **40% de matières ~ses** 40% fat; **corps ~** glyceride **2.** (*gros*) fat **3.** (*graisseux*) greasy; (*chaussée*) slippery; (*terre, boue*) slimy **4.** (*imprimé*) **en** (**caractère**) **~** in bold **5.** BOT **plante ~se** succulent **6.** (*épais:*

G

voix) deep; (*rire*) throaty; (*toux*) loose
grassement [gRasmɑ̃] *adv* (*payer*) generously
grassouillet(te) [gRasujɛ, jɛt] *adj inf* plump
gratifiant(e) [gRatifjɑ̃, jɑ̃t] *adj* (*travail*) rewarding; **effet** ~ gratifying effect
gratification [gRatifikasjɔ̃] *f* bonus
gratifier [gRatifje] <1> *vt* ~ **qn d'une récompense** to give sb a reward; ~ **qn d'un sourire** to reward sb with a smile
gratin [gRatɛ̃] *m* **1.** GASTR gratin **2.** *sans pl, inf* (*haute société*) upper crust
gratiné(e) [gRatine] *adj* **1.** GASTR au gratin **2.** *inf* (*extraordinaire: raclée*) harsh; (*aventure*) wild
gratiner [gRatine] <1> **I.** *vi* to brown **II.** *vt* (**faire**) ~ **qc** to brown sth under the grill
gratis [gRatis] *adj, adv inf* free
gratitude [gRatityd] *f* gratitude
gratte-ciel [gRatsjɛl] *m inv* skyscraper
grattement [gRatmɑ̃] *m* scratching
gratte-papier [gRatpapje] <gratte-papier(s)> *mf péj* pen-pusher *Brit*, pencil pusher *Am*
gratter [gRate] <1> **I.** *vi* **1.** (*racler*) to scratch **2.** (*récurer*) to scrape off **3.** (*démanger*) to itch; **ça me gratte à la jambe** my leg's itching **II.** *vt* (*racler*) to scratch; (*mur, table, carottes, sol*) to scrape; (*allumette*) to strike **III.** *vpr* **se** ~ **qc** to scratch sth; **se** ~ **jusqu'au sang** to scratch oneself raw ►**tu peux toujours te** ~**!** *inf* you can whistle for it!
grattoir [gRatwaR] *m* scraper
grat(t)ouiller [gRatuje] <1> **I.** *vi* to itch **II.** *vt* ~ **qn** to make sb itch
gratuit(e) [gRatɥi, ɥit] *adj* **1.** (*gratis*) free; **à titre** ~ free of charge **2.** (*arbitraire: affirmation, supposition*) unwarranted; (*accusation*) unfounded; (*acte*) unmotivated; (*cruauté*) gratuitous
gratuité [gRatɥite] *f* **1.** (*caractère gratuit*) free nature **2.** (*caractère arbitraire: d'une affirmation*) unwarranted nature; (*d'un acte*) unmotivated nature
gratuitement [gRatɥitmɑ̃] *adv* **1.** (*gratis*) free **2.** (*sans motif: affirmer*) wantonly; (*agir*) without motivation; (*commettre un crime*) gratuitously
gratuitiel [gRatɥisjɛl] *m Québec* INFOR freeware
gravats [gRavɑ] *mpl* rubble
grave [gRav] **I.** *adj* **1.** (*sérieux*) serious; (*nouvelles*) bad; **blessé** ~ seriously injured; **ce n'est pas** ~ it doesn't matter **2.** (*digne: assemblée*) solemn **3.** LING **accent** ~ grave accent **4.** (*profond*) low; (*voix a.*) deep **II.** *m* **les** ~**s et les aigus** the low and the high registers
gravement [gRavmɑ̃] *adv* **1.** (*dignement*) gravely; (*marcher*) solemnly **2.** (*fortement*) seriously
graver [gRave] <1> **I.** *vt* **1.** (*tracer en creux*) ~ **qc sur/dans qc** to engrave sth on/in sth **2.** (*à l'eau-forte*) ~ **qc sur cuivre/sur bois** to etch sth on copper/wood **3.** (*fixer*) ~ **qc dans sa mémoire** to imprint sth on one's memory **II.** *vpr* **se** ~ **dans la mémoire de qn** to be engraved on sb's memory
graveur [gRavœR] *m* INFOR ~ **de CD-ROM/DVD** CD-ROM/DVD writer
graveur, -euse [gRavœR, -øz] *m, f* ART engraver
gravier [gRavje] *m* gravel
gravillon [gRavijɔ̃] *m* bit of gravel
gravir [gRaviR] <8> *vt* to climb
gravitation [gRavitasjɔ̃] *f* gravitation
gravité [gRavite] *f* **1.** (*sévérité*) solemnity; **avec** ~ seriously; (*regarder*) solemnly **2.** (*importance: d'une situation*) seriousness; (*d'une catastrophe, sanction, d'un problème*) gravity; **un accident sans** ~ a minor accident **3.** PHYS gravity
graviter [gRavite] <1> *vi* ~ **autour de qn/qc** to revolve around sb/sth
gravure [gRavyR] *f* **1.** *sans pl* (*technique*) engraving; (*à l'eau-forte*) etching **2.** (*œuvre*) engraving; (*sur cuivre*) copperplate engraving; (*sur bois*) woodcutting; (*à l'eau-forte*) etching **3.** (*reproduction*) plate
gré [gRe] **de** ~ **ou de force** (whether) by choice or by force; **de bon** ~ willingly; **bon** ~ **mal** ~ whether you like it or not; **de mauvais** ~ grudgingly; **de mon/son plein** ~ of my/his own free will; **savoir** ~ **à qn de qc** *soutenu* to be grateful to sb for sth; **trouver qn/qc à son** ~ to find sb/sth to one's taste; **au** ~ **de sa fantaisie** as her fancy takes her; **au** ~ **de qn** (*de l'avis de*) according to sb's opinion; (*selon les désirs de*) according to sb's wishes; **contre le** ~ **de qn** against sb's wishes
grec [gRɛk] *m* **le** ~ **ancien/moderne** ancien/modern Greek; *v. a.* **français**
grec, grecque [gRɛk] *adj* Greek
Grec, Grecque [gRɛk] *m, f* Greek
Grèce [gRɛs] *f* **la** ~ Greece
gréco-latin(e) [gRekolatɛ̃, in] *adj* Greek and Latin **gréco-romain(e)** [gRekoRɔmɛ̃, ɛn] <gréco-romains> *adj* Graeco-Roman *Brit*, Greco-Roman *Am*
gredin(e) [gRədɛ̃, in] *m(f)* rascal; **petit** ~**!** little rascal!
gréement [gRemɑ̃] *m sans pl* **1.** NAUT rigging **2.** (*matériel*) kit
greffe [gRɛf] *f* **1.** MED transplant **2.** BOT grafting; (*greffon*) graft
greffer [gRefe] <1> **I.** *vt* **1.** MED ~ **qc à qn** to transplant sth into sb **2.** BOT ~ **qc sur qc** to graft sth on to sth **II.** *vpr* **se** ~ **sur qc** to graft on to sth
greffier, -ière [gRefje, -jɛR] *m, f* clerk of the court
grégaire [gRegɛR] *adj* **instinct** ~ herd instinct
grège [gRɛʒ] *adj* beige grey *Brit*, beige gray *Am*; *v. a.* **bleu**
grégorien(ne) [gRegɔRjɛ̃, jɛn] *adj* Gregorian

grêle [gʀɛl] I. *adj* spindly; (*apparence*) lanky; (*son, voix*) thin II. *f* hail
grêlé(e) [gʀele] *adj* pockmarked
grêler [gʀele] <1> *vi impers* **il grêle** it is hailing
grêlon [gʀɛlɔ̃] *m* hailstone
grelot [gʀəlo] *m* small bell
grelottant(e) [gʀəlɔtɑ̃, ɑ̃t] *adj* shivering
grelotter [gʀəlɔte] <1> *vi* ~ **de fièvre** to shiver with fever
grenade [gʀənad] *f* 1. MIL grenade 2. BOT pomegranate
Grenade [gʀənad] *f* Grenada
grenadien(ne) [gʀənadjɛ̃, ɛn] *adj* Grenadan
Grenadien(ne) [gʀənadjɛ̃, ɛn] *m(f)* Grenadan
grenadine [gʀənadin] *f* grenadine
grenat [gʀəna] *adj inv* dark red
grenier [gʀənje] *m* (*d'une maison*) attic; (*d'une ferme*) loft
grenouille [gʀənuj] *f* 1. (*rainette*) frog 2. *fig, inf* ~ **de bénitier** Holy Joe
grenouillère [gʀənujɛʀ] *f* sleepsuit *Brit,* sleepers *Am*
grenu(e) [gʀəny] *adj* (*peau, roche*) coarse-grained; (*marbre, papier*) grained; (*cuir*) textured
grès [gʀɛ] *m* 1. (*roche*) sandstone 2. (*poterie*) stoneware; **cruche en** ~ stoneware pitcher
grésil [gʀezil] *m* fine hail
grésillement [gʀezijmɑ̃] *m* crackling; (*de la friture*) sizzling
grésiller [gʀezije] <1> *vi* to sizzle; **la radio/le disque/téléphone grésille** the radio/record/telephone is crackling
greubons [gʀøbɔ̃] *mpl Suisse* (*petits résidus solides qui se forment quand le lard fond*) *residue from melted bacon fat*
grève [gʀɛv] *f* strike; **appel à la** ~ strike call; ~ **sur le tas/de la faim** sit-down/hunger strike; ~ **du zèle** work-to-rule *Brit;* **être en** ~, **faire** ~ to be on strike; **se mettre en** ~ to go on strike; **ouvrier en** ~ striking worker; **entreprise en** ~ strikebound company
grever [gʀəve] <4> *vt* ~ **un budget de dépenses** to weigh down a budget with expenditures
gréviste [gʀevist] *mf* striker; ~**s de la faim** hunger strikers
gribiche [gʀibiʃ] *adj* **sauce** ~ gribiche sauce (*mayonnaise with chopped eggs and capers*)
gribouillage [gʀibujaʒ] *m* scribble; **faire des** ~**s sur qc** to scribble on sth
gribouiller [gʀibuje] <1> *vt, vi* to scribble
gribouillis [gʀibuji] *m v.* **gribouillage**
grief [gʀijɛf] *m* **avoir des** ~**s contre qn** to have grievances against sb
grièvement [gʀijɛvmɑ̃] *adv* seriously
griffe [gʀif] *f* 1. (*ongle pointu*) claw; **faire ses** ~**s** to sharpen one's claws 2. (*marque*) stamp 3. (*signature*) signature 4. *Belgique* (*égratignure, éraflure*) scratch ▸**toutes** ~**s dehors** ready to pounce; **arracher qn des** ~**s de qn** to snatch sb from sb's clutches; **être entre les** ~**s de qn** to be between the jaws of sb; **montrer les** ~**s** to show one's claws; **porter la** ~ **de qn** to carry the stamp of sb; **reconnaître la** ~ **de qn** to recognize the stamp of sb; **rentrer ses** ~**s** to draw in one's claws; **tomber entre les** ~**s de qn** to fall into sb's clutches
griffé(e) [gʀife] *adj* (*vêtement*) designer
griffer [gʀife] <1> *vt* to scratch
griffonnage [gʀifɔnaʒ] *m* scribble
griffonner [gʀifɔne] <1> *vt, vi* to scribble
griffure [gʀifyʀ] *f* scratch
grignoter [gʀiɲɔte] <1> I. *vi* (*personne*) to nibble; (*animal*) to gnaw II. *vt* 1. (*manger du bout des dents*) ~ **qc** (*personne*) to nibble sth; (*animal*) to gnaw at sth; (*entièrement*) to eat away at sth 2. (*restreindre: capital, libertés*) to erode; (*espaces*) to eat away at
grigou [gʀigu] *m inf* skinflint
gril [gʀil] *m* griddle ▸**être sur le** ~ *inf* to be on tenterhooks
grillade [gʀijad] *f* grill; **faire des** ~**s** to grill some meat
grillage [gʀijaʒ] *m* 1. (*treillis métallique*) wire netting 2. (*clôture*) wire fencing
grillager [gʀijaʒe] <2a> *vt* ~ **une fenêtre** to put wire netting on a window; ~ **un jardin** to put wire fencing around a garden
grille [gʀij] *f* 1. (*clôture*) railings 2. (*porte*) gate 3. (*treillis*) grille; (*d'un château fort*) portcullis; (*d'un four*) grate 4. (*tableau*) ~ **d'horaires** schedule; ~ **des rémunérations** [*o* **salaires**] salary scale; ~ **des tarifs** price scale; ~ **des programmes de télévision** television schedules *pl;* ~ **de loto** lottery card; ~ **de mots croisés** crossword puzzle
grille-pain [gʀijpɛ̃] *m inv* toaster
griller [gʀije] <1> I. *vi* 1. (*cuire: viande, poisson*) to grill; (*pain*) to toast; **faire** ~ to grill; (*café, châtaignes*) to roast; (*pain*) to toast 2. (*brûler*) ~ **d'envie de** +*infin* to have a burning desire to +*infin* 3. *inf* (*avoir chaud*) to boil II. *vt* 1. (*faire cuire*) to cook; (*café, châtaignes*) to roast; (*pain*) to toast 2. (*détruire*) ~ **qc** (*soleil, feu*) to burn sth; **le gel a grillé les bourgeons** the frost damaged the buds 3. ELEC **être grillé** to have blown 4. (*brûler: feu rouge*) to run 5. *inf* (*fumer*) to smoke ▸**être grillé auprès de qn** *inf* to have no chance with sb
grillon [gʀijɔ̃] *m* cricket
grimaçant(e) [gʀimasɑ̃, ɑ̃t] *adj* grimacing
grimace [gʀimas] *f* grimace; **faire la** ~ to make a face; **faire des** ~**s** to make funny faces
grimacer [gʀimase] <2> *vi* to grimace; ~ **de douleur** to grimace in pain
grimer [gʀime] <1> I. *vt* ~ **qn** to make sb up II. *vpr* **se** ~ to make oneself up
grimpant(e) [gʀɛ̃pɑ̃, ɑ̃t] *adj* **rosier** ~ climbing rose
grimper [gʀɛ̃pe] <1> I. *vi* 1. (*escalader, monter*) ~ **sur une paroi** to climb a wall; ~

G

sur le toit/à [*o* **dans**] **l'arbre/à l'échelle** to climb on the roof/up the tree/up the ladder; ~ **à l'assaut de l'Everest** to launch an attempt on Everest; ~ **le long de qc** (*plante*) to climb along sth; ~ **dans la montagne** (*route*) to climb up a mountain; **ça grimpe dur!** it's a hard climb! **2.** (*augmenter*) to soar **II.** *vt* (*escalier*) to climb; ~ **la côte** to climb the hill

grimpette [gʀɛ̃pɛt] *f inf* steep little climb

grimpeur, **-euse** [gʀɛ̃pœʀ, -øz] *m, f* **1.** (*alpiniste*) climber **2.** (*cycliste*) hill specialist

grinçant(e) [gʀɛ̃sɑ̃, ɑ̃t] *adj* (*ton*) squeaky; (*humour*) darkly humourous *Brit,* darkly humorous *Am*

grincement [gʀɛ̃smɑ̃] *m* (*d'une roue, porte*) squeaking; (*de dents*) grinding

grincer [gʀɛ̃se] <2> *vi* to grate; (*parquet*) to creak; (*craie*) to scrape ►~ **des dents** (*de colère*) to gnash one's teeth; (*dans son sommeil*) to grind one's teeth

grincheux, **-euse** [gʀɛ̃ʃø, -øz] **I.** *adj* (*enfants*) whining; (*personne*) grumpy **II.** *m, f* misery

gringalet [gʀɛ̃galɛ] *m péj* runt

gringe [gʀɛ̃ʒ] *adj Suisse* (*grincheux*) grumpy

griotte [gʀijɔt] *f* Morello cherry

grippal(e) [gʀipal, o] <-aux> *adj* flu

grippe [gʀip] *f* flu ►**prendre qn en** ~ to take a dislike to sb

grippé(e) [gʀipe] *adj* flu-ridden; **être** ~ to have the flu

gripper [gʀipe] <1> *vi, vpr* (**se**) ~ to jam; (*moteur, système*) to seize up

grippe-sou [gʀipsu] <grippe-sous> *m inf* skinflint

gris(e) [gʀi, gʀiz] *adj* grey *Brit,* gray *Am;* ~ **anthracite** anthracite grey

grisaille [gʀizɑj] *f* **1.** (*monotonie*) dullness; (*de la vie quotidienne*) monotony **2.** (*caractère terne: de l'aube, du paysage*) greyness *Brit,* grayness *Am*

grisant(e) [gʀizɑ̃, ɑ̃t] *adj* (*succès*) exhilarating; (*parfum, vin*) intoxicating

grisâtre [gʀizɑtʀ] *adj* greyish *Brit,* grayish *Am*

gris-bleu [gʀiblø] *adj inv* blue-grey *Brit,* blue-gray *Am*

grisé [gʀize] *m* grey tint *Brit,* gray tint *Am*

griser [gʀize] <1> **I.** *vt, vi* to intoxicate; (*flatteries, succès, bonheur*) to overwhelm; **se laisser** ~ **par la vitesse** to be intoxicated by speed **II.** *vpr* (*s'étourdir*) **se** ~ **de qc** to get drunk on sth

griserie [gʀizʀi] *f* intoxication

grison(ne) [gʀizɔ̃, ɔn] *adj* of the Grisons

Grison(ne) [gʀizɔ̃, ɔn] *m(f)* person from the Grisons

grisonnant(e) [gʀizɔnɑ̃, ɑ̃t] *adj* greying *Brit,* graying *Am*

grisonner [gʀizɔne] <1> *vi* to be going grey *Brit,* to be going gray *Am*

Grisons [gʀizɔ̃] *mpl* **les** ~ the Graubünden

grisou [gʀizu] *m* **coup de** ~ firedamp explosion

gris-vert [gʀivɛʀ] *adj inv* green-grey *Brit,* green-gray *Am*

grive [gʀiv] *f* thrush ►**faute de ~s, on mange des merles** *prov* you must cut your coat according to your cloth

grivois(e) [gʀivwa, waz] *adj* saucy

grizzli, **grizzly** [gʀizli] *m* grizzly bear

Groenland [gʀɔɛnlɑ̃:d] *m* **le** ~ Greenland

grog [gʀɔg] *m* hot toddy

groggy [gʀɔgi] *adj inv, inf* groggy

grogne [gʀɔɲ] *f* rumbling

grognement [gʀɔɲmɑ̃] *m* (*du cochon*) grunting; (*de l'ours, du chien*) growl; (*d'une personne*) grunt

grogner [gʀɔɲe] <1> *vi* **1.** (*pousser son cri: chien, ours*) to growl; (*cochon*) to grunt **2.** (*ronchonner*) ~ **contre** [*o* **après**] **qn** to grumble about sb

grognon(ne) [gʀɔɲɔ̃, ɔn] *adj* grumpy; (*enfant*) grouchy

groin [gʀwɛ̃] *m* (*du porc*) snout

grommeler [gʀɔmle] <3> **I.** *vi* to mutter; ~ **dans sa barbe** to mumble under one's breath **II.** *vt* ~ **des injures contre qn** to mutter insults about sb

grondement [gʀɔ̃dmɑ̃] *m* (*d'un canon, du tonnerre*) rumbling; (*d'un torrent, d'un moteur*) roar; (*d'un chien*) growl

gronder [gʀɔ̃de] <1> **I.** *vi* **1.** (*émettre un son menaçant*) to roar; (*canon*) to rumble; (*chien*) to growl **2.** (*être près d'éclater: révolte*) to brew **II.** *vt* to scold

groom [gʀum] *m* bellboy

gros [gʀo] **I.** *m* **1.** COM bulk; **commerçant en** ~ wholesale merchant; **prix de** ~ wholesale price **2.** (*la plus grande partie*) **le** ~ **du travail** the bulk of the work; **le** ~ **de la troupe** the main body of the army; **le** ~ **de l'orage est passé** the worst of the storm is over; **faire le plus** ~ to do the main things ►**en** ~ COM in bulk; (*à peu près*) more or less; (*dans l'ensemble*) on the whole **II.** *adv* **1.** (*beaucoup*) a lot; (*jouer, parier*) for high stakes; **je donnerais** ~ **pour savoir …** I would give anything to know … **2.** (*grand: écrire*) big ►**il y a** ~ **à parier que** it is a safe bet that

gros(se) [gʀo, gʀos] **I.** *adj* **1.** (*épais*) thick; (*manteau, couverture*) heavy; (*poitrine, lèvres*) big; (*foie*) enlarged; ~ **comme le poing** as big as a fist **2.** (*de taille supérieure*) big; **en** ~ **caractères** in big letters **3.** (*corpulent*) fat **4.** (*intense: fièvre*) high; (*sécheresse*) serious; (*appétit*) large; (*soupir, averse*) heavy; (*voix*) loud; (*bises*) big **5.** (*important: dépenses, dégâts*) heavy; (*client*) important; (*faute, opération*) big; (*récolte*) large; **acheter par ~ses quantités** to buy in bulk **6.** (*extrême: buveur, mangeur*) big; (*joueur*) heavy; (*fainéant*) great; ~ **bêta** [*o* **nigaud**]**!** *inf* big idiot! **7.** (*peu raffiné*) crude; ~ **rouge** rough red wine **8.** (*exagéré: histoire*) exaggerated; **c'est un peu ~!** it is a bit much! **9.** (*pé-*

nible: travaux) difficult; ~ **œuvre** big job **10.** (*plein*) ~ **de chagrin** full of grief; **le cœur ~ de désirs** heart full of desire **11.** (*houleux: mer*) rough **12.** (*enceinte: femme*) pregnant **II.** *m(f)* fat person

groseille [gʀozɛj] *f* currant; ~ **à maquereau** gooseberry

groseillier [gʀozeje] *m* redcurrant bush; ~ **à maquereau** gooseberry bush

gros-porteur [gʀopɔʀtœʀ] <gros-porteurs> **I.** *adj* **avion** ~ jumbo jet **II.** *m* jumbo (jet)

grossesse [gʀosɛs] *f* pregnancy; **test de** ~ pregnancy test

grosseur [gʀosœʀ] *f* **1.** (*dimension*) size; (*d'un fil*) thickness **2.** (*boule*) lump

grossier, **-ière** [gʀosje, -jɛʀ] *adj* **1.** (*imparfait: instrument*) crude; (*réparation*) superficial; (*imitation*) poor; (*manières, mensonge*) bad; (*personne*) crass; (*ruse, plaisanterie*) unsubtle; (*erreur*) stupid **2.** (*malpoli: personne*) rude; **se montrer ~ envers qn** to be rude to sb; **quel ~ personnage!** what a rude individual! **3.** *postposé* (*vulgaire*) vulgar

grossièrement [gʀosjɛʀmɑ̃] *adv* **1.** (*de façon imparfaite*) crudely; (*emballer, réparer, exécuter, imiter*) clumsily; (*se tromper*) grossly; (*calculer*) roughly **2.** (*de façon impolie*) impolitely; (*répondre*) rudely; (*insulter*) grossly

grossièreté [gʀosjɛʀte] *f* **1.** *sans pl* (*qualité*) coarseness; **agir avec** ~ to act coarsely; **répondre avec** ~ to reply rudely **2.** (*remarque*) coarse comment

grossir [gʀosiʀ] <8> **I.** *vi* **1.** (*devenir plus gros: personne, animal*) to become fatter; (*point, nuage*) to get bigger; (*fruit*) to swell; (*ganglions, tumeur*) to grow; **le sucre fait** ~ sugar is fattening **2.** (*augmenter en nombre: foule, nombre*) to get bigger **3.** (*augmenter en intensité: bruit faible*) to get louder **II.** *vt* **1.** (*rendre plus gros*) to make fatter; ~ **un objet** (*loupe, microscope*) to magnify an object **2.** (*augmenter en nombre: foule, nombre de chômeurs*) to swell; (*équipe*) to get bigger **3.** (*exagérer: événement, fait*) to exaggerate

grossissant(e) [gʀosisɑ̃, ɑ̃t] *adj* **1.** (*flot*) swelling; (*foule, nombre*) growing **2.** (*qui fait paraître plus gros: miroir, verre*) enlarging

grossissement [gʀosismɑ̃] *m* **1.** (*d'une personne*) weight gain; (*d'un muscle*) enlargement **2.** (*en optique*) magnification **3.** (*enflure*) swelling; (*d'une tumeur*) growth **4.** (*augmentation de volume: d'un fleuve*) swelling; (*d'une fortune*) enlargement; ~ **du capital** capital growth **5.** (*augmentation en nombre*) (big) increase **6.** (*exagération*) exagerration

grossiste [gʀosist] *mf* wholesaler

grosso modo [gʀosomɔdo] *adv* more or less; (*expliquer, décrire*) in rough terms; (*calculer, estimer*) roughly; **il y avait 200 personnes** ~ there were roughly 200 people

grotesque [gʀɔtɛsk] *adj* grotesque

grotte [gʀɔt] *f* cave

grouillant(e) [gʀujɑ̃, jɑ̃t] *adj* **1.** (*foule, masse*) milling; **le marché est ~ de monde/d'activité** the market is teeming with people/activity **2.** (*populeux*) heaving; **le bistrot est ~ de monde** the bistro is swarming with people

grouiller [gʀuje] <1> **I.** *vi* (*foule*) to mill about; **la place grouille de touristes** the square was teeming with tourists **II.** *vpr inf* **se** ~ to hurry up

groupe [gʀup] *m* **1.** group; **réduction de** ~ group reduction; **travail en** ~ group work; **par ~s de quatre** in groups of four; ~ **de rock** rock band; ~ **de pression** pressure group; ~ **sanguin** blood group [*o* type] **2.** (*ensemble de choses*) ~ **électrogène** generating set

groupement [gʀupmɑ̃] *m* ~ **syndical/professionnel** union/professional organization; ~ **de capitaux** capital organization; ~ **d'entreprises** company group; ~ **d'intérêts** interest group; ~ **d'achat** bulk-buying organization

grouper [gʀupe] <1> **I.** *vt* **1.** (*réunir: personnes, objets, idées*) to group together; (*ressources*) to pool **2.** (*classer*) to categorize; ~ **dans une catégorie** to put into a category **II.** *vpr* **se** ~ to gather; (*personnes, partis*) to form a group; **se ~ autour de qn** to gather around sb

groupie [gʀupi] *mf* groupie

groupuscule [gʀupyskyl] *m péj* small group

gruau [gʀyo] *m* groats *pl;* **farine de** ~ fine wheat flour

grue [gʀy] *f* crane

gruger [gʀyʒe] <2a> *vt* **1.** (*duper*) to swindle **2.** *Québec* (*grignoter*) to nibble

grumeau [gʀymo] <x> *m* lump; **faire des ~x** to go lumpy

grunge *m* **la mode** ~ grunge fashion

grutier, **-ière** [gʀytje, -jɛʀ] *m, f* crane driver

gruyère [gʀyjɛʀ] *m* Gruyère cheese

GTI [ʒetei] *abr de* (**automobile**) **grand tourisme à injection** GTI

Guadeloupe [gwadlup] *f* **la** ~ Guadeloupe

gué [ge] *m* ford; **traverser à** ~ to ford a river

guenilles [gənij] *fpl* rags

guenon [gənɔ̃] *f* female monkey; *v. a.* **singe**

guépard [gepaʀ] *m* cheetah

guêpe [gɛp] *f* wasp

guêpier [gepje] *m* wasps' nest ►**se <u>fourrer</u> dans un** ~ to land oneself in trouble

guère [gɛʀ] *adv* **1.** (*pas beaucoup*) **ne ~ manger** to hardly eat anything; **ne plus ~ lire** to hardly read any more; **n'être ~ poli** to be by no means polite; **ne ~ se soucier de qc** to not worry much about sth; **il n'y a ~ de monde** there's hardly anyone; **ça ne va ~ mieux** things are hardly any better; **ce n'est ~ pire** it's not really any worse; **on ne lui donne ~ plus de 40 ans** he doesn't look much more than 40 years old; ~ **plus** not much more **2.** (*pas souvent*) **ne faire plus ~ qc** to not do sth much more; **cela ne se dit** ~ that is not often said **3.** (*pas longtemps*) **ça ne dure** ~ it doesn't last long **4.** (*seulement*) **je ne peux** ~ **demander qu'à mes parents** I can only ask my parents

guéri(e) [geʀi] *adj* être ~, to be better

guéridon [geʀidɔ̃] *m* pedestal table

guérilla [geʀija] *f* guerilla warfare

guérillero, guérilléro [geʀijeʀo] *m* guerilla (fighter)

guérir [geʀiʀ] <8> **I.** *vt* ~ **qn de qc** to cure sb of sth **II.** *vi* to get better; (*plaie, blessure*) to heal; (*rhume*) to get better **III.** *vpr* **1.** MED **se** ~ to be cured; (*tout seul*) to cure oneself **2.** (*se débarrasser*) **se** ~ **de qc** to be cured of sth

guérison [geʀizɔ̃] *f* (*processus, résultat*) recovery; (*d'une blessure*) healing; **être en voie de** ~ to be on the road to recovery

guérisseur, -euse [geʀisœʀ, -øz] *m, f* healer; (*rebouteux*) quack

guérite [geʀit] *f* **1.** MIL sentry box **2.** CONSTR workman's hut

Guernesey [gɛʀnəzɛ] **(l'île de)** ~ (the island of) Guernsey

guerre [gɛʀ] *f* **1.** (*lutte armée entre groupes/États*) war; **la Grande** ~, **la** ~ **de 14** the First World War, the Great War; **la** ~ **de l'Indépendance américaine** the War of Independence *Brit*, the American Revolution *Am;* **la** ~ **du Viêtnam** the Vietnam war; ~ **sainte** holy war; ~ **économique** economic warfare; ~ **des étoiles** Star Wars; **ministre de la** ~ Minister for War; **déclarer la** ~ to declare war; **entrer en** ~ **contre un pays** to engage in war against a country; **faire la** ~ **à qn/à un pays** to fight sb/a country; **partir pour la** ~ to leave for war **2.** *fig* **déclarer la** ~ **à qc** to declare war on sb; **faire la** ~ **à qc** to wage war on sth; **partir en** ~ **contre qc** to declare war on sth ►**de** ~ **lasse, il a cédé** tired of fighting, he gave in; **à la** ~ **comme à la** ~ you have to make the best of things

Guerre [gɛʀ] *f* **la Première** ~ **mondiale** the First World War, the Great War; **la Seconde** ~ **mondiale** the Second World War

guerrier, -ière [gɛʀje, -jɛʀ] **I.** *adj* warlike; **exploits** ~**s** war exploits **II.** *m, f* warrior

guerroyer [gɛʀwaje] <6> *vi soutenu* ~ **contre qn** to wage war on sb

guet [gɛ] **faire le** ~ to be on watch

guet-apens [gɛtapɑ̃] *m inv* ambush

guêtre [gɛtʀ] *f* gaiter; (*d'un danseur*) legwarmer

guetter [gete] <1> *vt* **1.** (*épier*) to watch **2.** (*attendre: occasion, signal*) to watch for; (*personne*) to wait for **3.** (*menacer*) ~ **qn** (*maladie, danger, mort*) to threaten sb

gueulante [gœlɑ̃t] *f* **pousser une** ~ **contre qn** *inf* to kick up a row against sb

gueule [gœl] *f* **1.** (*bouche d'un animal*) mouth **2.** *inf* (*figure*) face; **avoir une bonne/sale** ~ to look nice/horrible **3.** *inf* (*bouche humaine*) **avoir une grande** ~ to have a big mouth; **être une grande** ~ to be a big mouth; (**ferme**) **ta** ~! shut it! ►**avoir la** ~ **de bois** *inf* to have a hangover; **faire une** ~ **d'enterrement** *inf* to have a gloomy face; **se jeter dans la** ~ **du loup** to throw oneself into the lion's jaw; **avoir de la** ~ *inf* to look great; **casser la** ~ **à qn** *inf* to smash sb's face in; **se casser la** ~ *inf* (*personne*) to fall flat on one's face; **faire la** ~ **à qn** *inf* to be in a bad mood with sb; **faire une sale** ~ *inf* to pull [*o* make] a face; **se fendre la** ~ *inf* to laugh one's head off; **se foutre de la** ~ **de qn** *inf* to make fun of sb; **se soûler la** ~ *inf* to get blind drunk

gueuler [gœle] <1> **I.** *vi inf* **1.** (*crier*) to yell **2.** (*protester*) to kick up a fuss **II.** *vt inf* to bellow

gueuleton [gœltɔ̃] *m inf* blow-out

gui [gi] *m* mistletoe

guibolle [gibɔl] *f inf* pin

guichet [giʃɛ] *m* counter; ~ **d'information** information desk; ~ **automatique** (**d'une banque**) cash machine, ATM *Am* ►**jouer à** ~**s fermés** to play to packed houses

guide [gid] **I.** *mf* **1.** (*cicérone*) guide; ~ **touristique** tourist guide; ~ **de montagne** mountain guide **2.** (*conseiller*) advisor **II.** *m* guidebook; ~ **touristique/gastronomique** tourist/restaurant guide **III.** *fpl* reins

guider [gide] <1> *vt* **1.** (*indiquer le chemin, diriger, accompagner*) to guide; **se laisser** ~ **par qc** to be guided by sth **2.** (*conseiller*) to advise

guidon [gidɔ̃] *m* handlebars *pl*

guigne [giɲ] *f inf* bad luck

guigner [giɲe] <1> *vt* to eye

guignol [giɲɔl] *m* puppet; **faire le** ~ to clown about

guili [gili] *m* **faire des** ~**s à qn** *inf* to tickle sb

Guillaume [gijoːm(ə)] *m* HIST ~ **Tell** William Tell; ~ **le Conquérant** William the Conqueror

guillemets [gijmɛ] *mpl* quotation marks; **entre** ~ in quotation marks

guilleret(te) [gijʀɛ, ɛt] *adj* **1.** (*gai*) perky **2.** (*frétillant*) lively

guillotine [gijɔtin] *f* guillotine

guillotiner [gijɔtine] <1> *vt* to guillotine

guimauve [gimov] *f* **1. pâte de** ~ *marshmallow* **2.** BOT marsh mallow **3.** (*mièvrerie*) soppiness; **histoire/film/chanson à la** ~ soppy story/film/song ►**être mou comme de la** ~ to be soft like jelly; **sa main est molle comme de la** ~ his hand's are soft like jelly

guimbarde [gɛ̃baʀd] *f* **1.** MUS Jew's harp **2.** *inf* (*voiture*) jalopy, banger *Brit*

guincher [gɛ̃ʃe] <1> *vi inf* to dance

guindé(e) [gɛ̃de] *adj* starchy

Guinée [gine] *f* **la** ~ Guinea

guinéen(ne) [gineɛ̃, ɛn] *adj* Guinean

Guinéen(ne) [gineɛ̃, ɛn] *m(f)* Guinean

guingois [gɛ̃gwa] **de** ~ askew

guinguette [gɛ̃gɛt] *f* dance hall

guirlande [giʀlɑ̃d] *f* garland; ~ **lumineuse**

fairy lights

guise [giz] à **ma/sa** ~ as I like/he/she/it likes; **à votre ~!** as you like!; **en ~ de** by way of

guitare [gitaʀ] *f* guitar

guitariste [gitaʀist] *mf* guitarist

gus [gys] *m inf* guy

gustatif, **-ive** [gystatif, -iv] *adj* gustatory; **papilles gustatives** taste buds

guttural(e) [gytyʀal, o] <-aux> *adj* guttural

Guyana [gɥijana] *m* **le** ~ Guyana

guyanais(e) [gɥijanɛ, ɛz] *adj* Guyanese

Guyanais(e) [gɥijanɛ, ɛz] *m(f)* Guyanese

Guyane [gɥijan] *f* **la** ~ Guiana

gym [ʒim] *f inf abr de* **gymnastique**

gymnase [ʒimnɑz] *m* **1.** (*halle*) gymnasium **2.** *Suisse* (*école secondaire, lycée*) secondary school

gymnaste [ʒimnast] *mf* gymnast

gymnastique [ʒimnastik] *f* gymnastics + *vb sing*

gynéco [ʒineko] *mf inf abr de* **gynécologue**

gynécologie [ʒinekɔlɔʒi] *f* gynaecology *Brit*, gynecology *Am*

gynécologue [ʒinekɔlɔg] *mf* gynaecologist *Brit*, gynecologist *Am*

gypse [ʒips] *m* gypsum

gyrophare [ʒiʀofaʀ] *m* revolving light

H

H, **h** [aʃ, ˊaʃ] *m inv* H, h; ~ **aspiré/muet** aspirate/silent h; ~ **comme Henri** h as in Harry *Brit*, h as in How *Am*; (*on telephone*) h for Harry *Brit*, h for How *Am*

h *abr de* **heure**

ha [ˊa] *abr de* **hectare** ha

habile [abil] *adj* **1.** (*adroit: personne, mains*) skilful *Brit*, skillful *Am*; **être ~ au tricot** to be good at knitting **2.** (*malin*) clever

habileté [abilte] *f* **1.** *sans pl* (*adresse*) skill; ~ **de main** manual skill **2.** (*ruse*) trick

habilitation [abilitasjɔ̃] *f* **1.** JUR capacitation **2.** (*autorisation officielle*) authorization

habilité(e) [abilite] *adj* **être ~ à** + *infin* to be authorized to + *infin*

habiliter [abilite] <1> *vt* JUR to authorize

habillé(e) [abije] *adj* **1.** (*vêtu: personne*) dressed; **être ~ d'un short** to be wearing shorts **2.** (*de fête: vêtement*) smart

habillement [abijmɑ̃] *m* (*ensemble des vêtements*) clothing; **industrie de l'~** clothing industry

habiller [abije] <1> **I.** *vt* **1.** (*vêtir*) to dress **2.** (*déguiser*) ~ **qn en qc** to dress sb up as sth **3.** (*fournir en vêtements*) to clothe **4.** (*recouvrir, décorer*) to cover **II.** *vpr* **1.** (*se vêtir*) **s'~** to dress (oneself); (*mettre des vêtements de cérémonie*) to dress up; **s'~ de noir/soie** to dress in black/silk **2.** (*se déguiser*) **s'~ en fée/homme** to dress up as a fairy/a man **3.** (*acheter ses vêtements*) **s'~ de neuf** to buy new clothes

habilleur, **-euse** [abijœʀ, -jøz] *m, f* THEAT dresser

habit [abi] *m* **1.** *pl* (*vêtements*) clothes *pl* **2.** (*costume de fête*) dress; (*de fée, de soldat*) costume **3.** (*uniforme*) dress

habitable [abitabl] *adj* (in)habitable

habitacle [abitakl] *m* **1.** AUTO (*de voiture*) passenger compartment **2.** (*poste de pilotage: de petit avion, d'avion de chasse*) cockpit; (*d'avion de ligne*) flight deck

habitant(e) [abitɑ̃, ɑ̃t] *m(f)* **1.** (*occupant: d'un pays, d'une ville*) inhabitant; (*d'un immeuble, d'une maison*) occupant **2.** *Québec* (*paysan*) farmer ►**loger chez l'~** to stay in a private house

habitat [abita] *m* **1.** BOT, ZOOL habitat **2.** GEO settlement **3.** (*conditions de logement*) housing conditions

habitation [abitasjɔ̃] *f* **1.** (*demeure*) home **2.** (*logis*) house; ~ **à loyer modéré** ≈ council flat *Brit*, public housing unit *Am*

habiter [abite] <1> **I.** *vi* to live; ~ **à la campagne/en ville/à Rennes** to live in the country/in (the) town/ in Rennes; ~ **au numéro 17** to live at number 17; ~ **dans un appartement/une maison** to live in a flat/a house *Brit*, to live in an apartment/a house *Am* **II.** *vt* **1.** (*occuper*) ~ **une maison/caravane** to live in a house/a caravan; GEO (*île, région*) to inhabit; ~ **(le) 17, rue Leblanc** to live at (number) 17, rue Leblanc **2.** *fig, soutenu* ~ **qn/qc** (*passion, sentiment*) to abide in sb/sth

habitude [abityd] *f* **1.** (*pratique*) habit; **avoir l'~ de qc** to get used to sth; (*s'y connaître*) to be used to sth; **avoir l'~ de faire qc** to be in the habit of doing sth; **faire perdre une ~ à qn** to break sb of a habit; **d'~** usually; **plus tôt que d'~** earlier than (is) usual **2.** (*coutume*) custom

habitué(e) [abitɥe] *m(f)* (*d'un magasin, restaurant*) regular (customer)

habituel(le) [abitɥɛl] *adj* usual

habituellement [abitɥɛlmɑ̃] *adv* **1.** (*d'habitude*) usually **2.** (*selon la coutume*) normally

habituer [abitɥe] <1> **I.** *vt* **1.** (*accoutumer*) ~ **qn/un animal à qc** to get sb/an animal used to sth **2.** (*avoir l'habitude*) **être habitué à qc** to be used to sth **II.** *vpr* **s'~ à qn/qc** to get used to sb/sth

hâbleur, **-euse** [ˊɑblœʀ, -øz] **I.** *adj* bragging **II.** *m, f* braggart

hache [ˊaʃ] *f* (*à manche long*) axe *Brit*, ax *Am*; (*à manche court*) hatchet ►**déterrer/enterrer la ~ de guerre** to take up/bury the hatchet; **mettre la ~ dans qc** *Québec* (*détruire qc*) to wreck sth

haché(e) [ˊaʃe] *adj* **1.** (*coupé menu: fines herbes, légume*) chopped; (*viande*) minced

H

Brit, ground *Am* **2.** (*entrecoupé*) jerky
hacher [ˊaʃe] <1> *vt* **1.** (*couper: fines herbes, légumes*) to chop; (*viande*) to mince *Brit,* to grind *Am* **2.** (*entrecouper: phrase, discours*) to interrupt
hachis [ˊaʃi] *m* **1.** (*chair à saucisse*) mince *sans pl Brit,* hamburger *sans pl Am* **2.** (*plat*) ~ **de légumes** chopped vegetables
hachisch [ˊaʃiʃ] *m v.* **hashish**
hachoir [ˊaʃwaʀ] *m* **1.** (*couteau*) chopper; (*avec lame courbe*) chopping knife **2.** (*machine*) ~ **à viande** (meat) mincer *Brit,* meat grinder *Am*
hachure ['aʃyʀ] *f* hatching *no pl*
hachurer [ˊaʃyʀe] <1> *vt* (*diagramme, chaussée*) to hatch
hachures [ˊaʃyʀ] *fpl* (*d'un diagramme, de la chaussée*) hatching *sans pl*
haddock [ˊadɔk] *m* GASTR smoked haddock
hagard(e) [ˊagaʀ, aʀd] *adj* wild
haie [ˊɛ] *f* **1.** (*clôture*) hedge **2.** SPORT hurdle; (*équitation*) fence; **gagner aux 100 mètres ~s** to win the 100 metres hurdles *Brit,* to win the 100 meter hurdles *Am* **3.** (*rangée: de personnes*) row
haillon [ˊɑjɔ̃] *m gén pl* rag
haine [ˊɛn] *f* hatred *sans pl*
haineux, -euse [ˊɛnø, -øz] *adj* **1.** (*plein de haine*) full of hatred **2.** (*plein de méchanceté*) malevolent
hainuyer, -ère [ɛnɥije, ɛʀ] *adj* of Hainaut; *v. a.* **ajaccien**
Hainuyer, -ère [ɛnɥije, ɛʀ] *m, f* person from Hainaut; *v. a.* **Ajaccien**
haïr [ˊaiʀ] *vt irr* to hate
haïssable [ˊaisabl] *adj* (*personne, comportement*) loathsome; (*temps*) atrocious
Haïti [aiti] Haiti
haïtien(ne) [aitiɛ̃, ɛn] *adj* Haitian
Haïtien(ne) [aitiɛ̃, ɛn] *m(f)* Haitian
halage [ˊalaʒ] *m* **1.** (*par un bateau*) towing **2.** (*par des hommes, des chevaux*) hauling **3.** *Québec* (*action de sortir le bois en grumes de la forêt*) timber hauling
hâle [ˊɑl] *m* tan
hâlé(e) [ˊɑle] *adj* (sun)tanned
haleine [alɛn] *f sans pl* (*souffle*) breath *sans pl;* **mauvaise** ~ bad breath; **reprendre** ~ to get one's breath back; (*s'arrêter*) to have a breather ▸**travail de <u>longue</u>** ~ long and demanding job
haler [ˊale] <1> *vt* **1.** NAUT (*corde, bouée*) to haul in **2.** (*remorquer: péniche*) to tow **3.** *Québec* (*tirer*) to haul
hâler [ˊɑle] <1> *vt* to tan
haletant(e) [ˊal(ə)tɑ̃, ɑ̃t] *adj* (*personne, animal, respiration*) panting; **je voyais sa poitrine ~e** I could see her heaving chest; **être** ~ to pant; **être** ~ **de soif/de curiosité** to be gasping with thirst/curiosity
halètement [ˊalɛtmɑ̃] *m* panting *sans pl*
haleter [ˊal(ə)te] <4> *vt* to pant
hall [ˊol] *m* (*d'immeuble*) (entrance) hall; (*d'hôtel*) foyer; (*de gare*) concourse
halle [ˊal] *f* **1.** (*partie d'un marché*) covered market **2.** HIST **les Halles** *former central food market in Paris* **3.** *Suisse* ~ **de gymnastique** (*gymnase*) gym(nasium)
hallebarde [ˊalbaʀd] *f* halberd ▸**il <u>pleut</u>** [*o* **<u>tombe</u>**] **des ~s** *inf* it's pouring down
hallucinant(e) [a(l)lysinɑ̃, ɑ̃t] *adj* staggering
hallucination [a(l)lysinasjɔ̃] *f* MED hallucination ▸**<u>avoir</u> des ~s** *inf* to be seeing things
halluciné(e) [a(l)lysine] *adj* **1.** (*qui a des hallucinations: drogué, fou*) suffering from hallucinations **2.** (*bizarre*) weird
halluciner [alysine] <1> *vi inf* **j'hallucine!** I'm seeing things!
hallucinogène [a(l)lysinɔʒɛn] **I.** *adj* hallucinogenic **II.** *m* hallucinogen
halo [ˊalo] *m* **1.** ASTR halo **2.** PHOT halation
halogène [alɔʒɛn] **I.** *m* CHIM halogen **II.** *app* halogen
halte [ˊalt] **I.** *f* **1.** (*pause*) stop; (*repos*) break; **faire une** ~ (*s'arrêter*) to (come to a) stop; (*se reposer*) to have a break **2.** CHEMDFER halt **II.** *interj* **~!** stop!
haltère [altɛʀ] *m* dumbbell
haltérophile [alteʀɔfil] *mf* weightlifter
hamac [ˊamak] *m* hammock
hamburger [ˊɑ̃buʀgœʀ, ˊɑ̃bœʀgœʀ] *m* GASTR hamburger
hameau [ˊamo] <x> *m* hamlet
hameçon [amsɔ̃] *m* fish-hook *Brit,* fishhook *Am*
hampe¹ [ˊɑ̃p] *f* **1.** (*d'une lance*) shaft; (*d'un drapeau*) pole **2.** BOT scape **3.** (*trait vertical*) stroke
hampe² [ˊɑ̃p] *f* **1.** (*poitrine: d'un cerf*) breast **2.** (*ventre: d'un bœuf*) flank
hamster [ˊamstɛʀ] *m* ZOOL hamster
han [ˊɑ̃] **I.** *m* grunt **II.** *interj* **~!** oof!
hanche [ˊɑ̃ʃ] *f* ANAT hip; **balancer les ~s** to sway one's hips
handball, hand-ball [ˊɑ̃dbal] *m sans pl* SPORT handball *sans pl*
handballeur, -euse [ˊɑ̃dbalœʀ, -øz] *m, f* SPORT handball player
handicap [(ˊ)ɑ̃dikap] *m* handicap
handicapant(e) ['ɑ̃dikapɑ̃, ɑ̃t] *adj* disabling
handicapé(e) [ˊɑ̃dikape] **I.** *adj* handicapped **II.** *m(f)* MED disabled person; ~ **physique** physically handicapped person
handicaper [ˊɑ̃dikape] <1> *vt* to handicap
hangar [ˊɑ̃gaʀ] *m* **1.** AGR, CHEMDFER shed **2.** (*entrepôt*) warehouse **3.** AVIAT ~ **à avions** aircraft hangar **4.** NAUT ~ **à bateaux** boathouse **5.** *Québec* (*abri de bois pour le chauffage*) wood shed
hanneton [ˊan(ə)tɔ̃] *m* ZOOL cockchafer
hanté(e) ['ɑ̃te] *adj* haunted
hanter [ɑ̃te] <1> *vt* **1.** (*fréquenter*) to haunt **2.** (*obséder*) ~ **qn** (*idée, souvenir*) to haunt sb
hantise [ˊɑ̃tiz] *f* dread
happer [ˊape] <1> *vt* **1.** (*saisir brusque-*

ment) ~ **qn/qc** (*train, voiture*) to hit sb/sth **2.** (*attraper*) ~ **qc** (*animal, oiseau*) to snap sth up

happy end [ˊapiɛnd] <happy ends> *m o f* happy ending

hara-kiri [ˊaʀakiʀi] <hara-kiris> *m* hara-kiri *sans pl;* (**se**) **faire** ~ to commit hara-kiri

harangue [ˊaʀɑ̃g] *f* harangue

haranguer [ˊaʀɑ̃ge] <1> *vt* to harangue

haras [ˊaʀɑ] *m* stud farm

harassant(e) [aʀasɑ̃, ɑ̃t] *adj* exhausting

harassé(e) [ˊaʀase] *adj* exhausted

harasser [ˊaʀase] <1> *vt* to exhaust; **être harassé de travail** to be exhausted from working

harcèlement [ˊaʀsɛlmɑ̃] *m* **1.** MIL **guerre de** ~ war of harassment; **tir de** ~ harassing fire **2.** (*tracasserie*) harassment

harceler [ˊaʀsəle] <4> *vt* **1.** (*poursuivre*) to pursue **2.** (*importuner*) to harass

hardes [ˊaʀd] *fpl* **1.** *péj* (*guenille*) old clothes **2.** *Québec* (*vêtements*) clothes

hardi(e) [ˊaʀdi] *adj* **1.** (*audacieux: personne, entreprise*) bold; (*réponse*) daring **2.** (*original: imagination, pensée*) bold

hardiesse [ˊaʀdjɛs] *f* **1.** (*audace: d'une personne, d'une entrprise*) boldness; (*d'une réponse*) daring **2.** (*originalité: de l'imagination, d'une pensée*) boldness

hardiment [ˊaʀdimɑ̃] *adv* **1.** (*courageusement*) boldly **2.** (*carrément: parler, regarder*) fearlessly **3.** (*à la légère: partir, s'engager*) rashly **4.** (*effrontément*) brazenly

hard rock [aʀdʀɔk] *m* MUS **le** ~ hard rock

hardware [ˊaʀdwɛʀ] *m* INFOR hardware

harem [ˊaʀɛm] *m* harem

hareng [ˊaʀɑ̃] *m* **1.** (*poisson*) herring **2.** GASTR ~ **saur** smoked herring

hargne [ˊaʀɲ] *f* **1.** (*comportement agressif*) bad temper *sans pl* **2.** (*méchanceté*) spite *sans pl*

hargneux, -euse [ˊaʀɲø, -øz] *adj* **1.** (*agressif: personne, caractère, ton*) bad-tempered; (*chien*) vicious **2.** (*méchant*) spiteful

haricot [ˊaʀiko] *m* (*légume*) bean; ~ **vert** green bean ►**c'est la fin des ~s!** *inf* that's the last straw!

harissa [(ˊ)aʀisa] *f* GASTR harissa (*hot pepper paste*)

harmonica [aʀmɔnika] *m* MUS harmonica

harmonie [aʀmɔni] *f* **1.** MUS harmony **2.** (*accord*) harmony; **être en** ~ **avec qc** (*idées, opinion*) to be in harmony with sth; (*comportement, vêtement*) to be in keeping with sth

harmonieux, -euse [aʀmɔnjø, -jøz] *adj* harmonious; (*instrument, voix*) melodious

harmonique [aʀmɔnik] *adj* MUS harmonic

harmonisation [aʀmɔnizasjɔ̃] *f* harmonization

harmoniser [aʀmɔnize] <1> **I.** *vt* to harmonize **II.** *vpr* **s'**~ to harmonize

harmonium [aʀmɔnjɔm] *m* MUS harmonium

harnaché(e) ['aʀnaʃe] *adj* **1.** (*accoutré*) rigged out **2.** (*équipé*) ~ **d'appareils photo** festooned with cameras

harnachement [ˊaʀnaʃmɑ̃] *m* **1.** (*harnais: d'un animal*) harnessing *sans pl* **2.** *péj* (*accoutrement*) rig-out

harnacher [ˊaʀnaʃe] <1> *vt* (*mettre le harnais à: animal*) to harness

harnais [ˊaʀnɛ] *m* **1.** (*équipement: d'un cheval*) harness **2.** (*sangles: d'un pilote*) harness; (*d'un plongeur*) rig

harnois ['aʀnwa] *m Québec v.* **harnais**

harpe [ˊaʀp] *f* MUS harp

harpie [ˊaʀpi] *f* **vieille** ~ *péj* old witch

harpiste [ˊaʀpist] *mf* MUS harpist

harpon [ˊaʀpɔ̃] *m* harpoon

harponner [ˊaʀpɔne] <1> *vt* **1.** (*à la pêche: poisson*) to harpoon **2.** *inf* (*attraper: malfaiteur*) to collar

hasard [ˊazaʀ] *m* **1.** (*évènement fortuit, fatalité*) chance; **il faut faire la part du** ~ always expect the unexpected **2.** *pl* (*aléas, risque*) **les ~s de la guerre** the hazards of war ►**à tout** ~ just in case; **essayer qc à tout** ~ to try sth on the off chance; **au** ~ at random; **comme par** ~ *iron* curiously enough; **par** ~ (*se rencontrer*) by chance; (*laisser tomber un verre*) by accident

hasarder [ˊazaʀde] <1> **I.** *vt* (*tenter, avancer: démarche, remarque, question*) to hazard **II.** *vpr* **1.** (*s'aventurer*) **se** ~ **dans un quartier/la rue** to venture (out) into a district/the street **2.** (*se risquer à*) **se** ~ **à faire qc** to risk doing sth

hasardeux, -euse [ˊazaʀdø, -øz] *adj* hazardous; (*affirmation*) rash

hasch [ˊaʃ] *m abr de* **haschich** *inf* hash *sans pl*

haschich, haschisch [ˊaʃiʃ] *m* hashish *sans pl*

hâte [ˊɑt] *f* haste; **à la** ~ hastily; **sans** ~ unhurriedly; **avoir** ~ **de** +*infin* to be in a hurry to +*infin;* **j'ai** ~ **de te revoir** I can't wait to see you again

hâter [ˊɑte] <1> **I.** *vt* to hasten **II.** *vpr* **se** ~ to hurry

hâtif, -ive [ˊɑtif, -iv] *adj* **1.** (*trop rapide: décision, réponse*) hasty; (*travail*) hurried **2.** (*précoce: croissance, développement*) precocious; (*fruit, légume*) early

hauban [ˊobɑ̃] *m* (*d'un voilier*) shroud; (*d'un chapiteau de cirque, d'un pont*) stay

haubert ['obɛʀ] *m* hauberk

hausse [ˊos] *f* **1.** (*action: des prix, salaires*) increase **2.** (*processus*) rise; **être en nette** ~ to be rising sharply **3.** FIN **jouer à la** ~ to speculate on a rising market

haussement [ˊosmɑ̃] *m* ~ **d'épaules** shrug (of the shoulders)

hausser [ˊose] <1> **I.** *vt* **1.** (*surélever: mur*) to raise; ~ **une maison** to increase the height of a house **2.** (*amplifier*) ~ **le ton** [*o* **la voix**] to

H

raise one's voice **3.** (*augmenter: prix*) to raise **4.** (*soulever: sourcils*) to raise; ~ **les épaules** to shrug (one's shoulders) **II.** *vpr* **se ~ de toute sa taille** to draw oneself up to one's full height; **se ~ sur la pointe des pieds** to stand (up) on tiptoe

haut [´o] **I.** *adv* **1.** (*opp: bas: sauter*) high **2.** (*ci-dessus*) **voir plus ~** see above **3.** (*fort, franchement*) out loud **4.** (*à un haut degré*) **un fonctionnaire ~ placé** a high-ranking official; **viser trop ~** to aim too high **5.** MUS **chanter trop ~** to sing sharp ▶**parler ~ et clair** to speak out; (*sans ambiguïté*) to make oneself perfectly clear; **regarder** [*o* **traiter**] **qn de ~** to look down on sb; **d'en ~** from above; **en ~** at the top; (*étage supérieur*) upstairs; **en ~ de** at the top of **II.** *m* **1.** (*hauteur*) height; **avoir un mètre de ~** to be one metre high *Brit,* to be one meter high *Am* **2.** (*altitude*) top; **être à un mètre de ~** to be one metre up *Brit,* to be one meter up *Am;* **du ~ de …** from the top of …; **appeler du ~ de la tribune/du balcon** to call down from the gallery/balcony **3.** (*sommet, opp: bas*) top; **l'étagère du ~** the top shelf; **les voisins du ~** the upstairs neighbours *Brit,* the upstairs neighbors *Am* ▶**des ~s et des bas** ups and downs

haut(e) [´o, ´ot] *adj* **1.** (*grand*) high; **être ~ de plafond** (*pièce*) to have a high ceiling; **de ~e taille** tall; **le plus ~ étage** the top floor **2.** (*en position élevée: nuage*) high **3.** GEO (*montagne, plateau*) high; (*région, Rhin*) upper; **marée ~e** high tide; **la mer est ~e** it is high tide; **en ~e mer** on the open sea; **la ville ~e** the upper (part of the) town **4.** (*intense, fort*) *a.* ELEC high; **courant à ~e tension** high-voltage current; **à voix ~e** out loud **5.** (*élevé: prix*) high **6.** (*supérieur: fonctionnaire*) senior; **~ commandement** MIL high command; **la ~e société** high society; **au plus ~ niveau** at the highest level; **en ~ lieu** in high places **7.** (*très grand*) great; **jouir d'une ~e considération** to be highly thought of; **être de la plus ~e importance** to be of the highest importance

hautain(e) [´otɛ̃, ɛn] *adj* haughty

hautbois [´obwa] *m* MUS oboe

haut-de-forme [´od(ə)fɔʀm] *m inv* top hat

haute [´ot] *f inf* **la ~** the upper crust

haute-fidélité [´otfidelite] **I.** *f sans pl* hi-fi *sans pl* **II.** *adj inv* (*chaîne*) hi-fi

hautement [´otmɑ̃] *adv* highly; **pays ~ industrialisé** highly-industrialized country

haute-technologie *f* high technology

hauteur [´otœʀ] *f* **1.** (*grandeur, altitude*) height; **quelle est la ~ de ce mur?** what's the height of this wall?; **la ~ est de 3 mètres** the height is 3 metres *Brit,* the height is 3 meters *Am* **2.** SPORT **saut en ~** high jump **3.** (*même niveau*) **être à ~ des yeux** to be at eye level; **à la ~ de qc** (*au même niveau que*) (on a) level with sth; (*dans les environs de*) in the area of sth **4.** (*colline*) hill(top); **~s** heights **5.** (*noblesse*) loftiness **6.** (*arrogance*) haughtiness ▶**être à la ~ de qc** to be equal to sth

haut-fond [´ofɔ̃] <hauts-fonds> *m* shallow **haut-le-cœur** [´ol(ə)kœʀ] *m inv* **avoir un ~** to feel sick **haut-le-corps** [´ol(ə)kɔʀ] *m inv* **avoir un ~** to jump **haut-lieu** [´oljø] <hauts-lieux> *m* **un ~ touristique** a tourist Mecca **haut-parleur** [´opaʀlœʀ] <haut-parleurs> *m* loudspeaker

havane [´avan] **I.** *adj inv* (*couleur*) tobacco (brown) **II.** *m* (*cigare*) Havana

Havane [´avan] *f* **la ~** Havana

havre [´avʀ] *m soutenu* haven

Havre [´avʀ] *m* **Le ~** Le Havre; **vivre/aller au ~** to live in/to go to Le Havre; **venir du ~** to come from Le Havre

Haye [ɛ] *f* **La ~** The Hague

hayon [´ɛjɔ̃] *m* AUTO tailgate; **voiture à ~ arrière** hatchback

hé [he, ´e] *interj* (*pour appeler*) hey!

heaume [´om] *m* helmet

hebdo *m inf v.* **hebdomadaire**

hebdomadaire [ɛbdɔmadɛʀ] **I.** *adj* (*réunion, revue*) weekly; **"fermeture ~ le lundi"** "closed on Mondays" **II.** *m* (*journal, magazine*) weekly

hébergement [ebɛʀʒəmɑ̃] *m* (*d'un ami*) putting up; (*d'un réfugié*) taking in

héberger [ebɛʀʒe] <2a> *vt* **1.** (*loger provisoirement: ami*) to put up **2.** (*accueillir: réfugié*) to take in

hébété(e) [ebete] *adj* dazed

hébétement [ebetmɑ̃] *m* stupor

hébraïque [ebʀaik] *adj* Hebrew

hébreu [ebʀø] <x> **I.** *adj féminin: israélite, juive* Hebrew **II.** *m* Hebrew; *v. a.* **français** **2.** *inf* **c'est de l'~** it's all Greek to me, it's double Dutch to me *Brit*

Hébreux [ebʀø] *mpl* **les ~** the Hebrews

Hébrides [ebʀid(ə)] *fpl* **les (îles) ~** the Hebrides

HEC [´aʃøse] *f abr de* (**école des**) **hautes études commerciales** *prestigious French business school*

hécatombe [ekatɔ̃b] *f* slaughter

hectare [ɛktaʀ] *m* hectare **hectolitre** [ɛktɔlitʀ] *m* hectolitre *Brit,* hectoliter *Am*

hégémonie [eʒemɔni] *f* hegemony

hein [´ɛ̃] *interj inf* **1.** (*comment?*) eh? **2.** (*renforcement de l'interrogation*) **que vas-tu faire, ~?** what are you going to do (then), eh? **3.** (*marque l'étonnement*) **~? qu'est-ce qui se passe?** eh, what's going on here (then)? **4.** (*n'est-ce pas?*) **tu en veux bien, ~?** you'd like to, wouldn't you?; **il fait froid, ~?** it's cold, isn't it?

hélas [elas] *interj soutenu* alas

héler [´ele] <5> *vt* (*porteur, taxi*) to hail

hélice [elis] *f* **1.** TECH (*d'avion, de bateau*) propeller **2.** MAT helix; **escalier en ~** spiral staircase

hélicoïdal(e) [elikɔidal, o] <-aux> *adj* (*escalier*) spiral

hélicoptère [elikɔptɛʀ] *m* helicopter

héliomarin(e) [eljɔmaʀɛ̃, in] *adj* MED (*cure*) sun and sea air
héliport [elipɔʀ] *m* heliport
héliporté(e) [elipɔʀte] *adj* transported by helicopter
hélitreuillé(e) [elitʀœje] *adj* **être** ~ to be winched aboard
hélium [eljɔm] *m* CHIM helium
hellénique [elenik, ɛllenik] *adj* Hellenic
helvétique [ɛlvetik] *adj* Swiss; **la Confédération** ~ the Swiss Federal Republic
hem [hɛm, ˈɛm] *interj* **1.** (*hé, holà*) hey! **2.** (*hein*) eh? **3.** (*hum*) hmm
hématome [ematom] *m* MED bruise; (*sérieux*) haematoma *Brit*, hematoma *Am*
hémicycle [emisikl] *m* **1.** (*demi-cercle*) semi-circle; (*d'un théâtre, parlement*) hemicycle; **en** ~ in a semi-circle **2.** (*salle d'une assemblée nationale*) **l'**~ the chamber **3.** (*bancs d'une assemblée nationale*) **l'**~ ≈ the benches *Brit*, ≈ the House floor *Am*
hémiplégie [emipleʒi] *f* MED hemiplegia
hémiplégique [emipleʒik] MED **I.** *adj* hemiplegic **II.** *mf* hemiplegic
hémisphère [emisfɛʀ] *m* GEO, ANAT hemisphere
hémisphérique [emisfeʀik] *adj* hemispheric(al)
hémoglobine [emɔglɔbin] *f* MED haemoglobin *Brit*, hemoglobin *Am*
hémophile [emɔfil] MED **I.** *adj* haemophiliac *Brit*, hemophiliac *Am* **II.** *mf* haemophiliac *Brit*, hemophiliac *Am*
hémophilie [emɔfili] *f* MED haemophilia *Brit*, hemophilia *Am*
hémorragie [emɔʀaʒi] *f* **1.** MED haemorrhage *Brit*, hemorrhage *Am* **2.** (*perte en hommes*) ~ **démographique** haemorrhage of the population *Brit*, hemorrhage of the population *Am*
hémorroïde [emɔʀɔid] *f gén pl* MED haemorrhoid *Brit*, hemorrhoid *Am*
henné [ˈene] *m* (*arbuste, colorant*) henna
hennir [ˈeniʀ] <8> *vi* to neigh
hennissement [ˈenismɑ̃] *m* whinny
hep [ˈɛp, hɛp] *interj* hey!
hépatique [epatik] MED **I.** *adj* hepatic; **colique** ~ biliary colic **II.** *mf* person suffering from a liver complaint
hépatite [epatit] *f* MED ~ **virale** viral hepatitis
héraldique [eʀaldik] *adj* heraldic; **science** ~ heraldry
héraut [ˈeʀo] *m soutenu* herald
herbacé(e) [ɛʀbase] *adj* herbaceous
herbage [ɛʀbaʒ] *m* (*herbe, pré*) pasture
herbe [ɛʀb] *f* **1.** BOT grass *sans pl;* **mauvaise** ~ weed **2.** MED, GASTR herb; **fines** ~**s** mixed herbs; **les** ~**s de Provence** Provençal mixed herbs (*parsley, thyme, oregano and bay*) ►**couper l'**~ **sous le(s) pied(s) de qn** to cut the ground from under sb's feet
herbeux, -euse [ɛʀbø, -øz] *adj* grassy
herbicide [ɛʀbisid] **I.** *adj* **produit** ~ weedkiller **II.** *m* weedkiller
herbier [ɛʀbje] *m* (*collection, livre*) herbarium
herbivore [ɛʀbivɔʀ] **I.** *adj* herbivorous **II.** *m* herbivore
herboriser [ɛʀbɔʀize] <1> *vi* to collect plants
herboriste [ɛʀbɔʀist] *mf* herbalist
hercule [ɛʀkyl] *m* **avoir une force d'**~ to have the strength of ten men
Hercule [ɛʀkyl(ə)] *m* Hercules ►**être fort comme** ~ to be a Hercules
herculéen(ne) [ɛʀkyleɛ̃, ɛn] *adj* herculean
hère [ˈɛʀ] *m* **pauvre** ~ poor devil
héréditaire [eʀeditɛʀ] *adj* hereditary
hérédité [eʀedite] *f* **1.** BIO heredity *sans pl;* **avoir une** ~ **chargée** [*o* **une lourde** ~] to have disturbing hereditary influences **2.** JUR right of inheritance
hérésie [eʀezi] *f* heresy
hérétique [eʀetik] **I.** *adj* heretical **II.** *mf* heretic
hérissé(e) [ˈeʀise] *adj* **1.** (*dressé*) (standing) on end; (*barbe*) bristly; ~ **de poils** bristling with hairs **2.** (*piquant: cactus*) prickly
hérisser [ˈeʀise] <1> **I.** *vt* **1.** (*dresser: poils, piquants*) to bristle; (*plumes*) to ruffle **2.** (*faire dresser*) **la peur lui a hérissé les poils** fear made its fur stand on end **3.** (*remplir*) ~ **qc de qc** to spike sth with sth **4.** (*irriter*) ~ **qn** to ruffle sb's feathers **II.** *vpr* **se** ~ **1.** (*se dresser: cheveux, poils*) to stand on end **2.** (*dresser ses poils, plumes: chat*) to bristle; (*oiseau*) to ruffle its feathers **3.** (*se fâcher*) to bristle
hérisson [ˈeʀisɔ̃] *m* ZOOL hedgehog
héritage [eʀitaʒ] *m* **1.** (*succession, biens*) inheritance; **laisser qc en** ~ **à qn** to bequeath sth to sb **2.** *fig* (*d'une civilisation, de coutumes*) heritage
hériter [eʀite] <1> *vt, vi* ~ (**qc**) **de qn** to inherit (sth) from sb
héritier, -ière [eʀitje, -jɛʀ] *m, f* **1.** heir *m*, heiress *f* **2.** (*fils*) **son** ~ *inf* his son and heir
hermaphrodite [ɛʀmafʀɔdit] *m* BIO hermaphrodite
hermétique [ɛʀmetik] *adj* **1.** (*étanche: fermeture, joint*) hermetic; (*à l'air*) airtight; (*à l'eau*) watertight **2.** (*impénétrable: poésie, secret*) impenetrable; (*écrivain*) obscure; **visage** ~ closed expression
hermétiquement [ɛʀmetikmɑ̃] *adv* hermetically
hermine [ɛʀmin] *f* **1.** ZOOL stoat **2.** (*fourrure*) ermine
hernie [ˈɛʀni] *f* MED hernia; ~ **discale** slipped disc *Brit*, slipped disk *Am*
Hérode [eʀɔd(ə)] *m* Herod ►**être vieux comme** ~ to be (as) old as Methuselah
héroïne[1] [eʀɔin] *f* (*drogue*) heroin
héroïne[2] [eʀɔin] *f v.* **héros**
héroïnomane [eʀɔinɔman] *mf* heroin addict

H

héroïque [eʀɔik] *adj* **1.** (*digne d'un héros*) heroic **2.** (*légendaire*) **les temps ~s du cinéma** the great days of the cinema

héroïsme [eʀɔism] *m* heroism

héron [ˊeʀɔ̃] *m* heron

héros, **héroïne** [ˊeʀo, eʀɔin] *m, f* hero *m*, heroine *f*

herpès [ɛʀpɛs] *m* MED herpes

herse [ˊɛʀs] *f* **1.** AGR harrow **2.** (*grille d'entrée: d'une forteresse*) portcullis

hertz [ɛʀts] *m inv* ELEC hertz

hésitant(**e**) [ezitɑ̃, ɑ̃t] *adj* (*personne, pas, voix*) hesitant; (*électeur*) wavering

hésitation [ezitasjɔ̃] *f* **1.** (*incertitude*) hesitation **2.** (*arrêt*) **avec ~** (*réciter, répondre*) hesitatingly; **sans ~** without hesitation

hésiter [ezite] <1> *vi* to hesitate

hétéro [eteʀo] **I.** *adj abr de* **hétérosexuel**(**le**) *inf* hetero **II.** *mf abr de* **hétérosexuel**(**le**) *inf* hetero

hétéroclite [eteʀɔklit] *adj* (*collection, ensemble*) motley; (*objets*) sundry; (*œuvre, bâtiment*) heterogeneous

hétérogène [eteʀɔʒɛn] *adj* heterogeneous

hétérosexuel(**le**) [eteʀosɛksɥɛl] *adj, m(f)* heterosexual

hêtre [ˊɛtʀ] *m* **1.** (*arbre*) beech (tree) **2.** (*bois*) beech (wood)

heu [ˊø] *interj* **1.** (*pour ponctuer à l'oral*) hmm!; **vous êtes Madame, ~ … – Madame Giroux!** you are Madame, um … – Madame Giroux! **2.** (*embarras*) er!; **~ … comment dirais-je?** er! … how can I put it?

heure [œʀ] *f* **1.** (*mesure de durée*) hour; **une ~ et demie** an hour and a half; **une demi-~** half an hour; **une ~ de cours** (*pour l'élève*) an hour's lesson; (*pour le professeur*) an hour's teaching; **24 ~s sur 24** 24 hours a day; **pendant deux ~s** for two hours; **des ~s** (**entières**) for hours (on end); **travailler/être payé à l'~** to work/be paid by the hour; **une ~ de retard** an hour's delay **2.** (*indication chiffrée*) **dix ~s du matin/du soir** ten o'clock in the morning/in the evening; **à trois ~s** at three o'clock; **il est trois ~s/trois ~s et demie** it's three o'clock/half past three; **6 ~s moins 20** 20 to 6 **3.** (*point précis du jour*) **il est quelle ~?** *inf* what time is it?; **vous avez l'~, s'il vous plaît?** have you got the time, please?; **regarder l'~** to look at the time; **à quelle ~?** (at) what time?; **à la même ~** at the same time **4.** (*distance*) **être à deux ~s de qc** to be two hours (away) from sth **5.** (*moment dans la journée*) **~ de fermeture** closing time; **~ d'affluence** AUTO rush hour; COM busy period; **~s de réception au public** public admission times; **à ~ fixe** at a set time; **à toute ~** at any time (of the day); **à cette ~-ci** at this time; **à l'~** on time; **en première ~** at the first opportunity; **il est l'~ de** +*infin* it's time to +*infin;* **jusqu'à une ~ avancée** till late; **arriver avant l'~** to arrive early **6.** (*moment dans le cours des événements*) **des ~s mémorables** memorable times; **traverser des ~s critiques/difficiles** to go through critical/difficult times; **problèmes de l'~** problems of the moment; **l'~ est grave** these are difficult times; **à l'~ actuelle** (*en ce moment précis*) at this moment; (*à l'époque actuelle*) at this moment (in time) ▸**l'~ H** zero hour; **de bonne ~** early; **les nouvelles de dernière ~** stop-press news; **à cette ~** *Belgique* (*maintenant*) at present; **être/ne pas être à l'~** (*personne*) to be/not to be on time; (*montre*) to be right/wrong; **tout à l'~** (*il y a peu de temps*) just now; (*dans peu de temps*) shortly; **à tout à l'~!** (*bientôt*) see you (soon)!; (*plus tard*) see you (later)!; **sur l'~** at once

> In France, there are no official **heures de fermeture** and they can vary between towns and areas. Usually, shops close at 7 p.m. Department stores and supermarkets usually stay open later, until 9 p.m. Shops are open all day on Saturdays and delicatessens and bakeries open on Sunday mornings. Many shops are closed on Mondays.

heureusement [øʀøzmɑ̃] *adv* **1.** (*par bonheur*) fortunately **2.** (*favorablement*) **se terminer ~** to have a happy ending

heureux, **-euse** [øʀø, -øz] **I.** *adj* **1.** (*rempli de bonheur: personne, vie, souvenir*) happy; **être ~ de qc** to be happy with sth; **être ~ de** +*infin* to be happy to +*infin* **2.** (*chanceux*) fortunate; **être ~ au jeu** to be lucky at cards **3.** (*favorable: issue, coïncidence, résultat*) happy; (*circonstances, réponse*) favourable *Brit,* favorable *Am* **4.** (*réussi: effet, formule, mélange*) happy ▸**encore ~!** (it's) just as well! **II.** *m, f* **faire un ~** *inf* to make somebody very happy

heurt [ˊœʀ] *m* **1.** (*conflit*) clash **2.** *soutenu* (*impact, coup: d'un portail*) slam

heurter [ˊœʀte] <1> **I.** *vi* **~ à la porte** to knock at the door **II.** *vt* **1.** (*entrer rudement en contact*) **~ qn** (*à pied*) to bump into sb; (*en voiture*) to hit sb **2.** (*choquer: personne, sentiments*) to offend **3.** (*être en opposition avec*) **~ les intérêts de qn** to clash with sb's interests; **~ les convenances** to go against convention **III.** *vpr* **1.** (*se cogner contre*) **se ~ à** [*o* **contre**] **qn/qc** (*personne, véhicule*) to bump into sb/sth; **se ~** to bump into each other **2.** (*buter contre*) **se ~ à qc** (*problème, refus*) to come up against sth **3.** (*entrer en conflit*) **se ~ avec qn** (*personne*) to clash with sb; **se ~** (*personnes*) to clash (with each other)

heurtoir [ˊœʀtwaʀ] *m* (*d'une porte*) (door)knocker

hexagonal(**e**) [ɛgzagɔnal, o] <-aux> *adj* **1.** hexagonal **2.** (*concerne l'Hexagone français: problème, frontières*) French

hexagone [ɛgzagon, ɛgzagɔn] *m* hexagon

Hexagone [ɛgzagon, ɛgzagɔn] *m* **l'~** ≈ France (*because of its georaphical shape*)

hexamètre [ɛgzamɛtʀ] *m* LIT hexameter
hiatus [´jatys] *m* LING hiatus
hibernation [ibɛʀnasjɔ̃] *f* hibernation
hiberner [ibɛʀne] <1> *vi* to hibernate
hibou [´ibu] <x> *m* owl
hic [´ik] *m inf* snag
hideur [´idœʀ] *f* hideousness *sans pl*
hideux, -euse [´idø, -øz] *adj* hideous
hier [jɛʀ] *adv* **1.** (*la veille*) yesterday; **la matinée d'**~ yesterday morning **2.** (*passé récent*) **vous ne vous connaissez que d'**~ you've hardly known each other any time at all
hiérarchie [jeʀaʀʃi] *f* hierarchy
hiérarchique [´jeʀaʀʃik] *adj* hierarchic(al); **par la voie** ~ through official channels
hiéroglyphe [´jeʀɔglif] *m* hieroglyphic
hi-fi [´ifi] *abr de* **High Fidelity I.** *adj inv* hi-fi; **chaîne** ~ hi-fi system **II.** *f sans pl* hi-fi *sans pl*
high tech [´ajtɛk] **I.** *adj inv* hi-tech **II.** *f sans pl* hi-tech *sans pl*
hilarant(e) [ilaʀɑ̃, ɑ̃t] *adj* hilarious
hilare [ilaʀ] *adj* (*personne*) jovial; (*visage*) beaming
hilarité [ilaʀite] *f sans pl* hilarity *sans pl*
hindi [´indi, indi] *m* Hindi; *v. a.* **français**
hindou(e) [ɛ̃du] *adj* Hindu
hindouisme [ɛ̃duism] *m* Hinduism
hip [´ip] *interj* ~ ~ ~**! hourra!** hip, hip hurray!
hippie [´ipi] <hippies> **I.** *adj* hippie **II.** *mf* hippie
hippique [ipik] *adj* equine; **concours** ~ horse show
hippisme [ipism] *m* horse riding *Brit,* horseback riding *Am*
hippocampe [ipɔkɑ̃p] *m* ZOOL seahorse
hippodrome [ipodʀom] *m* racecourse
hippopotame [ipɔpɔtam] *m* ZOOL hippopotamus
hirondelle [iʀɔ̃dɛl] *f* swallow
hirsute [iʀsyt] *adj* (*tête*) tousled; (*barbe*) shaggy
hispanique [ispanik] *adj* Hispanic
hispanisme [ispanism] *m* Hispanicism
hispano-américain(e) [ispanoameʀikɛ̃, ɛn] <hispano-américains> *adj* Spanish-American
hispanophone [ispanɔfɔn] **I.** *adj* Spanish-speaking; **être** ~ to be a Spanish-speaker **II.** *mf* Spanish-speaker
hisser [´ise] <1> **I.** *vt* (*drapeau, voile*) to hoist **II.** *vpr* (*grimper*) **se** ~ **sur le mur** to heave oneself (up) onto the wall
histoire [istwaʀ] *f* **1.** *sans pl* (*science, événements*) history *no pl* **2.** (*récit, conte, blague, propos mensonger*) story **3.** *inf* (*suite d'événements*) story; (*affaire*) business; **le meilleur de l'**~ the best part of the story; **c'est toujours la même** ~**, avec toi!** it's always the same (old) story with you! **4.** *gén pl, inf* (*complications*) fuss *no pl;* (*problèmes*) trouble *no pl;* **faire toute une** ~ **pour qc** to make a big fuss about sth; **vie sans** ~**s** uncomplicated life ►~ <u>de</u> *+infin inf* just to *+infin;* **cette** ~**-<u>là</u>** (*dont il est question*) that story
histoire-fiction [istwaʀ fiksjɔ̃] <histoires-fictions> *f* **1.** (*futuriste*) futurist novel **2.** (*imaginaire*) fiction
historien(ne) [istɔʀjɛ̃, jɛn] *m(f)* historian
historique [istɔʀik] **I.** *adj* (*événement, monument*) historic; (*document, roman*) historical **II.** *m* (*d'un mot, d'une institution*) history; (*d'une affaire*) review
historiquement [istɔʀikmɑ̃] *adv* historically
hitlérien(ne) [itleʀjɛ̃, jɛn] *adj* HIST Hitlerian
hit-parade [´itpaʀad] <hit-parades> *m* **1.** (*meilleures chansons*) **le** ~ the charts **2.** *fig* top ten
HIV [´aʃive] *m* MED *abr de* **Human Immunodeficiency Virus** HIV
hiver [ivɛʀ] *m* winter; **station de sports d'**~ winter sports resort; *v. a.* **automne**
hivernage [ivɛʀnaʒ] *m* wintering
hivernal(e) [ivɛʀnal, o] <-aux> *adj* **1.** (*de l'hiver*) winter **2.** (*comme en hiver*) wintry
hiverner [ivɛʀne] <1> *vi* to winter
HLM [´aʃɛlɛm] *m o f inv abr de* **habitation à loyer modéré** (*appartement*) ≈ council flat *Brit,* ≈ public housing unit *Am* (*low-rent, state-owned accommodation*)*;* (*immeuble*) ≈ (block of) council flats *Brit,* ≈ public housing *Am*
hobby [´ɔbi] <hobbies> *m* hobby
hochement [´ɔʃmɑ̃] *m* ~ **de tête** (*pour approuver*) nod (of the head); (*pour désapprouver*) shake of the head
hocher [´ɔʃe] <1> *vt* ~ **la tête** (*pour approuver*) to nod (one's head); (*pour désapprouver*) to shake one's head
hochet [´ɔʃɛ] *m* (*jouet*) rattle
hockey [´ɔkɛ] *m* hockey
holà [´ɔla] **I.** *interj* ~**! pas si vite!** hold on! not so fast! **II.** *m* <u>mettre</u> **le** ~ **à qc** to put a stop to sth
holding [´ɔldiŋ] *m o f* COM holding company
hold-up [´ɔldœp] *m inv* hold-up
hollandais [´ɔllɑ̃dɛ] *m* Dutch; *v. a.* **français**
hollandais(e) [´ɔllɑ̃dɛ, ɛz] *adj* Dutch
Hollandais(e) [´ɔllɑ̃dɛ, ɛz] *m(f)* Dutchman, Dutchwoman *m, f*
Hollande [´ɔllɑ̃d] *f* **la** ~ Holland
holocauste [olokost] *m* (*génocide*) holocaust
homard [´ɔmaʀ] *m* GASTR, ZOOL lobster
home ['om] *m Belgique* (*centre d'accueil, d'hébergement*) hostel
homéopathe [ɔmeɔpat, omeopat] *mf* MED homeopath
homéopathie [ɔmeɔpati] *f* MED homeopathy
homérique [ɔmeʀik] *adj* **1.** (*poèmes*) Homeric **2.** *fig* (*rire*) hearty
home-trainer [´omtʀɛnœʀ] <home-trainers> *m* exercise bike
homicide [ɔmisid] *m* JUR murder, homicide *Am;* ~ **involontaire** manslaughter; ~ **volon-**

H

taire murder, homicide *Am*

hommage [ɔmaʒ] *m* **1.** (*témoignage de respect, œuvre ou manifestation en l'honneur de qn*) tribute **2.** *pl, soutenu* (*compliments*) respects; **mes ~s, Madame!** (*à la rencontre*) ≈ how do you do?; (*au revoir*) ≈ goodbye!

homme [ɔm] *m* man; **vêtements d'~** [*o* **pour ~s**] menswear; ~ **politique** politician; ~ **de loi** lawyer; ~ **de main** hired man; (*dans des besognes criminelles*) henchman; ~ **d'État** statesman ►~ **à tout faire** odd-job man, handyman; **entre ~s** (as) man to man

homme-grenouille [ɔmgʀənuj] <hommes-grenouilles> *m* frogman

homme-sandwich [ɔmsɑ̃dwitʃ] <hommes-sandwichs> *m* sandwich man

homo [omo] **I.** *adj abr de* **homosexuel(le)** *inf* gay **II.** *mf abr de* **homosexuel(le)** *inf* gay man, woman *m, f;* **~s** gays

homogène [ɔmɔʒɛn] *adj* homogeneous

homogénéiser [ɔmɔʒeneize] <1> *vt* GASTR, CHIM to homogenize

homogénéité [ɔmɔʒeneite] *f* homogeneity

homologue [ɔmɔlɔg] *adj* (*équivalent*) homologous

homologuer [ɔmɔlɔge] <1> *vt* **1.** (*reconnaître officiellement: prix*) to authorize; (*record*) to ratify **2.** (*déclarer conforme aux normes: siège-auto*) to license

homonyme [ɔmɔnim] *m* **1.** LING homonym **2.** (*personne*) namesake

homosexualité [ɔmɔsɛksɥalite] *f* homosexuality

homosexuel(le) [ɔmɔsɛksɥɛl] **I.** *adj* homosexual **II.** *m(f)* homosexual

hongre [ˊɔ̃gʀ] *adj* (*cheval*) gelded

Hongrie [ˊɔ̃gʀi] *f* **la ~** Hungary

hongrois [ˊɔ̃gʀwa] *m* Hungarian; *v. a.* **français**

hongrois(e) [ˊɔ̃gʀwa, waz] *adj* Hungarian

Hongrois(e) [ˊɔ̃gʀwa, waz] *m(f)* Hungarian

honnête [ɔnɛt] *adj* **1.** (*probe: personne*) honest; (*commerçant, entreprise*) respectable **2.** (*franc: personne*) honest; **être ~ avec soi-même** to be honest with oneself **3.** (*honorable: conduite, intention, propos*) honourable *Brit,* honorable *Am;* (*méthode*) fair **4.** (*vertueux*) honest **5.** (*acceptable: prix, repas, résultat*) reasonable

honnêtement [ɔnɛtmɑ̃] *adv* **1.** (*convenablement: payer, gagner sa vie*) honestly **2.** (*loyalement, avec probité: gérer une affaire*) honourably *Brit,* honorably *Am*

honnêteté [ɔnɛtte] *f* **1.** (*probité, franchise: d'une personne*) honesty **2.** (*honorabilité: d'une conduite, intention, d'un propos*) decency

honneur [ɔnœʀ] *m* **1.** *sans pl* (*principe moral*) honour *Brit,* honor *Am;* **promettre sur l'~ que qn a fait qc** to promise on one's honour that sb has done sth **2.** *sans pl* (*réputation*) credit; **être tout à l'~ de qn** to do sb great credit **3.** (*privilège*) honour *Brit,* honor *Am;* **nous avons l'~ de vous faire part de ...** *form* we are pleased to inform you of ...; **j'ai l'~ de solliciter un poste de ...** *form* I wish to apply for the post of ...; **j'ai l'~ de vous informer que qn a fait qc** *form* I am writing to inform you that sb has done sth; **à toi l'~!** after you! **4.** *pl* (*marques de distinctions*) honours *Brit,* honors *Am;* **rendre les derniers ~s à qn** *form* to pay one's final tribute to sb **5.** (*considération*) **faire un grand ~ à qn en faisant qc** to do sb a great honour by doing sth *Brit,* to do sb a great honor by doing sth *Am* ►**faire les ~s de la maison à qn** (*accueillir somptueusement*) to roll out the red carpet for sb; (*faire visiter les lieux*) to show sb round (the house); **être à l'~** to have the place of honour *Brit,* to have the place of honor *Am;* **faire ~ à un repas** to do justice to a meal; **en quel ~?** *iron* in aid of what?

honorabilité [ɔnɔʀabilite] *f* respectability

honorable [ɔnɔʀabl] *adj* **1.** (*estimable: personne, profession*) honourable *Brit,* honorable *Am* **2.** (*respectable, suffisant*) respectable

honoraire [ɔnɔʀɛʀ] **I.** *adj* honorary; **professeur ~** professor emeritus **II.** *mpl* fee(s)

honorer [ɔnɔʀe] <1> **I.** *vt* **1.** (*traiter avec considération, respecter, célébrer*) *a.* COM to honour *Brit,* to honor *Am* **2.** (*faire honneur à*) ~ **qn** (*sentiments, conduite*) to be a credit to sb **II.** *vpr* **s'~ d'être qc** to pride oneself (up) on being sth

honorifique [ɔnɔʀifik] *adj* honorary

honte [ˊɔ̃t] *f* **1.** (*déshonneur*) disgrace; **(c'est) la ~!** *inf* it's a disgrace! **2.** *sans pl* (*sentiment d'humiliation*) shame; **avoir ~ de qn/qc** to be ashamed of sb/sth ►**faire ~ à qn** to make sb (feel) ashamed; **mourir de ~** to die of shame

honteux, **-euse** [ˊɔ̃tø, -øz] *adj* (*acte, défaite, sentiment*) shameful; **être ~ de qc** to be ashamed of sth

hop [ˊɔp] *interj* **1.** (*pour faire sauter*) come on, jump!; **~ là!** (*quand qn ou qc va tomber*) oops(-a-daisy)! **2.** (*pour marquer une action brusque*) **allez ~!** come on, off you go!

hôpital [ɔpital, o] <-aux> *m* hospital

hoquet [ˊɔkɛ] *m* hiccup; **avoir le ~** to have (the) hiccups

hoqueter [ˊɔkte] <3> *vi* **1.** (*avoir le hoquet*) to hiccup **2.** (*sangloter*) to gulp

horaire [ɔʀɛʀ] **I.** *adj* hourly **II.** *m* **1.** (*répartition du temps*) timetable; **~ de travail** hours of work; **~ mobile** [*o* **flexible**] flexitime **2.** (*tableau: des cours, trains, bus*) timetable; (*des vols*) schedule

horde [ˊɔʀd] *f* horde

horizon [ɔʀizɔ̃] *m* **1.** *sans pl* (*ligne*) horizon **2.** (*étendue*) view; **changer d'~** to have a change of scenery **3.** (*perspective*) horizon; **ouvrir des ~s insoupçonnés à qn** to open (up) undreamt-of horizons for sb

horizontal(e) [ɔʀizɔ̃tal, o] <-aux> *adj* horizontal

horizontale [ɔʀizɔ̃tal] *f* **1.** MAT horizontal **2.** (*position*) **être à l'**~ to be horizontal

horizontalement [ɔʀizɔ̃talmɑ̃] *adv* horizontally

horloge [ɔʀlɔʒ] *f* (*appareil*) clock ►~ parlante speaking clock

horloger, **-ère** [ɔʀlɔʒe, -ɛʀ] **I.** *adj* watchmaking **II.** *m, f* watchmaker

horlogerie [ɔʀlɔʒʀi] *f* **1.** (*secteur économique*) watchmaking; (*commerce*) watchmaking business **2.** (*magasin*) ~ **bijouterie** jeweller's *Brit,* jeweler's *Am* (*specializing in clocks and watches*)

hormonal(**e**) [ɔʀmɔnal, o] <-aux> *adj* hormonal

hormone [ɔʀmɔn] *f* hormone

horodateur [ɔʀɔdatœʀ] *m* (*au parking*) ticket machine

horoscope [ɔʀɔskɔp] *m* horoscope

horreur [ɔʀœʀ] *f* **1.** (*sensation d'épouvante, de dégoût*) horror; ~ **de la violence** horror of violence; **faire** ~ **à qn** to disgust sb; **film d'**~ horror film **2.** (*atrocité: d'un crime, supplice*) horror **3.** (*aversion*) **avoir** ~ **de qn/qc** (*haïr*) to hate sb/sth; **j'ai** ~ **des souris/ordinateurs** I can't stand mice/computers **4.** *pl* (*grossièretés, actions infâmes*) dreadful things

horrible [ɔʀibl] *adj* **1.** (*abominable: spectacle, meuble*) horrible; (*acte, accident, cris*) terrible **2.** (*extrême, très mauvais*) terrible

horriblement [ɔʀibləmɑ̃] *adv* (*triste, cher, chaud, mal*) horribly

horrifiant(**e**) [ɔʀifjɑ̃, ɑ̃t] *adj* horrifying

horrifier [ɔʀifje] <1> *vt* to horrify

horripilant(**e**) [ɔʀipilɑ̃, ɑ̃t] *adj* exasperating

horripiler [ɔʀipile] <1> *vt* ~ **qn** *inf* to exasperate sb, to get sb's back up *Brit*

hors [ˊɔʀ] *prep* **1.** (*à l'extérieur de*) ~ **de** outside; **tomber/être projeté** ~ **de qc** to fall/be thrown out of sth; ~ **d'ici!** get out of here! **2.** (*au-delà de*) ~ **d'atteinte** [*o* **de portée**] out of reach ►~ **de** combat out of action; ~ **de** danger out of danger; ~ **de** prix exorbitant; **être** ~ **de** soi to be beside oneself (with anger)

hors-bord [ˊɔʀbɔʀ] *m inv* **1.** (*moteur*) outboard **2.** (*bateau*) speedboat **hors-d'œuvre** [ˊɔʀdœvʀ] *m inv* GASTR starter **hors-jeu** [ˊɔʀʒø] *m inv* SPORT offside **hors-la-loi** [ˊɔʀlalwa] *m inv* outlaw **hors-piste** ['ɔʀpist] *m inv* **faire du** ~ to ski off-piste

hortensia [ɔʀtɑ̃sja] *m* BOT hydrangea

horticole [ɔʀtikɔl] *adj* horticultural

horticulteur, **-trice** [ɔʀtikyltœʀ, -tʀis] *m, f* horticulturist

horticulture [ɔʀtikyltyʀ] *f* horticulture

hospice [ɔspis] *m* home

hospitalier, **-ière** [ɔspitalje, -jɛʀ] *adj* **1.** (*à l'hôpital*) hospital **2.** (*accueillant*) hospitable

hospitalisation [ɔspitalizasjɔ̃] *f* hospitalization

hospitaliser [ɔspitalize] <1> *vt* to hospitalize

hospitalité [ɔspitalite] *f* hospitality

hostie [ɔsti] *f* REL host

hostile [ɔstil] *adj* **être** ~ **à qn/qc** to be hostile to(wards) sb/sth

hostilité [ɔstilite] *f* hostility

hosto [ɔsto] *m inf abr de* **hôpital**

hot-dog ['ɔtdɔg] <hot-dogs> *m* hot dog

hôte [ot] **I.** *mf* (*d'une personne, d'un hôtel*) guest **II.** *m* INFOR host (computer)

hôte, **hôtesse** [ot, otɛs] *m(f) soutenu* (*maître de maison*) host, hostess *m, f*

hôtel [ɔtɛl, otɛl] *m* **1.** (*hôtellerie*) hotel **2.** (*riche demeure*) mansion ►~ Matignon *offices of the Prime Minister of the French Republic;* ~ **de** ville town hall

hôtelier, **-ière** [otəlje, ɔtəlje, -jɛʀ] **I.** *adj* hotel; **industrie hôtelière** hotel business **II.** *m, f* hotelier

hôtellerie [otɛlʀi, ɔtɛlʀi] *f* (*profession*) hotel business

hôtesse [otɛs] *f* **1.** *v.* **hôte 2.** (*profession*) ~ **d'accueil** (*d'une entreprise, d'un hôtel*) receptionist; (*dans une exposition*) hostess; ~ **de l'air** air hostess

hotte [ˊɔt] *f* **1.** (*appareil d'aspiration: d'une cheminée*) hood; ~ **aspirante** cooker hood *Brit,* range hood *Am* **2.** (*panier*) basket

hou [ˊu] *interj* **1.** (*pour faire honte*) tut tut!; (*pour conspuer*) boo! **2.** (*pour faire peur*) boo! ►~, ~! hey (there)!

houblon [ˊublɔ̃] *m* **1.** (*plante*) hop **2.** (*ingrédient de la bière*) hops *pl*

houe [ˊu] *f* hoe

houille [ˊuj] *f* coal

houiller, **-ère** [ˊuje, -ɛʀ] *adj* coal

houle [ˊul] *f* swell

houlette [ˊulɛt] **sous la** ~ **de qn** under the guidance of sb

houleux, **-euse** [ˊulø, -øz] *adj* **1.** (*agité par la houle: mer*) stormy **2.** (*troublé: séance*) stormy; (*assemblée*) tumultuous

houligan ['uligan] *m* hooligan

houppe [ˊup] *f* ~ **de cheveux** tuft of hair

houppette [ˊupɛt] *f* (powder) puff

hourra [ˊuʀa] **I.** *interj* hurray! **II.** *m* cheer; **pousser des** ~**s** to cheer

houspiller [ˊuspije] <1> *vt* ~ **qn** to tell sb off

housse [ˊus] *f* cover; ~ **de siège/couette** seat/duvet cover

houx [ˊu] *m* BOT holly

hovercraft [ˊɔvœʀkʀaft] *m* hovercraft

HS [aʃɛs] *abr de* **hors service: être** ~ *inf* to be beat, to be all in

HT [aʃte] *adv abr de* **hors taxes** net of tax

hublot [ˊyblo] *m* (*d'un bateau*) porthole; (*d'un avion, appareil ménager*) window

huche [ˊyʃ] *f* chest; ~ **à pétrir** kneading trough; ~ **à pain** bread bin *Brit,* breadbox *Am*

hue [ˊy] *interj* **1.** (*avancer*) gee up! **2.** (*tourner à droite*) gee!

huées [ˊɥe] *fpl* (*cris de réprobation*) boos

huer [ˊɥe] <1> *vt* to boo

huguenot(**e**) [ˊygno, ɔt] *m(f)* Huguenot

H

huile [ɥil] *f* oil; ~ **d'olive/de tournesol** olive/sunflower oil; ~ **solaire** suntan oil; **peint à l'**~ painted in oils ►**jeter de l'**~ **sur le feu** to add fuel to the flames
huilé(e) [ɥile] *adj* oiled
huiler [ɥile] <1> *vt* (*mécanisme*) to oil; (*moule*) to grease
huileux, **-euse** [ɥilø, -øz] *adj péj* **1.** (*plat, surface*) oily **2.** (*gras: cheveux, peau*) greasy **3.** (*pollué*) **des eaux huileuses** oil-contaminated water
huis [ɥi] **à** ~ **clos** behind closed doors; JUR in camera
huissier [ɥisje] *m* **1.** JUR (*officier ministériel*) bailiff **2.** (*appariteur*) usher
huit [ˊɥit, *devant une consonne* ˊɥi] **I.** *adj* eight **II.** *m inv* eight ►**le grand** ~ the big dipper *Brit,* the roller coaster *Am; v. a.* **cinq**
huitaine [ˊɥitɛn] *f* **1.** (*ensemble d'environ huit éléments*) **une** ~ **de personnes/pages** about eight people/pages **2.** (*une semaine*) **dans une** ~ in a week or so
huitante [ˊɥitɑ̃t] *adj Suisse* (*quatre-vingts*) eighty; *v. a.* **cinq, cinquante**
huitième [ˊɥitjɛm] **I.** *adj antéposé* eighth **II.** *mf* **le/la** ~ the eighth **III.** *m* **1.** (*fraction*) eighth **2.** SPORT ~ **de finale** round before the quarterfinal; *v. a.* **cinquième**
huitièmement [ˊɥitjɛmmɑ̃] *adv* eighthly
huître [ɥitʀ] *f* oyster
hulotte [ˊylɔt] *f* tawny owl
hululement [ˊylylmɑ̃] *m* hooting
hululer [ˊylyle] <1> *vi* (*oiseau de nuit*) to hoot
hum [ˊœm] *interj* (*pour exprimer le doute, la gêne, une réticence*) hmm! ►~, ~**!** ahem!
humain(e) [ymɛ̃, ɛn] *adj* **1.** (*propre à l'homme: chair, dignité, vie*) human; **les êtres** ~**s** human beings **2.** (*compatissant, sensible*) humane
humainement [ymɛnmɑ̃] *adv* **1.** (*avec humanité: traiter*) humanely **2.** (*avec les capacités humaines*) **faire tout ce qui est** ~ **possible** to do all that is humanly possible
humaniser [ymanize] <1> **I.** *vt* (*conditions de vie, travail*) to humanize **II.** *vpr* **s'**~ to become more human
humaniste [ymanist] **I.** *adj* humanist(ic) **II.** *mf* humanist
humanitaire [ymanitɛʀ] *adj* (*aide, organisation*) humanitarian
humanité [ymanite] *f* humanity
humanités [ymanite] *fpl Belgique* (*études secondaires* (*classiques, modernes ou techniques*)) secondary education
humanoïde [ymanɔid] *adj, m* humanoid
humble [œ̃bl] *adj* humble
humblement [œ̃bləmɑ̃] *adv* **1.** humbly; **faire** ~ **remarquer que qn a fait qc** to humbly point out that sb has done sth **2.** (*sans prétention: vivre*) modestly
humecter [ymɛkte] <1> **I.** *vt* (*doigts, timbre, linge*) to moisten **II.** *vpr* **s'**~ **les lèvres** to moisten one's lips
humer [ˊyme] <1> *vt* (*plat*) to smell; ~ **l'air** (*personne*) to breathe in the air; (*animal*) to sniff the air
humérus [ymeʀys] *m* ANAT humerus
humeur [ymœʀ] *f* **1.** (*état d'âme*) mood; **être de bonne/mauvaise** ~ to be in a good/bad mood; **être/se sentir d'**~ **à faire qc** to be/feel in the mood for doing sth **2.** (*tempérament*) temper **3.** (*irritation*) (bad) temper; **répondre avec** ~ to reply crossly ►**passer son** ~ **sur qn** to take out one's bad temper on sb
humide [ymid] *adj* **1.** (*qui a pris l'humidité*) damp **2.** METEO (*climat, temps*) humid; **il fait une chaleur** ~ it's muggy; **il fait un froid** ~ it's cold and damp
humidifier [ymidifje] <1> *vt* to humidify
humidité [ymidite] *f* humidity
humiliant(e) [ymiljɑ̃, jɑ̃t] *adj* humiliating
humiliation [ymiljasjɔ̃] *f* humiliation
humilier [ymilje] <1> **I.** *vt* to humiliate **II.** *vpr* **s'**~ **devant qn** to humble oneself before sb
humilité [ymilite] *f* humility
humoriste [ymɔʀist] *mf* humorist
humoristique [ymɔʀistik] *adj* humorous
humour [ymuʀ] *m* humour *Brit,* humor *Am*
humus [ymys] *m* humus
huppe [ˊyp] *f* (*d'oiseau*) crest
huppé(e) [ˊype] *adj* **1.** ZOOL crested **2.** *inf* (*de haut rang: personne, restaurant*) classy
hure [ˊyʀ] *f* **1.** (*tête*) head **2.** GASTR brawn *Brit,* headcheese *Am*
hurlant(e) [ˊyʀlɑ̃, ɑ̃t] *adj* howling
hurlement [ˊyʀləmɑ̃] *m* (*d'un animal, d'une personne, du vent*) howl(ing); (*de la foule*) roar(ing); (*de freins*) squeal(ing)
hurler [ˊyʀle] <1> **I.** *vi* **1.** (*pousser des hurlements: animal, personne*) to howl; (*foule*) to roar; ~ **de douleur/rage** to howl with pain/rage **2.** (*produire un son semblable à un hurlement: vent*) to howl; (*freins*) to squeal **II.** *vt* (*injures*) to yell; (*menaces*) to scream
hurluberlu(e) [yʀlybɛʀly] *m(f) inf* oddball
hurrah [ˊuʀa] *interj v.* **hourra**
hussard [ˊysaʀ] *m* MIL hussar
hussarde [ˊysaʀd] **à la** ~ roughly
hutte [ˊyt] *f* hut
hybride [ibʀid] **I.** *adj* hybrid; **solution** ~ compromise solution **II.** *m* BIO hybrid
hydrant [idʀɑ̃] *m,* **hydrante** [idʀɑ̃t] *f Suisse* (*borne d'incendie*) fire hydrant
hydratant(e) [idʀatɑ̃, ɑ̃t] *adj* moisturizing
hydrate [idʀat] *m* CHIM hydrate; ~ **de calcium** calcium hydrate
hydrater [idʀate] <1> **I.** *vt* **1.** (*en cosmétique*) to moisturize **2.** CHIM to hydrate **II.** *vpr* CHIM **s'**~ to become hydrated
hydraulique [idʀolik] **I.** *adj* hydraulic; **énergie** ~ water power **II.** *f sans pl* hydraulics
hydravion [idʀavjɔ̃] *m* seaplane
hydrocarbure [idʀokaʀbyʀ] *m* CHIM hydro-

carbon
hydrocution [idʀɔkysjɔ̃] *f* MED immersion syncope
hydroélectrique, **hydro-électrique** [idʀoelɛktʀik] *adj* hydroelectric; **centrale ~** hydroelectric power station
hydrogène [idʀɔʒɛn] *m* CHIM hydrogen
hydroglisseur [idʀoglisœʀ] *m* jetfoil
hydrographie [idʀɔgʀafi] *f* hydrography
hydrophile [idʀɔfil] *adj* **coton ~** cotton wool
hyène [jɛn, ˊjɛn] *f* ZOOL hyena
hygiène [iʒjɛn] *f sans pl* **1.** (*bonnes conditions sanitaires*) hygiene *sans pl;* **les services d'~** the public health department **2.** (*soin: des cheveux, d'un bébé*) care *sans pl;* **articles d'~** toiletries
hygiénique [iʒjenik] *adj* **1.** (*de propreté*) hygienic; **papier ~** toilet paper **2.** (*sain*) healthy
hygrométrie [igʀɔmetʀi] *f* hygrometry
hymen [imɛn] *m* ANAT hymen
hymne [imn] *m* MUS hymn
hyper [ipɛʀ] *m abr de* **hypermarché**
hyperglycémie [ipɛʀglisemi] *f* MED hyperglycaemia *Brit,* hyperglycemia *Am*
hyperlien [ipɛʀljɛ̃] *m* INFOR hyperlink
hypermarché [ipɛʀmaʀʃe] *m* superstore
hypermétrope [ipɛʀmetʀɔp] *adj* long-sighted
hypersensible [ipɛʀsɑ̃sibl] *adj* hypersensitive
hypertendu(**e**) [ipɛʀtɑ̃dy] *adj inf* **1.** (*très stressé*) **être ~** (*personne*) to be stressed out **2.** (*difficile: ambiance*) very tense
hypertension [ipɛʀtɑ̃sjɔ̃] *f* MED high blood pressure
hypertexte [ipɛʀtɛkst] *m* INFOR hypertext
hypertrophie [ipɛʀtʀɔfi] *f* MED, BIO hypertrophy
hypertrophié(**e**) [ipɛʀtʀɔfje] *adj* hypertrophied
hypnose [ipnoz] *f* hypnosis
hypnotiser [ipnɔtize] <1> *vt* to hypnotize
hypocalorique [ipokalɔʀik] *adj* low-calorie
hypocondriaque [ipɔkɔ̃dʀijak] *adj péj* (*personne*) hypochondriac
hypocrisie [ipɔkʀizi] *f* hypocrisy
hypocrite [ipɔkʀit] **I.** *adj* hypocritical **II.** *mf* hypocrite
hypoglycémie [ipoglisemi] *f* MED hypoglycaemia *Brit,* hypoglycemia *Am*
hypophyse [ipɔfiz] *f* ANAT pituitary gland
hypotension [ipotɑ̃sjɔ̃] *f* MED low blood pressure
hypothécaire [ipɔtekɛʀ] *adj* FIN **prêt ~** mortgage (loan)
hypothèque [ipɔtɛk] *f* mortgage
hypothéquer [ipɔteke] <5> *vt* **1.** FIN (*maison*) to mortgage; (*créance*) to secure (by mortgage) **2.** (*engager*) **~ l'avenir** to sign away one's future
hypothermie [ipotɛʀmi] *f* MED hypothermia
hypothèse [ipɔtɛz] *f* **1.** (*supposition*) hypothesis **2.** (*éventualité, cas*) **dans l'~ où ...** on the assumption that ...; **dans cette ~** on this assumption
hypothétique [ipɔtetik] *adj* hypothetical
hystérie [isteʀi] *f* hysteria
hystérique [isteʀik] **I.** *adj* hysterical **II.** *mf* hysterical person

I

I, i [i] *m inv* I, i; **~ comme Irma** i as in Isaac *Brit,* i as in Item *Am;* (*on telephone*) i for Isaac *Brit,* i for Item *Am*
ibid. [ibid] *adv abr de* **ibidem** ibid
ibidem [ibidɛm] *adv* ibidem
ibis [ibis] *m* ibis
iceberg [ajsbɛʀg, isbɛʀg] *m* iceberg
ici [isi] *adv* **1.** (*lieu*) here; **~ et là** here and there; (**à partir**) **d'~** from here; **les gens d'~** the people (from round) here; **par ~ on croit ...** round here people think ...; **d'~ à Paris/au musée** from here to Paris/the museum; **près/loin d'~** near/a long way from here; **sortez d'~!** get out of here!; **viens ~ immédiatement!** come here right now!; **je suis venu jusqu'~** I came (all the way) here; **viens par ~** come over here; (*monter*) come up here; (*descendre*) come down here; **passer par ~** to come this way; **Madame la directrice, ~ présente, va ...** The director, who is here with us, will ... **2.** (*temporel*) **jusqu'~** up till now; **d'~** from now; **d'~ peu** very soon; **d'~ là** between now and then; **d'~ (à) 2010/(à) demain/(à) lundi** between now and 2010/tomorrow/Monday; **d'~ (à) la semaine prochaine** between now and next week; **d'~ une semaine/quelques semaines** a week/a few weeks from now; **d'~ (à ce) qu'il accepte, cela peut durer** as for him agreeing, don't hold your breath; **mais d'~ à ce qu'il abandonne, je n'aurais jamais imaginé!** but I never thought he'd actually give up!
icône [ikon] *f* INFOR icon
iconoclaste [ikɔnɔklast] *mf* iconoclast
id. [id] *abr de* **idem** id
idéal [ideal, o] <-aux *o* s> *m* **1.** (*modèle*) ideal; **~ de justice/liberté/beauté** ideal of justice/freedom/beauty; **personne sans ~** person with no ideals **2.** *sans pl* (*le mieux*) **l'~ serait qu'elle revienne** the ideal thing would be for her to come back; **dans l'~** ideally
idéal(**e**) [ideal, o] <-aux *o* s> *adj inf* (*rêvé, imaginaire: femme, solution, société, beauté*) ideal; **des vacances ~es** a perfect holiday *Brit,* a perfect vacation *Am*
idéaliser [idealize] <1> *vt* to idealize
idéalisme [idealism] *m* idealism
idéaliste [idealist] *mf* idealist
idée [ide] *f* **1.** (*projet, inspiration, suggestion,*

opinion) idea; ~ **lumineuse** brilliant idea; **être plein d'~s** to be full of ideas; ~ **de génie** brainwave; **donner l'~ à qn de faire qc** to give sb the idea of doing sth; **quelle drôle d'~!** what a funny idea!; **tu as de ces ~s!** you have some funny ideas!; **avoir les/des ~s larges** to be broad-minded; **avoir une haute ~ de qn/soi-même** to have a high opinion of sb/oneself; ~ **fixe** obsession; **~s noires** gloomy thoughts; **si je suis/perds le fil de mes ~s** if I follow/lose my train of thought; **se faire à l'~ que qn est mort** to get used to the idea of sb being dead; **il faut te changer les ~s** you should put everything out of your mind; **se faire une ~ de qc** to have a (particular) idea of sth; **ne pas avoir la moindre ~ de qc** to have absolutely no idea of sth; **aucune ~!** no idea!; **on n'a pas ~!**, **a-t-on ~!** you have no idea! **2.**(*esprit*) **cela m'est venu à l'~** it occurred to me; **il m'est venu à l'~ de la voir** it occurred to me to see her ►**se faire des ~s** (*s'imaginer des choses*) to imagine things; (*se faire des illusions*) to have another thing coming

idem [idɛm] *adv* (*de même*) likewise

identifiant [idɑ̃tifjɑ̃] *m* INFOR identifier; ~ **d'utilisateur** user identification

identification [idɑ̃tifikasjɔ̃] *f* ~ **à qn** identification with sb

identifier [idɑ̃tifje] <1> **I.** *vt* to identify **II.** *vpr* **s'~ à qn/qc** to identify oneself with sb/sth

identique [idɑ̃tik] *adj* identical; **être ~ à qc** to be identical to sth; **il reste toujours ~ à lui-même** he's the same as ever

identité [idɑ̃tite] *f* (*d'une personne*) identity; **sous une fausse ~** under a false identity

idéologie [ideɔlɔʒi] *f* ideology

idéologique [ideɔlɔʒik] *adj* ideological

idiomatique [idjɔmatik] *adj* idiomatic

idiot(e) [idjo, idjɔt] **I.** *adj* idiotic; **être complètement ~** to be a complete idiot ►**je ne veux pas mourir ~** I don't want everything in life to pass me by **II.** *m(f)* idiot; **tu me prends pour un ~?** do you take me for some kind of idiot?; ~ **du village** *inf* village idiot ►**faire l'~** (*faire mine de ne pas comprendre*) to act stupid; (*vouloir amuser, se conduire stupidement*) to fool around

idiotie [idjɔsi] *f* idiocy *no pl;* **dire des ~s** to talk rubbish [*o* nonsense]; **faire des ~s** to act like an idiot; **faire l'~ de** +*infin* to be stupid enough to +*infin*

idole [idɔl] *f* idol; **faire de qn son ~** to idolize sb

idylle [idil] *f* **1.** idyll **2.**(*amour tendre*) romance; **l'~ d'un été** a summer romance

if [if] *m* yew

IFOP [ifɔp] *m abr de* **Institut français d'opinion publique** *French public opinion institute*

igloo, iglou [iglu] *m* igloo

ignare [iɲaʀ] *adj* ignorant; **être ~ en qc** to be an ignoramus when it comes to sth

ignifugé(e) [iɲifyʒe] *adj* fireproofed

ignoble [iɲɔbl] *adj* disgraceful; (*taudis*) sordid; **des procédés/propos ~s** shameful things to do/say

ignominie [iɲɔmini] *f soutenu* **1.**(*acte*) disgraceful act **2.**(*opprobre*) ignominy; **se couvrir d'~** to disgrace oneself

ignorance [iɲɔʀɑ̃s] *f* ignorance; **être dans l'~ de qc** to be ignorant of sth

ignorant(e) [iɲɔʀɑ̃, ɑ̃t] **I.** *adj* **1.**(*inculte*) ignorant; **être ~ en qc** to know nothing about sth **2.**(*qui n'est pas au courant*) **être ~ des événements** to know nothing of events **II.** *m(f)* ignoramus; **faire l'~** to feign ignorance; **parler en ~ de qc** to speak without any knowledge of sth

ignorer [iɲɔʀe] <1> **I.** *vt* **1.**(*opp: savoir*) not to know; **ne pas ~ qc** to be aware of sth; **n'~ rien de qc** to know all about sth **2.**(*négliger*) to ignore ►**nul n'est censé ~ la loi** ignorance of the law is no excuse; **afin que nul n'en ignore** so that all may know of it **II.** *vpr* **s'~ 1.**(*feindre de ne pas se connaître*) to ignore each other **2.**(*devoir être connu*) **qc ne s'ignore pas** sth is well known

iguane [igwan] *m* iguana

il [il] *pron pers* **1.**(*masc, personne*) he **2.**(*masc, objet*) it **3.** *interrog, non traduit* **Louis a-t-~ ses clés?** has Louis got his keys? **4.**(*répétitif*) ~ **est beau, ce costume** this suit's nice; **regarde le soleil, ~ se couche** look at the sun, it's setting; **l'oiseau, ~ fait cui-cui** birds go tweet-tweet **5.** *impers* it; ~ **est possible qu'elle vienne** it's possible she may come; ~ **pleut** it's raining; ~ **faut que je parte** I've got to go; ~ **y a deux ans** two years ago; ~ **paraît qu'elle vit là-bas** apparently she lives there; *v. a.* **avoir**

île [il] *f* island; **les ~s Malouines** Falkland Islands; **l'~ de Man** Isle of Man; **l'~ de Wight** Isle of Wight; **l'~ du Prince-Edouard** Prince Edward Island

Île-de-France [ildəfʀɑ̃s] *f* **l'~** the Île-de-France (*the area surrounding Paris*)

illégal(e) [i(l)legal, o] <-aux> *adj* illegal

illégalement [i(l)legalmɑ̃] *adv* illegally

illégalité [i(l)legalite] *f* illegality

illégitime [i(l)leʒitim] *adj* **1.**(*enfant, demande*) illegitimate **2.**(*non justifié*) unwarranted

illettré(e) [i(l)letʀe] *adj, m(f)* illiterate

illettrisme [iletʀism] *m* illiteracy

illicite [i(l)lisit] *adj* illicit; **concurrence ~** unfair competition

illico [i(l)liko] *adv inf* right now ►**~ presto** this instant

illimité(e) [i(l)limite] *adj* **1.**(*sans bornes: confiance, pouvoirs*) unlimited; (*reconnaissance*) boundless **2.**(*indéterminé: durée, congé*) indefinite

illisible [i(l)lizibl] *adj* **1.**(*indéchiffrable: écriture*) illegible **2.**(*incompréhensible: article,*

roman) unreadable
illogique [i(l)lɔʒik] *adj* illogical
illumination [i(l)lyminasjɔ̃] *f* **1.** (*action d'éclairer: d'une rue, d'un quartier*) lighting; (*au moyen de projecteurs*) floodlighting **2.** *pl* (*lumières festives*) illuminations *pl*
illuminé(**e**) [i(l)lymine] *adj* **1.** (*très éclairé*) lit up; (*au moyen de projecteurs*) floodlit **2.** (*radieux: visage*) illuminated
illuminer [i(l)lymine] <1> **I.** *vt* **1.** (*éclairer*) ~ **un endroit** (*lustre*) to light up a place **2.** (*faire resplendir*) **la colère illumine ses yeux** anger makes his eyes blaze; **la fierté/la joie illumina ses traits** pride/joy lit up his face **II.** *vpr* **s'**~ **1.** (*s'éclairer vivement: vitrine*) to be lit up; (*monument*) to be floodlit **2.** (*resplendir: personne*) to light up; **à cette nouvelle, son visage s'est illuminé** her face lit up at the news; **ses yeux s'illuminaient de joie/colère** her eyes lit up with joy/anger
illusion [i(l)lyzjɔ̃] *f* (*erreur*) illusion; ~ **d'optique** optical illusion; **se faire des ~s sur qn/qc** to have illusions about sth
illusionniste [i(l)lyzjɔnist] *mf* illusionnist
illusoire [i(l)lyzwaʀ] *adj* illusory; (*promesse*) deceptive; **rêve** ~ empty dream
illustrateur, **-trice** [i(l)lystʀatœʀ, -tʀis] *m, f* illustrator
illustration [i(l)lystʀasjɔ̃] *f* illustration
illustre [i(l)lystʀ] *adj* illustrious
illustré [i(l)lystʀe] *m* magazine
illustré(**e**) [i(l)lystʀe] *adj* illustrated; **journal** ~ magazine
illustrer [i(l)lystʀe] <1> **I.** *vt* **1.** (*orner*) ~ **qc de qc** to illustrate sth with sth **2.** (*enrichir*) ~ **qc de qc** to illustrate sth with sth **II.** *vpr* **s'**~ **1.** (*se rendre célèbre*) to win acclaim **2.** *péj* (*se faire remarquer*) to distinguish oneself
îlot [ilo] *m* **1.** (*petite île*) islet **2.** (*pâté de maisons*) block **3.** (*groupe isolé*) island
ils [il] *pron pers* **1.** (*pl masc ou mixte*) they **2.** *interrog, non traduit* **les enfants sont-~ là?** are the children here? **3.** (*répétitif*) **regarde les paons comme ~ sont beaux** look how beautiful the peacocks are; *v. a.* **il**
image [imaʒ] *f* **1.** (*dessin*) picture; ~ **de marque** (brand) image **2.** (*reflet*) *a. fig* image; **se faire une ~ de qn/qc** to have an image of sb/sth ►**sage comme une** ~ as good as gold; **à l'~ de qn/qc** in the image of sb/sth
imagé(**e**) [imaʒe] *adj* (*langage*) colourful *Brit*, colorful *Am*; (*style*) full of imagery
imagerie [imaʒʀi] *f* TECH, MED imaging ►~ **populaire** popular imagery
imaginable [imaʒinabl] *adj* imaginable
imaginaire [imaʒinɛʀ] **I.** *adj* imaginary **II.** *m* **l'**~ the imagination
imaginatif, **-ive** [imaʒinatif, -iv] *adj* imaginative
imagination [imaʒinasjɔ̃] *f* imagination; **dépasser l'**~ to be beyond the imagination; **vous ne manquez pas d'~!** you've got a good imagination!
imaginer [imaʒine] <1> **I.** *vt* **1.** (*se représenter, supposer*) to imagine; ~ **de faire qc** to imagine doing sth **2.** (*inventer*) to think up **II.** *vpr* **1.** (*se représenter*) **s'**~ **qn/qc autrement** to imagine sb/sth differently **2.** (*se voir*) **s'**~ **à la plage/dans vingt ans** to imagine oneself at the beach/in twenty years' time **3.** (*croire faussement*) **s'**~ **qc** to imagine sth
imam [imam] *m* imam
imbattable [ɛ̃batabl] *adj* unbeatable
imbécile [ɛ̃besil] **I.** *adj* idiotic **II.** *mf* cretin; **faire l'**~ (*vouloir paraître stupide*) to act stupid; (*se conduire stupidement*) to act like a fool ►**il n'y a que les ~s qui ne changent pas d'avis** only fools never change their mind
imbécillité [ɛ̃besilite] *f* **1.** (*manque d'intelligence, action stupide*) idiocy **2.** (*chose stupide*) **une** ~ a totally stupid thing to do; **faire des ~s** to act like a total idiot; **il ne dit que des ~s** he talks total rubbish [*o* nonsense]
imberbe [ɛ̃bɛʀb] *adj* beardless
imbibé(**e**) [ɛ̃bibe] *adj inf* pickled
imbiber [ɛ̃bibe] <1> **I.** *vt* **1.** to soak; **des chaussures imbibées d'eau** soaking wet shoes; **imbibé de sang** bloodsoaked **2.** *péj, inf* **être imbibé d'alcool** to be a boozer **II.** *vpr* **1. s'**~ **de qc** to become soaked with sth **2.** *péj, inf* **s'**~ **d'alcool** to hit the bottle
imbriquer [ɛ̃bʀike] <1> **I.** *vt* (*pièces, tuiles*) to fit together; **être imbriqué dans qc** to be fitted into sth **II.** *vpr* **s'**~ **1.** (*se chevaucher: plaques, tuiles*) to fit together **2.** (*s'enchevêtrer*) to be interlinked; **s'**~ **dans qc** to get caught up in sth
imbroglio [ɛ̃bʀɔglijo, ɛ̃bʀɔljo] *m* imbroglio
imbu(**e**) [ɛ̃by] *adj souvent péj* ~ **de soi-même** full of oneself; **être** ~ **de préjugés** to be steeped in prejudice; **être** ~ **de principes** to have staunch principles
imbuvable [ɛ̃byvabl] *adj* **1.** (*boisson*) undrinkable **2.** *inf* (*détestable*) appalling; **c'est** ~ it stinks
IME [iɛmø] *m abr de* **Institut monétaire européen** EMI
imitateur, **-trice** [imitatœʀ, -tʀis] *m, f* **1.** (*personne qui imite*) imitator **2.** (*comédien*) impressionist
imitation [imitasjɔ̃] *f* **1.** (*action*) imitation; **à l'**~ **de qn/qc** in imitation of sb/sth **2.** (*plagiat*) copy **3.** (*contrefaçon: d'une signature*) forgery; (**en**) ~ imitation ►**pâle** ~ pale imitation
imiter [imite] <1> *vt* **1.** (*reproduire*) to imitate; (*pour amuser*) to mimic **2.** (*prendre pour modèle*) to imitate; **un exemple à** ~ an example to follow **3.** (*singer, reproduire*) to mimic; (*signature*) to forge **4.** (*avoir l'aspect de*) ~ **qc** to look like sth
immaculé(**e**) [imakyle] *adj* **1.** immaculate; **être d'une blancheur ~e** [*o* **d'un blanc** ~] to be spotlessly white **2.** (*honneur*) unsullied; (*âme, réputation*) spotless
immangeable [ɛ̃mɑ̃ʒabl] *adj* inedible

immanquable [ɛ̃mɑ̃kabl] *adj* **1.** (*inévitable*) inescapable **2.** (*infaillible: cible*) unmissable

immanquablement [ɛ̃mɑ̃kabləmɑ̃] *adv* unfailingly

immatériel(le) [i(m)mateʀjɛl] *adj* **1.** immaterial **2.** (*léger, aérien*) ethereal

immatriculation [imatʀikylasjɔ̃] *f* (*d'un étudiant, d'une voiture*) registration; ~ **d'un commerçant au registre du commerce** trader's entry in the trade register; ~ **à la Sécurité sociale** Socical Security membership

immatriculé(e) [imatʀikyle] *adj* registered; **être** ~ (*voiture*) to have a registration number; **être** ~ **dans la Savoie** to have a Savoy registration number

immatriculer [imatʀikyle] <1> *vt* to register; **se faire** ~ **à l'université** to register at university; **faire** ~ **une voiture** to register a car

immature [imatyʀ] *adj* immature

immédiat [imedja] *m* immediate future

immédiat(e) [imedja, jat] *adj* **1.** (*très proche*) immediate; (*contact*) direct; (*soulagement, effet*) instantaneous; **dans l'avenir** ~ in the immediate future **2.** (*sans intermédiaire*) direct **3.** (*qui s'impose: question*) vital; **mesures** ~**es** immediate steps

immédiatement [imedjatmɑ̃] *adv* **1.** (*tout de suite*) immediately **2.** (*sans intermédiaire*) directly

immense [i(m)mɑ̃s] *adj* immense

immensément [i(m)mɑ̃semɑ̃] *adv* (*riche*) immensely

immensité [i(m)mɑ̃site] *f* immensity; **devant** ~ **de la tâche** in the face of this immense task

immergé(e) [imɛʀʒe] *adj* (*rocher, terres*) submerged

immersion [imɛʀsjɔ̃] *f* immersion; (*d'un câble*) laying; (*d'un sous-marin*) diving; (*de déchets radioactifs*) dumping; (*des terres*) submersion

immettable [ɛ̃metabl] *adj* (*vêtement*) unwearable

immeuble [imœbl] *m* building; ~ **à usage locatif** block of rented properties; ~ **de bureaux** office building

immigrant(e) [imigʀɑ̃, ɑ̃t] **I.** *adj* immigrant **II.** *m(f)* immigrant

immigration [imigʀasjɔ̃] *f* immigration

immigré(e) [imigʀe] **I.** *adj* immigrant **II.** *m(f)* immigrant

immigrer [imigʀe] <1> *vi* to immigrate

imminent(e) [iminɑ̃, ɑ̃t] *adj* imminent; (*conflit, danger*) impending; **être** ~ to be imminent

immiscer [imise] <2> *vpr* **s'**~ **dans qc** to interfere in sth

immobile [i(m)mɔbil] *adj* **1.** (*fixe*) still; (*personne*) motionless; (*partie, pièce*) fixed **2.** (*qui n'évolue pas*) immovable

immobilier [imɔbilje] *m* **l'**~ real estate; **travailler dans l'**~ to work in real estate

immobilier, -ière [imɔbilje, -jɛʀ] *adj* (*annonce, société, vente, ensemble*) property; (*saisie*) of property; (*crise, placement*) in property; (*revenus*) from property; **agent/agence** ~(**-ière**) real estate agent/agency; **biens** ~**s** real estate; **crédit** ~ mortgage; **promoteur** ~ property developer

immobilisation [imɔbilizasjɔ̃] *f* **1.** (*arrêt: d'un véhicule*) stopping; (*d'une machine*) stoppage; **attendez l'**~ **totale du convoi!** wait until the train comes to a complete stop!; **entraîner l'**~ **de la circulation** to bring traffic to a complete stop **2.** MED (*d'un membre, d'une fracture*) immobilization

immobiliser [imɔbilize] <1> **I.** *vt* **1.** (*stopper: camions*) to stop; (*circulation*) to bring to a standstill **2.** (*paralyser: personne*) to paralyse *Brit,* to paralyze *Am;* **immobilisé de peur** paralysed with fear **3.** MED, SPORT to immobilize; ~ **qn** (*fracture, grippe*) to keep sb out of action **II.** *vpr* **s'**~ (*personne, machine, train*) to come to a halt; **s'**~ **de peur** to be paralysed with fear *Brit,* to be paralyzed by fear *Am;* **s'**~ **de surprise** to stop dead in surprise

immobilisme [imɔbilism] *m* resistance to change

immobilité [imɔbilite] *f* **1.** (*inertie*) stillness **2.** (*immuabilité*) immovability

immoler [imɔle] <1> *vt* ~ **qn/un animal à qn/qc** to sacrifice sb/an animal to sb/sth

immonde [i(m)mɔ̃d] *adj* **1.** (*d'une saleté extrême*) foul **2.** (*répugnant: crime, action*) sordid; (*personne*) squalid; (*propos*) vile

immondices [i(m)mɔ̃dis] *fpl* refuse

immoral(e) [i(m)mɔʀal, o] <-aux> *adj* immoral

immoralité [i(m)mɔʀalite] *f* immorality

immortaliser [imɔʀtalize] <1> **I.** *vt* to immortalize **II.** *vpr* **s'**~ **par qc** to immortalize oneself through sth

immortalité [imɔʀtalite] *f* immortality

immortel(le) [imɔʀtɛl] *adj* **1.** REL immortal **2.** *soutenu* (*impérissable: amour, gloire, monument*) eternal; (*souvenir, principe*) undying; (*personne*) immortal

immuable [imɥabl] *adj* immutable; (*sourire*) unchanging; **rester** ~ **dans ses convictions** to remain firm in one's convictions

immuniser [imynize] <1> *vt a. fig* ~ **qn contre qc** to immunize sb against sth

immunité [imynite] *f* immunity

impact [ɛ̃pakt] *m* (*heurt, influence*) impact; **point d'**~ (*d'une balle*) point of impact; ~ **publicitaire/médiatique** advertising/media impact; **avoir de l'**~ **sur qn/qc** to have an impact on sb/sth; (*intervention, nouvelle*) to make an impact on sb/sth

impair [ɛ̃pɛʀ] *m* **1.** (*opp: pair*) odd numbers; **miser sur l'**~ (*à la roulette*) to bet on the odd numbers **2.** (*gaffe*) blunder; **commettre un** ~ to make a blunder

impair(e) [ɛ̃pɛʀ] *adj* odd

imparable [ɛ̃paʀabl] *adj* (*argument,*

riposte) unanswerable; (*coup, tir*) unstoppable
impardonnable [ɛ̃paʀdɔnabl] *adj* (*erreur, faute*) inexcusable; **elle est ~ de se tromper encore** its unforgiveable of her to make another mistake
imparfait [ɛ̃paʀfɛ] *m* imperfect; **à l'~** in the imperfect
impartial(e) [ɛ̃paʀsjal, jo] <-aux> *adj* impartial
impartialité [ɛ̃paʀsjalite] *f* impartiality; **avec ~** impartially ►**en toute ~** completely impartial
impasse [ɛ̃pɑs] *f* (*rue*) dead end ►**s'engager dans une ~** to get into an impasse; **être dans l'~** to be in an impasse; **faire l'~ sur qc** to give up on sth
impassibilité [ɛ̃pasibilite] *f* impassiveness; **l'~ de son visage** his impassive face; **garder son ~** to remain impassive
impassible [ɛ̃pasibl] *adj* (*personne, visage*) impassive; **rester ~** to show no emotion
impatiemment [ɛ̃pasjamɑ̃] *adv* impatiently
impatience [ɛ̃pasjɑ̃s] *f* impatience; **je brûle d'~ de partir** I can't wait to go; **avec ~** impatiently
impatient(e) [ɛ̃pasjɑ̃, jɑ̃t] **I.** *adj* impatient; **je suis ~ de te voir** I can't wait to see you **II.** *m(f)* impatient person
impatienter [ɛ̃pasjɑ̃te] <1> **I.** *vt* **~ qn avec qc** to irritate sb with sth; **vous commencez à m'~** you're beginning to get on my nerves **II.** *vpr* **s'~ de qc** to get impatient with sth; **s'~ contre qn/qc** to lose patience with sb/sth
impec [ɛ̃pɛk] *inf,* **impeccable** [ɛ̃pekabl] *adj* **1.** (*très propre*) spotless **2.** (*irréprochable*) faultless; (*attitude, conduite*) exemplary **3.** *inf* (*parfait*) **~!** perfect
impénétrable [ɛ̃penetʀabl] *adj* impenetrable; **être ~ aux balles** to be bulletproof; **il est ~ à ce qui l'entoure** he's impervious to everything around him
impénitent(e) [ɛ̃penitɑ̃, ɑ̃t] *adj* unrepentant; **être un fumeur ~** to be an unashamed smoker
impensable [ɛ̃pɑ̃sabl] *adj* unthinkable
imper [ɛ̃pɛʀ] *m inf abr de* **imperméable**
impératif [ɛ̃peʀatif] *m* **1.** *souvent pl* (*nécessité*) constraint; **les ~s de la mode** the dictates of fashion **2.** LING imperative
impérativement [ɛ̃peʀativmɑ̃] *adv* **1.** (*obligatoirement*) absolutely; **il faut ~ que qn fasse qc** (*subj*) sb absolutely must do sth **2.** (*nécessairement*) of necessity **3.** (*avec autorité*) imperiously
impératrice [ɛ̃peʀatʀis] *f* empress; *v. a.* **empereur**
imperceptible [ɛ̃pɛʀsɛptibl] *adj* **1.** (*indécelable*) imperceptible; **être ~ à l'oreille** to be too faint to hear; **être ~ à l'œil** to be imperceptible to the (naked) eye **2.** (*infime, minime*) minute
imperceptiblement [ɛ̃pɛʀsɛptibləmɑ̃] *adv* imperceptibly
imperfection [ɛ̃pɛʀfɛksjɔ̃] *f* **1.** *sans pl* (*opp: perfection*) imperfection **2.** *souvent pl* (*défaut: d'une matière, d'un roman, plan*) flaw; (*d'un visage, de la peau*) blemish
impérial(e) [ɛ̃peʀjal, jo] <-aux> *adj* **1.** (*d'empereur: sceptre, pouvoir*) imperial; **dignité ~e** imperial majesty **2.** (*dominateur, altier*) majestic
impérialisme [ɛ̃peʀjalism] *m* imperialism
impérialiste [ɛ̃peʀjalist] **I.** *adj* imperialist(ic) **II.** *mf* imperialist
impérieux, -euse [ɛ̃peʀjø, -jøz] *adj* **1.** (*autoritaire*) imperious **2.** (*pressant*) imperative; (*nécessité, réalité*) compelling; **rendre qc ~** to make sth urgent
impérissable [ɛ̃peʀisabl] *adj* imperishable
imperméabiliser [ɛ̃pɛʀmeabilize] <1> *vt* to waterproof; **ce produit imperméabilise les chaussures** the product makes shoes waterproof
imperméable [ɛ̃pɛʀmeabl] **I.** *adj* **1.** (*sol*) impermeable; (*tissu, toile*) waterproof **2.** (*insensible*) **~ à des arguments** impervious to argument; **~ à l'art/à un sentiment** untouched by art/a feeling **II.** *m* raincoat
imperméable [ɛ̃pɛʀmeabl] **I.** *adj* (*sol*) impermeable; (*tissu, toile*) waterproof **II.** *m* raincoat
impersonnel(le) [ɛ̃pɛʀsɔnɛl] *adj* impersonal
impertinence [ɛ̃pɛʀtinɑ̃s] *f* impertinence *no pl;* **avec ~** impertinently; **arrête tes ~s!** don't be so impertinent!
impertinent(e) [ɛ̃pɛʀtinɑ̃, ɑ̃t] **I.** *adj* impertinent **II.** *m(f)* impertinent person
imperturbable [ɛ̃pɛʀtyʀbabl] *adj* imperturbable
impétueux, -euse [ɛ̃petɥø, -øz] *adj* **1.** (*fougueux*) impetuous **2.** (*qui prend des risques*) rash; (*orateur*) fiery
impétuosité [ɛ̃petɥozite] *f soutenu* **1.** (*fougue*) impetuosity; (*d'une passion*) impulsiveness **2.** (*violence*) ferocity
impie [ɛ̃pi] **I.** *adj soutenu* impious **II.** *mf soutenu* **1.** ungodly person **2.** (*blasphémateur*) blasphemer
impitoyable [ɛ̃pitwajabl] *adj* (*personne*) pitiless; (*critique, jugement*) merciless; (*haine*) unrelenting; (*regard*) without pity
impitoyablement [ɛ̃pitwajabləmɑ̃] *adv* mercilessly
implacable [ɛ̃plakabl] *adj* (*ennemi, juge, destin*) implacable; (*soleil*) merciless; (*film, critique, mal*) relentless
implant [ɛ̃plɑ̃] *m* implant; **~ capillaire** hair implant
implantation [ɛ̃plɑ̃tasjɔ̃] *f* **1.** setting up; (*d'une population*) introduction **2.** MED implanting
implanter [ɛ̃plɑ̃te] <1> **I.** *vt* **1.** (*introduire*) *a.* MED to implant; **être implanté** (*industrie*) to be implanted; (*personne*) to be settled in; (*arbre*) to be established; (*système*) to be running **2.** (*enraciner*) **être implanté dans qc**

I

(*habitudes, préjugés*) to be ingrained **II.** *vpr* **s'~ 1.** (*se fixer*) to be implanted; (*immigrants*) to settle; (*parti politique*) to become established **2.** (*s'installer: idées, préjugés*) to become ingrained; (*usages*) to become established

implémenter [ɛ̃plemɑ̃te] <1> *vt* INFOR to implement

implication [ɛ̃plikasjɔ̃] *f* **1.** *gén pl* (*conséquence*) implications *pl* **2.** (*mise en cause*) ~ **de qn dans qc** sb's implication in sth

implicite [ɛ̃plisit] *adj* implicit; **mais c'était le sens ~ de ses propos** yes but that was what he implied

implicitement [ɛ̃plisitmɑ̃] *adv* implicitly

impliquer [ɛ̃plike] <1> **I.** *vt* **1.** (*signifier, avoir pour conséquence*) to imply **2.** (*demander*) ~ **de la concentration** to involve concentration **3.** (*mêler*) ~ **qn dans qc** to involve sb in sth **II.** *vpr* **s'~ dans qc** to get involved in sth

implorer [ɛ̃plɔʀe] <1> *vt* to implore

impoli(e) [ɛ̃pɔli] **I.** *adj* ~ **envers qn** impolite to sb **II.** *m(f)* impolite person

impolitesse [ɛ̃pɔlitɛs] *f* impoliteness *no pl;* **avec** ~ impolitely

impondérable [ɛ̃pɔ̃deʀabl] **I.** *adj* (*événement*) imponderable; **facteurs ~s** imponderables **II.** *m gén pl* imponderable

impopulaire [ɛ̃pɔpylɛʀ] *adj* unpopular; **se rendre** ~ to make oneself unpopular

impopularité [ɛ̃pɔpylaʀite] *f* unpopularity

import [ɛ̃pɔʀ] *m abr de* **importation**

importable¹ [ɛ̃pɔʀtabl] *adj* (*qu'on peut importer*) importable

importable² [ɛ̃pɔʀtabl] *adj* (*immettable*) unwearable; **ce complet est devenu** ~ this suit is not fit to be worn any more

importance [ɛ̃pɔʀtɑ̃s] *f* **1.** (*rôle*) importance; **de la dernière** ~ of the highest importance; **accorder de l'~ à qc** to grant importance to sth; **se donner de l'~** *péj* to think oneself important; **être d'~** to be of some importance; **prendre de l'~** to take on some importance; **sans** ~ of no importance **2.** (*ampleur*) size

important [ɛ̃pɔʀtɑ̃] *m* important thing

important(e) [ɛ̃pɔʀtɑ̃, ɑ̃t] **I.** *adj* **1.** (*considérable*) important; **quelque chose d'~** something important **2.** (*gros*) considerable; (*dégâts*) large-scale; (*somme, quantité*) large **3.** *péj* self-important; **prendre des airs ~s** to put on airs of importance **II.** *m(f)* **faire l'~** *péj* to act important

importateur, -trice [ɛ̃pɔʀtatœʀ, -tʀis] **I.** *adj* **un pays ~ de blé** a wheat-importing country **II.** *m, f* importer

importation [ɛ̃pɔʀtasjɔ̃] *f* **1.** (*commerce*) importing **2.** (*produit*) import; **marchandise d'~** imported product; **c'est de la viande d'~** it's imported meat

importer¹ [ɛ̃pɔʀte] <1> *vt* to import

importer² [ɛ̃pɔʀte] <1> *vi* **1.** (*être important*) **la seule chose qui importe, c'est que ...** the only thing that matters is that ...; **cela importe peu/beaucoup** that's very/not very important; **peu importe que** +*subj* it doesn't matter if; **peu importe(nt) les difficultés!** never mind the difficulties; **qu'importe qc** who cares about sth; **qu'importe si qn fait qc** what does it matter if sb does sth **2.** (*intéresser*) ~ **fort peu à qn** to be of very little importance to sb; **ce qui m'importe, c'est ...** the important thing for me is ... ►**n'importe comment** no matter how; **n'importe lequel/laquelle** any; (*des deux*) either; **n'importe** (*cela m'est égal*) it doesn't matter; (*néanmoins*) even so; **n'importe où** anywhere; **n'importe quand** any time; **n'importe quel** + *subst* any; **acheter à n'importe quel prix** to buy at any price; **n'importe qui** anybody; **n'importe quoi** anything; **dire n'importe quoi** to talk nonsense

import-export [ɛ̃pɔʀɛkspɔʀ] <imports-exports> *m* import-export (business)

importun(e) [ɛ̃pɔʀtœ̃, yn] **I.** *adj soutenu* (*arrivée, visite, visiteur*) untimely; (*curiosité, demande*) unwelcome; (*plainte, lamentation*) bothersome **II.** *m(f) soutenu* nuisance

importuner [ɛ̃pɔʀtyne] <1> *vt soutenu* to trouble

imposable [ɛ̃pozabl] *adj* taxable; **n'être pas** ~ to be non-taxable

imposant(e) [ɛ̃pozɑ̃, ɑ̃t] *adj* **1.** (*majestueux*) imposing **2.** (*considérable*) impressive; (*somme*) hefty

imposé(e) [ɛ̃poze] *adj* (*prix, date*) fixed; **le minimum ~ par la loi** the minimum set by the law

imposer [ɛ̃poze] <1> **I.** *vt* **1.** (*exiger: décision*) to impose; (*repos*) to order; ~ **qc à qn** to impose sth on sb **2.** (*prescrire: date*) to set; ~ **qc à qn** to impose sth on sb; ~ **à qn de** +*infin* to force sb to +*infin* **3.** (*faire accepter de force*) ~ **le silence à qn** to impose silence on sb; ~ **sa volonté à qn** to impose one's will on sb; **il sait ~ son autorité** he knows how to establish his authority **4.** (*faire reconnaître: produit*) to establish **5.** FIN (*personne, revenu, marchandise*) to tax; **être imposé sur qc** (*personne*) to be taxed on sth **II.** *vpr* **1.** (*devenir indispensable*) **s'~ à qn** (*repos*) to be vital for sb; (*solution*) to force itself on sb; (*prudence*) to be required of sb; **ça s'impose** that's a matter of course; **ça ne s'imposait vraiment pas** that wasn't really necessary **2.** (*être importun*) **s'~** to impose oneself **3.** (*se faire reconnaître*) **s'~** to stand out **4.** (*se donner comme devoir*) **s'~ qc** to impose sth on oneself; **il s'est imposé de ne plus fumer** he forced himself to stop smoking

impossibilité [ɛ̃pɔsibilite] *f* impossibility; **il y a ~ à ce que qn fasse qc** (*subj*) there is no possibility of sb doing sth; **être dans l'~ de** +*infin* to be unable to +*infin;* **mettre qn dans l'~ de** +*infin* to make it impossible for sb to

+*infin*

impossible [ɛ̃pɔsibl] **I.** *adj* **1.** (*irréalisable, insupportable*) impossible; **être ~ à qn** to be impossible for sb; **rendre la vie ~ à qn** to make life impossible for sb **2.** *inf* (*invraisemblable*) ridiculous; **à des heures ~s** at the most ridiculous hours **II.** *m* impossible; **tenter l'~** to try to do the impossible

imposteur [ɛ̃pɔstœʀ] *m* impostor

impôt [ɛ̃po] *m* tax; **~ sur le revenu** (**des personnes physiques**) income tax; **~ sur les salaires** tax on salaries; **~ foncier** property tax; **~s locaux** local authority tax

In France, **impôt** is not deducted on a monthly basis. It is paid at the end of the year in a lump sum for the past year.

impotent(**e**) [ɛ̃pɔtɑ̃, ɑ̃t] **I.** *adj* crippled **II.** *m(f)* cripple

impraticable [ɛ̃pʀatikabl] *adj* **1.** (*route, piste, sentier*) impassible; (*terrain de sport*) unplayable **2.** (*irréalisable*) impracticable; (*méthode*) impractical

imprécis(**e**) [ɛ̃pʀesi, iz] *adj* imprecise; (*souvenir, contour*) vague; (*limites*) unclear; (*évaluation*) inaccurate; **n'avoir que des souvenirs fort ~ de qc** to have only the faintest recollection of sth

imprécision [ɛ̃pʀesizjɔ̃] *f* vagueness

imprégner [ɛ̃pʀeɲe] <5> **I.** *vt* **1.** (*imbiber: bois*) to impregnate; (*étoffe*) to soak; **~ un tampon de qc** to soak a wad of cloth in sth; **l'odeur imprègne la pièce** the smell pervades the room **2.** (*marquer*) **~ qn** (*atmosphère*) to leave its mark on sb; (*sentiment*) to fill sb; **l'amertume imprégnait ses paroles** his words were filled with bitterness; **être imprégné de préjugés** to be imbued with prejudice; **être imprégné d'un souvenir** to be filled with a memory; **une lettre imprégnée d'ironie** a letter suffused with irony **II.** *vpr* **s'~ d'eau** to soak up water; **s'~ d'une odeur** to be filled with a smell

imprenable [ɛ̃pʀənabl] *adj* (*forteresse, château*) impregnable; (*vue*) clear

imprésario <s *o* imprésarii> [ɛ̃pʀezaʀjo, ɛ̃pʀesaʀjo, -ʀii] *m* impresario

impression [ɛ̃pʀesjɔ̃] *f* (*sentiment*) impression; **avoir l'~ que ...** to have the impression that ..; **faire une forte ~ sur qn** to make a strong impression on sb; **laisser à qn une ~** to leave sb an impression ▶**une ~ de <u>déjà-vu</u>** an impression of déjà-vu

impressionnable [ɛ̃pʀesjɔnabl] *adj* impressionnable

impressionnant(**e**) [ɛ̃pʀesjɔnɑ̃, ɑ̃t] *adj* **1.** (*imposant*) impressive **2.** (*considérable*) remarkable

impressionner [ɛ̃pʀesjɔne] <1> *vt* **~ qn** to impress sb; (*films d'horreur*) to upset sb; **se laisser ~ par qn/qc** to feel intimidated by sb/sth

impressionnisme [ɛ̃pʀesjɔnism] *m* Impressionnism

impressionniste [ɛ̃pʀesjɔnist] **I.** *adj* impressionnistic; (*école, mouvement*) impressionist **II.** *mf* Impressionnist

imprévisible [ɛ̃pʀevizibl] **I.** *adj* unforseeable; (*personne*) unpredictable **II.** *m* **l'~** the unforseeable

imprévoyance [ɛ̃pʀevwajɑ̃s] *f* lack of foresight; **quelle ~!** such lack of foresight!

imprévoyant(**e**) [ɛ̃pʀevwajɑ̃, jɑ̃t] *adj* lacking in foresight

imprévu [ɛ̃pʀevy] *m* **1.** (*ce à quoi on ne s'attend pas*) **l'~** the unexpected; **j'aime l'~** I like to be surprised; **des vacances pleines d'~s** a holiday with lots of surprises **2.** (*fâcheux*) unexpected incident; **il y a eu un ~** something (unexpected) cropped up; **en cas d'~** in the event of any (unexpected) problem

imprévu(**e**) [ɛ̃pʀevy] *adj* unexpected

imprimante [ɛ̃pʀimɑ̃t] *f* INFOR printer; **~ à jet d'encre/à laser/thermique** ink-jet/laser/thermal printer

imprimé [ɛ̃pʀime] *m* **1.** (*formulaire*) form **2.** (*tissu*) print **3.** (*ouvrage imprimé*) printed matter

imprimé(**e**) [ɛ̃pʀime] *adj* printed

imprimer [ɛ̃pʀime] <1> *vt* to print; **~ ses pas sur la neige** to leave one's footprints in the snow

imprimerie [ɛ̃pʀimʀi] *f* **1.** (*technique*) printing **2.** (*établissement*) print shop

imprimeur, **-euse** [ɛ̃pʀimœʀ, -øz] *m, f* printer

improbable [ɛ̃pʀɔbabl] *adj* improbable

improductif, **-ive** [ɛ̃pʀɔdyktif, -iv] **I.** *adj* unproductive; (*efforts*) fruitless **II.** *m, f* unproductive citizen

impromptu(**e**) [ɛ̃pʀɔ̃pty] *adj* (*repas*) impromptu; **un discours ~** an off-the-cuff speech; **visite ~e** surprise visit

imprononçable [ɛ̃pʀɔnɔ̃sabl] *adj* unpronounceable

impropre [ɛ̃pʀɔpʀ] *adj* **1.** inappropriate **2.** (*inapte*) **~ à qc** unfit for sth

improvisation [ɛ̃pʀɔvizasjɔ̃] *f* improvisation

improvisé(**e**) [ɛ̃pʀɔvize] *adj* improvised; (*excursion*) impromptu

improviser [ɛ̃pʀɔvize] <1> **I.** *vt, vi* to improvise; **~ une excuse** to think up a quick excuse **II.** *vpr* **1.** (*opp: se préparer*) **s'~** to be improvised; **un tel discours ne s'improvise pas** you can't make up a speech like that as you go along **2.** (*devenir subitement*) **s'~ infirmière** to take on the role of nurse; **on ne s'improvise pas artiste** you don't turn into a painter just like that

improviste [ɛ̃pʀɔvist] **à l'~** unexpectedly; **prendre qn à l'~** to catch sb unawares; **arriver à l'~** to arrive without warning

imprudemment [ɛ̃pʀydamɑ̃] *adv* unwisely

imprudence [ɛ̃pʀydɑ̃s] *f* carelessness; (*en*

prenant des risques) rashness; **par** ~ carelessly; **avoir l'~ de** +*infin* to be foolish enough to +*infin;* **regretter ~ de ses propos** to regret one's rash words

imprudent(e) [ɛ̃pʀydɑ̃, ɑ̃t] I. *adj* 1.(*négligent*) foolish 2.(*dangereux*) rash II. *m(f)* careless fool

impudence [ɛ̃pydɑ̃s] *f* impudence *no pl*

impuissance [ɛ̃pɥisɑ̃s] *f* 1.(*faiblesse*) powerlessness; **être dans l'~ de** +*infin* to be powerless to +*infin;* **être réduit à l'~** to be left powerless; **les malfaiteurs furent rapidement réduits à l'~** the wrongdoers were soon foiled 2.(*sur le plan sexuel*) impotence

impuissant [ɛ̃pɥisɑ̃] *m* impotent man

impuissant(e) [ɛ̃pɥisɑ̃, ɑ̃t] *adj* 1.(*faible*) powerless; (*effort*) hopeless; **être ~ face à qc** to be powerless in the face of sth 2.(*sexuellement*) impotent

impulsif, -ive [ɛ̃pylsif, -iv] I. *adj* impulsive II. *m, f* man , woman of impulse *m*

impulsion [ɛ̃pylsjɔ̃] *f* 1. *a.* TECH, ELEC impulse 2.(*incitation*) impetus ►**sous l'~ de qn** spurred on by sb; **sous l'~ d'un sentiment** driven on by a feeling; **agir sous l'~ de la vengeance** to act out an urge for vengeance

impunément [ɛ̃pynemɑ̃] *adv* with impunity

impuni(e) [ɛ̃pyni] *adj* unpunished

impunité [ɛ̃pynite] *f* impunity; **en toute ~** with complete impunity

impur(e) [ɛ̃pyʀ] *adj* 1.impure; (*eau, air*) polluted; (*race*) mongrel 2.REL (*animal*) unclean 3.*soutenu* (*immoral*) impure

impureté [ɛ̃pyʀte] *f* impurity; **à cause de l'~ de l'air** because of the polluted air

imputer [ɛ̃pyte] <1> *vt* 1.~ **la faute à qn/qc** to impute a fault to sb/sth; ~ **une défaite à qn/qc** to make sb/sth responsible for a defeat 2.(*porter en compte*) ~ **une dépense à un budget** to charge an expense to a budget; **les dépenses seront imputées sur les frais généraux** expenditure will be allocated to overheads

imputrescible [ɛ̃pytʀesibl] *adj* rot-proof

in [in] *adj inv, inf* hip

inabordable [inabɔʀdabl] *adj* (*lieu*) unreachable; (*personne*) unapproachable; **des loyers ~s** rents people can't afford

inacceptable [inaksɛptabl] *adj* unacceptable

inaccessible [inaksesibl] *adj* 1.(*hors d'atteinte: sommet*) inaccessible; ~ **à qn/qc** out of reach to sb/sth; **la côte/l'île est ~ aux bateaux** the coast/the island cannot be reached by boat 2.(*inabordable: personne*) unapproachable 3.(*insensible*) **être ~ à qc** to be impervious to sth 4.(*trop cher*) beyond one's means; **les loyers sont ~s** the rents are out of people's reach 5.(*incompréhensible*) impenetrable; **ce sont des poèmes pratiquement ~s** the poems are virtually unintelligible

inaccoutumé(e) [inakutyme] *adj soutenu* ~ **à qc** unaccustomed to sth

inachevé(e) [inaʃ(ə)ve] *adj* unfinished; **la symphonie ~e de Schubert** Schubert's Unfinished Symphony

inactif, -ive [inaktif, -iv] I. *adj* 1.(*oisif*) idle; **ne pas rester ~** not to remain idle; (*au repos: personne*) not to keep still; **être ~** (*personne*) to be out of work 2.(*inefficace*) ineffective II. *m, f* **les ~s** the non-working population

inaction [inaksjɔ̃] *f* inaction

inactivité [inaktivite] *f* 1.(*d'une personne*) inactivity; (*d'un commerce, des affaires*) standstill 2.ADMIN **en ~** not in active service

inadaptation [inadaptasjɔ̃] *f* ~ **à qc** failure to adapt to sth

inadapté(e) [inadapte] I. *adj* 1.(*médicament*) inappropriate; ~ **à qc** unsuited to sth; **mener une vie ~e à ses ressources** to have a lifestyle that doesn't correspond to one's means 2.PSYCH maladjusted II. *m(f)* maladjusted person

inadéquat(e) [inadekwa, kwat] *adj soutenu* inappropriate; ~ **à qc** unsuited to sth

inadmissible [inadmisibl] *adj* unacceptable

inadvertance [inadvɛʀtɑ̃s] *f soutenu* 1.(*négligence*) inadvertence *no pl* 2.(*erreur d'inattention*) oversight; **par ~** inadvertently

inaliénable [inaljenabl] *adj* inalienable

inaltérable [inalteʀabl] *adj* 1.**la couleur est ~ au lavage/à la lumière** the colour will not fade in the wash/in sunlight *Brit,* the color will not fade in the wash/in sunlight *Am;* **substance ~ à l'air/à la chaleur** air-resistant/heat-resistant substance 2.(*immuable: santé*) unfailing; (*conviction*) unshakeable; **rester ~** (*sentiment*) to stand fast; **être d'un ~ optimisme** to be unfailingly optimistic

inamovible [inamɔvibl] *adj* 1.fixed; (*fonctionnaire*) irremovable 2.*iron* (*éternel: chapeau, sourire*) glued-on; **être vraiment ~** (*personne*) to be part of the furniture

inanimé(e) [inanime] *adj* 1.(*sans vie*) inanimate 2.(*évanoui*) unconscious

inanition [inanisjɔ̃] *f* **mourir/tomber d'~** to die of/faint with hunger; **se laisser mourir d'~** to starve oneself to death

inaperçu(e) [inapɛʀsy] *adj* **passer ~** to pass unnoticed; **tu ne vas pas passer ~, comme ça!** you're going to make yourself noticed!

inapplicable [inaplikabl] *adj* (*théorie*) inapplicable; (*mesure*) unenforceable; ~ **à qc** not applicable to sth; **cette mesure est ~ à la réalité** this measure cannot be enforced in the real world

inappréciable [inapʀesjabl] *adj* 1.invaluable 2.(*difficile à évaluer*) imperceptible

inapte [inapt] *adj* 1.~ **à qc** unsuitable for sth; ~ **à faire qc** incapable of doing sth; ~ **au travail** unfit for work 2.MIL unfit

inattaquable [inatakabl] *adj* unassailable

inattendu [inatɑ̃dy] *m* **l'~** the unexpected

inattendu(e) [inatɑ̃dy] *adj* unexpected

inattentif, -ive [inatɑ̃tif, -iv] *adj* 1.(*distrait*) inattentive 2.(*insouciant*) ~ **à qc** heedless of sth

inattention [inatɑ̃sjɔ̃] *f* (*distraction*) lack of attention; **une faute d'**~ careless mistake; **par** ~ carelessly

inaudible [inodibl] *adj* inaudible; *péj* painful to the ears; **ici, les émissions de cette station sont** ~**s** that station's broadcasts can hardly be heard round here ►**cette musique est vraiment** ~ this music is not worth listening to

inaugural(e) [inogyʀal, o] <-aux> *adj* inaugural

inauguration [inogyʀasjɔ̃] *f* (*d'une exposition, d'une usine, route, de locaux*) opening; (*d'une statue, plaque commémorative, d'un monument*) unveiling; (*d'une ligne aérienne*) inauguration

inaugurer [inogyʀe, inɔgyʀe] <1> *vt* **1.** (*ouvrir solennellement: exposition, bâtiment, usine, locaux, école, route*) to open; (*monument, plaque commémorative*) to unveil; (*ligne aérienne*) to inaugurate **2.** (*introduire: période, politique, ère*) to inaugurate; (*méthode*) to launch **3.** (*utiliser pour la première fois: maison, machine, voiture*) to inaugurate

inavouable [inavwabl] *adj* unmentionable; (*mœurs*) shameful; (*motifs*) dishonorable

inavoué(e) [inavwe] *adj* (*sentiment, amour*) unavowed; (*acte, crime*) unconfessed

inca [ɛ̃ka] *adj* **l'Empire** ~ the Inca Empire

incalculable [ɛ̃kalkylabl] *adj* **1.** (*considérable*) incalculable; (*nombre*) countless **2.** (*imprévisible*) incalculable; **les difficultés risquent d'être** ~**s** there may be too many difficulties to count

incandescence [ɛ̃kɑ̃desɑ̃s] *f* incandescence; **chauffer qc jusqu'à l'**~ to heat sth until it is white hot; **lampe à** ~ incandescent lamp; **manchon à** ~ incandescent mantle; **en** ~ incandescent

incandescent(e) [ɛ̃kɑ̃desɑ̃, ɑ̃t] *adj* incandescent

incapable [ɛ̃kapabl] **I.** *adj* incapable; **c'est un homme tout à fait** ~ the man is completely hopeless **II.** *mf* incompetent

incapacité [ɛ̃kapasite] *f* **1.** (*inaptitude*) incapacity; ~ **de** +*infin* inability to +*infin*; **être dans l'**~ **de** +*infin* to be unable to +*infin* **2.** (*convalescence*) disability; **j'ai eu 3 mois d'**~ I've had three months' leave; ~ **de travail** work disability; ~ **d'exercice** incapacity

incarcération [ɛ̃kaʀseʀasjɔ̃] *f* incarceration

incarcérer [ɛ̃kaʀseʀe] <5> *vt* to incarcerate

incarner [ɛ̃kaʀne] <1> **I.** *vt* to embody; (*rôle*) to take **II.** *vpr* **1.** REL **s'**~ **dans** [*o* **en**] **qn/qc** to become incarnate in sb/sth **2.** (*se matérialiser*) **s'**~ **en qn/dans qc** to be embodied in sb/in sth; **leur idéal s'est incarné dans cette nouvelle secte** this new sect embodied their ideal **3.** (*entrer dans la chair*) **s'**~ (*ongle*) to become ingrown

incartade [ɛ̃kaʀtad] *f* escapade; (*d'un cheval*) swerve

Incas [ɛ̃ka] *mpl* **les** ~ the Incas

incassable [ɛ̃kɑsabl] *adj* unbreakable

incendiaire [ɛ̃sɑ̃djɛʀ] **I.** *adj* **1.** incendiary; **projectiles** ~**s** incendiary bombs **2.** (*virulent: article, discours*) inflammatory **3.** (*aguicheur: œillade, lettre*) passionate; **blonde** ~ blonde bombshell **II.** *mf* **1.** arsonist **2.** (*agitateur*) trouble-maker

incendie [ɛ̃sɑ̃di] *m* fire ►~ **criminel** arson

incendier [ɛ̃sɑ̃dje] <1> *vt* **1.** (*mettre en feu*) to set on fire **2.** *inf* (*engueuler*) ~ **qn** to give sb hell; **se faire** ~ **par qn** to get hell from sb

incertain(e) [ɛ̃sɛʀtɛ̃, ɛn] *adj* **1.** (*opp: assuré, décidé*) uncertain; **être** ~ **sur la conduite à suivre** to be uncertain about what should be done; **être** ~ **de pouvoir** +*infin* to be unsure about being able to +*infin* **2.** (*douteux*) uncertain; (*temps*) unsettled; **la date est encore** ~**e** there is still some uncertainty about the date

incertitude [ɛ̃sɛʀtityd] *f* uncertainty; **laisser qn dans l'**~ to leave sb in a state of uncertainty

incessamment [ɛ̃sesamɑ̃] *adv* shortly

incessant(e) [ɛ̃sesɑ̃, ɑ̃t] *adj* (*bruit, pluie*) incessant; (*réclamations, critiques, coups de fil*) unending; (*efforts*) ceaseless

inceste [ɛ̃sɛst] *m* incest

incident [ɛ̃sidɑ̃] *m* **1.** (*anicroche*) incident; ~ **de parcours** setback; ~ **technique** technical hitch **2.** (*péripétie*) episode ►**l'**~ **est clos** the matter is closed

incident(e) [ɛ̃sidɑ̃, ɑ̃t] *adj* incidental; **une question/remarque** ~**e** a question/remark in passing

incinération [ɛ̃sineʀasjɔ̃] *f* incineration; (*d'un cadavre*) cremation

incinérer [ɛ̃sineʀe] <5> *vt* (*cadavre*) to cremate; (*ordures ménagères*) to incinerate

inciser [ɛ̃size] <1> *vt* (*abcès*) to lance; (*écorce, peau*) to incise; (*arbre*) to tap

incision [ɛ̃sizjɔ̃] *f a.* MED incision

incisive [ɛ̃siziv] *f* incisor

incitation [ɛ̃sitasjɔ̃] *f* ~ **à qc** incitement to sth

inciter [ɛ̃site] <1> *vt* ~ **qn à l'action/au travail** to spur sb on to act/work; ~ **qn à l'achat** to push sb to buy; ~ **qn à la méfiance** to cause mistrust in sb

incivique [ɛ̃sivik] *mf Belgique* (*collaborateur*) collaborator

inclassable [ɛ̃klɑsabl] *adj* **1.** (*hors catégorie*) unclassifiable **2.** (*admirable*) unique

inclinable [ɛ̃klinabl] *adj* reclining

inclinaison [ɛ̃klinɛzɔ̃] *f* (*déclivité: d'une pente, route*) incline; (*d'un toit, mur*) slope

inclination [ɛ̃klinasjɔ̃] *f* **1.** ~ **à** [*o* **pour**] **qc** inclination to sth **2.** (*affection*) ~ **pour qn** liking for sb **3.** (*geste*) bow

incliné(e) [ɛ̃kline] *adj* **1.** (*pentu: pente, terrain*) sloping; (*toit*) pitched; **plan** ~ ramp; (*sur le trottoir*) dropped kerb *Brit,* dropped curb

Am **2.** (*penché*) leaning; (*tête*) bending; ~ **vers qc** leaning towards sth

incliner [ɛ̃kline] <1> **I.** *vt* (*buste, corps*) to bow; (*bouteille*) to tilt; (*dossier d'une chaise*) to lean; ~ **la tête** to bow one's head; (*pour acquiescer*) to nod one's head **II.** *vpr* **1.** (*se courber*) **s'~ devant qn/qc** to bow to sb/sth **2.** (*céder*) **s'~ devant qn/qc** to yield to sb/sth

inclure [ɛ̃klyʀ] *vt irr* **1.** (*joindre, ajouter*) ~ **qc dans qc** (*dans une enveloppe*) to enclose sth in sth; (*dans une liste*) to include sth in sth; ~ **qc dans un contrat** to insert sth in a contract **2.** (*contenir, comprendre*) to include

inclus(e) [ɛ̃kly, ɛ̃klyz] *adj* included; **jusqu'au dix mars** ~ until 10 March inclusive; **le service est** ~ service is included

incognito [ɛ̃kɔɲito] **I.** *adv* incognito **II.** *m* anonymity; **garder l'~** to remain anonymous; **dans l'~** anonymously

incohérence [ɛ̃kɔeʀɑ̃s] *f* **1.** (*caractère illogique, contradictoire*) inconsistency **2.** (*inintelligibilité*) incoherence

incohérent(e) [ɛ̃kɔeʀɑ̃, ɑ̃t] *adj* **1.** (*contradictoire*) inconsistent **2.** (*bizarre*) incoherent

incollable [ɛ̃kɔlabl] *adj* **1.** (*qui ne colle pas*) **du riz** ~ non-stick rice **2.** *inf* (*imbattable*) unbeatable

incolore [ɛ̃kɔlɔʀ] *adj* colourless *Brit,* colorless *Am*

incomber [ɛ̃kɔ̃be] <1> *vi* ~ **à qn** (*devoirs, responsabilité, travail*) to be incumbent on sb; (*frais, réparations*) to be sb's responsibility

incommode [ɛ̃kɔmɔd] *adj* **1.** uncomfortable **2.** (*peu pratique*) inconvenient; (*heure, outil*) awkward

incommoder [ɛ̃kɔmɔde] <1> *vt* ~ **qn** (*bruit, fumée*) to bother sb; (*chaleur*) to make sb feel uncomfortable; **j'étais incommodé par le bruit** I was bothered by the noise

incomparable [ɛ̃kɔ̃paʀabl] *adj* incomparable

incomparablement [ɛ̃kɔ̃paʀabləmɑ̃] *adv* (*jouer, chanter, mieux*) incomparably; ~ **bien** extraordinarily well

incompatibilité [ɛ̃kɔ̃patibilite] *f* ~ (**entre**) **des choses/personnes** incompatibility of things/people; **il y a** ~ **entre deux fonctions** the two functions are incompatible

incompatible [ɛ̃kɔ̃patibl] *adj* incompatible; **~s entre eux** mutually incompatible

incompétence [ɛ̃kɔ̃petɑ̃s] *f* lack of competence; *péj* incompetence; ~ **en qc** ignorance where sth is concerned

incompétent(e) [ɛ̃kɔ̃petɑ̃, ɑ̃t] *adj* ignorant; *péj* incompetent; **être** ~ **en qc** to be incompetent in sth

incomplet, -ète [ɛ̃kɔ̃plɛ, -ɛt] *adj* incomplete; (*œuvre, travail*) unfinished

incompréhensible [ɛ̃kɔ̃pʀeɑ̃sibl] *adj* incomprehensible; (*paroles*) unintelligible; **un mystère** ~ a mystery beyond our understanding

incompréhensif, -ive [ɛ̃kɔ̃pʀeɑ̃sif, -iv] *adj* unsympathetic; **se montrer** ~ **à l'égard de qn** to show sb no understanding

incompréhension [ɛ̃kɔ̃pʀeɑ̃sjɔ̃] *f* lack of understanding; ~ **entre deux/plusieurs personnes** mutual misunderstanding

incompris(e) [ɛ̃kɔ̃pʀi, iz] **I.** *adj* misunderstood **II.** *m(f)* misunderstood person

inconcevable [ɛ̃kɔ̃svabl] *adj* **1.** (*inimaginable*) inconceivable **2.** (*incroyable*) incredible; **il est** ~ **d'imaginer que ce soit vrai** (*subj*) it is impossible to imagine it being true

inconditionnel(le) [ɛ̃kɔ̃disjɔnɛl] **I.** *adj* unconditional; **être** ~ **de qn/qc** to be a big fan of sb/sth **II.** *m(f)* enthusiast; **un** ~ **des sports d'hiver** a winter sports fanatic

inconfort [ɛ̃kɔ̃fɔʀ] *m* **1.** (*d'un logement*) lack of comfort; (*d'un siège*) uncomfortableness **2.** (*délicat: d'une position, situation*) awkwardness

inconfortable [ɛ̃kɔ̃fɔʀtabl] *adj* **1.** (*sans confort*) uncomfortable **2.** (*déplaisant: situation*) awkward

inconfortablement [ɛ̃kɔ̃fɔʀtabləmɑ̃] *adv* uncomfortably

incongru(e) [ɛ̃kɔ̃gʀy] *adj* (*ton*) unseemly; (*situation*) incongruous; (*conversation*) out of place

incongruité [ɛ̃kɔ̃gʀɥite] *f* (*d'une remarque*) inappropriateness; (*d'un geste, d'une parole, d'un ton*) unseemliness; (*d'une situation*) incongruousness; **commettre** [*o* **faire**] **des ~s** to behave in an unseemly way

inconnu [ɛ̃kɔny] *m* **l'~** the unknown

inconnu(e) [ɛ̃kɔny] **I.** *adj* **1.** (*ignoré*) unknown **2.** (*nouveau: émotion*) (hitherto) unknown; (*odeur, parfum*) strange **II.** *m(f)* **1.** (*étranger*) stranger **2.** (*qui n'est pas célèbre*) unknown; **être un** ~ **pour qn** to be unknown to sb ▶**illustre** ~ *iron* famous unknown

inconnue [ɛ̃kɔny] *f* MAT unknown

inconsciemment [ɛ̃kɔ̃sjamɑ̃] *adv* **1.** (*sans s'en rendre compte*) unconsciously **2.** PSYCH subconsciously **3.** (*à la légère*) thoughtlessly

inconscience [ɛ̃kɔ̃sjɑ̃s] *f* **1.** (*légèreté*) thoughtlessness **2.** (*irresponsabilité*) recklessness **3.** (*ignorance*) **l'~ du danger** ignorance of the danger **4.** (*évanouissement*) unconsciousness

inconscient [ɛ̃kɔ̃sjɑ̃] *m* PSYCH unconscious

inconscient(e) [ɛ̃kɔ̃sjɑ̃, jɑ̃t] **I.** *adj* **1.** (*évanoui*) unconscious **2.** (*qui ne se rend pas compte*) **être** ~ **de qc** to be unaware of sth **3.** (*machinal, irréfléchi*) automatic; (*effort, élan*) unconscious **II.** *m(f)* (*irresponsable*) thoughtless person

inconséquent(e) [ɛ̃kɔ̃sekɑ̃, ɑ̃t] *adj* **1.** inconsistent **2.** (*irréfléchi*) thoughtless

inconsidéré(e) [ɛ̃kɔ̃sideʀe] *adj* thoughtless

inconsistant(e) [ɛ̃kɔ̃sistɑ̃, ɑ̃t] *adj* **1.** (*fragile, léger*) flimsy **2.** (*mou: caractère, personne*) shallow **3.** (*trop liquide*) watery; (*crème*) thin

inconsolable [ɛ̃kɔ̃sɔlabl] *adj* **1.** (*désespéré*) disconsolate; ~ **de qc** inconsolable over sth **2.** (*déchirant: chagrin, malheur, peine*) inconsolable

inconstant(e) [ɛ̃kɔ̃stɑ̃, ɑ̃t] *adj* fickle

incontestable [ɛ̃kɔ̃tɛstabl] *adj* indisputable; (*principe, réussite, droit*) unquestionable; (*fait, preuve, qualité*) undeniable; **il est ~ que c'est cher** it's undeniably expensive

incontestablement [ɛ̃kɔ̃tɛstabləmɑ̃] *adv* undeniably

incontesté(e) [ɛ̃kɔ̃tɛste] *adj* undoubted; (*champion, leader*) undisputed; (*personne*) recognized

incontinence [ɛ̃kɔ̃tinɑ̃s] *f* MED incontinence; ~ **d'urine** [*o* **urinaire**] enuresis

incontournable [ɛ̃kɔ̃tuʀnabl] *adj* (*fait, exigence*) unavoidable; **ce problème est ~** there is no getting round this problem; **cet homme est ~** the man is inescapable

incontrôlable [ɛ̃kɔ̃tʀolabl] *adj* **1.** (*invérifiable*) unverifiable **2.** (*irrépressible: besoin, envie, mouvement*) uncontrollable; (*passion*) ungovernable; (*attirance*) irresistible **3.** (*ingouvernable*) out of control; **devenir ~** to get out of control

inconvenant(e) [ɛ̃kɔ̃v(ə)nɑ̃, ɑ̃t] *adj* **1.** (*déplacé: conduite, proposition*) improper **2.** (*indécent*) indecent

inconvénient [ɛ̃kɔ̃venjɑ̃] *m* **1.** (*opp: avantage*) disadvantage; (*d'une situation*) drawback **2.** *gén pl* (*conséquence fâcheuse*) consequences **3.** (*obstacle*) **l'~, c'est que c'est cher** the problem is, it's expensive ▶**il n'y a pas d'~ à faire qc/à ce que qc soit fait** (*subj*) there is no problem about doing sth/sth being done; **ne pas voir d'~ à qc/à ce que qn fasse qc** (*subj*) to have no objection to sth/to sb doing sth; **sans ~** without difficulty; (*sans danger*) safely

incorporer [ɛ̃kɔʀpɔʀe] <1> **I.** *vt* **1.** GASTR, TECH (*mélanger*) ~ **qc à qc** to blend sth in to sth; ~ **délicatement les blancs battus en neige** fold in the stiffly beaten egg whites **2.** (*intégrer*) ~ **qn/qc dans** [*o* **à**] **qc** to incorporate sb/sth into sth; ~ **qc dans un récit** to bring sth into a story **3.** MIL ~ **qn dans qc** to enlist sb in sth **II.** *vpr* **s'~ à qc** (*personne*) to fit into sth; (*liquide, substance*) to blend into sth

incorrect(e) [ɛ̃kɔʀɛkt] *adj* **1.** (*défectueux: expression, style*) inappropriate; (*montage*) incorrect; (*réponse*) wrong; **une lecture ~e d'un compteur** an incorrect meter reading **2.** (*inconvenant*) improper; (*langage, ton*) impolite **3.** (*impoli*) impolite; **se montrer ~** to behave impolitely **4.** (*déloyal*) ~ **en qc/avec qn** underhand about sth/with sb

incorrection [ɛ̃kɔʀɛksjɔ̃] *f* **1.** (*faute, manque de correction*) incorrectness *no pl* **2.** (*impolitesse*) improper behaviour *no pl*

incorrigible [ɛ̃kɔʀiʒibl] *adj* incorrigible

incorruptible [ɛ̃kɔʀyptibl] **I.** *adj* **1.** incorruptible **2.** (*matériau, substance*) rot-proof; **bois rendu ~ à l'humidité** damp-proofed wood **II.** *mf* incorruptible (person)

incrédule [ɛ̃kʀedyl] *adj* incredulous; **rester ~** to remain unconvinced

incrédulité [ɛ̃kʀedylite] *f* incredulity; **avec ~** incredulously

increvable [ɛ̃kʀəvabl] *adj* **1.** *inf* (*infatigable: personne*) never-tiring; (*appareil, voiture*) everlasting; **être vraiment ~** to go on for ever **2.** (*qui ne peut être crevé: pneu, ballon*) puncture-proof

incriminer [ɛ̃kʀimine] <1> *vt* **1.** to incriminate **2.** (*mettre en cause*) to call into question; ~ **l'honnêteté de qn** to question sb's honesty; **être incriminée** to be implicated; **la chose incriminée** the thing under attack

incroyable [ɛ̃kʀwajabl] *adj* (*extraordinaire, bizarre*) incredible; **c'est ~ de voir à quel point tout a changé** it's incredible to see how much everything's changed; **si ~ que cela puisse paraître** incredible as it may appear ▶~ **mais vrai** incredible but true

incroyant(e) [ɛ̃kʀwajɑ̃, jɑ̃t] **I.** *adj* unbelieving **II.** *m(f)* unbeliever

incrustation [ɛ̃kʀystasjɔ̃] *f* INFOR pop-up window

incrusté(e) [ɛ̃kʀyste] *adj* **être ~ de qc** to be encrusted with sth

incruster [ɛ̃kʀyste] <1> **I.** *vt* ART to inlay; ~ **qc de diamants/mosaïques** to inlay diamonds/mosaics in sth **II.** *vpr* **1.** *inf* (*s'installer à demeure*) **s'~ chez qn** to settle in at sb's place **2.** (*adhérer fortement*) **s'~** (*coquillage*) to become embedded; (*odeur*) to hang around **3.** (*se graver*) **ce souvenir s'est incrusté dans mon esprit** the memory has engraved itself in my mind

incubation [ɛ̃kybasjɔ̃] *f a.* MED incubation

inculpé(e) [ɛ̃kylpe] *m(f)* JUR accused

inculper [ɛ̃kylpe] <1> *vt* ~ **qn de qc** to accuse sb of sth

inculquer [ɛ̃kylke] <1> *vt* ~ **qc à qn** to instil sth into sb *Brit*, to instill st into sb *Am*

inculte [ɛ̃kylt] *adj* **1.** (*non cultivé*) uncultivated **2.** (*ignare*) ignorant

incurable [ɛ̃kyʀabl] *adj* **1.** MED incurable **2.** (*incorrigible*) incorrigible; (*ignorance*) hopeless; (*paresse*) chronic

incursion [ɛ̃kyʀsjɔ̃] *f* **1.** (*raid, intrusion*) incursion **2.** (*passage rapide*) foray

incurvé(e) [ɛ̃kyʀve] *adj* curved

Inde [ɛ̃d] *f* **l'~** India; **de l'~** Indian

indécence [ɛ̃desɑ̃s] *f* **1.** (*d'une personne*) effrontery **2.** (*inconvenance*) indecency **3.** *pl* (*actes*) indecent behaviour *no pl Brit*, indecent behavior *no pl Am* **4.** *pl* (*propos*) indecent talk *no pl*

indécent(e) [ɛ̃desɑ̃, ɑ̃t] *adj* **1.** indecent **2.** (*déplacé*) out of place; (*joie*) unseemly; **avoir une chance ~e** to have the luck of the devil; **il est ~ que tu ries** it's out of place for you to laugh

indéchiffrable [ɛ̃deʃifʀabl] *adj* **1.** (*illisible*)

indecipherable **2.** (*incompréhensible*) unintelligible; (*monde*) incomprehensible; (*énigme*) unfathomable; (*visage*) impenetrable

indécis(e) [ɛ̃desi, iz] *adj* **1.** (*hésitant*) undecided; **être ~ sur qc** to be undecided about sth; **être ~ entre qc et qc** to be hesitating between sth and sth **2.** (*douteux: question*) undecided; (*résultat, victoire*) uncertain; (*temps*) unsettled

indécision [ɛ̃desizjɔ̃] *f* (*doute*) uncertainty; *péj* indecision; **~ sur qc** uncertainty over sth; **dans l'~ il préfère attendre** while there is any uncertainty, he prefers to wait

indéfendable [ɛ̃defɑ̃dabl] *adj* indefensible

indéfini(e) [ɛ̃defini] *adj* **1.** (*indéterminé*) ill-defined **2.** (*illimité: espace, nombre, progrès, temps*) indefinite

indéfiniment [ɛ̃definimɑ̃] *adv* indefinitely

indéfinissable [ɛ̃definisabl] *adj* indefinable

indélébile [ɛ̃delebil] *adj* (*ineffaçable, perpétuel*) indelible; (*couleur, encre*) permanent

indélicat(e) [ɛ̃delika, at] *adj* **1.** (*malhonnête*) dishonest **2.** (*grossier*) indelicate

indemne [ɛ̃dɛmn] *adj* unscathed

indemnisation [ɛ̃dɛmnizasjɔ̃] *f* indemnification; (*dédommagement versé par l'État*) compensation; **~ des dommages de guerre** compensation for war damage

indemniser [ɛ̃dɛmnize] <1> *vt* **1.** (*rembourser*) to reimburse **2.** (*compenser*) **~ qn pour qc** to compensate sb for sth

indemnité [ɛ̃dɛmnite] *f* **1.** (*réparation*) compensation **2.** (*forfait*) indemnity; **~ de guerre** war indemnity **3.** (*prime*) allowance; (*d'un maire, conseiller régional*) salary; **~ de chômage** unemployment benefit; **~ de déplacement/logement** travel/housing allowance

indéniable [ɛ̃denjabl] *adj* undeniable; **il est ~ que c'est vrai** it's undeniably true

indéniablement [ɛ̃denjabləmɑ̃] *adv* undeniably

indépendamment [ɛ̃depɑ̃damɑ̃] *adv* (*en dehors de cela*) apart from everything else ►**~ de qc** (*outre*) apart from sth; (*abstraction faite de*) disregarding sth; (*sans dépendre de*) independently of sth

indépendance [ɛ̃depɑ̃dɑ̃s] *f* (*liberté, autonomie*) independence; **~ d'idées** independent ideas; **en toute ~ d'esprit** with a completely independent mind; **la guerre de l'~ grecque** the Greek War of Independence; **accéder à l'~** to achieve independence; **proclamer son ~** to declare independence

indépendant(e) [ɛ̃depɑ̃dɑ̃, ɑ̃t] *adj* **1.** (*libre, souverain, indocile*) independent **2.** (*à son compte*) self-employed; (*artiste, architecte, photographe, collaborateur, journaliste*) freelance **3.** (*séparé: chambre*) self-contained; (*questions, systèmes*) separate **4.** (*sans liaison avec*) **~ de qn/qc** independent of sb/sth; **pour des raisons ~es de notre volonté** for reasons beyond our control

Indes [ɛ̃d] *f* **les ~** Indies

indescriptible [ɛ̃dɛskʀiptibl] *adj* indescribable

indésirable [ɛ̃deziʀabl] **I.** *adj* undesirable **II.** *mf* undesirable

indestructible [ɛ̃dɛstʀyktibl] *adj* (*personne, construction*) indestructible; (*foi, solidarité*) steadfast; (*liaison, amour*) enduring; (*impression*) indelible

indétermination [ɛ̃detɛʀminasjɔ̃] *f* **1.** (*indécision*) hesitancy **2.** (*permanente*) indecisiveness **3.** (*imprécision*) vagueness

indéterminé(e) [ɛ̃detɛʀmine] *adj* **1.** (*non précisé*) indeterminate; (*date*) unspecified **2.** (*incertain*) uncertain; (*sens, termes*) vague **3.** (*indistinct*) vague **4.** (*indécis*) **être ~ sur qc** to be undecided about sth

index [ɛ̃dɛks] *m* **1.** (*doigt*) index finger **2.** (*table alphabétique*) index

indicateur, -trice [ɛ̃dikatœʀ, -tʀis] **I.** *adj* **panneau ~** information board; **poteau ~** signpost; **borne ~** milestone *Brit*, mile marker *Am* **II.** *m, f* **~ de police** police informer

indicatif [ɛ̃dikatif] *m* **1.** TEL prefix; **~ départemental** area code; **l'~ de la France** the code for France **2.** LING indicative

indicatif, -ive [ɛ̃dikatif, -iv] *adj* **1.** (*qui renseigne*) indicative; (*vote*) straw poll; (*prix*) suggested; **à titre ~** simply for information; **ce chiffre n'est qu'~** this figure is simply an indication **2.** LING **mode ~** indicative (mood)

indication [ɛ̃dikasjɔ̃] *f* **1.** (*information*) information *no pl;* **une ~ sur qc** (some) information about sth; **sur les ~s de qn** acting on information from sb **2.** (*signalisation: d'une adresse, d'un numéro, prix*) indication; (*d'un virage dangereux*) sign **3.** (*prescription*) direction **4.** (*indice*) **~ de qc** indicator of sth ►**sauf ~ contraire** unless otherwise directed

indice [ɛ̃dis] *m* **1.** (*signe*) indication **2.** (*trace*) clue **3.** (*preuve*) evidence *no pl;* JUR piece of evidence **4.** ECON, FIN index; **~ des prix** price index **5.** TV **~ d'écoute** ratings *pl*

indien(ne) [ɛ̃djɛ̃, jɛn] *adj* Indian

Indien(ne) [ɛ̃djɛ̃, jɛn] *m(f)* Indian

indifféremment [ɛ̃difeʀamɑ̃] *adv* **1.** (*pareillement*) equally well **2.** (*sans juger*) without discrimination

indifférence [ɛ̃difeʀɑ̃s] *f* **1.** (*insensibilité, apathie*) indifference **2.** (*détachement*) disinterest

indifférent(e) [ɛ̃difeʀɑ̃, ɑ̃t] **I.** *adj* **1.** (*insensible: attitude, personne*) indifferent; (*mère*) unfeeling; **regard ~** look of indifference; **être ~ à qc** to be indifferent to sth; **être ~ à une personne** to show indifference to a person; **laisser qn ~** to leave sb unmoved **2.** (*égal*) **être ~ à qn** (*personne*) to be of no importance to sb; (*choix, sort, avis*) not to matter to sb **II.** *m(f)* indifferent person

indigène [ɛ̃diʒɛn] **I.** *adj* **1.** *a.* BOT, ZOOL indigenous **2.** (*opp: blanc*) native **II.** *mf* native

indigénisme [ɛ̃diʒenism] *m* Indigenism (*lit-

erary movement in Haiti emphasizing its African heritage)

indigéniste [ɛ̃diʒenist] *adj* Indigenist (*writer emphasizing Haiti's African heritage*)

indigent(e) [ɛ̃diʒɑ̃, ʒɑ̃t] **I.** *adj* **1.** (*personne*) destitute **2.** (*faible*) feeble **II.** *m(f)* pauper; **les ~s** the destitute

indigeste [ɛ̃diʒɛst] *adj* (*cuisine, nourriture*) indigestible

indigestion [ɛ̃diʒɛstjɔ̃] *f* indigestion; **avoir une ~ de qc** to have indigestion from eating sth

indignation [ɛ̃diɲasjɔ̃] *f* indignation

indigne [ɛ̃diɲ] *adj* **1.** (*qui ne mérite pas*) **être ~ de qn/qc** to be unworthy of sb/sth; **être ~ de** +*infin* to be unworthy to +*infin* **2.** (*inconvenant*) **être ~ de qn** (*action, attitude, sentiment*) to be unworthy of sb **3.** (*odieux*) disgraceful; (*époux, fils*) unworthy; **c'est une mère ~** she's not fit to be a mother

indigné(e) [ɛ̃diɲe] *adj* **~ de qc** indignant over sth

indigner [ɛ̃diɲe] <1> *vpr* **s'~ contre qn/qc** to get indignant with sb/over sth

indigo [ɛ̃digo] *m inv* indigo

indiqué(e) [ɛ̃dike] *adj* **1.** (*conseillé*) advisable **2.** (*adéquat*) right; **être tout ~** to be ideal; **le Louvre est le lieu tout ~** the Louvre is the perfect place **3.** (*fixé*) appointed; (*date*) agreed

indiquer [ɛ̃dike] <1> *vt* **1.** (*désigner*) **~ qc à qn** to show sb sth; (*écriteau, flèche*) to indicate sth to sb; **~ qn/qc de la main** to point to sb/sth; **qu'indique le panneau?** what does it say on the sign? **2.** (*recommander*) **~ qn/qc à qn** to suggest sb/sth to sb **3.** (*dire*) **~ à qn qc** to tell sb about sth; (*expliquer*) to explain sth to sb; **~ à qn comment y aller/ce que cela représente** to tell sb how to get there/what that represents **4.** (*révéler*) **~ qc/que qn est passé** to show sth/that sb has been here **5.** (*marquer: adresse*) to write down; (*lieu*) to mark ▸ **rien n'indique qu'il est** [*o* **soit**] **parti** there's nothing to indicate that he's gone; **tout indique qu'il n'est plus là** everything points to his having left

indirect(e) [ɛ̃diʀɛkt] *adj* indirect; **par des moyens ~s** by indirect means

indirectement [ɛ̃diʀɛktəmɑ̃] *adv* indirectly

indiscipline [ɛ̃disiplin] *f* indiscipline; **pour ~** for disobeying orders

indiscipliné(e) [ɛ̃disipline] *adj* undisciplined

indiscret, -ète [ɛ̃diskʀɛ, -ɛt] **I.** *adj* **1.** (*curieux: personne*) inquisitive; (*yeux*) prying **2.** (*bavard*) indiscreet; **des commérages ~s** blabbering gossip **3.** (*inconvenant*) indiscreet; (*familiarité, démarche*) intrusive; (*présence*) uncalled for **II.** *m, f* (*personne bavarde*) gossip; (*personne curieuse*) inquisitive person

indiscrétion [ɛ̃diskʀesjɔ̃] *f* **1.** (*curiosité, tendance à divulguer*) indiscretion; **sans ~, peut-on savoir si ...** without wishing to pry, could I ask if ... **2.** (*acte*) indiscretion; (*bavardage*) indiscreet word; **j'ai commis beaucoup d'~s** I have committed many indiscretions

indiscutable [ɛ̃diskytabl] *adj* (*fait*) undeniable; (*succès, supériorité, réalité*) undoubted; (*personne, crédibilité*) unquestionable; (*témoignage*) irrefutable; **il est ~ que** it is undeniable that

indiscutablement [ɛ̃diskytabləmɑ̃] *adv* indisputably

indispensable [ɛ̃dispɑ̃sabl] **I.** *adj* indispensable; (*précautions*) vital; (*devoir*) unavoidable; **il est ~ de** +*infin*/**que qc soit fait** (*subj*) it is essential to +*infin*/that sth is done; **il est ~ que nous prenions une assurance** it is vital that we take out insurance; **être ~ à qn/qc** [*o* **pour qc**] to be indispensible to sb/for sth **II.** *m* **l'~** the absolute essentials; **faire l'~** to do the essential things

indisponible [ɛ̃dispɔnibl] *adj* unavailable

indisposer [ɛ̃dispoze] <1> *vt* **1.** to antagonize; **~ les gens contre soi** to alienate people **2.** (*incommoder*) **la chaleur/l'odeur l'indispose** he is upset [*o* indisposed] by the heat/the smell

indisposition [ɛ̃dispozisjɔ̃] *f* **1.** indisposition **2.** (*règles*) period

indissociable [ɛ̃disɔsjabl] *adj* indissociable

indistinct(e) [ɛ̃distɛ̃, ɛ̃kt] *adj* (*murmure, vision, voix*) indistinct; (*couleur*) vague; (*objet*) unclear

individu [ɛ̃dividy] *m* individual; **drôle d'~** *a. péj* strange individual

individualisation [ɛ̃dividɥalizasjɔ̃] *f* personalization

individualiser [ɛ̃dividɥalize] <1> **I.** *vt* **1.** (*personnaliser: appartement, voiture*) to personalize; **~ son attitude** to adapt one's attitude to the individual; **~ son style** to develop one's own style **2.** (*particulariser*) to individualize **II.** *vpr* **s'~** **1.** (*se différencier: cellule*) to differentiate; (*forme, manière, style*) to become more individual **2.** (*s'accentuer*) to become more distinctive

individualisme [ɛ̃dividɥalism] *m* individualism

individualiste [ɛ̃dividɥalist] **I.** *adj* **1.** PHILOS individualist **2.** *péj* self-centred *Brit,* self-centered *Am* **II.** *mf* **1.** (*non conformiste*) individualist **2.** *péj* self-centred person *Brit,* self-centered person *Am*

individualité [ɛ̃dividɥalite] *f* individuality; (*nouveauté*) originality; **avoir un style d'une forte ~** to have a highly individual style

individuel(le) [ɛ̃dividɥɛl] **I.** *adj* individual; (*propriété, responsabilité, initiative*) personal; (*maison*) private **II.** *m(f)* (*sportif*) individual

individuellement [ɛ̃dividɥɛlmɑ̃] *adv* individually

indivisible [ɛ̃divizibl] *adj* indivisible

Indochine [ɛ̃dɔʃin] *f* HIST **l'~** Indochina

indo-européen(ne) [ɛ̃doœʀɔpeɛ̃, ɛn]

<indo-européens> *adj* Indo-european
indolence [ɛ̃dɔlɑ̃s] *f* indolence
indolent(e) [ɛ̃dɔlɑ̃, ɑ̃t] **I.** *adj* indolent; (*geste*) lethargic **II.** *m(f)* indolent person
indolore [ɛ̃dɔlɔʀ] *adj* painless
indomptable [ɛ̃dɔ̃tabl] *adj* (*animal*) untameable
Indonésie [ɛ̃donezi] *f* l'~ Indonesia
indonésien [ɛ̃donezjɛ̃] *m* Indonesian; *v. a.* **français**
indonésien(ne) [ɛ̃donezjɛ̃, ɛn] *adj* Indonesian
Indonésien(ne) [ɛ̃donezjɛ̃, ɛn] *m(f)* Indonesian
indu(e) [ɛ̃dy] *adj* **1.** unseemly; **à des heures ~es** at all hours **2.** (*optimisme*) undue; (*réclamation, reproches*) unwarranted
indubitable [ɛ̃dybitabl] *adj* indubitable; **il est ~ que c'est le meilleur** he's indubitably the best
induire [ɛ̃dɥiʀ] *vt irr* **1.** ~ **qn/qc à** +*infin* to induce sb/sth to +*infin;* ~ **qn/qc à qc** to lead sb/sth into sth; ~ **qn en erreur** to mislead sb **2.** (*tirer comme conclusion*) ~ **qc de qc** to infer sth from sth; ~ **de qc que ...** to infer from sth that ... **3.** (*provoquer*) ~ **qc** to lead to sth
indulgence [ɛ̃dylʒɑ̃s] *f* **1.** (*en jugeant*) ~ **pour** [*o* **envers**] **qn/pour qc** lenience with sb/over sth **2.** (*bienveillance*) *a.* REL indulgence; **avec** ~ indulgently; **sans** ~ harshly
indulgent(e) [ɛ̃dylʒɑ̃, ʒɑ̃t] *adj* indulgent; (*en punissant*) lenient; **être ~ envers l'accusé** to be lenient with the accused
industrialisation [ɛ̃dystʀijalizasjɔ̃] *f* industrialization
industrialiser [ɛ̃dystʀijalize] <1> **I.** *vt* (*région, pays, agriculture*) to industrialize; (*découverte*) to commercialize; ~ **un nouveau produit** to put a new product on the market **II.** *vpr* **s'~** (*pays, région, secteur*) to be industrialized
industrie [ɛ̃dystʀi] *f* industry; **l'~ cinématographique** the cinema industry; **l'~ du livre** the publishing industry
industriel(le) [ɛ̃dystʀijɛl] **I.** *adj* industrial; (*pain*) factory-produced **II.** *m(f)* industrialist
industriellement [ɛ̃dystʀijɛlmɑ̃] *adv* industrially; **fabriqué** ~ mass-produced
inébranlable [inebʀɑ̃labl] *adj* **1.** (*solide: position*) unassailable **2.** (*inflexible*) steadfast; (*résolution*) unwavering; **être ~ dans sa résolution** to be steadfast in one's resolve; **être ~ dans ses convictions** to have unwavering convictions
inédit [inedi] *m* **1.** (*ouvrage*) unpublished work **2.** (*chose nouvelle*) novelty
inédit(e) [inedi, it] *adj* **1.** (*non publié*) unpublished **2.** (*nouveau*) novel
ineffaçable [inefasabl] *adj* **1.** (*indélébile: empreinte, trace*) indelible; (*couleur*) unfading **2.** (*inoubliable*) indelible
inefficace [inefikas] *adj* (*démarche*) ineffective; (*employé, machine*) inefficient
inefficacité [inefikasite] *f* (*d'une démarche, d'un secours*) ineffectiveness; (*d'un pouvoir, service administratif, cadre*) inefficiency
inégal(e) [inegal, o] <-aux> *adj* **1.** (*différent*) unequal; **de grandeur ~e** of different sizes **2.** (*changeant*) uneven; **être d'une humeur** ~ to be moody
inégalable [inegalabl] *adj* (*qualité*) matchless
inégalé(e) [inegale] *adj* unequalled
inégalement [inegalmɑ̃] *adv* unequally; (*sans régularité*) unevenly
inégalitaire [inegalitɛʀ] *adj* **une société** ~ *a non-egalitarian society;* **politique fiscale** ~ biased tax policy
inégalité [inegalite] *f* **1.** (*différence*) disparity; **l'~ entre l'offre et la demande** the difference between supply and demand **2.** (*disproportion*) unevenness; (*des forces*) imbalance; ~ **des chances** inequality of opportunity
inélégant(e) [inelegɑ̃, ɑ̃t] *adj* **1.** inelegant **2.** (*discourtois*) ill-mannered
inéluctable [inelyktabl] *adj* unavoidable; (*destin, sort, mort*) inescapable
inéluctablement [inelyktabləmɑ̃] *adv* inescapably
inepte [inɛpt] *adj* inept
ineptie [inɛpsi] *f* ineptitude *no pl;* **dire des ~s** to talk stupid nonsense
inépuisable [inepɥizabl] *adj* **1.** (*intarissable*) inexhaustible **2.** (*infini: indulgence, patience*) endless; (*curiosité*) boundless
inerte [inɛʀt] *adj* **1.** (*sans vie, expression: corps, membre, visage*) lifeless **2.** PHYS inert
inertie [inɛʀsi] *f a.* PHYS inertia
inespéré(e) [inɛspeʀe] *adj* unexpected
inesthétique [inɛstetik] *adj* unsightly
inestimable [inɛstimabl] *adj* incalculable; (*objet*) priceless
inévitable [inevitabl] **I.** *adj* **1.** (*certain, fatal*) inevitable; (*accident*) unavoidable **2.** (*nécessaire*) inescapable; (*opération*) unavoidable; **il est ~ que cela se produise** it is inevitable that it will happen **3.** *antéposé, iron* (*habituel*) inevitable **II.** *m* **l'~** the inevitable
inévitablement [inevitabləmɑ̃] *adv* inevitably
inexact(e) [inɛgzakt] *adj* **1.** (*erroné: renseignement, résultat*) inaccurate; (*calcul, théorie*) incorrect **2.** (*déformé: traduction, citation, récit*) inaccurate; **très ~/le plus ~** quite/altogether inaccurate; **non, c'est ~** no, that's wrong; **il est ~ de** +*infin* it is incorrect to +*infin* **3.** (*opp: ponctuel: personne*) unpunctual
inexactitude [inɛgzaktityd] *f* **1.** (*erreur*) inaccuracy **2.** (*manque de ponctualité*) unpunctuality
inexcusable [inɛkskyzabl] *adj* inexcusable; (*personne*) unforgiveable; **il est ~ de faire ça** it is unforgiveable of him to do that

inexistant(e) [inɛgzistɑ̃, ɑ̃t] *adj* 1.(*qui n'existe pas, imaginaire*) non-existent; **la télévision était encore ~e** television did not exist then 2. *péj* (*nul*) non-existent; (*résultat*) appalling; (*aide*) not worth speaking of
inexorable [inɛgzɔʀabl] *adj* inexorable; (*volonté*) unbending; (*vieillesse, fuite du temps*) relentless
inexpérience [inɛkspeʀjɑ̃s] *f* lack of experience
inexpérimenté(e) [inɛkspeʀimɑ̃te] *adj* inexperienced
inexplicable [inɛksplikabl] *adj* inexplicable
inexpliqué(e) [inɛksplike] *adj* unexplained
inexploité(e) [inɛksplwate] *adj* (*gisement, richesses*) untapped; (*talent*) unexploited
inexploré(e) [inɛksplɔʀe] *adj* unexplored
inexpressif, -ive [inɛkspʀesif, -iv] *adj* (*regard, visage*) inexpressive
inexprimable [inɛkspʀimabl] *adj* inexpressible
in extremis [inɛkstʀemis] I. *adv* at the last moment II. *adj inv* (*sauvetage, succès*) last-minute
infaillibilité [ɛ̃fajibilite] *f* infallibility
infaillible [ɛ̃fajibl] *adj* 1.(*fiable*) infallible; (*instrument*) unerring; (*signe*) sure 2.(*prévu*) inevitable; (*accident*) unavoidable 3.(*qui ne peut se tromper*) infallible; (*instinct*) unerring
infaisable [ɛ̃fəzabl] *adj* impracticable
infamant(e) [ɛ̃famɑ̃, ɑ̃t] *adj* infamous; (*supplice*) ignominious; **peine** ~ *conviction depriving a person of their civil rights;* **il n'est pas ~ de faire qc** there's no disgrace in doing sth
infâme [ɛ̃fam] *adj a. antéposé* 1.(*honteux, indigène: acte, conduite, trahison*) heinous; (*métier, entremetteur, spéculateur*) ignominious 2.(*odieux*) loathsome 3.(*répugnant*) foul; (*logis, hôtel*) appalling
infamie [ɛ̃fami] *f* 1.(*déshonneur, bassesse*) infamy 2.(*calomnie*) (vile) slander 3.(*action*) vile deed
infanterie [ɛ̃fɑ̃tʀi] *f* MIL infantry; **d'~** infantry
infanticide [ɛ̃fɑ̃tisid] I. *adj* **mère ~** *mother who kills her child* II. *mf* child-killer III. *m* infanticide
infantile [ɛ̃fɑ̃til] *adj* infantile
infarctus [ɛ̃faʀktys] *m* MED infarction; ~ **du myocarde** coronary (thrombosis)
infatigable [ɛ̃fatigabl] *adj* tireless; (*amour, patience*) untiring
infect(e) [ɛ̃fɛkt] *adj* 1.(*répugnant*) vile; (*nourriture*) foul; (*lieu, logement*) sordid 2. *inf* (*ignoble*) lousy
infecté(e) [ɛ̃fɛkte] *adj* infected
infecter [ɛ̃fɛkte] <1> *vpr* MED **s'~** to get infected
infectieux, -euse [ɛ̃fɛksjø, -jøz] *adj* infectious
infection [ɛ̃fɛksjɔ̃] *f* infection
inférieur(e) [ɛ̃feʀjœʀ] I. *adj* 1.(*dans l'espace*) lower; **les étages ~s** the lower floors 2.(*en qualité*) inferior; **être ~ à qn/qc** to be inferior to sb/sth; **se sentir ~** to feel inferior; **~ en intelligence** less intelligent 3.(*en quantité*) ~ **à qn/qc** less than sb/sth; **huit est ~ à dix** eight is less than ten; ~ **en nombre** smaller in number II. *m(f)* inferior; **être l'~ de qn en qc** to be infcrior to sb in sth
infériorité [ɛ̃feʀjɔʀite] *f* 1.(*en qualité, rang*) inferiority; **en position d'~** in a position of weakness 2.(*moindre quantité*) smaller number; ~ **en poids** lighter weight
infernal(e) [ɛ̃fɛʀnal, o] <-aux> *adj* 1. MYTH infernal; **divinité ~e** god of the underworld 2.(*diabolique: complot, entreprise*) diabolical; **machine ~e** explosive device 3.(*insupportable: sort, temps*) foul; **cet enfant est ~** the child is a holy terror 4.(*endiablé*) infernal; (*logique, progrès*) relentless; **cycle ~** vicious circle; **un rythme ~** a furious pace
infesté(e) [ɛ̃fɛste] *adj* **être ~ de qc** to be infested with sth
infidèle [ɛ̃fidɛl] I. *adj* 1.(*perfide*) unfaithful; **être ~ à qn** to be unfaithful to sb; **être ~ à sa parole** to be untrue to one's word; **être ~ à ses devoirs** to fail to carry out one's duty 2.(*inexact: récit*) inaccurate; (*narrateur, mémoire*) unreliable; (*traduction*) unfaithful 3. REL infidel II. *mf* REL infidel
infidélité [ɛ̃fidelite] *f* 1. *sans pl* (*déloyauté*) disloyalty 2.(*action: d'un conjoint*) infidelity; (*d'un ami*) betrayal; **faire des ~s à qn** to be unfaithful to sb 3.(*inexactitude*) error; (*d'une description*) inaccuracy; ~ **à la description des faits** failure to give a correct account of the facts
infiltration [ɛ̃filtʀasjɔ̃] *f* 1.(*d'un liquide, gaz*) infiltration; **pénétrer par ~** to infiltrate 2. MED injection
infiltrer [ɛ̃filtʀe] <1> I. *vt* to infiltrate II. *vpr* 1. **s'~** to infiltrate; (*lumière*) to filter through; (*vent*) to get in 2. MED **s'~** to be injected 3.(*noyauter*) **s'~ dans qc** to infiltrate sth
infime [ɛ̃fim] *adj* 1. tiny 2.(*situé au plus bas d'une hiérarchie*) lowly
infini [ɛ̃fini] *m* MAT **tendre vers l'~** to tend towards inifinity ►**à l'~** for ever and ever
infini(e) [ɛ̃fini] *adj* 1.(*qui n'a pas de limite*) *a.* MAT infinite 2.(*immense: distance, nombre*) vast; (*étendue, durée, longueur*) immense 3.(*extrême*) infinite; (*reconnaissance*) deepest; (*richesses*) immeasurable 4.(*interminable: lutte*) never-ending; (*propos, temps*) endless
infiniment [ɛ̃finimɑ̃] *adv* 1.(*sans borne*) infinitely 2.(*extrêmement*) immensely; (*regretter*) deeply 3.(*beaucoup de*) ~ **de tendresse/d'attention** the utmost tenderness/attention
infinité [ɛ̃finite] *f* 1.(*caractère de ce qui est infini*) infinity 2.(*très grand nombre*) **une ~ de choses** an infinite number of things
infinitif [ɛ̃finitif] *m* infinitive
infinitif, -ive [ɛ̃finitif, -iv] *adj* **proposition**

infinitive infinitive clause; **le mode** ~ the infinitive

infirme [ɛ̃fiʀm] **I.** *adj* (*à la suite d'un accident*) disabled; (*pour cause de vieillesse*) infirm; ~ **de qc** to be crippled with sth **II.** *mf* disabled person; ~ **de guerre** war invalid

infirmerie [ɛ̃fiʀməʀi] *f* infirmary; (*d'une école*) sick bay

infirmier, **-ière** [ɛ̃fiʀmje, -jɛʀ] *m, f* nurse; **école d'infirmières** nursing college

infirmité [ɛ̃fiʀmite] *f* **1.** disability **2.** (*imperfection*) weakness

inflammable [ɛ̃flamabl] *adj* inflammable

inflammation [ɛ̃flamasjɔ̃] *f* inflammation; ~ **de la gorge/des bronches** inflamed throat/airways

inflation [ɛ̃flasjɔ̃] *f* inflation

inflexible [ɛ̃flɛksibl] *adj* inflexible; (*sévérité, volonté, résistance*) unyielding

infliger [ɛ̃fliʒe] <2a> *vt* **1.** (*donner*) ~ **une amende à qn pour qc** to fine sb for sth; ~ **un châtiment à qn** to punish sb **2.** (*faire subir: coups, récit*) to inflict; (*politique*) to impose; ~ **sa présence à qn** to inflict one's presence on sb

influençable [ɛ̃flyɑ̃sabl] *adj* easy to influence

influence [ɛ̃flyɑ̃s] *f* (*effet, autorité*) influence; (*des mesures, d'un médicament*) effect; **des luttes d'**~ struggles for influence; **sous l'**~ **de la colère** in the grip of anger; **sous l'**~ **de la boisson** under the influence of drink; **avoir de l'**~ to have influence; **avoir/exercer de l'**~ **sur qn/qc** to have/exert influence over sb/sth; **subir l'**~ **de qn** to be influenced by sb; **sous** ~ under influence

influencer [ɛ̃flyɑ̃se] <2> *vt* ~ **qn** to influence sb; (*mesures*) to have an effect on sb

influent(**e**) [ɛ̃flyɑ̃, ɑ̃t] *adj* influential

influer [ɛ̃flye] <1> *vi* ~ **sur qc** to influence sth

info [ɛ̃fo] *f inf abr de* **information** piece of news; **les** ~**s** the news

infogroupe [ɛ̃fogʀup] *m* INFOR newsgroup

infonaute [ɛ̃fonot] *mf* INFOR [Net] surfer

informateur, **-trice** [ɛ̃fɔʀmatœʀ, -tʀis] *m, f* informer

informaticien(**ne**) [ɛ̃fɔʀmatisjɛ̃, jɛn] *m(f)* computer scientist

informatif, **-ive** [ɛ̃fɔʀmatif, -iv] *adj* **1.** (*riche en informations*) informative **2.** (*destiné à informer: publicité*) informational; **brochure informative** information brochure; **réunion informative** briefing session

information [ɛ̃fɔʀmasjɔ̃] *f* **1.** (*renseignement*) piece of information; **prendre des** ~**s sur qn/qc** to obtain information about sb/sth; **une réunion d'**~ a briefing session **2.** *souvent pl* (*nouvelles*) news; **les** ~**s de vingt heures** the eight o'clock news; ~**s sportives/routières** sports/travel news; **magazine d'**~ news magazine **3.** *sans pl* (*fait d'informer*) information; **assurer l'**~ **de qn en matière de qc** to keep sb informed about sth; **faire de l'**~ to give out information **4.** (*ensemble des médias*) information media **5.** *pl* INFOR, TECH information

informatique [ɛ̃fɔʀmatik] **I.** *adj* **industrie** ~ computer industry; **saisie** ~ data capture **II.** *f* computer science

informatisation [ɛ̃fɔʀmatizasjɔ̃] *f* (*d'une entreprise*) computerization

informatisé(**e**) [ɛ̃fɔʀmatize] *adj* (*poste de travail*) computerized; **fichier** ~ computer file; **gestion** ~ computer assisted management; **communication/système** ~(**e**) computer-based communication/system

informatiser [ɛ̃fɔʀmatize] <1> **I.** *vt* to computerize **II.** *vpr* **s'**~ to be computerized

informe [ɛ̃fɔʀm] *adj* **1.** (*sans forme, laid*) shapeless; (*être*) misshapen **2.** (*ébauché*) rough; (*plan*) ill-defined

informer [ɛ̃fɔʀme] <1> **I.** *vt* to inform; **des personnes/milieux bien informé**(**e**)**s** well-informed people/circles **II.** *vi* to inform **III.** *vpr* **s'**~ **de qc** (*poser des questions*) to inquire about sth; (*se renseigner*) to inform oneself about sth; **s'**~ **sur qn** (*sa santé*) to ask after sb; (*son caractère*) to find out about sb; **s'**~ **si qn a fait qc** to find out if sb has done sth

infos *fpl inf* **les** ~ the news

infraction [ɛ̃fʀaksjɔ̃] *f* offence *Brit,* offense *Am;* ~ **au code de la route** driving offence; **c'est une** ~ **à la loi** it's an offence

infranchissable [ɛ̃fʀɑ̃ʃisabl] *adj* impassible

infrarouge [ɛ̃fʀaʀuʒ] **I.** *adj* infrared **II.** *m* infrared radiation; **système à** ~**s** heat-seeking system

infrastructure [ɛ̃fʀastʀyktyʀ] *f* infrastructure; ~ **routière** highway infrastructure

infréquentable [ɛ̃fʀekɑ̃tabl] *adj péj* (*personne*) that one does not associate with; (*pays*) pariah; **il est devenu** ~ he has put himself beyond the pale; **se rendre** ~ to put oneself beyond the pale

infructueux, **-euse** [ɛ̃fʀyktɥø, -øz] *adj* fruitless

infuser [ɛ̃fyze] <1> **I.** *vt* **1.** to infuse **2.** (*communiquer: courage*) to instil *Brit,* to instill *Am* **II.** *vi* (*tisane, thé*) to brew

infusion [ɛ̃fyzjɔ̃] *f* infusion; ~ **de camomille** camomile [*o* chamomile] tea

ingénier [ɛ̃ʒenje] <1a> *vpr* **s'**~ **à** +*infin* to endeavour to +*infin Brit,* to endeavor to +*infin Am*

ingénierie [ɛ̃ʒeniʀi] *f* engineering; **une entreprise d'**~ an engineering company

ingénieur [ɛ̃ʒenjœʀ] *m* engineer

ingénieux, **-euse** [ɛ̃ʒenjø, -jøz] *adj* ingenious

ingéniosité [ɛ̃ʒenjozite] *f* ingenuity; **déployer des trésors d'**~ to bring all one's ingenuity to bear

ingénu(**e**) [ɛ̃ʒeny] **I.** *adj* **1.** (*sans malice*) ingenuous **2.** (*naïf*) naive **II.** *m(f)* naive person

ingénue [ɛ̃ʒeny] *f* THEAT ingénue; **jouer les**

~**s** to play ingénue roles

ingérence [ɛ̃ʒeʀɑ̃s] *f* (*d'un magistrat*) intervention; ~ **dans qc** interference in sth

ingérer [ɛ̃ʒeʀe] <5> **I.** *vt* (*médicament*) to ingest; (*aliment*) to absorb **II.** *vpr* **s'~ dans qc** to interfere in sth

ingouvernable [ɛ̃guvɛʀnabl] *adj* (*pays, peuple*) ungovernable; (*parlement*) unruly

ingrat(e) [ɛ̃gʀa, at] **I.** *adj* **1.** (*opp: reconnaissant*) ~ **envers qn** ungrateful to sb **2.** (*infructueux: métier, sujet*) thankless; (*vie*) unrewarding **3.** (*dépourvu de charme: visage*) unlovely **II.** *m(f)* ungrateful wretch

ingratitude [ɛ̃gʀatityd] *f* (*d'une personne*) ingratitude; (*d'une tâche*) thanklessness; **faire preuve d'~** to show ingratitude

ingrédient [ɛ̃gʀedjɑ̃] *m* ingredient

inguérissable [ɛ̃geʀisabl] *adj* (*maladie*) incurable

ingurgiter [ɛ̃gyʀʒite] <1> *vt* **1.** (*avaler: nourriture*) to guzzle down; (*boisson*) to gulp down; **faire ~ qc à qn** to force sth down sb **2.** (*apprendre: connaissances, science*) to cram into one's head; **faire ~ un poème à qn** to force a poem down sb's throat

inhabitable [inabitabl] *adj* (*région*) uninhabitable; (*maison*) unfit for habitation

inhabité(e) [inabite] *adj* uninhabited; (*appartement*) empty

inhabituel(le) [inabitɥɛl] *adj* unusual

inhalation [inalasjɔ̃] *f a.* MED inhalation; **faire une ~** to have an inhalation

inhaler [inale] <1> *vt* MED to inhale

inhérent(e) [ineʀɑ̃, ɑ̃t] *adj a.* PHILOS **être ~ à qc** to be inherent in sth

inhibition [inibisjɔ̃] *f* inhibition

inhospitalier, -ière [inɔspitalje, -jɛʀ] *adj* (*personne, lieu*) inhospitable; (*chambre*) uninviting

inhumain(e) [inymɛ̃, ɛn] *adj* inhuman

inhumation [inymasjɔ̃] *f* burial

inhumer [inyme] <1> *vt* to bury

inimaginable [inimaʒinabl] *adj* unimaginable

inimitable [inimitabl] *adj* inimitable

inimitié [inimitje] *f* enmity

inintelligible [inɛ̃teliʒibl] *adj* unintelligible

ininterrompu(e) [inɛ̃teʀɔ̃py] *adj* uninterrupted; (*série*) unbroken; (*spectacle*) non-stop

initial(e) [inisjal, jo] <-aux> *adj* (*cause, choc, lettre*) initial; (*état, position*) original; (*feuillets*) first

initiale [inisjal] *f* initial

initialement [inisjalmɑ̃] *adv* initially

initialisation [inisjalizasjɔ̃] *f* INFOR initialization

initiateur, -trice [inisjatœʀ, -tʀis] *m, f* originator; (*d'une mode*) pioneer; (*d'une organisation*) founder

initiation [inisjasjɔ̃] *f* initiation; **cours d'~** introductory course; ~ **à qc** introduction to sth

initiative [inisjativ] *f* (*idée première, dynamisme*) initiative; **avoir l'~ de qc** to have the idea for sth; **de sa/leur propre ~** of her/their own initiative; **avoir de l'~** to have initiative

initié(e) [inisje] **I.** *adj* initiated **II.** *m(f)* initiate

initier [inisje] <1a> **I.** *vt* **1.** ~ **qn à un art** to introduce sb to an art; ~ **qn à un secret** to initiate sb into a secret **2.** REL ~ **qn à qc** to initiate sb into sth **II.** *vpr* **s'~ à qc** to initiate oneself to sth; **s'~ à un métier** to learn a trade

injecter [ɛ̃ʒɛkte] <1> *vt* to inject

injection [ɛ̃ʒɛksjɔ̃] *f* injection; **moteur à ~** injection engine; **voiture à ~** car with fuel injection

injoignable [ɛ̃ʒwaɲabl] *adj* **elle est ~** she can't be reached

injure [ɛ̃ʒyʀ] *f* insult; **abreuver qn d'~** to shower sb with abuse

injurier [ɛ̃ʒyʀje] <1> **I.** *vt* to insult; ~ **la mémoire de qn** to be an insult to sb's memory **II.** *vpr* **s'~** to insult each other

injurieux, -euse [ɛ̃ʒyʀjø, -jøz] *adj* offensive

injuste [ɛ̃ʒyst] *adj* unfair

injustement [ɛ̃ʒystəmɑ̃] *adv* **1.** (*à tort*) unfairly **2.** (*iniquement*) unjustly

injustice [ɛ̃ʒystis] *f* injustice; **avec ~** unjustly

injustifié(e) [ɛ̃ʒystifje] *adj* unjustified

inlassable [ɛ̃lɑsabl] *adj* untiring

inlassablement [ɛ̃lɑsabləmɑ̃] *adv* untiringly

inné(e) [i(n)ne] *adj* innate

innocemment [inɔsamɑ̃] *adv* innocently

innocence [inɔsɑ̃s] *f* **1.** (*naïveté*) innocence; **abuser de l'~ de qn** to take advantage of sb's innocence; **en toute ~** in all innocence **2.** (*caractère inoffensif*) harmlessness

innocent(e) [inɔsɑ̃, ɑ̃t] **I.** *adj* **1.** (*opp: coupable*) innocent; **être ~ de qc** to be not guilty of sth **2.** (*inoffensif*) **l'article n'est pas ~** the article is disingenuous; **ce n'est pas ~ si qn fait qc** it is no accident if sb does sth **II.** *m(f)* innocent; **faire l'~** to play the innocent

innocenter [inɔsɑ̃te] <1> *vt* ~ **qn de vol** to clear sb of theft

innombrable [i(n)nɔ̃bʀabl] *adj* innumerable

innommable [i(n)nɔmabl] *adj* unspeakable

innovateur, -trice [inɔvatœʀ, -tʀis] **I.** *adj* (*méthode, politique*) innovative; **action innovatrice** innovation; **être ~** to be innovative **II.** *m, f* innovator

innovation [inɔvasjɔ̃] *f* innovation

innover [inɔve] <1> **I.** *vt* to create **II.** *vi* ~ **en (matière de) qc** to innovate in the field of sth

inoccupé(e) [inɔkype] *adj* **1.** (*vide: place, terrain*) vacant; (*maison*) unoccupied **2.** (*oisif*) unoccupied

inoculer [inɔkyle] <1> *vt* **1.** MED ~ **qc à qn** to inoculate sb with sth **2.** (*transmettre*) ~ **qc à qn** to infect sb with sth

inodore [inɔdɔʀ] *adj* odourless *Brit,* odorless *Am*

inoffensif, -ive [inɔfɑ̃sif, -iv] *adj* (*personne*) inoffensive; (*piqûre, remède*) harmless

inondation [inɔ̃dasjɔ̃] *f* **1.** (*débordement*

I

d'eaux) flood; (*d'un fleuve*) flooding **2.** (*afflux massif: de machandises, produits*) flood

inondé(e) [inɔ̃de] *adj* **1.** (*recouvert d'eau*) flooded **2.** *fig* ~ **de soleil** bathed in sunlight

inonder [inɔ̃de] <1> **I.** *vt* **1.** (*couvrir d'eaux*) to flood; **être inondé** (*personnes*) to be flooded (out) **2.** (*tremper*) ~ **qn/qc de qc** to soak sb/sth with sth; ~ **qn/qc** (*chose*) to pour down sb/sth **3.** (*submerger*) ~ **qn de qc** to swamp sb with sth; ~ **un pays de qc** to flood a country with sth; ~ **les rues** to pour into the streets **II.** *vpr* **s'**~ **de qc** to soak oneself with sth

inopiné(e) [inɔpine] *adj* unexpected

inopportun(e) [inɔpɔʀtœ̃, yn] *adj* inopportune

inoubliable [inublijabl] *adj* unforgettable

inouï(e) [inwi] *adj* **1.** (*inconnu*) unheard of **2.** *inf* (*formidable*) **être** ~ (*personne*) to be beyond belief

inox [inɔks] *abr de* **inoxydable I.** *m inv* stainless steel **II.** *app inv* (*acier*) stainless; (*cuve, tambour*) stainless steel

inoxydable [inɔksidabl] *adj* stainless

inqualifiable [ɛ̃kalifjabl] *adj* unspeakable

inquiet, -ète [ɛ̃kjɛ, -ɛt] **I.** *adj* **1.** (*anxieux*) worried; **c'est un caractère** ~ he's a worrier; **ne sois pas** ~**!** don't worry!; **être** ~ **de qc** to be worried about sth **2.** (*qui dénote l'appréhension: regard, attente*) anxious **II.** *m, f* worrier

inquiétant(e) [ɛ̃kjetɑ̃, ɑ̃t] *adj* **1.** (*alarmant*) worrying; **devenir** ~ to cause anxiety **2.** (*patibulaire*) disturbing

inquiéter [ɛ̃kjete] <5> **I.** *vt* to worry **II.** *vpr* **1.** (*s'alarmer*) **s'**~ to be disturbed **2.** (*se soucier de*) **s'**~ **au sujet de la fille/la maison** to worry about the girl/the house; **s'**~ **de savoir si/qui** to be anxious to know if/who

inquiétude [ɛ̃kjetyd] *f* anxiety; **plonger qn dans l'**~ to cast sb into a state of anxiety; **avoir des** ~**s au sujet de la fille/la maison** to be worried about the girl/the house; **être sans** ~ **sur qc** to be unconcerned about sth

insaisissable [ɛ̃sezisabl] *adj* **1.** unseizable **2.** *inf* (*qu'on ne parvient pas à rencontrer*) elusive **3.** (*qui échappe à toute influence*) slippery **4.** (*imperceptible*) imperceptible; (*ton*) hard to distinguish; **les différences les plus** ~**s** barely perceptible differences **5.** (*fuyant: rêve*) fleeting; (*horizon*) unreachable **6.** JUR non-seizable

insalubre [ɛ̃salybʀ] *adj* (*climat*) unhealthy; (*quartier*) insalubrious

insanité [ɛ̃sanite] *f* (*d'une personne*) insanity; (*d'un propos, d'un acte*) absurdity; **dire des** ~**s** to make absurd remarks

insatiable [ɛ̃sasjabl] *adj* (*personne, curiosité*) insatiable; (*soif*) unquenchable

insatisfaction [ɛ̃satisfaksjɔ̃] *f* ~ **devant qc** dissatisfaction over sth

insatisfait(e) [ɛ̃satisfɛ, ɛt] **I.** *adj* **1.** (*mécontent*) ~ **de qn/qc** dissatisfied with sb/sth **2.** (*inassouvi*) unsatisfied **II.** *m(f)* **c'est un éternel** ~ he's never satisfied

inscription [ɛ̃skʀipsjɔ̃] *f* **1.** (*texte*) inscription; (*d'un poteau indicateur*) words **2.** (*immatriculation*) registration; **les** ~**s sont closes le 31 mars** the final date for registration is 31 March; ~ **d'un élève à une école** enrolment of a pupil at a school *Brit,* enrollment of a pupil at a school *Am;* ~ **de qn à un concours** sb's entry in a competition; ~ **de qn à un club** sb's joining a club

inscrire [ɛ̃skʀiʀ] *irr* **I.** *vt* **1.** (*noter*) ~ **qc dans un carnet/sur une enveloppe** to write sth down in a notebook/on an envelope; ~ **qc à l'ordre du jour** to put sth on the agenda; **être inscrit dans ma mémoire** to be engraved in my memory; **être inscrit sur mon visage** to be written on my face **2.** (*immatriculer*) ~ **qn à une école/dans un club** to enrol sb at a school/in a club *Brit,* to enroll sb at a school/in a club *Am;* ~ **qn sur une liste** to put sb on a list; (*pour prendre rendez-vous*) to put sb on a waiting list; **être inscrit à la faculté** to be at university *Brit,* to be in college *Am;* **être inscrit dans un club** to be a member of a club **II.** *vpr* **1.** (*s'immatriculer*) **s'**~ **à une école** to enrol at a school *Brit,* to enroll at a school *Am;* **s'**~ **à une faculté** to register at a university; **s'**~ **à un parti/club** to join a party/club; **s'**~ **sur une liste** to put one's name down on a list; **se faire** ~ **au tennis** to join the tennis club **2.** (*s'insérer dans*) **s'**~ **dans le cadre de qc** (*décision, mesure, projet*) to come within the context of sth **3.** (*apparaître*) **s'**~ **sur l'écran** to appear on the screen

inscrit(e) [ɛ̃skʀi, it] **I.** *part passé de* **inscrire II.** *adj* (*candidat, député, électeur*) registered **III.** *m(f)* person (registered); (*à un examen*) (registered) candidate; (*à un parti*) (registered) member; (*sur une liste électorale*) (registered) voter; (*à une faculté*) (registered) student

insecte [ɛ̃sɛkt] *m* insect

insecticide [ɛ̃sɛktisid] **I.** *adj* **poudre** ~ insecticidal powder **II.** *m* insecticide

insectivore [ɛ̃sɛktivɔʀ] **I.** *adj* insectivorous **II.** *m* insectivore

insécurité [ɛ̃sekyʀite] *f* **1.** (*sentiment, risque*) insecurity **2.** (*danger pour le public*) low public safety

INSEE [inse] *m abr de* **Institut national de la statistique et des études économiques** *French national institute of economic and statistical information*

insémination [ɛ̃seminasjɔ̃] *f* insemination

insensé(e) [ɛ̃sɑ̃se] *adj* insane ►**c'est** ~**!** it's sheer madness!

insensibilisation [ɛ̃sɑ̃sibilizasjɔ̃] *f* anaesthesia *Brit,* anesthsia *Am*

insensibiliser [ɛ̃sɑ̃sibilize] <1> *vt* **1.** to anaesthetize *Brit,* to anesthetize *Am* **2.** *fig* **être insensibilisé à qc** to be impervious to sth

insensibilité [ɛ̃sɑ̃sibilite] *f* **1.** (*physique*) insensibility **2.** (*morale*) insensitivity

insensible [ɛ̃sɑ̃sibl] *adj* **1.** (*physiquement*) **être** ~ (*personne*) to be unconscious; (*lèvres, membre*) to be numb; ~ **à la douleur/chaleur** to be insensitive to pain/heat **2.** (*moralement*) insensitive; ~ **aux compliments** impervious to compliments; **laisser qn** ~ to leave sb unmoved

insensiblement [ɛ̃sɑ̃sibləmɑ̃] *adv* (*imperceptiblement*) imperceptibly

inséparable [ɛ̃sepaʀabl] *adj* (*amis, idées*) inseparable; **être** ~ **de qc** to be inseparable from sth

insérer [ɛ̃seʀe] <5> **I.** *vt* to insert **II.** *vpr* **s'**~ **dans qc** (*personne*) to integrate with sth

insertion [ɛ̃sɛʀsjɔ̃] *f* ~ **dans qc** integration into sth; **centre** (**d'hébergement et**) **d'**~ rehabilitation centre *Brit,* rehabilitation center *Am;* **l'**~ **sociale de qn** sb's social integration

insidieux, -euse [ɛ̃sidjø, -jøz] *adj a.* MED insidious

insigne [ɛ̃siɲ] *m* badge; (*d'un ordre*) emblem

insignifiance [ɛ̃siɲifjɑ̃s] *f* insignificance

insignifiant(**e**) [ɛ̃siɲifjɑ̃, jɑ̃t] *adj* insignificant; (*paroles*) trivial

insinuation [ɛ̃sinɥasjɔ̃] *f* insinuation

insinuer [ɛ̃sinɥe] <1> **I.** *vt* (*laisser entendre*) insinuate **II.** *vpr* **1.** (*pénétrer*) **s'**~ **dans qc** to work one's way into sth **2.** (*se glisser*) **s'**~ **dans qc** (*personne*) to insinuate oneself into sth; (*idée, sentiment*) to creep into sth; **s'**~ **dans l'esprit de qn** to creep into sb's mind

insipide [ɛ̃sipid] *adj* **1.** tasteless **2.** (*ennuyeux*) insipid

insistance [ɛ̃sistɑ̃s] *f* insistance; ~ **à faire qc** insistance on doing sth; ~ **à ne pas** +*infin* insistent refusal to +*infin;* **avec** ~ insistently

insistant(**e**) [ɛ̃sistɑ̃, ɑ̃t] *adj* (*ton, regard*) insistent; (*rumeur*) persistent; (*curiosité*) stubborn

insister [ɛ̃siste] <1> *vi* **1.** (*pour persuader*) ~ **sur qc** to insist on sth; ~ **à faire qc** to insist on doing sth; **inutile d'**~ there's no use insisting; **n'insistez pas!** don't insist; **je n'ai pas insisté** I didn't insist any more **2.** (*persévérer*) to keep on trying **3.** (*mettre l'accent sur*) ~ **sur qc** to stress sth ▶**sans** ~ without making a fuss

insociable [ɛ̃sɔsjabl] *adj soutenu* antisocial

insolation [ɛ̃sɔlasjɔ̃] *f* (*coup de chaleur*) sunstroke *no pl*

insolence [ɛ̃sɔlɑ̃s] *f* **1.** (*impertinence*) insolence; **avec** ~ insolently **2.** (*arrogance*) arrogance

insolent(**e**) [ɛ̃sɔlɑ̃, ɑ̃t] **I.** *adj* **1.** (*impertinent*) insolent **2.** (*arrogant*) arrogant **3.** (*provocant*) unashamed **II.** *m(f)* insolent person; **petit** ~ insolent little so-and-so

insolite [ɛ̃sɔlit] *adj* (*inhabituel*) unusual

insoluble [ɛ̃sɔlybl] *adj* insoluble

insolvable [ɛ̃sɔlvabl] *adj* insolvent

insomniaque [ɛ̃sɔmnjak] **I.** *adj* insomniac; **être** ~ to have insomnia **II.** *mf* insomniac

insomnie [ɛ̃sɔmni] *f* insomnia *no pl;* **avoir des** ~**s** to have insomnia

insondable [ɛ̃sɔ̃dabl] *adj* (*abîme*) bottomless; (*mystère, pensée*) unfathomable; (*douleur*) immeasurable; (*bêtise*) abysmal

insonoriser [ɛ̃sɔnɔʀize] <1> *vt* to soundproof

insouciance [ɛ̃susjɑ̃s] *f* carefree attitude; **vivre dans l'**~ to have a carefree existence

insouciant(**e**) [ɛ̃susjɑ̃, jɑ̃t] **I.** *adj* (*heureux*) carefree; (*imprévoyant*) unconcerned; **être** ~ **du lendemain** not to think about tomorrow; **être** ~ **du danger** heedless of (the) danger **II.** *m(f) péj* careless person

insoupçonné(**e**) [ɛ̃supsɔne] *adj* unsuspected

insoutenable [ɛ̃sutnabl] *adj* (*insupportable*) unbearable

inspecter [ɛ̃spɛkte] <1> *vt* to inspect

inspecteur, -trice [ɛ̃spɛktœʀ, -tʀis] *m, f* inspector; ~ **de police** police inspector; ~ **des finances** state auditor, *checking finances of state bodies;* ~ **des écoles maternelles** preschool inspector, *for pre-primary institutions;* ~ **des travaux finis** *iron* last-minute helper; ~ **des Ponts et Chaussées** public works inspector, *controlling French public highway projects;* ~ **du travail** factory inspector; ~ **général** ECOLE schools inspector; ~ **pédagogique régional** ECOLE regional schools inspector; ~ **d'Académie** ECOLE regional director of education; ~ **primaire** primary schools inspector

inspection [ɛ̃spɛksjɔ̃] *f* **1.** (*contrôle*) inspection **2.** (*corps de fonctionnaires*) inspectorate; ~ **des Finances** state auditors, *checking finances of state bodies;* ~ **du Travail** factory inspectorate; ~ **académique** ≈ education authority; ~ **générale** ECOLE *schools inspectorate;* ~ **primaire** ECOLE *primary schools inspectorate;* ~ **régionale** ECOLE local schools authority

inspiration [ɛ̃spiʀasjɔ̃] *f a.* MED inspiration; **avoir la bonne/mauvaise** ~ **de faire qc** to have the good/bad idea of doing sth; **avoir de l'**~**/manquer d'**~ to have/lack inspiration; **chercher l'**~ to seek inspiration; **suivre son** ~**/l'**~ **de qn** to act on one's/sb's inspiration; **faire** [*o* **prendre**] **une grande** ~ to breathe in deeply ▶**selon l'**~ **du moment** as the mood takes one; **d'**~ **médiévale/orientale** of medieval/oriental inspiration; **sous l'**~ **de qn/qc** inspired by sb/sth

inspiré(**e**) [ɛ̃spiʀe] *adj* ~ **de qc** inspired by sth

inspirer [ɛ̃spiʀe] <1> **I.** *vt* **1.** ANAT to breathe in **2.** (*susciter*) ~ **du dégoût** to make one feel disgust; ~ **de l'inquiétude** to be worrying; ~ **de la confiance** (*personne*) to inspire confidence; ~ **le dégoût à qn** to disgust sb; ~ **la prudence à qn** to incline sb to prudence **3.** (*suggérer*) ~ **une idée à qn** to give sb an idea; ~ **un roman à qn** to give sb the idea for a novel; ~ **à qn de faire qc** to give sb the idea of doing sth **4.** (*être à l'origine de: œuvre, per-*

I

sonnage de roman) to inspire; (*décision*) to prompt; **être inspiré par qc** (*chose*) to be inspired by sth; **être inspiré par qn** (*opération, attentat, conjuration*) to be inspired by sb **5.** (*rendre créatif*) ~ **qn** to inspire sb **6.** *inf* (*plaire*) **son idée m'inspirait/ne m'inspirait pas du tout** I went for/didn't go at all for her idea **II.** *vpr* **s'**~ **de qn/qc** to be inspired by sb/sth; **un film qui s'inspire d'un roman** a film inspired by a novel **III.** *vi* to breathe in

instabilité [ɛ̃stabilite] *f* instability; ~ **des prix** price instability; **l'**~ **du temps/de la situation** the unsettled weather/situation; ~ **ministérielle** instability within the cabinet

instable [ɛ̃stabl] *adj* unstable; (*temps*) unsettled; (*personne*) restless

installateur, **-trice** [ɛ̃stalatœʀ, -tʀis] *m, f* installer

installation [ɛ̃stalasjɔ̃] *f* **1.** (*mise en place*) installation; (*d'un meuble*) assembly; (*d'un campement*) setting up; ~ **de l'eau/du gaz** installation of water/gas **2.** *gén pl* (*équipement*) equipment; ~**s électriques/sanitaires** (*fils/tuyaux*) wiring/plumbing; (*prises/lavabos*) electrical/bathroom fittings; ~ **de fortune** makeshift arrangements **3.** (*emménagement*) moving in

installé(**e**) [ɛ̃stale] *adj* **1.** (*aménagé: appartement*) furnished; (*atelier*) fitted out; **être bien** ~ to be well fitted out **2.** (*qui jouit d'une situation confortable*) comfortably off; **c'est un homme** ~ he's comfortable; **être** ~ to be set up in life

installer [ɛ̃stale] <1> **I.** *vt* **1.** (*mettre en place sous terre: câbles, tuyaux*) to lay **2.** (*mettre en place chez qn: câbles, tuyaux, téléphone*) to put in; (*eau courante, électricité*) to install; (*meuble*) to assemble; (*barrage*) to build **3.** (*caser, loger*) ~ **qn/qc quelque part** to put sb/sth somewhere; ~ **qn dans un fauteuil** to settle sb in an armchair; ~ **qn dans un lit** to put sb to bed; **être installé en Bretagne** to live in Brittany **4.** (*établir officiellement*) to install **II.** *vpr* **1.** (*s'asseoir*) **s'**~ to sit (down); (*commodément*) to settle (oneself) **2.** (*se loger*) **s'**~ to settle; **s'**~ **chez qn** to move in with sb; **s'**~ **à la campagne** to go and live in the country **3.** (*s'établir*) **s'**~ to set up; (*commerçant, patron d'un restaurant*) to open up

instamment [ɛ̃stamɑ̃] *adv* insistently

instance [ɛ̃stɑ̃s] *f* **1.** *gén pl* authority; **les** ~**s dirigeantes** the authorities **2.** JUR (*poursuite en justice*) proceedings *pl;* **introduire une** ~ to start proceedings **3.** (*insistance*) insistence; **avec** ~ insistently; **sur** [*o* **devant**] **les** ~**s de qn** in the face of sb's entreaties ►**être en** ~ **de qc** to be in the process of sth; **être en** ~ **de divorce** to be waiting for a divorce; **être en** ~ to be pending; **être en** ~ **à la poste** (*courrier, lettre*) in the post

instant [ɛ̃stɑ̃] *m* moment; **à chaque** ~ (*d'ici peu*) at any moment; (*constamment*) all the time; **au même** ~ at the same moment; **vivre dans l'**~ to live for the moment; **à l'**~ (**même**) at that (very) moment; (*tout de suite*) straight away; **à l'**~ **où qn a fait qc** at the moment when sb did sth; **dans l'**~ (**même**) in no time; **dans un** ~ in a moment; **dès l'**~ **que qn a fait qc** from the moment sb did sth; **dès l'**~ **où qn a fait qc** (*puisque*) once sb does sth; (*dès que*) from the moment sb did sth; **de tous les** ~**s** constant; **d'un** ~ **à l'autre** from one minute to the next; **en un** ~ in an instant; **par** ~**s** at moments; **pour l'**~ for the moment; (**pendant**) **un** ~ for a moment; **un** ~**!** one moment!

instantané(**e**) [ɛ̃stɑ̃tane] *adj* **1.** (*immédiat: réaction, réponse*) instant; (*mort*) instantanous; **être** ~ (*réponse*) to come instantly; (*mort*) to be immediate; **l'effet du médicament est** ~ the drug acts instantly **2.** GASTR (*café*) instant; **potage/soupe** ~(**e**) instant soup

instantanément [ɛ̃stɑ̃tanemɑ̃] *adv* instantly

instauration [ɛ̃stɔʀasjɔ̃] *f* (*d'un gouvernement*) establishment; (*d'un processus*) starting

instaurer [ɛ̃stɔʀe] <1> **I.** *vt* (*gouvernement*) to establish; (*mode*) to start; (*liens*) to create; (*processus*) to set up **II.** *vpr* **s'**~ to be established; (*état d'esprit*) to be created; (*doute*) to be raised; **s'**~ **entre des personnes** (*collaboration*) to be set up; (*débat*) to open up

instigateur, **-trice** [ɛ̃stigatœʀ, -tʀis] *m, f* instigator; **c'est l'**~ **du complot** he's behind the plot

instiguer [ɛ̃stige] <1> *vt Belgique* (*pousser, inciter*) to incite

instinct [ɛ̃stɛ̃] *m* (*tendance innée*) instinct; ~ **de propriété** instinct to possess; **d'**[*o* **par**] ~ by instinct; ~ **des affaires** business instinct

instinctif, **-ive** [ɛ̃stɛ̃ktif, -iv] *adj* instinctive

instinctivement [ɛ̃stɛ̃ktivmɑ̃] *adv* instinctively

instit [ɛ̃stit] *mf fam abr de* **instituteur** (primary) teacher

instituer [ɛ̃stitɥe] <1> **I.** *vt* **1.** (*organisation, ordre*) to establish **2.** (*établir en fonction*) to institute **3.** (*nommer par testament: héritier, légataire*) to appoint **II.** *vpr* **1.** **s'**~ to become established **2.** (*s'ériger en*) **s'**~ **qn** to set oneself up as sb

institut [ɛ̃stity] *m* institute; **Institut de France** *Institute comprising the five Academies or learned societies, including the Académie française;* ~ **universitaire de formation des maîtres** *training college for primary school teachers;* **Institut universitaire de technologie** technological university; ~ **de beauté** beauty salon

instituteur, **-trice** [ɛ̃stitytœʀ, -tʀis] *m, f* (primary) teacher; ~ **spécialisé** ≈ special needs teacher

institution [ɛ̃stitysjɔ̃] *f* **1.** (*établissement d'enseignement*) school **2.** (*création, fondation*) creation; (*d'un régime*) founding;

(*d'une mesure, d'un usage*) institution **3.** (*chose instituée*) *a.* POL institution

Institut monétaire européen *m* European Monetary Institute

instructif, -ive [ɛ̃stʀyktif, -iv] *adj* instructive

instruction [ɛ̃stʀyksjɔ̃] *f* **1.** (*enseignement*) education; ~ **civique** civics **2.** (*prescription*) *a.* MIL, ADMIN instruction **3.** *gén pl* (*mode d'emploi*) instructions

instruire [ɛ̃stʀɥiʀ] *irr* **I.** *vt* **1.** (*enfants*) to teach; (*adultes*) to train; ~ **qn dans une science** to instruct sb in a science **2.** (*informer*) ~ **qn d'une nouvelle** to inform sb of some news **3.** JUR ~ **une affaire** to investigate a matter; ~ **contre qn** to investigate sb **II.** *vi* (*chose*) to educate **III.** *vpr* **1. s'~ dans une langue** to teach oneself a language **2.** JUR **s'~** to be under investigation

instruit(e) [ɛ̃stʀɥi, it] *adj* educated

instrument [ɛ̃stʀymɑ̃] *m* **1.** (*outil*) instrument; ~ **de travail** tool **2.** MUS ~ **de musique** musical instrument; **jouer d'un** ~ to play an instrument **3.** (*moyen*) tool; ~ **de propagande** propaganda tool; ~ **de sélection** tool for selection

instrumental(e) [ɛ̃stʀymɑ̃tal, o] <-aux> *adj* instrumental

instrumentiste [ɛ̃stʀymɑ̃tist] *mf* MUS instrumentalist

insu [ɛ̃sy] **à l'~ de qn** without sb knowing; **à l'~ de tout le monde** unknown to anyone

insubmersible [ɛ̃sybmɛʀsibl] *adj* unsinkable

insubordination [ɛ̃sybɔʀdinasjɔ̃] *f a.* MIL insubordination; ~ **ouvrière** revolt by the workers

insuccès [ɛ̃syksɛ] *m* failure

insuffisamment [ɛ̃syfizamɑ̃] *adv* insufficiently; **travailler/dormir** ~ not to work/sleep enough

insuffisance [ɛ̃syfizɑ̃s] *f* **1.** inadequacy; ~ **de la récolte** inadequate harvest **2.** (*faiblesse*) weakness **3.** MED ~ **hépatique/rénale** liver/kidney failure

insuffisant(e) [ɛ̃syfizɑ̃, ɑ̃t] *adj* **1.** (*en quantité*) insufficient; (*moyens, personnel*) inadequate; (*nombre, dimension*) too small; **être en nombre** ~ to be insufficient in number; **être** ~ to not be enough; (*nombre, dimension*) to be too small **2.** (*en qualité*) inadequate; (*candidat, élève*) weak; (*travail*) poor

insulaire [ɛ̃sylɛʀ] **I.** *adj* insular; **administration** ~ island administration **II.** *mf* islander

insuline [ɛ̃sylin] *f* insulin

insultant(e) [ɛ̃syltɑ̃, ɑ̃t] *adj* insulting; **être** ~ **pour qn/qc** to be insulting to sb/sth

insulte [ɛ̃sylt] *f* ~ **à la mémoire de qn/religion** insult to the memory of sb/to religion

insulter [ɛ̃sylte] <1> **I.** *vt* to insult **II.** *vpr* **s'~** (*personnes*) to insult each other

insupportable [ɛ̃sypɔʀtabl] *adj* **1.** (*intolérable*) unbearable **2.** (*désagréable: caractère*) insufferable

insurgé(e) [ɛ̃syʀʒe] *adj, m(f)* rebel

insurger [ɛ̃syʀʒe] <2a> *vpr* **1. s'~ contre qn/qc** to rise up against sb/sth **2.** (*protester*) **s'~ contre qc** to challenge sth

insurmontable [ɛ̃syʀmɔ̃tabl] *adj* unsurmountable

insurrection [ɛ̃syʀɛksjɔ̃] *f* insurrection

intact(e) [ɛ̃takt] *adj* intact

intarissable [ɛ̃taʀisabl] *adj* (*eau, puits, verve*) inexhaustible; (*pleurs*) endless; (*personne, bavard*) never silent; **il est** ~ **sur qc** he can go on for ever about sth

intégral(e) [ɛ̃tegʀal, o] <-aux> *adj* (*audition, texte*) full; (*horreur*) utter; **bronzage** ~ full-body tan; **nu** ~ complete nudity

intégrale [ɛ̃tegʀal] *f* **1.** MAT integral **2.** LIT, MUS complete works *pl*

intégralement [ɛ̃tegʀalmɑ̃] *adv* in full

intégralité [ɛ̃tegʀalite] *f* entirety; **le bâtiment/projet dans son** ~ the whole [*o* entire] building/project; **en** ~ in full

intégration [ɛ̃tegʀasjɔ̃] *f* **1.** (*union: économique, européenne, politique*) integration **2.** (*assimilation*) ~ **dans qc** integration into sth **3.** *inf* (*admission*) ~ **à qc** admission to sth

intègre [ɛ̃tɛgʀ] *adj* (*vie, juge*) honest; (*personne*) upright

intégrer [ɛ̃tegʀe] <5> *vpr* **s'~ à** [*o* **dans**] **qc** (*personne, chose*) to integrate into sth

intégrisme [ɛ̃tegʀism] *m* fundamentalism

intégriste [ɛ̃tegʀist] **I.** *adj* fundamentalist **II.** *mf* fundamentalist

intégrité [ɛ̃tegʀite] *f* **1.** (*d'une vie, personne*) integrity **2.** (*intégralité: d'une personne, d'un édifice*) soundness; (*d'un honneur, territoire, d'une œuvre*) integrity; **conserver l'~ de ses facultés** to have kept all one's faculties

intellectuel(le) [ɛ̃telɛktɥɛl] **I.** *adj* **1.** (*mental*) mental **2.** (*sollicitant l'intelligence*) intellectual **II.** *m(f)* intellectual

intellectuellement [ɛ̃telɛktɥɛlmɑ̃] *adv* intellectually

intelligemment [ɛ̃teliʒamɑ̃] *adv* intelligently

intelligence [ɛ̃teliʒɑ̃s] *f* **1.** (*entendement*) *a.* INFOR intelligence; **avec** ~ intelligently; **faire preuve de beaucoup d'~** to show great intelligence; ~ **artificielle** artificial intelligence **2.** (*compréhension*) ~ **d'une personne** understanding of a person **3.** (*personne*) intellect

intelligent(e) [ɛ̃teliʒɑ̃, ʒɑ̃t] *adj* intelligent; **c'est ~!** *iron* that's clever!

intelligible [ɛ̃teliʒibl] *adj* intelligible

intello [ɛ̃telo] *mf péj, fam abr de* **intellectuel** intellectual

intempéries [ɛ̃tɑ̃peʀi] *fpl* bad weather

intempestif, -ive [ɛ̃tɑ̃pɛstif, -iv] *adj* **1.** (*allusion, gaieté*) untimely; (*zèle*) misplaced; (*curiosité, demande*) inopportune **2.** (*accidentel: alarme*) false

intenable [ɛ̃t(ə)nabl] *adj* **1.** (*intolérable*)

unbearable **2.** (*indéfendable*) untenable **3.** (*insupportable: adulte, enfant*) unruly; (*classe*) rowdy; **être** ~ to be out of control

intendance [ɛ̃tɑ̃dɑ̃s] *f* **1.** supplies division; MIL Supply Corps; ~ **universitaire** university finance department **2.** (*bureaux de l'intendant*) bursary **3.** *inf* (*questions matérielles et économiques*) finances; **faire** [*o* **s'occuper**] **de l'**~ to handle the finances ▸**l'**~ **suit** the practical questions will be dealt with in due course

intendant [ɛ̃tɑ̃dɑ̃] *m* **1.** HIST steward **2.** MIL quartermaster

intendant(e) [ɛ̃tɑ̃dɑ̃, ɑ̃t] *m(f)* **1.** bursar **2.** (*régisseur*) steward; (*d'une entreprise*) manager

intense [ɛ̃tɑ̃s] *adj* **1.** (*fort*) intense **2.** (*dense: activité*) intense; (*circulation*) heavy

intensif, -ive [ɛ̃tɑ̃sif, -iv] *adj* intensive; **culture intensive** intensive farming

intensification [ɛ̃tɑ̃sifikasjɔ̃] *f* intensification; (*des efforts, de la production*) stepping up

intensifier [ɛ̃tɑ̃sifje] <1> **I.** *vt* to intensify; (*efforts, production*) to step up; (*chute des cours*) to accelerate **II.** *vpr* **s'**~ to intensify; (*production*) to be stepped up; **le froid s'intensifie** the cold is getting more intense

intensité [ɛ̃tɑ̃site] *f* (*d'un regard, sentiment, de la chaleur, lumière*) intensity; ~ **lumineuse** brightness; **de faible/d'une grande** ~ low-/high-intensity; (*lumière*) faint/brilliant; (*moment*) dull/intense; **un courant de faible/d'une grande** ~ a low/high voltage current; ~ **du courant** current

intenter [ɛ̃tɑ̃te] <1> *vt* JUR ~ **un procès à** [*o* **contre**] **qn** to take sb to court

intention [ɛ̃tɑ̃sjɔ̃] *f* **1.** (*volonté*) intention; **une histoire part d'une bonne** ~ an incident starts with good intentions; **agir dans une bonne** ~ to act with good intentions; **avoir de bonnes/mauvaises** ~**s à l'égard de qn** to be well-intentioned/ill-intentioned towards sb; **c'est l'**~ **qui compte** it's the thought that counts; **sans** ~ unintentionally; **c'était sans** ~ no harm was meant **2.** (*but*) **à cette** ~ to this end ▸**à l'**~ **de qn** for sb

intentionné(e) [ɛ̃tɑ̃sjɔne] *adj* **être bien/mal** ~ **à l'égard de qn** to be well-intentioned/ill-intentioned towards sb; **il a l'air mal** ~ he looks as if he's up to no good

intentionnel(le) [ɛ̃tɑ̃sjɔnɛl] *adj* intentional; **être** ~ to be deliberate; JUR to be premeditated

intentionnellement [ɛ̃tɑ̃sjɔnɛlmɑ̃] *adv* intentionally; JUR deliberately

interactif, -ive [ɛ̃tɛʀaktif, -iv] *adj* interactive

interaction [ɛ̃tɛʀaksjɔ̃] *f a.* INFOR interaction

intercalaire [ɛ̃tɛʀkalɛʀ] **I.** *adj* **jour** ~ intercalary day; **feuillet** ~ insert; **fiche** ~ divider **II.** *m* insert

intercaler [ɛ̃tɛʀkale] <1> **I.** *vt* (*citation, exemple*) to insert; ~ **un rendez-vous dans une semaine/entre 2 dates** to fit in an appointment in a week/between two dates **II.** *vpr* **s'**~ **dans une liste** to be inserted on a list; **s'**~ **entre des personnes** (*coureur*) to squeeze in between two people

intercéder [ɛ̃tɛʀsede] <5> *vi* ~ **pour** [*o* **en faveur de**] **qn auprès de qn** to intercede for sb with sb

intercepter [ɛ̃tɛʀsɛpte] <1> *vt* to intercept

interception [ɛ̃tɛʀsɛpsjɔ̃] *f* interception

interchangeable [ɛ̃tɛʀʃɑ̃ʒabl] *adj* interchangeable

interclasse [ɛ̃tɛʀklas] **I.** *m* ECOLE break **II.** *app* (*match*) interclass

intercommunautaire [ɛ̃tɛʀkɔmynotɛʀ] *adj* **décisions** ~**s** Community decisions

interdiction [ɛ̃tɛʀdiksjɔ̃] *f* prohibition; ~ **de stationnement aux camions** no parking for lorries *Brit,* no parking for trucks *Am;* ~ **de pénétrer sur le chantier/de stationner/de fumer** no entry to the site/parking/smoking; **lever une** ~ to remove a prohibition

interdire [ɛ̃tɛʀdiʀ] *irr* **I.** *vt* **1.** (*défendre*) ~ **à qn de** +*infin* to forbid sb to +*infin* **2.** (*empêcher*) to preclude; ~ **à qn de faire qc** to stop sb doing sth; **qc interdit le sport/le travail à qn** sth stops sb doing sport/working; **rien n'interdit de faire ça** nothing stops you from doing that **3.** (*empêcher l'accès de*) ~ **sa porte à qn** to bar sb from one's door **II.** *vpr* **s'**~ **qc** to deny oneself sth; **s'**~ **qc/de faire qc** to abstain from doing sth

interdisciplinaire [ɛ̃tɛʀdisiplinɛʀ] *adj* interdisciplinary

interdit [ɛ̃tɛʀdi] *m* taboo

interdit(e) [ɛ̃tɛʀdi, it] *adj* forbidden; (*film*) banned; **chantier** ~ no entry to site; **passage** ~ **sauf aux riverains** no entry except for residents; ~ **aux moins de 16 ans** under 16 not admitted; ~ **aux chiens** no dogs allowed; ~ **au public** no entry; **il est** ~ **à qn de** +*infin* sb is not allowed to +*infin;* **être** ~ **d'antenne** to be banned from the air; **être** ~ **de séjour** to be under an exclusion order

intéressant(e) [ɛ̃teʀesɑ̃, ɑ̃t] **I.** *adj* **1.** (*digne d'intérêt*) interesting; **chercher à se rendre** ~ to seek attention; **ne pas être/être peu** ~ *péj* to be of little/no interest **2.** (*avantageux: prix, affaire*) attractive; ~ **pour qn** worth sb's while; **il est** ~ **pour qn de** +*infin* it's worth sb's while to +*infin;* **être** ~ **à faire** to be worth doing; **c'est** ~ **à signaler** it's worth pointing out **II.** *m(f)* **faire l'**~ *péj* to show off

intéressé(e) [ɛ̃teʀese] **I.** *adj* **1.** (*captivé*) interested **2.** (*concerné*) concerned **3.** (*égoïste*) self-interested **II.** *m(f)* **1.** (*personne concernée*) person concerned **2.** (*personne qui s'intéresse à qc*) interested person

intéresser [ɛ̃teʀese] <1> **I.** *vt* **1.** (*captiver*) to interest; ~ **un enfant à un jeu** to interest a child in a game; **être intéressé à faire qc** to be interested in doing sth; **rien ne l'intéresse** she's not interested in anything; **cause tou-**

jours, tu m'intéresses! *iron, inf* keep talking, I'm fascinated!; **est-ce que ça t'intéresse** [*o* **t'intéresserait**] **de voir ce film?** are you interested in seeing this film? **2.** (*concerner*) to concern **II.** *vpr* **s'~ à qn/qc** to be interested in sb/sth; **elle s'est intéressée à mon cas** she took an interest in my case

intérêt [ɛ̃teʀɛ] *m* **1.** (*attention, importance, attrait*) ~ **pour qn/qc** interest in sb/sth; **avec** ~ with interest; **sans** ~ without any interest; **porter de l'~ à qn** to show an interest in sb; **prêter ~ à qc** to take an interest in sth; **un film/livre sans** (**aucun**) ~ a film/book of no interest; **gagner de l'~/perdre son ~** to be of greater/less interest; **ne présenter aucun ~** (*proposition*) to be of no interest; **offrir peu d'~** (*travail*) to be of little interest; **ne pas trouver le moindre ~ à qc** to find nothing interesting in sth **2.** (*importance*) significance; **du plus haut ~** of the greatest significance **3.** *souvent pl* (*cause*) interest; **dans l'~ général** in the public interest; **défendre les ~s de qn** to defend sb's interests **4.** (*avantage*) **par ~** out of self-interest; **dans l'~ de qn** in sb's (own) interest; **dans l'~ de qc** in the interests of sth; **tu devrais te taire dans ton propre ~** you should keep quiet for your own good; **ne pas voir l'~ de faire qc** to see no point in doing sth; **quel ~ y a-t-il à faire ça?** what's the point of doing that?; **elle a** (**tout**) **~ à refuser** it's in her own best interest to refuse; **trouver son ~ dans qc** to find sth worth one's while **5.** *souvent pl* (*rendement*) interest; **7% d'~** 7% interest; **avec/sans ~(s)** with/without interest; **avec ~ annuel de 10%** with 10% interest per annum **6.** *pl* (*part*) **avoir des ~s dans une affaire** to have an interest in a business ►**il promet de revenir et** (**il**) **y a ~!** *inf* he's promised to come back and he'd better!

interface [ɛ̃tɛʀfas] *f* INFOR interface; ~ **graphique** graphic interface; ~ **utilisateur** user interface

intérieur [ɛ̃teʀjœʀ] *m* **1.** (*opp: extérieur: d'un bâtiment*) interior; (*d'un objet*) inside; **à l'~** (*dedans*) inside; (*opp: en plein air*) indoors; **à l'~ de** inside; **à l'~ d'une noix** inside a walnut; **à l'~ du magasin** inside the shop; **à l'~ de la ville** within the city; **être fermé de l'~** to be locked from inside **2.** (*aménagement: d'une maison, d'un magasin*) interior (design) **3.** (*logement*) home; **femme d'~** house-proud woman **4.** (*espace, pays*) interior; **à l'~ des terres** inland **5.** (*ministère*) **à l'Intérieur** at the Ministry of the Interior

intérieur(**e**) [ɛ̃teʀjœʀ] *adj* **1.** (*opp: extérieur*) interior **2.** (*concernant un pays*) domestic; **dette ~e** domestic debt **3.** PSYCH inner

intérieurement [ɛ̃teʀjœʀmɑ̃] *adv* **1.** (*au-dedans*) inside **2.** (*dans l'esprit: rire, se révolter*) inwardly

intérim [ɛ̃teʀim] *m* **1.** (*fonction, durée*) interim; **par ~** (*provisoirement*) in the interim; **directeur/ministre par ~** acting director/minister; **assurer** [*o* **faire**] **l'~** to deputize; **faire de l'~** [*o* **des ~s**] to temp **2.** (*organisation*) temping; **travail par ~** temp work; **agence de travail par ~** temping agency

intérimaire [ɛ̃teʀimɛʀ] **I.** *adj* **1.** (*par intérim: directeur, ministre*) acting; (*gouvernement, charge, fonction*) interim **2.** (*temporaire*) **employé/salarié ~** temporary employee/worker; **secrétaire ~** temp **II.** *mf* **1.** (*remplaçant*) temp **2.** (*employé ~*) temporary employee

interjection [ɛ̃tɛʀʒɛksjɔ̃] *f* interjection

interligne [ɛ̃tɛʀliɲ] *m* (line) spacing; MUS space; **double ~** double spacing

interlocuteur, -trice [ɛ̃tɛʀlɔkytœʀ, -tʀis] *m, f* **votre ~** the person you are talking to; POL, COM negotiating partner

interloqué(**e**) [ɛ̃tɛʀlɔke] *adj* stunned

intermède [ɛ̃tɛʀmɛd] *m a.* MUS, THEAT interlude

intermédiaire [ɛ̃tɛʀmedjɛʀ] **I.** *adj* (*couleur, ton*) intermediate; (*espace, niveau, époque*) intervening; (*solution*) compromise; **position ~** (*d'un fauteuil*) intermediate position; **position ~ entre un parti et l'autre** POL halfway position between two parties **II.** *mf* **1.** (*médiateur*) intermediary **2.** COM middleman **III.** *m* **par l'~ de qn/qc** through; **sans ~** directly

interminable [ɛ̃tɛʀminabl] *adj* interminable

interminablement [ɛ̃tɛʀminabləmɑ̃] *adv* interminably

intermittence [ɛ̃tɛʀmitɑ̃s] *f* intermittence; (*sans la continuité voulue*) irregularity; **par ~** intermittently; *péj* by fits and starts

intermittent(**e**) [ɛ̃tɛʀmitɑ̃, ɑ̃t] *adj* (*travail*) occasional; (*douleur*) intermittent

internat [ɛ̃tɛʀna] *m* **1.** (*élèves*) boarders **2.** (*pension*) boarding **3.** (*établissement*) boarding school

international(**e**) [ɛ̃tɛʀnasjɔnal, o] <-aux> **I.** *adj* international **II.** *m(f)* SPORT international

internationalement [ɛ̃tɛʀnasjɔnalmɑ̃] *adv* internationally; **connu ~** known all over the world

internaute [ɛ̃tɛʀnot] **I.** *adj* Internet **II.** *mf* cybernaut; ~ **novice** newbie

interne [ɛ̃tɛʀn] **I.** *adj* internal **II.** *mf* **1.** ECOLE boarder **2.** MED junior doctor *Brit*, intern *Am*

interner [ɛ̃tɛʀne] <1> *vt* **1.** POL ~ **qn dans un camp** to intern sb in a camp **2.** MED to commit

Internet [ɛ̃tɛʀnɛt] *m* Internet; **accéder à ~** to access the Internet; **commercer sur ~** to do business over the Internet

internetais [ɛ̃tɛʀnətɛ] *adj* INFOR Netspeak

interpellation [ɛ̃tɛʀpelasjɔ̃] *f* (*arrestation*) arrest (*for questioning*)**; il y a eu une dizaine d'~s** about ten people were taken in for questioning

interpeller [ɛ̃tɛʀpəle] <1> **I.** *vt* **1.** (*arrêter*) ~ **qn** (*police*) to detain sb (for questioning) **2.** (*sommer de s'expliquer*) ~ **un témoin sur un accident** to question a witness about an

I

accident **3.** (*apostropher*) ~ **qn** to call out to sb; (*avec brusquerie*) to yell at sb **II.** *vpr* **s'~** (*s'apostropher*) to yell at each other
interphone® [ɛ̃tɛʀfɔn] *m* intercom; **parler à qn par l'~** to speak to sb over the intercom
interplanétaire [ɛ̃tɛʀplanetɛʀ] *adj* interplanetary
interposer [ɛ̃tɛʀpoze] <1> **I.** *vt* ~ **qc entre le lit et le lavabo** to put sth between the bed and the basin **II.** *vpr* **1. s'~ dans qc** to intervene in sth **2.** (*se placer*) **s'~** to interpose; **s'~ entre deux personnes** to put onself between two people
interprétariat [ɛ̃tɛʀpʀetaʀja] *m* interpreting
interprétation [ɛ̃tɛʀpʀetasjɔ̃] *f* interpretation
interprète [ɛ̃tɛʀpʀɛt] *mf* **1.** MUS player **2.** CINE, THEAT actor **3.** (*traducteur*) interpreter; **faire l'~, servir d'~** to interpret **4.** (*porte-parole*) spokesman, spokeswoman *m, f*
interpréter [ɛ̃tɛʀpʀete] <5> **I.** *vt* **1.** MUS, CINE, THEAT to play; (*de façon personnelle*) to interpret **2.** (*expliquer, traduire*) to interpret **3.** (*comprendre*) ~ **qc en bien/mal** to take sth the right/wrong way **II.** *vpr* **s'~ de plusieurs façons** to have several interpretations
interro *f inf* test
interrogateur, **-trice** [ɛ̃teʀɔgatœʀ, -tʀis] **I.** *adj* questioning **II.** *m, f* examiner
interrogatif [ɛ̃teʀɔgatif] *m* interrogative
interrogatif, **-ive** [ɛ̃teʀɔgatif, -iv] *adj* **1.** (*air, regard*) questioning **2.** LING interrogative
interrogation [ɛ̃teʀɔgasjɔ̃] *f* **1.** (*question*) question **2.** ECOLE test **3.** (*action de questionner*) interrogation
interrogative [ɛ̃teʀɔgativ] *f* interrogative clause
interrogatoire [ɛ̃teʀɔgatwaʀ] *m* (*de la police*) interview; **subir un ~** to be interviewed
interrogeable [ɛ̃teʀɔʒabl] *adj* ~ **à distance** (*répondeur*) with remote access
interroger [ɛ̃teʀɔʒe] <2a> **I.** *vt* **1.** (*questionner*) ~ **qn sur un sujet** to question sb on a subject; (*pour un sondage*) to poll sb on a subject; ~ **qn sur son alibi** to question sb about their alibi; **40 % des personnes interrogées** 40 % of those questioned; ~ **qn du regard** to give sb a questioning look **2.** (*consulter: banque de données, répondeur*) to check **3.** (*examiner: conscience*) to examine **II.** *vpr* **s'~ sur qn/qc** to wonder about sb/sth
interrompre [ɛ̃teʀɔ̃pʀ] *irr* **I.** *vt* **1.** (*couper la parole, déranger*) to interrupt; ~ **qn dans un discours** to interrupt sb's speech **2.** (*arrêter: activité*) to interrupt; (*grossesse*) to terminate; (*silence*) to break; **être interrompu** (*trafic*) to be disrupted **II.** *vpr* **s'~** (*personne*) to break off; (*discussion, film*) to close; (*conversation*) to stop; **ne vous interrompez pas pour moi!** dont stop talking just for me!
interrupteur [ɛ̃teʀyptœʀ] *m* switch
interruption [ɛ̃teʀypsjɔ̃] *f* **1.** (*arrêt définitif*) end; ~ (**volontaire**) **de grossesse** termination (of pregnancy); **décider l'~ du match** to decide to stop the match **2.** (*arrêt provisoire*) interruption; **sans ~** continuously; **un magasin ouvert sans ~** a shop open all day; ~ **de deux heures/trois mois** two hour/three month break
intersection [ɛ̃tɛʀsɛksjɔ̃] *f* **1.** (*de routes*) intersection; (*de voies ferrées*) crossing **2.** GEOM intersection
intersidéral(e) [ɛ̃tɛʀsideʀal, o] <-aux> *adj* interstellar
interstellaire [ɛ̃tɛʀstelɛʀ] *adj* interstellar
interstice [ɛ̃tɛʀstis] *m* chink
intervalle [ɛ̃tɛʀval] *m* **1.** (*écart*) gap; (*espace de temps*); ~ **de temps** interval; **à ~s réguliers** at regular intervals; **à huit jours d'~** (*après huit jours*) a week later; (*séparés de huit jours*) a week apart; **dans l'~** in the meanwhile; **par ~s** at intervals **2.** MUS interval
intervenir [ɛ̃tɛʀvəniʀ] <9> *vi* **1.** (*entrer en action: police, pompiers*) to intervene; ~ **dans un débat/une affaire** to intervene in a debate/an affair; ~ **en faveur d'un collègue auprès de qn** to intervene with sb on behalf of a colleague **2.** (*prendre la parole*) to speak **3.** (*survenir: accord*) to be reached; (*contretemps*) to occur; (*fait*) to happen; **un accord/évènement est intervenu** there has been an agreement/an event
intervention [ɛ̃tɛʀvɑ̃sjɔ̃] *f* **1.** (*action*) intervention **2.** (*prise de parole*) speech **3.** MED operation
intervertir [ɛ̃tɛʀvɛʀtiʀ] <8> *vt* (*lettres, mots*) to invert; (*rôles*) to reverse
interview [ɛ̃tɛʀvju] *f* interview
interviewer [ɛ̃tɛʀvjuve] <1> *vt* to interview
intestin [ɛ̃tɛstɛ̃] *m souvent pl* intestine; ~ **grêle** small intestine; **gros ~** large intestine
intestinal(e) [ɛ̃tɛstinal, o] <-aux> *adj* intestinal; **transit ~** digestion
intime [ɛ̃tim] *adj* **1.** (*secret*) intimate; (*hygiène, toilette*) personal; (*vie, chagrin*) private; **journal ~** private diary; **la personnalité ~ de X** X's private personality **2.** (*privé: cérémonie, dîner*) quiet **3.** (*confortable: atmosphère, lieu*) intimate; **faire ~** to have an intimate feel **4.** (*étroit, proche: ami, rapports*) close; **être ~ avec qn** to be on close terms with sb
intimement [ɛ̃timmɑ̃] *adv* **1.** (*profondément*) **je suis ~ convaincu que …** I am firmly convinced that … **2.** (*étroitement*) ~ **lié** intimately linked
intimer [ɛ̃time] <1> *vt* ~ **à un subordonné** (**l'ordre**) **de** +*infin* to instruct a subordinate to +*infin*
intimidant(e) [ɛ̃timidɑ̃, ɑ̃t] *adj* intimidating
intimidé(e) [ɛ̃timide] *adj* overawed
intimider [ɛ̃timide] <1> *vt* to intimidate
intimité [ɛ̃timite] *f* **1.** (*vie privée*) privacy; **dans l'~** (*se marier*) at a private ceremony;

(*déjeûner*) with friends; **dans la plus stricte** ~ in the strictest privacy **2.** (*relation étroite*) intimacy **3.** (*confort: d'un salon*) comfort

intituler [ɛ̃tityle] <1> **I.** *vt* ~ **un livre "Mémoires"** to title a book "Memoirs"; **être intitulé "Mémoires"** to be entitled "Memoirs" **II.** *vpr* **s'~ "Mémoires"** to be entitled "Memoirs"

intolérable [ɛ̃tɔleʀabl] *adj* intolerable

intolérance [ɛ̃tɔleʀɑ̃s] *f* (*sectarisme*) intolerance

intolérant(e) [ɛ̃tɔleʀɑ̃, ɑ̃t] *adj* intolerant

intonation [ɛ̃tɔnasjɔ̃] *f souvent pl* tone; **les ~s de sa voix** the tone of her voice; **prendre des ~s douces en parlant à qn** to speak softly to sb; **trouver les ~s justes** to find the right tone of voice

intouchable [ɛ̃tuʃabl] **I.** *adj fig* untouchable; **il se croyait** ~ he thought he was untouchable **II.** *mf* untouchable

intoxication [ɛ̃tɔksikasjɔ̃] *f* **1.** (*empoisonnement*) poisoning; ~ **alimentaire** food poisoning; ~ **au mercure** mercury poisoning **2.** (*influence*) brainwashing

intoxiqué(e) [ɛ̃tɔksike] *adj* **être ~ par une substance/un aliment** to be poisoned by a substance/a food; **être ~ par une drogue/la télé** to be addicted to a drug/the TV; **être ~ par la publicité** to be brainwashed by advertising

intoxiquer [ɛ̃tɔksike] <1> **I.** *vt* **1.** (*empoisonner*) to poison; **être légèrement intoxiqué** (*pompier*) to be suffering from smoke inhalation **2.** (*pervertir*) ~ **la population** (*émission, télévision*) to poison people's minds; (*publicité*) to brainwash people **II.** *vpr* **s'~** to poison oneself

intracommunautaire [ɛ̃tʀakɔmynɔtɛʀ] *adj* (*échanges*) within the community

intraduisible [ɛ̃tʀadɥizibl] *adj* (*auteur, expression*) untranslatable; (*réaction, sentiment*) impossible to express

intraitable [ɛ̃tʀɛtabl] *adj* inflexible; ~ **sur le règlement** unbending about the rules

intramusculaire [ɛ̃tʀamyskylɛʀ] *adj* intramuscular

intranet [ɛ̃tʀanɛt] *m* intranet

intransigeance [ɛ̃tʀɑ̃ziʒɑ̃s] *f* intransigence

intransigeant(e) [ɛ̃tʀɑ̃ziʒɑ̃, ʒɑ̃t] *adj* uncompromising

intransitif, -ive [ɛ̃tʀɑ̃zitif, -iv] *adj* intransitive

intransportable [ɛ̃tʀɑ̃spɔʀtabl] *adj* (*chose*) untransportable; (*personne*) unable to travel

intraveineuse [ɛ̃tʀavɛnøz] *f* intravenous injection

intraveineux, -euse [ɛ̃tʀavɛnø, -øz] *adj* intravenous

intrépide [ɛ̃tʀepid] *adj* **1.** (*courageux*) intrepid **2.** (*audacieux*) unashamed

intrépidité [ɛ̃tʀepidite] *f* fearlessness; (*audace*) boldness

intrigant(e) [ɛ̃tʀigɑ̃, ɑ̃t] **I.** *adj* scheming **II.** *m(f)* schemer

intrigue [ɛ̃tʀig] *f* **1.** CINE, LIT, THEAT plot **2.** (*manœuvre*) intrigue **3.** (*liaison*) ~ **amoureuse** love affair

intriguer [ɛ̃tʀige] <1> **I.** *vt* **1.** (*travailler*) to puzzle **2.** (*piquer la curiosité*) to intrigue; **intrigués, les policiers tentaient ...** intrigued, the police were trying ... **II.** *vi* to scheme

introduction [ɛ̃tʀɔdyksjɔ̃] *f* introduction; **chapitre d'~** introductory chapter; **quelques mots d'~** a few words of introduction; **en ~** by way of introduction; **l'~ de la peste en Europe** the introduction of the plague to Europe

introduire [ɛ̃tʀɔdɥiʀ] *irr* **I.** *vt* **1.** (*personne*) to show in; (*objet*) to insert; (*liquide, gaz*) to introduce; ~ **qn dans une pièce** to show sb into a room; ~ **qn chez une famille** to introduce sb to a family; ~ **une clé dans qc** to insert a key into sth; ~ **une pièce de monnaie dans qc** to insert a coin in sth; ~ **du tabac en contrebande** to smuggle in tobacco **2.** (*faire adopter: mode*) to introduce **II.** *vpr* **1.** (*se faire admettre*) **s'~ dans une famille/un milieu** to gain entry to a family/a circle **2.** (*s'infiltrer*) **s'~ dans une maison** to get into a house; **s'~ au milieu des invités** to mingle among the guests; **s'~ dans qc** (*eau, fumée*) to seep into sth; (*impureté*) to get into sth **3.** (*se mettre*) **s'~ qc dans le nez/les oreilles** to put sth in one's nose/ears **4.** (*être adopté*) **s'~ dans un pays** (*usage, mode*) to be introduced in a country

introuvable [ɛ̃tʀuvabl] *adj* (*perdu: chose, personne*) nowhere to be found

intrus(e) [ɛ̃tʀy, yz] **I.** *adj* intruding; (*visiteur*) unwelcome **II.** *m(f)* intruder ►**cherchez l'~** find the odd one out

intrusion [ɛ̃tʀyzjɔ̃] *f* ~ **dans une maison/discussion** intrusion into a house/in a discussion; **faire ~ chez qn/dans une maison** to intrude on sb/into sb's home

intuitif, -ive [ɛ̃tɥitif, -iv] **I.** *adj* intuitive **II.** *m, f* person of intuition

intuition [ɛ̃tɥisjɔ̃] *f* intuition; **procéder par ~** to work on one's intuition

intuitivement [ɛ̃tɥitivmɑ̃] *adv* intuitively

inusable [inyzabl] *adj* hard-wearing

inusité(e) [inyzite] *adj* uncommon

inutile [inytil] **I.** *adj* useless; (*effort, mesure*) pointless; **être ~ à qn** to be no use to sb; **se sentir ~** to feel useless; **si ma présence est ~, ...** if there is no point in my being here, ...; **il est/n'est pas ~ de faire qc/que qn fasse qc** (*subj*) it's pointless/worthwhile doing sth/for sb to do sth; ~ **d'espérer de l'aide** it's no good hoping for help; ~ **de (te/vous) dire qu'il l'a fait** I hardly need tell you that he did it; ~ **d'insister!** it's no good insisting! **II.** *m* **l'~** the useless **III.** *mf* useless creature

inutilement [inytilmɑ̃] *adv* **1.** (*sans utilité*) uselessly **2.** (*en vain*) pointlessly

inutilisable [inytilizabl] *adj* **1.**(*qui n'offre aucune utilité*) useless **2.**(*dont on ne peut se servir*) unusable; **mon ordinateur est actuellement** ~ my computer's out of action at the moment
inutilisé(e) [inytilize] *adj* unused
inutilité [inytilite] *f* pointlessness; **j'ai compris l'**~ **de ma présence ici** I see there's no point in my being here
invaincu(e) [ɛ̃vɛ̃ky] *adj* (*sportif*) unbeaten; (*sommet*) unconquered
invalidant(e) [ɛ̃validɑ̃, ɑ̃t] *adj* disabling
invalide [ɛ̃valid] **I.** *adj* disabled **II.** *mf* disabled person
invalidité [ɛ̃validite] *f* **1.**(*d'une personne*) disability; **pension d'**~ disability allowance **2.** JUR invalidity; **frapper qc d'**~ to declare sth invalid
invariable [ɛ̃vaʀjabl] *adj* **1.**(*qui ne change pas*) *a.* LING invariable **2.**(*qu'on ne peut changer*) unchangeable
invasion [ɛ̃vɑzjɔ̃] *f* MIL *a. fig* invasion; ~ **de touristes** tourist invasion
invectiver [ɛ̃vɛktive] <1> **I.** *vt* to insult **II.** *vpr* **s'**~ to insult each other
invendable [ɛ̃vɑ̃dabl] *adj* unsaleable; **il est** ~ it can't be sold
inventaire [ɛ̃vɑ̃tɛʀ] *m* **1.** JUR (*des biens*) inventory **2.** COM stocklist; **faire l'**~ to inventory, to stocktake *Brit* **3.**(*revue*) inventory, stocktaking *Brit*
inventer [ɛ̃vɑ̃te] <1> *vt* to invent; **ça ne s'invente pas** you couldn't make it up
inventeur, **-trice** [ɛ̃vɑ̃tœʀ, -tʀis] *m, f* inventor; **ce sont les ~s de ce procédé** they are the ones who invented this process
inventif, **-ive** [ɛ̃vɑ̃tif, -iv] *adj* inventive
invention [ɛ̃vɑ̃sjɔ̃] *f* **1.** invention; **l'**~ **de ce procédé date de 1850** the process was invented in 1850; **de mon/son** ~ of my invention **2.**(*imagination*) inventiveness **3.**(*mensonge*) lie; **c'est une** ~ **de sa part!** she's made it all up!; **ce sont des ~s pures et simples!** it is all a tissue of lies!
invérifiable [ɛ̃veʀifjabl] *adj* unverifiable
inverse [ɛ̃vɛʀs] **I.** *adj* opposite; MAT inverse **II.** *m* opposite; **c'est l'**~ **qui est vrai** the opposite is true; **à l'**~ conversely; **à l'**~ **de qn/qc** contrary to sb/sth
inversement [ɛ̃vɛʀsəmɑ̃] *adv* conversely; **et/ou** ~ and/or vice-versa
inverser [ɛ̃vɛʀse] <1> **I.** *vt* (*mots, phrases*) to turn round; (*évolution, mouvement, rôles*) to reverse; ~ **l'ordre des mots** to turn the order of the words around **II.** *vpr* **s'**~ (*mouvement, tendance*) to be reversed
inversion [ɛ̃vɛʀsjɔ̃] *f a.* LING inversion
invertébré [ɛ̃vɛʀtebʀe] *m* invertebrate
investigation [ɛ̃vɛstigasjɔ̃] *f* investigation
investir [ɛ̃vɛstiʀ] <8> **I.** *vt* **1.** FIN ~ **son argent dans qc** to invest one's money in sth **2.** *fig* ~ **du temps/du travail dans qc** to invest time/work in sth **II.** *vi* ECON, FIN to invest; ~ **dans de nouvelles machines** to invest in new machines **III.** *vpr* **s'**~ **dans qc** to involve oneself deeply in sth
investissement [ɛ̃vɛstismɑ̃] *m* **1.** ECON, FIN investment; **les dépenses d'**~ investment expenses **2.**(*engagement*) ~ **de qn dans une activité** sb's involvement in an activity
investisseur [ɛ̃vɛstisœʀ] *m* investor
invétéré(e) [ɛ̃veteʀe] *adj* inveterate
invincible [ɛ̃vɛ̃sibl] *adj* (*personne, armée*) invincible; (*courage, détermination*) insuperable; (*charme, envie*) irresistible
invisible [ɛ̃vizibl] *adj* invisible; ~ **à l'œil nu** invisible to the naked eye
invitation [ɛ̃vitasjɔ̃] *f* invitation; ~ **à une manifestation/au restaurant/à déjeuner** invitation to a demonstration/a meal out/to lunch; **sans** ~ uninvited; ~ **à la débauche** invitation to debauchery; **à** [*o* **sur**] **l'**~ **de qn** at sb's invitation
invite [ɛ̃vit] *m* INFOR prompt; ~ **de commande** command prompt
invité(e) [ɛ̃vite] *m(f)* guest; ~ **d'honneur** guest of honour *Brit,* guest of honor *Am*
inviter [ɛ̃vite] <1> *vt* **1.**(*convier*) ~ **qn à** +*infin* to invite sb to +*infin;* ~ **qn à danser** to ask sb for a dance; ~ **qn à un anniversaire** to invite sb to a birthday party; ~ **qn chez soi** to invite sb over (to one's place); **vous venez? c'est moi qui invite!** are you coming? it's my treat! **2.**(*prier*) ~ **qn à** +*infin* to ask sb to +*infin;* ~ **qn à entrer** to ask sb in; **être invité à** +*infin* to be requested to +*infin* **3.**(*inciter à*) ~ **qn à une discussion** to invite sb to take part in a discussion; ~ **qn à** +*infin* to call on sb to +*infin;* ~ **à la réflexion** (*événements*) to call for reflection
in vitro [invitʀo] *adj, adv inv* in vitro
invivable [ɛ̃vivabl] *adj* unbearable
involontaire [ɛ̃vɔlɔ̃tɛʀ] *adj* (*erreur, mouvement, réflexion*) involuntary; (*spectateur, témoin*) unwitting; (*offense*) unintended
involontairement [ɛ̃vɔlɔ̃tɛʀmɑ̃] *adv* (*sursauter*) involuntarily; (*voir*) unwittingly; (*offenser*) unintentionally
invoquer [ɛ̃vɔke] <1> *vt* **1.**(*se servir de: raison, excuse*) to put forward; (*circonstance atténuante*) to plead; ~ **le prétexte de qc** to put sth forward as a pretext **2.** *soutenu* (*implorer*) to invoke
invraisemblable [ɛ̃vʀɛsɑ̃blabl] *adj* **1.**(*qui ne semble pas vrai: histoire, argument*) improbable **2.**(*incroyable*) incredible
invraisemblance [ɛ̃vʀɛsɑ̃blɑ̃s] *f* improbability; (*contradiction*) implausibility
invulnérable [ɛ̃vylneʀabl] *adj* invulnerable; ~ **aux attaques** invulnerable to attack
iode [jɔd] *m* iodine
IRA [iʀa] *f abr de* **Irish Republican Army** IRA
irai [iʀɛ] *fut de* **aller**
Irak [iʀak] *m* **l'**~ Iraq
irakien(ne) [iʀakjɛ̃, jɛn] *adj* Iraqi

Irakien(ne) [iʀakjɛ̃, jɛn] *m(f)* Iraqi
Iran [iʀɑ̃] *m* l'~ Iran
iranien(ne) [iʀanjɛ̃, jɛn] *adj* Iranian
Iranien(ne) [iʀanjɛ̃, jɛn] *m(f)* Iranian
Iraq [iʀak] *m v.* **Irak**
irascible [iʀasibl] *adj* irascible
iris [iʀis] *m* ANAT, BOT iris
irisé(e) [iʀize] *adj* iridescent
irlandais [iʀlɑ̃dɛ] *m* Irish; **l'~ gaélique** Irish Gaelic; *v. a.* **français**
irlandais(e) [iʀlɑ̃dɛ, ɛz] *adj* Irish
Irlandais(e) [iʀlɑ̃dɛ, ɛz] *m(f)* Irishman, Irishwoman *m, f*; **les ~** the Irish
Irlande [iʀlɑ̃d] *f* **l'~** Ireland; **la république** [*o* **l'État libre**] **d'~** Republic of Ireland, Irish Republic; **l'~ du Nord** Northern Ireland
ironie [iʀɔni] *f* irony; **dire qc par ~** to say sth ironically
ironique [iʀɔnik] *adj* ironic
ironiquement [iʀɔnikmɑ̃] *adv* ironically
ironiser [iʀɔnize] <1> *vi* **~ sur qn/qc** to be ironic about sb/sth
irradier [iʀadje] <1a> **I.** *vi* (*douleur, lumière*) to radiate **II.** *vt* to irradiate
irrationnel [iʀasjɔnɛl] *m* **l'~** the irrational
irrationnel(le) [iʀasjɔnɛl] *adj* irrational
irrattrapable [iʀatʀapabl] *adj* irretrievable
irréalisable [iʀealizabl] *adj* unrealizable
irréalisme [iʀealism] *m* lack of realism
irréaliste [iʀealist] *adj* unrealistic
irréconciliable [iʀekɔ̃siljabl] *adj* irreconcilable
irrécupérable [iʀekypeʀabl] *adj* (*voiture, ferraille*) unreclaimable; **être ~** (*voiture*) to be a write-off *Brit,* to be totaled *Am;* (*réfrigérateur*) to be beyond repair
irrécusable [iʀekyzabl] *adj* (*juge, témoin*) unimpeachable; (*témoignage, preuve*) undeniable
irréductible [iʀedyktibl] *adj* (*ennemi, personne*) invincible; (*obstacle, opposition*) unsurmountable; (*volonté*) indomitable
irréel(le) [iʀeɛl] *adj* unreal
irréfléchi(e) [iʀefleʃi] *adj* thoughtless; (*personne*) unthinking; (*spontané*) impulsive
irréfutable [iʀefytabl] *adj* irrefutable
irrégularité [iʀegylaʀite] *f* **1.** (*inégalité*) irregularity; *pl* (*d'une surface, d'un terrain*) unevenness **2.** (*manque de régularité: d'un élève, d'une équipe*) uneven performance; **l'~ de ses résultats** her uneven results **3.** *gén pl* (*illégalité*) irregularity; (*d'une situation*) illegality
irrégulier, -ère [iʀegylje, -ɛʀ] *adj* **1.** (*inégal*) irregular; (*écriture, terrain*) uneven; **avoir des horaires ~s** to keep irregular hours **2.** (*discontinu: rythme, vitesse*) irregular; (*sommeil*) fitful; (*effort, travail, élève, sportif, résultats*) erratic **3.** (*illégal: absence, opération, procédure*) unauthorized; (*situation*) irregular; **des opérations irrégulières** unauthorized operations **4.** LING (*pluriel, verbe*) irregular
irrégulièrement [iʀegyljɛʀmɑ̃] *adv* **1.** (*inégalement*) unevenly **2.** (*illégalement*) illegally; (*s'absenter*) without authorization
irrémédiable [iʀemedjabl] **I.** *adj* (*aggravation*) irreversible; (*défaite*) irretrievable; (*erreur, défaut*) irreparable; (*mal*) incurable; (*malheur*) beyond remedy; (*situation*) irremediable **II.** *m* **l'~** the irreparable
irremplaçable [iʀɑ̃plasabl] *adj* irreplaceable; (*instant*) unrepeatable
irréparable [iʀepaʀabl] **I.** *adj* (*objet, machine*) beyond repair; (*dommage, perte*) irreparable; (*erreur*) irretrievable **II.** *m* **l'~** the irreparable
irrépressible [iʀepʀesibl] *adj* irrepressible
irréprochable [iʀepʀɔʃabl] *adj* (*vie, mère*) beyond reproach; (*travail*) faultless; (*linge*) spotless
irrésistible [iʀezistibl] *adj* **1.** (*impérieux*) irresistible; (*logique*) compelling **2.** (*qui fait rire*) uproarious; **il est ~!** (*personne*) he's such a laugh!
irrésistiblement [iʀezistibləmɑ̃] *adv* (*attirer, évoquer*) irresistibly; (*avancer*) relentlessly
irrésolu(e) [iʀezɔly] *adj* (*personne, caractère*) irresolute; (*problème, question*) unresolved
irrespirable [iʀɛspiʀabl] *adj* stifling
irresponsabilité [iʀɛspɔ̃sabilite] *f* irresponsibility; JUR immunity
irresponsable [iʀɛspɔ̃sabl] **I.** *adj* (*comportement, personne*) irresponsible; JUR incapable **II.** *mf* irresponsible person
irréversible [iʀevɛʀsibl] **I.** *adj* irreversible **II.** *m* **l'~** the irreversible
irrévocable [iʀevɔkabl] *adj* (*jugement, décision*) irrevocable; (*volonté*) unalterable
irrigation [iʀigasjɔ̃] *f* irrigation
irriguer [iʀige] <1> *vt* AGR to irrigate
irritable [iʀitabl] *adj* irritable
irritant(e) [iʀitɑ̃, ɑ̃t] *adj a.* MED irritating; **substance ~e** irritant
irritation [iʀitasjɔ̃] *f* **1.** (*énervement*) irritation **2.** MED inflammation; **~ de la gorge** inflammation of the throat
irrité(e) [iʀite] *adj* irritated; **être ~ contre qn** to be irritated at sb
irriter [iʀite] <1> **I.** *vt* to irritate; **je ne voulais pas vous ~** I didn't mean to irritate you; **ce produit n'irrite pas la peau** the product does not irritate the skin **II.** *vpr* **1.** (*s'énerver*) **s'~ de qc/contre qn** to get annoyed at sth/with sb **2.** MED **s'~** to become inflamed
irruption [iʀypsjɔ̃] *f* **après son ~ dans la pièce** after she burst into the room; **l'~ de la deuxième guerre mondiale** the breakout of the Second World War; **faire ~** (*personne*) to burst in; (*eau*) to flood in
islam [islam] *m* **l'~** Islam
Islam [islam] *m* **l'~** Islam
islamique [islamik] *adj* islamic
islamiste [islamist] *adj, mf* Islamist
islandais [islɑ̃dɛ] *m* Icelandic; *v. a.* **français**

islandais(e) [islɑ̃dɛ, ɛz] *adj* Icelandic
Islandais(e) [islɑ̃dɛ, ɛz] *m(f)* Icelander
Islande [islɑ̃d] *f* **l'**~ Iceland
ISO [izo] *f abr de* **International Standards Organization** ISO
isolant [izɔlɑ̃] *m* insulator; ~ **thermique et phonique** thermal and sound insulation *no pl;* ~ **d'étanchéité** waterproofing *no pl*
isolant(e) [izɔlɑ̃, ɑ̃t] *adj* CONSTR, ELEC insulating
isolation [izɔlasjɔ̃] *f* insulation
isolationnisme [izɔlasjɔnism] *m* isolationism
isolé(e) [izɔle] *adj* **1.** (*éloigné, unique: endroit, maison*) isolated; **ce cas n'est pas** ~ this is not an isolated case **2.** (*seul: personne, maison*) lonely; (*bâtiment, arbre*) solitary; **vivre très** ~ to live a very solitary life **3.** TECH, ELEC insulated
isolement [izɔlmɑ̃] *m* **1.** (*solitude*) isolation **2.** ELEC, TECH insulation
isolément [izɔlemɑ̃] *adv* in isolation
isoler [izɔle] <1> **I.** *vt* **1.** (*séparer des autres*) *a.* BIO, CHIM to isolate; ~ **un quartier** (*police*) to seal off an area; **être isolé du reste du monde** (*village*) to be cut off from the rest of the world **2.** TECH, ELEC ~ **qc de l'humidité** to insulate sth from dampness **3.** (*considérer à part*) ~ **qc** to take sth on its own **II.** *vi* ~ **de qc** (*matériau*) to insulate from sth **III.** *vpr* **s'**~ **de qn/qc** to isolate oneself from sb/sth; **s'**~ **du monde** to cut oneself off from the world
isoloir [izɔlwaʀ] *m* polling booth *Brit,* voting booth *Am*
isotherme [izɔtɛʀm] *adj* **1. bouteille/sac** ~ insulated flask/bag; **camion** ~ refrigerated lorry *Brit,* refrigerated truck *Am* **2.** METEO isothermal
Israël [isʀaɛl] *m* **l'**~ Israel
israélien(ne) [isʀaeljɛ̃, jɛn] *adj* Israeli
Israélien(ne) [isʀaeljɛ̃, jɛn] *m(f)* Israeli
israélite [isʀaelit] **I.** *adj* Israelite **II.** *mf* Israelite
issu(e) [isy] *adj* **1.** (*né de*) **être** ~ **d'une famille modeste** to be from a modest family; **être** ~ **de sang royal** to be of royal blood **2.** (*résultant de*) **être** ~ **de qc** to arise from sth
issue [isy] *f* **1.** (*sortie*) exit; ~ **de secours** emergency exit; **chemin/route/voie sans** ~ dead end; (*signalisation*) no through road **2.** (*solution*) outcome; **sans** ~ (*problème*) with no solution; (*situation*) at a standstill; (*avenir*) with no prospects **3.** (*fin*) end; **avoir une** ~ **fatale/heureuse** to end in tragedy/happily; **à l'**~ **de qc** at the end of sth
isthme [ism] *m* isthmus
Italie [itali] *f* **l'**~ Italy
italien [italjɛ̃] *m* Italian; *v. a.* **français**
italien(ne) [italjɛ̃, jɛn] *adj* Italian
Italien(ne) [italjɛ̃, jɛn] *m(f)* Italian
italique [italik] **I.** *m* **en** ~**(s)** in italics **II.** *adj* italic
itinéraire [itineʀɛʀ] *m* **1.** (*parcours*) itinerary **2.** *fig* path; **son** ~ **biographique** the path his life took
itinérant(e) [itineʀɑ̃, ɑ̃t] *adj* itinerant; **théâtre** ~ touring theatre *Brit,* touring theater *Am*
IUFM [iyɛfɛm] *m abr de* **institut universitaire de formation des maîtres** *training college for primary teachers*
IUT [iyte] *m abr de* **institut universitaire de technologie** polytechnic
IVG [iveʒe] *f abr de* **interruption volontaire de grossesse** termination of pregnancy
ivoire [ivwaʀ] *m* ivory
ivoirien(ne) [ivwaʀjɛ̃, jɛn] *adj* Ivorian
Ivoirien(ne) [ivwaʀjɛ̃, jɛn] *m(f)* Ivorian
ivre [ivʀ] *adj* drunk; **légèrement** ~ a bit drunk; ~ **mort** blind drunk
ivresse [ivʀɛs] *f* drunkenness; ~ **au volant** drunk driving; **en état d'**~ under the influence of alcohol
ivrogne [ivʀɔɲ] *mf* drunk
ivrognerie [ivʀɔɲʀi] *f* drunkenness
ixième [iksjɛm] *adj* umpteenth

J

J, j [ʒi] *m inv* J, j; ~ **comme Joseph** j as in Jack *Brit,* j as in Jig *Am;* (*on telephone*) j for Jack *Brit,* j for Jig *Am*
j' [ʒ] *pron v.* **je**
jacasser [ʒakase] <1> *vi* (*pie, personne*) to chatter
jachère [ʒaʃɛʀ] *f* **1.** (*procédé agricole*) practice of fallowing land **2.** (*terre*) fallow land
jacinthe [ʒasɛ̃t] *f* hyacinth
jacter [ʒakte] <1> *vi inf* to blather
jade [ʒad] *m* jade
jadis [ʒadis] *adv* formerly
jaguar [ʒagwaʀ] *m* jaguar
jaillir [ʒajiʀ] <8> *vi* **1.** (*gicler: eau*) to gush out; (*sang*) to spurt out; (*flammes*) to shoot up; (*éclair*) to flash **2.** (*fuser: rires*) to burst out **3.** (*surgir: personne*) to spring up [*o* out] **4.** (*se manifester: vérité, idée*) to emerge
jaillissement [ʒajismɑ̃] *m* (*de pétrole*) gushing out; (*de larmes*) welling up; (*de flammes*) shooting up
jais [ʒɛ] *m* (*en minéralurgie*) jet ►**de** ~ jet-black
jalon [ʒalɔ̃] *m* **1.** (*piquet*) marker **2.** *souvent pl* (*repère*) landmark; **poser les** ~**s de qc** to lay the foundations of [*o* for] sth
jalonner [ʒalɔne] <1> *vt* **1.** (*tracer: terrain*) to mark out **2.** (*border*) ~ **un jardin** (*piquets*) to mark off a garden; (*arbustes*) to line a garden **3.** (*marquer*) ~ **une carrière** (*succès*) to punctuate
jalousement [ʒaluzmɑ̃] *adv* **1.** (*avec envie*) enviously **2.** (*avec soin*) jealously
jalouser [ʒaluze] <1> **I.** *vt* ~ **qn** to be jealous

of sb **II.** *vpr* **se** ~ to be jealous of each other

jalousie [ʒaluzi] *f* **1.** (*en amour, amitié*) jealousy **2.** (*envie*) envy

jaloux, **-ouse** [ʒalu, -uz] **I.** *adj* **1.** (*en amour, amitié*) ~ **de qn** jealous of sb **2.** (*envieux*) ~ **de qn/qc** envious of sb/sth **3.** (*très attaché*) **être** ~ **de sa réputation** to be jealous of one's reputation **II.** *m, f* **1.** (*en amour, amitié*) jealous person **2.** (*envieux*) envious person; **faire des** ~ to make people jealous

jamaïcain(e), **jamaïquain(e)** [ʒamaikɛ̃, ɛn] *adj* Jamaican

Jamaïquain(e) [ʒamaikɛ̃, ɛn] *m(f)* Jamaican

Jamaïque [ʒamaik] *f* **la** ~ Jamaica

jamais [ʒamɛ] *adv* **1.** *avec construction négative* (*en aucun cas*) never; ~ **plus** [*o* **plus** ~] never again **2.** (*seulement*) only; **ça ne fait** ~ **que deux heures qu'il est parti** he left only two hours ago **3.** *avec construction positive ou interrogative* (*un jour*) ever; **si** ~ **elle donne de l'argent** if ever she should give money **4.** (*dans une comparaison*) **pire que** ~ worse than ever ►**à** (**tout**) ~ *soutenu* forever

jambe [ʒɑ̃b] *f* leg; **les ~s croisées** with one's legs crossed; **se dégourdir les ~s** to stretch one's legs; **traîner la** ~ to trudge along ►**prendre ses ~s à son cou** to take to one's heels; **ça me fait une belle ~!** *iron, inf* a (fat) lot of good that does me!; **ne plus avoir de ~s** *inf* to be on one's last legs; **à toutes ~s** in a rush

jambière [ʒɑ̃bjɛʀ] *f* legging

jambon [ʒɑ̃bɔ̃] *m* ham; ~ **de Paris** cooked ham; ~ **beurre** (*buttered*) *ham sandwich*

jambonneau [ʒɑ̃bɔno] <x> *m* ham knuckle

jante [ʒɑ̃t] *f* rim

janvier [ʒɑ̃vje] *m* January; *v. a.* **août**

Japon [ʒapɔ̃] *m* **le** ~ Japan

japonais [ʒapɔnɛ] *m* Japanese; *v. a.* **français**

japonais(e) [ʒapɔnɛ, ɛz] *adj* Japanese

Japonais(e) [ʒapɔnɛ, ɛz] *m(f)* Japanese

jappement [ʒapmɑ̃] *m* yap; **~s** yapping *no pl*

japper [ʒape] <1> *vi* to yap

jaquette [ʒakɛt] *f* **1.** (*couverture: d'un livre*) dust jacket **2.** COUT (*d'homme*) morning coat; (*de femme*) jacket

jardin [ʒaʀdɛ̃] *m* garden; ~ **potager** vegetable garden; ~ **public** (public) park ►~ **secret** private domain

jardinage [ʒaʀdinaʒ] *m* gardening

jardiner [ʒaʀdine] *vi* to do some gardening

jardinier, **-ière** [ʒaʀdinje, -jɛʀ] **I.** *adj* (*plante*) garden **II.** *m, f* gardener

jardinière [ʒaʀdinjɛʀ] *f* **1.** GASTR mixed vegetables **2.** (*bac à plantes*) window box

jargon [ʒaʀgɔ̃] *m péj* **1.** (*charabia*) gibberish **2.** (*langue technique*) jargon

jarre [ʒaʀ] *f* (earthenware) jar

jarret [ʒaʀɛ] *m* (*chez l'homme*) back of the leg; (*chez l'animal*) hock; ~ **de veau** shin of veal

jaser [ʒaze] <1> *vi* ~ **sur qn/qc** to gossip about sb/sth

jasmin [ʒasmɛ̃] *m* jasmine

jauge [ʒoʒ] *f* ~ **d'essence** petrol gauge *Brit,* gas gauge *Am;* ~ (**de niveau**) **d'huile** dipstick

jauger [ʒoʒe] <2a> *vt* **1.** TECH to measure **2.** (*apprécier*) to size up

jaunâtre [ʒonɑtʀ] *adj* yellowish

jaune [ʒon] **I.** *adj* yellow; ~ **d'or** golden yellow **II.** *m* **1.** (*couleur*) yellow; ~ **pâle/foncé** pale/dark yellow; ~ **paille** straw coloured *Brit,* straw colored *Am* **2.** (*partie d'un œuf*) (egg) yolk **III.** *adv* **rire** ~ to give a forced laugh

jaunir [ʒoniʀ] <8> **I.** *vi* to turn yellow; (*papier*) to yellow **II.** *vt* ~ **un tissu** (*lumière*) to turn a material yellow; (*nicotine*) to stain a material yellow

jaunisse [ʒonis] *f* jaundice ►**en faire une** ~ *inf* to be furious

java [ʒava] *f popular dance* ►**faire la** ~ *inf* to rave it up

javel [ʒavɛl] *f sans pl* bleach

javelliser [ʒavelize] <1> *vt* (*eau*) to chlorinate

javelot [ʒavlo] *m* javelin

jazz [dʒɑz] *m* jazz; **musicien de** ~ jazz musician

jazzman [dʒɑzman, -mɛn] <s *o* -men> *m* jazzman

je [ʒə, ʒ] <j'> *pron pers* I; **moi,** ~ **m'appelle Jean** my name is Jean; **que vois-~?** what do I see there?

jean [dʒin] *m* **1.** (*tissu*) denim **2.** *sing o pl* (*pantalon*) (pair of) jeans

jean-foutre [ʒɑ̃futʀ] *m inv, inf* good-for-nothing

Jeanne [ʒaːn(ə)] *f* HIST ~ **d'Arc** Joan of Arc

jeep® [dʒip] *f* Jeep®

je-m'en-foutiste [ʒ(ə)mɑ̃futist] *inv* **I.** *adj inf* **elle est plutôt** ~ she just couldn't give a damn **II.** *mf inf: person with a couldn't-give-a-damn attitude*

jérémiade [ʒeʀemjad] *f souvent pl, inf* moaning

jerrican(e), **jerrycan** [(d)ʒeʀikan] *m* jerry can

jersey [ʒɛʀzɛ] *m* jersey; **tricoter en** ~ (**endroit**) to knit in stocking stitch *Brit,* to knit in stockinette stitch *Am*

Jersey [ʒɛʀzɛ] (**l'île de**) ~ (the island of) Jersey

jésuite [ʒezɥit] **I.** *adj* Jesuit **II.** *m* REL Jesuit

Jésus-Christ [ʒezykʀi] *m* Jesus Christ

jet [ʒɛ] *m* **1.** (*giclée: d'un tuyau*) jet; ~ **d'eau** fountain **2.** (*action*) throwing; (*d'un filet*) casting **3.** (*résultat*) throw; **recevoir un** ~ **de gravillons** to be hit by a load of grit **4.** (*distance*) **à un** ~ **de pierre** a stone's throw away **5.** (*jaillissement*) ~ **de vapeur** jet of steam **6.** (*en métallurgie*) casting; **d'un seul** ~ in one piece ►**à** ~ **continu** nonstop; **le premier** ~ the first draft; **du premier** ~ at the first attempt; **traduire d'un** (**seul**) ~ to translate in one go

jetable [ʒ(ə)tabl] *adj* disposable

J

jeté [ʒ(ə)te] *m* **1.** (*action*) throwing **2.** (*résultat*) throw **3.** (*étoffe*) ~ **de lit** bedspread; ~ **de table** runner

jetée [ʒ(ə)te] *f* jetty

jeter [ʒ(ə)te] <3> **I.** *vt* **1.** (*lancer*) to throw; ~ **un ballon/une pierre à qn** to throw a ball to sb/a stone at sb **2.** (*lâcher: pistolet*) to drop; (*sonde*) to cast; (*bouée*) to throw **3.** (*se débarrasser de*) to throw away; (*liquide*) to pour away; (*lest*) to jettison **4.** *inf* (*vider: importun*) to chuck out; (*employé*) to fire; ~ **qn sur le pavé** to throw sb out (onto the streets) **5.** (*pousser*) ~ **qn à terre** to throw sb to the ground **6.** (*mettre rapidement*) ~ **qc sur ses épaules** to fling sth over one's shoulders **7.** (*mettre en place: passerelle*) to set up; ~ **les bases de qc** to lay the foundations of sth **8.** (*émettre: étincelles*) to throw out; ~ **mille feux** to sparkle brilliantly; ~ **un vif éclat** to shine brightly **9.** (*répandre: trouble*) to stir up; (*désordre*) to spread; ~ **le discrédit sur qn** to bring discredit on sb **10.** (*dire: remarque*) to throw in; ~ **des cris** to cry out; ~ **des insultes à qn** to hurl insults at sb ►~ **un regard/(coup d')œil à qn** to glance at sb; (*pour surveiller*) to keep an eye on sb; **en** ~ *inf* to be really something; **n'en jetez plus!** *inf* stop it! **II.** *vpr* **1.** (*s'élancer*) **se** ~ to throw oneself; **se** ~ **en arrière** to jump back; **se** ~ **à genoux** to throw oneself down on one's knees; **se** ~ **à plat ventre/sous un train** to throw oneself down/in front of a train; **se** ~ **au cou de qn** to fling oneself around sb's neck; **se** ~ **contre un arbre** to crash into a tree; **se** ~ **à l'eau** to jump into the water; *fig* to take the plunge **2.** (*s'engager*) **se** ~ **à l'assaut de qc** to launch into sth **3.** (*déboucher*) **se** ~ **dans qc** to flow into sth **4.** (*être jetable*) **se** ~ to be disposable **5.** (*s'envoyer*) **se** ~ **des injures à la figure** to hurl insults at each other

jeton [ʒ(ə)tɔ̃] *m* **1.** JEUX counter **2.** (*plaque à la roulette*) chip **3.** TEL token ►**faux** ~ *inf* phoney; **avoir les ~s** *inf* to be scared stiff; **donner** [*o* **ficher**] **les ~s à qn** *inf* to put the wind up sb *Brit*

jeu [ʒø] <x> *m* **1.** (*fait de s'amuser*) play, playing; ~ **de dés** game of dice; ~ **de rôle(s)** role play; ~ **d'équipe/radiophonique** team/radio game; ~ **de patience** puzzle; ~ **de piste** treasure hunt; **jouer le** ~ to play the game; **par** ~ for fun; **c'est pas du ~!** *inf* that's not fair! **2.** (*boîte, partie*) game; ~ **vidéo/de construction** video/building game; **qui mène le ~?** who's leading? **3.** SPORT (*manière de jouer*) game; ~ **de jambes** footwork; **avoir un** ~ **défensif** to play a defensive game **4.** (*lieu du jeu*) ~ **de boules** *bowling ground without grass;* ~ **de quilles** skittle alley *Brit,* ninepin alley *Am;* **terrain de ~x** playground; SPORT playing field; **le ballon est hors** ~ the ball is out of play; **remettre le ballon en** ~ to put the ball back into play; **mettre qn hors** ~ to put sb offside **5.** (~ *d'argent*) ~ **de hasard** game of chance; **faites vos ~x!** place your bets!; **se ruiner au** ~ to gamble away all one's money **6.** (*série*) ~ **de clés** set of keys; ~ **de caractères/puces** character/chip set **7.** (*interaction*) ~ **des alliances** interplay of alliances **8.** (*manège: du destin*) game; ~ **de l'amour** love-play; ~ **de bourse** stock market transactions *pl* **9.** (*habileté*) **jouer double** ~ to play a double game; **ce petit** ~ this little game **10.** (*action facile*) **c'est un** ~ **d'enfant** it's child's play; **avoir beau** ~ to have it easy ►**les forces (mises) en** ~ the forces at work; **jouer franc** ~ to play fair; **jouer le grand** ~ to pull out all the stops; **se prendre à son propre** ~ to be caught at one's own game; **être vieux** ~ to be old-fashioned; **entrer dans le** ~ **de qn** to play sb's game; **faire le** ~ **de qn** to play into sb's hands; **les ~x sont faits** the die is cast; (*au casino*) les jeux sont faits; **mettre sa vie en** ~ to risk one's life

jeu-concours [ʒøkɔ̃kuʀ] <jeux-concours> *m* competition

jeudi [ʒødi] *m* Thursday; ~ **saint** Maundy Thursday; *v. a.* **dimanche**

jeun [ʒœ̃] **venez à** ~ come without having eaten or drunk anything; **à prendre à** ~ to be taken on an empty stomach

jeune [ʒœn] **I.** *adj* **1.** (*opp: vieux*) young **2.** *antéposé* (*cadet*) **ma** ~ **sœur** my younger sister; **le** ~ **Durandol** Durandol junior **3.** (*inexpérimenté*) inexperienced; **être** ~ **dans le métier** to be new to the trade **4.** *postposé* (*comme un jeune*) **faire** ~ to look young **5.** *antéposé* (*d'enfance*) **dès son plus** ~ **âge** from his/her earliest years **6.** *postposé* (*nouveau: vin*) young ►**c'est un peu ~!** *inf* that's not much! **II.** *mf* **1.** (*personne*) young man/girl **2.** *pl* (*jeunes gens*) young people

jeûne [ʒøn] *m* REL, MED fast

> The **Jeûne fédéral** is a Swiss thanksgiving day that has taken place every third Sunday in September since 1832. Cinemas and entertainment centres have shorter opening hours than usual. Plum tart is traditionally eaten on this day.

jeûner [ʒøne] <1> *vi* to fast

jeunesse [ʒœnɛs] *f* **1.** (*état*) youthfulness **2.** (*période*) youth **3.** (*personnes jeunes*) young people; **une** ~ *inf* (young) girl **4.** (*nouveauté, fraîcheur*) youthfulness

jeunot(te) [ʒœno, ɔt] **I.** *adj* young **II.** *m(f) inf* young lad/girl

JF [ʒiɛf] *abr de* **jeune fille** girl

JH [ʒiaʃ] *abr de* **jeune homme** young man

JO [ʒio] **I.** *mpl abr de* **jeux Olympiques** Olympics **II.** *m abr de* **Journal officiel** *official publication giving announcements and information about laws*

joaillerie [ʒɔajʀi] *f* **1.** (*bijouterie*) jeweller's shop *Brit,* jewelry store *Am* **2.** (*art, métier*) jewellery-making *Brit,* jewelry-making *Am*

3. (*marchandises*) jewellery *Brit*, jewelry *Am*

joaillier, **-ière** [ʒɔaje, -jɛʀ] **I.** *m, f* jeweller *Brit*, jeweler *Am* **II.** *app* **ouvrier-~** goldsmith

job [dʒɔb] *m inf* job

jobard(e) [ʒɔbaʀ, aʀd] **I.** *adj* gullible **II.** *m(f)* sucker

jobardise [ʒɔbaʀdiz] *f* gullibility

jockey [ʒɔkɛ] *m* jockey

Joconde [ʒɔkɔ̃:d(ə)] *f* **la ~** the Mona Lisa

jodler [jɔdle] <1> *vi* to yodel

jogging [(d)ʒɔgiŋ] *m* **1.** (*footing*) jogging; **faire du ~** to go jogging **2.** (*survêtement*) track suit

joie [ʒwa] *f* **1.** (*bonheur*) joy; **cri de ~** cry of joy; **avec ~** with delight; **~ de vivre** joie de vivre; **~ de posséder** pride in possession; **être au comble de la** [*o* **fou de**] **~** to be overjoyed; **je m'en fais une (telle) ~** I'm (so) looking forward to it; **pleurer/sauter de ~** to weep/jump for joy; **être en ~** to be delighted **2.** *pl* (*plaisirs*) pleasures *pl;* **sans ~s** joyless ►**c'est pas la ~** *inf* things could be better

joindre [ʒwɛ̃dʀ] *irr* **I.** *vt* **1.** (*faire se toucher*) to join; (*mains*) to clasp; (*talons*) to put together **2.** (*relier*) to link **3.** (*rassembler*) **~ des efforts** to combine efforts **4.** (*ajouter*) **~ qc à un dossier** to add sth to a file; **~ le geste à la parole** to suit the action to the word **5.** (*atteindre: personne*) to reach **II.** *vi* (*fenêtre*) to shut properly; (*lattes*) to fit properly **III.** *vpr* **1.** (*s'associer*) **se ~ à qn/qc** to join sb/sth; **joignez-vous à nous** come (over) and join us **2.** (*participer à*) **se ~ à une conversation** to join in a conversation **3.** (*se toucher*) **se ~** to touch

joint [ʒwɛ̃] *m* **1.** (*espace*) joint **2.** (*garniture: d'un couvercle*) seal; (*d'un robinet*) washer; **~ d'étanchéité** seal ►**chercher/trouver le ~** to look for/to find the answer

joint(e) [ʒwɛ̃, ɛ̃t] **I.** *part passé de* **joindre** **II.** *adj* **1.** (*adhérent*) **mains ~es** clasped hands; **pieds ~s** feet together **2.** (*commun: efforts, compte*) joint **3.** (*ajouté*) enclosed; **pièce ~e** enclosure **4.** (*sans jeu*) fitting tightly together; **des fenêtres mal ~es** windows which don't close properly **5.** (*bien assemblés: planches*) fitted flush

jointif, **-ive** [ʒwɛ̃tif, -iv] *adj* (*planches*) butt-jointed

jointure [ʒwɛ̃tyʀ] *f* joint

jojo [ʒoʒo] **I.** *m* **un affreux ~** a horrible character **II.** *adj inv, inf* (*joli*) **ne pas être ~** to not be very nice

joker [(d)ʒɔkɛʀ] *m* joker

joli(e) [ʒɔli] *adj* **1.** (*agréable: voix*) pleasant; (*intérieur, vêtement d'homme*) nice; (*chanson, vêtement de femme*) nice, pretty **2.** (*considérable*) nice; (*position*) good **3.** *iron* **un ~ monsieur** a nasty type; **un ~ gâchis** a fine mess; **c'est du ~!** that's great!

joliment [ʒɔlimɑ̃] *adv* **1.** (*agréablement*) nicely **2.** (*très*) *a. iron* really; **tu as ~ travaillé!** you've done a really good job!

jonc [ʒɔ̃] *m* rush; **canne de ~** cane

joncher [ʒɔ̃ʃe] <1> **I.** *vt* to strew; **~ le chemin de fleurs** to strew the path with flowers **II.** *vpr* **se ~ de qc** to be strewn with sth

jonction [ʒɔ̃ksjɔ̃] *f* **1.** (*liaison*) *a.* TECH, ELEC junction; (*de routes*) (road) junction; (*de fleuves*) confluence; (*de voies ferrées*) points *pl;* **gare de ~** railway junction **2.** (*action*) link-up

jongler [ʒɔ̃gle] <1> *vi* to juggle; **~ avec les chiffres** to juggle the figures

jonglerie [ʒɔ̃gləʀi] *f péj* (*manœuvre*) juggling

jongleur, **-euse** [ʒɔ̃glœʀ, -øz] *m, f* juggler; **c'est un habile ~ de mots** he knows how to juggle words around

jonque [ʒɔ̃k] *f* junk

jonquille [ʒɔ̃kij] **I.** *f* daffodil **II.** *adj inv* (bright) yellow

Jordanie [ʒɔʀdani] *f* **la ~** Jordan

jordanien(ne) [ʒɔʀdanjɛ̃, jɛn] *adj* Jordanian

Jordanien(ne) [ʒɔʀdanjɛ̃, jɛn] *m(f)* Jordanian

jouable [ʒwabl] *adj* **1.** MUS playable **2.** (*faisable*) feasible

joual [ʒwal] <s> *m* joual; *v. a.* **français**

joual(e) [ʒwal] <s> *adj* joual

joue [ʒu] *f* **1.** ANAT cheek; **~s rebondies** chubby cheeks; **avoir les ~s creuses** to be hollow-cheeked **2.** *pl* (*parois latérales: d'un fauteuil*) side panels ►**se caler les ~s** *inf* to have a good feed; **en ~!** take aim!; **tenir qn/qc en ~** to train one's gun on sb/sth

jouer [ʒwe] <1> **I.** *vi* **1.** (*s'amuser*) *a.* SPORT, MUS to play; **~ au foot** to play football; **~ du piano** to play the piano; **faire ~ qn** to organize a game for sb; **à toi/vous de ~!** it's your turn! **2.** *fig* **~ avec les sentiments de qn** to play with sb's feelings; **c'est pour ~** I'm only joking **3.** THEAT, CINE **~ dans qc** to act in sth **4.** (*affecter d'être*) **~ à qn** to play at being sb **5.** FIN **~ à la bourse** to speculate on the stock exchange **6.** (*miser*) **~ sur qc** to bank on sth **7.** (*risquer*) **~ avec sa santé** to gamble with one's health **8.** (*intervenir: mesure*) to apply; (*relations*) to count; **~ de son influence** to use one's influence; **faire ~ une clause** to apply a clause; **~ du couteau** to use a knife ►**ça a joué en ma faveur** that has worked in my favour *Brit*, that has worked in my favor *Am;* **bien joué!** (*au jeu*) well played!; *fig* well done!; **~ serré** to play it tight **II.** *vt* **1.** JEUX, MUS (*carte, revanche*) to play; (*pion*) to move; **je joue atout cœur** hearts are trumps **2.** (*miser*) to back **3.** (*risquer: sa tête*) to risk; (*sa réputation*) to stake **4.** THEAT, CINE (*pièce*) to stage; (*rôle*) to play; **quelle pièce joue-t-on?** what play is on? **5.** (*feindre*) **~ la surprise** to feign surprise; **~ la comédie** to put on an act ►**rien n'est encore joué** nothing is settled yet **III.** *vpr* **1.** (*se moquer*) **se ~ de qn** to deceive sb, to have sb on; **se ~ des lois** to scoff at the law **2.** (*être joué*) **se ~** (*film*) to be shown;

J

(*spectacle*) to be on **3.** (*se dérouler*) **se ~** (*crime*) to happen **4.** (*se décider*) **se ~** (*avenir*) to be at stake ►**en se jouant** without trying

jouet [ʒwɛ] *m* **1.** (*jeu*) toy; **marchand de ~s** toyshop owner **2.** (*proie*) **être le ~ du vent** to be at the mercy of the wind; **être le ~ d'une illusion** to be the victim of an illusion

jouette [ʒwɛt] *adj Belgique* (*qui ne pense qu'à jouer*) playful

joueur, **-euse** [ʒwœʀ, -øz] **I.** *adj* (*animal, enfant, tempérament*) playful **II.** *m, f* JEUX, SPORT player; **se montrer beau ~** to prove to be a good loser; **être mauvais ~** to be a bad loser; **c'est un ~ malchanceux** he's an unlucky gambler

joufflu(**e**) [ʒufly] *adj* chubby-cheeked

joug [ʒu] *m* **1.** AGR yoke **2.** (*contrainte: d'une loi*) force; (*du mariage*) yoke; **tomber sous le ~ de qn** to come under sb's yoke

jouir [ʒwiʀ] <8> *vi* **1.** (*apprécier*) **~ de la vie** to enjoy life **2.** (*disposer de*) **~ de privilèges/d'une bonne santé** to enjoy privileges/good health; **~ d'une réputation intacte** to have a good reputation; **~ d'un bien** to own a property; **~ d'une fortune** to be wealthy; **~ d'une grande faveur auprès de qn** to be very popular with sb **3.** (*sexuellement*) to have an orgasm

jouissance [ʒwisɑ̃s] *f* **1.** (*plaisir*) pleasure; **être avide de ~s** to be pleasure-loving **2.** (*usage*) **la ~ d'un immeuble** the use of a building **3.** (*orgasme*) orgasm

jouisseur, **-euse** [ʒwisœʀ, -øz] **I.** *adj* sensualist **II.** *m, f* sensualist

jouissif, **-ive** [ʒwisif, -iv] *adj* enjoyable

joujou [ʒuʒu] <x> *m enfantin* toy; **faire ~** to play

jour [ʒuʀ] *m* **1.** (*24 heures*) day; **par ~** daily, a day; **tous les ~s** every day; **star d'un ~** fleeting celebrity **2.** (*opp: nuit*) day; **dormir le ~** to sleep during the day; **être de ~** MIL to be on day duty **3.** (*opp: obscurité*) daylight; **faux ~** deceptive light; **il fait** (**grand**) **~** it's (broad) daylight; **le ~ baisse/se lève** it's getting dark/light; **~ naissant** dawn; **au petit ~** at dawn; **sous un ~ favorable** in a favourable light *Brit,* in a favorable light *Am* **4.** (*jour précis*) day; **le ~ J** (on) D-day; **le ~ de Noël** (on) Christmas Day; **~ des Rois** Twelfth Night; **~ du Seigneur** Sabbath; **les ~s de marché/de pluie** (on) market/rainy days; **un ~ qu'il pleuvra** on a rainy day; **plat du ~** today's special; **goût du ~** current tastes *pl;* **œuf du ~** fresh egg; **être dans un bon ~** to be in a good mood; **notre entretien de ce ~** our discussion today; **~ pour ~** to the day; **porter la tenue des grands ~s** to be festively dressed **5.** (*période vague*) **à ce ~** to date; **un de ces ~s** one of these days; **de nos ~s** these days; **l'autre ~** *inf* the other day; **un ~ ou l'autre** some day; **habit de tous les ~s** workaday clothes *pl;* **tous les ~s que** (**le bon**) **Dieu fait** day in day out **6.** *pl, soutenu* (*vie*) **ses ~s sont comptés** his/her days are numbered; **finir ses ~s à l'hospice** to end one's days in a home; **vieux ~s** old age **7.** (*interstice*) gap; **clôture à ~** openwork fence ►**c'est le ~ et la nuit** there's (absolutely) no comparison; **d'un ~ à l'autre** (*soudain*) from one day to the next; (*sous peu*) any day now; **au grand ~** for all to see; **donner ses huit ~s à qn** to give a week's notice to sb; **se montrer sous son vrai ~** to show one's true colours *Brit,* to show one's true colors *Am;* **donner le ~ à qn** to bring sb into the world; **demain, il fera ~** tommorrow is another day; **mettre qc à ~** to update sth; **se mettre à ~ dans qc** to bring oneself up to date on sth; **mettre au ~** to bring to light; **mettre des antiquités au ~** to unearth antiquities; **percer qn/qc à ~** to see through sb/sth; **voir le ~** (*personne*) to come into the world; (*projet*) to see the light of day; **au ~ le ~** one day at a time; (*précairement*) from hand to mouth

Jourdain [ʒuʀdɛ̃] *m* **le ~** Jordan

journal [ʒuʀnal, o] <-aux> *m* **1.** PRESSE newspaper; **~ de mode** fashion magazine **2.** (*bureaux*) newspaper office **3.** (*mémoire*) **~ intime** private diary; **~ de bord** NAUT ship's log **4.** (*média non imprimé*) **~ filmé** newsreel; **~ télévisé** television news *pl*

journalier, **-ière** [ʒuʀnalje, -jɛʀ] **I.** *adj* daily **II.** *m, f* AGR day labourer *Brit,* day laborer *Am*

journalisme [ʒuʀnalism] *m* journalism

journaliste [ʒuʀnalist] *mf* journalist

journalistique [ʒuʀnalistik] *adj* journalistic

journée [ʒuʀne] *f* **1.** (*durée du jour, temps de travail*) day; **pendant la ~** during the day; **~ de grève** day of strike action; **~s d'études** seminar; **~ de 8 heures** 8-hour day; **~ continue** continuous working day **2.** (*salaire*) day's wages *pl* **3.** (*recette*) day's takings *pl;* **faire une ~/des ~s** to work as a day labourer *Brit,* to work as a day laborer *Am;* **travailler/être payé à la ~** to work/to be paid by the day **4.** (*distance*) **à une ~ de marche/voyage** a day's walk/journey away; **c'est à trois ~s de train** it's a three-day journey by train ►**toute la sainte ~** all day long

joute [ʒut] *f* **1.** SPORT **~ nautique** water tournament **2.** (*rivalité*) duel; **~ oratoire** (verbal) sparring match

jouvence [ʒuvɑ̃s] *f* **cure de ~** rejuvenation cure; **eau de ~** waters of youth

jouvenceau, **-elle** [ʒuvɑ̃so, -ɛl] <x> *m, f iron* **1.** (*jeune homme*) youth **2.** (*jeune fille*) maiden

jovial(**e**) [ʒɔvjal, jo] <s *o* -aux> *adj* jovial

jovialement [ʒɔvjalmɑ̃] *adv* jovially

jovialité [ʒɔvjalite] *f* joviality

joyau [ʒwajo] <x> *m a. fig* jewel

joyeusement [ʒwajøzmɑ̃] *adv* happily

joyeux, **-euse** [ʒwajø, -jøz] *adj* (*chant*) joyful; (*personne*) cheerful; (*compagnie*) merry; **être de joyeuse humeur** to be in a joyful mood; **être tout ~** to be overjoyed; **joyeuse**

fête! many happy returns!; ~ **anniversaire!** happy birthday!

JT [ʒite] *m abr de* **journal télévisé** television news

jubilation [ʒybilasjɔ̃] *f* jubilation

jubilé [ʒybile] *m* jubilee

jubiler [ʒybile] <1> *vi* to be jubilant

jucher [ʒyʃe] <1> **I.** *vt* ~ **sur qc** to perch on sth **II.** *vi* (*oiseau*) to perch **III.** *vpr* **se** ~ **sur qc** to perch on sth

judaïque [ʒydaik] *adj* Jewish; (*loi*) Judaic

judaïsme [ʒydaism] *m* Judaism

judas [ʒyda] *m* ARCHIT peephole

judéo-chrétien(**ne**) [ʒydeokʀetjɛ̃, ɛn] *adj* Judaeo-christian *Brit,* Judeo-Christian *Am*

judiciaire [ʒydisjɛʀ] *adj* judicial; (*casier*) police [*o* criminal] record; **police** ~ ≈ Criminal Investigation Department

judicieusement [ʒydisjøzmɑ̃] *adv* judiciously

judicieux, **-euse** [ʒydisjø, -jøz] *adj* judicious

judo [ʒydo] *m* judo

judoka [ʒydoka] *mf* judoka

juge [ʒyʒ] *mf* **1.** (*magistrat*) judge; **aller devant le**(**s**) ~(**s**) to go to court; ~ **des enfants** ≈ juvenile magistrate *Brit;* ~ **d'instruction** examining magistrate; ~ **d'instance** justice of the peace **2.** (*arbitre*) referee; **je vous laisse** [*o* **en fais**] ~ I'll let you be the judge; **être mauvais** ~ to be a bad judge **3.** SPORT ~ **d'arrivée** finishing judge; ~ **de touche** linesman **4.** JEUX ~ **d'un concours** judge ▶**être** (**à la fois**) ~ **et partie** to be both judge and judged

jugé [ʒyʒe] **au** ~ by guesswork; **répondre au** ~ to guess

juge-arbitre [ʒyʒaʀbitʀ] <juges-arbitres> *m* referee

jugement [ʒyʒmɑ̃] *m* **1.** JUR (*action de juger*) judgement; **faire passer qn en** ~ to put sb on trial; **une affaire passe en** ~ a case is (being) heard **2.** (*sentence*) sentence; ~ **par défaut** judgement **3.** (*discernement, opinion*) judgement; **porter des** ~**s trop sommaires sur qn/qc** to judge sb/sth too hastily

jugeote [ʒyʒɔt] *f inf* commonsense ▶**ne pas avoir pour deux sous de** ~ to have not an ounce of commonsense

juger [ʒyʒe] <2a> **I.** *vt* **1.** JUR ~ **un litige** to rule in a dispute; ~ **qn pour vol** to try sb for theft; ~ **qn coupable** to find sb guilty **2.** (*arbitrer*) ~ **un différend** to arbitrate in a dispute **3.** (*évaluer: livre, situation*) to judge **4.** (*estimer*) to consider **II.** *vi* **1.** JUR to judge; **le tribunal jugera** the court will decide **2.** (*estimer*) ~ **de qc** to assess sth; **autant qu'on puisse en** ~ as far as one can judge; **à en** ~ **par qc** judging by sth **3.** (*s'imaginer*) ~ **de qc** to imagine sth **III.** *vpr* (*s'estimer*) **se** ~ **incapable/perdu** to consider oneself incapable/lost

juguler [ʒygyle] <1> *vt* (*inflation*) to curb; (*fièvre*) to lower; (*révolte*) to suppress; (*désir, personne*) to repress

juif, **-ive** [ʒɥif, -iv] *adj* Jewish

Juif, **-ive** [ʒɥif, -iv] *m, f* Jew; **le** ~ **errant** the Wandering Jew

juillet [ʒɥijɛ] *m* July; *v. a.* **août**

juin [ʒɥɛ̃] *m* June; *v. a.* **août**

juke-box [ʒykbɔks] *m inv* jukebox

jules [ʒyl] *m inf* (*amoureux, mari*) man, guy

Juliette [ʒyljɛt(ə)] *f* **Roméo et** ~ Romeo and Juliet

jumeau, **-elle** [ʒymo, -ɛl] <x> **I.** *adj* twin; **des lits** ~**x** twin beds; **des maisons jumelles** semi-detached houses **II.** *m, f* **1.** (*besson*) twin; **vrais/faux** ~**x** identical/fraternal twins **2.** (*frère*) twin brother **3.** (*sœur*) twin sister **4.** (*sosie*) double

jumelage [ʒymlaʒ] *m* twinning

jumelé(**e**) [ʒymle] *adj* (*lié culturellement*) **des villes** ~**es** twin towns *Brit,* sister cities *Am*

jumeler [ʒymle] <3> *vt* POL (*deux villes*) to twin

jumelles [ʒymɛl] *fpl* (*en optique*) binoculars *pl;* ~ **de théâtre** opera glasses *pl*

jument [ʒymɑ̃] *f* mare

jumping [dʒœmpiŋ] *m* show jumping

jungle [ʒœ̃gl, ʒɔ̃gl] *f* jungle

junior [ʒynjɔʀ] **I.** *adj* (*catégorie*) junior; **mode** ~ junior fashion **II.** *mf* junior; **le championnat des** ~**s** the junior championship

junte [ʒœ̃t] *f* junta

jupe [ʒyp] *f* skirt; ~ **droite/plissée** straight/pleated skirt

jupe-culotte [ʒypkylɔt] <jupes-culottes> *f* culottes *pl*

jupe-portefeuille [ʒyppɔʀtəfœj] *f* wraparound skirt

Jupiter [ʒypitɛr] *m* ASTR, HIST Jupiter

jupon [ʒypɔ̃] *m* petticoat ▶**courir le** ~ to womanize

Jura [ʒyʀa] *m* **le** ~ the Jura (Mountains)

jurassien(**ne**) [ʒyʀasjɛ̃, jɛn] *adj* of the Jura (Mountains)

jurassique [ʒyʀasik] **I.** *adj* GEO **période** ~ Jurassic period **II.** *m* GEO Jurassic

juré(**e**) [ʒyʀe] **I.** *adj a. fig* sworn **II.** *m(f)* JUR juror

jurer [ʒyʀe] <1> **I.** *vt* **1.** (*promettre, affirmer*) ~ **à ses parents de** +*infin* to swear to one's parents to +*infin;* **faire** ~ **à un collègue de** +*infin* to make a colleague swear to +*infin;* **je te** [*o* **vous**] **jure!** *inf* honestly!; **je te** [*o* **vous**] **jure que oui/non!** yes, really/no, not at all! **2.** (*se promettre*) ~ **la mort de qn** to vow to kill sb; ~ **de se venger** to swear vengeance **3.** (*croire*) **j'aurais juré que c'était toi** I could have sworn that it was you; **ne** ~ **que par qn/qc** to swear by sb/sth **II.** *vi* **1.** (*pester*) ~ **contre** [*o* **après**] **qn/qc** to swear at sb/sth **2.** (*détonner*) ~ **avec qc** to clash with sth **3.** (*affirmer*) ~ **de qc** to swear to sth; **je n'en jurerais pas** I wouldn't swear to it **4.** (*croire*) **il ne faut** ~ **de rien** you never can tell **III.** *vpr*

J

1. (*se promettre mutuellement*) **se ~ qc** to swear sth to one another **2.** (*décider*) **se ~ de** +*infin* to vow to +*infin*

juridiction [ʒyʀidiksjɔ̃] *f a.* JUR jurisdiction; **avoir recours à la ~ supérieure** to appeal to a higher court; **le tribunal de votre ~** the court in which you have jurisdiction

juridique [ʒyʀidik] *adj* **1.** (*judiciaire*) judicial **2.** (*qui a rapport au droit*) legal; **vide ~** gap in the law; **faire des études ~s** to study law

juridiquement [ʒyʀidikmɑ̃] *adv* **1.** (*en justice*) judicially; (*demander*) in court **2.** (*légalement*) legally

jurisconsulte [ʒyʀiskɔ̃sylt] *mf* legal adviser

jurisprudence [ʒyʀispʀydɑ̃s] *f* case law; **faire ~** to set a (legal) precedent

juriste [ʒyʀist] *mf* lawyer

juron [ʒyʀɔ̃] *m* swear word

jury [ʒyʀi] *m* **1.** JUR jury; **président du ~** foreman of the jury **2.** ART, SPORT panel of judges **3.** ECOLE, UNIV board of examiners

jus [ʒy] *m* **1.** (*suc: d'un fruit, d'une viande*) juice; **rendre du ~** to be juicy **2.** *inf* (*café*) coffee **3.** *inf* (*courant*) juice ►**laisser mijoter qn dans son ~** *inf* to let sb stew in his own juice; **ça vaut le ~!** *inf* it's worth it!; **au ~!** *inf* in you go/he goes!

jusqu'au-boutiste [ʒyskobutist] **I.** *adj* **être ~** to always go to extremes; **politique ~** hard-line policy **II.** *mf* hard-liner

jusque [ʒysk] <jusqu'> **I.** *prep* **1.** (*limite de lieu*) as far as; **grimper jusqu'à 3000 m** to climb up to 3,000 metres *Brit,* to climb up to 3,000 meters *Am;* **jusqu'aux genoux** up to one's knees; **viens jusqu'ici!** come up to here!; **jusqu'où?** how far? **2.** (*limite de temps*) until; **jusqu'à midi/au soir** until midday/the evening; **jusqu'ici/en mai** until now/May **3.** (*y compris*) even; **tous jusqu'au dernier** every last one; **~ dans** even in **4.** (*au plus*) **jusqu'à concurrence de 200 euros** up to 200 euros; **jusqu'à dix personnes** up to ten people **5.** (*limite*) **jusqu'à un certain point** up to a (certain) point; **jusqu'à quel point** to what extent; **jusqu'où** as far as **6.** (*assez pour*) **manger jusqu'à en être malade** to eat to the point of being sick; **il va jusqu'à prétendre que c'est moi** he goes so far as to claim that it's me **II.** *conj* **jusqu'à ce qu'il vienne** until he comes

jusque-là [ʒuskla] *adv* **1.** (*jusqu'à ce moment-là*) until then **2.** (*jusqu'à cet endroit*) that far; **va ~!** go up to there!

justaucorps [ʒystokɔʀ] *m* SPORT body stocking; **~ de gymnastique** leotard

juste [ʒyst] **I.** *adj* **1.** (*équitable*) just; (*condition*) fair; **ce n'est pas ~** it's not fair **2.** *antéposé* (*fondé*) justified; **avoir de ~s raisons de se réjouir** to have good reason to be delighted **3.** (*trop court: vêtement*) too short **4.** (*trop étroit*) too tight; (*ouverture*) narrow **5.** (*à peine suffisant*) barely enough **6.** (*exact*) correct; (*heure*) right; **c'est ~!** that's (quite) right!; **à 8 heures ~(s)** at 8 o'clock on the dot; **apprécier qc à sa ~ valeur** to appreciate the true worth of sth **7.** (*pertinent*) pertinent **8.** MUS (*note*) true; (*voix, instrument*) in tune; **le piano n'est pas ~** the piano is out of tune **II.** *m* REL just man **III.** *adv* **1.** (*avec exactitude*) accurately; (*penser*) logically; (*raisonner*) soundly; **parler ~** to find the right words; **dire ~** to be right; **deviner ~** to guess right(ly); **le calcul tombe ~** the calculation works out exactly **2.** (*exactement, seulement*) just; **il habite ~ à côté** he lives just next door; **il a plu ~ ce qu'il fallait** it rained just enough **3.** (*à peine: mesurer*) exactly; **au plus ~** just enough; **cela entre ~** that barely fits in; **tout ~** hardly ►**être un peu ~** *inf* (*avoir peu d'argent*) to be short of cash; **au ~** exactly; **comme de ~** as usual

justement [ʒystəmɑ̃] *adv* **1.** (*à bon droit*) rightly **2.** (*pertinemment: remarquer*) correctly; (*penser*) logically; (*raisonner*) soundly **3.** (*exactement*) exactly **4.** (*précisément*) precisely

justesse [ʒystɛs] *f* **1.** (*précision*) accuracy **2.** (*pertinence*) aptness; (*d'un raisonnement*) soundness; **s'exprimer avec ~** to express oneself appropriately ►**de ~** only just

justice [ʒystis] *f* **1.** (*principe*) justice; **agir avec ~** to act justly **2.** (*loi*) law; **rendre la ~** to dispense justice; **obtenir ~** to obtain justice **3.** (*juridiction*) jurisdiction; **en ~** in court; **assigner qn en ~** to summon sb to appear in court ►**être raide comme la ~** *inf* to be (as) stiff as a board; **ce n'est que ~** it's only right and proper; **faire ~ à son mérite** to acknowledge his/her merit; **se faire ~** (*se suicider*) to take one's life; (*se venger*) to take the law into one's own hands; **il faut lui rendre cette ~** to his credit it must be said

justicier, -ière [ʒystisje, -jɛʀ] *m, f* **1.** (*redresseur de torts*) righter of wrongs; **se poser en ~** to set oneself up as judge **2.** (*vengeur*) avenger

justifiable [ʒystifjabl] *adj* justifiable

justificatif [ʒystifikatif] *m* **1.** (*preuve*) documentary evidence; **~ d'identité** identity papers *pl* **2.** PRESSE specimen copy

justificatif, -ive [ʒystifikatif, -iv] *adj* PRESSE (*exemplaire*) specimen

justification [ʒystifikasjɔ̃] *f* **1.** (*explication: d'un acte, d'une conduite*) justification **2.** (*preuve*) proof; (*d'un paiement*) receipt

justifier [ʒystifje] <1> **I.** *vt* **1.** (*donner raison à, expliquer*) *a.* TYP, INFOR to justify; **rien ne justifie tes craintes** your fears are unjustified; **justifié à droite/gauche** to justify to the right/left **2.** (*disculper*) to vindicate **3.** (*prouver*) **~ une créance** to justify a claim; **pouvez-vous ~ vos affirmations?** can you prove your assertions? **II.** *vi* **~ d'un paiement/de son identité** to give proof of payment/of one's identity **III.** *vpr* **1.** (*se disculper*) **se ~ de qc auprès de qn** to justify oneself to

sb about sth **2.** (*s'expliquer*) **se ~ par qc** to be justified by sth
jute [ʒyt] *m* jute
juter [ʒyte] <1> *vi* to be juicy
juteux, **-euse** [ʒytø, -øz] *adj* **1.** (*opp: sec: fruit*) juicy **2.** *inf* (*lucratif*) lucrative
juvénile [ʒyvenil] *adj* youthful
juxtaposer [ʒykstapoze] <1> *vt* to juxtapose
juxtaposition [ʒykstapozisjɔ̃] *f* juxtaposition

K

K, k [kɑ] *m inv* K, k; **~ comme Kléber** k as in King; (*on telephone*) k for King
kabyle [kabil] **I.** *adj* Kabylian **II.** *m* Kabylian; *v. a.* **français**
kaki [kaki] **I.** *adj inv* khaki **II.** *m sans pl* khaki
kaléidoscope [kaleidɔskɔp] *m* kaleidoscope
kangourou [kɑ̃guʀu] *m* kangaroo
kaolin [kaɔlɛ̃] *m* kaolin
kapok [kapɔk] *m* kapok
karaoké [kaʀaɔke] *m* karaoke
karaté [kaʀate] *m* karate
karatéka [kaʀateka] *mf* **être ~** (*expert*) to be a karate expert; (*apprenant*) to do karate
kart [kaʀt] *m* go-kart
karting [kaʀtiŋ] *m* go-karting; **piste de ~** go-karting track
kascher [kaʃɛʀ] *adj* kosher
kayak [kajak] *m* kayak
kelvin [kɛlvin] *m* kelvin
Kenya [kenja] *m* **le ~** Kenya
kényan(e) [kenjɑ̃, an] *adj* Kenyan
Kényan(e) [kenjɑ̃, an] *mf* Kenyan
képi [kepi] *m* kepi
kermesse [kɛʀmɛs] *f* **1.** (*fête de bienfaisance*) charity fête **2.** *Belgique, Nord* (*fête patronale*) fair
kérosène [keʀozɛn] *m* kerosene
ketchup [kɛtʃœp] *m* ketchup
KGB [kaʒebe] *m abr de* **Komitet Gossoudarstvennoï Bezopasnosti** KGB
khâgne [kaɲ] *f inf: preparatory class for entrance to the École normale supérieure*
kibboutz [kibuts, kibutsim] <kibboutz(im)> *m* kibbutz
kidnapper [kidnape] <1> *vt* to kidnap
kidnappeur, **-euse** [kidnapœʀ, -øz] *m, f* kidnapper
kidnapping [kidnapiŋ] *m* kidnapping
kif-kif [kifkif] *m* **c'est ~** (**bourricot**) *inf* it comes to the same thing
kiki [kiki] *m inf* **c'est parti, mon ~** here we go; **serrer le ~ à qn** to throttle sb
kilo [kilo] *m abr de* **kilogramme** kilo
kilogramme [kilɔgʀam] *m* kilogramme *Brit*, kilogram *Am*
kilohertz [kiloɛʀts] *m* kilohertz
kilométrage [kilɔmetʀaʒ] *m* (*d'une voiture*) mileage
kilomètre [kilɔmɛtʀ] *m* kilometre *Brit*, kilometer *Am;* **140 ~s à l'heure** [*o* **~s-heure**] 140 kilometres an hour; **~ carré** square kilometre
kilomètre-heure [kilɔmɛtʀœʀ] <kilomètres-heure> *m* kilometre per hour *Brit*, kilometer per hour *Am*
kilométrique [kilɔmetʀik] *adj* (*mesure, prix de revient*) by kilometre *Brit*, by kilometer *Am;* (*distance*) in kilometres; **borne ~** kilometre marker *Brit*, kilometer marker *Am*
kilo-octet [kiloɔktɛ] <kilo-octets> *m* kilobyte
kilotonne [kilotɔn] *f* kiloton
kilowatt [kilowat] *m* kilowatt
kilowattheure [kilowatœʀ] *m* kilowatt-hour
kilt [kilt] *m* kilt; (*pour femme*) *skirt that is pleated at the back only*
kimono [kimɔno] **I.** *m* kimono **II.** *app inv* **manches/robe ~** kimono sleeves/dress
kiné [kine] *mf inf abr de* **kinésithérapeute** physical therapist, physio *Brit*
kinési [kinezi] *mf inf abr de* **kinésithérapeute** physical therapist, physio *Brit*
kinésithérapeute [kineziteʀapøt] *mf* physiotherapist
kiosque [kjɔsk] *m* (*lieu de vente*) kiosk; **~ à friandises/de fleuriste** sweet/flower stall; **~ à journaux** newspaper kiosk
kir® [kiʀ] *m* kir; **~ royal** kir royal (*champagne with blackcurrant liqueur*)
Kiribati [kiʀibati] *f* Kiribati
kirsch [kiʀʃ] *m* kirsch
kit [kit] *m* kit
kitchenette [kitʃənɛt] *f* kitchenette
kit(s)ch [kitʃ] *adj inv* kitsch
kitticien(ne) [kitisiɛ̃, ɛn] *adj* Kittsian
Kitticien(ne) [kitisiɛ̃, ɛn] *m(f)* Kittsian
kiwi [kiwi] *m* kiwi
klaxon® [klaksɔn] *m* horn; **donner un coup/petit coup de ~** to honk, to give a hoot/toot *Brit*
klaxonner [klaksɔne] <1> *vi* to honk (one's horn), to hoot (one's horn) *Brit*
kleenex® [klinɛks] *m* Kleenex®, tissue
km *abr de* **kilomètre** km
Ko [kɑo] *m abr de* **kilo-octet** kb
KO [kɑo] *adj inv, inf abr de* **knock-out** **1.** (*assommé*) knocked-out; SPORT KO'd; **mettre qn ~** to KO sb; **le choc l'a mis ~** he was knocked out by the blow **2.** (*épuisé*) shattered; **mettre qn ~** to shatter sb
koala [kɔala] *m* koala (bear)
kouglof [kuglɔf] *m* kugelhopf, *ring-shaped fruit loaf*
Koweït [kɔwɛt] *m* **le ~** Kuwait
koweïtien(ne) [kɔwɛtjɛ̃, jɛn] *adj* Kuwaiti
Koweïtien(ne) [kɔwɛtjɛ̃, jɛn] *m(f)* Kuwaiti

krach [kRak] *m* FIN crash
kurde [kyRd] I. *adj* Kurdish II. *m* Kurdish; *v. a.* français
Kurde [kyRd] *m, f* Kurd
Kurdistan [kyRdistɑ̃] *m* **le** ~ Kurdistan
Kuwait [kɔwɛt] *m v.* **Koweït**
kyrielle [kiRjɛl] *f inf* **une** ~ **d'enfants** a crowd of children; **une** ~ **d'injures** a stream of insults; **une** ~ **de bêtises** *one mistake after the other;* **ils sont une** ~ **à postuler pour ce poste** there's a whole crowd of them after this job
kyste [kist] *m* cyst

L

L, l [ɛl] *m inv* L, l; ~ **comme Louis** l as in Lucy *Brit,* l as in Love *Am;* (*on telephone*) l for Lucy *Brit,* l for love *Am*
l *abr de* **litre** litre *Brit,* liter *Am*
l' *art, pron v.* **le, la**
la¹ [la] <*devant voyelle ou h muet* l'> I. *art déf* the II. *pron pers, fém* 1. (*personne*) her; **il** ~ **voit/l'aide** he sees/helps her 2. (*animal ou objet*) it; **là-bas, il y a une mouche/ma ceinture,** ~ **vois-tu?** there's a fly/my belt over there, can you see it? 3. *avec un présentatif* ~ **voici** [*o* **voilà**]**!** here it/she is!
la² [la] *m inv* MUS A, lah *Brit,* la *Am;* **donner le** ~ to set the tone; *v. a.* **do**
là¹ [la] *adv* 1. (*avec déplacement à distance*) (over) there 2. (*avec/sans déplacement à proximité/distance*) there; **passer par** ~ to go that way; **de** ~ from there; **quelque part par** ~ (*en montrant du doigt*) somewhere over there; (*dans une région*) somewhere around there 3. (*ici, avec une personne à qui on parle*) here; **je suis** ~ here I am; **peux-tu être** ~ **à six heures?** can you be here [*o* come] at six o'clock? 4. (*à ce moment-là*) **à partir de** ~ from then on; ~ **je m'en vais** I'm just going 5. (*alors*) then ►**les choses en sont** ~ that's how things stand
là² [la] *interj* now
LA [ɛle] *abr de* **Los Angeles** LA
là-bas [labɑ] *adv* 1. (*avec déplacement à distance*) over there 2. (*avec l'endroit précisé*) over; ~ **à Paris** in Paris
label [labɛl] *m* (*marque de qualité*) brand (name); (*vêtements*) label
labo [labo] *m inf* lab
laboratoire [labɔRatwaR] *m* (*salle*) laboratory; ~ **de langues/d'analyses** language/analysis laboratory
laborieux, -euse [labɔRjø, -jøz] *adj* 1. (*pénible*) laborious; (*recherche*) painstaking; **eh bien, c'est** ~**!** *inf* it's hard going! 2. (*travailleur: classes, masses*) working; (*personne*) industrious; (*vie*) hardworking
labour [labuR] *m* 1. digging 2. (*avec une charrue*) ploughing *Brit,* plowing *Am;* **cheval de** ~ plough horse 3. *pl* (*terres labourées*) ploughed fields *Brit,* plowed fields *Am*
labourer [labuRe] <1> *vt* 1. AGR to plough *Brit,* to plow *Am* 2. (*creuser*) to slash into
labyrinthe [labiRɛ̃t] *m* 1. (*dédale*) labyrinth 2. (*complication*) maze
lac [lak] *m* lake; ~ **de Constance** Lake Constance; ~ **Léman** Lake Geneva; ~ **de Neuchâtel** Lake Neuchâtel; ~ **des Quatre-Cantons** Lake Lucerne; ~ **Érié** Lake Erie; ~ **Supérieur** Lake Superior; **les Grands** ~**s** the Great Lakes
lacer [lase] <2> I. *vt* to tie (up) II. *vpr* **se** ~ **devant** (*chaussures*) to lace up along the front
lacérer [laseRe] <5> *vt* 1. (*déchirer*) to rip 2. (*taillader*) ~ **le visage à qn** to slash sb's face
lacet [lasɛ] *m* 1. (*cordon*) (shoe)lace; **à** ~**s** with laces 2. (*virage*) bend; **route en** ~(**s**) winding road
lâchage [lɑʃaʒ] *m inf* (*abandon*) desertion
lâche [lɑʃ] I. *adj* 1. (*poltron, méprisable*) cowardly 2. (*détendu: corde*) slack II. *mf* coward
lâchement [lɑʃmɑ̃] *adv* 1. (*peureusement*) in a cowardly way 2. (*de façon méprisable*) ~, **il ...** like the coward he is, he ...
lâcher [lɑʃe] <1> I. *vt* 1. (*laisser aller involontairement*) to let go of 2. (*laisser aller délibérément*) to release; ~ **une bêtise/un mot** to come out with something silly/a word 3. *inf* (*abandonner*) to abandon; **le moteur lâche qn** the motor let sb down; **ne pas** ~ **qn** (*rhume, idée*) not to let go of sb; **tout** ~ *inf* to drop everything II. *vi* to give way; (*corde*) to break
lâcheté [lɑʃte] *f* 1. (*couardise*) cowardice; **par** ~ out of cowardice 2. (*bassesse*) lowness
lâcheur, -euse [lɑʃœR, -øz] *m, f inf* **être** ~ to let people down
laconique [lakɔnik] *adj* laconic; (*réponse*) concise
lacrymogène [lakRimɔʒɛn] *adj* **gaz** ~ teargas
lacté(e) [lakte] *adj* 1. GASTR (*bouillie*) milk; **régime** ~ milk diet 2. MED **fièvre** ~**e** milk fever
lacune [lakyn] *f* gap
lacustre [lakystR] *adj* lacustrian; **cité** ~ lakeside village (*on stilts*)
là-dedans [lad(ə)dɑ̃] *adv* 1. (*lieu*) inside; **je ne reste pas** ~ I am not staying in there 2. (*direction*) into 3. (*en parlant d'une affaire*) **n'avoir rien à voir** ~ to have nothing to do with it; **pourquoi me suis-je embarqué** ~**?** why did I get involved?
là-dessous [lad(ə)su] *adv* 1. (*dessous*) underneath 2. *fig* behind; **qu'y a-t-il** ~**?** what's the story?
là-dessus [lad(ə)sy] *adv* 1. (*direction, ici*) on here 2. (*direction, là-bas*) on there 3. (*à ce sujet*) about that; **compte** ~ count on it 4. (*sur ce*) on that matter
lagon [lagɔ̃] *m* lagoon

lagune [lagyn] *f* lagoon

là-haut [lao] *adv* **1.** (*au-dessus: direction, dans le ciel*) up there **2.** (*au-dessus: lieu*) on top

La Haye [la´ɛ] The Hague

laïc, **-que** [laik] *adj v.* **laïque**

laïciser [laisize] <1> *vt* to laicize

laïcité [laisite] *f* secularity; (*de l'enseignement*) non-religion stance

> In France, the principle of **laïcité** is strictly upheld and the church has been separate from the state since 1905. There is no religious education in schools.

laid(e) [lɛ, lɛd] *adj* **1.** (*opp: beau*) ugly; **être ~ à faire peur** [*o* **comme un pou**] to be as ugly as sin *inf* **2.** (*moralement: action, défaut*) mean

laideron [lɛdʀɔ̃] *m* ugly duckling

laideur [lɛdœʀ] *f* ugliness

laie [lɛ] *f* forest track

lainage [lɛnaʒ] *m* **1.** (*étoffe*) wool **2.** (*vêtement*) wool(len) *Brit,* wool(en) *Am;* **jupe en/de ~** wool(len) skirt; **mettre un ~** to put on a jumper *Brit,* to put on a sweater *Am*

laine [lɛn] *f* **1.** (*fibre*) wool; **gilet de ~** wool jacket **2.** (*vêtement*) **une petite ~** a light cardigan **3.** (*laine minérale*) **~ de verre** glass wool

laineux, **-euse** [lɛnø, -øz] *adj* woolly

laïque [laik] *adj* layperson, layman *m,* laywoman *f*

laisse [lɛs] *f* (*lanière*) lead *Brit,* leash *Am;* **tenir un animal en ~** to keep an animal on a lead

laissé-pour-compte, **-ée-pour-compte** [lesepuʀkɔ̃t] <laissés-pour-compte> **I.** *adj* (*rejeté: personne*) rejected **II.** *m, f* (*exclu*) reject

laisser [lese] <1> **I.** *vt* **1.** (*faire rester*) to leave; **~ qn perplexe** to puzzle sb; **~ qn tranquille** to leave sb alone; **~ qn à ses illusions** to not disillusion sb **2.** (*accorder: choix*) to give; **~ la vie à qn** to spare sb's life; **~ la parole à qn** to let sb speak **3.** (*ne pas prendre*) to leave; **~ une route à sa droite** to go past a turning on one's right *Brit,* to go past a turn on one's right *Am* **4.** (*réserver: part de tarte*) to reserve; **~ qc à qn** to leave sth for sb **5.** (*quitter*) **je te/vous laisse!** I'm off!; **je l'ai laissé en pleine forme** when I last saw him he was in great shape **6.** (*déposer: personne*) to drop **7.** (*oublier*) to leave **8.** (*produire: traces, auréoles*) to leave **9.** (*remettre*) to leave; **~ ses enfants à qn** to leave one's children with sb; **laisse-moi le soin de ...** permit me to ... **10.** (*léguer*) **~ qc à qn** to bequeath sth to sb **II.** *aux* (*permettre*) **~ qn/qc** + *infin* to allow sb/sth to + *infin* ▶ **~ <u>faire</u>** to do nothing; **se ~ <u>faire</u>** (*subir*) not to put up a fight; **laisse-toi faire!** (*pour décider qn*) go on! *inf;* **<u>se</u> ~ boire** (*vin*) to go down well

laisser-aller [leseale] *m inv* carelessness

laisser-faire [lesefɛʀ] *m inv* laissez-faire policy

laissez-passer [lesepɑse] *m inv* pass

lait [lɛ] *m* **1.** (*aliment*) milk; **~ en poudre** powdered milk; **~ de vache** cow's milk; **~ condensé/entier** condensed/whole milk; **~ longue conservation** long-life milk; **petit ~** whey **2.** (*liquide laiteux*) lotion; **~ de toilette** (*pour le corps*) body lotion; (*pour le visage*) beauty lotion ▶ **boire du <u>petit</u> ~** to lap it up; **se boire comme du petit ~** to be easy to drink

laitage [lɛtaʒ] *m* milk products

laiterie [lɛtʀi] *f* **1.** (*industrie*) dairy industry **2.** (*secteur économique*) dairy farming

laiteux, **-euse** [lɛtø, -øz] *adj* milky

laitier, **-ière** [letje, -jɛʀ] *m, f* dairyman, dairywoman *m, f*

laiton [lɛtɔ̃] *m* brass

laitue [lety] *f* lettuce

laïus [lajys] *m inf* great spiel; **faire un ~** *iron* to make a long speech; **faire tout un ~ à qn** to go on and on to sb

lama [lama] *m* **1.** (*animal*) llama; **laine de ~** llama wool **2.** (*moine*) lama

lambeau [lɑ̃bo] <x> *m* scrap; **en ~x** in rags

lambin(e) [lɑ̃bɛ̃, in] *adj* dawdler

lambiner [lɑ̃bine] <1> *vi* to dawdle

lambris [lɑ̃bʀi] *m* **1.** (*boiserie*) panelling *Brit,* paneling *Am;* **revêtir de ~** to panel; **en ~** panelled *Brit,* paneled *Am* **2.** (*en stuc, marbre*) casing

lame [lam] *f* blade; **~ de couteau/scie** knife/saw blade

lamé [lame] *m* lamé; **robe en ~** lamé dress; **en ~ argent/or** silver/gold lamé

lamé(e) [lame] *adj* lamé; **tissu ~ argent/or** silver/gold lamé fabric

lamelle [lamɛl] *f* **1.** (*petite lame*) strip **2.** (*tranche fine*) slice

lamentable [lamɑ̃tabl] *adj* **1.** (*pitoyable: état, mine, salaire*) pitiful; (*ton, voix*) miserable; (*résultats, travail*) appalling **2.** (*honteux*) shameful

lamentations [lamɑ̃tasjɔ̃] *fpl* lamentations; **cessez vos ~!** stop moaning!

lamenter [lamɑ̃te] <1> *vpr* **se ~ sur qc** to moan about sth

laminer [lamine] <1> *vt* **1.** TECH to laminate **2.** (*écraser*) to squeeze; (*résistance*) to crush; **se faire ~ par qn** (*équipe, parti, troupe*) to be beaten hollow by sb; **être laminé** to be thrashed

laminoir [laminwaʀ] *m* IND rolling mill

lampadaire [lɑ̃padɛʀ] *m* **1.** (*lampe sur pied*) standard lamp *Brit,* floor lamp *Am* **2.** (*réverbère*) street lamp **3.** (*sur l'autoroute*) motorway light *Brit,* freeway light *Am*

lampe [lɑ̃p] *f* **1.** (*appareil*) lamp; **~ de bureau/chevet** desk/bedside lamp; **~ de poche** torch *Brit,* flashlight *Am;* **~ témoin** warning light **2.** (*ampoule*) bulb; **~ fluo-**

rescente fluorescent lamp
lampée [lɑ̃pe] *f inf* swig; **une bonne** ~ a big swig; **boire qc à grandes ~s** to swig sth down
lampion [lɑ̃pjɔ̃] *m* Chinese lantern
lampiste [lɑ̃pist] *mf peu usité, inf* dogsbody *Brit,* gofer *Am;* **encore une fois, on s'en prend au** ~ as usual, they go for the dogsbody
lamproie [lɑ̃pʀwa] *f* lamprey
lance [lɑ̃s] *f* **1.**(*arme*) spear **2.**(*tuyau*) hose; ~ **à eau/d'incendie** water/fire hose
lancée [lɑ̃se] *f* way; **sur ma/sa** ~ in my/his/her/its stride
lance-flammes [lɑ̃sflam] *m inv* flame-thrower
lancement [lɑ̃smɑ̃] *m* **1.**(*envoi*) *a.* COM launch; **prix de** ~ launch price **2.** INFOR start-up
lance-pierre [lɑ̃spjɛʀ] <lance-pierres> *m* catapult ►**manger avec un** ~ *inf* to shovel one's meal down
lancer [lɑ̃se] <2> **I.** *vt* **1.**(*projeter: jambe*) to fling; (*fusée*) to launch; (*coup*) to throw; ~ **de la lave** (*volcan*) to spew out lava **2.**(*faire connaître: mode, mouvement*) to launch; ~ **un acteur** to set an actor on the road to fame **3.**(*donner de l'élan: moteur, voiture*) to start; (*marque, produit, entreprise*) to launch; ~ **qn/un animal sur qn** to set sb/an animal on sb; ~ **la police sur qn/qc** to set the police on sb/sth; **quand il est lancé, on ne l'arrête plus** once he's got going, you can't stop him **4.**(*inaugurer: programme, campagne, projet*) to launch **5.**(*envoyer: nouvelle*) to send; (*ultimatum*) to give **6.**(*émettre: accusation, menace*) to hurl; ~ **un appel à qn** to (launch an) appeal to sb **7.** INFOR to start up **II.** *vpr* **1.**(*se précipiter*) **se** ~ **sur le lit** to leap onto the bed; **se** ~ **à la poursuite de qn** to dash after sb; **allez, lance-toi!** go on, go for it! *inf* **2.**(*s'engager*) **se** ~ **dans qc** to embark on sth; **se** ~ **dans une discussion** to get involved in a discussion; **se** ~ **dans le cinéma** to launch oneself into film *Brit,* to launch oneself into the movies *Am* **III.** *m* SPORT throw; (*du poids*) shot put; ~ **de javelot** throwing the javelin
lanceur [lɑ̃sœʀ] *m* AVIAT launcher
lancinant(e) [lɑ̃sinɑ̃, ɑ̃t] *adj* (*cuisant: douleur*) shooting
landau [lɑ̃do] <s> *m* (*pour enfant*) pram *Brit,* baby carriage *Am*
lande [lɑ̃d] *f* moor
Landes [lɑ̃d] *fpl* **les** ~ the Landes, *region in the South-West of France*
langage [lɑ̃gaʒ] *m* **1.**(*idiome*) *a.* INFOR language; ~ **des sourds-muets** sign language; ~ **de programmation** programming language **2.**(*jargon*) jargon ►**tenir un double** ~ **à qn** to tell sb different things at different times
langer [lɑ̃ʒe] <2a> *vt* ~ **un bébé** to change a baby's nappy *Brit,* to change a baby's diaper *Am*
langoureux, -euse [lɑ̃guʀø, -øz] *adj* languid
langouste [lɑ̃gust] *f* crayfish *Brit,* rock lobster *Am*
langoustine [lɑ̃gustin] *f* Dublin Bay prawn
langue [lɑ̃g] *f* **1.** ANAT tongue; **tirer la** ~ **à qn** to stick out one's tongue at sb **2.**(*langage*) language; ~ **étrangère/maternelle** foreign/mother tongue; ~ **verte** underworld slang ►~ **de bois** political doublespeak; **tourner sept fois sa** ~ **dans sa bouche avant de parler** to think before one speaks; **donner sa** ~ **au chat** to give up; **ne pas avoir la** ~ **dans sa poche** to never be at a loss for words; **être mauvaise** ~ to be a nasty gossip; **avoir la** ~ **bien pendue** to have a ready tongue; **tenir sa** ~ to hold one's tongue
langue-de-chat [lɑ̃gdəʃa] <langues-de-chat> *f* langue de chat
languedocien(ne) [lɑ̃g(ə)dɔsjɛ̃, ɛn] *adj* of the Languedoc
Languedocien(ne) [lɑ̃g(ə)dɔsjɛ̃, ɛn] *m(f)* person from the Languedoc
languette [lɑ̃gɛt] *f* (*patte: d'une chaussure*) tongue; (*d'une boîte*) strip
languir [lɑ̃giʀ] <8> **I.** *vi* **1.**(*s'enliser: conversation*) to flag **2.**(*patienter*) **faire** ~ **qn** to make sb wait **II.** *vpr* **se** ~ **de qn** to pine for sb
languissant(e) [lɑ̃gisɑ̃, ɑ̃t] *adj* **1.**(*action, récit, ton*) listless; (*conversation*) flagging; (*regard*) languid; **ton de voix** ~ languid tone of voice **2.**(*défaillant: santé*) failing; (*affaires, personne*) ailing
lanière [lanjɛʀ] *f* strip
lanterne [lɑ̃tɛʀn] *f* lantern ►~ **rouge** rear light *Brit,* taillight *Am;* **éclairer la** ~ **de qn** to enlighten sb
lanterner [lɑ̃tɛʀne] <1> *vi* **1.**(*traîner*) to dawdle **2.**(*attendre*) **faire** ~ **qn** to keep sb hanging aroud
lapalissade [lapalisad] *f* statement of the obvious
laper [lape] <1> *vt* to lap up
lapereau [lapʀo] <x> *m* young rabbit
lapidaire [lapidɛʀ] *adj* succinct
lapider [lapide] <1> *vt* **1.**(*attaquer*) to stone **2.**(*tuer*) to stone (to death)
lapin [lapɛ̃] *m* ZOOL, GASTR rabbit; ~ **de garenne** wild rabbit; **courir comme un** ~ to run like the wind; *v. a.* **lapine** ►**le coup du** ~ whiplash; **chaud** ~ *inf* horny so-and-so; **poser un** ~ **à qn** *inf* to stand sb up
lapine [lapin] *f* ZOOL rabbit; *v. a.* **lapin**
lapinisme [lapinism] *m fam* overbreeding
laps [laps] *m* ~ **de temps** time lapse
lapsus [lapsys] *m* slip
laquais [lakɛ] *m* lackey
laque [lak] *f* **1.**(*pour les cheveux*) hair spray **2.**(*peinture*) lacquer
laqué(e) [lake] *adj* **1.**(*peint*) lacquered **2.** GASTR **canard** ~ Peking duck
laquelle [lakɛl] *pron v.* **lequel**
laquer [lake] <1> *vt* ~ **qc en blanc/noir** to lacquer sth in black/white
larbin [laʀbɛ̃] *m péj, inf* flunkey; **avoir une mentalité de** ~ to have the mind of a flunkey
lard [laʀ] *m* bacon; ~ **gras** streaky bacon; ~

maigre back bacon ▸**ne pas savoir si c'est du ~ ou du cochon** to not know where one stands; **n'être ni ~ ni cochon** to be neither one thing nor the other; **gros ~** fat lump

larder [laʀde] <1> *vt* **1.** GASTR to lard **2.** (*blesser*) **~ qn d'une lance** to run through sb with a lance; **les bras lardés de piqûres de seringue** with arms covered in needle marks

lardon [laʀdɔ̃] *m* GASTR lardon

large [laʀʒ] **I.** *adj* **1.** (*opp: étroit*) wide; (*cercle*) large; **être ~ de carrure** to have a large build; **être ~ d'épaules** to have broad shoulders; **~ de 10 mètres** 10 metres wide *Am,* 10 meters wide *Am* **2.** (*ample: vêtement*) loose **3.** (*important*) big; (*champ d'action, diffusion*) wide; **un ~ débat** a wide-ranging debate; **de ~s extraits** extensive extracts **4.** (*ouvert: acception, sens*) broad; **avoir les idées ~s** to be open-minded; **~ d'esprit** broad-minded **II.** *adv* (*calculer*) on the generous side; **voir ~** to think big ▸**ne pas en mener ~** *inf* to have one's heart in one's boots **III.** *m* **1.** (*haute mer*) open sea **2.** (*largeur*) **un champ de 30 mètres de ~** a field 30 metres wide *Brit,* a field 30 meters wide *Am* ▸**prendre le ~** *inf* (*s'enfuir*) to clear off; (*s'esquiver*) to sneak away; **au ~ de la côte** off the coast

largement [laʀʒəmɑ̃] *adv* **1.** (*opp: étroitement*) wide **2.** (*amplement*) **vous avez ~ le temps** you have plenty of time; **~ assez** more than enough; **~ trop** far too much **3.** (*généreusement*) generously **4.** (*au minimum*) at least; **il est ~ onze heures** it's well past eleven o'clock **5.** *inf* (*assez*) **c'est ~ suffisant** it is more than enough; **il y en a déjà ~** there is already enough

largesse [laʀʒɛs] *f* **1.** *pl* (*dons*) gifts; **faire des ~s** to bestow gifts **2.** *soutenu* (*générosité*) largesse

largeur [laʀʒœʀ] *f* **1.** (*dimension*) width **2.** (*opp: mesquinerie*) **~ d'esprit** generosity of spirit ▸**dans les grandes ~s** *inf* well and truly

larguer [laʀge] <1> *vt* **1.** NAUT (*ancre*) to slip; (*voile*) to unfurl **2.** AVIAT to release; (*parachutistes, troupes*) to drop **3.** *inf* (*laisser tomber: projets, travail*) to give up; **~ un ami** to dump a friend

larme [laʀm] *f* **1.** (*pleur*) tear; **en ~s** in tears **2.** *inf* (*goutte*) drop ▸**avoir la ~ à l'œil** to have a tear in one's eye; **avoir des ~s dans la voix** to sob; **avoir les ~s aux yeux** to have tears in one's eyes; **avoir la ~ facile** to cry easily; **fondre en ~s** to dissolve into tears

larmoyer [laʀmwaje] <6> *vi* **1.** (*œil*) to weep; (*voix*) to whine; **faire ~ qn** to make sb weep **2.** (*pleurnicher*) **~ sur qc** to weep over sth

larve [laʀv] *f* **1.** ZOOL larva **2.** (*personne déchue*) worm *inf*

larvé(e) [laʀve] *adj a.* MED latent; (*inflation*) creeping; (*guerre*) waiting to break out

laryngite [laʀɛ̃ʒit] *f* laryngitis

larynx [laʀɛ̃ks] *m* larynx

las(se) [lɑ, lɑs] *adj* (*personne*) tired; (*geste*) weary

lasagne [lazaɲ] <(s)> *f* lasagne [*o* lasagna]

lascif, -ive [lasif, -iv] *adj* lascivious

laser [lazɛʀ] **I.** *m* laser **II.** *app* compact disc; **platine ~** compact disc player

lassant(e) [lɑsɑ̃, ɑ̃t] *adj* tiresome; **les enfants, vous êtes ~s!** you children are so tiring!

lasser [lɑse] <1> **I.** *vt* to tire; **~ la patience de qn** to wear sb's patience thin **II.** *vpr* **se ~ de qc** to tire of sth; **sans se ~** without tiring oneself

lassitude [lɑsityd] *f* **1.** (*fatigue physique*) fatigue **2.** (*fatigue morale*) weariness; **accepter par ~** to agree out of weariness

lasso [laso] *m* lasso; **prendre au ~** to lasso

latent(e) [latɑ̃, ɑ̃t] *adj* latent

latéral(e) [lateʀal, o] <-aux> *adj* (*de côté*) lateral; **porte ~e** side door

latex [latɛks] *m* latex

latin [latɛ̃] *m* Latin; *v. a.* **français** ▸**j'y perds mon ~** I can't make head or tail of it

latin(e) [latɛ̃, in] *adj* **1.** Latin **2.** (*opp: anglo-saxon, orthodoxe*) latin

latinisme [latinism] *m* latinism

latiniste [latinist] *mf* **1.** (*étudiant, élève*) Latin student **2.** (*spécialiste*) latinist

latino-américain(e) [latinoameʀikɛ̃, ɛn] <latino-américains> *adj* Latin-American

Latino-américain(e) [latinoameʀikɛ̃, ɛn] <Latino-américains> *m(f)* Latin-American

latitude [latityd] *f* **1.** GEO latitude; **être à 45° de ~ nord** to be at latitude 45° north **2.** *pl* (*régions*) **sous nos ~s** in our regions **3.** (*liberté*) **toute ~** complete freedom

latte [lat] *f* (*planche*) slat

laudatif, -ive [lodatif, -iv] *adj* laudatory

lauréat(e) [lɔʀea, at] **I.** *adj* award-winning; **les élèves/étudiants ~s** prize-winning students **II.** *m(f)* award-winner; **~ du prix Nobel** Nobel prize winner

laurier [lɔʀje] *m* **1.** BOT bay tree **2.** GASTR bay **3.** *pl* (*gloire*) praise; **s'endormir sur ses ~s** to rest on one's laurels

laurier-rose [lɔʀjeʀoz] <lauriers-roses> *m* oleander

lausannois(e) [lɔzanwa, waz] *adj* of Lausanne; *v. a.* **ajaccien**

Lausannois(e) [lɔzanwa, waz] *m(f)* person from Lausanne; *v. a.* **Ajaccien**

lavable [lavabl] *adj* washable; **~ en machine** machine-washable; **~ uniquement à la main** handwash only

lavabo [lavabo] *m* **1.** (*cuvette*) washbasin **2.** *pl* (*toilettes*) toilets

lavage [lavaʒ] *m* washing; **au ~** in the wash; **au troisième ~** during the third wash ▸**~ de cerveau** brainwashing; **~ d'estomac** stomach pumping

lavande [lavɑ̃d] *f* lavender

L

lave [lav] *f* lava
lave-glace [lavglas] <lave-glaces> *m* windscreen washer *Brit,* windshield washer *Am;* **donner un coup de** ~ to wash the windscreen **lave-linge** [lavlɛ̃ʒ] *m inv* washing machine
lavement [lavmɑ̃] *m* **1.** MED enema **2.** REL washing
laver [lave] <1> **I.** *vt* **1.** (*nettoyer*) to clean; (*vaisselle, sol*) to wash; (*mur*) to wash (down); ~ **qc à la machine** to machine-wash sth; ~ **qc à la serpillière** to mop sth; ~ **qc à l'éponge** to sponge sth (down); ~ **qc à la main** to hand-wash sth; ~ **qc au lave-vaisselle** to wash sth in the dishwasher **2.** (*disculper*) ~ **qn d'un soupçon** to clear sb of a suspicion **II.** *vpr* **1.** (*se nettoyer*) **se** ~ to wash (oneself); **se** ~ **les dents** to brush one's teeth **2.** (*être lavable*) **se** ~ to be washable; **se** ~ **à 90°** washes at 90°
laverie [lavʀi] *f* laundry; ~ **automatique** laundrette *Brit,* laundromat *Am*
lavette [lavɛt] *f* **1.** (*chiffon*) dish cloth **2.** *inf* (*personne*) drip **3.** *Suisse* (*gant*) facecloth *Brit,* washcloth *Am*
laveur, **-euse** [lavœʀ, -øz] *m, f* ~ **de carreaux** window cleaner; ~ **de voitures** car washer
laveuse [lavøz] *f Québec* (*lave-linge*) washing machine
lave-vaisselle [lavvɛsɛl] *m inv* dishwasher
lavoir [lavwaʀ] *m* washhouse
laxatif [laksatif] *m* laxative
laxatif, **-ive** [laksatif, -iv] *adj* laxative; **être** ~ to have a laxative effect
laxisme [laksism] *m* laxism
laxiste [laksist] *adj* overindulgent
layette [lɛjɛt] *f* layette
le [lə] <*devant voyelle ou h muet* l'> **I.** *art déf* the **II.** *pron pers, masc* **1.** (*personne*) **elle** ~ **voit/l'aide** she sees/helps him **2.** (*animal ou objet*) **là-bas, il y a un cochon/sac,** ~ **vois-tu?** there's a pig/bag over there, can you see it? **3.** (*valeur neutre*) **je** ~ **comprends** I understand; **je l'espère!** I hope so! **4.** *avec un présentatif* ~ **voici/voilà!** here/there he [*o* it] is!
lé [le] *m* (*d'une étoffe, d'un papier peint*) length
leader [lidœʀ] **I.** *m* leader; **être** ~ **du classement** to be at the top in the table **II.** *adj inv* leader
leasing [liziŋ] *m* leasing
lèche [lɛʃ] *f inf* **faire de la** ~ **à qn** to lick sb's boots
lèche-botte [lɛʃbɔt] <lèche-bottes> *mf inf* bootlicker **lèche-cul** [lɛʃky] <lèche-culs> *mf vulg* arse-licker *Brit,* ass kisser *Am*
lécher [leʃe] <5> **I.** *vt* (*assiette, cuillère, bol, plat*) to lick (clean); (*visage, glace*) to lick; (*lait*) to lap up **II.** *vpr* **se** ~ **les lèvres** to lick one's lips
lèche-vitrines [lɛʃvitʀin] *m sans pl* window shopping; **faire du** ~ to go window shopping
leçon [l(ə)sɔ̃] *f a.* ECOLE lesson; **servir de** ~ **à qn** to be a lesson to sb
lecteur [lɛktœʀ] *m* **1.** MEDIA player; ~ **de son** music player; ~ **de cassettes/CD** tape/CD player; ~ **laser vidéo** video disc player **2.** INFOR drive; ~ **de CD-ROM/disquettes/DVD** CD-ROM/disk/DVD drive; ~ **optique** optical character reader; **introduire une disquette dans le** ~ **de disquette** to insert a floppy disk into the disk drive
lecteur, **-trice** [lɛktœʀ, -tʀis] *m, f* **1.** (*liseur, personne qui fait la lecture*) reader **2.** UNIV, ECOLE teaching assistant
lecture [lɛktyʀ] *f* **1.** (*action de lire*) reading; **aimer la** ~ to like reading **2.** (*action de lire à haute voix*) reading out loud; **faire la** ~ **de qc à qn** to read sth to sb; **donner** ~ **de qc** to read sth out **3.** (*qc qui se lit*) *a.* CINE, TV, INFOR reading; **il lui a donné de la** ~ he gave her something to read; ~ **optique** optical character reading
ledit, **ladite** [lədi, ladit, ledi, ledit] <lesdit(e)s> *adj antéposé* the aforesaid
légal(e) [legal, o] <-aux> *adj* legal; (*fête*) public; (*heure*) standard
légalement [legalmɑ̃] *adv* legally
légaliser [legalize] <1> *vt* **1.** (*autoriser*) to legalize **2.** (*authentifier*) to authenticate
légalité [legalite] *f* (*respect de la loi*) legality; **sortir de la** ~ to step beyond the law
légataire [legatɛʀ] *mf* legatee; ~ **universel** sole legatee
légendaire [leʒɑ̃dɛʀ] *adj* **1.** (*mythique: animal*) mythical; (*figure, histoire*) legendary **2.** (*célèbre*) famous
légende [leʒɑ̃d] *f* **1.** (*mythe*) legend; **un personnage de** ~ a legendary character **2.** (*explication: d'une carte, d'un plan*) key; (*d'une photo*) caption
léger, **-ère** [leʒe, -ɛʀ] *adj* **1.** (*opp: lourd*) light; (*vêtement*) light(weight); **poids** ~ lightweight **2.** (*de faible intensité*) slight; (*peine*) mild; (*doute, soupçon*) faint; (*couche de neige*) thin; **blessures** ~**s** slight injuries **3.** (*insouciant*) **d'un cœur** ~ with a light heart **4.** *péj* (*superficiel*) thoughtless ►**à la légère** thoughtlessly; **tout prendre à la légère** to take nothing seriously
légèrement [leʒɛʀmɑ̃] *adv* **1.** (*un peu, vraiment*) slightly **2.** (*avec des choses légères*) lightly; **s'habiller** ~ to wear summer clothes **3.** (*avec grâce, délicatement*) nimbly; **marcher plus** ~ to tread more lightly
légèreté [leʒɛʀte] *f* **1.** (*faible poids*) lightness **2.** (*insouciance*) frivolity **3.** (*superficialité*) thoughtlessness
légiférer [leʒifeʀe] <5> *vi* to legislate
Légion [leʒjɔ̃] *f* **1.** MIL ~ **étrangère** Foreign Legion **2.** (*décoration*) ~ **d'honneur** Legion of Honour *Brit,* Legion of Honor *Am*

The **Légion étrangère** was formed in France in 1831, in connection with the colonialization of Algeria. This powerful and unrelenting army can be brought in rapidly and without parliamentary consent. Half of the soldiers are French and half non-French. The majority of them are stationed in France, the rest overseas.

légionnaire [leʒjɔnɛʀ] I. *m* 1. HIST legionary 2. MIL legionnaire II. *mf* (*membre de la Légion d'Honneur*) member of the Legion of Honour *Brit*, member of the Legion of Honor *Am*
législateur, **-trice** [leʒislatœʀ, -tʀis] *m, f* legislator
législatif, **-ive** [leʒislatif, -iv] *adj* legislative
législation [leʒislasjɔ̃] *f* legislation
législatives [leʒislativ] *fpl* general election + *vb sing*
légiste [leʒist] *mf* legist
légitime [leʒitim] *adj a.* JUR legitimate; **femme** ~ lawful wife
légitimement [leʒitimmɑ̃] *adv* rightly; JUR legitimately
légitimer [leʒitime] <1> *vt* 1. (*justifier*) to justify 2. JUR to legitimate
légitimité [leʒitimite] *f* legitimacy; **en toute** ~ completely legitimately
legs [lɛ(g)] *m* JUR bequest; **faire un** ~ **à un musée** to make a bequest to a museum
léguer [lege] <5> *vt* JUR ~ **qc à qn** to bequeath sth to sb
légume [legym] I. *m* vegetable; ~**s secs** pulses II. *f* **une** <u>**grosse**</u> ~ *inf* a big cheese
légumier, **-ière** [legymje, -jɛʀ] *m, f Belgique* (*marchand*) produce merchant, greengrocer *Brit*
légumineuse [legyminøz] *f* legume
leitmotiv <- *o* e> [lajtmɔtif, lɛtmɔtiv] *m* leitmotiv [*o* leitmotif]
lendemain [lɑ̃dmɛ̃] *m* 1. *sans pl* (*jour suivant*) **le** ~ the following day; **le** ~ **soir** the following evening; **du jour au** ~ from one day to the next 2. (*temps qui suit*) **au** ~ **du mariage** after the wedding 3. (*avenir*) future ►**il ne faut jamais** <u>**remettre**</u> **au** ~ **ce qu'on peut faire le jour même** *prov* one should never put off until tomorrow what can be done today *prov*
lénifiant(e) [lenifjɑ̃, jɑ̃t] *adj* soothing
lent(e) [lɑ̃, lɑ̃t] *adj* slow; (*esprit*) slow-witted; **aller à pas** ~**s** to go slowly
lentement [lɑ̃tmɑ̃] *adv* slowly ►~, **mais** <u>**sûrement**</u> slowly but surely
lenteur [lɑ̃tœʀ] *f* slowness; ~ **d'esprit** slow-wittedness; **se déplacer avec** ~ to move slowly
lentille [lɑ̃tij] *f* 1. BOT, GASTR lentil 2. (*en optique*) lens; ~**s de contact** contact lenses
Léonard [leɔnaːʀ] *m* HIST ~ **de Vinci** Leonardo da Vinci
léopard [leɔpaʀ] *m* 1. ZOOL leopard; ~ **femelle** leopardess 2. (*fourrure*) leopard-skin
lepénisme [løpenism] *m: right wing political ideology instigated by Jean-Marie Le Pen*
lèpre [lɛpʀ] *f* MED leprosy
lépreux, **-euse** [lepʀø, -øz] I. *adj* 1. MED leprous 2. (*rongé*) flaking II. *m, f* leper
lequel, **laquelle** [ləkɛl, lakɛl, lekɛl] <lesquels, lesquelles> I. *pron interrog* which; **regarde cette fille! – laquelle?** look at that girl! – which one?; ~/**laquelle d'entre vous ...?** which of you ...?; **auxquels de ces messieurs devrai-je m'adresser?** to which of these gentlemen should I speak?; **demandez à l'un de vos élèves, n'importe** ~**!** ask any of your students, doesn't matter which!; **je ne sais lesquels prendre!** I don't know which ones to take! II. *pron rel* 1. (*se rapportant à une personne*) who(m); **la concierge, laquelle ...** the caretaker, who ...; **la personne à laquelle je fais allusion** the person to whom I am referring; **les grévistes, au nombre desquels il se trouve** the strikers, among whom there is 2. (*se rapportant à un animal, un objet*) which; **la situation délicate dans laquelle nous nous trouvons** the delicate situation in which we find ourselves; **la liberté, au nom de laquelle ...** freedom, in whose name ...
les [le] I. *art déf* the II. *pron pers, pl* 1. (*personnes, animaux, objets*) them 2. *avec un présentatif* they; ~ **voici/voilà !** here/there they are!
lesbien(ne) [lɛzbjɛ̃, jɛn] *adj* lesbian
lesbienne [lɛzbjɛn] *f* lesbian
léser [leze] <5> *vt* 1. (*désavantager*) to damage; **partie lésée** injured party 2. (*nuire*) ~ **les intérêts de qn** to be against sb's interests
lésiner [lezine] <1> *vi* ~ **sur qc** to skimp on sth
lésion [lezjɔ̃] *f* lesion
lésothan(ne) [lezotɑ̃, an] *adj* Mosotho
Lésothan(ne) [lezotɑ̃, an] *m(f)* Mosotho
Lesotho [lezoto] *m* **le** ~ Lesotho
lessivable [lesivabl] *adj* washable
lessive [lesiv] *f* 1. (*détergent*) detergent; ~ **en poudre/liquide** washing powder/liquid 2. (*lavage, linge à laver*) washing; **jour de** ~ washday; **faire la** ~ to do the washing
lessiver [lesive] <1> *vt* 1. (*nettoyer: pièce, sol*) to wash; (*murs*) to wash (down) 2. *inf* (*épuiser*) **être lessivé** to be worn out
lest [lɛst] *m* ballast
leste [lɛst] *adj* 1. (*vif*) sprightly 2. (*grivois*) crude
lester [lɛste] <1> I. *vt* 1. (*garnir de lest*) to ballast; **être lesté de qc** to be ballasted with sth 2. *inf* (*remplir*) ~ **ses poches** to line one's pockets II. *vpr inf* **se** ~ to stuff oneself; **se** ~ **l'estomac** to feed one's face
léthargie [letaʀʒi] *f* lethargy; **sortir qn de sa** ~ to shake sb out of their lethargic state
letton [lɛtɔ̃] *m* Latvian; *v. a.* **français**
letton(e) [lɛtɔ̃, ɔn] *adj* Latvian
Letton(e) [lɛtɔ̃, ɔn] *m(f)* Latvian

L

Lettonie [lɛtɔni] *f* **la** ~ Latvia

lettre [lɛtʀ] *f* **1.** (*missive, signe graphique*) letter; ~ **d'affaires/d'amour/de menaces** business/love/threatening letter; ~ **de candidature** letter of application; **mettre une** ~ **à la poste** to post a letter; **par** ~ by post; **c'est en grosses** ~**s dans les journaux** it's made the headlines **2.** *pl* UNIV (*opp: sciences*) arts; **professeur de** ~**s** French teacher **3.** *sans pl* (*sens strict*) **à la** ~ to the letter; **prendre qc à la** ~ to take sth literally ▶**passer comme une** ~ **à la poste** *inf* to go off smoothly; (*proposition*) to be accepted easily; **en toutes** ~**s** (*opp: en chiffres*) in words; (*sans abréviation*) in full; (*écrit noir sur blanc*) in black and white; (*sans doute possible*) definitely

leucémie [løsemi] *f* MED leukaemia *Brit,* leukemia *Am*

leur[1] [lœʀ] *pron pers, inv* **1.** (*personnes, animaux, objets*) them **2.** (*avec un sens possessif*) **le cœur** ~ **battait fort** their hearts were beating fast; *v. a.* **me**

leur[2] [lœʀ] <leurs> **I.** *dét poss* their; *v. a.* **ma, mon II.** *pron poss* **1. le/la** ~ their; **les** ~**s** theirs; *v. a.* **mien 2.** *pl* (*ceux de leur famille*) **les** ~**s** their family; (*leurs partisans*) their people; **vous êtes des** ~**s** you are with them; *v. a.* **mien** ▶**ils y mettent du** ~ they pull their weight

leurre [lœʀ] *m* **1.** (*artifice*) illusion **2.** (*à la peche, à la chasse*) lure; MIL decoy

leurrer [lœʀe] <1> **I.** *vt* to delude; **se laisser** ~ **par qc** to be taken in by sth **II.** *vpr* **se** ~ to delude oneself

leurs [lœʀ] *v.* **leur**

levage [ləvaʒ] *m* **1.** GASTR (*d'une pâte*) rising **2.** (*action de soulever*) lifting

levain [ləvɛ̃] *m* (*pour pain, pour gâteau*) leaven; **pain au/sans** ~ leavened/unleavened bread

levant [ləvɑ̃] *m* (*est*) east

levée [l(ə)ve] *f* collection; **heures de** ~ collection times

lever [l(ə)ve] <4> **I.** *vt* **1.** (*soulever*) to lift; (*jambe, tête, visage*) to raise; ~ **la main** to raise one's hand; ~ **les yeux vers qn** to look up at sb; **ne pas** ~ **le nez de son livre** not to look up from one's book **2.** (*sortir du lit*) ~ **un enfant/un malade** to get a child/a sick person out of bed; **faire** ~ **qn** to make sb get up **3.** (*faire cesser*) **être levé** (*séance*) to come to an end **II.** *vpr* **se** ~ **1.** (*se mettre debout, sortir du lit*) to get up; **se** ~ **de table** to leave the table **2.** (*commencer à paraître: lune, soleil*) to rise; (*jour, aube*) to break **3.** (*se soulever: rideau, main*) to go up **4.** (*commencer à s'agiter: mer*) to rise; (*vent*) to get up **5.** (*devenir meilleur: temps, brouillard*) to clear **III.** *vi* **1.** (*gonfler: pâte*) to rise **2.** (*pousser*) to come up **IV.** *m* **au** ~ **du soleil** at sunrise; ~ **du jour** daybreak

lève-tard [lɛvtaʀ] *mf inv, inf* late riser **lève-tôt** [lɛvto] *mf inv, inf* early riser **lève-vitre** [lɛvvitʀ] <lève-vitres> *m* window lever

levier [ləvje] *m* (*tige de commande, pour lever*) lever; ~ **de commande/de** (**changement de**) **vitesse** control/gear lever; **faire** ~ **sur qc** to lever sth up ▶**être aux** ~**s de commande** to be in control

levraut [ləvʀo] *m* leveret

lèvre [lɛvʀ] *f* **1.** ANAT lip; ~ **inférieure/supérieure** lower/upper lip; **la cigarette aux** ~**s** a cigarette between one's lips **2.** *pl* (*parties de la vulve*) labia ▶**ne pas desserrer les** ~**s** not to open one's mouth

lévrier [levʀije] *m* greyhound

levure [l(ə)vyʀ] *f a.* CHIM yeast; ~ **de boulanger** bakers' yeast; ~ **chimique/de bière** dried/brewers' yeast

lexicographie [lɛksikɔgʀafi] *f* lexicography

lexique [lɛksik] *m* **1.** (*dictionnaire bilingue*) lexicon; (*en fin d'ouvrage*) glossary **2.** (*vocabulaire*) lexis

lézard [lezaʀ] *m* lizard

lézarde [lezaʀd] *f* crack

lézardé(e) [lezaʀde] *adj* cracked

lézarder[1] [lezaʀde] <1> *vi inf* to bask in the sun

lézarder[2] [lezaʀde] <1> *vt, vpr* (**se**) ~ to crack

liaison [ljɛzɔ̃] *f* **1.** (*contact*) contact; ~ **radio/téléphonique** radio/telephone link; **mettre qn en** ~ **avec qn** to put sb in contact with sb; **restons en** ~**!** (let's) stay in touch!; **travailler en** ~ **étroite avec qn** to work in close contact with sb **2.** (*enchaînement*) connection; **sans** ~ **avec le reste** without any connection to the rest **3.** LING liaison **4.** (*relation amoureuse*) affair

liane [ljan] *f* creeper

liant [ljɑ̃] *m* **1.** (*d'un métal*) flexibility **2.** (*substance: d'un vernis*) binder

liant(e) [ljɑ̃, ljɑ̃t] *adj* sociable; **avoir l'esprit** ~ to have a sociable outlook

liasse [ljas] *f* (*de documents*) bundle; (*de billets*) wad

Liban [libɑ̃] *m* **le** ~ Lebanon

libanais [libanɛ] *m* Lebanese; *v. a.* **français**

libanais(e) [libanɛ, ɛz] *adj* Lebanese

Libanais(e) [libanɛ, ɛz] *m(f)* Lebanese

libeller [libele] <1> *vt* (*remplir, rédiger: chèque*) to make out; (*contrat*) to draw up

libellule [libelyl] *f* dragonfly

libéral(e) [libeʀal, o] <-aux> **I.** *adj* liberal **II.** *m(f)* POL Liberal

libéralisme [libeʀalism] *m* **1.** ECON, POL free market philosophy **2.** (*tolérance*) liberalism

libérateur, -trice [libeʀatœʀ, -tʀis] **I.** *adj* liberating **II.** *m, f* liberator

libération [libeʀasjɔ̃] *f* **1.** (*mise en liberté*) release **2.** (*délivrance*) *a. fig* liberation; **la** ~ **de la femme** Women's Liberation

Libération [libeʀasjɔ̃] *f* **la** ~ the Liberation *(the liberation of French territory occupied by German troops during the Second World War)*

libéré(e) [libeʀe] *adj* (*émancipé*) liberated

libérer [libeʀe] <5> **I.** *vt* **1.** (*relâcher*) to discharge **2.** (*délivrer*) to free **3.** (*décharger*) ~ **qn de sa dette** to relieve sb of his debt; ~ **qn d'une promesse** to release sb from a promise **4.** (*dégager: voie*) to unblock **5.** (*rendre disponible: chambre*) to free; **cela me libérerait un peu de temps** that will give me some time **II.** *vpr* **1.** (*se délivrer*) **se** ~ **de ses liens** to free oneself from one's ties; **se** ~ **de ses soucis** to relieve oneself of one's worries **2.** (*se rendre libre*) **se** ~ to get away **3.** (*devenir vacant*) **se** ~ (*poste, place*) to become free

Libéria [libeʀia] *m* **le** ~ Liberia

libérien(ne) [libeʀjɛ̃, ɛn] *adj* Liberian

Libérien(ne) [libeʀjɛ̃, ɛn] *m(f)* Liberian

liberté [libɛʀte] *f* **1.** *sans pl* (*opp: oppression, emprisonnement*) freedom, liberty; **mise en** ~ **d'un prisonnier politique** release of a political prisoner; **en** ~ (*opp: en captivité*) in the wild; (*opp: en prison*) free; **être en** ~ **provisoire/surveillée** to be on bail/probation; **rendre la** ~ **à qn** to give someone back his freedom **2.** *sans pl* (*loisir*) leisure; **quelques heures/jours de** ~ a few hours/days off **3.** (*droit, indépendance, absence de contrainte*) freedom; ~**s syndicales** union rights; **laisser toute** ~ **à qn** to give sb complete freedom; **parler en toute** ~ to speak freely ▸**Liberté, Égalité, Fraternité** Liberty, Equality, Fraternity; **prendre des** ~**s avec qn** (*être trop familier*) to take liberties with sb; (*sexuellement*) to take advantage of sb

libido [libido] *f* libido

libraire [libʀɛʀ] *mf* bookseller

librairie [libʀeʀi] *f* bookshop *Brit,* bookstore *Am;* **en** ~ in bookshops

librairie-papeterie [libʀɛʀipapɛtʀi] <librairies-papeteries> *f* book and stationery shop

libre [libʀ] *adj* **1.** *a.* POL free; **la «zone** ~**»** the unoccupied zone (*the parts of French territory unoccupied by German troops during the Second World War*)**;** **elle est** ~ **de ses choix** she's free to make her own choices; **ne pas être** ~ (*personne*) not to be available **2.** (*opp: marié: personne*) single **3.** (*sans contrainte: discussion, esprit*) open; **être** ~ **de tout préjugé/engagement** to be free of any prejudice/commitment **4.** (*opp: entravé: cheveux*) loose; **laisser la taille/le cou** ~ (*robe*) to be loose-waisted/wide-necked **5.** (*autorisé*) **entrée** ~ please come in **6.** ECOLE, UNIV independent **7.** SPORT **exercices/figures** ~**s** freestyle

librement [libʀəmɑ̃] *adv* freely; **respirer plus** ~ to breathe more easily

libre-service [libʀəsɛʀvis] <libres-services> *m* **1.** (*magasin*) self-service shop **2.** (*restaurant*) self-service restaurant **3.** *sans pl* (*système de vente*) self-service

Libye [libi] *f* **la** ~ Libya

licence [lisɑ̃s] *f* **1.** UNIV degree; ~ **ès sciences** science degree; **faire une** ~ **d'allemand** to do a German degree **2.** COM, JUR licence *Brit,* license *Am;* ~ **de débit de boisson** bar licence; **fabriqué sous** ~ manufactured under licence **3.** SPORT permit; **joueur titulaire d'une** ~ authorized player

> The **licence** is an academic qualification, awarded after three years of university study in France, four in Belgium. In Switzerland, it is an academic qualification for humanities, economics and legal faculties.

licencié(e) [lisɑ̃sje] *adj* **1.** UNIV graduate **2.** (*renvoyé*) fired

licenciement [lisɑ̃simɑ̃] *m* dismissal; ~ **collectif** mass redundancy *Brit,* mass lay-offs *Am;* ~ **économique** redundancy *Brit,* lay-off *Am*

licencier [lisɑ̃sje] <1> *vt* to fire

lichen [likɛn] *m* BOT lichen

lichette [liʃɛt] *f Belgique* (*petite attache servant à suspendre un vêtement, un torchon*) tag

licorne [likɔʀn] *f* unicorn

lie [li] *f* (*dépôt*) deposit; ~ **de vin** wine sediment

lié(e) [lje] *adj* (*proche*) **être** ~ **avec qn** to be friendly with sb

Liechtenstein [liʃtɛnʃtajn] *m* **le** ~ Liechtenstein

lie-de-vin [lidvɛ̃] *adj inv* wine-coloured *Brit,* wine-colored *Am*

liège [ljɛʒ] *m* cork; **bouchon de** ~ cork

Liège [ljɛʒ] Liège

liégeois(e) [ljeʒwa, waz] *adj* of Liège; *v. a.* **ajaccien**

Liégeois(e) [ljeʒwa, waz] *m(f)* person from Liège; *v. a.* **Ajaccien**

lien [ljɛ̃] *m* **1.** (*attache*) tie; (*chaîne*) link **2.** (*rapport*) *a.* INFOR link; ~ **entre deux/plusieurs choses** link between two/several things **3.** (*ce qui unit*) ~ **affectif** emotional tie; ~ **de parenté** family ties; **nouer des** ~**s avec qn** to tighten a bond with sb

lier [lje] <1> **I.** *vt* **1.** (*attacher*) ~ **qn/qc à qc** to tie sb/sth to sth **2.** (*assembler*) ~ **les mots** to join words up **3.** (*mettre en relation*) **être lié à qc** to be linked to sth **4.** (*unir*) ~ **qn/qc à qn/qc** to bind sb/sth to sb/sth **5.** (*astreindre*) **être lié par un serment** to be bound by an oath **II.** *vpr* **se** ~ **avec qn** to make friends with sb

lierre [ljɛʀ] *m* ivy

liesse [ljɛs] *f soutenu* jubilation; **être en** ~ to be jubilant

lieu[1] [ljø] <x> *m* **1.** (*endroit*) place; ~ **de séjour** place of residence; ~ **de naissance/travail** place of birth/work; ~ **de rencontre** meeting place **2.** *pl* (*endroit précis*) **sur les** ~**x de l'accident** at the scene of the accident; **être déjà sur les** ~**x** (*police*) to already be at the scene **3.** (*endroit particulier*) **haut** ~ **de la Résistance** shrine of the Resistance; **en haut** ~ in high places; **en** ~ **sûr** (*à l'abri*) in a safe place; (*en prison*) in prison **4.** (*dans une suc-*

L

cession) **en premier/second** ~ in the first/second place; **en dernier** ~ finally **5.** (*place*) **avoir** ~ to take place; **tenir** ~ **de qc à qn** to serve sb as sth; **au** ~ **de qc** instead of sth **6.** (*raison*) **il n'y a pas** ~ **de s'inquiéter** there is no reason to worry; **donner** ~ **à qc** (*provoquer*) to cause sth; (*fournir l'occasion de*) to give rise to sth

lieu² [ljø] <s> *m* ZOOL ~ **jaune** pollack; ~ **noir** coalfish

lieu commun [ljøkɔmœ̃] <~x ~s> *m* commonplace

lieu-dit <lieux-dits> *m*, **lieudit** [ljødi] <s> *m* place (*introduces place name*); **le car s'arrête au** ~ **de la "Pierre du Diable"** the coach stops at the (place called) "Pierre du Diable"

lieue [ljø] *f* (*mesure*) *a.* NAUT league ►**à cent** ~**s à la ronde** for miles around; **être à cent** [*o* **mille**] ~**s de faire qc** to have no idea of doing sth; **nous étions à cent** [*o* **mille**] ~**s de penser que ...** it never crossed our mind that ...

lieutenant [ljøt(ə)nɑ̃] *m* **1.** MIL lieutenant **2.** (*adjoint*) second in command

lieutenant-colonel [ljøt(ə)nɑ̃kɔlɔnɛl] *m* MIL lieutenant-colonel

lièvre [ljɛvʀ] *m* ZOOL hare ►**courir deux/plusieurs** ~**s à la fois** to have more than one/several irons in the fire *inf;* **courir comme un** ~ to run like the wind; **lever un** ~ to start something off

lifting [liftiŋ] *m* facelift; **se faire faire un** ~ to have a facelift

ligament [ligamɑ̃] *m* ANAT ligament

ligérien(ne) [liʒeʀjɛ̃, ɛn] *adj* of the Loire

Ligérien(ne) [liʒeʀjɛ̃, ɛn] *m(f)* person from the Loire Valley

ligne [liɲ] *f* **1.** (*trait, limite réelle, forme*) *a.* CHEMDFER, ELEC, TEL line; ~ **d'arrivée/de départ** finishing/starting line *Brit,* finish/starting line *Am;* ~ **de but** goal line; **une** ~ **de métro** an underground line *Brit,* a subway line *Am;* **être en** ~ TEL to be on the phone; INFOR to be on line; **gardez la** ~**!** *Québec* (*ne quittez pas*) hold the line! **2.** (*limite imaginaire*) ~ **d'horizon** horizon; ~ **de tir** line of fire **3.** (*suite de mots*) *a.* INFOR line; **de huit** ~**s** eight lines long; **à la** ~**!** new line!; ~ **commentaire/de commande** comment/command line; **en/hors** ~ on-/off-line **4.** *sans pl* (*silhouette*) figure; **avoir/garder la** ~ to have/keep a trim figure **5.** (*ensemble de produits cosmétiques*) line **6.** (*point*) **les grandes** ~**s de l'ouvrage** the main outline of the work **7.** (*direction*) ~ **droite** straight line; **5 km en** ~ **droite** 5 km as the crow flies; **la dernière** ~ **droite avant l'arrivée** the home straight *Brit,* the home stretch *Am* **8.** (*à la pêche*) (fishing) line **9.** (*rangée*) *a.* MIL row; **se mettre en** ~ to line up **10.** (*filiation*) **en** ~ **directe** in a direct line **11.** *Belgique* **la** ~ **des cheveux** (*la raie*) the parting *Brit,* the part *Am* ►**entrer en** ~ **de compte** to have to be taken into account; **prendre qc en** ~ **de compte** to take sth into account; **hors** ~ off-line; **sur toute la** ~ from start to finish

lignée [liɲe] *f* (*descendance*) lineage

ligneux, -euse [liɲø, -øz] *adj* woody

ligoter [ligɔte] <1> *vt* **1.** (*attacher*) to tie up **2.** (*priver de liberté*) **être ligoté** to be imprisoned

ligue [lig] *f* league

Ligue [lig] *f* ~ **des droits de l'homme** League of Human Rights

liguer [lige] <1> *vpr* **se** ~ **contre qn** to conspire together against sb

lilas [lila] *adj inv, m* lilac

lilliputien(ne) [li(l)lipysjɛ̃, jɛn] *adj, m(f)* Lilliputian

lillois(e) [lilwa, waz] *adj* of Lille; *v. a.* **ajaccien**

Lillois(e) [lilwa, waz] *m(f)* person from Lille; *v. a.* **Ajaccien**

limace [limas] *f* slug

limande [limɑ̃d] *f* dab

lime [lim] *f* (*outil*) file; ~ **à ongles** nail file

limer [lime] <1> **I.** *vt* (*ongles, clé, métal*) to file; (*bois*) to plane **II.** *vpr* **se** ~ **les ongles** to file one's nails

limier [limje] *m* **1.** (*chien de chasse*) bloodhound **2.** (*détective*) sleuth; **être un fin** ~ to be a shrewd detective

limitation [limitasjɔ̃] *f* limitation; ~ **des armements** arms limitation; ~ **de vitesse** speed limit; ~ **des naissances** birth control; **sans** ~ **de temps** with no time limit

limite [limit] **I.** *app* **1.** (*extrême: âge, poids, prix, vitesse*) maximum; (*cas*) borderline **2.** (*presque impossible*) very difficult; **ce cas me paraît** ~ this case seems nearly impossible to me **3.** *inf* (*pas terrible*) **être** ~ to be borderline **II.** *f* **1.** (*démarcation*) boundary **2.** (*dans le temps*) deadline; ~ **pour les inscriptions** deadline for registration **3.** (*borne*) *a.* MAT limit; **sans** ~**s** (*ambition, vanité*) boundless; (*pouvoir*) limitless; **être à la** ~ **du supportable** to be just barely tolerable; **atteindre les** ~**s du ridicule** to be completely ridiculous; **dépasser les** ~**s** to overstep the mark; **il y a des** ~**s** there are limits; **dans les** ~**s du possible** subject to what is possible ►**à la** ~ at a pinch; **à la** ~**, je ferais mieux de ...** in a way, I'd do better to ...; **à la** ~**, on croirait que ...** one would almost think that ...

limité(e) [limite] *adj* limited

limiter [limite] <1> **I.** *vt* **1.** (*délimiter*) to limit **2.** (*restreindre*) ~ **qc à l'essentiel** to restrict sth to what is essential; ~ **les dégâts** to limit the damage **II.** *vpr* **se** ~ **dans qc** (*en mangeant, buvant, dans son comportement*) to be careful when it comes to sth; **je me limiterai à dire ceci** I'll do no more than say this

limitrophe [limitʀɔf] *adj* neighbouring *Brit,* neighboring *Am;* **les pays** ~**s de la France** countries bordering on France; **les villes** ~**s**

de l'Allemagne the towns on the German border

limoger [limɔʒe] <2a> *vt inf* to sideline

limon [limɔ̃] *m* (*terre*) silt

limonade [limɔnad] *f* lemonade

limougeaud(e) [limuʒo, od] *adj* of Limoges; *v. a.* **ajaccien**

Limougeaud(e) [limuʒo, od] *m(f)* person from Limoges; *v. a.* **Ajaccien**

limousin(e) [limuzɛ̃, in] *adj* of the Limousin

Limousin(e) [limuzɛ̃, in] *m(f)* person from the Limousin

limousine [limuzin] *f* limousine

limpide [lɛ̃pid] *adj* **1.** (*pur*) limpid; (*regard*) lucid; (*air*) clear; **des yeux d'un bleu** ~ clear blue eyes **2.** (*intelligible*) clear

limpidité [lɛ̃pidite] *f* (*pureté*) limpidity; (*de l'air*) clearness

lin [lɛ̃] *m* **1.** BOT flax **2.** (*fibre textile*) linen

linceul [lɛ̃sœl] *m* shroud

linéaire [lineɛʀ] *adj* **1.** (*droit*) linear **2.** (*simple*) simplistic; **vision trop** ~ **de la science** a rather blinkered vision of science

linge [lɛ̃ʒ] *m* **1.** *sans pl* (*vêtements*) clothing; **du** ~ **de rechange/de toilette** clean/bathroom linen; **avoir du** ~ **à laver** to have clothes to wash **2.** (*morceau de tissu*) cloth ►**il faut laver son** ~ **sale en <u>famille</u>** one should not wash one's dirty linen in public; **<u>blanc</u> comme un** ~ as white as a sheet

lingerie [lɛ̃ʒʀi] *f* **1.** *sans pl* (*dessous*) ~ **féminine** lingerie **2.** (*local*) linen room

lingot [lɛ̃go] *m* **1.** (~ *d'or*) gold ingot **2.** (*masse de métal*) ingot

linguiste [lɛ̃gɥist] *mf* linguist

linguistique [lɛ̃gɥistik] **I.** *adj* **1.** (*relatif à la science du langage*) linguistic **2.** (*relatif à la langue*) **communauté/famille** ~ speech community/family **II.** *f* linguistics + *vb sing*

linoléum [linɔleɔm] *m* linoleum

linotte [linɔt] *f* linnet

linteau [lɛ̃to] <x> *m* ARCHIT lintel

lion [ljɔ̃] *m* lion; *v. a.* **lionne**

Lion [ljɔ̃] *m* Leo; *v. a.* **Balance**

lionceau [ljɔ̃so] <x> *m* lion cub

lionne [ljɔn] *f* lioness; *v. a.* **lion**

lipide [lipid] *m* lipid

liquéfier [likefje] <1> **I.** *vt* to liquefy **II.** *vpr* **se** ~ (*gaz*) to condense; (*solide*) to melt

liqueur [likœʀ] *f* liqueur

liquidation [likidasjɔ̃] *f* **1.** (*solde*) sale; ~ **totale du stock** closing down sale **2.** JUR (*d'une succession, d'un compte*) liquidation

liquide [likid] **I.** *adj* **1.** (*fluide*) liquid; **être trop** ~ (*sauce*) to be too thin **2.** (*disponible*) **argent** ~ cash **II.** *m* **1.** (*fluide*) liquid; ~ **vaisselle/de frein(s)** washing up/brake fluid; **les** ~**s et les solides** liquids and solids **2.** *sans pl* (*argent*) cash; **en** ~ in cash

liquider [likide] <1> *vt* **1.** COM (*marchandise*) to sell off; (*stock*) to liquidate **2.** *inf* (*se débarrasser: adversaire*) to eliminate; (*dossier*) to get rid of; **voilà une affaire (de) liquidée** that's the end of that **3.** *inf* (*tuer*) to eliminate; **se faire** ~ to be eliminated **4.** *inf* (*finir: boisson, nourriture*) to clear **5.** JUR (*société*) to liquidate; (*compte*) to settle

liquoreux, -euse [likɔʀø, -øz] *adj* **vin** ~ dessert wine

lire[1] [liʀ] *irr* **I.** *vi* to read; **elle sait** ~ she can read; ~ **à haute voix** to read aloud; ~ **dans les lignes de la main de qn** to read sb's palm; ~ **dans les pensées de qn** to read sb's thoughts **II.** *vt* to read; **c'est à** ~**!** it is a must-read! *inf;* **en espérant vous/te** ~ **bientôt** hoping to hear from you soon; **à te** ~ from what you write **III.** *vpr* **1.** (*se déchiffrer*) **l'hébreu se lit de droite à gauche** Hebrew reads from right to left **2.** (*se comprendre*) **ce texte peut se** ~ **de deux manières** this text can be interpreted in two ways **3.** (*se deviner*) **la surprise se lisait sur son visage** surprise was written all over his face ►**qc/ça se <u>laisse</u>** ~ sth/it is very easy to read

lire[2] [liʀ] *f* lira

lis[1] [lis] *m* lily

lis[2] [li] *indic prés de* **lire**

lisais [lizɛ] *imparf de* **lire**

lisant [lizɑ̃] *part prés de* **lire**

Lisbonne [lisbɔn] Lisbon

liseré [liz(ə)ʀe] *m,* **liséré** [lizeʀe] *m* border

liseron [lizʀɔ̃] *m* BOT bindweed

lisez [lize] *indic prés et impératif de* **lire**

lisible [lizibl] *adj* legible; **ne pas être** ~ to be illegible

lisiblement [lizibləmɑ̃] *adv* legibly

lisière [lizjɛʀ] *f* **1.** COUT selvage **2.** (*limite*) edge; (*d'un champ*) boundary

lisons [lizɔ̃] *indic prés et impératif de* **lire**

lisse [lis] *adj* smooth

lissé(e) [lise] *adj* (*cheveux*) smoothed down

lisser [lise] <1> **I.** *vt* to smooth; (*papier*) to smooth (out) **II.** *vpr* **se** ~ **les cheveux/la moustache** to smooth down one's hair/moustache *Brit,* to smooth down one's hair/mustache *Am*

liste [list] *f* (*nomenclature*) list; ~ **électorale** electoral register; ~ **de mariage** wedding list; **faire la** ~ **de qc** to list sth; **les** ~**s des inscriptions sont closes** registrations are closed ►**être sur (la)** ~ **<u>rouge</u>** to be ex-directory *Brit,* to be unlisted *Am*

lister [liste] <1> *vt* to list

listing [listiŋ] *m* listing

lit[1] [li] *m* **1.** (*meuble*) bed; ~ **d'enfant/de camp** child's/camp bed; ~ **pour deux personnes** double bed; **aller au** ~ to go to bed; **mettre qn au** ~ to put sb to bed; **au** ~**!** bed!; **être cloué au** ~ to be confined to bed **2.** (*creux: d'une rivière*) bed; **sortir de son** ~ to burst its banks ►**du <u>premier</u>/<u>second</u>** ~ from the first/second marriage

lit[2] [li] *indic prés de* **lire**

litchi [litʃi] *m* lychee

literie [litʀi] *f* **1.** (*sommier et matelas*) bed **2.** (*linge*) bedding; **le rayon** ~ the bedding department

litière [litjɛʀ] *f* litter; (*d'un cheval, d'une vache*) bedding; ~ **pour chats** cat litter *Brit,* kitty litter *Am*

litige [litiʒ] *m* **1.**(*contestation*) dispute; **régler un** ~ to settle a dispute **2.** JUR lawsuit

litre [litʀ] *m* **1.**(*mesure*) litre *Brit,* liter *Am* **2.**(*bouteille*) litre bottle *Brit,* liter bottle *Am*

littéraire [liteʀɛʀ] **I.** *adj* literary **II.** *mf* **1.**(*opp: scientifique*) literary type **2.**(*étudiant, professeur*) student/teacher of literature

littéral(e) [liteʀal, o] <-aux> *adj* (*traduction, sens*) literal; (*copie*) exact

littéralement [liteʀalmɑ̃] *adv* literally

littérature [liteʀatyʀ] *f* literature

littoral [litɔʀal, o] <-aux> *m* coast

littoral(e) [litɔʀal, o] <-aux> *adj* coastal

Lituanie [litɥani] *f* **la** ~ Lithuania

lituanien [litɥanjɛ̃] *m* Lithuanian; *v. a.* **français**

lituanien(ne) [litɥanjɛ̃, jɛn] *adj* Lithuanian

Lituanien(ne) [litɥanjɛ̃, jɛn] *m(f)* Lithuanian

liturgie [lityʀʒi] *f* liturgy

Liverpool [livəʀpul] Liverpool; **habitant de** ~ Liverpudian

livide [livid] *adj* livid; (*lèvres*) blue-tinged; (*lumière*) pale

living [liviŋ] *m,* **living-room** [liviŋʀum] <living-rooms> *m* living room

livrable [livʀabl] *adj* which can be delivered

livraison [livʀɛzɔ̃] *f* delivery; ~ **à domicile** home delivery; **payable à la** ~ cash on delivery

livre¹ [livʀ] *m* **1.**(*ouvrage*) book; ~ **d'enfant** [*o* **pour enfants**] children's book; ~ **d'images** picture book; ~ **de poche** paperback; ~ **de cuisine** cookery book *Brit,* cookbook *Am;* ~ **d'histoire/d'anglais** history/English book; ~ **scolaire** school book; ~ **de lecture** reading book; ~ **à succès** bestseller **2.** *sans pl* (*industrie*) **le** ~ the book trade; **salon du** ~ book fair **3.**(*registre*) ~ **de caisse** cashbook; ~ **d'or** visitors' book ►**à** ~ **ouvert** at sight

livre² [livʀ] *f* **1.**(*unité monétaire anglaise*) pound; ~ **sterling** pound sterling **2.** *Québec* (*unité de masse valant 0,453 kg*) pound

livrer [livʀe] <1> **I.** *vt* **1.**(*fournir*) to deliver; **se faire** ~ **qc** to have sth delivered **2.**(*remettre*) ~ **qn à la police** to hand over sb to the police **3.**(*dénoncer*) to give away **4.**(*abandonner*) ~ **qn à la mort** to send sb to his death; **être livré à soi-même** to be left alone **5.**(*dévoiler*) to reveal **II.** *vpr* **1.**(*se rendre*) **se** ~ **à qn** to give oneself up to sb **2.**(*se confier*) **se** ~ **à qn** to confide in sb **3.**(*se consacrer*) **se** ~ **à un sport** to practise a sport *Brit,* to practice a sport *Am;* **se** ~ **à une enquête** to take up an investigation; **se** ~ **à ses occupations habituelles** to be immerse oneself in one's usual occupations

livret [livʀɛ] *m* (*registre*) booklet; ~ (**de caisse**) **d'épargne** bankbook; ~ **de famille** family record book; ~ **militaire** military record; ~ **scolaire** school report

livreur, **-euse** [livʀœʀ, -øz] *m, f* delivery person

lobby <lobbies *o* s> [lɔbi] *m* lobby

lobe [lɔb] *m* ANAT, BOT lobe; ~ **de l'oreille** ear lobe

local [lɔkal, o] <-aux> *m* **des locaux** (*salles*) premises *pl;* (*bureaux*) offices *pl;* **des locaux à usage commercial** commercial premises

local(e) [lɔkal, o] <-aux> *adj* local; **1 h 30 heure** ~**e** 1.30am local time *Brit,* 1:30 a.m. local time *Am*

localement [lɔkalmɑ̃] *adv* **1.**(*par endroits*) in places **2.**(*à un endroit précis*) locally

localiser [lɔkalize] <1> **I.** *vt* **1.**(*situer*) ~ **qc sur la carte** to locate sth on the map **2.**(*circonscrire*) to localize **II.** *vpr* **se** ~ (*conflit, épidémie*) to be confined

localité [lɔkalite] *f* town

locataire [lɔkatɛʀ] *mf* tenant; **être** ~ to rent

location [lɔkasjɔ̃] *f* **1.**(*bail: d'une habitation, d'un terrain, d'une voiture*) renting; **voiture de** ~ hire car *Brit,* rental car *Am;* **prendre/donner un appartement en** ~ to rent an apartment **2.**(*maison à louer*) **prendre une** ~ **pour les vacances** to rent a house for the holidays

location-vente [lɔkasjɔ̃vɑ̃t] <locations-ventes> *f* hire purchase *Brit,* installment plan *Am;* **en** ~ on hire purchase *Brit,* in installments *Am*

lock-out [lɔkaut] *m inv* lockout

locomotion [lɔkɔmosjɔ̃] *f* locomotion

locomotive [lɔkɔmɔtiv] *f* TECH locomotive

locuteur, **-trice** [lɔkytœʀ, -tʀis] *m, f* speaker; ~ **natif** native speaker

locution [lɔkysjɔ̃] *f* phrase

loden [lɔdɛn] *m* Loden (coat)

loft [lɔft] *m* loft

loge [lɔʒ] *f* **1.**(*pièce: d'un concierge*) lodge; (*d'un acteur*) dressing room **2.** THEAT box ►**être aux premières** ~**s** to be in the front row

logement [lɔʒmɑ̃] *m* **1.**(*habitation*) accommodation *no pl;* (*appartement*) flat *Brit,* apartment *Am;* (*maison*) house; MIL quarters *pl;* (*chez un civil*) billet; ~ **de deux pièces** two room apartment; ~ **de fonction** *housing provided by one's employer;* ~ **provisoire** provisional housing **2.**(*secteur*) **le** ~ housing; **crise du** ~ housing crisis; **politique en matière de** ~ housing policy

loger [lɔʒe] <2a> **I.** *vi* (*séjourner: personne*) to live **II.** *vt* **1.**(*héberger*) ~ **qn** to put sb up **2.**(*contenir: hôtel*) to accommodate **3.**(*envoyer avec une arme*) ~ **une balle dans la tête de qn** to put a bullet through sb's head **III.** *vpr* **1.**(*trouver un logement*) **se** ~ **chez un ami** to stay at a friend's house **2.**(*se placer*) **se** ~ **entre deux vertèbres** (*balle*) to lodge between two vertebrae

logeur, **-euse** [lɔʒœʀ, -ʒøz] *m, f* landlord, landlady *m, f*

loggia [lɔdʒja] *f* loggia

logiciel [lɔʒisjɛl] *m* software *no pl;* ~ **libre** [*o* **gratuit**] freeware; ~ **anti-virus** anti-virus software; ~ **de courrier électronique** email software; ~ **de traitement de texte** wordprocessing software; ~ **de navigation** browser

logicien(**ne**) [lɔʒisjɛ̃, jɛn] *m(f)* logician

logique [lɔʒik] **I.** *adj* logical **II.** *f* PHILOS, MAT logic; **manquer de** ~ to lack logic; **être dans la** ~ **des choses** to be in the nature of things; **en toute** ~ logically

logiquement [lɔʒikmɑ̃] *adv* **1.** (*normalement*) logically **2.** (*rationnellement*) rationally

logo(**type**) [lɔgɔ(tip)] *m* logo

loi [lwa] *f* **1.** (*prescription légale*) *a.* PHYS, MAT law; **la** ~ **du talion** lex talionis; **j'ai la** ~ **pour moi** I have the law on my side **2.** (*ordre imposé*) rules; (*par Dieu*) law; **dicter sa** ~ [*o* **faire la** ~] to lay down the law; **la** ~ **du moindre effort** the line of least resistance; **c'est la** ~ **des séries** once things happen, they keep happening

loin [lwɛ̃] *adv* **1.** (*distance*) far; ~ **d'ici** a long way from here; **au** ~ in the distance; **de** ~ from a distance; **aller** ~ **de sa ville natale** to go far from one's place of birth; **c'est encore assez** ~ it is still quite a long way; **plus** ~ farther **2.** *fig* far; **il ira** ~ he will go far; **j'irais même plus** ~ I would go even further; **voir plus** ~ **page 28** see below page 28; **elle revient de** ~ she had a close shave *Brit,* she had a close call *Am* **3.** (*dans le temps*) far; **il n'est pas très** ~ **de minuit** it's very nearly midnight; **de** ~ **en** ~ here and there **4.** (*au lieu de*) ~ **de faire qc** far from doing sth; ~ **de cela** far from that ►~ **s'en <u>faut</u>** not by a longshot; **<u>de</u>** ~ by far; ~ **<u>de</u> là** far from it

lointain(**e**) [lwɛ̃tɛ̃, ɛn] *adj* **1.** (*dans l'espace*) faraway **2.** (*dans le temps: avenir*) far off; (*époque, souvenir*) distant **3.** (*indirect*) distant **4.** (*détaché, absent: personne*) remote; (*regard*) faraway

loir [lwaʀ] *m* dormouse ►**<u>dormir</u> comme un** ~ to sleep like a log

loisir [lwaziʀ] *m* **1.** *sing o pl* (*temps libre*) leisure *no pl;* **heures de** ~ free time **2.** (*passe-temps*) hobby

lombaire [lɔ̃bɛʀ] **I.** *adj* **région** ~ lumbar region **II.** *f* lumbar vertebra *pl*

londonien(**ne**) [lɔ̃dɔnjɛ̃, jɛn] *adj* Londoner

Londonien(**ne**) [lɔ̃dɔnjɛ̃, jɛn] *m(f)* Londoner

Londres [lɔ̃dʀ] London; **le Grand** ~ Greater London; **la police de** ~ the Metropolitain Police *Brit*

long [lɔ̃] **I.** *adv* **qc en dit** ~ **sur qc** sth speaks volumes about sth; **en savoir** ~ **sur qc** to know a lot about sth **II.** *m* **en** ~ lengthways; **de** ~ **en large** to and fro; **en** ~ **et en large** in great detail; **tout au** ~ **du parcours** all along the way; **tout au** ~ **de sa vie** throughout his life; **avoir 2 km de** ~ to be 2 km long; **tomber de tout son** ~ to fall headlong; **tout le** ~ **du mur** all along the the wall

long, **longue** [lɔ̃, lɔ̃g] *adj* long; ~ **de 5 km** 5 km long; **une ~ue habitude** a long-standing habit; **ce sera** ~ it'll take a long time; **être** ~ **à faire qc** to be slow in doing sth

longer [lɔ̃ʒe] <2a> *vt* **1.** (*border*) ~ **qc** (*mur*) to border sth; (*sentier, rivière*) to run alongside sth **2.** (*se déplacer le long de*) ~ **qc** (*bateau, véhicule*) to travel along sth; (*personne*) (*à pied*) to walk along sth; (*en voiture*) to travel along sth

longévité [lɔ̃ʒevite] *f* **1.** (*longue durée de vie*) longevity **2.** (*durée de vie*) life expectancy

longiligne [lɔ̃ʒiliɲ] *adj* (*personne*) rangy

longitude [lɔ̃ʒityd] *f* longitude; **43° de** ~ **est/ouest** longitude 43° east/west

longtemps [lɔ̃tɑ̃] *adv* (*un temps long*) for a long time; **il y a** ~ a long time ago; **j'en ai pour** ~ it'll take me a long time; **je n'en ai pas pour** ~ I won't be long; **être à Paris pour** ~ to be in Paris for a long time; **elle n'est pas là pour** ~ she's not here for long; **aussi** ~ **que ...** as long as ...; ~ **avant/après qc** long before/after sth

longue [lɔ̃g] **I.** *adj v.* **long II.** *f* **<u>à</u> la** ~ eventually

longuement [lɔ̃gmɑ̃] *adv* at length; (*s'étendre sur un sujet*) in detail; (*étudier*) for a long time

longueur [lɔ̃gœʀ] *f* length; **avoir une** ~ **de 10 cm, avoir 10 cm de** ~ to be 10 cm in length; **plier en** ~ to fold lengthwise; ~ **d'onde** wavelength ►**avoir une** ~ **d'<u>avance</u> sur qn** to be way ahead of sb; **être sur la même** ~ **d'<u>onde</u>** *inf* to be on the same wavelength; **<u>avoir</u> des ~s** to have tiresome moments; **<u>traîner</u> en** ~ to drag on; **<u>à</u>** ~ **d'année/de journée** all year/day

longue-vue [lɔ̃gvy] <longues-vues> *f* telescope

look [luk] *m* (*d'une personne*) appearance ►**avoir un** ~ **d'<u>enfer</u>** *inf* to look great

looping [lupiŋ] *m* AVIAT loop; **faire un** ~ to loop the loop

lopin [lɔpɛ̃] *m* ~ **de terre** plot of land

loquace [lɔkas] *adj* talkative

loque [lɔk] *f* **1.** (*vêtement*) rags; **en ~s** in rags **2.** *péj* (*personne*) wreck **3.** *Belgique, Nord* (*reste d'étoffe, morceau d'étoffe usé, déchiré*) scrap **4.** *Belgique* (*peau à la surface du lait bouilli*) skin

loquet [lɔkɛ] *m* latch; **mettre le** ~ to put the door on the latch

lorgner [lɔʀɲe] <1> *vt* **1.** (*reluquer*) to eye *inf* **2.** (*convoiter*) ~ **qc** to have one's eye on sth

lorgnette [lɔʀɲɛt] *f* spyglass ►**regarder qc par le petit <u>bout</u> de la** ~ to have a very narrow view of sth

lorgnon [lɔʀɲɔ̃] *m* **1.** (*face-à-main*) lorgnette **2.** (*pince-nez*) pince-nez

loriot [lɔʀjo] *m* oriole

lorrain(e) [lɔʀɛ̃, ɛn] *adj* of Lorraine

Lorrain(e) [lɔʀɛ̃, ɛn] *m(f)* person from Lorraine

Lorraine [lɔʀɛn] *f* **la** ~ Lorraine

lors [lɔʀ] *adv* ~ **de notre arrivée** at the time of our arrival; ~ **d'un congrès** during a conference; **depuis** ~ since then; **dès** ~ (*à partir de ce moment-là*) from then on; (*de ce fait*) in that case; **dès** ~ **que qn a fait qc** once sb does sth

lorsque [lɔʀsk(ə)] <lorsqu'> *conj* when

losange [lɔzɑ̃ʒ] *m* lozenge; **en** (**forme de**) ~ diamond-shaped

lot [lo] *m* **1.** (*prix*) prize; ~ **de consolation** consolation prize; **gagner le gros** ~ to hit the jackpot **2.** (*assortiment*) batch; (*aux enchères*) lot **3.** (*parcelle*) parcel **4.** INFOR **traitement par** ~**s** batch processing **5.** JUR (*part*) share

loterie [lɔtʀi] *f* **1.** (*jeu*) lottery; **gagner à la** ~ to win the lottery **2.** (*hasard*) chance

Lothaire [lɔtɛːʀ(ə)] *m* Lothario

loti(e) [lɔti] *adj* **être bien/mal** ~ to be well/badly off

lotion [losjɔ̃] *f* lotion; ~ **capillaire/après-rasage** hair/after-shave lotion

lotir [lɔtiʀ] <8> *vt* **1.** (*diviser en lots*) ~ **qc** to divide sth into lots **2.** (*mettre en possession d'un lot*) ~ **qn de qc** to endow sb with sth

lotissement [lɔtismɑ̃] *m* (*ensemble immobilier*) housing estate

loto [lɔto] *m* (*jeu de société*) lotto

Loto [lɔto] *m* (*loterie*) **le tirage du** ~ the lottery results; **jouer au** ~ to play the lottery; **jouer au** ~ **sportif** ≈ to do the pools

lotte [lɔt] *f* monkfish

lotus [lɔtys] *m* lotus

louable[1] [lwabl] *adj* (*digne de louange*) praiseworthy

louable[2] [lwabl] *adj* (*pièce, appartement, maison*) rentable

louange [lwɑ̃ʒ] *f* **1.** *soutenu* (*glorification*) praise; **digne de** ~ worthy of praise **2.** *gén pl* (*paroles*) praise **3.** (*gloire*) **chanter les** ~**s de qn/qc** to sing the praises of sb/sth

loubard(e) [lubaʀ, aʀd] *m(f) inf* hooligan

louche[1] [luʃ] *adj* (*douteux, suspect*) dubious; (*passé*) shady; (*affaire, histoire, personne*) suspicious

louche[2] [luʃ] *f* (*ustensile*) ladle

loucher [luʃe] <1> *vi* **1.** MED to squint **2.** *inf* (*lorgner*) ~ **sur qn** to eye up sb; ~ **sur l'héritage** to have one's eye on an inheritance

louer[1] [lwe] <1> *vt* to praise

louer[2] [lwe] <1> **I.** *vt* to rent; **à** ~ for rent **II.** *vpr* **se** ~ (*appartement, voiture, chambre*) to be rented (out)

loueur, -euse [lwœʀ, -øz] *m, f* ~ **de chambres** landlord *m*, landlady *f*; ~ **de voitures** car rental agent

Louisiane [lwizjan(ə)] *f* **la** ~ Louisiana

loup [lu] *m* **1.** (*mammifère*) wolf; *v. a.* **louve** **2.** (*poisson*) ~ (**de mer**) sea bass **3.** *fig* **jeune** ~ young Turk **4.** (*masque*) eye mask **5.** *inf* (*terme d'affection*) **mon** ~ my love ►**quand on parle du** ~ **on en voit la queue** speak of the devil (and he will appear); **être connu comme le** ~ **blanc** to be known everywhere

loupe [lup] *f* magnifying glass ►**examiner/regarder qc à la** ~ to examine/look at sth under a microscope

louper [lupe] <1> **I.** *vt inf* **1.** (*ne pas réussir: examen*) to fail; **être loupé** (*soirée*) to be ruined; (*mayonnaise, gâteau*) to be spoiled **2.** (*manquer*) to miss **II.** *vi inf* (*échouer: projet, tentative*) to fail; **ça n'a pas loupé** it happened all right

lourd(e) [luʀ, luʀd] **I.** *adj* **1.** *a. antéposé* (*de grand poids*) heavy **2.** (*pesant: jambes, paupières, tête*) heavy; **avoir l'estomac** ~ to feel bloated; **avoir le cœur** ~ to have a heavy heart **3.** *a. antéposé* (*oppressant: chaleur*) sultry; **il fait** ~ it is sultry **4.** *a. antéposé* (*important: impôts, dettes*) heavy **5.** *a. antéposé* (*pénible: tâche*) serious; **emploi du temps très** ~ very busy timetable **6.** (*chargé*) ~ **de menaces/signification** full of threats/meaning **7.** (*gauche*) heavy; (*compliment, plaisanterie*) heavy-handed **8.** (*opp: fin, délicat*) heavy **9.** *a. antéposé* (*grave*) gerious **10.** *a. antéposé* (*sévère: défaite, peine*) severe **11.** (*profond: sommeil*) deep **12.** (*dense: terre, liquide*) dense **II.** *adv* **peser** ~ to be heavy ►**pas** ~ *inf* not much

lourdaud(e) [luʀdo, od] **I.** *adj* clumsy **II.** *m(f)* dimwit

lourdement [luʀdəmɑ̃] *adv* heavily; (*se tromper*) seriously; (*insister*) strenuously

lourdeur [luʀdœʀ] *f* **1.** (*pesanteur*) **des** ~**s d'estomac** a bloated feeling **2.** (*caractère massif*) heaviness

loutre [lutʀ] *f* **1.** ZOOL otter **2.** (*fourrure*) otterskin

Louvain [luvɛ̃] Leuven

louve [luv] *f* she-wolf; *v. a.* **loup**

louveteau [luvto] <x> *m* **1.** ZOOL wolf cub **2.** (*jeune scout*) cub scout

louvoyer [luvwaje] <6> *vi* **1.** (*tergiverser*) to hedge **2.** NAUT to tack

lover [lɔve] <1> *vpr* **se** ~ to coil up

loyal(e) [lwajal, jo] <-aux> *adj* (*ami*) loyal; (*services*) faithful; (*conduite, procédés*) fair; (*adversaire*) honest

loyalement [lwajalmɑ̃] *adv* (*reconnaître*) in all honesty; (*être dévoué*) loyally; (*régler un différend, se battre*) fairly

loyauté [lwajote] *f* loyalty; (*d'un adversaire, d'un procédé*) honesty

loyer [lwaje] *m* rent

lu(e) [ly] *part passé de* **lire**

lubie [lybi] *f* craze; **avoir des** ~**s** to have one's whims

lubrifiant [lybʀifjɑ̃] *m* lubricant

lubrifier [lybʀifje] <1a> *vt* to lubricate

lubrique [lybʀik] *adj* lustful; (*propos, scène, spectacle*) lewd

lucarne [lykaʀn] *f* (*petite fenêtre*) dormer

window; (*d'une entrée, d'un mur, cachot*) small window

lucide [lysid] *adj* **1.** (*clairvoyant: intelligence, jugement*) clear-sighted **2.** (*conscient*) conscious

lucidité [lysidite] *f* (*conscience*) consciousness; **des moments de** ~ moments of lucidity

luciole [lysjɔl] *f* firefly

lucratif, **-ive** [lykʀatif, -iv] *adj* lucrative

ludique [lydik] *adj* **activités ~s** play activity

ludothèque [lydɔtɛk] *f* toy library

lueur [lɥœʀ] *f* **1.** (*faible clarté, signe passager*) glimmer; (*des braises*) glow; **à la ~ d'une bougie** by candlelight; ~ **d'espoir** glimmer of hope **2.** (*éclat fugitif dans le regard*) ~ **de colère/joie** gleam of anger/joy

luge [lyʒ] *f* sledge *Brit*, sled *Am*; **faire de la** ~ to sledge *Brit*, to sled *Am*

lugubre [lygybʀ] *adj* lugubrious; (*personne, pensée*) gloomy; (*paysage*) dismal

lui [lɥi] **I.** *pron pers* **1.** (*personne masc ou fém*) **je ~ ai demandé s'il/si elle venait** I asked him/her if he/she was coming **2.** (*animal, objet masc ou fém*) it **3.** (*avec un sens possessif*) **le cœur ~ battait fort** his/her heart was beating hard; *v. a.* **me II.** *pron pers, masc* **1.** *inf* him; **tu veux l'aider, ~?** do you want to help HIM?; **à ~ seul** him alone **2.** (*soi*) himself; **il ne pense qu'à ~** he thinks only of himself

lui-même [lɥimɛm] *pron pers* himself; ~ **n'en savait rien** he himself did not know anything about it; **il est venu de ~** he came by his own choice; **M. X? – ~!** Mr X? – himself!

luire [lɥiʀ] *vi irr* **1.** (*briller*) to shine **2.** (*réfléchir la lumière: feuilles*) to glimmer; (*lac, rosée*) to glisten **3.** (*exprimer*) ~ **de désir/colère** (*yeux*) to glow

luisant(**e**) [lɥizɑ̃, ɑ̃t] *adj* shining; (*yeux*) (*de joie*) shining; (*de colère*) gleaming; ~ **de fièvre** bright with fever

lumbago [lœ̃bago] *m* lumbago

lumière [lymjɛʀ] *f* **1.** (*clarté naturelle, éclairage*) light; ~ **du soleil** sunlight; ~ **du jour** daylight; ~ **de la lune** moonlight **2.** *pl* (*connaissances*) knowledge; **j'aurais besoin de vos ~s** I need your advice **3.** (*personne intelligente*) **être une ~** to be a bright spark; **ne pas être une ~** not to be too bright **4.** (*ce qui permet de comprendre*) **faire la ~ sur une affaire** to get to the bottom of a matter; **jeter une ~ nouvelle sur qc** to shed new light on sth

lumignon [lymiɲɔ̃] *m* small light

luminaire [lyminɛʀ] *m* (*lampe*) lamp

lumineux, **-euse** [lyminø, -øz] *adj* **1.** (*qui répand la lumière*) luminous; (*enseigne, rayon*) neon **2.** (*brillant, éclatant: couleur, yeux*) bright; (*regard*) luminous; (*teint*) translucent **3.** (*clair: pièce, appartement*) light

luminosité [lyminozite] *f* **1.** (*éclat lumineux: du ciel, d'une couleur*) luminosity **2.** (*clarté: d'une pièce, d'un appartement*) brightness

lunaire [lynɛʀ] *adj* **1.** ASTR **sol** ~ lunar surface **2.** (*qui ressemble à la lune*) **paysage** ~ lunar landscape; **visage** ~ moonlike face **3.** (*extravagant: projet*) fanciful; (*rêve*) fantastic; **personnage** ~ whimsical character

lunatique [lynatik] *adj* (*personne*) lunatic; (*humeur*) quirky

lunch [lœntʃ] <(e)s> *m* buffet

lundi [lœ̃di] *m* Monday; ~ **de Pâques/Pentecôte** Easter/Whit Monday; *v. a.* **dimanche**

lune [lyn] *f* moon; **nouvelle/pleine** ~ new/full moon

luné(**e**) [lyne] *adj inf* **être bien/mal** ~ to be in a good/bad mood

lunette [lynɛt] *f* **1.** *pl* (*verres*) glasses; **~s noires** dark glasses; **~s de plongée** goggles; **~s de soleil** sunglasses; **mettre ses ~s** to put one's glasses on **2.** (*instrument*) sight **3.** (*petite fenêtre: d'un toit*) skylight; ~ **arrière** AUTO rear window **4.** (*anneau: des WC*) toilet seat

lupin [lypɛ̃] *m* lupin

lurette [lyʀɛt] *f* **il y a belle ~ que qn a fait qc** *inf* sb did sth ages ago, sb did sth donkey's years ago *Brit*; **depuis belle** ~ *inf* ages ago, donkey's years ago *Brit*

luron [lyʀɔ̃, ɔn] *m* **joyeux** ~ *inf* fun-loving character

lus [ly] *passé simple de* **lire**

lustre [lystʀ] *m* (*lampe*) ceiling light

lustrer [lystʀe] <1> *vt* (*faire briller: voiture*) to shine; ~ **sa fourrure/son poil** (*animal*) to lick one's fur

luth [lyt] *m* lute

luthier [lytje] *m* (stringed-)instrument maker

lutin [lytɛ̃] *m* elf

lutte [lyt] *f* **1.** (*combat*) fight; ~ **contre/pour qn/qc** fight against/for sb/sth; ~ **antidrogue** fight against drugs; ~ **des classes** class struggle; **la ~ pour la vie** the fight for life; **être en ~ contre qn** to be in conflict with sb; **entrer en ~** to go into battle **2.** SPORT wrestling; **faire de la ~** to wrestle; ~ **suisse** [*o* **à la culotte**] *Suisse* Swiss wrestling

> The **lutte suisse** is a wrestling match held in a ring, whereby each fighter aims to bring the other down by seizing his leather shorts.

lutter [lyte] <1> *vi* **1.** (*combattre*) to fight; (*se démener*) to struggle; ~ **contre la mort** to fight death; ~ **contre le sommeil/le vent** to fight against sleep/the wind **2.** (*mener une action*) ~ **contre qc** to fight against sth

lutteur, **-euse** [lytœʀ, -øz] *m, f* **1.** SPORT wrestler **2.** (*battant*) fighter

luxation [lyksasjɔ̃] *f* (*de l'épaule, de la hanche*) dislocation

luxe [lyks] *m* **1.** (*opp: nécessité*) luxury; **c'est du ~!** this is luxury!; **ce n'est pas du ~** *inf* it's a necessity **2.** (*coûteux*) **de** ~ luxury; **magasin de** ~ shop selling luxury goods

Luxembourg [lyksɑ̃buʀ] *m* **1.** (*ville*) Luxembourg **2.** (*pays*) **le** (**Grand-Duché du**) ~

(the Grand Duchy of) Luxembourg **3.** (*à Paris*) **le** (**palais du**) ~ *the seat of the French Senate in Paris;* **le** (**jardin du**) ~ *the Luxembourg Gardens*

luxembourgeois(**e**) [lyksɑ̃buʀʒwa, waz] *adj* Luxembourg

Luxembourgeois(**e**) [lyksɑ̃buʀʒwa, waz] *m(f)* Luxembourger

luxer [lykse] <1> *vpr* **se** ~ **l'épaule** to dislocate one's shoulder

luxueux, -euse [lyksɥø, -øz] *adj a. antéposé* luxurious; **hôtel** ~ luxury hotel

luxuriant(**e**) [lyksyʀjɑ̃, jɑ̃t] *adj* (*végétation*) lush

luzerne [lyzɛʀn] *f* alfalfa

lycée [lise] *m* **1.** secondary school *Brit,* high school *Am;* ~ **d'enseignement général et technologique** technology school; ~ **professionnel** [*o* **technique**] technical school; **être prof au** ~ to be a secondary school teacher; **aller au** ~ to go to secondary school **2.** *Belgique* (*établissement secondaire pour filles*) girls' school

> At the end of "collège", students aged 15 or 16 can go to a **lycée**. There are three classes, "seconde", "première" and "terminale", and at the end, students sit the "baccalauréat".

lycéen(**ne**) [liseɛ̃, ɛn] *m(f)* secondary school pupil *Brit,* high school student *Am*

lycra® [likʀa] *m* Lycra®; **en** ~ Lycra

lymphatique [lɛ̃fatik] *adj* **1.** MED **système** ~ lymphatic system **2.** (*flegmatique: personne*) apathetic; (*constitution, tempérament*) sluggish

lymphe [lɛ̃f] *f* lymph

lyncher [lɛ̃ʃe] <1> *vt* to lynch

lynx [lɛ̃ks] *m* lynx

Lyon [ljɔ̃] Lyons

lyonnais(**e**) [ljɔnɛ, ɛz] *adj* of Lyons; *v. a.* **ajaccien**

Lyonnais(**e**) [ljɔnɛ, ɛz] *m(f)* person from Lyons; *v. a.* **Ajaccien**

lyophiliser [ljɔfilize] <1> *vt* to freeze-dry; **café lyophilisé** freeze-dried coffee

lyre [liʀ] *f* lyre

lyrique [liʀik] *adj* **1.** MUS, LITT lyric **2.** (*passionné*) lyrical

lys [lis] *m v.* **lis**

M

M, m [ɛm] *m inv* M, m; ~ **comme Marcel** m as in Mary *Brit,* m as in Mike *Am;* (*on telephone*) m for Mary *Brit,* m for Mike *Am*

m [ɛm] *abr de* **mètre** m

M. <MM.> *m abr de* **Monsieur** Mr *Brit,* Mr. *Am*

m' *pron v.* **me**

ma [ma, me] <mes> *dét poss* my ►~ **pauvre!** you poor thing!

mac [mak] *m inf abr de* **maquereau** pimp

Mac [mak] *m* INFOR *abr de* **Macintosh** Mac; **travailler sur un** ~ to work on a Mac

macabre [makɑbʀ] *adj* macabre; **humour** ~ black humour *Brit,* black humor *Am*

macadam [makadam] *m* (*revêtement routier*) tarmac

macaron [makaʀɔ̃] *m* GASTR macaroon

macaroni [makaʀɔni] *m* **1.** GASTR macaroni **2.** *péj, inf* (*Italien*) wop, eyetie *pej*

macédoine [masedwan] *f* GASTR ~ **de fruits** fruit salad; ~ **de légumes** diced mixed vegetables

Macédoine [masedwan(ə)] *f* **la** ~ Macedonia

macédonien [masedɔnjɛ̃] *m* Macedonian

macédonien(**ne**) [masedɔnjɛ̃, ɛn] *adj* Macedonian

Macédonien(**ne**) [masedɔnjɛ̃, ɛn] *m(f)* Macedonian

macération [maseʀasjɔ̃] *f* GASTR maceration

macérer [maseʀe] <5> *vi, vt* GASTR to macerate

mâche [mɑʃ] *f* lamb's lettuce *Brit,* corn salad *Am*

mâcher [mɑʃe] <1> *vt* (*mastiquer*) to chew; (*rongeur*) to gnaw

machette [maʃɛt] *f* machete

machiavélique [makjavelik] *adj* Machiavellian

mâchicoulis [mɑʃikuli] *m* machicolation

machin [maʃɛ̃] *m inf* (*truc*) thingummy *Brit,* whatchamacallit *Am*

Machin(**e**) [maʃɛ̃, in] *m inf* what's-his-name, her-name *m, f*

machinal(**e**) [maʃinal, o] <-aux> *adj* mechanical

machinalement [maʃinalmɑ̃] *adv* mechanically

machination [maʃinasjɔ̃] *f* plot; **de sombres ~s** dark dealings

machine [maʃin] *f* (*appareil*) appliance; ~ **à café** coffee machine; ~ **à coudre/à sous** sewing/slot machine; ~ **à écrire** typewriter; ~ **à laver** washing machine, washer *Am;* **écrire/taper à la** ~ to type ►**faire** ~ **arrière** to backpedal

machine-outil [maʃinuti] <machines-outils> *f* machine tool

machinerie [maʃinʀi] *f* **1.** (*équipement*) machinery **2.** (*salle des machines: d'un navire*) engine room

machinisme [maʃinism] *m* mechanization

machiniste [maʃinist] *mf* **1.** THEAT stagehand; MEDIA grip **2.** (*conducteur*) driver

machisme [mat(t)ʃism] *m* machismo

machiste [mat(t)ʃist] **I.** *adj* chauvinist **II.** *m* chauvinist

macho [matʃo] *m inf* macho

mâchoire [mɑʃwaʀ] *f* **1.** ANAT (*d'un mammi-*

fère) jaw; (*d'un insecte*) mandibule **2.** *pl* TECH jaws

mâchonner [mɑʃɔne] <1> *vt* **1.** (*mâcher, mordiller: cigare, crayon, paille, brin d'herbe*) to chew **2.** (*marmonner*) to mumble

mâchouiller [mɑʃuje] <1> *vt inf* to chew on

maçon(ne) [masɔ̃, ɔn] *m(f)* (*ouvrier*) bricklayer

maçonnerie [masɔnʀi] *f* **1.** (*ouvrage maçonné*) masonry **2.** (*secteur*) building **3.** (*franc-maçonnerie*) Freemasonry

macroordinateur [makʀoɔʀdinatœʀ] *m* INFOR mainframe

maculé(e) [makyle] *adj* **être ~ de qc** to be stained with sth

Madagascar [madagaskaʀ] *f* Madagascar; **à ~** in Madagascar

madame [madam, medam] <mesdames> *f* **1.** *souvent non traduit* (*femme à qui on s'adresse*) Madam *iron;* **bonjour ~** good morning; **bonjour Madame Larroque** good morning Mrs Larroque; **bonjour mesdames** good morning ladies; **Mesdames, mesdemoiselles, messieurs!** Ladies and Gentlemen! **2.** (*profession*) **Madame la Duchesse/le juge/le professeur/la Présidente** Madam **3.** (*sur une enveloppe*) **Madame Dupont** Mrs Dupont *Brit,* Mrs. Dupont *Am* **4.** (*en-tête*) (**Chère**) **Madame,** Dear Madam; **Madame, Monsieur,** Sir, Madam,; **Madame, Mademoiselle, Monsieur,** Mr, Mrs, Miss *Brit,* Mr., Mrs., Miss *Am*

madeleine [madlɛn] *f* GASTR madeleine ►<u>**pleurer**</u> **comme une Madeleine** to cry like a baby

mademoiselle [mad(ə)mwazɛl, med(ə)mwazɛl] <mesdemoiselles> *f* **1.** *souvent non traduit* (*jeune femme à qui on s'adresse*) Miss; **bonjour ~** good morning; **bonjour Mademoiselle Larroque** good morning Miss Larroque; **bonjour mesdemoiselles** good morning ladies; **Mesdames, mesdemoiselles, messieurs!** Ladies and Gentlemen! **2.** (*sur une enveloppe*) **Mademoiselle Aporé** Miss Aporé **3.** (*en-tête*) (**Chère**) **Mademoiselle,** Dear Madam; **Madame, Mademoiselle, Monsieur,** Mr, Mrs, Miss *Brit,* Mr., Mrs., Miss *Am*

> In France, unmarried women are called **Mademoiselle**, and married women **Madame**. At a certain age, this is also a compliment.

madère [madɛʀ] *m* Madeira

Madrid [madʀid] Madrid

madrier [madʀije] *m* beam

madrilène [madʀilɛn] *adj* **le climat ~** the Madrid climate

maestria [maɛstʀija] *f* mastery; **avec ~** brilliantly

maf(f)ia [mafja] *f* Mafia

maf(f)ieux, -euse [mafjø, -øz] *adj* Mafia

Maf(f)ieux, -euse [mafjø, -øz] *m, f* Mafioso

magasin [magazɛ̃] *m* **1.** (*boutique*) shop *Brit,* store *Am;* **~ spécialisé** specialist shop *Brit,* specialty store *Am;* **grand ~** department store; **~ d'alimentation/d'usine** food/factory shop *Brit,* food store/factory store *Am;* **tenir un ~** to run a shop **2.** (*entrepôt: d'un port*) warehouse; MIL arsenal; **en ~** in stock; **~ à blé** wheat hopper **3.** THEAT **~ des accessoires** props department **4.** TECH, PHOT magazine

magasinage [magazinaʒ] *m* **1.** COM storing **2.** *Québec* (*shopping*) shopping

magasiner [magazine] <1> *vi Québec* (*faire des courses*) to go shopping

magazine [magazin] *m* PRESSE, CINE, TV magazine; **~ électronique** webzine

mage [maʒ] **I.** *m* magus **II.** *app* **les Rois ~s** the Three Magi

Maghreb [magʀɛb] *m* **le ~** the Maghreb

> The **Maghreb** consists of the North African countries of Algeria, Morocco, Tunisia and Lybia, the first three of which were once under French control and are today marked by French culture. Because of the colonial history, there are many "maghrébins" living in France.

maghrébin(e) [magʀebɛ̃, in] *adj* North African

Maghrébin(e) [magʀebɛ̃, in] *m(f)* North African

magicien(ne) [maʒisjɛ̃, jɛn] *m(f)* **1.** (*sorcier*) wizard **2.** (*illusionniste*) magician

magie [maʒi] *f* **1.** (*pratiques occultes*) witchcraft **2.** (*séduction*) magic; **c'est de la ~!** it's magic!; **comme par ~** as if by magic

magique [maʒik] *adj* **1.** (*surnaturel*) **baguette ~** magic wand **2.** (*merveilleux*) magical

magistral(e) [maʒistʀal, o] <-aux> *adj* **1.** (*fameux, génial*) masterly; (*réussite*) brilliant **2.** *iron* (*grand: claque, coup de pied, raclée*) almighty; **un bide ~** a stupendous flop **3.** (*doctoral: ton, air*) learned **4.** UNIV, ECOLE **cours ~** lecture; **enseignement ~** lectures *pl* **5.** MED **un médicament ~** a magistral

magistrat [maʒistʀa] *m* ADMIN, JUR magistrate (*besides presiding judges, French magistrats include examining magistrates and mayors and councillors*)

magistrature [maʒistʀatyʀ] *f* **1.** (*fonction judiciaire*) magistracy (*rank of elected officials and presiding and investigating magistrates*)*;* **la ~ suprême** the presidency **2.** (*corps des magistrats*) the judiciary (*including investigating and presiding judges*)

magma [magma] *m* **1.** GEO magma **2.** (*bouillie*) mush

magnanime [maɲanim] *adj* magnanimous

magnat [maɲa] *m* **~ du pétrole/de la presse** oil/press baron

magner [maɲe] <1> *vpr inf* **se ~** to hurry up

magnésium [maɲezjɔm] *m* magnesium

magnétique [maɲetik] *adj* magnetic
magnétiser [maɲetize] <1> *vt* **1.** PHYS to magnetize **2.** (*fasciner*) to mesmerize
magnétisme [maɲetism] *m* **1.** PHYS magnetism **2.** (*fascination*) **subir le ~ de qn** to be under sb's charm
magnéto *inf,* **magnétophone** [maɲetɔfɔn] *m* **1.** (*à cassettes*) cassette recorder **2.** (*à bandes*) tape recorder
magnétoscope [maɲetɔskɔp] *m* video, VCR
magnificence [maɲifisɑ̃s] *f* **1.** (*somptuosité*) magnificence **2.** *soutenu* (*prodigalité*) lavishness
magnifique [maɲifik] *adj a. antéposé* **1.** (*très beau*) attractive; (*temps*) magnificent **2.** (*somptueux*) magnificent; (*femme*) gorgeous
magnifiquement [maɲifikmɑ̃] *adv* magnificently; (*se tirer de*) masterfully
magnolia [maɲɔlja] *m* magnolia
magnum [magnɔm] *m* magnum
magot [mago] *m inf* nest egg; **il a amassé un petit/joli ~** he's got a little/tidy bit put away
magouillage [magujaʒ] *m inf,* **magouille** [maguj] *f péj* scheming; **~ électorale** vote-fixing
magouiller [maguje] <1> *vi* to fiddle
magrébin(e) [magʀebɛ̃, in] *adj v.* **maghrébin**
Magrébin(e) [magʀebɛ̃, in] *m(f) v.* **Maghrébin**
maharadjah [maaʀadʒa] *m* Maharajah
mai [mɛ] *m* May ▸**en ~, fait ce qu'il te plaît** *prov* never cast a clout until May is out; *v. a.* **août**
maïeur [majœʀ] *m Belgique* (*maire*) mayor
maigre [mɛgʀ] **I.** *adj* **1.** (*opp: gros*) thin **2.** GASTR lean; (*bouillon*) clear; **lait ~** skimmed milk *Brit,* skim milk *Am* **3.** *antéposé* (*faible*) poor; (*chance*) slim; (*profit*) meagre *Brit,* meager *Am* **4.** *a. antéposé* (*peu abondant: végétation*) sparse; (*récolte*) poor; (*repas*) light **II.** *mf* thin person
maigreur [mɛgʀœʀ] *f* **1.** (*opp: embonpoint*) thinness; **être d'une ~ effrayante** to be frighteningly thin **2.** (*pauvreté: d'un sol*) poorness **3.** (*opp: abondance: d'un profit, des revenus*) meagreness *Brit,* meagerness *Am* **4.** (*rareté: de la végétation*) sparseness
maigrichon(ne) [megʀiʃɔ̃, ɔn] *adj inf v.* **maigrelet**
maigrir [megʀiʀ] <8> **I.** *vi* to lose weight; **il a maigri de figure** his face has slimmed down; **~ de cinq kilos** to loose five kilos **II.** *vt* **~ qn** to make sb look slimmer
maille [mɑj] *f* **1.** COUT stitch; **filet à fines ~s** finely-stitched net; **~ filée** ladder *Brit,* run *Am* **2.** (*maillon: d'une chaîne, armure*) link ▸**glisser entre les ~s (du filet)** to slip through the net
mailler [mɑje] <1> *vt Suisse* (*tordre*) to warp
maillet [majɛ] *m* mallet
maillon [mɑjɔ̃] *m* (*anneau*) link ▸**être un ~ de la chaîne** to be a link in the chain
maillot [majo] *m* **1.** (*pour se baigner*) **~ de bain** (*de femme*) swimsuit; (*d'homme*) swimming trunks; **~ de bain une pièce/deux pièces** one-/two-piece swimsuit **2.** SPORT football shirt **3.** (*sous-vêtement*) **~ de corps** vest
main [mɛ̃] *f* **1.** ANAT, SPORT hand; **battre des ~s** to clap one's hands; **se donner la ~** to hold hands; (*aider*) to help one another out; **passer de ~ en ~** to go from hand to hand; **prendre qn par la ~** to take sb by the hand; **serrer la ~ à qn** to shake sb's hand; **tendre la ~ à qn** to reach out to sb; **être fait (à la) ~** to be handmade; **sac à ~** handbag, purse *Am;* **frein à ~** hand brake *Brit,* parking brake *Am;* **écrire à la ~** to write (by hand); **(la) ~ dans la ~** hand in hand; **de la ~** directly; **de la ~ même de l'auteur** from the author's own hand; **à deux ~s** with both hands; **ramasser qc à pleines ~s** to pick up handfuls of sth; **jouer à quatre ~s** to play four-handed; **les ~s en l'air!, haut les ~s!** hands up! **2.** (*style: d'un artiste, maître*) style; **de ~ de maître** with a master's hand **3.** JEUX lead; **avoir la ~** to be in the lead ▸**donner un coup de ~ à qn** to give sb a hand; **tomber aux ~s de l'ennemi** to fall into the hands of the enemy; **j'en mettrais ma ~ au feu** I would stake my life on it; **mettre la ~ à la pâte** *inf* to lend a hand; **il met la ~ au porte-monnaie** he puts his hand in his pocket; **prendre qn la ~ dans le sac** to catch sb red-handed; **du cousu ~** handstitched; **gagner qc haut la ~** to win sth hands down; **voter à ~ levée** to vote by a show of hands; **avoir les ~s libres** to have a free hand; **à ~s nues** with bare fists; **de première/seconde ~** firsthand/secondhand; **remettre qc à qn en ~s propres** to give sth to sb personally; **avoir qc sous la ~** to have sth on hand; **ils peuvent se donner la ~** *iron* they are two of a kind; **être aux ~s de qn** to be at sb's hands; **il se fait la ~** he's getting the knack; **je m'en lave les ~s!** I wash my hands of it!; **passer la ~** (*transmettre ses pouvoirs*) to stand down; **il perd la ~** he's losing his touch; **en venir aux ~s** to come to blows; **de la ~ à la ~** directly
main-d'œuvre [mɛ̃dœvʀ] <mains-d'œuvre> *f* workforce
main-forte [mɛ̃fɔʀt] *f* **prêter ~ à qn** to help sb out
maintenance [mɛ̃tnɑ̃s] *f* maintenance
maintenant [mɛ̃t(ə)nɑ̃] *adv* **1.** *a. en tête de phrase* (*en ce moment, cela dit*) now; **dès ~** as of now **2.** (*actuellement*) today **3.** (*désormais*) henceforth
maintenir [mɛ̃t(ə)niʀ] <9> **I.** *vt* **1.** (*conserver: ordre, offre, contrat, politique*) to maintain; (*tradition*) to preserve; **~ un rendez-vous** to keep a meeting **2.** (*soutenir*) to keep; **~ sa tête hors de l'eau** to keep one's head out of the water **3.** (*contenir*) to hold; ~

les prix to hold prices **4.** (*affirmer*) to claim; ~ **que qc est vrai** to claim [*o* maintain] that sth is true **II.** *vpr* **se** ~ to persist; (*institution*) to live on; (*paix*) to hold; (*santé, prix*) to remain steady; **se** ~ **au second tour** (*candidat*) to survive to the second round; **se** ~ **en surface** to stay on the surface

maintien [mɛ̃tjɛ̃] *m* **1.** (*conservation*) upholding; (*des libertés, traditions*) preservation; (*d'un contrat*) maintenance **2.** (*attitude*) bearing **3.** (*soutien*) support

maire [mɛʀ] *mf* mayor

mairie [meʀi] *f* **1.** (*hôtel de ville*) town hall, city hall *Am* **2.** (*administration*) town council *Brit,* city council *Am* **3.** (*fonction de maire*) mayoralty

mais [mɛ] **I.** *conj* but **II.** *adv* **1.** (*pourtant, renforcement, impatience*) but; **tu ne m'aimes pas – ~ si!** you don't love me – yes I do!; ~ **encore** but besides **2.** *inf* (*indignation*) **non ~, tu me prends pour ...** for goodness sake, do you take me for ... **III.** *m* but

maïs [mais] *m* AGR maize, corn; GASTR sweetcorn

maison [mɛzɔ̃] **I.** *f* **1.** (*habitation*) house **2.** (*famille*) family; **être de la** ~ to be part of the family **3.** (*entreprise*) company; ~ **mère** parent company; ~ **de couture** fashion house; ~ **de disques** record shop; ~ **d'édition** publishing house; ~ **de jeux** gambling club; **avoir quinze ans de** ~ to have worked in the company for fifteen years **4.** (*bâtiment*) ~ **de maître** family mansion; ~ **d'arrêt** prison; ~ **de repos/retraite** convalescent/retirement home; ~ **des jeunes et de la culture** community youth and arts centre *Brit,* community youth and arts center *Am* ▸~ close brothel; **c'est gros comme une** ~ it's as big as a house **II.** *app inv* **1.** (*particulier à une* ~) in-house; (*esprit, genre*) house **2.** (*opp: industriel: pâté*) home-made

Maison-Blanche [mɛzɔ̃blɑ̃ʃ] *f sans pl* **la** ~ the White House

maisonnée [mɛzɔne] *f* household

maisonnette [mɛzɔnɛt] *f* small house; (*pour jeux*) Wendy house *Brit,* playhouse *Am*

maître [mɛtʀ] **I.** *m* ART, LIT master; **coup de** ~ master stroke; ~ **à penser** intellectual guide; **passer** ~ **dans l'art de faire qc** *fig* to become a (past) master in the art of doing sth **II.** *mf* UNIV ~ **de conférences** senior lecturer

maître, -esse [mɛtʀ, -ɛs] **I.** *adj* **1.** (*principal*) **œuvre maîtresse** master work **2.** (*qui peut disposer de*) **être** ~ **de son destin** to be master of one's destiny; **être** ~ **de soi** to be in control of oneself **II.** *m, f* **1.** (*chef*) master; ~ **des lieux** master of the house; ~ **de maison** host; ~ **d'hôtel** maître d'hôtel; **régner en** ~ to reign supreme **2.** (*patron*) instructor; ~ **nageur** swimming instructor **3.** ECOLE (*à l'école primaire*) teacher **4.** (*propriétaire: d'un chien*) master

maître chanteur [mɛtʀəʃɑ̃tœʀ] *m* blackmailer

maîtresse [mɛtʀɛs] **I.** *adj v.* **maître II.** *f* (*liaison*) mistress

maîtrise [metʀiz] *f* **1.** (*contrôle*) control; ~ **de fabrication** manufacturing control; ~ **d'une langue** mastery of a language **2.** (*habileté*) mastery **3.** (*sang-froid*) ~ **de soi** self-control **4.** UNIV master's degree **5.** (*grade*) supervisors *pl*

> The **maîtrise** is awarded after the completion of a "licence" after four years of university study and the submission of a "mémoire", or dissertation. It is a prerequisite for the admission to a "C.A.P.E.S", an "agrégation" and a "doctorat".

maîtriser [metʀize] <1> **I.** *vt* **1.** (*dominer, dompter: situation, difficulté, sujet*) to master; ~ **qn/qc** to bring sb/sth under control **2.** (*contenir: émotion, passion*) to suppress; (*réactions*) to control; (*larmes*) to force back **II.** *vpr* **se** ~ to control oneself

Majesté [maʒɛste] *f* **Votre** ~ Your Majesty

majestueux, -euse [maʒɛstɥø, -øz] *adj* majestic

majeur [maʒœʀ] *m* ANAT middle finger

majeur(e) [maʒœʀ] **I.** *adj* **1.** (*très important: difficulté, intérêt, événement*) major **2.** (*le plus important*) main; **son défaut** ~ his main fault **3.** *antéposé* (*la plupart*) **la ~e partie du temps** most of the time **4.** JUR **être** ~ to be of age **5.** (*apte à se diriger: peuple*) responsible **6.** MUS major; **do/ré/mi/fa** ~ C/D/E/F major ▸**être** ~ **et vacciné** *inf* to be old enough to take care of oneself **II.** *m(f)* JUR adult

major [maʒɔʀ] *m* **1.** ECOLE, UNIV top student; **être** ~ to be first in one's year *Brit,* to be top of one's class *Am* **2.** MIL adjutant

majoration [maʒɔʀasjɔ̃] *f* ADMIN, COM (*d'un prix*) increase; (*des impôts*) surcharge; ~ **de 10%** 10% increase

majorer [maʒɔʀe] <1> *vt* to increase; ~ **une facture de 3,5%** to add 3.5% on to a bill

majorette [maʒɔʀɛt] *f* majorette

majoritaire [maʒɔʀitɛʀ] *adj* **1.** POL **scrutin** ~ ballot requiring a majority; **être** ~ (*parti*) to be in the majority **2.** JUR, COM **associé** ~ associate with a majority holding

majoritairement [maʒɔʀitɛʀmɑ̃] *adv* as a majority

majorité [maʒɔʀite] *f* **1.** (*majeure partie*) majority; **la** ~ **de** the majority of; **en** ~ mostly; **les Français pensent dans leur** ~ **...** the majority of the French think that ... **2.** JUR majority

Majorque [maʒɔʀk(ə)] Majorca

majuscule [maʒyskyl] **I.** *adj* capital **II.** *f* capital; **en ~s (d'imprimerie)** in capitals

mal[1] [mal] **I.** *adv* **1.** badly; **ça va** ~ **finir!** it will end badly!; **le moment est vraiment** ~ **choisi** this really is not the best moment **2.** (*pas dans le bon ordre, de la bonne façon,* *de manière immorale*) **il s'y prend** ~ he is going about it the wrong way; **il a ~ tourné** he's gone wrong **3.** (*de manière inconvenante*) ~ **répondre** to reply rudely **4.** (*de manière défavorable*) **être ~ vu** to be frowned upon ▶**ça la fout** ~ *inf* it looks bad; **pas** ~ *avec ou sans nég* (*assez bien*) not bad; (*passablement, assez*) enough; *sans nég, inf* (*opp: très peu*) quite a few; **je m'en fiche pas** ~ I couldn't care less **II.** *adj inv* **1.** (*mauvais, immoral*) **faire quelque chose/ne rien faire de** ~ to do something/nothing bad; **j'ai dit quelque chose de ~?** did I say something wrong? **2.** (*malade: se sentir*) ill **3.** (*pas à l'aise*) **être** ~ to be uncomfortable **4.** (*en mauvais termes*) **être ~ avec qn** to be on bad terms with sb

mal² [mal, mo] <maux> *m* **1.** *a.* REL **le** ~ evil **2.** *sans pl* (*action, parole, pensée mauvaise*) harm; **faire du ~ à qn** to harm sb; **je n'en pense pas de** ~ I don't think badly of him/her/it; **sans penser à** ~ without meaning any harm; **dire du ~ de qn** to say bad things about sb; **il n'y a pas de ~ à qc** there is no harm in sth **3.** *sans pl* (*maladie, malaise*) illness; ~ **de l'air** airsickness; ~ **de mer** seasickness; ~ **des montagnes** altitude sickness **4.** (*souffrance physique*) ~ **de tête** headache; ~ **de ventre** stomach ache; **il a ~ à la main** his hand hurts; **avoir ~ à la jambe** to have a sore leg; (**se**) **faire** ~ to hurt (oneself); **ces chaussures me font ~ aux pieds** these shoes hurt my feet **5.** (*souffrance morale*) **faire** ~ to hurt; ~ **de vivre** depression; ~ **du pays** homesickness; **qn/qc me fait ~ au cœur** sb/sth makes me feel sick **6.** (*calamité*) disaster **7.** *sans pl* (*peine*) difficulty; **il a du ~ à supporter qc** he has difficulty putting up with sth; **se donner un ~ de chien pour** *+infin inf* to bend over backwards to *+infin* **8.** *sans pl* (*dégât*) damage; **le travail ne fait pas de ~ à qn** hard work never hurt anyone; **prendre son ~ en patience** to grin and bear it; **mettre qc à** ~ to damage sth **9.** (*manque*) **un peintre en ~ d'inspiration** a painter suffering from a lack of inspiration ▶**elle ne ferait pas de ~ à une mouche** *inf* she wouldn't hurt a fly; **le ~ est fait** the damage is done

malabar [malabaʀ] *m inf* hulk

malade [malad] **I.** *adj* **1.** (*souffrant*) ill; **tomber** ~ to fall ill; **être ~ du sida** to suffer from AIDS; **être ~ du cœur** to have a heart complaint **2.** (*bouleversé*) ~ **de jalousie/d'inquiétude** to be sick with jealousy/worry **3.** *inf* (*cinglé*) **être** ~ to be crazy **4.** (*en mauvais état: économie, entreprise*) in a bad way **II.** *mf* **1.** (*personne souffrante*) invalid; **grand** ~ seriously ill person; ~ **mental** mentally ill person **2.** (*patient*) patient

maladie [maladi] *f* **1.** (*affection*) illness; ~ **de cœur/peau** heart/skin complaint; ~ **infantile/mentale** childhood/mental illness; **être en** ~ to be off work sick **2.** (*manie*) mania; **il a la ~ de tout ranger** he has a mania for tidying everything, he is a clean freak *Am* ▶**faire une ~ de qc** *inf* to make a mountain out of sth

maladif, -ive [maladif, -iv] *adj* **1.** (*souffreteux: personne*) sickly; (*air, pâleur*) unhealthy **2.** (*maniaque: besoin, peur*) pathological

maladresse [maladʀɛs] *f* **1.** (*gaucherie: d'un comportement, geste*) clumsiness; (*de caresses, d'un style*) awkwardness **2.** (*bévue, gaffe*) blunder

maladroit(e) [maladʀwa, wat] **I.** *adj* **1.** (*opp: habile, leste: geste, personne*) clumsy; (*caresses, style, personne*) awkward **2.** *fig* (*parole, remarque*) tactless **II.** *m(f)* **1.** (*personne malhabile*) butterfingers **2.** (*gaffeur*) blunderer

maladroitement [maladʀwatmɑ̃] *adv* (*gauchement*) clumsily; **s'exprimer** ~ to be tactless

malaise [malɛz] *m* **1.** MED faintness; **avoir un** ~ to feel faint **2.** (*crise*) discontent; ~ **politique/social** political/social unrest

malaisé(e) [maleze] *adj* difficult; **il est ~ de faire qc** sth is difficult [*o* hard] to do

Malaisie [malezi] *f* **la** ~ Malaysia

malaria [malaʀja] *f* malaria

Malawi [malawi] *m* Malawi

malawite [malawit(ə)] *adj* Malawian

Malawite [malawit(ə)] *mf* Malawian

malaxer [malakse] <1> *vt* (*argile, beurre*) to knead; (*ciment, mortier*) to mix

malchance [malʃɑ̃s] *f* misfortune

malchanceux, -euse [malʃɑ̃sø, -øz] *adj* (*personne*) unlucky

Maldives [maldiːv(ə)] *fpl* **les** ~ the Maldives *pl*

mâle [mɑl] *adj, m* male

malédiction [malediksjɔ̃] *f* **1.** (*fatalité, action de maudire*) malediction **2.** (*malheur*) curse

maléfice [malefis] *m soutenu* evil spell

maléfique [malefik] *adj soutenu* evil

malencontreux, -euse [malɑ̃kɔ̃tʀø, -øz] *adj* inopportune

malentendant(e) [malɑ̃tɑ̃dɑ̃, ɑ̃t] *m(f)* person with hearing difficulties; **les ~s** the hard of hearing

malentendu [malɑ̃tɑ̃dy] *m* misunderstanding

malfaçon [malfasɔ̃] *f* **1.** (*à l'usine*) defect **2.** (*mauvais travail*) defective workmanship

malfaisant(e) [malfəzɑ̃, ɑ̃t] *adj* **1.** (*nuisible: animal, être*) harmful **2.** (*pernicieux*) evil

malfaiteur, -trice [malfɛtœʀ, -tʀis] *m, f* criminal

malformation [malfɔʀmasjɔ̃] *f* malformation; ~ **du cœur** malformed heart

malfrat [malfʀa] *m inf* **un petit** ~ a little crook

malgache [malgaʃ(ə)] **I.** *m* Malagasy; *v. a.* **français II.** *adj* Malagasy

Malgache [malgaʃ(ə)] *mf* Malagasy

malgré [malgʀe] *prep* 1.(*en dépit de*) despite; ~ **tout** despite everything 2.(*contre le gré de*) ~ **moi/elle/lui** against my/her/his will 3.(*sans le vouloir*) **j'ai entendu ~ moi ce que vous venez de dire** I couldn't help hearing what you just said

malhabile [malabil] *adj* awkward

malheur [malœʀ] *m* 1.(*événement pénible*) misfortune; **si jamais il m'arrivait ~** if ever anything bad happened to me 2. *sans pl* (*malchance*) bad luck; **par ~** through bad luck 3.(*tort*) **avoir le ~ de** +*infin* to be foolish enough to +*infin* ►**le ~ des uns fait le bonheur des autres** *prov* one man's joy is a another man's sorrow; **un ~ ne vient jamais seul** *prov* it never rains but it pours; **faire un ~** *inf* (*faire un scandale*) to go mad; (*avoir un gros succès*) to be a big hit; **(ne) parle pas de ~!** *inf* don't tempt fate; **oiseau de ~** bird of ill omen

malheureusement [maløʀøzmɑ̃] *adv* (*hélas*) unfortunately

malheureux, **-euse** [maløʀø, -øz] I. *adj* 1.(*qui souffre: personne, air*) unhappy 2. *a. antéposé* (*regrettable, fâcheux*) regrettable; (*incident, suites, initiative, parole*) unfortunate 3.(*malchanceux: candidat, joueur*) unlucky; **être ~ au jeu/en amour** to be unlucky in sport/love 4. *antéposé* (*insignifiant*) wretched 5. *antéposé* (*infortuné: victime*) unfortunate II. *m, f* 1.(*indigent*) needy person 2.(*infortuné*) poor soul

malhonnête [malɔnɛt] *adj* 1.(*indélicat, déloyal*) dishonest 2. *iron* rude

malhonnêtement [malɔnɛtmɑ̃] *adv* dishonestly

malhonnêteté [malɔnɛtte] *f* dishonesty

mali [mali] *m Belgique* (*déficit*) deficit

Mali [mali] *m* **le ~** Mali

malice [malis] *f* 1.(*espièglerie*) mischief; **avec ~** archly 2.(*méchanceté*) spite

malicieux, **-euse** [malisjø, -jøz] *adj* (*espiègle*) mischievous; (*méchant*) malicious

malien(ne) [maljɛ̃, ɛn] *adj* Malian

Malien(ne) [maljɛ̃, ɛn] *m(f)* Malian

malin, **maligne** [malɛ̃, maliɲ] I. *adj* 1.(*astucieux: personne*) shrewd; (*sourire*) cunning; (*air*) smart 2. *a. antéposé* (*méchant*) sly; (*influence*) malicious 3. MED (*tumeur*) malignant II. *m, f* (*personne astucieuse*) crafty person; **faire le ~** to show off; **gros ~!** *iron* clever stick!; **petit ~** crafty one

malingre [malɛ̃gʀ] *adj* puny

malintentionné(e) [malɛ̃tɑ̃sjɔne] *adj* ill-intentioned

malle [mal] *f* trunk ►**se faire la ~** *inf* to make oneself scarce

malléable [maleabl] *adj* 1.(*souple: personne*) flexible 2. TECH (*argile*) pliable; (*métal*) malleable

mallette [malɛt] *f* 1.(*porte-documents*) briefcase 2. *Belgique* (*cartable d'écolier*) satchel

malmener [malməne] <4> *vt* 1.(*rudoyer*) to manhandle 2.(*critiquer*) to criticize 3. MIL, SPORT (*bousculer*) ~ **qn** to give sb a hard time

malnutrition [malnytʀisjɔ̃] *f* malnutrition

malodorant(e) [malɔdɔʀɑ̃, ɑ̃t] *adj* foul-smelling

malotru(e) [malɔtʀy] *m(f)* lout

malpoli(e) [malpɔli] I. *adj inf* (*mal élevé*) discourteous; (*enfant*) rude II. *m(f) inf* rude person

malpropre [malpʀɔpʀ] I. *adj* (*sale*) dirty II. *mf inf* **traiter qn comme un ~** to treat sb like dirt

malsain(e) [malsɛ̃, ɛn] *adj* unhealthy

malt [malt] *m* malt

Malte [malt(ə)] *f* Malta

maltraitance [maltʀɛtɑ̃s] *f* abuse

maltraiter [maltʀete] <1> *vt* 1.(*brutaliser*) to mistreat 2.(*critiquer*) to slam

malus [malys] *m* claim surcharge

malveillance [malvɛjɑ̃s] *f* 1.(*hostilité*) ill will; **avec ~** spitefully 2.(*intention de nuire*) malevolence

malveillant(e) [malvɛjɑ̃, ɑ̃t] *adj* spiteful

malvoyant(e) [malvwajɑ̃, ɑ̃t] *m(f)* partially sighted person

maman [mamɑ̃] *f* 1.(*mère*) mother; **future ~** mother-to-be 2.(*appellation*) mummy *Brit*, mommy *Am*

mamelle [mamɛl] *f* ANAT (*de la chèvre, vache*) udder; (*de la chienne, chatte, lapine*) teat

mamelon [mam(ə)lɔ̃] *m* 1. ANAT nipple 2. GEO hillock

mamie [mami] *f inf* granny

mammifère [mamifɛʀ] *mf* mammal

mammouth [mamut] *m* mammoth

mamy [mami] *f v.* **mamie**

manager[1] [manadʒɛʀ, manadʒœʀ] *m* ECON, SPORT manager; THEAT agent

manager[2] [mana(d)ʒe] <2a> *vt* to manage

manche[1] [mɑ̃ʃ] *f* 1. COUT (*d'un vêtement*) sleeve 2.(*aux courses*) round 3.(*au ski*) leg 4. JEUX game ►**faire la ~** to beg

manche[2] [mɑ̃ʃ] *m* 1.(*poignée*) handle 2. MUS (*d'une guitare, d'un violon*) neck ►**se débrouiller comme un ~ pour qc** *inf* to make a pig's ear of sth

Manche [mɑ̃ʃ] *f* **la ~** the English Channel

Manchester [mɑ̃ʃɛstɛːʀ] Manchester; **habitant de ~** Mancunian; **agglomération de ~** Greater Manchester

manchette [mɑ̃ʃɛt] *f* 1.(*poignet: d'une chemise*) cuff 2. SPORT forearm blow 3. COUT false sleeve 4. TECH headline

manchon [mɑ̃ʃɔ̃] *m* 1. muff 2. TECH (*bague, cylindre*) sleeve 3. TECH (*d'une lampe*) mantle

manchot [mɑ̃ʃo] *m* (*pingouin*) penguin

manchot(e) [mɑ̃ʃo, ɔt] I. *adj* (*amputé d'un bras*) one-armed II. *m(f)* (*personne*) person with one arm

mandarine [mɑ̃daʀin] *f* mandarin

mandat [mɑ̃da] *m* 1.(*mission*) mandate

M

2. JUR ~ **d'arrêt** arrest warrant 3. COM, FIN postal order *Brit,* money order *Am*

mandater [mɑ̃date] <1> *vt* 1. JUR, POL ~ **un avocat pour** *+infin* to appoint a lawyer to *+infin;* **être mandaté** to be duly appointed 2. FIN (*payer*) ~ **qc** to pay sth by money order

mandibule [mɑ̃dibyl] *f* ZOOL (*pièce buccale*) mandible ▶**jouer des ~s** *inf* to munch away

mandoline [mɑ̃dɔlin] *f* mandolin

mandragore [mɑ̃dʀagɔʀ] *f* mandrake

manège [manɛʒ] *m* 1. (*attraction foraine*) roundabout *Brit,* merry-go-round *Am* 2. (*agissements*) ruse

manette [manɛt] *f* INFOR ~ **de jeu** joystick

mangeable [mɑ̃ʒabl] *adj* edible

mangeaille [mɑ̃ʒaj] *f inf* grub

mangeoire [mɑ̃ʒwaʀ] *f* manger

manger [mɑ̃ʒe] <2a> I. *vt* 1. (*se nourrir de, absorber*) to eat 2. (*ronger: mites, rouille, lèpre*) to eat away 3. *iron* (*dévorer*) to devour 4. (*dilapider: capital, héritage, temps*) to swallow up 5. (*consommer: essence*) to guzzle 6. *inf* (*ne pas articuler: mots*) to mumble II. *vi* (*personne, animal*) to eat; **inviter qn à ~** to invite sb to dinner; **donner à ~ à un bébé/aux vaches** to feed a baby/the cows III. *vpr* **qc se mange chaud/avec les doigts** sth is eaten hot/with one's fingers

mange-tout [mɑ̃ʒtu] *app inv* **pois ~** mange-touts, string beans; **haricots ~** mange-tout beans

mangeur, -euse [mɑ̃ʒœʀ, -ʒøz] *m, f* **gros ~** big eater

mangouste [mɑ̃gust] *f* (*animal*) mongoose

mangue [mɑ̃g] *f* mango

maniabilité [manjabilite] *f* (*d'une voiture*) manoeuvrability *Brit,* maneuverability *Am;* (*d'un appareil, d'une machine*) ease of use; (*d'un livre, outil*) handiness

maniable [manjabl] *adj* (*voiture, appareil, machine*) easy to handle; (*livre, outil*) handy

maniaque [manjak] I. *adj* 1. (*pointilleux: soin*) fanatical; (*personne*) fussy 2. MED, PSYCH (*euphorie*) maniacal II. *mf* 1. (*personne trop méticuleuse*) fanatic; **être un ~ de l'ordre** to be fanatical about tidiness, to be a clean freak *Am* 2. MED, PSYCH maniac; **~ sexuel** sex maniac

manichéisme [manikeism] *m* Manicheism

manie [mani] *f* 1. (*tic*) habit 2. *a.* MED, PSYCH (*mania*) ~ **de la propreté** mania for cleanliness; ~ **de la persécution** persecution mania

maniement [manimɑ̃] *m* 1. (*manipulation*) handling; (*d'un appareil*) use 2. (*gestion: des affaires*) management 3. (*maîtrise: d'une langue*) use

manier [manje] <1> *vt* 1. (*se servir de, utiliser, maîtriser*) to use; (*appareil*) to handle; ~ **l'ironie/l'humour** to use irony/humour *Brit,* to use irony/humor *Am* 2. (*manipuler, avoir entre les mains*) ~ **qn/qc** to manipulate sb/sth 3. (*gérer*) ~ **de grosses sommes d'argent** to manage large sums of money

manière [manjɛʀ] *f* 1. (*façon*) way; ~ **de faire qc** way of doing sth; **avoir la ~** to have the knack; **à la ~ de qn/qc** like sb/sth; **à ma/sa ~** in my/her own way; **de ~ brutale/rapide** brutally/quickly; **d'une certaine ~** in a way; **d'une ~ générale** generally; **d'une ~ ou d'une autre** in one way or another; **de toute ~** in any case; **de ~ à** *+infin* so as to *+infin;* **de ~ (à ce) qu'il soit satisfait** (*subj*) so that he's satisfied; **de quelle ~?** how?; **en aucune ~** not at all 2. *pl* (*comportement*) manners; **faire des ~s** to put on airs; **en voilà des ~s!** what a way to behave! 3. (*style: d'un artiste, écrivain*) manner 4. LING **adverbe/complément de ~** adverb/complement of manner ▶**la ~ forte** stong measures *pl;* **employer la ~ forte** to be tough

maniéré(e) [manjeʀe] *adj* mannered; (*ton, personne*) affected

manif [manif] *f abr de* **manifestation** *inf* demo

manifestant(e) [manifɛstɑ̃, ɑ̃t] *m(f)* demonstrator

manifestation [manifɛstasjɔ̃] *f* 1. POL demonstration 2. (*événement*) event 3. (*expression: d'un sentiment*) expression; (*d'une humeur*) show; (*de joie, amitié*) demonstration; **les ~s d'une maladie** the symptoms of an illness

manifeste [manifɛst] I. *adj* obvious; (*vérité*) evident II. *m* POL, LIT manifesto

manifestement [manifɛstəmɑ̃] *adv* obviously

manifester [manifɛste] <1> I. *vt* to show II. *vi* to demonstrate III. *vpr* **se ~** 1. (*se révéler*) to appear; (*crise*) to arise 2. (*se faire connaître*) to make oneself known; (*candidat*) to put oneself forward 3. (*s'exprimer*) to express oneself 4. (*se montrer: personne*) to appear

manigance [manigɑ̃s] *f gén pl* scheme

manigancer [manigɑ̃se] <2> *vt* to scheme

manioc [manjɔk] *m* cassava

manipulation [manipylasjɔ̃] *f* 1. (*maniement: d'une machine, d'un ordinateur*) use; (*d'un outil, d'un produit, d'une substance*) handling 2. *pl* (*expériences*) experiments 3. (*prestidigitation*) sleight of hand 4. *péj* (*manœuvre: de la foule, l'opinion*) manipulation *no pl*

manipuler [manipyle] <1> *vt* 1. (*manier: outil*) to use; (*substance*) to handle 2. *péj* (*fausser*) to manipulate; (*écritures, résultats*) to fiddle 3. (*influencer*) to manipulate

manivelle [manivɛl] *f* AUTO starting handle

mannequin [mankɛ̃] *m* 1. (*pour le tailleur, la vitrine*) dummy 2. (*pour le peintre, sculpteur, de mode*) model

manœuvre [manœvʀ] I. *f* 1. (*maniement: d'une machine*) operation; (*d'un véhicule*) handling; **fausse ~** error; *fig* wrong move 2. (*action, exercice*) *a.* MIL manoeuvre *Brit,* maneuver *Am;* ~ **d'évitement** avoiding action; ~ **de diversion** diversion 3. *péj* (*agis-*

sement, machination) ploy; **les ~s dilatoires** stalling tactics **II.** *m* labourer *Brit,* laborer *Am*

manœuvrer [manœvʀe] <1> **I.** *vt* **1.** (*faire fonctionner: machine*) to operate; (*outil*) to use **2.** (*conduire: véhicule*) to drive **3.** *péj* (*manipuler*) to manipulate **II.** *vi* **1.** (*agir habilement*) *a.* MIL to manoeuvre *Brit,* to maneuver *Am* **2.** AUTO to manoeuvre the car *Brit,* to maneuver the car *Am*

manoir [manwaʀ] *m* manor

manomètre [manɔmɛtʀ] *m* manometer

manouche [manuʃ] *mf inf* Gypsy

manquant(e) [mɑ̃kɑ̃, ɑ̃t] *adj* (*pièce, somme, article*) missing; (*personne*) absent

manque [mɑ̃k] *m* **1.** (*carence*) lack; **~ à gagner** loss of earnings; **un enfant en ~ d'affection** a child lacking affection **2.** *pl* (*lacunes*) failings **3.** (*défauts*) faults **4.** (*vide*) gap **5.** MED (*privation*) withdrawal; **être en** (**état de**) **~** to have withdrawal symptoms

manqué(e) [mɑ̃ke] *adj* **1.** (*raté: occasion, rendez-vous*) missed; (*roman*) failed; (*photo*) spoilt **2.** *postposé, iron, inf* failed

manquer [mɑ̃ke] <1> **I.** *vt* **1.** (*rater, laisser passer: but, bus, train, marche*) to miss; **une occasion à ne pas ~** a chance not to be missed **2.** (*se venger*) **ne pas ~ qn** to not let sb get away with it **3.** (*opp: réussir: examen*) to fail **4.** (*opp: assister à: film, réunion*) to miss; (*cours, école*) to skip; **~ la classe** to skip class ►**ne pas en ~ <u>une</u>** *inf* to never miss a chance to put one's foot in it **II.** *vi* **1.** (*être absent*) to be missing **2.** (*faire défaut, être insuffisant, ne pas avoir assez de*) **commencer à ~** to start to run out; **qc te manque pour** *+infin* you don't have sth to *+infin;* **qn/qc manque de qn/qc** sb/sth is lacking sb/sth; **tu ne manques pas de toupet!** you've got some nerve! **3.** (*regretter de ne pas avoir*) **mes enfants/les livres me manquent** I miss my children/books **4.** (*rater: attentat, tentative*) to fail **5.** (*ne pas respecter*) **il manque à sa parole/promesse** he fails to keep his word/promise; **~ à ses devoirs/obligations** to neglect one's duty/obligations **6.** (*faillir*) **~** (**de**) **faire qc** to almost do sth **7.** (*ne pas omettre*) **ne pas ~ de** *+infin* to be sure to *+infin* ►**ça n'a <u>pas</u> manqué!** it was bound to happen!; **il ne manquait <u>plus</u> que ça** that's all we needed **III.** *vpr* **1.** (*rater son suicide*) **se ~** to make a mess of one's suicide bid **2.** (*ne pas se rencontrer*) **se ~ de 5 minutes** to miss each other by 5 minutes

mansarde [mɑ̃saʀd] *f* garret

mansardé(e) [mɑ̃saʀde] *adj* attic; **chambre ~e** attic room; **être ~** to have a sloping roof

mante [mɑ̃t] *f* **1.** ZOOL **~** (**religieuse**) praying mantis **2.** *fig* **~ religieuse** man-eater

manteau [mɑ̃to] <x> *m* coat

manucure [manykyʀ] *mf* manicurist

manuel [manɥɛl] *m* **1.** (*livre didactique*) handbook; **~ scolaire** textbook **2.** (*manuel d'utilisation*) manual

manuel(le) [manɥɛl] **I.** *adj* manual **II.** *m(f)* **1.** (*personne qui travaille de ses mains*) manual worker **2.** (*personne douée de ses mains*) practical type

manufacture [manyfaktyʀ] *f* factory; **~ de tapisseries** tapestry workshop

manufacturé(e) [manyfaktyʀe] *adj* manufactured

manuscrit [manyskʀi] *m* manuscript

manuscrit(e) [manyskʀi, it] *adj* (*écrit à la main*) handwritten

manutention [manytɑ̃sjɔ̃] *f* **1.** (*manipulation*) handling **2.** (*local*) storehouse

manutentionnaire [manytɑ̃sjɔnɛʀ] *mf* warehouse worker

maous(se) [maus] *adj inf* enormous; **brochet ~** whopping great pike

mappemonde [mapmɔ̃d] *f* **1.** (*carte*) map of the world **2.** (*globe terrestre*) globe

maquer [make] <1> *vt inf* (*être le souteneur de*) **~ une femme** to be a woman's pimp; **être maquée** to have a man; (*prostituée*) to have a pimp

maquereau[1] [makʀo] <x> *m* ZOOL mackerel

maquereau[2] [makʀo] <x> *m inf* (*souteneur*) pimp

maquette [makɛt] *f* **1.** (*modèle réduit, jouet*) model; **~ d'avion/de bateau** model aeroplane/boat *Brit,* model airplane/boat *Am* **2.** TYP paste-up; (*d'une couverture*) art work **3.** (*projet*) mock up **4.** ART sketch

maquillage [makijaʒ] *m* **1.** (*se maquiller, produits de beauté*) make-up **2.** (*falsification: de documents*) faking; (*d'une voiture*) disguising

maquiller [makije] <1> **I.** *vt* **1.** (*farder*) **~ qn** to make sb up **2.** (*falsifier*) to fake; (*vérité*) to doctor; (*voiture*) to disguise; **~ un meurtre en suicide** to make a murder look like suicide **II.** *vpr* (*se farder*) **se ~** to put on one's make-up

maquilleur, **-euse** [makijœʀ, -jøz] *m, f* make-up artist

maquis [maki] *m* **1.** BOT scrubland **2.** (*groupe de résistance*) underground; HIST Maquis (*resistance movement in the Second World War*)*;* **prendre le ~** to join the Resistance

maquisard(e) [makizaʀ, aʀd] *m(f)* HIST resistance fighter (*in the Second World War*)

marabout [maʀabu] *m* **1.** ZOOL marabou **2.** REL marabout

maraîcher, **-ère** [maʀeʃe, -ɛʀ] **I.** *adj* **région maraîchère** market gardening area; **des produits ~s** market garden produce **II.** *m, f* market gardener

marais [maʀɛ] *m* marsh

marasme [maʀasm] *m* **1.** (*stagnation*) slump; **~ des affaires** slump in business **2.** (*découragement*) depression

marathon [maʀatɔ̃] *m, app a.* SPORT, POL marathon

marâtre [maʀɑtʀ] *f fig* wicked stepmother

marbre [maʀbʀ] *m* **1.** (*pierre, objet, statue*) marble **2.** (*plateau: d'une cheminée*) marble mantel; (*d'une commode*) marble top **3.** *fig* **cœur de** ~ heart of stone; **visage de** ~ stony face; **être/rester de** ~ to be/remain indifferent

marbré(e) [maRbRe] *adj* **1.** (*veiné*) marbled; **gâteau** ~ marble cake **2.** (*marqué*) **être** ~ (*par des coups*) to be marked; (*par le froid*) to be mottled

marbrer [maRbRe] <1> *vt* (*décorer de veines*) to marble

marbrier, -ière [maRbRije, -ijɛR] **I.** *adj* marble **II.** *m, f* monumental mason

marbrure [maRbRyR] *f* **1.** (*décoration: d'une boiserie, de la tranche d'un livre, d'un papier*) marbling **2.** (*marque violacée*) blotch

marc [maR] *m* **1.** (*résidu*) marc; ~ **de pommes/raisins** apple/grape marc; ~ **de café/thé** coffee/tea dregs **2.** (*eau de vie*) marc

marcassin [maRkasɛ̃] *m* ZOOL young wild boar

marchand(e) [maRʃɑ̃, ɑ̃d] **I.** *adj* **1.** (*qui transporte des marchandises: marine, navire*) merchant **2.** (*où se pratique le commerce*) **rue** ~**e** market street; **galerie** ~**e** shopping arcade **3.** (*dans le commerce*) **valeur** ~**e** market value **II.** *m(f)* **1.** (*commerçant*) tradesman; ~ **ambulant** travelling salesman *Brit*, traveling salesman *Am* **2.** *fig* ~ **d'illusions** illusion-monger; ~ **de rêve** dream-merchant; ~ **de sable** sandman; ~ **de tapis** *péj* tough bargainer

marchandage [maRʃɑ̃daʒ] *m* **1.** (*discussion*) bargaining **2.** (*tractation*) dealings

marchander [maRʃɑ̃de] <1> **I.** *vt* ~ **le prix/un tapis** to bargain over the price/a carpet **II.** *vi* to bargain

marchandise [maRʃɑ̃diz] *f* merchandise

marche[1] [maRʃ] *f* **1.** (*action*) *a.* SPORT walking; **se mettre en** ~ (*personnes*) to make a move; (*cortège, caravane*) to set off; ~ **à suivre** procedure **2.** (*allure*) gait; (*d'un navire*) sailing **3.** (*trajet*) walk **4.** MIL, POL march; **une** ~ **pacifique/de protestation** a peace/protest march; **faire** ~ **sur qc** to march upon sth **5.** (*mouvement continu: d'une étoile*) course; (*d'une caravane, d'un véhicule*) movement; **dans le sens de la** ~ facing the engine; **en** ~ **arrière** in reverse **6.** (*fonctionnement: d'une entreprise, horloge*) working; (*d'une machine*) functioning; **le moteur est en** ~ the engine's running; **mettre une machine/un appareil en** ~ to start up a machine/device **7.** MUS march ►**faire** ~ **arrière** to backpedal; AUTO to reverse; **être en** ~ (*démocratie*) to be on the march

marche[2] [maRʃ] *f* (*d'un escalier*) stair; (*d'un véhicule, devant une maison*) step

marché [maRʃe] *m* **1.** (*lieu de vente, opérations financières, l'offre et la demande, clientèle potentielle*) market; ~ **aux puces** flea market; ~ **des capitaux** money market; ~ **en croissance** growth market; **le** ~ **unique** the single market **2.** (*contrat*) bargain; **conclure un** ~ **avec qn/qc** to strike a deal with sb/sth; ~ **conclu!** it's a deal! ►**bon** ~ *inv* cheap; **par-dessus le** ~ on top of all that

marchepied [maRʃəpje] *m* **1.** (*marche*) step **2.** (*escabeau*) steps *pl* ►**servir de** ~ **à qn** to be a stepping stone for sb

marcher [maRʃe] <1> *vi* **1.** (*se déplacer*) to walk; ~ **à reculons** to walk backwards; ~ **à la rencontre de qn** to walk towards sb **2.** MIL ~ **sur la ville/Paris** to march on the town/Paris **3.** (*poser le pied*) ~ **sur/dans qc** to step on/in sth **4.** *fig* ~ **sur/dans qc** to tread on/in sth **5.** (*être en activité: métro, bus*) to run; ~ **à l'essence/l'électricité** to run on petrol/electricity *Brit*, to run on gas/electricity *Am* **6.** (*fonctionner*) to function; (*montre, télé, machine*) to work **7.** (*réussir: affaire, film*) to be a success; (*études*) to go well; (*procédé*) to work **8.** *inf* (*croire naïvement*) to be taken in; **faire** ~ **qn** to take sb in **9.** *inf* (*être d'accord*) **je marche** (**avec vous**) OK!; **ça marche!** (*au restaurant*) coming up!

marcheur, -euse [maRʃœR, -øz] *m, f a.* SPORT walker; POL marcher

mardi [maRdi] *m* Tuesday; *v. a.* **dimanche** ►~ **gras** Shrove Tuesday, Pancake Tuesday *Brit*; (*carnaval*) mardi gras

mare [maR] *f* **1.** (*eau stagnante*) pond **2.** (*après la pluie*) puddle **3.** (*flaque*) ~ **de sang/d'huile** pool of blood/oil

marécage [maRekaʒ] *m* marsh

marécageux, -euse [maRekaʒø, -ʒøz] *adj* marshy; (*plante*) marsh

maréchal(e) [maReʃal, o] <-aux> *m* marshal; ~ **de camp** brigadier; ~ **des logis** sergeant; ~ **des logis-chef** staff sergeant

maréchal-ferrant [maReʃalfeRɑ̃] <maréchaux-ferrants> *m* blacksmith

marée [maRe] *f* (*mouvements de la mer*) tide; **à** ~ **basse/haute** at low/high tide **2.** ~ **humaine** surge of people; ~ **noire** oil slick

marelle [maRɛl] *f* ≈ hopscotch

marennes [maRɛn] *f* Marennes oyster

mareyeur, -euse [maRɛjœR, -jøz] *m, f* fish wholesaler

margaille [maRgɑj] *f Belgique* **1.** *fam* (*bagarre, mêlée bruyante*) scuffle **2.** (*désordre*) mess

margarine [maRgaRin] *f* margarine

marge [maRʒ] *f* **1.** (*espace blanc, délai*) margin; ~ **d'erreur** margin of error; ~ **bénéficiaire** profit margin **2.** *fig* **vivre en** ~ **de la société** to live cut off from society

margelle [maRʒɛl] *f* coping

marginal(e) [maRʒinal, o] <-aux> **I.** *adj* **1.** (*accessoire*) marginal **2.** (*en marge de la société, peu orthodoxe*) **être** ~ to be on the fringes (of society) **II.** *m(f)* **1.** (*asocial*) dropout **2.** (*en marge de la société*) fringe member of society

marguerite [maRgəRit] *f* daisy

mari [maRi] *m* husband

mariage [maRjaʒ] *m* **1.** (*institution, union*)

marriage; ~ **blanc** unconsummated marriage; ~ **de raison** marriage of convenience; **demander qn en** ~ to ask sb's hand in marriage; **faire un riche** ~ to marry somebody rich **2.** (*cérémonie*) wedding **3.** (*vie conjugale*) married life; **fêter les 25/10 ans de** ~ to celebrate 25/10 years of marriage **4.** (*de plusieurs choses*) marriage **5.** (*combinaison*) combination

Mariannes-du-Nord [maʀjan(ə) dy nɔʀ] *fpl* Northern Mariana Islands

marié(e) [maʀje] **I.** *adj* **être** ~ to be married **II.** *m(f)* **1.** (*le jour du mariage*) **les ~s** the married couple **2.** (~ *depuis peu*) **jeune** ~ newlywed *Brit,* newlywed *Am;* **les jeunes ~s** the newly-weds

marier [maʀje] <1> **I.** *vt* **1.** (*procéder au mariage de, donner en mariage*) ~ **qn avec qn** to marry sb to sb **2.** *Belgique, Nord, Québec* (*épouser*) to marry **3.** (*combiner*) to combine; (*couleurs, goûts, parfums*) to marry **II.** *vpr* **1.** (*contracter mariage*) **se** ~ **avec qn** to marry sb **2.** (*s'harmoniser*) **se** ~ **(ensemble)** to blend; **se** ~ **avec qc** to marry with sth

marihuana, **marijuana** [maʀiʀwana] *f* marijuana

marin [maʀɛ̃] *m* sailor

marin(e) [maʀɛ̃, in] *adj* **1.** (*relatif à la mer*) sea **2.** (*relatif au marin: costume*) sailor

marinade [maʀinad] *f* marinade; ~ **de saumon** marinaded salmon

marine [maʀin] **I.** *f* navy **II.** *adj gén inv* navy (blue)

mariner [maʀine] <1> **I.** *vt* GASTR to marinate **II.** *vi* **1.** GASTR (*aliment*) to marinate **2.** *inf* (*attendre*) to wait around

marinier, -ière [maʀinje, -jɛʀ] *m, f* bargee *Brit,* bargeman *Am*

marionnette [maʀjɔnɛt] *f* puppet

maritalement [maʀitalmɑ̃] *adv* **vivre** ~ to live as husband and wife

maritime [maʀitim] *adj* **1.** (*du bord de mer*) seaside; (*région, ville*) coastal **2.** (*relatif au commerce par mer*) maritime; (*transport, compagnie*) shipping

marjolaine [maʀʒɔlɛn] *f* marjoram

mark [maʀk] *m* mark

marketing [maʀkɛtiŋ] *m* marketing

marmaille [maʀmɑj] *f inf* kids *pl*

marmelade [maʀməlad] *f* (*de pommes, d'abricots*) jam, jelly *Am;* (*d'oranges*) marmelade

marmite [maʀmit] *f* cooking pot; ~ **norvégienne** haybox ▸**faire bouillir la** ~ to keep the pot boiling

marmonner [maʀmɔne] <1> *vt, vi* to mutter

marmot [maʀmo] *m* **1.** *inf* (*petit garçon*) kid **2.** *pl* (*petits enfants*) kids

marmotte [maʀmɔt] *f* marmot

Maroc [maʀɔk] *m* **le** ~ Morocco

marocain(e) [maʀɔkɛ̃, ɛn] *adj* Moroccan

Marocain(e) [maʀɔkɛ̃, ɛn] *m(f)* Moroccan

maroquinerie [maʀɔkinʀi] *f* **1.** (*boutique*) leather shop **2.** (*fabrication*) leather working; (*commerce*) leather trade **3.** (*articles en cuir*) leather goods *pl*

marotte [maʀɔt] *f* hobby; **avoir la** ~ **de (faire) qc** to have a craze for (doing) sth; **le nettoyage est une** ~ **chez elle** she's an obsessive cleaner

marquant(e) [maʀkɑ̃, ɑ̃t] *adj* (*important: fait, événement*) outstanding; (*personnage, œuvre*) striking; (*souvenir*) vivid

marque [maʀk] *f* **1.** (*trace, repère*) *a.* LING mark; (*de coups de fouet*) wound **2.** (*tache*) stain **3.** SPORT marker; **à vos ~s!** on your marks! **4.** (*témoignage*) ~ **de confiance** sign of trust; ~ **de respect** mark of respect **5.** (*signe distinctif*) sign; (*au fer rouge*) signal; **porter la** ~ **de l'artiste/son génie** to have the artist's stamp/mark of his genius **6.** COM brand; ~ **déposée** registered trademark; **produit de** ~ branded product **7.** (*insigne*) badge **8.** (*score*) score; **ouvrir la** ~ open the scoring; **la** ~ **était de 2 à 1** the score was 2 to 1 ▸**il trouve ses ~s** he's getting his bearings; **personnage/invité de** ~ distinguished person/visitor

marqué(e) [maʀke] *adj* **1.** (*net: curiosité, traits du visage*) marked; (*préférence, différence*) distinct; (*trait*) pronounced **2.** (*traumatisé*) **être** ~ to be marked

marquer [maʀke] <1> **I.** *vt* **1.** (*indiquer, distinguer, laisser une trace sur, représenter*) to mark; (*heure, degré*) to show; ~ **qc d'un trait/d'une croix** to mark a line/cross on sth; **il a marqué son époque** (*personne, événement*) he/it left his/its mark **2.** (*souligner: rythme*) to beat; (*paroles*) to stress; **pour** ~ **cet événement** to mark this event **3.** (*respecter: feu rouge*) to respect; ~ **un temps d'arrêt** (*dans un discours, dans un mouvement*) to pause **4.** (*inscrire, noter*) to write; **le prix marqué** the marked price **5.** SPORT to mark; (*but*) to score **II.** *vi* **1.** (*jouer un rôle important*) ~ **dans qc** to have an impact on sth; **un fait qui marquera dans l'histoire** a deed which will go down in history **2.** (*laisser une trace: bouteille*) to leave a mark; (*tampon*) to stamp; (*crayon*) to mark

marqueterie [maʀkɛtʀi] *f* ART marquetry

marqueur [maʀkœʀ] *m* **1.** (*crayon*) *a.* INFOR marker **2.** (*marqueur fluorescent*) highlighter

marquis(e) [maʀki, iz] *m(f)* marquess

marquise [maʀkiz] *f* (*auvent*) awning

marraine [maʀɛn] *f* godmother

marrant(e) [maʀɑ̃, ɑ̃t] *adj inf* funny

marre [maʀ] *adv inf* **en avoir** ~ **de qn/qc** to be fed up with sb/sth

marrer [maʀe] <1> **I.** *vpr* **se** ~ *inf* to laugh **II.** *vi* **faire** ~ **qn** to make sb laugh

marron [maʀɔ̃] **I.** *m* (*fruit*) chestnut; **~s glacés** marrons glacés **II.** *adj inv* brown

> **Marrons** can be bought in tins in France and can be used to make sauces. Chestnut jam is

M

another favorite. In winter, roasted chestnuts can be bought on the streets.

marronnier (**d'Inde**) [maʀɔnje dɛ̃d] *m* horse chestnut
mars [maʀs] *m* **1.** (*mois*) March; *v. a.* **août** **2.** ASTR Mars
marseillais(**e**) [maʀsɛjɛ, jɛz] *adj* of Marseille(s); *v. a.* **ajaccien**
Marseillais(**e**) [maʀsɛjɛ, ɛz] *m(f)* person from Marseille(s); *v. a.* **Ajaccien**
Marseillaise [maʀsɛjɛz] *f* **la** ~ the Marseillaise (*the French national anthem*)

The **Marseillaise** has been the French national anthem since 1795. It was composed in 1792 by C.J. Rouget de Lisle as a war song for the Rhine army. It was also sung at the time of the revolution by a freedom group from Marseilles as it marched to Paris to take part in an uprising, hence the name.

Marseille [maʀsɛj(ə)] Marseille(s)
marsouin [maʀswɛ̃] *m* ZOOL porpoise
marsupial [maʀsypjal, jo] <-aux> *m* ZOOL marsupial
marsupial(**e**) [maʀsypjal, jo] <-aux> *adj* marsupial; **poche ~e** marsupium
marteau [maʀto] <x> **I.** *m* hammer; ~ **piqueur** pneumatic drill **II.** *adj inf* loopy
martèlement [maʀtɛlmɑ̃] *m* **1.** (*coups de marteau*) hammering **2.** (*bruit cadencé: des obus, pas*) pounding
marteler [maʀtəle] <4> *vt* **1.** (*frapper*) to hammer **2.** (*scander*) to hammer out
martial(**e**) [maʀsjal, jo] <-aux> *adj* **1.** (*de guerrier: air*) martial **2.** (*de guerre*) **cour ~e** court martial; **loi ~e** martial law; **arts martiaux** martial arts
Martien(**ne**) [maʀsjɛ̃, jɛn] *m(f)* Martian
martinet[1] [maʀtinɛ] *m* (*fouet*) lash
martinet[2] [maʀtinɛ] *m* ZOOL swift
martingale [maʀtɛ̃gal] *f* **1.** COUT half-belt **2.** JEUX winning formula
Martiniquais(**e**) [maʀtinikɛ, ɛz] *m(f)* person from Martinique
Martinique [maʀtinik] *f* **la** ~ Martinique
martre [maʀtʀ] *f* ZOOL marten
martyr(**e**) [maʀtiʀ] **I.** *adj* (*enfant*) battered; (*mère*) stricken; (*pays, peuple*) martyred **II.** *m(f)* (*personne sacrifiée*) martyr
martyre [maʀtiʀ] *m* **1.** REL martyr **2.** (*grande douleur*) agony; **souffrir le** ~ to suffer in agony
martyriser [maʀtiʀize] <1> *vt* (*faire souffrir*) to bully
marxisme [maʀksism] *m* Marxism
mas [mɑ] *m* cottage (*in southeastern France*)
mascara [maskaʀa] *m* mascara
mascarade [maskaʀad] *f* **1.** (*bal masqué*) masked ball; ART, HIST masquerade **2.** (*accoutrement*) weird outfit ►**être une vraie** ~ (*procès*) to be an utter farce
mascotte [maskɔt] *f* mascot
masculin [maskylɛ̃] *m* LING masculine
masculin(**e**) [maskylɛ̃, in] *adj* male
masculinité [maskylinite] *f* masculinity
maso [mazo] *abr de* **masochiste** **I.** *adj inv, inf* **être** ~ to be a masochist **II.** *mf inv, inf* masochist
masochisme [mazɔʃism] *m* masochism
masochiste [mazɔʃist] **I.** *adj* masochistic **II.** *mf* masochist
masque [mask] *m* **1.** (*objet*) mask; ~ **à gaz** gas mask; **arracher son** ~ **à qn** to unmask sb **2.** (*air, face*) front
masqué(**e**) [maske] *adj* **1.** (*recouvert d'un masque*) masked **2.** (*dissimulé: feux*) obscured; (*virage, sortie*) hidden
masquer [maske] <1> **I.** *vt* (*dissimuler, recouvrir d'un masque*) to conceal; MIL to camouflage; (*odeur, visage*) to mask; (*lumière*) to obscure; (*vérité*) to hide **II.** *vpr* **1.** (*mettre un masque*) **se** ~ to put on a mask; **se** ~ **le visage** to hide one's face **2.** (*se dissimuler*) **se** ~ **derrière/sous qc** to hide behind/under sth
massacrant(**e**) [masakʀɑ̃, ɑ̃t] *adj* **être d'humeur ~e** to be in a foul mood
massacre [masakʀ] *m* **1.** (*tuerie*) massacre **2.** (*travail mal fait*) mess
massacrer [masakʀe] <1> **I.** *vt* **1.** (*tuer sauvagement: peuple*) to massacre; (*animaux*) to slaughter **2.** *inf* (*démonter, mettre à mal*) ~ **qn** to make mincemeat out of sb **3.** *inf* (*détériorer*) ~ **qc** to make a mess of sth **II.** *vpr* **se faire** ~ to be massacred
massage [masaʒ] *m* massage
masse [mas] *f* **1.** (*volume*) mass; **les ~s populaires** the workig classes; **ce genre de films, ça me plaît pas des ~s** *inf* I don't really go for this type of film **2.** ECON ~ **monétaire** money supply; ~ **salariale** wage bill **3.** ART **dans la** ~ from the block
masser[1] [mase] <1> **I.** *vt* (*grouper*) to gather together; (*troupes*) to mass **II.** *vpr* (*se grouper*) **se** ~ to assemble
masser[2] [mase] <1> *vt* (*faire un massage à*) to massage
masseur, **-euse** [masœʀ, -øz] *m, f* masseur, masseuse *m, f*
massif [masif] *m* **1.** BOT clump **2.** GEO massif
massif, **-ive** [masif, -iv] *adj* **1.** (*lourd: carrure, meuble*) heavy; (*esprit*) strong; (*bâtiment, visage*) huge **2.** (*pur: argent, bois*) solid **3.** (*important*) massive; (*doses*) huge
massivement [masivmɑ̃] *adv* **1.** (*en nombre: démissionner, licencier, partir*) en masse; **la population a** ~ **repondu oui au référendum** the people gave an overwhelming yes in the referendum **2.** (*à haute dose*) in huge doses
mass media [masmedja] *mpl* mass media
massue [masy] **I.** *f* mace **II.** *app inv* sledgehammer
mastic [mastik] **I.** *m* **1.** (*pâte: du vitrier*)

putty; (*du menuisier*) filler **2.** TYP transposition **II.** *adj inv* (*beige clair*) putty-coloured *Brit,* putty-colored *Am*

mastication [mastikasjɔ̃] *f* chewing

mastiquer[1] [mastike] <1> *vt, vi* ANAT to chew

mastiquer[2] [mastike] <1> *vt* TECH (*vitre*) to putty; (*trou, fuite*) to stop up

mastoc [mastɔk] *adj inv, inf* (*personne*) hefty; (*meuble, voiture, statue*) massive

mastodonte [mastɔdɔ̃t] *m* **1.** (*chose énorme*) mammoth; (*camion*) juggernaut; (*personne énorme*) giant **2.** ZOOL mastodon

masturbation [mastyʀbasjɔ̃] *f* masturbation

masturber [mastyʀbe] <1> *vt, vpr* (**se**) ~ to masturbate

masure [mɑzyʀ] *f* hovel

mat [mat] **I.** *adj inv* JEUX checkmated **II.** *m* JEUX checkmate

mât [mɑ] *m* pole

mat(**e**) [mat] *adj* **1.** (*sans reflet, sourd: bruit, son*) dull; (*or, argent*) matt **2.** (*opp: pâle: peau, teint*) dark

matador [matadɔʀ] *m* matador

match [matʃ] <(e)s> *m* match; ~ **de boxe** boxing match; ~ **nul** draw, tie *Am*

matelas [matlɑ] *m* **1.** (*pièce de literie*) mattress; ~ **pneumatique** air bed *Brit,* air mattress *Am;* ~ **à ressorts** sprung mattress *Brit,* spring mattress *Am* **2.** (*couche épaisse*) layer

matelassé(**e**) [matlase] *adj* padded

matelot [matlo] *m* sailor

mater [mate] <1> *vt* **1.** (*faire s'assagir*) to subdue **2.** (*réprimer, vaincre*) to bring under control; (*révolte, rébellion*) to quash

matérialisation [mateʀjalizasjɔ̃] *f* materialization

matérialiser [mateʀjalize] <1> **I.** *vt* **1.** (*concrétiser*) to realize; ~ **une idée** to bring an idea to life **2.** (*signaliser*) to mark; ~ **sur l'écran** to show on the screen **II.** *vpr* **se** ~ to materialize

matérialisme [mateʀjalism] *m* materialism

matérialiste [mateʀjalist] **I.** *adj a.* PHILOS materialistic **II.** *mf a.* PHILOS materialist

matériau [mateʀjo] <x> *m* **1.** (*matière*) material; ~**x de construction** construction materials **2.** *sans pl, fig* equipment

matériel [mateʀjɛl] *m* **1.** (*équipement, assortiment d'un magasin*) equipment **2.** INFOR hardware

matériel(**le**) [mateʀjɛl] *adj* **1.** (*concret, qui concerne des objets*) material **2.** (*qui concerne l'argent: ennui, conditions*) financial; (*civilisation*) materialistic **3.** PHILOS materialistic

matériellement [mateʀjɛlmɑ̃] *adv* **1.** (*sur le plan financier*) financially **2.** (*pour des raisons matérielles*) practically; **je n'en ai ~ pas le temps** I simply haven't got the time

maternel(**le**) [matɛʀnɛl] *adj* **1.** (*de/pour la mère*) motherly; (*tendresse, instinct*) maternal **2.** (*du côté de la mère: grand-père*) maternal; (*biens*) mother's **3.** ECOLE **école ~le** nursery school

maternelle [matɛʀnɛl] *f* nursery school

> **La maternelle** is a nursery for children aged 2 or more. The children stay there the whole day. They eat there at lunch time and have beds for naps after eating. They are introduced to reading, writing and arithmetics through games, in order to prepare them for primary school.

maternellement [matɛʀnɛlmɑ̃] *adv* maternally

materner [matɛʀne] <1> *vt péj* to baby

maternité [matɛʀnite] **I.** *f* **1.** (*bâtiment*) maternity hospital **2.** (*faculté d'engendrer*) pregnancy **3.** (*condition de mère*) motherhood **4.** ART (*tableau*) *painting of mother and child;* (*de la vierge*) Madonna and child **II.** *app* maternity

mathématicien(**ne**) [matematisjɛ̃, jɛn] *m(f)* mathematician

mathématique [matematik] **I.** *adj* mathematical **II.** *fpl* mathematics

matheux, -euse [matø, -øz] *m, f inf* **1.** (*élève/étudiant en maths*) maths student *Brit,* math student *Am* **2.** (*personne douée en maths*) mathematical genius

math(**s**) [mat] *fpl inf abr de* **mathématique**

matière [matjɛʀ] *f* **1.** (*substance*) material; ~ **organique** organic matter; ~ **première** raw material **2.** PHILOS, PHYS, ART matter **3.** (*sujet, thème*) *a.* ECOLE subject; (*d'une discussion*) theme; **en ~ de sport/finances/d'impôts** in the matter of sport/finances/tax

matin [matɛ̃] **I.** *m* (*début du jour, matinée*) morning; **le** ~ in the morning; **un ~ de juillet** a July morning; **du ~ au soir** from morning until night; **de bon** ~ early in the morning; **ce** ~ this morning; **chaque** ~, **tous les ~s** every morning; **au petit** ~ early in the morning; **6/11 heures du** ~ 6/11 o'clock in the morning; **l'équipe du** ~ the morning shift ►**un de ces quatre ~s** one of these days; **être du** ~ (*être en forme le matin*) to be an early bird; (*être de l'équipe du matin*) to be on the morning shift **II.** *adv* **mardi** ~ Tuesday morning; ~ **et soir** morning and evening; (*tout le temps*) from morning till night

matinal(**e**) [matinal, o] <-aux> *adj* **1.** (*du matin*) morning **2.** (*qui se lève tôt*) **être** ~ to be an early riser; (*ponctuellement*) to be up early

matinée [matine] *f* **1.** (*matin*) morning **2.** CINE, THEAT, MUS matinée; **aller en** ~ to go to the matinée [*o* the afternoon performance] ►**faire la grasse** ~ to sleep in

matou [matu] *m* ZOOL tom

matraquage [matʀakaʒ] *m* **1.** (*coups de matraque*) **le ~ des manifestants par la police** the beating up of the demonstrators by the police **2.** MEDIA (*intoxication*) (media) hype; ~ **publicitaire** advertising overkill; **résister au** ~ to resist brainwashing

matraque [matʀak] *f* cosh *Brit,* billy club *Am*

matraquer [matʀake] <1> *vt* **1.** (*frapper*) ~ **qn** to cosh sb *Brit,* to beat sb with a billy club *Am* **2.** (*escroquer*) ~ **qn** to rip sb off; **se faire** ~ to get ripped off **3.** MEDIA (*répéter avec insistance: auditeur, téléspectateur*) to browbeat; (*produit, chanson*) to plug **4.** (*critiquer*) to hammer

matriarcat [matʀijaʀka] *m* matriarchy

matrimonial(**e**) [matʀimɔnjal, jo] <-aux> *adj* matrimonial; **agence ~e** marriage bureau; **régime** ~ marriage settlement

mature [matyʀ] *adj* mature

maturité [matyʀite] *f* **1.** *a.* BOT, BIO maturity; **venir à** ~ to come to maturity **2.** *Suisse* (*examen correspondant au baccalauréat*) baccalaureate (secondary school examinations)

maudire [modiʀ] <8> *vt* to curse

maudit(**e**) [modi, it] **I.** *adj* **1.** *antéposé* (*fichu*) blasted **2.** *postposé* (*réprouvé: poète, écrivain*) accursed **3.** *postposé* (*funeste*) disastrous; (*lieu*) cursed **II.** *m(f)* (*rejeté*) damned soul

maure [mɔʀ] *adj* HIST Moor

mauresque [mɔʀɛsk] *adj* Moorish

Maurice [mɔʀis(ə)] *f* (**l'île**) ~ Mauritius

mauricien(**ne**) [mɔʀisjɛ̃, ɛn] *adj* Mauritian

Mauricien(**ne**) [mɔʀisjɛ̃, ɛn] *m(f)* Mauritian

Mauritanie [mɔʀitani] *f* **la** ~ Mauritania

mausolée [mozɔle] *m* mausoleum

maussade [mosad] *adj* sullen; (*ciel*) dark; (*humeur*) morose; (*temps, paysage*) gloomy

mauvais [movɛ] **I.** *adv* bad; **il fait** ~ the weather is bad **II.** *m* **1.** (*ce qui est mauvais*) bad part **2.** (*personne*) **les bons et les** ~ the good and the bad

mauvais(**e**) [movɛ, ɛz] *adj* **1.** *antéposé* bad; (*action*) wrong; **la balle est ~e** the ball is out; **être** ~ **en qc** to be bad at sth; **c'est** ~ **pour la santé** it is bad for your health; **ne pas avoir un** ~ **fond** to not be bad deep down **2.** (*méchant: intention, regard*) spiteful; (*sujet*) bad; (*sourire*) nasty **3.** (*agité*) **la mer est ~e** the sea is rough

mauve [mov] *adj, m* (*couleur*) mauve

mauviette [movjɛt] *f* (*personne chétive*) weakling; *inf* (*poule mouillée*) wimp

max [maks] *m inf abr de* **maximum**

maxi [maksi] *adj inv* maxi

maxillaire [maksilɛʀ] *m* MED jaw; ~ **supérieur/inférieur** upper/lower jaw

maximal(**e**) [maksimal, o] <-aux> *adj* maximum

maxime [maksim] *f* maxim

maximum [maksimɔm, -ma] <*s o* maxima> **I.** *adj* maximum **II.** *m* maximum; JUR maximum sentence; **il fait le** ~ he's doing everything he can; **au grand** ~ at the very most; **s'amuser/s'éclater/travailler un** ~ *inf* to have great fun/laugh a lot/work incredibly hard

mayen [majɛ̃] *m Suisse* (*pâturage d'altitude moyenne avec bâtiment, où le bétail séjourne au printemps et en automne*) spring and autumn pasture

mayeur *v.* **maïeur**

mayonnaise [majɔnɛz] *f* mayonnaise

Mayotte [majɔt(ə)] Mayotte

mazot [mazo] *m Suisse* (*petit bâtiment rural*) farm building

mazout [mazut] *m* heating oil

mazurka [mazyʀka] *f* mazurka

me [mə] <*devant voyelle ou h muet* m'> *pron pers* **1.** me; **il m'explique le chemin** he's explaining the way to me **2.** *avec être, devenir, sembler, soutenu* to me; **cela** ~ **semble bon** that seems fine to me; **son amitié m'est chère** his/her/its friendship is dear to me; **ça m'est bon de rentrer au pays** it does me good to return to my home country; **le café m'est indispensable** I can't do without coffee **3.** *avec les verbes pronominaux* **je** ~ **nettoie** I'm cleaning myself up; **je** ~ **nettoie les ongles** I'm cleaning my nails; **je** ~ **fais couper les cheveux** I'm having my hair cut **4.** (*avec un sens possessif*) **le cœur** ~ **battait fort** my heart was beating hard **5.** *avec un présentatif* ~ **voici** [*o* **voilà**]**!** here I am!

méandre [meɑ̃dʀ] *m* **1.** (*d'un cours d'eau, d'un chemin*) twist **2.** *pl, fig* (*de la pensée, de la phrase*) twists and turns; **les ~s de la diplomatie** the maze of diplomacy

mec [mɛk] *m inf* guy, bloke *Brit*

mécanicien(**ne**) [mekanisjɛ̃, jɛn] *m(f)* mechanic

mécanique [mekanik] **I.** *adj* **1.** (*automatique*) mechanical **2.** *inf* (*technique: difficulté*) technical **II.** *f* mechanics

mécaniquement [mekanikmɑ̃] *adv* mechanically

mécanisation [mekanizasjɔ̃] *f* mechanization

mécaniser [mekanize] <1> *vpr* **se** ~ to mechanize

mécanisme [mekanism] *m* mechanism; ~ **de change** currency exchange mechanism

mécano [mekano] *m inf abr de* **mécanicien** mechanic

mécénat [mesena] *m* sponsorship; ~ **d'entreprise** corporate sponsorship

mécène [mesɛn] *m* (*protecteur des arts*) patron; (*personne qui soutient*) sponsor

méchamment [meʃamɑ̃] *adv* **1.** (*cruellement*) cruelly **2.** *inf* (*très*) very; (*amoché*) badly

méchanceté [meʃɑ̃ste] *f* **1.** *sans pl* (*cruauté*) cruelty; **regarder qn avec** ~ to look at sb nastily **2.** (*acte, parole*) spiteful

méchant(**e**) [meʃɑ̃, ɑ̃t] **I.** *adj* **1.** (*opp: gentil*) nasty; (*enfant*) naughty; (*animal*) vicious; **être** ~ **avec qn** to be nasty to sb; (*enfant*) to be disobedient to sb; **attention, chien ~!** beware of the dog! **2.** *antéposé* (*sévère*) harsh; (*soleil, mer*) nasty **3.** *antéposé, inf* (*extraordinaire*) serious **II.** *m(f)* bad person; **Aline, tu es une ~e!** Aline, you are a bad girl!

mèche [mɛʃ] *f* **1.** (*cordon: d'une bougie*) wick **2.** (*touffe*) ~ **de cheveux** lock of hair ►**vendre la** ~ to let the cat out of the bag; **être de** ~ **avec qn** *inf* to be in league with sb

méchoui [meʃwi] *m* **1.** (*mouton*) whole roast sheep **2.** (*repas*) barbecue; **faire un** ~ to have a barbecue

méconduire [mekɔ̃dɥiʀ] *vpr* **se** ~ *Belgique* (*se conduire mal*) to misbehave

méconnaissable [mekɔnɛsabl] *adj* unrecognizable

méconnu(e) [mekɔny] *adj* unrecognized

mécontent(e) [mekɔ̃tɑ̃, ɑ̃t] **I.** *adj* ~ **de qn/qc** dissatisfied with sb/sth; **elle n'est pas ~e de quitter la ville** she's not unhappy about leaving the town **II.** *m(f)* malcontent

mécontentement [mekɔ̃tɑ̃tmɑ̃] *m* discontent; **se sentir plein de** ~ to feel highly discontented

mécontenter [mekɔ̃tɑ̃te] <1> *vt* ~ **qn** (*déplaire*) to displease; (*contrarier, irriter*) to annoy

médaille [medaj] *f* badge; (*décoration*) medal; ~ **d'or** gold medal

médaillé(e) [medaje] **I.** *adj* decorated **II.** *m(f)* medal holder; SPORT medallist *Brit,* medalist *Am*

médaillon [medajɔ̃] *m* GASTR, ART medallion

médecin [medsɛ̃] *m* **1.** doctor; ~ **de famille** family doctor; ~ **légiste** forensic surgeon **2.** *Suisse* (*chirugien*) ~ **dentiste** dental surgeon

médecine [medsin] *f* medecine; **exercer la** ~ to practise medecine *Brit,* to practice medecine *Am;* ~ **douce/générale** alternative/general medecine; ~ **du travail** occupational medecine

média [medja] *m* medium; **les ~s** the media

médian(e) [medjɑ̃, jan] *adj* **ligne ~e** median line

médiane [medjan] *f* GEOM (*d'un triangle*) median

médiateur, -trice [medjatœʀ, -tʀis] **I.** *adj* **1.** (*de conciliation*) mediatory **2.** MAT mediating **II.** *m, f* mediator

médiathèque [medjatɛk] *f* multimedia library

médiation [medjasjɔ̃] *f* (*d'un conflit*) mediation; ~ **des négociations** arbitration of negotiations

médiatique [medjatik] *adj* (*image, sport, personne, campagne*) media

médiatisation [medjatizasjɔ̃] *f* mediatization

médiatisé(e) [medjatize] *adj* **un événement** ~ a heavily covered media event

médiatiser [medjatize] <1> *vt* to mediatize; (*excessivement*) to hype

médical(e) [medikal, o] <-aux> *adj* medical

médicament [medikamɑ̃] *m* medicine

médicinal(e) [medisinal, o] <-aux> *adj* **plantes ~es** medicinal plants

médiéval(e) [medjeval, o] <-aux> *adj* medieval

médiocre [medjɔkʀ] **I.** *adj* **1.** (*petit: salaire*) meagre *Brit,* meager *Am* **2.** (*minable*) mediocre; (*sol*) poor; (*vie*) sad **3.** (*faible: élève*) poor **4.** *péj* (*peu intelligent*) thick; (*mesquin*) mean; **d'un intérêt** ~ of little interest; **des esprits ~s** small-minds **II.** *mf* second-rater **III.** *m* nonentity

médiocrement [medjɔkʀəmɑ̃] *adv* **1.** (*assez peu*) not very well **2.** (*assez mal*) poorly

médiocrité [medjɔkʀite] *f* **1.** (*insuffisance en quantité*) inadequacy **2.** (*insuffisance en qualité*) mediocrity; (*d'une vie*) insignificance

médire [mediʀ] *vi irr* ~ **de qn** to speak ill of sb

médisance [medizɑ̃s] *f* gossip *no pl*

médisant(e) [medizɑ̃, ɑ̃t] *adj* (*commentaires*) slanderous; **être** ~ to say bad things about people; **tenir des propos ~s sur qn** to run sb down; **c'est une personne ~e** they're a gossip

méditation [meditasjɔ̃] *f* **1.** (*réflexion*) thought **2.** REL meditation

méditer [medite] <1> **I.** *vi* **1.** (*réfléchir*) ~ **sur qc** to think about sth **2.** REL to meditate **II.** *vt* **1.** (*réfléchir sur*) ~ **qc** to meditate on sth **2.** (*projeter*) to contemplate

Méditerranée [mediteʀane] *f* **la (mer)** ~ the Mediterranean (Sea)

méditerranéen(ne) [mediteʀaneɛ̃, ɛn] **I.** *adj* Mediterranean **II.** *m(f)* sb from the Mediterranean region

médium [medjɔm] *m* medium

médius [medjys] *m* middle finger

méduse [medyz] *f* jellyfish

médusé(e) [medyze] *adj* dumbfounded

meeting [mitiŋ] *m* meeting

méfait [mefɛ] *m* **1.** (*faute*) wrongdoing **2.** *gén pl* (*conséquence néfaste*) **les ~s de l'alcool/du journalisme** the harm caused by alcohol/journalism

méfiance [mefjɑ̃s] *f* distrust

méfiant(e) [mefjɑ̃, jɑ̃t] *adj* **être** ~ **à l'égard de qn** to be suspicious about sb

méfier [mefje] <1> *vpr* **1.** (*être soupçonneux*) **se** ~ **de qn/qc** to be wary of sb/sth **2.** (*faire attention*) **se** ~ to watch out; **méfiez-vous!** be careful!

méga-hertz [megaɛʀts] *m inv* megahertz

mégalo [megalo] *adj inf abr de* **mégalomane** power-crazed

mégalomane [megalɔman] *adj, mf* megalomaniac

méga-octet [megaɔktɛ] <méga-octets> *m* INFOR megabyte

mégaphone [megafɔn] *m* megaphone

mégarde [megaʀd] **par** ~ accidentally

mégère [meʒɛʀ] *f* shrew

M

mégot [mego] *m inf* cigarette butt

mégoter [megɔte] <1> *vi inf* ~ **sur qc** to skimp on sth

meilleur [mɛjœʀ] **I.** *adv* better; **il fait** ~ the weather is better **II.** *m* **le** ~ the best; **garder le** ~ **pour la fin** to save the best until last ►**pour le** ~ **et pour le pire** for better or for worse; **donner le** ~ **de soi-même** to give the best of oneself

meilleur(e) [mɛjœʀ] **I.** *adj* **1.** *comp de* **bon** better; **acheter qc** ~ **marché** to buy sth cheaper **2.** *superl* **le/la** ~**(e) élève** the best pupil; **je vous adresse mes ~s vœux** I send you my best wishes **II.** *m(f)* **le/la** ~**(e) de la classe** the top of the class ►**j'en passe et des ~es** that's not all, I could go on

Mél. [mel] INFOR *abr de* **messagerie électronique**

mélancolie [melɑ̃kɔli] *f* melancholy

mélancolique [melɑ̃kɔlik] *adj* melancholy

mélange [melɑ̃ʒ] *m* **1.** (*action*) mixing **2.** (*résultat*) blend ►**il fait des ~s** he mixes his drinks

mélangé(e) [melɑ̃ʒe] *adj* mixed; (*couleur*) blended

mélanger [melɑ̃ʒe] <2a> **I.** *vt* **1.** (*mêler*) ~ **du café et du lait** to mix coffee and milk **2.** (*mettre en désordre*) to mix up **3.** (*confondre*) to muddle **II.** *vpr* **se** ~ to mix

mélangeur [melɑ̃ʒœʀ] *m* (**robinet**) ~ mixer tap

mélasse [melas] *f* **1.** (*résidu*) molasses **2.** *inf* (*brouillard*) pea soup; (*mélange confus*) muddle; (*boue*) muck ►**être dans la** ~ *inf* to be in a mess

mêlé(e) [mele] *adj* **1.** (*mélangé, composite*) mixed **2.** (*impliqué*) **être** ~ **à une affaire** to be caught up in an affair

mêlée [mele] *f* **1.** (*corps à corps*) brawl; (*dans un débat d'idées*) fray **2.** (*conflit*) **entrer/se jeter dans la** ~ to launch oneself into the fray **3.** (*personnes mêlées*) mixture; (*choses mêlées*) muddle **4.** SPORT scrum

mêler [mele] <1> **I.** *vt* **1.** (*mélanger, allier*) to mix; (*voix*) to mingle; (*ingrédients*) to blend; ~ **la réalité et la fiction** (*récit*) to confuse fact and fiction; ~ **l'utile à l'agréable** to combine business with pleasure **2.** (*ajouter*) ~ **des détails pittoresques à un récit** to add in colourful details to a story *Brit,* to add in colorful details to a story *Am* **3.** (*mettre en désordre*) to muddle; (*fils*) to mix up; (*cartes*) to shuffle **4.** (*impliquer*) ~ **qn à qc** to involve sb in sth **II.** *vpr* **1.** (*se mélanger*) **se** ~ **à qc** to mix with sth **2.** (*joindre*) **se** ~ **à un groupe** to join a group; **se** ~ **à la foule** to mingle with the crowd **3.** (*participer*) **se** ~ **à la conversation/au jeu** to join in the conversation/the game **4.** *péj* (*s'occuper*) **se** ~ **de qc** to meddle with sth

mêle-tout [mɛltu] *m inv, Belgique* (*personne qui se mêle de tout, qui est indiscrète*) nosy parker *Brit*

mélèze [melɛz] *m* larch

méli-mélo [melimelo] <mélis-mélos> *m inf* muddle

mélo [melo] **I.** *m péj, inf abr de* **mélodrame** **II.** *adj inv, péj, inf abr de* **mélodramatique**

mélodie [melɔdi] *f* melody

mélodieux, -euse [melɔdjø, -jøz] *adj* melodious

mélodramatique [melɔdʀamatik] *adj* melodramatic

mélodrame [melɔdʀam] *m* melodrama

mélomane [melɔman] **I.** *adj* music-loving **II.** *mf* music-lover

melon [m(ə)lɔ̃] *m* melon

membrane [mɑ̃bʀan] *f* membrane

membre [mɑ̃bʀ] **I.** *m* **1.** ANAT, ZOOL limb; ~ **antérieur/postérieur** fore/hind limb **2.** (*adhérent*) *a.* MAT member; ~ **à part entière** full member ►**trembler de tous ses ~s** to tremble all over **II.** *app* **État ~/pays** ~ member state/country

même [mɛm] **I.** *adj* **1.** (*identique, simultané*) same **2.** (*semblable*) same; **c'est la** ~ **chose** it is the same thing **3.** (*en personne*) **être la gaieté/la bonne humeur** ~ to be happiness/good humour itself *Brit,* to be happiness/good humor itself *Am* **4.** (*pour renforcer*) **c'est cela** ~ **qui ...** it is that very thing which ... **II.** *pron indéf* **le/la** ~ the same **III.** *adv* **1.** (*de plus, jusqu'à*) even; ~ **pas** not even **2.** (*précisément*) **ici** ~ at this very place; **et, par là ~, il s'accuse** and by the very fact of saying so he's making an admission; **je le ferai aujourd'hui** ~ I will do it this very day **3.** *inf* (*en plus*) ~ **que c'est vrai** and what's more, it's true ►**être à** ~ **de** *+infin* to be able to *+infin;* **à** ~ **le sol** on the bare ground; **vous de** ~**!** *soutenu* and you likewise!; **il en est de** ~ **pour qn/qc** it is the same for sb/sth; **de** ~ **que son frère** just like his brother; **tout de** ~ all the same

mémé [meme] *f inf* granny; **faire** ~ (*personne*) to look old; (*robe*) to look old-fashioned

mémère [memɛʀ] *f inf* **1.** *enfantin* (*grand-mère*) grandma **2.** *péj* (*femme d'un certain âge*) old girl; **faire** ~ to look old-fashioned

mémoire[1] [memwaʀ] *f* **1.** (*capacité*) memory; **avoir la** ~ **des chiffres/dates** to have a good memory for figures/dates; **si j'ai bonne** ~ if my memory serves me; **il se remet qc en** ~ he reminds himself of sth; **pour** ~ for the record; **faire qc à la** ~ **de qn** to do sth in sb's memory **2.** INFOR memory; ~ **cache/centrale** cache/core memory; ~ **externe/interne** external/internal store; ~ **morte** [*o* **en lecture seule**] read only memory; ~ **RAM** random access memory; ~ **ROM** read only memory; ~ **tampon** buffer; ~ **virtuelle** virtual storage; ~ **vive** [*o* **à accès direct**] random access memory

mémoire[2] [memwaʀ] *m* **1.** *pl* (*journal*) memoir **2.** (*dissertation*) dissertation **3.** (*exposé*) paper

mémorable [memɔʀabl] *adj* **1.** (*qui fait date*) memorable **2.** (*inoubliable*) unforgettable

mémoriser [memɔʀize] <1> *vt* **1.** (*apprendre*) to memorize **2.** INFOR to store

menaçant(e) [mənasɑ̃, ɑ̃t] *adj* menacing; (*décision, ciel, geste*) threatening

menace [mənas] *f* (*parole, geste, danger*) threat; **des ~s de mort** death threats

menacé(e) [mənase] *adj* threatened

menacer [mənase] <2> **I.** *vt* **1.** (*faire peur avec, faire des menaces de*) **~ qn d'une arme/du poing** to threaten sb with a weapon/fist; **~ qn de mort/de faire qc** to threaten sb with death/doing sth **2.** (*constituer une menace pour*) to menace; (*santé*) to threaten **II.** *vi* to threaten

ménage [menaʒ] *m* **1.** (*entretien de la maison*) housework; **faire le ~** (*nettoyer*) to do the housework; *inf* (*réorganiser*) to sort things out; **faire des ~s** to do cleaning **2.** (*vie commune*) **être/se mettre en ~ avec qn** to live with/move in with sb **3.** (*couple*) married couple **4.** (*famille*) family ►**faire bon/mauvais ~ avec qn/qc** to get on well/badly with sb/sth

ménagement [menaʒmɑ̃] *m* **1.** (*réserve*) consideration; **sans ~** brutally **2.** *gén pl* (*égard*) **avec de grands ~s** with the utmost consideration

ménager [menaʒe] <2a> **I.** *vt* **1.** (*employer avec mesure: revenus*) to economize; (*forces*) to conserve; **~ ses paroles** to use words sparingly **2.** (*traiter avec égards pour raisons de santé*) **~ qn** to be gentle with sb **3.** (*traiter avec égards par respect ou intérêt*) **~ qn** to handle sb with care **II.** *vpr* **1.** (*prendre soin de soi*) **se ~** to take care of oneself **2.** (*se réserver*) **se ~ du temps** to keep some time for oneself

ménager, -ère [menaʒe, -ɛʀ] *adj* household

ménagère [menaʒɛʀ] *f* **1.** (*femme*) housewife **2.** (*service de couverts*) cutlery set

ménagerie [menaʒʀi] *f* **1.** (*animaux*) menagerie **2.** (*lieu d'exposition*) zoo

mendiant(e) [mɑ̃djɑ̃, jɑ̃t] *m(f)* beggar

mendicité [mɑ̃disite] *f* **1.** (*action*) begging **2.** (*condition*) **réduire qn à la ~** to reduce sb to beggary

mendier [mɑ̃dje] <1> **I.** *vi* to beg **II.** *vt* **~ de l'argent/du pain** to beg for money/bread

menée [məne] *f Suisse* (*congère*) snowdrift

mener [məne] <4> **I.** *vt* **1.** (*amener*) to take; **~ un enfant à l'école/chez le médecin** to take a child to school/the doctor's; **~ les troupes au combat** to lead the troops into combat **2.** (*conduire, faire agir*) to lead; **~ une entreprise à la ruine/faillite** to lead a company into ruin/bankruptcy; **seul l'intérêt le mène** he is led solely by interest **3.** (*diriger*) to direct; (*négociations*) to lead **4.** (*administrer*) to manage **II.** *vi* to lead; **~ (par) deux à zéro** to lead two to zero

meneur, -euse [mənœʀ, -øz] *m, f* leader; *péj* agitator; **~ de jeu** SPORT key player; RADIO, TV quizmaster; **~ d'hommes** leader of men

menhir [meniʀ] *m* menhir

méninge [menɛ̃ʒ] *f* ANAT brain ►**il se creuse les ~s** *inf* he's racking his brains

méningite [menɛ̃ʒit] *f* MED meningitis ►**ne pas risquer d'**[*o* **ne pas aller**]**attraper une ~** *inf* not to overtax onself

ménopause [menopoz] *f* menopause

menotte [mənɔt] *f pl* handcuffs *pl;* **passer les ~s à qn** to handcuff sb

mensonge [mɑ̃sɔ̃ʒ] *m* **1.** (*opp: vérité*) lie; **raconter un ~ à qn** to (tell a) lie to sb **2.** *sans pl* (*action, habitude*) lying; **vivre dans le ~** to live a lie

mensonger, -ère [mɑ̃sɔ̃ʒe, -ɛʀ] *adj* (*propos*) untrue; (*promesse*) false

menstruel(le) [mɑ̃stʀyɛl] *adj* menstrual; **cycle ~** menstrual cycle; **flux ~** menstrual flow

mensualiser [mɑ̃sɥalize] <1> *vt* **1.** (*rémunérer*) **~ qn** to pay sb monthly **2.** (*verser chaque mois*) **~ qc** to pay sth monthly

mensualité [mɑ̃sɥalite] *f* **1.** monthly payment; **payer par ~s** to pay monthly **2.** (*salaire*) monthly salary

mensuel [mɑ̃sɥɛl] *m* monthly publication

mensuel(le) [mɑ̃sɥɛl] *adj* monthly

mensuellement [mɑ̃sɥɛlmɑ̃] *adv* monthly

mensuration [mɑ̃syʀasjɔ̃] *f* **1.** (*action de mesurer*) to measure **2.** *pl* (*dimensions du corps*) vital statistics

mental [mɑ̃tal] *m sans pl* spirit

mental(e) [mɑ̃tal, o] <-aux> *adj* (*psychique, intellectuel, de tête*) mental; (*prière*) silent; **calcul ~** mental arithmetic

mentalement [mɑ̃talmɑ̃] *adv* mentally

mentalité [mɑ̃talite] *f* mentality

menteur, -euse [mɑ̃tœʀ, -øz] **I.** *adj* (*personne*) lying **II.** *m, f* liar

menthe [mɑ̃t] *f* mint; **~ poivrée** peppermint

mentholé(e) [mɑ̃tɔle] *adj* (*dentifrice*) mint; (*cigarette*) menthol

mention [mɑ̃sjɔ̃] *f* **1.** (*fait de signaler*) mention; **faire ~ de qn/qc** to mention sb/sth **2.** (*indication*) comment; **rayer les ~s inutiles** delete as appropriate **3.** ECOLE, UNIV grade; **avec (la) ~ bien** ≈ with grade B pass

mentionner [mɑ̃sjɔne] <1> *vt* to mention

mentir [mɑ̃tiʀ] <10> *vi* to lie; **~ à qn** to lie to sb ►**il ment comme il respire** he lies through his teeth

menton [mɑ̃tɔ̃] *m* chin

menu[1] [məny] *m* **1.** (*repas*) meal; **~ enfant** children's meal **2.** (*carte au restaurant, à la cantine*) *a.* INFOR menu; **~ contextuel/déroulant** context/pull-down menu; **barre de ~** menu-bar **3.** *inf* (*programme: d'une réunion*) agenda

menu[2] [məny] *adv* **haché/coupé ~** chopped/cut finely

menu(e) [məny] *adj postposé* **1.** (*frêle: personne*) slender; (*jambes, bras*) slim; (*taille*)

M

thin **2.** *antéposé* (*qui a peu d'importance: détails, occupations*) minor; (*soucis, dépenses*) petty **3.** *souvent antéposé* (*qui a peu de volume*) fine; (*souliers*) thin; (*bruits*) slight

menuet [mənɥɛ] *m* minuet

menuiserie [mənɥizʀi] *f* **1.** *sans pl* (*métier*) carpentry **2.** (*atelier*) joiner's workshop

menuisier [mənɥizje] *m* carpenter

mépris [mepʀi] *m* **1.** (*opp: estime*) contempt **2.** (*opp: prise en compte*) disregard

méprisable [mepʀizabl] *adj* despicable

méprisant(e) [mepʀizɑ̃, ɑ̃t] *adj* contemptuous

méprise [mepʀiz] *f* mistake

mépriser [mepʀize] <1> *vt* **1.** (*opp: estimer*) to look down on **2.** (*opp: prendre en compte: insultes*) to ignore; ~ **la loi** to treat the law with disdain

mer [mɛʀ] *f* **1.** (*étendue d'eau, littoral*) sea; ~ **d'huile** calm sea; **en haute** ~ on the high seas; ~ **Égée** Aegean (Sea); ~ **du Nord** North Sea; ~ **Noire/Rouge** Black/Red Sea; ~ **Caspienne** Caspian Sea; ~ **des Caraïbes** Caribbean Sea; **prendre la** ~ to put out to sea; **expédier par** ~ to send by sea; **passer ses vacances à la** ~ to spend one's holidays by the sea **2.** (*eau de* ~) seawater **3.** (*marée*) **quand la** ~ **est basse/haute** when the tide is low/high **4.** (*grande quantité*) ~ **de documents** wave of documents ►**ce n'est pas la** ~ **à boire!** it's not asking the impossible!

mercantile [mɛʀkɑ̃til] *adj péj* mercenary

mercatique [mɛʀkatik] *f* marketing

mercenaire [mɛʀsənɛʀ] *m, f* mercenary

mercerie [mɛʀsəʀi] *f* **1.** (*magasin*) haberdasher's shop *Brit,* notions store *Am* **2.** (*commerce, marchandises*) haberdashery *Brit,* notions *Am*

merci [mɛʀsi] **I.** *interj* **1.** (*pour remercier*) thank you; ~ **bien** thank you very much; ~ **à vous pour tout** thank you for everything **2.** (*pour exprimer l'indignation, la déception*) thanks **II.** *m* thank you; **un grand** ~ **à vous de nous avoir aidés** a big thanks to you for having helped us; **il ne m'a jamais dit un** ~ he did not thank me once **III.** *f* **être à la** ~ **de qn/qc** to be at the mercy of sb/sth; **sans** ~ without mercy

mercredi [mɛʀkʀədi] *m* Wednesday; ~ **des Cendres** Ash Wednesday; *v. a.* **dimanche**

mercure [mɛʀkyʀ] *m* mercury

Mercure [mɛʀkyʀ] *f* ASTR, HIST Mercury

mercurochrome® [mɛʀkyʀokʀom] *m* Mercurochrome®

merde [mɛʀd] **I.** *f* **1.** *vulg* shit **2.** *inf* (*ennui*) problem **3.** *inf* (*saleté*) crap **4.** *inf* (*personne, chose sans valeur*) shit; **ne pas se prendre pour une** ~ *inf* he thinks the sun shines out of his arse *Brit,* he thinks the sun shines out of his ass *Am, vulg;* **c'est de la** ~**, ce stylo** this pen's a piece of shit ►**il est dans la** ~ **jusqu'au cou** *inf* he's in the shit up to his neck; **foutre la** ~ *inf* to wreak havoc; **temps/boulot de** ~ *inf* crappy weather/job **II.** *interj inf* ~ **alors!** shit!

merder [mɛʀde] <1> *vi inf* to mess up

merdeux, -euse [mɛʀdø, -øz] **I.** *m, f inf* **petit** ~ little shit; (*enfant*) brat **II.** *adj inf* **se sentir** (**tout**) ~ to feel crappy

merdier [mɛʀdje] *m inf* **1.** (*désordre*) mess; (*pièce*) pigsty **2.** (*situation complexe*) shambles

merdique [mɛʀdik] *adj inf* crappy

mère [mɛʀ] **I.** *f* **1.** (*femme*) mother; ~ **poule** mother hen; ~ **au foyer** housewife (and mother); ~ **porteuse** surrogate mother; **ne pas pouvoir être** ~ to be unable to have children **2.** REL ~ **supérieure** Mother Superior; **ma** ~ Mother **II.** *app* **maison** ~ parent company; **fille** ~ unmarried mother

merguez [mɛʀgɛz] *f: spicy sausage from North Africa*

méridien [meʀidjɛ̃] *m* meridian

méridional(e) [meʀidjɔnal, o] <-aux> *adj* **1.** (*du Midi de la France*) southern **2.** (*du Bassin méditerranéen*) Mediterranean; **être une caractéristique** ~**e** to be typical of the South **3.** (*au/du sud*) southern; **côte** ~**e d'un pays** south coast of a country

meringue [məʀɛ̃g] *f* meringue

mérinos [meʀinos] *m* **1.** (*mouton*) merino sheep **2.** (*laine*) merino wool

merise [məʀiz] *f* wild cherry

merisier [məʀizje] *m* **1.** (*arbre*) wild cherry **2.** (*bois*) cherry; **en** [*o* **de**] ~ cherry **3.** *Québec* (*bouleau à écorce foncé*) *type of birch*

méritant(e) [meʀitɑ̃, ɑ̃t] *adj* deserving

mérite [meʀit] *m* **1.** (*qualité, vertu de qn*) merit; **elle a bien du** ~ all credit to her **2.** *sans pl* (*valeur*) worth **3.** (*avantage: d'un appareil, d'une organisation*) advantage

Mérite [meʀit] *m* (*distinction*) **le** ~ the Order of Merit

mériter [meʀite] <1> *vt* **1.** (*avoir droit à qc*) to deserve; ~ **de réussir/d'être récompensé** to deserve to succeed/to be reimbursed **2.** (*valoir*) to be worth; **cela mérite réflexion** that deserves some thought

méritoire [meʀitwaʀ] *adj* meritorious

merlan [mɛʀlɑ̃] *m* whiting

merle [mɛʀl] *m* blackbird ►~ **blanc** impossible creature; **siffler comme un** ~ to sing like a lark

mérou [meʀu] *m* grouper

merveille [mɛʀvɛj] *f* wonder; (*d'une création*) marvel; **à** ~ beautifully; **faire** (**des**) ~(**s**) to work wonders ►**la huitième** ~ **du monde** the eighth wonder of the world

merveilleusement [mɛʀvɛjøzmɑ̃] *adv* marvellously *Brit,* marvelously *Am*

merveilleux, -euse [mɛʀvɛjø, -jøz] **I.** *adj* **1.** (*exceptionnel*) marvellous *Brit,* marvelous *Am;* (*très beau*) beautiful **2.** *postposé* (*surnaturel, magique*) **monde/lampe** ~(**-euse**) magic world/lamp **II.** *m* **le** ~ the supernatural; **le** ~ **de qc** the extraordinary thing about sth

mes [me] *dét poss v.* **ma**, **mon**

mésalliance [mezaljɑ̃s] *f* **faire une** ~ to marry beneath one

mésange [mezɑ̃ʒ] *f* tit; ~ **bleue** blue tit; ~ **charbonnière** great tit

mésaventure [mezavɑ̃tyʀ] *f* misadventure

mesdames [medam] *fpl v.* **madame**

mesdemoiselles [medmwazɛl] *fpl v.* **mademoiselle**

mésentente [mezɑ̃tɑ̃t] *f* dissension

mesquin(e) [mɛskɛ̃, in] *adj* **1.** (*étriqué: pensée, milieu*) mean-minded; (*vie*) petty **2.** (*avare*) mean; **ça fait** ~ that looks mean

mesquinerie [mɛskinʀi] *f* **1.** *sans pl* (*étroitesse*) pettiness; **avec** ~ mean-mindedly **2.** *sans pl* (*avarice*) meanness **3.** (*attitude, action*) small-mindedness *no pl*

message [mesaʒ] *m* **1.** (*nouvelle*) news; ~ **publicitaire** advertisement **2.** (*note écrite, communication solennelle*) *a.* INFOR, TEL message; ~ **d'erreur** error message

messager, **-ère** [mesaʒe, -ɛʀ] *m, f* messenger

messagerie [mesaʒʀi] *f* message service; ~ **électronique** electronic mail

messe [mɛs] *f* mass; ~ **de mariage** nuptial mass; ~ **de minuit** midnight mass ►**dire des ~s basses** to mutter

messie [mesi] *m* messiah

messieurs [mesjø] *mpl v.* **monsieur**

messin(e) [mesɛ̃, in] *adj* of Metz; *v. a.* **ajaccien**

Messin(e) [mesɛ̃, in] *m(f)* person from Metz; *v. a.* **Ajaccien**

mesure [m(ə)zyʀ] *f* **1.** (*action: d'une surface*) measurement **2.** (*dimension*) measurement; (*de la température*) measure; **~s de qn** sb's measurements; **prendre les ~s de qn** to take sb's measurements; **prendre les ~s d'une pièce** to measure a room **3.** (*unité, récipient, contenu, élément de comparaison, limite, disposition*) measure; **l'homme est la ~ de toutes choses** man is the measure of all things; **outre** ~ beyond measure; ~ **disciplinaire** disciplinary measures; **par** ~ **de sécurité** as a safety precauthion; **par** ~ **d'économie** for the sake of economy; **prendre des ~s** to take steps **4.** (*modération*) **avec** ~ in moderation; **il manque de** ~ **dans ses paroles** he lacks moderation in what he says **5.** MUS tempo; **battre la** ~ to beat time ►**à** ~ as; **dans la** ~ **du possible** as far as possible; **dans une certaine** ~ to some extent; **être en** ~ **de** +*infin* to be able to +*infin;* **costume sur ~(s)** custom-tailored suit; **emploi du temps sur ~(s)** customized timetable

mesuré(e) [məzyʀe] *adj* (*ton*) steady; (*pas*) measured; (*personne*) moderate

mesurer [məzyʀe] <1> **I.** *vi* (*avoir pour mesure*) to measure; ~ **1 m 70 de haut/de large/de long** to be 1.7 m tall/wide/long; **combien mesures-tu?** how tall are you? **II.** *vt* **1.** (*déterminer les dimensions*) to measure **2.** (*évaluer*) to assess; (*conséquences, risque*) to measure; ~ **qn des yeux** to weigh up sb **3.** (*modérer: paroles, propos*) to weigh **III.** *vpr* **1.** (*se comparer à*) **se** ~ **à qn** to compare oneself with sb **2.** (*être mesurable*) **se** ~ **en mètres/litres** to be measured in metres/litres *Brit,* to be measured in meters/liters *Am*

métairie [meteʀi] *f* tenant farming (*where the landlord takes a share of the crop*)

métal [metal, o] <-aux> *m* metal

métallique [metalik] *adj* metallic; **fil** ~ metal wire

métallisé(e) [metalize] *adj* metallic

métallurgie [metalyʀʒi] *f sans pl* **1.** (*industrie*) metallurgical industry; ~ **lourde** heavy metal industry; ~ **de transformation** mechanical construction industry **2.** (*technique*) metallurgy

métallurgique [metalyʀʒik] *adj* metallurgial; **industrie** ~ the metal industry

métallurgiste [metalyʀʒist] *mf* **1.** (*ouvrier*) metal worker **2.** (*industriel*) metallurgist

métamorphose [metamɔʀfoz] *f* metamorphosis

métamorphoser [metamɔʀfoze] <1> **I.** *vt* **1.** (*changer en bien*) to transform **2.** MYTH ~ **qn en animal/statue** to turn sb into an animal/a statue **II.** *vpr* **1.** BIO, ZOOL **se** ~ (*insecte, têtard*) to be metamorphosed **2.** (*changer en bien*) **se** ~ to be transformed; **se** ~ **en qn** to be transformed into sb

métaphore [metafɔʀ] *f* metaphor

métaphorique [metafɔʀik] *adj* metaphorical; **emploi** ~ metaphorical use

métaphysique [metafizik] **I.** *adj a.* PHILOS metaphysical **II.** *f* **1.** PHILOS metaphysics + *vb sing* **2.** *sans pl* (*spéculations*) abstract consideration

métayer, **-ère** [meteje, -ɛʀ] *m, f* tenant farmer (*who gives a share of the crop to the landlord*)

météo [meteo] *inv abr de* **météorologique**, **météorologie**

météore [meteɔʀ] *m* meteor ►**passer comme un** ~ to have a brief meteoric career

météorite [meteɔʀit] *m o f* meteorite

météorologie [meteɔʀɔlɔʒi] *f* meteorology

météorologique [meteɔʀɔlɔʒik] *adj* meteorological

méthode [metɔd] *f* **1.** (*technique*) method **2.** (*manuel*) ~ **de piano/guitare** piano/guitar manual; ~ **de comptabilité/langue** accountancy/language learning manual **3.** *sans pl, inf* (*manière de faire, logique*) way; **chacun sa ~!** to each his own!

méthodique [metɔdik] *adj* methodical

méthodiquement [metɔdikmɑ̃] *adv* methodically

méticuleux, **-euse** [metikylø, -øz] *adj* meticulous

métier [metje] *m* **1.** (*profession*) occupation; **être architecte de son** ~ to be an architect by trade; **apprendre/exercer un** ~ to learn/

practice a profession; **être du** ~ to be in the trade; **qu'est-ce que vous faites comme ~?**, **quel ~ faites-vous?** what is your job? **2.** *pl* (*ensemble de métiers*) **les ~s du bois/de la restauration** the wood/catering trades **3.** *sans pl* (*secteur d'activité: d'une entreprise*) business **4.** *sans pl* (*rôle*) **il fait son** ~ he is doing his job **5.** *sans pl* (*technique*) technique; (*habileté*) skill; **avoir du** ~ to have practical experience; **connaître son** ~ to know what one is doing **6.** TECH ~ **à tisser** weaving loom ►**exercer le plus vieux ~ du monde** to be in the oldest profession

métis [metis] *m* (*personne*) half-caste

métis(se) [metis] *adj* (*personne*) half-caste

métissé(e) [metise] *adj* (*animal*) crossbred

métrage [metʀaʒ] *m* CINE **court** ~ short (film); **long** ~ feature film

mètre [mɛtʀ] *m* **1.** (*unité de mesure*) metre *Brit*, meter *Am;* ~ **cube/carré** cubic/square metre; **par 500 ~s de fond** 500 metres down; **à cinquante ~s d'ici** fifty metres from here **2.** (*instrument*) metre rule *Brit*, meter ruler *Am* **3.** SPORT **le 110 ~s haies** the 110 metre hurdles *Brit*, the 110 meter hurdles *Am;* **piquer un cent ~s** *inf* to sprint

métrique [metʀik] *adj* metric

métro [metʀo] *m* underground (train system) *Brit*, subway *Am;* ~ **souterrain/aérien** underground train system/elevated railway; ~ **urbain** urban underground system *Brit*, urban subway system *Am;* **en** ~ by underground *Brit*, by subway *Am* **2.** (*station*) underground station *Brit*, subway station *Am*

> The Parisian **métro** is one of the oldest in Europe (since 1900). All the lines run from around 5.30 a.m. until about half past midnight. Recently, the newest underground line, Meteor, has been opened, featuring driverless trains and fully automatic systems from the arrival at the platform to the closing of the doors.

métronome [metʀɔnɔm] *m* metronome

métropole [metʀɔpɔl] *f* (*grande ville*) big city; ~ **du cinéma** movie capital; ~ **financière** financial centre *Brit*, financial center *Am*

Métropole [metʀɔpɔl] *f sans pl* **la** ~ (Metropolitan) France

métropolitain [metʀɔpɔlitɛ̃] *m* **1.** *form* (*métro*) underground railway **2.** REL metropolitan

métropolitain(e) [metʀɔpɔlitɛ̃, ɛn] *adj* **1.** GEO metropolitan; **la France ~e** metropolitan France **2.** REL **l'église ~e** the mother church

mets [mɛ] *m* dish

mettable [mɛtabl] *adj* wearable

metteur [metœʀ] *m* TV, THEAT, CINE ~ **en scène** director

mettre [mɛtʀ] *irr* **I.** *vt* **1.** (*placer, poser*) to put; (*à plat, couché, horizontalement*) to lay; (*debout, verticalement*) to stand; (*assis*) to sit; (*suspendre*) to hang; ~ **les mains en l'air** to put one's hands up **2.** (*déposer, entreposer*) ~ **une voiture au garage/parking** to leave a car in the garage/car park *Brit*, to leave a car in the garage/parking garage *Am;* ~ **à la fourrière** to impound; ~ **qc à l'abri** to leave sth in the shade **3.** (*jeter*) ~ **qc à la poubelle/au panier** to throw sth in the bin/basket **4.** (*ajouter, conditionner*) ~ **trop de sel dans la soupe** to put too much salt in the soup; ~ **de la farine en sacs** to bag flour; ~ **du vin en bouteilles** to bottle wine **5.** (*répandre*) ~ **du beurre sur une tartine** to butter some bread; ~ **du cirage sur ses chaussures** to put polish on one's shoes; ~ **de la crème sur ses mains** to put cream on one's hands **6.** (*ajuster, adapter*) ~ **un nouveau moteur** to run in a new motor *Brit*, to break in a new motor *Am* **7.** (*coudre*) ~ **un bouton à une veste** to sew [*o* put] a button on a jacket **8.** (*introduire*) to insert; ~ **une lettre dans une enveloppe** to put a letter into an envelope **9.** (*écrire*) write; ~ **un nom sur une liste** to put a name on a list; ~ **une note à qn** to write a note to sb **10.** (*nommer, inscrire, classer*) ~ **qn au service clients** to put sb in customer services; ~ **ses enfants à l'école privée** to put one's children in a private school; ~ **au-dessus/en-dessous de qn/qc** to put above/below sb/sth **11.** (*revêtir*) ~ **qc** (*vêtement, chaussures, chapeau, lunettes, bijou, bague, maquillage*) to put sth on; (*lentilles de contact*) to put sth in; (*broche*) to pin sth on **12.** (*consacrer*) ~ **deux heures/une journée à faire un travail** to take two hours/a day to do a job; ~ **ses espoirs dans un projet/une étude** to put one's hopes on a project/study; **tu as mis le temps!** you took your time! **13.** (*investir*) ~ **beaucoup d'argent/300 euros dans un projet/une maison** to put a lot of money/300 euros in a project/house **14.** (*transformer*) ~ **qc en allemand/anglais** to translate sth into German/English; ~ **qc au propre** to copy sth out neatly; ~ **qc en forme** to get sth into shape **15.** (*faire fonctionner*) ~ **qc** to turn sth on; ~ **la radio/télé plus fort** to turn up the radio/television **16.** (*régler*) ~ **une montre à l'heure** to set a watch to the right time **17.** (*installer: rideaux, papier peint*) to hang; (*moquette*) to lay; (*électricité*) to install **18.** (*faire*) ~ **qc à cuire/à chauffer/à bouillir** to cook/heat/boil sth **19.** (*envoyer*) ~ **une fléchette dans la cible** to get a dart in the bull's-eye; ~ **le ballon dans les buts** to put the ball in the goal; **je lui ai mis mon poing dans la figure** *inf* I punched him in the face **20.** (*admettre*) **mettons/mettez qu'elle l'ait fait** let's assume that she did it **21.** INFOR ~ **à jour** to update **22.** *fig* ~ **un peu de fantaisie dans sa vie** to bring a bit of fantasy into one's life **II.** *vpr* **1.** (*se placer*) **se ~ debout/assis** to get up/sit down; **se ~ à genoux** to kneel down; **se ~ au garde-à-vous** to stand to attention; **se ~ à la disposition de qn/qc** to put oneself at sb's/sth's disposal **2.** (*placer sur soi*) **se ~ un chapeau sur la tête** to put a hat on one's head; **il se met les doigts dans le nez** he put his fingers in his nose **3.** (*se ranger*) **se ~ dans l'armoire/à droite** to go in the cupboard/on the right **4.** (*porter*) **se ~ en pantalon/rouge** to put on a pair of trousers/red clothes; **se ~ du parfum** to put on some perfume **5.** (*commencer à*) **se ~ au travail** to get down to work; **bon, je m'y mets** OK, I'll get down to it **6.** (*pour exprimer le changement d'état*) **se ~ au courant de qc** to bring oneself up to date on sth; **se ~ en colère** to get angry; **se ~ en route** to set off; **se ~ en place** (*réforme, nouvelle politique*) to be put in place **7.** (*se coincer*) **se ~ dans qc** to get caught in sth **8.** *inf* **se ~ avec qn** (*coéquipiers, amoureux*) to get together with sb; (*en ménage*) to move in with sb **9.** *inf* (*boire trop*) **s'en ~ jusque-là** to drink loads **10.** *fig* **mets-toi bien ça dans le crâne!** get that into your head!

meuble [mœbl] *m* (*mobilier*) piece of furniture; **~s** furniture + *vb sing;* **~s de jardin** garden furniture; **~s de rangement** storage units ►**sauver les ~s** to salvage what one can from the wreckage

meublé [mœble] *m* **1.** (*chambre*) furnished room **2.** (*appartement*) furnished flat *Brit,* furnished apartment *Am*

meublé(e) [mœble] *adj* furnished

meubler [mœble] <1> **I.** *vt* **1.** (*garnir de meubles*) to furnish **2.** (*constituer le mobilier*) **un lit et une chaise meublent la chambre** a bed and a chair furnish the room **3.** (*remplir: silence, conversation*) to fill **II.** *vpr* **se ~** to buy furniture

meuf [mœf] *f vulg* woman

meuglement [møgləmɑ̃] *m* mooing

meugler [møgle] <1> *vi* to moo

meule[1] [møl] *f* **1.** (*d'un moulin*) millstone **2.** (*pour aiguiser*) grindstone; (*pour polir*) polishing wheel **3.** GASTR round; **~ de gruyère** a gruyère round

meule[2] [møl] *f* AGR rick; **~ de foin** haystack

meunier [mønje] *m Québec* (*poisson d'eau douce*) bullhead

meunier, -ère [mønje, jɛʀ] *m, f* miller *m,* miller's wife *f*

meure [mœʀ] *subj prés de* **mourir**

meurent [mœʀ], **meurs** [mœʀ], **meurt** [mœʀ] *indic prés de* **mourir**

meurtre [mœʀtʀ] *m* murder; **~ avec préméditation** premeditated murder

meurtri(e) [mœʀtʀi] *adj* bruised

meurtrier, -ière [mœʀtʀije, -ijɛʀ] **I.** *adj* murderer; (*accident, coup*) fatal; (*carrefour, route*) lethal **II.** *m, f* murderer

meurtrissure [mœʀtʀisyʀ] *f* bruise

meus [mø] *indic prés de* **mouvoir**

Meuse [møz] *f* **la ~** the Meuse

meut [mø] *indic prés de* **mouvoir**

meute [møt] *f a. fig* pack

meuve [møv] *subj prés de* **mouvoir**

meuvent [mœv] *indic prés de* **mouvoir**

mévente [mevɑ̃t] *f* poor sales *pl*

mexicain(e) [mɛksikɛ̃, ɛn] *adj* Mexican

Mexicain(e) [mɛksikɛ̃, ɛn] *m(f)* Mexican

Mexico [mɛksiko] Mexico City

Mexique [mɛksik] *m* **le ~** Mexico

MF [ɛmɛf] *mpl abr de* **millions de francs** MF

mi [mi] *m inv* E; (*dans la gamme*) mi; *v. a.* **do**

miam-miam [mjammjam] *interj inf* yum yum

miaou [mjau] *interj* miaow *Brit,* meow *Am*

mi-août [miut] *f sans pl* **à la ~** in mid-August

miaulement [mjolmɑ̃] *m* mewing *no pl*

miauler [mjole] <1> *vi* to mew

mi-avril [miavʀil] *f sans pl* **à la ~** in mid-April

mi-bas [miba] *m inv* knee-high

mica [mika] *m* MIN mica

mi-carême [mikaʀɛm] <mi-carêmes> *f* mid-Lent Thursday

miche [miʃ] *f* **1.** (*pain*) cob loaf **2.** *pl, inf* (*fesses*) butt, bum *Brit*

Michel-Ange [mikɛlɑ̃:ʒ(ə)] *m* Michelangelo

mi-chemin [miʃmɛ̃] **à ~** midway

Mickey [mikɛ] *m* Mickey Mouse

mi-clos(e) [miklo, kloz] *adj* half-closed; **un bourgeon ~** a half-open bud

micmac [mikmak] *m inf* **1.** (*manigance*) funny business; **cette affaire de pots-de-vin est un sacré ~** this corruption business is one hell of a carry-on *Brit* **2.** *sans pl* (*affaire embrouillée*) palaver

mi-corps [mikɔʀ] **jusqu'à ~** as far as the waist; **portrait à ~** half-length portrait

micro [mikʀo] *abr de* **microphone, micro-ordinateur, micro-informatique**

microbe [mikʀɔb] *m* **1.** BIO germ **2.** *inf* (*avorton*) runt

microbien(ne) [mikʀɔbjɛ̃, jɛn] *adj* microbial; **infection ~ne** bacterial infection

microclimat [mikʀoklima] *m* microclimate

microfiche [mikʀofiʃ] *f* microfiche

microfilm [mikʀofilm] *m* microfilm

micro-informatique [mikʀoɛ̃fɔʀmatik] *f sans pl* computer science

Micronésie [mikʀɔnezi] *f* **la ~** Micronesia

micronésien(ne) [mikʀɔnezjɛ̃, ɛn] *adj* Micronesian

Micronésien(ne) [mikʀɔnezjɛ̃, ɛn] *m(f)* Micronesian

micro-onde [mikʀoɔ̃d] <micro-ondes> *f* microwave; **four à ~s** microwave oven **micro-ondes** [mikʀoɔ̃d] *m inv* (*four*) microwave **micro-ordinateur** [mikʀoɔʀdinatœʀ] <micro-ordinateurs> *m* PC

microphone [mikʀɔfɔn] *m* microphone, mike *inf*

microprocesseur [mikʀɔpʀɔsɛsœʀ] *m* INFOR microprocessor

microscope [mikʀɔskɔp] *m* microscope

microscopique [mikʀɔskɔpik] *adj* micro-

M

scopic

micro-trottoir [mikʀotʀɔtwaʀ] <micros-trottoirs> *m* public opinion, vox pop *Brit*

miction [miksjɔ̃] *f* MED micturition

mi-cuisse [mikɥis] **à** ~ up to one's thighs **mi-décembre** [midesɑ̃bʀ] *f sans pl* **à la** ~ in mid-December

midi [midi] *m* **1.** *inv, sans art ni autre dét* (*heure*) twelve o'clock; (*mi-journée*) midday, noon; **à** ~ at twelve o'clock; **entre** ~ **et deux** between twelve and two o'clock; **mardi/demain** ~ Tuesday/tomorrow at twelve o'clock **2.** (*moment du déjeuner*) lunchtime; **ce** ~ today at lunchtime; **le repas de** ~ lunch **3.** (*sud*) south ►**chercher** ~ **à quatorze heures** to complicate things; **entre l'heure de** ~ *Belgique* (*à midi*) at midday

Midi [midi] *m* **le** ~ the South of France

mie [mi] *f sans pl* (*de pain*) soft part

miel [mjɛl] *m* honey

mielleux, **-euse** [mjɛlø, -øz] *adj* honeyed

mien(**ne**) [mjɛ̃, mjɛn] *pron poss* **1.** **le/la** ~(**ne**) mine; **les** ~**s** mine; **cette maison est la** ~**ne** this house is mine **2.** *pl* (*ceux de ma famille*) **les** ~**s** my family; (*mes partisans*) my circle ►**j'y mets du** ~ I pull my weight

miette [mjɛt] *f* **1.** (*aliment: de pain, gâteau*) crumb; **ne pas en laisser une** ~ not to leave a crumb **2.** (*petit fragment*) **être réduit en** ~**s** (*verre, porcelaine*) to be smashed to smithereens

mieux [mjø] **I.** *adv comp de* **bien** **1.** better; **qn va** ~ sb is better; **pour** ~ **dire** in other words; **on ferait** ~ **de réfléchir avant de parler** one would do better to think before speaking; **aimer** ~ *+infin* to prefer to *+infin;* **plus il s'entraîne,** ~ **il joue** the more he trains, the better he plays; **qn n'en fait que** ~ **qc** sb just does sth better **2.** *en loc conj* **d'autant** ~ **que qn fait qc** all the better that sb does sth **3.** *en loc adv* **ce chapeau lui va on ne peut** ~ this hat suits him/her so well; **de** ~ **en** ~ better and better; **tant** ~ **pour qn!** so much the better for sb ►**il vaut** ~ **qu'elle fasse qc** (*subj*) it would be better if she did sth; ~ **vaut tard que jamais** *prov* better late than never **II.** *adv superl de* **bien** **1.** + *verbe* **c'est lui qui travaille le** ~ he is the one who works the hardest; **c'est ce qu'on fait de** ~ it is what we do best **2.** + *adj* **il est le** ~ **disposé à nous écouter** he is the most prepared to listen to us; **un exemple des** ~ **choisis** a perfectly chosen example **3.** *en loc verbale* **le** ~ **serait de ne rien dire** the best thing would be to say nothing; **elle fait du** ~ **qu'elle peut** she does her best **4.** *en loc adv* **il travaille de son** ~ he is working his hardest **5.** *en loc prép* **au** ~ **de vos intérêts** in your best interests **III.** *adj comp de* **bien** **1.** (*en meilleure santé*) **il la trouve** ~ he thinks she is better **2.** (*plus agréable d'apparence*) **elle est** ~ **les cheveux courts** she looks better with short hair **3.** (*plus à l'aise*) **vous serez** ~ **dans le fauteuil** you would be more comfortable in the armchair **4.** (*préférable*) **c'est** ~ **ainsi** it is better this way **IV.** *adj superl de* **bien** **1.** (*le plus réussi*) **c'est avec les cheveux courts qu'elle est le** ~ she looks best with her hair short **2.** *en loc verbale* **il est au** ~ **avec qn** he's well in with sb **V.** *m* **1.** (*une chose meilleure*) **trouver** ~ to find (something) better **2.** (*amélioration*) **un léger** ~ a slight improvement; **il y a du** ~ there is some improvement

mièvre [mjɛvʀ] *adj* (*sourire*) mawkish; (*livre, peinture*) sentimental; (*paroles, personne*) vapid

mi-février [mifevʀije] *f sans pl* **à la** ~ in mid-February **mi-figue**, **mi-raisin** [mifig, miʀɛzɛ̃] (*sourire*) wry

mignon(**ne**) [miɲɔ̃, ɔn] **I.** *adj* **1.** (*agréable à regarder*) cute **2.** *inf* (*gentil*) kind **II.** *m(f)* **mon/ma** ~(**ne**) sweetheart

migraine [migʀɛn] *f* MED migraine

migrateur, **-trice** [migʀatœʀ, -tʀis] *adj* migratory

migration [migʀasjɔ̃] *f* migration

mi-hauteur [miˊotœʀ] **à** ~ halfway up **mi-jambe** [miʒɑ̃b] **à** ~ as far as the knee(s) **mi-janvier** [miʒɑ̃vje] *f sans pl* **à la** ~ in mid-January

mijoter [miʒɔte] <1> **I.** *vt* **1.** (*faire cuire lentement*) to simmer **2.** *inf* (*manigancer*) ~ **qc** to cook sth up; ~ **de** *+infin* to be hatching plans to *+infin;* ~ **qc contre qn** to cook sth up for sb **II.** *vi* **1.** (*cuire lentement*) to simmer; **faire** ~ **un ragoût** to simmer a stew **2.** *inf* (*attendre*) **laisser** ~ **qn** to let sb stew

mi-juillet [miʒɥijɛ] *f sans pl* **à la** ~ in mid-July **mi-juin** [miʒɥɛ̃] *f sans pl* **à la** ~ in mid-June

mil [mil] *adj* thousand; **en** (**l'an**) ~ **neuf cent soixante-trois** in nineteen sixty-three

Milan [milɑ̃] Milan

milanais(**e**) [milanɛ, ɛz] *adj* **1.** (*de Milan*) Milanese **2.** GASTR **escalope** (**à la**) ~**e** escalope milanaise

mile [majl] *m* mile

milice [milis] *f* **1.** (*police*) militia **2.** *Belgique* (*service militaire*) national [*o* military] service

milicien [milisjɛ̃] *m Belgique* (*soldat qui fait son service militaire*) conscript

milieu [miljø] <x> *m* **1.** *sans pl* (*dans l'espace, dans le temps*) *a.* SPORT middle; **en plein** ~ **de la rue** right in the middle of the road; **le bouton du** ~ the middle button; **au** ~ **de la nuit/de l'après-midi/du film** in the middle of the night/afternoon/film; ~ **de terrain** midfield **2.** *sans pl* (*moyen terme*) medium **3.** (*environnement*) *a.* BIO, SOCIOL environment; **le** ~ **ambiant** the atmosphere; **les** ~**x populaires** the working class **4.** *sans pl* (*criminels*) **le** ~ the underworld

militaire [militɛʀ] **I.** *adj* army; (*opération, discipline, service*) military **II.** *mf* (*personne*) serviceman; ~ **de carrière** career serviceman

militant(**e**) [militɑ̃, ɑ̃t] **I.** *adj* militant **II.** *m(f)* militant

militariser [militaʀize] <1> *vpr* **se** ~ to militarize

militariste [militaʀist] *mf* militarist

militer [milite] <1> *vi* **1.** (*être militant*) to be a militant **2.** (*lutter*) ~ **pour/contre qc** to fight for/against **3.** (*plaider*) ~ **en faveur de/contre qn/qc** (*argument, comportement*) to militate for/against sb/sth

millage [milaʒ] *m Québec* (*action de mesurer en milles*) mileage

mille¹ [mil] **I.** *adj* **1.** (*chiffre, nombreux*) thousand; ~ **un** a thousand and one; **billet de ~ marks** thousand mark note *Brit,* thousand mark bill *Am* **2.** (*dans l'indication de l'ordre*) **page ~** page one thousand **II.** *m inv* **1.** (*cardinal*) one thousand **2.** (*cible*) bull's-eye; **taper (en plein) dans le ~** to hit the bull's-eye ▶**des ~ et des cents** *inf* tons of money; **je vous le donne en ~** you'll never guess; *v. a.* **cinq, cinquante**

mille² [mil] *m* NAUT ~ **marin** nautical mile

millefeuille [milfœj] *m* ≈ vanilla slice

millénaire [mileneʀ] **I.** *adj* thousand-year old; (*très vieux*) ancient **II.** *m* millennium

mille-pattes [milpat] *m inv* millipede

millésimé(e) [milezime] *adj* (*vin*) vintage; **une bouteille de Bordeaux ~e** a bottle of vintage Bordeaux

milliard [miljaʀ] *m* billion (*thousand million*); **des ~(s) de personnes/choses** billions of people/things

milliardaire [miljaʀdɛʀ] *mf* billionaire

millième [miljɛm] **I.** *adj antéposé* thousandth **II.** *mf* **le/la ~** the thousandth **III.** *m* (*fraction*) thousandth; *v. a.* **cinquième**

millier [milje] *m* **un/deux ~(s) de personnes/choses** one/two thousand people/things; **des ~s de personnes/choses** thousands of people/things; **des ~s et des ~s** thousands and thousands; **par ~s** by thousands

milligramme [miligʀam] *m* milligram

millimètre [milimɛtʀ] *m* millimetre *Brit,* millimeter *Am*

millimétré(e) [milimetʀe] *adj* **papier ~** ≈ maths paper *Brit,* ≈ graph paper *Am* (*with millimetre squares*)

million [miljɔ̃] *m* **un/deux ~(s) de personnes/choses** one/two million people/things; **des ~s de personnes/choses** millions of people/things; **des ~s de bénéfices** millions in profits; **des ~s et des ~s** millions and millions; *v. a.* **cinq, cinquante**

millionnaire [miljɔnɛʀ] *mf* millionaire

mi-long, -longue [milɔ̃, -lɔ̃g] <mi-longs> *adj* mid-length **mi-lourd** [miluʀ] *m* light heavyweight **mi-mai** [mimɛ] *f sans pl* **à la ~** in mid-May **mi-mars** [mimaʀs] *f sans pl* **à la ~** in mid-March

mime [mim] **I.** *mf* **1.** (*acteur*) mime artist **2.** (*imitateur*) mimic **II.** *m sans pl* (*activité*) mime

mimer [mime] <1> *vt* **1.** THEAT to mime **2.** (*imiter*) to mimic

mimétisme [mimetism] *m a.* ZOOL (*imitation parfaite*) mimicry

mimique [mimik] *f* **1.** *sans pl* (*jeu de physionomie*) funny face **2.** (*expression particulière*) **avoir une ~ expressive pour dire qc à qn** to make sth clear to sb by one's expression

mimolette [mimɔlɛt] *f: type of mild cheese*

mimosa [mimoza] *m* mimosa

minable [minabl] **I.** *adj* **1.** (*misérable: lieu*) shabby; (*aspect*) run-down **2.** (*médiocre*) pathetic **II.** *mf* loser

minaret [minaʀɛ] *m* minaret

minauder [minode] <1> *vi* to simper

mince [mɛ̃s] **I.** *adj* **1.** (*fin*) thin **2.** (*élancé*) slim; ~ **comme un fil** as thin as a rake **3.** (*modeste*) slender; (*preuve, résultat*) slim; **ce n'est pas une ~ affaire** it's no easy task **II.** *adv* thinly **III.** *interj inf* (*pour exprimer le mécontentement*) ~ **(alors)**! blast it!

minceur [mɛ̃sœʀ] *f sans pl* **1.** (*finesse: d'une feuille, couverture*) thinness **2.** (*sveltesse: d'une personne, de la taille*) slimness

mincir [mɛ̃siʀ] <8> *vi* to get slimmer

mine¹ [min] *f* **1.** *sans pl* (*aspect du visage*) expression; **avoir bonne ~** to look well; *iron, inf* (*avoir l'air ridicule*) to look stupid; **avoir mauvaise/une petite ~** to look ill/off-colour *Brit;* **faire bonne/grise ~ à qn** to give sb a warm/cool reception; **ne pas payer de ~** to be not much to look at **2.** *sans pl* (*allure*) appearance ▶**avoir une ~ de papier mâché** to look like death warmed up *Brit,* to look like death warmed over *Am;* ~ **de rien** *inf* (*sans se gêner*) all casually; (*malgré les apparences*) you'd never think it but

mine² [min] *f* **1.** (*gisement*) mine **2.** *a. fig* (*souterraine, lieu aménagé, source*) mine; ~ **de renseignements** mine of information

mine³ [min] *f* (*d'un crayon*) lead

mine⁴ [min] *f* MIL mine

miner [mine] <1> *vt* **1.** MIL to mine **2.** (*ronger*) ~ **qc** to eat away at sth **3.** (*affaiblir*) to weaken

minerai [minʀɛ] *m* ore; ~ **de fer/d'aluminium** iron/aluminium ore *Brit,* iron/aluminum ore *Am*

minéral [mineʀal, o] <-aux> *m* mineral

minéral(e) [mineʀal, o] <-aux> *adj* mineral

minéralogie [mineʀalɔʒi] *f* mineralogy

minéralogique [mineʀalɔʒik] *adj* **1.** AUTO **plaque ~** registration plate *Brit,* license plate *Am;* **numéro ~** registration number *Brit,* license number *Am* **2.** MIN mineralogical; **collection ~** mineral collection

minerval [minɛʀval] *m Belgique* (*frais de scolarité payés par les élèves de certaines écoles*) school fees *pl*

minerve [minɛʀv(ə)] *f* MED surgical collar

minet [minɛ] *m péj* pussy

minet(te) [minɛ, ɛt] *m(f)* **1.** *inf* (*chat*) pussy **2.** (*mot tendre*) **mon (gros/petit) ~** my sweetie pie

minette [minɛt] *f* (*jeune fille*) chick

mineur [minœʀ] *m* miner

mineur(e) [minœʀ] **I.** *adj* (*peu important*) *a.* JUR, MUS minor; **des enfants ~s** minors; **mode ~** minor mode **II.** *m(f)* JUR minor; **interdit aux ~s** forbidden to people under 18 years old

mini [mini] *adj inv, inf* (*mode*) mini

miniature [minjatyʀ] **I.** *f* miniature; **en ~** in miniature **II.** *app* **voiture ~** toy car

miniaturisation [minjatyʀizasjɔ̃] *f* miniaturization

miniaturiser [minjatyʀize] <1> *vt* to miniaturize

minier, -ière [minje, -jɛʀ] *adj* **société minière** mining company; **catastrophe minière** mining disaster; **région minière** mining area; **bassin ~** mineral field; **exploitation minière** mine

minigolf [minigɔlf] *m* miniature golf; (*terrain*) miniature golf course

minijupe [miniʒyp] *f* miniskirt

minimal(e) [minimal, o] <-aux> *adj* minimal

minime [minim] *adj* minor; (*dégâts, dépenses*) minimal

minimiser [minimize] <1> *vt* to minimize

minimum [minimɔm, minima] <s *o* minima> **I.** *adj* minimum **II.** *m* **1.** *sans pl* (*plus petite quantité, somme la plus faible, niveau le plus bas, valeur la plus basse*) minimum; **un ~ de points** a minimum number of points; **un ~ de risques** the fewest possible risks; **avoir un ~ vital** to have barely enough to live on; **s'il avait un ~ de savoir-vivre/d'argent** *inf* if he had just a little knowledge/money **2.** *sans pl* JUR minimum sentence

ministère [ministɛʀ] *m* **1.** (*bâtiment, portefeuille*) ministry *Brit,* department *Am;* **~ du Travail** Ministry of Employment *Brit,* Department of Labor *Am;* **~ de l'Intérieur** Ministry of the Interior; **~ des Affaires étrangères** Foreign Ministry, State Department *Am* **2.** (*cabinet, gouvernement*) government

ministériel(le) [ministeʀjɛl] *adj* **1.** (*d'un ministère, d'un ministre*) ministerial; **arrêté ~** ministerial decree; **portefeuille ~** minister's portfolio **2.** (*du gouvernement*) government; **remaniement ~** cabinet reshuffle **3.** (*du ministre*) ministerial

ministre [ministʀ] *mf* POL minister *Brit,* secretary *Am;* **Premier ~** Prime Minister, Premier; **~ des Affaires étrangères** Minister of Foreign Affairs *Brit,* Secretary of State *Am;* **~ d'Etat** Minister without Portfolio; **Madame le** [*o* **la**] **~** Minister

> The **Premier ministre** in France is the head of the government and is charge of its activities. He remains in office for five years. He is authorized to enforce guidelines and regulations in areas which are unregulated. He suggests the appointment and dismissal of Ministers to the President and is responsible for Parliament.

minitel® [minitɛl] *m* minitel

> The **minitel** gives access to a partially free electronic telephone directory as well as numerous pay services such as journey planners, credit card shopping or information about companies and authorities. Each service has a four-figure code, usually beginning with the number 36.

minium [minjɔm] *m* red lead

minoritaire [minɔʀitɛʀ] **I.** *adj* minority; **être ~s** to be in the minority **II.** *mf* POL **les ~s** the minority (party)

minorité [minɔʀite] *f* minority; **~ pénale** legal infancy

Minorque [minɔʀk(ə)] Minorca

minoterie [minɔtʀi] *f* (*moulin*) flour mill; (*meunerie*) flour milling

minou [minu] *m* **1.** *enfantin* (*chat*) pussy **2.** (*terme d'affection*) **mon ~** sweetie

mi-novembre [minɔvɑ̃bʀ] *f sans pl* **à la ~** in mid-November

minuit [minɥi] *m sans pl ni dét* midnight; **à ~ et demi** at half past midnight

minus [minys] *mf inf* washout

minuscule [minyskyl] **I.** *adj* **1.** (*très petit*) minute **2.** (*en écriture*) small; **lettres ~s** small letters **II.** *f* (*lettre*) small letter

minutage [minytaʒ] *m* timing

minute [minyt] *f* minute; **la ~ de vérité** the moment of truth; **d'une ~ à l'autre** from one moment to another; **information/modification de dernière ~** last-minute information/modification; **à la ~** just this very moment; (*tout de suite*) straight away; **je vous demande une ~ d'attention** could I have your attention for one minute?

minuter [minyte] <1> *vt* (*organiser*) to time

minuterie [minytʀi] *f* timer

minuteur [minytœʀ] *m* timer

minutie [minysi] *f sans pl* **1.** (*précision*) detail **2.** (*soin*) meticulousness

minutieux, -euse [minysjø, -jøz] *adj* meticulous; (*personne, examen*) thorough; (*exposé, description*) detailed; **avec un soin ~** with meticulous care

mi-octobre [miɔktɔbʀ] *f sans pl* **à la ~** in mid-October

mirabelle [miʀabɛl] *f* **1.** (*fruit*) mirabelle (plum) **2.** (*eau-de-vie*) plum brandy

miracle [miʀakl] **I.** *m* miracle; **par ~** miraculously **II.** *app inv* miracle; **solution/recette ~** miracle solution/formula

miraculé(e) [miʀakyle] **I.** *adj* miracle **II.** *m(f)* **c'est un ~** (*d'une maladie*) he's made a miraculous recovery; (*d'un accident*) he had a miraculous escape

miraculeux, -euse [miʀakylø, -øz] *adj* miraculous

mirador [miʀadɔʀ] *m* (*d'une prison*) watchtower; (*à la chasse*) perch

mirage [miʀaʒ] *m* (*vision*) mirage

mire [miʀ] *f* **1.** MEDIA test card **2.** TECH (*d'un arpenteur*) surveyor's rod

miro [miʀo] *adj inf* blind as a bat

mirobolant(**e**) [miʀɔbɔlɑ̃, ɑ̃t] *adj inf* fantastic

miroir [miʀwaʀ] *m* mirror

miroitant(**e**) [miʀwatɑ̃, ɑ̃t] *adj soutenu* gleaming

miroiter [miʀwate] <1> *vi* **1.** to gleam **2.** *fig* **faire ~ qc à qn** to dangle sth in front of sb

mis [mi] *passé simple de* **mettre**

mis(**e**) [mi, miz] **I.** *part passé de* **mettre** **II.** *adj* **être bien ~** to be well dressed

misanthrope [mizɑ̃tʀɔp] *mf* misanthrope

mise [miz] *f* **1.** JEUX bet **2.** FIN outlay **3.** *sans pl* (*habillement*) clothing **4.** (*fait de mettre*) **~ à feu** (*d'une fusée*) launch; **~ à jour** updating; **~ à la retraite** retirement; **~ à mort** killing; **~ à prix** reserve price, upset price *Am*; **~ en circulation d'une monnaie** (putting into) circulation of a currency; **~ en garde** warning; **~ en liberté** release; **~ en marche** switching on; **~ en œuvre** implementation; **~ en page**(**s**) make-up; **~ en pratique** putting into practice; **~ en scène** CINE production; *a.* THEAT staging; (*dans la vie privée*) performance **5.** INFOR **~ à jour** update; **~ en page** page layout; **~ en réseau** networking **6.** *Suisse* (*vente aux enchères*) auction

mi-septembre [misɛptɑ̃bʀ] *f sans pl* **à la ~** in mid-September

miser [mize] <1> **I.** *vi* **1.** (*parier sur*) **~ sur un animal/sur le rouge** to bet on an animal/the red; **~ 8 contre 1** to place an 8 to 1 bet **2.** *inf* (*compter sur*) **~ sur qn/qc pour** *+infin* to rely on sb/sth to *+infin* **II.** *vt* **1.** (*jouer*) **~ 100 euros sur un cheval** to bet 100 euros on a horse **2.** *Suisse* (*acheter aux enchères*) to buy at auction; (*vendre aux enchères*) to sell at auction

misérable [mizeʀabl] *adj* **1.** (*pauvre: personne, famille*) poverty-stricken; (*logement, aspect*) shabby **2.** (*pitoyable*) pitiful **3.** *antéposé* (*malheureux*) miserable

misérablement [mizeʀabləmɑ̃] *adv* **1.** (*dans la pauvreté*) in misery **2.** (*pitoyablement*) miserably

misère [mizɛʀ] *f* **1.** (*détresse*) misery **2.** *gén pl* (*souffrances*) woes; **faire des ~s à qn** *inf* to torment sb ►**salaire/traitement de ~** starvation wage; **~ de ~!** misery me!

miséreux, **-euse** [mizeʀø, -øz] **I.** *adj* (*mendiant*) destitute; (*quartier*) poverty-stricken **II.** *m, f* down-and-out

misogyne [mizɔʒin] **I.** *adj* misogynistic **II.** *m* misogynist

missel [misɛl] *m* missal

missile [misil] *m* missile

mission [misjɔ̃] *f* **1.** (*tâche culturelle, dangereuse, officielle*) *a.* MIL mission; **~ de reconnaissance** MIL, AVIAT reconnaissance mission; **j'ai reçu ~ d'aller à Rome** I have been ordered to go to Rome; **en ~** POL on a mission; COM on business **2.** (*délégation*) delegation **3.** (*vocation*) mission

missionnaire [misjɔnɛʀ] *mf* missionary

missive [misiv] *f soutenu* missive

mistral [mistʀal] <s> *m* Mistral

mit [mi] *passé simple de* **mettre**

MIT [ɛmajti] *m abr de* **Massachusetts Institute of Technology** MIT

mitaine [mitɛn] *f Québec* (*moufle*) mitten

mite [mit] *f* moth

mité(**e**) [mite] *adj* moth-eaten

mi-temps [mitɑ̃] **I.** *f inv* SPORT half-time **II.** *m inv* (*travail*) part-time; **travailler à ~** to work part-time

mîtes [mit] *passé simple de* **mettre**

miteux, **-euse** [mitø, -øz] **I.** *adj* (*immeuble, lieu*) dingy; (*personne*) seedy; (*habit, meuble*) tatty **II.** *m, f inf* seedy individual

mitigé(**e**) [mitiʒe] *adj* (*réaction, sentiments*) mixed; (*accueil, zèle, impression*) lukewarm

mitonner [mitɔne] <1> **I.** *vt inf* **1.** GASTR to simmer **2.** (*planifier*) **~ qc** (*affaire*) to cook sth up; (*avenir*) to plot sth; (*devoir, problème*) to slave over sth **II.** *vi inf* to simmer

mitoyen(**ne**) [mitwajɛ̃, jɛn] *adj* (*cloison*) partition; (*maison*) semi-detached; **mur ~** party wall; **être ~ avec** [*o* **de**] **qc** to be next to sth

mitraille [mitʀɑj] *f* **1.** (*projectiles*) grapeshot **2.** (*pluie de balles*) hail of bullets

mitrailler [mitʀɑje] <1> *vt* **1.** (*tirer*) to machine gun **2.** *inf* (*photographier*) **~ qn/qc** to take shot after shot of sb/sth

mitraillette [mitʀɑjɛt] *f* sub-machine gun

mitre [mitʀ] *f* REL mitre *Brit,* miter *Am*

mi-voix [mivwa] **à ~** in an undertone

mixage [miksaʒ] *m* mixing

mixer [mikse] <1> *vt* to mix

mixeur [miksœʀ] *m* mixer

mixte [mikst] *adj* **1.** (*pour les deux sexes: chorale, classe*) mixed **2.** (*formé d'éléments différents: mariage, végétation, salade*) mixed; (*commission*) joint; (*cuisinière*) combination

mixture [mikstyʀ] *f* **1.** CHIM, MED mixture **2.** *péj* (*boisson*) concoction

MJC [ɛmʒise] *f abr de* **maison des jeunes et de la culture** community youth and arts centre *Brit,* community youth and arts center *Am*

MLF [ɛmɛlɛf] *m abr de* **Mouvement de libération des femmes** Women's Liberation Movement

Mlle [madmwazɛl] <s> *f abr de* **Mademoiselle** Miss

MM. [mesjø] *mpl abr de* **Messieurs** Messrs *Brit,* Messrs. *Am*

Mme [madam] <s> *f abr de* **Madame** Mrs *Brit,* Mrs. *Am*

Mo [ɛmo] *m abr de* **méga-octet** MB

mob [mɔb] *f inf abr de* **mobylette**

mobile [mɔbil] **I.** *adj* **1.** (*opp: fixe*) moving **2.** (*non sédentaire: forces de police, population*) mobile **3.** (*changeant: regard*) changing; (*yeux*) darting **II.** *m* **1.** (*motif*) motive; **avoir pour ~ l'argent/l'amour** to have money/love as a motive **2.** PHYS moving body **3.** ART mobile

mobilier [mɔbilje] *m* (*ameublement*) furniture

mobilier, -ière [mɔbilje, -jɛʀ] *adj* moveable; (*crédit, saisie*) transferable; (*vente*) personal property

mobilisation [mɔbilizasjɔ̃] *f a.* MIL mobilization

mobiliser [mɔbilize] <1> **I.** *vt* **1.** (*rassembler*) to assemble **2.** MIL to mobilize; (*réservistes*) to call up **II.** *vi* MIL to mobilize **III.** *vpr* **se ~** to take action

mobilité [mɔbilite] *f* (*opp: immobilité*) mobility

mobylette [mɔbilɛt] *f* scooter

mocassin [mɔkasɛ̃] *m* moccassin

moche [mɔʃ] *adj inf* **1.** (*laid*) ugly **2.** (*regrettable*) rotten

mocheté [mɔʃte] *f inf* **1.** (*laideur*) ugliness **2.** (*chose laide*) eyesore **3.** (*personne laide*) fright

modalité [mɔdalite] *f* **1.** *pl* (*procédure*) methods *pl* **2.** MUS modality **3.** JUR clause

mode¹ [mɔd] **I.** *f* **1.** (*goût du jour*) fashion; **à la ~** in fashion; **être passé de ~** to be out of fashion **2.** (*métier*) fashion trade **3.** GASTR **à la ~ de qc** in the style of sth **II.** *app* fashion

mode² [mɔd] *m* **1.** (*méthode*) **~ d'emploi** directions for use; **~ de production** production method; **~ de gouvernement** form of government; **~ de pensée** way of thinking; **~ de transport/d'expression** mode of transport/expression *Brit,* mode of transportation/expression *Am;* **~ de paiement** method of payment **2.** LING mood **3.** MUS mode **4.** INFOR **~ de paysage** (*orientation d'une page*) landscape

modelage [mɔd(ə)laʒ] *m* modelling *Brit,* modeling *Am*

modèle [mɔdɛl] **I.** *m* **1.** (*référence, maquette*) *a.* LING, TYP model; **prendre ~ sur qn** to model oneself on sb; **faire qc sur le ~ de qc** to model sth on sth; **~ réduit** scale model **2.** COUT, ART pattern ►**~ déposé** registered design **II.** *adj* (*exemplaire*) model

modelé [mɔd(ə)le] *m* (*d'une sculpture, du visage*) contours; (*du terrain*) relief

modeler [mɔd(ə)le] <4> **I.** *vt* **1.** (*pétrir: poterie*) to model; (*pâte*) to mould *Brit,* to mold *Am* **2.** (*façonner: caractère, relief*) to shape **II.** *vpr* **se ~ sur qn/qc** to model oneself on sb/sth

modélisme [mɔdelism] *m* modelling *Brit,* modeling *Am*

modéliste [mɔdelist] *mf* **1.** COUT designer **2.** (*adepte du modélisme*) model maker

modem [mɔdɛm] *m* INFOR *v.* **MODulateur DÉModulateur** modem

modération [mɔdeʀasjɔ̃] *f* moderation; **faire/consommer qc avec ~** to do/consume sth in moderation

modéré(e) [mɔdeʀe] **I.** *adj* **1.** (*raisonnable: vent, froid, opinion*) moderate; (*prix*) reasonable **2.** (*médiocre: désir, résultat*) average; (*enthousiasme, succès*) moderate; (*optimisme*) restrained **II.** *m(f)* POL moderate

modérément [mɔdeʀemɑ̃] *adv* moderately

modérer [mɔdeʀe] <5> **I.** *vt* (*tempérer: personne*) to restrain; (*ambitions, colère, dépenses*) to control; (*passion*) to curb; (*vitesse*) to reduce; (*désirs*) to temper **II.** *vpr* **se ~** to restrain oneself

moderne [mɔdɛʀn] **I.** *adj* up-to-date; (*pays*) progressive; (*idée, histoire*) modern; **les temps ~s** modern times **II.** *m* modern style

modernisation [mɔdɛʀnizasjɔ̃] *f* modernization

moderniser [mɔdɛʀnize] <1> **I.** *vt* to modernize **II.** *vpr* **se ~** (*ville, pays*) to modernize; (*personne*) to bring oneself up to date

modernisme [mɔdɛʀnism] *m* modernism

modernité [mɔdɛʀnite] *f* modernity; (*d'une pensée*) progressiveness

modeste [mɔdɛst] **I.** *adj* modest **II.** *mf* unassuming person

modestie [mɔdɛsti] *f* modesty

modifiable [mɔdifjabl] *adj* modifiable; (*conduite, personne*) changeable; **le texte reste ~** the text can still be changed

modification [mɔdifikasjɔ̃] *f* modification; **apporter des ~s à qc** to make changes to sth

modifier [mɔdifje] <1> **I.** *vt a.* LING to modify **II.** *vpr* **se ~** to be modified

modique [mɔdik] *adj* modest

modulation [mɔdylasjɔ̃] *f* modulation

module [mɔdyl] *m* INFOR **~ d'extension** plug-in

moduler [mɔdyle] <1> **I.** *vt* **1.** RADIO, TEL to modulate **2.** (*adapter*) adjust; **les peines doivent être modulées en fonction des délits** sentences should fit the crime **II.** *vi* MUS to modulate

moelle [mwal, mwɛl] *f* ANAT, BOT marrow; **~ épinière** spinal chord

moelleux [mwɛlø] *m* **1.** (*souplesse: d'un lit, d'un tapis*) softness **2.** (*au goût: d'un vin*) mellowness

moelleux, -euse [mwɛlø, -øz] *adj* **1.** (*au toucher*) soft **2.** (*au goût, agréable: vin, son, voix*) mellow

moellon [mwalɔ̃, mwɛlɔ̃] *m* rubble

mœurs [mœʀ(s)] *fpl* **1.** (*coutumes: d'une personne, société*) customs; (*d'un animal*) habits; **entrer dans les ~** to become common **2.** (*règles morales*) morals; **une personne de bonnes/mauvaises ~** a person of high/low moral standards **3.** (*façon de vivre*) ways

mohair [mɔɛʀ] *m, app inv* mohair

moi [mwa] I. *pron pers* 1. *inf* (*pour renforcer*) ~, **je n'ai pas ouvert la bouche** I never opened my mouth; **c'est** ~ **qui l'ai dit** I'm the one who said it; **il veut m'aider,** ~**?** he wants to help ME? 2. *avec un verbe à l'impératif* **regarde-**~ look at me; **donne-**~ **ça!** give me that! 3. *avec une préposition* **avec/sans** ~ with/without me; **à** ~ **seul** by myself; **la maison est à** ~ the house is mine; **c'est à** ~ **de décider** it is for me to decide; **c'est à** ~**!** it's mine! 4. *dans une comparaison* me; **tu es comme** ~ you're like me; **plus fort que** ~ stronger than me 5. (*emphatique*) **c'est** ~**!** (*me voilà, je suis le responsable*) it's me; **et** ~**(, alors)?** *inf* and what about me?; **que ferais-tu si tu étais** ~**?** what would you do if you were me? ►**à** ~**!** help! II. *m* PHILOS, PSYCH ego

moignon [mwaɲɔ̃] *m* stump

moi-même [mwamɛm] *pron pers* myself; **je suis venu de** ~ it came of my own accord

moindre [mwɛ̃dʀ] *adj antéposé* 1. (*inférieur: inconvénient, degré, étendue*) lesser; (*prix, qualité*) lower 2. (*le plus petit*) **le** ~ **bruit** the slightest noise; **le** ~ **mal** the lesser evil; **ne pas avoir le** ~ **diplôme** to not have the least qualification; **ce serait la** ~ **des choses/des politesses** it would be the least you could do/be common courtesy

moine [mwan] *m* monk; **se faire** ~ to become a monk

moineau [mwano] <x> *m* sparrow

moins [mwɛ̃] I. *adv* 1. less; **rouler** ~ **vite** to drive slower; **les enfants de** ~ **de 13 ans** children under 13 years old; **se situer à** ~ **de 3,6 %** to be less than 3.6 %; ~ **...** ~ **...** the less ... the less ...; ~ **..., plus ...** the less ..., the more ... 2. *superl* **le** ~ the least ►**en** ~ **de deux** *inf* in a jiffy; **à** ~ **de faire qc** unless you do sth; **à** ~ **que qn ne fasse qc** (*subj*) unless sb does sth; **au** ~ at least; **(tout) au** ~ at the very least; **d'autant** ~ **que** the less so because; **de** ~, **en** ~ (*argent*) less; (*enfants*) fewer; **il a un an de** ~ **que moi** he is one year younger than me; **de** ~ **en** ~ less and less; **du** ~ at least; ~ **que rien** (*gagner, payer*) next to nothing II. *prep* 1. (*soustraction*) less; **tous les pays** ~ **la France** every country except France 2. (*heure*) to; **il est midi** ~ **vingt/le quart** it is twenty/a quarter to twelve 3. (*température*) minus; **il fait** ~ **3** it is minus 3 III. *m* 1. (*minimum*) least; **le** ~ **de matière** the smallest piece of matter 2. (*signe*) minus

moire [mwaʀ] *f* COUT (*tissu*) moiré

mois [mwa] *m* month; **le** ~ **de janvier/mars** the month of January/March; **les** ~ **en r** the months with an r in them; **au** ~ monthly; **au** ~ **de janvier/d'août** in January/August; **elle est dans son deuxième** ~ she is in her second month (of pregnancy); **le premier/cinq/dernier du/de ce** ~ the first/fifth/last day of the/this month

Moïse [mɔiːz(ə)] *m* Moses

moisi [mwazi] *m* mould *Brit,* mold *Am*

moisi(e) [mwazi] *adj* mouldy *Brit,* moldy *Am*

moisir [mwaziʀ] <8> *vi* 1. (*se gâter*) to mould *Brit,* to mold *Am* 2. (*être inutilisé: voiture, meuble*) to rot; (*argent, capital*) to stagnate; (*talent*) to go to waste 3. *inf* (*croupir: personne*) to stagnate

moisissure [mwazisyʀ] *f* mould *Brit,* mold *Am*

moisson [mwasɔ̃] *f* 1. AGR harvest 2. (*grande quantité*) **une** ~ **de souvenirs/d'images** a wealth of memories/pictures

moissonner [mwasɔne] <1> I. *vt* 1. AGR to harvest 2. (*recueillir: documents, images, souvenirs, idées, renseignements*) to gather; (*lauriers*) to collect II. *vi* to harvest

moissonneur, -euse [mwasɔnœʀ, -øz] *m, f* harvester

moite [mwat] *adj* sticky

moiteur [mwatœʀ] *f* stickiness; (*humidité*) dampness

moitié [mwatje] *f* 1. (*partie, milieu*) half; **la** ~ **du temps/de l'année** half the time/year; ~ **moins/plus** half less/more; **à** ~ **ivre/convaincu** half drunk/convinced; **à** ~ **prix** half-price; **ne jamais rien faire à** ~ to do nothing by halves; **de** ~ by half; **pour** ~ half to blame 2. *iron* (*épouse*) other half

moka [mɔka] *m* GASTR 1. (*café*) mocha 2. (*gâteau*) mocha gateau

mol [mɔl] *adj v.* **mou**

molaire [mɔlɛʀ] *f* ANAT molar

moldave [mɔldaːv(ə)] *adj* Moldovan

Moldave [mɔldaːv(ə)] *mf* Moldovan

Moldavie [mɔldavi] *f* **la** ~ Moldova

molécule [mɔlekyl] *f* molecule

molester [mɔlɛste] <1> *vt* to harass; (*physiquement*) to manhandle; **se faire** ~ **par qn** to be harassed by sb; (*physiquement*) to be manhandled by sb

molette [mɔlɛt] *f* 1. (*outil*) roller 2. (*pièce d'une mécanisme*) wheel 3. (*roue de l'éperon*) rowel

mollard [mɔlaʀ] *m inf* gob of (spit)

mollasson(ne) [mɔlasɔ̃, ɔn] I. *adj inf* sluggish II. *m(f) inf* lazybones

molle [mɔl] *adj v.* **mou**

mollement [mɔlmɑ̃] *adv* 1. (*confortablement: allongé, installé*) languidly; (*tomber*) limply; **les jours s'écoulent** ~ the days go gently by 2. (*sans ardeur: protester, réagir*) feebly

mollesse [mɔlɛs] *f* 1. (*indolence*) lethargy 2. (*laxisme*) weakness 3. (*douceur: d'un matelas, des contours, traits*) softness; (*d'une poignée de main*) limpness

mollet [mɔlɛ] *m* ANAT calf

molletonné(e) [mɔltɔne] *adj* quilted

mollir [mɔliʀ] <8> *vi* 1. (*fléchir: personne, ennemi*) to yield; (*créancier, vendeur*) to placate; (*courage*) to wane; (*jambes*) to give way; **faire** ~ **qn** to soften sb 2. (*perdre de sa force: vent*) to abate 3. (*se ramollir: cire, beurre*) to soften

M

mollo [mɔlo] *adv inf* ~! easy now!; **y aller** ~ to go easy
mollusque [mɔlysk] *m* ZOOL mollusc *Brit*, mollusk *Am*
môme [mom] *mf inf* kid
moment [mɔmɑ̃] *m* **1.** (*instant*) moment; **au dernier/même** ~ at the last/same moment; **à ce** ~**-là** at that moment; **à** [*o* **pour**] **un** ~ for a moment; **à tout/aucun** ~ at any/no time; **attendre qn/qc à tout** ~ to be expecting sb/sth at any moment; **au** ~ **de la chute du mur de Berlin** at the time of the fall of the Berlin Wall; **au** ~ **de partir, je me suis aperçu ...** as I was about to leave, I noticed ...; **à mes/ses** ~**s perdus** in my/his/her idle moments; **à partir du** ~ **où qn a fait qc** from the moment sb did sth; **dans un** ~ in a moment; **la mode du** ~ the fashion of the moment; **du** ~ **que qn fait qc** the moment sb does sth; **d'un** ~ **à l'autre** from one moment to another; **en ce** ~ at the moment; **pour le** ~ for the moment; **par** ~**s** from time to time; **sur le** ~ at the time; **un** ~**!** one moment!; **au bon** ~ at the right time; **le** ~ **présent** the present time; **être dans un de ses mauvais** ~**s** to be in a bad mood; **passer un bon** ~ to have a good time; **il vit ses derniers** ~**s** his life is ebbing away; **ce fut un grand** ~ it was a great moment **2.** (*occasion*) opportunity; **attendre le** ~ **opportun** to wait for the right moment; **le bon/mauvais** ~ the right/wrong time; **le** ~ **venu** when the time comes; **à un** ~ **donné** at a given moment; **c'est le** ~ **ou jamais** it's now or never; **c'est le** ~ **de** + *infin* this is the moment to + *infin*; **ce n'est pas le** ~ this is not the right time
momentané(e) [mɔmɑ̃tane] *adj* (*désir, ennui*) short-lived; (*effort*) brief; (*arrêt, espoir, gêne*) momentary
momentanément [mɔmɑ̃tanemɑ̃] *adv* for a moment
momie [mɔmi] *f* mummy
mon [mɔ̃, me] <mes> *dét poss* my; ~ **Dieu!** my God!; ~ **Père** Father; ~ **colonel** Sir; **à** ~ **avis** in my opinion; **à** ~ **approche** as I approach(ed) ▶ ~ **amour/chéri** my love; ~ **œil!** I bet!; ~ **pauvre!** you poor thing!
Monaco [mɔnako] Monaco
monarchie [mɔnaʀʃi] *f* monarchy

> Belgium is a **monarchie parlementaire** and the King is the head of the state. He appoints and dismisses the federal Ministers and State Secretary. He practises his legislative powers with the Chamber and the Senate.

monarchique [mɔnaʀʃik] *adj* monarchist; (*État*) monarchical; **user de son autorité/pouvoir** ~ (*reine*) to use the monarch's authority/power
monarchiste [mɔnaʀʃist] *adj, mf* monarchist
monarque [mɔnaʀk] *m* monarch
monastère [mɔnastɛʀ] *m* monastery
monastique [mɔnastik] *adj* monastic
monceau [mɔ̃so] <x> *m* **1.** (*tas*) mound **2.** (*grande quantité*) pile; **un** ~ **de vieux livres** a pile of old books; **des** ~**x de lettres** piles of letters
mondain(e) [mɔ̃dɛ̃, ɛn] **I.** *adj* society; **chronique** ~**e** society gossip **II.** *m(f)* socialite
mondaine [mɔ̃dɛn] *f inf* (*police*) vice squad
mondanité [mɔ̃danite] *f* **1.** (*goût pour la vie mondaine*) love of society life **2.** *pl* (*la vie mondaine*) society life
monde [mɔ̃d] *m* **1.** (*univers*) world; ~ **du rêve** realm of dreams; **le** ~ **des vivants** the land of the living; **plaisirs du** ~ worldly pleasures; **être encore/ne plus être de ce** ~ to be still/no longer with us; **être seul au** ~ to be alone in the world; **courir le** ~ to roam the world **2.** (*groupe social*) **dans le** ~ **enseignant/intellectuel** in teaching/intellectual circles; **le** ~ **rural** the rural community; ~ **du travail/des affaires** world of work/business **3.** (*foule*) crowd; **peu/beaucoup de** ~ not many/a lot of people; **un** ~ **fou** crowds of people; **pas grand** ~ not many people; **tout ce** ~**!** all these people! **4.** (*société*) **tout le** ~ **en parle** everyone is talking about it; **c'est à tout le** ~ it belongs to everyone ▶ **il y a du** ~ **au balcon** *inf* she is stacked!; **l'autre** ~ the next world; **je vais le mieux du** ~ I am perfectly fine; **pas le moins du** ~ not in the least; **c'est un** ~**!** *inf* if that does not beat all!; **depuis que le** ~ **existe** since the dawn of time; **mettre qn au** ~ to give birth to sb; **pour rien au** ~ not for anything
mondial [mɔ̃djal] *m* SPORT world championship
mondial(e) [mɔ̃djal, jo] <-aux> *adj* worldwide; (*économie, politique*) world
mondialement [mɔ̃djalmɑ̃] *adv* worldwide
mondialisation [mɔ̃djalizasjɔ̃] *f* globalization
monégasque [mɔnegask] *adj* Monacan
Monégasque [mɔnegask] *mf* Monacan
monétaire [mɔnetɛʀ] *adj* (*marché, politique*) financial; (*union, unité*) monetary
mongol [mɔ̃gɔl] *m* Mongolian; *v. a.* **français**
mongol(e) [mɔ̃gɔl] *adj* Mongolian
Mongol(e) [mɔ̃gɔl] *m(f)* Mongolian
Mongolie [mɔ̃gɔli] *f* **la** ~ Mongolia
mongolien(ne) [mɔ̃gɔljɛ̃, jɛn] **I.** *adj* MED Down's Syndrome **II.** *m(f)* MED Down's child [*o* sufferer]
moniteur [mɔnitœʀ] *m* (*écran*) monitor; ~ **de 15 pouces** 15-inch monitor
moniteur, -trice [mɔnitœʀ, -tʀis] *m, f* ~ **de colonies** camp supervisor; ~ **d'auto-école** driving instructor; ~ **de sport** instructor
monnaie [mɔnɛ] *f* **1.** ECON, FIN money; ~ **d'échange** currency; **fausse** ~ counterfeit money; ~ **électronique** e-cash **2.** (*devise*) currency; ~ **nationale/unique** national/single currency **3.** (*petites pièces*) **menue** ~ small change; **la** ~ **de 100 euros** change for 100

euros; **faire la ~ sur qc à qn** to give sb change for sth; **ça va, j'ai la ~** it's all right, I have change **4.** (*argent rendu*) change **5.** (*pièce*) coin ►**rendre à qn la ~ de sa pièce** to repay sb in kind; **~ de singe** empty promise; **c'est ~ courante** it's common practice

monnayer [mɔneje] <7> **I.** *vt* **1.** (*tirer argent de*) to turn into cash **2.** (*tirer profit*) **~ qc** to sell sth **II.** *vpr* **se ~** to be a saleable commodity

mono [mɔnɔ] *mf inf abr de* **moniteur, monitrice**

monocle [mɔnɔkl] *m* monocle

monogame [mɔnogam] *adj* monogamous

monolingue [mɔnolɛ̃g] *adj* monolingual

monologue [mɔnɔlɔg] *m* monologue

monologuer [mɔnɔlɔge] <1> *vi* **1.** (*parler pour soi*) to hold forth **2.** (*parler tout seul*) to talk to oneself

monoparental(e) [monopaʀɑ̃tal, o] <-aux> *adj* (*famille, autorité*) single parent

monopole [mɔnɔpɔl] *m* **1.** ECON monopoly **2.** (*exclusivité*) **avoir le ~ de qc** to have a monopoly on sth

monopoliser [mɔnɔpɔlize] <1> *vt* to monopolize

monoski [mɔnoski] *m* monoski

monospace [mɔnɔspas] *m* monospace

monosyllabe [mɔnosi(l)lab] *m* LING monosyllable; **par ~s** monosyllabically

monothéisme [mɔnoteism] *m* monotheism

monotone [mɔnɔtɔn] *adj* monotonous; (*style, vie*) dreary

monotonie [mɔnɔtɔni] *f* (*d'un discours, d'une voix*) monotony; (*de la vie, du style*) dreariness

monsieur [məsjø, mesjø] <messieurs> *m* **1.** *souvent non traduit* (*homme à qui on s'adresse*) Sir; **bonjour ~** good morning; **bonjour Monsieur Larroque** good morning Mr Larroque; **bonjour messieurs** good morning gentlemen; **Mesdames, mesdemoiselles, messieurs!** Ladies and Gentlemen!; **messieurs et chers collègues ...** gentlemen and colleagues ...; **Monsieur le Professeur Dupont/le Président François** Professor Dupont/President François; **Monsieur Untel** Mister So-and-so **2.** (*sur une enveloppe*) **Monsieur Pujol** Mister Pujol **3.** (*en-tête*) **(Cher) Monsieur,** Dear Sir; **Madame, Monsieur,** Sir, Madam,; **Madame, Mademoiselle, Monsieur,** Mr, Mrs, Miss *Brit,* Mr., Mrs., Miss *Am;* **messieurs dames** Ladies and Gentlemen **4.** (*un homme*) **un ~** a gentleman; **Monsieur Tout-le-monde** the average man

monstre [mɔ̃stʀ] **I.** *m* **1.** (*animal fantastique*) monster **2.** (*personne laide*) freak **3.** (*personne moralement abjecte*) brute **4.** (*construction laide*) eyesore **5.** BIO, ZOOL freak of nature ►**~ sacré** CINE, THEAT superstar **II.** *adj inf* gigantic

monstrueux, -euse [mɔ̃stʀyø, -øz] *adj* **1.** (*difforme*) freakish **2.** (*colossal*) massive **3.** (*ignoble*) monstrous

monstruosité [mɔ̃stʀyozite] *f* (*caractère ignoble*) monstrousness

mont [mɔ̃] *m* GEO mount; **le ~ Sinaï/Carmel** Mount Sinai/Carmel; **le ~ Cervin** the Matterhorn; **le ~ Blanc** Mont Blanc ►**promettre ~s et merveilles** to promise the moon

montage [mɔ̃taʒ] *m* **1.** (*assemblage: d'un appareil, d'une pièce de vêtement*) assembly; (*d'un bijou*) mounting; (*d'une tente*) pitching **2.** CINE, TV, THEAT, TYP editing; (*d'une maquette*) assembly; (*d'une opération*) organization; (*d'une page*) make-up; (*d'une pièce de théâtre*) production; (*d'une exposition*) setting up

montagnard(e) [mɔ̃taɲaʀ, aʀd] **I.** *adj* mountain **II.** *m(f)* mountain dweller

montagne [mɔ̃taɲ] *f a. fig* mountain; **en haute ~** high up in the mountains; **habiter la ~** to live in the mountains; **versant de la ~** mountainside ►**gros comme une ~** *inf* as big as a house; **~s russes** roller coaster; **(se) faire une ~ de qc/rien** to make a mountain out of sth/a molehill

montagneux, -euse [mɔ̃taɲø, -øz] *adj* mountainous

montant [mɔ̃tɑ̃] *m* **1.** (*somme*) sum; (*total*) total **2.** (*pièce verticale: d'un lit*) post; (*d'une porte*) jamb; (*d'une échelle*) upright

montant(e) [mɔ̃tɑ̃, ɑ̃t] *adj* (*chemin*) uphill; (*col*) high; (*mouvement*) upward; **colonne ~e** rising main; **garde ~e** MIL relief guard; **marée ~e** rising tide; **la génération ~e** the rising generation

monte [mɔ̃t] *f* **1.** (*manière de monter un cheval*) horsemanship **2.** ZOOL mounting

monté(e) [mɔ̃te] *adj* (*à cheval*) on horseback ►**être bien/mal ~ en qc** to be well/ill equipped with sth; **être ~ contre qn** to be angry with sb

monte-charge [mɔ̃tʃaʀʒ] *m inv* goods lift *Brit,* freight elevator *Am*

montée [mɔ̃te] *f* **1.** (*fait de croître: des eaux*) rising; (*de la colère, de l'islam, d'un parti*) rise; (*d'un danger, du mécontentement, de la violence*) increase; **~ en puissance** (*d'un moteur*) increase in power; (*d'une idéologie*) stunning rise; **la ~ des prix/de la température** the rise in prices/in temperature **2.** (*poussée: de la sève*) rise **3.** (*côte, pente*) hill **4.** (*action de monter*) climb; (*d'un avion, ballon*) ascent; **la ~ des marches** climbing the steps

monter [mɔ̃te] <1> **I.** *vi* **1.** *être* (*grimper*) to go up; (*vu d'en haut*) to come up; (*alpiniste*) to climb up; **~ sur une échelle** to climb a ladder; **~ à une tribune/en chaire** to stand up at the rostrum/in the pulpit; **~ dans sa chambre** to go (up) to one's room; **~ par l'ascenseur** to take the lift up *Brit,* to take the elevator up *Am;* **~ jusqu'à qc** (*eau, robe*) to reach sth; **~ à 200 km/h** to go up to 200 km/h **2.** (*chevaucher*) **~ à cheval/bicyclette/moto** to ride a horse/

bike/motorbike **3.** *être* (*prendre place dans*) ~ **dans une voiture** to get into a car; ~ **dans un train/avion/bus** to get on a train/plane/bus **4.** *être* (*aller vers le nord*) to go up **5.** *être* (*s'élever: avion, flammes, soleil*) to rise; (*route, chemin*) to go up **6.** *avoir o être* (*augmenter de niveau: baromètre, mer, sève*) to rise; (*lait*) to come; (*impatience, bruits*) to increase; **les larmes lui montent aux yeux** tears came to his eyes **7.** *avoir o être* (*augmenter: actions, croissance*) to increase; (*pression*) to grow **8.** *être* (*passer à l'aigu: ton, voix*) to get higher **9.** *avoir o être* (*faire une ascension sociale*) to go up in the world; **c'est une étoile qui monte** he's a rising star **II.** *vt avoir* **1.** (*gravir: personne*) to go up; (*vu d'en haut*) to come up; (*échelle*) to climb **2.** (*porter en haut, vu d'en bas*) ~ **qc** to take sth up; (*porter en haut, vu d'en haut*) to bring sth up **3.** GASTR ~ **qc** to whisk sth up **4.** (*chevaucher*) to mount **5.** (*couvrir*) to mount **6.** (*augmenter: prix*) to increase; ~ **le son** to turn up the sound **7.** (*organiser: affaire*) to organize; (*association, projet*) to set up; (*opération*) to mount; (*pièce de théâtre*) to stage; (*film*) to make; (*spectacle*) to put together **8.** (*fomenter: coup, complot*) to organize; (*histoire*) to make up **9.** TECH (*assembler, installer: échafaudage*) to erect; (*tente*) to pitch; (*maison*) to set up; (*mur*) to build; (*pneu*) to fit **10.** (*exciter*) ~ **le coup à qn** to take sb for a ride **III.** *vpr* (*atteindre*) **se** ~ **à 2000 euros** to come to 2000 euros

monteur, **-euse** [mɔ̃tœʀ, -øz] *m, f* **1.** TECH fitter **2.** CINE editor

montgolfière [mɔ̃gɔlfjɛʀ] *f* hot air balloon

monticule [mɔ̃tikyl] *m* (*colline*) mound

montpelliérain(**e**) [mɔ̃pəljeʀɛ̃, ɛn] *adj* of Montpellier; *v. a.* **ajaccien**

Montpelliérain(**e**) [mɔ̃pəljeʀɛ̃, ɛn] *m(f)* person from Montpellier; *v. a.* **Ajaccien**

montre [mɔ̃tʀ] *f* watch; ~ **à quartz** quartz watch ▶~ **en main** exactly; **course contre la** ~ race against the clock

Montréal [mɔ̃ʀeal] Montreal

montréalais(**e**) [mɔ̃ʀealɛ, ɛz] *adj* from Montreal

Montréalais(**e**) [mɔ̃ʀealɛ, ɛz] *m(f)* personal from Montreal

montre-bracelet [mɔ̃tʀəbʀaslɛ] <montres-bracelets> *f* wrist watch

montrer [mɔ̃tʀe] <1> **I.** *vt* to show; ~ **la sortie à qn** to show sb the exit **II.** *vpr* **1.** (*prouver*) **il se** ~ **qc** he proves himself to be sth **2.** (*apparaître*) **se** ~ to appear; **se** ~ **à son avantage** to show oneself off to one's best advantage

montreur, **-euse** [mɔ̃tʀœʀ, -øz] *m, f* ~ **de marionnettes** puppeteer; ~ **d'ours** bear leader

monture [mɔ̃tyʀ] *f* **1.** (*animal*) mount **2.** (*en optique*) frame **3.** (*bijou*) setting

monument [mɔnymɑ̃] *m* **1.** (*mémorial*) memorial; ~ **funéraire** funeral monument; ~ **aux morts** memorial; (*aux soldats morts pendant la guerre*) war memorial **2.** (*édifice*) monument; **être classé** ~ **historique** to be listed as an historic building; ~ **public** civic building **3.** *fig, inf* **c'est un** ~ **d'orgueil/de bêtise** he is monumentally proud/stupid

monumental(**e**) [mɔnymɑ̃tal, o] <-aux> *adj* **1.** (*imposant*) monumental **2.** *inf* (*énorme: erreur*) colossal; (*orgueil*) monumental; **être d'une bêtise ~e** to be monumentally stupid

moquer [mɔke] <1> *vpr* **1.** (*ridiculiser*) **se** ~ **de qn/qc** to make fun of sb/sth **2.** (*dédaigner*) **se** ~ **du qu'en dira-t-on** not to care what people say; **se** ~ **de faire qc** to not care about doing sth; **je m'en moque pas mal** I really couldn't care less **3.** (*tromper*) **se** ~ **du monde** to have (some) nerve

moquerie [mɔkʀi] *f* jeer; **les ~s** mockery

moquette [mɔkɛt] *f* (fitted) carpet

moqueur, **-euse** [mɔkœʀ, -øz] **I.** *adj* (*air*) mocking; **être très** ~ to always make fun of people **II.** *m, f* mocker

moral [mɔʀal, o] <-aux> *m* **1.** (*état psychologique*) morale; **le** ~ **de l'armée/la population** the army's/population's morale **2.** (*vie psychique*) **au** ~ mentally ▶**avoir le** ~ **à zéro** to feel really down; **avoir le** ~ to be in good spirits; **ne pas avoir le** ~ to be in low spirits; **remonter le** ~ **à qn** to boost sb's morale

moral(**e**) [mɔʀal, o] <-aux> *adj* moral

morale [mɔʀal] *f* **1.** (*principes*) morality **2.** (*éthique*) ethic ▶**faire la** ~ **à qn** to lecture sb

moralement [mɔʀalmɑ̃] *adv* **1.** (*sur le plan spirituel*) on an emotional level **2.** (*relatif, conformément à la morale*) morally; (*agir, se conduire*) with integrity

moralisateur, **-trice** [mɔʀalizatœʀ, -tʀis] **I.** *adj* (*enseignement, influence*) moralizing; (*histoire, récit*) elevating; (*personne, ton*) sanctimonious **II.** *m, f* moralizer

moraliser [mɔʀalize] <1> **I.** *vi* to moralize **II.** *vt* to lecture

moraliste [mɔʀalist] **I.** *adj* moralistic **II.** *mf* moralist

moralité [mɔʀalite] *f* **1.** (*valeur morale*) morality **2.** (*leçon*) moral

morbide [mɔʀbid] *adj* (*malsain: goût, littérature*) morbid; (*imagination*) gruesome

morceau [mɔʀso] <x> *m* **1.** (*fragment*) piece; **sucre en ~x** lump sugar; **mettre un livre en ~x** to pull a book to pieces; ~ **par** ~ bit by bit **2.** (*viande*) cut; **bas ~x** cheap cuts; ~ **de choix** choice cut **3.** ART piece ▶**lâcher le** ~ *inf* to come clean; **manger un** ~ to have a bite (to eat); **recoller les ~x** to patch things up

morceler [mɔʀsəle] <3> **I.** *vt* ~ **qc** to divide sth up; (*terrain, héritage*) to parcel sth up **II.** *vpr* **se** ~ (*propriété, terrain*) to be split up

morcellement [mɔʀsɛlmɑ̃] *m* **1.** (*de terres, d'un terrain*) dividing up **2.** (*dispersion*) splitting up

mordant(**e**) [mɔʀdɑ̃, ɑ̃t] *adj* **1.** (*incisif*)

incisive; (*personne, trait d'esprit*) sharp; (*ton, voix*) cutting; (*vent*) biting **2.** (*qui entame: corrosif*) destructive; (*lime*) sharp

mordiller [mɔʀdije] <1> *vt* ~ **qc** to chew on sth

mordoré(e) [mɔʀdɔʀe] *adj* bronze

mordre [mɔʀdʀ] <14> **I.** *vi* **1.** (*attaquer*) to bite **2.** (*se laisser prendre*) ~ **à l'appât** to bite; *fig* to take the bait **3.** (*prendre goût*) ~ **à qc** to take to sth **4.** (*enfoncer les dents*) ~ **dans qc** to bite into sth **5.** (*pénétrer*) ~ **dans qc** to eat into sth **6.** (*empiéter*) ~ **sur qc** to go past sth **II.** *vt* **1.** (*serrer avec les dents*) to bite; ~ **qn à l'oreille/la jambe** to bite sb's ear/leg **2.** (*empiéter sur: démarcation*) to go past **III.** *vpr* **se** ~ **la langue** to bite one's tongue

mordu(e) [mɔʀdy] **I.** *part passé de* **mordre** **II.** *adj* **1.** (*amoureux*) **être** ~ **de qn** to be in love with sb **2.** *inf* (*passionné*) **être** ~ **de qc** to be mad about sth **III.** *m(f) inf* ~ **de musique/sport** music/sports fan

morfal(e) [mɔʀfal] <s> **I.** *adj inf* greedy **II.** *m(f) inf* greedy-guts

morfondre [mɔʀfɔ̃dʀ] <14> *vpr* **se** ~ **1.** (*s'ennuyer*) to fret **2.** (*languir*) to mope; **être morfondu** to be dejected

morgue [mɔʀg] *f* **1.** (*institut médico-légal*) morgue **2.** (*salle d'hôpital*) mortuary

moribond(e) [mɔʀibɔ̃, ɔ̃d] **I.** *adj* **être** ~ to be dying **II.** *m(f)* dying man, woman *m, f*

morille [mɔʀij] *f* morel

morne [mɔʀn] *adj* bleak; (*vie, paysage*) dismal; (*regard*) sullen

morose [mɔʀoz] *adj* (*personne, situation*) morose; (*temps, air*) sullen

morosité [mɔʀozite] *f* moroseness; ~ **économique** depressed economy

morphine [mɔʀfin] *f* morphine

morphinomane [mɔʀfinɔman] **I.** *adj* addicted to morphine **II.** *mf* morphine addict

morphologie [mɔʀfɔlɔʒi] *f* morphology

morpion [mɔʀpjɔ̃] *m inf* (*pou*) flea

mors [mɔʀ] *m* bit ►**prendre le** ~ **aux dents** (*cheval*) to get the bit between its teeth; (*personne*) (*s'emporter*) to fly into a rage; (*s'y mettre avec énergie*) to swing into action

morse[1] [mɔʀs] *m* ZOOL walrus

morse[2] [mɔʀs] **I.** *m* Morse code; **envoyer un message en** ~ to send a message in Morse code **II.** *adj* **l'alphabet** ~ the Morse alphabet

morsure [mɔʀsyʀ] *f* **1.** (*action de mordre, plaie*) bite **2.** (*d'un insecte*) sting

mort [mɔʀ] *f* (*décès, destruction*) death ►**faire qc la** ~ **dans l'âme** to do sth with a heavy heart; **tu vas attraper la** ~ *inf* you will catch your death; **être blessé à** ~ to be mortally wounded; **se donner la** ~ to take one's own life; **frapper qn à** ~ to beat sb to death; **à ~! à ~!** die! die!; ~ **au tyran!** death to the tyrant!; **en vouloir à** ~ **à qn** to hate sb (with a vengeance); **s'ennuyer à** ~ to be bored to death

Mort [mɔʀ] *f* **la** ~ Death

mort(e) [mɔʀ, mɔʀt] **I.** *part passé de* **mourir** **II.** *adj* **1.** (*décédé, sans animation, hors d'usage*) dead **2.** *inf* (*épuisé*) **être** ~ to be dead beat; **être** ~ **de fatigue** to be exhausted **3.** (*avec un fort sentiment de*) **être** ~ **de honte/peur** to be mortified/scared stiff **4.** (*éteint: yeux, regard*) lifeless; (*feu*) out **5.** (*qui n'existe plus: langue*) dead ►**être** ~ **et enterré** to be dead and buried; **être laissé pour** ~ to be left for dead; **tomber raide** ~ to drop stone dead **III.** *m(f)* **1.** (*défunt*) dead person; **les ~s de la guerre** those killed in the war **2.** (*dépouille*) dead body ►**être un** ~ **en sursis** to be living on borrowed time; **être un** ~ **vivant** to be more dead than alive; **faire le** ~ (*comme si on était mort*) to play dead; (*ne pas répondre*) to lie low

mortadelle [mɔʀtadɛl] *f* mortadella

mortalité [mɔʀtalite] *f* mortality

mort-aux-rats [mɔʀoʀa] *f inv* rat poison

mortel(le) [mɔʀtɛl] **I.** *adj* **1.** (*sujet à la mort*) mortal **2.** (*causant la mort*) fatal **3.** (*extrême, pénible: frayeur, haine*) mortal; (*froid, chaleur*) deathly; (*pâleur, ennemi, silence*) deadly **4.** *inf* (*ennuyeux*) deadly **II.** *m(f) souvent pl* mortal

mortellement [mɔʀtɛlmɑ̃] *adv* **1.** mortally **2.** (*extrêmement: vexé*) deeply; ~ **ennuyeux** deadly boring

mortier [mɔʀtje] *m* mortar

mortifié(e) [mɔʀtifje] *adj* mortified

mort-né(e) [mɔʀne] <mort-nés> **I.** *adj* (*enfant*) stillborn; (*projet, entreprise*) abortive **II.** *m(f)* stillborn

mortuaire [mɔʀtɥɛʀ] **I.** *adj* funeral; **chambre** ~ death chamber; **registre** ~ register of deaths; **habits** ~ grave clothes; **salon** ~ *Québec* (*entreprise de pompes funèbres*) funeral parlour *Brit*, funeral parlor *Am* **II.** *f Belgique* (*maison du défunt*) house of the deceased

morue [mɔʀy] *f* **1.** ZOOL ~ **séchée/fraîche/fumée** dried/fresh/smoked cod; **huile de foie de** ~ cod liver oil **2.** *vulg* (*prostituée*) whore

morve [mɔʀv] *f* mucus

morveux, **-euse** [mɔʀvø, -øz] **I.** *adj* (*nez*) runny; (*enfant*) snotty *inf* **II.** *m, f péj, inf* snotty kid

mosaïque [mɔzaik] *f* **1.** (*image*) mosaic **2.** *fig* ~ **de peuples** patchwork of peoples

Moscou [mɔsku] Moscow

moscovite [mɔskɔvit] *adj* Muscovite

Moscovite [mɔskɔvit] *mf* Muscovite

Moselle [mozɛl] *f* **la** ~ the Moselle

mosquée [mɔske] *f* mosque

mot [mo] *m* **1.** (*moyen d'expression*) word; **gros** ~ swear word; ~ **composé** compound; **les ~s me manquent** I'm speechless; **chercher ses ~s** to look for the right words; **c'est le** ~ **juste** it is the right word; **à ces ~s** with these words; ~ **pour** ~ word for word **2.** (*message*) message; ~ **d'excuse** excuse

M

note; ~ **d'ordre** slogan; ~ **de félicitations** letter of congratulions; **laisser un ~ à qn** to leave a message for sb **3.** (*parole mémorable*) saying **4.** *a.* INFOR ~ **de passe** password; ~ **de passe de messagerie** email password **5.** JEUX **faire des ~s croisés** to do crossword puzzles ►**le fin ~ de l'affaire** the real story; **avoir un ~ sur le bout de la langue** to have a word on the tip of one's tongue; **dire deux ~s à qn** to give sb a piece of one's mind; **expliquer/raconter qc en deux ~s** to explain/tell sth briefly; **avoir son ~ à dire** to have something to say; **sans ~ dire** without a word; **se donner le ~** to pass the word round; **avoir des ~s avec qn** *inf* to have words with sb; **avoir toujours le ~ pour rire** to be a joker; **je lui en toucherai un ~** I will have a word with her about it; ~ **à ~** word for word; **en un ~** (**comme en cent**) in a word

motard(e) [mɔtaʀ] *m(f) inf* **1.** (*motocycliste*) motorcyclist, biker **2.** (*policier*) motorcycle policeman *Brit,* motorcycle cop *Am*

mot-clé [mokle] <mots-clés> *m* keyword

motel [mɔtɛl] *m* motel

moteur [mɔtœʀ] **I.** *m* **1.** TECH motor; ~ **à explosion** internal combustion engine; ~ **à réaction** jet engine; ~ **diesel** diesel engine **2.** (*cause*) **être le ~ de qc** (*concurrence*) to be the catalyst for sth; (*personne*) to be the driving force behind sth **3.** INFOR ~ **de recherche** search engine **II.** *app* **bloc ~** engine block; **frein ~** engine braking

moteur, -trice [mɔtœʀ, -tʀis] *adj* (*muscle, nerf*) motor; (*force, roue*) driving

motif [mɔtif] *m* **1.** (*raison*) motive **2.** *pl* (*dans un jugement*) grounds **3.** (*ornement*) motif **4.** (*modèle*) pattern

motion [mosjɔ̃] *f* motion; ~ **de censure** censure motion

motivant(e) [mɔtivɑ̃, ɑ̃t] *adj* motivating

motivation [mɔtivasjɔ̃] *f* **1.** (*justification*) ~ **de qc** motivation for sth **2.** ECON **lettre de ~** application letter

motivé(e) [mɔtive] *adj* **1.** (*justifié*) justified; **absence non ~e** unexplained absence **2.** (*stimulé: personne*) motivated

motiver [mɔtive] <1> *vt* **1.** (*justifier*) to justify **2.** (*causer*) to cause **3.** (*stimuler*) to motivate

moto [moto] *f abr de* **motocyclette**

motocross, moto-cross [motokʀɔs] *m inv* motocross

motoculteur [motokyltœʀ] *m* Rotavator® *Brit,* rototiller *Am*

motocyclisme [motosiklism] *m* motorbike racing

motocycliste [motosiklist] **I.** *adj* motorcycling **II.** *mf* motorcyclist

motoneige [motonɛʒ] *f* snowmobile

motorisé(e) [motoʀize] *adj* motorized

motoriser [motoʀize] <1> *vt* to motorize

motrice [mɔtʀis] *f* power unit

mots-croisiste [mokʀwazist] *mf* crossword enthusiast

motte [mɔt] *f* (*de beurre*) slab; (*de gazon*) turf; ~ **de terre** clod of earth

motus [mɔtys] *interj* not a word!; ~ **et bouche cousue!** don't breathe a word!

mot-valise [movaliz] <mots-valises> *m* portmanteau word

mou [mu] *m* **1.** *inf* (*personne*) sluggish person **2.** (*qualité*) softness

mou, molle [mu, mɔl] <*devant un nom masculin commençant par une voyelle ou un h muet* mol> **I.** *adj* **1.** (*opp: dur*) soft; **chapeau ~** trilby *Brit,* fedora *Am* **2.** (*flasque*) flabby **3.** (*amorphe, faible: personne, geste*) feeble; (*résistance, protestations*) weak **4.** (*sourd: bruit*) muffled **II.** *adv* (*jouer*) tiredly

mouchard(e) [muʃaʀ, aʀd] *m(f)* **1.** (*rapporteur*) informer **2.** *péj* (*indicateur de police*) snitch

moucharder [muʃaʀde] <1> **I.** *vi inf* to snitch **II.** *vt inf* ~ **qn** to sneak on sb; (*à la police*) to grass on sb *Brit,* to narc on sb *Am*

mouche [muʃ] *f* **1.** (*animal, a. pour la pêche*) fly **2.** (*centre: d'une cible*) bull's eye **3.** (*en cosmétique*) beauty spot ►**quelle ~ l'a piqué?** what has got into him/her?

moucher [muʃe] <1> **I.** *vt* ~ (**le nez à**) **qn** to blow sb's nose **II.** *vpr* **se ~** (**le nez**) to blow one's nose

moucheron [muʃʀɔ̃] *m* **1.** ZOOL midge **2.** *inf* (*petit enfant*) kid

moucheté(e) [muʃte] *adj* (*animal, pelage*) spotted; (*tissu, laine*) flecked

mouchoir [muʃwaʀ] *m* ~ **de poche** pocket handkerchief; ~ **en papier** tissue, kleenex *Am;* ~ **en tissu** handkerchief

moudre [mudʀ] *vt irr* to grind

moue [mu] *f* pout

mouette [mwɛt] *f* seagull

moufle [mufl] *f* mitten

mouflon [muflɔ̃] *m* mouflon

moufter [mufte] <1> *vi v.* **moufeter**

mouillage [mujaʒ] *m* **1.** (*action de mouiller*) wetting **2.** (*coupage*) watering down **3.** NAUT (*emplacement*) moorings *pl;* **rester au ~** to ride at anchor **4.** NAUT (*mise à l'eau: d'un navire*) launch; (*d'une mine*) laying; **le ~ de l'ancre** dropping anchor

mouillé(e) [muje] *adj* **1.** (*trempé*) wet **2.** (*plein d'émotion: voix*) emotional **3.** (*plein de larmes: regard, yeux*) tearful **4.** LING palatal

mouiller [muje] <1> **I.** *vt* **1.** (*humecter*) to wet **2.** (*tremper*) to soak; **se faire ~** to get soaked **3.** GASTR ~ **un rôti avec du bouillon** to baste a roast with stock **4.** NAUT (*ancre*) to cast; (*mines*) to lay **5.** *inf* (*compromettre*) ~ **qn dans qc** to implicate sb in sth **II.** *vi* **1.** (*jeter l'ancre*) to cast anchor **2.** *inf* (*avoir peur*) to be scared to death **III.** *vpr* **1.** (*passer sous l'eau*) **se ~** to get wet; **se ~ les mains** to get one's hands wet **2.** (*se tremper*) **se ~** to get soaked **3.** (*s'humecter: yeux*) to brim with tears **4.** *inf* (*se compromettre*) **se ~ dans qc** to get

involved in sth **5.** *inf* (*s'engager*) **se ~ pour qn/pour** +*infin* to put oneself on the line for sb/to +*infin*
mouillette [mujɛt] *f* soldier
moulage [mulaʒ] *m* **1.** (*action de mouler*) moulding *Brit,* molding *Am* **2.** (*empreinte, objet*) cast
moulant(e) [mulɑ̃, ɑ̃t] *adj* tight
moule[1] [mul] *m* **1.** (*forme*) *a.* GASTR mould *Brit,* mold *Am* **2.** (*empreinte*) cast **3.** (*modèle*) **être fait sur le même ~** to come from the same mould *Brit,* to come from the same mold *Am*
moule[2] [mul] *f* mussel
mouler [mule] <1> *vt* **1.** (*fabriquer*) to mould *Brit,* to mold *Am* **2.** (*prendre un moulage de*) **~ un buste** to cast a bust **3.** (*coller à*) **des vêtements qui moulent le corps** clothes which hug the body
moulin [mulɛ̃] *m* mill; **~ à café** coffee mill; **~ à vent** windmill ►**être un ~ à paroles** *inf* to be a chatterbox; **on entre ici comme dans un ~** you can just walk in
mouliné(e) [muline] *adj* liquidized
mouliner [muline] <1> *vt* GASTR to grate
moulinet [mulinɛ] *m* PECHE reel ►**faire des ~s avec qc** to twirl sth
moulinette [mulinɛt] *f* vegetable mill
moulu(e) [muly] **I.** *part passé de* **moudre** **II.** *adj* **1.** (*en poudre*) ground **2.** *inf* (*fourbu*) **être ~** (**de fatigue**) to be dead beat
moulure [mulyʀ] *f* moulding *Brit,* mold *Am*
moumoute [mumut] *f inf* **1.** (*perruque*) wig **2.** (*veste*) fleece (jacket)
mourant(e) [muʀɑ̃, ɑ̃t] **I.** *adj* (*musique, son*) faint; (*personne, feu, lumière*) dying; **être ~** to be dying **II.** *m(f)* dying person
mourir [muʀiʀ] *vi irr être* **1.** (*cesser d'exister: personne, animal, plante*) to die; (*fleuve*) to dry up; **~ de ses blessures** to die of one's wounds; **~ de chagrin/soif** to die of grief/thirst; **~ de faim** to starve to death; **~ de froid** to freeze to death; **~ dans un accident de voiture** to die in a car crash; **il est mort assassiné/empoisonné** he was murdered/poisoned; **elle est morte noyée** she drowned **2.** (*venir de ~*) **être mort** to have died **3.** (*tuer*) to kill; **tu vas faire ~ ta mère de chagrin** you're going to make your mother die of grief **4.** (*disparaître peu à peu*) to die out; (*voix, bruit, feu*) to die down ►**c'est à ~ de rire** you'd die laughing; **se sentir malade à ~** to feel seriously ill; **s'ennuyer à ~** to be bored to death
mouroir [muʀwaʀ] *m péj* old folks' home
mousquetaire [muskətɛʀ] *m* musketeer
mousqueton [muskətɔ̃] *m* karabiner
moussant(e) [musɑ̃, ɑ̃t] *adj* foaming
mousse[1] [mus] **I.** *f* **1.** (*écume*) froth; **~ à raser** shaving foam **2.** BOT moss **3.** GASTR mousse **4.** (*matière*) foam **II.** *app inv* **vert ~** moss green
mousse[2] [mus] *m* cabin boy
mousseline [muslin] **I.** *f* muslin; **une ~** a muslin cloth **II.** *app inv* **pommes ~** potato purée; **sauce ~** sauce mousseline
mousser [muse] <1> *vi* **1.** (*produire de la mousse*) to foam; **faire ~** to lather **2.** *inf* (*vanter*) **faire ~ qn/qc** to sing the praises of sb/sth; **il s'est fait ~ auprès de son chef** he tried to make himself look good in front of his boss
mousseux [musø] *m* sparkling wine
mousson [musɔ̃] *f* monsoon
moussu(e) [musy] *adj* mossy
moustache [mustaʃ] *f* **1.** moustache *Brit,* mustache *Am* **2.** (*du chat*) whiskers
moustachu(e) [mustaʃy] *adj* (*homme*) wearing a moustache *Brit,* wearing a mustache *Am;* (*lèvre supérieure*) with a moustache *Brit,* with a mustache *Am*
moustachu [mustaʃy] *m* man with a moustache *Brit,* man with a mustache *Am*
moustiquaire [mustikɛʀ] *f* **1.** (*rideau*) mosquito net **2.** (*à la fenêtre, à la porte*) mosquito screen
moustique [mustik] *m* **1.** ZOOL mosquito **2.** *péj* (*enfant*) little squirt **3.** *péj* (*personne malingre*) scrawny person
moût [mu] *m* (*du vin*) must; (*de la bière*) wort
moutarde [mutaʀd] **I.** *f* mustard **II.** *app inv* mustard
mouton [mutɔ̃] *m* **1.** ZOOL sheep **2.** (*peau*) sheepskin **3.** (*viande*) mutton **4.** (*écume*) white horse *Brit,* whitecap *Am* **5.** (*poussière*) bit of fluff **6.** (*nuages*) fluffy cloud **7.** (*personne douce*) lamb ►**revenons à nos ~s** let's get back to the point
moutonner [mutɔne] <1> **I.** *vi* (*mer, vagues*) to be topped with white foam; (*collines*) to roll; **les nuages moutonnent dans le ciel** there are fleecy clouds in the sky **II.** *vpr* **se ~** (*mer*) to be topped with white foam; (*ciel*) to roll
mouture [mutyʀ] *f* **1.** (*action de moudre: du café*) grinding; (*des céréales*) milling **2.** (*produit de l'opération*) **une ~ fine** (*du café*) finely ground coffee; (*des céréales*) finely milled flour **3.** *péj* (*reprise*) rehash **4.** (*version*) draft; **première ~** first draft
mouvant(e) [muvɑ̃, ɑ̃t] *adj* **1.** (*ondoyant: foule*) heaving; (*champs de blé*) swaying; (*ombre*) moving; (*flamme*) wavering **2.** (*changeant: pensée, univers*) changing; (*situation*) unsettled **3.** (*sans stabilité: terrain*) unstable; **sables ~s** quicksand
mouvement [muvmɑ̃] *m* **1.** (*action, partie de l'œuvre*) movement **2.** (*impulsion*) reaction; **~ de colère/d'humeur** burst of anger/bad temper; **~ d'impatience** impatient gesture **3.** (*animation*) activity **4.** ECON (*de marchandises, capitaux, fonds*) movement; **~ des prix** price trend; **~ de baisse** downturn; **~ de hausse** upturn **5.** ADMIN (*changement d'affectation*) move **6.** GEO **~ de terrain** undulation

7. (*évolution*) trend; ~ **d'opinion** movement of opinion; ~ **d'idées** intellectual movement 8. MUS (*tempo*) movement ►**il est libre de ses ~s** he is free to come and go as he pleases

mouvementé(e) [muvmɑ̃te] *adj* 1. (*agité*) stormy; (*vie*) turbulent; (*poursuite, récit*) eventful 2. (*accidenté*) uneven

mouvoir [muvwaʀ] *irr* I. *vt* 1. **faire ~** to move; **être mû par qc** to be moved by sth 2. (*être poussé*) **être mû par l'intérêt/la pitié** to be prompted by self-interest/pity II. *vpr* **se ~** to move

moyen [mwajɛ̃] *m* 1. (*procédé, solution*) means; ~ **d'action** means of action; **essayer par tous les ~s de** +*infin* to try everything to +*infin;* **par le ~ de** by means of; **au ~ de qc** using sth 2. (*manière*) way 3. *pl* (*capacités physiques*) strength 4. *pl* (*capacités intellectuelles*) faculties; **être en (pleine) possession de ses ~s** to have all one's faculties; **par ses propres ~s** by himself 5. *pl* (*ressources financières*) means; **vivre au-dessus de ses ~s** to live above one's means; **c'est au-dessus de mes ~s** I cannot afford it; **il/elle a les ~s!** *inf* he/she can afford it! 6. *souvent pl* (*instruments*) **~s publicitaires** advertising resources; ~ **de transport/contrôle** means of transport/control ►**se débrouiller avec les ~s du bord** to make do; **employer les grands ~s** to resort to drastic measures; **pas ~!** no way!

moyen(ne) [mwajɛ̃, jɛn] *adj* 1. (*intermédiaire, en proportion*) medium; (*classe*) middle; **à ~ terme** in the medium term; *v. a.* **moyenne** 2. (*ni bon, ni mauvais*) average 3. (*du type courant*) standard; **le Français ~** the average Frenchman

Moyen Âge, Moyen-Âge [mwajɛnɑʒ] *m* Middle Ages *pl*

moyenâgeux, -euse [mwajɛnɑʒø, -jøz] *adj a. péj* medieval

moyennant [mwajɛnɑ̃] *prep* ~ **une récompense/un petit service** in return for a reward/small favour *Brit,* in return for a reward/small favor *Am;* ~ **2000 euros** for 2000 euros ►~ **quoi** in return for which

moyenne [mwajɛn] *f* 1. MAT, ECOLE average; **la ~ d'âge** the average age; **en ~** on average; **avoir la ~ en qc** to get a pass mark in sth *Brit,* to get a passing grade in sth *Am* 2. (*type le plus courant*) standard

moyennement [mwajɛnmɑ̃] *adv* moderately

Moyen-Orient [mwajɛnɔʀjɑ̃] *m* **le ~** the Middle East

moyeu [mwajø] <x> *m* hub

MST [ɛmɛste] *f abr de* **maladie sexuellement transmissible** STD

mû, mue [my] *part passé de* **mouvoir**

mucosité [mykozite] *f* mucus *no pl*

mue [my] *f* 1. ZOOL (*de l'oiseau*) moulting *Brit,* molting *Am;* (*du serpent*) sloughing; (*d'un mammifère*) shedding 2. ANAT breaking *Brit,* changing *Am*

muer [mɥe] <1> *vi* 1. ZOOL (*oiseau*) to moult *Brit,* to molt *Am;* (*serpent*) to slough; (*mammifère*) to shed 2. (*changer de timbre*) **sa voix** [*o* il] **mue** his voice is breaking *Brit,* his voice is changing *Am*

muesli [mysli] *m* muesli

muet(te) [mɥɛ, mɥɛt] I. *adj* silent; ~ **d'admiration/de surprise** speechless with admiration/surprise; **le cinéma ~** silent films II. *m(f)* mute

muezzin [mɥɛdzin] *m* muezzin

muffin [mœfin] *m Québec* (*petit cake rond très léger*) muffin

mufle [myfl] *m* 1. (*du chien*) muzzle; (*de la vache, du mouton*) muffle 2. (*goujat*) lout

muflerie [myfləʀi] *f* loutishness

mugir [myʒiʀ] <8> *vi* (*bovin*) to moo; (*vent, sirène*) to howl; (*mer, flots*) to roar

mugissement [myʒismɑ̃] *m* 1. (*cri de bovin*) mooing 2. (*bruit du vent, d'une sirène*) howl 3. (*bruit de la mer*) roar

muguet [mygɛ] *m* lily of the valley

> On May 1 **du muguet** is sold on every street. This is given as a gift to bring luck and and as a sign of affection.

mulâtre, mulâtresse [mylɑtʀ, mylɑtʀɛs] I. *adj* mulatto II. *m, f* mulatto

mule¹ [myl] *f* ZOOL (she)-mule ►**être têtu comme une ~** to be as stubborn as a mule

mule² [myl] *f* (*pantoufle*) mule

mulet [mylɛ] *m* ZOOL (he)-mule ►**être chargé comme un ~** *inf* to be loaded like a packhorse

muletier, -ière [myltje, -jɛʀ] I. *adj* **sentier** [*o* **chemin**] ~ mule track II. *m, f* mule driver

mulot [mylo] *m* field mouse

multicolore [myltikɔlɔʀ] *adj* multicoloured *Brit,* multicolored *Am*

multiculturel(le) [myltikyltyʀɛl] *adj* multicultural

multifenêtrage [mytifənɛtʀaʒ] *m* INFOR 1. (*fractionnement d'une page web en plusieurs éléments*) frames 2. (*technique de manier plusieurs fenêtres sur un écran dont chacune correspond à un programme différent*) multi-windowing

multilingue [myltilɛ̃g] *adj* multilingual

multimédia [myltimedja] I. *adj inv* CINE, TV, INFOR multimedia II. *m* **le ~** multimedia

multinationale [myltinasjɔnal] *f* (*entreprise*) multinational

multiple [myltipl] I. *adj* 1. (*nombreux*) numerous 2. (*maints, varié: occasions, aspects, raisons, cas*) many; **à de ~s reprises** on many occasions 3. (*complexe*) *a.* MAT, TECH multiple; **être ~ de qc** to be a multiple of sth II. *m* **être le ~ de qc** to be the multiple of sth

multiplexe [myltiplɛks] I. *adj* multiplex II. *m* multiplex

multipliable [myltiplijabl] *adj* multipliable

multiplication [myltiplikasjɔ̃] *f* BOT, MAT

multiplication
multiplicité [myltiplisite] *f* multiplicity
multiplier [myltiplije] <1> I. *vt* 1. MAT, BOT to multiply; ~ **sept par trois** to multiply seven by three 2. (*augmenter le nombre de: efforts, attaques*) to increase II. *vpr* **se** ~ to multiply
multiprogrammation [myltipʀɔgʀamasjɔ̃] *f* INFOR concurrent programming
multiracial(e) [myltiʀasjal, jo] <-aux> *adj* multiracial
multitude [myltityd] *f* 1. (*grand nombre*) mass 2. (*foule*) multitude
muni(e) [myni] *adj* **être** ~ **de qc** to have sth; ~ **d'un dictionnaire** with a dictionary
municipal(e) [mynisipal, o] <-aux> *adj* 1. (*communal*) municipal; (*élections*) local; **conseil** ~ town council *Brit,* city council *Am* 2. (*de la ville*) town
municipalité [mynisipalite] *f* 1. (*administration*) town council *Brit,* city council *Am* 2. (*commune*) municipality
munir [myniʀ] <8> I. *vt* ~ **qn/qc de piles** to provide sb/sth with batteries II. *vpr* **se** ~ **de qc** to provide oneself with sth; *fig* to arm oneself with sth
munitions [mynisjɔ̃] *fpl* ammuntion
munster [mɛ̃stɛʀ] *m* munster (*small, round, strong-flavoured cheese*)
muqueuse [mykøz] *f* mucous membrane
mur [myʀ] *m* wall ►**franchir le** ~ **du son** to break the sound barrier; **raser les** ~**s** to hug the walls; (*se faire tout petit*) to curl up
mûr(e) [myʀ] *adj* (*fruit*) ripe; (*pays*) mature; (*pour qc*) ready
muraille [myʀɑj] *f* wall
mural(e) [myʀal, o] <-aux> *adj* wall
mûre [myʀ] *f* 1. (*fruit de la ronce*) blackberry 2. (*fruit du mûrier*) mulberry
mûrement [myʀmɑ̃] *adv* at length
murer [myʀe] <1> I. *vt* 1. TECH to block up 2. (*isoler: avalanche*) to block; **être muré dans le silence** to be immured in silence II. *vpr* **se** ~ **chez soi** to shut oneself away at home; **se** ~ **dans sa douleur** to immure oneself in one's pain
muret [myʀɛ] *m* low wall
mûrir [myʀiʀ] <8> I. *vi* to ripen; (*projet, idée*) to develop II. *vt* 1. (*rendre mûr: fruit*) to ripen 2. (*rendre sage*) to mature 3. (*méditer*) to nurture
murmure [myʀmyʀ] *m* 1. (*chuchotement*) murmur 2. *pl* (*protestation*) murmurings
murmurer [myʀmyʀe] <1> I. *vi* (*chuchoter, protester*) to murmur II. *vt* ~ **qc à qn** to murmur sth to sb; **on murmure qu'ils sont amants** the rumour is that they're lovers *Brit,* the rumor is that they're lovers *Am*
mus [my] *passé simple de* **mouvoir**
musaraigne [myzaʀɛɲ] *f* shrew
musarder [myzaʀde] <1> *vi* to dawdle
musc [mysk] *m* musk
muscade [myskad] *f* nutmeg
muscadet [myskadɛ] *m* Muscadet
muscat [myska] *m* 1. (*raisin*) muscat grape 2. (*vin*) muscatel wine
muscle [myskl] *m* muscle ►**avoir des** ~**s d'acier** to have muscles of steel; **avoir du** ~ (*économie, entreprise*) to be in good shape; *inf* (*personne*) to have plenty of muscle
musclé(e) [myskle] *adj* 1. (*athlétique*) muscular 2. *fig, inf* (*gouvernement, discours, politique*) tough 3. (*vif: style*) vigorous 4. *inf* (*compliqué*) **le problème était plutôt** ~ it was a tough problem
muscler [myskle] <1> *vt* ~ **qn** to develop sb's muscles; ~ **le dos/les jambes** to develop the back/leg muscles
musculaire [myskylɛʀ] *adj* muscular
musculation [myskylasjɔ̃] *f* body building
musculature [myskylatyʀ] *f* muscle structure
muse [myz] *f* muse
museau [myzo] <x> *m* (*du chien*) muzzle; (*du porc, poisson*) snout
musée [myze] *m* museum
museler [myzle] <3> *vt* 1. (*mettre une muselière*) to muzzle 2. (*bâillonner*) to silence
muselière [myzəljɛʀ] *f* muzzle
muser [myze] <1> *vi Belgique* (*faire un bruit sourd à bouche fermée* (*chahut, protestation*)) to give a disgruntled mmmm
musette [myzɛt] I. *f* 1. lunchpack 2. MUS musette II. *app* (*orchestre, valse*) led by the accordeon; **bal** ~ *popular dance with a band led by the accordeon*
muséum [myzeɔm] *m* natural history museum
musical(e) [myzikal, o] <-aux> *adj* musical; **comédie** ~**e** musical
music-hall [myzikol] <music-halls> *m* 1. (*spectacle*) variety show 2. (*établissement*) music hall
musicien(ne) [myzisjɛ̃, jɛn] I. *adj* musical II. *m(f)* musician
musique [myzik] *f* (*art, harmonie*) music; **mettre qc en** ~ to set sth to music ►**connaître la** ~ *inf* to know the story; **en avant la** ~**!** *inf* here we go!
mustang [mystɑ̃g] *m* mustang
musulman(e) [myzylmɑ̃, an] *adj* muslim
Musulman(e) [myzylmɑ̃, an] *m(f)* Muslim
mutant(e) [mytɑ̃, ɑ̃t] *adj, m(f)* mutant
mutation [mytasjɔ̃] *f* 1. BIO mutation 2. ADMIN transfer 3. (*changement*) change; **société en** ~ changing society
muter [myte] <1> *vt* ADMIN to transfer
mutilation [mytilasjɔ̃] *f* mutilation
mutilé(e) [mytile] *m(f)* disabled person; ~ **de guerre** disabled ex-serviceman *Brit,* disabled veteran *Am*
mutiler [mytile] <1> I. *vt a. fig* to mutilate II. *vpr* **se** ~ to mutilate oneself
mutin(e) [mytɛ̃, in] I. *adj* mischievous II. *m(f)* rebel
mutiner [mytine] <1> *vpr* **se** ~ to mutiny
mutinerie [mytinʀi] *f* mutiny

mutisme [mytism] *m* silence
mutuel(le) [mytɥɛl] *adj* (*réciproque*) mutual
mutuelle [mytɥɛl] *f* supplemental insurance, ≈ Friendly Society *Brit* (*providing top-up health insurance*)
mutuellement [mytɥɛlmɑ̃] *adv* mutually
mycologie [mikɔlɔʒi] *f* mycology
mygale [migal] *f* tarantula
myope [mjɔp] I. *adj* short-sighted II. *mf* short-sighted person
myopie [mjɔpi] *f a. fig* short-sightedness
myosotis [mjɔzɔtis] *m* forget-me-not
myriade [miʀjad] *f* myriad; **~s d'étoiles** myriad of stars
myrtille [miʀtij] *f* blueberry
mystère [mistɛʀ] *m* 1. (*secret*) secret; **s'entourer de ~** to shroud oneself in secrecy 2. (*énigme*) mystery; **être un ~ pour qn** to be a mystery to sb ▶ **~ et boule de gomme!** *iron* I haven't a clue!
mystérieusement [misteʀjøzmɑ̃] *adv* 1. (*en secret*) secretively 2. (*inexplicablement, d'une façon mystérieuse*) mysteriously
mystérieux [misteʀjø] *m* **le ~** mysterious
mystérieux, -euse [misteʀjø, -jøz] I. *adj* mysterious II. *m, f* **faire le ~** to be secretive
mysticisme [mistisism] *m* mysticism
mystificateur, -trice [mistifikatœʀ, -tʀis] I. *adj* hoax; **intention mystificatrice** intent to deceive II. *m, f* hoaxer
mystification [mistifikasjɔ̃] *f* hoax; (*imposture*) myth
mystifier [mistifje] <1> *vt* to fool
mystique [mistik] *adj* 1. (*religieux*) mystical 2. (*exalté, fervent*) mystic
mythe [mit] *m* myth
mythique [mitik] *adj* mythical; (*imaginaire*) imaginary; **récit ~** myth; **la générosité ~ de qn** sb's fabled generosity
mythologie [mitɔlɔʒi] *f* mythology
mythologique [mitɔlɔʒik] *adj* mythological
mythomane [mitɔman] I. *adj* mythomaniac II. *mf* mythomaniac

N

N, n [ɛn] I. *m inv* N, n; **~ comme Nicolas** n as in Nelly *Brit,* n as in Nan *Am;* (*on telephone*) n for Nelly *Brit,* n for Nan *Am* II. *f: road equivalent to a British 'A' road or to a state highway in the U.S.*
n' *v.* **ne**
na [na] *interj enfantin* so there
nabot(e) [nabo, ɔt] *m(f)* dwarf
nacelle [nasɛl] *f* 1. gondola; (*coque carénée*) nacelle; (*d'un appareil de levage*) cradle 2. (*partie mobile: d'un landau, d'une poussette*) carriage
nacre [nakʀ] *f* mother of pearl
nacré(e) [nakʀe] *adj* pearly
nage [naʒ] *f* swimming; (*façon de nager*) stroke; **~ libre/sur le dos** freestyle/backstroke ▶ **à la ~** swimming; **traverser qc à la ~** to swim across sth; **être en ~** to be in a sweat
nageoire [naʒwaʀ] *f* fin
nager [naʒe] <2a> I. *vi* 1. (*se mouvoir dans l'eau, baigner*) to swim 2. *fig* **~ dans le bonheur** to be overjoyed 3. (*flotter*) **~ sur qc** to float in sth 4. *inf* (*être au large*) **elle nage dans le pull** the sweater is miles too big for her 5. *inf* (*ne pas comprendre*) to be lost II. *vt* to swim; (*crawl*) to do
nageur, -euse [naʒœʀ, -ʒøz] I. *m, f* swimmer II. *app* **maître ~** lifeguard
naguère [nagɛʀ] *adv soutenu* formerly
naïf, naïve [naif, naiv] *adj* 1. *péj* (*crédule*) gullible 2. (*naturel*) naïve
nain(e) [nɛ̃, nɛn] I. *adj* (*personne*) dwarf II. *m(f)* dwarf
naissance [nɛsɑ̃s] *f* 1. (*venue au monde, apparition*) birth; **à la ~** at birth 2. (*origine*) source ▶ **donner ~ à un enfant** to give birth to a child; **aveugle/muet/sourd de ~** blind/mute/deaf from birth; **Français de ~** French by birth
naître [nɛtʀ] *vi irr être* 1. (*venir au monde*) to be born; **être né musicien** to be a born musician 2. (*apparaître: crainte, désir, soupçon, difficulté*) to arise; (*idée*) to be born 3. (*être destiné à*) **être né pour qn/qc** to be made for sb/sth
naïvement [naivmɑ̃] *adv* naïvely
naïveté [naivte] *f* innocence; **avoir la ~ de** +*infin* to be naïve enough to +*infin;* **être d'une grande ~** to be very naïve
Namibie [namibi] *f* **la ~** Namibia
namibien(ne) [namibjɛ̃, ɛn] *adj* Namibian
Namibien(ne) [namibjɛ̃, ɛn] *m(f)* Namibian
namurois(e) [namyʀw, waz] *adj* of Namur; *v. a.* **ajaccien**
Namurois(e) [namyʀwa, waz] *m(f)* person from Namur; *v. a.* **Ajaccien**
nana [nana] *f inf* chick
nantais(e) [nɑ̃tɛ, ɛz] *adj* of Nantes; *v. a.* **ajaccien**
Nantais(e) [nɑ̃tɛ, ɛz] *m(f)* person from Nantes; *v. a.* **Ajaccien**
nanti(e) [nɑ̃ti] I. *adj* rich II. *m(f)* rich person
naphtaline [naftalin] *f* **boules de ~** mothballs
napoléon [napɔleɔ̃] *m* FIN napoleon
Napoléon [napɔleɔ̃] *m* Napoleon
napoléonien(ne) [napɔleɔnjɛ̃, jɛn] *adj* Napoleonic
nappe [nap] *f* 1. (*linge*) tablecloth 2. (*vaste étendue: d'eau*) sheet; (*de brouillard*) blanket; **~ de pétrole** oil slick
napper [nape] <1> *vt* GASTR **~ qc de chocolat** to cover sth in chocolate
napperon [napʀɔ̃] *m* mat
naquis [naki] *passé simple de* **naître**
narcisse [naʀsis] *m* BOT narcissus

narcissique [naʀsisik] *adj* narcissistic
narcissisme [naʀsisism] *m* narcissism
narcodollars [naʀkodɔlaʀ] *mpl* narcodollars
narcose [naʀkoz] *f* narcosis
narcotique [naʀkɔtik] **I.** *adj* narcotic **II.** *m* narcotic
narcotrafic [naʀkotʀafik] *m* drug traffic
narguer [naʀge] <1> *vt* to flout; (*agacer*) to laugh at
narine [naʀin] *f* nostril
narquois(e) [naʀkwa, waz] *adj* sardonic
narrateur, -trice [naʀatœʀ, -tʀis] *m, f* narrator
narratif, -ive [naʀatif, -iv] *adj* narrative
narration [naʀasjɔ̃] *f* (*actvité*) narration; (*histoire*) narrative
NASA [naza] *f abr de* **National Aeronautics and Space Administration** NASA
nasal(e) [nazal, o] <-aux> *adj* LING nasal
nasale [nazal] *f* LING nasal
nase [nɑz] *adj inf* **1.** (*cassé: chose*) bust **2.** (*épuisé*) beat, knackered *Brit*
naseau [nazo] <x> *m* nostril
nasillard(e) [nazijaʀ, jaʀd] *adj* nasal
natal(e) [natal] <s> *adj* (*langue, terre*) native; **maison/ville ~e** house/town where one was born
natalité [natalite] *f* birth rate
natation [natasjɔ̃] *f* swimming
natel [natɛl] *m Suisse* (*téléphone portable*) mobile (phone) *Brit*, cellphone *Am*
natif, -ive [natif, -iv] **I.** *adj* **être ~ de Toulouse** to be a native of Toulouse **II.** *m, f* native; **les ~s du Cancer** Cancerians
nation [nasjɔ̃] *f* **1.** (*peuple*) nation **2.** (*pays*) country; **la Nation** the Nation; **les Nations unies** the United Nations
national(e) [nasjɔnal, o] <-aux> *adj* **1.** (*de l'État*) national; **fête ~e** national holiday **2.** (*opp: local, régional: entreprise*) state-owned; **route ~e** *road equivalent to a British 'A' road or to a state highway in the U.S.*

> The 14th July is France's **fête nationale** to celebrate the storming of the Bastille in 1789. On this day, the towns are decorated with flags and a military parade takes place on the Champs-Elysées. At 10 p.m., fireworks go off all over France. Belgium's national holiday is 21st July, the birthday of Leopold I.

Nationale [nasjɔnal] *f: road equivalent to a British 'A' road or to a state highway in the U.S.*
nationalisation [nasjɔnalizasjɔ̃] *f* nationalization
nationaliser [nasjɔnalize] <1> *vt* to nationalize
nationalisme [nasjɔnalism] *m* nationalism
nationaliste [nasjɔnalist] **I.** *adj* nationalist **II.** *mf* nationalist
nationalité [nasjɔnalite] *f* nationality
national-socialisme [nasjɔnalsɔsjalism] *m sans pl* National Socialism
national-socialiste [nasjɔnalsɔsjalist] <nationaux-socialistes> **I.** *adj* National Socialist **II.** *m, f* National Socialist
Nativité [nativite] *f* **la ~** the Nativity
natte [nat] *f* **1.** (*cheveux*) plait *Brit*, braid *Am*; **se faire une ~** to plait one's hair *Brit*, to braid one's hair *Am* **2.** (*tapis*) (straw) mat
natter [nate] <1> *vt* (*cheveux, paille*) to plait, to braid *Am*
naturalisation [natyʀalizasjɔ̃] *f* POL naturalization; **demande de ~** application for naturalization
naturalisé(e) [natyʀalize] **I.** *adj* naturalized **II.** *m(f)* naturalized citizen
naturaliser [natyʀalize] <1> *vt* **~ qn français** to grant sb French citizenship; **se faire ~** to become naturalized
naturaliste [natyʀalist] **I.** *adj* **1.** ART, LIT, PHILOS naturalistic **2.** (*scientifique*) **savant ~** naturalist **II.** *mf* naturalist
nature [natyʀ] **I.** *f* **1.** (*environnement, caractère*) nature **2.** ART **~ morte** still life ►**être dans la ~ des <u>choses</u>** to be in the nature of things; **ne pas être <u>gâté</u> par la ~** *inf* to be no oil painting; **<u>petite</u> ~** *inf* delicate flower; **<u>de</u>** [*o* **<u>par</u>**] **~** naturally; **<u>plus</u> vrai que ~** larger than life **II.** *adj inv* **1.** (*sans assaisonnement: café, thé*) black; (*yaourt*) plain **2.** *inf* (*simple*) simple
naturel [natyʀɛl] *m* **1.** (*caractère*) nature; **son bon ~** his/her good nature **2.** (*spontanéité*) naturalness ►**être <u>d'un</u> ~ jaloux/timide** to be naturally jealous/shy
naturel(le) [natyʀɛl] *adj* **1.** (*opp: artificiel, inné*) natural; (*père*) biological; (*produit*) organic **2.** (*simple: manières, personne, style*) simple
naturellement [natyʀɛlmɑ̃] *adv* **1.** (*bien entendu*) of course; **~!** naturally! **2.** (*opp: artificiellement, de façon innée, aisément*) naturally **3.** (*spontanément*) easily **4.** (*automatiquement*) automatically
naturisme [natyʀism] *m* naturism
naturiste [natyʀist] **I.** *adj* naturist **II.** *mf* naturist
naufrage [nofʀaʒ] *m* NAUT wreck ►**<u>faire</u> ~** (*bateau, projet*) to be wrecked
naufragé(e) [nofʀaʒe] *m(f)* shipwrecked person
Nauru [nɔʀu] *f* Nauru
nauséabond(e) [nozeabɔ̃, ɔ̃d] *adj* **1.** putrid **2.** (*ordurier: œuvre, spectacle*) nauseating
nausée [noze] *f* **1.** (*haut-le-cœur*) bout of nausea; **j'ai la ~** [*o* **des ~s**] I feel nauseous **2.** (*dégoût*) disgust ►**cette personne/cette odeur me <u>donne</u> la ~** this person/smell makes me feel sick
nautique [notik] *adj* **ski ~** waterskiing; **sport ~** watersports *pl*
naval(e) [naval] <s> *adj* naval; **chantier ~** shipyard

N

Navale [naval] *f* (*École* ~) Naval Academy
navet [navɛ] *m* **1.** BOT turnip **2.** *péj, inf* (*œuvre sans valeur*) piece of rubbish; (*mauvais film*) flop; **être un** ~ to be a flop
navette [navɛt] *f* shuttle; **faire la** ~ **entre son lieu de travail et son domicile** to commute between one's place of work and home
navetteur, **-euse** [navøtœʀ, -øz] *m, f Belgique (personne qui fait régulièrement la navette par un moyen de transport collectif, entre son domicile et son lieu de travail)* commuter
navigable [navigabl] *adj* navigable
navigant(e) [navigɑ̃, ɑ̃t] **I.** *adj* AVIAT **personnel** ~ flying personnel; NAUT sea-going personnel **II.** *m(f)* **les** ~**s** AVIAT flying personnel; NAUT sea-going personnel
navigateur [navigatœʀ] *m* INFOR browser; ~ **Web** Web browser
navigateur, **-trice** [navigatœʀ, -tʀis] *m, f* **1.** NAUT sailor **2.** AUTO, AVIAT navigator
navigation [navigasjɔ̃] *f* **1.** NAUT shipping; ~ **à** (**la**) **voile** sailing **2.** AUTO, AVIAT navigation; ~ **spatiale** space navigation
naviguer [navige] <1> *vi* **1.** AVIAT to fly **2.** NAUT to sail **3.** INFOR ~ **sur le Web** to surf the Web
navire [naviʀ] *m* ship; ~ **de commerce** merchantman; ~ **pétrolier** oil tanker
navrant(e) [navʀɑ̃, ɑ̃t] *adj* **c'est** ~**!** it is a shame!
navré(e) [navʀe] *adj* **être** ~ **de qc** to be (terribly) sorry about sth
naze [nɑz] *adj v.* **nase**
nazi(e) [nazi] *abr de* **national-socialiste I.** *adj* Nazi **II.** *m(f)* Nazi
nazisme [nazism] *m abr de* **national-socialisme** nazism
NB [ɛnbe] *abr de* **nota bene** N.B.
NBC *adj inv abr de* **nucléaire-biologique-chimique** MIL NBC
NDLR [ɛndeɛlɛʀ] *abr de* **note de la rédaction** editor's note
NDT [ɛndete] *abr de* **note du traducteur** translator's note
ne [nə] <*devant voyelle ou h muet* n'> *adv* **1.** (*avec autre mot négatif*) **il** ~ **mange pas le midi** he doesn't eat at lunchtime; **elle n'a guère d'argent** she has hardly any money; **je** ~ **fume plus** I don't smoke any more; **je** ~ **me promène jamais** I never go for walks; **je** ~ **vois personne** I can't see anyone; **personne** ~ **vient** nobody comes; **je** ~ **vois rien** I can't see anything; **rien** ~ **va plus** no more bets; **il n'a ni frère ni sœur** he has no brothers or sisters; **tu n'as aucune chance** you have no chance **2.** *sans autre mot négatif, soutenu* **je n'ose le dire** I dare not say it **3.** (*seulement*) **je** ~ **vois que cette solution** this is the only solution I can see; **il n'y a pas que vous qui le dites** you're not the only one to say so
né(e) [ne] **I.** *part passé de* **naître II.** *adj souvent écrit avec un trait d'union* (*de naissance*) née; **Madame X,** ~**e Y** Mrs X, née Y
néanmoins [neɑ̃mwɛ̃] *adv* nonetheless
néant [neɑ̃] **I.** *m* nothingness ▶**tirer qn du** ~ to draw sb out of oblivion **II.** *pron* (*rien*) **signes particuliers:** ~ distinguishing marks: none
nébuleuse [nebyløz] *f* **1.** ASTR nebula **2.** (*amas diffus*) **être à l'état de** ~ to be still at the idea stage
nébuleux, **-euse** [nebylø, -øz] *adj* **1.** METEO overcast **2.** (*confus, flou*) nebulous; (*projet, idées, discours*) woolly
nécessaire [nesesɛʀ] **I.** *adj a.* PHILOS, MAT (*indispensable*) **être** ~ **à qc** to be necessary for sth; **le dévouement si** ~ the devotion that is so necessary **II.** *m* **1.** (*opp: superflu*) **le** ~ what is required **2.** (*étui*) ~ **à ongles** nail kit
nécessairement [nesesɛʀmɑ̃] *adv* necessarily
nécessité [nesesite] *f* necessity ▶**de première** ~ absolutely essential; **être dans la** ~ **de** *+infin* to need to *+infin*
nécessiter [nesesite] <1> *vt* to require
nécessiteux, **-euse** [nesesitø, -øz] **I.** *adj* needy **II.** *m, f* needy person; **les** ~ the needy
nec plus ultra [nɛkplysyltʀa] *m inv* last word
nécrologie [nekʀɔlɔʒi] *f* obituary
nécrologique [nekʀɔlɔʒik] *adj* **avis** ~ obituary; **rubrique** ~ obituary section
nectar [nɛktaʀ] *m* nectar
nectarine [nɛktaʀin] *f* nectarine
néerlandais [neɛʀlɑ̃dɛ] *m* Dutch; *v. a.* **français**
néerlandais(e) [neɛʀlɑ̃dɛ, ɛz] *adj* Dutch
Néerlandais(e) [neɛʀlɑ̃dɛ, ɛz] *m(f)* Dutchman, Dutchwoman *m, f*
néerlandophone [neɛʀlɑ̃dɔfɔn] **I.** *adj* **1.** (*aux Pays-Bas*) Dutch-speaking; **être** ~ to be a Dutch-Speaker **2.** (*en Belgique*) Flemish-speaking; **être** ~ to be a Flemish-Speaker **II.** *mf* **1.** (*aux Pays-Bas*) Dutch-speaker **2.** (*en Belgique*) Flemish-speaker
nef [nɛf] *f* ARCHIT nave
néfaste [nefast] *adj* harmful; (*régime, décision*) ill-fated; **être** ~ **à qn/qc** to be a disaster for sb/sth
négatif [negatif] *m* PHOT negative
négatif, **-ive** [negatif, -iv] *adj* negative
négation [negasjɔ̃] *f* LING negation
négationnisme [negasjɔnism] *m* negationism
négationniste [negasjɔnist] *mf* negationist
négative [negativ] *f* **répondre par la** ~ to reply in the negative; (*refuser*) to refuse
négativement [negativmɑ̃] *adv* negatively; **répondre** ~ to reply in the negative
négligé(e) [negliʒe] *adj* (*intérieur*) neglected; (*style, travail*) careless; (*tenue*) sloppy
négligeable [negliʒabl] *adj* negligible; (*élément, facteur*) inconsiderable; (*détail, moyens*) insignificant

négligemment [neglizamɑ̃] *adv* **1.** (*nonchalamment*) casually **2.** (*sans soin*) carelessly
négligence [neglizɑ̃s] *f* **1.** *sans pl* (*manque d'attention*) negligence; JUR criminal negligence; **par** ~ negligently **2.** (*omission*) oversight; (*faute légère*) error
négligent(e) [neglizɑ̃, zɑ̃t] *adj* (*élève*) careless; (*employé*) negligent
négliger [neglize] <2a> **I.** *vt* **1.** (*se désintéresser de, délaisser*) to neglect; (*occasion*) to miss; (*conseil, détail, fait*) to disregard **2.** (*omettre de faire*) ~ **de** +*infin* to fail to +*infin* **II.** *vpr* **se** ~ to neglect oneself
négoce [negɔs] *m soutenu* trade; **faire du** ~ **avec qn** to trade with sb
négociant(e) [negɔsjɑ̃, jɑ̃t] *m(f)* trader; ~ **en gros** wholesaler
négociation [negɔsjasjɔ̃] *f gén pl* negotiation
négocier [negɔsje] <1> **I.** *vi* POL ~ **avec qn** to negotiate with sb **II.** *vt* **1.** COM, JUR, POL ~ **la capitulation avec qn** (*discuter*) to discuss surrender with sb; (*obtenir après discussion*) to negotiate surrender with sb **2.** COM, FIN, AUTO to negotiate
nègre [nɛgʀ] *m péj* Negro ►**travailler comme un** ~ to work like a slave
négresse [negʀɛs] *f péj* Negress
négrier, -ière [negʀije, -jɛʀ] **I.** *adj* **capitaine/vaisseau** ~ slave captain/ship **II.** *m, f* **1.** HIST slaver **2.** (*exploiteur*) slave driver
négro [negʀo] *m péj, inf* nigger
neige [nɛʒ] *f* **1.** METEO snow **2.** GASTR **battre les blancs** (**d'œufs**) **en** ~ to beat the egg whites until they form stiff peaks ►**être blanc comme** ~ to be a white as snow
neiger [neʒe] <2a> *vi impers* **il neige** it's snowing
neigeux, -euse [nɛʒø, -ʒøz] *adj* snowy
nem [nɛm] *m* small spring roll
néné [nene] *m inf* boob
nénuphar [nenyfaʀ] *m* water lily
néologisme [neɔlɔʒism] *m* neologism
néon [neɔ̃] *m* **1.** CHIM neon **2.** (*tube fluorescent*) neon light
néonazi(e) [neonazi] **I.** *adj* neo-Nazi **II.** *m(f)* neo-Nazi
néophyte [neɔfit] *mf* novice; (*nouveau converti*) neophyte
néoprène® [neɔpʀɛn] *m* neoprene
néo-zélandais(e) [neozelɑ̃dɛ, dɛz] *adj* New Zealand
Néo-zélandais(e) [neozelɑ̃dɛ, dɛz] *m(f)* New Zealander
néphrétique [nefʀetik] *adj* **coliques** ~**s** renal colic
Neptune [nɛptyn] *f* ASTR Neptune
nerf [nɛʀ] *m* **1.** ANAT, MED nerve **2.** *pl* PSYCH nerves; **avoir les** ~**s fragiles** to be highly strung; **avoir des** ~**s d'acier** [*o* **les** ~**s à toute épreuve**] to have nerves of steel; **avoir les** ~**s à vif** to be on edge; **être sur les** ~**s** *inf* to be keyed up; **être malade des** ~**s** to suffer from nerves ►**passer ses** ~**s sur qn/qc** *inf* to take it out on sb; **taper sur les** ~**s à qn** *inf* to get on sb's nerves; **vivre sur les** ~**s** *inf* to live on one's nerves; **un peu de** ~**!**, **du** ~**!** *inf* buck up!
nerveusement [nɛʀvøzmɑ̃] *adv* **1.** nervously **2.** (*avec vigueur*) energetically; **démarrer** ~ to start vigorously **3.** (*sur le plan nerveux*) **être épuisé** ~ to be suffering from nervous exhaustion
nerveux, -euse [nɛʀvø, -øz] **I.** *adj* **1.** ANAT, MED (*spasme, troubles*) nervous **2.** (*irritable*) irritable; (*animal, personne*) touchy **3.** (*émotif*) emotional **4.** (*vigoureux: animal, personne*) energetic; (*style*) vigorous; (*moteur, voiture*) responsive **II.** *m, f* highly-strung person; **c'est un grand** ~ he's very highly strung
nervosité [nɛʀvozite] *f* nervousness
nervure [nɛʀvyʀ] *f* **1.** BOT, ZOOL vein **2.** ARCHIT, TECH, TYP rib
n'est-ce-pas [nɛspɑ] *adv* **1.** (*invitation à acquiescer*) **c'est vrai,** ~**?** it's true, isn't it?; **vous viendrez,** ~**?** you'll come, won't you? **2.** (*renforcement*) of course
net(te) [nɛt] **I.** *adj* **1.** *postposé* (*propre*) clean; (*copie, intérieur*) neat **2.** *postposé* (*précis*) precise; (*position, réponse*) exact **3.** *a. antéposé* (*évident*) clear; (*amélioration, différence, tendance*) distinct **4.** *postposé* (*distinct: dessin, écriture, souvenir*) clear; (*contours, image*) sharp; (*cassure, coupure*) clean **5.** *inf* (*opp: cinglé*) sharp **6.** *postposé* COM, FIN **salaire** ~ net salary; **être** ~ **d'impôt** to be net of taxes **II.** *adv* **1.** (*brusquement: se casser*) cleanly; (*s'arrêter*) dead; **être tué** ~ to be killed instantly **2.** (*franchement: dire, refuser*) straight out **3.** COM net
Net [nɛt] *m* **le** ~ the Net
netiquette [netikɛt] *f* INFOR netiquette
nettement [nɛtmɑ̃] *adv* **1.** (*sans ambiguïté*) clearly **2.** (*distinctement*) distinctly; (*se détacher*) sharply; (*se souvenir*) clearly **3.** (*largement*) markedly
netteté [nɛtte] *f* **1.** (*précision*) neatness **2.** (*caractère distinct, franc*) clearness; (*des contours, d'une image*) cleanness
nettoyage [netwajaʒ] *m* **1.** (*lavage*) cleaning; ~ **à sec** dry-cleaning **2.** MIL, POL cleaning up
nettoyer [netwaje] <6> **I.** *vt* **1.** (*laver*) to clean; ~ **la table à l'eau/avec la brosse** to clean the table with water/a brush; ~ **à fond la maison** to clean the house from top to bottom **2.** *inf* (*ruiner*) ~ **qn** to clean sb out **3.** *inf* (*épuiser*) ~ **qn** to wear sb out **II.** *vpr* **se** ~ (*personne, animal*) to wash oneself
neuchâtelois(e) [nøʃatwa, waz] *adj* of Neuchâtel; *v. a.* **ajaccien**
Neuchâtelois(e) [nøʃatwa, waz] *m(f)* person from Neuchâtel; *v. a.* **Ajaccien**
neuf[1] [nœf] *adj* nine; *v. a.* **cinq**
neuf[2] [nœf] *m* new ►**il y a du** ~ something new has happened
neuf, neuve [nœf, nœv] *adj* new; **flambant**

N

~ brand new ▸**quelque chose/rien de ~** something/nothing new

neurasthénie [nøʀasteni] *f* neurasthenia; (*pessimisme*) depression; **faire de la ~** to be depressed

neurasthénique [nøʀastenik] *adj* depressed

neurochirurgie [nøʀoʃiʀyʀʒi] *f* neurosurgery

neurochirurgien(ne) [nøʀoʃiʀyʀʒjɛ̃, jɛn] *m(f)* neurosurgeon

neurologie [nøʀɔlɔʒi] *f* neurology

neurologique [nøʀɔlɔʒik] *adj* neurological

neurologue [nøʀɔlɔg] *mf* neurologist

neurone [nøʀon] *m* **1.** BIO, INFOR neuron **2.** *pl* (*cerveau*) brain

neutraliser [nøtʀalize] <1> **I.** *vt* **1.** (*empêcher d'agir: concurrent, système*) to neutralize **2.** (*mettre hors d'état de nuire: ennemi, gang*) to overpower **II.** *vpr* **se ~** (*influences, produits*) to cancel each other out

neutraliste [nøtʀalist] **I.** *adj* neutralist **II.** *mf* neutralist

neutralité [nøtʀalite] *f* **1.** (*impartialité*) neutrality; (*d'un livre, rapport, enseignement*) impartiality **2.** POL, CHIM, ELEC neutrality

neutre [nøtʀ] **I.** *adj* **1.** (*impartial*) neutral **2.** (*qui ne choque pas*) *a.* POL, CHIM, ELEC neutral **3.** (*asexué*) *a.* LING, ZOOL neuter; **être du genre ~** to be neuter **II.** *m* **1.** *pl* POL neutral nations **2.** LING neuter noun **3.** ELEC neutral

neutron [nøtʀɔ̃] *m* neutron

neuvième [nœvjɛm] *adj antéposé* ninth; *v. a.* **cinquième**

névé [neve] *m* névé

neveu [n(ə)vø] <x> *m* nephew

névicien(ne) [nevisjɛ̃, ɛn] *adj* Nevisian

Névicien(ne) [nevisjɛ̃, ɛn] *m(f)* Nevisian

névralgie [nevʀalʒi] *f* **1.** (*douleur du nerf*) neuralgia; **~ sciatique** sciatica **2.** (*mal de tête*) headache

névralgique [nevʀalʒik] *adj* **1.** MED neuralgic; **centre ~** nerve centre *Brit,* nerve center *Am* **2.** (*sensible: point*) sensitive spot

névrite [nevʀit] *f* neuritis

névrose [nevʀoz] *f* neurosis

névrosé(e) [nevʀoze] **I.** *adj* neurotic **II.** *m(f)* neurotic

névrotique [nevʀɔtik] *adj* neurotic

new-look [njuluk] **I.** *adj inv* (*politique, style*) new-look **II.** *m inv* new look

newton [njutɔn] *m* newton

newtonien(ne) [njutɔnjɛ̃, jɛn] *adj* Newtonian

New York [nujɔʀk] New York

new-yorkais(e) [nujɔʀkɛ, kɛz] *adj* New York

New-Yorkais(e) [nujɔʀkɛ, kɛz] *m(f)* New Yorker

nez [ne] *m* nose; **saigner du ~** to have a nosebleed ▸**se voir comme le ~ au milieu de la figure** *inf* to stick out a mile; **avoir le ~ fin** to have a flair for business; **avoir du ~ pour qc** *inf* to have an instinct for sth; **avoir le ~ dans les livres/mots croisés** *inf* to have one's nose stuck in a book/the crosswords; **se bouffer** [*o* **se manger**] **le ~** *inf* to be at each other's throats; **se casser le ~** *inf* to come a cropper; **fourrer son ~ dans qc** *inf* to poke one's nose into sth; **pendre au ~ à qn** to loom over sb; **piquer du ~** *inf* (*s'endormir*) to doze off; (*descendre à pic*) to go into a nosedive; **(re)tomber sur le ~ de qn** *inf* to backfire on sb; **~ à ~** face to face; **raccrocher au ~ de qn** to hang up on sb; **rire au ~ de qn** to laugh in sb's face; **devant** [*o* **sous**] **le ~ de qn** *inf* under sb's nose

NF [ɛnɛf] *f abr de* **norme française** *official French mark of approval for manufactured goods*

ni [ni] *conj* **1.** *après une autre nég* **il ne sait pas dessiner ~ peindre** he can neither draw nor paint, he can't draw or paint; **il n'a rien vu ~ personne** he saw nothing and nobody, he didn't see anything or anybody; **rien de fin ~ de distingué** nothing elegant or distinguished **2.** *entre deux négations* **je ne l'aime ~ ne l'estime** I neither like nor respect him **3.** (*alternative négative*) **~ l'un ~ l'autre** neither one nor the other; **~ plus ~ moins que** neither more nor less than

Niagara [njagaʀa] *m* **les chutes du ~** Niagara Falls

niais(e) [njɛ, njɛz] **I.** *adj* foolish; (*style*) inane **II.** *m(f)* fool

niaisement [njɛzmɑ̃] *adv* inanely

niaiserie [njɛzʀi] *f* **1.** (*simplicité*) inanity **2.** (*chose sotte*) silly nonsense *no pl*

niaiseux, -euse [njɛzø, -øz] *adj Québec* (*niais, sot*) soft

niche [niʃ] *f* **1.** (*abri*) kennel **2.** (*alcôve*) niche

nichée [niʃe] *f* **1.** ZOOL brood **2.** (*jeunes animaux*) litter **3.** *inf* (*enfants*) brood

nicher [niʃe] <1> **I.** *vi* **1.** (*nidifier*) to nest **2.** *inf* (*habiter*) to settle **II.** *vpr* **se ~ dans un arbre** to nest in a tree

nichon [niʃɔ̃] *m inf* boob

nickel [nikɛl] **I.** *m* nickel **II.** *adj inv, inf* (*impeccable*) spotless

nickelé(e) [nikle] *adj* nickel-plated

Nicosie [nikozi] Nicosia

nicotine [nikɔtin] *f* nicotine

nid [ni] *m* ZOOL nest; **~ d'aigle** eyrie *Brit,* aerie *Am*

nièce [njɛs] *f* niece

nième [ɛnjɛm] *adj v.* **énième**

nier [nje] <1> **I.** *vt* (*contester, refuser l'idée de*) to deny; **~ qu'on mente** to deny that one is lying **II.** *vi* to deny the claim(s)

Niger [niʒɛʀ] *m* **le ~** Niger

Nigeria [niʒeʀja] *m* **le ~** Nigeria

nigérian(e) [niʒeʀjɑ̃, jan] *adj* Nigerian

Nigérian(e) [niʒeʀjɑ̃, jan] *m(f)* Nigerian

nigérien(ne) [niʒeʀjɛ̃, jɛn] *adj* Nigerien

Nigérien(ne) [niʒeʀjɛ̃, jɛn] *m(f)* Nigerien

night-club [najtklœb] <night-clubs> *m* nightclub

nihiliste [niilist] I. *adj* nihilistic II. *mf* nihilist
Nil [nil] *m* **le** ~ the Nile
n'importe [nɛ̃pɔʀt] *v.* **importer**
niôle [ɲol] *f v.* **gnôle**
nippes [nip] *fpl inf* gear
nippon, -o(n)ne [nipɔ̃, -ɔn] *adj* Japanese
Nippon, -o(n)ne [nipɔ̃, -ɔn] *m, f* Japanese
niquer [nike] <1> *vt vulg* to fuck
nirvana [niʀvana] *m* nirvana
nitouche [nituʃ] *f* sainte ~ goody-goody; **avec son air de sainte** ~ with her goody-goody ways
nitrate [nitʀat] *m* nitrate
nitroglycérine [nitʀogliseʀin] *f* nitroglycerine
niveau [nivo] <x> *m* **1.** (*hauteur*) *a.* TECH level; ~ **à bulle** spirit level **2.** (*degré*) level; ~ **culturel** [*o* **de culture**] level of culture; ~ **de vie** standard of living ▸**au plus haut** ~ at the highest level; **au** ~ **de qn/qc** (*hauteur*) at the level of sb/sth; (*près de*) by sb/sth; (*valeur*) on the level of sb/sth; **au** ~ **local/national/émotionnel** on a local/national/emotional level; **au** ~ **de l'U.E.** at the E.U. level; **au niveau (de la) sécurité** as for security
niveler [nivle] <3> *vt* to even out; (*sol, terrain*) to level
nivellement [nivɛlmɑ̃] *m* **1.** *a.* TECH levelling *Brit*, leveling *Am*; **instrument de** ~ level **2.** (*égalisation*) evening out
nivologue [nivɔlɔg] *mf* nivologist
noble [nɔbl] I. *adj* noble II. *mf* nobleman, noblewoman *m, f*; **les** ~**s** the nobles
noblement [nɔbləmɑ̃] *adv* **1.** nobly **2.** (*dignement*) with dignity
noblesse [nɔblɛs] *f* nobility
noce [nɔs] *f a. pl* wedding ▸**convoler en justes** ~**s** *iron* to be wed; **faire la** ~ *inf* to live it up
noceur, -euse [nɔsœʀ, -øz] *m, f* reveller *Brit*, reveler *Am*
nocif, -ive [nɔsif, -iv] *adj* harmful
nocivité [nɔsivite] *f* harmfulness
noctambule [nɔktɑ̃byl] I. *adj* **fêtard/noceur** ~ party-goer/reveller out late *Brit*, partygoer/reveler out late *Am* II. *mf* night owl
nocturne [nɔktyʀn] I. *adj* nocturnal II. *f* (*manifestation* ~) evening demonstration; **en** ~ late-night
Noël [nɔɛl] *m* **1.** REL Christmas; **arbre de** ~ Christmas tree; **nuit de** ~ Christmas Eve; **joyeux** ~ Merry Christmas **2.** (*période de* ~) Christmas time ▸~ **au balcon, Pâques au tison** *prov* a mild Christmas means a cold Easter

> For French children, **Noël** is 25th December. Presents are opened after breakfast. The adults exchange presents last, as an aperitif is drunk before lunch. The evening before, the 24th, the whole family goes to midnight mass. 26th December is not a public holiday.

nœud [nø] *m* **1.** (*boucle, vitesse, protubérance*) *a.* NAUT, BOT knot; **double** ~ double knot; ~ **papillon** bow tie **2.** (*point essentiel: d'une pièce, d'un roman, d'un débat*) crux
noie [nwa] *indic et subj prés de* **noyer**
noierai [nwaʀe] *fut de* **noyer**
noir [nwaʀ] *m* **1.** (*couleur, vêtement*) black; (*de deuil*) mourning; **habillé en** ~ dressed in black **2.** (*obscurité*) dark; **dans le** ~ in the dark **3.** *inf* (*café*) espresso **4.** PHOT ~ **et blanc** black and white ▸~ **sur blanc** in black and white; **broyer du** ~ to be all gloom and doom; **peindre tout en** ~ to paint a black picture; **au** ~ on the black market; **travail au** ~ moonlighting
noir(e) [nwaʀ] *adj* **1.** (*opp: blanc; illégal, satanique*) black; (*ciel*) dark; ~ **comme l'encre** as black as ink **2.** (*foncé: lunettes*) dark; (*raisin*) black; **blé** ~ buckwheat; **la rue est** ~**e de monde** the street is teeming with people **3.** (*propre à la race*) black; **l'Afrique** ~**e** black Africa **4.** (*obscur*) dark **5.** (*sinistre*) dark; (*humour*) black **6.** LIT, CINE **film** ~ film noir; **série** ~**e** thriller series
Noir(e) [nwaʀ] *m(f)* black (person)
noirâtre [nwaʀɑtʀ] *adj* blackish
noiraud(e) [nwaʀo, od] I. *adj* dark II. *m(f)* dark-skinned person
noirceur [nwaʀsœʀ] *f* **1.** (*perfidie*) blackness **2.** (*caractère sinistre*) darkness
noircir [nwaʀsiʀ] <8> I. *vt* **1.** (*salir*) to dirty **2.** (*colorer: étoffe*) to blacken **3.** (*dénigrer*) ~ **la réputation de qn** to blacken sb's reputation **4.** (*couvrir d'écriture: cahier, feuille*) to cover II. *vi* (*façade, fruit*) to go black; (*ciel, peau*) to darken; (*bois, couleur*) to discolour *Brit*, to discolor *Am* III. *vpr* **se** ~ (*façade*) to go black; (*ciel*) to darken; (*bois, couleur*) to discolour *Brit*, to discolor *Am*
noire [nwaʀ] *f* MUS crotchet *Brit*, quarter note *Am*
noise [nwaz] *f* **chercher** ~ [*o* **des** ~**s**] **à qn** to pick a quarrel with sb
noisetier [nwaztje] *m* hazel tree
noisette [nwazɛt] I. *f* **1.** (*fruit*) hazelnut **2.** GASTR **une** ~ **de beurre** a knob of butter II. *adj inv* hazel
noix [nwa] *f* **1.** (*fruit*) walnut **2.** *péj* (*individu stupide*) idiot **3.** (*viande*) fillet **4.** (*quantité*) **une** ~ **de beurre** a knob of butter ▸**à la** ~ **(de coco)** *inf* pathetic
nom [nɔ̃] *m* **1.** (*dénomination*) name; **quel est le** ~ **de ...?** what's the name of ...?; **je ne le connais que de** ~ I only know him by name; **donner son** ~ **à qn/qc** to give one's name to sb/sth **2.** LING noun; ~ **composé** compound noun ▸~ **d'un chien!**, ~ **d'une pipe!** heavens!; ~ **de Dieu (de** ~ **de Dieu)!** my God!; ~ **à coucher dehors** *inf* name you wouldn't believe; **porter bien/mal son** ~ to suit/not suit one's name; **traiter qn de tous les** ~**s** to call sb every name under the sun; **au** ~ **du Père, du Fils et du Saint-Esprit** in the

N

name of the Father, Son and Holy Spirit

nomade [nɔmad] **I.** *adj* **1.** (*opp: sédentaire*) nomadic; ZOOL migratory **2.** (*errant*) wandering **II.** *mf* nomad

no man's land [nomanslɑ̃d] *m inv* no man's land

nombre [nɔ̃bʀ] *m* number; **en grand** ~ in large numbers

nombreux, **-euse** [nɔ̃bʀø, -øz] *adj* numerous; (*foule, clientèle, famille*) large; **ils sont ~ à faire qc** many of them do sth

nombril [nɔ̃bʀil] *m* navel

nomenclature [nɔmɑ̃klatyʀ] *f* **1.** (*entrées: d'un dictionnaire*) word list **2.** (*terminologie*) nomenclature

nominal(e) [nɔminal, o] <-aux> *adj* nominal

nominatif, **-ive** [nɔminatif, -iv] *m* LING nominative

nomination [nɔminasjɔ̃] *f* (*désignation*) nomination; ~ **à un poste de directeur/de professeur** appointment to the position of manager/teacher

nominé(e) [nɔmine] *adj* nominated

nommément [nɔmemɑ̃] *adv* by name

nommer [nɔme] <1> *vt* **1.** (*appeler: chose*) to call; **une femme nommée Laetitia** a woman named Laetitia **2.** (*citer*) to name; **quelqu'un que je ne nommerai pas** somebody who will remain anonymous **3.** (*désigner*) to designate; (*avocat, expert*) to appoint; ~ **qn à un poste/à une fonction** to appoint sb to a job/position

non [nɔ̃] **I.** *adv* **1.** (*réponse*) no; **je pense que ~** I don't think so, I think not; **moi ~, mais** not me, but; **ah ~!** no!; **ça ~!** certainly not!; **mais ~!** (*atténuation*) of course not!; (*insistance*) definitely not!; (**oh**) **que ~!** *inf* definitely not! **2.** (*opposition*) not; **je n'y vais pas – moi ~ plus** I'm not going – nor am I; **il n'en est pas question ~ plus** it's also out of the question; **~ seulement ..., mais** (**encore**) not only ..., but also **3.** *inf* (*sens interrogatif*) **vous venez, ~?** you're coming, aren't you?; **~, pas possible!** no, I don't believe it! **4.** (*sens exclamatif*) **~, par exemple!** for goodness sake!; **~ mais** (**alors**)! *inf* honestly!; **~, mais dis donc!** *inf* really! **5.** (*qui n'est pas*) **~ négligeable** not inconsiderable; **~ polluant** non-polluting **II.** *m inv* no; **48 % de ~** 48 % noes; **répondre par un ~ catégorique** to reply with a categorical no

nonagénaire [nɔnaʒenɛʀ] **I.** *adj* nonagenarian; **être ~** (*avoir 90 ans*) to be ninety; (*être âgé de 91 à 99 ans*) to be in one's nineties **II.** *mf* nonagenarian

non-agression [nɔnagʀesjɔ̃] <non-agressions> *f* **pacte de ~** non-aggression pact

nonante [nɔnɑ̃t] *adj Belgique, Suisse* (*quatre-vingt-dix*) ninety; *v. a.* **cinq, cinquante**

non-assistance [nɔnasistɑ̃s] <non-assistances> *f* **~ à personne en danger** failure to assist a person in danger

nonchalance [nɔ̃ʃalɑ̃s] *f* **1.** nonchalance; **avec ~** nonchalantly **2.** (*lenteur*) listlessness; **avec ~** listlessly

nonchalant(e) [nɔ̃ʃalɑ̃, ɑ̃t] *adj* **1.** nonchalant **2.** (*lent*) listless

non-conformiste [nɔ̃kɔ̃fɔʀmist] <non-conformistes> *adj, mf* nonconformist **non-croyant(e)** [nɔ̃kʀwajɑ̃, jɑ̃t] <non-croyants> **I.** *adj* non-believing **II.** *m(f)* nonbeliever **non-dit** [nɔ̃di] <non-dits> *m* **le ~** the unsaid **non-fumeur**, **-euse** [nɔ̃fymœʀ, -øz] <non-fumeurs> *m, f* non-smoker **non-lieu** [nɔ̃ljø] <non-lieux> *m* dismissal of charges

nonne [nɔn] *f* nun

non-respect [nɔ̃ʀɛspɛ] <non-respects> *m* disrespect; **~ de la loi** failure to respect the law **non-sens** [nɔ̃sɑ̃s] *m inv* **1.** (*absurdité*) nonsense **2.** ECOLE meaningless word **non-stop** [nɔnstɔp] **I.** *adj inv* non-stop **II.** *m inv* **1.** CINE, TV non-stop broadcasting **2.** (*vol*) **en ~** non-stop **non-violence** [nɔ̃vjɔlɑ̃s] <non-violences> *f* non-violence **non-violent(e)** [nɔ̃vjɔlɑ̃, ɑ̃t] <non-violents> **I.** *adj* non-violent **II.** *m(f)* supporter of non-violence **non-voyant(e)** [nɔ̃vwajɑ̃, jɑ̃t] <non-voyants> *m(f)* visually handicapped person

nord [nɔʀ] **I.** *m* (*point cardinal*) north; **au ~ de qc** to the north of sth; **être exposé au ~** to have northerly exposure; **dans le ~ de** in the north of; **du ~** from the north; **vers le ~** towards the north ►**perdre le ~** (*perdre son calme*) to blow one's top; (*perdre la raison*) to go mad; **elle perd pas le ~** she's got her head screwed on **II.** *adj inv* north; (*banlieue, latitude*) northern

Nord [nɔʀ] **I.** *m* North; **le grand ~** the far North; **l'Europe du ~** Northern Europe; **le ~ canadien** the North of Canada; **dans le ~** (*dans la région*) in the North; (*vers la région*) to the North **II.** *adj inv* **l'hémisphère ~** the Northern hemisphere; **le pôle ~** the North Pole

nord-africain(e) [nɔʀafʀikɛ̃, ɛn] <nord-africains> *adj* North African **Nord-Africain(e)** [nɔʀafʀikɛ̃, ɛn] <Nord-Africains> *m(f)* North African **nord-américain(e)** [nɔʀameʀikɛ̃, ɛn] <nord-américains> *adj* North American **nord-coréen(ne)** [nɔʀkɔʀeɛ̃, ɛn] <nord-coréens> *adj* North Korean **Nord-Coréen(ne)** [nɔʀkɔʀeɛ̃, ɛn] <Nord-Coréens> *m(f)* North Korean **nord-est** [nɔʀɛst] *m inv* northeast **Nord-Est** [nɔʀɛst] *m inv* northeast

nordique [nɔʀdik] *adj* Nordic

Nordique [nɔʀdik] *mf* Nordic

nord-ouest [nɔʀwɛst] *m inv* northwest **Nord-Ouest** [nɔʀwɛst] *m inv* northwest **Nord-Sud** [nɔʀsyd] *adj inv* North-South **nord-vietnamien(ne)** [nɔʀvjɛtnamjɛ̃, jɛn] <nord-vietnamiens> *adj* HIST North Vietnamese **Nord-Vietnamien(ne)** [nɔʀvjɛtnamjɛ̃, jɛn] <Nord-Vietnamiens> *m(f)* HIST North Vietnamese

normal(e) [nɔʀmal, o] <-aux> *adj* **1.** (*ordinaire*) normal; **redevenir** ~ to return to normal **2.** (*compréhensible*) normal; **il est/n'est pas ~ que** +*subj*/**de** +*infin* it is/is not all right for sb to +*infin* **3.** (*sain*) normal

normale [nɔʀmal] *f* **1.** (*état habituel*) normal situation **2.** (*norme*) norm; **des capacités au-dessus de la ~** above-normal capacities **3.** METEO **~s saisonnières** seasonal norms

normalement [nɔʀmalmɑ̃] *adv* **1.** (*conformément aux normes*) normally **2.** (*selon toute prévision*) all being well

normalien(ne) [nɔʀmaljɛ̃, jɛn] *m(f): student or graduate of the Ecole Normale Supérieure*

normalisation [nɔʀmalizasjɔ̃] *f* **1.** (*standardization*) standardization **2.** POL (*retour à la normale*) normalization

normaliser [nɔʀmalize] <1> **I.** *vt* **1.** (*standardiser*) to standardize **2.** (*rendre normal*) to normalize **II.** *vpr* **les relations/la situation se normalise(nt)** the relationships are/situation is getting back to normal

normand(e) [nɔʀmɑ̃, ɑ̃d] *adj* Norman

Normand(e) [nɔʀmɑ̃, ɑ̃d] *m(f)* Norman

Normandie [nɔʀmɑ̃di] *f* **la ~** Normandy

norme [nɔʀm] *f* norm; **rester dans la/être hors ~** to remain within/to be outside normal limits

Norvège [nɔʀvɛʒ] *f* **la ~** Norway

norvégien [nɔʀveʒjɛ̃] *m* Norwegian; *v. a.* **français**

norvégien(ne) [nɔʀveʒjɛ̃, jɛn] *adj* Norwegian

Norvégien(ne) [nɔʀveʒjɛ̃, jɛn] *m(f)* Norwegian

nos [no] *dét poss v.* **notre**

nostalgie [nɔstalʒi] *f* nostalgia; **avoir la ~ de qc** to be nostalgic about sth

nostalgique [nɔstalʒik] *adj* nostalgic

nota (bene) [nɔta(bene)] *m inv* nota bene

notable [nɔtabl] **I.** *adj* notable **II.** *mf* worthy

notablement [nɔtabləmɑ̃] *adv* notably

notaire [nɔtɛʀ] *m* notary

notamment [nɔtamɑ̃] *adv* **1.** (*particulièrement*) notably **2.** *Belgique* (*nommément*) specifically

notarié(e) [nɔtaʀje] *adj* (*acte*) in due legal form

notation [nɔtasjɔ̃] *f* **1.** notation; **~ musicale** musical notation; **~ sténographique** shorthand **2.** ADMIN evaluation; ECOLE grading

note [nɔt] *f* **1.** (*communication, annotation*) *a.* ECOLE, MUS note; **~ de bas de page** footnote **2.** (*facture*) bill; **~ de 100 euros** bill for 100 euros ►**fausse ~** MUS wrong note; (*maladresse*) sour note; **forcer la ~** to overdo it; **prendre bonne ~ de qc** to take good note of sth; **prendre qc en ~** (*inscrire*) to take a note of sth; (*prendre conscience*) to take note of sth

In French schools, work is graded from A to E, or given a **note** out of 10 or 20.

noter [nɔte] <1> *vt* **1.** (*inscrire*) to write down **2.** (*remarquer*) to note; **notez-le bien, notons-le** note this **3.** ADMIN, ECOLE to mark *Brit*, to grade *Am*; (*employé*) to rate; **~ qn/qc 12 sur 20** to mark sb/sth 12 out of 20 **4.** (*souligner*) **~ qc d'une croix** to mark sth with a cross

notice [nɔtis] *f* **1.** (*mode d'emploi*) **~ (explicative)** instructions **2.** (*préface*) note

notifier [nɔtifje] <1a> *vt* (*jugement*) to notify; **~ qc à qn** to notify sb of sth

notion [nosjɔ̃] *f* **1.** (*idée, conscience*) **la ~ de l'heure** [*o* **du temps**] the notion of time **2.** *pl* (*connaissances*) basic knowledge; **avoir des ~s de qc** to have a basic knowledge of sth

notoire [nɔtwaʀ] *adj* (*criminel*) notorious; (*bêtise, inconduite*) well-known; **il est ~ qu'il l'a fait** it's common knowlege that he did it

notoriété [nɔtɔʀjete] *f* **1.** (*renommée: d'une personne, œuvre*) fame **2.** (*caractère connu*) notoriety; **être de ~ publique** to be common knowledge

notre [nɔtʀ, no] <nos> *dét poss* **1.** our; *v. a.* **ma, mon 2.** REL **Notre Père qui êtes aux cieux** Our Father, who art in heaven

nôtre [notʀ] *pron poss* **1. le/la/les ~(s)** our; *v. a.* **mien 2.** *pl* (*ceux de notre famille*) **les ~s** our folks; (*nos partisans*) our people; **il est des ~s** he's one of us; *v. a.* **mien** ►**à la (bonne) ~!** *inf* to us!

Notre-Dame [nɔtʀədam] *f inv* **1.** REL Our Lady **2.** (*à Paris*) Notre Dame

nouba [nuba] *f inf* party; **faire la ~ toute la nuit** to party all night

noué(e) [nwe] *adj* **avoir la gorge ~e** to have a lump in one's throat; **avoir l'estomac ~** to feel dreadful in the pit of one's stomach

nouer [nwe] <1> **I.** *vt* **1.** (*faire un nœud avec*) to knot **2.** (*entourer d'un lien*) to do up; (*paquet, bouquet*) to tie up **3.** (*établir: alliance*) to form; (*contact, relation, amitié*) to strike up **4.** (*paralyser*) **l'émotion/les sanglots lui a/ont noué la gorge** emotion/sobs choked him; **l'angoisse lui a noué l'estomac** anxiety gave him a dreadful feeling in the pit of his stomach **II.** *vpr* **1.** (*se serrer*) **sa gorge se noua en voyant cela** he felt a lump in his throat when he saw it **2.** (*s'attacher*) **se ~ autour du cou** to be tied around the neck; (*accidentellement*) to get tied around one's neck **3.** LIT, THEAT **l'intrigue se noue** the plot reaches a climax

noueux, -euse [nwø, -øz] *adj* knotty; (*doigt, main*) gnarled

nougat [nuga] *m* nougat

nougatine [nugatin] *f* nougatine

nouille [nuj] **I.** *f* **1.** GASTR noodle **2.** *inf* oaf **II.** *adj* **1.** *inf* (*empoté*) clumsy **2.** *inf* (*tarte*) idiot

N

nounou [nunu] *f enfantin* 1. (*nourrice*) nanny 2. (*garde d'enfant*) babysitter, childminder *Brit*

nounours [nunuʀs] *m enfantin* teddy bear

nourrice [nuʀis] *f* 1. (*gardienne*) nanny 2. (*bidon*) jerry can

nourricier, -ière [nuʀisje, -jɛʀ] *adj* (*adoptif*) foster

nourrir [nuʀiʀ] <8> I. *vt* 1. (*donner à manger à: personne, animal*) to feed; ~ **qn au biberon/à la cuillère** to bottle-feed/spoon-feed sb; ~ **qn au sein** to breast-feed sb; **être bien/mal nourri** to be well-/under-fed 2. (*faire vivre*) ~ **qn** to provide for sb ▶**être nourri et logé** to have bed and board II. *vi* to be nourishing III. *vpr* (*s'alimenter*) **se** ~ **de qc** to feed on sth; **bien se** ~ to eat well

nourrissant(e) [nuʀisɑ̃, ɑ̃t] *adj* nourishing

nourrisson [nuʀisɔ̃] *m* infant

nourriture [nuʀityʀ] *f* (*produits*) food; ~ **pour animaux** animal food

nous [nu] I. *pron pers* 1. *sujet* we; **vous avez fini, mais pas** ~ you've finished but we haven't; ~ **autres** the rest of us 2. *complément d'objet direct et indirect* us 3. *avec être, devenir, sembler, soutenu* **cela** ~ **semble bon** that seems fine to us; *v. a.* **me** 4. *avec les verbes pronominaux* **nous** ~ **punissons** we're punishing ourselves; **nous** ~ **voyons souvent** we see each other often; **nous** ~ **nettoyons les ongles** we're cleaning our nails 5. *inf* (*pour renforcer*) ~, ~ **n'avons pas** [*o* **on n'a pas** *inf*] **ouvert la bouche** we never opened our mouths; **c'est** ~ **qui l'avons dit** we're the ones who said it; **il veut** ~ **aider,** ~**?** he wants to help US? 6. (*avec un sens possessif*) **le cœur** ~ **battait fort** our hearts were beating fast 7. *avec un présentatif* ~ **voici** [*o* **voilà**]**!** here we are! 8. *avec une préposition* **avec/sans** ~ with/without us; **à** ~ **deux** between the two of us; **la maison est à** ~ the house is ours; **c'est à** ~ **de décider** it's for us to decide; **c'est à** ~**!** it's our turn! 9. *dans une comparaison* us; **vous êtes comme** ~ you're like us; **plus fort que** ~ stronger than us 10. (*je*) ~**, Roi de France** We, the King of France 11. *inf* (*signe d'intérêt*) **comment allons-**~**?** how are we? II. *m* we; **le** ~ **de majesté** the royal We

nous-même [numɛm] <nous-mêmes> *pron pers* 1. (*nous en personne*) ~**s n'en savions rien** we know nothing; **nous sommes venus de** ~**s** we came of our own accord 2. (*j'ai froid – nous aussi*) I'm cold – so are we; *v. a.* **moi-même**

nouveau [nuvo] <x> *m* **du** ~ new ▶**à** [*o* **de**] ~ again

nouveau, nouvelle [nuvo, nuvɛl, nuvɛl] <*devant un nom masculin commençant par une voyelle ou un h muet* nouvel, x> I. *adj* 1. (*récent*) new; **rien de** ~ nothing new 2. *antéposé* (*répété*) another; **une nouvelle fois** another time 3. *antéposé* (*de fraîche date*) **les** ~**x venus** the newcomers ▶**tout beau, tout** ~ *prov* everything's new and lovely; **c'est** ~ (**ça**)! *inf* that's new! II. *m, f* new man, new woman *m, f*

Nouveau-Brunswick [nuvobʀœsvik] *m* **le** ~ New Brunswick

Nouveau-Mexique [nuvomɛksik(ə)] *m* **le** ~ New Mexico

nouveau-né(e) [nuvone] <nouveau-nés> I. *adj* newborn II. *m(f)* newborn

nouveauté [nuvote] *f* 1. (*en librairie*) new book; (*en salle*) new film; (*voiture, avion*) new model 2. (*innovation*) novelty; **c'est une** ~ it is a novelty

nouvel(le) [nuvɛl] *adj v.* **nouveau**

nouvelle [nuvɛl] *f* 1. (*événement*) piece of news; (*information*) piece of information; **connaissez-vous la** ~**?** have you heard the news? 2. *pl* (*renseignements sur qn*) **avoir des** ~**s de qn** to have news from sb; **donner de ses** ~**s** to tell sb one's news; **prendre des** ~**s de qn** to ask about sb 3. *pl* CINE, TV news + *vb sing* 4. LIT short story ▶**pas de** ~**s, bonnes** ~**s** *prov* no news is good news; **aux dernières** ~ the last I heard; **tu m'en diras/vous m'en direz des** ~**s** tell me what you think of this; **tu auras/il aura de mes** ~**s!** you'll/he'll be hearing from me!; *v. a.* **nouveau**

Nouvelle-Angleterre [nuvɛlɑ̃glətɛːʀ(ə)] *f* **la** ~ New England **Nouvelle-Calédonie** [nuvɛlkaledoni] *f* **la** ~ New Caledonia **Nouvelle-Écosse** [nuvɛlekɔs(ə)] *f* **la** ~ Nova Scotia

nouvellement [nuvɛlmɑ̃] *adv* newly

Nouvelle-Orléans [nuvɛlɔʀleɑ̃] *f* **la** ~ New Orleans **Nouvelles-Galles du Sud** [nuvɛl(ə)gal(ə)dysyd] *fpl* **les** ~ New South Wales **Nouvelle-Zélande** [nuvɛlzelɑ̃d] *f* **la** ~ New Zealand

novateur, -trice [nɔvatœʀ, -tʀis] I. *adj* innovative II. *m, f* innovator

novembre [nɔvɑ̃bʀ] *m* November; *v. a.* **août**

novice [nɔvis] I. *adj* **être** ~ **dans qc** to be a novice at sth II. *mf* 1. (*débutant*) beginner 2. REL novice

noyade [nwajad] *f* drowning

noyau [nwajo] <x> *m* 1. BOT stone 2. PHYS, BIO nucleus; GEO core 3. (*groupe humain*) nucleus; ~ **de manifestants** core of demonstrators; ~ **dur** hard core shareholders

noyé(e) [nwaje] I. *adj* drowned II. *m(f)* drowned man, woman *m, f*

noyer¹ [nwaje] *m* 1. (*arbre*) walnut tree 2. (*bois*) walnut

noyer² [nwaje] <6> I. *vt* 1. (*tuer, oublier*) to drown 2. (*inonder*) to flood; ~ **qc sous l'eau** to drown sth with water 3. GASTR to water down 4. AUTO to flood II. *vpr* (*mourir*) **se** ~ to drown

nu [ny] *m* ART nude

nu(e) [ny] *adj* 1. (*sans vêtement*) naked; **les pieds** ~**s** barefoot; **se mettre torse** ~ to strip to the waist 2. (*non protégé: fil électrique, lame*) bare ▶**mettre qc à** ~ (*à découvert*) to lay sth bare; (*découvrir*) to strip sth; **mettre son cœur à** ~ to lay bare one's heart

nuage [nɥaʒ] *m* **1.** (*nébulosité, amas*) cloud **2.** (*très petite quantité*) **un** ~ **de lait** a drop of milk ▸**être dans les** ~**s** to be in the clouds; **être** [*o* **marcher**] **sur un** ~ to be on cloud nine; **ciel sans** ~(**s**) cloudless sky; **bonheur/amitié sans** ~(**s**) untroubled happiness/friendship

nuageux, -euse [nɥaʒø, -ʒøz] *adj* METEO cloudy

nuance [nɥɑ̃s] *f* **1.** (*gradation de couleur*) shade; (*détail de couleur*) nuance **2.** (*légère différence*) nuance; POL shade of opinion; **à quelques** ~**s près** apart from a few minor differences

nuancé(e) [nɥɑ̃se] *adj* nuanced; (*chant, style*) finely shaded

nuancer [nɥɑ̃se] <2> *vt* ~ **qc** to put nuances in sth; MUS to colour sth *Brit,* to color sth *Am;* ART to tone sth; (*couleur*) to shade sth; ~ **son style** to put subtle variations in one's style; ~ **sa pensée** to qualify one's thought

nuancier [nɥɑ̃sje] *m* colour chart *Brit,* color chart *Am*

nucléaire [nykleɛʀ] **I.** *adj* nuclear **II.** *m* nuclear technology

nudisme [nydism] *m* nudism; **pratiquer le** ~ to be a nudist

nudiste [nydist] **I.** *adj* nudist **II.** *mf* nudist

nudité [nydite] *f* **1.** (*absence de vêtement*) nudity; **couvrir sa** ~ to cover one's nakedness **2.** (*dépouillement*) bareness **3.** ART nude ▸**s'étaler dans toute sa** ~ to be laid bare to the world; **l'horreur dans toute sa** ~ undisguised horror

nuée [nɥe] *f* (*grand nombre*) horde

nues [ny] **porter qn aux** ~ to praise sb to the skies; **tomber des** ~ to be dumbfounded

nuire [nɥiʀ] *vi irr* ~ **à qn/qc** to damage sb/sth

nuisance [nɥizɑ̃s] *f* enviromental nuisance; ~**s sonores** noise pollution

nuisible [nɥizibl] *adj* (*influence, habitude*) harmful; (*gaz*) noxious; **animaux/insectes** ~**s** pests; **être** ~ **à qc** to be harmful to sth

nuit [nɥi] *f* **1.** (*espace de temps, nuité*) night; **bonne** ~**!** good night!; **mardi, dans la** ~ in the course of Tuesday night **2.** (*obscurité*) darkness; **la** ~ **tombe** night is falling; **il fait/commence à faire** ~ it is dark/beginning to get dark; **il fait** ~ **noire** it's pitch black **3.** (*temps d'activité*) **de** ~ night; **être de** ~ to be on nights; **faire la** ~ to be the nightwatchman ▸**la** ~ **porte conseil** *prov* it is best to sleep on it; ~ **blanche** sleepless night; ~ **de noces** wedding night; **les Mille et Une Nuits** the Thousand and One Nights; **faire sa** ~ to sleep through (the night)

nul(le) [nyl] **I.** *adj* **1.** (*mauvais: discours, film, devoir*) lousy; **il est** ~ **en physique** (*médiocre*) he's no good at physics; (*incompétent*) he's hopeless at physics **2.** (*ennuyeux, raté*) **c'était** ~**, cette fête** that party was awful **3.** *inf* (*crétin*) **c'est** ~**/t'es** ~ **d'avoir fait qc** it's/you're stupid to do sth **4.** SPORT nil; (*égalité*) drawn; **match** ~ draw **5.** (*minime: risque, différence*) non-existent; **être quasiment** ~ to be practically non-existent **6.** MAT zero **7.** JUR, POL (*élection, testament*) null and void **II.** *pron indéf, soutenu* ~ **ne** nobody **III.** *m(f)* idiot

nullard(e) [nylaʀ, aʀd] **I.** *adj inf* (*incompétent*) **être** ~ **en anglais** to be useless in English **II.** *m(f) inf* hopeless case

nullement [nylmɑ̃] *adv* (*aucunement*) not at all; (*en aucun cas*) in any way

nullité [nylite] *f* **1.** (*manque de valeur, incompétence*) uselessness; **être d'une parfaite** ~ to be completely useless [*o* hopeless] **2.** (*personne*) nonentity **3.** JUR nullity

numéral [nymeʀal, o] <-aux> *m* LING numeral

numéral(e) [nymeʀal, o] <-aux> *adj* **1.** (*symbole, système, lettres*) numeral; (*cartes*) number **2.** LING (*adjectif*) numeral

numérateur [nymeʀatœʀ] *m* numerator

numération [nymeʀasjɔ̃] *f* **1.** MAT (*comptage*) counting; (*système*) notation; ~ **binaire/décimale** binary/decimal system **2.** MED count; ~ **globulaire** [*o* **sanguine**] blood count

numérique [nymeʀik] *adj* **1.** (*exprimé en nombre*) numerical **2.** INFOR, TEL digital; **des données** ~**s** digital data; **utiliser un codage** ~ to encode digitally

numérisé [nymeʀize] *adj* INFOR digitized

numériser [nymeʀize] <1> *vt* INFOR to digitize

numériseur [nymeʀizœʀ] *m* INFOR scanner, digitizer

numéro [nymeʀo] *m* **1.** (*nombre*) number; **le** ~ **de la rue/de la page** the street/page number; ~ **de téléphone** telephone number; **faire** [*o* **composer**] **un** ~ to dial a number; ~ **vert** freephone number *Brit,* toll-free number *Am* **2.** PRESSE issue **3.** (*spectacle*) number **4.** *inf* (*personne*) character ▸**faire son** ~ **à qn** *inf* to put on one's act for sb; ~ **un** number one; **ennemi** ~ **un** enemy number one; **souci/problème** ~ **un** number one worry/problem

numérotation [nymeʀɔtasjɔ̃] *f* numbering; ~ **à 10 chiffres** 10-digit phone numbering

numéroter [nymeʀɔte] <1> *vt* to number

numerus clausus [nymeʀysklozys] *m inv* quota

numismatique [nymismatik] **I.** *adj* numismatic **II.** *f* numismatics + *vb sing*

nu-pieds [nypje] **I.** *adj inv* barefoot **II.** *mpl* (*chaussures*) flip-flops

nuptial(e) [nypsjal, jo] <-aux> *adj* (*messe*) nuptial; (*anneau*) wedding; (*chambre, lit*) marriage; **cérémonie** ~**e** wedding ceremony; **bénédiction** ~**e** nuptial blessing

nuque [nyk] *f* nape of the neck

nurse [nœʀs] *f* nanny

N

nu-tête [nytɛt] *adj inv* bare-headed
nutritif, **-ive** [nytʀitif, -iv] *adj* **1.** (*nourricier*) nourishing; (*qualité, valeur, substance*) nutritional **2.** MED **besoins ~s** nutritive requirements
nutrition [nytʀisjɔ̃] *f* nutrition
nylon® [nilɔ̃] *m* nylon®
nymphe [nɛ̃f] *f* nymph
nymphomane [nɛ̃fɔman] **I.** *adj* nymphomaniac **II.** *f* nymphomaniac
nymphomanie [nɛ̃fɔmani] *f* nymphomania

O

O, **o** [o] *m inv* O, o; ~ **comme Oscar** o as in Oliver *Brit,* o as in Oboe *Am;* (*on telephone*) o for Oliver *Brit,* o for Oboe *Am*
O. *abr de* **ouest**
ô [o] *interj* oh
oasis [ɔazis] *f* oasis
obéir [ɔbeiʀ] <8> *vi* **1.** (*se soumettre*) ~ **à qn** to obey sb; ~ **à une loi/un ordre** to obey a law/an order; **se faire ~ de qn** to be obeyed by sb **2.** (*céder à*) ~ **à sa conscience/son instinct** to follow one's conscience/instinct
obéissance [ɔbeisɑ̃s] *f* ~ **à qn/qc** obedience to sb/sth
obéissant(**e**) [ɔbeisɑ̃, ɑ̃t] *adj* obedient
obélisque [ɔbelisk] *m* obelisk
obèse [ɔbɛz] **I.** *adj* obese **II.** *mf* obese person
obésité [ɔbezite] *f* obesity
objecter [ɔbʒɛkte] <1> *vt* to object; ~ **qc à qn** to advance sth to sb as an objection; **avoir quelque chose/ne rien avoir à ~ à qc** to have an objection/no objection against sth
objecteur [ɔbʒɛktœʀ] *m* ~ **de conscience** conscientious objector
objectif [ɔbʒɛktif] *m* **1.** (*but*) objective **2.** (*en optique*) **a.** PHYS, PHOT lens
objectif, **-ive** [ɔbʒɛktif, -iv] *adj* objective
objection [ɔbʒɛksjɔ̃] *f* objection; **faire une ~** to make an objection; **soulever une ~** to raise an objection; **si vous n'y voyez pas d'~** if you have no objection; ~ **de conscience** conscientious objection
objectivement [ɔbʒɛktivmɑ̃] *adv* objectively
objectivité [ɔbʒɛktivite] *f* objectivity
objet [ɔbʒɛ] *m* **1.** (*chose*) **a.** LING object; ~ **d'art** objet d'art; ~ **de curiosité/de convoitise** object of curiosity/desire **2.** (*but*) purpose; **avoir qc pour ~** to have the aim of sth ►**~s trouvés** lost property office *Brit,* lost and found *Am*
obligation [ɔbligasjɔ̃] *f* **1.** (*nécessité*) **a.** JUR obligation; ~ **de** +*infin* obligation to +*infin;* **être dans l'~ de** +*infin* to be obliged to +*infin;* ~ **alimentaire** maintenance obligation **2.** *pl* (*devoirs*) obligations; (*devoirs civiques, scolaires*) duties; **ses ~s de citoyen/de père de famille** his duties as a citizen/father; **les ~s militaires** liability for military service **3.** FIN bond ►**sans ~ de la part de qn** with no obligation on sb's part; **sans ~ d'achat** with no obligation to buy
obligatoire [ɔbligatwaʀ] *adj* **1.** (*exigé*) compulsory; **présence ~** compulsory attendance; **rendre qc ~** to make sth compulsory **2.** *inf* (*inévitable*) inevitable
obligatoirement [ɔbligatwaʀmɑ̃] *adv* **1.** (*nécessairement*) **ils étudient ~ deux langues modernes** they are required to study two modern languages; **devoir ~** +*infin* to be obliged to +*infin;* **il faut ~ qc** sth is a strict requirement **2.** *inf* (*forcément*) inevitably; **ça devait ~ arriver!** of course, it had to happen!
obligé(**e**) [ɔbliʒe] *adj* **1.** (*nécessaire*) vital; (*inévitable*) inevitable **2.** (*reconnaissant*) **être ~ à qn de qc** to be obliged to sb for sth
obligeance [ɔbliʒɑ̃s] *f* (*prévenance*) consideration; (*serviabilité*) helpfulness; **avoir l'~ de** +*infin* to be kind enough to +*infin*
obligeant(**e**) [ɔbliʒɑ̃, ʒɑ̃t] *adj* **1.** (*complaisant: paroles, termes, offre*) kind; (*personne*) obliging **2.** (*serviable*) helpful
obliger [ɔbliʒe] <2a> **I.** *vt* **1.** (*forcer*) to force; ~ **qn à** +*infin* to force sb to +*infin;* **on était bien obligés!** we had to! **2.** (*contraindre moralement, rendre service à*) to oblige **II.** *vpr* (*s'engager*) **s'~ à faire qc** to commit oneself to doing sth
oblique [ɔblik] *adj* oblique
obliquer [ɔblike] <1> *vi* to cut across; (*route*) to turn off
oblitérer [ɔbliteʀe] <5> *vt* to obliterate
oblong, **-ongue** [ɔblɔ̃, -ɔ̃g] *adj* oblong
obnubiler [ɔbnybile] <1> *vt* **1.** (*obscurcir: esprit, pensée*) to cloud; **obnubilé par les préjugés** clouded by prejudice; **se laisser ~ par qn/qc** to let sb/sth cloud one's judgment **2.** (*obséder*) to obsess
obole [ɔbɔl] *f* offering; **verser son ~** to make a small contribution
obscène [ɔpsɛn] *adj* obscene
obscénité [ɔpsenite] *f* obscenity
obscur(**e**) [ɔpskyʀ] *adj* **1.** (*sombre*) dark **2.** (*incompréhensible, inconnu*) obscure
obscurcir [ɔpskyʀsiʀ] <8> **I.** *vt* (*assombrir*) to darken **II.** *vpr* **1.** (*devenir obscur*) **s'~** (*ciel*) to darken; **le jour s'obscurcit** the day is growing dark; **le temps s'obscurcit** the sky is growing dark **2.** (*se brouiller*) **ma vue s'obscurcit** my sight is growing dim
obscurcissement [ɔpskyʀsismɑ̃] *m* (*du ciel*) darkening; (*de la vue*) dimming
obscurément [ɔpskyʀemɑ̃] *adv* **1.** (*vaguement*) obscurely; (*deviner, sentir*) in an obscure way **2.** (*de façon peu claire*) vaguely
obscurité [ɔpskyʀite] *f* **1.** (*absence de lumière*) darkness **2.** (*manque de clarté: d'une affaire*) obscurity **3.** (*anonymat*) **vivre dans/sortir de l'~** to live in/emerge from obscurity

obsédant(e) [ɔpsedɑ̃, ɑ̃t] *adj* (*voix, musique*) haunting; **idée ~e** obsessive idea
obsédé(e) [ɔpsede] *m(f)* **1.** (*par le sexe*) sex maniac **2.** (*fanatique*) obsessive
obséder [ɔpsede] <5> *vt* to obsess; (*souci, remords*) to haunt
obsèques [ɔpsɛk] *fpl* funeral; ~ **nationales** state funeral
obséquieux, -euse [ɔpsekjø, -jøz] *adj* obsequious
observable [ɔpsɛʀvabl] *adj* observable
observateur, -trice [ɔpsɛʀvatœʀ, -tʀis] **I.** *adj* (*personne, regard, esprit*) observant **II.** *m, f* observer
observation [ɔpsɛʀvasjɔ̃] *f* observation; **faire des ~s à qn sur qc** to make an observation about sth to sb; **être en ~** to be under observation; **mettre qn en ~** to put sb under observation
observatoire [ɔpsɛʀvatwaʀ] *m* **1.** GEO, ASTR, METEO observatory **2.** MIL observation post **3.** ECON economic research institute
observer [ɔpsɛʀve] <1> **I.** *vt* **1.** (*regarder attentivement*) ~ **qn faire qc** to watch sb doing sth **2.** (*surveiller*) to observe **3.** (*remarquer*) to notice; **faire ~ qc à qn** to point sth out to sb **4.** (*respecter: coutume, attitude*) to respect; (*discrétion, règle*) to observe; (*jeûne*) to keep; ~ **une minute de silence à la mémoire de qn/qc** to observe a minute's silence in memory of sb/sth **II.** *vi* to observe **III.** *vpr* **s'~ 1.** (*se surveiller*) to watch each other **2.** (*s'épier*) to spy on each other
obsession [ɔpsesjɔ̃] *f* obsession
obsessionnel(le) [ɔpsesjɔnɛl] *adj* obsessive
obstacle [ɔpstakl] *m* obstacle; **faire ~ à qn/qc** to hinder sb/sth; **constituer un ~ à qc** to be an obstacle to sth
obstination [ɔpstinasjɔ̃] *f* **1.** (*entêtement*) obstinacy **2.** (*persévérance*) persistence; ~ **dans le travail** dogged hard work
obstiné(e) [ɔpstine] **I.** *adj* **1.** (*entêté*) obstinate **2.** (*persévérant*) persistent **3.** (*incessant: toux*) stubborn **II.** *m(f)* obstinate individual
obstinément [ɔpstinemɑ̃] *adv* **1.** (*avec entêtement*) obstinately **2.** (*avec persévérance*) doggedly
obstiner [ɔpstine] <1> *vpr* **s'~ dans qc** to persist in sth; **s'~ sur un détail/un problème** to keep worrying over a detail/problem
obstruer [ɔpstʀye] <1> **I.** *vt* to block **II.** *vpr* **s'~** to get blocked
obtempérer [ɔptɑ̃peʀe] <5> *vi* to obey; ~ **à un ordre** to comply with [*o* obey] an order; **refus d'~** refusal to comply
obtenir [ɔptəniʀ] <9> *vt* **1.** (*recevoir*) to get; (*avantage*) to obtain; ~ **de qn que** +*subj* to get sb to +*infin* **2.** (*parvenir à*) to obtain; (*examen*) to pass; (*majorité, total*) to achieve
obtention [ɔptɑ̃sjɔ̃] *f* (*d'un résultat*) achieving; (*d'un examen*) passing; (*d'une pièce administrative*) obtaining
obturer [ɔptyʀe] <1> *vt* to seal; (*dent*) to fill
obtus(e) [ɔpty, yz] *adj a.* MAT obtuse
obus [ɔby] *m* shell
oc [ɔk] *m* **langue d'~** langue d'oc
occasion [ɔkazjɔ̃] *f* **1.** (*circonstance (favorable)*) opportunity; **c'est l'~ ou jamais** it's now or never; **à la première ~** at the earliest opportunity **2.** COM (*offre avantageuse*) bargain; **voiture d'~** secondhand car *Brit,* used car *Am;* **le marché de l'~** the secondhand market **3.** (*cause*) **être l'~ de qc** to be the cause of sth ►**les grandes ~s** special occasions; **à l'~** on occasion; **à l'~ de qc** on the occasion of sth
occasionnel(le) [ɔkazjɔnɛl] *adj* occasional; (*travail*) casual
occasionnellement [ɔkazjɔnɛlmɑ̃] *adv* occasionally
occasionner [ɔkazjɔne] <1> *vt* to cause
occident [ɔksidɑ̃] *m* (*opp: orient*) west
Occident [ɔksidɑ̃] *m* POL **l'~** the West
occidental(e) [ɔksidɑ̃tal, o] <-aux> *adj* **1.** GEO, POL Western **2.** (*opp: oriental*) western
Occidental(e) [ɔksidɑ̃tal, o] <-aux> *m(f)* **1.** (*opp: Oriental*) Westerner **2.** POL West; **les Occidentaux** the western countries
occitan [ɔksitɑ̃] *m* Occitan; *v. a.* **français**
occitan(e) [ɔksitɑ̃, an] *adj* Occitan
occulte [ɔkylt] *adj* **1.** (*ésotérique*) occult **2.** (*secret*) secret
occulter [ɔkylte] <1> *vt* **1.** (*dissimuler: difficulté, problème*) to hide; (*vision*) to obscure **2.** (*cacher à la vue: phare, lumière*) to occult
occultisme [ɔkyltism] *m* occultism
occupant(e) [ɔkypɑ̃, ɑ̃t] **I.** *adj* MIL occupying **II.** *m(f)* **1.** MIL **l'~** the occupier **2.** (*habitant: d'une chambre, d'une voiture*) occupant; (*des lieux*) occupier
occupation [ɔkypasjɔ̃] *f* **1.** (*activité*) occupation **2.** (*métier*) job **3.** MIL, HIST occupation; **l'armée d'~** the occupying army; **l'Occupation** the Occupation
occupé(e) [ɔkype] *adj* **1.** (*opp: inoccupé: personne*) busy; (*place, toilettes, ligne téléphonique*) engaged; (*chambre d'hôtel*) occupied; **être ~ à qc** to be busy doing sth **2.** MIL, POL (*pays, usine*) occupied
occuper [ɔkype] <1> **I.** *vt* **1.** (*remplir: place*) to occupy; (*temps*) to spend; ~ **ses loisirs à faire qc** to spend one's free time doing sth **2.** (*habiter: appartement*) to occupy **3.** (*exercer: emploi, poste*) to hold; (*fonction*) to occupy **4.** (*employer*) ~ **qn à qc** to occupy sb for sth **5.** MIL, POL (*pays, usine*) to occupy **II.** *vpr* **1.** (*s'employer*) **s'~ de littérature/politique** to be involved in literature/politics **2.** (*prendre en charge*) **s'~ de qn/qc** to take care of sb/sth; **occupe-toi de tes affaires!** mind your own business! ►**t'occupe (pas)!** *inf* none of your business!
océan [ɔseɑ̃] *m* ocean; **l'~ Atlantique/Indien/Pacifique** the Atlantic/Indian/Pacific Ocean
Océanie [ɔseani] *f* **l'~** Oceania

océanique [ɔseanik] *adj* oceanic
océanographie [ɔseanɔɡʀafi] *f* oceanography
océanologie [ɔseanɔlɔʒi] *f* oceanology
océanologue [ɔseanɔlɔɡ] *mf* oceanologist
ocelot [ɔslo] *m* ocelot
ocre [ɔkʀ] **I.** *f* (*colorant*) ochre **II.** *adj inv* ochre
octane [ɔktan] *m* octane
octante [ɔktɑ̃t] *adj Belgique, Suisse* eighty; *v. a.* **cinq, cinquante**
octave [ɔktav] *f* octave; **faire des ~s** to play octaves; **jouer qc à l'~** to play sth an octave higher [*o* lower]
octet [ɔktɛ] *m* byte
octobre [ɔktɔbʀ] *m* October; **la révolution d'~ en Russie** HIST the October Revolution in Russia; *v. a.* **août**
octogénaire [ɔktɔʒenɛʀ] *adj, mf* octogenarian
octroi [ɔktʀwa] *m* **l'~ de qc** the granting of sth
octroyer [ɔktʀwaje] <6> **I.** *vt* **~ un délai/un répit/une somme d'argent à qn** to grant sb an extension/respite/a sum of money; **~ une faveur à qn** to do sb a favour *Brit,* to do sb a favor *Am* **II.** *vpr* **s'~ qc** to claim sth
oculaire [ɔkylɛʀ] *adj* **1.** ANAT ocular; **globe ~** eyeball **2.** (*visuel*) **témoin ~** eyewitness
oculiste [ɔkylist] *mf* eye specialist
ode [ɔd] *f* ode
odeur [ɔdœʀ] *f* smell; **sans ~** odourless *Brit,* odorless *Am;* **je sens une ~ de brûlé** I can smell burning
odieux, -euse [ɔdjø, -jøz] *adj* **1.** (*ignoble: personne*) obnoxious; (*caractère*) odious **2.** (*insupportable: personne*) unbearable
odorant(e) [ɔdɔʀɑ̃, ɑ̃t] *adj* scented
odorat [ɔdɔʀa] *m* sense of smell
œcuménisme [ekymenism] *m* ecumenism
œdème [ødɛm, edɛm] *m* oedema *Brit,* edema *Am*
œil [œj, jø] <yeux> *m* **1.** ANAT eye; **lever/baisser les yeux** to raise/lower one's eyes; **se maquiller les yeux** to put on eye make-up **2.** (*regard*) look; **il la cherche/suit des yeux** his eyes seek her out/follow her **3.** (*regard averti*) eye; **avoir l'~ à tout** to keep an eye on everything **4.** (*regard rapide*) **jeter un coup d'~ au journal/à l'heure** to glance at the newspaper/time; **au premier coup d'~** at first glance **5.** (*vision, vue*) **regarder qn d'un ~ envieux/méchant** to give someone a jealous/malicious look **6.** (*jugement*) **d'un ~ critique** with a critical eye; **ne plus voir les choses du même ~** to no longer see things in the same way **7.** (*judas*) spyhole ▸**avoir un ~ au beurre noir** to have a black eye; **loin des yeux, loin du cœur** *prov* out of sight, out of mind; **ne pas avoir les yeux dans sa poche** not to miss a thing; **coûter les yeux de la tête** to cost an arm and a leg; **qn a les yeux plus grands que le ventre** *inf* sb has eyes bigger than his stomach; **pour les beaux yeux de qn** *inf* to be nice to sb; **ne pas avoir froid aux yeux** to have a sense of adventure; **à l'~ nu** to the naked eye; **cela crève les yeux** *inf* it's staring you in the face; **ne dormir que d'un ~** to sleep with one eye open; **faire de l'~ à qn** *inf* to make eyes at sb; **fermer les yeux sur qc** to turn a blind eye to sth; **ouvrir l'~** to keep one's eyes open; **ouvrir les yeux à qn sur qc** to open sb's eyes about sth; **se rincer l'~** *inf* to get an eyeful; **cela saute aux yeux** it's staring you in the face; **taper dans l'~ de qn** *inf* to catch sb's eye, to take sb's fancy *Brit;* **avoir qn à l'~** *inf* to have an eye on sb; **aux yeux de qn** in sb's eyes; **sous l'~ de qn** under sb's eye; **mon ~!** *inf* my foot!
œil-de-bœuf [œjdəbœf] <œils-de-bœuf> *m* bull's eye
œillade [œjad] *f* (*clin d'œil*) wink; **jeter des ~s à qn** to wink at sb
œillère [œjɛʀ] *f* eyebath *Brit,* eyecup *Am* ▸**avoir des ~s** to wear blinkers
œillet[1] [œjɛ] *m* BOT carnation; **~ d'Inde** French marigold
œillet[2] [œjɛ] *m* **1.** (*petit trou: d'une chaussure*) eyelet **2.** (*renfort métallique*) grommet
œnologie [enɔlɔʒi] *f* oenology *Brit,* enology *Am*
œsophage [ezɔfaʒ] *m* oesophagus *Brit,* esophagus *Am*
œuf [œf, ø] *m* **1.** ZOOL, GASTR egg; **~s de poisson** spawn; **~s brouillés/à la coque** scrambled/boiled eggs; **~ au plat** fried egg; **~ à la neige** floating island **2.** (*qui a la forme d'un ~*) **~ à repriser** darning egg; **~ de Pâques** Easter egg ▸**mettre tous ses ~s dans le même panier** to put all one's eggs in one basket; **être plein comme un ~** (*salle*) to be full to bursting; **va te faire cuire un ~!** *inf* go take a running jump!; **dans l'~** in the bud; **quel ~!** *inf* what an idiot!
œuvre [œvʀ] **I.** *f* **1.** ART, LIT, TECH work; **~ d'art** work of art; **les ~s complètes d'un auteur** the complete works of an author **2.** (*résultat: de l'érosion, du temps*) work **3.** *pl* (*actes*) deeds **4.** (*organisation caritative*) **~ de bienfaisance** charity; **les bonnes ~s** charities ▸**être à l'~** to be at work; **mettre en ~** to implement; **se mettre à l'~** to get down to work **II.** *m* **être à pied d'~** to be ready to start working; **le gros ~** the shell
offensant(e) [ɔfɑ̃sɑ̃, ɑ̃t] *adj* offensive
offense [ɔfɑ̃s] *f* (*affront*) offence *Brit,* offense *Am;* **faire une ~ à qn** to offend sb
offensé(e) [ɔfɑ̃se] **I.** *adj* offended **II.** *m(f)* offended party
offenser [ɔfɑ̃se] <1> **I.** *vt* (*outrager*) to offend **II.** *vpr* (*se vexer*) **s'~ de qc** to take offence at sth *Brit,* to take offense at sth *Am*
offenseur [ɔfɑ̃sœʀ] *m* offender
offensif, -ive [ɔfɑ̃sif, -iv] *adj* offensive
offensive [ɔfɑ̃siv] *f* offensive; **prendre l'~** to take the offensive; **passer à l'~** to go on the

offensive; **lancer une ~ contre qn/qc** to launch an offensive against sb/sth

office [ɔfis] *m* **1.** (*agence, bureau*) office; **~ du tourisme** tourist information office **2.** REL service **3.** (*fonction, charge*) office **4.** (*pièce*) kitchen ▸**les bons ~s de qn** sb's good offices; **faire ~ de qc** (*personne*) to act as sth; (*chose*) to serve as sth; **d'~** (*par voie d'autorité*) officially; (*en vertu d'un règlement*) automatically; (*sans demander*) without any consultation

officiel(le) [ɔfisjɛl] **I.** *adj* official; **de source ~le** from official sources **II.** *m(f)* official

officiellement [ɔfisjɛlmɑ̃] *adv* officially

officier [ɔfisje] *m* **1.** ADMIN, JUR **~ d'état civil** registrar **2.** MIL officer **3.** (*titulaire d'une distinction*) **~ de la Légion d'honneur** Officer of the Legion of Honour *Brit*, Officer of the Legion of Honor *Am*; **~ de l'ordre du mérite** Officer of the Order of Merit

officieux, -euse [ɔfisjø, -jøz] *adj* unofficial

offrande [ɔfʀɑ̃d] *f* REL offering

offrant [ɔfʀɑ̃] *m* **le plus ~** the highest bidder

offre [ɔfʀ] *f* **1.** (*proposition*) offer; ECON supply; **~ de paix/d'emplois** offer of peace/job advertisement **2.** (*aux enchères*) bid

offrir [ɔfʀiʀ] <11> **I.** *vt* **1.** (*faire un cadeau*) **~ qc à qn** to give sb sth **2.** (*proposer*) **~ le bras à qn** to offer sb one's arm; **~ à qn de faire qc** to offer to do sth for sb; **je vous offre 20 euros pour le vase** I'll offer you 20 euros for the vase; **il nous a offert le déjeuner** he gave us lunch **3.** (*comporter: avantages, inconvénients*) to have; (*difficulté*) to present **II.** *vpr* **1.** (*se présenter*) **s'~ à qn/qc** to reveal oneself to sb/sth **2.** (*se proposer*) **s'~ pour** +*infin* to volunteer to +*infin* **3.** (*s'accorder*) to treat oneself; **s'~ des vacances** to take oneself on holiday *Brit*, to treat oneself to a vacation *Am*

offusquer [ɔfyske] <1> **I.** *vt* to offend **II.** *vpr* **s'~ de qc** to take offence at sth *Brit*, to take offense at sth *Am*

ogive [ɔʒiv] *f* **1.** MIL warhead **2.** ARCHIT diagonal rib

ogre, ogresse [ɔgʀ, ɔgʀɛs] *m, f* **1.** (*géant vorace dans les contes de fées*) ogre *m*, ogress *f* **2.** *inf* (*gourmand*) pig ▸**manger comme un ~** *inf* to eat like a horse

oh [o] **I.** *interj* oh **II.** *m inv* **pousser des ~ et des ah de surprise** to ooh and aah with surprise

ohé [oe] *interj* hey

oie [wa] *f* **1.** (*oiseau*) goose **2.** *inf* (*personne niaise*) silly goose

oignon [ɔɲɔ̃] *m* **1.** GASTR onion **2.** BOT bulb ▸**aux petits ~s** *inf* first-rate; **c'est pas mes/tes ~s** *inf* it is none of my/your business; **occupe-toi de tes ~s!** *inf* mind your own business!

oiseau [wazo] <x> *m* **1.** (*en ornithologie*) bird **2.** *péj* (*type*) character ▸**~ de mauvais augure** [*o* **de malheur**] bird of ill omen; **petit à petit, l'~ fait son nid** *prov* slowly and surely wins the race; **à vol d'~, Marseille est à 200 kilomètres de Lyon** as the crow flies, Marseilles is 200 kilometres from Lyons *Brit*, as the crow flies, Marseilles is 200 kilometers from Lyons *Am*

oisellerie [wazɛlʀi] *f* bird shop

oiseux, -euse [wazø, -øz] *adj* pointless

oisif, -ive [wazif, -iv] **I.** *adj* idle **II.** *m, f* idler

oisillon [wazijɔ̃] *m* fledgling

oisiveté [wazivte] *f* idleness

OK [ɔke] *abr de* **oll korrect** OK

olé [ɔle] **I.** *interj* olé **II.** *adj inv, inf* **~ ~** naughty

oléagineux [ɔleaʒinø] *m* oil-producing plant

oléagineux, -euse [ɔleaʒinø, -øz] *adj* oil-producing

oléoduc [ɔleɔdyk] *m* oil pipeline

olfactif, -ive [ɔlfaktif, -iv] *adj* olfactory

olive [ɔliv] **I.** *f* olive **II.** *adj inv* olive

olivier [ɔlivje] *m* **1.** (*arbre*) olive tree **2.** (*bois*) olive wood

OLP [oɛlpe] *f abr de* **Organisation de libération de la Palestine** PLO

olympiade [ɔlɛ̃pjad] *f* Olympiad

olympien(ne) [ɔlɛ̃pjɛ̃, jɛn] *adj* Olympian

olympique [ɔlɛ̃pik] *adj* Olympic

ombilical(e) [ɔ̃bilikal, o] <-aux> *adj* (*cordon*) umbilical

ombrage [ɔ̃bʀaʒ] *m* **1.** (*feuillage*) shade **2.** (*offense*) offence *Brit*, offense *Am*

ombragé(e) [ɔ̃bʀaʒe] *adj* shady

ombrager [ɔ̃bʀaʒe] <2a> *vt* to shade

ombrageux, -euse [ɔ̃bʀaʒø, -ʒøz] *adj* (*susceptible: caractère*) prickly; (*personne*) touchy

ombre [ɔ̃bʀ] *f* **1.** (*opp: soleil*) shade; **à l'~** in the shade; **~s chinoises** shadowgraphs **2.** (*soupçon*) **il n'y a pas l'~ d'un doute/soupçon** there is not a shadow of a doubt/suspicion; **sans l'~ d'une hésitation** without a hint of hesitation **3.** (*maquillage*) **~ à paupières** eyeshadow ▸**il y a une ~ au tableau** there is a fly in the ointment; **faire de l'~ à qn** to overshadow sb; **mettre qn à l'~** *inf* to lock sb up; **vivre dans l'~ de qn** to live in sb's shadow

ombrelle [ɔ̃bʀɛl] *f* parasol

omelette [ɔmlɛt] *f* GASTR omlette; **~ aux champignons/au fromage** mushroom/cheese omlette

omettre [ɔmɛtʀ] *vt irr* **1.** (*négliger*) **~ de** +*infin* to omit [*o* fail] to +*infin* **2.** (*oublier*) **~ qn/qc** to leave sb/sth out

omis [ɔmi] *passé simple de* **omettre**

omis(e) [ɔmi, iz] *part passé de* **omettre**

omission [ɔmisjɔ̃] *f* **1.** (*fait d'omettre qc, chose omise: d'un mot, détail*) omission **2.** (*fait d'omettre de faire qc, acte omis*) oversight

omnibus [ɔmnibys] **I.** *m* CHEMDFER stopping train **II.** *app* (*train*) stopping

omnipotent(e) [ɔmnipɔtɑ̃, ɑ̃t] *adj* omnipotent

omniprésent(e) [ɔmnipʀezɑ̃, ɑ̃t] *adj* omnipresent

omniscient(**e**) [ɔmnisjɑ̃, jɑ̃t] *adj* omniscient

omnisports [ɔmnispɔʀ] *adj inv* general purpose; (*club, salle*) sports

omnivore [ɔmnivɔʀ] *adj* omnivorous

omoplate [ɔmɔplat] *f* shoulder blade

on [ɔ̃] *pron pers* **1.** (*tout le monde*) people; (*toute personne*) one, you; ~ **dit qu'elle l'a fait** they say that she did it; **en France, ~ boit du vin** in France, people drink wine; **après un moment, on n'y pense plus** after a while you don't think about it any more; **on peut imaginer une autre solution** another solution can be envisaged **2.** (*quelqu'un*) somebody; ~ **vous demande au téléphone** somebody wants to speak to you on the telephone; **j'attends qu'**~ [*o* **que l'**~] **apporte le dessert** I'm waiting for the dessert to come **3.** *inf* (*nous*) we; ~ **s'en va!** off we go!; **nous,** ~ **veut bien!** we would love to!; ~ **fait ce qu'**~ [*o* **que l'**~] **peut** we're doing what we can **4.** *inf* (*tu, vous*) you; **alors Marie,** ~ **s'en va déjà?** so Marie, are you off already? **5.** *inf* (*il(s), elle(s)*) **qu'**~ [*o* **que l'**~] **est jolie aujourd'hui!** aren't they pretty today! **6.** (*je, moi*) **oui, oui,** ~ **va le faire!** yeah, yeah, I'll do it!

once [ɔ̃s] *f* **1.** (*une très petite quantité*) **une ~ de bon sens** an ounce of common sense **2.** (*mesure de poids*) ounce

oncle [ɔ̃kl] *m* uncle

onctueux, **-euse** [ɔ̃ktɥø, -øz] *adj* **1.** (*moelleux, lisse: potage, sauce*) smooth **2.** (*doux au toucher*) smooth; (*crème*) creamy

onctuosité [ɔ̃ktɥozite] *f* (*d'un potage, d'une sauce*) smoothness; (*d'une crème*) creaminess

onde [ɔ̃d] *f* **1.** PHYS, RADIO wave; **~s courtes/moyennes** short/medium wave; **petites/grandes ~s** short/long wave; **passer sur les ~s** to be broadcast on the radio **2.** *pl* (*ondulation: blé, foule*) waves ►**être sur la même longueur d'~s** *inf* to be on the same wavelength

ondée [ɔ̃de] *f* shower

on-dit [ɔ̃di] *m inv* hearsay

ondulation [ɔ̃dylasjɔ̃] *f* **1.** (*mouvement onduleux, ligne sinueuse: du blé, des vagues*) undulation; **les ~s du terrain** the undulations of the land **2.** (*vagues: des cheveux*) waves *pl*

ondulé(**e**) [ɔ̃dyle] *adj* (*cheveux*) wavy; (*route, surface*) undulating; (*carton, tôle*) corrugated

onduler [ɔ̃dyle] <1> **I.** *vi* **1.** (*ondoyer: blé, vague*) to undulate; (*serpent*) to slither **2.** (*être sinueux: route*) to snake; (*cheveux*) to wave **II.** *vt* (*cheveux*) to wave

onéreux, **-euse** [ɔneʀø, -øz] *adj* expensive; (*loyer, marchandise*) costly; **à titre** ~ against payment

ongle [ɔ̃gl] *m* ANAT nail; **~s des pieds et des mains** fingernails and toenails; **se faire les ~s** to do one's nails

onglée [ɔ̃gle] *f* **j'ai l'**~ the tips of my fingers are frozen numb

onglet [ɔ̃glɛ] *m* **1.** (*encoche*) tab **2.** (*entaille: d'un canif, d'une règle*) groove

onomatopée [ɔnɔmatɔpe] *f* LING onomatopoeia

ont [ɔ̃] *indic prés de* **avoir**

Ontario [ɔ̃taʀjo] *m* **l'**~ Ontario

ONU [ony] *f abr de* **Organisation des Nations unies** U.N.

onze [ɔ̃z] **I.** *adj* eleven **II.** *m inv* eleven; *v. a.* **cinq**

onzième [ɔ̃zjɛm] **I.** *adj antéposé* eleventh **II.** *mf* **le/la** ~ the eleventh **III.** *m* (*fraction*) eleventh; *v. a.* **cinquième**

opale [ɔpal] *f* opal

opaline [ɔpalin] *f* (*matière, objet*) opaline

opaque [ɔpak] *adj* **1.** (*opp: transparent*) opaque **2.** (*dense: brouillard*) thick; (*obscurité*) impenetrable

opéra [ɔpeʀa] *m* opera

opérable [ɔpeʀabl] *adj* operable

opéra-comique [ɔpeʀakɔmik] <opéras-comiques> *m* comic opera

opérant(**e**) [ɔpeʀɑ̃, ɑ̃t] *adj* effective

opérateur [ɔpeʀatœʀ] *m* INFOR, MAT operator; ~ **du système** system operator; ~ **de téléphonie numérique mobile** digital mobile telephone network operator

opérateur, **-trice** [ɔpeʀatœʀ, -tʀis] *m, f* **1.** TECH, TEL operator; ~ **de saisie** keyboard operator **2.** FIN dealer

opération [ɔpeʀasjɔ̃] *f* **1.** MED, MAT, MIL operation; ~ **de publicité** publicity campaign; ~ **de police/sauvetage** police/rescue operation; **l'**~ **ville propre** anti-litter campaign **2.** (*transaction*) deal; **~s boursières** stock transactions

opérationnel(**le**) [ɔpeʀasjɔnɛl] *adj* operational

opératoire [ɔpeʀatwaʀ] *adj* MED (*bloc, technique*) operating; (*choc, dépression*) post-operative

opéré(**e**) [ɔpeʀe] *m(f)* patient

opérer [ɔpeʀe] <5> **I.** *vt* **1.** MED ~ **qn de qc** to operate on sb for sth; ~ **qn du rein** to operate on sb's kidney **2.** (*provoquer*) ~ **un changement** to bring about a change **3.** (*réaliser: choix*) to make; (*réforme*) to achieve **II.** *vi* **1.** (*produire: charme, médicament*) to work **2.** (*procéder*) to act **III.** *vpr* **s'**~ **1.** (*se réaliser*) to happen **2.** MED to be operated on

opérette [ɔpeʀɛt] *f* MUS operetta

ophtalmo *inf,* **ophtalmologiste** [ɔftalmɔlɔʒist] *mf,* **ophtalmologue** [ɔftalmɔlɔg] *mf* opthalmologist

opinel® [ɔpinɛl] *m* Opinel knife® (*type of penknife*)

opiner [ɔpine] <1> *vi* ~ **de la tête** to nod one's assent; ~ **à qc** to agree to sth

opiniâtre [ɔpinjɑtʀ] *adj* **1.** (*obstiné: travail, efforts*) dogged; (*résistance, haine*) unrelenting; (*personne, caractère*) obstinate **2.** (*tenace: fièvre, toux*) stubborn

opiniâtreté [ɔpinjɑtʀəte] *f* **1.** (*persévérance*) persistence **2.** (*entêtement*) stubbornness

opinion [ɔpinjɔ̃] *f* **1.** (*avis*) opinion; **avoir une ~ sur un sujet** to have an opinion on a subject; **se faire une ~** to form an opinion **2.** (*jugement collectif*) **l'~ publique** public opinion; **l'~ française** French public opinion **3.** *gén pl* (*convictions*) **(à) chacun ses ~s** to each his own; **liberté d'~** freedom of opinion

opiomane [ɔpjɔman] *mf* opium addict

opium [ɔpjɔm] *m* opium

opportun(e) [ɔpɔʀtœ̃, yn] *adj* (*démarche, intervention*) timely; **en temps ~** at the right time; **au moment ~** at the right moment

opportunément [ɔpɔʀtynemɑ̃] *adv* opportunely

opportuniste [ɔpɔʀtynist] **I.** *adj* opportunist **II.** *mf* opportunist

opportunité [ɔpɔʀtynite] *f* **1.** (*bien-fondé*) timeliness **2.** (*occasion*) opportunity

opposant(e) [ɔpozɑ̃, ɑ̃t] **I.** *m(f)* opponent; **les ~s à qn/qc** the opponents to sb/sth **II.** *adj* (*qui s'oppose à*) *a.* JUR opposing

opposé [ɔpoze] *m* opposite ►**à l'~** (*dans l'autre direction*) the other way; (*au contraire*) directly opposite; **à l'~ de qn/qc** unlike sb/sth

opposé(e) [ɔpoze] *adj* **1.** (*d'en face*) *a.* PHYS opposing; MAT opposite **2.** (*contraire: avis, intérêt*) conflicting; (*caractère, goût*) opposing **3.** (*hostile*) **être ~ à qc** to be opposed to sth

opposer [ɔpoze] <1> **I.** *vt* **1.** (*comparer*) **~ des personnes/des choses** to compare people/things; **~ qn/qc et [*o* à] qn/qc** to compare sb/sth with sb/sth **2.** MIL **le conflit oppose les deux nations** the conflict opposes the two nations **3.** SPORT **ce match oppose l'équipe X à [*o* et] l'équipe Y** this match pits team X against team Y **4.** (*répondre par*) **~ un refus à qn** to refuse sb **5.** (*objecter*) **~ des arguments/raisons à qn/qc** to put forward arguments/reasons against sb/sth **II.** *vpr* **1.** (*faire obstacle*) **s'~ à qn/qc** to oppose sb/sth **2.** (*faire contraste*) **s'~** to contrast

opposition [ɔpozisjɔ̃] *f* **1.** (*résistance*) **~ à qc** opposition to sth; **faire/mettre ~ à qc** to oppose sth; **faire de l'~** to mount opposition **2.** (*différence: des opinions, caractères*) clash; **des ~s d'intérêt** conflict of interest; **être/entrer en ~ avec qn sur un point particulier** to be opposed to/oppose sb over a particular point **3.** (*combat*) **~ de deux adversaires** opposition of two adversaries **4.** POL the opposition; **les partis/journaux d'~** the opposition parties/newspapers ►**faire ~ à un paiement** to countermand a payment; **faire ~ à un chèque** to stop a cheque *Brit,* to stop payment on a check *Am;* **en ~** at odds; **par ~** in contrast; **par ~ à qn/qc** (*contrairement*) in contrast to sb/sth; (*par défi*) as opposed to sb/sth

oppressant(e) [ɔpʀesɑ̃, ɑ̃t] *adj* oppressive

oppressé [ɔpʀese] *adj* unable to breathe

oppresser [ɔpʀese] <1> *vt* **1.** (*angoisser: sentiment, souvenir*) to oppress **2.** (*suffoquer: chaleur, temps*) to stifle

oppresseur, -euse [ɔpʀesœʀ] *m, f* oppressor

oppression [ɔpʀesjɔ̃] *f* **1.** (*tyrannie, angoisse*) oppression **2.** (*suffocation*) stifling feeling

opprimé(e) [ɔpʀime] *m(f)* victim; **les ~s** the oppressed

opprimer [ɔpʀime] <1> *vt* to oppress

opter [ɔpte] <1> *vi* **~ pour qc** to opt for sth

opticien(ne) [ɔptisjɛ̃, jɛn] *m(f)* optician

optimal(e) [ɔptimal, o] <-aux> *adj* optimum

optimisme [ɔptimism] *m* optimism

optimiste [ɔptimist] **I.** *adj* optimistic **II.** *mf* optimist

option [ɔpsjɔ̃] *f* **1.** (*choix*) choice **2.** ECOLE option, elective *Am* **3.** (*promesse d'achat*) **prendre une ~ sur une maison** to take an option on a house **4.** AUTO optional extra

optique [ɔptik] **I.** *adj* (*nerf*) optic; (*verre, centre*) optical **II.** *f* **1.** (*science, lentille*) optics + *vb sing;* **appareils/instruments d'~** optical devices/instruments **2.** (*point de vue*) perspective; **dans [*o* vu sous] cette ~** in this perspective

opulence [ɔpylɑ̃s] *f* **1.** (*richesse*) wealth **2.** (*ampleur: des formes*) fullness

opulent(e) [ɔpylɑ̃, ɑ̃t] *adj* **1.** (*très riche: personne, pays*) rich; (*vie*) opulent **2.** (*plantureux: formes, poitrine*) ample

opus [ɔpys] *m* opus

opuscule [ɔpyskyl] *m* opuscule

or[1] [ɔʀ] **I.** *m* gold; **d'~/en ~** made of gold ►**pour tout l'~ du monde** for all the tea in China; **être cousu d'~** to be very rich; **rouler sur l'~** to be rolling in money; **affaire en ~** a bargain; **caractère/personne en ~** wonderful character/person; **sujet en ~** superb subject **II.** *app inv* **1.** (*couleur*) *a.* FIN gold **2.** COM **les bijoux ~** gold jewellery *Brit,* gold jewelry *Am*

or[2] [ɔʀ] *conj* **1.** (*dans un syllogisme*) now **2.** (*transition*) but

oracle [ɔʀakl] *m* oracle

orage [ɔʀaʒ] *m* **1.** METEO storm; **le temps est à l'~** there's a storm coming **2.** (*dispute*) upset ►**il y a de l'~ dans l'air** *inf* there's a storm brewing

orageux, -euse [ɔʀaʒø, -ʒøz] *adj* **1.** METEO stormy; (*pluie*) thundery; (*nuage*) thunder **2.** (*agité, houleux: adolescence, époque*) turbulent; (*discussion*) stormy

oraison [ɔʀɛzɔ̃] *f* REL **1.** (*lecture*) oration **2.** (*méditation*) prayer ►**~ funèbre** funeral oration

oral [ɔʀal, o] <-aux> *m* oral (exam)

oral(e) [ɔʀal, o] <-aux> *adj* **1.** (*opp: écrit*) oral **2.** (*buccal: cavité*) oral; **prendre par voie ~e** take by mouth **3.** PSYCH (*stade*) oral

oralement [ɔʀalmɑ̃] *adv* orally

orange [ɔʀɑ̃ʒ] **I.** *f* orange; ~ **amère/sanguine** bitter/blood orange; **glace à l'~** orange ice-cream; **confiture d'~** orange marmelade **II.** *m* **1.** (*couleur*) orange **2.** AUTO amber *Brit,* yellow *Am;* **le feu passe/est à l'~** the lights are changing to/are on amber; **passer à l'~** (*voiture*) to go through on amber **III.** *adj inv* orange

orangé [ɔʀɑ̃ʒe] *m* orangey colour *Brit,* orangey color *Am*

orangé(e) [ɔʀɑ̃ʒe] *adj* orangey

orangeade [ɔʀɑ̃ʒad] *f* orangeade

oranger [ɔʀɑ̃ʒe] *m* orange tree

orangeraie [ɔʀɑ̃ʒʀɛ] *f* orange grove

orangerie [ɔʀɑ̃ʒʀi] *f* orangery

orang-outan(g) [ɔʀɑ̃utɑ̃] <orangs-outan(g)s> *m* orang-utan *Brit,* orangutan *Am*

orateur, -trice [ɔʀatœʀ, -tʀis] *m, f* speaker

orbite [ɔʀbit] *f* **1.** ANAT (eye-)socket **2.** ASTR orbit **3.** (*sphère d'influence*) **être dans l'~ de qn** to be in sb's sphere of influence

Orcades [ɔʀkad(ə)] *fpl* **les îles ~** the Orkney Isles; **les ~ du Sud** South Orkney + *vb sing*

orchestral(e) [ɔʀkɛstʀal, o] <-aux> *adj* orchestral

orchestre [ɔʀkɛstʀ] *m* **1.** MUS orchestra; ~ **à cordes** string orchestra; ~ **de cuivres** brass band **2.** (*emplacement*) stalls *pl;* **fosse d'~** orchestra pit **3.** THEAT, CINE (*place de devant*) stalls seat; (*public assis devant*) front stalls *pl*

orchestrer [ɔʀkɛstʀe] <1> *vt* **1.** MUS to orchestrate **2.** (*organiser: campagne de presse, de publicité*) to orchestrate; (*manifestation*) to organize

orchidée [ɔʀkide] *f* orchid

ordinaire [ɔʀdinɛʀ] **I.** *adj* **1.** (*habituel: événement, fait*) ordinary; (*réaction, geste*) usual **2.** (*courant: produit*) everyday **3.** *péj* (*médiocre*) average ▸**ça, alors, c'est pas ~!** *inf* that is unusual **II.** *m* **1.** (*banalité, habitude*) ordinary; **une intelligence au-dessus de l'~** an above-average intelligence; **ça change de l'~** that's a change; **comme à l'~** as usual; **d'~** ordinarily **2.** (*menu habituel*) everyday menu

ordinairement [ɔʀdinɛʀmɑ̃] *adv* ordinarily

ordinal [ɔʀdinal, o] <-aux> *m* ordinal (number)

ordinal(e) [ɔʀdinal, o] <-aux> *adj* ordinal

ordinateur [ɔʀdinatœʀ] *m* computer; ~ **personnel** personal computer; ~ **portable** laptop computer; ~ **de table** desktop computer; **assisté par ~** computer-assisted; **travailler sur ~** to work on computer; **éteindre l'~** to shut down the computer; **mettre l'~ sous tension** [*o* **en marche**] to turn on the computer

ordination [ɔʀdinasjɔ̃] *f* ordination

ordinogramme [ɔʀdinɔgʀam] *m* flow chart

ordonnance [ɔʀdɔnɑ̃s] *f* **1.** MED prescription; **médicament délivré sur ~** prescription medicine **2.** JUR order **3.** (*disposition: d'une phrase*) structure; (*d'un poème, d'un tableau*) layout; (*d'une cérémonie*) organization; (*d'un appartement, repas*) order

ordonné(e) [ɔʀdɔne] *adj* **1.** (*méthodique: personne*) methodical **2.** (*qui a de l'ordre*) orderly **3.** (*opp: confus: vie*) orderly; (*maison*) tidy

ordonnée [ɔʀdɔne] *f* MAT ordinate

ordonner [ɔʀdɔne] <1> **I.** *vt* **1.** (*arranger*) to arrange; MAT to arrange in order **2.** (*commander*) ~ **qc à qn** to order sth for sb; MED to prescribe sth for sb; ~ **que** +*subj* to order sb to +*infin* **3.** REL to ordain **II.** *vpr* (*s'organiser*) **mes idées se sont ordonnées** my ideas are organized

ordre¹ [ɔʀdʀ] *m* **1.** (*caractère ordonné: d'une pièce, personne*) tidiness; **avoir de l'~** to be tidy; **mettre sa chambre en ~** to tidy one's room **2.** (*classement, organisation, stabilité sociale, association honorifique, congrégation*) *a.* BOT, ZOOL, HIST order; **par ~ alphabétique** in alphabetical order; **tiercé dans l'~** tiercé in the right order; **faire régner l'~** to keep order; **rappeler qn à l'~** to call sb to order; **rentrer dans l'~** to return to normal **3.** (*genre*) nature; **d'~ politique/économique** of a political/economic nature **4.** (*association*) association; REL order ▸**c'est dans l'~ des <u>choses</u>** it's in the order of things; **un ~ de <u>grandeur</u>** a rough idea; **dans le même ~ d'<u>idées</u>** while we're on the subject; **dans un autre ~ d'<u>idées</u>** in a different way; **mettre <u>bon</u> ~ à qc** to sort sth out; **<u>de</u> l'~ de** of roughly; **<u>de</u> premier/deuxième ~** first-/second-rate; **<u>en</u> ~** in order

ordre² [ɔʀdʀ] *m* **1.** (*commandement*) order; **donner l'~ à qn de** +*infin* to give sb the order to +*infin;* **être aux ~s de qn** to be at sb's orders; **être sous les ~s de qn** to be under sb's command; **à vos ~s!** yes sir!; ~ **de mission** order to travel; ~ **de route** marching orders **2.** (*directives*) order; **sur ~ du médecin** on doctor's orders; ~ **de grève** strike call **3.** (*commande*) order; ~ **d'achat/de vente** purchase/sale order; **par ~** by order ▸~ **du <u>jour</u>** agenda; **être à l'~ du jour** to be on the agenda; **jusqu'à <u>nouvel</u> ~** until further instructions; **<u>à</u> l'~ de** payable to

ordure [ɔʀdyʀ] *f* **1.** *pl* (*détritus, objets usés*) rubbish *no pl Brit,* garbage *no pl Am;* **jeter/mettre qc aux ~s** to throw sth away **2.** *inf* (*personne*) swine; **se conduire comme une ~** to behave like a bastard **3.** *pl* (*propos obscènes*) filth *no pl*

ordurier, -ière [ɔʀdyʀje, -jɛʀ] *adj* filthy

orée [ɔʀe] *f* (*d'un bois, d'une forêt*) edge ▸**<u>à</u> l'~ de qc** (*au début de*) on the verge of sth; **à l'~ de la forêt** (*en lisière de*) on the edge of the forest

oreille [ɔʀɛj] *f* **1.** ANAT ear; **des ~s décollées** protruding ears **2.** (*ouïe*) **avoir l'~ fine** (*entendre bien*) to have a good sense of hearing;

(*percevoir les nuances*) to have a sharp ear; **avoir l'~ juste** [*o* **de l'~**] to have a good ear (for music) **3.** (*appuie-tête*) headrest; **un fauteuil à ~s** a wing-chair ►**avoir les ~s en feuille de chou** *inf* to have cauliflower ears; **n'être pas tombé dans l'~ d'un sourd** not to fall on deaf ears; (*conseil, proposition*) to be taken notice of; **être dur d'~** to be hard of hearing; **faire la sourde ~** to turn a deaf ear; **casser** [*o* **(é)chauffer**] **les ~s à qn** to deafen sb; **dormir sur ses deux ~s** to sleep soundly; **dresser** [*o* **tendre**] **l'~** to prick up one's ears; **n'écouter que d'une ~** to listen with half an ear; **je ne l'entends pas de cette ~** I'm not having it; **prêter l'~ à qn/qc** to listen to sb/sth; **rebattre les ~s à qn avec qc** to go on about sth to sb; **se faire tirer l'~** to need a lot of persuading; **jusqu'aux ~s** up to one's eyes

oreiller [ɔʀeje] *m* pillow

oreillette [ɔʀɛjɛt] *f* **1.** ANAT auricle **2.** COUT earflap; **à ~s** with earflaps

oreillons [ɔʀɛjɔ̃] *mpl* mumps

ores [ɔʀ] **d'~ et déjà** *soutenu* already

orfèvre [ɔʀfɛvʀ] *mf* goldsmith

orfèvrerie [ɔʀfɛvʀəʀi] *f* **1.** (*travail*) gold work **2.** (*art*) goldsmithing **3.** (*objet*) gold plate *no pl*

organe [ɔʀgan] *m* **1.** ANAT organ; **les ~s de la digestion/respiration** the respiratory/digestive organs **2.** (*porte-parole*) mouthpiece **3.** (*instrument*) instrument **4.** (*voix*) organ **5.** ADMIN **les ~s directeurs** [*o* **dirigeants**] **d'un parti** the leadership of a party

organigramme [ɔʀganigʀam] *m* **1.** ADMIN organizational chart **2.** INFOR flow chart

organique [ɔʀganik] *adj* organic

organisateur [ɔʀganizatœʀ] *m* INFOR organizer

organisateur, -trice [ɔʀganizatœʀ, -tʀis] **I.** *adj* organizing **II.** *m, f* organizer; (*d'une manifestation, d'un voyage*) leader; **tes talents d'~** your organizational skills

organisation [ɔʀganizasjɔ̃] *f* organization; **avoir une bonne ~ de son emploi du temps** to have a well-organized timetable; **l'~ des services** the structure of services; **~ syndicale** trade union organization *Brit,* labor union organization *Am*

organisé(e) [ɔʀganize] *adj* **1.** (*structuré, méthodique*) organized; **être ~ dans son travail** to be organized in one's work **2.** *inf* (*manifeste*) **c'est du vol ~!** it's daylight robbery! *Brit,* it's highway robbery! *Am*

organiser [ɔʀganize] <1> **I.** *vt* **1.** (*préparer, planifier*) to organize **2.** (*structurer*) to set up **II.** *vpr* **s'~ pour qc** to get organized for sth; **savoir s'~** to know how to organize oneself

organisme [ɔʀganism] *m* **1.** BIO organism **2.** ADMIN organization; **~ de crédit/tourisme** credit/tourist company

organiste [ɔʀganist] *mf* organist

orgasme [ɔʀgasm] *m* orgasm

orge [ɔʀʒ] *f* barley

orgie [ɔʀʒi] *f* **1.** (*débauche*) orgy **2.** *iron* (*profusion, excès: de bonbons, de glaces*) profusion; **~ de couleurs** riot of colours *Brit,* riot of colors *Am*

orgue [ɔʀg] **I.** *m* organ; **~ de Barbarie** barrel organ; **tenir l'~** to play the organ **II.** *fpl* organ + *vb sing*

orgueil [ɔʀgœj] *m* **1.** (*fierté*) pride **2.** (*prétention*) arrogance

orgueilleux, -euse [ɔʀgøjø, -jøz] **I.** *adj* **1.** (*fier*) proud **2.** (*prétentieux*) arrogant **II.** *m, f* proud person

Orient [ɔʀjɑ̃] *m* **l'~** the Orient

orientable [ɔʀjɑ̃tabl] *adj* swivelling; (*lampe*) adjustable; (*antenne, bras*) movable

oriental(e) [ɔʀjɑ̃tal, o] <-aux> *adj* **1.** (*situé à l'est d'un lieu*) eastern **2.** (*relatif à l'Orient*) oriental

Oriental(e) [ɔʀjɑ̃tal, o] <-aux> *m(f)* Oriental

orientation [ɔʀjɑ̃tasjɔ̃] *f* **1.** (*position: d'une maison*) aspect; (*du soleil, d'un phare, de lamelles, d'une antenne, d'un avion, navire*) direction; **changer l'~ d'une lampe** to change the position of a lamp **2.** (*tendance, direction: d'une enquête, d'un établissement*) tendency; (*d'une campagne, d'un parti politique*) trend; **l'~ de sa pensée** the trend of her thought; **les nouvelles ~s de la médecine** the new trends in medecine **3.** PSYCH, ECOLE guidance

orienté(e) [ɔʀjɑ̃te] *adj* oriented

orienter [ɔʀjɑ̃te] <1> **I.** *vt* **1.** (*diriger: carte, plan*) to turn; **~ une antenne/un phare vers** [*o* **sur**] **qc** to position [*o* turn] an antenna/headlight towards sth **2.** (*guider*) **~ une activité/conversation vers qc** to turn an activity/conversation toward sth; **~ un touriste/visiteur vers qc** to direct a tourist/visitor towards sth **3.** PSYCH, ECOLE to guide **4.** MAT (*droite, grandeur*) to orient **II.** *vpr* **1.** (*a. fig*) **s'~** to find one's bearings **2.** (*se tourner vers*) **s'~ vers qc** to turn towards sth; **s'~ au nord** (*vent*) to move round to the north

orienteur, -euse [ɔʀjɑ̃tœʀ, -øz] *m, f* careers adviser *Brit,* career counselor *Am*

orifice [ɔʀifis] *m* orifice; (*d'une canalisation*) opening; (*d'un tuyau*) mouth; **les ~s naturels du corps** the natural orifices of the body

oriflamme [ɔʀiflɑm] *f* standard; HIST oriflamme

origan [ɔʀigɑ̃] *m* oregano

originaire [ɔʀiʒinɛʀ] *adj* **être ~ d'une ville/d'un pays** to originally come from a town/country

originairement [ɔʀiʒinɛʀmɑ̃] *adv* originally

original [ɔʀiʒinal, o] <-aux> *m* original

original(e) [ɔʀiʒinal, o] <-aux> **I.** *adj* **1.** (*premier: édition, titre*) first **2.** (*inédit, personnel, authentique: texte, version, gravure, idée*) original **3.** *péj* (*bizarre*) eccentric **II.** *m(f)* eccentric; **arrête de faire l'~!** stop being so weird!

originalité [ɔʀiʒinalite] *f* **1.** (*nouveauté*) novelty **2.** (*élément original*) originality **3.** *péj* (*bizarrerie: d'une personne*) eccentricity

origine [ɔʀiʒin] *f* **1.** (*commencement*) beginning; **à l'~** in the beginning; **dès l'~** from the beginning **2.** (*cause: d'un échec*) cause; **quelle est l'~ de ...?** what caused this ...? **3.** (*ascendance, provenance*) origin ►**des ~s à nos jours** from its origins to the present day; **avoir son ~ dans qc, tirer son ~ de qc** to originate from sth; (*coutume*) to have its origins in sth; **être à l'~ de qc** (*personne*) to be behind sth; **être à l'~ d'un mal** (*chose*) to be the cause of an evil; **appellation/certificat d'~** label/certificate of origin; **un mot d'~ grecque/belge** a word of Greek/Belgian origin; **être d'~ française/ouvrière** to have French origins/a working-class background; **d'~ paysanne/noble** from peasant/noble stock

originel(le) [ɔʀiʒinɛl] *adj* original

originellement [ɔʀiʒinɛlmɑ̃] *adv* originally

oripeaux [ɔʀipo] *mpl* **1.** rags **2.** (*apparence trompeuse*) flashy cloak

ORL [oɛʀɛl] **I.** *mf abr de* **oto-rhino-laryngologiste** E.N.T. specialist **II.** *f abr de* **oto-rhino-laryngologie** E.N.T.

orléanais(e) [ɔʀleanɛ, ɛz] *adj* of Orleans; *v. a.* **ajaccien**

Orléanais(e) [ɔʀleanɛ, ɛz] *m(f)* person from Orleans; *v. a.* **Ajaccien**

Orléans [ɔʀleɑ̃] Orleans

orme [ɔʀm] *m* elm

ormeau [ɔʀmo] <x> *m* **1.** BOT elm **2.** ZOOL abalone

ornement [ɔʀnəmɑ̃] *m* **1.** (*chose décorative*) ornament; **arbre/plante d'~** ornamental tree/plant **2.** (*décoration*) adornment; ARCHIT, ART embellishment; **sans ~s** plain

ornemental(e) [ɔʀnəmɑ̃tal, o] <-aux> *adj* (*style, motif*) decorative; (*plante*) ornamental; **ne pas être très ~** not to be very attractive

ornementation [ɔʀnəmɑ̃tasjɔ̃] *f* ornamentation

ornementer [ɔʀnəmɑ̃te] <1> *vt* to ornament

orner [ɔʀne] <1> **I.** *vt* **1.** (*parer*) to adorn; (*style, vérité*) to embellish **2.** (*servir d'ornement*) to decorate; **être orné de qc** (*objet, vêtements*) to be decorated with sth; (*mur, pièce, salle*) to be adorned with sth **II.** *vpr* **s'~ de qc** (*personne*) to adorn oneself with sth; (*chose*) to be decorated with sth

ornière [ɔʀnjɛʀ] *f* rut ►**sortir de l'~** (*se tirer d'une situation difficile*) to get out of the woods; (*échapper à la routine*) to get out of a rut

ornithologie [ɔʀnitɔlɔʒi] *f* ornithology

ornithologue [ɔʀnitɔlɔg] *mf v.* **ornithologist**

ornithorynque [ɔʀnitɔʀɛ̃k] *m* duck-billed platypus

oronge [ɔʀɔ̃ʒ] *f* agaric; (*amanite des Césars*) Caesar's mushroom; **fausse ~** fly agaric

orphelin(e) [ɔʀfəlɛ̃, in] **I.** *adj* orphan; **se trouver ~** to become an orphan; **~ de père** fatherless; **~ de mère** motherless; **être ~ de père et de mère** to be orphaned **II.** *m(f)* orphan

orphelinat [ɔʀfəlina] *m* orphanage

orphéon [ɔʀfeɔ̃] *m* **1.** (*chorale*) male voice choir; **d'enfants** children's choir **2.** (*fanfare*) brass band

ORSEC [ɔʀsɛk] *abr de* **Organisation des secours** *Organisation dealing with major civil emergencies*

orteil [ɔʀtɛj] *m* toe

ORTF [oɛʀteɛf] *m abr de* **Office de radiodiffusion et télévision française** *former French broadcasting service*

orthodontiste [ɔʀtodɔ̃tist] *mf* orthodontist

orthodoxe [ɔʀtɔdɔks] **I.** *adj* **1.** (*conforme à l'opinion générale, au dogme*) orthodox; **être assez peu ~** to be somewhat unorthodox; **il n'est pas très ~ de** *+infin* it's rather unorthodox to *+infin* **2.** REL Orthodox; **~ russe** Russian Orthodox ►**ne pas être/paraître très ~** to be/seem very unorthodox **II.** *mf* **1.** REL (*chrétien d'une Église orientale*) Orthodox **2.** REL (*opp: hérétique*) orthodox believer **3.** (*légaliste*) orthodox member; **les ~s du parti** the orthodox wing of the party

orthographe [ɔʀtɔgʀaf] *f* spelling; **quelle est l'~ de votre nom?** how do you spell your name?; **réforme de l'~** spelling reform; **avoir une bonne ~** to be good at spelling; **les fautes d'~** spelling mistakes

orthographier [ɔʀtɔgʀafje] <1> *vt* to spell; **comment ce mot est-il orthographié?** how is this word spelled?

orthographique [ɔʀtɔgʀafik] *adj* (*signe*) orthographical; (*règle, système*) spelling

orthopédique [ɔʀtɔpedik] *adj* orthopaedic *Brit*, orthopedic *Am*

orthopédiste [ɔʀtɔpedist] *mf* orthopaedist *Brit*, orthopedist *Am*

orthophoniste [ɔʀtɔfɔnist] *mf* speech therapist

ortie [ɔʀti] *f* (stinging) nettle

orvet [ɔʀvɛ] *m* slow-worm *Brit*, slowworm *Am*

os [ɔs, o] <os> *m* **1.** (*matière*) *a.* ANAT bone; **~ à moelle** marrowbone; **~ de seiche** cuttlebone; **en ~** bone **2.** *pl* (*ossements, restes*) bones ►**ne pas faire de vieux ~** (*ne pas rester longtemps*) not to stay long; *inf* (*mourir rapidement*) not to be long for this world; **il y a un ~** *inf* there's a snag; **tomber sur un ~** *inf* to come across a snag

OS [oɛs] *mf abr de* **ouvrier(-ière) spécialisé(e)** unskilled worker

oscar [ɔskaʀ] *m* **~ de qc** Oscar for sth; (*récompense*) prize for sth

oscillation [ɔsilasjɔ̃] *f* **1.** (*fluctuation: d'un navire*) rocking; (*de la température, tension artérielle*) fluctuation **2.** ELEC, PHYS oscillation

osciller [ɔsile] <1> *vi* **1.** (*balancer*) to oscillate; (*personne*) to rock; (*tête*) to shake; (*flamme*) to flicker; (*pendule*) to swing **2.** (*hésiter, varier*) ~ **entre qc et qc** (*personne*) to waver between sth and sth; (*chose*) to fluctuate between sth and sth

osé(e) [oze] *adj* **1.** (*téméraire*) daring; (*démarche, expédition*) risky **2.** (*choquant*) bold

oseille [ozɛj] *f* **1.** BOT sorrel **2.** *inf* (*argent*) bread, dosh *Brit*

oser [oze] <1> **I.** *vt* **1.** (*risquer*) to dare; **je n'ose penser ce qui serait arrivé si ...** I dare not think what would have happened if ... **2.** (*se permettre de*) **j'ose espérer que ...** I hope that ...; **si j'ose dire** if I may say so **II.** *vi* to dare

osier [ozje] *m* willow; **panier/meubles en** ~ wicker basket/furniture

Oslo [ɔslo] Oslo

ossature [ɔsatyʀ] *f* **1.** frame; **une ~ grêle/robuste** a fragile/sturdy frame; **l'~ de la tête** the bone structure of the head **2.** (*charpente: d'un bateau, immeuble, appareil*) framework; **être doté d'une solide** ~ (*machine*) to have a sturdy frame(work) **3.** (*éléments constitutifs*) structure; (*d'une société*) fabric

osselet [ɔslɛ] *m pl* JEUX jacks

ossements [ɔsmɑ̃] *mpl* bones

osseux, -euse [ɔsø, -øz] *adj* **1.** (*relatif aux os*) bone **2.** (*maigre: corps, main*) bony

ossuaire [ɔsɥɛʀ] *m* (*tas d'ossements, catacombes*) ossuary

ostendais(e) [ɔstɑ̃dɛ, ɛz] *adj* of Ostend; *v. a.* **ajaccien**

Ostendais(e) [ɔstɑ̃dɛ, ɛz] *m(f)* person from Ostend; *v. a.* **Ajaccien**

ostensible [ɔstɑ̃sibl] *adj* (*mépris*) patent; (*geste*) conspicuous

ostensiblement [ɔstɑ̃sibləmɑ̃] *adv* conspicuously; (*manifester*) clearly

ostentation [ɔstɑ̃tasjɔ̃] *f* (*affectation, étalage indiscret*) ostentation; **avec** ~ ostentatiously; **faire ~ de qc** to make a show of sth; **mettre de l'~ dans qc** to be ostentatious about sth

ostentatoire [ɔstɑ̃tatwaʀ] *adj* ostentatious

ostréiculture [ɔstʀeikyltyʀ] *f* oyster farming

otage [ɔtaʒ] *m* hostage

OTAN [ɔtɑ̃] *f abr de* **Organisation du traité de l'Atlantique Nord** NATO

otarie [ɔtaʀi] *f* sea lion

ôter [ote] <1> **I.** *vt* **1.** (*retirer*) to remove; ~ **sa chemise/ses gants** to take one's shirt/gloves off; ~ **un vase de la table** to remove a vase from the table; ~ **un noyau d'une cerise** to remove a stone from a cherry *Brit,* to remove a pit from a cherry *Am* **2.** (*faire disparaître*) ~ **un goût/une odeur** to get rid of a taste/smell; ~ **ses scrupules/remords à qn** to rid sb of their scruples/feelings of remorse **3.** (*débarrasser*) ~ **qc** (*menottes, pansements*) to take sth off; (*prendre: objet, envie*) to take sth away; (*illusion*) to dispel; **cela n'ôte rien à tes mérites** that does not detract from your merit **4.** (*retrancher*) ~ **un nom d'une liste** to take a name off a list; **4 ôté de 9 égale 5** 4 from 9 equals 5 **II.** *vpr* (*s'écarter*) **s'~** to get out of the way ►**ôte-toi de là que je m'y mette!** *iron, inf* move out of the way!

otite [ɔtit] *f* ear infection

oto-rhino [ɔtɔʀino] <oto-rhinos> *mf abr de* **oto-rhino-laryngologiste** ear, nose and throat specialist

oto-rhino-laryngologiste [ɔtɔʀinolaʀɛ̃gɔlɔʒist] <oto-rhino-laryngologistes> *mf* ear, nose and throat specialist

ottoman(e) [ɔtɔmɑ̃, an] *adj* **l'Empire** ~ the Ottoman Empire

ou [u] *conj* **1.** (*alternative, approximation, en d'autres termes*) or; ~ (**bien**) or; ~ (**bien**) ... ~ (**bien**) ... either ... or ...; **c'est l'un ~ l'autre** it's one or the other **2.** (*sinon*) ~ (**alors**) otherwise; **tu m'écoutes, ~ alors tu ...** listen to me, or out you ...

où [u] **I.** *pron* **1.** (*spatial*) where; **là** ~ where; **je le suis partout ~ il va** I follow him everywhere he goes; **d'~ il vient** where he comes from; (*duquel*) which it comes from; **jusqu'~** how far; **par ~ il faut aller** the way to go; **le chemin par ~ nous sommes passés** the way we came **2.** (*temporel: jour, matin, soir*) when, on which; (*moment*) when, at which; (*année, siècle*) in which **3.** (*abstrait*) **à l'allure ~ il va** at the speed he's going at; **au prix ~ j'ai acheté cet appareil** at the price I payed for this camera; **dans l'état ~ tu es** in the state you're in **II.** *adv interrog* **1.** (*spatial*) where; ~ **s'arrêter?** where does one stop?; ~ **aller?** where can we go?; **d'~ êtes-vous?** where are you from?; **jusqu'~** *a. fig* how far; **par** ~ which way **2.** (*abstrait*) ~ **en étais-je?** where was I?; ~ **voulez-vous en venir?** what are you leading up to? **III.** *adv indéf* **1.** (*là où*) where; **par ~ que vous passiez** wherever you went; ~ **les choses se gâtent, c'est lorsque ...** where things go wrong, it's because ... **2.** (*de là*) **d'~ que vienne le vent** wherever the wind comes from; **d'~ l'on peut conclure que ...** from which one can conclude that ...; **d'~ mon étonnement** hence my surprise

ouah [wa] *interj* **1.** (*cri du chien*) woof! **2.** (*exprime l'admiration ou la joie*) ~**!** wow!

ouais [ˈwɛ] *adv inf* **1.** (*oui*) yeah **2.** (*sceptique*) oh yeah? **3.** (*hourra!*) ~**!** hooray!

ouananiche [wananiʃ] *f Québec* (*saumon d'eau douce*) salmon trout

ouate [wat] *f* ~ (**hydrophile**) cotton wool ►**être élevé dans la** ~ to wrapped up in cotton wool

ouaté(e) [wate] *adj* (*bruit, pas*) muffled; (*atmosphère*) cocooned; **les bruits nous arrivent ~s** the sounds we could hear were muffled

ouater [wate] <1> *vt* to quilt

O

oubli [ubli] *m* **1.** (*perte du souvenir*) forgetfulness; ~ **de son nom** forgetting her name; **tomber dans l'**~ to be forgotten **2.** (*étourderie*) oversight; **réparer un** ~ to make up for an oversight; **par** ~ due to an oversight **3.** (*lacune*) lapse (of memory) **4.** (*manquement à: du devoir filial, d'une promesse, règle*) neglect; ~ **du devoir** neglect of duty **5.** (*détachement volontaire*) ~ **de soi-même** selflessness

oublier [ublije] <1> **I.** *vt* **1.** (*ne plus se rappeler*) to forget; **être oublié par qn/qc** to be forgotten by sb/sth; **qc ne doit pas faire** ~ **que ...** sth must not let us forget that ... **2.** (*négliger*) to forget; **se sentir oublié** to feel forgotten; **n'oubliez pas le guide** don't forget the guide; **il ne faudrait pas** ~ **que** one must not forget that; **sans** ~ **le patron/les accessoires** without forgetting the boss/the accessories **3.** (*omettre*) to omit; (*mot, virgule*) to leave out; **avoir oublié qn dans son testament** to have left sb out of [*o* forgotten sb in] one's will **4.** (*évacuer de son esprit: injure, querelle*) to forget **5.** (*manquer à*) to neglect; ~ **un devoir/une obligation** to neglect a duty/obligation **6.** (*laisser par inadvertance*) ~ **qc** to leave sth behind ►**se faire** ~ to keep out of sight **II.** *vpr* **1.** (*sortir de l'esprit*) **qn/qc s'oublie** sb/sth is forgotten **2.** (*ne pas penser à soi*) **s'**~ not to think of oneself; **ne pas s'**~ to remember number one **3.** (*se laisser aller*) **s'**~ to forget oneself **4.** (*faire ses besoins*) **s'**~ (*personne, animal*) to have an accident

oubliettes [ublijɛt] *fpl* **1.** (*placard*) **aux** ~ in cold storage **2.** (*cachot*) dungeon

ouèbe [wɛb] *m inf* (world wide) web

oued [wɛd] *m* wadi

ouest [wɛst] **I.** *m* **l'**~ the west; **à** [*o* **dans**] **l'**~ in the west; **à** [*o* **vers**] **l'**~ to the west; **à l'**~ **de qc** west of sth; **vent d'**~ westerly wind; **les régions de l'**~ the western regions **II.** *adj inv* westerly; (*banlieue, longitude, partie*) western

Ouest [wɛst] *m* West; **les pays de l'**~ the West; **les gens de l'**~ Westerners; **le conflit entre l'Est et l'**~ the conflict between East and West

ouest-allemand(**e**) [wɛstalmɑ̃, ɑ̃d] <ouest-allemands> *adj* West German **ouest-nord-ouest** [wɛstnɔʀwɛst] *m sans pl* west-northwest **ouest-sud-ouest** [wɛstsydwɛst] *m sans pl* west-southwest

ouf [ˊuf] *interj* phew; **faire** ~ to catch one's breath

Ouganda [ugɑ̃da] *m* **l'**~ Uganda

ougandais(**e**) [ugɑ̃dɛ, dɛz] *adj* Ugandan

Ougandais(**e**) [ugɑ̃dɛ, dɛz] *m(f)* Ugandan

oui [ˊwi] **I.** *adv* **1.** (*opp: non*) yes; ~ **ou non?** yes or no?; **répondre par** ~ **ou par non** to give a yes or no reply **2.** (*intensif*) yes indeed; **ah** [*o* **ça**] ~, (**alors**)! oh yes!; **hé** ~! oh yes!; ~ **ou merde?** *inf* yes or no?; **alors, tu arrives,** ~? *inf* so are you coming then?; **que** ~! *inf* I should say so! **3.** (*substitut d'une proposition*) **croire/penser que** ~ to believe/think so; **craindre/dire que** ~ to fear/say so; **je dirais que** ~ I would think so **II.** *m inv* **1.** (*approbation*) yes; ~ **à qn/qc** yes to sb/sth **2.** (*suffrage*) aye ►**pour un** ~ (**ou**) **pour un non** at the least thing

ouï-dire [ˊwidiʀ] *m inv* hearsay; **apprendre qc par** ~ to hear sth at secondhand

ouïe [wi] *f* (*sens*) hearing; ZOOL gill

ouille [ˊuj] *interj* ouch!

ouistiti [ˊwistiti] *m* **1.** ZOOL marmoset **2.** *inf* (*zigoto*) oddball; **être un drôle de** ~ *inf* to be an oddball

ouragan [uʀagɑ̃] *m* **1.** (*tempête*) hurricane **2.** (*déchaînement*) storm; **un** ~ **de clameurs** a storm of protest **3.** (*personne déchaînée*) whirlwind ►**arriver en** [*o* **comme un**] ~ to arrive like a whirlwind

ourlé(**e**) [uʀle] *adj* hemmed

ourler [uʀle] <1> *vt* to hem

ourlet [uʀlɛ] *m* hem

ours [uʀs] **I.** *m* **1.** ZOOL bear; ~ **blanc** [*o* **polaire**]/**brun** polar/brown bear; *v. a.* **ourse** **2.** (*jouet d'enfant*) **un** ~ **en peluche** a teddy bear **3.** *inf* (*misanthrope*) old bear; **vivre comme un** ~ to be at odds with the world ►~ **mal léché** *inf* grumpy so-and-so **II.** *adj inv, inf* gruff

ourse [uʀs] *f* she-bear; *v. a.* **ours** ►**la Grande/Petite Ourse** the Great/Little Bear, the Big/Little Dipper *Am*

oursin [uʀsɛ̃] *m* sea urchin

ourson [uʀsɔ̃] *m* bear cub

oust(**e**) [ˊust] *interj inf* **1.** (*pour chasser qn*) buzz off! **2.** (*pour presser qn*) hurry up!

outil [uti] *m* (*instrument, moyen*) *a.* INFOR tool; ~ **agricole/de recherche** farming/research tool

outillage [utijaʒ] *m* (*d'un artisan, fermier, jardinier*) tools *pl;* (*d'un atelier, d'une usine*) equipment; **une usine d'**~ a tool-making factory

outillé(**e**) [utije] *adj* **être** ~ **pour qc** to have the (right) tools for sth

outiller [utije] <1> **I.** *vt* to equip; **être outillé pour** *+infin* to be equipped to *+infin;* (*établissement*) to be fitted out to *+infin* **II.** *vpr* **s'**~ **en/pour qc** to kit oneself out as/for sth

outrage [utʀaʒ] *m* insult; ~ **à agent** insulting a police officer; ~ **à magistrat** contempt of court; ~ **aux bonnes mœurs** affront to public decency; ~ **à la pudeur** indecent exposure

outrager [utʀaʒe] <2a> *vt* to offend; **d'un air outragé** with an outraged look

outrance [utʀɑ̃s] *f* extravagance; **à** ~ to excess; **la guerre à** ~ all-out war; **avec** ~ extravagantly

outrancier, **-ière** [utʀɑ̃sje, -jɛʀ] *adj* extreme

outre[1] [utʀ] *f* (*sac*) goatskin ►**être gonflé** [*o* **plein**] **comme une** ~ to be full to bursting

outre[2] [utʀ] **I.** *prep* (*en plus de*) as well as; ~ **le fait que cela est connu** besides the fact that it is known **II.** *adv* **en** ~ moreover

outré(e) [utʀe] *adj* **1.** (*indigné*) outraged **2.** (*excessif*) overdone

outre-Atlantique [utʀatlɑ̃tik] *adv* across the Atlantic

outrecuidance [utʀəkɥidɑ̃s] *f soutenu* **1.** (*impertinence*) impertinence **2.** (*fatuité*) self-importance

outre-Manche [utʀəmɑ̃ʃ] *adv* across the Channel

outremer [utʀəmɛʀ] **I.** *m* **1.** (*en minéralogie*) lapis lazuli **2.** (*bleu*) ultramarine **II.** *adj inv* ultramarine

outre-mer [utʀəmɛʀ] *adv* overseas

outrepasser [utʀəpɑse] <1> *vt* (*droits, limites, pouvoir*) to overstep; (*ordre*) to exceed

outrer [utʀe] <1> *vt* **1.** (*exagérer*) to exaggerate; ~ **son jeu** (*acteur*) to overact; **être outré** (*portrait*) to be exaggerated **2.** (*scandaliser*) to outrage

outre-Rhin [utʀəʀɛ̃] *adv* across the Rhine

outre-tombe [utʀətɔ̃b] *adv* beyond the grave

outsider [autsajdœʀ] *m* outsider

ouvert(e) [uvɛʀ, ɛʀt] **I.** *part passé de* **ouvrir** **II.** *adj* open; (*robinet*) on; **être grand** ~ (*yeux*) to be wide open; **être** ~ **à qn/qc** to be open to sb/sth

ouvertement [uvɛʀtəmɑ̃] *adv* openly

ouverture [uvɛʀtyʀ] *f* **1.** (*action d'ouvrir, fait de rendre accessible au public, inauguration*) opening; (*d'un robinet*) turning on; **l'~ de cette porte est automatique** this door opens automatically; **les jours/heures d'~** opening days/times; **l'~ au public** opening to the public **2.** (*commencement*) opening; **la séance d'~** opening session **3.** (*orifice*) opening; (*d'un volcan*) mouth **4.** (*attitude ouverte*) openness; ~ **d'esprit** openmindedness; **ton ~ sur le monde** your opening on to the world; **l'~ sur l'Europe** opening up to Europe **5.** *pl* (*avance, proposition: de négociations, paix*) overtures **6.** MUS overture **7.** PHOT aperture **8.** COM, JUR (*d'un compte, d'une information judiciaire*) reading; (*d'un crédit*) setting up; (*d'une succession*) reading **9.** INFOR ~ **d'une session** login ►**faire l'~** *inf* (*d'un magasin*) to open up; (*de la saison*) to go out on the opening day

ouvrable [uvʀabl] *adj* working

ouvrage [uvʀaʒ] **I.** *m* **1.** (*objet fabriqué*) work; ~ **de sculpture** sculpture **2.** (*livre*) ~ **d'histoire** historical work **3.** (*travail*) piece of work; COUT work; **table à** ~ worktable; **se mettre à l'~** to start work ►~ **d'art** work of art **II.** *f inf* **de la belle** ~ a nice piece of work

ouvragé(e) [uvʀaʒe] *adj* finely worked; (*signature*) elaborate

ouvrant(e) [uvʀɑ̃, ɑ̃t] *adj v.* **toit**

ouvré(e) [uvʀe] *adj* (*jour*) working

ouvre-boîte [uvʀəbwat] <ouvre-boîtes> *m* tin-opener *Brit,* can opener *Am* **ouvre-bouteille** [uvʀ(ə)butɛj] <ouvre-bouteilles> *m* bottle opener

ouvreur, -euse [uvʀœʀ, øz] *m, f* CINE, THEAT usher

ouvrier, -ière [uvʀije, -ijɛʀ] **I.** *adj* (*classe, mouvement, quartier, syndicat*) working-class; (*conflit, législation, condition*) industrial; (*militant*) labour *Brit,* labor *Am* **II.** *m, f* (*travailleur manuel*) worker; ~ **d'usine/spécialisé** factory/unskilled worker; ~ **professionnel** [*o* **qualifié**] skilled worker

ouvrière [uvʀijɛʀ] *f* (*abeille, termite, fourmi*) worker

ouvrir [uvʀiʀ] <11> **I.** *vt* **1.** (*opp: fermer, écarter, déployer, rendre accessible, fonder, créer, inaugurer, commencer, percer*) *a.* SPORT, JUR, FIN to open; (*à clé*) to unlock; ~ **grand ses oreilles** to pin back one's ears; ~ **le bec** to open one's mouth; ~ **un crédit à qn** to set up a loan for sb **2.** *inf* (*faire fonctionner: chauffage, télé, robinet, gaz*) to turn on **3.** (*débloquer, frayer*) ~ **une issue/un passage à qn/qc** to open up a way out/way through for sb/sth; ~ **à la navigation** to open to shipping **4.** (*être en tête de: marche, procession*) to lead; ~ **une liste** to head a list **5.** (*provoquer une blessure*) ~ **qc** (*jambe, ventre, crâne*) to cut sth open ►**l'~** *inf* to open one's mouth **II.** *vi* **1.** (*donner sur*) ~ **sur qc** to open on to sth **2.** (*être accessible au public, être rendu accessible au public*) ~ **le lundi** to open on Mondays; ~ **à 15 h** to open at 3 p.m. **3.** (*commencer*) ~ **par qc** to begin with sth **III.** *vpr* **1.** (*opp: se fermer*) **s'~** to open; (*vêtement*) to unfasten; (*foule*) to part; **mal s'~** to open wrongly **2.** (*devenir accessible à*) **s'~ au commerce** to open up for trade; **s'~ à l'extérieur** [*o* **au monde**] to open up to the outside world **3.** (*commencer*) **s'~ par qc** to begin with sth; (*exposition, séance*) to open with sth **4.** (*se blesser*) **s'~ les veines** to slash one's wrists; **s'~ la lèvre** to split one's lip; **s'~ la jambe/le crâne** to cut one's leg/one's head open

ovaire [ɔvɛʀ] *m* ANAT, BOT ovary

ovale [ɔval] **I.** *adj* oval **II.** *m* oval

ovation [ɔvasjɔ̃] *f* ovation; **faire une ~ à qn** to give sb an ovation

ovationner [ɔvasjɔne] <1> *vt* ~ **qn** to give sb an ovation; **se faire ~ par qn** to be given an ovation by sb

overdose [ɔvœʀdoz, ɔvɛʀdoz] *f* overdose

ovin [ɔvɛ̃] *m* sheep

ovin(e) [ɔvɛ̃, in] *adj* (*race*) ovine

ovipare [ɔvipaʀ] **I.** *adj* egg-laying; (*reproduction*) oviparous; **être** ~ to lay eggs **II.** *m* egg-layer

OVNI [ɔvni] *m abr de* **objet volant non identifié** UFO

ovulation [ɔvylasjɔ̃] *f* ovulation

ovule [ɔvyl] *m* **1.** ovum **2.** BOT ovule **3.** MED pessary

oxydation [ɔksidasjɔ̃] *f* oxydation

oxyde [ɔksid] *m* oxide; ~ **de carbone** carbon monoxide

oxyder [ɔkside] <1> *vt, vpr* (**s'**)~ to oxidize

oxygène [ɔksiʒɛn] *m* **1.** CHIM oxygen **2.** (*air pur*) fresh air **3.** (*souffle nouveau*) new lease on life

oxygéné(**e**) [ɔksiʒene] *adj* (*cheveux*) bleached; **eau ~e** hydrogen peroxide

oxygéner [ɔksiʒene] <5> **I.** *vt* (*cheveux*) to bleach **II.** *vpr* **s'~** to bleach one's hair

ozone [ozon, ɔzɔn] *f* ozone

P

P, p [pe] *m inv* P, p; **~ comme Pierre** p as in Peter

PACA [paka] *f abr de* (**région**) **Provence-Alpes-Côte d'Azur** Provence-Alpes-Côte d'Azur region

pachyderme [paʃidɛʀm, pakidɛʀm] *m* elephant

pacifier [pasifje] <1a> *vt* to pacify

pacifique [pasifik] *adj* peaceful; (*personne, pays, peuple*) peace-loving

Pacifique [pasifik] *m* **le ~** the Pacific

pacifiste [pasifist] **I.** *adj* pacifist **II.** *mf* pacifist

pack [pak] *m* pack

pacotille [pakɔtij] *f* **1.** (*mauvaise marchandise*) rubbish; **de ~** cheap; *fig* rubbishy **2.** (*bijoux*) cheap jewellery *Brit*, cheap jewelry *Am*

PACS [paks] *m abr de* **pacte civil de solidarité** *formal civil contract between a non-married heterosexual or homosexual couple*

pacte [pakt] *m* pact; **~ d'alliance** treaty of alliance; **le ~ de Varsovie** HIST the Warsaw Pact

pactiser [paktize] <1> *vi* **1. ~ avec qn** to come to terms with sb **2.** (*transiger*) **~ avec qc** (*crime*) to condone sth; (*conscience*) to smother sth

pactole [paktɔl] *m* gold mine; **~ du loto** lottery jackpot; **c'est le ~** it's a gold mine

paella [pae(l)ja, paela] *f* paella

paf [paf] **I.** *interj* **1.** (*bruit*) wham **2.** *inf* (*et toc*) so there **II.** *adj inv, inf* plastered

pagaïe, pagaille [pagaj] *f inf* mess ▸**mettre la ~ dans qc** to mess sth up; **en ~** in a mess; (*en quantité*) by the bucketload

paganisme [paganism] *m* paganism

pagayer [pageje] <7> *vi* to paddle

page [paʒ] *f* **1.** (*feuillet*) page; **la ~ des sports d'un journal** the sports page in a newspaper; (**en**) **~ 20** on page 20; **la ~ de publicité** the adverts page *Brit*, the ads page *Am* **2.** RADIO, TV **la ~ de publicité** the adverts *Brit*, commercials *Am* **3.** (*événement, épisode*) **une ~ glorieuse de l'histoire** a glorious page in history **4.** INFOR **~ d'accueil/personnelle** [*o* **perso**] home page; **~s visitées** pages visited; **~ Web** [*o* **sur la toile**] Web page; **accéder à une ~** to visit a page; **bas de ~** page bottom; **pied/haut de ~** footer/header; **~ de codes** code page ▸**~ blanche** blank page; **première ~** first page; **tourner la ~** to let bygones be bygones; (*pour recommencer*) to turn over a new leaf

pagination [paʒinasjɔ̃] *f* pagination

pagne [paɲ] *m* loincloth

pagode [pagɔd] **I.** *f* pagoda; **toit en ~** pagoda roof **II.** *app inv* **des manches ~** pagoda sleeves

paie[1] [pɛ] *f* (*d'un ouvrier, salarié*) pay

paie[2] [pɛ] *indic et subj prés de* **payer**

paiement [pɛmɑ̃] *m* payment

païen(**ne**) [pajɛ̃, jɛn] **I.** *adj* **1.** pagan **2.** *soutenu* (*impie*) heathen **II.** *m(f)* **1.** pagan **2.** *soutenu* (*impie*) heathen; **jurer comme un ~** to swear like a trooper

paierai [pɛʀɛ] *fut de* **payer**

paillasse [pajas] *f* **1.** straw mattress **2.** (*plan de travail*) draining board; (*dans un labo*) work surface ▸**crever** [*o* **trouer**] **la ~ à qn** *inf* to cut sb up

paillasson [pajasɔ̃] *m* doormat

paille [pɑj] *f* **1.** *inv* (*chaume, tiges tressées*) straw **2.** (*pour boire*) (drinking) straw ▸**tirer à la courte ~** to draw straws

paillé(**e**) [paje] *adj* (*chaise*) straw-bottomed

pailleté(**e**) [pajte] *adj* sequined

paillette [pɑjɛt] *f* **1.** COUT sequin; **des ~s argentées/d'or** silver/gold sequins **2.** (*lamelle: d'or*) speck; (*de mica, soude, soudure*) flake **3.** (*petite particule*) **en ~s** in flakes; **de la lessive/du savon en ~s** washing/soap flakes

paillote [pɑjɔt] *f* straw hut

pain [pɛ̃] *m* **1.** *inv* (*aliment*) bread; **~ de seigle** rye bread **2.** (*miche*) loaf; **~ de seigle** rye loaf; **un ~ d'un kilo** a kilo loaf; **~ au chocolat** pain au chocolat, *chocolate-filled croissant* **3.** GASTR (*de poisson, légumes*) loaf ▸**ôter** [*o* **retirer**] **à qn le ~ de la bouche** to take the bread out of sb's mouth; **avoir du ~ sur la planche** *inf* to have a lot on one's plate; **petit ~** (bread) roll; **être** (**mis**) **au ~ sec** to be put on bread and water; **gagner son ~** to earn one's living; **elle ne mange pas de ce ~-là** she's not having any of that; **ça ne mange pas de ~** *inf* it won't hurt

pair [pɛʀ] *m* **aller de ~ avec qc** to go hand in hand with sth; **une jeune fille au ~** an au pair (girl); **un jeune homme au ~** a male au pair; **hors** (**de**) **~** unrivalled

pair(**e**) [pɛʀ] *adj* **1.** (*divisible par deux*) even **2.** (*au nombre de deux*) in pairs

paire [pɛʀ] *f* **1.** (*de chaussures, gants, lunettes*) pair; **donner une ~ de claques** [*o* **de gifles**] **à qn** to slap sb's face **2.** (*aux cartes*) pair ▸**c'est une autre ~ de manches** *inf* that's another story; **les deux font la ~** *inf* they're two of a kind

paisible [pezibl] *adj* peaceful

paisiblement [peziblǝmɑ̃] *adv* peacefully

paître [pɛtʀ] *vi, vt irr* to graze; **faire** [*o* **mener**] ~ **des animaux** to graze animals

paix [pɛ] *f* **1.** (*opp: guerre, entente*) peace; **des manifestations en faveur de la** ~ peace demonstrations **2.** (*traité*) peace treaty **3.** (*tranquillité*) **la** ~! *inf* quiet!; **avoir la** ~ to have some peace (and quiet); **laisser qn en** ~ to leave sb in peace ►**faire la** ~ **avec qn** to make (one's) peace with sb; **qu'il repose en** ~! may he rest in peace!

Pakistan [pakistɑ̃] *m* **le** ~ Pakistan

pakistanais(**e**) [pakistanɛ, ɛz] *adj* Pakistani

Pakistanais(**e**) [pakistanɛ, ɛz] *m(f)* Pakistani

palabrer [palabʀe] <1> *vi* to go on (and on)

palabres [palabʀ] *fpl* talk *no pl*

palace [palas] *m* luxury hotel

palais[1] [palɛ] *m* palace; ~ **de l'Elysée** Elysée Palace (*residence of the French President*); ~ **des Papes** Popes' Palace; ~ **des sports** sports stadium

palais[2] [palɛ] *m* ANAT palate ►**avoir le** ~ **fin** to have a delicate palate

Palais [palɛ] *m* ~ **fédéral** *Suisse* Federal Houses of Parliament

palan [palɑ̃] *m* hoist

palanquin [palɑ̃kɛ̃] *m* palanquin

pale [pal] *f* (*d'un aviron, d'une rame, hélice*) blade

pâle [pɑl] *adj* pale

palefrenier, **-ière** [palfʀənje, -jɛʀ] *m, f* ostler

paléontologie [paleɔ̃tɔlɔʒi] *f* palaeontology *Brit*, paleontology *Am*

Palestine [palɛstin] *f* **la** ~ Palestine

palestinien(**ne**) [palɛstinjɛ̃, jɛn] *adj* Palestinian

Palestinien(**ne**) [palɛstinjɛ̃, jɛn] *m(f)* Palestinian

palet [palɛ] *m* **1.** SPORT puck **2.** (*pour jouer à la marelle*) quoit **3.** GASTR *large round chocolate filled with chocolate cream*

paletot [palto] *m* jacket (*thick knitted*); **il m'est tombé sur le** ~ *inf* he jumped on me

palette [palɛt] *f* **1.** (*plateau de chargement*) pallet **2.** (*ensemble de couleurs, ustensile du peintre*) palette **3.** (*gamme*) ~ **de produits** range of products **4.** (*raquette*) ~ **de ping-pong** *Québec* ping-pong bat

pâleur [pɑlœʀ] *f* (*d'une personne, du ciel*) paleness; (*d'un malade*) pallor

pâlichon(**ne**) [pɑliʃɔ̃, ɔn] *adj inf* (*personne*) a bit pale; (*soleil*) watery; (*sourire*) wan

palier [palje] *m* (*plateforme d'escalier*) landing; **habiter sur le même** ~ to live on the same floor

pâlir [pɑliʀ] <8> *vi* (*devenir pâle*) to turn pale ►~ **d'envie** to go green with envy

palissade [palisad] *f* fence

palissandre [palisɑ̃dʀ] *m* rosewood

palliatif [paljatif] *m* **1.** (*mesure provisoire*) stopgap **2.** MED palliative

palliatif, **-ive** [paljatif, -iv] *adj* palliative

pallier [palje] <1a> *vt* **1.** (*compenser*) ~ **qc par qc** to make up for sth with sth **2.** (*atténuer*) ~ **les effets de la crise par qc** to alleviate the effects of the crisis with sth

palmarès [palmaʀɛs] *m* **1.** (*liste des lauréats*) list of (prize)winners **2.** (*ensemble des succès: d'un sportif*) record; (*d'un romancier*) list of bestsellers; (*d'un cinéaste, acteur*) list of successes

palme [palm] *f* **1.** BOT palm leaf **2.** SPORT flipper; ~ **de plongée** diving flipper **3.** (*symbole de victoire*) palm; **remporter la** ~ to win the crown; **décerner la** ~ **à qn** to award the prize to sb **4.** (*décoration*) ~**s académiques** *award for services to teaching*

Palme [palm] *f* ~ **d'or** Palme d'or (*top prize at the Cannes film festival*)

palmé(**e**) [palme] *adj* (*feuille*) palmate; **pied** ~/**patte** ~**e** webbed foot

palmeraie [palməʀɛ] *f* palm grove

palmier [palmje] *m* **1.** BOT palm tree **2.** GASTR *heart-shaped pastry*

palmipède [palmipɛd] **I.** *adj* **oiseau** ~ web-footed bird **II.** *m* palmiped

palombe [palɔ̃b] *f* woodpigeon

pâlot(**te**) [pɑlo, ɔt] *adj* pale-looking

palourde [paluʀd] *f* clam

palper [palpe] <1> *vt* **1.** (*toucher: tissu, fruit, billet de banque*) to feel **2.** MED ~ **l'abdomen à qn** to palpate sb's abdomen

palpitant(**e**) [palpitɑ̃, ɑ̃t] *adj* thrilling

palpiter [palpite] <1> *vi* **1.** (*cœur*) to beat; (*de joie*) to race **2.** (*se contracter: animal*) to quiver; (*paupière*) to flutter; (*narine*) to flare **3.** (*scintiller: flamme, lumière*) to flicker

paluche [palyʃ] *f inf* **1.** paws; **ôte donc tes** ~**s de là!** get your paws off that! **2.** (*grossière et forte*) mitt

paludisme [palydism] *m* malaria

pâmer [pɑme] <1> *vpr* **se** ~ **de joie** to be overjoyed; **se** ~ **d'amour pour qn** to swoon with love for sb; **se** ~ **d'admiration pour qn**/**qc** to swoon over sb/sth

pampa [pɑ̃pa] *f* GEO pampas

pamphlet [pɑ̃flɛ] *m* lampoon

pamplemousse [pɑ̃pləmus] *m* GASTR grapefruit

pan [pɑ̃] *m* **1.** (*basque: d'une chemise, d'un manteau*) tail; **se promener**/**être en** ~**s de chemise** to walk around with/have just one's shirt on **2.** (*partie: de mur*) side; (*d'un immeuble, d'une affiche*) part

panacée [panase] *f* panacea

panache [panaʃ] *m* **1.** (*bravoure*) panache **2.** (*plumet*) plume **3.** (*coiffure, plumes en forme de* ~) plumes *pl* **4.** (*nuage*) ~ **de fumée** plume of smoke

panaché [panaʃe] *m* shandy

Panamá [panama] Panama City; **Canal de** ~ Panama Canal

panaris [panaʀi] *m* whitlow

pancarte [pɑ̃kaʀt] *f* notice; (*d'un manifestant*) placard; ~ **électorale**/**publicitaire** elec-

P

tion/publicity poster

pancréas [pɑ̃kʀeɑs] *m* pancreas

panda [pɑ̃da] *m* ZOOL panda

panégyrique [paneʒiʀik] *m* panegyric; **faire le ~ de qn/qc** to laud sb/sth to the skies

panier [panje] *m* **1.** (*corbeille*) basket; **~ à provisions** shopping basket; **~ à salade** salad shaker **2.** (*contenu*) **~ de cerises** basket of cherries **3.** PHOT magazine **4.** (*au basketball*) basket ►**mettre deux personnes dans le même ~** to lump two people together; **lui, c'est un vrai ~ percé!** he's such a spendthrift!

panière [panjɛʀ] *f* large (two-handled) basket

panier-repas [panjeʀəpɑ] <paniers-repas> *m* packed lunch

panini [panini] *m* panini

panique [panik] **I.** *f* panic; **être pris de ~** to panic; **pas de ~!** don't panic! **II.** *adj* (*peur, terreur*) panic-stricken

paniquer [panike] <1> **I.** *vt inf* **~ qn** to scare the wits out of sb, to put the wind up sb *Brit;* **être paniqué de devoir** *+infin* to be panicking about having to *+infin* **II.** *vi inf* to panic **III.** *vpr* **se ~** to panic

panne [pan] *f* **1.** (*arrêt de fonctionnement*) breakdown; **~ de courant** [*o* **d'électricité**] power failure; **~ de moteur** engine failure; **tomber en ~** (*automobiliste, voiture, moteur, machine*) to break down; **être en ~** (*automobiliste, voiture, moteur*) to have broken down; (*machine*) to be not not working **2.** *inf* (*arrêt*) **être** [*o* **rester**] **en ~** (*personne*) to be stuck; (*projet, travail*) to have come to a halt **3.** *inf* (*manque*) **je suis en ~ de café** I've run out of coffee

panneau [pano] <x> *m* **1.** AUTO **~ de signalisation** road sign **2.** AVIAT, CHEMDFER **~ horaire** (*des arrivées*) arrivals board; (*des départs*) departures board **3.** (*pancarte*) board; **~ d'affichage** (*pour petites annonces, résultats*) notice board *Brit,* bulletin board *Am;* (*pour publicité*) hoarding *Brit,* billboard *Am* **4.** (*au basketball*) backboard **5.** TECH **~ solaire** solar panel ►**tomber/donner dans le ~** to fall/walk right into the trap

panonceau [panɔ̃so] <x> *m* sign

panoplie [panɔpli] *f* **1.** **~ d'armes** armoury *Brit,* armory *Am;* **~ de médicaments** range of medicines; **~ de sanctions** array of sanctions **2.** (*jouet*) **~ d'infirmière/de magicien** nurse's/magician's outfit

panorama [panɔʀama] *m* panorama

panoramique [panɔʀamik] *adj* panoramic; (*restaurant*) with a panoramic view; **écran ~** CINE wide screen

panosse [panɔs] *f Suisse* (*serpillière*) floorcloth

panse [pɑ̃s] *f* **1.** (*d'une vache, brebis*) stomach **2.** *inf* (*ventre*) belly; **s'en mettre plein** [*o* **se remplir**] **la ~** *inf* to stuff one's face

pansement [pɑ̃smɑ̃] *m* **1.** (*action*) **faire un ~ à qn** to bandage sb up **2.** (*compresse*) dressing; **~ adhésif** (sticking) plaster *Brit,* Band-Aid® *Am*

panser [pɑ̃se] <1> *vt* **1.** (*soigner: blessé, jambe, blessure, plaie*) to bandage; **~ la main de qn** to bandage sb's hand **2.** (*guérir: blessure morale, peine*) to heal **3.** (*brosser: cheval*) to groom

pantalon [pɑ̃talɔ̃] *m* (pair of) trousers *Brit,* (pair of) pants *Am*

panthère [pɑ̃tɛʀ] *f* ZOOL panther

pantin [pɑ̃tɛ̃] *m* **1.** (*marionnette*) jumping jack **2.** *fig* **gesticuler comme un ~** to wave one's arms about like a madman; **faire de qn un ~** to make sb one's puppet

pantois(e) [pɑ̃twa, waz] *adj* speechless; **laisser qn ~** to leave sb speechless; **rester ~** to be left speechless

pantomime [pɑ̃tɔmim] *f* **1.** *sans pl* (*jeu du mime*) mime **2.** (*pièce mimée*) mime (show) **3.** (*comédie*) scene

pantouflard(e) [pɑ̃tuflaʀ, aʀd] *inf* **I.** *adj* stay-at-home **II.** *m(f)* stay-at-home

pantoufle [pɑ̃tufl] *f* (carpet) slipper

PAO [peɑo] *f abr de* **production** (**ou publication**) **assistée par ordinateur** CAD

paon [pɑ̃] *m* ZOOL peacock ►**fier comme un ~** (as) proud as a peacock

papa [papa] *m* dad(dy)

papal(e) [papal, o] <-aux> *adj* papal

papauté [papote] *f* papacy

papaye [papaj] *m* pawpaw, papaya

pape [pap] *m* **1.** REL pope **2.** (*d'un mouvement, d'une organisation*) leading light; (*du jazz*) high priest

papelard [paplaʀ] *m inf* **1.** (*feuille*) (bit of) paper **2.** *pl* (*papiers d'identité*) papers

paperasse [papʀas] *f péj* **1.** (*papiers inutiles à lire*) (useless) papers *pl,* bumf *Brit* **2.** (*papiers à remplir*) forms *pl* **3.** (*grosse quantité de papiers*) stack of paper(s)

paperasserie [papʀasʀi] *f péj* **1.** (*papiers inutiles à lire*) paperwork, bumf *Brit* **2.** (*papiers à remplir*) paperwork

papeterie [papɛtʀi] *f* **1.** (*magasin*) stationer's (shop) **2.** (*fabrication*) paper-making (industry) **3.** (*usine*) paper mill

papetier, -ière [pap(ə)tje, -jɛʀ] **I.** *adj* **industrie papetière** paper industry **II.** *m, f* **1.** (*vendeur*) stationer **2.** (*fabricant*) paper manufacturer

papi [papi] *m enfantin, inf v.* **papy**

papier [papje] *m* **1.** *sans pl* (*matière*) paper; **bout/feuille/morceau de ~** bit/sheet/piece of paper; **~ à en-tête** headed (note)paper; **~ à musique** manuscript paper *Brit,* music paper *Am;* **~ hygiénique** toilet paper; **~ peint** wallpaper **2.** *sans pl* (*feuille de métal*) **~ (d')aluminium** aluminium foil *Brit,* aluminum foil *Am* **3.** (*feuille*) piece of paper; (*à remplir*) form **4.** (*article*) article **5.** (*document*) paper **6.** *pl* (*papiers d'identité*) papers ►**réglé comme du ~ à musique** (as) regular as clockwork; **être dans les petits ~s de qn** to be in sb's good books [*o* good graces]

papier-filtre [papjefiltʀ] <papiers-filtres> *m* filter paper **papier-toilette** [papjetwalɛt] <papiers-toilette> *m* toilet paper

papille [papij] *f* taste bud; **être un plaisir pour les ~s (gustatives)** to be a treat for the taste buds

papillon [papijɔ̃] *m* **1.** ZOOL butterfly; **~ de nuit** moth **2.** SPORT (**nage**) ~ butterfly (stroke); **200 m** ~ 200 metres butterfly **3.** *inf* (*contravention*) (parking) ticket

papillonner [papijɔne] <1> *vi* to flit around

papillote [papijɔt] *f* **1.** (*pour les bonbons*) sweet paper *Brit,* candy wrapper *Am* **2.** GASTR **en** ~ *cooked wrapped in greaseproof paper or foil*

papilloter [papijɔte] <1> *vi* (*paupières*) to flutter; (*yeux*) to blink

papoter [papɔte] <1> *vi* to chatter

papouan-néo-guinéen, papouanne-néo-guinéenne [papuɑ̃neɔgineɛ̃, ɛn] *adj* Papua New Guinean

Papouan-Néo-Guinéen, Papouanne-Néo-Guinéenne [papuɑ̃neɔgineɛ̃, ɛn] *m, f* Papua New Guinean

Papouasie-Nouvelle-Guinée [papwazinuvɛlgine] *f* Papua New Guinea

papouille [papuj] *f inf* tickling *no pl*

paprika [papʀika] *m* GASTR paprika

papy [papi] *m enfantin, inf* grandad

papyrus [papiʀys] *m* papyrus

pâque [pɑk] *f* **la ~ (juive)** Passover

paquebot [pakbo] *m* NAUT liner

pâquerette [pɑkʀɛt] *f* BOT daisy ▸**au ras des ~s** *inf* (*humour*) pretty basic

Pâques [pɑk] **I.** *m* Easter; **lundi/œuf/vacances de ~** Easter Monday/egg/holidays ▸**à ~ ou à la Trinité** *iron* never in a month of Sundays **II.** *fpl* Easter; **joyeuses ~!** Happy Easter!

> At **Pâques** French children are told that church bells which have not been during the previous days return from Rome and drop chocolate eggs, bells and other goodies. In France, only Easter Sunday is a public holiday.

paquet [pakɛ] *m* **1.** (*boîte*) packet; (*de café, sucre*) bag; (*de cigarettes*) packet *Brit,* pack *Am;* (*de linge, vêtements*) bundle **2.** (*colis*) parcel **3.** *inf* (*grande quantité: de billets*) wad; (*d'eau*) torrent; (*de neige*) heap **4.** (*au rugby: d'avants*) pack **5.** INFOR package ▸**être un ~ de graisse** *inf* to be a fat lump; **être un ~ de nerfs** *inf* to be a bundle of nerves; **être un ~ d'os** *inf* to be nothing but skin and bone; **faire ses ~s** to pack one's bags; **mettre le ~** *inf* to pull out all the stops; (*payer beaucoup*) to spare no expense

paquet-cadeau [pakɛkado] <paquets-cadeaux> *m* gift-wrapped parcel; **vous pouvez me faire un ~?** could you gift-wrap it for me?

paqueté(e) [pak(ə)te] *adj Québec* (*trop plein, rempli à l'excès*) full to bursting

par [paʀ] *prep* **1.** (*grâce à l'action de, au moyen de*) by; **tout faire ~ soi-même** to do everything by oneself; **~ chèque/carte bancaire** by cheque/debit card; **~ tous les moyens** using all possible means **2.** (*origine*) **un oncle ~ alliance** an uncle by marriage; **descendre de qn ~ sa mère** to descend from sb on one's mother's side **3.** *gén sans art* (*cause, motif*) through; **~ sottise/devoir** out of stupidity/duty **4.** (*à travers, via*) **regarder ~ la fenêtre** to look out of the window; **venir ~ le chemin le plus court** to come (by) the shortest way; **est-il passé ~ ici?** did he come this way? **5.** (*localisation*) **habiter ~ ici/là** to live around here/there (somewhere); **~ 5 mètres de fond** at a depth of 5 metres *Brit,* at a depth of 5 meters *Am;* **être assis ~ terre** to be sitting on the ground; **tomber ~ terre** to fall to the ground **6.** (*distribution, mesure*) by; **un ~ un** one by one; **heure ~ heure** hour by hour; **~ moments** at times; **~ centaines/milliers** in their hundreds/thousands **7.** (*durant, pendant*) **~ temps de brouillard** in fog; **~ temps de pluie** in wet weather; **~ les temps qui courent** these days; **~ le passé** in the past **8.** (*dans des exclamations, serments*) **~ pitié, aidez-moi!** for pity's sake, help me! ▸**~ contre** on the other hand

para [paʀa] *m abr de* **parachutiste** para

parabole [paʀabɔl] *f* **1.** REL parable **2.** MAT parabola **3.** (*antenne*) satellite dish

parabolique [paʀabɔlik] *adj* parabolic; **antenne ~** TEL satellite dish

parachever [paʀaʃ(ə)ve] <4> *vt* **~ qc** (*finir*) to finish sth off; (*perfectionner*) to put the finishing touches to sth

parachutage [paʀaʃytaʒ] *m* **1. ~ de vivres/de soldats** parachuting in of food/soldiers **2.** (*nomination inattendue*) **les employés n'apprécient pas beaucoup le ~ de ce patron** the workers are not pleased about being landed with this boss

parachute [paʀaʃyt] *m* parachute; **sauter en ~** to parachute

parachuter [paʀaʃyte] <1> *vt* **1. ~ qn/qc** to parachute sb/sth in **2.** *inf* (*nommer de manière inattendue*) **~ qn à un poste** to drop sb into a job; **on nous a parachuté un nouveau directeur** they've landed us with a new manager

parachutisme [paʀaʃytism] *m* parachuting

parachutiste [paʀaʃytist] **I.** *adj* MIL **troupes ~s** paratroops; **unité ~** paratroop unit **II.** *mf* **1.** MIL paratrooper **2.** SPORT parachutist

parade [paʀad] *f* **1.** (*défense*) parry **2.** (*défilé*) parade **3.** *fig* **trouver la ~ à un argument** to counter an argument

paradis [paʀadi] *m* paradise ▸**tu ne l'emporteras pas au ~** you won't get away with that

paradisiaque [paʀadizjak] *adj* heavenly

paradoxal(e) [paʀadɔksal, o] <-aux> *adj*

P

paradoxical
paradoxalement [paʀadɔksalmɑ̃] *adv* paradoxically
paradoxe [paʀadɔks] *m* paradox
paraffine [paʀafin] *f* paraffin
parages [paʀaʒ] *mpl* **dans les** ~ in the area
paragraphe [paʀagʀaf] *m a.* TYP (*alinéa: d'un devoir, texte*) paragraph
paraître [paʀɛtʀ] *irr* **I.** *vi* **1.** (*sembler*) ~ +*infin* to appear to +*infin;* **cela me paraît (être) une erreur** it looks like a mistake to me **2.** (*apparaître: personne*) to appear **3.** (*être publié: journal, livre*) to come out; **faire ~ qc** (*maison d'édition*) to bring sth out; (*auteur*) to have sth published **4.** (*être visible: sentiment*) to show **5.** (*se mettre en valeur*) **aimer ~** to like to show off; **désir de ~** desire to be noticed **II.** *vi impers* **il me paraît difficile de** +*infin* it strikes me as difficult to +*infin;* **il lui paraît impossible que** +*subj* it seems impossible to him that ►**il paraît que qn va** +*infin* it seems that sb is going to +*infin;* (*soi-disant*) sb is apparently going to +*infin;* **il paraîtrait que ...** it would seem that ...; **il paraît que oui!** so it seems!; **il n'y paraîtra plus** nobody will notice it; **sans qu'il y paraisse** without it showing
parallèle [paʀalɛl] **I.** *adj* **1.** (*en double*) *a.* MAT parallel **2.** (*non officiel: marché, police*) unofficial **II.** *f* MAT parallel (line) **III.** *m* parallel
parallèlement [paʀalɛlmɑ̃] *adv* **1.** (*dans l'espace*) in parallel **2.** (*dans le temps*) at the same time
parallélépipède [paʀalelepipɛd] *m* GEOM parallelepiped; ~ **rectangle** right-angled parallelepiped
parallélisme [paʀalelism] *m* **1.** AUTO alignment; ~ **des roues** wheel alignment; GEOM parallelism **2.** (*correspondance*) ~ **entre qc et qc** parallel between sth and sth
parallélogramme [paʀalelɔgʀam] *m* GEOM parallelogram
paralysé(e) [paʀalize] **I.** *adj* (*bras, personne*) paralysed *Brit,* paralyzed *Am;* **il est ~ des jambes** his legs are paralysed **II.** *m(f)* paralytic
paralyser [paʀalize] <1> *vt* to paralyse *Brit,* to paralyze *Am;* **être paralysé par la peur** to be paralysed with fear
paralysie [paʀalizi] *f* paralysis
paralytique [paʀalitik] *adj, mf* paralytic
paramètre [paʀamɛtʀ] *m* parameter
parano [paʀano] *inf,* **paranoïaque** [paʀanɔjak] **I.** *adj* paranoid **II.** *mf* **être ~** to be paranoid
parapente [paʀapɑ̃t] *m* **1.** (*parachute rectangulaire*) parachute **2.** (*sport*) paragliding
parapet [paʀapɛ] *m* parapet
parapharmacie [paʀafaʀmasi] *f: shop selling health and beauty products*
paraphe [paʀaf] *m* initials *pl*
parapluie [paʀaplɥi] *m* umbrella
parasite [paʀazit] **I.** *adj* parasitic(al) **II.** *m* **1.** (*profiteur*) *a.* BIO parasite **2.** *pl* RADIO, TV interference *no pl*
parasiter [paʀazite] <1> *vt* **1.** BIO ~ **qn/qc** (*champignon, insecte, ver*) to be a parasite of sb/sth **2.** (*vivre aux dépens de*) ~ **qn/qc** to live off sb/sth **3.** RADIO, TV ~ **qc,** to interfere with sth
parasol [paʀasɔl] *m* parasol
parastatal(e) [paʀastatal, o] <-aux> *adj Belgique* (*semi-public(que)*) semi-public
paratonnerre [paʀatɔnɛʀ] *m* lightning conductor
paravent [paʀavɑ̃] *m* screen
parc [paʀk] *m* **1.** (*jardin*) park; ~ **botanique** botanic(al) garden(s); ~ **d'attractions** amusement park **2.** (*région protégée*) ~ **naturel** nature reserve; ~ **national** national park **3.** (*bassin d'élevage*) ~ **à huîtres/moules** oyster/mussel bed **4.** (*pour bébé*) playpen **5.** (*emplacement*) ~ **des expositions** exhibition centre *Brit,* exhibition hall *Am*
parcelle [paʀsɛl] *f* (*terrain*) parcel of land
parce que [paʀskə] *conj* because ►**~!** because!
parchemin [paʀʃəmɛ̃] *m* **1.** (*peau d'animal, texte*) parchment **2.** *inf* (*diplôme universitaire*) diploma
par-ci [paʀsi] **~, par-là** here and there
parcimonie [paʀsimɔni] *f* parsimony; **distribuer/donner qc avec ~** to distribute/give sth parsimoniously; **accorder ses éloges avec ~** to be sparing in one's praise
parcmètre [paʀkmɛtʀ] *m* parking meter
parcourir [paʀkuʀiʀ] *vt irr* **1.** (*accomplir: trajet, distance*) to cover **2.** (*traverser, sillonner: ville, rue*) to go through; (*en tous sens: ville*) to go all over; (*rue*) to go up and down; (*région, pays*) to travel through; (*en tous sens: région, pays*) to travel the length and breadth of; ~ **une région** (*navire*) to sail through a region; (*ruisseau*) to run through a region; (*objet volant*) to fly through a region **3.** (*examiner rapidement: journal, lettre*) to glance through; ~ **qc des yeux** [*o* **du regard**] to run one's eye over sth
parcours [paʀkuʀ] *m* **1.** (*trajet: d'un véhicule*) journey; (*d'un fleuve*) course **2.** SPORT (*piste*) course; (*épreuve*) round **3.** *fig* ~ **du combattant** obstacle course
par-delà [paʀdəla] *prep* (*de l'autre côté de*) beyond; ~ **les problèmes** over and above the problems **par-derrière** [paʀdɛʀjɛʀ] *adv* **1.** (*opp: par-devant: attaquer, emboutir*) from behind **2.** (*dans le dos de qn*) ~ **qn** behind sb; *fig* (*raconter, critiquer*) behind sb's back **par-dessous** [paʀdəsu] *prep, adv* under(neath) **par-dessus** [paʀdəsy] **I.** *prep* over (the top of) **II.** *adv* over (the top)
pardessus [paʀdəsy] *m* overcoat
pardi [paʀdi] *interj* **~!** of course!; **c'est qu'il y trouve son intérêt, ~!** it's serves his own interest, of course![*o* what do you think!]
pardon [paʀdɔ̃] *m* forgiveness; REL pardon;

demander ~ à qn to apologize to sb ▶**mille ~(s)!** (I'm) terribly sorry; **~?** (I beg your) pardon?

pardonnable [paʀdɔnabl] *adj* pardonable; **il est ~** (*personne*) he can be forgiven

pardonner [paʀdɔne] <1> **I.** *vt* (*absoudre*) **~ qc à qn** to forgive sb for sth ▶**pardonne-moi/pardonnez-moi** excuse me **II.** *vi* **1.** (*être fatal*) **ne pas ~** (*maladie, poison, erreur*) to be very unforgiving **2.** (*absoudre*) to forgive

paré(e) [paʀe] *adj* **être ~ contre qc** to be prepared for sth

pare-balles [paʀbal] **I.** *adj inv* bullet-proof **II.** *m inv* bullet shield **pare-brise** [paʀbʀiz] *m inv* AUTO windscreen *Brit,* windshield *Am* **pare-chocs** [paʀʃɔk] *m inv* AUTO **~ arrière/avant** rear/front bumper **pare-feu** [paʀfø] **I.** *adj inv* **dispositif ~** fire prevention device; **porte ~** fire door **II.** *m inv* **1.** (*pare-étincelles*) fireguard **2.** (*en forêt*) firebreak

pareil(le) [paʀɛj] **I.** *adj* **1.** (*identique*) the same; **être ~ à** [*o* **que**] **qn/qc** to be the same as sb/sth **2.** (*tel*) **une voiture/idée/vie ~le** such a car/an idea/a life, a car/an idea/a life like that **II.** *m(f) pl, péj* (*semblable*) **vous et vos ~s** you and your kind ▶**c'est du ~ au même** *inf* it makes no difference; **rendre la ~le à qn** to pay sb back; **sans ~** unparalleled **III.** *adv inf* (*s'habiller*) the same

pareillement [paʀɛjmɑ̃] *adv* **1.** (*également*) likewise; **Bonne Année! – à vous ~!** Happy New Year! – and the same to you! **2.** (*de la même façon*) the same

parent [paʀɑ̃] *m* parent

parent(e) [paʀɑ̃, ɑ̃t] *m(f)* (*personne de la famille*) relative

parental(e) [paʀɑ̃tal, o] <-aux> *adj* parental

parenté [paʀɑ̃te] *f* **1.** (*lien familial, analogie*) relationship **2.** (*ensemble des parents*) relations *pl*

parenthèse [paʀɑ̃tɛz] *f* **1.** TYP, MAT bracket **2.** (*digression*) parenthesis **3.** (*incident*) interlude ▶**soit dit entre ~s** incidentally; **mettre qc entre ~s** to put sth in brackets; (*oublier provisoirement*) to set sth aside

paréo [paʀeo] *m* pareo

parer [paʀe] <1> **I.** *vt* (*attaque, coup*) to ward off; (*argument*) to counter **II.** *vi* **~ à qc** to ward off sth

pare-soleil [paʀsɔlɛj] *m inv* AUTO sun visor

paresse [paʀɛs] *f* laziness

paresser [paʀese] <1> *vi* **~ au** [*o* **dans son**] **lit** to laze around in bed

paresseux, -euse [paʀesø, -øz] **I.** *adj* lazy; (*attitude*) casual **II.** *m, f* lazy person

parfait [paʀfɛ] *m* **1.** LING perfect **2.** GASTR parfait; **~ au café** coffee parfait

parfait(e) [paʀfɛ, ɛt] *adj* **1.** (*sans défaut*) perfect; (*beauté*) flawless **2.** (*qui répond exactement à un concept*) perfect; (*discrétion*) absolute; (*ignorance*) complete **3.** *antéposé* (*modèle: gentleman, idiot*) perfect; (*crapule, filou*) utter

parfaitement [paʀfɛtmɑ̃] *adv* **1.** (*de façon parfaite*) perfectly; **parler ~ français** to speak perfect French **2.** (*tout à fait: idiot, ridicule*) perfectly **3.** (*oui, bien sûr*) absolutely

parfois [paʀfwa] *adv* sometimes

parfum [paʀfœ̃] *m* **1.** (*substance*) perfume **2.** (*odeur*) scent **3.** GASTR flavour *Brit,* flavor *Am* ▶**être au ~** *inf* to be in the know; **mettre qn au ~** *inf* to put sb in the picture

parfumé(e) [paʀfyme] *adj* **1.** (*qui a une bonne odeur*) scented **2.** (*qui a bon goût*) **très ~** full of flavour *Brit,* full of flavor *Am* **3.** (*avec du parfum*) **femme trop ~e** woman wearing too much perfume **4.** (*aromatisé*) **glace ~e au chocolat** chocolate flavoured ice cream *Brit,* chocolate flavored ice cream *Am*

parfumer [paʀfyme] <1> **I.** *vt* **1.** (*donner une bonne odeur à*) to perfume **2.** GASTR (*glace, crème*) to flavour *Brit,* to flavor *Am* **II.** *vpr* **se ~** to put perfume on; (*habituellement*) to use perfume

parfumerie [paʀfymʀi] *f* **1.** (*magasin*) perfume shop **2.** (*usine, fabrication*) perfumery **3.** (*produits*) perfumes *pl*

parfumeur, -euse [paʀfymœʀ, -øz] *m, f* **1.** (*fabricant*) perfumer **2.** (*propriétaire d'une parfumerie*) perfumery owner

pari [paʀi] *m* bet

paria [paʀja] *m* pariah

parier [paʀje] <1> **I.** *vt* **~ qc à qn** to bet sb sth; **~ qc sur qn/qc** to bet sth on sb/sth; **tu paries que j'y arrive!** you bet I'll do it! **II.** *vi* to bet; **~ sur qn/qc** to bet on sb/sth; **~ aux courses** to bet on horses

parieur, -euse [paʀjœʀ, -jøz] *m, f* better

parigot(e) [paʀigo, ɔt] *adj inf* Parisian

Paris [paʀi] *m* Paris

paris-brest [paʀibʀɛst] <paris-brest(s)> *m* GASTR Paris-Brest (*choux pastry ring filled with cream*)

parisien(ne) [paʀizjɛ̃, jɛn] *adj* (*banlieue, métro, mode*) Paris *avant subst;* (*personne, société, vie*) Parisian

Parisien(ne) [paʀizjɛ̃, jɛn] *m(f)* Parisian

parjure [paʀʒyʀ] **I.** *adj* disloyal **II.** *mf* traitor **III.** *m* betrayal; **commettre un ~** to commit an act of betrayal

parka [paʀka] *m o f* parka, anorak

parking [paʀkiŋ] *m* AUTO car park *Brit,* parking lot *Am*

parlant(e) [paʀlɑ̃, ɑ̃t] *adj* **1.** (*éloquent: geste, regard*) eloquent; (*description, exemple*) vivid; (*preuve*) clear; **ces chiffres sont ~s** these figures speak for themselves **2. le cinéma ~** [*o* **les films ~s**] the talkies; **horloge ~e** speaking clock

parlement [paʀləmɑ̃] *m* parliament

Parlement [paʀləmɑ̃] *m* **~ européen** European Parliament

parlementaire [paʀləmɑ̃tɛʀ] **I.** *adj* parliamentary **II.** *mf* **1.** (*député*) Member of Parliament; (*aux Etats-Unis*) Congressman, -woman *m, f Am;* ~ **européen** Member of the European Parliament **2.** (*médiateur*) mediator

parlementer [paʀləmɑ̃te] <1> *vi* **1.** (*négocier*) ~ **avec qn** to negotiate with sb **2.** (*discuter*) to talk (at length)

parler [paʀle] <1> **I.** *vi* **1.** (*prendre la parole*) to talk **2.** (*exprimer*) to speak; ~ **avec les mains** to use one's hands when talking; ~ **par gestes** to use sign language **3.** (*converser, discuter*) ~ **de qn/qc avec qn** to talk about sb/sth with sb **4.** (*entretenir*) ~ **de qn/qc à qn** (*dans un but précis*) to talk about sb/sth to sb; (*raconter*) to tell sb about sb/sth **5.** (*adresser la parole*) ~ **à qn** to speak to sb **6.** (*avoir pour sujet*) ~ **de qn/qc** (*article, film, journal, livre*) to be about sb/sth; (*brièvement*) to mention sb/sth **7.** (*en s'exprimant de telle manière*) **généralement/légalement parlant** generally/legally speaking ▸**faire** ~ **de soi** to get oneself talked about; **sans** ~ **de qn/qc** not to mention sb/sth; **moi qui vous parle** *inf* I myself **II.** *vt* **1.** (*être bilingue: langue*) to speak **2.** (*aborder un sujet*) ~ **affaires/politique** to talk business/politics **III.** *vpr* **1.** (*être employé*) **se** ~ (*langue*) to be spoken **2.** (*s'entretenir: personnes*) to talk to each other; **se** ~ **à soi-même** to talk to oneself **3.** (*s'adresser la parole*) **ne plus se** ~ not to speak to each other any more **IV.** *m* **1.** (*manière*) speech **2.** (*langue régionale*) dialect

parleur, **-euse** [paʀlœʀ, -øz] *m, f* talker; **beau** ~ *péj* smooth talker

parloir [paʀlwaʀ] *m* (*d'une prison, d'un internat, hôpital*) visiting room; (*d'un couvent, d'une école*) parlour *Brit,* parlor *Am*

parlot(t)e [paʀlɔt] *f* **faire la** ~ **avec qn** to chat with sb

parme¹ [paʀm] *adj inv* (*mauve*) violet

parme² [paʀm] *m inv* (*jambon de Parme*) Parma ham

parmesan [paʀməzɑ̃] *m* parmesan

parmi [paʀmi] *prep* (*entre*) among(st); ~ **la foule** in the crowd

parodie [paʀɔdi] *f* parody

parodier [paʀɔdje] <1a> *vt* to parody

paroi [paʀwa] *f* **1.** (*d'un récipient, véhicule, d'une baignoire*) side; (*d'une caverne*) wall **2.** (*cloison*) partition **3.** ANAT wall; ~ **abdominale** abdominal lining **4.** (*roc, muraille*) wall

paroisse [paʀwas] *f* parish ▸**prêcher pour sa** ~ *inf* to look after number one

paroissial(e) [paʀwasjal, jo] <-aux> *adj* **église** ~**e** parish church

paroissien(ne) [paʀwasjɛ̃, jɛn] *m(f)* parishioner

parole [paʀɔl] *f* **1.** *souvent pl* (*mot*) word; **une** ~ **célèbre** a famous saying; **la** ~ **de Dieu** the word of God; **assez de** ~**s!** (that's) enough talking! **2.** (*promesse*) ~ **d'honneur** word of honour *Brit,* word of honor *Am;* **c'est un homme de** ~ he's a man of his word; **tu peux la croire sur** ~ you can take her word for it; **manquer à sa** ~ to go back on one's word **3.** *sans pl* (*faculté de parler*) speech; **perdre/retrouver la** ~ to lose/recover one's speech **4.** *sans pl* (*fait de parler*) **ne plus adresser la** ~ **à qn** not to speak to sb any more; **couper la** ~ **à qn** to cut sb short **5.** *sans pl* (*droit de parler*) **demander/prendre la** ~ to ask/begin to speak; **avoir la** ~ to be speaking; **donner la** ~ **à qn** to invite sb to speak; **refuser la** ~ **à qn** to refuse sb permission to speak; **retirer la** ~ **à qn** to stop sb speaking; **temps de** ~ speaking time **6.** *pl* MUS (*de chanson classique*) words; (*de chanson populaire*) lyrics ▸**être** ~ **d'évangile pour qn** to be the gospel (truth) to sb; **ce n'est pas** ~ **d'évangile** it's not gospel; **prêcher** [*o* **porter**] **la bonne** ~ *a.* REL to spread the word; **ma** ~**!** (*je le jure!*) cross my heart!; (*exprimant l'étonnement*) my word!

parolier, **-ière** [paʀɔlje, -jɛʀ] *m, f* (*d'un opéra, d'une œuvre musicale*) librettist; (*d'une chanson*) lyric writer

paroxysme [paʀɔksism] *m* (*d'un sentiment, d'une crise*) height; (*d'une maladie*) paroxysm; **être au** ~ **de la colère/douleur** to be beside oneself with anger/grief; **le bruit est au** [*o* **à son**] ~ the noise was at its height

parpaing [paʀpɛ̃] *m* CONSTR breeze-block *Brit,* cinder block *Am*

parquer [paʀke] <1> *vt* **1.** (*animaux*) to pen **2.** *péj* (*entasser*) ~ **des personnes dans qc** to shut people up in sth **3.** (*garer: véhicule*) to park

parquet [paʀkɛ] *m* (parquet) floor

parrain [paʀɛ̃] *m* **1.** REL godfather **2.** (*celui qui parraine qn/qc: d'un athlète, festival, théâtre*) sponsor; (*d'un artiste, projet, d'une fondation*) patron; (*d'une entreprise, initiative*) promoter **3.** *fig* (*de la mafia*) godfather

parrainage [paʀɛnaʒ] *m* (*d'un athlète, festival, théâtre*) sponsorship; (*d'un artiste, projet, d'une fondation*) patronage; (*d'une entreprise, initiative*) promotion

parrainer [paʀene] <1> *vt* **1.** (*apporter son soutien à: athlète, festival, théâtre*) to sponsor; (*artiste, projet, fondation*) to support; (*entreprise, initiative*) to promote **2.** (*introduire*) to sponsor

parraineur, **-euse** [paʀɛnœʀ, -øz] *m, f* sponsor

parricide [paʀisid] **I.** *adj* **fils** ~ (*quant au père*) parricide; (*quant à la mère*) matricide; **crime** ~ parricide **II.** *m* (*quant au père*) parricidal; (*quant à la mère*) matricidal **III.** *mf* (*quant au père*) parricide; (*quant à la mère*) matricide

parsemé(e) [paʀsəme] *adj* **être** ~ **de qc** to be strewn with sth

parsemer [paʀsəme] <4> *vt* **1.** (*répandre*) ~ **un gâteau de qc** to sprinkle a cake with sth; ~ **son devoir/son discours de qc** to pepper one's homework/one's speech with sth **2.** (*être répandu sur*) ~ **le sol** to be strewn around on the ground

part [paʀ] *f* **1.** (*portion*) share; (*de gâteau*) piece; (*de légumes*) portion **2.** (*partie*) part **3.** (*participation*) ~ **dans qc** part in sth; **avoir ~ à qc** to be involved in sth; **prendre ~ à qc** to take part in sth; **prendre ~ aux frais** to make a contribution towards the costs **4.** FIN share ▸**faire la ~ des choses** to take everything into account; **autre ~** *inf* somewhere else; **d'autre ~** moreover; **d'une ~ …, d'autre ~ …** on the one hand …, on the other (hand) …; **de ~ et d'autre de qn/qc** on both sides of sb/sth; **citoyen à ~ entière** full citizen; **un Français à ~ entière** person with full French citizenship; **nulle ~** nowhere; **de toute(s) ~(s)** from all sides; **faire ~ de qc à qn** to inform sb of sth; **prendre qn à ~** to take sb aside; **cas/place à ~** unique case/place; **classer/ranger qc à ~** to file sth/put sth away separately; **mettre qc à ~** to put sth aside; **à ~ lui/cela** apart from him/that; **à ~ que qn a fait qc** *inf* apart from the fact that sb has done sth; **de ma/sa ~** from me/him; **de la ~ de qn** (*au nom de*) on behalf of sb; **donner à qn le bonjour de la ~ de qn** to give sb sb's regards; **pour ma/sa ~** as far as I/he's concerned

partage [paʀtaʒ] *m* **1.** (*division: d'un terrain, gâteau, butin*) dividing up **2.** (*répartition: d'un trésor, d'aliments*) sharing out; (*d'un appartement*) sharing; (*des voix*) distribution; **il y a ~ des responsabilités entre les deux conducteurs** both drivers are jointly responsible ▸**régner sans ~** to rule absolutely; **autorité/pouvoir sans ~** absolute authority/power

partager [paʀtaʒe] <2a> **I.** *vt* **1.** (*diviser: gâteau, pièce, terrain*) to divide (up); **~ qc en qc** to divide sth (up) into sth **2.** (*répartir*) **~ qc entre des personnes/choses/qc et qc** to share sth (out) between people/things/sth and sth **3.** (*avoir en commun: appartement, frais, bénéfices, passions, goûts, responsabilité*) to share **4.** (*s'associer à*) **~ l'avis de qn** to share sb's point of view; **~ la surprise de qn** to be just as surprised as sb; **être partagé** (*frais*) to be shared; (*avis*) to be divided; (*plaisir, amour*) to be mutual **5.** (*donner une part de ce que l'on possède*) **~ qc avec qn** to share sth with sb **6.** (*hésiter*) **être partagé entre qc et qc** to be torn between sth and sth **7.** (*être d'opinion différente*) **ils sont partagés sur qc/en ce qui concerne qc** they are divided on sth/as far as sth is concerned **II.** *vpr* **1.** (*se diviser*) **se ~ en qc** to be divided into sth **2.** (*se répartir*) **se ~ qc** to share sth between themselves; **se ~ entre** (*voix*) to be divided between

partagiciel [paʀtaʒisjɛl] *m Québec* INFOR shareware

partance [paʀtɑ̃s] **être en ~** (*avion*) to be about to take off; (*train*) to be about to depart; (*bateau*) to be about to sail; **le train en ~ pour Paris** the Paris train

partant(e) [paʀtɑ̃, ɑ̃t] **I.** *adj inf* **être ~ pour qc** to be ready for sth; **je suis ~!** count me in! **II.** *m(f)* **1.** (*opp: arrivant*) person leaving **2.** SPORT starter; **non ~** non-runner

partenaire [paʀtənɛʀ] *mf* partner

partenariat [paʀtənaʀja] *m* partnership; **en ~** in partnership

parterre [paʀtɛʀ] *m* **1.** **~ de fleurs** flower bed **2.** THEAT orchestra, stalls *pl Brit;* **prendre des places au ~** to get seats in the stalls

parti [paʀti] *m* **1.** POL party; **~ de droite/gauche** right-wing/left-wing party **2.** (*camp*) **se ranger du ~ de qn** to side with sb **3.** (*personne à marier*) match ▸**~ pris** prejudice; **prendre ~ pour qn** to take sb's side; **prendre ~ contre qn** to side against sb; **prendre son ~** to make up one's mind; **prendre son ~ de qc** to come to terms with sth; **prendre le ~ de** +*infin* to make up one's mind to +*infin;* **tirer ~ de qc** to make the most of sth

parti(e) [paʀti] *part passé de* **partir**

partial(e) [paʀsjal, jo] <-aux> *adj* (*juge*) biased; (*critique*) prejudiced

partialité [paʀsjalite] *f* partiality; **agir avec ~** to act in a biased way

participant(e) [paʀtisipɑ̃, ɑ̃t] **I.** *adj* **personnes ~es** participants **II.** *m(f)* (*à une débat*) participant; (*à un concours*) entrant

participation [paʀtisipasjɔ̃] *f* **1.** (*présence, contribution*) participation; **~ électorale** turnout at the polls **2.** (*partage*) **~ aux bénéfices** profit-sharing **3.** (*droit de regard*) involvement

participe [paʀtisip] *m* LING participle

participer [paʀtisipe] <1> *vi* **1.** (*prendre part*) **~ à une réunion/à un colloque** to take part in a meeting/in a seminar **2.** (*collaborer*) **~ à la conversation** to join in the conversation **3.** (*payer*) **~ aux frais** to contribute to the costs

particulariser [paʀtikylaʀize] <1> *vpr* **se ~ en faisant qc** to stand out by doing sth

particularisme [paʀtikylaʀism] *m* particularity

particularité [paʀtikylaʀite] *f* **1.** (*caractère*) particularity **2.** (*caractéristique*) distinctive feature; **qn/qc a la ~ de …** a distinctive feature of sb/sth is that …

particule [paʀtikyl] *f* **1.** (*grain*) *a.* LING particle; **~ de sable** particle of sand; **~ élémentaire** elementary particle **2.** (*préposition*) **~ nobiliaire** nobiliary particle (*de, as in de Beauvoir, de Gaulle*)**;** **porter un nom à ~** to have a name beginning with de

particulier [paʀtikylje] *m* **1.** (*personne privée*) individual **2.** ADMIN, COM private individual; **vente aux ~s** private sale

particulier, -ière [paʀtikylje, -jɛʀ] *adj* **1.** (*spécifique: aspect, exemple*) particular; (*trait*) characteristic; **"signes ~s (néant)"** "distinguishing features (none)" **2.** (*spécial*) particular; (*aptitude, cas*) special **3.** (*privé: conversation, leçon, secrétaire*) private **4.** (*étrange*) peculiar; **être d'un genre ~** to be rather odd ▸**en ~** (*en privé*) in private; (*notamment*) in particular; (*séparément*) sep-

P

arately

particulièrement [paʀtikyljɛʀmɑ̃] *adv* particularly; **je n'y tiens pas** ~ I'm not particularly keen

partie [paʀti] *f* **1.** (*part*) part; **la majeure** ~ **du temps** most of the time; **en** ~ partly; **en grande** ~ largely; **faire** ~ **de qc** to be part of sth **2.** *pl, inf* (*les ~s sexuelles masculines*) a man's privates **3.** JEUX, SPORT game **4.** (*divertissement*) ~ **de chasse/pêche** shooting/fishing party **5.** (*adversaire*) ~**s belligérantes** warring factions ►**faire une** ~ **de jambes en l'air** *inf* to have it off; **faire** ~ **des meubles** to be part of the furniture; **ce n'est pas une** ~ **de plaisir** it's no picnic; **la** ~ **est jouée** the die is cast; **être** ~ **prenante** to take part; **être de la** ~ to join in; (*s'y connaître*) to know a thing or two

partiel [paʀsjɛl] *m* UNIV mid-year exam *Brit,* midterm exam *Am*

partiel(le) [paʀsjɛl] *adj* partial; (*information*) incomplete; **élection** ~**le** ≈ by-election; **chômage** ~ short-time working; **travail à temps** ~ part-time work; **examen** ~ mid-year exam *Brit,* midterm exam *Am*

partielle [paʀsjɛl] *f* (*élection*) by-election

partiellement [paʀsjɛlmɑ̃] *adv* partially

partir [paʀtiʀ] <10> *vi être* **1.** (*s'en aller*) to go; (*voiture, train, avion*) to leave; (*lettre*) to go (off); ~ **en courant** to run away; ~ **en ville** to go into town; **être parti pour** (**ses**) **affaires** to be away on business; ~ **en vacances** to go (away) on holiday *Brit,* to take a vacation *Am;* ~ **en voyage** to go (away) on a trip; ~ **à la recherche de qn/qc** to go (off) looking for sb/sth; ~ **chercher qn** to go and get sb **2.** (*après un séjour*) to leave **3.** (*démarrer: coureur, moteur*) to start; **c'est parti!** *inf* we're off! **4.** (*sauter, exploser: fusée, coup de feu*) to go off **5.** (*se mettre à*) ~ **dans de grandes explications** to launch into long explanations **6.** (*disparaître: douleur*) to go (away); (*odeur*) to go; (*tache*) to come out; **ce veston part en lambeaux** this jacket is falling apart **7.** (*mourir*) to pass away **8.** (*venir de*) **ce train part de Berlin** this train leaves from Berlin; **la deuxième personne en partant de la gauche** the second person from the left **9.** (*dater de*) **l'abonnement part de février** the subscription runs from February **10.** (*commencer une opération*) ~ **d'un principe/d'une idée** to start from a principle/from an idea ►**à** ~ **de** from

partisan(e) [paʀtizɑ̃, an] **I.** *adj* (*favorable à*) **être** ~ **de qc** to be in favour of sth *Brit,* to be in favor of sth *Am* **II.** *m(f)* supporter; (*d'une idée*) advocate

partitif, -ive [paʀtitif, -iv] *adj* partitive

partition [paʀtisjɔ̃] *f* **1.** MUS score; **jouer sans** ~ to play without music **2.** (*division*) partition **3.** INFOR (*action de diviser un disque en domaines*) partition; ~ **de mémoire** memory partitioning

partout [paʀtu] *adv* **1.** (*en tous lieux*) everywhere; **un peu** ~ here and there; ~ **où ...** wherever ... **2.** SPORT **on en est à trois** ~ it's three all

parure [paʀyʀ] *f* **1.** (*bijoux*) jewels; ~ **de diamants** set of diamonds **2.** (*ensemble de pièces de linge*) ~ **en soie** set of silk underwear; ~ **de lit** set of bed linen

parution [paʀysjɔ̃] *f* publication

parvenir [paʀvəniʀ] <9> *vi être* **1.** (*atteindre*) ~ **à une maison/au sommet** to reach a house/the summit **2.** (*arriver*) ~ **à qn** (*colis, lettre*) to reach sb; (*bruit*) to reach sb's ears; **faire** ~ **une lettre à qn** to get a letter to sb **3.** (*réussir à obtenir*) ~ **à la gloire** to attain glory; ~ **à convaincre qn** to manage to persuade sb **4.** (*atteindre naturellement*) ~ **à un âge avancé** to reach an advanced age; **être parvenu au terme de sa vie** to have reached the end of one's life

parvenu(e) [paʀvəny] *adj, m(f)* upstart

parvis [paʀvi] *m* square (*in front of a cathedral or other important building*)

pas[1] [pɑ] *m* **1.** (*enjambée*) step; **au** ~ **de charge** at the charge; **au** ~ **de course/de gymnastique** at a run/a jog trot; **marcher d'un bon** ~ to walk at a good pace **2.** *pl* (*trace*) footprints; **revenir** [*o* **retourner**] **sur ses** ~ to retrace one's steps **3.** (*allure: d'une personne*) pace; (*d'un cheval*) walk; **marcher au** ~ to march **4.** (~ *de danse*) dance step **5.** (*entrée*) ~ **de la porte** doorstep; **sur le** ~ **de la porte** on the doorstep ►**avancer à** ~ **de géant** to progress by leaps and bounds; **à** ~ **de loup** stealthily; **faire les cent** ~ to pace up and down; **à deux** ~ a stone's throw away; **faux** ~ faux pas; **faire un faux** ~ to make a silly mistake; (*par indiscrétion*) to commit a faux pas; **à** ~ **feutrés** stealthily; **se sortir** [*o* **se tirer**] **d'un mauvais** ~ to get oneself out of a tight spot; **céder le** ~ **à qn** to give precedence to sb; **franchir** [*o* **sauter**] **le** ~ to take the plunge; **marcher sur les** ~ **de qn** to follow in sb's footsteps; **marquer le** ~ to mark time; **mettre qn au** ~ to bring sb into line; ~ **à** ~ step by step; **de ce** ~ straightaway

pas[2] [pɑ] *adv* **1.** (*négation*) **ne** ~ **croire** not to believe; (**ne**) ~ **de ...** no ...; **il ne fait** ~ **son âge** he doesn't look his age; **j'ai** ~ **le temps** *inf* I haven't got (the) time; (**ne**) ~ **beaucoup/assez de ...** not a lot of/enough ... **2.** *sans verbe* ~ **de réponse** no reply; ~ **bête!** *inf* not a bad idea!; **absolument** ~! absolutely not!; ~ **encore** not again; ~ **du tout** not at all; ~ **que je sache** not as far as I know; ~ **toi?** aren't you? **3.** *avec un adj* not; **une histoire** ~ **ordinaire** an unusual story; **c'est vraiment** ~ **banal!** that's really something unusual!

pascal [paskal] <s> *m* INFOR Pascal

Pas de Calais [padøkalɛ] *m* **le** ~ the Straits of Dover

passable [pɑsabl] *adj* ECOLE fair; **mention** ~ ≈ passmark

passablement [pasabləmɑ̃] *adv* **1.**(*pas trop mal*) reasonably; **jouer ~ d'un instrument** to play an instrument reasonably well **2.**(*beaucoup*) **il lui a fallu ~ de courage pour le faire** he needed quite a bit of courage to do it

passage [pasaʒ] *m* **1.**(*venue*) **observer le ~ des voitures** to watch the cars go by; **observer le ~ des oiseaux** to watch the birds fly by; **"~ interdit"** "no entry"; **~ protégé** *priority given to traffic on the main road;* **personne de ~** someone who is passing through; **il y a du ~** *inf*(*personnes*) there are a lot of coming and going; (*circulation*) there's a lot of traffic **2.**(*court séjour*) **lors de son dernier ~ chez X** when he was at last at X's **3.**(*avancement*) **lors du ~ d'un élève en classe supérieure** when a pupil moves up to the next class; **~ au grade de capitaine** promotion to captain **4.**(*transformation*) transition; **~ de l'enfance à l'adolescence** passage from childhood to adolescence **5.**(*voie pour piétons*) passage(way); **~ clouté** [*o* **pour piétons**] pedestrian crossing; **les valises encombrent le ~** the cases are blocking the way **6.** CHEMDFER **~ à niveau** level crossing *Brit,* grade crossing *Am* **7.**(*galerie marchande*) (shopping) arcade **8.**(*fragment: d'un roman, morceau musical*) passage ►**céder le ~ à qn/qc** to let sb go first; **au ~** (*en chemin*) on the way past; (*soit dit en passant*) by the way

passager, -ère [pasaʒe, -ɛʀ] **I.** *adj* **1.**(*de courte durée*) fleeting; (*beauté, bonheur*) passing; (*pluies*) occasional **2.**(*très fréquenté: lieu, rue*) busy **II.** *m, f* passenger; **~ avant** front passenger

passant [pasɑ̃] *m* (*d'une ceinture*) (belt) loop

passant(e) [pasɑ̃, ɑ̃t] *m(f)* passer-by

passe [pas] *f* SPORT pass; **~ mal ajustée** bad pass ►**être dans une bonne ~** to be doing all right; **être dans une mauvaise ~** to be going through a bad patch; **être en ~ de faire qc** to be on one's way to doing sth

passé [pase] **I.** *m* **1.**(*temps révolu*) past; **par le ~** in the past; **tout ça c'est du ~** *inf* that's all in the past (now) **2.** LING past tense; **~ simple** past historic; **~ composé** perfect **II.** *prep* (*après*) **~ minuit** after midnight; **~ la frontière** once past the border

passé(e) [pase] *adj* **1.**(*dernier*) last **2.**(*révolu*) past; (*angoisse*) former **3.**(*délavé: couleur*) faded **4.**(*plus de*) **il est midi ~/deux heures ~es** it's past midday [*o* noon]/two o'clock

passe-droit [pasdʀwa] <passe-droits> *m* special privilege **passe-montagne** [pasmɔ̃taɲ] <passe-montagnes> *m* balaclava **passe-partout** [paspaʀtu] **I.** *adj inv, fig* all-purpose **II.** *m inv* **1.**(*clé*) skeleton key **2.** ART passe-partout **passe-passe** [paspas] *m v.* **tour passe-plat** [paspla] <passe-plats> *m* (serving) hatch

passeport [paspɔʀ] *m* passport

passer [pase] <1> **I.** *vi avoir o être* **1.**(*se déplacer*) to pass; (*aller*) to go past; (*venir*) to come past; **laisser ~ qn/une voiture** to let sb/a car past **2.**(*desservir: bus, métro, train*) to stop; **le bus va bientôt ~** the bus will be here soon **3.**(*s'arrêter un court instant*) **~ chez qn** to call (in) on sb; **~ à la poste** to go to the post office **4.**(*avoir un certain trajet*) **~ au bord de qc** (*route, train*) to go round the edge of sth; **~ dans une ville** (*automobiliste, voiture*) to go through a town; (*rivière*) to flow through a town; **~ devant qn/qc** to go past sb/sth; **~ entre deux maisons** (*personne*) to pass between two houses; (*route*) to run between two houses; **~ par Francfort** (*automobiliste, route*) to go through Frankfurt; (*avion*) to go via Frankfurt; **~ par la porte** to go through the door; **~ sous qc** to go under sth; **~ sur un pont** to go over a bridge; **~ sur l'autre rive** to cross (over) on to the other bank **5.**(*traverser en brisant*) **~ à travers le pare-brise** to go through the windscreen; **~ à travers la glace** to fall through the ice **6.**(*réussir à franchir: personne, animal, véhicule*) to get through; (*objet, meuble*) to fit through **7.**(*s'infiltrer par, filtrer*) **~ à travers qc** (*eau, lumière*) to go through sth **8.**(*se trouver*) **où est passée ta sœur/la clé?** where's your sister/the key got to? **9.**(*changer*) **~ de la salle à manger au salon** to go from the dining room into the sitting room; **~ de maison en maison** to go from house to house; **~ en seconde** AUTO to change into second; **le feu passe au rouge** the lights are changing to red; **le feu passe du vert à l'orange** the lights are changing from green to amber *Brit,* the lights are changing from green to yellow *Am* **10.**(*aller définitivement*) **~ dans le camp ennemi** to go over to the enemy camp **11.**(*être consacré à*) **60% du budget passent dans les traitements** 60% of the budget goes on salaries **12.**(*faire l'expérience de*) **~ par des moments difficiles** to have some hard times; **il est passé par la Légion étrangère** he was in the Foreign Legion **13.**(*utiliser comme intermédiaire*) **~ par qn** to go through sb **14.**(*être plus/moins important*) **~ avant/après qn/qc** to come before/after sb/sth **15.**(*avoir son tour, être présenté*) to go; **faire ~ qn avant/après les autres** to let sb go before/after the others; **~ à un examen** to go for an examination; **~ à la radio/télé** to be on the radio/TV; **le film passe au Rex** the film is showing at the Rex **16.**(*être accepté*) ECOLE **~ en sixième** to go into year seven *Brit,* to go into the seventh grade *Am;* **le candidat est passé à l'examen** the candidate has passed the exam; **la plaisanterie est bien/mal passée** the joke went down/didn't go down well; **la pièce de théâtre n'est pas passée** the play was a failure

17. (*ne pas tenir compte de, oublier*) ~ **sur les détails** to pass over the details; **passons!** let's say no more! **18.** JEUX to pass **19.** (*s'écouler: temps*) to pass; **on ne voyait pas le temps** ~ we didn't see the time go by **20.** (*disparaître*) to go; (*colère*) to die down; (*chagrin*) to pass (off); (*mode*) to die out; (*pluie*) to passed over; (*orage*) to blow over; (*couleur*) to fade; **ça te passera** you'll get over it **21.** (*devenir*) ~ **capitaine/directeur** to become a captain/director **22.** ~ **pour qc** (*être pris pour*) to be taken for sth; (*avoir la réputation de*) to be regarded as sth **23.** (*présenter comme*) **faire ~ qn pour qc** to make sb out to be sth ►~ **outre à qc** to disregard sth; **ça passe ou ça casse!** *inf* (it's) all or nothing! **II.** *vt avoir* **1.** (*donner: sel, photo*) to pass; (*consigne, travail, affaire*) to pass on; ~ **un message à qn** to give sb a message; ~ **la grippe/un virus à qn** to give sb (the) flu/a virus **2.** (*prêter*) ~ **un livre à qn** to lend sb a book **3.** SPORT ~ **la balle à qn** to pass sb the ball **4.** (*au téléphone*) ~ **qn à qn** to put sb on to sb **5.** ECOLE, UNIV (*examen*) to sit; ~ **un examen avec succès** to pass an exam **6.** (*vivre, occuper*) ~ **ses vacances à Rome** to spend one's holidays in Rome; **des nuits passées à boire** nights of drinking **7.** (*présenter: film, diapositives*) to show; (*disque, cassette*) to put on **8.** (*franchir: rivière, seuil, montagne*) to cross; (*obstacle*) to overcome; (*en sautant: obstacle*) to jump over; (*tunnel, écluse, mur du son*) to go through; (*frontière*) to cross (over); **faire ~ la frontière à qn** to get sb over the border **9.** (*faire mouvoir*) ~ **sa tête à travers le grillage/par la portière** to stick one's head through the railings/round the door; ~ **le chiffon sur l'étagère** to dust the bookshelf **10.** (*étaler, étendre*) ~ **une couche de peinture sur qc** to give sth a coat of paint **11.** (*faire subir une action*) ~ **qc sous le robinet** to rinse sth under the tap **12.** GASTR (*sauce, soupe, thé*) to strain **13.** (*calmer*) ~ **sa colère sur qn/qc** to work off one's anger on sb **14.** (*sauter* (*volontairement*): *chapitre, page*) to skip; (*son tour*) to miss **15.** (*oublier*) leave out; ~ **les détails** to leave out the details **16.** (*permettre*) ~ **tous ses caprices à qn** to indulge sb's every whim **17.** (*enfiler*) ~ **un pull** to slip on a sweater **18.** AUTO (*vitesse*) ~ **la seconde** to change into second **19.** COM, JUR (*accord, convention*) to reach; (*contrat*) to sign; ~ **un marché** to do [*o* make] a deal **III.** *vpr* **1.** (*s'écouler*) **le temps/le jour se passe** time/the day goes by **2.** (*avoir lieu*) to happen; **que s'est-il passé?** what (has) happened?; **que se passe-t-il?** what's going on? **3.** (*se dérouler*) **se** ~ (*action, histoire, manifestation*) to take place; **l'accident s'est passé de nuit** the accident happened at night; **si tout se passe bien** if everything goes well **4.** (*se débrouiller sans*) **se ~ de qn/qc** to do without sb/sth; **voilà qui se passe de commentaires!** that speaks for itself! **5.** (*renoncer à*) **se ~ de faire qc** to go without doing sth **6.** (*se mettre*) **se ~ de la crème sur le visage** to put cream on one's face; **se ~ la main sur le front/dans les cheveux** to wipe one's hand across one's forehead/run one's hand through one's hair ►**ça ne se passera pas comme ça!** *inf* not if I have anything to do with it!

passereau [pasʀo] <x> *m* passerine

passerelle [pasʀɛl] *f* **1.** (*pont*) footbridge **2.** NAUT gangway; (*pont supérieur*) bridge **3.** AVIAT (*téléscopique*) aircraft boarding tunnel; (*amovible*) (boarding) steps **4.** ECOLE **classe** ~ conversion course (*allowing students to move from one course to another*)

passe-temps [pastɑ̃] *m inv* pastime

passeur, **-euse** [pasœʀ, -øz] *m, f* **1.** (*sur un bac*) ferryman *m*, ferrywoman *f* **2.** (*à la frontière*) smuggler; ~ **de drogues** drugs runner

passible [pasibl] *adj* COM, JUR **être ~ d'une amende/peine** (*personne*) to be liable to a fine/penalty; (*délit*) to be punishable by a fine/penalty

passif [pasif] *m* LING passive; **au** ~ in the passive

passif, **-ive** [pasif, -iv] *adj* passive

passion [pasjɔ̃] *f* passion; ~ **du sport** passion for sport; ~ **de la liberté** passionate desire for freedom; ~ **du pouvoir** lust for power; **vivre une ~ avec qn** to have a passionate affair with sb

passionnant(e) [pasjɔnɑ̃, ɑ̃t] *adj* fascinating

passionné(e) [pasjɔne] **I.** *adj* passionate; **être ~ de qc** to have a passion for sth **II.** *m(f)* enthusiast; ~ **de cinéma** film buff

passionnel(le) [pasjɔnɛl] *adj* **crime** ~ crime of passion; **drame** ~ (*au théâtre, cinéma*) dramatic love story; (*vécu*) tragic event; **état** ~ hyperemotional state

passionnément [pasjɔnemɑ̃] *adv* passionately

passionner [pasjɔne] <1> **I.** *vt* to fascinate **II.** *vpr* **se ~ pour qc** to be fascinated by sth

passivement [pasivmɑ̃] *adv* passively

passivité [pasivite] *f* passivity

passoire [paswaʀ] *f* sieve ►**ma mémoire est une vraie ~!** I have a memory like a sieve!

pastaga [pastaga] *m Midi* pastis

pastel [pastɛl] *m, app inv* (*couleur*) pastel

pastèque [pastɛk] *f* watermelon

pasteur [pastœʀ] *m* **1.** (*prêtre*) pastor **2.** (*berger*) shepherd

pasteuriser [pastœʀize] <1> *vt* to pasteurize

pastiche [pastiʃ] *m* pastiche

pasticher [pastiʃe] <1> *vt* ~ **qc** (*auteur*) to do a pastiche of sth; (*film*) to be a pastiche of sth

pastille [pastij] *f* **1.** MED lozenge; ~ **de menthe** (pepper)mint **2.** (*gommette*) ~ **autocollante** sticker; ~ **verte** *small sticker for* *vehicles with catalytic converters, allowing them to be driven when pollution leads to traffic restrictions* **3.** INFOR button

pastis [pastis] *m* pastis (*anise-flavoured alcoholic aperitif*)

pataquès [patakɛs] *m* **1.** LING incorrect liaison **2.** (*situation confuse*) muddle

patate [patat] *f* **1.** *inf* (*pomme de terre*) spud; ~ **douce** sweet potato **2.** *Québec* (*pomme frite*) ~**s frites** chips *Brit,* (French) fries *Am* **3.** *inf* (*imbécile*) dope ►**en avoir gros sur la** ~ *inf* to be very upset

patati [patati] *interj inf* **et** ~**! et patata!** and so on and so forth!

patatras [patatʀa] *interj* ~**!** crash (bang)!

pataud(e) [pato, od] **I.** *adj* clumsy **II.** *m(f)* oaf

pataugeoire [patoʒwaʀ] *f* paddling pool

patauger [patoʒe] <2a> *vi* **1.** (*marcher*) to squelch around **2.** (*barboter*) to paddle **3.** (*ne pas suivre: élève*) not to follow **4.** *inf* (*s'empêtrer*) to be getting nowhere

patchwork [patʃwœʀk] *m* **1.** COUT patchwork **2.** *fig* **un** ~ **de nationalités** an assortment of nationalities

pâte [pɑt] *f* **1.** GASTR (*à tarte*) pastry; (*à pain*) dough; ~**s alimentaires** pasta *no pl;* **fromage à** ~ **molle/dure** soft/hard cheese **2.** (*substance molle*) paste; ~ **à modeler** ≈ Plasticine® *Brit,* ≈ Playdough® *Am*

pâté [pɑte] *m* **1.** GASTR pâté; ~ **de campagne** farmhouse pâté; ~ **en croûte** pâté en croute (*pâté baked in pastry and served in slices*) **2.** (*tache d'encre*) (ink) blot **3.** (*sable moulé*) ~ **de sable** sand pie **4.** (*ensemble*) ~ **de maisons** block (of houses) **5.** *Belgique* (*petit gâteau à la crème*) cream cake

pâtée [pɑte] *f* pet food; ~ **pour chat** catfood; ~ **pour chien** dogfood

patelin [patlɛ̃] *m inf* (out-of the-way) village

patente [patɑ̃t] *f Québec* (*objet quelconque*) whatsit

patère [patɛʀ] *f* (*portemanteau*) coathook

paternalisme [patɛʀnalism] *m* paternalism

paternaliste [patɛʀnalist] *adj* paternalistic

paternel(le) [patɛʀnɛl] *adj* paternal

paternité [patɛʀnite] *f* paternity

pâteux, **-euse** [pɑtø, -øz] *adj* (*sauce*) thickish; (*pain, masse*) stodgy; (*langue*) furry

pathétique [patetik] **I.** *adj* pathetic; (*roman*) moving **II.** *m* pathos

pathologique [patɔlɔʒik] *adj* pathological

patiemment [pasjamɑ̃] *adv* patiently

patience [pasjɑ̃s] *f* patience; **avoir de la** ~ to have patience; **n'avoir aucune patience** to be extremely impatience; **prendre** ~ to be patient; ~**!** don't be so impatient! ►**une** ~ **d'ange** the patience of a saint

patient(e) [pasjɑ̃, ɑ̃t] **I.** *adj* patient; **c'est un esprit** ~ he/she is a patient man/woman **II.** *m(f)* MED patient

patienter [pasjɑ̃te] <1> *vi* to wait; **faire** ~ **qn** to ask sb to wait; (*au téléphone*) to ask sb to hold

patin [patɛ̃] *m* ~ **à glace** ice skate; ~ **à roulettes** roller skate; ~ **en ligne** in-line skate, rollerblade; **faire du** ~ **à glace/à roulettes** to ice-skate/roller-skate ►**rouler un** ~ **à qn** *inf* to French-kiss sb

patinage [patinaʒ] *m* ~ **sur glace** ice-skating; ~ **à roulettes** roller-skating

patine [patin] *f* patina

patiner[1] [patine] <1> *vi* **1.** SPORT to skate **2.** AUTO (*embrayage*) to slip; (*roue*) to spin; (*véhicule*) to be stuck with the wheels spinning **3.** (*ne pas progresser*) to be stalled

patiner[2] [patine] <1> **I.** *vt* ~ **qc** (*recouvrir de patine*) to add a finish to sth; **des statues patinées par le temps** statues with the patina of time **II.** *vpr* **se** ~ to develop a patina

patinette [patinɛt] *f* scooter (*for a child*)

patineur, **-euse** [patinœʀ, -øz] *m, f* skater; ~ **à roulettes** roller skater; ~ **en ligne** in-line skater

patinoire [patinwaʀ] *f* **1.** (*piste de patinage*) skating rink **2.** (*endroit glissant*) ice rink

patio [patjo, pɑsjo] *m* patio

pâtir [pɑtiʀ] <8> *vi* ~ **de qc** to suffer from sth; ~ **des erreurs de qn** to pay for sb's mistakes

pâtisserie [pɑtisʀi] *f* **1.** (*magasin*) cake shop **2.** (*métier*) the confectionery business **3.** (*gâteaux*) cakes and pastries *pl* **4.** (*préparation de gâteaux*) cake and pastry making

pâtissier, **-ère** [pɑtisje, -ɛʀ] *m, f* pastrycook

patois [patwa] *m* patois

patraque [patʀak] *adj inf* **être** [*o* **se sentir**] ~ to feel out of sorts

patriarcat [patʀijaʀka] *m* patriarchate

patriarche [patʀijaʀʃ] *m* patriarch

patrie [patʀi] *f* **1.** (*nation*) homeland; **mourir pour la** ~ to die for one's country **2.** (*lieu de naissance*) birthplace **3.** (*berceau*) **la** ~ **des arts** the cradle of the arts

patrimoine [patʀimwan] *m* **1.** (*biens de famille*) *a.* BIO inheritance; ~ **génétique** [*o* **héréditaire**] genotype **2.** (*bien commun*) heritage

patriote [patʀijɔt] **I.** *adj* patriotic **II.** *mf* patriot

patriotique [patʀijɔtik] *adj* patriotic

patriotisme [patʀijɔtism] *m* patriotism

patron(ne) [patʀɔ̃, ɔn] *m(f)* **1.** (*employeur*) employer; **les grands** ~**s de l'industrie** the captains of industry **2.** (*chef*) boss **3.** (*propriétaire*) owner **4.** (*gérant*) manager **5.** (*artisan*) ~ **boulanger** master baker **6.** (*leader: d'une organisation*) head; **le** ~ **des** ~**s** the head of the employers' federation **7.** REL patron

patronage [patʀɔnaʒ] *m* patronage

patronal(e) [patʀɔnal, o] <-aux> *adj* **1.** (*du patron*) employer's; (*des patrons*) employers' **2.** REL **fête** ~**e** *feast of the saint one is named after, celebrated like a birthday*

patronat [patʀɔna] *m* **le** ~ the employers *pl*

patronner [patʀɔne] <1> *vt* (*personne*) to

P

sponsor; (*candidature, entreprise, initiative*) to support

patrouille [patʀuj] *f* patrol; ~ **de police** police patrol

patrouiller [patʀuje] <1> *vi* to be on patrol

patte¹ [pat] *f* **1.** (*jambe: d'un animal*) leg **2.** (*extrémité: d'un chien, chat, ours*) paw **3.** *inf* (*jambe*) leg; **être bas** [*o* **court**] **sur ~s** to have short legs **4.** *inf* (*main*) hand ▸**pantalon à ~s d'éléphant** (pair of) baggy trousers; **~s de mouche** spidery handwriting; **faire ~ de velours** to be all charm; **bas les ~s!** *inf* hands off!; **montrer ~ blanche** to show that one has the right credentials; **avoir une ~ folle** *inf* to have a game leg; **en avoir plein les ~s** *inf* to be fed up; **à quatre ~s** *inf* on all fours; **tirer dans les ~s de qn** *inf* to give sb a hard time

patte² [pat] *f Suisse* **1.** (*chiffon*) duster **2.** (*torchon*) tea towel *Brit*, dishtowel *Am*

patte-d'oie [patdwa] <pattes-d'oie> *f* **1.** *pl* (*rides*) crow's feet *pl* **2.** (*carrefour en Y*) Y-junction

pâturage [pɑtyʀaʒ] *m* (*herbage*) pasture

paume [pom] *f* **1.** ANAT (*de la main*) palm **2.** SPORT **jeu de ~** real tennis

paumé(e) [pome] *inf* **I.** *adj* **1.** (*perdu: lieu, village*) god-forsaken; **il est ~** he hasn't got a clue where he is **2.** (*désorienté*) mixed up **3.** (*socialement inadapté*) **être complètement ~** to be completely screwed up **II.** *m(f)* **c'est un ~** he's completely screwed up

paumer [pome] <1> **I.** *vt inf* to lose **II.** *vpr inf* **se ~** to get lost

paupière [popjɛʀ] *f* ANAT eyelid

paupiette [popjɛt] *f* ~ **de veau** stuffed veal escalope

pause [poz] *f* **1.** (*interruption*) break **2.** MUS pause **3.** SPORT half-time

pause-café [pozkafe] <pauses-café> *f inf* coffee break

pauvre [povʀ] **I.** *adj* **1.** (*opp: riche*) poor; (*mobilier, vêtement*) shabby; (*végétation*) sparse; (*style*) weak; **être ~ en graisse/oxygène** to be low in fat/oxygen **2.** *antéposé* (*médiocre: argument, salaire, orateur*) poor **3.** *antéposé* (*digne de pitié*) poor; (*sourire*) weak; **mon ~ ami, si tu savais** if only you knew; **~ France!** poor old France! **4.** *inf* ~ **type** (*malheureux*) poor guy; (*minable*) loser; ~ **idiot** silly fool **II.** *mf* **1.** (*sans argent*) poor man *m*, poor woman *f* **2.** (*idiot*) ~ **d'esprit** half-wit

pauvrement [povʀəmɑ̃] *adv* (*vêtu, meublé*) shabbily

pauvreté [povʀəte] *f* poverty; (*du sol*) poorness; (*d'une habitation, du mobilier*) shabbiness; **la ~ de votre style** your impoverished style

pavage [pavaʒ] *m* paving

pavaner [pavane] <1> *vpr* **se ~** to strut about

pavé [pave] *m* **1.** (*dalle*) paving stone **2.** (*revêtement*) paving **3.** *péj, inf* (*livre*) weighty tome **4.** (*morceau de viande*) ~ **de bœuf** thick steak **5.** INFOR ~ **numérique** numeric keypad

paver [pave] <1> *vt* to pave

pavillon [pavijɔ̃] *m* **1.** (*maison particulière*) house; ~ **de banlieue** house in the suburbs **2.** (*petite maison dans un jardin*) summerhouse; ~ **de chasse** hunting lodge **3.** (*bâtiment: d'un hôpital*) block; (*d'un château*) wing; ~ **central** central section **4.** NAUT flag

pavoiser [pavwaze] <1> *vi inf* (*se réjouir*) to rejoice

pavot [pavo] *m* poppy

payable [pɛjabl] *adj* payable; ~ **fin juillet** (*somme*) payable by the end of July; (*objet*) that must be paid for by the end of July

payant(e) [pɛjɑ̃, ɑ̃t] *adj* **1.** (*opp: gratuit*) where you have to pay; **l'entrée est ~e** you have to pay to go in; **c'est ~** you have to pay **2.** (*rentable: entreprise, coup*) profitable; **c'est une politique ~e** it's a policy that will pay off **3.** (*qui paie: hôte, spectateur*) paying

paye [pɛj] *v.* **paie**

payement [pɛjmɑ̃] *v.* **paiement**

payer [peje] <7> **I.** *vt* **1.** (*acquitter, rétribuer*) to pay; ~ **par chèque/en espèces** to pay by cheque/in cash *Brit*, to pay by check/in cash *Am*; ~ **qn à l'heure** to pay sb by the hour **2.** (*verser de l'argent pour: maison, service*) to pay for; **faire ~ qc à qn mille euros** to charge sb a thousand euros for sth **3.** (*récompenser*) to reward; ~ **qn de sa peine** to pay sb for his trouble; **il était bien/mal payé de cela** he made some money/didn't make much out of it **4.** (*offrir*) ~ **qc à qn** to buy sth for sb; ~ **un coup à qn** *inf* to treat sb **5.** (*expier*) ~ **qc de qc** to pay for sth with sth; **tu me le paieras!** you'll pay for this! ▸**je suis payé pour le savoir** it's my business to know that **II.** *vi* **1.** (*régler*) to pay **2.** (*être rentable*) to pay; (*politique, tactique*) to pay off; **le crime ne paie pas** crime doesn't pay **3.** (*expier*) ~ **pour qn/qc** to pay for what sb did/sth **III.** *vpr* **1.** *inf* (*s'offrir*) **se ~ qc** to buy oneself sth **2.** *inf* (*se prendre*) **se ~ un arbre** to wrap one's car round a tree **3.** (*passif*) **la commande se paie à la livraison** orders are to be paid for on delivery ▸**se ~ la tête de qn** *inf* (*tourner en ridicule*) to take the mickey out of sb; (*tromper*) to pull sb's leg

payeur, -euse [pɛjœʀ, -øz] **I.** *adj* **organisme/service ~** claims department/office **II.** *m, f* payer

pays [pei] *m* **1.** (*nation, État*) country; ~ **membres de l'UE** member countries of the EU; ~ **en voie de développement/d'industrialisation** developing/industrializing country **2.** *sans pl* (*région*) region; **mon ~ natal** the area where I was born; **être du ~** to be local; **les gens du ~** the local people; **saucisson/vin de ~** local sausage/wine **3.** *sans pl* (*patrie*) native country **4.** *sans pl* (*terre d'élection*) **c'est le ~ du vin** it's wine country

5. (*milieu favorable à*) ~ **de légumes** vegetable-growing area; ~ **d'élevage** cattle-breeding area **6.** GEO area; **plat** ~ flat country(side) **7.** (*village*) village; **un petit** ~ **perdu** a small isolated village ▸**être en** ~ **de connaissance** (*connaître la matière, le lieu*) to be on home ground; (*être connu*) to be among friends; **il se conduit comme** (**si il était**) **en** ~ **conquis** he acts as if he owns the place; **voir du** ~ to get around

paysage [peizaʒ] *m* landscape ▸**cela fait bien dans le** ~ **de faire qc** *inf* it looks good if you do sth

paysagiste [peizaʒist] **I.** *mf* **1.** (*en horticulture*) landscape gardener **2.** ART landscape artist **II.** *app* landscape

paysan(**ne**) [peizɑ̃, an] **I.** *adj* **1.** (*agricole: monde, problème*) farming; (*revendication*) farmers' **2.** (*rural: mœurs, vie*) country **3.** *péj* (*rustre: air, manières*) rustic **II.** *m(f)* **1.** (*agriculteur*) farmer **2.** *péj* **quel** ~**!** what a peasant!

Pays-Bas [peibɑ] *mpl* **les** ~ the Netherlands

Pays de Galles [pɛidəgal] *m* Wales

Pays de la Loire [pɛidəlalwaːʀ] *m* Loire Valley

PC [pese] *m* **1.** *abr de* **personal computer** INFOR PC; ~ **de poche** hand-held **2.** *abr de* **poste de commandement** MIL headquarters

PCF [peseɛf] *m abr de* **Parti communiste français** French Communist Party

PCV [peseve] *abr de* **à percevoir: appeler en** ~ to reverse the charges *Brit,* to make a collect call *Am*

PDG [pedeʒe] *m inf abr de* **Président-directeur général** chairman and managing director *Brit,* chairman and chief executive officer *Am*

péage [peaʒ] *m* **1.** (*lieu*) tollbooth **2.** (*taxe*) toll; **route à** ~ toll road, turnpike *Am;* **pont à** ~ toll bridge

> Many French autoroutes are toll roads, with **péage** booths at regular intervals.

peau [po] <x> *f* **1.** (*épiderme: d'une personne*) skin **2.** *pl* (*morceaux desséchés*) ~**x autour des ongles** cuticles; ~**x mortes** dead skin *no pl* **3.** (*cuir*) hide **4.** (*enveloppe, pellicule: d'une banane, tomate, du lait*) skin; (*d'une orange, pomme*) peel ▸**attraper qn par la** ~ **du cou** [*o* **du dos**] *inf* to grab sb by the scruff of the neck; **coûter** [*o* **valoir**] **la** ~ **des fesses** *inf* to cost an arm and a leg; **n'avoir que la** ~ **et les os** [*o* **sur les os**] to be nothing but skin and bone(s); **entrer** [*o* **se mettre**] **dans la** ~ **du personnage** to get (right) into the part; **ne pas donner cher de la** ~ **de qn** *inf* not to give much for sb's chances; **avoir la** ~ **dure** *inf* (*personne*) to be thick-skinned; **vieille** ~ *péj, inf* old crone; **j'aurai ta/leur** ~**!** *inf* I'll get you/them!; **avoir qc dans la** ~ *inf* to have sth in one's blood; **avoir qn dans la** ~ *inf* to be crazy about sb; **défendre sa** ~ to fight for one's life; **entrer dans la** ~ **de qn** to put oneself in sb's shoes; **être bien/mal dans sa peau** to feel good/bad about oneself; **faire la** ~ **à qn** *inf* to bump sb off; **y laisser sa** [*o* **la**] ~ *inf* to get killed; **risquer sa** ~ **pour qn/qc** *inf* to risk one's neck for sb/sth; **tenir à sa** ~ *inf* to value one's life

Peau-Rouge [poʀuʒ] <Peaux-Rouges> *mf* redskin

pêche¹ [pɛʃ] *f* peach; ~ **Melba** peach Melba ▸**avoir la** ~ *inf* to be on form *Brit,* to be in form *Am;* **se fendre la** ~ *inf* to laugh one's head off

pêche² [pɛʃ] *f sans pl* **1.** (*profession*) fishing; ~ **au saumon/au thon** salmon/tuna fishing; ~ **à la baleine** whaling; **produit de la** ~ catch **2.** (*loisir*) fishing; (*à la ligne*) angling; ~ **à la mouche** fly fishing; ~ **au lancer** rod and reel fishing; **aller à la** ~ to go fishing **3.** (*période*) fishing season **4.** (*réserve*) fishing grounds *pl* **5.** (*prises*) catch

péché [peʃe] *m* sin ▸**c'est son** ~ **mignon** it's her weakness

pêcher¹ [peʃe] <1> **I.** *vi* to go fishing; (*avec une canne*) to go angling [*o* fishing] **II.** *vt* **1.** (*être pêcheur de*) ~ **qc** to fish for sth **2.** (*attraper: poisson, crustacé, grenouille*) to catch **3.** *inf* (*chercher*) ~ **qc** (*idée, histoire*) to dig sth up; (*costume, vieux meuble*) to pick sth up; **où a-t-elle pêché** (**l'idée**) **que ...** where did she get the idea that ...

pêcher² [peʃe] *m* peach (tree)

pécheur, **pécheresse** [peʃɛʀ, peʃʀɛs] *m, f* sinner

pêcheur, **-euse** [pɛʃɛʀ, -øz] *m, f* **1.** (*professionnel*) fisherman *m,* fisherwoman *f* **2.** (*à la ligne*) angler

pectoral(**e**) [pɛktɔʀal, o] <-aux> *adj* **1.** ANAT, ZOOL **région** ~**e** pectoral area; **nageoire** ~**e** pectoral fin **2.** MED **sirop** ~ cough syrup

pectoraux [pɛktɔʀo] *mpl* ANAT pectoral muscles

pécule [pekyl] *m sans pl* nest egg

pécuniaire [pekynjɛʀ] *adj* financial

pédagogie [pedagɔʒi] *f* **1.** (*science*) education **2.** (*méthode d'enseignement*) educational methods *pl* **3.** *sans pl* (*qualité*) teaching ability

pédagogique [pedagɔʒik] *adj* educational; (*matériel*) teaching; (*exposé, résumé*) well-presented; **avoir un sens** ~ to be a natural teacher

pédagogue [pedagɔg] **I.** *mf* **1.** (*enseignant*) teacher **2.** (*spécialiste*) educationalist **II.** *adj* **être** ~ to be a good teacher

pédale [pedal] *f* **1.** (*levier pour le pied: d'une bicyclette, voiture, poubelle*) pedal; ~ **de frein** brake pedal **2.** *péj, inf* (*homosexuel*) queer ▸**s'emmêler les** ~**s** *inf* to get in a muddle; **perdre les** ~**s** *inf* to lose it

pédaler [pedale] <1> *vi* **1.** (*bicyclette*) to pedal; ~ **debout** to stand on the pedals **2.** *inf*

P

(*faire vite*) to get a move on
pédalier [pedalje] *m* **1.** (*d'une bicyclette*) pedals *pl* and chain drive **2.** MUS pedalboard
pédalo® [pedalo] *m* pedalo *Brit,* pedal boat *Am;* **faire du** ~ to go out in a pedalo
pédant(e) [pedɑ̃, ɑ̃t] **I.** *adj péj* pedantic **II.** *m(f) péj* pedant
pédé [pede] *m péj, inf abr de* **pédéraste** queer, fag *Am*
pédéraste [pedeʀast] *m* (*homosexuel*) homosexual
pédestre [pedɛstʀ] *adj* **randonnée** ~ ramble; **sentier** ~ footpath
pédiatre [pedjatʀ] *mf* paediatrician *Brit,* pediatrician *Am*
pédicure [pedikyʀ] *mf* chiropodist *Brit,* podiatrist *Am*
pedigree [pedigʀe] *m* pedigree
pédophile [pedɔfil] *mf* paedophile *Brit,* pedophile *Am*
PEGC [peøʒese] *mf abr de* **professeur d'enseignement général des collèges** schoolteacher
pègre [pɛgʀ] *f sans pl* underworld
peigne [pɛɲ] *m* comb; ~ **fin** fine-tooth comb; ~ **à manche/de poche** tail/pocket comb; **se donner un coup de** ~ to run a comb through one's hair ►**passer au** ~ **fin** (*livre, témoignage*) to go over with a fine-tooth comb; (*région*) to comb
peigner [peɲe] <1> **I.** *vt* (*cheveux, chien*) to comb; ~ **qn** to comb sb's hair **II.** *vpr* **se** ~ to comb one's hair
peignoir [pɛɲwaʀ] *m* dressing gown *Brit,* robe *Am*
peinard(e) [pɛnaʀ, aʀd] *adj inf* (*personne*) laid-back; (*boulot, vie*) cushy; (*coin*) quiet
peindre [pɛ̃dʀ] *irr* **I.** *vi* (*au pinceau*) to paint **II.** *vt* ~ **qc en rouge/jaune** to paint sth red/yellow ►**être peint** *péj* to be heavily made-up **III.** *vpr* **se** ~ **sur le visage de qn** (*angoisse, joie*) to be written on sb's face
peine [pɛn] **I.** *f* **1.** (*chagrin, douleur*) sorrow; **des ~s de cœur** troubles of the heart; **avoir de la ~/beaucoup de** ~ to be upset/very upset; **faire de la** ~ **à qn** to upset sb **2.** JUR sentence; ~ **de mort** death penalty; **défense d'entrer sous** ~ **de poursuites** trespassers will be prosecuted **3.** (*effort, difficulté*) trouble; **avoir de la ~/beaucoup de** ~ **à faire qc** to have trouble/a lot of trouble doing sth; **donnez-vous** [*o* **prenez** (**donc**)] **la** ~ **d'entrer** *form* (please) do come in; **ne vous donnez pas cette** ~ please don't bother; **ne pas épargner sa** ~ to go to a great deal of trouble; **avec** ~ with difficulty; **sans** ~ without (any) difficulty; **pour la/sa** ~ (*en récompense*) for one's trouble; (*en punition*) as a punishment ►**être bien en** ~ **de** +*infin* to be hard pressed to +*infin;* **être dur à la** ~ to be a hard worker; **c'est bien la** ~ **de faire qc** *iron* what's the point of doing sth; **n'être pas en** ~ **pour faire qc** to have no difficulty (in) doing sth; **en être pour sa** ~ to get nothing for one's trouble; **sous** ~ **de ...** on pain of ...; **roule doucement sous** ~ **de glisser** drive slowly or you'll slip **II.** *adv* **1.** (*très peu*) **à** ~ hardly **2.** (*tout au plus*) **à** ~ only just; **il y a à** ~ **huit jours** scarcely a week ago **3.** (*juste*) **avoir à** ~ **commencé/fini** to have just started/finished **4.** (*aussitôt*) **à** ~ **...** no sooner ... ►**à** ~**!** *iron* you don't say!
peiner [pene] <1> **I.** *vi* **1.** (*avoir des difficultés*) ~ **à/pour faire qc** to have trouble doing sth; ~ **sur un problème** to struggle with a problem **2.** (*avoir des problèmes: moteur, voiture*) to labour *Brit,* to labor *Am* **II.** *vt* ~ **qn** (*nouvelle, refus*) to upset sb; (*décevoir*) to disappoint sb; (*faire de la peine à*) to hurt sb
peint(e) [pɛ̃, ɛ̃t] *adj* painted ►**papier** ~ wallpaper
peintre [pɛ̃tʀ] *m* painter; ~ **en bâtiment** painter and decorator
peinture [pɛ̃tyʀ] *f* **1.** (*couleur*) paint; ~ **à l'eau** watercolour *Brit,* watercolor *Am;* ~ **à l'huile** oil paint **2.** (*couche, surface peinte*) paintwork; ~ **fraîche!** wet paint! **3.** *sans pl* (*action*) painting; ~ **au pistolet** spray-painting **4.** *sans pl* ART painting; **école de** ~ school of painting; **musée de** ~ art gallery **5.** (*toile*) painting; ~ **murale** wall painting; ~ **à l'huile** oil painting **6.** *sans pl* (*description, évocation*) portrayal; **faire la** ~ **de qc** to portray sth ►**je ne peux pas le voir en** ~ *inf* I can't stand (the sight of) him
peinturlurer [pɛ̃tyʀlyʀe] <1> **I.** *vt inf* to daub; **être peinturluré de qc** to be daubed with sth **II.** *vpr inf* **se** ~ **le visage** to put on thick make-up
péjoratif, -ive [peʒɔʀatif, -iv] *adj* pejorative
péjorativement [peʒɔʀativmɑ̃] *adv* pejoratively
pékinois [pekinwa] *m* (*chien*) pekinese, pekingese
PEL [peøɛl] *m abr de* **plan d'épargne logement** *savings plan for buying property*
pelage [pəlaʒ] *m* (*d'un animal*) coat
pelé [pəle] *m Belgique* (*partie du gîte à la noix*) *part of the topside of beef*
pelé(e) [pəle] **I.** *adj* (*personne*) bald(-headed) **II.** *m(f)* **quatre** [*o* **trois**] **~s et un tondu** *inf* one man and a dog
pêle-mêle [pɛlmɛl] *adv* all jumbled up; **les choses sont** ~ everything's all over the place
peler [pəle] <4> **I.** *vi* **1.** (*perdre sa peau*) to peel **2.** *inf* (*avoir froid*) to be freezing (cold) **II.** *vt* to peel **III.** *vpr* **se** ~ **facilement** to peel easily
pèlerin [pɛlʀɛ̃] *m* REL pilgrim
pèlerinage [pɛlʀinaʒ] *m* **1.** (*voyage*) pilgrimage **2.** (*lieu*) place of pilgrimage
pélican [pelikɑ̃] *m* pelican
pelisse [pəlis] *f* pelisse
pelle [pɛl] *f* shovel; (*d'un jardinier*) spade; ~ **mécanique** mechanical digger; ~ **à tarte** cake

slice ►**on les** <u>**ramasse**</u> **à la** ~ *inf* there are piles of them; (**se**) <u>**ramasser**</u> [*o* **se** <u>**prendre**</u>] **une** ~ *inf* to fall flat on one's face; <u>**rouler**</u> **une** ~ **à qn** *inf* to give sb a French kiss

pelletée [pɛlte] *f* **1.** (*contenu d'une pelle*) **une** ~ **de sable** a shovelful of sand; (*dans le jardin, à la plage*) a spadeful of sand **2.** *inf* (*bordée*) **une** ~ **d'injures** a torrent of abuse

pelleteuse [pɛltøz] *f* digger

pellicule [pelikyl] *f* **1.** PHOT, CINE film; ~ **couleur** colour film *Brit,* color film *Am;* ~ **noir et blanc** black-and-white film **2.** (*mince couche: de poussière, givre, crème, pétrole*) film **3.** *souvent pl* (*peau morte*) dandruff

pelote [p(ə)lɔt] *f* **1.** (*boule de fils*) ball **2.** SPORT ~ **basque** pelota

peloter [p(ə)lɔte] <1> **I.** *vt inf* to paw; **se faire** ~ **par qn** to be groped by sb **II.** *vpr inf* **se** ~ to paw each other

peloton [p(ə)lɔtɔ̃] *m* **1.** SPORT, POL, ECON pack; **être dans le** ~ **de tête** to be in with the front runners; **être dans le** ~ **de queue** to be trailing behind **2.** MIL squad; (*de sapeurs-pompiers*) contingent; ~ **de gendarmerie** police squad; ~ **d'exécution** firing squad

pelotonner [p(ə)lɔtɔne] <1> *vpr* **1.** (*se mettre en boule*) **se** ~ to curl up **2.** (*se blottir*) **se** ~ **contre qn/qc** to snuggle up to sb/sth; **se** ~ **sous les draps** to snuggle down under the sheets

pelouse [p(ə)luz] *f* lawn

peluche [p(ə)lyʃ] *f* **1.** (*matière*) plush; **ours en** ~ teddy (bear) **2.** (*jouet*) soft toy **3.** (*poil*) fluff **4.** (*poussière*) piece of fluff **5.** (*d'un pull*) pill

pelucher [p(ə)lyʃe] <1> *vi* (*tissu, vêtement*) to pill

pelucheux, -euse [p(ə)lyʃø, -øz] *adj* fluffy

pelure [p(ə)lyʀ] *f* **1.** (*d'un fruit, légume*) peeling **2.** *inf* (*manteau*) coat; **enlever sa** ~ to take one's coat off

pénal(**e**) [penal, o] <-aux> *adj* (*code*) penal; **affaire/procédure** ~**e** criminal matter/proceedings *pl;* **droit** ~ criminal law

pénalisation [penalizasjɔ̃] *f* **1.** (*pénalité*) penalty **2.** (*désavantage*) penalization

pénaliser [penalize] <1> *vt* **1.** SPORT to penalize **2.** (*désavantager: classe, religion*) to discriminate against; ~ **qn/qc de qc** to penalize sb/sth by sth **3.** (*sanctionner*) to punish **4.** (*sanctionner d'une amende*) to fine

pénalité [penalite] *f a.* SPORT penalty; **coup de pied de** ~ penalty kick; **tirer le coup de pied de** ~ to take the penalty (kick)

penalty <s *o* -ies> [penalti] *m* (*tir au but*) penalty

penaud(**e**) [pəno, od] *adj* **1.** (*honteux*) sheepish; **s'en aller tout** ~ to go off looking sheepish **2.** (*contrit*) contrite **3.** (*déçu*) crestfallen

penchant [pɑ̃ʃɑ̃] *m* ~ **à qc** tendency towards sth; ~ **pour qc** liking for sth

penché(**e**) [pɑ̃ʃe] *adj* **1.** (*écriture*) slanting; **être** ~ (*mur, tour*) to lean (over); (*bouteille*) to be tipping; (*tableau*) to be tilting; **la tour** ~**e de Pise** the Leaning Tower of Pisa **2.** (*être courbé vers*) **être** ~ **sur qn/qc** to be leaning over sb/sth; ~ **sur ses livres** bent over one's books

pencher [pɑ̃ʃe] <1> **I.** *vi* **1.** (*perdre l'équilibre*) to tip (over); (*arbre*) to tilt; (*bateau*) to list; **le vent fait** ~ **l'arbre** the tree is bending over in the wind **2.** (*ne pas être droit*) to lean sideways; ~ **à droite** to lean to the right **3.** (*se prononcer pour*) ~ **pour qc** to incline to favour sth **II.** *vt* (*bouteille, carafe*) to tip; (*table, chaise*) to tilt; ~ **la tête** (*en avant, sur qc*) to bend one's head (forward); (*de honte*) to hang one's head; (*sur le côté*) to put one's head on on side; ~ **la tête en arrière** to tip one's head back **III.** *vpr* **1.** (*baisser*) **se** ~ to bend down; **se** ~ **par la fenêtre** to lean out of the window **2.** (*examiner*) **se** ~ **sur un problème** to look into a problem

pendaison [pɑ̃dɛzɔ̃] *f* hanging; **mort par** ~ death by hanging

pendant [pɑ̃dɑ̃] **I.** *prep* **1.** (*pour indiquer une durée*) for; ~ **trois jours/plusieurs années** for three days/several years; **marcher** ~ **des kilomètres et des kilomètres** to walk for miles and miles **2.** (*au cours de, simultanément à*) during; **c'était avant le cours ou** ~**?** was it before or during the lesson?; ~ **ce temps** meanwhile; ~ **longtemps** for a long time **II.** *conj* **1.** (*tandis que*) ~ **que** while **2.** (*aussi longtemps que*) ~ **que** as long as ►~ **que tu y** <u>**es**</u> *iron* while you're at it; ~ **que j'y** <u>**pense**</u> while I think of it

pendant(**e**) [pɑ̃dɑ̃, ɑ̃t] *adj* **1.** (*tombant*) hanging; (*langue*) hanging out; **oreilles** ~**es** floppy ears **2.** (*ballant: jambes*) dangling; **rester les bras** ~**s** to stand around inanely **3.** JUR (*procès, affaire*) pending

pendentif [pɑ̃dɑ̃tif] *m* (*bijou*) pendant

penderie [pɑ̃dʀi] *f* **1.** (*garde-robe*) wardrobe **2.** (*placard mural*) (fitted) wardrobe *Brit,* closet *Am* **3.** (*armoire*) cupboard

pendouiller [pɑ̃duje] <1> *vi inf* to dangle

pendre [pɑ̃dʀ] <14> **I.** *vi être* **1.** (*être suspendu*) to hang; ~ **à qc** to be hanging on sth; ~ **de qc** to be hanging from sth **2.** (*tomber: cheveux, guirlande*) to hang down; (*joues*) to sag; **laisser** ~ **ses jambes** to dangle one's legs **II.** *vt* **1.** (*accrocher*) ~ **qc au portemanteau/dans l'armoire** to hang sth (up) on the coat rack/in the cupboard **2.** (*mettre à mort*) ~ **qn à un arbre** to hang sb from a tree; **être pendu** to be hanged ►**je** <u>**veux**</u> (**bien**) **être pendu si ...** I'll be damned if ... **III.** *vpr* **1.** (*s'accrocher*) **se** ~ **à une branche** to hang from a branch; **se** ~ **au cou de qn** to throw one's arms around sb's neck; (*par crainte*) to cling to sb **2.** (*se suicider*) **se** ~ to hang oneself

pendu [pɑ̃dy] *m* JEUX **jouer au** ~ to play hangman

pendu(**e**) [pɑ̃dy] **I.** *part passé de* **pendre**

P

II. *adj inf* (*agrippé*) **être ~ aux lèvres de qn** to hang on sb's every word; **être ~ au téléphone** to always be on the phone **III.** *m(f)* hanged man *m*, hanged woman *f*

pendule [pɑ̃dyl] **I.** *f* clock; **~ murale/de cuisine** wall/kitchen clock ►**remettre les ~s à l'heure** to set the record straight **II.** *m* (*d'un sourcier*) pendulum

pendulette [pɑ̃dylɛt] *f* clock

pénétrant(e) [penetʀɑ̃, ɑ̃t] *adj* **1.** (*qui transperce: froid*) bitter; (*air*) bitterly cold; (*pluie*) drenching **2.** (*fort: odeur*) strong **3.** (*aigu: regard*) penetrating

pénétration [penetʀasjɔ̃] *f* **1.** *sans pl* (*action*) penetration **2.** *sans pl* (*perspicacité*) insight

pénétré(e) [penetʀe] *adj* (*ton, air*) earnest; **dire qc d'un ton** [*o* **sur un ton**] **~** to say sth in deeply serious tones; **être ~ de son sujet** to know one's subject backwards; **~ de son importance** [*o* **de soi-même**] full of self-importance

pénétrer [penetʀe] <5> **I.** *vi* **1.** (*entrer*) **~ dans qc** (*personne, véhicule, armée*) to enter sth; (*par la force, abusivement*) to break into sth; (*balle*) to penetrate sth; **~ sur un marché** to break into a market **2.** (*prendre place*) **~ dans qc** (*idée*) to sink into sth; (*habitude*) to establish itself in sth **3.** (*s'insinuer*) **~ dans qc** (*odeur, liquide, crème, vent*) to get into sth; (*soleil*) to shine into sth; **~ à travers qc** to go through sth **II.** *vt* **1.** (*transpercer*) **~ qc** to penetrate sth; **~ qn** (*froid, humidité*) to go right through sb; (*regard*) to penetrate sb **2.** (*imprégner: mode, habitude*) to become established in **3.** (*découvrir: mystère, secret*) to penetrate; (*intentions, sens*) to fathom

pénible [penibl] *adj* **1.** (*fatigant, difficile*) hard; (*chemin*) rough; (*respiration*) laboured *Brit*, labored *Am*; **il est ~ à qn de** +*infin* it's very hard for sb to +*infin* **2.** (*douloureux: heure, moment*) painful; (*circonstance, événement*) distressing; **être ~ à qn** to be painful for sb **3.** (*désagréable: sujet, circonstance*) unpleasant; **il m'est ~ de constater que …** I am sorry to find that … **4.** (*agaçant: personne, caractère*) tiresome; **c'est ~!** isn't it awful!; **il est vraiment ~** *inf* he's a real pain (in the neck)

péniblement [penibləmɑ̃] *adv* **1.** (*difficilement*) with difficulty **2.** (*tout juste*) just about

péniche [peniʃ] *f* barge

pénichette [peniʃɛt] *f* riverboat

pénicilline [penisilin] *f* penicillin

péninsule [penɛ̃syl] *f* peninsula; **la ~ balkanique/ibérique** the Balkan/Iberian Peninsula

pénis [penis] *m* penis

pénitence [penitɑ̃s] *f* penitence; (*sacrement*) penance; **faire ~** to do penance

pénitentiaire [penitɑ̃sjɛʀ] *adj* **régime ~** prison regime; **établissement ~** prison; **personnel ~** prison staff; **colonie ~** penal colony

Pennsylvanie [pɛnsilvani] *f* **la ~** Pennsylvania

pénombre [penɔ̃bʀ] *f* **1.** half-light **2.** ASTR penumbra

pensable [pɑ̃sabl] *adj* **ne pas être ~** to be unthinkable

pensant(e) [pɑ̃sɑ̃, ɑ̃t] *adj* thinking

pensée¹ [pɑ̃se] *f* **1.** (*idée*) thought; **être absorbé dans ses ~s** to be deep in thought; **aller jusqu'au bout de sa ~** (*achever sa réflexion*) to follow one's thoughts through to their conclusion; (*réaliser ses intentions*) to see one's thoughts through; **loin de moi la ~ que …** far be it from me to think that … **2.** *sans pl* (*opinion*) thinking; **je partage votre ~ là-dessus** I share your opinion on that **3.** *sans pl* PHILOS (*raison*) thought; (*façon de penser*) thinking **4.** (*esprit*) mind; **je suis en ~ avec vous** my thoughts are with you **5.** *sans pl* (*philosophie: chrétienne, marxiste*) thinking; **la ~ de Gandhi/Nietzsche** the thought of Gandhi/Nietzsche; **libre ~** free thinking **6.** (*réflexion brève*) thought

pensée² [pɑ̃se] *f* BOT pansy

penser [pɑ̃se] <1> **I.** *vi* **1.** (*réfléchir*) to think; **faculté de ~** capacity for thought; **~ à qc** to think of sth **2.** (*juger*) **~ différemment sur qc** to think differently about sth **3.** (*songer à*) **~ à qn/qc** to think about sb/sth; **sans ~ à mal** without meaning any harm **4.** (*ne pas oublier*) **~ à qn/qc** to remember sb/sth; **~ à** +*infin* to remember to +*infin*; **faire ~ à qn/qc** to remind one of sb/sth **5.** (*s'intéresser à*) **~ aux autres** to think of others ►**je pense bien!** *inf* I should hope so!; **donner** [*o* **laisser**] **à ~** to make one think; **laisser à ~ que …** to let it be thought that …; **mais j'y pense …** but I was just thinking …; **tu n'y penses pas!** *inf* you don't mean it!; (**là**) **où je pense** *inf* you know where; **tu penses!** *inf* (*tu plaisantes*) you must be joking!; (*et comment*) you bet! **II.** *vt* **1.** to think; **~ qn intelligent/sincère** to consider sb intelligent/sincere; **c'est bien ce que je pensais** that's exactly what I was thinking; **je pense que oui/que non** I think/don't think so; **vous pensez bien que …** *inf* you can well imagine that … **2.** (*avoir l'intention de*) **~ faire qc** to be thinking of doing sth; **que pensez-vous faire à présent?** what are you planning now? ►**n'en penser pas moins** to draw one's own conclusions; **cela me fait ~ que …** that reminds me that …; **pensez que …** (*tenez compte*) to think that …; (*imaginez*) you can well imagine that …

penseur, -euse [pɑ̃sœʀ, -øz] *m, f* thinker; **libre ~** freethinker

pensif, -ive [pɑ̃sif, -iv] *adj* thoughtful

pension [pɑ̃sjɔ̃] *f* **1.** (*allocation*) pension; **~ alimentaire** (*en cas de divorce*) alimony; (*à un enfant naturel*) maintenance **2.** ECOLE boarding (school); **mettre qn en ~** to send sb to boarding school **3.** (*petit hôtel*) guesthouse **4.** (*hébergement*) board and lodging(s); ~

complète full board; **être en ~ chez qn** to be boarding with sb
pensionnaire [pɑ̃sjɔnɛʀ] *mf* **1.** ECOLE boarder **2.** (*dans un hôtel*) resident **3.** (*dans une famille*) lodger
pensionnat [pɑ̃sjɔna] *m* boarding school
pensionné(e) [pɑ̃sjɔne] *m(f)* pensioner
pente [pɑ̃t] *f* (*d'une route, colline, d'un terrain*) slope; (*d'un toit*) pitch; **monter la ~** to climb (up) the hill; **en ~** sloping; **descendre/monter en ~ douce/raide** to slope gently/steeply downwards/upwards ▶**être sur une ~ dangereuse** *inf* to be on a slippery slope; **être sur une mauvaise ~** to be going downhill; **remonter la ~** to get back one one's feet again
Pentecôte [pɑ̃tkot] *f* Whit(sun) *Brit,* Pentecost *Am;* **les vacances de (la) ~** the Whit(sun) holiday(s) *Brit,* Pentecost vacation *Am*
pénurie [penyʀi] *f* (*pavreté*) penury *no pl;* (*manque*) shortage; **~ d'eau/vivres** water/food shortage; **~ d'argent/de capitaux** lack of money/capital; **~ de personnel** staff shortage; **~ de logements** housing shortage; **il y a (une) ~ de qc** there's a shortage of sth
pépé [pepe] *m inf* grandpa
pépée [pepe] *f inf* chick
pépère [pepɛʀ] **I.** *adj inf* (*vie*) cosy; (*travail*) cushy; **un petit coin ~** a cosy little spot **II.** *m* **1.** *enfantin, inf* (*grand-père*) grandad **2.** *inf* oldster, old-timer *Am;* (*enfant*) bonny child *Brit,* cute kid *Am;* **un gros ~** a fat old guy
pépier [pepje] <1a> *vi* to twitter
pépin [pepɛ̃] *m* **1.** (*graine: d'un raisin, d'une pomme*) pip; **sans ~s** seedless; **fruits à ~** seeded fruit **2.** *inf* (*ennui, difficulté*) hitch; **j'ai eu un gros ~** I've had big trouble **3.** *inf* (*parapluie*) umbrella, brolly *Brit*
pépinière [pepinjɛʀ] *f* **1.** nursery **2.** (*vivier*) **~ de savants/jeunes talents** a breeding ground for scholars/young talent
pépite [pepit] *f* **~ d'or** gold nugget
péquenaud(e) [pɛkno, od] **I.** *adj péj, inf* peasant **II.** *m(f) péj, inf* yokel
perçant(e) [pɛʀsɑ̃, ɑ̃t] *adj* (*cri, regard, voix*) piercing; (*froid*) bitter; (*esprit*) penetrating
percée [pɛʀse] *f* **1.** (*dans une forêt*) clearing; (*dans un mur*) opening; **faire [o ouvrir] une ~ dans la forêt** to make a clearing in the forest **2.** SPORT, ECON, MIL breakthrough; **~ technologique/politique** technological/political breakthrough
percement [pɛʀsəmɑ̃] *m* (*d'une cloison, rue, d'un mur*) building; (*d'une fenêtre, porte*) opening up; (*d'un tunnel*) digging
perce-neige [pɛʀsənɛʒ] <perce-neige(s)> *m o f* snowdrop
percepteur [pɛʀsɛptœʀ] *m* (*fonctionnaire*) tax collector; (*administration*) taxman
perceptible [pɛʀsɛptibl] *adj* (*détail, mouvement, son, amélioration*) perceptible
perception [pɛʀsɛpsjɔ̃] *f* perception; (*des couleurs, odeurs*) sense
percer [pɛʀse] <2> **I.** *vi* **1.** (*apparaître: dent*) to come through; **le soleil perce à travers les nuages** the sun is breaking through the clouds **2.** (*transparaître*) **~ dans qc** (*sentiment, ironie*) to show in sth **3.** (*devenir populaire: artiste*) to make a name for oneself **II.** *vt* **1.** (*forer: trou*) to make; (*avec une perceuse*) to drill **2.** (*faire des trous dans*) **~ qc d'un trou/de trous** to make a hole/holes in sth; (*avec une perceuse*) to drill a hole/holes in sth **3.** (*perforer: mur, tôle*) to make a hole in; (*coffre-fort*) to break open; (*abcès, ampoule*) to burst; (*avec une lame*) to lance; (*pneu, tympan*) to burst; (*oreille, narine*) to pierce; (*tonneau*) to broach; **être percé** (*chaussette, chaussure, poche*) to have holes in; (*d'un seul trou*) to have a hole in **4.** (*creuser une ouverture dans: mur, rocher*) to make an opening in **5.** (*traverser: ligne, front*) to break through; **~ la foule** to make one's way through the crowd **6.** (*déchirer: nuages*) to break through; (*obscurité, silence*) to pierce; **~ les oreilles [o les tympans] à qn** (*bruit*) to make sb's ears ring **7.** (*découvrir: mystère, secret*) to penetrate
perceuse [pɛʀsøz] *f* drill
percevoir [pɛʀsəvwaʀ] <12> *vt* **1.** (*avec l'oreille*) to hear; (*avec les yeux*) to see **2.** (*concevoir: évolution, problème, gêne, nuance*) to see; (*vérité, intention*) to understand; **être mal perçu par qn** (*mesure, projet, loi, intention*) to meet with sb's disapproval; (*problème*) to be poorly understood by sb; **~ qn comme un perturbateur** to see sb as a troublemaker **3.** (*recevoir, encaisser: indemnité, honoraires, interêts*) to receive; (*loyer, cotisation*) to collect **4.** (*prélever*) to collect
perche[1] [pɛʀʃ] *f* ZOOL perch
perche[2] [pɛʀʃ] *f* **1.** pole; (*d'un téléski*) rod; MEDIA boom **2.** SPORT **la ~, le saut à la ~** (*épreuve*) pole vault; (*sport*) pole vaulting ▶**grande ~** *inf* beanpole; **saisir la ~ que l'on vous tend** to take the help that's been offered; **tendre la ~ à qn** to throw sb a line
perché(e) [pɛʀʃe] *adj* perched
percher [pɛʀʃe] <1> **I.** *vi* (*oiseau*) to perch **II.** *vt inf* (*mettre*) **~ qc sur qc** to stick sth on sth **III.** *vpr* **se ~** to perch
perchiste [pɛʀʃist] *mf* **1.** SPORT pole vaulter **2.** MEDIA boom operator **3.** (*en ski*) ski lift attendant
perchoir [pɛʀʃwaʀ] *m* **1.** perch; (*des poules*) roost **2.** *inf* (*lieu élevé*) perch; **descends de ton ~!** get down from your high chair! **3.** *inf* POL *Speaker's chair in the French Parliament*
perclus(e) [pɛʀkly, yz] *adj* **être ~ de rhumatismes** to be crippled with rhumatism; **être ~ de douleurs** to be all aches and pains
percolateur [pɛʀkɔlatœʀ] *m* percolator
perçu(e) [pɛʀsy] *part passé de* **percevoir**
percussion [pɛʀkysjɔ̃] *f* percussion; **la ~, les instruments à ~** percussion instruments; **perforeuse à ~** hammer drill
percussionniste [pɛʀkysjɔnist] *mf* MUS per-

P

cussionnist
percutant(e) [pɛʀkytɑ̃, ɑ̃t] *adj* powerful
percuter [pɛʀkyte] <1> **I.** *vi* ~ **contre qc** to crash into sth **II.** *vt* to strike; ~ **qn** (*avec la voiture*) to crash into sb
perdant(e) [pɛʀdɑ̃, ɑ̃t] **I.** *adj* (*billet, numéro, cheval*) losing; **être** ~ to lose out; **partir** ~ to be doomed to failure **II.** *m(f)* loser
perdition [pɛʀdisjɔ̃] *f* **navire en** ~ ship in distress
perdre [pɛʀdʀ] <14> **I.** *vi* ~ **au jeu/au loto/aux élections** to lose at the tables/on the lottery/in the elections ►**y** ~ COM to make a loss **II.** *vt* **1.** to lose; (*date, nom*) to forget **2.** (*cesser d'avoir: réputation, estime, vitesse*) to lose; (*habitude*) to get out of; ~ **de son prestige** to lose some of one's prestige; **n'avoir rien à** ~ **dans qc** to have nothing to lose by sth **3.** (*se voir privé d'une partie de soi*) to lose; **il perd la vue/l'ouïe** his sight/hearing is failing; ~ **le goût de qc** to lose one's taste for sth **4.** (*laisser s'échapper: sang*) to lose; **tu perds ton pantalon** your trousers are falling down *Brit,* your pants are falling down *Am;* **elle perdait une de ses chaussures** one of her shoes was coming off **5.** (*gaspiller: du temps, une heure*) to waste; ~ **une occasion** to miss an opportunity; **faire** ~ **une heure à qn** to waste an hour of sb's time **6.** (*rater*) ~ **qc en ne faisant pas qc** [*o* **à ne pas faire qc**] to miss sth by not doing sth; **tu n'y perds rien!** you haven't missed anything! **7.** (*ruiner*) ~ **qn** to be the ruin of sb ►**tu ne perds rien pour attendre!** you're not getting off so lightly!; **ne pas en** ~ **une miette** to let nothing escape one **III.** *vpr* **1.** (*s'égarer*) **se** ~ **dans la/en forêt** to get lost in the/a forest; **se** ~ **en route** (*colis, lettre*) to get lost in the post **2.** (*s'attarder à*) **se** ~ **dans des explications** to get bogged down in explanations **3.** (*se plonger*) **se** ~ **dans ses pensées** to be lost in thought **4.** (*disparaître*) **se** ~ (*sens, bonnes habitudes*) to be lost; (*coutume, tradition, métier*) to be dying out **5.** (*faire naufrage*) **se** ~ to sink; **un bateau s'est perdu** a boat has been lost **6.** (*se gâter*) **se** ~ (*fruits, légumes*) to go bad; (*récolte*) to be lost **7.** (*rester inutilisé*) **se** ~ (*ressources*) to go to waste; (*initiative, occasion*) to be lost ►**il y a des gifles qui se perdent** *inf* someone needs a clip round the ear; **je m'y perds** I can't make head (n)or tail of it
perdreau [pɛʀdʀo] <x> *m* young partridge
perdrix [pɛʀdʀi] *f* partridge; ~ **grise** partridge; ~ **rouge** red-legged partridge
perdu(e) [pɛʀdy] **I.** *part passé de* **perdre** **II.** *adj* **1.** lost **2.** (*qui a été égaré: objet*) lost; (*chien*) stray; (*sans propriétaire*) abandoned **3.** (*gaspillé, manqué*) **soirée/temps/argent de** ~ waste of an evening/of time/of money; **place de** ~ wasted space; **occasion de** ~ wasted opportunity **4.** (*de loisir*) **à mes heures ~es** [*o* **moments ~s**] in my spare time **5.** (*isolé: pays, coin, endroit*) out-of-the-way **6.** (*non consigné: bouteille*) non-returnable; (*emballage*) disposable **7.** (*mourant*) dying
perdurer [pɛʀdyʀe] *vi Belgique* (*continuer*) to carry on
père [pɛʀ] *m* **1.** (*géniteur*) father; **Durand** ~ Durand senior; **de** ~ **en fils** from father to son **2.** (*créateur, fondateur: d'une idée, théorie, d'un projet*) father; (*d'une institution*) founder **3.** *inf* (*monsieur*) **le** ~ **Dupont** old (man) Dupont ►**tel** ~**, tel fils** like father, like son; ~ **Fouettard** bogeyman; ~ **Noël** Father Christmas *Brit,* Santa Claus *Am*
Père [pɛʀ] *m* REL **Notre** ~ Our Father
pérégrinations [peʀegʀinasjɔ̃] *fpl* peregrinations; (*pour des démarches*) travels
péremptoire [peʀɑ̃ptwaʀ] *adj* peremptory
pérennité [peʀenite] *f sans pl* endurance
perf [pɛʀf] *f abr de* **perfusion** drip *Brit,* IV *Am*
perfection [pɛʀfɛksjɔ̃] *f sans pl* perfection; **être une** ~ to be absolutely perfect; **à la** ~ to perfection
perfectionné(e) [pɛʀfɛksjɔne] *adj* (*machine, dispositif*) advanced; **très** ~ sophisticated
perfectionnement [pɛʀfɛksjɔnmɑ̃] *m* improvement; (*d'un système, appareil, d'une technique*) development; **apporter des ~s à qc** to improve sth; **stage de** ~ advanced training course; **classe de** ~ ECOLE advanced class
perfectionner [pɛʀfɛksjɔne] <1> **I.** *vt* to improve; (*système, technique, appareil*) to develop; (*mettre au point*) to perfect **II.** *vpr* **se** ~ to improve; (*système, technique, appareil*) to be developed; (*être mis au point*) to be perfected; **se** ~ **en français** (*personne*) to improve one's French; **se** ~ **dans/en qc** (*personne*) to increase one's knowledge of/in sth
perfectionnisme [pɛʀfɛksjɔnism] *m* perfectionism
perfectionniste [pɛʀfɛksjɔnist] *mf, adj* perfectionist
perforation [pɛʀfɔʀasjɔ̃] *f* **1.** MED perforation; **une** ~ **du tympan** a perforated eardrum; **une** ~ **intestinale** INFOR a perforated intestine **2.** (*trou*) perforation; (*d'un film*) sprocket hole
perforatrice [pɛʀfɔʀatʀis] *f* card punch
perforé(e) [pɛʀfɔʀe] *adj* **1.** (*percé*) **avoir le tympan** ~ to have a perforated eardrum **2.** (*qui a de petits trous*) punched; **carte ~e** punch card
perforer [pɛʀfɔʀe] <1> *vt* to pierce; (*percer d'un trou*) to punch; (*percer de trous réguliers*) to perforate
perforeuse [pɛʀfɔʀøz] *f* card punch
performance [pɛʀfɔʀmɑ̃s] *f a.* SPORT performance; **~s** (*d'une machine, voiture*) performance + *vb sing;* **réaliser de bonnes ~s** to get good results
performant(e) [pɛʀfɔʀmɑ̃, ɑ̃t] *adj* (*appareil, technique*) high-performance; (*entreprise, industrie, produit*) successful; (*cadre, manager*) effective

perfusion [pɛʀfyzjɔ̃] *f* MED drip; **être sous ~** to be on a drip *Brit,* to be on an IV *Am;* **mettre qn sous ~** to put sb on a drip

pergola [pɛʀgɔla] *f* pergola

péricliter [peʀiklite] <1> *vi* (*affaire, commerce*) to be in decline; **son commerce périclite** his business is going downhill

péridurale [peʀidyʀal] *f* epidural

périf [peʀif] *m inf abr de* **périphérique**

périgourdin(e) [peʀiguʀdɛ̃, in] *adj* from the Perigord

périlleux, -euse [peʀijø, -jøz] *adj* **1.** (*dangereux*) perilous **2.** (*délicat: sujet*) dangerous

périmé(e) [peʀime] *adj* **1.** (*carte, visa, garantie*) expired; **un médicament ~** a medicine that has gone past its use-by date; **un yaourt ~** a yoghurt that has passed its eat-by date **2.** (*démodé, dépassé: conception, institution*) outdated; **être ~** to be outdated [*o* out of date]

périmer [peʀime] <1> *vi* **être périmé** (*carte, passeport, visa, billet*) to have expired; **laisser ~ un billet** to let a ticket run out

période [peʀjɔd] *f* **1.** (*époque*) time; **la ~ classique** the classical period **2.** (*espace de temps*) period; **une ~ d'un an** a period of a year; **~ électorale** election time; **~ de double circulation** (*concernant l'euro*) dual circulation period; **~ de transition** (*concernant l'euro*) transition period; **~ de (la) vie** period of one's life; **~ d'activité** (*durée d'un emploi*) time employed; **~ d'essai** trial period; **par ~(s)** from time to time

périodicité [peʀjɔdisite] *f* periodicity; **avoir une ~ semestrielle** (*revue*) to appear twice a year

périodique [peʀjɔdik] **I.** *adj* **1.** (*cyclique*) *a.* PRESSE periodical **2.** (*hygiénique*) **serviette ~** sanitary towel **II.** *m* PRESSE periodical

périodiquement [peʀjɔdikmɑ̃] *adv* periodically

péripétie [peʀipesi] *f* event; **vie pleine de ~s** eventful life

périph [peʀif] *m inf abr de* **périphérique**

périphérie [peʀifeʀi] *f* **1.** MAT (*d'un cercle*) circumference **2.** (*banlieue*) outskirts; **habiter à la ~ de la ville** to live in the suburbs of the town; **l'immobilier dans la ~** property in the suburbs

périphérique [peʀifeʀik] **I.** *adj* **1.** (*extérieur*) **quartier ~** outlying area **2.** CINE, TV **poste/radio/station ~** private transmitter/radio/station (*transmitting from just outside the French border*) **II.** *m* **1.** (*boulevard*) **le ~ de Paris** the Paris ring road *Brit,* the Paris beltway *Am;* **~ intérieur/extérieur** inner/outer ring road **2.** INFOR peripheral; **~ son** sound device; **~ d'entrée/de sortie** input/output device

périphrase [peʀifʀɑz] *f* periphrasis

périple [peʀipl] *m* **1.** *soutenu* HIST voyage **2.** (*voyage par voie de terre*) expedition; **un ~ chinois/en Chine** a Chinese expedition/an expedition to China

périr [peʀiʀ] <8> *vi* **1.** *soutenu* to perish; **~ noyé** to drown; **faire ~ qn** to kill; **~ d'ennui** to die of boredom **2.** *soutenu* (*disparaître: bateau, civilisation, empire*) to perish; (*plante*) to die; (*marchandises*) to be lost; (*souvenir*) to vanish

périscope [peʀiskɔp] *m* periscope

périssable [peʀisabl] *adj* (*denrée*) perishable

péristyle [peʀistil] *m* peristyle

péritel [peʀitɛl] *adj inv* **prise ~** Scart socket

péritonite [peʀitɔnit] *f* peritonitis

perle [pɛʀl] *f* **1.** pearl; (*boule*) bead; **~ naturelle** natural pearl **2.** *inf* (*erreur*) howler **3.** (*chose de grande valeur*) jewel ►**c'est une ~ rare** she is a gem

perler [pɛʀle] <1> *vi* (*sueur*) to stand out in beads

perlimpinpin [pɛʀlɛ̃pɛ̃pɛ̃] *m inf* **poudre de ~** quack cure-all

permanence [pɛʀmanɑ̃s] *f* **1.** ADMIN, MED duty; **assurer** [*o* **tenir**] **la ~/être de ~** to be on duty **2.** (*bureau*) duty office; **~ électorale** electiopn headquarters *pl* **3.** ECOLE study room ►**en ~** (*siéger*) permanently; (*surveiller*) continuously

permanent(e) [pɛʀmanɑ̃, ɑ̃t] *adj* **1.** (*constant, continu*) permanent; (*contrôle, collaboration, liaison, formation*) ongoing; (*tension, troubles*) continuous; **cinéma ~** *cinema showing the same film throughout the day;* **ici le spectacle est ~** the show here is continuous; **spectacle/cinéma ~ de ... à ...** continuous show/films from ... to ... **2.** (*opp: spécial, extraordinaire: envoyé, représentant, personnel*) permanent; (*armée*) standing

permanente [pɛʀmanɑ̃t] *f* perm

perme [pɛʀm] *f inf* **1.** MIL *abr de* **permission** leave **2.** ECOLE *abr de* **permanence** study

perméable [pɛʀmeabl] *adj* **1.** GEO, PHYS, BIO permeable; **~ à l'eau** water-permeable **2.** (*ouvert*) **être ~ à qc** (*personne*) to be easily influenced by sth; (*frontière*) to be easily penetrated by sth

permettre [pɛʀmɛtʀ] *irr* **I.** *vt impers* **1.** (*être autorisé*) **il est permis à qn de** +*infin* sb is authorized to +*infin* **2.** (*être possible*) **il est permis à qn de** +*infin* sb is able to +*infin;* **est-il permis d'être aussi bête!** nobody's any right to be that stupid! **II.** *vt* **1.** (*autoriser*) **~ à qn de** +*infin* to authorize sb to +*infin;* (*donner droit à*) to entitle sb to +*infin;* **~ que qn** +*subj* to authorize sb to +*infin;* **c'est permis par la loi** it is permitted by law; **vous permettez?** may I?; **vous permettez que je fasse qc?** (*subj*) may I do sth? **2.** (*rendre possible*) **~ à qn de** +*infin* (*chose*) to allow sb to +*infin;* **si le temps le permet** if the weather/time allows ►**permettez!/tu permets!** sorry! **III.** *vpr* **1.** (*s'accorder*) **se ~ une fantaisie** to indulge oneself **2.** (*oser*) **se ~ une plaisanterie** to dare to tell a joke; **se ~ bien des choses** to take a lot of liberties

permis [pɛʀmi] *m* **1.**(*document du permis de conduire*) driving licence *Brit,* driver's license *Am;* (*examen du permis de conduire*) driving test; ~ **moto** motorbike licence; **échouer au** ~ to fail one's driving test **2.**(*licence*) ~ **de chasse/pêche** hunting/fishing permit; ~ **de construire** planning permission *Brit,* building permit *Am* **3.**(*autorisation*) ~ **de séjour** residence permit

permis(e) [pɛʀmi, z] *part passé de* **permettre**

permissif, -ive [pɛʀmisif, -iv] *adj* SOCIOL, PSYCH permissive

permission [pɛʀmisjɔ̃] *f* **1.** *sans pl* (*autorisation*) ~ **de** +*infin* permission to +*infin;* ~ **de minuit** late pass **2.** MIL leave

permutation [pɛʀmytasjɔ̃] *f* **1.** *a.* MAT, CHIM, LING permutation **2.** ADMIN (*de fonctionnaires, d'employés*) interchange

permuter [pɛʀmyte] <1> **I.** *vi* ~ **avec qn** to switch with sb; **deux personnes permutent** two people switch round **II.** *vt* to switch round; MAT, CHIM, LING to permutate

pernicieux, -euse [pɛʀnisjø, -jøz] *adj* pernicious

péroné [peʀɔne] *m* fibula

pérorer [peʀɔʀe] <1> *vi péj* to hold forth

Pérou [peʀu] *m* **le** ~ Peru ►**ce n'est pas le** ~ it's hardly a fortune

perpendiculaire [pɛʀpɑ̃dikylɛʀ] *adj* **être** ~ **à qc** to be perpendicular to sth

perpète [pɛʀpɛt] *inf* **1.**(*pour toujours*) **être condamné à** ~ to get life; **attendre jusqu'à** ~ to wait for ever **2.**(*très loin*) **aller à** ~ to go miles; **habiter à** ~ to live at the back of beyond; **jusqu'à** ~ to the ends of the earth

perpétrer [pɛʀpetʀe] <5> *vt* JUR (*crime*) to perpetrate

perpétuel(le) [pɛʀpetɥɛl] *adj* (*angoisse, difficultés*) perpetual; (*murmure, lamentations*) incessant

perpétuellement [pɛʀpetɥɛlmɑ̃] *adv* perpetually

perpétuer [pɛʀpetɥe] <1> **I.** *vt* (*tradition, souvenir*) to perpetuate; (*nom*) to carry on; **servir à** ~ **l'espèce** to continue the species **II.** *vpr* **se** ~ (*abus, injustices, tradition*) to be perpetuated; (*espèce*) to survive

perpétuité [pɛʀpetɥite] *f* **à** ~ in perpetuity; (*condamnation*) for life; **être condamné à** ~ to receive a life sentence

perplexe [pɛʀplɛks] *adj* (*personne, mine*) perplex; **rendre qn** ~ to puzzle sb

perplexité [pɛʀplɛksite] *f* perplexity; **plonger qn dans la plus grande** ~ to leave sb thoroughly perplexed

perquisition [pɛʀkizisjɔ̃] *f* search (*by police*)

perquisitionner [pɛʀkizisjɔne] <1> **I.** *vi* to carry out a search **II.** *vt* to search

perron [pɛʀɔ̃] *m* steps *pl*

perroquet [pɛʀɔkɛ] *m* **1.**(*oiseau, personne*) parrot; **répéter qc comme un** ~ to repeat sth parrot-fashion **2.**(*boisson*) *drink made from pastis and mint syrup*

perruche [pɛʀyʃ, peʀyʃ] *f* budgerigar

perruque [pɛʀyk, peʀyk] *f* wig

persan [pɛʀsɑ̃] *m* Persian; *v. a.* **français**

persan(e) [pɛʀsɑ̃, an] *adj* Persian

Persan(e) [pɛʀsɑ̃, an] *m(f)* Persian

perse [pɛʀs] **I.** *adj* HIST Persian **II.** *m* HIST Persian; *v. a.* **français**

Perse [pɛʀs] **I.** *m, f* HIST Persian **II.** *f* **la** ~ Persia

persécuté(e) [pɛʀsekyte] **I.** *adj* persecuted **II.** *m(f)* persecuted person

persécuter [pɛʀsekyte] <1> *vt* to persecute

persécution [pɛʀsekysjɔ̃] *f* persecution

persévérance [pɛʀseveʀɑ̃s] *f* perseverance

persévérant(e) [pɛʀseveʀɑ̃, ɑ̃t] *adj* persevering

persévérer [pɛʀseveʀe] <5> *vi* to persever; ~ **dans ses efforts** to persever in one's efforts; ~ **dans une recherche** to persever in a search; ~ **à faire qc** to persist in doing sth

persienne [pɛʀsjɛn] *f* shutter

persil [pɛʀsi] *m* parsley

persistance [pɛʀsistɑ̃s] *f* persistence; ~ **dans qc** persistence in sth

persistant(e) [pɛʀsistɑ̃, ɑ̃t] *adj* **1.** persistent **2.** BOT evergreen

persister [pɛʀsiste] <1> *vi* (*persévérer*) ~ **dans qc** to persist in sth; ~ **dans un projet** to persevere in a project; ~ **à faire qc** to persist in doing sth ►**qn persiste et signe** sb sticks to what they say

perso [pɛʀsɔ] *adj inf abr de* **personnalisé, personnel**

personnage [pɛʀsɔnaʒ] *m* **1.** ART, LIT character; CINE *a.* part; **les ~s de Walt Disney** Walt Disney characters; **jouer le** ~ **d'un voleur** to play the part of a thief **2.**(*rôle*) image; **soigner son** ~ to polish one's image **3.**(*individu*) individual; **un grossier** ~ an uncouth individual **4.**(*personnalité*) celebrity; **~s politiques** political figures

personnalisation [pɛʀsɔnalizasjɔ̃] *f* personalization

personnalisé(e) [pɛʀsɔnalize] *adj* personalized

personnaliser [pɛʀsɔnalize] <1> *vt* **1.**(*adapter*) to personalize **2.**(*rendre personnel*) ~ **qc** to give a personal touch to sth

personnalité [pɛʀsɔnalite] *f* (*caractère, personne*) personality; **avoir une forte** [*o* **de la**] ~ to have a strong personality

personne[1] [pɛʀsɔn] *f* **1.**(*individu, être humain*) *a.* LING person; **dix ~s** ten people; ~ **âgée** elderly person; **les ~s âgées** the elderly; **la** ~ **qui/les ~s qui** the person/people who; **je respecte sa** ~ I respect his/her dignity; **tu ne penses qu'à ta** ~ you think only of yourself; **satisfait de sa** ~ satisfied with oneself **2.**(*femme*) woman; (*jeune fille*) girl ►~ **à charge** dependent; **grande** ~ grown-up; **par** ~ **interposée** through a third party; **tierce** ~

third party; **en** ~ in person

personne² [pɛʀsɔn] *pron indéf* **1.** (*opp: quelqu'un*) nobody, no one; **il n'y a** ~ there's nobody there; ~ **d'autre** nobody else **2.** (*quelqu'un*) anybody, anyone; **une place sans presque** ~ a place with nearly nobody ►**plus rapide que** ~ faster than anybody

personnel [pɛʀsɔnɛl] *m* staff; (*d'une entreprise*) personnel; ~ **enseignant** teaching staff

personnel(le) [pɛʀsɔnɛl] *adj* **1.** (*individuel*) personal; **à titre** ~ personally **2.** LING (*forme, pronom*) personal; **mode** ~ finite mode

personnellement [pɛʀsɔnɛlmɑ̃] *adv* personally

personnifié(e) [pɛʀsɔnifje] *adj* personified

personnifier [pɛʀsɔnifje] <1a> *vt* **1.** to personify **2.** (*incarner*) to embody

perspective [pɛʀspɛktiv] *f* **1.** MAT, ART perspective **2.** (*éventualité, horizon*) ~ **insoupçonnée** unexpected prospect; **une** ~ **réjouissante** a joyful prospect; ~**s d'avenir** prospects for the future; **ouvrir des** ~**s** to widen one's horizons; **à la** ~ **de qc** at the prospect of sth; **dans cette** ~ with this in view **3.** (*panorama*) view **4.** (*point de vue*) point of view; **changer de** ~ to change one's point of view ►**en** ~ ART in perspective; (*en vue*) in prospect

perspicace [pɛʀspikas] *adj* **1.** (*sagace*) perspicacious **2.** (*très capable d'apercevoir*) clear-sighted; (*observation*) observant; **d'un œil** [*o* **regard**] ~ with a perceptive eye

perspicacité [pɛʀspikasite] *f* (*d'une prévision*) clear-sightedness; (*d'une remarque*) perspicaciousness

persuadé(e) [pɛʀsɥade] *adj* convinced

persuader [pɛʀsɥade] <1> **I.** *vt* ~ **qn de qc** to persuade sb of sth; ~ **qn de** +*infin* (*intellectuellement*) to convince sb to +*infin;* (*sentimentalement*) to persuade sb to +*infin;* ~ **qn que qn a fait qc** to convince sb that sb did sth **II.** *vpr* **se** ~ **de qc** to convince oneself of sth; **se** ~ **que qn a fait qc** to convince oneself that sb did sth

persuasif, -ive [pɛʀsɥazif, -iv] *adj* persuasive

persuasion [pɛʀsɥazjɔ̃] *f* **1.** (*action*) persuasion; **puissance de** ~ power of persuasion **2.** (*conviction*) belief

perte [pɛʀt] *f* **1.** (*privation*) *a.* COM loss; **en cas de** ~ if lost; ~ **du sommeil** lack of sleep; ~ **de mémoire** memory loss; ~ **de temps/d'argent** waste of time/money; ~ **d'autorité/de prestige** loss of authority/prestige **2.** (*ruine, financière*) ruin **3.** (*déchet*) waste **4.** *pl* (*morts*) losses ►**renvoyer avec** ~ **et fracas** to throw out; **à** ~ **de vue** (*très loin*) as far as the eye can see; (*interminablement*) interminably; **en pure** ~ fruitlessly; **courir à sa** ~ to be on the road to ruin; **à** ~ at a loss

pertinemment [pɛʀtinamɑ̃] *adv* pertinently; **tu le sais** ~ you know it full well

pertinence [pɛʀtinɑ̃s] *f* pertinence; (*d'un argument, raisonnement*) relevance; **parler avec** ~ to speak pertinently; **conseiller qn avec** ~ to advise sb wisely

pertinent(e) [pɛʀtinɑ̃, ɑ̃t] *adj* pertinent

perturbant(e) [pɛʀtyʀbɑ̃, ɑ̃t] *adj* disturbing

perturbateur, -trice [pɛʀtyʀbatœʀ, -tʀis] **I.** *adj* disruptive **II.** *m, f* troublemaker

perturbation [pɛʀtyʀbasjɔ̃] *f* disruption

perturbé(e) [pɛʀtyʀbe] *adj* **1.** (*troublé: personne*) perturbed **2.** (*dérangé: service*) interrupted; (*monde*) upside-down; (*trafic*) disrupted

perturber [pɛʀtyʀbe] <1> *vt* (*service*) to disrupt; (*personne*) to disturb

péruvien(ne) [peʀyvjɛ̃, ɛn] *adj* Peruvian

Péruvien(ne) [peʀyvjɛ̃, ɛn] *m(f)* Peruvian

pervenche [pɛʀvɑ̃ʃ] **I.** *f* **1.** BOT periwinkle **2.** *inf* (*contractuelle*) traffic warden **II.** *app inv* periwinkle blue

pervers(e) [pɛʀvɛʀ, ɛʀs] **I.** *adj* perverse **II.** *m(f)* pervert

perversion [pɛʀvɛʀsjɔ̃] *f a.* PSYCH perversion; (*des coutumes*) corruption; (*de l'odorat, du goût*) distortion

pervertir [pɛʀvɛʀtiʀ] <8> *vt* **1.** (*corrompre*) to pervert **2.** (*altérer*) to corrupt; (*goût*) to distort

pesamment [pəzamɑ̃] *adv* heavily; (*sans grâce*) clumsily

pesant [pəzɑ̃] *m* **valoir son** ~ **d'or** *inf* to be worth one's weight in gold

pesant(e) [pəzɑ̃, ɑ̃t] *adj* heavy

pesanteur [pəzɑ̃tœʀ] *f* **1.** PHYS gravity; **accélération de la** ~ acceleration of gravity **2.** *pl* (*inertie*) sluggishness **3.** (*manque de finesse*) clumsiness

pesée [pəze] *f* weighing; SPORT weigh-in

pèse-lettre [pɛzlɛtʀ] <pèse-lettre(s)> *m* letter scales **pèse-personne** [pɛzpɛʀsɔn] <pèse-personne(s)> *m* scales *pl*

peser [pəze] <4> **I.** *vt* (*mesurer le poids, estimer*) to weigh; (*marchandises, ingrédients*) to weigh out ►**emballez, c'est pesé** *inf* it's a deal; **tout bien pesé** all things considered **II.** *vi* **1.** (*avoir un certain poids*) to weigh; **ne rien** ~ to weigh nothing; ~ **lourd** to be heavy; ~ **2 milliards d'euros** *inf* to cost 2 billion euros **2.** (*être lourd*) to be heavy **3.** (*exercer une pression*) ~ **sur/contre qc** to lean on sth; **le gâteau lui pèse sur l'estomac** the cake is a weight on his stomach **4.** (*accabler*) **ce climat me pèse** this climate is weighing me down; **des soupçons pèsent sur lui** worried weigh him down; **des remords pesaient sur elle** remorse weighed her down **5.** (*influencer*) ~ **sur qn/qc** to influence sb/sth **III.** *vpr* **se** ~ to weigh oneself

peseta [pezeta] *f* peseta

pessimiste [pesimist] **I.** *adj* pessimistic **II.** *m, f* pessimist

peste [pɛst] *f* **1.** MED plague **2.** (*personne ou chose*) pain ►**craindre/éviter qn/qc comme la** ~ to fear/avoid sb/sth like the plague; **se** __**méfier**__ **de qn/qc comme de la** ~ to be highly suspicious of sb/sth

pester [pɛste] <1> *vi* ~ **contre qn/qc** to curse sb/sth

pesticide [pɛstisid] **I.** *adj* pesticidal **II.** *m* pesticide

pestiféré(e) [pɛstifeʀe] **I.** *adj* plague-stricken **II.** *m(f)* plague victim; *fig* pariah

pestilentiel(le) [pɛstilɑ̃sjɛl] *adj* pestilential; **une odeur ~le** a foul smell

pet [pɛ] *m inf* fart; **faire** [*o* **lâcher**] **un** ~ to let out a fart ►(**toujours**) **avoir un** ~ **de** __**travers**__ (*être mal luné*) to be always out of sorts; (*être malade*) to be always in a bad way; **ne pas** __**valoir**__ **un** ~ (**de lapin**) to be worthless

pétale [petal] *m* petal

pétanque [petɑ̃k] *f* petanque

pétarade [petaʀad] *f* crackle; (*d'une mobylette*) backfire

pétarader [petaʀade] <1> *vi* to crackle; (*mobylette*) to backfire

pétard [petaʀ] *m* **1.** (*explosif*) firecracker **2.** *inf* (*cigarette de haschich*) joint **3.** *inf* (*postérieur*) bum *Brit,* ass *Am* ►**être/se mettre** __**en**__ ~ *inf* to be/get in a fury

pétasse [petas] *f inf* cow

péter [pete] <5> **I.** *vi inf* **1.** (*faire un pet*) to break wind **2.** (*éclater*) to explode; (*verre, assiette*) to smash; (*ampoule*) to blow **II.** *vt inf* to bust; **j'ai pété la couture de mon pantalon** I've split the seam of my trousers

pète-sec [pɛtsɛk] **I.** *adj inv, inf* (*air*) high-handed **II.** *m, f inv, inf* tyrant

péteux, -euse [petø, -øz] *m, f inf* chicken-hearted

pétillant(e) [petijɑ̃, jɑ̃t] *adj* (*gazeux, brillant*) sparkling; **des yeux ~s de malice/gaieté** eyes shining with evil/happiness

pétiller [petije] <1> *vi* **1.** (*faire des bulles*) to fizz; (*champagne*) to sparkle; **boisson qui pétille** fizzy drink **2.** (*être bouillant de*) ~ **de gaieté/de malice** sparkling with happiness/evil

petit(e) [p(ə)ti, it] **I.** *adj* **1.** (*opp: grand*) small; (*lumière*) faint; **au** ~ **jour** in the early morning; **à ~e vitesse** slowly **2.** (*de courte durée*) short; **faire un** ~ **salut/sourire** give a little wave/smile **3.** (*de basse extraction*) **le** ~ **peuple** the lower classes **4.** (*jeune*) young; ~ **chat** kitten; ~ **Jésus** baby Jesus; **les ~es classes** the younger classes **5.** (*terme affectueux*) little; (*mots*) sweet; ~ **chou** little darling; **ton** ~ **mari** your darling husband; ~ **copain** [*o* **ami**] boyfriend **6.** (*condescendant*) **jouer au** ~ **chef** to play the boss **7.** (*mesquin, bas, vil: esprit*) mean; (*intérêts*) petty **8.** (*médiocre: vin, année, cru*) average; (*santé*) poor **9.** (*pour atténuer*) little; **une ~e heure** a bit less than an hour **10.** (*miniature*) ~**(e)s soldats/voitures** toy soldiers/cars ►**se** __**faire**__ **tout** ~ to keep out of sight **II.** *m(f)* **1.** (*enfant*) child **2.** ZOOL **les ~s du lion** the lions young ►__**mon**__ **~/**__**ma**__ **~e** my friend; **~, ~, ~!** kitty, kitty, kitty! **III.** *adv* **voir** ~ to think small ►~ __**à**__ ~ little by little; __**en**__ ~ in miniature; (*écrire*) in small letters

petit-beurre [p(ə)tibœʀ] <petits-beurre> *m* petit beurre *Brit,* butter cookie *Am* **petit-bourgeois, petite-bourgeoise** [p(ə)tibuʀʒwa, p(ə)titbuʀʒwaz] <petits-bourgeois> **I.** *adj péj* lower middle-class **II.** *m, f péj* petit-bourgeois **petit-déj** *inf,* **petit-déjeuner** [p(ə)tideʒœne] <petits-déjeuners> *m* breakfast **petite-fille** [p(ə)titfij] <petites-filles> *f* granddaughter

petitesse [pətitɛs] *f* **1.** smallness; (*des revenus*) modesty **2.** (*mesquinerie*) meanness **3.** (*acte, parole*) pettiness *no pl*

petit-fils [p(ə)tifis] <petits-fils> *m* grandson **petit-four** [p(ə)tifuʀ] <petits-fours> *m* petit four **petit-gris** [pətigʀi] <petits-gris> *m* garden snail

pétition [petisjɔ̃] *f* petition

petit-lait [p(ə)tilɛ] <petits-laits> *m* whey ►__**boire**__ **du** ~ to lap it up; **se** __**boire**__ **comme du** ~ to go down well; __**boire**__ **qc comme du** ~ to knock sth back **petit-pois, petit pois** [pətipwa] <petits-pois> *m* pea; **les petits-pois** GASTR petits pois **petits-enfants** [p(ə)tizɑ̃fɑ̃] *mpl* grandchildren **petit-suisse** [p(ə)tisɥis] <petits-suisses> *m: small pot of plain fromage frais*

pétoche [petɔʃ] *f inf* **avoir la** ~ to have the wind up

peton [pətɔ̃] *m inf* foot

pétrel [petʀɛl] *m* petrel

pétrifié(e) [petʀifje] *adj* (*changé en pierre, médusé*) petrified; ~ **de terreur** petrified with fear

pétrifier [petʀifje] <1a> **I.** *vt* **1.** (*changer en pierre*) to petrify **2.** (*méduser, figer*) to petrify; (*timidité*) to paralyse *Brit,* to paralyze *Am;* ~ **qn de terreur** to scare sb rigid with terror **II.** *vpr* **se** ~ **1.** (*se changer en pierre*) to petrify **2.** (*se figer*) to be petrified; (*sourire*) to freeze

pétrin [petʀɛ̃] *m inf* (*difficultés*) mess; **être dans le** ~ to be in a mess; **se fourrer dans le** ~ to get into a mess

pétrir [petʀiʀ] <8> *vt* (*malaxer*) to knead

pétrodollars [petʀodɔlaʀ] *mpl* petrodollars

pétrole [petʀɔl] **I.** *m* oil **II.** *app* (*bleu, vert*) dark blue-green

pétrolier [petʀɔlje] *m* (*navire*) oil tanker

pétrolier, -ière [petʀɔlje, -jɛʀ] *adj* oil

pétrolifère [petʀɔlifɛʀ] *adj* oil-bearing

P et T [peete] *pl abr de* **Postes et Télécommunications** *French national post and telecommunications organization*

pétulant(e) [petylɑ̃, ɑ̃t] *adj* (*personne*) exuberant; (*joie*) wild

pétunia [petynja] *m* BOT petunia

peu [pø] **I.** *adv* **1.** (*opp: beaucoup, très*) not … much; *avec un adj ou un adv* not very; **je lis** ~ I don't read much; **j'y vais** ~ I don't go there often [*o* much]; **être** ~ **aimable** to be unfriendly; ~ **avant/après** shortly before/

after; **avant** [*o* **d'ici**] [*o* **sous**] ~ soon; **il est parti depuis** ~ he's only recently left; **bien/trop** ~ very little/too little; ~ **de temps/d'argent** little time/money; ~ **de voitures/jours** few cars/days; **en** ~ **de temps** in a very short time **2.** (*rarement*) ~ **souvent** rarely ▸**c'est** ~ **dire** that's something of an understatement; **ce n'est pas** ~ **dire** that is saying something; ~ **à** ~ bit by bit; **à** ~ **près** more or less; **de** ~ just **II.** *pron indéf* (*peu de personnes, peu de choses*) few; ~ **importe** it doesn't really matter **III.** *m* **le** ~ **de temps/d'argent qu'il me reste** the little time/money that I have left; **le** ~ **de personnes/choses** the few people/things; **le** ~ **que j'ai vu** the little I've seen; **un** ~ **de beurre/bonne volonté** a little butter/good will; **un** ~ **de monde** a few people ▸**un** ~ **partout** all over the place; (**et**) **pas qu'un** ~**!** not half!; **pour un** ~ **elle partait** she was very nearly leaving; **pour si** ~ for so little; **pour** ~ **que** +*subj* so long as; **si** ~ **qu'on lui donne, ...** however little he is given, ...; **tant soit** ~ slightly; **attends un** ~ **que je t'attrape** *inf* just you wait; **un** ~ **que j'ai raison!** you bet I'm right!

peuchère [pøʃɛʀ] *interj Midi* oh dear (oh dear)!

peuplade [pœplad] *f* people

peuple [pœpl] *m* people; **le** ~ **chrétien** the Christian people; **le** ~ **palestinien** the Palestinian people; **le** ~ **élu** the chosen people ▸**ils se moquent du** ~ *inf* who do they think they are?

peuplé(e) [pœple] *adj* populated; (*région*) inhabited

peuplement [pœpləmɑ̃] *m* **1.** (*action de peupler*) populating; (*avec des animaux*) stocking; (*avec des plantes, arbres*) planting **2.** (*densité*) population

peupler [pœple] <1> **I.** *vt* **1.** (*pourvoir*) ~ **un lieu de prisonniers** to populate a place with prisoners; **la guerre peupla les camps de réfugiés** the war filled the camps with refugees; ~ **un lieu d'animaux** to stock a place with animals; ~ **un lieu de plantes/d'arbres** to plant a place with plants/trees **2.** (*habiter*) ~ **un pays/une région** to populate a country/a region; ~ **un immeuble** to move into a block of flats *Brit,* to move into an apartment building *Am* **II.** *vpr* **1.** (*se pourvoir*) **se** ~ **de nouveaux habitants** to acquire a new population **2.** (*se remplir*) **se** ~ **de rires joyeux** to be filled with cheerful laughter

peuplier [pøplije] *m* poplar tree

peur [pœʀ] *f* fear; **la** ~ **du ridicule** fear of ridicule; **avoir** ~ **de faire qc** to be frightened of doing sth; **avoir** ~ **pour qn** to be frightened for sb; **avoir** ~ **pour sa vie/santé** to fear for one's life/health; **avoir** ~ **que qn fasse qc** (*subj*) to be frightened that sb might do sth; **faire** ~ **à qn** to frighten sb ▸**avoir eu plus de** ~ **que de mal** to have been more frightened than anything else; **n'ayons pas** ~ **des mots** let's not be afraid of straight talking; **avoir une** ~ **bleue** to be scared stiff; **j'ai bien** ~ **que qn ait fait qc** (*subj*) I'm rather afraid that sb has done sth; **à faire** ~ frighteningly; **prendre** ~ to take fright; **par** ~ **du ridicule/des critiques** for fear of ridicule/criticism; **de** ~ **de faire qc/que qn fasse qc** (*subj*) for fear of doing sth/that sb might do sth

peureux, -euse [pœʀø, -øz] **I.** *adj* fearful **II.** *m, f* fearful person

peut [pø] *indic prés de* **pouvoir**

peut-être [pøtɛtʀ] *adv* **1.** (*éventuellement*) perhaps, maybe; ~ **que qn va faire qc** perhaps sb will do sth; ~ **bien** perhaps **2.** (*environ*) maybe **3.** (*marque de doute*) perhaps; **ce médicament est** ~ **efficace, mais ...** this medecine may well be effective, but ...

peuvent [pœv], **peux** [pø] *indic prés de* **pouvoir**

phacochère [fakɔʃɛʀ] *m* ZOOL warthog

phalange¹ [falɑ̃ʒ] *f* ANAT phalanx

phalange² [falɑ̃ʒ] *f* **1.** POL falange **2.** HIST (*formation de combat*) phalanx

phallus [falys] *m* phallus

pharaon [faʀaɔ̃] *m* HIST pharoah

phare [faʀ] *m* **1.** (*projecteur*) headlight; ~ **antibrouillard** fog lamp *Brit,* fog light *Am* **2.** (*tour*) lighthouse

pharmaceutique [faʀmasøtik] *adj* pharmaceutical; **préparation** ~ pharmaceutical

pharmacie [faʀmasi] *f* **1.** (*boutique*) chemist *Brit,* drugstore *Am;* ~ **de garde** duty chemist *Brit,* duty pharmacy *Am* **2.** (*science*) pharmacy **3.** (*armoire*) medicine cabinet

pharmacien(ne) [faʀmasjɛ̃, jɛn] *m(f)* pharmacist, chemist *Brit*

pharyngite [faʀɛ̃ʒit] *f* MED pharyngitis

pharynx [faʀɛ̃ks] *m* ANAT pharynx

phase [fɑz] *f* phase; (*d'une maladie*) stage

phénicien [fenisjɛ̃] *m* Phoenician

phénicien(ne) [fenisjɛ̃, jɛn] *adj* Phoenician

Phénicien(ne) [fenisjɛ̃, jɛn] *m(f)* Phoenician

phénix [feniks] *m* phoenix

phénoménal(e) [fenɔmenal, o] <-aux> *adj a.* PHILOS phenomenal

phénomène [fenɔmɛn] *m* **1.** (*fait*) phenomenon **2.** *inf* (*individu*) freak

Philadelphie [filadɛlfi] Philadelphia; **habitant de** ~ Philadelphian

philanthrope [filɑ̃tʀɔp] *mf* philanthropist

philatélie [filateli] *f* **1.** (*science*) philately **2.** (*hobby*) stamp collecting

philatéliste [filatelist] *mf* philatelist

philippin(ne) [filipɛ̃, in] *adj* Philippine

Philippin(ne) [filipɛ̃, in] *m(f)* Filipino

Philippines [filipin] *fpl* **les** ~ the Philippines

philosophe [filɔzɔf] **I.** *mf* philosopher **II.** *adj* philosophical

philosopher [filɔzɔfe] <1> *vi* to philosophize

philosophie [filɔzɔfi] *f* philosophy

philosophique [filɔzɔfik] *adj* philosophical

phobie [fɔbi] *f* **1.** (*aversion*) **avoir la** ~ **de qc**

P

to loathe sth **2.** PSYCH phobia

phocéen(ne) [fɔseɛ̃, ɛn] *adj* **cité ~ne** Marseille(s); **l'équipe ~ne** the Marseille team

phonétique [fɔnetik] **I.** *f* phonetics + *vb sing* **II.** *adj* phonetic

phoque [fɔk] *m* seal

phosphate [fɔsfat] *m a.* CHIM phosphate

phosphore [fɔsfɔʀ] *m* CHIM phosphorus

phosphorescent(e) [fɔsfɔʀesɑ̃, ɑ̃t] *adj* **1.** PHYS phosphorescent **2.** (*luisant: balles*) luminous; (*brume*) glowing; (*mer*) gleaming

photo [fɔto] *f abr de* **photographie** **1.** (*cliché*) photo; **~ couleur** colour photo *Brit,* color photo *Am;* **~ noir et blanc** black and white photo; **~ de famille/d'identité** family/passport photo; **faire une ~** to take a photo; **prendre qn/qc en ~** to take a photo of sb/sth; **en ~** in photos **2.** (*art*) photography; **faire de la ~** to be a photograper ►**tu veux ma ~?** *inf* do you want my autograph?

photocomposition [fɔtokɔ̃pozisjɔ̃] *f* photocomposition

photocopie [fɔtɔkɔpi] *f* photocopy

photocopier [fɔtɔkɔpje] <1> *vt* to photocopy

photocopieur [fɔtɔkɔpjœʀ] *m,* **photocopieuse** [fɔtɔkɔpjøz] *f* photocopier

photocopillage [fɔtɔkɔpijaʒ] *m* unauthorized photocopying

photogénique [fɔtɔʒenik] *adj* photogenic

photographe [fɔtɔgʀaf] *mf* photographer

photographie [fɔtɔgʀafi] *f* **1.** (*activité*) photography **2.** (*image*) photograph

photographier [fɔtɔgʀafje] <1> *vt* **1.** PHOT to photograph **2.** (*mémoriser*) to memorize

photographique [fɔtɔgʀafik] *adj* photographic; **appareil ~** camera; **épreuve ~** print

photomaton® [fɔtɔmatɔ̃] *m* photo booth

photomontage [fɔtomɔ̃taʒ] *m* photomontage

photothèque [fɔtɔtɛk] *f* picture library

phrase [fʀɑz] *f* sentence ►**~ toute faite** stock phrase

phrygien [fʀiʒjɛ̃] *adj v.* **bonnet**

physicien(ne) [fizisjɛ̃, jɛn] *m(f)* physicist

physiologie [fizjɔlɔʒi] *f* physiology

physiologique [fizjɔlɔʒik] *adj* physiological

physionomie [fizjɔnɔmi] *f* **1.** facial expression; **jeux de ~** facial contortions **2.** (*apparence*) **~ d'un pays/d'un objet** appearance of a country/an object

physionomiste [fizjɔnɔmist] **I.** *adj* **être ~** to be good at faces **II.** *mf* physiognomist

physique [fizik] **I.** *adj* physical **II.** *m* **1.** (*aspect extérieur*) physical appearance; **avoir un beau ~** to look good **2.** (*constitution*) **grâce à son ~ robuste** thanks to his robust constitution ►**il/elle a le ~ de l'emploi** he/she looks the part; **avoir un ~** to have a certain something **III.** *f* physics

physiquement [fizikmɑ̃] *adv* physically; **être très bien ~** to be physically attractive

piaf [pjaf] *m inf* sparrow

piaffer [pjafe] <1> *vi* **1.** (*cheval*) to paw the ground **2.** (*s'agiter*) **~ sur place** to be mad with impatience

piaillement [pjɑjmɑ̃] *m* (*d'un oiseau*) to squawk; (*d'un enfant*) to squeal; (*d'une femme*) to screech

piailler [pjɑje] <1> *vi* (*animal*) to cheep; (*enfant*) to whine; (*femme*) to wail

pianiste [pjanist] *mf* pianist

piano [pjano] **I.** *m* MUS piano; **~ à queue** grand piano; **jouer du ~** to play the piano **II.** *adv* softly; **(y) aller ~** *inf* to go easy; **vas-y ~** easy does it

piano-bar [pjanobaʀ] <pianos-bars> *m* piano bar

pianoter [pjanɔte] <1> *vi* **1.** (*jouer sans talent*) **~ sur un piano** to tinkle away at the piano **2.** (*taper comme un débutant*) to tap at the keyboard; **~ sur un ordinateur/sur un minitel** to tap away on a computer/minitel **3.** (*tapoter du bout des doigts*) **~ sur la table/vitre** to drum one's fingers on the table/window

piastre [pjastʀ] *f Québec, inf* (*dollar*) dollar

piaule [pjol] *f inf* room

PIB [peibe] *m abr de* **produit intérieur brut** GDP

pic [pik] *m* (*sommet*) peak ►**tomber à ~** to happen at just the right moment; (*personne*) to turn up at the right moment; **à ~** steeply; **couler à ~** to sink to the bottom

picard(e) [pikaʀ, aʀd] *adj* Picard

Picard(e) [pikaʀ, aʀd] *m(f)* Picard

Picardie [pikaʀdi] *f* **la ~** Picardy

pichet [piʃɛ] *m* jug

pickpocket [pikpɔkɛt] *m* pickpocket

picoler [pikɔle] <1> *vi inf* to drink (*too much alcohol*)

picorer [pikɔʀe] <1> **I.** *vi* **1.** (*becqueter: animal*) to peck **2.** (*grignoter: personne*) to nibble; **~ dans son assiette** to pick at one's food **II.** *vt* **1.** (*becqueter: animal*) **~ qc** to peck at sth **2.** (*grignoter*) **~ qc dans l'assiette de qn** to pick at sth in sb else's plate

picotement [pikɔtmɑ̃] *m* **1.** (*dans la gorge*) tickling **2.** (*sur la peau*) smarting **3.** (*dans les yeux*) stinging

picoter [pikɔte] <1> *vt* **la fumée (me) picote les yeux** the smoke is stinging my eyes; **le froid picote/les orties picotent la peau** the cold/nettles sting your skin; **les herbes picotent les mollets** the grass makes your legs sting; **ça me picote le nez** that tickles my nose

picto-charantais(e) [piktɔʃaʀɑ̃tɛ, ɛz] *adj* of Poitou-Charentes

Picto-charantais(e) [piktɔʃaʀɑ̃tɛ, ɛz] *m(f)* person from Poitou-Charentes

pie [pi] *f* **1.** (*oiseau*) magpie **2.** *inf* (*femme*) chatterbox

pièce [pjɛs] *f* **1.** (*salle*) room **2.** (*monnaie*) **~ de monnaie** coin; **~ d'un euro** one euro coin; **~s (en) euro** euro coins **3.** THEAT **~ de théâtre** play **4.** MUS piece **5.** (*document*) paper; **~ d'identité** proof of identity *no pl;* **les ~s** documents; **les ~s du procès** the trial documents; **~ justificative** proof; **~ d'archives** archive document; **~ à conviction** piece of evidence **6.** (*élément constitutif*) part; (*d'une collection, d'un trousseau*) piece; **~ de mobilier** piece of furniture; **~ de musée** museum piece **7.** (*quantité*) **~ de viande** cut of meat **8.** (*pour rapiécer*) patch **9.** (*unité*) **acheter/vendre à la ~** to buy/sell separately ▶**~ de rechange** [*o* **détachée**] spare part; **~ rapportée** *péj* odd man out; **être tout d'une ~** to be all of a piece; **c'est un homme tout d'une ~** he's a man who speaks his mind; **tout d'une ~** stiffly; **créer qc de toutes ~s** to make sth out of bits and pieces; **construire qc de toutes ~s** to build sth from nothing; **être inventé de toutes ~s** to be a lie from start to finish; **donner la ~ à qn** *inf* to tip sb; **mettre/tailler qn/qc en ~s** to pull/hack sb/sth to pieces; **aux ~s** at piece rate; **travailler aux ~s** to do piecework; **être payé aux ~s** to be paid on piecework

pied [pje] *m* **1.** (*opp: tête*) foot; **~ plat** flat foot; **à ~** on foot; **au ~!** heel! **2.** (*support: d'un lit*) leg; (*microphone*) stand **3.** (*partie inférieure: d'une chaussette, d'un bas*) foot **4.** (*base*) foot; (*d'un champignon*) stalk; **au ~ d'une colline/d'un mur** at the foot of a hill/against a wall; **mettre qc au ~ de qc** to put sth at the foot of sth; **être au ~ de qc** to be at the foot of sth **5.** (*plant*) **~ de salade/poireau** lettuce/leek; **~ de vigne** vine **6.** (*pas*) **marcher d'un ~ léger** to walk with a spring in one's step; **ils s'en vont/marchent du même ~** they set off/walk in step ▶**traiter qn sur un ~ d'égalité** to treat sb as an equal; **prendre qc au ~ de la lettre** to take sth literally; **mettre qn au ~ du mur** to put sb's back to the wall; **avoir bon ~ bon œil** to be as fit as a fiddle; **avoir/rouler le ~ au plancher** to have/drive with one's foot hard down; **mettre les ~s dans le plat** (*commettre une gaffe*) to put one's foot in it; **mettre ~ à terre** to set foot on land; **vouloir être à cent ~s sous terre** to wish the ground would open up and swallow one; **avoir/garder les (deux) ~s sur terre** to have/keep both feet on the ground; **des ~s à la tête** from head to toe; **avoir un ~ dans la tombe** to have one foot in the grave; **partir du bon/mauvais ~** to get off to a good/bad start; **se lever du ~ gauche** [*o* **du mauvais ~**] to get out of the wrong side of the bed; **faire un cours au ~ levé** to make up a lesson as one goes along; **faire un discours au ~ levé** to make an off-the-cuff speech; **remplacer qn au ~ levé** to stand in for sb at the last minute; **~s nus** barefoot; **avoir ~** to be in one's depth; **casser les ~s à qn** *inf* to get on sb's nerves; **s'emmêler les ~s** to get one's feet caught; **être sur ~** to be up and about; **ça lui fait les ~s** *inf* that serves her right; **lever le ~** (*s'enfuir*) to run away; (*ralentir*) to ease of the accelerator; **marcher sur les ~s de qn** (*faire mal*) to tread on sb's feet; (*embêter*) to tread on sb's toes; **mettre les ~s quelque part** to set footsomewhere; **mettre un projet sur ~** to set up a project; **mettre une entreprise sur ~** to set up a company; **perdre ~** (*se noyer, ne plus comprendre*) to get out of one's depth; **prendre/reprendre ~** to gain/regain a footing; **remettre qn/qc sur ~** to stand sb/sth up again; **ne pas savoir sur quel ~ danser** not to know what to do; **sortir de qc les ~s devant** to leave sth feet first; **traîner les ~s** to drag one's feet; **tomber** [*o* **se jeter**] **aux ~s de qn** to fall at sb's feet; **se traîner** [*o* **ramper**] **aux ~s de qn** to grovel at sb's feet; **~ de nez** insult; **faire un ~ de nez à qn** to thumb one's nose at sb

pied-à-terre [pjetatɛʀ] *m inv* pied-à-terre

pied-de-mouton [pjedmutɔ̃] <pieds-de-mouton> *m* wood hedgehog

piédestal [pjedɛstal, o] <-aux> *m* pedestal ▶**descendre/tomber** [*o* **dégringoler**] **de son ~** to come down from/fall off one's pedestal; **faire tomber qn de son ~** to knock sb off their pedestal; **mettre** [*o* **placer**] **qn sur un ~** to put sb on a pedestal

pied-noir [pjenwaʀ] <pieds-noirs> **I.** *mf inf* pied-noir **II.** *adj* pied-noir

piège [pjɛʒ] *m* trap; **~ à souris** mousetrap; **prendre un animal au ~** to catch an animal in a trap; **prendre qn au ~** to trap sb; **tendre un ~** to set a trap; **tendre un ~ à qn** to set a trap for sb; **tomber dans le/un ~** to fall in the/a trap ▶**qc/c'est un ~ à cons** *inf* it's a con; **se prendre/être pris à son propre ~** to get/be caught in one's own trap

piégé(e) [pjeʒe] *adj* **engin ~** boobytrap; **valise/lettre/voiture ~e** suitcase/letter/car bomb

piéger [pjeʒe] <2a, 5> *vt* **1.** (*attraper: animal*) to trap **2.** (*tromper*) **~ qn** to catch sb out; **se faire ~ par qn** to be caught out by sb; **se laisser ~** to get caught out; (*par de bonnes paroles*) to be taken in

pierre [pjɛʀ] *f* **1.** (*caillou*) stone; **~ ponce** pumice stone **2.** (*pierre précieuse*) gem ▶**faire d'une ~ deux coups** to kill two birds with one stone; **jour à marquer d'une ~ blanche** red-letter day; **~ tombale** tombstone; **poser la première ~ de qc** to lay the first stone of sth; **jeter la (première) ~ à qn** to throw the first stone at sb; **cœur de ~** heart of stone

pierreries [pjɛʀʀi] *fpl* precious stones

pierreux, -euse [pjeʀø, -øz] *adj* **1.** (*couvert de pierres, qui ressemble à de la pierre*) stony **2.** (*poire*) gritty

pierrot [pjeʀo] *m* pierrot

piété [pjete] *f* REL piety

piétinement [pjetinmɑ̃] *m* **1.** (*bruit*) stamping; (*mouvement*) stamping around **2.** (*stagnation*) standstill; **vu le ~ des négociations**

given the standstill in [*o* the lack of progress in] the negotiations

piétiner [pjetine] <1> I. *vi* 1. (*trépigner*) ~ **de colère** [*o* **rage**]/**d'impatience** to stamp one's feet in anger/with impatience 2. (*avancer péniblement*) to be at a standstill; ~ **sur place** to stand about 3. (*ne pas progresser*) to mark time II. *vt* 1. (*marcher sur: sol, neige*) to tread on; (*pelouse*) to trample; ~ **qc de rage** to trample on sth in rage 2. (*ne pas respecter*) ~ **qc** to trample on sth

piéton(ne) [pjetɔ̃, ɔn] *m(f)* pedestrian

piéton(ne) [pjetɔ̃, ɔn] *adj*, **piétonnier**, **-ière** [pjetɔnje, -jɛʀ] *adj* (*zone, rue*) pedestrian

pieu [pjø] <x> *m* 1. stake 2. *inf* (*lit*) bed; **au ~!** bedtime!

pieuter [pjøte] <1> I. *vi inf* to crash II. *vpr inf* **se ~** to turn in

pieuvre [pjœvʀ] *f* 1. ZOOL octopus 2. (*personne*) vampire

pieux, **-euse** [pjø, -jøz] *adj* 1. REL pious 2. *antéposé, soutenu* (*respectueux: affection, souvenir*) respectful

pif¹ [pif] *m inf* hooter ▸**au** ~ at a rough guess; **estimer qc au** ~ to make a guesstimate of sth

pif² [pif] *interj* ~**!** ~ [*o* **paf**]**!** (*bruit d'une gifle*) slap! slap!; (*bruit d'une détonation*) bang! bang!

pifomètre [pifɔmɛtʀ] *v.* **pif**

pige [piʒ] *f* 1. *pl, inf* (*année*) **avoir 40 ~s** to be 40; **à 53 ~s, …** when you've hit 53, … 2. MEDIA **être payé à la** ~ to be paid freelance rates; **travailler à la** ~ to work freelance

pigeon [piʒɔ̃] *m* 1. ZOOL pigeon; ~ **voyageur** homing pigeon 2. *inf* (*dupe*) **être le ~ dans l'affaire** to be the mug [*o* sucker] in the matter; **cherchez un autre ~!** find another sucker!

pigeonner [piʒɔne] <1> *vt inf* ~ **qn** to take sb for a ride; **se faire ~ par qn** to be taken for a ride by sb

pigeonnier [piʒɔnje] *m* pigeon loft

piger [piʒe] <2a> *vt, vi inf* to get it; **ne rien** ~ not to get anything

pigiste [piʒist] *mf* freelance

pigment [pigmɑ̃] *m* pigment

pigmentation [pigmɑ̃tasjɔ̃] *f* (*de la peau*) pigmentation

pignon [piɲɔ̃] *m* 1. ARCHIT gable 2. TECH (*roue dentée*) cogwheel; (*petite roue*) pinion 3. BOT, GASTR (*graine*) pine kernel ▸**avoir** ~ **sur rue** to be established; (*attitude méprisable*) to be common currency

pignouf [piɲuf] *m inf* slob

pile¹ [pil] *f* 1. (*tas*) pile 2. ELEC battery; **fonctionner à ~s** to be battery-operated 3. *Midi* (*évier*) sink

pile² [pil] *adv* 1. (*avec précision: arriver*) on the dot; ((*s'*)*arrêter*) dead 2. (*brusquement: (s')arrêter*) suddenly 3. (*au bon moment: arriver*) right on time; **ça tombe ~!** that's perfect timing! 4. (*exactement*) **à 10 heures** ~ at 10 o'clock on the dot ▸~ **poil** *inf* exactly

pile³ [pil] *f* **le côté** ~ tails; ~ **ou face?** heads or tails?; **on va jouer ça à ~ ou face!** we'll toss for it!

piler [pile] <1> I. *vt* to crush II. *vi inf* (*voiture*) to slam on the brakes

pileux, **-euse** [pilø, -øz] *adj* hair; **système** ~ hair

pilier [pilje] *m* 1. ARCHIT pillar 2. SPORT prop

pillage [pijaʒ] *m* pillage; **livrer** [*o* **mettre**] **une ville au** ~ to pillage a town

pillard(e) [pijaʀ, jaʀd] I. *adj* (*nomades, soldats*) pillaging; (*oiseaux*) plundering II. *m(f)* pillager

piller [pije] <1> *vt* 1. (*mettre à sac*) to loot 2. (*plagier*) ~ **un auteur** to plagiarize an author

pilleur, **-euse** [pijœʀ, -jøz] *m, f* looter

pilon [pilɔ̃] *m* 1. (*instrument*) *a.* MED pestle 2. (*jambe artificielle*) peg-leg 3. GASTR drumstick ▸**mettre** [*o* **passer**] **un livre au** ~ to pulp a book

pilonner [pilɔne] <1> *vt* 1. MIL to pound; (*aviation, pilote*) to bombard 2. (*écraser au pilon: ingrédients*) to crush; (*livres*) to pulp

pilori [pilɔʀi] *m* pillory ▸**clouer** [*o* **mettre**] **qn/qc au** ~ to pillory sb/sth

pilotage [pilɔtaʒ] *m* piloting

pilote [pilɔt] I. *adj* 1. (*qui ouvre la voie: projet, essai*) pilot 2. (*expérimental*) test 3. (*exemplaire*) model 4. NAUT (*bateau, navire*) prototype II. *mf* 1. AVIAT pilot; ~ **de ligne** airline pilot 2. AUTO driver; ~ **de course** racing driver; ~ **d'essai** test pilot III. *m* 1. (*dispositif*) ~ **automatique** automatic pilot 2. INFOR driver

piloter [pilɔte] <1> *vt* 1. AUTO (*avion, navire*) to pilot; (*voiture*) to drive 2. INFOR to drive

pilotis [pilɔti] *m* pile; **des maisons sur** ~ houses on stilts

pilule [pilyl] *f* MED pill; **la** ~ the pill ▸**la ~ est dure à avaler** it's a bitter pill to swallow

pimbêche [pɛ̃bɛʃ] *f* stuck-up woman

piment [pimɑ̃] *m* 1. GASTR pepper; ~ **doux** sweet pepper; ~ **en poudre** chilli powder *Brit,* chili powder *Am* 2. (*piquant*) spice; **donner du ~ à qc** to spice sth up; **trouver du ~ à qc** to find sth rather piquant

pimenté(e) [pimɑ̃te] *adj* spicy

pimenter [pimɑ̃te] <1> *vt* 1. GASTR ~ **qc** to add chilli to sth *Brit,* to add chili to sth *Am* 2. *fig* ~ **qc** to add spice to sth

pimpant(e) [pɛ̃pɑ̃, ɑ̃t] *adj* smart (as a new pin)

pin [pɛ̃] *m* pine (tree); ~ **sylvestre** Scots pine *Brit,* Scotch pine *Am;* ~ **parasol** stone pine

pinacle [pinakl] **porter qn au** ~ to laud sb to the skies

pinailler [pinaje] <1> *vi inf* ~ **sur qc** to quibble over sth

pince [pɛ̃s] *f* 1. TECH pair of pliers 2. ZOOL claw 3. COUT **pantalon à ~s** front-pleated trousers 4. (*épingle*) ~ **à linge** clothes peg *Brit,* clothespin *Am* 5. (*instrument d'épilation*) ~ **à épiler** tweezers *pl*

pincé(e) [pɛ̃se] *adj* **1.**(*hautain*) starchy; (*sourire, ton*) stiff **2.**(*serré: nez, narines*) thin; (*lèvres*) tight

pinceau [pɛ̃so] <x> *m* brush ►**se mélanger** [*o* **s'emmêler**] **les ~x** *inf* to get mixed up

pincée [pɛ̃se] *f* pinch

pincement [pɛ̃smɑ̃] *m* **1.**(*des lèvres*) pursing; (*des narines*) tightening **2.** MUS plucking **3.** AGR (*des branches*) pruning back; (*bourgeons*) pinching out ►**avec un (petit) ~ au cœur** with a twinge; **avoir un (petit) ~ au cœur** to feel a twinge

pincer [pɛ̃se] <2> **I.** *vt* **1.**(*faire mal: personne*) to pinch; (*crabe, écrevisse*) to nip; **~ la joue/le bras à qn** to pinch sb's cheek/arm; (*crabe, écrevisse*) to nip sb's cheek/arm **2.**(*serrer fortement*) **~ la bouche** to clamp one's mouth shut; **~ les lèvres** to purse one's lips **3.** *inf* (*arrêter*) to catch; **se faire ~ par qn** to get caught by sb **II.** *vpr* **1.**(*se blesser, se serrer la peau*) **se ~** to pinch oneself; **se ~ le doigt** to get one's finger caught **2.**(*boucher*) **se ~ le nez** to hold one's nose **III.** *vi* **pince-moi, je rêve!** pinch me, I'm dreaming!; **en ~ pour qn** *inf* to be gone on sb

pince-sans-rire [pɛ̃ssɑ̃ʀiʀ] **I.** *mf inv* **c'est un/une ~** he has true deadpan humour *Brit,* he has true deadpan humor *Am* **II.** *adj inv* deadpan

pincette [pɛ̃sɛt] *f* pair of tongs ►**ne pas être à prendre avec des ~s** *inf* to be like a bear with a sore head

pinède [pinɛd] *f* pine forest

pingouin [pɛ̃gwɛ̃] *m* penguin; (*oiseau arctique*) auk

ping-pong [piŋpɔ̃g] *m inv* table tennis [*o* ping pong]

pingre [pɛ̃gʀ] **I.** *adj inf* stingy **II.** *mf inf* skinflint, tightwad *Am*

pinotte [pinɔt] *f Québec, inf* (*cacahuète*) peanut

pin-pon [pɛ̃pɔ̃] *interj* wah-wah (*imitation of a two-tone siren*)

pin's [pins] *m inv* pin (*worn on clothes*)

pinson [pɛ̃sɔ̃] *m* chaffinch ►**gai comme un ~** happy as a lark

pintade [pɛ̃tad] *f* guinea fowl

pintadeau [pɛ̃tado] <x> *m* young guinea fowl

pinte [pɛ̃t] *f* **1.**(*en France*) ≈ quart (*0.93 litre*) **2.**(*système impérial*) pint **3.** *Québec* (*1,136 l*) quart (*1.136 litre*) **4.** *Suisse* (*café, bistrot*) cafe

pinté(e) [pɛ̃te] *adj inf* plastered

pin up [pinœp] *f inv* pin-up

pioche [pjɔʃ] *f* **1.**(*outil*) pick; **à coups de ~** with a pick **2.** JEUX stock

piocher [pjɔʃe] <1> **I.** *vt* **1.**(*creuser*) to dig **2.** *inf* (*étudier*) **~ qc** to slog away at sth, to grind away at sth *Am* **3.** JEUX to take a card [*o* domino] **4.**(*dénicher*) **~ un renseignement** to pick up a piece of information **II.** *vi* **1.**(*creuser*) to dig **2.** *inf* (*étudier*) to slog away **3.** JEUX to take a card; (*prendre un domino*) to take a domino **4.** *inf* (*puiser*) **~ dans ses économies** to dip into one's savings **5.**(*chercher pour saisir, se servir*) **~ dans le plat de hors-d'œuvre** to dip into the platter of hors-d'œuvre; **~ dans une pile de livres** to dip into a pile of books

piolet [pjɔlɛ] *m* ice-axe

pion [pjɔ̃] *m* JEUX pawn

pion(ne) [pjɔ̃, pjɔn] *m(f) inf* ECOLE supervisor

pioncer [pjɔ̃se] <2> *vi inf* to have a doze

pionnier, -ière [pjɔnje, -jɛʀ] *m, f* (*de la médecine, de l'aviation*) pioneer; **être un ~ dans un domaine** to be a pioneer in a field

pipe [pip] *f* pipe

pipeau [pipo] <x> *m* **1.** MUS reed pipe **2.**(*appeau*) bird call ►**c'est du ~** *inf* it's all moonshine

pipeline [pajplajn, piplin] *m* pipeline

piper [pipe] <1> **I.** *vi* **ne pas ~** not to breath a word **II.** *vt* (*dés*) to load; (*cartes*) to mark

pipette [pipɛt] *f* pipette

pipi [pipi] *m inf enfantin* wee-wee *Brit,* pee-pee *Am;* **faire ~** to go for a wee ►**c'est du ~ de chat** it's pathetic; (*en parlant d'une boisson*) it's like dishwater

pipi-room [pipiʀum] <pipi-rooms> *m iron, inf* loo *Brit,* bathroom *Am*

piquant [pikɑ̃] *m* **1.**(*épine*) thorn; (*de ronce*) prickle **2.**(*agrément*) **avoir du ~** (*récit, livre*) to be spicy; **le ~ de l'histoire, c'est qu'il l'a cru** the best thing about the story is that he believed it

piquant(e) [pikɑ̃, ɑ̃t] *adj* **1.**(*pointu: joue, plante*) prickly; (*rose*) thorny **2.** GASTR (*moutarde, radis*) hot; (*odeur*) pungent; (*goût, sauce*) spicy **3.**(*mordant: air, bise, froid*) biting

pique [pik] *m* JEUX spade; **valet de ~** jack of spades

piqué [pike] **descendre en ~** to nose-dive

pique-assiette [pikasjɛt] <pique-assiette(s)> *mf inf* scrounger **pique-nique** [piknik] <pique-niques> *m* picnic **pique-niquer** [piknike] <1> *vi* to picnic **pique-niqueur, -euse** [piknikœʀ, -øz] <pique-niqueurs> *m, f* picnicker

piquer [pike] <1> **I.** *vt* **1.**(*faire une piqûre: personne, guêpe, moustique*) to sting; (*serpent, puce*) to bite **2.**(*donner la mort*) **~ un animal** to put an animal down **3.**(*prendre/fixer avec un objet pointu: olive, papillon*) to stick **4.**(*enfoncer par le bout*) **~ une aiguille dans qc** to jab a needle into sth **5.**(*picoter: yeux, visage*) to sting; **~ la peau** to prickle; **~ la langue** to tingle on one's tongue **6.** *inf* (*faire brusquement*) **~ un cent mètres** to do a hundred metre sprint; **~ une colère/une crise** to fly into a rage/have a fit; **~ une crise de larmes** to burst out crying; **~ un fard** to go red; **~ un roupillon/une tête** to have a nap **7.** *inf* (*voler*) to pinch **8.** *inf* (*arrêter, attraper*) to catch **II.** *vi* **1.**(*faire une piqûre: moustique,* *aiguille*) to sting; (*serpent, puce*) to bite **2.** (*descendre*) ~ **sur qc** to swoop down on sth **3.** (*se diriger*) ~ **sur qn/qc** to head for sb/sth **4.** (*irriter un sens: fumée, ortie*) to sting; (*moutarde, radis*) to be hot; (*barbe, pull*) to prickle; (*froid, vent*) to bite; (*eau gazeuse*) to fizz **III.** *vpr* **1.** (*se blesser*) **se ~ avec une aiguille/à un rosier** to prick oneself with a needle/on a rosebush; **se ~ avec des orties** to get stung oneself by (stinging) nettles **2.** (*se faire une injection*) **se ~** to inject oneself; (*drogué*) to shoot up; **se ~ à qc** to inject oneself with sth; (*drogué*) to shoot up with sth

piquet [pikɛ] *m* (*pieu: de parc, jardin*) post; (*de tente*) peg ▸**raide comme un ~** as stiff as a poker; **être/rester planté comme un ~** *inf* to stand doing nothing; **aller au ~** ECOLE to go to the corner; **~ de grève** picket line

piquette [pikɛt] *f* **1.** *péj* (*mauvais vin*) plonk **2.** *inf* (*défaite cuisante*) thrashing

piquouse [pikuz] *f inf* jab

piqûre [pikyʀ] *f* **1.** (*blessure: d'épingle*) stab; (*de guêpe*) sting; (*de moustique*) bite **2.** MED injection; **faire une ~ à qn** to give sb an injection

piranha [piʀana] *m* piranha

pirate [piʀat] **I.** *m* **1.** NAUT pirate **2.** AVIAT **~ de l'air** hijacker **3.** AUTO **~ de la route** carjacker **II.** *adj* pirate

pirater [piʀate] <1> *vt* to pirate

pire [piʀ] **I.** *adj* **1.** (*plus mauvais*) worse; **rien de ~ que** nothing worse than; **de ~ en ~** worse and worse **2.** (*le plus mauvais*) **le/la ~ élève** the worst pupil **II.** *m* **le ~** the worst; **s'attendre au ~** to expect the worst; **au ~** if the worst comes to the worst

pirogue [piʀɔg] *f* dugout canoe

pirouette [piʀwɛt] *f* **1.** (*culbute: d'un acrobate, danseur, cheval*) pirouette **2.** (*volte-face*) about-face, about-turn *Brit* ▸**répondre** [*o* **s'en tirer**] **par une ~** to evade the question

pis [pi] *m* udder

pis-aller [pizale] *m inv* **être un ~** to be better than nothing

pisciculture [pisikyltyʀ] *f* fish farming

piscine [pisin] *f* swimming pool

pissenlit [pisɑ̃li] *m* dandelion

pisser [pise] <1> *vi inf* to (have a) piss

pisseux, **-euse** [pisø, -øz] *adj* **1.** *inf* (*imprégné d'urine*) piss-soaked **2.** (*terne*) wishy-washy

pissotière [pisɔtjɛʀ] *f inf* urinal

pistache [pistaʃ] *f, adj inv* pistachio

piste [pist] *f* **1.** (*trace: d'un cambrioleur, suspect*) trail; (*d'un animal*) tracks *pl* **2.** (*indice*) clue **3.** AVIAT runway; **~ d'atterrissage/de décollage** landing/take-off runway **4.** AUTO **~ cyclable** cycle lane; **~ cavalière** bridle path **5.** (*au ski*) slope; **~ de ski de fond** cross-country ski track **6.** (*grand ovale à l'hippodrome*) course, track; (*grand ovale au vélodrome/circuit automobile*) track; **~ d'essai** test track; **cyclisme sur ~/épreuve sur ~** course cycling/course test **7.** (*espace pour le patinage*) rink; (*espace pour la danse*) floor; (*espace au cirque*) ring **8.** (*chemin dans le désert*) track; (*chemin à la montagne*) path **9.** CINE, TV track ▸**brouiller les ~s** to confuse the issue; **entrer en ~** to come on to the scene

pisteur, **-euse** [pistœʀ, -øz] *m, f* ski patroller

pistil [pistil] *m* BOT pistil

pistolet [pistɔlɛ] *m* **1.** (*arme*) pistol; **~ à eau** water pistol; **~ d'alarme** alarm gun **2.** (*pulvérisateur*) spray **3.** *Belgique* (*petit pain rond*) bread roll

pistolet-mitrailleur [pistɔlɛmitʀɑjœʀ] <pistolets-mitrailleurs> *m* submachine gun

piston [pistɔ̃] *m inf* (*favoritisme*) string-pulling

pistonner [pistɔne] <1> *vt inf* **~ qn** to pull strings for sb; **se faire ~ par qn** to have sb pull strings

pitance [pitɑ̃s] *f soutenu* portion

piteux, **-euse** [pitø, -øz] *adj* (*air, apparence*) pitiful; (*état*) pathetic; (*résultat*) miserable

pitié [pitje] *f* (*compassion*) pity; (*miséricorde*) mercy; **par ~** for pity's sake; **agir/combattre sans ~** to act/fight mercilessly; **être sans ~** to be merciless; **avoir/prendre ~ de qn** to have/take pity on sb; **Seigneur, prends ~ de nous!** Lord, have mercy on us!; **faire ~ à qn** to make sb feel sorry for one; *péj* to be pitiful; **prendre qn/qc en ~** to take pity on sb/sth

piton [pitɔ̃] *m* **1.** (*crochet*) hook; SPORT piton **2.** GEO peak **3.** *Québec* (*bouton*) button **4.** *Québec* (*touche: d'un ordinateur, téléphone*) key; (*d'une télécommande*) button

pitonnage [pitɔnaʒ] *m Québec, inf* (*zapping*) channel-hopping *Brit,* channel surfing *Am*

pitonner [pitɔne] <1> *vi Québec* (*tapoter sur des touches*) to twiddle at the keys

pitoyable [pitwajabl] *adj* **1.** (*qui inspire la pitié: aspect, état, état, personne*) pitiful **2.** (*piteux*) pitiful; (*niveau de vie, résultat*) miserable

pitre [pitʀ] *m* clown; **faire le ~** to play the clown

pitrerie [pitʀəʀi] *f souvent pl* clowning; **faire des ~s** to clown around

pittoresque [pitɔʀɛsk] *adj* picturesque

pive [piv] *f Suisse* (*fruit des conifères*) pine cone

pivert [pivɛʀ] *m* green woodpecker

pivoine [pivwan] *f* peony ▸**rouge comme une ~** as red as a beetroot *Brit,* beet red *Am*

pivot [pivo] *m* **1.** TECH (*pour une dent*) post **2.** (*agent principal: d'une entreprise*) kingpin

pivotant(e) [pivɔtɑ̃, ɑ̃t] *adj* revolving

pivoter [pivɔte] <1> *vi* **~ sur qc** to revolve around sth; **faire ~ qc** to pivot sth

pixel [piksɛl] *m* INFOR pixel

pizza [pidza] *f* pizza; **morceau de ~ au**

fromage slice of cheese pizza
pizzeria [pidzeʀja] *f* pizzeria
PJ [peʒi] *f abr de* **Police judiciaire** ≈ CID
placard [plakaʀ] *m* (*armoire*) cupboard; ~ **à balais** broom cupboard ►**mettre qn/qc au** ~ *inf* to lock sb up
placarder [plakaʀde] <1> *vt* ~ **un mur** to stick posters up all over a wall
place [plas] *f* **1.** (*lieu public*) square; ~ **de l'église/du marché** church/market square; **sur la** ~ **publique** in public **2.** (*endroit approprié*) place; **à la** ~ **de qc** in place of sth; **sur** ~ on the spot; **être à sa** ~ to be in the right place; **être en** ~ (*installé*) to be installed; (*en fonction*) to be in place; **mettre les meubles/une machine en** ~ to install furniture/a machine; **se mettre en** ~ to be set up; **se mettre à la** ~ **de qn** to put oneself in sb else's shoes **3.** (*endroit quelconque*) spot; **être/rester cloué sur** ~ to be/remain rooted to the spot; **prendre la** ~ **de qc** to take the place of sth; **il ne reste pas** [*o* **tient**] **en** ~ he can't keep still **4.** (*espace*) room; **tenir/prendre de la** ~ to take up room; **gagner de la** ~ to gain some space **5.** (*emplacement réservé*) space; ~ **assise** seat; ~ **debout** standing room; ~ **de stationnement** parking space; **y a-t-il encore une** ~ (**de**) **libre?** is there another seat free? **6.** (*billet*) seat; ~ **de cinéma/concert** cinema/concert ticket; **louer des** ~**s** to book seats **7.** (*emploi*) position **8.** *Belgique, Nord* (*pièce*) room **9.** *Québec* (*endroit, localité*) place ►**avoir/obtenir sa** ~ **au soleil** to have/get one's place in the sun; **les** ~**s sont chères** *inf* there is a lot of competition; **faire** ~ **à qn/qc** to give way to sb/sth; **remettre qn à sa** ~ to put sb in his place; **en** ~**!** ECOLE places!; SPORT get into position!; **être/figurer en bonne** ~ **pour** +*infin* to be/look in a good position to +*infin;* **laisser qn sur** ~ to leave sb behind
placé(e) [plase] *adj* **1.** (*situé*) **être bien/mal** ~ (*objet*) to be well/awkwardly placed; (*terrain*) to be well/badly situated; (*spectateurs*) to be well/badly seated; **c'est de la fierté mal** ~**e!** it's misplaced pride!; **être bien/mal** ~ **pour répondre** to be in a good/bad position to reply; **tu es mal** ~ **pour me faire des reproches!** you're in no position to criticize me! **2.** SPORT placed; **être bien/mal** ~ to be placed high/low; **jouer** ~ to back a horse each way *Brit,* to bet a horse to place *Am* **3.** (*dans une situation*) **être haut** ~ to be high up; **fonctionnaire haut** ~ high-ranking official
placement [plasmɑ̃] *m* **1.** investment; ~ **à terme** term investment; **faire un** ~ **obligataire/en actions** to invest in bonds/stocks **2.** MED internment **3.** (*embauche*) placement **4.** *Belgique* (*action de placer*) placing
placer [plase] <2> **I.** *vt* **1.** (*mettre*) ~ **qc sur l'étagère** to put sth on the shelf **2.** (*installer: sentinelle*) to place; ~ **les spectateurs/les invités** to seat the spectators/guests; ~ **un enfant dans une famille d'acceuil** to place a child with a foster family **3.** (*introduire: anecdote, remarque*) to put in; ~ **une idée dans qc** to put an idea in sth; **ne pas pouvoir** ~ **un mot** [*o* **ne pas arriver à en** ~ **une**] to not be able to get a word in **4.** (*mettre dans une situation professionnelle*) ~ **un ami dans une entreprise comme qc** to get a friend a job in a company as sth **5.** FIN (*argent, capitaux, économies*) to invest **II.** *vpr* **1.** (*s'installer*) **se** ~ to take up a position; (*debout*) to stand **2.** (*se situer*) **se** ~ **dans le cas où ...** to suppose that ... **3.** (*avoir sa place désignée*) **se** ~ **devant/à côté de qc** (*meuble, objet, obstacle*) to belong in front of/next to sth **4.** (*prendre un certain rang*) **se** ~ **deuxième** to be placed second
placide [plasid] *adj* calm
plafond [plafɔ̃] *m* **1.** (*opp: plancher*) ceiling **2.** (*limite supérieure*) ceiling; (*d'un crédit*) limit ►**sauter au** ~ *inf* to hit the roof
plafonner [plafɔne] <1> **I.** *vi* (*atteindre son maximum*) to peak **II.** *vt* **1.** CONSTR ~ **qc** to put a ceiling in sth **2.** FIN to cap
plafonnier [plafɔnje] *m* ceiling light
plage [plaʒ] *f* **1.** (*rivage*) beach; **les** ~**s de la Seine** the beaches along the Seine; ~ **de galets/sable** pebble/sandy beach; **robe de** ~ beach dress; **serviette de** ~ beach towel; **sur la** ~ on the beach; **être/aller à la** ~ to be at/go to the beach **2.** (*station balnéaire*) resort **3.** AUTO ~ **arrière** back shelf
plagiaire [plaʒjɛʀ] *mf* plagiarist
plagiat [plaʒja] *m* plagiarism *no pl*
plagier [plaʒje] <1a> *vt* to plagiarize
plagiste [plaʒist] *mf* beach attendant
plaid [plɛd] *m* plaid
plaider [plede] <1> **I.** *vt* **1.** JUR ~ **la cause de qn** to plead sb's case; **être plaidé** (*cause*) to be heard **2.** JUR (*faire valoir: irresponsabilité, incompétence*) to plead; ~ **coupable/non-coupable** to plead guilty/not guilty; ~ **que l'accusé est très jeune** to plead that the defendant is very young **II.** *vi* **1.** JUR (*faire une plaidoirie: avocat*) to plead; ~ **pour/contre qn** to plead for/against sb **2.** JUR (*intenter un procès*) ~ **contre qn** to take court action against sb **3.** (*appuyer*) ~ **pour** [*o* **en faveur de**] **son fils auprès de qn** to speak up for one's son with sb; ~ **contre qn/qc** to speak against sb/sth **4.** (*être à l'avantage*) ~ **pour** [*o* **en faveur de**] **qn** (*passé*) to be in sb's favour *Brit,* to be in sb's favor *Am*
plaidoirie [plɛdwaʀi] *f* **1.** JUR speech for the defence *Brit,* speech for the defense *Am* **2.** (*défense*) defence *Brit,* defense *Am;* ~ **pour** [*o* **en faveur de**] **qn/qc** in defence of sb/sth
plaidoyer [plɛdwaje] *m* speech for the defence *Brit,* speech for the defense *Am*
plaie [plɛ] *f* **1.** (*blessure*) wound **2.** (*malheur*) bad luck; **quelle** ~**!** *inf* what bad luck! **3.** *inf* (*personne*) nuisance
plaignant(e) [plɛɲɑ̃, ɑ̃t] **I.** *adj* **partie** ~**e** plaintiff **II.** *m(f)* plaintiff
plain(e) [plɛ̃, ɛn] *adj* **tapis** ~ *Belgique*

P

(*moquette*) (fitted) carpet

plaindre [plɛ̃dʀ] *irr* **I.** *vt* (*s'apitoyer sur*) ~ **qn** to pity sb; (*être solidaire de*) to feel sorry for sb; **je te plains vraiment/sincèrement** I really/sincerely feel sorry for you **II.** *vpr* **1.** (*se lamenter*) **se** ~ **de qc** to moan about sth **2.** (*protester*) **se** ~ **de qn/qc à l'arbitre** to complain about sb/sth to the referee

plaine [plɛn] *f* plain

plain-pied [plɛ̃pje] *m sans pl* **être de** ~ to be on the same level

plainte [plɛ̃t] *f* **1.** (*gémissement*) moan; **des** ~**s** moaning **2.** (*récrimination*) *a.* JUR complaint; **déposer une** ~ [*o* **porter** ~] **contre qn auprès du tribunal pour le vacarme** to press charges against sb for excessive noise

plaintif, -ive [plɛ̃tif, -iv] *adj* plaintive

plaire [plɛʀ] *irr* **I.** *vi* **1.** (*être agréable*) **qc plaît à qn** sb likes sth; ~ **aux spectateurs** to please the audience **2.** (*charmer*) **il lui plaît** she fancies him; **les brunes me plaisent davantage** I like brunettes better **3.** (*convenir*) ~ **à qn** (*idée, projet*) to suit sb **4.** (*être bien accueilli: chose*) to be appreciated ►**qn a tout pour** ~ *iron* sb who gets on people's nerves **II.** *vi impers* (*être agréable*) **il plaît à l'enfant de faire qc** the child likes doing sth; **vous plairait-il de venir dîner?** would you like to come to dinner?; **comme il te/vous plaira** as you like; **quand ça te/vous plaira** whenever you like ►**s'il te/vous plaît** please; *Belgique* (*voici*) here you are **III.** *vpr* **1.** (*se sentir à l'aise*) **se** ~ **avec qn** to enjoy sb's company; **se** ~ **au Canada** to like being in Canada **2.** (*s'apprécier*) **se** ~ (*personnes*) to like each another; **se** ~ **avec qc** to enjoy being with sth **3.** (*prendre plaisir*) **il se plaît à faire qc** he likes doing sth

plaisance [plɛzɑ̃s] *f* NAUT (**navigation de**) ~ boating; (*à voile*) sailing; **port de** ~ sailing harbour *Brit,* sailing harbor *Am*

plaisancier, -ière [plɛzɑ̃sje, jɛʀ] *m, f* amateur sailor

plaisant(e) [plɛzɑ̃, ɑ̃t] *adj* **1.** pleasant; **être** ~ **à l'œil** [*o* **au regard**] to be pleasing to the eye **2.** (*amusant*) amusing

plaisanter [plɛzɑ̃te] <1> *vi* **1.** (*blaguer*) to joke; **je ne plaisante pas!** I'm not joking!; ~ **sur** [*o* **à propos de**] **qc** to joke about sth; **je ne suis pas d'humeur à** ~ I'm in no mood for jokes **2.** (*dire par jeu*) **ne pas** ~ **sur la discipline/avec l'exactitude** to be strict about discipline/punctuality; **tu plaisantes!** you're joking!

plaisanterie [plɛzɑ̃tʀi] *f* (*blague*) joke; ~ **de mauvais goût** joke in bad taste; **par** ~ for fun; **aimer la** ~ to like jokes; **dire qc sur le ton de la** ~ to say sth laughingly ►**les** ~**s les plus courtes sont les meilleures** brevity is the soul of wit

plaisantin [plɛzɑ̃tɛ̃] *m* **1.** (*blagueur*) joker; **petit** ~ clown **2.** *péj* (*fumiste*) fake

plaisir [plezіʀ] *m* **1.** (*joie, distraction*) pleasure; ~ **de faire qc** pleasure of doing sth; **il a** ~ **à faire qc** he enjoys of doing sth; **éprouver** [*o* **prendre**] **un malin** ~ **à faire qc** to get a kick out of doing sth; **faire** ~ **à qn** to please sb; (*rendre service à qn*) to do sb a favour *Brit,* to do sb a favor *Am;* **maintenant fais-moi le** ~ **de te taire!** now, do me a favour and shut up!; **elle prend** (**du**) ~ **à qc** she takes pleasure in sth; **souhaiter à qn bien du** ~ *iron* to wish sb joy; **faire** ~ **à voir** to be a pleasure to see; **par** [*o* **pour le**] ~ for pleasure **2.** (*jouissance sexuelle*) **se donner du** ~ to pleasure each other **3.** *pl* (*sentiment agréable*) **menus** ~**s** entertainment; **les** ~**s de la table** the pleasures of the table; **courir après les** ~**s** to be a pleasure-seeker ►**bon** ~ wish; **décider qc selon son bon** ~ to decide on sth as one sees fit; **faire durer le** ~ to make the pleasure last; **au** ~**!** *inf* see you soon!; **avec grand** ~ with great pleasure

plan [plɑ̃] *m* **1.** (*représentation graphique, projet*) plan; ~ **de travail** work plan; ~ **d'action** plan of action **2.** (*canevas: d'un devoir, livre, d'une dissertation*) plan **3.** CINE, TV shot; (*cadrage*) frame; ~ **fixe** static shot; **gros** ~, ~ **rapproché** close-up; **au premier** ~ in the foreground **4.** *inf* (*projet de sortie*) **j'ai un** ~ **d'enfer!** I have a great idea! **5.** (*niveau*) **sur le** ~ **national/régional** on a national/regional level; **passer au second** ~ to drop into the background; **de premier** ~ leading; **de second** ~ second-rate; **sur le** ~ **moral** morally (speaking); **sur le** ~ **de qc** as regards sth **6.** (*surface*) ~ **d'eau** stretch of water; ~ **de travail** (*dans une cuisine*) work surface ►**tirer son** ~ *Belgique* (*se débrouillier*) to manage; **laisser qn en** ~ *inf* to leave sb high and dry; **laisser qc en** ~ to drop sth

planche [plɑ̃ʃ] *f* **1.** (*pièce de bois*) plank; ~ **à dessin/à repasser** drawing/ironing board **2.** (*scène*) **les** ~**s** the boards; **brûler les** ~**s** to give a good performance; **monter sur les** ~**s** to tread the boards **3.** SPORT ~ **à roulettes** skateboard; ~ **à voile** (*objet*) sailboard; (*sport*) windsurfing

plancher [plɑ̃ʃe] *m* floor ►**le** ~ **des vaches** *iron, inf* dry land; **débarrasser le** ~ *inf* to beat it

planchiste [plɑ̃ʃist] *mf* windsurfer

plancton [plɑ̃ktɔ̃] *m* plankton

planer [plane] <1> *vi* **1.** (*voler*) *a.* AVIAT to glide **2.** (*peser*) ~ **sur qn/qc** (*danger, soupçons*) to hang over sb/sth; **laisser** ~ **le doute sur qc** to leave lingering doubt about sth **3.** *inf* (*rêver*) to have one's head in the clouds **4.** *inf* (*être sous effet euphorisant*) to be spaced out; (*sous l'effet d'une drogue*) to be high

planétaire [planetɛʀ] *adj* **1.** (*mondial*) global **2.** ASTR planetary

planétarium [planetaʀjɔm] *m* planetarium

planète [planɛt] *f* planet; **la** ~ **Terre** the planet Earth

planeur [planœʀ] *m* glider

planification [planifikasjɔ̃] *f* planning
planifier [planifje] <1> *vt* to plan
planisphère [planisfɛʀ] *m* planisphere
planning [planiŋ] *m* **1.** (*calendrier*) calendar **2.** (*planification*) planning; ~ **familial** family planning
planque [plɑ̃k] *f inf* **1.** (*cachette*) hiding place **2.** (*travail tranquille*) easy work; **c'est la ~!** it is cushy number! **3.** (*lieu protégé*) hideout
planqué(e) [plɑ̃ke] *m(f) péj, inf* stashed away
planquer [plɑ̃ke] <1> *vt, vpr inf* (**se**) ~ to hide
plant [plɑ̃] *m* **1.** (*jeune plante*) seedling; ~ **de vigne** young vine; ~ **de laitue** lettuce seedling **2.** (*plantation*) ~ **d'asperges** asparagus bed
plantage [plɑ̃taʒ] *m* INFOR crash
plantaire [plɑ̃tɛʀ] *adj* plantar; **voûte** ~ arch of the foot
plantation [plɑ̃tasjɔ̃] *f* **1.** (*exploitation agricole*) plantation; ~ **de café** coffee plantation **2.** (*action*) planting; **faire des ~s** to plant
plante [plɑ̃t] *f* plant
planté(e) [plɑ̃te] *adj* (*debout et immobile*) **être/rester ~ là** to just stand there; **être** [*o* **rester**] **~ là à attendre** to be standing there waiting
planter [plɑ̃te] <1> **I.** *vt* **1.** (*mettre en terre*) to plant **2.** (*garnir de*) ~ **un jardin de/en qc** to plant a garden with sth; **avenue plantée d'arbres** tree-lined avenue **3.** (*enfoncer: pieu, piquet*) to drive in; ~ **un clou dans le mur** to hammer a nail into the wall; ~ **ses griffes dans le bras à qn** (*chat*) to sink one's claws into sb's arm **4.** (*dresser: tente*) to pitch; (*échelle, drapeau*) to put up **5.** *inf* (*abandonner*) ~ **qn là** to drop sb; *fig* to dump sb **II.** *vpr* **1.** *inf* (*se tromper*) **se ~ dans qc** to screw up over sth; **se ~ à un examen** to screw up in an exam **2.** (*se mettre*) **se ~ une aiguille dans la main** to stick a needle in one's hand; **se ~ dans le mur** (*couteau, flèche*) to stick in the wall **3.** *inf* (*se poster*) **se ~ dans le jardin** to take up one's post in the garden; **se ~ devant** [*o* **en face de**] **qn** to position oneself in front of sb **4.** *inf* (*avoir un accident*) *a.* INFOR **se ~** to crash
planteur [plɑ̃tœʀ] *m* planter
plantureux, -euse [plɑ̃tyʀø, -øz] *adj* **1.** (*repas*) copious **2.** (*bien en chair: femme*) buxom; (*poitrine*) ample **3.** (*fertile: région, terre*) fertile; (*année*) bumper
plaque [plak] *f* **1.** (*matériau plat*) sheet **2.** (*présentation*) ~ **de beurre** pack of butter; ~ **de chocolat** slab of chocolate **3.** (*couche*) ~ **de verglas** sheet of ice **4.** MED patch **5.** (*pièce de métal: d'une porte, rue*) plaque; (*d'un policier*) badge; ~ **commémorative** commemorative plaque; ~ **minéralogique** registration plate *Brit,* license plate *Am* **6.** (*décoration*) plaque **7.** GASTR (*d'une cuisinière*) hob; ~ **chauffante** [*o* **électrique**] hotplate **8.** GEO plate ▶~ **tournante** turntable *fig,* nerve centre; **être à côté de la ~** *inf* to have got it all wrong; **mettre à côté de la ~** *inf* to be off target

> On French **plaques minéralogiques** the last two numbers indicate where the vehicle is from. So the 78 at the end of plate number 6785 MN 78 shows that a car is registered in the Yvelines (postal code 78...).

plaqué [plake] *m* (*bois*) veneer; (*métal*) plate; **c'est du ~ chêne** it's oak-veneered; **bijoux en ~ or** gold-plated jewellery
plaqué(e) [plake] *adj* ~ (**en**) **argent/or** silver/gold-plated; ~ **chêne** oak-veneered
plaquer [plake] <1> **I.** *vt* **1.** *inf* (*abandonner: conjoint*) to dump; ~ **un emploi** to pack in a job; **tout ~** to pack it all in; ~ **son petit ami/fiancé** to dump one's boyfriend/fiancé **2.** (*aplatir*) ~ **ses cheveux** to plaster one's hair down **3.** (*coller*) **la pluie plaquait sa robe sur ses jambes** the rain made her dress cling to her legs **4.** (*serrer contre*) ~ **qn contre le mur/au mur** to pin sb up against/to the wall **5.** SPORT to tackle **II.** *vpr* (*se serrer*) **se ~ contre qc** to hold oneself against sb
plaquette [plakɛt] *f* **1.** (*petite plaque*) plaque; ~ **de marbre/métal** marble/metal plaque **2.** GASTR (*présentation*) ~ **de chocolat** bar of chocolate; ~ **de beurre** pack of butter *Brit,* stick of butter *Am;* ~ **de pilules** strip of pills **3.** MED platelet **4.** (*livre*) booklet; (*brochure*) brochure **5.** AUTO **~s de frein** brake pad
plastic [plastik] *m* plastic explosive
plastifier [plastifje] <1a> *vt* to coat with plastic
plastiquage [plastikaʒ] *m v.* **plasticage**
plastique [plastik] **I.** *m* plastic; **en ~** plastic **II.** *adj inv* plastic
plastiquer [plastike] <1> *vt* to bomb
plat [pla] *m* **1.** (*récipient creux*) dish; (*récipient plat*) plate; ~ **à viande** meat dish **2.** (*contenu*) **un ~ de lentilles** a dish of lentils **3.** (*mets, élément d'un repas*) course; ~ **principal** [*o* **de résistance**] main course; ~ **du jour** dish of the day; ~ **de poisson/légumes** fish/vegetable dish; **de bons petits ~s** tasty little dishes; ~ **garni** main course with vegetables ▶**mettre les petits ~s dans les grands** to lay on a grand meal; **faire tout un ~ de qc** *inf* to make a song and dance about sth
plat(e) [pla, plat] *adj* **1.** (*égal, opp: arrondi*) flat; (*mer*) smooth **2.** (*peu profond, peu haut: assiette, chaussure, talon*) flat; **mettre/poser qc à ~** to lay sth down flat **3.** (*fade: conversation*) dull **4.** (*obséquieux*) **faire de ~es excuses** to make an abject apology **5.** (*vidé de son contenu*) **être à ~** (*pneu, batterie*) to be flat; *inf* (*épuisé*) to be run-down ▶**mettre une question/un problème à ~** to examine a question/problem closely
platane [platan] *m* plane tree
plateau [plato] <x> *m* **1.** (*support*) tray; ~ **à**

P

fromages cheeseboard **2.** GASTR ~ **de fruits de mer** seafood platter; ~ **de fromages** cheeseboard **3.** (*partie plate: d'une balance*) pan **4.** GEO plateau; ~ **continental** continental shelf **5.** CINE, TV set; (*invités*) line-up; **sur le ~/hors du ~** on the set/off the set

plateau-repas [platoʀ(ə)pa] <plateaux-repas> *m* (*chez soi*) TV dinner; (*dans les transports*) meal on a tray

platebande, plate-bande [platbɑ̃d] <plates-bandes> *f* (flower) bed ▸**marcher sur les plates-bandes de qn** *inf* to tread on sb's toes

plateforme, plate-forme [platfɔʀm] <plates-formes> *f* **1.** AUTO, CHEMDFER, INFOR, TECH platform; ~ **de forage** drilling platform **2.** GEO ~ **continentale** [*o* **littorale**] continental shelf

platine[1] [platin] **I.** *m* platinum **II.** *app inv* platinum

platine[2] [platin] *f* **1.** platen; (*d'un microscope*) stage; (*d'une serrure*) plate **2.** MEDIA (*d'un électrophone*) turntable; (*d'un lecteur cassettes*) deck; ~ **laser** CD player

platitude [platityd] *f* **1.** *sans pl* triteness **2.** (*propos*) platitude

platonique [platɔnik] *adj* (*amour*) platonic

plâtre [plɑtʀ] *m* (*matériau*) *a.* MED plaster; **mur en ~** plaster wall; **avoir un bras dans le ~** to have an arm in plaster *Brit*, to have an arm in a cast *Am* ▸**essuyer les ~s** *inf* to put up with all the teething trouble

plâtré(e) [plɑtʀe] *adj* in plaster

plâtrer [plɑtʀe] <1> *vt* **1.** (*couvrir de plâtre*) to plaster; (*trou, fissure*) to fill **2.** (*mettre dans le plâtre*) to plaster

plâtrier, -ière [plɑtʀije, -jɛʀ] *m, f* plasterer

plausible [plozibl] *adj* plausible

play-back [plɛbak] *m inv* lip-synching

play-boy [plɛbɔj] <play-boys> *m* playboy

plébiscite [plebisit] *m* plebiscite

plébisciter [plebisite] <1> *vt* **1.** POL to elect by plebiscite **2.** (*approuver*) ~ **qn** to endorse sb massively

plein [plɛ̃] **I.** *adv* **1.** *inf* (*beaucoup*) **avoir ~ d'argent/d'amis** to have loads of money/friends **2.** (*exactement*) **en ~ dans l'œil/sur la table/dans la soupe** right in the eye/on the table/in the soup; **en ~ devant** straight ahead **3.** (*au maximum*) **tourner à ~** to turn fully; **utiliser une machine à ~** to get full use from a machine ▸**mignon/gentil tout ~** *inf* just too cute/kind **II.** *prep* **de l'argent ~ les poches** tons of money **III.** *m* (*de carburant*) fill-up; **faire le ~** to fill the tank; **le ~, s'il vous plaît!** fill it up, please ▸**battre son ~** to be in full swing

plein(e) [plɛ̃, plɛn] *adj* **1.** (*rempli*) full; (*journée, vie*) busy; **à moitié ~** half-full; **être ~ de bonne volonté/de joie** to be full of good will/joy; **être ~ de santé** to be bursting with health; **être ~ à craquer** to be full to bursting **2.** (*rond: joues, visage*) round **3.** (*sans réserve*) **à ~s bras/à ~es mains** in armfuls/handfuls; **mordre à ~es dents dans une pomme** to bite deeply into an apple; **respirer à ~s poumons** to breathe deeply **4.** (*au maximum de*) **à ~s bords** full to the brim; **à ~ régime** [*o* **rendement**], **à ~e vapeur** at full power **5.** (*au plus fort de*) **en ~ été/hiver** in the middle of summer/winter; **en ~ jour** in broad daylight; **en ~e nuit** in the middle of the night; **en ~ soleil** in full sun **6.** (*au milieu de*) **être en ~ travail** to be in the middle of working; **viser en ~ cœur** to aim straight at the heart; **en ~e rue** out in the road; **en ~e obscurité** in complete darkness; **en ~e lumière** in full sunlight; **en ~ vol** in full flight; **en ~ essor** booming; **être en ~ boum** to be rushed off one's feet **7.** (*sans vide: trait*) continuous; (*bois, porte*) solid **8.** *antéposé* (*total: victoire*) total; (*succès, confiance*) complete; **avoir ~e conscience de qc** to be fully aware of sth **9.** (*entier: jour, mois*) whole **10.** (*gravide*) pregnant

pleinement [plɛnmɑ̃] *adv* fully

plénitude [plenityd] *f* fullness

pléonasme [pleɔnasm] *m* pleonasm

pléthore [pletɔʀ] *f sans pl, soutenu* ~ **de qc** plethora of sth; COM glut of sth; **il y a ~ de candidats** there's a mass of candidates

pleurer [plœʀe] <1> **I.** *vi* **1.** (*verser des larmes, crier: personne, bébé*) to cry; (*œil*) to water; **faire ~ qn** to make sb cry; **la poussière me fait ~** the dust makes my eyes water; ~ **de rage** to cry with rage; ~ **de rire** to weep with laughter **2.** (*se lamenter*) ~ **sur qn/qc** to lament over sb/sth; ~ **sur son sort** to bemoan one's lot **3.** (*réclamer*) to whine; **aller ~ auprès de qn** to go moaning to sb; ~ **après qc** *inf* to go begging for sth **4.** (*extrêmement*) **triste à (faire) ~** so sad you could cry; **maigre à (faire) ~** pitifully thin; **bête à ~** painfully stupid **II.** *vt* **1.** (*regretter*) ~ **qn** to mourn for sb; ~ **sa jeunesse** to mourn one's youth **2.** (*verser*) ~ **des larmes de joie/sang** to cry tears of joy/blood; ~ **toutes les larmes de son corps** to cry one's eyes out

pleureuse [plœʀøz] *f* mourner

pleurnichard(e) [plœʀniʃaʀ, aʀd] *adj inf v.* **pleurnicheur**

pleurnicher [plœʀniʃe] <1> *vi inf* **1.** to whimper **2.** (*se lamenter*) to whine

pleurnicheur, -euse [plœʀniʃœʀ, -øz] **I.** *adj inf* **1.** (*qui pleure*) snivelling **2.** (*qui se lamente*) whining **II.** *m, f inf* **1.** (*qui pleure*) crybaby **2.** (*qui se lamente*) whiner

pleurs [plœʀ] *mpl soutenu* tear; **être en ~** to be in tears

pleuvoir [pløvwaʀ] *irr* **I.** *vi impers* **il pleut de grosses gouttes** it's raining heavily ▸**qu'il pleuve ou qu'il vente** come rain or shine **II.** *vi* **1.** (*s'abattre: coups, reproches*) to rain down **2.** (*arriver en abondance*) **les mauvaises nouvelles pleuvent en ce moment** there's no end to bad news at the moment

Plexiglas® [plɛksiglas] *m* Perspex® *Brit,* Plexiglas® *Am*

pli [pli] *m* **1.** (*pliure*) pleat; (*du papier*) fold; **faire le ~ d'un pantalon** to put a crease in a pair of trousers; **jupe à ~s** pleated skirt **2.** (*mauvaise pliure*) (**faux**) ~ crease; **cette veste fait des ~s/un ~** this jacket creases **3.** *sans pl* (*forme*) **avoir un beau ~** to have a good shape **4.** JEUX **faire un ~** to take a trick **5.** *Belgique* (*raie formée par les cheveux*) parting *Brit,* part *Am* ▸**prendre un mauvais ~** to get into a bad habit; **ça ne fait pas un ~** *inf* there is no doubt (about it); **prendre le ~ de faire qc** to get into the habit of doing sth

pliable [plijabl] *adj* pliable

pliant(e) [plijɑ̃, jɑ̃t] *adj* folding

plie [pli] *f* plaice

plier [plije] <1> **I.** *vt* **1.** (*replier: papier, tissu*) to fold; (*linge, tente*) to fold up; **un papier plié en quatre** a piece of paper folded into four **2.** (*refermer*) to close; (*journal, carte routière*) to fold up **3.** (*fléchir: bras, jambe*) to flex **4.** (*courber*) to bend; **la neige plie les arbres** the snow is making the trees bend; **être plié par l'âge** to be bent over by age; **être plié par la douleur** to be doubled up in pain **II.** *vi* **1.** (*se courber*) ~ **sous le poids de qc** to bend with the weight of sth **2.** (*céder*) to yield; ~ **devant l'autorité du chef** to yield to the leader's authority **III.** *vpr* **1.** (*être pliant*) **se ~** to fold **2.** (*se soumettre*) **se ~ à la volonté de qn** to yield to sb's will

plinthe [plɛ̃t] *f* plinth

plissé(e) [plise] *adj* **1.** COUT pleated **2.** GEO **chaîne ~e** folded chain **3.** (*ridé*) wrinkled

plissement [plismɑ̃] *m* **1.** (*du front*) creasing; **avoir un ~ d'yeux** to screw up ones eyes; **avoir un ~ de la bouche** to pucker up one's lips **2.** GEO fold

plisser [plise] <1> **I.** *vt* **1.** (*couvrir de faux plis*) to crease **2.** (*froncer: front*) to crease; (*yeux*) to screw up; (*nez*) to wrinkle; (*bouche*) to pucker; **une ride plissa son front** a wrinkle creased his brow **II.** *vi* to wrinkle; (*lin, tissu*) to crease

pliure [plijyʀ] *f* **1.** (*du bras, genou*) bend; (*d'un ourlet, tissu, papier*) fold **2.** (*pliage: d'un papier, tissu*) folding

plomb [plɔ̃] *m* **1.** (*métal*) lead; **lourd comme du ~** as heavy as lead; **sans ~** (*essence*) unleaded **2.** (*fusible*) fuse **3.** (*pour la chasse*) lead shot *no pl;* **du ~** shot **4.** (*à la pêche*) sinker ▸**avoir du ~ dans la tête** to have some sense; **ne pas avoir de ~ dans la tête** to be empty-headed; **à ~** straight; **ciel de ~** leaden sky; **sommeil de ~** heavy sleep; **j'ai des jambes de ~** my legs feel like a dead weight; **par un soleil de ~** under a blazing sun

plombage [plɔ̃baʒ] *m* **1.** MED (*d'une dent*) filling **2.** (*action de sceller*) sealing

plomberie [plɔ̃bʀi] *f sans pl* plumbing

plombier [plɔ̃bje] *m* plumber

plonge [plɔ̃ʒ] *f* **faire la ~** *inf* to do the washing up

plongé(e) [plɔ̃ʒe] **I.** *part passé de* **plonger** **II.** *adj* **1.** (*absorbé*) immersed **2.** (*entouré*) **être ~ dans l'obscurité** to be surrounded by darkness

plongeant(e) [plɔ̃ʒɑ̃, ʒɑ̃t] *adj* (*décolleté*) plunging; **une vue ~e sur le parc** a view from above over the park

plongée [plɔ̃ʒe] *f* **1.** (*action de plonger*) diving **2.** SPORT ~ **sous-marine** scuba diving; **faire de la ~** to go scuba diving

plongeoir [plɔ̃ʒwaʀ] *m* diving board

plongeon [plɔ̃ʒɔ̃] *m* **1.** SPORT dive **2.** (*chute*) fall; **faire un ~** to take a nose-dive

plonger [plɔ̃ʒe] <2a> **I.** *vi* **1.** (*s'immerger*) to plunge; ~ **à la recherche de qc** to plunge into [*o* immerse oneself in] the search for sth **2.** (*faire un plongeon*) ~ **dans l'eau** (*personne, oiseau*) to dive into the water; (*voiture*) to plunge into the water; **tu plonges ou tu ne plonges pas?** are you diving or not? **3.** (*sombrer*) ~ **dans le désespoir/la dépression** to plunge into desperation/depression **II.** *vpr* **se ~ dans ses pensées** to immerse oneself in one's thoughts

plongeur, -euse [plɔ̃ʒœʀ, -ʒøz] *m, f* **1.** SPORT diver **2.** (*dans un restaurant*) dishwasher

plouc [pluk] **I.** *mf péj, inf* **être un ~** to be vulgar, to be a hick *Am* **II.** *adj péj, inf* vulgar, hick *Am*

plouf [pluf] *interj, m* splash

ployer [plwaje] <6> *vi soutenu* ~ **sous le poids de qc** to bend under the weight of sth

plu¹ [ply] *part passé de* **plaire**

plu² [ply] *part passé de* **pleuvoir**

plugiciel [plyʒisjɛl] *m* INFOR plug-in

pluie [plɥi] *f* **1.** METEO rain; **saison des ~s** rainy season; **jours/temps de ~** rainy days/weather; **sous la ~** in the rain; **le temps est à la ~** it's going to rain **2.** *sans pl* (*grande quantité*) shower ▸**après la ~ le beau temps** *prov* every cloud has a silver lining; **faire la ~ et le beau temps** to call the shots; **ne pas être né** [*o* **tombé**] **de la dernière ~** not to have been born yesterday

plumage [plymaʒ] *m* plumage

plumard [plymaʀ] *m inf* bed

plume [plym] *f* **1.** (*penne*) feather **2.** (*pour écrire*) quill ▸**laisser** [*o* **perdre**] **des ~s** to come off badly; **voler dans les ~s à** [*o* **de**] **qn** *inf* to go for sb

plumeau [plymo] <x> *m* feather duster

plumer [plyme] <1> *vt* (*animal*) to pluck; (*personne*) to fleece

plumet [plymɛ] *m* plume

plupart [plypaʀ] *f sans pl* **la ~ des élèves/femmes mariées** most pupils/married women; **la ~ d'entre nous/eux/elles** most of us/them; **la ~ sont venus** most of them came; **dans la ~ des cas** in most cases; **la ~ du temps** most of the time ▸**pour la ~** for the

P

most part

pluriel [plyʀjɛl] *m* plural

plus¹ [ply] *adv* **1.** (*opp: encore*) **il n'est ~ très jeune** he's no longer very young; **il ne l'a ~ jamais vu** he has never seen him since; **il ne pleut ~ du tout** it's completely stopped raining; **il ne neige presque ~** it has nearly stopped snowing; **il n'y a ~ personne** there's nobody left; **nous n'avons ~ rien à manger** we have nothing left to eat; **il ne dit ~ un mot** he didn't say another word; **elle n'a ~ un sou** she hasn't a penny left; **ils n'ont ~ d'argent/de beurre** they have no more money/butter; **nous n'avons ~ du tout de pain** we have no bread left at all **2.** (*seulement encore*) **on n'attend ~ que vous** we're only waiting for you now; **il ne manquait ~ que ça** that was all we needed **3.** (*pas plus que*) **non ~** neither

plus² [ply(s)] **I.** *adv* **1.** (*davantage*) **être ~ dangereux/bête que lui** to be more dangerous/stupid than him; **deux fois ~ âgé/cher qu'elle** twice as old/expensive as her; **~ tard/tôt/près/lentement qu'hier** later/earlier/nearer/slower than yesterday **2.** (*dans une comparaison*) **je lis ~ que toi** I read more than you; **ce tissu me plaît ~ que l'autre** I like this fabric more than the other one **3.** (*très*) **il est ~ qu'intelligent** he is extremely intelligent; **elle est ~ que contente** she is more than happy ►**~ que jamais** more than ever; **~ ou moins** more or less; **le vin est bon, ni ~ ni moins** the wine is good, nothing more nothing less; **c'est une dame on ne peut ~ charmante** she is the most charming lady **II.** *adv emploi superl* **le/la ~ rapide/important(e)** the fastest/most important; **le ~ intelligent des élèves** the most intelligent pupil; **c'est le ~ intelligent d'eux** he is the most intelligent of all of them; **le ~ vite/souvent** the fastest/most often; **le ~ tard possible** as late as possible; **c'est lui qui lit le ~** he reads the most; **le ~ d'argent/de pages** the most money/pages; **le ~ possible de choses/personnes** as many things/people as possible; **il a pris le ~ de livres/d'argent qu'il pouvait** he took as many books/much money as he could ►**au ~ tôt/vite** as soon as possible; **tout au ~** at the very most

plus³ [plys, ply] *adv* more; **pas ~** no more; **~ d'une heure/de 40 ans** more than one hour/40 years; **les enfants de ~ de 12 ans** children over 12 years old; **il est ~ de minuit** it's after midnight; **tu as de l'argent? – ~ qu'il n'en faut** do you have any money? – more than enough; **~ de la moitié** more than half; **j'ai dépensé ~ d'argent que je ne le pensais** I have spent more money than I thought; **~ le temps passe, ~ l'espoir diminue** as time passes, hope fades ►**~ il réfléchit, (et) moins il a d'idées** the more he thinks, the fewer ideas he has; **moins il l'aimait, (et) ~ il lui disait qu'il l'aimait** the less he loved her, the more he told her that he loved her; **de ~** furthermore; **un jour/une assiette de ~** another day/plate; **une fois de ~** once more; **boire de ~ en ~** to drink more and more; **de ~ en ~ beau** more and more beautiful; **de ~ en ~ vite** faster and faster; **en ~** as well; **il est moche, et il est bête en ~** he is ugly, and he is stupid too; **être en ~** (*en supplément*) to be extra; (*de trop*) to be surplus; **en ~ de qc** as well as sth; **sans ~** and no more

plus⁴ [plys] **I.** *conj* **1.** (*et*) and; **2 ~ 2 font 4** 2 and 2 make 4; **le loyer ~ les charges** rent plus charges **2.** (*quantité positive*) **~ quatre degrés** plus four degrees **II.** *m* **1.** MAT plus sign **2.** (*avantage*) plus

plus⁵ [ply] *passé simple de* **plaire**

plusieurs [plyzjœʀ] **I.** *adj antéposé, pl* several **II.** *pron pl* people; **~ m'ont raconté cette histoire** several people have told me this story; **~ d'entre nous/de ces journaux** several of us/of these newspapers ►**à ~ ils ont pu ...** several of them together were able to ...

plus-que-parfait [plyskəpaʀfɛ] <plus-que-parfaits> *m* pluperfect

plut [ply] *passé simple de* **pleuvoir**

plutonium [plytɔnjɔm] *m* plutonium

plutôt [plyto] *adv* **1.** (*de préférence*) **prendre ~ l'avion que le bateau** to take the plane rather than the boat; **cette maladie affecte ~ les enfants** this illness affects mainly children **2.** (*au lieu de*) **~ que de parler, il vaudrait mieux que vous écoutiez** rather than speaking, it would be better if you listened **3.** (*mieux*) **~ mourir que (de) fuir** better to die than flee **4.** (*et pas vraiment*) **être paresseux ~ que sot** to be lazy rather than silly; **elle n'est pas méchante, ~ lunatique** she is not bad, temperamental rather **5.** (*assez*) **être ~ gentil** to be quite kind; **c'est ~ bon signe** it is rather a good sign; **~ mal/lentement** fairly badly/slowly **6.** *inf* (*très*) very **7.** (*plus exactement*) **ou ~** or rather

pluvial(e) [plyvjal, o] <-aux> *adj* **eaux ~es** rainwater *no pl*

pluvieux, -euse [plyvjø, -jøz] *adj* rainy; **par temps ~** in wet weather

PM [peɛm] *abr de* **post meridiem** p.m.

PME [peɛmø] *f abr de* **petites et moyennes entreprises** SMB

PMU [peɛmy] *m abr de* **Pari mutuel urbain** ≈ the tote *Brit,* ≈ OTB *Am* (*horse betting system*)

PNB [peɛnbe] *m abr de* **produit national brut** G.N.P.

pneu [pnø] *m* tyre *Brit,* tire *Am;* **avoir un ~ crevé** to have a flat tyre

pneumatique [pnømatik] *adj* inflatable

pneumonie [pnømɔni] *f* pneumonia *no pl*

poche¹ [pɔʃ] *f* **1.** (*cavité, sac*) bag; **~ de thé** *Québec* (*sachet de thé*) teabag **2.** (*compartiment*) pocket **3.** ANAT **avoir des ~s sous les yeux** to have bags under one's eyes ►**connaître qn/qc comme sa ~** to know sb/sth like the back of one's hand; **en être de sa** ~ *inf* to be out of pocket; **payer de sa** ~ to pay out of one's own pocket; **se remplir les** ~**s** to fill one's pockets; **lampe de** ~ torch *Brit,* flashlight *Am*

poche² [pɔʃ] *m inf* paperback

poche³ [pɔʃ] *f Suisse* (*cuillère à pot, louche*) ladle

poché(e) [pɔʃe] *adj* **1.** (*gonflé et bleu*) **œil** ~ black eye **2.** GASTR **œuf** ~ poached egg

poche-revolver [pɔʃʀevɔlvɛʀ] <poches-revolver> *f* pocket revolver

pochette [pɔʃɛt] *f* **1.** (*étui: de disque*) sleeve **2.** (*mouchoir de veste*) pocket handkerchief **3.** (*petit sac*) clutch bag

pochette-surprise [pɔʃɛtsyʀpʀiz] <pochettes-surprises> *f* lucky bag

pochoir [pɔʃwaʀ] *m* stencil

podium [pɔdjɔm] *m a.* SPORT podium; **monter sur le** ~ to mount the podium

poêle¹ [pwal] *f* GASTR frying pan

poêle² [pwal] *m* stove; ~ **à mazout/à bois** oil/wood-burning stove

poème [pɔɛm] *m* poem

poésie [pɔezi] *f* poetry

poète [pɔɛt] *m* **1.** (*écrivain*) poet **2.** (*rêveur*) dreamer

poétique [pɔetik] *adj* poetic

pognon [pɔɲɔ̃] *m sans pl, inf* dough

poids [pwɑ] *m* **1.** (*mesure, objet, charge, responsabilité*) weight; **quel** ~ **faites-vous?** how much do you weigh?; **acheter/vendre au** ~ to buy/sell by weight; **perdre/prendre du** ~ to lose/gain weight; **surveiller son** ~ to watch one's weight; **être un grand** ~ **pour qn** to be a heavy weight for sb; **se sentir délivré d'un grand** ~ to feel relieved of a great burden **2.** *sans pl* (*importance*) force; **un argument de** ~ a forceful argument; **le** ~ **économique d'un pays** the economic force of a country; **donner du** ~ **à qc** to give weight to sth; **être de peu de** ~ to be lightweight **3.** *sans pl* (*influence*) influence; **un homme de** ~ a man of influence **4.** AUTO ~ **lourd** heavy goods vehicle *Brit,* freight vehicle *Am* ►**avoir** [*o* **se sentir**] **un** ~ **sur l'estomac** to have a weight on one's stomach; **faire le** ~ COM to make up the weight; **faire le** ~ **devant qn/qc** to be a match for sb/sth

poignant(e) [pwaɲɑ̃, ɑ̃t] *adj* (*scène*) poignant; (*douleur*) heartbreaking

poignard [pwaɲaʀ] *m* dagger

poignarder [pwaɲaʀde] <1> *vt* to stab

poigne [pwaɲ] *f* grip ►**avoir de la** ~ to have a strong grip; *fig* to have an iron fist; **homme/femme à** ~ strong man/woman; ~ **de fer** (*force, autorité*) iron fist; **régner avec une** ~ **de fer** to rule with an iron fist

poignée [pwaɲe] *f* **1.** (*manche*) *a.* INFOR handle; (*d'une épée*) hilt; (*dans le bus, la baignoire*) grab-handle **2.** (*quantité*) handful; **une** ~ **de riz/de jeunes gens** a handful of rice/young people ►**à** [*o* **par**] (**pleines**) ~**s** in handfuls; ~ **de main** handshake

poignet [pwaɲɛ] *m* wrist

poil [pwal] *m* **1.** ANAT hair; **les** ~**s de la barbe** the bristles [*o* hairs] of a beard; **il n'a pas de** ~**s** he hasn't any hair on his chest **2.** ZOOL coat; **à** ~ **ras/long** smooth-/long-haired; **manteau en** ~ **de lapin/renard** rabbitskin/fox fur coat; **le chat perd ses** ~**s** the cat's moulting **3.** (*filament*) bristle; (*d'un tapis, d'une moquette*) pile **4.** *inf* (*un petit peu*) **un** ~ **de gentillesse** an ounce of kindness; **ne pas avoir un** ~ **de bon sens** to not have an iota of common sense ►**reprendre du** ~ **de la bête** (*se rétablir*) to perk up again; (*se ressaisir*) to get one's strength back; **être de bon/mauvais** ~ *inf* to be in a good/bad mood; **de tout** ~, **de tous** ~**s** *inf* of all sorts; ~ **à gratter** itching powder; **à** ~ *inf* stark naked; **se mettre à** ~ to strip off; **au** ~**!** *inf* great!

poiler [pwale] <1> *vpr inf* **se** ~ to die laughing

poilu(e) [pwaly] *adj* hairy

poinçon [pwɛ̃sɔ̃] *m* **1.** awl; (*d'un graveur*) stylus **2.** (*estampille: d'un orfèvre*) hallmark

poinçonner [pwɛ̃sɔne] <1> *vt* to stamp; (*orfèvre*) to hallmark; (*faire un trou*) to punch

poindre [pwɛ̃dʀ] *vi irr, soutenu* (*apparaître: jour, aube*) to break

poing [pwɛ̃] *m* fist ►**envoyer** [*o* **mettre**] **son** ~ **dans la figure à qn** *inf* to punch sb in the face; **taper du** ~ **sur la table, donner un coup de** ~ **sur la table** to bang one's fist on the table; **dormir à** ~**s fermés** to sleep like a log

point [pwɛ̃] *m* **1.** (*ponctuation*) mark *Brit,* period *Am;* ~**s de suspension** suspension points; ~ **d'exclamation/d'interrogation** exclamation/question mark; **c'est le grand** ~ **d'interrogation** that's the big question **2.** (*lieu*) ~ **de départ** point of departure; ~ **de repère** landmark; *fig* reference; ~ **de vente** sales point **3.** MAT point; ~ **d'intersection** point of intersection **4.** (*dans une notation*) point **5.** (*partie: d'ordre du jour*) point; ~ **de détail** point of detail; **être d'accord sur tous les** ~**s** to agree on all points; ~ **par** ~ point by point **6.** GEO **les quatre** ~**s cardinaux** the four points of the compass; ~ **culminant** peak **7.** POL ~ **chaud** trouble spot ►**qn se fait un** ~ **d'honneur de** +*infin,* **qn met un/son** ~ **d'honneur à** +*infin* sb makes it a point of honour to +*infin Brit,* sb makes it a point of honor to +*infin Am;* **mettre les** ~**s sur les i à qn** to dot the i's and cross the t's; ~ **de vue** viewpoint; (*opinion*) point of view; **à mon** ~ **de vue** in my opinion; **d'un certain** ~ **de vue** from a certain point of view; **au** [*o* **du**] ~ **de vue de qc** from the point of view of sth; **au** ~ **de vue scientifique** from a scientific viewpoint; **c'est un bon/mauvais** ~ **pour qn/qc** it is a plus/minus for sb/sth; **jusqu'à un certain** ~ (*relativement*) to a certain extent; **avoir raison jusqu'à un certain** ~ to be right up to

P

a point; **ça va jusqu'à un certain** ~ *inf* it's OK up to a point; ~ **commun** something in common; **n'avoir aucun** ~ **commun avec qn** to have nothing in common with sb; ~ **faible/fort** weak/strong point; **au plus haut** ~ extremely; **être mal en** ~ in a bad way; **être toujours au même** ~ to still be in the same situation; ~ **noir** (*comédon*) blackhead; (*grave difficulté*) problem; (*lieu d'accidents*) blackspot; **à (un) tel** ~ [*o* **à un** ~ **tel**] **que qn fait qc** to such an extent that sb did sth; **être au** ~ (*procédé*) to be perfected; (*voiture*) to be tuned; **être sur le** ~ **de** +*infin* to be just about to +*infin;* **faire le** ~ **de la situation** (*journal*) to give an update on the situation; **mettre au** ~ (*régler*) to tune; (*préparer dans les détails*) to develop; **mettre une technique au** ~ to perfect a technique; **mettre qc au** ~ **avec qn** (*s'entendre avec qn sur qc*) to settle sth with sb; (*éclaircir*) to sort sth out with sb; **partir à** ~ to leave at the right moment; **tomber à** ~ to happen just at the right moment; **je voudrais ma viande à** ~ I would like my meat cooked medium; **légumes/pâtes à** ~ vegetables/pasta al dente; **fruit/fromage à** ~ ripe fruit/cheese; **arriver** [*o* **venir**] **à** ~ to arrive at the right time; **comment a-t-il pu en arriver à ce** ~(**-là**)? how could he have got to this state?; **au** ~ **qu'on a dû faire qc/que qn fait** [*o* **fasse** (*subj*)] **qc** to the point where we had to do sth/that sb does sth; **le** ~ **sur qn/qc** (*dans un journal télévisé*) the update on sb/sth

pointage [pwɛ̃taʒ] *m* check; (*d'une liste*) checking off; **faire le** ~ **d'un colis** to check in a package; **faire le** ~ **des bulletins de vote** to count the voting papers

pointe [pwɛ̃t] *f* **1.** (*extrémité*) point; **la** ~ **de l'île** the headland of the island **2.** (*objet pointu*) spike **3.** (*clou*) tack **4.** (*de danse*) point; **faire des** ~**s** to dance on points **5.** (*petite quantité de*) **une** ~ **de cannelle** a pinch of cinnamon; **une** ~ **de méchanceté** a touch of evil; **une** ~ **d'ironie** a hint of irony; **une** ~ **d'accent** a hint of an accent ►**faire des** ~**s** (**de vitesse**) **de** [*o* **à**] **200/230 km/heure** to hit 200/230 km/hr; **être à la** ~ **de qc** to be at the forefront of sth; **vitesse de** ~ top speed; **heures de** ~ rush-hour; **de** [*o* **en**] ~ leading; **technologie/équipe de** ~ leading-edge technology/team; **notre société est en** ~**/reste une entreprise de** ~ our company is/remains at the cutting edge; **marcher sur la** ~ **des pieds** to tiptoe; **se mettre sur la** ~ **des pieds** to stand on tiptoe

pointer [pwɛ̃te] <1> **I.** *vi* **1.** ECON (**aller**) ~ (*ouvrier, employé*) to clock in; (*chômeur*) to sign on **2.** (*au jeu de boules*) to aim for the jack **3.** INFOR ~ **sur une icône** to point on a icon **II.** *vt* **1.** (*diriger vers*) ~ **qc sur/vers qn/qc** to train sth on sb/sth; ~ **son/le doigt sur qn** to point one's finger at sb **2.** (*au jeu de boules*) ~ **une boule** to throw a bowl **III.** *vpr inf* **se** ~ to turn up

pointeur [pwɛ̃tœʀ] *m* INFOR ~ **de la souris** mouse pointer

pointillé [pwɛ̃tije] *m* dotted line; **être en** ~(**s**) to appear in outline

pointilleux, -euse [pwɛ̃tijø, -jøz] *adj* **être** ~ **sur qc** [*o* **en matière de qc**] to be particular about sth

pointu(e) [pwɛ̃ty] **I.** *adj* **1.** (*acéré*) razor sharp **2.** (*grêle et aigu*) shrill **3.** (*très poussé: formation*) intensive; (*analyse*) in-depth; (*sujet*) specialized **II.** *adv* **parler** ~ to have a northern French accent

pointure [pwɛ̃tyʀ] *f* (shoe) size; **quelle est votre** ~**?** what's your size?

point-virgule [pwɛ̃viʀgyl] <points-virgules> *m* semi-colon

poire [pwaʀ] *f* pear

poireau [pwaʀo] <x> *m* leek

poireauter [pwaʀote] <1> *vi inf* **faire** ~ **les gens** to keep people kicking their heels

poirier [pwaʀje] *m* pear tree ►**faire le** ~ to do a headstand

pois [pwɑ] *m* pea; ~ **cassés** split peas; ~ **chiche** chick pea; **petit** ~ petit pois ►**à** ~ spotted; **à gros** ~**s** with large spots

poison [pwazɔ̃] **I.** *m* poison **II.** *mf inf* **1.** (*personne*) nuisance **2.** (*enfant insupportable*) horror

poisse [pwas] *f* bad luck; **porter la** ~ **à qn** *inf* to be a jinx on sb; **quelle** ~**!** what bad luck!

poisseux, -euse [pwasø, -øz] *adj* sticky

poisson [pwasɔ̃] *m* ZOOL fish; ~ **rouge** goldfish ►**être comme un** ~ **dans l'eau** to be in one's element; **engueuler qn comme du** ~ **pourri** *inf* to call sb all the names under the sun; ~ **d'avril** April Fool's Day; ~ **d'avril!** April fool!; **faire un** ~ **d'avril à qn** to play an April fool's joke on sb

On the first of April, people play practical jokes and the traditional children's **poisson d'avril** is to cut out paper fish and try to stick them on people's backs without being noticed.

poissonnerie [pwasɔnʀi] *f* (*boutique*) fish shop

poissonneux, -euse [pwasɔnø, -øz] *adj* full of fish

poissonnier, -ière [pwasɔnje, -jɛʀ] *m, f* fish merchant, fishmonger *Brit*

Poissons [pwasɔ̃] *m* Pisces; *v. a.* **Balance**

poitevin(e) [pwat(ə)vɛ̃, in] *adj* of Poitiers; *v. a.* **ajaccien**

Poitevin(e) [pwat(ə)vɛ̃, in] *m(f)* person from Poitiers; *v. a.* **Ajaccien**

Poitou [pwatu] *m* **le** ~ Poitou

poitrail [pwatʀaj] *m* (*d'un cheval, d'un chien*) breast

poitrine [pwatʀin] *f* **1.** (*d'un homme*) chest; (*d'une femme*) breast; **le tour de** ~ (*d'un homme*) chest measurement; (*d'une femme*) bust measurement **2.** GASTR breast

poivre [pwavʀ] *m sans pl* pepper; ~ **de**

Cayenne Cayenne pepper
poivré(e) [pwavʀe] *adj* **1.** (*épicé*) spicy **2.** (*évoquant l'odeur, le goût du poivre: parfum, menthe*) peppery
poivrer [pwavʀe] <1> **I.** *vt* ~ **qc** to add pepper to sth **II.** *vi* to add pepper
poivrière [pwavʀijɛʀ] *f* pepperpot; (*moulin*) pepper mill
poivron [pwavʀɔ̃] *m* sweet pepper *Brit,* bell pepper *Am*
poix [pwɑ] *f* pitch
poker [pɔkɛʀ] *m* (*jeu, partie*) poker
polaire [pɔlɛʀ] *adj* GEO polar
polaque [pɔlak] *adj péj, inf* Polak *pej*
Polaque [pɔlak] *mf péj, inf* Polak *pej*
polar [pɔlaʀ] *m inf* detective story
polariser [pɔlaʀize] <1> **I.** *vt* **1.** ~ **l'attention** to focus attention **2.** (*concentrer*) ~ **son attention sur un problème** to focus one's attention on a problem **3.** PHYS, ELEC to polarize **II.** *vpr* **se** ~ **sur qn/qc** to focus on sb/sth
polaroïd® [pɔlaʀɔid] *m* **1.** (*appareil*) Polaroïd® *camera* **2.** (*photo*) Polaroïd®
polder [pɔldɛʀ] *m* polder
pôle [pol] *m* GEO pole; ~ **Nord/Sud** North/South Pole
polémique [pɔlemik] **I.** *adj* polemical **II.** *f* polemic
polémiquer [pɔlemike] <1> *vi* ~ **contre qn/qc** to inveigh against sb/sth
poli(e) [pɔli] *adj* polite
police[1] [pɔlis] *f sans pl* police; ~ **judiciaire** ≈ Criminal Investigation Department; ~ **municipale/nationale** local/national police force; ~ **privée** private police force; ~ **secrète** secret police; ~ **de l'air et des frontières** border police [*o* patrol]; ~ **de la route** traffic police; ~ **des mœurs** vice squad; ~ **secours** ≈ emergency services ►faire **la** ~ to keep order
police[2] [pɔlis] *f* **1.** (*contrat*) ~ **d'assurance** insurance policy **2.** INFOR ~ **de caractères** font
policier, -ière [pɔlisje, -jɛʀ] **I.** *adj* **chien/état** ~ police dog/state; **roman/film** ~ detective novel/film; **femme** ~ policewoman **II.** *m, f* police officer
poliment [pɔlimɑ̃] *adv* politely
polio [pɔljo] *inf,* **poliomyélite** [pɔljɔmjelit] *f* polio, poliomyelitis
polir [pɔliʀ] <8> *vt* to polish
polisson(ne) [pɔlisɔ̃, ɔn] **I.** *adj* **1.** mischievous; (*chanson*) saucy; (*regard*) cheeky **2.** (*espiègle*) roguish; **elle est ~ne** she's a rogue **II.** *m(f)* rascal
politesse [pɔlitɛs] *f* **1.** *sans pl* (*courtoisie*) politeness; **manquer de** ~ to be impolite; **faire qc par** ~ to do sth out of politeness **2.** *pl* (*propos*) polite remarks; (*comportements*) gestures of politeness; **se faire des ~s** to exchange polite remarks
politicien(ne) [pɔlitisjɛ̃, jɛn] *m(f)* politician
politique [pɔlitik] **I.** *adj* political **II.** *f* **1.** POL politics + *vb sing;* ~ **économique/extérieure/intérieure/sociale** economic/foreign/home/social politics; ~ **de droite/gauche** right-/left-wing politics; **faire de la** ~ to be involved in politics **2.** (*ligne de conduite*) policy; **pratiquer la** ~ **de l'autruche** to stick one's head in the sand; **pratiquer la** ~ **du moindre effort** to take the easy way out **III.** *mf* **1.** (*gouvernant*) politician **2.** (*prisonnier politique*) political prisoner **3.** (*domaine politique*) politics
politiquement [pɔlitikmɑ̃] *adv* politically
pollen [pɔlɛn] *m* pollen
polluant [pɔlɥɑ̃] *m* pollutant
polluant(e) [pɔlɥɑ̃, ɑ̃t] *adj* polluting; **non** ~ non-polluting
polluer [pɔlɥe] <1> *vt, vi* to pollute
pollueur, -euse [pɔlɥœʀ, -øz] **I.** *adj* polluting **II.** *m, f* polluter
pollution [pɔlysjɔ̃] *f* pollution; ~ **atmosphérique** [*o* **de l'air**] atmospheric pollution; ~ **des eaux** water pollution
polo [pɔlo] *m* **1.** (*chemise*) polo shirt **2.** SPORT polo
Pologne [pɔlɔɲ] *f* **la** ~ Poland
polonais [pɔlɔnɛ] *m* Polish; *v. a.* **français**
polonais(e) [pɔlɔnɛ, ɛz] *adj* Polish
Polonais(e) [pɔlɔnɛ, ɛz] *m(f)* Pole
polonaise [pɔlɔnɛz] *f* MUS polonaise
poltron(ne) [pɔltʀɔ̃, ɔn] **I.** *adj* faint-hearted **II.** *m(f)* coward
polyculture [pɔlikyltyʀ] *f* mixed farming
polyester [pɔliɛstɛʀ] *m, app inv* polyester
polygame [pɔligam] **I.** *adj* polygamous **II.** *m* polygamist
polyglotte [pɔliglɔt] *adj, mf* polyglot
polygone [pɔligɔn] *m* **1.** polygon **2.** MIL shooting range
Polynésie française [pɔlinezifʀɑ̃sɛz] *f* **la** ~ French Polynesia
polysémique [pɔlisemik] *adj* polysemous
polytechnicien(ne) [pɔlitɛknisjɛ̃, jɛn] *m(f): student or graduate of the Ecole polytechnique*
polytechnique [pɔlitɛknik] *f* (**École**) ~ *engineering college, officially a military academy*
polythéiste [pɔliteist] **I.** *adj* polytheistic **II.** *mf* polytheist
polyvalent(e) [pɔlivalɑ̃, ɑ̃t] **I.** *adj* **1.** multipurpose; (*sérum, vaccin*) polyvalent; **salle ~e** all-purpose hall **2.** CHIM polyvalent **3.** *Québec* **école ~e** (*école secondaire dispensant l'enseignement général et l'enseignement professionnel*) *secondary school providing normal and vocational education* **II.** *m(f)* FIN tax inspector
polyvalente [pɔlivalɑ̃t] *f Québec* (*école secondaire dispensant l'enseignement général et l'enseignement professionnel*) *secondary school providing normal and vocational education*
pomélo [pɔmelo] *m* pink grapefruit
pommade [pɔmad] *f* ointment ►passer **de**

la ~ **à qn** to butter sb up

pomme [pɔm] *f* **1.** (*fruit*) apple **2.** (*pomme de terre*) **~s dauphines** pommes dauphine **3.** ANAT **~ d'Adam** Adam's apple **4.** BOT **~ de pin** pine cone ►**être grand** [*o* **haut**] **comme trois ~s** to be knee-high to a grasshopper; **être/tomber dans les ~s** to have fainted/faint; **pour ma ~** *inf* down to yours truly; **la vaisselle, ça va encore être pour ma ~!** yours truly's going to be lumbered with the dishes again!

pomme de terre [pɔmdətɛʀ] <pommes de terre> *f* potato

pommette [pɔmɛt] *f souvent pl* cheekbone

pommier [pɔmje] *m* apple tree

pompe [pɔ̃p] *f* **1.** (*machine*) pump; **~ à essence** petrol pump *Brit,* gas pump *Am;* **~ à incendie** fire engine **2.** *inf* (*chaussure*) shoe **3.** *inf* SPORT press-ups *Brit,* push-ups *Am;* **faire des ~s** to do press-ups ►**avoir un coup de ~** *inf* to feel suddenly exhausted; **être** [*o* **marcher**] **à côté de ses ~s** *inf* to be out of it

pomper [pɔ̃pe] <1> *vi* **1.** (*puiser*) to pump **2.** *inf* ECOLE **~ sur qn** to copy from sb

pompeux, **-euse** [pɔ̃pø, -øz] *adj* pompous

pompier [pɔ̃pje] *m* fireman ►**fumer comme un ~** to smoke like a chimney

pompiste [pɔ̃pist] *mf* petrol pump attendant *Brit,* gas station attendant *Am*

pompon [pɔ̃pɔ̃] *m* pompom ►**décrocher le ~** *inf* to take the cake

pomponner [pɔ̃pɔne] <1> **I.** *vt* **~ qn** to doll sb up **II.** *vpr* **se ~** to doll oneself up

ponce [pɔ̃s] *f* pumice

poncer [pɔ̃se] <2> *vt* to sand down

ponceuse [pɔ̃søz] *f* sander; **~ à détail** detail sander

poncho [pɔ̃(t)ʃo] *m* poncho

poncif [pɔ̃sif] *m* cliché

ponctualité [pɔ̃ktɥalite] *f* punctuality

ponctuation [pɔ̃ktɥasjɔ̃] *f* punctuation; **signes de ~** punctuation marks

ponctuel(le) [pɔ̃ktɥɛl] *adj* **1.** (*exact*) punctual **2.** (*momentané*) occasional; (*unique*) one-off

ponctuer [pɔ̃ktɥe] <1> *vt* **1.** LING, MUS to punctuate; **ce texte est bien/mal ponctué** this text is well/badly punctuated **2.** (*souligner*) **~ qc de qc** to punctuate sth with sth

pondération [pɔ̃deʀasjɔ̃] *f* **1.** level-headedness **2.** (*en statistique*) *a* ECON weighting **3.** POL balance; **~ des pouvoirs** checks and balances

pondéré(e) [pɔ̃deʀe] *adj* **1.** level-headed; **esprit ~** a steady mind **2.** (*en statistique*) weighted

pondeuse [pɔ̃døz] *f* **1.** (*poule*) layer **2.** (*femme*) fast breeder

pondre [pɔ̃dʀ] <14> *vt, vi* to lay

poney [pɔnɛ] *m* pony

pongiste [pɔ̃ʒist] *mf* table tennis player

pont [pɔ̃] *m* **1.** ARCHIT, NAUT bridge; **~ basculant/suspendu/routier** bascule/suspension/road bridge **2.** (*vacances*) **faire le ~** to make it a long weekend (*by taking extra days off after or before a public holiday*) ►**couper les ~s avec qn/qc** to burn one's bridges with sb/sth; **jeter un ~ entre qc et qc** to build a bridge between sth and sth

ponte¹ [pɔ̃t] *f* **1.** laying **2.** (*œufs*) clutch

ponte² [pɔ̃t] *m inf* bigwig; **~ de la finance** big name in finance

pontife [pɔ̃tif] *m* **1.** *souvent péj, inf* bigwig; **~ de la critique/littérature** critical/literary pundit; **~s de la Faculté** big names in medicine **2.** REL pontiff; **souverain ~** supreme pontiff

pontifical(e) [pɔ̃tifikal, o] <-aux> *adj* pontifical

pontificat [pɔ̃tifika] *m* REL pontificate **pont-levis** [pɔ̃l(ə)vi] <ponts-levis> *m* drawbridge

ponton [pɔ̃tɔ̃] *m* **1.** (*appontement*) landing stage **2.** (*plate-forme flottante*) pontoon

pop [pɔp] *adj inv* pop

pop-corn [pɔpkɔʀn] *m inv* popcorn

pope [pɔp] *m* Orthodox priest

popote [pɔpɔt] **I.** *f inf* cooking; **faire la ~** to do the cooking **II.** *adj inv, inf* **être très ~** to be the home-loving type

populace [pɔpylas] *f péj* rabble

populaire [pɔpylɛʀ] *adj* **1.** (*du peuple*) **république ~** people's republic **2.** (*destiné à la masse*) popular; **bal ~** local dance **3.** (*plébéien: goût*) common; **quartier ~** working-class area; **classes ~s** working classes; **être d'origine ~** to have a working-class background **4.** (*qui plaît*) well-liked; (*personne*) popular

popularité [pɔpylaʀite] *f* popularity

population [pɔpylasjɔ̃] *f* population; **~ du globe** world population

populeux, **-euse** [pɔpylø, -øz] *adj* (*rue*) crowded; (*cité*) densely populated

porc [pɔʀ] *m* **1.** ZOOL pig **2.** (*chair*) pork; **pur ~** pure pork **3.** *péj, inf* (*personne*) swine

porcelaine [pɔʀsəlɛn] *f* **1.** (*matière*) porcelain **2.** (*vaisselle*) china; **~ de Saxe** Dresden china

porcelet [pɔʀsəlɛ] *m* piglet

porc-épic [pɔʀkepik] <porcs-épics> *m* **1.** porcupine **2.** (*individu*) prickly individual

porche [pɔʀʃ] *m* porch

porcherie [pɔʀʃəʀi] *f* pigsty

porcin(e) [pɔʀsɛ̃, in] **I.** *adj* **1. élevage ~** pig farm **2.** *fig* (*sourire, visage*) piglike; **yeux ~s** piggy eyes **II.** *mpl* pigs

pore [pɔʀ] *m* pore ►**suer la vanité/l'arrogance par tous les ~s** to ooze vanity/arrogance at every pore

poreux, **-euse** [pɔʀø, -øz] *adj* porous

porno [pɔʀno] *inf abr de* **pornographie**, **pornographique**

pornographie [pɔʀnɔgʀafi] *f* pornography

pornographique [pɔʀnɔgʀafik] *adj* pornographic

port¹ [pɔʀ] *m* NAUT, INFOR port; **~ fluvial/maritime** river/sea port; **~ de pêche** fishing port; ~ **jeu/parallèle/série/imprimante** game/parallel/serial/printer port ▸**arriver à** __**bon**__ ~ to arrive safe and sound; ~ __**d'attache**__ port of registry; *fig* base

port[2] [pɔʀ] *m* **1.** (*fait de porter: d'un vêtement, casque, objet*) wearing; ~ **obligatoire de la ceinture de sécurité** seatbelts must be worn **2.** COM carriage; (*d'une lettre*) postage; ~ **dû/payé** postage due/paid; **franco de ~ et d'emballage** carriage and packing paid **3.** (*allure: d'une personne*) bearing; ~ **de tête** the way one holds one's head

portable [pɔʀtabl] **I.** *adj* portable **II.** *m* **1.** TEL mobile (phone) *Brit,* cellphone *Am* **2.** INFOR laptop (computer)

portage [pɔʀtaʒ] *m Québec* (*action de porter une embarcation d'un cours d'eau à l'autre*) portage

portail [pɔʀtaj] <s> *m* **1.** (*porte*) gate **2.** INFOR portal

portant(e) [pɔʀtɑ̃, ɑ̃t] *adj* **être bien/mal** ~ to be in good/poor health

portatif, -ive [pɔʀtatif, -iv] *adj* portable

porte [pɔʀt] *f* **1.** (*ouverture, panneau mobile*) door; (*plus grand*) gate; ~ **de garage** garage door; ~ **du four/de la maison** oven/front door; ~ **de devant/derrière** front/back door; **voiture à deux ~s** two-door car; ~ **de secours** emergency exit; ~ **de service** tradesman's entrance; ~ **d'embarquement** departure gate; ~ **cochère** carriage entrance; **à la** ~ at the door; *Belgique* (*dehors, à l'extérieur*) outside; **de ~ en ~** from door to door; **forcer la ~** to force the door open; **claquer** [*o* **fermer**] **la ~ au nez de qn** to slam the door in sb's face **2.** (*entrée: d'un château, d'une ville*) gate; ~ **de Clignancourt** Porte de Clignancourt; ~ **de Bourgogne** gateway to Burgundy ▸**trouver ~** __**close**__ to find nobody at home; **être aimable** [*o* **souriant**]**/poli comme une ~ de** __**prison**__ to be like a bear with a sore head; **entrer par la** __**grande**__**/**__**petite**__ ~ to start at the top/bottom; **enfoncer une ~** __**ouverte**__ [*o* **des ~s** __**ouvertes**__] to state the obvious; **laisser la ~** __**ouverte**__ **à qc** to leave the way open for sth; **toutes les ~s lui sont** __**ouvertes**__ every door is open to him; (**journée**) **~s** __**ouvertes**__ open day; __**écouter**__ **aux ~s** to eavesdrop; __**fermer**__ [*o* __**refuser**__]**/**__**ouvrir**__ **sa ~ à qn** to close/open the door to sb; __**forcer**__ **la ~ de qn** to force one's way into sb's home; __**frapper**__ **à la ~ de qn** to knock at sb's door; __**frapper**__ **à la bonne ~** to come to the right person; __**frapper**__ **à la mauvaise ~** to come to the wrong person; __**mettre**__ [*o* __**foutre**__ *inf*] **qn à la ~** to kick sb out; __**prendre**__ **la ~** to leave; __**à**__ **la ~!** get out!; __**à**__ [*o* __**devant**__] **ma ~** nearby; **ce n'est pas la ~ à** __**côté!**__ it's a good way off!; __**entre**__ **deux ~s** briefly

porte-à-faux [pɔʀtafo] **en ~** (*mur*) out of true; (*roche*) overhanging; *fig* (*personne*) in an awkward position **porte-à-porte** [pɔʀtapɔʀt] *m inv* door-to-door; **faire du ~** (*quêteur*) to go around knocking on doors; (*marchand ambulant*) to sell door-to-door **porte-avions** [pɔʀtavjɔ̃] *m inv* aircraft carrier **porte-bagages** [pɔʀtbagaʒ] *m inv* **1.** (*sur un deux-roues*) rack **2.** (*dans un train*) luggage rack **porte-bonheur** [pɔʀtbɔnœʀ] *m inv* good-luck charm **porte-cartes** [pɔʀtəkaʀt] *m inv* **1.** (*pour les cartes routières*) map wallet **2.** (*pour les documents personnels*) card wallet **porte-clés** [pɔʀtəkle] *m inv* key ring *Brit,* key chain *Am* **porte-couteau** [pɔʀtkuto] <porte-couteau(x)> *m* knife rest **porte-documents** [pɔʀtdɔkymɑ̃] *m inv* briefcase

portée [pɔʀte] *f* **1.** (*distance*) range; **à ~ de vue** within sight; **à ~ de voix/de la main** within earshot/reach; **à la ~ de qn** within sb's reach; **hors de la ~ de qn** out of sb's reach **2.** (*effet: d'un acte, événement*) consequences *pl;* (*d'un argument, de paroles*) impact **3.** MUS stave **4.** ZOOL litter **5.** (*aptitude, niveau*) **c'est au-dessus** [*o* **hors**] **de ma ~** it is beyond me; **être à la ~ de qn** (*livre, discours*) to be suitable for sb; **cet examen est à votre ~** this exam is within your capabilities; **être hors de** (**la**) **~ de qn** (*livre*) to be beyond sb's understanding; (*examen, travail*) to be beyond sb's capabilities; **mettre qc à la ~ de qn** to make sth accessible to sb **6.** (*accessibilité*) **être à la ~ de qn** to be available to everyone; **à la ~ de toutes les bourses** suitable for all budgets

porte-fenêtre [pɔʀtfənɛtʀ] <portes-fenêtres> *f* French door

portefeuille [pɔʀtəfœj] *m* wallet

porte-jarretelles [pɔʀtʒaʀtɛl] *m inv* suspender belt

portemanteau [pɔʀtmɑ̃to] <x> *m* hat stand; (*mobile*) coat-hanger; (*crochets au mur*) coat-rack

porte-monnaie [pɔʀtmɔnɛ] *m inv* purse; **avoir le ~ bien garni** *fig* to be well-off **porte-parapluies** [pɔʀtpaʀaplɥi] *m inv* umbrella stand **porte-parole** [pɔʀtpaʀɔl] *m inv* **1.** (*personne*) spokesperson **2.** (*journal*) mouthpiece

porter [pɔʀte] <1> **I.** *vt* **1.** (*tenir*) to carry **2.** (*endosser: responsabilité, faute*) to shoulder; **faire ~ qc à qn** to make sb shoulder sth **3.** *a. fig* (*apporter: en allant*) to take; (*en venant*) to bring; (*lettre, colis*) to deliver; (*attention*) to attract; (*assistance, secours*) to give; **la nuit porte conseil** it's best to sleep on it **4.** (*diriger*) ~ **son regard/ses yeux sur qn/qc** to turn towards/one's eyes towards sb/sth; ~ **son choix sur qc** to choose sth; ~ **ses pas vers la porte** to turn one's feet towards the door; ~ **le verre à ses lèvres** to bring the glass to one's lips; ~ **la main au chapeau** to touch one's hat with one's hand; ~ **la main à sa poche** to put one's hand in one's pocket; ~ **qn quelque part** to take sb somewhere **5.** (*avoir sur soi: vêtement, lunettes*) to wear; (*nom, titre*) to carry; ~ **la barbe/les cheveux longs** to have a beard/long hair **6.** (*révéler:*

P

traces) to reveal; (*marque de fabrique*) to carry **7.** (*ressentir*) ~ **de l'amitié/de l'amour à qn/qc** to show friendship/love for sb; ~ **de l'intérêt à qn/qc** to show an interest in sb/sth; ~ **de la haine à qn/qc** to hate sb/sth; ~ **de la reconnaissance à qn** to be grateful to sb **8.** (*inscrire*) **être porté malade** to be reported as ill; **être porté disparu** to be reported missing; **se faire** ~ **absent** to go absent **9.** (*avoir en soi*) ~ **de la haine en soi** to feel hatred in oneself **II.** *vi* **1.** (*avoir pour objet*) ~ **sur qc** (*action, effort*) to be concerned with sth; (*discours*) to be about sth; (*revendications, divergences, étude*) to concern sth; (*question, critique*) to revolve around sth **2.** (*avoir telle étendue*) ~ **sur qc** to concern sth; (*préjudice*) to extend to sth **3.** (*faire effet: coup, critique*) to hit home; (*conseil*) to have its effect **4.** (*avoir une certaine portée: voix*) to carry; **cette arme à feu porte à ...** this firearm has a range of ... **5.** (*reposer sur*) ~ **sur qc** (*édifice, poids*) to be supported by sth; (*accent*) to fall on sth **6.** (*heurter*) **c'est son front qui a porté** his forehead took the blow; **sa tête a porté sur un tabouret** his head hit a stool **III.** *vpr* **1.** (*aller*) **se** ~ **bien/mal** to be well/unwell; **se** ~ **comme un charme** to be fighting fit **2.** (*se présenter comme*) **se** ~ **acquéreur de qc** to offer to buy sth; **se** ~ **candidat** to come forward as a candidate; **se** ~ **volontaire** to volunteer **3.** (*se diriger*) **se** ~ **sur qn/qc** (*regard, choix, soupçon*) to fall on sb/sth; **se** ~ **vers qc** (*personne*) to go towards sb/sth **4.** (*être porté*) **se** ~ **en été/hiver** (*vêtements*) to be worn in summer/winter; **se** ~ **beaucoup en ce moment** to be fashionable at the moment

porte-savon [pɔʀtsavɔ̃] <porte-savon(s)> *m* soapdish **porte-serviettes** [pɔʀtsɛʀvjɛt] *m inv* towel rail

porteur, **-euse** [pɔʀtœʀ, -øz] *m, f* messenger

porte-voix [pɔʀtəvwa] *m inv* loud hailer; *fig* megaphone ▶**en** ~ cupped around one's mouth

portier, **-ière** [pɔʀtje, -jɛʀ] *m, f* porter

portière [pɔʀtjɛʀ] *f* CHEMDFER, AUTO door

portillon [pɔʀtijɔ̃] *m* (*de passage à niveau*) gate; (*du métro parisien*) ticket barrier ▶**ça se bouscule** [*o* **presse**] **au** ~ *inf* people are queueing up! *Brit,* people are lining up! *Am*

portion [pɔʀsjɔ̃] *f* GASTR portion

portique [pɔʀtik] *m* **1.** ARCHIT portico **2.** SPORT crossbeam; (*pour enfants*) climbing frame **3.** TECH ~ (**à signaux**) signal gantry

porto [pɔʀto] *m* port

portoricain(**ne**) [pɔʀtɔʀikɛ̃, -ɛn] *adj* Puerto Rican

Portoricain(**ne**) [pɔʀtɔʀikɛ̃, -ɛn] *m(f)* Puerto Rican

Porto Rico [pɔʀtoʀiko] Puerto Rico

portrait [pɔʀtʀɛ] *m* **1.** ART, PHOT portrait; ~ **fidèle** good likeness; **faire le** ~ **de qn** (*peindre*) to paint a portrait of sb; (*faire une photo*) to take a portrait shot of sb; **se faire tirer le** ~ *inf* to have one's photo taken **2.** (*description: d'une personne*) profile; (*d'une société*) portrait; **faire le** ~ **de qn** to paint a picture of sb ▶**se faire esquinter le** ~ *inf* to get one's face smashed in; **être tout le** ~ **de qn** to be the spitting image of sb

portrait-robot [pɔʀtʀɛʀɔbo] <portraits-robots> *m* **1.** Identikit picture® *Brit,* police sketch *Am* **2.** (*caractéristiques*) profile

portuaire [pɔʀtɥɛʀ] *adj* **installations** ~**s** harbour facilities *Brit,* harbor facilities *Am*

portugais [pɔʀtygɛ] *m* Portuguese; *v. a.* **français**

portugais(**e**) [pɔʀtygɛ, ɛz] *adj* Portuguese

Portugais(**e**) [pɔʀtygɛ, ɛz] *m(f)* Portuguese

portugaise [pɔʀtygɛz] *f* GASTR Portuguese oyster ▶**avoir les** ~**s ensablées** *inf* to be as deaf as a post

Portugal [pɔʀtygal] *m* **le** ~ Portugal

pose [poz] *f* **1.** (*attitude*) posture; ART, PHOT pose **2.** PHOT (*exposition*) exposure; (*photo*) photo; **temps de** ~ exposure time

posé(**e**) [poze] *adj* calm ▶**bien/mal** ~ MUS steady/unsteady

posément [pozemɑ̃] *adv* calmly

poser [poze] <1> **I.** *vt* **1.** (*mettre: livre, main, bagages*) to put down; (*échelle*) to lean; (*pieds*) to place; ~ **qc par terre** to put sth down on the ground **2.** MAT (*opération*) to write; (*équation*) to set down **3.** (*installer: moquette*) to lay; (*rideau, tapisserie*) to hang; (*serrure*) to install **4.** (*énoncer: définition, principe*) to set out; (*devinette*) to set; (*question*) to ask; (*condition*) to lay down **5.** (*soulever: problème, question*) to put **6.** *Belgique, Québec* (*commettre, accomplir un acte*) ~ **un acte** to carry out an act **II.** *vi* ~ **pour qn/qc** to pose for sb/sth **III.** *vpr* **1.** (*exister*) **se** ~ (*question, difficulté, problème*) to arise; **se** ~ **des problèmes** to think about problems; **il se pose la question si ...** he's wondering if ... **2.** (*cesser de voler*) **se** ~ **dans/sur qc** (*insecte, oiseau, avion*) to land in/on sth **3.** (*se fixer*) **se** ~ **sur qc** (*regard, yeux*) to turn towards sth; (*main*) to touch sth **4.** (*s'appliquer*) **se** ~ **facilement** (*moquette*) to be easy to lay; (*papier peint, rideau*) to be easy to hang

poseur, **-euse** [pozœʀ, -øz] **I.** *adj* affected **II.** *m, f* **1.** ~ **de carrelages** tiler; ~ **de parquet** floor layer; ~ **d'affiches** billsticker **2.** (*pédant*) poser; **être** ~ to be a poser

positif, **-ive** [pozitif, -iv] *adj* positive

position [pozisjɔ̃] *f* (*emplacement, posture, en danse, situation*) position; (*dans une course*) place; **arriver en première/dernière** ~ (*coureur, candidat*) to come in first place/last; **la** ~ **debout** standing; **en** ~ **allongée** [*o* **couchée**] lying down; **se mettre en** ~ **allongée/assise** to lie/sit down ▶**être en** ~ **de force** to be in a position of strength;

être dans une ~ **intéressante** *Belgique* (*être enceinte*) to be in a certain condition

positivement [pozitivmɑ̃] *adv* positively

posologie [pozɔlɔʒi] *f* dosage

posséder [pɔsede] <5> *vt* **1.** (*avoir*) to possess **2.** (*disposer de: expérience, talent, mémoire, réflexes*) to have; ~ **la vérité** to know the truth **3.** *inf* (*rouler*) to take in

possesseur [pɔsesœʀ] *m* owner; (*d'une action, d'un diplôme, d'un secret*) holder

possessif [pɔsesif] *m* possessive

possessif, -ive [pɔsesif, -iv] *adj* possessive

possession [pɔsesjɔ̃] *f* possession; **avoir qc en sa** ~ to have sth in one's possession; **entrer en** ~ **de qc** to take possession of sth

possibilité [pɔsibilite] *f* **1.** (*éventualité*) possibility **2.** *pl* (*moyens matériels*) means; (*moyens intellectuels*) abilities

possible [pɔsibl] **I.** *adj* **1.** (*faisable, éventuel, indiquant une limite: cas, mesures*) possible; (*projet*) feasible; **il est** ~ **qu'il vienne** he may come; **les tomates les plus grosses** ~**s** the biggest possible tomatoes; **autant que** ~ as much as possible **2.** *inf* (*supportable*) **ne pas être** ~ (*personne*) to be impossible ►~ **et imaginable** possible; (**c'est**) **pas** ~! *inf* I don't believe it! **II.** *m* **faire** (**tout**) **son** ~ **pour faire qc/pour que qn** +*subj* to do everything one can to make sth happen/for sb to +*infin;* **être gentil/doué au** ~ to be as kind/gifted as can be

possiblement [pɔsibləmɑ̃] *adv Québec* (*d'une manière possible*) possibly

postal(e) [pɔstal, o] <-aux> *adj* **carte** ~**e** postcard; **code** ~ postcode *Brit,* zip code *Am*

postcommunisme [pɔstkɔmynism] *m* postcommunism

postcommuniste [pɔstkɔmynist] *mf* postcommunist

poste¹ [pɔst] *f* (*bâtiment, administration*) post office; **mettre à la** ~ to post; **par la** ~ by post *Brit,* by mail *Am* ►~ **aérienne** airmail; ~ **restante** poste restante *Brit,* general delivery *Am*

poste² [pɔst] *m* **1.** (*emploi*) job; (*dans une hiérarchie*) position; ~ **de diplomate/de directeur** diplomatic/managerial post; ~ **de professeur** teaching job; **être en** ~ **à Berlin/au ministère** to have a position in Berlin/at the ministry **2.** (*lieu de travail*) workplace **3.** (*appareil*) set; ~ **de radio/de télévison** radio/television set **4.** (*lieu*) ~ **de douane/de contrôle** customs/control post; ~ **d'incendie** fire point; ~ **d'essence/de police** filling/police station; ~ **de pilotage** cockpit; ~ **frontière/de secours** border/first-aid post **5.** MIL post; ~ **de commandement** headquarters; ~ **d'observation** observation post; ~ **d'écoute** listening station **6.** TEL telephone; ~ **téléphonique** telephone extension **7.** INFOR ~ **de travail** work station

posté(e) [pɔste] *adj* IND **travail** ~ shift work

poste-clé [pɔstəkle] <postes-clés> *m* key job

poste-frontière [pɔstəfʀɔ̃tjɛʀ] <postes-frontières> *m* border post

poster¹ [pɔste] <1> *vt* to post

poster² [pɔstɛʀ] *m* poster

postérieur [pɔsteʀjœʀ] *m inf* posterior

postérieurement [pɔsteʀjœʀmɑ̃] *adv* subsequently; ~ **à qc** after sth

postérité [pɔsteʀite] *f* **1.** descendents; (*d'un artiste, d'une œuvre*) followers **2.** (*futur*) posterity; **passer à la** ~ to go down to posterity

posthume [pɔstym] *adj* (*enfant, œuvre*) posthumous; **à titre** ~ posthumously

postier, -ière [pɔstje, -jɛʀ] *m, f* postal worker; **grève des** ~**s** postal workers' strike

postillon [pɔstijɔ̃] *m* spit; **envoyer des** ~**s à qn** to splutter at sb

postposer [pɔstpoze] <1> *vt Belgique* (*remettre qc à plus tard*) to postpone

post-scriptum [pɔstskʀiptɔm] *m inv* postscript

postuler [pɔstyle] <1> **I.** *vt* **1.** ~ **un emploi** to apply for a job **2.** (*en logique*) to postulate **II.** *vi* ~ **à qc** to apply for sth

posture [pɔstyʀ] *f* posture ►**être en bonne/mauvaise** ~ to be be in a good/awkward position; **financièrement, il est dans une mauvaise** ~ he's in bad shape financially; **être en** ~ **de** +*infin* to be in a position to +*infin*

pot [po] *m* **1.** (*en terre, en plastique*) pot; (*en verre*) jar; (*en métal*) tin; ~ **à eau/à lait** water/milk jug; ~ **de confiture/miel** jar of jam/honey; **petit** ~ **pour bébé** jar of baby food; **mettre des plantes en** ~ to pot plants **2.** *inf* (*chance*) **c'est pas de** ~! hard luck!; **avoir du** ~**/ne pas avoir de** ~ to be lucky/unlucky **3.** *inf* (*consommation*) drink; (*réception*) drinks party; (*d'adieu*) farewell party; **payer un** ~ **à qn** to buy sb a drink; **prendre un** ~ to have a drink **4.** (*pot de chambre*) chamberpot; (*pour enfant*) potty ►~ **de colle** *inf* leech; **découvrir/dévoiler le** ~ **aux roses** to find out what's been happening; **payer les** ~**s cassés** to pick up the tab; ~ **catalytique** catalytic converter; ~ **d'échappement** exhaust pipe; **être sourd comme un** ~ to be as deaf as a post; **tourner autour du** ~ to beat about [*o* around] the bush

potable [pɔtabl] *adj* potable; (*eau*) drinking

potache [pɔtaʃ] *m inf* schoolkid

potage [pɔtaʒ] *m* soup

potager [pɔtaʒe] *m* vegetable garden

potager, -ère [pɔtaʒe, -ɛʀ] *adj* vegetable

potasse [pɔtas] *f* potassium hydroxide; (*engrais chimique*) potash; **mines de** ~ potash mines

potasser [pɔtase] <1> **I.** *vt inf* ~ **un examen** to swot for an exam *Brit,* to cram for a test *Am;* ~ **un discours** to work hard on a speech; ~ **un livre** to work through a book **II.** *vi inf* to swot, to cram

pot-au-feu [pɔtofø] **I.** *adj inv, inf* **être** ~ to be the home-loving type *Brit,* to be a homebody *Am* **II.** *m inv* GASTR **1.** beef stew **2.** (*viande*) stewing beef **pot-de-vin** [podvɛ̃] <pots-de-vin> *m* bribe

pote [pɔt] *m inf* mate *Brit,* buddy *Am*

poteau [pɔto] <x> *m* post; ~ **d'arrivée/départ** finishing/starting post; ~ **électrique/télégraphique** electricity/telegraph pole; ~ **indicateur** signpost

potelé(e) [pɔtle] *adj* chubby; (*bras*) plump

potence [pɔtɑ̃s] *f* **1.** gallows *pl* **2.** (*support*) bracket

potentiel [pɔtɑ̃sjɛl] *m* potential

potentiel(le) [pɔtɑ̃sjɛl] *adj* potential

poterie [pɔtʀi] *f* pottery

potiche [pɔtiʃ] *f* **1.** (potbellied) vase **2.** (*figurant*) puppet

potier, -ière [pɔtje, -jɛʀ] *m, f* potter

potin [pɔtɛ̃] *m* **1.** *souvent pl* gossip *no pl* **2.** *inf* (*bruit*) row

potion [posjɔ̃] *f* potion

potiquet [pɔtikɛ] *m Belgique* (*petit pot, récipient*) pot

potiron [pɔtiʀɔ̃] *m* pumpkin

pou [pu] <x> *m* louse ▸**chercher des ~x à qn** to be out to make trouble for sb; **fier** [*o* **orgueilleux**] **comme un** ~ *inf* as proud as a peacock; **laid comme un** ~ *inf* as ugly as sin

pouah [pwa] *interj* yuck!

poubelle [pubɛl] *f* **1.** (*dans la cuisine*) bin **2.** (*devant la porte*) dustbin *Brit,* garbage can *Am*

pouce [pus] **I.** *m* **1.** (*doigt: de la main*) thumb; (*du pied*) big toe **2.** (*mesure*) inch **3.** *Québec* (*auto-stop*) **faire du** ~ to hitchhike ▸**donner un coup de** ~ **à qc** to give sth a boost; **ne pas céder d'un** ~ to not give an inch; **se tourner les ~s** *inf* to twiddle one's thumbs; **ne pas avancer d'un** ~ to make no progress; **ne pas reculer d'un** ~ to not back down an inch; **manger sur le** ~ *inf* to eat on the run **II.** *interj enfantin* truce!

poudre [pudʀ] *f* **1.** (*fines particules*) powder; **sucre en** ~ caster sugar; ~ **à laver** washing powder **2.** (*produit cosmétique*) face powder ▸**prendre la ~ d'escampette** to take to one's heels; **jeter de la** ~ **aux yeux à qn** to try to impress sb; **il n'a pas inventé la** ~ *inf* he'll never set the world on fire; **ça sent la** ~ things could turn nasty; ~ **de perlimpinpin** *inf* magical cure-all

poudrer [pudʀe] <1> **I.** *vt* to powder **II.** *vpr* **se** ~ to put powder on; **se** ~ **le nez** to powder one's nose

poudrerie [pudʀəʀi] *f Québec* (*tourbillons de neige*) blizzard

poudreuse [pudʀøz] *f* powder snow

poudreux, -euse [pudʀø, -øz] *adj* **1.** dusty **2.** (*en poudre*) powdery

poudrier [pudʀije] *m* powder compact

poudrière [pudʀijɛʀ] *f* **1.** *fig* powder keg **2.** (*magasin*) powder magazine

pouf¹ [puf] **I.** *m* pouf **II.** *interj* thud

pouf² [puf] *m Belgique* (*dette*) debt ▸**acheter à** ~ (*à crédit*) to buy on the never-never *Brit,* to buy on an installment plan *Am;* **taper à** ~ (*deviner*) to guess

pouffer [pufe] <1> *vi* ~ (**de rire**) to burst out laughing

pouilleux, -euse [pujø, -jøz] *adj* **1.** lousy **2.** (*sordide: endroit, quartier*) seedy **3.** GEO barren

poulailler [pulaje] *m* henhouse

poulain [pulɛ̃] *m* foal

poularde [pulaʀd] *f* fattened hen

poule [pul] *f* **1.** (*femelle du coq*) hen **2.** (*poulet*) chicken ▸**quand les ~s auront des dents** when pigs start to fly; ~ **mouillée** wimp; **se coucher avec les ~s** to go to bed early; **se lever avec les ~s** to be an early riser; **ma** ~ *inf* my dear

poulet [pulɛ] *m* chicken

poulette [pulɛt] **I.** *f inf* chick **II.** *app* **sauce** ~ (*sauce made from eggs, butter and cream*)

pouliche [puliʃ] *f* filly

poulie [puli] *f* NAUT, TECH pulley; (*emboîtée*) block; ~ **fixe** fixed block; ~ **folle** loose pulley

poulpe [pulp] *m* octopus

pouls [pu] *m* pulse; **prendre le** ~ **de qn** to take sb's pulse ▸**prendre** [*o* **tâter**] **le** ~ **de qn/qc** to take the pulse of sb/sth

poumon [pumɔ̃] *m* lung; **à pleins ~s** at the top of one's voice; (*respirer*) deeply ▸**cracher ses ~s** *inf* to cough up one's lungs

poupe [pup] *f* stern

poupée [pupe] *f* doll; **jouer à la** ~ to play dolls

poupon [pupɔ̃] *m* baby

pouponner [pupɔne] <1> **I.** *vi inf* to play mummy **II.** *vt* ~ **qn** to fuss over sb

pouponnière [pupɔnjɛʀ] *f* nursery

pour [puʀ] **I.** *prep* **1.** for; **j'en ai** ~ **une heure!** I'll be an hour!; **être grand** ~ **son âge** to be tall for one's age **2.** (*en direction de*) for; **partir** ~ **Paris/l'étranger** to leave for Paris/to go abroad; ~ **où?** where to? **3.** (*en faveur de*) ~ **qn/qc** for sb/sth; **être** ~ **faire qc** to be for doing sth **4.** (*quant à*) as for; ~ **moi** as for me **5.** (*à cause de*) for; **merci** ~ **votre cadeau!** thank you for your present; **remercier qn** ~ **avoir fait qc** to thank sb for having done sth **6.** (*à la place de*) for **7.** (*comme*) as; **prendre** ~ **femme** to take as sb's wife; **j'ai** ~ **principe de faire** it's a principle with me to do; **avoir** ~ **effet** to have as an effect **8.** (*pour ce qui est de*) ~ **être furieux, je le suis!** I am so furious!; ~ **autant que je sache** as far as I know **9.** (*dans le but de*) ~ +*infin* (in order) to +*infin;* **ce n'est pas** ~ **me déplaire** it's something I'm quite pleeased about; ~ **que tu comprennes** so that you understand; **il est trop jeune** ~ +*infin* he's too young to +*infin* ▸**œil** ~ **œil, dent** ~ **dent** an eye for an eye, a tooth for a tooth **II.** *m* **le** ~ **et le contre** the pros and cons

pourboire [puʀbwaʀ] *m* tip

pourcentage [puʀsɑ̃] *m* **1.** *a.* COM ~ **sur qc**

mark-up on sth; ~ **de bénéfices** cut of the profits; **travailler/être payé au** ~ to work/be paid on a commission basis **2.** (*proportion pour cent*) percentage

pourchasser [puʀʃase] <1> *vt* to pursue

pourlécher [puʀleʃe] <5> *vpr* to lick one's lips; *v. a.* **babines**

pourparlers [puʀpaʀle] *mpl* negotiations; **engager des** [*o* **entrer en**] ~ **avec qn** to start negotiations with sb; **être en** ~ **avec qn** to be in negotiations with sb

pourpre [puʀpʀ] *adj* purple

pourquoi [puʀkwa] **I.** *conj* (*pour quelle raison, à quoi bon*) why; ~ **continuer/chercher?** why carry on/look? ►**c'est** ~ that's why; **c'est** ~**?** *inf* why's that? **II.** *adv* why; **je me demande bien** ~ I wonder why; **voilà** ~ that's why; ~ **pas?** [*o* **non?**] why not? **III.** *m inv* **1.** (*raison*) **le** ~ **de qc** the reason for sth; **chercher le** ~ **et le comment** to look for the how and why **2.** (*question*) question why

pourri [puʀi] *m* **1.** (*pourriture*) **ça sent le** ~ **dans cette pièce!** there's a rotten smell in this room! **2.** *péj* (*homme corrompu*) crook

pourri(e) [puʀi] *adj* **1.** (*putréfié: fruit, œuf, arbre, planche*) rotten; (*poisson, viande*) bad; (*cadavre*) rotting **2.** (*infect*) rotten; **quel temps** ~**!** what rotten weather! **3.** (*corrompu: personne, société*) corrupt **4.** (*gâté: enfant*) spoilt

pourrir [puʀiʀ] <8> **I.** *vi* **1.** (*se putréfier: œuf, arbre, planche, fruit*) to rot; (*poisson*) to go bad; (*cadavre*) to decompose **2.** *inf* (*croupir*) ~ **en prison/dans la misère** to rot in prison/misery; **il pourrit dans cet emploi/ce village** he is wasting away in this job/village **II.** *vt* (*aliment*) to go bad; (*bois, végétaux, fruit*) to rot; (*enfant*) to getting spoilt

pourriture [puʀityʀ] *f* **1.** rot; (*processus*) rotting; **odeur de** ~ rotting smell **2.** (*dans une cave*) **odeur de** ~ smell of rot **3.** (*corruption: de la société, d'un régime*) rottenness; (*des mœurs*) corruptness **4.** *péj* (*homme corrompu*) swine **5.** *péj* (*femme corrompue*) bitch **6.** BOT ~ **noble** noble rot

poursuite [puʀsɥit] *f* **1.** pursuit; **être à la** ~ **de qn** to be in pursuit of sb; **se lancer** [*o* **se mettre**] **à la** ~ **de qn** to set off in pursuit of sb **2.** (*recherche*) **la** ~ **de la fortune/de la gloire/du bonheur** the pursuit of fortune/glory/happiness; **la** ~ **de la vérité** the search for truth **3.** *gén pl* JUR ~**s judiciaires** legal proceedings; ~**s pénales** criminal proceedings; **engager des** ~**s contre qn** to start proceedings against sb **4.** (*continuation: de négociations, d'un travail*) continuation; **décider la** ~ **de la guerre** to decide to carry on the war **5.** SPORT pursuit

poursuivant(e) [puʀsɥivɑ̃, ɑ̃t] **I.** *adj* JUR **partie** ~**e** plaintiff **II.** *m(f)* **1.** pursuer **2.** JUR plaintiff

poursuivre [puʀsɥivʀ] *irr* **I.** *vt* **1.** (*courir après*) to pursue **2.** (*harceler*) ~ **qn** (*personne*) to harass sb; (*souvenir, images, remords*) to hound sb **3.** (*rechercher: bonheur, gloire, idéal*) to seek; (*but*) to aim for; (*vérité*) to pursue; ~ **l'argent** to chase after money **4.** (*continuer*) to continue; (*combat, enquête*) to pursue **II.** *vi* **1.** (*continuer*) to continue a story; ~ **sur un sujet** to continue on a subject **2.** (*persévérer*) to persevere **III.** *vpr* **se** ~ to continue; (*enquête, grève*) to carry on

pourtant [puʀtɑ̃] *adv* **1.** (*marque l'opposition, le regret*) however **2.** (*marque l'étonnement*) all the same; **c'est** ~ **facile!** it's easy though!

pourtour [puʀtuʀ] *m* **1.** perimeter; **un** ~ **de 50 mètres** a 50 metre perimeter *Brit,* a 50-meter perimeter *Am* **2.** (*bords*) edge

pourvoi [puʀvwa] *m* ~ (**en appel**) appeal; ~ **en cassation** appeal (*to the court of Cassation*)

pourvoir [puʀvwaʀ] *irr* **I.** *vt* ~ **de** [*o* **en**] **provisions/marchandises** to supply with food/goods; ~ **qn d'une beauté/intelligence exceptionnelle** to give sb exceptional beauty/intelligence; ~ **qn d'une recommandation** to provide sb with a recommendation; ~ **un poste** to fill a post **II.** *vi* ~ **à qc** to provide for sth; ~ **à l'entretien de la famille** to provide for the family's upkeep **III.** *vpr* **1. se** ~ **de provisions/vêtements** to provide onself with food/clothing; **se** ~ **d'armes** to arm oneself **2.** JUR **se** ~ **devant qc** to appeal to sth; **se** ~ **en appel/cassation** to lodge an appeal/an appeal with the court of Cassation; **se** ~ **en révision** to request a review

pourvu [puʀvy] *conj* **1.** (*souhait*) just so long as; ~ **que nous ne manquions pas le train!** let's hope have don't miss the train! **2.** (*condition*) **pourvu que cela vous convienne** provided that that suits you

pousse [pus] *f* **1.** *a.* BOT shoot; ~**s de bambou** bamboo shoots **2.** (*développement*) growth; (*d'une dent*) emergence; **la** ~ **des cheveux** hair growth

poussé(e) [puse] *adj* (*étude, technique*) advanced; (*discussion, enquête*) extensive; (*travail*) intensive; (*précision*) exhaustive

pousser [puse] <1> **I.** *vt* **1.** (*déplacer*) to push; (*troupeau*) to drive **2.** (*pour ouvrir*) ~ **la porte/la fenêtre** to push the door/window open; (*pour fermer*); ~ **la porte/la fenêtre** to shut the door/window **3.** (*ouvrir en claquant*) ~ **la porte/la fenêtre** to throw the door/window open; (*fermer en claquant*); ~ **la porte/la fenêtre** to slam the door/window shut **4.** (*bousculer*) ~ **qn/qc du coude/pied** to nudge sb/sth with one's elbow/foot **5.** (*entraîner: courant, vent*) to push **6.** (*stimuler: candidat, élève, cheval*) to urge on; ~ **un moteur/une machine** to work an engine/a machine hard; **l'intérêt/l'ambition le pousse** he's driven by self-interest/ambition **7.** (*inciter à*) ~ **qn à** +*infin* to push sb to +*infin;* (*envie, intérêt, ambition*) to drive sb to

P

+*infin;* ~ **qn à la consommation** to encourage sb to consume; ~ **qn au crime** to drive sb to crime **8.** (*diriger*) ~ **qn vers qc/qn** to push sb towards sth/sb **9.** (*émettre: cri, soupir*) to let out; ~ **des cris de joie** to shout with joy; ~ **des gémissements** to whimper; **en** ~ **une** *inf* to sing a song **10.** (*exagérer*) ~ **qc à l'extrême/trop loin** to push sth to extremes/too far; ~ **la jalousie/la gentillesse jusqu'à faire qc** to carry jealousy/kindness to the point of doing sth **11.** (*approfondir*) ~ **plus loin les études/recherches** to further study/research **12.** (*poursuivre: enquête, recherches*) to pursue **13.** (*cultiver*) **faire** ~ **des salades/légumes** to grow lettuce/vegetables; **faire** ~ **des fleurs** to grow flowers **14.** (*grandir*) **se laisser** ~ **les cheveux/la barbe** to let one's hair/beard grow **II.** *vi* **1.** (*croître*) to grow; **sa première dent a poussé** his first tooth is out **2.** (*faire un effort pour accoucher, pour aller à la selle*) to push **3.** (*aller*) ~ **jusqu'à Toulon** to press on as far as Toulon **4.** *inf* (*exagérer*) to overdo it **III.** *vpr* **se** ~ **1.** (*s'écarter*) to shift; **pousse-toi un peu!** (*sur un banc*) move up a bit!; (*pour laisser un passage*) out of the way! **2.** (*se bousculer*) to jostle each other

poussette [pusɛt] *f* (*voiture d'enfant*) pushchair *Brit,* stroller *Am*

poussière [pusjɛʀ] *f* dust; **faire la** ~ to do the dusting; **avoir une** ~ **dans l'œil** to have something in one's eye ►**réduire qn/qc en** ~ to reduce sb/sth to dust; **tomber en** ~ to crumble into dust; **2000 euros et des** ~**s** *inf* just over 2000 euros

poussiéreux, -euse [pusjeʀø, -øz] *adj* dusty

poussif, -ive [pusif, -iv] *adj* (*personne, moteur*) wheezy; (*cheval*) broken-winded

poussin [pusɛ̃] *m* chick

poussoir [puswaʀ] *m* (*d'une montre, sonnette*) button

poutre [putʀ] *f* **1.** ARCHIT (*de bois*) beam; ~**s apparentes** exposed beams **2.** ARCHIT (*de métal*) girder **3.** SPORT beam

poutrelle [putʀɛl] *f* **1.** (*de bois*) beam **2.** (*de métal*) girder

poutser [putse] <1> *vt Suisse* (*nettoyer*) to clean

pouvoir[1] [puvwaʀ] *irr* **I.** *aux* **1.** (*être autorisé*) can, may; **tu peux aller jouer** you may go and play; **il ne peut pas venir** he can't come; **puis-je fermer la fenêtre?** may I close the window? **2.** (*être capable de*) can, to be able to; **j'ai fait ce que j'ai pu** I did what I could; **je ne peux pas m'empêcher de tousser** I cannot stop coughing **3.** (*éventualité*) **elle peut/pourrait être en France** she may/might be in France; **quel âge peut-il bien avoir?** how old can he be?; **c'est une chose qui peut arriver** it's something that happens **4.** (*suggestion*) **tu peux me prêter ton vélo?** could you please lend me your bike?; **tu aurais pu nous le dire plus tôt!** you could have told us sooner! ►**je ne peux pas de ma mère** *Belgique* (*elle ne m'en donne pas la permission*) my mother won't let me **II.** *aux impers* **il peut/pourrait pleuvoir** it could/might rain; **il aurait pu y avoir un accident** there could have been an accident; **cela peut arriver** that may happen; **il peut se faire que** +*subj* it could happen that **III.** *vt* (*être capable de*) ~ **quelque chose pour qn** to be able to do something for sb; **ne rien** ~ **faire pour qn** not to be able to do anything for sb ►**on ne peut mieux** it's the best there is; **chanter on ne peut mieux** to sing incomparably; **n'en plus** ~ **de qc** not to be able to take any more of sth; **je n'y peux rien** (*ne peux y porter remède*) I can't do anything about it; (*ne suis pas responsable*) it's nothing to do with me; **on peut dire que qn a bien fait qc** sb certainly did sth well; **le moins qu'on puisse dire** the least that can be said; **qu'est-ce que cela peut te faire?** what's that got to do with you?; **ne rien** ~ **(y) faire** not to be able to do anything about it **IV.** *vpr impers* **cela se peut/pourrait** that is/could be possible; **non, ça ne se peut pas** no, that's impossible; **il se pourrait qu'elle vienne** she might come

pouvoir[2] [puvwaʀ] *m* **1.** POL power; **le parti au** ~ the party in power; **arriver au** ~ to come to power; **prendre le** ~ to seize power **2.** (*autorité, influence*) ~ **sur qn** power over sb; **tenir qn en son** ~ to hold sb in one's power **3.** ECON ~ **d'achat** purchasing power

praire [pʀɛʀ] *f* clam

prairie [pʀeʀi] *f* meadow

praline [pʀalin] *f* **1.** ~ **grillée** caramelized peanut **2.** *Belgique* (*bonbon au chocolat*) chocolate

praliné [pʀaline] *m* praline

praliné(e) [pʀaline] *adj* (*amande, noisette*) sugared; (*crème, glace*) praline

praticable [pʀatikabl] **I.** *adj* **1.** (*chemin, gué*) passable; (*terrain de sport*) playable **2.** (*exécutable: opération, projet*) practicable; (*moyen*) practical **3.** ARCHIT, THEAT (*fenêtre, décor*) practicable **II.** *m* **1.** THEAT prop **2.** CINE, TV dolly

praticien(ne) [pʀatisjɛ̃, jɛn] *m(f)* *a.* MED practitioner

pratiquant(e) [pʀatikɑ̃, ɑ̃t] **I.** *adj* practising *Brit,* practicing *Am;* **être très** ~ to go to church regularly; **être peu** ~ not to go to church very often **II.** *m(f)* practising member *Brit,* practicing member *Am;* **cette religion compte 20 millions de** ~**s** 20 million people practise this religion

pratique [pʀatik] **I.** *adj* **1.** (*commode*) handy; (*solution*) practical; (*emploi du temps*) convenient **2.** (*réaliste*) practical; **n'avoir aucun sens** ~ to be not at all practical; **être un esprit** ~ to have a practical mind; **dans la vie** ~ in real life **3.** (*opp: théorique*) practical;

travaux ~s lab work **II.** *f* **1.** (*opp: théorie, procédé*) practice; **dans la** [*o* **en**] ~ in practice; **mettre en** ~ to put into practice; **c'était une ~ courante** it was common practice **2.** (*expérience*) practical experience; **avoir la ~ du métier** to be experienced in a profession; **~ de la conduite** driving experience **3.** (*coutume*) practice

pratiquement [pʀatikmɑ̃] *adv* **1.** (*en réalité*) in practice **2.** (*presque*) practically

pratiquer [pʀatike] <1> **I.** *vt* **1.** (*exercer, mettre en pratique*) to practise *Brit,* to practice *Am;* ~ **le tennis/golf** to play tennis/golf; ~ **le yoga** to do yoga; **les prix qu'ils pratiquent** their prices **2.** (*faire: trou*) to make; (*opération*) to carry out **II.** *vi* MED, REL to practise *Brit,* to practice *Am*

pré [pʀe] *m* field

préado [pʀeado] *m, f inf abr de* **préadolescent**

préadolescence [pʀeadɔlesɑ̃s] *f* preadolescence

préadolescent(e) [pʀeadɔlesɑ̃, ɑ̃t] *m(f)* preadolescent, pre-teenager

préalable [pʀealabl] **I.** *adj* (*entretien, question*) preliminary; **je voudrais votre accord/avis** ~ I'd like your prior agreement/opinion **II.** *m* preliminary; **sans** (**aucun**) ~ without any preliminaries ▶**au** ~ previously

préalablement [pʀealabləmɑ̃] *adv* previously; ~ **à qc** prior to sth

préambule [pʀeɑ̃byl] *m* **1.** (*entrée en matière*) *a.* JUR preamble **2.** (*prélude*) prelude ▶**sans** ~ without any preliminaries

préau [pʀeo] <x> *m* courtyard; (*d'une école*) playground shelter

préavis [pʀeavi] *m a.* JUR notice; **délai de** ~ period of notice; ~ **de licenciement** redundancy notice; **être licencié sans** ~ to be made redundant without notice; **donner son** ~ to give (in) one's notice; ~ **de grève** strike notice; **sans** ~ without notice

précaire [pʀekɛʀ] *adj* **1.** (*position, situation*) precarious; (*emploi*) with no security; (*bonheur, santé, paix*) fragile **2.** JUR **possession** ~ precarious tenure

précarité [pʀekaʀite] *f a.* JUR (*d'une situation*) precariousness; (*d'un emploi*) lack of security; (*d'un bonheur*) fragility

précaution [pʀekosjɔ̃] *f* **1.** (*disposition*) precaution **2.** (*prudence*) caution; **par** ~ as a precaution; **s'entourer de ~s** to take every possible precaution

précédemment [pʀesedamɑ̃] *adv* previously

précédent(e) [pʀesedɑ̃, ɑ̃t] *adj* previous; **le jour** ~ the day before

précéder [pʀesede] <5> **I.** *vt* **1.** (*dans le temps, dans l'espace*) to precede; **le jour qui précédait leur départ** the day preceding their departure; **l'article précède le nom** the article precedes the noun **2.** (*devancer*) ~ **qn** to go in front of sb **3.** (*devancer en voiture*) ~ **qn** to be in front of sb; **je vais vous** ~ **pour ...** I am going to drive on ahead of you to ...; **elle m'a précédé de quelques minutes** she was ahead of me by a few minutes **II.** *vi* to precede; **les jours qui précédaient** the preceding days

précepte [pʀesɛpt] *m a.* REL precept; **les ~s en usage dans la société** society's precepts

précepteur, -trice [pʀesɛptœʀ, -tʀis] *m, f* tutor

préchauffer [pʀeʃofe] <1> *vt* (*four*) to preheat; (*diesel*) to warm

prêcher [pʀeʃe] <1> **I.** *vt* (*l'Évangile, croisade*) to preach; (*fraternité, haine*) to advocate; **tu peux toujours ~ la bonne parole, ...** *iron* you can preach to people as much as you like, ... **II.** *vi* REL to preach

prêchi-prêcha [pʀeʃipʀeʃa] *m inv, péj* sermonizing

précieusement [pʀesjøzmɑ̃] *adv* carefully

précieux, -euse [pʀesjø, -jøz] *adj* precious

préciosité [pʀesjozite] *f* **1.** affectation; **la ~ du style de cet auteur** this author's mannered style **2.** LIT preciosity

précipice [pʀesipis] *m* precipice

précipitamment [pʀesipitamɑ̃] *adv* hurriedly; (*partir, s'enfuir*) in a rush

précipitation [pʀesipitasjɔ̃] *f* **1.** (*hâte*) haste; (*d'un départ, d'une décision*) hurry; **sans** ~ unhurriedly; **avec** ~ in haste; **partir avec** ~ to rush off **2.** *pl* METEO rainfall *no pl*

précipité(e) [pʀesipite] *adj* **1.** (*hâtif: fuite, départ*) hurried; (*décision*) rushed **2.** (*accéléré: pas, rythme, respiration*) rapid

précipiter [pʀesipite] <1> **I.** *vt* **1.** (*jeter*) ~ **qn de l'escalier** to throw sb down the stairs; ~ **la voiture contre un arbre** to smash the car into a tree **2.** (*plonger*) ~ **qn dans le malheur** to plunge sb into misery; ~ **qn dans les bras de qn** to throw sb into sb's arms **3.** (*accélérer: pas, démarche*) to quicken **4.** (*brusquer: départ, décision*) to hasten; **il ne faut rien** ~ we must not be hasty **5.** CHIM to precipitate **II.** *vi* CHIM to precipitate **III.** *vpr* **1.** (*s'élancer*) **se ~ de qc** to jump from sth; **se ~ dans le vide** to throw oneself into the void **2.** (*se jeter*) **se ~ à la porte/dans la rue** to dash to the door/into the street; **se ~ sur qn/dans les bras de qn** to rush up to sb/into sb's arms; **il s'est précipité à mon secours** he raced to my rescue **3.** (*s'accélérer*) **se** ~ to speed up; **les événements se précipitent** the pace of events quickened **4.** (*se dépêcher*) **se** ~ to hurry; **ne nous précipitons pas!** let's not be in too much of a hurry!

précis(e) [pʀesi, iz] *adj* **1.** (*juste*) precise; **à 10 heures ~es** at exactly [*o* precisely] 10 o'clock **2.** (*net*) particular

précisément [pʀesizemɑ̃] *adv* precisely

préciser [pʀesize] <1> **I.** *vt* **1.** (*donner des précisions: point, fait*) to state; (*intention, idée*) to make clear; (*date, lieu*) to specify; **précisez!** be specific! **2.** (*souligner*) to point out **II.** *vpr* **se** ~ to take shape; (*menace, idée,*

situation) to become clear
précision [pʀesizjɔ̃] *f* **1.** (*justesse*) preciseness; (*d'un geste, d'un instrument*) precision; **être/ne pas être d'une grande** ~ to be/not be very precise **2.** (*netteté: des contours, d'un trait*) distinctness **3.** *souvent pl* (*détail*) detail
précoce [pʀekɔs] *adj* **1.** (*plante, variété, gelée*) early **2.** (*prématuré: rides, sénilité, mariage*) premature **3.** (*en avance: enfant, sentiment*) precocious
précocité [pʀekɔsite] *f* (*d'un fruit*) earliness; (*d'une gelée, de l'hiver*) early arrival; (*d'un enfant*) precociousness
préconçu(e) [pʀekɔ̃sy] *adj* **1.** *péj* (*idée, opinion*) preconceived **2.** (*préétabli: plan*) premeditated
préconiser [pʀekɔnize] <1> *vt* to advocate
précurseur [pʀekyʀsœʀ] **I.** *adj seulement m* **événement** ~ **de qc** event that gives warning of sth; **signe** ~ **de qc** warning sign of sth; **l'éclair est (le signe)** ~ **de l'orage** the lightning is the warning of the storm **II.** *m* precursor
prédateur, **-trice** [pʀedatœʀ, -tʀis] **I.** *adj* **animal** ~ predatory animal; **être** ~ **de qc** to prey on sth **II.** *m, f* predator
prédécesseur [pʀedesesœʀ] *m* predecessor
prédestiné(e) [pʀedɛstine] *adj* **être** ~ **à qc** to be predestined for sth
prédicateur, **-trice** [pʀedikatœʀ, -tʀis] *m, f* preacher
prédiction [pʀediksjɔ̃] *f* prediction
prédilection [pʀedilɛksjɔ̃] *f* predilection; **avoir une** ~ **pour qn/qc** to have a fondness for sb/sth; **auteur/sport de** ~ favourite author/sport *Brit,* favorite author/sport *Am*
prédire [pʀediʀ] *vt irr* to predict
prédisposer [pʀedispoze] <1> *vt a.* MED ~ **qn à qc** to predispose sb to sth; **son éducation le prédispose à être sévère** the way he was brought up makes him prone to be severe; ~ **qn en faveur de qn** to be predisposed in sb's favour *Brit,* to be predisposed in sb's favor *Am;* **être prédisposé à qc/à faire qc** to be prone to sth/to doing sth
prédit(e) [pʀedi, it] *part passé de* **prédire**
prédominer [pʀedɔmine] <1> *vi* (*avis, préoccupation, sport*) to be prevalent; (*couleur, impression*) to predominate; (*personne, pays*) to prevail; **aujourd'hui les nuages prédomineront** today will be mainly cloudy
préexister [pʀeɛgziste] <1> *vi* to pre-exist; ~ **à qn/qc** to pre-exist sb/sth
préfabriqué [pʀefabʀike] *m* **1.** prefabricated material **2.** (*bâtiment*) prefab
préfabriqué(e) [pʀefabʀike] *adj* **1.** TECH prefabricated; **maison** ~**e** prefab **2.** *péj* (*faux: accusation*) concocted; (*sourire*) artificial
préface [pʀefas] *f* preface
préfacer [pʀefase] <2> *vt* to preface
préfectoral(e) [pʀefɛktɔʀal, o] <-aux> *adj* **administration** ~**e** administration by prefect; **arrêté** ~ prefect's decree; **par mesure** ~**e** by order (of the prefect)
préfecture [pʀefɛktyʀ] *f* prefecture; ~ **de police** police headquarters
préférable [pʀefeʀabl] *adj* **être** ~ **à qc** to be preferable; **il est** ~ **de se taire** it is preferable [*o* better] to say nothing; **il est** ~ **que je m'en aille** I had better go
préféré(e) [pʀefeʀe] **I.** *adj* (*ami*) best; (*chanteur*) favourite *Brit,* favorite *Am* **II.** *m(f)* favourite *Brit,* favorite *Am*
préférence [pʀefeʀɑ̃s] *f* preference; **avoir une** ~ [*o* **des** ~**s**] **pour qn/qc** to have a preference for sb/sth; **avoir la** ~ **sur qn** to be preferred over sb ►**de** ~ preferably; **de** ~ **à qc** in preference to sth
préférer [pʀefeʀe] <5> *vt* ~ **qn/qc à qn/qc** to prefer sth/sb to sth/sb else; **je préfère que tu le fasses** (*subj*) I would prefer you to do it
préfet [pʀefɛ] *m* **1.** prefect; ~ **de police** chief of police **2.** *Belgique* (*directeur d'athénée, de lycée*) principal

> A **préfet** represents the government and state authorities in a Département. He is supported by the police and has mayoral duties and is responsible for the decisions taken in the districts. Prefects were first introduced by Napoleon.

préfète [pʀefɛt] *f* **1.** prefect (*woman*) **2.** *Belgique* (*directrice d'athénée, de lycée*) principal
préfigurer [pʀefigyʀe] <1> *vt* to prefigure
préfixe [pʀefiks] *m* prefix
préhistoire [pʀeistwaʀ] *f* prehistory
préhistorique [pʀeistɔʀik] *adj* HIST prehistoric
préjudice [pʀeʒydis] *m* harm; ~ **financier** financial loss; **causer** [*o* **porter**] **un** ~ **à qn** to harm sb; **porter** ~ **à la tranquillité de qc** to disturb the tranquility of sth; **subir un** ~ to be harmed ►**au** ~ **de qn/qc** to the detriment of sb/sth; **sans** ~ **de qc** without prejudice to sth
préjudiciable [pʀeʒydisjabl] *adj* ~ **à qn/qc** prejudicial to sb/sth; **une erreur** ~ a prejudicial error
préjugé [pʀeʒyʒe] *m* prejudice; **avoir un** ~ **contre qn** to be prejudiced against sb ►**bénéficier d'un** ~ **favorable** to be favourably considered *Brit,* to be favorably considered *Am*
prélasser [pʀelɑse] <1> *vpr* **se** ~ to lounge about *Brit,* to lounge around *Am*
prélat [pʀela] *m* prelate
prélèvement [pʀelɛvmɑ̃] *m* **1.** (*d'eau*) drawing; (*de sang*) taking; (*d'organe*) removal; **faire un** ~ **de tissu/de sang** to take a tissue/blood sample **2.** FIN deduction; ~ **bancaire** standing order; ~ **automatique** standing order; (*pour une facture*) direct debit; ~ **fiscal** tax levy; ~**s obligatoires** compulsory deductions, ≈ stoppages **3.** (*somme retenue*) deduction **4.** (*retrait, somme retirée*) withdrawal

prélever [pRel(ə)ve] <4> *vt* (*somme, pourcentage*) to take off; (*taxe*) to deduct; (*organe, tissu*) to remove; (*sang*) to take; ~ **de l'argent sur le compte** to withdraw money from the account

préliminaire [pReliminɛR] **I.** *adj* preliminary; (*discours*) introductory **II.** *mpl* preliminaries; ~**s de la paix** preliminary peace talks

prélude [pRelyd] *m* **1.** MUS prelude **2.** (*début*) ~ **de qc** prelude to sth

prématuré(**e**) [pRematyRe] **I.** *adj* premature; **enfant** ~ premature baby; **il est/serait** ~ **de** +*infin* it is/would be premature to +*infin* **II.** *m(f)* premature baby

prématurément [pRematyRemɑ̃] *adv* prematurely

préméditation [pRemeditasjɔ̃] *f* **1.** forethought; **agir sans la moindre** ~ to act without thinking **2.** JUR premeditation; **avec** ~ (*agir*) with intent; (*meutre*) premeditated

prémédité(**e**) [pRemedite] *adj* (*crime*) premeditated; (*réponse, réaction*) thought-out

premier [pRəmje] *m* first ▸**les** ~**s seront les derniers** the last shall be first; **jeune** ~ romantic male lead; **en** ~ (*avant les autres*) first; (*pour commencer*) firstly

premier, **-ière** [pRəmje, -jɛR] *adj* **1.** *antéposé* (*opp: dernier*) first; (*page*) front; ~ **venu** le the first to arrive; (*n'importe qui*) anybody; **en** ~ **lieu** in the first place; **dans les** ~**s temps** at the beginning; *v. a.* **cinquième 2.** (*principal: besoins, rudiments*) basic; (*objectif, rôle*) main; (*qualité*) primary; **au** ~ **plan** in the foreground; **être aux premières loges** to have a grandstand view; **marchandises de** ~ **choix** [*o* **première qualité**] top quality products

première [pRəmjɛR] *f* **1.** (*vitesse*) first gear **2.** ECOLE ≈ year twelve *Brit,* eleventh grade *Am* **3.** (*manifestation sans précédent*) first; ~ **mondiale** world first **4.** THEAT, CINE première; **grande** ~ grand première **5.** AUTO first class; **billet de** ~ first class ticket ▸**être de** ~ to be first class; **être de** ~ **pour qc** *inf* (*personne*) to be brilliant at sth

premièrement [pRəmjɛRmɑ̃] *adv* **1.** (*en premier lieu*) in the first place **2.** (*et d'abord*) firstly

prémonition [pRemɔnisjɔ̃] *f* premonition

prémonitoire [pRemɔnitwaR] *adj* **1.** MED (*symptômes, signe*) premonitory **2.** (*qui constitue une prémonition*) **faire un rêve** ~ to have a premonitory dream

prémunir [pRemyniR] <8> **I.** *vt* **1.** (*prévenir*) ~ **qn contre qc** to warn sb against sth **2.** (*protéger*) ~ **qn contre qc** to protect sb against sth **II.** *vpr* **se** ~ **contre qc** to guard against sth

prenant(**e**) [pRənɑ̃, ɑ̃t] *adj* **1.** (*captivant: film, livre*) absorbing **2.** (*absorbant: travail, activité*) time-consuming

prénatal(**e**) <s *o* -aux> [pRenatal, o] *adj* prenatal; **congé** ~ maternity leave

prendre [pRɑ̃dR] <13> **I.** *vt avoir* **1.** to take; ~ **qc dans qc** to take sth from sth; ~ **qn par le bras** to take sb by the arm **2.** (*absorber: boisson, café, sandwich*) to have; (*médicament*) to take; **vous prendrez bien quelque chose?** will you have something? **3.** (*aller chercher*) ~ **qn chez lui/à la gare** to pick sb up at their house/the station **4.** (*emporter: manteau, parapluie*) to take **5.** AUTO (*train, métro, ascenseur, avion*) to take; ~ **le volant** to drive **6.** (*capturer: gibier*) to shoot; (*poisson, mouches*) to catch; (*forteresse, ville*) to take; **se faire** ~ to be captured; **être pris dans qc** to be caught in sth **7.** (*se laisser séduire*) **se laisser** ~ **par qn/à qc** to be taken in by sb/sth **8.** (*surprendre*) to catch; ~ **qn sur le fait** to catch sb red-handed; **on ne m'y prendra plus!** I won't be caught out next time! **9.** (*acheter*) to buy; (*chambre, couchette*) to take; ~ **de l'essence** to get petrol *Brit,* to get gas *Am* **10.** (*accepter*) ~ **qn comme locataire** to take sb as a tenant; ~ **qn comme cuisinier** to take on sb as a chef **11.** (*noter, enregistrer: empreintes, notes*) to take; (*adresse, nom*) to take down; (*renseignements*) to take in; ~ **un rendez-vous** to make an appointment; ~ **des nouvelles de qn** to ask about sb; ~ **sa température** to take one's temperature **12.** (*adopter: décision*) to make; (*précautions, mesure*) to take; (*air innocent*) to put on; (*ton menaçant*) to adopt; ~ **l'apparence/la forme de qc** to take on the appearance/form of sth **13.** (*acquérir: couleur, goût de rance*) to acquire; (*nouveau sens*) to take on; ~ **du courage** to take courage; ~ **du poids** to gain weight; ~ **du ventre** to get a bit of a paunch **14.** MED ~ **froid** to catch cold; **être pris d'un malaise** to feel faint **15.** (*s'accorder: plaisir, repos*) to have; (*des congés, vacances*) to take; ~ **sa retraite** to retire **16.** (*coûter*) **ce travail me prend tout mon temps** this work takes up all my time **17.** (*prélever, faire payer: argent, pourcentage*) to take; (*commission, cotisation*) to charge; **être pris sur le salaire** to be taken off one's salary **18.** *inf* (*recevoir, subir*) ~ **une averse** to get caught in a shower; ~ **des coups/des reproches** to be on the wrong end of a beating/criticism; ~ **la balle/porte en pleine figure** to get hit right in the face by the ball/by the door **19.** (*traiter: personne*) to handle; (*problème*) to deal with; ~ **qn par la douceur** to use the gentle approach on sb; ~ **qn par les sentiments** to appeal to sb's feelings **20.** (*considérer comme*) ~ **qc pour prétexte** to use sth as an excuse; **pour qui me prends-tu?** who do you take me for? **21.** (*assaillir: doute, faim, panique*) to strike; (*colère, envie*) to come over; **être pris par le doute/la panique** to be seized by doubt/panic **22.** LING (*s'écrire*) **ce mot prend deux l/une cédille** there are two ls/a cedilla in this word ▸**tel est pris qui croyait** ~ *prov* it's the biter bit; **c'est à** ~ **ou à laisser** take it or leave it; **à tout** ~ on the whole; ~ **qc sur soi** to take

P

sth on oneself; ~ **sur soi de** +*infin* to take it on oneself to +*infin;* **qu'est-ce qui te/lui prend?** what's got into ou/him? **II.** *vi* **1.** (*réussir*) **avec moi, ça ne prend pas!** *inf* it won't wash with me! **2.** *avoir* (*s'enflammer: feu*) to take hold **3.** *avoir o être* (*durcir: ciment, mayonnaise*) to set **4.** *avoir* (*se diriger*) ~ **à gauche/droite** (*personne*) to go left/right; (*chemin*) to turn left/right **5.** *avoir* (*faire payer*) ~ **beaucoup/peu** to charge a lot/little; ~ **cher/bon marché** to be expensive/cheap; ~ **cher de l'heure** to be expensive by the hour **III.** *vpr* **1.** (*s'accrocher*) **se** ~ **le doigt dans la porte** to catch one's finger in the door **2.** (*se considérer*) **se** ~ **trop au sérieux** to take oneself too seriously **3.** (*procéder*) **s'y** ~ **bien/mal avec qn** to deal with sb the right/wrong way; **s'y** ~ **bien/mal avec qc** to handle sth well/badly; **s'y** ~ **à trois reprises** to have three goes at doing sth **4.** (*en vouloir*) **s'en** ~ **à qn/qc** to blame sb/sth **5.** (*s'attaquer*) **s'en** ~ **à qn/qc** to lay into sb/sth **6.** (*être pris*) **se** ~ (*médicament*) to be taken; **se** ~ **au filet/à la ligne** (*poisson*) to be caught in a net/on a line **7.** (*se tenir*) **se** ~ **par le bras** to take each other's arm

preneur, **-euse** [pʀənœʀ, -øz] *m, f* buyer; **ce tableau me plaît, je suis** ~ I like this painting, I'll have it; **trouver** ~ **pour qc** to find a buyer for sth

prénom [pʀenɔ̃] *m* first name

prénommer [pʀenɔme] <1> **I.** *vt* ~ **qn Julien** to name sb Julien **II.** *vpr* **se** ~ **Julia** to be called Julia

préoccupant(**e**) [pʀeɔkypɑ̃, ɑ̃t] *adj* worrying

préoccupation [pʀeɔkypasjɔ̃] *f* **1.** (*souci*) worry **2.** (*occupation*) preoccupation

préoccupé(**e**) [pʀeɔkype] *adj* preoccupied; **avoir l'air** ~ to look worried; **être** ~ **de faire qc** to be worried about doing sth

préoccuper [pʀeɔkype] <1> **I.** *vt* **1.** (*inquiéter*) to worry; **l'avenir/la situation me préoccupe** I'm concerned about the future/the situation **2.** (*absorber: problème, affaire*) to preoccupy **II.** *vpr* **se** ~ **de qn/qc** to worry about sb/sth; **se** ~ **de faire qc** to worry about doing sth

prépa [pʀepa] *f abr de* **classe préparatoire** *class preparing the entrance examinations for the Grandes Ecoles*

préparatifs [pʀepaʀatif] *mpl* preparations; ~ **de la fête** party preparations

préparation [pʀepaʀasjɔ̃] *f* **1.** (*mise au point*) *a.* CHIM, MED preparation; (*d'un discours, plan*) drafting; (*d'un complot*) hatching; **avoir qc en** ~ to have sth in the pipeline **2.** (*entraînement*) ~ **au Tour de France** training for the Tour de France **3.** ECOLE **classe de** ~ preparation class; **la** ~ **à l'examen** preparation for the exam

préparatoire [pʀepaʀatwaʀ] *adj* **1.** (*qui prépare*) preparatory **2.** ECOLE **cours** ~ *first year in primary school;* **classe** ~ *class preparing students for the entrance exams to the Grandes Ecoles*

préparer [pʀepaʀe] <1> **I.** *vt* **1.** (*confectionner*) to prepare; **plat préparé** ready-made meal **2.** (*apprêter: affaires, bagages, terre*) to prepare; (*chambre, voiture*) to get ready; (*gibier, poisson, volaille*) to dress **3.** (*mettre au point: fête, plan, voyage*) to plan; ~ **un piège à qn** to lay a trap for sb **4.** (*travailler à: cours, discours, leçon*) to prepare; (*nouvelle édition, roman, thèse*) to work on; (*bac, concours*) to prepare for **5.** (*réserver*) ~ **un rhume/une grippe** to be coming down with a cold/the flu; ~ **une déception/des ennuis à qn** *iron* to have a disappointment/trouble in store for sb; **que nous prépare-t-il?** what has he got in store for us? **6.** (*entraîner*) **j'y étais préparé** I was prepared [*o* ready] for it **II.** *vpr* **1.** (*se laver, se coiffer, s'habiller*) **se** ~ to get ready **2.** (*faire en sorte d'être prêt*) **se** ~ **à un examen/une compétition** to prepare for an exam/a competition **3.** *soutenu* (*être sur le point de*) **se** ~ **à** +*infin* to be getting ready to +*infin* **4.** (*approcher*) **se** ~ (*événement*) to near; (*orage*) to brew; (*grandes choses, tragédie*) to approach

prépondérance [pʀepɔ̃deʀɑ̃s] *f* (*suprématie: d'un groupe, parti, d'une nation*) predominance; (*d'une croyance, idée*) prevalence; **la** ~ **du rendement sur** [*o* **par rapport à**] **la qualité** the greater importance given to output over quality

prépondérant(**e**) [pʀepɔ̃deʀɑ̃, ɑ̃t] *adj* (*influence, part, rôle*) predominant; (*voix*) prevailing; **occuper une place** ~**e** to play a dominant role

préposé(**e**) [pʀepoze] *m(f)* **1.** (*facteur*) postman *m,* postwoman *f* **2.** ADMIN ~ **des douanes** customs officer; ~ **des postes** post office worker **3.** (*responsable de*) ~**e aux vestiaires** cloakroom attendant; **le** ~**/la** ~**e aux tickets** the person in charge of tickets; ~ **à la circulation** traffic warden

préposition [pʀepozisjɔ̃] *f* preposition

prépuce [pʀepys] *m* prepuce

préretraite [pʀeʀ(ə)tʀɛt] *f* early retirement; **départ en** ~ early retirement; **être en** ~ to have taken early retirement; **être mis en** ~ to be given early retirement

prérogative [pʀeʀɔgativ] *f* prerogative

près [pʀɛ] **I.** *adv* (*à une petite distance, dans peu de temps*) near ►**de** ~ **ou de loin** whichever way you look at it; **ni de** ~ **ni de loin** in no way shape or form; **qn n'en est pas/plus à qc** ~ another sth's not going to make any difference to sb now/at this stage; **ne pas y regarder de trop** ~ *inf* not to take too close a look; **à cela** ~ **que qn a fait qc** if is wasn't for the fact that sb did sth; **à la minute** ~ to the minute; **à peu** (**de choses**) ~ approximately; (*ressembler*) nearly; **l'hôtel était à peu** ~ **vide/calme** the hotel was nearly empty/quite quiet; **rater le bus à quelques secondes** ~ to miss the bus by a few seconds; **à une exception/quelques détails** ~ apart from one exception/some details; **au centimètre** ~ to the centimetre *Brit,* to the centimeter *Am;* **regarder de** ~ to watch closely; **voir qc de** ~ to see sth close up; **frôler qc de (tout/très)** ~ to come within an inch of sth; **(se) suivre de** ~ (*événements*) to happen close together **II.** *prep* **1.** (*à côté de*) ~ **d'une personne/d'un lieu** near (to) a person/place; **habiter** ~ **de chez qn** to live near sb; ~ **du bord** near the edge **2.** (*à peu de temps de*) **être** ~ **du but** to be near one's goal; **être** ~ **de la retraite** to be close to retirement **3.** (*presque*) ~ **de** nearly ▶**ne pas être** ~ **de faire qc** to have no intention of doing sth

présage [prezaʒ] *m* **1.** (*signe annonciateur*) omen; **heureux/mauvais** ~ good/bad omen; **être un** ~ **de malheur** to be an omen of misfortune; **être** ~ **de chaleur/de pluie** to be a sign of heat/rain **2.** (*prédiction*) prediction; **tirer un** ~ **de qc** (*interpréter*) to see sth as an omen; (*prédire*) to use sth to make a prediction

présager [prezaʒe] <2a> *vt* **1.** ~ **qc** (*être un signe annonciateur: vent, beau temps, pluie*) to be a sign of; **cela ne présage rien de bon** that's an ominous sign **2.** (*prévoir: personne*) to foresee; (*indice*) to announce; **laisser** ~ **une catastrophe** to portend a disaster

presbyte [prɛsbit] **I.** *adj* long-sighted *Brit,* farsighted *Am* **II.** *mf* long-sighted person *Brit,* farsighted person *Am*

presbytère [prɛsbitɛr] *m* presbytery

prescription [prɛskripsjɔ̃] *f* **1.** (*ordre formel*) instruction; (*morale*) dictate; **~s officielles** official instructions **2.** MED (*traitement prescrit*) prescription; (*action de prescrire*) prescribing; ~ **médicale** doctor's prescription; **médicament délivré sur** ~ **médicale** drug dispensed only on a doctor's prescription **3.** JUR prescription; ~ **pénale** statute of limitations; **il y a** ~ the statute of limitations applies

prescrire [prɛskrir] *irr* **I.** *vt* **1.** (*ordonner*) to order; (*comportement, démarche*) to lay down; (*mesures*) to dictate; ~ **à qn de** +*infin* to instruct sb to +*infin;* **jour/délai prescrit** the prescribed day/period of notice **2.** MED ~ **qc à qn contre qc** to prescribe sb sth for sth; **ne pas dépasser la dose prescrite** do not exceed the prescribed dose **3.** JUR (*acquérir: bien, propriété*) to obtain by prescription **4.** JUR (*abolir*) **être prescrit** (*dette, peine*) to lapse **II.** *vpr* **1.** MED **se** ~ to be prescribed **2.** JUR **se** ~ (*dette, peine, rente*) to lapse

présence [prezɑ̃s] *f* (*opp: absence, personnalité*) presence; **avoir de la** ~ to have presence ▶ ~ **d'esprit** presence of mind

présent [prezɑ̃] *m* present; **pour le** ~ for the present ▶**à** ~ at present; **à** ~ **qu'il est parti** now that he has gone; **dès à** ~ here and now; **jusqu'à** ~ until now

présent(e) [prezɑ̃, ɑ̃t] **I.** *adj* **1.** (*opp: absent: personne*) present; **les personnes ~es** those present **2.** (*qui existe*) **avoir qc** ~ **à l'esprit/à la mémoire** to have sth in one's mind/memory **3.** (*actuel: circonstances, état, temps*) current; **à la minute/l'heure ~e** at the present moment/time **II.** *m(f)* (*personne*) person present

présentable [prezɑ̃tabl] *adj* presentable

présentateur, -trice [prezɑ̃tatœr, -tris] *m, f* (*des informations, du journal télévisé*) newsreader *Brit,* newscaster *Am;* (*d'un programme*) presenter; (*d'une émission, discussion*) host

présentation [prezɑ̃tasjɔ̃] *f* **1.** presentation; (*d'un programme*) presentation **2.** (*fait d'introduire qn*) **les ~s** the introductions

présenter [prezɑ̃te] <1> **I.** *vt* **1.** (*faire connaître*) to introduce; (*cheval, troupe*) to present; ~ **qn à un juge** to present sb to a judge **2.** RADIO, TV (*émission*) to present; (*programme*) to introduce; ~ **le journal télévisé** to present the news **3.** (*décrire*) ~ **qn/qc comme qn/qc** to portray sb/sth as sb/sth **4.** (*montrer: billet, carte d'identité, document*) to present; ~ **le dos** to have one's back turned **5.** (*soumettre: problème, théorie, travail*) to submit; (*exprimer: critique, objection, condoléances, félicitations, regrets*) to offer; ~ **ses excuses à qn** to present one's excuses to sb **6.** (*donner une apparence*) to present; **c'est bien présenté** it is well presented **7.** (*avoir*) to have; ~ **un danger/des dangers** to present danger/; ~ **un aspect rugueux/humide** to look rough/damp **8.** (*offrir*) to offer; (*plat, rafraîchissement, fleurs, bouquet*) to present **9.** (*proposer: devis, dossier, projet de loi*) to present; (*addition, facture*) to submit; (*motion, demande*) to propose **II.** *vi* ~ **bien/mal** *inf* to look good/awful **III.** *vpr* **1.** (*décliner son identité*) **se** ~ **à qn** to introduce oneself to sb **2.** (*se rendre, aller, venir*) **se** ~ **chez qn** to go to sb's house; **se** ~ **chez un employeur** to go to see an employer **3.** (*être candidat*) **se** ~ **à un examen** to take an exam; **se** ~ **pour un emploi** to apply for a job **4.** (*apparaître, exister, surgir*) **se** ~ (*problème, difficulté, obstacle*) to arise; **se** ~ **à l'esprit de qn** to come to sb's mind **5.** (*paraître, avoir un certain aspect*) **se** ~ **sous forme de cachets** to be in tablet form; **ça se présente bien!** that bodes well!

présentoir [prezɑ̃twar] *m* display stand

préservatif [prezɛrvatif] *m* condom

préservation [prezɛrvasjɔ̃] *f* (*des biens, récoltes, de la santé*) protection; (*d'une espèce, de monuments, de l'environnement*) conservation; **campagne en vue de la** ~ **des animaux en voie de disparition** endangered animal conservation campaign

préserver [prezɛrve] <1> **I.** *vt* **1.** (*protéger*) ~ **qn de la contamination/du froid/du danger** to protect sb from contamination/the

P

cold/danger; ~ **qc du froid/de l'humidité** to keep sth in a warm/dry place **2.** (*garder intact: secret*) to keep; (*intérêts*) to look after; (*information*) to keep confidential **II.** *vpr* **se ~ de qc** to guard against sth

présidence [pʀezidɑ̃s] *f* presidency

président(e) [pʀezidɑ̃, ɑ̃t] *m(f)* **1.** (*personne qui dirige: d'une association, commission, d'un comité, jury, congrès*) chair; (*d'une université*) chancellor; (*d'un tribunal*) presiding judge; (*d'une entreprise*) president; (*d'une assemblée*) speaker **2.** *Suisse* (*maire dans les cantons de Valais et de Neuchâtel*) mayor

Président(e) [pʀezidɑ̃, ɑ̃t] *m(f)* (*chef de l'État*) the President; **le ~ de la République française** the President of the French Republic

> The **Président de la République** is the French head of state and is elected directly by the people for an office of seven years ("le septennat") following a majority victory. The President and the government do not have to be from the same political party.

président-directeur général, présidente-directrice générale [pʀezidɑ̃diʀɛktœʀʒeneʀal] <présidents-directeurs généraux> *m, f* chairman and managing director *Brit,* chief executive officer *Am*

présidentiel(le) [pʀezidɑ̃sjɛl] *adj* presidential

présidentielle [pʀezidɑ̃sjɛl] *f gén pl* presidential elections

présider [pʀezide] <1> **I.** *vt* **1.** (*mission*) to lead; ~ **un dîner/banquet** to preside at a dinner/banquet **2.** (*diriger*) ~ **une assemblée/séance** to chair a meeting/session; **être présidé par qn** (*réunion, assemblée, débat, délibération*) to be chaired by sb **II.** *vi* **1.** (*diriger: président*) to be in the chair **2.** (*surveiller*) ~ **aux préparatifs d'une fête** to supervise the preparations for a celebration

présomption [pʀezɔ̃psjɔ̃] *f* **1.** (*supposition*) presumption; **avoir de fortes ~s que qn a fait qc** to have strong suspicions that sb did sth **2.** JUR ~ **d'innocence/de paternité** presumption of innocence/legitimacy; ~ **de faute** [*o* **culpabilité**] presumption of guilt

présomptueux, -euse [pʀezɔ̃ptɥø, -øz] **I.** *adj* presumptuous **II.** *m, f* arrogant individual

presque [pʀɛsk] *adv* nearly; **tout le monde ou ~** everyone or nearly everyone; **je ne l'ai ~ pas entendu** I could hardly hear him; **je ne connais ~ personne** I know hardly anyone; **il pleurait ~** he was nearly crying

presqu'île [pʀɛskil] *f* peninsula

pressant(e) [pʀɛsɑ̃, ɑ̃t] *adj* **1.** (*urgent*) urgent **2.** (*insistant*) insistent; **se faire ~** to become increasingly insistent

presse [pʀɛs] *f* (*journaux*) press; ~ **écrite** press; ~ **à grand tirage** popular press; ~ **féminine** women's magazines; ~ **sportive** sports press; ~ **nationale/régionale** national/regional press; ~ **mensuelle** monthly magazines; ~ **quotidienne** daily newspapers ►**avoir bonne/mauvaise ~** to have a good/bad press

pressé(e)[1] [pʀese] *adj* (*qui se hâte*) **d'un pas ~** in a hurry; **être ~ d'arriver** to be in a hurry to arrive

pressé(e)[2] [pʀese] *adj* (*citron, orange*) freshly-squeezed

presse-bouton [pʀɛsbutɔ̃] *adj inv* (*usine, cuisine*) push-button **presse-citron** [pʀɛssitʀɔ̃] <presse-citrons> *m* lemon squeezer

pressentiment [pʀesɑ̃timɑ̃] *m* presentiment; **avoir le ~ de qc** to have a foreboding of sth; **avoir le ~ qu'il va pleuvoir** to have the feeling that it will rain

pressentir [pʀesɑ̃tiʀ] <10> *vt* **1.** to sense; ~ **qu'il va pleuvoir** to sense that it is going to rain; **il laisse ~ son mécontentement** he's making it clear that he will not be pleased **2.** *soutenu* (*sélectionner*) ~ **qn pour qc** to approach sb over sth

presse-papiers [pʀɛspapje] *m inv* paperweight; INFOR clipboard

presser[1] [pʀese] <1> **I.** *vt* (*hâter: cadence, pas*) to speed up; (*affaire, choses, personne*) to rush; (*départ, événement*) to hasten **II.** *vi* (*affaire*) to be urgent; **le temps presse** time is short ►**ça presse!** *inf* it's urgent! **III.** *vpr* **se ~** to hurry; **se ~ de** +*infin* to hasten to +*infin*

presser[2] [pʀese] <1> **I.** *vt* **1.** (*pour extraire un liquide, serrer avec les mains: fruit, jus, éponge*) to squeeze; (*pis d'une vache, raisin*) to press; ~ **qn contre soi/sa poitrine** to press sb against one/to one's chest **2.** (*comprimer*) ~ **qn contre le mur** to squash sb against the wall **II.** *vpr* **1.** (*se serrer*) **se ~ contre qn/qc** to squash up against sb/sth **2.** (*se bousculer*) **se ~ vers la sortie** to rush for the exit

pressing [pʀesiŋ] *m* **1.** (*teinturerie*) dry cleaner's **2.** SPORT pressure; **faire un ~** to put pressure on

pression [pʀɛsjɔ̃] *f* **1.** (*contrainte*) *a.* MED, METEO, PHYS pressure; **zone de haute/basse ~** high/low pressure zone; **subir des ~s** to be under pressure **2.** (*bouton*) press stud **3.** (*bière*) **bière (à la) ~** draught beer *Brit,* draft beer *Am* ►**être sous ~** to be under pressure

pressoir [pʀɛswaʀ] *m* **1.** (*machine*) press; (*pour le raisin*) wine press; ~ **à olives** olive press **2.** (*lieu*) press-house

pressurer [pʀesyʀe] <1> **I.** *vt* **1.** (*exploiter: contribuable, peuple*) to squeeze **2.** (*presser: pommes, raisin, olives*) to press; (*orange, citron*) to squeeze **II.** *vpr inf* **inutile de te ~ les méninges** it's no use racking your brains

pressurisé(e) [pʀesyʀize] *adj* pressurized

prestance [pʀɛstɑ̃s] *f* (*d'une personne*) presence; **avoir de la ~** to have good bearing

prestation [pʀɛstasjɔ̃] *f* **1.** THEAT, SPORT performance; ~ **télévisée** televised performance; **faire une excellente ~** to give an excellent performance **2.** *gén pl* (*services fournis*) services *pl;* ~ **en nature** payment in kind **3.** *pl* (*sommes versées*) benefits; ~**s familiales** family allowances (*including maternity and child benefit*); ~**s locatives** service charges (*on property*); ~**s sociales** social security allowances; ~**s de maladie** sickness benefit; ~**s d'invalidité** invalidity benefit; ~**s de vieillesse** old age pension

preste [pʀɛst] *adj soutenu* (*geste, main, mouvement*) deft; (*personne*) nimble

prestidigitateur, **-trice** [pʀɛstidiʒitatœʀ, -tʀis] *m, f* conjurer

prestidigitation [pʀɛstidiʒitasjɔ̃] *f* conjuring; **tour de** ~ conjuring trick

prestige [pʀɛstiʒ] *m* prestige

prestigieux, **-euse** [pʀɛstiʒjø, -jøz] *adj* (*lieu, événement, carrière, métier, école*) prestigious; (*objet, produits, artiste, scientifique*) renowned

présumé(**e**) [pʀezyme] *adj* (*auteur*) presumed

présumer [pʀezyme] <1> **I.** *vt* to assume; ~ **une issue heureuse/de bons résultats** to expect a happy outcome/good results; **je présume que tu es d'accord** I assume you agree **II.** *vi* **trop** ~ **de ses forces** to overtax oneself

prêt [pʀɛ] *m* **1.** (*action de prêter*) lending **2.** (*crédit, chose prêtée*) loan; ~ **à intérêt** interest-bearing loan

prêt(**e**) [pʀɛ, pʀɛt] *adj* **1.** (*préparé*) ~ **à cuire** ready to cook; ~ **à rôtir** oven-ready; **fin** ~ *inf* all set; **à vos marques;** ~**s? partez!** one your marks, get set, go! **2.** (*disposé*) ~ **à** +*infin* ready to +*infin*

prêt-à-porter [pʀɛtapɔʀte] *m sans pl* ready-to-wear

prétendant(**e**) [pʀetɑ̃dɑ̃, ɑ̃t] *m(f)* (*candidat*) ~ **à un poste** candidate for a post; ~ **au trône** pretender to the throne

prétendre [pʀetɑ̃dʀ] <14> *vt* **1.** (*affirmer*) to claim; **à ce qu'on prétend, il est ...** according to what people say, he is ... **2.** (*avoir la prétention de*) to seek; **je ne prétends pas vous convaincre** I do not seek to convince you

prétendu(**e**) [pʀetɑ̃dy] *adj antéposé* supposed; (*justice, liberté*) so-called

prête-nom [pʀɛtnɔ̃] <prête-noms> *m* figurehead

prétentieusement [pʀetɑ̃sjøzmɑ̃] *adv* pretentiously

prétentieux, **-euse** [pʀetɑ̃sjø, -jøz] **I.** *adj* (*personne, ton*) pretentious **II.** *m, f* pretentious individual

prétention [pʀetɑ̃sjɔ̃] *f* **1.** *sans pl* (*vanité*) pretentiousness; **maison sans** ~ unpretentious house; **repas sans** ~ simple meal; **avoir/ne pas avoir la** ~ **de** +*infin* to claim/not claim to +*infin;* **ce diplôme n'a pas la** ~ **de remplacer ...** this certificate does not seek to replace ... **2.** *gén pl* (*ce à quoi on prétend*) expectation; **avoir des** ~**s** to have expectations

prêter [pʀete] <1> **I.** *vt* **1.** (*avancer pour un temps: livre, voiture, parapluie*) to lend **2.** (*attribuer*) ~ **une intention à qn** to claim sb has an intention **II.** *vi* **1.** (*donner matière à*) ~ **à équivoque** to be ambiguous; ~ **à rire** to be laughable **2.** (*consentir un prêt*) ~ **à 8 %** to lend at 8 % **III.** *vpr* **1.** (*consentir*) **se** ~ **à un jeu** to get involved in a game **2.** (*être adapté à*) **se** ~ **à qc** to lend itself to sth

prêteur, **-euse** [pʀɛtœʀ, -øz] **I.** *adj* **être** ~ to lend things easily **II.** *m, f* lender; ~ **sur gages** pawnbroker

prétexte [pʀetɛkst] *m* (*raison apparente*) pretext; (*excuse*) excuse; **mauvais** ~ lame excuse; **sous aucun** ~ on no account; **sous** ~ **de manque de temps, elle est ...** using lack of time as an excuse, she is ...

prétexter [pʀetɛkste] <1> *vt* to give as an excuse; **elle prétexte qu'elle n'a pas le temps** she says that she hasn't got the time

prêtre [pʀɛtʀ] *m* REL priest

preuve [pʀœv] *f* **1.** (*indice probant, démonstration*) ~ **de qc** proof of sth; ~ **en main** concrete proof; **jusqu'à** ~ **du contraire** until there is proof to the contrary **2.** MAT ~ **par neuf** casting out of the nines ►<u>**faire**</u> ~ **de bonne volonté/courage** to show good will/courage; <u>**faire**</u> ~ **d'entêtement** to be stubborn; <u>**faire**</u> **ses** ~**s** (*élève*) to prove oneself; (*méthode*) to prove itself

prévaloir [pʀevalwaʀ] *irr* **I.** *vi soutenu* (*argument, opinion, droits, volonté*) to prevail; ~ **sur** [*o* **contre**] **qc** (*argument, opinion, volonté*) to prevail over sth; **les diplômes prévalent sur l'expérience** qualifications count for more than experience; **faire** ~ **son opinion/point de vue** to assert one's opinion/point of view; **faire** ~ **ses droits** to successfully assert one's rights; **il faut faire** ~ **la qualité sur la quantité** quality must win out over quantity **II.** *vpr soutenu* **1.** (*tirer avantage*) **se** ~ **de sa fortune** to take advantage of one's fortune **2.** (*se flatter*) **se** ~ **de ses titres** to vaunt one's titles

prévenance [pʀev(ə)nɑ̃s] *f* consideration; **être plein de** ~**s** to be full of consideration; **n'avoir aucune** ~ **pour qn** to show no consideration for sb

prévenant(**e**) [pʀev(ə)nɑ̃, ɑ̃t] *adj* (*personne, manières*) considerate; **être** ~ **avec** [*o* **envers**] **qn** to be considerate with sb

prévenir [pʀev(ə)niʀ] <9> **I.** *vt* **1.** (*aviser*) to tell; (*médecin, police*) to inform; ~ **qn de qc** to inform sb of sth **2.** (*avertir*) to warn; **tu es prévenu!** you have been warned! **II.** *vi* to warn; **arriver sans** ~ (*événement*) to happen without warning

préventif, **-ive** [pʀevɑ̃tif, -iv] *adj* preventative

prévention [pʀevɑ̃sjɔ̃] *f* **1.** (*mesures préventives*) prevention **2.** (*idée préconçue*) prejudice; **avoir des** ~**s contre qn/qc** to be

P

prejudiced against sb/sth

Prévention [pʀevɑ̃sjɔ̃] *f* (*organisme*) **la ~ routière** *road safety organization*

prévenu(e) [pʀev(ə)ny] **I.** *adj* **1.** JUR **être ~** to be charged; **être ~ d'un délit** to be charged with a crime **2.** (*qui a des préventions*) **être ~ contre qn/qc** to be biased against sb/sth; **être ~ en faveur de qn/qc** to be biased in favour of sb/sth *Brit,* to be biased in favor of sb *Am* **II.** *m(f)* JUR accused

prévisible [pʀevizibl] *adj* predictable; **difficilement ~** difficult to foresee

prévision [pʀevizjɔ̃] *f* (*d'un comportement, événement, phénomène*) prediction; (*des dépenses, recettes*) forecast; **les ~s météorologiques** the weather forecast; **au-delà de toute ~** beyond all expectations; **en ~ du départ** in anticipation of one's departure

prévisionnel(le) [pʀevizjɔnɛl] *adj* (*mesures, étude, analyse*) forward-looking; (*coûts*) projected

prévoir [pʀevwaʀ] *vt irr* **1.** (*envisager ce qui va se passer*) to foresee; **il faut ~ les conséquences de ses actes** one must consider the consequences of one's acts; **laisser ~ un malheur** to warn of an impending misfortune; **plus beau/moins cher que prévu** more beautiful/cheaper than expected **2.** (*projeter*) to plan; **leur arrivée est prévue pour 3 heures** their arrival is expected at 3 o'clock **3.** (*envisager*) to arrange for; (*casse-croûte, couvertures*) to provide; **c'est prévu** it is planned; **tout est prévu pour ton arrivée** everything is set up for your arrival

prévoyance [pʀevwajɑ̃s] *f* (*aptitude à prévoir*) foresight; **faire preuve de ~ pour le temps de la vieillesse** to make provision for one's old age; **manquer de ~** to lack foresight

prévoyant(e) [pʀevwajɑ̃, jɑ̃t] *adj* (*qui prend des précautions*) prudent; (*qui est apte à anticiper*) far-sighted; **des mesures ~es** contingency measures

prie-Dieu [pʀidjø] *m inv* prie-dieu

prier [pʀije] <1> **I.** *vt* **1.** REL to pray **2.** (*inviter, solliciter*) **~ qn de** *+infin* to ask sb to *+infin;* **se faire ~** to have people beg; **sans se faire ~** without waiting to be asked twice **3.** (*ordonner*) **~ qn de** *+infin* to order sb to *+infin* ►**je vous prie d'agréer mes sincères salutations/sentiments les meilleurs** yours sincerely; **je t'en/vous en prie** (*fais/faites donc*) go ahead; (*s'il te/vous plaît*) please; (*il n'y a pas de quoi, après un remerciement*) you're welcome; (*il n'y a pas de quoi, après une excuse*) it's nothing; **je te/vous prie!** please! **II.** *vi* REL **~ pour qn/qc** to pray for sb/sth

prière [pʀijɛʀ] *f* **1.** REL prayer; **faire sa ~** to say one's prayers **2.** (*demande*) plea; **à la ~ de qn** at sb's request; **j'ai une ~ à vous faire!** I have a request to make!; **~ d'essuyer ses pieds!** please wipe your feet! ►**tu peux faire ta ~!** *iron* say your prayers!

primaire [pʀimɛʀ] **I.** *adj* primary; **inspecteur ~** primary school inspector **II.** *m* ECOLE primary school; **être en ~** to be at primary school

primate [pʀimat] *m pl* ZOOL primate

primauté [pʀimote] *f* (*supériorité*) **~ de qc sur qc** primacy of sth over sth

prime [pʀim] *f* **1.** (*allocation, en complément du salaire*) bonus; (*subvention payée par l'État*) subsidy; **~ de fin d'année** Christmas bonus; **~ de risque** danger money; **~ de transport** transport allowance **2.** (*somme à payer*) **~ d'assurance** insurance premium ►**en ~** on top

primer [pʀime] <1> *vt* to award a prize; **film/livre primé** award-winning film/book

primesautier, -ière [pʀimsotje, -jɛʀ] *adj soutenu* impulsive

primeurs [pʀimœʀ] *fpl* early fruit and vegetables

primevère [pʀimvɛʀ] *f* primrose

primitif, -ive [pʀimitif, -iv] **I.** *adj* **1.** (*originel*) original; (*sentiment, passion*) initial; **état ~** original state; **les sept couleurs primitives** the seven colours of the spectrum *Brit,* to seven colors of the spectrum *Am;* **les terrains ~s** GEO primeval formations **2.** (*initial: préoccupation, projet*) original; MED early; **concept ~** basic concept; **proposition primitive** basic proposition; **cancer ~** cancer at an early stage **3.** SOCIOL primitive; **hommme ~** primitive man **4.** (*rudimentaire: installation, procédé*) primitive **5.** *péj* (*fruste: esprit, personne*) unsophisticated **6.** LING **langue primitive** primitive language; **mot ~** primitive word; **sens ~ d'un mot** original sense of a word; **concept ~** basic concept; **les temps ~s d'un verbe** the basic tenses of a verb **II.** *m, f* ART (*peintre*) primitive

primo [pʀimo] *adv* firstly

primordial(e) [pʀimɔʀdjal, jo] <-aux> *adj* **1.** (*essentiel: importance, rôle*) primordial; **être ~ pour qn/qc** to be paramount for sb/sth; **il est ~ que vous soyez à l'heure** it is vital for you to be on time **2.** (*fondamental*) fundamental; **droit ~** fundamental right

prince, princesse [pʀɛ̃s, pʀɛ̃sɛs] *m, f* prince, princess *m, f;* **~ charmant** prince charming; **~ héritier** crown prince ►**être bon ~** to be generous; **vivre comme un ~** to live like a king

princesse [pʀɛ̃sɛs] *f v.* **prince**

princier, -ière [pʀɛ̃sje, -jɛʀ] *adj* princely

principal [pʀɛ̃sipal, o] <-aux> *m* (*l'important*) **le ~** the main thing

principal(e) [pʀɛ̃sipal, o] <-aux> **I.** *adj* **1.** (*le plus important*) principal **2.** (*premier dans une hiérarchie*) **les principaux intéressés dans cette histoire** the ones most directly involved in this business; **les raisons ~es** the main reasons; **rôle ~ d'un film** leading role in a film **3.** LING **proposition ~e** main clause **II.** *m(f)* ECOLE principal

principale [pʀɛ̃sipal] *f* LING main clause

principalement [pʀɛ̃sipalmɑ̃] *adv* mainly

principauté [pʀɛ̃sipote] *f* principality
principe [pʀɛ̃sip] *m* **1.** (*règle de conduite*) *a.* PHYS, MAT principle; ~ **fondamental** fundamental principle; **avoir des ~s** to have scruples; **qn a pour ~ de** +*infin* it's a principle with sb to +*infin* **2.** (*hypothèse*) assumption; **poser des ~s** to make working assumptions ►**en** ~ in principle [*o* theory]; **par** ~ on principle; **pour le** ~ on principle
printanier, -ière [pʀɛ̃tanje, -jɛʀ] *adj* (*atmosphère, tenue*) spring; **robe printanière** summer dress
printemps [pʀɛ̃tɑ̃] *m* spring
prioritaire [pʀijɔʀitɛʀ] **I.** *adj* **1.** (*qui passe en premier*) priority; **être** ~ to have priority **2.** AUTO **être** ~ (*automobiliste, route*) to have the right of way **II.** *mf* (*personne*) person with priority; AUTO person who has the right of way
priorité [pʀijɔʀite] *f* priority; ~ **sur qn/qc** priority over sb/sth; **en** ~ as a priority; **avoir la** ~ to have priority; AUTO to have right of way; **il y a ~ à droite** vehicles coming from the right have the right of way
pris [pʀi] *passé simple de* **prendre**
pris(e) [pʀi, pʀiz] **I.** *part passé de* **prendre** **II.** *adj* **1.** (*occupé*) **être** ~ (*place*) to be taken; **avoir les mains ~es** to have one's hands full **2.** (*emploi du temps complet: personne*) busy **3.** (*en proie à*) **être ~ de peur/de panique** to be stricken with fear/panic; **être ~ d'envie de** +*infin* to get a great urge to +*infin*
prise [pʀiz] *f* **1.** (*action de prendre avec les mains*) hold; **maintiens bien la ~!** keep tight hold! **2.** (*poignée, objet que l'on peut empoigner*) grip; **lâcher** ~ to let go; *fig* to loosen one's grip **3.** (*animal capturé*) catch **4.** ELEC ~ **de courant** electrical socket; ~ **multiple** adaptor **5.** CINE shooting **6.** (*pincée: de tabac*) pinch; (*de drogue*) snort **7.** MED ~ **de sang** blood sample; **se faire faire une ~ de sang** to have a blood sample taken **8.** (*action d'assumer*) ~ **en charge** ADMIN *acceptance of medical costs by Social Security* **9.** *fig* ~ **de conscience** realization
prisé(e) [pʀize] *adj soutenu* appreciated
prisme [pʀism] *m* prism
prison [pʀizɔ̃] *f* prison
prisonnier, -ière [pʀizɔnje, -jɛʀ] **I.** *adj* (*en détention*) **être** ~ to be being held prisoner; (*soldat*) to be being held captive **II.** *m, f* prisoner; ~ **de guerre** prisoner of war; **faire qn** ~ to take sb prisoner
privation [pʀivasjɔ̃] *f* **1.** *soutenu* (*suppression*) deprivation; (*de la liberté, des droits civiques*) loss **2.** *pl* (*sacrifice*) privation; **vie de ~s** life of hardship
privatiser [pʀivatize] <1> *vt* to privatize
privé [pʀive] *m* **1.** (*vie privée*) private life; **dans le** ~ in private; **déclarations/conversation en** ~ private declarations/conversation; **confier qc à qn en** ~ to confide sth to sb in private **2.** ECON private sector
privé(e) [pʀive] **I.** *adj* (*opp: public*) private; **il est ici à titre** ~ he is here in a private capacity **II.** *m(f) inf* (*détective*) private detective
priver [pʀive] <1> **I.** *vt* **1.** (*refuser à*) ~ **qn de liberté** to deprive sb of their freedom **2.** (*faire perdre à*) ~ **qn de tous ses moyens** to leave sb completely helpless; **être privé d'électricité** to be without electricity **3.** (*frustrer*) ~ **qn de qc** to deprive sb of sth; **je ne veux pas vous** ~ I don't want to deprive you **II.** *vpr* **1.** (*se restreindre*) **se ~ pour qn** to make sacrifices for sb **2.** (*renoncer*) **se ~ de cigarettes/dessert** to deny oneself cigarettes/dessert; **se ~ de fumer** to go without smoking ►**ne pas se ~ de faire qc** to make sure one does sth
privilège [pʀivilɛʒ] *m* privilege
privilégié(e) [pʀivileʒje] **I.** *adj* (*avantagé*) privileged **II.** *m(f)* privileged person
privilégier [pʀivileʒje] <1> *vt* **1.** (*avantager*) to favour *Brit,* to favor *Am* **2.** (*donner la priorité*) ~ **qc** to lay great stress on sth
prix [pʀi] *m* **1.** (*coût, contrepartie*) price; ~ **d'ami** special price; ~ **coûtant** cost price; **dernier** ~ final offer; ~ **d'achat/de détail** purchase/retail price; ~ **de gros** wholesale price; **à ~ d'or** for a small fortune; **à bas** ~ cheaply; **à moitié** ~ half-price; **à ~ salé** at an steep price; **hors de** ~ terrifically expensive; **vendre au ~ fort** to charge the full price; **le ~ de la gloire/du succès** the price of glory/success; **à tout/aucun** ~ not at any/at any price **2.** (*valeur*) **de** ~ valuable; **ne pas avoir de** ~ to be priceless **3.** (*distinction, lauréat*) *a.* SPORT prize; ~ **d'interprétation** prize for best actor; ~ **Nobel** Nobel prize; **être un ~ Nobel de littérature/médecine** to be a Nobel prizewinner for litterature/medecine ►**c'est le même** ~ *inf* it comes to the same thing; **payer le ~ fort** to pay the full price; **mettre la tête de qn à** ~ to put a price on sb's head; **y mettre le** ~ to pay what it costs
Prix [pʀi] *m* **Grand** ~ (**automobile**) Grand Prix
prix-choc [pʀiʃɔk] <prix-chocs> *m* fantastic reductions
pro [pʀo] *mf inf abr de* **professionnel** pro
probabilité [pʀɔbabilite] *f* probability; **calcul des ~s** probability theory; **selon toute** ~ in all probability
probable [pʀɔbabl] *adj* probable
probablement [pʀɔbabləmɑ̃] *adv* probably; ~ **qu'il dira oui** he will probably say yes
probant(e) [pʀɔbɑ̃, ɑ̃t] *adj* (*argument, explication, raison*) convincing; (*document, témoignage*) probative
probatoire [pʀɔbatwaʀ] *adj* **période/stage** ~ probationary period/training period; **test** ~ preliminary test
probité [pʀɔbite] *f* (*d'un employé, fonctionnaire, serviteur*) honesty; (*du langage, de la pensée*) integrity
problématique [pʀɔblematik] **I.** *adj* (*qui pose problème*) problematic **II.** *f* issues *pl*

P

problème [pʀɔblɛm] *m* problem; **enfant/peau à ~s** *inf* problem child/skin; **ça me pose un ~** [*o* **des ~s**] that's a bit of a problem for me; (**y a**) **pas de ~!** *inf* no problem!; **faux ~** non-problem; **les ~s de circulation/stationnement** traffic/parking problems; **~ du logement/chômage** housing/unemployment problems; **~ de géométrie/de physique** geometry/physics problem

procédé [pʀɔsede] *m* **1.** (*méthode*) process; **~ de fabrication** manufacturing process **2.** *souvent pl* (*façon d'agir*) behaviour *Brit,* behavior *Am;* **user de bons/mauvais ~s à l'égard de qn** to behave well/badly towards sb

procéder [pʀɔsede] <5> *vi* (*agir*) to proceed; **~ par ordre** to do things in order

procédure [pʀɔsedyʀ] *f* **1.** (*marche à suivre*) procedure; **~s d'urgence** emergency procedures; **quelle est la ~ à suivre?** what is the correct procedure? **2.** JUR (*action en justice*) proceedings *pl;* **~ civile/pénale** civil/criminal proceedings; (*ensemble des règles juridiques*) civil/criminal law; **code de ~ pénale** penal code

procès [pʀɔsɛ] *m* JUR (*civil*) lawsuit; (*criminel*) trial; **être en ~ avec qn** to be involved in a lawsuit with sb ►**faire le ~ de qn/qc** to put sb/sth on trial

processeur [pʀɔsesœʀ] *m* INFOR processor

procession [pʀɔsesjɔ̃] *f a.* REL procession; **en ~** in procession

processus [pʀɔsesys] *m* **1.** (*évolution*) *a.* MED progress; (*biologique, physiologique*) process **2.** TECH (*ensemble d'opérations*) process; **~ de fabrication** manufacturing process

procès-verbal [pʀɔsɛvɛʀbal, o] <procès-verbaux> *m* **1.** (*contravention*) parking ticket; **dresser un ~ à qn** to give sb a parking ticket **2.** (*compte rendu: d'une réunion, séance*) minutes *pl* **3.** JUR (*constat*) report; **~ de perquisition** search report

prochain [pʀɔʃɛ̃] *m* (*être humain*) neighbour *Brit,* neighbor *Am*

prochain(e) [pʀɔʃɛ̃, ɛn] **I.** *adj* **1.** (*suivant*) next; **en août ~** next August **2.** *postposé* (*proche: arrivée, départ*) impending; (*mort*) imminent; (*avenir*) near **II.** *m(f)* (*personne ou chose suivante*) next one

prochaine [pʀɔʃɛn] *f inf* **1.** (*station*) next station **2.** (*fois*) **à la ~!** see you soon!

prochainement [pʀɔʃɛnmɑ̃] *adv* soon

proche [pʀɔʃ] **I.** *adj* **1.** (*à proximité: lieu*) near; **être ~ de qc** to be near sth; **un restaurant tout ~** a nearby restaurant; **la ville la plus ~** the nearest town; **~s l'un de l'autre** near to one another **2.** *antéposé* (*d'à côté: voisin*) next-door **3.** (*imminent*) imminent **4.** (*récent: événement, souvenir*) recent **5.** *antéposé* (*de parenté étroite: cousin, parent*) close; **être ~ de qn** (*par la pensée*) to be close to sb **6.** (*voisin*) **être ~ de qc** (*langue*) to be closely related to sth; (*prévision, attitude*) to be not far removed from sth ►**de ~ en ~** step by step **II.** *mf* **1.** (*ami intime*) close friend **2.** *mpl* (*parents*) **les ~s de qn** sb's close relatives [*o* family]

Proche-Orient [pʀɔʃɔʀjɑ̃] *m* **le ~** the Near East

proclamation [pʀɔklamasjɔ̃] *f* **1.** (*annonce publique*) announcement; (*de la république*) proclamation **2.** (*manifeste*) decree

proclamer [pʀɔklame] <1> **I.** *vt* **1.** (*affirmer, désigner comme: conviction, vérité*) to proclaim; (*innocence*) to declare; **~ qn empereur/roi** to proclaim sb emperor/king **2.** (*annoncer publiquement*) to announce; (*état de siège, république*) to declare **II.** *vpr* (*se déclarer*) **se ~ indépendant** to declare one's independence; **se ~ république autonome** to proclaim autonomy as a republic

procuration [pʀɔkyʀasjɔ̃] *f* proxy; COM power of attorney; **donner ~ à qn pour** +*infin* to give sb power of attorney to +*infin*

procurer [pʀɔkyʀe] <1> **I.** *vt* **1.** (*faire obtenir*) **~ qc à qn** to obtain sth for sb **2.** (*apporter: joie, ennuis*) to bring **II.** *vpr* (*obtenir*) **se ~ un travail** to get (oneself) a job

procureur [pʀɔkyʀœʀ] *m* JUR prosecutor; **~ général** public prosecutor

Procureur [pʀɔkyʀœʀ] *m* JUR **~ de la République** state prosecutor

prodigalité [pʀɔdigalite] *f* **1.** (*caractère dépensier*) extravagance **2.** *pl* (*dépenses excessives*) extravagance(s)

prodige [pʀɔdiʒ] *m* **1.** (*miracle*) miracle **2.** (*merveille*) marvel; **faire des ~s** to work wonders **3.** (*personne très douée*) prodigy ►**tenir du ~** to be astounding

prodigieusement [pʀɔdiʒjøzmɑ̃] *adv* (*beau, difficile*) fantastically; (*doué, intéressant*) incredibly; (*agacer, s'ennuyer*) beyond belief

prodigieux, **-euse** [pʀɔdiʒjø, -jøz] *adj* (*bêtise, effort, force*) prodigious; (*personne*) extraordinary

prodigue [pʀɔdig] *adj* **1.** (*dépensier*) extravagant **2.** (*généreux*) **être ~ de compliments** to be lavish with one's compliments; **il n'est pas ~ de paroles** to be a man of few words **3.** *postposé* (*qui a quitté sa famille: fils, père*) prodigal

prodiguer [pʀɔdige] <1> **I.** *vt* **1.** (*distribuer généreusement: biens*) to lavish; **~ le temps/l'énergie** to be lavish with one's time/energy; **~ des conseils/compliments à qn** to lavish advice/compliments on sb; **~ des paroles à qn** to shower words on sb; **~ son temps à qn/qc** to lavish time on sb/sth; **~ des soins à qn** to lavish care on sth **2.** (*gaspiller*) **~ qc à qn** to waste sth on sb **II.** *vpr* **se ~** to give of oneself unstintingly

producteur, **-trice** [pʀɔdyktœʀ, -tʀis] **I.** *adj* COM producing; **~ de blé** wheat-growing; **pays ~ de gaz naturel/charbon** natural gas-/coal-producing country; **les pays ~s de pétrole** the oil-producing countries **II.** *m, f* **1.** AGR grower **2.** (*fabricant*) manufacturer **3.** CINE, RADIO, TV producer

productif, -ive [pRɔdyktif, -iv] *adj* productive

production [pRɔdyksjɔ̃] *f* **1.** (*fait de produire*) production **2.** (*fabrication: de produits manufacturés*) production; **~ de voitures** car production; **~ d'électricité/énergie** electricity/energy generation **3.** (*exploitation*) **~ de blé/fruits** wheat-/fruit-growing; **~ de viande** meat production **4.** (*quantité produite*) production; (*d'énergie*) generation; AGR yield **5.** CINE, RADIO, TV production

productivité [pRɔdyktivite] *f* **1.** (*rendement: d'une usine, d'un employé, ouvrier*) productivity **2.** (*rentabilité: d'un service, impôt*) profitability

produire [pRɔdɥiR] *irr* **I.** *vt* **1.** ECON (*matières premières, produits manufacturés*) to produce; (*électricité*) to generate **2.** AGR, GEO (*cultivateur, arbre*) to grow; (*pays, région, terre*) to yield **II.** *vi* FIN to return **III.** *vpr* **se ~ 1.** (*survenir*) to happen; (*changement*) to take place; **le silence s'est produit** there was silence **2.** (*se montrer en public*) to appear in public **3.** (*se montrer sur la scène*) to appear on stage

produit [pRɔdɥi] *m* **1.** ECON, CHIM, BIO, MAT product; **~ alimentaire** foodstuff; **~s de beauté** cosmetics; **~ de première nécessité** vital commodities **2.** (*rapport, bénéfice*) **~ brut/net** gross/net profit; **~ intérieur brut** gross domestic product; **~ national brut** gross national product

proéminent(e) [pRɔeminɑ̃, ɑ̃t] *adj* (*front, menton, nez*) prominent

pro-européen(ne) [pRoøRɔpeɛ̃, ɛn] *m(f)* pro-European

prof *inf v.* **professeur**

profanation [pRɔfanasjɔ̃] *f* profanation

profane [pRɔfan] **I.** *adj* **1.** (*ignorant: auditoire, public*) lay; **je suis ~ en la matière** I'm uninitiated in the subject **2.** (*opp: religieux: musique*) profane; (*fête, monde*) secular **II.** *mf* (*non initié*) layman *m*, laywoman *f*; **les ~s** the uninitiated **III.** *m* REL **le ~** the profane

profaner [pRɔfane] <1> *vt* to profane

proférer [pRɔfeRe] <5> *vt* (*paroles, menaces*) to utter; **être proféré par qn** to be uttered by sb

professeur [pRɔfesœR] *mf* **1.** ECOLE teacher; **~ de lycée** school teacher; **~ des écoles** primary school teacher; **~ de français/de piano** French/piano teacher **2.** UNIV (*avec chaire*) professor; (*sans chaire*) lecturer

profession [pRɔfesjɔ̃] *f* profession; **exercer la ~ de qc** to follow the profession of sth

professionnalisme [pRɔfesjɔnalism] *m* professionalism

professionnel(le) [pRɔfesjɔnɛl] **I.** *adj* **1.** (*relatif à un métier: conscience, qualification, vie*) professional; (*cours, enseignement*) vocational; **lycée ~** technical school **2.** (*opp: amateur: écrivain, journaliste*) professional **3.** (*compétent*) adept **II.** *m(f)* **1.** (*homme de métier, personne compétente*) professional; **~ du tourisme/de l'enseignement** tourism/education professional **2.** SPORT **passer ~** *inf* to turn professional

professionnelle [pRɔfesjɔnɛl] *f inf* (*prostituée*) prostitute

professorat [pRɔfesɔRa] *m* teaching; **~ de mathématiques** mathematics teaching

profil [pRɔfil] *m* **1.** (*relief*) outline; **de ~** in outline **2.** (*silhouette, aptitudes*) *a.* INFOR profile; **~ utilisateur** user profile ▶**montrer son meilleur ~** to show one's best side

profilage [pRɔfilaʒ] *m* profiling

profiler [pRɔfile] <1> **I.** *vt* **1.** TECH to shape **2.** (*représenter en profil: corniche, édifice*) to profile; **~ un visage** to draw an outline of a face **3.** (*faire ressortir*) **le (mont) Cervin profilait au loin sa silhouette** the Matterhorn stood outlined in the distance **II.** *vpr* **se ~ 1.** (*se détacher: édifice, nuages, silhouette*) to stand out **2.** (*s'esquisser: ennuis, obstacles, solution*) to loom on the horizon

profit [pRɔfi] *m* **1.** COM, FIN profit **2.** (*avantage*) advantage; **mettre à ~ une situation pour** +*infin* to take advantage of a situation to +*infin;* **au ~ de qn/qc** (*concert*) in aid of sb/sth; (*activités*) for sb/sth

profitable [pRɔfitabl] *adj* **1.** (*avantageux: action*) beneficial; **être ~ à qn** (*avis, voyage, leçon*) to be of benefit to sb **2.** (*rentable: affaire*) profitable

profiter [pRɔfite] <1> *vi* **1.** (*tirer avantage de*) **~ d'une situation/d'une occasion** to take advantage of a situation/an opportunity **2.** (*être utile à*) **~ à qn** to benefit sb; (*repos, vacances*) to do sb good **3.** *inf* (*se fortifier*) to thrive; (*enfant*) to grow **4.** (*tirer un profit*) **~ dans un marché** to make a profit from a market

profiteur, -euse [pRɔfitœR, -øz] *m, f péj* profiteer

profond(e) [pRɔfɔ̃, ɔ̃d] **I.** *adj* **1.** (*qui s'enfonce loin*) deep; **~ de 50 m** 50 metres deep *Brit*, 50 meters deep *Am* **2.** (*très grand*) great; (*révérence, sommeil, nuit*) deep; (*sentiment*) profound; **dans la nuit ~e** in the dark of (the) night **3.** *postposé* (*caché: cause*) underlying; (*signification*) deep; (*tendance*) deep-rooted; **la France ~e** rural France **4.** (*opp: superficiel, léger: esprit, penseur, regard*) profound; (*pensée, réflexion, soupir, voix*) deep **5.** *postposé* MED (*arriéré, débile*) seriously; **handicapé ~** severely handicapped **II.** *adv* (*creuser, planter*) deep

profondément [pRɔfɔ̃demɑ̃] *adv* **1.** (*d'une manière profonde: s'incliner*) deeply; (*creuser, pénétrer*) deep **2.** (*beaucoup: respirer, aimer, réfléchir*) deeply; (*dormir*) soundly; (*influencer, ressentir*) profoundly; (*souhaiter*) sincerely; **se tromper ~** to be pro-

P

foundly mistaken **3.** *antéposé* (*très, tout à fait: choqué, ému, touché, vexé*) deeply, greatly; (*convaincu, différent*) profoundly

profondeur [pRɔfɔ̃dœR] *f* **1.** (*distance*) depth; **50 m de** ~ a depth of 50 metres *Brit,* a depth of 50 meters *Am* **2.** (*intensité: d'une voix*) deepness; (*d'un regard*) depth ►**en** ~ (*connaissance*) in-depth

profusion [pRɔfyzjɔ̃] *f* (*abondance*) profusion; (*de cadeaux*) abundance; **une** ~ **de lumières** a profusion of lights; **être baigné dans une** ~ **de lumière** to be bathed in a profusion of light ►**à** ~ in profusion

progéniture [pRɔʒenityR] *f* **1.** LIT (*descendance*) progeny **2.** *iron* (*enfants*) offspring

programmable [pRɔgRamabl] *adj* INFOR, TECH programmable

programmation [pRɔgRamasjɔ̃] *f* CINE, RADIO, TV, TECH, INFOR programming; **langage de** ~ programming language

programme [pRɔgRam] *m* **1.** (*objectif planifié*) plan; (*étapes*) programme *Brit,* program *Am;* ~ **d'action** plan of action; ~ **de recherches** research programme **2.** (*livret*) programme *Brit,* program *Am;* CINE, TV guide; **être au** ~ to be on **3.** ECOLE syllabus **4.** UNIV course ►**vaste** ~! *iron* that will take some doing!; **être au** ~ to be on the programme; CINE, TV to be on; **être hors** ~ not to be on the programme; ECOLE not to be on the syllabus; **c'est tout un** ~ that's quite a business

programmer [pRɔgRame] <1> *vt* **1.** CINE, TV to schedule **2.** THEAT to show **3.** (*établir à l'avance: journée, réjouissances, vacances*) to plan; **être programmé à dix heures** to be planned for ten o'clock **4.** TECH (*calculatrice*) to program; ~ **une machine à laver sur qc** to set a washing machine to sth

programmeur, **-euse** [pRɔgRamœR, -øz] *m, f* programmer

progrès [pRɔgRɛ] *m a.* ECOLE progress *no pl;* **faire des** ~ **en qc** to make progress in sth ►**il y a du** ~ *inf* there's progress; **on n'arrête pas le** ~ *inf* progress never stops

progresser [pRɔgRese] <1> *vi* **1.** (*s'améliorer*) to progress; (*conditions de vie*) to improve **2.** (*augmenter: difficultés*) to increase; (*prix, salaires*) to rise **3.** (*s'étendre: épidémie, incendie, inondation, idées*) to spread **4.** (*avancer: armée, explorateur, sauveteur, véhicule*) to advance

progressif, **-ive** [pRɔgResif, -iv] *adj* (*amélioration, évolution, transformation*) gradual; (*développement, difficulté, amnésie, paralysie*) progressive

progression [pRɔgRɛsjɔ̃] *f* **1.** (*amélioration*) progress; (*des conditions de vie, du bien-être*) improvement **2.** (*augmentation: du chômage, de l'alcoolisme*) increase; (*des prix, salaires*) rise **3.** (*extension, développement*) spread **4.** (*marche en avant: d'un explorateur, sauveteur, véhicule, d'une armée*) progress **5.** MAT progression

progressiste [pRɔgResist] *adj, mf* progressive

progressivement [pRɔgResivmɑ̃] *adv* progressively; (*procéder*) gradually

prohibé(**e**) [pRɔibe] *adj* forbidden

prohibitif, **-ive** [pRɔibitif, -iv] *adj* **1.** **tarif** ~ prohibitive rate **2.** JUR prohibitory

proie [pRwa] *f* (*opp: prédateur, victime*) prey ►**être en** ~ **à qc** to be plagued by sth

projecteur [pRɔʒɛktœR] *m* **1.** (*de cinéma, diapositives*) projector **2.** (*d'un bateau*) searchlight; (*d'un monument, stade*) floodlight ►**braquer les** ~**s sur qn/qc** to put the spotlight on sb/sth; **les** ~**s sont braqués sur qn/qc** the spotlight is on sb/sth

projectile [pRɔʒɛktil] *m* projectile; MIL missile

projection [pRɔʒɛksjɔ̃] *f* **1.** CINE, OPT projection; (*de diapositives, d'un film*) showing **2.** (*lancement: de lave*) ejection; (*de liquide, vapeur*) discharge; (*de pierres*) volley **3.** GEO, MAT, PSYCH projection

projectionniste [pRɔʒɛksjɔnist] *mf* projectionist

projet [pRɔʒɛ] *m* **1.** (*intention*) plan; (*programme*) project; ~ **de vacances** holiday plan; ~ **de film** plan for a film; ~ **de construction** building project **2.** (*ébauche, esquisse*) draft; ~ **de contrat** draft contract; ~ **de loi** bill

projeter [pRɔʒ(ə)te] <3> **I.** *vt* **1.** (*faire un projet*) to plan **2.** (*éjecter*) to throw; (*fumée*) to give off; (*étincelles*) to throw off **II.** *vpr* (*se refléter*) **se** ~ (*ombre, silhouette*) to be outlined

prolétaire [pRɔletɛR] **I.** *adj* working-class, proletarian *form* **II.** *mf* proletarian

prolétariat [pRɔletaRja] *m* proletariat

prolifération [pRɔlifeRasjɔ̃] *f* proliferation

proliférer [pRɔlifeRe] <5> *vi* to proliferate; (*crimes*) to multiply

prolifique [pRɔlifik] *adj* prolific

prolixe [pRɔliks] *adj* verbose

prolo [pRolo] *abr de* **prolétaire** **I.** *adj péj, inf* working class; (*sans manières*) common; **faire** ~ to have no class **II.** *mf péj, inf* prole

prologue [pRɔlɔg] *m* **1.** *a.* LIT, MUS, THEAT (*introduction*) prologue **2.** *fig* ~ **à un événement** prelude to an event

prolongation [pRɔlɔ̃gasjɔ̃] *f* **1.** (*allongement: d'un congé, délai, d'une trêve*) extension **2.** SPORT extra time *Brit,* overtime *Am* ►**jouer les** ~**s** SPORT to play extra time *Brit,* to play in overtime *Am; iron* to hang around

prolongé(**e**) [pRɔlɔ̃ʒe] *adj* (*de longue durée: arrêt, séjour*) lengthy; (*cri, rire*) long-drawn-out; (*débat, exposition au soleil*) prolonged; (*effort*) sustained

prolongement [pRɔlɔ̃ʒmɑ̃] *m* **1.** (*continuation*) continuation; (*d'une route*) extension **2.** (*appendice*) extension **3.** *gén pl* (*suites: d'une affaire, décision, d'un événement*) repercussions; **l'affaire aura des** ~**s** the affair will have repercussions

prolonger [pʀɔlɔ̃ʒe] <2a> **I.** *vt* **1.** (*faire durer davantage*) to prolong **2.** (*rendre plus long*) to extend; (*rue*) to continue **II.** *vpr* **se ~ 1.** (*durer: débat, séance*) to go on; (*trêve*) to hold out; (*effet, séjour*) to last; (*maladie*) to continue **2.** (*s'étendre en longueur: chemin, rue*) to continue

promenade [pʀɔm(ə)nad] *f* **1.** (*balade à pied*) walk; (*balade en bateau*) sail; (*balade à cheval*) ride; ~ **en voiture** drive; ~ **à/en vélo** bike ride; **faire faire une ~ à qn** to take sb for a walk **2.** (*lieu où l'on se promène en ville*) promenade **3.** (*lieu où l'on se promène à la campagne*) walk

promener [pʀɔm(ə)ne] <4> **I.** *vt* **1.** (*accompagner*) ~ **qn/un animal** to take sb/an animal for a walk **2.** (*laisser errer*) ~ **ses doigts sur le clavier** to strum the keyboard; ~ **son regard sur la plaine** to cast one's eyes over the plain ►**ça <u>me</u>/<u>le</u> promènera** *inf* it will get me/him out for a while **II.** *vpr* **1.** (*faire une promenade*) (**aller**) **se ~** (*animal, personne*) to go for a walk; (*à cheval*) to go for a ride; (*en bateau*) to go for a sail; **se ~ en voiture** to go for a drive; **se ~ à vélo** [*o* **en**] to go for a bike ride **2.** *fig* **se ~** (*rivière*) to run; (*chaussettes, livres, outils*) to lie about; (*imagination, regards*) to wander

promeneur, **-euse** [pʀɔm(ə)nœʀ, -øz] *m, f* walker

promesse [pʀɔmɛs] *f* (*engagement*) promise ►~ **en l'<u>air</u>** [*o* **de <u>Gascon</u>**] empty promise

prometteur, **-euse** [pʀɔmɛtœʀ, -øz] *adj* promising

promettre [pʀɔmɛtʀ] *irr* **I.** *vt* (*s'engager à, laisser présager*) to promise; ~ **une visite à qn** to promise to visit sb; ~ **le secret à qn** to promise to keep sb's secret; **ça je te le promets!** that I can promise you! ►**c'est promis <u>juré</u>** *inf* it's a promise **II.** *vi* **1.** (*faire une promesse*) to promise **2.** (*être prometteur*) to be promising ►**<u>ça</u> promet!** *iron* that's promising! **III.** *vpr* (*prendre la résolution de*) **se ~ de** +*infin* to promise oneself to +*infin*

promis(e) [pʀɔmi, iz] *adj* **être ~ à qn/qc** to be destined for sb/sth

promiscuité [pʀɔmiskɥite] *f* ~ **d'un taudis** the lack of privacy in a slum; ~ **du métro** overcrowding in the metro

promo [pʀomo] *f inf abr de* **promotion** year

promontoire [pʀɔmɔ̃twaʀ] *m* promontory

promoteur, **-trice** [pʀɔmotœʀ, -tʀis] *m, f* CONSTR ~ (**immobilier**) developer

promotion [pʀɔmosjɔ̃] *f* **1.** (*avancement*) promotion **2.** (*progression*) ~ **sociale** social advancement **3.** ECOLE year **4.** (*produit en réclame*) special offer

promotionnel(le) [pʀɔmosjɔnɛl] *adj* **1.** (*en promotion: produit*) on offer *Brit*, on sale *Am*; **vente ~le** promotional sale **2.** (*pour préparer la promotion: argument*) promotional; **matériel ~** promotional material

promouvoir [pʀɔmuvwaʀ] *vt irr* **1.** (*élever en grade*) ~ **un mécanicien** (**à la fonction de**) **contremaître** to promote a mechanic foreman **2.** (*soutenir: politique, recherche*) to further **3.** COM (*produit*) to promote

prompt(e) [pʀɔ̃(pt), pʀɔ̃(p)t] *adj* **1.** *antéposé* (*rapide: rétablissement*) rapid; (*décision*) swift; (*changement, départ*) sudden **2.** *postposé* (*geste*) quick; (*conclusion*) speedy **3.** *soutenu* (*vif: répartie*) ready; **avoir l'esprit ~** to be quick-witted; **être ~** (*réaction*) to come quickly; **il est ~ à l'injure** insults come quickly to his lips

promptitude [pʀɔ̃(p)tityd] *f soutenu* **1.** (*rapidité*) quickness; (*d'un changement, départ*) suddenness; **la ~ des secours** the speed with which help arrived **2.** (*vivacité: d'une réaction*) speed; (*d'une personne*) quick-wittedness; (*d'un esprit*) readiness; **la ~ de ses réparties** his lightning wit; ~ **à** +*infin* readiness to +*infin*

promulguer [pʀɔmylge] <1> *vt* (*loi, décret, édit*) to promulgate

prôner [pʀone] <1> *vt* to advocate

pronom [pʀɔnɔ̃] *m* pronoun

pronominal [pʀɔnɔminal, o] <-aux> *m* reflexive verb

pronominal(e) [pʀɔnɔminal, o] <-aux> *adj* pronominal; (*verbe*) reflexive

prononcé [pʀɔnɔ̃se] *m* JUR (*d'un arrêt, d'une sentence*) pronouncement

prononcé(e) [pʀɔnɔ̃se] *adj* (*trait, accent, goût pour qc*) pronounced; (*parfum*) strong

prononcer [pʀɔnɔ̃se] <2> **I.** *vt* **1.** (*articuler*) to pronounce **2.** (*dire, exprimer: parole*) to say; (*souhait*) to express; (*discours, plaidoyer*) to give **II.** *vpr* **1.** (*être articulé*) **se ~** (*lettre, mot, nom*) to be pronounced **2.** (*prendre position*) **se ~ pour/contre qn/qc** to pronounce oneself for/against sb/sth **3.** (*formuler son point de vue, diagnostic*) **se ~ sur qc** to give an opinion on sth

prononciation [pʀɔnɔ̃sjasjɔ̃] *f* **1.** LING pronunciation **2.** JUR pronouncement

pronostic [pʀɔnɔstik] *m* forecast

propagande [pʀɔpagɑ̃d] *f* propaganda ►**<u>faire</u> de la ~ à/pour qn/qc** to push sb/sth; POL to campaign for sb/sth

propagateur, **-trice** [pʀɔpagatœʀ, -tʀis] *m, f* propagator

propagation [pʀɔpagasjɔ̃] *f* **1.** (*extension*) propagation **2.** (*diffusion: d'une idée, nouvelle*) spreading

propager [pʀɔpaʒe] <2a> **I.** *vt* (*diffuser: idée, nouvelle*) to spread **II.** *vpr* **se ~** to spread

propane [pʀɔpan] *m* propane (gas)

Prophète [pʀɔfɛt] *m* **le ~** the Prophet (*Muhammed*)

prophète, **-esse** [pʀɔfɛt, -ɛs] *m, f* prophet ►**nul n'est ~ en son <u>pays</u>** *prov* a prophet is without honour in his own country *Brit*, a prophet is without honor in his own country *Am*

prophétie [pʀɔfesi] *f a.* REL prophesy

prophétique [pʀɔfetik] *adj* prophetic
propice [pʀɔpis] *adj* favourable *Brit,* favorable *Am*
proportion [pʀɔpɔʀsjɔ̃] *f* **1.** (*rapport*) proportion; **en ~ de qc** in proportion to sth **2.** *pl* (*taille, volume: d'une personne, d'un texte, édifice*) proportions; (*d'une recette*) quantities; **dans des ~s inattendues** in unexpected proportions ▶**toutes ~s gardées** relatively speaking
proportionné(e) [pʀɔpɔʀsjɔne] *adj* proportionate; **être ~ à qc** to be in proportion [*o* proportionate] to sth
proportionnel(le) [pʀɔpɔʀsjɔnɛl] *adj* proportional; **être ~ à qc** to be proportional to sth
proportionnelle [pʀɔpɔʀsjɔnɛl] *f* POL **la ~** proportional representation
proportionnellement [pʀɔpɔʀsjɔnɛlmɑ̃] *adv* proportionally
propos [pʀɔpo] *m gén pl* (*paroles*) words; **tenir des ~ inacceptables** to say unacceptable things ▶**bien/mal à ~** at the right/wrong time; **à tout ~** constantly; **à ~ de tout et de rien** for no reason; **juger à ~ de** +*infin* to think it appropriate to +*infin;* **à ce ~** in this connection; **hors de ~** irrelevant; **à quel ~?** on what subject?; **à ~** well-timed; **à ~ de qc** about sth
proposer [pʀɔpoze] <1> **I.** *vt* **1.** (*soumettre: plan, projet*) to propose; (*devoir, question, sujet*) to set; (*idée*) to suggest; (*décret, loi*) to put forward; **~ une nouvelle loi** (*gouvernement*) to propose a new law **2.** (*offrir: marchandise, paix, récompense, activité*) to offer; (*spectacle*) to propose **3.** (*présenter*) **~ qn pour un poste/comme collaborateur** to put sb forward for a job/as a partner **II.** *vpr* **1.** (*avoir pour objectif*) **se ~ un but** to set oneself a goal **2.** (*offrir ses services*) **se ~ à qn comme chauffeur** to offer sb one's services as a chauffeur
proposition [pʀɔpozisjɔ̃] *f* **1.** (*offre*) offer; **~ d'emploi** job offer; **~ de loi** private bill **2.** *pl* (*avances*) **des ~s** a proposition **3.** MAT proposition **4.** LING clause
propre[1] [pʀɔpʀ] **I.** *adj* **1.** (*opp: sale*) clean **2.** (*soigné: travail, intérieur, personne, tenue*) neat **3.** (*opp: incontinent: enfant*) toilet-trained; (*animal*) house-trained **4.** (*honnête: affaire, argent*) honest **5.** (*non polluant*) environmentally-friendly ▶**me/le voilà ~!** *inf* I'm/he's in a real mess! **II.** *m* **c'est du ~!** *inf* what a mess!; **mettre qc au ~** to copy out sth neatly
propre[2] [pʀɔpʀ] **I.** *adj* **1.** *antéposé* (*à soi*) own **2.** *postposé* (*exact: mot, terme*) proper; (*sens*) literal; **le sens ~ d'un mot** the literal meaning of a word **3.** (*particulier: biens, capitaux*) separate **II.** *m* **1.** (*particularité*) particularity **2.** LING **au ~ et au figuré** literally and figuratively **3.** (*propriété*) **en ~** as personal property
proprement [pʀɔpʀəmɑ̃] *adv* **1.** (*avec soin*) cleanly; (*manger*) properly **2.** (*avec honnêteté*) honestly
propreté [pʀɔpʀəte] *f* **1.** (*opp: saleté*) cleanliness **2.** (*caractère non polluant*) cleanness
propriétaire [pʀɔpʀijetɛʀ] *mf* **1.** (*possesseur*) owner; (*d'un animal*) master **2.** (*opp: locataire*) landlord **3.** (*bailleur*) lessor
propriété [pʀɔpʀijete] *f* **1.** (*domaine, immeuble*) ownership **2.** (*chose possédée*) property
propulser [pʀɔpylse] <1> **I.** *vt* **1.** (*projeter*) to propel **2.** *fig, inf* **~ qn à un poste** to propel sb into a job **II.** *vpr inf* (*jouer des coudes*) **se ~ jusque dans les premiers rangs** to thrust onself into the front row
propulsion [pʀɔpylsjɔ̃] *f* propulsion; **à ~ atomique** [*o* **nucléaire**] nuclear-powered
prorogation [pʀɔʀɔgasjɔ̃] *f* **1.** (*prolongation*) extension **2.** (*report*) deferment
prosaïque [pʀozaik] *adj* prosaic
proscrire [pʀɔskʀiʀ] *vt irr* **1.** (*interdire*) to ban **2.** HIST, POL (*bannir*) to banish; **~ qn d'un pays** to banish sb from a country
proscrit(e) [pʀɔskʀi, it] **I.** *adj* banished **II.** *m(f)* exile; HIST outlaw
prose [pʀoz] *f* **a.** LIT prose; **~ administrative** *péj* officialese
prosélytisme [pʀɔzelitism] *m* proselytism
prospecter [pʀɔspɛkte] <1> *vt* **1.** (*explorer*) to explore **2.** COM to canvass **3.** MIN to prospect
prospection [pʀɔspɛksjɔ̃] *f* **1.** COM canvassing; **faire de la ~** to go canvassing **2.** MIN prospecting
prospectus [pʀɔspɛktys] *m* prospectus
prospère [pʀɔspɛʀ] *adj* (*affaires, commerce, entreprise*) flourishing; (*mine, personne, santé*) prosperous; **période ~** period of prosperity
prospérer [pʀɔspeʀe] <5> *vi* **1.** (*réussir: affaires, commerce, entreprise*) to flourish **2.** (*croître, bien se porter*) to thrive
prospérité [pʀɔspeʀite] *f* **1.** (*richesse*) prosperity **2.** *soutenu* (*santé*) good health
prostate [pʀɔstat] *f* prostate
prosterner [pʀɔstɛʀne] <1> *vpr* **se ~ devant qn/qc** **1.** (*s'incliner profondément*) to bow low before sb/sth **2.** (*s'humilier*) to grovel to sb/sth
prostitué(e) [pʀɔstitɥe] *m(f)* prostitute
prostituer [pʀɔstitɥe] <1> **I.** *vt* **1. ~ une femme à qn** to prostitute a woman to sb **2.** *soutenu* (*déshonorer: art, talent*) to prostitute **II.** *vpr* **se ~** **a.** *fig* to prostitute oneself
prostitution [pʀɔstitysjɔ̃] *f* prostitution
prostré(e) [pʀɔstʀe] *adj* prostrate
protagoniste [pʀɔtagɔnist] *mf* protagonist
protecteur, -trice [pʀɔtɛktœʀ, -tʀis] **I.** *adj* **1.** (*défenseur*) protective; ECON, POL protectionist **2.** (*condescendant: air, ton*) patronizing **II.** *m, f* **1.** (*défenseur*) guardian **2.** (*mécène*) patron
protection [pʀɔtɛksjɔ̃] *f* **1.** (*défense*) ~

contre qc protection against sth; ~ **de l'enfance** child welfare; ~ **de l'environnement** environmental protection **2.** (*appui*) **avoir de hautes ~s** to have friends in high places **3.** (*élément protecteur*) safety device ►~ **sociale** social welfare; **mesures de** ~ protective measure

protégé(e) [pʀɔteʒe] **I.** *adj* (*site, territoire*) protected; (*passage*) priority **II.** *m(f)* (*favori*) protégé

protéger [pʀɔteʒe] <2a, 5> **I.** *vt* **1.** (*défendre*) ~ **qn/qc de/contre qn/qc** to protect sb/sth from sb/sth **2.** (*patronner: arts, carrière, sport*) to patronize; (*carrière, sport*) to sponsor **II.** *vpr* (*se défendre*) **se** ~ **contre qn/qc** to protect oneself from sb/sth

protège-tibia [pʀɔtɛʒtibja] <protège-tibias> *m* shin pad *Brit*, shin guard *Am*

protéine [pʀɔtein] *f* protein

protestant(e) [pʀɔtɛstɑ̃, ɑ̃t] *adj, m(f)* Protestant

protestantisme [pʀɔtɛstɑ̃tism] *m* protestantism

protestation [pʀɔtɛstasjɔ̃] *f* (*plainte*) protest; ~ **écrite** written complaint

protester [pʀɔtɛste] <1> *vi* (*s'opposer à*) to protest

prothèse [pʀɔtɛz] *f* **1.** (*organe artificiel*) prosthesis; ~ **dentaire** denture **2.** (*technique*) prosthetics + *vb sing*

prothésiste [pʀɔtezist] *mf* prosthetic technician; ~ **dentaire** dental technician

protocolaire [pʀɔtɔkɔlɛʀ] *adj* (*cérémonie, invitation, visite*) formal; **problème/question** ~ problem/question of protocol; **être/ne pas être** ~ to be keen/not too keen on etiquette

protocole [pʀɔtɔkɔl] *m* protocol

proton [pʀɔtɔ̃] *m* proton

protonotaire [pʀɔtonɔtɛʀ] *m* *Québec* (*fonctionnaire chargé de l'enregistrement des actes dans un bureau régional*) ≈ registrar

prototype [pʀɔtɔtip] *m* prototype

protubérance [pʀɔtybeʀɑ̃s] *f* **1.** (*saillie*) bulge **2.** ANAT protuberance **3.** ASTR prominence

proue [pʀu] *f* prow

prouesse [pʀuɛs] *f* (*exploit*) exploit ►**faire des ~s** to to do great work; *iron* to hit the heights

prout [pʀut] *m inf* pfft; **faire (un)** ~ to fart

prouver [pʀuve] <1> **I.** *vt* **1.** (*démontrer*) to prove; **il est prouvé que c'est vrai** it's been proved to be true; **il n'est pas prouvé que ce soit vrai** (*subj*) it hasn't been proved to be true **2.** (*montrer: amour*) to prove; (*reconnaissance*) to demonstrate; (*réponse, conduite*) to show **II.** *vpr* **se** ~ **1.** (*se convaincre: personne*) to prove oneself **2.** (*être démontrable: chose*) to be demonstrated

provenance [pʀɔv(ə)nɑ̃s] *f* (*origine*) origin ►**être en ~ de ...** to be from; **de même** ~ (*marchandises*) from the same source; **de toute** ~ from everywhere

provençal [pʀɔvɑ̃sal] *m* Provençal; *v. a.* **français**

provençal(e) [pʀɔvɑ̃sal, o] <-aux> *adj* Provençal

Provençal(e) [pʀɔvɑ̃sal, o] <-aux> *m(f)* Provençal

provençale [pʀɔvɑ̃sal] *f* GASTR **à la** ~ Provençale

Provence [pʀɔvɑ̃s] *f* **la** ~ Provence

provenir [pʀɔv(ə)niʀ] <9> *vi* **1.** (*venir de*) ~ **de qn/qc** to come from sb/sth **2.** (*être la conséquence de*) ~ **de qc** to result from; (*idée, sentiment*) to arise from

proverbe [pʀɔvɛʀb] *m* proverb; **comme dit le** ~ according to the proverb

proverbial(e) [pʀɔvɛʀbjal, jo] <-aux> *adj* proverbial

providence [pʀɔvidɑ̃s] *f* **1.** (*chance*) piece of luck **2.** REL providence **3.** *soutenu* (*personne secourable*) **être la ~ de qn** to save sb's life

providentiel(le) [pʀɔvidɑ̃sjɛl] *adj* **1.** (*personne*) providential; (*rencontre, voyage, pluie, nouvelle*) timely **2.** REL providential

province [pʀɔvɛ̃s] *f* province ►**la Belle Province** Quebec; **faire très** ~ *inf* to be very provincial

> In Belgium, there are seven **provinces**, which are similar to the French Départements. They have some autonomy but are overseen by the Federal state, communities and regions.

provincial(e) [pʀɔvɛ̃sjal, jo] <-aux> **I.** *adj* **1.** (*opp: parisien: air, manières, rythme, vie*) provincial **2.** *Québec* (*opp: fédéral: mesures, décision*) Provincial **II.** *m(f)* Provincial

proviseur [pʀɔvizœʀ] *m* **1.** headteacher *Brit*, principal *Am* **2.** *Belgique* (*adjoint du préfet* (*directeur de lycée*)) vice-principal

provision [pʀɔvizjɔ̃] *f* **1.** *pl* (*vivres*) provisions **2.** (*réserve*) ~ **d'eau** water reserves; **faire ~ de qc** to get in a stock of sth

provisoire [pʀɔvizwaʀ] **I.** *adj* **1.** (*opp: définitif*) *a.* JUR provisional; (*solution, mesure, installation*) temporary; (*bonheur, liaison*) fleeting **2.** (*intérimaire: gouvernement*) interim **II.** *m* **c'est du** ~ it's temporary

provisoirement [pʀɔvizwaʀmɑ̃] *adv* temporarily; **asseyez-vous là** ~ sit there for the moment

provoc [pʀɔvɔk] *f inf abr de* **provocation**

provocant(e) [pʀɔvɔkɑ̃, ɑ̃t] *adj* provocative

provocateur, -trice [pʀɔvɔkatœʀ, -tʀis] **I.** *adj* provocative; **agent** ~ agent provocateur **II.** *m, f* agitator

provocation [pʀɔvɔkasjɔ̃] *f* (*défi*) provocation; **faire de la** ~ to be provocative

provoquer [pʀɔvɔke] <1> **I.** *vt* **1.** (*causer*) to prompt; (*changement*) to bring about; (*colère, gaieté*) to provoke; (*mort, accident, explosion, révolte, désordre*) to cause **2.** (*énerver, aguicher*) to provoke **II.** *vpr* **se** ~ to provoke each other

proxénète [pʀɔksenɛt] *m* procurer

proximité [pʀɔksimite] *f* proximity; **à ~ de qc** near (to) sth ▸ **les magasins de ~** local shops

pruche [pʀyʃ] *f Québec* (*connifère apparenté au sapin*) hemlock spruce

prudemment [pʀydamɑ̃] *adv* **1.** (*avec précaution*) carefully **2.** (*par précaution*) wisely

prudence [pʀydɑ̃s] *f* caution; **avoir la ~ de** +*infin* to have the good sense to +*infin*

prudent(e) [pʀydɑ̃, ɑ̃t] *adj* (*personne*) careful; (*précaution*) prudent; (*pas*) cautious

prud'homme [pʀydɔm] *m: member of an industrial tribunal*

prune [pʀyn] *f* (*fruit*) plum ▸ **pour des ~s** *inf* for nothing

pruneau [pʀyno] <x> *m* **1.** GASTR prune **2.** *Suisse* (*quetsche*) plum

prunelle [pʀynɛl] *f* **1.** BOT sloe **2.** (*liqueur*) sloe liqueur **3.** (*eau-de-vie*) sloe gin **4.** ANAT pupil ▸ **tenir à qc comme à la ~ de ses yeux** to treat sth as one's greatest treasure

prunier [pʀynje] *m* plum tree ▸ **secouer qn comme un ~** *inf* to shake sb hard

prunus [pʀynys] *m* flowering cherry

prurit [pʀyʀit] *m* pruritus

PS [peɛs] *m* **1.** *abr de* **Parti socialiste** *French socialist party* **2.** *abr de* **post-scriptum** P.S.

psaume [psom] *m* psalm

pseudonyme [psødɔnim] *m* psuedonym

pseudo-savant [psødosaɑ̃] *m* pseudo-scientist

psy [psi] *mf inf abr de* **psychanalyste, psychiatre, psychologue** shrink

psychanalyse [psikanaliz] *f* psychoanalysis

psychanalyser [psikanalize] <1> *vt* to psychoanalyse *Brit*, to psychoanalyze *Am*; **se faire ~** to undergo psychoanalysis

psychanalyste [psikanalist] *mf* psychoanalyst

psychiatre [psikjatʀ] *mf* psychiatrist

psychiatrie [psikjatʀi] *f* psychiatry

psychiatrique [psikjatʀik] *adj* psychiatric

psychique [psiʃik] *adj* psychic

psycho [psikɔ] *f inf*, **psychologie** [psikolɔʒi] *f* psychology

psychologique [psikolɔʒik] *adj* psychological

psychologiquement [psikolɔʒikmɑ̃] *adv* psychologically

psychologue [psikolɔg] **I.** *adj* perceptive **II.** *mf* psychologist

psychose [psikoz] *f* MED psychosis; (~ *collective*) general hysteria

psychosomatique [psikosɔmatik] *adj* psychosomatic

psychothérapie [psikoteʀapi] *f* psychotherapy

psychotique [psikotik] *adj, mf* psychotic

PTT [petete] *mpl abr de* **Postes, Télégraphes, Téléphones** *French national postal and telecommunications company*

pu [py] *part passé de* **pouvoir**

puant(e) [pɥɑ̃, ɑ̃t] *adj* **1.** (*lieu*) stinking **2.** *inf* (*odieux*) insufferable

puanteur [pɥɑ̃tœʀ] *f* stink

pub¹ [pyb] *f inf abr de* **publicité**

pub² [pœb] *m* (*bar*) pub

puberté [pybɛʀte] *f* puberty

pubis [pybis] *m* pubis

public [pyblik] *m* **1.** (*assistance*) audience; (*spectateurs*) public; (*lecteurs*) readership; (*auditeurs*) listeners; **être bon ~** to be easy to please; **le grand ~** the general public **2.** (*tous*) public; **en ~** (*en présence de personnes*) in public

public, -ique [pyblik] *adj* (*commun, de l'État*) public; (*école*) state; **la rumeur publique veut que ce soit vrai** (*subj*) rumours going round say it's true *Brit*, rumors going around say it's true *Am*

publication [pyblikasjɔ̃] *f* publication

publiciste [pyblisist] *mf* publicist

publicitaire [pyblisitɛʀ] *adj* **pancarte ~** billboard; **vente ~** promotional sale

publicité [pyblisite] *f* **1.** CINE, TV (*dans la presse*) advertising; (*à la radio, télé*) commercial; **une page de ~** (*dans la presse*) a page of advertisements; (*à la radio, télé*) a commercial break **2.** (*réclame*) advertisement **3.** *sans pl* (*métier*) advertising **4.** *sans pl* (*action de rendre public*) publicity

publier [pyblije] <1> *vt* **1.** (*faire paraître: auteur, éditeur*) to publish **2.** (*rendre public*) to publicize; (*nouvelle*) to publish; (*communiqué*) to release

publiquement [pyblikmɑ̃] *adv* publicly

puce [pys] *f* **1.** ZOOL flea; **le marché aux ~s** the flea market **2.** INFOR chip; **ordinateur à ~ unique** single chip computer **3.** (*terme d'affection*) **viens, ma ~!** come here, dear! ▸ **mettre la ~ à l'oreille de qn** to get sb thinking; **secouer les ~s à qn** *inf* (*réprimander*) to tell sb off; (*dégourdir*) to wake sb up; **se secouer les ~s** to wake up

puceau, pucelle [pyso, pysɛl] <x> **I.** *adj inf* virgin **II.** *m, f inf* virgin

Pucelle [pysɛl] *f* **la ~ d'Orléans** the Maid of Orleans

puceron [pys(ə)ʀɔ̃] *m* greenfly

pudeur [pydœʀ] *f* **1.** (*décence*) modesty **2.** (*délicatesse*) decency; **ayez la ~ de vous taire!** have the decency to shut up!

pudique [pydik] *adj* **1.** (*chaste: comportement, personne, geste*) modest **2.** (*plein de réserve: personne*) discreet

pudiquement [pydikmɑ̃] *adv* **1.** (*par euphémisme*) discreetly **2.** (*chastement*) modestly

puer [pɥe] <1> **I.** *vi péj* to stink; **il pue des pieds** his feet stink **II.** *vt* **1.** *péj* (*empester*) ~ **le renfermé** to smell musty **2.** *péj, inf* (*porter l'empreinte de*) ~ **le fric** to stink of money

puériculteur, -trice [pɥeʀikyltœʀ, -tʀis] *m, f* nursery nurse

puéril(e) [pɥeʀil] *adj* puerile

puérilité [pɥeʀilite] *f* **1.** *sans pl* (*caractère puéril*) puerility **2.** (*chose peu digne d'un adulte*) childish nonsense *no pl;* **vraiment c'est d'une ~!** really, this is so childish!

pugilat [pyʒila] *m* fist fight

puis¹ [pɥi] *adv* then; **et ~ après** [*o* **quoi**]**?** *inf* so what?; **et ~ quoi encore!?** *inf* and what now?; **et ~** (*en outre*) and anyway

puis² [pɥi] *indic prés de* **pouvoir**

puiser [pɥize] <1> **I.** *vt* **1. ~ de l'eau dans qc** to draw water from sth **2.** *soutenu* (*aller chercher*) **~ dans la tristesse la force de vivre** to draw the strength to live from one's sadness **II.** *vi* **~ dans ses réserves** to draw on one's reserves

puisque [pɥisk(ə)] <puisqu'> *conj* since; **mais puisqu'elle est malade!** but she's ill, for heaven's sake!; **puisqu'il le faut!** if we must!

puissamment [pɥisamɑ̃] *adv* **1.** (*avec des moyens efficaces*) greatly **2.** (*à un haut degré*) powerfully

puissance [pɥisɑ̃s] *f* power; (*des éléments, du vent*) strength; **volonté de ~** lust for power; **grande ~** major power; **dix ~ deux** ten to the power of two

puissant(e) [pɥisɑ̃, ɑ̃t] **I.** *adj* **1.** (*d'une grande force*) strong **2.** (*qui a du pouvoir, qui a un grand potentiel économique ou militaire*) powerful **3.** (*très efficace*) potent **II.** *mpl* **les ~s** the powers

puisse [pɥis] *subj prés de* **pouvoir**

puits [pɥi] *m* **1.** (*pour l'eau*) well **2.** (*pour l'exploitation d'un gisement: d'une mine*) shaft; **~ de pétrole** oil well

pull [pyl] *m inf,* **pull-over** [pylɔvɛʀ, pylɔvœʀ] <pull-overs> *m* sweater

pulluler [pylyle] <1> *vi* **1.** (*être en grand nombre*) **des personnes/animaux pullulent** it's teeming with people/animals; **le gibier pullule ici** it's swarming with game round here **2.** (*être plein de*) **l'article pullulait d'inexactitudes** the article was a mass of inaccuracies **3.** (*proliférer*) to proliferate; **faire ~ des animaux** to make animals breed prolifically

pulmonaire [pylmɔnɛʀ] *adj* **tuberculose ~** pulmonary tuberculosis

pulpe [pylp] *f* (*chair*) pulp; **~ dentaire** dental pulp; **~ des doigts** the pad of the fingers

pulpeux, -euse [pylpø, -øz] *adj* (*lèvres*) full; (*femme*) curvaceous

pulsation [pylsasjɔ̃] *f* **1.** (*battement: du cœur*) beat; (*du pouls*) beating; **le nombre de ~s à la minute** the number of beats per minute; **son pouls bat à 80 ~s à la minute** his pulse is 80 to the minute **2.** ELEC pulsation; ELEC pulsatance

pulsion [pylsjɔ̃] *f* impulse; **~ sexuelle** sexual urge [*o* impulse]

pulvérisateur [pylveʀizatœʀ] *m* spray; **~ nasal/buccal** nasal/oral spray

pulvérisation [pylveʀizasjɔ̃] *f* spraying; (*d'un produit médicamenteux*) pulverization; **la ~ d'un produit détachant** spraying on a stain remover

pulvériser [pylveʀize] <1> *vt* **1.** (*vaporiser*) spray; **peinture à ~** spray paint **2.** (*réduire à néant*) to demolish **3.** *inf* (*battre très largement: adversaire*) to pulverize; (*armée*) to crush; (*record*) to smash **4.** (*réduire en poudre*) to pulverize

puma [pyma] *m* puma

punaise [pynɛz] *f* **1.** ZOOL bug **2.** (*petit clou*) drawing pin

punch [pœnʃ] *m inv* (*dynamisme*) drive; **avoir du ~** *inf* to have drive

punir [pyniʀ] <8> *vt* **1.** (*châtier*) **~ qn d'une peine d'emprisonnement** to punish sb with a prison sentence **2.** (*sévir*) **être puni de mort** to be punishable by death **3.** (*opp: récompenser*) **te voilà bien puni!** serves you right!

punitif, -ive [pynitif, -iv] *adj* punitive; *v.* **expédition**

punition [pynisjɔ̃] *f* punishment

punk [pœ̃k, pœnk] *adj inv, mf* (*personne*) punk

pupille¹ [pypij, pypil] *f* ANAT pupil

pupille² [pypij, pypil] *mf* ward; **~ de la Nation** *child of a member of the armed forces who dies in service;* **~ de l'État** *child in state care*

pupitre [pypitʀ] *m* **1.** INFOR console **2.** MUS (*d'un musicien, choriste*) music stand; (*d'un chef d'orchestre*) rostrum; (*d'un piano*) music rest **3.** (*meuble à plan incliné*) desk

pur(e) [pyʀ] *adj* **1.** (*non altéré: air, eau*) pure **2.** (*non mélangé*) neat **3.** (*authentique: vérité*) plain; (*hasard, méchanceté*) sheer; **mais c'est de la folie ~e!** but it's sheer madness! **4.** (*opp: appliqué: recherche, science, mathématiques*) pure **5.** (*innocent: cœur, amour*) innocent; (*regard*) clear; (*jeune fille*) pure; (*intentions*) honorable **6.** (*harmonieux: ligne, son*) flowing; (*profil*) flawless; (*langue, style*) pure ▶ **~ et <u>simple</u>** pure and simple; **un "non" ~ et simple** a straight "no"

purée [pyʀe] *f* purée; **~ de pommes de terre** mashed potatoes

purement [pyʀmɑ̃] *adv* purely; **~ et simplement** purely and simply

pureté [pyʀte] *f* **1.** (*opp: souillure*) purity **2.** (*perfection*) flawlessness **3.** (*innocence: des intentions*) honourableness *Brit,* honorableness *Am;* (*d'un regard, de l'enfance*) innocence

purgatif [pyʀgatif] *m* purgative

purgatif, -ive [pyʀgatif, -iv] *adj* **être ~** to be a purgative

purgatoire [pyʀgatwaʀ] *m* purgatory

purge [pyʀʒ] *f* **1.** (*action de vidanger: d'un radiateur*) bleeding; (*d'une huile, tuyauterie, chaudière*) draining; **robinet de ~** drainage valve **2.** POL, MED purge

purger [pyʀʒe] <2a> **I.** *vt* **1.** (*vidanger: conduite, tuyauterie, chaudière, huile*) to drain;

(*radiateur*) to bleed; ~ **qc d'eau** to drain the water from sth **2.** JUR (*peine*) to serve **3.** MED ~ **qn** to purge; **être purgé** to take a purge **4.** POL ~ **un parti de ses éléments subversifs** to purge the subversive elements in a party **II.** *vpr* **se** ~ to take a purge; (*animal*) to purge itself

purifier [pyʀifje] <1> **I.** *vt* to purify **II.** *vpr* **se** ~ **de qc** to cleanse oneself of sth

purin [pyʀɛ̃] *m* slurry

purisme [pyʀism] *m* purism

puriste [pyʀist] **I.** *adj* puristic **II.** *mf* purist

puritain(e) [pyʀitɛ̃, ɛn] **I.** *adj* **1.** puritan **2.** HIST Puritan **II.** *m(f)* **1.** puritan **2.** HIST Puritan

pur-sang [pyʀsɑ̃] <pur(s)-sang(s)> *m* thoroughbred

purulent(e) [pyʀylɑ̃, ɑ̃t] *adj* MED (*infection*) purulent; (*plaie*) suppurating

pus[1] [py] *m* pus

pus[2] [py] *passé simple de* **pouvoir**

pustule [pystyl] *f* pustule

putain [pytɛ̃] **I.** *f* **1.** *péj, vulg* whore; **faire la** ~ *vulg* (*se prostituer*) to walk the streets; *inf* (*s'avilir*) to sell out **2.** *péj, inf* ~ **de voiture** bloody car **II.** *interj* **1.** *inf* (*exprime la colère*) bugger *Brit,* dammit *Am;* (*exprime l'étonnement, l'incrédulité*) bugger me **2.** *Midi, inf* (*forme d'insistance*) ~**!** god! ►~ (**de bordel**) **de merde** *inf* bloody hell *Brit,* goddamn (son of a bitch) *Am*

pute [pyt] *f péj, vulg* whore

putois [pytwa] *m* polecat *Brit,* skunk *Am*

putréfaction [pytʀefaksjɔ̃] *f* (*d'un corps*) putrefaction; **cadavre en** ~ putrefying body; **dans un état** [*o* **en état**] **de** ~ **avancé** in a state of advanced putrefaction

putride [pytʀid] *adj* putrid

putsch [putʃ] *m* putsch

puzzle [pœzl, pœzœl] *m* jigsaw (puzzle)

PV [peve] *m abr de* **procès-verbal** report

pygmée [pigme] *adj* (*langue, littérature*) pygmy; **campement de** ~**s** pygmy encampment; **populations** ~**s** pygmy peoples

pyjama [piʒama] *m* pyjama; **en** ~(**s**) in pyjamas

pylône [pilon] *m* TECH, ARCHIT pylon; ~ **électrique** electicity pylon

pyramide [piʀamid] *f* pyramid; ~ **des âges** population pyramid

pyrénéen(ne) [piʀeneɛ̃, ɛn] *adj* Pyrenean

Pyrénéen(ne) [piʀeneɛ̃, ɛn] *m(f)* Pyrenean

Pyrénées [piʀene] *fpl* **les** ~ the Pyrenees

pyrex® [piʀɛks] *m* pyrex®

pyromane [piʀɔman] **I.** *adj* pyromaniac **II.** *mf* arsonist; PSYCH pyromaniac

python [pitɔ̃] *m* python

Q

Q, q [ky] *m inv* Q, q; ~ **comme Quintal** q as in Queenie *Brit,* q as in Queen *Am;* (*on telephone*) q for Queenie *Brit,* q for Queen *Am*

QCM [kyseɛm] *m abr de* **questionnaire à choix multiple** multiple choice question paper

QG [kyʒe] *m abr de* **quartier général** headquarters

QI [kyi] *m abr de* **quotient intellectuel** *inv* IQ

qu' [k] *v.* **que**

quadrature [k(w)adʀatyʀ] *f* squaring

quadrilatère [k(w)adʀilatɛʀ] *m* quadrilateral

quadrillage [kadʀijaʒ] *m* **1.** (*encadrement, action d'implanter un réseau*) covering; ~ **électoral** electoral division; **organiser un véritable** ~ **de la population** MED to organize the entire population into areas **2.** (*opération militaire, policière*) ~ **de qc** setting up controls throughout sth **3.** (*d'un papier*) squaring off; (*d'un tissu*) check patterning

quadrillé(e) [kadʀije] *adj* squared

quadriller [kadʀije] <1> *vt* **1.** (*procéder à une opération militaire, policière*) ~ **qc** to set up controls in sth **2.** (*tracer des lignes*) ~ **qc** to square sth off

quadrupède [k(w)adʀypɛd] **I.** *adj* four-footed **II.** *m* quadruped

quadruple [k(w)adʀypl] **I.** *adj* quadruple; **une** ~ **rangée de chaises** four rows of chairs **II.** *m* **le** ~ **du prix** four times the price; **il me l'a rendu au** ~ he gave it back to me fourfold

quadrupler [k(w)adʀyple] <1> **I.** *vi* (*se multiplier par quatre*) to increase fourfold **II.** *vt* (*multiplier par quatre*) ~ **qc** to increase sth fourfold

quadruplés, -ées [k(w)adʀyple] *mpl, fpl* quadruplets

quai [ke] *m* **1.** (*d'une gare, station de métro*) platform **2.** (*pour accoster*) quay **3.** (*voie publique*) embankment; **les** ~**s de la Seine** the banks of the Seine

qualificatif, -ive [kalifikatif, -iv] **I.** *adj* LING **adjectif** ~ qualifying adjective **II.** *m* (*expression*) qualifier

qualification [kalifikasjɔ̃] *f* **1.** SPORT qualification; **match de** ~ qualifier **2.** (*expérience*) ~ **professionnelle** professional qualification

qualifié(e) [kalifje] *adj* **1.** (*compétent: personne*) qualified **2.** (*formé*) skilled

qualifier [kalifje] <1> *vpr* SPORT **se** ~ **pour qc** to qualify for sth

qualitatif, -ive [kalitatif, -iv] *adj* (*analyse*) qualitative; **différence qualitative** qualitative difference

qualité [kalite] *f* quality; **de première** ~ top quality; ~**s morales** moral qualities

quand [kɑ̃] **I.** *adv* when; **depuis/jusqu'à** ~**?** since/till when?; **de** ~ **date ce livre?** when did this book come out? **II.** *conj* **1.** when;

quand elle arrivera when she arrives **2.** *inf* (*le moment où, le fait que*) when **3.** (*exclamatif*) ~ **je pense que ...!** when I think that ...! ►~ **même** (*malgré cela*) still; *inf* (*tout de même*) all the same; **tu aurais ~ même pu avertir** you could still have let us know

quant [kɑ̃t] *prep* (*pour ce qui concerne*) ~ **à qn/qc** as for sb/sth; ~ **à moi** as for me

quant-à-soi [kɑ̃taswa] *m inv* **rester sur son ~** to remain aloof

quantitatif, -ive [kɑ̃titatif, -iv] *adj* quantitative

quantité [kɑ̃tite] *f* **1.** (*nombre*) quantity; (*au sujet d'objets dénombrables, de personnes*) number; **être ~ négligeable** to be of no importance **2.** (*grand nombre*) (**une**) ~ **de personnes/choses** a large number of people/things; (**des**) ~**s de personnes/de choses** a great many people/things; (**des**) ~**s** a great many; **en ~** in large numbers

quarantaine [kaʀɑ̃tɛn] *f* **1.** (*environ quarante*) **une ~ de personnes/pages** about forty people/pages **2.** (*âge approximatif*) **avoir la ~** [*o* **une ~ d'années**] to be around forty; **approcher de la ~** to be getting on for forty; **avoir largement dépassé la ~** to be well over forty **3.** MED quarantine; *v. a.* **cinquantaine**

quarante [kaʀɑ̃t] **I.** *adj* forty; ~ **et un** forty-one; **semaine de ~ heures** forty-hour week **II.** *m inv* **1.** (*cardinal*) forty **2.** (*taille de confection*) **faire du ~** to take a size forty ►**les Quarante** *the forty members of the Académie française; v. a.* **cinq, cinquante**

quarantième [kaʀɑ̃tjɛm] **I.** *adj antéposé* fortieth **II.** *mf* **le/la ~** the fortieth **III.** *m* (*fraction*) fortieth; *v. a.* **cinquième**

quart [kaʀ] *m* **1.** (*quatrième partie d'un tout*) quarter; **trois ~s** three quarters; ~ **de finale** quarter final; ~ **de siècle** quarter of a century **2.** GASTR (*25 cl*) quarter litre *Brit,* quarter liter *Am* **3.** (*15 minutes*) quarter; **un ~ d'heure** quarter of an hour; (*dans le décompte des heures*) quarter; **il est 3 heures et/un ~** it's a quarter past three; **il est 4 heures moins le ~** it's a quarter to four **4.** (*partie appréciable*) quarter; **je n'ai pas fait le ~ de ce que je voulais faire** I haven't done half of what I wanted to; **les trois ~s de qc** the best part of sth; **les trois ~s du temps** most of the time ►**au ~ de poil** *inf* perfectly; **au ~ de tour** straight off; **passer un mauvais** [*o* **sale**] **~ d'heure** to have a miserable time

quartier [kaʀtje] *m* **1.** (*partie de ville*) district; ~ **résidentiel** residential area; **le Quartier latin** the Latin Quarter **2.** (*lieu où l'on habite, habitants*) neighbourhood *Brit,* neighborhood *Am;* **les gens du ~** the people living here **3.** *Suisse* (*banlieue*) ~ **périphérique** suburb ►**avoir ~ libre** (*être autorisé à sortir*) to have time to oneself; **ne pas faire de ~** to give no quarter

quart-monde [kaʀmɔ̃d] <quarts-mondes> *m* **1.** (*pauvreté*) **le ~** poverty; (*personnes défavorisées*) the poor **2.** (*pays les plus pauvres*) the Fourth World

quarto [kwaʀto] *adv soutenu* fourthly

quartz [kwaʀts] *m* quartz; **montre à ~** quartz watch

quasi [kazi] *adv* nearly; ~ **mort** as good as dead

quasi-certitude [kazisɛʀtityd] *f* practical certainty

quasiment [kazimɑ̃] *adv inf* practically

quasi-totalité [kazitɔtalite] <quasi-totalités> *f* **la ~ des enfants** virtually all the children

quaternaire [kwatɛʀnɛʀ] **I.** *adj* **ère ~** Quaternary era **II.** *m* Quaternary

quatorze [katɔʀz] **I.** *adj* (*cardinal*) fourteen ►**c'est reparti comme en ~** here we go again **II.** *m inv* fourteen; *v. a.* **cinq**

quatorzième [katɔʀzjɛm] **I.** *adj antéposé* fourteenth **II.** *mf* **le/la ~** the fourteenth **III.** *m* (*fraction*) fourteenth; *v. a.* **cinquième**

quatre [katʀ(ə)] **I.** *adj* (*cardinal*) four ►**monter l'escalier ~ à ~** to bound up the stairs four at a time; **descendre l'escalier ~ à ~** to dash down the stairs four at a time; **manger comme ~** to eat like a wolf; **boire comme ~** to drink like a fish; **un de ces ~** (**matins**) *inf* one of these days **II.** *m inv* four; *v. a.* **cinq**

quatre-heures [katʀœʀ] *m inv, inf* snack, tea *Brit* **quatre-quarts** [kat(ʀə)kaʀ] *m inv: large sponge cake* **quatre-quatre** [katkatʀə] *m o f inv* AUTO four-wheel drive

quatre-vingt [katʀəvɛ̃] <quatre-vingts> **I.** *adj* ~**s** eighty; ~ **mille** eighty thousand **II.** *m* ~**s** eighty; *v. a.* **cinq, cinquante**

quatre-vingt-dix [katʀəvɛ̃dis] **I.** *adj* ninety **II.** *m inv* ninety; *v. a.* **cinq, cinquante**

quatre-vingt-dixième [katʀəvɛ̃dizjɛm] <quatre-vingt-dixièmes> **I.** *adj antéposé* ninetieth **II.** *mf* **le/la ~** the ninetieth **III.** *m* (*fraction*) ninetieth; *v. a.* **cinquième**

quatre-vingtième [katʀəvɛ̃tjɛm] <quatre-vingtièmes> **I.** *adj antéposé* eightieth **II.** *mf* **le/la ~** the eightieth **III.** *m* (*fraction*) eightieth; *v. a.* **cinquième**

quatre-vingt-onze [katʀəvɛ̃ɔ̃z] **I.** *adj* ninety-one **II.** *m inv* ninety-one; *v. a.* **cinq, cinquante**

quatre-vingt-un, -une [katʀəvɛ̃œ̃, -yn] *adj, m inv* eighty-one; *v. a.* **cinq, cinquante**

quatre-vingt-unième [katʀəvɛ̃ynjɛm] **I.** *adj antéposé* eighty-first **II.** *mf* **le/la ~** the eighty-first **III.** *m* (*fraction*) eighty-first; *v. a.* **cinquième**

quatrième [katʀijɛm] **I.** *adj antéposé* fourth **II.** *mf* **le/la ~** the fourth **III.** *f* ECOLE fourth; *v. a.* **cinquième**

quatrièmement [katʀijɛmmɑ̃] *adv* fourthly

quatuor [kwatɥɔʀ] *m* **1.** (*œuvre, musiciens*) quartet; ~ **à cordes** string quartet **2.** *inf* (*clique*) foursome

que [kə] <qu'> **I.** *conj* **1.** (*introduit une com-*

plétive) that; **je ne crois pas qu'il vienne** I don't think (that) he'll come **2.** (*dans des formules de présentation*) **peut-être** ~ perhaps **3.** (*dans des questions*) **qu'est-ce ~ c'est?** what is it?; **qu'est-ce que c'est ~ ça?** *inf* what's that?; **quand/où est-ce ~ tu pars?** when/where are you going? **4.** (*reprend une conjonction de subordination*) **si tu as le temps et qu'il fait beau** if you've got the time and the weather's nice **5.** (*introduit une proposition de temps*) **ça fait trois jours qu'il est là** he's been here for four days now **6.** (*introduit une proposition de but*) so (that); **taisez-vous qu'on entende l'orateur!** keep quiet so we can hear the speaker! **7.** (*pour comparer*) **plus/moins/autre ...** ~ more/less/other than; (**tout**) **aussi ...** ~ as ... as; **autant de ...** ~ as many [*o* much] ... as; **tel** ~ such as **8.** (*seulement*) only; **il ne fait ~ travailler** all he does is work; **il n'est arrivé qu'hier** he only arrived yesterday; **la vérité, rien ~ la vérité** the truth and nothing but the truth **II.** *adv* (*comme*) (**qu'est-ce**) ~ **c'est beau!** how lovely it is! **III.** *pron rel* **1.** (*complément direct se rapportant à un substantif*) which, that; **ce** ~ what; **chose** ~ which; **quoi ~ tu dises** whatever you (may) say **2.** (*après une indication de temps*) **un jour qu'il faisait beau** one day when it was fine; **toutes les fois qu'il vient** every time he comes; **le temps ~ la police arrive, ...** by the time the police arrive, ... **IV.** *pron interrog* **1.** (*quelle chose?*) what?; **qu'est-ce ~ ...?** what ...?; **ce** ~ what **2.** (*attribut du sujet*) what; ~ **deviens-tu?** how are you doing?; **qu'est-ce ~ ...?** what ...?; **ce** ~ what **3.** (*quoi*) What ▸**qu'est-ce qui vous prend?** what's the matter with you?

Québec [kebɛk] *m* **1.** (*ville*) Quebec **2.** (*région*) **le** ~ Quebec

québécisme [kebesism] *m* French-Canadianism

québécois(e) [kebekwa, waz] *adj* Quebec

Québécois(e) [kebekwa, waz] *m(f)* Quebecker

quel(le) [kɛl] **I.** *adj* **1.** (*dans une question*) what; (*lequel*) which; ~ **temps fait-il?** what's the weather like?; **~le heure est-il?** what's time is it?; ~ **est le plus grand des deux?** which (one) is bigger?; **je me demande ~le a pu être sa réaction** I wonder what his reaction was; ~ **que soit son choix** (*subj*) whatever he chooses; **~les que soient les conséquences, ...** whatever the consequences (may be), ... **2.** (*exclamation*) what; ~ **dommage!** what a shame!; ~ **talent!** what talent! **II.** *pron* which; **de nous deux, ~ est le plus grand?** which of us is taller?

quelconque [kɛlkɔ̃k] *adj* **1.** (*n'importe quel*) **un ...** ~ any **2.** (*ordinaire*) run-of-the-mill; (*médiocre*) indifferent

quelque [kɛlk] **I.** *adj indéf, antéposé* **1.** *pl* (*plusieurs*) some, a few; **à ~s pas d'ici** not far from here **2.** *pl* (*petit nombre*) **les ~s fois où ...** the few times that ... **II.** *adv* ~ **peu** somewhat; **et ~(s)** *inf* **10 kg et ~s** just over ten kilograms; **cinq heures et ~(s)** just after five o'clock

quelque chose [kɛlkəʃoz] *pron* something; ~ **de beau** something beautiful; **c'est déjà ~!** that's something ▸**apporter un petit ~ à qn** *inf* to bring sb a little something; **prendre un petit ~** *inf* (*une collation*) to have a bite (to eat); (*un petit verre*) to have a quick drink; **il a dû y avoir ~ entre qn et qn** there must have been something going on between sb and sb; **c'est ~** (**tout de même**)! *inf* really!; **être pour ~ dans qc** to have something to do with sth; ~ **comme** something like

quelquefois [kɛlkəfwa] *adv* sometimes

quelque part [kɛlkpaʀ] *adv* somewhere

quelques-uns, -unes [kɛlkəzœ̃, -yn] *pron indéf* **1.** (*un petit nombre de personnes*) a few **2.** (*certaines personnes*) some people **3.** (*certains*) **quelques-unes des personnes/choses** some of the people/things; **j'en ai mangé ~/quelques-unes** I ate some

quelqu'un [kɛlkœ̃] *pron indéf* (*une personne*) somebody, someone; ~ **d'autre** somebody else

quémander [kemɑ̃de] <1> *vt* ~ **qc** to beg for sth; ~ **des secours à qn** to try to wheedle help out of sb

qu'en-dira-t-on [kɑ̃diʀatɔ̃] *m inv* **se moquer du** ~ not to care about gossip [*o* what people say]

quenelle [kənɛl] *f* GASTR quenelle (*poached meat or fish dumpling in sauce*); **~s de veau/brochet** veal/pike quenelles

quenotte [kənɔt] *f enfantin, inf* tooth, toothy peg *Brit*

quéquette [kekɛt] *f enfantin, inf* willy

querelle [kəʀɛl] *f* quarrel; **une ~ sur qc** a quarrel over sth; **provoquer une** ~ to lead to a quarrel; ~ **de famille** family quarrel; ~ **d'amoureux** lovers' quarrel [*o* tiff]; **la ~ des Anciens et des Modernes** *debate over literary styles in the 17th century* ▸**~s de clocher** petty quarrels; **~s byzantines** abstruse arguments; **chercher ~ à qn** (*provoquer*) to goad sb into an argument; (*chercher à provoquer*) to egg sb on; **embrasser** [*o* **épouser**] **la ~ de qn** to take sb's side; **vider une** ~ *soutenu* to settle a quarrel

quereller [kəʀele] <1> *vpr* **se ~ avec qn à propos de qc** to quarrel with sb over sth

qu'est-ce que [kɛskə] *pron interrog* what

qu'est-ce qui [kɛski] *pron interrog* who

question [kɛstjɔ̃] *f* **1.** (*demande*) *a.* INFOR question; **la ~ est: ...** the question is, ...; **poser une ~ à qn** to ask sb a question; **sans poser de ~s** without asking questions; (**re**)**mettre qc en** ~ to call sth into question; **~s courantes** frequently asked questions **2.** (*problème*) **c'est une ~ de temps** it's a question [*o* matter] of time; **c'est** (**toute**) **la** ~ that's the big question; **ce n'est pas la** ~ that's not the question [*o* issue] **3.**(*domaine*) **c'est une ~ d'habitude** it's a question of habit **4.**(*ensemble de problèmes soulevés*) question; **la ~ du chômage/pétrole** the unemployment/oil question [*o* issue]; **la ~ du trou d'ozone** the issue of the ozone layer ►**il est ~ de qn/qc** (*il s'agit de*) it's a matter of sb/sth; (*on parle de*) people are talking about sb/sth; **il n'est pas ~ de qc** there's no question of sth; **hors de ~** out of the question; **pas ~!** *inf* no way!; **~ qc, ...** *inf* as for sth, ...

questionnaire [kɛstjɔnɛʀ] *m* **1.**(*formulaire*) question paper; **~ à choix multiple** multiple choice question paper **2.**(*série de questions*) questionnaire

questionner [kɛstjɔne] <1> *vt* (*interroger*) **~ qn sur qc** to question sb about sth

question-piège [kɛstjɔ̃pjɛʒ] <questions-pièges> *f* trick question

quête [kɛt] *f* (*collecte d'argent*) collection; **faire la ~** (*dans la rue: association*) to do a collection; (*chanteur des rues*) to pass the hat around

quêter [kete] <1> *vi* **~ pour qn/qc** to make a collection for sb/sth

quetsche [kwɛtʃ] *f* **1.**(*fruit*) quetsche plum **2.**(*eau-de-vie*) plum brandy

queue [kø] *f* **1.** ZOOL tail **2.** BOT stalk **3.**(*manche: d'une casserole, poêle*) handle; **~ de billard** billiard cue *Brit,* pool cue *Am* **4.** AUTO (*d'un train, métro*) rear **5.** *inf* (*pénis*) cock **6.**(*file de personnes*) queue; **faire la ~** to queue (up) *Brit,* to line up *Am;* **se mettre à la ~** to get in the queue ►**être rond comme une ~ de pelle** *inf* to be blind drunk; **faire une ~ de poisson à qn** to cut sb up; **n'avoir ni ~ ni tête** to make no sense; **à la ~ basse** *inf* with one's tail between one's legs

qui [ki] **I.** *pron rel* **1.**(*comme sujet se rapportant à une chose*) which, that; (*comme sujet se rapportant à une personne*) who, that; **toi ~ sais tout** you who think you know it all; **le voilà ~ arrive** here he comes; **j'en connais ~ ...** i know someone who ...; **c'est lui/elle ~ a fait cette bêtise** he/she was the one that did this stupid thing; **ce ~ ...** (*servant de sujet*) what; (*se rapportant à une phrase principale*) which; **ce ~ se passe est grave** what's going on is serious; **chose ~ ...** something which ... **2.**(*comme complément, remplace une personne*) **la dame à côté de ~ tu es assis/tu t'assois** the lady (that) you're sitting/you sit next to; **l'ami dans la maison de ~ ...** the friend in whose house ...; **la dame à ~ c'est arrivé** the lady it happened to **3.**(*celui qui*) whoever; **~ fait qc ...** (*introduisant un proverbe, dicton*) he who does sth ... ►**c'est à ~ criera le plus fort** everyone was trying to shout louder than the others; **~ que tu sois** (*subj*) whoever you are; **je ne veux être dérangé par ~ que ce soit** (*subj*) I don't want to be disturbed by anybody **II.** *pron interrog* **1.**(*qu'est-ce que*) **~ ...?** who ...?; **~ ça?** who's that ...?; **~ c'est qui est là?** who's there? **2.**(*question portant sur la personne complément direct*) **~ ...?** who, whom *form;* **~ as-tu vu?** who did you see?; **~ croyez-vous?** who do you believe? **3.**(*question portant sur la personne complément indirect*) **à/avec ~ as-tu parlé?** who did you speak to/with?; **pour ~ as-tu voté?** who did you vote for?; **chez ~ est la réunion?** whose house is the meeting at? **4.**(*marque du sujet, personne ou chose*) **qui est-ce ~ ...?** who ...?; **qu'est-ce ~ ...?** what ...?

quiche [kiʃ] *f* **~** (**lorraine**) quiche (lorraine)

quiconque [kikɔ̃k] **I.** *pron rel* (*celui qui*) **~ veut venir** anyone who wants to come **II.** *pron indéf* (*personne*) **hors de question que ~ sorte** there's no question of anyone leaving; **elle ne veut recevoir d'ordres de ~** she won't take orders from anyone

qui est-ce que [kiɛskə] *pron interrog* (*question portant sur une personne en position complément*) **~ ...?** who, whom *form;* **avec/pour ~ tu l'as fait?** who did you do it with/for?

qui est-ce qui [kiɛski] *pron interrog* (*question portant sur une personne en position sujet*) **~ ...?** who ...?

quignon [kiɲɔ̃] *m* **~** (**de pain**) chunk of bread

quille [kij] *f* **1.** JEUX skittle *Brit,* ninepin *Am;* **jouer aux ~s** to play skittles **2.** *inf* (*fin du service militaire*) demob *Brit;* (*sortie de prison*) getting out

quilleur, -euse [kijœʀ, -øz] *m, f Québec* (*personne qui joue aux quilles*) skittles player *Brit,* ninepins player *Am*

quincaillerie [kɛ̃kɑjʀi] *f* hardware store

quinconce [kɛ̃kɔ̃s] *m* **en ~** in a quincunx

quinine [kinin] *f* (*médicament*) quinine; **comprimés de ~** quinine tablets

quinquagénaire [kɛ̃kaʒenɛʀ, kɥɛ̃kwaʒenɛʀ] **I.** *adj* **homme/femme ~** fifty-year-old man/woman; **être ~** to be fifty **II.** *mf* (*personne*) fifty-year-old

quinquennal(e) [kɛ̃kenal, o] <-aux> *adj* (*qui a lieu tous les cinq ans*) quinquennial

quinquennat [kɛ̃kena] *m* five-year mandate

quintal [kɛ̃tal, o] <-aux> *m* quintal

quinte [kɛ̃t] *f* MED **~ de toux** fit of coughing

quinté [kɛ̃te] *m: bet on five horses*

quintette [k(ɥ)ɛ̃tɛt] *m* quintet

quintupler [kɛ̃typle] <1> **I.** *vi* (*se multiplier par cinq*) to increase fivefold **II.** *vt* (*multiplier par cinq*) **~ qc** to increase sth fivefold

quintuplés, -ées [kɛ̃typle] *mpl, fpl* quintuplets

quinzaine [kɛ̃zɛn] *f* **1.**(*environ quinze*) **une ~ de personnes/pages** around fifteen people/pages **2.**(*deux semaines*) **revenir dans une ~** (**de jours**) to come back in two weeks [*o* a fortnight *Brit*]; **la première ~ de janvier** the first half [*o* two weeks] of January

quinze [kɛ̃z] **I.** *adj* fifteen; **tous les ~ jours**

Q

every two weeks **II.** *m inv* **1.** (*cardinal*) fifteen **2.** SPORT **le ~ d'Irlande** the Ireland team; *v. a.* **cinq**

quinzième [kɛ̃zjɛm] **I.** *adj antéposé* fifteenth **II.** *mf* **le/la ~** the fifteenth **III.** *m* (*fraction*) fifteenth; *v. a.* **cinquième**

quiproquo [kipʀɔko] *m* mistake; **~ entre le mari et l'amant** confusion over the identities of the husband and the lover

quittance [kitɑ̃s] *f* receipt; **faire une ~ à qn** to give sb a receipt

quitte [kit] *adj* **1.** (*sans dettes*) **être ~ de qc** to be clear of sth **2.** (*au risque de*) **~ à faire qc** even if it means doing sth

quitter [kite] <1> *vt* **1.** (*prendre congé de, rompre avec, sortir de, partir de*) to leave; **ne quittez pas** TEL hold the line; **~ l'école** to leave school; **ils ont quitté Paris** they've left Paris **2.** (*ne plus rester sur*) **la voiture a quitté la route** the car went off the road **3.** INFOR **~ un logiciel** [*o* **un programme**] to quit a program

qui-vive [kiviv] *m inv* **être/rester sur le ~** to be/stay on the alert

quoi [kwa] **I.** *pron rel* **1.** (*annexe d'une phrase principale complète*) **..., ce à ~ il ne s'attendait pas** ..., which he didn't expect; **ce en ~ elle se trompait** ..., but she was mistaken there **2.** (*dans une question indirecte*) **elle ne comprend pas ce à ~ on fait allusion** she doesn't understand what they're alluding to; **ce sur ~ je veux que nous discutions** what I want us to discuss **3.** (*comme pronom relatif*) **à/de ~ ...** to/about which ...; **voilà de ~ je voulais te parler** that's what I wanted to talk to you about; **voilà à ~ je pensais** that's what I was thinking about **4.** (*cela*) **..., après ~ ...** ..., after which ... **5.** (*ce qui est nécessaire pour*) **de ~ faire qc** the things need for doing sth; **as-tu de ~ écrire?** have you got something to write with?; **elle n'a pas de ~ vivre** she has nothing to live on; **il y a de ~ s'énerver, non?** it's enough to make you mad, isn't it?; **il est très fâché – il y a de ~!** he's really angry – he's every reason to be!; **il n'y a pas de ~ rire** it's nothing to laugh about ►**il n'y a pas de ~!** you're welcome; **avoir de ~** *inf* to have means; **~ que ce soit** (*subj*) anything; **si tu as besoin de ~ que ce soit, ...** (*subj*) if there's anything you need, ...; **elle n'a jamais dit ~ que ce soit** (*subj*) she never said anything (at all); **~ qu'il en soit** (*subj*) be that as it may; **comme ~** *inf* (*pour dire*) saying; **comme ~ on peut se tromper!** which just goes to show you can make mistakes!; **~ que** whatever **II.** *pron interrog* **1.** + *prép* **à ~ penses-tu** [*o* **est-ce que tu penses**]**?** what are you thinking about?; **dites-nous à ~ cela sert** tell us what it's for; **de ~ n'est-elle pas capable/a-t-elle besoin?** is there anything she's not capable of/she needs?; **cette chaise est en ~?** *inf* what's this chair made of?; **par ~ commençons-nous?** where do we begin? **2.** *inf* (*qu'est-ce que*) what?; **c'est ~, ce truc?** what is this thing?; **tu sais ~?** you know what?; **~ encore?** what's that?; **tu es idiot, ou ~?** *inf* are you stupid or what? **3.** (*qu'est-ce qu'il y a de ...?*) **~ de neuf?** what's new?; **~ de plus facile/beau que ...?** is there anything easier/lovelier than ...? **4.** *inf* (*comment?*) what? ►**de ~(, de ~)?** *inf* what's all this? **III.** *interj* **1.** (*marque la surprise: comment!*) **~!** what! **2.** *inf* (*en somme*) **..., ~!** ..., eh!; **il n'est pas bête, il manque un peu d'intelligence, ~!** he's not stupid, he's just not very clever, you know!

quoique [kwak(ə)] *conj* although

quolibet [kɔlibɛ] *m* taunt

quota [k(w)ɔta] *m* quota

quote-part [kɔtpaʀ] <quote-parts> *f* share

quotidien(ne) [kɔtidjɛ̃, jɛn] **I.** *adj* **1.** (*journalier*) daily; **vie ~ne** daily life; (*train-train*) everyday life **2.** (*banal: tâches*) everyday **II.** *m* **1.** (*journal*) daily (paper); **un ~ du matin/soir** a morning/evening daily **2.** (*vie quotidienne*) daily life; (*train-train*) everyday life

quotidiennement [kɔtidjɛnmɑ̃] *adv* daily

quotient [kɔsjɑ̃] *m* quotient

R

R, r [ɛʀ] *m inv* R, r; **rouler les ~** to roll one's Rs; **~ comme Raoul** r for Robert *Brit,* r for Roger *Am*

rab [ʀab] *m inf* **il y a du ~** there's some left over; **faire du ~** to do overtime

rabâchage [ʀabɑʃaʒ] *m* **1.** (*répétition fastidieuse: d'une leçon*) constantly going over things; **faire du ~** to keep churning out the same stuff **2.** (*radotage*) rambling on; **c'est du ~** it's always the same old thing

rabâcher [ʀabɑʃe] <1> *vt* (*ressasser*) **~ la même chose à qn** to keep coming out with the same old thing (to sb)

rabais [ʀabɛ] *m* discount; **faire 20 % de ~** to take 20 % off; **au ~** (*avec réduction de prix*) at a reduced price; (*de mauvaise qualité*) second-rate; **travailler au ~** to work for next to nothing; **vente au ~** cut-price sale

rabaisser [ʀabese] <1> *vt* (*dénigrer*) to belittle; **~ ses exigeances** to lower one's expectations

rabat [ʀaba] *m* **1.** (*partie rabattue: d'une poche, enveloppe*) flap; **faire un joli ~** (*en faisant le lit à la française*) to fold the sheet down nicely **2.** (*revers de col: d'une toge*) bands *pl*

rabat-joie [ʀabaʒwa] *mf inv* killjoy

rabatteur [ʀabatœʀ] *m* (*d'une moissonneuse*) reel

rabattre [ʀabatʀ] *irr* **I.** *vt* **1.** (*refermer*) **~ qc**

to put sth down; ~ **le capot de la voiture** to close the bonnet **2.** (*faire retomber*) **le vent rabattait la pluie sur le toit** the wind was driving the rain against the roof **3.** (*faire un rabais*) **le commerçant rabat 5 % sur le prix affiché** the shopkeeper's taking 5 % off the marked price **4.** (*à la chasse*) ~ **le gibier** to drive game **5.** COUT ~ **les mailles de son tricot** to decrease the stitches of one's knitting ▶~ **le caquet à qn** to shut sb up; **en** ~ to climb down; (*changer d'avis*) to change one's tune **II.** *vpr* **se** ~ **1.** (*changer de direction*) to cut in; **le coureur s'est rabattu à la corde** the runner moved over to the inside lane **2.** (*accepter faute de mieux*) **se** ~ **sur qn/qc** to fall back on sb/sth

rabbin [ʀabɛ̃] *m* REL rabbi

rabibocher [ʀabibɔʃe] <1> **I.** *vt inf* **1.** (*réconcilier*) ~ **un couple** to get a couple back together **2.** (*rafistoler*) to patch up **II.** *vpr inf* **se** ~ to get back together (again)

râble [ʀɑbl] *m* **1.** ANAT back **2.** GASTR ~ **de lapin à la moutarde** saddle of hare with mustard ▶**tomber sur le** ~ **à qn** *inf* to lay into sb

râblé(e) [ʀɑble] *adj* (*personne*) stocky; (*animal*) broad-backed

rabot [ʀabo] *m* plane

raboter [ʀabɔte] <1> *vt* TECH (*planche*) to plane (down)

rabougri(e) [ʀabugʀi] *adj* (*personne*) stunted; (*plante*) shrivelled

rabrouer [ʀabʀue] <1> *vt* to snub

racaille [ʀakɑj] *f* scum

raccard [ʀakaʀ] *m Suisse* (*grange à blé*) wheat barn

raccommodage [ʀakɔmɔdaʒ] *m* (*réparation*) mending; **faire du** ~ to do some mending

raccommoder [ʀakɔmɔde] <1> **I.** *vt* (*réparer: linge*) to mend; (*chaussettes*) to darn **II.** *vpr inf* **se** ~ to get back together

raccompagner [ʀakɔ̃paɲe] <1> *vt* ~ **qn à la maison** (*à pied*) to walk sb home; (*en voiture*) to drive sb home

raccord [ʀakɔʀ] *m* **1.** (*jonction*) join **2.** (*retouche*) touch up **3.** (*enchaînement*) continuity; CINE link shot **4.** (*joint*) link ▶**faire un** ~ *inf* (*de maquillage*) to fix one's make-up

raccordement [ʀakɔʀdəmɑ̃] *m* linking; ELEC connecting

raccorder [ʀakɔʀde] <1> **I.** *vt* (*joindre: tuyaux, routes*) to connect; ~ **une ville à la ligne de TGV** to link a town to the TGV line; **il faut** ~ **les différents plans** CINE the various shots need to be linked; ~ **qn au réseau** TEL to connect sb **II.** *vpr* **se** ~ **à qc 1.** (*se relier: route, voie de chemin de fer*) to link up to sth **2.** (*se rapporter: événement*) to tie in with sth

raccourci [ʀakuʀsi] *m a.* INFOR shortcut; ~ **clavier** keyboard shortcut

raccourcir [ʀakuʀsiʀ] <8> **I.** *vt* (*rendre plus court: texte, vêtement*) to shorten **II.** *vi* **1.** (*devenir plus court*) to get shorter **2.** (*au lavage: vêtement*) to shrink

raccrocher [ʀakʀɔʃe] <1> **I.** *vi* **1.** TEL to hang up **2.** *inf* SPORT (*renoncer: professionnel*) to retire **II.** *vpr* (*se cramponner*) **se** ~ **à qn/qc** to grab hold of sb/sth

race [ʀas] *f* **1.** (*groupe ethnique*) race **2.** (*espèce zoologique, sorte*) breed; **quelle sale** ~**!** *péj* what a rotten lot!; **être de la même** ~ to be of the same breed; **je suis de la** ~ **des gens qui sont toujours optimistes** I'm one of those people who are always optimistic; **cheval de** ~ thoroughbred horse; **chien/chat de** ~ pedigree dog/cat

racé(e) [ʀase] *adj* **1.** (*cheval*) thoroughbred; (*chien, chat*) pedigree **2.** (*personnes*) well-bred

rachat [ʀaʃa] *m* **1.** JUR, FIN buying back; (*d'une rente*) redemption; (*d'un titre*) transfer **2.** (*pardon: d'une faute*) reparation; (*d'un péché*) expiation **3.** (*salut*) redemption **4.** (*libération sous caution*) ransoming **5.** (*d'une entreprise*) buyout

racheter [ʀaʃte] <4> **I.** *vt* **1.** (*acheter en plus*) ~ **du vin** to buy some more wine **2.** (*acheter d'autrui*) ~ **une table à qn** to buy a table from sb **3.** (*se libérer de*) ~ **une dette** to redeem a debt **II.** *vpr* **se** ~ **d'un crime** to make amends for a crime

rachitique [ʀaʃitik] *adj* **1.** MED suffering from rickets **2.** (*chétif: personne*) puny

racial(e) [ʀasjal, jo] <-aux> *adj* **haine** ~**e** racial hatred

racine [ʀasin] *f* (*origine*) *a.* BOT root; **la** ~ **du mal** the root of the problem ▶**prendre** ~ to take root

racisme [ʀasism] *m* (*théorie des races, hostilité*) racism; ~ **anti-jeunes** prejudice against young people

raciste [ʀasist] *adj, mf* racist

racket [ʀakɛt] *m* racket

racketter [ʀakete] <1> *vt* to run a protection racket; ~ **qn** to extort money from sb

racketteur, -euse [ʀakɛtœʀ, -øz] *m, f* racketeer

raclée [ʀɑkle] *f inf* **1.** (*volée de coups*) hiding **2.** (*défaite*) thrashing

racler [ʀɑkle] <1> **I.** *vt* **1.** (*nettoyer, frotter*) to scrape; **le garde-boue racle le pneu** the mudguard [*o* fender *Am*] is scraping against the tyre [*o* tire *Am*]; (*casserole*) to scrape; (*boue, croûte*) to scrape off **2.** (*ratisser: sable*) to rake **II.** *vpr* **se** ~ **la gorge** to clear one's throat

raclette [ʀɑklɛt] *f* **1.** GASTR (*spécialité, fromage*) raclette (*cheese melted and served on potatoes*) **2.** (*grattoir*) scraper

racolage [ʀakɔlaʒ] *m* **1.** (*recrutement*) touting; **faire du** ~ to tout **2.** (*action d'une prostituée*) solliciting

racoler [ʀakɔle] <1> *vt* (*électeurs, adeptes*) to canvass; ~ **des clients** to tout for customers; (*prostituée*) to solicit

racontar [ʀakɔ̃taʀ] *m gén pl, inf* piece of gossip; ~**s** gossip

R

raconter [ʀakɔ̃te] <1> *vt* **1.** (*narrer*) ~ **une histoire à qn** to tell sb a story; ~ **un voyage** to relate a journey **2.** (*dire à la légère*) ~ **des histoires** to talk nonsense; **c'est du moins ce qu'elle raconte** at least, that's what she says ►~ **sa vie à qn** *inf* to tell sb one's life story; **j'au perdu mon porte-feuille, je te/vous raconte pas!** *inf* I lost my wallet, I'll spare you the details!

radar [ʀadaʀ] **I.** *m* radar **II.** *app* **contrôle-~** speed trap

rade [ʀad] *f* harbour *Brit,* harbor *Am* ►**être/rester en** ~ *inf* to be/have been left stranded

radeau [ʀado] <x> *m* raft; ~ **de fortune** makeshift raft; ~ **de sauvetage** life raft

radiateur [ʀadjatœʀ] *m* (*de chauffage central*) *a.* AUTO radiator

radiation [ʀadjasjɔ̃] *f* **1.** PHYS radiation **2.** (*action de rayer*) removal; ~ **du barreau** disbarment; ~ **des listes électorales** removal from the electoral register

radical [ʀadikal, o] <-aux> *m* LING root

radical(**e**) [ʀadikal, o] <-aux> *adj* **1.** (*total*) drastic; (*refus*) total **2.** (*énergique*) radical **3.** (*foncier*) fundamental; **instinct** ~ basic instinct; **principe** ~ radical principle; **islam** ~ radical Islam

radicalement [ʀadikalmɑ̃] *adv* **1.** (*entièrement*) completely **2.** (*absolument*) **des opinions** ~ **opposées** radically opposed views

radicaliser [ʀadikalize] <1> **I.** *vt* (*conflit*) to intensify; (*position*) to harden; ~ **une opinion/théorie** to make an opinion/theory more radical **II.** *vpr* **se** ~ (*parti, régime, théorie*) to become more radical; (*conflit*) to intensify; (*position*) to harden

radier [ʀadje] <1> *vt* (*candidat, nom*) to remove; ~ **un avocat du barreau** to disbar a lawyer; ~ **un médecin** to strike off a doctor

radieux, **-euse** [ʀadjø, -jøz] *adj* radiant

radin(**e**) [ʀadɛ̃, in] **I.** *adj inf* (*avare*) tightfisted **II.** *m(f) inf* skinflint, tightwad *Am*

radiner [ʀadine] <1> *vpr inf* **allez, radinetoi!** come on, get a move on!

radinerie [ʀadinʀi] *f inf* stinginess

radio [ʀadjo] *f* **1.** (*poste*) radio; **allumer/éteindre la** ~ to turn on/off the radio **2.** (*radiodiffusion*) radio (broadcasting); **passer à la** ~ (*personne*) to be on the radio; (*chanson*) to get played on the radio **3.** (*station*) radio station; ~ **locale libre** independent local radio (station) **4.** MED X-ray; **passer une** ~ to have an X-ray

radioactif, **-ive** [ʀadjoaktif, -iv] *adj* radioactive

radioactivité [ʀadjoaktivite] *f* radioactivity

radioamateur, **-trice** [ʀadjoamatœʀ, -tʀis] *m, f* radio ham

radiodiffusé(**e**) [ʀadjodifyze] *adj* broadcast (on radio)

radiographie [ʀadjɔgʀafi] *f* MED **1.** (*procédé*) radiography **2.** (*cliché*) X-ray

radiographier [ʀadjɔgʀafje] <1a> *vt* MED (*malade, organe*) to X-ray; **se faire** ~ to be X-rayed

radiologue [ʀadjɔlɔg] *mf* radiologist

radiophonique [ʀadjɔfɔnik] *adj* **pièce** ~ radio play

radio-réveil [ʀadjoʀevɛj] <radios-réveils> *m* clock radio **radio-taxi** [ʀadjotaksi] <radio-taxis> *m* radio cab

radiotélévisé(**e**) [ʀadjotelevize] *adj* **message** ~ **du chef de l'État** message from the Head of State broadcast simultaneously on radio and television

radis [ʀadi] *m* radish; ~ **noir** black radish **2. ça ne vaut pas un** ~ *inf* it's not worth a penny [*o* red cent *Am*]

radium [ʀadjɔm] *m* radium

radotage [ʀadɔtaʒ] *m* **1.** (*rabâchage*) rambling **2.** *inf* (*papotage*) babbling

radoter [ʀadɔte] <1> *vi* **1.** (*rabâcher*) to keep harping on **2.** (*déraisonner*) to witter on

radoucir [ʀadusiʀ] <8> *vpr* **se** ~ **1.** (*se calmer: personne*) to soften **2.** METEO (*température, temps*) to get milder

radoucissement [ʀadusismɑ̃] *m* **1.** (*apaisement*) soothing; (*de l'humeur*) calming; (*de la voix*) softening **2.** (*de la température*) rise; (*du temps*) warming

RAF [ɛʀaɛf] *f abr de* **Royal Air Force** RAF

rafale [ʀafal] *f* METEO gust; ~ **de neige** flurry of snow; ~ **de vent/pluie** gust of wind/rain; **le vent souffle en ~s** it's blustery

raffermir [ʀafɛʀmiʀ] <8> *vpr* **se** ~ (*devenir ferme: voix*) to steady; (*peau, muscles*) to tone up; (*chair*) to firm up

raffinage [ʀafinaʒ] *m* refining

raffiné(**e**) [ʀafine] *adj* (*délicat*) subtle; (*goût, cuisine, personne*) refined; (*esprit*) discriminating

raffinement [ʀafinmɑ̃] *m* **1.** (*délicatesse: du goût, des manières, d'une personne*) refinement **2.** *pl* (*recherche*) niceties; (*d'une toilette*) sophistication + *vb sing* **3.** (*manifestation extrême d'un sentiment*) ~ **de cruauté** refined cruelty

raffiner [ʀafine] <1> *vt* **1.** ECON (*pétrole, sucre, métaux, papier*) to refine **2.** (*affiner: goût, langage*) to polish

raffinerie [ʀafinʀi] *f* ~ **de pétrole/sucre** oil/sugar refinery

raffoler [ʀafɔle] <1> *vi* ~ **de qn/qc** to be wild about sb/sth

raffut [ʀafy] *m inf* racket ►**faire du** ~ (*faire un scandale*) to kick up a stink

rafiot [ʀafjo] *m inf* tub; **un vieux** ~ an old tub

rafistoler [ʀafistɔle] <1> *vt inf* (*chaussures, meuble*) to patch up

rafle [ʀafl] *f* (*arrestation*) raid; **être pris dans une** ~ to be caught in a raid

rafler [ʀafle] <1> *vt inf* **1.** (*voler: bijoux*) to run off with **2.** (*remporter: prix*) to walk off with

rafraîchir [ʀafʀeʃiʀ] <8> *vpr* **se** ~ **1.** (*deve-

nir plus frais: air, temps, température) to get colder **2.** (*boire*) to have a cool drink **3.** (*se laver, arranger sa toilette, son maquillage*) to freshen up

rafraîchissant(**e**) [ʀafʀeʃisɑ̃, ɑ̃t] *adj* **1.** (*apportant la fraîcheur: boisson, averse, brise*) refreshing **2.** (*tonifiant*) invigorating

rafraîchissement [ʀafʀeʃismɑ̃] *m* **1.** (*boisson*) cold drink **2.** INFOR **vitesse de ~ de la mémoire** memory refresh rate

rafting [ʀaftiŋ] *m* **faire du ~** to go white-water rafting

ragaillardir [ʀagajaʀdiʀ] <8> *vt* (*boisson, repos*) to perk up; (*nouvelle*) to buck up

rage [ʀaʒ] *f* **1.** (*colère*) rage; **être fou de ~** to be absolutely furious **2.** (*passion*) passion; **la ~ de vivre** an insatiable lust for life **3.** MED **la ~** rabies

rageant(**e**) [ʀaʒɑ̃, ɑ̃t] *adj* **c'est ~** *inf* it's maddening

rager [ʀaʒe] <2a> *vi inf* to be furious

rageur, **-euse** [ʀaʒœʀ, -ʒøz] *adj* bad-tempered

rageusement [ʀaʒøzmɑ̃] *adv* furiously

ragot [ʀago] *m inf* bit of gossip; **des ragots** gossip

ragoût [ʀagu] *m* stew; **~ de mouton/veau** mutton/veal stew

ragoûtant(**e**) [ʀagutɑ̃, ɑ̃t] *adj* **être peu ~** (*personne*) to be rather unsavoury [*o* unsavory *Am*]; (*repas, plat*) to be unappetizing; **c'est ~ ce que vous faites-là!** that's disgusting!

raï [ʀaj] *m* raï (*popular style of youth music from Algeria*)

raid [ʀɛd] *m* MIL raid; **~ aérien** air raid

raide [ʀɛd] **I.** *adj* **1.** (*rigide: personne, corps, membre*) stiff; (*cheveux*) straight **2.** (*escarpé: chemin, escalier, pente*) steep **3.** *inf* (*fort: alcool*) rough; (*café*) strong **4.** *inf* (*ivre*) plastered **II.** *adv* **1.** (*en pente*) steeply **2.** (*brusquement*) **étendre qn ~** to lay sb out cold; **tomber ~ mort** to drop stone dead; **tuer qn ~** to kill sb outright

raideur [ʀɛdœʀ] *f* **1.** (*rigidité*) stiffness; **saluer qn avec ~** to greet sb stiffly **2.** (*du chemin, de l'escalier*) steepness **3.** (*rigidité: des principes*) rigidness

raidillon [ʀedijɔ̃] *m* steep path

raidir [ʀediʀ] <8> **I.** *vt* (*tendre, durcir*) to stiffen; (*muscles*) to tense **II.** *vpr* **se ~** **1.** (*se tendre: drap, tissu, membres, personne*) to go stiff; (*corde*) to be pulled taut; (*muscles*) to tense **2.** (*résister*) to brace oneself; **se ~ contre le destin** to stand firm against fate

raie[1] [ʀɛ] *f* (*ligne*) line

raie[2] [ʀɛ] *indic et subj prés de* **rayer**

raierai [ʀɛʀɛ] *fut de* **rayer**

raifort [ʀɛfɔʀ] *m* horseradish

rail [ʀɑj] *m* CHEMDFER, TECH rail; **sortir des ~s** to come off the rails

raillerie [ʀɑjʀi] *f* **1.** (*fait de plaisanter*) mockery **2.** *pl* (*propos moqueurs*) mockery

rainette [ʀɛnɛt] *f* tree frog

rainure [ʀenyʀ] *f* groove

raisin [ʀɛzɛ̃] *m* grape; **~s secs** raisins

raison [ʀɛzɔ̃] *f* **1.** (*motif, sagesse*) reason; **~ d'être** raison d'être; **~ de vivre** reason for living; **avoir de bonnes/mauvaises ~s** to have good/bad reasons; **avoir de fortes ~s de penser que** to have good reason to think that; **ce n'est pas une ~ pour faire qc** that's no excuse for doing sth; **avoir ses ~s** to have one's reasons; **ramener qn à la ~** to bring sb back to their senses **2.** (*facultés intellectuelles*) mind; **avoir toute sa ~** to be in one's right mind; **perdre la ~** to lose one's mind ►**la ~ du plus fort est toujours la meilleure** *prov* might is right; **pour la bonne ~ que je le veux** simply because I want it; **à plus forte ~, je ne le ferai pas** all the more reason why I won't do it; **à tort ou à ~** rightly or wrongly; **avoir ~** to be right; **donner ~ à qn** to agree that sb is right; **entendre ~** to listen to reason; **se faire une ~** to resign oneself; **pour quelle ~?** why?; **pour une ~ ou pour une autre** for one reason or another

raisonnable [ʀɛzɔnabl] *adj* (*sage*) reasonable

raisonnement [ʀɛzɔnmɑ̃] *m* (*façon de penser, argumentation*) reasoning; **~ analogique/déductif** analogical/deductive reasoning

raisonner [ʀɛzɔne] <1> *vi* **1.** (*penser*) to think **2.** (*enchaîner des arguments*) to reason **3.** (*discuter*) **~ sur qc** to argue about sth

rajeunir [ʀaʒœniʀ] <8> **I.** *vt* **1.** (*rendre plus jeune*) to rejuvenate **2.** (*attribuer un âge plus moins avancé à*) **vous me rajeunissez de dix ans!** you're making me out to be ten years younger than I really am!; **ça ne nous rajeunit pas!** *iron* doesn't make us any younger, does it! **II.** *vi* **1.** (*se sentir plus jeune*) to feel younger **2.** (*sembler plus jeune*) to seem younger

rajeunissant(**e**) [ʀaʒœnisɑ̃, ɑ̃t] *adj* **une coupe ~e** a cut that makes you look younger; **traitement ~** rejuvenating treatment

rajeunissement [ʀaʒœnismɑ̃] *m* **1.** rejuvenation; **cure de ~** course of rejuvenating treatment **2.** (*d'une théorie, d'un ouvrage*) updating; (*d'une institution*) modernization; **~ du personnel** bringing in younger staff

rajouter [ʀaʒute] <1> *vt* **~ une phrase à qc** to add a sentence to sth; **il faut ~ du sel/sucre** it needs salt/sugar ►**en ~** *inf* to lay it on a bit thick

rajuster [ʀaʒyste] <1> *vt* (*remettre en place: vêtement, lunettes*) to adjust

râlant [ʀɑlɑ̃] *adj* **c'est ~** *inf* it's enough to drive you mad

râle[1] [ʀɑl] *m* (*du mourant*) rattle; (*du poumon*) rale

râle[2] [ʀɑl] *m* ZOOL rail

ralenti [ʀalɑ̃ti] *m* **1.** CINE, TV **au ~** in slow motion; **l'entreprise fonctionne au ~** the company is running under capacity **2.** AUTO

R

idling speed; **tourner au** ~ (*moteur*) to idle

ralentir [Ralɑ̃tiR] <8> I. *vt* to slow down; (*zèle, activité*) to slacken II. *vi* (*marcheur, véhicule, progrès, croissance*) to slow down III. *vpr* **se** ~ 1.(*devenir plus lent: allure, mouvement*) to slow down 2.(*diminuer: ardeur, effort, zèle*) to flag; (*production, croissance*) to slacken off

ralentissement [Ralɑ̃tismɑ̃] *m* 1.(*perte de vitesse: de l'allure, de la marche, circulation*) reduction in speed 2.(*diminution*) reduction

râler [Rɑle] <1> *vi* (*grogner*) ~ **contre qn/qc** to moan about sb/sth; **faire** ~ **qn** to make sb angry

râleur, **-euse** [RɑlœR, -øz] I. *adj inf* grouchy II. *m, f inf* moaner

ralliement [Ralimɑ̃] *m* 1. MIL rallying; **signe/point de** ~ rallying sign/point 2.(*adhésion*) ~ **à une cause** espousal of a cause; ~ **à un mouvement/parti** joining a movement/party

rallier [Ralje] <1a> I. *vt* 1.(*gagner: adeptes, groupe, sympathisants*) ~ **qn** to win sb over; **cette proposition a rallié tous les suffrages** this proposal won everybody's approval 2.(*unir des personnes pour une cause commune*) to rally; ~ **des personnes autour de qn/qc** to rally people around sb/sth 3.(*rejoindre*) ~ **une unité** to rejoin a unit; ~ **la côte** to haul in for the coast; ~ **son poste** to return to one's post; **les matelots ont rallié le bord** the sailors have rejoined ship 4.(*rassembler*) to rally II. *vpr* **se** ~ **à l'avis de qn** to be won over to sb's view

rallonge [Ralɔ̃ʒ] *f* 1.(*d'une table*) leaf 2. ELEC extension lead *Brit*, extension cord *Am*

rallonger [Ralɔ̃ʒe] <2a> *vt* to lengthen

rallumer [Ralyme] <1> *vt* (*allumer: feu, cigarette*) to relight; (*lampe, lumière*) to switch on again; (*électricité*) to turn on again

rallye [Rali] *m* rally

RAM [Ram] *f abr de* **Random Access Memory** RAM

ramadan [Ramadɑ̃] *m* Ramadan

ramassage [Ramɑsaʒ] *m* 1.(*collecte*) collecting; ~ **des vieux papiers** clearing litter 2.(*récolte: des fruits*) picking; (*des pommes de terre*) digging up; (*du foin*) gathering 3. ECOLE ~ **scolaire** school bus service; **service/car de** ~ school bus/coach

ramasse-miettes [Ramɑsmjɛt] *m inv* table tidy *Brit*, silent butler *Am* **ramasse-poussière** [RamɑspusjɛR] <ramasse-poussière(s)> *m Belgique, Nord* (*pelle à poussière*) dustpan

ramasser [Ramɑse] <1> I. *vt* 1.(*collecter: bois mort, coquillages*) to gather; (*champignons*) to pick; (*ordures, copies*) to collect; ~ **pas mal d'argent** to make quite a bit of money 2. *inf* (*embarquer*) **se faire** ~ **par la police** to get nabbed by the police 3.(*relever une personne qui est tombée*) ~ **qn qui est ivre mort** to pick up sb who's dead drunk 4.(*prendre ce qui est tombé par terre*) to pick up ►~ **qn dans le ruisseau** *péj* to pick sb up out of the gutter II. *vpr* **se** ~ *inf* (*tomber*) to fall flat on one's face

ramassis [Ramɑsi] *m péj* (*amas*) jumble; (*bande*) bunch

rambarde [Rɑ̃baRd] *f* rail

ramdam [Ramdam] *m inf* racket

rame[1] [Ram] *f* (*en horticulture*) stake

rame[2] [Ram] *f* (*aviron*) oar; **rejoindre la côte à la** ~ to row back to the coast ►**ne pas en ficher une** ~ *inf* not to do a damn thing, to do bugger all *Brit*

rame[3] [Ram] *f* CHEMDFER train

rameau [Ramo] <x> *m* 1. BOT *a. fig* branch 2. REL **le Dimanche des Rameaux/les Rameaux** Palm Sunday 3. ANAT ramification

ramener [Ramne] <4> I. *vt* 1.(*reconduire*) ~ **qn chez soi** to take sb back home 2.(*faire revenir, amener avec soi: beau temps*) to bring back; ~ **qn à la vie** to bring sb back to life; ~ **qn à de meilleurs sentiments** to bring sb round to a more generous point of view; ~ **qn à la raison** to bring sb back to their senses; ~ **qn/qc de Paris** to bring sb/sth back from Paris 3.(*rétablir*) ~ **la paix** to restore peace ►**la** ~ *inf* (*être prétentieux*) to show off; (*vouloir s'imposer*) to stick one's oar in; ~ **tout à soi** (*être égocentrique*) to see everything in relation to oneself II. *vpr inf* (*arriver*) **se** ~ to show up

ramer[1] [Rame] <1> *vi* 1. NAUT to row 2. *inf* (*peiner*) to sweat

ramer[2] [Rame] <1> *vt* (*en horticulture*) to stake

rameur [RamœR] *m* rower

rami [Rami] *m* rummy

ramier [Ramje] *m* wood pigeon

ramification [Ramifikasjɔ̃] *f* ramification

ramifier [Ramifje] <1a> *vpr* **se** ~ **en qc** to branch out into sth

ramollir [RamɔliR] <8> I. *vt* (*rendre mou: cuir, beurre*) to soften II. *vpr* **se** ~ 1.(*asphalte, beurre, biscuit*) to turn soft 2.(*s'affaiblir: ardeur, courage, volonté*) to weaken; (*os*) to get weak; **son cerveau se ramollit** she's getting weak in the head

ramollo [Ramɔlo] I. *adj* 1. *péj* (*gâteux*) weak in the head 2. *inf* (*mou*) **être/se sentir** ~ to be/feel all washed-out II. *mf* 1. *péj* (*gâteux*) dodderer 2. *inf* (*mollasson*) wash-out

ramonage [Ramɔnaʒ] *m* cleaning; (*de la cheminée*) sweeping

ramoner [Ramɔne] <1> *vt* (*pipe*) to clean; (*cheminée*) to sweep

ramoneur, **-euse** [RamɔnœR, -øz] *m, f* chimney sweep

rampe [Rɑ̃p] *f* 1.(*rambarde: d'un escalier*) banister; (*à l'extérieur*) 2.(*plan incliné*) ramp; ~ **d'accès** approach ramp 3.(*montée*) slope 4.(*lumières*) lights; THEAT footlights; ~ **de projecteurs** row of spotlights 5. ~ **de lancement** launchpad ►**passer la** ~ THEAT to come across (to the audience)

ramper [ʀɑ̃pe] <1> *vi* **1.** (*progresser par reptation: animal, enfant*) to crawl **2.** (*pousser: lierre, vigne*) to creep **3.** (*s'insinuer*) to lurk; **le danger/mal rampe, il est partout** danger/evil is lurking everywhere; **un feu qui rampe** a latent fire; **l'inquiétude rampe en moi** worry's gnawing away at me **4.** (*s'abaisser: personnes*) ~ **devant qn** to crawl to sb

rancard [ʀɑ̃kaʀ] *m inf* (*rendez-vous*) meeting

rancarder [ʀɑ̃kaʀde] <1> **I.** *vt* **1.** *vulg* (*renseigner*) ~ **qn** to tip sb off **2.** *inf* (*donner un rendez-vous à*) ~ **qn** to fix a date with sb **II.** *vpr* **se** ~ *vulg* (*se renseigner*) to get the low-down

rancart [ʀɑ̃kaʀ] *m* **mettre qc au** ~ *inf* to chuck sth out; **une table bonne à mettre au** ~ a table that should be junked; **votre projet, vous pouvez le mettre au** ~ you can forget about your project; **mettre qn au** ~ *inf* to throw sb on the scrapheap

rance [ʀɑ̃s] **I.** *adj* rancid **II.** *m* **sentir le ~/avoir un goût de** ~ to smell/taste rancid

ranch [ʀɑ̃tʃ] <(e)s> *m* ranch

rancir [ʀɑ̃siʀ] <8> *vi* to go rancid

rancœur [ʀɑ̃kœʀ] *f soutenu* resentment

rançon [ʀɑ̃sɔ̃] *f* **1.** (*rachat*) ransom **2.** (*prix*) **la** ~ **de la gloire/du succès/progrès** the price of fame/success/progress

rançonner [ʀɑ̃sɔne] <1> *vt* (*racketter*) to fleece

rancune [ʀɑ̃kyn] *f* **garder** ~ **à qn de qc** to hold a grudge against sb for sth ►**sans ~!** no hard feelings!

rancunier, **-ière** [ʀɑ̃kynje, -jɛʀ] *adj* vindictive; **être** ~ to bear grudges

randonnée [ʀɑ̃dɔne] *f* **faire une** ~ **à pied/skis/bicyclette** to go for a hike/cross-country skiing/a bicycle ride

randonneur, **-euse** [ʀɑ̃dɔnœʀ, -øz] *m, f* hiker

rang [ʀɑ̃] *m* **1.** (*suite de personnes ou de choses*) line; **en** ~ **par deux** in rows of two; **mettez-vous en ~!** line up! **2.** (*rangée de sièges*) row; **se placer au premier** ~ to sit in the front row **3.** (*position dans un ordre ou une hiérarchie*) rank **4.** (*condition*) station; **le** ~ **social** social standing; **garder/tenir son** ~ to maintain one's position in society

rangé(**e**) [ʀɑ̃ʒe] *adj* tidy

rangée [ʀɑ̃ʒe] *f* row

rangement [ʀɑ̃ʒmɑ̃] *m* **1.** (*fait de ranger: d'une pièce, d'un meuble*) tidying; (*du linge, d'objets*) putting away; **faire du** ~ to tidy [*o* clean] up **2.** (*possibilités de ranger*) storage space **3.** (*classement*) storage unit

ranger [ʀɑ̃ʒe] <2a> **I.** *vt* **1.** (*mettre en ordre: maison, tiroir*) to tidy up **2.** (*mettre à sa place: objet, vêtements*) to put away **3.** (*classer: dossiers, fiches*) to file (away) **II.** *vi* **il passe son temps à** ~ he spends his time tidying up **III.** *vpr* **se** ~ **1.** (*s'écarter: piéton*) to stand aside; (*véhicule*) to pull over **2.** (*se mettre en rang*) to line up **3.** (*devenir plus sérieux: personnes*) to settle down

ranimer [ʀanime] <1> *vt* **1.** (*ramener à la vie: noyé, personne évanouie*) to revive **2.** (*revigorer: amour, feu*) to rekindle; (*espoir, forces*) to renew

rap [ʀap] *m* rap

rapace [ʀapas] **I.** *adj* **1.** (*avide*) rapacious; **oiseau** ~ bird of prey **2.** (*cupide: homme d'affaires, usurier*) money-grubbing **II.** *m* (*oiseau*) bird of prey

rapatrié(**e**) [ʀapatʀije] *m(f)* repatriate

rapatriement [ʀapatʀimɑ̃] *m* **1.** (*transfert de personnes*) repatriation **2.** (*transfert de biens: des fonds, bénéfices*) transfer home; ~ **des capitaux** return of capital

rapatrier [ʀapatʀije] <1> *vt* (*ramener: personne*) to repatriate; (*objet*) to send home

râpe [ʀɑp] *f* **1.** GASTR grater; ~ **à fromage** cheese grater **2.** TECH rasp

râpé(**e**) [ʀɑpe] *adj* (*carotte, fromage*) grated ►**c'est** ~ *inf* so much for that!

râper [ʀɑpe] <1> *vt* (*fromage, betteraves, carottes*) to grate

rapetisser [ʀap(ə)tise] <1> **I.** *vt* **1.** (*rendre plus petit*) ~ **qc** to make sth smaller; (*vêtement*) to shorten sth **2.** (*dévaloriser*) to belittle **II.** *vi* to grow smaller; (*jour*) to shorten **III.** *vpr* **se** ~ **1.** (*devenir plus petit*) to grow smaller **2.** (*se dévaloriser*) to belittle oneself

râpeux, **-euse** [ʀɑpø, -øz] *adj* rough

raphia [ʀafja] *m* raffia

rapiat(**e**) [ʀapja, jat] **I.** *adj inf* stingy **II.** *m(f) inf* skinflint, tightwad *Am*

rapide [ʀapid] **I.** *adj* **1.** (*d'une grande vitesse*) fast; (*manière, progrès, réponse*) rapid; (*geste, intelligence, personne*) quick; **une réaction** ~ a speedy reaction **2.** (*expéditif: décision, démarche*) hasty; (*visite*) hurried **II.** *m* **1.** (*train*) express train **2.** (*cours d'eau*) rapid

rapidement [ʀapidmɑ̃] *adv* quickly; **parcourir le journal** ~ to have a quick glance at the newspaper

rapidité [ʀapidite] *f* (*vitesse*) speed; **agir avec la** ~ **de l'éclair** to act with lightning speed

rapidos [ʀapidɔs] *adv abr de* **rapidement** pronto

rapiécer [ʀapjese] <2, 5> *vt* to patch up

raplapla [ʀaplapla] *adj inv, inf* **1.** (*fatigué*) washed-out **2.** (*aplati*) flat; (*matelas*) sunken; (*soufflé*) collapsed

rappel [ʀapɛl] *m* **1.** (*remise en mémoire, panneau de signalisation*) reminder **2.** (*admonestation*) ~ **à l'ordre** call to order; POL naming; ~ **à la raison** call to reason **3.** FIN ~ **de cotisation** payment of contribution arrears; ~ **de salaire** back pay **4.** THEAT curtain call; **il y a eu trois ~s** there were three curtain calls **5.** MED booster

rappeler [ʀap(ə)le] <3> **I.** *vt* **1.** (*remémorer, évoquer: souvenir*) to remind; ~ **une date à qn** to remind sb of a date; ~ **à qn que c'est**

lundi to remind sb that it is Monday; ~ **un enfant/tableau à qn** to remind sb of a child/painting **2.** (*appeler pour faire revenir*) to call back; **les acteurs ont été rappelés plusieurs fois** the actors had several curtain calls **3.** TEL ~ **qn** to phone sb back **II.** *vi* TEL to phone back **III.** *vpr* **se** ~ **qn/qc** to remember sb/sth; **elle se rappelle que nous étions venus** she remembers that we had come

rappliquer [raplike] <1> *vi inf* to turn up again

rapport [rapɔʀ] *m* **1.** (*lien*) link; ~ **entre deux ou plusieurs choses** connection between two or several things; ~ **de cause à effet** relation of cause and effect; ~ **qualité-prix** value for money **2.** (*relations*) relationship; ~**s d'amitié/de bon voisinage** friendly/neighbourly [*o* neighborly *Am*] relations; **les** ~**s franco-allemands** Franco-German relations **3.** *pl* (*relations sexuelles*) (sexual) relations; **avoir des** ~**s avec qn** to have sex with sb **4.** (*compte rendu*) report; **rédiger un** ~ **sur qn/qc** to draw up a report on sb/sth; ~ **de police** police report; ~ **de recherche** research paper ►<u>**avoir**</u> ~ **à qc** to be about sth; **sous** <u>**tous**</u> **les** ~**s** in every respect; <u>**en**</u> ~ **avec** (*qui correspond à*) in keeping with; **mettre qc en** ~ **avec** (*en relation avec*) to relate sth to; <u>**par**</u> ~ **à qn/qc** (*en ce qui concerne*) regarding sb/sth; (*proportionnellement*) compared to sb/sth

rapporté(e) [rapɔʀte] *adj* (*poche*) sewn-on; (*élément*) added; **une pièce** ~**e** *fig, inf* an odd man out

rapporter [rapɔʀte] <1> **I.** *vt* **1.** (*ramener, rendre*) ~ **un livre à qn** to bring a book back to sb; ~ **un livre à la bibliothèque** to return a book to the library **2.** (*être profitable*) ~ **qc** (*action, activité*) to yield sth; (*métier*) to bring in sth **3.** *péj* (*répéter pour dénoncer*) to report **II.** *vpr* (*être relatif à*) **se** ~ **à qc** to relate to sth

rapporteur [rapɔʀtœʀ] *m* protractor

rapporteur, **-euse** [rapɔʀtœʀ, øz] *m, f* **1.** (*qui répète*) taleteller **2.** (*qui fait un rapport*) rapporteur

rapproché(e) [rapʀɔʃe] *adj* **1.** close; **combat** ~ close combat; **la protection** ~**e d'un chef d'état** tight security for a head of state; **à une date aussi** ~**e** so close in the future **2.** (*répété*) frequent; (*intervalles*) short

rapprochement [rapʀɔʃmɑ̃] *m* **1.** coming closer **2.** (*réconciliation*) coming together; (*d'idées, de points de vue*) rapprochement; ~ **franco-anglais** rapprochement between France and England **3.** (*analogie*) connection; (*comparaison: de textes*) comparison; **faire le** ~ **entre deux événements** to draw a parallel between two events

rapprocher [rapʀɔʃe] <1> **I.** *vt* **1.** (*avancer: objets, chaises*) to bring closer; **rapproche ta chaise de la table/de moi!** move your chair closer to the table/me! **2.** (*réconcilier: ennemis, familles brouillées*) to reconcile; **ce drame nous a beaucoup rapprochés** this tragedy brought us closer together **3.** (*mettre en parallèle: idées, thèses*) to compare **II.** *vpr* **1.** (*approcher*) **se** ~ **de qn/qc** to approach sb/sth; **rapproche-toi de moi!** come closer!; **l'orage/le bruit se rapproche de nous** the storm/noise is getting closer (to us) **2.** (*sympathiser*) **se** ~ to be reconciled

rapproprier [rapʀɔpʀije] <1> *vpr Belgique, Nord* (*mettre des vêtements propres*) **se** ~ to put clean things on

rapt [ʀapt] *m* abduction; ~ **d'enfant** child abduction

raquer [ʀake] <1> *vi inf* to foot the bill

raquette [ʀakɛt] *f* **1.** SPORT bat; ~ **de tennis** tennis racket **2.** (*semelle pour la neige*) snowshoe

rare [ʀɑʀ] *adj* **1.** (*opp: fréquent: animal, édition, variété, objet, mot*) rare; **il est** ~ **qu'elle fasse des erreurs** (*subj*) she rarely makes mistakes **2.** (*exceptionnel*) unusual **3.** (*peu nombreux*) few; **ses rares amis** her few friends ►**se** <u>**faire**</u> ~ to become scarce

raréfier [ʀaʀefje] <1a> **I.** *vt* PHYS to rarefy **II.** *vpr* **se** ~ (*touristes, gibier, argent, marchandise*) to get scarcer; (*air, oxygène*) to get thinner

rarement [ʀɑʀmɑ̃] *adv* rarely

rareté [ʀɑʀte] *f* **1.** scarcity; **la** ~ **des touristes/visiteurs** the dearth of tourists/visitors; **être d'une extrème** ~ to be extremely scarce **2.** (*chose précieuse*) rarity

rarissime [ʀaʀisim] *adj* extremely rare

ras [ʀɑ] *m* ~ **du** <u>**cou**</u> crew-neck; **au** ~ **des** <u>**pâquerettes**</u> intellectually undemanding; <u>**à**</u> ~ cut short; <u>**au**</u> ~ **de qc** passing just next to sth; **au** ~ **de l'eau** skimming the surface

RAS [ɛʀɑɛs] *abr de* **rien à signaler** (*sur un certificat médical*) nothing to report

ras(e) [ʀɑ, ʀɑz] **I.** *adj* (*barbe, cheveux, herbe*) short; (*étoffe*) short-pile; **à poil** ~ short-hair; **avoir les cheveux** ~ to have close-cropped hair **II.** *adv* (*coupé, taillé, tondu*) short; **la haie est taillée** ~ the hedge is clipped short

rasade [ʀɑzad] *f* glassful; **se verser une** ~ **de vin** to pour oneself a glass of wine

rasant(e) [ʀɑzɑ̃, ɑ̃t] *adj* **1.** OPT low; MIL low-built; **tir** ~ grazing fire **2.** *inf* (*ennuyeux*) boring

rascasse [ʀaskas] *f* scorpion fish

rase-mottes [ʀɑzmɔt] *inv* <u>**voler**</u> **en** [*o* <u>**faire**</u> **du**] ~ to hedgehop

raser [ʀɑze] <1> **I.** *vt* **1.** (*tondre*) to shave; (*cheveux*) to shave off; **être rasé de près/de frais** to be close-shaven/freshly shaven **2.** (*effleurer*) ~ **les murs** to hug the walls; ~ **le sol** (*oiseaux, projectiles*) to skim the ground **3.** (*détruire: bâtiment, quartier*) to raze **4.** *inf* (*ennuyer*) to bore **II.** *vpr* **1.** (*se couper ras*) **se** ~ to shave; **se** ~ **la barbe/la tête** to shave off one's beard/hair; **se** ~ **les jambes** to shave one's legs **2.** *inf* (*s'ennuyer*) **se** ~ to be bored

raseur, **-euse** [ʀɑzœʀ, -øz] *m, f inf* bore;

(*casse-pieds*) pain in the neck

ras-le-bol [ʀɑl(ə)bɔl] *m inv, inf* **en avoir ~ de qc** to be sick and tired of sth; **~!** I've had it up to here!

rasoir [ʀɑzwaʀ] **I.** *m* razor **II.** *adj inf* **qu'il est ~!** what a bore he is!

rassasié(e) [ʀasazje] *adj* **être ~** to have had one's fill

rassemblement [ʀasɑ̃bləmɑ̃] *m* **1.** (*de documents, d'objets épars*) collection **2.** (*regroupement*) union; POL alliance; MIL parade; **~!** fall in!

rassembler [ʀasɑ̃ble] <1> **I.** *vt* **1.** (*réunir: documents, objets épars*) to collect; (*troupeau*) to gather; **deux cents pièces sont rassemblées au musée ...** the museum has a collection of two hundred items ... **2.** (*regrouper: troupes, soldats*) to rally; **~ des personnes** (*personne*) to gather together; **ce parti rassemble les mécontents** this party draws all the malcontents **3.** (*faire appel à: forces, idées*) to gather; (*courage*) to summon; **j'ai du mal à ~ mes idées** [*o* **esprits**] I just can't collect my thoughts **4.** (*remonter: charpente, mécanisme*) to reassemble **II.** *vpr* **se ~** (*badauds, foule, participants*) to gather; (*écoliers, soldats*) to assemble

rasseoir [ʀaswaʀ] *vpr irr* **se ~** to sit down again; **va te ~!** go back to your seat!

rasséréner [ʀaseʀene] <5> **I.** *vt* **~ qn** to restore sb's serenity; **je suis rasséréné** my mind is at rest **II.** *vpr* **se ~** (*personne*) to have one's serenity restored; (*ciel, visage*) to clear

rassis, rassie [ʀasi] *adj* **1.** (*qui n'est plus frais: pain, pâtisserie*) stale **2.** (*pondéré: personne*) calm

rassurant(e) [ʀasyʀɑ̃, ɑ̃t] *adj* (*nouvelle*) reassuring; (*visage*) comforting; **se montrer ~** to be reassuring; **c'est ~!** *iron* that's very reassuring!

rassurer [ʀasyʀe] <1> **I.** *vt* to reassure; **ne pas être rassuré** to feel worried; **je ne me sens pas rassuré dans sa voiture** I don't feel very safe in his car **II.** *vpr* **se ~** to reassure oneself; **rassurez-vous!** don't worry!; **que l'on se rassure** set your minds at rest

rasta [ʀasta] **I.** *adj inv, inf* Rasta **II.** *mf inf* Rasta

rat [ʀa] *m* ZOOL rat ►**~ de bibliothèque** bookworm; **s'ennuyer comme un ~ mort** to be bored stiff

ratage [ʀataʒ] *m* flop; **être un ~ complet** (*entreprise*) to be a total flop

ratatiné(e) [ʀatatine] *adj* **1.** (*rapetisé*) shrivelled *Brit*, shriveled *Am* **2.** *inf* (*fichu*) totalled *Brit*, totaled *Am*

ratatiner [ʀatatine] <1> *vt* (*rabougrir: fruit*) to shrivel; (*visage*) to wizen

ratatouille [ʀatatuj] *f* ratatouille

rate [ʀat] *f* ANAT spleen

raté(e) [ʀate] *m(f)* failure

râteau [ʀɑto] <x> *m* rake

râtelier [ʀɑtəlje] *m* **1.** AGR rack **2.** *inf* (*dentier*) false teeth *pl* **3.** (*support*) rack ►**manger à tous les ~s** to take advantage of everyone and everything

rater [ʀate] <1> **I.** *vt* **1.** (*manquer: cible, occasion, train*) to miss **2.** (*ne pas réussir*) **~ sa vie** to make a mess of one's life; **tu vas tout faire ~!** you're going to spoil everything!; **j'ai raté la mayonnaise** I messed up the mayonnaise; **~ son examen** to fail one's exam; **être raté** to be ruined; (*photos*) to be spoilt **3. il n'en rate pas une!** he's always putting his foot in it!; **ne pas ~ qn** to fix sb **II.** *vi* (*affaire, coup, projet*) to fail **III.** *vpr* **1.** *inf* (*mal se suicider*) **il s'est raté** he bungled his suicide attempt **2.** (*ne pas se voir*) **se ~** to miss one another

ratification [ʀatifikasjɔ̃] *f* ratification; **~ de vente** sales confirmation

ratifier [ʀatifje] <1> *vt* (*loi, traité*) to ratify

rating [ʀatiŋ, ʀetiŋ] *m* ECON rating

ration [ʀasjɔ̃] *f* ration; **vous avez tous eu la même ~** you've all had the same; **~ de pain/viande** bread/meat ration; **~ alimentaire** food intake; **arrête, il a eu sa ~!** stop, he's had his share!

rationaliser [ʀasjɔnalize] <1> *vt* to rationalize

rationalité [ʀasjɔnalite] *f* rationality; **dépourvu de toute ~** devoid of meaning

rationnel(le) [ʀasjɔnɛl] *adj a.* MAT (*comportement, pensée, organisation, méthode*) rational; (*alimentation*) sensible; **c'est un esprit ~** she's got a rational mind

rationnellement [ʀasjɔnɛlmɑ̃] *adv* rationally

rationnement [ʀasjɔnmɑ̃] *m* rationing

rationner [ʀasjɔne] <1> *vt* to ration; **~ qn** to put sb on rations

ratisser [ʀatise] <1> **I.** *vt* **1. ~ une allée/une platebande** to rake over a path/a border; (**~** *l'herbe/des feuilles mortes*) to rake up the grass/dead leaves **2.** MIL to comb **3.** *inf* (*piller*) to pinch; **il s'est fait ~ au jeu** he got cleaned out at the tables **II.** *vi* to rake

raton [ʀatɔ̃] *m* **1.** ZOOL **~ laveur** raccoon **2.** *Québec* (*chat sauvage*) wild cat

R.A.T.P. [ɛʀɑtepe] *f abr de* **Régie autonome des transports parisiens** *Paris public transport system*

rattachement [ʀataʃmɑ̃] *m* **1.** ADMIN, POL **~ de l'Alsace-Lorraine à la France** incorporation of Alsace-Lorraine into France; **~ à une commune** incorporation in a commune; **~ de qn à un service** sb's attachment to a department **2.** (*liaison*) connection; **le ~ de ces deux questions s'impose** these two questions have to be examined together

rattacher [ʀataʃe] <1> *vt* **1.** (*renouer*) to retie; (*lacet, ceinture, jupe*) to do up again **2.** (*annexer*) **~ un territoire à un pays** to bring a territory under the jurisdiction of a country

ratte [ʀat] *f* ratte (*type of potato*)

R

rattrapage [ʀatʀapaʒ] *m* **1.** (*d'une maille*) picking up **2.** ECOLE (*remise à niveau*) remedial work; **classe de** ~ remedial class; **cours de** ~ remedial classes *pl* **3.** ECOLE, UNIV (*repêchage*) passing, letting through; **examen de** ~ resit; **oral de** ~ second oral (exam); **avoir son bac au** ~ to get one's bac after a second oral **4.** (*rajustement: des salaires*) adjustment **5.** IND, COM ~ **des heures perdues/du retard** making up for hours lost/the delay

rattraper [ʀatʀape] <1> **I.** *vt* **1.** (*rejoindre*) ~ **qn** to catch sb up **2.** (*regagner: temps perdu, retard*) to make up for; (*sommeil*) to catch up on; (*pertes*) to recover **3.** (*retenir*) to catch hold of; ~ **qn par le bras/le manteau** to grab hold of sb's arm/coat **II.** *vpr* **1.** (*se raccrocher*) **se** ~ **à une branche** to grab hold of a branch **2.** (*compenser, réparer, corriger une erreur*) **se** ~ to make up

rature [ʀatyʀ] *f* crossing out

raturé(e) [ʀatyʀe] *adj* full of crossings out; **une lettre ~e** a deleted letter

raturer [ʀatyʀe] <1> *vt* to cross out; (*corriger*) to make an alteration

rauque [ʀok] *adj* (*son, toux*) throaty; (*cri, voix*) hoarse

ravagé(e) [ʀavaʒe] *adj inf* barmy *Brit,* nuts

ravager [ʀavaʒe] <2a> *vt* (*pays, ville*) to lay waste; (*cultures*) to devastate

ravages [ʀavaʒ] *mpl* **1.** (*dégâts*) devastation + *vb sing;* ~ **de la grêle/de l'orage** devastation caused by the hail/storm **2.** (*effets néfastes: de l'alcool, de la drogue*) **la drogue fait des** ~ **dans ce quartier** drug abuse is rife in this district ►**faire des** ~ to wreak havoc; **il fait des ~!** he's a real heartbreaker!

ravalement [ʀavalmɑ̃] *m* cleaning; (*avec du crépi*) roughcasting

ravaler [ʀavale] <1> *vt* **1.** (*retenir: larmes, émotion*) to hold back **2.** (*nettoyer: façade*) to restore

rave [ʀɛv] *f* rave

ravi(e) [ʀavi] *adj* delighted; **avoir l'air** ~ to look pleased; **être** ~ **de** +*infin* to be delighted to +*infin*

ravier [ʀavje] *m* hors d'œuvres dish

ravigoter [ʀavigɔte] <1> *vt inf* ~ **qn** (*nouvelle, alcool, douche, repas*) to buck sb up; **se sentir ravigoté par une sieste** to feel refreshed by an afternoon nap

ravin [ʀavɛ̃] *m* ravine

raviner [ʀavine] <1> *vt* GEO to gully

raviole [ʀavjɔl] *f* **des ~s** ravioli + *vb sing*

ravioli [ʀavjɔli] *m* ravioli *no pl*

ravir [ʀaviʀ] <8> *vt* **1.** to delight; **ta visite me ravit** I'm delighted about your visit; **ces vacances me ravissent** these holidays are a delight **2.** *soutenu* (*enlever*) ~ **qc à qn** (*honneur, trésor*) to rob sb of sth; **la mort nous a ravi notre enfant** death has stolen away our child ►**à** ~ ravishingly

raviser [ʀavize] <1> *vpr* **se** ~ to change one's mind

ravissant(e) [ʀavisɑ̃, ɑ̃t] *adj* beautiful; (*femme*) ravishingly beautiful

ravissement [ʀavismɑ̃] *m a.* REL rapture; **avec** ~ rapturously; **plonger qn dans le** ~ to send sb into raptures

ravisseur, -euse [ʀavisœʀ, -øz] *m, f* kidnapper

ravitaillement [ʀavitajmɑ̃] *m* **1.** (*approvisionnement: de la population, des troupes*) supplying; **assurer le** ~ **de qn en charbon** to supply sb with coal; **aller au** ~ to go for fresh supplies **2.** (*denrées alimentaires*) food supplies **3.** MED ~ **d'urgence** emergency feeding **4.** AVIAT ~ **en vol** in-flight refuelling [*o* refueling *Am*]

ravitailler [ʀavitaje] <1> **I.** *vt* ~ **qn en essence** to supply sb with petrol; ~ **les avions en vol** to refuel planes in flight **II.** *vpr* **se** ~ **en qc** to get (fresh) supplies of sth

raviver [ʀavive] <1> **I.** *vt* (*espoir, souvenir*) to reawaken; (*couleur, vieilles blessures*) to revive; (*feu*) to rekindle; ~ **une douleur** (*personne*) to revive a sorrow **II.** *vpr* **se** ~ (*douleur*) to revive; (*inquiétude, pessimisme*) to be revived; **mes regrets se sont ravivés quand ...** my regrets returned when ...

ravoir [ʀavwaʀ] *vt irr, défec, toujours à l'infin* **1.** (*récupérer*) to get back **2.** *inf* (*détacher*) ~ **qc** (*casserole, cuivres, vêtements*) to get sth clean

rayé(e) [ʀeje] *adj* **1.** (*zébré*) striped; (*papier*) lined **2.** (*éraflé: disque, vitre*) scratched

rayer [ʀeje] <7> *vt* **1.** (*érafler: disque, vitre*) to scratch **2.** (*biffer: mot, nom*) to cross out **3.** (*supprimer*) ~ **qn/qc de la liste** to strike sb's name/sth off the list; ~ **qn des cadres** to dismiss sb; ~ **un souvenir de sa mémoire** to blot out a memory

rayon [ʀɛjɔ̃] *m* **1.** (*faisceau*) ray; ~ **laser** laser beam; ~ **de lumière** shaft of light **2.** *pl* (*radiations*) radiation *no pl;* **~s X** X-rays; **~s ultraviolets/infrarouges** ultraviolet/infrared rays **3.** (*étagère: d'une armoire*) shelf; **ranger ses livres dans les ~s d'une bibliothèque** to put away one's books on the shelves of a bookcase **4.** COM department; ~ **d'alimentation** food department; **c'est tout ce qu'il me reste en** ~ that's all we have left in stock **5.** (*distance*) **dans un** ~ **de plus de 20 km** within a radius of more than 20 km **6.** (*d'une roue*) spoke ►~ **de soleil** ray of sunshine; **en connaître un** ~ **en politique** he really knows a thing or two about politics; **c'est mon** ~ that's my department

rayonnage [ʀɛjɔnaʒ] *m* shelving *no pl*

rayonnant(e) [ʀɛjɔnɑ̃, ɑ̃t] *adj* **1.** radiant; **par un soleil** ~ in glorious sunshine; ~ **de santé/joie** radiant with health/joy **2.** (*en étoile*) radiating **3.** ARCHIT, ART **gothique** ~ High Gothic; **chapelles ~es** radiating chapels **4.** PHYS **chaleur** radiant; MED (*douleur*) radiating

rayonnement [ʀɛjɔnmɑ̃] *m* **1.** (*d'une civilisation, d'un pays*) influence **2.** (*aura*) radiance

3. (*lumière*) radiance; **le ~ solaire** the radiance of the sun 4. PHYS radiation

rayonner [ʀɛjɔne] <1> *vi* (*irradier*) **~ de joie** to be radiant with joy; **~ de santé** to be blooming with health

rayure [ʀejyʀ] *f* 1. stripe; **à ~s** striped 2. (*éraflure*) scratch 3. TECH (*d'une arme à feu*) groove

raz-de-marée [ʀɑdəmaʀe] *m inv* GEO tidal wave; **~ électoral** *fig* landslide victory

razzia [ʀa(d)zja] *f* raid; **faire une ~ sur qc** to raid sth

R.D.A. [ɛʀdeɑ] *f* HIST *abr de* **République démocratique allemande** GDR

ré [ʀe] *m inv* MUS (*note*) D; (*en solfiant*) re; *v. a.* **do**

réacteur [ʀeaktœʀ] *m* 1. AVIAT jet engine 2. PHYS, CHIM reactor; **~ nucléaire** nuclear reactor

réaction [ʀeaksjɔ̃] *f* 1. reaction; **~ à une catastrophe/un spectacle** reaction to a disaster/show; **~ en chaîne** chain reaction; **en ~ contre qn/qc** as a reaction against sb/sth; **avoir des ~s rapides/un peu lentes** to have good/bad reflexes 2. (*transformation chimique ou physique*) CHEM, PHYS, AVIAT **propulsion par ~** jet propulsion

réactionnaire [ʀeaksjɔnɛʀ] *adj, mf* reactionary

réactiver [ʀeaktive] <1> *vt* (*alliance, idéologie, amitié*) to revive; (*feu*) to rekindle; MED (*maladie, sérum*) to reactivate

réactualiser [ʀeaktɥalize] <1> *vt* to update; (*débat*) to relaunch

réadaptation [ʀeadaptasjɔ̃] *f* re-education; (*d'un handicapé*) rehabilitation; **~ à la vie civile/au travail** readjustment to civilian life/work

réadapter [ʀeadapte] <1> *vt* 1. (*réaccoutumer*) **~ qn à la vie professionnelle** to help sb readjust to working life 2. MED (*articulation, muscle*) to re-educate

réafficher [ʀeafiʃe] <1> *vt* INFOR **~ les copies des pages visitées** to display copies of pages visited

réaffirmer [ʀeafiʀme] <1> *vt* (*intention, volonté*) to reassert; **je réaffirme que les choses se sont passées ainsi** I reaffirm that that's how things happened

réagir [ʀeaʒiʀ] <8> *vi* 1. (*répondre spontanément*) **~ à qc** to react to sth; **~ mal aux antibiotiques** to react badly to antibiotics 2. *a.* MED (*s'opposer à*) **~ contre une idée** to react against an idea; **~ contre une menace** to react against a threat; **~ contre une infection** (*organisme*) to react against an infection

réajuster [ʀeaʒyste] <1> *vt v.* **rajuster**

réalisable [ʀealizabl] *adj* feasible; (*rêve*) attainable

réalisateur, **-trice** [ʀealizatœʀ, -tʀis] *m, f* CINE, TV director

réalisation [ʀealizasjɔ̃] *f* 1. (*exécution*) carrying out 2. CINE, RADIO, TV directing

réaliser [ʀealize] <1> I. *vt* 1. (*accomplir: ambition*) to achieve; (*projet, intention, menace, travail, réforme*) to carry out; (*rêve, désir*) to fulfil *Brit,* fulfill *Am;* (*effort*) to make; (*exploit*) to perform 2. (*effectuer: plan, maquette, achat, vente, progrès*) to make; **~ des économies** to make savings; **~ des bénéfices** to make a profit 3. (*se rendre compte de*) **~ l'ampleur de son erreur** to realize the extent of one's mistake 4. CINE, RADIO, TV (*faire*) to direct II. *vi* to realize; **est-ce que tu réalises vraiment?** do you really understand?; **j'ai du mal à ~** it's hard for me to realize III. *vpr* **se ~** (*projet*) to be carried out; (*rêve, vœu*) to come true; (*ambition*) to be achieved

réalisme [ʀealism] *m* realism; **le roman manque de ~** the book is not very realistic

réaliste [ʀealist] I. *adj* realistic; ART, LIT realist II. *m, f* realist

réalité [ʀealite] *f* (*réel, chose réelle*) reality; **devenir ~** to become reality; (*rêve, souhait*) to come true; **la ~ dépasse la fiction** truth is stranger than fiction ►**en ~** in fact

réaménagement [ʀeamenaʒmɑ̃] *m* (*d'un site*) redevelopment

réaménager [ʀeamenaʒe] <2a> *vt* (*site*) to redevelop; **~ les rues en zone piétonne** to pedestrianize the streets

réanimation [ʀeanimasjɔ̃] *f* 1. (*technique*) resuscitation 2. (*service*) **service de ~** intensive care unit; **être en ~** to be in intensive care

réanimer [ʀeanime] <1> *vt* to resuscitate

réapparaître [ʀeapaʀɛtʀ] *vi irr avoir o être* to reappear

réapparition [ʀeapaʀisjɔ̃] *f* reappearance

réapprendre [ʀeapʀɑ̃dʀ] <13> *vt* (*leçon, poésie*) to relearn; **~ à marcher** to learn how to walk again

réapprovisionner [ʀeapʀɔvizjɔne] <1> I. *vt* to restock II. *vpr* **se ~ en chocolat** to stock up on chocolate

réarmer [ʀeaʀme] <1> I. *vi* to rearm II. *vt* (*fusil, pistolet*) to cock; (*appareil photo*) to wind on; (*troupes, pays*) to rearm; (*navire*) to refit

rebaptiser [ʀ(ə)batize] <1> *vt* to rename

rébarbatif, **-ive** [ʀebaʀbatif, -iv] *adj* (*air, mine*) forbidding; (*style*) off-putting; (*sujet, tâche*) daunting

rebattre [ʀəbatʀ] *vt irr* **~ les oreilles à qn de qc** to keep harping on to sb about sth

rebattu(**e**) [ʀəbaty] *adj* (*citation, sujet*) hackneyed

rebelle [ʀəbɛl] I. *adj* 1. (*insurgé: populations, troupes*) rebel; **~ à la patrie/à un souverain** rebel against the homeland/a sovereign 2. (*récalcitrant: enfant*) rebellious; (*fièvre, maladie, animal*) stubborn; (*cheveux, mèche*) unruly; **avoir l'esprit ~** to have a rebellious spirit; **être ~ au latin/à la géographie** to be allergic to Latin/georaphy; **ce virus est ~ à tous les remèdes** this virus defies all treatments II. *mf* rebel

rebeller [ʀ(ə)bele] <1> *vpr* **se ~ contre qc**

R

to rebel against sth
rébellion [Rebeljɔ̃] *f* **1.**~ **contre qn/qc** rebellion against sb/sth; **entrer en** ~ **contre qn** to rebel against sb **2.**(*rebelles*) rebels
rebiffer [R(ə)bife] <1> *vpr inf* **se** ~ **contre qn/qc** to rebel against sb/sth
rebiquer [R(ə)bike] <1> *vi inf* to stick up
reblochon [Rəblɔʃɔ̃] *m: full-flavoured camembert-type cheese*
reboisement [R(ə)bwazmɑ̃] *m* reafforestation
reboiser [R(ə)bwaze] <1> *vt, vi* to reafforest
rebond [R(ə)bɔ̃] *m* rebound; **faux** ~ awkward bounce
rebondi(e) [R(ə)bɔ̃di] *adj* (*croupe, fesses, femme, formes*) well-rounded; (*porte-monnaie*) fat; (*ventre*) ample; (*bouteille, cruche*) potbellied; **un bébé aux joues ~es** a baby with plump cheeks
rebondir [R(ə)bɔ̃diR] <8> *vi* ~ **contre qc** (*balle, ballon*) to bounce off sth
rebondissement [R(ə)bɔ̃dismɑ̃] *m* **nouveau** ~ **dans l'affaire X!** new development in the X case!; **le** ~ **de l'architecture gothique** the sudden revival of Gothic architecture
rebord [R(ə)bɔR] *m* rim; (*d'une cheminée, fenêtre*) ledge; (*d'un meuble*) edge
reboucher [R(ə)buʃe] <1> *vt* (*bouteille, récipient*) to recork; (*tranchée*) to fill in again
rebours [R(ə)buR] **1.**(*à rebrousse-poil*) **caresser un chien à** ~ to stroke a dog the wrong way; **compter à** ~ to count backwards **2.**MIL **compte à** ~ countdown **3.***fig* **comprendre à** ~ to get the wrong end of the stick; **prendre qn à** ~ to rub sb up the wrong way; **faire qc à** ~ to do sth the wrong way round
reboutonner [R(ə)butɔne] <1> **I.** *vt* to rebutton **II.** *vpr* **se** ~ to do one's buttons up again
rebrousse-poil [R(ə)bRuspwal] **à** ~ (*caresser, lisser*) the wrong way; **prendre qn à** ~ *inf* to rub sb up the wrong way
rebrousser [R(ə)bRuse] <1> *vt* (*cheveux, poils*) to ruffle; **brossez le tapis en rebroussant les poils** brush the carpet against the pile
rebuffade [R(ə)byfad] *f* rebuff; **essuyer une** ~ to be rebuffed
rébus [Rebys] *m* rebus; (*casse-tête*) puzzle
rebut [Rəby] *m* **1.**scrap; (*objets*) junk **2.***péj* (*racaille*) **le(s)** ~**(s) de la société** the dregs of society ▸**aller au** ~ to be scrapped; **de** ~ **marchandise de** ~ rejects
rebutant(e) [R(ə)bytɑ̃, ɑ̃t] *adj* repulsive; (*décourageant*) disheartening
rebuter [R(ə)byte] <1> **I.** *vt* **1.**(*repousser*) to disgust **2.**(*décourager*) ~ **qn** (*démarche, travail*) to dishearten; **rien ne le rebute** nothing makes him downhearted **II.** *vpr* **se** ~ to be disheartened
récalcitrant(e) [RekalsitRɑ̃, ɑ̃t] **I.** *adj* **1.**(*enfant*) rebellious; (*animal*) stubborn; **se montrer** [*o* **être**] ~ **à qc** to be stubbornly opposed to sth; **ne sois pas aussi ~!** don't be so stubborn! **2.** *inf* (*pas facilement arrangeable: boutons, machine, outil*) awkward **II.** *m(f)* recalcitrant
recaler [R(ə)kale] <1> *vt inf* ECOLE to fail; **se faire** ~ **en math** to fail maths *Brit,* to flunk math *Am*
récapitulation [Rekapitylasjɔ̃] *f* recapitulation; **faire** [*o* **procéder à**] **la** ~ **de qc** to recapitulate sth
récapituler [Rekapityle] <1> *vt* to recapitulate; ~ **sa journée** to sum up one's day
recauser [R(ə)koze] <1> *vi inf* ~ **d'une idée à qn** to talk to sb about an idea again; **elle ne m'en a jamais recausé** she never spoke to me about it again
recel [Rəsɛl] *m* receiving; ~ **de cadavre** concealment of death; ~ **de malfaiteur/de criminel** harbouring [*o* harboring *Am*] a wrongdoer/criminal
receler [Rəs(ə)le, R(ə)səle], **recéler** [R(ə)sele] <4> *vt* **1.**JUR to receive; ~ **un malfaiteur** to harbour [*o* harbor *Am*] a wrongdoer/criminal **2.**(*renfermer: fond marin, sous-sol*) to hold; **ce texte recèle des erreurs** the text contains errors
receleur, -euse [Rəs(ə)lœR, -øz, R(ə)səlœR, -øz] *m, f,* **recéleur, -euse** [R(ə)selœR, -øz] *m, f* receiver (of stolen goods), fence *inf*
récemment [Resamɑ̃] *adv* recently
recensement [R(ə)sɑ̃smɑ̃] *m* **1.**(*dénombrement détaillé d'habitants*) ADMIN **faire le** ~ **de la population** to take a census of the population **2.**(*inventaire*) inventory
recenser [R(ə)sɑ̃se] <1> *vt* **1.**(*population*) to take a census of **2.**(*dénombrer*) to take stock of; ~ **les ressources d'une région** to list the resources of a region
récent(e) [Resɑ̃, ɑ̃t] *adj* (*événement, période, passé*) recent; **leur divorce est tout** ~ they've only recently got divorced
recentrer [R(ə)sɑ̃tRe] <1> **I.** *vt* POL to revise; TECH to realign **II.** *vi* SPORT to centre [*o* center *Am*] again
récépissé [Resepise] *m* receipt; ~ **de dépôt** receipt (*for a deposit*); ~ **d'envoi** receipt (*for an article sent by post*)
réceptacle [Resɛptakl] *m* **1.**(*des eaux*) catchment basin; (*d'objets hétéroclites*) container **2.**BOT receptacle
récepteur [Resɛptœr] *m* **1.**RADIO receiver; ~ **de radio** radio receiver **2.**TEL ~ (**téléphonique**) receiver **3.**PHYSIOL, BIO (*auditif, olfactif*) receptor; LING receiver **4.**(*transformateur*) transformer
réception [Resɛpsjɔ̃] *f* **1.** *a.* TV, RADIO (*fête*) reception; **donner une** ~ to hold a reception **2.**(*accueil*) welcome; **faire bonne/mauvaise** ~ **à qn** to give sb a warm/cold welcome **3.**(*guichet d'accueil*) reception; (*hall d'accueil*) reception area **4.**SPORT (*de ballon*) catching; (*d'un sauteur*) landing
réceptionner [Resɛpsjɔne] <1> *vt* **1.**to

receive; ~ **des marchandises** to take delivery of goods **2.** SPORT (*ballon*) to catch

réceptionniste [ʀesɛpsjɔnist] *mf* receptionist

récession [ʀesesjɔ̃] *f* recession

recette [ʀ(ə)sɛt] *f* **1.** GASTR *a. fig* recipe **2.** *sans pl* COM takings *pl* **3.** *pl* COM (*opp: dépenses*) receipts; **~s budgétaires** budgetary revenue

receveur, -euse [ʀəs(ə)vœʀ, -øz, ʀ(ə)səvœʀ, -øz] *m, f* **1.** ~ **des impôts** tax collector **2.** MED recipient; ~ **universel** universal recipient

recevoir [ʀəs(ə)vwaʀ, ʀ(ə)səvwaʀ] <12> **I.** *vt* **1.** (*obtenir en récompense, bénéficier de, accepter*) to receive; **être bien/mal reçu** to be well/badly received; **je n'ai pas de conseil/leçon à ~ de vous** I don't need advice/lessons from you; **recevez, cher Monsieur/chère Madame, l'expression de mes sentiments distingués/mes sincères salutations** *form* yours faithfully **2.** (*obtenir en cadeau*) to get, be given; ~ **une décoration** to receive a decoration; ~ **une poupée en cadeau** to be given a doll as a present **3.** (*percevoir*) to be paid; ~ **un bon salaire** to get a good salary **4.** (*accueillir*) to welcome; ~ **qn à dîner** to have sb over for dinner; **j'ai reçu la visite de ma sœur** I received a visit from my sister; **être reçu à l'Élysée** to be invited to the Élysée Palace **5.** (*subir: coup, projectile*) to get; **j'ai reçu la pluie** I got caught in the rain; **c'est moi qui ai tout reçu** (*coups*) I got the worst of it; ~ **une correction** to get a beating; **elle a reçu le ballon sur la tête** she got hit on the head by the ball **6.** (*admettre*) ~ **qn dans un club/une école** to admit sb into a club/school; **être reçu à un examen** to pass an exam; **les candidats reçus** the successful candidates **7.** (*contenir*) **pouvoir ~ des personnes** (*salle*) to hold people; **cet hôtel peut ~ 80 personnes** this hotel can accommodate 80 people; **cette tente peut ~ 3 personnes** this tent can sleep 3 people ▶**se faire** (**bien/drôlement**) ~ *inf* to get told off **II.** *vi* **1.** (*donner une réception*) to entertain **2.** SPORT (*jouer sur son terrain*) **Lyon reçoit Montpellier** Lyon is playing Montpellier at home

rechange [ʀ(ə)ʃɑ̃ʒ] *m* **prendre un ~** to take a change of clothes ▶**pièce de ~** spare part; **roue de ~** spare wheel *Brit,* spare tire *Am;* **solution de ~** alternative; **chaussures de ~** extra pair of shoes

réchapper [ʀeʃape] <1> *vi* ~ **de l'incendie** to escape the fire

recharge [ʀ(ə)ʃaʀʒ] *f* **1.** ELEC (*processus*) recharging **2.** (*cartouche: d'arme*) reload; (*d'un stylo à bille*) refill

rechargeable [ʀ(ə)ʃaʀʒabl] *adj* (*briquet, stylo*) refillable; **briquet/rasoir non ~** disposable lighter/razor

recharger [ʀ(ə)ʃaʀʒe] <2a> **I.** *vt* (*arme*) to reload; (*briquet, stylo*) to refill; (*accumulateurs, batterie*) to recharge **II.** *vpr* ELEC **se ~** to recharge

réchaud [ʀeʃo] *m* stove; ~ **à gaz** camping stove

réchauffé [ʀeʃofe] *m* GASTR reheated food; **ça doit être du ~** it must have been heated up again **2.** *fig* **ça sent le ~!** there's nothing new about it!

réchauffé(e) [ʀeʃofe] *adj* hackneyed

réchauffement [ʀeʃofmɑ̃] *m* warming up; (*des relations, d'une amitié*) improvement; **annoncer un ~ des températures** to forecast a rise in temperatures; ~ **de la planète** global warming

réchauffer [ʀeʃofe] <1> **I.** *vt* **1.** GASTR (**faire**) ~ **qc** to heat sth up (again) **2.** (*donner de la chaleur à: corps, membres*) to warm up; **ce bouillon m'a bien réchauffé** this broth has warmed me up; **cela m'a réchauffé le cœur** *fig* it warmed (the cockles of) my heart **II.** *vpr* **1.** (*devenir plus chaud*) **se ~** (*temps, température, eau, planète*) to get warmer; **les océans se sont réchauffés** ocean temperatures have risen **2.** (*retrouver sa chaleur*) **se ~** (*pieds, mains*) to warm up; **se ~ les doigts/pieds** to warm up one's fingers/feet

rêche [ʀɛʃ] *adj* **1.** (*vin, texture*) rough; (*fruit*) bitter **2.** *soutenu* (*rude: personne*) prickly

recherche [ʀ(ə)ʃɛʀʃ] *f* **1.** (*quête*) *a.* INFOR search; **la ~ d'un livre** the search for a book; **être à la ~ d'un appartement/de qn** to be looking for a flat/sb; **la ~ du bonheur** the pursuit of happiness; ~ **documentaire en ligne** on-line information retrieval **2.** *gén pl* (*enquête*) investigation; **abandonner les ~s** to give up the search; **faire des ~s sur qc** to carry out an investigation into sth; **la ~ d'un criminel** the hunt for a criminal **3.** *sans pl* MED, ECOLE, UNIV research; **faire de la ~ scientifique/fondamentale** to do scientific/basic research

recherché(e) [ʀ(ə)ʃɛʀʃe] *adj* **1.** (*demandé: acteur, produit*) in great demand; (*livre*) highly sought-after **2.** (*raffiné: style*) mannered; (*expression*) studied; (*plaisir*) exquisite

rechercher [ʀ(ə)ʃɛʀʃe] <1> *vt* **1.** (*chercher à trouver*) ~ **un nom/une amie** to look for a name/a friend; ~ **un terroriste** to hunt for a terrorist; ~ **l'albumine dans les urines** to look for the presence of albumin in the urine; ~ **où/quand/comment/si c'est arrivé** to try to determine where/when/how/if it happened; **être recherché pour meurtre/vol** to be wanted for murder/theft **2.** (*reprendre*) **aller ~ qn/qc** to go and fetch sb/sth

rechigner [ʀ(ə)ʃiɲe] <1> *vi* ~ **à faire un travail** to be reluctant to do a task; **travailler en rechignant** to work with a sour face

rechute [ʀ(ə)ʃyt] *f* MED relapse; **avoir une ~** to (have a) relapse

rechuter [ʀ(ə)ʃyte] <1> *vi a.* MED to have a relapse

R

récidive [ʀesidiv] *f a.* MED relapse

récidiver [ʀesidive] <1> *vi* MED to relapse

récidiviste [ʀesidivist] I. *adj* recidivist; **être ~** to be a habitual [*o* repeat *Am*] offender II. *mf* JUR (*au second délit*) second offender; (*après plusieurs délits*) habitual [*o* repeat *Am*] offender

récif [ʀesif] *m* reef; **~ corallien/frangeant** coral/fringing reef

récipient [ʀesipjɑ̃] *m* container

réciprocité [ʀesipʀɔsite] *f* reciprocity; **accord de ~** reciprocal agreement; **il y a ~** it's the same on both sides

réciproque [ʀesipʀɔk] I. *adj* mutual; (*accord, aide*) reciprocal II. *f* 1. reverse; **s'attendre à la ~** to expect the same (treatment); **la ~ n'est pas toujours vraie** the converse is not always true 2. MAT reciprocal

réciproquement [ʀesipʀɔkmɑ̃] *adv* 1. (*mutuellement*) **ils s'admirent ~** they admire each other 2. (*inversement*) **et ~** and vice versa

réciproquer [ʀesipʀɔke] <1> *vt Belgique* (*adresser en retour*) **~ des vœux** to return good wishes

récit [ʀesi] *m* story; (*narration*) account; **~ d'aventures** adventure story; **faire un ~ circonstancié de qc** to give a detailed account of sth

récital [ʀesital] <s> *m* recital; **~ poétique/de piano/de violon/de chanson/de danse** poetry/piano/violin/song/dance recital

récitation [ʀesitasjɔ̃] *f* ECOLE recitation; **leçon de ~** work to be recited by heart

réciter [ʀesite] <1> *vt* (*leçon, poème*) to recite

réclamation [ʀeklamasjɔ̃] *f* 1. (*plainte*) complaint; **déposer une ~** to lodge a complaint 2. (*demande*) claim 3. (*service*) **les ~s** complaints department 4. TEL **téléphoner aux ~s** to ring the engineers *Brit*, to call repairs *Am*

réclame [ʀeklam] *f* (*publicité*) advertising; **faire de la ~ pour qn/qc** to advertise sth ►**en ~** on special offer

réclamer [ʀeklame] <1> I. *vt* 1. (*solliciter: argent*) to ask for; (*aide, silence*) to call for 2. (*demander avec insistance*) to demand; **je réclame la parole!** I ask to speak! 3. (*revendiquer*) to demand; **~ une augmentation à qn** to ask sb for a raise 4. (*nécessiter: patience, soin, temps*) to require II. *vi* to complain

reclasser [ʀ(ə)klase] <1> *vt* 1. (*réaffecter: employé, ouvrier*) to redeploy; (*chômeur*) to place 2. (*réajuster: fonctionnaire*) to regrade 3. (*remettre en ordre*) to reorder; (*dossiers*) to reclassify

réclusion [ʀeklyzjɔ̃] *f* JUR imprisonment; **~ criminelle** imprisonment; **être condamné à la ~ criminelle à perpétuité** to be sentenced to life imprisonment

recoiffer [ʀ(ə)kwafe] <1> *vpr* **se ~** to redo one's hair

recoin [ʀəkwɛ̃] *m* corner; **fouiller jusque dans les moindres ~s** to search every nook and cranny

recoller [ʀ(ə)kɔle] <1> *vt* 1. (*coller à nouveau: enveloppe*) to stick back down; (*étiquette, timbre*) to stick back on 2. (*raccommoder: morceaux, vase cassé*) to stick back together 3. *inf* (*remettre*) **~ qn en prison** to stick sb back in prison 4. *inf* (*redonner*) **on m'a racollé une amende** I've had another fine slapped on me

récoltant(e) [ʀekɔltɑ̃, ɑ̃t] I. *adj* **viticulteur ~** wine-producer; **propriétaire ~** grower II. *m(f)* grower

récolte [ʀekɔlt] *f* 1. (*activité*) harvest 2. (*produits récoltés*) **~ des abricots/pommes de terre** apricot/potato crop

récolter [ʀekɔlte] <1> *vt* 1. AGR to harvest 2. (*recueillir: argent*) to collect; (*contraventions, coups, ennuis*) to get; (*points, voix*) to pick up ►**~ ce qu'on a <u>semé</u>** to reap what one has sown

recommandable [ʀ(ə)kɔmɑ̃dabl] *adj* commendable; **un type très peu ~** a rather disreputable character

recommandation [ʀ(ə)kɔmɑ̃dasjɔ̃] *f* 1. (*appui*) recommendation; **lettre de ~** letter of recommendation; **sur la ~ de qn** on sb's recommendation 2. (*conseil*) advice; **faire des ~s à qn** to give sb some advice

recommandé [ʀ(ə)kɔmɑ̃de] *m* (*lettre, paquet*) ≈ recorded *Brit*, ≈ registered *Am*; **en ~** ≈ by recorded delivery *Brit*, ≈ by registered mail *Am*

recommander [ʀ(ə)kɔmɑ̃de] <1> *vt* 1. (*conseiller*) to advise; **~ à qn de** +*infin* to advise sb to +*infin*; **être recommandé** to be advisable; **je recommande ce film** I recommend this film; **il est recommandé de** +*infin* it is advisable to +*infin*; **ce vin est à ~ aux amateurs de blanc** this wine is recommended for people who like white wine 2. (*appuyer: candidat*) to recommend

recommencement [ʀ(ə)kɔmɑ̃smɑ̃] *m* renewal; (*de la pluie*) fresh onset; **la vie est un éternel ~** life is a series of new beginnings

recommencer [ʀ(ə)kɔmɑ̃se] <2> I. *vt* 1. (*reprendre*) to start again; (*combat, lutte*) to resume; **~ un récit depuis le début** to begin a story again at the beginning 2. (*refaire*) **~ sa vie** to make a fresh start; **tout est à ~** everything has to be done all over again; **si c'était à ~, ...** if I could have it over again... 3. (*répéter: erreur*) to make again; (*expérience*) to have again; **ne recommence jamais ça!** don't ever do that again! II. *vi* (*reprendre, se remettre à*) to start again; **les cours ont recommencé** the new term has started; **la pluie recommence (à tomber)** it's starting to rain again; **~ à espérer/marcher** to begin to hope/walk again; **il recommence à neiger** it's starting to snow again ►**(et voilà que) <u>ça</u> recommence!** here we go again!

récompense [ʀekɔ̃pɑ̃s] *f* 1. (*matérielle*)

reward **2.** ECOLE, SPORT (*prix*) award; **obtenir la ~ de qc** to win the award for sth; **mériter une ~** to deserve an award; **en ~ de qc** in return for

récompenser [ʀekɔ̃pɑ̃se] <1> *vt* (*personne*) to reward; **~ qn d'un effort/loyauté** to reward sb for their efforts/loyalty

recomposer [ʀ(ə)kɔ̃poze] <1> **I.** *vt* to reconstruct; (*numéro de téléphone*) to redial **II.** *vpr* **se ~** POL to re-form

recomposition [ʀ(ə)kɔ̃pozisjɔ̃] *f* **1.** (*reconstitution*) reconstruction; (*d'une chanson*) recomposition **2.** POL re-forming

recompter [ʀ(ə)kɔ̃te] <1> **I.** *vi* to recount **II.** *vt* **~ une addition** to add up a bill again; (*opération*) to recheck

réconciliation [ʀekɔ̃siljasjɔ̃] *f* reconciliation

réconcilier [ʀekɔ̃silje] <1> **I.** *vt* (*personnes, choses*) to reconcile; **~ qn avec le père/une idée** to reconcile sb with their father/an idea **II.** *vpr* **se ~** (*personnes*) to make up; (*pays*) to be reconciled; **se ~ avec qn/qc** to be reconciled with sb/sth; **se ~ avec soi-même** to learn to live with oneself

reconduire [ʀ(ə)kɔ̃dɥiʀ] *vt irr* **~ qn chez lui** to see someone (back) home; **~ à la frontière** to escort sb back to the border; **~ qn en voiture à la gare** to drive sb back to the station

réconfort [ʀekɔ̃fɔʀ] *m* comfort; **avoir besoin de ~** to need comforting

réconfortant(e) [ʀekɔ̃fɔʀtɑ̃, ɑ̃t] *adj* **1.** (*rassurant*) reassuring; (*consolant*) comforting; (*stimulant*) invigorating; **être pour qn une personne ~e** to be a source of comfort for sb **2.** (*fortifiant*) fortifying

réconforter [ʀekɔ̃fɔʀte] <1> *vt* **1.** (*consoler*) to comfort; (*rassurer*) to reassure; (*stimuler*) to cheer up; **~ qn par une lettre** to comfort sb with a letter; **cela m'a bien réconforté** it made me feel much better **2.** (*fortifier*) to fortify

reconnaissable [ʀ(ə)kɔnɛsabl] *adj* recognizable

reconnaissance [ʀ(ə)kɔnɛsɑ̃s] *f* **1.** *a.* POL (*gratitude*) gratitude; (*fait d'admettre les mérites de qn*) recognition; **un geste de ~** a mark of gratitude; **en ~ de qc** (*pour remercier*) in appreciation of; (*pour honorer*) in recognition of **2.** JUR, ADMIN **~ de dette** acknowledgement of a debt; **~ d'enfant** (*par le père*) legal recognition of a child **3.** (*exploration, prospection: d'un pays, terrain, de la situation de l'ennemi*) reconnaissance; **faire une ~** to go on reconnaissance; **avion/patrouille de ~** reconnaissance aircraft/patrol; **partir en ~** to go off on reconnaissance **4.** INFOR **~ optique de caractères/vocale** optical character/voice recognition

reconnaissant(e) [ʀ(ə)kɔnɛsɑ̃, ɑ̃t] *adj* grateful

reconnaître [ʀ(ə)kɔnɛtʀ] *irr* **I.** *vt* **1.** (*identifier*) to recognize; **je reconnais bien là ta paresse** that's just typical of you, you're so lazy; **~ qn à son style** to recognize sb by their style; **savoir ~ un faucon d'un aigle** to be able to tell a falcon from an eagle **2.** (*admettre: innocence, qualité*) to recognize; (*erreur, faute*) to admit; **~ la difficulté de la tâche** to recognize the difficulty of the task; **il faut ~ que nous sommes allés trop loin** we have to admit that we have gone too far **3.** (*admettre comme légitime: droit*) to recognize; **~ qn comme chef** to recognize sb as a leader **4.** JUR **~ qn innocent** to recognize sb's innocence **5.** (*être reconnaissant de: service, bienfait*) to recognize; **il faut lui ~ ses qualités** we must recognize his qualities **II.** *vpr* **1.** (*se retrouver*) **se ~ dans sa ville** to find one's way around one's town; **je me reconnais dans le comportement de mon fils** I can see myself in the way my son behaves **2.** (*être reconnaissable*) **se ~ à qc** to be recognizable by sth **3.** (*s'avouer*) **se ~ coupable/vaincu** to confess to being guilty/beaten

reconnu(e) [ʀəkɔny] **I.** *part passé de* **reconnaître** **II.** *adj* **1.** (*admis: chef*) acknowledged; (*fait*) accepted; **il est ~ que ce médicament est très efficace** this medicine is known to be very effective **2.** (*de renom*) **~ pour qc** well-known for sth

reconquérir [ʀ(ə)kɔ̃keʀiʀ] *vt irr* (*pays*) to reconquer; (*amour, dignité, pouvoir*) to win back

reconquête [ʀ(ə)kɔ̃kɛt] *f* (*d'un pays*) reconquest; (*la dignité, du pouvoir*) recovery; (*de l'amour*) winning back

reconsidérer [ʀ(ə)kɔ̃sideʀe] <5> *vt* to reconsider

reconstituer [ʀ(ə)kɔ̃stitɥe] <1> **I.** *vt* **1.** (*remettre dans l'ordre: texte*) to restore; (*faits*) to reconstruct; (*puzzle*) to piece together; (*scène, bataille*) to recreate **2.** (*reformer, réorganiser: organisation*) to reform; **~ une fortune** to rebuild a fortune **3.** (*restaurer*) to reconstruct; (*vieux quartier, édifice*) to restore **4.** BIO to regenerate; **~ ses forces en mangeant** to build up one's strength again by eating **II.** *vpr* **se ~** (*armée, parti*) to re-form; (*organe*) to regenerate

reconstitution [ʀ(ə)kɔ̃stitysjɔ̃] *f* (*d'un texte*) rewriting; (*d'une association*) re-forming; (*d'un puzzle*) piecing together; (*des faits*) reconstruction; **~ de carrière** career record; **~ historique** reconstruction of history

reconstruction [ʀ(ə)kɔ̃stʀyksjɔ̃] *f* reconstruction

reconstruire [ʀ(ə)kɔ̃stʀɥiʀ] *vt irr* (*ville, édifice*) to reconstruct; **~ une fortune** to rebuild a fortune; **~ sa vie** to rebuild one's life

reconversion [ʀ(ə)kɔ̃vɛʀsjɔ̃] *f* **1.** (*recyclage*) **suivre un stage de ~ en informatique** to do an IT-retraining course **2.** ECON **~ industrielle** industrial redevelopment; **~ économique d'une entreprise** economic turnround [*o* turnaround *Am*] of a company

reconvertir [R(ə)kɔ̃vɛRtiR] <8> **I.** *vt* **1.** (*adapter*) ~ **un entrepôt en usine** to reconvert a warehouse into a factory; **être reconverti en qc** to be converted into sth **2.** (*recycler*) ~ **le personnel à l'informatique** to retrain the staff in IT **II.** *vpr* **se** ~ (*personne*) to retrain; (*usine*) to be put to a new use; **se** ~ **dans la médecine** to retrain as a doctor

recopier [R(ə)kɔpje] <1> *vt* **1.** (*transcrire*) to copy out **2.** (*mettre au propre*) to write up **3.** INFOR ~ **un fichier sur une disquette à qn** to copy a file onto a floppy disk for sb

record [R(ə)kɔR] **I.** *m a.* SPORT (*performance*) record; ~ **d'affluence/de production** record audience numbers/production; **battre tous les ~s** to beat all records; **établir un** ~ to set a record **II.** *app inv* **vitesse** ~ record speed; **en un temps** ~ in record time

recordman [R(ə)kɔRdman] <s> *m* (men's) record holder

recordwoman [R(ə)kɔRdwuman] <s> *f* (women's) record holder

recoucher [R(ə)kuʃe] <1> **I.** *vt* (*personne*) to put back to bed; (*objet*) to lay down again **II.** *vpr* **se** ~ to go back to bed

recoudre [R(ə)kudR] *vt irr* **1.** COUT to sew up (again); ~ **un bouton** to sew a button back on **2.** MED to restitch; (*opéré*) to stitch up again; ~ **qc à un blessé** to stitch sth back onto an injured person

recoupement [R(ə)kupmɑ̃] *m* crosscheck; **faire un ~/des ~s** to crosscheck

recouper [R(ə)kupe] <1> **I.** *vt* **1.** (*couper de nouveau: vêtement*) to recut; ~ **un morceau à qn** to cut another piece for sb **2.** (*confirmer*) ~ **qc** (*témoignage, renseignement*) to confirm sth **II.** *vpr* **se** ~ (*coïncider: chiffres*) to add up; (*faits*) to tie

recourbé(e) [R(ə)kuRbe] *adj* (*bec*) curved; **cils ~s** curling eyelashes; **nez** ~ hooknose

recourir[1] [R(ə)kuRiR] *vi irr* **1.** (*coureur*) to run again; (*cycliste, coureur automobile*) to race again **2.** (*retourner*) ~ **à la maison** (*une seconde fois*) to run back to the house; **je recours aussitôt vous chercher** (*revenir*) I'll dash back to fetch you

recourir[2] [R(ə)kuRiR] *vi irr* ~ **à qn/qc** to have recourse to sb/sth; ~ **à la violence** to resort to violence; ~ **à une aide/un emprunt** to seek help/a loan

recours [R(ə)kuR] *m* **1.** (*utilisation*) ~ **à qc** recourse to sth; ~ **à la violence** resorting to violence; **avoir** ~ **à qn** to turn to sb; **avoir** ~ **à la violence** to resort to violence; **avoir** ~ **à des mesures conservatoires** to have recourse to protective measures **2.** (*ressource, personne*) resort; **c'est sans** ~ there's nothing we can do about it; **il n'y a aucun** ~ **contre cette décision** there's no way of changing this decision; **en dernier** ~ as a last resort

recouvrement [R(ə)kuvRəmɑ̃] *m* **1.** FIN (*de l'impôt, des impayés*) collection; **somme mise en** ~ amount payable **2.** CONSTR lap

recouvrer [R(ə)kuvRe] <1> *vt* FIN (*impôt, cotisation*) to collect; (*effet de commerce, créance*) to recover

recouvrir [R(ə)kuvRiR] <11> *vt* **1.** (*couvrir entièrement*) to cover; ~ **un mur de papier peint** to paper a wall; **être recouvert de buée/crépi/neige/givre** to be covered in condensation/roughcast/snow/frost **2.** (*couvrir à nouveau*) ~ **un fauteuil** to recover an armchair; ~ **le toit de tuiles** to retile the roof; ~ **un enfant** to cover up a child again **3.** (*inclure*) **une étude qui recouvre partiellement des domaines très divers** a study which touches on a wide range of fields

recracher [R(ə)kRaʃe] <1> **I.** *vi* to spit again **II.** *vt* **1.** (*expulser*) ~ **qc** to spit sth back out **2.** *inf* (*répéter: leçon*) to regurgitate

récré [RekRe] *f inf,* **récréation** [RekReasjɔ̃] *f* **1.** ECOLE break *Brit,* recess *Am;* **aller en** ~ to go out for break; **les enfants sont en** ~ the children are having break **2.** (*délassement*) recreation; (*pause*) break

récrimination [RekRiminasjɔ̃] *f souvent pl* recrimination

récriminer [RekRimine] <1> *vi* ~ **contre qn/qc** to complain loudly about sb

récrire [RekRiR] *vt irr* **1.** (*rewriter*) to rewrite **2.** (*répondre*) ~ **une lettre à qn** to write another letter to sb

recroqueviller [R(ə)kRɔk(ə)vije] <1> *vpr* **1.** (*se rétracter*) **se** ~ to hunch up; (*fleur*) to curl up **2.** (*se tasser*) **se** ~ to shrink; (*avec l'âge*) to shrivel up; **se** ~ **dans les bras de qn** to snuggle up in sb's arms; **se** ~ **sur un objet** to hunch over an object; **se** ~ **sur son passé** to take refuge in one's past

recrudescence [R(ə)kRydesɑ̃s] *f* (*épidémie*) further outbreak; (*fièvre*) new bout; **une** ~ **de la criminalité** a new crime wave

recrutement [R(ə)kRytmɑ̃] *m* recruitment; **cabinet de** ~ recruitment agency

recruter [R(ə)kRyte] <1> **I.** *vt a.* MIL, POL to recruit; ~ **qn comme technicien** to take sb on as a technician **II.** *vi a.* MIL to recruit; **on recrute dans la police** the police are recruiting **III.** *vpr* (*provenir de*) **les interprètes se recrutent généralement dans les milieux multilingues** interpreters generally come from multilingual backgrounds

recta [Rɛkta] *adv* **payer** ~ to pay on the spot

rectangle [Rɛktɑ̃gl] **I.** *m* rectangle **II.** *adj* (*triangle, trapèze*) right-angled

rectangulaire [Rɛktɑ̃gylɛR] *adj* rectangular

recteur [Rɛktœr] *m* **1.** ECOLE rector (*chief education officer in an académie*) **2.** REL rector

recteur, -trice [Rɛktœr, tRis] *m, f Québec* (*chef d'une université*) rector (*head of a university*)

rectificatif [Rɛktifikatif] *m* correction; ~ **à une loi** amendment to a law

rectificatif, -ive [Rɛktifikatif, -iv] *adj* **note**

rectificative correction

rectification [ʀɛktifikasjɔ̃] *f* (*d'un texte, d'une déclaration*) correction; (*d'une erreur*) rectification; (*d'une route*) straightening

rectifier [ʀɛktifje] <1> *vt* **1.** (*corriger*) to correct; ~ **les défauts d'un produit** to iron out the flaws in a product **2.** (*redresser: route, tracé*) to straighten; (*position*) to correct **3.** (*rendre conforme: cravate*) to adjust; ~ **la position** to correct one's stance

rectiligne [ʀɛktiliɲ] *adj* rectilinear; **parfaitement** ~ perfectly straight

recto [ʀɛkto] *m* front; **voir au** ~ see other side; ~ **verso** on both sides (of the page)

rectorat [ʀɛktɔʀa] *m* **1.** (*fonction*) rectorate **2.** (*bureaux*) ≈ local education offices

rectum [ʀɛktɔm] *m* rectum

reçu [ʀ(ə)sy] *m* (*quittance*) receipt

reçu(e) [ʀ(ə)sy] **I.** *part passé de* **recevoir** **II.** *adj* **1.** (*couramment admis*) accepted; **idée ~e** commonplace idea **2.** ECOLE **14 candidats sont ~s sur les 131 qui se sont présentés** of the 131 candidates who took the exam, 14 passed **III.** *m(f)* ~ **à un examen** successful candidate in an exam

recueil [ʀəkœj] *m* (*ensemble*) collection; ~ **de poèmes** anthology of poems; ~ **de documents** collection of documents

recueillement [ʀ(ə)kœjmɑ̃] *m* contemplation; (*religieux*) meditation; **avec** ~ with reverence

recueillir [ʀ(ə)kœjiʀ] *irr* **I.** *vt* **1.** (*réunir: documents*) to collect **2.** (*obtenir: signatures*) to obtain; ~ **des applaudissements** to win applause; ~ **tous les suffrages** to win everybody's approval; **il n'a recueilli aucun bénéfice de ses vacances** he didn't benefit at all from his holiday **3.** (*accueillir*) to welcome; ~ **des réfugiés** to take in refugees **4.** (*enregistrer: déposition*) to take down; (*opinion*) to record **II.** *vpr* **se** ~ to gather one's thoughts; **se ~ sur la tombe d'un ami** to spend some moments in silence at a friend's grave

recuire [ʀ(ə)kɥiʀ] *vt irr* to recook; (*cuire plus*) to cook longer

recul [ʀ(ə)kyl] *m* **1.** (*éloignement dans le temps, l'espace*) distance; (*d'une voiture*) reversing; **le siège n'a pas assez de** ~ you can't push the seat back far enough **2.** (*réflexion*) **avec le** ~ with the benefit of hindsight; **prendre du** ~ to step back **3.** FIN fall; ~ **de la livre** the fall of the pound

reculer [ʀ(ə)kyle] <1> **I.** *vi* **1.** (*opp: avancer: véhicule*) to back up, to reverse *Brit;* (*personne*) to step back; (*involontairement*) to draw back; ~ **devant le danger** to retreat in the face of danger; **faire ~ qn** to force sb back; **faire ~ un animal** to move an animal back; ~ **de deux pas** to take two steps backwards **2.** (*renoncer*) to shrink back; ~ **devant une obligation** to back away from an obligation; **faire ~ qn** to make sb back down; **rien ne me fera ~** nothing will stop me; **ne ~ devant rien** not to flinch at anything; **il ne recule devant rien** he'll stop at nothing **3.** (*diminuer: chômage*) to come down; (*influence*) to be on the decline; **faire ~ le chômage** to bring employment down ▸ ~ **pour mieux sauter** to put off the inevitable **II.** *vt* (*meuble*) to move back; (*mur*) to push back; (*frontière*) to extend; (*véhicule*) to back up, to reverse *Brit;* (*rendez-vous*) to postpone; (*décision, échéance*) to put off **III.** *vpr* **se** ~ to take a step back; **recule-toi!** get back!

reculons [ʀ(ə)kylɔ̃] **à** ~ backwards; **sortir à ~ d'une salle** to back out of a room; **aller à l'école à** ~ to creep unwillingly to school; **avancer à** ~ to be getting nowhere

récupérable [ʀekypeʀabl] *adj* **1.** (*réutilisable*) **reusable** (*objets*) salvageable; (*heure, congé*) recoverable; **des vêtements ~s** clothes that are still wearable; **ces heures sup sont ~s sous forme de congé** extra holiday [*o* vacation *Am*] will be given in lieu of this overtime **2.** (*amendable*) **ce délinquant est** ~ this delinquent can be rehabilitated; **ne plus être** ~ to be beyond redemption

récupération [ʀekypeʀasjɔ̃] *f* **1.** (*reprise de possession: des biens, des forces*) recovery **2.** (*réutilisation: de la feraille*) salvage; (*des chiffons*) reprocessing; (*du verre*) recycling; ~ **des vieux papiers** paper recycling **3.** (*recouvrement: des heures de cours, d'une journée de travail*) making up **4.** POL (*d'un mouvement politique, d'idées*) hijacking

récupérer [ʀekypeʀe] <5> **I.** *vi* to recuperate **II.** *vt* **1.** (*reprendre: argent, biens*) to recover **2.** *inf* (*retrouver: stylo prêté*) to get back **3.** *inf* (*aller chercher*) to pick up **4.** (*recouvrer: journée de travail*) to make up for; (*sous forme de congés*) to get back **5.** POL (*mouvement, idée*) to hijack

récurer [ʀekyʀe] <1> *vt* to scour

recyclable [ʀ(ə)siklabl] *adj* ECOL recyclable

recyclage [ʀ(ə)siklaʒ] *m* **1.** ECOL (*d'une entreprise*) reorientation; (*d'une personne*) retraining **2.** (*nouveau traitement: de l'air, l'eau*) recycling

recyclé(e) [ʀəsikle] *adj* recycled

recycler [ʀ(ə)sikle] <1> **I.** *vt* **1.** ECOL (*déchets, verre, eau*) to recycle **2.** (*reconvertir*) to retrain; (*mettre à jour*) to send on a refresher course; (*élève*) reorientate **II.** *vpr* (*se reconvertir*) **se** ~ to retrain; (*entreprise*) to readapt itself; **se ~ dans l'enseignement** to retrain as a teacher

rédacteur, -trice [ʀedaktœʀ, -tʀis] *m, f* writer; ~ **en chef** editor; ~ **publicitaire** copywriter

rédaction [ʀedaksjɔ̃] *f* **1.** (*écriture: d'un article*) writing; (*d'une encyclopédie*) compilation **2.** PRESSE (*lieu*) editorial office; (*équipe*) editorial staff **3.** ECOLE composition

reddition [ʀedisjɔ̃] *f* surrender

redécouvrir [ʀ(ə)dekuvʀiʀ] <11> *vt* to rediscover

R

redéfinir [R(ə)definiR] <8> *vt* to redefine

redemander [R(ə)dəmɑ̃de, Rəd(ə)mɑ̃de] <1> *vt* ~ **un livre** (*le même*) to ask for a book again; (*le sien*) to ask for a book back; (*un autre*) to ask for another book; ~ **de la sauce** to ask for more sauce; ~ **toujours du chocolat** to keep asking for more chocolate; ~ **une bouteille de vin** to ask for another bottle of wine; **si tu veux encore du poulet, tu n'as qu'à en** ~ If you want more chicken, all you have to do is ask; **en** ~ to beg for more; *iron* to ask for more

redémarrer [R(ə)demaRe] <1> *vi* **1.** (*repartir*) to start again **2.** *fig* (*entreprise*) to relaunch; (*production, machines*) to start up again; **faire** ~ **l'économie** to restart the economy; **faire** ~ **un chantier** to restart work on a building site

redéployer [R(ə)deplwaje] <6> **I.** *vt* (*industrie, économie*) to restructure; (*personnel, forces*) to redeploy **II.** *vpr* **se** ~ (*secteur économique*) to reorganize

redescendre [R(ə)desɑ̃dR] <14> **I.** *vt avoir* **1.** (*vu d'en haut*) to go down; (*échelle*) to climb down; (*en courant: escalier*) to run down; (*en escaladant: escalier, échelle*) to climb down; (*voiture*) to drive down; (*vu d'en bas*) to come down **2.** (*porter vers le bas*) ~ **qn/qc au marché** to take sb/sth down to the market; ~ **qn/qc d'un arbre** to get sb/sth back down from a tree **II.** *vi être* (*baromètre, fièvre*) to fall again; (*marée*) to go out again; (*rue*) to go back down

redevable [R(ə)dəvabl, Rəd(ə)vabl] **I.** *adj* **1.** FIN **être** ~ **à qn d'une somme** to owe an amount to sb; **être** ~ **de l'impôt** to be liable to tax **2.** (*tenu à reconnaissance*) **être** ~ **à qn d'un service** to be indebted to sb for a favour [*o* favor *Am*]; **être** ~ **à qn d'un succès** to owe one's success to sb **II.** *mf* taxpayer

redevance [R(ə)dəvɑ̃s, Rəd(ə)vɑ̃s] *f* **1.** TEL rental charge; ~ **télé** ≈ licence [*o* license *Am*] fee **2.** (*taxe*) tax

redevenir [R(ə)dəv(ə)niR] <9> *vi* to become again; **être redevenu soi-même** to be one's old self again

rediffuser [R(ə)difyze] <1> *vt* ~ **une série** to show a series again

rédiger [Rediʒe] <2a> *vt* (*contrat, procès-verbal*) to draft; (*revue*) to write

redingote [R(ə)dɛ̃gɔt] *f* tailored coat; HIST frock coat

redire [R(ə)diR] *vt irr* (*répéter: histoire*) to tell again; (*rapporter*) to repeat ►<u>avoir</u>/<u>trouver</u> **à** ~ **à qc** to find fault with sth

rediscuter [R(ə)diskyte] <1> *vt* to discuss again; **nous en rediscuterons** we'll talk about it again

redistribuer [R(ə)distRibɥe] <1> *vt* (*répartir*) to redistribute; (*cartes*) to deal again

redite [R(ə)dit] *f* repetition

redondant(e) [R(ə)dɔ̃dɑ̃, ɑ̃t] *adj* superfluous

redonner [R(ə)dɔne] <1> *vt* **1.** (*rendre*) to give back; ~ **de l'espoir/des forces/courage** to restore hope/strength/courage; **ça te redonnera du tonus** that will build your strength back up **2.** (*donner à nouveau: cours*) to give again; ~ **du travail à qn** to give sb more work; **ça m'a redonné soif** it made me thirsty again; **ça m'a redonné envie de jouer du piano** it made me want to play the piano again **3.** (*resservir*) ~ **des légumes à qn** to give sb another helping of vegetables; ~ **à boire à qn** to give sb more to drink **4.** (*refaire*) ~ **forme à une chose** to give sth back its shape; ~ **une couche** (**de peinture**) **à qc** to give sth another coat of paint

redormir [R(ə)dɔRmiR] *vi irr* (*plus longtemps*) to go back to sleep; **je ne pourrai pas** ~ **de la nuit** I'll never be able to get to sleep again

redoubler [R(ə)duble] <1> **I.** *vt* **1.** ECOLE ~ **une année** to repeat a year **2.** (*accroître*) ~ **d'efforts** to step up one's efforts; (*douleur*) to intensify **II.** *vi* to increase

redoutable [R(ə)dutabl] *adj* (*arme, maladie, adversaire*) fearsome; (*phénomène*) formidable; **avoir l'air** ~ to look formidable

redouter [Rədute] <1> *vt* ~ **qn/qc** to dread sb/sth; ~ **de grossir** to dread putting on weight; (*devant le risque immédiat*) to be afraid of putting on weight

redoux [Rədu] *m* (*après l'hiver*) thaw; ~ **passager** mild spell

redressement [R(ə)dRɛsmɑ̃] *m* **1.** (*d'un poteau, buste, axe, d'une route*) straightening; (*d'une tôle*) beating out; **procéder au** ~ **de qc** to straighten sth; **être excellent pour le** ~ **du buste** to be excellent for firming up the bust **2.** (*relèvement: d'une économie, d'une entreprise, des finances*) recovery; (*d'une situation*) straightening out **3.** FIN (*d'un compte, de l'imposition*) adjustment **4.** ELEC rectification ►~ <u>**fiscal**</u> tax adjustment

redresser [R(ə)dRese] <1> **I.** *vt* **1.** (*remettre droit: buste, corps*) to straighten; (*tête*) to lift up; ~ **qn sur son oreiller** to prop sb up against their pillow **2.** (*rétablir*) to put right; ~ **l'euro** to achieve the recovery of the euro; ~ **le pays/l'économie** to get the country/the economy back on its feet again; ~ **une entreprise déficitaire** to turn a company around **3.** (*rediriger: voiture*) to straighten up **II.** *vpr* **se** ~ **1.** (*se mettre droit*) to stand up straight; (*se mettre assis*) to sit up straight; **redresse-toi!** (*personne assise*) sit up straight!; (*personne debout*) stand up straight! **2.** (*se relever: pays, ville, économie*) to recover; (*situation*) to correct itself; (*avion*) to flatten out

redresseur [R(ə)dRɛsœR] *m* ELEC rectifier

réduction [Redyksjɔ̃] *f* **1.** (*diminution*) reduction; **du personnel** staff cuts; ~ **de peine** reduction of sentence; ~ **d'impôts** tax cut **2.** (*rabais*) ~ **de 5 % sur un manteau** 5 % off a coat; ~**s étudiants** student concessions; ~

de prix price cut; **faire une** ~ **à qn** to give sb a reduction

réduire [ʀedɥiʀ] *irr* **I.** *vt* **1.** (*diminuer*) *a.* GASTR to reduce; (*salaire, texte, personnel*) to cut; (*temps de travail, peine*) to shorten; (*risques*) to lessen; (*chômage*) to bring down **2.** (*transformer*) ~ **qc en bouillie** to reduce sth to a pulp **II.** *vpr* **se** ~ **à qc** to boil down to; (*montant*) to amount to sth

réduit(e) [ʀedɥi, it] *adj* **1.** (*miniaturisé: échelle, modèle*) small-scale **2.** (*diminué: prix*) cut; (*tarif*) reduced; (*vitesse*) low

réécrire [ʀeekʀiʀ] *vt irr v.* **récrire**

réécriture [ʀeekʀityʀ] *f* rewriting

rééducation [ʀeedykasjɔ̃] *f* **1.** (*d'un malade*) physiotherapy treatment *Brit,* physical therapy *Am;* (*d'un membre*) reeducation **2.** (*d'un délinquant*) rehabilitation; (*d'un mineur*) reeducation

réel [ʀeɛl] *m* **le** ~ reality

réel(le) [ʀeɛl] *adj* **1.** (*véritable*) real; (*danger*) genuine; **c'est un fait** ~ it's a fact **2.** FIN (*salaire*) actual

réélire [ʀeeliʀ] *vt irr* ~ **qn à la présidence** to re-elect sb president

réellement [ʀeɛlmɑ̃] *adv* really

rééquilibrer [ʀeekilibʀe] <1> *vt* to restabilize; ~ **une majorité** to restore a stable majority

réexpédier [ʀeɛkspedje] <1a> *vt* ~ **un colis à qn à Rouen** (*au destinataire*) to forward a parcel to sb in Rouen; (*à l'expéditeur*) to send a parcel back to sb in Rouen

refaire [ʀ(ə)fɛʀ] *vt irr* **1.** (*faire de nouveau*) to do again; (*plat, lit*) to make again; (*article*) to rewrite; (*addition*) to add up again; (*nœud*) to retie; ~ **du bruit** to make more noise **2.** (*recommencer: travail, dessin*) to redo; ~ **la même faute** to repeat the same mistake; ~ **un petit tour du parc** to go for another quick walk around the park; ~ **du sport** to do [*o* play] sport again; **c'est à** ~ it should to be done again; **si c'était à** ~**, je ne ferais pas médecine** if I could start all over again, I wouldn't do medicine **3.** (*remettre en état: meuble*) to restore; (*toit*) to redo; (*chambre*) to redecorate; ~ **la peinture de qc** to repaint sth; **se faire** ~ **le nez** to have one's nose remodelled

réfection [ʀefɛksjɔ̃] *f* repairing; (*d'une statue*) restoration; **travaux de** ~ repair work

réfectoire [ʀefɛktwaʀ] *m* (*d'une école*) dining hall; (*d'une caserne, usine, d'un hôpital*) canteen

référence [ʀefeʀɑ̃s] *f* **1.** (*renvoi*) reference; (*en bas de page*) footnote; ADMIN, COM reference number; **faire** ~ **à qn/qc** to refer to sb/sth; **faire** ~ **à qn dans un livre** to make a reference [*o* refer] to sb in a book; **en** ~ **à qc** in reference to sth **2.** (*modèle*) **faire figure de** ~ **pour qn** to be seen as a model for sb; **être une** ~ to be a recommendation; **il n'est pas une** ~ *iron* he's nothing to go by; **ouvrage de** ~ reference book; **lettre de** ~ testimonial

référencé(e) [ʀefeʀɑ̃se] *adj* referenced

référendum [ʀefeʀɑ̃dɔm] *m* referendum

référer [ʀefeʀe] <5> **I.** *vi* **en** ~ **à un supérieur** to refer back to a superior; **en** ~ **au tribunal** to submit to a court **II.** *vpr* **1.** (*faire référence à*) **se** ~ **à qn/qc** to refer to sb/sth **2.** (*s'en remettre à*) **s'en** ~ **à qn/qc** to refer the matter to sb/sth

refermer [ʀ(ə)fɛʀme] <1> **I.** *vt* **1.** (*opp: ouvrir*) to close; (*porte*) to shut **2.** (*verrouiller*) ~ **qc à clé** to lock sth **II.** *vpr* **se** ~ to close; (*plaie*) to heal up; **se** ~ **sur qn** (*porte*) to close on sb

refiler [ʀ(ə)file] <1> *vt inf* ~ **un objet sans valeur à qn** to palm off a worthless object on sb; **il m'a refilé la grippe** he gave me his flu

réfléchi(e) [ʀefleʃi] *adj* **1.** (*raisonnable: action*) well thought-out; (*jugement*) well-considered **2.** LING reflexive

réfléchir [ʀefleʃiʀ] <8> *vi* **1.** (*penser*) to think; **donner à** ~ (*chose*) to give food for thought; **demander à** ~ (*personne*) to need time to think things over **2.** (*cogiter*) ~ **à qc** to think about sth; **réfléchissez à ce que vous faites** think about what you're doing ►**tout bien réfléchi** after careful consideration; **c'est tout réfléchi** my mind is made up

reflet [ʀ(ə)flɛ] *m* **1.** (*représentation, image réfléchie*) reflection; **être le** ~ **de qc** to be the reflection of sth; **être le** ~ **de qn** to be the image of sb; **n'être qu'un pâle** ~ **de qc** to be the pale reflection of sth **2.** (*éclat: d'une étoffe*) shimmer; (*du soleil*) reflection

refléter [ʀ(ə)flete] <5> **I.** *vt* to reflect; ~ **le bonheur** to glow with happiness **II.** *vpr* **1.** (*se réfléchir*) **se** ~ **dans l'eau** to be reflected in the water **2.** (*transparaître*) **se** ~ **dans un objet** to be mirrored in an object

réflexe [ʀeflɛks] *m* **1.** ANAT reflex **2.** (*réaction rapide*) reaction; **avoir de bons** ~**s** to have good reflexes; ~ **de professeur** a typical teacher's reaction; **manquer de** ~ to be slow to react; **il a eu le** ~ **de courir** instinctively he ran

réflexion [ʀeflɛksjɔ̃] *f* **1.** (*analyse*) thought; **après mûre** ~ after careful consideration; **son idée demande** ~ his idea deserves thought **2.** (*remarque*) remark; **faire des** ~**s à qn sur un sujet** to make comments to sb about a subject; **je te dispense de tes** ~**s** I can do without your comments; **ma mère me fait toujours des** ~**s sur mon comportement** my mother's always complaining about my behaviour [*o* behavior *Am*] ►~ **faite** (*en fin de compte*) on reflection; (*changement d'avis*) on second thoughts

refluer [ʀ(ə)flye] <1> *vi* (*foule*) to surge back; (*eaux, liquide*) to flow back; (*mer*) to ebb; (*sang*) to return; **faire** ~ **qn** to push sb back

reflux [ʀəfly] *m* **1.** ebb **2.** (*recul: de la foule*) backward surge; (*d'un électorat*) falling away; (*des aliments*) repeating

R

reforestation [ʀəfɔʀɛstasjɔ̃] *f* reforestation
réformateur, **-trice** [ʀefɔʀmatœʀ, -tʀis] **I.** *m, f* **1.** reformer **2.** HIST, REL Reformer **II.** *adj* reforming
réforme [ʀefɔʀm] *f* **1.** ADMIN, POL reform; **~s sociales** social reforms; **~ de l'orthographe** spelling reform **2.** MIL discharge **3.** HIST **la Réforme** the Reformation
réformé(e) [ʀefɔʀme] **I.** *adj* **1.** MIL (*soldat*) declared unfit for service **2.** REL reformed **II.** *m(f)* **1.** MIL discharged soldier **2.** REL Protestant
réformer [ʀefɔʀme] <1> *vt* **1.** (*modifier*) to reform **2.** MIL to discharge; (*appelé*) to declare unfit for service
refoulé(e) [ʀ(ə)fule] **I.** *adj* repressed **II.** *m(f)* *inf* repressed person
refouler [ʀ(ə)fule] <1> *vt* **1.** (*repousser: attaque, envahisseur*) to push back; (*foule*) to drive back; (*intrus*) to turn back; (*demande*) to reject **2.** (*réprimer*) to hold back; **~ sa colère** to keep one's anger in check; (*pulsion*) to repress; (*souvenir*) to suppress; (*larmes*) to choke back
réfractaire [ʀefʀaktɛʀ] **I.** *adj* **1. être ~ à une influence** to be impervious to an influence; **être ~ à une maladie** to have resistance to an illness; **être ~ à la musique** to have no feeling for music **2.** (*rebelle: conscrit*) rebellious; (*maladie*) stubborn **II.** *m* HIST *Frenchman during the Second World War refusing to work in Germany*
refrain [ʀ(ə)fʀɛ̃] *m* **1.** MUS chorus **2.** (*rengaine*) song; **c'est toujours le même ~** it's always the same old story; **change de ~!** give it a rest!
refréner, **réfréner** [ʀefʀene] <5> **I.** *vt* (*inmpatience, envies*) to curb **II.** *vpr* **se ~** to check oneself
réfrigérant(e) [ʀefʀiʒeʀɑ̃, ɑ̃t] *adj* **1. appareil ~** refrigerator **2.** (*glacial*) icy
réfrigérateur [ʀefʀiʒeʀatœʀ] *m* refrigerator; **~-congélateur combiné** fridge-freezer
refroidir [ʀ(ə)fʀwadiʀ] <8> **I.** *vt* **1.** (*faire baisser la température de*) to cool down **2.** (*décourager*) **~ qn** to dampen sb's spirits **II.** *vi* (*devenir plus froid: moteur, aliment*) to cool down; (*devenir trop froid*) to get cold; **mettre qc à ~** to leave sth to cool down **III.** *vpr* **se ~** (*devenir plus froid: chose*) to cool off; (*devenir trop froid*) to get cold; **le temps s'est refroidi** it's getting colder
refroidissement [ʀ(ə)fʀwadismɑ̃] *m* **1.** AUTO, TECH (*de l'air, l'eau*) cooling; **tour de ~** cooling tower **2.** MED cold; **attraper un ~** to catch a cold **3.** (*diminution*) cooling (off)
refuge [ʀ(ə)fyʒ] *m* **1.** (*abri, échappatoire*) refuge; **chercher/trouver ~ quelque part** to seek/find shelter somewhere; **chercher/trouver (un) ~ dans la drogue** to seek/find refuge in drugs **2.** (*pour animaux*) sanctuary **3.** (*dans une rue*) traffic island
réfugié(e) [ʀefyʒje] *m(f)* refugee
réfugier [ʀefyʒje] <1> *vpr* **se ~ chez qn** to take refuge with sb
refus [ʀ(ə)fy] *m* (*résistance*) refusal; **~ d'obéissance** insubordination; **~ de priorité** refusal to give way; **ce n'est pas de ~** *inf* I wouldn't say no
refuser [ʀ(ə)fyze] <1> **I.** *vt* **1.** (*opp: accepter*) to refuse; (*invitation*) to decline; (*cadeau*) to refuse; (*manuscrit*) to reject; **~ qc en bloc/tout net** to refuse sth outright/flatly **2.** (*opp: accorder: objet, permission, entrée*) to refuse; (*compétence*) to deny; **elle m'a refusé la priorité** she didn't give way to me; **je lui refuse toute intelligence** I can't believe that he has any intelligence **II.** *vi* to resist **III.** *vpr* **1.** (*se priver de*) **se ~ un plaisir** to deny oneself a pleasure; **elle ne se ~ rien!** *iron* she certainly does herself well! **2.** (*être décliné*) **se ~** (*une offre qui ne se refuse pas*) an offer you can't refuse; **ça ne se refuse pas** you can't say no to that
réfuter [ʀefyte] <1> *vt* to refute
regagner [ʀ(ə)gaɲe] <1> *vt* **1.** (*amitié, faveurs*) to regain; (*argent*) to get back; (*en travaillant: argent*) to earn again; (*temps perdu*) to make up for; MIL (*terrain*) to recover; **~ le terrain perdu** to make up lost ground **2.** (*aller de nouveau*) **~ sa place** to return to one's seat **3.** (*rentrer*) **~ sa maison/son pays** to return home/to one's country
regain [ʀəgɛ̃] *m* **1.** (*renouveau: d'optimisme*) surge; (*de santé*) return; **~ d'espoir** new hope; **~ de jeunesse** renewed youth **2.** AGR second crop
régal [ʀegal] *m* delight; **mon grand ~, c'est la tarte aux pommes** I absolutely adore apple tart; **c'est un ~ pour les yeux** it's a sight for sore eyes
régaler [ʀegale] <1> *vpr* **1.** (*savourer*) **se ~** to have a delicious meal; **on va se ~** we'll really enjoy this **2.** (*éprouver un grand plaisir*) **se ~ en faisant qc** to have a great time doing sth
regard [ʀ(ə)gaʀ] *m* look; **~ d'envie** envious look; **avec un ~ de convoitise** with a greedy stare; **adresser un ~ à qn** to look at sb; **attirer les ~s de qn sur qc** to draw sb's attention to sth; **dévorer qn/qc du ~** to look hungrily at sb; **fusiller qn du ~** to give sb a withering look; **lancer un ~/des ~s à qn** to look at sb
regardant(e) [ʀ(ə)gaʀdɑ̃, ɑ̃t] *adj* **être ~ sur qc** to be careful with sth
regarder [ʀ(ə)gaʀde] <1> **I.** *vt* **1.** (*contempler*) to look at; (*observer, suivre des yeux avec attention*) to watch; **~ la mer pendant des heures** to look at the sea for hours; **~ tomber la pluie** to watch the rain falling; **il la regarde faire** he's watching her do it; **~ la télévision** [*o* **la télé** *inf*] to watch television; **as-tu regardé le match?** did you watch the game? **2.** (*consulter rapidement*) to look over; (*courrier*) to look through; (*numéro, mot*) to

look up; ~ **sa montre** to check one's watch **3.**(*vérifier: mécanisme*) to check **4.**(*envisager, considérer: situation, être*) to consider; ~ **qn comme un ami** to regard sb as a friend **5.**(*concerner*) **ça ne te regarde pas!** *iron* that's none of your business!; (*être l'affaire de qn*) this doesn't concern you!; **je fais ce qui me regarde** this is my buiness ▶**regarde-moi cet imbécile!** *inf* what an idiot!; **tu ne m'as pas (bien) regardé!** *inf* you must be joking!; **regardez-moi ça!** *inf* just look at that! **II.** *vi* (*s'appliquer à voir*) to look; **tu n'as pas bien <regardé>** you haven't looked properly; ~ **dans un livre** to look in a book **III.** *vpr* **1.**(*se contempler*) **se** ~ **dans qc** to look at oneself in sth **2.**(*se mesurer du regard*) **se** ~ (*personnes*) to look at each other ▶**tu (ne) t'es (pas) regardé!** *inf* you should take a good look at yourself!

régate [ʀegat] *f* regatta

régence [ʀeʒɑ̃s] *f* regency

Régence [ʀeʒɑ̃s] **I.** *f* **la** ~ the Regency (*under Philippe d'Orléans, 1715–1723*) **II.** *app inv* **style** ~ Regency

Régent [ʀeʒɑ̃] *m* **le** ~ the Regent (*Philippe d'Orléans*)

régent(e) [ʀeʒɑ̃, ʒɑ̃t] **I.** *adj* regent; **prince** ~ Prince Regent **II.** *m(f)* **1.**(*gouvernant d'une monarchie*) regent **2.** *Belgique* (*enseignant des trois années du secondaire inférieur*) teacher (*in the first three years of secondary school*)

régenter [ʀeʒɑ̃te] <1> **I.** *vi* to rule **II.** *vt* ~ **qn/qc** to rule over sb/sth; **vouloir tout** ~ to want to run the show

reggae [ʀege] *m* reggae

régicide [ʀeʒisid] **I.** *adj* regicidal **II.** *mf* regicide

régie [ʀeʒi] *f* **1.** CINE, THEAT, TV production team **2.** TV, RADIO (*local*) control room **3.** ADMIN **en** ~ under state control

régime [ʀeʒim] *m* **1.**(*système*) system of government; ~ **capitaliste/militaire** capitalist/military régime; **opposants au** ~ opponents of the régime; **l'Ancien Régime** HIST the Ancien Régime **2.** MED diet; ~ **végétarien/diététique** vegetarian/health food diet; **il est au** ~ **sec** he's on an alcohol-free diet; **être au** ~ to be dieting; **mettre qn au** ~ to put sb on a diet; **se mettre au** ~ to go on a diet

régiment [ʀeʒimɑ̃] *m* **1.** MIL regiment **2.**(*quantité*) mass(es); **avoir un** ~ **de cousins** to have a whole army of cousins; **il y en a pour tout un** ~ *inf* there's enough for a whole army

région [ʀeʒjɔ̃] *f a.* ADMIN (*contrée*) region; ~ **agricole/équatoriale/polaire** agricultural/equatorial/polar region; ~ **frontalière** frontier zone; **la** ~ **parisienne** the area around Paris, Greater Paris

régional(e) [ʀeʒjɔnal, o] <-aux> *adj* (*relatif à une région*) regional

régionalisme [ʀeʒjɔnalism] *m* regionalism

régisseur, -euse [ʀeʒisœʀ, -øz] *m, f* CINE, TV assistant director; THEAT stage manager

registre [ʀəʒistʀ] *m* **1.** *a.* LING (*livre*) register; ~ **d'état civil** ≈ register of births, marriages and deaths; ~ **de notes** mark book *Brit,* grade book *Am;* ~**s de comptabilité** ledger **2.** MUS range; **un** ~ **aigu/grave** a high/low pitch **3.** INFOR **base de** ~**s** system registry

réglable [ʀeglabl] *adj* adjustable

réglage [ʀeglaʒ] *m* **1.**(*mise au point: d'un moteur*) tuning; (*d'une montre*) adjustment; **système de** ~ control system **2.**(*tracé: d'un papier*) lines *pl*

règle [ʀɛgl] *f* **1.**(*loi*) rule; **les** ~ **du jeu** the rules of the game; **échapper à la** ~ to be an exception to the rule; **être en** ~ to be in order; **se faire une** ~ **de** +*infin* to make it a rule to +*infin;* **en** ~ **générale** as a rule; **dans les** ~**s de l'art** according to the rule book; **faire partie des** ~**s du métier** to be one of the rules of the trade; ~ **d'or** golden rule **2.**(*instrument*) ruler

règlement [ʀɛgləmɑ̃] *m* **1.**(*discipline*) regulations *pl;* ~ **intérieur** (*d'une entreprise*) company regulations; (*d'une organisation, assemblée*) house rules; (*d'une école*) school rules; ~ **de police** bye-law **2.**(*différend*) ~ **de compte(s)** settling of scores; (*meutre*) gangland killing; **nous avons eu un** ~ **de comptes** we settled some scores between us **3.**(*paiement*) payment; **faire un** ~ **par chèque** to settle by cheque [*o* check *Am*]; **faire un** ~ **en espèces** to pay in cash

réglementaire [ʀɛgləmɑ̃tɛʀ] *adj* **1.**(*taille, tenue, uniforme*) regulation; **ce n'est pas très** ~ it's against regulations **2.** JUR statutory; **dispositions** ~**s** regulations

réglementation [ʀɛgləmɑ̃tasjɔ̃] *f* **1.**(*du code de la route, commerce, travail*) regulation **2.**(*fixation: des taux de change, loyers, salaires*) control; ~ **des prix** price control(s)

réglementer [ʀɛgləmɑ̃te] <1> *vt* to regulate

régler [ʀegle] <5> **I.** *vt* **1.**(*résoudre*) to settle; (*problème*) to sort out; (*conflit, différend*) to resolve; **c'est une affaire réglée** it's all settled now **2.**(*payer: facture*) to pay **3.**(*réguler*) to regulate; (*circulation*) to control; (*montre*) to set **4.**(*fixer: modalités, programme*) to decide on; **son sort est déjà réglé** his fate is already sealed **II.** *vi* to pay **III.** *vpr* **1.**(*se résoudre*) **l'affaire se règle** it's sorting itself out **2.**(*être mis au point*) **se** ~ to be adjusted

règles [ʀɛgl] *fpl* period; **avoir ses** ~ to have one's period

réglisse [ʀeglis] **I.** *f* (*plante*) liquorice *Brit,* licorice *Am* **II.** *m o f* (*bonbon*) liquorice; (*bâton*) stick of liquorice

réglo [ʀeglo] *adj inf* straight; **c'est** ~**!** that's OK!; **c'est un type** ~**!** he's an OK guy!

règne [ʀɛɲ] *m* **1.**(*souveraineté: d'un régime*) rule; (*d'un roi, souverain*) reign; **que ton** ~

vienne! Thy kingdom come!; **sous le ~ de qn** under sb's reign **2.** (*influence prédominante*) rule; **c'est le ~ de qc** sth rules **3.** BOT, ZOOL kingdom

régner [ʀeɲe] <5> *vi* ~ **sur qc** (*prince, roi*) to reign over sth

regonfler [ʀ(ə)gɔ̃fle] <1> *vt* **1.** (*gonfler à nouveau: ballon, chambre à air*) to reinflate; (*avec la bouche: ballon*) to blow up again; ~ **un pneu** to pump a tyre [*o* tire *Am*] back up **2.** *inf* (*tonifier*) ~ **qn** to buck sb up; ~ **le moral de qn** to boost sb's morale; **être regonflé** (**à bloc**) to be back on top form

regorger [ʀ(ə)gɔʀʒe] <2a> *vi* (*abonder*) ~ **d'argent** (*personne*) to be rolling in money; ~ **de personnes/choses** (*marché, magasin, pièce*) to be packed with people/things

régresser [ʀegʀese] <1> *vi* to regress

régression [ʀegʀesjɔ̃] *f* **1.** (*diminution: d'une douleur, épidémie, d'une mentalité, société, histoire*) decline; (*d'une production, des ventes, accidents*) fall; ~ **intellectuelle** mental decline; **être en** ~ to be in decline **2.** BIO, PSYCH, GEO regression

regret [ʀ(ə)gʀɛ] *m* **1.** (*nostalgie*) **le(s)** ~**(s) de qc** missing sth; **se complaire dans le ~ du passé** to wallow in nostalgia; ~**s éternels** sadly missed **2.** (*contrariété*) **avoir le ~ de faire qc** to regret to (have to) do sth; **ne pas avoir de ~s** to have no regrets; **je suis au ~ de faire qc** I regret to (have to) do sth; **au grand ~ de qn** to sb's deep regret; **tous mes ~s** you have my sympathy **3.** (*remords*) ~ **de qc** regret over sth; **ne manifester aucun** ~ to show no regrets ►**à** ~ (*partir*) regretfully; (*accepter*) reluctantly; **allez, sans ~!** come on now, no looking back!

regrettable [ʀ(ə)gʀetabl] *adj* regrettable

regretter [ʀ(ə)gʀete] <1> **I.** *vt* **1.** (*se repentir de, déplorer*) to regret; **je regrette de ne pas être venu avec vous** I'm sorry that I didn't come with you **2.** (*déplorer l'absence de*) ~ **sa jeunesse** to be nostalgic for one's youth **II.** *vi* **je regrette** I'm sorry

regroupement [ʀ(ə)gʀupmɑ̃] *m* grouping (together); (*de forces, personnes*) rallying; ~ **familial** JUR *immigrants' right to have their families join them*

regrouper [ʀ(ə)gʀupe] <1> **I.** *vt* (*mettre ensemble*) to bring together; (*personnes*) to gather together **II.** *vpr* **se ~ autour de qn** to group together around sb; (*se ~ dans un but commun*) to join forces with a common objective; **regroupez-vous pour la photo** gather together for the photo

régulariser [ʀegylaʀize] <1> *vt* **1.** (*mettre en ordre*) to sort out; (*acte administratif*) to put in order; (*situation* (*de couple*)) to regularize **2.** (*adjuster*) to regulate

régularité [ʀegylaʀite] *f* **1.** (*harmonie: d'une façade*) evenness; (*d'un dessin, des traits du visage*) proportion **2.** (*ponctualité: d'un acte, repas*) regularity **3.** (*conformité aux règles, légalité*) lawfulness

régulier, **-ière** [ʀegylje, -jɛʀ] *adj* **1.** *a.* LIT, LING (*équilibré: vie, habitudes*) regular **2.** (*constant: effort*) steady; (*résultats, vitesse*) consistent **3.** (*à périodicité fixe: avion, train, ligne*) scheduled; **manger à des heures régulières** to eat at regular times **4.** (*légal: gouvernement*) legitimate; (*tribunal*) official; **être en situation régulière** to have one's papers in order

régulièrement [ʀegyljɛʀmɑ̃] *adv* (*périodiquement*) regularly

réhabilitation [ʀeabilitasjɔ̃] *f* rehabilitation

réhabiliter [ʀeabilite] <1> **I.** *vt* **1.** JUR to clear; ~ **qn dans ses fonctions** to reinstate sb **2.** (*réinsérer*) to rehabilitate **3.** (*remettre à l'honneur*) ~ **qc** to bring sth back into favour [*o* favor *Am*]; ~ **la mémoire de qn** to clear sb's name **II.** *vpr* **se ~** to clear one's name

réhabituer [ʀeabitɥe] <1> **I.** *vt* ~ **un enfant à qn/qc** (*personne*) to get a child used to sb/sth again; ~ **un élève à faire qc** to get a pupil used to doing sth again **II.** *vpr* **se ~ à qn/qc** to get used to sb/sth again; **se ~ à faire qc** to get used to doing sth again

rehausser [ʀəose] <1> *vt* **1.** (*surélever: clôture, plancher, plafond*) to raise; ~ **un édifice** to increase the height of a building **2.** (*majorer: forfait fiscal, impôt*) to raise; (*monnaies*) to revalue **3.** (*mettre en valeur*) to set off; (*mérite, prestige, réputation*) to enhance; ~ **une chemise de dentelle** to set off a lace blouse; ~ **un avocat aux yeux de qn** to enhance a lawyer's reputaion with sb

rein [ʀɛ̃] *m* **1.** (*organe*) kidney **2.** *pl* (*bas du dos*) (lower) back; **j'ai mal aux ~s** my lower back hurts

réincarnation [ʀeɛ̃kaʀnasjɔ̃] *f* reincarnation; **la ~ de sa mère** (*portrait*) the image of his mother; (*personnification*) his mother come back to life

réincarner [ʀeɛ̃kaʀne] <1> *vpr* REL **se ~ dans qc** (*âme*) to be reincarnated in sb

reine [ʀɛn] *f* *a.* JEUX queen

reine-claude [ʀɛnklod] <reines-claudes> *f* greengage

reinette [ʀɛnɛt] *f* reinette (*type of apple, the preferred variety for making tarte Tatin*)

réinfecter [ʀeɛ̃fɛkte] <1> *vpr* **se ~** (*blessure, plaie*) to reinfect

réinitialiser [ʀeinisjalize] <1> *vt* INFOR to reset

réinscription [ʀeɛ̃skʀipsjɔ̃] *f* reregistration

réinscrire [ʀeɛ̃skʀiʀ] *irr* **I.** *vt* (*mettre à nouveau sur une liste*) (**faire**) ~ **qn/qc sur une liste** to put sb/sth back on a list; (**faire**) ~ **qn dans une nouvelle école** to put sb in a new school **II.** *vpr* **se** (**faire**) ~ **sur une liste** to put oneself back on a list; **se** (**faire**) ~ **à l'université** ADMIN to reregister at university; (*reprendre ses études*) to go back to university [*o* college *Am*]

réinsertion [ʀeɛ̃sɛʀsjɔ̃] *f* (*d'un délinquant*)

rehabilitation

réintégrer [Reɛ̃tegRe] <5> *vt* **1.**(*revenir dans*) ~ **une place** to return to a seat; ~ **sa cellule/maison** to return to one's cell/house **2.**(*rétablir*) ~ **qn dans un groupe** to bring sb back into a group; ~ **qn dans la société** to reintegrate sb into society

réinventer [Reɛ̃vɑ̃te] <1> *vt* (*appareil*) to reinvent; (*monde*) to remake; (*solidarité, partage, relations*) to rediscover

réitérer [ReiteRe] <5> *vt* to reiterate

rejaillir [R(ə)ʒajiR] <8> *vi* **1.**(*retomber*) ~ **sur qn/qc** (*honte, faute*) to be put on sb/sth; (*bienfait, gloire, renommée*) to be reflected on sb/sth **2.**(*jaillir avec force: boue*) to splash; (*liquide*) to spurt out; (*lumière*) to burst out

rejet [R(ə)ʒɛ] *m* **1.**(*refus*) *a.* MED rejection; **réaction de** ~ rejection response **2.** *pl* (*déchets*) waste **3.** AGR sucker **4.** LING (*d'un verbe*) end position

rejeter [Rəʒ(ə)te] <3> **I.** *vt* **1.**(*refuser*) to reject; (*circonstances atténuantes*) to disregard; **être rejeté** to be rejected; (*exclu d'une communauté*) to be cast out **2.**(*évacuer*) ~ **qc** (*déchets*) to throw sth out; (*épaves*) to throw sth up; (*nourriture*) to vomit sth **3.**(*se décharger de*) ~ **une responsabilité sur qn/qc** to push a responsibility off on sb; ~ **une faute sur qn/qc** to put the blame on sb/sth **4.**(*repousser*) ~ **la tête** to throw one's head back; ~ **les épaules** to pull one's shoulders back; ~ **la terre** to throw earth back up **II.** *vpr* **1.**(*faire un mouvement du corps*) **se** ~ **en arrière** to jump back **2.**(*s'accuser*) **se** ~ **la faute** (**l'un l'autre**) to blame each other

rejeton [Rəʒ(ə)tɔ̃, R(ə)ʒətɔ̃] *m* **1.** AGR sucker **2.** *inf* (*descendant*) kid

rejoindre [R(ə)ʒwɛ̃dR] *irr* **I.** *vt* **1.**(*regagner: personne*) to meet again; ~ **son domicile/un lieu** to return to one's home/a place **2.**(*déboucher*) ~ **une route** (*route*) to rejoin a road; (*automobiliste*) to get back onto a road **3.**(*rattraper*) ~ **qn** to catch up with sb; **vas-y, je te rejoins** go on, I'll catch up with you **II.** *vpr* **se** ~ **1.**(*être d'accord: idées, points de vue*) to be very close; (*personnes*) to be in agreement **2.**(*se réunir: personnes*) to meet up; (*choses*) to meet

réjoui(**e**) [Reʒwi] *adj* cheerful

réjouir [Reʒwir] <8> *vpr* **se** ~ **de faire qc** to be delighted to do sth; (*à l'avance*) to look forward to doing sth; **se** ~ **à l'idée de ...** to be thrilled at the idea of ...

réjouissance [Reʒwisɑ̃s] *f* **1.**(*joie*) rejoicing **2.** *pl* (*festivités*) festivities

réjouissant(**e**) [Reʒwisɑ̃, ɑ̃t] *adj* cherful; (*histoire, spectacle*) entertaining; **c'est** ~**!** *iron* that's just fine!

relâche [Rəlɑʃ] *f* (*répit*) **un moment de** ~ a moment's rest; **poursuivre/combattre sans** ~ to pursue/fight sth relentlessly; **travailler/harceler sans** ~ to work/harass unremittingly

relâchement [R(ə)lɑʃmɑ̃] *m* laxity

relâcher [R(ə)lɑʃe] <1> *vt* **1.**(*desserrer*) to loosen; (*muscles*) to relax **2.**(*libérer*) to free **3.**(*cesser de tenir*) ~ **qc** to let go of sth

relais [R(ə)lɛ] *m* SPORT relay; **le** ~ **quatre fois cent mètres** the four by one hundred metres [*o* meter *Am*] relay ►**prendre le** ~ **de qn/qc** to take over from sb/sth

relance [R(ə)lɑ̃s] *f* **1.**(*nouvel essor*) revival; (*de la consommation*) boost; ~ **économique** reflation of the economy **2.** SPORT new attack **3.**(*aux cartes*) raise; **faire une** ~ to raise the stakes

relancer [R(ə)lɑ̃se] <2> *vt* **1.**(*donner un nouvel essor à: mouvement*) to relaunch; (*idée*) to revive; (*économie, production, investissement, immobilier*) to boost **2.** *inf* (*harceler*) to badger; (*client, débiteur*) to chase up

relater [R(ə)late] <1> *vt* (*événement, fait*) to relate; (*aventure*) to recount; **les faits relatés par la presse** the facts reported by the press

relatif [R(ə)latif] *m* LING relative pronoun

relatif, -ive [R(ə)latif, -iv] *adj* **1.**(*opp: absolu*) relative **2.**(*partiel*) relative; **être d'une relative discrétion** to be not absolutely discreet **3.**(*en liaison avec*) **être** ~ **à qn/qc** to relate to sb/sth; ~ **à qn/qc** concerning sb/sth **4.** *postposé* LING relative

relation [R(ə)lasjɔ̃] *f* **1.**(*rapport*) relation **2.** *pl* (*rapport entre personnes*) relationship; **des ~s amicales/tendues** a friendly/tense relationship; **~s d'affaires** business relationship; **avoir une** ~ **amoureuse/des ~s amoureuses avec qn** to be romantically involved with sb; **avoir de bonnes/mauvaises ~s avec qn** to have a good/bad relationship with sb; **par ~s** through connections **3.**(*lien logique*) relation; ~ **de cause à effet** relation of cause and effect **4.**(*personne de connaissance*) contact ►**~s publiques** public relations; **en** ~ in contact

relative [R(ə)lativ] *f* LING relative clause

relativement [R(ə)lativmɑ̃] *adv* (*dans une certaine mesure: facile, honnête, rare*) relatively

relativiser [R(ə)lativize] <1> *vt* ~ **qc** to put sth into perspective

relativité [R(ə)lativite] *f* PHILOS, PHYS relativity; **théorie de la** ~ theory of relativity

relaver [R(ə)lave] <1> *vt* **1.**(*laver de nouveau*) ~ **qc** to wash sth again **2.** *Suisse* (*laver*) to wash

relax [Rəlaks] *adj inv, inf* laid-back

relaxant(**e**) [R(ə)laksɑ̃, ɑ̃t] *adj* relaxing

relaxation [R(ə)laksasjɔ̃] *f a.* PHYSIOL relaxation; **exercice de** ~ relaxation exercise

relaxer [R(ə)lakse] <1> **I.** *vt* **1.**(*décontracter*) to relax **2.** JUR to free **II.** *vpr* **se** ~ to relax

relayer [R(ə)leje] <7> **I.** *vt* (*remplacer*) ~ **qn** to take over from sb; **se faire** ~ **par qn** (*personne*) to hand over to sb **II.** *vpr* **se** ~ **pour faire qc** to do sth in turns

relecture [R(ə)lɛktyR] *f* rereading; TYP check-

R

ing

reléguer [ʀ(ə)lege] <5> *vt* **1.** (*mettre à l'écart*) to relegate; ~ **qn dans une maison de retraite** to send sb off to an old people's home; ~ **qn au second plan** to push sb into the background; ~ **un élève au fond de la classe** to send a pupil to the back of the class; **équipe reléguée en seconde division** team relegated to the second division **2.** HIST to banish

relent [ʀ(ə)lɑ̃] *m* **1.** (*mauvaise odeur*) stink; **dégager des ~s d'alcool** to stink of alcohol **2.** *soutenu* (*trace*) **un ~/des ~s de qc** a strong smell of sth

relève [ʀ(ə)lɛv] *f* relief; **assurer** [*o* **prendre**] **la ~** (*assurer la succession*) to take over; **la ~ est assurée** (*succession*) there will be someone to take over; (*génération montante*) there will be others to take over

relevé [ʀəl(ə)ve, ʀ(ə)ləve] *m* **1.** FIN ~ **de compte** account statement; ~ **d'identité bancaire** *slip giving bank account details* **2.** (*liste, facture détaillée*) statement; ~ **de gaz/téléphone** gas/telephone bill; ~ **de notes** exam results; **procéder au ~ du compteur** to read the meter **3.** CONSTR (*d'un terrain*) survey; **faire un ~ de terrain** to survey a piece of land

relevé(**e**) [ʀəl(ə)ve, ʀ(ə)ləve] *adj* **1.** GASTR (*plat, sauce*) spicy **2.** *soutenu* (*noble: langage*) elevated

relever [ʀəl(ə)ve] <4> **I.** *vt* **1.** (*redresser: chaise, objet tombé*) to pick up; (*blessé*) to lift; ~ **qn** to help sb back up **2.** (*remonter*) ~ **qc** (*col, siège, strapontin, cheveux*) to put sth up; (*store, chaussettes*) to pull sth up; ~ **sa voile** to lift one's veil **3.** (*noter: adresse, renseignement, observation*) to note; (*compteur*) to read; ~ **l'électricité/le gaz** to read the electricity/gas meter **II.** *vi* **1.** (*se remettre*) ~ **de maladie** to recover after being ill **2.** (*dépendre de*) ~ **de la compétence de qn** to fall in sb's sphere of competence; ~ **du miracle** to be miraculous **III.** *vpr* **se** ~ (*se remettre debout*) to get up

relief [ʀəljɛf] *m* **1.** GEO, ART, ARCHIT relief **2.** (*saillie*) **sans ~** flat; **carte/impression en ~** relief map/printing; **motif/caractères en ~** raised design/characters ►<u>**mettre**</u> **qc en ~** to accentuate sth

relier [ʀəlje] <1> *vt* **1.** (*réunir: personnes, choses*) to connect; ~ **un appareil à un autre** to connect one piece of equipment to another **2.** LING (*préposition*) to link; ~ **une subordonnée à qc** to link a subordinate clause to sth **3.** TECH (*livre*) to bind; **une édition reliée** (**en**) **cuir** a leather-bound edition

relieur, **-euse** [ʀəljœʀ, -jøz] *m, f* binder

religieuse [ʀ(ə)liʒjøz] **I.** *adj v.* **religieux II.** *f* **1.** REL nun **2.** GASTR cream puff

religieusement [ʀ(ə)liʒjøzmɑ̃] *adv* religiously; (*se marier*) in church

religieux [ʀ(ə)liʒjø] *m* religious; (*moine*) monk

religieux, **-euse** [ʀ(ə)liʒjø, -jøz] *adj* REL (*personne, habit, opinions, vie, tradition, art, ordre*) religious; (*cérémonie, mariage, musique, chant*) church

religion [ʀ(ə)liʒjɔ̃] *f* religion; **appartenir à la ~ protestante** to be a Protestant

reliquat [ʀəlika] *m* FIN, JUR remainder

relique [ʀəlik] *f* REL, BIO relic

relire [ʀ(ə)liʀ] *irr* **I.** *vt* (*lettre, roman*) to reread; (*pour vérifier une référence: passage*) to check **II.** *vpr* **se** ~ to read over one's work

reliure [ʀəljyʀ] *f* binding; ~ **pleine peau** full leather binding

reloger [ʀ(ə)lɔʒe] <2a> **I.** *vt* to rehouse **II.** *vpr* (**trouver à**) **se** ~ to find a new place to live

reluire [ʀ(ə)lɥiʀ] *vi irr* to gleam; **faire ~ qc** to make sth gleam

reluisant(**e**) [ʀ(ə)lɥizɑ̃, ɑ̃t] *adj* **1.** (*brillant*) shining; ~ **de graisse** shiny with grease; **être ~ de propreté** to gleam **2.** (*réjouissant: perspective, situation, résultat*) brilliant; (*avenir*) shining

reluquer [ʀ(ə)lyke] <1> *vt inf* (*personne, poste*) to eye

remâcher [ʀ(ə)mɑʃe] <1> *vt* **1.** (*ressasser*) ~ **qc** to brood over sth **2.** ZOOL to ruminate

remake [ʀimɛk] *m* remake

remanier [ʀ(ə)manje] <1a> *vt* **1.** (*modifier*) to reorganize; (*quartier*) to rebuild; (*manuscrit, pièce*) to revise **2.** POL (*cabinet, ministère*) to reshuffle; (*comité, direction*) to restructure; (*constitution*) to revise

remaquiller [ʀ(ə)makije] <1> **I.** *vt* ~ **qn** to do sb's make-up again **II.** *vpr* **se** ~ to do one's make-up again

remarcher [ʀ(ə)maʀʃe] <1> *vi* to work again

remarier [ʀ(ə)maʀje] <1> *vpr* **se** ~ **avec qn** to get remarried to sb

remarquable [ʀ(ə)maʀkabl] *adj* remarkable; **être ~ par sa taille/intelligence** to be remarkably tall/intelligent

remarquablement [ʀ(ə)maʀkabləmɑ̃] *adv* (*beau, intelligent*) remarkably; (*jouer, se porter, réussir*) brilliantly

remarque [ʀ(ə)maʀk] *f* remark; **faire une ~ à qn sur qc** to remark on sth to sb; **en faire la ~ à qn** to remark on it to sb

remarquer [ʀ(ə)maʀke] <1> **I.** *vt* **1.** (*apercevoir*) to notice **2.** (*distinguer*) ~ **qn/qc par qc** to notice sb/sth because of sth **3.** (*noter*) to notice; **faire ~ qc à qn** to draw sb's attention to sb; **se faire ~** *péj* to draw attention to oneself; **sans se faire ~** without being noticed; **remarque, je m'en fiche!** mind you, I couldn't care less!; **remarque, il a essayé** he did try, though **II.** *vpr* **se** ~ to be noticeable

remballer [ʀɑ̃bale] <1> **I.** *vt* **1.** (*opp: déballer*) to pack up **2.** *inf* (*garder pour soi*) to save; **remballe tes commentaires!** keep your comments to yourself! **II.** *vi* to pack up

rembarquer [Rɑ̃baRke] <1> **I.** *vt* to reload; (*passagers*) to re-embark **II.** *vi* to re-embark **III.** *vpr* **1.** MIL, NAUT **se ~** to re-embark **2.** *inf* (*s'engager de nouveau*) **se ~ dans qc** to get involved in sth again; **se laisser ~ dans qc** to get mixed up in sth again

rembarrer [Rɑ̃bɑRe] <1> *vt inf* **~ qn** to tell sb where to get off; **se faire ~** to get told where to go

remblai [Rɑ̃blɛ] *m* embankment; (*matériau en terre*) ballast; (*en caillou*) hardcore *Brit*

rembobiner [Rɑ̃bɔbine] <1> *vt, vi* to rewind

rembourrer [Rɑ̃buRe] <1> *vt* **1.** (*matelasser*) **~ un siège avec qc** to stuff a seat with sth; **faire ~ des fauteuils** to have armchairs reupholstered; **~ les épaules de qn** to pad sb's shoulders **2.** *fig* **être bien rembourré** to be well-padded

remboursement [Rɑ̃buRsəmɑ̃] *m* (*d'un emprunt, d'une dette*) repayment; (*des frais*) reimbursement; **contre ~** cash with order

rembourser [Rɑ̃buRse] <1> *vt* to repay; **~ une dette/un emprunt à qn** to repay a debt/a loan to sb; **ce médicament n'est pas remboursé** this medicine is not reimbursed (*by the Sécurité Sociale*)*;* **ça rembourse à peine les frais de fonctionnement** it barely covers operating costs; **je te rembourserai demain!** I'll pay you back tomorrow!; **remboursez! remboursez!** *iron* we want our money back!

rembrunir [Rɑ̃bRyniR] <8> *vpr* **se ~** (*traits, visage, ciel*) to darken; **elle se rembrunit** her face darkened; **le temps se rembrunit** it's clouding over

remède [R(ə)mɛd] *m* (*moyen de lutte*) remedy; (*d'un problème*) cure; **~ miracle** miracle cure; **~ contre l'inflation** cure for inflation ►**~ de cheval** drastic remedy; **le ~ est pire que le mal** the cure is worse than the disease

remédier [R(ə)medje] <1> *vi* **~ à une maladie** to find a cure for an illness; **~ à un problème** to remedy a problem

remémorer [R(ə)memɔRe] <1> *vpr* **se ~ qc** to recall sth

remerciement [R(ə)mɛRsimɑ̃] *m* (*activité*) thanking; **des ~s** thanks *pl;* **adresser ses ~s à qn** to express one's thanks to sb; **avec tous mes/nos ~s** with all my/our thanks; **lettre de ~** letter of thanks; (*pour un cadeau*) thank-you letter

remercier [R(ə)mɛRsje] <1> *vt* (*dire merci à*) **~ qn/qc de qc** to thank sb/sth for sth; **~ qn/qc de faire qc** to thank sb/sth for doing sth

remettre [R(ə)mɛtR] *irr* **I.** *vt* **1.** (*replacer*) **~ qc** to put sth back; **~ un bouton** to sew a button back on; **~ qc debout** to stand sth up again; **~ à cuire** to leave sth to cook some more; **~ qn sur la bonne voie** to put sb back on the right track **2.** (*rétablir*) **~ qn/faire ~ qn en liberté** to free sb; **~ une machine/un moteur en marche** to restart a machine/an engine; **~ qc en ordre** to sort sth out; **~ qc à neuf** to restore sth; **~ sa montre à l'heure** to set one's watch right **3.** (*donner*) **~ qc** (*récompense, prix*) to give sth; (*démission, devoir*) to hand sth in; **~ un paquet à qn** to give a parcel to sb **4.** (*rajouter: ingrédient*) to add (more); **~ de l'huile dans le moteur** to put more oil in the engine; **~ du sel dans les légumes** to put more salt in the vegetables; **~ du rouge à lèvres** to put more lipstick on **5.** (*ajourner*) **~ une décision à la semaine prochaine** to leave [*o* postpone] a decision till the following week; **~ un jugement à l'année prochaine** to defer a judgment till the following year **6.** (*porter de nouveau*) **~ qc** to put sth back on **7.** (*confier*) **~ un enfant à qn** to entrust a child to sb **8.** *Belgique* (*rendre la monnaie*) to give change; **~ sur 100 euros** to give change out of 100 euros **9.** *Belgique* (*vendre, céder*) to sell; **maison à ~** house for sale ►**~ ça** *inf* to do it all over again; **en ~** *inf* to overdo it **II.** *vpr* **1.** (*recouvrer la santé*) **se ~ de qc** to get over sth; **remettez-vous maintenant!** get a grip on yourself now! **2.** (*recommencer*) **se ~ au travail** to get back to work; **se ~ en mouvement** to start again; **se ~ à faire qc** to start doing sth again **3.** METEO **le temps se remet au beau/à la pluie** it's turning nice/rainy again; **il se remet à pleuvoir** the rain's starting again **4.** (*se replacer*) **se ~ en tête du groupe** to return to the top of the group; **se ~ debout/sur ses jambes** to get back up/to one's feet again; **se ~ à table** to return to the table **5.** (*se réconcilier*) **se ~ avec qn** *inf* to get back together with sb; **ils se sont remis ensemble** they've got back together again

réminiscence [Reminisɑ̃s] *f* reminiscence

remise [R(ə)miz] *f* **1.** (*dépôt, attribution: d'une clé, d'une rançon*) handing over; (*d'une décoration, d'un cadeau*) presentation; (*d'une lettre, d'un paquet*) delivery; (*en mains propres*) handing over **2.** (*dispense, grâce*) reduction; **~ de peine** reduction of sentence **3.** (*rabais*) discount; **faire une ~ de 5 % à qn** to give sb a 5 % discount **4.** (*local*) shed ►**~ en état** restoration; **~ en forme** getting back in shape; **centre de ~ en forme** health farm; **~ à jour** updating; **~ à jour des connaissances** updating of one's knowledge; **~ en marche** restarting; **~ en marche de l'économie** jump-starting the economy

rémission [Remisjɔ̃] *f* remission ►**sans ~** (*traitement*) pitiless; (*punir*) pitilessly

remmener [Rɑ̃m(ə)ne] <4> *vt* **~ qn** (*en venant*) to bring sb back; (*en allant*) to take sb back

remontant [R(ə)mɔ̃tɑ̃] *m* tonic

remontant(e) [R(ə)mɔ̃tɑ̃, ɑ̃t] *adj* **1.** (*fortifiant*) invigorating **2.** (*en horticulture*) reflowering

remontée [R(ə)mɔ̃te] *f* **1.** (*action: d'une côte, pente*) climb; (*d'un mineur, plongeur*) return to the surface; SPORT recovery **2.** (*hausse: des eaux, d'une popularité, d'une*

R

action) rise **3.** (*machine*) ~ **mécanique** ski lift

remonte-pente [R(ə)mɔ̃tpɑ̃t] <remonte-pentes> *m* ski-lift

remonter [R(ə)mɔ̃te] <1> **I.** *vi* **1.** *être* (*monter à nouveau*) ~ **dans une chambre/de la cuisine** to go back up to a bedroom/from the kitchen; ~ **à Paris** to go back to Paris; ~ **en bateau/à la nage** to sail/swim back up; ~ **sur l'échelle** to get back on the ladder; ~ **sur scène** to return to the stage; ~ *+infin* (*vu d'en bas*) to go back up to *+infin;* (*vu d'en haut*) to come back up to *+infin* **2.** *être* (*reprendre place*) ~ **à bicyclette** to get back on one's bicycle; ~ **en voiture** to get back in the car; ~ **à bord** to go back on board **3.** *avoir* (*s'élever de nouveau*) to go back up **4.** *avoir* (*s'améliorer*) ~ **dans l'estime de qn** to rise in sb's esteem **5.** *être* (*glisser vers le haut: jupe, vêtement*) to ride up; (*col*) to stand up **6.** *avoir* (*dater de*) ~ **au mois dernier/à l'année dernière** (*événement, fait*) to have occurred last month/last year; **cela remonte au siècle dernier** that goes back to the last century; **cet incident remonte à quelques jours** this incident happened a few days ago **II.** *vt avoir* **1.** ~ **qc** (*parcourir à pieds*) to go up sth; (*parcourir dans un véhicule*) to drive up sth; (*à la nage: fleuve, rivière*) to swim up sth **2.** (*relever*) ~ **qc** (*col*) to turn sth up; (*chaussettes, pantalon, manches*) to pull sth up; (*bas du pantalon*) to hitch sth up; (*étagère, tableau, mur*) to raise sth; ~ **une note** ECOLE to increase a mark [*o* grade *Am*] **3.** (*rapporter du bas*) ~ **une bouteille de la cave à son père** to bring a bottle up from the cellar to one's father **4.** (*porter vers le haut*) ~ **la valise au grenier** to take the suitcase up to the attic **5.** (*faire marcher*) ~ **qc** (*mécanisme, montre*) to wind sth up; **être remonté** *iron* (*excité*) to be full of beans; **être remonté contre qn** (*fâché*) to be mad with sb **6.** (*opp: démonter*) ~ **qc** (*appareil*) to put sth back together; (*roue, robinet*) to put sth back on **7.** (*remettre en état: affaires*) to boost; (*mur*) to rebuild; ~ **qn** (*physiquement*) to make sb feel better; (*moralement*) to give sb a boost; ~ **le moral de qn** to cheer sb up

remontoir [R(ə)mɔ̃twaR] *m* winder; **montre à** ~ wind-up watch

remontrance [R(ə)mɔ̃tRɑ̃s] *f* reproof; **faire des ~s à qn** to reprove sb

remords [R(ə)mɔR] *m* remorse *no pl;* **des ~s** remorse; **avoir des** ~ to feel remorse; **pas de ~?** no regrets?

remorque [R(ə)mɔRk] *f* (*d'un véhicule*) trailer

remorquer [R(ə)mɔRke] <1> *vt* (*voiture*) to tow; **se faire** ~ to get a tow

remorqueur [R(ə)mɔRkœR] *m* tug

rémoulade [Remulad] *f* rémoulade

remous [R(ə)mu] *m* **1.** (*tourbillon: de l'air, eau*) eddy; (*d'un bateau*) wash; (*d'une foule*) swirl **2.** (*agitation*) stir *no pl;* **provoquer** [*o* **causer**] **des** ~ to cause a stir; **les ~ de la politique** political turbulence

rempailler [Rɑ̃paje] <1> *vt* to reseat (*with straw*)

rempart [Rɑ̃paR] *m* MIL rampart; (*d'une ville*) wall

rempiler [Rɑ̃pile] <1> **I.** *vt* ~ **qc** to pile sth up again **II.** *vi inf* to re-enlist; ~ **pour trois ans** to re-enlist for three years

remplaçant(e) [Rɑ̃plasɑ̃, ɑ̃t] *m(f)* MED locum; ECOLE supply teacher *Brit,* substitute teacher *Am;* SPORT substitute

remplacement [Rɑ̃plasmɑ̃] *m* (*intérim*) temping; **faire des ~s** to temp

remplacer [Rɑ̃plase] <2> **I.** *vt* **1.** (*changer, tenir lieu de*) to replace **2.** (*prendre la place de*) ~ **qn** to take over from sb **II.** *vpr* **se** ~ to be replaced

rempli(e) [Rɑ̃pli] *adj* **1.** (*plein*) full; ~ **de personnes** full of people; **tasse ~e de thé** cup full of tea **2.** (*rond*) plump **3.** (*occupé: journée, vie*) full; (*emploi du temps*) busy

remplir [Rɑ̃pliR] <8> **I.** *vt* **1.** (*rendre plein*) ~ **un carton de choses** to fill a box with things; ~ **une valise de vêtements** to pack a case full of clothes **2.** (*occuper*) to fill **3.** (*compléter*) ~ **un formulaire** to fill in [*o* out *Am*] a form; ~ **un chèque** to write out a cheque [*o* check *Am*] **4.** (*réaliser, répondre à: mission, contrat, conditions*) to fulfil *Brit,* to fulfill *Am* **II.** *vpr* **se** ~ **de personnes/liquide** to fill with people/liquid

remplissage [Rɑ̃plisaʒ] *m* **1.** (*fait de remplir*) filling **2.** *péj* (*développement inutile*) padding

remplumer [Rɑ̃plyme] <1> *vpr inf* **se** ~ **1.** (*grossir*) to fill out again **2.** (*financièrement*) to improve one's bank balance

remporter [Rɑ̃pɔRte] <1> *vt* **1.** (*reprendre*) ~ **qc** to take sth back; **faire** ~ **une livraison** to send back a delivery **2.** (*gagner*) to win

remuant(e) [Rəmɥɑ̃, ɑ̃t] *adj* **1.** (*turbulent*) restless **2.** (*entreprenant*) full of energy

remue-ménage [R(ə)mymenaʒ] *m inv* **un** ~ a commotion; **faire du** ~ to cause a commotion

remuer [Rəmɥe] <1> **I.** *vi* (*bouger*) to move (around) **II.** *vt* **1.** (*bouger*) to move; (*hanches*) to swing; ~ **les oreilles** (*chien*) to wiggle one's ears; ~ **la queue** to wag its tail **2.** (*mélanger: mayonnaise, sauce, café*) to stir; (*salade*) to toss **3.** (*émouvoir*) to move **III.** *vpr* **se** ~ **1.** (*bouger*) to move **2.** (*faire des efforts*) to go to a lot of trouble

rémunérateur, -trice [RemyneRatœR, -tRis] *adj* remunerative; **être très** ~ to be very lucrative

rémunération [RemyneRasjɔ̃] *f* remuneration

rémunérer [RemyneRe] <5> *vt* to pay, remunerate *form*

renâcler [R(ə)nɑkle] <1> *vi* ~ **à** [*o* **devant**] **qc** to grumble about sth; ~ **à faire qc** to grumble about doing sth

renaissance [ʀ(ə)nɛsɑ̃s] *f* **1.** (*vie nouvelle*) rebirth **2.** HIST, ART **la Renaissance** the Renaissance

renaître [ʀ(ə)nɛtʀ] *vi irr, défec* **1.** (*reparaître: espoir*) to revive; (*désir, doute*) to return; (*difficultés, dispute*) to resurface; **faire ~ l'espoir chez qn** to give sb new hope; **faire ~ le conflit** to revive the conflict **2.** (*reprendre vigueur: fleur, économie, pays*) to revive; (*jour*) to dawn again **3.** REL, MYTH to be born again

rénal(e) [ʀenal, o] <-aux> *adj* **la fonction ~e** kidney function

renard [ʀ(ə)naʀ] *m* (*animal, fourrure*) fox ►**fin** ~ shrewd customer; **vieux** ~ sly old devil

renardière [ʀ(ə)naʀdjɛʀ] *f Québec* (*élevage de renards*) fox farm

renchérir [ʀɑ̃ʃeʀiʀ] <8> **I.** *vi* **1.** (*faire de la surenchère*) to make a higher bid **2.** (*devenir plus cher*) to become dearer **3.** (*faire une enchère supérieure*) ~ **sur qn** to go one better than sb **II.** *vt* ~ **qc** to make sth dearer

rencontre [ʀɑ̃kɔ̃tʀ] *f* **1.** (*fait de se rencontrer*) meeting; ~ **secrète** secret meeting **2.** (*entrevue*) meeting; ~ **au sommet** summit meeting **3.** SPORT fixture; ~ **de football/boxe** football/boxing match; ~ **d'athlétisme** athletics meeting *Brit,* track and field meet *Am* ►**faire une mauvaise** ~ to have an unpleasant encounter; **aller/venir à la ~ de qn** to go/come to meet sb; **faire la ~ de qn** to meet sb

rencontrer [ʀɑ̃kɔ̃tʀe] <1> **I.** *vt* **1.** (*croiser, avoir une entrevue, faire la connaissance de*) *a.* SPORT to meet **2.** (*être confronté à*) to encounter **II.** *vpr* **se** ~ to meet; **il les a fait se** ~ they met through him

rendement [ʀɑ̃dmɑ̃] *m* **1.** (*production: d'une terre, d'un champ, d'une exploitation agricole*) yield; (*d'un puits de pétrole, d'une machine*) output; **des terres d'un bon** ~ land that crops well **2.** FIN yield; **des placements à fort/faible** ~ high-/low-yield investments **3.** (*efficacité: d'une personne*) output **4.** PHYS efficiency

rendez-vous [ʀɑ̃devu] *m inv* **1.** (*rencontre officielle*) appointment; **avoir ~ avec qn** to have an appointment with sb; **donner un ~ à qn** to give sb an appointment; **prendre ~ avec qn** to make an appointment with sb; **prendre ~ chez qn** to make an appointment with sb; **sur** ~ by appointment **2.** (*rencontre avec un ami*) meeting; **avoir ~ avec qn** to be meeting sb; **se donner** ~ to arrange to meet; **donner un ~ à qn** to arrange to meet sb; ~ **à 8 heures/à la gare** see you at 8 o'clock/at the station **3.** (*rencontre entre amoureux*) date **4.** (*lieu de rencontre*) meeting place ►**être au** ~ (*soleil*) to shine; (*élément prévu*) to turn up on cue

rendormir [ʀɑ̃dɔʀmiʀ] *irr* **I.** *vt* ~ **qn** to send sb back to sleep **II.** *vpr* **se** ~ to go back to sleep

rendre [ʀɑ̃dʀ] <14> **I.** *vt* **1.** (*restituer*) ~ **qc** to give sth back **2.** (*donner en retour*) to return; ~ **la monnaie sur 100 euros** to give the change from a 100 euros **3.** (*rapporter*) ~ **qc** (*article défectueux*) to take sth back **4.** (*donner*) ~ **son devoir** to hand in one's homework **5.** (*redonner*) ~ **la liberté/la vue à qn** to give sb back their freedom/their sight; ~ **l'espoir/le courage à qn** to give sb new hope/courage **6.** (*faire devenir*) ~ **qc plus facile** to make sth easier; ~ **qn triste/joyeux** to make sb sad/happy; ~ **qc public** to make sth public; ~ **qc moins compliqué** to make sth less complicated; **c'est à vous ~ fou!** it'd drive you mad! **7.** JUR (*jugement, verdict, arrêt*) to give **8.** (*vomir*) ~ **qc** to bring sth back up **II.** *vi* (*vomir*) to vomit **III.** *vpr* **1.** (*capituler*) **se** ~ to surrender; **se ~ à l'évidence** *fig* to accept the obvious **2.** (*aller*) **se ~ chez qn/à son travail** to go to see sb/to work

rendu(e) [ʀɑ̃dy] *part passé de* **rendre**

rêne [ʀɛn] *f* rein ►**lâcher les ~s** to slacken the reins; **prendre les ~s de qc** to take control of sth

renégocier [ʀənegɔsje] <1> *vt, vi* to renegotiate

renfermé [ʀɑ̃fɛʀme] *m* **sentir le** ~ to smell musty

renfermé(e) [ʀɑ̃fɛʀme] *adj* withdrawn

renfermer [ʀɑ̃fɛʀme] <1> **I.** *vt* to hold **II.** *vpr* **se ~ sur soi-même** to withdraw into oneself

renflé(e) [ʀɑ̃fle] *adj* bulging

renflouer [ʀɑ̃flue] <1> *vt* **1.** NAUT to refloat **2.** (*fournir des fonds*) ~ **qn/qc** to bail sb/sth out

renfoncement [ʀɑ̃fɔ̃smɑ̃] *m* recess

renforcé(e) [ʀɑ̃fɔʀse] *adj* reinforced

renforcement [ʀɑ̃fɔʀsəmɑ̃] *m* reinforcement; (*d'une couleur, de l'amour, de la haine*) strengthening

renforcer [ʀɑ̃fɔʀse] <2> **I.** *vt* **1.** (*consolider*) to reinforce **2.** (*intensifier*) to strengthen; (*couleur*) to enliven; ~ **le son** to increase the sound; ~ **ses efforts** to redouble one's efforts **3.** (*affermir: paix*) to consolidate; (*position, sentiment, soupçon*) to strengthen **4.** (*confirmer*) ~ **qn dans son opinion** to reinforce sb's opinion **II.** *vpr* **1.** (*devenir plus efficace*) **se ~ de qn** (*groupe*) to be joined by sb **2.** (*s'affermir*) **se** ~ to be reinforced; (*popularité*) to increase

renfort [ʀɑ̃fɔʀ] *m* **1.** *souvent pl* (*personnes*) helpers *pl* **2.** (*supplément*) **~s en nourriture/matériel** supplies of food/material **3.** COUT lining **4.** ARCHIT reinforcement; **mettre un ~ contre qc** to add reinforcement against sth **5.** AUTO ~ **latéral** (**de sécurité**) side impact bar ►**à grand ~ de gestes/statistiques** with the aid of a good many gestures/statistics

renfrogné(e) [ʀɑ̃fʀɔɲe] *adj* sullen

rengaine [ʀɑ̃gɛn] *f inf* **1.** (*chanson*) tune **2.** (*propos*) line; **c'est toujours la même** ~ it's always the same old story

R

rengorger [Rɑ̃gɔRʒe] <2a> *vpr* **se ~ de son succès** to be full of oneself after one's success; **se ~ de faire qc** to preen oneself when one does sth

reniement [Rənimɑ̃] *m* (*du passé*) disowning; (*d'une promesse*) going back on; (*de la foi*) renunciation

renier [Rənje] <1> **I.** *vt* (*promesse*) to break; (*idée, passé*) to disown; **~ sa foi** to renounce one's faith **II.** *vpr* **se ~** to withdraw

renifler [R(ə)nifle] <1> **I.** *vi* to sniff **II.** *vt* **1.** (*sentir, aspirer*) to sniff **2.** *inf* (*pressentir*) to smell

rennais(e) [Rɛnɛ, ɛz] *adj* of Rennes; *v. a.* **ajaccien**

Rennais(e) [Rɛnɛ, ɛz] *m(f)* person from Rennes; *v. a.* **Ajaccien**

renne [Rɛn] *m* reindeer

renom [R(ə)nɔ̃] *m* renown; **en** [*o* **de**] **grand ~** renowned

renommé(e) [R(ə)nɔme] *adj* renowned; **~ pour** renowned for

renommée [R(ə)nɔme] *f* **1.** *sans pl* (*célébrité*) renown **2.** (*réputation*) fame; **de ~ mondiale** world-famous

renon [Rənɔ̃] *m Belgique* (*résiliation d'un bail*) notice

renoncement [R(ə)nɔ̃smɑ̃] *m* **1. ~ à qc** renouncement of sth **2.** (*sacrifice*) renunciation; **esprit de ~** spirit of self-sacrifice; **mener une vie de ~** to live a life of self-sacrifice

renoncer [R(ə)nɔ̃se] <2> **I.** *vi* **1.** (*abandonner*) **~ à qc** to give sth up; **~ au monde/aux plaisirs** to renounce the world/pleasure; **~ à sa foi** to renounce one's faith; **~ à fumer/boire** to give up smoking/drinking **2.** (*refuser un droit*) **~ à qc** to renounce sth **II.** *vt Belgique* **1.** (*résilier: bail*) to end **2.** (*donner congé à*) **~ un locataire** to give a tenant notice (to quit)

renoncule [Rənɔ̃kyl] *f* buttercup

renouer [Rənwe] <1> *vi* **~ avec qn** to take up with sb again; **~ avec qc** (*habitude*) to take up sth again; (*tradition*) to revive sth

renouveau [R(ə)nuvo] *m* renew; **qc connaît un ~ d'intérêt** there is renewed interest in sth

renouvelable [R(ə)nuv(ə)labl] *adj* **1.** (*prolongeable*) renewable **2.** (*rééligible*) eligible for re-election **3.** (*qui peut être répété*) repeatable **4.** (*inépuisable: énergie*) renewable

renouveler [R(ə)nuv(ə)le] <3> **I.** *vt* **1.** (*remplacer*) to renew; **~ des députés/un parlement** to elect new deputies/a new parliament; **~ sa garde-robe** to renew one's wardrobe **2.** (*répéter*) **~ une offre/une promesse à qn** to renew an offer/a promise to sb; **~ une question à qn** to ask sb a question again; **~ sa candidature** (*à un emploi*) to reapply; POL to stand again **3.** (*prolonger: bail, passeport*) to renew **4.** (*rénover*) to renovate; **~ l'aspect de qc** to give sth a new look; **version renouvelée** new version **II.** *vpr* **se ~ 1.** (*être remplacé*) BIO to be renewed; POL to be re-elected **2.** (*se reproduire*) to happen again **3.** (*innover: artiste, style*) to renew oneself

renouvellement [R(ə)nuvɛlmɑ̃] *m* **1.** (*remplacement*) renewal; **~ de l'air** air change **2.** (*répétition*) repetition **3.** (*prolongation*) extension **4.** (*rénovation: de la conception, d'un genre, style*) renewal

rénovateur, -trice [Renɔvatœr, -tRis] **I.** *adj* reformist **II.** *m, f* reformer

rénovation [Renɔvasjɔ̃] *f* **1.** (*remise à neuf*) renovation **2.** (*modernisation*) updating

rénover [Renɔve] <1> *vt* **1.** (*remettre à neuf*) to renovate; (*meuble*) to restore **2.** (*moderniser*) **~ qc** to bring sth up to date

renseignement [Rɑ̃sɛɲmɑ̃] *m* **1.** (*information*) **un ~** some [*o* a piece of] information; **à titre de ~** for your information; **de plus amples ~s** further information [*o* details] **2.** TEL **les ~s** directory enquiries *Brit*, information *Am* **3.** MIL intelligence; **les ~s généraux** Intelligence Service (*of the Police*)

renseigner [Rɑ̃seɲe] <1> **I.** *vt* to inform; **~ qn sur un élève** (*document*) to tell sb about a pupil **II.** *vpr* **se ~ sur qn/qc** to find out about sb/sth

rentabiliser [Rɑ̃tabilize] <1> *vt* **~ qc** to make sth profitable

rentabilité [Rɑ̃tabilite] *f* ECON profitability

rentable [Rɑ̃tabl] *adj* **1.** profitable **2.** *inf* (*qui vaut la peine*) **être ~** to be worthwhile

rente [Rɑ̃t] *f* **1.** (*revenu*) private income *no pl;* **~ viagère** life annuity; **vivre de ses ~s** to live off one's private income **2.** (*emprunt d'État*) bond; **~ perpétuelle** irredeemable securities

rentier, -ière [Rɑ̃tje, -jɛR] *m, f* person with private means

rentrée [Rɑ̃tRe] *f* **1.** ECOLE new term; **le jour de la ~** the day the schools go back; **aujourd'hui, c'est la ~** (**des classes**) the schools go back today **2.** UNIV start of the new academic year **3.** (*après les vacances d'été*) **à la ~** after the summer break; **la ~ politique** the return of parliament; **la ~ théâtrale** *the start of the new theatre season;* **faire sa ~** POL to start the new session of parliament **4.** (*come-back*) comeback; **faire sa ~** to make one's comeback **5.** (*fait de rentrer*) return; **~ dans l'atmosphère** re-entry into the atmosphere **6.** (*somme d'argent*) money coming in *no pl;* **~s** income **7.** (*mise à l'abri*) bringing in

> **La rentrée** is the period after the two-month-long summer holidays, when the new school and university terms begin and political and cultural activity resumes.

rentrer [Rɑ̃tRe] <1> **I.** *vi être* **1.** (*retourner chez soi*) to go back, return; **comment rentres-tu?** how are you getting back?; **~ au pays natal** to return to the country where one was born **2.** (*repartir chez soi*) to go home; (*revenir chez soi*) to come home; **~ de l'école**

to come home from school; **à peine rentré, il ...** the moment he got back home, he ...; **elle est déjà rentrée?** is she back already? **3.** (*entrer à nouveau, vu de l'intérieur*) to come back in; (*vu de l'extérieur*) to go back in **4.** (*reprendre son travail: professeurs, députés, écoliers*) to go back; (*parlement*) to reconvene **5.** (*entrer*) **faire ~ qn** (*vu de l'intérieur*) to bring sb in; (*vu de l'extérieur*) to take sb in; **~ dans un café** to go into a café; **~ sans frapper** to enter without knocking; **~ par la fenêtre** to get in by the window; **l'eau/le voleur rentre dans la maison** water/the thief is getting inside the house **6.** (*s'insérer*) **~ dans une valise/un tiroir** to fit in a suitcase/a drawer; **~ les uns dans les autres** (*tubes*) to fit inside each other **7.** (*être inclus dans*) **~ dans qc** to go in sth; **faire ~ qc dans une catégorie** to put sth in a category **8.** (*devenir membre*) **~ dans la police/une entreprise** to join the police/a business; **~ dans les ordres/au couvent** to take orders/the veil; **faire ~ qn dans une entreprise** to take sb into a business **9.** (*commencer à étudier*) **~ en fac** to start university [*o* college *Am*] **10.** (*percuter*) **~ dans qc** to hit sth; (*conducteur*) to run into sth **11.** COM, FIN (*article, créances*) to come in; **faire ~ des commandes/des impôts** to bring in orders/taxes **12.** (*recouvrer*) **~ dans ses droits** to recover one's rights; **~ dans ses frais** to cover one's costs ►**elle lui est rentré <u>dedans</u>** *inf* she laid into him **II.** *vt avoir* **1.** (*ramener à l'intérieur: table, foin*) to bring in; (*tête, ventre*) to pull back; **~ son chemisier dans la jupe** to tuck one's blouse into one's skirt; **~ la voiture au garage** to put the car in the garage; **~ son cou dans les épaules** to hunch one's shoulders **2.** (*enfoncer*) **~ la clé dans la serrure** to put the key in the lock **3.** (*refouler: larmes, rage*) to hold in; (*déception*) to hide **III.** *vpr* **se ~ dedans** to lay into each other

renversant(e) [ʀɑ̃vɛʀsɑ̃, ɑ̃t] *adj inf* astonishing

renverse [ʀɑ̃vɛʀs] *f* **tomber à la ~** (*en arrière*) to fall backwards; (*de surprise*) to be staggered

renversé(e) [ʀɑ̃vɛʀse] *adj* **1.** (*stupéfait*) staggered **2.** (*à l'envers*) upside down **3.** (*penché vers la gauche: écriture*) slanting to the left

renversement [ʀɑ̃vɛʀsəmɑ̃] *m* **1.** (*changement complet*) reversal; (*de tendance*) swing **2.** POL defeat; (*par un coup d'État*) overthrow **3.** (*mise à l'envers*) inversion

renverser [ʀɑ̃vɛʀse] <1> **I.** *vt* **1.** (*faire tomber*) **~ un vase** to knock over a vase; **~ un piéton** to run over a pedestrian; **~ des arbres** (*tempête*) to blow down trees **2.** (*répandre*) to spill **3.** (*réduire à néant: obstacles*) to scatter **4.** POL to defeat; (*ordre établi*) to overthrow **5.** (*pencher en arrière*) **~ le corps** to lean back; **~ la tête** to throw back one's head **6.** (*retourner*) **~ qc** to turn sth upside down **7.** (*inverser: ordre des mots, fraction*) to invert; (*situation, image*) to reverse **8.** *inf* (*étonner*) **ça me renverse** I'm staggered **II.** *vpr* **1.** (*se pencher en arrière*) **se ~** to lean back; **se ~ sur le dos** to lie down on one's back **2.** (*se retourner*) **se ~** to spill; (*bateau*) to capsize

renvoi [ʀɑ̃vwa] *m* **1.** (*réexpédition*) return **2.** SPORT return **3.** (*licenciement*) dismissal **4.** ECOLE, UNIV expulsion **5.** (*indication*) **~ à qc** reference to sth **6.** JUR, POL **~ devant qc/en qc** sending before/to sth **7.** (*ajournement*) **~ à qc** postponement until sth **8.** (*rot*) belch; **avoir des ~s** to belch

renvoyer [ʀɑ̃vwaje] <6> *vt* **1.** (*envoyer à nouveau*) **~ une lettre à un client** to send a new letter to a customer **2.** SPORT to return **3.** (*retourner: compliment*) to return; **~ l'ascenseur** to send the lift [*o* elevator *Am*] back **4.** (*réexpédier*) to return **5.** (*licencier*) to dismiss **6.** ECOLE to expel **7.** UNIV **~ un étudiant** to send down a student **8.** (*éconduire*) **~ qn** to send sb away **9.** (*adresser*) **~ à qn** to send back to sb **10.** JUR, POL **~ qn devant la cour d'assises** to send sb for trial at the Crown court; **~ qc en cour de cassation** to refer sth to the appeals court **11.** (*ajourner*) **~ qc à plus tard/à une date ultérieure** to leave sth till later/till a later date

réoccuper [ʀeɔkype] <1> *vt* to reoccupy

réorganisation [ʀeɔʀganizasjɔ̃] *f* reorganization

réorganiser [ʀeɔʀganize] <1> *vt, vpr* (**se**) ~ to reorganize

réorientation [ʀeɔʀjɑ̃tasjɔ̃] *f* reorientation

réorienter [ʀeɔʀjɑ̃te] <1> **I.** *vt* **1.** (*changer d'orientation*) to reorientate **2.** ECOLE **~ les élèves vers la littérature** to redirect pupils towards literature **II.** *vpr* **se ~ vers une branche** to turn to a new field

réouverture [ʀeuvɛʀtyʀ] *f* reopening

repaire [ʀ(ə)pɛʀ] *m* den ►**c'est un ~ de <u>brigands</u>** *iron, inf* it's a den of thieves

repaître [ʀəpɛtʀ] *vpr irr* **se ~ de qc** to feed on sth

répandre [ʀepɑ̃dʀ] <14> **I.** *vt* **1.** (*laisser tomber*) **~ qc par terre/sur la table** to spread sth on the ground/the table; (*du liquide*) to pour sth on the ground/the table; (*par mégarde*) to spill sth on the ground/the table **2.** (*être source de*) **~ qc** to give out sth **3.** (*épandre*) **~ qc** (*gaz*) to give off sth **4.** (*faire connaître, susciter, verser: nouvelle, peur, eaux*) to spread **II.** *vpr* **1.** (*s'écouler*) **se ~** to spread; (*par accident*) to spill **2.** (*se disperser*) **se ~** to spread out **3.** (*se dégager*) **se ~** (*chaleur, fumée, odeur*) to spread; (*son*) to carry **4.** (*se propager*) **se ~** (*épidémie*) to spread **5.** (*se manifester*) **se ~ sur qc** to spread over sth **6.** (*envahir*) **se ~** to spread **7.** (*proférer*) **se ~ en louanges sur l'écrivain** to sing the praises of the writer

répandu(e) [ʀepɑ̃dy] **I.** *part passé de*

répandre II. *adj* 1. (*épars*) ~ **sur qc** strewn over sth 2. (*courant*) widespread

réparable [ʀepaʀabl] *adj* (*panne, objet*) repairable; **la faute/perte est** ~ you can make up for the mistake/loss

reparaître [ʀ(ə)paʀɛtʀ] *vi irr* 1. *avoir* (*se montrer de nouveau*) to reappear 2. *avoir o être* PRESSE (*journal, livre*) to reappear

réparateur, -trice [ʀepaʀatœʀ, -tʀis] I. *adj* (*sommeil*) refreshing II. *m, f* repairer; (*d'appareils*) repairman, engineer *Brit*

réparation [ʀepaʀasjɔ̃] *f* 1. *sans pl* (*remise en état*) repair; (*d'un accroc*) mending; (*d'une fuite*) stopping; **atelier de** ~ repair shop; **frais de** ~ repair costs; **être en** ~ to be being repaired 2. (*endroit réparé*) repair 3. *pl* ARCHIT repair work 4. *sans pl* (*correction*) correction 5. *sans pl* (*compensation*) reparation 6. *sans pl* MED (*des forces*) restoration; (*des tissus*) repair 7. (*dédommagement*) reparation; **demander** ~ **à un État de qc** to seek reparation from a state for sth; **obtenir** ~ **de qc** to obtain reparation for sth 8. *pl* POL reparations ►**obtenir** ~ **de qc** to obtain redress for sth; **surface/coup de pied de** ~ SPORT penalty area/kick

réparer [ʀepaʀe] <1> *vt* 1. (*remettre en état: maison, route, dégât*) to repair; (*accroc, fuite*) to mend 2. (*rattraper*) ~ **qc** to make up for sth 3. (*régénérer: forces*) to recoup; (*santé*) to mend

reparler [ʀ(ə)paʀle] <1> I. *vi* ~ **de qn/qc** to speak about sth again; **on reparlera bientôt de lui** you're going to hear more of him; ~ **à qn** to speak to sb again ►**on en reparlera** *inf* we'll talk about it another time II. *vpr* **se** ~ to talk to each other again

repartie, répartie [ʀepaʀti] *f* **avoir de la** ~ to have a sense of repartee

repartir [ʀ(ə)paʀtiʀ] <10> *vi être* 1. (*se remettre à avancer*) to set off again 2. (*s'en retourner*) to leave; **vous voulez déjà** ~? you're leaving already? 3. (*fonctionner à nouveau: moteur, chauffage, machine*) to start again; (*discussion, dispute, affaire*) to start up again ►**et c'est reparti** (**pour un tour**)! *inf* here we go again!

répartir [ʀepaʀtiʀ] <10> I. *vt* 1. (*partager*) ~ **un butin/bénéfice/une somme** to divide up booty/profit/money; ~ **les touristes entre les deux bus** to split the tourists between two coaches 2. (*diviser*) ~ **en groupes** to divide into groups 3. (*disposer*) ~ **des troupes aux endroits stratégiques** to place troops at strategic positions; ~ **des choses sur les étagères** to spread things over the shelves 4. (*étaler*) ~ **qc sur le corps/sur toute la semaine** to spread sth over the body/the whole week; **les travaux sont répartis sur deux ans** the work is spread out over two years II. *vpr* 1. (*se partager*) **ils se répartissent les élèves/la responsabilité** they divide the pupils/the resposbibility among themselves 2. (*être partagé*) **se** ~ to be distributed; **le travail se répartit comme suit** the work will be allocated as follows 3. (*se diviser*) **se** ~ **en groupes** to be divided into groups

répartition [ʀepaʀtisjɔ̃] *f* 1. (*partage*) distribution; **la** ~ **des revenus en France** income distribution in France; ~ **des frais/rôles entre trois personnes** allocation of costs/roles among three people; **la** ~ **des élèves entre les classes est la suivante** the pupils are divided up between the classes as follows 2. (*division*) **la** ~ **des touristes en groupes** the division of tourists into groups 3. (*disposition: des troupes*) positioning 4. (*étalement: d'une crème, lotion*) spreading; (*d'un programme*) scheduling 5. (*localisation: de pièces, salles*) allocation

reparution [ʀ(ə)paʀysjɔ̃] *f* reappearance

repas [ʀ(ə)pɑ] *m* (*nourriture, ensemble de plats, fait de manger*) meal; **faire un** ~ **sommaire** to have a quick meal; **faire un bon** ~ to have a good meal; **aimer les bons** ~ to like to eat well; **partager le** ~ **de qn** to share sb's meal; **cinq** ~ **par jour** five meals a day; **prendre ses** ~ **au restaurant** to eat (one's meals) at a restaurant; **donner un grand** ~ to give a big dinner; **c'est l'heure du** ~ it's time to eat

repassage [ʀ(ə)pɑsaʒ] *m* 1. ironing; **faire du** ~ to do some ironing 2. (*aiguisage*) sharpening

repasser[1] [ʀ(ə)pɑse] <1> I. *vi avoir* to iron II. *vt* 1. (*défriper*) to iron 2. (*aiguiser*) to sharpen III. *vpr* **se** ~ to iron; **bien/mal se** ~ to be easy/hard to iron; **ne pas se** ~ to be non-iron *Brit*

repasser[2] [ʀ(ə)pɑse] <1> I. *vi être* 1. (*revenir*) to come by again; **ne pas** ~ **par la même route** not to go by the same way 2. (*passer à nouveau: plat*) to be passed round again; (*film*) to be showing again; ~ **devant les yeux de qn** (*souvenirs*) to pass again before sb's eyes 3. (*revoir le travail de*) ~ **derrière qn** to check sb's work 4. (*retracer*) ~ **sur qc** to go over sth again ►**il peut toujours** ~! *inf* in his dreams! II. *vt avoir* 1. (*franchir de nouveau*) ~ **qc** to cross sth again 2. (*refaire: examen*) to resit 3. (*remettre*) ~ **une couche de peinture sur qc** to give sth another coat of paint; ~ **le plat au four** to put the dish back in the oven 4. (*redonner*) ~ **qc** (*plat, outil*) to hand sth back; ~ **le standard à qn** to return sb to the switchboard; **je te repasse papa** I'll give you back to Dad 5. (*rejouer*) ~ **qc** to put sth on again 6. (*passer à nouveau*) ~ **qc dans sa tête** [*o* **son esprit**] to go over sth again in one's mind 7. (*réviser*) ~ **qc** to go through sth again 8. *inf* (*donner*) ~ **un travail à qn** to hand a job on to sb; ~ **une maladie à qn** to give sb a disease

repasseuse [ʀ(ə)pɑsøz] *f* 1. (*femme*) ironer 2. (*machine*) ironing machine

repayer [ʀ(ə)peje] <7> *vt* to repay

repêchage [ʀ(ə)pɛʃaʒ] *m* 1. (*fait de retirer de l'eau*) fishing out 2. ECOLE, UNIV passing (*borderline candidates*); (*examen*) second chance exam 3. SPORT repechage

repêcher [ʀ(ə)peʃe] <1> *vt* 1. (*retirer de l'eau*) ~ **qc** to fish sth out 2. *inf* ECOLE, UNIV ~ **qn** to push sb through (*in borderline cases*); (*par examen complémentaire*) to give sb a second chance 3. SPORT to let through by repechage

repeindre [ʀ(ə)pɛ̃dʀ] *vt irr* to repaint

repenser [ʀ(ə)pɑ̃se] <1> I. *vi* ~ **à qc** to think of sb again; **je vais y** ~ I'll give it some more thought II. *vt* to rethink

repenti(e) [ʀ(ə)pɑ̃ti] *adj* (*buveur, fumeur*) reformed; (*malfaiteur, terroriste*) repentant

repentir [ʀ(ə)pɑ̃tiʀ] I. *m* repentance II. <10> *vpr* **se** ~ **de qc/d'avoir fait qc** to repent sth/doing sth

repérage [ʀ(ə)peʀaʒ] *m* 1. (*localisation*) location 2. CINE location scouting; **faire des ~s** to scout for locations

répercussion [ʀepɛʀkysjɔ̃] *f* 1. (*effet*) *a.* PHYS repercussion; **avoir des ~s négatives** to have negative repercussions; **avoir peu de ~s sur qc** to have little repercussion on sth 2. ECON, FIN ~ **de qc** passing on of sth

répercuter [ʀepɛʀkyte] <1> I. *vt* 1. (*réfléchir*) to reflect; (*son*) to send back 2. ECON, FIN ~ **qc sur les consommateurs** to pass sth on to consumers; ~ **qc sur les prix des marchandises** to put sth on to the cost of goods 3. (*transmettre*) ~ **qc** to pass sth on II. *vpr* 1. (*être réfléchi*) **se** ~ to be reflected 2. (*se transmettre à*) **se** ~ **sur qc** to be passed on to sth

repère [ʀ(ə)pɛʀ] I. *m* 1. (*signe*) marker; **tracer des ~s sur qc** to put markers on sth 2. (*trait*) mark II. *app* **borne** ~ landmark; **des dates** ~ landmark dates

repérer [ʀ(ə)peʀe] <5> I. *vt* 1. *inf* (*découvrir*) to spot; **se faire** ~ to be spotted; **se faire** ~ **par qn** to be spotted by sb 2. CINE (*lieux*) to scout for 3. MIL (*localiser*) to locate II. *vpr inf* 1. (*se retrouver, s'orienter*) **se** ~ **dans qc** to find one's way around 2. (*se remarquer*) **se** ~ to stand out

répertoire [ʀepɛʀtwaʀ] *m* 1. index 2. (*carnet*) address book 3. THEAT repertoire 4. INFOR directory; ~ **principal** main directory 5. *inf* (*grand nombre*) repertoire

répertorier [ʀepɛʀtɔʀje] <1> *vt* 1. (*inscrire dans un répertoire*) to list 2. (*classer*) ~ **des personnes/choses** to classify people/things

répéter [ʀepete] <5> I. *vt* 1. (*redire*) to repeat; **répète après moi: ...** repeat after me: ...; **ne pas se faire** ~ **les choses deux fois** not to need telling twice; ~ **à son fils de** +*infin* to keep telling one's son to +*infin;* **je vous l'ai répété cent fois déjà** I've told you a hundred times already; **combien de fois vous ai-je répété que...?** how many times have I told you that...? 2. (*rapporter*) to tell; (*propos*) to repeat; **ne va pas le ~!** don't tell a soul! 3. (*refaire*) ~ **qc** to do sth again 4. (*mémoriser*) to learn 5. THEAT, MUS to rehearse 6. (*plagier*) to copy II. *vi* 1. (*redire*) **répète un peu!** say that again! 2. THEAT to rehearse III. *vpr* 1. (*redire les mêmes choses*) **se** ~ to repeat oneself 2. (*se raconter*) **se** ~ (*histoire*) to be told; **se** ~ **qc** to tell oneself sth 3. (*se redire la même chose*) **se** ~ **qc/que** to keep telling oneself sth/that 4. (*être reproduit, se reproduire*) **se** ~ to happen again

répétitif, -ive [ʀepetitif, -iv] *adj* repetitive; **faire des gestes ~s** to make repetitive movements

répétition [ʀepetisjɔ̃] *f* 1. (*redite*) repetition 2. (*mémorisation: d'un rôle, morceau*) learning 3. THEAT, MUS rehearsal; ~ **générale** dress rehearsal; **être en** ~ to be in rehearsal 4. (*renouvellement, reproduction: d'un accident*) recurrence; (*d'un exploit*) repeating ▸**faire des otites à** ~ *inf* to have one ear infection after the other

repeupler [ʀ(ə)pœple] <1> I. *vt* 1. (*peupler à nouveau*) to repopulate 2. (*regarnir: forêt*) to replant; ~ **qc d'animaux** to renew the animal population of sth II. *vpr* **se** ~ to be repopulated

repiquage [ʀ(ə)pikaʒ] *m* 1. BOT ~ **de qc** bedding sth out 2. CINE, TV copying; **faire un** ~ **de cassettes** to copy cassettes 3. PHOT touching up

repiquer [ʀ(ə)pike] <1> *vt* 1. BOT ~ **qc** to bed sth out 2. CINE, TV to copy 3. PHOT ~ **qc** to touch sth up 4. *inf* (*attraper de nouveau*) ~ **qn** to catch sb again; **il a été repiqué à voler** he was caught stealing again

répit [ʀepi] *m* 1. (*pause*) rest; **sans** ~ nonstop 2. (*délai supplémentaire*) breathing space [*o* room]

replacement [ʀ(ə)plasmɑ̃] *m* repositioning

replacer [ʀ(ə)plase] <2> I. *vt* 1. (*remettre à sa place*) to replace 2. (*situer*) ~ **un événement dans son époque** to put an event into its historical context II. *vpr* **se** ~ **dans qc** to take up one's position again in sth

replanter [ʀ(ə)plɑ̃te] <1> *vt* to replant

replat [ʀəpla] *m* projecting ledge

replâtrer [ʀ(ə)plɑtʀe] <1> *vt* 1. (*plâtrer de nouveau*) to replaster 2. *inf* (*raccommoder*) ~ **qc** to patch sth up

replet, -ète [ʀəplɛ, -ɛt] *adj* plump; (*visage*) chubby

repleuvoir [ʀəplœvwaʀ] *vi irr, impers* **il repleut** it's raining again

repli [ʀəpli] *m* 1. *pl* (*ondulations: d'un drapeau, de la peau*) fold; (*d'une rivière, d'un intestin*) bend; ~ **de terrain** fold in the terrain 2. (*retraite*) withdrawal 3. FIN, ECON fall 4. (*isolement: d'un pays*) withdrawal; ~ **sur soi-même** withdrawal into oneself 5. COUT fold

repliable [ʀ(ə)plijabl] *adj* folding

replier [ʀ(ə)plije] <1> I. *vt* 1. (*plier à nouveau*) to refold 2. (*plier sur soi-même*) ~ **qc**

R

(*bas de pantalon, manche, feuille*) to roll sth up; (*coin d'une page*) to fold sth down; (*mètre rigide*) to fold sth up **3.** (*rabattre*) ~ **qc** (*jambes, pattes*) to fold sth; (*ailes, couteau, lame*) to fold sth away; (*couverture, drap*) to fold sth down; **les jambes repliées** with one's legs folded **4.** MIL to withdraw **II.** *vpr* **1.** (*faire retraite*) **se** ~ to fall back **2.** (*se protéger*) **se** ~ **sur qc** to fall back on sth **3.** (*se plier*) **se** ~ to fold **4.** (*se ramasser*) **se** ~ (*animal*) to curl up **5.** (*se renfermer*) **se** ~ (*pays*) to withdraw; **se** ~ **sur soi-même** to withdraw into oneself

réplique [Replik] *f* **1.** (*réponse*) rejoinder; **avoir la** ~ **facile** to have an answer to everything **2.** (*objection, réaction*) ~ **à qc** answer to sth **3.** THEAT cue **4.** ART replica ►**donner la** ~ **à qn** THEAT to give sb their cue; (*répondre*) to answer sb back; **être la vivante** ~ **de qn** to be the spitting image of sb; **sans** ~ unanswerable; (*obéir*) with no arguments

répliquer [Replike] <1> **I.** *vi* **1.** (*répondre*) to reply **2.** (*protester, répondre avec impertinence*) to retort **II.** *vt* ~ **la même chose à sa mère** to answer the same thing back to one's mother; ~ **qc à un argument** to reply sth to an argument

replonger [R(ə)plɔ̃ʒe] <2a> **I.** *vi* **1.** (*faire un plongeon*) ~ **dans la piscine** to dive back into the swimming pool **2.** (*aller au fond de l'eau*) ~ **dans le bassin** to dive into the pool **II.** *vt* **1.** (*plonger à nouveau*) ~ **les rames dans l'eau** to dip the oars back in the water; ~ **la main dans sa poche** to put one's hand back in one's pocket **2.** (*précipiter à nouveau*) ~ **les gens/la région dans la misère** to plunge people/the region back into misery **III.** *vpr* **se** ~ **dans qc** to reimmerse oneself in sth

répondant [Repɔ̃dɑ̃] *m* **avoir du** ~ to have money; (*de la répartie*) to always have a ready reply

répondant(e) [Repɔ̃dɑ̃, ɑ̃t] *m(f)* (*garant*) guarantor

répondeur [Repɔ̃dœR] *m* answering machine; ~ **interrogeable à distance** answering machine with remote access

répondeur, -euse [Repɔ̃dœR, -øz] *adj* (*impertinent*) **un enfant** ~ a child that answers back

répondeur-enregistreur [Repɔ̃dœRɑ̃Rəʒistʀœʀ] <répondeurs-enregistreurs> *m* answering machine

répondre [Repɔ̃dR] <14> **I.** *vi* **1.** (*donner une réponse*) to answer, to reply; ~ **par qc** to answer with sth; ~ **à une lettre** to reply to a letter; ~ **à une question** to reply to [*o* answer] a question; **ne pas** ~ **à des injures** not to reply to insults; ~ **par monosyllabes** to give a monosyllabic reply; ~ **en souriant/en haussant les épaules** to answer with a smile/a shrug of one's shoulders **2.** (*réagir*) **ne pas** ~ **au téléphone** not to answer the telephone **3.** (*être impertinent*) ~ **à qn** to answer sb back **II.** *vt* ~ **qc à qn** to reply sth to sb; ~ **oui** to answer yes; **réponds-moi!** answer me!; **que dois-je** ~ **à ça?** what am I supposed to say to that?; **avoir quelque chose/n'avoir rien à** ~ to have something/nothing to say in reply; ~ **à qn de** +*infin* to reply by telling sb to +*infin*

réponse [Repɔ̃s] *f* ~ **à qc** reply [*o* answer] to sth; **avoir** ~ **à tout** to have an answer to everything; **rester sans** ~ to remain unanswered

report [RəpɔR] *m* **1.** (*renvoi*) *a.* MIL postponement; (*d'une échéance*) deferment, postponement; ~ **à une date ultérieure** postponement till a later date **2.** (*inscription*) carrying forward **3.** POL (*de voix*) transfer **4.** PHOT, TYP transfer

reportage [R(ə)pɔRtaʒ] *m* report; ~ **télévisé** television report

reporter¹ [R(ə)pɔRtɛR, R(ə)pɔRtœR] *mf* reporter

reporter² [R(ə)pɔRte] <1> **I.** *vt* (*différer*) to postpone; ~ **qc à une date ultérieure** to postpone sth till a later date **II.** *vpr* (*se référer*) **se** ~ **à qc** to refer to sth; **se** ~ **à la page 13** see page 13

repos [R(ə)po] *m* **1.** (*détente*) rest; **prendre un peu de** ~ to have a little rest **2.** (*congé*) **une journée de** ~ a day off; **il a pris une matinée/3 jours de** ~ he took a morning/three days off ►**ce n'est pas de tout** ~ (*fatigant*) it's no rest cure

reposant(e) [R(ə)pozɑ̃, ɑ̃t] *adj* relaxing; (*lieu*) restful; ~ **pour la vue/l'esprit** restful for the eyes/the mind

reposé(e) [R(ə)poze] *adj* rested; **elle a le teint/l'esprit** ~ she has a refreshed complexion/mind

reposer¹ [R(ə)poze] <1> **I.** *vt* **1.** (*poser à nouveau*) ~ **qc** to put sth back **2.** (*répéter*) ~ **la question** to ask the question again; ~ **le problème** to raise the problem again **II.** *vi* (*être fondé sur*) ~ **sur une hypothèse/des observations** to be based on a hypothesis/observations **III.** *vpr* **se** ~ (*se poser à nouveau: problème, question*) to come up again

reposer² [R(ə)poze] <1> **I.** *vt* (*délasser*) to relax; **il lit, ça le repose** he's reading, he finds it relaxing **II.** *vpr* (*se délasser*) **se** ~ to rest

repose-tête [R(ə)poztɛt] <repose-tête(s)> *m* headrest

repoussant(e) [R(ə)pusɑ̃, ɑ̃t] *adj* revolting; **être d'une laideur ~e** to be sickeningly ugly

repousser¹ [R(ə)puse] <1> **I.** *vt* **1.** (*écarter: attaque, ennemi*) to repel; ~ **des coups/un agresseur** to ward off blows/an attacker; ~ **la foule** to drive back the crowd; ~ **des cartons** to push boxes out of the way **2.** (*écarter avec véhémence*) ~ **des papiers** to push some papers away; ~ **qn sur le côté** to push sb aside **3.** (*refuser: aide, arguments, conseil*) to ignore; (*demande*) to refuse **4.** (*remettre à sa place: meuble*) ~ **qc** to push sth back **5.** (*différer*) to postpone **II.** *vpr* **se** ~ to repel each other

repousser² [R(ə)puse] *vi* (*croître de nou-*

veau) to grow back; **laisser ~ sa barbe/ses cheveux** to let one's beard/hair grow back

répréhensible [ʀepʀeɑ̃sibl] *adj* (*acte*) reprehensible

reprendre [ʀ(ə)pʀɑ̃dʀ] <13> **I.** *vt* **1.** (*récupérer*) **~ qc** (*objet prêté, parole, emballage, territoire, ville*) to take sth back; (*place*) to go back to sth; (*objet déposé*) to pick sth up; **~ un employé** to take a worker back on; **~ ses enfants à l'école** to pick up one's children after school; **~ sa voiture et rentrer chez soi** to pick up one's car and go back home; **~ la voiture/le volant après un accident** to get back in the car/go back to driving after an accident **2.** (*retrouver*) **~ contact** to get back in touch; **~ ses habitudes** to get back into one's old habits; **~ son nom de jeune fille** to start using one's maiden name again; **~ confiance/espoir/courage** to get new confidence/hope/courage; **~ conscience** to regain consciousness; **~ des couleurs** to get some colour [*o* color *Am*] back in one's cheeks; **~ des forces** to get one's strength back **3.** COM, ECON **~ qc** (*fonds de commerce, entreprise*) to take sth over; (*marchandise usagée*) to take sth back **4.** (*continuer après une interruption: promenade*) to continue; **~ sa fonction** to return to one's post; **~ un travail** to go back to some work; **~ sa parole** to take back one's word; **~ sa lecture** to go back to one's reading; **~ un récit** to go back to a story; **~ la route** to get back on the road; **~ (le chemin de) l'école** to set off for school again; **~ son cours** (*conversation*) to pick up again; (*vie*) to go back to normal **5.** (*recommencer*) **~ la lecture/le récit de qc** to begin reading/telling sth again; **tout ~ à zéro** to start all over again from scratch **6.** (*corriger: article, chapitre*) to rework; **~ un élève** to correct a pupil; **~ une faute** to point out a mistake; **~ un travail** to go back over some work **7.** COUT to alter; **~ qc** (*rétrécir*) to take sth in; (*raccourcir*) to take sth up; (*agrandir*) to let sth out; (*rallonger*) to let sth down **8.** (*se resservir de*) **~ de la viande/du gâteau** to have some more meat/cake **9.** (*s'approprier*) **~ une idée/suggestion** to take up an idea/suggestion ►**ça me/le reprend** *iron* I'm/he's at it again; **que je ne t'y reprenne pas!** don't let me catch you doing that again!; **on ne m'y reprendra plus** I won't be caught out again **II.** *vi* **1.** (*se revivifier: affaires, convalescent*) to pick up; (*vie*) to return to normal **2.** (*recommencer: douleurs, musique, pluie, conversation*) to start up again; (*classe, cours*) to start again **3.** (*enchaîner*) to go on **4.** (*répéter*) **je reprends: ...** to go back to what I was saying: ... **III.** *vpr* **1.** (*se corriger*) **se ~** to correct oneself **2.** (*s'interrompre*) **se ~** to stop **3.** *soutenu* (*recommencer*) **se ~ à faire qc** to start doing sth again; **s'y ~ à deux fois pour** *+infin* to have to make a second attempt before one manages to *+infin* **4.** (*se ressaisir*) **se ~** to pull oneself together

représailles [ʀ(ə)pʀezɑj] *fpl* reprisals; **exercer des** [*o* **user de**] **~ contre qn** to take reprisals against sb; **s'attendre à des ~ de la part de qn** to expect reprisals from sb; **en ~ à qc** for sth; **par ~** in retaliation

représentant(e) [ʀ(ə)pʀezɑ̃tɑ̃, ɑ̃t] *m(f)* representative; **~ en papier/livres** paper/book rep; **~ de commerce** sales representative; **la Chambre des ~s** *Belgique* the House of Representatives (*the lower house of the Belgian Parliament*)

représentatif, -ive [ʀ(ə)pʀezɑ̃tatif, -iv] *adj* **a.** POL **~ de qn/qc** representative of sb/sth; **être ~ de sa génération** to be typical of one's generation

représentation [ʀ(ə)pʀezɑ̃tasjɔ̃] *f* **1.** (*description*) representation **2.** THEAT performance

représenter [ʀ(ə)pʀezɑ̃te] <1> **I.** *vt* **1.** (*décrire*) to represent; **~ qn comme qc** to make sb out to be sth **2.** (*correspondre à: progrès, révolution, travail, autorité*) to represent **3.** JUR, POL, COM to represent **II.** *vpr* **1.** (*s'imaginer*) **se ~ qn/qc** to imagine sb/sth **2.** (*survenir à nouveau*) **se ~** (*occasion, possibilité, problème*) to come up again **3.** POL **se ~ à qc** to stand for sth again

répressif, -ive [ʀepʀesif, -iv] *adj* repressive

répression [ʀepʀesjɔ̃] *f* **1.** JUR suppression **2.** POL, PSYCH repression

réprimande [ʀepʀimɑ̃d] *f* reprimand; **faire une ~ à qn** to reprimand sb

réprimander [ʀepʀimɑ̃de] <1> *vt* to reprimand

réprimer [ʀepʀime] <1> *vt* **1.** (*retenir*) to suppress; (*larmes*) to hold back **2.** JUR, POL to suppress

repris de justice [ʀ(ə)pʀid(ə)ʒystis] *m inv* ex-convict

reprise [ʀ(ə)pʀiz] *f* **1.** (*recommencement: d'une activité, des hostilités*) resumption; (*du froid*) return; (*d'une chanson*) cover; (*d'une émission*) rerun; (*d'un film*) new showing **2.** SPORT start of the second half **3.** MUS reprise **4.** COM (*essor*) upturn **5.** COM (*rachat: d'un appareil, d'une voiture*) trade-in; (*d'un fonds de commerce, d'une usine*) takeover; (*de mobilier*) *payment for furniture left, etc.*; **pas de ~!** no exchanges! **6.** COM (*retour: d'une marchandise, de bouteilles*) return **7.** (*réutilisation: d'une idée, suggestion*) re-examination **8.** AUTO acceleration **9.** MIL, POL (*d'un territoire, siège*) recovery **10.** COUT (*d'une chaussette*) darn; (*d'une chemise, d'un drap, pantalon*) patch **11.** (*en équitation*) riding lesson **12.** SPORT (*deuxième mi-temps*) second half; (*en boxe*) round ►**à deux/trois ~s** twice/three times; **à plusieurs** [*o* **diverses**] **~s** several times

réprobateur, -trice [ʀepʀɔbatœʀ, -tʀis] *adj* reproachful

réprobation [ʀepʀɔbasjɔ̃] *f* **1.** disapproval

R

2. REL reprobation

reproche [R(ə)pRɔʃ] *m* reproach; **faire un ~ à qn** to reproach sb

reprocher [R(ə)pRɔʃe] <1> **I.** *vt* (*faire grief de*) **~ qc à qn** to reproach sb with sth; **~ à qn de faire qc** to reproach sb with doing sth; **avoir qc à ~ à qn** to have sth to reproach sb with **II.** *vpr* **se ~ qc/de faire qc** to blame oneself for sth/for doing sth; **avoir qc à se ~** to have done sth to feel guilty about

reproducteur, -trice [R(ə)pRɔdyktœR, -tRis] *adj* **organe ~** reproductive organ; **taureau ~** stud bull

reproduction [R(ə)pRɔdyksjɔ̃] *f* (*copie*) reproduction

reproduire [R(ə)pRɔdɥiR] *vpr irr* **se ~** (*se répéter*) to happen again

réprouver [RepRuve] <1> *vt* **1.** to condemn **2.** REL (*personne*) to reprobate; **être réprouvé** to be damned

reptile [Rɛptil] *m* reptile; **les ~s** the reptiles

repu(e) [Rəpy] *adj* **1.** (*rassasié*) sated **2.** (*gavé*) **être ~ de lecture** to have one's fill of reading

républicain(e) [Repyblikɛ̃, ɛn] *adj, m(f)* republican

république [Repyblik] *f* republic; **République démocratique allemande** German Democratic Republic; **République fédérale d'Allemagne** Federal Republic of Germany; **République française** French Republic; **République populaire de Chine** People's Republic of China; **République centrafricaine** Central African Republic ►**on est en ~** it's a free country

> The figure of Marianne, a woman with a red cap, symbolizes the **république** as opposed to the monarchy.

répudier [Repydje] <1a> *vt* (*idées, principes, conjoint*) to repudiate; (*legs, nationalité*) to renounce

répugnance [Repyɲɑ̃s] *f* **1.** (*aversion*) repugnance; **avoir de la ~ pour qc** to feel loathing for sth; **~ à qc** loathing for sth; **éprouver de la ~ à faire qc** to find doing sth repugnant **2.** (*hésitation*) reluctance; **~ pour qc** reluctance over sth; **éprouver de la ~ à** *+infin* to be loath to *+infin*

répugnant(e) [Repyɲɑ̃, ɑ̃t] *adj* repulsive; **d'une laideur ~e** repulsively ugly

répugner [Repyɲe] <1> *vi* **1.** (*dégoûter*) **~ à qn** (*nourriture, personne*) to repel sb; (*action, idée, malhonnêteté*) to revolt sb **2.** (*n'avoir pas envie*) **~ à qc** to be reluctant about sth; **ça me répugne de le faire** I'm loath to do it

répulsion [Repylsjɔ̃] *f* **1.** (*aversion*) repugnance; **soulever la ~ de qn** to repel sb; **~ pour qn/qc** repugnance for sb/sth; **avoir de la ~ pour qn** to find sb repulsive **2.** (*dégoût*) disgust **3.** PHYS repulsion

réputation [Repytasjɔ̃] *f* **1.** (*honneur*) repute **2.** (*renommée*) reputation; **~ mondiale** worldwide reputation; **avoir bonne/mauvaise ~** to have a good/bad reputation; **la ~ de qn n'est plus à faire** *a. iron* sb's reputation is only too well known; **se faire une ~** to earn a reputation (for oneself)

réputé(e) [Repyte] *adj* (*connu*) reputed; **ce professeur est ~ pour être sévère** that teacher has a reputation for being strict

requérir [RəkeRiR] *irr* **I.** *vt* **1.** (*nécessiter*) to require **2.** (*solliciter*) **~ l'aide de qn** to seek sb's help **3.** (*exiger: explication, justification*) to demand; (*avion spécial, protection*) to request **4.** JUR **~ une peine** to call for a sentence **II.** *vi* to make one's closing speech

requête [Rəkɛt] *f* INFOR search

requin [Rəkɛ̃] *m* ZOOL shark

requinquer [R(ə)kɛ̃ke] <1> **I.** *vt inf* **~ qn** to buck sb up; **être requinqué** to feel a lot better **II.** *vpr inf* **se ~** to buck oneself up

requis(e) [Rəki, iz] **I.** *part passé de* **requérir** **II.** *adj* required **III.** *m(f)* labour conscript *Brit,* labor conscript *Am*

réquisitionner [Rekizisjɔne] <1> *vt* (*requérir: biens, hommes*) to requisition ►**être réquisitionné pour faire la vaisselle** *inf* to be volunteered to do the dishes

réquisitoire [RekizitwaR] *m* **1.** JUR (*réquisition*) instruction **2.** JUR (*discours*) closing speech (*by prosecution*) **3.** *fig* **~ contre qn** indictment of sb

R.E.R. [ɛRøɛR] *m abr de* **réseau express régional** (*express train service for the Paris region*)

resaler [Rəsale] <1> *vt* **~ qc** to put more salt in sth

rescapé(e) [Rɛskape] **I.** *adj* **personne ~e** survivor **II.** *m(f)* survivor

rescousse [Rɛskus] *f* **venir à la ~ de qn** to come to sb's rescue

réseau [Rezo] <x> *m* (*structure, organisation*) *a.* INFOR network; **~ ferroviaire/routier** rail/road network; **~ téléphonique/radiophonique** telephone/radio network; **~ d'espionnage/de la mafia** espionage/mafia network; **le ~ Internet** the Internet; **~ local** local network

réservation [RezɛRvasjɔ̃] *f* reservation

réserve [RezɛRv] *f* **1.** (*provision*) reserve; **faire des ~s pour l'hiver** to lay in reserves for the winter **2.** (*lieu protégé*) reserve; **~ indienne** Indian reservation; **~ naturelle/botanique** nature/botanical reserve; **~ ornithologique** bird sanctuary; **~ de chasse** hunting preserve ►**avoir des ~s** *iron* to have reserves of fat to fall back on

réservé(e) [RezɛRve] *adj* **1.** (*discret*) reserved **2.** (*limité à certains*) **~ aux handicapés/autobus** reserved for the disabled/buses

réserver [RezɛRve] <1> **I.** *vt* **1.** (*garder: place*) to keep; **~ le meilleur pour la fin** to keep the best for the last **2.** (*retenir*) to reserve; (*voyage*) to book; **~ un billet d'avion** to book a plane ticket **II.** *vpr* (*se ménager*) **se ~ pour le dessert** to leave room for dessert; **se ~ pour une meilleure occasion** to hold back for a better opportunity; **se ~ pour plus tard** to save oneself for later

réservoir [ʀezɛʀvwaʀ] *m* **1.** (*cuve*) tank; **~ d'eau** water tank; **~ d'air/d'air comprimé** air/compressed air tank **2.** (*lac, barrage*) reservoir **3.** (*réserve*) **~ de main-d'œuvre/matières premières** reserves of labour [*o* labor *Am*]/raw materials; **~ d'images** hoard of images

résidence [ʀezidɑ̃s] *f* **1.** (*domicile*) residence; **lieu de ~** place of residence; **~ principale** main residence **2.** (*appartement pour les vacances*) holiday appartment **3.** (*maison pour les vacances*) holiday home **4.** (*immeuble*) **~ universitaire** hall of residence *Brit*, dormitory *Am*; **~ pour personnes âgées** old persons' home; **~ pour handicapés** home for the disabled

résident(e) [ʀezidɑ̃, ɑ̃t] *m(f)* (*étranger*) resident; **les ~s allemands en France** Germans residing in France

résidentiel(le) [ʀezidɑ̃sjɛl] *adj* **1.** (*d'habitation*) **zone ~le** residential area **2.** (*de standing*) fashionable

résider [ʀezide] <1> *vi* (*habiter*) to reside; **les étrangers qui résident en France** foreigners residing in France

résidu [ʀezidy] *m* **1.** CHIM residue; **~s de combustion/fission** residue of combustion/fission **2.** MAT remainder

résignation [ʀeziɲasjɔ̃] *f* resignation; **avec ~** with resignation; **la ~ à qc** resignation to sth

résigné(e) [ʀeziɲe] *adj* resigned; **~ à son sort** resigned to one's fate

résigner [ʀeziɲe] <1> *vpr* **se ~** to resign oneself; **se ~ à faire qc** to resign oneself to doing sth

résilier [ʀezilje] <1> *vt* to cancel

résine [ʀezin] *f* resin; **~ synthétique** [*o* **artificielle**] synthetic resin

résineux [ʀezinø] *m* resiniferous tree; **les ~** conifers; **forêt de ~** conifer forest

résineux, -euse [ʀezinø, -øz] *adj* resinous; **bois ~** resinous wood

résistance [ʀezistɑ̃s] *f* (*opposition*) resistance; **la Résistance** HIST the Resistance

résistant(e) [ʀezistɑ̃, ɑ̃t] **I.** *adj* (*robuste: matériau*) resistant; (*étoffe*) hard-wearing; (*personne, plante, animal*) tough; **l'acier est plus ~ que le fer** steel is tougher than iron **II.** *m(f)* HIST member of the Resistance

résister [ʀeziste] <1> *vi* **1.** (*s'opposer*) **~ à qn** to resist sb; **~ à un désir/une passion/tentation** to resist a desire/passion/temptation **2.** (*supporter*) **résister à qc** to withstand sth; **~ au feu** to be fireproof; **~ au lavage** to be washable

resituer [ʀəsitɥe] <1> *vt* to resituate

résolu(e) [ʀezɔly] **I.** *part passé de* **résoudre** **II.** *adj* (*air, personne*) determined; (*ton*) resolute; **être ~ à qc** to be determined on sth; **être ~ à** *+infin* to be determined to *+infin*

résolument [ʀezɔlymɑ̃] *adv* resolutely

résolution [ʀezɔlysjɔ̃] *f* **1.** (*décision*) decision; **prendre une ~** to take a decision; **prendre des ~s** to make decisions; **prendre de bonnes ~s** to make good resolutions; **prendre la ~ de** *+infin* to resolve to *+infin* **2.** INFOR resolution

résonance [ʀezɔnɑ̃s] *f* **1.** (*répercussion*) echo; **avoir une grande ~ dans l'opinion** to strike a chord in public opinion **2.** (*connotation*) overtones *pl*

résonner [ʀezɔne] <1> *vi* (*salle*) to resonate; **~ de qc** to resound with sth

résorber [ʀezɔʀbe] <1> **I.** *vt* (*inflation, chômage, surplus*) to bring down; (*déficit*) to reduce; (*tumeur, abcès*) to resorb **II.** *vpr* **se ~** (*chômage, inflation, surplus*) to come down; (*déficit*) to be reduced; (*embouteillage*) to be going down; (*abcès, tumeur*) to be resorbed

résoudre [ʀezudʀ] *irr* **I.** *vt* **1.** (*trouver une solution: conflit, problème*) to resolve; (*mystère*) to solve **2.** (*décider*) **~ de** *+infin* to decide to *+infin;* **~ qn à** *+infin* to induce sb to *+infin* **II.** *vpr* (*se décider*) **se ~ à faire qc** to reconcile oneself to doing sth

respect [ʀɛspɛ] *m* (*égards*) respect; **~ de qn/qc** respect for sb/sth; **devoir le ~ à qn** to owe sb respect; **manquer de ~ à qn** to fail to show sb respect; **par ~ pour qn/qc** out of respect for sb/sth

respectable [ʀɛspɛktabl] *adj* **1.** (*digne de respect*) respectable; (*motif, scrupule*) honorable **2.** (*assez important*) considerable

respecter [ʀɛspɛkte] <1> *vt* **1.** (*avoir des égards pour*) to respect; **être respecté** to be respected; **se faire ~ par qn** to get sb's respect **2.** (*observer: forme, tradition, normes*) to respect; **~ un engagement** to stand by a commitment

respectif, -ive [ʀɛspɛktif, -iv] *adj* respective

respectivement [ʀɛspɛktivmɑ̃] *adv* respectively

respectueusement [ʀɛspɛktɥøzmɑ̃] *adv* respectfully

respectueux, -euse [ʀɛspɛktɥø, -øz] *adj* respectful; **être ~ de qc** (*mettre en pratique*) to abide by sth; (*attacher de l'importance*) to show respect for [*o* respect] sth; **être ~ de la loi** to be law-abiding; **être ~ d'une autre religion/de l'environnement** to respect another religion/the environment; **être ~ envers qn** to show sb respect; **je vous présente mes respectueuses salutations/mes hommages** (*à la fin d'une lettre*) Yours faithfully

respiration [ʀɛspiʀasjɔ̃] *f* breathing; **~ artificielle** artificial respiration; **couper la ~ à qn** to stop sb from breathing; **retenir sa ~** to hold one's breath

respiratoire [ʀɛspiʀatwaʀ] *adj* **voies ~s** airways; **organes/maladies/troubles ~s** respiratory organs/illnesses; **sous assistance ~** receiving artificial respiration; **appareil ~** (*organes*) repiratory system; (*masque*) breathing apparatus

respirer [ʀɛspiʀe] <1> *vi* **1.** (*inspirer*) to breathe; **respirez fort!** take a deep breath! **2.** (*se détendre*) to rest **3.** (*être rassuré*) to breathe easy

resplendir [ʀɛsplɑ̃diʀ] <8> *vi soutenu* **1.** (*rayonner*) to shine **2.** (*briller*) **~ de propreté** to gleam

resplendissant(**e**) [ʀɛsplɑ̃disɑ̃, ɑ̃t] *adj* **1.** (*brillant*) shining; **d'un blanc ~** shining white; **le sol est ~** the floor is gleaming **2.** (*éclatant: beauté*) radiant; **~ de beauté** radiantly beautiful; **~ de santé** glowing with health; **être doté d'une santé ~e** to glow with health; **avoir une mine ~e** [*o* **être ~**] to look splendid; **~ de bonheur/joie** to be radiant with with happiness/joy

responsabiliser [ʀɛspɔ̃sabilize] <1> **I.** *vt* **~ qn** to give sb a sense of responsibility **II.** *vpr* **se ~** to become more responsible

responsabilité [ʀɛspɔ̃sabilite] *f* **1.** (*culpabilité*) responsibility; **avoir une ~ dans qc** to share some responsibility for sth **2.** JUR responsibility; **~ collective** collective responsibility; **~ civile** civil liability; (*assurance*) civil liability insurance **3.** (*charge de responsable*) **~ de qc** responsibility for sth; **avoir/prendre des ~s** to have/take on responsibilities; **avoir de grosses ~s** to have big responsibilities; **avoir la ~ de qn/qc** to be responsible for sb/sth; **décliner/rejeter toute ~** to accept no responsibility; **sous la ~ de qn** under sb; **il a plusieurs employés sous sa ~** he is responsible for several employees under him **4.** (*conscience*) sense of responsibility

responsable [ʀɛspɔ̃sabl] **I.** *adj* **1.** (*coupable*) **être ~ de qc** to be responsible for sth **2.** JUR (*civilement, pénalement*) responsible; **être ~ de qn/qc devant qn** to be answerable for sb/sth to sb; **être ~ de ses actes** to be responsible for one's actions **3.** (*chargé de*) **~ de qc** responsible for sth **4.** (*conscient: attitude, acte, personne*) responsible **II.** *mf* **1.** (*auteur*) person responsible; **les ~s** those responsible **2.** (*personne compétente*) person in charge; (*d'une organisation, entreprise*) leader; **~ d'un parti/syndicat** party/union leader; **~ politique** politician; **~ technique** technician

resquille [ʀɛskij] *f inf* **1.** wangling; **faire de la ~** to wangle one's way in **2.** (*voyager sans payer*) **faire de la ~** to dodge the fare **3.** (*dans une file d'attente*) **faire de la ~** to jump the queue *Brit*, to cut in line *Am*

resquiller [ʀɛskije] <1> **I.** *vi inf* **1.** to wangle **2.** (*voyager sans payer*) to dodge the fare **3.** (*dans une file d'attente*) to jump the queue *Brit*, to cut in line *Am* **II.** *vt* **~ qc** *inf* to wangle sth

resquilleur, **-euse** [ʀɛskijœʀ, -jøz] *m, f inf* **1.** wangler **2.** (*voyageur sans ticket*) fare dodger **3.** (*dans une file d'attente*) queue jumper *Brit*, person who takes cuts in line *Am*

ressac [ʀəsak] *m* backwash

ressaisir [ʀ(ə)seziʀ] <8> *vpr* (*se maîtriser*) **se ~** to take hold of oneself

ressasser [ʀ(ə)sase] <1> *vt* **~ des pensées moroses** to dwell on morbid thoughts

ressemblance [ʀ(ə)sɑ̃blɑ̃s] *f* resemblance; **avoir une ~ avec qc** to bear a resemblance to sth; **il y a une très grande ~ entre X et Y** there's a strong resemblance between X and Y

ressemblant(**e**) [ʀ(ə)sɑ̃blɑ̃, ɑ̃t] *adj* lifelike; **vous n'êtes pas très ~ sur cette photo** this photo isn't a very good likeness (of you)

ressembler [ʀ(ə)sɑ̃ble] <1> **I.** *vi* **1.** (*être semblable*) **~ à qn** to resemble sb **2.** (*être semblable physiquement*) **~ à qn/sth** to look like [*o* resemble] sb/sth **3.** *inf* (*être digne de*) **~ à qn** to be typical of [*o* just like] sb; **ça te ressemble de faire ça** it's just like you to do that ►**<u>à</u> quoi ça ressemble!** *inf* (*c'est nul*) what's this supposed to be?; **<u>à</u> quoi ça ressemble de faire ça?** *inf* (*qu'est-ce que ça veut dire*) what's the idea of doing that?; **<u>à</u> quoi il ressemble, ton nouveau copain?** so what's your new boyfriend like?; **regarde un peu <u>à</u> quoi tu ressembles!** *inf* take a look at yourself! **II.** *vpr* **1.** (*être semblables*) **se ~** to be alike **2.** (*être semblables physiquement*) **se ~** to resemble each other ►**qui se ressemble s'<u>assemble</u>** *prov* birds of a feather flock together *prov*

ressemeler [ʀ(ə)səm(ə)le] <3> *vt* to (re)sole

ressentiment [ʀ(ə)sɑ̃timɑ̃] *m* resentment; **éprouver du ~ à l'égard de qn** to feel resentment towards sb; **ne garder aucun ~ à qn** to bear sb no ill will

ressentir [ʀ(ə)sɑ̃tiʀ] <10> *vt* to feel; **se faire ~ sur qc** to have an effect on sth

resserrer [ʀ(ə)seʀe] <1> **I.** *vt* **1.** (*serrer plus fort: boulon, vis, ceinture*) to tighten **2.** (*fortifier: amitié, relations*) to strengthen **II.** *vpr* **se ~ 1.** (*devenir plus étroit*) to narrow; (*personnes*) to close in; (*cercle d'amis, groupe*) to draw in **2.** (*se fortifier: amitié, relations*) to grow stronger

resservir [ʀ(ə)sɛʀviʀ] *irr* **I.** *vt* **1. ~ qc** (*plat de la veille*) to serve sth up again; (*plat réussi*) to make sth again; **~ qn** to serve sb again **2.** *péj* (*radoter*) **~ qc** to dish sth up again **II.** *vi* (*revenir en usage*) to be used again; **ces emballages me resserviront** I can use the packing again in the future **III.** *vpr* **1.** (*reprendre*) **se ~ en/de qc** to have more of sth **2.** (*réutiliser*) **se ~ de qc** to reuse sth

ressort[1] [ʀ(ə)sɔʀ] *m* **1.** (*pièce métallique*) spring; **les ~s de suspension d'une voiture** a car's suspension springs; **~ à boudin/lame** coil/leaf spring; **articulation à ~** spring joint **2.** (*énergie*) drive; **sans ~** with no drive ►**<u>faire</u> ~** to act as a spring; **se redresser**

comme mû par un ~ to spring up with a jerk

ressort² [R(ə)sɔR] *m* ADMIN, JUR jurisdiction; **en premier** ~ on first appeal; **en dernier** ~ on final appeal; **jugement en premier/dernier** ~ JUR judgement of first/final instance; **être du** ~ **de qn/qc** to be the responsibility of sb/sth; **ce n'est pas de mon** ~ it's outside my responsibility

ressortir [R(ə)sɔRtiR] <10> **I.** *vi être* **1.** (*sortir à nouveau: personne*) (*vu de l'intérieur*) to go out again; (*vu de l'extérieur*) to come out again **2.** (*contraster*) ~ **sur qc** (*couleur, qualité*) to stand out against sth; **faire** ~ **qc** (*mettre en relief*) to bring sth out **3.** *inf* (*renouer*) ~ **avec qn** to go out with sb again **II.** *vt avoir* **1.** (*remettre d'actualité*) ~ **un projet** to revive a project; ~ **un modèle** to bring back a model **2.** (*remettre dehors*) ~ **qc** (*meubles de jardin*) to get sth back out; **peux-tu** ~ **l'agenda?** can you get the diary back out?

ressortissant(e) [R(ə)sɔRtisɑ̃, ɑ̃t] *m(f)* national; **les** ~**s étrangers résidant en France** foreign nationals residing in France

ressource [R(ə)suRs] *f* **1.** *pl* (*moyens*) means; (*de l'État*) funds; ~**s naturelles** natural resources; ~**s personnelles** private income; **sans** ~**s** with no means of support **2.** *sans pl* (*recours*) **tu es ma seule** ~ you are the only one I can turn to; **en dernière** ~ as a last resort; **sans** ~ with nowhere to turn ►**avoir de la** ~ to have strength in reserve

ressuscité(e) [Resysite] *m(f)* **1.** REL **le Ressuscité** the risen Christ **2.** *fig* **vous êtes un vrai** ~**!** you look like death warmed over!

ressusciter [Resysite] <1> **I.** *vi* **1.** *être* REL **être ressuscité** to be risen **2.** *avoir* (*renaître: malade, nature*) to come back to life; (*pays, entreprise*) to revive; (*idéologie, projet*) to be revived **II.** *vt avoir* **1.** REL to raise **2.** (*régénérer, faire revivre*) ~ **qc** (*entreprise, pays, nature*) to bring sth back to life; (*idéologie, mode*) to revive sth; ~ **un malade** to bring a sick person back to life; **être ressuscité** (*malade, entreprise, pays*) to come back to life; (*idéologie*) to be revived

restant [Rɛstɑ̃] *m* rest; **le** ~ **de la journée** the rest of the day; ~ **de poulet/tissu** leftover chicken/cloth

restaurant [Rɛstɔʀɑ̃] *m* restaurant; **aller au** ~ to eat out; ~ **universitaire** university canteen; ~ **du cœur** *canteen run by volunteers for poor and homeless people during the winter*

restaurateur, -trice [Rɛstɔratœʀ, -tris] *m, f* **1.** (*aubergiste*) restaurant owner **2.** (*personne qui remet en état*) restorer; ~ **de bâtiments/tableaux** building/picture restorer

restauration [Rɛstɔrasjɔ̃] *f* **1.** ARCHIT, ART (*remise en état*) restoration **2.** (*hôtellerie*) catering; (*commerce*) restaurant trade; ~ **rapide** fast food **3.** INFOR restoration

restaurer [Rɛstɔre] <1> **I.** *vt* **1.** (*remettre en état, rétablir*) ~/**faire** ~ **qc** to restore sth **2.** POL (*droits, ordre, paix, monarchie, régime*) to restore; (*coutume, habitude*) to revive **3.** MED (*fonction*) to restore; (*organisme*) to repair; ~ **ses forces/sa santé** to get one's strength/health back **4.** (*nourrir*) to feed; **j'ai de quoi vous** ~ I've got enough to feed you **II.** *vpr* **se** ~ to have something to eat

reste [Rɛst] *m* **1.** (*reliquat*) **le** ~ **de la journée/du temps/de ma vie** the rest of the day/the time/my life; **tout le** ~ all the rest; **un** ~ **de tissu** a scrap of cloth; **un** ~ **d'amour/de pitié** a scrap of love/pity **2.** MAT remainder **3.** *pl* (*reliefs: d'un repas*) leftovers; **ne pas laisser beaucoup de** ~**s** not to leave much ►**avoir de beaux** ~**s** *iron* to still be a fine figure of a woman; **partir sans demander son** ~ to take off without making a fuss; **faire le** ~ to do the rest; **du** ~ besides; **pour le** ~ as for the rest

rester [Rɛste] <1> **I.** *vi être* **1.** (*demeurer, ne pas s'en aller*) to stay; ~ **au lit** to stay in bed; ~ **chez soi** to stay at home; ~ **(à) dîner** to stay for dinner; ~ **sans parler/manger/bouger** to stay silent/hungry/still **2.** (*continuer à être*) to stay; ~ **debout/assis toute la journée** to be standing/sitting all day; ~ **immobile** to keep still **3.** (*subsister*) to remain; **ça m'est resté** (*dans ma mémoire*) I've never forgotten it; (*dans mes habitudes*) it's stuck with me; **beaucoup de choses restent à faire** much remains to be done **4.** (*ne pas se libérer de*) ~ **sur un échec** never to get over a failure ►**en** ~ **là** to stop there; **y** ~ to meet one's end **II.** *vi impers être* **1.** (*être toujours là*) **il reste du vin** there's some wine left; **il n'est rien resté** there was nothing left; **il ne me reste (plus) que toi/cinquante euros** all I've got left is you/fifty euros **2.** (*ne pas être encore fait*) **je sais ce qu'il me reste à faire** I know what's left for me to do; **reste à savoir si ...** it remains to be decided if ...

restituer [Rɛstitɥe] <1> *vt* **1.** (*rendre*) ~ **un livre à un ami** to give a book back to a friend **2.** MEDIA to reproduce **3.** (*reconstituer: inscription, texte, fresque*) to restore **4.** (*libérer, dégager*) **être restitué sous forme de chaleur** (*énergie*) to be released as heat

resto [Rɛsto] *m inf abr de* **restaurant**

restoroute® [RɛstoRut] *f* roadside restaurant; (*de l'autoroute*) motorway restaurant *Brit*, truck stop *Am*

restreindre [RɛstRɛ̃dR] *irr* **I.** *vt* to restrict; (*champ d'action, crédit, étude, ambition*) to limit; (*quantité, production, dépenses*) to cut **II.** *vpr* **se** ~ **1.** (*s'imposer des restrictions*) to limit oneself; **se** ~ **dans ses dépenses** to restrict one's spending; **se** ~ **sur la nourriture** to cut down on food **2.** (*diminuer: ambition*) to die down; (*champ d'action, sens d'un mot*) to be restricted; (*dépenses, production, quantité*) to go down

restreint(e) [RɛstRɛ̃, ɛ̃t] **I.** *part passé de*

R

restreindre **II.** *adj* limited; ~ **à un petit cercle/certaines personnes** restricted to a small circle/certain people

restriction [ʀɛstʀiksjɔ̃] *f* **1.** (*limitation: des libertés*) curtailment; (*des dépenses, de la consommation, production*) limiting; ~ **des importations/exportations** import/export limits *pl;* **mesures de** ~ restrictions **2.** *pl* (*rationnement*) restrictions; **les ~s** rationing *no pl;* **~s d'électricité/d'eau** electricity/water rationing; **~s budgétaires** budget restrictions **3.** (*réserve*) reservation; **apporter des ~s à qc** to express some qualifications about sth; **faire** [*o* **émettre**] **des ~s** to express reservations; **sans faire de ~s** unreservedly; **avec des ~s** with certain reservations; **sans** ~ without reservation

restructuration [ʀəstʀyktyʀasjɔ̃] *f* restructuring

restructurer [ʀəstʀyktyʀe] <1> *vt* to restructure

résultat [ʀezylta] *m* **1.** MAT, SPORT, ECON, POL, ECOLE result; (*d'un problème*) solution; (*d'une intervention*) outcome; **les ~s des élections** the election results **2.** (*conséquence, chose obtenue*) result; **avoir de bons/mauvais ~s** to have good/bad results; **avoir pour** ~ **une augmentation des prix** to result in an increase in prices; **c'est déjà un** ~ something at least has been achieved; **n'obtenir aucun** ~ to achieve nothing; **obtenir quelques ~s** to get some results ►**sans** ~ to no effect

résulter [ʀezylte] <1> **I.** *vi* ~ **d'un conflit/d'une situation/réunion/discussion** to arise from a conflict/situation/meeting/discussion **II.** *vi impers* **il résulte de ce renseignement que qn a fait qc** this information tells us that sb did sth; **il en résulte/est résulté une grande confusion** this leads/led to a great deal of confusion; **il en résulte/est résulté que qn a fait qc** the outcome is/was that sb did sth; **qu'en résultera-t-il?** what will be the outcome?

résumé [ʀezyme] *m* summary ►**en** ~ in short; **en** ~**: ...** to put things briefly: ...

résumer [ʀezyme] <1> *vt* (*récapituler*) to summarize; ~ **qc en une page** to summarize sth in one page

résurrection [ʀezyʀɛksjɔ̃] *f* resurrection; **la Résurrection** the Resurrection

rétablir [ʀetabliʀ] <8> **I.** *vt* **1.** (*remettre en fonction: communication, courant*) to restore; (*contact, liaison*) to re-establish; **être rétabli** (*communication, contact*) to be re-established; (*trafic*) to be moving again **2.** (*restaurer: confiance, équilibre, ordre*) to restore; (*monarchie, faits*) to re-establish; ~ **la vérité** to get back down to the truth **3.** MED ~ **qn** to bring sb back to health; **être rétabli** to be better **II.** *vpr* **se** ~ **1.** (*guérir: personne, pays*) to recover; **en voie de se** ~ on one's way to recovery **2.** (*revenir: calme, silence*) to return; (*trafic*) to return to normal

rétablissement [ʀetablismɑ̃] *m* (*d'un malade*) recovery; **bon** ~**!** get well soon!; **souhaiter un bon** ~ **à qn** to wish sb a complete recovery

rétamé(e) [ʀetame] *adj inf* **1.** (*fatigué*) worn out **2.** (*ruiné*) wrecked **3.** (*mort*) dead

retape [ʀ(ə)tap] *f inf* hype; **faire la** ~ to be on the game; **faire (de) la** ~ **pour qc** (*agent publicitaire*) to tout for sth; (*publicité*) to plug sth

retaper [ʀ(ə)tape] <1> **I.** *vt* **1.** (*remettre en état*) ~ **qc** (*maison, voiture*) to fix sth up; (*lit*) to straighten sth **2.** *inf* (*rétablir*) ~ **un malade** to set a sick person up again **II.** *vpr inf* **se** ~ **à la mer/la montagne** to have a break at the seaside/in the mountains

retard [ʀ(ə)taʀ] *m* **1.** (*arrivée tardive*) late arrival; **un** ~ **d'une heure** being an hour late; **avec une heure/dix minutes de** ~ an hour/ten minutes late; **arriver en** ~ to arrive late; **avoir du** ~**/deux minutes de** ~ to be late/two minutes late; **avoir du** ~ **sur son planning** to be behind schedule; **être en** ~ **de dix minutes** to be ten minutes late **2.** (*réalisation tardive*) **avoir du** ~ **dans un travail/paiement** to be behind on a job/with a payment; **être en** ~ **d'un mois pour (payer) le loyer** to be a month late with the rent **3.** (*développement plus lent*) slow(er) progress; ECOLE lack of progress; **malgré leur retard** despite their being behind; **présenter un** ~ **de langage/de croissance** to be late developing in terms of language/growth; **être en** ~ **sur son temps** to be behind the times

retardataire [ʀ(ə)taʀdatɛʀ] **I.** *adj* (*invité*) late; (*idées, méthodes, théorie*) outdated; **élève** ~ latecomer (*in school*) **II.** *mf* latecomer

retardement [ʀ(ə)taʀdəmɑ̃] *m* **bombe à** ~ time bomb; **dispositif à** ~ timer device; **à** ~ (*rire, se fâcher*) a bit late; (*féliciter*) belatedly; **comprendre à** ~ to be slow on the uptake

retarder [ʀ(ə)taʀde] <1> **I.** *vt* **1.** (*mettre en retard: personne, véhicule*) to delay; ~ **l'arrivée de qn** to delay sb's arrival; ~ **le départ du train** to hold up the departure of the train **2.** (*ralentir, empêcher*) ~ **qn** to hold sb up; ~ **qn dans son travail/ses préparatifs** to hold up sb's work/preparations **II.** *vi* (*être en retard*) ~ **d'une heure** (*montre, horloge*) to be an hour slow

retenir [ʀ(ə)təniʀ, ʀət(ə)niʀ] <9> **I.** *vt* **1.** (*maintenir en place*) ~ **qn/qc** (*objet, bras, personne qui glisse*) to hold on to sb/sth; (*foule, personne*) to hold sb/sth back; ~ **qn par la manche** to hold on to sb's sleeve **2.** (*empêcher d'agir*) ~ **qn** to hold sb back; **retiens/retenez-moi, ou je fais un malheur** hold on to me or I'll do something I shouldn't; **je ne sais pas ce qui me retient de le gifler** I don't know what's stopping me from slapping him **3.** (*empêcher de tomber*) to hold **4.** (*garder*) to keep; **je ne te retiens pas plus longtemps** I won't keep you any longer;

~ **qn prisonnier/en otage** to keep sb prisoner/hostage; **j'ai été retenu** I was held up **5.** (*requérir*) ~ **l'attention** to claim one's attention **6.** (*réserver: chambre, place*) to reserve; (*table*) to book **7.** (*se souvenir de*) to remember; **retenez bien la date** don't forget that date **8.** (*réprimer: colère, cri, geste*) to restrain; (*larmes, sourire*) to hold back; (*souffle*) to hold **9.** (*accepter, choisir: candidature*) to accept; ~ **une proposition** to accept a suggestion **10.** (*prélever*) ~ **un montant sur le salaire** to withhold some money out of wages; ~ **les impôts sur le salaire** to stop tax out of wages ►**je te/le/la retiens!** *inf* I won't forget you/him/her in a hurry! **II.** *vpr* **1.** (*s'accrocher*) **se** ~ **à qn/qc pour** +*infin* to hold on to sb/sth to +*infin* **2.** (*s'empêcher*) **se** ~ to restrain oneself; **se** ~ **pour ne pas rire** to keep oneself from laughing **3.** (*contenir ses besoins naturels*) **se** ~ to hold on

retentir [ʀ(ə)tɑ̃tiʀ] <8> *vi* **1.** (*résonner: bruit, cri, cloche, chant*) to ring out; ~ **d'applaudissements** to ring with applause; ~ **d'appels/de cris** to be filled with calls/cries **2.** (*affecter*) ~ **sur le caractère/la santé de qn** to have an effect on sb's character/health

retentissant(e) [ʀ(ə)tɑ̃tisɑ̃, ɑ̃t] *adj* **1.** (*fort, sonore: cri, voix*) ringing; (*bruit, claque*) resounding **2.** (*fracassant: déclaration, succès*) resounding; (*scandale, discours*) sensational

retentissement [ʀ(ə)tɑ̃tismɑ̃] *m* **1.** (*répercussion: d'un discours, de mesures politiques, d'une affaire*) repercussions *pl* **2.** (*éclat: d'un film, d'une œuvre*) impact; **avoir un grand** ~ to have a great impact

retenue [ʀ(ə)təny, ʀət(ə)ny] *f* **1.** (*prélèvement*) ~ **sur les salaires/les revenus** deduction from salaries/incomes; **opérer** [*o* **faire**] **une** ~ **de 10% sur le salaire de qn** to stop 10% out of sb's salary; **la** ~ **pour la Sécurité sociale** Social Security stoppages **2.** (*modération*) restraint; **avoir de la** ~ to have self-control; **n'avoir aucune** [*o* **manquer de**] ~ to have no self-control; **avec** ~ with restraint; **se conduire avec** ~ to behave with restraint; **sans** ~ without any restraint **3.** MAT number to carry **4.** ECOLE detention; **attraper une** ~/**être en** ~ to get/be in detention; **avoir trois heures de** ~ to have three hours' detention; **mettre un élève en** ~ to keep a pupil in **5.** (*bouchon*) hold-up **6.** TECH (*barrage*) damming **7.** (*maintien: d'une marchandise*) retention

réticence [ʀetisɑ̃s] *f* reluctance; **avec** ~ reluctantly

réticent(e) [ʀetisɑ̃, ɑ̃t] *adj* reluctant

rétif, -ive [ʀetif, -iv] *adj* stubborn

rétine [ʀetin] *f* retina

retiré(e) [ʀ(ə)tiʀe] *adj* (*solitaire: lieu*) secluded; **mener une vie** ~**e** to live a secluded life; **vivre complètement** ~ **du monde** to live far away from the rest of the world

retirer [ʀ(ə)tiʀe] <1> **I.** *vt* **1.** (*enlever*) ~ **qc** (*vêtement, montre*) to take sth off; ~ **ses lunettes** to take one's glasses off; ~ **qc du commerce** to withdraw sth from sale; ~ **qc du catalogue/programme** to remove sth from the catalogue/the programme; ~ **son jouet à qn** to take sb's toy away from them; ~ **sa confiance à qn** to no longer have confidence in sb; ~ **le permis à qn** to take away sb's licence **2.** (*faire sortir*) ~ **qc** to take sth out; ~ **un gâteau du moule** to take a cake out of a tin [*o* pan *Am*]; ~ **la clé de la serrure** to take the key out of the lock; ~ **qn de l'école** to take sb out of school; ~ **qn des décombres** to pull sb out from under the rubble **3.** (*prendre possession de: argent*) to withdraw; (*billet*) to collect; ~ **de l'argent à la banque/d'un compte** to withdraw money from the bank/an account; ~ **ses bagages de la consigne** to get one's bags out of the left luggage [*o* baggage check *Am*] **4.** (*ramener en arrière*) ~ **qc** (*main, tête*) to move sth away; ~ **des troupes** to withdraw troops **5.** (*annuler: déclaration, paroles, candidature, offre*) to withdraw **6.** (*obtenir*) ~ **des avantages de qc** to get benefits from sth; ~ **un bénéfice de qc** to make a profit out of sth; ~ **qc d'une expérience** to get sth out of an experience **7.** (*extraire*) ~ **de l'huile d'une substance** to get oil from a substance; ~ **du minerai/du charbon** to extract ore/coal **8.** (*tirer de nouveau*) ~ **un coup de feu** to fire another shot **9.** (*faire un second tirage*) **faire** ~ **une photo** (*meilleur tirage*) to have a photo printed again; (*double*) to get a reprint of a photo **II.** *vi* to fire again **III.** *vpr* **1.** (*partir*) **se** ~ to withdraw; **se** ~ **dans sa chambre** to withdraw to one's room; **se** ~ **à la campagne** to go off to live in the country **2.** (*annuler sa candidature*) **se** ~ to withdraw **3.** (*prendre sa retraite*) **se** ~ to retire **4.** (*reculer*) **se** ~ (*armée, ennemi*) to withdraw; (*eau, mer*) to go out; **retire-toi d'ici!** get out of here! **5.** (*quitter*) **se** ~ **de la vie publique/des affaires** to leave public life/business; **se** ~ **du jeu** to leave the game

retombée [ʀ(ə)tɔ̃be] *f* **1.** *pl* (*répercussions*) fallout + *vb sing;* **les** ~**s médiatiques/publicitaires de qc** the media/advertising fallout from sth **2.** (*impact*) impact

retomber [ʀ(ə)tɔ̃be] <1> *vi être* **1.** (*tomber à nouveau*) to fall back; ~ **dans l'oubli/la misère** to fall back into oblivion/misery; ~ **dans la délinquance/la drogue** to get back into delinquency/drugs; ~ **sur le même sujet** to come back to the same subject **2.** (*tomber après s'être élevé*) to fall down again; (*ballon*) to come back down; (*capot*) to fall back down; (*fusée*) to fall back to earth; **se laisser** ~ to drop back **3.** (*baisser: curiosité, enthousiasme*) to dwindle; (*fièvre, cote de popularité*) to fall; ~ **au niveau d'il y a trois ans** (*consommation*) to fall back to the level of three years ago **4.** (*redevenir*) ~ **amoureux** to fall in love again; ~ **malade/enceinte** to get ill/pregnant again **5.** METEO (*brouillard*) to come down again; **la pluie/la neige retombe** it's raining/snowing again **6.** (*échoir à*) ~ **sur qn** to fall on sb; **cela va me ~ dessus** it's all going to land on me; **faire ~ la faute sur qn** to land sb with the blame for sth; **faire ~ la responsabilité sur qn/qc** to make sb/sth out to be responsible **7.** (*revenir, rencontrer*) ~ **au même endroit** to come back to the same place; ~ **sur qn** to come across sb again

rétorquer [RetɔRke] <1> *vt* to retort; ~ **un bon mot à un adversaire/à qc** to come back with a smart answer to an opponent/to sth; **il n'a rien rétorqué** he made no answer; ~ **à qn que qn a fait qc** to answer sb that sb did sth

retors(e) [Rətɔr, ɔrs] *adj* crafty

rétorsion [RetɔRsjɔ̃] *f* **user de** ~ to retaliate; **des mesures de** ~ retaliation + *vb sing*

retouche [R(ə)tuʃ] *f* **1.** (*d'un vêtement*) alteration; **faire une ~ à une jupe** to alter a skirt **2.** INFOR ~ **d'image** image retouching

retoucher [R(ə)tuʃe] <1> **I.** *vt* **1.** (*corriger: vêtement*) to alter **2.** (*être remboursé*) ~ **mille euros** to get a thousand euros back **II.** *vi* **1.** (*toucher de nouveau*) ~ **à qc** to touch sth again **2.** (*regoûter à*) ~ **à l'alcool** to go back to drinking

retour [R(ə)tuR] **I.** *m* **1.** (*opp: départ*) return; (*chemin*) way back; (*à la maison*) way home; (*voyage*) return journey; (*à la maison*) journey home; **prendre le chemin du ~** to set off back; **au ~** on the way back; (*en avion*) on the flight back; (*à l'arrivée*) when one gets back; **au ~ du service militaire** coming back from national service; **de ~ à la maison** back home; **être de ~** to be back **2.** (*à un état antérieur*) ~ **à la nature** return to nature; (*slogan*) back to nature; ~ **à l'Antiquité** return to Antiquity; ~ **à la politique/terre** return to politics/the land; ~ **au calme** return to a state of calm; ~ **en arrière** flashback **3.** (*réapparition*) ~ **de la grippe** new outbreak of flu; **un ~ du froid** a new cold spell; **la mode des années 60 est de ~** sixties fashions are back; ~ **en force** return in strength **4.** (*billet*) return (ticket); **un aller et ~ pour Paris** a return for Paris **5.** CINE, TV rewind; **touche de ~ rapide** fast rewind button ►**c'est un juste ~ des choses** it's only fair; **par ~ du courrier** by return of post; ~ **à l'expéditeur!** return to sender!; *inf* (*rendre la pareille*) same to you!; ~ **éternel** eternal recurrence **II.** *app* **match ~** return match

retournement [R(ə)tuRnəmɑ̃] *m* turnround; ~ **de la conjoncture** reversal of the economic position; ~ **de l'opinion** turnround in opinion; **un ~ de la situation** turnround in the situation

retourner [R(ə)tuRne] <1> **I.** *vt avoir* **1.** (*mettre dans l'autre sens*) ~ **qc** (*matelas, omelette, viande, cartes*) to turn sth over; (*caisse, tableau, verre*) to turn sth upside down **2.** (*mettre à l'envers*) ~ **qc** (*vêtement*) to turn sth inside out; (*manche, bas de pantalon*) to roll up sth; **être retourné** (*vêtement*) to be inside out; (*col*) to be turned up **3.** (*orienter en sens opposé*) ~ **une critique à qn** to turn sb's criticism back against them; ~ **un compliment à qn** to return the compliment to sb; ~ **la situation en faveur de qn** to turn the situation back in sb's favour; ~ **l'opinion en sa faveur** to bring public opinion around **4.** (*faire changer d'opinion*) ~ **qn** to bring sb around; ~ **qn contre un projet** to turn sb against a project; ~ **qn en faveur d'une amie** to win sb over to a friend **5.** (*renvoyer*) ~ **une lettre à l'expéditeur** to return a letter to the sender; ~ **des marchandises** to send goods back **6.** *inf* (*bouleverser: maison, pièce*) to turn upside down; (*personne*) to shake; **le film m'a retourné** I was shaken by the film; **j'en suis tout retourné** I'm all shaken (up) **II.** *vi être* **1.** (*revenir*) to return; (*en partant*) to go back; (*en revenant*) to come back; (*en avion*) to fly back; ~ **sur ses pas** to retrace one's steps; ~ **chez soi** to go back home **2.** (*aller de nouveau*) ~ **à la montagne/chez qn** to go back to the mountains/to sb's house **3.** (*se remettre à*) ~ **à son travail** to get back to work; (*après une maladie, des vacances*) to go back to [*o* return] work **III.** *vpr être* **1.** (*se tourner dans un autre sens*) **se ~** (*personne*) to turn over; (*voiture, bateau*) to overturn; **se ~ sans cesse dans son lit** to toss and turn in one's bed **2.** (*tourner la tête*) **se ~** to look back; **tout le monde se retournait sur leur passage** all heads turned as they went by; **se ~ vers qn/qc** to look back at sb/sth **3.** (*prendre parti*) **se ~ en faveur de/contre qn** to side with/turn against sb; **se ~ contre qn** JUR to take action against sb **4.** (*prendre un nouveau cours*) **se ~ contre qn** (*acte, action*) to backfire on sb **5.** (*se tordre*) **se ~ l'épaule** to dislocate one's shoulder; **se ~ le doigt/bras** to twist one's finger/arm **6.** (*repartir*) **s'en ~ dans son pays natal/en France** to go back to one's native country/to France ►**s'en retourner comme on est venu** to leave just as one came

retracer [R(ə)tRase] <2> *vt* **1.** (*raconter*) to relate; (*histoire*) to retrace **2.** (*tracer à nouveau*) to redraw

rétracter [RetRakte] <1> **I.** *vt* (*rentrer*) to retract **II.** *vpr* **se ~ 1.** ANAT, TECH to retract **2.** (*se dédire*) to withdraw (one's statement); JUR to retract

retrait [R(ə)tRɛ] *m* **1.** (*action de retirer: d'argent, d'un projet de loi, d'une candidature*) withdrawal; (*des bagages, d'un billet*) collection **2.** (*suppression: d'une autorisation*) withdrawal; ~ **du permis** (**de conduire**) driving ban

retraite [R(ə)tRɛt] *f* **1.** (*cessation du travail*) retirement; **l'âge de la ~** retirement age; ~

anticipée early retirement; **être à la** ~ to be retired; **mettre qn à la** ~ to retire sb; **partir à la** ~, **prendre sa** ~ to retire **2.** (*pension*) pension; ~ **complémentaire** (*assurance*) pension (plan)

retraité(e) [R(ə)tRete] **I.** *adj* (*à la retraite*) retired **II.** *m(f)* retired person

retraitement [R(ə)tRɛtmɑ̃] *m* (*des combustibles nucléaires*) reprocessing; (*des déchets*) recycling; **centre/usine de** ~ **des déchets nucléaires** nuclear reprocessing plant/works; ~ **des vieux papiers** recycling of used paper

retranchement [R(ə)tRɑ̃ʃmɑ̃] *m* retrenchment ▸**forcer** [*o* **poursuivre**] [*o* **pousser**] **qn** (**jusque**) **dans ses** (**derniers**) ~**s** to get sb's back against the wall

retrancher [R(ə)tRɑ̃ʃe] <1> **I.** *vt* **1.** (*retirer*) ~ **une somme/un nombre de qc** to deduct a sum/a number from sth; ~ **un mot/passage d'un texte** to cut a word/passage from a text **2.** (*séparer des autres*) **vivre retranché** to live cut off from others **II.** *vpr* **1.** MIL **se** ~ to entrench oneself **2.** (*se protéger*) **se** ~ **derrière la loi** to hide behind the law; **se** ~ **dans sa douleur** to hide away in one's sorrow

retransmettre [R(ə)tRɑ̃smɛtR] *vt irr* to broadcast; (*émission*) to show; ~ **qc en direct** to broadcast sth live; ~ **qc en différé** to show a recording of sth

retransmission [R(ə)tRɑ̃smisjɔ̃] *f* broadcast; ~ **en direct** live broadcast; ~ **en différé** broadcast recording; **la** ~ **du match aura lieu en direct/en différé** there will be live/recorded coverage of the match

retravailler [R(ə)tRavaje] <1> **I.** *vi* (*reprendre le travail*) to go back to work **II.** *vt* (*discours, texte*) to rework; (*matière, minerai*) to reprocess; ~ **une question** to think some more about a question

rétrécir [RetResiR] <8> **I.** *vt* (*rendre plus étroit*) to narrow; ~ **une bague/une jupe** to take in a ring/a skirt **II.** *vi, vpr* (*laine, tissu*) to shrink; **le pull a rétréci au lavage** the sweater shrank in the wash

rétrécissement [RetResismɑ̃] *m* **1.** (*resserrement: de la laine, d'un tissu*) shrinking; (*de la pupille, rue*) contraction; ~ **de la vallée** narrowing of the valley **2.** MED stricture

rétribuer [RetRibɥe] <1> *vt* (*personne*) to pay; (*travail, service*) to pay for

rétribution [RetRibysjɔ̃] *f* payment; (*d'un service, travail*) remuneration

rétro [RetRo] *abr de* **rétrograde** **I.** *adj inv* (*démodé*) old-fashioned; (*mode*) retro **II.** *adv* (*s'habiller*) in retro clothing

rétroactes [RetRoakt] *mpl Belgique* (*antécédents*) background + *vb sing*

rétroactif, **-ive** [RetRoaktif, -iv] *adj* retroactive; **avoir un effet** ~ to be retroactive; (*loi*) to be retrospective; **une augmentation avec effet** ~ **à partir du 1**^er^ an increase retroactive to the first

rétrofusée [RetRofyze] *f* retrorocket

rétrograde [RetRogRad] *adj* **1.** (*arriéré*) backward-looking **2.** ASTR, MAT retrograde

rétrograder [RetRogRade] <1> *vi* AUTO ~ **de troisième en seconde** to change [*o* shift *Am*] down to second

rétroprojecteur [RetRopRɔʒɛktœR] *m* overhead projector

rétrospectif, **-ive** [RetRɔspɛktif, -iv] *adj* (*tourné vers le passé: examen, étude*) retrospective; **jeter un regard** ~ **sur qc** to take a backward glance at sth

rétrospective [RetRɔspɛktiv] *f* **1.** ART retrospective **2.** CINE season **3.** *Québec* (*retour en arrière dans un film*) flashback

rétrospectivement [RetRɔspɛktivmɑ̃] *adv* retrospectively; (*avoir peur, être jaloux*) looking back

retroussé(e) [R(ə)tRuse] *adj* (*nez*) turned-up; (*lèvres*) curled

retrousser [R(ə)tRuse] <1> *vt* ~ **qc** (*manche, bas de pantalon*) to roll sth up; (*moustache*) to curl sth; ~ **les lèvres** to curl one's lips; ~ **les babines** to bare one's teeth

retrouvailles [R(ə)tRuvɑj] *fpl* reunion + *vb sing*

retrouver [R(ə)tRuve] <1> **I.** *vt* **1.** (*récupérer*) to find; ~ **sa fonction/place** to return to one's post/seat; ~ **son utilité** to become useful again; **j'ai retrouvé mon portefeuille** I've found my wallet **2.** (*rejoindre*) ~ **qn** to meet (up with) sb; **attendez-moi, je vous retrouve dans un quart d'heure** wait for me, I'll be back in a quarter of an hour **3.** (*recouvrer*) ~ **l'équilibre** to get one's balance back; ~ **la foi/ses forces** to get one's faith/strength back; ~ **son calme** to calm down again; ~ **la santé** to return to health; **elle a retrouvé le sourire/le sommeil/l'espoir** she has been able to smile/sleep/hope again **4.** (*redécouvrir: situation, travail, marchandise*) to find; **tu auras du mal à** ~ **une occasion aussi favorable** you won't find another opportunity as good as this one **5.** (*reconnaître*) **je te retrouve tel que je t'ai toujours connu** you're just the same as you always were; **je retrouve bien là mon mari!** that's my husband all right! **II.** *vpr* **1.** (*se réunir*) **se** ~ (*personnes*) to meet; **se** ~ **au bistro** to meet at the bistro; **j'espère qu'on se retrouvera bientôt** I hope we'll see each other again soon **2.** (*se présenter de nouveau*) **se** ~ (*occasion, circonstance*) to turn up again **3.** (*être de nouveau*) **se** ~ **dans la même situation** to find oneself back in the same situation; **se** ~ **devant les mêmes difficultés** to be confronted with the same difficulties; **se** ~ **seul/désemparé** to find oneself alone/at a loss **4.** (*finir*) **se** ~ **en prison/dans le fossé** to end up in prison/in the ditch; **se** ~ **sur le pavé** to end up on the streets **5.** (*retrouver son chemin*) **se** ~ **dans une ville inconnue** to find one's way in a city one doesn't know; **j'ar-**

rive toujours à me ~ I always manage to find my way around **6.** (*voir clair*) **s'y** ~ to make sense of it; **je n'arrive pas à m'y** ~ I can't make any sense of all this; **s'y** ~ **dans ses calculs** to get one's sums to work out; **s'y** ~ **dans des explications** to make some sense of explanations ►**comme on se retrouve!** it's a small world!; **on se retrouvera!** *inf* (*menace*) we'll meet again!

rétroviseur [ʀetʀɔvizœʀ] *m* rear view mirror; ~ **extérieur/intérieur** wing/interior mirror

réunification [ʀeynifikasjɔ̃] *f* (*de nations, d'États*) reunification; **la** ~ **de l'Allemagne** German reunification

réunifier [ʀeynifje] <1> *vt* to reunify; **l'Allemagne réunifiée** reunited Germany

réunion [ʀeynjɔ̃] *f* **1.** (*séance*) meeting; (*après une longue période*) reunion; (*rassemblement politique/public*) union; ~ **de famille** family gathering; ~ **de parents d'élèves** PTA meeting; ~ **d'information** briefing session; **être en** ~ to be in a meeting **2.** (*ensemble, rapprochement*) merging; (*d'États*) union; (*cercle: d'amis*) gathering; (*convocation*) getting together; **la** ~ **des membres de la famille** getting the family together

Réunion [ʀeynjɔ̃] *f* (**l'île de**) **la** ~ Reunion (Island)

réunir [ʀeyniʀ] <8> **I.** *vt* **1.** (*mettre ensemble: objets, papiers*) to gather; (*faits, preuves, arguments*) to collect; **les conditions sont réunies pour que la tension baisse** conditions are right for a lowering of tension **2.** (*cumuler*) ~ **un maximum d'avantages** to combine as many advantages as possible; ~ **toutes les conditions exigées** to meet all the requirements **3.** (*rassembler*) ~ **des personnes** (*personne*) to bring people together; ~ **des documents dans un classeur** to collect documents in a file **II.** *vpr* **se** ~ (*se rassembler: personnes*) to gather

réussi(e) [ʀeysi] *adj* **1.** (*couronné de succès*) successful; (*examen*) with good results; **être vraiment** ~ to be a real success **2.** (*bien exécuté*) successful; **ne pas être très réussi** to be a bit of a flop ►**c'est** ~**!** *iron* well done!

réussir [ʀeysiʀ] <8> **I.** *vi* **1.** (*aboutir à un résultat: chose*) to be a success; ~ **bien/mal** to be/not be a success **2.** (*parvenir au succès*) ~ **dans la vie/dans les affaires** to succeed in life/business; ~ **à l'/un examen** to pass the/an exam; **tout lui réussit** he makes a success of everything **3.** (*être capable de*) **il réussit à** +*infin a. iron* he manages to +*infin;* **j'ai réussi à la convaincre** I managed to persuade him **II.** *vt* **1.** (*bien exécuter*) to manage; ~ **son effet** to achieve the effect one wants **2.** (*réaliser avec succès: épreuve, examen*) to pass; ~ **sa vie** to make a success of one's life

réussite [ʀeysit] *f* (*bon résultat, succès*) success; ~ **sociale** social success; ~ **d'une tentative** the success of an attempt

revaloir [ʀ(ə)valwaʀ] *vt irr* **je te/vous/lui revaudrai ça, je te/vous le revaudrai/je le lui revaudrai** (*en bien*) I'll make it up to you/him; (*en mal*) I'll get even with you/him

revaloriser [ʀ(ə)valɔʀize] <1> *vt* **1.** (*opp: déprécier*) ~ **qc** to raise the standing of sth **2.** FIN (*monnaie*) to revalue; (*rente, traitement, salaire*) to raise

revanche [ʀ(ə)vɑ̃ʃ] *f* (*vengeance*) revenge; JEUX, SPORT (*match*) return match; **j'ai gagné! tu veux qu'on fasse la** ~**?** (*subj*) I've won! do you want your revenge?; **prendre sa** ~ to get one's revenge; SPORT to play a return match ►**en** ~ (*par contre*) on the other hand; (*en contrepartie*) in exchange

rêvasser [ʀɛvase] <1> *vi péj* to daydream

rêve [ʀɛv] *m* dream; **beau/mauvais** ~ nice/bad dream; **faire un** ~ to have a dream; **fais de beaux** ~**s!** sweet dreams!; **une voiture de** ~ a dream car; **la femme/la maison/le métier de mes** ~**s** the woman/house/job of my dreams ►**prendre ses** ~**s pour des réalités** to confuse dreams and reality; **c'est le** ~ *inf* it's just perfect

rêvé(e) [ʀeve] *adj* perfect; (*solution*) ideal; **la femme/l'homme** ~**(e)** the woman/man of one's dreams

revêche [ʀəvɛʃ] *adj* (*caractère*) sour; (*personne*) sour-tempered; **être d'humeur** ~ to be in a sour mood

réveil [ʀevɛj] *m* **1.** (*réveille-matin*) alarm clock; **mettre le** ~ **à 6 heures** to set the alarm for six o'clock **2.** (*retour à la réalité*) awakening; **un** ~ **douloureux** a painful awakening

réveiller [ʀeveje] <1> **I.** *vt* **1.** (*sortir du sommeil, ramener à la réalité*) ~ **qn** to wake sb up; **être réveillé** to be awake; **être bien réveillé** to be wide awake; **je suis mal réveillé** I haven't woken up properly; **être à moitié réveillé** to be still half asleep **2.** (*raviver: curiosité, jalousie, cupidité*) to awaken; (*appétit*) to excite; (*rancune*) to reawaken **II.** *vpr* **se** ~ **1.** (*sortir du sommeil*) to wake up **2.** (*se raviver*) to reawaken; (*appétit*) to return; **dès que la douleur se réveillera** when the pain starts up again **3.** (*se ranimer: souvenir*) to reawaken; (*volcan*) to awake

réveillon [ʀevɛjɔ̃] *m: night before Christmas or New Year, or a meal or party to celebrate it;* **fêter le** ~ **de Noël/du nouvel an** to celebrate Christmas Eve/New Year's Eve

réveillonner [ʀevɛjɔne] <1> *vi* (*fêter Noël/le nouvel an*) to celebrate Christmas Eve/New Year's Eve

révélateur [ʀevelatœʀ] *m* **1.** (*chose qui dévoile*) **être le** ~ **de qc** to reveal sth **2.** PHOT developer

révélation [ʀevelasjɔ̃] *f* **1.** (*dévoilement*) revelation; **faire la** ~ **d'un projet** to reveal a project; **retarder la** ~ **de l'intention de qn** to delay the revelation of sb's intention; **faire une** ~ (*révéler un fait/projet*) to make a revelation;

faire des ~s à un collègue sur un projet to tell a colleague about a project; **avoir des ~s à faire à ses parents sur le mariage** to have things to tell one's parents about marriage **2.** (*mise en lumière: d'un artiste, talent*) discovery; (*d'une tendance*) revelation; **être la ~ du ski** to be skiing's new discovery **3.** (*aveu*) disclosure; **je n'ai plus aucune ~ à vous faire** I have no more to tell you **4.** (*découverte, surprise*) discovery; **avoir la ~ de qc** to discover sth; **avoir une ~** to have a brainwave **5.** REL **la Révélation** Revelation; **c'est la ~** *iron* what a revelation!

révéler [revele] <5> *vt* (*divulguer*) to reveal; **~ ses intentions/opinions/projets à qn** to reveal one's intentions/opinions/plans to sb; **~ de nouveaux faits/le scandale** (*enquête, journal*) to bring new facts/the scandal to light

revenant [rəv(ə)nɑ̃] *m* ghost; **des histoires de ~s** ghost stories

revenant(e) [rəv(ə)nɑ̃, ɑ̃t] *m(f) inf* stranger; **tiens, (voilà) un ~!** *iron* hello stranger!

revendeur, -euse [r(ə)vɑ̃dœr, -øz] *m, f* dealer; **~ de drogue** drug dealer; **être ~ de livres anciens** antiquarian book dealer

revendication [r(ə)vɑ̃dikasjɔ̃] *f* demand; JUR, POL claim; **des ~s salariales/syndicales** pay/union demands; **une lettre de ~** a letter putting forward one's claims; **journée de ~** day of action; **présenter une ~** to put in a claim

revendiquer [r(ə)vɑ̃dike] <1> *vt* **1.** (*réclamer: droit, augmentation de salaire*) to demand **2.** (*assumer: responsabilité*) to claim; **l'attentat a été revendiqué par la Maffia/n'a pas été revendiqué** the Mafia/nobody has claimed responsibilty for the attack

revendre [r(ə)vɑ̃dr] <14> *vt* **1.** (*vendre d'occasion*) **~ un piano à un collègue** to sell a piano to a colleague **2.** *fig* **avoir de l'énergie à ~** to have bags of energy

revenir [r(ə)vənir, rəvnir] <9> *vi être* **1.** (*venir de nouveau: personne, lettre*) to come back; (*printemps*) to return; **~ +*infin*** to come back to +*infin* **2.** (*rentrer*) to return; **~ en avion/en voiture/à pied** to fly/drive/walk back; **je reviens dans un instant** I'll be back in a moment **3.** (*recommencer*) **~ à un projet/sujet** to come back to a theme/subject; **~ à de meilleurs sentiments** to return to a better frame of mind **4.** (*réexaminer*) **~ sur un sujet/le passé** to go back over a subject/the past; **~ sur une affaire/un scandale** *péj* to rake over an affair/a scandal again; **ne revenons pas là-dessus!** let's not go over that again! **5.** (*se dédire de*) **~ sur une opinion** to change one's opinion; **~ sur une décision** to change a decision **6.** (*se présenter à nouveau à l'esprit*) **~ à qn** to come back to sb **7.** (*être déçu par*) **~ de ses illusions** to lose one's illusions **8.** (*équivaloir à*) **cela revient au même** it comes to the same thing; **cela revient à dire que qn a fait qc** it's like saying sb did sth **9.** (*coûter au total*) **~ à 100 euros** to come to a 100 euros; **~ à 100 euros à qn** to cost sb a 100 euros; **~ cher/meilleur marché** to work out expensive/cheaper **10.** GASTR **faire ~ le lard** to brown the bacon; **faire ~ les oignons/les légumes** to brown the onions/vegetables ▸**je n'en reviens pas ~ de son attitude** *inf* I can't get over her attitude; **elle revient de loin** it was a close thing (for her)

revenu [r(ə)vəny, rəvny] *m* income; **~ minimum d'insertion** *basic income paid to the jobless*

rêver [reve, rɛve] <1> *vi* **1.** (*avoir un rêve*) **~ de qn/qc** to dream about sb/sth **2.** (*désirer*) **~ de qc/de faire qc** to dream of sth/of doing sth **3.** (*divaguer*) **te prêter de l'argent? tu rêves!** lend you money? in your dreams!

réverbération [revɛrberasjɔ̃] *f* (*de la chaleur, lumière*) reflection; (*du son*) reverberation

réverbère [revɛrbɛr] *m* **1.** (*éclairage*) streetlight **2.** TECH reflector

réverbérer [revɛrbere] <5> **I.** *vt* (*réfléchir: chaleur, lumière*) to reflect; (*son*) to send back **II.** *vpr* **se ~** (*son*) to reverberate; (*chaleur, lumière*) to be reflected

reverdir [r(ə)vɛrdir] <8> **I.** *vi* to grow green again **II.** *vt* to soak

révérence [reverɑ̃s] *f* (*salut cérémonieux: d'un homme*) bow; (*d'une femme*) curtsey ▸**tirer sa ~** *iron* to walk off; **il a tiré sa ~** (*mourir*) he's bowed out

révérer [revere] <5> *vt soutenu* to revere

rêverie [rɛvri] *f* **1.** (*méditation*) reverie **2.** *pl, péj* (*chimères*) daydreams

revers [r(ə)vɛr] *m* **1.** (*dos*) back; (*d'une étoffe*) wrong side; (*de la main*) back; **balayer qc d'un ~ de main** to clear sth away with the back of one's hand **2.** (*échec*) setback **3.** (*en tennis*) backhand **4.** (*repli: d'un pantalon, d'une manche*) turn-up; (*d'un manteau*) cuff; (*d'un col*) lapel ▸**c'est le ~ de la médaille** that's the other side of the coin; **prendre qn/qc à ~** MIL to take sb/sth from the rear

reverser [r(ə)vɛrse] <1> *vt* **1.** (*verser davantage*) **~ une boisson à qn** to pour sb another drink; **~ un liquide dans un récipient** to pour more liquid into a container **2.** FIN **~ une somme à qn sur un compte** to pay back a sum into sb's account

réversible [revɛrsibl] *adj* **1.** reversible **2.** FIN, JUR revertible

revêtement [r(ə)vɛtmɑ̃] *m* (*couche protectrice*) covering; (*d'une route, poêle, d'un chemin, four*) surface

revêtir [r(ə)vetir] *irr* **I.** *vt* **1.** (*endosser*) to don **2.** (*poser un revêtement*) **~ une surface de liège/bois** to cover a surface with cork/wood; **~ un sol de moquette** to carpet a floor; **~ un mur de boiseries** to panel a surface; **~ un mur de carrelage/crépi** to tile/roughcast a wall **3.** (*recouvrir: papier peint,*

R

moquette, pavés, neige) to cover **4.** (*prendre, avoir: apparence, caractère, formes*) to take on; ~ **une importance particulière** to take on particular importance **5.** *soutenu* (*habiller*) ~ **qn d'un manteau** to clothe sb in a coat **6.** *soutenu* (*investir*) ~ **qn d'un pouvoir/d'insignes** to invest sb with a power/with insignia; **être revêtu de qc** to be invested with sth **7.** *soutenu* (*dissimuler*) ~ **des mensonges d'une apparence d'honnêteté** to cloak lies in an appearance of truth **8.** ADMIN, JUR ~ **un document d'un sceau** to append a seal to a document; ~ **un document d'une signature** to add a signature to a document **II.** *vpr* (*s'habiller*) **se** ~ **d'un manteau** to don a coat

rêveur, -euse [ʀɛvœʀ, -øz] **I.** *adj* **1.** (*songeur*) dreamy; **avoir l'esprit** ~ to be a dreamer **2.** (*perplexe*) **ça me laisse ~!** *inf* it makes you wonder! **II.** *m, f* dreamer

revient [ʀəvjɛ̃] *m v.* **prix**

revigorer [ʀ(ə)vigɔʀe] <1> **I.** *vt* **1.** (*ragaillardir: air frais, repas, boisson*) to revive; (*discours, promesse*) to hearten **2.** (*ranimer: idée, doctrine*) to revitalize; ~ **une entreprise** to put new life into a business **II.** *vi* to invigorate

revirement [ʀ(ə)viʀmɑ̃] *m* (*d'un goût*) total change; (*d'une tendance, d'une situation*) reversal

réviser [ʀevize] <1> *vt, vi* ECOLE to revise

révision [ʀevizjɔ̃] *f* **1.** (*modification: d'une opinion, d'un jugement*) revision **2.** *pl* ECOLE revision *no pl;* **faire ses ~s** to revise

révisionniste [ʀevizjɔnist] *adj, mf* revisionist

revivre [ʀ(ə)vivʀ] *irr* **I.** *vi* (*être revigoré*) to come back to life **II.** *vt* (*vivre à nouveau*) to relive

révocation [ʀevɔkasjɔ̃] *f* (*d'un fonctionnaire*) dismissal; (*d'un contrat*) revocation; ~ **de l'Édit de Nantes** the Revocation of the Edict of Nantes

revoici [ʀ(ə)vwasi] *prep inf* **me/le** ~ here I am/he is again

revoilà [ʀ(ə)vwala] *prep inf* **me/le** ~ I'm/he's back; ~ **Nadine!** Nadine's back!

revoir [ʀ(ə)vwaʀ] *irr* **I.** *vt* **1.** (*voir à nouveau*) ~ **qn/qc** to see sb/sth again; **au** ~ goodbye **2.** (*regarder de nouveau*) ~ **qn/qc** to look at sb/sth again **3.** (*se souvenir*) **je la revois** I can see her now **II.** *vpr* **se** ~ **1.** (*se retrouver*) to meet up **2.** (*se souvenir de soi*) **se** ~ **jeune** (*vieillard*) to see oneself as young man (again)

révoltant(e) [ʀevɔltɑ̃, ɑ̃t] *adj* revolting

révolte [ʀevɔlt] *f* (*émeute*) revolt

révolté(e) [ʀevɔlte] **I.** *adj* in revolt **II.** *m(f)* rebel

révolter [ʀevɔlte] <1> **I.** *vt* (*individu*) to disgust; (*crime, injustice*) to revolt **II.** *vpr* **se** ~ **contre qn/qc 1.** (*s'insurger*) to rebel against sb/sth **2.** (*s'indigner*) to be revolted by sb/sh

révolu(e) [ʀevɔly] *adj* **1.** (*époque, temps*) gone by **2.** ADMIN (*achevé*) **à dix-huit ans ~s** at over eighteen; **au bout de deux ans ~s** after a full two years

révolution [ʀevɔlysjɔ̃] *f* (*changement*) revolution; ~ **culturelle** cultural revolution

Révolution [ʀevɔlysjɔ̃] *f* HIST **la** ~ the Revolution

révolutionnaire [ʀevɔlysjɔnɛʀ] *adj, mf* revolutionary

révolutionner [ʀevɔlysjɔne] <1> *vt* **1.** (*transformer radicalement*) to revolutionize **2.** *inf* (*bouleverser*) ~ **qn** (*nouveau venu, nouvelle*) to shake sb up; (*film, reportage*) to shake sb

revolver [ʀevɔlvɛʀ] *m* revolver

révoquer [ʀevɔke] <1> *vt* **1.** ADMIN (*destituer*) (**faire**) ~ **qn pour une faute** to dismiss sb for a fault **2.** JUR (*annuler*) to revoke

revouloir [ʀ(ə)vulwaʀ] *vt irr, inf* ~ **qc** to want sth again

revoyure [ʀ(ə)vwajyʀ] **à la ~!** *inf* bye for now!

revue [ʀ(ə)vy] *f* (*magazine*) review; ~ **spécialisée** specialist review; ~ **illustrée** illustrated magazine; ~ **de presse** press review

révulser [ʀevylse] <1> **I.** *vt* to revolt **II.** *vpr* (*visage*) to contort; (*yeux*) to roll

rewriting [ʀiʀajtiŋ, ʀəʀajtiŋ] *m* rewriting

rez-de-chaussée [ʀed(ə)ʃose] *m inv* (*niveau inférieur*) ground floor *Brit,* first floor *Am;* **habiter au** ~ to live on the ground floor

rez-de-jardin [ʀed(ə)ʒaʀdɛ̃] *m inv* garden flat *Brit,* garden apartment *Am*

RF [ɛʀɛf] *f abr de* **République française** French Republic

RFA [ɛʀɛfa] *f abr de* **République fédérale d'Allemagne: la** ~ Germany; (*avant 1989*) West Germany

rhabiller [ʀabije] <1> *vpr* **se** ~ (*remettre ses vêtements*) to get dressed (again) ▸**tu peux aller te** ~ *inf* forget it!

rhésus [ʀezys] *m* MED rhesus; (**facteur**) ~ **positif/négatif** rhesus positive/negative

rhétorique [ʀetɔʀik] **I.** *adj* rhetorical **II.** *f* **1.** (*art de bien parler*) rhetoric **2.** *Belgique* (*terminale*) final year (*of secondary school*)

Rhin [ʀɛ̃] *m* **le** ~ the Rhine

rhinocéros [ʀinɔseʀɔs] *m* rhinocerus

rhizome [ʀizom] *m* rhizome

rhodanien(ne) [ʀɔdanjɛ̃, ɛn] *adj* of the Rhône

Rhodanien(ne) [ʀɔdanjɛ̃, ɛn] *m(f)* person from the Rhône Valley

Rhodes [ʀɔd] (**l'île de**) ~ (the island of) Rhodes

rhododendron [ʀɔdɔdɛ̃dʀɔ̃] *m* rhododendron

Rhône [ʀon] *m* **le** ~ the Rhône

rhubarbe [ʀybaʀb] *f* rhubarb

rhum [ʀɔm] *m* rum

rhumatismal(e) [ʀymatismal, o] <-aux> *adj* rheumatic

rhumatisme [ʀymatism] *m* rheumatism *no pl*

rhume [Rym] *m* **1.**(*coup de froid*) cold; **attraper un** ~ to catch a cold **2.** ~ **des foins** hay fever

ri [Ri] *part passé de* **rire**

riais [R(i)jɛ] *imparf de* **rire**

riant(e) [R(i)jɑ̃, jɑ̃t] *part prés de* **rire**

RIB [Rib] *m abr de* **relevé d'identité bancaire** *slip showing details of a bank account*

ribambelle [Ribɑ̃bɛl] *f inf* ~ **de touristes** horde of tourists; ~ **de livres** pile of books; ~ **de noms** string of names; ~ **d'enfants** swarm of children

ricanement [Rikanmɑ̃] *m* **1.**(*rire sarcastique*) snigger, snicker *Am* **2.**(*rire stupide*) cackle

ricaner [Rikane] <1> *vi* **1.**(*avec mépris*) to snigger, snicker *Am* **2.**(*bêtement*) to giggle

Richard [Riʃa:R] *m* HIST ~ **Cœur de Lion** Richard the Lionheart

riche [Riʃ] **I.** *adj* **1.**(*opp: pauvre*) rich **2.**(*nourrissant: aliment, nourriture*) rich; ~ **en calories/vitamines** rich [*o* high] in calories/vitamins **II.** *mf* rich person; **nouveau** ~ nouveau riche

richement [Riʃmɑ̃] *adv* (*décoré, vêtu, meublé*) richly; (*vivre*) in style; **être** ~ **marié** to be in a rich marriage

richesse [Riʃɛs] *f* **1.**(*fortune*) wealth *no pl* **2.** *pl* (*ressources*) wealth *no pl;* (*d'un musée*) treasures **3.**(*bien*) blessing

richissime [Riʃisim] *adj inf* fabulously rich

ricocher [Rikɔʃe] <1> *vi* ~ **sur qc** to ricochet off sth; **faire** ~ **une pierre sur l'eau** to skim a stone on the water

ric-rac [RikRak] *adv inf* (*avec une exactitude rigoureuse*) **payer** ~ to pay on the nail

rictus [Riktys] *m* grimace; ~ **de colère** angry grimace

ride [Rid] *f* (*pli*) wrinkle

ridé(e) [Ride] *adj* wrinkled

rideau [Rido] <x> *m* **1.**(*voile*) curtain **2.** THEAT curtain **3.** HIST **le** ~ **de fer** the Iron Curtain

rider [Ride] <1> **I.** *vt* **1.**(*marquer de rides: peau, front*) to line; (*eau*) to make ripples in **2.** NAUT (*cordage*) to tighten **II.** *vpr* **se** ~ (*front, peau, pomme*) to wrinkle; (*eau*) to ripple

ridicule [Ridikyl] **I.** *adj* (*personne, vêtement, conduite*) ridiculous **II.** *m* (*moqueries*) ridicule; (*absurdité*) ridiculousness; **le** ~ **de cette situation** the ridiculousness of this situation; **avoir peur du** ~ to be afraid of ridicule; **couvrir qn/se couvrir de** ~ to cover sb/oneself in ridicule; **tourner qc en** ~ to ridicule sth

ridiculiser [Ridikylize] <1> **I.** *vt* to ridicule **II.** *vpr* **se** ~ to make onself ridiculous

ridule [Ridyl] *f* small wrinkle

rie [Ri] *subj prés de* **rire**

rien [Rjɛ̃] **I.** *pron indéf* **1.**(*aucune chose*) nothing; **c'est ça ou** ~ it's that or nothing; **ça ne vaut** ~ it's worthless; ~ **d'autre** nothing else; ~ **de nouveau/mieux** nothing new/better; **il n'y a plus** ~ there's nothing left **2.**(*seulement*) ~ **que la chambre coûte 400 euros** the room alone costs 400 euros; ~ **que d'y penser** just thinking about it **3.**(*quelque chose*) anything; **être incapable de** ~ **dire** to be unable to say anything; **rester sans** ~ **faire** to do nothing ►**j'en <u>ai</u>** ~ **à cirer** *inf* I couldn't care less; **ce n'<u>est</u>** ~ it's nothing; **comme si de** ~ **n'<u>était</u>** as if there was nothing the matter; **elle n'<u>est</u> pour** ~ **dans ce problème** this problem has nothing to do with her; **<u>de</u>** ~! my pleasure!; **blessure <u>de</u>** ~ **du tout** just a tiny scratch; ~ **<u>du</u> tout** nothing at all; ~ **<u>que</u> ça!** *iron* (*pas plus*) just that!; (*c'est abuser*) is that all? **II.** *m* **1.**(*très peu de chose*) trifle **2.**(*un petit peu*) tiny bit; **un** ~ **de cognac** a drop of brandy; **un** ~ **trop large/moins fort** *inf* a tiny bit too wide/less loud ►**en un** ~ **de <u>temps</u>** in no time; **<u>comme</u> un** ~ *inf* as if it was nothing

rient [Ri] *indic prés de* **rire**

riesling [Rislinŋ] *m* Riesling

rieur, -euse [R(i)jœR, R(i)jøz] **I.** *adj* laughing **II.** *m, f* laugher

riez [R(i)je] *indic prés et impératif de* **rire**

rigide [Riʒid] *adj* **1.**(*opp: flexible*) rigid; (*carton*) stiff **2.**(*sévère*) strict

rigidité [Riʒidite] *f* **1.**(*opp: flexibilité*) rigidity; (*d'un carton*) stiffness **2.** ANAT (*d'un cadavre, muscle*) stiffness; (*du pénis*) hardness **3.**(*rigueur*) rigidity

rigolade [Rigɔlad] *f inf* fun ►**c'<u>est</u> de la** ~ (*c'est facile*) it's child's play; (*c'est pour rire*) it's just a bit of fun; (*ça ne vaut rien*) it's rubbish; **<u>prendre</u> qc à la** ~ to make a joke of sth; **prendre un examen à la** ~ to treat an exam as a joke

rigole [Rigɔl] *f* channel; ~ **d'écoulement** drainage channel; **creuser des** ~**s** to cut channels

rigoler [Rigɔle] <1> *vi inf* **1.**(*rire*) to laugh; **faire** ~ **qn** to make sb laugh **2.**(*s'amuser*) to have fun **3.**(*plaisanter*) ~ **avec qn/qc** to have a laugh with sb/sth; **pour** ~ for a laugh; **je (ne) rigole pas!** it's no joke! ►**tu me <u>fais</u>** ~! *iron* don't make me laugh!

rigolo(te) [Rigɔlo, ɔt] **I.** *adj inf* (*amusant*) funny **II.** *m(f) inf* (*homme amusant*) funny guy

rigoureusement [RiguRøzmɑ̃] *adv* **1.**(*sévèrement*) severely **2.**(*précisément*) rigorously **3.**(*absolument: exact*) absolutely; (*interdit, authentique*) completely; ~ **vrai** totally true

rigoureux, -euse [RiguRø, -øz] *adj* **1.**(*sévère*) strict **2.**(*exact, précis*) rigorous **3.** *antéposé* (*absolu: exactitude*) absolute; (*interdiction, authenticité*) total **4.**(*dur: climat, froid, hiver*) rigorous

rigueur [RigœR] *f* **1.**(*sévérité*) strictness; (*d'une punition*) harshness; **appliquer la loi avec** ~ to apply the law strictly **2.**(*austérité*) austerity; ~ **économique** economic rigour *Brit,* economic rigor *Am;* ~ **salariale** strict

R

wage control **3.** (*précision*) rigour *Brit,* rigor *Am* **4.** (*épreuve: d'un climat*) rigour *Brit,* rigor *Am;* (*d'une captivité*) harshness ►**tenir** ~ **à qn de qc** to hold sth against sb; **à la** ~ (*tout au plus*) at most; (*si besoin est*) at a pinch; **une tenue correcte est de** ~ correct dress is essential

rillettes [ʀijɛt] *fpl: potted meat*

rime [ʀim] *f* rhyme

rimer [ʀime] <1> *vi* ~ **avec qc** to rhyme with sth ►**à quoi riment ces excentricités?** what's all this nonsense supposed to mean?; **ne** ~ **à rien** to make no sense

rimmel [ʀimɛl] *m* mascara

rinçage [ʀɛ̃saʒ] *m* rinsing

rince-doigts [ʀɛ̃sdwa] *m inv* **1.** (*bol*) finger bowl **2.** (*papier*) wipe

rincer [ʀɛ̃se] <2> **I.** *vt* **1.** (*laver*) to rinse **2.** *inf* (*doucher*) **se faire** ~ to have a shower **II.** *vpr* **se** ~ **la bouche** to rinse one's mouth

ring [ʀiŋ] *m* SPORT ring

ringard(e) [ʀɛ̃gaʀ, aʀd] **I.** *adj inf* uncool **II.** *m(f) inf* has-been

rions [ʀ(i)jɔ̃] *indic prés et impératif de* **rire**

RIP [ʀip] *m abr de* **relevé d'identité postal** *slip showing details of a post-office bank account*

riposte [ʀipɔst] *f* **1.** riposte; **être prompt à la** ~ to have a ready repartee **2.** SPORT riposte **3.** MIL counter-attack

riposter [ʀipɔste] <1> **I.** *vi* **1.** (*répondre*) *a.* SPORT to riposte; ~ **à une attaque verbale** to come back against a verbal attack **2.** MIL to counter-attack **II.** *vt* (*rétorquer*) ~ **qc** to answer back sth

ripou <s *o* x> [ʀipu] **I.** *adj inf* scummy **II.** *m inf* bent copper

riquiqui [ʀikiki] *adj inv, inf* (*pièce*) poky; (*chapeau*) shabby; (*portion*) stingy; **faire** ~ to look shabby [*o* stingy]

rire [ʀiʀ] *irr* **I.** *vi* **1.** (*opp: pleurer*) to laugh; **faire** ~ **qn** to make sb laugh; **laisse(z)-moi** ~**!** *iron* don't make me laugh! **2.** (*se moquer*) ~ **de qn/qc** to laugh at sb/sth **3.** (*s'amuser*) to have a laugh **4.** (*plaisanter*) to joke; **tu veux** ~**!** you're joking! ►~ **dans sa barbe** to laugh up one's sleeve; **sans** ~**?** no kidding? **II.** *m* **1.** (*action de rire*) laugh; **des** ~**s** laughter *no pl* **2.** (*hilarité*) laughter; **fou** ~ giggling

ris[1] [ʀi] *indic prés et passé simple de* **rire**

ris[2] [ʀi] *m* GASTR ~ **de veau** calf sweetbread

ris[3] [ʀi] *m* NAUT reef

risée [ʀize] *f* **être la** ~ **des voisins/du quartier** to be the laughing stock of the neighbours/the neighbourhood *Brit* [*o* the neighbors/the neighborhood *Am*]

risible [ʀizibl] *adj* **1.** (*ridicule*) laughable **2.** (*drôle*) comic

risque [ʀisk] *m* **1.** (*péril*) risk; **au** ~ **de déplaire** at the risk of upsetting you; **courir un** ~**/des** ~**s** to run a risk/risks **2.** *pl* (*préjudice possible*) risk; **les** ~**s du métier** *inf* the risks of the job ►**à mes/tes** ~**s et périls** at my/your own risk

risqué(e) [ʀiske] *adj* (*hasardeux*) risky

risquer [ʀiske] <1> *vt* **1.** (*mettre en danger*) to risk **2.** (*s'exposer à*) ~ **le renvoi/la prison** to risk being sacked/going to prison; ~ **la mort** to risk death; **il ne risque rien** there's no risk **3.** (*tenter, hasarder*) to chance; ~ **le coup** to chance it; ~ **un coup d'œil** to risk a glance ►**ça (ne) risque pas!** *inf* not likely; **ça ne risque pas de m'arriver** no fear of that happening to me

risque-tout [ʀiskətu] *mf inv* daredevil

rissoler [ʀisɔle] <1> **I.** *vt* (*beignets*) to brown; (*pommes de terre*) to sauté; **pommes rissolées** sauté potatoes **II.** *vi* (*pommes de terre, beignets*) to brown

ristourne [ʀistuʀn] *f* (*sur achat*) reduction

rit [ʀi] *indic prés de* **rire**

rital(e) [ʀital] <s> *m péj, inf* wop *pej*

rite [ʀit] *m* **1.** (*coutume*) ritual **2.** REL, SOCIOL (*cérémonial*) rite

ritournelle [ʀituʀnɛl] *f* ritornello ►**c'est toujours la même** ~ it's always the same old story

rituel [ʀitɥɛl] *m* REL, SOCIOL ritual

rituel(le) [ʀitɥɛl] *adj a.* REL, SOCIOL ritual

rivage [ʀivaʒ] *m* shore

rival(e) [ʀival, o] <-aux> *adj, m(f)* rival

rivaliser [ʀivalize] <1> *vi* **1.** (*soutenir la comparaison*) ~ **avec qn** to vie with sb; ~ **avec qc** to compare with sth **2.** (*se disputer la palme*) ~ **d'élégance** to try to outdo each other in elegance

rivalité [ʀivalite] *f* rivalry; ~**s de clocher** petty rivalries

rive [ʀiv] *f* bank; ~ **droite/gauche** right/left bank

river [ʀive] <1> *vt* **1.** TECH (*clou, pointe*) to clinch; (*rivet*) to fix; (*chaîne, plaque*) to rivet; ~ **qc à un support** to rivet sth onto a support **2.** (*clouer*) ~ **qn** (*travail, maladie*) not to let sb go; **la peur me rivait sur mon fauteuil/sur place** fear held me glued to my seat/the spot; **être rivé à/devant la télé** to be glued to the TV; **le regard rivé sur eux/l'horizon** with her eyes fixed on them/the horizon

riverain(e) [ʀiv(ə)ʀɛ̃, ɛn] **I.** *adj* (*sur l'eau*) waterside; ~ **de qc** alongside sth **II.** *m(f)* (*voisin*) resident

rivet [ʀivɛ] *m* rivet

Riviera [ʀivjɛʀa] *f* **la** ~ the Riviera

rivière [ʀivjɛʀ] *f* (*cours d'eau*) river

rixe [ʀiks] *f* scuffle

riz [ʀi] *m* rice; ~ **au curry** curried rice; ~ **au lait** ≈ rice pudding; ~ **complet** brown rice; ~ **long** long-grain rice

rizière [ʀizjɛʀ] *f* paddy field

R.M.I. [ɛʀɛmi] *m abr de* **revenu minimum d'insertion**

RMIste, RMiste [ɛʀɛmist] *v.* **érémiste**

R.N. [ɛʀɛn] *f abr de* **route nationale**

R.N.I.S. [ɛʀɛniɛs] *m abr de* **réseau de numérique à intégration de service** ISDN

roast-beef [Ro:stbi:f] *m v.* **rosbif**

robe [Rɔb] *f* (*vêtement féminin*) dress; ~ **de plage/du soir** beach/evening dress; **se mettre en** ~ to put on a dress

robe de chambre [Rɔb də ʃɑ̃bR] *f* dressing gown

robinet [Rɔbinɛ] *m* tap; ~ **d'eau/du gaz** water/gas tap

robot [Rɔbo] *m* **1.** (*machine automatique*) robot **2.** (*appareil ménager*) (food) processor

robotique [Rɔbɔtik] *f* robotics + *vb sing*

robotisé(**e**) [Rɔbɔtize] *adj* automated

robotiser [Rɔbɔtize] <1> *vt* to automate; ~ **qn** to turn sb into a robot

robuste [Rɔbyst] *adj* (*personne, plante*) hardy; (*appétit*) hearty; (*foi*) robust

robustesse [Rɔbystɛs] *f* robustness; (*d'une personne, plante*) sturdiness; (*de la foi*) firmness

roc [Rɔk] *m* (*pierre, personne*) rock ►**des convictions dures comme un** ~ rock-solid views; **solide comme un** ~ solid as a rock

rocade [Rɔkad] *f* communications line

rocaille [Rɔkaj] **I.** *adj* **style** ~ rocaille style **II.** *f* **1.** (*cailloux*) loose stones **2.** ART rocaille

rocailleux, -euse [Rɔkajø, -jøz] *adj* **1.** (*pierreux*) stony **2.** (*sans grâce: style*) rough **3.** (*rauque*) growly

rocambolesque [Rɔkɑ̃bɔlɛsk] *adj* fantastic

roche [Rɔʃ] *f* GEO rock

rocher [Rɔʃe] *m* rock

Rocheuses [Rɔʃøz] *fpl* **les** ~ the Rockies

rocheux, -euse [Rɔʃø, -øz] *adj* rocky

rock [Rɔk] *adj* **concert de** ~ rock concert

rock(**-and-roll**) [RɔkɛnRɔl] *m inv* rock('n roll)

rocker [Rɔkœr] *m*, **rockeur, -euse** [Rɔkœr, -øz] *m, f* **1.** MUS (*musicien*) rock musician **2.** (*admirateur*) rock fan **3.** *inf* (*jeune*) youngster

rocking-chair [Rɔkiŋ(t)ʃɛR] <rocking-chairs> *m* rocking chair

rococo [Rɔkɔko] **I.** *adj* **1.** ART **style** ~ rococo style **2.** *péj* outdated **II.** *m* rococo

rodage [Rɔdaʒ] *m* **1.** (*adaptation*) acclimatization; (*d'un employé*) breaking in **2.** AUTO (*d'un moteur*) running in **3.** TECH (*opération: des cames, soupapes*) grinding ►**être en** ~ (*voiture*) to be running in *Brit,* be breaking in *Am;* (*organisation, entreprise*) to be at the running in stage

rodéo [Rɔdeo] *m* **1.** (*des cowboys*) rodeo **2.** *inf* (*avec moto, voiture*) joyride

roder [Rɔde] <1> *vt* **1.** AUTO, TECH ~ **qc** (*moteur, voiture, engrenages*) to run sth in *Brit,* to break sth in *Am;* (*cames, soupapes*) to grind **2.** (*mettre au point*) ~ **un spectacle** to get a show on its feet; ~ **des méthodes** to get methods working smoothly; **l'actrice est** (**bien**) **rodée** the actress knows her stuff

rôder [Rode] <1> *vi* ~ **dans les parages** to wander about

rôdeur, -euse [Rodœr, -øz] *m, f* prowler

rogne [Rɔɲ] *f inf* anger ►**se mettre** [*o* **se ficher**] [*o* **se foutre**] **en** ~ **contre qn** *inf* to get into a blazing temper

rogner [Rɔɲe] <1> **I.** *vt* **1.** (*couper: ongles*) to cut; (*griffes, ailes*) to clip; (*page, pièce, plaque*) to trim **2.** (*mordre sur*) ~ **les salaires/les revenus** to gnaw at wages/income **II.** *vi* ~ **sur qc** to cut down on sth

rognon [Rɔɲɔ̃] *m* GASTR kidney

rognure [RɔɲyR] *f* ~**s de papier/carton/cuir/viande** scraps of paper/cardboard/leather/meat; ~**s de métal** metal shavings; ~**s d'ongles** nail clippings

roi [Rwa] *m* **1.** (*souverain, a. dans les jeux*) king **2.** (*premier*) ~ **du pétrole** oil tycoon; **le** ~ **des imbéciles** a prize oaf ►**galette** [*o* **gâteau** *Midi*] **des Rois** Twelfth Night cake; **heureux comme un** ~ happy as a king; **être plus royaliste que le** ~ to be more Roman than the Pope; **tirer les** ~**s** to eat the Twelfth Night cake

> The **gâlette des Rois** is a flat cake full of marzipan. In the South of France the **gâteau des Rois** is a sweet ring with candied fruit. In both types, there is a small figure, the "fève", and whoever finds it becomes the 'king'.

Roi-Soleil [sɔlɛj] *m inv* **le** ~ the Sun King

roitelet [Rwat(ə)lɛ] *m* **1.** ZOOL wren **2.** (*roi*) kinglet

rôle [Rol] *m* **1.** THEAT, CINE role; **le premier** ~ the main role; ~ **de composition/de figurant** character/extra part **2.** (*fonction*) role ►**avoir le beau** ~ to have it easy

roller [Rɔlœr] *m* Rollerblade®; **paire de** ~**s** pair of rollerblades; **faire du** ~ to blade

roller, -euse [Rɔlœr, øz] *m, f* (*patineur*) rollerblader

ROM [Rɔm] *f inv abr de* **Read Only Memory** ROM

romain(**e**) [Rɔmɛ̃, ɛn] *adj* Roman

Romain(**e**) [Rɔmɛ̃, ɛn] *m(f)* Roman

roman [Rɔmɑ̃] *m* **1.** LIT novel; ~ **épistolaire/policier** epistolary/detective novel **2.** ARCHIT, ART Romanesque

roman(**e**) [Rɔmɑ̃, an] *adj* ARCHIT, ART Romanesque

romance [Rɔmɑ̃s] *f* **1.** MUS romance **2.** (*chanson sentimentale*) ballad ►**pousser la** ~ *iron* to sing a song

romanche [Rɔmɑ̃ʃ] **I.** *adj* **langue** ~ Romansh **II.** *m* Romansh; *v. a.* **français**

romancier, -ière [Rɔmɑ̃sje, -jɛR] *m, f* novelist

romand(**e**) [Rɔmɑ̃, ɑ̃d] *adj* **la Suisse** ~**e** French-speaking Switzerland

Romand(**e**) [Rɔmɑ̃, ɑ̃d] *m(f)* French-speaking Swiss

romanesque [Rɔmanɛsk] **I.** *adj* **1.** (*digne du roman: histoire*) fantastic; (*aventures, amours*) storybook **2.** (*sentimental*) romantic **3.** *postposé* (*propre au roman: technique*) novelistic **II.** *m* **le** ~ fiction; **se réfugier dans le** ~ to take refuge in fiction

roman-feuilleton [ʀɔmɑ̃fœjtɔ̃] <romans-feuilletons> *m* **1.** LIT serialized novel **2.** (*histoire à rebondissements*) saga

romanichel(le) [ʀɔmaniʃɛl] *m(f) péj* gypsy

roman-photo [ʀɔmɑ̃fɔto] <romans-photos> *m* photo novel

romantique [ʀɔmɑ̃tik] *adj, mf* romantic

romantisme [ʀɔmɑ̃tism] *m* **1.** LIT Romanticism **2.** (*grande sensibilité*) romanticism

romarin [ʀɔmaʀɛ̃] *m* rosemary

rombière [ʀɔ̃bjɛʀ] *f inf* old bird

Rome [ʀɔm] Rome

rompre [ʀɔ̃pʀ] *irr* **I.** *vt* (*interrompre*) ~ **qc** (*fiançailles, pourparlers, relations*) to break sth off **II.** *vi* (*se séparer*) ~ **avec qn** to break it off with sb; ~ **avec une tradition** to break with a tradition

rompu(e) [ʀɔ̃py] **I.** *part passé de* **rompre** **II.** *adj* (*très fatigué*) worn out ►**parler à <u>bâtons</u>** ~**s** to have a good chat

romsteak, **romsteck** [ʀɔmstɛk] *m* rump steak

ronce [ʀɔ̃s] *f pl* (*épineux*) brambles

rond [ʀɔ̃] **I.** *m* **1.** (*cercle*) ring **2.** (*trace ronde*) ring; ~**s de fumée** smoke ring; ~ **de serviette** napkin ring **3.** *inf* (*argent*) **n'avoir pas un** ~ not to have a bean **II.** *adv* **avaler qc tout** ~ to swallow sth whole; **ne pas tourner** ~ (*personne*) *inf* to have sth the matter with one

rond(e) [ʀɔ̃, ʀɔ̃d] *adj* **1.** (*circulaire*) round **2.** (*rebondi*) round; (*personne*) plump **3.** (*net: chiffre, compte*) round **4.** *inf* (*ivre*) sozzled

ronde [ʀɔ̃d] *f* **1.** (*tour de surveillance*) round; ~ **de police** police patrol **2.** (*danse*) round (dance); **faire la** ~ to dance in a ring **3.** (*danseurs*) ring **4.** MUS semibreve *Brit,* whole note *Am* **5.** (*écriture*) round hand ►**<u>à</u> la** ~ (*aux alentours*) around; **faire passer qc à la** ~ (*tour à tour*) to pass sth round

rondelet(te) [ʀɔ̃dlɛ, ɛt] *adj* **1.** (*rondouillard*) tubby **2.** (*coquet: somme, salaire*) tidy

rondelle [ʀɔ̃dɛl] *f* GASTR slice; ~ **de carottes/pommes de terre** carrot/potato slice; **concombre coupé en** ~**s** sliced cucumber

rondement [ʀɔ̃dmɑ̃] *adv* **1.** (*tambour battant*) briskly **2.** (*franchement*) bluntly

rondeur [ʀɔ̃dœʀ] *f* **1.** (*forme ronde*) plumpness; ~**s** curves; **la** ~ **de ses joues** her plump cheeks; **la** ~ **de son visage** her round face; ~**s de l'enfance** puppy fat *Brit,* baby fat *Am* **2.** *sans pl* (*franchise*) bluntness; **parler avec** ~ to speak bluntly

rondin [ʀɔ̃dɛ̃] *m* log; **des** ~**s de sapin** pine logs; **cabane en** ~**s** log cabin

rond-point [ʀɔ̃pwɛ̃] <ronds-points> *m* roundabout *Brit,* traffic circle *Am*

ronflement [ʀɔ̃fləmɑ̃] *m* **1.** (*respiration*) snore **2.** (*grondement: d'un avion, poêle*) roar; (*d'un orgue*) throb

ronfler [ʀɔ̃fle] <1> *vi* **1.** (*respirer: personne*) to snore **2.** *inf* (*dormir*) to snore away

ronger [ʀɔ̃ʒe] <2a> **I.** *vt* **1.** (*grignoter*) to gnaw **2.** (*miner*) to sap; **être rongé par la maladie** to be ravaged by illness; **être rongé de remords** to suffer the pangs of remorse **II.** *vpr* **1.** (*se grignoter*) **se** ~ **les ongles** to bite one's nails **2.** (*se tourmenter*) **se** ~ **d'inquiétude** to worry oneself sick

rongeur, **-euse** [ʀɔ̃ʒœʀ, -øz] *m* rodent

ronron [ʀɔ̃ʀɔ̃] *m* **1.** (*ronronnement: du chat*) purr(ing) **2.** *inf* (*d'une machine, d'un moteur*) drone **3.** *inf* (*monotonie*) **le** ~ **de la vie quotidienne** the daily grind

ronronnement [ʀɔ̃ʀɔnmɑ̃] *m* purring *no pl,* purr

ronronner [ʀɔ̃ʀɔne] <1> *vi* (*chat*) to purr; **ronronner de satisfaction** to purr with satisfaction

roquefort [ʀɔkfɔʀ] *m* roquefort (*blue cheese made with sheeps' milk*)

rosace [ʀozas] *f* rose window

rosbif [ʀɔzbif] *m* GASTR roast beef

rose[1] [ʀoz] *f* BOT rose ►**<u>frais</u> comme une** ~ fresh as a daisy; **<u>envoyer</u> qn sur les** ~**s** *inf* to send sb packing

rose[2] [ʀoz] **I.** *adj* **1.** (*rouge pâle*) pink **2.** (*érotique: messagerie*) sex; **téléphone** ~ sex chatline **II.** *m* pink; ~ **saumon** salmon pink; ~ **bonbon** candy pink ►**<u>voir</u> la vie/tout en** ~ to see life/things through rose-tinted glasses

rosé [ʀoze] *m* (*vin*) rosé (wine)

rosé(e) [ʀoze] *adj* rosé

roseau [ʀozo] <x> *m* reed; **être souple comme un** ~ to bend like a reed

rosée [ʀoze] *f* dew

roseraie [ʀozʀɛ] *f* rose garden

rosette [ʀozɛt] *f* **1.** (*ornement, décoration*) bow **2.** GASTR *type of sausage* **3.** BOT rosette

rosier [ʀozje] *m* rose tree; ~ **grimpant/nain** climbing/dwarf rose (tree)

rosse [ʀɔs] **I.** *adj* **1.** (*mordant: critique, satire*) vicious **2.** (*méchant: personne*) nasty **3.** (*sévère*) tough **II.** *f inf* (*personne*) **quelle vieille** ~**!** what a horrible old so-and-so!

rosser [ʀɔse] <1> *vt* **1.** ~ **qn** to thrash; **se faire** ~ **par qn** to get a thrashing from sb **2.** SPORT **se faire** ~ **par qn** to get thrashed by sb

rossignol [ʀɔsiɲɔl] *m* **1.** (*oiseau*) nightingale **2.** *inf* COM piece of junk **3.** (*passe-partout*) skeleton key

rot [ʀo] *m* (*renvoi*) belch; **faire/lâcher un** ~ to belch; (*bébé*) to burp

rotation [ʀɔtasjɔ̃] *f* **1.** (*mouvement*) rotation **2.** AVIAT, NAUT roound trip **3.** (*série périodique d'opérations*) ~ **des stocks** stock rotation; ~ **du personnel/du capital** staff/capital turnover

rotative [ʀɔtativ] *f* press

roter [ʀɔte] <1> *vi inf* to belch

rôti [ʀoti] *m* roast; ~ **de bœuf/porc/veau** roast beef/pork/veal

rotin [ʀɔtɛ̃] *m* cane; **des meubles en** ~ cane

furniture

rôtir [ʀotiʀ, ʀɔtiʀ] <8> **I.** *vt a. inf* GASTR (*brûler*) to roast **II.** *vi* **1.** GASTR to roast; **faire ~ qc** to roast sth **2.** *inf* (*être exposé au soleil*) to fry in the sun **III.** *vpr inf* **se (faire) ~** to fry in the sun

rôtisserie [ʀɔtisʀi] *f* **1.** (*magasin*) rotisserie **2.** (*restaurant*) steakhouse

rôtissoire [ʀɔtiswaʀ] *f* rotisserie

rotonde [ʀɔtɔ̃d] *f* rotunda

rotule [ʀɔtyl] *f* ANAT kneecap ►**je suis sur les ~s** *inf* my legs won't carry me

roturier, **-ière** [ʀɔtyʀje, -jɛʀ] **I.** *adj* HIST common **II.** *m, f* HIST commoner

rouage [ʀwaʒ] *m* **1.** (*élément constituant*) **n'être qu'un ~** to be just a cog in the wheels; **les ~s** the workings **2.** TECH cog

roublard(**e**) [ʀublaʀ, aʀd] **I.** *adj inf* wily **II.** *m(f) inf* wily devil

roublardise [ʀublaʀdiz] *f* wiliness

rouble [ʀubl] *m* rouble

roucoulades [ʀukulad] *fpl*, **roucoulement** [ʀukulmɑ̃] *m* **1.** (*du pigeon, de la tourterelle*) cooing *no pl* **2.** *pl, fig, inf* (*propos tendres*) sweet nothings

roucouler [ʀukule] <1> **I.** *vi* **1.** ZOOL to coo **2.** *iron* (*tenir des propos tendres*) to bill and coo **II.** *vt iron* to murmur

roue [ʀu] *f* **1.** (*partie d'un véhicule*) wheel; **~ arrière/avant** rear/front wheel; **~ de secours** AUTO spare wheel **2.** TECH wheel; **la ~ du moulin** the mill wheel **3.** (*supplice*) **la ~** the wheel ►**être la cinquième ~ du carrosse** to be surplus to requirements

roué(**e**) [ʀwe] *adj* (*rusé*) sly

rouennais(**e**) [ʀwanɛ, ɛz] *adj* of Rouen; *v. a.* **ajaccien**

Rouennais(**e**) [ʀwanɛ, ɛz] *m(f)* person from Rouen; *v. a.* **Ajaccien**

rouer [ʀwe] <1> *vt* **1.** (*rosser*) **~ qn de coups** to thrash sb **2.** HIST **être roué** to be broken on the wheel

rouet [ʀwɛ] *m* spinning wheel

rouge [ʀuʒ] **I.** *adj* **1.** (*de couleur rouge*) red; **poisson ~** goldfish **2.** (*congestionné*) red; **~ de colère** red with anger; **~ comme une écrevisse** red as a lobster **3.** (*incandescent*) red (hot); **la braise est encore ~** the embers are still glowing red **4.** POL red **5.** (*délicat*) **journée classée ~ pour le trafic routier** peak traffic day **II.** *m* **1.** (*couleur*) red; **le feu est au ~** the light's red **2.** *inf* (*vin*) red (wine); **un verre de ~** a glass of red; **gros ~** *inf* cheap red wine **3.** (*fard*) rouge; **~ à lèvres** lipstick; **se mettre du ~** to put some rouge on **III.** *adv* **se fâcher tout ~** to get hot under the collar; **voir ~** to see red

rougeâtre [ʀuʒɑtʀ] *adj* reddish; **brun ~** reddish brown

rougeaud(**e**) [ʀuʒo, od] **I.** *adj* ruddy **II.** *m(f)* **un gros ~** a big red-faced individual

rouge-gorge [ʀuʒgɔʀʒ] <rouges-gorges> *m* robin

rougeole [ʀuʒɔl] *f* measles

rougeoyant(**e**) [ʀuʒwajɑ̃, jɑ̃t] *adj* (*cendres*) glowing; (*reflet*) gleaming red

rougeoyer [ʀuʒwaje] <6> *vi* blazing

rouget [ʀuʒɛ] *m* **1.** (*poisson*) mullet; **~ barbet** red mullet; **~ grondin** gurnard **2.** (*maladie*) erysipelas

rougeur [ʀuʒœʀ] *f* **1.** (*carnation rouge*) red face; (*quand on rougit*) blushing *no pl;* **la ~ de son nez** his red nose; **la ~ de ses yeux** her bloodshot eyes; **sa ~ trahissait son émotion** his blushing gave his feelings away **2.** (*tache*) red patch; **~s** rash + *vb sing*

rougi(**e**) [ʀuʒi] *adj* red

rougir [ʀuʒiʀ] <8> *vi* **1.** (*exprimer une émotion: personne*) to blush; **~ de confusion/plaisir** to blush with embarrassment/pleasure; **~ de colère** to get red with anger **2.** (*avoir honte*) **~ de qn** to be ashamed of sb; **faire ~ qn** to make sb ashamed **3.** (*devenir rouge*) to go red

rouille [ʀuj] *f* rust

rouillé(**e**) [ʀuje] *adj* **1.** (*couvert de rouille*) rusty **2.** (*sclérosé*) rusty; (*muscles*) stiff

rouiller [ʀuje] <1> *vi* (*se couvrir de rouille*) to rust

roulant(**e**) [ʀulɑ̃, ɑ̃t] *adj* **1.** (*sur roues*) **fauteuil ~** wheelchair **2.** CHEMDFER **personnel ~** train crews *pl* **3.** (*mobile*) moving; **escalier ~** escalator; **tapis ~** (*pour passagers*) moving walkway; (*dans une usine*) conveyor belt

roulé(**e**) [ʀule] *adj* **col ~** polo neck ►**bien ~** *inf* with a good figure

rouleau [ʀulo] <x> *m* **1.** (*bigoudi*) roller **2.** (*bande enroulée*) roll; **un ~ de pièces** a tube of coins; **~ de cuivre** a roll of copper **3.** TECH (*cylindre*) **~ compresseur** steamroller; **~ de peintre** paint roller **4.** (*vague*) roller **5.** SPORT roll

roulement [ʀulmɑ̃] *m* **1.** (*bruit sourd: du tonnerre*) roll; (*du train*) rumble; **~ de tambour** drum roll **2.** (*mouvement: des yeux*) rolling; (*des épaules*) swinging; **marcher avec des ~s de hanches** to swing one's hips as one walks **3.** (*alternance*) rotation **4.** (*circulation: des capitaux, fonds*) turnover **5.** TECH bearing; **~ à aiguilles/billes/rouleaux** needle/ball/roller bearing **6.** (*circulation*) **~ des voitures/poids lourds** car/heavy vehicle movement

rouler [ʀule] <1> **I.** *vt* **1.** (*faire avancer*) to roll; (*brouette, poussette*) to push **2.** (*enrouler*) to roll; **~ un parapluie/une crêpe** to roll up an umbrella/a pancake **3.** (*enrouler, enrober*) **~ qc dans la farine** to roll sth in flour **4.** *inf* (*tromper*) to trick; **se faire ~ par qn** to be done by sb **5.** (*faire tourner une partie du corps: épaules*) to sway; (*hanches*) to swing **II.** *vi* **1.** (*se déplacer sur roues: objet*) to roll; (*voiture*) to go; (*conducteur*) to drive; **on roulait vite** we were going fast; **~ en 2 CV** to drive a 2 CV **2.** (*tourner sur soi*) to roll; **~ sous la table** (*personne*) to fall under the table ►**ça roule** *inf* everything's

R

fine!; **allez roulez!** *inf* here we go! **III.** *vpr* (*se vautrer*) **se ~ par terre/dans l'herbe** to roll on the ground/in the grass; **c'est vraiment à se ~ par terre** it'd drive you around the bend

roulette [Rulɛt] *f* **1.** (*petite roue*) wheel; **patins à ~s** roller skates **2.** (*jeu*) roulette; **~ russe** Russian roulette ►**marcher comme sur des ~s** *inf* to go off without a hitch

roulis [Ruli] *m* rolling

roulotte [Rulɔt] *f* caravan

roumain [Rumɛ̃] *m* Romanian; *v. a.* **français**

roumain(e) [Rumɛ̃, ɛn] *adj* Romanian

Roumain(e) [Rumɛ̃, ɛn] *m(f)* Romanian

Roumanie [Rumani] *f* **la ~** Romania

round [Raund, Rund] *m* SPORT *a. fig* round

roupettes [Rupɛt] *fpl inf* balls, goolies *Brit*

roupie [Rupi] *f* FIN rupee

roupiller [Rupije] <1> *vi inf* to snooze

roupillon [Rupijɔ̃] *m inf* nap; **piquer un ~** to have a nap [*o* a snooze]

rouquin(e) [Rukɛ̃, in] **I.** *adj* (*personne*) redheaded; (*cheveux*) red **II.** *m(f)* redhead

rouspéter [Ruspete] <4> *vi inf* **~ contre qn/qc** to grumble about sb/sth; **se faire ~** to get bawled out

rousseur [RusœR] *f* reddishness

roussi [Rusi] *m* **ça sent le ~** (*sentir le brûlé*) there's a smell of burning; (*être suspect*) things look dodgy

routard(e) [RutaR, aRd] *m(f)* backpacker

route [Rut] *f* **1.** (*voie*) road; **la ~ de Paris** the Paris road; **~ nationale/départementale** major/secondary road; **~ secondaire** secondary road **2.** (*voyage*) travel; **trois heures de ~** (*en voiture*) three hours' driving; (*à pied*) three hours' walk; **être en ~ pour Paris** to be on the way to Paris; **bonne ~!** drive safely! **3.** (*itinéraire, chemin*) way; NAUT, AVIAT path; **demander sa ~** to ask one's way; **être sur la bonne ~** to be going the right way ►**faire fausse ~** to go the wrong way; (*se tromper*) to be on the wrong track; **faire de la ~** to be on the roads a lot; **mettre qc en ~** to get sth started; **en ~!** off we go!

routier, -ière [Rutje, -jɛR] **I.** *adj* (*relatif à la route*) road; **prévention routière** road safety **II.** *m, f* (*camionneur*) lorry driver *Brit,* trucker *Am*

routine [Rutin] *f a.* INFOR routine; **contrôle/visite de ~** routine check/visit

rouvrir [RuvRiR] <11> **I.** *vt, vi* to reopen **II.** *vpr* **se ~** (*porte*) to open again; (*blessure, plaie, débat*) to be reopened

roux [Ru] *m* **1.** (*couleur*) reddish brown **2.** GASTR roux

roux, rousse [Ru, Rus] **I.** *adj* (*personne*) redheaded; (*cheveux*) red; (*barbe, feuillage*) reddish; (*pelage, robe de cheval*) russet **II.** *m, f* (*personne*) redhead

royal(e) [Rwajal, o] <-aux> *adj* **1.** (*propre à un roi*) royal; **prince ~/princesse ~e** prince/princess royal **2.** (*digne d'un roi*) regal **3.** (*parfait: indifférence*) utter; (*paix*) perfect

royalement [Rwajalmɑ̃] *adv* **1.** (*magnifiquement: vivre*) like a king **2.** *inf* (*complètement*) **je m'en moque ~** I couldn't give a damn

royaume [Rwajom] *m* (*monarchie*) kingdom

Royaume-Uni [Rwajomyni] *m* **le ~** the United Kingdom

royauté [Rwajote] *f* **1.** (*régime*) monarchy **2.** (*fonction*) royalty

RPR [ɛRpeɛR] *m abr de* **Rassemblement pour la république** *French political party of the right*

RSVP [ɛRɛsvepe] *abr de* **répondez s'il vous plaît** RSVP

ruade [Rɥad] *f* kick; **le cheval a décoché** [*o* **lancé**] **une ~** the horse kicked

ruban [Rybɑ̃] *m* **1.** (*bande de tissu*) ribbon **2.** (*insigne de décoration*) **~ de la Légion d'honneur** ribbon [*o* riband] of the Legion of Honour **3.** (*autres matériaux*) tape; **~ magnétique** *a.* INFOR magnetic tape; **~ adhésif** adhesive tape

rubéole [Rybeɔl] *f* German measles

rubis [Rybi] *m* (*pierre précieuse*) ruby

rubrique [RybRik] *f* **1.** PRESSE (*section*) page(s); (*article*) column; **~ littéraire/sportive** the book/sports page(s); **~ des spectacles** the entertainment section **2.** (*titre, catégorie*) heading

ruche [Ryʃ] *f* hive

rude [Ryd] *adj* **1.** (*pénible: climat, montée*) hard **2.** (*rugueux: peau, surface, étoffe*) rough **3.** (*fruste: personne*) rough; (*manières*) rough and ready; (*traits*) rugged **4.** *antéposé* (*redoutable: gaillard*) hearty **5.** *antéposé, inf* (*sacré: appétit*) hearty

rudement [Rydmɑ̃] *adv inf* (*sacrément*) awfully; **avoir ~ peur** to have the scare of one's life

rudesse [Rydɛs] *f* **1.** (*dureté: d'une personne*) roughness; **la ~ de son langage/ses manières** his rough language/manners **2.** (*rigueur: des conditions de vie*) harshness; **la ~ du climat/de l'hiver** the harsh climate/winter

rudimentaire [Rydimɑ̃tɛR] *adj* (*sommaire: connaissances, installation*) basic

rudiments [Rydimɑ̃] *mpl* basics; **avoir des ~ de français** to have basic French

rudoyer [Rydwaje] <6> *vt* **~ qn** to treat sb harshly

rue [Ry] *f* **1.** (*artère*) street; **~ commerçante/à sens unique** shopping/one-way street; **~ piétonne** pedestrians only street; **en pleine ~** right out in the street; **dans la ~** in the street; **traîner dans les ~s** to hang around in the streets **2.** (*ensemble des habitants*) **toute la ~ la connaît** the whole street knows her ►**courir les ~s** (*personne*) to wander through the streets; (*chose*) to be perfectly ordinary; **ça ne court pas les ~s** you don't find a lot of them around

ruée [Rɥe] *f* rush; **~ vers l'issue de secours**

rush for the emergency exit; ~ **vers l'or** gold rush

ruelle [Rɥɛl] *f* lane

ruer [Rɥe] <1> **I.** *vi* (*cheval, âne*) to kick **II.** *vpr* **se ~ sur qn/qc** to rush at sb/sth; **se ~ dans la rue/vers la sortie** to dash into the street/towards the exit; **la foule se rua vers la frontière** the crowd rushed towards the border

rugby [Rygbi] *m* rugby

rugbyman <s *o* -men> [Rygbiman, -mɛn] *m* rugby player

rugir [RyʒiR] <8> **I.** *vi* **1.** to bellow; ~ **de colère** to roar with anger **2.** (*mugir, gronder*) to roar; **faire ~ son moteur** to rev one's engine **II.** *vt* (*insultes, menaces*) to bellow

rugissement [Ryʒismɑ̃] *m* **1.** (*d'un fauve*) roar **2.** (*hurlement*) **pousser des ~s** to bellow; **~s de colère** angry roaring *no pl* **3.** (*grondement: de la tempête, du vent, d'un moteur*) roar

rugueux, **-euse** [Rygø, -øz] *adj* rough

ruine [Rɥin] *f* **1.** *pl* (*décombres*) ruins **2.** (*édifice délabré*) ruin **3.** (*personne*) wreck **4.** (*destruction*) **en ~(s)** in ruins; **tomber en ~(s)** to go to ruin; **menacer de tomber en ~(s)** to be in danger of falling down **5.** (*perte de biens*) ruin; **courir à la ~** to be heading for ruin

ruiner [Rɥine] <1> **I.** *vt* **1.** (*dépouiller de sa richesse*) to ruin **2.** (*détruire*) to ruin; ~ **tous les espoirs de qn** to dash all sb's hopes **3.** (*coûter cher*) **ça (ne) va pas te ~** *inf* it won't ruin you **II.** *vpr* **se ~ pour qn** to bankrupt oneself for sb

ruineux, **-euse** [Rɥinø, -øz] *adj* (*voiture, voyage*) ruinously expensive; (*dépense*) ruinous; **avoir des goûts ~** to have wildly expensive tastes; **ce n'est pas ~** it won't break the bank

ruisseau [Rɥiso] <x> *m* stream

ruisselant(e) [Rɥis(ə)lɑ̃, ɑ̃t] *adj* **1.** (*coulant*) streaming; ~ **de pluie** streaming with rain **2.** (*couvert*) ~ **de sueur/de sang** dripping with sweat/blood; ~ **d'humidité** dripping wet

ruisseler [Rɥis(ə)le] <3> *vi* **1.** (*couler*) to stream **2.** (*être couvert de*) ~ **de sueur** to be dripping with sweat; ~ **d'humidité** (*murs*) to be dripping wet; **ses joues ruisselaient de larmes** tears were streaming down his cheeks

ruissellement [Rɥisɛlmɑ̃] *m* **1.** stream **2.** *fig* ~ **de lumières** stream of light + *vb sing*

rumeur [RymœR] *f* (*bruit qui court*) rumour *Brit,* rumor *Am;* **la ~ publique** rumour; **faire courir une ~** to spread a rumour

ruminant [Ryminɑ̃] *m* ruminant

ruminer [Rymine] <1> **I.** *vt* **1.** (*ressasser*) to ponder; ~ **son chagrin** to brood over one's sorrows **2.** ZOOL to ruminate **II.** *vi* to chew the cud

rumsteck *m v.* **romsteak**

rupestre [RypɛstR] *adj* rock

rupin(e) [Rypɛ̃, in] **I.** *adj inf* (*personne, appartement*) posh **II.** *m(f) inf* filthy rich guy

rupture [RyptyR] *f* **1.** (*cassure*) break **2.** (*déchirure: d'une corde*) breaking; (*d'un tendon, d'une veine*) severing **3.** (*annulation: de fiançailles*) breaking off; ~ **de contrat/traité** breach of contract/a treaty **4.** (*séparation*) break-up

rural(e) [RyRal, o] <-aux> **I.** *adj* (*vie, région*) country; (*exploitation, économie*) rural; **pays ~** country area; **domaine ~** country estate **II.** *m(f)* country person

ruse [Ryz] *f* (*subterfuge*) ruse

rusé(e) [Ryze] **I.** *adj* crafty **II.** *m(f)* crafty individual

ruser [Ryze] <1> *vi* to use trickery

russe [Rys] *adj, m* Russian; *v. a.* **français**

Russe [Rys] *mf* Russian; ~ **blanc** White Russian

Russie [Rysi] *f* **la ~** Russia

rustine [Rystin] *f* tyre patch *Brit,* tire patch *Am*

rustique [Rystik] *adj* (*mobilier, objets, outils*) rustic; (*personne, vie, coutumes*) country; (*arbre, plante*) hardy

rustre [RystR] **I.** *adj* boorish **II.** *m* lout

rut [Ryt] *m* rut; **en ~** in rut

rutilant(e) [Rytilɑ̃, ɑ̃t] *adj* sparkling

RV [ɛRve] *m abr de* **rendez-vous** meeting

rythme [Ritm] *m* **1.** MUS rhythm **2.** (*allure, cadence*) rate; **ne pas pouvoir suivre le ~** not to be able to keep up; **au ~ de qc** at the rate of sth **3.** (*mouvement régulier*) ~ **cardiaque/respiratoire** cardiac/respiratory rate

rythmé [Ritme] *adj* rhythmical

rythmer [Ritme] <1> *vt* (*cadencer*) ~ **qc** to mark the rhythm of sth

rythmique [Ritmik] **I.** *adj* rhythmical; **section/guitare ~** rhythm section/guitar **II.** *f* **1.** (*danse*) rhythmics + *vb sing* **2.** (*cadence*) rhythm

S

S, s [ɛs] *m inv* S, s; ~ **comme Suzanne** s for Sugar ►**virage en S** zigzag bend

s *f inv abr de* **seconde** s

S *abr de* **sud**

s' *v.* **se, si**

sa [sa, se] <ses> *dét poss* (*d'un homme*) his; (*d'une femme*) her; (*d'une chose, d'un animal*) its; *v. a.* **ma**

Sa [sa, se] <Ses> *dét poss, avec un titre, form* ~ **Majesté** (*reine*) Her Majesty; (*roi*) His Majesty

SA [ɛsɑ] *f abr de* **société anonyme** limited company

sabbat [saba] *m* REL sabbath; **jour du ~** Sabbath day

sabbatique [sabatik] *adj* sabbatical

sablage [sɑblaʒ] *m* sanding

sable [sɑbl] **I.** *m* sand; ~**s mouvants** quicksand **II.** *adj inv* sandy

sablé [sɑble] *m* GASTR ≈ shortbread biscuit [*o* cookie *Am*]

sablé(e) [sɑble] *adj* GASTR **gâteau** ~ ≈ shortbread biscuit [*o* cookie *Am*]; **pâte** ~**e** rich shortcrust pastry

sabler [sɑble] <1> *vt* **1.** (*couvrir de sable*) to sand **2.** *fig* ~ **le champagne** to crack open a bottle of champagne

sableuse [sɑbløz] *f* (*appareil pour couvrir de sable*) sander

sableux, -euse [sɑblø, -øz] *adj* sandy

sablonneux, -euse [sɑblɔnø, -øz] *adj* sandy

sabord [sabɔʀ] *m* scuttle ►**mille** ~**s!** *inf* blistering barnacles!

saborder [sabɔʀde] <1> **I.** *vt* **1.** (*projet*) to scupper; ~ **une entreprise** to wind up a business **2.** NAUT (*bateau, flotte*) to scuttle **II.** *vpr* **se** ~ **1.** (*patron*) to shut down; (*candidat*) to do for oneself **2.** NAUT to scuttle one's ship

sabot [sabo] *m* **1.** (*chaussure*) clog **2.** ZOOL hoof **3.** (*pour les véhicules*) ~ **de Denver** wheel clamp *Brit,* Denver boot *Am* ►**je te vois venir avec tes gros** ~**s** I can see you coming; **faire qc comme un** ~ to be a dud at sth

sabotage [sabɔtaʒ] *m* sabotage

saboter [sabɔte] <1> *vt* **1.** (*détruire volontairement*) *a. fig* to sabotage **2.** (*bâcler*) to botch

saboteur, -euse [sabɔtœʀ, -øz] *m, f* saboteur

sabre [sɑbʀ] *m* (*arme*) SPORT sabre *Brit,* saber *Am* ►**le** ~ **et le goupillon** *inf* the army and the church

sabrer [sɑbʀe] <1> *vt* **1.** (*biffer*) to strike out **2.** (*raccourcir*) to hack at **3.** (*ouvrir*) ~ **le champagne** to open the champagne, (traditionally by removing the cork with a blow from a sabre) **4.** *inf* (*bâcler*) ~ **qc** to make a hash of sth

sac[1] [sak] **I.** *m* **1.** bag; ~ **à pommes de terre** potato sack; ~ **à linge** laundry bag; ~ **postal** mail bag; **mettre en** ~**s** to put into bags; ~ **congélation** freezer bag; ~ **aspirateur** vacuum bag; ~ **de couchage** sleeping bag; ~ **à main** handbag *Brit,* purse *Am;* ~ **à provisions** shopping bag; ~ **d'écolier** school bag; ~ **de marin** kitbag *Brit,* kit bag *Am;* ~ **de plage/sport/voyage** beach/sport/travel bag; ~ **à dos** rucksack, backpack; ~ **à malice(s)** bag of tricks **2.** *inf* (*dix francs ou mille anciens francs*) *ten francs* ►~ **d'embrouilles** [*o* **de nœuds**] *inf* can of worms; **l'affaire est/c'est dans le** ~ *inf* the thing's/it's in the bag; **mettre qn dans le même** ~ to tar sb with the same brush; **vider son** ~ *inf* to get everything off one's chest **II.** *app inv* (*robe*) dress

sac[2] [sak] *m* (*pillage*) sack; **mettre à** ~ to sack

saccade [sakad] *f* jolt; **par** ~**s** jerkily

saccadé(e) [sakade] *adj* (*respiration, rire*) halting; (*bruit*) staccato

saccage [sakaʒ] *m* **1.** (*pillage*) destruction **2.** (*dévastation*) havoc

saccager [sakaʒe] <2a> *vt* (*dévaster*) to wreck; (*récolte*) to destroy

SACEM [sasɛm] *f abr de* **Société des auteurs, compositeurs et éditeurs de musique** *French association responsible for the management of royalties*

sacerdoce [sasɛʀdɔs] *m* **1.** REL priesthood **2.** (*vocation*) vocation

sachant [saʃɑ̃] *part prés de* **savoir**

sache [saʃ] *subj prés de* **savoir**

sachet [saʃɛ] *m* bag; (*petit emballage fermé*) sachet; ~ **de bonbons** bag of sweets; ~ **de lavande** sachet of lavender

sacoche [sakɔʃ] *f* **1.** (*sac*) bag; ~ **de cycliste** saddlebag **2.** *Belgique* (*sac à main* (*de femme*)) handbag

sac-poubelle [sakpubɛl] <sacs-poubelles> *m* bin bag *Brit,* garbage bag *Am*

sacquer [sake] <1> *vt inf* **1.** (*renvoyer*) to fire; **se faire** ~ to get fired **2.** (*noter sévèrement*) ~ **qn** to give sb a lousy mark [*o* grade *Am*]; **se faire** ~ to get a lousy mark **3.** (*détester*) **je ne peux pas la** ~ I can't stand (the sight of) her

sacraliser [sakʀalize] <1> *vt* ~ **qc** to look on sth as sacred

sacre [sakʀ] *m* **1.** (*cérémonie religieuse: d'un souverain, évêque*) consecration **2.** (*consécration: du printemps*) rite **3.** *Québec* (*jurement, formule de juron*) swearword

sacré [sakʀe] *m* sacred

sacré(e) [sakʀe] *adj* **1.** REL sacred; (*édifice*) holy **2.** *fig* (*horreur, terreur*) holy **3.** (*inviolable: droits, lois*) sacred; **pour lui, le sommeil, c'est** ~ his sleep is sacred as far as he's concerned **4.** *antéposé, inf* (*maudit*) ~ **nom d'un chien!** hell! **5.** *antéposé, inf* (*satané*) damned; (*farceur, gaillard, talent*) real; **avoir un** ~ **toupet** to have one hell of a nerve; **cette** ~**e Lina a encore gagné!** Lina has gone and won again!

sacrebleu [sakʀəblø] *interj* my goodness!

Sacré-Cœur [sakʀekœʀ] *m sans pl* Sacred Heart

sacrement [sakʀəmɑ̃] *m* sacrament; **derniers** ~**s** last rites; **saint** ~ Blessed Sacrament

sacrément [sakʀemɑ̃] *adv inf* damned

sacrer [sakʀe] <1> *vt* **1.** (*introniser*) to consecrate **2.** (*déclarer*) ~ **qn le meilleur acteur de sa génération** to hail sb as the best actor of his generation; **être sacré le meilleur roman de l'année** to be declared the best novel of the year

sacrifice [sakʀifis] *m* sacrifice; **faire le** ~ **de qc pour qc** to sacrifice sth for sth; **sens du** ~ sense of sacrifice ►**Saint Sacrifice** Holy Sacrifice of the Mass

sacrifié(e) [sakʀifje] *m(f)* sacrificed; (*prix*) giveaway

sacrifier [sakʀifje] <1> **I.** *vt* **1.** (*renoncer à*) ~ **qc pour** [*o* **à**] **qc** to sacrifice sth for sth; ~ **qc**

à ses intérêts to sacrifice sth to one's personal interests; ~ **qc pour faire qc** to sacrifice sth for sth **2.** (*négliger: personnage, rôle*) to neglect **3.** COM (*marchandises*) to give away; (*prix*) to slash **4.** REL to sacrifice **II.** *vpr* **se ~ pour ses enfants/pour la patrie** to sacrifice oneself for one's children/for one's country; **se ~ à des idées** to subscribe blindly to ideas

sacrilège [sakʀilɛʒ] **I.** *adj* **a.** REL sacrilegious **II.** *m* **a.** REL (*profanation*) sacrilege **III.** *mf* (*personne*) perpetrator of sacrilege

sacristain, -tine [sakʀistɛ̃, -tin] *m, f* sacristan

sacristie [sakʀisti] *f* sacristy

sacro-saint(e) [sakʀosɛ̃, sɛ̃t] <sacro-saints> *adj iron* sacrosanct

sadique [sadik] **I.** *adj* sadistic **II.** *mf* sadist

sadisme [sadism] *m* sadism

sadomaso [sadomazo] *inv, inf,* **sadomasochiste** [sadomazɔʃist] **I.** *adj* sadomasochistic **II.** *mf* sado-masochist

safari [safaʀi] *m* safari

safari-photo [safaʀifɔto] <safaris-photos> *m* camera safari

safran [safʀɑ̃] **I.** *m* **1.** GASTR, BOT saffron **2.** (*couleur*) saffron (yellow) **II.** *adj inv* saffron (yellow)

sagace [sagas] *adj* sagacious

sagacité [sagasite] *f* sagacity

sagaie [sagɛ] *f* assegai

sage [saʒ] **I.** *adj* **1.** (*avisé: conseil, personne*) wise **2.** (*docile: écolier, enfant*) well-behaved **3.** (*chaste: jeune fille*) good **4.** (*décent, modéré: goût, vêtement*) restrained **II.** *m* wise man; **conseil des ~s** advisory commission

sage-femme [saʒfam] <sages-femmes> *f* midwife

sagement [saʒmɑ̃] *adv* **1.** (*raisonnablement*) wisely **2.** (*modérément: user*) wisely **3.** (*docilement*) quietly **4.** (*chastement*) modestly

sagesse [saʒɛs] *f* wisdom; **agir avec ~** to act wisely; **voix de la ~** voice of wisdom; **avoir la ~ de** +*infin* to have the good sense to +*infin* ▶**~ des nations** traditional wisdom

Sagittaire [saʒitɛʀ] *m* Sagittarius; *v. a.* **Balance**

sagouin(e) [sagwɛ̃, in] *m(f) inf* (*personne malpropre*) slob

Sahara [saaʀa] *m* **le ~** the Sahara

saharien(ne) [saaʀjɛ̃, jɛn] *adj* Saharan

saharienne [saaʀjɛn] *f* safari jacket

Sahel [saɛl] *m* **le ~** the Sahel

saignant(e) [sɛɲɑ̃, ɑ̃t] *adj* (*rouge: bifteck, viande*) rare

saignement [sɛɲmɑ̃] *m* (*perte de sang, fait de saigner*) bleeding; **les ~s de nez** nosebleeds

saigner [seɲe] <1> **I.** *vi* to bleed; **~ du nez** to have a nosebleed ▶**ça va ~!** the fur will fly! **II.** *vt* **1.** MED to bleed **2.** (*tuer: animal*) to kill; (*personne*) to bleed **3.** (*exploiter*) **~ qn** to bleed sb white **III.** *vpr* **se ~ pour qn** to bleed oneself white for sb

saillant [sajɑ̃] *m* (*d'un bastion*) salient; (*d'une frontière*) projection

saillant(e) [sajɑ̃, jɑ̃t] *adj* **1.** (*protubérant: corniche*) projecting; (*pommettes*) high; (*veine, yeux, muscle*) protruding; (*front, menton*) protuberant; (*angle*) salient **2.** (*important: événement*) salient; (*trait*) notable

saillir[1] [sajiʀ] *vi irr, défec* (*corniche*) to project; (*veines, yeux, muscle*) to stand out; (*menton, os, front*) to protrude

saillir[2] [sajiʀ] <8> *vt* to serve

sain(e) [sɛ̃, sɛn] *adj* **1.** (*en bonne santé, salubre, normal, de bon aloi: affaire, gestion*) healthy; (*constitution, politique, lectures, idées*) sound **2.** (*non abîmé*) sound ▶**~ et sauf** safe and sound

saindoux [sɛ̃du] *m* lard

saint(e) [sɛ̃, sɛ̃t] **I.** *adj* **1.** REL holy; **~es huiles** holy oils; **le ~ sacrifice de la messe** the Holy Sacrifice of the Mass; **jeudi ~** Maundy Thursday; **vendredi ~** Good Friday; **samedi ~** Easter Saturday **2.** *antéposé* (*inspiré par la piété*) **une ~e colère** an almighty rage **II.** *m(f)* REL saint; **~ patron** patron saint; **le culte des ~s** the worship of saints; **les ~s de glace** *the 11th, 12th and 13th of May, when frost is traditionally expected;* **le ~ des saints** the Holy of Holies ▶**ne pas savoir à quel ~ se vouer** not to know which way to turn

Saint(e) [sɛ̃, sɛ̃t] *adj* **le ~ Sépulcre** the Holy Sepulchre; **la ~e Vierge** the Blessed Virgin; **les ~es Écritures** the Holy Scriptures

Saint-Barthélémy [sɛ̃baʀtelemi] *f sans pl* **la ~** the Saint Bartholomew's Day massacre

saint-bernard [sɛ̃bɛʀnaʀ] <saint-bernard(s)> *m* **1.** (*chien*) St Bernard **2.** (*âme secourable*) good samaritan **saint-cyrien(ne)** [sɛ̃siʀjɛ̃, jɛn] <saint-cyriens> *m(f): military cadet from the St. Cyr academy* **Saint-Domingue** [sɛ̃dɔmɛ̃:g(ə)] Santo Domingo **Sainte-Catherine** [sɛ̃tkatʀin] *f sans pl* **elle coiffe ~** she's 25 and unmarried **Sainte-Hélène** [sɛ̃telɛn(ə)] GEO Saint Helena **Sainte-Lucie** [sɛ̃tlysi] *f* Saint Lucia **sainte-nitouche** [sɛ̃tnituʃ] <saintes-nitouches> *f* goody-goody **Saint-Esprit** [sɛ̃tɛspʀi] *m sans pl* **le ~** the Holy Spirit

sainteté [sɛ̃tte] *f* holiness

Sainteté [sɛ̃tte] *f* **Sa/Votre ~** His/Your Holiness

saint-frusquin [sɛ̃fʀyskɛ̃] *m inv, inf* clobber **saint-gallois, saint-galloise** [sɛ̃galwa, waz] *adj* of Saint-Gall; *v. a.* **ajaccien** **Saint-Gallois, Saint-Galloise** [sɛ̃galwa, waz] *m, f* person from Saint-Gall; *v. a.* **Ajaccien** **saint-glinglin** [sɛ̃glɛ̃glɛ̃] *f sans pl, inf* **à la ~** one fine day **saint-honoré** [sɛ̃tɔnɔʀe] *m inv pastry topped with cream and meringue* **Saint-Jean** [sɛ̃ʒɑ̃] *f sans pl* **la ~** Midsummer's Day **Saint-Jean-Baptiste** [sɛ̃ʒɑ̃batist] *m* St John the Baptist

La Saint-Jean-Baptiste on 24 July is the national holiday of French Canada (more important for French Canadians than the Canadian national holiday, "Confederation Day" on 1 July) and there is dancing round high piles of logs.

Saint-Kitts-et-Nevis [sɛ̃kitsenevis] *m* Saint Kitts-Nevis **Saint-Laurent** [sɛ̃lɔʀɑ̃] *m* Saint Lawrence **saint-lucien(ne)** [sɛ̃lysjɛ̃, ɛn] *adj* Saint Lucian **Saint-Lucien(ne)** [sɛ̃lysjɛ̃, ɛn] *m(f)* Saint Lucian **Saint-Marin** [sɛ̃maʀɛ̃] *m* San Marino **Saint-Nicolas** [sɛ̃nikɔla] *f sans pl* **la** ~ St Nicholas's Day **Saint-Père** [sɛ̃pɛʀ] <Saints-Pères> *m* Holy Father **Saint-Pierre** [sɛ̃pjɛʀ] *m sans pl* Saint Peter's (Basilica) **Saint-Pierre-et-Miquelon** [sɛ̃pjɛʀemikəlɔ̃] *m* Saint Pierre and Miquelon **Saint-Siège** [sɛ̃sjɛʒ] *m* the Holy See **Saint-Sylvestre** [sɛ̃silvɛstʀ] *f sans pl* New Year's Eve **Saint-Vincent-et-les-Grenadines** [sɛ̃vɛ̃sɑ̃elegʀənadin(ə)] *m* Saint Vincent and the Grenadines

sais [sɛ] *indic prés de* **savoir**

saisie [sezi] *f* **1.** JUR seizure; ~ **immobilière** seizure of property; ~ **mobilière** distraint *Brit*, distress *Am* **2.** (*confiscation*) seizure **3.** INFOR data entry; (*chez l'imprimeur*) keyboarding; ~ **de données** data input; ~ **de l'écran** screenshot

saisir [seziʀ] <8> **I.** *vt* **1.** (*prendre*) ~ **qn par les épaules/le chien par le collier** to take hold of sb by the shoulders/the dog by the collar; ~ **qn à bras le corps** to seize sb bodily **2.** (*attraper: ballon, corde*) to catch **3.** (*mettre à profit: chance*) to grab; (*occasion*) to seize **4.** (*comprendre*) to catch; ~ **au vol une partie de la conversation** to catch [*o* overhear] a part of the conversation in passing **5.** (*impressionner*) ~ **qn** (*beauté, ressemblance, changement*) to strike sb **6.** GASTR (*viande*) to seal **7.** (*confisquer*) to seize **8.** JUR (*commission*) to submit a case to; ~ **un tribunal d'une affaire** to refer a case to a tribunal **9.** INFOR to input **II.** *vpr* **se** ~ **de qc** to seize sth

saisissant(e) [sezisɑ̃, ɑ̃t] *adj* (*qui surprend: beauté, changement, différence*) striking; (*froid*) biting

saisissement [sezismɑ̃] *m* **1.** (*frisson*) chill **2.** (*émotion*) astonishment; **de** ~ with astonishment; **il resta muet de** ~ he couldn't speak for shock

saison [sɛzɔ̃] *f* season; **belle/mauvaise** ~ summer/winter; **en toute(s)** ~**(s)** at any time of year; **il n'y a plus de** ~**s** *inf* the weather doesn't match the seasons any more; **fruits de** ~ fruit in season; ~ **des amours** mating season; ~ **des foins** haymaking time; **en/hors** ~ in/out of season

saisonnier, -ière [sɛzɔnje, -jɛʀ] **I.** *adj* (*propre à la saison, limité à la saison*) seasonal **II.** *m, f* seasonal worker

sait [sɛ] *indic prés de* **savoir**

salade [salad] *f* **1.** BOT lettuce; GASTR salad; ~ **niçoise** salade niçoise; ~ **de tomates/fruits** tomato/fruit salad; ~ **de saison** seasonal salad **2.** *inf* (*confusion*) muddle **3.** *pl, inf* (*mensonges*) fairy tales ►**vendre sa** ~ **à qn** *inf* to give sb a sales pitch

saladier [saladje] *m* salad bowl

salage [salaʒ] *m* (*contre le verglas: des routes*) salting, gritting *Brit*

salaire [salɛʀ] *m* **1.** (*rémunération*) salary; (*d'un ouvrier*) pay; ~ **minimum interprofessionnel de croissance** minimum wage; ~ **de misère** starvation wage **2.** (*récompense*) reward

salamandre [salamɑ̃dʀ] *f* salamander

salami [salami] *m* salami

salant [salɑ̃] *adj v.* **marais**

salarial(e) [salaʀjal, jo] <-aux> *adj* **politique ~e** pay policy

salarié(e) [salaʀje] **I.** *adj* (*travail*) paid; (*personne*) salaried **II.** *m(f)* salaried worker

salaud [salo] **I.** *adj inf* **être** ~ to be a bastard **II.** *m inf* bastard

sale [sal] **I.** *adj* **1.** (*opp: propre*) dirty **2.** *antéposé, inf* (*vilain, louche*) low; (*type, temps*) lousy; (*coup*) dirty; **il a une** ~ **gueule** (*il est malade*) he looks awful; (*il est méchant*) he looks nasty **II.** *m inf* **être au** ~ to be in the wash

salé [sale] **I.** *m* **petit** ~ salt pork **II.** *adv* **manger** ~ to eat salty food

salé(e) [sale] *adj* **1.** (*contenant du sel: beurre, cacahuètes*) salted; (*eau*) salt; **être trop** ~ (*soupe*) to be too salty **2.** (*opp: sucré*) savoury **3.** *inf* (*corsé: histoire*) juicy

salement [salmɑ̃] *adv* **1.** (*opp: proprement*) **manger** ~ to be a sloppy eater; **travailler** ~ to make a mess working; **gagner** ~ to win by trickery **2.** *inf* (*très*) damned

saler [sale] <1> **I.** *vi* **1.** GASTR to add salt **2.** TECH to salt [*o* grit *Brit*] the roads **II.** *vt* **1.** GASTR to salt **2.** TECH (*route*) to salt, to grit *Brit* **3.** *inf* (*corser*) ~ **l'addition** to bump up the bill

saleté [salte] *f* **1.** (*malpropreté*) dirtiness **2.** (*chose sale*) dirt *no pl;* **faire des ~s partout** to make a mess everywhere **3.** *sans pl* (*crasse*) filth **4.** *inf* (*objet sans valeur*) piece of junk **5.** *inf* (*maladie*) nasty bug; **ramasser une** ~ to pick sth up **6.** *inf* (*friandise*) junk *no pl* **7.** (*obscénité*) filthy name ►**faire des ~s** (*animal*) to mess; ~ **d'ordinateur/de Maurice!** *inf* bloody computer/Maurice!

salière [saljɛʀ] *f a. inf* salt cellar

saligaud [saligo] *m inf* swine

salir [saliʀ] <8> **I.** *vt* ~ **qc** to make sth dirty **II.** *vpr* **se** ~ (*se souiller, devenir sale*) to get dirty; **se** ~ **les mains** to get one's hands dirty

salissant(e) [salisɑ̃, ɑ̃t] *adj* **1.** dirty; **des travaux/jeux ~s** dirty jobs/games **2.** (*qui se salit*) **être** ~ to show the dirt

salive [saliv] *f* saliva ►**avaler sa** ~ to keep

one's mouth shut; **gaspiller sa ~** *inf* to waste one's breath

saliver [salive] <1> *vi* **1.** (*baver*) to salivate **2.** (*convoiter*) ~ **d'envie de faire un tour en moto** to be dying to go for a motorbike ride; ~ **d'impatience** to seethe with impatience; **laisser qn ~ d'impatience** to leave sb dying of impatience; **faire ~ qn** to make sb drool

salle [sal] *f* **1.** (*pièce*) room; ~ **à manger/de séjour** dining/living room; ~ **d'attente/de jeux** waiting/games room; ~ **d'audience** courtroom; ~ **de bains** bathroom; ~ **de cinéma** cinema; ~ **de classe** classroom; ~ **de réanimation/de réunion** recovery/conference room; ~ **des fêtes** village hall; ~ **des pas perdus** waiting hall; ~ **d'étude** prep room; ~ **d'opération** operating theatre *Brit,* operating room *Am;* ~ **polyvalente** multi-use hall; **faire du sport en ~** to do indoor sports **2.** (*cinéma*) cinema; **~s obscures** cinemas **3.** (*spectateurs*) audience ▸**faire ~ comble** to have a full house

salmonelle [salmɔnɛl] *f* salmonella

salmonellose [salmɔneloz] *f* salmonellosis

Salomon [salɔmɔ̃] *fpl* **les îles ~** Solomon Islands

salomonais(**e**) [salɔmɔnɛ, nɛz] *adj* Solomon Island

Salomonais(**e**) [salɔmɔnɛ, nɛz] *m(f)* Solomon Islander

salon [salɔ̃] *m* **1.** (*salle de séjour*) living room **2.** (*mobilier*) living-room suite; ~ **de jardin** set of garden furniture **3.** (*salle d'hôtel pour les clients*) lounge **4.** (*salle d'hôtel pour des conférences, réunions*) function room **5.** (*commerce*) ~ **de coiffure** hairdresser's; ~ **de thé** tea-room

Salon [salɔ̃] *m* ~ **du jouet** toy exhibition; ~ **de l'Auto**(**mobile**) motor show

salopard [salɔpaʀ] *m inf* bastard; **bande de ~s** bastards

salope [salɔp] *f* **1.** *vulg* (*débauchée*) slut, slag *Brit* **2.** *inf* (*garce*) bitch

saloper [salɔpe] <1> *vt inf* **1.** (*bâcler*) to botch **2.** (*salir*) to mess up

saloperie [salɔpʀi] *f inf* **1.** (*objet sans valeur*) piece of junk; **vendre de la ~** to sell junk **2.** *gén pl* (*saletés*) dirt **3.** (*mauvaise nourriture*) muck *no pl Brit,* garbage *no pl Am* **4.** (*maladie*) nasty bug **5.** (*méchanceté*) dirty trick; **faire une ~ à qn** to play a dirty trick on sb **6.** (*obscénité*) filthy remark ▸**c'est de la ~** it's rubbish *Brit,* it's garbage *Am;* ~ **d'ordinateur/de bagnole** lousy computer/car

salopette [salɔpɛt] *f* (pair of) overalls

salsa [salsa] *f* salsa

salsifis [salsifi] *m* GASTR salsify

saltimbanque [saltɛ̃bɑ̃k] *mf* acrobat; (*dans une foire*) fairground performer

salubre [salybʀ] *adj* healthy

salubrité [salybʀite] *f* **1.** (*caractère sain: du climat*) healthiness; (*de l'air*) clearness; (*d'un logement*) cleanliness **2.** (*hygiène*) hygiene **3.** ADMIN ~ **publique** public health

saluer [salɥe] <1> **I.** *vt* **1.** (*dire bonjour*) ~ **qn** to say hello to sb; ~ **qn de la main** to wave hello to sb **2.** (*dire au revoir*) ~ **qn** to say goodbye to sb **3.** (*rendre hommage*) to salute **4.** (*accueillir*) to welcome; ~ **qn par des sifflets** to greet sb with whistles; **être salué par des applaudissements** to be greeted by applause **5.** *soutenu* (*considérer*) ~ **Brassens comme chef de file de la chanson française** to hail Brassens as the number one in French song **6.** MIL ~ **un supérieur/le drapeau** to salute a superior/the flag **II.** *vi* **1.** THEAT to bow **2.** MIL to salute

salut[1] [saly] **I.** *m* **1.** (*salutation*) greeting; **faire un ~ de la main** to wave a greeting; **sans un ~** without a wave [*o* word] **2.** MIL ~ **aux supérieurs/au drapeau** salute to one's superiors/flag **II.** *interj* **1.** *inf* (*bonjour*) **~!** hi! **2.** *inf* (*au revoir*) **~!** ciao!

salut[2] [saly] *m* **1.** (*sauvegarde*) safety **2.** REL salvation **3.** POL ~ **public** state security

salutaire [salytɛʀ] *adj* salutary; (*décision*) helpful; **ce séjour m'a été ~** this stay has done me good; ~ **à qn/qc** (*avantageux*) beneficial to sb/sth; (*secourable*) helpful to sb/sth

salutations [salytasjɔ̃] *fpl form* salutations; **je vous prie/nous vous prions d'agréer, Madame/Monsieur, mes/nos ~s distinguées** yours sincerely; **veuillez agréer, Madame la Présidente, mes respectueuses ~s** yours faithfully

salve [salv] *f* volley

samba [sɑ̃mba] *f* samba

samedi [samdi] *m* Saturday; *v. a.* **dimanche**

Samoa [samɔa] *fpl* **les îles ~** Samoan Islands; **les ~s occidentales** Western Samoa

samoan(**ne**) [samɔɑ̃, an] *adj* Samoan

Samoan(**ne**) [samɔɑ̃, an] *m(f)* Samoan

samouraï [samuʀaj] *m* samurai

SAMU [samy] *m abr de* **Service d'aide médicale d'urgence** ambulance service; (*médecin*) emergency doctor; **appeler le ~** to call an ambulance

sanatorium [sanatɔʀjɔm] *m* sanatorium

sanction [sɑ̃ksjɔ̃] *f* **1.** (*punition*) penalty; ECOLE punishment; **mériter une ~** to deserve punishment; **être passible d'une ~** to be liable to a penalty **2.** ECON, POL sanction

sanctionner [sɑ̃ksjɔne] <1> **I.** *vt* (*punir*) to punish; ECON to levy sanctions on **II.** *vi* to punish

sanctuaire [sɑ̃ktɥɛʀ] *m a.* REL sanctuary

sandale [sɑ̃dal] *f* sandal

sandalette [sɑ̃dalɛt] *f* sandal

sandwich [sɑ̃dwitʃ] <(e)s> *m* GASTR sandwich; ~ **au jambon** ham sandwich ▸**prendre qn en ~** *inf* to sandwich sb

Sandwich [sɑ̃dwitʃ] *fpl* **les îles ~ du Sud** South Sandwich Islands

sang [sɑ̃] *m* **1.** ANAT blood; **donner son ~** to give blood; **être en ~** to be covered in blood;

S

se gratter jusqu'au ~ to scratch oneself raw **2.** (*race*) blood **3.** (*vie*) life; **payer qc de son** ~ to pay for sth with one's life ▶**suer** ~ **et eau** to sweat blood; **avoir du** ~ **sur les mains** to have blood on one's hands; **ne pas avoir de** ~ **dans les veines** *inf* to be spineless; **avoir le** ~ **chaud** to be hot-blooded; **du** ~ **frais** [*o* **neuf**] fresh blood; **se faire du mauvais** ~ to get in a state; **baigner dans son** ~ to lie in a pool of blood; **se ronger les** ~**s** *inf* to agonize

sang-froid [sɑ̃fʀwa] *m sans pl* **1.** (*maîtrise de soi*) sang-froid; **garder/perdre son** ~ to keep/to lose one's head **2.** (*froideur*) cool; **agir avec** ~ to act coolly; **de** ~ in cold blood

sanglant(e) [sɑ̃glɑ̃, ɑ̃t] *adj* **1.** (*saignant*) bleeding **2.** (*violent*) cruel; (*rencontre, match*) bloody

sangle [sɑ̃gl] *f* strap; ~ **d'une selle** girth of a saddle

sanglier [sɑ̃glije] *m* boar

sanglot [sɑ̃glo] *m* sob; **avec des** ~**s dans la voix** sobbing; **éclater en** ~**s** to burst out sobbing; **être en** ~**s** to be sobbing

sangloter [sɑ̃glɔte] <1> *vi* to sob

sangria [sɑ̃gʀija] *f* sangria

sangsue [sɑ̃sy] *f* leech

sanguin(e) [sɑ̃gɛ̃, in] *adj* **1.** ANAT **plasma** ~ blood plasma **2.** (*coloré*) red; **orange** ~**e** blood orange **3.** (*impulsif*) impulsive; (*type*) fiery

sanguinaire [sɑ̃ginɛʀ] *adj* **1.** bloodthirsty **2.** *soutenu* (*sanglant*) bloody

sanguine [sɑ̃gin] *f* (*orange*) blood orange

sanguinolent(e) [sɑ̃ginɔlɑ̃, ɑ̃t] *adj* (*mucosité*) mixed with blood; (*plaie*) covered in blood

sanisette® [sanizɛt] *f* Superloo®, *coin operated toilet Brit*

sanitaire [sanitɛʀ] **I.** *adj* health; (*mesure*) sanitary; **installations** ~**s** bathroom plumbing *no pl;* **cordon** ~ cordon sanitaire; **les services** ~**s** public health services **II.** *m gén pl* bathroom installations

sans [sɑ̃] **I.** *prep* without; ~ **arrêt** continually; ~ **but** aimless; **partir** ~ **fermer la porte**/~ **que tu le saches** to leave without closing the door/you knowing; **la situation n'est pas** ~ **nous inquiéter** the situation does worry us; **vous n'êtes pas** ~ **savoir que** you must know that ▶~ **plus** and thats all; ~ **quoi** otherwise **II.** *adv inf* without; **il va falloir faire** ~ we'll have to manage without

sans-abri [sɑ̃zabʀi] *m inv* homeless person **sans-culotte** [sɑ̃kylɔt] <sans-culottes> *m* sans-culotte **sans-emploi** [sɑ̃zɑ̃plwa] *m inv* unemployed person **sans-faute** [sɑ̃fot] *m inv* clear round; SPORT faultless performance **sans-fil** [sɑ̃fil] *m inv* cordless phone **sans-gêne** [sɑ̃ʒɛn] **I.** *adj inv* inconsiderate **II.** *m sans pl* (*désinvolture*) lack of consideration **III.** *mf inv* (*personne désinvolte*) inconsiderate person **sans-le-sou** [sɑ̃lsu] *mf inv, inf* penniless person **sans-logis** [sɑ̃lɔʒi] *mf inv, soutenu* homeless person

sansonnet [sɑ̃sɔnɛ] *m* ZOOL starling

sans-papiers [sɑ̃papje] *mf inv: immigrant without legal papers*

santé [sɑ̃te] *f* **1.** (*opp: malade*) health; **être bon pour la** ~ to be healthy; **avoir une** ~ **de fer** to have a iron constitution; **être en bonne/mauvaise** ~ to be in good/poor health; **comment va la** ~**?** how are you? **2.** ADMIN **la** ~ **publique** public health; **les services de** ~ the health services; **profession de la** ~ health care profession ▶**se refaire une** ~ *inf* to get one's health back; **respirer la** ~ *inf* to exude good health; **à la** ~ **de qn** to sb's good health; **à ta** ~**!** good health!

Santé [sɑ̃te] *f* **le ministre de la** ~ the Minister for Health

santiag [sɑ̃tjag] *f inf* cowboy boot

santon [sɑ̃tɔ̃] *m* Christmas crib figure

saoudien(ne) [saudjɛ̃, jɛn] *adj* Saudi Arabian

Saoudien(ne) [saudjɛ̃, jɛn] *m(f)* Saudi Arabian

saoul(e) [su, sul] *adj v.* **soûl**

saouler [sule] <1> *vt v.* **soûler**

saper [sape] <1> *vpr inf* **se** ~ to get dressed up

sapeur-pompier [sapœʀpɔ̃pje] <sapeurs-pompiers> *m* firefighter; **femme** ~ firewoman; **les sapeurs-pompiers** the fire brigade

saphir [safiʀ] *adj inv* sapphire

sapin [sapɛ̃] **I.** *m* fir tree; ~ **de Noël** Christmas tree **II.** *app inv* deal

saquer [sake] <1> *vt v.* **sacquer**

sarabande [saʀabɑ̃d] *f* **1.** *inf* (*chahut*) racket **2.** MUS saraband

sarbacane [saʀbakan] *f* peashooter

sarcasme [saʀkasm] *m* sarcasm; (*remarque*) sarcastic remark

sarcastique [saʀkastik] *adj* sarcastic

sarcler [saʀkle] <1> *vt* to weed

sarcophage [saʀkɔfaʒ] *m* sarcophagus

Sardaigne [saʀdɛɲə] *f* **la** ~ Sardinia

sardine [saʀdin] *f* sardine ▶**serrés comme des** ~**s en boîte** *inf* squashed together like sardines

sari [saʀi] *m* sari

SARL [ɛsaɛʀɛl] *f abr de* **société à responsabilité limitée** limited liability company

sarment [saʀmɑ̃] *m* climbing stem

sarrasin [saʀazɛ̃] *m* buckwheat

sas [sas] *m* **1.** (*dans une écluse*) lock **2.** (*pièce intermédiaire*) double doorway (*for security*)

satané(e) [satane] *adj antéposé* **1.** (*maudit*) damned, bloody **2.** (*sacré*) ~ **farceur!** you old joker!

satanique [satanik] *adj a.* REL satanic; (*ruse*) wicked

satellite [satelit] **I.** *m* satellite **II.** *adj* **ville** ~ satellite town

satiété [sasjete] *f* satiety; (*dégoût*) surfeit; **à** ~ till one has had one's fill; (*jusqu'au dégoût*) ad nauseam; **manger à** ~ to eat one's fill

satin [satɛ̃] *m* satin; **peau de** ~ silky-smooth skin
satiné [satine] *m* **1.**(*aspect luisant*) sheen **2.**(*douceur: de la peau*) silky-smoothness
satiné(e) [satine] *adj* satin-like
satire [satiʀ] *f* satire; **faire la** ~ **de qn/qc** (*pièce, texte*) to satirize sb/sth
satirique [satiʀik] *adj* satirical
satisfaction [satisfaksjɔ̃] *f* satisfaction; **à la** ~ **générale** to everybody's satisfaction ►**donner** ~ **à qn** to give sb satisfaction; **obtenir** ~ to get satisfaction
satisfaire [satisfɛʀ] *irr* **I.** *vt* **1.**(*contenter: personne*) to satisfy **2.**(*assouvir: soif*) to slake; (*faim*) to satisfy **3.**(*donner droit à*) ~ **une réclamation** to uphold a complaint **II.** *vi* ~ **à une obligation** to fulfil an obligation *Brit,* to fulfill an obligation *Am* **III.** *vpr* **1.**(*se contenter*) **se** ~ **de qc** to be satisfied with sth **2.**(*uriner*) **se** ~ to relieve oneself **3.**(*prendre son plaisir*) **se** ~ to have one's pleasure; (*par la masturbation*) to pleasure oneself
satisfaisant(e) [satisfəzɑ̃, ɑ̃t] *adj* satisfactory
satisfait(e) [satisfɛ, ɛt] *adj* **être** ~ **de qn/qc** to be satisfied with sb/sth
saturation [satyʀasjɔ̃] *f* **1.** saturation; **manger du chocolat jusqu'à** ~ to eat all the chocolate one wants **2.**(*surcharge: d'une rue*) jamming; (*d'un standard téléphonique*) overload **3.** CHIM, PHYS saturation; (*d'un réacteur*) overload ►**arriver** [*o* **être**] **à** ~ *a.* CHIM to reach saturation point
saturé(e) [satyʀe] *adj* **1.**(*plein: route*) congested **2.**(*surcharger*) **être** ~ (*standard*) to be overloaded; (*marché*) to be saturated **3.**(*plus que rassasier*) **je suis** ~ **de poisson** *inf* I'm fed up with fish; **être** ~ **de publicité** to be glutted with advertising
saturer [satyʀe] <1> *vt* **1.**(*soûler*) to swamp **2.**(*surcharger*) to overload
Saturne [satyʀn] *f* Saturn
satyre [satiʀ] *m* **1.** lecher **2.** MYTH satyr
sauce [sos] *f* GASTR sauce; ~ **béchamel/chasseur** white/chasseur sauce; ~ **vinaigrette** salad dressing; ~ **au vin** wine sauce; **viande en** ~ meat in a sauce ►**la** ~ **fait passer le poisson** *inf* a bit of sugar helps the medicine go down; **mettre qc à toutes les** ~**s** *inf* to serve sth up to suit any occasion; **être mis à toutes les** ~**s** to be served up whatever the occasion
saucée [sose] *f inf* downpour
saucer [sose] <2> *vt* **1.**(*essuyer*) ~ **qc** to mop up the sauce from sth **2.** *inf* (*tremper*) **être saucé/se faire** ~ to be/get soaked
saucière [sosjɛʀ] *f* sauceboat
sauciflard [sosiflaʀ] *m inf* sausage
saucisse [sosis] *f* GASTR sausage
saucisson [sosisɔ̃] *m* GASTR sausage; ~ **sec** dry sausage ►**être ficelé comme un** ~ (*mal vêtu*) to be dressed like nothing on earth; (*être serré*) to be bursting out of one's clothes
sauf [sof] *prep* **1.**(*à l'exception de*) except; ~ **que tu es trop jeune** except that you're too young **2.**(*à moins de*) ~ **erreur de ma part** unless I am mistaken; ~ **imprévu** unless anything unforeseen happens; ~ **avis contraire** unless advised otherwise
saugrenu(e) [sogʀəny] *adj* peculiar
saule [sol] *m* willow; ~ **pleureur** weeping willow
saumâtre [somɑtʀ] *adj* **1.** briny **2.** *inf* (*désagréable: impression*) unpleasant; (*plaisanterie*) off-colour *Brit,* off-color *Am*
saumon [somɔ̃] **I.** *m* salmon **II.** *adj inv* salmon **III.** *app* **rose** ~ salmon pink
saumoné(e) [somɔne] *adj* **truite** ~**e** salmon trout
saumure [somyʀ] *f* brine
sauna [sona] *m* sauna
saupoudrer [sopudʀe] <1> *vt* **1.** GASTR ~ **qc de sucre/sel** to sprinkle sth with sugar/salt; ~ **qc de farine** to dust sth with flour **2.** FIN ~ **les crédits** to give funds out sparingly
saurai [sɔʀɛ] *fut de* **savoir**
saut [so] *m* **1.**(*bond*) jump; ~ **de la mort** leap of death; ~ **de l'ange** swallow dive *Brit,* swan dive *Am* **2.** SPORT ~ **à la perche** pole vaulting; ~ **à la corde** skipping *Brit,* jumproping *Am;* ~ **en longueur** long jump; ~ **en parachute/en chute libre** parachute/free-fall jump; ~ **de haies** hurdling; ~ **d'obstacles** obstacle race; ~ **périlleux** somersault **3.** INFOR break ►**au** ~ **du lit** on getting up; **prendre qn au** ~ **du lit** to find sb just out of bed; **faire le** ~ to take the plunge; **faire un** ~ **chez qn** *inf* to drop [*o* pop] round to see sb
saute [sot] *f* ~ **de température** jump in temperature; ~ **d'humeur** mood swing; ~ **d'image** flicker
sauté [sote] *m* ~ **de veau** sauté of veal
saute-mouton [sotmutɔ̃] *m inv* leapfrog; **jouer à** ~ to play leapfrog
sauter [sote] <1> **I.** *vi* **1.**(*bondir*) to jump; (*sautiller*) to hop; (~ *vers le haut*) to jump up; ~ **du lit** to leap out of bed; ~ **par la fenêtre/d'un train** to jump out of the window/a train **2.** SPORT to jump; ~ **en parachute** to do a parachute jump; ~ **à la corde** to skip *Brit,* to jump rope *Am* **3.**(*se précipiter*) ~ **sur l'occasion** to jump at the opportunity; ~ **sur le prétexte** to grab the excuse **4.**(*passer brusquement*) ~ **d'un sujet à l'autre** to leap from one subject to another; **un élève qui saute du CP en CE2** a pupil who jumps from year 2 to year 4 [*o* from first to third grad *Am*] **5.**(*jaillir: bouchon*) to pop (out); (*bouton*) to fly off; (*chaîne*) to snap **6.**(*exploser: bâtiment, pont, bombe*) to blow up; **faire** ~ **qn/qc** to blow sb/sth up **7.** ELEC (*fusibles, plombs*) to blow **8.** *inf* (*ne pas avoir lieu: classe, cours*) to go by the board **9.** GASTR **faire** ~ **qc** to sauté sth; **des pommes de terre sautées** sauté potatoes **10.**(*clignoter: image*) to flicker **11.**(*annuler*) **faire** ~ **une contravention** to cancel a fine

S

II. *vt* 1. (*franchir*) ~ **un fossé/mur** to leap over a ditch/wall 2. (*omettre: étape, page, classe, repas*) to skip; (*mot*) to leave out 3. *inf* (*avoir des relations sexuelles*) to screw

sauterelle [sotʀɛl] *f* grasshopper

sauteur, -euse [sotœʀ, -øz] *m, f* SPORT jumper

sauteuse [sotøz] *f* GASTR sauté pan

sautiller [sotije] <1> *vi* to hop

sautoir [sotwaʀ] *m* 1. SPORT jumping pit 2. (*collier*) chain; **porter qc en** ~ to wear sth on a chain ►**en** ~ crossed

sauvage [sovaʒ] I. *adj* 1. (*hors norme: camping, vente*) unofficial; (*grève*) wildcat; (*concurrence*) unfair 2. (*opp: domestique*) wild 3. (*à l'état de nature: côte, lieu, pays*) wild 4. (*violent*) violent; (*haine, horde*) savage; (*cris*) wild II. *mf* 1. (*solitaire*) recluse 2. (*brute, indigène*) savage ►**comme un** ~ *Québec* (*impoliment*) like a little savage

sauvagement [sovaʒmɑ̃] *adv* savagely; (*frapper, traiter*) brutally

sauvagerie [sovaʒʀi] *f* 1. savagery 2. (*insociabilité*) unsociableness

sauvegarde [sovgaʀd] *f* 1. (*protection*) protection; ~ **de l'emploi** employment protection 2. INFOR backup; **faire la** ~ **d'un fichier** to save a file

sauvegarder [sovgaʀde] <1> *vt* 1. (*protéger*) to protect; (*relations, image de marque*) to maintain 2. INFOR to save

sauve-qui-peut [sovkipø] *m inv* panic

sauver [sove] <1> I. *vt* (*porter secours, sauvegarder*) a. INFOR to save; ~ **qn/qc de qc** to save sb/sth from sth; ~ **la vie à qn** to save sb's life; **il a été sauvé par sa ceinture de sécurité** he was saved by his seatbelt ►~ **les meubles** to salvage what one can from the wreckage II. *vi* to save ►**sauve qui peut!** run for your life! III. *vpr* 1. (*échapper à*) **se** ~ **d'un mauvais pas** to get out of a tight spot 2. (*s'enfuir*) **se** ~ to escape 3. *inf* (*s'en aller*) **se** ~ to dash 4. (*déborder*) **se** ~ to boil over

sauvetage [sov(ə)taʒ] *m* rescue

sauveteur [sov(ə)tœʀ] *m* rescuer

sauvette [sovɛt] *f* **à la** ~ *inf* hastily; (*secrètement*) on the sly; **se marier à la** ~ to elope

sauveur [sovœʀ] I. *adj* saving II. *m* a. REL saviour *Brit,* savior *Am*

savamment [savamɑ̃] *adv* 1. skilfully *Brit,* skillfully *Am* 2. (*avec érudition*) learnedly 3. (*par expérience*) **parler** ~ **du chômage** to speak of about unemployment from (personal) experience

savane [savan] *f* 1. (*prairie*) savannah 2. *Québec* (*terrain marécageux*) swamp

savant(e) [savɑ̃, ɑ̃t] I. *adj* 1. (*érudit*) learned; **être** ~ **en histoire** to be a learned historian; **c'est trop** ~ **pour moi** it's all above my head 2. *antéposé, péj* (*discussion*) highbrow; (*calcul*) complex 3. (*habile*) skilful *Brit,* skillful *Am;* **c'est un** ~ **dosage** it's a careful balance 4. (*dressé*) performing II. *m(f)* 1. (*lettré*) scholar 2. (*scientifique*) scientist

savate [savat] *f* worn-out; (*chaussure*) old shoes ►**traîner la** ~ *inf* to hang around; (*vivoter*) to be down at heel

saveur [savœʀ] *f* 1. (*goût*) flavour *Brit,* flavor *Am;* **avoir une** ~ **âcre/douce** to have a pungent/sweet flavour; **sans** ~ tasteless 2. (*attrait: d'une nouveauté, d'un interdit*) lure

Savoie [savwa] *f* **la** ~ Savoy

savoir [savwaʀ] *irr* I. *vt* 1. (*être au courant, connaître, être conscient: leçon, rôle, détails*) to know; ~ **qc de** [*o* **sur**] **qn/qc** to know sth about sb/sth; ~ **la nouvelle par les journaux/sa famille** to find out the news through the papers/one's family; **faire** ~ **à qn que tout va bien** to let sb know that everything is fine; **tâcher d'en** ~ **davantage** to try to get to know more about it 2. (*être capable de*) ~ **attendre/dire non** to be able to wait/say no; **je ne saurais vous renseigner** I cannot help you 3. *Belgique, Nord* (*pouvoir*) **ne pas** ~ **venir à l'heure** not to be able to arrive on time ►~ **y faire** *inf* to know how to handle things; **elle ne sait plus où se mettre** *inf* she doesn't know where to put herself; **je ne veux rien** ~ I just don't want to know; **à** ~ that is; **on ne sait jamais** you never know; **en** ~ **quelque chose** to know sth about the matter; **n'en rien** ~ to know nothing II. *vi* to know ►**pas que je sache** not that I know; **pour autant que je sache!** for all I know III. *vpr* 1. (*être connu*) **se** ~ to be known 2. (*avoir conscience*) **se** ~ **en danger/malade** to know that one is in danger/ill IV. *m* knowledge

savoir-faire [savwaʀfɛʀ] *m inv* savoir-faire

savoir-vivre [savwaʀvivʀ] *m inv* manners *pl*

savon [savɔ̃] *m* 1. (*savonnette*) soap; ~ **de Marseille** household soap 2. *inf* (*réprimande*) telling-off; **passer un** ~ **à qn** to give sb a good telling-off; **prendre un** (**bon**) ~ to get told off

savonner [savɔne] <1> *vt, vpr* (**se**) ~ to soap (oneself)

savonnette [savɔnɛt] *f* bar of soap

savonneux, -euse [savɔnø, -øz] *adj* soapy; **eau savonneuse** soapy water

savourer [savuʀe] <1> *vt, vi* to savour *Brit,* savor *Am*

savoureux, -euse [savuʀø, -øz] *adj* delicious

saxe [saks] *m* Dresden china *no pl*

Saxe [saks] *f* **la** ~ Saxony

saxo [sakso] I. *m* sax II. *mf* sax player

saxon [saksɔ̃] *m* Saxon; *v. a.* **français**

saxon(ne) [saksɔ̃, ɔn] *adj* Saxon

Saxon(ne) [saksɔ̃, ɔn] *m(f)* Saxon

saxophone [saksɔfɔn] *m* saxophone

saxophoniste [saksɔfɔnist] *mf* saxophonist

saynète [sɛnɛt] *f* playlet

sbire [sbiʀ] *m* henchman

scabreux, -euse [skabʀø, -øz] *adj* 1. (*osé: conversation, histoire, allusion*) unsavoury

2. *soutenu* (*risqué: question, thème*) risky
scalp [skalp] *m* scalp
scalpel [skalpɛl] *m* scalpel
scalper [skalpe] <1> *vt* to scalp
scandale [skɑ̃dal] *m* **1.** (*éclat*) scandal; **presse à ~** gutter press **2.** (*indignation*) outrage **3.** (*tapage*) disturbance; **~ sur la voie publique** disturbing the peace ▸**faire** ~ to cause a scandal
scandaleusement [skɑ̃daløzmɑ̃] *adv* **1.** (*honteusement*) scandalously **2.** (*outrageusement*) outrageously; (*exagéré, sous-estimé*) grossly
scandaleux, **-euse** [skɑ̃dalø, -øz] *adj* **1.** (*honteux*) scandalous; (*prix, propos*) outrageous **2.** (*qui exploite le scandale*) **la chronique scandaleuse** the scandal pages
scandaliser [skɑ̃dalize] <1> **I.** *vt* to shock **II.** *vpr* **se ~ de qc** to be shocked at sth; **se ~ que j'aie dit la vérité** to be shocked that I told the truth
scander [skɑ̃de] <1> *vt* (*slogans*) to chant
scandinave [skɑ̃dinav] *adj* Scandinavian
Scandinave [skɑ̃dinav] *mf* Scandinavian
Scandinavie [skɑ̃dinavi] *f* **la ~** Scandinavia
scannage [skanaʒ] *m* INFOR **faire un ~** to scan
scanner [skane] <1> *vt* to scan
scanner [skanɛʀ] *m*, **scanneur** [skanœʀ] *m* scanner; **~ à main/à plat** hand-held/flatbed scanner
scaphandre [skafɑ̃dʀ] *m* (*pour scaphandrier*) diving suit; (*pour astronaute*) spacesuit; **le ~ autonome** Aqua-Lung®
scaphandrier, **-ière** [skafɑ̃dʀije, -jɛʀ] *m, f* diver
scarabée [skaʀabe] *m* beetle
scarlatine [skaʀlatin] *f* scarlet fever
scarole [skaʀɔl] *f* escarole
sceau [so] <x> *m* seal ▸**sous le ~ du secret** under the seal of secrecy
scélérat(e) [seleʀa, at] *m(f) soutenu* villain
sceller [sele] <1> *vt* **1.** TECH (*crochet, couronne dentaire*) to fix; (*pierre, barreaux, dalle*) to embed **2.** (*confirmer solennellement, fermer hermétiquement*) to seal; (*engagement*) to confirm **3.** (*authentifier par un sceau*) to seal
scellés [sele] *mpl* seals; **mettre les ~** to fix seals (*on a house, vehicle, etc so that evidence in an investigation cannot be tampered with*); **apposer les ~ sur qc** to put seals on sth; **lever les ~** to remove the seals; **sous ~** under seal
scénario [senaʀjo, senaʀi] <s *o* scénarii> *m* **1.** (*script: d'un film*) screenplay; (*d'une pièce de théâtre*) script; (*d'un roman*) scenario **2.** (*déroulement prévu*) scenario; **c'est toujours le même ~** it is always the same old routine
scénariste [senaʀist] *mf* scriptwriter
scène [sɛn] *f* **1.** (*spectacle*) scene; **~ d'amour** love scene **2.** (*querelle*) scene; **~ de jalousie** fit of jealousy; **~ de ménage** domestic fight; **faire une ~** to make a scene; **faire une ~ à qn** to have a big row with sb **3.** (*estrade*) stage; **entrer en ~** to come on stage; **mettre une histoire en ~** to stage a story; **mettre une pièce de théâtre en ~** to direct a play; **en ~!** on stage! **4.** (*décor, cadre: d'un crime, drame*) scene
scénique [senik] *adj* (*gestuelle, traitement*) dramatic; **indications ~s** stage directions
scepticisme [sɛptisism] *m a.* PHILOS scepticism *Brit*, skepticism *Am*
sceptique [sɛptik] **I.** *adj* sceptical *Brit*, skeptical *Am* **II.** *mf* sceptic *Brit*, skeptic *Am*
sceptre [sɛptʀ] *m* sceptre *Brit*, scepter *Am*
schah [ʃa] *m* shah
schéma [ʃema] *m* **1.** (*abrégé*) outline **2.** (*dessin*) diagram; **~ de montage** assembly diagram
schématique [ʃematik] *adj* **1.** *péj* (*sommaire*) oversimplified **2.** (*simplifié: représentation*) schematic
schématiquement [ʃematikmɑ̃] *adv* schematically
schématiser [ʃematize] <1> *vt* to schematize
schilling [ʃiliŋ] *m* schilling
schisme [ʃism] *m* schism
schiste [ʃist] *m* schist
schizophrène [skizɔfʀɛn] *adj, mf* schizophrenic
schizophrénie [skizɔfʀeni] *f* schizophrenia
schlinguer [ʃlɛ̃ge] <1> *vi inf* to stink
schmolitz [ʃmɔlits] *m Suisse* **faire ~** to call each other "tu"

> **faire schmolitz** is a ritual in which people make the transition from calling each other "vous" to "tu". They link arms holding glasses and down their drinks in one.

schnaps [ʃnaps] *m* schnapps
schnock, **schnoque** [ʃnɔk] *m inf* **vieux ~** old fart
schuss [ʃus] *m* schuss; **descendre tout ~** *inf* to schuss down
sciatique [sjatik] **I.** *adj* **nerf ~** sciatic nerve **II.** *f* sciatica
scie [si] *f* saw; **~ circulaire** circular saw; **~ à bois** wood saw; **~ à découper** fretsaw
sciemment [sjamɑ̃] *adv* knowingly
science [sjɑ̃s] *f* **1.** (*domaine scientifique*) science **2.** (*disciplines scolaires*) **les ~s** the sciences; **faculté des ~s** science faculty **3.** (*savoir faire*) expertise **4.** (*érudition*) knowledge ▸**avoir la ~ infuse** *inf* to know without being told
science-fiction [sjɑ̃sfiksjɔ̃] *f inv* science fiction; **roman/film de ~** science fiction novel/film
scientifique [sjɑ̃tifik] **I.** *adj* scientific **II.** *mf* **1.** (*savant*) scientist **2.** (*élève*) science student
scientifiquement [sjɑ̃tifikmɑ̃] *adv* scien-

tifically

scientologie [sjɑ̃tɔlɔʒi] *f* scientology; **Église de ~** Church of Scientology

scier [sje] <1> *vt* **1.** (*couper*) to saw; (*arbres*) to saw down **2.** *inf* (*estomaquer*) to bore; **être scié** to be bored rigid

scierie [siʀi] *f* sawmill

scinder [sɛ̃de] <1> **I.** *vt* (*parti*) to split; (*question, problème*) to divide; **scindé en deux** split in two **II.** *vpr* **se ~ en qc** to split up into sth

scintillant(e) [sɛ̃tijɑ̃, jɑ̃t] *adj* sparkling

scintillement [sɛ̃tijmɑ̃] *m* sparkle; (*d'une image télévisée*) flicker

scintiller [sɛ̃tije] <1> *vi* to sparkle

scission [sisjɔ̃] *f* split; **faire ~** to split away

sciure [sjyʀ] *f* sawdust

sclérose [skleʀoz] *f* **1.** (*encroûtement*) ossification **2.** MED sclerosis; **~ en plaques** multiple sclerosis

scléroser [skleʀoze] <1> **I.** *vt* (*personne*) to ossify; (*initiatives*) to paralyse *Brit*, paralyze *Am* **II.** *vpr* **1.** (*se figer*) **se ~** (*société*) to become ossified; **se ~ dans ses habitudes** to become stuck in one's ways **2.** MED **se ~** to become sclerotic

scolaire [skɔlɛʀ] *adj* **1.** (*relatif à l'école: succès, année*) school; **échec ~** failure at school **2.** *péj* (*livresque*) starchy; **parler un allemand ~** to speak school German

scolarisation [skɔlaʀizasjɔ̃] *f* **1.** schooling **2.** (*équipement en écoles*) availability of schooling

scolariser [skɔlaʀize] <1> *vt* **1.** (*admettre dans une école*) to school **2.** (*doter d'écoles*) **~ un pays/une région** to build schools in a country/region

scolarité [skɔlaʀite] *f* schooling; (*période*) time at school

scoliose [skɔljoz] *f* scoliosis

scolopendre [skɔlɔpɑ̃dʀ] *f* **1.** ZOOL centipede **2.** BOT hart's-tongue

scoop [skup] *m* scoop

scooter [skutœʀ, skutɛʀ] *m* scooter; **~ des mers/des neiges** jetski/snowmobile

scorbut [skɔʀbyt] *m* scurvy

score [skɔʀ] *m* score; **mener au ~** to be ahead

scories [skɔʀi] *fpl* slag

scorpion [skɔʀpjɔ̃] *m* ZOOL scorpion

Scorpion [skɔʀpjɔ̃] *m* Scorpio; *v. a.* **Balance**

scotch® [skɔtʃ] *m sans pl* (*adhésif*) Sellotape®, Scotch tape®

scotcher [skɔtʃe] <1> *vt* to sellotape *Brit*, tape; (*pour fermer*) to tape [*o* sellotape *Brit*] down

scout(e) [skut] **I.** *adj* scout **II.** *m(f)* boy scout, girl scout *m, f*

scoutisme [skutism] *m* scouting; **faire du ~** (*enfant*) to be a scout; (*adulte*) to be a scout leader

scrabble® [skʀabl] *m* Scrabble®

scribe [skʀib] *m* scribe

script [skʀipt] *m* **1.** CINE, THEAT script **2.** (*écriture*) printing; **en ~** printed

scripte [skʀipt] *f* script

scrupule [skʀypyl] *m* **1.** *souvent pl* (*hésitation*) scruple; **avoir des ~s à faire qc** to have scruples about doing sth **2.** (*souci*) **un ~ d'exactitude** scrupulous attention to accuracy

scrupuleusement [skʀypyløzmɑ̃] *adv* scrupulously

scrupuleux, -euse [skʀypylø, -øz] *adj* scrupulous; **peu ~** unscrupulous

scruter [skʀyte] <1> *vt* (*horizon*) to scan; (*pénombre*) to peer into; (*conscience*) to examine

scrutin [skʀytɛ̃] *m* ballot; **~ majoritaire** election on majority basis

sculpter [skylte] <1> **I.** *vt* to scuplt; (*bois*) to carve; **~ qc dans du marbre** to sculpt sth in marble **II.** *vi* to scuplt

sculpteur [skyltœʀ] *m* sculptor; **~ sur bois** woodcarver

sculpture [skyltyʀ] *f* **la ~** sculpture; **la ~ sur pierre** stone sculpture; **la ~ sur bois** woodcarving

SDF [ɛsdeɛf] *m, f abr de* **sans domicile fixe** homeless person

SDN [ɛsdeɛn] *f abr de* **Société des Nations** League of Nations

se [sə] <*devant voyelle ou h muet* **s'**> *pron pers* **1.** himself/herself; **il/elle ~ regarde dans le miroir** he/she looks at himself/herself in the mirror; **il/elle ~ demande s'il/si elle a raison** he/she asks if he's/she's right **2.** (*l'un l'autre*) each other; **ils/elles ~ suivent/font confiance** they follow/trust each other **3.** *avec les verbes pronominaux* **ils/elles ~ nettoient** they clean each themselves up; **il/elle ~ nettoie les ongles** he/she cleans his/her nails

séance [seɑ̃s] *f* **1.** CINE, THEAT showing **2.** (*période*) session; **~ de pose** sitting; **~ de spiritisme** séance **3.** (*réunion*) meeting; **en ~** in session; **lever la ~** to end the meeting; (*interrompre*) to suspend the meeting **4.** *inf* (*scène*) scene ►**~ tenante** without further ado

séant [seɑ̃] *adj v.* **seyant**

seau [so] <x> *m* bucket ►**il pleut à ~x** *inf* it's bucketing down

SEBC [ɛsøbese] *m abr de* **Système européen de banques centrales** ECBS

sec [sɛk] **I.** *adv* **1.** (*fort: démarrer*) sharply; (*frapper*) hard **2.** (*abondamment: boire*) a lot ►**aussi ~** *inf* (*répondre*) straight off **II.** *m* **étang à ~** dried-up pond; **mettre qc à ~** to drain sth; **mettre qc au ~** to put sth in a dry place; **tenir qc au ~** to keep sth in a dry place ►**être à ~** to be flat broke

sec, sèche [sɛk, sɛʃ] *adj* **1.** (*opp: humide*) dry **2.** (*déshydraté: figue*) dried; **légumes ~s** pulses; **raisins ~s** raisins **3.** (*opp: gras: bras*) lean; (*peau, cheveu, toux*) dry **4.** (*brusque: rire*) dry; **coup ~** snap **5.** (*opp: aimable: refus*) curt; (*réponse, lettre, merci*) terse; (*ton, cœur, personne*) cold **6.** (*sobre: style*) dry **7.** SPORT (*jeu, placage*) straight **8.** (*pur: whisky, gin*) neat **9.** (*opp: doux: champagne, vin*) dry **10.** JEUX (*atout, valet*) singleton

sécateur [sekatœʀ] *m* pair of secateurs [*o* pruning shears]; (*grand*) pair of shears

sécession [sesesjɔ̃] *f* POL, HIST secession; **faire ~** to secede

séchage [seʃaʒ] *m* drying

sèche-cheveux [sɛʃʃəvø] *m inv* hair drier

sèche-linge [sɛʃlɛ̃ʒ] *m inv* tumble-dryer

sèche-mains [sɛʃmɛ̃] *m inv* hand-dryer

sèchement [sɛʃmɑ̃] *adv* (*démarrer*) briskly; (*frapper, tirer*) sharply; (*refuser, répondre*) curtly

sécher [seʃe] <5> **I.** *vt* **1.** (*rendre sec*) to dry **2.** *inf* (*ne pas assister à*) to skip **II.** *vi* **1.** (*devenir sec*) to dry; **mettre le linge à ~** to put the washing out to dry **2.** (*se déshydrater: bois, plante, terre*) to dry out; (*fleur, fruits*) to dry up **3.** *inf* (*ne pas savoir*) to be stumped; **~ en histoire** to be stumped in history **III.** *vpr* **se ~** to dry oneself; **se ~ les mains/les cheveux** to dry one's hands/one's hair

sécheresse [sɛʃʀɛs] *f* dryness; METEO drought

sécheuse [seʃøz] *f Québec* (*sèche-linge*) tumble dryer

séchoir [seʃwaʀ] *m* dryer

second [s(ə)gɔ̃] *m* (*dans une charade*) second

second(e) [s(ə)gɔ̃, ɔ̃d] *adj antéposé* **1.** (*deuxième*) second; **en ~ lieu** in second place **2.** (*qui n'a pas la primauté*) second; **au ~ plan** in the background; **de ~ ordre** second-rate **3.** (*nouveau: jeunesse, nature, vie*) second; *v. a.* **cinquième**

secondaire [s(ə)gɔ̃dɛʀ] **I.** *adj* secondary **II.** *m* ECOLE **le ~** secondary education

seconde [s(ə)gɔ̃d] **I.** *adj v.* **second** **II.** *f* **1.** (*unité de temps*) *a.* MAT, MUS, AUTO second **2.** ECOLE year eleven *Brit*, tenth grade *Am* **3.** AUTO second class; **billet de ~** second-class ticket

seconder [s(ə)gɔ̃de] <1> *vt* **~ qn dans son travail** to aid sb in his/her work; **être secondé par qn** to be helped by sb

secouer [s(ə)kwe] <1> **I.** *vt* **1.** (*agiter*) to shake; **~ qn pour le réveiller** to shake sb to wake him up; **~ la poussière de la veste** to shake the dust from one's jacket **2.** (*ballotter: explosion, bombardement*) to rock; (*autobus, avion, personne*) to shake **3.** (*traumatiser: émotion*) to shake ►**il n'en a <u>rien</u> à ~ de qc** *inf* he couldn't care less about sth **II.** *vpr inf* **se ~** **1.** (*s'ébrouer*) to shake oneself **2.** (*réagir*) to get going

secourir [s(ə)kuʀiʀ] *vt irr* to help

secourisme [s(ə)kuʀism] *m* first aid; **faire du ~** to do first aid

secouriste [s(ə)kuʀist] *mf* first-aider

secours [s(ə)kuʀ] *m* **1.** (*sauvetage*) help; (*organisme*) aid organization; (*en montagne*) rescue service; **les ~** the rescue services; **donner les premiers ~ aux accidentés** to give first aid to accident victims **2.** (*aide*) help; **appeler qn à son ~** to call to sb for help; **porter** [*o* **prêter**] **~ à qn** to help sb; **aller** [*o* **courir**]/**voler au ~ de qn/qc** to fly to sb's/sth's aid; **sortie de ~** emergency exit; **au ~!** help! **3.** (*subvention*) grant

secousse [s(ə)kus] *f* **1.** (*choc*) jolt; **par ~s** bumpily **2.** POL upheaval

secret [səkʀɛ] *m* **1.** (*cachotterie, mystère*) secret; **~ d'alcôve** intimate secret; **~ de Polichinelle** *inf* open secret; **garder un ~** to keep a secret; **ne pas avoir de ~ pour qn** to keep no secrets from sb **2.** *sans pl* (*confidentialité*) confidentiality; **~ de la confession** seal of the confessional; **garder le ~ sur qc** [*o* **de qc**] to maintain silence over sth ►**être dans le ~ des <u>dieux</u>** to be in on the secret; **l'astrologie n'<u>a</u> plus de ~ pour elle** astrology holds no secrets for her; **<u>être</u> dans le ~/dans le ~ de qn** to be in on the secret/sb's secret; **<u>mettre</u> qn dans le ~** to let sb in on the secret; **cadenas/serrure <u>à</u> ~** combination padlock/lock; **<u>en</u> grand ~** in great secrecy

secret, **-ète** [səkʀɛ, -ɛt] *adj* **1.** (*caché*) secret; **garder qc ~** to keep sth secret **2.** *soutenu* (*renfermé*) confidential

secrétaire [s(ə)kʀetɛʀ] **I.** *mf* secretary; **~ de direction** personal assistant; **~ de mairie** chief executive; **~ d'État aux Affaires étrangères/à la Guerre** Secretary of State for Foreign Affairs/War **II.** *m* secretary

secrétariat [s(ə)kʀetaʀja] *m* **1.** (*service administratif*) secretariat; **~ général des Nations Unies** general secretariat of the United Nations; **~ d'État** office of the secretary of state **2.** (*fonction officielle*) secretaryship **3.** (*emploi de secrétaire*) secretarial work **4.** (*bureau*) secretary's office

secrètement [səkʀɛtmɑ̃] *adv* secretly

sécréter [sekʀete] <5> *vt* **1.** ANAT to secrete **2.** (*engendrer*) to exude; **~ l'ennui/la fatigue** to exude boredom/tedium

sécrétion [sekʀesjɔ̃] *f* secretion

sectaire [sɛktɛʀ] *adj, mf* sectarian; **je ne suis pas ~** I'm not fanatical about it

secte [sɛkt] *f* **1.** (*groupe organisé*) sect **2.** *péj* (*clan*) clan

secteur [sɛktœʀ] *m* **1.** (*domaine*) *a.* ECON sector; **~ d'économie** economic sector **2.** (*coin*) *a.* ADMIN, POL, ELEC area; **~ sauvegardé** conservation area; **panne de ~** area outage **3.** MIL **~ de recrutement** recruitment zone

section [sɛksjɔ̃] *f* **1.** ADMIN, POL department; (*d'une voie ferrée*) section; (*d'un parcours*) stretch **2.** (*branche*) JUR branch; ECOLE course **3.** (*groupe*) **~ d'un syndicat** union group; MIL section; **~s spéciales** special sections **4.** MED amputation

sectionnement [sɛksjɔnmɑ̃] *m* severing

sectionner [sɛksjɔne] <1> **I.** *vt* **1.** (*couper: artère, fil*) to sever **2.** (*subdiviser: circonscrip-*

tion, groupe) to divide up **II.** *vpr* **se** ~ (*câble, fil*) to be severed

sécu [seky] *f abr de* **Sécurité sociale** Social Security

séculaire [sekylɛʀ] *adj* age-old

sécularisation [sekylaʀizasjɔ̃] *f* secularization

séculier, **-ière** [sekylje, -jɛʀ] *adj* secular

secundo [səgɔ̃do] *adv* secondly

sécurisant(e) [sekyʀizɑ̃, ɑ̃t] *adj* (*atmosphère, climat*) reassuring; **être** ~ to be reassuring

sécuriser [sekyʀize] <1> *vt* ~ **qn** to give sb a feeling of security; **ne pas se sentir très sécurisé** not to feel very secure

sécurité [sekyʀite] *f* **1.** (*opp: danger*) safety; (*au moyen de mesures organisées*) security; **règles/conseils de** ~ safety rules/advice; **être en** ~ to be safe **2.** (*sentiment*) security; **se sentir en** ~ to feel secure **3.** POL, ECON ~ **de l'emploi** job security; ~ **civile** civil defence *Brit,* civil defense *Am;* ~ **publique** law and order; ~ **routière** road safety ►**jouer la** ~ to put safety at risk; **en toute** ~ in complete safety

Sécurité [sekyʀite] *f* ~ **sociale** social security

sédatif [sedatif] *m* sedative; (*qui calme la douleur*) painkiller

sédentaire [sedɑ̃tɛʀ] *adj* sedentary

sédiment [sedimɑ̃] *m* GEO sediment

séditieux, **-euse** [sedisjø, -jøz] **I.** *adj soutenu* seditious; (*troupes*) insurgent **II.** *m, f soutenu* insurgent

sédition [sedisjɔ̃] *f soutenu* sedition

séducteur, **-trice** [sedyktœʀ, -tʀis] **I.** *adj* seductive **II.** *m, f* seducer, seductress *m, f*

séduction [sedyksjɔ̃] *f* **1.** (*pouvoir de séduire*) seduction; (*par le talent*) charm; **un discours plein de** ~ a speech full of charm; **succomber à la** ~ **de qn** to succumb to sb's charm **2.** (*attrait*) appeal

séduire [sedɥiʀ] *irr* **I.** *vt* **1.** (*tenter*) to charm **2.** (*plaire à: personne*) to appeal to; **être séduit par une idée** to be won over by an idea **II.** *vi* to charm

séduisant(e) [sedɥizɑ̃, ɑ̃t] *adj* seductive; (*personne*) charming; (*projet, proposition*) attractive; (*style*) appealing

segment [sɛgmɑ̃] *m* **1.** GEOM segment **2.** AUTO ~ **de frein** brake shoe; ~ **de piston** piston ring

segmenter [sɛgmɑ̃te] <1> *vt* (*sujet, surface*) to segment; ~ **en plusieurs parties** to split into several parts

ségrégation [segʀegasjɔ̃] *f* segregation

ségrégationniste [segʀegasjɔnist] **I.** *adj* (*idée, article, journal*) segregationist; (*politique, problème*) of segregation; (*troubles*) due to segregation **II.** *mf* segregationist

seiche [sɛʃ] *f* ZOOL cuttlefish; **os de** ~ cuttlebone

seigle [sɛgl] *m* rye

seigneur [sɛɲœʀ] *m* **1.** HIST lord **2.** (*personnage puissant*) ~ **de la finance** financial baron; ~ **de l'industrie** captain of industry ►**à tout** ~ **tout honneur** *prov* credit where credit is due; **grand** ~ fine gentleman; **jouer** [*o* **faire**] **le grand** ~ to act like a lord; **vivre en grand** ~ to live like a lord

Seigneur [sɛɲœʀ] *m* REL **le** ~ the Lord

sein [sɛ̃] *m* ANAT breast; **donner le** ~ **à un enfant, nourrir un enfant au** ~ to breastfeed a child

Seine [sɛn] *f* **la** ~ the Seine

seing [sɛ̃] *m* **acte sous** ~ **privé** private agreement

séisme [seism] *m a. fig* earthquake

seize [sɛz] *adj* sixteen; *v. a.* **cinq**

seizième [sɛzjɛm] **I.** *adj antéposé* sixteenth **II.** *m* **1.** (*fraction*) sixteenth **2.** SPORT ~ **de finale** *fourth round before the final of a competition; v. a.* **cinquième**

séjour [seʒuʀ] *m* **1.** (*fait de séjourner*) stay; (*vacances*) holiday *Brit,* vacation *Am;* **faire un** ~ **en Italie** to go to Italy; **mes ~s en Italie** my time in [*o* visits to] Italy **2.** (*salon*) living room

séjourner [seʒuʀne] <1> *vi* to stay

sel [sɛl] *m* **1.** GASTR, CHIM salt; ~ **de cuisine/table** cooking/table salt; **gros** ~ rock salt; **~s de bain** bath salts; **les ~s** smelling salts **2.** (*piquant*) spice; (*d'une histoire*) wit ►**ne pas manquer de** ~ (*histoire, remarque*) to have a certain wit

sélectif, **-ive** [selɛktif, -iv] *adj* selective

sélection [selɛksjɔ̃] *f* **1.** SPORT, ZOOL, BIO (*fait de choisir, choix*) selection; **faire une** ~ to choose **2.** (*choix avec règles et critères*) selection; **critères de** ~ selection criteria; **match de** ~ selection match; **test** [*o* **épreuve**] **de** ~ trial; **bouton de** ~ TECH selection button

sélectionné(e) [selɛksjɔne] *m(f)* SPORT selected player

sélectionner [selɛksjɔne] <1> *vt* (*choisir*) *a.* INFOR to select

sélectionneur, **-euse** [selɛksjɔnœʀ, -øz] *m, f* selector

self [sɛlf] *m inf* self-service restaurant

self-service [sɛlfsɛʀvis] <self-services> *m* **1.** (*magasin*) self-service shop **2.** (*restaurant*) self-service restaurant

selle [sɛl] *f* **1.** (*siège*) *a.* GASTR saddle **2.** *pl* (*matières fécales*) stools

seller [sele] <1> *vt* to saddle

sellette [sɛlɛt] *f* **mettre qn sur la** ~ to put sb in the hot seat

sellier, **-ière** [selje, -jɛʀ] *m, f* saddler

selon [s(ə)lɔ̃] *prep* **1.** (*conformément à*) ~ **votre volonté/les instructions** in accordance with your wishes/the instructions **2.** (*en fonction de, d'après*) ~ **l'humeur/mes moyens** according to one's mood/my means; ~ **leur âge et leur taille** according to their age and height; **c'est** ~ *inf* it depends; ~ **moi** in my opinion

semailles [s(ə)mɑj] *fpl* sowing + *vb sing;*

(*graines*) seeds

semaine [s(ə)mɛn] *f* (*sept jours*) week; **la ~ de trente-cinq heures** the thirty-five hour week; **à la ~** weekly; **en ~** during the week ►**il le fera la ~ des quatre jeudis** *inf* he'll never do it in a month of Sundays

sémantique [semɑ̃tik] **I.** *adj* semantic **II.** *f* semantics + *vb sing*

sémaphore [semafɔʀ] *m* **1.** NAUT semaphore **2.** CHEMDFER semaphore signal

semblable [sɑ̃blabl] **I.** *adj* **1.** (*pareil*) similar; **rien de ~** nothing like it **2.** *antéposé* (*tel*) such; **une ~ désinvolture** such casualness **3.** (*ressemblant*) like; **~ à qn/qc** like sb/sth **II.** *mf* **1.** (*prochain*) fellow being **2.** (*congénère*) **lui et ses ~s** him and his kind

semblant [sɑ̃blɑ̃] *m* **un ~ de jardin** a garden of sorts; **un ~ de bonheur/vérité** a semblance of happiness/truth; **retrouver un ~ de calme** to find some sort of calm ►**faire ~ de dormir** to pretend to be asleep; **elle ne pleure pas: elle fait juste ~!** she's not crying: she's just pretending!; **faire ~ de rien** *inf* to pretend to take no notice

sembler [sɑ̃ble] <1> **I.** *vi* **~ préoccupé** to seem preoccupied; **tu me sembles nerveux** you seem nervous (to me) **II.** *vi impers* **1.** (*paraître*) **il semble que …** it seems that …; **il semblerait que …** it would appear that … **2.** (*avoir l'impression de*) **il me semble bien vous avoir déjà rencontré** I have the feeling I've already met you **3.** (*paraître*) **il me semble, à ce qu'il me semble** it seems to me; **semble-t-il** so it seems

semelle [s(ə)mɛl] *f* sole; **~ de cuir** leather sole; **~ intérieure** insole ►**être de la (vraie) ~** (*bifteck, escalope*) to be as tough as leather; **ne pas avancer d'une ~** not to move an inch forward; **ne pas céder** [*o* **reculer**] **d'une ~** not to give an inch; **ne pas lâcher** [*o* **quitter**] **qn d'une ~** to stick to sb like a leech

semence [s(ə)mɑ̃s] *f* **1.** AGR seeds *pl;* **~ de blé** wheat seed **2.** (*sperme*) seed **3.** (*clou*) tack

semer [s(ə)me] <4> **I.** *vi* to sow **II.** *vt* **1.** AGR to sow; **cette plate-bande est semée de pensées** this border is sown with pansies **2.** (*joncher: confettis, fleurs*) to strew; **être semé de pétales de roses** to be strewn with rose petals; **une robe semée de diamants** a diamond-studded dress **3.** (*propager: discorde, zizanie*) to sow; (*terreur, panique*) to bring **4.** (*truffer*) **~ un texte de citations** to sprinkle a text with quotations; **être semé de difficultés** to be strewn with difficulties **5.** (*se débarrasser de*) to get rid of **6.** *inf* (*égarer*) to lose

semestre [s(ə)mɛstʀ] *m* half-year; UNIV semester; **par ~** half-yearly

semestriel(le) [s(ə)mɛstʀijɛl] *adj* (*assemblée*) six-monthly; (*bulletin, revue*) biannual

semi-conserve [s(ə)mikɔ̃sɛʀv] <semi-conserves> *f* semi-preserve **semi-consonne** [səmikɔ̃sɔn] *f* semiconsonant

sémillant(e) [semijɑ̃, jɑ̃t] *adj iron, soutenu* spirited

séminaire [seminɛʀ] *m* seminary

séminariste [seminaʀist] *m* seminarist

semi-remorque [səmiʀ(ə)mɔʀk] <semi-remorques> **I.** *m* articulated lorry *Brit,* semi(trailer) *Am* **II.** *f* (*remorque*) trailer

semis [s(ə)mi] *m* **1.** *pl* sowing + *vb sing;* (*plants*) seedlings **2.** (*motif décoratif*) pattern

sémite [semit] *adj* Semitic

semonce [səmɔ̃s] *f* rebuke; **coup de ~** warning shot

semoule [s(ə)mul] **I.** *f* GASTR semolina ►**pédaler dans la ~** *inf* to flounder; (*police, enquêteurs*) to be at a dead end **II.** *app* (*sucre*) caster

sempiternel(le) [sɑ̃pitɛʀnɛl] *adj antéposé* eternal; (*chapeau, costume*) timeless

sénat [sena] *m* POL, HIST senate

Sénat [sena] *m* **le ~** the Senate

> The **Sénat** is the upper house of the French Parliament and sits in the Palais de Luxembourg. There are 295 senators, elected for nine years. New laws can only be come in to force with the agreement of both chambers.

sénateur, -trice [senatœʀ, tʀis] *m, f* senator

sénatoriales [senatɔʀjal] *fpl* senate elections

Sénégal [senegal] *m* **le ~** Senegal

sénégalais(e) [senegalɛ, ɛz] *adj* Senegalese

Sénégalais(e) [senegalɛ, ɛz] *m(f)* Senegalese

sénescence [senesɑ̃s] *f* senescence

sénile [senil] *adj* senile

sénilité [senilite] *f* senility

senior [senjɔʀ] **I.** *adj* (*équipe*) senior **II.** *mf* **1.** (*sportif plus âgé*) senior **2.** (*vieillard*) **les ~s** the over-50s

sens¹ [sɑ̃s] *m* (*signification*) meaning; **un mot à double ~** a word with a double meaning; **au ~ large/figuré** in a broad/figurative sense; **être dépourvu de tout ~** [*o* **n'avoir aucun ~**] to have no meaning; **être plein de ~** to be full of meaning

sens² [sɑ̃s] *m* **1.** (*direction*) direction; **dans le ~ de la longueur** lengthwise; **dans le ~ des aiguilles d'une montre** clockwise; **dans tous les ~** all over the place; **partir dans tous les ~** to go in all directions; **en ~ inverse** the other way; **aller/rouler en ~ inverse** to go/drive in the other direction; **revenir en ~ inverse** to come back the other way round; **caresser dans le ~ du poil** to stroke the right way **2.** (*idée*) sense; **dans le ~ de qn/qc** along the same lines as sb/sth; **aller dans le même ~** to go the same way; **aller dans le ~ d'un compromis** to work towards a compromise; **aller dans le bon ~** (*personne*) to heading in the right direction; **le ~ de l'Histoire** the tide of history; **donner des ordres dans**

ce ~ to give orders along these lines **3.** AUTO ~ **giratoire** roundabout *Brit,* traffic circle *Am;* ~ **unique** one-way street; ~ **interdit** one-way street; (*panneau*) no entry; **rouler en** ~ **interdit** to drive the wrong way up a one-way street ►~ **dessus dessous** upside-down; **raisonnements à** ~ **unique** one-sided arguments; **en ce** ~ **que ...** in the sense that ...; **en un** (**certain**) ~ in a way

sens³ [sɑ̃s] *m* sense; **avoir le** ~ **du rythme** to have a sense of rhythm; ~ **de l'humour** sense of humour [*o* humor *Am*]; ~ **de l'orientation** sense of direction; ~ **de la répartie** gift of repartee ►**reprendre ses** ~ to regain consciousness; **tomber sous le** ~ to stand to reason; **à mon** ~ to my mind

sensas(**s**) [sɑ̃sɑs] *adj inv, inf abr de* **sensationnel**

sensation [sɑ̃sasjɔ̃] *f* sensation; (*émotion*) feeling; **avoir une** ~ **de chaleur** to get a feeling of warmth; ~ **de brûlure** burning sensation; **avoir une** ~ **de malaise** to feel weak ►~**s fortes** thrills; **faire** ~ to create a sensation; **presse à** ~ tabloid press

sensationnel [sɑ̃sasjɔnɛl] *m* sensational

sensationnel(**le**) [sɑ̃sasjɔnɛl] *adj* sensational

sensé(**e**) [sɑ̃se] *adj* sensible

sensibilisation [sɑ̃sibilizasjɔ̃] *f* ~ **à qc** awareness of sth

sensibiliser [sɑ̃sibilize] <1> *vt* ~ **qn à** [*o* **sur**] **qc** to make sb aware of sth

sensibilité [sɑ̃sibilite] *f* **1.** PSYCH (*d'une personne*) sensitiveness; **être d'une grande** ~ to be very sensitive **2.** ANAT sensitivity; **être d'une extrême** ~ to be very sensitive; ~ **au froid** sensitive to cold

sensible [sɑ̃sibl] *adj* **1.** (*émotif, fragile, opp: indifférent, délicat*) sensitive; **être** ~ **aux attentions** to notice kindnesses; **être très** ~ **de la gorge** to have a very delicate throat **2.** (*perceptible*) noticeable **3.** (*fin: odorat, ouïe*) sensitive **4.** PHILOS sensory; (*univers, monde*) physical

sensiblement [sɑ̃sibləmɑ̃] *adv* noticeably

sensiblerie [sɑ̃sibləʀi] *f* sentimentality

sensoriel(**le**) [sɑ̃sɔʀjɛl] *adj* (*vie, organe, nerf*) sense; (*éducation, information*) sensory

sensualité [sɑ̃sɥalite] *f* sensuality

sensuel(**le**) [sɑ̃sɥɛl] *adj* sensual

sentence [sɑ̃tɑ̃s] *f* **1.** JUR sentence **2.** (*adage*) maxim

sentencieux, **-euse** [sɑ̃tɑ̃sjø, -jøz] *adj* sententious

senteur [sɑ̃tœʀ] *f soutenu* scent

senti(**e**) [sɑ̃ti] *adj* **un discours bien** ~ a very direct speech; **vérité bien** ~**e** home-truth

sentier [sɑ̃tje] *m* path; ~ **de grande randonnée** long-distance footpath ►**sortir des** ~**s battus** to go off the beaten track

sentiment [sɑ̃timɑ̃] *m* **1.** (*émotion*) feeling **2.** (*sensibilité*) emotion **3.** (*conscience*) ~ **de sa valeur** awareness of one's worth **4.** (*impression*) feeling; **le** ~ **d'être un raté** the feeling of being a loser **5.** *pl* (*formule de politesse*) **mes meilleurs** ~**s** my best wishes **6.** *pl* (*tendance*) disposition; **avoir de bons/mauvais** ~**s à l'égard de qn** to be well/badly disposed towards sb ►**partir d'un bon** ~ to have good intentions; **prendre qn par les** ~**s** to appeal to sb's feelings

sentimental(**e**) [sɑ̃timɑ̃tal, o] <-aux> **I.** *adj* **1.** (*sensible: nature, personne*) romantic **2.** (*amoureux: problème, vie*) love **3.** (*opp: rationnel: attachement, réaction, valeur*) sentimental **4.** *péj* (*avec sensibilité*) sentimental; (*film*) soppy **II.** *m(f)* sentimentalist

sentinelle [sɑ̃tinɛl] *f* sentry ►**en** ~ on sentry duty

sentir [sɑ̃tiʀ] <10> **I.** *vt* **1.** (*humer*) to smell **2.** (*goûter*) to taste **3.** (*ressentir*) to feel; **je sens la fatigue me gagner** I feel tiredness coming over me **4.** (*avoir une odeur*) ~ **la fumée** to smell of smoke; **ça sent le brûlé** there's a smell of burning; **cette pièce sent le renfermé** this room smells musty **5.** (*avoir un goût*) ~ **l'ail/la vanille** to taste of garlic/vanilla **6.** (*annoncer*) **ça sent la neige** there's snow in the air **7.** (*pressentir*) to feel; ~ **qu'il va pleuvoir** to feel that it's going to rain **8.** (*rendre sensible*) **faire** ~ **son autorité à qn** to make sb feel one's authority; **faire** ~ **à qn qu'il est allé trop loin** to make sb realize that he has gone too far ►**je ne peux pas la** ~ I can't stand her **II.** *vi* **1.** (*avoir une odeur*) to smell; ~ **bon** to smell good **2.** (*puer*) to stink; **il sent des pieds** his feet stink **III.** *vpr* **1.** (*se trouver*) **se** ~ **fatigué** to feel tired **2.** (*être perceptible*) **qc se sent** (*amélioration, changement, effet*) sth can be felt; **se faire** ~ (*conséquences, effet*) to start to be felt ►**ne pas se** ~ **bien** *inf* not to feel well; **se** ~ **mal** to feel ill; **ils ne peuvent pas se** ~ they can't stand each other; **ne plus se** ~ **de joie/bonheur** to be beside oneself with joy/happiness

séparation [sepaʀasjɔ̃] *f* **1.** (*action de séparer*) separation; (*de convives*) parting; (*de manifestants*) dispersion **2.** JUR (*de biens*) separate ownership (*of property by marriage partners*); ~ **de corps** legal separation; ~ **de fait** voluntary separation **3.** POL separation **4.** (*distinction*) dividing line **5.** (*cloison*) (**mur de**) ~ dividing wall

séparatiste [sepaʀatist] *adj, mf* separatist

séparé(**e**) [sepaʀe] *adj* separate

séparément [sepaʀemɑ̃] *adv* (*examiner*) separately; (*vivre*) apart

séparer [sepaʀe] <1> **I.** *vt* **1.** (*désunir, détacher, diviser*) to separate; ~ **qc en deux groupes** to divide sth into two groups; ~ **un enfant de ses parents** to take a child away from his parents **2.** (*être interposé entre*) to separate; **la Manche sépare la France de la Grande-Bretagne** the Channel separates France from Great-Britain **3.** (*différencier: idées, théories, problèmes*) to distinguish between; ~ **la théorie de la pratique** to differentiate between theory and practice **II.** *vpr* **1.** (*se défaire de*) **se ~ de qc** to part with sth; **se ~ de qn** to let sb go **2.** (*se diviser*) **se ~ de qc** (*route*) to leave sth; **se ~ en qc** (*rivière, route*) to split into sth; **nos routes se séparent** we're going our separate ways **3.** (*se détacher*) **se ~** to break up; **se ~ de qc** to break off from sth **4.** (*se disperser*) **se ~** to disperse

sept [sɛt] *adj* seven; *v. a.* **cinq**

septante [sɛptɑ̃t] *adj Belgique, Suisse* (*soixante-dix*) seventy; *v. a.* **cinq, cinquante**

septantième [sɛ̃ptɑ̃tjɛm] *adj antéposé, Belgique, Suisse* (*soixante-dixième*) seventieth; *v. a.* **cinquième**

septembre [sɛptɑ̃bʀ] *m* September; *v. a.* **août**

septennat [sɛptena] *m* seven-year period; POL seven-year (presidential) mandate

septentrional(e) [sɛptɑ̃tʀijɔnal, o] <-aux> *adj* northern

septicémie [sɛptisemi] *f* MED septicaemia *Brit,* septicemia *Am*

septième [sɛtjɛm] *adj antéposé* seventh; *v. a.* **cinquième**

septièmement [sɛtjɛmmɑ̃] *adv* seventhly

septique [sɛptik] *adj* MED septic

septuagénaire [sɛptɥaʒenɛʀ] *adj, mf* septuagenarian

sépulture [sepyltyʀ] *f* **1.** (*acte*) burial **2.** (*tombeau*) tomb

séquelle [sekɛl] *f* (*d'un accident, d'une maladie*) after-effect

séquence [sekɑ̃s] *f* **1.** CINE, TV, LING sequence **2.** INFOR string

séquentiel(le) [sekɑ̃sjɛl] *adj* INFOR sequential

séquestration [sekɛstʀasjɔ̃] *f* (*de biens*) impoundment; ~ **de personne** illegal confinement; ~ **d'enfant** child kidnapping

séquestrer [sekɛstʀe] <1> *vt* **1.** JUR (*biens*) to impound **2.** (*enfermer: personne*) to imprison; (*otage*) to hold

sera [səʀa], **serai** [səʀɛ] *fut de* **être**

seras [səʀa] *fut de* **être**

serbe [sɛʀb] **I.** *adj* Serb(ian) **II.** *m* Serb(ian); *v. a.* **français**

Serbe [sɛʀb] *mf* Serb(ian)

Serbie [sɛʀbi] *f* **la ~** Serbia

serein(e) [səʀɛ̃, ɛn] *adj* serene; (*objectif*) dispassionate

sereinement [səʀɛnmɑ̃] *adv* serenely; (*agir, juger*) dispassionately

sérénade [seʀenad] *f* **1.** MUS serenade **2.** (*concert*) **donner une ~ à qn** to serenade sb **3.** *inf* (*scène*) fuss **4.** *inf* (*charivari*) racket

sérénité [seʀenite] *f* serenity; **en toute ~** quite calmly

serez [səʀe] *fut de* **être**

serf, serve [sɛʀ(f), sɛʀv] **I.** *adj* **la condition serve** serfdom **II.** *m, f* serf

sergent [sɛʀʒɑ̃] *m* sergeant

série [seʀi] *f* **1.** (*ensemble: de casseroles, volumes*) set; ~ **spéciale d'un ouvrage** special edition of a work **2.** (*succession*) string **3.** CINE, TV series **4.** COM **véhicule de ~** mass-produced vehicle ▸~ **noire** (*roman*) crime thriller; (*succession de malheurs*) string of disasters; **fabriquer qc en ~** to mass-produce sth; **tueur en ~** serial killer; **hors ~** (*extraordinaire*) outstanding; ECON custom-built

sérieusement [seʀjøzmɑ̃] *adv* **1.** (*vraiment: croire, penser*) seriously **2.** (*avec sérieux: agir, travailler*) conscientiously; **vous parlez ~?** are you serious? **3.** (*gravement*) seriously

sérieux [seʀjø] *m* **1.** (*fiabilité, conscience*) reliability; (*d'une entreprise, d'un projet*) seriousness; (*d'un employé*) conscientiousness **2.** (*air grave, gravité: d'une situation, d'un état*) seriousness; **garder son ~** to keep a straight face ▸**prendre qc au ~** to take sth seriously; **se prendre au ~** to take oneself seriously

sérieux, -euse [seʀjø, -jøz] *adj* **1.** (*opp: inconséquent*) serious; **pas ~, s'abstenir** no time wasters **2.** (*grave, opp: plaisantin*) serious; **être atteint d'une maladie sérieuse** to suffer from a serious illness **3.** (*digne de confiance*) reliable; (*promesse*) genuine **4.** (*consciencieux: élève, apprenti*) conscientious **5.** (*digne d'intérêt: problème*) genuine; (*renseignement*) reliable **6.** (*approfondi: études, recherches, travail*) worthwhile **7.** *a. antéposé* (*fort: différence, somme*) considerable; (*raison*) good **8.** (*sage*) earnest

serin [s(ə)ʀɛ̃] *m* canary

seriner [s(ə)ʀine] <1> *vt inf* (*rabâcher*) ~ **qc à un enfant** to drum sth into a child

seringue [s(ə)ʀɛ̃g] *f* MED syringe

serment [sɛʀmɑ̃] *m* (*engagement solennel*) oath; ~ **sur l'honneur** solemn oath; ~ **professionnel** professional oath; ~ **d'Hippocrate** MED Hippocratic oath; **prêter ~** to take an oath; **faire un faux ~** to make a false oath; **sous ~** under oath

sermon [sɛʀmɔ̃] *m* **1.** REL sermon **2.** *péj* (*discours moralisateur*) lecture; **faire un ~ à qn** to lecture sb

sermonner [sɛʀmɔne] <1> *vt* (*réprimander*) ~ **qn** to lecture sb; **se faire ~** to get a lecture

séronégatif, -ive [seʀonegatif, -iv] *adj* HIV-negative

séropositif, -ive [seʀopozitif, -iv] **I.** *adj* seropositive; (*en parlant du sida*) HIV positive **II.** *m, f* person who is seropositive; (*atteint du sida*) person who is HIV positive

séropositivité [seʀopozitivite] *f* **constater la ~ de qn** to confirm sb as seropositive; (*due au virus du sida*) to confirm sb as HIV positive; **un film qui traite de la ~** a film about HIV

serpe [sɛʀp] *f* AGR billhook ▸**un visage/personnage taillé à la** [*o* **à coups de**] ~ a rugged face/character; **faire qc à la ~** to do sth in a slapdash way

serpent [sɛʀpɑ̃] *m* **1.** (*reptile*) snake; ~ **à**

S

lunettes Indian cobra; ~ **à sonnettes** rattlesnake **2.** (*personne mauvaise*) **langue de ~** evil gossip **3.** ECON **~ monétaire européen** European currency snake

serpenter [sɛʀpɑ̃te] <1> *vi* (*chemin, rivière, vallée*) to meander; **le sentier montait en serpentant** the path wound its way up

serpentin [sɛʀpɑ̃tɛ̃] *m* (*ruban*) streamer

serpette [sɛʀpɛt] *f* pruning knife

serpillière [sɛʀpijɛʀ] *f* floorcloth; **passer la ~** to clean up the floor

serpolet [sɛʀpɔlɛ] *m* wild thyme

serrage [sɛʀaʒ] *m* tightening; **le ~ de ce nœud est trop fort** this knot's been pulled too tight

serre [sɛʀ] *f* AGR greenhouse; (*serre chauffée*) hothouse; **fruits/légumes de ~** greenhouse fruits/vegetables

serré [seʀe] *adv* **1.** (*avec prudence*) **jouer ~** to play a tight game; *fig* to play it tight **2.** (*avec peu de moyens: vivre*) on a tight budget **3.** (*brèvement: écrire*) in a cramped hand

serré(e) [seʀe] *adj* **1.** (*fort: café, alcool*) strong **2.** (*petit: budget, délai*) tight **3.** (*dense: forêt, foule*) dense; **en rangs ~s** in serried ranks; **des mailles ~es** close stitches **4.** (*rigoureux: débat, discussion*) closely-argued; (*combat, course*) close; (*style*) taut **5.** (*fauché: train de vie*) impoverished; **être ~** to be pressed for cash

serrer [seʀe] <1> **I.** *vt* **1.** (*tenir en exerçant une pression*) to squeeze; **~ qn/qc dans ses bras/contre soi** to hold sb/sth in one's arms/against oneself; **~ qn à la gorge** to strangle sb **2.** (*contracter: dents, mâchoires, poings*) to clench; (*lèvres*) to tighten; **avoir la gorge serrée** to have a lump in one's throat; **il a le cœur serré devant qc** sth brings a lump to his throat; **~ les fesses** *fig, inf* to be scared stiff **3.** (*rendre très étroit: ceinture, nœud*) to tighten **4.** (*se tenir près de*) **~ qn/qc** to keep close behind sb/sth; **~ une femme** *fig* to chat a woman up; **~ qn/qc contre un mur** to wedge sb/sth against a wall; **serre bien ta droite!** keep to the right! **5.** (*rapprocher: invités*) to squeeze up; **~ les lignes/les mots** to pack the lines/words closer together; **~ les rangs** to close ranks; **être serrés** (*personnes, objets*) to be squashed together **6.** (*restreindre: budget*) to cut back; (*dépenses*) to cut back on; **~ les délais** to bring the deadlines forward **II.** *vi* **~ à droite/à gauche** to keep to the right/left **III.** *vpr* **se ~ 1.** (*se rapprocher: personnes*) to squeeze up; **se ~ contre qn** to squeeze up against sb; **serrons-nous autour du feu!** let's huddle around the fire! **2.** (*se contracter*) **sa gorge se serre** his throat tightened ►**se ~ la** ceinture *inf* to tighten one's belt

serre-tête [sɛʀtɛt] *m inv* **1.** (*bandeau*) headband **2.** SPORT skullcap

serrure [seʀyʀ] *f* lock; **~ de sûreté** security lock

serrurerie [seʀyʀʀi] *f* **1.** (*objet*) ironwork *no pl* **2.** (*métier*) locksmithing

serrurier, -ière [seʀyʀje, -jɛʀ] *m, f* locksmith

sertir [sɛʀtiʀ] <8> *vt* **1.** (*enchâsser: diamant, pierre précieuse*) to set; **~ qc dans un diadème** to set sth in a tiara **2.** TECH to crimp

sérum [seʀɔm] *m* PHYSIOL, MED serum; **~ antidiphtérique/antirabique** anti-diphtheric/anti-rabies serum; **~ antivenimeux/antitétanique** anti-venom/anti-tetanus serum; **~ physiologique** saline solution

servante [sɛʀvɑ̃t] *f* maid

serveur [sɛʀvœʀ] *m* INFOR server; **~ de courrier** mail server

serveur, -euse [sɛʀvœʀ, -øz] *m, f* (*employé*) waiter

serviable [sɛʀvjabl] *adj* helpful

service [sɛʀvis] *m* **1.** (*au restaurant, bar, à l'hôtel, dans un magasin*) service; **manger au premier/second ~** to eat at the first/second sitting; **le ~ est assuré jusqu'à ...** (*au restaurant*) meals are served until ... **2.** (*pourboire*) service charge; **(le) ~ (est) compris** (the) service charge (is) included **3.** *pl* (*aide*) services; **se passer des ~s de qn** *form* to dispense with sb's services **4.** (*organisme officiel*) **~ administratif** (*d'État*) administrative department; (*d'une commune*) administrative service; **~s de l'immigration** immigration department; **~ du feu** *Suisse* fire brigade *Brit*, fire department *Am*; **~ d'ordre** marshals *pl*; **le ~ public** the public services *pl*; **entreprise du ~ public** national utility company; **~ de santé** health service; **les ~s sociaux** social services; **~s spéciaux/secrets** special/secret services **5.** (*département*) department; **~ (des) achats** purchasing department; **~ après-vente** after-sales service; **~ administratif/~s administratifs** (*d'une entreprise*) adminstration department/departments; **~ (de) dépannage** breakdown service; **~ du personnel** personnel department **6.** MED department; **~ de cardiologie/d'urologie** cardiology/urology department; **~ de réanimation** intensive care unit; **~ des urgences** accident and emergency (department) *Brit*, emergency room *Am* **7.** MIL national service; **~ civil** non-military national service; **être bon pour le ~** to be fit for military service; **faire son ~ (militaire)** to do one's national [*o* military] service **8.** (*activité professionnelle*) duty; **pendant le ~** while on duty; **heures de ~** hours on duty; **être de ~** to be on duty **9.** ECON (*prestations*) service **10.** (*action de servir*) service; **~ de l'État** service of the State; **escalier de ~** service staircase **11.** (*faveur*) favour *Brit*, favor *Am*; **demander un ~ à qn** to ask sb a favour; **rendre ~ à qn** to do sb a favour; **qu'y a-t-il pour votre ~?** how can I help you? **12.** (*assortiment pour la table*) set; **~ à fondue/raclette** fondue/raclette set; **~ à thé** tea set **13.** (*engagement au tennis, au volley-ball*) service **14.** REL ~ (**religieux**) (religious) service; ~ **funèbre** funeral service ▶**à ton/votre** ~**!** at your service!; ~ **en ligne** on-line service; **entrer en** ~ (*unité de production*) to come into service; **mettre qc en** ~ to put sth into operation; **hors** ~ out of order

serviette [sɛʀvjɛt] *f* **1.** (*pour la toilette*) towel; ~ **de plage /de bain** beach/bath towel; ~ **hygiénique** sanitary towel *Brit*, sanitary napkin *Am* **2.** (*serviette de table*) napkin; ~ **en papier** paper napkin **3.** (*attaché-case: d'un homme, d'une femme d'affaires*) briefcase

servile [sɛʀvil] *adj* **1.** (*obséquieux, trop fidèle*) servile **2.** *postposé* HIST **condition** ~ serfdom; **travail** ~ servile work

servir [sɛʀviʀ] *irr* **I.** *vt* to serve; **on lui sert le petit-déjeuner au lit** they serve him breakfast in bed; **c'est servi!** *inf* ready!; **on vous sert, Madame/Monsieur?** are you being served Madam/Sir?; **qu'est-ce que je vous sers?** what would you like? ▶**on n'est jamais si bien servi que par soi-même** *prov* if you want a job done properly, do it yourself **II.** *vi* **1.** (*être utile: voiture, outil, conseil, explication*) to be useful; **ça me sert à la réparation/à faire la cuisine** (*machine, outil*) I use it for doing repairs/for cooking; **à quoi cet outil peut-il bien** ~**?** what can this tool be used for?; **rien ne sert de t'énerver** it's no use getting annoyed **2.** (*tenir lieu de*) ~ **de guide à qn** to be a guide for sb; **ça te servira de leçon!** that'll teach you a lesson!; **cela lui sert de prétexte** he uses that as an excuse **3.** (*être utilisable*) to be usable; **ce vélo peut encore/ne peut plus** ~ this bike can still/no longer be used **4.** SPORT (*au tennis, au volleyball*) to serve ▶**rien ne sert de courir, il faut partir à point** *prov* more haste, less speed **III.** *vpr* **1.** (*utiliser*) **se** ~ **d'un copain/article pour** *+infin* to use a friend/article to *+infin;* **se** ~ **de ses relations** to use one's acquaintances; **ne pas savoir se** ~ **de ses dix doigts** to be all thumbs **2.** (*prendre soi-même qc*) **se** ~ to help oneself; **se** ~ **des légumes** to help oneself to vegetables **3.** (*être servi*) **ce vin se sert frais** this wine should be served chilled

serviteur [sɛʀvitœʀ] *m* (*domestique*) servant

servitude [sɛʀvityd] *f* **1.** *pl* (*contraintes*) constraints **2.** (*esclavage*) slavery; **réduire qn à la** ~ to enslave sb **3.** JUR (*obligation*) easement; ~ **de passage** right of way

ses [se] *dét poss v.* **sa, son**

sésame [sezam] *m* **1.** BOT sesame **2.** (*passepartout*) key ▶**Sésame, ouvre-toi** open Sesame

session [sesjɔ̃] *f* **1.** (*séance*) sitting; ~ **d'examens** exam session **2.** INFOR session; **ouvrir/clore une** ~ to log on/off

set [sɛt] *m* **1.** SPORT set; ~ **gagnant** winning set **2.** (*nécessaire*) ~ **de rasage** shaving kit

setter [setɛʀ] *m* ~ **irlandais** Irish setter

seuil [sœj] **I.** *m* **1.** (*pas de la porte*) doorstep; **rester sur le** ~ **de la porte** to remain on the doorstep; **franchir le** ~ to step through the door **2.** (*limite*) threshold; ~ **auditif** auditory threshold; ~ **de pauvreté** poverty line; ~ **de rentabilité** break-even point **II.** *app inv* **valeur/salaire** ~ threshold value/salary

seul(e) [sœl] **I.** *adj* **1.** (*sans compagnie*) alone; **tout** ~ all alone; **être** ~ **à** ~ to be alone with each other; **parler à qn** ~ **à** ~ to speak to sb privately; **parler tout** ~ to speak to oneself; **eh vous, vous n'êtes pas** ~**!** there are other people here, you know!; **ça descend tout** ~ *inf* it goes down a treat **2.** (*célibataire*) single **3.** *antéposé* (*unique*) single; ~ **et unique** one and only; **une** ~**e fois** once; **être** ~ **de son espèce** to be unique; **déclarer d'une** ~**e voix** to unanimously declare; **pour la** ~**e raison que ...** for the single reason that ... **4.** (*uniquement*) only; **il est** ~ **capable de le faire** he alone is able to do it; ~**s les invités sont admis** only guests are admitted; ~ **le résultat importe** only the result is important **II.** *m(f)* **le/la** ~(**e**) the only one; **vous n'êtes pas le** ~ **à ...** you're not the only one to ...; **un/une** ~(**e**) only one

seulement [sœlmɑ̃] *adv* just ▶**non** ~ **..., mais** (**encore**) not only ..., but; **pas** ~ *soutenu* not just; **si** ~ if only

sève [sɛv] *f* BOT sap

sévère [sevɛʀ] *adj* **1.** (*rigoureux: climat*) harsh; (*critique, jugement*) severe; (*concurrence*) strong; (*lutte*) hard; (*sélection*) rigorous **2.** (*grave: crise, pertes*) severe; (*échec*) terrible

sévèrement [sevɛʀmɑ̃] *adv* **1.** (*durement: punir, critiquer*) severely; (*éduquer, juger*) harshly; (*battu*) heavily **2.** (*gravement*) seriously

sévérité [seveʀite] *f* severity; (*d'une critique, d'un verdict, climat*) harshness; **être d'une grande** ~ to be very severe; **un regard d'une telle** ~ **que ...** a look so severe that ...; **style d'une grande** ~ very severe style

sévices [sevis] *mpl* physical abuse; **exercer des** ~ **sur qn** to abuse sb

sévir [seviʀ] <8> *vi* **1.** (*punir*) ~ **contre qn/qc** to take strong measures against sb/sth **2.** (*exercer ses ravages: malfaiteur, professeur*) to be on the loose; (*fléau*) to be unleashed; (*grippe*) to rage; (*doctrine*) to be taken seriously

sevrage [səvʀaʒ] *m* weaning

sevrer [səvʀe] <1> *vt* (*cesser d'allaiter*) to wean

sèvres [sɛvʀ] *m* Sèvres porcelain; (*objet*) *object made out of Sèvres porcelain*

sexagénaire [sɛksaʒenɛʀ] **I.** *adj* **un homme/une femme** ~ a sixty-year-old (man/woman); **être** ~ to be sixty years old **II.** *mf* sixty-year-old

sex-appeal [sɛksapil] <sex-appeals> *m* sex appeal

sexe [sɛks] *m* **1.** (*catégorie, sexualité*) sex

2. (*organe*) sex organs ►**discuter du ~ des anges** to discuss futilities

sexisme [sɛksism] *m* sexism

sexiste [sɛksist] *adj, mf* sexist

sexologue [sɛksɔlɔg] *mf* sexologist

sex-shop [sɛksʃɔp] <sex-shops> *m* sex shop **sex-symbol** [sɛkssɛ̃bɔl] <sex-symbols> *m* sex symbol

sextant [sɛkstɑ̃] *m* sextant

sexualité [sɛksɥalite] *f* sexuality; **les perversions de la ~** sexual perversions

sexuel(le) [sɛksɥɛl] *adj* **1.** (*relatif à la sexualité*) sexual; (*éducation*) sex **2.** (*relatif au sexe*) sex

sexuellement [sɛksɥɛlmɑ̃] *adv* sexually

sexy [sɛksi] *adj inv, inf* sexy

seyant(e) [sɛjɑ̃, jɑ̃t] **I.** *part prés de* **seoir** **II.** *adj* becoming

Seychelles [sɛʃɛl(ə)] *fpl* **les ~** the Seychelles

shah [ʃa] *m* shah

shampo(o)ing [ʃɑ̃pwɛ̃] *m* shampoo; **~ colorant** wash-in hair dye; **faire un ~ à qn** to shampoo sb's hair

shampouiner [ʃɑ̃pwine] <1> *vt v.* **shampooiner**

shérif [ʃeʀif] *m* sheriff

Shetland [ʃɛtlɑ̃:d] *fpl* **les Îles ~** the Shetland Islands; **les Îles ~ du Sud** the South Shetland Islands

shoot [ʃut] *m* shot

shooter [ʃute] <1> **I.** *vi* SPORT to shoot **II.** *vt* SPORT (*penalty, corner*) to take **III.** *vpr inf* **1.** (*se droguer*) **se ~ à qc** to shoot up with sth **2.** *iron* **se ~ au champagne** to drink champagne

shop(p)ing [ʃɔpiŋ] *m* **faire du ~** to do some shopping

short [ʃɔʀt] *m* shorts *pl;* **~ de foot** football shorts

show [ʃo] *m* show

showbiz [ʃobiz], **show-business** [ʃobiznɛs] *m inf sans pl* show business

si¹ [si] <*devant voyelle ou h muet* **s'**> **I.** *conj* **1.** (*condition, hypothèse*) if; **~ je ne suis pas là, partez sans moi** if I'm not there, leave without me; **~ j'étais riche, ...** if I were rich, ...; **~ j'avais su!** if I'd only known! **2.** (*opposition*) if; **~ toi tu es mécontent, moi, je ne le suis pas!** even if you're unhappy, I'm not! **3.** (*éventualité*) if; **~ nous profitions du beau temps?** how about taking advantage of the good weather? **4.** (*désir, regret*) if only; **ah ~ je les tenais!** if only I'd got them!; **~ seulement tu étais venu hier!** if only you'd come yesterday! ►**~ ce n'est ...** if not ...; **~ ce n'est qn/qc** apart from sb/sth; **~ c'est ça** *inf* if that's how it is **II.** *m inv* (*hypothèse*) if; **avec des ~, on mettrait Paris en bouteille** if ifs and ands were pots and pans there'd be no need for tinkers

si² [si] *adv* **1.** (*dénégation*) yes; **il ne vient pas – mais ~!** he's not coming – yes he is!; **tu ne peux pas venir – mais ~!** you can't come – yes I can! **2.** (*tellement*) so; **ne parle pas ~ bas!** don't speak so quietly; **une ~ belle fille** such a pretty girl; **elle était ~ impatiente qu'elle ne tenait plus en place** she was so impatient that she couldn't sit still **3.** (*aussi*) **~ ... que** as ... as; **il n'est pas ~ intelligent qu'il le paraît** he's not as intelligent as he seems ►**~ bien que** so mush so that; **j'en avais assez, ~ bien que je suis partie** I'd had enough, so much so that I left; **il viendra pas – oh que ~!** he won't come – oh yes he will!

si³ [si] *adv* (*interrogation indirecte*) if

si⁴ [si] *m inv* MUS ti; *v. a.* **do**

siamois [sjamwa] *m* (*chat*) Siamese

siamois, es [sjamwa, waz] *mpl, fpl* (*jumeaux*) **des ~(es)** Siamese [*o* conjoined] twims

Sibérie [sibeʀi] *f* **la ~** Siberia

sibérien(ne) [sibeʀjɛ̃, jɛn] *adj* Siberian

Sibérien(ne) [sibeʀjɛ̃, jɛn] *m(f)* Siberian

sibyllin(e) [sibilɛ̃, in] *adj* enigmatic

SICAV [sikav] *f abr de* **société d'investissement à capital variable** (*société*) ≈ unit trust *Brit,* ≈ mutual fund *Am*

Sicile [sisil] *f* **la ~** Sicily

sicilien [sisiljɛ̃] *m* Sicilian; *v. a.* **français**

sicilien(ne) [sisiljɛ̃, jɛn] *adj* Sicilian

Sicilien(ne) [sisiljɛ̃, jɛn] *m(f)* Sicilian

SIDA [sida] *m abr de* **syndrome d'immunodéficience acquise** AIDS

side-car [sidkaʀ] <side-cars> *m* (*motocyclette plus side-car*) motorbike and sidecar

sidérer [sideʀe] <5> *vt inf* to stagger

sidérurgie [sideʀyʀʒi] *f* steel industry

sidérurgique [sideʀyʀʒik] *adj* steel-manufacturing; (*usine, produit*) steel; **bassin/groupe ~** steel-producing region/group

siècle [sjɛkl] *m* **1.** (*période de cent ans*) century; **de ~ en ~** from century to century; **au IIIᵉ ~ avant J.C.** in the 3rd century B.C. **2.** (*période remarquable*) **le ~ de Louis XIV/de Périclès** the age of Louis XIV/Pericles; **le ~ de l'atome** the atomic age **3.** (*période très longue*) age; **depuis des ~s** for ages; **il y a des ~s que je ne t'ai vu** *inf* I haven't seen you for ages; **mais ça fait un ~ de ça!** but that was ages ago! ►**du ~** *inf* (*combat, marché, inondation*) of the century

Siècle [sjɛkl] *m* **le ~ des Lumières** the Enlightenment; **le Grand ~** the 17th century

siège [sjɛʒ] *m* **1.** (*meuble, au Parlement*) *a.* POL seat; **~ avant/arrière** AUTO front/back seat; **~ pour enfant** child seat; **~ pliant** folding chair **2.** (*résidence: d'une organisation*) headquarters; **~ social** registered office

siéger [sjeʒe] <2a, 5> *vi* **1.** (*avoir un siège: députés, procureur*) to sit **2.** (*tenir séance*) to be in session

sien(ne) [sjɛ̃, sjɛn] *pron poss* **1. le ~/la ~ne/les ~s** (*d'une femme*) hers; (*d'un homme*) his; *v. a.* **mien** **2.** *pl* (*ceux de sa famille*) **les ~s** his [*o* her] family; (*ses partisans*) his [*o* her] kind ►**faire des ~nes** *inf* to play up; **à la**

(**bonne**) ~**ne!** *iron, inf* cheers!; **y mettre du** ~ to pull one' weight

sierra-léonais(**e**) [sjɛʀaleɔnɛ, nɛz] *adj* Sierra Leonean

Sierra-Léonais(**e**) [sjɛʀaleɔnɛ, nɛz] *m(f)* Sierra Leonean

Sierra Leone [sjɛʀaleɔn(ə)] *f* **la** ~ Sierra Leone

sieste [sjɛst] *f* siesta

sifflement [sifləmɑ̃] *m* whistling; (*du serpent, de la vapeur*) hissing; ~ **d'oreilles** ringing in the ears; ~ **d'admiration** whistle of admiration

siffler [sifle] <1> **I.** *vi* to whistle; (*gaz, vapeur, serpent*) to hiss; **elle a les oreilles qui sifflent** there's a ringing in her ears **II.** *vt* **1.** (*appeler*) ~ **son copain/chien** to whistle for one's friend/dog; ~ **une fille** to whistle at a girl **2.** (*signaler en sifflant*) to blow the whistle; ~ **le départ de la course/la fin du match** to blow the starting/final whistle **3.** (*huer*) to boo; **se faire** ~ to bet booed **4.** (*moduler: chanson, mélodie*) to whistle **5.** *inf* (*boire: verre*) to knock back

sifflet [siflɛ] *m* **1.** (*instrument*) whistle; **coup de** ~ blast on the whistle **2.** *pl* (*huées*) booing ▸**couper le** ~ **à qn** *inf* (*couper la parole*) to shut sb up; **ça me coupe le** ~**!** I'm speechless!

siffleux [siflø] *m Québec* (*marmotte*) marmot

siffloter [siflɔte] <1> *vt, vi* to whistle a tune

sigle [sigl] *m* abbreviation

signal [siɲal, o] <-aux> *m a.* INFOR signal; **donner le** ~ **du départ** to give the signal for departure; ~ **sonore** sound signal; ~ **d'alarme** alarm; **déclencher le** ~ **d'alarme** to set off the alarm; ~ **de détresse** distress signal; ~ **de validation** enabling signal

signalement [siɲalmɑ̃] *m* description

signaler [siɲale] <1> *vt* **1.** (*attirer l'attention sur*) to point out; ADMIN (*fait nouveau, perte, vol*) to report; ~ **un détail/une erreur à qn** to point out a detail/a mistake to sb **2.** (*marquer par un signal*) ~ **la direction à qn** (*carte, écriteau, balise*) to signpost the way for sb **3.** (*indiquer*) ~ **l'existence de qc** to show the existence of sth ▸**rien à** ~ nothing to report

signalisation [siɲalizasjɔ̃] *f* (*d'un aéroport, port*) (*par lumière*) beaconing; (*d'une route*) (*par panneaux*) roadsigns *pl;* (*au sol*) markings *pl;* **feux de** ~ traffic lights

signataire [siɲatɛʀ] *adj, mf* signatory

signature [siɲatyʀ] *f* **1.** (*action*) signing **2.** (*marque d'authenticité*) signature; **apposer sa** ~ **au bas de qc** to sign at the bottom of sth; ~ **légalisée** authenticated signature

signe [siɲ] *m* **1.** (*geste, indice*) sign; ~ **de** (**la**) **croix** sign of the cross; **faire le** ~ **de la croix/un** ~ **de croix** to make the/a sign of the cross; ~ **de la main** a gesture; (*pour saluer*) wave; ~ **de tête affirmatif** nod; ~ **de tête négatif** shake of the head; **faire** ~ **à qn** (*pour signaler qc*) to give sb a sign; (*pour contacter qn*) to get in touch with sb; **faire un** ~ **de la tête à son partenaire** to nod to one's partner; **faire** ~ **à son fils de** +*infin* to gesture to one's son to +*infin;* **faire** ~ **que oui/non** (*de la tête*) to nod/shake one's head; (*d'un geste*) to say yes/no with one's hand; ~ **avant-coureur** *a.* MED early warning sign **2.** (*trait distinctif*) mark; ~**s particuliers: néant** distinguishing marks: none; ~**s extérieurs de richesse** signs of conspicuous wealth **3.** LING, MAT ~ **de ponctuation** punctuation mark; ~ **négatif/positif** negative/positive sign; ~ **d'égalité/de multiplication** equals/multiplication sign **4.** (*en astrologie*) sign; ~ **du zodiaque** sign of the zodiac ▸**elle n'a pas donné** ~ **de vie** there's been no sign of life from her; **c'est bon/mauvais** ~ it's a good/bad sign

signer [siɲe] <1> *vt* **1.** (*apposer sa signature*) to sign; ~ **qc de son nom/de sa main** to sign one's name on sth/sth in one's own hand **2.** (*produire sous son nom: œuvre, pièce*) to produce; (*tableau*) to sign ▸**c'est signé qn** *inf* it's got sb's fingerprint's all over it

signet [siɲɛ] *m* INFOR bookmark

significatif, -ive [siɲifikatif, -iv] *adj* (*date, décision, fait*) significant; (*geste, silence, sourire*) meaningful; **être** ~ **de qc** to reflect sth

signification [siɲifikasjɔ̃] *f* (*sens*) meaning

signifier [siɲifje] <1> *vt* **1.** (*avoir pour sens*) to mean; **qu'est-ce que cela signifie?** what does that mean? **2.** (*faire connaître*) ~ **une intention à qn** to make an intention known to sb; ~ **une décision à qn** JUR to notify sb of a decision ▸**qu'est-ce que ça signifie?** what's that supposed to mean?

silence [silɑ̃s] *m sans pl* (*absence de bruit, absence de paroles, d'information*) silence; (*calme*) stillness; ~ **de mort** deathly hush; **le** ~ **se fait dans la salle** a hush falls over the room; **le** ~ **des enfants m'inquiète** I'm worried about hearing no noise from the children; **quel** ~**!** how quiet it is!; ~**! on tourne!** quiet! action!; ~ **gêné/éloquent** an embarrassed/eloquent silence; ~ **glacial** icy hush; **garder le** ~ **sur qc** to keep quiet about sth; **passer qc sous** ~ not to mention sth; **réduire qn au** ~ to reduce sb to silence; **rompre le** ~ to break the silence ▸**la parole est d'argent, mais le** ~ **est d'or** *prov* (speech is silver,) silence is golden

silencieusement [silɑ̃sjøzmɑ̃] *adv* **1.** (*sans bruit*) silently **2.** (*en secret*) secretly

silencieux [silɑ̃sjø] *m* silencer *Brit,* muffler *Am*

silencieux, -euse [silɑ̃sjø, -jøz] *adj* **1.** (*opp: bruyant*) silent **2.** (*où règne le silence*) silent **3.** (*peu communicatif: personne*) quiet; (*majorité*) silent; **rester** ~ to remain silent

silex [silɛks] *m* GEO flint

silhouette [silwɛt] *f* **1.** (*allure, figure indistincte*) figure **2.** (*contour*) outline **3.** (*dessin*) silhouette

silicone [silikɔn] *m* silicone

silicose [silikoz] *f* silicosis

sillage [sijaʒ] *m* NAUT wake; (*d'un avion*) slipstream; ~ **de l'eau** wash ▸**marcher dans le ~ de qn** to follow in sb's footsteps; **rester dans le ~ de qn** to remain in sb's shadow; **entraîner qn/qc dans son ~** to pull sb/sth along in one's wake; **dans le ~ de ces événements** in the wake of these events; **dans le ~ du ministère de la Culture ...** following the lead of the Ministry of Culture ...

sillon [sijɔ̃] *m* **1.** AGR furrow; **creuser/tracer/ouvrir un ~** to dig/mark out/plough [*o* plow *Am*] a furrow **2.** (*trace longitudinale*) trace; (*ride*) furrow; ANAT fissure; **des larmes tracèrent deux ~s humides sur ses joues** tears drew two wet lines down his cheeks **3.** (*piste: d'un disque*) groove

sillonner [sijɔne] <1> *vt* (*traverser*) ~ **une ville** (*personnes, touristes*) to go to and fro across a town; (*canaux, routes*) to criss-cross a town; ~ **le ciel** (*avions, éclairs*) to go back and forth across the sky

silo [silo] *m* silo

simagrées [simagʀe] *fpl* playacting

simiesque [simjɛsk] *adj* simian

similaire [similɛʀ] *adj* similar

simili [simili] *m* imitation

similitude [similityd] *f* (*analogie*) similarity

simoun [simun] *m* simoon

simple [sɛ̃pl] **I.** *adj* **1.** (*facile*) simple; **rien de plus ~ à réaliser!** nothing simpler!; **le plus ~, c'est ...** the simplest thing is to ... **2.** (*modeste*) unaffected; (*personne, revenus, famille*) modest **3.** (*non multiple: feuille, nœud*) single; **un aller ~ pour Paris, s'il vous plaît** a single [*o* one-way ticket *Am*] to Paris please **4.** *postposé* LING, CHIM simple **5.** *antéposé* (*rien d'autre que: formalité, remarque*) simple; **un simple regard/coup de téléphone** just a look/phone call; **"sur ~ appel"** "just call" **6.** (*naïf*) simple ▸**c'est (bien) ~** *inf* it's perfectly simple; **écoute, c'est ~, si tu ...** listen, it's simple, if you ...; **si tu fais ça, c'est bien ~, je te quitte!** if you do that, I'll simply leave you!; **c'est bien ~, il ne m'écoute jamais!** he never listens to me, that's all there is to it!; **tu penses que tu vas t'en tirer comme ça, mais ce serait trop ~!** you think you'll get away with it, but that'd be too easy! **II.** *m* **1.** SPORT singles; **un ~ dames/messieurs** a ladies'/men's singles match **2.** (*personne naïve*) ~ **d'esprit** simple soul ▸**passer du ~ au double** to double

simplement [sɛ̃pləmɑ̃] *adv* **1.** (*sans affectation: s'exprimer, se vêtir*) simply; (*recevoir, se comporter*) unpretentiously **2.** (*seulement*) simply; **tout ~** (*sans plus*) just; (*absolument*) quite simply

simplet(te) [sɛ̃plɛ, ɛt] *adj* **1.** (*niais*) simple **2.** (*simpliste*) simplistic; (*intrigue, question, raisonnement*) naive; (*roman*) unsophisticated

simplicité [sɛ̃plisite] *f* **1.** (*opp: complexité*) simplicity; **être d'une extrême/de la plus grande ~** to be very/utterly simple; **être d'une ~ enfantine** to be child's play **2.** (*naturel*) plainness; **être resté d'une grande ~** to have stayed very simple; **parler avec ~** to speak plainly; **recevoir qn en toute ~** to give sb a simple welcome **3.** (*naïveté*) simpleness; **avoir la ~ de croire qc** to be simple enough to believe sth

simplificateur, **-trice** [sɛ̃plifikatœʀ, -tʀis] *adj* simplifying; **cette explication est simplificatrice** this explanation oversimplifies things; **avoir l'esprit très ~** to tend to oversimplify

simplification [sɛ̃plifikasjɔ̃] *f* simplification

simplifier [sɛ̃plifje] <1> **I.** *vt* to simplify **II.** *vpr* **se ~ la vie** to simplify life (for oneself)

simpliste [sɛ̃plist] *adj* simplistic

simulacre [simylakʀ] *m* (*action simulée*) pretence *Brit,* pretense *Am;* **un ~ de combat** a mock fight

simulateur, **-trice** [simylatœʀ, -tʀis] *m, f* **1.** (*trompeur*) shammer **2.** (*qui simule une maladie*) malingerer

simulation [simylasjɔ̃] *f* **1.** (*reconstitution*) simulation; **jeu de ~** simulation game **2.** (*action de simuler un sentiment*) pretence *Brit,* pretense *Am* **3.** (*action de simuler une maladie*) malingering

simulé(e) [simyle] *adj* feigned; **un appel de détresse ~** a hoax distress call

simuler [simyle] <1> *vt* **1.** (*feindre*) to feign **2.** (*reconstituer*) to simulate

simultané(e) [simyltane] *adj* simultaneous

simultanéité [simyltaneite] *f* simultaneity

simultanément [simyltanemɑ̃] *adv* simultaneously

sincère [sɛ̃sɛʀ] *adj* **1.** (*franc, loyal: aveu*) sincere; (*ami, repentir, explication, réponse*) honest **2.** (*véritable: condoléances*) sincere; **croyez à mes plus ~s regrets** my sincerest regrets; **veuillez agréer mes plus ~s salutations** yours sincerely

sincèrement [sɛ̃sɛʀmɑ̃] *adv* **1.** (*franchement: avouer, dire*) honestly; (*regretter*) sincerely; **il est ~ désolé de qc** he is deeply sorry about sth; ~**, tu ne veux pas y aller?** do you honestly not want to go? **2.** (*à franchement parler*) honestly

sincérité [sɛ̃seʀite] *f* (*franchise: des aveux, d'une personne, d'un sentiment*) sincerity; (*d'une explication, réponse*) frankness; **en toute ~** quite sincerely

sinécure [sinekyʀ] *f* sinecure ▸**ce n'est pas une ~, c'est pas une ~** *inf* it's no walk in the park

sine qua non [sinekwanɔn] *adj v.* **condition**

Singapour [sɛ̃gapuʀ] Singapore

singapourien(ne) [sɛ̃gapuʀjɛ̃, ɛn] *adj* Singaporean

Singapourien(ne) [sɛ̃gapuʀjɛ̃, ɛn] *m(f)*

Singaporean

singe [sɛ̃ʒ] *m* **1.** ZOOL monkey; **grand** ~ great ape; **l'homme descend du** ~ humankind is decended from the apes; *v. a.* **guenon** **2.** *inf* (*personne laide*) horror **3.** *inf* (*personne qui imite*) mimic; **faire le** ~ *inf* to monkey about [*o* around] ►**être poilu comme un** ~ *inf* to be as hairy as an ape

singer [sɛ̃ʒe] <2a> *vt* **1.** (*imiter*) ~ **qn/qc** to take sb/sth off **2.** (*feindre: sentiment, intérêt*) to feign

singerie [sɛ̃ʒʀi] *f pl, inf* (*grimaces, pitreries*) antics; **faire des ~s** to play the fool

singulariser [sɛ̃gylaʀize] <1> *vpr* **se ~ par qc** to distinguish oneself by sth

singularité [sɛ̃gylaʀite] *f* **1.** *sans pl* (*caractère original*) singularity; **présenter une** ~ to have a distinct feature **2.** *pl* (*excentricité*) peculiarity

singulier [sɛ̃gylje] *m* singular

singulier, -ière [sɛ̃gylje, -jɛʀ] *adj* **1.** (*bizarre*) strange **2.** (*étonnant*) singular **3.** LING singular

singulièrement [sɛ̃gyljɛʀmɑ̃] *adv* **1.** (*étrangement*) strangely **2.** (*fortement*) singularly

sinistre [sinistʀ] **I.** *adj* **1.** (*lugubre*) gloomy; **avoir l'air** ~ to look gloomy **2.** (*inquiétant: projet*) sinister **3.** (*terrible: nouvelle, spectacle*) gruesome **II.** *m* (*catastrophe*) disaster; (*réclamation*) claim; **maîtriser un** ~ to bring a disaster under control

sinistré(e) [sinistʀe] **I.** *adj* (*bâtiment*) disaster-stricken; (*zone, région*) disaster; **personnes ~es à la suite des inondations** flood disaster victims **II.** *m(f)* victim

sinon [sinɔ̃] *conj* **1.** (*dans le cas contraire*) otherwise **2.** (*si ce n'est*) **que faire ~ attendre?** what shall we do but wait?; **à quoi sert la clé ~ à faire qc** what use is a key apart from doing sth; **aucun roman ~ "Madame Bovary"** no novel except "Madame Bovary"; **il ne s'intéresse à rien ~ à la musique** he's not interested in anything apart from music; ~ **... du** [*o* **au**] **moins** (*en tout cas*) if not ... at least

sinueux, -euse [sinɥø, -øz] *adj* **1.** (*ondoyant*) winding **2.** (*compliqué*) tortuous

sinuosité [sinɥozite] *f* **1.** (*formes sinueuses*) curves **2.** (*détours*) **les ~s de la pensée** the twists and turns of thought

sinus[1] [sinys] *m* ANAT sinus; ~ **frontal/maxillaire** frontal/maxillary sinus

sinus[2] [sinys] *m* GEOM sine

sinusite [sinyzit] *f* sinusitis

siphon [sifɔ̃] *m* **1.** (*tube courbé*) siphon; (*d'un évier, des W.-C.*) U-bend **2.** GEO sump **3.** (*bouteille*) siphon

siphonné(e) [sifɔne] *adj inf* **être** ~ to be cracked

sire [siʀ] *m* **triste** ~ *péj* unsavoury [*o* unsavory *Am*] character

Sire [siʀ] *m* Sire

sirène [siʀɛn] *f* **1.** (*signal*) siren; ~ **d'alarme** alarm siren; **les ~s sonnent** the sirens are going off **2.** (*femme poisson*) mermaid **3.** *iron* (*symbole de séduction*) **chant des ~s** siren song

sirocco [siʀɔko] *m* sirocco

sirop [siʀo] *m* **1.** (*liquide sucré*) *a.* MED syrup; ~ **de citron/framboise/fraise** lemon/raspberry/strawberry syrup; **pêches au** ~ peaches in syrup; ~ **contre la toux** cough syrup **2.** (*boisson diluée*) cordial

siroter [siʀɔte] <1> *vt inf* to sip

sirupeux, -euse [siʀypø, -øz] *adj* (*boisson*) syrupy

sismique [sismik] *adj* **secousse** ~ earth tremor

sismographe [sismɔgʀaf] *m* seismograph ►**avoir une sensibilité de ~ à qc** to be hypersensitive to sth

site [sit] *m* **1.** (*paysage*) place; (*région*) area; ~ **classé** conservation area; ~ **touristique** place of interest; ~ **historique/naturel** historical/natural site; ~ **sauvage** wild place **2.** (*lieu d'activité*) ~ **archéologique/olympique** archeological/Olympic site **3.** INFOR site; ~ **(sur) Internet**, ~ **Web** website; **s'offrir un ~ sur Internet** to get oneself a website ►~ **propre** bus lane

sitôt [sito] **I.** *adv* **pas de** ~ not for a while; **elle ne recommencera pas de** ~ *iron* she won't do that again in a hurry **II.** *conj* ~ **entré/arrivé** as soon as he came in/arrived ►~ **dit,** ~ **fait** no sooner said than done

situation [sitɥasjɔ̃] *f* **1.** (*état: d'une personne*) position; ~ **de famille** marital status; **la ~ sociale de qn** sb's social standing; **des ~s sociales** (*des cas sociaux*) social cases; **dans ma** ~ in my situation; **agir en ~ de légitime défense** to act in self-defence [*o* -defense *Am*]; **remettre qc en** ~ to put sth back in context **2.** (*état conjoncturel*) *a.* ECON, FIN situation; **la ~ de l'emploi en France** the employment situation in France **3.** (*emploi*) post; **avoir une belle** ~ to have a good job; **se faire une** ~ to work one's way into a good job

situé(e) [sitɥe] *adj* situated

situer [sitɥe] <1> **I.** *vt* **1.** (*localiser dans l'espace par la pensée*) ~ **son film/l'action de son roman à Paris** to set one's film/one's novel in Paris; **je ne situe pas très bien ce lieu** I can't quite place this place; **pouvez-vous ~ l'endroit précis où ...?** can you locate the exact place where ...? **2.** (*localiser dans le temps*) ~ **qc en l'an ...** to place sth in the year ... **3.** *inf* (*définir: personne*) ~ **qn** to work sb out **II.** *vpr* **se ~ 1.** (*se localiser dans l'espace*) to be situated **2.** (*se localiser dans le temps*) **se ~ en l'an ...** to take place in the year ... **3.** (*se localiser à un certain niveau*) **se ~ entre 25 et 35%** to fall between 25 and 35%; **se ~ à un niveau inférieur/supérieur** to be at a lower/higher level **4.** (*se définir*) **se**

~ to be placed; **se ~ par rapport à qc** to be in relation to sth
six [sis, *devant une voyelle* siz, *devant une consonne* si] *adj* six; *v. a.* **cinq**
sixième [sizjɛm] **I.** *adj antéposé* sixth **II.** *f* ECOLE year seven *Brit,* sixth grade *Am; v. a.* **cinquième**
skaï [skaj] *m* Skaï®, *imitation leather*
skate [skɛt] *inf,* **skate-board** [skɛtbɔʀd] <skate-boards> *m* skateboard; **faire du ~** to go skateboarding
sketch [skɛtʃ] <(e)s> *m* sketch
ski [ski] *m* **1.** (*objet*) ski; **aller quelque part à ~s** to ski somewhere **2.** (*sport*) skiing; **~ de fond** cross-country skiing; **~ de randonnée** ski touring; **~ hors piste** off-piste skiing; **~ alpin** Alpine skiing; **~ artistique/acrobatique** artistic/acrobatic skiing; **~ nordique** Nordic skiing; **~ nautique** water-skiing; **aller au ~** *inf,* **faire du ~** to go skiing; **des chaussures de ~** ski boots; **station de ~** ski resort
skiable [skjabl] *adj* (*neige, piste*) skiable; (*domaine, saison*) skiing
skier [skje] <1> *vi* to ski
skieur, -euse [skjœʀ, -jøz] *m, f* skier; **~ de fond/hors piste** cross-country/off-piste skier
skin(head) [skin(ɛd)] *m* skinhead
skipper [skipœʀ] *m* skipper
slalom [slalɔm] *m* **1.** (*épreuve de ski*) slalom; **~ spécial/(super-)géant** special/giant slalom **2.** (*en canoë-kayak*) **~ nautique** slalom canoeing **3.** (*parcours sinueux*) slalom; **faire du ~** to weave in and out; **en ~** dodging in and out
slalomer [slalɔme] <1> *vi* **1.** SPORT to slalom **2.** (*zigzaguer*) to weave in and out
slash [slaʃ] *m* slash
slave [slav] *adj* Slavic
Slave [slav] *mf* Slav
slip [slip] *m* briefs *pl;* **~ (de bain)** swimming costume ▶**se retrouver en ~** *inf* to lose one's shirt
slogan [slɔgɑ̃] *m* slogan
slovaque [slɔvak] **I.** *adj* Slovak **II.** *m* Slovak; *v. a.* **français**
Slovaque [slɔvak] *mf* Slovak
Slovaquie [slɔvaki] *f* **la ~** Slovakia
slovène [slɔvɛn] **I.** *adj* Slovene **II.** *m* Slovene; *v. a.* **français**
Slovène [slɔvɛn] *mf* Slovene
Slovénie [slɔveni] *f* **la ~** Slovenia
slow [slo] *m* slow dance
smala [smala] *f iron, inf* tribe
smash [sma(t)ʃ] *m* smash
SME [ɛsɛmø] *m abr de* **Système monétaire européen** EMS
SMIC [smik] *m abr de* **salaire minimum interprofessionnel de croissance** minimum wage; **payé au ~** paid the minimum wage

> The **SMIC** came into force in 1970 to protect the purchasing power of job seekers. There is a minimum gross hourly wage for permanent staff. It increases annually by at least 50% of the average wage raise.

smicard(e) [smikaʀ, aʀd] *m(f) inf* minimum wage earner
SMIG [smig] *m abr de* **salaire minimum interprofessionnel garanti** guaranteed minimum wage
smoking [smɔkiŋ] *m* dinner jacket *Brit,* tuxedo *Am*
snack [snak] *m,* **snack-bar** [snakbaʀ] <snack-bars> *m* snack bar
SNCF [ɛsɛnseɛf] *f abr de* **Société nationale des chemins de fer français** SNCF (*French national railway company*)
snob [snɔb] **I.** *adj* snobbish **II.** *mf* snob
snober [snɔbe] <1> *vt* (*personne*) to snub; **~ qc** (*invitation, repas*) to turn one's nose up at sth
snobisme [snɔbism] *m* snobbery
sobre [sɔbʀ] *adj* sober; **être ~ dans ses explications** to give explanations sparingly; **être ~ dans ses gestes** to be restrained in one's use of gestures
sobrement [sɔbʀəmɑ̃] *adv* soberly
sobriété [sɔbʀijete] *f* **1.** (*tempérance: d'une personne*) soberness; (*d'un animal*) modest needs *pl;* **la ~ de sa vie** her modest lifestyle; **la ~ au volant** soberness at the wheel; **la ~ de ses déclarations** her restrained declarations; **la ~ de ses gestes** the restraint in her gestures **2.** (*modération*) **~ en toutes choses** temperance in all things; **~ dans ses explications** her bare explanations **3.** (*discrétion: d'un style*) sobriety
sobriquet [sɔbʀikɛ] *m* nickname
sociable [sɔsjabl] *adj* **1.** (*aimable*) sociable **2.** SOCIOL social; **l'homme est de nature ~** humans are social animals
social [sɔsjal, jo] <-aux> *m* **1.** (*questions sociales*) social issues **2.** (*politique*) social policy
social(e) [sɔsjal, jo] <-aux> *adj* social; **aide ~e** benefits *pl Brit,* ≈ welfare *Am;* **les logements sociaux** public housing; **avantage ~** welfare benefit
social-démocrate, sociale-démocrate [sɔsjaldemɔkʀat, sɔsjodemɔkʀat] <sociaux-démocrates> *adj, m, f* Social Democrat
social-démocratie [sɔsjaldemɔkʀasi] <social-démocraties> *f* social democracy
socialement [sɔsjalmɑ̃] *adv* socially
socialisation [sɔsjalizasjɔ̃] *f* **1.** POL collectivization **2.** PSYCH socialization
socialiser [sɔsjalize] <1> *vt* POL to collectivize; PSYCH to socialize
socialisme [sɔsjalism] *m* socialism; **~ d'État** state socialism
socialiste [sɔsjalist] *adj, mf* socialist
socialo [sɔsjalo] *mf inf abr de* **socialiste**
socialo-communiste [sɔsjalokɔmynist]

<socialo-communistes> *adj* social communist

sociétaire [sɔsjetɛʀ] *mf* member

société [sɔsjete] *f* **1.**(*communauté*) society; ~ **de consommation** consumer society; **problème de** ~ social problem **2.** ECON company; ~ **à responsabilité limitée** limited liability company; ~ **anonyme** public limited company; ~ **civile** non-trading company **3.**(*society*) ~ **littéraire/savante** literary/learned society **4.**(*ensemble de personnes*) society; **la bonne** ~ polite society; **les gens de la bonne** ~ polite society; **la haute** ~ high society

Société [sɔsjete] *f* POL ~ **des Nations** League of Nations

socioculturel(le) [sɔsjokyltyʀɛl] *adj* sociocultural **socio-économique** [sɔsjoekɔnɔmik] <socio-économiques> *adj* socioeconomic **socio-éducatif, -ive** [sɔsjoedykatif, iv] <socio-éducatifs> *adj* socioeducational **sociolinguistique** [sɔsjolɛ̃gɥistik] **I.** *f* sociolinguistics **II.** *adj* sociolinguistic

sociologie [sɔsjɔlɔʒi] *f* sociology

sociologique [sɔsjɔlɔʒik] *adj* sociological

sociologiquement [sɔsjɔlɔʒikmɑ̃] *adv* sociologically

sociologue [sɔsjɔlɔg] *mf* sociologist

sociopolitique [sɔsjopɔlitik] *adj* sociopolitical **socio-professionnel(le)** [sɔsjopʀɔfesjɔnɛl] <socio-professionnels> **I.** *adj* socio-professional **II.** *m(f)* (*responsable*) socio-professional

socle [sɔkl] *m* **1.**(*d'une lampe, d'un vase*) base; (*d'une statue, colonne*) plinth **2.** GEO platform; ~ **continental** continental platform

socquette [sɔkɛt] *f* ankle sock

soda [sɔda] *m* (*boisson aromatisée*) soft drink

sodomie [sɔdɔmi] *f* sodomy

sodomiser [sɔdɔmize] <1> *vt* to sodomize

sœur [sœʀ] **I.** *f* **1.**(*opp: frère, objet semblable*) sister; ~ **de lait** foster sister; ~ **d'infortune** *soutenu* fellow sufferer **2.** REL nun; **ma** ~ Sister; **bonne** ~ *inf* nun; **se faire (bonne)** ~ to become a nun ►**et ta** ~**(, elle bat le beurre)**? *inf* get lost! **II.** *adj* **1.**(*semblable: civilisation, âme*) sister **2.**(*apparentés*) **être** ~**s** (*choses*) to be sisters

sœurette [sœʀɛt] *f* little sister

sofa [sɔfa] *m* sofa

SOFRES [sɔfʀɛs] *f abr de* **Société française d'enquêtes par sondages** *French public opinion poll company*

software [sɔftwɛʀ, sɔftwaʀ] *m* software

soi [swa] **I.** *pron pers avec une préposition* oneself; **chez** ~ at home; **malgré** ~ despite oneself ►**en** ~ in itself; **un genre en** ~ a separate genre **II.** *m* self; **la conscience du** ~ self-awareness

soi-disant [swadizɑ̃] **I.** *adj inv, antéposé* so-called **II.** *adv* supposedly; ~ **qu'il serait en vacances** *inf* he was supposedly on holiday [*o* vacation *Am*]

soie [swa] *f* **1.**(*tissu*) silk; ~ **grège/sauvage** raw/wild silk; **peinture sur** ~ silk painting **2.**(*poils*) bristle; **en** ~**s de sanglier** boar-bristle

soierie [swaʀi] *f* **1.** silk; **commerce de la** ~ silk trade **2.**(*industrie*) silk production **3.**(*usine*) silk mill

soif [swaf] *f* **1.**(*besoin de boire*) thirst; **avoir** ~ to be thirsty; (*plante*) to need watering; **donner** ~ **à qn** to make sb thirsty; **boire à sa** ~ to drink one's fill **2.**(*désir*) ~ **d'indépendance/de vengeance** thirst for independence/for vengeance; ~ **de vivre** zest for life ►**il fait** ~ *inf* it gives you a thirst; **laisser qn sur sa** ~ (*livre, spectacle, personne*) to leave sb wanting more; **mourir de** ~ to be dying of thirst; **rester sur sa** ~ (*avoir encore* ~) to be still thirsty; (*rester insatisfait*) to be unsatisfied; **boire jusqu'à plus** ~ *inf* to drink one's fill

soignant(e) [swaɲɑ̃, ɑ̃t] *adj* **personnel** ~ nursing staff

soigné(e) [swaɲe] *adj* **1.**(*impeccable: personne*) neat; (*travail*) careful **2.** *péj, inf* **attraper un rhume** ~ to have a stinking cold; **l'addition est** ~**e** the bill's astronomical

soigner [swaɲe] <1> **I.** *vt* **1.**(*traiter: médecin*) to treat; (*infirmier*) to look after; ~ **son rhume à la maison** to treat one's cold at home; **se faire** ~ to get treatment **2.**(*avoir soin de: animal, plante, personne*) to look after; (*mains, chevelure, plante*) to take care of; (*travail, repas, style, tenue*) to take care over; **savoir** ~ **ses invités** to look after one's guests **3.** *iron, inf* (*forcer l'addition: client*) to swindle **4.**(*maltraiter*) ~ **qn** to give sb the works ►**va [*o* tu devrais] te faire** ~! *inf* you must be mad [*o* crazy]! **II.** *vpr* **1.**(*essayer de se guérir*) **se** ~ to treat oneself; **se** ~ **tout seul** to look after oneself **2.** *iron* (*avoir soin de soi*) **se** ~ to take good care of oneself **3.**(*pouvoir être soigné*) **se** ~ **par [*o* avec] une thérapie** to be treatable by a therapy ►**ça se soigne!** *inf* there's a cure for that!; **la paresse, ça se soigne** laziness can be fixed

soigneur, -euse [swaɲœʀ, -øz] *m, f* SPORT trainer; (*d'un boxeur*) second

soigneusement [swaɲøzmɑ̃] *adv* (*travailler, installer, éviter*) carefully; (*ranger*) neatly

soigneux, -euse [swaɲø, -øz] *adj* **1.**(*appliqué*) meticulous; (*ordonné*) neat; **être** ~ **dans son travail** to be meticulous in one's work **2.**(*soucieux*) **être** ~ **de ses affaires** to take care of one's belongings; **être** ~ **de sa personne** to take care over one's appearance **3.** *soutenu* (*minutieux: recherches*) careful

soi-même [swamɛm] *pron pers* oneself; **le respect de** ~ self-respect

soin [swɛ̃] *m* **1.** *sans pl* (*application*) care; (*ordre et propreté*) tidiness; **avec beaucoup de** ~ with great care **2.** *pl* (*traitement médical*) treatment; ~**s à domicile** home treatment; **les premiers ~s** first aid; **donner des ~s à qn** to treat sb; **donner les premiers ~s** to give first aid **3.** *pl* (*hygiène*) **~s du visage/corps** facial/body care + *vb sing* **4.** *sans pl* (*responsabilité*) **confier à un voisin le ~ de la maison** to get a neighbour to look after the house *Brit,* to get a neighbor to look after the house *Am;* **laisser à sa mère le ~ de** *+infin* to leave one's mother to *+infin* **5.** *pl* (*attention*) attention ▸**aux bons ~s de qn** care of sb; **être aux petits ~s pour qn** to wait on sb hand and foot

soir [swaʀ] **I.** *m* evening; **le ~ tombe** evening is falling; **au ~** in the evening; **hier au ~** yesterday evening; **pour le repas de ce ~** for this evening's meal; **8 heures du ~** 8 o'clock in the evening; **le ~** in the evening; **un beau ~** one fine evening; **l'autre ~** the other evening ▸**du matin au ~** from morning till night; **le Grand Soir** the Big Night; **être du ~** *inf* (*être en forme le soir*) to be a night owl; (*être de l'équipe du soir*) to be on night duty **II.** *adv* evening; **hier ~** yesterday evening; **mardi ~** Tuesday evening

soirée [swaʀe] *f* **1.** (*fin du jour*) evening; **en ~** in the evening; **demain en ~** tomorrow evening; **en fin de ~** at the end of the evening; **toute la ~** all evening; **dans la ~** in the evening; **lundi dans la ~, dans la ~ de lundi** on Monday evening **2.** (*fête*) party; **~ dansante/costumée** dance/fancy dress ball; **tenue de ~** evening dress **3.** THEAT, CINE evening performance; **en ~** in the evening

sois [swa] *subj prés de* **être**

soit **I.** [swat] *adv* (*d'accord*) very well; **eh bien ~!** very well then! **II.** [swa] *conj* **1.** (*alternative*) **~ ..., ~ ...** either ..., or ...; **~ qu'il soit malade, ~ qu'il n'ait pas envie** (*subj*) whether he's ill, or he doesn't want to **2.** (*c'est-à-dire*) that is

soixantaine [swasɑ̃tɛn] *f* **1.** (*environ soixante*) **une ~ de personnes/pages** about sixty people/pages **2.** (*âge approximatif*) **avoir la ~** [*o* **une ~ d'années**] about sixty years old; **approcher de la ~** to approach sixty; **avoir largement dépassé la ~** to be well past sixty

soixante [swasɑ̃t] *adj* sixty; **~ et un** sixty-one; **~ et onze** seventy-one; *v. a.* **cinq, cinquante**

soixante-dix [swasɑ̃tdis] *adj* seventy; *v. a.* **cinq, cinquante**

soixante-dixième [swasɑ̃tdizjɛm] <soixante-dixièmes> *adj antéposé* seventieth; *v. a.* **cinquième**

soixante-huitard(e) [swasɑ̃tɥitaʀ, -aʀd] <soixante-huitards> *m(f): person who took part in the events of May 1968*

soixantième [swasɑ̃tjɛm] *adj antéposé* sixtieth; *v. a.* **cinquième**

soja [sɔʒa] *m* soya

sol¹ [sɔl] *m* **1.** (*terre*) soil **2.** (*croûte terrestre*) ground; **personnel au ~** AVIAT ground staff **3.** (*plancher: d'une pièce, maison*) floor; **exercices au ~** SPORT floor exercises **4.** (*territoire*) soil ▸**le ~ se déroba sous les pieds de qn** the ground gave way under sb's feet

sol² [sɔl] *m inv* MUS so; *v. a.* **do**

solaire [sɔlɛʀ] *adj* **1.** (*utilisant la force du soleil*) *a.* ASTR solar; **cadran ~** sundial **2.** (*protégeant du soleil*) **huile ~** suntan oil

soldat [sɔlda] *m* soldier; **~ de plomb** tin soldier; **jouer aux petits ~s** to play soldiers ▸**jouer au petit ~ avec qn** *inf* to act big

Soldat [sɔlda] *m* **le ~ inconnu** the Unknown Soldier

soldate [sɔldat] *f inf* woman soldier

solde¹ [sɔld] *m* **1.** *pl* (*marchandises*) sale goods; **dans les ~s de lainage** in the woollen sales **2.** (*braderie*) sale; **~s d'été/d'hiver** summer/winter sales; **en ~** on offer *Brit,* on sale *Am* **3.** (*balance*) balance; **~ débiteur/créditeur** debit/credit balance

solde² [sɔld] *f* (*d'un soldat, matelot*) pay ▸**être à la ~ de qn** to be in sb's pay

soldé(e) [sɔlde] *adj* reduced

solder [sɔlde] <1> **I.** *vt* **1.** COM to sell at cut price; **~ tout son stock** to reduce the prices on all one's stock **2.** FIN (*dette*) to settle; (*fermer: compte*) to close **II.** *vpr* **se ~ par un échec/succès** (*conférence, tentative*) to end in success/failure; **se ~ par un bénéfice/déficit** (*budget, compte, opération*) to show a profit/loss

solderie [sɔldəʀi] *f* discount store

sole [sɔl] *f* (*poisson*) sole

soleil [sɔlɛj] *m* **1.** ASTR sun; **~ de minuit** midnight sun; **~ couchant/levant** setting/rising sun; **au ~ levant** at sunrise **2.** (*rayonnement*) sunshine; (*temps ensoleillé*) sunny; **se mettre au ~** to go into the sunshine; **déteindre au ~** to fade in the sun; **un coin au ~** a sunny corner; **il fait ~** it's sunny; **prendre le ~** to sunbathe **3.** (*fleur*) (**grand**) **~** sunflower **4.** (*acrobatie*) somersault; **grand ~** grand circle; **faire un ~** (*personne*) to somersault; (*voiture*) to flip over ▸**ôte-toi de mon ~!** get out of my sight!

solennel(le) [sɔlanɛl] *adj* (*officiel, grave: cérémonie, occasion, obsèques*) solemn; **rendre des honneurs ~s à qn** to pay homage to sb

solennellement [sɔlanɛlmɑ̃] *adv* (*jurer, s'exprimer*) solemnly; (*promettre*) formally

solennité [sɔlanite] *f* solemnity; **avec ~** solemnly

Soleure [sɔlœʀ] Solothurn; **le canton de ~** Canton Solothurn

soleurois(e) [sɔləʀwa, waz] *adj* of Soleure; *v. a.* **ajaccien**

Soleurois(e) [sɔləʀwa, waz] *m(f)* person from Soleure; *v. a.* **Ajaccien**

solfège [sɔlfɛʒ] *m* **1.** (*théorie*) musical theory **2.** (*livre*) music primer

soli [sɔli] *pl de* **solo**

solidaire [sɔlidɛʀ] *adj* **1.** (*lié*) **être ~(s)** to stand together; **se montrer ~(s)** to show solidarity; **être ~ de** [*o* **avec**] **qn/de qc** to be behind sb/sth **2.** (*interdépendant*) **être ~s** (*questions, phénomènes*) interdependent; (*mécanismes, matériaux*) linked; **être ~ de qc** to be linked to sth **3.** JUR (*cautionnement, obligation*) joint and several; (*contrat*) joint; **caution ~** joint deposit; **être ~ des actes de qn** to be liable for sb's acts

solidariser [sɔlidaʀize] <1> *vpr* **se ~** to show solidarity

solidarité [sɔlidaʀite] *f* solidarity

solide [sɔlid] **I.** *adj* **1.** (*opp: liquide*) solid **2.** (*résistant: construction, outil*) sturdy; (*matériau*) strong; (*personne, santé*) robust **3.** (*sûr: connaissances, bon sens*) sound; (*amitié, base*) firm; (*source*) reliable; (*position*) strong **4.** (*robuste, vigoureux*) sturdy; **ne pas être très ~ sur ses jambes** to not be very steady on one's legs **5.** *antéposé, inf* (*substantiel: fortune, repas, coup de poing*) hefty; (*appétit*) hearty **II.** *m* **1.** MAT, PHYS solid **2.** (*aliments*) **du ~** solids **3.** *inf* (*chose sûre, résistante*) **c'est du ~!** it's good solid stuff!

solidement [sɔlidmã] *adv* **1.** (*fermement: fixer*) firmly; (*construire*) solidly; **tenir ~ le bout d'une corde** to hold the end of the string tightly **2.** (*durablement: s'établir, s'installer, attaché*) firmly; (*structurer*) solidly

solidifier [sɔlidifje] <1a> **I.** *vt* (*liquide, corps gazeux*) to solidify **II.** *vpr* **se ~** (*lave*) to solidify; (*cire, ciment, névé*) to harden

solidité [sɔlidite] *f* **1.** (*robustesse: d'une machine, d'un meuble*) sturdiness; (*d'un tissu, vêtement*) strength; (*d'une personne*) robustness; (*d'un nœud*) tightness; **être d'une grande ~** (*ouvrage*) to be very sound; **avoir la ~ d'un roc** (*personne*) to be as solid as a rock **2.** (*stabilité*) soundness **3.** (*sérieux: d'un argument, raisonnement*) soundness

soliste [sɔlist] *mf* soloist

solitaire [sɔlitɛʀ] **I.** *adj* **1.** (*seul: vie*) solitary; (*vieillard*) lonely; (*caractère*) solitary **2.** (*isolé: maison*) isolated **3.** (*désert: parc, chemin*) deserted; (*demeure*) lonely **II.** *mf* solitary person; (*ermite*) recluse ►__en__ ~ alone; **un tour du monde en ~** a solo round-the-world trip **III.** *m* (*diamant, jeu*) solitaire

solitude [sɔlityd] *f* **1.** (*isolement*) loneliness **2.** (*tranquillité, lieu solitaire*) solitude

solliciter [sɔlisite] <1> *vt form* (*demander: audience, explication, emploi*) to seek; **~ une autorisation de qn** to ask sb for authorization; **~ de qn des dommages et intérêts** to demand damages from sb

solliciteur, **-euse** [sɔlisitœʀ, -øz] *m, f* supplicant

sollicitude [sɔlisityd] *f* solicitude; **avec ~** solicitously

solo <s *o* soli> [sɔlo, sɔli] **I.** *m* solo; **~ de piano** piano solo; **en ~** (*chanter, jouer*) solo; (*escalader*) alone; **escalade en ~** solo climb **II.** *adj inv* **violon ~** solo violin

solstice [sɔlstis] *m* solstice; **~ d'été/d'hiver** summer/winter solstice

soluble [sɔlybl] *adj* **1.** (*pouvant être dissout: substance*) soluble; **~ dans l'eau** water soluble **2.** (*pouvant être résolu*) **être ~** (*problème*) to be solvable

solution [sɔlysjɔ̃] *f* **1.** (*issue*) *a.* CHIM, MED solution; **~ à un** [*o* **d'un**] **problème** solution to a problem; **~ de facilité** easy way out; **~ de repli** fallback solution; **~ miracle** miracle solution **2.** (*résultat*) solution; **trouver la ~ d'une équation** to find the solution to an equation **3.** (*réponse: d'une énigme, d'un rébus*) answer ►**~ __finale__** HIST, POL Final Solution

solvable [sɔlvabl] *adj* (*client, pays, demande, marché*) solvent; **client/pays non ~** insolvent customer/country; **débiteur non ~** insolvent debtor

solvant [sɔlvã] *m* solvent

somatique [sɔmatik] *adj* somatic

sombre [sɔ̃bʀ] *adj* **1.** (*obscur: lieu, nuit*) dark; **il fait ~** it's dark **2.** (*foncé*) **un bleu/rouge ~** dark blue/red; **gris ~** dark grey [*o* gray *Am*] **3.** (*sinistre: heure, année*) dark; (*avenir, réalité, tableau*) dismal; (*pensée*) gloomy **4.** (*triste: roman, visage*) grim; (*caractère, personne*) sombre **5.** *antéposé, inf* (*lamentable: histoire*) dark

sombrer [sɔ̃bʀe] <1> *vi* **1.** (*faire naufrage*) to sink; **~ au fond de la mer** to sink to the bottom of the sea **2.** (*se perdre: personne*) **~ dans la folie** to sink into madness

sommaire [sɔmɛʀ] **I.** *adj* **1.** (*court: analyse, réponse, exposé*) brief **2.** (*élémentaire, rapide: examen*) cursory; (*réparation, repas*) quick **3.** (*expéditif: exécution, justice, procédure*) summary **II.** *m* **1.** (*table des matières*) table of contents **2.** (*résumé*) summary

sommairement [sɔmɛʀmã] *adv* **1.** (*brièvement*) briefly **2.** (*simplement*) quickly **3.** (*de façon expéditive: juger qn*) summarily

sommation [sɔmasjɔ̃] *f* **1.** *a.* JUR summons; (*de satisfaire à une obligation*) demand; **recevoir ~ de payer qc** to receive a demand for sth **2.** MIL warning; **les ~s d'usage** [*o* **réglementaires**] the normal warning; **tirer sans ~** to fire without warning

somme[1] [sɔm] *f* **1.** (*quantité d'argent*) sum **2.** (*total*) total; (*des angles*) sum; **faire la ~ de qc** to calculate the total of sth **3.** (*ensemble*) amount; **la ~ des dégâts/des besoins** the total damage/requirements ►__en__ ~, ~ __toute__ all in all

somme[2] [sɔm] *m* (*sieste*) nap; **piquer un ~** *inf* to take a nap

sommeil [sɔmɛj] *m* **1.** (*fait de dormir*) sleep; (*envie de dormir*) sleepiness; **avoir ~** to be sleepy; **tomber de ~** to be asleep on one's feet; **être réveillé en plein ~** to be woken from a deep sleep; **dans le premier ~** in the first hours of sleep **2.** (*inactivité*) sleep; **être en ~** to be asleep; **laisser qc en ~** to leave sth in abeyance ►**dormir du ~ du __juste__** *iron* to sleep the sleep of the just

sommeiller [sɔmeje] <1> *vi* (*somnoler*) to doze

sommelier, **-ière** [sɔməlje, -jɛʀ] *m, f* sommelier, wine waiter

sommelière [sɔməljɛʀ] *f Suisse* (*serveuse de café ou de restaurant*) waitress

sommer [sɔme] <1> *vt* JUR ~ **qn de** [*o* **à**] **comparaître** to summon sb to appear

sommes [sɔm] *indic prés de* **être**

sommet [sɔmɛ] *m* **1.** (*faîte: d'une montagne*) summit; (*d'une tour, hiérarchie, d'un arbre, toit*) top; (*d'une pente, vague*) crest; (*d'un crâne*) crown **2.** (*apogée*) height; **être au ~ de la gloire** to be at the height one's fame **3.** POL summit; ~ **européen** European summit; **accord/négociation au ~** summit agreement/negotiation

sommier [sɔmje] *m* base; ~ **avec pieds** divan base *Brit;* ~ **à lattes** slatted base; ~ **à ressorts** spring base; ~ **tapissier** sprung base

sommité [sɔ(m)mite] *f* expert; ~ **de la médecine/de la science** leading doctor/scientist; **les ~s du monde politique** the big names in the political world

somnambule [sɔmnɑ̃byl] **I.** *adj* sleepwalking **II.** *mf* sleepwalker

somnifère [sɔmnifɛʀ] *m* soporific; (*cachet, pilule*) sleeping pill

somnolence [sɔmnɔlɑ̃s] *f* **1.** (*demi-sommeil*) drowsiness; **être gagné par la ~** to give way to sleep; **tirer qn de sa ~** to rouse sb from their slumbers **2.** (*inertie: d'une ville*) sleepiness; (*d'une personne, vie, conscience*) lethargy

somnolent(**e**) [sɔmnɔlɑ̃, ɑ̃t] *adj* **1.** (*à moitié endormi*) drowsy; (*ville*) sleepy **2.** (*amorphe: conscience, esprit*) lethargic

somnoler [sɔmnɔle] <1> *vi* (*dormir à moitié*) to doze

somptueusement [sɔ̃ptɥøzmɑ̃] *adv* sumptuously

somptueux, **-euse** [sɔ̃ptɥø, -øz] *adj* (*résidence, vêtement*) magnificent; (*repas*) sumptuous; (*cadeau*) lavish

son[1] [sɔ̃] **I.** *m* sound; **au ~ de l'accordéon** to the accordeon; **baisser le ~** to turn the volume down; **synchroniser le ~ et l'image** to synchronize sound and picture ►**~ de cloche** story; **n'entendre qu'un ~ de cloche** to hear just one side of the story **II.** *app* (**spectacle**) **~ et lumière** son et lumière (show)

son[2] [sɔ̃, se] <ses> *dét poss* **1.** (*d'une femme*) her; (*d'un homme*) his; (*d'un objet, animal*) its; *v. a.* **mon 2.** *après un indéfini* one's, your; **c'est chacun ~ tour** everyone takes a turn

Son [sɔ̃, se] <Ses> *dét poss, avec un titre, form* ~ **Altesse Royale** (*princesse*) Her Royal Highness; (*prince*) His Royal Highness

sonate [sɔnat] *f* sonata; ~ **pour piano** piano sonata

sondage [sɔ̃daʒ] *m* **1.** (*enquête*) poll; ~ **d'opinion** opinion poll **2.** (*contrôle rapide*) survey; **faire quelques ~s dans qc** to sound people out on sth

sonde [sɔ̃d] *f* MED probe; (*cathéter*) catheter

sonder [sɔ̃de] <1> *vt* **1.** ADMIN (*personnes, intentions*) to poll; ~ **l'opinion** to survey public opinion **2.** (*interroger insidieusement: personne*) to sound out **3.** (*pénétrer: conscience, cœur, sentiments*) to probe; ~ **l'avenir** to probe into the future

songer [sɔ̃ʒe] <2a> **I.** *vi* (*penser*) ~ **à qn/qc** to think of sb/sth; (*réfléchir*) to think about sb/sth; ~ **à faire qc** to think about doing sth **II.** *vt* **tout cela est bien étrange, songeait-il** that is all very strange, he thought to himself

songerie [sɔ̃ʒʀi] *f soutenu* dreaming *no pl*

songeur, **-euse** [sɔ̃ʒœʀ, -ʒøz] *adj* **1.** (*perdu dans ses pensées*) pensive **2.** (*perplexe*) **être ~** to be puzzled; **laisser qn ~** to leave sb wondering

sonnant(**e**) [sɔnɑ̃, ɑ̃t] *adj* **à minuit ~/à 4 heures ~es** at the stroke of midnight/4 o'clock

sonné(**e**) [sɔne] *adj* **1.** *inf* (*cinglé*) mad, crazy **2.** *inf* (*groggy*) punch-drunk **3.** (*annoncé par la cloche*) **il est minuit ~/4 heures ~es** it is midnight/4 o'clock exactly ►**avoir cinquante ans <u>bien</u> ~s** *inf* to be on the wrong side of fifty

sonner [sɔne] <1> **I.** *vt* **1.** (*tirer des sons de: cloche*) to ring; (*clairon*) to blow; ~ **trois coups** to ring three times **2.** (*annoncer*) ~ **l'alarme** (*personne, sirène*) to sound the alarm **3.** (*appeler*) ~ **qn** to ring for sb **4.** *inf* (*étourdir, secouer*) to shake; (*coup, maladie, nouvelle*) to knock out; **être sonné** to be groggy **5.** *inf* (*réprimander*) **se faire ~ par qn** to be told off by sb ►**on** (**ne**) **t'a <u>pas</u> sonné** *inf* nobody asked you **II.** *vi* **1.** (*produire un son: cloche, réveil, téléphone*) to ring; (*angélus, trompette*) to sound **2.** (*produire un effet*) ~ **bien** (*proposition*) to sound good; ~ **juste** to sound in tune; (*film*) to ring true; ~ **faux** (*aveux*) to sound false **3.** (*être annoncé: heure*) to strike; (*fin*) to come; **midi/minuit sonne** noon/midnight strikes; **la récréation sonne** the bell for break [*o* recess bell *Am*] rings; **quand sonne l'heure de qc** when it is time for sth **4.** (*s'annoncer*) to ring **5.** (*tinter: monnaie, clés*) to jingle; (*marteau*) to ring; **faire ~ qc** to make sth ring

sonnerie [sɔnʀi] *f* **1.** (*appel sonore*) ring **2.** (*mécanisme: d'un réveil*) ring; ~ **électrique** electric alarm; **remonter la ~ d'un réveil** to reset the alarm on an alarm clock

sonnet [sɔnɛ] *m* sonnet

sonnette [sɔnɛt] *f* (*d'une porte d'entrée*) doorbell; ~ **d'alarme** alarm bell ►**<u>tirer</u> la ~ d'alarme** to sound the alarm bell; **<u>tirer</u> les ~s** (*pour s'amuser*) to ring doorbells and run away, to play ding-dong ditch *Am;* (*pour demander de l'aide*) to ring everybody's bell

sonore [sɔnɔʀ] *adj* **1.** (*retentissant: voix, rire*) ringing; (*gifle, baiser*) loud **2.** (*relatif au son*) **onde ~** soundwave; **bande/piste ~**

soundtrack; **ambiance/fond** ~ background noise; **nuisances ~s** noise pollution *no pl* **3.** (*qui résonne: lieu, voûte*) echoing **4.** LING (*consonne*) voiced

sonorisation [sɔnɔʀizasjɔ̃] *f* (*d'un film*) adding the sound track; (*d'une salle*) fitting a sound system; (*équipement*) sound system

sonoriser [sɔnɔʀize] <1> *vt* ~ **un film** to add the sound track to a film; ~ **une salle** to put a sound system in a hall

sonorité [sɔnɔʀite] *f* **1.** (*qualité sonore: d'un instrument, d'une voix*) tone; (*d'un transistor*) sound; (*d'une salle*) acoustics *pl* **2.** (*résonance*) sonority **3.** LING voicing

sonothèque [sɔnɔtɛk] *f* sound effects library

sont [sɔ̃] *indic prés de* **être**

sophistiqué(e) [sɔfistike] *adj* sophisticated

sophistiquer [sɔfistike] <1> *vt* (*perfectionner*) ~ **qc** to make sth more sophisticated

soporifique [sɔpɔʀifik] *adj* **1.** sleep-inducing; **cachet** ~ sleeping pill **2.** (*endormant, ennuyeux*) soporific

soprane [sɔpʀan] *mf* soprano

soprano[1] <s *o* soprani> [sɔpʀano, sɔpʀani] *m* (*voix*) soprano

soprano[2] [sɔpʀano] *mf* soprano

sorbet [sɔʀbɛ] *m* sorbet; ~ **(au) citron** lemon sorbet

sorbetière [sɔʀbətjɛʀ] *f* ice cream maker

sorbier [sɔʀbje] *m* service tree; ~ **commun** [*o* **des oiseleurs**] rowan (tree)

sorcellerie [sɔʀsɛlʀi] *f* **1.** sorcery **2.** (*chose incompréhensible*) piece of sorcery; **c'est** [*o* **ça tient**] **de la** ~ it's witchcraft!

sorcier, -ière [sɔʀsje, -jɛʀ] **I.** *m, f* socerer *m*, witch *f* **II.** *adj* **ce n'est pas bien** ~ it is not really difficult

sordide [sɔʀdid] *adj* **1.** (*répugnant: quartier, ruelle*) squalid **2.** (*ignoble*) sordid

sort [sɔʀ] *m* **1.** (*condition*) lot; (*situation*) situation **2.** (*destinée, hasard*) fate; **quel a été le** ~ **de ton ami/votre voiture?** what became of your friend/your car?; **connaître le même** ~ **que** to suffer the same fate as; **abandonner qn à son triste** ~ to abandon sb to their fate; **c'est le** ~ **qui décidera** fate will decide; **le** ~ **a tourné** fate has turned; **tirer le vainqueur/les numéros gagnants au** ~ to draw lots for the winner/winning numbers ►**faire un** ~ **à un gigot/à une bouteille** *inf* to polish off a joint of meat/bottle; **le** ~ **en est jeté** the die is cast

sortable [sɔʀtabl] *adj inf* presentable

sortant(e) [sɔʀtɑ̃, ɑ̃t] **I.** *adj* **1.** (*en fin de mandat: coalition, député, ministre*) outgoing **2.** (*tiré au sort*) **les numéros ~s** the numbers which come up **II.** *m(f)* (*député*) incumbent; (*ministre*) outgoing minister; **les entrants et les ~s** those coming in and those leaving

sorte [sɔʀt] *f* type, sort; **plusieurs ~s de pommes** several types of apples; **toutes ~s de personnes/choses** all sorts of people/things; **des disques de toutes ~s** all sorts of records; **ne plus avoir de marchandises d'aucune** ~ to no goods left at all ►**en quelque** ~ in some way; **faire en** ~ **que tout se passe bien** to ensure that all goes well; **de la** ~ of the sort

sortie [sɔʀti] *f* **1.** (*action de sortir: d'une personne*) exit; (*action de quitter: d'une personne*) departure; ~ **de prison/d'hôpital** getting out of prison/hospital; **la** ~ **de piste** AUTO coming off the track **2.** (*promenade*) walk; (*en voiture, à bicyclette*) ride; (*excursion*) outing; **la première** ~ **depuis une maladie** the first outing since an illness; **être de** ~ (*personne*) to have a day off; **tu es de** ~ **aujourd'hui?** is it your day off today? **3.** (*lieu par où l'on sort: d'un bâtiment, d'une autoroute, d'un garage*) exit; ~ **de secours** emergency exit; ~ **de l'usine** factory exit; ~ **des artistes** stage door **4.** (*fin: d'un spectacle, d'une saison*) end; ~ **de l'école/des bureaux** end of the school/working day; **à la** ~ **de l'usine** at the end of the factory day **5.** (*parution: d'une publication*) publication; (*d'un disque, d'un film*) release; (*d'un nouveau modèle, véhicule*) launch; **la** ~ **de ce film est prévue pour le mois prochain** this film should be released next month **6.** SPORT (*d'un ballon*) going into touch; (*d'un gardien*) leaving the goal; ~ **(de but)** going into touch behind the goal **7.** (*exportation: de capitaux, devises*) export **8.** INFOR (*output*) output; (*édition*); ~ **(sur imprimante)** printing ►**fausse** ~ THEAT sham exit; **attendre qn à la** ~ *inf* to wait for sb outside

sortilège [sɔʀtilɛʒ] *m* spell; (*moyen*) charm; **se débarrasser du** ~ **de qn** to free oneself from sb's spell

sortir [sɔʀtiʀ] <10> **I.** *vi être* **1.** (*partir*) to go out; (*venir*) to come out; ~ **par la fenêtre** to leave through the window; **faire** ~ **qn** to make sb leave; **faire** ~ **un animal** to get an animal out; **laisser** ~ **qn** to let sb out **2.** (*quitter*) ~ **du magasin** to leave the shop; (*venir*) to come out of the shop; ~ **du lit** to get out of bed; **d'où sors-tu?** where did you come from?; ~ **de chez ses amis** to come out of one's friends' house; **elle vient justement de** ~ **d'ici** she's just this minute left; **à quelle heure sors-tu du bureau?** what time do you leave the office?; ~ **de prison** to get out of prison; **en sortant du théâtre** after the theatre *Brit,* after the theater *Am;* ~ **du garage** (*voiture*) to leave the garage; ~ **de la piste/route** to leave the track/road; **la faim fait** ~ **le loup du bois** hunger will drive him out **3.** (*quitter son domicile*) to go out; ~ **de chez soi** to leave one's home; ~ **faire les courses** to go out shopping; **faire** ~ **un enfant/un animal** to put an animal/a child out; **laisser** ~ **un enfant/un animal** to let an animal/child out **4.** (*se divertir*) to go out; ~ **en boîte/en ville** to go to a nightclub/into town **5.** *inf* (*avoir une relation amoureuse avec*) ~ **avec qn** to go out with sb **6.** (*en terminer avec*) ~ **d'une période diffi-**

S

cile to come through a difficult period; **ne pas être encore sorti d'embarras** not to be out of the woods yet; **être à peine sorti de convalescence** to hardly be through convalescence **7.** (*être tel après un événement*) ~ **indemne d'un accident** to come out of an accident unscathed; ~ **vainqueur/vaincu d'un concours** to to emerge as the winner/loser in a competition **8.** (*faire saillie*) ~ **de qc** to stick out of sth; **les yeux lui sortaient de la tête** *fig* his eyes were popping out of their sockets **9.** COM (*capitaux, devises*) to leave **10.** (*s'écarter*) ~ **du sujet/de la question** to get off the subject/question; **ça m'était complètement sorti de l'esprit** it had gone completely out of my head **11.** SPORT ~ **en touche** to go into touch; **être sorti en touche** to have gone into touch **12.** (*être issu de*) ~ **de qc** to come from sth; ~ **de l'école de musique** to have studied at the music school **13.** (*apparaître: bourgeons, plante*) to come up; (*dent*) to come through; ~ **de terre** to come up out of the ground **14.** (*paraître: livre*) to be published; (*film, disque*) to be released; (*nouveau modèle, voiture*) to be launched; **vient de** ~ just released; ~ **sur les écrans** to be released in the cinemas **15.** JEUX (*numéro*) to come up ►(**mais**) **d'où tu sors?** *inf* where've you been?; **ne pas en** ~ *inf* not to be able to cope **II.** *vt avoir* **1.** (*mener dehors*) to put out; (*porter dehors*) to take out; **ça vous sortira** it'll get you out **2.** (*expulser*) to get rid of **3.** (*libérer*) ~ **qn d'une situation difficile** to get sb out of a difficult situation; ~ **qn de l'ordinaire** (*chose*) to get sb out of the everyday routine **4.** (*retirer d'un lieu*) to get out; ~ **ses disques/les robes légères** to get out one's records/summer dresses; ~ **qc d'un sac/d'un tiroir/d'une valise** to get sth out of a bag/drawer/suitcase; **ne pas arriver à** ~ **qc** to be unable to get sth out; ~ **la voiture du garage** to get the car out of the garage; ~ **les mains de ses poches** to take one's hands out of one's pockets **5.** COM ~ **des marchandises** to take goods out; (*en fraude*) to smuggle goods out **6.** (*lancer sur le marché: nouveau modèle, véhicule, film, livre, disque*) to launch **7.** *inf* (*débiter: âneries, sottises*) to come out with; ~ **des âneries à qn** to come out with idiotic things in front of sb **8.** *inf* (*éliminer*) to knock out; **se faire** ~ **par qn** to get knocked out by sb **9.** *inf* (*tirer: numéro, carte*) to take **III.** *vpr être* **1.** (*se tirer*) **se** ~ **d'une situation/d'un piège** to get oneself out of a situation/trap **2.** (*réussir*) **s'en** ~ to manage; (*échapper à un danger, un ennui*) to get by; (*survivre*) to pull through; **je ne m'en sors plus** (*fam*) I can't cope any more **IV.** *m* **au** ~ **du lit** when one gets out of bed; **au** ~ **d'une réunion** at the end of a meeting

SOS [ɛsoɛs] *m* **1.** (*appel*) S.O.S. **2.** (*organisation*) ~ **médecins** emergency doctors on call; ~ **dépannage** emergency /repair service; ~ **Racisme/femmes battues** *organization for victims of racism/for battered women* ►**lancer un** ~ to put out an S.O.S.

sosie [sɔzi] *m* double

sot(te) [so, sɔt] *adj* stupid

sottise [sɔtiz] *f* **1.** (*acte sot*) **faire une** ~ to do something stupid **2.** *sans pl* (*caractère sot*) stupidity; **avoir la** ~ **de** +*infin* to be stupid enough to +*infin* **3.** (*paroles niaises*) **dire une** ~/**des** ~**s** to say something stupid/talk nonsense

sou [su] *m pl, inf* money; **ça en fait des** ~**s!** *inf* that's a lot of money! ►**ne pas avoir un** ~ **en poche** *inf* to be flat broke; **propre comme un** ~ **neuf** as clean as a new pin; **être beau comme un** ~ **neuf** to be a picture; **de quatre** ~**s** cheap; **L'Opéra de quat'** ~**s** The Threepenny Opera; **ne pas avoir** [*o* **être sans**] **le** ~ *inf* to be penniless; **compter ses** ~**s** *inf* to count one's pennies; (*être avare*) to count the pennies; **un** ~ (**c'**)**est un** ~ *prov* every penny counts; **être près de ses** ~**s** *inf* to be tight-fisted; **ne pas être rigolo pour un** ~ not to be the least bit funny

soubassement [subasmɑ̃] *m* CONSTR foundation; GEO bedrock

soubresaut [subʀəso] *m* **1.** (*cahot: d'un véhicule*) jolt; (*d'un cheval*) start; **faire un** ~ (*cheval*) to start **2.** (*tressaillement*) shudder; ~**s d'agonie** death throes; **avoir un** ~ **de peur** to start with fear **3.** POL, ECON jolt

souche [suʃ] *f* **1.** BOT stock; ~ **de vigne** vine stock **2.** (*famille*) descent; **français de** ~ native French; **les Marseillais de** ~ real Marseille people; **de vieille** ~ of old stock; **une famille de vieille** ~ an old family; **être de** ~ **paysanne** to come from peasant stock **3.** LING root; **être de** ~ **grecque** (*langue*) to come from Greek **4.** BIO colony **5.** (*talon*) stub **6.** (*partie de cheminée*) stack ►**dormir comme une** ~ to sleep like a log; **faire** ~ to start a line; **rester** (**planté**) **comme une** ~ to stand there like an idiot

souci [susi] *m* **1.** *souvent pl* (*inquiétude*) worry; **se faire du** ~ **pour qn/qc** to worry about sb/sth; **sans** ~ free of worry **2.** (*préoccupation*) concern **3.** (*respect*) **le** ~ **de la vérité/perfection** concern for the truth/perfection; **par** ~ **de vérité** for the sake of the truth; **par** ~ **d'égalité** for equality's sake

soucier [susje] <1> *vpr* **se** ~ **de qn/de la nourriture** to worry about sb/food; **se** ~ **de l'avenir** to worry about the future; **se** ~ **de l'heure** to be worried about the time; **ne pas se** ~ **de la vérité** to have no regard for the truth

soucieux, -euse [susjø, -jøz] *adj* **1.** (*inquiet: personne, air, ton*) worried **2.** (*préoccupé*) **être** ~ **de qn/de l'avenir** to be concerned about sb/the future; **être** ~ **de la vérité** to have respect for the truth

soucoupe [sukup] *f* saucer ►~ **volante** flying saucer

soudain(**e**) [sudɛ̃, ɛn] **I.** *adj* (*événement, geste*) sudden; (*sentiment*) unexpected; **ce fut très** ~ it was very sudden **II.** *adv* suddenly
soudainement [sudɛnmɑ̃] *adv* suddenly
soudaineté [sudɛnte] *f* suddenness; **la** ~ **de sa mort** his sudden death; **la** ~ **de ton revirement** the way you changed your mind so suddenly
Soudan [sudɑ̃] *m* **le** ~ Sudan
soudanais(**e**) [sudanɛ, nɛz] *adj* Sudanese
Soudanais(**e**) [sudanɛ, nɛz] *m(f)* Sudanese
souder [sude] <1> **I.** *vt* **1.** TECH to weld; (*braser: pièces*) to solder **2.** (*réunir: gens, amis*) to bond; **être** [*o* **rester**] **soudés** to be close **3.** (*attacher*) **être soudé** to be attached; **être soudé à sa région natale** to be tied [*o* attached] to the place one was born; **avoir les pieds soudés au plancher** to have one's feet firmly on the ground **4.** MED, ANAT, BOT **être soudé** to be joined; **pour** ~ **les deux parties de l'os** to join the two parts of the bone **II.** *vpr* **se** ~ to unite
soudoyer [sudwaje] <6> *vt* to bribe; **des assassins soudoyés** hired assassins
soudure [sudyʀ] *f* **1.** (*action*) welding; (*brasure*) soldering; (*substance*) solder; ~ **autogène** weld **2.** (*résultat*) weld; (*brasure*) joint **3.** BIO (*d'os*) suture **4.** (*liaison*) **assurer la** ~ **entre deux choses** to bridge the gap between two things; **faire la** ~ **avec qc** to bridge the gap with sth
soufflant(**e**) [suflɑ̃, ɑ̃t] *adj* **machine** ~**e** blower; **brosse à cheveux** ~**e** hot air brush
souffle [sufl] *m* **1.** (*respiration*) breathing; (*action, capacité pulmonaire*) breath; **le dernier** ~ the last breath; ~ **au cœur** heart murmur; **avoir le** ~ **court** to be short of breath; **arriver le** ~ **haletant** to arrive gasping for breath; **éteindre les bougies d'un unique** ~ to blow out the candles in one puff; **il faut du** ~ you have a lot of breath; **manquer de** ~ to be short of breath; **perdre le** ~ to get out of breath **2.** (*déplacement d'air: d'une explosion, d'un incendie, ventilateur*) blast **3.** (*vent*) puff; (*d'air*) breath **4.** (*vitalité*) energy; (*persévérance*) perseverence; **il faut du** ~ you need energy; **second** ~ second wind **5.** (*mouvement créateur: d'un écrivain, poète, d'une œuvre, histoire*) inspiration; **le** ~ **créateur de Dieu** the breath of God ▶ **avoir du** ~ to have a lot of breath; **couper le** ~ **à qn** to take sb's breath away; **être à couper le** ~ to be breathtaking; **ne pas manquer de** ~ to be long-winded; **reprendre son** ~ (*respirer*) to get one's breath back; (*se calmer*) to calm down; **dans un** ~ in a breath; **d'un** ~ by a whisker [*o* hair *Am*]
soufflé [sufle] *m* GASTR soufflé; ~ **au fromage** cheese soufflé
soufflé(**e**) [sufle] *adj inf* (*stupéfait*) (**en**) **être** ~ to be amazed
souffler [sufle] <1> **I.** *vi* **1.** METEO (*vent*) to blow; **ça souffle** it's blowing hard **2.** (*insuffler de l'air*) ~ **sur/dans qc** to blow on/into sth **3.** (*haleter*) to gasp **4.** (*se reposer*) to get one's breath back **5.** (*prendre du recul*) **laisser** ~ **qn** to give sb a rest **II.** *vt* **1.** (*éteindre*) to blow out **2.** (*déplacer en soufflant*) to blow away; ~ **la poussière dans les yeux** to blow dust into one's eyes; ~ **la fumée au visage de qn** to blow smoke into sb's face **3.** *inf* (*enlever*) ~ **une affaire à qn** to pinch a deal from sb; ~ **un pion** JEUX to huff a draught *Brit,* to jump a checker *Am* **4.** (*détruire*) to blast **5.** (*dire discrètement*) ~ **un secret à qn** to whisper a secret to sb; ~ **un poème à l'oreille de qn** to whisper a poem into sb's ear **6.** THEAT to prompt **7.** *inf* (*stupéfier*) to stagger **8.** TECH ~ **le verre** to blow glass
soufflerie [sufləʀi] *f* **1.** fan **2.** AVIAT, AUTO wind tunnel
soufflet [suflɛ] *m* **1.** (*instrument*) bellows + *vb sing* **2.** (*partie pliante*) bellows + *vb sing;* **classeur à** ~ concertina file *Brit,* accordion file *Am*
souffleur, **-euse** [suflœʀ, -øz] *m, f* THEAT prompter
souffleuse [sufløz] *f Québec* (*chasse-neige qui projette la neige à distance*) snow blower
souffrance [sufʀɑ̃s] *f* suffering
souffrant(**e**) [sufʀɑ̃, ɑ̃t] *adj* (*indisposé*) **être** ~ to be unwell
souffre-douleur [sufʀədulœʀ] *mf inv* punch bag
souffreteux, **-euse** [sufʀətø, -øz] *adj* sickly
souffrir [sufʀiʀ] <11> **I.** *vi* **1.** (*avoir mal, être malheureux*) to suffer; **faire** ~ **qn** to make sb suffer; ~ **de la tête/de l'estomac/des reins** to have a headache/stomach problems/kidney problems; ~ **du froid/de la faim** to suffer from the cold/with hunger; ~ **d'être seul** to feel very lonely; **ses dents le font** ~ his teeth give him a lot of trouble **2.** (*être endommagé à cause de*) ~ **du gel** (*cultures*) to suffer from frost-damage; ~ **d'une grave crise** (*pays*) to suffer from a serious crisis; **sa réputation souffre de ce scandale** his reputation has been damaged by this scandal **3.** *inf* (*avoir des difficultés*) **il a souffert pour avoir l'examen** he had a hard time passing the exam **II.** *vt* **1.** (*endurer*) to bear **2.** (*admettre*) to allow
soufre [sufʀ] **I.** *adj inv* **jaune** ~ sulphur yellow *Brit,* sulfur yellow *Am* **II.** *m* sulphur *Brit,* sulfur *Am* ▶ **sentir le** ~ to smack of heresy
souhait [swɛ] *m* **1.** (*désir*) wish; **exprimer le** ~ **de** +*infin* to express a desire to +*infin* **2.** (*très, très bien*) **joli à** ~ extremely pretty; **paisible à** ~ very peaceful; **marcher à** ~ (*entreprise, affaire*) to work perfectly ▶ **à tes/vos** ~**s!** bless you!
souhaitable [swɛtabl] *adj* desirable
souhaiter [swete] <1> *vt* **1.** (*désirer*) ~ **qc** to wish for sth; ~ **que tout se passe bien** to hope that everything goes well; **nous souhaitons manger** we would like to eat; **je souhaiterais t'aider davantage** I would like to

S

help you more **2.** (*espérer pour quelqu'un*) ~ **bonne nuit à qn** to bid sb goodnight; ~ **beaucoup de bonheur à qn** to wish sb lots of happiness; ~ **bien des choses pour la nouvelle année à qn** to wish sb all the best for the new year; ~ **un joyeux anniversaire à qn** to wish sb a happy birthday

souillon [sujɔ̃] *f* (*personne malpropre*) slut

souk [suk] *m* **1.** (*bazar*) souk **2.** *inf* (*désordre*) shambles + *vb sing*

soûl [su] *m* **tout mon/ton** ~ as much as I/you can

soûl(e) [su, sul] *adj inf* (*ivre*) drunk; **être complètement** ~ to be completely drunk

soulagement [sulaʒmɑ̃] *m* relief; **un soupir de** ~ a sigh of relief

soulager [sulaʒe] <2a> **I.** *vt* to relieve **II.** *vpr* **1.** (*se défouler*) **se** ~ **en faisant qc** to find relief by doing sth **2.** *inf* (*satisfaire un besoin naturel*) **se** ~ to relieve oneself

soûler [sule] <1> **I.** *vt* **1.** (*enivrer*) ~ **qn à la bière/au whisky** to get sb drunk on beer/whiskey; **ça soûle!** that's strong stuff! **2.** (*tourner la tête*) ~ **qn** to make sb's head spin **II.** *vpr* **1.** (*s'enivrer*) **se** ~ **à la bière/au whisky** to get drunk on beer/whiskey **2.** (*se griser*) **se** ~ **de musique** to get intoxicated by music

soulèvement [sulɛvmɑ̃] *m* **1.** (*révolte*) uprising **2.** GEO upheaval

soulever [sul(ə)ve] <4> *vt* **1.** (*lever: poids*) to lift **2.** (*relever légèrement*) to lift up **3.** (*susciter: problème, question*) to raise

soulier [sulje] *m* **1.** (*chaussure à semelle résistante*) shoe **2.** *Québec* (*chaussure*) shoe ►**être dans ses petits ~s** to be uneasy

souligner [suliɲe] <1> *vt* **1.** (*tirer un trait sous*) to underline; **souligné de deux traits** double underlined; **souligné en rouge** underlined in red; ~ **l'importance de qc** to underline the importance of sth **2.** (*accentuer, marquer*) to emphasize

soumettre [sumɛtʀ] *irr* **I.** *vt* **1.** (*asservir*) ~ **un joueur à qn/qc** to subject a player to sb/sth **2.** (*faire subir*) ~ **qn à des tests/analyses** to subject sb to tests/analyses **3.** (*présenter*) ~ **une idée/un projet à qn** to submit an idea/project to sb **II.** *vpr* **1.** (*obéir*) **se** ~ **à la loi/à une décision** to submit to the law/a decision **2.** (*se plier à, suivre*) **se** ~ **à un entraînement spécial** to put oneself through special training

soumis(e) [sumi,-z] **I.** *part passé de* **soumettre II.** *adj* **1.** (*docile*) dutiful **2.** (*assujetti*) ~ **à l'impôt** liable to tax; **non** ~ **à l'impôt** free of tax

soumission [sumisjɔ̃] *f* **1.** (*obéissance*) submissiveness **2.** (*reddition: des rebelles, d'un pays*) surrender; **faire (sa)** ~ **à qn** to surrender to sb **3.** COM tender

soupape [supap] *f* valve

soupçon [supsɔ̃] *m* **1.** (*suspicion*) suspicion; **de graves ~s** grave suspicions; **être au-dessus de tout** ~ to be above all suspicion; **éveiller les ~s de qn** to arouse sb's suspicions **2.** (*très petite quantité: de sel, poivre*) pinch; (*d'ironie*) sprinkling

soupçonner [supsɔne] <1> *vt* (*suspecter*) ~ **qn de vol** to suspect sb of theft

soupçonneux, **-euse** [supsɔnø, -øz] *adj* suspicious

soupe [sup] *f* **1.** (*potage*) soup; **assiette/cuillère à** ~ soup dish/spoon; ~ **à l'oignon/de légumes** onion/vegetable soup; **à la ~!** *inf* come and get it! **2.** (*neige fondue*) slush **3.** (*organisme charitable*) ~ **populaire** soup kitchen ►**être trempé comme une** ~ *inf* soaked to the skin; **cracher dans la** ~ *inf* to bite the had that feeds you

soupente [supɑ̃t] *f* (*en haut d'une pièce*) loft; (*sous l'escalier*) cupboard

souper[1] [supe] *m* **1.** (*repas tard dans la nuit*) supper **2.** *Belgique, Québec, Suisse* (*dîner*) dinner

souper[2] [supe] <1> *vi* **1.** (*prendre un souper*) to have supper **2.** *Belgique, Québec, Suisse* (*dîner*) to have dinner; **vous restez à ~?** will you stay to dinner? ►**en avoir soupé de qc** *inf* to have had it up to here with sth

soupeser [supəze] <4> *vt* **1.** (*peser*) to feel the weight of **2.** (*évaluer*) ~ **qc** to weigh sth up; ~ **des arguments** to weigh (up) the arguments

soupière [supjɛʀ] *f* tureen

soupir [supiʀ] *m* (*signe d'émotion*) sigh; **pousser un** ~ **de soulagement** to give a sigh of relief

soupirail [supiʀaj, o] <-aux> *m* basement window

soupirant [supiʀɑ̃] *m iron* suitor

soupirer [supiʀe] <1> *vi* to sigh

souple [supl] *adj* **1.** (*opp: rigide*) supple; (*tissu*) soft **2.** (*agile: bras, jambes, personne*) supple **3.** (*adaptable*) flexible

souplesse [suplɛs] *f* (*adaptabilité*) flexibility; (*d'une personne*) suppleness

source [suʀs] **I.** *f* **1.** (*point d'eau*) spring; ~ **thermale/d'eau minérale** thermal/mineral water spring; **eau de** ~ spring water **2.** (*naissance d'un cours d'eau*) source; **prendre sa** ~ **en Suisse** to rise in Switzerland **3.** PHYS, OPT ~ **lumineuse/d'énergie** light/energy source **4.** (*origine de l'information*) **de** ~ **sûre/bien informée** from a reliable/well-informed source ►**couler de** ~ to come naturally **II.** *app* INFOR **langage/programme** ~ source language/program

sourceur, **-euse** *m, f* COM sourcing expert

sourcil [suʀsi] *m* eyebrow ►**froncer les ~s** to knit one's brow

sourcilier, **-ière** [suʀsilje, -jɛʀ] *adj v.* **arcade**

sourciller [suʀsije] <1> *vi* **sans** ~ without turning a hair

sourd(e) [suʀ, suʀd] **I.** *adj* **1.** (*qui n'entend pas*) deaf; ~ **d'une oreille** deaf in one ear **2.** (*étouffé: bruit*) muffled **II.** *m(f)* deaf person

sourdement [suʀdəmɑ̃] *adv soutenu* **1.** (*avec un bruit sourd*) dully **2.** (*secrètement*) silently
sourdine [suʀdin] *f* **1.** MUS (*dispositif*) mute; **en ~** softly **2.** *fig* **mettre la ~** *inf* (*faire moins de bruit*) to quieten down
sourdingue [suʀdɛ̃g] *adj péj, inf* cloth-eared
sourd-muet, **sourde-muette** [suʀmɥɛ, suʀd(ə)mɥɛt] <sourds-muets> *m, f* deaf-mute
souriant(e) [suʀjɑ̃, jɑ̃t] *adj* smiling
souricière [suʀisjɛʀ] *f* **1.** (*piège à souris*) mousetrap **2.** (*traquenard*) trap
sourire [suʀiʀ] **I.** *m* smile; **faire un ~** to give a smile; **faire un ~ à qn** to give sb a smile; **avoir le ~** *inf* to have a smile on one's face; **garder le ~** to keep smiling **II.** *vi irr* **1.** (*avoir un sourire*) to smile **2.** (*adresser un sourire*) **~ à qn** to smile at sb
souris [suʀi] *f* a. INFOR mouse
sournois(e) [suʀnwa, waz] **I.** *adj* **1.** (*hypocrite*) sly **2.** (*insidieux*) underhand **II.** *m(f)* sly character
sournoisement [suʀnwazmɑ̃] *adv* **1.** (*pas franchement: observer*) on the sly **2.** (*insidieusement*) underhandedly
sous [su] *prep* **1.** (*spatial, manière, dépendance, causal*) under **2.** (*temporel, pour exprimer un délai*) **~ huitaine** within a week; **~ peu** shortly **3.** METEO in **4.** MED on; **être ~ perfusion** to be on a drip *Brit*
sous-alimenté(e) [suzalimɑ̃te] *adj* undernourished **sous-bois** [subwɑ] *m inv* undergrowth *no pl*
souscription [suskʀipsjɔ̃] *f* **1.** subscription **2.** FIN (*d'actions, obligations*) application
souscrire [suskʀiʀ] *irr* **I.** *vi* **1.** (*participer financièrement*) to subscribe; **~ pour 5000 euros** to contribute 5000 euros **2.** (*s'engager à acheter*) **~ à une encyclopédie** to subscribe to an encyclopedia; **~ à un emprunt** FIN to subscribe to a loan **3.** *soutenu* (*donner son approbation à*) **~ à qc** to go along with sth **II.** *vt* **1.** (*signer et s'engager à payer*) to sign; (*police d'assurance, abonnement*) to take out **2.** FIN (*actions, obligations*) **~ qc** to apply for sth
sous-cutané(e) [sukytane] *adj* subcutaneous **sous-développé(e)** [sudev(ə)lɔpe] <sous-développés> *adj* under-developed **sous-développement** [sudev(ə)lɔpmɑ̃] <sous-développements> *m* under-development **sous-directeur**, **-trice** [sudiʀɛktœʀ, -tʀis] <sous-directeurs> *m, f* deputy manager **sous-entendre** [suzɑ̃tɑ̃dʀ] <14> *vt* (*dire implicitement*) to imply **sous-entendu(e)** [suzɑ̃tɑ̃dy] <sous-entendus> *m* insinuation; **parler par sous-entendus** to insinuate **sous-estimer** [suzɛstime] <1> *vt* to underestimate **sous-évaluer** [suzevalɥe] <1> *vt* to undervalue **sous-fifre** [sufifʀ] <sous-fifres> *m* underling **sous-louer** [sulwe] <1> *vt* to sublet **sous-marin** [sumaʀɛ̃] <sous-marins> *m* submarine **sous-officier** [suzɔfisje] <sous-officiers> *m* non-commissioned officer **sous-payer** [supeje] <7> *vt* to underpay **sous-préfecture** [supʀefɛktyʀ] <sous-préfectures> *f* sub-prefecture **sous-préfet, Mme le sous-préfet** [supʀefɛ] <sous-préfets> *m, f* sub-prefect **sous-produit** [supʀɔdɥi] <sous-produits> *m* (*produit dérivé*) by-product
soussigné(e) [susiɲe] *adj, m(f)* JUR undersigned
sous-sol [susɔl] <sous-sols> *m* basement **sous-tasse** [sutɑs] *f Belgique, Suisse* (*soucoupe*) saucer **sous-titre** [sutitʀ] <sous-titres> *m* subtitle **sous-titré(e)** [sutitʀe] *adj* subtitled; **version originale ~e** original language version with subtitles **sous-titrer** [sutitʀe] <1> *vt* to subtitle
soustraction [sustʀaksjɔ̃] *f* **1.** JUR removal **2.** MAT subtraction; **faire une ~** to do a subtraction
soustraire [sustʀɛʀ] *irr* **I.** *vi* to subtract **II.** *vpr* **se ~ à une obligation** to shirk an obligation
sous-traitant [sutʀɛtɑ̃] <sous-traitants> *m* subcontractor **sous-verre** [suvɛʀ] *m inv* glass mount **sous-vêtement** [suvɛtmɑ̃] <sous-vêtements> *m* **des sous-vêtements** underwear *no pl*
soutane [sutan] *f* cassock
soute [sut] *f* (*d'un avion, bateau*) hold; **~ à charbon** coal bunker; **~ à bagages** baggage hold
soutenance [sut(ə)nɑ̃s] *f* UNIV viva *Brit,* defense *Am* (*for a thesis*)
souteneur [sut(ə)nœʀ] *m* procurer
soutenir [sut(ə)niʀ] <9> *vt* **1.** (*porter, aider, prendre parti pour*) to support **2.** (*maintenir debout, en bonne position*) to hold up **3.** ECON (*monnaie*) to prop up **4.** (*affirmer*) **~ que c'est la vérité** to maintain that it is the truth **5.** (*résister à*) **~ le regard de qn** to withstand the gaze of sb
soutenu(e) [sut(ə)ny] **I.** *part passé de* **soutenir** **II.** *adj* **1.** (*régulier: attention, effort*) sustained **2.** (*avec des effets de style: style, langue*) formal
souterrain [suteʀɛ̃] *m* underpass
souterrain(e) [suteʀɛ̃, ɛn] *adj* (*sous terre*) underground; **passage ~** underpass
soutien [sutjɛ̃] *m* **1.** (*aide, appui*) support; **~ de famille** breadwinner; **apporter son ~ à qn** to support sb **2.** ECOLE **cours de ~** remedial lessons *pl*
soutien-gorge [sutjɛ̃gɔʀʒ] <soutiens-gorge(s)> *m* bra
soutif [sutif] *m inf* bra
soutirer [sutiʀe] <1> *vt* (*escroquer*) **~ de l'argent à qn** to get money out of sb
souvenir[1] [suv(ə)niʀ] <9> *vpr* **1.** (*se rappeler, se remémorer*) **se ~ de qn/qc** to

S

remember sb/sth; **il se souvient à qui il a parlé** he remembers who he spoke to **2.** (*se venger*) **je m'en souviendrai!** I'll remember this!

souvenir² [suv(ə)niʀ] **I.** *m* **1.** (*image dans la mémoire, ce qui rappelle qn/qc*) memory; **si mes ~s sont exacts, …** is my memory is right, …; **garder un bon/mauvais ~ de qn/qc** to have good/bad memories of sb/sth; **en ~ de qc/qn** in memory of sth/sb **2.** (*objet touristique*) souvenir **II.** *app* **photo-~** souvenir photo

souvent [suvɑ̃] *adv* often; **le plus ~** most often

souverain(**e**) [suv(ə)ʀɛ̃, ɛn] **I.** *adj* **1.** (*État, puissance, peuple*) sovereign; **être ~** (*assemblée, cour, juge*) to have supreme authority **2.** (*suprême: bien, bonheur, indifférence, mépris*) supreme **3.** (*très efficace: remède*) sovereign **II.** *m(f)* sovereign

souverainement [suv(ə)ʀɛnmɑ̃] *adv* **1.** (*extrêmement*) supremely **2.** (*en toute indépendance*) with supreme authority

souveraineté [suv(ə)ʀɛnte] *f* (*d'un État, peuple*) sovereignty

soviétique [sɔvjetik] *adj* Soviet; **l'Union ~** the Soviet Union

Soviétique [sɔvjetik] *mf* Soviet; **les ~s** the Soviets

soyeux, **-euse** [swajø, -jøz] *adj* **1.** (*doux*) silky **2.** (*brillant*) shiny

SPA [ɛspea] *f abr de* **Société protectrice des animaux** animal protection society

spacieux, **-euse** [spasjø, -jøz] *adj* spacious

spaghettis [spageti] *mpl* spaghetti + *vb sing*

sparadrap [spaʀadʀa] *m* elastoplast® *Brit,* Band-Aid® *Am*

spasme [spasm] *m* spasm

spasmodique [spasmɔdik] *adj* spasmodic

spatial(**e**) [spasjal, jo] <-aux> *adj* space

spationaute [spasjonot] *mf* astronaut

spatiotemporel(**le**) [spasjotɑ̃pɔʀɛl] *adj* spatiotemporal

spatule [spatyl] *f* **1.** (*ustensile*) spatula **2.** (*bout d'un ski*) tip

spécial(**e**) [spesjal, jo] <-aux> *adj* **1.** (*opp: général*) special; **équipement ~** specialist equipment; **rien de ~** nothing special **2.** (*bizarre*) strange

spécialement [spesjalmɑ̃] *adv* **1.** (*en particulier*) especially **2.** (*tout exprès*) specially **3.** *inf* (*pas vraiment*) **tu as faim? – non, pas ~** are you hungry? – no, not particularly

spécialisation [spesjalizasjɔ̃] *f* specialization

spécialisé(**e**) [spesjalize] *adj* **être ~ dans qc** to be specialized in sth

spécialiser [spesjalize] <1> **I.** *vt* **~ qn dans un domaine précis** to train sb as a specialist in a particular field **II.** *vpr* **se ~ dans** [*o* **en**] **qc** to specialize in sth

spécialiste [spesjalist] *mf* **1.** (*expert*) expert; **~ de l'art moderne** modern art expert **2.** (*technicien*) *a.* MED specialist

spécialité [spesjalite] *f* speciality

spécification [spesifikasjɔ̃] *f* specification

spécificité [spesifisite] *f* specificity

spécifier [spesifje] <1> *vt* to specify; (*loi*) to stipulate; **~ que …** to specify that …

spécifique [spesifik] *adj* specific

spécifiquement [spesifikmɑ̃] *adv* specifically

spécimen [spesimɛn] *m* **1.** (*exemplaire*) specimen **2.** (*exemplaire publicitaire*) specimen copy

spectacle [spɛktakl] *m* **1.** (*ce qui s'offre au regard*) spectacle; **~ de la nature** spectacle of nature **2.** THEAT, CINE, TV show; **aller au ~** to go to a show **3.** (*show-business*) **le monde du ~** the entertainment world **4.** (*avec de gros moyens*) **à grand ~** spectacular

spectaculaire [spɛktakylɛʀ] *adj* spectacular

spectateur, **-trice** [spɛktatœʀ, -tʀis] *m, f* **1.** THEAT, SPORT spectator **2.** (*observateur*) onlooker

spectre [spɛktʀ] *m* **1.** spectrum; **~ solaire/sonore** solar/sound spectrum; **antibiotique à large ~** broad-spectrum antibiotic **2.** *a. fig* (*fantôme*) spectre

spéculateur, **-trice** [spekylatœʀ, -tʀis] *m, f* speculator

spéculatif, **-ive** [spekylatif, -iv] *adj* speculative; **gain ~** speculative gain

spéculation [spekylasjɔ̃] *f* speculation; **faire des ~s sur qc** to speculate about sth

spéculer [spekyle] <1> *vi* **1.** FIN, COM **~ sur qc** to speculate about sth **2.** (*compter sur*) **~ sur qc** to bank on sth

speech [spitʃ] *m* speech

speed [spid] *adj,* **speedé**(**e**) [spide] *adj* **1.** *inf* (*agité*) hyper **2.** (*par des amphétamines*) on speed

spéléologie [speleɔlɔʒi] *f* **1.** (*science*) speleology **2.** (*loisirs*) pot-holing *Brit,* spelunking *Am*

spéléologue [speleɔlɔg] *mf* potholer *Brit,* spelunker *Am*

spermatozoïde [spɛʀmatɔzɔid] *m* sperm

sperme [spɛʀm] *m* sperm

spermicide [spɛʀmisid] *adj* spermicide

sphère [sfɛʀ] *f* **1.** (*en science*) sphere **2.** (*domaine*) field; (*d'influence*) sphere

sphérique [sfeʀik] *adj* spherical

sphinx [sfɛ̃ks] *m* **1.** sphinx **2.** ZOOL (*papillon*) hawk moth

spinnaker [spinakɛʀ] *m* spinnaker

spirale [spiʀal] *f* spiral; **cahier à ~** spiral-bound notebook; **~ de prix** price spiral

spiritisme [spiʀitism] *m* spiritualism

spiritualité [spiʀitɥalite] *f* REL, PHILOS spirituality

spirituel(**le**) [spiʀitɥɛl] *adj* **1.** (*plein d'esprit*) witty **2.** (*qui se rapporte à l'esprit*) *a.* REL spiritual

spirituellement [spiʀitɥɛlmɑ̃] *adv* (*avec esprit*) wittily

spiritueux [spiʀitɥø] *m* spirituous
spitant(e) [spitɑ̃, ɑ̃t] *adj Belgique* (*pétillant*) sparkling
spleen [splin] *m* spleen
splendeur [splɑ̃dœʀ] *f a. iron* splendour *no pl Brit,* splendor *no pl Am;* **être une** ~ to be magnificent
splendide [splɑ̃did] *adj* splendid
spoiler [spɔjlɛʀ] *m* spoiler
spolier [spɔlje] <1a> *vt* ~ **qn de qc** to despoil sb of sth
spongieux, -euse [spɔ̃ʒjø, -jøz] *adj a.* ANAT spongy; (*sol*) sponge-like
sponsor [spɔ̃sɔʀ, spɔnsɔʀ] *m* sponsor
sponsoring [spɔ̃sɔʀiŋ] *m,* **sponsorisation** [spɔ̃sɔʀizasjɔ̃] *f* sponsoring
sponsoriser [spɔ̃sɔʀize] <1> *vt* to sponsor
spontané(e) [spɔ̃tane] *adj* spontaneous
spontanéité [spɔ̃taneite] *f* spontaneity
spontanément [spɔ̃tanemɑ̃] *adv* spontaneously
sporadique [spɔʀadik] *adj* sporadic
sport [spɔʀ] **I.** *adj inv* (*coupe*) casual; **s'habiller** ~ to dress casually **II.** *m* sport; ~ **de combat/de compétition** combat/competitive sport; ~ **professionnel** professional-level sport; **faire du** ~ to do [*o* play] sport [*o* sports *Am*]; **chaussures de** ~ sports shoes; ~**s nautiques** water sports; ~ **d'hiver** winter sport; **pratiquer plusieurs** ~**s** to do several sports ▶**ça, c'est du** ~ that's no fun
sportif, -ive [spɔʀtif, -iv] **I.** *adj* **1.** (*de sport*) **pages sportives d'un journal** sports pages of a newspaper **2.** (*de compétition*) **danse/natation sportive** competitive dancing/swimming **3.** (*qui fait du sport*) athletic **4.** (*typique de qui fait du sport: allure, démarche*) sporty **II.** *m, f* sportsman, sportswoman *m, f*
spot [spɔt] *m* **1.** (*lampe, projecteur*) light spot **2.** (*message publicitaire*) ~ **publicitaire** commercial
spray [spʀɛ] *m* **1.** (*pulvérisation*) spray **2.** (*atomiseur*) aerosol
sprint [spʀint] *m* **1.** (*course sur petite distance*) sprint **2.** (*fin de course*) ~ **final** final sprint
sprinter[1] [spʀintɛʀ] *m v.* **sprinteur**
sprinter[2] [spʀinte] <1> *vi* to sprint
sprinteur, -euse [spʀintœʀ, -øz] *m, f* sprinter
squale [skwal] *m* shark
square [skwaʀ] *m* square
squash [skwaʃ] *m* squash
squatter[1] [skwatœʀ] *m* squatter
squatter[2] [skwate] <1> *vt* to squat
squelette [skəlɛt] *m* ANAT, ARCHIT *a. fig* skeleton
squelettique [skəletik] *adj* **être** ~ (*très maigre*) to be skin and bone
Sri Lanka [sʀilɑ̃ka] *m* **le** ~ Sri Lanka
stabiliser [stabilize] <1> **I.** *vt* **1.** (*consolider, équilibrer*) to consolidate **2.** (*rendre stable, éviter toute fluctuation*) to stabilize **II.** *vpr* (*devenir stable*) **se** ~ to stabilize
stabilité [stabilite] *f* ECON, POL ~ **des prix** price stability
stable [stabl] *adj* **1.** (*ferme, équilibré*) stable; (*terrain*) consolidated **2.** (*durable, qui ne varie pas*) stable
stade [stad] *m* **1.** SPORT stadium; ~ **olympique** Olympic stadium **2.** (*phase*) stage
stage [staʒ] *m* **1.** (*en entreprise*) **faire un** ~ to do a period of work experience *Brit,* to do an internship *Am;* ~**s** (*sur un CV*) work experience **2.** (*séminaire*) course; ~ **de perfectionnement** advanced training course; ~ **d'initiation à qc** introductory course in sth **3.** (*période avant la titularisation*) trial period
stagiaire [staʒjɛʀ] **I.** *adj* trainee **II.** *mf* (*en entreprise*) trainee
stagnant(e) [stagnɑ̃, ɑ̃t] *adj a.* ECON (*dormant*) stagnant; **eaux** ~**es** stagnant water + *vb sing*
stagnation [stagnasjɔ̃] *f* stagnation
stagner [stagne] <1> *vi* to stagnate
stalactite [stalaktit] *f* stalactite
stalagmite [stalagmit] *f* stalagmite
stalinien(ne) [stalinjɛ̃, jɛn] *adj, mf* Stalinist
stalinisme [stalinism] *m* Stalinism
stalle [stal] *f a.* REL stall
stand [stɑ̃d] *m* **1.** (*dans une exposition*) stand **2.** (*dans une fête*) stall; ~ **de tir** shooting range **3.** SPORT ~ **de ravitaillement** pit
standard[1] [stɑ̃daʀ] *m* TEL switchboard
standard[2] [stɑ̃daʀ] **I.** *adj inv* standard **II.** *m* standard; ~ **de sécurité** security norms; ~ **de vie** standard of living
standardisation [stɑ̃daʀdizasjɔ̃] *f a.* IND standardization
standardiser [stɑ̃daʀdize] <1> *vt* to standardize
standardiste [stɑ̃daʀdist] *mf* switchboard operator
standing [stɑ̃diŋ] *m* **1.** (*niveau de vie*) standing **2.** (*confort*) **hôtel de** (**grand**) ~ luxury hotel
staphylocoque [stafilɔkɔk] *m* staphylococcus
star [staʀ] *f* star; ~ **de cinéma** film star
starter [staʀtɛʀ] *m* **1.** AUTO choke; **mettre le** ~ to pull the choke out; ~ **automatique** automatic choke **2.** SPORT starter; **coup de pistolet du** ~ shot from the starting pistol
station [stasjɔ̃] *f* **1.** AUTO service station; ~ **de taxis** taxi rank **2.** CINE, TV station **3.** TECH, REL station; ~ **d'épuration** water-treatment plant; ~ (**d'**)**essence** petrol station *Brit,* gas station *Am;* ~ **météorologique** weather station; ~ **orbitale/spatiale** orbiting/space station; ~ **radar** radar tracking station; **les quatorze** ~**s du chemin de Croix** the fourteen Stations of the Cross **4.** (*pour le tourisme*) ~ **balnéaire/de sports d'hiver** sea/winter sports resort; ~ **thermale** thermal spa
stationnaire [stasjɔnɛʀ] *adj* (*qui n'évolue pas*) stationary

S

stationnement [stasjɔnmɑ̃] *m* **1.**(*fait de sationner*) parking; **voitures en ~** parked cars; **ticket/disque de ~** parking ticket/permit; **~ payant** pay parking; **~ interdit** no parking; **panneau de ~ interdit** no parking sign **2.** *Québec* (*parc de stationnement*) car park *Brit,* parking lot *Am*

stationner [stasjɔne] <1> *vi* (*être garé*) to be parked; **interdiction de ~** no parking

station-service [stasjɔ̃sɛʀvis] <stations-service(s)> *f* service station

statistique [statistik] **I.** *adj* statistical **II.** *f* (*science*) statistics + *vb sing;* **faire des ~s** to do statistics

statue [staty] *f* statue; **la ~ de la Liberté** the Statue of Liberty

statuer [statɥe] <1> *vi* **~ sur qc** to rule on sth

statuette [statɥɛt] *f* statuette

statufier [statyfje] <1a> *vt* **1.** *inf*(*élever une statue à*) **~ qn** to erect a statue of sb **2.**(*pétrifier*) to petrify; **être statufié** to be petrified

statu quo [statykwo] *m inv* status quo

stature [statyʀ] *f* **1.**(*taille*) height; **de ~ moyenne** of medium height; **de haute ~** tall **2.**(*envergure*) stature

statut [staty] *m* **1.** *a.* ADMIN status; **~ de fonctionnaire** civil servant status; **~ social** social status **2.** *pl* JUR (*d'une association, société*) statutes

steak [stɛk] *m* steak

stèle [stɛl] *f* stele

stellaire [stelɛʀ] *adj* **lumière ~** stellar light; **les influences ~s** the influence of the stars

sténo [steno] *abr de* **sténodactylo, sténographie**

sténodactylo [stenodaktilo] *mf* shorthand typist

sténographie [stenɔgʀafi] *f* shorthand

steppe [stɛp] *f* steppe

stéréo [steʀeo] **I.** *adj inv abr de* **stéréophonique: chaîne ~** stereo **II.** *f abr de* **stéréophonie** stereo

stéréophonie [steʀeɔfɔni] *f* stereophony

stéréophonique [steʀeɔfɔnik] *adj* stereophonic

stéréotype [steʀeɔtip] *m* stereotype

stéréotypé(e) [steʀeɔtipe] *adj* stereotyped

stérile [steʀil] *adj* sterile

stérilet [steʀilɛ] *m* IUD

stérilisation [steʀilizasjɔ̃] *f* sterilization

stériliser [steʀilize] <1> *vt* to sterilize

stérilité [steʀilite] *f* **1.** AGR barrenness; BIO sterility **2.**(*absence de microbes*) sterility **3.** ART, LIT *a. fig* sterility

sternum [stɛʀnɔm] *m* sternum, breastbone

stéthoscope [stetɔskɔp] *m* stethoscope

steward [stiwaʀt] *m* steward

stick [stik] *m* stick; **~ à lèvres** lipstick

stimulant [stimylɑ̃] *m* **1.**(*médicament*) stimulant **2.**(*incitation*) stimulus

stimulant(e) [stimylɑ̃, ɑ̃t] *adj* stimulating

stimulateur [stimylatœʀ] *m* **~ cardiaque** pacemaker

stimuler [stimyle] <1> *vt* **1.**(*activer, augmenter*) to stimulate **2.**(*encourager*) to encourage

stipuler [stipyle] <1> *vt* **1.** JUR to stipulate **2.**(*préciser: personne*) to specify; **l'annonce stipule** [*o* **il est stipulé dans l'annonce**] **que ...** the advertisement stipulates that ...

stock [stɔk] *m* **1.** COM stock; **avoir qc en ~** to have sth in stock; **~ de marchandises** stock of goods **2.**(*réserve*) supply; **~ de sucre** supply of sugar **3.** *inf* (*grande quantité*) **garde ce stylo, j'en ai tout un ~** keep that pen, I've got lots

stocker [stɔke] <1> *vt* **1.**(*mettre en réserve*) to stock **2.** INFOR **~ les données sur une disquette** to store data on a disk

Stockholm [stɔkˊɔlm] Stockholm

stoïque [stɔik] *adj* stoic

stomacal(e) [stɔmakal, o] <-aux> *adj* **douleurs ~es** stomach pains

stomatologie [stɔmatɔlɔʒi] *mf* stomatology

stop [stɔp] **I.** *interj* (*halte, dans un télégramme*) stop; **~ à l'inflation** end inflation **II.** *m* **1.**(*panneau*) stop sign; (*feu*) red light **2.** AUTO (*feu arrière*) brake light **3.** *inf* (*autostop*) **faire du ~** to hitchhike; **en ~** hitchhiking **III.** *app* **panneau ~** stop sign

stopper [stɔpe] <1> *vt, vi* to stop

store [stɔʀ] *m* **1.**(*rideau à enrouler, à lamelles*) blind **2.**(*rideau de magasin*) awning

strabisme [stʀabism] *m* squinting; **avoir un ~** to have a squint

strangulation [stʀɑ̃gylasjɔ̃] *f* strangulation

strapontin [stʀapɔ̃tɛ̃] *m* **1.**(*siège*) flap seat **2.**(*place secondaire*) minor position

Strasbourg [stʀasbuʀ] Strasbourg

strasbourgeois(e) [stʀasbuʀʒwa, waz] *adj* of Strasbourg; *v. a.* **ajaccien**

Strasbourgeois(e) [stʀasbuʀʒwa, waz] *m(f)* person from Strasbourg; *v. a.* **Ajaccien**

stratagème [stʀataʒɛm] *m* stratagem

strate [stʀat] *f* stratum

stratégie [stʀateʒi] *f* strategy; **jeu de ~** strategy game

stratégique [stʀateʒik] *adj* strategic

stratifié [stʀatifje] *m* stratified

stratosphère [stʀatɔsfɛʀ] *f* stratosphere

stress [stʀɛs] *m* stress

stressant(e) [stʀesɑ̃, ɑ̃t] *adj* stressful

stressé(e) [stʀese] *adj* stressed

stresser [stʀese] <1> **I.** *vt* to put under stress **II.** *vi* (*personne*) to stress

stretch [stʀɛtʃ] *m* stretch fabric

strict(e) [stʀikt] *adj* **1.**(*sévère*) strict; **être très ~ sur le règlement** to be very strict about the rules **2.**(*rigoureux: principe, observation, respect*) strict **3.** *antéposé* (*exact*) **c'est la ~e vérité** it's the exact truth **4.** *antéposé* (*absolu*) minimum; **le ~ nécessaire** the bare minimum; **dans la plus ~e intimité** in the strictest privacy **5.**(*littéral*) **au sens ~** in the strict sense (of the term) **6.** (*sobre: vêtement, tenue*) sober

strictement [stʀiktəmɑ̃] *adv* **1.** (*pour renforcer, littéralement, au sens restreint*) strictly; **c'est ~ pareil** it's exactly the same **2.** (*sobrement*) **~ vêtu** soberly dressed

strident(e) [stʀidɑ̃, ɑ̃t] *adj* strident

strie [stʀi] *f rare au sing* **1.** (*en relief*) **les ~s** stria **2.** (*de couleur*) streaks

string [stʀiŋ] *m* G-string

strip-tease [stʀiptiz] <strip-teases> *m* striptease

strip-teaseur, -euse [stʀiptizœʀ, -øz] <strip-teaseurs> *m, f* stripper

strophe [stʀɔf] *f* verse

structure [stʀyktyʀ] *f* **1.** (*organisation*) structure; **~ de la personnalité** personality structure; **réforme de ~** structural reform **2.** (*lieu, service social*) **~ d'accueil** welcome facilities

structurel(le) [stʀyktyʀɛl] *adj* structural

structurer [stʀyktyʀe] <1> **I.** *vt* to structure **II.** *vpr* **se ~** to be structured

stuc [styk] *m* stucco; **~ de marbre** marble stucco

studieux, -euse [stydjø, -jøz] *adj* **1.** (*appliqué*) studious **2.** (*consacré au travail, aux études: vacances, soirée*) study

studio [stydjo] *m* (*logement*) *a.* CINE, TV studio; **~ de télévision/cinéma** television/film studio; **~ d'enregistrement** recording studio; **à vous, les ~s** now back to the studio

stup [styp] *m inf abr de* **stupéfiant** drug

stupéfaction [stypefaksjɔ̃] *f* (*étonnement*) amazement

stupéfait(e) [stypefɛ, ɛt] *adj* (*étonné*) amazed

stupéfiant [stypefjɑ̃] *m* drug

stupéfiant(e) [stypefjɑ̃, jɑ̃t] *adj* amazing

stupéfié(e) [stypefje] *adj* (*très étonné*) amazed

stupéfier [stypefje] <1> *vt* (*étonner*) to amaze

stupeur [stypœʀ] *f* (*étonnement*) amazement; **être frappé de ~** to be stunned

stupide [stypid] *adj* stupid

stupidement [stypidmɑ̃] *adv* stupidly

stupidité [stypidite] *f* stupidity

style [stil] *m* **1.** (*écriture*) *a.* ART, LIT, LING style **2.** (*genre*) type; (*d'un vêtement*) style; **des meubles de ~** period furniture **3.** (*manière personnelle*) style; **~ de vie** lifestyle; **avoir du ~** to have style; **arriver en retard, c'est bien dans son ~!** arriving late, that's him all over!

stylé(e) [stile] <1> *adj* well-trained

stylet [stilɛ] *m* stylet

stylisé(e) [stilize] *adj* stylized

styliste [stilist] *mf* stylist

stylistique [stilistik] **I.** *adj* stylistic **II.** *f* stylistics + *vb sing*

stylo [stilo] *m* pen; **~ (à) plume** fountain pen; **~ (à) bille** ball-point pen

stylo-feutre [stiloføtʀ] <stylos-feutres> *m* felt-tipped pen

su [sy] *part passé de* **savoir**

suaire [sɥɛʀ] *m* **le saint ~** the Holy Shroud

suave [sɥav] *adj* suave; (*couleur, ton*) mellow; (*sourire*) sweet; (*voix, forme*) smooth

subalterne [sybaltɛʀn] **I.** *adj* **1.** (*inférieur*) junior **2.** (*secondaire*) subordinate **II.** *mf* subordinate

subconscient [sybkɔ̃sjɑ̃] *m* subconscious

subdiviser [sybdivize] <1> *vt* to subdivide

subdivision [sybdivizjɔ̃] *f* subdivision

subir [sybiʀ] <8> *vt* **1.** (*être victime de*) to suffer **2.** (*endurer*) to undergo; (*événements*) to go through; (*conséquences*) to suffer **3.** (*être soumis à*) **~ le charme/l'influence** to be under the spell/influence; **~ une opération/un interrogatoire** to undergo an operation/questioning **4.** (*être l'objet de*) **~ des modifications** to be modified **5.** *inf* (*devoir supporter: personne*) to put up with

subit(e) [sybi, it] *adj* sudden

subitement [sybitmɑ̃] *adv* suddenly

subjectif, -ive [sybʒɛktif, -iv] *adj* subjective

subjectivité [sybʒɛktivite] *f* subjectivity

subjonctif [sybʒɔ̃ktif] *m* subjunctive

subjuguer [sybʒyge] <1> *vt* (*fasciner*) to enthrall

sublime [syblim] **I.** *adj* **1.** (*admirable*) wonderful **2.** (*d'une haute vertu*) sublime **II.** *m* sublime

submerger [sybmɛʀʒe] <2a> *vt* **1.** (*inonder: digue, rives*) to submerge; (*plaine, terres*) to flood **2.** (*envahir*) **~ qn de qc** to swamp sb with sth

submersible [sybmɛʀsibl] *adj* (*navire, sous-marin*) submersible; **terre ~** land prone to flooding

subodorer [sybɔdɔʀe] <1> *vt inf* to scent

subordination [sybɔʀdinasjɔ̃] *f* subordination

subordonné(e) [sybɔʀdɔne] **I.** *m(f)* subordinate **II.** *adj* (*proposition*) subordinate

subordonnée [sybɔʀdɔne] *f* subordinate clause

subordonner [sybɔʀdɔne] <1> *vt* **~ une décision à qc** to subordinate a decision to sth; **être subordonné à qn/qc** to be subordinate to sb/sth

subside [sybzid] *m* subsidy

subsidiaire [sybzidjɛʀ, sypsidjɛʀ] *adj* subsidiary

subsistance [sybzistɑ̃s] *f* subsistence

subsister [sybziste] <1> *vi* **1.** (*subvenir à ses besoins*) to subsist **2.** (*demeurer: doute, erreur*) to remain; **~ de qc** to live on sth

substance [sypstɑ̃s] *f* **1.** (*matière*) matter **2.** (*essentiel: d'un article, livre*) substance; **en ~** in substance

substantiel(le) [sypstɑ̃sjɛl] *adj* **1.** (*nourrissant*) filling **2.** (*important*) substantial

substantif [sypstɑ̃tif] *m* noun

substituer [sypstitɥe] <1> **I.** *vt* **~ un collègue/un mot à un autre** to substitute a colleague/one word for another **II.** *vpr* **se ~ à qn** to take sb's place

substitut [sypstity] *m* **1.** (*remplacement*) **être le ~ de qn/qc** to be the substitute for sb/sth **2.** JUR **~ du procureur** deputy prosecutor

substitution [sypstitysjɔ̃] *f* substitution

subterfuge [syptɛʀfyʒ] *m* subterfuge

subtil(e) [syptil] *adj* (*personne*) discerning; (*distinction, nuance, parfum*) subtle

subtilement [syptilmɑ̃] *adv* subtly

subtiliser [syptilize] <1> *vt* **~ un livre à qn** to steal a book away from sb

subtilité [syptilite] *f soutenu* subtlety

subvenir [sybvəniʀ] <9> *vi* **~ à qc** to provide for sth

subvention [sybvɑ̃sjɔ̃] *f* grant

subventionné(e) [sybvɑ̃sjɔne] *adj* subsidized

subventionner [sybvɑ̃sjɔne] <1> *vt* to subsidize

subversif, -ive [sybvɛʀsif, -iv] *adj* subversive

suc [syk] *m* juice

succédané [syksedane] *m* substitute

succéder [syksede] <5> **I.** *vi* **1.** (*venir après*) **~ à qc** to follow sth **2.** (*assurer la succession*) **~ à qn** to succeed sb **3.** (*hériter*) to succeed to **II.** *vpr* **se ~** to follow one another

succès [syksɛ] *m* **1.** (*opp: échec*) **~ en qc** success in sth; **avoir un ~ fou** *inf* to be a big hit; **avoir du ~ auprès de qn** to have success with sb; **être couronné de ~** to be crowned with success; **remporter un ~** to have a success; **à ~** hit **2.** (*conquête amoureuse*) conquest **3.** SPORT, MIL victory

successeur [syksesœʀ] *m* successor

successif, -ive [syksesif, -iv] *adj* successive

succession [syksesjɔ̃] *f* succession; **prendre la ~ de qn/qc** to succeed sb/sth; **droits de ~** inheritance tax

successivement [syksesivmɑ̃] *adv* successively

succinct(e) [syksɛ̃, ɛ̃t] *adj* **1.** succinct; **soyez ~!** be brief! **2.** (*peu abondant*) **un repas ~** a frugal meal

succion [sy(k)sjɔ̃] *f* suction; (*d'une plaie, blessure*) sucking

succomber [sykɔ̃be] <1> *vi* **1.** (*mourir*) **~ à qc** to die of sth **2.** (*être vaincu*) **~ sous qc** to be overcome by sth; **~ sous le poids de qc** to give way under the weight of sth **3.** (*céder à*) **~ à la tentation/au charme de qn/qc** to give in to the temptation/charm of sb/sth

succulent(e) [sykylɑ̃, ɑ̃t] *adj* succulent

succursale [sykyʀsal] *f* branch

sucer [syse] <2> **I.** *vt* to suck **II.** *vpr* **se ~** to be sucked

sucette [sysɛt] *f* (*bonbon*) lollipop

suçon [sysɔ̃] *m Québec* (*sucette*) lollipop

sucre [sykʀ] *m* sugar; (*morceau*) sugar lump; **~ candi** sugar candy; **~ cristallisé** granulated sugar; **~ glace** icing sugar *Brit,* powdered sugar *Am;* **~ en morceaux/en poudre** lump/caster sugar; **~ de canne** cane sugar ►**casser du ~ sur le dos de qn** *inf* to gossip about sb; **être tout ~ tout miel** to be all sweetness and light

sucré(e) [sykʀe] *adj* sweet; (*par addition de sucre*) sugared

sucrer [sykʀe] <1> **I.** *vt* **1.** (*mettre du sucre*) to sugar; (*thé, café*) to put sugar in **2.** *inf* (*supprimer*) **~ l'argent de poche à un enfant** to stop a child's pocket money **II.** *vi* (*rendre sucré*) to sweeten **III.** *vpr inf* **se ~** to line one's pockets

sucrerie [sykʀəʀi] *f* **1.** (*friandise*) sweet **2.** *Québec* (*fabrique de sucre d'érable*) maple sugar works

sucrette® [sykʀɛt] *f* sweetener

sucrier [sykʀije] *m* sugar bowl

sucrier, -ière [sykʀije, -ijɛʀ] *adj* sugar; (*région*) sugar-producing

sud [syd] **I.** *m* south; **au ~** (*dans/vers la région*) in the south; (*vers le point cardinal*) to the south; **au ~ de qc** south of sth; **dans le ~ de** in the south of; **du ~** southern; **vers le ~** towards the south **II.** *adj inv* south; (*banlieue, latitude*) southern

Sud [syd] **I.** *m* South; **l'Europe du ~** Southern Europe; **dans le ~** (*dans la région*) in the South; (*vers la région*) to the South; **l'autoroute du ~** the southern motorway [*o* highway]; **les gens du ~** the Southerners **II.** *adj inv* **l'hémisphère ~** the Southern hemisphere; **le pôle ~** the South Pole

sud-africain(e) [sydafʀikɛ̃, ɛn] <sud-africains> *adj* South African **Sud-Africain(e)** [sydafʀikɛ̃, ɛn] <Sud-Africains> *m(f)* South African **sud-américain(e)** [sydameʀikɛ̃, ɛn] <sud-américains> *adj* South American **Sud-Américain(e)** [sydameʀikɛ̃, ɛn] <Sud-Américains> *m(f)* South American **sud-coréen(ne)** [sydkɔʀeɛ̃, ɛn] <sud-coréens> *adj* South Korean **Sud-Coréen(ne)** [sydkɔʀeɛ̃, ɛn] <Sud-Coréens> *m(f)* South Korean **sud-est** [sydɛst] *inv* **I.** *m* south-east *Brit,* southeast *Am* **II.** *adj* south-east *Brit,* southeast *Am;* **vent ~** southeaster **sud-ouest** [sydwɛst] *inv* **I.** *m* south-west *Brit,* southwest *Am* **II.** *adj* south-west *Brit,* southwest *Am;* **vent ~** southwester **sud-vietnamien(ne)** [sydvjɛtnamjɛ̃, jɛn] <sud-vietnamiens> *adj* HIST South Vietnamese **Sud-Vietnamien(ne)** [sydvjɛtnamjɛ̃, jɛn] <Sud-Vietnamiens> *m(f)* HIST South Vietnamese

Suède [sɥɛd] *f* **la ~** Sweden

suédois [sɥedwa] *m* Swedish; *v. a.* **français**

suédois(e) [sɥedwa, waz] *adj* Swedish

Suédois(e) [sɥedwa, waz] *m(f)* Swede

suée [sɥe] *f inf* sweat; **attraper une (bonne) ~** to work up a good sweat

suer [sɥe] <1> *vi* **1.** (*transpirer*) **~ de qc** to sweat with sth **2.** (*se donner beaucoup de mal*) **~ sur qc/pour faire qc** to sweat over/doing sth

sueur [sɥœʀ] *f* sweat; **avoir des ~s** to be in a sweat; **être en ~** to be bathed in sweat ►**à la ~ de son front** by the sweat of one's brow; **avoir des ~s froides** to be in a cold sweat

suffire [syfiʀ] *irr* **I.** *vi* **1.** (*être assez*) to be enough **2.** (*satisfaire*) **~ aux besoins de qn** to meet sb's needs; **~ aux obligations** to meet the requirements **II.** *vi impers* **il suffit d'une fois** once is enough; **il suffit que vous soyez là pour qu'il se calme** you just have to be there for him to calm down; **ça suffit (comme ça)!** *inf* that's enough! **III.** *vpr* **se ~ à soi-même** to be self-sufficient

suffisamment [syfizamɑ̃] *adv* **~ grand** big enough; **~ affranchie** with enough stamps; **~ de temps/livres** enough time/books; **~ à boire** enough to drink

suffisant(e) [syfizɑ̃, ɑ̃t] *adj* (*nombre, techniques*) sufficient, enough; (*résultat, somme*) satisfactory; **une place ~e** enough room; **ne pas être ~** not to be enough; **~ pour** *+infin* sufficient to *+infin*

suffixe [syfiks] *m* suffix

suffocant(e) [syfɔkɑ̃, ɑ̃t] *adj* (*fumée, odeur*) suffocating; (*chaleur*) stifling

suffoquer [syfɔke] <1> **I.** *vt* **1.** (*étouffer*) to suffocate **2.** (*stupéfier*) to stun **II.** *vi* **1.** (*perdre le souffle*) to gasp for breath **2.** (*ressentir une vive émotion*) **~ de colère** to choke with anger

suffrage [syfʀaʒ] *m* **1.** (*voix*) vote; **~ universel** universal suffrage; **les ~s exprimés** valid votes **2.** *pl* (*approbation*) approval *no pl;* **remporter tous les ~s** to meet with universal approval

suggérer [sygʒeʀe] <5> *vt* to suggest; **~ un voyage/une solution à qn** to suggest a trip/a solution to sb

suggestif, -ive [sygʒɛstif, -iv] *adj* **1.** (*érotique*) suggestive **2.** (*évocateur*) evocative

suggestion [sygʒɛstjɔ̃] *f* suggestion; **faire une ~ à qn** to make a suggestion to sb

suicidaire [sɥisidɛʀ] *adj* suicidal

suicide [sɥisid] **I.** *m* **1.** (*mort volontaire*) suicide **2.** (*entreprise suicidaire*) suicide mission; **c'est du ~** it's suicide **II.** *app* (*opération, commando, avion*) suicide

suicider [sɥiside] <1> *vpr* **se ~** to commit suicide

suie [sɥi] *f* soot

suinter [sɥɛ̃te] <1> *vi* **~ de qc** (*eaux*) to ooze with sth; (*mur*) to run with sth; (*plaie*) to weep sth

suis [sɥi] *indic prés de* **être**

suisse [sɥis] **I.** *adj* Swiss; **~ romand** Swiss French **II.** *m* **1.** (*gardien d'église*) verger **2.** *Québec* (*écureuil rayé* (*sur la longueur*)) chipmunk ►**petit ~** GASTR fromage frais; **boire/manger en ~** *inf* to drink/eat alone

Suisse [sɥis] **I.** *f* **la ~** Switzerland **II.** *mf* Swiss; **c'est un ~ allemand/romand** he's a German-/French-speaking Swiss

Suissesse [sɥisɛs] *f* Swiss woman; **~ romande** Swiss-French woman

suite [sɥit] *f* **1.** (*ce qui vient après: d'une lettre, d'un roman*) rest; **raconter la ~ de l'affaire** to tell what happened next; **attendre la ~** to wait for what is to follow **2.** (*succession: d'événements, de nombres*) sequence; (*d'objets, de personnes*) series **3.** (*conséquence*) consequence; **sans ~** with no repercussions **4.** (*nouvel épisode*) next episode; **la ~ au prochain numéro** to be continued in the next issue **5.** (*cohérence*) coherence **6.** (*appartement*) suite **7.** INFOR **~ bureautique** office suite ►**tout de ~** straightaway; **tout de ~ avant/après** immediately before/after; **donner ~ à qc** to follow up sth; **entraîner qn à sa ~** to drag sb along behind one; **faire ~ à qc** to follow up on sth; **prendre la ~ de qn/qc** to succeed sb/sth; **~ à qc** further to sth; **à la ~ de qc** following sth; **et ainsi de ~** and so on; **de ~** in a row; **par la ~** afterwards; **par ~ de qc** as a result of sth

suivant [sɥivɑ̃] *prep* **1.** (*conformément à, en fonction de*) according to **2.** (*le long de*) along

suivant(e) [sɥivɑ̃, ɑ̃t] **I.** *adj* **1.** (*qui vient ensuite*) next **2.** (*ci-après*) following **II.** *m(f)* next one; **au ~!** next please!

suivi [sɥivi] *m* (*d'une affaire*) follow-up; (*d'un produit*) monitoring; **~ médical** aftercare

suivi(e) [sɥivi] *adj* **1.** (*continu*) steady; (*effort*) sustained **2.** (*cohérent: conversation, raisonnement*) coherent; (*politique*) consistent

suivre [sɥivʀ] *irr* **I.** *vt* **1.** (*aller derrière, se conformer à*) to follow; **~ la mode** to follow fashion; **faire ~ qn** to have sb followed **2.** (*venir ensuite*) **~ qn sur une liste** to come after sb on a list; **l'hiver suit l'automne** winter follows autumn **3.** (*hanter*) to shadow **4.** ECOLE (*classe, cours*) to attend **5.** (*observer: actualité, affaire, compétition*) to follow; **~ un élève/malade** to follow the progress of a pupil/patient **6.** COM (*article, produit*) to keep in stock **7.** (*comprendre*) to follow ►**être à ~** (*personne*) to be worth watching; (*exemple*) to be followed **II.** *vi* **1.** (*venir après*) to follow **2.** (*réexpédier*) **faire ~ qc** to forward sth **3.** (*être attentif*) to follow **4.** (*assimiler*) to copy **III.** *vi impers* **comme suit** as follows **IV.** *vpr* **se ~ 1.** (*se succéder*) to follow each other **2.** (*être cohérent*) to be in the right order

sujet [syʒɛ] *m* **1.** (*thème*) *a.* LING, PHILOS subject; (*d'un examen*) question **2.** (*cause*) cause; **sans ~** without reason **3.** (*individu*) subject; **brillant ~** brilliant student; **~ d'élite** exceptionally brilliant student; **mauvais ~** bad boy ►**c'est à quel ~?** *inf* what is it about?; **à ce ~** on this subject; **au ~ de qn/qc** about sb/sth

sujet(te) [syʒɛ, ʒɛt] *adj* **être ~ à qc/à** *+infin* to be prone to sth/to *+infin*

sultan [syltɑ̃] *m* sultan

summum [sɔ(m)mɔm] *m* **1.** (*apogée: d'une civilisation, de la gloire*) height **2.** *iron* (*comble*) limit; **le ~ de qc** the height of sth

S

super[1] [sypɛʀ] *m abr de* **supercarburant** four-star *Brit,* premium *Am;* ~ **sans plomb/plombé** super unleaded/leaded petrol

super[2] [sypɛʀ] *adj inv, inf* super

superbe [sypɛʀb] *adj* (*repas, vin, temps, performance, résultat*) superb; (*corps, enfant*) magnificent; **tu as une mine** ~ you look great

superbement [sypɛʀbəmɑ̃] *adv* superbly

supercarburant [sypɛʀkaʀbyʀɑ̃] *m* high-octane petrol *Brit,* high-octane gas *Am*

supercherie [sypɛʀʃəʀi] *f* trick

supérette [sypeʀɛt] *f* mini-market

superficie [sypɛʀfisi] *f* (*d'un terrain, pays*) area; (*d'un appartement*) surface area; **unité de** ~ area measurement

superficiel(le) [sypɛʀfisjɛl] *adj* superficial

superficiellement [sypɛʀfisjɛlmɑ̃] *adv* superficially

superflu [sypɛʀfly] *m* excess; (*luxe*) luxuries *pl*

superflu(e) [sypɛʀfly] *adj* superfluous

supérieur [sypeʀjœʀ] *m* higher education

supérieur(e) [sypeʀjœʀ] **I.** *adj* **1.** (*plus haut dans l'espace: lèvre, mâchoire*) upper **2.** (*plus élevé dans la hiérarchie*) superior; (*animal, plante*) greater; (*cadre*) senior; **enseignement** ~ higher education; **d'ordre** ~ higher **3.** (*de grande qualité*) superior **4.** (*qui dépasse*) **être** ~ **à qn par la vitesse/en vitesse** to be faster than sb; ~ **en nombre** greater in number; ~ **par la qualité** better quality; **être** ~ **à la moyenne** to be above average **5.** (*prétentieux: air, regard, ton*) superior **II.** *m(f)* *a.* REL superior

supériorité [sypeʀjɔʀite] *f* ~ **sur qn/qc** superiority over sb/sth; **complexe de** ~ superiority complex

superlatif [sypɛʀlatif] *m* superlative

supermarché [sypɛʀmaʀʃe] *m* supermarket

superposé(e) [sypɛʀpoze] *adj* (*livres, pierres*) superimposed; **lits ~s** bunk beds

superposer [sypɛʀpoze] <1> **I.** *vt* **1.** (*faire chevaucher*) to superimpose **2.** (*empiler*) to stack **II.** *vpr* **1.** (*se recouvrir*) **se** ~ (*figures géométriques, images*) to be superimposed **2.** (*s'ajouter*) **se** ~ **à qc** (*couche*) to be superimposed on sth

superposition [sypɛʀpozisjɔ̃] *f* (*action de superposer*) superimposing

superproduction [sypɛʀpʀɔdyksjɔ̃] *f* spectacular

supersonique [sypɛʀsɔnik] **I.** *adj* supersonic **II.** *m* supersonic aircraft

superstitieux, -euse [sypɛʀstisjø, -jøz] *adj* superstitious

superstition [sypɛʀstisjɔ̃] *f* superstition

superviser [sypɛʀvize] <1> *vt* to supervise; (*travail*) to oversee

superviseur [sypɛʀvizœʀ] *m* INFOR supervisor

supplanter [syplɑ̃te] <1> *vt* to supplant

suppléant(e) [sypleɑ̃, ɑ̃t] **I.** *adj* (*député, juge*) deputy; (*instituteur*) supply **II.** *m(f)* replacement; MED locum

suppléer [syplee] <1> **I.** *vt* (*personne*) to replace **II.** *vi* **1.** (*remplacer*) ~ **à la main d'œuvre par le recours à la machine** to replace workers with machines **2.** (*compenser*) ~ (**à**) **un défaut par qc** to make up for a fault with sth

supplément [syplemɑ̃] *m* **1.** (*surplus*) extra; ~ **de salaire** bonus; **en** ~ extra **2.** (*publication: d'un journal, dictionnaire, d'une revue*) supplement **3.** (*somme d'argent à payer*) extra charge; CHEMDFER supplement; **un ~ de 100 euros** 100 euros extra

supplémentaire [syplemɑ̃tɛʀ] *adj* extra; **heures ~s** overtime + *vb sing*

supplication [syplikasjɔ̃] *f* supplication

supplice [syplis] *m* torture ▸**être au** ~ to be in agony; **mettre qn au** ~ to put sb through agony

supplier [syplije] <1> *vt* ~ **qn de** +*infin* to beg sb to +*infin*

support [sypɔʀ] *m* **1.** (*soutien*) support; (*d'un meuble, d'une statue*) stand **2.** INFOR ~ **d'information** data medium

supportable [sypɔʀtabl] *adj* bearable

supporter[1] [sypɔʀte] <1> **I.** *vt* **1.** (*psychiquement*) to bear; ~ **de** +*infin* to bear to +*infin;* **il supporte mal ~/ne supporte pas ~ qu'elle fasse qc** (*subj*) he can hardly bear/can't bear her doing sth; **je ne peux pas le** ~ I can't bear it **2.** (*physiquement: alcool, chaleur*) to tolerate; (*douleur, opération*) to stand; **elle ne supporte pas ~ l'avion/la vue du sang** she can't stand planes/the sight of blood; ~ **la chaleur** (*plat*) to be heat-proof **3.** (*subir: affront, avanies, échec*) to suffer; ~ **les conséquences de qc** to suffer [*o* endure] the consequences of sth **4.** (*soutenir: pilier*) to support **5.** SPORT ~ **qn/qc** (*donner son appui*) to support sb/sth **II.** *vpr* **se** ~ to stand each other

supporter[2] [sypɔʀtɛʀ] *m,* **supporteur, -trice** [sypɔʀtœʀ, -tʀis] *m, f* supporter

supposé(e) [sypoze] *adj* supposed

supposer [sypoze] <1> *vt* **1.** (*imaginer*) to suppose; **je suppose qu'il va revenir** I suppose he'll come back; **supposons qu'elle dise non** +*subj* let's suppose she says no **2.** (*présumer*) to assume **3.** (*impliquer*) to presuppose

supposition [sypozisjɔ̃] *f* assumption

suppositoire [sypozitwaʀ] *m* suppository

suppression [sypʀesjɔ̃] *f* **1.** (*d'une subvention, difficulté, d'un objet*) removal; (*d'une phrase*) deletion; (*de personnel, d'emplois*) cutting; (*d'une administration, usine*) closing **2.** (*abrogation*) abolition

supprimer [sypʀime] <1> **I.** *vt* **1.** (*enlever*) ~ **un avantage/emploi à qn** to take away sb's benefit/job; ~ **le permis à qn** to revoke sb's license **2.** (*abolir: libertés, peine de mort*) to abolish **3.** (*faire disparaître*) to get rid of **4.** (*tuer*) to eliminate **II.** *vpr* **se** ~ to kill oneself

suppurer [sypyʀe] <1> *vi* to suppurate
suprématie [sypʀemasi] *f* supremacy
suprême [sypʀɛm] I. *adj* (*bonheur, cour, instance, pouvoir*) supreme; (*degré*) highest II. *m* GASTR ~ **de volaille/poissons** chicken/fish supreme
sur [syʀ] *prep* **1.** (*position*) on; (*au-dessus de*) over; **marcher ~ la capitale** to march on the capital **2.** (*temporel*) ~ **le soir** towards the evening; ~ **ses vieux jours** in his later years; ~ **le coup** (*immédiatement*) immediately; (*au début*) at first; ~ **ce je vous quitte** and now I must leave you **3.** (*successif*) **coup ~ coup** shot after shot **4.** (*causal*) ~ **sa recommandation** on his/her recommendation; ~ **présentation d'une pièce d'identité** on presentation of a form of identification **5.** (*modal*) **ne me parle pas ~ ce ton!** don't speak to me like that!; ~ **mesure** tailor-made; ~ **le mode mineur** in a minor key; ~ **l'air de ...** to the tune of ... **6.** (*au sujet de*) about **7.** (*proportionnalité, notation, dimension*) **neuf fois ~ dix** nine times out of ten; **un enfant ~ deux** one child in two; **faire 5 mètres ~ 4** to measure 5 metres by four *Brit,* to measure 5 meters by four *Am*
sûr(**e**) [syʀ] *adj* **1.** (*convaincu, certain*) ~ **de qn/qc** sure of sb/sth; **être ~ de faire qc/que ...** to be sure of doing sth/that ...; **j'en suis ~** I am sure (of it) **2.** (*sans danger*) safe; **en lieu ~** in a safe place **3.** (*digne de confiance*) trustworthy; (*temps*) reliable **4.** (*solide: arme*) sturdy; (*base, main*) steady; (*raisonnement, instinct*) sound ►**bien ~** of course; **bien ~ que oui** *inf* of course; **bien ~ que non** *inf* of course not; **être ~ et certain** to be absolutely sure; **rien n'est moins ~** it's by no means certain; **le plus ~ est de** +*infin* the safest thing is to +*infin;* **c'est ~** *inf* definitely; **pas** (**si**) **~!** *inf* it's not so sure!
surabondance [syʀabɔ̃dɑ̃s] *f* superabundance; ~ **de produits** overabundance of products
surabondant(**e**) [syʀabɔ̃dɑ̃, ɑ̃t] *adj* superabundant
suraigu(**ë**) [syʀegy] *adj* very high-pitched; (*douleur*) very intense
suralimentation [syʀalimɑ̃tasjɔ̃] *f* overeating
suranné(**e**) [syʀane] *adj* (*style*) outmoded; (*beauté, charme*) antiquated
surbooking [syʀbukiŋ] *m* overbooking
surcharge [syʀʃaʀʒ] *f* **1.** (*excès de charge*) overloading **2.** (*excédent de poids*) excess load; ~ **de bagages** excess luggage **3.** (*surcroît*) ~ **des programmes scolaires** overloading of the school syllabus
surchargé(**e**) [syʀʃaʀʒe] *adj* **1.** (*trop chargé*) overloaded **2.** *fig* **être ~ de travail** to be overworked
surcharger [syʀʃaʀʒe] <2a> *vt* to overload
surchauffé(**e**) [syʀʃofe] *adj* **1.** (*trop chauffé*) overheated **2.** (*surexcité*) overexcited; **imagination ~e** overactive imagination
surchauffer [syʀʃofe] <1> *vt* to overheat
surclasser [syʀklɑse] <1> *vt* to outclass; **être surclassé** to be outclassed
surcroît [syʀkʀwɑ] *m* **un ~ de travail/passagers** extra work/passengers; **un ~ d'honnêteté/de scrupules** excessive honesty/scruples ►**de** [*o* **par**] ~ *soutenu* moreover
surdité [syʀdite] *f* deafness
surdose [syʀdoz] *f* overdose
surdoué(**e**) [syʀdwe] I. *adj* (highly) gifted II. *m(f)* prodigy
sureau [syʀo] *m* elder
surélevé(**e**) [syʀelve] *adj* raised
surélever [syʀelve] <4> *vt* to raise
sûrement [syʀmɑ̃] *adv* certainly
surenchère [syʀɑ̃ʃɛʀ] *f* **1.** (*exagération*) overstatement; ~ **électorale** competing electoral promises; **faire de la ~** to try to outdo the others **2.** COM overbidding
surenchérir [syʀɑ̃ʃeʀiʀ] <8> *vi* to bid higher; (*en rajouter*) to raise one's bid; ~ **sur qn/qc** to top sb/sth
surendetté(**e**) [syʀɑ̃dete] *adj* deeply in debt
surendettement [syʀɑ̃dɛtmɑ̃] *m* excessive debt
surestimer [syʀɛstime] <1> *vt* (*immeuble*) to overvalue; (*force, puissance, personne, valeur*) to overestimate
sûreté [syʀte] *f* **1.** (*précision*) sureness **2.** (*sécurité*) safety; **épingle/serrure de ~** safety pin/lock; **mettre qn/qc en ~** to put sb/sth in a safe place; **pour plus de ~** for greater security
surévaluer [syʀevalɥe] <1> *vt* (*personne*) to overestimate; (*immeuble, nombre, prix*) to overvalue
surexcitation [syʀɛksitasjɔ̃] *f* overexcitement
surexcité(**e**) [syʀɛksite] *adj* overexcited
surf [sœʀf] *m* **1.** (*sport*) surfing; (*sur la neige*) snowboarding; **faire du ~** to go surfing; (*sur la neige*) to go snowboarding **2.** (*planche pour l'eau*) surfboard; (*planche pour la neige*) snowboard **3.** INFOR surfing; **faire du ~ sur le Net** to surf (the Web)
surface [syʀfas] *f* **1.** (*aire*) area; (*d'un appartement, d'une pièce*) surface area; ~ **de réparation** SPORT penalty area; ~ **corrigée** JUR amended area **2.** (*couche superficielle*) surface; **à la ~** on the surface **3.** INFOR ~ **de travail** user surface ►**grande ~** hypermarket; **faire ~** to surface; **refaire ~** to resurface; **en ~** on the surface
surfait(**e**) [syʀfɛ, ɛt] *adj* (*auteur, œuvre*) overrated; **une réputation ~e** an exaggerated reputation
surfer [sœʀfe] <1> *vi* (*sur l'eau*) *a.* INFOR to surf; ~ **sur le Web** to surf the Web
surfeur, -euse [sœʀfœʀ, -øz] *m, f* **1.** (*sur l'eau*) *a.* INFOR surfer **2.** (*sur la neige*) snowboarder
surfing [sœʀfiŋ] *m* INFOR surfing; **faire du ~**

S

sur le Net to surf the Web

surgelé(e) [syʀʒəle] *adj* (deep-)frozen

surgeler [syʀʒəle] <4> *vt* to (deep-)freeze

surgelés [syʀʒəle] *mpl* frozen foods

surgir [syʀʒiʀ] <8> *vi* to appear; (*arbres*) to rise up; (*difficulté*) to crop up

surhomme [syʀɔm] *m* superman

surhumain(e) [syʀymɛ̃, ɛn] *adj* superhuman

surimi [syʀimi] *m* crabstick

sur-le-champ [syʀləʃɑ̃] *adv* on the spot

surlendemain [syʀlɑ̃dmɛ̃] *m* two days later; **le ~ de qc** two days after sth

surligner [syʀliɲe] <1> *vt a.* INFOR to mark

surmenage [syʀmənaʒ] *m* (*intellectuel, scolaire*) overwork; (*physique*) overexertion

surmené(e) [syʀməne] *adj* overworked

surmener [syʀməne] <4> **I.** *vt* to overwork **II.** *vpr* **se ~** to be overworked

surmonter [syʀmɔ̃te] <1> **I.** *vt* to surmount **II.** *vpr* **se ~ 1.** (*se maîtriser*) to control oneself **2.** (*être maîtrisé: timidité*) to be overcome

surnager [syʀnaʒe] <2a> *vi* **1.** to float on the surface **2.** *fig* to linger on

surnaturel(le) [syʀnatyʀɛl] *adj a.* REL supernatural

surnom [syʀnɔ̃] *m* **1.** (*sobriquet*) nickname **2.** (*qualificatif*) name

surnombre [syʀnɔ̃bʀ] *m* surplus

surnommer [syʀnɔme] <1> *vt* **~ qn Junior** to nickname sb Junior

suroffre [syʀɔfʀ] *f* COM higher bid

suroît [syʀwa] *m* **1.** (*chapeau*) sou'wester **2.** METEO southwesterly (wind)

surpasser [syʀpɑse] <1> *vpr* **se ~** to excel oneself

surpayer [syʀpeje] <1> *vt* (*personne*) to overpay; **~ qc** to pay too much for sth

surpeuplé(e) [syʀpœple] *adj* (*pays*) overpopulated; (*salle*) overcrowded

surpeuplement [syʀpœpləmɑ̃] *m* (*d'un pays*) overpopulation; (*d'une salle*) overcrowding

surplace [syʀplas] *m* (*d'une économie*) stagnation; (*d'un gouvernement*) standstill; **faire du ~** to be marking time

surplomb [syʀplɔ̃] *m* overhang; **étage en ~** overhanging floor

surplomber [syʀplɔ̃be] <1> *vt* **~ qc** (*étage, lumière*) to overhang sth

surplus [syʀply] *m* (*d'une somme, récolte*) surplus; **~ d'un stock/de marchandises** surplus stock/products ►**au ~** moreover

surpopulation [syʀpɔpylasjɔ̃] *f* overpopulation

surprenant(e) [syʀpʀənɑ̃, ɑ̃t] *adj* surprising

surprendre [syʀpʀɑ̃dʀ] <13> **I.** *vt* **1.** (*étonner*) to surprise; **être surpris de qc/que** +*subj* to be surprised about sth/that **2.** (*prendre sur le fait*) **~ qn à faire qc** to catch sb doing sth **3.** (*découvrir: complot, secret*) to discover; (*conversation*) to overhear **4.** (*prendre au dépourvu*) **~ qn dans son bureau** to surprise sb in their office **5.** (*prendre à l'improviste*) **la pluie nous a surpris** the rain caught us by surprise **II.** *vpr* **se ~ à faire qc** to catch oneself doing sth

surpris(e) [syʀpʀi, iz] *part passé de* **surprendre**

surprise [syʀpʀiz] *f* (*étonnement, chose inattendue*) surprise; **faire la ~ à qn** to surprise sb; **à la grande ~ de qn** to everyone's great surprise; **avec/par ~** with/in surprise

surproduction [syʀpʀɔdyksjɔ̃] *f* overproduction

surréaliste [syʀʀealist] **I.** *adj* **1.** ART, LIT surrealist **2.** *inf* (*extravagant*) surreal **II.** *mf* surrealist

sursaut [syʀso] *m* **1.** (*haut-le-corps*) jump; **avoir un ~ de surprise** to jump in surprise **2.** start; **se réveiller en ~** to wake up with a start **3.** (*élan: de colère*) blaze; (*d'énergie*) burst

sursauter [syʀsote] <1> *vi* to jump; **faire ~ qn** (*personne, nouvelle, bruit*) to startle sb

sursis [syʀsi] *m* **1.** (*délai*) extension; (*pour payer*) postponement **2.** JUR reprieve

surtaxe [syʀtaks] *f* surcharge

surtaxer [syʀtakse] <1> *vt* to surcharge

surtout [syʀtu] *adv* **1.** (*avant tout*) above all **2.** *inf* (*d'autant plus*) **j'ai peur de lui, ~ qu'il est si fort** I'm scared of him, with him being so strong ►**~ pas** definitely not

surveillance [syʀvɛjɑ̃s] *f* (*contrôle: de la police*) surveillance; (*des travaux, études*) supervision; **être sous étroite/haute ~** to be under tight/close surveillance; **service de ~** security

surveillant(e) [syʀvɛjɑ̃, jɑ̃t] *m(f)* supervisor; (*de prison*) warder *Brit*, prison guard *Am*; (*de magasin*) security guard; **~e de salle** MED ward sister *Brit*, head nurse *Am*

surveillé(e) [syʀveje] *adj* **1.** ECOLE (*étude*) supervised **2.** JUR **liberté ~** probation

surveiller [syʀveje] <1> *vt* **1.** (*prendre soin de*) **~ un enfant** to watch over a child; **~ un malade** to care for a patient **2.** (*suivre l'évolution*) to watch; (*éducation des enfants*) to oversee **3.** (*garder*) to watch **4.** (*assurer la protection de*) to keep watch on **5.** GASTR to watch **6.** ECOLE (*élèves*) to supervise; (*examen*) to invigilate *Brit*, to proctor *Am*

survenir [syʀvəniʀ] <9> *vi être* (*événement, incident, changement*) to occur; (*complications*) to arise

survêt *m inf*, **survêtement** [syʀvɛtmɑ̃] *m* overgarment; SPORT track suit

survie [syʀvi] *f* **1.** (*maintien en vie*) survival **2.** REL afterlife

survivant(e) [syʀvivɑ̃, ɑ̃t] **I.** *adj* surviving **II.** *m(f)* (*rescapé*) survivor

survivre [syʀvivʀ] *vi irr* **1.** (*demeurer en vie*) **~ à qc** to survive sth **2.** (*vivre plus longtemps que*) **~ à qn/qc** to survive sb/sth

survol [syʀvɔl] *m* **1.** (*fait de voler*) overflying **2.** *fig* **rapide ~ d'un problème** quick overview of a problem

survoler [syʀvɔle] <1> *vt* **1.** AVIAT to fly over **2.** (*examiner: article*) to skim through; (*question*) to skim over

survolté(e) [syʀvɔlte] *adj* overexcited

sus [sy(s)] *adv* ~ **à l'ennemi!** at them!

susceptibilité [sysɛptibilite] *f* touchiness

susceptible [sysɛptibl] *adj* **1.** (*ombrageux*) touchy **2.** (*en mesure de*) **il est ~ de faire qc** he could do sth

susciter [sysite] <1> *vt* **1.** (*faire naître*) to arouse; (*querelle*) to provoke **2.** (*provoquer: obstacle*) to create; (*troubles*) to cause

suspect(e) [syspɛ, ɛkt] **I.** *adj* **1.** (*louche*) **être ~ à qn** to be suspicious to sb **2.** (*soupçonné*) **être ~ de qc** to be suspected of sth **3.** (*douteux*) suspect **II.** *m(f)* suspect

suspecter [syspɛkte] <1> *vt* (*soupçonner*) to suspect

suspendre [syspɑ̃dʀ] <14> *vt* **1.** (*accrocher*) ~ **qc au porte-manteau/au mur** to hang sth on the coat stand/on the wall **2.** (*rester collé à*) **être suspendu à la radio** to be glued to the radio; **être suspendu aux lèvres de qn** to hang on sb's every word **3.** (*interrompre: séance, réunion, paiement*) to suspend **4.** (*remettre: décision*) to put off; (*jugement*) to defer **5.** (*destituer: fonctionnaire, joueur*) to suspend

suspendu(e) [syspɑ̃dy] *adj* **1.** AUTO **bien/mal ~** with good/bad suspension **2.** (*en hauteur: jardin*) hanging; **pont ~** suspension bridge

suspens [syspɑ̃] **procès/dossier en ~** trial/file that is pending; **le projet est en ~** the project is in abeyance

suspense [syspɛns] *m* suspense; **à ~** suspense

suspension [syspɑ̃sjɔ̃] *f* **1.** suspension; (*d'une réunion*) adjournment; ~ **d'armes** short ceasefire **2.** ADMIN, AUTO suspension **3.** (*luminaire*) light fitting **4.** (*installation*) suspension ►**en** ~ *a.* CHIM, PHYS in suspension

suspente [syspɑ̃t] *f Suisse* (*boucle de ganse permettant de suspendre un vêtement, un torchon*) tag

suspicieux, -euse [syspisjø, -jøz] *adj* suspicious

suspicion [syspisjɔ̃] *f* suspicion; ~ **légitime** reasonable suspicion; **avoir des ~s de qc envers un employé** to suspect an employee of sth

susurrer [sysyʀe] <1> **I.** *vt* ~ **des mots à qn/à l'oreille de qn** to whisper words to sb/in sb's ear **II.** *vi* (*personne*) to whisper; (*source*) to babble; (*vent*) to murmur

suture [sytyʀ] *f* MED, ANAT suture

svelte [svɛlt] *adj* svelte

SVP [ɛsvepe] *abr de* **s'il vous plaît**

swasi(e) [swazi] *adj* Swazi

Swasi(e) [swazi] *m(f)* Swazi

Swaziland [swazilɑ̃:d] *m* **le** ~ Swaziland

sweat-shirt [switʃœʀt] <sweat-shirts> *m* sweatshirt

syllabe [sil(l)ab] *f* syllable

sylvestre [silvɛstʀ] *adj* forest

sylviculture [silvikyltyʀ] *f* forestry

symbiose [sɛ̃bjoz] *f* symbiosis

symbole [sɛ̃bɔl] *m* **1.** (*image*) *a.* CHIM, MAT symbol **2.** REL Creed

symbolique [sɛ̃bɔlik] **I.** *adj* **1.** (*emblématique*) symbolic **2.** (*très modique*) nominal **II.** *f* symbology

symboliser [sɛ̃bɔlize] <1> *vt* to symbolize

symétrie [simetʀi] *f a.* MAT symmetry

symétrique [simetʀik] *adj a.* MAT symmetrical; ~ **de qc** symmetrical to sth

sympa [sɛ̃pa] *adj inf abr de* **sympathique**

sympathie [sɛ̃pati] *f* **1.** (*inclination*) ~ **pour qn/qc** liking sb/sth; **inspirer la** ~ to be likeable **2.** (*lors d'un deuil*) sympathy

sympathique [sɛ̃patik] *adj* **1.** (*aimable: personne, animal*) friendly **2.** *inf* (*personne, plat*) nice; (*accueil*) warm; (*ambiance*) pleasant

sympathisant(e) [sɛ̃patizɑ̃, ɑ̃t] **I.** *adj* sympathetic **II.** *m(f)* sympathizer

sympathiser [sɛ̃patize] <1> *vi* ~ **avec qn** to get on well with sb

symphonie [sɛ̃fɔni] *f* symphony

symphonique [sɛ̃fɔnik] *adj* (*orchestre*) symphonic

symptôme [sɛ̃ptom] *m* **1.** (*indice*) sign **2.** MED symptom

synagogue [sinagɔg] *f* (*édifice*) synagogue

synchronisation [sɛ̃kʀɔnizasjɔ̃] *f* synchronization

synchroniser [sɛ̃kʀɔnize] <1> *vt* to synchronize; **ne pas être synchronisé** to be out of sync

syncope [sɛ̃kɔp] *f* fainting fit; **avoir une** [*o* **tomber en**] ~ to faint

syncopé(e) [sɛ̃kɔpe] *adj* LING, MUS syncopated

syndical(e) [sɛ̃dikal, o] <-aux> *adj* trade union

syndicaliste [sɛ̃dikalist] **I.** *adj* union **II.** *mf* (trade) unionist

syndicat [sɛ̃dika] *m* **1.** (~ *de salariés*) trade union **2.** (*pour les touristes*) ~ **d'initiative** tourist office

syndiquer [sɛ̃dike] <1> *vpr* **se** ~ to join a union

synonyme [sinɔnim] **I.** *adj* **être ~ de qc** to be synonymous with sth **II.** *m* synonym

syntagme [sɛ̃tagm] *m* phrase; ~ **nominal/verbal** noun/verb phrase

syntaxe [sɛ̃taks] *f* **1.** LING syntax **2.** *Belgique* (*première année du secondaire supérieur*) *second-to-last year of secondary school*

synthèse [sɛ̃tɛz] *f* synthesis; (*exposé d'ensemble*) summary; **faire la ~ de qc** to summarize sth ►~ **vocale** voice synthesis; **résine/produit de** ~ synthetic resin/product

synthétique [sɛ̃tetik] **I.** *adj* (*matériau*) artificial; (*fibres, caoutchouc*) synthetic **II.** *m* synthetic

synthétiser [sɛ̃tetize] <1> *vt a.* BIO, CHIM to synthesize

S

synthétiseur [sɛ̃tetizœʀ] *m* MUS synthesizer
syphilis [sifilis] *f* syphilis
Syrie [siʀi] *f* **la** ~ Syria
systématique [sistematik] **I.** *adj* systematic **II.** *f* systematics + *vb sing*
systématiquement [sistematikmɑ̃] *adv* systematically
système [sistɛm] *m* **1.** (*structure*) system; ~ **de vie** approach to life; ~ **international d'unités** International System of Units **2.** *inf* (*combine*) way; **connaître le** ~ *inf* to know the system; ~ **D** *inf* resourcefulness **3.** (*institution*) system **4.** INFOR ~ **informatique/d'exploitation** computing/operating system; ~ **de gestion de base de données** database management system; ~ **expert** expert system **5.** AUTO ~ **de guidage** guidance system; ~ **de signalisation** (*feux*) traffic lights *pl;* (*signaux de route*) road signs *pl;* (*marques*) road markings *pl* ▶**taper sur le** ~ **à qn** *inf* to get on sb's nerves
Système européen de banques centrales *m* European Central Banking System
Système monétaire européen *m* European Monetary Systen

T

T, t [te] *m inv* T, t; **en t** T-shaped; ~ **comme Thérèse** t for Tommy *Brit,* t for Tare *Am*
t *f abr de* **tonne** t.
t' *pron v.* **te, tu**
ta [ta, te] <tes> *dét poss* your; *v. a.* **ma**
tabac [taba] **I.** *m* **1.** (*plante, produit*) tobacco; ~ **à priser** snuff **2.** *inf* (*magasin*) tobacconist('s shop) *Brit,* tobacco shop *Am* ▶**faire un** ~ *inf* to be a great success; **passer qn à** ~ *inf* to beat sb up **II.** *adj inv* buff

> In France, cigarettes are available only from a licenced distributor in a **tabac**, either a small shop or a counter in a cafe. They also sell stamps, car tax stickers, postal orders, bus and metro tickets etc.

tabagie [tabaʒi] *f* **1.** (*endroit enfumé*) tobacco den **2.** *Québec* (*bureau de tabac*) tobacconist('s shop) *Brit,* tobacco shop *Am*
tabagisme [tabaʒism] *m* nicotine addiction; ~ **passif** passive smoking
tabasser [tabase] <1> **I.** *vt inf* ~ **qn** to beat sb up **II.** *vpr inf* **se** ~ (*personnes*) to beat each other up
tabernacle [tabɛʀnakl] *m* REL tabernacle
tablar(d) [tablaʀ] *m Suisse* (*étagère*) shelf
table [tabl] *f* **1.** (*meuble, tablée, tableau*) table; (*d'autel*) altar stone; **dresser** [*o* **mettre**] **la** ~ to lay [*o* set] the table; **être à** ~ to be having a meal; **à** ~**!** come and eat!; ~ **d'hôte** buffet meal; ~ **d'écoute** wire tapping apparatus; **je suis sur** ~ **d'écoute** my line is tapped; **service de** ~ table linen; ~ **des matières** table of contents **2.** (*nourriture*) food **3.** (*tablette*) ~ **mortuaire** mortuary slab ▶~ **ronde** round table; **se mettre à** ~ (*aller manger*) to sit down to eat; *inf* (*avouer sa faute*) to own up
tableau [tablo] <x> *m* **1.** (*cadre*) picture; (*peinture*) painting **2.** (*scène, paysage*) scene **3.** ECOLE board; ~ **noir** blackboard **4.** (*panneau*) *a.* INFOR table; ~ **indicateur de vitesse** speedometer; ~ **de service** work notice board; ~ **de bord** (*d'une voiture*) dashboard; (*d'un bateau, avion*) instrument panel **5.** (*présentation graphique*) chart **6.** (*présentoir mural*) ~ **des clés** key rack; ~ **des fusibles** fuse box ▶**gagner sur les deux** ~**x** to win all ways round; **miser sur les deux** ~**x** to hedge one's bets; ~ **d'honneur** ECOLE roll of honour *Brit,* honor roll *Am*
tablée [table] *f* table (*people*)
tabler [table] <1> *vi* ~ **sur qc** to count on sth
tablette [tablɛt] *f* **1.** (*plaquette*) block **2.** (*planchette: d'un lavabo, d'une armoire*) shelf; HIST tablet; ~ **de chocolat** bar of chocolate **3.** *Québec* (*bloc de papier à lettres*) writing pad
tableur [tablœʀ] *m* INFOR spreadsheet
tablier [tablije] *m* **1.** (*vêtement*) apron; (*d'un écolier*) overall **2.** (*plaque protectrice: d'une cheminée*) shutter **3.** AUTO bulkhead
tabou [tabu] *m* taboo
tabou(e) [tabu] *adj* **1.** (*interdit*) taboo **2.** (*intouchable*) untouchable
taboulé [tabule] *m* tabbouleh
tabouret [tabuʀɛ] *m* **1.** (*petit siège*) stool **2.** (*support pour les pieds*) footstool
tac [tak] *m* ~ ~ **d'une mitrailleuse** the rattle of a machine gun ▶**répondre du** ~ **au** ~ to answer back smartly
tache [taʃ] *f* **1.** (*salissure*) stain; ~ **de rousseur** freckle; ~ **de vin** (*sur la peau*) strawberry birthmark **2.** (*flétrissure*) blot **3.** (*impression visuelle*) patch; (*de couleur, peinture*) spot ▶**faire** ~ **d'huile** to gain ground; **faire** ~ to stick out like a sore thumb
tâche [taʃ] *f* **1.** (*besogne*) work **2.** (*mission*) task ▶**être dur à la** ~ to be a hard worker; **à la** ~ (*au travail*) on the job; (*selon le travail rendu*) on piecework rates
taché(e) [taʃe] *adj* stained; ~ **de sang** bloodstained
tacher [taʃe] <1> **I.** *vi* to stain **II.** *vt* **1.** (*faire des taches sur*) to stain **2.** (*moucheter*) ~ **la peau de qc** to mark the skin of sth **3.** (*souiller*) to sully **III.** *vpr* **se** ~ (*tissu*) to get stained; (*personne*) to get dirty
tâcher [taʃe] <1> *vi* **1.** (*s'efforcer*) ~ **de** +*infin* to endeavour to +*infin Brit,* to endeavor to +*infin Am* **2.** (*faire en sorte*) ~ **que qc (ne) se produise (pas)** to ensure that sth (does not) happen
tacheté(e) [taʃte] *adj* spotted

tacheter [taʃte] <3> *vt* to speckle
tachymètre [takimɛtʀ] *m* tachometer
tacite [tasit] *adj* tacit
tacitement [tasitmɑ̃] *adv* tacitly
taciturne [tasityʀn] *adj* taciturn
tacle [takl] *m* tackle
tacon [takɔ̃] *m Suisse* (*pièce servant à raccommoder les vêtements*) patch
tacot [tako] *m inf* AUTO jalopy, banger *Brit*
tact [takt] *m* tact; **avoir du/manquer de** ~ to have/lack tact
tacticien(**ne**) [taktisjɛ̃, jɛn] *m(f)* tactician
tactile [taktil] *adj* tactile; (*écran*) touch-sensitive
tactique [taktik] **I.** *adj* tactical **II.** *f* tactic
t{nia [tenja] *m* tapeworm
taffetas [tafta] *m* taffeta
tag [tag] *m* tag
taguer [tage] <1> *vi* to tag
tagueur, **-euse** [tagœʀ, -øz] *m, f* tagger
taie [tɛ] *f* (*d'un oreiller*) pillow case
taillader [tɑjade] <1> **I.** *vt* (*sièges*) to slash; (*rôti*) to hack at **II.** *vpr* **se** ~ **le doigt** to slash one's finger
taille¹ [tɑj] *f* **1.** (*hauteur: d'une personne*) height **2.** (*dimension, importance, pointure*) size; **de** ~ *inf* considerable; **la** ~ **en dessous** the next size down; **quelle** ~ **faites-vous?** what size are you? **3.** (*partie du corps, d'un vêtement*) waist ►**être de** ~ **à faire qc** to be capable of doing sth; **ne pas être à sa** ~ (*vêtement*) to be the wrong size; (*personne*) to be no match for her
taille² [tɑj] *f* **1.** (*sculpture: d'un diamant, d'une pierre*) cut; (*du bois*) carving **2.** BOT coppice
taillé(**e**) [tɑje] *adj* **1.** (*bâti*) ~ **en qc** built like sth **2.** (*destiné*) ~ **pour qc** to be made for sth
taille-crayon [tɑjkʀɛjɔ̃] <taille-crayon(s)> *m* pencil sharpener
tailler [tɑje] <1> **I.** *vt* **1.** (*couper: arbre*) to prune; (*crayon*) to sharpen; (*ongles*) to trim; (*pierre*) to hew; (*diamant*) to cut; (*pièce de bois*) to carve **2.** (*découper: robe*) to cut out **3.** (*creuser*) ~ **un trou dans qc** to make a hole in sth **II.** *vpr* **1.** (*conquérir*) **se** ~ **une place au soleil** to earn oneself a place in the sun **2.** (*se couper*) **se** ~ **la barbe** to trim one's beard
tailleur [tɑjœʀ] *m* **1.** (*couturier*) tailor **2.** (*tenue*) suit ►**être assis en** ~ to be sitting cross-legged
tailleur, **-euse** [tɑjœʀ, -jøz] *m, f* (*ouvrier*) cutter; ~ **de pierre** stone cutter
tailleur-pantalon [tɑjœʀpɑ̃talɔ̃] <tailleurs-pantalons> *m* trouser suit
taillis [taji] *m* copse
tain [tɛ̃] *m* silvering; **glace sans** ~ two-way mirror
taire [tɛʀ] *irr* **I.** *vpr* **1.** (*être silencieux, faire silence*) **se** ~ to be silent **2.** (*s'abstenir de parler*) **se** ~ **sur qc** to keep quiet about sth **II.** *vt* **1.** (*celer*) to hush up **2.** (*refuser de dire: vérité*) to conceal; ~ **ses raisons** to keep quiet about one's reasons **III.** *vi* **faire** ~ **qn** to shut sb up
taiseux, **-euse** [tɛzø, -øz] *m, f Belgique* (*personne qui ne parle guère*) silent type
Taiwan [tajwan] Taiwan
talc [talk] *m* talc
talent [talɑ̃] *m* talent; **avoir du** ~ to be talented
talentueux, **-euse** [talɑ̃tɥø, -øz] *adj* talented
talisman [talismɑ̃] *m* talisman
talkie-walkie [tokiwolki] <talkies-walkies> *m* walkie-talkie
Talmud [talmyd] *m* **le** ~ the Talmud
taloche [talɔʃ] *f* **1.** *inf* clout; **donner** [*o* **flanquer**] **une** ~ **à qn** to give sb a clip round the ear **2.** TECH float
talon [talɔ̃] *m* **1.** (*pièce de chaussure, chaussette*) *a.* ANAT heel; ~ **aiguille** stiletto heel **2.** (*bout*) crust; (*d'un jambon, fromage*) heel **3.** (*partie non détachable d'une feuille de carnet*) stub **4.** TECH (*d'un ski*) tail **5.** JEUX talon ►**il a qn sur ses** ~**s** he's got sb on his heels; **être sur les** ~**s de qn** to be (hot) on sb's heels
talonnade [talɔnad] *f* SPORT back-heel
talonner [talɔne] <1> *vt* **1.** (*suivre de près*) to pursue **2.** (*harceler: personne*) to hound **3.** (*frapper du talon au rugby/football*) to heel (the ball)
talquer [talke] <1> *vt* ~ **qc** to put talcum powder on sth
talus [taly] *m* embankment
TAM [teɑɛm] *f abr de* **toile d'araignée mondiale** WWW
tambouille [tɑ̃buj] *f inf* grub *no pl*
tambour [tɑ̃buʀ] *m* **1.** MUS, TECH, ARCHIT (*d'un frein, treuil, lave-linge*) drum; (*d'une montre*) barrel **2.** (*musicien*) drummer **3.** (*tourniquet*) revolving door ►**sans** ~ **ni trompette** without any fuss; ~ **battant** briskly
tambourin [tɑ̃buʀɛ̃] *m* tambourine
tambouriner [tɑ̃buʀine] <1> *vi* ~ **à/sur qc** to drum on sth
tamis [tami] *m* **1.** (*crible*) sieve **2.** SPORT strings *pl* ►**passer une région au** ~ to comb a region
Tamise [tamiz] *f* **la** ~ the Thames
tamisé(**e**) [tamize] *adj* **1.** (*passé au tamis*) sieved **2.** *fig* **lumière** ~**e** soft light
tamiser [tamize] <1> *vt* **1.** (*passer au tamis*) to sieve **2.** (*filtrer: lumière*) to filter
tampon [tɑ̃pɔ̃] **I.** *m* **1.** (*en coton*) wad **2.** (*périodique*) tampon **3.** (*à récurer*) scouring pad **4.** (*pansement*) pad **5.** (*cachet*) stamp **6.** (*bouchon*) plug **7.** CHEMDFER buffer ►~ **buvard** blotter **II.** *app inv* buffer
tamponner [tɑ̃pɔne] <1> **I.** *vt* **1.** (*essuyer*) to mop up **2.** (*nettoyer: plaie*) to dab **3.** (*heurter*) ~ **qc** (*voiture*) to crash into sth **4.** (*timbrer*) to stamp **II.** *vpr* (*se heurter*) **se** ~ (*voitures*) to smash into each other
tamponneur, **-euse** [tɑ̃pɔnœʀ, -øz] *adj* (*véhicule*) bumper

tam-tam [tamtam] <tam-tams> *m* **1.** MUS tomtom **2.** (*tapage*) fuss

tandem [tɑ̃dɛm] *m* **1.** (*cycle*) tandem **2.** (*duo*) pair

tandis que [tɑ̃dikə] *conj +indic* while

tangage [tɑ̃gaʒ] *m* NAUT pitching

tangent(e) [tɑ̃ʒɑ̃, ʒɑ̃t] *adj* **1.** (*très juste*) close; (*élève*) borderline **2.** MAT tangent

tangente [tɑ̃ʒɑ̃t] *f* MAT tangent ►**prendre la** ~ to make oneself scarce

tangentiel(le) [tɑ̃ʒɑ̃sjɛl] *adj* tangential

Tanger [tɑ̃ʒe] Tangier

tangible [tɑ̃ʒibl] *adj* tangible

tango [tɑ̃go] **I.** *m* tango **II.** *adj inv* tangerine

tanguer [tɑ̃ge] <1> *vi* **1.** NAUT to pitch **2.** *inf* (*tituber*) to stagger **3.** *inf* (*vaciller*) ~ **autour de qn** (*objets*) to spin around sb

tanière [tanjɛʀ] *f* **1.** (*repère: d'un animal*) den; (*d'un malfaiteur*) lair **2.** (*lieu retiré*) retreat

tanin [tanɛ̃] *m* tannin

tank [tɑ̃k] *m* tank

tannage [tanaʒ] *m* tanning

tanner [tane] <1> *vt* **1.** (*préparer des peaux*) to tan **2.** *inf* (*harceler: personne*) to hassle **3.** (*hâler: visage*) to weather

tannerie [tanʀi] *f* **1.** (*opérations*) tanning **2.** (*établissement*) tannery

tanneur, -euse [tanœʀ, -øz] *m, f* tanner

tannin [tanɛ̃] *m v.* **tanin**

tant [tɑ̃] **I.** *adv* **1.** (*tellement*) so much **2.** (*une telle quantité*) ~ **de choses/fois** so many things/times; **une voiture comme il y en a** ~ a perfectly ordinary car **3.** (*autant*) ~ **qu'il peut** as much as he can; **ne pas en demander** ~ to not ask so much **4.** (*aussi longtemps que*) ~ **que tu seras là** as long as you're there; ~ **que j'y suis** while I'm here **5.** (*dans la mesure où*) ~ **qu'à faire la vaisselle, tu peux aussi ...** since you're doing the washing up, you might as well... ►~ **qu'à faire** *inf* might as well; **en** ~ **que** as; ~ **pis!** *inf* hard luck! **II.** *m* (*date*) **le** ~ such a date

tante [tɑ̃t] *f* **1.** (*parente*) aunt **2.** *vulg* (*homosexuel*) queer

tantième [tɑ̃tjɛm] **I.** *adj* **le** ~ **jour du mois** on such a date in the month **II.** *m* percentage

tantinet [tɑ̃tinɛ] **un** ~ a tiny bit

tantôt [tɑ̃to] *adv* **1.** (*en alternance*) ~ **à pied** ~ **à vélo** sometimes on foot, sometimes by bike **2.** *Belgique* (*tout à l'heure*) later

Tanzanie [tɑ̃zani] *f* **la** ~ Tanzania

tanzanien(ne) [tɑ̃zanjɛ̃, ɛn] *adj* Tanzanian

Tanzanien(ne) [tɑ̃zanjɛ̃, ɛn] *m(f)* Tanzanian

taon [tɑ̃] *m* ZOOL horsefly

tapage [tapaʒ] *m* **1.** (*vacarme*) racket **2.** (*publicité*) talk

tapageur, -euse [tapaʒœʀ, -ʒøz] *adj* (*liaison, vie*) raucous; (*enfant*) rowdy; (*publicité*) blazing; (*toilette*) loud

tapant(e) [tapɑ̃, ɑ̃t] *adj* sharp

tape [tap] *f* slap

tape-à-l'œil [tapalœj] *inv* **I.** *adj* (*toilette*) flashy **II.** *m* show

taper [tape] <1> **I.** *vi* **1.** (*donner des coups*) to beat; ~ **à la porte** to knock at the door; ~ **sur qn** to beat sb **2.** (*frapper*) ~ **de la main sur la table** to bang one's hand on the table; ~ **dans le ballon** to kick the ball; ~ **des mains** to clap **3.** (*dactylographier*) to type **4.** *inf* (*dire du mal de*) ~ **sur qn** to run sb down **5.** *inf* (*cogner: soleil*) to beat down ►~ **à côté** *inf* to be wide of the mark **II.** *vt* **1.** (*battre: tapis*) to beat; (*personne, animal*) to hit; (*amicalement*) to tap **2.** (*cogner*) ~ **le pied contre qc** to stub one's foot on sth **3.** (*frapper de*) ~ **la table du poing** to bang one's fist on the table **4.** (*produire en tapant*) ~ **trois coups à la porte** to knock three times at the door **5.** (*dactylographier*) to type **6.** INFOR (*texte, code, 3615*) to enter **III.** *vpr* (*se frapper*) **c'est à se** ~ **la tête contre les murs!** it'd drive you up the wall! ►**je m'en tape** *inf* I couldn't care less

tapette [tapɛt] *f* **1.** (*petite tape*) tap **2.** (*ustensile pour les tapis*) carpet beater **3.** (*ustensile pour les mouches*) fly swatter **4.** (*piège*) trap

tapin [tapɛ̃] **faire le** ~ *vulg* to be on the game

tapinois [tapinwa] **s'approcher en** ~ to creep up; **agir en** ~ to act on the quiet

tapioca [tapjɔka] *m* tapioca

tapir¹ [tapiʀ] *m* tapir

tapir² [tapiʀ] <8> *vpr* **se** ~ **sous/derrière qc** (*animal, personne*) to hide away under/behind sth

tapis [tapi] *m* **1.** (*textile protecteur*) rug **2.** JEUX baize **3.** (*vaste étendue*) carpet **4.** INFOR ~ (**pour**) **souris** mouse pad ►~ **roulant** conveyor belt; (*pour bagages*) carousel; **aller au** ~ SPORT to go out for the count; **envoyer qn au** ~ SPORT to floor sb; **mettre qc sur le** ~ to bring sth up for discussion; **revenir sur le** ~ (*sujet, thème*) to come back up for discussion

tapis-brosse [tapibʀɔs] <tapis-brosses> *m* doormat

tapisser [tapise] <1> *vt* **1.** (*revêtir: mur, pièce*) to wallpaper; (*fauteuil*) to upholster **2.** (*recouvrir: lierre, mousse*) to carpet

tapisserie [tapisʀi] *f* **1.** (*revêtement*) wallpaper **2.** (*pose du papier peint*) wallpapering **3.** ART (*activité*) tapestry-making; (*tapis*) tapestry ►**faire** ~ to be a wallflower

tapissier, -ière [tapisje, -jɛʀ] *m, f* **1.** paperhanger **2.** (*pour fauteuils*) upholsterer **3.** ART tapestry maker **4.** (*marchand*) interior decorator

tapoter [tapɔte] <1> *vt* (*taper à petits coups répétés: joues*) to pat

taquet [takɛ] *m* **1.** (*cale*) wedge **2.** (*verrou*) bolt **3.** TECH tab stop; CHEMDFER scotch

taquin(e) [takɛ̃, in] **I.** *adj* (*caractère, personne*) teasing **II.** *m(f)* tease

taquiner [takine] <1> **I.** *vt* **1.** (*s'amuser à agacer*) to tease **2.** (*faire légèrement souffrir: choses*) to bother **II.** *vpr* **se** ~ to tease each other

taquinerie [takinʀi] *f* teasing *no pl*

tarabiscoté(e) [taʀabiskɔte] *adj* ornate; (*histoire*) convoluted

tarabuster [taʀabyste] <1> *vt* **1.** (*importuner*) to bother **2.** (*causer de l'inquiétude*) ~ **qn** (*choses*) to worry sb

taratata [taʀatata] *interj inf* nonsense

tard [taʀ] **I.** *adv* (*tardivement*) late; **le plus ~ possible** as late as possible; **au plus ~** at the latest; **pas plus ~ que ...** no later than ... ▶**mieux vaut ~ que jamais** *prov* better late than never **II.** *m* **sur le ~** late in the day

tarder [taʀde] <1> *vi* **1.** (*traîner*) to be late; **sans ~** without delay; **~ à faire qc** to delay doing sth **2.** (*se faire attendre*) to take a long time; **tu ne vas pas ~ à t'endormir** you'll soon be asleep

tardif, -ive [taʀdif, -iv] *adj* **1.** (*qui vient, qui se fait tard*) belated **2.** AGR (*fruits, fleurs*) late

tardivement [taʀdivmɑ̃] *adv* late

tare [taʀ] *f* **1.** (*défaut: d'une personne, société*) flaw **2.** MED defect **3.** (*poids de l'emballage, contrepoids*) tare; **faire la ~** to allow for the tare

taré(e) [taʀe] **I.** *adj* **1.** *inf* (*idiot*) sick in the head **2.** MED degenerate **II.** *m(f)* **1.** *inf* (*idiot*) sicko **2.** MED degenerate

tarentule [taʀɑ̃tyl] *f* tarantula

targette [taʀʒɛt] *f* bolt

tari(e) [taʀi] *adj* dried up

tarif [taʀif] *m* (*barème*) rate; (*d'une réparation*) cost

tarifer [taʀife] <1> *vt* **~ la marchandise** to set the price for the goods

tarification [taʀifikasjɔ̃] *f* COM pricing

tarir [taʀiʀ] <8> **I.** *vi* (*cesser de couler*) to dry up **II.** *vt* (*assécher*) **~ qc** to dry sth up **III.** *vpr* **se ~** (*s'assécher*) to dry up

tarot [taʀo] *m* **1.** (*jeu*) tarot; (*carte*) tarot card **2.** (*en cartomancie*) Tarot

tartare [taʀtaʀ] *adj* **1.** HIST **les populations ~s** the Tartars **2.** GASTR **steak ~** steak tartare

Tartare [taʀtaʀ] *mf* HIST Tartar

tarte [taʀt] **I.** *f* **1.** GASTR tart; **~ aux cerises/prunes** cherry/plum tart **2.** *inf* (*gifle*) slap **II.** *adj inf* daft

tartelette [taʀtəlɛt] *f* tartlet

tartine [taʀtin] *f* **1.** GASTR **~ beurrée** piece of bread and butter; **~ grillée** piece of toast **2.** *péj, inf* (*long développement*) **écrire des ~s** to write reams

tartiner [taʀtine] <1> *vt* GASTR to spread

tartre [taʀtʀ] *m* fur; (*des dents*) tartar

tartuf(f)e [taʀtyf] **I.** *m* hypocrite **II.** *adj* hypocritical

tas [tɑ] *m* **1.** (*amas*) heap **2.** *inf* (*beaucoup de*) **un ~ de choses/personnes** loads *pl* of things/people

Tasmanie [tasmani] *f* **la ~** Tasmania

tasmanien(ne) [tasmanjɛ̃, ɛn] *adj* Tasmanian

Tasmanien(ne) [tasmanjɛ̃, ɛn] *m(f)* Tasmanian

tasse [tɑs] *f* **1.** (*contenu*) cup; **~ de thé** cup of tea **2.** (*récipient*) **~ à thé** teacup ▶**ce n'est pas ma ~ de thé** *inf* it is not my cup of tea

tassé(e) [tɑse] *adj* **un café/pastis bien ~** a good strong coffee/pastis

tassement [tɑsmɑ̃] *m* **1.** (*affaissement: des neiges*) drifting; (*des sédiments, de terrain*) subsidence **2.** (*affermissement: du sol*) packing **3.** MED (*des vertèbres*) compression **4.** (*diminution*) drop

tasser [tɑse] <1> **I.** *vt* **1.** (*comprimer*) to compress; (*paille, foin*) to pack **2.** (*en tapant: neige, sable, terre*) to pack down **II.** *vpr* **se ~** **1.** (*s'affaisser*) to settle **2.** *inf* (*s'arranger: difficulté, chose*) to sort itself out; (*ennui, querelle*) to settle down

tatami [tatami] *m* tatami

tatane [tatan] *f inf* shoe

tâter [tɑte] <1> **I.** *vt* to feel ▶**~ le terrain** to see how the land lies **II.** *vi* (*faire l'expérience*) **~ de qc** to have a taste of sth **III.** *vpr* **se ~** *inf* (*hésiter*) to be in two minds

tatie [tati] *f inf* aunty

tatillon(ne) [tatijɔ̃, jɔn] **I.** *adj* finicky **II.** *m(f)* nit-picker

tâtonnement [tɑtɔnmɑ̃] *m* **1.** (*essai hésitant*) tentative step **2.** (*marche incertaine*) groping along *no pl*

tâtonner [tɑtɔne] <1> *vi* **1.** (*chercher en hésitant*) to grope around **2.** (*se déplacer sans voir*) to grope one's way along

tâtons [tɑtɔ̃] *mpl* **chercher qc à ~** to grope around for sth

tatou [tatu] *m* armadillo

tatouage [tatwaʒ] *m* **1.** (*action*) tattooing **2.** (*dessin sur la peau*) tattoo

tatoué(e) [tatwe] *adj* tattooed

tatouer [tatwe] <1> *vt* to tattoo

tatoueur, -euse [tatwœʀ, -øz] *m, f* tattoo artist

taudis [todi] *m* (*logement misérable*) slum

taulard(e) [tolaʀ, aʀd] *m(f) vulg* con

taule [tol] *f* **1.** *vulg* (*prison*) nick *Brit*, pen *Am*; **faire de la ~** [*o* **être en ~**] to do [*o* be doing] time **2.** *inf* (*chambre*) room

taupe [top] *f* ZOOL mole

taupinière [topinjɛʀ] *f* molehill

taureau [tɔʀo] <x> *m* ZOOL bull

Taureau [tɔʀo] <x> *m* Taurus; *v. a.* **Balance**

tauromachie [tɔʀɔmaʃi] *f* bullfighting

taux [to] *m* **1.** (*pourcentage administrativement fixé*) rate **2.** (*mesure statistique*) *a.* MED level; (*en évolution*) rate; **~ d'activité/de chômage** employment/unemployment rate; **~ de change/d'intérêt** exchange/interest rate; **~ de conversion** *pl* conversion rates; **~ de natalité/de mortalité** birth/mortality rate; **~ de cholestérol/sucre** cholesterol/sugar level **3.** TECH **~ de compression** compression ratio

taverne [tavɛʀn] *f* **1.** (*gargote*) inn **2.** HIST tavern **3.** *Québec* (*débit de boissons réservé* *aux hommes*) tavern (*for men only*)

tavernier, **-ière** [tavɛʀnje, -jɛʀ] *m, f* innkeeper

tavillon [tavijɔ̃] *m Suisse* (*petit bardeau servant à recouvrir les toits*) wooden roof tile

taxable [taksabl] *adj* **1.** (*imposable*) taxable **2.** (*à la douane*) dutiable

taxation [taksasjɔ̃] *f* FIN (*des marchandises, produits, prix*) taxation; ~ **des salaires** taxing of salaries

taxe [taks] *f* (*impôt*) tax; ~ **professionnelle** local business tax; ~ **de séjour** tourist tax; ~ **à la valeur ajoutée** value added tax; **toutes ~s comprises** tax included; **hors ~s** duty free; (*sans T.V.A.*) V.A.T. free

taxer [takse] <1> *vt* **1.** (*imposer*) to tax **2.** (*fixer le prix: marchandise, produit*) to fix the price of

taxi [taksi] *m* **1.** (*véhicule*) taxi **2.** *inf* (*chauffeur*) cabby

taxiphone® [taksifɔn] *m* public telephone

Tchad [tʃad] *m* **le** ~ Chad

tchadien(**ne**) [tʃadjɛ̃, ɛn] *adj* Chadian

Tchadien(**ne**) [tʃadjɛ̃, ɛn] *m(f)* Chadian

tchador [tʃadɔʀ] *m* (*vêtement long*) chador

tchao [tʃao] *interj inf* bye

tchat [tʃat] *m* INFOR chat

tchatcher [tʃatʃe] <1> *vi inf* to chatter, to natter *Brit*

tchécoslovaque [tʃekɔslɔvak] *adj* HIST Czechoslovakian

Tchécoslovaque [tʃekɔslɔvak] *mf* HIST Czechoslovak

Tchécoslovaquie [tʃekɔslɔvaki] *f* HIST Czechoslovakia

tchèque [tʃɛk] **I.** *adj* Czech; **la République** ~ the Czech Republic **II.** *m* Czech; *v. a.* **français**

Tchèque [tʃɛk] *mf* Czech

TD [tede] *mpl abr de* **travaux dirigés** tutorial class

te [tə] <*devant voyelle ou h muet* **t'**> *pron pers* you; *v. a.* **me**

té [te] *m* **1.** (*règle*) T-square **2.** TECH (*ferrure*) T-bracket

technicien(**ne**) [tɛknisjɛ̃, jɛn] *m(f)* (*professionnel qualifié, expert*) technician

technicité [tɛknisite] *f* technical nature

technico-commercial(**e**) [tɛknikokɔmɛʀsjal, jo] <technico-commerciaux> **I.** *adj* technical sales **II.** *m(f)* COM technical sales advisor

technique [tɛknik] **I.** *adj* (*ouvrage, revue, terme*) technical; **lycée** ~ technology college **II.** *m* ECOLE technical education **III.** *f* technique

techniquement [tɛknikmɑ̃] *adv* technically

techno [tɛknɔ] **I.** *adj* **musique** ~ techno music **II.** *f* techno

technocrate [tɛknɔkʀat] *mf péj* technocrat

technologie [tɛknɔlɔʒi] *f* technology; ~ **de pointe** cutting-edge technology

technologique [tɛknɔlɔʒik] *adj* technological

teck [tɛk] *m* teak

teckel [tekɛl] *m* dachshund

teenager [tinɛdʒœʀ] *mf* teenager

tee-shirt [tiʃœʀt] <tee-shirts> *m* T-shirt

Téfal® [tefal] *adj inv* Tefal®

téflon® [teflɔ̃] *m* Teflon®

tégéviste [teʒevist] *mf* TGV driver

teigne [tɛɲ] *f* **1.** ZOOL tineid **2.** MED ringworm **3.** *inf* (*personne méchante*) pain

teigneux, **-euse** [tɛɲø, -øz] **I.** *adj inf* scabby **II.** *m, f* **1.** *inf* (*hargneux*) nasty piece of work **2.** MED ringworm sufferer

teindre [tɛ̃dʀ] *irr* **I.** *vt* to dye; (*bois*) to stain; ~ **qc en rouge/noir** to dye sth red/black **II.** *vpr* (*se colorer les cheveux*) **se** ~ **en brun** to dye one's hair brown

teint [tɛ̃] *m* (*couleur de la peau*) complexion ▶**bon** ~ *iron* staunch; **grand** ~ colourfast *Brit,* colorfast *Am*

teint(**e**) [tɛ̃, ɛ̃t] **I.** *part passé de* **teindre** **II.** *adj* dyed

teinte [tɛ̃t] *f* (*couleur*) shade

teinté(**e**) [tɛ̃te] *adj* **1.** (*coloré*) tinted **2.** *fig, soutenu* ~ **de nostalgie** tinged with nostalgia

teinter [tɛ̃te] <1> **I.** *vt* (*colorer*) to dye **II.** *vpr* **1.** (*se colorer*) **se** ~ **de roux** to take on a reddish tinge **2.** (*se nuancer*) **son discours se teintait d'ironie/d'amertume** his/her speech was tinged with irony/bitterness

teinture [tɛ̃tyʀ] *f* **1.** (*colorant*) dye **2.** MED ~ **d'arnica/d'iode** tincture of arnica/of iodine **3.** (*fait de teindre*) dyeing

teinturerie [tɛ̃tyʀʀi] *f* **1.** (*magasin*) dry cleaner's **2.** (*industrie*) dry cleaning

teinturier, **-ère** [tɛ̃tyʀje, -ɛʀ] *m, f* **1.** (*commerçant*) **porter qc chez le** ~ to take sth to the dry cleaner's **2.** (*artisan*) dyer

tel(**le**) [tɛl] **I.** *adj indéf* **1.** (*semblable, si fort/grand*) **un** ~/**une** ~**le ...** such a ...; **de** ~(**s**) ... such ... **2.** (*ainsi*) ~**le n'est pas mon intention** that is not my intention; ~ **père,** ~ **fils** like father, like son **3.** (*comme*) ~ **que qn/qc** such as [*o* like] sb/sth; **un homme** ~ **que lui** a man like him **4.** (*un certain*) ~ **jour et à** ~**le heure** on such a day at such a time ▶**passer pour** ~ to be thought of as such; **en tant que** ~ as such; **rendre qc** ~ **quel** *inf* to return sth as it is; **il n'y a rien de** ~ there's nothing like it **II.** *pron indéf* **si** ~ **ou** ~ **te dit ...** if anybody tells you ...

tél. *m abr de* **téléphone** tel.

télé [tele] *f inf abr de* **télévision** TV; **à la** ~ on TV

téléachat [teleaʃa] *m* teleshopping

télébenne [telebɛn] *f,* **télécabine** [telekabin] *f* cable car

télécarte [telekaʀt] *f* phonecard

téléchargement [teleʃaʀʒmɑ̃] *m* INFOR download

télécharger [teleʃaʀʒe] *vt* ~ **qc** (*vers l'aval*) to download sth; (*vers l'amont*) to upload sth

Télécom [telekɔm] **France** ~ France Telecom (*French national telecommunications company*)

télécommande [telekɔmɑ̃d] *f* (*boîtier, procédé: d'une télé, d'un magnétoscope*) remote control

télécommandé(e) [telekɔmɑ̃de] *adj* (*jouet*) remote-control; **être ~** to be remote-controlled

télécommander [telekɔmɑ̃de] <1> *vt* **~ qc 1.** TECH to operate sth by remote control **2.** (*organiser à distance*) to mastermind sth (from a distance)

télécommunication [telekɔmynikasjɔ̃] *f gén pl* (*administration, technique*) telecommunication

télécoms [telekɔm] *fpl inf abr de* **télécommunications**

téléconférence [telekɔ̃feʀɑ̃s] *f* videoconference

télécopie [telekɔpi] *f* fax

télécopieur [telekɔpjœʀ] *m* fax machine

télédétection [teledetɛksjɔ̃] *f* remote sensing; **~ par satellite** satellite sensing

télédiffuser [teledifyze] <1> *vt* to broadcast (on television)

télédiffusion [teledifyzjɔ̃] *f* television broadcasting

télédistribution [teledistʀibysjɔ̃] *f* wired broadcasting

téléenseignement [teleɑ̃sɛɲəmɑ̃] *m* distance learning

téléfax [telefaks] *m* fax

téléférique [telefeʀik] *m v.* **téléphérique**

téléfilm [telefilm] *m* television film *Brit,* TV movie *Am*

télégénique [teleʒenik] *adj* telegenic

télégramme [telegʀam] *m* telegram

télégraphe [telegʀaf] *m* telegraph

télégraphie [telegʀafi] *f* telegraphy

télégraphier [telegʀafje] <1> *vt* **1.** (*envoyer un message en morse*) to wire **2.** NAUT to telegraph

télégraphique [telegʀafik] *adj* **1.** TEL telegraph **2.** (*abrégé: style*) telegraphic

télégraphiste [telegʀafist] *mf* telegraphist

téléguidage [telegidaʒ] *m* remote control

téléguidé(e) [telegide] *adj* **1.** (*guidé à distance*) remote-controlled **2.** *fig, inf* **attentats ~s de l'étranger** attacks masterminded from outside the country

téléguider [telegide] <1> *vt* **~ qc 1.** (*diriger à distance*) to operate sth by radio control **2.** *inf* (*influencer à distance*) to mastermind sth (from a distance)

téléinformatique [teleɛ̃fɔʀmatik] *f* remote access computing

télématique [telematik] **I.** *adj* telematic **II.** *f* telematics

téléobjectif [teleɔbʒɛktif] *m* telephoto lens

télépaiement [telepɛmɑ̃] *m* electronic payment

télépathe [telepat] *mf* telepath

télépathie [telepati] *f* telepathy

télépathique [telepatik] *adj* telepathic

télépendulaire [telepɑ̃dylɛʀ] *m* telecommuter

téléphérique [telefeʀik] *m* cable car

téléphone [telefɔn] *m* telephone; **~ à touches** push-button phone; **~ sans fil** cordless phone; **~ portable** mobile (phone) *Brit,* cellphone *Am;* **~ à cartes** cardphone; **~ visuel** videophone; **~ arabe** *iron* grapevine; **appeler/avoir qn au ~** to call sb on the phone; **être au ~** to be on the phone

téléphoner [telefɔne] <1> **I.** *vt* (*transmettre par téléphone*) **~ une nouvelle à une amie** to tell a friend news over the phone **II.** *vi* (*parler au téléphone*) to telephone; **~ à qn** to (tele)phone sb **III.** *vpr* **se ~** to (tele)phone each other

téléphonie [telefɔni] *f* telephony; **~ numérique mobile** digital mobile telephony

téléphonique [telefɔnik] *adj* telephonic; **cabine ~** telephone box *Brit,* telephone booth *Am*

téléphoniste [telefɔnist] *mf* telephonist

téléport [telepɔʀ] *m* teleport

téléreportage [teleʀ(ə)pɔʀtaʒ] *m* (*activité*) television reporting; (*rapport*) (television) news report

télescopage [teleskɔpaʒ] *m* concertinaing

télescope [teleskɔp] *m* telescope

télescoper [telɛskɔpe] <1> **I.** *vt* (*heurter violemment*) to crush **II.** *vpr* (*se percuter*) **se ~** to concertina (into each other)

télescopique [telɛskɔpik] *adj* ASTR, TECH telescopic

téléscripteur [teleskʀiptœʀ] *m* teleprinter *Brit,* teletypewriter *Am*

télésexe [telesɛks] *m* INFOR cybersex

télésiège [telesjɛʒ] *m* chair lift; **prendre le ~** to take the chair lift

téléski [teleski] *m* ski lift

téléspectateur, -trice [telespɛktatœʀ, -tʀis] *m, f* (television) viewer

télésurveillance [telesyʀvɛjɑ̃s] *f* remote surveillance

Télétel® [teletɛl] *m: electronic telephone directory*

Télétex® [teletɛks] *m* ≈ Teletext®

télétexte [teletɛkst] *m* teletext

téléthon [teletɔ̃] *m* telethon

télétraitement [teletʀɛtmɑ̃] *m* INFOR teleprocessing

télétransmission [teletʀɑ̃smisjɔ̃] *f* remote transmission

télétravail [teletʀavaj] *m* telecommuting

télétype® [teletip] *m* Teletype®

télévendeur, -euse [televɑ̃dœʀ, -øz] *m, f* telemarketer

télévente [televɑ̃t] *f* telemarketing, telesales

télévisé(e) [televize] *adj* televised; **journal ~** television news

téléviser [televize] <1> *vt* to televise

téléviseur [televizœʀ] *m* television (set)

télévision [televizjɔ̃] *f* **1.** (*organisme, technique, programmes*) television; **regarder la ~** to watch television; **à la ~** on television; **~ par**

T

câble/satellite cable/satellite television **2.** (*chaîne*) **chaîne de** ~ television channel **3.** (*récepteur*) television (set) **4.** *Québec* ~ **communautaire** (*temps de télévision et moyens de réalisation mis à la disposition de collectivités, de groupes, pour la présentation de certaines émissions*) community television

télévisuel(le) [televizɥɛl] *adj* television

télex [telɛks] *m inv* telex

télexer [telɛkse] <1> *vt* to telex

télexiste [telɛksist] *mf* telex operator

tellement [tɛlmɑ̃] *adv* **1.** (*si*) so; **ce serait** ~ **mieux** it'd be so much better **2.** (*tant*) so much **3.** (*beaucoup*) **pas/plus** ~ *inf* (*venir, aimer*) not much/much now; (*boire, manger, travailler*) not that much/much any more **4.** *inf* (*tant de*) **avoir** ~ **d'amis/de courage** to have so many friends/so much courage **5.** (*parce que*) because; **on le comprend à peine** ~ **il parle vite** you can hardly understand him he speaks so fast

tellurique [telyʀik] *adj* (*courant, prospection*) telluric

téméraire [temeʀɛʀ] *adj* **1.** (*audacieux*) daring **2.** (*imprudent: entreprise, jugement*) foolhardy

témérité [temeʀite] *f* temerity

témoignage [temwaɲaʒ] *m* **1.** (*déposition*) evidence *no pl Brit,* testimony *no pl Am;* **faire un faux** ~ to lie under oath **2.** (*récit*) account; **selon divers ~s, ...** according to a number of witnesses, ... **3.** (*manifestation*) expression; ~ **d'affection** sign of affection; **en** ~ **de ma reconnaissance** to express my gratitude

témoigner [temwaɲe] <1> **I.** *vi* **1.** (*déposer*) ~ **en faveur de/contre qn** to testify in favour of/against sb *Brit,* to testify in favor of/against sb *Am* **2.** (*faire un récit*) to give an account **II.** *vt* **1.** (*attester, jurer*) ~ **avoir vu l'accusé** to testify that one saw the accused **2.** (*exprimer*) to express; ~ **son attachement à qn** to show one's fondness for sb

témoin [temwɛ̃] **I.** *m* **1.** witness; ~ **oculaire** eyewitness; ~ **à charge/décharge** witness for the prosecution/defence *Brit,* witness for the prosecution/defense *Am;* **faux** ~ perjurer **2.** (*preuve*) **être (un)** ~ **de qc** to be proof of sth **3.** SPORT baton **4.** (*voyant lumineux*) warning light **II.** *app* **lampe** ~ warning light; **appartement** ~ show apartment

tempe [tɑ̃p] *f* temple

tempérament [tɑ̃peʀamɑ̃] *m* (*caractère*) temperament ►**vente à** ~ COM sale on instalments *Brit,* installment plan *Am*

tempérance [tɑ̃peʀɑ̃s] *f* temperance

tempérant(e) [tɑ̃peʀɑ̃, ɑ̃t] *adj* temperate

température [tɑ̃peʀatyʀ] *f* ANAT, METEO, PHYS temperature; ~ **ambiante** ambient temperature; ~ **d'ébullition/de fusion** boiling/melting point ►**avoir de la** ~ to have a temperature; **prendre la** ~ **de qn** to take sb's temperature; **prendre la** ~ **d'un groupe** to sound out a group

tempéré(e) [tɑ̃peʀe] *adj* **1.** (*modéré*) *a.* METEO temperate **2.** MUS tempered

tempérer [tɑ̃peʀe] <5> **I.** *vt* **1.** METEO to moderate **2.** (*modérer: enthousiasme*) to temper; (*ardeur*) to calm; (*douleur, peine*) to soothe **II.** *vpr soutenu* **se** ~ to be tempered

tempête [tɑ̃pɛt] *f a. fig* storm; ~ **de neige** snowstorm; ~ **d'applaudissements/de rires** storm of applause/laughter

tempêter [tɑ̃pete] <1> *vi* ~ **contre qn/qc** to rant and rave against sb/sth

tempétueux, -euse [tɑ̃petɥø, -øz] *adj fig* tempestuous

temple [tɑ̃pl] *m* temple; (*protestant*) church

tempo [tɛmpo] *m a.* MUS tempo

temporaire [tɑ̃pɔʀɛʀ] *adj* temporary; **à titre** ~ for the time being

temporairement [tɑ̃pɔʀɛʀmɑ̃] *adv* temporarily

temporel(le) [tɑ̃pɔʀɛl] *adj a.* LING, REL temporal

temporellement [tɑ̃pɔʀɛlmɑ̃] *adv* temporally

temporisateur [tɑ̃pɔʀizatœʀ] *m* TECH timer

temporisation [tɑ̃pɔʀizasjɔ̃] *f* delaying

temporiser [tɑ̃pɔʀize] <1> *vi* to delay

temps[1] [tɑ̃] *m* **1.** (*durée, déroulement du temps, moment, période*) time; **passer tout son** ~ **à faire qc** to spend all one's time doing sth; **avoir tout son** ~ to have plenty of time; ~ **libre** free time; **à plein** ~ full time; **emploi à** ~ **complet** full-time job; **emploi à** ~ **partiel** part-time job; **le bon vieux** ~ the good old days **2.** *pl* (*époque*) times **3.** (*saison*) **le** ~ **des cerises/moissons** the cherry/harvest season **4.** LING tense **5.** TECH stroke; **moteur à deux** ~ two-stroke engine **6.** MUS beat ►**le** ~ **c'est de l'argent** *prov* time is money; **en** ~ **et lieu** in due course; **en deux** ~ **trois mouvements** in two shakes; **la plupart** [*o* **les trois quarts**] **du** ~ most of the time; **le plus clair de mon/ton** ~ the better part of my/your time; **ces derniers** ~ lately; **trouver le** ~ **long** (*s'impatienter*) to find it hard to wait; (*s'ennuyer*) to find that time weighs heavily; ~ **mort** slack period; SPORT injury time; **dans un premier** ~ initially; **dans un second** ~ subsequently; **tout le** ~ all the time; **il y a un** ~ **pour tout** there is a (right) time for everything; **n'avoir qu'un** ~ not to last; **il est (grand)** ~ **de** +*infin*/**qu'il parte** it is high time to +*infin*/ that he left; **il était** ~! about time!; **mettre du** ~ **à faire qc** to take a (terribly) long time doing sth; **passer le** ~ to pass the time; **à** ~ in time; **faire qc à** ~ **perdu** to do sth in one's spare time; **ces** ~**-ci** these days; **dans le** ~ in the old days; **de** ~ **en** ~ from time to time; **de tout** ~ from time immemorial; **depuis le** ~ it's been a such long time; **depuis le** ~ **que ...** considering how long ...; **depuis ce** ~**-là** since then; **en même** ~ at the same time; **en** ~ **de crise/guerre** in times of crisis/war; **en** ~ **de paix** in peacetime; en ~ **normal** [*o* **ordinaire**] under normal circumstances; en **peu de** ~ in a short time

temps² [tɑ̃] *m* METEO weather; **il fait beau/mauvais** ~ the weather is good/bad; **quel** ~ **fait-il?** what's the weather like? ►**un** ~ **à ne pas mettre un chien** [*o* **le nez**] **dehors** *inf* lousy weather; **par tous les** ~ in all weathers

tenable [t(ə)nabl] *adj* **ne pas être** ~ to be unbearable; (*position, point de vue*) to be untenable

tenace [tənas] *adj* **1.** (*persistant*) persistent; (*haine*) deep-seated; (*croyance*) deep-rooted **2.** (*obstiné: personne, résistance*) tenacious

ténacité [tenasite] *f* **1.** (*obstination*) stubbornness **2.** (*persévérance*) tenacity **3.** (*persistance*) tenacity; (*d'un préjugé*) doggedness

tenailler [tənaje] <1> *vt* ~ **qn** (*faim*) to gnaw at sb; **le remords la tenaille** she is racked with remorse

tenailles [t(ə)naj] *fpl* pliers

tenancier, **-ère** [tənɑ̃sje, -ɛʀ] *m, f* manager

tenant(e) [tənɑ̃, ɑ̃t] *m(f)* SPORT **le** ~ **de la coupe** the cup-holder; **le** ~ **du titre** the reigning champion ►**les** ~**s et les aboutissants** the ins and outs; **d'un seul** ~ in one piece

tendance [tɑ̃dɑ̃s] *f* **1.** (*propension*) tendency; ~ **à la rêverie** tendency to daydream **2.** (*opinion*) leaning **3.** (*orientation*) trend ►**avoir** ~ **à** +*infin* to tend to +*infin*

tendancieux, **-euse** [tɑ̃dɑ̃sjø, -øz] *adj* tendentious

tendeur [tɑ̃dœʀ] *m* (*câble pour fixer*) elastic strap

tendineux, **-euse** [tɑ̃dinø, -øz] *adj* **1.** (*coriace*) stringy **2.** ANAT tendinous

tendinite [tɑ̃dinit] *f* tendinitis

tendon [tɑ̃dɔ̃] *m* tendon; **le** ~ **d'Achille** Achilles tendon

tendre¹ [tɑ̃dʀ] <14> **I.** *vt* **1.** (*raidir*) to tighten **2.** (*installer: tapisserie*) to hang **3.** (*présenter: bras*) to stretch out; (*cou*) to crane; (*joue*) to offer ►~ **la main** to hold out one's hand; ~ **la main à qn** to give sb a hand **II.** *vpr* (*se raidir*) **se** ~ to tighten; (*relations*) to become strained **III.** *vi* **1.** (*aboutir à*) ~ **à** +*infin* to tend to +*infin;* ~ **vers zéro/l'infini** to tend towards zero/infinity **2.** (*viser à*) ~ **à qc** to aim for sth

tendre² [tɑ̃dʀ] **I.** *adj* **1.** (*opp: dur*) soft; (*peau, viande*) tender **2.** (*affectueux*) fond; (*ami*) loving **3.** (*jeune, délicat*) tender **4.** (*léger: couleur*) soft **II.** *mf* **c'est un** ~ he's soft-hearted

tendrement [tɑ̃dʀəmɑ̃] *adv* gently; (*aimer*) tenderly

tendresse [tɑ̃dʀɛs] *f* **1.** *sans pl* (*affection*) affection; **avoir de la** ~ **pour qn** to feel affection for sb **2.** *sans pl* (*douceur*) tenderness; **regarder qn avec** ~ to look tenderly at sb **3.** *pl* (*marques d'affection*) affection *no pl*

tendreté [tɑ̃dʀəte] *f* tenderness

tendu(e) [tɑ̃dy] **I.** *part passé de* **tendre II.** *adj* **1.** (*nerveux*) tense **2.** (*difficile: relations*) strained

ténèbres [tenɛbʀ] *fpl* REL tenebrae

ténébreux [tenebʀø] *m* **un beau** ~ *iron* a handsome but sombre youth

ténébreux, **-euse** [tenebʀø, -øz] *adj soutenu* (*malaisé à comprendre*) dark

Ténérife, **Tenerife** [teneʀif] Tenerife

teneur [tənœʀ] *f* **1.** (*contenu exact*) contents **2.** (*proportion*) content; **avoir une forte** ~ **en plomb/fer** to have a high lead/iron content

ténia [tenja] *m* tapeworm

tenir [t(ə)niʀ] <9> **I.** *vt* **1.** (*avoir à la main, dans les bras ...*) to hold **2.** (*maintenir dans la même position*) to keep **3.** (*rester dans un lieu*) ~ **la chambre/le lit** to stay in one's bedroom/in bed **4.** (*avoir: article, marchandise*) to have (in stock) **5.** MUS (*note*) to hold **6.** (*avoir sous son contrôle*) ~ **son cheval** to control one's horse **7.** (*s'occuper de: hôtel, magasin, maison*) to run; (*comptes*) to keep **8.** (*assumer: conférence, meeting*) to hold; (*rôle*) to have **9.** (*avoir reçu*) ~ **une information de qn** to have information from sb **10.** (*occuper: largeur, place*) to take up **11.** (*résister à*) ~ **l'eau** to be watertight **12.** (*habiter*) ~ **qn** (*jalousie, colère, envie*) to have sb in its grip **13.** (*être contraint*) **être tenu à qc** to be held to sth; **être tenu de** +*infin* to be obliged to +*infin* **14.** (*respecter: parole, promesse*) to keep; (*pari*) to carry off **15.** (*énoncer*) ~ **des propos racistes** to make racist comments **16.** (*juger*) ~ **un chanteur pour un talent** to consider a singer to be talented ►~ **lieu de qc** to act as sth **II.** *vi* **1.** (*être attaché*) ~ **à qn** to care about sb **2.** (*vouloir absolument*) ~ **à faire qc/à ce que tout soit en ordre** (*subj*) to insist on doing sth/that everything be in order **3.** (*être fixé*) to stay up **4.** (*être cohérent: raisonnement, théorie, argument*) to stand up; (*histoire*) to hold water **5.** (*être contenu dans*) ~ **dans une voiture** to fit in a car **6.** (*se résumer*) ~ **en un mot** to come down to one word **7.** (*durer*) to last **8.** (*ressembler à*) ~ **de qn** to take after sb; ~ **de qc** to be reminiscent of sth ►~ **bon** to hold out; **tiens/tenez!** well!; **tiens! il pleut** hey! it's raining **III.** *vpr* **1.** (*se prendre*) **se** ~ **par la main** to hold hands **2.** (*s'accrocher*) **se** ~ **à qc** to hold on to sth **3.** (*rester, demeurer*) **se** ~ **debout/assis/couché** to be standing/sitting/in bed **4.** (*se comporter*) **se** ~ to behave **5.** (*avoir lieu*) **se** ~ **dans une ville/le mois prochain** (*réunion, conférence*) to be held in a town/the following month **6.** (*être cohérent*) **se** ~ (*événements, faits*) to hold together **7.** (*se limiter à*) **s'en** ~ **à qc** to confine oneself to sth **8.** (*respecter*) **se** ~ **à qc** to respect sth **9.** (*se considérer comme*) **se** ~ **pour qc** to consider oneself (as) sth ►**se le** ~ **pour dit** to be warned **IV.** *vi impers* (*dépendre de*) **ça tient à qn/qc** it depends on sb/sth

tennis [tenis] **I.** *m* **1.** SPORT tennis; **jouer au** ~ to play tennis; ~ **de table** table tennis

T

2. (*court*) tennis court **II.** *mpl o fpl* (*chaussures*) tennis shoes

tennis-elbow [tenisɛlbo] <tennis-elbows> *m* tennis elbow

tennisman [tenisman, -mɛn] <s *o* -men> *m* tennis player

ténor [tenɔʀ] **I.** *m* **1.** (*soliste*) tenor **2.** (*grande figure*) leading figure; **un ~ du barreau** a big name at the bar **II.** *adj* **le saxophone ~** the tenor saxophone

tenseur [tɑ̃sœʀ] *adj* **muscle ~** tensor

tensioactif, -ive [tɑ̃sjoaktif, -iv] *adj* CHIM **produit ~** surface-active product

tension [tɑ̃sjɔ̃] *f* **1.** (*état tendu*) *a.* TECH, PHYS tension **2.** ELEC voltage; **ligne à haute ~** high-voltage line **3.** MED pressure; **avoir** [*o* **faire**] **de la ~** to have high blood pressure

tentaculaire [tɑ̃takylɛʀ] *adj* **1.** ZOOL tentacular **2.** *fig* (*ville*) sprawling

tentacule [tɑ̃takyl] *m* ZOOL tentacle

tentant(e) [tɑ̃tɑ̃, ɑ̃t] *adj* tempting

Tentateur [tɑ̃tatœʀ] *m* (*diable*) **le ~** the Tempter

tentateur, -trice [tɑ̃tatœʀ, -tʀis] **I.** *adj* (*séducteur*) tempting **II.** *m, f* (*personne*) seducer

tentation [tɑ̃tasjɔ̃] *f a.* REL temptation

tentative [tɑ̃tativ] *f* attempt; **~ de meurtre/viol/vol** JUR attempted murder/rape/robbery

tente [tɑ̃t] *f* tent; **monter une ~** to put up a tent

tenter [tɑ̃te] <1> *vt* **1.** (*allécher*) to tempt **2.** (*essayer*) to try; **~ de** +*infin* to try to +*infin*

tenture [tɑ̃tyʀ] *f* **1.** (*tapisserie*) hanging **2.** (*rideau*) curtain **3.** (*pour funérailles*) funeral hanging

tenu(e) [t(ə)ny] **I.** *part passé de* **tenir II.** *adj* **1.** (*obligé*) **être ~ au secret professionnel** to be bound by professional secrecy; **être ~ de** +*infin* to be obliged to +*infin* **2.** (*propre*) **être bien/mal ~** (*maison*) to be well/badly kept

ténu(e) [teny] *adj* **1.** (*peu perceptible: son, bruit*) faint; (*nuance, distinction*) fine **2.** (*fin: fil*) thin

tenue [t(ə)ny] *f* **1.** (*comportement*) behaviour *Brit,* behavior *Am;* **avoir de la ~/manquer de ~** to have good/no manners; **un peu de ~!** manners, please! **2.** (*vêtements*) outfit; **se mettre en ~** to change; **~ de soirée** evening dress **3.** MIL uniform; **~ de campagne** [*o* **combat**] combat dress **4.** (*gestion: d'une maison, restaurant*) running; **la ~ des livres de comptes** the bookkeeping **5.** (*réunion: d'un congrès, d'une assemblée*) holding **6.** AUTO **~ de route** road-holding

tequila [tekila] *f* tequila

ter [tɛʀ] *adv* **habiter au 12 ~** to live at 12b

tercet [tɛʀsɛ] *m* LING tercet

térébenthine [teʀebɑ̃tin] *f* turpentine; **essence de ~** turpentine oil

tergal® [tɛʀgal] *m* ≈ Terylene®; **pantalon de** [*o* **en**] **~** Terylene trousers

tergiversation [tɛʀʒivɛʀsasjɔ̃] *f gén pl* **1.** (*hésitation*) vacillation **2.** *pl* (*faux-fuyants*) prevarication + *sing vb*

tergiverser [tɛʀʒivɛʀse] <1> *vi* **1.** (*user de faux-fuyants*) to prevaricate **2.** (*hésiter*) to vacillate

terme[1] [tɛʀm] *m* **1.** (*fin: d'un stage, voyage, travail*) end; **toucher à son ~** (*stage, soirée*) to come to an end **2.** (*date limite*) term; **à court/moyen/long ~** in the short/medium/long term; **naissance avant ~** premature birth **3.** ECON **marché à ~** futures market; **vente à ~** forward sale **4.** (*échéance*) due date **5.** (*loyer*) rental term ▶ **mener qc à son ~** to bring sth to completion; **mettre un ~ à qc** to put an end to sth

terme[2] [tɛʀm] *m* **1.** (*mot*) term **2.** *pl* (*formule: d'un contrat, d'une loi*) terms ▶ **trouver un moyen ~** to find a middle way; **être en bons/mauvais ~s avec qn** to be on good/bad terms with sb; **en d'autres ~s** in other terms

terminaison [tɛʀminɛzɔ̃] *f* ending

terminal [tɛʀminal, o] <-aux> *m* terminal

terminal(e) [tɛʀminal, o] <-aux> *adj* (*phase*) final

terminale [tɛʀminal] *f* ECOLE year 13 *Brit,* senior year *Am;* **être en ~** to be in one's last year (at school)

> The final year of secondary education is called **terminale** in France and "rhétorique" in Belgium. Belgian students in this year are called "les rhétos".

terminer [tɛʀmine] <1> **I.** *vt* **1.** (*finir*) to finish **2.** (*passer la fin de, être le dernier élément de: soirée, vacances*) to end **II.** *vi* **~ de lire le journal** to finish reading the newspaper; **en ~ avec un sujet/une tâche** to finish with a subject/task; **pour ~, ...** to end with, ... **III.** *vpr* **se ~** (*année, vacances, stage*) to end; **bien/mal se ~** to end well/badly

terminologie [tɛʀminɔlɔʒi] *f* terminology

terminus [tɛʀminys] *m* terminus

termite [tɛʀmit] *m* termite

termitière [tɛʀmitjɛʀ] *f* termite hill

ternaire [tɛʀnɛʀ] *adj* ternary

terne [tɛʀn] *adj* **1.** (*sans éclat: œil, cheveux, regard*) lifeless; (*teint, visage*) pale; (*couleur*) drab; (*miroir, glace*) dull; (*métal*) tarnished **2.** (*monotone: personne, conversation, journée*) dull; (*vie, style*) drab

terni(e) [tɛʀni] *adj* (*couleur, coloris*) dull; (*métal, chandelier*) tarnished

ternir [tɛʀniʀ] <8> **I.** *vt* **1.** (*défraîchir: rideau, tissu, couleur*) to fade; (*métal*) to tarnish **2.** (*nuire à: honneur*) to blemish **II.** *vpr* **se ~** (*rideau, tissu, couleur, coloris*) to go dull; (*métal, chandelier*) to become tarnished

terrain [teʀɛ̃] *m* **1.** (*parcelle*) ground *no pl,* piece of ground **2.** AGR land *no pl,* piece of land; (*un ~ à bâtir*) some building land **3.** (*espace* *réservé*) ~ **de camping** camping site; ~ **de jeu** playground **4.** (*sol*) **un** ~ **plat/accidenté** (some) flat/undulating land; **un** ~ **vague** some wasteland; **véhicule tout** ~ all-terrain vehicle **5.** *gén pl* GEO formation **6.** (*domaine*) field **7.** MIL terrain ▸**trouver** ~ **d'entente avec qn** to find common ground with sb; **être sur un** ~ **glissant** to be on shaky ground; **aller sur le** ~ to go into the field; **céder du** ~ *a. fig* to give ground; **connaître le** ~ to know the terrain; **être sur son** ~ to be on home ground; **homme/femme de** ~ man/woman with direct experience

terrasse [teʀas] *f* **1.** (*plateforme en plein air*) *a.* GEO terrace **2.** (*toit plat*) (**toit en**) ~ flat roof

terrassement [teʀasmɑ̃] *m* **1.** (*travaux*) excavation works **2.** (*matériaux déplacés*) earthworks

terrasser [teʀase] <1> *vt* **1.** (*vaincre*) to bring down **2.** (*accabler, tuer*) ~ **qn** (*mauvaise nouvelle*) to overwhelm sb; (*émotion, fatigue*) to strike sb down; **être terrassé par une embolie/un infarctus** to be struck down by an embolism/a coronary

terrassier [teʀasje] *m* labourer *Brit,* laborer *Am*

terre [tɛʀ] *f* **1.** *sans pl* (*le monde*) **la** ~ the earth **2.** *sans pl* (*croûte terrestre*) **la** ~ the ground; **sous** ~ underground **3.** (*matière*) soil **4.** (*terre cultivable*) land; ~ **battue** packed earth; **légumes de pleine** ~ vegetables grown in soil **5.** *gén pl* (*propriété*) estate **6.** (*contrée, pays*) country; ~ **d'élection** (*d'une personne*) chosen country of residence **7.** (*continent*) ~ **ferme** terra firma **8.** *sans pl* (*vie à la campagne*) **la** ~ the land **9.** *sans pl* (*argile*) clay; ~ **cuite** (*matière*) terracotta **10.** *sans pl* ELEC earth *Brit,* ground *Am;* **mise à la** ~ earthing *Brit,* grounding *Am* **11.** (*opp: ciel*) earth; **être sur** ~ to be on earth ▸**revenir** [*o* **redescendre**] **sur** ~ *inf* to come back down to earth; **par** ~ on the ground; **être par** ~ (*projet, plan*) to be in ruins

Terre [tɛʀ] *f sans pl* (*planète*) **la** ~ (the) Earth

terre à terre [tɛʀatɛʀ] *adj inv* (*personne*) down-to-earth; (*préoccupations*) day-to-day

terreau [teʀo] *m sans pl* compost

terre-neuve [tɛʀ(ə)nœːv(ə)] *m* Newfoundland (dog)

Terre-neuve [tɛʀ(ə)nœːv(ə)] Newfoundland

terre-plein [tɛʀplɛ̃] <terre-pleins> *m* earthwork; ~ **central** (*îlôt directionnel*) central reservation

terrer [teʀe] <1> **I.** *vt* (*pommes de terre, asperges*) to earth up; (*pelouse*) to earth over **II.** *vpr* **se** ~ **1.** (*se cacher: animal*) to crouch down; (*fuyard, criminel*) to lie low; (*soldat*) to lie flat **2.** (*vivre reclus*) to hide oneself away

terrestre [teʀɛstʀ] *adj* **1.** (*de la Terre*) **la croûte/surface** ~ the earth's crust/surface **2.** (*sur la terre: espèce*) terrestrial; (*vie*) on earth **3.** (*opp: aquatique, marin*) **animal** ~ land animal **4.** (*opp: aérien, maritime*) ground **5.** (*de ce bas monde: plaisirs, séjour*) earthly

terreur [teʀœʀ] *f* **1.** (*peur violente, terrorisme*) terror **2.** (*personne terrifiante*) **être une** ~ *inf* (*personne*) to be a bully; (*enfant*) to be a terror

terreux, -euse [teʀø, -øz] *adj* **1.** (*de la terre: goût, odeur*) earthy **2.** (*sali de terre: mains, chaussures, salade*) muddy; (*route*) dirt **3.** (*pâle: façade*) muddy; (*visage*) ashen

terrible [teʀibl] **I.** *adj* **1.** (*qui inspire de la terreur: crime*) terrible; (*catastrophe*) dreadful; (*jugement, année*) awful; (*personnage, arme*) fearsome **2.** (*très intense*) tremendous **3.** (*turbulent*) dreadful **4.** *inf* (*super*) terrific **II.** *adv inf* fantastically

terriblement [teʀibləmɑ̃] *adv* dreadfully; (*dangereux, sévère*) terribly

terrien(ne) [teʀjɛ̃, ɛn] **I.** *adj* **1.** (*qui possède des terres*) **il est propriétaire** ~ he's a landowner **2.** (*opp: citadin*) **traditions/mœurs** ~**nes** country traditions/customs; **mes racines** ~**nes** my roots in the country **II.** *m(f)* (*habitant de la Terre*) earthling

terrier [tɛʀje] *m* (*de renard*) earth; (*de lapin*) burrow; (*de blaireau*) sett

terrier, -ère [tɛʀje, -ɛʀ] *m, f* (*chien*) terrier

terrifiant(e) [teʀifjɑ̃, ɑ̃t] *adj* incredible; (*nouvelle*) terrifying

terrifier [teʀifje] <1> *vt* to terrify

terril [teʀi(l)] *m* slag heap

terrine [teʀin] *f* terrine; ~ **de lapin** rabbit terrine

territoire [teʀitwaʀ] *m* (*d'un animal, pays, d'une nation*) territory; (*d'une ville*) area; (*d'un juge, évêque*) jurisdiction; ~ **d'outre-mer** overseas territory

Territoire antarctique australien *m* Australian Antarctic Territory

Territoire de la Capitale Australienne *m* Australian Capital Territory

Territoire-du-North *m* Northern Territory

Territoire du Yukon *m* Yukon Territory

Territoires du Nord-Ouest *m* Northwest Territories

territorial(e) [teʀitɔʀjal, jo] <-aux> *adj* territorial

territorialité [teʀitɔʀjalite] *f* territoriality

terroir [teʀwaʀ] *m* soil; **vin/accent du** ~ country wine/accent; **écrivain/poète du** ~ rural author/poet

terrorisant(e) [teʀɔʀizɑ̃, ɑ̃t] *adj* terrifying

terroriser [teʀɔʀize] <1> *vt* (*faire très peur*) to terrorize

terrorisme [teʀɔʀism] *m* terrorism

terroriste [teʀɔʀist] *adj, mf* terrorist

tertiaire [tɛʀsjɛʀ] **I.** *adj* (*emploi, activité*) tertiary **II.** *m* **le** ~ the tertiary sector

tertiarisation [tɛʀsjaʀizasjɔ̃] *f* ECON tertiarization

tertio [tɛʀsjo] *adv* thirdly

tertre [tɛʀtʀ] *m* **1.** (*butte*) mound **2.** (*sur une sépulture*) ~ **funéraire** funeral mound

T

tes [te] *dét poss v.* **ta**, **ton**
Tessin [tesɛ̃] *m* **le** ~ Ticino
tessiture [tesityʀ] *f* MUS tessitura
tesson [tesɔ̃] *m* **~s de bouteille** broken glass + *sing vb*
test [tɛst] *m* test; ~ **de dépistage du sida** [*o* **de séropositivité**] AIDS test; ~ **de grossesse** pregnancy test
testable [tɛstabl] *adj* testable
testament [tɛstamɑ̃] *m* JUR will
Testament [tɛstamɑ̃] *m* **l'Ancien/le Nouveau** ~ the Old/New Testament
testamentaire [tɛstamɑ̃tɛʀ] *adj* **l'héritier** ~ the heir specified in the will
tester [tɛste] <1> *vt* (*mettre à l'épreuve*) to test
testeur [tɛstœʀ] *m* (*appareil*) tester
testeur, **-euse** [tɛstœʀ, -øz] *m, f* tester
testicule [tɛstikyl] *m* testicle
testostérone [tɛstosteʀɔn] *f* testosterone
tétanie [tetani] *f* tetany
tétanique [tetanik] *adj* **1.** (*atteint du tétanos: malade*) tetanus **2.** (*musculaire: contraction*) tetanic
tétaniser [tetanize] <1> *vpr* **se** ~ (*muscle, membre*) to paralyse *Brit,* to paralyze *Am*
tétanos [tetanos] *m* **1.** (*maladie*) tetanus **2.** (*contraction du muscle*) lockjaw
têtard [tɛtaʀ] *m* ZOOL tadpole
tête [tɛt] *f* **1.** ANAT, BOT head; **baisser/courber la** ~ to lower/bend one's head **2.** (*mémoire, raison*) **ne pas avoir de** ~ *inf* to be empty-headed; **perdre la** ~ (*devenir fou*) to lose one's mind; (*perdre son sang-froid*) to lose one's head **3.** (*mine, figure*) **avoir une bonne** ~ *inf* to have a friendly face; **avoir une sale** ~ *inf* (*avoir mauvaise mine*) to look awful; (*être antipathique*) to look unpleasant **4.** (*longueur*) **avoir** [*o* **faire**] **une** ~ **de moins/plus que qn** to be a head shorter/taller than sb **5.** (*vie*) **jouer** [*o* **risquer**] **sa** ~ to risk one's neck **6.** (*personne*) ~ **couronnée** crowned head; ~ **de linotte** [*o* **en l'air**] *inf* scatterbrain; ~ **de mule** [*o* **cochon**] *inf* pain; ~ **de Turc** whipping boy **7.** (*chef*) **être la** ~ **de qc** *inf* to be the head of sth **8.** (*première place*) head; (*les premiers*) top; **wagon de** ~ leading wagon; **prendre la** ~ **d'un gouvernement/d'une entreprise** to take over at the head of a government/company; **prendre la** ~ **de la classe** to become the top of the class; **à la** ~ **de qc** at the top of sth **9.** (*début: d'un chapitre, d'une liste*) beginning **10.** (*extrémité: d'un clou, d'une épingle*) head; (*d'un champignon*) top; ~ **d'un lit** bedhead; ~ **d'un arbre** top of a tree; ~ **de ligne** terminus **11.** TECH ~ **chercheuse d'une fusée** homing device on a rocket; ~ **de lecture** (*d'un magnétophone*) play-back head; ~ **nucléaire** nuclear warhead **12.** INFOR ~ **de lecture-écriture** read-write head **13.** SPORT header **14.** *Belgique* GASTR ~ **pressée** (*fromage de* ~) (pork) brawn *Brit,* head cheese *Am* ►**être à la** ~ **du client** *inf* to depend on who's paying; **avoir la** ~ **de l'emploi** *inf* (*acteur*) to look the part; **agir** ~ **baissée** to act blindly; **se jeter dans qc** ~ **baissée** to rush headlong into sth; **avoir la** ~ **dure** to be a blockhead; **garder la** ~ **froide** to keep a cool head; **avoir la grosse** ~ *inf* to be big-headed; **faire qc à** ~ **reposée** to do sth with a clear head; **avoir toute sa** ~ to have all one's wits about one; **ne plus avoir toute sa** ~ not to be all there any more; **avoir la** ~ **à ce qu'on fait** to have one's mind on the job; **en avoir par-dessus la** ~ *inf* to have had it up to here; **ne pas se casser la** ~ not to go to much trouble; **j'en suis sûr, ma** ~ **à couper** I'm sure of that, I'd swear to it; **enfoncer qc dans la** ~ **de qn** to get sth into sb's thick head; **faire la** ~ **à qn** *inf* to sulk at sb; **n'en faire qu'à sa** ~ to just suit oneself; **se mettre en** ~ **de** +*infin* to take it into one's head to +*infin;* **se mettre dans la** ~ **que ...** to get it into one's head that ...; **se monter la** ~ *inf* to get worked up; **monter à la** ~ **de qn** (*vin, succès*) to go to sb's head; **passer au-dessus de la** ~ **de qn** to go over sb's head; **se payer la** ~ **de qn** *inf* to make fun of sb; **piquer une** ~ **dans qc** *inf* (*plonger*) to have a splash in sth; (*tomber*) to bang one's head into sth; **redresser** [*o* **relever**] **la** ~ to lift up one's head high; **il a une** ~ **qui ne me revient pas** *inf* I don't like the look of him; **ne pas savoir où donner de la** ~ *inf* not to know where to turn; (**faire**) **tourner la** ~ **à qn** (*personne*) to turn sb's head; (*succès, gloire, vin*) to go to sb's head; (*manège*) to make sb's head spin
tête-à-queue [tɛtakø] *m inv* **faire un** ~ (*voiture*) to spin round **tête-à-tête** [tɛtatɛt] *m inv* (*entretien*) tête-à-tête **tête-bêche** [tɛtbɛʃ] *adv* head to foot; **être couchés** ~ to sleep at opposite ends of the bed **tête-de-nègre** [tɛtdənɛgʀ] **I.** *adj inv* chocolate brown **II.** *f* chocolate-covered meringue
tétée [tete] *f* **1.** (*action de téter*) sucking **2.** (*repas*) feed; **donner la** ~ **à un bébé** to feed a baby
téter [tete] <5> **I.** *vt* ~ **le sein** to feed (at the breast); ~ **le biberon** to have a (bottle) feed; ~ **sa mère** (*bébé*) to feed (at the breast); (*chaton*) to suckle **II.** *vi* to feed; **donner à** ~ **à un animal** to feed an animal
tétine [tetin] *f* **1.** (*biberon*) teat *Brit,* nipple *Am* **2.** (*sucette pour calmer*) dummy *Brit,* pacifier *Am*
téton [tetɔ̃] *m inf a.* TECH (*sein*) nipple
tétraèdre [tetʀaɛdʀ] *m* MAT tetrahedron
tétralogie [tetʀalɔʒi] *f* LIT tetralogy
tétraplégie [tetʀapleʒi] *f* quadriplegia
tétraplégique [tetʀapleʒik] *adj, mf* quadriplegic
tétras [tetʀɑ(s)] *m* grouse
têtu(**e**) [tety] **I.** *adj* stubborn ►**être** ~ **comme une mule** to be as stubborn as a mule **II.** *m(f)* stubborn person
texan(**ne**) [tɛksɑ̃, an] *adj* Texan

Texan(**ne**) [tɛksɑ̃, an] *m(f)* Texan
tex-mex [tɛksmɛks] *adj inv, m sans pl* tex-mex
texte [tɛkst] *m* text ▸**cahier de ~s** homework notebook
textile [tɛkstil] **I.** *adj* textile **II.** *m* **1.** (*matière*) textile **2.** *sans pl* (*industrie*) textiles
texto [tɛksto] *adv inf* word for word
textuel(**le**) [tɛkstɥɛl] *adj* (*copie, réponse, contenu*) exact; (*traduction*) literal
textuellement [tɛkstɥɛlmɑ̃] *adv* literally; (*répéter*) word for word; (*reproduire*) verbatim
texture [tɛkstyʀ] *f* texture
TF1 [teɛfœ̃] *f abr de* **Télévision Française 1ère chaîne** *French private television channel*
TGV [teʒeve] *m inv abr de* **train à grande vitesse** high speed train
thaï [taj] *m* Thai; *v. a.* **français**
thaï(**e**) [taj] *adj* **langues ~es** Thai languages
Thaï(**e**) [taj] *m(f)* Thai
thaïlandais(**e**) [tajlɑ̃dɛ, ɛz] *adj* Thai
Thaïlandais(**e**) [tajlɑ̃dɛ, ɛz] *m(f)* Thai
Thaïlande [tajlɑ̃d] *f* **la ~** Thailand
thalasso [talaso] *f inf,* **thalassothérapie** [talasoteʀapi] *f* thalassotherapy
thé [te] *m* tea ▸**prendre le ~ avec qn** to have tea with sb
théâtral(**e**) [teɑtʀal, o] <-aux> *adj* (*effet, geste*) theatrical
théâtralement [teɑtʀalmɑ̃] *adv fig* theatrically
théâtre [teɑtʀ] *m* **1.** (*édifice, spectacle*) theatre *Brit,* theater *Am;* **~ de verdure** open-air theatre **2.** (*art dramatique, genre littéraire*) drama; **école de ~** drama school **3.** (*œuvres*) plays **4.** (*lieu: des combats, d'une dispute*) scene
théière [tejɛʀ] *f* teapot
théine [tein] *f* theine
théisme [teism] *m* REL theism
thématique [tematik] **I.** *adj* thematic; (*soirée*) theme **II.** *f* themes *pl*
thème [tɛm] *m* **1.** (*sujet: d'une discussion*) theme; (*d'une peinture*) subject **2.** ECOLE prose (*translation out of French*) **3.** MUS theme **4.** (*en astrologie*) **~ astral** birth chart
théocratie [teɔkʀasi] *f* theocracy
théocratique [teɔkʀatik] *adj* theocratic
théologie [teɔlɔʒi] *f* theology
théologien(**ne**) [teɔlɔʒjɛ̃, ɛn] *m(f)* theologian
théologique [teɔlɔʒik] *adj* theological
théorème [teɔʀɛm] *m* theorem; **~ de Pythagore** Pythagorus' theorem
théoricien(**ne**) [teɔʀisjɛ̃, ɛn] *m(f)* theorist
théorie [teɔʀi] *f* theory
théorique [teɔʀik] *adj* theoretical
théoriquement [teɔʀikmɑ̃] *adv* **1.** (*logiquement*) in theory **2.** (*par une théorie: fondé, justifié*) theoretically
théoriser [teɔʀize] <1> **I.** *vt* to theorize **II.** *vi* **~ sur qn/qc** to theorize about sb/sth
thérapeute [teʀapøt] *mf* therapist
thérapeutique [teʀapøtik] **I.** *adj* therapeutic **II.** *f* **1.** (*science*) therapeutics + *sing vb* **2.** (*traitement*) therapy
thérapie [teʀapi] *f* therapy; **être en ~** to be in therapy
thermal(**e**) [tɛʀmal, o] <-aux> *adj* **source ~e** hot spring; **station ~e** spa
thermalisme [tɛʀmalism] *m* thermal baths *pl*
thermes [tɛʀm] *mpl* **1.** (*dans une station thermale*) thermal baths **2.** HIST thermae
thermique [tɛʀmik] **I.** *adj* thermal **II.** *f* heat sciences
thermoactif, -ive [tɛʀmoaktif, -iv] *adj* thermoactive **thermodynamique** [tɛʀmodinamik] **I.** *adj* thermodynamic **II.** *f* thermodynamics + *sing vb* **thermoélectrique** [tɛʀmoelɛktʀik] *adj* thermoelectric
thermomètre [tɛʀmɔmɛtʀ] *m* **1.** (*instrument*) thermometer **2.** *fig* (*de l'opinion, la conjoncture*) gauge
thermonucléaire [tɛʀmonykleɛʀ] *adj* thermonuclear
thermos® [tɛʀmos] *m o f* Thermos® *flask Brit,* Thermos® *Am*
thermostat [tɛʀmɔsta] *m* thermostat
thésard(**e**) [tezaʀ, aʀd] *m(f) inf* Ph.D. student
thésaurisation [tezɔʀizasjɔ̃] *f* hoarding
thésauriser [tezɔʀize] <1> *vt, vi* to hoard
thésaurus, thesaurus [tezɔʀys] *m* thesaurus
thèse [tɛz] *f* **1.** (*point de vue défendu*) argument **2.** UNIV (*recherches, ouvrage*) thesis; (*soutenance*) viva; **~ de troisième cycle** doctoral thesis; (*thèse de doctorat d'État*) state doctoral thesis (*leading to promotion in higher education*)
thon [tɔ̃] *m* tuna
thonier [tɔnje] *m* tuna boat
Thora [tɔʀa] *f* (*Pentateuque*) Torah
thoracique [tɔʀasik] *adj* thoracic; **cage ~** ribcage
thorax [tɔʀaks] *m* thorax
thriller [sʀilœʀ] *m* thriller
thrombose [tʀɔ̃boz] *f* thrombosis
thune [tyn] *f inf* **avoir de la ~** to have dough; **n'avoir pas/plus une ~** not to have a bean/a bean left
Thurgovie [tyʀgɔvi] *f* **la ~** Thurgau
thuya [tyja] *m* thuja
thym [tɛ̃] *m* thyme
thyroïde [tiʀɔid] **I.** *adj* **glande ~** thyroid gland **II.** *f* thyroid
thyroïdien(**ne**) [tiʀɔidjɛ̃, ɛn] *adj* thyroid
tiare [tjaʀ] *f* **1.** (*coiffe*) tiara **2.** (*dignité papale*) papal tiara
Tibet [tibe] *m* **le ~** Tibet
tibétain [tibetɛ̃] *m* Tibetan; *v. a.* **français**
tibétain(**e**) [tibetɛ̃, ɛn] *adj* Tibetan
Tibétain(**e**) [tibetɛ̃, ɛn] *m(f)* Tibetan
tibia [tibja] *m* shin

T

tic [tik] *m* **1.**(*contraction nerveuse*) ~ **nerveux** nervous tic **2.**(*manie*) habit
ticket [tikɛ] *m* ticket; ~ **de caisse** (till) receipt; ~ **de cinéma/quai** cinema/platform ticket ▸**avoir un ~ avec qn** *inf* to make a hit with sb
ticket-repas [tikɛ-Rəpa] <tickets-repas> *m,* **ticket-restaurant**® [tikɛ-Rɛstɔʀɑ̃] *m* luncheon voucher® *Brit,* meal ticket *Am*
tic-tac [tiktak] *m inv* ticking
tie-break [tajbRɛk] <tie-breaks> *m* tie-break
tiédasse [tjedas] *adj péj* lukewarm
tiède [tjɛd] *adj* **1.**(*entre le chaud et le froid: gâteau, lit*) warm; (*eau, café, repas*) lukewarm **2.**(*de peu d'ardeur: engagement, accueil, soutien*) half-hearted; (*sentiment, foi*) lukewarm
tièdement [tjɛdmɑ̃] *adv* half-heartedly
tiédeur [tjedœR] *f* **1.**(*chaleur modérée: de la température, de l'air, d'un hiver*) mildness; (*de l'eau*) warmth **2.**(*manque d'ardeur: d'un sentiment, accord, d'une participation*) half-heartedness
tiédir [tjediR] <8> **I.** *vi* **1.**(*refroidir*) to cool down **2.**(*se réchauffer*) to warm up **II.** *vt* **1.**(*réchauffer*) to heat up; (*mains*) to warm up **2.**(*refroidir*) to cool down
tiédissement [tjedismɑ̃] *m* **1.**(*réchauffement*) warming up **2.**(*refroidissement*) cooling down
tien(**ne**) [tjɛ̃, ɛn] *pron poss* **1.**(*ce que l'on possède*) **le ~/la ~ne/les ~s** yours; *v. a.* **mien 2.** *pl* (*ceux de ta famille*) **les ~s** your family; (*tes partisans*) your friends ▸**à la ~ne(, Étienne)!** *inf* cheers!; **tu pourrais y mettre du ~!** you could put some effort into it!
tiendrai [tjɛ̃dRɛ] *fut de* **tenir**
tienne [tjɛn] *subj prés de* **tenir**
tiennent [tjɛn] *indic prés et subj prés de* **tenir**
tiens, tient [tjɛ̃] *indic prés de* **tenir**
tierce [tjɛRs] *f* **1.** JEUX, SPORT tierce **2.** MUS third
tiercé [tjɛRse] *m* **1.** SPORT *French betting system: betters forecast the first three horses in a race* **2.**(*série de trois éléments arrivant en tête*) **le ~ gagnant/vainqueur de qc** the top/winning three in sth
tiers [tjɛR] *m* **1.**(*fraction*) third **2.**(*tierce personne*) **un ~** a third person; **assurance au ~** third party insurance ▸**~ payant** *direct payment by insurers for medical treatment;* **~ provisionnel** interim tax payment

> The **tiers provisionnel** is due on 31 January and 30 April and amounts to a third of the previous year's income tax.

tiers, tierce [tjɛR, tjɛRs] *adj* third
tiers-monde [tjɛRmɔ̃d] *m sans pl* **le ~** the Third World **tiers-mondisme** [tjɛRmɔ̃dism] *m* support for the Third World **tiers-mondiste** [tjɛRmɔ̃dist] <tiers-mondistes> **I.** *adj* (*actions*) Third World **II.** *mf* Third World supporter
tif [tif] *m inf souvent pl* hair + *sing vb*
TIG [teiʒe] *m abr de* **travaux d'intérêt général** paid community work
tige [tiʒ] *f* **1.**(*pédoncule: d'une fleur, feuille*) stem; (*d'une céréale, graminée*) stalk **2.**(*partie mince et allongée*) rod; (*d'une clé*) shank; (*d'une botte*) leg
tignasse [tiɲas] *f inf* hair
tigre [tigR] *m* tiger; *v. a.* **tigresse**
tigré(**e**) [tigRe] *adj* (*pelage*) striped; (*chat*) tabby; (*cheval*) piebald *Brit,* pinto *Am*
tigresse [tigRɛs] *f* tigress; *v. a.* **tigre**
tilde [tild(e)] *m* tilde
tilleul [tijœl] *m* **1.** BOT linden tree **2.**(*infusion*) lime-blossom tea
tilt [tilt] *m* (*d'un flipper*) tilt ▸**ça a fait ~ dans ma tête** the penny dropped
timbale [tɛ̃bal] *f* **1.**(*gobelet*) tumbler **2.**(*contenu*) cup **3.** MUS kettledrum ▸**décrocher la ~** *inf* to hit the jackpot
timbrage [tɛ̃bRaʒ] *m* (*oblitération*) post-marking
timbre[1] [tɛ̃bR] *m* **1.**(*vignette, cachet*) stamp; **~ fiscal** tax stamp **2.** MED research stamp
timbre[2] [tɛ̃bR] *m* (*qualité du son*) timbre; (*d'une flûte, voix*) tone
timbré(**e**)[1] [tɛ̃bRe] *adj* stamped
timbré(**e**)[2] [tɛ̃bRe] *adj inf* (*un peu fou*) cracked
timbre-amende [tɛ̃bRamɑ̃d] <timbres-amendes> *m: stamp bought to pay a parking fine* **timbre-poste** [tɛ̃bRəpɔst] <timbres-poste> *m* postage stamp
timbrer [tɛ̃bRe] <1> *vt* to stamp
timide [timid] **I.** *adj* **1.**(*timoré, de peu d'audace*) shy **2.**(*craintif: sourire, voix*) timid; (*manières, air*) bashful **II.** *mf* timid person
timidement [timidmɑ̃] *adv* **1.**(*modestement*) shyly **2.**(*craintivement*) timidly
timidité [timidite] *f* (*d'une personne*) shyness; (*d'une démarche, avancée*) timidity
timing [tajmiŋ] *m* timing
timonerie [timɔnRi] *f* NAUT **1.**(*lieu*) wheelhouse **2.**(*matelots*) wheelhouse crew **3.**(*service*) steering and braking system
timonier [timɔnje] *m* NAUT helmsman
timoré(**e**) [timɔRe] *péj* **I.** *adj* fearful **II.** *m(f)* fearful person
tintamarre [tɛ̃tamaR] *m* racket; **faire du ~** to make a racket
tintement [tɛ̃tmɑ̃] *m* (*d'une cloche, sonnette, d'un grelot*) ringing; (*de verres, de bouteilles*) clinking
tinter [tɛ̃te] <1> *vi* (*cloche*) to ring; (*grelot, clochette*) to tinkle; (*verres, bouteilles*) to clink
tintin [tɛ̃tɛ̃] *m* **~!** tough!; **tu peux faire ~!** tough on you!
tintouin [tɛ̃twɛ̃] *m inf* **1.**(*vacarme*) din **2.**(*souci, tracas*) worry
TIP [tip] *m abr de* **titre interbancaire de paiement** payment slip

tipi [tipi] *m* tepee
Tipperary du Nord North Tipperary
Tipperary du Sud South Tipperary
tique [tik] *f* tick
tiquer [tike] <1> *vi inf* to raise an eyebrow
tir [tiʀ] *m* **1.** MIL fire; (*prolongé*) firing; ~ **à blanc** firing blank rounds **2.** SPORT shot; ~ **au but** goal shot; (*penalty*) penalty kick; ~ **à l'arc** archery **3.** (*projectile tiré*) shot **4.** (*stand*) **stand de** ~ rifle range **5.** (*forain*) **stand de** ~ shooting gallery ▸**rectifier** [*o* **rajuster**] **le** ~ to change tack
TIR [tiʀ] *pl abr de* **transports internationaux routiers** TIR
tirade [tiʀad] *f* **1.** *souvent péj* (*paroles*) tirade **2.** THEAT monologue
tirage [tiʀaʒ] *m* **1.** (*action de tirer au sort*) ~ **au sort** draw **2.** FIN (*d'un chèque*) drawing **3.** TYP, ART, PHOT printing; (*ensemble des exemplaires*) impression **4.** (*transvasement: d'un vin, d'une liqueur*) decanting **5.** (*arrivée d'air: d'une cheminée, d'un poêle*) draught *Brit,* draft *Am* ▸**il y a du** ~ **entre eux** *inf* things are tense between them
tiraillement [tiʀɑjmɑ̃] *m* **1.** *gén pl* (*sensation douloureuse*) gnawing pain **2.** (*conflit chez une personne*) agonizing *no pl* **3.** (*conflit entre plusieurs personnes*) friction
tirailler [tiʀɑje] <1> **I.** *vt* **1.** (*tirer à petits coups*) to tug; (*pli*) to pull at **2.** (*harceler*) **être tiraillé entre deux choses** to be torn between two things **II.** *vi* to shoot at random
tirailleur [tiʀɑjœʀ] *m* skirmisher
tirant [tiʀɑ̃] *m* **1.** (*cordon*) string **2.** (*partie latérale: d'une chaussure*) boot-strap **3.** NAUT ~ **d'eau** draught *Brit,* draft *Am*
tire¹ [tiʀ] **vol à la** ~ pickpocketing
tire² [tiʀ] *f Québec* (*sirop d'érable très épaissi, ayant la consistance du miel*) maple toffee *Brit,* maple taffy *Am*
tiré [tiʀe] *m* ~ **à part** off-print
tiré(e) [tiʀe] *adj* (*fatigué*) drawn; **avoir les traits ~s** to look drawn
tire-au-flanc [tiʀoflɑ̃] *mf inv* layabout **tire-botte** [tiʀbɔt] <tire-bottes> *m* **1.** (*planchette*) boot-jack **2.** (*crochet*) book-hook **tire-bouchon, tirebouchon** [tiʀbuʃɔ̃] <tire-bouchons> *m* corkscrew ▸**avoir des boucles en** ~ to have ringlets; **queue en** ~ curly tail **tire-bouchonner, tirebouchonner** [tiʀbuʃɔne] <1> *vi* (*chaussettes*) to crumple down round one's ankles **tire-d'aile** [tiʀdɛl] *adv* **à** ~ swiftly **tire-fesses** [tiʀfɛs] *m inv, inf* ski-tow; **prendre le** ~ to take the ski-tow **tire-lait** [tiʀlɛ] *m inv* breast-pump **tire-larigot** [tiʀlaʀigo] *adv* **à** ~ *inf* to one's heart's content **tire-ligne** [tiʀliɲ] <tire-lignes> *m* drawing pen
tirelire [tiʀliʀ] *f* moneybox; **casser sa** ~ **pour acheter qc** *inf* to break open the piggy bank to buy sth
tirer [tiʀe] <1> **I.** *vt* **1.** (*exercer une force de traction: signal d'alarme, chasse d'eau*) to pull; (*vers le bas: jupe, manche*) to pull down; (*vers le haut: chaussettes, collant*) to pull up; (*pour lisser: drap, collant*) to smooth; (*pour tendre/maintenir tendu: corde, toile*) to tighten; ~ **la sonnette** to ring the bell **2.** (*tracter: chariot, véhicule, charge*) to draw **3.** (*éloigner*) to draw away **4.** (*fermer: rideau*) to pull; (*ouvrir: tiroir, porte coulissante*) to pull open; ~ **la porte** to pull the door to; ~ **le verrou de qc** (*pour fermer*) to bolt sth; (*pour ouvrir*) to unbolt sth **5.** (*aspirer*) ~ **une longue bouffée** to take a deep breath **6.** (*lancer un projectile: balle, coup de fusil, revolver*) to fire **7.** (*toucher, tuer: perdrix, lièvre*) to shoot **8.** (*tracer, prendre au hasard: trait, ligne, carte, numéro, lettre*) to draw **9.** (*faire sortir*) ~ **qn du lit** to get sb out of bed; ~ **qn de son sommeil** to rouse sb from sleep; ~ **qn du pétrin** to get sb out of a mess; ~ **une citation/un extrait d'un roman** to take a quote/extract from a novel **10.** (*emprunter à*) ~ **son origine de qc** (*coutume*) to have its origins in sth **11.** (*déduire*) ~ **une conclusion/leçon de qc** to draw a conclusion/learn a lesson from sth **12.** FIN (*chèque*) to draw **13.** PHOT, ART, TYP (*film, négatif, photo, ouvrage, estampe, lithographie*) to print **14.** (*transvaser: vin*) to decant ▸**on ne peut rien** ~ **de qn** you can get nothing out of sb **II.** *vi* **1.** (*exercer une traction*) ~ **sur les rênes de son cheval** to pull on the reins of one's horse **2.** (*aspirer*) ~ **sur sa pipe/cigarette** to puff on one's pipe/cigarette **3.** (*gêner: peau, cicatrice*) to pull **4.** (*à la chasse*) *a.* MIL to shoot **5.** (*au football*) to shoot **6.** (*avoir une certaine ressemblance avec*) ~ **sur qc** (*couleur*) to verge on sth; ~ **sur qn** *Belgique, Nord* to resemble sb **7.** TYP ~ **à 2000 exemplaires** to have a circulation of 2000 **8.** (*avoir du tirage*) **bien/mal** ~ (*cheminée, poêle*) to draw well/badly **III.** *vpr* **1.** *inf* (*s'en aller*) **se** ~ to push off **2.** (*se sortir*) **se** ~ **d'une situation/d'embarras** to get out of a situation/trouble **3.** (*se blesser*) **se** ~ **une balle dans la tête** to put a bullet in one's head ▸**il s'en tire bien** *inf* (*à la suite d'une maladie*) he's pulling through; (*à la suite d'un accident*) he's all right; (*à la suite d'un ennui*) he's out of the woods; (*réussir*) he's managing pretty well
tiret [tiʀɛ] *m* **1.** (*dans un dialogue, au milieu d'une phrase*) dash **2.** (*à la fin, au milieu d'un mot*) hyphen
tirette [tiʀɛt] *f Belgique* (*fermeture à glissière*) zip *Brit,* zipper *Am*
tireur, -euse [tiʀœʀ, -øz] *m, f* **1.** MIL, SPORT (*avec une arme*) marksman *m,* markswoman *f;* ~ **d'élite** trained marksman **2.** SPORT (*au football*) striker; (*au basket*) shooter; ~ **à l'arc** archer **3.** FIN (*d'un chèque, d'une lettre de change*) drawer
tiroir [tiʀwaʀ] *m* drawer ▸**racler les fonds de** ~**(s)** to scrape one's last pennies together
tiroir-caisse [tiʀwaʀkɛs] <tiroirs-

T

caisses> *m* cash till

tisane [tizan] *f* herbal tea; ~ **de verveine** verbena tea; ~ **à la menthe** mint tea

tisanière [tizanjɛʀ] *f* teapot (*for herbal tea*)

tison [tizɔ̃] *m* brand

tisonner [tizɔne] <1> *vt* to poke

tisonnier [tizɔnje] *m* poker

tissage [tisaʒ] *m* **1.** (*activité manuelle, industrie*) weaving; ~ **des tapis** carpet weaving **2.** (*usine*) mill

tisser [tise] <1> *vt* **1.** (*fabriquer par tissage, transformer en tissu: tapis, laine*) to weave **2.** (*constituer*) ~ **sa toile** (*araignée*) to spin a web **3.** (*ourdir: intrigue*) to build

tisserand(e) [tisʀɑ̃, ɑ̃d] *m(f)* weaver

tissu [tisy] *m* **1.** (*textile*) fabric; ~ **éponge** towelling *Brit*, toweling *Am* **2.** (*enchevêtrement: de contradictions, d'intrigues*) tissue; (*d'inepties*) catalogue *Brit*, catalog *Am* **3.** BIO tissue **4.** SOCIOL ~ **social** social fabric

titan [titɑ̃] *m* titan; **travail de** ~ Herculean task

titane [titan] *m* CHIM titanium

titanesque [titanɛsk] *adj* (*travail*) titanic; (*entreprise, œuvre*) massive

titi [titi] *m inf* ~ **parisien** Paris street urchin

titiller [titije] <1> *vt* **1.** (*chatouiller*) to tickle **2.** *inf* (*asticoter*) **l'envie de tout raconter la titille** she's taken by the idea of telling all

titrage [titʀaʒ] *m* (*action de titrer*) titling

titre [titʀ] *m* **1.** (*intitulé, qualité, trophée*) title; (*d'un chapitre*) heading; (*article de journal*) headline; **faire les gros ~s de qc** CINE, TV to make the headlines on sth **2.** (*pièce justificative*) certificate; ~ **de transport** ticket **3.** (*valeur, action*) security ►**à <u>juste</u>** ~ rightly; **<u>à</u> ce** ~ as such; **<u>à</u>** ~ **de qc** as sth

titré(e) [titʀe] *adj* (*personne*) titled

titrer [titʀe] <1> *vt* (*donner un titre à*) ~ **qc sur cinq colonnes** (*journal*) to splash sth as a headline across five columns

titubant(e) [titybɑ̃, ɑ̃t] *adj* (*démarche*) unsteady; (*ivrogne*) staggering

tituber [titybe] <1> *vi* ~ **d'ivresse** to stagger drunkenly

titulaire [titylɛʀ] **I.** *adj* **1.** (*en titre: professeur, instituteur*) with tenure **2.** (*détenteur*) **être ~ d'un poste/diplôme** to be the holder of a position/diploma **II.** *mf* **1.** ECOLE, UNIV, ADMIN incumbent **2.** (*détenteur*) ~ **de la carte/du poste** cardholder/postholder

titularisation [titylaʀizasjɔ̃] *f* tenure; **demande de** ~ application for tenure

titulariser [titylaʀize] <1> *vt* (*fonctionnaire*) to appoint permanently; ~ **un professeur** to give a lecturer tenure

TNP [teɛnpe] *m abr de* **Théâtre national populaire** *one of France's national theatres*

TNT [teɛnte] *m abr de* **trinitrotoluène** TNT

toast [tost] *m* piece of toast

toasteur [tostœʀ] *m* toaster

toboggan [tɔbɔgɑ̃] *m* **1.** TECH chute **2.** (*piste glissante*) slide **3.** *Québec* (*traîneau sans patins, fait de planches minces recourbées à l'avant*) toboggan

toc [tɔk] *m inf* (*imitation*) **du** ~ junk; **en** ~ fake

tocade [tɔkad] *f* fad

tocard [tɔkaʀ] *m inf* **1.** (*personne*) loser **2.** (*cheval*) old nag

tocard(e) [tɔkaʀ, aʀd] *adj inf* tacky

toccata [tɔkata] *f* MUS toccata

tocsin [tɔksɛ̃] *m* alarm; **sonner le** ~ to sound the alarm

toge [tɔʒ] *f* gown; HIST toga

Togo [tɔgo] *m* **le** ~ Togo

togolais(e) [tɔgolɛ, ɛz] *adj* Togolese

Togolais(e) [tɔgolɛ, ɛz] *m(f)* Togolese

tohu-bohu [tɔybɔy] *m inv, inf* confusion

toi [twa] *pron pers* **1.** *inf* (*pour renforcer*) you; ~**, tu n'as pas ouvert la bouche** YOU haven't opened your mouth; **c'est** ~ **qui l'as dit** you're the one who said it; **il veut t'aider,** ~**?** he wants to help YOU? **2.** *avec un verbe à l'impératif* **regarde-**~ look at yourself; **imagine-**~ **en Italie** imagine yourself in Italy; **lave-**~ **les mains** wash your hands **3.** *avec une préposition* **avec/sans** ~ with/without you; **à** ~ **seul** (*parler*) just to you **4.** *dans une comparaison* you; **je suis comme** ~ I'm like you; **plus fort que** ~ stronger than you **5.** (*emphatique*) **c'est** ~**?** is that you?; **si j'étais** ~ if I were you; *v. a.* **moi**

toile [twal] *f* **1.** (*tissu*) cloth **2.** (*pièce de tissu*) piece of cloth **3.** *fig* ~ **de fond** backdrop **4.** ART, NAUT canvas **5.** INFOR ~ **(d'araignée) mondiale** World Wide Web ►~ **d'<u>araignée</u>** spider web; (*poussière*) cobweb; **<u>tisser</u> sa** ~ to spin its web

Toile [twal] *f* Web

toilettage [twaletaʒ] *m* **1.** (*d'un chat, chien*) grooming; **salon de** ~ grooming parlour *Brit*, grooming parlor *Am* **2.** *inf* (*retouche*) tidying up

toilette [twalɛt] *f* **1.** (*soins corporels*) washing; **faire sa** ~ (*personne*) to have a wash; (*animal*) to wash itself **2.** (*nettoyage: d'un édifice, monument*) cleaning **3.** (*vêtements*) outfit **4.** *pl* (*W.-C.*) toilet; **aller aux ~s** to go to the toilet

toiletter [twalete] <1> *vt* (*chat, chien*) to groom

toi-même [twamɛm] *pron pers* (*toi en personne*) yourself; *v. a.* **moi-même**

toiser [twaze] <1> **I.** *vt* ~ **qn** to look sb up and down **II.** *vpr* **se** ~ to look each other up and down

toison [twazɔ̃] *f* **1.** (*pelage*) coat **2.** (*chevelure*) mop **3.** (*poils*) growth ►**la <u>Toison</u> d'or** HIST the Golden Fleece

toit [twa] *m* roof

toiture [twatyʀ] *f* roof

Tokyo [tɔkjo] Tokyo

tôle [tol] *f* **1.** (*en métallurgie*) sheet metal **2.** AUTO bodywork

tolérable [tɔleʀabl] *adj* tolerable; (*douleur*)

bearable

tolérance [tɔleʀɑ̃s] *f* tolerance; ~ **à qc** tolerance of sth

tolérant(**e**) [tɔleʀɑ̃, ɑ̃t] *adj* tolerant

tolérer [tɔleʀe] <5> **I.** *vt* **1.** (*autoriser: infraction, pratique*) to tolerate **2.** (*supporter*) *a.* MED to tolerate; (*douleur*) to bear **II.** *vpr* (*se supporter*) **se** ~ to tolerate each other

tollé [tɔle] *m* outcry

TOM [tɔm] *mpl abr de* **territoire d'outremer** *French overseas territory*

The **TOM** are the four corporate areas of the French Republic, which were established in 1946. They include Wallis and Futuna, French Polynesia, New Caledonia and the "Southern and Antarctic lands".

tomate [tɔmat] *f* tomato

tombal(**e**) [tɔ̃bal, o] <s *o*-aux> *adj* funerary

tombant(**e**) [tɔ̃bɑ̃, ɑ̃t] *adj* hanging; (*épaules*) sloping

tombe [tɔ̃b] *f* grave

tombeau [tɔ̃bo] <x> *m* tomb

tombée [tɔ̃be] *f* ~ **de la nuit** [*o* **du jour**] nightfall

tomber [tɔ̃be] <1> *vi être* **1.** (*chuter, s'abattre*) to fall; ~ **en arrière**/**en avant** to fall backwards/forwards; ~ **dans les bras de qn** to fall into sb's arms; ~ (**par terre**) to fall; (*échafaudage*) to collapse **2.** (*être affaibli*) **je tombe de fatigue**/**sommeil** I'm ready to drop I'm so tired/sleepy **3.** (*se détacher: cheveux, dent*) to fall out; (*feuille, masque*) to fall **4.** (*arriver: nouvelle, télex*) to arrive; **qc tombe un lundi** sth falls on a Monday **5.** (*descendre: nuit, soir, neige, pluie, averse*) to fall; (*foudre*) to strike **6.** THEAT (*rideau*) to fall **7.** (*être vaincu*) to fall; (*dictateur, gouvernement*) to be brought down; (*record*) to be smashed **8.** MIL (*mourir*) to fall **9.** (*baisser: vent*) to drop; (*colère, enthousiasme, exaltation*) to fade **10.** (*disparaître, échouer: obstacle*) to disappear; (*plan, projet*) to fall through **11.** (*pendre*) to hang; **bien**/**mal** ~ (*vêtement*) to hang well/badly **12.** *inf* (*se retrouver*) ~ **enceinte** to become pregnant; ~ **d'accord** to agree **13.** (*être pris*) ~ **dans un piège** to fall into a trap **14.** (*être entraîné*) ~ **dans l'oubli** to sink into oblivion **15.** (*concerner par hasard*) ~ **sur qn** to happen to sb; (*sort*) to choose sb **16.** (*rencontrer, arriver par hasard*) ~ **sur un article** to come across an article; ~ **sur qn** to bump into sb **17.** (*abandonner*) **laisser** ~ **un projet**/**une activité** to drop a project/an activity **18.** (*se poser*) ~ **sur qn**/**qc** (*conversation*) to come round to sb/sth; (*regard*) to light upon sb/sth **19.** *inf* (*attaquer*) ~ **sur qn** to lay into sb ►**<u>bien</u>**/**<u>mal</u>** ~ to be a bit of good/bad luck; **ça tombe bien**/**mal** that's handy/a nuisance

tombola [tɔ̃bɔla] *f* tombola, raffle

tome [tɔm] *m* volume

tom(**m**)**e** [tɔm] *f* tomme (*hard cheese*)

ton[1] [tɔ̃] *m* **1.** (*manière de s'exprimer, couleur*) *a.* MUS tone; **d'un** [*o* **sur un**] ~ **convaincu** with conviction **2.** (*timbre: d'une voix*) tone; **baisser**/**hausser le** ~ to lower/raise one's voice ►**il est de <u>bon</u>** ~ **de** +*infin* it is polite to +*infin*

ton[2] [tɔ̃, te] <tes> *dét poss* (*à toi*) your; *v. a.* **mon** ►**ne fais pas** ~ **<u>malin</u>!** don't get clever!

tonalité [tɔnalite] *f* **1.** TEL dialling tone *Brit,* dial tone *Am* **2.** (*timbre, impression d'ensemble*) *a.* LING tone

tondeuse [tɔ̃døz] *f* **1.** (*pour les cheveux, la barbe*) clippers *pl* **2.** (*pour le jardin*) ~ (**à gazon**) lawnmower

tondre [tɔ̃dʀ] <14> *vt* to shear; (*gazon*) to mow; (*haie*) to cut

tondu(**e**) [tɔ̃dy] **I.** *part passé de* **tondre** **II.** *adj* (*personne, tête, cheveux*) close-cropped; (*pelouse, pré*) mown; (*haie*) clipped

tong [tɔ̃g] *f* thong

Tonga [tɔ̃ga] *fpl* **les** ~ Tonga + *vb sing*

tonifier [tɔnifje] <1> **I.** *vt* (*cheveux, peau*) to condition; (*organisme, personne, muscles*) to tone up; (*esprit, personne*) to stimulate **II.** *vi* to tone up

tonique [tɔnik] **I.** *adj* **1.** (*revigorant: froid*) fortifying; (*boisson*) tonic **2.** (*stimulant: idée, lecture*) stimulating **3.** LING (*syllabe, voyelle*) accented **II.** *m* MED tonic

tonitruant(**e**) [tɔnitʀyɑ̃, ɑ̃t] *adj* thundering; (*voix*) booming

tonnage [tɔnaʒ] *m* tonnage; ~ **brut**/**net** gross/net tonnage

tonne [tɔn] *f* **1.** (*unité*) ton **2.** *inf* (*énorme quantité*) loads *pl* ►**en <u>faire</u> des** ~**s** *inf* to overdo it

tonneau [tɔno] <x> *m* **1.** (*récipient*) barrel **2.** (*accident de voiture*) somersault **3.** (*acrobatie aérienne*) barrel roll

tonnelet [tɔnlɛ] *m* keg

tonnelier, -ière [tɔnəlje, -jɛʀ] *m, f* cooper

tonnelle [tɔnɛl] *f* bower

tonner [tɔne] <1> **I.** *vi* **1.** (*retentir: artillerie, canons*) to thunder **2.** (*parler*) ~ **contre qc** to thunder against sth **II.** *vi impers* **il tonne** it's thundering

tonnerre [tɔnɛʀ] *m* **1.** METEO thunder **2.** (*manifestation bruyante*) ~ **de protestations** thunder of protests; ~ **d'applaudissements** thunderous applause ►**fille**/**type**/**voiture <u>du</u>** ~ *inf* great girl/guy/car

tonsure [tɔ̃syʀ] *f* **1.** REL tonsure **2.** *inf* (*calvitie*) bald patch

tonte [tɔ̃t] *f* **1.** (*action*) shearing; (*d'un gazon*) mowing; (*d'une haie*) clipping **2.** (*époque*) shearing-time

tonton [tɔ̃tɔ̃] *m enfantin* uncle

tonus [tɔnys] *m* **1.** (*dynamisme*) energy **2.** ANAT ~ **musculaire** muscle tone

top [tɔp] **I.** *adj inv, antéposé* ~ **model** supermodel **II.** *m* **1.** RADIO beep **2.** (*signal de départ*) ~ (**de départ**) starting signal **3.** SPORT get set

T

4. *inf* (*niveau maximum*) **le** ~ the best

topo [tɔpo] *m inf* **1.** (*exposé oral, écrit*) piece **2.** *péj* (*répétition ennuyeuse*) spiel

topologie [tɔpɔlɔʒi] *f* topology

topométrie [tɔpɔmetʀi] *f* topometry

toponyme [tɔpɔnim] *m* place name

toponymie [tɔpɔnimi] *f* toponymy

toque [tɔk] *f* (*coiffure: d'un juge, magistrat*) cap; (*d'un cuisinier*) chef's hat

toqué(e) [tɔke] **I.** *adj inf* (*cinglé*) cracked **II.** *m(f) inf* nutcase

Torah [tɔʀa] *f* Torah

torche [tɔʀʃ] *f* **1.** (*flambeau*) (flaming) torch **2.** (*lampe électrique*) torch *Brit,* flashlight *Am*

torché(e) [tɔʀʃe] *adj inf* (*bâclé*) botched ►**être bien** ~ to be a nice job

torcher [tɔʀʃe] <1> **I.** *vt* **1.** *inf* (*essuyer*) to wipe **2.** *inf* (*bâcler*) to bodge **II.** *vpr inf* **se** ~ (**le derrière**) to wipe one's bottom

torchis [tɔʀʃi] *m* cob

torchon [tɔʀʃɔ̃] *m* **1.** (*tissu*) cloth; **donner un coup de** ~ **sur/à qc** to dry/dust sth **2.** *inf* (*mauvais journal*) rag **3.** (*sale travail*) mess ►**il ne faut pas mélanger les ~s et les serviettes** *inf* you've got to be sure you're comparing like with like

tordant(e) [tɔʀdɑ̃, ɑ̃t] *adj inf* (*drôle*) hilarious

tord-boyaux [tɔʀbwajo] *m inv, inf* rotgut

tordre [tɔʀdʀ] <14> **I.** *vt* **1.** (*serrer en tournant: linge*) to wring; (*brins, fils*) to twist **2.** (*plier*) to bend; **être tordu** (*jambe, nez, règle*) to be twisted **3.** (*déformer*) ~ **la bouche/les traits de qn** to twist sb's mouth/features **II.** *vpr* **1.** (*faire des contorsions*) **se** ~ **de douleur** to double up with pain; **se** ~ **de rire** to double up with laughter **2.** (*se luxer*) **se** ~ **un membre** to dislocate a limb

tordu(e) [tɔʀdy] **I.** *part passé de* **tordre** **II.** *adj inf* (*esprit, personne, idée*) twisted **III.** *m(f) inf* weirdo

toréador [tɔʀeadɔʀ] *m* toreador

toréer [tɔʀee] <1> *vi* to fight a bull

torero [tɔʀeʀo] *m* bullfighter

tornade [tɔʀnad] *f* tornado

torpédo [tɔʀpedo] *f* AUTO, HIST open touring car

torpeur [tɔʀpœʀ] *f* torpor

torpille [tɔʀpij] *f* MIL torpedo

torpiller [tɔʀpije] <1> *vt* (*faire échouer*) *a.* MIL to torpedo

torpilleur [tɔʀpijœʀ] *m* torpedo boat

torréfier [tɔʀefje] <1> *vt* to roast

torrent [tɔʀɑ̃] *m* (*cours d'eau, flot abondant*) torrent; ~ **de boue** torrent of mud; ~ **de larmes** flood of tears ►**il pleut à ~s** it's pouring down

torrentiel(le) [tɔʀɑ̃sjɛl] *adj* (*pluies*) torrential

torride [tɔʀid] *adj* **1.** (*brûlant*) burning; (*chaleur*) scorching **2.** (*passionné*) torrid

tors(e) [tɔʀ, tɔʀs] *adj* (*fil*) twisted; (*jambes*) crooked; (*colonne*) wreathed

torsade [tɔʀsad] *f* twist

torsader [tɔʀsade] <1> *vt* (*brins, cheveux*) to twist

torse [tɔʀs] *m* **1.** (*poitrine*) chest **2.** ANAT, ART torso

torsion [tɔʀsjɔ̃] *f* (*déformation: de la bouche, des traits*) twisting

tort [tɔʀ] *m* **1.** (*erreur*) error; **avoir** ~ to be wrong; **avoir grand** ~ **de** +*infin* to be very wrong to +*infin* **2.** (*préjudice*) wrong; (*moral*) harm; **faire du** ~ **à qn/qc** to harm sb/sth ►**à** ~ **ou à raison** rightly or wrongly; **à** ~ **et à travers** anyhow; **parler à** ~ **et à travers** to talk complete nonsense

torticolis [tɔʀtikɔli] *m* stiff neck

tortillard [tɔʀtijaʀ] *m inf* local train

tortiller [tɔʀtije] <1> **I.** *vt* (*cheveux*) to twiddle; (*cravate, mouchoir*) to twiddle with **II.** *vi* ~ **des hanches/fesses** to wiggle one's hips/bottom ►**y a pas à** ~ *inf* there's no two ways about it **III.** *vpr* **se** ~ (*personne*) to fidget; (*animal*) to squirm

tortionnaire [tɔʀsjɔnɛʀ] *mf* torturer

tortue [tɔʀty] *f* **1.** ZOOL tortoise; (*de mer*) turtle **2.** *inf* (*personne très lente*) slowcoach *Brit,* slowpoke *Am*

tortueux, -euse [tɔʀtɥø, -øz] *adj* **1.** (*sinueux: chemin*) winding; (*escalier, ruelle*) twisting **2.** (*retors: conduite*) tortuous; (*manœuvres*) devious

torture [tɔʀtyʀ] *f* **1.** (*supplice*) torture **2.** (*souffrance*) torment ►**mettre qn à la** ~ to torture sb

torturer [tɔʀtyʀe] <1> **I.** *vt* **1.** (*supplicier*) to torture **2.** (*faire souffrir: douleur, doute, faim, jalousie, remords*) to torment **3.** (*déformer*) **être torturé par qc** (*traits, visage*) to be twisted with sth **II.** *vpr* **se** ~ to torment oneself

tôt [to] *adv* **1.** (*de bonne heure*) early **2.** (*à une date ou une heure avancée, vite*) soon; **plus** ~ sooner; **le plus** ~ **possible** as soon as possible ►~ **ou tard** sooner or later; **pas plus** ~ **… que** no sooner … than

total [tɔtal, o] <-aux> *m* (*somme*) total ►**faire le** ~ **de qc** to add sth up; **au** ~ (*en tout*) all in all; (*somme toute*) in total

total(e) [tɔtal, o] <-aux> *adj* **1.** (*absolu: maîtrise, désespoir*) complete; (*obscurité, ruine*) total **2.** FIN, MAT (*hauteur, somme*) total

totalement [tɔtalmɑ̃] *adv* totally; (*détruit, ruiné*) completely

totaliser [tɔtalize] <1> *vt* ~ **qc** **1.** (*additionner*) to add sth up **2.** (*atteindre: nombre, points, voix, habitants*) to total sth up

totalitaire [tɔtalitɛʀ] *adj* totalitarian

totalité [tɔtalite] *f* whole

totem [tɔtɛm] *m* totem

toucan [tukɑ̃] *m* toucan

touchant(e) [tuʃɑ̃, ɑ̃t] *adj* (*émouvant*) moving; (*situation, histoire*) touching

touche [tuʃ] *f* **1.** INFOR, MUS (*d'un accordéon, piano*) key; ~ **Alternative** Alt key; ~ **Contrôle** CTRL; ~ **Echappement** ESC; ~ **Entrée**

ENTER; ~ **Espace** SPACE; ~ **Insertion** INS; ~ **Majuscule** SHIFT; ~ **'page précédente/suivante'** PgUp/PgDn key; ~ **Retour arrière** BACKSPACE; ~ **Retour** RETURN; ~ **Suppression** DEL; ~ **Tabulation** TAB; **presser la ~ F1** to press F1; ~ **d'effacement** BACKSPACE; ~ [**de**] **Fonction** FUNCTION; ~ **verrouillage majuscule** caps lock **2.** (*coup de pinceau*) stroke **3.** (*à la pêche*) bite **4.** (*en escrime*) hit; (*au football, rugby: ligne*) touchline; (*au football: sortie du ballon*) throw-in; (*au rugby: sortie du ballon*) line-out ▸**faire une** ~ *inf* to be a hit; **sur la** ~ (*au bord du terrain*) on the bench; *inf* (*à l'écart*) on the sidelines

touche-à-tout [tuʃatu] *mf inv, inf* **c'est un** ~ **1.** (*enfant*) he can't keep his hands of anything **2.** (*personne aux activités multiples*) he's a jack of all trades **3.** (*personne aux talents multiples*) he dabbles in all sorts of things

toucher [tuʃe] <1> **I.** *vt* **1.** (*porter la main sur, entrer en contact avec: ballon, fond, sol, plafond*) to touch **2.** (*être contigu à*) to adjoin **3.** (*frapper: balle, coup, explosion*) to hit; (*mesure, politique*) to affect **4.** (*concerner*) to concern; (*histoire, affaire*) to involve **5.** (*émouvoir: critique, reproche*) to affect; (*drame, deuil, scène*) to move **6.** (*recevoir: argent, ration, commission, pension, traitement*) to receive; (*à la banque: chèque*) to cash **7.** (*contacter, atteindre: personne, port, côte*) to reach **II.** *vi* **1.** (*porter la main sur*) ~ **à qc** to touch sth **2.** (*se servir de*) ~ **à ses économies** to use one's savings **3.** (*tripoter*) ~ **à qn** to lay a finger on sb **4.** (*modifier*) ~ **au règlement** to change the rules **5.** (*concerner*) ~ **à un domaine** to be connected with a field **6.** (*aborder*) ~ **à un problème/sujet** to broach a problem/subject **7.** (*être proche de*) ~ **à un lieu/objet** to be nearing a place/an object; ~ **à sa fin** to near its end **III.** *vpr* **se** ~ (*personnes*) to touch; (*immeubles, localités, propriétés*) to be next to each other **IV.** *m* **1.** MUS, SPORT touch **2.** (*impression*) feel ▸**au** ~ by touch

touffe [tuf] *f* tuft

touffu(**e**) [tufy] *adj* (*épais*) thick; (*sourcils*) bushy; (*végétation*) dense

toujours [tuʒuʀ] *adv* **1.** (*constamment*) always **2.** (*encore*) still **3.** (*en toutes occasions*) always **4.** (*malgré tout*) still ▸**qn peut** ~ **faire qc** sb can always do sth; **depuis** ~ always

toulousain(**e**) [tuluzɛ̃, ɛn] *adj* of Toulouse; *v. a.* **ajaccien**

Toulousain(**e**) [tuluzɛ̃, ɛn] *m(f)* person from Toulouse; *v. a.* **Ajaccien**

toupet [tupɛ] *m* **1.** (*touffe*) tuft of hair **2.** *inf* (*culot*) nerve

toupie [tupi] *f* **1.** (*jouet*) spinning top **2.** TECH spindle moulder *Brit*, spindle molder *Am*

tour¹ [tuʀ] *f* **1.** (*monument*) *a.* MIL tower; ~ **de contrôle** control tower; ~ **de forage** drilling rig; ~ **de guet** watchtower; **la** ~ **Eiffel** the Eiffel tower **2.** (*immeuble*) tower block **3.** JEUX castle, rook ▸**c'est une vraie** ~ *inf* he's massive

tour² [tuʀ] *m* **1.** (*circonférence*) outline; ~ **des yeux** eyeline; ~ **de cou** neck measurement; ~ **de hanches/poitrine** hip/chest measurement **2.** (*brève excursion*) trip; **faire un** ~ (*à pied*) to go for a walk; (*en voiture*) to go for a drive; (*à vélo*) to go for a ride; ~ **de France** SPORT Tour de France; HIST tour of France; ~ **d'horizon** survey **3.** (*succession alternée*) ~ **de garde** turn on duty; **c'est au** ~ **de qn de** *+infin* it's sb's turn to *+infin* **4.** (*rotation*) revolution **5.** (*duperie*) trick **6.** (*tournure*) expression **7.** (*exercice habile*) stunt; ~ **de force** feat of strength; (*exploit moral*) achievement; ~ **de prestidigitation** [*o* **de magie**] magic trick; **avoir le** ~ **de main** to have the knack **8.** (*séance*) performance; ~ **de chant** song recital **9.** POL round; ~ **de scrutin** round of voting ▸**faire le** ~ **du cadran** to sleep round the clock; **en un** ~ **de main** in no time at all; **à** ~ **de rôle** in turn; **jouer un** ~ **à qn** to play a trick on sb; **prendre un** ~ **désagréable/inquiétant** to become unpleasant/worrying; **c'est un** ~ **à prendre** it's a knack you pick up

tourbe [tuʀb] *f* AGR peat

tourbière [tuʀbjɛʀ] *f* peat bog

tourbillon [tuʀbijɔ̃] *m* **1.** (*vent*) whirlwind; ~ **de neige** swirl of snow **2.** (*masse d'eau*) whirlpool **3.** (*colonne tournoyante*) ~ **de sable** eddy of sand **4.** (*agitation*) ~ **de la vie** hustle and bustle of life

tourbillonnement [tuʀbijɔnmɑ̃] *m* (*tournoiement: de feuilles, fumée*) swirl

tourbillonner [tuʀbijɔne] <1> *vi* (*eaux, feuilles*) to eddy; (*fumée, neige, poussière*) to swirl

Tour de Londres *f* **la** ~ the Tower of London

tourelle [tuʀɛl] *f* **1.** turret **2.** MIL, NAUT gun turret

tourisme [tuʀism] *m* **1.** tourism; ~ **vert** ecotourism; **agence de** ~ travel agency; **office de** ~ tourist office **2.** AUTO **voiture de grand** ~ saloon car *Brit*, 4-door sedan *Am*

touriste [tuʀist] *mf* tourist

touristique [tuʀistik] *adj* tourist

tourmente [tuʀmɑ̃t] *f soutenu* (*tempête*) storm

tourmenté(**e**) [tuʀmɑ̃te] *adj* **1.** (*angoissé*) tormented **2.** (*compliqué: côte, formes, paysages*) rugged; (*style*) tortured **3.** (*agité: mer*) rough; (*vie*) turbulent

tourmenter [tuʀmɑ̃te] <1> **I.** *vt* **1.** (*tracasser: ambition, envie, jalousie*) to torment; (*doute, remords, scrupules*) to plague **2.** (*importuner*) ~ **qn de qc** to harass sb with sth **II.** *vpr* **se** ~ to worry oneself sick

tournage [tuʀnaʒ] *m* **1.** CINE shooting **2.** TECH turning

tournant [tuʀnɑ̃] *m* **1.** (*virage*) bend **2.** (*changement*) turning point

T

tournant(**e**) [turnɑ̃, ɑ̃t] *adj* (*qui peut tourner: plaque, pont, scène*) revolving

tourné(**e**) [turne] *adj* (*aigri*) off; (*sauce, vin*) sour ▸**article**/**lettre** **bien**/**mal** ~ well/badly-written article/letter

tournebouler [turnəbule] <1> *vt inf* to bewilder; ~ **la cervelle** [*o* **l'esprit**] [*o* **les idées**] **à qn** to put sb's head in a spin; **être tourneboulé** to be in a spin

tourne-disque [turnədisk] <tourne-disques> *m* record player

tournedos [turnədo] *m* GASTR tournedos steak

tournée [turne] *f* **1.** (*circuit: d'un artiste, conférencier*) tour; **être en** ~ to be on tour **2.** *inf* (*au café*) round

tournemain [turnəmɛ̃] *m* **en un** ~ in next to no time

tourner [turne] <1> **I.** *vt* **1.** (*mouvoir en rond, orienter, détourner*) to turn; ~ **la lampe vers la gauche**/**le haut** to turn the lamp to the left/upwards; ~ **le dos à qn**/**qc** to turn one's back on sb/sth **2.** (*retourner: page*) to turn; (*disque, feuille*) to turn over **3.** (*contourner, en voiture, à vélo*) to round **4.** (*formuler*) to phrase **5.** (*transformer*) ~ **qn**/**qc en ridicule** to make a laughing stock of sb/sth; ~ **qc à son avantage** to turn sth to one's advantage **6.** CINE to shoot **7.** TECH to throw; (*bois*) to turn **II.** *vi* **1.** (*pivoter sur son axe*) to turn **2.** (*avoir un déplacement circulaire: personne, animal*) to turn; **la terre tourne autour du soleil** the earth revolves around the sun **3.** (*fonctionner*) to run; ~ **à vide** (*machine*) to be on but not working; (*moteur*) to idle; ~ **à plein rendement** [*o* **régime**] to be working at full capacity; **faire** ~ **un moteur** to run an engine **4.** (*avoir trait à*) **la conversation tourne autour de qn**/**qc** the conversation centred [*o* centered *Am*] on sb/sth **5.** (*bifurquer*) to turn off **6.** (*s'inverser*) to turn around; (*vent*) to change; **ma chance a tourné** my luck has changed [*o* turned] **7.** (*évoluer*) ~ **à**/**en qc** to change to/into sth; (*événement*) to turn into sth; **le temps tourne au beau** the weather's turning fine **8.** (*devenir aigre: crème, lait*) to turn **9.** CINE to shoot **10.** (*approcher*) ~ **autour de qc** (*prix, nombre*) to be around sth ▸~ **bien**/**mal** (*personne, chose*) to turn out well/badly **III.** *vpr* **1.** (*s'adresser à, s'orienter*) **se** ~ **vers qn**/**qc** to turn to sb/sth **2.** (*changer de position*) **se** ~ **vers qn**/**de l'autre côté** to turn towards sb/to the other side

tournesol [turnəsɔl] *m* sunflower

tournevis [turnəvis] *m* screwdriver

tournicoter [turnikɔte] <1> *vi inf,* **tourniquer** [turnike] <1> *vi inf* to hover around

tourniquet [turnikɛ] *m* **1.** (*barrière*) turnstile **2.** (*porte*) revolving door **3.** (*pour arroser*) sprinkler **4.** (*présentoir*) revolving stand

tournis [turni] *m inf* dizziness

tournoi [turnwa] *m* tournament

tournoiement [turnwamɑ̃] *m* whirling; (*des feuilles*) swirling

tournoyer [turnwaje] <6> *vi* to whirl; (*plus vite*) to spin

tournure [turnyr] *f* **1.** (*évolution*) development; **prendre bonne** ~ to take a turn for the better **2.** LING form; (*idiomatique*) expression **3.** (*apparence*) bearing ▸~ **d'esprit** turn of mind; **prendre** ~ to take shape

tour-opérateur [turɔperatœr] <tour-opérateurs> *m* tour operator

tourteau[1] [turto] <x> *m* ZOOL crab

tourteau[2] [turto] <x> *m* AGR cattle-cake

tourtereau [turtəro] <x> *m* **1.** *pl, iron* (*amoureux*) lovebird **2.** (*oiseau*) young turtle-dove

tourterelle [turtərɛl] *f* turtledove

tourtière [turtjɛr] *f Québec* (*tourte à base de porc*) *type of pork pie*

tous [tu, tus] *v.* **tout**

Toussaint [tusɛ̃] *f* **la** ~ All Saints' Day

> In France **la Toussaint** is a public holiday. People visit cemeteries and lay flowers, usually chrysanthemums, on family graves.

tousser [tuse] <1> *vi* **1.** (*avoir un accès de toux*) to cough **2.** (*s'éclaircir la gorge, pour avertir*) to clear one's throat **3.** (*avoir des ratés: moteur*) to splutter

toussoter [tusɔte] <1> *vi* **1.** (*tousser légèrement*) to have a slight cough **2.** (*pour avertir, de gêne*) to clear one's throat

tout [tu] **I.** *adv* **1.** (*totalement*) ~ **simple**/**bête** quite simple/easy; **le** ~ **premier**/**dernier** the very first/last; **c'est** ~ **autre chose** it's not the same thing at all **2.** (*très, vraiment*) very; ~ **près de** very near to; ~ **autour** (**de**) all around **3.** (*aussi*) ~**e maligne qu'elle soit, ...** (*subj*) as crafty as she may be ... **4.** *inv* (*en même temps*) ~ **en faisant qc** while doing sth **5.** (*en totalité*) completely; **tissu** ~ **laine**/**soie** pure wool/silk material ▸~ **d'un coup** (*en une seule fois*) in one go; (*soudain*) suddenly; ~ **à fait** exactly; **être** ~ **à fait charmant** to be completely charming; **c'est** ~ **à fait possible** it is perfectly possible; ~ **de suite** straight away; **c'est** ~ **comme** *inf* it's the same thing; ~ **de même** all the same; **le** ~ **Paris** the whole of Paris society **II.** *m* **1.** (*totalité*) whole **2.** (*ensemble*) **le** ~ everything ▸(**pas**) **du** ~! not at all!; **elle n'avait pas du** ~ **de pain** she had no bread at all

tout(**e**) [tu, tut, tus/tu, tut] <tous, toutes> **I.** *adj indéf* **1.** *sans pl* (*entier*) ~ **le temps**/**l'argent** all the time/money; ~ **le monde** everybody; ~**e la journée** all day; ~ **ce bruit** all this noise; **nous avons** ~ **notre temps** we have all the time we need **2.** *sans pl* (*tout à fait*) **c'est** ~ **le contraire** it's exactly the opposite **3.** *sans pl* (*seul, unique*) **c'est** ~ **l'effet que ça te fait** is that all it does to you? **4.** *sans pl* (*complet*) **j'ai lu** ~ **Balzac** I have read all

Balzac's works; ~ **Londres** the whole of London; **à ~ prix** at any price; **à ~e vitesse** at top speed **5.** *sans pl* (*quel qu'il soit*) ~ **homme** all men *pl;* **de ~e manière** in any case **6.** *pl* (*l'ensemble des*) **~es les places** all the seats; **tous les jours** every day; **dans tous les cas** in any case **7.** *pl* (*chaque*) **tous les quinze jours/deux jours** every two weeks/two days **8.** *pl* (*ensemble*) **nous avons fait tous les cinq ce voyage** all five of us made the trip **9.** *pl* (*la totalité des*) **à tous égards** in all respects; **de tous côtés** (*arriver*) from everywhere; (*regarder*) from all around; **de ~es sortes** of all kinds; **un film tous publics** a universal film; **chiffon ~ usage** multi-use cloth **II.** *pron indéf* **1.** *sans pl* (*opp: rien*) everything **2.** *pl* (*opp: personne/aucun*) everybody/everything; **un film pour tous** a film for everyone; **nous tous** all of us; **tous/~es ensemble** all together **3.** *sans pl* (*l'ensemble des choses*) ~ **ce qui bouge** anything that moves ▶**il/elle a ~ pour lui/elle** *inf* he/she has got everything going for him/her; **et c(e n)'est pas ~!** and that's not all!; **être ~ pour qn** to be everything to sb; **c(e n)'est pas ~ (que) de** *+infin* it's not enough just to *+infin;* **~ est bien qui finit bien** *prov* all's well that ends well; **et ~ (et ~)** *inf* and everything; **~ ou rien** all or nothing; **en ~** (*au total*) in all; (*dans toute chose*) in every respect; **en ~ et pour ~** all in all

tout-à-l'égout [tutalegu] *m sans pl* mains sewer

toutefois [tutfwa] *adv* however

toutou [tutu] *m enfantin* (*chien*) doggy ▶**suivre qn comme un ~** *inf* to follow sb around like a poodle

tout-petit [tup(ə)ti] <tout-petits> *m* small child

Tout-Puissant [tupɥisɑ̃] *m* REL **le ~** the Almighty

tout-puissant, toute-puissante [tupɥisɑ̃, tutpɥisɑ̃t] <tout-puissants> **I.** *adj* omnipotent **II.** *m, f* (*souverain absolu*) all-poweful figure

tout-terrain [tuteʀɛ̃] <tout-terrains> **I.** *adj* all-terrain, four-wheel drive; **vélo ~** mountain bike **II.** *m* (*véhicule*) all-terrain [*o* four-wheel drive] vehicle

tout-venant [tuv(ə)nɑ̃] *m inv* **le ~ 1.** (*gens banals*) anybody **2.** (*choses courantes*) ordinary stuff

toux [tu] *f* cough

toxicité [tɔksisite] *f* toxicity

toxico [tɔksikɔ] *mf abr de* **toxicomane**

toxicologique [tɔksikɔlɔʒik] *adj* toxicological

toxicologue [tɔksikɔlɔg] *mf* toxicologist

toxicomane [tɔksikɔman] **I.** *adj* addicted to drugs **II.** *mf* drug addict

toxicomanie [tɔksikɔmani] *f* drug addiction

toxique [tɔksik] *adj* toxic; (*gaz*) poisonous

TP [tepe] *mpl* **1.** *abr de* **travaux pratiques** practical work **2.** *abr de* **travaux publics** civil engineering

trac [tʀak] *m inf* fear; **avoir le ~** to have stage fright

tracas [tʀaka] *m* worry; **se faire du ~** to worry

tracasser [tʀakase] <1> **I.** *vt* to worry; (*administration*) to harass **II.** *vpr* **se ~ pour qn/qc** to worry about sb/sth

tracasserie [tʀakasʀi] *f gén pl* bother *no pl*

tracassier, -ière [tʀakasje, -jɛʀ] *adj* (*administration, bureaucratie*) pettifogging

trace [tʀas] *f* **1.** (*empreinte*) tracks *pl* **2.** (*marque laissée, quantité minime*) trace; (*cicatrice*) mark; (*de fatigue*) sign; **disparaître sans laisser de ~s** to disappear without a trace **3.** (*voie tracée*) path; (*au ski*) track ▶**marcher sur les ~s de qn** to follow in sb's footsteps; **suivre qn à la ~** to follow sb's trail

tracé [tʀase] *m* **1.** (*parcours*) route **2.** (*plan, dessin*) layout **3.** (*graphisme*) line

tracer [tʀase] <2> *vt* **1.** (*dessiner*) to draw; (*chiffre, mot*) to write **2.** (*frayer: piste, route*) to open up **3.** (*décrire: portrait, tableau*) to paint

traceur [tʀasœʀ] *m* **1.** CHIM, MED, RADIO tracer **2.** INFOR plotter

trachée(-artère) [tʀaʃeaʀtɛʀ] <trachées(-artères)> *f* windpipe

trachéite [tʀakeit] *f* tracheitis

trachéotomie [tʀakeɔtɔmi] *f* tracheotomy

tract [tʀakt] *m* handout; **~ publicitaire** flier

tractable [tʀaktabl] *adj* towable

tracté(e) [tʀakte] *adj* tractor-drawn

tracter [tʀakte] <1> *vt* to tow

tracteur [tʀaktœʀ] *m* tractor

traction [tʀaksjɔ̃] *f* **1.** TECH traction **2.** AUTO drive; **~ avant/arrière** front-/rear-wheel drive **3.** SPORT (*à la barre, aux anneaux*) pull-up **4.** CHEMDFER engine service

tradition [tʀadisjɔ̃] *f* **1.** (*coutume*) tradition **2.** *sans pl a.* REL (*coutumes transmises*) tradition **3.** JUR transfer ▶**dans la grande ~ de qn/qc** in the great tradition of sb/sth; **être de ~** to be a tradition

traditionnel(le) [tʀadisjɔnɛl] *adj* **1.** (*conforme à la tradition*) traditional **2.** (*habituel*) usual

traditionnellement [tʀadisjɔnɛlmɑ̃] *adv* **1.** (*selon la tradition*) traditionally **2.** (*habituellement*) usually **3.** (*comme toujours*) as always

traducteur [tʀadyktœʀ] *m* INFOR translator; **~ de poche** pocket translator

traducteur, -trice [tʀadyktœʀ, -tʀis] *m, f* (*interprète*) translator

traduction [tʀadyksjɔ̃] *f* **1.** (*dans une autre langue*) translation; **~ en anglais** translation into English **2.** (*expression: d'un sentiment*) expression

traduire [tʀadɥiʀ] *irr* **I.** *vt* **1.** (*dans une autre langue*) **~ de l'anglais en français** to translate from English into French **2.** (*exprimer*) ~

une pensée/un sentiment (*chose*) to convey a thought/feeling; (*personne*) to express a thought/feeling **3.** JUR ~ **en justice** to bring sb up before the courts **II.** *vpr* **1.** (*être traduisible*) **se** ~ **en qc** to translate into sth **2.** (*s'exprimer*) **se** ~ **par qc** (*sentiment*) to be conveyed by sth

traduisible [tʀadɥizibl] *adj* translatable

trafic [tʀafik] *m* **1.** (*circulation*) traffic **2.** *péj* (*commerce*) trade; ~ **de drogues** drug trafficking **3.** *inf* (*activité suspecte*) funny business

traficoter [tʀafikɔte] <1> *vt inf* **1.** (*falsifier*) to fake; (*produit*) to doctor **2.** (*bricoler*) ~ **un appareil** to fix an appliance **3.** (*manigancer*) to plot

trafiquant(e) [tʀafikɑ̃, ɑ̃t] *m(f)* trafficker; ~ **de drogue** drug trafficker

trafiquer [tʀafike] <1> *vt inf* **1.** (*falsifier: comptes*) to fiddle; ~ **un moteur/produit** to tamper with a product/engine **2.** (*bricoler*) to fix **3.** (*manigancer*) to plot

tragédie [tʀaʒedi] *f* tragedy

tragédien(ne) [tʀaʒedjɛ̃, jɛn] *m(f)* tragic actor, actress *m, f*

tragique [tʀaʒik] **I.** *adj* (*auteur, accident*) tragic **II.** *m sans pl* (*genre littéraire, gravité*) tragedy

tragiquement [tʀaʒikmɑ̃] *adv* tragically

trahir [tʀaiʀ] <8> **I.** *vt* **1.** (*tromper*) to betray; (*femme*) to be unfaithful to **2.** (*révéler*) to give away **3.** (*dénaturer: auteur, pièce*) to be unfaithful to **4.** (*lâcher: sens*) to misrepresent **II.** *vi* to be a traitor **III.** *vpr* **se** ~ **par une action/un geste** to give oneself away with an action/a gesture

trahison [tʀaizɔ̃] *f* **1.** (*traîtrise*) treachery; (*d'une femme*) betrayal **2.** (*falsification: d'une œuvre*) misrepresentation

train [tʀɛ̃] *m* **1.** CHEMDFER train; ~ **express/omnibus/rapide** express/slow/fast train; ~ **à grande vitesse** high speed train; ~ **électrique/à vapeur** electric/steam train; **le** ~ **en direction/venant de Lyon** the train to/from Lyons; **prendre le** ~ to take the train **2.** (*allure*) pace; ~ **de sénateur** stately pace; **à ce** ~ at this rate; ~ **de vie** lifestyle **3.** (*jeu*) train; ~ **de roues/pneus** set of wheels/tyres *Brit,* set of wheels/tires *Am;* ~ **d'atterrissage** landing gear **4.** (*série: de textes, négociations*) batch; ~ **de réformes** set of reforms; ~ **d'expulsions/de licenciements** batch of expulsions/redundancies [*o* layoffs *Am*] **5.** AUTO ~ **avant/arrière** front/rear axle unit ►**prendre le** ~ **en marche** to climb on the bandwagon; **mener grand** ~ to live in style; **être en** ~ **de faire qc** to be doing sth; **en** ~ in shape; **mettre qc en** ~ to get sth under way; **mettre qn en** ~ (*moralement*) to get sb going; (*physiquement*) to warm sb up

traînant(e) [tʀɛnɑ̃, ɑ̃t] *adj* **1.** (*lent*) slow; (*démarche*) shuffling **2.** (*qui traîne à terre: ailes*) trailing

traînard(e) [tʀɛnaʀ, aʀd] *m(f) inf* (*lambin*) straggler

traîne [tʀɛn] *f* COUT train ►**à la** ~ lagging behind

traîneau [tʀɛno] <x> *m* sleigh

traînée [tʀene] *f* (*trace*) tracks; (*d'une étoile filante*) tail ►**comme une** ~ **de poudre** like wildfire

traînement [tʀɛnmɑ̃] *m* trailing; (*de pieds*) dragging

traîner [tʀene] <1> **I.** *vt* **1.** (*tirer*) to pull; (*jambe*) to drag **2.** (*emmener de force*) to drag **3.** (*être encombré de: personne*) to be unable to shake off; ~ **qc avec soi** to carry sth around with one **4.** (*ne pas se séparer de*) ~ **une idée** to be stuck with an idea **II.** *vi* **1.** (*lambiner: personne*) to lag behind; (*discussion, maladie, procès*) to drag on **2.** (*vadrouiller: personne*) to hang about [*o* around] **3.** (*être en désordre*) to lie around **4.** (*pendre à terre*) to drag **5.** (*être lent*) **elle a l'accent qui traîne** she has a drawl **III.** *vpr* **1.** (*se déplacer difficilement*) **se** ~ to drag oneself around **2.** (*se forcer*) **se** ~ **pour** +*infin* to have to force oneself to +*infin*

train-ferry [tʀɛ̃feʀi] <train-ferrys *o* train-ferries> *m* train ferry

training [tʀeniŋ] *m* (*entraînement*) training

train-train [tʀɛ̃tʀɛ̃] *m sans pl, inf* boring routine

traire [tʀɛʀ] *vt irr, défec* to milk

trait [tʀɛ] *m* **1.** (*ligne*) line **2.** (*caractéristique*) trait; (*distinctif, dominant*) characteristic; (*d'une époque, d'un individu*) feature **3.** *gén pl* (*lignes du visage*) feature **4.** (*preuve*) act **5.** MUS run **6.** LING feature; ~ **d'union** LING hyphen; (*lien*) link ►~ **de génie** brainwave; **boire qc à longs** ~**s** to gulp sth down; **avoir** ~ **à qc** to relate to sth; (*film, livre*) to deal with sth; **tirer un** ~ **sur qc** (*renoncer*) to draw a line under sth; **d'un** ~ in one go; ~ **pour** ~ exactly

traitant(e) [tʀɛtɑ̃, ɑ̃t] *adj* (*shampoing, lotion*) medicated; **votre médecin** ~ the doctor treating you

traite [tʀɛt] *f* **1.** (*achat à crédit*) ~ **de qc** instalment for sth **2.** AGR (*des vaches*) milking **3.** (*trafic*) trade; **la** ~ **des noirs/blanches** the slave/white slave trade ►(**tout**) **d'une** (**seule**) ~ all in one go

traité [tʀete] *m* **1.** POL treaty; ~ **de Maastricht** Maastricht Treaty; ~ **de Versailles** Treaty of Versailles **2.** (*ouvrage*) treatise

traitement [tʀɛtmɑ̃] *m* **1.** MED, TECH treatment **2.** (*façon de traiter: du chômage, d'un problème, d'une question*) handling **3.** (*comportement*) treatment; ~ **de faveur** preferential treatment **4.** (*de l'eau, de déchets radioactifs*) processing **5.** INFOR ~ **multitâche** multitask processing; ~ **de l'information** [*o* **des données**] data processing; ~ **de texte** word processing; ~ **par lots** batch processing **6.** (*rémunération*) salary

traiter [tʀete] <1> **I.** *vt* **1.** (*se comporter envers, analyser*) *a.* MED to treat; **se faire** ~

pour qc to get treatment for sth **2.** (*qualifier*) ~ **qn de fou/menteur** to call sb mad/a liar **3.** (*régler: dossier*) to process; ~ **une affaire/question** to deal with some business/an issue **4.** TECH (*déchets*) to process; (*eaux*) to treat; (*pétrole*) to refine; **oranges non traitées** unwaxed oranges **5.** INFOR (*données, texte*) to process **II.** *vi* **1.** (*avoir pour sujet*) ~ **de qc** to deal with sth; (*film*) to be about sth **2.** (*négocier*) ~ **avec qn** to negotiate with sb **III.** *vpr* (*être réglé*) **se** ~ to be dealt with

traiteur [tʀɛtœʀ] *m* delicatessen; (*à domicile*) caterer

traître, -esse [tʀɛtʀ, -ɛs] **I.** *adj* **1.** (*qui trahit*) treacherous **2.** (*sournois*) underhand; (*escalier, virage*) treacherous; (*paroles*) threatening **II.** *m, f* (*traitor*) ~ **à qn/qc** traitor to sb/sth ►**en** ~ underhandedly

traîtrise [tʀetʀiz] *f* **1.** (*déloyauté*) treachery **2.** (*acte perfide*) act of treachery **3.** (*danger caché*) treacherousness

trajectoire [tʀaʒɛktwaʀ] *f* **1.** (*parcours: d'un véhicule*) path; (*d'un projectile*) trajectory; (*d'une planète*) orbit **2.** (*carrière*) career path

trajet [tʀaʒɛ] *m* journey; (*d'une artère, d'un nerf*) course

tralala [tʀalala] *m inf* fuss; **surtout pas de** ~ please no fuss; **avec tout le** ~ with the whole works; **et tout le** ~ the whole works ►**en grand** ~ in grand fashion; **se mettre en grand** ~ to put one one's finery

tram [tʀam] *m inf abr de* **tramway**

trame [tʀam] *f* **1.** (*ensemble de fils*) weft **2.** (*base: d'un récit, film, livre*) framework; **sur cette** ~ against this background ►**usé jusqu'à la** ~ worn threadbare

tramer [tʀame] <1> **I.** *vt* **1.** (*ourdir: coup*) to plot; (*complot*) to hatch **2.** (*tisser*) to weave **II.** *vpr* **se** ~ **contre qn/qc** (*intrigue*) to be plotted against sb/sth; (*complot*) to be hatched against sb/sth

tramontane [tʀamɔ̃tan] *f* tramontana

trampoline [tʀɑ̃pɔlin] *m* trampoline

tramway [tʀamwɛ] *m* tram

tranchant [tʀɑ̃ʃɑ̃] *m* **1.** (*côté coupant*) cutting edge **2.** (*mordant: d'un argument*) impact; (*d'un reproche*) force ►**être à double** ~ to be double-edged

tranchant(e) [tʀɑ̃ʃɑ̃, ɑ̃t] *adj* **1.** (*coupant*) sharp **2.** (*péremptoire: reproche*) sharp; (*personne*) curt **3.** (*trop vif*) cutting

tranche [tʀɑ̃ʃ] *f* **1.** (*portion*) slice **2.** (*subdivision: de travaux*) section; (*de remboursement*) instalment *Brit,* installment *Am;* ~ **d'âge** age group; ~ **de revenus** salary bracket; ~ **de vie** slice of life **3.** (*bord: d'une pièce de monnaie, d'une planche, d'un livre*) edge **4.** (*viande*) piece ►**s'en payer une** ~ *inf* to have a great time

tranché(e) [tʀɑ̃ʃe] *adj* sliced

tranchée [tʀɑ̃ʃe] *f* (*fossé*) *a.* MIL trench

trancher [tʀɑ̃ʃe] <1> **I.** *vt* **1.** (*couper au couteau*) to cut; (*mettre en tranches*) to slice; (*enlever*) to cut off; (*couper à l'épée*) to slash **2.** (*résoudre: différend, débat*) to settle **II.** *vi* (*décider*) ~ **en faveur de qn/qc** to decide in favour [*o* favor *Am*] of sb/sth

tranchoir [tʀɑ̃ʃwaʀ] *m* **1.** (*planche*) chopping board **2.** (*couteau*) chopper

tranquille [tʀɑ̃kil] **I.** *adj* **1.** (*calme, paisible*) quiet **2.** (*en paix*) **être** ~ (*personne*) to have peace; **laisser qn** ~ to leave sb alone **3.** (*rassuré*) at ease **4.** (*assuré: conviction, courage*) quiet **5.** *iron, inf* (*certain*) **là, je suis** ~ I'm sure of that ►**pouvoir dormir** ~ to be able to sleep easy; **se tenir** ~ to keep quiet **II.** *adv inf* **1.** (*facilement*) easily **2.** (*sans crainte*) with no worries

tranquillement [tʀɑ̃kilmɑ̃] *adv* **1.** (*paisiblement, avec maîtrise de soi*) peacefully; (*vivre*) quietly **2.** (*sans risque*) safely **3.** (*sans se presser*) calmly

tranquillisant [tʀɑ̃kilizɑ̃] *m* tranquilizer

tranquillisant(e) [tʀɑ̃kilizɑ̃, ɑ̃t] *adj* tranquilizing

tranquilliser [tʀɑ̃kilize] <1> **I.** *vt* to reassure **II.** *vpr* **se** ~ to put one's mind at ease

tranquillité [tʀɑ̃kilite] *f* **1.** (*calme*) tranquility; (*d'un lieu, de la mer, rue*) calmness **2.** (*sérénité*) peace; (*matérielle*) security ►**en toute** ~ with complete peace of mind

tranquillos [tʀɑ̃kilos] *adv inf* calmly

transaction [tʀɑ̃zaksjɔ̃] *f* COM transaction; ~ **boursière** stock exchange dealing

transactionnel(le) [tʀɑ̃zaksjɔnɛl] *adj* JUR compromise

transalpin(e) [tʀɑ̃zalpɛ̃, in] *adj* transalpine

transat, transatlantique [tʀɑ̃zatlɑ̃tik] **I.** *adj* transatlantic **II.** *m* **1.** (*paquebot*) (transatlantic) liner **2.** (*chaise*) deskchair **III.** *f* transatlantic race

transbahuter [tʀɑ̃sbayte] <1> **I.** *vt inf* to shift **II.** *vpr inf* **se** ~ **à la maison** to drag oneself home

transbordement [tʀɑ̃sbɔʀdəmɑ̃] *m a.* NAUT (*d'une cargaison*) shipment; (*de passagers*) transfer

transborder [tʀɑ̃sbɔʀde] <1> *vt* (*marchandises*) to ship; (*personnes*) to transfer; NAUT (*personnes*) to transfer by sea

transbordeur [tʀɑ̃sbɔʀdœʀ] **I.** *adj* **navire** ~ transporter ship **II.** *m* (*car-ferry*) ferry

transcendance [tʀɑ̃sɑ̃dɑ̃s] *f* transcendency

transcendant(e) [tʀɑ̃sɑ̃dɑ̃, ɑ̃t] *adj* **1.** (*remarquable*) exceptional; **ne pas être** ~ (*personne*) to be nothing special **2.** PHILOS, REL, MAT transcendental

transcendantal(e) [tʀɑ̃sɑ̃dɑ̃tal, o] <-aux> *adj* transcendental

transcender [tʀɑ̃sɑ̃de] <1> **I.** *vt* (*dépasser*) to transcend **II.** *vpr* **se** ~ to transcend oneself

transcoder [tʀɑ̃skɔde] <1> *vt* to transcode

transcodeur [tʀɑ̃skɔdœʀ] *m* transcoder

transcription [tʀɑ̃skʀipsjɔ̃] *f* **1.** (*copie*)

transcript **2.** LING, MUS, BIO transcription

transcrire [tʀɑ̃skʀiʀ] *vt irr* **1.** (*copier: manuscrit, texte*) to copy out; (*message oral*) to write down **2.** ADMIN, JUR, LING, BIO, MUS to transcribe

transculturel(le) [tʀɑ̃skyltyʀɛl] *adj* intercultural

transdisciplinaire [tʀɑ̃sdisiplinɛʀ] *adj* interdisciplinary

transe [tʀɑ̃s] *f* **1.** *pl* (*affres*) agony + *vb sing* **2.** (*état second*) trance

transept [tʀɑ̃sɛpt] *m* transept

transférable [tʀɑ̃sfeʀabl] *adj* transferable

transférer [tʀɑ̃sfeʀe] <5> *vt* **1.** (*déplacer*) *a.* FIN to transfer; (*cendres, dépouille*) to translate; **nos bureaux ont été transférés** we have moved offices; ~ **une somme à qn** to transfer a sum of money to sb **2.** JUR to convey

transfert [tʀɑ̃sfɛʀ] *m* (*déplacement*) transfer

transfiguration [tʀɑ̃sfigyʀasjɔ̃] *f* (*transformation*) transfiguration

Transfiguration [tʀɑ̃sfigyʀasjɔ̃] *f* REL **la** ~ the Transfiguration

transfiguré(e) [tʀɑ̃sfigyʀe] *adj* transformed

transfigurer [tʀɑ̃sfigyʀe] <1> *vt* to transfigure; (*visage, réalité*) to transform

transfo [tʀɑ̃sfo] *m inf abr de* **transformateur**

transformable [tʀɑ̃sfɔʀmabl] *adj* **être ~ en qc** to be convertible into sth; (*aspect*) to be transformable into sth

transformateur [tʀɑ̃sfɔʀmatœʀ] *m* ELEC transformer

transformation [tʀɑ̃sfɔʀmasjɔ̃] *f* **1.** (*changement*) change; (*d'une maison, pièce*) transformation; (*de matières premières*) conversion **2.** (*métamorphose*) ~ **en qc** change into sth **3.** SPORT conversion

transformer [tʀɑ̃sfɔʀme] <1> **I.** *vt* **1.** (*modifier*) to change; (*entreprise*) to transform; (*vêtement*) to alter; (*matière première*) to convert **2.** (*opérer une métamorphose*) ~ **une pièce en bureau** to convert a room into an office **3.** SPORT (*pénalité, penalty*) to score; (*essai*) to convert **4.** MAT to transform **II.** *vpr* **1.** (*changer*) **se** ~ to change **2.** (*changer de nature*) **se** ~ **en jeune homme sérieux** to turn into a serious young man **3.** CHIM, PHYS **l'eau se transforme en glace** water is transformed into ice

transfuge [tʀɑ̃sfyʒ] *mf* renegade

transfusé(e) [tʀɑ̃sfyze] *m(f)* transfused

transfuser [tʀɑ̃sfyze] <1> *vt* (*sang*) to transfuse; ~ **qn** to give sb a blood transfusion

transfusion [tʀɑ̃sfyzjɔ̃] *f* transfusion

transgresser [tʀɑ̃sgʀese] <1> *vt* (*loi*) to break

transgression [tʀɑ̃sgʀesjɔ̃] *f* ~ **d'une interdiction** breaking of a ban

transhumer [tʀɑ̃zyme] <1> *vi* (*animal*) to move to summer grazing

transi(e) [tʀɑ̃zi] *adj* **1.** (*paralysé*) ~ **de froid/peur** rigid with cold/fear **2.** *fig* **amoureux** ~ lovelorn youth

transiger [tʀɑ̃ziʒe] <2a> *vi* (*faire un compromis*) ~ **avec qn/qc** to compromise with sb/sth; ~ **avec un collègue** to meet a colleague half-way; ~ **sur un point** to compromise on a point

transistor [tʀɑ̃zistɔʀ] *m* RADIO, ELEC transistor

transit [tʀɑ̃zit] *m* COM, ANAT transit ►**en** ~ in transit

transitaire [tʀɑ̃zitɛʀ] *adj* transit

transiter [tʀɑ̃zite] <1> *vi* ~ **par qc** to pass through sth in transit; (*en avion*) to fly through sth

transitif, -ive [tʀɑ̃zitif, -iv] *adj* transitive; **verbe ~ direct/indirect** direct/indirect transitive verb

transition [tʀɑ̃zisjɔ̃] *f* MUS, CINE, PHYS (*passage*) ~ **de l'enfance à qc** transition from childhood to sth; **sans** ~ suddenly ►**de** ~ transitional

transitoire [tʀɑ̃zitwaʀ] *adj* transitory; (*période*) provisional

transitoirement [tʀɑ̃zitwaʀmɑ̃] *adv* temporarily

translation [tʀɑ̃slasjɔ̃] *f* MAT translation

translittération [tʀɑ̃sliteʀasjɔ̃] *f* transliteration

translucide [tʀɑ̃slysid] *adj* translucid

translucidité [tʀɑ̃slysidite] *f* transparency

transmanche [tʀɑ̃smɑ̃ʃ] *adj* **trafic** ~ cross-Channel traffic

transmetteur [tʀɑ̃smetœʀ] *m* transmitter

transmettre [tʀɑ̃smɛtʀ] *irr* **I.** *vt* **1.** (*léguer*) to hand down **2.** (*faire parvenir: message*) to transmit; (*renseignement, ordre*) to pass on **3.** (*en science*) *a.* RADIO, TEL, TV to transmit **4.** BIO, MED ~ **une maladie à qn** to pass on a disease to sb **II.** *vpr* **1.** (*se passer*) **se** ~ **une maladie/des nouvelles** to pass a disease/some news on to each other **2.** (*se communiquer*) **se** ~ (*secret, maladie*) to be passed on; (*métier*) to be taught

transmissible [tʀɑ̃smisibl] *adj* **1.** MED transmitted **2.** JUR transmissible

transmission [tʀɑ̃smisjɔ̃] *f* **1.** (*passation*) handing on; ~ **de l'autorité à qn** conferment of authority on sb **2.** (*diffusion*) *a.* INFOR ~ **d'une information à qn** passing on of information to sb; ~ **d'une lettre à qn** forwarding of a letter to sb; ~ **de données** data transmission; ~ **de pensée** thought transmission **3.** RADIO, TEL, TV broadcasting **4.** SPORT (*d'un ballon*) passing **5.** BIO, MED, TECH, AUTO transmission

transmutation [tʀɑ̃smytasjɔ̃] *f* PHYS, CHIM transmutation

transparaître [tʀɑ̃spaʀɛtʀ] *vi irr* (*forme, jour, idées, sentiment*) to show through

transparence [tʀɑ̃spaʀɑ̃s] *f* **1.** (*opp: opacité: du cristal, verre*) transparency; (*de l'air, de l'eau*) clearness **2.** (*absence de secret*) openness; (*d'une allusion*) transparency

transparent [tʀɑ̃spaʀɑ̃] *m* transparency; (*pour rétroprojecteur*) overhead

transparent(e) [tʀɑ̃spaʀɑ̃, ɑ̃t] *adj* **1.** (*opp: opaque*) transparent; (*air, eau*) clear; **papier ~** see-through paper **2.** (*sans secret*) open; (*affaire, négociation*) transparent **3.** (*limpide: regard, yeux*) limpid; (*personne*) open **4.** (*évident*) obvious; (*allusion*) transparent

transpercer [tʀɑ̃spɛʀse] <2> *vt* (*percer, passer au travers: regard, balle*) to pierce; **~ qc** (*pluie*) to soak through sth; (*froid*) to go through sth

transpiration [tʀɑ̃spiʀasjɔ̃] *f* **1.** (*processus*) perspiring **2.** (*sueur*) perspiration; (*soudaine*) sweat

transpirer [tʀɑ̃spiʀe] <1> *vi* **1.** (*suer*) to perspire **2.** *inf* (*se donner du mal*) **~ sur qc** to sweat over sth

transplantable [tʀɑ̃splɑ̃tabl] *adj* MED, AGR transplantable

transplantation [tʀɑ̃splɑ̃tasjɔ̃] *f* **1.** BIO, MED (*d'un organe*) transplant **2.** AGR transplantation **3.** (*déplacement: d'une population*) transplanting

transplanté(e) [tʀɑ̃splɑ̃te] *m(f)* **1.** MED transplant patient **2.** (*d'une autre région/ville*) *person who has been relocated*

transplanter [tʀɑ̃splɑ̃te] <1> **I.** *vt* **1.** BIO, MED, AGR to transplant **2.** (*déplacer: population*) to resettle **II.** *vpr* **se ~** to resettle

transport [tʀɑ̃spɔʀ] *m* **1.** (*acheminement*) transport; (*d'énergie*) carrying **2.** *pl* **les ~s** transport *Brit,* transportation *Am;* **~s aériens/routiers** air/road transport; **le ministre des ~s** the Minister of Transport ▸**entreprise de ~** haulage company *Brit,* trucking company *Am;* **moyens de ~** means of transport; **~s en commun** public transport *Brit,* public transportation *Am*

transportable [tʀɑ̃spɔʀtabl] *adj* (*marchandise*) transportable; (*blessé, malade*) fit to be moved

transporter [tʀɑ̃spɔʀte] <1> *vt* **1.** (*acheminer: voyageur, blessé, prisonnier*) to transport **2.** TECH (*énergie, son*) to carry **3.** (*transférer*) to bring; (*scène, action*) to shift

transporteur [tʀɑ̃spɔʀtœʀ] *m* **1.** TECH conveyor **2.** (*entreprise*) haulage company *Brit,* trucking company *Am*

transposable [tʀɑ̃spozabl] *adj* **1.** (*qui peut être transposé*) adaptable **2.** MUS transposable

transposer [tʀɑ̃spoze] <1> *vt* **1.** (*transférer*) to adapt **2.** MUS (*morceau*) to transpose

transposition [tʀɑ̃spozisjɔ̃] *f* **1.** (*transfert, dans une autre époque*) adaptation **2.** MUS transposition

transsexuel(le) [tʀɑ̃(s)sɛksɥɛl] *adj, m(f)* transsexual

transvaser [tʀɑ̃svɑze] <1> *vt* to decant

transversal(e) [tʀɑ̃svɛʀsal, o] <-aux> *adj* transversal; **rue ~e** road running across

transversale [tʀɑ̃svɛʀsal] *f* **1.** (*itinéraire*) cross-country route **2.** (*route*) side street

transversalement [tʀɑ̃svɛʀsalmɑ̃] *adv* across

trapèze [tʀapɛz] *m* **1.** MAT trapezium **2.** SPORT trapeze **3.** ANAT trapezius

trapéziste [tʀapezist] *mf* trapeze artist

trapézoïdal(e) [tʀapezɔidal, o] <-aux> *adj* trapezoid

trappe [tʀap] *f* **1.** (*ouverture*) hatch; (*dans le plancher*) *a.* THEAT trap door; **~ d'évacuation** exit door **2.** (*piège*) trap ▸**passer à la ~** to be shown the door

trappeur [tʀapœʀ] *m* trapper

trapu(e) [tʀapy] *adj* squat

traque [tʀak] *f* (*du gibier*) tracking; (*d'un malfaiteur*) tracking down; (*d'une vedette*) hounding

traquenard [tʀaknaʀ] *m* trap

traquer [tʀake] <1> *vt* (*abus, injustices*) to hunt down; (*voleur*) to track down; (*vedette*) to hound

traumatique [tʀomatik] *adj* traumatic

traumatisant(e) [tʀomatizɑ̃, ɑ̃t] *adj* traumatic

traumatiser [tʀomatize] <1> *vt* **1.** (*choquer*) to traumatize **2.** MED **~ qn** to cause sb trauma

traumatisme [tʀomatism] *m* trauma

traumatologie [tʀomatɔlɔʒi] *f* **1.** (*science*) traumatology **2.** (*service*) trauma unit

traumatologiste [tʀomatɔlɔʒist] *mf* trauma specialist; (*chirurgien*) emergency service specialist

travail [tʀavaj, o] <-aux> *m* **1.** (*activité*) work; **travaux dirigés** [*o* **pratiques**] ECOLE tutorial class; **un ~ d'amateur** piece of amateur workmanship; **~ de force/de fourmi** heavy/painstaking work; **~ d'équipe** team work **2.** (*tâche*) task **3.** (*activité professionnelle*) job; **~ (au) noir** undeclared work; **se mettre au ~** to get down to work; **~ à la chaîne** assembly-line work; **~ à plein temps/à temps partiel** full-time/part-time work; **travaux d'utilité collective** paid community work **4.** *pl* (*ensemble de tâches*) **les travaux domestiques/ménagers** housework; **travaux d'urbanisme** town planning **5.** ECON labour *Brit,* labor *Am* **6.** (*façonnage*) working; **~ de la pâte** working the dough **7.** (*fonctionnement*) working **8.** (*effet*) work; **~ de l'érosion/de la fermentation** process of erosion/fermentation **9.** PHYS work **10.** ADMIN **travaux publics** civil engineering; **ingénieur des travaux publics** civil engineer; **travaux!** work in progress! **11.** HIST **travaux forcés** hard labour *Brit,* hard labor *Am* ▸**mâcher le ~ à qn** to do all the hard work for sb; **se tuer au ~** to work oneself to death

travailler [tʀavaje] <1> **I.** *vi* **1.** (*accomplir sa tâche*) to work **2.** (*exercer un métier*) to work; **~ à son compte** to work for oneself **3.** (*s'exercer*) to practise; (*sportif*) to train **4.** (*viser un but*) **~ à un reportage/sur un projet** to work on a report/project; **~ à satisfaire les**

T

clients to work to satisfy the customers **5.** (*fonctionner: esprit, muscle*) to work; **faire ~ sa tête** (*l'utiliser*) to use one's head; (*réfléchir beaucoup*) to use one's mind **6.** (*subir des modifications*) to work; (*cidre, vin*) to ferment **II.** *vt* **1.** to work; (*pâte, terre*) to work; (*phrase, style*) to work on; **travaillé à la main** hand-made **2.** (*s'entraîner à*) to train; (*morceau de musique*) to practise *Brit*, practice *Am* **3.** (*tourmenter*) ~ **qn** to worry sb; (*douleur, fièvre*) to torment sb; (*problème, question*) to preoccupy sb **4.** (*opp: chômer*) **les jours travaillés** working days; **les jours non travaillés** holidays

travailleur, -euse [tʀavajœʀ, -jøz] **I.** *adj* hard-working **II.** *m, f* **1.** (*salarié*) worker; ~ **de force** labourer *Brit*, laborer *Am*; ~ **indépendant** self-employed worker **2.** (*personne laborieuse*) hard worker

travailliste [tʀavajist] **I.** *adj* POL **parti** ~ Labour Party **II.** *mf* **les ~s** Labour + *vb sing*

travée [tʀave] *f* **1.** (*d'une église, d'un théâtre, amphithéâtre*) row **2.** ARCHIT bay

travelling [tʀavliŋ] *m* CINE dolly

travelo [tʀavlo] *m inf* drag queen

travers [tʀavɛʀ] *m* (*petit défaut*) failing ▶ **à ~ champs** across fields; **prendre qc de ~** to take sth the wrong way; **regarder qn de ~** (*avec suspicion*) to look askance at sb; (*avec animosité*) to give sb a dirty look; **à ~ qc, au ~ de qc** (*en traversant*) across sth; (*par l'intermédiaire de*) through sth; **passer à ~ les mailles du filet** *inf* to slip through the net; **à ~ les siècles** down the centuries; **à ~ le monde** across the world; **de ~** (*en biais*) crooked; (*mal*) wrong; **en ~** across

traversable [tʀavɛʀsabl] *adj* crossable

traverse [tʀavɛʀs] *f* **1.** CHEMDFER sleeper *Brit*, tie *Am* **2.** TECH crosspiece; (*d'une fenêtre*) transom

traversée [tʀavɛʀse] *f* (*franchissement*) **la ~ d'une rue/d'un pont** crossing a road/bridge; **la ~ d'une région/d'une ville en voiture** driving through a region/town ▶ ~ **du désert** wilderness years *pl*

traverser [tʀavɛʀse] <1> *vt* **1.** (*franchir*) to cross; ~ **qc à pied** to walk across sth; ~ **qc en voiture** to drive across sth; ~ **qc à vélo** to ride across sth; ~ **qc à la nage** to swim across sth; **faire ~ qn** to help sb across **2.** (*se situer en travers de: route, fleuve, pont*) to cross **3.** (*transpercer*) to pierce; (*clou*) to go through **4.** (*subir*) to go through **5.** (*se manifester dans*) **cette idée lui traverse l'esprit** the idea crosses her mind **6.** (*fendre*) to slice through **7.** (*barrer*) **une balafre lui traversait le front** a scar ran across his forehead

traversier [tʀavɛʀsje] *m Québec* (*bac*) ferry

traversier, -ière [tʀavɛʀsje, -jɛʀ] *adj* running across; **flûte traversière** transverse flute

traversin [tʀavɛʀsɛ̃] *m* bolster

travesti [tʀavɛsti] *m* **1.** (*homosexuel*) transvestite **2.** (*rôle pour un homme*) trouser role; (*rôle pour une femme*) drag role; (*artiste*) drag artist

travesti(e) [tʀavɛsti] *adj* fancy dress

travestir [tʀavɛstiʀ] <8> *vt* **1.** (*falsifier*) to misrepresent; (*voix*) to disguise **2.** (*déguiser*) ~ **qn en fée** to dress sb up as a fairy

travestissement [tʀavɛstismɑ̃] *m* **1.** (*déformation*) misrepresentation; (*de la vérité, réalité*) travesty; (*de la voix*) disguising **2.** (*déguisement*) dressing up

traviole [tʀavjɔl] *inf* **mettre qc de ~** to put sth askew; **comprendre/faire qc de ~** to get/do sth all wrong; **regarder qn/qc de ~** to look askance at sb/sth

trayeuse [tʀɛjøz] *f* (*machine*) milking machine

trébuchant(e) [tʀebyʃɑ̃, ɑ̃t] *adj* **1.** (*chancelant*) tottering; (*ivrogne*) staggering **2.** (*hésitant: voix*) faltering; (*diction*) halting

trébucher [tʀebyʃe] <1> *vi* **1.** (*buter*) ~ **sur une pierre** to stumble over a stone **2.** (*être arrêté par*) **faire ~ qn** to trip sb up

trèfle [tʀɛfl] *m* **1.** BOT clover **2.** JEUX clubs *pl* **3.** (*figure*) shamrock **4.** ARCHIT trefoil

treillage [tʀɛjaʒ] *m* trellis; (*clôture*) lattice

treille [tʀɛj] *f* **1.** (*tonnelle*) vine arbour [*o* arbor *Am*] **2.** (*vigne*) climbing vine

treillis[1] [tʀɛji] *m* **1.** CONSTR lattice work **2.** (*clôture en bois*) lattice; (*en métal*) wire mesh; (*du garde-manger*) mesh **3.** (*grillage*) wire mesh

treillis[2] [tʀɛji] *m* MIL fatigues *pl*

treize [tʀɛz] **I.** *adj* thirteen **II.** *m inv* thirteen; *v. a.* **cinq**

treizième [tʀɛzjɛm] **I.** *adj antéposé* thirteenth **II.** *mf* **le/la ~** the thirteenth **III.** *m* (*fraction*) thirteenth; *v. a.* **cinquième**

tréma [tʀema] **I.** *m* dieresis **II.** *app* **e/i/u ~** e/i/u dieresis; **a/o/u ~** (*en allemand*) a/o/u umlaut

tremblant(e) [tʀɑ̃blɑ̃, ɑ̃t] *adj* trembling; (*lueur*) flickering

tremble [tʀɑ̃bl] *m* aspen

tremblement [tʀɑ̃bləmɑ̃] *m* **1.** (*frissonnement*) shiver; (*des jambes*) shaking; (*d'une lumière, flamme*) flickering; **~s de fièvre** feverish shivering + *vb sing*; ~ **de terre** earthquake **2.** (*vibration*) shaking; (*des feuilles*) trembling; **avec des ~ dans la voix** with a trembling voice

trembler [tʀɑ̃ble] <1> *vi* **1.** (*frissonner*) to shiver; (*flamme, lumière*) to flicker; ~ **de colère** to shake with rage **2.** (*vibrer*) to tremble; (*voix*) to quaver **3.** (*avoir peur*) to tremble; **faire ~ qn** to make sb tremble

tremblote [tʀɑ̃blɔt] *f* shivering; **avoir la ~** *inf* (*de peur, froid*) to have the shivers; (*de vieillesse*) to have the shakes

trembloter [tʀɑ̃blɔte] <1> *vi* (*de peur, froid*) to shiver a bit; (*de vieillesse*) to shake a bit

trémousser [tʀemuse] <1> *vpr* **se ~** (*dan-*

seur) to wiggle; (*enfant*) to wriggle

trempe [tʀɑ̃p] *f* **1.** (*fermeté*) stature **2.** *inf* (*correction*) hiding **3.** TECH (*de l'acier, du verre*) quenching

trempé(e) [tʀɑ̃pe] *adj* **1.** (*mouillé*) soaked; ~ **de sueur** dripping with sweat **2.** TECH (*acier, verre*) tempered ▸**bien** ~ sturdy

tremper [tʀɑ̃pe] <1> **I.** *vt* **1.** (*mouiller*) to soak; (*sol*) to wet **2.** (*humecter: grains, semence*) to soak **3.** (*plonger*) ~ **sa plume dans l'encre** to dip one's pen in the ink; ~ **son croissant dans son café au lait** to dunk one's croissant in one's coffee **4.** TECH (*acier*) to temper **II.** *vi* **1.** (*rester immergé*) **laisser** ~ **des légumes secs** to soak pulses **2.** (*participer à*) ~ **dans qc** to be involved in sth

trempette [tʀɑ̃pɛt] *f inf* dip; **faire** ~ **dans le lac** to have a dip in the lake

tremplin [tʀɑ̃plɛ̃] *m* **1.** SPORT diving-board; (*au ski*) ski-jump **2.** (*aide, soutien*) springboard

trentaine [tʀɑ̃tɛn] *f* **1.** (*environ trente*) **une** ~ **de personnes/pages** about thirty people/pages **2.** (*âge approximatif*) **avoir la** ~ to be about thirty years old; **approcher de la** ~ to be nearly thirty years old

trente [tʀɑ̃t] **I.** *adj* thirty **II.** *m inv* thirty; *v. a.* **cinq, cinquante**

trentenaire [tʀɑ̃tnɛʀ] *adj* thirty-year-old; **prescription** ~ thirty-year statute of limitations

trente-six [tʀɑ̃tsis] **I.** *adj* **1.** (*chiffre*) thirty-six; *v. a.* **cinq** **2.** *inf* (*une grande quantité*) loads ▸**voir** ~ **chandelles** to see stars **II.** *m inf* **tous les** ~ **du mois** once in a blue moon

trentième [tʀɑ̃tjɛm] **I.** *adj antéposé* thirtieth **II.** *mf* **le/la** ~ the thirtieth **III.** *m* (*fraction*) thirtieth; *v. a.* **cinquième**

trépidant(e) [tʀepidɑ̃, ɑ̃t] *adj* **1.** (*saccadé*) frenetic **2.** (*fébrile*) throbbing

trépidation [tʀepidasjɔ̃] *f* **1.** (*mouvement*) vibration **2.** (*fébrilité*) bustle

trépider [tʀepide] <1> *vi* to vibrate

trépied [tʀepje] *m* **1.** (*siège*) (three-legged) stool **2.** (*support*) trivet; (*d'un appareil photo*) tripod

trépignement [tʀepiɲmɑ̃] *m* stamping of feet

trépigner [tʀepiɲe] <1> *vi* ~ **d'impatience** to stamp one's feet with impatience

très [tʀɛ] *adv* very; (*nécessaire*) extremely; **avoir** ~ **faim/peur** to be very hungry/frightened; **faire** ~ **attention** to be very careful

trésor [tʀezɔʀ] *m* **1.** (*richesse enfouie*) treasure **2.** *pl* (*richesses*) treasures **3.** (*source précieuse*) **dépenser des** ~**s d'ingéniosité** to expend boundless ingenuity **4.** ADMIN, FIN **Trésor (public)** (*moyens financiers*) Treasury; (*bureau*) Treasury Department

trésorerie [tʀezɔʀʀi] *f* **1.** (*budget*) finances **2.** (*gestion: d'une entreprise*) accounts; (*budget*) budget **3.** ADMIN, FIN accounts; (*bureau*) accounts department; (*gestion du budget de l'État*) public revenue office

trésorier, -ière [tʀezɔʀje, -jɛʀ] *m, f* treasurer

tressaillement [tʀesajmɑ̃] *m* start; (*du corps*) shiver; **elle eut un** ~ **de joie** she quivered with joy

tressaillir [tʀesajiʀ] *vi irr* to quiver; (*maison*) to shake; (*cœur*) to flutter

tressauter [tʀesote] <1> *vi* **1.** (*être secoué: personne*) to be jolted; (*dans un véhicule*) to be tossed about **2.** (*sursauter*) to jump; (*dans son sommeil, ses pensées*) to start

tresse [tʀɛs] *f* plait *Brit,* braid *Am*

tresser [tʀese] <1> *vt* to plait *Brit,* to braid *Am*

tréteau [tʀeto] <x> *m* **1.** (*support*) trestle **2.** THEAT **les** ~**x** the boards

treuil [tʀœj] *m* winch

trêve [tʀɛv] *f* **1.** (*répit*) respite **2.** (*arrêt des hostilités*) truce ▸**mettre une** ~ **à qc** to call a halt to sth; ~ **de plaisanteries!** seriously now!

tri [tʀi] *m* **1.** (*choix*) sorting; ~ **des déchets** waste sorting; **faire le** ~ **de qc** to sort sth **2.** (*à la poste*) sorting **3.** INFOR **effectuer un** ~ **croissant/décroissant** to sort by increasing/decreasing order

triade [tʀijad] *f* triad

triage [tʀijaʒ] *m* CHEMDFER marshalling; **gare de** ~ marshalling yard

trial [tʀijal] *m* **1.** (*moto*) trial bike **2.** (*course*) scramble

triangle [tʀijɑ̃gl] *m* **1.** MAT, MUS triangle **2.** AUTO ~ **de présignalisation** warning triangle

triangulaire [tʀijɑ̃gylɛʀ] **I.** *adj* **1.** (*à trois côtés*) triangular **2.** (*à trois: accord, débat*) three-sided **II.** *f* POL three-cornered contest

triathlonien(ne) [tʀi(j)atlɔnjɛ̃, jɛn] *m(f)* triathlete

tribal(e) [tʀibal, o] <-aux> *adj* tribal

tribord [tʀibɔʀ] *m* starboard

tribu [tʀiby] *f* **1.** SOCIOL tribe **2.** *iron* (*grande famille*) clan

tribulations [tʀibylasjɔ̃] *fpl* tribulations; **il n'est pas au bout de ses** ~ his troubles aren't over yet

tribunal [tʀibynal, o] <-aux> *m* **1.** (*juridiction*) court; ~ **administratif** *court dealing with internal affairs in the French civil service;* ~ **correctionnel** magistrates' court; ~ **de commerce** commercial court; ~ **fédéral** *Suisse* (*cour suprême de la Suisse*) supreme court; ~ **de grande instance** ≈ Crown court; ~ **de police** police court; ~ **d'instance** magistrates' court; ~ **pour enfants** juvenile court **2.** (*bâtiment*) court building *Brit,* courthouse *Am* **3.** REL ~ **suprême** judgement of God

tribune [tʀibyn] *f* **1.** (*estrade*) platform; POL rostrum **2.** (*galerie surélevée*) gallery; SPORT (*d'un champ de courses, stade*) (grand)stand **3.** (*lieu d'expression*) forum; (*dans un journal*) opinion page ▸**monter à la** ~ to stand up to speak

tribut [tRiby] *m* **1.** HIST tribute **2.** (*sacrifice*) price; **le ~ payé à la route est très lourd** the roads take a heavy toll

tributaire [tRibytɛR] *adj* tributary

tricentenaire [tRisɑ̃tnɛR] **I.** *adj* three-hundred-year-old **II.** *m* (*d'une personne, d'un événement*) tercentenary

triche [tRiʃ] *f inf* cheating; **c'est** [*o* **y a**] **de la ~** that's cheating

tricher [tRiʃe] <1> *vi* **1.** (*frauder*) to cheat; **~ aux cartes/à l'examen** to cheat at cards/in an exam **2.** (*tromper*) **~ sur le prix** to overcharge

tricherie [tRiʃRi] *f* cheating

tricheur, **-euse** [tRiʃœR, -øz] **I.** *adj* **être ~** to be a cheat **II.** *m, f* swindler; (*au jeu, à l'examen*) cheat; (*aux cartes*) card sharp

tricolore [tRikɔlɔR] **I.** *adj* **1.** (*bleu, blanc, rouge*) red, white and blue **2.** (*français: succès*) French **3.** (*de trois couleurs*) three-coloured *Brit,* three-colored *Am* **II.** *mpl* SPORT **les ~s** the French team

tricot [tRiko] *m* **1.** (*vêtement*) sweater; (*gilet tricoté*) cardigan; **~ de corps** vest *Brit,* undershirt *Am* **2.** TECH (*étoffe*) knitwear **3.** (*action*) knitting

tricoter [tRikɔte] <1> **I.** *vt* to knit; **tricoté à la main/à la machine** hand-/machine-knitted **II.** *vi* (*faire du tricot*) to knit; **aiguille à ~** knitting needle ▸**~ des jambes** *inf* to run like mad

tricycle [tRisikl] *m* tricycle

trident [tRidɑ̃] *m* **1.** (*à la pêche*) fish-spear **2.** AGR three-pronged fork **3.** HIST trident

triennal(**e**) [tRijenal, o] <-aux> *adj* **1.** (*qui dure trois ans*) three-year-long **2.** (*qui a lieu tous les trois ans*) three-yearly

trier [tRije] <1> *vt* to sort; (*choisir*) to select

trieur, **-euse** [tRijœR, -jøz] *m* **1.** MIN grader **2.** AGR sorter

trigo *inf,* **trigonométrie** [tRigɔnɔmetRi] *f* trigonometry

trigonométrique [tRigɔnɔmetRik] *adj* trigonometric(al)

trilatéral(**e**) [tRilateRal, o] <-aux> *adj* ECON, POL trilateral

trilingue [tRilɛ̃g] **I.** *adj* trilingual **II.** *mf* trilingual person

trille [tRij] *m* trill

trimaran [tRimaRɑ̃] *m* trimaran

trimbal(**l**)**er** [tRɛ̃bale] <1> **I.** *vt inf* **~ qc** to cart sth around **II.** *vpr inf* **se ~ dans les rues** to wander the streets

trimer [tRime] <1> *vi* to slave away

trimestre [tRimɛstR] *m* **1.** (*période de trois mois*) quarter; ECOLE term **2.** (*somme*) quarter

trimestriel(**le**) [tRimɛstRijɛl] *adj* (*paiement, publication*) quarterly

trimestriellement [tRimɛstRijɛlmɑ̃] *adv* on a quarterly basis

tringle [tRɛ̃gl] *f* rod

trinidadien(**ne**) [tRinidadjɛ̃, ɛn] *adj* Trinidadian

Trinidadien(**ne**) [tRinidadjɛ̃, ɛn] *m(f)* Trinidadian

Trinité [tRinite] *f* **1.** REL Trinity; **la Sainte ~** the Holy Trinity **2.** GEO (**l'île de**) **la ~** Trinidad

Trinité-et-Tobago [tRiniteetɔbago] Trinidad and Tobago

trinquer [tRɛ̃ke] <1> *vi* **~ à la santé de qn** to drink to sb's health

trio [tRijo] *m a.* MUS trio

triomphal(**e**) [tRijɔ̃fal, o] <-aux> *adj* triumphal; (*accueil*) triumphant

triomphalement [tRijɔ̃falmɑ̃] *adv* triumphantly

triomphalisme [tRijɔ̃falism] *m* triumphalism; (*après un succès*) overconfidence

triomphant(**e**) [tRijɔ̃fɑ̃, ɑ̃t] *adj* triumphant

triomphateur, **-trice** [tRijɔ̃fatœR, -tRis] **I.** *adj* (*air, nation, parti*) triumphant **II.** *m, f* triumphant victor

triomphe [tRijɔ̃f] *m* triumph

triompher [tRijɔ̃fe] <1> *vi* **1.** (*remporter une victoire, faire un triomphe: personne, vérité, doctrine, mode*) to triumph **2.** (*crier victoire*) to rejoice

tripartite [tRipaRtit] *adj* tripartite; **gouvernement ~** three-party government

tripatouillage [tRipatujaʒ] *m inf* messing aroung; (*économique, électorale*) fiddling

tripe [tRip] *f* **1.** *pl* GASTR tripe **2.** *pl, inf* (*boyau, ventre de l'homme*) guts ▸**prendre qn aux ~s** *inf* (*nouvelle, accident*) to get sb right there; (*misère, violence*) to have a profound impact on sb; **faire qc avec ses ~s** *inf* (*avec enthousiasme*) to put everything one's got into sth; (*intuitivement*) to do sth from the heart

triphasé [tRifɑze] *m* three-phase current

triphasé(**e**) [tRifɑze] *adj* three-phase

triple [tRipl] **I.** *adj* triple **II.** *m* **le ~ du prix** three times the price; **le ~ de temps** three times as long

triplé [tRiple] *m* SPORT treble *Brit;* (*trois victoires de suite*) triple success

triplement [tRipləmɑ̃] **I.** *adv* **1.** (*trois fois*) three times over **2.** (*tout à fait*) trebly; (*vrai*) in three ways **II.** *m* **1.** (*multiplication*) tripling **2.** (*agrandissement*) threefold increase; (*d'une autoroute, voie*) trebling

tripler [tRiple] <1> **I.** *vt* **1.** (*multiplier par trois*) to triple **2.** (*agrandir de trois éléments: autoroute*) to treble **II.** *vi* to triple

triplés, **-ées** [tRiple] *mpl, fpl* triplets

triporteur [tRipɔRtœR] *m* delivery tricycle

tripoter [tRipɔte] <1> **I.** *vt* **1.** (*triturer: fruits*) to finger; **~ des crayons/des pièces** to fiddle with pencils/coins; **~ une radio** to play with a radio **2.** (*toucher avec insistance*) **~ qc** to fiddle with sth **II.** *vi* **1.** (*fouiller*) **~ dans un tiroir** to rummage about in a drawer **2.** (*trafiquer*) to be involved in funny business **III.** *vpr* **1.** (*se caresser*) **se ~** to play with oneself **2.** (*triturer*) **se ~ la barbe en parlant** to fiddle with one's beard while speaking

trique [tRik] *f* (*gourdin*) cudgel ▸**être sec**

comme un coup de ~ to be as skinny as a rake

trisomie [tʀizɔmi] *f* Down's syndrome

triste [tʀist] *adj* **1.** *a. antéposé* (*affligé, affligeant*) sad; **avoir l'air** ~ to look sad; **avoir** ~ **mine** to be a sorry sight **2.** *a. antéposé* gloomy **3.** *antéposé, péj* (*déplorable: époque, mémoire*) dreadful; (*affaire*) sorry; (*résultats*) awful ▸**ne pas être** ~ *inf* (*personne*) to be a laugh a minute; (*soirée, voyage*) to be eventful

tristement [tʀistəmɑ̃] *adv* **1.** (*d'un air triste: regarder*) sorrowfully; (*parler, raconter*) sadly **2.** (*de façon lugubre*) gloomily **3.** (*cruellement*) cruelly

tristesse [tʀistɛs] *f* **1.** (*état de mélancolie*) sadness **2.** (*chagrin*) sorrow

tristounet(te) [tʀistunɛ, ɛt] *adj inf* sad; (*temps*) dreary

trithérapie [tʀiteʀapi] *f* MED triple therapy

triton [tʀitɔ̃] *m* ZOOL newt

trituration [tʀityʀasjɔ̃] *f* **1.** (*mastication*) grinding up **2.** TECH (*broyage*) crushing; (*pilage*) pounding; (*malaxage*) kneading

triturer [tʀityʀe] <1> *vt* **1.** (*broyer*) to crush; (*aliments, médicament, sel*) to grind (up) **2.** (*tripoter: mouchoir*) to twist; ~ **son crayon/sa veste** to fiddle with one's pencil/jacket

trivial(e) [tʀivjal, jo] <-aux> *adj* **1.** (*vulgaire*) crude **2.** (*ordinaire*) mundane **3.** (*évident*) trite

trivialement [tʀivjalmɑ̃] *adv* crudely

trivialité [tʀivjalite] *f* **1.** (*vulgarité*) crudeness **2.** (*banalité*) mundaneness

troc [tʀɔk] *m* **1.** (*échange*) swap **2.** (*système économique*) **le** ~ barter

troène [tʀɔɛn] *m* privet

troglodyte [tʀɔglɔdit] **I.** *adj v.* **troglodytique II.** *m* **1.** (*habitant d'une grotte*) cave dweller, troglodyte **2.** (*oiseau*) wren

troglodytique [tʀɔglɔditik] *adj* **habitations ~s** cave dwellings

trogne [tʀɔɲ] *f inf* mug

trognon [tʀɔɲɔ̃] *m* core; (*de chou*) stalk

troïka [tʀɔika] *f* troïka

trois [tʀwɑ] **I.** *adj* three ▸**en** ~ **mots** in a word **II.** *m inv* three; *v. a.* **cinq**

trois-étoiles [tʀwɑzetwal] **I.** *adj inv* three-star **II.** *m inv* **1.** (*hôtel*) three-star hotel **2.** (*restaurant*) three-star restaurant **trois-huit** [tʀwɑɥit] *mpl inv* **faire les** ~ to operate three eight-hour shifts

troisième [tʀwɑzjɛm] **I.** *adj antéposé* third; **le** ~ **âge** (*période de vie*) retirement years *pl;* (*personnes âgées*) senior citizens *pl;* **le** ~ **cycle** postgraduate courses *Brit,* graduate school *Am* **II.** *mf* **le/la** ~ the third **III.** *f* ECOLE year ten *Brit,* eighth grade *Am; v. a.* **cinquième**

troisièmement [tʀwɑzjɛmmɑ̃] *adv* thirdly

trois-mâts [tʀwɑmɑ] *m inv* three-master

trois-pièces [tʀwɑpjɛs] *m inv* **1.** (*appartement*) three-room flat *Brit,* three-room apartment *Am* **2.** COUT **costume** ~ three-piece suit

trolleybus [tʀɔlɛbys] *m* trolley bus

trombe [tʀɔ̃b] *f* **1.** (*forte averse*) cloudburst **2.** METEO whirlwind ▸**en** ~ *inf* at top speed; **passer en** ~ to race by

trombone [tʀɔ̃bɔn] **I.** *m* **1.** MUS trombone **2.** (*attache*) paper clip **II.** *mf* trombonist

trompe [tʀɔ̃p] *f* **1.** MUS trumpet **2.** AUTO horn **3.** HIST squinch **4.** ZOOL snout; (*d'un insecte*) proboscis **5.** *souvent pl* ANAT tube **6.** TECH ~ **à eau/à mercure** water/mercury pump

trompe-l'œil [tʀɔ̃plœj] *m inv* ART trompe-l'œil

tromper [tʀɔ̃pe] <1> **I.** *vt* **1.** (*duper*) to trick; ~ **qn sur le prix** to overcharge sb **2.** (*être infidèle à*) ~ **qn avec qn** to cheat on sb with sb **3.** (*déjouer*) ~ **qc** to escape from sth **4.** (*décevoir*) ~ **l'attente/l'espoir de qn** to disappoint sb's expectations/hopes **5.** (*faire oublier*) ~ **qc** to keep sth at bay; (*faim, soif*) to stave off sth **II.** *vi* to deceive **III.** *vpr* **1.** (*faire erreur*) **se** ~ to make a mistake; **se** ~ **dans son calcul** to get one's calculations wrong **2.** (*confondre*) **se** ~ **de direction** to take the wrong direction; **se** ~ **de numéro** to get the wrong number ▸**c'est à s'y** ~ you'd hardly know the difference

tromperie [tʀɔ̃pʀi] *f* deception

trompette [tʀɔ̃pɛt] **I.** *f* MUS trumpet ▸**nez en** ~ turned-up nose **II.** *m* **1.** MUS trumpet player **2.** MIL bugler

trompettiste [tʀɔ̃petist] *mf* trumpet player

trompeur, **-euse** [tʀɔ̃pœʀ, -øz] *adj* (*promesse*) empty; (*distance, résultats*) deceptive; (*ressemblance*) illusory; (*personne*) deceitful; (*discours*) misleading

trompeusement [tʀɔ̃pøzmɑ̃] *adv* deceitfully

tronc [tʀɔ̃] *m* **1.** BOT, ANAT trunk **2.** ARCHIT (*d'une colonne*) shaft **3.** ECOLE ~ **commun** (*cycle commun*) common-core syllabus; (*partie de programme commune*) UNIV compulsory module

troncation [tʀɔ̃kasjɔ̃] *f* (*mot tronqué*) truncated word

tronche [tʀɔ̃ʃ] *f inf* head; (*visage*) face; **avoir une sale** ~ to have an ugly mug

tronçon [tʀɔ̃sɔ̃] *m* **1.** (*partie*) section; (*d'une voie ferrée, route, autoroute*) stretch **2.** (*morceau coupé*) segment; (*d'une colonne*) section

tronçonner [tʀɔ̃sɔne] <1> *vt* **1.** (*diviser en tronçons*) to divide up **2.** (*découper*) to cut up **3.** (*scier*) to saw up

tronçonneuse [tʀɔ̃sɔnøz] *f* chain saw

trône [tʀon] *m* throne

trôner [tʀone] <1> *vi* to sit enthroned; (*tableau*) to have pride of place

tronquer [tʀɔ̃ke] <1> *vt* (*détail*) to cut out; (*conclusion*) to shorten; (*texte, citation*) to abridge; (*données*) to cut down

trop [tʀo] *adv* **1.** (*de façon excessive*) too; (*manger, faire*) too much **2.** (*en quantité excessive*) ~ **de temps/travail** too much time/work **3.** (*pas tellement*) **ne pas** ~ **aimer**

qc not to like sth much; **ne pas ~ savoir** not to be too sure; **je n'ai pas ~ envie** I don't really feel like it ►**c'est ~!** it's too much
trophée [tʀɔfe] *m* trophy
tropical(e) [tʀɔpikal, o] <-aux> *adj* tropical
tropique [tʀɔpik] *m* **1.** GEO tropic **2.** (*région tropicale*) **les ~s** the tropics
Tropique [tʀɔpik] *m* **~ du Cancer/du Capricorne** Tropic of Cancer/of Capricorn
trop-perçu [tʀopɛʀsy] <trop-perçus> *m* **1.** ADMIN overpayment **2.** COM excess payment
trop-plein [tʀoplɛ̃] <trop-pleins> *m* **1.** TECH (*tuyau d'évacuation*) overflow **2.** (*surplus*) surplus **3.** (*excès*) **un ~ d'amour/d'énergie** overflowing love/boundless energy
troquer [tʀɔke] <1> *vt* to swap
trot [tʀo] *m* **1.** (*allure*) trot **2.** (*discipline*) **course de ~ attelé** trotting race
trotte [tʀɔt] *f inf* quite a way
trotter [tʀɔte] <1> *vi* **1.** *inf* (*aller à petits pas: animal*) to scamper; (*personne*) to scurry **2.** (*aller au trot: cheval*) to trot
trotteur, -euse [tʀɔtœʀ, -øz] *m, f* (*cheval*) trotter
trotteuse [tʀɔtøz] *f* (sweep) second hand
trottiner [tʀɔtine] <1> *vi* to jog along; (*enfant*) to toddle about
trottinette [tʀɔtinɛt] *f* toy scooter
trottoir [tʀɔtwaʀ] *m* pavement *Brit,* sidewalk *Am*
trou [tʀu] *m* **1.** (*cavité*) hole; (*d'une aiguille*) eye; **~ de la serrure** keyhole **2.** (*moment de libre*) gap **3.** (*déficit*) gap; **~ (dans la couche) d'ozone** hole in the ozone layer **4.** (*vide: d'un témoignage, d'une œuvre*) gap; **~ de mémoire** memory lapse
troubadour [tʀubaduʀ] *m* troubadour
troublant(e) [tʀublɑ̃, ɑ̃t] *adj* **1.** (*déconcertant*) disconcerting; (*élément*) troubling **2.** (*inquiétant: événement, fait*) perturbing **3.** (*étrange: événement, mystère*) unsettling **4.** (*qui inspire le désir*) arousing
trouble[1] [tʀubl] **I.** *adj* **1.** (*opp: limpide: image, vue*) blurred; (*liquide*) cloudy; (*lumière*) dull **2.** (*équivoque: période*) dismal **II.** *adv* **voir ~** to have blurred vision
trouble[2] [tʀubl] *m* **1.** *pl* MED disorder; (*psychiques, mentaux*) distress *no pl* **2.** *pl* (*désordre: politiques, sociaux*) unrest **3.** (*désarroi*) confusion **4.** (*agitation*) turmoil
trouble-fête [tʀubləfɛt] <trouble-fêtes> *mf* spoilsport
troubler [tʀuble] <1> **I.** *vt* **1.** (*gêner fortement*) to disrupt **2.** (*perturber*) to bother **3.** (*déranger*) to disturb **4.** (*émouvoir*) to unsettle; (*sexuellement*) to arouse **5.** MED (*digestion, facultés mentales*) to disturb **6.** (*altérer la clarté: atmosphère, ciel*) to cloud; **~ l'eau** to make the water cloudy **II.** *vpr* **se ~** (*devenir trouble*) to become cloudy; (*mémoire*) to become blurred
troué(e) [tʀue] *adj* **chaussettes ~es** socks with holes in
trouée [tʀue] *f* (*ouverture*) gap; (*d'une forêt*) clearing
trouer [tʀue] <1> *vt* **~ qc 1.** (*faire un trou*) to make a hole in sth **2.** (*faire plusieurs trous*) to make holes in sth **3.** (*traverser: rayon de lumière*) to break through sth
troufion [tʀufjɔ̃] *m inf* soldier
trouillard(e) [tʀujaʀ, jaʀd] **I.** *adj inf* yellow **II.** *m(f) inf* coward
trouille [tʀuj] *f inf* **ficher** [*o* **flanquer**] **la ~ à qn** to scare the hell out of sb
troupe [tʀup] *f* **1.** MIL troop **2.** THEAT troupe
troupeau [tʀupo] <x> *m* herd
trousse [tʀus] *f* (*étui à compartiments*) case; **~ à outils** toolkit; **~ d'écolier** pencil case; **~ de toilette** [*o* **voyage**] toilet bag ►**avoir qn à ses ~s** to have sb hot on one's heels; **être aux ~s de qn** to be hot on sb's heels
trousseau [tʀuso] <x> *m* **1.** (*clés*) bunch of keys **2.** (*vêtements*) clothes *pl;* (*d'une mariée*) trousseau
trouvaille [tʀuvɑj] *f* find
trouvé(e) [tʀuve] *adj* **objets ~s** lost property *no pl;* **excuse toute ~e** ready-made excuse
trouver [tʀuve] <1> **I.** *vt* **1.** (*découvrir, avoir le sentiment*) to find; **~ étrange qu'elle ait fait qc** (*subj*) to find it strange that she did sth **2.** (*voir*) **~ du plaisir à faire qc** to take pleasure in doing sth; **aller/venir ~ qn** to go/come and find sb **II.** *vpr* **1.** (*être situé*) **se ~** to be **2.** (*être*) **se ~ bloqué/coincé** to find oneself stuck; **se ~ dans l'obligation de partir** to be compelled to leave **3.** (*se sentir*) **se ~ bien/mal** to feel good/uncomfortable **4.** (*exprime la coïncidence*) **ils se trouvent être nés le même jour** they turned out to have been born on the same day **5.** (*se rencontrer*) **un bon job se trouve toujours** one can always find a good job **III.** *vpr impers* **1.** (*par hasard*) **il se trouve que je suis libre** it so happens I'm free **2.** (*on trouve, il y a*) **il se trouve toujours un pour faire qc** there's always one who'll do sth ►**si ça se trouve, il va pleuvoir** *inf* it may well rain
trouvère [tʀuvɛʀ] *m* (*troubadour*) trouvère (*wandering medieval poet in northern France*)
truand [tʀyɑ̃] *m* crook
truander [tʀyɑ̃de] <1> *vt inf* to swindle
truc [tʀyk] *m* **1.** *inf* (*chose*) thingummyjig **2.** *inf* (*personne*) what's-his-name, what's-her-name *m, f;* **c'est Truc, tu sais** it's you know, what's-his-name, it's you know, what's-her-name *m, f* **3.** *inf* (*combine*) trick **4.** (*tour*) trick ►**c'est mon ~** *inf* it's my thing
trucage [tʀykaʒ] *m* **1.** (*falsification: de statistiques, de la réalité*) doctoring; (*des élections*) fixing **2.** CINE, PHOT effect
trucider [tʀyside] <1> *vt inf* **~ qn** to knock sb off
truculence [tʀykylɑ̃s] *f* raciness
truculent(e) [tʀykylɑ̃, ɑ̃t] *adj* racy
truelle [tʀyɛl] *f* trowel

truffe [tRyf] *f* **1.** BOT, GASTR truffle **2.** (*museau*) nose
truffé(e) [tRyfe] *adj* **1.** (*garni de truffes*) truffled **2.** *fig* **être ~ de qc** to be crammed with sth
truffer [tRyfe] <1> *vt* **1.** GASTR ~ **qc** to garnish sth with truffles **2.** *fig* ~ **un texte de citations** to pepper a text with quotations
truie [tRɥi] *f* sow
truite [tRɥit] *f* trout
truquage [tRykaʒ] *m v.* **trucage**
truquer [tRyke] <1> *vt* to fix; (*comptes*) to fiddle
trust [tRœst] *m* ECON trust
tsar [tsaR] *m* tsar, czar
tsarine [tsaRin] *f* tsarina, czarina
tsariste [tsaRist] *adj* tsarist, czarist
tsé-tsé [tsetse] *adj inv v.* **mouche**
TSF [teɛsɛf] *f abr de* **télégraphie sans fil** wireless telegraphy
t-shirt [tiʃœRt] *m abr de* **tee-shirt**
tsigane [tsigan] **I.** *adj* **musique** ~ Hungarian gypsy music **II.** *mf* Hungarian gypsy
tsvp *abr de* **tournez s'il vous plaît** PTO
TTC [tetese] *abr de* **toutes taxes comprises** inc.
tu [ty] <*devant voyelle ou h muet* t'> **I.** *pron pers* you **II.** *m* **dire ~ à qn** to use "tu" with sb
tu(e) [ty] *part passé de* **taire**
tuba [tyba] *m* **1.** MUS tuba **2.** SPORT snorkel
tube[1] [tyb] *m* **1.** (*tuyau, emballage à presser*) *a.* ELEC tube; ~ **à essai** test tube **2.** ANAT ~ **digestif** digestive tract
tube[2] [tyb] *m inf* (*chanson*) hit
tubercule [tybɛRkyl] *m* BOT tubercle
tuberculeux, -euse [tybɛRkylø, -øz] **I.** *adj* (*personne*) tuberculous **II.** *m, f* MED tuberculosis patient
tuberculose [tybɛRkyloz] *f* tuberculosis
tubéreux, -euse [tybeRø, -øz] *adj* BOT tuberous
tubulaire [tybylɛR] *adj* (*lampe*) tubular
tubulure [tybylyR] *f* **1.** (*ensemble de tubes*) piping **2.** (*conduit*) pipe **3.** TECH ~ **d'alimentation** supply pipe
TUC [tyk] *m abr de* **travail d'utilité collective** paid community work
tucard(e) [tykaR, kaRd] *m(f)* paid community worker
tuciste [tysist] *m, f v.* **tucard**
tué(e) [tɥe] *m(f)* **il y a eu deux blessés et un ~** there were two people injured and one person killed
tue-mouche(s) [tymuʃ] **I.** *adj inv* **papier ~** fly-paper **II.** *m* fly agaric
tuer [tɥe] <1> **I.** *vt* **1.** (*donner la mort à*) to kill; (*gibier*) to shoot; **se faire ~** to get killed **2.** (*nuire à: espoir, environnement*) to ruin; (*initiative*) to kill off **II.** *vi* to kill **III.** *vpr* **1.** (*être victime d'un accident*) **se ~** to get killed **2.** (*se donner la mort*) **se ~** to kill oneself **3.** (*se fatiguer*) **se ~ à faire qc** to wear oneself out doing sth
tuerie [tyRi] *f* slaughter
tue-tête [tytɛt] *adv* **à ~** at the top of one's voice
tueur, -euse [tɥœR, -øz] *m, f* killer
tuf [tyf] *m* tuff
tuile [tɥil] *f* **1.** (*petite plaque: d'un toit*) tile **2.** *inf* (*événement fâcheux*) stroke of bad luck **3.** GASTR *thin biscuit* (*cookie*)
tuilerie [tɥilRi] *f* tilery
tulipe [tylip] *f* tulip
tulle [tyl] *m* tulle
tuméfié(e) [tymefje] *adj* swollen
tumeur [tymœR] *f* tumour *Brit,* tumor *Am*
tumulte [tymylt] *m* (*d'une foule*) commotion; (*des flots, d'un orage*) tumult; (*des passions*) turmoil; (*de la rue, de la ville*) (*agitation*) hustle and bustle; (*bruit*) hubbub
tumultueux, -euse [tymyltɥø, -øz] *adj* **1.** (*agité: passion*) tumultuous; (*période, vie*) stormy; (*discussion*) agitated; (*flots*) turbulent **2.** (*bruyant*) loud
tuner [tynœR] *m* tuner
tungstène [tœ̃kstɛn] *m* CHIM tungsten
tunique [tynik] *f* **1.** (*vêtement ample*) smock **2.** MIL tunic
Tunisie [tynizi] *f* **la ~** Tunisia
tunisien(ne) [tynizjɛ̃, jɛn] *adj* Tunisian
Tunisien(ne) [tynizjɛ̃, jɛn] *m(f)* Tunisian
tunnel [tynɛl] *m* **1.** (*galerie*) tunnel **2.** (*période difficile*) **le bout du ~** the end of the tunnel
tuque [tyk] *f Québec* (*bonnet de laine à bords roulés en forme de cône surmonté d'un gland ou d'un pompon*) tuque (*woollen hat*)
turban [tyRbɑ̃] *m* turban
turbine [tyRbin] *f* turbine
turbo[1] [tyRbo] *adj inv* turbo
turbo[2], **turbocompresseur** [tyRbokɔ̃pResœR] *m* turbocharger
turboréacteur [tyRboReaktœR] *m* turbojet
turbot [tyRbo] *m* turbot
turbotrain [tyRbotRɛ̃] *m* turbotrain
turbulence [tyRbylɑ̃s] *f* **1.** (*agitation*) *a.* PHYS, METEO turbulence **2.** (*caractère*) boisterousness
turbulent(e) [tyRbylɑ̃, ɑ̃t] *adj* **1.** (*agité*) turbulent **2.** (*rebelle*) rebellious
turc [tyRk] *m* Turkish; *v. a.* **français**
turc(que) [tyRk] *adj* Turkish
Turc(que) [tyRk] *m(f)* Turk
turf [tœRf, tyRf] *m* racecourse
turfiste [tœRfist, tyRfist] *mf* racing fan, racegoer
turlupiner [tyRlypine] <1> *vt inf* to bother
turpitude [tyRpityd] *f gén pl* depravity *no pl*
turque [tyRk] **W.-C. à la ~** stand-up toilet; *v. a.* **turc**
Turquie [tyRki] *f* **la ~** Turkey
turquoise [tyRkwaz] **I.** *f* (*pierre*) turquoise **II.** *m* (*couleur*) turquoise **III.** *adj inv* turquoise
tus [ty] *passé simple de* **taire**
tutélaire [tytelɛR] *adj* JUR tutelary

T

tutelle [tytɛl] *f* **1.** (*protection abusive*) tutelage **2.** JUR (*d'un mineur, aliéné*) guardianship **3.** ADMIN, POL protection; **en** [*o* **sous**] ~ under protection ►**prendre qn sous sa** ~ JUR to become the guardian of sb; (*protéger*) to take sb under one's wing
tuteur [tytœʀ] *m* (*support*) stake
tuteur, -trice [tytœʀ, -tʀis] *m, f* **1.** JUR (*d'un mineur*) guardian **2.** ECOLE, UNIV tutor
tutoiement [tytwamɑ̃] *m* use of "tu"
tutorat [tytɔʀa] *m* tutorial system
tutoyer [tytwaje] <6> **I.** *vt* ~ **qn** to use "tu" with sb **II.** *vpr* **se** ~ to call each other "tu"
tutu [tyty] *m* tutu
Tuvalu [tyvaly] *m* Tuvalu
tuyau [tɥijo] <x> *m* **1.** (*tube rigide*) pipe; (*tube souple*) tube; (*d'une cheminée*) flue; ~ **d'alimentation** supply pipe; ~ **d'arrosage** garden hose; ~ **d'échappement** exhaust (pipe) **2.** *inf* (*conseil*) tip
tuyauter [tɥijote] <1> *vt inf* ~ **qn** to tip sb off
tuyauterie [tɥijotʀi] *f* (*d'une installation, chaudière*) piping
TV [teve] *f abr de* **télévision** TV
TVA [teveɑ] *f abr de* **taxe à la valeur ajoutée** V.A.T
tweed [twid] *m* tweed; **une jupe en** [*o* **de**] ~ a tweed skirt
tympan [tɛ̃pɑ̃] *m* **1.** ANAT eardrum **2.** ARCHIT tympanum
type [tip] **I.** *m* **1.** (*archétype, modèle*) type **2.** (*genre*) sort; **avoir le** ~ **chinois** to look Chinese **3.** (*individu quelconque*) guy ►**du troisième** ~ of the third kind **II.** *app inv* typical
typé(e) [tipe] *adj* **un allemand très** ~ a very typical-looking German
typhoïde [tifɔid] *adj, f* typhoid
typhon [tifɔ̃] *m* typhoon
typhus [tifys] *m* typhus fever
typique [tipik] *adj* typical
typiquement [tipikmɑ̃] *adv* typically
typographe [tipɔgʀaf] *mf* typographer
typographie [tipɔgʀafi] *f* typography
typographique [tipɔgʀafik] *adj* typographical
tyran [tiʀɑ̃] *m* tyrant
tyrannie [tiʀani] *f* (*despotisme, influence excessive*) tyranny
tyrannique [tiʀanik] *adj* tyrannical
tyranniser [tiʀanize] <1> *vt* to bully
tyrolienne [tiʀɔljɛn] *f* MUS yodel
tzar [tsaʀ] *m v.* **tsar**
tzarine [tsaʀin] *f v.* **tsarine**
tzigane [tsigan] *adj v.* **tsigane**

U

U, u [y] *m inv* U, u; ~ **comme Ursule** u for Uncle ►**en u** U-shaped
ubiquité [ybikɥite] *f v.* **don**
UCT [ysete] *f abr de* **Unité Centrale de Traitement** CPU
UDF [ydeɛf] *f abr de* **Union pour la démocratie française** *centre-right French political party*
UDR [ydeɛʀ] *f abr de* **Union des démocrates pour la République** *French political party*
UEFA [yefa] *f abr de* **Union of European Football Associations** UEFA
UEM [yøɛm] *f abr de* **Union économique et monétaire** EMU
UHT [yaʃte] *abr de* **ultra-haute température** UHT
Ukraine [ykʀɛn] *f* **l'**~ Ukraine
ukrainien [ykʀɛnjɛ̃] *m* Ukrainian; *v. a.* **français**
ukrainien(ne) [ykʀɛnjɛ̃, jɛn] *adj* Ukrainian
Ukrainien(ne) [ykʀɛnjɛ̃, jɛn] *m(f)* Ukrainian
ulcère [ylsɛʀ] *m* ulcer
ulcérer [ylseʀe] <5> *vt* to sicken
ULM [yɛlɛm] *m abr de* **ultra-léger motorisé** microlight
ultérieur(e) [ylteʀjœʀ] *adj* later
ultérieurement [ylteʀjœʀmɑ̃] *adv* later; (*regretter*) subsequently
ultimatum [yltimatɔm] *m* ultimatum
ultime [yltim] *adj a. antéposé* ultimate; (*ironie*) final
ultra [yltʀa] *mf* (*extrémiste de droite/gauche*) right-wing/left-wing extremist
ultrachic [yltʀaʃik] *adj inf* hyper chic
ultraconfidentiel(le) [yltʀakɔ̃fidɑ̃sjɛl] *adj inf* top secret
ultraconservateur, -trice [yltʀakɔ̃sɛʀvatœʀ, -tʀis] *adj inf* ultraconservative
ultraléger, -ère [yltʀaleʒe, -ɛʀ] *adj* ultralight
ultramoderne [yltʀamɔdɛʀn] *adj* ultramodern
ultrapériphérique [yltʀapeʀifeʀik] *adj* remote
ultrarapide [yltʀaʀapid] *adj inf* high-speed
ultrasensible [yltʀasɑ̃sibl] *adj inf* highly sensitive
ultrason [yltʀasɔ̃] *m* ultrasound
ultraviolet [yltʀavjɔlɛ] *m* ultraviolet; **les ~s** ultraviolet rays
ultraviolet(te) [yltʀavjɔlɛ, ɛt] *adj* ultraviolet
Ulysse [ylis(ə)] *m* Ulysses
UME [yɛmø] *f abr de* **Union monétaire européenne** EMU
un [œ̃] **I.** *adj* one ►**c'est tout** ~ it's all the same; **ne faire qu'**~ to be as one; **elle n'a fait ni ~e ni deux, elle a refusé** she refused straight off **II.** *m inv* one **III.** *adv* firstly; **~, je suis fatigué, deux, j'ai faim** for one thing I'm

tired, for another I'm hungry; *v. a.* **cinq**

un(e) [œ̃, yn] **I.** *art indéf* **1.** (*un certain*) a, an; **avec ~ grand courage** with great courage **2.** (*intensif*) **il y a ~ (de ces) bruit** it's so noisy; **ce type est d'~ culot!** this guy's got some nerve! **II.** *pron* **1.** (*chose/personne parmi d'autres*) one; **en connaître ~ qui ...** to know somebody who ...; **être l'~ de ceux qui ...** to be one of those who ... **2.** (*chose/personne opposée à une autre*) **les ~s ... et les autres ...** some people ... and others ...; **ils sont assis en face l'~ de l'autre** they're sitting opposite each other; **ils sont aussi menteurs l'~ que l'autre** one's as big a liar as the other; **s'injurier l'~ l'autre** to insult each other ►**l'~ dans l'autre** by and large; **l'~ ou l'autre** one or the other; **comme pas ~** extremely; **et d'~!** *inf* and that's that!; **~ par ~** one after the other

unanime [ynanim] *adj* unanimous

unanimement [ynanimmɑ̃] *adv* unanimously

unanimité [ynanimite] *f* unanimity ►**à l'~** unanimously

une [yn] **I.** *art v.* **un II.** *f* **1.** (*première page du journal*) front page **2.** (*premier sujet*) main news ►**c'était moins ~!** *inf* it was a close call!

UNEF [ynɛf] *f abr de* **Union nationale des étudiants de France** *French students' union*

UNESCO [ynɛsko] *f abr de* **United Nations Educational, Scientific and Cultural Organization** UNESCO

uni(e) [yni] *adj* **1.** (*sans motifs*) plain; (*unicolore*) self-coloured *Brit,* self-colored *Am* **2.** (*en union*) **~s par qc** united by sth **3.** (*lisse: surface*) smooth; (*chemin*) even

UNICEF [ynisɛf] *m abr de* **United Nations International Children's Emergency Fund** UNICEF

unicolore [ynikɔlɔʀ] *adj* self-coloured *Brit,* self-colored *Am*

unième [ynjɛm] *adj* **vingt et ~** twenty first

unificateur, -trice [ynifikatœʀ, -tʀis] *adj* unifying

unification [ynifikasjɔ̃] *f* unification; (*des tarifs*) standardization; (*de l'Allemagne*) reunification

unifier [ynifje] <1 a> **I.** *vt* **1.** (*unir*) to unify; (*partis*) to unite **2.** (*uniformiser: programmes*) to standardize **II.** *vpr* **s'~** to unite

uniforme [ynifɔʀm] **I.** *adj* **1.** (*pareil*) uniform **2.** (*standardisé*) standardized **3.** (*invariable: vitesse*) steady; (*vie*) monotonous; (*mouvement, paysage*) uniform **II.** *m* uniform

uniformément [ynifɔʀmemɑ̃] *adv* **1.** (*de façon monotone*) uniformly **2.** (*sans incident*) uneventfully

uniformisation [ynifɔʀmizasjɔ̃] *f* standardization

uniformiser [ynifɔʀmize] <1> *vt* to standardize

uniformité [ynifɔʀmite] *f* **1.** (*similitude: des mœurs, produits*) uniformity **2.** (*monotonie*) monotony

unijambiste [yniʒɑ̃bist] **I.** *adj* one-legged **II.** *mf* one-legged man *m,* one-legged woman *f*

unilatéral(e) [ynilateʀal, o] <-aux> *adj* unilateral; **stationnement ~** parking on one side only

unilatéralement [ynilateʀalmɑ̃] *adv a.* POL unilaterally

unilingue [ynilɛ̃g] *adj* monolingual

union [ynjɔ̃] *f* **1.** (*alliance*) union; **en ~ avec qn** in union with sb **2.** (*vie commune*) union; **~ conjugale** marital union **3.** (*juxtaposition: des éléments*) combination **4.** (*association*) association; **~ syndicale** federation of trade unions

Union économique [ynjɔ̃ ekɔnɔmik] *f* economic union

Union européenne [ynjɔ̃ øʀɔpeɛn] *f* European Union

unioniste [ynjɔnist] *m Québec* (*membre du parti de l'Union nationale*) unionist (*member of the National Union Party*)

Union monétaire [ynjɔ̃ mɔnetɛʀ] *f* monetary union

Union Soviétique [ynjɔ̃ sɔvjetik] *f* HIST Soviet Union

unique [ynik] *adj* **1.** (*seul*) only; (*monnaie*) single; **un prix ~** one price; **enfant ~** only child; **à voie ~** single-lane; **rue à sens ~** one-way street **2.** (*exceptionnel*) unique

uniquement [ynikmɑ̃] *adv* **1.** (*exclusivement*) exclusively **2.** (*seulement*) only

unir [yniʀ] <8> **I.** *vt* **1.** (*associer*) to unite **2.** (*marier*) **~ deux personnes** to join two people in matrimony **3.** (*combiner*) to combine **4.** (*relier*) **~ les gens** (*chemin de fer, langage*) to link people **II.** *vpr* **1.** (*s'associer*) **s'~** to unite **2.** (*se marier*) **s'~** to marry **3.** (*se combiner*) **s'~ à qc** to join with sth

unisexe [ynisɛks] *adj* unisex

unisson [ynisɔ̃] *m a.* MUS unison; **être à l'~ de qc** to be in accord with sth; **se mettre à l'~ de qn** to adopt sb's point of view

unitaire [ynitɛʀ] *adj* **1.** (*simple*) *a.* MAT, PHYS unitary **2.** POL (*revendications*) common; (*mouvement*) unified **3.** COM (*production*) unit

unité [ynite] *f* **1.** (*cohésion*) *a.* POL (*d'une famille, classe*) unity; (*d'un texte*) cohesion; **~ d'action** unity of action; **~ de vues** unanimous view **2.** MAT, MIL unit; **~ de réanimation** resuscitation unit **3.** INFOR, TECH **~ centrale** central processing unit; **~ de stockage** storage device; **~ de bande magnétique** tape streamer; **~ de disque** disk drive; **~ de sortie** output device **4.** COM **prix à l'~** unit price

univers [univɛʀ] *m* **1.** ASTR universe **2.** (*milieu*) world

universaliser [ynivɛʀsalize] <1> **I.** *vt* to universalize **II.** *vpr* **s'~** to become universal

universalité [ynivɛʀsalite] *f* universality

universel(le) [ynivɛʀsɛl] *adj* **1.** (*opp: particulier*) universal **2.** (*mondial*) world; **exposition**

U

~**le** world exhibition **3.** (*tous usages: remède*) all-purpose; **clé ~le** adjustable spanner [*o* wrench *Am*]

universellement [ynivɛʀsɛlmɑ̃] *adv* **1.** universally **2.** (*mondialement*) all over the world; ~ **connu** known everywhere (in the world)

universitaire [ynivɛʀsitɛʀ] **I.** *adj* university; (*titre*) academic; **résidence** ~ hall of residence *Brit*, residence hall *Am*; **diplôme** ~ degree; **restaurant** ~ university canteen **II.** *mf* academic

université [ynivɛʀsite] *f* university; ~ **d'été** summer school

Untel, **Unetelle** [ɛ̃tɛl, yntɛl] *m, f* so-and-so

uploader [œplode] *vt* INFOR to upload

uranium [yʀanjɔm] *m* uranium

Uranus [yʀanys] *f* Uranus

urbain(**e**) [yʀbɛ̃, ɛn] *adj* urban

urbanisation [yʀbanizasjɔ̃] *f* urbanization

urbaniser [yʀbanize] <1> **I.** *vt* (*région, zone*) to urbanize **II.** *vpr* **s'**~ to be urbanized

urbanisme [yʀbanism] *m* town planning *Brit*, city planning *Am*

urbaniste [yʀbanist] *mf* urban planner

urée [yʀe] *f* urea

urgence [yʀʒɑ̃s] *f* **1.** (*caractère urgent*) urgency; **il y a** ~ it's urgent; **d'**~ immediately **2.** (*cas urgent*) matter of urgency; MED emergency; **les ~s** the casualty department *Brit*, the emergency room *Am*; **le secours de première** ~ first aid

urgent(**e**) [yʀʒɑ̃, ʒɑ̃t] *adj* urgent; **~!** it's urgent!

urger [yʀʒe] <2a> *vi* **ça urge!** *inf* it's urgent!

urinaire [yʀinɛʀ] *adj* urinary

urine [yʀin] *f* urine

uriner [yʀine] <1> *vi* to urinate

urinoir [yʀinwaʀ] *m* urinal

urne [yʀn] *f* **1.** (*boîte*) ballot box; **les ~s** the ballot box **2.** (*vase funéraire*) (funeral) urn

urologie [yʀɔlɔʒi] *f* urology

URSS [yɛʀɛsɛs] *f* HIST *abr de* **Union des républiques socialistes soviétiques** USSR

urticaire [yʀtikɛʀ] *f* hives ►**donner de l'~ à qn** *inf* to drive sb mad

US [yɛs] *f abr de* **Union sportive** sports association

us [ys] *mpl* ~ **et coutumes** habits and customs

USA [yɛsɑ] *mpl abr de* **United States of America** USA

usage [yzaʒ] *m* **1.** (*utilisation*) use; **à l'~ de qn/qc** for sb/sth; **hors d'~** unusable; **méthode en** ~ method in use; **être d'~ courant** to be in common use **2.** (*façon de se servir, consommation*) *a.* JUR use; ~ **de faux** use of forged documents **3.** (*faculté*) **retrouver l'~ de la vue** to recover one's sight; **perdre l'~ de la parole** to lose the power of speech **4.** (*coutume*) custom; **c'est contraire aux ~s** it's against common practice; **c'est l'~ de** +*infin* it's customary to +*infin* ►**à l'~** with use

usagé(**e**) [yzaʒe] *adj* worn; (*pile*) used

usager, **-ère** [yzaʒe, -ɛʀ] *m, f* user; ~ **de la route** road user

usant(**e**) [yzɑ̃, ɑ̃t] *adj* wearing

usé(**e**) [yze] *adj* (*détérioré*) worn; (*semelles*) worn-down

user [yze] <1> **I.** *vt* **1.** (*détériorer*) ~ **qc** to wear sth out; (*roche*) to wear sth away **2.** (*épuiser*) ~ **qn** to wear sb out **3.** (*consommer*) to use **II.** *vi* ~ **d'un droit** to exercise a right; ~ **de termes de métier** to use professional terms ►~ **et abuser de qc** to use and abuse sth **III.** *vpr* **s'**~ to wear out; **s'~ à qc** to wear oneself out with sth; **s'~ les yeux** to ruin one's eyesight

usine [yzin] *f* factory; ~ **d'automobiles** car factory

usité(**e**) [yzite] *adj* common(ly used)

ustensile [ystɑ̃sil] *m* (*de cuisine*) utensil; (*de jardinage*) tool

usuel(**le**) [yzɥɛl] *adj* usual; (*emploi*) normal; (*mot*) common; (*objet*) everyday

usuellement [yzɥɛlmɑ̃] *adv soutenu* commonly

usufruit [yzyfʀɥi] *m* usufruct

usure [yzyʀ] *f* **1.** (*détérioration*) wear and tear **2.** (*état*) wear **3.** (*érosion*) wearing away **4.** (*affaiblissement*) wearing out ►**avoir qn à l'~** *inf* to wear sb down

usurier, **-ière** [yzyʀje, -jɛʀ] *m, f* usurer

usurpateur, **-trice** [yzyʀpatœʀ, -tʀis] *m, f* usurper

usurpation [yzyʀpasjɔ̃] *f* **1.** (*appropriation*) usurpation **2.** POL usurping

usurper [yzyʀpe] <1> *vt* ~ **le pouvoir/un titre** to usurp power/a title

ut [yt] *m inv* MUS C

utérus [yteʀys] *m* womb

utile [ytil] **I.** *adj* (*profitable*) useful **II.** *m* **joindre l'~ à l'agréable** to combine business with pleasure

utilement [ytilmɑ̃] *adv* usefully; **conseiller ~ qn** to give sb some useful advice

utilisable [ytilizabl] *adj* usable; **ce n'est plus** ~ it's no longer usable

utilisateur, **-trice** [ytilizatœʀ, -tʀis] *m, f a.* INFOR user

utilisation [ytilizasjɔ̃] *f* use

utiliser [ytilize] <1> *vt* **1.** (*se servir de*) to use **2.** (*recourir à: avantage*) to make use of; (*moyen, mot*) to use **3.** (*exploiter: personne*) to use; (*restes*) to use up

utilitaire [ytilitɛʀ] **I.** *adj* **1.** (*susceptible d'être utilisé*) utilitarian; (*objet*) functional; (*véhicule*) commercial **2.** (*intéressé: calculs*) useful **II.** *m* **1.** INFOR utility **2.** AUTO commercial vehicle

utilité [ytilite] *f* **1.** (*aide*) use **2.** (*caractère utile*) usefulness; **association reconnue d'~ publique** ≈ non-profit-making organization; **je n'en ai pas l'~** I haven't any use for it

utopie [ytɔpi] *f* utopia

utopique [ytɔpik] *adj* utopian

UV [yve] **I.** *mpl abr de* **ultraviolets** UV rays **II.** *f abr de* **unité de valeur** UNIV credit

V

V, **v** [ve] *m inv* V, v; ~ **comme Victor** v for Victor ►**décolleté en V** V-neck
va [va] *indic prés de* **aller**
vacance [vakɑ̃s] *f* **1.** *pl* (*période*) holiday *Brit,* vacation *Am;* ~**s scolaires** school holidays; **être en** ~**s** to be on holiday; **bonnes** ~**s!** have a good holiday!; **partir en** ~**s** to go on holiday **2.** (*poste*) vacancy

In France the **vacances scolaires** are staggered by one week according to area. The country is divided into three zones (A, B and C) running from north to south.

vacancier, **-ière** [vakɑ̃sje, -jɛʀ] *m, f* holidaymaker *Brit,* vacationer *Am*
vacant(e) [vakɑ̃, ɑ̃t] *adj* vacant
vacarme [vakaʀm] *m* racket
vacation [vakasjɔ̃] *f* (*rémunération*) fee
vaccin [vaksɛ̃] *m* vaccine; ~ **contre le tétanos** tetanus vaccine
vaccinal(e) [vaksinal, o] <-aux> *adj* **complication** ~**e** post-vaccination complication
vaccination [vaksinasjɔ̃] *f* vaccination
vacciner [vaksine] <1> *vt* MED to vaccinate
vache [vaʃ] **I.** *f* **1.** ZOOL cow **2.** (*cuir*) cowhide ►**années/période de** ~**s grasses/maigres** prosperous/lean years/period; **la** ~**!** *inf* hell! **II.** *adj inf* (*méchant*) mean
vachement [vaʃmɑ̃] *adv inf* damned, bloody *Brit*
vacher, **-ère** [vaʃe, -ɛʀ] *m, f* cowherd, cowgirl *m, f*
vacherie [vaʃʀi] *f inf* nastiness *no pl;* **des** ~**s** lousy tricks
vacherin [vaʃʀɛ̃] *m* **1.** (*fromage*) vacherin cheese **2.** (*dessert*) vacherin
vacillant(e) [vasijɑ̃, jɑ̃t] *adj* shaky; (*lumière*) flickering
vaciller [vasije] <1> *vi* (*personne*) to stagger; (*poteau*) to sway; (*lumière*) to flicker
vacuité [vakɥite] *f* emptiness
vadrouille[1] [vadʀuj] *f* **être en** ~ *inf* to be roaming around
vadrouille[2] [vadʀuj] *f Québec* (*balai à franges*) *long-handled duster*
va-et-vient [vaevjɛ̃] *m inv* **1.** (*mouvement alternatif*) comings and goings *pl* **2.** ELEC two-way switch
vagabond(e) [vagabɔ̃, ɔ̃d] **I.** *adj* **1.** (*errant*) roving **2.** (*sans règles*) roaming **II.** *m(f)* (*sans domicile fixe*) vagrant
vagabonder [vagabɔ̃de] <1> *vi* (*errer*) to roam
vagin [vaʒɛ̃] *m* vagina
vaginal(e) [vaʒinal, o] <-aux> *adj* vaginal
vagissement [vaʒismɑ̃] *m* wail
vague[1] [vag] **I.** *adj* **1.** *a. antéposé* (*indistinct*) vague **2.** *antéposé* (*lointain*) faraway **3.** (*ample: manteau*) loose **II.** *m* (*imprécision*) vagueness; **rester dans le** ~ to be terribly vague
vague[2] [vag] *f* GEO, METEO (*a. afflux*) wave
vaguement [vagmɑ̃] *adv* **1.** (*opp: précisément*) vaguely **2.** (*un peu*) **avoir l'air** ~ **surpris** to seem slightly surprised
vahiné [vaine] *f* Tahitian (woman)
vaillance [vajɑ̃s] *f* courage
vaillant(e) [vajɑ̃, ʒɑ̃t] *adj* brave
vaille [vaj] *subj prés de* **valoir**
vain(e) [vɛ̃, vɛn] *adj* (*inutile*) vain ►**en** ~ in vain
vaincre [vɛ̃kʀ] *irr* **I.** *vi soutenu* to prevail **II.** *vt soutenu* **1.** MIL (*pays*) to conquer **2.** MIL, SPORT (*adversaire*) to defeat **3.** (*surmonter*) to overcome
vaincu(e) [vɛ̃ky] **I.** *part passé de* **vaincre** **II.** *adj* defeated; **s'avouer** ~ to admit defeat **III.** *m(f)* (*perdant*) **les** ~**s** the defeated; SPORT the losers
vainement [vɛnmɑ̃] *adv* vainly
vainqueur [vɛ̃kœʀ] **I.** *adj* (*victorieux*) victorious **II.** *m* **1.** MIL, POL victor **2.** SPORT winner
vairon [vɛʀɔ̃] *adj* **yeux** ~**s** wall eyes
vais [vɛ] *indic prés de* **aller**
vaisseau[1] [vɛso] <x> *m* ANAT vessel
vaisseau[2] [vɛso] <x> *m* **1.** NAUT vessel **2.** AVIAT ~ **spatial** spacecraft **3.** ARCHIT nave
vaisselier [vɛsəlje] *m* dresser
vaisselle [vɛsɛl] *f* **1.** (*service de table*) crockery, dishes *pl* **2.** (*objets à nettoyer*) dishes *pl,* washing-up *Brit;* **faire** [*o* **laver**] **la** ~ to do the dishes
val [val, vo] <vaux> *m* valley
valable [valabl] *adj a.* JUR, COM valid
valablement [valabləmɑ̃] *adv* **1.** (*légitimement*) validly **2.** (*convenablement*) reasonably **3.** (*d'une manière efficace*) effectively
Valais [valɛ] *m* **le** ~ the Valais
valaisan(e) [valɛzɛ̃, ɛn] *adj* of the Valais
Valaisan(e) [valɛzɛ̃, ɛn] *m(f)* person from the Valais
valdinguer [valdɛ̃ge] <1> *vi inf* ~ **contre qc** to smash into sth
valence [valɑ̃s] *f* CHIM valency *Brit,* valence *Am*
valériane [valeʀjan] *f* valerian
valet [valɛ] *m* **1.** (*domestique*) valet **2.** JEUX jack
Valette [valɛt(ə)] *f* La ~, Valletta
valeur [valœʀ] *f* **1.** (*prix*) *a.* MAT, MUS, JEUX value; ~ **marchande** market value; **de** ~ of value **2.** (*pour le courrier*) **envoyer qc en** ~ **déclarée** to send sth value declared **3.** FIN (*cours*) value; (*titre*) security **4.** ECON value; ~ **ajoutée** value added; ~ **d'échange** exchange value **5.** (*importance*) value; **accorder** [*o* **attacher**] **de la** ~ **à qc** to value sth; **mettre qn en** ~ to show sb to advantage; **mettre qc en** ~ to show sth off **6.** (*équivalent*) **la** ~ **d'un litre** a litre's worth *Brit,* a liter's worth *Am*
valeureux, **-euse** [valœʀø, -øz] *adj* valiant
validation [validasjɔ̃] *f* (*certification*) *a.*

INFOR validation

valide [valid] *adj* **1.** (*bien portant: personne*) able-bodied **2.** (*valable: papier*) valid

valider [valide] <1> *vt* (*certifier*) *a.* INFOR to validate

validité [validite] *f* validity

valise [valiz] *f* suitcase; **faire sa** ~ to pack one's suitcase

vallée [vale] *f* valley

vallon [valɔ̃] *m* small valley

vallonné(e) [valɔne] *adj* undulating

valoche [valɔʃ] *f inf* case

valoir [valwaʀ] *irr* **I.** *vi* **1.** (*coûter*) to be worth; **combien ça vaut?** how much is it worth? **2.** (*mettre en avant*) **faire ~ un argument** to press an argument **II.** *vt* **1.** (*avoir de la valeur*) to be worth; ~ **qc** to be worth sth; **ne pas ~ grand-chose** not to be worth much **2.** (*être valable*) to apply; **autant vaut** [*o* **vaudrait**] **faire qc** you might as well do sth **3.** (*être équivalent à*) *a.* JEUX to be worth; **rien ne vaut un bon lit quand on est fatigué** there's nothing like a good bed when you're tired **4.** (*mériter*) to deserve; **cette ville vaut le détour** this town is worth going out of your way to see **5.** (*avoir pour conséquence*) ~ **qc à qn** to earn sb sth; **qu'est-ce qui nous vaut cet honneur?** to what do we owe this honour? [*o* honor? *Am*] **III.** *vpr* **se ~ 1.** COM to be worth the same; **ces deux vases se valent** there's not much to choose between these two vases **2.** (*être comparable: personnes, choses*) to be the same

valorisant(e) [valɔʀizɑ̃, ɑ̃t] *adj* enriching

valorisation [valɔʀizasjɔ̃] *f* (*d'une région*) development; (*des déchets*) recovery

valoriser [valɔʀize] <1> *vt* ECON (*région*) to develop; (*déchets*) to recover

valse [vals] *f* waltz

valser [valse] <1> *vi* to waltz

valseur, -euse [valsœʀ, -øz] *m, f* waltzer

valve [valv] *f* TECH, ZOOL valve

valves [valv] *fpl Belgique* (*tableau d'affichage, généralement sous vitrine*) notice board

valvule [valvyl] *f* valve

vamp [vɑ̃p] *f* vamp

vamper [vɑ̃pe] <1> *vt* (*fam*) to vamp

vampire [vɑ̃piʀ] *m* vampire

vampiriser [vɑ̃piʀize] *vt inf* ~ **qn** to suck the blood out of sb

van [vɑ̃] *m* horsebox *Brit,* horse trailer *Am*

vandale [vɑ̃dal] *mf* (*destructeur*) vandal

vandaliser [vɑ̃dalize] <1> *vt* to vandalize

vandalisme [vɑ̃dalism] *m* vandalism

vanille [vanij] *f* GASTR, BOT vanilla

vanité [vanite] *f* vanity; **être d'une immense ~** to be incredibly vain

vaniteux, -euse [vanitø, -øz] *adj* vain

vanne [van] *f* **1.** NAUT (*d'une écluse*) sluice **2.** *inf* (*plaisanterie*) **lancer des ~s à qn** to make digs at sb

vanné(e) [vane] *adj inf* (*personne*) dead-beat

vannerie [vanʀi] *f* **1.** (*fabrication*) basketry **2.** (*objets*) wickerwork

vannier [vanje] *m* basket maker

vantail [vɑ̃taj, o] <-aux> *m* leaf

vantard(e) [vɑ̃taʀ, aʀd] **I.** *adj* boastful **II.** *m(f)* boaster

vantardise [vɑ̃taʀdiz] *f* boasting

vanter [vɑ̃te] <1> **I.** *vt* to praise; **~ la marchandise** to talk up the goods **II.** *vpr* **se ~ de qc** to boast of sth

Vanuatu [vanwatu] *m* Vanuatu

vanuatuan(ne) [vanwatuɑ̃, an] *adj* Vanuatuan

Vanuatuan(ne) [vanwatuɑ̃, an] *m(f)* Vanuatuan

va-nu-pieds [vanypje] *mf inv* tramp

vapes [vap] *fpl* **être dans les ~** *inf* to be in a daze

vapeur [vapœʀ] **I.** *f* **1.** (*buée*) **~ d'eau** steam **2.** (*énergie*) **bateau à ~** steamboat; **machine à ~** steam-driven machine **3.** *pl* (*émanation*) fumes; **~s d'essence** petrol fumes *Brit,* gasoline fumes *Am* ►**renverser la ~** to backpedal; **à toute ~** full steam ahead **II.** *m* steamer

vaporeux, -euse [vapɔʀø, -øz] *adj* (*tissu, cheveux*) gossamer

vaporisateur [vapɔʀizatœʀ] *m* spray

vaporisation [vapɔʀizasjɔ̃] *f* (*d'un parfum, d'une plante*) spraying

vaporiser [vapɔʀize] <1> **I.** *vt* (*pulvériser, imprégner*) to spray; **~ les cheveux avec de la laque** to put on some hairspray **II.** *vpr* **se ~ qc sur le visage** to spray sth on one's face

vaquer [vake] <1> *vi* **~ à ses occupations** to attend to one's affairs

varappe [vaʀap] *f* rock-climbing; **faire de la ~** to go rock-climbing

varech [vaʀɛk] *m* kelp

vareuse [vaʀøz] *f* (*blouse*) pea jacket

variable [vaʀjabl] **I.** *adj* **1.** (*opp: constant*) variable **2.** METEO changeable; **vent ~** variable wind **II.** *f* variable

variante [vaʀjɑ̃t] *f* (*forme différente*) variant

variateur [vaʀjatœʀ] *m* **~ de lumière** dimmer; **~ de vitesse** speed variator

variation [vaʀjasjɔ̃] *f* **1.** (*changement*) change **2.** (*écart*) *a.* MAT, BIO variation **3.** MUS **une ~ sur le thème du printemps** a variation on the theme of spring

varice [vaʀis] *f souvent pl* varicose vein

varicelle [vaʀisɛl] *f* chickenpox

varié(e) [vaʀje] *adj* **1.** (*divers*) varied **2.** (*très différent: arguments*) various

varier [vaʀje] <1> **I.** *vi* **1.** (*évoluer*) to change **2.** (*être différent*) to vary **II.** *vt* (*diversifier, changer*) to vary

variété [vaʀjete] *f* **1.** (*diversité, changement*) *a.* ZOOL, BOT variety **2.** *pl* THEAT variety **3.** *pl* CINE, TV variety programme *Brit,* variety program *Am*

variole [vaʀjɔl] *f* smallpox

variolique [vaʀjɔlik] *adj* smallpox

Varsovie [vaʀsɔvi] Warsaw

vas [va] *indic prés de* **aller**
vasculaire [vaskylɛʀ] *adj* ANAT, MED vascular
vase[1] [vɑz] *m* **1.** (*récipient*) vase **2.** PHYS **le principe des ~s communicants** the principle of communicating vessels
vase[2] [vɑz] *f* mud
vaseline [vazlin] *f* Vaseline®
vaseux, -euse [vɑzø, -øz] *adj* **1.** (*boueux*) muddy **2.** *inf* (*confus*) muddled **3.** *inf* (*mal en point*) **être complètement ~** to be completely dazed
vasistas [vazistɑs] *m* ARCHIT opening window
vasouiller [vazuje] <1> *vi inf* to flounder
vasque [vask] *f* basin
vassal(e) [vasal, o] <-aux> *m(f)* HIST vassal
vaste [vast] *adj antéposé* **1.** (*immense*) immense; (*spacieux: appartement*) vast **2.** (*ample: vêtement*) huge **3.** (*puissant: organisation*) vast
va-t-en-guerre [vatɑ̃gɛʀ] *m inv* warmonger
Vatican [vatikan] *m* **le ~** the Vatican
vaudeville [vodvil] *m* vaudeville
vaudois(e) [vodwa, waz] *adj* of the Vaud
Vaudois(e) [vodwa, waz] *m(f)* person from the Vaud
vaudou [vodu] *m inv* voodoo
vaudrai [vodʀɛ] *fut de* **valoir**
vau-l'eau [volo] *adv* **aller à ~** to be going downhill fast
vaurien(ne) [voʀjɛ̃, jɛn] *m(f)* good-for-nothing
vaut [vo] *indic prés de* **valoir**
vautour [votuʀ] *m* vulture
vautrer [votʀe] <1> *vpr* (*s'étendre*) **se ~** to sprawl
vaux [vo] *indic prés de* **valoir**
va-vite [vavit] *adv inf* **à la ~** in a rush
VDQS [vedekyɛs] *m abr de* **vin délimité de qualité supérieure** *guaranteed quality wine*
veau [vo] <x> *m* **1.** ZOOL calf; **~ marin** seal **2.** GASTR veal
vecteur [vɛktœʀ] *m* **1.** MAT vector **2.** (*support*) **~ de culture** vehicle for culture
vectoriel(le) [vɛktɔʀjɛl] *adj* MAT, INFOR vector
vécu [veky] *m* **le ~** real life; **son ~** her experience of life
vécu(e) [veky] **I.** *part passé de* **vivre** **II.** *adj* **1.** (*réel*) true-life **2.** (*éprouvé*) **bien ~** happy; **mal ~** traumatic
vécus [veky] *passé simple de* **vivre**
vedette [vədɛt] **I.** *f* **1.** (*rôle principal*) star; **avoir** [*o* **tenir**] **la ~** to play the starring role **2.** (*personnage connu*) star **3.** (*centre de l'actualité*) **avoir** [*o* **tenir**] **la ~** to be in the limelight **II.** *app* **1.** **mannequin ~** supermodel **2.** CINE, TV **émission ~** flagship programme *Brit*, flagship program *Am*
végétal [veʒetal, o] <-aux> *m* vegetable
végétal(e) [veʒetal, o] <-aux> *adj* vegetable
végétarien(ne) [veʒetaʀjɛ̃, jɛn] **I.** *adj* vegetarian **II.** *m(f)* vegetarian
végétatif, -ive [veʒetatif, -iv] *adj* ANAT vegetative
végétation [veʒetasjɔ̃] *f* **1.** BOT vegetation **2.** *pl* MED adenoids
végéter [veʒete] <5> *vi* (*plante*) to grow; (*personne*) to vegetate
véhémence [veemɑ̃s] *f* (*d'une discussion*) vehemence
véhément(e) [veemɑ̃, ɑ̃t] *adj* vehement
véhicule [veikyl] *m* **1.** (*support*) *a.* AUTO vehicle **2.** (*agent de transmission: d'une maladie*) vector; (*d'une information*) medium
véhiculer [veikyle] <1> *vt* **1.** AUTO to transport **2.** (*transmettre: maladie, savoir*) to transmit; (*émotions*) to convey
veille [vɛj] *f* **1.** day before; **la ~ au soir** the evening of the day before; **la ~ de Noël** Christmas Eve **2.** (*fait de ne pas dormir*) wakefulness **3.** (*garde de nuit*) night watch ►**à la ~ de qc** on the eve of sth; **en ~** standby
veillée [veje] *f* **1.** (*soirée*) evening **2.** (*dans la nuit*) vigil
veiller [veje] <1> **I.** *vi* **1.** (*faire attention à*) **~ à qc** to attend to sth; **~ à +infin** to be sure to +*infin* **2.** (*surveiller*) to be on watch; **~ sur qn/qc** to watch over sb/sth **3.** (*ne pas dormir*) to stay awake **II.** *vt* **~ qn** to watch over sb
veilleur [vɛjœʀ] *m* **~ de nuit** night watchman
veilleuse [vɛjøz] *f* **1.** (*petite lampe*) nightlight **2.** *pl* (*feu de position*) sidelights **3.** (*flamme: d'un réchaud*) pilot light; **mettre la flamme en ~** to turn the heat right down ►**se mettre en ~** to put one's sidelights on
veinard(e) [vɛnaʀ, aʀd] *m(f) inf* lucky devil
veine [vɛn] *f* **1.** ANAT vein **2.** (*inspiration*) vein **3.** *inf* (*chance*) luck **4.** (*veinure*) veining
veiné(e) [vene] *adj* (*peau, marbre*) veined; (*bois*) grained
veineux, -euse [vɛnø, -øz] *adj* veined
velcro® [vɛlkʀo] *m* Velcro®
véliplanchiste [veliplɑ̃ʃist] *mf* windsurfer
velléitaire [veleitɛʀ] *adj* indecisive
velléité [veleite] *f soutenu* vague desire
vélo [velo] *m* **1.** (*bicyclette*) bicycle; **à** [*o* **en** *inf*] **~** by bike **2.** (*activité*) cycling
vélocité [velɔsite] *f* velocity
vélodrome [velodʀom] *m* velodrome
vélomoteur [velomɔtœʀ] *m* moped
véloski [veloski] *m* skibob
velours [v(ə)luʀ] *m* **1.** (*tissu*) velvet; **~ côtelé** corduroy **2.** (*douceur: d'une pêche*) bloom
velouté [vəlute] *m* (*douceur: d'une peau*) velvet; (*d'un vin*) smoothness; (*d'un potage*) creaminess; (*de la voix*) silkiness
velouté(e) [vəlute] *adj* **1.** (*doux au toucher*) velvet-soft **2.** GASTR smooth **3.** (*d'aspect doux: teint*) velvety
velu(e) [vəly] *adj* hairy
venaison [vənɛzɔ̃] *f* venison
vénal(e) [venal, o] <-aux> *adj* venal; *péj* (*personne*) mercenary
venant [vənɑ̃] *m* **à tout ~** to everybody

vendable [vɑ̃dabl] *adj* saleable

vendange [vɑ̃dɑ̃ʒ] *f souvent pl* (*récolte*) grape harvest + *vb sing*

vendanger [vɑ̃dɑ̃ʒe] <2a> **I.** *vi* to pick grapes **II.** *vt* (*raisin*) to pick; ~ **les vignes** to pick the grapes from the vines

vendangeur, -euse [vɑ̃dɑ̃ʒœʀ, -ʒøz] *m, f* grape-picker

Vendée [vɑ̃de] *f* **la** ~ the Vendée

vendetta [vɑ̃deta, vɑ̃dɛtta] *f* vendetta

vendeur, -euse [vɑ̃dœʀ, -øz] **I.** *m, f* **1.** (*opp: acheteur*) seller **2.** (*marchand dans un magasin*) (sales) assistant; ~ **de légumes** vegetable merchant **II.** *adj* **1.** (*qui fait vendre*) **un argument** ~ an argument that sells **2.** (*qui vend*) **les pays ~s de pétrole** oil-selling countries

vendre [vɑ̃dʀ] <14> **I.** *vi* COM to sell; **faire** ~ to boost sales; **être à** ~ to be for sale **II.** *vt* to sell; ~ **qc aux enchères** to auction sth **III.** *vpr* **1.** COM **se** ~ to be sold; **se** ~ **bien/mal** to sell well/badly **2.** *fig* **se** ~ (*candidat*) to sell oneself

vendredi [vɑ̃dʀədi] *m* Friday; ~ **saint** Good Friday; *v. a.* **dimanche**

vendu(e) [vɑ̃dy] **I.** *part passé de* **vendre** **II.** *adj* (*corrompu*) traitor

vénéneux, -euse [venenø, -øz] *adj* poisonous

vénérable [veneʀabl] *adj* venerable

vénération [veneʀasjɔ̃] *f* veneration

vénérer [veneʀe] <5> *vt* to revere

vénérien(ne) [veneʀjɛ̃, jɛn] *adj* venereal

vénézolan(e) [venezolɑ̃, an] *adj* Venezuelan

Vénézolan(e) [venezolɑ̃, an] *m(f)* Venezuelan

Venezuela [venezɥɛla] *m* **le** ~ Venezuela

vengeance [vɑ̃ʒɑ̃s] *f* vengeance

venger [vɑ̃ʒe] <2a> **I.** *vt* to avenge **II.** *vpr* **se** ~ **de qn/qc** to take revenge on sb/for sth

vengeur, -geresse [vɑ̃ʒœʀ, -ʒ(ə)ʀɛs] *adj* vengeful

venimeux, -euse [vənimø, -øz] *adj* poisonous

venin [vənɛ̃] *m* venom

venir [v(ə)niʀ] <9> **I.** *vi être* **1.** (*arriver, se situer dans un ordre*) to come; **viens avec moi!** come with me!; **faire** ~ **le médecin** to call out the doctor; **faire** ~ **les touristes** to bring in the tourists; **à** ~ to come **2.** (*se présenter à l'esprit*) **l'idée m'est venue de chercher dans ce livre** I had the idea of looking in this book **3.** (*parvenir, étendre ses limites*) ~ **jusqu'à qn/qc** to reach sb/sth **4.** (*arriver*) to arrive; (*nuit*) to fall; **laisser** ~ **qn/qc** to let sb/sth come; **alors, ça vient?** *inf* ready yet? **5.** (*se développer: plante*) to grow **6.** (*provenir*) ~ **d'Angleterre** to come from England; **ce mobilier lui vient de sa mère** this furniture came to him from his mother **7.** (*découler, être la conséquence*) ~ **de qc** to come from sth **8.** (*aboutir à*) **où veut-il en ~?** what is he getting at? **II.** *aux être* **1.** (*se déplacer pour*) **je viens manger** I'm coming to dinner **2.** (*avoir juste fini*) **je viens juste de finir** I've just finished **3.** (*être conduit à*) **s'il venait à passer par là** if he should go that way; **elle en vint à penser qu'il (le) faisait exprès** she got to the stage of thinking he was doing it on purpose **III.** *vi impers être* **1. il viendra un temps où** there will come a time when **2.** (*provenir*) **de là vient que qn a fait qc** the result of this is that sb did sth; **d'où vient que qn a fait qc?** how come sb did sth?

Venise [v(ə)niz] Venice

vénitien [venisjɛ̃] *m* Venetian; *v. a.* **français**

vénitien(ne) [venisjɛ̃, jɛn] *adj* Venetian; **blond** ~ strawberry blond

Vénitien(ne) [venisjɛ̃, jɛn] *m(f)* Venetian

vent [vɑ̃] *m* **1.** (*courant d'air*) *a.* METEO, NAUT wind; ~ **du nord** north wind; **il y a du** ~ it's windy; **à tous les ~s** to the four winds; **instrument à** ~ wind instrument **2.** (*tendance*) **dans le** ~ fashionable ►**quel <u>bon</u> ~ vous/t'amène?** *iron* what brings you here?; **<u>avoir</u> eu ~ de qc** to have wind of sth

vente [vɑ̃t] *f* **1.** (*action*) sale; ~ **au détail** retail; ~ **par correspondance** mail order; **mettre qc en** ~ to put sth on sale **2.** (*service*) sales **3.** *pl* (*chiffre d'affaires*) sales **4.** (*réunion où l'on vend*) ~ **aux enchères** (*action*) auctioning; (*réunion*) auction

venté(e) [vɑ̃te] *adj* windswept

venter [vɑ̃te] <1> *vi impers* **il vente** it's windy

venteux, -euse [vɑ̃tø, -øz] *adj* windy

ventilateur [vɑ̃tilatœʀ] *m* fan

ventilation [vɑ̃tilasjɔ̃] *f* **1.** (*aération*) ventilation **2.** (*répartition: du courrier*) sorting

ventiler [vɑ̃tile] <1> *vt* **1.** (*aérer: pièce*) to ventilate **2.** (*répartir*) ~ **des dépenses sur plusieurs mois** to spread spending over several months

ventilo [vɑ̃tilo] *m inf abr de* **ventilateur** fan

ventouse [vɑ̃tuz] *f* **1.** (*dispositif*) suction pad; **faire** ~ to adhere **2.** ZOOL, BOT sucker **3.** MED cupping glass

ventral(e) [vɑ̃tʀal, o] <-aux> *adj* **douleurs ~es** stomach pains

ventre [vɑ̃tʀ] *m* stomach; **avoir mal au** ~ to have stomach ache; **prendre du** ~ to get a paunch [*o* gut] ►**courir** ~ **à <u>terre</u>** to go at top speed; **<u>avoir</u> quelque chose dans le** ~ to have guts

ventrée [vɑ̃tʀe] *f inf* **s'en mettre une** ~ to pig out

ventricule [vɑ̃tʀikyl] *m* ventricle

ventriloque [vɑ̃tʀilɔk] **I.** *adj* **être** ~ to be a ventriloquist **II.** *mf* ventriloquist

ventripotent(e) [vɑ̃tʀipɔtɑ̃, ɑ̃t] *adj* potbellied

ventru(e) [vɑ̃tʀy] *adj* potbellied

venu(e) [v(ə)ny] **I.** *part passé de* **venir** **II.** *adj* **bien** ~ (*conseil*) timely; **mal** ~ unwelcome **III.** *m(f)* **nouveau** ~ newcomer

venue [v(ə)ny] *f* arrival

vêpres [vɛpʀ] *fpl* REL vespers
ver [vɛʀ] *m* worm; ~ **blanc** grub; ~ **de terre** earthworm; ~ **luisant** glow-worm; ~ **solitaire** tapeworm; ~ **à soie** silkworm; **être mangé** [*o* **piqué**] **aux** ~**s** (*bois, fruit*) to be worm-eaten ▸**tirer les** ~**s du** nez **à qn** to worm information out of sb; nu **comme un** ~ *inf* as naked as the day one was born
véracité [veʀasite] *f* truth
véranda [veʀɑ̃da] *f* conservatory
verbal(**e**) [vɛʀbal, o] <-aux> *adj* verbal
verbalement [vɛʀbalmɑ̃] *adv* verbally
verbaliser [vɛʀbalize] <1> **I.** *vi* ~ **contre qn** to report sb **II.** *vt* (*mettre une contravention*) to book
verbatim [vɛʀbatim] **I.** *adv* verbatim **II.** *m* verbatim report
verbe [vɛʀb] *m* LING verb
verbeux, **-euse** [vɛʀbø, -øz] *adj* verbose
verbiage [vɛʀbjaʒ] *m péj* verbiage
verdâtre [vɛʀdɑtʀ] *adj* greenish
verdeur [vɛʀdœʀ] *f* (*acidité*) tartness; (*d'un vin*) acidity
verdict [vɛʀdikt] *m* verdict; ~ **d'acquittement** not guilty verdict
verdir [vɛʀdiʀ] <8> **I.** *vi* (*nature*) to turn green **II.** *vt* ~ **qc** to turn sth green
verdoyant(**e**) [vɛʀdwajɑ̃, jɑ̃t] *adj* green
verdure [vɛʀdyʀ] *f* **1.** (*végétation*) greenery; **un tapis de** ~ a green carpet **2.** (*légumes*) greens *pl*
véreux, **-euse** [veʀø, -øz] *adj* **1.** (*gâté par les vers: fruit*) worm-eaten **2.** (*douteux: personne*) corrupt
verge [vɛʀʒ] *f* **1.** ANAT penis **2.** (*baguette*) rod
verger [vɛʀʒe] *m* orchard
verglacé(**e**) [vɛʀglase] *adj* icy
verglas [vɛʀglɑ] *m* black ice
vergogne [vɛʀgɔɲ] *f* **sans** ~ shameless
vergue [vɛʀg] *f* yard
véridique [veʀidik] *adj* (*information*) genuine; (*histoire*) true
vérifiable [veʀifjabl] *adj* verifiable
vérificateur [veʀifikatœʀ] *m* INFOR ~ **orthographique** spell checker
vérificateur, **-trice** [veʀifikatœʀ, -tʀis] *m, f* controller
vérification [veʀifikasjɔ̃] *f* **1.** (*contrôle*) verification **2.** (*confirmation*) confirmation
vérifier [veʀifje] <1> **I.** *vt* **1.** (*contrôler*) to verify **2.** (*confirmer*) to confirm **II.** *vpr* **se** ~ (*soupçon*) to be confirmed
vérin [veʀɛ̃] *m* TECH jack
véritable [veʀitabl] *adj* **1.** *a. postposé* (*réel, authentique: cuir, perles*) real **2.** *antéposé* (*vrai*) true
véritablement [veʀitabləmɑ̃] *adv* **1.** (*réellement*) genuinely **2.** (*à proprement parler*) truly
vérité [veʀite] *f* **1.** (*opp: mensonge, connaissance du vrai*) truth **2.** *sans pl* (*réalisme*) realism **3.** *sans pl* (*sincérité*) truthfulness ▸**il n'y a que la** ~ **qui** blesse *prov* the truth hurts; **à la** ~ to tell the truth; **en** ~ in fact
verjus [vɛʀʒy] *m* verjuice
verlan [vɛʀlɑ̃] *m* backslang
vermeil [vɛʀmɛj] *m* vermilion
vermeil(**le**) [vɛʀmɛj] *adj* (*tein*) rosy
vermicelle [vɛʀmisɛl] *m* vermicelli
vermifuge [vɛʀmifyʒ] *adj* **remède** ~ worm powder
vermillon [vɛʀmijɔ̃] *adj inv, m* vermilion
vermine [vɛʀmin] *f sans pl* (*parasites, racaille*) vermin
vermoulu(**e**) [vɛʀmuly] *adj* worm-eaten
vermout(**h**) [vɛʀmut] *m* vermouth
verni(**e**) [vɛʀni] *adj* **1.** (*ongles, bois*) varnished; (*peinture*) glossy; **chaussures** ~**es** patent leather shoes **2.** *inf* (*chanceux*) **on peut dire qu'il est** ~ he's a lucky devil
vernir [vɛʀniʀ] <8> **I.** *vt* (*bois, peinture*) to varnish **II.** *vpr* **se** ~ **les ongles** to put nail varnish on
vernis [vɛʀni] *m* **1.** (*laque*) varnish; ~ **à ongles** nail varnish **2.** (*aspect brillant*) shine **3.** (*façade*) veneer
vernissage [vɛʀnisaʒ] *m* **1.** (*action*) varnishing **2.** (*inauguration*) preview
vernissé(**e**) [vɛʀnise] *adj* glazed
vernisser [vɛʀnise] <1> *vt* to glaze
vérole [veʀɔl] *f inf* pox; **petite** ~ smallpox
vérolé(**e**) [veʀɔle] *adj* INFOR infected by a virus
véronique [veʀɔnik] *f* speedwell
verrai [vɛʀɛ] *fut de* **voir**
verrat [vɛʀa] *m* boar
verre [vɛʀ] *m* **1.** (*matière, récipient, contenu*) glass; ~ **à vitre** window glass; ~ **de sécurité** safety glass; ~ **à pied** stem glass; **deux** ~**s de vin** two glasses of wine; **prendre un** ~ to have a drink **2.** (*objet: d'une montre*) glass; (*en optique*) lens; ~ **de contact** contact lens
verrée [veʀe] *f Suisse* (*moment d'une réunion où l'on offre à boire*) drinks *pl*
verrerie [vɛʀʀi] *f* **1.** (*fabrication*) glass-making **2.** (*objets*) glassware **3.** (*fabrique*) glassworks + *vb sing*
verrier [vɛʀje] *m* glassworker
verrière [vɛʀjɛʀ] *f* **1.** (*toit*) glass roof **2.** (*paroi*) glass wall
verroterie [vɛʀɔtʀi] *f* glass jewellery
verrou [veʀu] *m* **1.** (*loquet*) bolt **2.** (*serrure*) lock
verrouillage [veʀujaʒ] *m* **1.** (*fermeture*) locking; (*d'un ordinateur*) lockout; ~ **central** [*o* **centralisé**] central locking **2.** (*blocage*) blocking
verrouiller [veʀuje] <1> *vt* **1.** (*fermer*) *a.* INFOR to lock **2.** POL, SPORT (*bloquer*) to block
verrue [veʀy] *f* MED wart
vers[1] [vɛʀ] *prep* **1.** (*en direction de*) ~ **qn/qc** towards [*o* toward *Am*] sb/sth **2.** (*aux environs de: lieu*) around **3.** (*aux environs de: temps*) about; ~ **midi** about midday
vers[2] [vɛʀ] *m* verse *no pl;* **faire des** ~ to write verse; **en** ~ in verse

V

versant [vɛʀsɑ̃] *m* (*pente*) slope; (*d'un toit*) side

versatile [vɛʀsatil] *adj* (*personne, caractère*) fickle; (*humeur*) changeable

versatilité [vɛʀsatilite] *f* fickleness

verse [vɛʀs] *f* **il pleut à ~** it's pouring

Verseau [vɛʀso] <x> *m* Aquarius; *v. a.* **Balance**

versement [vɛʀsəmɑ̃] *m* payment; (*sur un compte*) deposit

verser [vɛʀse] <1> **I.** *vt* **1.** (*faire couler*) **~ de l'eau à qn** to pour sb some water; **~ du riz dans un plat** to pour rice into a dish **2.** (*payer*) **~ une somme à qn** to pay a sum to sb; **~ qc sur un compte** to deposit sth in an account **3.** (*ajouter*) **~ qc au dossier** to add sth to a file **II.** *vi* **1.** (*basculer*) to overturn **2.** (*faire couler*) **cette cafetière verse bien** this coffeepot pours well

verset [vɛʀsɛ] *m* REL (*de la Bible, du Coran*) verse

verseur, **-euse** [vɛʀsœʀ, -øz] *adj* **bec ~** pouring spout

verseuse [vɛʀsøz] *f* coffeepot

versificateur, **-trice** [vɛʀsifikatœʀ, -tʀis] *m, f* **1.** (*poète*) poet **2.** *péj* rhymester

versification [vɛʀsifikasjɔ̃] *f* versification

versifier [vɛʀsifje] <1> **I.** *vi* to write verse **II.** *vt* to put into verse

version [vɛʀsjɔ̃] *f* **1.** (*interprétation*) **a.** MUS, THEAT, CINE version; **en ~ originale sous-titrée** in the original language with sub-titles; **ma ~ de ce qui c'est passé** my version of what happened **2.** (*modèle*) model; **la ~ 5 portes d'une voiture** the 5-door model of a car **3.** ECOLE unseen (*translation into French*)

verso [vɛʀso] *m* back

vert [vɛʀ] *m* green; **~ foncé/pâle/tendre** dark/pale/soft green; **le feu est passé au ~** the traffic lights have gone green; **passer au ~** (*voiture*) to get through on green

vert(e) [vɛʀ, vɛʀt] **I.** *adj* **1.** (*de couleur verte, écologiste*) green **2.** (*blême*) **~ de peur** white with fear; **~ de jalousie** green with envy **3.** (*de végétation*) **espaces ~s** green spaces **4.** (*à la campagne*) **classe ~e** school camp **5.** (*opp: mûr: fruit*) unripe; (*vin*) young **6.** (*opp: sec: bois, légumes*) green **7.** (*vaillant: vieillard*) sprightly **8.** (*agricole*) **l'Europe ~e** green Europe **II.** *m(f)* (*écologiste*) green

vertébral(e) [vɛʀtebʀal, o] <-aux> *adj* **colonne ~e** spinal column

vertèbre [vɛʀtɛbʀ] *f* vertebra

vertébré [vɛʀtebʀe] *m* vertebrate

vertébré(e) [vɛʀtebʀe] *adj* vertebrate

vertement [vɛʀtəmɑ̃] *adv* sharply

vertical(e) [vɛʀtikal, o] <-aux> *adj* vertical

verticale [vɛʀtikal] *f* vertical line

verticalement [vɛʀtikalmɑ̃] *adv* vertically

vertige [vɛʀtiʒ] *m* **1.** *sans pl* (*peur du vide*) vertigo; **être sujet au ~** to suffer from vertigo **2.** (*malaise*) dizzy spell; **il a le ~** he's having a dizzy spell; **donner le ~ à qn** (*personne, situation*) to make sb's head spin; (*hauteur*) to make sb dizzy **3.** (*égarement*) fever; **~ du pouvoir** lure of power

vertigineux, **-euse** [vɛʀtiʒinø, -øz] *adj* breathtaking

vertu [vɛʀty] *f* **1.** (*qualité*) virtue **2.** *sans pl* (*moralité*) virtue **3.** (*pouvoir*) power ►**en ~ de** by virtue of; **en ~ de la loi** in accordance with the law

vertueux, **-euse** [vɛʀtɥø, -øz] *adj* virtuous

verve [vɛʀv] *f* eloquence; **être en ~** (*personne*) to be in top form; **avec beaucoup de ~** with verve

verveine [vɛʀvɛn] *f* verbena

vésicule [vezikyl] *f* **1.** ANAT vesicle; **~ biliaire** gall-bladder **2.** MED blister

vespasienne [vɛspazjɛn] *f* urinal

vessie [vesi] *f* bladder ►**faire prendre à qn des ~s pour des lanternes** *inf* to pull the wool over sb's eyes

veste [vɛst] *f* **1.** (*vêtement court, veston*) jacket **2.** (*gilet*) cardigan

vestiaire [vɛstjɛʀ] *m* cloakroom *Brit*, coat check *Am*

vestibule [vɛstibyl] *m* (*d'un appartement*) lobby; (*d'une maison*) hall

vestige [vɛstiʒ] *m souvent pl* trace

vestimentaire [vɛstimɑ̃tɛʀ] *adj* **dépenses ~s** spending on clothes

veston [vɛstɔ̃] *m* jacket

vêtement [vɛtmɑ̃] *m* garment; **des ~s** clothes

vétéran(e) [veteʀɑ̃, an] *m(f)* **1.** MIL veteran **2.** (*personne expérimentée*) old hand **3.** *pl* SPORT veterans

vétérinaire [veteʀinɛʀ] **I.** *adj* veterinary **II.** *mf* vet *Brit*, veterinarian *Am*

vétille [vetij] *f* trifle

vêtir [vetiʀ] *vpr irr, soutenu* **se ~** to dress oneself; **se ~ de qc** to dress in sth

veto [veto] *m inv* veto; **droit de ~** right of veto

vét(t)étiste [vetetist] *mf* mountain biker

vêtu(e) [vety] **I.** *part passé de* **vêtir** **II.** *adj* dressed; **~ de qc** wearing sth

veuf, **veuve** [vœf, vœv] **I.** *adj* widowed **II.** *m, f* widower, widow *m, f*

veuille [vœj] *subj prés de* **vouloir**

veulent [vœl] *indic prés de* **vouloir**

veut [vø] *indic prés de* **vouloir**

veuvage [vœvaʒ] *m* (*d'un veuf*) widowerhood; (*d'une veuve*) widowhood

veuve [vœv] *v.* **veuf**

veux [vø] *indic prés de* **vouloir**

vexant(e) [vɛksɑ̃, ɑ̃t] *adj* **1.** (*blessant*) hurtful **2.** (*rageant*) annoying

vexation [vɛksasjɔ̃] *f* humiliation

vexer [vɛkse] <1> **I.** *vt* to offend **II.** *vpr* **se ~ de qc** to be offended by sth

VF [veɛf] *f abr de* **version française** French version

VHS [veaʃɛs] *abr de* **Video Home System** VHS

via [vja] *prep* via

viabilisé(e) [vjabilize] *adj* with services (laid on)

viabiliser [vjabilize] <1> *vt* (*terrain*) to service

viabilité [vjabilite] *f* **1.** (*état d'une route: d'une route*) practicability **2.** (*aménagement: d'un terrain*) availability of services **3.** (*aptitude à vivre*) viability

viable [vjabl] *adj* viable

viaduc [vjadyk] *m* viaduct

viager [vjaʒe] *m* life annuity

viager, -ère [vjaʒe, -ɛʀ] *adj* life

viande [vjɑ̃d] *f* meat

viander [vjɑ̃de] <1> *vpr inf* **se ~** to get smashed up

viatique [vjatik] *m* **1.** (*équipement de voyage*) provisions (for a journey) *pl* **2.** REL viaticum

vibrant(e) [vibʀɑ̃, ɑ̃t] *adj* vibrating; **~ de colère** shaking with anger

vibraphone [vibʀafɔn] *m* vibraphone

vibration [vibʀasjɔ̃] *f* (*d'une voix, corde*) resonance; (*d'un moteur*) vibration

vibrato [vibʀato] *m* vibrato

vibratoire [vibʀatwaʀ] *adj* vibratory

vibrer [vibʀe] <1> **I.** *vi* **1.** (*trembler: voix, corde*) to resonate; (*mur, moteur*) to vibrate **2.** (*trahir une émotion*) **~ de colère** (*personne*) to shake with anger **II.** *vt* (*béton*) to vibrate

vibromasseur [vibʀomasœʀ] *m* **1.** MED massager **2.** (*objet érotique*) vibrator

vicaire [vikɛʀ] *m* curate; **~ général** vicar-general

vice [vis] *m* (*anomalie*) defect; **~ de construction** building fault

vice-consul [viskɔ̃syl] <vice-consuls> *m* vice-consul

vicelard(e) [vislaʀ, aʀd] *inf* **I.** *adj* **1.** (*malin: personne*) devious **2.** (*vicieux: histoire*) sleazy; (*personne, air*) sly **II.** *m(f)* dirty old so-and-so

vice-président(e) [vispʀezidɑ̃, ɑ̃t] <vice-présidents> *m(f)* vice-president **vice-roi, vice-reine** [visʀwa, visʀɛn] <vice-rois> *m* viceroy, vicereine *m, f*

vice versa [vis(e)vɛʀsa] *adv* **et ~** and vice versa

vicier [visje] <1> *vt* (*goût, relations*) to spoil; **air vicié** polluted air

vicieux, -euse [visjø, -jøz] **I.** *adj* **1.** (*obsédé sexuel: personne, air*) lecherous **2.** *inf* (*vache, tordu: coup, personne*) devious **3.** (*rétif: cheval*) vicious **4.** SPORT (*balle, tir*) nasty **II.** *m, f* **1.** (*cochon*) pervert **2.** *inf* (*homme tordu*) double-dealer

vicinal [visinal, o] <-aux> *adj* **chemin ~** byroad

vicomte, -esse [vikɔ̃t, -ɛs] *m, f* viscount *m*, viscountess *f*

victime [viktim] *f* **1.** (*blessé, mort*) casualty **2.** (*personne/chose qui subit*) victim

victoire [viktwaʀ] *f* **~ sur qn/qc** victory over sb/sth

victorieux, -euse [viktɔʀjø, -jøz] *adj* victorious

victuailles [viktɥaj] *fpl* food + *vb sing*

vidange [vidɑ̃ʒ] *f* **1.** (*action: d'un circuit*) emptying; AUTO oil change **2.** (*dispositif: d'un évier*) waste outlet **3.** *pl* (*effluents*) sewage + *vb sing* **4.** *Belgique* (*verre consigné*) returns *pl* **5.** *pl, Belgique* (*bouteilles vides* (*consignées ou non*)) empties

vidanger [vidɑ̃ʒe] <2a> *vt* **1.** AUTO **faire ~ une voiture** to change the oil in a car **2.** (*vider*) to drain

vide [vid] **I.** *adj* **1.** (*opp: plein*) empty **2.** (*opp: riche: discussion*) empty; **~ de qc** devoid of sth **3.** (*opp: occupé*) vacant **II.** *m* **1.** *sans pl* (*abîme*) void **2.** PHYS vacuum; **emballé sous ~** vacuum-packed **3.** (*espace vide*) gap **4.** (*néant*) void ►**faire le ~** (*débarrasser*) to clear everything away; (*évacuer ses soucis*) to empty one's mind; **parler dans le ~** (*personne n'écoute*) to waste one's breath; (*sans objet*) to talk rubbish

vidéo [video] **I.** *f* (*technique, film, émission*) video **II.** *adj inv* video

vidéocassette [videokasɛt] *f* videocassette

vidéoclip [videoklip] *m* video

vidéoconférence [videokɔ̃feʀɑ̃s] *f* videoconference

vidéodisque [videodisk] *m* videodisc

vidéophone [videofɔn] *m* videophone

vide-ordures [vidɔʀdyʀ] *m inv* waste disposal

vidéosurveillance [videosyʀvɛjɑ̃s] *f* video surveillance

vidéotex® [videotɛks] *m* videotex®

vidéothèque [videotɛk] *f* video (rental) shop

vidéotransmission [videotʀɑ̃smisjɔ̃] *f* video transmission

vide-poches [vidpɔsch] <vide-poches> *m* **1.** AUTO glove compartment; (*latéral*) tidy; (*au dos du siège*) seat pocket **2.** (*récipient*) tidy

vider [vide] <1> **I.** *vt* **1.** (*retirer, voler le contenu de*) to empty; **~ un bassin de son eau** to empty the water from a bowl **2.** (*verser: bouteille, boîte*) to empty **3.** (*faire s'écouler: substance liquide*) to drain; (*substance solide*) to empty **4.** (*consommer*) **~ son verre** to drain one's glass **5.** *inf* (*expulser*) to throw out **6.** *inf* (*fatiguer*) **être vidé** to be exhausted **7.** GASTR (*poisson*) to clean **II.** *vpr* **1.** (*perdre son contenu*) **se ~** (*bouteille*) to be emptied; (*ville*) to empty **2.** (*s'écouler*) **se ~ dans le caniveau** (*eaux usées*) to drain into the gutter

videur, -euse [vidœʀ, -øz] *m, f* bouncer

vie [vi] *f* **1.** (*existence, biographie*) life; **revenir à la ~** (*reprendre conscience*) to come back to life; (*reprendre goût à la vie*) to start living again; **être en ~** to be alive; **être sans ~** to be lifeless **2.** (*façon de vivre*) life; **la ~ active**

work; **voir la ~ en rose** to see life through rose-tinted spectacles; **c'est la ~!** that's life! ►**à la ~, à la mort** to the end; **gagner sa ~** to earn a living; **refaire sa ~ avec qn** to make a new life with sb; **à ~** for life

vieil [vjɛj] *adj v.* **vieux**

vieillard [vjɛjaʀ] *m* old man

vieille [vjɛj] *v.* **vieux**

vieilleries [vjɛjʀi] *fpl* old-fashioned things; (*vêtements*) old-fashioned clothes

vieillesse [vjɛjɛs] *f* **1.** (*opp: jeunesse*) old age **2.** *sans pl* (*personnes âgées*) **la ~** the elderly *pl*

vieilli(e) [vjeji] *adj* aged

vieillir [vjɛjiʀ] <8> **I.** *vi* **1.** (*prendre de l'âge: personne*) to grow old; (*chose*) to age; (*fromage, vin*) to mature **2.** *péj* (*diminuer: personne*) to age **3.** (*se démoder*) to become old-fashioned; **être vieilli** to be old-fashioned **II.** *vt* (*faire paraître plus vieux: coiffure, vêtements*) to date **III.** *vpr* **se ~** (*se faire paraître plus vieux*) to make oneself look older

vieillissant(e) [vjɛjisɑ̃, ɑ̃t] *adj* aging

vieillissement [vjɛjismɑ̃] *m* (*d'une personne, population*) ageing *Brit,* aging *Am;* (*d'une idéologie*) dating

vieillot(te) [vjɛjo, jɔt] *adj* quaint

viendrai [vjɛ̃dʀɛ] *fut de* **venir**

vienne [vjɛn] *subj prés de* **venir**

Vienne [vjɛn] Vienna

viennent [vjɛn] *indic prés de* **venir**

viennois(e) [vjɛnwa, waz] *adj* Viennese

Viennois(e) [vjɛnwa, waz] *m(f)* Viennese

viennoiserie [vjɛnwazʀi] *f: pastry made with yeast, such as a croissants or brioche*

viens, vient [vjɛ̃] *indic prés de* **venir**

vierge [vjɛʀʒ] *adj* **1.** (*non défloré: fille, garçon*) virgin **2.** (*intact: disquette, page*) blank; (*film*) unexposed **3.** (*inexploré: espace*) unexplored; **la forêt ~** virgin forest **4.** (*pur: laine*) new **5.** GEO **les Îles ~s** Virgin Islands

Vierge [vjɛʀʒ] *f* **1.** REL **la ~ Marie** the Virgin Mary; **la Sainte ~** the Blessed Virgin **2.** ASTR Virgo; *v. a.* **Balance**

Viêt-nam, Vietnam [vjɛtnam] *m* Vietnam; **le ~ du Nord/Sud** North/South Vietnam

vietnamien [vjɛtnamjɛ̃] *m* Vietnamese; *v. a.* **français**

vietnamien(ne) [vjɛtnamjɛ̃, jɛn] *adj* Vietnamese

Vietnamien(ne) [vjɛtnamjɛ̃, jɛn] *m(f)* Vietnamese

vieux [vjø] **I.** *adv* (*faire, s'habiller*) old; **faire ~** (*coiffure, habits*) to look old **II.** *m* (*choses anciennes*) old stuff

vieux, vieille [vjø, vjɛj] <*devant un nom masculin commençant par une voyelle ou un h muet* vieil> **I.** *adj* **1.** *antéposé* old **2.** *antéposé, inf* (*sale: con, schnock*) old ►**se faire ~** to make onself look old; **vivre ~** to live to a ripe old age **II.** *m, f* **1.** (*vieille personne*) old person; **un petit ~/une petite vieille** *inf* a little old man/woman **2.** *inf* (*mère/père*) old man *m,* old girl *f;* **mes ~** my folks ►**mon (petit) ~!** *inf* my friend!

vif [vif] *m* **le ~ du sujet** the heart of the matter; **au ~** to the quick; **sur le ~** from real life

vif, vive [vif, viv] *adj* **1.** (*plein de vie: personne*) lively **2.** (*rapide*) fast; **avoir l'esprit ~** to be quick-witted **3.** (*intense: douleur*) sharp; (*soleil*) brilliant; (*froid*) biting; (*couleur*) vivid; (*lumière*) bright **4.** *antéposé* (*profond: regret, intérêt*) deep; (*souvenir*) vivid; (*plaisir, chagrin*) intense; (*impression*) lasting **5.** (*vivant*) alive; **eau vive** running water **6.** (*coupant, nu: angle*) acute; **plaie à ~** open wound

vigie [viʒi] *f* **1.** (*en marine*) look-out **2.** (*surveillance*) watch

vigilance [viʒilɑ̃s] *f* vigilance

vigilant(e) [viʒilɑ̃, ɑ̃t] *adj* (*personne*) vigilant; **attention ~e** careful attention; **d'un œil ~** with a watchful eye; **malgré des soins ~s** despite watchful care

vigile [viʒil] *mf* security guard

vigne [viɲ] *f* **1.** BOT vine; **pied de ~** vine **2.** (*vignoble*) vineyard **3.** *sans pl* (*activité viticole*) winegrowing

vigneron(ne) [viɲ(ə)ʀɔ̃, ɔn] **I.** *adj* **activité ~ne** winegrowing **II.** *m(f)* winegrower

vignette [viɲɛt] *f* **1.** (*attestant un paiement*) label **2.** (*image*) illustration **3.** (*petite illustration*) vignette **4.** HIST (*d'une automobile*) tax sticker

vignoble [viɲɔbl] *m* **1.** (*terrain*) vineyard **2.** *sans pl* (*ensemble de ~s*) vineyards *pl*

vigoureusement [viguʀøzmɑ̃] *adv* vigorously

vigoureux, -euse [viguʀø, -øz] *adj* **1.** (*fort*) strong **2.** (*ferme, énergique: coup, mesure*) vigorous

vigueur [vigœʀ] *f* **1.** (*énergie: d'une personne*) strength; **sans ~** feeble **2.** (*véhémence: d'un argument*) force; (*d'une réaction*) strength; **avec ~** vigorously ►**en ~** in force

Viking [vikiŋ] *m* Viking

vilain [vilɛ̃] *m* (*grabuge*) **il va y avoir du ~** things are going to get nasty

vilain(e) [vilɛ̃, ɛn] *adj* **1.** (*laid*) ugly **2.** *antéposé* (*sale, inquiétant: mot, coup*) nasty; **jouer un ~ tour à qn** to play an nasty trick on sb **3.** *antéposé, enfantin* (*personne, animal*) naughty **4.** *antéposé* (*désagréable: temps*) lousy

vilainement [vilɛnmɑ̃] *adv* **1.** (*laidement*) in an ugly way; **il est ~ bâti** he's not got a nice build **2.** (*désagréablement: parler, se conduire*) nastily **3.** (*gravement*) horribly

vilebrequin [vilbʀəkɛ̃] *m* AUTO crankshaft

villa [villa] *f* villa

village [vilaʒ] *m* village

villageois(e) [vilaʒwa, waz] *m(f)* villager

village-vacances [vilaʒvakɑ̃s] *m* holiday village *Brit,* vacation village *Am*

ville [vil] *f* **1.** (*agglomération*) town; **~ jumelée** twin town *Brit,* sister city *Am* **2.** (*quartier*) area; **vieille ~** old town **3.** (*opp: la campagne*) la ~ the city **4.** (*municipalité*) town; (*plus grande*) city ►**en** ~ in town

ville-dortoir [vildɔʀtwaʀ] <villes-dortoirs> *f* dormitory town *Brit,* bedroom community *Am*

villégiature [vi(l)leʒjatyʀ] *f* (*vacances*) holiday *Brit,* vacation *Am*

ville-satellite [vilsatelit] <villes-satellites> *f* satellite town

vin [vɛ̃] *m* wine; ~ **blanc/rosé/rouge** white/rosé/red wine; ~ **de pays** local wine ►**quand le ~ est tiré, il faut le boire** *prov* as you make your bed, you must lie in it; **cuver son** ~ *inf* to sleep it off

vinaigre [vinɛgʀ] *m* vinegar ►**tourner au** ~ to turn sour

vinaigrer [vinegʀe] <1> *vt* ~ **qc** to add vinegar to sth

vinaigrette [vinɛgʀɛt] *f* vinaigrette

vinasse [vinas] *f inf* cheap wine, plonk *Brit*

vindicatif, -ive [vɛ̃dikatif, -iv] *adj* vindictive

vineux, -euse [vinø, øz] *adj* (*couleur*) of wine

vingt [vɛ̃] **I.** *adj* **1.** (*cardinal*) twenty **2.** (*dans l'indication des époques*) **les années** ~ the twenties **II.** *m inv* twenty; *v. a.* **cinq**

vingtaine [vɛ̃tɛn] *f* **1.** (*environ vingt*) **une** ~ **de personnes/pages** about twenty people/pages **2.** (*âge approximatif*) **avoir la** ~ [*o* **une** ~ **d'années**] to be about twenty

vingt-et-un [vɛ̃teœ̃] *inv* **I.** *adj* twenty-one; *v. a.* **cinq II.** *m* JEUX **quatre cent** ~ blackjack

vingtième [vɛ̃tjɛm] **I.** *adj antéposé* twentieth **II.** *mf* **le/la** ~ the twentieth **III.** *m* (*fraction, siècle*) twentieth; *v. a.* **cinquième**

vinicole [vinikɔl] *adj* **région** ~ wine-producing region

vinification [vinifikasjɔ̃] *f* vinification

vinifier [vinifje] <1> *vt, vi* to vinify

vînmes [vɛ̃m], **vinrent** [vɛ̃ʀ], **vins** [vɛ̃], **vint** [vɛ̃], **vîntes** [vɛ̃t] *passé simple de* **venir**

vioc [vjɔk] *v.* **vioque**

viol [vjɔl] *m* rape

violacé(e) [vjɔlase] **I.** *adj* purplish; (*main*) blue with cold **II.** *fpl* violaceae

violateur, -trice [vjɔlatœʀ, -tʀis] *m, f* (*d'un secret, domicile*) violator; (*d'un lieu sacré*) desecrator; ~ **des lois** law-breaker

violation [vjɔlasjɔ̃] *f* **1.** (*trahison: d'un secret, serment*) violation; ~ **des correspondances** opening of private corresponence **2.** (*effraction*) ~ **de domicile** forced entry **3.** (*profanation: d'un lieu sacré*) desecration

viole [vjɔl] *f* viol

violemment [vjɔlamɑ̃] *adv* violently

violence [vjɔlɑ̃s] *f* **1.** (*brutalité*) violence; **par la** ~ violently **2.** (*acte de* ~) act of violence; **se faire** ~ to force oneself **3.** (*virulence: du comportement, d'une tempête*) violence

violent(e) [vjɔlɑ̃, ɑ̃t] *adj* violent

violenter [vjɔlɑ̃te] <1> *vt* ~ **qn** to sexually assault sb

violer [vjɔle] <1> *vt* **1.** (*abuser de*) to rape; **se faire** ~ **par qn** to be raped by sb **2.** (*transgresser: droit, traité*) to violate; (*promesse*) to break; (*secret*) to betray **3.** (*profaner: frontière*) to violate; (*lieu sacré*) to desecrate

violet [vjɔlɛ] *m* purple

violet(te) [vjɔlɛ, ɛt] *adj* purple

violette [vjɔlɛt] *f* BOT violet

violeur, -euse [vjɔlœʀ, -øz] *m, f* rapist

violon [vjɔlɔ̃] *m* violin

violoncelle [vjɔlɔ̃sɛl] *m* cello

violoncelliste [vjɔlɔ̃selist] *mf* cellist

violoniste [vjɔlɔnist] *mf* violinist

vioque [vjɔk] **I.** *adj inf* old **II.** *mf inf* old man, old girl *m, f*

VIP [veipe, viajpi] *m inv abr de* **Very Important Person** *inf* V.I.P.

vipère [vipɛʀ] *f* viper

virage [viʀaʒ] *m* **1.** (*tournant*) turn **2.** (*changement: d'une politique*) U-turn **3.** CHIM ~ **au bleu/rouge** change to blue/red ►**faire un** ~ (*route*) to bend

virago [viʀago] *f* virago

viral(e) [viʀal, o] <-aux> *adj* viral; **avoir une origine ~e** to be caused by a virus

virée [viʀe] *f inf* spin

virement [viʀmɑ̃] *m* FIN transfer (of money)

virer [viʀe] <1> **I.** *vi* (*véhicule*) to turn; (*temps, visage, couleur*) to change; (*personne*) to turn around **II.** *vt* **1.** FIN ~ **une somme à qn/ sur le compte de qn** to transfer a sum to sb/sb's account **2.** *inf* (*renvoyer*) to fire **3.** *inf* (*se débarrasser de*) to get rid of

virevolter [viʀvɔlte] <1> *vi* to twirl

virginal(e) [viʀʒinal, o] <-aux> *adj soutenu* virginal

Virginie [viʀʒini] *f* **la** ~ Virginia

Virginie-Occidentale *f* **la** ~ West Virginia

virginité [viʀʒinite] *f* virginity

virgule [viʀgyl] *f* comma

viril(e) [viʀil] *adj* (*mâle*) virile; (*attitude*) manly

viriliser [viʀilize] <1> *vt* **1.** (*opp: féminiser*) ~ **qn/qc** to make sb/sth more male **2.** MED ~ **qn** to create male characteristics in sb

virilité [viʀilite] *f* **1.** ANAT masculinity **2.** (*caractère viril*) virility

virole [viʀɔl] *f* ferrule

virologiste [viʀɔlɔʒist] *mf,* **virologue** [viʀɔlɔg] *mf* virologist

virtuel(le) [viʀtɥɛl] *adj* **1.** (*possible*) possible; (*réussite*) potential **2.** INFOR virtual

virtuellement [viʀtɥɛlmɑ̃] *adv* (*pratiquement*) virtually

virtuose [viʀtɥoz] *mf* MUS virtuoso

virtuosité [viʀtɥozite] *f* (*d'un pianiste*) virtuosity

virulence [viʀylɑ̃s] *f* **1.** (*véhémence: d'une critique*) viciousness **2.** MED (*d'un microbe*) virulence

virulent(e) [viʀylɑ̃, ɑ̃t] *adj* **1.** (*véhément*) vicious **2.** MED (*microbe*) virulent; (*poison*)

potent
virus [viʀys] *m* MED, INFOR virus
vis[1] [vis] *f* screw; ~ **platinée** AUTO contact point
vis[2] [vi] *indic prés de* **vivre**
vis[3] [vi] *passé simple de* **voir**
visa [viza] *m* **1.** (*autorisation de résider*) visa; ~ **d'entrée/de sortie** entry/exit visa **2.** (*signature*) initials *pl*
visage [vizaʒ] *m* face; **à** ~ **humain** with a human face
Visage [vizaʒ] *m* ~ **pâle** paleface
visagiste® [vizaʒist] *mf* stylist
vis-à-vis [vizavi] **I.** *prep* **1.** (*en face de*) ~ **de l'église** opposite the church **2.** (*envers*) ~ **de qn/qc** towards sb/sth **3.** (*comparé à*) ~ **de qn/qc** next to sb/sth **II.** *adv* **être/se trouver** ~ to be/find themselves face to face **III.** *m inv* (*personne*) person opposite; (*immeuble*) building opposite
viscéral(e) [viseʀal, o] <-aux> *adj* **1.** (*profond: peur*) deep-rooted **2.** ANAT visceral
viscère [visɛʀ] *f* organ; **les** ~**s** the intestines
viscosité [viskozite] *f* **1.** (*moiteur: de la peau*) stickiness **2.** PHYS (*d'un liquide*) viscosity
visée [vize] *f* **1.** (*action: d'une arme*) taking aim; (*d'un appareil*) aim **2.** *pl* (*dessein*) ~**s sur qc** designs on sth
viser[1] [vize] <1> **I.** *vi* **1.** (*avec une arme*) to take aim **2.** (*avoir pour but*) ~ **au succès** to aim for success; ~ **haut** to aim high **II.** *vt* **1.** (*mirer: tireur*) to aim **2.** (*ambitionner: carrière*) to aim at **3.** (*concerner*) ~ **qn/qc** (*remarque*) to be directed at sb/sth; (*mesure*) to be aimed at sb/sth **4.** (*chercher à atteindre*) to set one's sights on
viser[2] [vize] <1> *vt* (*mettre un visa sur: document*) to initial; ~ **un passeport** to put a visa in a passport
viseur [vizœʀ] *m* sight
visibilité [vizibilite] *f* visibility
visible [vizibl] *adj* **1.** (*qui peut être vu*) visible; ~ **à l'œil nu** visible to the naked eye; **être** ~ (*personne*) to be available **2.** (*évident*) obvious
visiblement [viziblәmɑ̃] *adv* evidently
visière [vizjɛʀ] *f* eyeshade; (*d'une casquette*) peak
visioconférence [vizjɔkɔ̃feʀɑ̃s] *f* INFOR videoconference
vision [vizjɔ̃] *f* **1.** (*faculté, action de voir qc*) sight **2.** (*conception, perception avec appareil*) view **3.** (*apparition*) *a.* REL vision
visionnaire [vizjɔnɛʀ] **I.** *adj* (*intuitif, halluciné*) visionary **II.** *mf* (*intuitif*) *a.* REL visionary
visionner [vizjɔne] <1> *vt* (*film, diapositives*) to view
visionneuse [vizjɔnøz] *f* (*appareil*) *a.* INFOR viewer
visiophone [vizjɔfon] *m* INFOR video phone
visite [vizit] *f* **1.** (*action de visiter*) visit; (*d'un musée*) tour; ~ **guidée** guided tour; **rendre** ~ **à qn** to visit sb; **en** ~ on a visit **2.** (*inspection: des bagages*) inspection **3.** MED (*d'un médecin*) consultation; ~ **médicale** medical check-up
visiter [vizite] <1> **I.** *vt* **1.** (*explorer*) *a.* COM, REL to visit **2.** MED (*malades*) to call on **II.** *vi* to visit **III.** *vpr* **se** ~ to visit each other
visiteur, **-euse** [vizitœʀ, -øz] *m, f* **1.** (*personne qui visite*) visitor **2.** (*métier*) ~ **des douanes** customs inspector
vison [vizɔ̃] *m* mink
visonnière [vizɔnjɛʀ] *f Québec* (*élevage de visons*) mink farm
visqueux, **-euse** [viskø, -øz] *adj* (*liquide*) viscous; (*peau*) sticky
visser [vise] <1> **I.** *vt, vi* to screw on **II.** *vpr* **se** ~ to be screwed on
visu [vizy] **de** ~ with one's own eyes
visualisation [vizɥalizasjɔ̃] *f* visualization; INFOR display; ~ **de la page** page preview
visualiser [vizɥalize] <1> *vt* to visualize; (*écran*) to display
visuel [vizɥɛl] *m* INFOR visual display unit
visuel(le) [vizɥɛl] *adj* (*mémoire, panneau*) visual
visuellement [vizɥɛlmɑ̃] *adv* (*quant à la vue, de visu*) visually
vit[1] [vi] *indic prés de* **vivre**
vit[2] [vi] *passé simple de* **voir**
vital(e) [vital, o] <-aux> *adj* vital
vitalité [vitalite] *f* vitality
vitamine [vitamin] *f* vitamin
vitaminé(e) [vitamine] *adj* vitamin-enriched
vite [vit] *adv* fast; **ce sera** ~ **fait** it'll soon be done; **faire** ~ to hurry; **au plus** ~ as quickly as possible
vîtes [vit] *passé simple de* **voir**
vitesse [vitɛs] *f* **1.** (*rapidité*) speed; **à la** ~ **de 100 km/h** at a speed of 100 km/h; ~ **maximale** AUTO speed limit; **en grande** ~ (*pour le courrier*) *a.* CHEMDFER express **2.** (*promptitude*) quickness **3.** AUTO gear; (*d'un vélo*) speed; **changer de** ~ to change gears ▸**à la** ~ **grand V** *inf* at top speed; **prendre** [*o* **gagner**] **qn de** ~ to beat sb; **à toute** ~ as fast as possible; **en** (**quatrième**) ~ *inf* at top speed

> On French motorways, the **vitesse maximale** is 130 kilometres per hour. In villages and towns it is 50, on dual carriageways 110, and on country roads 90.

viticole [vitikɔl] *adj* **production** ~ wine production
viticulteur, **-trice** [vitikyltœʀ, -tʀis] *m, f* winegrower
viticulture [vitikyltyʀ] *f* winegrowing
vitrage [vitʀaʒ] *m* windows *pl*
vitrail [vitʀaj, o] <-aux> *m* stained-glass window
vitre [vitʀ] *f* **1.** (*carreau*) pane of glass **2.** (*fenêtre*) window
vitré(e) [vitʀe] *adj* glass
vitrer [vitʀe] <1> *vt* to glaze

vitrerie [vitʀəʀi] *f* **1.** (*activité*) glazing **2.** (*marchandise*) glass
vitreux, -euse [vitʀø, -øz] *adj* (*yeux*) glassy
vitrier [vitʀije] *m* glazier
vitrifier [vitʀifje] <1> *vt* **1.** (*action: substance*) to glaze **2.** (*recouvrir: parquet*) to varnish
vitrine [vitʀin] *f* **1.** (*étalage*) (shop) window **2.** (*armoire vitrée*) display cabinet
vitriol [vitʀijɔl] *m fig* **critique au ~** vitriolic criticism
vitrioler [vitʀijɔle] <1> *vt* **~ qn** to throw vitriol at sb
vitrocéramique [vitʀoseʀamik] *f* vitreous ceramic
vitupérer [vitypeʀe] <5> *vi* **~ contre qn** to inveigh against sb
vivable [vivabl] *adj* (*personne*) that one can live with; (*monde*) fit to live in
vivace [vivas] *adj* **1.** BOT (*plante*) hardy **2.** (*tenace: foi*) steadfast; (*haine*) undying
vivacité [vivasite] *f* **1.** (*promptitude*) vivacity; **~ d'esprit** quick-wittedness **2.** (*brusquerie: d'un langage*) sharpness **3.** (*intensité: d'une couleur*) vividness; (*d'une émotion*) intensity
vivant [vivɑ̃] *m* **1.** (*personne en vie*) living person; **bon ~** bon viveur **2.** REL **les ~s** the living ▶**du ~ de qn** when sb was alive; (*d'un mort*) in sb's lifetime
vivant(e) [vivɑ̃, ɑ̃t] *adj* **1.** (*en vie: personne, animal*) living; **être encore ~** to still be alive **2.** (*animé: souvenir*) clear; (*rue*) lively **3.** (*expressif*) life-like
vivarium [vivaʀjɔm] *m* vivarium
vivat [viva] *m gén pl* cheer
vive [viv] **I.** *adj v.* **vif II.** *interj* **~ la mariée/la liberté!** long live the bride/freedom!
vivement [vivmɑ̃] **I.** *adv* **1.** (*intensément: intéresser*) keenly; (*regretter*) deeply **2.** (*brusquement: parler*) sharply **3.** (*avec éclat: briller*) brightly **II.** *interj* (*souhait*) **~ les vacances!** I can't wait for the holidays! [*o* until vacation! *Am*]
vivier [vivje] *m* **1.** (*étang*) fishpond **2.** (*bac*) fish-tank
vivifiant(e) [vivifjɑ̃, jɑ̃t] *adj* invigorating
vivifier [vivifje] <1> *vt* **1.** (*stimuler*) to enliven; (*personne, plante*) to invigorate **2.** (*animer: région, ville*) to bring new life to
vivipare [vivipaʀ] *adj* ZOOL viviparous
vivisection [vivisɛksjɔ̃] *f* vivisection
vivoir [vivwaʀ] *m Québec* (*salon, pièce commune dans un appartement*) living room
vivoter [vivɔte] <1> *vi inf* to struggle along; (*avec des petits moyens*) to live from hand to mouth
vivre [vivʀ] *irr* **I.** *vi* **1.** (*exister*) to live; **elle vit encore** she's still alive **2.** (*habiter, mener sa vie*) to live; **~ bien/pauvrement** to live well/in poverty **3.** (*subsister*) **~ de son salaire/ses rentes** to live on one's salary/private income; **faire ~ qn** to support sb **4.** (*persister: coutume*) to live on **5.** (*être plein de vie: portrait*) to be alive; (*rue*) to be lively ▶**il faut bien ~** you have to live; **qui vivra verra** *prov* what will be will be **II.** *vt* **1.** (*passer: moment*) to spend; (*vie*) to live **2.** (*être mêlé à: événement*) to live through **3.** (*éprouver intensément: époque*) to live in **III.** *mpl* supplies ▶**couper les ~s à qn** to cut off sb's allowance
vizir [viziʀ] *m* vizier
vlan [vlɑ̃] *interj inf* bang!
VO [veo] *f abr de* **version originale** original language version
vocabulaire [vɔkabylɛʀ] *m* vocabulary
vocal(e) [vɔkal, o] <-aux> *adj* vocal
vocalique [vɔkalik] *adj* vowel
vocalisation [vɔkalizasjɔ̃] *f* vocalization
vocalise [vɔkaliz] *f* singing exercise
vocaliser [vɔkalize] <1> **I.** *vi* to practise [*o* practice *Am*] singing **II.** *vt* (*consonne*) to vocalize **III.** *vpr* **se ~** (*consonne*) to be vocalized
vocatif [vɔkatif] *m* vocative
vocation [vɔkasjɔ̃] *f* **1.** (*disposition*) calling; **il faut avoir la ~!** *inf* you have to have the calling! **2.** (*destination: d'une personne, d'un peuple*) destiny **3.** REL vocation; **avoir la ~** to have a vocation
vocifération [vɔsifeʀasjɔ̃] *f souvent pl* cry of anger
vociférer [vɔsifeʀe] <5> **I.** *vi* to give a cry of anger; **~ contre qn** to scream at sb **II.** *vt* (*ordre*) to scream
vocodeur [vɔkɔdœʀ] *m* INFOR vocoder
vodka [vɔdka] *f* vodka
vœu [vø] <x> *m* **1.** (*désir*) wish **2.** *pl* (*souhaits*) wishes **3.** REL vow
vogue [vɔg] *f* vogue; **en ~** fashionable
voici [vwasi] **I.** *adv* here is/are; **~ mon père et voilà ma mère** here are my father and mother **II.** *prep soutenu* **1.** (*il y a*) **~ quinze ans que son fils a fait qc** it's fifteen years (now) since his son did sth **2.** (*depuis*) **~ bien des jours que j'attends** I've been waiting for several days now **III.** *interj soutenu* **1.** (*réponse*) here you are **2.** (*présentation*) here's, here are
voie [vwa] *f* **1.** (*passage*) way; **~ d'accès** access road; **~ de garage** siding; **~ sans issue** no through road **2.** (*file: d'une route*) lane; **~ d'eau** NAUT (*brèche*) leak **3.** CHEMDFER **~ ferrée** railway track *Brit,* railroad track *Am* **4.** (*moyen de transport*) **par ~ aérienne** by air; **par ~ postale** by post; **la ~ des ondes** the air waves *pl* **5.** (*filière*) means; **la ~ de la réussite** the road to success **6.** (*ligne de conduite*) path; **s'engager sur la ~ du mal** to set out on the path of evil; **~ de fait** (*violence*) assault; **~ de recours** JUR course of appeal **7.** ANAT (*conduit*) tract; **~s respiratoires** airways **8.** ASTR **~ lactée** Milky Way ▶**par ~ de conséquence** as a result; **être en bonne ~** (*affaire*) to be well under way; **être en ~ de guérison** to be on one's way to recovery

V

voilà [vwala] I. *adv* 1. (*opp: voici*) there; voici ma maison, et ~ le jardin here's my house and there's the garden 2. (*pour désigner*) ~ mes amis there are my friends; ~ pour toi that's for you; ~ pourquoi/où ... that's why/where ...; et ~ tout and that's all; la jeune femme que ~ the young woman over there; en ~ une histoire! what a story!; me ~/te ~ here I am/you are 3. *explétif* ~ que la pluie se met à tomber and then it starts to rain; et le ~ qui recommence there he goes again; en ~ assez! that's enough! ►~ ce que c'est de faire une bêtise *inf* that's what comes of doing something stupid; nous y ~ here we are II. *prep* 1. (*il y a*) ~ quinze ans que son enfant a fait qc it's been fifteen years since her child did sth 2. (*depuis*) ~ bien une heure que j'attends I've been waiting for over an hour now III. *interj* 1. (*réponse*) there you are 2. (*présentation*) this is 3. (*naturellement*) et ~! so there!

voilage [vwalaʒ] *m* net curtain

voile¹ [vwal] *m* 1. (*foulard, léger écran*) *a. fig* veil; prendre le ~ REL to take the veil; ~ de brume veil of mist 2. (*tissu fin, pour cacher*) net 3. PHOT fog 4. MED shadow

voile² [vwal] *f* 1. NAUT sail; bateau à ~s sailing boat *Brit,* sailboat *Am* 2. SPORT la ~ sailing; faire de la ~ to go sailing

voilé(e)¹ [vwale] *adj* (*couvert d'un voile, dissimulé: femme, statue, allusion*) veiled

voilé(e)² [vwale] *adj* (*déformé: planche*) warped; être ~ (*roue*) to be buckled

voilement [vwalmɑ̃] *m* (*d'une planche*) warping; (*d'une roue*) buckling

voiler¹ [vwale] <1> I. *vpr* se ~ 1. (*se dissimuler*) to hide one's face; (*avec un voile*) to wear a veil 2. (*perdre sa clarté: ciel, horizon*) to grow cloudy; (*regard*) to mist over; (*voix*) to become husky II. *vt* (*cacher: visage*) to veil

voiler² [vwale] <1> I. *vpr* (*se fausser*) se ~ (*roue*) to buckle II. *vt* (*fausser: roue, étagère*) to buckle

voilette [vwalɛt] *f* (hat) veil

voilier [vwalje] *m* 1. NAUT sailing boat *Brit,* sailboat *Am* 2. (*fabricant*) sail maker

voilure [vwalyʀ] *f* 1. NAUT sails *pl* 2. AVIAT canopy

voir [vwaʀ] *irr* I. *vt* 1. to see; je l'ai vu comme je vous vois I saw him as (clearly as) I can see you; ~ qn/qc faire qc to see sb/sth do sth; en ~ (de dures) *inf* to have some hard times; faire ~ à qn qu'il se trompe (*personne*) to show sb that he is mistaken; ~ venir la catastrophe to see disaster coming 2. (*montrer*) fais-moi donc ~ ce que tu fais! show me what you're doing! 3. (*rencontrer, rendre visite à: personne*) to see; aller/venir ~ qn to go/come and see sb 4. (*examiner: dossier, leçon*) to look at; ~ page 6 see page 6 5. (*se représenter*) ~ qc/qn sous un autre jour to see sb/sth in a different light; je vois ça (d'ici)! *inf* I can just imagine! 6. (*trouver*) ~ une solution à qc to see a solution to sth 7. (*apparaître*) faire/laisser ~ sa déception à qn to show sb/let sb see one's disappointment ►je voudrais bien t'y/vous y ~ *inf* I'd like to see you in the same position; on aura tout vu! *inf* isn't that the limit!; avoir quelque chose/n'avoir rien à ~ avec [*o* dans] cette histoire to be involved in/have nothing to do with this business; ~ qc venir to see sth coming II. *vi* 1. (*percevoir par la vue*) tu (y *inf*) vois sans tes lunettes? can you see without your glasses? 2. (*prévoir*) ~ grand/petit to think big/small 3. (*constater*) to see; on verra bien we'll see 4. (*veiller*) il faut ~ à ce que +*subj* we have to see that 5. *inf* (*donc*) essaie/regarde ~! just try/look! ►à toi de ~ it's up to you; pour ~ to see (what happens); vois-tu you see III. *vpr* 1. (*être visible*) se ~ bien la nuit (*couleur*) to stand out at night 2. (*se rencontrer*) se ~ to saw each other 3. (*se produire*) se ~ (*phénomène*) to happen; ça ne s'est jamais vu it's unheard of 4. (*se trouver*) se ~ contraint de +*infin* to find oneself obliged to +*infin* 5. (*constater*) se ~ mourir to realize one is dying; il s'est vu refuser l'entrée he was turned away 6. (*s'imaginer*) se ~ faire qc to see oneself doing sth

voire [vwaʀ] *adv* ~ (même) not to say

voirie [vwaʀi] *f* 1. (*routes*) roads *pl* 2. (*entretien des routes*) road maintenance; (*service administratif*) highway department 3. (*enlèvement des ordures*) refuse collection *Brit,* garbage collection *Am* 4. (*dépotoir*) refuse dump *Brit,* garbage dump *Am*

voisin(e) [vwazɛ̃, in] I. *adj* 1. (*proche: maison*) neighbouring *Brit,* neighboring *Am;* (*rue*) next; (*pièce*) adjoining; région ~e de la frontière border region; être ~ de qc to be next to sth 2. (*analogue: sens*) similar; (*espèce animale*) related; être ~ de qc to be akin to sth II. *m(f)* (*dans une rue, un immeuble*) neighbour *Brit,* neighbor *Am;* passe à ton ~! pass it on to the person next to you!

voisinage [vwazinaʒ] *m* 1. (*voisins*) neighbourhood *Brit,* neighborhood *Am;* des relations de bon ~ neighbourly [*o* neighborly *Am*] terms 2. (*proximité*) nearness 3. (*environs*) vicinity

voisiner [vwazine] <1> *vi* ~ avec qn/qc to be next to sb/sth

voiture [vwatyʀ] *f* 1. AUTO car; ~ particulière private car; ~ de course racing car *Brit,* racecar *Am;* ~ de location/d'occasion hire/second-hand car *Brit,* rental/used car *Am;* ~ d'enfant pram *Brit,* baby carriage *Am* 2. CHEMDFER carriage *Brit,* (railroad) car *Am* 3. (*véhicule attelé*) cart; ~ à cheval horse-drawn carriage 4. (*véhicule utilitaire*) ~ de livraison/de dépannage delivery/recovery vehicle; ~ d'infirme disabled vehicle ►en ~! all aboard!

voiture-balai [vwatyʀbalɛ] <voitures-balais> *f* SPORT support car **voiture-bar**

[vwatyʀbaʀ] <voitures-bars> *f* CHEMDFER buffet car **voiture-lit** [vwatyʀli] <voiture(s)-lits> *f* sleeper *Brit,* sleeping car *Am* **voiture-radio** [vwatyʀʀadjo] <voitures-radio> *f* radio car **voiture-restaurant** [vwatyʀʀɛstɔʀɑ̃] <voitures-restaurants> *f* restaurant car

voix [vwɑ] *f* **1.** (*organe de la parole, du chant*) *a.* MUS voice; **d'une ~ forte** in a loud voice; **à ~ basse** in a low voice; **avoir la ~ fausse/juste** to sing in tune/out of tune; **~ de ténor** tenor voice; **à une/deux ~** in one/two parts **2.** (*son: d'un animal*) voice; (*d'un instrument, du vent*) sound **3.** POL (*suffrage*) vote; **d'une seule ~** as one **4.** (*opinion: du peuple, de la conscience*) voice; **écouter la ~ d'un ami** to heed the words of a friend; **faire entendre la ~ de qn** to make sb's voice heard **5.** LING voice; **~ passive/active** passive/active voice ▸**avoir ~ au chapitre** to have a say in the matter; **de vive ~** personally; **élever la ~** to raise one's voice

vol[1] [vɔl] *m* **1.** ZOOL, AVIAT flight; (*formation*) flock; **~ de nuit** night flight; **~ libre** hang-gliding **2.** SPORT **~ à voile** gliding ▸**à ~ d'oiseau** as the crow flies; **en ~ plané** gliding; **prendre son ~** (*oiseau, adolescent*) to leave the nest; **rattraper qc au ~** to catch sth in midair

vol[2] [vɔl] *m* (*larcin*) theft; (*avec violence*) robbery; **~ à main armée** armed robbery; **~ avec effraction** burglary

volage [vɔlaʒ] *adj* (*personne, humeur*) fickle; (*époux*) faithless; **être d'humeur ~** to have a fickle humour *Brit,* to have a fickle humor *Am;* **cœur ~** flighty heart

volaille [vɔlɑj] *f* poultry

volailler, **-ère** [vɔlɑje, -ɛʀ] *m, f* poultry farmer

volant [vɔlɑ̃] *m* **1.** AUTO steering wheel; **être au ~** to be behind the wheel; **se mettre au/prendre le ~** to get behind/take the wheel **2.** TECH flywheel **3.** (*garniture: d'un rideau*) flounce **4.** SPORT shuttlecock **5.** *pl* AVIAT (*personnel volant*) flight crew

volant(**e**) [vɔlɑ̃, ɑ̃t] *adj* flying

volatil(**e**) [vɔlatil] *adj* **1.** CHIM volatile **2.** *soutenu* (*qui disparaît: bien*) transient

volatile [vɔlatil] *m* fowl

volatilisation [vɔlatilizasjɔ̃] *f* **1.** CHIM volatilization **2.** (*disparition*) disappearance

volatiliser [vɔlatilize] <1> **I.** *vt* to volatilize **II.** *vpr* **se ~ 1.** CHIM to volatilize **2.** (*disparaître*) to vanish

volatilité [vɔlatilite] *f* volatility

vol-au-vent [vɔlovɑ̃] *m inv* vol-au-vent

volcan [vɔlkɑ̃] *m* volcano

volcanique [vɔlkanik] *adj* volcanic

volcanologue [vɔlkanɔlɔg] *mf* vulcanologist

volée [vɔle] *f* **1.** (*groupe*) **une ~ de moineaux** a flock of sparrows **2.** (*décharge, raclée*) **une ~ de projectiles/de coups** a volley of projectiles/of blows **3.** SPORT volley; **monter à la ~** to come up to the net **4.** *Suisse* (*élèves d'une même promotion*) year ▸**~ de bois vert** savage attack; **acteur/journaliste de haute ~** top-flight actor/journalist; **prendre sa ~** to spread one's wings; **à la ~** (*au passage*) in mid-air; **à toute ~** with all one's strength

voler[1] [vɔle] <1> *vi* **1.** (*se mouvoir dans l'air, être projeté*) to fly; **~ au vent** (*feuilles*) to fly around in the wind; **faire ~ des feuilles** to blow leaves around **2.** (*courir*) to fly along

voler[2] [vɔle] <1> **I.** *vt* **1.** (*dérober*) to steal **2.** (*tromper*) **~ qn sur la quantité** to cheat sb on the quantity ▸**il ne l'a pas volé** *inf* he was asking for that **II.** *vi* to steal

volet [vɔlɛ] *m* **1.** (*persienne*) shutter; **~ roulant** roller shutter **2.** (*feuillet: d'une pièce administrative*) section **3.** (*panneau: d'un triptyque*) wing **4.** AVIAT, TECH, AUTO flap **5.** (*partie: d'un plan*) point **6.** INFOR **~ de protection contre l'écriture** write-protect tab ▸**trier des personnes/choses sur le ~** to hand-pick people/things

voleter [vɔlte] <4> *vi* (*voltiger*) to flutter

voleur, **-euse** [vɔlœʀ, -øz] **I.** *adj* (*qui dérobe*) light-fingered **II.** *m, f* thief; **~ à la tire** pickpocket; **~ de grand chemin** highwayman ▸**au ~!** stop thief!; **partir** [*o* **filer**] **comme un ~** to sneak away

volière [vɔljɛʀ] *f* aviary

volley(**-ball**) [vɔlɛ(bol), vɔlɛ(bal)] *m sans pl* volleyball

volleyer [vɔleje] <1> *vi* to volley

volleyeur, **-euse** [vɔlɛjœʀ, -jøz] *m, f* **1.** (*joueur de volley*) volleyball player **2.** SPORT volleyer

volontaire [vɔlɔ̃tɛʀ] **I.** *adj* **1.** (*voulu*) deliberate; **incendie ~** arson **2.** (*non contraint*) voluntary; **engagé ~** volunteer **3.** (*décidé*) determined; *péj* (*personne*) wilful *Brit,* willful *Am* **II.** *mf* **1.** *a.* MIL volunteer **2.** *péj* (*personne têtue*) wilful person *Brit,* willful person *Am*

volontairement [vɔlɔ̃tɛʀmɑ̃] *adv* **1.** (*exprès*) *a.* JUR deliberately **2.** (*de son plein gré*) voluntarily

volontariat [vɔlɔ̃taʀja] *m* **1.** (*bénévolat*) voluntary service **2.** MIL volunteering

volontarisme [vɔlɔ̃taʀism] *m* voluntarism

volonté [vɔlɔ̃te] *f* **1.** (*détermination*) will **2.** (*désir*) wish **3.** (*énergie*) willpower ▸**avec la meilleure ~ du monde** with the best will in the world; **à ~** as desired

volontiers [vɔlɔ̃tje] *adv* **1.** (*avec plaisir*) willingly; (*réponse*) with pleasure **2.** (*souvent*) readily

volt [vɔlt] *m* volt

voltage [vɔltaʒ] *m* ELEC voltage

volte-face [vɔltəfas] *f inv* about-turn *Brit,* about-face *Am*

voltige [vɔltiʒ] *f* **1.** (*au cirque*) **numéro de haute ~** acrobatics routine **2.** AVIAT aerobatics **3.** (*équitation*) stunt riding

voltiger [vɔltiʒe] <2a> *vi* **1.** (*voler çà et là*)

V

to flit about **2.** (*flotter légèrement*) **faire ~ qc** to make sth flutter

voltigeur, **-euse** [vɔltiʒœʀ, -ʒøz] *m, f* **1.** (*acrobate au trapèze*) trapeze artist **2.** (*acrobate sur un cheval*) stunt rider

voltmètre [vɔltmɛtʀ] *m* voltmeter

volubile [vɔlybil] *adj* voluble

volubilité [vɔlybilite] *f* volubility

volume [vɔlym] *m* volume

volumétrique [vɔlymetʀik] *adj* volumetric

volumineux, **-euse** [vɔlyminø, -øz] *adj* (*dossier*) voluminous; (*paquet*) bulky

volumique [vɔlymik] *adj* **masse ~** density

volupté [vɔlypte] *f* **1.** (*plaisir sensuel*) sensual pleasure **2.** (*plaisir sexuel*) sexual pleasure **3.** (*plaisir intellectuel*) delight

voluptueusement [vɔlyptɥøzmɑ̃] *adv* voluptuously

voluptueux, **-euse** [vɔlyptɥø, -øz] **I.** *adj* voluptuous **II.** *m, f* voluptuous person

volute [vɔlyt] *f* **1.** (*spirale*) curl **2.** ARCHIT scroll

vomi [vɔmi] *m inf* vomit

vomir [vɔmiʀ] <8> *vt, vi* to vomit

vomissement [vɔmismɑ̃] *m* **1.** (*action*) vomiting **2.** (*vomissure*) vomit *no pl*

vomissure [vɔmisyʀ] *f souvent pl* vomit *no pl*

vomitif [vɔmitif] *m* MED emetic

vomitif, **-ive** [vɔmitif, -iv] *adj* MED emetic

vont [vɔ̃] *indic prés de* **aller**

vorace [vɔʀas] *adj* (*animal, personne*) voracious

voracement [vɔʀasmɑ̃] *adv* voraciously

voracité [vɔʀasite] *f* voracity

vortex [vɔʀtɛks] *m* vortex

vos [vo] *dét poss v.* **votre**

Vosges [voʒ] *fpl* **les ~** the Vosges

votant(e) [vɔtɑ̃, ɑ̃t] *m(f)* (*participant au vote, électeur*) voter

votation [vɔtasjɔ̃] *f Suisse* (*vote*) vote

vote [vɔt] *m* **1.** (*adoption: des crédits*) voting; (*d'un projet de loi*) passing **2.** (*suffrage*) *a.* POL vote; **~ de confiance** vote of confidence; **~ par correspondance** postal vote *Brit,* absentee ballot *Am*

voter [vɔte] <1> **I.** *vi* **~ contre/pour qn/qc** to vote against/for sb/sth; **~ sur qc** to vote on sth; **~ à main levée** to vote by a show of hands **II.** *vt* (*crédits*) to vote; (*loi*) to pass

votre [vɔtʀ] <vos> *dét poss* (*à une/plusieurs personne(s) vouvoyée(s), à plusieurs personnes tutoyées*) your; **à ~ avis** in your opinion; *v. a.* **ma, mon**

Votre [vɔtʀ] <vos> *dét poss, form* **~ Majesté** Your Majesty

vôtre [votʀ] *pron poss* **1. le/la ~** yours; *v. a.* **mien 2.** *pl* (*ceux de votre famille*) **les ~s** your family; (*vos partisans*) your friends; **il est des ~s?** is he one of yours?; *v. a.* **mien** ►**à la (bonne) ~!** *inf* here's to you!

vouer [vwe] <1> **I.** *vt* **1.** (*condamner*) to doom; **~ qn/qc à l'échec** to doom sb/sth to fail **2.** (*consacrer: temps*) to devote **3.** REL **~ qc à un saint/une sainte** to devote sth to a saint **4.** (*ressentir*) **~ de la haine à qn** to vow hatred toward sb **II.** *vpr* **se ~ à qn/qc** to dedicate oneself to sb/sth

vouloir [vulwaʀ] *irr* **I.** *vt* **1.** (*exiger*) to want; **que lui voulez-vous?** what do you want from him? **2.** (*souhaiter*) **il veut/voudrait ce gâteau/deux kilos de pommes** he wants/would like this cake/two kilos of apples; **il voudrait être médecin** he would like to be a doctor **3.** (*consentir à*) **veux-tu/voulez-vous** [*o* **veuillez**] [*o* **voudriez-vous**] **prendre place** (*poli*) would you like to take a seat; (*impératif*) please take a seat **4.** (*attendre: décision, réponse*) to expect; **que veux-tu/voulez-vous que je te/vous dise?** what am I supposed to say? **5.** (*nécessiter: soins*) to require **6.** (*faire en sorte*) **le hasard a voulu qu'il parte ce jour-là** as fate would have it he left that day **7.** (*prétendre*) to claim; **la loi veut que tout délit soit puni** (*subj*) the law expects every crime to be punished ►**bien ~ que qn** +*subj* to be quite happy for sb to +*infin;* **il l'a voulu!** he asked for it! **II.** *vi* **1.** (*être disposé*) to be willing **2.** (*souhaiter*) to wish **3.** (*accepter*) **ne plus ~ de qn** not to want anything more to do with sb; **ne plus ~ de qc** not to want sth any more **4.** (*avoir des griefs envers*) **en ~ à un collègue de qc** to hold sth against a colleague **5.** (*avoir des visées sur*) **en ~ à qc/qn** to have designs on sth/sb ►**(moi,) je veux bien** (*volontiers*) I'd love to; (*concession douteuse*) I don't mind; **en ~** *inf* to play to win; **de l'argent/des cadeaux en veux-tu, en voilà!** money/presents galore! **III.** *vpr* **se ~ honnête** to like to think of oneself as honest ►**s'en ~ de qc** to feel bad about sth

voulu(e) [vuly] **I.** *part passé de* **vouloir II.** *adj* **1.** (*requis: effet*) desired; (*moment*) required; **en temps ~** in due course **2.** (*délibéré*) deliberate; **c'est ~** *inf* it's all on purpose

vous [vu] **I.** *pron pers, 2. pers. pl, pers, forme de politesse* **1.** *sujet, complément d'objet direct et indirect* you **2.** *avec être, devenir, sembler, soutenu* **si cela ~ semble bon** if you approve; *v. a.* **me 3.** *avec les verbes pronominaux* **vous ~ nettoyez (les ongles)** you clean your nails; **vous vous voyez dans le miroir** you see yourself in the mirror **4.** *inf* (*pour renforcer*) **~, vous n'avez pas ouvert la bouche** YOU haven't opened your mouth; **c'est ~ qui l'avez dit** you're the one who said it; **il veut ~ aider, ~?** he wants to help YOU? **5.** (*avec un sens possessif*) **le cœur ~ battait fort** your heart was beating fast **6.** *avec un présentatif* you; **~ voici** [*o* **voilà**]**!** here you are! **7.** *avec une préposition* **avec/sans ~** with/without you; **à ~ deux** (*parler, donner*) to both of you; (*faire qc*) between the two of you; **la maison est à ~?** is the house yours?; **c'est à ~ de décider** it's for you to decide; **c'est à ~!** it's your turn! **8.** *dans une comparaison* you;

nous sommes comme ~ we're like you; **plus fort que** ~ stronger than you **II.** *pron* **1.** (*on*) you; ~ **ne pouvez même pas dormir** you can't even sleep **2.** ((*à*) *quelqu'un*) **des choses qui** ~ **gâchent la vie** things which ruin your life **III.** *m* **dire** ~ **à qn** to call sb "vous"

vous-même [vumɛm] <vous-mêmes> *pron pers, 2. pers. pl, pers, forme de politesse* **1.** (*toi et toi en personne*) ~ **n'en saviez rien** YOU know nothing about it; **vous êtes venus de vous-mêmes** you came of your own free will **2.** (*toi et toi aussi*) yourself; **vous-mêmes** yourselves; *v. a.* **nous-même**

voussure [vusyʀ] *f* arching; ~ **de la fenêtre** arch of the window

voûte [vut] *f* **1.** ARCHIT vault **2.** ANAT ~ **crânienne** dome of the skull **3.** (*ciel*) ~ **étoilée** starry sky

voûté(e) [vute] *adj* **1.** (*en forme de voûte: salle*) vaulted **2.** (*courbé*) round-shouldered

voûter [vute] <1> **I.** *vt* **1.** ARCHIT to arch; **être vouté** to be vaulted **2.** (*courber*) to curve; **l'âge avait voûté son dos** age had bent his back **II.** *vpr* **se** ~ to become round-shouldered

vouvoiement [vuvwamɑ̃] *m* calling sb "vous"

vouvoyer [vuvwaje] <6> **I.** *vt* ~ **qn** to call sb "vous" **II.** *vpr* **se** ~ to call each other "vous"

voyage [vwajaʒ] *m* **1.** (*le fait de voyager*) travel; ~ **en avion/train** air/train travel **2.** (*trajet*) journey; ~ **aller/retour** single/return journey **3.** *inf* (*trip*) trip

voyager [vwajaʒe] <2a> *vi* **1.** (*aller en voyage*) to travel **2.** COM ~ **pour une entreprise** to travel for a company **3.** (*être transporté: marchandises*) to travel

voyageur, -euse [vwajaʒœʀ, -ʒøz] **I.** *adj* **être d'humeur voyageuse** to have a wayfaring nature **II.** *m, f* **1.** (*personne qui voyage*) traveller *Brit,* traveler *Am* **2.** (*dans un avion/sur un bateau*) passenger **3.** COM ~ **de commerce** commercial traveller [*o* traveler *Am*]

voyagiste [vwajaʒist] *m* tour operator

voyais [vwajɛ] *imparf de* **voir**

voyance [vwajɑ̃s] *f* (*occultisme*) clairvoyance

voyant [vwajɑ̃] *m* indicator light

voyant(e) [vwajɑ̃, jɑ̃t] **I.** *part prés de* **voir** **II.** *adj* (*qui se remarque*) garish **III.** *m(f)* **1.** (*devin*) visionary **2.** (*opp: aveugle*) sighted person

voyelle [vwajɛl] *f* vowel

voyeur, -euse [vwajœʀ, -jøz] *m, f* (*amateur de scènes lubriques*) voyeur

voyeurisme [vwajœʀism] *m* **1.** (*perversion du voyeur*) voyeurism **2.** (*curiosité*) curiosity

voyez [vwaje], **voyons** [vwajɔ̃] *indic prés et impératif de* **voir**

voyou [vwaju] **I.** *adj* **il/elle est un peu** ~ he/she is a bit of a lout **II.** *m* **1.** (*délinquant*) lout **2.** (*garnement*) brat

VPC [vepese] *f abr de* **vente par correspondance** mail order

vrac [vʀak] *m* **en** ~ (*en grande quantité*) in bulk; (*non emballé*) loose; **des idées en** ~ some ideas off the top of my head

vrai [vʀɛ] **I.** *m* **le** ~ the truth; **être dans le** ~ to be right; **il y a du** ~ there's some truth ►**à dire** ~ [*o* **à** ~ **dire**] in fact; **pour de** ~ *inf* for real **II.** *adv* **dire** [*o* **parler**] ~ to speak the truth; **faire** ~ to look real

vrai(e) [vʀɛ] *adj* **1.** (*véridique*) true; (*événement*) real **2.** *postposé* (*conforme à la réalité: personnage, tableau*) true to life **3.** *antéposé* (*authentique*) real; (*cause*) true **4.** *antéposé* (*digne de ce nom*) true **5.** *antéposé* (*convenable: méthode, moyen*) proper ►**il n'en est pas moins** ~ **qu'il est trop jeune** it's nevertheless true that he's too young; **pas** ~**?** *inf* right?; ~ **de** ~ *inf* the real thing; ~**!** true!; ~**?** is that so?

vraiment [vʀɛmɑ̃] *adv* really

vraisemblable [vʀɛsɑ̃blabl] *adj* **1.** (*plausible*) convincing **2.** (*probable*) likely

vraisemblablement [vʀɛsɑ̃blabləmɑ̃] *adv* most likely

vraisemblance [vʀɛsɑ̃blɑ̃s] *f* **1.** (*crédibilité*) plausibility **2.** (*probabilité*) likelihood

vrille [vʀij] *f* **1.** TECH gimlet **2.** AVIAT spin **3.** BOT tendril ►**en** ~ in a spin

vrillé(e) [vʀije] *adj* **1.** BOT tendrilled **2.** (*tordu*) twisted

vriller [vʀije] <1> **I.** *vi* (*avion*) to spiral; (*cordon, fil*) to twist **II.** *vt* to bore into

vrombir [vʀɔ̃biʀ] <8> *vi* to throb

vroom, vroum [vʀum] *interj* vroom!

VRP [veɛʀpe] *mf abr de* **voyageurs, représentants, placiers** *inv* rep

vs *prep abr de* **versus** vs.

VSOP [veɛsope] *m abr de* **Very Superior Old Pale** VSOP

VTC [vetese] *m abr de* **vélo tout-chemin** hybrid bicycle

VTT [vetete] *m abr de* **vélo tout-terrain** **1.** (*vélo*) mountain bike **2.** (*sport*) mountain biking

vu [vy] **I.** *prep* in view of **II.** *conj* ~ **qu'il est malade ...** since he's ill ... **III.** *m* **au** ~ **et au su de tous** publicly; **c'est du déjà** ~ we've seen it all before; **c'est du jamais** ~ it's unheard of **IV.** *adv* **ni** ~ **ni connu** with no one any the wiser

vu(e) [vy] **I.** *part passé de* **voir** **II.** *adj* **1.** *pas de forme féminine* (*compris*) all right; (**c'est**) ~**?** *inf* (is it) OK? **2.** (*d'accord*) OK **3.** *form* (*lu*) read **4.** (*observé*) **la remarque est bien/mal** ~**e** it's a judicious/careless remark **5.** (*apprécié*) **être bien/mal** ~ **de qn** to be well-thought-of/disapproved of by sb ►**c'est tout** ~**!** *inf* it's a foregone conclusion

vue [vy] *f* **1.** (*sens*) eyesight; **sa** ~ **d'aigle** her eagle eyes *pl* **2.** (*regard, spectacle: d'une personne, du sang*) sight; **perdre qn/qc de** ~ to lose sight of sb/sth **3.** (*panorama, photo, peinture, conception*) view; ~ **d'ensemble** *fig* overview; **les** ~**s de qn** sb's views **4.** (*visées*)

avoir qn/qc en ~ to have sb/sth in one's sights ►**à** ~ **de nez** *inf* roughly; **à** ~ **d'œil** before one's eyes; **dessiner à** ~ to draw from sight; **garder qn à** ~ to detain sb; **à la** ~ **de qn** (*sous le regard de qn*) with sb looking on; **en** ~ (*visible*) in view; (*tout proche*) in sight; (*célèbre*) prominent; **en** ~ **de** (**faire**) **qc** with a view to (doing) sth

vulcanisation [vylkanizasjɔ̃] *f* vulcanization

vulcaniser [vylkanize] <1> *vt* to vulcanize

vulgaire [vylgɛʀ] **I.** *adj* **1.** (*grossier*) vulgar **2.** *antéposé* (*quelconque*) common **3.** *postposé* (*populaire*) popular **II.** *m* **le** ~ the common people; **tomber dans le** ~ to lapse into vulgarity

vulgairement [vylgɛʀmɑ̃] *adv* **1.** (*grossièrement*) vulgarly **2.** (*couramment: dire, se nommer*) commonly

vulgarisateur, -trice [vylgaʀizatœʀ, -tʀis] **I.** *adj* popularizing **II.** *m, f* **jouer le rôle de** ~ **de qc** to popularize sth

vulgarisation [vylgaʀizasjɔ̃] *f* popularization; **revue de** ~ magazine for a wider public

vulgariser [vylgaʀize] <1> **I.** *vt* to popularize **II.** *vpr* **se** ~ to become popularized

vulgarité [vylgaʀite] *f* (*grossièreté, parole vulgaire: d'un langage*) vulgarity; (*d'une personne*) coarseness

vulnérabilité [vylneʀabilite] *f* vulnerability; **la** ~ **de ma situation** the precarity of my situation

vulnérable [vylneʀabl] *adj* vulnerable; (*situation*) precarious

vulve [vylv] *f* **la** ~ the vulva

W

W, w [dubləve] *m inv* W, w; ~ **comme William** w as in William; (*on telephone*) w for William

wagnérien(ne) [vagneʀjɛ̃, jɛn] **I.** *adj* **opéra** ~ Wagnerian opera **II.** *m(f)* Wagnerian

wagon [vagɔ̃] *m* CHEMDFER carriage

wagon-citerne [vagɔ̃sitɛʀn] <wagons-citernes> *m* tank wagon

wagon-lit [vagɔ̃li] <wagons-lits> *m* sleeping car

wagon-restaurant [vagɔ̃ʀɛstɔʀɑ̃] <wagons-restaurants> *m* restaurant car

walkie-talkie [wokitoki, wɔlkitɔlki] *m v.* **talkie-walkie**

walkman® [wɔkman] *m* Walkman®

wallon(ne) [walɔ̃] **I.** *adj* Walloon **II.** *m* **le** ~ Walloon; *v. a.* **français**

Wallon(ne) [walɔ̃] *m(f)* Walloon

Wallonie [walɔni] *f* **la** ~ Wallonia

wap [wap] *adj* WAP

warning [waʀniŋ] *m* warning

Washington [waʃiŋtɔn] *m* **1.** (*État*) **le** ~ Washington **2.** (*ville*) Washington DC.

water-polo [watɛʀpɔlo] <water-polos> *m* water polo

watt [wat] *m* watt

wattheure [watœʀ] *m* watt-hour

W.-C. [vese] *mpl abr de* **water-closet(s)** WC

Web, WEB [vɛb] *m* **le** ~ the Web

Webmane [vɛbman] *mf* webmaniac

Webcam [vɛbkam] *f* web camera

Webmestre [vɛbmɛstʀ] *m* webmaster

webnaute [vɛbnot] *mf* [web] surfer

week-end [wikɛnd] <week-ends> *m* weekend

welsch(e) [vɛlʃ] *adj Suisse, iron* French-speaking (*from Switzerland*)

Welsch(e) [vɛlʃ] *m(f) Suisse, iron* French-speaker (*from Switzerland*)

western [wɛstɛʀn] *m* western

white-spirit [wajtspiʀit] *m inv* white spirit

World Wide Web *m* World Wide Web

X, x [iks] *m inv* **1.** (*lettre*) X, x; ~ **comme Xavier** x for Xmas **2.** *inf* (*plusieurs*) **x fois** Heaven knows how many times **3.** (*Untel*) X; **contre X** against persons unknown **4.** CINE **film classé X** ≈ 18 film *Brit,* X-rated movie *Am*

xénophobe [gzenɔfɔb] **I.** *adj* xenophobic **II.** *mf* xenophobe

xylophone [ksilɔfɔn] *m* xylophone

Y

Y, y [igʀɛk] *m inv* Y, y; ~ **comme Yvonne** y for Yellow *Brit,* y for Yoke *Am*

y [i] **I.** *adv* there **II.** *pron pers* (*à/sur cela*) **s'y entendre** to manage; **ne pas y tenir** not to be very keen

yacht [jɔt] *m* yacht

yaourt [jauʀt] *m* yoghurt

Yémen [jemɛn] *m* **le** ~ Yemen

yen [jɛn] *m* yen

yeux [jø] *mpl v.* **œil**

yiddish [jidiʃ] **I.** *adj inv* Yiddish **II.** *m* **le** ~ Yiddish; *v. a.* **français**

yog[h]ourt [jɔgurt] *m v.* **yaourt**

yougoslave [jugɔslav] *adj* Yugoslav

Yougoslave [jugɔslav] *mf* Yugoslav

Yougoslavie [jugɔslavi] *f* **la** ~ Yugoslavia; **République fédérale de** ~ Federal Republic of Yugoslavia

youpi, youppie [jupi] *interj* yippee

Z

Z, z [zɛd] *m inv* Z, z; ~ **comme Zoé** z for Zebra

Zaïre [zaiʀ] *m* HIST **le** ~ Zaïre

zaïrois(e) [zaiʀwa] *adj* HIST Zaïrean

Zaïrois(e) [zaiʀwa] *m(f)* HIST Zaïrean

Zambie [zɑ̃bi] *f* **la** ~ Zambia

zambien(ne) [zɑ̃bjɛ̃] *adj* Zambian

Zambien(ne) [zɑ̃bjɛ̃] *m(f)* Zambian

zapper [zape] <1> *vi* to zap

zèbre [zɛbʀ] *m* ZOOL zebra

zébré(e) [zebʀe] *adj* **1.** (*rayé*) striped **2.** (*marqué*) streaked

zèle [zɛl] *m* zeal; **faire du** ~ *péj* to go over the top

zélé(e) [zele] *adj* zealous

zénith [zenit] *m a. fig* zenith

ZEP [zɛp] *f abr de* **zone d'éducation prioritaire** ≈ education action zone

zéro [zeʀo] **I.** *num* **1.** *antéposé* (*aucun*) no **2.** *inf* (*nul*) useless **II.** *m* **1.** *inv* (*nombre*) nought *Brit*, naught *Am* **2.** *fig a.* METEO, PHYS zero **3.** ECOLE **avoir** ~ **sur dix/sur vingt** nought [*o* zero *Am*] out of ten/twenty **4.** (*rien*) nothing **5.** (*personne incapable*) dead loss

zeste [zɛst] *m a. fig* zest

zézayer [zezeje] <7> *vi* to lisp

zieuter [zjøte] <1> *vt inf* to eye

zigouiller [ziguje] <1> *vt inf* (*tuer*) to waste

zigzag [zigzag] *m* zigzag

zigzaguer [zigzage] <1> *vi* to zigzag

Zimbabwe [zimbabwe] *m* **le** ~ Zimbabwe

zimbabwéen(ne) [zimbabweɛ̃] *adj* Zimbabwean

Zimbabwéen(ne) [zimbabweɛ̃] *m(f)* Zimbabwean

zinc [zɛ̃g] *m* **1.** zinc **2.** *inf* (*comptoir*) counter **3.** *inf* (*avion*) plane

zingueur [zɛ̃gœʀ] *m* zinc worker

zinzin [zɛ̃zɛ̃] *adj inf* loopy

zip® [zip] *m* zip *Brit*, zipper *Am*

zizi [zizi] *m enfantin, inf* willy *Brit*, peter *Am*

zodiaque [zɔdjak] *m* zodiac

zonard(e) [zonaʀ] **I.** *adj inf* inner-city **II.** *m(f) péj, inf* (*marginal*) dropout

zone [zon] *f* **1.** *a.* GEO zone; ~ **d'influence** sphere of influence **2.** (*monétaire*) area; ~ **euro** eurozone **3.** INFOR ~ **de dialogue** dialogue zone

zoo [z(o)o] *m* zoo

zoologique [zɔɔlɔʒik] *adj* zoological; **parc** ~ zoo

zozoter [zɔzɔte] <1> *vi inf* to lisp

zut [zyt] *interj inf* drat

Supplément I

Correspondance personnelle 584

Correspondance commerciale 606

Formules courantes dans la correspondance 618

Expressions utiles 621

Supplement I

Private correspondence 584

Business correspondence 606

Useful expressions in letters 618

Useful phrases 621

Correspondance personnelle
Private correspondence

A l'office du tourisme: demande de documentation

M. et Mme Norbert Petit
5, rue du Dr Chaussier
21000 Dijon

Comité Départemental
du Tourisme du Finistère
11, rue Théodore-Le-Hars
29104 Quimper cedex

Dijon, le 2 février 2002

Messieurs,

Je désire passer mes vacances avec ma famille dans la région de Quimper en juillet.

C'est pourquoi je vous serais reconnaissant de bien vouloir m'envoyer une documentation sur les sites touristiques et les hôtels de cette région.

D'avance, je vous remercie de votre réponse.

Je vous prie de croire, Messieurs, à ma considération distinguée.

Petit

Je désire passer mes vacances ...	*I wish to spend my holidays ...*
envoyer une documentation	*to send details*

Note: French writers put both their name and address at the top left of the page, with the name and address of the other person below and to the left.

Tourist office: asking for information

65 Rogers Road,
Rickland
GN8 4BY

2 February 2002

England Tourist Board
New Park
Southbridge
Kent
XP1 7TU

Dear Sirs,

My family and I wish to spend our holidays in the South-East during July.

Could you kindly send me details of places of interest and hotels.

With thanks,

Yours faithfully,

John Roberts

A noter: Les Anglais mettent rarement le nom de famille en haut de la lettre. L'adresse de l'expéditeur est en haut à droite, celle du destinataire à gauche. On signera John Roberts ou J. Roberts, mais jamais Roberts tout court.

Réserver une chambre d'hôtel

Monsieur,

Je vous remercie de votre dépliant me donnant tous les détails sur les conditions de séjour dans votre hôtel.

Je vous prie de réserver pour ma femme, moi-même et nos deux filles deux chambres avec douche et W. C., l'une à deux lits, l'autre à un grand lit, en demi-pension, du 2 au 15 juillet compris.

D'avance je vous remercie de votre confirmation.

Veuillez recevoir, Monsieur, l'assurance de mes sentiments distingués.

Petit

votre dépliant me donnant tous les détails — *your leaflet giving details*

Je vous prie de réserver … — *I would like to book …*

Booking a room in a hotel

Dear Sirs,

Thank you for your leaflet giving details about your hotel.

I would like to book two double rooms with bathroom at half-board from 2 to 15 July inclusive, one for my wife and myself with double bed, and one with twin beds for my two daughters.

I would be grateful if you could confirm this booking.

Yours sincerely,

John Roberts

Demander des renseignements pour une location de vacances

Monsieur,

L'office du tourisme m'a envoyé la liste et le descriptif des gîtes ruraux de votre ville et ses environs.

L'appartement meublé que vous proposez m'intéresse particulièrement. Je souhaiterais le louer pour une période d'un mois à compter du premier juillet. Mais j'aimerais, avant de me décider, quelques renseignements supplémentaires.

Pourriez-vous me préciser si les charges (gaz, électricité et autres taxes) sont comprises dans le prix de la location ; et quel serait le montant des arrhes à verser ? Est-ce que la literie est fournie ? Et enfin, est-ce que les animaux sont admis ?

Dans l'attente de votre réponse, je vous prie de recevoir, Monsieur, l'assurance de mes sincères salutations.

Petit

la liste et le descriptif des gîtes ruraux	*a detailed list of holiday lettings*
un appartement meublé	*a furnished apartment*
pour une période d'un mois à compter du premier juillet	*for one month from 1 July*
Pourriez-vous me préciser si ...	*Could you tell me if ...*
le prix de la location	*the rent*
le montant des arrhes à verser	*the deposit*
Est-ce que la literie est fournie ?	*Is bedding provided?*

Information about a holiday apartment

Dear Sir,

The tourist office has sent me details of holiday lettings in and around your town and I am particularly interested in your furnished apartment. I would like to rent it for one month from 1 July. However I should be grateful for some further details before making a final decision

Could you tell me if bills (gas, electricity and any taxes) are included in the rent? What deposit do you require? Is bedding provided? And finally, are pets welcome?

Yours sincerely,

John Roberts

Réserver une location de vacances

Monsieur,

Je vous remercie de votre prompte réponse.

Ayant pris connaissance des renseignements complémentaires que vous avez eu l'amabilité de me communiquer, je vous confirme ma décision de louer votre appartement du premier au trente juillet inclus.

Ci-joint vous trouverez un chèque de 1 500 francs, à valoir comme arrhes. Le solde, c'est-à-dire 7 000 francs, vous en sera réglé le jour de notre arrivée, le premier juillet.

Dans l'attente de votre réponse, je vous prie de recevoir, Monsieur, l'assurance de mes sincères salutations.

Petit

P.S. : Vous voudrez bien nous préciser où prendre les clés de l'appartement, le jour de notre arrivée.

... que vous avez eu l'amabilité de nous communiquer	*... that you have kindly sent*
je vous confirme ma décision de louer	*I confirm that we have decided to rent*
à valoir comme arrhes	*as a deposit*
Le solde vous en sera réglé ...	*We will pay the balance ...*
Vous voudrez bien nous préciser où ...	*Kindly let us know where ...*

Booking a holiday apartment

Dear Mr Hill,

Thank you for answering my letter so quickly.

I have read through the information and I can now confirm that we have decided to rent your apartment from 1 to 30 July inclusive.

I enclose a cheque for £150; amd we will pay the balance of £700 on our arrival on 1 July.

Yours sincerely,

John Roberts

PS: Kindly let us know where to pick up the keys to the apartment on the day of our arrival.

Carte de vacances

Chère Elisabeth, Cher Pascal,

Un très grand bonjour de la Martinique où depuis une semaine nous profitons du soleil et du sable chaud à l'ombre des cocotiers et des gommiers. Nous avons déjà goûté à toutes les spécialités culinaires. Et que dire du merveilleux rhum martiniquais ?! Bref, des vacances de rêve, même si l'hôtel est, certes confortable, mais très bruyant. Nous espérons que vous allez bien tous les deux et que vous ne souffrez pas trop des grands froids du nord de la métropole.

Grosses bises.

Monique et François

M. et Mme Canevet
23, rue Gilbert

75000 Paris

Holiday postcard

Here we are in Barbados. There's plenty of sun, sand and palm trees. The beach suits me fine, but Peter keeps trying to tempt me off the beach to join him for some water-skiing. The hotel is good and the food is delicious, but the disco can be rather noisy if you want an early night! We have another week here before we head back home to a British winter. We hope that you're both well and we'll see you soon.

Love from

Maggie and Peter

Gemma and John Roberts
65 Rogers Road
Rickland
GN8 4BY

Vœux de fin d'année (à de très bons amis)

Chère Chantal, Cher Robert,

Un très grand merci de vos vœux de fin d'année.

A mon tour, je vous souhaite un très joyeux Noël et une excellente année 2002, en espérant qu'elle vous apporte toutes les joies et les satisfactions que vous attendez.

A très bientôt à Paris ou en Angleterre.

Bises

Marie et Edouard

Christmas and New Years Wishes

Dear Julia and Robert,

Wishing you both a very Merry Christmas and an excellent New Year, hoping that it brings you all the joy and success you wish for.

Hope to see you soon over here or back home in the States.

Love from

Maddie and Neil

Vœux de fin d'année (à des connaissances)

MADAME PREVOST-PREUX

Avocat au barreau de Cambrai

vous présente, ainsi qu'à votre famille, ses vœux de bonne et heureuse année.

Amicalement vôtre

Prevost-Preux

Christmas Greetings – for businesses

A very Happy Christmas and good wishes for the New Year

from

Elaine Goodman

Goodman and Hart
Solicitors
48 High Street
Rickland
GN8 4SK

Carte d'anniversaire

Cher Daniel,

26 juillet : une année de plus... Mais peu importe, tu es et resteras toujours jeune.

Nous te souhaitons de tout cœur un très joyeux anniversaire.

Si nous n'habitions pas aussi loin, nous t'aurions apporté nous-mêmes notre petit cadeau : la poste s'en chargera. Nous espérons qu'il arrivera à temps. Encore une fois : bon anniversaire (arrose-le bien !)

Nous t'embrassons affectueusement.

Sophie et Michel

Nous te souhaitons de tout cœur un très joyeux anniversaire.	*We wish you a very happy birthday.*

Birthday card

Dear Simon,

Happy Birthday! But I can't believe it's a year since the last one!

It's far too long since we got together and it's a real shame that we won't be around for the celebrations. We hope you like our little present and that you'll have a good time on the day.

Love from

Sophie and Mike

Répondre à un faire-part de décès (à des connaissances)

M. et Mme Thibaut

ont appris avec émotion la perte cruelle qui
vous frappe et vous présentent leurs très
sincères condoléances.

Thibaut

leurs très sincères condoléances — *our sincere condolences*

Condolences

We were deeply saddened to hear of your sad loss and wish to offer our sincere condolences

With our deepest sympathy,

James and Barbara Thornton

Invitation

Chers amis,

Depuis un mois nous sommes installés dans notre nouvelle maison à Saint-Benin, un petit village très pittoresque du nord de la France.

Nous serions très heureux de vous y accueillir pour le week-end de la Pentecôte. Le samedi soir nous pendrons la crémaillère avec tous nos amis. Nous aimerions que vous soyez de la partie.

Ci-joint un plan pour ne pas vous perdre.

En espérant une réponse positive de votre part, nous vous adressons toutes nos amitiés.

Elisabeth et Pascal

nous pendrons la crémaillère	*we're throwing a house-warming party*
Ci-joint un plan	*We have enclosed a map*
En espérant une réponse positive de votre part …	*Hoping that you can make it …*

Invitation

Dear Angela and Martin,

It's just over a month since we moved into our new house at Bennington. We like it here in the north of England, and it's very picturesque.

Would you be able to come and stay with us for the holiday weekend? We're throwing a house-warming party on Saturday night and would be very happy if you could be there.

We have enclosed a map so that you don't get lost.

Hoping that you can make it.

With warm regards,

Elizabeth and Paul

Accepter une invitation

Chers amis,

C'est évidemment avec un très grand plaisir que nous acceptons votre gentille invitation. Nous nous faisons une joie de vous revoir.

Nous arriverons donc le vendredi soir et repartirons le lundi matin.

Merci pour le plan.

Nous profitons de cette courte réponse pour vous féliciter de votre nouvelle demeure.

Nos sincères amitiés.

Annie et Bernard

Nous nous faisons une joie de vous revoir. *We're really looking forward to seeing you again.*

Accepting an invitation

Dear Elizabeth and Paul,

Of course we would be delighted to accept your kind invitation and we're really looking forward to seeing you again.

We should get there early on Friday evening we'll be off again on Monday morning. Thanks for the map.

Congratulations on your new home.

With warmest regards

Angela and Martin

Refuser une invitation

Chers amis,

Votre aimable invitation nous a beaucoup touchés et nous vous en remercions vivement.

Malheureusement, nous avons déjà pris des engagements familiaux qui ne nous permettent pas de nous libérer ce week-end-là. Dommage !

Nous aurions été très heureux de vous revoir, mais peut-être qu'une autre occasion de nous réunir se présentera bientôt.

Recevez, Chers amis, notre meilleur souvenir.

Anne et Bernard

Nous avons déjà pris des engagements familiaux. *We already have family commitments.*

Dear Elizabeth and Paul,

We were delighted to receive your kind invitation and would like to thank you very much.

We're terribly sorry but we already have family commitments that prevent us getting away on that weekend. Shame! It would have been great to get out into the country for a break.

We're terribly sorry we won't be seeing you, let's hope there'll be another chance to get together in the near future.

With our best wishes,

Angela and Martin

Remerciements après un séjour

Chère Madame, Cher Monsieur,

Nous voulons vous remercier bien sincèrement de nous avoir si gentiment et si chaleureusement reçus.

Nous n'oublierons jamais tous les merveilleux moments passés en votre compagnie. Grâce à toutes les excursions que vous avez eu la gentillesse d'organiser pour nous, nous avons pu découvrir pour la première fois votre ville, votre région et une autre manière de vivre.

Veuillez dire à vos voisins, Monsieur et Madame Lebeau, que nous gardons un excellent souvenir de toutes les parties de boule faites ensemble.

Nous vous remercions encore pour tout et espérons avoir bientôt le plaisir de vous faire visiter, à notre tour, notre pays.

Nous vous prions de recevoir, Chère Madame, Cher Monsieur, nos salutations amicales.

John Good

de nous avoir si gentiment et si chaleureusement reçus	*for the warm welcome you gave us*
les merveilleux moments passés en votre compagnie	*the wonderful time we spent with you*
nous gardons un excellent souvenir de …	*we won't forget …*

Thanks after staying in someone's home

Dear Mr and Mrs Shaw,

We would like to say a big thank you for the warm welcome you gave us.

We had a wonderful time while we were with you. We have many happy memories of our outings in Exeter and its surroundings and I hope you'll enjoy the photographs we took.

Would you please thank all your friends, especially Bob and Sandra Carter from the tennis club, who did so much to make our stay enjoyable.

It was a holiday to remember and I hope it will not be too long before we are able to welcome you to our country.

Yours sincerely,

Jacques Lunel

Faire-part de mariage et invitation

M. et Mme Lempereur
et M. et Mme Lesur

ont le plaisir de vous faire part du mariage de leurs enfants,

Isabelle et Victor.

Ils vous prient d'assister à la bénédiction nuptiale qui leur sera donnée le samedi 12 juin 2001 à 11 heures en l'église Sainte-Catherine à Lille.

M. et Mme Lempereur
et M. et Mme Lesur

recevront à l'issue de la cérémonie religieuse

au Manoir Le Vent, Lille

R.S.V.P.

à l'issue de la cérémonie religieuse	*following the ceremony*
R.S.V.P. (Répondez, s'il vous plaît)	*R.S.V.P.*

Marriage announcement

Mr and Mrs Henry Grant

request the pleasure of your company at the marriage of their daughter Christine to Mr Robin Davies

at St Anne's Church, Lewes on Saturday 17 June at 11 a.m.

and at the reception afterwards at

Hollyoak Manor, Kingston

R.S.V.P

Invitation à un mariage (à de bons amis)

Chère Marie-Claire, Cher Jean,

Je prends ma plus belle plume pour vous annoncer la grande nouvelle : Isabelle se marie ! Mais vous avez sûrement déjà lu le petit carton joint à cette lettre.

Nous espérons de tout cœur que vous nous ferez le plaisir d'assister à ce mariage. Nous serions tellement heureux de vous avoir parmi nous. Ce sera l'occasion de nous revoir et de faire la fête ensemble. Nous comptons sur votre présence.

Quant à l'hébergement, ne vous inquiétez pas ! Tout sera prêt.

En attendant le plaisir de vous revoir, nous vous envoyons nos sincères amitiés.

Thérèse et Bernard Lempereur

... que vous nous ferez le plaisir d'assister à ce mariage	*... that you will be able to come to the wedding*
Ce sera l'occasion de nous revoir.	*It will be good to see each other again.*
Nous comptons sur votre présence.	*We are counting on you.*

Wedding invitation

Dear Helen and Mark,

I've got some news for you: Christine is getting married! You'll be getting the invitation card in the post soon.

We really hope that you you can come to the wedding. We would be delighted to have you with us. It would be good to see each other again and celebrate together. We are counting on you.

Don't worry about where to stay, we'll take care of everything.

We hope to see you again soon,

With our very best wishes,

Lorna and Henry Grant

Accepter l'invitation au mariage

Chère Christine, Cher Christian

Nous avons été très touchés de votre gentille invitation à l'occasion du mariage de votre fille Isabelle, que nous acceptons bien entendu avec le plus grand plaisir. Nous serons heureux de pouvoir complimenter le jeune couple.

Nous vous remercions d'avoir pensé à nous et nous réjouissons déjà de vous revoir après tous ces mois de silence. Mais comme vous le savez, nos occupations professionnelles nous accaparent énormément et les semaines passent si vite!

En espérant que toute la famille se porte bien, nous vous disons à très bientôt.

Amicalement à vous.

Marie-Claire et Jean

P.S.: Peut-être pourriez-vous nous suggérer un cadeau de mariage qui serait susceptible de plaire aux jeunes époux. Merci d'avance.

… que nous acceptons avec le plus grand plaisir	*… which we are delighted to accept*
après tous ces mois de silence	*after so many months*
nos occupations professionnelles nous accaparent énormément	*our professional lives keep us so busy*
suggérer un cadeau de mariage qui serait susceptible de plaire aux jeunes époux	*suggest a wedding gift that the newlyweds would like*

Acceptance of a wedding invitation

Dear Lorna and Henry

We were very so pleased to hear about Christine's wedding, and delighted to get your invitation. Of course we shall be coming and look forward to seeing the young couple and giving them our best wishes.

Things have been terribly busy at work over the past few months. Time passes too quickly and it's easy to lose touch with our friends, so it will be lovely to see you all again.

We hope that everyone is keeping well and we will see you soon.

With warmest regards,

Helen and Mark

P.S. Do you have any ideas for a wedding gift that Christine and Robin might like? We'd be very grateful for suggestions.

Remerciements pour un cadeau de mariage

Chers amis,

Comment vous remercier pour le superbe cadeau que vous avez eu la gentillesse de nous faire à l'occasion de notre mariage ?

Nous avons été très touchés par votre geste. Vous nous avez vraiment gâtés.

Merci encore, Chers amis, et croyez à notre sincère amitié.

Sophie et Marc

le superbe cadeau que vous avez eu la gentillesse de nous faire	*the wonderful present that you gave us*
Vous nous avez vraiment gâtés.	*It was really too much.*

Thanks for a wedding gift

Dear Helen and Mark

Thank you so much for the wonderful present that you gave us for our wedding.

We were very touched by your kindness. It was really too much.

Thank you once again.

With our love,

Christine and Robin

Remerciements pour un cadeau d'anniversaire

Chère Sophie, Cher Michel,

Votre cadeau est bien arrivé le bon jour et à la bonne heure.

Mille mercis. Vraiment c'est trop. Vous me mettez presque dans l'embarras. Vous saviez que rien ne me ferait plus plaisir et vous ne perdez pas une occasion de me prouver votre affection qui est, comme vous le savez, réciproque.

Encore une fois merci et à très bientôt.

Je vous embrasse bien fort.

Daniel

Mille mercis.	*Thank you so much.*
Vous me mettez presque dans l'embarras.	*I'm almost overwhelmed.*

Thanks for a birthday present

Dear Sophie and Mike,

You always remember my birthday – even though I'd rather forget about it now!

Thank you so much your present – really you shouldn't have. It made my day: you certainly know what I like! It will remind me of you, but don't think I really need any reminder. I could never forget good friends like you.

Thanks once again, and I hope it won't be too long before we see each other.

Love

Simon

Correspondance commerciale
Business correspondence

Passation de commande

Monsieur René Fourt
46, bd du Général-de-Gaulle
59100 Roubaix

Roseraie Paul Guallot
Domaine de La Source
38460 Chamagnieu

Objet: Commande

Roubaix, le 10 mars 2002

Monsieur,

A la suite de notre entretien téléphonique de ce matin je vous confirme ma commande des rosiers suivants:

Désignation	Quantité
Rose mousse „Goethe“	10
Rose de Damas „Celsina“	5
Rose de Chine „Perle d'or“	6

La facture sera payée par virement bancaire.

Je vous serais reconnaissant de bien vouloir me livrer, comme convenu, sous huitaine.

Veuillez agréer, Monsieur, l'expression de mes salutations distinguées.

René Fourt

Ordering

46, Ambrose Crescent
Silhurst
CW3 8DS

Hitchfield Electronics
Chingleford
QN4 6RT

10 March 2002

Dear Sir,

Re. Printer supplies

Further to our telephone conversation this morning, I would like to confirm my order for the following items:

Type	Quantity
Printer cable, code HX398	1
Inkjet cartridges, black, code HW 546	2
Colour cartridge, code HW 756	1

Please debit my credit card, no. 1111 2222 3333 4444, expiry date 02/04

I understand that you deliver within three working days.

Yours faithfully,

Ronald Grieves

Accuser réception d'une commande

Céramique – CERPOR – Porcelaine
15, rue Marie Curie
13006 Marseille
Tel. : 04.91.56.91.11

Ets Casserole
11, rue du Colombier
45032 Orléans

Marseille, le 18 avril 2002

Messieurs,

Nous avons bien reçu votre commande n° 32 du 15 courant et vous en remercions.

Soyez assurés que nous apporterons tous nos soins à son excécution.

Nous acceptons vos conditions de livraison et de paiement, à savoir :
Livraison : avant le 12 mai, franco de port, par service routier.
Règlement : dans les 60 jours à compter de la date de facturation, sans escompte.

Conditions particulières : nous vous reconnaissons, dès maintenant, le droit de refuser les articles qui ne vous seraient pas livrés d'ici au 12 mai.

Toujours dévoués à vos ordres, nous vous prions d'agréer, Messieurs, l'expression de nos sentiments distingués.

ABlaise

Anne Blaise
Service des Ventes

Confirming receipt of an order

PWP Ceramics
15, Highbridge Road
Mingley
WP9 7SA
Tel.: 024 4825 3147

Hailingbury plc
11, Foghard Way
Hocksmore
TQ3 6BV

18 April 2002

Dear Sirs,

Thank you for your order number 32 dated 15 April.

This order will be dealt with and shipped as soon as possible

Our standard payment and delivery conditions apply, i.e.

Delivery: by 12 May, carriage paid, by courier service.
Payment: within 60 days of the billing date, without discount.

All goods should be inspected on delivery.

Yours faithfully,

A Black

Anne Black
Sales Department

Réclamations

Raoul Germain
38, cours Napoléon
45032 Orléans

Orléans, le 20 avril 2002

Madame,

Les articles commandés par lettre en date du 22 mars me sont bien parvenus.

Cependant, j'ai constaté parmi ceux-ci que l'article référencé 36 A n° 5 présentait un défaut de fabrication: ce qui est inacceptable pour un article de ce prix.

Je vous le renvoie donc à vos frais et vous demande de le remplacer sans délai.

Avec mes remerciements, veuillez agréer, Madame, l'expression de mes salutations distinguées.

Raoul Germain

Complaints

38, Swinburne Avenue
Hawdrey
MY7 9PL

20 April 2002

Dear Madam

I have received the items ordered by letter dated 22March.

However, further inspection has revealed a defect in the cooler unit, part reference PL-00274/B and this prevents its use in the manufacturing process.

I would be therefore be grateful if you would supply a replacement unit a.s.a.p. Please advise us when you will be able to deliver and collect the defective item from us.

Yours faithfully,

C Benson

Charles Benson

Lettre de candidature

Ann Roberts
65 Rogers Road,
Rickland
GN8 4BY

Rickland, le 3 novembre 2002

Objet: Lettre de candidature au poste de secrétaire-assistante

Madame, Monsieur,

Comme suite à votre annonce parue dans «le Monde» de ce jour, je pose ma candidature au poste de secrétaire-assistante des ventes que vous proposez au sein de votre entreprise.

Je suis actuellement à la recherche d'un emploi à temps complet qui puisse me permettre de développer mes qualités d'organisation et d'utiliser mes connaissances en anglais (langue maternelle), français et allemand que j'ai pu approfondir au cours de plusieurs séjours ou stages à l'étranger. De par mon emploi actuel j'ai acquis une bonne maîtrise de l'informatique.

Veuillez trouver ci-joint mon curriculum vitae.

Je me tiens à votre disposition pour un entretien au jour et à l'heure qui vous conviendront.

Je vous prie de croire, Madame, Monsieur, à l'expression de mes sentiments distingués.

Ann Roberts

Application letter

Chantal Leroy
10, rue St. Léonard
17000 La Rochelle

3 November 2002

Dear Sir or Madam,

Re: Application for post of Secretary/Personal Assistant

With reference to your advertisement in today's *Guardian*, I would like to apply for the position of Secretary/Personal Assistant to the Sales Manager.

I am currently looking for full-time work that will allow me to develop my organizational skills and to use my French (mother tongue), English and German which I have been able to practise during several visits and training programmes abroad. My current position has enabled me to acquire sound computing skills.

I enclose my curriculum vitae.

Please do not hesitate to contact me to arrange a suitable time for an interview.

Yours faithfully,

Chantal Leroy

Lettre de candidature spontanée

Ann Roberts
65 Rogers Road,
Rickland
GN8 4BY

Rickland, le 1er septembre 2002

Monsieur le Directeur,

La réputation de votre entreprise est à la mesure de la qualité de ses produits et de son dynamisme. J'ai appris que vous étiez sur le point d'adopter une nouvelle politique marketing: domaine qui m'intéresse particulièrement.

Dans la société où je travaille actuellement j'ai organisé le service publicité, et en trois ans sa notoriété a été multiplié par deux (voir C.V. joint).

Mes expériences professionnelles, mes qualités de rigueur et d'organisation, mais aussi ma créativité me donnent à penser que je corresponds au profil exigé par une fonction au sein de votre équipe.

De plus, je parle couramment anglais (langue maternelle), français et allemand.

Si cette offre est susceptible de vous intéresser, je me tiens à votre disposition pour un prochain rendez-vous.

Dans cette attente, je vous prie de croire, Monsieur le Directeur, à l'assurance de ma considération distinguée.

Ann Roberts

Unsolicited application letter

François Ripou
6, rue de la Victoire
14104 Lisieux
Tel. : 02.13.12.92.01

1 September 2002

Dear Sir,

I have been following the performance of your company and have been particularly interested by press reports that you are currently overhauling your overseas marketing strategy.

Over the past three years I have been closely involved in the restructuring of our advertising department, which has led to an 80 % increase in public awareness of our brands at home, and a 50 % increase in overseas sales. You will find full details of my work and responsibilities in the enclosed CV.

I am proud of my achievements and I believe that my professionalism, creativity and discipline could be a major asset to your organization.

I hope that we will be able to meet and discuss this further.

Yours faithfully,

François Ripou

Curriculum vitæ

Ann Roberts
65 Rogers Road,
Rickland
GN8 4BY

Née le 2 juillet 1970
Nationalité britannique
Célibataire

TRILINGUE (ANGLAIS, FRANÇAIS, ALLEMAND)

4 années d'école primaire en France et fréquents séjours dans le pays
année de stage chez Sama en Allemagne

FORMATION

1992	A Levels (Anglais, Français, Allemand, Histoire)
1994	Highfield Tertiary College (cours de secrétariat)
1998	BA Français & Etudes Commerciales, Université de Brighton (équivalent Licence)

EXPERIENCE PROFESSIONNELLE

Depuis octobre 1999	Secrétaire-assistante du Directeur Export de la Société RIGMONT (groupe informatique) Fonctions : • suivi des commandes • contacts avec les filiales à l'étranger • prospection de la clientèle étrangère
Avril – août 1999	Stagiaire chez PUBLICAT, agence de Presse à Strasbourg, au secrétariat de direction (maîtrise de la mise en page informatique)
Octobre 1995 – juin 1996	Stagiaire chez Sama à Cologne en Allemagne : correspondancière (allemand et anglais)

DIVERS

Animatrice du club informatique dans une Maison des Jeunes

Sports : gymnastique, judo

Curriculum vitae

Chantal Leroy
10, rue St. Léonard
17000 La Rochelle
Tel. 05.46.43.12.83

Date of Birth: 02/07/1970
French
Single

EDUCATION & TRAINING

1991	Brevet de Technician Supérieur – International Business (=NVQ)
1990	Cours Pigier (shorthand and typing)
1988	Baccalaureate (= A levels in Economics, Maths, French, English)

PROFESSIONAL EXPERIENCE

Since October 1999	Personal assistant to the Export Director of a software company	
	Responsibilities:	Follow-up of orders Contacts with subsidiaries abroad Canvassing foreign clients
April – August 1999	Trainee at Publicat, press agency in Strasbourg, in the office of the director's secretary (learning computer page layout techniques)	
October 1997 – March 1998	Trainee at Sama in Cologne, Germany, in Customer Relations, dealing with telephone enquiries in three languages	

LANGUAGES

Trilingual: French, English, German
4 years' primary education in Great Britain and frequent holidays
6 months as a trainee for Sama in Germany

OTHER INTERESTS

Volunteer helper with a local disabled group
Sports: gymnastics, judo

Formules courantes dans la correspondance

Useful expressions in letters

L'appel

At the beginning of a letter

Vous écrivez ...	When you're writing ...
... à une bonne connaissance ou à des amis • Dear Mark, • Dear Janet,	**... to someone you know or to a friend** • Mon cher Louis, • Ma chère Caroline, • Bien chers tous,
... à une ou plusieurs personnes que vous connaissez (très) bien • Dear Colleague, • Dear Mark and Janet, • Dear Norman,	**... to someone you know (very) well** • Cher collègue, Chère collègue, • Chers collègues, • Chers amis, • Chère Chantal,
... à une personne que vous connaissez personnellement ou avec qui vous avez des relations commerciales régulières • Dear Mrs Arnold, • Dear Mr Arnold,	**... to someone you know or to business contacts** • Madame, • Monsieur, • Chère Madame Dupont, • Cher Monsieur Dupont,
... à une société ou à une personne dont vous ne connaissez ni le nom ni le sexe • Dear Sir or Madam, • Dear Sirs,	**... to companies or organizations** • Madame, Monsieur, • Messieurs, • Mesdames, Messieurs,
... à une personne dont vous connaissez le titre • Dear Sir, • Dear Madam, • Dear Doctor, *(pour un médecin)*	**... to someone whose title you know** • Madame la Présidente, • Monsieur le Président, • Madame la Directrice, • Monsieur le Directeur, • Maître, *(to a lawyer)* • Docteur, *(to a doctor)* • Monsieur le Chef du Personnel,

La formule de politesse

Ending a letter

Très amical :	Very informally :
(With) Warmest regards,	Affectueuses pensées.
Love,	• Bons baisers. • Grosses bises. • Je t'embrasse bien fort/de tout cœur/ affectueusement.

Amical :	Informally :
With best wishes,	Soyez assuré/e de ma sincère amitié.
Yours ever,	• Sincèrement à toi. • Bien à vous.
(With) kind regards,	(Avec) Toutes mes amitiés.
Regards,	Amicalement.
Yours,	Avec mon amical souvenir.
Yours with best wishes,	Je t'adresse mes amicales pensées.

Amical et pour de courts messages :	Informal or short messages :
Yours truly,	Sincères salutations.
Yours sincerely,	• Veuillez agréer nos meilleurs sentiments. • Salutations distinguées. • Bien/Très sincèrement.
Best wishes,	• Amicalement vôtre. • Bien cordialement.

Formel mais amical :	Formal :
• Yours sincerely, *(Si la lettre commence par "Dear Mr/Mrs ...")* • Yours faithfully, *(Si la lettre commence par "Dear Sir/Madam")*	• Nous vous prions de croire, ..., à l'assurance de nos sentiments distingués. • Nous vous prions d'agréer, ..., l'expression de nos sentiments distingués. *(A woman should avoid using „sentiments" when addressing a man!)* • Nous vous prions d'agréer/de recevoir, ..., nos salutations distinguées. • Veuillez agréer, ..., nos salutations distinguées. • Agréez, ..., nos salutations distinguées. *(This ending is fairly formal on account of the imperative!)*

Très respectueux :	When you do not know the name of the person you are writing to :
Yours faithfully,	• Je vous prie d'agréer, ..., l'assurance de ma respectueuse considération. • Nous vous prions de croire, ..., à l'expression de nos sentiments respectueux/les plus dévoués. • Je vous prie d'agréer, ..., les assurances de ma haute/respectueuse considération. • Veuillez accepter/Je vous prie d'agréer, Madame, l'expression de mes respectueux hommages/l'hommage de mon respect. *(only of a man to a woman)*

A des clients :	To customers :
• Yours sincerely, *(Si la lettre commence par "Dear Mr/Mrs ...")* • Yours faithfully, *(Si la lettre commence par "Dear Sir/Madam")*	• Nous vous présentons/adressons, ..., nos salutations les plus empressées/dévouées. • Nous vous prions de croire, ..., à l'assurance de nos sentiments dévoués. • Veuillez agréer, ..., l'expression de mon sincère dévouement.

Expressions utiles / Useful phrases

L'heure / Time

L'heure	Time
Quelle heure est-il?	What time is it?
Vous avez l'heure, s'il vous plaît?	Could you tell me the time please?
Il est exactement une heure.	It's one o'clock exactly.
Il est environ … … trois heures. … trois heures cinq. … trois heures et quart. … trois heures vingt-cinq. … trois heures et demie. … quatre heures moins vingt-cinq. … quatre heures moins le quart. … midi/minuit.	It's nearly … … three o'clock. … five past three. … quarter past three. … twenty-five minutes past three. … half past three. … twenty-five minutes to four. … quarter to four. … twelve o'clock midday/midnight.
Il est déjà quatre heures passées.	It's already after four (o'clock).
Viens entre quatre et cinq heures.	Come between four and half past (four).

Salutations, présentations, départ / Greetings, Introductions, Farewell

Salutations, présentations, départ	Greetings, Introductions, Farewell
Bonjour!	Good morning! Hello! Good day! (*Aus*)
Bonsoir!	Good evening!
Salut!	Hello! Hi!
Je m'appelle Becker.	My name is Becker.
Comment allez-vous/vas-tu? (Comment) ça va?	How are you?
Bien, merci. Et vous-même/Et toi?	Fine, thanks! And you?
Au revoir!	Goodbye!
Salut! Tchao!	Bye!
À demain!	Until tomorrow!
À tout à l'heure!	See you later!
Amusez-vous/Amuse-toi bien!	Enjoy yourself!/Have fun!
Bonne nuit!	Goodnight!
Donnez/Donne bien le bonjour à Mme Durand de ma part.	Say hello to Ms Durand for me.

Rendez-vous / Appointments

Rendez-vous	Appointments
Est-ce que je peux vous/t'inviter à manger?	May I invite you to a meal?
Vous avez/Tu as des projets pour demain?	Do you already have plans for tomorrow?
On se voit à quelle heure?	When are we meeting?
Je peux passer vous/te prendre, si vous voulez/tu veux ?	Can I pick you up?
On se retrouve à neuf heures devant le cinéma.	Let's meet in front of the cinema at nine o'clock.

Demandes et remerciements / Please and Thank-You Expressions

Demandes et remerciements	Please and Thank-You Expressions
Oui, je veux bien.	Yes, please.
Non, merci.	No, thanks.
Merci, bien volontiers!	Thanks, my pleasure!
Merci, vous de même! [*o* vous aussi!]	Thanks, same to you!
Pourriez-vous m'aider, s'il vous plaît?	Can you help me please?
Je vous en prie [*o* De rien]!	My pleasure!
Merci beaucoup!	Many thanks!
Il n'y a pas de quoi.	It's not worth mentioning.

Excuses, regrets / Apologies, Regrets

Excuses, regrets	Apologies, Regrets
Excusez-moi/Excuse-moi!	Excuse me!
Je vous/te dois des excuses.	I must apologise!
Je suis vraiment navré [*o* désolé]!	I am very sorry!
Ce n'est pas ce que j'ai voulu dire!	I did not mean it like that!
Dommage!	Pity!
C'est bien triste!	That is sad!

Vœux et félicitations / Wishes and congratulations

Vœux et félicitations	Wishes and congratulations
Toutes mes félicitations!	Congratulations!
Bonne chance!	Good luck!
Je vous/te souhaite un prompt rétablissement!	Get well soon!
Bonnes vacances!	Have a great holiday!
Joyeuses Pâques!	Happy Easter!
Joyeux Noël et bonne année!	Merry Christmas and a Happy New Year!
Joyeux anniversaire!	Happy birthday!
Tous mes meilleurs vœux pour votre/ton anniversaire!	Best wishes on your birthday!
Je croise les doigts pour toi.	I'll keep my fingers crossed for you.

Demander son chemin / Asking Directions

Demander son chemin	Asking Directions
Pardon, Mme/Mlle/M., pour aller à … , s'il vous plaît?	Excuse me, how do I get to …?
Pourriez-vous m'indiquer le chemin pour aller à …?	Can you tell me, how I get to the … ?
Vous allez tout droit jusqu'à …	Straight ahead until …
Ensuite, vous tournez à droite, au feu.	Turn right at the traffic lights.
Vous suivez les panneaux.	Follow the signs.
Vous ne pouvez pas vous tromper.	You cannot miss it.
Quel bus faut-il prendre pour aller à …?	Which bus goes to …?
C'est bien le bus pour …?	Is this the right bus to …?
C'est à combien de kilomètres d'ici?	How far is it?
Vous n'êtes pas sur la bonne route.	You are at the wrong place.
Il faut retourner à …	You need to go back to …

Au restaurant / In a Restaurant

Au restaurant	In a Restaurant
Je voudrais retenir une table pour quatre personnes.	I would like to reserve a table for four people.
Je voudrais une table pour deux personnes, s'il vous plaît.	A table for two, please.
Est-ce que cette table/place est libre?	Is this table/place free?
Je prendrai …	I will take …
Est-ce que vous pourriez nous apporter encore un peu de pain, s'il vous plaît?	Could we have some more bread please?
L'addition, sil vous plaît.	I'd like to pay.
Je paie le tout.	All together please.
Vous faites des notes séparées, s'il vous plaît.	Seperate bills please.

Faire des courses / Shopping

Faire des courses	Shopping
Où est-ce qu'on peut acheter …?	Where can I find …?
Vous pourriez m'indiquer un magasin d'épicerie fine/d'alimentation?	Can you recommend a delicatessen/food-store?
On vous sert?	Are you beeing served?
Je regarde, merci.	Thanks, I'm just looking around.
Vous désirez?	What would you like?
Donnez-moi…, s'il vous plaît	Could I please have …
Je voudrais …	I would like …
Et avec ça?	Would you like anything else?
Vous acceptez les cartes de crédit?	Do you accept credit cards?
Vous pourriez me l'emballer?	Could you wrap it up for me?

A la banque / At the Bank

A la banque	At the Bank
Je voudrais changer 100 francs en euros.	I would like to exchange 100 francs into euros.
Je voudrais encaisser ce chèque de voyage.	I would like to cash this travellers cheque.
Quelle est la somme maximale que je peux retirer?	What is the maximum limit on the cheque?
Je voudrais retirer 200 euros de mon compte.	I would like to withdraw 200 euros from my account.
Vous avez une pièce d'identité, s'il vous plaît?	May I see your ID?
Votre signature, s'il vous plaît.	Your signature please!

A la poste / At the Post Office

A la poste	At the Post Office
Où se trouve la boîte aux lettres la plus proche/ le bureau de poste le plus proche?	Where is the nearest postbox/postoffice?
Quel est le tarif d'affranchissement des lettres pour la France?	How much is a letter to France?
Trois timbres, s'il vous plaît.	Three stamps please.
Je voudrais envoyer un télégramme.	I would like to send a telegram.
Je voudrais une Télécarte, s'il vous plaît.	I would like a telephone card.
Est-ce que je peux envoyer un fax à Paris d'ici?	Can I send a fax to Paris from here?

Téléphoner / Making a Phone Call

Téléphoner	Making a Phone Call
Où est la cabine téléphonique la plus proche?	Where is the nearest telephone box?
Quel est l'indicatif de la France?	What's the international dialling code for France?
Je voudrais un numéro en PCV.	I would like to make a reverse-charge call.
Allô? Qui est à l'appareil?	Hello, who's speaking?
Est-ce que je pourrais parler à Mme Durand, s'il vous plaît?	May I please speak to Ms Durand?
Je vous le/la passe.	Connecting now!
Ne quittez pas.	Please hold the line.
Je suis désolé, elle n'est pas là.	I am sorry, she is not here.
Vous voulez laisser un message?	Would you like to leave a message?
Je rappellerai.	I'll call again later.
Il n'y a pas d'abonné au numéro que vous avez demandé.	The number you have called has not been recognised.

A

A, a [eɪ] <-'s *o* -s> *n* **1.** (*letter*) A *m*, a *m*; ~ **as in Andrew** *Brit*, ~ **as in Apple** *Am* (*on telephone*), ~ **for Andrew** *Brit*, ~ **for Apple** *Am* a comme Anatole **2.** MUS do *m* **3.** SCHOOL très bonne note; **an ~ student** *Am, Aus* un élève brillant **4.** (*place, position*) **to go from A to B** aller d'un point à l'autre; **from A to Z** de A à Z

a [ə] *indef art* (+ *consonant*) (*single, not specified*) un(e); **I'm a photographer/beginner** je suis photographe/débutant; **a Ron Tyler phoned** un certain Ron Tyler a téléphoné

A *n* ELEC *abbr of* **amp**

AAA *n abbr of* **Amateur Athletics Association** *fédération d'athlétisme britannique*

aback [ə'bæk] *adv* **to be taken ~** être sidéré

abandon [ə'bændən] **I.** *vt* **1.** laisser; **to ~ equipment** abandonner du matériel; **to ~ ship** quitter le navire **2.** (*give up*) abandonner; **to ~ a plan** laisser tomber un projet; **to ~ a game** abandonner une partie **3.** (*desert*) déserter; **to ~ sb to their fate** abandonner qn à son destin **4.** (*lose self-control*) **to ~ oneself to sth** s'abandonner à qc **II.** *n no pl* abandon *m*

abandoned *adj* **1.** (*left*) abandonné(e) **2.** *pej* (*wicked*) dévergondé(e)

abashed [ə'bæʃt] *adj* décontenancé(e); ~ **at sth** confus par qc

abate [ə'beɪt] **I.** *vi form* se calmer **II.** *vt form* (*lessen*) atténuer

abattoir ['æbətwɑːʳ] *n* abattoir *m*

abbess ['æbes] *n* REL abbesse *f*

abbey ['æbi] *n* abbaye *f*

abbot ['æbət] *n* REL abbé *m*

abbreviate [ə'briːvɪeɪt] *vt* abréger

abbreviation [əˌbriːvɪ'eɪʃn] *n* abréviation *f*

ABC[1] [ˌeɪbiː'siː] *n pl, Am* **1.** (*alphabet*) ABC *m*; **as easy as ~** simple comme bonjour **2.** (*rudiments*) b, a, ba *m*

ABC[2] [ˌeɪbiː'siː] *n* **1.** *Aus* TV **the ~** *abbr of* **Australian Broadcasting Corporation** *chaîne de télévision australienne* **2.** *Am* TV *abbr of* **American Broadcasting Corporation** *chaîne de télévision américaine*

abdicate ['æbdɪkeɪt] **I.** *vi* abdiquer **II.** *vt* (*give up*) renoncer à; **to ~ the throne/a right** renoncer au trône/à un droit; **to ~ a responsibility** refuser une responsabilité

abdication [ˌæbdɪ'keɪʃn] *n* **1.** (*giving up throne*) abdication *f* **2.** *no pl* (*renunciation*) renonciation *f*; ~ **of a right** renonciation à un droit

abdomen ['æbdəmən] *n* abdomen *m*

abdominal [æb'dɒmɪnl, *Am:* -'dɑːmə-] *adj* abdominal(e)

abduct [æb'dʌkt] *vt* enlever

abduction [æb'dʌkʃn] *n* (*kidnap*) enlèvement *m*

aberration [ˌæbə'reɪʃn] *n* aberration *f*

abet [ə'bet] <-tt-> *vt* inciter; **to ~ a crime** être complice d'un crime

abeyance [ə'beɪəns] *n no pl* **to be in ~** en suspens

abhor [əb'hɔːʳ, *Am:* æb'hɔːr] <-rr-> *vt* abhorrer

abhorrence [əb'hɒrəns, *Am:* æb'hɔːr-] *n no pl* aversion *f*; **to regard sth with ~** avoir qc en horreur

abide [ə'baɪd] **I.** *vt* supporter **II.** <-d *o* abode, -d *o* abode> *vi* (*respect*) **to ~ by a rule/an agreement** respecter un règlement/un accord

ability [ə'bɪlətɪ] <-ies> *n* **1.** *no pl* (*capability*) capacité *f*; **to the best of one's ~** de son mieux **2.** *no pl* (*talent*) aptitude *f* **3.** *pl* (*skills*) compétences *fpl*

abject [ə'bleɪz] *adj* **1.** (*humble*) servile; **an ~ apology** de plates excuses **2.** (*extreme*) abject(e); ~ **coward** misérable lâche *m*; ~ **misery** misère noire

ablaze [ə'bleɪz] *adj* **1.** en feu; **to be ~** flamber **2.** *fig* enflammé(e)

able ['eɪbl] *adj* **1.** <more *o* better ~, most *o* best ~> (*having the ability*) capable; **to be ~ to** +*infin* pouvoir +*infin*, savoir +*infin Belgique*; **to be ~ to swim/drive** savoir nager/conduire **2.** <abler, ablest *o* more ~, most ~> (*clever*) apte

able-bodied *adj* valide

ABM *n abbr of* **anti-ballistic missile** missile *m* antimissile

abnormal [æb'nɔːml, *Am:* -'nɔːr-] *adj* anormal(e)

abnormality [ˌæbnə'mælɪtɪ, *Am:* -nɔːr-'mæləṭɪ] <-ies> *n* **1.** (*feature*) anomalie *f* **2.** *no pl* (*unusualness*) anormalité *f*

aboard [ə'bɔːd, *Am:* ə'bɔːrd] **I.** *adv* à bord; **all ~!** RAIL en voiture! **II.** *prep* à bord de; **the passengers ~ the train/ship** les passagers dans le train/à bord du navire; **to come** [*o* **go**] **~ a boat/airplane** embarquer [*o* monter] sur un bateau/dans un avion; **to welcome sb ~ sth** accueillir qn à bord de qc

abode [ə'bəʊd, *Am:* ə'boʊd] **I.** *pt, pp of* **abide II.** *n iron, form* demeure *f*; **of no fixed ~** sans domicile fixe

abolish [ə'bɒlɪʃ, *Am:* -ɑːl-] *vt* abolir; (*tax*) supprimer

abolition [əbəl'ɪʃn] *n no pl* abolition *f*

abominable [ə'bɒmɪnəbl, *Am:* ə'bɑːm-] *adj* abominable

abominate [ə'bɒmɪneɪt, *Am:* ə'bɑːm-] *vt form* abominer

abomination [əˌbɒmɪ'neɪʃn, *Am:* ə'bɑːm-] *n* **1.** *no pl, form* (*detestation*) horreur *f* **2.** (*thing*) abomination *f*

aboriginal [ˌæbə'rɪdʒənl] *adj* aborigène

Aborigine [ˌæbə'rɪdʒɪnɪ] *n* Aborigène *mf*

abort [ə'bɔːt, *Am:* ə'bɔrt] **I.** *vt* **1.** MED **to ~ a baby** avorter d'un bébé; **to ~ a pregnancy** interrompre une grossesse **2.** (*call off*) annuler; **to ~ a flight/mission** interrompre un vol/une mission **II.** *vi* MED avorter; (*miscarry*) faire une fausse couche

abortion [ə'bɔːʃn, *Am:* ə'bɔr-] *n* MED avortement *m;* **to have an ~** se faire avorter

abortive [ə'bɔːtɪv, *Am:* ə'bɔːrt̬ɪv] *adj* (*attempt, coup*) manqué(e)

abound [ə'baʊnd] *vi* abonder; **to ~ with sth** abonder de qc

about [ə'baʊt] **I.** *prep* **1.** (*on subject of*) à propos de; **a book ~ sth** (*un livre sur qc*), **to talk ~ cinema** parler de cinéma; **to talk ~ it** en parler; **I'm calling ~ the job** j'appelle au sujet du travail; **it's all ~ winning** ce qu'il faut, c'est gagner; **while he's ~ it** *Brit, inf* pendant qu'il y est **2.** (*surrounding*) **round ~ sb/sth** tout autour de qn/qc **3.** (*through, over*) **scattered ~ the house** éparpillé dans la maison; **to go ~ a place** parcourir un lieu en tous sens **4.** (*characteristic of*) **what I like ~ him** ce que j'aime en lui **5.** (*with*) **do you have any stamps ~ you?** *Brit, form* avez-vous des timbres sur vous? ►**to go ~ (doing) sth** aller (faire qc); **don't go ~ telling everybody** ne va pas raconter à tout le monde; **how** [*o* **what**] **~ him?** et lui?; **how** [*o* **what**] **~ doing sth?** et si nous faisions qc?; **what ~ sth?** et qc?; **what ~ the taxes?** et les impôts? **II.** *adv* **1.** (*around*) **all ~** tout autour; **to leave things lying ~ somewhere** laisser traîner des affaires quelque part; **to be the other way ~** être l'inverse **2.** (*approximately*) **at ~ 3:00** vers 3 h; **~ 5 years ago** il y a environ 5 ans; **~ twenty** une vingtaine; **~ my size** à peu près ma taille; **round ~ 5 km** environ 5 km; **~ here** quelque part par ici; **to be somewhere ~** être dans les parages; **just ~ enough of sth** à peine assez de qc; **I've had ~ enough!** j'en ai assez!; **that's ~ it** [*o* **all**] **for today** ça suffira pour aujourd'hui **3.** (*almost*) presque; **to be (just) ~ ready to** +*infin* être presque prêt à +*infin* **4.** (*willing to*) **not to be ~ to** +*infin* ne pas être prêt à +*infin; s. a.* **out, up**

about-face [ə'baʊtfeɪs] *n Am, Aus,* **about-turn** [ə'baʊttɜːn, *Am:* -tɜːrn] *n Aus, Brit* **1.** demi-tour *m* **2.** *fig* revirement *m*

above [ə'bʌv] **I.** *prep* **1.** (*over*) au-dessus de; **the hills ~ the town** les collines au-dessus de la ville; **~ suspicion** au-dessus de tout soupçon **2.** (*greater than, superior to*) **those ~ the age of 70** ceux de plus de 70 ans; **~ average** supérieur à la moyenne; **~ (and beyond) sth** (très) au-delà de qc; **over and ~ that** en plus de cela **3.** (*more important than*) **~ all** par-dessus tout; **she's ~ such quarrels** elle est au-dessus de ce genre de disputes; **he is not ~ begging** il irait jusqu'à mendier **4.** (*louder than*) **to shout ~ the noise** crier par-dessus le bruit **5.** GEO (*upstream*) en amont de; (*north of*) au nord de ►**to be ~ sb** [*o* **sb's head**] dépasser qn **II.** *adv* (*on top of*) **up ~** ci-dessus; **the skies up ~ were cloudless** le ciel était clair; **from ~** *a.* REL d'en haut **III.** *adj* (*previously mentioned*) précité(e); **the words ~** les mots ci-dessus **IV.** *n* **the ~** le(la) susdit(e)

aboveboard *adj* honnête

above-mentioned *adj form* mentionné(e) ci-dessus

abrasion [ə'breɪʒn] *n* **1.** MED égratignure *f* **2.** *no pl* TECH frottement *m*

abrasive [ə'breɪsɪv] **I.** *adj* **1.** (*scratching*) abrasif(-ive) **2.** (*not polite*) caustique **II.** *n* abrasif *m*

abreast [ə'brest] *adv* **1.** (*side by side*) côte à côte; **three ~** en ligne de trois; **~ of sb/sth** à la hauteur de qn/qc **2.** (*up to date*) **to keep ~ of sth** se tenir au courant de qc

abridge [ə'brɪdʒ] *vt* TYP raccourcir; **to ~ a book/script** abréger un livre/scénario

abridgement, abridgment *n* TYP **1.** (*version*) version *f* abrégée **2.** *no pl* (*act*) abrégement *m*

abroad [ə'brɔːd, *Am:* ə'brɑːd] *adv* **1.** à l'étranger **2.** *fig, form* **there is a rumour ~ that ...** le bruit court que ...

abrupt [ə'brʌpt] *adj* **1.** (*sudden*) soudain(e); **~ end** fin *f* abrupte **2.** (*brusque*) brutal(e); **~ reply** réponse brusque **3.** (*steep*) escarpé(e); **~ slope** pente escarpée

ABS [ˌeɪbiː'es] *n abbr of* **anti-lock braking system** ABS *m*

abscess ['æbses] *n* MED abcès *m*

abscond [əb'skɒnd, *Am:* -'skɑːnd] *vi* prendre la fuite; **to ~ with sb/sth** s'enfuir avec qn/qc

abseil ['æbsaɪl] *Aus, Brit* **I.** *vi* SPORT **to ~ (down sth)** descendre qc en rappel **II.** *n* SPORT descente *f* en rappel

absence ['æbsəns] *n* **1.** *no pl* (*not being there*) absence *f;* **~ from school** absence de l'école **2.** (*period away*) absence *f;* **in sb's ~** en l'absence de qn **3.** *no pl* (*lack*) manque *m;* **in the ~ of sth** faute de qc ►**~ makes the heart grow fonder** *prov* la distance renforce l'affection

absent¹ ['æbsənt] *adj* (*not there*) absent(e); **an ~ stare** un regard absent; **humour is (sadly) ~** l'humour brille par son absence

absent² [æb'sent] *vt form* **to ~ oneself from sth** s'absenter de qc

absentee [ˌæbsən'tiː] *n* absent(e) *m(f)*

absenteeism *n no pl* absentéisme *m*

absentee landlord *n* propriétaire *m* absent

absent-minded [ˌæbsənt'maɪndɪd] *adj* distrait(e)

absolute ['æbsəluːt] **I.** *adj a.* POL, MAT absolu(e) **II.** *n* PHILOS absolu *m*

absolutely *adv* absolument

absolution [ˌæbsə'luːʃn] *n no pl, form* REL absolution *f;* **to give sb ~** donner l'absolution à qn

absolutism ['æbsəluːtɪzəm, *Am:* -səluːt̬-] *n no pl* POL absolutisme *m*

absolve [əb'zɒlv, *Am:* -'zɑːlv] *vt form* **to ~ sb of sth** absoudre qn de qc

absorb [əb'sɔːb, *Am:* -'sɔːrb] *vt* **1.** (*take into itself*) absorber **2.** (*understand*) assimiler **3.** (*engross*) absorber

absorbed *adj* absorbé(e)

absorbent [əb'sɔːbənt, *Am:* -'sɔːrb-] *adj* absorbant(e)
absorbing *adj* absorbant(e); ~ **book** livre *m* captivant; ~ **activity** activité *f* prenante
absorption [əb'sɔːpʃn] *n no pl* **1.** (*absorbing*) absorption *f* **2.** (*deep thought*) concentration *f*
abstain [əb'steɪn] *vi* s'abstenir
abstemious [əb'stiːmɪəs] *adj* frugal(e)
abstention [əb'stenʃn] *n* abstention *f*
abstinence ['æbstɪnəns] *n no pl* abstinence *f;* ~ **from sth** abstention *f* de qc
abstract[1] ['æbstrækt] **I.** *adj a.* ART abstrait(e) **II.** *n* **1.** PHILOS **the** ~ l'abstrait *m* **2.** (*summary*) résumé *m* **3.** ART œuvre *f* abstraite
abstract[2] [əb'strækt] *vt* (*summarize: book*) résumer
abstracted *adj* distrait(e)
abstraction [əb'strækʃn] *n* abstraction *f*
abstruse [əb'struːs] *adj* obscur(e)
absurd [əb'sɜːd, *Am:* -'sɜːrd] *adj* absurde
absurdity [əb'sɜːdətɪ, *Am:* -'sɜːrdət̬ɪ] <-ies> *n* absurdité *f*
abundance [ə'bʌndəns] *n no pl* abondance *f;* **in** ~ à profusion
abundant [ə'bʌndənt] *adj* abondant(e); ~ **evidence/detail** abondance *f* de preuves/détails
abuse[1] [ə'bjuːs] *n* **1.** *no pl* (*insolent language*) injure *f;* **a stream of** ~ un torrent d'injures; **a term of** ~ une injure **2.** *no pl* SOCIOL comportement *m* abusif; **child** ~ sévices *mpl* sur les enfants; **sexual/mental** ~ sévice *m* sexuel/mental **3.** *no pl* (*misuse*) abus *m;* **substance/alcohol** ~ abus d'alcool/de substances toxiques **4.** (*infringement*) violation *f*
abuse[2] [ə'bjuːz] *vt* **1.** (*misuse*) abuser de; **to** ~ **one's authority** abuser de son autorité; **to** ~ **sb's trust** abuser de la confiance de qn **2.** (*infringe*) violer **3.** (*mistreat*) maltraiter; (*child*) exercer des sévices sur **4.** (*verbally*) injurier
abusive [ə'bjuːsɪv] *adj* injurieux(-euse); ~ **to sb** grossier envers qn
abysmal [ə'bɪzməl] *adj* abominable
abyss [ə'bɪs] *n* **1.** abîme *m* **2.** *fig* catastrophe *f;* **on the edge of an** ~ au bord du gouffre
AC [ˌeɪ'siː] *n* ELEC *abbr of* **alternating current** CA *m*
a/c *n abbr of* **account** C *m*
academic [ˌækə'demɪk] **I.** *adj* **1.** SCHOOL scolaire **2.** UNIV universitaire; (*person*) studieux(-euse); ~ **year** année *f* universitaire, année académique *Belgique, Québec, Suisse* **3.** (*theoretical*) théorique **4.** (*irrelevant*) hors de propos **II.** *n* UNIV universitaire *mf*
academy [ə'kædəmɪ] <-ies> *n* **1.** (*institution*) école *f* **2.** *Am, Scot* (*school*) collège *m*
Acadia [ə'keɪdiə] *n* HIST l'Acadie *f*
Acadian **I.** *adj* acadien(ne) **II.** *n* **1.** (*person*) Acadien(ne) *m(f)* **2.** LING acadien *m; s. a.* **English**
ACAS ['eɪˌkæs] *n Brit abbr of* **Advisory, Conciliation, and Arbitration Service** *service traitant des problèmes entre employés et employeurs*
accede [æk'siːd] *vi* **1.** *form* (*agree*) consentir; **to** ~ **to a demand** accéder à une demande **2.** *form* (*take up: to* ~ *a the throne*) accéder au trône
accelerate [ək'seləreɪt] **I.** *vi* **1.** AUTO accélérer **2.** *fig* s'accélérer **II.** *vt* accélérer
acceleration [əkˌselə'reɪʃn] *n no pl a.* PHYS accélération *f*
accelerator [ək'seləreɪtə[r], *Am:* -eɪt̬ɚ] *n a.* PHYS acccélérateur *m*
accent[1] ['æksənt, *Am:* -sent] *n* **1.** (*pronunciation*) accent *m;* **a broad** ~ un accent prononcé **2.** (*mark*) accent *m* **3.** LIT, MUS accentuation *f*
accent[2] [æk'sent] *vt* **1.** LIT, MUS accentuer **2.** *fig* souligner; **to** ~ **an aspect** mettre l'accent sur un aspect
accentuate [ək'sentʃʊeɪt] *vt* accentuer
accept [ək'sept] **I.** *vt* **1.** (*take*) accepter; **to** ~ **a gift/an offer** accepter un cadeau/une offre **2.** (*believe*) admettre **3.** (*resign oneself to*) se résigner; **to** ~ **one's fate** se soumettre à son destin **4.** (*welcome*) accepter; **to** ~ **sb as sth** accepter qn en tant que qc **II.** *vi* (*say yes*) accepter
acceptable *adj* **1.** (*agreeable*) acceptable; **not** ~ **to sb** inadmissible pour qn **2.** (*welcome*) bienvenu(e) **3.** (*satisfactory*) satisfaisant(e)
acceptance [ək'septəns] *n* acceptation *f;* ~ **speech** discours de remerciement
access ['ækses] **I.** *n no pl* **1.** (*way into*) accès *m;* **to deny sb** ~ **to sth** refuser à qn l'accès à qc **2.** INFOR accès *m* **3.** LAW droit *m* de visite **II.** *vt* INFOR accéder; **to** ~ **a file** accéder à un dossier
accessibility [ækˌsesə'bɪlətɪ, *Am:* -ət̬ɪ] *n no pl, a. fig* accessibilité *f*
accessible [ək'sesəbl] *adj* **1.** (*easy to get to*) accessible **2.** (*approachable*) abordable
accession [æk'seʃn] *n no pl, form* accession *f;* ~ **to the throne** accession au trône
accessory [ək'sesərɪ] <-ies> *n* **1.** (*for outfit, toy*) accessoire *m* **2.** *fig* fioriture *f* **3.** LAW complice *mf;* ~ **to sth before/after the fact** complice de qc par instigation/assistance
access provider *n* fournisseur *m* d'accès **access road** *n* voie *f* d'accès **access time** *n* INFOR temps *m* d'accès
accident ['æksɪdənt] *n* accident *m;* **car/road** ~ accident *m* de voiture/de la route; ~ **insurance** assurance *f* accidents; **by** ~ (*accidentally*) accidentellement; (*by chance*) par hasard; **it was no** ~ **that ...** ce n'était pas un hasard que ... ►~**s will happen** ce sont des choses qui arrivent; **it was an** ~ **waiting to happen** cela devait forcément arriver
accidental [ˌæksɪ'dentl, *Am:* -t̬l] **I.** *adj* accidentel(le); ~ **discovery** découverte *f* fortuite **II.** *n* MUS accident
accidentally *adv* accidentellement; (*by*

chance) par hasard

acclaim [ə'kleɪm] **I.** *vt* acclamer; **~ed as sth** proclamer qn qc; **a highly ~ed performance** une interprétation très acclamée **II.** *n no pl* acclamations *fpl;* **to great ~** avec grand succès

acclimate ['æklɪmeɪt, *Am:* -lə-] *vt, vi Am s.* **acclimatize**

acclimation [ˌæklaɪ'meɪʃn] *n no pl, Am s.* **acclimatization**

acclimatisation *n Aus, Brit,* **acclimatization** [əˌklaɪmətaɪ'zeɪʃn] *n no pl* acclimatation *f;* **~ to a new environment** acclimatation *f* à un nouveau milieu

acclimatize [ə'klaɪmətaɪz] **I.** *vi* s'acclimater; **to ~ to sth** s'habituer à qc **II.** *vt* **to ~ sb** acclimater qn; **to get ~d to (doing) sth** s'habituer à (faire) qc

accommodate [ə'kɒmədeɪt, *Am:* -'kɑː-] *vt* **1.** (*give place to stay*) héberger **2.** *form* (*store*) contenir **3.** *form* (*help*) aider **4.** *form* (*supply*) **to ~ sb with sth** pourvoir qn avec qc **5.** *form* (*adapt*) **to ~ oneself to sth** s'accommoder de qc

accommodating *adj* accommodant(e)

accommodation [əˌkɒmə'deɪʃn, *Am:* -kɑː-] *n* **1.** *no pl, Aus, Brit* (*place to stay*) logement *m* **2.** *pl, Am* (*lodgings*) logement *m* **3.** (*seat on plane*) place *f* **4.** *form* (*compromise*) compromis *m*

accompaniment *n* accompagnement *m;* **piano/violin ~** accompagnement au piano/au violon; **to the ~ of sth** au son de qc; **to the ~ of boos/cheers** au son des huées/des cris de joie

accompanist *n* MUS accompagnateur, -trice *m, f*

accompany [ə'kʌmpənɪ] <-ie-> *vt* **1.** (*go with*) accompagner **2.** MUS **to ~ sb on the violin** accompagner qn au violon

accomplice [ə'kʌmplɪs, *Am:* -'kɑːm-] *n* complice *mf*

accomplish [ə'kʌmplɪʃ, *Am:* -'kɑːm-] *vt* accomplir

accomplished *adj* accompli(e); **a highly ~ pianist/performance** un pianiste/une interprétation remarquable

accomplishment *n* **1.** *no pl* (*completion*) accomplissement *m;* **~ of an aim** réalisation *f* d'un but **2.** (*skill*) talent *m* **3.** (*achievement*) **what an ~!** c'est une réussite!

accord [ə'kɔːd, *Am:* -'kɔːrd] **I.** *n* **1.** (*treaty*) accord *m* **2.** *no pl* (*agreement*) accord *m;* **with one ~** d'un commun accord ►**of one's <u>own</u> ~** de soi-même **II.** *vt form* **to ~ sb sth** accorder qc à qn **III.** *vi* **to ~ with sth** s'accorder avec qc

accordance [ə'kɔːdəns, *Am:* -'kɔːrd-] *prep* **in ~ with** en accord avec

accordingly [ə'kɔːdɪŋlɪ, *Am:* -'kɔːrd-] *adv* **1.** (*appropriately*) de façon appropriée **2.** (*therefore*) donc

according to *prep* **1.** (*as told by*) **~ her/what I read** d'après elle/ce que j'ai lu; **sth goes ~ plan** qc se passe comme prévu; **~ all appearances** selon toute apparence **2.** (*as basis*) **~ the law** conformément à la loi **3.** (*as instructed by*) **~ the recipe** suivant la recette **4.** (*depending on*) en fonction de; **to classify ~ size** classer par taille

accordion [ə'kɔːdɪən, *Am:* -'kɔːrd-] *n* accordéon *m*

accost [ə'kɒst, *Am:* -'kɑːst] *vt form* accoster

account [ə'kaʊnt] **I.** *n* **1.** FIN compte *m;* **current ~, checking ~** *Am* compte courant; **savings ~** compte épargne; **to pay sth into an ~, to deposit sth in an ~** déposer qc sur un compte; **to draw money out of an ~** débiter un compte **2.** (*credit service*) **to put sth on one's ~** mettre qc sur sson compte **3.** (*bill*) **to settle an ~** régler une facture **4.** *pl* (*financial records*) la comptabilité; **to keep ~s** tenir les livres de comptes **5.** (*customer*) compte client; **we lost the BT ~** nous avons perdu le budget BT **6.** (*description*) compte-rendu *m;* **the police ~ of events** le compte-rendu de la police; **to give an ~ of sth** faire le récit de qc; **by all ~s** au dire de tout le monde **7.** (*cause*) **on ~ of sth** *no pl* en raison de qc; **on sb's ~** à cause de qn; **on that ~** en tenant compte de cela; **on no ~** en aucun cas **8.** *no pl* (*consideration*) **to take sth into ~** prendre qc en considération; **to take no ~ of sth** ne pas tenir compte de qc **9.** *no pl, form* (*importance*) **of little/no ~** sans grande/aucune importance **10.** *no pl* (*responsibility*) **on one's own ~** de son propre chef ►**to give a <u>good</u> ~ of oneself** bien s'acquitter; **to be <u>called</u> to ~** devoir se justifier; **to <u>turn</u> sth to ~** tirer parti de qc **II.** *vt form* (*consider*) **to ~ sb sth** considérer qn qc

◆**account for** *vt* **1.** (*explain: situation, difference*) expliquer; (*spending, conduct*) justifier; (*missing things or people*) retrouver **2.** (*constitute*) représenter

accountability [əˌkaʊntə'bɪlɪtɪ, *Am:* -kaʊnṱə'bɪləṱɪ] *n no pl* **~ to sb** responsabilité *f* envers qn

accountable *adj* **to be ~ to sb for sth** être responsable de qc envers qn

accountancy [ə'kaʊntənsɪ, *Am:* -'kaʊnṱnsɪ] *n no pl* comptabilité *f*

accountant [ə'kaʊntənt] *n* comptable *mf;* **a chartered ~, a certified public ~** *Am* expert comptable *mf*

account(s) book *n* livre *m* de comptes

account holder *n* titulaire *m* d'un compte

accredit [ə'kredɪt] *vt* accréditer; **~ed members of the press** les journalistes accrédités; **~ed to sth** attribué à qc

accrue [ə'kruː] *vi* **1.** *form* FIN s'accumuler **2.** *form* (*be received by*) **to ~ to sb** revenir à qn

accumulate [ə'kjuːmjʊleɪt] **I.** *vt* accumuler **II.** *vi* s'accumuler

accumulation [əˌkjuːmjʊ'leɪʃn] *n* **1.** *no pl* (*collecting*) accumulation *f* **2.** *no pl* (*growth*) accroissement *m* **3.** (*quantity: of evidence*) accumulation *f; pej* amas *m*

A

accumulator [əˈkjuːmjʊleɪtəʳ] *n* **1.** *Aus, Brit* (*battery*) accumulateur *m* **2.** (*bet*) pari *m* avec report
accuracy [ˈækjərəsɪ, *Am:* -jɚəsɪ] *n no pl* **1.** (*correct aim*) précision *f* **2.** (*correctness: of report*) justesse *f;* (*of data*) exactitude *f*
accurate [ˈækjərət, *Am:* -jɚət] *adj* **1.** (*on target*) précis(e) **2.** (*correct*) exact(e)
accusation [ˌækjuːˈzeɪʃn] *n* accusation *f;* **to bring an ~ against sb** accuser qn de
accusative [əˈkjuːzətɪv, *Am:* -t̬ɪv] **I.** *n* accusatif, -ive *m, f;* **in the ~** à l'accusatif *m* **II.** *adj* accusatif
accuse [əˈkjuːz] *vt* accuser; **to stand ~d of sth/doing sth** être accusé de qc/de faire qc
accused *n* LAW prévenu(e) *m(f)*
accustom [əˈkʌstəm] *vt* **to ~ sb to sth** habituer qn à qc
accustomed *adj* **1.** (*used*) habitué(e); **to be ~ to sth/doing sth** être habitué à qc/à faire qc; **to become ~ to sth** s'accoutumer à qc **2.** (*usual*) coutumier
ace [eɪs] **I.** *n* **1.** (*card*) as *m;* **~ of hearts/clubs/spades/diamonds** as de cœur/trèfle/pique/carreau **2.** (*expert*) as *m* **3.** (*in tennis*) service *m* gagnant **II.** *adj* **1.** *inf* **~ driver** as du volant; **~ pilot** pilote d'élite **2.** *inf* (*excellent*) excellent(e) **III.** *vt inf* SPORT **to ~ sb** écraser qn
acetate [ˈæsɪteɪt] *n no pl* acétate *m*
acetic [əˈsiːtɪk, *Am:* əˈsiːt̬ɪk] *adj* acétique
acetylene [əˈsetəliːn, *Am:* əˈset̬ə-] *n no pl* acétylène *m*
ache [eɪk] **I.** *n* douleur *f; fig* peine *f;* **~s and pains** douleurs *fpl* **II.** *vi* **1.** (*have pain: patient*) souffrir; (*part of body*) faire mal **2.** *fig* **to be aching for sth/to** *+infin* mourir d'envie de qc/de *+infin*
achieve [əˈtʃiːv] *vt* (*aim*) atteindre; (*promotion, independence*) obtenir; (*ambition*) réaliser; **to ~ nothing** n'arriver à rien; **crying ~s nothing** pleurer ne sert à rien; **to ~ fame** se faire un nom; **to ~ success** réussir
achievement *n* **1.** (*feat*) exploit *m* **2.** *no pl* (*achieving: of aim*) atteinte *f;* (*of promotion, independence*) obtention *f;* (*of ambition*) réalisation *f*
achiever *n* personne qui réussit
acid [ˈæsɪd] **I.** *n* **1.** CHEM acide *m* **2.** *no pl, inf* (*LSD*) acide *m* **II.** *adj* **1.** CHEM acide; **~ rain** pluies acides; **~ stomach** acidité gastrique **2.** (*sour-tasting*) acide; **~ drop** bonbon acidulé **3.** (*sarcastic*) caustique; (*remark*) acerbe; (*voice*) aigre **4.** (*conclusive*) **~ test** épreuve décisive
acidic [əˈsɪdɪk] *adj* acide
acidify [əˈsɪdɪfaɪ] <-ie-> *vt* acidifier
acknowledge [əkˈnɒlɪdʒ, *Am:* -ˈnɑːlɪdʒ] *vt* **1.** (*admit*) admettre; (*mistake*) avouer; **to ~ that ...** reconnaître que ... **2.** (*show recognition of: admirers*) saluer; **to ~ the applause** remercier pour les applaudissements **3.** (*thank for*) être reconnaissant pour; **to ~ one's sources** citer ses sources **4.** (*reply to*) répondre à; **to ~ receipt of sth** accuser réception de qc
acknowledgement, acknowledgment *n* **1.** *no pl* (*admission, recognition*) reconnaissance *f;* (*of guilt*) aveu *m* **2.** (*reply*) accusé *m* de réception **3.** (*greeting*) signe *m* **4.** *pl* (*in book*) remerciements *mpl*
acne [ˈæknɪ] *n no pl* acné *f*
acorn [ˈeɪkɔːn, *Am:* ˈeɪkɔrn] *n* gland (de chêne) *m*
acoustic [əˈkuːstɪk] **I.** *adj* acoustique **II.** *npl* acoustique *f*
acoustic coupler *n* INFOR coupleur *m* acoustique **acoustic guitar** *n* guitare *f* acoustique **acoustic nerve** *n* nerf *m* auditif
acquaint [əˈkweɪnt] *vt* **to ~ sb with sth** mettre qn au courant de qc; **to become ~ed with the facts** prendre connaissance des faits; **to become ~ed with sb** faire la connaissance de qn
acquaintance [əˈkweɪntəns] *n* **1.** (*person*) connaissance *f* **2.** *no pl* (*relationship*) relations *fpl;* **to make sb's ~** faire la connaissance de qn **3.** *no pl, form* (*knowledge*) **his ~ with the city** sa connaissance de la ville
acquiesce [ˌækwɪˈes] *vi form* acquiescer; **to ~ in sth** donner son accord sur qc
acquiescence [ˌækwɪˈesns] *n no pl, form* acquiescement *m;* **~ in sth** consentement *m* à qc
acquiescent [ˌækwɪˈesnt] *adj form* consentant(e)
acquire [əˈkwaɪəʳ, *Am:* -ˈkwaɪɚ] *vt* acquérir; **~d characteristic** caractère acquis; **it's an ~d taste** c'est qc qu'on apprend à aimer
acquired immunity *n no pl* MED immunité *f* acquise
acquisition [ˌækwɪˈzɪʃn] *n* acquisition *f;* **recent ~s** acquisitions récentes
acquisitive [əˈkwɪzətɪv, *Am:* -ət̬ɪv] *adj pej* avide
acquit [əˈkwɪt] <-tt-> *vt* **1.** LAW acquitter; **to ~ sb of a charge** décharger qn d'une accusation **2.** (*perform*) **to ~ oneself well/badly** bien/mal s'en tirer **3.** FIN s'acquitter de
acquittal [əˈkwɪtl, *Am:* -ˈkwɪt̬-] *n* LAW *no pl* acquittement *m*
acre [ˈeɪkəʳ, *Am:* ˈeɪkɚ] *n* **1.** (*unit*) acre *f* **2.** *pl, + sing vb, inf* (*a large amount*) des hectares *mpl*
acreage [ˈeikrədʒ] *n no pl* superficie *f*
acrid [ˈækrɪd] *adj* **1.** âcre **2.** *fig* (*tone*) acerbe
acrimonious [ˌækrɪˈməʊnɪəs, *Am:* -ˈmoʊnɪ-] *adj* acrimonieux(-euse); (*debate*) acerbe
acrimony [ˈækrɪmənɪ, *Am:* -moʊnɪ] *n no pl, form* **1.** (*feeling*) acrimonie *f* **2.** (*attitude*) aigreur *f*
acrobat [ˈækrəbæt] *n* acrobate *mf*
acrobatic [ˌækrəˈbætɪk, *Am:* -ˈbæt̬ɪk] *adj* acrobatique
across [əˈkrɒs, *Am:* əˈkrɑːs] **I.** *prep* **1.** (*on other side of*) **~ sth** de l'autre côté de qc; **just**

~ **the street** juste en face; ~ **from sb/sth** en face de qn/qc **2.** (*from one side to other*) **to walk** ~ **the bridge** traverser le pont; **to swim/drive/crawl** ~ **sth** traverser qc à la nage/en voiture/en rampant; **to write sth** ~ **sth** écrire qc en travers de qc; **to go** ~ **the sea to France** aller en France en traversant la mer; **a road** ~ **the desert** une route à travers le désert; ~ **country** à travers champs; **voters** ~ **America** les électeurs à travers l'Amérique **3.** (*on*) **surprise flashed** ~ **her face** la surprise passa sur son visage **4.** (*find unexpectedly*) **to come** [*o* **run**] ~ **sb/sth** tomber sur qn/qc ►~ **the board** (*increase taxes*) pour tous; **he excels** ~ **the board** il excelle dans tout **II.** *adv* **1.** (*one side to other*) **to run/swim** ~ traverser en courant/à la nage; **to be 2m** ~ avoir 2 mètres de large **2.** (*from one to another*) **to get sth** ~ **to sb** faire comprendre qc à qn

act [ækt] **I.** *n* **1.** (*action*) acte *m;* **an** ~ **of God** catastrophe *f* naturelle; **the sexual** ~ l'acte sexuel **2.** (*performance*) numéro *m* **3.** *fig* **it's all an** ~ c'est du cinéma **4.** THEAT acte *m* **5.** LAW, POL loi *f* ►**he's a hard** ~ **to follow** on ne peut pas l'égaler; **to catch sb in the** ~ prendre qn sur le fait; **to do a disappearing** ~ faire disparaître qn/qc; **to get in on the** ~ se mettre dans le mouvement; **get one's** ~ **together** *inf* faire un effort **II.** *vi* **1.** (*take action*) agir; **to** ~ **as sth** servir de qc; **to** ~ **for sb** agir au nom de qn **2.** *inf* (*behave*) se comporter; **to** ~ **like sth** se conduire en qc; **he ~s as if he knows everybody** il fait comme si il connaît tout le monde **3.** THEAT jouer **4.** (*pretend*) jouer la comédie **III.** *vt* **1.** THEAT tenir le rôle de; **to** ~ **the king** incarner le roi **2.** (*pretend*) **to** ~ **a part** jouer un rôle

◆**act on** *vt* (*advice, instructions*) agir selon; (*information*) agir à partir de

◆**act out** *vt* **to** ~ **a dream** vivre un rêve

◆**act up** *vi* (*child*) mal se conduire; (*car, machine*) faire des siennes; **my knee is acting up on me** mon genou me joue des tours

acting I. *adj* suppléant **II.** *n no pl* (*performance, pretence*) jeu; (*career*) le théâtre; (*interpretation*) interprétation *f*

action ['ækʃn] *n* **1.** *no pl* (*activeness*) action *f;* **plan of** ~ plan d'action; **a man of** ~ un homme d'action; **to get into** ~ entrer en action; **to put a plan into** ~ mettre un projet à exécution; **out of** ~ hors service; **the government must take strong** ~ le gouvernement doit prendre des mesures fermes **2.** (*act*) action *f;* (*movement*) gestes *mpl* **3.** *no pl* LIT, CINE action *f* **4.** *no pl* MIL engagement *m;* **to be in** ~ être engagé; **to go into** ~ engager le combat; **to be killed/missing in** ~ être tué/avoir disparu au combat; **to see** ~ combattre **5.** (*battle*) combat *m* **6.** *no pl* (*way of working*) effet *m* **7.** (*mechanism*) mécanisme *m* **8.** LAW procès *m;* ~ **for libel** plainte en diffamation **9.** *no pl, inf* (*exciting events*) activité *f;* **there is a lot of** ~ **here** ça bouge beaucoup ici ►**to want a piece of the** ~ *inf* vouloir une part du gâteau; **~s speak louder than words** *prov* les actes en disent plus long que les paroles

action-packed *adj* plein d'action **action replay** *n Brit* TV répétition *f* immédiate d'une séquence

activate ['æktɪveɪt] *vt* **1.** (*set going: system, machine*) actionner; **to** ~ **an alarm** déclencher une alarme **2.** CHEM activer

active ['æktɪv] *adj* actif(-ive); (*volcano*) en activité; **in the** ~ **voice** à l'actif; **to be** ~ **in sth** être actif au sein de qc; **to see** ~ **service** combattre; **to give** ~ **consideration to sth** examiner sérieusement qc

activist *n* POL activiste *mf*

activity [æk'tɪvətɪ, *Am:* -ət̬ɪ] <-ies> *n* **1.** *no pl* (*opp: passivity*) activité *f* **2.** *pl* (*pursuit*) occupation *f;* **activities for the children** des activités pour les enfants

actor ['æktəʳ, *Am:* -tɚ] *n* acteur, actrice *m, f*

actress ['æktrɪs] *n* actrice *f*

actual ['æktʃʊəl] *adj* réel; **in** ~ **fact** en fait; **the** ~ **details** les détails exacts; **it's the** ~ **car he bought** c'est précisément la voiture qu'il a achetée; **I do little** ~ **teaching** je fais peu d'enseignement à proprement parler

actually ['æktʃʊlɪ] *adv* **1.** (*in fact*) en fait, vraiment; **I wasn't** ~ **there** en fait, je n'étais pas là; **he** ~ **lied/fell asleep** il est allé jusqu'à mentir/s'endormir; ~ **I wonder if ...** je me demande bien si ... **2.** (*used politely*) à vrai dire; **You're Scottish, aren't you – Irish,** ~ vous êtes écossais, n'est-ce pas? – irlandais, plus précisément

actuary ['æktʃuəri] *n* actuaire *mf*

acumen ['ækjʊmən, *Am:* ə'kju:-] *n no pl* sagacité *f*

acupuncture ['ækjʊpʌŋktʃəʳ, *Am:* -tʃɚ] *n no pl* acupuncture *f*

acute [ə'kju:t] **I.** *adj* **1.** (*serious: illness, pain*) aigu(ë); (*difficulties*) grave; (*nervousness, anxiety*) vif(vive); **an** ~ **sense of embarrassment/injustice** un profond sentiment de gêne/d'injustice; **an** ~ **shortage of sth** une sévère pénurie de qc **2.** (*sharp: sense*) fin(e); (*observation*) perspicace **3.** (*clever*) avisé(e) **4.** MAT, LING (*angle, accent*) aigu(ë) **II.** *n* LING accent *m* aigu

ad [æd] *n inf abbr of* **advertisement**

AD [ˌeɪ'di:] *adj abbr of* **Anno Domini** ap JC

adagio [ə'dɑ:dʒɪəʊ, *Am:* ə'dɑ:dʒoʊ] **I.** *adv* adagio **II.** *adj* adagio **III.** *n* adagio *m*

Adam ['ædəm] *n no art* Adam *m* ►**not to know sb from** ~ ne connaître qn ni d'+ve ni d'Adam

adamant ['ædəmənt] *adj* inflexible; ~ **about** (*fact*) catégorique sur; (*rule*) intransigeant sur; ~ **refusal** refus ferme

Adam's apple *n* ANAT pomme *f* d'Adam

adapt [ə'dæpt] **I.** *vt* adapter; **to** ~ **sth for sth** adapter qc à qc **II.** *vi* s'adapter

adaptable *adj* adaptable

adaptation [ˌædæp'teɪʃn] *n* adaptation *f*
adapter, **adaptor** [ə'dæptəʳ, *Am:* -ɚ] *n* 1. LIT auteur *m* d'une adaptation 2. ELEC adaptateur *m*
add [æd] I. *vt* ajouter; **with ~ed calcium** avec calcium rajouté II. *vi* faire des additions
◆**add up** I. *vt* additionner II. *vi* 1. MAT faire des additions; **to ~ to** s'élever à; **it all adds up** ça chiffre 2. *fig* **it all adds up to a delicate situation/a fantastic result** tout ça fait une situation délicate/un résultat fantastique; **it all adds up** je comprends tout
adder ['ædəʳ, *Am:* 'ædɚ] *n* vipère *f*
addict ['ædɪkt] *n* intoxiqué(e) *m(f)*; **drug ~** toxicomane *mf*; *fig* fana *mf*; **a fitness/telly ~** un(e) accro de la forme/de la télé
addicted *adj* adonné(e); **to be ~ to sth** s'adonner à qc; *fig* ne pas pouvoir se passer de qc
addiction [ə'dɪkʃən] *n* 1. *no pl* dépendance *f*; **drug ~** toxicomanie *f* 2. *fig* **~ to sth** passion *f* de qc
addictive [ə'dɪktɪv] *adj* qui crée une dépendance ►**it's highly ~** c'est comme une drogue
adding-machine ['ædɪŋmə'ʃiːn] *n* machine *f* à calculer
addition [ə'dɪʃn] *n* 1. *no pl a.* MAT addition *f* 2. (*added thing*) ajout *m*; **there's an ~ to the family** la famille s'agrandit 3. (*as well*) **in ~** de plus; **in ~ to sth** en plus de qc
additional [ə'dɪʃənl] *adj* additionnel(le)
additionally [ə'dɪʃənəlɪ] *adv* en outre
additive ['ædɪtɪv, *Am:* -ət̬ɪv] *n* additif *m*
address[1] [ə'dres, *Am:* 'ædres] *n* 1. (*place of residence*) *a.* INFOR adresse *f*; **home ~** adresse privée 2. (*speech*) discours *m* 3. (*title*) **form of ~** titre *m*
address[2] [ə'dres] *vt* 1. (*write address on*) adresser; **to ~ sth to sb** adresser qc à qn 2. (*speak to*) **to ~ sb** adresser la parole à qn; **she ~ed the remark to Paul** sa remarque était destinée à Paul 3. (*use title*) **to ~ sb as 'Your Highness'** appeler qn 'Votre Altesse' 4. (*give attention to: problem*) aborder 5. (*in golf*) **to ~ the ball** viser la balle
address book *n* carnet *m* d'adresses
adenoids ['ædɪnɔɪdz, *Am:* 'ædnɔɪdz] *npl* ANAT végétations *fpl*
adept [ə'dept] *adj* habile
adequate ['ædɪkwət] *adj* 1. (*supply*) suffisant(e); (*room*) convenable 2. (*person*) compétent(e)
adhere [əd'hɪəʳ, *Am:* -'hɪr] *vi* adhérer; **to ~ to** (*surface, religion*) adhérer à; (*rules*) observer
adherence [əd'hɪərəns, *Am:* -'hɪrns] *n no pl* adhérence *f*
adherent [əd'hɪərənt] *n form* adhérent(e) *m(f)*
adhesive [əd'hiːsɪv] I. *adj* adhésif(-ive); **~ tape** *Am* sparadrap *m*; *Brit* ruban *m* adhésif II. *n no pl* (*glue*) colle *f*
adjacent [ə'dʒeɪsnt] *adj* 1. (*next to each other*) attenant(e) 2. *a.* MAT adjacent(e)
adjective ['ædʒɪktɪv] *n* adjectif *m*
adjoin [ə'dʒɔɪn] I. *vt* avoisiner II. *vi form* être contigu
adjoining *adj* contigu(ë)
adjourn [ə'dʒɜːn, *Am:* -'dʒɜːrn] I. *vt* ajourner II. *vi* s'arrêter; (*court, parliament*) lever la séance
adjust [ə'dʒʌst] I. *vt* 1. TECH régler; (*salaries*) redresser; (*size*) ajuster; (*language, rules*) adapter 2. (*rearrange: clothes*) réajuster 3. (*adapt*) **to ~ sth to sth** adapter qc en fonction de qc II. *vi* **to ~ to sth** (*person*) s'adapter à qc; (*machine*) se régler sur qc
adjustable *adj* réglable
adjustable spanner *n Aus, Brit* clé *f* anglaise
adjustment *n* 1. (*mental*) adaptation *f* 2. (*mechanical*) réglage *m*
adjutant ['ædʒʊtənt] *n* aide *mf* de camp
ad-lib [ˌæd'lɪb] I. <-bb-> *vt, vi* improviser II. *n* improvisation *f*
administer [əd'mɪnɪstəʳ, *Am:* -stɚ] *vt* 1. POL (*city*) administrer; (*affairs, business*) gérer 2. (*dispense*) donner; (*law*) appliquer; (*medicine, sacrament*) administrer; (*first aid*) apporter
administrate [əd'mɪnɪstreɪt] *vt* gérer
administration [ədˌmɪnɪ'streɪʃn] *n* 1. *no pl* (*organization*) administration *f*; **time spent on ~** temps consacré aux tâches administratives 2. (*management*) gestion *f*; **the ~** la direction 3. *Am* (*term of office*) mandat *m* 4. *Am* (*president and cabinet*) gouvernement *m*
administrative [əd'mɪnɪstrətɪv] *adj* administratif(-ive)
administrator [əd'mɪnɪstreɪtəʳ, *Am:* -tɚ] *n* administrateur, -trice *m, f*
admirable ['ædmərəbl] *adj* admirable
admiral ['ædmərəl] *n* amiral *m*
admiration [ˌædmə'reɪʃn] *n no pl* admiration *f*
admire [əd'maɪəʳ, *Am:* əd'maɪɚ] *vt* admirer
admirer [əd'mɪərəʳ, *Am:* -ɚ] *n* admirateur, -trice *m, f*
admissible [əd'mɪsəbl] *adj form* recevable
admission [əd'mɪʃn] *n* 1. (*act of entering, entrance, entrance fee*) entrée *f*; (*into school, college*) inscription *f*; (*into hospital*) admission *f* 2. (*acknowledgement*) aveu *m*
admit [əd'mɪt] <-tt-> *vt* 1. (*acknowledge*) avouer; (*defeat, error*) reconnaître; **to ~ one's guilt** s'avouer coupable; **to ~ having done sth** avouer avoir fait qc; **I ~ he's young, he's young, I ~** il est jeune, je l'admets 2. (*allow to enter: person*) admettre; (*air, water*) laisser passer; **she was ~ted to hospital** elle a été hospitalisée
admittance [əd'mɪtns] *n no pl* accès *m*; **no ~** accès interdit
admittedly [əd'mɪtɪdlɪ, *Am:* -'mɪt̬ɪdlɪ] *adv* **~ it's not easy** il faut reconnaître que ce n'est pas facile

admonish [əd'mɒnɪʃ] *vt form* admonester; **to ~ sb for doing sth** reprocher à qn de faire qc

admonishment, **admonition** [ˌædmə'nɪʃn] *n form* avertissement *m*

ado [ə'du:] *n no pl* **without further** [*o* **more**] **~** sans plus de cérémonie ▶**much ~ about nothing** beaucoup de bruit pour rien

adolescence [ˌædə'lesns] *n no pl* adolescence *f*

adolescent [ˌædə'lesnt] **I.** *adj* **1.** (*teenage: boys, girls*) adolescent(e); (*behaviour, fantasy*) d'adolescent **2.** *pej* puéril(e) **II.** *n* adolescent(e) *m(f)*

adopt [ə'dɒpt, *Am:* -'dɑ:pt] *vt* adopter; (*accent*) prendre; (*suggestion*) accepter; **to ~ a candidat** *Brit* choisir un candidat

adoption [ə'dɒpʃn, *Am:* -'dɑ:p-] *n* LAW adoption; **to have a child by ~** avoir un enfant adoptif

adorable [ˌə'dɔ:rəbl] *adj* adorable

adoration [ˌædə'reɪʃn] *n no pl a.* REL adoration *f*

adore [ə'dɔ:ʳ, *Am:* -'dɔ:r] *vt a.* REL adorer

adoring *adj* plein(e) d'adoration

adrenalin(**e**) [ə'drenəlɪn] *n no pl* adrénaline *f*

adrift [ə'drɪft] *adv* **to be ~** (*boat, sailor*) à la dérive; *fig* (*student, tourist*) perdu; **to be six points ~** être six points derrière ▶**to cast** [*o* **turn**] **sb/sth ~** abandonner qn/qc à son sort; **to come ~** *Brit, inf* (*seam, rope*) se détacher; (*plan, schedule*) aller à vau-l'eau

adroit [ə'drɔɪt] *adj* habile; **to be ~ at doing sth** faire qc avec habileté

adulation [ˌædjʊ'leɪʃn, *Am:* -dʒə-] *n no pl* adoration *f*

adult ['ædʌlt, *Am:* ə'dʌlt] **I.** *n* adulte *mf* **II.** *adj* adulte; (*film*) pour adultes

adult education *n no pl* formation *f* pour adultes

adulterate [ə'dʌltəreɪt, *Am:* -t̬əreɪt] *vt* falsifier; **to ~ wine** trafiquer du vin

adulterous [ə'dʌltərəs, *Am:* -t̬ɚ-] *adj* adultère

adultery [ə'dʌltərɪ, *Am:* -t̬ɚɪ] *n no pl* adultère *m*

advance [əd'vɑ:ns, *Am:* -'væ:ns] **I.** *vi* avancer **II.** *vt* **1.** (*develop: cause, interest*) faire avancer; (*video, tape*) avancer; **to ~ one's career** faire avancer sa carrière **2.** (*pay in advance*) avancer; **to ~ sb sth** avancer qc à qn **3.** (*put forward: idea, suggestion*) avancer **III.** *n* **1.** (*progress, forward movement*) progrès *m* **2.** FIN avance *f* **3.** *pl* (*sexual flirtation*) avances *fpl* ▶**to do sth in ~** faire qc à l'avance **IV.** *adj* préalable; **without ~ warning** sans avertissement préalable

advance booking *n* réservation *f*

advanced *adj* avancé(e); **~ search** recherche détaillée

advancement *n no pl* **1.** (*improvement*) progrès *m* **2.** (*promotion*) avancement *m*

advance notice *n no pl* préavis *m* **advance payment** *n* paiement *m* d'avance; (*of salary*) avance *f*

advantage [əd'vɑ:ntɪdʒ, *Am:* -'væ:nt̬ɪdʒ] *n a.* SPORT avantage *m*; **what's the ~ of doing that?** quel intérêt y a-t-il à faire ça?; **to give sb an ~ over sb** avantager qn par rapport à qn; **to take ~ of sb/sth** *a. pej* profiter de qn/qc; **to one's own ~** à son avantage

advantageous [ˌædvən'teɪdʒəs, *Am:* -væn'-] *adj* avantageux(-euse)

advent ['ædvənt] *n no pl* (*coming*) arrivée *f*

Advent ['ædvent] *n no pl* REL l'avent *m*

adventure [əd'ventʃəʳ, *Am:* -tʃɚ] *n* aventure *f*

adventure playground *n Brit* terrain *m* de jeu

adventurer *n a. pej* aventurier, -ère *m, f*

adventurous [əd'ventʃərəs] *adj* aventureux(-euse)

adverb ['ædvɜ:b, *Am:* -vɜ:rb] *n* adverbe *m*

adversary ['ædvəsərɪ, *Am:* -vɚserɪ] <-ies> *n* adversaire *mf*

adverse ['ædvɜ:s, *Am:* -vɜ:rs] *adj* défavorable

adversity [əd'vɜ:sətɪ, *Am:* -'vɜ:rsət̬ɪ] <-ies> *n* adversité *f*

advert ['ædvɜ:t, *Am:* -vɜ:rt] *n Brit* **1.** (*on TV, radio, in print*) pub *f* **2.** (*classified ad*) petite annonce *f*

advertise ['ædvətaɪz, *Am:* -vɚ-] **I.** *vt* **1.** (*publicize: product, event*) faire de la publicité pour; (*reduction, changes*) annoncer; (*in classified ads*) passer une annonce pour **2.** (*announce*) annoncer **II.** *vi* mettre une annonce; **to ~ for a secretary** mettre une annonce pour une secrétaire

advertisement [əd'vɜ:tɪsmənt, *Am:* ˌædvər'taɪzmənt] *n* publicité *f*; (*in newspaper*) (petite) annonce *f*; **it's not a good ~ for the school** *fig* ce n'est pas une bonne pub pour l'école

advertiser ['ædvətaɪzəʳ, *Am:* -vɚtaɪzɚ] *n* **1.** (*one who advertises*) annonceur, -euse *m, f* **2.** (*agency*) agence *f* de publicité

advertising *n* publicité *f*

advertising agency <-ies> *n* agence *f* de publicité **advertising campaign** *n* campagne *f* publicitaire **advertising media** *npl* moyens *mpl* publicitaires **advertising space** *n no pl* espace *m* publicitaire

advice [əd'vaɪs] *n no pl* **1.** (*suggestion, opinion*) conseil *m*; **some** [*o* **a piece of**] **~** un conseil; **to ask for ~ on sth** demander conseil au sujet de qc; **to give** [*o* **offer**] **sb ~** donner un conseil à qn; **to get professional ~** demander l'avis d'un professionnel **2.** ECON notification *f*

advisable *adj* conseillé(e); **it's ~** c'est recommandé

advise [əd'vaɪz] **I.** *vt* **1.** (*give advice to*) **to ~ sb to +infin** conseiller à qn de +*infin*; **to ~ sb against sth** déconseiller qc à qn; **to ~ sb on sth** conseiller qn sur qc **2.** (*inform*) **to ~ sb of sth** aviser qn de qc; **to ~ sb that ...** informer

A

qn que … **3.** (*suggest: prudence, firmness*) recommander **II.** *vi* donner (un) conseil; **to ~ against sth** déconseiller qc

adviser, **advisor** [əd'vaɪzəʳ, *Am:* -zɚ] *n* conseiller, -ère *m, f*

advisory [əd'vaɪzərɪ] *adj* consultatif(-ive); **in an ~ capacity** en tant que conseiller

advocate¹ ['ædvəkeɪt] *vt* préconiser

advocate² ['ædvəkət] *n* **1.** POL partisan(e) *m(f)*; **an ~ of women's rights** un défenseur des droits de la femme **2.** LAW avocat(e) *m(f)*

AEA *n Brit abbr of* **Atomic Energy Authority** AEN *f*

AEC *n Am abbr of* **Atomic Energy Commission** CEA *m*

Aegean [iː'dʒiːən] *n* **the ~** la mer Égée

aegis ['iːdʒɪs] *n no pl* **under the ~ of sb/sth** sous l'égide *f* de qn/qc

aeon ['iːən, *Am:* -ɑːn] *n* **~s ago** il y a une éternité

aerate ['eəreɪt, *Am:* 'ereɪt] *vt* **1.** (*expose to air*) aérer **2.** GASTR gazéifier

aerial ['eərɪəl, *Am:* 'erɪ-] **I.** *adj* aérien(ne) **II.** *n* antenne *f*

aerobics [eə'rəʊbɪks, *Am:* er'oʊ-] *n + sing v* aérobic *f*

aerodynamic [ˌeərəʊdaɪ'næmɪk, *Am:* ˌeroʊ-] *adj* aérodynamique

aerodynamics *n + sing v* aérodynamique *f*

aeronautic [ˌeərə'nɔːtɪk, *Am:* ˌerə'nɑːt̬ɪk] *adj* aéronautique; **~ engineering** aéronautique *f*

aeronautics *n + sing v* aéronautique *f*

aeroplane ['eərəpleɪn, *Am:* 'erə-] *n Aus, Brit* avion *m*

aerosol ['eərəsɒl, *Am:* 'erəsɑːl] *n* aérosol *m*

aesthetic [iːs'θetɪk(l), *Am:* es'θet̬-] *adj* esthétique

afar [ə'fɑːʳ, *Am:* -'fɑːr] *adv* loin; **from ~** de loin

affability [ˌæfə'bɪlətɪ, *Am:* -t̬ɪ] *n no pl* affabilité *f*

affable ['æfəbl] *adj* affable

affair [ə'feəʳ, *Am:* -'fer] *n* **1.** (*matter, business*) affaire *f*; **it's sb's own ~** cela ne regarde que qn; **~s of state** affaires d'état; **to meddle in sb's ~s** se mêler des affaires de qn; **it's an odd/sad state of ~s** c'est bizarre/lamentable; **the Dreyfus ~** l'affaire Dreyfus; **the whole ~ was a disaster** ça a été un désastre **2.** (*sexual relationship*) liaison *f* **3.** (*event, occasion*) **it was a quiet/grand ~** ça a été discret/grandiose

affect [ə'fekt] *vt* **1.** (*change*) affecter; (*concern*) toucher; **to be ~ed by sth** être touché par qc **2.** (*move*) affecter; **to be very ~ed** êtree très affecté **3.** *pej, form* (*simulate*) feindre; (*accent*) prendre

affectation [ˌæfek'teɪʃn] *n pej* affectation *f*

affected *adj pej* (*smile, manner*) hypocrite

affection [ə'fekʃn] *n* affection *f*

affectionate [ə'fekʃənət] *adj* affectueux(-euse)

affidavit [ˌæfɪ'deɪvɪt] *n* déclaration *f* écrite sous serment

affiliate [ə'fɪlɪeɪt] **I.** *vt* ECON affilier; **~d with sth** affilié à qc **II.** *vi* s'affilier **III.** *n* ECON filiale *f*

affiliation [əˌfɪlɪ'eɪʃn] *n* **1.** affiliation *f* **2.** *fig* attaches *fpl*

affinity [ə'fɪnətɪ, *Am:* -ət̬ɪ] <-ies> *n a.* CHEM, MAT affinité *f*; **to feel an ~ for sth** se sentir attiré par qc

affirm [ə'fɜːm, *Am:* -'fɜːrm] *vt* affirmer

affirmation [ˌæfə'meɪʃn, *Am:* -ɚ-] *n* **1.** (*assertion*) affirmation *f* **2.** LAW déclaration *f* sur l'honneur

affirmative [ə'fɜːmətɪv, *Am:* -'fɜːrmət̬ɪv] **I.** *adj* affirmatif(-ive) **II.** *n* approbation *f*; **to answer** [*o* **reply**] **in the ~** répondre par l'affirmative

affix ['æfɪks] **I.** *vt* **1.** (*attach*) attacher **2.** (*stick on*) coller **3.** (*clip on*) agrafer **4.** (*add: signature*) apposer **II.** <-es> *n* LING affixe *m*

afflict [ə'flɪkt] *vt* affliger; (*disease*) faire souffrir; **to be ~ed with sth** souffrir de qc

affliction [ə'flɪkʃn] *n* **1.** (*misfortune*) calamité *f*; **in ~** dans la détresse **2.** (*illness*) affliction *f*

affluence ['æflʊəns] *n no pl* abondance *f*; (*wealth*) richesse *f*

affluent ['æflʊənt] *adj* aisé(e); **~ society** société de consommation

afford [ə'fɔːd, *Am:* -'fɔːrd] *vt* **1.** (*have money or time for*) **to be able to ~ (to do) sth** pouvoir se permettre (de faire) qc; **I can't ~ it** je n'en ai pas les moyens; **he can't ~ to miss this opportunity** il ne peut pas se permettre de rater cette occcasion **2.** (*provide*) donner; **to ~ protection** offrir sa protection

affordable *adj* abordable

afforest [ə'fɒrɪst, *Am:* -'fɔːrəst] *vt* boiser

afforestation [əˌfɒrɪ'steɪʃn, *Am:* -ˌfɔːrə-] *n no pl* boisement *m*

affront [ə'frʌnt] **I.** *n* offense *f* **II.** *vt* offenser

Afghan ['æfgæn] **I.** *adj* afghan(e) **II.** *n* **1.** (*person*) Afghan(e) *m(f)* **2.** LING afghan *m*; *s. a.* **English**

Afghanistan [æf'gænɪstæn, *Am:* -ə-] *n* l'Afghanistan *m*

afield [ə'fiːld] *adv* **far ~** très loin

afloat [ə'fləʊt, *Am:* -'floʊt] **I.** *adj* **to be ~** être à flot **II.** *adv* **to keep ~** flotter; *fig* maintenir la tête hors de l'eau

afoot [ə'fʊt] *adj* **there's mischief/something ~** il se trame/prépare quelque chose

aforementioned [əˌfɔː'menʃnd, *Am:* -ˌfɔːr-], **aforesaid** [əˌfɔːsed, *Am:* -ˌfɔːr-] *form* **I.** *adj* (*in text*) mentionné(e) plus haut; (*in conversation*) déjà mentionné(e) **II.** <-> *n* **the ~** le(la) sus-nommé(e); (*of person mentioned in conversation*) la personne déjà mentionnée

afraid [ə'freɪd] *adj* **1.** (*scared, frightened*) effrayé(e); **to feel** [*o* **to be**] **~** avoir peur; **to be ~ of doing** [*o* **to do**] **sth** avoir peur de faire qc; **to be ~ of sb/sth** avoir peur de qn/qc; **to be ~ that** craindre que +*subj* **2.** (*sorry*) **I'm ~ so/**

not je crains que oui/que non; **I'm ~ she's out/she's refused** je suis désolé mais elle est sortie/elle a refusé

afresh [ə'freʃ] *adv* de [*o* à] nouveau; **to start ~** repartir à zéro

Africa ['æfrɪkə] *n no pl* l'Afrique *f*

African ['æfrɪkən] **I.** *adj* africain(e) **II.** *n* Africain(e) *m(f)*

Afrikaans [ˌæfrɪ'kɑːnts] *n* LING afrika(a)ns *m; s. a.* **English**

Afrikaner [ˌæfrɪ'kɑːnəʳ, *Am:* -ɚ] *n* Africaner *mf*

Afro-american **I.** *adj* afro-américain(e) **II.** *n* Afro-Américain(e) *m(f)*

after ['ɑːftəʳ, *Am:* 'æftɚ] **I.** *prep* **1.** après; **~ two days** deux jours plus tard; **~ meals** après manger; (**a**) **quarter ~ six** *Am* six heures et quart; **the day ~ tomorrow** après-demain; **~ 6 May** (*since then*) depuis le 6 mai; (*as from then*) à partir du 6 mai **2.** (*behind*) **to run ~ sb** courir après qn; **to go ~ one's goal** poursuivre son but; **to slam the door ~ one** claquer la porte derrière soi **3.** (*following*) **D comes ~ C** le D suit le C; **to have quarrel ~ quarrel** avoir dispute sur dispute; **hour ~ hour** pendant des heures **4.** (*trying to get*) **to be ~ sb/sth** chercher qn/qc; **the police are ~ him** la police le recherche; **what are you ~?** qu'est-ce que vous voulez? **5.** (*about*) **to ask ~ sb** demander des nouvelles de qn **6.** (*despite*) **~ all** après tout; **~ all this work** après tout ce travail **7.** (*similar to*) **drawing ~ Picasso** dessin *m* d'après Picasso; **to name sth/sb ~ sb** donner à qc/qn le nom de qn **II.** *adv* après; **soon ~** peu après; **the day ~** le lendemain **III.** *conj* après (que); **he spoke ~ she went out** il parla après qu'elle fut sortie; **I'll call him ~ I've taken a shower** je l'appellerai quand j'aurai pris une douche

aftereffect ['ɑːftərɪˌfekt, *Am:* 'æftɚ-] *n* répercussion *f*

afterlife ['ɑːftəlaɪf, *Am:* 'æftɚ-] *n no pl* vie *f* après la mort

aftermath ['ɑːftəmæθ, *Am:* 'æftɚmæθ] *n no pl* conséquences *fpl;* **in the ~ of sth** à la suite de qc

afternoon [ˌɑːftə'nuːn, *Am:* ˌæftɚ-] *n* après-midi *m o f inv;* **this ~** cet(te) après-midi; **in the ~** (dans) l'après-midi; **4 o'clock in the ~** 4 heures de l'après-midi; **good ~!** bonjour!; **Monday ~s** tous les lundis après-midi

after-sales service *n no pl* service *m* après-vente

aftershave ['ɑːftəʃeɪv, *Am:* 'æftɚ-] *n* lotion *f* après-rasage

aftertaste ['ɑːftəteɪst, *Am:* 'æftɚ-] *n* arrière-goût *m*

afterthought ['ɑːftəθɔːt, *Am:* 'æftɚθɑːt] *n sing* pensée *f* après coup ►**as an ~** après coup

afterward ['ɑːftəwəd, *Am:* 'æftɚwɚd] *adv Am,* **afterwards** ['ɑːftəwədz, *Am:* 'æftɚwɚdz] *adv* **1.** (*later*) après **2.** (*after something*) ensuite; **shortly ~** peu après

again [ə'gen] *adv* **1.** (*as a repetition*) encore; (*one more time*) de nouveau; **never ~** plus jamais; **once ~** une fois de plus; **yet ~** encore une fois; **not ~!** encore!; **he's at it ~** il recommence; **~ and ~** plusieurs fois **2.** (*anew*) **to start ~** recommencer à zéro ►**then ~** d'un autre côté

against [ə'genst] **I.** *prep* **1.** (*in opposition to*) contre; **~ all comers** envers et contre tous; **~ one's will** malgré soi; **to protect oneself ~ rain** se protéger de la pluie; **the odds are ~ sb/sth** les prévisions sont contraires à qn/qc **2.** (*in contact with*) **to lean ~ a tree** s'adosser à un arbre; **to run ~ a wall** percuter un mur **3.** (*in contrast to*) **~ the light** à contre-jour; **~ a green background** sur un fond vert **4.** (*in competition with*) **~ time/the clock** contre la montre; **the dollar rose/fell ~ the euro** le dollar a monté/a baissé par rapport à l'euro **5.** (*in exchange for*) contre ►**to have one's back ~ a wall** être au pied du mur; **to go ~ the grain for sb** aller à l'encontre de la nature de qn **II.** *adv a.* POL **to be for or ~** être pour ou contre

agate ['ægət] *n* agate *f*

age [eɪdʒ] **I.** *n* **1.** (*length of life*) âge *m;* **to be 16 years of ~** avoir 16 ans; **to feel one's ~** se sentir vieux/vieille; **to be under ~** être mineur; **the voting/retirement ~** l'âge du droit de vote/de la retraite; **~ of consent** âge légal de consentement; **old ~** vieillesse *f;* **at my ~** à mon âge **2.** *no pl* (*long existence*) âge *m* **3.** (*era*) époque *f;* **the digital ~** l'ère informatique **4.** *pl* (*a long time*) des siècles; **it's been ~s** ça fait des siècles **II.** *vt, vi* vieillir

aged¹ ['eɪdʒɪd] **I.** *adj* (*old*) vieux(vieille) **II.** *n* **the ~** *pl* les personnes âgées *fpl*

aged² [eɪdʒd] *adj* (*with an age of*) **children ~ 8 to 12** enfants âgés de 8 à 12 ans

age group *n* tranche *f* d'âge **ageless** *adj* (*person, face*) toujours jeune; (*style, clothes*) éternel(le) **age limit** *n* limite *f* d'âge

agency ['eɪdʒənsɪ] <-ies> *n* **1.** agence *f;* **employment ~** bureau *m* de placement; **estate ~** agence immobilière **2.** ADMIN organisme *m* **3.** *no pl, form* (*factor*) **through the ~ of sb** par l'intermédiaire de qn; **through the ~ of sth** sous l'effet de qc

agenda [ə'dʒendə] *n* **1.** (*list*) ordre *m* du jour; **to be on the ~** être à l'ordre du jour **2.** (*program*) programme *m* d'action

agent ['eɪdʒənt] *n* agent *m;* **insurance ~** agent d'assurance

age-old *adj* ancestral(e) **age-related** *adj* lié(e) à l'âge

aggravate ['ægrəveɪt] *vt* **1.** (*make worse*) aggraver **2.** *inf* (*irritate*) exaspérer

aggravating *adj inf* exaspérant(e)

aggravation [ˌægrə'veɪʃn] *n no pl, inf* **1.** (*worsening*) aggravation *f* **2.** (*annoyance*) contrariété *f*

aggregate¹ ['ægrɪgɪt] **I.** *n* FIN, ECON total *m* **II.** *adj* FIN, ECON total(e)

aggregate² ['ægrɪgeɪt] *vt* FIN, ECON faire le total de
aggression [ə'greʃn] *n no pl* **1.**(*feelings*) agressivité *f* **2.**(*violence*) aggression *f*
aggressive [ə'gresɪv] *adj* agressif(-ive)
aggressiveness *n no pl* agressivité *f*
aggressor [ə'gresəʳ, *Am:* -ɚ] *n* agresseur *m*
aggrieved [ə'gri:vd] *adj* **1.**(*hurt*) blessé(e) **2.**(*bitter*) chagriné(e)
aghast [ə'gɑ:st, *Am:* -'gæst] *adj* atterré(e)
agile ['ædʒaɪl, *Am:* 'ædʒl] *adj* **1.**(*in moving*) agile **2.**(*in thinking and acting*) habile; (*mind*) vif(vive)
agility [ə'dʒɪlətɪ, *Am:* -t̬ɪ] *n no pl* agilité *f*
agitate ['ædʒɪteɪt] **I.** *vt* **1.**(*make nervous*) inquiéter **2.**(*shake*) agiter **II.** *vi* **to ~ for/against sth** faire campagne pour/contre qc
agitation [ˌædʒɪ'teɪʃn] *n no pl a.* POL agitation *f;* **in a state of** (**great**) **~** dans un état de grande agitation
agitator ['ædʒɪteɪtəʳ, *Am:* -t̬ɚ] *n* agitateur, -trice *m, f*
AGM [ˌeɪ.dʒi:'em] *n* **1.** *abbr of* **air-to-ground missile** missile *m* air-sol **2.** *abbr of* **annual general meeting** assemblée *f* générale annuelle
ago [ə'gəʊ, *Am:* -'goʊ] *adv* **that was a long time ~** c'était il y a longtemps; **a minute/a year ~** il y a une minute/un an
agonize ['ægənaɪz] *vi* se tourmenter
agonized *adj* atroce; (*cry*) déchirant(e)
agonizing *adj* **1.**(*painful*) atroce; **to die an ~ death** mourir d'une mort atroce **2.**(*causing anxiety*) angoissant(e)
agony ['ægənɪ] <-ies> *n* douleur *f* atroce; **to be in ~** souffrir le martyre; **the ~ of sth** l'angoisse *f* de qc
agree [ə'gri:] **I.** *vi* **1.**(*share, accept idea*) **to ~ with sb** être d'accord avec qn; **~ to a suggestion** accepter une suggestion; **to ~ on sth** se mettre d'accord sur qc; **to ~ to sth** consentir à qc **2.**(*endorse*) **to ~ with sth** approuver qc **3.**(*be good for*) **to ~ with sb** être bon pour qn **4.**(*match up*) concorder **5.** LING s'accorder ►**sb couldn't ~ more with sb** qn est entièrement d'accord avec qn **II.** *vt* **1.**(*concur*) convenir de; **it is ~d that** il est convenu que +*subj;* **to be ~d on sth** être d'accord sur qc; **are we all ~d on that?** sommes-nous tous d'accord sur ce point ? **2.**(*accept view, proposal*) **I ~ that it's expensive, it's expensive, I ~** c'est cher, je suis d'accord; **to ~ to** +*infin* (*when asked*) accepter de +*infin;* (*by mutual decision*) se mettre d'accord pour +*infin;* **to ~ to differ** renoncer à discuter **3.** *Brit* (*accept*) accepter
agreeable *adj* **1.**(*acceptable*) **to be ~ to sb** convenir à qn **2.**(*pleasant*) agréable **3.**(*consenting*) **to be ~ to sth** être d'accord pour qc
agreement *n* **1.** *no pl* (*state of accord*) **to be in ~ with sb** être d'accord avec qn; **to reach ~** se mettre d'accord **2.** *a.* LING accord *m* **3.**(*pact*) accord *m* **4.**(*promise*) engagement *m;* **an ~ to** +*infin* un engagement à +*infin;* **America's ~ to send troops** l'engagement américain d'envoyer des troupes **5.** *no pl* (*approval*) accord *m;* **~ to do/for sth** accord de faire/pour qc
agricultural [ˌægrɪ'kʌltʃərəl] *adj* agricole
agriculture ['ægrɪkʌltʃəʳ, *Am:* -tʃɚ] *n no pl* agriculture *f*
agrotourism ['ægrəʊtʊərɪzəm] *n* agrotourisme *m*
aground [ə'graʊnd] *adv* NAUT **to go** [*o* **run**] **~ on sth** s'échouer sur qc
ah [ɑ:] *interj* ah
aha [ɑ:'hɑ:] *interj* ah ah
ahead [ə'hed] *adv* **1.**(*in front*) **straight ~** droit devant; **to drive on ~** partir devant (en voiture); **to send sth on ~** envoyer qc en avance; **to be ~** *fig* (*party, team*) mener **2.**(*for the future*) à venir; **to look ~** penser à l'avenir; **to plan sth a week ~** prévoir qc une semaine à l'avance
ahead of *prep* **1.**(*in front of*) **to walk ~ sb** marcher devant qn; **what is ~ us** *fig* ce qui nous attend **2.**(*before*) **way ~ sb/sth** longtemps avant qn/qc; **to do sth ~ sth** faire qc en prévision de qc; **~ time** (*decide*) à l'avance; (*arrive*) en avance; **to be a minute ~ sb** avoir une minute d'avance sur qn **3.**(*more advanced than*) **to be way ~ sb/sth** être très en avance sur qn/qc; **~ one's time** en avance sur son époque ►**to be ~ the game** avoir une longueur d'avance
AI [ˌeɪ'ai] *n* **1.** *abbr of* **artificial insemination** IA *f* **2.** *abbr of* **artificial intelligence** IA *f*
aid [eɪd] **I.** *n* aide; **in ~ of sb/sth** au profit de qn/qc; **to come/go to the ~ of sb** venir/aller au secours de qn; **with the ~ of** (*person*) avec l'aide de; (*thing*) à l'aide de; **international ~** secours *m* international ►**what's all this in ~ of?** *Brit, inf* c'est en quel honneur ? **II.** *vt* **to ~ sb with sth** aider qn à faire qc
AID *n* **1.** *Am abbr of* **Agency for International Development** **2.** *abbr of* **artificial insemination by donor** IAD
aid agency *n* association *f* caritative
aide [eɪd] *n* assistant(e) *m(f)*
AIDS [eɪdz] *n no pl abbr of* **Acquired Immune Deficiency Syndrome** SIDA
ailing ['eɪlɪŋ] *adj* mal en point
ailment ['eɪlmənt] *n* maladie *f*
aim [eɪm] **I.** *vi* **1.**(*point a weapon*) viser; **to ~ at sb/sth** viser qn/qc **2.**(*plan to achieve*) **to ~ at** [*o* **for**] **sth** viser qc; **to ~ at doing** [*o* **to do**] **sth** avoir l'intention de faire qc **II.** *vt* **1.**(*point a weapon*) **to ~ sth at sb/sth** (*gun, launcher*) pointer qc sur qn/qc; (*spear, missile*) braquer; (*blow*) tenter de porter **2.**(*direct at*) **to ~ sth at sb** (*criticism, remark*) destiner qc à qn **3.** *fig* **to be ~ed at doing sth** viser à faire qc **III.** *n* **1.** *no pl* (*plan to shoot*) manière de viser; **to take ~** viser **2.**(*goal*) but *m;* **to do sth with the ~ of doing sth** faire qc dans le but de faire qc

aimless ['eɪmlɪs] *adj* sans but

air [eəʳ, *Am:* er] **I.** *n* **1.** *a.* MUS air; **to fire into the ~** tirer en l'air; **by ~** par avion; **there was an ~ of menace/excitement** il y avait de la menace/de l'émotion dans l'air **2.** *no pl* TV, RADIO **to be off/on (the) ~** être hors antenne/à l'antenne ►**~s and graces** *pej* manières *fpl;* **to be floating on ~** être aux anges; **to be in the ~** se tramer; **to be up in the ~** être flou; **to give oneself ~s** *pej* se donner des airs **II.** *vt* **1.** TV, RADIO diffuser **2.** (*expose to air*) aérer **3.** (*let know*) faire connaître; **to ~ one's grievances** exposer ses griefs **III.** *vi* **1.** *Am* TV, RADIO passer **2.** (*be exposed to air*) s'aérer

air ambulance *n* ambulance *f* aérienne

airbag *n* airbag *m*

airborne ['eəbɔːn, *Am:* 'erbɔːrn] *adj* **1.** (*by wind*) emporté(e) par le vent **2.** (*by aircraft*) aéroporté(e) **3.** (*in the air*) **to be ~** être en vol; **to get ~** (*plane*) décoller; (*bird*) s'envoler **4.** (*working*) opérationnel(le)

air-conditioned ['eəkən'dɪʃnd, *Am:* 'erkənˌdɪʃnd] *adj* climatisé(e)

air conditioning ['eəkən'dɪʃnɪŋ, *Am:* 'erkənˌdɪʃnɪŋ] *n no pl* climatisation *f*

aircraft ['eəkrɑːft, *Am:* 'erkræft] <-> *n* avion *m*

aircraft carrier *n* porte-avions *m inv* **aircraft industry** *n no pl* industrie *f* aéronautique

air fare *n* tarif *m* des vols

airfield ['eəfiːld, *Am:* 'er-] *n* terrain *m* d'aviation

air force *n* armée *f* de l'air

airgun *n* fusil *m* à air comprimé

airline *n* compagnie *f* aérienne

airliner ['eəlaɪn, *Am:* 'er-] *n* avion *m* de ligne

airmail ['eəmeɪl, *Am:* 'er-] *n no pl* poste *f* aérienne; **to send sth (by) ~** envoyer qc par avion

airman ['eəmən, *Am:* 'er-] <-men> *n* aviateur, -trice *m, f*

airplane ['eəpleɪn, *Am:* 'er-] *n Am* avion *m*

air pollution *n* pollution *f* de l'air

airport ['eəpɔːt, *Am:* 'erpɔːrt] *n* aéroport *m* **air raid** *n* bombardement *m* aérien

airsick ['eəsɪk, *Am:* 'er-] *adj* **to get ~** attraper le mal de l'air

airsickness *n no pl* mal *m* de l'air

airspace ['eəspeɪs, *Am:* 'er-] *n no pl* espace *m* aérien

airstrip ['eəstrɪp, *Am:* 'er-] *n* piste *f*

airtight ['eətaɪt, *Am:* 'er-] *adj* hermétique

air traffic controller *n* aiguilleur, -euse *m, f* du ciel

air travel *n* voyages *mpl* par avion

airway ['eəweɪ, *Am:* 'er-] *n* **1.** ANAT voie *f* respiratoire **2.** (*route*) voie *f* aérienne **3.** (*airline*) compagnie *f* aérienne

airy ['eərɪ, *Am:* 'er-] *adj* **1.** (*spacious*) clair(e) **2.** (*light*) léger(-ère) **3.** (*lacking substance*) chimérique

aisle [aɪl] *n* allée *f;* (*of a church*) allée *f* centrale ►**to take sb down the ~** se marier avec qn

ajar [ə'dʒɑːʳ, *Am:* -'dʒɑːr] *adj* entrouvert(e)

a.k.a. [ˌeɪ.keɪ'eɪ, *Am:* 'æk.ə] *abbr of* **also known as** alias

akin [ə'kɪn] *adj* **to be ~ to sth** être semblable à qc

Alabama [ˌælə'bæmə] **I.** *n* l'Alabama *m* **II.** *adj* de l'Alabama

alarm [ə'lɑːm, *Am:* -'lɑːrm] **I.** *n* **1.** *no pl* (*worry*) inquiétude *f;* (*fright*) frayeur *f* **2.** (*warning*) alarme *f;* **a false ~** une fausse alerte; **give the ~** donner l'alarme; *a. fig* sonner l'alarme **3.** (*warning device*) alarme *f;* **burglar ~** alarme antivol **4.** (*clock*) réveil *m,* cadran *m Québec* **II.** *vt* **1.** (*worry*) inquiéter **2.** (*cause fear*) effrayer

alarm clock *n* réveil *m*

alarming *adj* **1.** (*worrying*) inquiétant(e) **2.** (*frightening*) alarmant(e)

alarmist I. *adj pej* alarmiste **II.** *n pej* alarmiste *mf*

alas [ə'læs] *interj* hélas

Alaska [ə'læskə] **I.** *n* l'Alaska *m* **II.** *adj* de l'Alaska

Albania [æl'beɪnɪə] *n* l'Albanie *f*

Albanian I. *adj* albanais(e) **II.** *n* **1.** (*person*) Albanais(e) *m(f)* **2.** LING albanais *m; s. a.* **English**

albatross ['ælbətrɒs, *Am:* -trɑːs] *n* albatros *m*

albeit [ɔːl'biːɪt] *conj* quoique

albino [æl'biːnəʊ, *Am:* -'baiːnoʊ] **I.** *adj* albinos **II.** *n* albinos *mf*

album ['ælbəm] *n* album *m*

alcohol ['ælkəhɒl, *Am:* -hɑːl] *n no pl* alcool *m*

alcohol-free *adj* sans alcool

alcoholic [ˌælkə'hɒlɪk, *Am:* -'hɑːlɪk] **I.** *n* alcoolique *mf* **II.** *adj* alcoolisé(e)

alcoholism *n no pl* alcoolisme *m*

alcove ['ælkəʊv, *Am:* -koʊv] *n* alcôve *f*

alder ['ɔːldəʳ, *Am:* -dɚ] *n* aulne *m*

ale [eɪl] *n* bière *f*

alert [ə'lɜːt, *Am:* -'lɜːrt] **I.** *adj* (*attentive*) alerte; (*watchful*) vigilant(e); (*wide-awake*) éveillé(e); **to be ~ to sth** être conscient de qc **II.** *n* **1.** (*alarm*) alerte *f* **2. to be on the ~ for sth** être en état d'alerte concernant qc *m* **III.** *vt* alerter; **to ~ sb to sth** avertir qn de qc

> Le **A level** ("Advanced Level") est un examen de fin d'année que passent les élèves de la sixième classe (l'équivalent de la terminale) au lycée. La plupart du temps, les élèves choisissent trois matières principales sur lesquelles ils seront examinés. Mais il est aussi possible de ne choisir qu'une seule matière. Après l'obtention du "A level", les élèves peuvent accéder à une université si les notes sont acceptables.

algae ['ælg] *n pl* algues *fpl*

algebra ['ældʒɪbrə] *n no pl* algèbre *f*

algebraic [ˌældʒɪ'breɪɪk] *adj* algébrique
Algeria [æl'dʒɪərɪə, *Am:* -'dʒɪ-] *n* l'Algérie *f*
Algerian I. *adj* algérien(ne) II. *n* (*person*) Algérien(ne) *m(f)*
Algiers [æl'dʒɪəz, *Am:* -'dʒɪrz] *n* Alger
ALGOL ['ægɒl, *Am:* -gɑːl] *n* INFOR *abbr of* **algorithmic language** ALGOL *m*
alias ['eɪlɪəs] I. *n* faux nom *m;* **to use an ~** utiliser un nom d'emprunt II. *prep* alias
alibi ['ælɪbaɪ] *n* alibi *m*
Alice band ['ælɪsˌbænd] *n Brit* serre-tête *m*
alien ['eɪlɪən] I. *adj* 1. (*foreign*) étranger(-ère) 2. (*strange*) étrange; **~ to sb** étranger à qn II. *n* 1. *form* (*foreigner*) étranger, -ère *m, f;* **an illegal ~** un clandestin 2. (*extra-terrestrial creature*) extra-terrestre *m*
alienate ['eɪlɪəneɪt] *vt* 1. éloigner; **to ~ sb from sb/sth** éloigner qn de qn/qc 2. LAW aliéner
alight[1] [ə'laɪt] *adj* 1. (*on fire*) allumé(e); **to set sth ~** mettre le feu à qc; **to get sth ~** allumer qc 2. (*shining brightly*) **to be ~ with sth** rayonner de qc
alight[2] [ə'laɪt] *vi* 1. (*get out*) **to ~ from a vehicle** descendre d'un véhicule 2. (*land*) atterrir
◆**alight on** *vi* **to ~ sth** tomber sur qc
align [ə'laɪn] *vt* 1. (*move into line*) aligner 2. (*support*) **to ~ oneself with sb/sth** se rallier à qn/qc
alignment *n no pl* alignement *m;* **to be out of ~** sortir de l'alignement
alike [ə'laɪk] I. *adj* 1. (*identical*) identique 2. (*similar*) semblable II. *adv* de la même façon; **men and women ~** les hommes comme les femmes
alimony ['ælɪmənɪ, *Am:* -moʊ-] *n no pl* pension *f* alimentaire
alive [ə'laɪv] *adj* 1. (*not dead*) vivant(e); **to keep sb ~** maintenir qn en vie; **to keep hope ~** garder espoir 2. (*active*) actif(-ive); **to come ~** (*city*) s'éveiller; **to be ~ with fleas/greenfly** être couvert de puces/de pucerons 3. (*aware*) **to be ~ to sth** être conscient de qc
alkali ['ælkəlaɪ] *n* alcali *m*
alkaline ['ælkəlaɪn] *adj* alcalin(e)
all [ɔːl] I. *adj* tout(e) *m(f),* tous *mpl,* toutes *fpl;* **~ the butter/my life** tout le beurre/toute ma vie; **~ the children/my cousins** tous les enfants/mes cousins; **~ children/animals** tous les enfants/les animaux; **with ~ possible speed** aussi vite que possible II. *pron* 1. (*everybody*) tous *mpl,* toutes *fpl;* **~ aboard!** tout le monde à bord!; **~ but one** tous sauf un(e); **they ~ refused** ils ont tous refusé; **he's got four daughters, ~ blue-eyed** il a quatre filles, toutes aux yeux bleus; **there were hundreds of children, ~ singing** il y avait des centaines d'enfants, tous chantaient; **the kindest of ~** le plus gentil de tous; **once and for ~** une fois pour toutes 2. (*everything*) tout; **most of ~** surtout; **the best of all** le meilleur; **for ~ I know** autant que je sache; **for ~ he may think** quoi qu'il en pense 3. (*the whole quantity*) tout; **they took/drunk it ~** ils ont tout pris/bu; **~ of France** toute la France; **it's ~ so different** tout est si différent; **it's ~ nonsense** c'est complètement absurde 4. (*the only thing*) tout; **~ I want is ...** tout ce que je veux, c'est ...; **that's ~ the equipment you need** c'est tout le matériel dont vous aurez besoin ▶**none at ~** (*people*) personne; (*of things*) aucun(e); (*of amount*) rien du tout; **not at ~** (*you're welcome*) il n'y a pas de quoi; (*in no way*) pas du tout; **not at ~ worried** pas du tout inquiet; **nothing at ~** rien du tout III. *adv* tout; **it's ~ wet/dirty** c'est tout mouillé/sale; **~ round** tout autour; **not as stupid as ~ that** pas si bête que cela; **~ the same** quand même; **I've ~ but finished** je suis à deux doigts d'avoir fini; **~ over the lawn** sur toute la pelouse; **~ over the country** dans tout le pays; **two ~** SPORT deux partout
all-around *adj Am s.* **all-round**
all-clear [ˌɔːl'klɪəʳ, *Am:* -'klɪr] *n* signal *m* de fin d'alerte
allegation [ˌælɪ'geɪʃn] *n* allégation *f*
allege [ə'ledʒ] *vt* prétendre
alleged *adj form* LAW (*attacker/attack*) présumé(e)
allegedly *adv* **he ~ did sth** il a prétendument fait qc
allegiance [ə'liːdʒəns] *n* allégeance *f*
allegory ['ælɪgərɪ, *Am:* -gɔːrɪ] <-ies> *n* allégorie *f*
alleluia [ˌælɪ'luːjə] I. *interj* alléluia II. *n* alléluia *m*
allergen ['ælədʒən, *Am:* -ɚ-] *n* allergène *m*
allergenic [ælə'dʒenɪk, *Am:* -ɚ-] *adj* allergène
allergic [ə'lɜːdʒɪk, *Am:* -'lɜːr-] *adj a. fig* allergique
allergy ['ælədʒɪ, *Am:* -ɚ-] <-ies> *n* allergie *f*
alleviate [ə'liːvɪeɪt] *vt* atténuer
alley ['ælɪ] *n* 1. (*narrow street*) ruelle *f;* **blind ~** impasse *f;* **~ cat** chat *m* de gouttière 2. (*path in garden*) allée *f*
alliance [ə'laɪəns] *n* alliance *f*
allied ['ælaɪd] *adj* allié(e)
Allied forces *n* Forces *fpl* Alliées
alligator ['ælɪgeɪtəʳ, *Am:* -t̬ɚ] *n* alligator *m*
allocate ['æləkeɪt] *vt* attribuer
allocation [ˌælə'keɪʃn] *n* 1. (*assignment*) attribution *f* 2. (*amount*) crédits *mpl*
allot [ə'lɒt, *Am:* -'lɑːt] <-tt-> *vt* allouer
allotment *n* 1. (*assignment*) attribution *f* 2. *Brit* (*plot of land*) lopin *m* de terre
all-out [ɔːl'aʊt] *adj* (*attack, commitment*) total(e)
allow [ə'laʊ] *vt* 1. (*permit*) permettre; **photography is not ~ed** il est interdit de prendre des photos; **to ~ sb sth** (*officially*) autoriser qc à qn; **to ~ oneself a holiday** s'autoriser des vacances; **to ~ enough time** laisser suffisamment de temps; **to ~ sb in/out** laisser entre/sortir qn; **to allow sb through** laisser passer

qn **2.** (*allocate*) accorder; (*when planning*) prévoir **3.** (*plan*) prévoir **4.** (*concede*) **to ~ that ...** reconnaître que ...

◆**allow for** *vi* tenir compte de; **to ~ sb being slow** tenir compte du fait que qn est lent; **to ~ sb being delayed** prévoir que qn pourrait avoir du retard

allowable *adj* autorisé(e)

allowance [ə'laʊəns] *n* **1.** (*permitted amount*) allocation *f;* **baggage ~** franchise *f* de bagages; **tax ~** abattement *m* fiscal **2.** (*money*) indemnité *f; Am* (*to child*) argent *m* de poche; (*to adult*) rente *f;* **cost-of-living/travel ~** indemnité *f* de logement/déplacement **3.** (*prepare for*) **to make ~(s) for sth** prendre qc en considération; **to make ~s for sb** être indulgent envers qn

alloy ['ælɔɪ] *n* alliage *m*

all-purpose [ɔːl'pɜːpəs, *Am:* -'pɜːr-] *adj* multi-usage

all right I. *adj* **1.** (*o.k.*) d'accord; **that's** [*o* **it's**] **~** c'est bien; **will it be ~ if she comes?** c'est o.k.si elle vient? **2.** (*good*) pas mal; (*mediocre*) potable; **I feel ~** je me sens bien **3.** (*normal*) **I feel ~** ça va; **is everything ~?** tout va bien?; **the driver was ~** (*safe*) le conducteur était sain et sauf **II.** *interj* **1.** (*expressing agreement*) d'accord; **~ quieten down** ça va, du calme **2.** *inf* (*after thanks or excuse*) **it's ~** de rien **III.** *adv* **1.** (*properly: work, progress*) comme il faut; **the party went ~** la fête s'est bien passée; **to get on ~ with sb** bien s'entendre avec qn **2.** *inf* (*definitely*) **he saw us ~** il nous a vus, c'est sûr

all-round [ˌɔːl'raʊnd] *adj* polyvalent; (*sportsman*) complet(-ète)

all-rounder [ɔːl'raʊndəʳ, *Am:* -dɚ] *n Aus, Brit* multi-talent *mf* **All Saints Day** *n no pl* Toussaint *f* **All Souls' Day** *n* la fête des Morts **all-time** *adj* (*record*) absolu; **to be at an ~ high/low** être au plus haut/au plus bas

allude [ə'luːd] *vi* **to ~ to sth** faire allusion à qc

alluring [ə'lʊərɪŋ, *Am:* -'lʊrɪŋ] *adj* attrayant(e)

allusion [ə'luːʒn] *n* allusion *f*

all-weather [ˌɔːl'weðəʳ] *adj* pour tous les temps

ally [ə'laɪ] **I.** <-ies> *n* allié(e) *m(f)* **II.** <-ie-> *vt* **to ~ oneself with** [*o* **to**] **sb** s'allier avec qn

almanac ['ɔːlmənæk] *n* almanach *m*

almighty [ɔːl'maɪtɪ, *Am:* -t̬ɪ] *adj inf* terrible

Almighty [ɔːl'maɪtɪ, *Am:* -t̬ɪ] *n* REL **the ~** le Tout-Puissant

almond ['ɑːmənd] *n* **1.** (*nut*) amande *f* **2.** (*tree*) amandier *m*

almost ['ɔːlməʊst, *Am:* -moʊst] *adv* presque; **I ~ fell asleep** j'ai failli m'endormir

aloe vera [ˌaləʊ'vɪərə, *Am:* -oʊ'vɪrə] *n* BOT aloès *m*

alone [ə'ləʊn, *Am:* -'loʊn] **I.** *adj* **1.** (*without others*) seul(e) **2.** (*only*) le(la) seul(e); **Paul ~ can do that** il n'y a que Paul qui puisse faire cela; **money ~ is not enough** l'argent tout seul ne suffit pas ►**not <u>even</u> sth, let ~ sth else** pas qc et encore moins qc d'autre **II.** *adv* tout(e) seul(e)

along [ə'lɒŋ, *Am:* -'lɑːŋ] **I.** *prep* **1.** (*on*) **all ~ sth** tout le long de qc; **sb walks ~ the road** qn marche sur la route **2.** (*during*) **~ the way** en cours de route **3.** (*beside*) **the trees ~ the path** les arbres bordant le chemin **4.** (*in addition to*) **~ with sth/sb** en plus de qc/qn **II.** *adv* **1.** (*going forward*) **to walk ~** marcher **2.** (*to a place*) **to come ~** venir; **are you coming ~?** tu viens?, tu viens avec? *Belgique;* **he'll be ~ in an hour** il viendra dans une heure **3.** (*the whole time*) **all ~** depuis le début

alongside [əˌlɒŋ'saɪd, *Am:* ə'lɑːŋsaɪd] **I.** *prep* **1.** *a.* NAUT **to stop ~ a quay** stopper le long d'un quai **2.** (*next to*) **~ sth** à côté de qc; **to draw up ~ sb** stopper à la hauteur de qn **3.** (*together with*) **to work ~ each other** travailler côte à côte; **to fight ~ sb** se battre aux côtés de qn; *s. a.* **along II.** *adv* **1.** (*next to*) côte à côte **2.** NAUT bord à bord; **to come ~** accoster

aloof [ə'luːf] *adj* distant(e)

aloud [ə'laʊd] *adv* (*read, think*) à voix haute; (*laugh*) fort

alpha ['ælfə] *n* **1.** (*greek letter*) alpha *m* **2.** *Brit* (*student mark*) très bonne note *f*

alphabet ['ælfəbet] *n* alphabet *m*

alphabetical [ˌælfə'betɪkl] *adj* alphabétique

alphanumeric [ˌælfənjuː'merɪk, *Am:* -nuː-] *adj* alphanumérique

alpha particle, **alpha ray** *n* PHYS alpha *m*

alpine ['ælpaɪn] **I.** *adj* alpin(e); (*scene*) alpestre **II.** *n* (*alpine plant*) plante *f* alpine

Alps [ælps] *npl* **the ~** les Alpes

already [ɔːl'redɪ] *adv* déjà

alright [ɔːl'raɪt] *s. a.* **all right**

Alsace [æl'sæs] *n* l'Alsace *f*

Alsatian [æl'seɪʃn] **I.** *adj* alsacien(ne) **II.** *n* **1.** (*person*) Alsacien(ne) *m(f)* **2.** LING alsacien *m; s. a.* **English 3.** *Am, Aus* (*large dog*) berger *m* allemand

also ['ɔːlsəʊ, *Am:* 'ɔːlsoʊ] *adv* aussi

altar ['ɔːltəʳ, *Am:* -t̬ɚ] *n* autel *m*

alter ['ɔːltəʳ, *Am:* -t̬ɚ] **I.** *vt* changer; (*building*) faire des travaux sur; (*clothes*) retoucher **II.** *vi* changer

alteration [ˌɔːltə'reɪʃn, *Am:* -t̬ə-] *n* changement *m;* (*to clothes*) retouches *fpl;* **an ~ to sth** une modification à qc

altercation [ˌɔːltə'keɪʃn, *Am:* -t̬ɚ-] *n* altercation *f*

alternate [ɔːl'tɜːnət, *Am:* -'t̬ɜːr-] **I.** *vi, vt* alterner **II.** *adj* **1.** (*by turns*) alterné(e); **on ~ days** un jour sur deux **2.** *Am* (*different, alternative*) alternatif(-ive)

alternating *adj* en alternance

alternative [ɔːl'tɜːnətɪv, *Am:* -'tɜːrnət̬ɪv] **I.** *n* alternative *f* **II.** *adj* alternatif(-ive)

alternatively *adv* sinon; (*as a substitute*) à défaut

alternator ['ɔːltəneɪtəʳ, *Am:* -tɚneɪt̬ɚ] *n* alternateur *m*

although [ɔːl'ðəʊ, *Am:* -'ðoʊ] *conj* bien que, quoique; **he is late ~ he left early** il est en retard bien qu'il soit parti à temps; **~ it's snowing, ...** malgré la neige, ...; **she didn't win ~ she should have** elle n'a pas gagné pourtant elle aurait du; *s. a.* **though**

altimeter ['æltɪmiːtəʳ, *Am:* æl'tɪmət̬ɚ] *n* altimètre *m*

altitude ['æltɪtjuːd, *Am:* -tətuːd] *n* altitude *f*

alto ['æltəʊ, *Am:* -toʊ] **I.** *n* **1.** (*woman*) contralto *m,* alto *f* **2.** (*viola or man*) alto *m* **II.** *adj* alto; **~ flute** flûte *f* alto; **~ clef** clé *f* d'ut

altogether [ˌɔːltə'geðəʳ, *Am:* -ɚ] *adv* **1.** (*completely*) entièrement; **a different matter** [*o* **thing**] **~** une tout autre chose; **not ~** pas complètement; **it is not ~ surprising** ce n'est pas du tout étonnant **2.** (*in total*) globalement

altruism ['æltruːɪzəm] *n no pl* altruisme *m*

altruistic [ˌæltruː'ɪstɪk] *adj* altruiste

aluminium [ˌæljʊ'mɪnɪəm] *n,* **aluminum** [ə'luːmɪnəm] *n Am no pl* aluminium

always ['ɔːlweɪz] *adv* toujours

Alzheimer's (**disease**) ['æltshaɪməʳ-, *Am:* 'ɑːltshaɪmɚ-] *n* maladie *f* d'Alzheimer

am [əm] *1st pers sing of* **be**

a.m. [ˌeɪ'em] *adv abbr of* **ante meridiem** *avant midi*

amalgam [ə'mælgəm] *n* amalgame *m*

amalgamate [ə'mælgəmeɪt] **I.** *vt* **1.** CHEM amalgamer **2.** (*merge*) fusionner **II.** *vi* **1.** CHEM s'amalgamer **2.** (*merge*) fusionner

amalgamation [əˌmælgə'meɪʃn] *n* **1.** *no pl* (*process*) fusionnement *m* **2.** (*result*) fusion *f;* (*metal*) amalgamation *f*

amass [ə'mæs] *vt* amasser

amateur ['æmətəʳ, *Am:* -tʃɚ] **I.** *n a. pej* amateur *m* **II.** *adj* amateur; **~ work/sport** travail/sport *m* d'amateur

amateurish ['æmətərɪʃ, *Am:* ˌæmə'tɜːrɪʃ] *adj pej* d'amateur

amaze [ə'meɪz] *vt* stupéfier; **to be ~d that sb comes** être très surpris que qn vienne

amazement *n no pl* stupéfaction *f*

amazing *adj* très surprenant(e); **truly ~** ahurissant(e)

Amazon ['æməzən, *Am:* -zɑːn] *n* **1.** (*female warrior*) amazone *f* **2.** (*river*) **the** (**river**) **~** l'Amazone *f;* **the ~ rain forest** la forêt amazonienne

ambassador [æm'bæsədəʳ, *Am:* -dɚ] *n* ambassadeur, -drice *m, f*

amber ['æmbəʳ, *Am:* -bɚ] **I.** *n* ambre *m* **II.** *adj* ambré(e); **the traffic light is at ~** *Brit* le feu est à l'orange; *s. a.* **blue**

ambidextrous [ˌæmbɪ'dekstrəs] *adj* ambidextre

ambiguity [ˌæmbɪ'gjuːətɪ, *Am:* -bə'gjuːət̬ɪ] <-ies> *n* ambiguïté *f*

ambiguous [æm'bɪgjʊəs] *adj* ambigu(ë)

ambition [æm'bɪʃn] *n* ambition *f*

ambitious [æm'bɪʃəs] *adj* ambitieux(-euse)

amble ['æmbl] **I.** *vi* aller tranquillement; **to ~ along/down/off** se promener/descendre/partir tranquillement **II.** *n no pl* promenade *f;* **a leisurely ~** une balade tranquille *f*

ambulance ['æmbjʊləns] *n* ambulance *f;* **~ crew** ambulanciers *mpl*

ambush ['æmbʊʃ] **I.** *vt* tendre une embuscade à; **to be ~ed** être pris dans une embuscade **II.** <-es> *n* embuscade *f;* **to be caught in an ~** être pris dans une embuscade; **to lie in ~** se tenir en embuscade; **to lie in ~ for sb** tendre une embuscade à qn

amen [ɑː'men, *Am:* eɪ'men] *interj* amen

amenable [ə'miːnəbl] *adj* (*pupil, dog*) docile; **to be ~ to suggestion** être ouvert aux suggestions; **to be ~ to sb doing sth** être prêt à accepter que qn fasse qc

amend [ə'mend] *vt* **1.** (*change*) modifier; (*law*) amender **2.** (*improve, correct*) rectifier

amendment *n* (*change, changed words*) modification *f;* (*to a bill*) amendement *m*

amends *n* **to make ~** se rattraper

amenities [ə'miːnətɪz, *Am:* -'menət̬ɪz] *n pl* équipement *m*

America [ə'merɪkə] *n* l'Amérique *f*

American [ə'merɪkən] **I.** *adj* américain(e) **II.** *n* **1.** (*person*) Américain(e) *m(f)* **2.** LING américain *m; s. a.* **English**

American Civil War *n* **the ~** la guerre de Sécession

americanism *n* américanisme *m*

americanize [ə'merɪkənaɪz] *vt* américaniser

American Revolution *n Am, Can* guerre *f* d'Indépendance américaine

amethyst ['æmɪθɪst] **I.** *n* améthyste *f* **II.** *adj inv* améthyste

amiability [ˌeɪmɪə'bɪlətɪ, *Am:* -t̬ɪ] *n no pl* amabilité *f*

amiable ['eɪmɪəbl] *adj* aimable

amicable ['æmɪkəbl] *adj* amical(e); (*divorce, settlement*) à l'amiable

amid [ə'mɪd(st)] *prep* **1.** (*surrounded by*) au milieu de **2.** (*during*) **~ the discussion** en pleine discussion

amiss [ə'mɪs] **I.** *adj* **something is ~** il y a quelque chose qui ne va pas **II.** *adv* **to take sth ~** mal prendre qc; **sth would not go ~** qc serait le bienvenu

ammeter ['æmɪtəʳ, *Am:* -t̬ɚ] *n* ampèremètre *m*

ammonia [ə'məʊnɪə, *Am:* -'moʊnjə] *n no pl* **1.** (*gas*) amoniac *m* **2.** (*solution*) amoniaque *f*

ammunition [ˌæmjʊ'nɪʃn, *Am:* -jə-] *n no pl* **1.** (*for firearms*) munitions; **~ depot** [*o* **dump**] dépôt *m* de munitions **2.** (*in debate*) armes *fpl*

amnesia [æm'niːzɪə, *Am:* -ʒə] *n no pl* amnésie *f;* **~ victim** amnésique *mf*

amnesty ['æmnəstɪ] <-ies> *n* amnistie *f*

amok [ə'mɒk, *Am:* -'mʌk], *adv* **to run ~** être pris de folie furieuse

among [ə'mʌŋ(st)] *prep* **1.** (*between*) **~ friends/yourselves** entre amis/vous; **to**

divide up sth ~ us partager qc entre nous **2.** (*as part of*) (**just**) **one ~ many** un parmi tant d'autres; **it's ~ my tasks** ça fait partie de mes tâches; **~ my favourite artists** parmi mes artistes préférés **3.** (*in a group*) **~ Scots** chez les Écossais **4.** (*in midst of*) **~ the flowers/pupils** au milieu des [*o* parmi les] fleurs/élèves **5.** (*in addition to*) **~ other things** entre autres choses

amoral [ˌeɪˈmɒrəl, *Am:* -ˈmɔːr-] *adj* amoral(e)

amorous [ˈæmərəs] *adj* amoureux(-euse)

amorphous [əˈmɔːfəs, *Am:* -ˈmɔːr-] *adj* amorphe; **~ mass** masse *f* informe

amortize [əˈmɔːtaɪz, *Am:* æmˈɔːr-] *vt Aus, Brit* ECON amortir

amount [əˈmaʊnt] **I.** *n* quantité *f;* **any ~ of** *inf* des tas de; **any ~ of people** beaucoup de monde; **a certain ~ of determination** une certaine dose de détermination; **large ~s of electricity** de grosses quantités d'électricité **II.** *vi* **1.** (*add up to*) **to ~ to sth** s'élever à qc **2.** (*mean*) revenir à qc **3.** *fig* **sb will never ~ to much** qn n'arrivera jamais à rien

amp. [æmp] *n abbr of* **ampere** A *m*

ampere [ˈæmpeəʳ, *Am:* -pɪr] *n form* ampère *m*

amphetamine [æmˈfetəmiːn] *n* amphétamine *f*

amphibian [æmˈfɪbɪən] *n* **1.** ZOOL amphibien *m* **2.** AUTO véhicule *m* amphibie

amphibious [æmˈfɪbɪəs] *adj* amphibie

amphitheater *n Am,* **amphitheatre** [ˈæmfɪˌθɪətəʳ, *Am:* -fəˌθɪːət̬ɚ] *n Aus, Brit* amphithéâtre *m*

ample [ˈæmpl] <-r, -st> *adj* **1.** (*plentiful*) largement assez de; **~ evidence** des preuves abondantes **2.** *iron* (*large*) gros(se); **~ bosom** poitrine opulente; **~ girth** corpulence *f*

amplifier [ˈæmplɪfaɪəʳ, *Am:* -ɚ] *n* amplificateur *m*

amplify [ˈæmplɪfaɪ] <-ie-> *vt* **1.** MUS amplifier **2.** (*enlarge upon*) développer

amply *adv* (*rewarded*) largement

amputate [ˈæmpjʊteɪt] **I.** *vt* **to ~ sb's right foot** amputer qn du pied droit **II.** *vi* amputer

amputee [ˌæmpjʊˈtiː] *n* amputé(e) *m(f)*

amulet [ˈæmjʊlɪt] *n* amulette *f*

amuse [əˈmjuːz] *vt* **1.** amuser **2.** (*occupy*) divertir; **to keep sb ~d** occuper qn; **to ~ oneself** se divertir

amusement *n* **1.** *no pl* (*state*) amusement *m;* **much to sb's ~** au grand amusement de qn **2.** (*pleasure*) divertissement *m;* **for one's own ~** pour son propre plaisir **3.** (*place*) **fairground ~** attraction *f*

amusement arcade *n Brit* galerie *f* de jeux

amusement park *n* parc *m* d'attractions

amusing *adj* amusant(e); (*situation*) comique

an [ən] *indef art* (+ *vowel*) un(e); *s. a.* **a**

anachronistic [əˌnækrəˈnɪstɪk] *adj* anachronique

anaemia [əˈniːmɪə] *n no pl* anémie *f*

anaemic [əˈniːmɪk] *adj* **1.** MED anémique **2.** *pej* (*weak*) faible; **~ performance** représentation *f* médiocre

anaesthesia [ˌænɪsˈθiːzɪə, *Am:* -əsˈθiːʒə] *n no pl* anesthésie *f*

anaesthetic [ˌænɪsˈθetɪk, *Am:* -ˈθet̬-] *n* anesthésique *m;* **under ~** sous anesthésie

anaesthetise [əˈniːsθətaɪz, *Am:* -ˈnes-] *vt Aus, Brit s.* **anaesthetize**

anaesthetist *n* anesthésiste *mf*

anaesthetize [əˈniːsθətaɪz, *Am:* -ˈnes-] *vt* anesthésier

anagram [ˈænəgræm] *n* anagramme *f*

analgesic [ˌænælˈdʒiːsɪk] **I.** *adj* analgésique **II.** *n* analgésique *m*

analog [ˈænəlɒg] *n Am s.* **analogue**

analogic [ˌænəˈlɒdʒɪk, *Am:* -ˈlɑː-], **analogical** *adj* analogique

analogous [əˈnæləgəs] *adj* analogue

analogue [ˈænəlɒg, *Am:* -lɑːg] *n Brit* analogue *m*

analogy [əˈnælədʒɪ] <-ies> *n* analogie *f;* **to draw an ~** établir un parallèle; **on the ~ of sth** sur le modèle de qc

analyse [ˈænəlaɪz] *vt Aus, Brit s.* **analyze**

analysis [əˈnæləsɪs] <-ses> *n* **1.** (*detailed examination*) analyse *f;* **in the last** [*o* **final**] **~** en dernière analyse **2.** (*psychoanalysis*) (psych)analyse *f*

analyst [ˈænʟəlɪst] *n* **1.** (*professional analyzer*) analyste *mf;* **food ~** chimiste *mf* alimentaire; **systems ~** analyste programmeur *m* **2.** (*psychoanalyst*) (psych)analyste *mf*

analytical [ˌænəˈlɪtɪkl, *Am:* -ˈlɪt̬-] *adj* analytique; **~ mind** esprit *m* d'analyse

analyze [ˈænəlaɪz] *vt* analyser; PSYCH (psych)analyser

anarchic [əˈnɑːkɪk, *Am:* ænˈɑːr-], **anarchical** *adj* anarchique

anarchist [ˈænəkɪst, *Am:* -ɚ-] **I.** *n* anarchiste *mf* **II.** *adj* anarchiste

anarchistic [ˌænəˈkɪstɪk, *Am:* -ɚ-] *adj* anarchique

anarchy [ˈænəkɪ, *Am:* -ɚ-] *n no pl* anarchie *f*

anatomical [ˌænəˈtɒmɪkl, *Am:* -ˈtɑː-] *adj* anatomique; **~ drawings/specimen** études/pièce d'anatomie

anatomy [əˈnætəmɪ, *Am:* -ˈnæt̬-] *n* **1.** *no pl* ANAT anatomie *f* **2.** <-ies> *iron* (*body*) anatomie *f* **3.** *no pl* (*analysis*) analyse *f*

ancestor [ˈænsestəʳ, *Am:* -sestɚ] *n* ancêtre *mf*

ancestral [ænˈsestrəl] *adj* ancestral(e)

ancestry [ˈænsestrɪ] <-ies> *n* ascendance *f;* **to be of Polish ~** être d'origine polonaise

anchor [ˈæŋkəʳ, *Am:* -kɚ] **I.** *n* **1.** (*object*) ancre *f;* **to be at ~** être au mouillage; **to drop/weigh ~** jeter/lever l'ancre **2.** *fig* point *m* d'ancrage; **the ~ of sth** la pièce maîtresse de qc; **to be sb's ~** être la planche de salut de qn **3.** TV, RADIO présentateur, -trice *m, f* **II.** *vt* **1.** (*fix firmly*) ancrer **2.** TV, RADIO présenter **III.** *vi* mouiller

anchorage [ˈæŋkərɪdʒ] *n* NAUT mouillage *m;*

seat belt ~ point point *m* d'ancrage de ceinture de sécurité

anchovy ['æntʃəvɪ, *Am:* -tʃoʊ-] <-ies> *n* anchois *m;* ~ **butter** beurre *m* d'anchois

ancient ['eɪnʃənt] **I.** *adj* **1.** (*old*) ancien(ne) **2.** HIST antique **3.** *inf* (*very old*) très vieux **II.** *n pl* (*people*) **the ~s** les Anciens *mpl*

ancillary [æn'sɪlərɪ, *Am:* 'ænsəlerɪ] *adj* auxiliaire; ~ **equipment** matériel *m* supplémentaire

and [ən] *conj* **1.** (*also*) et **2.** MAT plus; **four hundred ~ twelve** quatre cent douze **3.** (*then*) **to go ~ open the window** aller ouvrir la fenêtre **4.** (*increase*) **better ~ better** de mieux en mieux ►**wait ~ see** on verra; ~ **so on** et ainsi de suite

Andes ['ændi:z] *npl* **the ~** les Andes

Andorra [æn'dɔ:rə] *n* Andorre *f*

Andorran I. *adj* andorran(e) **II.** *n* Andorran(e) *m(f)*

anecdotal [ˌænɪk'dəʊtl, *Am:* -'doʊt̬l] *adj* anecdotique

anecdote ['ænɪkdəʊt, *Am:* -doʊt] *n* anecdote *f*

anemia *n Am s.* **anaemia**

anemic *adj Am s.* **anaemic**

anesthesia [ˌænɪs'θi:ʒə] *n Am s.* **anaesthesia**

anesthetic *n Am s.* **anaesthetic**

anesthetist *n Am s.* **anaesthetist**

anesthetize *vt Am s.* **anaesthetize**

anew [ə'nju:, *Am:* -'nu:] *adv* à [*o* de] nouveau; **to begin ~** recommencer

angel ['eɪndʒl] *n* **1.** *a.* REL ange *m;* **be an ~ and help me** tu serais un ange de m'aider **2.** (*financial sponsor*) mécène *m*

anger ['æŋgəʳ, *Am:* -gɚ] **I.** *n no pl* colère *f;* ~ **at sb/sth** colère contre qn/qc; **words said in ~** des mots dits sous l'empire de la colère **II.** *vt* mettre en colère; **to be ~ed by sth** être mis hors hors de soi par qc

angina [æn'dʒaɪnə] *n* MED angine *f;* ~ **pectoris** angine de poitrine

angle[1] ['æŋgl] **I.** *n* MAT angle *m;* **at an ~ of 45 degrees** (en) formant un angle de 45 degrés; **at an ~ to sth** en biais par rapport à qc; **to be hanging at an ~** (*picture*) être suspendu de travers **II.** *vt* (*mirror, light*) orienter

angle[2] ['æŋgl] **I.** *n* (*perspective*) angle *m;* **new ~** nouvelle perspective; **to be looking at sth from the wrong ~** considérer qc sous un mauvais angle **II.** *vt* **1.** (*aim*) **to ~ sth at sb/sth** viser qn/qc par qc **2.** (*slant*) orienter

angled *adj* tortueux(-euse); SPORT latéral(e); ~ **shot** tir *m* au centre

angler ['æŋgləʳ, *Am:* -glɚ] *n* pêcheur *m*

Anglican ['æŋglɪkən] **I.** *adj* anglican(e) **II.** *n* Anglican(e) *m(f)*

Anglicanism ['æŋglɪsɪzəm] *n no pl* anglicanisme *m*

anglicise ['æŋglɪsaɪz] *vt Aus, Brit* angliciser

anglicism *n* anglicisme *m*

anglicize ['æŋglɪsaɪz] *vt s.* **anglicise**

angling *n no pl* pêche *f* (à la ligne)

anglophile ['æŋgləʊfaɪl, *Am:* -glə-] **I.** *n* anglophile *mf* **II.** *adj* anglophile

anglophobia [ˌæŋgləʊ'fəʊbɪə, *Am:* -glə-] *n no pl* anglophobie *f*

anglophone I. *n* anglophone *mf* **II.** *adj* anglophone

Anglo-Saxon I. *n* **1.** HIST Anglo-Saxon(ne) *m(f)* **2.** *Am* (*person of English heritage*) Anglo-Saxon(ne) *m(f)* **3.** LING anglo-saxon *m* **II.** *adj* anglo-saxon(ne)

Angola [æŋ'gəʊlə, *Am:* -'goʊ-] *n* Angola *m*

Angolan [æŋ'gəʊlən, *Am:* -'goʊ-] **I.** *adj* angolais(e) **II.** *n* Angolais(e) *m(f)*

angora [æŋ'gɔ:rə, *Am:* -'gɔ:rə] *n* **1.** ZOOL ~ **cat** chat *m* angora **2.** *no pl* (*soft fibre*) laine *f* angora; ~ **sweater** pull-over en mohair

angrily *adv* en colère

angry ['æŋgrɪ] *adj* **1.** (*furious*) en colère; **to make sb ~** mettre qn en colère; **to be/get ~ with** [*o* **at**] **sb** être/se mettre en colère contre qn; **to be ~ about** [*o* **at**] **sth** être mis hors de soi par qc; **to be ~ that ...** être furieux que ...; ~ **crowd** foule hargneuse; **to exchange ~ words** échanger des propos injurieux **2.** (*stormy: sky*) orageux; (*sea*) houleux **3.** (*inflamed*) irrité; ~ **sore** plaie enflammée

anguish ['æŋgwɪʃ] *n no pl* angoisse *f;* **to be in ~ at sth** être angoissé par qc; **to cause sb ~** faire souffrir qn

angular ['æŋgjʊləʳ, *Am:* -lɚ] *adj* anguleux(-euse); (*face*) osseux(-euse)

animal ['ænɪml] **I.** *n* **1.** ZOOL animal *m;* **farm ~** animal de ferme **2.** (*person*) brute *f;* **to become an ~** devenir bestial ►**to be different ~s** être deux paires de manches; **a political ~** une bête de la politique; **there's no such ~!** ce n'est pas possible! **II.** *adj* animal(e); ~ **doctor** vétérinaire *mf;* ~ **trainer** dompteur, -euse *m, f;* ~ **spirits** vitalité *f*

animal husbandry *n no pl* élevage *m* **animal kingdom** *n no pl* **the ~** le règne animal

animate ['ænɪmeɪt] **I.** *adj* animé(e) **II.** *vt* animer

animated *adj* **1.** (*lively*) animé(e); ~ **discussion** vive discussion **2.** CINE ~ **cartoon** [*o* **film**] dessin animé

animation [ˌænɪ'meɪʃn] *n* **1.** *no pl* (*enthusiasm*) enthousiasme *m* **2.** (*energy*) vivacité *f* **3.** CINE animation *f;* **computer ~** animation informatisée

animator ['ænɪmeɪtəʳ, *Am:* -t̬ɚ] *n* animateur, -trice *m, f*

animosity [ˌænɪ'mɒsətɪ, *Am:* -'mɑ:sət̬ɪ] *n no pl* (*feeling*) animosité *f*

aniseed ['ænɪsi:d] *n no pl* **1.** graine *f* d'anis **2.** (*taste*) anis *m*

ankle ['æŋkl] *n* cheville *f*

ankle boots *pl n* bottines *fpl* **ankle-deep** *adj* à la cheville; **to be ~ in sth** avoir qc qui monte jusqu'aux chevilles **ankle-length** *adj* (*dress*) qui descend jusqu'aux chevilles **ankle sock** *n Brit* socquette *f* **ankle strap** *n* bride *f*

anklet ['æŋklɪt] *n* 1.(*chain*) bracelet *m* de cheville 2.*Am* (*sock*) socquette *f*

annalist ['ænəlɪst] *n* annaliste *mf*

annals ['ænlz] *npl* annales *fpl*

annex¹ [ə'neks] *vt* annexer

annex² ['æneks] *n Am s.* **annexe**

annexation [ˌænek'seɪʃn] *n* 1.*no pl* (*act*) annexation *f* 2.(*territory*) territoire *m* annexe

annexe ['æneks] *n* annexe *f;* **as an ~ to this file** en annexe de ce dossier; *fig* appendice *m*

annihilate [ə'naɪəleɪt] *vt* 1.annihiler 2.(*defeat*) anéantir

annihilation [əˌnaɪə'leɪʃn] *n* anéantissement *m*

anniversary [ˌænɪ'vɜːsərɪ, *Am:* -'vɜːr-] <-ies> *n* anniversaire *m;* **wedding ~** anniversaire de mariage; **~ party** fête *f* d'anniversaire; **golden ~** noces *fpl* d'or

annotate ['ænəteɪt] *vt* annoter; **~d edition** édition *f* critique

annotation [ˌænə'teɪʃn] *n* 1.*no pl* (*act of writing*) commentaire *m* 2.(*note*) note *f*

announce [ə'naʊns] *vt* annoncer

announcement *n* annonce *f*

announcer [ə'naʊnsəʳ, *Am:* -sɚ] *n* présentateur, -trice *m, f*

annoy [ə'nɔɪ] *vt* embêter; **it ~s me that/when ...** ça me contrarie que/quand ...; **stop ~ing me** arrête de m'embêter

annoyance *n* 1.*no pl* (*state*) mécontentement *m;* **much to sb's ~** au grand déplaisir de qn; **to hide one's ~** dissimuler sa contrariété 2.(*cause*) tracas *m*

annoying *adj* énervant(e); (*habit*) fâcheux(-euse); **the ~ thing about it is that ...** ce qui m'agace, c'est que ...

annual ['ænjʊəl] I. *adj* annuel(le); **~ rainfall** hauteur annuelle des précipitations II. *n* 1. TYP publication *f* annuelle 2. BOT plante *f* annuelle

annualised *adj Aus, Brit,* **annualized** *adj* annualisé(e)

annually *adv* annuellement

annuity [ə'njuːətɪ, *Am:* -'nuːət̬ɪ] <-ies> *n* 1.(*money*) annuité *f* 2.(*contract*) viager *m;* **~ policy** assurance *f* vieillesse

annul [ə'nʌl] <-ll-> *vt* annuler

annulment *n* annulation *f*

Annunciation [əˌnʌnsɪ'eɪʃn] *n* **the ~** l'Annonciation *f*

anodyne ['ænədaɪn] *adj form* 1.(*harmless*) inoffensif/ive 2.*pej* insignifiant

anoint [ə'nɔɪnt] *vt* 1.(*oil*) oindre 2. REL consacrer; **to ~ sb king** sacrer qn roi 3.*fig* **to ~ sb as one's successor** désigner qn comme son successeur

anomalous [ə'nɒmələs, *Am:* -'nɑː-] *adj form* anormal(e)

anomaly [ə'nɒməlɪ, *Am:* -'nɑː-] <-ies> *n* anomalie *f;* **statistical ~** irrégularité *f* des statistiques

anon [ə'nɒn, *Am:* -'nɑːn] *adv iron* **see you ~!** à tout à l'heure!, à tantôt! *Belgique*

anonymity [ˌænə'nɪmətɪ, *Am:* -t̬ɪ] *n no pl* anonymat *m*

anonymous [ə'nɒnɪməs, *Am:* -'nɑːnə-] *adj* 1.anonyme; **to remain ~** garder l'anonymat 2.*fig* **a rather ~ face** un visage assez banal

anonymously *adv* anonymement

anorexia [ˌɑnə'reksɪə] *n no pl* anorexie *f*

anorexic I. *adj* anorexique II. *n* anorexique *mf*

another [ə'nʌðəʳ, *Am:* -ɚ] I. *pron* 1.(*one more*) un(e) autre; **many ~** bien d'autres 2.(*mutual*) **one ~** l'un l'autre II. *adj* un(e) autre; **~ cake?** encore un gâteau?; **not that cake, ~ one** pas ce gâteau-là, un autre; **~ £30** 30£ de plus; **could he be ~ Mozart?** serait-il un second Mozart?

ansafone® *n,* **ansaphone**® ['ɑːnsəfəʊn, *Am:* 'ænsəfoʊn] *n Brit* répondeur *m*

answer ['ɑːnsəʳ, *Am:* 'æːnsɚ] I. *n* 1.(*reply*) réponse *f;* **~ to a letter/question** réponse à une lettre/question; **there was no ~** (*at door*) il n'y avait personne; (*to letter, on phone*) il n'y a pas eu de réponse; **this was the ~ to my prayers** c'était la réponse à mes prières 2.(*solution*) solution *f* II. *vt* 1.(*respond to: question*) répondre à; **to ~ the telephone/the call of sb** répondre au téléphone/à l'appel de qn; **to ~ a charge** réfuter une accusation; **to ~ the door(bell)** ouvrir la porte (au coup de sonnette); **to ~ prayers** exaucer des prières 2.(*fit, suit*) correspondre à; **to ~ a need / a description** répondre à un besoin / une description III. *vi* donner une réponse; **I phoned but nobody ~ed** j'ai téléphoné mais personne n'a répondu

◆**answer back** *vi* répondre (avec insolence)

◆**answer for** *vt* 1.(*be responsible*) **to ~ sb/sth** répondre de qn/qc; **to have a lot to ~** *pej* en avoir la lourde responsabilité 2.*Brit* (*vouch for*) **to ~ sb/sth** se porter garant de qn/qc

◆**answer to** *vt* 1.(*obey*) **to ~ sb** être responsable devant 2.(*fit*) **to ~ a description** correspondre à une description 3.(*be named*) **to ~ a name** répondre à un nom

answerable *adj* 1.(*responsible*) **to be ~ for sth** être responsable de qc 2.(*accountable*) **to be ~ to sb** être responsable devant qn

answering machine *n* répondeur *m*

answering service *n* service *m* de messagerie

answerphone ['ɑːnsəfəʊn, *Am:* 'æːnsɚfoʊn] *n Brit* répondeur *m*

ant [ænt] *n* fourmi *f*

antagonise *vt Aus, Brit s.* **antagonize**

antagonism [æn'tægənɪzəm] *n no pl* 1.(*of ideas, systems*) antagonisme *m* 2.(*behaviour, attitude*) hostilité *f*

antagonistic *adj* antagoniste; **to be ~ toward(s) sb/sth** être opposé à qn/qc

antagonize [æn'tægənaɪz] *vt* contrarier

Antarctic [æn'tɑːktɪk, *Am:* -'tɑːrk-] *n* **the ~** l'Antarctique *m*

Antarctic Circle *n* le cercle polaire antarctique **Antarctic Ocean** *n* l'océan *m* antarctique

anteater ['ænt,iːtəʳ, *Am:* -tɚ] *n* fourmilier *m*

antecedent [,æntɪ'siːdnt] **I.** *n* **1.** (*forerunner*) précurseur *m* **2.** *pl* (*past history*) antécédents *mpl* **3.** LING antécédent *m* **II.** *adj form* antérieur(e)

antedate [,æntɪ'deɪt, *Am:* 'ænt̬ɪdeɪt] *vt form* **1.** (*predate*) antidater **2.** (*precede*) précéder

antediluvian [,æntɪdɪ'luːvɪən, *Am:* -t̬ɪdə-] *adj a. fig, iron* antédiluvien(ne)

antelope ['æntɪləʊp, *Am:* -t̬loʊp] <-s *o* -> *n* antilope *f*

antenatal [,æntɪ'neɪtl, *Am:* -t̬ɪ-] **I.** *adj* prénatal(e); ~ **class** préparation *f* à l'accouchement **II.** *n inf* examen *m* prénatal

antenna¹ [æn'tenə] <-nae> *n* BIO antenne *f*

antenna² [æn'tenə] <-s> *n Am, Aus* (*aerial*) antenne *f;* **radio** ~ antenne de radio

antennae *n pl of* **antenna**

anteroom ['æntɪrʊm, *Am:* -t̬ɪruːm] *n* antichambre *f*

anthem ['ænθəm] *n a.* REL hymne *m o f*

anthill ['ænthɪl] *n a. fig* fourmilière *f*

anthology [æn'θɒlədʒɪ, *Am:* -θɑːlə-] <-ies> *n* anthologie *f;* ~ **of verse/short stories** recueil *m* de poèmes/nouvelles

anthracite ['ænθrəsaɪt] *n no pl* anthracite *f*

anthropoid ['ænθrəpɔɪd] **I.** *n* anthropoïde *m* **II.** *adj* anthropoïde

anthropological [,ænθrəpə'lɒdʒɪkl] *adj* anthropologique

anthropologist *n* anthropologue *mf*

anthropology [,ænθrə'pɒlədʒɪ, *Am:* -'pɑːlə-] *n no pl* anthropologie *f*

anti ['æntɪ, *Am:* 'ænt̬ɪ] **I.** *prep* contre **II.** *adj* **to be** ~ être contre

anti-abortion *adj* contre l'avortement; (*groupe*) anti-avortement; ~ **activist** adversaire *mf* de l'I.V.G. **anti-aircraft** *adj* antiaérien(ne); ~ **emplacement** position *f* de D.C.A. **antibacterial** *adj* antibactérien(ne)

antibiotic [,æntɪbaɪ'ɒtɪk, *Am:* -t̬ɪbaɪ'ɑːt̬ɪk] **I.** *n* antibiotique *m* **II.** *adj* antibiotique

antibody ['æntɪbɒdɪ, *Am:* -t̬ɪbɑːdɪ] <-ies> *n* anticorps *m*

Antichrist ['æntɪkraɪst, *Am:* -t̬ɪ-] *n* **the** ~ l'Antéchrist *m*

anticipate [æn'tɪsɪpeɪt, *Am:* -ə-] *vt* **1.** (*expect, foresee*) prévoir; **to** ~ **a lot of people** attendre beaucoup de monde; **to** ~ **trouble/that there will be trouble** je prévois des ennuis / qu'il y aura des ennuis; **an** ~**ed victory** une victoire prévu **2.** (*look forward to*) savourer à l'avance **3.** (*act in advance of*) anticiper

anticipation [æn,tɪsɪ'peɪʃn, *Am:* æn,tɪsə-] *n no pl* **1.** plaisir *m* anticipé; **eager** ~ attente impatiente **2.** (*expectation*) attente *f;* **in** ~ **of sth** dans l'attente de qc **3.** (*preemptive action*) sens *m* d'anticipation

anticlimactic *adj* décevant(e)

anticlimax [,æntɪ'klaɪmæks, *Am:* -t̬ɪ-] <-es> *n* déception *f;* **sense of** ~ sentiment *m* de désenchantement

anticlockwise [,æntɪ'klɒkwaɪz, *Am:* -t̬ɪ'klɑːk-] *adv Aus, Brit* dans le sens inverse des aiguilles d'une montre

anticoagulant [,æntɪkəʊ'ægjʊlənt, *Am:* -t̬ɪkoʊ'ægjə-] **I.** *n* anticoagulant *m* **II.** *adj* anticoagulant(e)

anticorrosive [,æntɪkə'rəʊsɪv] *n* produit *m* anticorrosion

antics ['æntɪks, *Am:* -t̬ɪks] *n pl* pitreries *fpl pej*

anticyclone [,æntɪ'saɪkləʊn, *Am:* ,ænt̬ɪ'saɪkloʊn] *n* anticyclone *m*

antidepressant [,æntɪdɪ'presənt, *Am:* -t̬ɪ-] **I.** *n* antidépresseur *m* **II.** *adj* antidépresseur

antidote ['æntɪdəʊt, *Am:* -t̬ɪdoʊt] *n* **an** ~ **for sth** un antidote à qc; **to be an** ~ **to sth** être l'antidote de qc

antifreeze ['æntɪfriːz, *Am:* -t̬ɪ-] *n no pl* antigel *m*

antigen ['æntɪdʒən, *Am:* -t̬ɪ-] *n* antigène *m*

Antigua and Barbuda [æn'tiːgə ənd bɑː'bjuːdə, *Am:* -bɑːr-] *n* Antigua-et-Barbuda *f*

Antiguan **I.** *adj* antiguais(e) et barbudien(ne) **II.** *n* Antiguais(e) et Barbudien(ne) *m*

antihistamine [,æntɪ'hɪstə,miːn, *Am:* -t̬ɪ-] *n* antihistaminique *m*

anti-inflammatory **I.** <-ies> *n* anti-inflammatoire *m* **II.** *adj* anti-inflammatoire

anti-knock [,æntɪ'nɒk, *Am:* 'ænt̬ɪ'nɑːk] **I.** *n no pl* antidétonant *m* **II.** *adj* antidétonant(e)

anti-lock [æntɪ'lɒk] *adj* antiblocage *inv*

anti-lock braking system *n* système *m* A.B.S

antimatter ['æntɪmætəʳ, *Am:* -t̬ɪmæt̬ɚ] *n no pl* antimatière *f*

anti-missile [,æntɪ'mɪsaɪl, *Am:* -t̬ɪ'mɪsl] *adj* antimissile

anti-nuclear *adj* antinucléaire

antioxidant [,æntɪ'ɒksɪdənt, *Am:* -t̬ɪ'ɑːk-] *n* antioxydant *m*

antipathetic *adj form* antipathique

antipathy [æn'tɪpəθɪ] <-ies> *n usu sing* antipathie *f*

antiperspirant [,æntɪ'pɜːspərənt, *Am:* -t̬ɪ'pɜːrspɚ-] **I.** *n* déodorant *m* anti-transpirant **II.** *adj* anti-transpirant(e)

Antipodean **I.** *adj* **1.** (*relating to people*) des Antipodes **2.** *Brit, iron: australien(ne) et/ou néo-zélandais(e)* **II.** *n Brit, iron: Australien(ne) et/ou Néo-zélandais(e)*

Antipodes [æn'tɪpədiːz] *npl Brit* **the** ~ les Antipodes *mpl*

antiquarian [,æntɪ'kweərɪən, *Am:* -t̬ə'kwerɪ-] **I.** *n* **1.** (*antique dealer*) antiquaire *mf* **2.** (*collector*) amateur *m* d'antiquités **II.** *adj* d'antiquaire; ~ **bookseller** antiquaire de livres anciens

antiquated ['æntɪkweɪtɪd, *Am:* -t̬əkweɪt̬ɪd] *adj pej* vétuste; (*attitude*) vieux jeu; **to feel** ~ *iron* se sentir décrépit

antique [æn'tiːk] I. *n* antiquité *f;* ~ **dealer** antiquaire *mf;* ~ **shop** magasin *m* d'antiquités II. *adj* ancien(ne)

antiquity [æn'tɪkwətɪ, *Am:* -t̬ɪ] *n* 1. *no pl* (*ancient times*) antiquité *f;* **the classical** ~ l'Antiquité classique 2. *no pl* (*great age*) ancienneté *f* 3. <-ies> (*relics*) antiquités *fpl*

anti-rust [ˌæntɪ'rʌst] *adj* antirouille *inv*

anti-Semitic [ˌæntɪsɪ'mɪtɪk, *Am:* -t̬ɪsə'mɪt̬-] *adj pej* antisémite

antiseptic [ˌæntɪ'septɪk, *Am:* -t̬ə-] I. *n* antiseptique *m* II. *adj* 1. (*free from infection*) aseptique 2. *fig, pej* stérile

anti-social [ˌæntɪ'səʊʃl, *Am:* -t̬ɪ'soʊ-] *adj* 1. (*harmful to society*) antisocial(e) 2. (*not sociable*) asocial(e)

antistatic [ˌæntɪ'stætɪk, *Am:* -t̬ɪ'stæt̬-] *adj* antistatique

anti-tank [ˌæntɪ'tæŋk, *Am:* -t̬ɪ-] *adj* antichar

antithesis [æn'tɪθəsɪs] <-ses> *n* **the** ~ **of** [*o* **to**] **sth** l'opposé *f* de qc

antithetic [ˌætɪ'θetɪk, *Am:* -t̬ə'θet̬ɪk], **antithetical** *adj form* antithétique; **to be** ~ **to sth** aller à l'encontre de qc

antitoxin [ˌæntɪ'tɒksɪn, *Am:* -tɪ'tɑːk-] *n* antitoxine *f*

anti-virus I. *adj* INFOR anti-virus; ~ **programme** utilitaire *m* anti-virus II. *n* INFOR antivirus *m*

antler ['æntləʳ, *Am:* -lɚ] *n* bois *mpl*

antonym ['æntənɪm, *Am:* -tnɪm] *n* antonyme *m*

Antwerp ['æntwɜːp, *Am:* -twɜːrp] *n* Anvers

anus ['eɪnəs] *n* anus *m*

anvil ['ænvɪl, *Am:* -vl] *n* enclume *f*

anxiety [æŋ'zaɪətɪ, *Am:* -t̬ɪ] *n* 1. (*concern*) anxiété *f;* **to feel** ~ être anxieux 2. (*desire*) ~ **to** +*infin* impatience à +*infin*

anxious ['æŋkʃəs] *adj* 1. (*concerned*) anxieux(-euse); **to keep an** ~ **eye on sth** surveiller qc avec anxiété 2. (*eager*) **to be** ~ **for sth/for sth to happen** avoir un fort désir de qc/que qc arrive; **to be** ~ **to** +*infin* tenir (beaucoup) à +*infin*

any ['enɪ] I. *adj* 1. (*some*) **do they have** ~ **money/more soup?** ont-ils de l'argent/encore de la soupe?; **if we see** ~ **bears, ...** si jamais on voit des ours, ...; ~ **questions?** des questions? 2. (*not important which*) ~ **glass will do** n'importe quel verre ira; **come at** ~ **time** viens/venez n'importe quand; **in** ~ **case** de toute façon 3. (*that may exist*) ~ **faults/trouble should be reported to me** tout problème/incident doit m'être signalé II. *adv* 1. (*not*) **he doesn't come** ~ **more** il ne vient plus; **I can't make it** ~ **simpler** je ne peux pas le simplifier davantage; **does he feel** ~ **better?** se sent-il mieux? 2. *Am* (*at all*) **it doesn't help him** ~ cela ne lui sert à rien III. *pron* 1. (*some*) **do** ~ **of you know?** l'un d'entre vous; **I saw two cars but he didn't see** ~ j'ai vu deux voitures mais il n'en a vu aucune; **if you want** ~, **take some/one** si tu en veux, prends-en 2. (*indefinite*) **buy** ~ **you see** achète ce que tu verras; **if you haven't got olive oil,** ~ **will do** su tu n'as pas d'huile d'olive, toute autre huile fera l'affaire

anybody ['enɪbɒdɪ, *Am:* -bɑːdɪ] *indef pron, sing* 1. (*someone*) **if** ~ **knows** si quelqu'un sait; **I've not seen** ~ **like that** je n'ai vu personne de tel 2. (*whoever*) ~ **can apply** n'importe qui peut postuler; **I can give them to** ~ **I like** je peux les donner à qui je veux; ~ **will do** le premier venu sera le bon; ~ **else** n'importe qui d'autre; ~ **but him** tout autre que lui ►**everybody <u>who</u> is** ~ *iron* tous les gens qui comptent; **it's** ~**'s <u>guess</u>** Dieu seul le sait; *s. a.* **somebody, nobody**

anyhow ['enɪhaʊ] *adv* 1. (*in any case*) de toute façon; *s. a.* **anyway** 2. (*in a disorderly way*) n'importe comment

anyone ['enɪwʌn] *pron s.* **anybody**

anything ['enɪθɪŋ] *indef pron, sing* 1. (*something*) **does she know** ~**?** est-ce qu'elle sait quelque chose?; **I don't know** ~ je ne sais rien; **hardly** ~ presque rien; **is there** ~ **new?** quoi de neuf?; ~ **else** quelque chose d'autre; **I didn't find** ~ **better** je n'ai rien trouvé de mieux 2. (*whatever*) tout; **they can choose** ~ **they like** ils peuvent choisir ce qu'ils veulent; **it is** ~ **but funny** cela n'a rien de drôle; ~ **and everything** tout et n'importe quoi ►**to be <u>as</u> hard/dry/loud as** ~ être qc comme tout; **as much as** ~ tout autant qu'autre chose; ~ **<u>but</u>!** au contraire!; **<u>for</u>** ~ (**in the world**) pour rien au monde; **to do sth <u>like</u>** ~ faire qc comme un fou; *s. a.* **something, nothing**

anyway ['enɪweɪ] *adv,* **anyways** ['enɪweɪz] *adv Am, inf* 1. (*in any case*) de toute façon; **I bought it** ~ je l'ai tout de même acheté 2. (*well*) enfin

anywhere ['enɪweəʳ, *Am:* -wer] *adv* 1. (*in any place*) n'importe où; ~ **in France** partout en France 2. (*some place*) **have you looked** ~ **else?** est-ce que tu as cherché ailleurs?; **you won't hear this** ~ **else** tu n'entendras cela nulle part ailleurs ►**<u>miles</u> from** ~ *inf* à des kilomètres de tout; **doing sth doesn't <u>get</u> you** ~ cela n'avance à rien de faire qc, il n'y a pas d'avance à faire qc *Belgique;* **we're not <u>getting</u>** ~ nous n'allons nulle part; **not to be** ~ **<u>near</u> as ...** *inf* être loin d'être aussi...; ~ **<u>between</u> £5 and £50** *inf* quelque chose entre 5£ et 50£

L'**Anzac Day** ("Australian and New Zealand Armed Corps"), le 25 avril, est en Australie et en Nouvelle-Zélande une journée nationale de deuil, célébrée par un service religieux et des marches funéraires, en commémoration du débarquement des "Anzacs" sur l'île turque de Gallipoli, lors de la Première Guerre mondiale, le 25 avril 1915, qui furent vaincus par la suite. L'importance symbolique de ce jour réside dans le fait que les Australiens ont combattu pour la première fois ouvertement hors de leur territoire en tant qu'unités de guerre australiennes.

a.o.b. [ˌeɪ.əʊ'biː, *Am:* -oʊ-] *abbr of* **any other business**
aorta [eɪ'ɔːtə, *Am:* -'ɔːrt̬ə] *n* aorte *f*
APA *n abbr of* **American Psychatric Association**
apart [ə'pɑːt, *Am:* -'pɑːrt] *adv* **1.** (*separated*) écarté(e); **six km** ~ à six km de distance; **to be born years** ~ être nés à des années d'intervalle; **to move** ~ (*crowd*) s'écarter **2.** (*separated from sb*) **when we're** ~ lorsque nous sommes séparés **3.** (*into pieces*) **to come** ~ se démonter; **to take sth** ~ démonter qc
apart from *prep* **1.** (*except for*) ~ **that** à part cela **2.** (*in addition to*) outre, en plus **3.** (*separate from*) **to live** ~ **sb** être séparé de qn; **to live** ~ **each other** vivre chacun de son côté
apartheid [ə'pɑːtheɪt, *Am:* -'pɑːrteɪt] *n no pl* apartheid *m*
apartment [ə'pɑːtmənt, *Am:* -'pɑːrt-] *n* appartement *m*
apartment building *n,* **apartment house** *n Am* (*block of flats*) immeuble *m* (locatif), conciergerie *f Québec*
apathetic [ˌæpə'θetɪk, *Am:* -'θet̬-] *adj* apathique
apathy ['æpəθɪ] *n no pl* ~ **about sth** apathie *f* vis-à-vis de qc
ape [eɪp] **I.** *n* ZOOL grand singe *m* ►**to go** ~ *Am, inf* être furax **II.** *vt* singer
aperture ['æpətʃəʳ, *Am:* -ətʃʊr] *n* PHOT ouverture *f*
apex ['eɪpeks] <-es *o* apices> *n* sommet *m*
aphorism ['æfərɪzəm, *Am:* -ɚ-] *n* aphorisme *m*
aphrodisiac [ˌæfrəʊ'dɪziæk, *Am:* -rə'-] *n* aphrodisiaque *m*
apiary ['eɪpɪərɪ, *Am:* -erɪ] *n* rucher *m*
apiece [ə'piːs] *adv* **to cost £2** ~ coûter £2 pièce; **I gave them £2** ~ je leur ai donné £2 chacun
apocalypse [ə'pɒkəlɪps, *Am:* -'pɑːkə-] *n no pl* (*disaster*) apocalypse *f*
Apocalypse [ə'pɒkəlɪps, *Am:* -'pɑːkə-] *n no pl* REL **the** ~ l'Apocalypse
apocalyptic [əˌpɒkə'lɪptɪk, *Am:* -ˌpɑːkə-] *adj* apocalyptique
apogee ['æpədʒiː, *Am:* -ə-] *n no pl* apogée *m*
apologetic [əˌpɒlə'dʒetɪk, *Am:* -ˌpɑːlə'dʒet̬-] *adj* **to be** ~ **about sth** s'excuser de qc
apologetically *adv* **to smile** ~ sourire d'un air contrit
apologize [ə'pɒlədʒaɪz, *Am:* -'pɑːlə-] *vi* **to** ~ **to sb for sth** s'excuser de qc auprès de qn; **to** ~ **profusely for doing sth** se confondre en excuses d'avoir fait qc
apology [ə'pɒlədʒɪ, *Am:* -'pɑːlə-] <-ies> *n* **1.** (*regret*) excuses *fpl;* **to be full of apologies** se confondre en excuses; **to demand an** ~ **from sb** exiger des excuses de la part de qn; **to owe sb an** ~ devoir des excuses à qn; **to send one's apologies to sb** prier qn d'accepter ses excuses **2.** *form* (*formal defence*) ~ **for sth** apologie *f* de qc ►**an** ~ **for a supper** *péj, inf* un semblant de souper
apoplectic [ˌæpə'plektɪk] *adj* **1.** apoplectique; (*attack*) d'apoplexie **2.** *iron* **to be** ~ **with fury** s'étrangler de rage
apostle [ə'pɒsl, *Am:* -'pɑːsl] *n* apôtre *m*
apostrophe [ə'pɒstrəfɪ, *Am:* -'pɑːstrə-] *n* apostrophe *f*
appal [ə'pɔːl] <-ll-> *vt* offusquer
Appalachian Mountains [ˌæpə'leɪtʃən-] *npl* les (monts) Appalaches *mpl*
appall [ə'pɔːl] *vt Am s.* **appal**
appalling *adj* **1.** (*shocking*) révoltant(e) **2.** (*terrible*) épouvantable; ~ **luck** chance inouïe
appallingly *adv* **1.** (*shockingly*) effroyablement **2.** (*terribly*) épouvantablement
apparatus [ˌæpə'reɪtəs, *Am:* -ə'ræt̬-] *n* **1.** *no pl* (*equipment*) équipement *m;* **diving** ~ SPORT équipement de plongée **2.** (*machine*) appareil *m*
apparel [ə'pærəl, *Am:* -'per-] *n no pl, form* (*clothing*) vêtements *mpl*
apparent [ə'pærənt, *Am:* -'pernt] *adj* **1.** (*clear*) évident(e); **it is** ~ **that …** il est clair que…; **for no** ~ **reason** sans raison apparente; **to be** ~ **to sb** être clair pour qn **2.** (*seeming*) apparent(e)
apparently *adv* apparemment
apparition [ˌæpə'rɪʃn] *n* apparition *f*
appeal [ə'piːl] **I.** *vi* **1.** (*attract*) **to** ~ **to sb/sth** plaire à qn/qc; **to** ~ **to the emotions/senses** faire appel aux émotions/sens; **the idea doesn't** ~ l'idée manque d'attrait **2.** LAW **to** ~ **against sth** faire appel contre qc; ~ **against a verdict** contester un verdict **3.** (*plead, call upon*) **to** ~ **to sb for sth** lancer un appel auprès de qn pour qc; **to** ~ **for advice/help** faire appel à des conseils/de l'aide; **to** ~ **for donations** faire appel à des dons **II.** *n* **1.** (*attraction*) attrait *m;* **sex** ~ sex appeal *m;* **to have** ~ attirer; **it has little** ~ **for young people** ça a peu d'attrait pour les jeunes **2.** LAW appel *m;* **to lodge an** ~ **against sth** faire appel contre qc **3.** (*request*) demande *f;* (*by charity*) appel *m;* **an** ~ **for calm** un appel au calme
appealing *adj* **1.** (*attractive: idea, smile*) attrayant(e); **to be** ~ **to sb** attirer qn; **there is something** ~ **about her** elle a quelque chose d'attrayant **2.** (*beseeching: eyes, look*) suppliant(e)
appealingly *adv* **1.** (*attractively: dress*) de façon attrayante; ~ **packaged** plaisamment emballé **2.** (*beseechingly*) **to look** ~ **at sb** regarder qn d'un air suppliant; **to speak** ~ parler de manière suppliante
appear [ə'pɪəʳ, *Am:* -'pɪr] *vi* **1.** (*become vis-*

ible) apparaître; (*on page, screen*) paraître **2.** (*seem*) paraître; **to ~ to be ...** sembler être ...; **it ~s to me that ...** il me semble que ...; **it ~s he's ill** apparemment, il est malade; **I think he's angry – so it ~s** je crois qu'il est en colère – on dirait, oui **3.** LAW (*as witness defendant*) comparaître; **to ~ in court** comparaître devant le tribunal; **to ~ for the defendant** représenter le prévenu **4.** (*perform*) **to ~ in a film** jouer dans un film; **he ~s briefly in the play** il fait une apparition dans la pièce **5.** (*be published*) sortir

appearance [əˈpɪərəns, *Am:* -ˈpɪrəns] *n* **1.** (*instance of appearing*) apparition *f;* **to put in** [*o* **make**] **an ~** faire acte de présence **2.** LAW comparution *f;* **court ~** comparution devant le tribunal **3.** (*looks*) apparence *f* **4.** (*aspect: of a place*) aspect *m;* (*of wealth*) apparence *f;* **he gave the ~ of being very busy** il donnait l'impression d'être très occupé **5.** (*performance*) entrée *f* en scène; **his first stage ~** ses débuts au théâtre; **~ on television** passage *m* à la télévision **6.** (*publication*) parution *f* ►**to all ~s, from all ~s** *Am* selon toute apparence; **~s can be deceptive** *prov* il ne faut pas se fier aux apparences *prov;* **to keep up ~s** sauver les apparences

appease [əˈpiːz] *vt form* **1.** (*pacify: person*) apaiser; (*conflict, disorder*) calmer **2.** (*relieve: hunger, pain*) apaiser

appeasement *n no pl* apaisement *m*

appellant [əˈpelənt] *n* LAW appelant(e) *m(f)*

append [əˈpend] *vt form* **to ~ sth to sth** joindre qc à qc

appendage [əˈpendɪdʒ] *n form* appendice *m*

appendicitis [əˌpendɪˈsaɪtɪs] *n no pl* appendicite *f*

appendix [əˈpendɪks] *n* **1.** <-es> ANAT appendice *m* **2.** <-dices *o* -es> TYP (*of a book*) appendice *m;* (*of a report*) annexe *f*

appetite [ˈæpɪtaɪt, *Am:* -ə-] *n* appétit *m;* **to give sb an ~** mettre qn en appétit; **to have an ~** avoir de l'appétit; **to ruin one's ~** se couper l'appétit

appetizer [ˈæpɪtaɪzəʳ, *Am:* -ətaɪzɚ] *n* **1.** (*snack*) amuse-gueule *m* **2.** *Am* (*first course*) entrée *f*

appetizing [ˈæpɪtaɪzɪŋ, *Am:* -ə-] *adj* **1.** (*enticing*) appétissant(e) **2.** (*attractive*) alléchant(e); (*thought*) attrayant(e)

applaud [əˈplɔːd, *Am:* -ˈplɑːd] *vi, vt* applaudir

applause [əˈplɔːz, *Am:* -ˈplɑːz] *n no pl* applaudissements *mpl;* **let's have a round of ~ for him** on l'applaudit bien fort

apple [ˈæpl] *n* pomme *f* ►**the ~ of one's eye** la prunelle de ses yeux

apple pie *n* tarte *f* aux pommes **2.** *fig* **in ~ order** impeccable **apple tree** *n* pommier *m*

appliance [əˈplaɪəns] *n* appareil *m;* **electrical ~s department** rayon *m* de l'électroménager; **household/electrical ~** appareil ménager/électrique; **surgical ~s** appareils orthopédiques

applicable [ˈæplɪkəbl] *adj* **~ to sb/sth** applicable à qn/qc

applicant [ˈæplɪkənt] *n* **1.** (*for job, admission*) candidat(e) *m(f)* **2.** ADMIN demandeur, -euse *m, f*

application [ˌæplɪˈkeɪʃn] *n* **1.** (*for job, membership*) candidature *f;* **job ~** demande *f* d'emploi; **to send off an ~** envoyer une candidature **2.** ADMIN demande *f* **3.** *no pl* (*relevance*) **to have particular ~ to sb/sth** s'appliquer en particulier à qn/qc **4.** (*coating*) couche *f;* (*of ointment*) application *f* **5.** INFOR application *f* **6.** *no pl* (*perseverance*) application *f*

application form *n* **1.** (*for job, admission*) formulaire *m* de candidature **2.** ADMIN formulaire *m* (*pour une demande*)

applied *adj* appliqué(e)

apply [əˈplaɪ] **I.** *vi* **1.** (*request*) **to ~ to sb/sth for a job/passport** faire une demande d'emploi/de passeport auprès de qn/qc; **he applied to join the army** il a posé sa candidature pour entrer dans l'armée **2.** (*submit an application*) **to ~ in writing** faire une demande écrite; **to ~ to Harvard/Oxford** présenter une demande d'inscription à Harvard/Oxford **3.** (*pertain*) s'appliquer; **to ~ to sb** concerner qn **II.** *vt* appliquer; **to ~ sth to sth** appliquer qc à qc; **to ~ the brakes** freiner; **to ~ pressure to sth** exercer une pression sur qc; **to ~ common sense** faire preuve de bon sens; **to ~ oneself** s'appliquer

appoint [əˈpɔɪnt] *vt* **1.** (*select*) **to ~ sb/sth to** +*infin* nommer qn/qc pour +*infin;* **to ~ sb as heir** désigner qn comme héritier **2.** *form* (*designate*) **to ~ a date** fixer une date

appointed *adj* **1.** (*selected*) nommé(e) **2.** *form* (*designated*) fixé(e) **3.** *form* (*equipped*) équipé(e)

appointment *n* **1.** (*selection*) **the ~ of sb as sth** la nomination de qn comme qc **2.** (*meeting, arrangement*) rendez-vous *m;* **to make an ~ with sb** prendre rendez-vous avec qn; **dental ~** rendez-vous chez le dentiste; **by ~ only** sur rendez-vous uniquement

apposite [ˈæpəzɪt] *adj form* (*remark*) pertinent(e)

apposition [ˌæpəˈzɪʃn] *n a.* LING apposition *f*

appraisal [əˈpreɪzl] *n* **1.** (*evaluation*) évaluation *f;* **to carry out an ~ of sth** faire une évaluation de qc; **job ~** évaluation professionnelle **2.** (*estimation: of damage(s)*) estimation *f*

appraise [əˈpreɪz] *vt* **1.** (*evaluate*) évaluer **2.** (*estimate*) estimer

appreciable [əˈpriːʃəbl] *adj* appréciable; (*change*) notable; (*difference*) sensible

appreciate [əˈpriːʃɪeɪt] **I.** *vt* **1.** (*value*) apprécier **2.** (*understand*) **to ~ the danger** être conscient du danger; **to ~ that ...** se rendre compte que ... **3.** (*be grateful for*) être reconnaissant pour; **I would ~ if you didn't tell her** j'aimerais que tu ne le lui dises pas **II.** *vi* monter; **to ~ (in value) by 25 %** prendre

25 % de valeur
appreciation [əˌpriːʃɪ'eɪʃn] *n no pl* **1.**(*gratitude*) appréciation *f* **2.**(*understanding*) compréhension *f;* **she has no ~ of the problem** elle ne comprend pas le problème **3.** FIN hausse *f*
appreciative [ə'priːʃɪətɪv] *adj* **1.**(*appreciating*) sensible **2.**(*grateful*) reconnaissant(e)
apprehend [ˌæprɪ'hend] *vt form* **1.**(*arrest*) appréhender **2.**(*comprehend*) saisir **3.**(*fear*) craindre
apprehension [ˌæprɪ'henʃn] *n no pl* **1.** *form* (*arrest*) arrestation *f* **2.** *no pl* (*anxiety*) appréhension *f*
apprehensive [ˌæprɪ'hensɪv] *adj* d'appréhension; **to be ~ about sth** appréhender qc; **to be ~ that ...** appréhender que ...
apprentice [ə'prentɪs, *Am:* -t̬ɪs] **I.** *n* apprenti(e) *m(f);* **~ carpenter** apprenti charpentier **II.** *vt* **to ~ sb to sb** placer qn en apprentissage chez qn
apprenticeship [ə'prentɪʃɪp, *Am:* -t̬əsʃɪp] *n* apprentissage *m*
approach [ə'prəʊtʃ, *Am:* -'proʊtʃ] **I.** *vt* **1.**(*get close(r) to*) s'approcher de; **she's ~ing 60** elle a pas loin de soixante ans; **it was ~ing 3 o'clock** il était presque 3 heures **2.**(*talk to*) je vais m'adresser au président; **to ~ sb/sth about sth** aborder qn/qc à propos de qc; **I've been ~ed by a publisher** j'ai reçu des propositions d'un éditeur **3.**(*deal with*) aborder **II.** *vi* s'approcher **III.** *n* **1.**(*coming, way of handling*) approche *f* **2.**(*onset*) **the ~ of retirement/evening** l'approche de la retraite/de la soirée **3.**(*access*) accès *m* **4.**(*proposition*) proposition *f*
approachable *adj* (*building*) accessible; (*person*) abordable
approach road *n* bretelle *f*
approbation [ˌæprə'beɪʃn] *n no pl, form* (*praise*) approbation *f*
appropriate [ə'prəʊprɪət, *Am:* -'proʊ-] **I.** *adj* (*suitable*) approprié(e); **~ to sth** approprié(e) à qc; **to find the ~ words** trouver les mots justes; **they didn't take the ~ action** ils n'ont pas pris les mesures appropriées; **the ~ time** le moment adéquat; **what an ~ name!** quel nom bien trouvé!; **to be ~ for sth** convenir pour qc; **I contacted the ~ official** j'ai contacté l'autorité compétente; **it wouldn't be ~ for her to say anything** ce serait inopportun pour elle de dire quoi que ce soit **II.** [ə'prəʊprɪeɪt, *Am:* -'proʊ-] *vt form* **1.**(*take*) s'approprier **2.** FIN **to ~ funds for sth** affecter des fonds à qc
appropriation [əˌprəʊprɪ'eɪʃn, *Am:* -ˌproʊ-] *n* **1.**(*taking*) appropriation *f;* FIN détournement *m* **2.**(*allotment*) affectation *f;* **~s** FIN crédits *mpl*
approval [ə'pruːvl] *n no pl* approbation *f;* **to meet with sb's ~** recevoir l'approbation de qn; **a nod of ~** un signe d'approbation ►**on ~** ECON à l'essai
approve [ə'pruːv] **I.** *vi* (*like*) approuver; **to ~ of sb** apprécier qn **II.** *vt* approuver
approved *adj* **1.**(*generally agreed*) reconnu(e) **2.**(*sanctioned*) agréé(e)
approvingly [ə'pruːvɪŋlɪ] *adv* **to smile ~** avoir un sourire approbateur
approximate¹ [ə'prɒksɪmət, *Am:* -'prɑːk-] *adj* approximatif(-ive)
approximate² [ə'prɒksɪmeɪt, *Am:* -'prɑːk-] **I.** *vt form* s'approcher de **II.** *vi form* **to ~ to sth** s'approcher de qc
approximately [ə'prɒksɪmətlɪ] *adv* approximativement
approximation [əˌprɒksɪ'meɪʃn, *Am:* -ˌprɑːk-] *n form* **1.**(*estimation*) approximation *f* **2.**(*semblance*) semblant *m*
APR *n abbr of* **annual percentage rate** taux *m* d'intérêt annuel
apricot ['eɪprɪkɒt, *Am:* -kɑːt] **I.** *n* **1.** BOT abricot *m;* **~ jam** confiture *f* d'abricot **2.** *no pl* (*colour*) abricot *m* **II.** *adj* abricot *inv*
April ['eɪprəl] *n* **1.**(*month*) avril *m;* **~ showers** giboulées *fpl* de mars **2.**(*indication of a date or period*) **during** [*o* **in**] **~** en avril; **at the beginning/end of** [*o* **in early/late**] **~** début/fin avril; **on the fourth of ~, on ~ the fourth** le 4 avril ►**an ~ fool** (*person*) victime d'un poisson d'avril
April Fool's Day *n no pl* le 1er avril
apron ['eɪprən] *n* **1.**(*clothing*) tablier *m* **2.** AVIAT **~ area** aire *f* de manœuvre ►**to be tied to one's mother's ~ strings** être dans les jupes de sa mère
apropos, a propos [ˌæprə'pəʊ, *Am:* -'poʊ] **I.** *prep* **~ (of) sth** *form* à propos de qc **II.** *adv* à propos **III.** *adj* opportun(e)
apse [æps] *n* ARCHIT abside *f*
apt [æpt] *adj* **1.**(*appropriate: remark*) juste; (*moment*) bon(ne); **~ at doing sth** (*pupil*) doué pour faire qc **2.**(*likely*) **~ to** +*infin* enclin à +*infin*
APT *n abbr of* **advanced passenger train** ≈ TGV *m*
aptitude ['æptɪtjuːd, *Am:* -tuːd] *n* aptitude *f;* **to have an ~ for sth** avoir un don pour qc
aptitude test *n* test *m* d'aptitude
aquaculture ['ækwəˌkʌltʃəʳ, *Am:* 'ɑːkwəˌkʌltʃɚ] *n* aquaculture *f*
aqualung, Aqua lung® ['ækwəlʌŋ] *n* scaphandre *m* autonome
aquamarine [ˌækwəmə'riːn, *Am:* ˌɑːkwə-] **I.** *n* **1.**(*stone*) aigue-marine *f* **2.** *no pl* (*colour*) bleu-vert *m* **II.** *adj* bleu-vert *inv*
aquarium [ə'kweərɪəm, *Am:* -'kwerɪ-] <-s *o* -ria> *n* aquarium *m*
Aquarius [ə'kweərɪəs, *Am:* -'kwerɪ-] *n* Verseau *m;* **to be (an) ~** être (du) Verseau; **to be born under ~** être né sous le signe du Verseau
aquatic [ə'kwætɪk, *Am:* -'kwæt̬-] *adj* **1.**(*water-related*) aquatique **2.** SPORT nautique
aqueduct ['ækwɪdʌkt] *n* aqueduc *m*
Aquitaine [ˌækwɪ'teɪn] *n* l'Aquitaine *f*
Arab ['ærəb, *Am:* 'er-] **I.** *adj* arabe; **the**

A

United ~ **Emirates** les Émirats arabes unis **II.** *n* (*person*) Arabe *mf*

arabesque [ˌærəˈbesk, *Am:* ˌer-] *n* arabesque *f*

Arabian [əˈreɪbɪən] *adj* arabe; **the ~ peninsula** la péninsule arabique

Arabic [ˈærəbɪk, *Am:* ˈer-] *n* LING arabe *m; s. a.* **English**

arable [ˈærəbl, *Am:* ˈer-] *adj* arable

arbiter [ˈɑːbɪtəʳ, *Am:* ˈɑːrbɪtɚ] *n* **1.** (*judge*) arbitre *mf* **2.** (*mediator*) médiateur, -trice *m, f*

arbitrary [ˈɑːbɪtrərɪ, *Am:* ˈɑːrbətrerɪ] *adj* arbitraire

arbitrate [ˈɑːbɪtreɪt, *Am:* ˈɑːrbə-] *vt, vi* arbitrer

arbitration [ˌɑːbɪˈtreɪʃn, *Am:* ˌɑːrbə-] *n no pl* arbitrage *m;* **to go to ~** s'en remettre à un arbitrage

arbitrator [ˈɑːbɪtreɪtəʳ, *Am:* ˈɑːrbə-] *n s.* **arbiter**

arbor *n Am, Aus s.* **arbour**

> Aux USA, on plante des arbres pour l'**Arbor Day**. Dans certains États, ce jour est férié. La date exacte de l'"Arbor Day" diffère selon les États, étant donné que la bonne période pour planter des arbres peut varier selon leur situation géographique.

arboriculture [ˈɑːbərɪˌkʌltʃəʳ, *Am:* ˈɑːrbɚɪˌkʌltʃɚ] *n* arboriculture *f*

arbour [ˈɑːbəʳ, *Am:* ˈɑːrbɚ] *n Aus, Brit* tonnelle *f*

arc [ɑːk, *Am:* ɑːrk] *n* arc *m*

arcade [ɑːˈkeɪd, *Am:* ɑːr-] *n* ARCHIT arcade *f;* (*for shopping*) galerie *f* marchande; (*for games*) galerie *f* de jeux

arch[1] [ɑːtʃ, *Am:* ɑːrtʃ] **I.** *n* arche *f;* ~ **of the foot** voûte *f* plantaire **II.** *vi* former une voûte; **sth ~s over sth** qc enjambe qc **III.** *vt* cintrer; **to ~ one's eyebrows** froncer les sourcils

arch[2] [ɑːtʃ, *Am:* ɑːrtʃ] <-er, -est> *adj* narquois(e); ~ **smile** sourire forcé

archaeological *adj* archéologique

archaeologist *n* archéologue *mf*

archaeology [ˌɑːkɪˈɒlədʒɪ] *n no pl* archéologie *f*

archaic [ɑːˈkeɪɪk, *Am:* ɑːr-] *adj* **1.** (*antiquated*) archaïque **2.** *iron, inf* (*old-fashioned*) démodé(e)

archangel [ˈɑːkeɪndʒl, *Am:* ˈɑːr-] *n* archange *m*

archbishop [ˌɑːtʃˈbɪʃəp, *Am:* ˌɑːrtʃ-] *n* archevêque *m*

archdiocese [ˌɑːtʃˈdaɪəsɪs, *Am:* ˌɑːrtʃ-] *n* archidiocèse *m*

arch-enemy [ˌɑːtʃˈen.ɪ.mli, *Am:* ˌɑːrtʃ-] <-ies> *n* ennemi(e) *m(f)* juré(e)

archeological [ˌɑːrkɪəˈlɑːdʒɪkl] *adj Am s.* **archaeological**

archeologist [ˌɑːrkɪˈɑːlədʒɪst] *n Am s.* **archaeologist**

archeology [ˌɑːrkɪˈɑːlədʒɪ] *n Am s.* **archaeology**

archer [ˈɑːtʃəʳ, *Am:* ˈɑːrtʃɚ] *n* archer, -ère *m, f*

archery [ˈɑːtʃərɪ, *Am:* ˈɑːr-] *n no pl* tir *m* à l'arc

archetype [ˈɑːkɪtaɪp, *Am:* ˈɑːr-] *n* archétype *m*

archipelago [ˌɑːkɪˈpeləgəʊ, *Am:* ˌɑːrkəˈpeləgoʊ] <-s *o* -es> *n* archipel *m*

architect [ˈɑːkɪtekt, *Am:* ˈɑːrkə-] *n a. fig* architecte *mf*

architecture [ˈɑːkɪtektʃəʳ, *Am:* ˈɑːrkətektʃɚ] *n no pl* architecture *f*

archive(s) [ˈɑːkaɪvz, *Am:* ˈɑːr-] *n a.* INFOR archive *f*

archivist [ˈɑːkɪvɪst, *Am:* ˈɑːrkaɪ-] *n* archiviste *mf*

archway [ˈɑːtʃweɪ, *Am:* ˈɑːrtʃ-] *n* arche *f*

arc lamp, **arc light** *n* lampe *f* à arc

Arctic [ˈɑːktɪk, *Am:* ˈɑːrk-] *n* **the ~** l'Arctique *m*

Arctic Circle *n* cercle *m* polaire arctique

Arctic Ocean *n* océan *m* arctique

arc welding *n* ELEC soudure *f* à l'arc

ardent [ˈɑːdnt, *Am:* ˈɑːr-] *adj* ardent(e); (*admirer*) fervent(e)

ardor *n Am, Aus,* **ardour** [ˈɑːdəʳ, *Am:* ˈɑːrdɚ] *n Aus, Brit no pl* ardeur *f*

arduous [ˈɑːdjʊəs, *Am:* ˈɑːrdʒu-] *adj* ardu(e)

are [əʳ] *vi s.* **be**

area [ˈeərɪə, *Am:* ˈerɪ-] *n* **1.** (*place: in town*) zone *f;* (*in country*) région *f;* (*in office, home*) espace *m;* **in country ~s** à la campagne; **the bar ~** le bar *m* **2.** (*field*) domaine *m* **3.** (*land surface*) superficie *f* **4.** MAT aire *f;* (*of circle*) surface *f*

area code *n Am, Aus s.* **dialling code**

arena [əˈriːnə] *n* **1.** SPORT arène *f* **2.** (*for circus*) piste *f* **3.** *fig* scène *f*

Argentina [ˌɑːdʒənˈtiːnə, *Am:* ˌɑːr-] *n* l'Argentine *f*

Argentinian [ˌɑːdʒənˈtɪnɪən, *Am:* ˌɑːr-] **I.** *adj* argentin(e) **II.** *n* Argentin(e) *m(f)*

arguably [ˈɑːgjuːəblɪ, *Am:* ˈɑːrg-] *adv* sans doute

argue [ˈɑːgjuː, *Am:* ˈɑːrg-] **I.** *vi* **1.** (*have argument*) se disputer; **to ~ about sth with sb** se disputer avec qn au sujet de qc **2.** (*discuss*) **to ~ with sb about sth** débattre avec qn de qc **3.** (*reason*) argumenter; **to ~ for/against a proposal** argumenter en faveur de/contre une proposition **II.** *vt* **1.** (*debate*) discuter; **to ~ that ...** alléguer que ... **2.** (*persuade*) **to ~ sb into/out of doing sth** convaincre qn de faire/ne pas faire qc

argument [ˈɑːgjʊmənt, *Am:* ˈɑːrgjə-] *n* **1.** (*disagreement*) dispute *f;* **to have an ~** se disputer **2.** (*discussion*) débat *m* **3.** (*reasons*) argument *m;* **an ~ against/for sth** un argument contre/pour qc; **the ~ that ...** la thèse selon laquelle ... **4.** CINE, LIT sujet *m*

argumentative [ˌɑːgjʊˈmentətɪv, *Am:* ˌɑːrgjəˈmenţəţɪv] *adj pej* ergoteur(-euse)

aria [ˈɑːrɪə] *n* MUS aria *f*

arid ['ærɪd, *Am:* 'er-] *adj* aride

Aries ['eəri:z, *Am:* 'eri:z] *n* Bélier *m; s. a.* **Aquarius**

arise [ə'raɪz] <arose, -n> *vi* **1.** (*come about*) se produire; (*difficulty*) surgir; (*doute*) apparaître; **to ~ from** provenir de **2.** *form* (*get up*) se lever

arisen [ə'rɪzn] *pp of* **arise**

aristocracy [ˌærɪ'stɒkrəsɪ, *Am:* ˌerə'stɑ:krə-] <-ies> *n + pl/sing vb* aristocratie *f*

aristocrat ['ærɪstəkræt, *Am:* ə'rɪs-] *n* aristocrate *mf*

aristocratic *adj* aristocratique

arithmetic [ə'rɪθmətɪk, *Am:* ˌerɪθ'metɪk] **I.** *n no pl* arithmétique *f;* **to do the ~** faire le calcul **II.** *adj* arithmétique

arithmetical [ˌærɪθ'metɪkl, *Am:* ˌerɪθ-'metɪkl] *adj s.* **arithmetic**

Arizona I. *n* l'Arizona *m* **II.** *adj* de l'Arizona

ark [ɑ:k, *Am:* ɑ:rk] *n no pl* REL arche *f;* **Noah's ~** l'arche de Noé

Ark [ɑ:k, *Am:* ɑ:rk] *n no pl* REL **the ~ of the Covenant** l'Arche d'Alliance

Arkansas ['ɑ:kənsɔ:, *Am:* 'ɑ:rkənsɑ:] **I.** *n* l'Arkansas *m* **II.** *adj* de l'Arkansas

arm¹ [ɑ:rm] *n* **1.** *a. fig* ANAT, GEO bras *m;* **to hold/take sb in one's ~s** porter/prendre qn dans ses bras; **~ in ~** bras dessus, bras dessous; **on sb's ~** au bras de qn **2.** (*sleeve*) manche *f* **3.** (*armrest*) accoudoir *m* **4.** (*for eyeglasses*) branche *f;* (*division*) branche *f* ►**to keep sb at ~'s length** tenir qn à distance; **to twist sb's ~** forcer la main à qn

arm² [ɑ:m, *Am:* ɑ:rm] MIL **I.** *vt* **1.** armer **2.** *fig* **to ~ oneself for/against sth** s'armer pour/contre qc **II.** *n pl* armes *fpl* ►**to lay down one's ~s** déposer les armes; **take up ~s against sb/sth** partir en guerre contre qn/qc

armament ['ɑ:məmənt, *Am:* 'ɑ:r-] *n* armement *m*

armature ['ɑ:mətʃʊəʳ, *Am:* 'ɑ:rmətʃɚ] *n* **1.** PHYS inducteur *m* **2.** ELEC induit *m* **3.** ZOOL armure *f*

armchair ['ɑ:mˌtʃeəʳ, *Am:* 'ɑ:rmˌtʃer] *n* fauteuil *m*

armchair politician *n* **to be an ~** faire de la politique de salon

armed *adj a. fig* armé(e)

armed forces *npl* **the ~** les forces *fpl* armées

armed robbery *n* vol *m* à main armée

Armenia [ɑ:mi:niə, *Am:* ɑ:r-] *n* l'Arménie *f*

Armenian I. *adj* arménien(ne) **II.** *n* **1.** (*person*) Arménien(ne) *m(f)* **2.** LING arménien *m; s. a.* **English**

armful ['ɑ:mfʊl, *Am:* 'ɑ:rm-] *n* brassée *f*

armhole ['ɑ:mhəʊl, *Am:* 'ɑ:rmhoʊl] *n* emmanchure *f*

arming ['ɑ:mɪŋ] *n* armement *m*

armistice ['ɑ:mɪstɪs, *Am:* 'ɑ:rmə-] *n* armistice *m*

armor *n Am, Aus,* **armour** ['ɑ:məʳ, *Am:* 'ɑ:rmɚ] *n no pl* **1.** ZOOL cuirasse *f* **2.** MIL armure *f*

armour-clad ['ɑ:mə'klæd] *adj* (*ship,*) cuirassé(e); (*vehicle, door*) blindé(e)

armoured *adj Brit* blindé(e)

armpit ['ɑ:mpɪt, *Am:* 'ɑ:rm-] *n* aisselle *f*

armrest ['ɑ:mrest, *Am:* 'ɑ:rm-] *n* accoudoir *m*

arms control *n* MIL contrôle *m* des armements **arms limitation** *s.* **arms control**

arms race *n* **the ~** la course aux armements

army ['ɑ:mɪ, *Am:* 'ɑ:r-] <-ies> *n* armée *f;* **to go into the ~** entrer dans l'armée; **to join the ~** s'engager; **an ~ base** une base militaire; **an ~ officer** un officier de l'armée de terre

aroma [ə'rəʊmə, *Am:* -'roʊ-] *n* arôme *m*

aromatherapy [əˌrəʊmə'θerəpɪ, *Am:* -ˌroʊ-] *n no pl* aromathérapie *f*

aromatic [ˌærə'mætɪk, *Am:* ˌerə'mæt-] *adj* aromatique

arose [ə'rəʊz, *Am:* ə'roʊz] *pt of* **arise**

around [ə'raʊnd] **I.** *prep Am, Aus s.* **round II.** *adv* **1.** (*round about*) autour; **all ~** tout autour **2.** (*in circumference*) **for 50 m ~** dans un rayon de 50 m; **for miles ~** à des lieues à la ronde **3.** (*aimlessly*) **to walk ~** se balader; **to stand** [*o* **hang**] **~** rester là sans but précis **4.** (*near by*) dans les parages; **is he ~?** est-il (par) là? **5.** (*in existence*) **she's been ~ for years** elle est là depuis toujours; **he's still ~** il est encore en vie; **how long have computers been ~?** depuis quand est-ce qu'il y a des ordinateurs?; **there are too many mosquitos ~ in summer** il ya trop de moustiques (dans les parages) en été ►**the right/wrong way ~** *Am, Aus* à l'endroit/l'envers; **to have been ~** *inf* n'être pas né d'hier; *s. a.* **up**

arouse [ə'raʊz] *vt* exciter

arr. *n abbr of* **arrival** arr.

arrange [ə'reɪndʒ] *vt a.* MUS arranger; (*event, meeting*) organiser; (*deal*) convenir de; **to ~ with sb to** +*infin* s'organiser avec qn pour +*infin;* **to ~ for sb to** +*infin* faire en sorte que qn +*subj;* **we ~d that she would do it** nous avions prévu qu'elle le ferait; **we ~d when she would do it** nous avions prévu quand elle le ferait; **I'll ~ everything** je m'occuperai de tout

arrangement *n a.* MUS arrangement *m;* (*placing*) disposition *f;* **to come to an ~ with sb** se mettre d'accord avec qn; **to make ~s for sth** faire ce qui est nécessaire pour qc; **I've got other ~s** j'ai d'autres plans

array [ə'reɪ] **I.** *n* **1.** (*display*) étalage *m;* **an ~ of people** un déploiement de gens **2.** *form* (*clothes*) atours *mpl* **3.** INFOR, MAT tableau *m* **II.** *vt* **1.** (*display*) **to be ~ed** s'étaler **2.** *form* (*clothe*) **to be ~ed in sth** être paré de qc

arrears [ə'rɪəz, *Am:* -'rɪrz] *npl* FIN arriéré *m* ►**in ~** en retard (de paiement); **to pay in ~** payer à terme

arrest [ə'rest] **I.** *vt a.* LAW arrêter; (*growth*) stopper **II.** *n* LAW **to place under ~** mettre en état d'arrestation

arresting *adj* fascinant(e)
arrival [ə'raɪvl] *n* arrivée *f*; **on sb's/sth's** ~ à l'arrivée de qn/qc; ~**s hall** zone *f* d'arrivée
arrive [ə'raɪv] *vi* arriver; **to** ~ **at a conclusion** parvenir à une conclusion
arriviste [ˌæriː'viːst, *Am:* ˌer-] *n* arriviste *mf*
arrogance ['ærəgəns, *Am:* 'er-] *n no pl* arrogance *f*
arrogant ['ærəgənt, *Am:* 'er-] *adj* arrogant(e)
arrow ['ærəʊ, *Am:* 'eroʊ] *n* flèche *f*
arrowhead *n* pointe *f* de flèche
arse [ɑːs, *Am:* ɑːrs] *n Aus, Brit, vulg* cul *m*
arsenal ['ɑːsənl, *Am:* 'ɑːr-] *n* arsenal *m*
arsenic ['ɑːsnɪk, *Am:* 'ɑːr-] *n no pl* arsenic *m*
arson ['ɑːsn, *Am:* 'ɑːr-] *n* incendie *m* criminel
art [ɑːt, *Am:* ɑːrt] *n* **1.** art *m* **2.** *pl* UNIV sciences *fpl* humaines; ~**s faculty** faculté *f* des lettres, faculté des arts *Québec*
art collection *n* (*paintings*) collection *f* de tableaux **art critic** *n* critique *mf* d'art **art dealer** *n* marchand(e) *m(f)* d'objets d'art
artefact ['ɑːtɪfækt] *n* artefact *m*
arterial [ɑː'tɪərɪəl, *Am:* ɑːr'tɪrɪ-] *adj* **1.** ANAT artériel(le) **2.** AUTO, RAIL ~ **road** grand axe *m*
arteriosclerosis [ɑːˌtɪərɪəʊsklə'rəʊsɪs, *Am:* ɑːrˌtɪrɪoʊsklə'roʊsəs] *n* athérosclérose *f*
artery ['ɑːtərɪ, *Am:* 'ɑːrt̬ɚ] <-ies> *n* artère *f*
artesian well [ɑː'tiːzɪən'wel, *Am:* ɑːr'tiːʒn'wel] *n* puits *m* artésien
artful ['ɑːtfl, *Am:* 'ɑːrt-] *adj* habile
art gallery *n* (*public*) musée *m*; (*selling work*) galerie *f* d'art
arthritic [ɑː'θrɪtɪk, *Am:* ɑːr'θrɪt̬-] **I.** *adj* arthritique **II.** *n* arthritique *mf*
arthritis [ɑː'θraɪtɪs, *Am:* ɑːr'θraɪt̬əs] *n no pl* arthrite *f*
artichoke ['ɑːtɪtʃəʊk, *Am:* 'ɑːrt̬ətʃoʊk] *n* artichaut *m*
article ['ɑːtɪkl, *Am:* 'ɑːrt̬ɪ-] *n* **1.** article *m* **2.** LAW **to do** ~**s** faire son stage (*expérience professionnelle chez un notaire ou un avocat en fin d'études*)
articulate I. [ɑː'tɪkjʊlət, *Am:* ɑːr'tɪkjə-] *adj* **1.** (*person*) éloquent(e) **2.** (*speech*) clair(e) **II.** [ɑː'tɪkjʊleɪt, *Am:* ɑːr'tɪkjə-] *vt form* **1.** (*express clearly*) exposer clairement; **to** ~ **one's opposition** exprimer son opposition; **to** ~ **an idea** formuler une idée **2.** *a.* LING articuler
articulated lorry *n* semi-remorque *m*
articulation [ɑːˌtɪkjʊ'leɪʃn, *Am:* ɑːrˌtɪkjə-] *n no pl* **1.** (*clear expression*) structure *f* **2.** LING articulation *f*
artifact ['ɑːrt̬əfækt] *n Am s.* **artefact**
artifice ['ɑːtɪfɪs, *Am:* 'ɑːrt̬ə-] *n form* artifice *m*
artificial [ˌɑːtɪ'fɪʃl, *Am:* ˌɑːrt̬ə-] *adj a. pej* artificiel(le)
artificial insemination *n* insémination *f* artificielle **artificial intelligence** *n* intelligence *f* artificielle
artificiality [ˌɑːtɪfɪʃɪ'ælətɪ, *Am:* ˌɑːrt̬əfɪʃɪ'ælət̬ɪ] *n no pl* artificialité *f*
artificial respiration *n* respiration *f* artificielle; **to give sb** ~ pratiquer la respiration artificielle sur qn
artillery [ɑː'tɪlərɪ, *Am:* ɑːr-] *n no pl* artillerie *f*
artilleryman [ɑː'tɪlərɪmən, *Am:* ɑːr'tɪlrɪmen] *n* artilleur *m*
artisan [ˌɑːtɪ'zæn, *Am:* 'ɑːrt̬əzn] *n* artisan(e) *m(f)*
artist ['ɑːtɪst, *Am:* 'ɑːrt̬əst-] *n* artiste *mf*
artiste [ɑː'tiːst, *Am:* ɑːr-] *n* artiste *mf*
artistic [ɑː'tɪstɪk, *Am:* ɑːr-] *adj* artistique
artistry ['ɑːtɪstrɪ, *Am:* 'ɑːrt̬ə-] *n no pl* talent *m* artistique
artless ['ɑːtlɪs, *Am:* 'ɑːrt-] *adj* naturel(le)
artwork ['ɑːtwɜːk, *Am:* 'ɑːrtwɜːrk] *n no pl* illustrations *fpl*
arty ['ɑːtɪ, *Am:* 'ɑːrt̬ɪ] <-ier, -iest> *adj pej, inf* **1.** (*person*) (du) genre artiste **2.** (*style*) bohème; ~ **film** film marginal
Aryan ['eərɪən, *Am:* 'erɪ-] HIST **I.** *adj* aryen(ne) **II.** *n* Aryen(ne) *m(f)*
as [əz] **I.** *prep* comme; **dressed** ~ **a clown** habillé en clown; **he's described as a hero** il est décrit comme un héros; **it's claimed** ~ **progress** on prétend que c'est du progrès; **I'm working/speaking as her deputy** je travaille/m'exprime en tant que son adjoint(e); **the king,** ~ **such** le roi, en tant que tel; ~ **a baby, I was ...** quand j'étais bébé, j'étais ...; **to use sth** ~ **a lever** utiliser qc en guise de levier **II.** *conj* **1.** (*in comparison*) que; **the same name** ~ **sth/sb** le même nom que qc/qn **2.** (*like*) comme; ~ **it is** tel quel; ~ **it is, I can't come** étant donné la situation, je ne pourrai pas venir; **he's angry enough** ~ **it is** il est déjà assez furieux comme ça; **I came** ~ **promised** je suis venu comme promis; **she was angry** ~ **we all were** elle était en colère comme nous tous; ~ **if it were true** comme si c'était vrai **3.** (*because*) puisque; ~ **he's here I'm going** étant donné qu'il est là, je pars **4.** (*while*) pendant que; (*simultaneously*) au fur et à mesure que **5.** (*although*) (~) **fine** ~ **the day is, ...** si belle que soit la journée, ...; **try** ~ **I would, I couldn't** j'ai eu beau essayer, je n'ai pas pu ▶ ~ **far** ~ (*to the extent that*) dans la mesure où; ~ **far** ~ **I am concerned** pour moi **III.** *adv* ~ **well** aussi; ~ **simple/simply** ~ aussi simple/simplement que; ~ **long as** aussi longtemps que; ~ **long** ~ **he's at home** (*provided*) tant qu'il est à la maison; ~ **much as** (*same amount*) autant que; (~) **much** ~ **I'd like to go** bien que j'aie très envie d'y aller; ~ **soon as** aussitôt que; ~ **for you/the music** quant à toi/à la musique
a.s.a.p. [ˌeɪ.es.eɪ'piː] *abbr of* **as soon as possible** dès que possible
asbestos [æz'bestɒs, *Am:* -təs] *n no pl* amiante *f*
ascend [ə'send] **I.** *vi* (*person*) monter; (*smoke*) s'élever **II.** *vt* (*stairs, cliff*) gravir ▶ **to** ~ **the throne** monter sur le trône
ascendancy *n no pl* ascendant *m*

ascendant *n no pl* ascendant *m*
ascendency *s.* **ascendancy**
ascendent *s.* **ascendant**
ascension [ə'senʃn] *n* (*going up*) ascension *f*
Ascension *n* REL **the** ~ l'Ascension *f*
ascertain [ˌæsə'teɪn, *Am:* -ɚ-] *vt form* établir
ascetic [ə'setɪk, *Am:* -'seṭ-] **I.** *n* ascète *mf* **II.** *adj* ascétique
asceticism [ə'setɪsɪzəm, *Am:* -'seṭə-] *n no pl* ascétisme *m*

> **Ascot** est un village dans le Berkshire où se trouve un hippodrome construit en 1711 sur l'ordre de la reine Anne. Le "Royal Ascot" est une course étalée sur quatre jours. Elle a lieu tous les ans en juin et la reine s'y rend la plupart du temps. L'"Ascot Gold Cup" est une course hippique de 4 km à laquelle participent des chevaux ayant plus de trois ans. Le "Royal Ascot" est aussi célèbre pour la mode extravagante qui s'affiche durant ces 4 jours.

ascribable [ə'skraɪbəbl] *adj* **to be ~ to sb/sth** être attribuable à qc/qn
ascribe [ə'skraɪb] *vt* **to ~ sth to sb/sth** attribuer qc à qn/qc
ascription [ə'skrɪpʃn] *n* attribution *f*
asexual [ˌeɪ'sekʃʊəl, *Am:* -ʃuəl] *adj* **1.** (*without involving sex*) asexuel(le) **2.** (*without sex organs*) *a. fig* asexué(e)
ash[1] [æʃ] *n no pl* (*powder*) cendre *f*
ash[2] [æʃ] *n* (*tree*) frêne *m*
ashamed [ə'ʃeɪmd] *adj* **to feel ~** avoir honte; **to be ~ of sb/sth** avoir honte de qn/qc; **to be ~ to** +*infin* avoir honte de +*infin*
ashore [ə'ʃɔːʳ] **I.** *adj* **1.** (*on land*) à terre **2.** (*towards land*) vers le rivage **II.** *adv* **1.** (*on land*) à terre **2.** (*towards land*) vers le rivage; **to be washed ~** échouer (sur le rivage)
ashtray ['æʃˌtreɪ] *n* cendrier *m*
Ash Wednesday *n* mercredi *m* des Cendres
Asia ['eɪʃə, *Am:* -ʒə] *n no pl* l'Asie *f;* **~ Minor** l'Asie mineure
Asian ['eɪʃn, *Am:* -ʒn], **Asiatic** [ˌeɪʃɪ'ætɪk, *Am:* -ˌʒi'æṭ-] **I.** *adj* **1.** (*from Asia*) asiatique **2.** *Brit* (*from Indian subcontinent*) *originaire du subcontinent indien* **II.** *n* **1.** (*from Asia*) asiatique *mf* **2.** *Brit* (*from Indian subcontinent*) *personne originaire du subcontinent indien*
aside [ə'saɪd] **I.** *n* aparté *m* **II.** *adv* **1.** (*to one side: put, move, look*) de côté **2.** (*thinking aloud*) en aparté **3.** (*ignoring*) **sth ~** qc mis(e) à part; **that ~, what do you think?** à part ça, qu'en penses-tu?
aside from *prep* **1.** (*except for*) à part **2.** (*away from*) **to turn ~ sb/sth** se détourner de qn/qc
ask [ɑːsk, *Am:* æsk] **I.** *vt* **1.** (*request*) demander; **~ your sister** demande à ta sœur; **to ~ sb a question about sth** poser à qn une question sur qc; **to ~ for advice** demander conseil; **to ~ sb a riddle** poser une devinette à qn; **to ~ sb to** +*infin* demander à qn de +*infin* **2.** (*expect*) **to ~ too much of sb** en demander trop à qn; **it's ~ing a lot** c'est demander beaucoup; **I'm asking £50 for it** j'en demande £50 **3.** (*invite*) inviter; **to ~ sb out/home** inviter qn à sortir/chez soi ▶**don't ~ me** qu'est-ce que j'en sais?; **you may well ~** vous pouvez bien poser la question; **if you ~ me** si tu veux/vous voulez mon avis **II.** *vi* **1.** (*request information*) se renseigner; **to ~ about sth** se renseigner sur qc **2.** (*make a request*) demander; **to ~ to** +*infin* demander à +*infin* ▶**I ~ you!** je vous/t'en prie!
◆**ask after** *vt* **to ~ sb** demander des nouvelles de qn
◆**ask for** *vt* (*food, object*) demander; **she's asking for you** (*person*) elle vous demande **2.** *inf* **to be asking for it** chercher qc; **you're asking for trouble** tu cherches les histoires
askance [ə'skæns] *adv* **to look ~ at sb/sth** jeter un regard désapprobateur sur qn/qc
askew [ə'skjuː] *adj* de travers
asking *n* **it's your's for the ~** tu n'as qu'à le demander pour l'avoir
asking price *n* prix *m* demandé
asleep [ə'sliːp] *adj* endormi(e); **to be ~** dormir; **to fall ~** s'endormir
asparagus [ə'spærəgəs, *Am:* -'sper-] *n no pl* asperge *f*
ASPCA [ˌeɪ.esˌpiː.siː'eɪ] *n abbr of* **American Society for Prevention of Cruelty to Animals** ≈ SPA *f*
aspect ['æspekt] *n* **1.** (*point of view, feature*) aspect *m* **2.** (*direction*) **with a southern ~** orienté(e) sud **3.** (*appearance*) air *m*
aspen ['æspən] *n* tremble *m*
asperity [æ'sperətɪ, *Am:* -əṭɪ] <-ies> *n form* aspérité *f*
aspersion [ə'spɜːʃn, *Am:* -'spɜːrʒn] *n form* **to cast ~s on sb/sth** dénigrer qc/qn
asphalt ['æsfælt, *Am:* -faːlt] **I.** *n* asphalte *m* **II.** *vt* asphalter
asphyxia [æs'fɪksɪə] *n no pl* asphyxie *f*
asphyxiate [əs'fɪksɪeɪt] *vi, vt form* asphyxier
aspiration [ˌæspə'reɪʃn] *n* aspiration *f*
aspire [ə'spaɪəʳ, *Am:* -'spaɪɚ] *vi* **to ~ to sth** aspirer à qc
aspirin ['æsprɪn] *n* aspirine *f;* **an ~** un cachet *m* d'aspirine
aspiring [ə'spaɪərɪŋ, *Am:* -'spaɪɚ-] *adj* **an ~ actor/poet** un(e) prétendant(e) à la carrière d'acteur/de poète
ass [æs] <-es> *n* âne *m;* **to make an ~ of oneself** se ridiculiser
assail [ə'seɪl] *vt* assaillir
assassin [ə'sæsɪn, *Am:* -ən] *n* assassin *m*
assassinate [ə'sæsɪneɪt] *vt* assassiner
assassination [əˌsæsɪ'neɪʃn] *n* assassinat *m*
assault [ə'sɔːlt] **I.** *n* **1.** MIL assaut *m;* **to make an ~ on sth** assaillir qc **2.** (*physical attack*) agression *f;* **indecent ~** attentat *m* à la pudeur; **sexual ~** violences *fpl* sexuelles **3.** (*attack*) attaque *f;* **an ~ on privilege/sb's reputation** *fig* une attaque contre les privilèges/contre la

réputation de qn **II.** *vt* **1.** MIL attaquer **2.** (*physically*) agresser; **to indecently ~ sb** se livrer à des violences sexuelles sur qn; **to ~ sb's senses** *fig* agresser les sens de qn

assault and battery *n* LAW coups *mpl* et blessures *fpl*

assemble [ə'sembl] **I.** *vi* se rassembler **II.** *vt* assembler

assembly [ə'semblɪ] <-ies> *n* **1.** *a.* POL assemblée *f* **2.** (*meeting*) réunion *f* **3.** *Brit* (*at school*) *rassemblement des élèves dans le hall pour des prières, des informations* **4.** *no pl* TECH assemblage *m*

assembly line *n* chaîne *f* de montage

assent [ə'sent] *n no pl, form* consentement *m;* **to give one's ~ to sth** consentir à qc

assert [ə'sɜːt, *Am:* -'sɜːrt] *vt* affirmer; (*authority, rights*) faire valoir; **to ~ oneself** s'affirmer

assertion [ə'sɜːʃn, *Am:* -'sɜːr-] *n* affirmation *f*

assertive [ə'sɜːtɪv, *Am:* -'sɜːrt̬ɪv] *adj* assuré(e); (*person*) qui a de l'assurance

assertiveness *n no pl* assurance *f*

assess [ə'ses] *vt* (*amount, quantity*) évaluer; (*damage, situation*) faire le bilan de; (*employee, student*) contrôler

assessment *n* évaluation *f;* (*of situation*) bilan *m;* (*of employee, student*) contrôle *m*

assessor [ə'sesəʳ, *Am:* -'sesɚ] *n* expert(e) *m(f)*

asset ['æset] *n* **1.** (*of value*) atout *m;* **an ~ to sth** un atout pour qc **2.** FIN avoir *m;* **liquid ~s** liquidités *fpl*

assiduity [ˌæsɪ'djuːətɪ, *Am:* -'duːət̬ɪ] *n no pl* assiduité *f*

assiduous [ə'sɪdjʊəs, *Am:* -'sɪdʒu-] *adj* assidu(e)

assign [ə'saɪn] *vt* **1.** (*appoint*) **to ~ sb to duties, ~ duties to sb** assigner des responsabilités à qn **2.** (*send elsewhere*) **to ~ sb to a post** affecter qn à un poste **3.** (*set aside*) affecter **4.** (*give*) **to ~ the blame for sth to sth** rejeter la responsabilité de qc sur qc; **to ~ importance to sth** accorder de l'importance à qc **5.** (*allocate*) attribuer **6.** INFOR transférer **7.** LAW **to ~ sth to sb** transmettre qc à qn

assignment *n* **1.** (*task*) mission *f* **2.** *no pl* (*attribution*) affectation *f* **3.** SCHOOL, UNIV devoir *m*

assimilate [ə'sɪməleɪt] **I.** *vt* assimiler **II.** *vi* **to ~ into sth** s'assimiler à qc

assimilation [əˌsɪmə'leɪʃn] *n no pl* assimilation *f*

assist [ə'sɪst] **I.** *vt* aider; (*process*) faciliter; **to ~ sb with sth** assister qn dans qc **II.** *vi* **to ~ with sth** aider dans qc

assistance [ə'sɪstəns] *n no pl* aide *f;* **to be of ~ to sb/sth** être une aide pour qn/qc; **to come to sb's ~** venir à l'aide de qn; **to give sb ~** prêter secours à qn

assistant [ə'sɪstənt] **I.** *n* **1.** (*helper*) aide *mf* **2.** *Brit* (*person*) (**shop** [*o* **sales**]) **~** vendeur, -euse *m, f* **3.** INFOR assistant *m;* **personal digital ~** assistant personnel de communication **II.** *adj* adjoint(e)

associate I. [ə'səʊʃɪət, *Am:* -'soʊʃɪɪt] *n* associé(e) *m(f)* **II.** [ə'səʊʃɪeɪt, *Am:* -'soʊ-] *adj Am* UNIV **~ professor** ≈ maître *m* assistant **III.** [ə'səʊʃɪeɪt, *Am:* -'soʊ-] *vt* **to ~ sb/sth with sth** associer qn/qc à qc; **to be ~d with sth** être associé à qc **IV.** *vi* **to ~ with sb** fréquenter qn

associated *adj* associé(e)

association [əˌsəʊsɪ'eɪʃn, *Am:* -ˌsoʊ-] *n* **1.** (*organization*) association *f* **2.** *no pl* (*romantic relationship*) relation *f* **3.** *no pl* (*involvement*) relations *mpl* **4.** (*mental connection*) association *f;* **it has ~s of poverty/success** cela a des connotations de pauvreté/réussite

assonance ['æsənəns] *n no pl* assonance *f*

assorted [ə'sɔːtɪd, *Am:* -'sɔːrt̬ɪd] *adj* **1.** (*mixed*) assorti(e) **2.** (*going well together*) **to be well/poorly ~** être bien/mal assortis

assortment [ə'sɔːtmənt, *Am:* -'sɔːrt-] *n* assortiment *m*

assume [ə'sjuːm, *Am:* -'suːm] *vt* **1.** (*regard as true*) supposer; **you're assuming he's telling the truth** tu supposes qu'il dit la vérité **2.** (*adopt*) adopter; (*air, pose*) prendre; (*role*) endosser **3.** (*undertake*) **to ~ office/power** prendre ses fonctions/le pouvoir; **to ~ massive proportions** prendre des proportions démesurées

assumed *adj* **~ name/identity** nom/identité d'emprunt

assumption [ə'sʌmpʃn] *n* **1.** (*supposition*) supposition *f;* **on the ~ that** en supposant que *+subj* **2.** (*hypothesis*) hypothèse *f* **3.** *no pl* (*taking over*) **~ of power** prise *f* de pouvoir

Assumption [ə'sʌmpʃn] *n* REL **the ~** l'Assomption *f*

assurance [ə'ʃʊərəns, *Am:* 'ʃʊrns] *n* assurance *f*

assure [ə'ʃʊəʳ, *Am:* -'ʃʊr] *vt* assurer; **let me ~ you that** je vous le garantis; **to ~ oneself of sth** s'assurer de qc

assured *adj* (*person, style*) plein(e) d'assurance

asterisk ['æstərɪsk] **I.** *n* astérisque *m* **II.** *vt* marquer d'un astérisque

astern [ə'stɜːn, *Am:* -'stɜːrn] *adv* **1.** NAUT en poupe **2.** (*behind*) **to be ~ of sb** être derrière qn **3.** (*backwards*) vers l'arrière

asteroid ['æstərɔɪd] *n* astéroïde *m*

asthma ['æsmə, *Am:* 'æz-] *n no pl* asthme *m;* **~ attack** crise *f* d'asthme

asthmatic [æs'mætɪk, *Am:* æz'mæt̬-] **I.** *n* asthmatique *mf* **II.** *adj* asthmatique

astonish [ə'stɒnɪʃ, *Am:* -'stɑːnɪʃ] *vt* étonner; **to be ~ed at sth** être étonné par qc

astonishing *adj* étonnant(e)

astonishment *n no pl* étonnement *m;* **to sb's ~** à la surprise de qn; **to do sth in ~** faire qc avec étonnement

astound [ə'staʊnd] *vt, vi* stupéfier

astray [ə'streɪ] *adv* **to go ~** s'égarer; **to lead sb ~** (*on journey*) détourner qn de son che-

A

min; (*misinform*) induire qn en erreur; (*morally*) détourner qn du droit chemin
astride [ə'straɪd] **I.** *prep* **to sit ~ a chair** être assis à cheval sur une chaise **II.** *adv* à califourchon
astringent [ə'strɪndʒənt] **I.** *n* astringent *m* **II.** *adj* **1.** (*skin-tightening*) astringent(e) **2.** *fig* acerbe
astrologer [ə'strɒlədʒəʳ, *Am:* -'strɑːlədʒɚ] *n* astrologue *mf*
astrological [ˌæstrə'lɒdʒɪkl, *Am:* -'lɑːdʒɪkl] *adj* astrologique; (*book*) d'astrologie
astrology [ə'strɒlədʒɪ, *Am:* -'strɑːlə-] *n no pl* astrologie *f*
astronaut ['æstrənɔːt, *Am:* -nɑːt] *n* astronaute *mf*
astronautics [ˌæstrə'nɔːtɪks, *Am:* -trə'nɑːt̬ɪks] *n no pl* astronautique *f*
astronomer [ə'strɒnəməʳ, *Am:* -'strɑːnəmɚ] *n* astronome *mf*
astronomical [ˌæstrə'nɒmɪkl, *Am:* -'nɑːmɪkl] *adj* astronomique
astronomy [ə'strɒnəmɪ, *Am:* -'strɑːnə-] *n no pl* astronomie *f*
astute [ə'stjuːt, *Am:* -'stuːt] *adj* astucieux(-euse)
astuteness *n no pl* astuce *f*
asylum [ə'saɪləm] *n* asile *m; fig* refuge *m*
at¹ [ət] *prep* **1.** (*in location of*) à; **~ home/school** à la maison/l'école; **~ the office** au bureau; **~ table** à table; **~ the window** devant la fenêtre; **~ the dentist's** chez le dentiste **2.** (*expressing time*) **~ the same time** en même temps; **~ the/no time** à ce moment-là/aucun moment; **to do one thing ~ a time** faire une chose à la fois; **~ noon/midnight/3 o'clock** à midi/minuit/3 heures; **~ night** (durant) la nuit; **~ Easter** à Pâques; **while I'm ~ it** pendant que j'y suis **3.** (*towards*) **he ran ~ me** il a foncé sur moi; **to point ~ people** montrer les gens du doigt; **to rush ~ sth/sb** se ruer sur qc/qn **4.** (*in reaction to*) **~ the sight of sth** en voyant qc **5.** (*in an amount of*) **~ all** en tout; **to buy sth ~ a pound** acheter qc pour une livre; **to sell sth ~ £10 a kilo** vendre qc 10£ le kilo; **~ 120 km/h** à 120 à l'heure **6.** (*in a state of*) **I'm not ~ my best/most alert** je ne suis pas vraiment en forme/très éveillé; **~ war/peace** en guerre/paix; **~ 20** à l'âge de 20 ans; **a child ~ play** un enfant en train de jouer; **to be ~ lunch** déjeuner **7.** (*in ability to*) **to be good/bad ~ French** être bon/mauvais en français; **to be ~ an advantage** avoir l'avantage **8.** (*repetition, persistence*) **to tug ~ the rope** tirer sur la corde; **to be on ~ sb to** *+infin* harceler qn pour *+infin;* **she's always on at me** elle est toujours après moi; **he's ~ it again** il recommence; **he's always ~ it** il n'arrête pas ►**~ all** *often not translated* **do you know her husband ~ all?** est-ce que vous connaissez son mari?; **thank you ~ – not ~ all!** merci – je vous en prie!; **not angry ~ all** pas du tout fâché; **he said nothing at ~** il n'a rien dit du tout; **nobody ~ all** absolument personne; **to hardly work/talk ~ all** il travaille/parle à peine; **~ that** de surcroît; **that's where it's ~** *inf* c'est comme ça aujourd'hui; **let's see where we're ~** voyons où nous en sommes
at² *s.* **at-sign**
atavism ['ætəvɪzəm, *Am:* 'æt̬-] *n no pl* atavisme *m*
atavistic ['ætəvɪstɪk, *Am:* 'æt̬-] *adj* atavique
ATC [ˌeɪ.tiː'siː] *n Brit abbr of* **Air Training Corps** *unité de préparation militaire pour l'armée de l'air*
ate [et] *pt of* **eat**
atheism ['eɪθɪɪzəm] *n no pl* athéisme *m*
atheist ['eɪθɪɪst] **I.** *n* athée *mf* **II.** *adj* athée
atheistic [ˌeɪθɪ'ɪstɪk] *adj s.* **atheist**
Athens ['æθənz] *n* Athènes
athlete ['æθliːt] *n* athlète *mf*
athlete's foot *n* pied *m* d'athlète
athletic [æθ'letɪk, *Am:* -'let̬-] *adj* **1.** SPORT athlétique; (*club*) d'athlétisme **2.** (*physically fit*) sportif(-ive); (*body*) athlétique
athletics *n + sing v, Brit* athlétisme *m;* **an ~ coach/track** un entraîneur/une piste d'athlétisme
Atlantic [ət'læntɪk, *Am:* -t̬ɪk] **I.** *n no pl* **the ~** l'Atlantique **II.** *adj* atlantique
atlas ['ætləs] <-es> *n* atlas *m*
ATM [ˌeɪtiː'em] *n abbr of* **Automated teller machine** DAB *m*
atmosphere ['ætməsfɪəʳ, *Am:* -fɪr] *n* atmosphère *f;* **a good working ~** une bonne ambiance de travail
atmospheric [ˌætməs'ferɪk] *adj* atmosphérique
atoll ['ætɒl, *Am:* -ɑːl] *n* atoll *m*
atom ['ætəm, *Am:* 'æt̬-] *n* **1.** PHYS atome *m* **2.** (*tiny amount*) brin *m*
atomic [ə'tɒmɪk, *Am:* -'tɑːmɪk] *adj* atomique
atomic bomb *n* bombe *f* atomique **atomic reactor** *n* réacteur *m* nucléaire
atomizer ['ætəmaɪzəʳ, *Am:* 'æt̬əmaɪzɚ] *n* atomiseur *m*
atone [ə'təʊn, *Am:* -'toʊn] *vi* **to ~ for sth** expier qc
atrocious [ə'trəʊʃəs, *Am:* -'troʊ-] *adj* atroce
atrocity [ə'trɒsətɪ] <-ies> *n* atrocité *f*
atrophy ['ætrəfɪ] <-ies> **I.** *n no pl* atrophie *f* **II.** *vi* s'atrophier
at-sign *n* INFOR ar(r)obas *m,* a *m* commercial
attach [ə'tætʃ] *vt* **1.** (*fix*) **to ~ sth to sth** attacher qc à qc **2.** (*connect*) **to ~ sth to sth** relier qc à qc **3.** *form* (*send as enclosure*) **to ~ sth to sth** joindre qc à qc; **to ~ a file** INFOR envoyer un fichier en attaché **4.** (*join*) **to ~ oneself to sb** se coller à qn **5.** (*assign*) **to be ~ed to sth** être affecté à qc **6.** (*associate*) **to ~ importance to sth** attacher de l'importance à qc
attaché [ə'tæʃeɪ, *Am:* ˌæt̬ə'ʃeɪ] *n* attaché(e) *m(f)*
attaché case *n* attaché-case *m*

attached *adj* **to be ~ to sb/sth** être attaché à qc/qn

attachment *n* **1.** (*fondness*) affection *f;* **to form an ~ to sb** se prendre d'affection pour qn **2.** *no pl* (*support*) attachement *m* **3.** INFOR attachement *m* **4.** *no pl* (*assignment*) **to be on ~ to sth** être affecté à qc **5.** (*attached device*) accessoire *m* **6.** LAW (*person*) arrestation *f;* (*property*) saisie *f*

attack [ə'tæk] **I.** *n* **1.** *a.* MIL, SPORT attaque *f;* (*of person*) agression *f;* **a terrorist/bomb ~** une attentat terroriste/à la bombe; **all-out ~** attaque tous azimuts; **to launch** [*o* **make**] **an ~ against** [*o* **on**] **sb/sth** lancer une attaque contre qn/qc; **to be** [*o* **to go**] **on the ~** passer à l'attaque; **to be** [*o* **come**] **under ~** être attaqué; **to launch an ~ on** (*town, base*) lancer une attaque sur; (*party, writer*) s'attaquer à **2.** MED crise *f;* **~ of asthma** crise d'asthme; **~ of giggles** crise de fou rire; **~ of hysteria** crise de nerfs; **~ of shyness** accès *m* de timidité ►**~ is the best form of defence** *prov* l'attaque est la meilleure défense **II.** *vt* **1.** attaquer; (*right*) porter atteinte à; **to ~ sb in sth street** agresser qn dans la rue **2.** (*tackle: problem, food*) s'attaquer à; **to ~ the fridge** dévaliser le frigo **III.** *vi* attaquer

attain [ə'teɪn] *vt* atteindre

attainable *adj* (*goal*) réalisable

attainment *n* **1.** *pl, form* (*results*) résultats *mpl* **2.** *pl, form* (*knowledge*) aquis *mpl*

attempt [ə'tempt] **I.** *n* (*try*) tentative *f;* **to make an ~ to** *+infin* essayer de *+infin* ►**an ~ on sb's life** une atteinte à la vie de qn **II.** *vt* tenter

attend [ə'tend] **I.** *vt* **1.** (*be present at*) assister à; **to ~ church** aller à l'église; **the fête was well ~ed** il y avait plein de monde à la kermesse; **a well-~ed seminar** un séminaire très suivi **2.** (*accompany*) assister **II.** *vi* **1.** (*be present*) être présent **2.** *form* (*listen carefully*) être attentif

attendance [ə'tendəns] *n* **1.** *no pl* (*being present*) présence *f;* **~ at classes** participation *f* aux cours **2.** (*people*) assistance *f;* **~ was poor** il y avait peu de monde **3.** (*help and care*) **to be in ~ on sb** soigner qn; (*accompany*) être au service de qn ►**to dance ~ on sb** être aux petits soins pour qn

attendant [ə'tendənt] **I.** *n* **1.** (*official*) employé(e) *m(f)* **2.** (*servant*) serviteur *m* **II.** *adj* **~ on sth** résultant de qc

attention [ə'tenʃn] *n no pl* **1.** attention *f;* **for the ~ of sb** à l'attention de qn; **to attract sb's ~** attirer l'attention de qn; **it has been brought to my ~ that** on a porté qc à mon attention; **to call ~ to sth** signaler qc; **to pay ~** faire attention **2.** (*care*) soins *mpl;* **medical ~** soins *mpl* médicaux **3.** MIL **to stand to ~** être au garde-à-vous; **~!** garde-à-vous!

attentive [ə'tentɪv, *Am:* -t̬ɪv] *adj* **to be ~ to sb/sth** être attentif à qn/qc

attenuate [ə'tenjʊeɪt] *vt form* atténuer

attest [ə'test] **I.** *vt* attester **II.** *vi* **~ to sth** témoigner de qc

attestation [ˌæte'steɪʃn, *Am:* ˌæt̬-] *n* attestation *f*

attic ['ætɪk, *Am:* 'æt̬-] *n* grenier *m*

attitude ['ætɪtju:d, *Am:* 'æt̬ətu:d] *n* **1.** (*manner*) attitude *f* **2.** (*opinion*) opinion *f;* **I take the ~ that** ma position est que **3.** (*position*) posture *f;* ART pose *f;* **to strike an ~** poser **4.** *inf* aplomb *m*

attorney [ə'tɜ:nɪ, *Am:* -'tɜ:r-] *n Am* avocat(e) *m(f)*

Attorney-General *n Am* ≈ ministre *m* de la justice

attract [ə'trækt] *vt* attirer

attraction [ə'trækʃn] *n* **1.** (*force, place of enjoyment*) attraction *f* **2.** *no pl* (*appeal*) attrait *m;* **~ to sb** attirance *f* pour qn

attractive [ə'træktɪv] *adj* **1.** (*good-looking*) *a. fig* séduisant(e) **2.** (*pleasant*) intéressant(e)

attribute[1] [ə'trɪbju:t] *vt* **1.** (*ascribe*) attribuer; **to ~ the blame to sb** attribuer la responsabilité à qn; **they ~d their success to being lucky** ils ont attribué leur réussite à la chance **2.** (*give credit for*) **to ~ sth to sb** accorder qc à qn

attribute[2] ['ætrɪbju:t] *n* **1.** (*characteristic*) attribut *m* **2.** LING épithète *f*

attributive [ə'trɪbjʊtɪv, *Am:* -jət̬ɪv] *adj* épithète

attrition [ə'trɪʃn] *n no pl* **1.** (*wearing down*) usure *f;* **war of ~** guerre d'usure **2.** *Am, Aus* ECON réduction *f* de personnel

aubergine ['əʊbəʒi:n, *Am:* 'oʊbɚ-] **I.** *n* aubergine *f* **II.** *adj* aubergine

auburn ['ɔ:bən, *Am:* 'ɑ:bɚn] *adj* auburn

auburn-haired *adj* **to be ~** avoir les cheveux auburn

auction ['ɔ:kʃn, *Am:* 'ɑ:kʃn] **I.** *n* vente *f* aux enchères, mise *f Suisse;* **to hold an ~** organiser une vente aux enchères; **to be sold at ~, to be sold by ~** *Brit* être vendu aux enchères, être misé *Suisse;* **to put sth up for ~** mettre qc aux enchères **II.** *vt* **to ~ sth (off)** vendre qc aux enchères

auctioneer [ˌɔ:kʃə'nɪəʳ, *Am:* ˌɑ:kʃə'nɪr] *n* commissaire-priseur *m*

audacious [ɔ:'deɪʃəs, *Am:* ɑ:-] *adj* (*bold*) audacieux(-euse)

audacity [ɔ:'dæsətɪ, *Am:* ɑ:'dæsət̬ɪ] *n no pl* (*boldness, cheek*) audace *f*

audible ['ɔ:dəbl, *Am:* 'ɑ:-] *adj* audible; **barely ~** presque inaudible

audience ['ɔ:dɪəns, *Am:* 'ɑ:-] *n* **1.** *sing or pl vb* (*people*) public *m;* TV téléspectateurs *mpl;* RADIO auditeurs *mpl;* LIT lecteurs *mpl;* THEAT, CINE spectateurs *mpl;* **~ participation** participation *f* du public; **~ ratings** indice *m* d'écoute **2.** (*formal interview*) audience *f*

audio [ˌɔ:dɪəʊ, *Am:* ˌɑ:dɪoʊ] *adj* audio; **~ tape** cassette audio

audiovisual [ˌɔ:dɪəʊ'vɪʒuəl, *Am:* ˌɑ:dɪoʊ-'vɪʒu-] *adj* audiovisuel(le)

A

audit[1] ['ɔːdɪt, *Am:* 'ɑː-] **I.** *n* audit *m* **II.** *vt* (*accounts*) vérifier
audit[2] ['ɔːdɪt, *Am:* 'ɑː-] *vt Am, Aus* (*attend*) **to ~ a course** assister à un cours comme auditeur libre
audition [ɔː'dɪʃn, *Am:* ɑː-] **I.** *n* audition *f;* **to hold an ~ for a part** faire passer une audition pour un rôle **II.** *vi, vt* auditionner
auditor ['ɔːdɪtəʳ, *Am:* 'ɑːdəţɚ] *n* **1.** COM commissaire *m* au comptes **2.** *Am* UNIV **external ~** auditeur *m* externe
auditorium [ˌɔːdɪ'tɔːrɪəm, *Am:* ˌɑːdə-] <-s *o* auditoria> *n* **1.** auditorium *m* **2.** (*hall*) salle *f* (de spectacle) **3.** *Am* UNIV amphithéâtre *m*
augment [ɔːg'ment, *Am:* ɑːg-] *vt form* (*income, supply*) augmenter; (*reservoir*) remplir
augmentation [ˌɔːgmen'teɪʃn, *Am:* ˌɑːg-] *n form* augmentation *f*
augur ['ɔːgəʳ, *Am:* 'ɑːgɚ] **I.** *vi* augurer; **to ~ badly/well for sb/sth** s'annoncer mal/bien pour qn/qc **II.** *vt* présager
August ['ɔːgəst, *Am:* 'ɑː-] *n* août *m; s. a.* **April**
aunt [ɑːnt, *Am:* ænt] *n* tante *f*
aura ['ɔːrə] *n* aura *f*
aural ['ɔːrəl] *adj* auditif(-ive)
aurora [ɔː'rɔːrə] *n* **~ borealis/australis** aurore *f* boréale/australe
auspices ['ɔːspɪsɪz, *Am:* 'ɑː-] *n pl* égide *f;* **under the ~ of sb** sous l'égide de qn
auspicious [ɔː'spɪʃəs, *Am:* ɑː-] *adj form* prometteur(-euse)
austere [ɔː'stɪəʳ, *Am:* ɑː'stɪr] *adj* austère
austerity [ɔː'sterətɪ, *Am:* ɑː'sterəţɪ] <-ies> *n* austérité *f*
Australia [ɒ'streɪlɪə, *Am:* ɑː'streɪlʒə] *n* l'Australie *f;* **South ~** l'Australie-Méridionale; **Western ~** l'Australie-Occidentale

> L'**Australia day** est un jour férié national célébré le 26 janvier en souvenir de la fondation de la première colonie britanique en 1788 à Sydney Cove. Pour les "Aborigènes", les premiers habitants de l'Australie, ce jour marque la date de l'invasion de leur pays. A cette occasion, on organise de nombreuses manifestations culturelles dans le but de rassembler les populations noires et blanches d'Australie.

Australian [ɒ'streɪlɪən, *Am:* ɑː'streɪlʒən] **I.** *adj* australien(ne) **II.** *n* **1.** (*person*) Australien(ne) *m(f)* **2.** LING australien *m; s. a.* **English**
Australian Antarctic Territory *n* le Territoire antarctique australien **Australian Capital Territory** *n* le Territoire de la Capitale Australienne
Austria ['ɒstrɪə, *Am:* 'ɑː-] *n* l'Autriche *f*
Austrian ['ɒstrɪən, *Am:* 'ɑː-] **I.** *adj* autrichien(ne) **II.** *n* Autrichien(ne) *m(f)*
authentic [ɔː'θentɪk, *Am:* ɑː'θenţɪk] *adj* authentique
authenticate [ɔː'θentɪkeɪt, *Am:* ɑː'θenţɪ-] *vt* authentifier
authentication [ɔːˌθentɪ'keɪʃn, *Am:* ɑːˌθenţɪ-] *n no pl* authentification *f*
authenticity [ˌɔːθən'tɪsətɪ, *Am:* ˌɑːθən'tɪsəţɪ] *n no pl* authenticité *f*
author ['ɔːθəʳ, *Am:* 'ɑːθɚ] **I.** *n* auteur *m* **II.** *vt Am* rédiger
authoritarian [ɔːˌθɒrɪ'teərɪən, *Am:* əːˌθɔːrə'terɪ-] **I.** *n* personne *f* autoritaire; **to be an ~** être autoritaire **II.** *adj* autoritaire
authoritative [ɔː'θɒrɪtətɪv, *Am:* ə'θɔːrəteɪţɪv] *adj* **1.** (*imperious*) autoritaire **2.** (*reliable*) qui fait autorité
authority [ɔː'θɒrətɪ, *Am:* əː'θɔːrəţɪ] <-ies> *n* **1.** *no pl* (*right to control*) autorité *f;* **to be in ~** avoir l'autorité; **to have ~ over sb** avoir une autorité sur qn **2.** *no pl* (*permission*) autorisation *f* **3.** (*specialist*) autorité *f;* **to be an ~ on sth** être une autorité sur qc; **a world ~ on the subject** une autorité mondiale sur le sujet **4.** (*organization*) administration *f;* **the authorities** les autorités; **education/health ~** *administration chargée des affaires scolaires/de santé* ►**to have sth on sb's ~** tenir qc de qn; **to have sth on good ~** savoir qc de source sûre
authorization [ˌɔːθəraɪ'zeɪʃn, *Am:* ˌɑːθɚɪ-] *n no pl* autorisation *f*
authorize ['ɔːθəraɪz, *Am:* 'ɑː-] *vt* autoriser
auto ['ɔːtəʊ, *Am:* 'ɑːţoʊ] *adj Am* automobile
autobiographical [ˌɔːtəbaɪə'græfɪkl, *Am:* ˌɑːţə-] *adj* autobiographique
autobiography [ˌɔːtəbaɪ'ɒgrəfɪ, *Am:* ˌɑːţəbaɪ'ɑːgrə-] *n* autobiographie *f*
auto-bronzer ['ɔːtəbrɒnzəʳ], **auto-bronzing cream** *n* autobronzant *m*
autocracy [ɔː'tɒkrəsɪ, *Am:* ɑː'tɑːkrə-] *n* autocratie *f*
autocrat ['ɔːtəkræt, *Am:* 'ɑːţə-] *n* autocrate *m*
autocratic [ˌɔːtə'krætik, *Am:* ˌɑːţə'kræţ-] *adj* autocratique
autograph ['ɔːtəgrɑːf, *Am:* 'ɑːţəgræf] **I.** *n* autographe *m;* **~ session** séance d'autographes **II.** *vt* signer
autoimmune [ˌɔːtəʊɪ'mjuːn, *Am:* ˌɑːţoʊ-] *adj* (*disease*) auto-immune
automate ['ɔːtəmeɪt, *Am:* 'ɑːţə-] *vt* automatiser
automated *adj* automatisé(e)
automatic [ˌɔːtə'mætɪk, *Am:* ˌɑːţə'mæţ-] **I.** *n* **1.** (*machine*) machine *f* automatique **2.** (*car*) voiture *f* automatique **3.** (*rifle*) automatique *m* **II.** *adj* automatique
automatic pilot *n* pilotage *m* automatique; **to be on ~** être sur pilote automatique; *fig* être comme un automate
automation [ˌɔːtə'meɪʃn, *Am:* ˌɑːţə-] *n no pl* automatisation *f*
automaton [ɔː'tɒmətən, *Am:* ɑː'tɑːmə-] *n* automate *m*
automobile ['ɔːtəməbiːl, *Am:* 'ɑːţəmoʊ-] *n Am* automobile *f;* **~ accident** accident *m* de

voiture; ~ **industry** industrie *f* automobile

automotive [ˌɔːtəˈməʊtɪv, *Am:* ˌɑːt̬əˈmoʊt̬ɪv] *adj* automobile

autonomous [ɔːˈtɒnəməs, *Am:* ɑːˈtɑːnə-] *adj* autonome

autonomy [ɔːˈtɒnəmɪ, *Am:* ɑːˈtɑːnə-] *n no pl* autonomie *f*

autopilot [ˈɔːtəʊˌpaɪlət, *Am:* ˈɑːt̬oʊ-] *n s. a.* **automatic pilot**

autopsy [ˈɔːtɒpsɪ, *Am:* ˈɑːtɑːp-] <-ies> *n* **1.** MED autopsie *f;* **to carry out an ~ on sb** pratiquer une autopsie sur qn **2.** *fig* analyse *f*

autumn [ˈɔːtəm, *Am:* ˈɑːt̬əm] *n* automne *m;* **in (the) ~** en automne

autumnal [ɔːˈtʌmnəl, *Am:* ɑː-] *adj* (*colours*) automnal(e); (*rain, equinox*) d'automne

Auvergne [əʊˈvəən, *Am:* oʊˈvern] *n* **the ~** l'Auvergne *f*

auxiliary [ɔːgˈzɪlɪərɪ, *Am:* ɑːgˈzɪljrɪ] <-ies> **I.** *n* **1.** HIST, LING auxiliaire *m* **2.** (*nurse*) aide *mf* soignant(e) **II.** *adj* auxiliaire

AV I. *adj abbr of* **audiovisual** audiovisuel(le) **II.** *n abbr of* **Authorized Version** version *f* autorisée (*de la Bible*)

av. *n abbr of* **average**

Av. *n abbr of* **avenue** Av. *f*

avail [əˈveɪl] **I.** *n* **to no ~** en vain **II.** *vt* **to ~ oneself of sth** profiter de qc

availability [əˌveɪləˈbɪləti, *Am:* -ət̬i] *n* **1.** *no pl* (*being available*) disponibilité *f* **2.** *Am* (*for journalists, photographers*) ≈ conférence *f* de presse

available *adj* **1.** disponible; **this product is ~ in various colours** ce produit existe en plusieurs couleurs; **to make onself ~** se libérer; **only ~ from pharmacies** disponible seulement en pharmacie **2.** *fig* libre

avalanche [ˈævəlɑːnʃ, *Am:* -æntʃ] *n a. fig* avalanche *f*

avant-garde [ˌævɒŋˈgɑːd, *Am:* ˌɑːvɑːntˈgɑːrd] **I.** *n + sing or pl vb* avant-garde *f* **II.** *adj* d'avant-garde

avarice [ˈævərɪs] *n no pl* cupidité *f;* **wealth beyond the dreams of ~** fortune colossale

avaricious [ˌævəˈrɪʃəs] *adj form* cupide

avenge [əˈvendʒ] *vt* venger; **to ~ an insult** se venger d'une insulte; **to ~ oneself on sb** se venger de qn

avenue [ˈævənjuː, *Am:* -nuː] *n* **1.** (*street*) avenue *f* **2.** *Brit* (*road to a house*) allée *f* **3.** (*possibility*) possibilité *f;* **to explore all ~s** explorer toutes les possibilités; **a new ~ of enquiry** une nouvelle piste

average [ˈævərɪdʒ] **I.** *n* (*standard*) moyenne *f;* **by an ~ of 10 %** de 10 % en moyenne; **on ~** en moyenne; **well above/below ~** bien au-dessus/en-dessous de la moyenne **II.** *adj* (*typical: income, person, ability*) moyen(ne); **~ rainfall** taux moyen de précipitations **III.** *vt* **1.** (*have a general value*) **to ~ 35 hours a week** travailler en moyenne 35 heures par semaine; **to ~ £15 000 per year** gagner en moyenne 15 000£ par an **2.** (*calculate*) faire la moyenne de

averse [əˈvɜːs, *Am:* -ˈvɜːrs] *adj* **to be ~ to sth** être opposé à qc; **I'm not ~ to good wine** je ne dis pas non au bon vin

aversion [əˈvɜːʃn, *Am:* -ˈvɜːrʒn] *n* aversion *f;* **to have an ~ to doing sth** détester faire qc

avert [əˈvɜːt, *Am:* -ˈvɜːrt] *vt* **1.** (*prevent*) éviter **2.** (*avoid*) **to ~ one's eyes from sth** détourner les yeux de qc

aviary [ˈeɪvɪərɪ, *Am:* -er-] *n* volière *f*

aviation [ˌeɪvɪˈeɪʃn] *n no pl* aviation *f;* **~ fuel** kérosène *m;* **~ industry** industrie *f* aéronautique

avid [ˈævɪd] *adj* (*reader, supporter*) passionné(e); (*desire*) ardent(e); **to be ~ for sth** être avide de qc

avidity [əˈvɪdətɪ, *Am:* -t̬ɪ] *n no pl* avidité *f*

avocado [ˌævəˈkɑːdəʊ, *Am:* -doʊ] <-s *o* -es> *n* BOT avocat *m*

avoid [əˈvɔɪd] *vt* éviter; **to ~ sb/sth like the plague** éviter qn/qc comme la peste; **to ~ doing sth** éviter de faire qc; **alcohol should be ~ed** éviter l'alcool; **you're ~ing the issue** tu esquives la question

avoidable *adj* évitable

avoidance *n no pl* prévention *f*

avowed [əˈvaʊd] *adj* déclaré(e)

AWACS [ˈeɪwæks] *n abbr of* **airborn warning and control system** awacs *m*

await [əˈweɪt] *vt* attendre; **eagerly/long ~ed** tant/longuement attendu

awake [əˈweɪk] <awoke, awoken *o* -d, awoken *Am*> **I.** *vi* **1.** se réveiller **2.** *fig* **to ~ to sth** prendre conscience de qc **II.** *vt* **1.** (*rouse from sleep: person*) réveiller **2.** (*restart: passion*) raviver **III.** *adj* **1.** éveillé(e); **wide ~** complètement réveillé; **to keep ~** rester éveillé; **to keep sb ~** empêcher qn de dormir; **to lie ~** ne pas dormir **2.** *fig* **to be ~ to sth** être conscient de qc

awakening *n no pl* réveil *m;* **~ of sb to sth** la prise de conscience de qn à propos de qc; **he's in for a rude ~** il va tomber de haut

award [əˈwɔːd, *Am:* -ˈwɔːrd] **I.** *n* **1.** (*prize*) prix *m;* **to be presented with an ~** recevoir un prix **2.** (*compensation*) dédommagement *m* **II.** *vt* (*prize*) décerner; (*damages, grant*) accorder; **she was ~ed a £500 grant** on lui a accordé une bourse de 500£

aware [əˈweəʳ, *Am:* -ˈwer] *adj* **1.** (*knowing*) **to be ~ that ...** être bien conscient que ...; **to be perfectly well ~ of sth** avoir pleinement conscience de qc; **as far as I'm ~** autant que je sache **2.** (*sense*) **to be ~ of sth** être conscient de qc **3.** (*well-informed*) **to be ecologically ~** avoir une conscience écologique

awareness *n no pl* conscience *f;* **to raise public ~ of a problem** sensibiliser le public à un problème; **environmental ~** conscience vis-à-vis de l'environnement

away [əˈweɪ] *adv* **1.** (*elsewhere*) **~ on holiday** parti en vacances **2.** (*in distance, opposite direction*) loin; **to be miles ~** être très loin; ~

from the town loin de la ville; **as far ~ as possible** aussi loin que possible; **to limp/ swim ~** s'éloigner en boitant/en nageant **3.** (*in future time*) **it's a week ~** c'est dans une semaine **4.** (*continuously*) **to write ~** écrire sans s'arrêter; **to be laughing ~** rire aux éclats

away fixture, **away game**, **away match** *n* match *m* à l'extérieur **away team** *n* équipe qui visite

awe [ɔː, *Am:* ɑː] **I.** *n no pl* crainte mêlée de respect; **to hold sb in ~**, **to stand in ~ of sb** craindre qn **II.** <-ing *Brit o* awing *Am*> *vt* **the public was ~d into silence by his speech** son discours força le respect silencieux du public

awe-inspiring ['ɔːɪnˌspaɪərɪŋ, *Am:* 'ɑː-] *adj* qui force le respect

awesome ['ɔːsəm, *Am:* 'ɑː-] *adj* **1.** (*impressive*) impressionnant(e) **2.** (*fearsome*) effrayant(e) **3.** *Am, inf* (*good*) super; **to look ~** avoir l'air super

awestricken ['ɔːˌstrɪkn, *Am:* 'ɑː-], **awestruck** ['ɔːstrʌk, *Am:* 'ɑː-] *adj* impressionné(e)

awful ['ɔːfl, *Am:* 'ɑː-] *adj* **1.** (*bad*) affreux(-euse); **it smells ~** ça pue; **you look ~** tu as très mauvaise mine; **she looks ~ in that skirt** cette jupe ne lui va vraiment pas; **I felt ~ for saying that** je m'en suis voulu d'avoir dit ça **2.** (*great*) **an ~ lot** (**of**) énormément (de)

awfully *adv* **1.** (*badly*) affreusement **2.** (*very*) vraiment; **an ~ long journey** un trajet interminable; **she's not ~ good at tennis** elle n'est pas terrible en tennis

awkward ['ɔːkwəd, *Am:* 'ɑːkwɚd] *adj* **1.** (*difficult*) difficile; **~ to do** difficile à faire; **an ~ customer** *inf* un type pas commode; **to make things ~ for sb** compliquer les choses pour qn; **it's an ~ time** c'est un moment difficile **2.** (*not skilful*) maladroit(e) **3.** (*embarrassed: silence*) gêné(e); (*question*) gênant(e); **I feel so ~ asking her** je me sens mal à l'aise de lui demander **4.** *Brit* (*unwilling*) **he's just being ~** il fait sa tête de cochon; **it's ~ of him to ...** ce n'est pas très coopératif de sa part de ...

awning ['ɔːnɪŋ, *Am:* 'ɑː-] *n* store *m;* (*of caravan*) auvent *m*

awoke [ə'wəʊk, *Am:* -'woʊk] *pt of* **awake**

awoken [ə'wəʊkən, *Am:* -'woʊ-] *pp of* **awake**

AWOL MIL *abbr of* **absent without** (**official**) **leave** être en absence illégale

awry [ə'raɪ] *adj* **1.** (*wrong*) de travers; **to go ~** aller de travers; **to send sth ~** mettre qc en l'air **2.** (*untidy*) dans tous les sens

ax *n, vt Am,* **axe** [æks] **I.** *n* hache *f* ▶**to get the ~** *inf* (*workers*) se faire virer; (*projects*) sauter; **to have an ~ to grind** agir par intérêt **II.** <axing> *vt* (*projects*) abandonner; (*job*) supprimer

axiom ['æksɪəm] *n form* axiome *m*

axis ['æksɪs] *n* MAT, POL axe *m*

axle ['æksl] *n* essieu *m*

ayatollah [ˌaɪjə'tɔlə, *Am:* ˌaɪə'toʊlə-] *n* ayatollah *m*

aye [aɪ] *interj Brit, Scot* oui

Ayes [aɪz] *n* POL **the ~** les voix pour

azalea [ə'zeɪlɪə, *Am:* -'zeɪljə] *n* azalée *f*

Azerbaijan [ˌæzəbaɪ'dʒɑːn, *Am:* ˌɑːzɚ-] *n* l'Azerbaïdjan *m*

Azerbaijani I. *adj* azerbaïdjanais(e) **II.** *n* Azerbaïdjanais(e) *m(f)*

azure ['æʒəʳ, *Am:* 'æʒɚ] **I.** *n* azur *m* **II.** *adj* azur

B

B, **b** [biː] <-'s *o* -s> *n* **1.** (*letter*) B *m,* b *m;* **~ as in Benjamin** *Brit,* **~ as in Boy** *Am,* **~ for Benjamin** *Brit,* **~ for Boy** *Am* (*on telephone*) b comme Berthe **2.** MUS si *m* **3.** SCHOOL bonne note

BA [ˌbiː'eɪ] *n abbr of* **Bachelor of Arts** ≈ licence *f* (*lettres et sciences humaines*)

baa [bɑː, *Am:* bæ] **I.** *n* bêlement *m* **II.** <-ed> *vi* bêler

babble ['bæbl] **I.** *n no pl* **1.** (*speech*) babillage *m;* **~ of voices** brouhaha *m* **2.** (*sound*) murmure *m* **II.** *vi* babiller

babe [beɪb] *n* **1.** (*baby*) bébé *m;* **newborn ~** nouveau-né *m* **2.** (*person*) naïf, -ive *m, f* **3.** *inf* (*girl*) poupée *f;* **hi ~!** salut ma belle!

baboon [bə'buːn, *Am:* bæb'uːn] *n* babouin *m*

baby ['beɪbi] **I.** *n* **1.** (*child, childish person*) bébé *m* **2.** (*suckling*) nourisson *m* **3.** (*youngest person*) benjamin *m* **4.** *inf* (*personal concern*) **it's your ~** c'est ton bébé **5.** *inf* (*affectionate address*) chéri(e) *m(f)* **II.** *adj* **1.** (*young*) bébé **2.** (*small*) tout petit

baby carriage *n Am* voiture *f* d'enfant **baby food** *n no pl* aliments *mpl* pour enfants

babysit ['beɪbɪsɪt] **I.** *vi* faire du babysitting **II.** *vt* garder

babysitter ['beɪbɪˌsɪtəʳ, *Am:* -ˌsɪt̬ɚ] *n* babysitter *mf*

bachelor ['bætʃələʳ, *Am:* -lɚ] *n* **1.** (*man*) célibataire *m* **2.** UNIV licencié(e) *m(f)*

Un **Bachelor's degree** est le plus souvent un premier diplôme universitaire que les étudiants obtiennent après trois ans d'études (voire quatre ou cinq ans dans certaines matières). Les diplômes les plus importants sont le "BA" ("Bachelor of Arts") pour des études en sciences humaines, le "BSc" ("Bachelor of Science") pour des études en sciences naturelles, le "BEd" ("Bachelor of Education") pour des études de pédagogie, le "LLB" ("Bachelor of Laws") pour des études de droit et le "BMus" ("Bachelor of Music") pour des études de musicologie.

bacillus [bə'sɪləs] <-li> *n* bacille *m*

back [bæk] **I.** *n* **1.** (*opp: front*) arrière *m;* (*of envelope*) dos *m;* (*of cupboard*) fond *m;* (*of paper*) verso *m;* **in the ~ of a car** à l'arrière d'une voiture; **~ to front** à l'envers; **at the ~ of sth, in ~ of sth** *Am* derrière qc; **at the ~** (*of a house, building*) derrière; **we were right at the ~** (*in queue*) nous étions tout au bout; (*in cinema*) nous étions tout à l'arrière; **to look at the ~ of the book** regarder à la fin du livre **2.** ANAT dos *m;* **to be on one's ~** être étendu sur le dos; **to turn one's ~** tourner le dos; **to turn one's ~ on sb/sth** *fig* laisser qn/qc derrière soi **3.** SPORT arrière *m* ►**to know sth like the ~ of one's hand** connaître qc comme le fond de sa poche; **to have sth at the ~ of one's mind** avoir qc derrière la tête; **to have one's ~ against the wall** être au pied du mur; **in the ~ of beyond** dans un coin perdu; **to get off sb's ~** ficher la paix à qn; **to get sb's ~ up** courir sur la haricot de qn; **to put one's ~ into sth** s'y mettre énergiquement; **behind sb's ~** dans le dos de qn; **to do sth behind sb's ~** faire qc dans le dos de qn **II.** *adj* **1.** (*rear*) arrière; **on the ~ page** sur la dernière page **2.** (*late*) **~ payments** paiements en retard; **~ tax** arriérés *mpl* d'impôt **3.** MED (*pain*) dans le dos; (*problems*) de dos **III.** *adv* **1.** (*to previous place, situation*) en arrière; **to bring ~ memories** rappeler des souvenirs; **to be ~** être de retour; **to come ~** revenir; **we're ~ where we started** nous retournons à la case départ; **to come ~ into fashion** redevenir à la mode; **to get there and ~** y aller et revenir; **to put sth ~** remettre qc à sa place; **to want sb ~** vouloir que qn revienne (*subj*); **to want sth ~** vouloir que qc soit rendu (*subj*) **2.** (*to the rear, behind*) vers l'arrière; **5 km ~** il y a 5 kilomètres; **to go ~ and forth between A and B** aller et venir entre A et B; **to lie ~** s'installer confortablement; **to look ~** regarder en arrière; **to sit ~** s'installer (confortablement); **to stand** (**well**) **~** reculer; **to throw ~ one's head** renverser sa tête en arrière **3.** (*in return*) en retour; **to hit sb ~** rendre les coups; **to hit ~** (**against sb**) riposter; **to read sth ~ to sb** relire qc à qn **4.** (*into past*) **a few years ~** il y a quelques années; **~ in 1980** en 1980; **to think ~** penser; **as far ~ as I can remember** aussi loin que je me souvienne (*subj*) ►**~ to the drawing board** retour à la case départ; **to get ~ at sb** prendre sa revanche sur qn **IV.** *vt* **1.** (*support*) soutenir; (*with money*) financer; (*with arguments, facts*) soutenir **2.** (*bet on: horse*) parier sur **3.** (*reverse*) **to ~ a car round the corner/into a space** faire marche arrière dans un tournant/pour se garer **4.** (*line, strengthen: curtains*) doubler; (*book*) couvrir ►**to ~ the wrong horse** parier sur le mauvais cheval

◆**back away** *vi* **to ~ from sb/sth** reculer devant qn/qc

◆**back down** *vi* **1.** descendre à reculons **2.** *fig* céder

◆**back up** **I.** *vi* faire marche arrière **II.** *vt* **1.** (*reverse*) faire reculer **2.** INFOR faire une sauvegarde de **3.** (*support*) soutenir **4.** (*confirm*) confirmer

backache ['bækeɪk] *n* mal *m* de dos

backbencher [ˌbæk'bentʃəʳ, *Am:* -tʃɚ] *n Brit* député *m* sans portefeuille

backbiting ['bækˌbaɪtɪŋ, *Am:* -t̬ɪŋ] *n no pl* médisances *fpl*

backbone ['bækbəʊn, *Am:* -boʊn] *n* **1.** ANAT colonne *f* vertébrale **2.** *fig* (*of an organization*) pilier *m* **3.** *no pl* (*strength of character*) courage *m*

backdate [ˌbæk'deɪt, *Am:* 'bækdeɪt] *vt* (*pay rise*) payer rétroactivement; (*cheque*) antidater

backdrop ['bækdrɒp, *Am:* -drɑːp] *n Brit* toile *f* de fond

backer ['bækəʳ, *Am:* -ɚ] *n* (*supporter*) **their ~s** les personnes qui les soutiennent; (**financial**) **~** bailleur, -euse *m, f* de fonds

backfire [ˌbæk'faɪəʳ, *Am:* -'faɪɚ] *vi* **1.** (*go wrong*) mal tourner; **his plans ~d on him** ses projets se sont retournés contre lui **2.** AUTO pétarader

backgammon [bæk'gæmən] *n no pl* jacquet *m*

background ['bækgraʊnd] **I.** *n* **1.** (*rear view*) fond *m;* **in the ~** à l'arrière-plan; **against a ~ of sth** sur un fond de qc **2.** (*to a situation*) contexte *m;* (*in society*) milieu *m* d'origine; (*of education, work*) profil *m;* **fill me in on the ~** explique-moi la situation; **what's her ~?** d'où est-ce qu'elle sort? **II.** *adj* (*information, knowledge*) de base; (*noise*) de fond; **background music** musique *f* d'ambiance

backhand ['bækhænd] *n no pl* revers *m*

backhander [ˌbæk'hændəʳ, *Am:* -ɚ] *n inf* pot-de-vin *m*

backing ['bækɪŋ] *n no pl* **1.** (*aid*) soutien *m* **2.** FASHION renfort *m* **3.** MUS accompagnement *m*

backlash ['bæklæʃ] *n* contrecoup *m;* **to provoke a ~** provoquer une forte réaction

backlog ['bæklɒg, *Am:* -lɑːg] *n* arriéré *m* de travail; **a ~ of cases/repairs** des affaires/des réparations en retard

back number *n* ancien numéro *m*

backpack ['bækpæk] **I.** *n Am* sac *m* à dos **II.** *vi* **to go ~ing** faire de la randonnée

backpacker *n* **1.** (*travelling*) adepte *mf* du trekking **2.** (*hiking*) randonneur, -euse *m, f*

back pay *n* rappel *m* de traitement [*o* salaire]

backpedal ['bækpedəl] *vi* <-ll-> (*on cycle*) pédaler en arrière; (*change one's mind*) assouplir sa position; **to ~ on sth** freiner sur qc

backside ['bæksaɪd] *n inf* postérieur *m* ►**a**

kick up in the ~ un coup de pied au cul; **to get off one's** ~ bouger ses fesses

backspace (**key**) ['bækspeɪs-] *n* touche *f* de rappel arrière

backstage [bæk'steɪdʒ] **I.** *adj* **1.** dans les coulisses **2.** *fig* secret **II.** *adv* derrière la scène

backstairs [ˌbæk'steəz, *Am:* ˌbæk'sterz] **I.** *n* escalier *m* de service **II.** *adj fig* ~ **deals** combines *fpl* de couloirs

backstroke ['bækstrəʊk, *Am:* -stroʊk] *n no pl* dos *m* crawlé

backtrack ['bæktræk] *vi* **1.** revenir sur ses pas **2.** *fig* revenir sur ses propos

backup ['bækʌp] **I.** *n* **1.** (*support*) renforts *mpl;* **the** ~ **team** les renforts *mpl* **2.** (*reserve*) **to have sth as a** ~ avoir un qc de secours; **a** ~ **camera** un appareil photo de secours **3.** INFOR (fichier *m* de) sauvegarde *f;* ~ **disk** copie *f* sur disque **II.** *vt* INFOR faire la sauvegarde de

backward ['bækwəd, *Am:* -wɚd] **I.** *adj* **1.** (*directed to the rear*) rétrograde **2.** (*slow in learning*) lent(e) **3.** (*underdeveloped*) arriéré(e) ►**not to be** ~ **in coming forward** ne pas être modeste **II.** *adv s.* **backwards**

backward-looking *adj* réactionnaire

backwards ['bækwədz, *Am:* -wɚdz] *adv* **1.** (*towards the back*) en arrière; **to go** ~ **and forwards** (*machine part*) aller d'avant en arrière; (*person*) faire l'aller-retour **2.** (*in reverse*) à reculons **3.** (*into past*) **to look** ~ remonter dans le passé ►**to bend over** ~ se couper en quatre; **to know sth** ~ connaître qc comme le dos de sa main

backwater ['bækˌwɔːtəʳ, *Am:* -ˌwɑːt̬ɚ] *n* **1.** (*river*) bras *m* de décharge **2.** *fig, pej* trou *m* perdu

backwoods ['bækwʊdz] **I.** *npl* forêts *fpl* de l'intérieur ►**in the** ~ dans un bled **II.** *adj* **1.** des forêts **2.** *fig* rustre

backwoodsman ['bækwʊdzmən] *n* <-men> **1.** colon *m* de l'arrière-pays **2.** *fig* péquenaud *m*

backyard *n* **1.** *Brit* (*yard*) arrière-cour *f* **2.** *Am* (*garden*) jardin *m* ►**in one's own** ~ tout près de chez soi

bacon ['beɪkən] *n* lard *m* ►**to bring home the** ~ faire bouillir la marmite

bacteria [bæk'tɪərɪə] *n pl of* **bacterium**

bacteriologist [bækˌtɪərɪ'ɒlədʒɪst, *Am:* -ˌtɪrɪ'ɑːlə-] *n* bactériologiste *mf*

bacterium [bæk'tɪərɪəm] <-ria> *n* bactérie *f*

bad [bæd] <worse, worst> **I.** *adj* **1.** (*opp: good*) mauvais(e); (*neighbourhood*) mal fréquenté(e); **sb's** ~ **points** les défauts de qn; ~ **luck** malchance *f;* **a** ~ **cheque** un chèque en bois; ~ **at history/tennis** mauvais en histoire/tennis; **to go from** ~ **to worse** aller de mal en pis; **not too** ~ pas trop mal; **not** ~**!** pas mal!; **too** ~ tant pis **2.** (*difficult*) ~ **times** temps *mpl* difficiles **3.** (*harmful*) **to be** ~ **for sth/sb** ne pas être bon pour qc/qn **4.** (*spoiled*) pourri(e) **5.** MED grave; **to have a** ~ **cold** avoir un bon rhume; **I have a** ~ **leg/back** j'ai des problèmes avec ma jambe/mon dos **6.** (*unacceptable*) **to use** ~ **language** dire des gros mots **II.** *adv inf* mal; **to feel** ~ se sentir mal; **to look** ~ avoir l'air malade **III.** *n no pl* mal *m;* **the** ~ les méchants; **to go to the** ~ courir à sa perte

badge [bædʒ] *n* insigne *m;* (*with slogan*) badge *m*

badger ['bædʒəʳ, *Am:* -ɚ] **I.** *n* blaireau *m* **II.** *vt* harceler

badly ['bædli] <worse, worst> *adv* **1.** (*poorly*) mal; **you didn't do too** ~ tu ne t'es pas trop mal débrouillé **2.** (*critically*) **to think** ~ **of sb** penser du mal de qn **3.** (*very much: want*) vraiment; **to be** ~ **in need of sth** avoir grand besoin de qc **4.** (*severely: hurt, affected*) gravement; ~ **defeated** battu à plate(s) couture(s)

badminton ['bædmɪntən] *n no pl* badminton *m*

baffle ['bæfl] *vt* (*confuse*) déconcerter

baffling *adj* (*confusing*) déconcertant(e)

bag [bæg] **I.** *n* **1.** sac *m;* (*of sweets*) sachet *m,* cornet *m Suisse* **2.** (*luggage*) sac *m* de voyage; **to pack one's** ~**s** faire ses bagages **3.** (*baggy skin*) poches *fpl* (sous les yeux) **4.** (*woman*) vieille grincheuse *f* **5.** (*game caught by hunter*) tableau *m* **6.** *pl, Aus, Brit, inf* **to have** ~**s of** avoir plein de ►**a** ~ **of bones** un sac d'os; **the whole** ~ **of tricks** tout le bataclan; **it's in the** ~ c'est du tout cuit **II.** *vt* <-gg-> **1.** (*put in bag*) mettre en sac **2.** *inf* (*obtain*) **to** ~ **sb sth** [*o* **sth for sb**] retenir qc pour qn **3.** (*hunt and kill*) abattre

baggage ['bægɪdʒ] *n no pl* **1.** (*luggage*) bagages *mpl;* **excess** ~ excédent *m* de bagages; ~ **reclaim area** secteur *m* de retrait des bagages **2.** MIL équipement *m*

baggage allowance *n* franchise *f* de bagage

baggage check *n Am* bulletin *m* de consigne **baggage handler** *n* bagagiste *m*

baggy ['bægi] *adj* trop ample; (*trousers*) trop grand(e)

bagpiper ['bægpaɪpəʳ, *Am:* -ɚ] *n* joueur *m* de cornemuse

bagpipes ['bægpaɪps] *npl* cornemuse *f*

Bahamas [bə'hɑːməz] *npl* **the** ~ [*o* **Bahama Islands**] les Bahamas *fpl*

Bahamian [bə'eɪmiən] **I.** *adj* bahamien(ne) **II.** *n* Bahamien(ne) *m(f)*

bail [beɪl] **I.** *n* caution *f;* **to jump** ~ se dérober à la justice; **to put up** ~ **for sb** se porter garant de qn; **to release sb on** ~ relâcher qn sous caution; **to set** ~ fixer la caution **II.** *vt* (*release*) libérer sous caution

◆**bail out** **I.** *vt* **1.** (*remove: water*) écoper **2.** (*rescue: person*) tirer d'affaire; (*company*) renflouer **II.** *vi* sauter

bailiff ['beɪlɪf] *n* huissier *m*

bait [beɪt] **I.** *n* **1.** SPORT appât *m* **2.** *fig* leurre *m;* **to swallow the** ~ mordre à l'hameçon **II.** *vt* **1.** (*put bait on*) amorcer **2.** (*harass*) harceler

3. (*annoy*) tourmenter

bake [beɪk] I. *n* gratin *m* II. *vi* 1. (*cook: meat, cake*) cuire au four; **I hardly ever ~** je fais rarement des gâteaux 2. *inf* (*be hot*) **to be baking** (*weather*) être torride; (*person*) crever de chaleur III. *vt* 1. (*cook*) cuire; **~d potato** pomme de terre en robe des champs 2. (*harden by heat*) durcir

baker ['beɪkəʳ, *Am:* -kɚ] *n* boulanger, -ère *m, f*

baker's shop *n* boulangerie *f*

bakery ['beɪkəri] *n* boulangerie *f*

baking I. *n no pl* cuisson *f* II. *adj* cuit(e)

baking powder *n* levure *f* chimique

balance ['bælənts] I. *n* 1. (*device*) balance *f* 2. *no pl, a. fig* équilibre *m;* **to lose one's ~** perdre l'équilibre 3. (*state of equality*) équilibre *m;* **to hold the ~ of power** être en position d'inverser l'équilibre des forces; **to strike a ~ between sth and sth** trouver le juste milieu entre deux choses; **to upset the ~** perturber l'équilibre; **on ~** tout compte fait 4. FIN solde *m;* **a healthy bank ~** un bon compte bancaire ►**to throw sb off ~** déconcerter qn II. *vi* 1. (*keep a steady position*) se tenir en équilibre 2. (*be equal*) s'équilibrer III. *vt* 1. (*compare*) **to ~ two things against each other** comparer les avantages de deux choses 2. (*keep in a position*) maintenir en équilibre; **to ~ sth on sth** tenir qc en équilibre sur qc; **to ~ each other** s'équilibrer 3. FIN (*books*) régler; (*budget*) équilibrer

◆**balance out** *vi* (*be equivalent*) se compenser

balanced *adj* (*diet*) équilibré(e); (*view, report, judgement*) pondéré(e)

balance of payments *n* balance *f* des paiements **balance of trade** *n* balance du commerce **balance sheet** *n* bilan *m*

balcony ['bælkəni] *n* balcon *m*

bald [bɔːld] *adj* 1. (*hairless*) chauve; **to go ~** se dégarnir; **~ as a coot** chauve comme un œuf 2. (*blunt*) simple 3. (*plain: facts*) brut(e)

bald-headed *adj* chauve

baldly [bɔːldli] *adv* sèchement

baldness ['bɔːldnɪs] *n no pl* calvitie *f*

bale [beɪl] I. *n* ballot *m* II. *vt* mettre en ballot

Balearic Islands *n* **the ~** les Iles *fpl* Baléares

Balearics [ˌbæli'ærɪks, *Am:* ˌbɑːli'-] *n* **the ~** les Baléares *fpl*

baleful [beɪlfʊl] *adj* sinistre; **a ~ glance** un regard torve

balk [bɔːk] I. *vi* hésiter; **to ~ at sth** hésiter devant qc II. *vt* contrarier

Balkan States *n* États *mpl* balkaniques

ball [bɔːl] *n* 1. GAMES (*for tennis, golf*) balle *f;* (*for football, rugby*) ballon coll *m* 2. (*round form*) boule *f;* **a ~ of string/wool** une pelote de ficelle/de laine; **to curl oneself into a ~** se rouler en boule 3. ANAT éminence *f;* **~ of the hand** thénar *m* 4. (*dance*) bal *m* ►**the ~ is in his court** la balle est dans son camp; **to be on the ~** avoir de la présence d'esprit; **to start the ~ rolling** mettre les choses en train; **to have a ~** bien s'amuser; **to play ~** jouer le jeu

ballad ['bæləd] *n* romance *f*

ballast ['bæləst] *n no pl* 1. (*heavy material*) lest *m* 2. (*gravel*) ballast *m*

ball bearing *n* roulement *m* à billes

ballet ['bæleɪ, *Am:* bæl'eɪ] *n* ballet *m*

ball field *n Am* terrain *m* de base-ball **ball game** *n Am* match *m* (*de base-ball*) ►**that's a whole new ~** c'est une autre histoire

ballistic [bə'lɪstɪk] *adj* ballistique

balloon [bə'luːn] I. *n* 1. GAMES ballon *m* 2. (*for flying*) montgolfière *f* 3. TYP (*in cartoons*) bulle *f* II. *vi* gonfler

balloonist *n* aéronaute *mf*

ballot ['bælət] I. *n* 1. (*process*) scrutin *m* 2. (*election*) vote *m;* **to put sth to the ~** soumettre qc au vote 3. (*paper*) bulletin *m* de vote II. *vi* voter III. *vt* appeler à voter

ballpoint (**pen**) [ˌbɔːlpɔɪnt (pen)] *n* stylo *m* (à) bille

ballroom ['bɔːlrʊm] *n* salle *f* de bal; **~ dancing** danse *f* de salon

balm [bɑːm] *n* baume *m*

balmy ['bɑːmi] <-ier, -iest> *adj* doux(douce)

Baltic ['bɔːltɪk] *n* **the ~** (**Sea**) la (mer) Baltique

balustrade [ˌbælə'streɪd, *Am:* 'bæl-] *n* balustrade *f*

bamboo [bæm'buː] *n no pl* bambou *m*

bamboozle [bæm'buːzl] *vt inf* 1. (*confuse*) laisser perplexe; **to be completely ~d** être complètement déboussolé 2. (*trick*) embobiner

ban [bæn] I. *n* ban *m;* **to place a ~ on sth** interdire II. *vt* <-nn-> (*person*) bannir; (*practice, guns*) interdire

banal [bə'nɑːl] *adj* banal(e)

banality [bə'næləti, *Am:* -əṭi] <-ies> *n* banalité *f*

banana [bə'nɑːnə, *Am:* -'nænə] *n* banane *f*

banana republic *n pej* république *f* bananière

band¹ [bænd] *n* 1. MUS orchestre *m;* (*pop group*) groupe *m;* **brass ~** fanfare *f* 2. (*group*) bande *f*

band² [bænd] I. *n* 1. (*strip*) bande *f;* **hat ~** ruban *m;* **head ~** bandeau *m;* **waist ~** ceinture *f* 2. (*range*) tranche *f;* **tax ~** tranche d'imposition 3. (*ring*) anneau *m;* **wedding ~** alliance *f* 4. (*section*) série *f;* **a ~ of light rain and showers** un passage de pluies légères et d'averses II. *vt* grouper

◆**band together** *vi* se grouper

bandage ['bændɪdʒ] I. *n* pansement *m* II. *vt* mettre un pansement à

B & B [ˌbiːənd'biː] *n abbr of* **bed and breakfast**

bandit ['bændɪt] *n* bandit *m*

bandmaster *n* chef *m* d'orchestre **bandsman** *n* <-men> membre *m* d'un orchestre **bandstand** *n* kiosque *m* à musique **bandwagon** *n* **to climb on the ~** prendre le train en marche

bandy¹ ['bændi] <-ier, -iest> *adj* (*legs*) arqué(e)

bandy² ['bændi] <-ies, -ied> *vt* échanger; **to ~ insults** s'envoyer des insultes

◆bandy about *vt* (*story*) faire circuler; (*names, figures*) lancer; (*ball*) se passer

bang [bæŋ] **I.** *n* **1.** (*explosion*) bang *m* **2.** (*blow*) coup *m* violent **3.** *pl, Am* (*fringe*) frange *f* **4.** *Am, vulg* (*sexual intercourse*) partie *f* de jambes en l'air **5.** *Am* (*drug dose*) dose *f* ►**to go with a ~** *inf* être un grand succès **II.** *adv* (*exactly*) **slap ~ into sth** en plein dans qc; **to halt ~ in the middle of the road** s'arrêter au beau milieu de la route; **~ on** en plein dans le mille; **~ up-to-date** parfaitement à jour ►**to go ~** exploser; **oh, well, ~ goes my pay rise** et voilà, envolée mon augmentation **III.** *interj* **bang!** bang! **IV.** *vi* (*hit*) claquer; **to ~ at the door** frapper à la porte **V.** *vt* **1.** (*hit*) **to ~ one's fist on the table** frapper du poing sur la table; **to ~ the receiver down** raccrocher brutalement; **to ~ one's knee/elbow** se cogner le genou/le coude **2.** (*cut hair*) **to ~ one's hair** *Am* se faire une frange **3.** *vulg* (*have sex with*) baiser ►**to ~ the drum for sth** faire de la pub pour qc

◆bang on *vt* **1.** (*hit: wall, nail*) cogner sur **2.** *inf* (*speak*) **to ~ about sth** ressasser qc

banger ['bæŋəʳ, *Am:* -ɚ] *n* **1.** *Brit, inf* (*car*) tacot *m* **2.** *Brit, inf* (*sausage*) saucisse *f* **3.** (*firework*) pétard *m*

Bangladesh [bæŋglə'deʃ] **I.** *n* le Bangladesh **II.** *adj* bangladais(e)

Bangladeshi [bæŋglə'deʃi] **I.** *n* Bangladais(e) *m(f)* **II.** *adj* bangladais(e)

bangle ['bæŋgl] *n* bracelet *m*

banish ['bænɪʃ] *vt* **to ~ sb from sth** exclure qn de qc; **to ~ sb from a country** bannir qn d'un pays; **he was ~ed to an island** il a été exilé dans une île

banishment *n no pl* bannissement *m*

banister ['bænɪstəʳ, *Am:* -əstɚ] *n* rampe *f* (d'escalier)

banjo ['bændʒəʊ] <-s *o* -oes> *n* banjo *m*

bank¹ [bæŋk] **I.** *n* banque *f;* **to pay sth into the ~** déposer qc à la banque; **to play ~** être la banque; **blood/data ~** banque du sang/de données **II.** *vi* **to ~ with ...** avoir un compte à ... **III.** *vt* (*deposit*) **to ~ money/valuables** déposer de l'argent/des objets de valeur

bank² [bæŋk] *n* (*row*) rangée *f*

bank³ [bæŋk] **I.** *n* **1.** (*edge: of river*) bord *m;* (*of land*) talus *m;* (*of road*) remblai *m;* **the river broke its ~s** la rivière est sorti de son lit **2.** (*elevation in water*) banc *m* **3.** AVIAT virage *m* incliné **4.** (*mass*) massif *m;* (*of cloud*) amoncellement *m;* (*of fog*) couche *f* **II.** *vi* AVIAT virer (sur l'aile) **III.** *vt* **1.** (*cover*) **to ~ the fire** couvrir le feu **2.** AVIAT **to ~ an aeroplane** faire virer un avion sur l'aile

◆bank on *vt* (*result, help*) compter sur; **to ~ sth happening** compter sur le fait que qc se passe (*subj*)

◆bank up I. *vi* s'amonceler **II.** *vt* entasser

bank account *n* compte *m* bancaire **bank book** *n* livret *m* (de banque) **bank card** *n* carte *f* bancaire **bank charges** *n* frais *mpl* bancaires **bank clerk** *n* employé(e) *m(f)* de banque

banker ['bæŋkəʳ, *Am:* -kɚ] *n* **1.** FIN banquier, -ère *m, f* **2.** GAMES banque *f*

bank holiday *n* **1.** *Brit* jour *m* férié **2.** *Am* jour *m* de fermeture des banques

banking *n* banque *f*

banking hours *npl* heures *fpl* d'ouverture des banques

bank manager *n* directeur, -trice *m, f* d'agence **banknote** *n* billet *m* de banque **bank rate** *n* taux *m* d'escompte **bank robber** *n* cambrioleur, -euse *m, f* (de banque) **bank robbery** *n* hold-up *m* (de banque)

bankrupt ['bæŋkrʌpt] **I.** *n* **to declare sb a ~** déclarer qn en faillite **II.** *vt* mettre en faillite **III.** *adj* **1.** (*insolvent: firm*) en faillite; **a ~ farmer/industrialist** un agriculteur/industriel qui a fait faillite; **to go ~** faire faillite **2.** *form* **to be morally ~** n'avoir aucune moralité

bankruptcy ['bæŋkrəptsi] <-ies> *n* faillite *f*

bank statement *n* relevé *m* de compte **bank transfer** *n* virement *m* bancaire

banner ['bænəʳ, *Am:* -ɚ] *n* **1.** (*flag*) bannière *f* **2.** (*slogan*) devise *f*

banner headline *n* gros titre *m*

banns [bænz] *npl* bans *mpl*

banquet ['bæŋkwɪt, *Am:* -kwət] **I.** *n* banquet *m* **II.** *vi* festoyer

banquet-hall, **banqueting-hall** *n* salle *f* des banquets

bantam ['bæntəm, *Am:* -t̬əm] *n* **1.** (*chicken*) poulet *m* nain (de Bantam) **2.** SPORT poids-coq *m*

banter ['bæntəʳ, *Am:* -t̬ɚ] **I.** *n* plaisanteries *fpl* **II.** *vi* plaisanter

baptise [bæp'taɪz] *vt Aus, Brit s.* **baptize**

baptism ['bæptɪzəm] *n* baptême *m*

baptismal ['bæptɪzməl] *adj* baptismal(e); **~ certificate** certificat *m* de baptême; **~ font** fonts *mpl* baptismaux

Baptist ['bæptɪst] *n* baptiste *mf;* **John the ~** Saint Jean-Baptiste

baptize [bæp'taɪz, *Am:* 'bæp-] *vt* baptiser; **to be ~d a Protestant/Catholic** être baptisé protestant/catholique; **I was ~d Charles** Charles est mon nom de baptême

bar¹ [bɑːʳ, *Am:* bɑːr] **I.** *n* **1.** (*elongated piece: of steel*) barre *f;* (*of chocolate*) tablette *f;* (*of gold*) lingot *m;* (*of soap*) savonnette *f* **2.** (*rod: of cage*) barreau *m* **3.** (*band: of light*) raie *f;* (*of colour*) bande *f* **4.** GASTR bar *m;* (*counter*) comptoir *m* **5.** LAW **to be called to the Bar** être inscrit au barreau **6.** MUS mesure *f;* **beats to [*o* in] the ~** temps par mesure; **~ line** barre *f* de mesure **7.** SPORT barre *f* **8.** (*heating element*) résistance *f* **9.** *fig* obstacle *m* **II.** *vt*

<-rr-> 1. (*fasten*) verrouiller 2. (*obstruct*) barrer; **to ~ the way** bloquer le passage; **to ~ the way to sth** faire obstacle à qc 3. (*prohibit*) **to ~ sb from sth/doing sth** défendre qc à qn/à qn de faire qc; **to be ~red from playing** être interdit de jeu

bar² [bɑːʳ, *Am:* bɑːr] *prep Brit* (*except for*) **~ sb/sth** excepté qn/qc; **~ none** sans exception

Bar [bɑːʳ, *Am:* bɑːr] *n* LAW **the ~** le barreau

barb [bɑːb, *Am:* bɑːrb] *n* 1. (*part of hook*) ardillon *m* 2. (*insult*) pointe *f*

Barbadian [bɑː'beɪdiən, *Am:* bɑːr-] I. *adj* barbadien(ne) II. *n* Barbadien(ne) *m(f)*

Barbados [bɑː'bəɪdɒs, *Am:* bɑːr'bəɪdoʊs] *n* la Barbade

barbarian [bɑː'beərɪən, *Am:* bɑːr'berɪ-] *n* barbare *mf*

barbaric [bɑː'bærɪk, *Am:* bɑːr'ber-] *adj* barbare

barbarity [bɑː'bærəti, *Am:* bɑːr'berəṱi] *n* <-ies> barbarie *f*

barbarous ['bɑːbərəs, *Am:* 'bɑːr-] *adj* barbare

barbecue ['bɑːbɪkjuː, *Am:* 'bɑːr-] I. *n* barbecue *m* II. *vt* griller au barbecue

barbed [bɑːbd, *Am:* bɑːrbd] *adj* 1. (*with barbs*) barbelé(e) 2. (*hurtful*) acéré(e)

barber ['bɑːbəʳ, *Am:* 'bɑːrbɚ] *n* coiffeur *m*, barbier *m Québec*

barbershop ['bɑːbəʃɒp, *Am:* 'bɑːrbɚʃɑːp] *n no pl* salon *m* de coiffure pour hommes

barbiturate [bɑː'bɪtjʊrɪt, *Am:* bɑːr'bɪtʃrət] *n* barbiturique *m*

bar code *n* code-barre *m* **bar code scanner** *n* lecteur *m* de code-barres

bare [beəʳ, *Am:* ber] I. *adj* 1. (*uncovered*) nu(e); **with my ~ hands** avec mes mains nues 2. (*empty*) vide; **stripped ~** (*room*) complètement vide; **to be ~ of sth** être dépouillé de qc 3. (*unadorned: fact*) brut(e); (*truth*) nu(e) 4. (*little: minimum*) strict(e); **the ~ necessities of life** le minimum vital ►**the ~ bones of a story** l'essentiel de l'histoire II. *vt* **to ~ one's head** se découvrir la tête; **to ~ one's heart/soul to sb** dévoiler son cœur/son âme à qn; **to ~ one's teeth** montrer les dents

bareback ['beəbæk, *Am:* 'ber-] *adj* dos nu; **~ rider** écuyer, -ère *m, f* de cirque

barefaced ['beəfeɪst, *Am:* 'ber-] *adj pej* éhonté(e)

barefoot ['beəfʊt, *Am:* 'ber-], **barefooted** *adj, adv* pieds nus

bareheaded *adj, adv* tête nue

barely ['beəli, *Am:* 'ber-] *adv* 1. (*hardly*) à peine 2. (*scantily: furnished*) pauvrement

bareness *n* (*of person*) nudité *f;* (*of thing*) dépouillement *m*

bargain ['bɑːgɪn, *Am:* 'bɑːr-] I. *n* 1. (*agreement*) marché *m;* **to drive a hard ~** marchander dur; **to strike a ~** conclure un marché 2. (*item*) affaire *f;* **a real ~** une bonne affaire ►**into the ~** par-dessus le marché II. *vi* 1. (*negotiate*) **to ~ for sth** négocier pour qc 2. (*exchange*) **to ~ away sth** brader qc; **I've ~ed away my freedom for it** j'ai renoncé à ma liberté pour ça

◆**bargain for, bargain on** *vi* compter sur; **to get more than one bargained for** *fig* en avoir plus que son compte

bargain basement *n* rayon *m* des bonnes affaires

bargaining *n* négociation *f;* **collective ~** négotiations *fpl* syndicales (*avec la direction*); **~ chip** monnaie *f* d'échange (*dans une négociation*)

bargain offer *n* offre *f* exceptionnelle **bargain price** *n* prix *m* avantageux **bargain sale** *n* soldes *fpl*

barge [bɑːdʒ, *Am:* bɑːrdʒ] I. *n* péniche *f* II. *vt* **to ~ one's way to the front** foncer vers l'avant

◆**barge in** *vi* faire irruption; **sorry to ~** désolé de vous interrompre

◆**barge into** *vi* faire irruption dans; **to ~ sb** bousculer qn

◆**barge through** *vi* pousser (tout le monde)

baritone ['bærɪtəʊn, *Am:* 'berətoʊn] I. *n* baryton *m* II. *adj* de baryton

bark¹ [bɑːk, *Am:* bɑːrk] I. *n* 1. ZOOL aboiement *m* 2. (*cough*) toux *f* sèche II. *vi, vt* aboyer ►**to ~ up the wrong tree** se tromper (de cible)

◆**bark out** *vt* **to ~ an order** aboyer un ordre

bark² [bɑːk, *Am:* bɑːrk] *n no pl* BOT écorce *f*

barkeeper ['bɑːkiːpəʳ, *Am:* 'bɑːrkiːpɚ] *n Am* 1. (*owner or manager*) patron(ne) *m(f)* 2. (*person serving drinks*) serveur, -euse *m, f*

barley ['bɑːli, *Am:* 'bɑːr-] *n no pl* orge *f*

barmaid ['bɑːmeɪd, *Am:* 'bɑːr-] *n* serveuse *f*

barman ['bɑːmən, *Am:* 'bɑːr-] *n* <-men> barman *m*

barn [bɑːn, *Am:* bɑːrn] *n* grange *f*

barn owl *n* effraie *f*

barnyard *n* basse-cour *f*

barometer [bə'rɒmɪtəʳ, *Am:* -'rɑːməṱɚ] *n* baromètre *m*

barometric [ˌbærəʊ'metrɪk], **barometrical** *adj* barométrique; (*pressure*) atmosphérique

baron ['bærən, *Am:* 'ber-] *n* 1. baron *m* 2. *fig* **drug ~** baron *m* de la drogue; **press ~** magnat *m* de la presse

baroness ['bærənɪs, *Am:* 'bernəs] *n* baronne *f*

baronet ['bærənɪt, *Am:* 'bernət] *n* baronnet *m*

baroque [bə'rɒk, *Am:* -'roʊk] *adj* baroque

barrack ['bærək, *Am:* 'ber-] I. *vi Aus* **to ~ for sth/sb** soutenir qn/qc II. *vt* chahuter

barracks *n pl* caserne *f*

barrage ['bærɑːʒ, *Am:* bə'rɑːʒ] *n* 1. MIL tir *m* de barrage 2. *fig* (*of questions*) déluge *m* 3. *Brit* (*barrier*) barrage *m*

barrel ['bærəl, *Am:* 'ber-] I. *n* 1. (*container*) tonneau *m* 2. (*measure*) baril *m* 3. (*part of gun*) canon *m* ►**to be a ~ of fun** être très marrant; **I wouldn't say he's a ~ of laughs** c'est pas un marrant; **to have sb over a ~** tenir qn à sa merci **II.** *vi* <-ll- *Brit o* -l- *Am*> *inf* (*drive fast*) foncer **III.** *vt* <-ll- *Brit o* -l- *Am*> mettre en fût

barrel organ *n* orgue *f* de barbarie

barren ['bærən, *Am:* 'ber-] *adj* stérile; (*landscape*) aride

barrenness *n* stérilité *f*

barricade [ˌbærɪ'keɪd, *Am:* ˌberə-] **I.** *n* barricade *f* **II.** *vt* barricader; **to ~ oneself into sth** se barricader dans qc

barrier ['bærɪəʳ, *Am:* 'berɪɚ] *n* barrière *f*

barrier cream *n Brit* crème *f* écran

barring ['bɑːrɪŋ] *prep* excepté; **~ error/the unexpected** sauf erreur/imprévu

barrister ['bærɪstəʳ, *Am:* 'berɪstɚ] *n Aus, Brit* avocat(e) *m(f)*

barrow ['bærəʊ, *Am:* 'beroʊ] *n* brouette *f*

bartender ['bɑːtendəʳ, *Am:* 'bɑːrtendɚ] *n* barman *m*, barmaid *f*

barter ['bɑːtəʳ, *Am:* 'bɑːrt̬ɚ] **I.** *n no pl* troc *m* **II.** *vi* **1.** faire du troc; **to ~ for sth with sth** troquer qc contre qc **2.** (*haggle*) marchander **III.** *vt* **to ~ sth for sth** troquer qc contre qc

basalt ['bæsɔːlt, *Am:* bə'sɔːlt] *n no pl* basalte *m*

base[1] [beɪs] **I.** *n* (*headquarters, supporting part*) base *f*; (*of statue*) socle *m*; (*of tree, post*) pied *m* ►**to be off ~** *Am, inf* dérailler; **to touch ~** *Am* prendre contact **II.** *vt* **1.** (*place, support*) *a.* MIL baser; **a Brighton-based firm** une société basée à Brighton **2.** (*develop using sth*) **to ~ sth on sth** baser qc sur qc; **the theory is ~d on evidence** sa théorie est construite sur des preuves; **to be ~d on a novel** être basé sur un roman

base[2] [beɪs] *adj* **1.** (*not honourable*) indigne; (*behaviour*) ignoble **2.** (*not pure: metal*) vil(e)

baseball ['beɪsbɔːl] *n* **1.** (*game*) base-ball *m* **2.** (*ball*) balle *f* de base-ball

baseless ['beɪslɪs] *adj* sans fondement; (*accusation*) injustifié(e)

baseline ['beɪslaɪn] *n* **1.** SPORT ligne *f* de fond **2.** (*basis*) base *f*

base rate *n Brit* taux *m* de base

bash [bæʃ] **I.** *n* **1.** (*blow*) coup *m* **2.** *inf* (*party*) fête *f* **II.** *vt* **1.** (*hit hard*) **to ~ sth against sth** cogner qc contre qc **2.** (*criticize*) démolir

◆**bash into** *vi insep* **to ~ sb/sth** rentrer dans qc/qn

◆**bash up** *vt inf* (*person*) donner une raclée à; (*car*) démolir

bashful ['bæʃfl] *adj* timide; **to feel ~ about doing sth** se sentir intimidé à l'idée de faire qc

bashfulness *n no pl* timidité *f*

BASIC ['beɪsɪk] *n* INFOR *abbr of* **Beginner's All-purpose Symbolic Instruction Code** BASIC *m*

basic *adj* **1.** (*fundamental*) fondamental(e); (*needs*) premier(-ère); **to be ~ to sth** être essentiel à qc; **the ~ idea is to …** l'idée essentielle est de; **the ~ facts** les faits principaux; **~ requirements** minimum requis **2.** (*lowest in level*) rudimentaire; **to have a ~ command of English** avoir des connaissances de base en anglais; **~ vocabulary** vocabulaire *m* de base **3.** CHEM basique

basically *adv* en fait

basic pay *n* salaire *m* de base

basil ['bæzəl, *Am:* 'beɪzəl] *n* basilic *m*

basilica [bə'zɪlɪkə, *Am:* -'sɪl-] *n* basilique *f*

basin ['beɪsn] *n* **1.** (*bowl*) cuvette *f* **2.** (*sink*) lavabo *m*

basis ['beɪsɪs] *n* <bases> base 1 *f*; **to be the ~ for** (*agreement, discussion, progress, plan*) être le point de départ de; (*calculation*) être la référence pour; **on the ~ of sth** sur la base de qc; **to do sth on a voluntary ~** faire qc en tant que bénévole

bask [bɑːsk, *Am:* bæsk] *vi* **1.** (*warm oneself*) **to ~ in the sun** se prélasser au soleil **2.** *fig* **to ~ in sb's approval** jouir de l'approbation de qn

basket ['bɑːskɪt, *Am:* 'bæskət] *n* panier *m* ►**to be a ~ case** *pej* être un paumé

basketball ['bɑːskɪtbɔːl, *Am:* 'bæskətbɔːl] *n* basket-ball *m*

bass[1] [beɪs] *n* **1.** (*instrument, voice*) basse *f*; **to sing ~** chanter la basse **2.** (*singer*) basse *f*

bass[2] [bæs] *n* bar *m*

bass drum *n* grosse caisse *f*

bassoon [bə'suːn] *n* basson *m*

bastard ['bɑːstəd, *Am:* 'bæstɚd] *n* **1.** bâtard *m* **2.** *fig, pej, vulg* salaud *m*; **to be a real ~ to sb** être un vrai salaud envers qn; **you ~!** salaud!; **to be a lucky** [*o Brit* **jammy**] **~** être un sacré veinard

baste [beɪst] *vt* **1.** (*moisten food*) arroser **2.** *Am, Aus* (*tack*) bâtir

bastion ['bæstɪən, *Am:* -tʃən] *n* bastion *m*; **a ~ of freedom** un bastion pour la liberté

bat[1] [bæt] *n* ZOOL chauve-souris *f* ►**to have ~s in the belfry** avoir une araignée au plafond; **like a ~ out of hell** comme un fou; **to leave like a ~ out of hell** partir comme si on avait le diable aux trousses; (**as**) **blind as a ~** myope comme une taupe

bat[2] [bæt] *vt* **to ~ one's eyelids at sb** battre des paupières pour qn ►**she didn't ~ an eyelid when …** elle n'a pas bronché quand …

bat[3] [bæt] **I.** *n* batte *f* ►**right off the ~** *Am* sur le champ; **to do sth off one's own ~** *Brit, inf* faire qc de sa propre initiative **II.** *vi* <-tt-> être à la batte **III.** *vt* <-tt-> **to ~ the ball** frapper la balle

batch [bætʃ] **I.** <-es> *n* (*from oven*) fournée *f*; (*of items, material*) lot *m*; (*of people*) groupe *m* **II.** *vt* **to ~ sth together** grouper qc

batch processing *n* INFOR traitement *m* par lots

bated ['beɪtɪd, *Am:* 'bæt̬-] *adj* **with ~ breath** en retenant son souffle

bath [bɑːθ, *Am:* bæθ] **I.** *n* **1.** (*water, wash*) bain *m*; **~ oil** huile *f* pour le bain; **to run sb a ~** faire couler un bain à qn; **to give sb/sth a ~** baigner qn/qc; **to have** [*o* **take**] **a ~** prendre un bain **2.** (*tub*) baignoire *f* **3.** (*container*) cuvette *f* **II.** *vi* se baigner **III.** *vt* baigner

bath cube *n Brit* cube *m* parfumé pour le bain

bathe [beɪð] **I.** *vi* **1.** (*swim*) se baigner **2.** *Am* (*bath*) prendre un bain **II.** *vt* **1.** MED baigner; **to ~ one's eyes** se rincer les yeux; **to ~ one's feet** prendre un bain de pieds **2.** *fig* baigner; **to be ~d in sweat/tears** être en nage/baigné de larmes

bathing *n no pl* baignade *f;* **to go ~** aller se baigner

bathrobe *n* peignoir *m* de bain **bathroom** *n* **1.** (*room with bath*) salle *f* de bain **2.** *Am, Aus* (*lavatory*) toilettes *fpl* **bath towel** *n* serviette *f* de bain **bathtub** *n Am* baignoire *f*

batik [bæt'iːk, *Am:* bə'tiːk] *n no pl* batik *m;* **~ cloth** tissu *m* batik

baton ['bætən, *Am:* bə'tɑːn] *n* **1.** MUS baguette *f* **2.** (*for majorette*) canne *f* **3.** SPORT témoin *m;* **~ change** passe *f* **4.** (*truncheon*) matraque *f;* **~ charge** assaut *m* à la matraque

baton round *n Brit* cartouche *f* en plastique

batsman ['bætsmən] <-men> *n* batteur, -euse *m, f*

Batswana *npl* les Botwanais

battalion [bə'tælɪən, *Am:* -jən] *n* bataillon *m*

batten ['bætn] **I.** *n* latte *f* **II.** *vt* latter **III.** *vi* **to ~ on sb** vivre aux crochets de qn

batter ['bætəʳ, *Am:* 'bæt̬ɚ] **I.** *n* pâte *f* **II.** *vt* battre **III.** *vi* **to ~ at the door** tambouriner à la porte; **to ~ against the rocks** battre les rochers

battered ['bætəd, *Am:* -ɚd] *adj* **1.** (*injured*) battu(e) **2.** (*damaged: car*) cabossé(e); (*furniture*) délabré(e) **3.** (*covered in batter*) en beignet; **~ fish** beignet *m* de poisson

battering ['bætərɪŋ, *Am:* 'bæt̬-] *n* **1.** (*attack*) **to give sb a ~** rouer qn de coups **2.** *inf* (*defeat*) **to take a ~** prendre une râclée

battery ['bætəri, *Am:* 'bæt̬-] <-ies> *n* **1.** ELEC pile *f;* **batteries not included** piles vendues séparément; **~-operated** (qui fonctionne) à piles **2.** (*large amount*) *a.* AUTO, MIL batterie *f*

battery charger *n* chargeur *m* **battery hen** *n Aus, Brit* poulet *m* de batterie

battle ['bætl, *Am:* 'bæt̬-] **I.** *n* (*combat*) bataille *f;* **to be killed in ~** être mort au combat; **to join ~** entrer dans le conflit; **~ of wits/words** joute *f* verbale/oratoire; **to do ~** s'opposer; **~ against/for sth** lutte *f* contre/pour qc; **to fight a ~ for sth** se battre pour qc ►**to lose the ~ but win the war** perdre une bataille mais pas la guerre; **it's half the ~** c'est la moitié du travail; **to fight a losing ~** livrer une bataille perdue d'avance **II.** *vi* **1.** (*fight*) **to ~ over sth** se battre pour qc **2.** *fig* **to ~ against/for sth** lutter contre/pour qc **III.** *vt* combattre

battle cry *n* cri *m* de guerre **battledress** *n no pl* tenue *f* de combat **battlefield, battleground** *n a. fig* champ *m* de bataille

battlements ['bætlmənts, *Am:* 'bæt̬-] *npl* remparts *mpl*

battleship ['bætlʃɪp, *Am:* 'bæt̬-] *n* cuirassé *m*

baud [bɔːd, *Am:* bɑːd] *n* INFOR **~ (rate)** baud *m*

baulk [bɔːk, *Am:* bɑːk] *vi s.* **balk**

bauxite ['bɔːksaɪt, *Am:* 'bɑːk-] *n no pl* bauxite *f*

bawdy ['bɔːdi, *Am:* 'bɑː-] <-ier, -iest> *adj* paillard(e)

bawl [bɔːl, *Am:* bɑːl] **I.** *vi* brailler; **to ~ at sb** hurler contre qn; **to ~ at sb to come** appeler qn en hurlant **II.** *vt* **to ~ one's eyes out** pleurer toutes les larmes de son corps

bay¹ [beɪ] *n* GEO baie *f*

bay² [beɪ] *n* BOT laurier *m*

bay³ [beɪ] *n* **1.** (*marked-off space*) emplacement *m;* **loading ~** aire *f* de chargement **2.** (*recess*) renfoncement *m*

bay⁴ [beɪ] *n* (*horse*) cheval *m* bai

bay⁵ [beɪ] **I.** *vi* **1.** (*bark*) aboyer **2.** *fig, pej* **to ~ for blood** être assoiffé de sang **II.** *n no pl, a. fig* **to be at ~** être aux abois; **to hold sth/sb at ~** tenir qc/qn à distance

Bay of Biscay [-'bɪskeɪ] *n* Golfe *m* de Gascogne

bayonet ['beɪənɪt, *Am:* ˌbeɪə'net] **I.** *n* baïonnette *f;* **to fix ~s** fixer la baïonnette au canon **II.** *vt* passer à la baïonnette

bay window *n* fenêtre *f* en saillie

bazaar [bə'zɑːʳ, *Am:* -'zɑːr] *n* **1.** bazar *m* **2.** (*event*) vente *f* de charité

BBC ['biːbiː'siː] *n abbr of* **British Broadcasting Corporation** BBC *f*

BC [ˌbiː'siː] **I.** *n abbr of* **British-Columbia** **II.** *adv abbr of* **before Christ** av JC

BCG [ˌbiːsiː'dʒiː] *n abbr of* **bacillus of Calmette and Guérin** BCG *m*

be [biː] <was, been> **I.** *vi* + *n/adj* **1.** (*expresses identity, position, place*) **he's ~ English/a dentist** il est anglais/dentiste; **it's a key** c'est une clef; **to ~ in Spain** être en Espagne; **the statues are in the Louvre** les statues se trouvent au Louvre **2.** (*expresses a state, situation*) **I'm cold/hungry** j'ai froid/faim; **my hands are cold** j'ai froid aux mains; **how are you? – I'm fine** comment vas-tu/allez-vous? – je vais bien; **~ quiet!** reste(z) tranquille!; **to ~ on a diet** faire un régime; **to ~ on the pill** prendre la pilule; **to ~ on benefit** [*o* **welfare** *Am*] toucher des allocations **3.** (*expresses calculation/price*) **two and two is four** deux et deux font quatre; **this book is 50p** ce livre fait 50 pence **4.** (*indicates age*) **how old is he? – he's twenty** quel âge a-t-il? – il a vingt ans **5.** (*take place*) **the meeting is next Tuesday** la réunion a lieu mardi prochain **6.** (*exist*) **there is/are …** il y a …; **let her ~!** laisse-la tranquille! **7.** (*impersonal use*) **what is it?** qu'est-ce que c'est?; **it's three** il est trois heures; **it's cold/windy** il fait froid/du vent; **it's rainy** il pleut; **it's fair** c'est juste; **what's it to ~?** ce sera?; **as it were** pour ainsi dire ▸the ~-all and end-all le but suprême; ~ that as it may malgré cela; so ~ it soit; far ~ it from sb to *+infin* loin de qn l'idée de *+infin; s.a.* off II. *aux* 1. (*expresses continuation*) **he's breathing** il respire; **she's still sleeping** elle est encore en train de dormir; **it's raining** il pleut 2. (*expresses possibility*) **can it ~ that ...?** *form* est-ce possible que *+subj* ?; **the exhibition is to ~ seen at the gallery** on peut voir l'exposition à la galerie; **what is he to do?** qu'est-il censé faire?; **may I ~ of service?** je peux vous aider? 3. (*expresses passive*) **to ~ discovered by sb** être découvert par qn; **to ~ left speechless** rester bouche bée; **I'm asked to come at seven** on me demande de venir à sept heures 4. (*expresses future*) **she's leaving tomorrow** elle part demain; **you are to wait here** vous devez attendre ici; **we are to meet at seven** on est censé se rencontrer à sept heures 5. (*expresses future in past*) **she was never to see her brother again** elle n'allait jamais plus revoir son frère 6. (*in conditionals*) **if sb were** [*o* **was**] **were to** *+infin*, ... si qn devait *+infin*, ...; **if he were to work harder, he'd get better grades** s'il travaillait plus, il aurait de meilleures notes; **were sb to** *+infin*, ... *form* si qn devait *+infin*, ...

beach [biːtʃ] *n* plage *f*

beachhead ['biːtʃhed] *n* tête *f* de pont

beachwear ['biːtʃweəʳ, *Am:* -wer] *n no pl* tenues *fpl* de plage

beach wrap *n* paréo *m*

beacon ['biːkən] *n* 1. (*light*) signal *m* lumineux 2. (*signal*) balise *f* 3. (*lighthouse*) phare *m* 4. (*guide*) flambeau *m*; **a ~ of hope** un symbole d'espoir

bead [biːd] *n a. fig* perle *f* ▸**to draw a ~ on sth** viser qc

beading ['biːdɪŋ] *n* baguette *f*

beady ['biːdi] <-ier, -iest> *adj pej* **to have one's ~ eye(s) on sb/sth** avoir qn/qc à l'œil

beak [biːk] *n* 1. ZOOL bec *m* 2. *inf* (*nose*) nez *m* crochu

beaker ['biːkəʳ, *Am:* -kɚ] *n* gobelet *m*

beam [biːm] I. *n* 1. (*stream of light*) rayon *m*; PHYS faisceau *m* (lumineux); **full ~** AUTO pleins phares *mpl* 2. *a.* SPORT poutre *f*; **exposed wooden ~s** des poutres apparentes 3. (*big smile*) grand sourire *m* ▸**to be off ~** être à côté de la plaque II. *vt* 1. (*transmit*) diffuser 2. (*send*) diriger III. *vi* 1. **to ~ down on sth/sb** rayonner sur qc/qn 2. (*smile*) sourire largement; **she was ~ing at me** elle me donnait un grand sourire

beaming *adj* rayonnant(e)

bean [biːn] *n* 1. (*seed*) haricot *m*, fève *f Québec*; **runner/green** [*o* **French**] **~s** haricots plats/verts; **baked ~s** *haricots blancs à la sauce tomate* 2. (*pod*) cosse *f* ▸**not to have a ~** *inf* ne pas avoir un radis; **to be full of ~s** ne pas tenir en place; **to spill the ~s to sb** vendre la mèche à qn

beanbag *n* (*seat*) coussin *m* sac

beansprouts *n* germes *mpl* de soja

bear¹ [beəʳ, *Am:* ber] *n* 1. ZOOL ours *m*; **a she ~** une ourse 2. *fig, inf* **to be like a ~ with a sore head** [*o* **like a real ~** *Am*] être d'une humeur massacrante

bear² [beəʳ, *Am:* ber] <bore, borne> I. *vt* 1. (*carry, display*) porter; **he bore himself with dignity** il s'est montré digne 2. (*bring: letter, news*) porter 3. (*endure, deal with*) **to ~ a load/the cost** supporter une charge/le coût; **to ~ the burden/the pain** supporter le poids/la douleur; **to ~ hardship** endurer des épreuves; **to ~ the blame** endosser la responsabilité; **I can't ~ the suspense** je ne supporte plus l'attente; **I can't ~ the idea** l'idée m'est insupportable; **it doesn't ~ close examination** ça ne résiste pas à l'examen 4. (*show*) **to ~ sb ill-will** en vouloir à qn; **to ~ an (uncanny) likeness to sb** avoir une (troublante) ressemblance avec qn 5. (*keep*) **to ~ sth/sb in mind** penser à qn/qc 6. <born> *pp in passive* (*give birth to*) **to ~ a baby** donner naissance à un enfant; **to ~ sb a child** donner un enfant à qn; **animals ~ young** les animaux se reproduisent 7. (*generate*) **to ~ fruit** donner des fruits; *fig* porter ses fruits 8. FIN, ECON **to ~ interest** rapporter un intérêt II. *vi* 1. (*move*) **to ~ east** prendre la direction est; **to ~ left/right** prendre à gauche/droite 2. (*have influence*) **to bring pressure to ~ on sb** faire pression sur qn

◆**bear down on** *vi* foncer sur

◆**bear out** *vt* (*evidence, idea*) confirmer; (*person*) donner raison à

◆**bear up** *vi* ne pas se laisser abattre; **~!** courage!

◆**bear with** *vi* supporter; **to ~ sb** être patient avec qn

bearable ['beərəbl, *Am:* 'berə-] *adj* supportable

beard [bɪəd, *Am:* bɪrd] *n* 1. (*hair*) barbe *f*; **to grow a ~** se laisser pousser une barbe; **to have a ~** porter la barbe 2. ZOOL bouc *m*

bearded *adj* barbu(e)

beardless ['bɪədləs, *Am:* 'bɪrd-] *adj* imberbe

bearer ['beərəʳ, *Am:* 'berɚ] *n* 1. (*messenger*) porteur, -euse *m, f* 2. (*owner: of title, cheque*) porteur, -euse *m, f*; (*of passport, licence*) titulaire *mf*

bearing ['beərɪŋ, *Am:* 'berɪŋ] *n* 1. (*exact position*) position *f*; **to plot one's ~s** tracer sa route; **to take a ~ on sth** s'orienter par rapport à qc; **to lose one's ~s** se désorienter; **to get one's ~s** *fig* s'orienter 2. (*posture*) maintien *m* 3. (*air*) allure *f* 4. TECH **ball ~** roulement *m* à billes 5. (*relevance*) influence *f*; **to have some ~ on sth** influer sur qc

bearskin ['beəskɪn, *Am:* 'ber-] *n* peau *f* d'ours

beast [biːst] *n* 1. (*animal*) bête *f*; **~ of burden** bête de somme; **the king of the ~s** le roi des animaux 2. *inf* (*person*) sale bête *f*; **to**

be a ~ to sb être une peste envers qn; **to bring out the ~ in sb** réveiller la bête qui sommeille en qn **3.** *fig* **a ~ of a day** une sale journée

beastly ['bi:stli] <-ier, -iest> *adj inf* dégueulasse; (*meal*) dégoûtant(e)

beat [bi:t] <beat, -en> **I.** *n* **1.** (*pulsation*) battement *m* **2.** MUS temps *m;* (*rhythm*) rythme *m;* **~s to** [*o* **in**] **the bar** temps par mesure; **a strong ~** un temps fort; **to dance to the ~ of the music** danser au rythme de la musique **3.** *sing* (*police working area*) secteur *m;* **he's on the ~** faire une patrouille à pied **4.** *fig* **to be off sb's ~** ne pas relever du domaine de qn **II.** *adj inf* épuisé(e); **to be dead ~** *Brit* être crevé **III.** *vt* **1.** (*strike*) battre; **to ~ sb to death** battre qn à mort; **to ~ sb black and blue** rouer qn de coups; **to ~ a confession out of sb** obtenir une confession de qn par la force **2.** (*mix food*) **to ~ eggs** battre des œufs **3.** (*cut through*) **to ~ a path** se frayer un passage **4.** (*defeat*) battre; **to comfortably ~ sb/sth** battre qn/qc haut la main; **to ~ sb/sth fair and square** battre qn/qc loyalement **5.** *inf* (*be better than*) **to ~ sth/sb** être meilleur que qc/qn; **nothing ~s sth** rien ne vaut qc ►**to ~ one's brains out** *inf* se creuser la cervelle; **to ~ the (living) daylights out of sb** *inf* tabasser qn; **to ~ sb at his/her own game** battre qn à son propre jeu; **to ~ the pants off sb** [*o* **sb hollow** *Brit*] *inf* battre qn à plate(s) couture(s); **to ~ a path to sb's door** sonner à la porte de qn; **to ~ a retreat** battre en retraite; **if you can't ~ them, join them** *prov* une alliance vaut mieux qu'une défaite; **it ~s me** ça me dépasse; **~ it** dégage; **to ~ sb to it** devancer qn **IV.** *vi* battre

◆**beat back** *vt always sep* repousser; **the blaze was beaten back** les flammes ont été repoussées

◆**beat down I.** *vi* (*hail, rain*) battre; (*sun*) taper; **the rain was beating down** il pleuvait à verse **II.** *vt always sep* faire baisser; **I managed to beat him down to £35** j'ai réussi à le faire descendre à 35£

◆**beat off** *vt* repousser

◆**beat up I.** *vt always sep* passer à tabac **II.** *vi Am* **to ~ on sb** passer qn à tabac

beaten ['bi:tn, *Am:* 'bi:t̬n] *adj* (*metal*) martelé(e); (*earth*) battu(e); **off the ~ track** [*o* **path** *Am*] hors des sentiers battus

beater ['bi:tə^r^, *Am:* 'bi:t̬ɚ] *n* **1.** GASTR batteur *m* **2.** (*for carpets*) tapette *f* **3.** (*in hunting*) rabatteur, -euse *m, f*

beatification [bɪˌætɪfɪ'keɪʃn, *Am:* -ˌæt̬ə-] *n* béatification *f*

beatify [bɪ'ætɪfaɪ, *Am:* -'æt̬ə-] *vt* béatifier

beating ['bi:tɪŋ, *Am:* 'bi:t̬ɪŋ] *n* **1.** (*getting hit*) **to give sb a ~** rouer qn de coups **2.** (*defeat*) **to take a ~** se faire battre à plate(s) couture(s); **sth will take some ~** qc est imbattable

beatnik ['bi:tnɪk] *n* beatnik *mf*

beautician [bju:'tɪʃn] *n* esthéticien(ne) *m(f)*

beautiful ['bju:tɪfl, *Am:* -t̬ə-] *adj* **1.** (*attractive*) beau(belle) **2.** (*excellent*) magnifique **3.** (*trendy*) **the ~ people** beautiful people *mpl*

beautify ['bju:tɪfaɪ, *Am:* -t̬ə-] *vt* **to ~ oneself** se refaire une beauté

beauty ['bju:ti, *Am:* -t̬i] <-ies> *n* beauté *f;* **to be a (real) ~** être d'une grande beauté; (*car*) être une (véritable) merveille

beauty contest, **beauty pageant** *n* concours *m* de beauté **beauty parlour** *n,* **beauty salon** *n,* **beauty shop** *n Am* institut *m* de beauté **beauty spot** *n* **1.** (*location*) site *m* **2.** (*face mark*) mouche *f*

beaver ['bi:və^r^, *Am:* -vɚ] **I.** *n* **1.** ZOOL castor *m* **2.** (*person*) **to work like a ~** travailler d'arrache-pied **II.** *vi inf* **to ~ away at sth** travailler d'arrache-pied à qc

becalmed [bɪ'kɑ:md] *adj* **to be ~** être encalminé; (*stagnating*) être en stagnation

became [bɪ'keɪm] *pt of* **become**

because [bɪ'kɒz, *Am:* -'kɑ:z] **I.** *conj* parce que; **~ I said that, I had to leave** j'ai dû partir pour avoir dit cela; **~ it's snowing** à cause de la neige; **not ~ I am sad, but ...** non que je sois triste (*subj*), mais ... **II.** *prep* **~ of me** à cause de moi; **~ of illness** pour cause de maladie; **~ of the fine weather** en raison du beau temps

beck [bek] *n Brit* (*brook*) ruisseau *m* ►**to be at sb's ~ and call** être à la disposition de qn

beckon ['bekən] **I.** *vt* **to ~ sb over** faire signe à qn de venir; **to ~ sb to join us** faire signe à qn de nous rejoindre **II.** *vi* (*signal*) **to ~ to sb** faire signe à qn; **fame ~ed** *fig* la gloire lui souriait

become [bɪ'kʌm] <became, become> **I.** *vi + adj/n* devenir; **to ~ extinct** disparaître; **to ~ angry** s'énerver; **to ~ convinced that ...** se laisser gagner par la conviction que ...; **to ~ interested in sth/sb** commencer à s'intéresser à qc/qn; **I wonder what became of him** je me demande ce qu'il est devenu **II.** *vt* (*dress*) aller à; (*attitude*) convenir à

becquerel [ˌbekə'rel] *n* becquerel *m*

bed [bed] *n* **1.** (*furniture*) lit *m;* **to get out of ~** se lever; **to go to ~** aller au lit; **to put sb to ~** mettre qn au lit; **in ~** au lit **2.** (*related to sexuality*) **good in ~** bon(ne) au lit; **to go to ~ with sb** coucher avec qn **3.** TYP **to put sth to ~** mettre qc sous presse **4.** (*flower patch*) parterre *m* **5.** (*bottom*) **sea ~** fond *m* de la mer; **river ~** lit *m* de la rivière ►**it's not a ~ of roses** ce n'est pas une partie de plaisir; **to get out of** [*o* **up on** *Am*] **the wrong side of the ~** se lever du mauvais pied

BEd [bi:'ed] *n abbr of* **Bachelor of Education** diplôme *m* universitaire de pédagogie

bed and breakfast *n* ≈ chambre *f* d'hôtes

bed down I. *vi* **1.** (*go to bed*) se coucher **2.** (*become established: team*) s'adapter; (*institution, performance*) commencer à bien rouler **II.** *vt* coucher

bedclothes ['bedkləʊðz] *npl* draps *mpl* et couvertures *fpl*
bedding ['bedɪŋ] **I.** *n no pl* **1.** (*bed*) literie *f* **2.** ZOOL litière *f* **II.** *adj* ~ **plant** plant *m* à repiquer
bedeck *vt* orner
bedevil [bɪ'devəl] <-ll- *Brit o* -l- *Am*> *vt* **1.** (*worry*) **to be ~ed by sth** être assailli par qc **2.** (*make problems*) **to ~ sb/sth** assaillir qn/qc **3.** (*complicate*) compliquer
bedfellow ['bed,feləʊ, *Am:* -oʊ] *n fig* **to make strange ~s** faire une drôle de paire
bedlam ['bedləm] *n no pl* chahut *m*
Bedouin ['bedʊɪn] **I.** *adj* bédouin(e) **II.** <-s *o* -> *n* **the ~(s)** les Bédouins
bedraggled [bɪ'drægld] *adj* **1.** (*wet*) trempé(e) **2.** (*untidy*) débraillé(e)
bedridden ['bed,rɪdn] *adj* alité(e)
bedrock ['bedrɒk, *Am:* -rɑːk] *n no pl* **1.** (*rock*) soubassement *m* **2.** (*basis*) base *f*
bedroom ['bedrʊm, *Am:* -ruːm] *n* chambre *f* à coucher; **guest ~** chambre d'amis; **a three-~ house** une maison avec trois chambres; **~ scene** scène *f* de lit; **to have ~ eyes** avoir un regard troublant
bedside ['bedsaɪd] *n no pl* chevet *m*
bedside lamp *n* lampe *f* de chevet **bedside manner** *n* comportement *m* auprès des malades **bedside table** *n* table *f* de chevet
bedsitter *n Brit,* **bed-sitting room** *n Brit, form* chambre *f* meublée
bedsore ['bedsɔːʳ, *Am:* -sɔːr] *n* escarre *f*
bedspread ['bedspred] *n* couvre-lit *m*
bedstead ['bedsted] *n* cadre *m* de lit
bedtime ['bedtaɪm] *n no pl* heure *f* du coucher; **it's (way) past my ~** je devrais déjà être au lit; **to have a hot milk at ~** boire un lait chaud avant d'aller au lit
bee [biː] *n* **1.** (*zool*) abeille *f;* **swarm of ~s** essaim *m* d'abeilles; **worker ~s** abeilles ouvrières; **to be stung by a ~** être piqué par une abeille **2.** *Am, Aus* (*group*) *cercle de personnes ayant une activité commune* ▸**to have a ~ in one's bonnet about sth** faire une fixation sur qc; **the ~s' knees** *Brit, inf* (*person*) le nombril du monde; (*thing*) le nec plus ultra; **to be a busy ~** *iron* être débordant d'activité
Beeb [biːb] *n no pl, Brit, inf abbr of* **British Broadcasting Corporation** BBC *f*
beech [biːtʃ] *n* hêtre *m;* **a ~ table** une table en (bois de) hêtre; **made of ~** en (bois de) hêtre
beef [biːf] **I.** *n* **1.** *no pl* (*meat*) bo<eu>f *m;* **minced ~** bo<eu>f haché; **roast ~** rôti *m* de bo<eu>f **2.** *inf* (*complaint*) revendication *f;* **what's his ~?** qu'est qu'il veut? **II.** *vi* **to ~ about sth** râler à cause de qc
beefburger ['biːf,bɜːgəʳ, *Am:* -,bɜːrgɚ] *n* steack *m* haché
beefsteak [,biːf'steɪk] *n* bifteck *m*
beefy ['biːfi] <-ier, -iest> *adj inf* costaud
beehive ['biːhaɪv] *n* ruche *f*
beeline ['biːlaɪn] *n no pl, inf* **to make a ~ for sth/sb** filer droit sur qc/qn
been [biːn, *Am:* bɪn] *pp of* **be**
beep [biːp] *n* bip *m*
beer [bɪəʳ, *Am:* bɪr] *n* bière *f*
beery ['bɪəri, *Am:* 'bɪr-] *adj* ~ **breath** haleine qui sent la bière
beeswax ['biːzwæks] *n* cire *f* d'abeille
beet [biːt] *n* betterave *f*
beetle ['biːtl, *Am:* -t̬l] *n* **1.** ZOOL scarabée *m* **2.** *inf* AUTO coccinelle *f*
beetle off *vi Brit, inf* détaler
beetroot ['biːtruːt] *n* betterave *f,* carotte *f* rouge *Suisse* ▸**go** [*o* **turn**] **as red as a ~** devenir rouge comme une tomate
befit [bɪ'fɪt] <-tt-> *vt form* convenir à; **as ~s a soldier** comme il convient à un soldat
befitting *adj form* approprié(e); **~ her new status** à la hauteur de son nouveau statut
before [bɪ'fɔːʳ, *Am:* -'fɔːr] **I.** *prep* **1.** (*earlier*) avant; **~ doing sth** avant de faire qc; **to wash one's hands ~ meals** se laver les mains avant de manger **2.** (*in front of*) devant; **~ our eyes** sous nos yeux **3.** (*preceding*) avant; **C comes ~ D** le C précède le D; **just ~ the bus stop** juste avant l'arrêt du bus **4.** (*having priority*) **to put sth ~ sth else** donner la priorité à qc sur qc d'autre **5.** (*facing sb*) **he has sth ~ him** il a qc qui l'attend ▸**business ~ pleasure** *prov* le travail d'abord, le plaisir après **II.** *adv* **1.** (*previously*) **I've seen it ~** je l'ai déjà vu; **I've not seen it ~** je ne l'ai jamais vu; **the day ~** la veille; **two days ~** l'avant-veille; **as ~** comme dans le passé **2.** (*in front*) **this word and the one ~** ce mot et le précédent **III.** *conj* **1.** (*at previous time*) avant (que); **he spoke ~ she** il parla avant qu'elle *+subj;* **he had a drink ~ he went** il a pris un verre avant de partir **2.** (*rather than*) **he'd die ~ he'd tell the truth** il mourrait plutôt que de dire la vérité **3.** (*until*) **it was a week ~ he came** il s'est passé une semaine avant qu'il ne vienne **4.** (*so that*) **to have to do sth ~ sb would do sth** devoir faire qc pour que qn fasse qc (*subj*)
beforehand [bɪ'fɔːhænd, *Am:* -'fɔːr-] *adv* **1.** (*in advance*) à l'avance **2.** (*earlier*) déjà
befriend [bɪ'frend] *vt* **1.** (*become friends with*) **to ~ sb** se lier d'amitié avec qn **2.** (*help*) être amical avec
beg [beg] <-gg-> **I.** *vt* **1.** (*seek charity*) quémander; **to ~ sb's pardon** s'excuser auprès de qn; **I ~ your pardon?** je vous demande pardon? **2.** (*humbly request*) implorer; **to ~ leave to** *+infin form* solliciter l'autorisation de *+infin;* **to ~ sb to** *+infin* supplier qn de *+infin;* **I ~ to inform you that…** il me faut vous informer que… ▸**to ~ the question** faire l'impasse sur l'essentiel **II.** *vi* **1.** (*seek charity*) mendier; **to ~ for sth** mendier qc **2.** (*humbly request*) implorer; **I ~ of you to** *+infin* je vous supplie de *+infin;* **to ~ for mercy** demander grâce; **I ~ to differ** *form* permettez-moi d'être d'un autre avis **3.** (*sit up: dog*) faire le beau ▸**to go ~ging** être dispo-

B

nible

began [bɪˈgæn] *pt of* **begin**

beggar [ˈbegəʳ, *Am:* -ɚ] **I.** *vt* ruiner; **to ~ oneself** se ruiner ►**to ~ belief** dépasser l'imagination **II.** *n* **1.** (*poor person*) mendiant(e) *m(f)* **2.** (*rascal*) voyou *m* ►**~s can't be choosers** *prov* faute de grives on mange des merles *prov;* **lucky ~** *Brit, inf* sacré veinard

begin [bɪˈgɪn] <-n-, began, begun> **I.** *vt* commencer; **to ~ work/a phase** commencer le travail/une phase; **to ~ a conversation** engager la conversation; **to ~ to count** [*o* **counting**] commencer à compter **II.** *vi* (*start*) commencer; **to ~ with** premièrement; **to ~ with a song** commencer par une chanson; **"well", he began …** "bon", commença-t-il …

◆**begin on** *vt insep* se mettre à

beginner [bɪˈgɪnəʳ, *Am:* -ɚ] *n* débutant(e) *m(f);* **absolute ~** novice *mf*

beginning I. *n* **1.** (*start*) commencement *m;* **at the ~** au début; **from ~ to end** du début à la fin; **to make a ~** faire ses débuts **2.** (*origin*) origine *f;* **the ~s of humanity** l'aube *f* de l'humanité **II.** *adj* initial(e)

begonia [bɪˈgəʊniə, *Am:* -ˈgoʊnjə] *n* bégonia *m*

begrudge [bɪˈgrʌdʒ] *vt* **1.** (*envy*) **to ~ sb sth** envier qc à qn **2.** (*be reluctant about*) **they ~d her every penny** ils lui ont reproché le moindre sou; **to ~ doing sth** faire qc à contrecœur

begun [bɪˈgʌn] *pp of* **begin**

behalf [bɪˈhɑːf, *Am:* -ˈhæf] *n no pl* **on ~ of** au nom [*o* de la part] de; **to act on ~ of sb** agir pour le compte de qn

behave [bɪˈheɪv] **I.** *vi* **1.** (*act: people*) se comporter; (*object, substance*) réagir; **to ~ calmly in a crisis** garder son calme pendant une crise; **to ~ strangely** se conduire bizarrement **2.** (*act in proper manner*) bien se tenir; **to ~ well/badly** se tenir bien/mal; **~!** (*to child*) tiens-toi bien!; *Brit* (*to adult*) un peu de tenue! **3.** (*function*) fonctionner; **the TV isn't behaving properly** la télé ne fonctionne pas très bien **II.** *vt* **to ~ oneself** se tenir bien

behavior *n Am, Aus,* **behaviour** [bɪˈheɪvjəʳ, *Am:* -vjɚ] *n Aus, Brit no pl* comportement *m;* **to be on one's best ~** bien se tenir

behaviorism *n Am, Aus,* **behaviourism** [bɪˈheɪvjərɪzəm] *n Aus, Brit no pl* béhaviorisme *m*

behaviour pattern *n* schéma *m* de comportement

behead [bɪˈhed] *vt* décapiter

behind [bɪˈhaɪnd] **I.** *prep* **1.** (*at the back of*) derrière; **right ~ sb/sth** juste derrière qn/qc; **~ the wheel** au volant; **~ the scenes** dans les coulisses **2.** (*hidden by*) **a face ~ a mask** un visage caché sous un masque **3.** (*responsible for*) **who is ~ that scheme?** qui se cache derrière ce projet?; **there is sth ~ this** il y a qc là-dessous **4.** (*in support of*) **to be ~ sb/sth all the way** soutenir qn/qc à cent pour cent **5.** (*late*) **~ time** en retard; **to be/get ~ schedule** être en/prendre du retard **6.** (*less advanced than*) **to be ~ sb/the times** être en retard sur qn/son temps **II.** *adv* **1.** (*at the back*) derrière; **the seat ~** le siège derrière; **to stay ~** rester en arrière; **to fall ~** prendre du retard; **to come ~** suivre **2.** (*late*) en arrière; **to be ~ with sth** être en retard en qc; **to get ~ in sth** prendre du retard dans qc; **my watch is an hour ~** ma montre retarde d'une heure **3.** (*where one was*) **to leave one's bag ~** oublier son sac; **to stay ~** rester après les autres **III.** *n* (*buttocks*) postérieur *m*

behindhand [bɪˈhaɪndhænd] *adv* **to be ~ with sth** être en retard pour qc

beige [beɪʒ] *adj, n* beige; *s. a.* **blue**

being [ˈbiːɪŋ] **I.** *pres p of* **be II.** *n* **1.** (*living thing*) être *m;* **~ from another planet** créature *f* extraterrestre **2.** (*existence*) **to bring sth into ~** concrétiser qc; **to come into ~** prendre naissance **III.** *adj* **for the time ~** pour l'instant

Belarus [beləˈrʌs] *n* la Biélorussie

belated [bɪˈleɪtɪd, *Am:* -t̬ɪd] *adj* tardif(-ive)

belch [beltʃ] **I.** *n* rot *m* **II.** *vi* avoir un renvoi **III.** *vt* **to ~ clouds of smoke** cracher des nuages de fumée

belfry [ˈbelfri] *n* (*tower*) beffroi *m;* (*of church*) clocher *m* ►**to have bats in the ~** avoir une araignée au plafond

Belgian [ˈbeldʒən] **I.** *adj* belge **II.** *n* Belge *mf*

Belgium [ˈbeldʒəm] *n* la Belgique

belie [bɪˈlaɪ] *irr vt* **1.** (*disprove*) réfuter **2.** (*disguise*) masquer

belief [bɪˈliːf] *n* **1.** (*conviction*) conviction; **it is my firm ~ that …** j'ai l'intime conviction que …; **to the best of my ~** pour autant que je sache (*subj*); **to be beyond ~** dépasser l'imagination; **in the ~ that …** convaincu que … **2.** REL foi *f;* **religious ~s** croyances *fpl* religieuses **3.** (*trust*) foi *f;* **your ~ in yourself** ta confiance en toi-même; **to shake sb's ~ in sth** ébranler la foi de qn en qc

believable [bɪˈliːvəbl] *adj* vraisemblable

believe [bɪˈliːv] *vt* **1.** (*presume true*) croire; **~ you me!** crois-moi/croyez-moi!; **to make ~ (that) …** prétendre que … **2.** (*show surprise*) **not to ~ one's eyes/ears** ne pas en croire ses yeux/oreilles; **not to ~ one's luck** ne pas en revenir; **seeing is believing** il faut le voir pour le croire **3.** (*think*) croire

◆**believe in** *vt* (*God, spirits, discipline, honesty*) croire en; **he believes in being …** il pense qu'il faut être …

believer [bɪˈliːvəʳ, *Am:* -vɚ] *n* **1.** REL croyant(e) *m(f)* **2.** (*convinced person*) adepte *mf*

belittle [bɪˈlɪtl, *Am:* -ˈlɪt̬-] <-tling> *vt* dénigrer; **to ~ oneself** se rabaisser

Belize [bəˈliːz] *n* le Belize

Belizean [bəˈliːzɪən] **I.** *adj* bélizien(ne) **II.** *n* Bélizien(ne) *m(f)*

bell [bel] *n* **1.** (*object*) cloche *f;* (*bicycle, door*) sonnette *f* **2.** (*signal*) timbre *m* ▸**alarm** [*o* **warning**] ~**s rang in sb's head** une petite lampe rouge s'est allumée dans la tête de qn; **that rings a** ~ ça me dit quelque chose; **as clear as a** ~ clair comme du cristal; **to give sb a** ~ *Brit, inf* passer un coup de fil à qn; **with** ~**s on** *Am, Aus, inf* dare-dare

belladonna [ˌbeləˈdɒnə, *Am:* -dɑːnə] *n no pl* belladonne *f*

bell-bottoms *n pl* pantalon *m* à pattes d'éléphant

bellboy [ˈbelbɔɪ] *n* groom *m*

bell-flower *n* clochette *f*

bellicose [ˈbelɪkəʊs, *Am:* -koʊs] *adj* belliqueux(-euse)

belligerent [bɪˈlɪdʒərənt] *adj* **1.** (*at war*) hostile; ~ **nation** pays belligérant **2.** (*aggressive*) querelleur(-euse)

bellow [ˈbeləʊ, *Am:* -oʊ] **I.** *vt* brailler **II.** *vi* **1.** (*animal*) mugir **2.** (*person*) hurler **III.** *n* hurlement *m;* **to give a** ~ **of rage/pain** pousser un hurlement de rage/douleur

bellows [ˈbeləʊz, *Am:* -oʊz] *npl* soufflet *m*

bell-push *n Brit* bouton *m* de sonnette

belly [ˈbeli] <-ies> *n inf* ventre *m;* (*of animal*) panse *f* ▸**to go** ~ **up** *inf* tourner court

belly out I. *vi* se gonfler **II.** *vt* gonfler

bellyache *inf* **I.** *n* mal *m* au ventre **II.** *vi* rouspéter **belly button** *n childspeak, inf* nombril *m* **belly dancer** *n* danseuse *f* du ventre **bellyflop** *n* SPORT plat *m* **bellyful** *n fig, inf* **to have had a** ~ **of sth** avoir ras-le-bol de qc **belly landing** *n* AVIAT atterrissage *m* sur le ventre

belong [bɪˈlɒŋ, *Am:* -ˈlɑːŋ] *vi* **1.** (*be the property*) **to** ~ **to sb** appartenir à qn **2.** (*be in right place*) se ranger; **to** ~ **together** aller ensemble; **to put sth back where it** ~**s** remettre qc à sa place; **this doesn't** ~ **here** cela n'a rien à faire ici; **to** ~ **to the family** faire partie de la famille; **to** ~ **to a club/church** appartenir à un club/une église; **they make us feel we don't** ~ *fig* ils nous font nous sentir étrangers

belongings *npl* affaires *fpl;* **personal** ~ effets personnels

Belorussian [beləˈrʌʃn] **I.** *adj* biélorusse **II.** *n* **1.** Biélorusse *mf* **2.** LING biélorusse *m; s. a.* **English**

beloved[1] [bɪˈlʌvɪd] *n no pl* bien-aimé(e) *m(f)*

beloved[2] [bɪˈlʌvd] *adj* bien-aimé(e); **to be** ~ **by sb** être chéri de qn

below [bɪˈləʊ, *Am:* -ˈloʊ] **I.** *prep* **1.** (*lower than, underneath*) ~ **the table/surface** sous la table/surface; ~ **us/sea level** au-dessous de nous/du niveau de la mer; **the sun sinks** ~ **the horizon** le soleil disparaît à l'horizon; **to bend** ~ **sth** ployer sous (le poids de) qc; **my legs are giving way** ~ **me** mes jambes ne me portent plus **2.** GEO **England is** ~ **Scotland** l'Angleterre est au sud de l'Écosse; **the river** ~ **the town** la rivière en aval de la ville **3.** (*less than*) ~ **freezing/average** au-dessous de zéro/de la moyenne; **it's 4 degrees** ~ **zero** il fait moins 4; **children** ~ **the age of twelve** les enfants de moins de douze ans **4.** (*inferior to*) **to be** ~ **sb in rank** être d'un rang inférieur à qn; **to work** ~ **sb** être subordonné à qn **II.** *adv* **1.** (*lower down*) **the family** ~ la famille du dessous; **the river** ~ la rivière en contre-bas; **there is sth** ~ en bas [*o* plus bas], il y a qc; **from** ~ venant d'en bas **2.** (*further in text*) **see** ~ voir ci-dessous **3.** REL **here** ~ ici-bas; **down** ~ en enfer

belt [belt] **I.** *n* **1.** *a.* SPORT, AUTO ceinture *f;* **a blow below the** ~ un coup bas **2.** TECH sangle *f* **3.** (*area*) zone *f;* **commuter** ~ grande banlieue **4.** *inf* (*punch*) gnon *m* ▸**to tighten one's** ~ se serrer la ceinture; **to have sth under one's** ~ avoir qc à son actif **II.** *vt* **1.** (*secure*) sangler **2.** *inf* (*hit*) flanquer un coup à **III.** *vi inf* se précipiter; **to** ~ **along** foncer

◆**belt out** *vt inf* chanter à pleine voix

◆**belt up** *vi* **1.** (*fasten*) attacher sa ceinture (de sécurité) **2.** *Brit, inf* (*shut up*) la boucler

beltway *n Am* (boulevard) périphérique *m*

bemoan [bɪˈməʊn, *Am:* -ˈmoʊn] *vt form* déplorer; **to** ~ **one's fate** se lamenter sur son sort

bemused [bɪˈmjuːzd] *adj* perplexe; **to be** ~ **by sth** être intrigué par qc

bench [bentʃ] *n* **1.** (*seat*) banc *m* **2.** SPORT **the** ~ la touche **3.** LAW **the** ~ [*o* **Bench**] (*judges*) la magistrature; (*judge trying a case*) la cour; **to approach the** ~ parler en privé à la cour; **to take the** ~ *Am* tenir séance (à la chambre) **4.** *pl, Brit* POL **the government/opposition** ~**es** les bancs de la majorité/de l'opposition **5.** (*workbench*) établi *m* **6.** *Aus* (*worktop*) plan *m* de travail

bend [bend] <bent, bent> **I.** *n* **1.** (*curve*) courbe *f;* (*in pipe*) coude *m;* **to take a** ~ AUTO prendre un virage **2.** *pl, inf* (*illness*) mal *m* des caissons ▸**to be round the** ~ avoir pété les plombs; **to drive sb round the** ~ faire sortir qn de ses gonds **II.** *vi* (*wood*) fléchir; (*path*) tourner; (*body*) courber; (*arm, leg*) se replier; (*frame*) se tordre **III.** *vt* (*make sth change direction*) **to** ~ **one's arms/knees** plier les bras/genoux; **to be bent double** être plié en deux; **to** ~ **one's head over a book** pencher la tête sur un livre ▸**to** ~ **sb's ear** glisser un mot à l'oreille de qn; **to** ~ **the law** contourner la loi; **to** ~ **the truth** déformer la vérité; **to** ~ **to sb's will** se plier à la volonté de qn

◆**bend back I.** *vt* redresser **II.** *vi* se pencher en arrière

◆**bend down** *vi* s'incliner

bended [ˈbendɪd] *adj form* **on** ~ **knee** un genou à terre ▸**to go down on** ~ **knees to sb** supplier qn à genoux

beneath [bɪˈniːθ] **I.** *prep* sous, au-dessous de; *s.* **below II.** *adv* (*lower down*) (au-)dessous, en bas

benediction [ˌbenɪˈdɪkʃn] *n* bénédiction *f*

benefactor ['benɪfæktəʳ] *n* bienfaiteur *m;* (*patron*) mécène *m;* (*donor*) donateur *m*

beneficence [bɪ'nefɪsns] *n no pl* bienfait *m*

beneficent [bɪ'nefɪsnt] *adj form* bienfaisant(e); (*person*) généreux(-euse); (*work*) caritatif(-ive)

beneficial *adj* profitable

beneficiary [ˌbenɪ'fɪʃəri] <-ies> *n* benéficiaire *mf*

benefit ['benɪfɪt] **I.** *n* **1.** (*profit*) avantage *m;* ~ **of independence** avantage *m* de l'indépendance; **to derive** (**much**) ~ **from sth** tirer profit de qc; **for the** ~ **of sb** pour qn; **with the** ~ **of hindsight** avec le recul; **to the** ~ **of sth/sb** au profit de qc/qn; **to give sb the** ~ **of the doubt** accorder à qn le bénéfice du doute **2.** (*welfare payment*) aide sociale; **housing/maternity** ~ allocation *f* logement/assurance *f* maternité; **to be on** ~ toucher des allocations; **social security** ~**s** prestations *fpl* de sécurité sociale **II.** <-t- *o* -tt-> *vi* **to** ~ **from sth** profiter de qc; **who do you think** ~**s from her death?** à qui croyez-vous que sa mort profiterait? **III.** <-t- *o* -tt-> *vt* profiter à

Benelux ['benɪlʌks] *n* **the** ~ **countries** le Bénélux

Benin [ben'i:n] *n* le Bénin

Beninese [beni'ni:z] **I.** *adj* béninois(e) **II.** *n* Béninois(e) *m(f)*

bent [bent] **I.** *pt, pp of* **bend II.** *n* ~ **for sth** dispositions *fpl* pour qc; **to follow one's** ~ suivre ses tendances *fpl* **III.** *adj* **1.** (*determined*) **to be** ~ **on sth** être déterminé à (faire) qc **2.** (*twisted*) tordu(e) **3.** (*stooped*) voûté(e) **4.** *inf* (*corrupt: police officer*) pourri(e)

benumbed *adj form* paralysé(e)

benzene ['benzi:n] *n no pl* benzène *m*

benzine ['benzi:n] *n* benzine *f*

bequeath [bɪ'kwi:ð] *vt* **to** ~ **sth to sb** léguer qc à qn

bequest [bɪ'kwest] *n* legs *m*

berate [bɪ'reɪt] *vt form* **to** ~ **sb** réprimander qn

bereavement [bɪ'ri:vmənt] *n* **1.** (*death*) deuil *m;* **to suffer a** ~ vivre un deuil **2.** (*loss*) perte *f*

bereft [bɪ'reft] *adj form* dépourvu(e); ~ **of hope** sans aucun espoir; **to feel** ~ se sentir abandonné

beret ['bereɪ, *Am:* bə'reɪ] *n* béret *m*

Bermuda [bɜ:'mju:də, *Am:* bɚ-] *n* les Bermudes

Bermuda shorts *n pl* bermuda *m*

berry ['beri] <-ies> *n* baies *fpl;* **to go** ~ **picking** aller cueillir des baies

berserk [bə'sɜ:k, *Am:* bɚ'sɜ:rk] *adj* fou furieux (folle furieuse); **to go** ~ être pris de folie furieuse

berth [bɜ:θ, *Am:* bɜ:rθ] **I.** *n* **1.** RAIL couchette *f* **2.** NAUT (*for sailor*) bannette *f;* (*for ship*) mouillage *m* ▶**to give sb/sth a <u>wide</u>** ~ se tenir à l'écart de qn/qc **II.** *vt* faire mouiller

beseech [bɪ'si:tʃ] <-ed, besought> *vt form* **to** ~ **sb to** +*infin* supplier qn de +*infin*

beset [bɪ'set] <-tt-, beset, beset> *vt* **1.** (*trouble*) ~ **by sth** assailli par qc; ~ **by worries** accablé de soucis **2.** MIL (*country*) assiéger **3.** (*affect*) ~ **by sth** tourmenté(e) par qc

beside [bɪ'saɪd] *prep* **1.** (*next to*) auprès de; **right** ~ **sb/sth** juste à côté de qn/qc **2.** (*together with*) **to work** ~ **sb** travailler aux côtés de qn **3.** (*in comparison to*) ~ **sth/sb** comparé à [*o* en comparaison de] qc/qn ▶**to be** ~ **<u>oneself</u> with joy/worry** être comme fou de joie/d'inquiétude; **to be** ~ **the <u>point</u>** n'avoir rien à voir; *s. a.* **besides**

besides [bɪ'saɪdz] **I.** *prep* **1.** (*in addition to*) outre; ~ **sth/sb** en plus de qc/sans compter qn **2.** (*except for*) hormis; ~ **sth/sb** à part qc/excepté qn **II.** *adv* **1.** (*in addition*) en outre; **many more** ~ bien d'autres encore **2.** (*else*) **nothing** ~ rien de plus **3.** (*moreover*) d'ailleurs

besiege [bɪ'si:dʒ] *vt* **1.** *a. fig* assiéger **2.** (*assail*) assaillir

besotted [bɪ'sɒtɪd, *Am:* 'sɑ:t̬ɪd] *adj* **1.** (*infatuated*) **to be** ~ **with sb/sth** être complètement entiché de qn/qc; **to be** ~ **with an idea** être possédé par une idée **2.** *form* (*intoxicated*) **to be** ~ **with sth** être enivré de qc

besought [bɪ'sɔ:t, *Am:* -'sɑ:t] *pt, pp of* **beseech**

best [best] **I.** *adj superl of* **good** meilleur(e); ~ **wishes** meilleurs vœux; ~ **friend** meilleur(e) ami(e); **to want what is** ~ vouloir ce qu'il y a de mieux; **it's** ~ **to** +*infin* il est préférable de +*infin;* **to act in sb's** ~ **interests** agir dans le meilleur intérêt de qn; **the** ~ **way** la meilleure façon ▶**the** ~ **<u>part</u>** la majeure partie; **to be sb's** ~ **<u>bet</u>** *inf* être ce que qn a de mieux à faire; **with the** ~ **<u>will</u> in the world** avec la meilleure volonté du monde **II.** *adv superl of* **well** mieux; **we'd** ~ **be going now** on ferait mieux d'y aller; **to do as** ~ **one can** faire de son mieux; **to do as one thinks** ~ agir au mieux; **your mother knows** ~**!** ta maman sait ce qui est mieux pour toi! **III.** *n no pl* **1.** (*the finest*) **the** ~ le meilleur, la meilleure *m, f;* **all the** ~**!** *inf* (*as toast*) santé!; (*saying goodbye*) à la prochaine!; (*wishing luck*) bonne chance!; **to turn out for the** ~ bien finir; **for the** ~ pour le mieux; **to be the** ~ **of friends** être les meilleurs amis du monde; **to be in the** ~ **of health** être en pleine santé; **to the** ~ **of my knowledge/power** autant que je sache/puisse (*subj*); **to be at one's** ~ être au meilleur de sa forme; **the garden's at its** ~ **in July** le jardin est dans toute sa splendeur en juillet; **to do/try one's level** [*o* **very**] ~ faire/essayer de son mieux; **to get the** ~ **out of sb** tirer le maximum de qn; **to want the** ~ vouloir ce qu'il y a de mieux **2.** (*perspective*) **at** ~ au mieux; **this is journalism at its** ~ ça c'est du vrai journalisme; ~ **of luck with your exams!** bonne chance pour ton examen!; **at the** ~ **of times** même quand tout va bien **3.** SPORT **to get the** ~

of sb *a. fig* triompher sur qn; **to play the ~ of three** jouer en trois sets ►**make the ~ of a bad <u>bargain</u>** *Am* [*o* **<u>job</u>** *Brit*] [*o* **<u>situation</u>**], **make the ~ of <u>things</u>** faire contre mauvaise fortune bon cœur **IV.** *vt form* battre

bestial ['bestɪəl, *Am:* -tʃl] *adj* bestial(e)

bestiality [ˌbestɪ'æləti, *Am:* -tʃi'æləţi] *n no pl* bestialité *f*

bestir [bɪ'stɜːʳ, *Am:* -'stɜːr] <-rr-> *vt form* **to ~ oneself** se démener

best man *n* ≈ garçon *m* d'honneur

bestow [bɪ'stəʊ, *Am:* -'stoʊ] *vt form* **to ~ sth (up)on sb** accorder qc à qn; **to ~ a name (up)on sb/sth** attribuer un nom à qn/qc

best-seller *n* best-seller *m*

bet [bet] <-tt-, bet *o* -ted, bet *o* -ted> **I.** *n* pari *m;* **to do sth for** [*o* **on** *Am*] **a ~** faire qc par défi; **to be the best ~** être ce qu'il ya de mieux à faire; **to be a good ~** être la meilleure des choses; **it's a safe ~ that ...** c'est sûr que ...; **to place a ~ on sth** parier sur qc; **to make a ~ with sb** parier avec qn **II.** *vt* parier; **to ~ sb anything he/she likes** *inf* parier à qn tout ce qu'il/elle veut ►**you can ~ your <u>boots</u>** [*o* **<u>ass</u>** *Am*] **that ...** *inf* tu peux parier ce que tu veux que ...; (**how much**) **do you <u>want</u> to ~?** tu paries (combien)?; **<u>I'll</u> ~!** *inf* et comment!; **<u>you</u> ~!** *inf* tu parles! **III.** *vi* parier; **to ~ heavily** parier gros; **to ~ on a horse** miser sur un cheval; **don't ~ on it!** *inf* ne compte pas dessus!

beta ['biːtə, *Am:* 'beɪţə] *adj* INFOR bêta; **~ version** version *f* bêta

beta blocker *n* béta-bloquant *m*

betray [bɪ'treɪ] *vt* trahir

betrayal [bɪ'treɪəl] *n* trahison *f*

better¹ ['betəʳ, *Am:* 'beţɚ] **I.** *adj comp of* **good 1.** (*finer, superior*) meilleur(e); **sb's ~ nature** le bon cœur de qn; **~ luck next time** plus de chance la prochaine fois; **it's ~ that way** c'est mieux comme ça; **far ~** beaucoup mieux; **to be ~ at sth** être meilleur à qc; **to be ~ at singing than sb** chanter mieux que qn; **to be ~ for sb/sth** être mieux pour qn/qc **2.** (*healthier*) **to be ~** aller mieux; **to be a bit ~** aller un peu mieux; **to get ~** (*improve*) aller mieux; (*be cured*) être guéri **3.** (*most of*) **the ~ part** la majeure partie ►**<u>discretion</u> is the ~ part of valour** *prov* mieux vaut ne pas se faire remarquer; **~ <u>late</u> than never** *prov* mieux vaut tard que jamais *prov;* **~ <u>safe</u> than sorry** *prov* mieux vaut prévenir que guérir *prov;* **to go <u>one</u> ~** faire mieux **II.** *adv comp of* **well 1.** (*manner*) mieux; **~ dressed/written** mieux habillé(e)/écrit(e); **to do much ~** faire beaucoup mieux; **to like sth much ~ than sth** aimer qc beaucoup plus que qc; **there is nothing ~ than ...** il n'y a rien de mieux que ...; **or ~ still ...** ou mieux encore ... **2.** (*degree*) plus; **to be ~-known for sth than sth** être surtout connu pour qc plutôt que pour qc **3.** (*more advisably*) **you'd do ~ to leave** tu ferais mieux de partir; **you had ~ do sth** il faut que tu fasses qc (*subj*); **to think ~ of it** changer d'avis (après réflexion) **III.** *n no pl* **1.** mieux *m;* **not to have seen ~** ne pas avoir vu mieux; **the more you do sth, the ~ it is** plus tu fais qc et meilleur c'est; **to change for the ~** changer en mieux; **to expect ~ of sb** s'attendre à mieux de qn; **the sooner, the ~** le plus tôt sera le mieux; **so much the ~** encore mieux **2.** *pl, fig* **sb's ~s** *ceux qui sont supérieurs à qn* ►**to <u>get</u> the ~ of sb** triompher de qn; **for ~ or (for) <u>worse</u>** pour le meilleur ou pour le pire **IV.** *vt* **1.** (*beat: time*) améliorer **2.** (*go further than*) renchérir sur **3.** (*in standing*) améliorer; **to ~ oneself** s'élever

better² *n* parieur, -euse *m, f*

betterment ['betəmənt] *n no pl* amélioration *f*

betting ['betɪŋ] *n no pl* (*making bets*) paris *mpl;* **~ on horses** paris sur les chevaux; **the state of the ~ is sth to sth** la côte est de qc contre qc ►**if I were a ~ <u>man</u>, ...** si je devais parier, ...; **<u>what's</u> the ~ that ... ?** *inf* quelles sont les chances que *+subj*?

betting office *n,* **betting shop** *n Brit* ≈ bureau *m* de P.M.U

bettor ['betəʳ, *Am:* 'beţɚ] *n Am s.* **better**

between [bɪ'twiːn] **I.** *prep* **1.** (*in middle of, within*) entre; **~ times** entre-temps **2.** (*in time*) **to eat ~ meals** manger entre les repas; **to wait ~ planes** attendre entre deux avions; **~ now and tomorrow** d'ici (à) demain **3.** (*interaction*) **a match ~ them** un match les opposant; **to do sth ~ the two of us** faire qc à nous deux; **~ ourselves** entre nous **4.** (*among*) **the 3 children have £10 ~ them** les 3 enfants ont 10£ en tout; **nothing will come ~ them** rien ne les séparera; **~ you and me** entre nous **5.** (*combination of*) **the mule is a cross ~ a donkey and a horse** le mulet est un croisement entre l'âne et le cheval **II.** *adv* au milieu, dans l'intervalle ►**few and <u>far</u> ~** rare, clairsemé; *s. a.* **in between**

bevel ['bevl] **I.** <-ll- *Brit o* -l- *Am*> *vt* biseauter **II.** *n* biseau *m*

beverage ['bevərɪdʒ] *n form* boisson *f,* breuvage *m Québec;* **alcoholic ~s** boissons alcoolisées

beware [bɪ'weəʳ, *Am:* 'wer] **I.** *vi* être prudent; **~!** soyez prudents!; **~ of pickpockets!** méfiez-vous des pickpockets!; **beware of the dog** attention, chien méchant; **to ~ of sb/sth** prendre garde à qn/qc; **to ~ of doing sth** prendre garde de ne pas faire qc **II.** *vt* se méfier de

bewilder [bɪ'wɪldəʳ, *Am:* -dɚ] *vt* **1.** (*puzzle*) dérouter **2.** (*greatly surprise*) abasourdir

bewildered *adj* déconcerté(e)

bewildering *adj* déconcertant(e)

bewilderment *n no pl* confusion *f;* **in ~** déconcerté(e)

bewitch [bɪ'wɪtʃ] *vt* **1.** (*put under spell*) *a. fig* ensorceler **2.** (*enchant, fascinate*) charmer

bewitching *adj* charmant(e)

beyond [bɪ'jɒnd, *Am:* -'ɑːnd] **I.** *prep* **1.** (*other side of*) ~ **the mountain** au-delà de la montagne; **don't go ~ the line!** ne dépasse pas la ligne!; ~ **the sea** outre-mer; **from ~ the grave** d'outre-tombe **2.** (*after*) ~ **the river/8 o'clock** après le fleuve/8 heures; **to stay ~ a week** rester plus d'une semaine; ~ **lunchtime** passé l'heure du repas **3.** (*further than*) **to see/go** (**way**) ~ **sth** voir/aller (bien) au-delà de qc; **it goes ~ a joke** ça n'a plus rien de drôle; ~ **the reach of sb** hors de la portée de qn; ~ **belief** incroyable; ~ **repair** irréparable; **he is ~ help** *iron, pej* on ne peut plus rien pour lui; ~ **the shadow of a doubt** sans le moindre doute; **to go ~ the point of no return** avoir atteint le point de non-retour **4.** (*too difficult for*) **to be ~ sb** dépasser qn; **it's ~ me** ça me dépasse; **it's ~ my abilities** c'est au-delà de mes compétences **5.** (*more than*) **to live ~ one's income** vivre au-dessus de ses moyens; **to value sth ~ all else** tenir à qc par-dessus tout; **to go ~ just doing sth** ne pas se limiter à faire qc **6.** *with neg or interrog* (*except for*) ~ **sth** à part qc **II.** *adv* **1.** (*past*) **the mountains ~** les montagnes au loin **2.** (*future*) **the next ten years and ~** la prochaine décennie et au-delà **III.** *n* **the ~** REL l'au-delà *m*

bhp *n abbr of* **brake horsepower**

biannual [ˌbaɪ'ænjʊəl] *adj* semestriel(le)

bias ['baɪəs] **I.** *n* **1.** (*prejudice*) préjugé *m;* **their ~ against/in favour of sb/sth** leurs prejugés contre/en faveur de qn/qc **2.** *no pl* (*one-sidedness*) partialité *f;* ~ **against sb/sth** parti pris contre qn/qc **3.** (*tendency*) tendance *f* **4.** *no pl* (*oblique line: of clothes*) biais *m;* ~**-cut**(**ting**) coupe *f* en biais; **on the ~** en biais **II.** <-ss- *Brit o* -s- *Am*> *vt* influencer; **to ~ sb towards/against sb/sth** influencer qn en faveur de/contre qn/qc

biased *adj Am,* **biassed** *adj Brit* (*report*) tendancieux(-euse); (*judge*) partial

bib [bɪb] *n* bavoir *m;* **to be in one's best ~ and tucker** être sur son trente et un

Bible ['baɪbl] *n* Bible *f*

biblical ['bɪblɪkl] *adj* biblique

bibliographic, **bibliographical** *adj* bibliographique

bibliography [ˌbɪblɪ'ɒgrəfi, *Am:* -'ɑːgrə-] <-ies> *n* bibliographie *f*

bicarbonate [ˌbaɪ'kɑːbənət, *Am:* -'kɑːr-] *n* bicarbonate *m;* ~ **of soda** bicarbonate de soude

bicentenary [ˌbaɪsen'tiːnəri, *Am:* baɪ-'sentner-] <-ies> *n,* **bicentennial** *Am* **I.** *n* bicentenaire *m* **II.** *adj* bicentenaire

biceps ['baɪseps] *npl* biceps *m*

bicker ['bɪkəʳ, *Am:* -ɚ] *vi pej* **to ~ with sb about sth** se chamailler avec qn au sujet de qc

bickering *n no pl, pej* chamailleries *fpl*

bicycle ['baɪsɪkl] *n* vélo *m;* ~ **ride** tour *m* de vélo; **to get on one's ~** monter à vélo; **to ride a ~** rouler à vélo; **by ~** à vélo

bid¹ [bɪd] <-dd-, bid *o* bade, bid *o* -den> *vt form* **1.** (*greet*) **to ~ sb good morning** dire bonjour à qn; **to ~ sb welcome** souhaiter la bienvenue à qn **2.** (*command*) **to ~ sb to** +*infin* ordonner à qn de +*infin* **3.** (*invite*) **to ~ sb to sth** convier qn à qc

bid² [bɪd] **I.** *n* **1.** (*offer*) offre *f* **2.** (*attempt*) tentative *f;* **a ~ for power** une tentative d'accéder au pouvoir **II.** <-dd-, bid, bid> *vi* faire une offre **III.** <-dd-, bid, bid> *vt* offrir

bidden ['bɪdn] *pp of* **bid**

bidder ['bɪdəʳ, *Am:* -ɚ] *n* (*for auction lot*) offrant *m;* (*for contract*) candidat *m* à un appel d'offre; **the highest ~** le plus offrant

bidding ['bɪdɪŋ] *n no pl* **1.** FIN les enchères *fpl;* **to open the ~** ouvrir les enchères **2.** *form* (*command*) requête *f;* **to do sb's ~** obéir à qn; **at sb's ~** à la demande de qn

bide [baɪd] *vt* **to ~ one's time** attendre le bon moment

biennial [baɪ'enɪəl] **I.** *adj* biennal(e); BIO bisannuel(le) **II.** *n* biennale *f*

bier [bɪəʳ, *Am:* bɪr] *n* bière *f*

bifocals [baɪ'fəʊklz, *Am:* 'baɪˌfoʊ-] *npl* lunettes *fpl* à double foyer

big [bɪg] <-ger, -gest> *adj* **1.** (*large*) grand(e); (*oversized*) gros(se); ~ **game** gros gibier *m;* **a ~ drop in prices** une forte baisse des prix; **a ~ eater** *inf* un gros mangeur; **to be a ~ spender** *inf* dépenser beaucoup; **a ~ tip** un gros pourboire; **the ~ toe** le gros orteil; **a ~ budget film** un film à gros budget; **the ~ger the better** plus c'est gros, meilleur c'est; **the ~gest-ever egg** le plus grand œuf (jamais vu) **2.** (*grown-up*) *a. fig* grand(e); ~ **boy/brother** grand garçon/frère **3.** (*important*) grand(e); **he's ~ in his country** il est célèbre dans son pays; **a ~ shot** *inf* un gros bonnet; **a ~ day** un grand jour; **to have ~ ideas** *inf* avoir de grandes idées; **she's ~** [*o* **a ~ name**] **in finance** elle est connue dans le monde de la finance **4.** *inf* (*great*) super; **in a ~ way** quelque chose de bien; **to be ~ on sth** *Am* être dingue de qc **5.** (*generous*) **it's really ~ of sb** *iron* c'est vraiment généreux de la part de qn ►**to be too ~ for one's boots** *pej, inf* avoir la grosse tête; **the ~ boys** les gros bonnets; ~ **deal!** *inf* et alors!; **no ~ deal** *inf* c'est rien; **what's the ~ idea?** *iron, inf* qu'est-ce que ça veux dire?; **to make it ~** *inf* avoir du succès

bigamist ['bɪgəmɪst] *n* bigame *mf*

bigamy ['bɪgəmi] *n no pl* bigamie *f*

Big Apple *n* **the ~** *New York*

Big Ben était à l'origine le surnom donné à la grande cloche de la tour de la "Houses of Parliament" coulée en 1856, surnom hérité du "Chief Commissionner of Works" de l'époque, Sir Benjamin Hall. De nos jours, ce nom est utilisé pour désigner la grande horloge et la tour. Le carillon de "Big Ben" sert de sonal à certains journaux télévisés et radiophoniques.

big business *n* les grandes entreprises *fpl;* **to be ~** être du business **Big Easy** *n* **the ~** *La Nouvelle-Orléans* **bighead** *n inf* **to be a ~** être gonflé **bigheaded** *adj inf* **to be ~** être gonflé

bigot ['bɪgət] *n* **to be a ~** être sectaire

bigoted *adj* sectaire

bigotry ['bɪgətri] *n no pl* sectarisme *m*

big top *n* chapiteau *m*

bigwig ['bɪgwɪg] *n inf* grosse *f*

bike [baɪk] **I.** *n* **1.** *inf* vélo *m;* **a child's ~** un vélo pour enfant; **a ~ lane** une piste cyclable; **to get on a ~** monter à vélo; **to ride a ~** rouler à vélo; **by ~** à vélo **2.** (*motorcycle*) moto *f* **II.** *vi inf* rouler à vélo

biker ['baɪkəʳ, *Am:* -kɚ] *n* motard *m*

bikini [bɪ'kiːni] *n* bikini *m*

bilateral [ˌbaɪ'lætərəl, *Am:* -'læt̬ɚl] *adj* bilatéral(e)

bilberry ['bɪlbəri, *Am:* -ber-] <-ies> *n* airelle *f*

bile [baɪl] *n no pl, a. fig* bile *f*

bilingual [baɪ'lɪŋgwəl] *adj* bilingue

bilious ['bɪliəs, *Am:* -jəs] *adj a. fig* bilieux(-euse)

bill[1] [bɪl] **I.** *n* **1.** (*invoice*) facture *f;* (*for meal*) addition *f;* **to put it on sb's ~** le mettre sur la note de qn; **to run up a ~** avoir une facture; **to foot the ~** payer la facture; *fig* payer les pots cassés **2.** *Am* (*bank-note*) billet *m* **3.** LAW projet *m* de loi **4.** (*poster*) affiche *f;* **to top the ~** être en tête d'affiche ►**to give sb/sth a clean ~ of health** trouver qn/qc en parfait état **II.** *vt* **1.** (*invoice*) facturer; **to ~ sb for sth** facturer qc à qn **2.** (*announce*) **to ~ sth as sth** déclarer qc comme qc

bill[2] [bɪl] **I.** *n* bec *m* **II.** *vi* **to ~ and coo** *iron* roucouler

billboard ['bɪlbɔːd, *Am:* -bɔːrd] *n Am, Aus s.* **hoarding** panneau *m* d'affichage

billfold ['bɪlfəʊld, *Am:* -foʊld] *n Am* portefeuille *m*

billiards ['bɪliədz, *Am:* '-jɚdz] *n no pl* billard *m*

billion ['bɪliən, *Am:* -jən] **I.** *n* milliard *m* **II.** *adj* milliard de

billow ['bɪləʊ, *Am:* -oʊ] **I.** *n* nuage *m* **II.** *vi* **to ~ (forth)** surgir; **to ~ (out)** se déployer

bill poster *n* colleur, -euse *m, f* d'affiches **billposting** *n* collage *m* d'affiches **bill sticker** *s.* **bill poster**

billy ['bɪli] <-ies> *n,* **billycan** *n Aus, Brit* gamelle *f*

billy goat *n* bouc *m*

bimbo ['bɪmbəʊ, *Am:* -boʊ] <-es *o* -s> *n pej, inf* minette *f*

bi-monthly [ˌbaɪ'mʌnθli] **I.** *adj* **1.** (*twice a month*) bimensuel(le) **2.** (*every two months*) bimestriel(le) **II.** *adv* **1.** (*twice a month*) deux fois par mois **2.** (*every two months*) tous les deux mois

bin [bɪn] **I.** *n* **1.** *Aus, Brit, a. fig* poubelle *f;* **to throw sth in the ~** jeter qc à la poubelle **2.** (*storage*) boîte *f;* **a bread ~** une huche à pain **II.** *vt Brit* jeter à la poubelle

binary ['baɪnəri] *adj* binaire

bind [baɪnd] **I.** *n inf* **it's a ~** c'est casse-pieds *mf;* **to be in a bit of a ~** *inf* être un peu dans le pétrin; **to put sb in a real ~** mettre qn dans le pétrin **II.** <bound, bound> *vi* lier **III.** <bound, bound> *vt* **1.** (*tie*) attacher; **to ~ sb/sth to sth** attacher qn/qc à qc; **to be bound hand and foot** être pieds et poings liés; **to be bound to sb** être attaché à qn **2.** (*unite*) **to ~ (together)** lier ensemble **3.** (*commit*) **to ~ sb to** *+infin* obliger qn à *+infin* **4.** TYP (*book*) relier **5.** (*when cooking*) lier

binder ['baɪndəʳ, *Am:* -dɚ] *n* **1.** (*file*) classeur *m* **2.** (*person*) relieur, -euse *m, f*

binding ['baɪndɪŋ] **I.** *n no pl* **1.** TYP reliure *f* **2.** FASHION ganse *f* **II.** *adj* obligatoire; **a ~ agreement** un accord qui engage

bindweed ['baɪndwiːd] *n no pl* liseron *m*

binge [bɪndʒ] *inf* **I.** *n* **drinking ~** beuverie *f;* **~-eating** crise *f* de boulimie; **shopping ~** fringale *f* d'achats; **to go on a ~** faire la bringue **II.** *vi* se gaver; **to ~ on sth** se gaver de qc

bingo ['bɪŋgəʊ, *Am:* -goʊ] **I.** *n no pl* bingo *m* **II.** *interj inf* **~!** et voilà!

bin liner *n* sac *m* poubelle

binoculars [bɪ'nɒkjʊləz, *Am:* -'nɑːkjələ-z] *npl* jumelles *fpl*

binomial [baɪ'nəʊmɪəl, *Am:* -'noʊ-] **I.** *n* binôme *m* **II.** *adj* binomial(e)

bio- [baɪəʊ, *Am:* -oʊ-] *in compounds* (*synthesis, climatic, magnetism*) bio-

biochemical [ˌbaɪəʊ'kemɪkl, *Am:* -oʊ-] *adj* biochimique

biochemist [ˌbaɪəʊ'kemɪst, *Am:* -oʊ-] *n* biochimiste *mf*

biochemistry [ˌbaɪəʊ'kemɪstri, *Am:* -oʊ-] *n no pl* biochimie *f*

biodegradable [ˌbaɪəʊdɪ'greidəbl, *Am:* -oʊ-] *adj* biodégradable

biodegrade [ˌbaɪəʊdɪ'greid, *Am:* -oʊ-] *vi* se biodégrader

biodetergent *n* détergent *m* biodégradable

biodiversity [ˌbaɪəʊdaɪ'vɜːsəti, *Am:* -oʊdɪ'vɜːrsət̬i] *n* bio-diversité *f*

biographical [ˌbaɪəʊ'græfɪkəl] *adj* biographique

biography [baɪ'ɒgrəfi, *Am:* -'ɑːgrə-] <-ies> *n* biographie *f*

biological [ˌbaɪə'lɒdʒɪkəl, *Am:* -'lɑːdʒɪ-] *adj* biologique

biologist [baɪ'ɒlədʒɪst, *Am:* -'ɑːlə-] *n* biologiste *mf*

biology [baɪ'ɒlədʒi, *Am:* -'ɑːlə-] *n no pl* biologie *f*

biomass [ˌbaiəmæs] *n* biomasse *f*

biophysics [ˌbaɪəʊ'fɪzɪks, *Am:* -oʊ-] *n no pl* biophysique *f*

biopsy ['baɪɒpsi, *Am:* -ɑːp-] *n* biopsie *f*

biorhythm ['baɪəriðəm, *Am:* -oʊ-] *n* biorythme *m*

biosphere ['baɪəsfiːəʳ, *Am:* -sfir] *n no pl* biosphère *f*
biotechnology [ˌbaɪəʊtek'nɒlədʒi, *Am:* -oʊtek'nɑːlə-] *n no pl* biotechnologie *f*
biotope ['baɪətəʊp, *Am:* -toʊp] *n* biotope *m*
bipartisan [ˌbaɪpɑːtɪ'zæn, *Am:* -'pɑːrţəzən] *adj* bipartite
biped ['baɪped] *n* bipède *m*
biplane ['baɪpleɪn] *n* biplan *m*
bipolar [ˌbaɪ'pəʊləʳ, *Am:* -'poʊlɚ] *adj* bipolaire
birch [bɜːtʃ, *Am:* bɜːrtʃ] **I.** *n* **1.** (*tree*) bouleau *m* **2.** (*stick*) fouet *m* **II.** *vt* fouetter
bird [bɜːd, *Am:* bɜːrd] *n* **1.** (*animal*) oiseau *m;* **caged** ~ oiseau en cage; **~-like** d'oiseau; **migrating** ~ oiseau migrateur **2.** *inf* (*person*) type *m;* **a strange** ~ un drôle d'oiseau **3.** *Aus, Brit, inf* (*girl*) nana *f;* **old** ~ *inf* vieille peau *f* ►**to know about the ~s and bees** savoir que les bébés ne naissent pas dans les choux; **~s of a feather flock together** *prov* qui se ressemble s'assemble *prov;* **a ~ in the hand is worth two in the bush** *prov* un tiens vaut mieux que deux tu l'auras *prov;* **to kill two ~s with one stone** faire d'une pierre deux coups *prov;* **to feel free as a** ~ se sentir libre comme l'air; **to give sb the** ~ envoyer paître qn; (**strictly**) **for the ~s** *Am, Aus, inf* être nul
birdcage *n* cage *f* à oiseaux
birdie ['bɜːdi, *Am:* 'bɜːr-] *n* **1.** *childspeak* cui-cui *m* **2.** *Am* (*shuttlecock*) volant *m* **3.** SPORT birdie *m* ►**watch the** ~ attention, le petit oiseau va sortir
birdseed *n no pl* graines *fpl* pour les oiseaux
bird's-eye view *n no pl* vue *f* aérienne
bird's-nest *n* nid *m* d'oiseau
birth [bɜːθ, *Am:* bɜːrθ] *n* naissance *f;* **at/from** ~ *no pl* à la/de naissance; **date/place of** ~ date/lieu de naissance; **to give** ~ **to sth** *a. fig* donner naissance à qc
birth certificate *n* acte *m* de naissance
birth control *n* contrôle *m* des naissances
birthday ['bɜːθdeɪ, *Am:* 'bɜːrθ-] *n* anniversaire *m;* **happy ~!** joyeux anniversaire!
birthday party *n* fête *f* d'anniversaire
birthday present *n* cadeau *m* d'anniversaire **birthday suit** *n inf* costume *m* d'Adam
birthmark *n* tache *f* de naissance **birthplace** *n* lieu *m* de naissance **birth rate** *n* taux *m* de natalité
birthstone *n* pierre *f* porte-bonheur
biscuit ['bɪskɪt] *n* **1.** *Aus, Brit* biscuit *m,* bonbon *m Belgique* **2.** *Am* (*soft round cake*) petit pain *m*

Le **Biscuits and gravy** qui est un plat originaire des États du Sud, se mange fréquemment au petit déjeuner aux USA. Les "Biscuits" sont une sorte de petits pains plats que l'on sert avec du "gravy" (une sauce de rôti). Dans certaines régions, on ne trouve les "biscuits and gravy" que dans les "truck stops" (les restaurants routiers).

bisect [baɪ'sekt, *Am:* 'baɪsekt] *vt* diviser en deux
bisection [baɪ'sekʃn] *n* bissection *f*
bisexual [ˌbaɪ'sekʃʊəl, *Am:* -ʃʊəl] **I.** *n* bisexuel(le) *m(f)* **II.** *adj* bisexuel(le)
bishop ['bɪʃəp] *n* **1.** REL évêque *m* **2.** (*chess piece*) fou *m*
bishopric ['bɪsəprɪk] *n* évêché *m*
bison ['baɪsən] *n* bison *m*
bit[1] [bɪt] *n* **1.** *inf* (*fragment*) morceau *m;* **a ~ of meat/cloth/land** un bout de viande/de tissu/terrain; **to fall to ~s** tomber en morceaux; ~ **by** ~ petit à petit; **to stay/wait for a** ~ *inf* rester/attendre pendant un instant **2.** (*some*) **a** ~ un peu; **a ~ of sth** un peu de qc; **not a** ~ pas du tout; **quite a ~ of sth** assez de qc; **a ~ more salt** un peu plus de sel ►**a ~ of a** **we have a ~ of a problem** on a un petit problème; **she's a ~ of a nuisance/philospher** elle est un peu embêtante/philioosphe; **it's a ~ of a lottery** c'est un peu comme une loterie
bit[2] [bɪt] *pt of* **bite**
bit[3] [bɪt] *n* **1.** (*for horses*) mors *m* **2.** (*tool*) mèche *f*
bit[4] [bɪt] *n* INFOR *abbr of* **BInary digiT** bit *m*
bitch [bɪtʃ] **I.** *n* **1.** ZOOL chienne *f* **2.** *inf* (*woman*) garce *f* **II.** *vi Am, inf* **to ~ about sb/sth** rouspéter contre qn/qc
bitchy ['bɪtʃi] *adj inf* mauvais(e)
bite [baɪt] **I.** <bit, bitten> *vt* mordre; (*insect*) piquer; **to ~ one's nails** se ronger les ongles; **to ~ one's lips** se mordre les lèvres; *fig* se mordre les doigts; **to ~ sth off** arracher qc avec les dents **II.** <bit, bitten> *vi* **1.** (*when eating, attacking*) mordre; (*insect*) piquer; **to ~ into/through sth** mordre dans/à travers qc; **sb/sth won't ~** (**you**) *iron* qn/qc ne va pas te mordre **2.** (*in angling*) mordre ►**once bitten twice shy** *prov* chat échaudé craint l'eau froide *prov* **III.** *n* **1.** (*of dog, snake*) morsure *f;* (*of insect*) piqûre *f; fig* (*of wind*) morsure *f;* (*of speech*) mordant *m;* (*of taste*) piquant *m* **2.** (*food*) bouchée *f;* **to have a ~ to eat** manger un morceau; **to take a big ~ of sth** prendre une grosse bouchée de qc; **to take a big ~ out of one's salary** *fig* prendre un gros morceau du salaire de quelqu'un **3.** (*in angling*) touche *f*
biting ['baɪtɪŋ, *Am:* -ţɪŋ] *adj a. fig* mordant(e)
bitten ['bɪtn] *pp of* **bite**
bitter ['bɪtəʳ, *Am:* 'bɪţɚ] **I.** <-er, -est> *adj* **1.** (*acrid*) *a. fig* amer(-ère); **it's a ~ pill to swallow** la pilule est dure à avaler **2.** (*intense: cold*) rude; (*wind*) glacial(e); (*fight*) féroce; (*dispute*) âpre; (*tone*) acerbe; **to the ~ end** jusqu'au bout **II.** *n Aus, Brit* bière *f* brune
bitterly *adv* **1.** (*painfully*) amèrement **2.** (*intensely*) extrêmement; **it's ~ cold** il fait rudement froid; (*suffer*) cruellement
bitterness *n no pl a.* GASTR amertume *f*
bitumen ['bɪtjʊmən, *Am:* bɪ'tuːmən] *n no pl* bitume *m*

bituminous [bɪ'tjuːmɪnəs, *Am:* -'tuː-] *adj* bitumineux(-euse)

bivalve ['baivælv] **I.** *n* bivalve *m* **II.** *adj* bivalve

bivouac ['bɪvʊæk, *Am:* -uæk] **I.** *n* bivouac *m* **II.** <-king, -ked> *vi* bivouaquer

biweekly [ˌbaɪ'wiːkli] **I.** *adj* **1.** (*occurring every two weeks*) bimensuel(le) **2.** (*occurring twice a week*) bihebdomadaire **II.** *adv* **1.** (*every two weeks*) tous les quinze jours **2.** (*twice a week*) deux fois par semaine

bizarre [bɪ'zɑːʳ, *Am:* -'zɑːr] *adj* bizarre

blab [blæb] <-bb-> *inf* **I.** *vt* **to ~ sth to sb** rapporter qc à qn **II.** *vi* **1.** (*reveal sth*) parler **2.** *Am* (*chat*) jaser

black [blæk] **I.** *adj* noir(e); **~ art** art *m* nègre; **~ arts** magie *f* noire; **Black Death** peste *f* noire; **~ tea** thé sans lait; **a ~ and white photo/television** une photo/télé en noir et blanc; **everything's ~ and white with her** pour elle tout est tout blanc ou tout noir **II.** *n* **1.** (*colour*) noir *m* **2.** (*person*) Noir *m* ►(**down**) **in ~ and white** écrit noir sur blanc **III.** *vt* noircir; (*shoes*) cirer; *s. a.* **blue**
◆**black out I.** *vi* s'évanouir **II.** *vt* obscurcir; (*through power failure*) priver de courant

blackball *vt* blackbouler **blackberry** <-ies> *n* mûre *f* **blackbird** *n* merle *m* **blackboard** *n* tableau *m* noir **black book** *n fig* liste *f* noire **blackcurrant** *n* cassis *m*

blacken ['blækən] *vt, vi* noircir

black eye *n* œil *m* au beurre noir **blackguard** *n pej* crapule *f* **blackhead** *n* MED point *m* noir **black hole** *n* trou *m* noir **black ice** *n* verglas *m*

blacking ['blækɪŋ] *n* cirage *m* noir

blackish ['blækɪʃ] *adj* noirâtre

blackjack ['blækˌdʒæk] *n* **1.** GAMES black-jack *m* **2.** *Am* (*cosh*) matraque *f*

blacklead *n* graphite *m* **blackleg** *n Brit* briseur, -euse *m, f* de grève **blacklist I.** *n* liste *f* noire **II.** *vt* mettre à l'index **blackmail I.** *n* chantage *m* **II.** *vt* faire chanter; **they ~ed me into buying them ice cream** ils m'ont menacé pour que je leur achète (*subj*) des glaces **blackmailer** *n* maître *m* chanteur **black mark** *n* **1.** SCHOOL mauvaise note *f* **2.** *fig* pénalité *f* **black market** *n* marché *m* noir **black marketeer** *n* trafiquant(e) *m(f)*

blackness ['blæknɪs] *n* **1.** (*colour*) noir *m* **2.** (*darkness*) obscurité *f* **3.** (*dirt*) saleté *f* **4.** *fig* noirceur *f*

blackout ['blækaʊt] *n* **1.** TV, RADIO interruption *f* **2.** (*censor, turning off of lights*) black-out *m* **3.** ELEC panne *f* de courant **4.** (*faint*) évanouissement *m* **5.** (*lapse of memory*) trou *m* de mémoire

black pudding *n Brit* boudin *m* noir **Black Sea** *n* **the ~** la Mer Noire **black sheep** *n fig* brebis *f* galeuse **blacksmith** *n* forgeron *m* **black spot** *n* point *m* noir; **an accident ~** un lieu connu pour ses accidents

bladder ['blædəʳ, *Am:* -ɚ] *n* ANAT vessie *f*

blade[1] [bleɪd] *n* lame *f;* (*on helicopter*) pale *f;* (*of wipers*) balai *m;* **~ of grass** brin *m* d'herbe

blade[2] [bleɪd] *vi inf* faire du roller

blah blah (**blah**) *interj inf* blablabla

blame [bleɪm] **I.** *vt* **to ~ sb/sth for sth** reprocher qc à qn; **to ~ sth on sb/sth** attribuer la responsabilité de qc à qn; **I ~ myself** je m'en veux **II.** *n no pl* reproches *mpl;* **to put the ~ on sb** mettre la faute sur le dos de qn; **to put the ~ on sb else** rejeter la faute sur qn d'autre

blameless ['bleɪmlɪs] *adj* irréprochable

blameworthy ['bleɪmwɜːði, *Am:* -wɜːr-] *adj form* blâmable

blanch [blɑːntʃ, *Am:* blænʃ] **I.** *vt a.* GASTR blanchir **II.** *vi* pâlir

blancmange [blə'mɒnʒ, *Am:* 'mɑːnʒ] *n no pl* blanc-manger *m*

bland [blænd] *adj* insipide

blandishments ['blændɪʃmənts] *npl* flatteries *fpl*

blank [blæŋk] **I.** *adj* **1.** (*empty*) blanc(blanche); (*tape*) vierge; **~ cheque** chèque *m* en blanc; **~ page** page *f* blanche; **a ~ space** un blanc; **my mind's gone ~** j'ai la tête vide **2.** (*impassive: expression look*) absent(e) **3.** (*complete: refusal*) total(e) **II.** *n* **1.** (*space*) blanc *m* **2.** (*cartridge*) balle *f* à blanc ►**to draw a ~** faire chou blanc

blanket ['blæŋkɪt] **I.** *n* (*cover*) couverture *f; fig* (*of snow*) couche *f;* (*of fog*) nappe *f* **II.** *vt* couvrir **III.** *adj* global(e); LING (*term*) général(e)

blare [bleəʳ, *Am:* bler] **I.** *vi* retentir **II.** *n no pl* beuglement *m*

blaspheme [blæs'fiːm, *Am:* 'blæsfiːm] *vi* blasphémer

blasphemer [blæs'fiːməʳ, *Am:* 'blæsfiːmɚ] *n* blasphémateur, -trice *m, f*

blasphemous ['blæsfəməs] *adj* blasphématoire

blasphemy ['blæsfəmi] *n no pl* blasphème *m*

blast [blɑːst, *Am:* blæst] **I.** *vt a. fig* faire sauter; **to ~ a tunnel through a mountain** utiliser des explosif pour creuser un tunnel à travers une montagne **II.** *vi* retentir **III.** *n* **1.** (*detonation*) détonation *f* **2.** (*gust of wind*) rafale *f* **3.** (*noise*) bruit *m* soudain; (*of whistle, horn*) coup *m;* **the radio was at full ~** la radio était à fond **4.** *inf* (*fun*) **it was a ~!** c'était génial! **IV.** *interj inf* **~ it!** merde alors!

blasted *adj inf* sacré(e); **a ~ idiot** une espèce d'idiot

blast furnace *n* haut fourneau *m* **blast-off** *n* (*of rocket*) lancement *m* **blast wave** *n* onde *f* de choc

blatant ['bleɪtnt] *adj pej* flagrant(e)

blaze [bleɪz] **I.** *n* **1.** (*fire: for warmth*) feu *m;* (*out of control*) incendie *m* **2.** (*conflagration*) embrasement *m* **3.** *fig* **a ~ of colour/light** un déploiement de couleurs/lumières; **in a ~ of publicity/glory** sous les trompettes de la publicité/de la gloire **II.** *vi* flamber **III.** *vt a. fig* **to ~ a trail** montrer la voie

◆**blaze away** *vi* **1.**(*burn*) flamboyer **2.**(*shoot*) **to ~ at sb** faire feu sur qn

◆**blaze up** *vi* s'embraser

blazer ['bleɪzəʳ, *Am:* -zɚ] *n* blazer *m*

blazing ['bleɪzɪŋ] *adj* (*fire*) vif(vive); (*heat, sun*) plein(e); (*building*) en feu; (*row*) violent(e)

bleach [bli:tʃ] **I.** *vt* **1.**(*whiten*) blanchir; (*hair*) décolorer; (*spot*) javelliser **2.**(*disinfect*) javelliser **II.** *n* agent *m* blanchissant; (*cleaning product*) eau *m* de Javel

bleachers ['bli:tʃəz, *Am:* -tʃɚz] *n pl, Am* gradins *mpl*

bleaching **I.** *n* blanchiment *m* **II.** *adj* blanchissant(e)

bleak [bli:k] *adj* morne

bleary ['blɪəri, *Am:* 'blɪri] *adj* <-ier, -iest> trouble

bleary-eyed [ˌblɪəri'aɪd, *Am:* 'blɪriaɪd] *adj fig* **to be ~** avoir les yeux bouffis

bleat [bli:t] **I.** *vi* **1.**bêler **2.***fig, pej* se plaindre **II.** *n* **1.**bêlement *m* **2.***fig* jérémiades *fpl*

bled [bled] *pt, pp of* **bleed**

bleed [bli:d] <bled, bled> **I.** *vi* saigner **II.** *vt* **1.** HIST saigner **2.** TECH, AUTO purger

bleeder ['bli:dəʳ, *Am:* -ɚ] *n* **1.** MED hémophile *mf* **2.** *fig, vulg* salopard *m*; **little ~** *inf* petit merdeux; **lucky ~** *inf* sacré veinard

bleeding **I.** *n* saignement *m* **II.** *adj Brit, vulg* foutu(e) **III.** *adv Brit, vulg* sacrément

bleep [bli:p] TECH **I.** *n* bip *m* **II.** *vi* faire bip **III.** *vt* appeler par bip

bleeper ['blɪ:pəʳ, *Am:* -pɚ] *n* récepteur d'appel *m*

blemish ['blemɪʃ] **I.** *n* imperfection *f*; **without ~** *a. fig* sans tache; **there is not a ~ on sth** qc n'a pas le moindre défaut **II.** *vt* tacher; (*reputation*) entacher; **~ed skin** peau *f* à problèmes

blench [blentʃ] *vi a. fig* blêmir

blend [blend] **I.** *n* mélange *m* **II.** *vt* mélanger; (*wine*) couper **III.** *vi* se mélanger; (*colours*) s'harmoniser; **to ~ with sth** se marier avec qc

blend in *vi* (*fabric*) être bien assorti; (*people*) être du même style

blender [blendəʳ, *Am:* -dɚ] *n* mixeur *m*

bless [bles] *vt* bénir; **~ you!** (*after sneeze*) à vos souhaits!; (*in thanks*) c'est tellement gentil!; **to be ~ed with sth** avoir le bonheur de posséder qc

blessed ['blesɪd] *adj* béni(e)

Blessed Virgin *n* REL **the ~** la Sainte Vierge

blessing ['blesɪŋ] *n* bénédiction *f*

blew [blu:] *pt of* **blow**

blight [blaɪt] **I.** *vt* **1.**gâcher **2.***fig* **to ~ sb's chances/hopes** ruiner les chances/les espérances de qn **II.** *n no pl* BOT rouille *f*; **to cast a ~ on sth** *fig* gâcher qc

blighter ['blaɪtəʳ, *Am:* -t̬ɚ] *n Brit, inf* type *m*

blimey ['blaɪmi] *interj Brit, inf* zut alors!

blind [blaɪnd] **I.** *n* **1.**(*window shade*) store *m* **2.**(*subterfuge*) prétexte *m* **3.** *pl* (*people*) **the ~** les aveugles *mpl* **4.** *Am* (*in hunting*) affût *m* **II.** *vt a. fig* aveugler; **to ~ sb to sth** aveugler qn devant qc **III.** *adj* **1.**(*unable to see*) aveugle; **~ in one eye** borgne; **to be ~ to sth** *a. fig* être aveugle à qc **2.**(*hidden*) sans visibilité; (*door*) dérobé(e) ►**as ~ as a bat** myope comme une taupe; **to turn a ~ eye to sth** fermer les yeux sur qc; **love is ~** l'amour est aveugle **IV.** *adv* à l'aveuglette; **~ drunk** *inf* complètement soûl

blind alley <-s> *n a. fig* impasse *m* **blind date** *n rendez-vous arrangé avec un(e) inconnu(e)*

blinder ['blaɪndəʳ, *Am:* -ɚ] *n* **1.** *inf* SPORT **to play a ~** jouer comme un chef; **a ~ of a goal** un but spectaculaire **2.** *pl, Am* (*on horses*) œillères *fpl*

blindfold ['blaɪndfəʊld, *Am:* -foʊld] **I.** *n* bandeau *m* **II.** *vt* bander les yeux à **III.** *adj* aux yeux bandés **IV.** *adv a. fig* les yeux fermés

blindly *adv* (*obey*) aveuglément

blind-man's buff *n* colin-maillard *m*

blindness *n* **1.** MED cécité *f* **2.** *fig* aveuglement *m*

blind spot *n* **1.** AUTO angle *m* mort **2.** *fig* point *m* faible

blink [blɪŋk] **I.** *vt* **1.** ANAT **to ~ one's eyes** cligner des yeux; **to ~ back tears** refouler ses larmes **2.**(*ignore*) **to ~ at sth** fermer les yeux sur qc **II.** *vi* cligner des yeux **III.** *n* (*act of blinking*) battement *m* des paupières; **in the ~ of an eye** *fig* en un clin d'œil ►**sth is on the ~** *inf* qc est détraqué

blinker ['blɪŋkəʳ, *Am:* -kɚ] *n* **1.**(*for horse*) œillère *f* **2.** AUTO clignotant *m*, clignoteur *m Belgique*

blinkered *adj péj* limité(e)

bliss [blɪs] *n* béatitude *f*; **it's ~!** c'est le paradis!

blissful ['blɪsfl] *adj* **1.** REL bienheureux(-euse) **2.** *a. fig* extrêmement heureux(-euse); (*smile, holiday*) merveilleux(-euse)

blister ['blɪstəʳ, *Am:* -tɚ] **I.** *n* **1.**(*on skin*) ampoule *f* **2.**(*on paint*) cloque *f* **3.**(*in glass*) bulle *f* **II.** *vt* provoquer des cloques sur **III.** *vi* (*paint, metal*) cloquer; (*skin*) avoir des ampoules

blistering *adj* (*attack*) féroce; (*heat*) torride

blister pak *n* emballage *m* coque

blitz [blɪts] **I.** *n no pl* bombardement *m* aérien; **to have a ~ on sth** *inf* s'attaquer à qc **II.** *vt a. fig* bombarder

blizzard ['blɪzəd] *n* tempête *f* de neige, poudrerie *f Québec*

bloated ['bləʊtɪd, *Am:* 'bloʊt̬ɪd] *adj a. fig* gonflé(e); **~ with pride** bouffi d'orgueil

bloater ['bləʊtəʳ, *Am:* 'bloʊt̬ɚ] *n* hareng *m* saur

blob [blɒb, *Am:* blɑ:b] *n* **1.**(*drop*) goutte *f* **2.**(*stain*) tache *f*

bloc [blɒk] *n* POL bloc *m*; **the Eastern ~** HIST le bloc de l'Est

block [blɒk, *Am:* blɑːk] **I.** *n* **1.** (*solid lump of sth*) bloc *m;* (*of wood*) tronçon *m* **2.** (*for executions*) billot *m;* **to go to the ~** monter à l'échaffaud; **to go on the ~** *Am* être mis aux enchères; **to put one's head on the ~** *fig* mettre sa tête à prix **3.** INFOR bloc *m* **4.** ARCHIT pâté *m* de maisons; **~ of flats** *Brit,* **apartment ~** *Am* immeuble *m,* conciergerie *f Québec;* **two ~s away** *Am* à deux rues d'ici **5.** (*barrier*) *a. fig* entrave *f;* **a ~ to sth** un obstacle à qc; **mental ~** PSYCH blocage *m* **6.** GAMES **building ~** cube *m* de construction **II.** *vt* (*road, passage*) bloquer; (*pipe*) boucher
◆**block off** *vt* (*road*) barrer
◆**block out** *vt* (*light*) bloquer; (*thoughts*) bloquer
◆**block up** *vt* boucher

blockade [blɒ'keɪd, *Am:* blɑː'keɪd] **I.** *n* blocus *m* **II.** *vt* bloquer

blockage ['blɒkɪdʒ, *Am:* 'blɑːkɪdʒ] *n* obstruction *f*

block and tackle *n* palan *m*

blockbuster ['blɒkˌbʌstəʳ, *Am:* 'blɑːkˌbʌstɚ] **I.** *n* grand succès *m;* (*book*) best-seller *m* **II.** *adj* à grand succès; (*film*) à grand spectacle

blockhouse ['blɒkhaʊs, *Am:* 'blɑːk-] *n* blockhaus *m*

bloke [bləʊk] *n Brit, inf* type *m*

blond(e) [blɒnd, *Am:* blɑːnd] **I.** *adj* (*hair*) blond(e); (*complexion*) de blond(e) **II.** *n* blond(e) *m(f);* **a natural ~** un(e) vrai(e) blond(e)

blood [blʌd] *n no pl a. fig* sang *m;* **to give ~** donner son sang ►**to have ~ on one's hands** avoir du sang sur les mains; **~ is thicker than water** la voix du sang est la plus forte; **bad ~** animosité *f;* **in cold ~** de sang froid; **to make sb's ~ run cold** glacer le sang de qn; **fresh ~** sang neuf; **to make sb's ~ boil** faire bouillir qn; **sb's ~ is up** qn est furieux; **to have sth in one's ~** avoir qc dans le sang

blood bank *n* MED banque *f* du sang **bloodcurdling** *adj* à (vous) glacer le sang **blood donor** *n* donneur, -euse *m, f* de sang **blood group** *n* groupe *m* sanguin **bloodhound** *n a. fig* limier *m*

bloodless *adj* **1.** (*without blood*) *a. fig* exsangue; (*pale*) blême **2.** (*without violence*) sans effusion de sang

blood poisoning *n* septicémie *f* **blood pressure** *n no pl* tension *f* artérielle; **high ~** hypertension *f;* **low ~** hypotension *f* **blood pudding** *n* boudin *m* **blood relation, blood relative** *n* parent(e) *m(f)* par le sang **bloodshed** *n* effusion *f* de sang **bloodshot** *adj* injecté(e) de sang **bloodstained** *adj* taché(e) de sang **bloodstream** *n* système *m* sanguin **bloodsucker** *n* sangsue *f* **blood sugar** *n* glucose *m* sanguin **blood test** *n* analyse *f* de sang **bloodthirsty** *adj* sanguinaire **blood transfusion** *n* transfusion *f* sanguine **blood vessel** *n* vaisseau *m* sanguin

bloody ['blʌdi] <-ier, -iest> *adj* **1.** (*with blood*) ensanglanté(e) **2.** *fig* sanglant(e) **3.** *Aus, Brit, inf* sacré(e); **~ book** foutu bouquin

bloody-minded [ˌblʌdi'maɪndɪd] *adj Brit, inf* buté(e); **to be ~** emmerder le monde

bloom [bluːm] **I.** *n* fleur *f;* **to be in full ~** être en fleur(s); **to come into ~** fleurir **II.** *vi a. fig* fleurir

bloomin', blooming *Brit* **I.** *adj inf* sacré(e) **II.** *adv inf* sacrément

blooming ['bluːmɪŋ] *adj a. fig* florissant(e)

blossom ['blɒsəm, *Am:* 'blɑːsəm] **I.** *n* fleur *f;* **apple ~** fleur de pommier **II.** *vi* **1.** (*flower*) fleurir **2.** *fig* **to ~ (out)** s'épanouir; **to ~ into sth** se transformer en qc

blot [blɒt, *Am:* blɑːt] **I.** *n a. fig* tache *f* **II.** *vt* **1.** (*mark*) tacher **2.** (*dry*) sécher au buvard ►**to ~ one's copybook** ternir sa réputation
◆**blot out** *vt* (*view*) boucher; (*thought, memory*) faire disparaître

blotch [blɒtʃ, *Am:* blɑːtʃ] **I.** *n* tache *f* **II.** *vt* barbouiller

blotchy ['blɒtʃi, *Am:* 'blɑːtʃi] <-ier, -iest> *adj* tacheté(e); (*complexion*) brouillé

blotter ['blɒtəʳ, *Am:* 'blɑːt̬ɚ] *n* buvard *m*

blotting paper ['blɒtɪŋˌpeɪpəʳ, *Am:* 'blɑːt̬ɪŋˌpeɪpɚ] *n no pl* papier *m* buvard

blotto ['blɒtəʊ, *Am:* 'blɑːt̬oʊ] *adj inf* (*drunk*) bourré(e)

blouse [blaʊz] *n* chemisier *m*

blow[1] [bləʊ, *Am:* bloʊ] **I.** <blew, -n> *vi* (*expel air*) souffler; (*whistle*) retentir; **to ~ in the wind** s'agiter dans le vent ►**to ~ hot and cold** tergiverser **II.** *vt* **1.** (*expel air*) **to ~ air into a tube** souffler de l'air dans un tube; **the paper was ~n over the wall** le vent a soulevé le papier par-dessus le mur; **to ~ one's nose** se moucher; **to ~ sb a kiss** envoyer un baiser à qn **2.** (*play: trumpet*) souffler dans ►**to ~ the gaff on sb** dénoncer qn; **to ~ one's own trumpet** chanter ses propres louanges; **to ~ the whistle on sb** *inf* dénoncer qn **III.** *n* souffle *m;* (*wind*) coup *m* de vent; **to give a ~** souffler; **to give one's nose a good ~** se moucher un bon coup

blow[2] [bləʊ, *Am:* bloʊ] **I.** *n a. fig* coup *m;* **at one ~** d'un coup; **to come to ~s** en venir aux mains; **to soften the ~** amortir le choc; **to strike a ~ for sth** marquer un coup pour qc **II.** <blew, -n> *vi* (*explode*) exploser; (*tyre*) éclater; (*fuse*) sauter; (*bulb*) griller **III.** *vt* **1.** (*destroy: fuse*) faire sauter; **to ~ sb's brains out** faire sauter la cervelle de qn **2.** *inf* (*spend*) claquer ►**to ~ a fuse** *inf* péter les plombs; **~ it!** *inf* zut!; **to ~ sb's mind** *inf* époustoufler qn; **to ~ one's top** *inf* piquer une crise
◆**blow away** **I.** *vt* **1.** (*remove*) souffler; (*wind*) emporter **2.** *inf* (*kill*) **to blow sb away** flinguer qn **3.** *fig, inf* **to be blown away** être stupéfait **4.** (*disappear*) s'envoler **II.** *vi* s'envoler
◆**blow down** **I.** *vi* s'abattre **II.** *vt* abattre

B

◆**blow off** I. *vt* emporter II. *vi* 1. (*fly away*) s'envoler 2. *childspeak, inf* (*fart*) péter 3. (*lose temper*) exploser

◆**blow out** I. *vt* 1. (*extinguish*) éteindre 2. (*puff out*) gonfler II. *vi* 1. (*be extinguished*) s'éteindre 2. (*explode*) exploser; (*tyre*) éclater; (*fuse*) sauter 3. (*fly*) s'envoler

◆**blow over** *vi* se calmer

◆**blow up** I. *vi a. fig* éclater; (*with anger*) s'emporter II. *vt* 1. (*fill with air*) gonfler 2. PHOT agrandir 3. (*destroy*) faire exploser 4. (*exaggerate*) gonfler; **it was blown up out of all proportion** ça a été gonflé exagérément

blow-dry ['bləʊˌdraɪ, *Am:* 'bloʊ-] I. *vt* **to ~ sb's hair** faire un brushing à qn II. *n* brushing *m*

blower ['bləʊəʳ, *Am:* 'bloʊɚ] *n Aus, Brit, inf* bigophone *m*

blowfly ['bləʊflaɪ, *Am:* 'bloʊ-] <-ies> *n* mouche *f* bleue

blowhole ['bləʊhəʊl, *Am:* 'bloʊhoʊl] *n* évent *m*

blowlamp ['bləʊlæmp, *Am:* 'bloʊ-] *n s.* **blowtorch**

blown [bləʊn, *Am:* 'bloʊn] *pp of* **blow**

blowout ['bləʊaʊt, *Am:* 'bloʊ-] *n* 1. *Brit, inf* (*meal*) gueuleton *m* 2. AUTO crevaison *f*

blowtorch ['bləʊtɔːtʃ, *Am:* 'bloʊtɔːrtʃ] *n* chalumeau *m*

blow-up ['bləʊʌp] *n* PHOT agrandissement *m*

blub [blʌb] <-bb-> *vi*, **blubber** *vi Brit, inf* pleurnicher

blubber ['blʌbəʳ, *Am:* -ɚ] *n* 1. (*of whale*) blanc *m* 2. *inf* (*fat*) graisse *f*

bludgeon ['blʌdʒən] I. *n* matraque *f* II. *vt* 1. matraquer 2. *fig* **to ~ sb into doing sth** forcer qn à faire qc

blue [bluː] I. *adj* 1. (*colour*) bleu(e); **a light/dark/bright/strong ~ skirt** une jupe bleu clair/foncé/vif/soutenu; **to turn ~** bleuir 2. *fig* **to feel ~** broyer du noir ►**once in a ~ moon** tous les trente-six du mois; **out of the ~** sans crier gare II. *n* bleu *m;* **sky ~** bleu ciel; **the door is painted ~** la porte est peinte en bleu; **to be a pale/deep ~** être d'un bleu pâle/profond

blueberry ['bluːbəri, *Am:* -ˌber-] <-ies> *n* myrtille *f*

blue-black *adj* bleu-noir *inv* **bluebottle** *n* mouche *f* bleue **blue-collar worker** *n* col-bleu *m inf* **Blue Flag** *n* pavillon *m* vert

blueish *adj* tirant sur le bleu

blue-pencil <-led, -ling> *vt* censurer

blueprint ['bluːprɪnt] *n a. fig* plan *m*

blues [bluːz] *npl* blues *m;* **to have the ~** *inf* avoir le cafard

bluff¹ [blʌf] I. *vi* bluffer II. *vt* **to ~ sb into doing sth** bluffer pour que qn fasse qc (*subj*); **to ~ one's way out of trouble** se sortir d'affaire en bluffant III. *n* bluff *m;* **to call sb's ~** prendre qn au mot

bluff² [blʌf] I. *n* à-pic *m* II. <-er, -est> *adj* à pic

bluffer ['blʌfəʳ, *Am:* -ɚ] *n* bluffeur, -euse *m, f*

bluish ['bluːɪʃ] *adj s.* **blueish**

blunder ['blʌndəʳ, *Am:* -dɚ] I. *n* gaffe *f;* **to commit a ~** faire une gaffe II. *vi* 1. (*make a mistake*) faire une gaffe 2. (*move*) **to ~ forward/around** avancer/tourner à l'aveuglette

blunderer *n* gaffeur, -euse *m, f*

blunt [blʌnt] I. *adj* 1. (*blade*) émoussé(e); **a ~ instrument** un instrument contondant 2. *fig* brusque II. *vt a. fig* émousser; **to ~ the impact of sth** atténuer l'impact de qc

bluntly *adv* brusquement; **to put it ~, ...** pour parler franchement, ...

bluntness *n no pl* brusquerie *f*

blur [blɜːʳ, *Am:* blɜːr] I. *vi* <-rr-> s'estomper II. *vt* <-rr-> *a. fig* brouiller; **to ~ a distinction** estomper la différence III. *n no pl* flou *m;* **to be a ~** *a. fig* être flou

blurb [blɜːb, *Am:* blɜːrb] *n no pl* résumé *m* de présentation

blurred [blɜːd, *Am:* blɜːrd] *adj* flou(e)

blurt out [blɜːt'aʊt, *Am:* blɜːrt'aʊt] *vt* laisser échapper

blush [blʌʃ] I. *vi* rougir II. *n* rougeur *f*

blusher ['blʌsəʳ, *Am:* -ɚ] *n* fard *m* à joues

blushing *adj* rougissant(e)

bluster ['blʌstəʳ, *Am:* -tɚ] I. *vi* 1. (*blow wind*) souffler en rafales 2. (*speak*) tempêter 3. (*boast*) fanfaronner II. *n no pl, no art* tapage *m*

BM *n abbr of* **British Museum** British *m* Museum

BMA *n abbr of* **British Medical Association** *association britannique des médecins*

BO [ˌbiː'əʊ, *Am:* -'oʊ] *n abbr of* **body odour** odeur *f* corporelle

boa ['bəʊə, *Am:* 'boʊə] *n a.* FASHION boa *m*

boar [bɔːʳ, *Am:* bɔːr] *n* sanglier *m*

board [bɔːd, *Am:* bɔːrd] I. *n* 1. (*wood*) planche *f* 2. (*blackboard*) tableau *m* 3. (*notice board*) panneau *m* d'affichage 4. GAMES (*for chess*) échiquier *m;* (*for draughts*) damier *m;* (*for other games*) jeu *m* 5. ADMIN conseil *m;* **~ of directors** conseil d'administration; **~ of education** *Am* conseil d'établissement; **~ of trade** *Brit* ministère *m* du commerce 6. (*in hotels*) **half ~** demi-pension *f;* **full ~** pension *f* complète; **~ and lodging** *Brit,* **room and ~** *Am* le gîte et le couvert 7. NAUT, AVIAT **to get on ~** monter à bord; (*bus, train*) monter dans, embarquer dans *Québec;* **to take on ~** embarquer; (*fact, situation*) prendre en compte ►**to let sth go by the ~** laisser tomber qc; **across the ~** à tous les niveaux; **to get sb on ~** s'assurer le soutien de qn; **on the ~** *Am* au programme; **to tread the ~s** faire du théâtre II. *vt* 1. (*cover*) **to ~ sth up** couvrir qc de planches; (*seal*) condamner qc 2. (*lodge*) prendre [*o* avoir] en pension 3. (*get on: plane, boat*) monter à bord de; (*bus*) monter dans, embarquer dans *Québec* III. *vi* (*in hotel*) être en pension; (*in school*) être pensionnaire; **to ~ with sb** être en pension chez qn

boarder ['bɔːdəʳ, *Am:* 'bɔːrdɚ] *n* SCHOOL interne *mf*
board game *n* jeu *m* de société (*comme les échecs ou le Monopoly*)
boarding *n* embarquement *m*
boarding card *n Brit* carte *f* d'embarquement **boarding house** *n* pension *f* **boarding pass** *n Am s.* **boarding card** **boarding school** *n* pensionnat *m*
boardroom *n* salle *f* de réunion **boardwalk** *n Am* promenade *f* (en planches)

La **Boardwalk** est une promenade sur berge dans la région d'Atlantic City. Plus des deux tiers de la promenade s'étendent dans Atlantic City même et le reste dans la région avoisinante au sud, Ventnor City. "The Boardwalk" est bordée d'hôtels, de restaurants, de magasins et de théâtres. La "Miss America Pageant" (l'élection de Miss America) a lieu tous les ans au mois de septembre dans le "Convention Center" situé sur "The Boardwalk".

boast [bəʊst, *Am:* boʊst] **I.** *vi* se vanter; **to ~ about** [*o* **of**] **sth** se vanter de qc **II.** *vt* **1. to ~ that ...** se vanter que ... **2.** (*have: university, industry*) s'enorgueuillir de; (*device, feature*) être équipé de **III.** *n* **it's just a ~** c'est de la frime; **my proudest ~** ma plus grande fierté
boaster *n pej* vantard(e) *m(f)*
boastful ['bəʊstfl, *Am:* 'boʊst-] *adj pej* vantard(e)
boat [bəʊt, *Am:* boʊt] *n* bateau *m* ►**to be in the same ~** être dans la même galère; **to rock the ~** jouer les trouble-fête
boathouse *n* hangar *m* à bateaux
boating ['bəʊtɪŋ, *Am:* 'boʊt̬ɪŋ] *n no pl* canotage *m*
boat people *npl* boat people *mpl* **boat race** *n* course *f* d'aviron

La **Boat Race**, course annuelle de bateaux, oppose un samedi du mois de mars, sur "the Thames" (La Tamise), des équipes de huit rameurs des universités d'Oxford et de Cambridge. Elle constitue un événement national suivi par 460 millions de spectacteurs dans le monde entier.

boatswain ['bəʊsən, *Am:* 'boʊ-] *n* maître *m* d'équipage
boat train *n train qui assure la correspondance avec un ferry* **boat trip** *n* promenade *f* en bateau
bob[1] [bɒb, *Am:* bɑːb] *n* coupe *f* au carré
bob[2] [bɒb, *Am:* bɑːb] <-bb-> **I.** *vi* s'agiter; **to ~ up** surgir; **to ~ up and down on water** danser sur l'eau **II.** *vt* **to ~ one's head** faire un signe de tête; **to ~ a curtsy to sb** faire une petite révérence à qn **III.** *n* **1.** (*movement*) petit coup *m;* (*as curtsy*) bref salut *m* **2.** (*weight*) plomb *m*
bob[3] [bɒb, *Am:* bɑːb] *n Brit, inf* shilling *m;* **to earn/have a ~ or two** gagner/avoir des sous
bob[4] [bɒb, *Am:* bɑːb] *n inf* SPORT *abbr of* **bobsleigh** bob *m*
bobbin ['bɒbɪn, *Am:* 'bɑːbɪn] *n* bobine *f*
bobble *n* pompon *m*
bobby ['bɒbi, *Am:* 'bɑːbi] <-ies> *n Brit* flic *m*
bobby pin *n Am, Aus s.* **hairgrip**
bobsled ['bɒbsled, *Am:* 'bɑːb-], **bobsleigh** *n* SPORT bobsleigh *m*
bode [bəʊd, *Am:* boʊd] **I.** *vi* **to ~ well/ill** être de bon/mauvais augure **II.** *vt* présager
bodge [bɒdʒ, *Am:* bɑːdʒ] *Brit* **I.** *n* boulot *m* mal fait **II.** *vt* **to ~ sth** (**up**) saboter qc
bodice ['bɒdɪs, *Am:* 'bɑːdɪs] *n* corsage *m*
bodily ['bɒdəli] **I.** *adj* corporel(le); (*strength*) physique; (*needs*) matériel(le) **II.** *adv a. fig* à bras-le-corps
body ['bɒdi, *Am:* 'bɑːdi] <-ies> *n* **1.** (*physical structure*) corps *m; fig* (*of wine*) corps *m;* (*of hair*) volume *m* **2.** (*group*) organisme *m;* **legislative ~** corps législatif **3.** (*amount*) masse *f;* (*of water*) étendue *f;* **~ of evidence** accumulation de preuves **4.** (*main part: car*) carrosserie *f;* (*plane*) fuselage *m* **5.** (*leotard*) body *m* ►**over my dead ~!** plutôt mourir!; **just enough to keep ~ and soul together** tout juste de quoi subsister
bodybuilding *no pl n* culturisme *m* **bodyguard** *n* garde *mf* du corps **body language** *n* langage *m* du corps **body lotion** *n* lait *m* pour le corps **body politic** *n no pl, form* POL corps *m* social **body search** *n* fouille *f* corporelle **bodysuit** *n* justaucorps *m* **bodywork** *n* carrosserie *f*
bog [bɒg, *Am:* bɑːg] *n* **1.** (*wet ground*) marécage *m;* **peat ~** tourbière *f* **2.** *Aus, Brit, inf* (*toilet*) chiottes *fpl*
bog down <-gg-> *vt* **to be/get bogged down in sth** *a. fig* s'enliser dans qc
bogey ['bəʊgi, *Am:* 'boʊ-] *n* **1.** (*fear*) spectre *m* **2.** *Brit, inf* (*mucus*) crotte *f* de nez
bogeyman *n* croque-mitaine *m*
boggle ['bɒgl, *Am:* 'bɑːgl] **I.** *vi* **the mind ~s** on croit rêver; **sb's mind ~s at sth** qn est époustouflé par qc **II.** *vt* **to ~ the mind** être époustouflant
boggy ['bɒgi, *Am:* 'bɑːgi] <-ier, -iest> *adj* marécageux(-euse); (*ground*) bourbeux(-euse)
bogus ['bəʊgəs, *Am:* 'boʊ-] *adj* faux(fausse)
bogy ['bəʊgi, *Am:* 'boʊ-] *n s.* **bogey**
bohemian [bəʊ'hiːmiən, *Am:* boʊ-] **I.** *n* bohémien(ne) *m(f)* **II.** *adj* bohémien(ne); **the ~ life** la vie de bohème; **to be ~** être bohème
boil [bɔɪl] **I.** *n* **1.** *no pl, no art* ébullition *f;* **to bring sth to a ~, to bring sth to the ~** *Brit* porter qc à ébullition; **to be on the ~** être en ébullition; **to go off the ~** cesser de bouillir **2.** MED furoncle *m* **II.** *vi* bouillir; **to let sth ~ dry** laisser le contenu de qc s'évaporer ►**to make sb's blood ~** mettre qn hors de lui; **to keep the pot ~ing** faire bouillir la marmite **III.** *vt* **1.** (*bring to boil*) faire bouillir; (*kettle*)

B

faire chauffer **2.** (*cook in water*) bouillir; ~**ed potatoes** pomme de terre à l'eau; ~**ed egg** œuf à la coque
◆**boil away** *vi* s'évaporer
◆**boil down** **I.** *vi* réduire **II.** *vt* faire réduire
◆**boil down to** *vi* revenir à
◆**boil over** *vi* **1.** (*rise and flow over*) déborder **2.** (*go out of control*) exploser; **to boil** (**over**) **with rage** bouillir de rage
◆**boil up** **I.** *vt* faire bouillir **II.** *vi fig* (*trouble, situation*) surgir

boiler ['bɔɪləʳ, *Am:* -lɚ] *n* chaudière *f*, fournaise *f Québec*

boilermaker *n* chaudronnier *m* **boiler room** *n* chaufferie *f* **boiler suit** *n Aus, Brit* bleu *m* de travail

boiling *adj* bouillant(e); **to be** ~ **with rage** *fig* bouillir de rage

boiling point *n* point *m* d'ébullition; **at** ~ à ébullition

boisterous ['bɔɪstərəs] *adj* énergique; (*wind*) violent(e); (*sea*) agité(e)

bold[1] [bəʊld, *Am:* boʊld] <-er, -est> *adj* **1.** (*brave, striking*) audacieux(-euse) **2.** (*aggressive*) arrogant(e)

bold[2] [bəʊld, *Am:* boʊld] *n* INFOR, TYP **in** ~ en caractères gras

boldness *n* audace *f*

bolero [bə'leərəʊ, *Am:* -'leroʊ] <-s> *n* boléro *m*

Bolivia [bə'lɪvɪə] *n* la Bolivie

Bolivian [bə'lɪvɪən] **I.** *adj* bolivien(ne) **II.** *n* Bolivien(ne) *m(f)*

bollard ['bɒlɑːd, *Am:* 'bɑːlɚd] *n* (*showing direction*) balise *f*; (*blocking entry*) bollard *m*

bolster ['bəʊlstəʳ, *Am:* 'boʊlstɚ] **I.** *n* traversin *m*, boudin *m Belgique, Nord* **II.** *vt* **to** ~ **sb/sth** (**up**) soutenir qn/qc; **to** ~ **sb's ego** gonfler l'ego de qn

bolt [bəʊlt, *Am:* boʊlt] **I.** *vi* décamper **II.** *vt* **1.** (*eat*) **to** ~ (**down**) **one's food** engloutir sa nourriture **2.** (*lock*) verrouiller **3.** (*fix*) **to** ~ **sth on**(**to**) **sth** (*with bolt*) fixer qc à qc; *fig* plaquer qc sur qc **III.** *n* **1.** (*for locking*) verrou *m* **2.** (*screw*) boulon *m* **3.** (*lightning*) éclair *m*; ~ **of lightning** coup *m* de foudre **4.** (*roll*) rouleau *m* **5.** (*escape*) **to make a** ~ **for it** décamper ►**like a** ~ **from the** <u>**blue**</u> comme un coup de tonnerre **IV.** *adv* **to sit** ~ **upright** s'asseoir bien droit

bolt-hole *n* refuge *m*; (*animal*) terrier *m*

bomb [bɒm, *Am:* bɑːm] **I.** *n* **1.** (*explosive*) bombe *f*; **the Bomb** la bombe atomique; **to drop a** ~ larguer une bombe; **to go like a** ~ *Brit, inf, a. fig* très bien marcher; **it looks as if a** ~ **had hit it** *fig* c'est un véritable champ de bataille **2.** *Am, inf* (*flop*) fiasco *m* ►**to** <u>**cost**</u> **a** ~ *Brit* coûter les yeux de la tête **II.** *vt* bombarder **III.** *vi* **to** ~ *inf* faire un flop
◆**bomb out** *vt* chasser par des bombardements

bombard [bɒm'bɑːd, *Am:* bɑːm'bɑːrd] *vt* **1.** MIL bombarder **2.** *fig* **to** ~ **sb with sth** bombarder qn de qc

bombardment [bɒm'bɑːdmənt, *Am:* bɑːm'bɑːrd-] *n a. fig* bombardement *m*

bombast ['bɒmbæst, *Am:* 'bɑːm-] *n no pl, no art* grandiloquence *f*

bombastic [bɒm'bæstɪk, *Am:* bɑːm-] *adj* pompeux(-euse)

bombed [bɒmd] *adj* **1.** bombardé(e) **2.** *Am, fig, inf* (*on drugs*) défoncé(e)

bombed-out *adj* **1.** (*bombed*) bombardé(e); **I was** ~ ma maison a été bombardée **2.** *inf* (*high*) défoncé(e)

bomber ['bɒməʳ, *Am:* 'bɑːmɚ] *n* **1.** (*plane*) bombardier *m* **2.** (*person*) poseur *m* de bombes

bomber jacket *n* blouson *m* d'aviateur

bombing *n* **1.** MIL bombardement *m* **2.** (*by terrorist*) attentat *m* à la bombe

bombproof *adj* blindé(e) **bombshell** *n* **1.** obus *m* **2.** *inf* (*woman*) canon *m*

bona fide [ˌbəʊnə'faɪdi, *Am:* ˌboʊ-] *adj* **1.** (*genuine*) authentique **2.** (*serious*) sérieux(-euse)

bonanza [bə'nænzə] *n a.* MIN filon *m*; **a price** ~ des prix massacrés; **a goals** ~ des buts à gogo; **a tourist/oil** ~ **for the town** un filon touristique/pétrolier pour la ville

bond [bɒnd, *Am:* bɑːnd] **I.** *n* **1.** (*emotional connection*) lien *m*; **the** ~**s of marriage** les liens du mariage **2.** (*certificate of debt*) obligation *f* **3.** (*written agreement*) engagement *m* **4.** *Am* (*bail*) caution *f* **5.** (*joint*) attache *f* **6.** COM **in** ~ sous douane **II.** *vt* **1.** (*unite*) **to** ~ **two things/people together** unir deux choses/personnes entre elles **2.** (*stick or bind*) coller **3.** COM entreposer **III.** *vi* (*people*) créer des liens; (*things*) adhérer

bondage ['bɒndɪdʒ, *Am:* 'bɑːn-] *n no pl* esclavage *m*

bonded *adj* COM en dépôt; ~ **warehouse** entrepôt *m* en douane

bond holder *n* FIN obligataire *m*

bone [bəʊn, *Am:* boʊn] **I.** *n* os *m*; (*of fish*) arête *f* **II.** *adj* ~-**handled knife** couteau *m* à manche d'os **III.** *vt* (*meat*) désosser; (*fish*) retirer les arêtes de

bone china *n* porcelaine *f* à l'os **bone fracture** *n* fracture *f* **bonehead** *n pej, inf* idiot(e) *m(f)* **bone idle**, **bone lazy** *adj pej* flemmard(e)

boneless *adj* (*fish*) sans arêtes; (*meat*) désossé(e)

bone meal *n* engrais *m* phosphaté **boneshaker** *n iron, inf* vieille carcasse *f*

bonfire ['bɒnfaɪəʳ, *Am:* 'bɑːnfaɪɚ] *n* feu *m* de joie

bonnet ['bɒnɪt, *Am:* 'bɑːnɪt] *n* **1.** (*hat*) bonnet *m* **2.** *Aus, Brit* AUTO capot *m*

bonny ['bɒni, *Am:* 'bɑːni] *adj Brit* joli(e)

bonus ['bəʊnəs, *Am:* 'boʊ-] *n* **1.** (*money*) prime *f* **2.** (*advantage*) avantage *m*

bony ['bəʊni, *Am:* 'boʊ-] *adj* <-ier, -iest> **1.** (*with prominent bones*) osseux(-euse)

2. (*full of bones: fish*) plein d'arêtes

boo [buː] I. *interj inf* hou II. *vi, vt* <-s, -ing, -ed> huer

boob [buːb] I. *n* 1. *inf* (*breast*) lolo *m* 2. *Brit, inf* (*blunder*) gaffe *f* 3. *Am s.* **booby** II. *vi Brit, inf* gaffer

booby ['buːbi] *n* crétin(e) *m(f)*

booby prize *n* prix *m* de consolation **booby-trap** I. *n* piège *m* II. *vt* tendre un piège à

book [bʊk] I. *n* (*for reading*) livre *m;* (*of stamps, tickets*) carnet *m;* **the ~s** COM livres *mpl* de compte; **to do the ~s** faire les comptes ▶**to be in sb's bad ~s** ne pas avoir la cote avec qn; **to be in sb's good ~s** être dans les petits papiers de qn; **to bring sb to ~** obliger qn à rendre des comptes; **in my ~** d'après moi; **to do things by the ~** faire les choses dans les règles II. *vt* 1. (*reserve*) réserver 2. FIN, COM inscrire; (*police*) dresser un P.V. à; SPORT donner un avertissement à III. *vi* réserver

◆**book in** I. *vi* s'enregistrer II. *vt* **to book sb in** réserver une chambre à qn

◆**book through** *vi* **to be booked through to Tokyo** avoir réservé un billet pour Tokyo

◆**book up** *vi, vt* réserver; **to be booked up** être complet

bookable ['bʊkəbl] *adj* que l'on peut réserver

bookbinder *n* relieur, -euse *m, f* **bookbinding** *n no pl* reliure *f* **bookcase** *n* bibliothèque *f* **book club** *n* club *m* du livre **bookend** *n* serre-livres *m*

bookie ['bʊki] *n inf abbr of* **bookmaker**

booking ['bʊkɪŋ] *n* (*for room, seat*) réservation *f*

booking clerk *n Brit* préposé *m* aux réservations **booking office** *n Brit* bureau *m* de location

bookish ['bʊkɪʃ] *adj pej* 1. (*person*) studieux(-euse) 2. (*style*) pédant(e)

bookkeeper *n* comptable *mf* **bookkeeping** *n no pl* comptabilité *f* **booklet** *n* brochure *f*

bookmaker ['bʊkˌmeɪkəʳ, *Am:* -kɚ] *n* bookmaker *m*

bookmark *n a.* INFOR signet *m* **bookplate** *n* ex-libris *m* **bookseller** *n* libraire *mf* **bookshelf** *n* étagère *f* **bookshop** *n* librairie *f* **bookstall** *n* kiosque *m* **bookstore** *n Am s.* **bookshop** **book token** *n Brit* bon *m* pour un livre **book trade** *n* librairie *f* **bookworm** *n* rat *m* de bibliothèque

boom¹ [buːm] I. *vi* être en pleine croissance II. *n* essor *m;* **a construction ~** un boom dans la construction; **the ~ years** les années glorieuses

boom² [buːm] I. *n* grondement *m* II. *vi* **to ~ (out)** résonner; **"come in", he ~ed** "entrez", dit-il d'une voix sonore III. *vt* faire retentir

boom³ [buːm] *n* 1. (*floating barrier*) barrage *m* flottant 2. (*for microphone*) perche *f* de micro

boomerang ['buːməræŋ] I. *n* boomerang *m* II. *vi* **to ~ on sb** retomber sur qn

boon [buːn] *n* bienfait *m;* **it's such a ~** c'est merveilleux

boor [bʊəʳ, *Am:* bʊr] *n pej* rustre *m*

boorish ['bɔːrɪʃ, *Am:* 'bʊrɪʃ] *adj pej* rustre

boost [buːst] I. *n* **to give a ~ to sth** donner un coup de fouet à qc II. *vt* (*economy, sales, shares*) relancer; (*hopes, chances*) accroître; (*speed, output*) augmenter; **to ~ sb's confidence** renforcer la confiance en soi-même de qn

booster [buːstəʳ, *Am:* -stɚ] *n* 1. (*improvement*) regain *m* 2. MED rappel *m* 3. RADIO amplificateur *m* 4. ELEC survolteur *m* 5. AVIAT fusée *f* auxiliaire 6. AUTO compresseur *m*

booster rocket *n* fusée *f* de lancement **booster seat** *n* AUTO siège *m* pour enfant

boot [buːt] I. *n* 1. (*footwear: calf-length*) botte *f;* (*short*) boot *f* 2. *Brit* AUTO coffre *m* 3. INFOR amorce *f;* **warm/cold ~** démarrage *m* à chaud/froid ▶**to get the ~** se faire virer; **to put the ~ in** y aller fort II. *vt* 1. *inf* (*kick*) **to ~ sth somewhere** envoyer qc quelque part (d'un coup de pied); **he ~ed the ball past the line** il donna un coup de pied dans la balle qu'il envoya au-delà de la ligne 2. INFOR **to ~** amorcer

◆**boot out** *vt inf* flanquer à la porte

◆**boot up** INFOR I. *vt* (*system, program, computer*) lancer II. *vi* démarrer

bootblack ['buːtblæk] *n* cireur *m* de chaussures

bootee ['buːtiː, *Am:* -t̬i] *n* bottillon *m*

booth [buːð] *n* 1. (*cubicle*) cabine *f;* **polling ~** isoloir *m* 2. (*stall at fair*) stand *m*

bootjack *n* tire-botte *m* **bootlace** *n* lacet *m* de botte

bootleg ['buːtleg] <-gg-> I. *adj* 1. (*sold illegallly*) de contrebande 2. (*illegally copied*) piraté(e) II. *vt* 1. (*sell illegallly*) vendre en contrebande 2. (*copy illegally*) pirater III. *vi* faire de la contrebande; (*media*) faire du piratage

bootlicker *n* lèche-botte *m,* frotte-manche *m Belgique* **boot maker** *n* bottier *m*

booty ['buːti, *Am:* -t̬i] *n* butin *m*

booze [buːz] I. *n inf* alcool *m* II. *vi inf* picoler

boozer ['buːzəʳ, *Am:* -ɚ] *n* 1. *inf* (*person*) poivrot(e) *m(f)* 2. *Brit, inf* (*pub*) bistro *m*

booze-up *n* beuverie *f*

border ['bɔːdəʳ, *Am:* 'bɔːrdɚ] I. *n* 1. (*frontier: of country*) frontière *f;* (*of estate, town*) limite *f;* **a ~ post** un poste frontalier 2. (*decoration*) bordure *f* II. *vt* border; **to be ~ed by Germany** avoir l'Allemagne pour pays limitrophe

◆**border on** *vt* (*country*) avoir pour pays limitrophe; *fig* (*madness, insolence*) friser

borderer *n* frontalier, -ère *m, f*

bordering *adj* avoisinant(e); (*country*) limitrophe

borderland ['bɔːdəlænd, *Am:* 'bɔːrdɚ-] *n*

zone *f* frontalière

borderline ['bɔːdəlaɪn, *Am:* 'bɔːrdɚ-] *n* ligne *f* de séparation

borderline case *n* cas *m* limite

bore[1] [bɔːʳ, *Am:* bɔːr] **I.** *n* **1.** (*thing*) barbe *f* **2.** (*person*) raseur, -euse *m, f* **II.** <-d> *vt* ennuyer

bore[2] [bɔːʳ, *Am:* bɔːr] **I.** *n* **1.** (*calibre*) calibre *m* **2.** (*deep hole*) forage *m* **II.** *vt* forer; **to ~ a hole** faire un trou

bored *adj* (*look*) plein d'ennui; **~ children** des enfants qui s'ennuient

boredom ['bɔːdəm, *Am:* 'bɔːr-] *n no pl* ennui *m*

borer *n* foret *m*

boric ['bɔːrɪk] *adj* borique

boring ['bɔːrɪŋ] *adj* ennuyeux(-euse), ennuyant(e) *Québec*

born [bɔːn, *Am:* bɔːrn] *adj a. fig* né(e); **to be ~** naître

born-again ['bɔːnəgen, *Am:* ˌbɔːrn-] *adj* REL régénéré(e)

borne [bɔːn, *Am:* bɔːrn] *pt of* **bear**

borough ['bʌrə, *Am:* 'bɜːroʊ] *n* municipalité *f*

borrow ['bɒrəʊ, *Am:* 'bɑːroʊ] *vt* emprunter

borrower *n* emprunteur, -euse *m, f*

borrowing *n no pl* emprunt *m*

Bosnia and Herzegovina *n* la Bosnie-Herzégovine

Bosnian ['bɒznɪən, *Am:* 'bɑːz-] **I.** *adj* bosniaque, bosnien(ne) **II.** *n* Bosniaque *mf,* Bosnien(ne) *m(f)*

bosom ['bʊzəm] *n* **1.** poitrine *f* **2.** *fig* cœur *m* ▸**in the ~ of one's family** *iron* au sein de sa famille

boss[1] [bɒs, *Am:* bɑːs] **I.** *n a. inf* chef *m* **II.** *vt pej, inf* **to ~ sb about** donner des ordres à qn

boss[2] [bɒs, *Am:* bɑːs] *adj Am, inf* merveilleux(-euse)

bossy ['bɒsi, *Am:* 'bɑːsi] <-ier, -iest> *adj pej* despotique

bosun ['bəʊsən, *Am:* 'boʊ-] *n s.* **boatswain**

botanical [bə'tænɪkəl] *adj* botanique

botanist ['bɒtənɪst, *Am:* 'bɑːtnɪst] *n* botaniste *mf*

botany ['bɒtəni, *Am:* 'bɑːtni] *n* botanique *f*

botch [bɒtʃ, *Am:* bɑːtʃ] *s.* **bodge**

botcher *n* saboteur, -euse *m, f*

botch-up *Aus, Brit s.* **bodge**

both [bəʊθ, *Am:* boʊθ] **I.** *adj, pron* tous (les) deux; **~ of them** l'un et l'autre; **~ of us** nous deux; **~ (the) brothers** les deux frères; **on ~ sides** de part et d'autre; **I bought ~ the computer and the printer** j'ai acheté les deux, l'ordinateur et l'imprimante; **~ he and his sister are ill** sa sœur et lui sont tous les deux malades **II.** *adv* **to be ~ sad and pleased** être à la fois triste et content

bother ['bɒðəʳ, *Am:* 'bɑːðɚ] **I.** *n* **1.** (*trouble*) ennui *m;* **to have some ~** avoir des ennuis **2.** (*annoyance*) **it's such a ~** c'est tellement embêtant; **it's no ~** il n'a pas de problème; **I don't want to be a ~** je ne veux pas déranger **II.** *vi* **not to ~ about sth** ne pas s'inquiéter de qc; **don't ~ to ring** ce n'est pas la peine de téléphoner; **I can't be ~ed** ça vaut pas la peine **III.** *vt* ennuyer, chicaner *Québec*

botheration *interj* **~!** flûte!

bothersome ['bɒðəsəm, *Am:* 'bɑːðɚ-] *adj* importun(e)

Botswana [ˌbɒt'swɑːnə, *Am:* bɑːt-] *n* le Botswana

bottle ['bɒtl, *Am:* 'bɑːt̬l] **I.** *n* **1.** (*container*) bouteille *f;* **a baby's ~** un biberon **2.** *Brit, inf* (*courage*) courage *m;* **he lost his ~** il s'est dégonflé **II.** *vt* **1.** *Brit* (*preserve in jars*) mettre en bocaux **2.** (*put into bottles*) mettre en bouteilles

◆**bottle out** *vi Brit, inf* se dégonfler; **to ~ of sth** se dégonfler devant qc

◆**bottle up** *vt* étouffer

bottle bank *n* conteneur *m* à verre **bottle brush** *n* goupillon *m*

bottled ['bɒtld, *Am:* 'bɑːt̬ld] *adj* en bouteille(s); (*fruit*) en bocaux; **~ water** eau minérale

bottle-feed *vt* nourrir au biberon **bottle-green** *adj* vert bouteille *inv* **bottle heater** *n* chauffe-biberon *m* **bottleneck** *n* **1.** (*place*) étranglement *m* **2.** (*delay*) embouteillage *m* **bottle party** <-ies> *n soirée où l'on apporte une bouteille* **bottle rack** *n* porte-bouteille(s) *m*

bottom ['bɒtəm, *Am:* 'bɑːt̬əm] **I.** *n* **1.** (*lowest part*) bas *m;* (*of pyjamas*) pantalon *m;* (*of the sea, a container*) fond *m;* **from top to ~** de haut en bas **2.** (*end: of street*) bout *m;* (*of the garden*) fond *m;* **to be (at the) ~ of one's class** être le dernier de sa classe; **to start at the ~** commencer en bas de l'échelle **3.** (*buttocks*) derrière *m* ▸**to mean sth from the ~ of one's heart** dire qc du fond du cœur; **to get to the ~ of sth** aller au fond des choses; **to be at the ~ of sth** être derrière qc; **at ~** au [*o* dans le] fond **II.** *adj* (*level*) d'en bas; (*jaw*) inférieur(e); **bottom end** partie *f* inférieure; **the ~ of the table** le bout de la table

bottomless ['bɒtəmləs, *Am:* 'bɑːt̬əm-] *adj* **1.** (*without limit*) sans fin **2.** (*very deep*) sans fond

bottom line *n* **the ~ is that** en dernière analyse; **what's the ~?** c'est quoi l'essentiel?

botulism ['bɒtjʊlɪzəm, *Am:* 'bɑːtʃə-] *n* botulisme *m*

bough [baʊ] *n* branche *f*

bought [bɔːt, *Am:* bɑːt] *pt of* **buy**

boulder ['bəʊldəʳ, *Am:* 'boʊldɚ] *n* bloc *m* de pierre

bounce [baʊnts] **I.** *n* **1.** (*springing action, rebound*) rebond *m;* **to catch a ball on the ~** prendre une balle au bond **2.** *no pl* (*spring*) bond *m* **3.** *no pl* (*bounciness: of hair, bed*) ressort *m* **4.** (*vitality, energy*) vitalité *f* **II.** *vi* **1.** (*spring into the air, rebound*) rebondir **2.** (*jump up and down*) bondir **3.** *inf* COM

(*cheque*) être refusé III. *vt* 1. (*cause to rebound*) faire rebondir; **to ~ a baby on one's knee** faire sauter un bébé sur ses genoux 2. *inf* COM **to ~ a cheque** refuser un chèque en bois
◆**bounce back** *vi* 1. rebondir 2. *fig* se remettre
bouncer ['baʊntsəʳ, *Am:* -sɚ] *n* videur, -euse *m, f*
bouncing *adj* rebondi(e); (*baby*) en pleine santé
bound[1] [baʊnd] I. *vi* bondir II. *n* bond *m;* **with one ~** d'un bond ►**by leaps and ~s** à pas de géant
bound[2] [baʊnd] I. *vt* **to be ~ed by sth** être bordé par qc II. *n pl* limites *fpl;* **to be** [*o* **go**] **beyond the ~s of possibility** dépasser les limites du possible; **to be within the ~s of the law** être légal; **to keep sth within ~s** maintenir qc dans des limites acceptables; **to know no ~s** être sans limites ►**out of ~s** interdit
bound[3] [baʊnd] *adj* **~ for** en route pour; **the Geneva-~ flight** le vol à destination de Genève
bound[4] [baʊnd] I. *pt, pp of* **bind** II. *adj* 1. (*sure*) **sth is ~ to happen** qc va certainement se produire; **he's ~ to come** c'est sûr qu'il viendra; **it was ~ to happen sooner or later** cela devait arriver tôt ou tard 2. (*obliged*) **to be ~ to** +*infin* être obligé de +*infin* ►**to be ~ and determined** *Am* être absolument résolu
boundary ['baʊndri] <-ies> *n* 1. (*line, division*) limite *f* 2. (*border: between countries*) frontière *f* 3. SPORT limites *fpl* du terrain 4. *fig* **to blur the bounderies between sth and sth** estomper les différences entre qc et qc
boundless ['baʊndlɪs] *adj* illimité(e)
bounty ['baʊnti, *Am:* -t̬i] <-ies> *n* (*reward*) prime *f*
bouquet [bʊ'keɪ, *Am:* boʊ-] *n* bouquet *m*
bout [baʊt] *n* 1. (*period*) crise *f;* **a ~ of coughing** une quinte de toux; **drinking ~** beuverie *f* 2. SPORT combat *m*
bovine ['bəʊvaɪn, *Am:* 'boʊ-] *adj* bovin(e)
bow[1] [bəʊ, *Am:* boʊ] *n* 1. (*weapon*) arc *m;* **to draw one's ~** tendre son arc 2. MUS archet *m* 3. (*slip-knot*) nœud *m* ►**to have more than one string to one's ~** avoir plus d'une corde à son arc
bow[2] [baʊ] *n* NAUT proue *f*
bow[3] [baʊ] I. *n* 1. salut *m;* **to give** [*o* **make**] **a ~ to sb** saluer qn 2. *fig* **to take one's final ~** faire ses adieux II. *vi* **to ~ to sb/sth** saluer qn/qc; (*defer*) s'en remettre à ►**to ~ and scrape** *pej* être obséquieux III. *vt* (*one's head*) baisser
◆**bow out** *vi* (*stop taking part*) tirer sa révérence
bowdlerise *vt Aus, Brit,* **bowdlerize** ['baʊdləraɪz, *Am:* 'boʊdləraɪz] *vt pej* expurger
bowel ['baʊəl] *n* MED intestin *m*
bowel movement *n* selles *fpl*
bowl[1] [bəʊl, *Am:* boʊl] *n* bol *m;* (*for mixing*) saladier *m;* **a ~ of soup** une assiette de soupe
bowl[2] [bəʊl, *Am:* boʊl] SPORT I. *n* 1. (*in bowling*) boule *f* 2. *pl* (*game*) boules *fpl;* **to play (at) ~s** jouer aux boules II. *vi* 1. (*in cricket*) servir 2. (*roll*) faire rouler la balle 3. (*play skittles*) jouer au bowling III. *vt* (*ball*) lancer; (*bowling ball*) faire rouler
◆**bowl out** *vt* mettre hors jeu
◆**bowl over** *vt* 1. (*knock over*) renverser 2. (*astonish*) stupéfier; **to be bowled over** être sidéré
Bowl [bəʊl, *Am:* boʊl] *n Am* (*building*) **the ~** l'amphithéâtre
bow-legged [ˌbəʊ'legd, *Am:* boʊ-] *adj* aux jambes arquées
bowler ['bəʊləʳ, *Am:* 'boʊlɚ] *n* 1. (*in cricket*) serveur *m* 2. SPORT (*in bowls*) joueur, -euse *m, f* de boules; (*in tenpin bowling*) joueur, -euse *m, f* de bowling 3. (*hat*) chapeau *m* melon
bowling *n no pl* 1. (*tenpins*) bowling *m;* (*outdoor*) boules (anglaises) *fpl* 2. (*in cricket*) service *m* de la balle; **to open the ~** être le premier à lancer
bowling alley *n* 1. (*building*) bowling *m* 2. (*track*) piste *f* de bowling **bowling green** *n terrain de boules en gazon*
bowman ['bəʊmən, *Am:* 'boʊ-] *n* archer *m*
bowstring ['bəʊstrɪŋ, *Am:* 'boʊ-] *n* corde *f* d'arc
bow tie *n* nœud *m* papillon **bow window** *n* fenêtre *f* en saillie **bow-wow** *childspeak* I. *interj* oua-oua! II. *n* toutou *m*
box[1] [bɒks, *Am:* bɑːks] *n* 1. (*container*) boîte *f;* (*of large format*) caisse *f;* **a (cardboard) ~** un carton; **chocolate ~** boîte de chocolats; **tool ~** boîte à outils 2. (*rectangular space*) case *f* 3. (*small space*) **to be just a ~** être grand comme un mouchoir de poche 4. THEAT loge *f* 5. *Aus, Brit* SPORT coquille *f* 6. *inf* (*television*) **the ~** la télé 7. (*box junction*) *zone d'intersection quadrillée en jaune* 8. *no pl* (*tree*) buis *m*
box[2] [bɒks, *Am:* bɑːks] I. *n* gifle *f;* **to give sb a ~ on the ears** gifler qn II. *vi* SPORT faire de la boxe III. *vt* 1. SPORT boxer 2. (*hit*) **to ~ someone's ears** gifler qn
◆**box in** *vt* coincer
◆**box up** *vt* mettre dans une boîte
box calf *n* box *m*
boxer ['bɒksəʳ, *Am:* 'bɑːksɚ] *n* 1. (*dog*) boxer *m* 2. (*person*) boxeur, -euse *m, f* 3. *pl s.* **boxer shorts**
boxer shorts *n pl* boxers *mpl*
boxing ['bɒksɪŋ, *Am:* 'bɑːksɪŋ] *n no pl* boxe *f*

Le **Boxing Day** est le 26 décembre. Ce nom date d'une époque où les apprentis collectaient après le premier jour de Noël un pour

B

boire dans des "boxes" (boîtes) auprès des clients de leur maître. Autrefois, on appelait aussi l'argent que l'on donnait pour Noël aux livreurs ou aux employés le "Christmas Box".

boxing gloves *npl* gants *mpl* de boxe **boxing match** *n* match *m* de boxe
box number *n* boîte *f* postale **box office** *n* guichet *m;* **a ~ hit** un succès au box-office
boy [bɔɪ] **I.** *n* garçon *m* ▸**the ~s in blue** *Brit, inf* la police; **a local ~** un jeune du coin; **to be one of the ~s** faire partie des copains; **~s will be ~s** *prov* il faut que jeunesse se passe *prov;* **the/our ~s** MIL les/nos gars **II.** *interj* **oh ~!** bon sang!
boycott ['bɔɪkɒt, *Am:* -kɑːt] **I.** *vt* boycotter **II.** *n* boycott *m;* **to put a ~ on sb/sth, to put sb/sth under a ~** boycotter qn/qc
boyfriend ['bɔɪfrend] *n* petit ami *m*
boyhood ['bɔɪhʊd] **I.** *n no pl* enfance *f;* (*as a teenager*) adolescence *f* **II.** *adj* d'enfance; (*as a teenager*) d'adolescence
boyish ['bɔɪɪʃ] *adj* enfantin; (*for a woman*) de garçon; (*enthusiasm*) juvénile
Bq *n abbr of* **becquerel** Bq *m*
BR [ˌbiːɑr, *Am:* -'ɑːr] *n abbr of* **British Rail** *compagnie des chemins de fer britanniques*
bra [brɑː] *n* soutien-gorge *m,* brassière *f Québec*
Brabant [brə'bænt] *n* le Brabant wallon
brace [breɪs] **I.** *vt* **1.** (*prepare*) **to ~ oneself for sth** se préparer à qc **2.** (*support*) consolider **II.** *n Brit* **1.** (*for teeth*) appareil *m* dentaire **2.** (*for back*) corset *m*
bracelet ['breɪslɪt] *n* bracelet *m*
braces *n pl* **1.** *Am, Aus* (*for teeth*) appareil *m* dentaire **2.** *Aus, Brit* (*suspenders*) bretelles *fpl* **3.** *Am* (*callipers*) appareil *m* orthopédique
bracken ['brækn] *n no pl* fougère *f*
bracket ['brækɪt] **I.** *n* **1.** *pl* TYP parenthèses *fpl;* **in (round) ~s** entre parenthèses; **square ~s** crochets *mpl* **2.** (*category*) **age ~** tranche *f* d'âge; **income/tax ~** fourchette *f* de salaire/d'imposition **3.** (*L-shaped piece*) équerre *f* **II.** *vt* **1.** TYP mettre entre parenthèses **2.** (*include in one group*) **to ~ two people together** regrouper deux personnes
brackish ['brækɪʃ] *adj* salé(e); (*water*) saumâtre
brag [bræg] <-gg-> **I.** *vi pej, inf* **to ~ about sth** se vanter de qc **II.** *vt pej, inf* **to ~ that ...** se vanter que ...
braid [breɪd] **I.** *n* **1.** *no pl* (*decoration*) galon *m* **2.** *Am* (*plait*) tresse *f* **II.** *vt Am* (*plait*) tresser
Braille [breɪl] *n no pl* braille *m*
brain [breɪn] **I.** *n* **1.** (*organ*) cerveau *m;* **use your ~(s)!** réfléchis! **2.** (*intelligence*) intelligence *f;* **to have ~s** [*o* **a good ~**] être intelligent **3.** *inf* (*person*) cerveau *m;* **the best ~s** les meilleurs talents ▸**to blow sb's ~s out** faire sauter la cervelle à qn; **to pick sb's ~s** *inf* sonder les connaissances de qn; **to have sth on the ~** *pej, inf* être obsédé par qc **II.** *vt inf* assommer; **to ~ oneself** se cogner **III.** *adj* cérébral(e)
brainchild *n no pl* idée *f* **brain-dead** *adj* en état de coma dépassé; **to declare sb ~** conclure à la mort cérébrale de qn **brain death** *n* mort *f* cérébrale **brain drain** *n* exode *m* des cerveaux **brain fever** *n* méningite *f*
brainless *adj* idiot(e); **~ idiot!** espèce d'idiot!
brain scan *n* scannographie *f* du cerveau
brainstorm ['breɪnstɔːm, *Am:* -stɔːrm] **I.** *vi* faire un brainstorming **II.** *vt* faire un brainstorming sur **III.** *n* **1.** *Brit, inf* (*lapse*) moment *m* d'égarement **2.** *Am* (*brainwave*) idée *f* de génie
brainstorming ['breɪnˌstɔːmɪŋ, *Am:* -ˌstɔːr-] *n no pl* brainstorming *m*
brain tumour *n* tumeur *f* au cerveau **brainwashing** *n* lavage *m* de cerveau **brainwave** *n inf* idée *f* lumineuse
brainy ['breɪni] <-ier, -iest> *adj* **to be ~** être une grosse tête
braise [breɪz] *vt* braiser
brake [breɪk] **I.** *n* **1.** AUTO frein *m;* **anti-lock ~s** freins ABS; **to apply** [*o* **put on**] **the ~s** freiner; **to release the ~** desserrer le frein; **to slam on the ~(s)** *inf* piler **2.** *fig* **to put a ~** [*o* **the ~s**] **on** freiner **II.** *vi* freiner
brake block *n* patin *m* de frein **brake fluid** *n* liquide *m* de frein **brake light** *n* feux *mpl* de freins **brake pedal** *n* pédale *f* de frein **brake shoe** *n* sabot *m* de frein
braking *n* freinage *m*
braking distance *n* distance *f* de freinage
bramble ['bræmbl] *n* **1.** (*bush*) ronce *f* **2.** (*berry*) mûre *f* **3.** *Am* (*wild bush*) roncier *m*
bran [bræn] *n no pl* (*of grain*) son *m*
branch [brɑːntʃ, *Am:* bræntʃ] **I.** *n* **1.** *a.* BOT branche *f* **2.** *Am* (*fork: of a river*) bras *m;* (*of a road*) embranchement *m* **3.** (*office: of bank*) agence *f;* (*of company, store*) succursale *f* **4.** (*division: of organization*) branche *f* **II.** *vi* **1.** se ramifier **2.** *fig* bifurquer
◆**branch off** *vi* **1.** (*fork*) bifurquer **2.** *fig* digresser; **to ~ from a subject** s'écarter d'un sujet
◆**branch out** *vi* **1.** (*enter a new field*) **to ~ into sth** étendre ses activités à qc; **to ~ on one's own** s'établir à son compte **2.** (*undertake new activities*) diversifier ses activités
branch line *n* ligne *f* secondaire **branch office** *n* succursale *f*
brand [brænd] **I.** *n* **1.** (*trade name*) marque *f* **2.** (*type*) genre *m;* **do you like his ~ of humour?** est-ce que tu aimes son humour? **3.** (*mark*) marque *f* (au fer) **II.** *vt* **1.** (*label*) **to be ~ed (as) sth** être catalogué comme qc **2.** (*mark*) **to ~ an animal** marquer un animal
brandish ['brændɪʃ] *vt* brandir
brand name ['brændneɪm] *n* marque *f*
brand-new [ˌbrænd'njuː] *adj* flambant neuf(neuve); (*baby*) nouveau-né(e)
brandy ['brændi] <-ies> *n* eau *f* de vie

brandy snap *n biscuit dur roulé, parfois fourré*

brash [bræʃ] *adj pej* **1.** (*cocky*) prétentieux(-euse) **2.** (*gaudy*) voyant(e)

brass [brɑːs, *Am:* bræs] **I.** *n* **1.** (*metal*) laiton *m* **2.** (*brass engraving*) cuivres *mpl* **3.** + *pl/sing vb, no pl* MUS **the ~** les cuivres *mpl* **II.** *adj* en laiton

brass band *n* ≈ fanfare *f* **brass instrument** *n* MUS cuivre *m* **brass plate** *n* plaque *f* de cuivre **brassware** *n* dinanderie *f*

brassy [ˈbrɑːsi, *Am:* ˈbræsi] <-ier, -iest> *adj* **1.** *a.* MUS cuivré(e) **2.** *pej* (*loud: voice*) braillard(e) **3.** *pej* (*cocky*) provoquant(e)

brat [bræt] *n pej, inf* sale gosse *mf*

bravado [brəˈvɑːdəʊ, *Am:* -doʊ] *n no pl* bravade *f*

brave [breɪv] **I.** *adj* courageux, -euse; **to give a ~ smile** sourire bravement ►**to put on a ~ face** ne rien laisser paraître **II.** *vt* braver

bravery [ˈbreɪvəri] *n no pl* bravoure *f*

brawl [brɔːl, *Am:* brɑːl] **I.** *n* bagarre *f* **II.** *vi* se bagarrer

brawling *n no pl* bagarres *fpl*

brawn [brɔːn, *Am:* brɑːn] *n no pl* **1.** (*strength*) muscles *mpl* **2.** *Aus, Brit* (*meat*) fromage *m* de tête, tête *f* pressée *Belgique*

brawny [ˈbrɔːni, *Am:* brɑː-] <-ier, -iest> *adj* musclé(e)

bray [breɪ] *vi* braire; **~ing laugh** rire *m* chevalin

brazen [ˈbreɪzn] *adj* éhonté(e); **a ~ hussy** *iron* une dévergondée

brazen out *vt* **to brazen it out** payer d'audace

brazier [ˈbreɪziəʳ, *Am:* -ʒɚ] *n* brasero *m*

Brazil [brəˈzɪl] *n* le Brésil

Brazilian [brəˈzɪliən, *Am:* -jən] **I.** *adj* brésilien(ne) **II.** *n* Brésilien(ne) *m(f)*

breach [briːtʃ] **I.** *n* **1.** (*infraction*) rupture *f*; **~ of** [*o* **in**] **an agreement** rupture d'un accord; **~ of confidence** [*o* **faith**] abus *m* de confiance; **~ of duty** manquement *m* à son devoir; **~ of the law** violation *f* de la loi; **~ of promise** rupture de promesse; **to be in ~ of contract** avoir enfreint son contrat **2.** (*estrangement*) brouille *f* **3.** (*opening*) brèche *f* **II.** *vt* **1.** (*break*) rompre **2.** (*infiltrate*) ouvrir une brèche dans

bread [bred] *n* pain *m*; **a loaf of ~** un pain; **to bake ~** faire du pain **2.** *inf* (*money*) oseille *f*

bread and butter I. *n* gagne-pain *m* **II.** *adj* de tous les jours **breadbasket** *n* **1.** (*container*) corbeille *f* à pain **2.** (*region*) grenier *m* à blé **breadcrumb** *n* **1.** (*small fragment*) miette *f* **2.** *pl* GASTR panure *f*; **to cover** [*o* **coat**] **sth with ~s** paner qc **bread roll** *n* petit pain *m*, pistolet *m Belgique*

breadth [bretθ] *n no pl, a. fig* largeur *f*; **~ of learning** étendue *f* des connaissances

breadwinner [ˈbredˌwɪnəʳ, *Am:* -ɚ] *n* soutien *m* de famille

break [breɪk] **I.** *n* **1.** (*gap*) trou *m*; (*crack*) fêlure *f*; (*into two parts*) fracture *f*; **a ~ in the clouds** une brèche dans les nuages **2.** (*interruption: in conversation, for snack*) pause *f*; (*in output*) interruption *f*; **commercial ~** pause de publicité; **to take a ~** prendre une pause; **to need a ~ from doing sth** avoir besoin de se reposer de qc; **a weekend ~** un week-end détente **3.** SCHOOL récréation *f* **4.** (*escape*) évasion *f*; **to make a ~** s'évader **5. ~ of day** lever *m* du jour **6.** (*opportunity*) chance *f*; **she got her big ~ in that film** elle a percé grâce à ce film **7.** SPORT **~** (**of serve**) break *m* ►**give me a ~!** fiche-moi la paix!; **to make the ~ from sb/sth** rompre avec qn/qc; **to make a clean** [*o* **complete**] **~** cesser complètement de se voir **II.** <broke, broken> *vt* **1.** (*shatter*) casser; **to ~ a nail/one's arm** se casser un ongle/le bras **2.** (*damage*) endommager **3.** *fig* **to ~ an alibi** écarter un alibi **4.** AVIAT **to ~ the sonic** [*o* **sound**] **barrier** passer le mur du son **5.** (*interrupt*) **to ~** (**off**) **sth** rompre qc; **to ~ one's step** [*o* **stride**] ralentir; MIL rompre le pas; **to ~ sb's fall** arrêter la chute de qn **6.** (*put an end to: record*) battre; (*strike*) casser; **to ~ a deadlock** [*o* **an impasse**] sortir d'une impasse; **to ~ a habit** se débarrasser d'une habitude; **to ~ sb of a habit** faire passer une habitude à qn; **to ~ the suspense** [*o* **tension**] mettre fin au suspense; **to ~ the peace** troubler la tranquillité; **to ~ sb's spirit** [*o* **will**] briser la résistance [*o* volonté] de qn **7.** SPORT **to ~ a tie** prendre l'avantage; **to ~ sb's serve** (*in tennis*) faire le break **8.** (*violate: law*) enfreindre; (*treaty*) rompre; (*date*) annuler; **to ~ a promise to sb** ne pas tenir sa parole envers qn **9.** (*forcefully end*) **to ~ sb's hold** se dégager de l'emprise de qn **10.** (*decipher: code*) déchiffrer **11.** (*make public*) annoncer; **to ~ the news to sb** apprendre la nouvelle à qn **12.** (*make change for: banknote*) entamer **13.** MIL **to ~ camp** lever le camp ►**to ~ one's back** [*o* **ass** *Am*] *inf* se briser le dos; **to ~ sb's back** être la fin de qn; **to ~ the back of sth** *Aus, Brit* faire le plus gros de qc; **to ~ the bank** *iron* faire sauter la banque; **to ~ bread** REL rompre le pain; **to ~ cover** quitter son abri; **to ~ fresh** [*o* **new**] **ground** innover; **to ~ sb's heart** briser le cœur de qn; **to ~ the ice** *inf* rompre la glace; **to ~ the mould** faire preuve d'innovation; **to ~ ranks** rompre les rangs; **to ~ wind** lâcher un vent **III.** <broke, broken> *vi* **1.** (*shatter*) se casser; **she broke under torture/the strain** *fig* elle a craqué sous la torture/le stress **2.** (*separate*) se démonter **3.** (*interrupt*) **shall we ~** (**off**) **for lunch?** si on faisait une pause pour le déjeuner? **4.** (*strike*) se briser; **the wave broke on the shore** la vague s'est brisée sur le rivage **5.** (*change sound: voice at puberty*) muer; (*with emotion*) se briser **6.** (*begin: storm, scandal*) éclater; (*day*) se lever **7.** SPORT commencer ►**to ~ even** rentrer dans ses frais; **to ~ free** s'évader; **to ~ loose**

s'échapper

◆**break away** *vi* 1.(*move*) to ~ **from sb** s'éloigner de qn; **old enough to** ~ *fig* assez grand pour voler de ses propres ailes 2.(*split off*) **to** ~ **from sb** se désolidariser de qn 3.(*separate*) **chunks of ice are breaking away from the iceberg** des blocs de glace se détachent de l'iceberg

◆**break down** I. *vi* 1.(*stop working*) tomber en panne; (*plan*) s'effondrer 2.(*dissolve*) décomposer; (*marriage*) se détériorer 3.(*lose control emotionally*) craquer 4.(*be analysed*) **to** ~ **into three parts** se décomposer en trois parties II. *vt* 1.(*force to open*) enfoncer 2.(*overcome: barrier*) faire tomber; (*resistance*) vaincre 3. CHEM dissoudre 4.(*separate*) **to** ~ **sth into sth** décomposer qc en qc

◆**break in** I. *vi* 1.(*enter*) entrer par effraction 2.(*interrupt*) intervenir II. *vt* 1.(*make comfortable*) **to break one's shoes in** faire ses chaussures 2. *Am* AUTO roder 3.(*tame*) dompter 4. *fig* **to** ~ **one's staff** laisser son personnel s'accoutumer

◆**break into** *vi* 1.(*enter*) **to** ~ **sth** s'introduire dans qc; **to** ~ **a car** forcer la portière d'une voiture 2.(*start doing*) **to** ~ **applause/a run** se mettre à applaudir/courir; **to** ~ **laughter/tears** éclater de rire/en sanglots 3.(*get involved in*) **to** ~ **advertising/the youth market** percer dans la publicité/le marché des jeunes 4.(*start using: savings, note, new packet*) entamer

◆**break off** I. *vt* 1.(*separate*) casser 2.(*end*) rompre II. *vi* 1.(*not stay attached*) se détacher 2.(*stop speaking*) s'interrompre

◆**break out** *vi* 1.(*escape*) s'évader 2.(*begin: epidemic, fire*) se déclarer; (*storm*) éclater 3.(*become covered with*) **to** ~ **in spots** se couvrir de boutons; **to** ~ **in (a) sweat** se mettre à transpirer

◆**break through** *vi* se frayer un chemin; (*army*) ouvrir une brèche; (*sun*) percer

◆**break up** I. *vt* 1.(*forcefully end*) **to** ~ **sth** interrompre 2.(*split up: coalition*) disperser; (*family*) désunir; (*company, organization*) diviser; (*gang*) démanteler; (*demonstrators*) disperser 3.(*dig up: ground*) retourner II. *vi* 1.(*end a relationship*) se séparer 2.(*come to an end: marriage*) se désagréger; (*meeting*) se terminer 3.(*fall apart*) s'effondrer 4.(*disperse*) se disperser 5. *Brit* SCHOOL être en vacances 6.(*lose signal*) **you're breaking up** je ne t'entends plus

◆**break with** *vt* rompre avec

breakable ['breɪkəbl] *adj* fragile

breakage ['breɪkɪdʒ] *n* casse *f*

breakaway ['breɪkəweɪ] *adj* dissident(e)

breakdown ['breɪkdaʊn] *n* 1.(*collapse*) échec *m;* (*of ceasefire*) rupture *f* 2. TECH panne *f* 3.(*division*) ventilation *f;* (*of expenses*) détail *m* 4.(*decomposition*) décomposition *f* 5. PSYCH dépression *f*

breakdown lorry *n Brit* dépanneuse *f*

breakdown service *n* service *m* de dépannage

breaker ['breɪkəʳ, *Am:* -kɚ] *n* (*wave*) déferlante *f*

breakfast ['brekfəst] I. *n* petit déjeuner *m;* **to have** ~ déjeuner; **to have sth for** ~ prendre qc au petit déjeuner II. *vi form* **to** ~ **on tea and toast** prendre du thé et des toasts au petit déjeuner

break-in *n* cambriolage *m*

breaking and entering *n* LAW effraction *f;* **to charge sb with** ~ condamner qn pour effraction **breaking point** *n* **to reach** ~ atteindre le point de rupture

breakneck ['breɪknek] *adj* **at** ~ **speed** à une allure folle

breakthrough ['breɪkθruː] *n* MIL percée *f;* (*in science, negotiations*) tournant *m*

breakup ['breɪkʌp] *n* (*of marriage*) échec *m;* (*of group*) dissolution *f;* (*of company, party*) division *f;* (*of empire*) effondrement *m*

breakwater ['breɪkwɔːtəʳ, *Am:* -ˌwɑːt̬ɚ] *n* brise-lames *m*

breast [brest] *n* 1. ANAT sein *m* 2.(*bird's chest*) gorge *f* 3. GASTR blanc *m* ►~ **is best** rien ne vaut l'allaitement maternel

breastbone *n* sternum *m* **breast cancer** *n* cancer *m* du sein **breast-feed** *vt, vi* allaiter **breast pocket** *n* poche *f* de poitrine **breast screening** *n* dépistage *m* du cancer du sein **breaststroke** *n no pl* brasse *f*

breath [breθ] *n* 1.(*air*) souffle *m;* **to be out of** ~ être à bout de souffle; **to be short of** ~ être essoufflé; **to catch one's** ~, **to get one's** ~ **back, to draw** ~ reprendre son souffle; **to gasp for** ~ étouffer; **to hold one's** ~ retenir sa respiration; **to take a deep** ~ respirer à fond 2.(*air exhaled*) haleine *f* 3.(*break*) **to go out for a** ~ **of fresh air** sortir prendre l'air 4.(*wind*) **a** ~ **of air** un souffle d'air 5. *fig* **in the same** [*o* **next**] ~ dans la foulée

breathalyse ['breθəlaɪz] *vt Aus, Brit* faire subir un alcootest à

breathalyser® *n Aus, Brit* alcootest *m*

breathalyze *vt Am s.* **breathalyse**

breathalyzer® *n Am s.* **breathalyser**

breathe [briːð] I. *vi* 1. ANAT respirer; **to** ~ **through one's nose** respirer par le nez 2. *fig* **to** ~ **more easily** respirer II. *vt* 1.(*exhale*) **to** ~ **air into sb's lungs** insuffler de l'air dans les poumons de qn; **to** ~ **garlic fumes** souffler des relents d'ail 2.(*whisper*) chuchoter 3.(*let out*) **to** ~ **a sigh of relief** soupirer de soulagement ►**to** ~ **(new) life into sth** redonner de la vie à qc; **to** ~ **down sb's neck** être sur le dos de qn; **not to** ~ **a word** ne pas souffler mot

◆**breathe in** I. *vi* inspirer II. *vt* inhaler; **to** ~ **fresh air** respirer l'air frais

◆**breathe out** I. *vi* expirer II. *vt* exhaler

breather ['briːðəʳ, *Am:* -ðɚ] *n* (*rest*) pause *f;* **to have a** ~ faire une pause

breathing *n no pl* respiration *f*

breathing apparatus *n* respirateur *m*

breathing room, **breathing space** *n* **1.**(*time*) répit *m;* **to need some** ~ avoir besoin de respirer **2.**(*space*) espace *m*

breathless *adj* à bout de souffle

breathtaking ['breθteɪkɪŋ] *adj* stupéfiant(e)

breath test *n* alcootest *m*

bred [bred] *pt, pp of* **breed**

breech [bri:tʃ] *n* (*of gun*) culasse *f*

breeches ['brɪtʃɪz] *npl* culotte *f;* **riding** ~ culotte de cheval

breed [bri:d] **I.**<bred, bred> *vt* **1.**(*grow*) faire pousser **2.**(*raise*) élever **3.**(*engender*) engendrer **II.**<bred, bred> *vi* ZOOL se reproduire **III.** *n* **1.** ZOOL race *f* **2.** BOT espèce *f* **3.** *inf* (*type of person*) race *f*

breeder ['bri:dəʳ, *Am:* -dɚ] *n* éleveur, -euse *m, f*

breeding *n no pl* **1.**(*farming*) élevage *m* **2.**(*good manners*) manières *fpl*

breeze [bri:z] **I.** *n* **1.**(*wind*) brise *f* **2.** *Am, inf* (*easy task*) **it's a** ~ c'est un jeu d'enfant **3.** *no pl* (*cinders*) fraisil *m* **II.** *vi* **to** ~ **in/past** entrer/passer avec nonchalance; **to** ~ **to victory** l'emporter haut la main

breeze block [brɪ:z blɒk] *n* moellon *m*

breezy ['bri:zi] <-ier, -iest> *adj* **1.**(*windy*) **it's** ~ il y a une bonne brise **2.**(*jovial*) jovial(e)

Breton ['bretən] **I.** *adj* breton(ne) **II.** *n* **1.**(*person*) Breton(ne) *m(f)* **2.** LING breton *m; s. a.* **English**

breve [bri:v] *n* LING, MUS brève *f*

breviary ['bri:vɪəri] <-ies> *n* bréviaire *m*

brevity ['brevəti, *Am:* -t̬i] *n no pl* **1.**(*shortness*) brièveté *f* **2.**(*conciseness*) concision *f*

brew [bru:] **I.** *n* **1.**(*beer*) bière *f* **2.**(*tea*) infusion *f;* **let's have a** ~ *inf* on se fait du thé **3.**(*concoction*) mixture *f* **4.** *fig* mélange *m* **II.** *vi* **1.**(*boil*) infuser **2.** *fig* (*storm*) se préparer **III.** *vt* (*beer*) brasser; **to** ~ **coffee/tea for sb** préparer du café/thé pour qn

◆**brew up I.** *vi* **1.** *Brit, inf* (*brew tea*) faire du thé **2.**(*develop*) se préparer **II.** *vt Brit, inf* **would you mind brewing up a cuppa?** tu veux bien me faire un thé?

brewer ['bru:əʳ, *Am:* -ɚ] *n* brasseur, -euse *m, f*

brewery ['brʊəri, *Am:* 'bru:ɚi] <-ies> *n* brasserie *f*

briar ['braɪəʳ, *Am:* 'braɪɚ] *n* églantier *m*

bribe [braɪb] **I.** *vt* soudoyer; **I ~d the children to come** j'ai soudoyé les enfants pour qu'ils viennent **II.** *n* pot *m* de vin

bribery ['braɪbəri] *n no pl* corruption *f*

bric-a-brac ['brɪkəbræk] *n no pl* bric-à-brac *m*

brick [brɪk] *n* **1.**(*block*) brique *f* **2.**(*house*) **to invest in ~s and mortar** investir dans la pierre ►**you can't make ~s without <u>straw</u>** *prov* à l'impossible nul n'est tenu *prov*

◆**brick in**, **brick up** *vt* murer

brickie ['brɪki] <-ies> *n Aus, Brit, inf,* **bricklayer** *n* maçon *m*

brickwork ['brɪkwɜ:k, *Am:* -wɜ:rk] *n no pl* briquetage *m*

brickworks, **brickyard** *n* briqueterie *f*

bridal ['braɪdəl] *adj* (*veil, wear*) de mariée; (*chamber*) nuptial(e)

bride ['braɪd] *n* **1.**(*fiancée*) future mariée *f* **2.**(*married*) jeune mariée *f;* **child** ~ très jeune mariée

bridegroom *n* **1.**(*fiancé*) futur marié *m* **2.**(*married*) jeune marié *m* **bridesmaid** *n* demoiselle *f* d'honneur

bridge [brɪdʒ] **I.** *n* **1.** ARCHIT, NAUT *a. fig* pont *m;* **suspension** ~ pont suspendu **2.** MED bridge *m* **3.** *no pl* ANAT arête *f* du nez **4.**(*part of glasses*) arcade *f* **5.** MUS chevalet *m* **6.** *no pl* GAMES bridge *m* **II.** *vt* **1.**(*build bridge*) construire un pont sur **2.**(*bring together*) **to** ~ **the gap between sb/sth and sb/sth** rapprocher qn/qc et qn/qc

bridging loan ['brɪdʒɪŋ'ləʊn, *Am:* -'loʊn] *n Aus, Brit* prêt *m* relais

bridle ['braɪdl] **I.** *n* bride *f* **II.** *vt* brider **III.** *vi* **to** ~ **at sth** s'indigner devant qc

bridle path, **bridleway** *n* piste *f* cavalière

brief [bri:f] **I.**<-er, -est> *adj* bref, brève **II.** *n* **1.**(*instructions*) instructions *fpl* **2.**(*case summary*) dossier *m;* **to prepare a** ~ préparer un dossier **3.** *Brit, inf* (*lawyer*) avocat(e) **4.** *pl* (*underpants*) slip *m* ►**<u>in</u>** ~ en bref **III.** *vt form* (*inform*) briefer; **to** ~ **sb on sth** mettre qn au courant de qc

briefcase ['bri:fkeɪs] *n* serviette *f,* calepin *m Belgique*

briefing *n* briefing *m;* **to conduct a** ~ tenir un briefing; **pre-flight** ~ dernières instructions *fpl*

briefly *adv* **1.**(*shortly*) brièvement **2.**(*in short*) en bref

briefness *n no pl* brièveté *f*

brier ['braɪəʳ, *Am:* 'braɪɚ] *n s.* **briar**

brigade [brɪ'geɪd] *n* MIL brigade *f*

brigadier [ˌbrɪgə'dɪəʳ] *n* MIL général *m* de brigade

bright [braɪt] **I.** *adj* **1.**(*light*) vif, vive; (*room*) clair(e); (*clothes*) de couleur(s) vive(s) **2.**(*shining*) brillant(e); (*day*) radieux, -euse **3.**(*sparkling*) éclatant(e) **4.**(*intelligent*) intelligent(e); (*idea*) bon(ne) **5.**(*cheerful*) jovial(e) **6.**(*promising*) brillant(e); **to look** ~ **for sb/sth** l'avenir s'annonce bien pour qn/qc ►**to look at the** ~ **<u>side</u> of sth** prendre les choses du bon côté; ~ **and <u>early</u>** de bon matin **II.** *n pl, Am* AUTO pleins phrares *mpl*

brighten (**up**) ['braɪtən('ʌp)] **I.** *vt* **1.**(*make brighter*) éclaircir **2.**(*make more promising*) améliorer **3.**(*make more cheerful*) égayer **II.** *vi* **1.**(*become cheerful*) s'égayer; (*eyes*) s'allumer; (*face*) s'animer **2.**(*become brighter or more promising*) s'améliorer; (*weather*) s'éclaircir

bright-eyed *adj* ~ **and bushy-tailed** en pleine forme

brightly *adv* **1.**(*not dimly*) vivement; (*shine*) intensément; **the sun shines** ~ le soleil est éclatant; **the fire burns** ~ le feu est vif

2.(*vividly*) de couleur(s) vive(s); ~ **coloured** aux couleurs vives 3.(*cheerfully*) gaiement

brightness *n no pl* 1.*a.* TV luminosité *f* 2.(*shining*) éclat *m* 3.TECH intensité *f*

bright spark *n inf* petit(e) futé(e) *m,f*

brill ['brɪl] I. *adj Aus, Brit, inf* sensass II. *interj Aus, Brit, inf* super

brilliance ['brɪlɪəns], **brilliancy** *n no pl* 1.(*cleverness*) génie *f* 2.(*brightness*) éclat *m*

brilliant ['brɪlɪənt, *Am:* -jənt] I. *adj* 1.(*shining*) éclatant(e) 2.(*clever*) brillant(e) 3.*Brit, inf* (*excellent*) super; (*success*) excellent(e); (*save*) superbe; ~ **at swimming/cooking** excellent en natation/cuisine II. *interj Brit, inf* super

brilliantly *adv* 1.(*with great skill*) brillamment 2.(*brightly*) **to shine** ~ briller avec éclat; ~ **lit** vivement éclairé

brim [brɪm] I. *n* bord *m;* **to fill sth to the** ~ remplir qc à ras bord II. <-mm-> *vi* **to** ~ **with sth** déborder de qc

brimful [ˌbrɪm'fʊl] *adj* plein(e) à ras bord; ~ **of life/health** débordant de vie/santé

brine [braɪn] *n no pl* eau *f* salée

bring [brɪŋ] <brought, brought> *vt* 1.(*come with, carry: things*) apporter; **I brought the box into the house** j'ai rentré la boîte dans la maison 2.(*take, cause to come: people*) amener; **the road ~s you to the village** la route vous mène au village; **this ~s me to the question of money** cela me conduit au sujet argent 3.(*cause to have or happen*) **to ~ sth to sb, to ~ sb sth** apporter qc à qn; **the books brought her fame and riches** les livres lui ont apporté gloire et richesse; **to ~ sth on oneself** s'attirer qc; **to ~ shame/discredit to sb** jeter la honte/le discrédit sur qn; **to ~ sb luck** porter chance à qn 4.LAW **to ~ a charge against sb** inculper qn; **to ~ a suit against sb** intenter un procès à qn; **to ~ a complaint against sb** porter plainte contre qn 5.(*force*) **to ~ oneself to** +*infin* se résoudre à +*infin* 6.FIN rapporter; **to ~ a profit** bien rapporter ▶**to ~ sth to sb's attention** attirer l'attention de qn sur qc; **to ~ sth to a climax** porter qc à son paroxysme; **to ~ sth to a close** mettre fin à qc; **to ~ sth under control** maîtriser qc; **to ~ sb up to date** mettre qn au courant; **to ~ sb face to face with sth** confronter qn à qc; **to ~ sth to fruition** concrétiser qc; **to ~ sb/sth to a halt** faire arrêter qn/qc; **to ~ sth home to sb** rendre qc plus réel à qn; **to ~ sb to justice** traduire qn en justice; **to ~ sth to sb's knowledge** porter qc à la connaissance de qn; **to ~ sb back to life** ramener qn à la vie; **to ~ sth to life** donner vie à qc; **to ~ to light** réveler; **to ~ sth to mind** rappeler qc; **to ~ sb to his/her senses** ramener qn à la raison; **to ~ tears to sb's eyes** faire venir les larmes aux yeux de qn; **to ~ up short** arrêter net

◆**bring about** *vt* 1.(*cause to happen*) provoquer 2.(*achieve*) amener

◆**bring along** *vt* (*food*) apporter; (*friend*) amener

◆**bring around** *vt Am s.* **bring round**

◆**bring back** *vt* 1.(*reintroduce*) ramener 2.(*return*) rapporter 3.(*call to mind: memories*) rappeler ▶**to ~ the colour to sb's cheeks** redonner des couleurs à qn

◆**bring down** *vt* 1.(*opp: bring up*) descendre 2.(*topple*) renverser 3.(*reduce*) faire baisser 4.(*fell: trees, shelves*) faire tomber 5.(*shoot down*) abattre 6.(*make sad*) décourager ▶**to ~ the house** (*with laughter*) faire rire tout le monde; (*by performance*) éblouir tout le monde; **to bring sb down a peg (or two)** remettre qn à sa place

◆**bring forth** *vt insep, form* (*document*) produire; (*laughter, idea*) déclencher

◆**bring forward** *vt* 1.FIN reporter 2.(*fix earlier time for*) avancer 3.(*suggest*) proposer

◆**bring in** *vt* 1.(*introduce*) introduire; **to ~ a bill** présenter un projet de loi; **to ~ a topic** lancer un sujet 2.(*call in, reap*) faire rentrer 3.(*earn*) rapporter; **to ~ a profit** rapporter du bénéfice 4.(*ask to participate*) faire intervenir 5.(*produce*) rendre

◆**bring into** *vt always sep* **to bring sth into sth** introduire qc dans qc; **to bring sb into sth** faire participer qn à qc; **not to bring sb into sth** laisser qn en dehors de qc ▶**to bring sth into focus/play** mettre qc au point/en jeu

◆**bring off** *vt* réussir

◆**bring on** *vt* 1.MED causer 2.(*cause to occur*) provoquer 3.(*send in to play: reserve, actor*) faire entrer

◆**bring out** *vt* 1.*Aus, Brit* (*encourage*) **to bring sb out** faire sortir qn 2.COM (*product*) lancer; (*book, film*) sortir 3.(*stress*) faire ressortir 4.(*utter*) **to ~ a few words** prononcer quelques mots

◆**bring over** *vt* amener

◆**bring round** *vt* 1.MED ranimer 2.(*persuade*) convaincre 3.(*invite*) amener

◆**bring to** *vt always sep* ranimer

◆**bring together** *vt* réunir; **to bring people together** rapprocher des gens

◆**bring up** *vt* 1.(*opp: bring down*) monter 2.(*rear*) **to bring sb up** élever qn; **well brouht up** bien élevé(e) 3.(*mention*) parler de; **to ~ sth for discussion** aborder qc 4.*inf* (*vomit*) rendre ▶**to ~ the rear** fermer la marche

brink [brɪŋk] *n no pl* bord *m;* **to drive sb to the ~** pousser qn à bout; **to drive sb to the ~ of tears** pousser qn au bord des larmes; **to be on the ~ of bankruptcy/war** être au bord de la faillite/à deux doigts de la guerre

briny ['braɪni] <-ier, -iest> I. *adj* saumâtre II. *n Brit, inf* **the ~** la grande bleue

briquet(te) [brɪ'ket] *n* briquette *f*

brisk [brɪsk] <-er, -est> *adj* 1.(*not sluggish*) vif, vive; (*walk, traffic*) rapide; **business is ~** les ventes vont bon train 2.(*refreshing*) vivifiant(e)

briskly *adv* **1.** (*quickly*) rapidement; (*walk*) d'un bon pas **2.** (*not sluggishly*) vivement
briskness *n no pl* vivacité *f;* (*of business, trading*) dynamisme *m*
bristle ['brɪsl] **I.** *n* poil *m;* ~ **brush** brosse *f* en soies de sanglier **II.** *vi* se hérisser
bristly ['brɪsli] <-ier, -iest> *adj* (*beard*) dru(e); (*face*) à la barbe qui pique
Britain ['brɪtən] *n s.* **Great Britain**
British ['brɪtɪʃ, *Am:* 'brɪt̬-] **I.** *adj* britannique **II.** *n pl* **the** ~ les Anglais; (*as nationality*) les Britanniques
British Broadcasting Corporation *n* BBC *f* **British Columbia** *n* la Colombie-Britannique **British English** *n* anglais *m* d'Angleterre
Britisher *n Am* Britannique *mf*
British Isles *n* îles *fpl* Britanniques **British Summer Time** *n heure d'été en Grande-Bretagne*
Briton ['brɪtn] *n* Britannique *mf*
Brittany ['brɪtæni] *n* la Bretagne
brittle ['brɪtl, *Am:* 'brɪt̬-] *adj* **1.** (*fragile*) cassant(e); (*layer of ice*) fragile **2.** (*unfriendly*) sec, sèche
broach [brəʊtʃ, *Am:* broʊtʃ] **I.** *vt* (*topic*) aborder **II.** *n Am* foret *m*
broad [brɔːd, *Am:* brɑːd] <-er, -est> *adj* **1.** (*wide*) large **2.** (*spacious*) vaste **3.** (*general*) grand(e); (*description*) large; **to be in** ~ **agreement** être d'accord sur presque tout **4.** (*wide-ranging: range, syllabus*) varié(e) **5.** (*strong*) fort(e) ▶**in** ~ **daylight** en plein jour; **to drop** ~ **hints** faire de lourdes allusions; **it's as** ~ **as long** c'est du pareil au même
broad bean *n* fève *f*
broadcast ['brɔːdkɑːst, *Am:* 'brɑːdkæst] **I.** *n* **1.** *no pl* (*process*) diffusion *f* **2.** (*programme*) émission **II.** <broadcast, broadcast *o* -ed, -ed> *vi Am* diffuser **III.** <broadcast, broadcast *o* -ed, -ed> *vt Am* **1.** (*transmit*) diffuser **2.** *fig, inf* (*fact*) crier sur les toits; (*rumour*) répandre
broadcaster *n* RADIO, TV animateur, -trice *m, f*
broadcasting *n no pl* **1.** (*process*) diffusion *f* **2.** (*programmes*) émissions *fpl*
broadcasting station *n* RADIO, TV émetteur *m*
broaden ['brɔːdn, *Am:* 'brɑː-] **I.** *vi* s'élargir **II.** *vt* élargir
broadly ['brɔːdli] *adv* **1.** (*generally*) d'une manière générale **2.** (*widely*) largement; **to smile** [*o* **grin**] ~ avoir un large sourire
broad-minded [ˌbrɔːd'maɪndɪd, *Am:* ˌbrɑːd-] *adj* **to be** ~ avoir les idées larges
broadsheet ['brɔːdʃiːt, *Am:* ˌbrɑːd-] *n Aus, Brit* **1.** (*newspaper*) journal *m* grand format **2.** (*sheet of paper*) tract *m*
broadside ['brɔːdsaɪd, *Am:* ˌbrɑːd-] *n* invective *f*

> **Broadway** est une grande rue dans New York City. C'est dans cette rue que se situe le célèbre quartier des théâtres qui porte le même nom. "Broadway" est synonyme du grand art théâtral américain et pratiquement toutes les pièces de théâtre de quelque importance y ont été jouées. Celles qui ne sont pas jouées dans ce quartier sont souvent des productions expérimentales ou à petit budget et on les appelle des "off-Broadway plays".

broccoli ['brɒkəli, *Am:* 'brɑːkl-] *n no pl* brocoli *m*
brochure ['brəʊʃəʳ, *Am:* broʊ'ʃʊr] *n* brochure *f*
brogue[1] [brəʊg, *Am:* broʊg] *n* chaussure *f* de marche
brogue[2] [brəʊg, *Am:* broʊg] *n* accent *m* irlandais
broil [brɔɪl] *vt Am* griller
broiler ['brɔɪləʳ, *Am:* -lɚ] *n* **1.** (*chicken*) poulet *m* à rôtir **2.** *Am* (*grill*) grill *m*
broke [brəʊk, *Am:* broʊk] **I.** *pt of* **break** **II.** *adj inf* fauché(e) ▶**to go** ~ faire faillite; **to go for** ~ jouer le tout pour le tout
broken ['brəʊkən, *Am:* 'broʊ-] **I.** *pp of* **break** **II.** *adj* **1.** (*damaged*) cassé(e); **the computer/fridge is** ~ l'ordinateur/le frigidaire est en panne **2.** (*defeated, crushed*) brisé(e) **3.** (*interrupted*) interrompu(e) **4.** LING ~ **Italien** mauvais italien **5.** (*weakened*) abattu(e); **to be in** ~ **health** avoir une santé délabrée; **to have a** ~ **spirit** avoir l'esprit abattu; **to come from a** ~ **home** venir d'une famille désunie
broken-down *adj* **1.** TECH en panne, brisé *Québec* **2.** (*dilapidated*) délabré(e) **broken-hearted** *adj* **to be** ~ avoir le cœur brisé
broker ['brəʊkəʳ, *Am:* 'broʊkɚ] **I.** *n* courtier *m* **II.** *vt* négocier
brokerage ['brəʊkərɪdʒ, *Am:* 'broʊ-] *n* courtage *m*
brolly ['brɒli, *Am:* 'brɑːli] <-ies> *n Aus, Brit, inf* pépin *m*
bromide ['brəʊmaɪd, *Am:* 'broʊ-] *n* **1.** CHEM bromure *m* **2.** (*platitude*) platitude *f*
bromine ['brəʊmiːn, *Am:* 'broʊ-] *n* brome *m*
bronchi ['brɒŋkaɪ] *n pl* bronches *fpl*
bronchial ['brɒŋkɪəl, *Am:* 'brɑːŋ-] *adj* des bronches
bronchitis [brɒŋ'kaɪtɪs, *Am:* brɑːŋ'kaɪt̬ɪs] *n no pl* bronchite *f*
bronze [brɒnz, *Am:* brɑːnz] *n* bronze *m*
Bronze Age **I.** *n* **the** ~ l'âge du bronze **II.** *adj* de l'âge du bronze
brooch [brəʊtʃ, *Am:* broʊtʃ] *n* broche *f*
brood [bruːd] **I.** *n* **1.** (*hatch*) couvée *f* **2.** *iron* (*children*) progéniture *f* **II.** *vi* **1.** (*ponder*) broyer du noir; **to** ~ **on a grievance** entretenir des griefs **2.** (*hatch*) couver **III.** *vt* couver
brooding *adj* sombre
broody ['bruːdi] <-ier, -iest> *adj* **1.** ZOOL prêt(e) à couver **2.** *fig, inf* **to feel** ~ avoir envie d'avoir des enfants **3.** (*mopy*) maussade

brook¹ [brʊk] *n* ruisseau *m*

brook² [brʊk] *vt form* admettre

broom [bruːm] *n* **1.**(*brush*) balai *m* **2.** *no pl* BOT genêt *m*

broomstick ['bruːmstɪk] *n* manche *m* à balai

broth [brɒθ, *Am:* brɑːθ] *n no pl* bouillon *m*

brothel ['brɒθl, *Am:* 'brɑːθl] *n* maison *f* close

brother ['brʌðəʳ, *Am:* -ɚ] *n* frère *m*

brotherhood ['brʌðəhʊd, *Am:* '-ɚ-] *n + pl/sing vb* fraternité *f*

brother-in-law ['brʌðərɪnlɔː, *Am:* -ɚɪnlɑː] <brothers-in-law *o* -s *Brit*> *n* beau-frère *m*

brotherly ['brʌðəli, *Am:* -ɚli] *adv* **1.**(*friendly*) **a ~ advice** un conseil d'ami **2.**(*fraternal*) fraternel(le)

brought [brɔːt, *Am:* brɑːt] *pp, pt of* **bring**

brow [braʊ] *n* **1.**(*forehead*) front *m* **2.**(*eyebrow*) sourcil *m* **3.**(*top*) sommet *m*

browbeat ['braʊbiːt] <browbeat, -en> *vt* intimider

brown [braʊn] **I.** *adj* brun(e), marron *inv;* (*hair*) chatain; *s. a.* **blue II.** *vi* (*leaves*) roussir; (*person*) bronzer ►**to be ~ed off** *inf* en avoir ras le bol **III.** *vt* brunir; (*meat*) faire dorer

brown ale *n* bière *f* brune **brown bread** *n* pain *m* bis

brownie ['braʊni] *n Am* brownie *m* (*friandise*)

Brownie ['braʊni] *n Brit* ≈jeannette *f* ►**to earn ~ points** *inf* gagner des bons points

brownish ['braʊnɪʃ] *adj* tirant sur le brun

brown paper *n* papier *m* kraft **brown rice** *n* riz *m* complet **brownstone** *n Am* **1.**(*sandstone*) grès *m* brun **2.**(*house*) maison *f* en grès brun **brown sugar** *n* sucre *m* brun

browse [braʊz] *vi* **1.**(*skim*) **to ~ through sth** feuilleter qc **2.**(*look around*) regarder **3.**(*graze*) brouter

browser [braʊzə, *Am:* -ɚ] *n* INFOR **1.**(*software*) logiciel *m* de navigation, fureteur *m Québec* **2.**(*function*) explorateur *m,* navigateur *m*

bruise [bruːz] **I.** *n* **1.** MED bleu *m* **2.**(*on fruit*) meurtrissure *m* **II.** *vt* **1.**(*injure outside of*) **to ~ one's arm** se faire un bleu au bras **2.**(*damage: fruit*) meurtrir **3.**(*hurt*) blesser **III.** *vi* se faire un bleu

bruiser ['bruːzəʳ, *Am:* -zɚ] *n iron, inf* **1.**(*brute*) brute *f* **2.**(*boxer*) cogneur *m*

bruising **I.** *n no pl* **1.**(*contusions*) contusions *fpl* **2.**(*beating*) **to take a ~** prendre une râclée **II.** *adj* violent(e)

brunch [brʌntʃ] *n* brunch *m*

Brunei ['bruːnaɪ] *n* le Brunei

Bruneian **I.** *adj* brunéien(ne) **II.** *n* Brunéien(ne) *m(f)*

brunette [bruː'net] *n* brune *f*

brunt [brʌnt] *n no pl* **1.**(*part*) **to take the ~ of sth** subir le plus lourd de qc **2.**(*impact*) choc *m*

brush [brʌʃ] **I.** *n* **1.**(*for hair*) brosse *f* **2.**(*broom*) balai *m* **3.**(*for painting*) pinceau *m* **4.**(*action*) **to give sth a ~** donner un coup de balai à qc; **to give one's teeth a ~** se brosser les dents **5.**(*encounter*) accrochage *m;* **to have a ~ with the law** avoir des démêlés avec la justice; **to have a ~ with death** frôler la mort **6.** *no pl* (*brushwood*) broussailles *fpl* **7.**(*fox's tail*) queue *f* **II.** *vt* **1.**(*clean*) brosser; **to ~ one's teeth/hair** se brosser les dents/cheveux **2.**(*remove*) **to ~ sth off** enlever qc à la brosse/au balai **3.**(*graze, touch lightly in passing*) effleurer; **to ~ against sb** frôler qn

◆**brush aside** *vt* **1.**(*move*) balayer (d'un seul geste) **2.**(*dismiss*) repousser

◆**brush away** *vt* **1.**(*wipe*) essuyer **2.**(*push to one side*) écarter

◆**brush off** *vt* **1.**(*rebuff, avoid*) repousser **2.**(*ignore*) écarter d'un geste

◆**brush up** *vt* **to ~ on sth** se rafraîchir la mémoire en qc

brush-off ['brʌʃɒf, *Am:* -ɑːf] *n* **to give sb the ~** envoyer qn sur les roses; **to get the ~ from sb** se faire envoyer sur les roses par qn

brushwood ['brʌʃwʊd] *n no pl* broussailles *fpl*

brusque [bruːsk, *Am:* brʌsk] *adj* brusque

brusqueness *n no pl* brusquerie *f*

Brussels ['brʌsəlz] *n* Bruxelles

Brussels sprouts *npl* choux *mpl* de Bruxelles

brutal ['bruːtəl, *Am:* -t̬əl] *adj* **1.**(*savage*) violent(e) **2.**(*frank*) brutal(e)

brutality [bruː'tæləti, *Am:* -əţi] *n* brutalité *f*

brutalize ['bruːtəlaɪz, *Am:* -t̬əl-] *vt Am* **1.**(*treat cruelly*) brutaliser **2.**(*make brutal*) rendre brutal

brute [bruːt] **I.** *n* brute *f* **II.** *adj* brutal(e); **by ~ force** par la force

brutish ['bruːtɪʃ, *Am:* -t̬ɪʃ] *adj* brutal(e)

BSc [ˌbiːes'siː] *n abbr of* **Bachelor of Science** licencié(e) *m(f)* ès sciences

BSE [ˌbiːes'iː] *n no pl abbr of* **bovine spongiform encephalopathy** ESB *f*

BST [ˌbiːes'tiː] *n abbr of* **British Summer Time** *heure d'été en Grande-Bretagne*

Btu *n abbr of* **British thermal unit** *unité égale à 252 calories*

bubble ['bʌbl] **I.** *n* bulle *f;* **to blow a ~** faire une bulle ►**to burst sb's ~** faire redescendre qn sur terre **II.** *vi* **1.**(*boil*) bouillonner **2.**(*sound*) glouglouter

◆**bubble over with** *vi* **to ~ joy** déborder de joie

bubble bath *n* bain *m* moussant **bubble gum** *n* chewing-gum *m* (*qui fait des bulles*)

bubbly ['bʌbli] *inf* **I.** *n* champagne *m* **II.** *adj* **1.**(*full of bubbles*) pétillant(e) **2.**(*lively*) plein(e) de vie

buccaneer [ˌbʌkə'nɪəʳ, *Am:* -'nɪr] *n* boucanier *m*

Bucharest [ˌbuːkə'rest, *Am:* '-] *n* Bucarest

buck¹ [bʌk] *n Am, Aus, inf* dollar *m* ►**to make a fast ~** gagner du fric facile

buck² [bʌk] *n no pl, inf* **to pass the ~** faire porter le chapeau à qn d'autre
buck³ [bʌk] <-(s)> **I.** *n* **1.** (*male*) mâle *m* **2.** (*kick*) ruade *f* **II.** *adj* mâle; **~ deer** cerf *m* **III.** *vi* lancer une ruade **IV.** *vt* se rebiffer
◆**buck up I.** *vi inf* **1.** (*cheer up*) se secouer **2.** (*hurry up*) se grouiller **II.** *vt* (*cheer up*) remonter le moral à ▸**to buck one's ideas up** se secouer un peu
bucket ['bʌkɪt] *n* **1.** (*pail*) seau *m;* **champagne ~** seau à champagne **2.** *pl, inf* (*a lot*) beaucoup; **to weep ~s** pleurer toutes les larmes de son corps ▸**to kick the ~** *inf* casser sa pipe
bucketful ['bʌkɪtfʊl] <-s *o* bucketsful> *n* **1. a ~ of water** un plein seau d'eau **2.** *pl, fig* des masses
bucket shop *n Brit, inf* agence *f* de voyages discompte
Buckingham Palace [ˌbʌkɪŋəm-] *n* le palais de Buckingham

Buckingham Palace est la résidence londonienne du monarque britannique. Le palais possède 600 pièces et fut construit de 1821 à 1830 par John Nash pour le roi George IV. Ce bâtiment fut inauguré en 1837 à l'occasion de l'intronisation de la reine Victoria.

buckle ['bʌkl] **I.** *n* boucle *f* **II.** *vt* **1.** (*fasten*) boucler; (*belt*) attacher **2.** (*bend*) déformer **III.** *vi* **1.** (*fasten*) s'attacher **2.** (*bend*) se déformer
◆**buckle down** *vi* s'y mettre; **to ~ to one's work** se mettre au travail
buckshot ['bʌkʃɒt, *Am:* -ʃɑːt] *n no pl* chevrotine *f*
buckskin ['bʌkskɪn] **I.** *n no pl* peau *f* de daim **II.** *adj* en daim
buckwheat ['bʌkwiːt] *n no pl* sarrasin *m*
bud¹ [bʌd] BOT **I.** *n* bourgeon *m* ▸**to be in ~** bourgeonner **II.** <-dd-> *vi* bourgeonner
bud² [bʌd] *n Am, inf* mon pote *m*
Buddha ['bʊdə, *Am:* 'buːdə] *n* Bouddha *m*
Buddhism ['bʊdɪzəm, *Am:* 'buːdɪ-] *n no pl* bouddhisme *m*
buddhist I. *n* bouddhiste *mf* **II.** *adj* bouddhiste
budding ['bʌdɪŋ] *adj* naissant(e)
buddy ['bʌdi] *n Am, inf* (*pal*) pote; **calm down, ~!** du calme, coco! *m*
budge [bʌdʒ] **I.** *vi* **1.** (*move*) bouger **2.** (*change opinion*) changer d'avis **II.** *vt* faire bouger
budgerigar ['bʌdʒərɪgɑːʳ, *Am:* -gɑːr] *n form* perruche *f*
budget ['bʌdʒɪt] **I.** *n* budget *m;* **to draw up a ~** établir un budget; **a ~ deficit** un déficit budgétaire **II.** *vt* prévoir dans le budget **2.** *Am* **to ~ one's time** planifier son temps **III.** *vi* préparer un budget; **to ~ for sth** prévoir qc dans le budget **IV.** *adj* (*cheap*) à prix intéressant; **a ~ airline** une compagnie aérienne pour budgets serrés
budgetary ['bʌdʒɪtəri] *adj* budgétaire
buff [bʌf] **I.** *n inf* mordu(e) *m(f);* **jazz ~** passionné de jazz ▸**in the ~** à poil **II.** *adj* **1.** (*leather*) en buffle **2.** (*light brown*) beige **III.** *vt* **to ~ (up) sth** polir qc
buffalo ['bʌfələʊ, *Am:* -əloʊ] <-(es)> *n* buffle *m*
buffer¹ ['bʌfəʳ, *Am:* -ɚ] **I.** *n* **1.** tampon *m* **2.** INFOR mémoire *f* tampon **II.** *vt* CHEM tamponner
buffer² ['bʌfəʳ, *Am:* -ɚ] *n Brit, inf* vieux fossile *m*
buffet¹ ['bʊfeɪ, *Am:* bə'feɪ] *vt* secouer
buffet² ['bʌfɪt] *n* buffet *m*
buffet car *n Brit* voiture-buffet *f*
buffoon [bə'fuːn] *n* bouffon *m*
bug [bʌg] **I.** *n* **1.** ZOOL punaise *f* **2.** *inf* (*insect*) insecte *m* **3.** MED microbe *m;* **there's a ~ going round** il y a un microbe qui circule **4.** (*fault*) défaut *m* **5.** INFOR bogue *m* **6.** TEL table *f* d'écoute; **to plant a ~** installer des micros **7.** *inf* (*enthusiasm*) virus *m* **II.** <-gg-> *vt* **1.** (*tap*) brancher sur table d'écoute **2.** *inf* (*annoy*) casser les pieds à
bugbear ['bʌgbeəʳ, *Am:* -ber] *n* bête *f* noire
bugger ['bʌgəʳ, *Am:* -ɚ] **I.** *n inf* **1.** (*person*) salaud *m* **2.** (*thing*) casse-pieds *m* **II.** *interj Aus, Brit, vulg* merde ▸**~ it/me** merde **III.** *vt vulg* foutre en l'air
◆**bugger off** *vi inf* foutre le camp
◆**bugger up** *vt vulg* foutre en l'air
buggery ['bʌgəri] *n no pl, vulg* sodomie *f*
bugging *n* (*of room, telephone*) mise *f* sur écoute
bugging system *n* système *m* d'écoute
buggy ['bʌgi] <-ies> *n* **1.** *Brit* (*pushchair*) poussette *f* **2.** *Am* (*pram*) landau *m* **3.** AUTO buggy *m* **4.** (*carriage*) boghei *m*
bugle ['bjuːgl] *n* clairon *m*
bugler ['bjuːgləʳ] *n* joueur, -euse *m, f* de clairon
build [bɪld] **I.** *n* charpente *f* **II.** <built, built> *vt* **1.** (*construct*) bâtir; (*car, ship*) construire; (*memorial*) édifier **2.** *fig* (*company*) établir; (*system*) créer; (*vocabulary*) augmenter; **to ~ a case against sb** constituer un dossier contre qn ▸**Rome wasn't built in a day** *prov* Rome ne s'est pas faite en un jour *prov* **III.** <built, built> *vi* **1.** (*construct*) construire **2.** (*increase*) augmenter
◆**build in** *vt* (*cupboard*) encastrer; (*security, penalty*) introduire
◆**build on** *vt* **1.** (*add*) ajouter **2.** (*develop from*) partir de
◆**build up I.** *vt* **1.** (*accumulate: reserves, surplus*) accumuler; (*collection*) développer; **to ~ speed** gagner de la vitesse **2.** (*strengthen*) développer; **to ~ sb's hopes** donner de l'espoir à qn **3.** (*develop*) développer **4.** (*hype*) faire du battage autour de **II.** *vi* (*increase*) s'accumuler; (*traffic*) augmenter; (*pressure*) monter; (*popularity*) grimper; (*business*) se développer

builder ['bɪldəʳ, *Am:* -dɚ] *n* maçon *m;* (*company*) entreprise *f* de bâtiment; **we've got the ~s in** on a des ouvirers à la maison

builder's yard *n* dépôt *m* de matériel de chantier

building *n* **1.** (*place*) bâtiment *m;* (*for offices, apartments*) immeuble *m;* **the administration** ~ le bâtiment de l'administration **2.** (*industry*) le bâtiment **3.** (*process*) construction *f*

building contractor *n* entrepreneur *m* en bâtiment **building site** *n* chantier *m* **building society** *n Aus, Brit* société *f* de crédit immobilier

build-up ['bɪldʌp] *n* **1.** (*increase, accumulation*) montée *f;* (*of waste, toxins*) accumulation *f;* (*of troops*) rassemblement *m;* (*of resentment, grievances*) accumulation *f;* **a traffic** ~ un engorgement **2.** (*hype*) battage *m* publicitaire

built [bɪlt] **I.** *pp, pt of* **build II.** *adj* construit(e); **well-~** (*house*) bien construit(e); (*person*) bien bâti(e); **slightly** ~ fluet(te)

built-in ['bɪlt'ɪn, *Am:* 'bɪltɪn] *adj* **1.** encastré(e) **2.** *fig* incorporé(e)

built-up ['bɪltʌp] *adj* **1.** ARCHIT urbanisé(e); ~ **area** agglomération *f* urbaine **2.** (*made higher*) ~ **heels** talons *mpl* compensés; ~ **shoes** chaussures *fpl* à semelle compensée

bulb [bʌlb] *n* **1.** BOT bulbe *m* **2.** ELEC ampoule *f*

bulbous ['bʌlbəs] *adj* **1.** BOT bulbeux(-euse) **2.** (*large: nose*) gros(se)

Bulgaria [bʌl'geərɪə, *Am:* -'gerɪ-] *n* la Bulgarie

Bulgarian [bʌl'geərɪən, *Am:* -'gerɪ-] **I.** *adj* bulgare **II.** *n* **1.** (*person*) Bulgare *mf* **2.** LING bulgare *m; s. a.* **English**

bulge [bʌldʒ] **I.** *vi* (*pocket*) être bourré; (*clothes*) faire des bourrelets; (*wall, surface*) faire une bosse *f;* **her eyes ~d in surprise** ses yeux étaient grand ouverts d'étonnement; **a pocket ~ing with sth** une poche bourrée de qc ▶**to be bulging at the seams** *inf* être plein à craquer; (*room, cinema*) être bondé **II.** *n* **1.** (*swelling*) gonflement *m* **2.** ECON hausse *f* à court terme **3.** HIST **the Battle of the Bulge** la bataille des Ardennes

bulging *adj* (*eyes*) globuleux(-euse); (*forehead, wall*) bombé(e)

bulimia [bʊlɪ:miə, *Am:* bju:'-], **bulimia nervosa** *n no pl* boulimie *f*

bulk [bʌlk] **I.** *n* **1.** *no pl* (*mass*) masse *f* **2.** *no pl* (*quantity*) volume *m;* **in** ~ (*buy*) en quantité; (*deliver*) en vrac **3.** *no pl* (*size*) grandeur *f;* (*body*) corpulence *f;* **ships of great** ~ des vaisseaux de grandes dimensions **4.** (*largest part*) majeure partie *f;* **the** ~ **of mankind** le commun des hommes **II.** *vi* **to** ~ **large** occuper une place importante

◆**bulk buy** *vi, vt* acheter en grosse quantité

bulk buying *n* ECON *no pl* achat *m* en gros

bulk cargo *n* NAUT cargaison *f* en vrac

bulkhead ['bʌlkhed] *n* NAUT cloison *f*

bulky ['bʌlki] <-ier, iest> *adj* **1.** (*large*) volumineux(-euse); (*person*) corpulent(e) **2.** (*awkwardly large*) encombrant(e)

bull¹ [bʊl] *n* **1.** (*male bovine*) taureau *m* **2.** (*male animal*) mâle *m* **3.** (*man*) **he is a ~ of a man** il est fort comme un taureau ▶**like a ~ in a china shop** comme un éléphant dans un magasin de porcelaine

bull² [bʊl] *n* **1.** *no pl, inf* (*nonsense*) foutaise *f* **2.** FIN haussier *m* **3.** *Brit* SPORT centre *m* de la cible

bulldog ['bʊldɒg, *Am:* -dɑ:g] *n* bouledogue *m*

bulldoze ['bʊldəʊz, *Am:* -doʊz] *vt* **1.** ARCHIT **to ~ sth** (**flat**) applatir qc; (*tear down*) démolir **2.** (*force*) **to ~ sb into doing sth** obliger qn à faire qc

bulldozer ['bʊldəʊzəʳ, *Am:* -doʊzɚ] *n* bulldozer *m*

bullet ['bʊlɪt] *n* **1.** MIL balle *f* **2.** TYP, INFOR puce *f* ▶**to bite the** ~ se forcer; **a** ~ **train** un train à grande vitesse (*au Japon*)

bullet-headed *adj* **1.** à la tête ronde **2.** *Am, fig* **to be** ~ être entêté

bulletin ['bʊlətɪn, *Am:* -əţɪn] *n* **1.** TV, CINE (**news**) ~ actualités *fpl* télévisées; (*on one topic*) communiqué *m* spécial **2.** (*newsletter*) bulletin *m* d'informations; **church** ~ journal *m* paroissial

bulletin board *n* **1.** *Am* (*board*) tableau *m* d'affichage; ADMIN tableau *m* d'annonces **2.** INFOR messagerie *f* électronique

bullet-proof vest *n* gilet *m* pare-balles

bullfight ['bʊlfaɪt] *n* combat *m* de taureaux

bullfighter ['bʊlfaɪtəʳ, *Am:* -ţɚ] *n* toréador *m*

bullfinch ['bʊlfɪntʃ] *n* bouvreuil *m*

bullion ['bʊlɪən, *Am:* -jən] *n no pl* **gold/silver** ~ or/argent en lingot(s) *m*

bull-neck *n* cou *m* de taureau

bullock ['bʊlək] *n* bœuf *m*

bullring ['bʊlrɪŋ] *n* arène *f*

bullseye *n* cible *f;* **to hit the** ~ *a. fig* faire mouche

bully ['bʊli] **I.** <-ies> *n* **1.** (*person*) tyran *m;* (*child*) brute *f* **2.** GASTR bœuf *m* en conserve **II.** <-ie-> *vi* être une brute **III.** <-ie-> *vt* victimiser; **to ~ sb into doing sth** contraindre qn par la menace à faire qc **IV.** *interj* ~ **for you!** *inf* tant mieux pour toi/vous!; *iron* bravo!

bulrush ['bʊlrʌʃ] <-es> *n* jonc *m*

bulwark ['bʊlwək, *Am:* -wɚk] *n* **1.** (*wall*) fortification *f* **2.** *fig* rempart *m*

bum [bʌm] **I.** *n* **1.** (*lazy person*) bon-à-rien *m,* bonne-à-rien *f* **2.** *Am* (*tramp*) clochard(e) *m(f)* **3.** *Aus, Brit, inf* (*bottom*) derrière *m* **4.** *Am* **to give sb the ~'s rush** *inf* virer qn à coups de pied au fesses **II.** <-mm-> *vt* **to ~ a ride** faire de l'auto-stop; **to ~ a cigarette from sb** *inf* taper qn d'une cigarette

bumbag *n* banane *f*

bumblebee ['bʌmblbi:] *n* bourdon *m*

bumf [bʌmf] *n no pl, Aus, Brit, inf* **1.** (*printed

matter) paperasses *fpl* **2.** (*paperwork*) paperasserie *f*

bump [bʌmp] **I.** *n* **1.** (*swelling*) bosse *f* **2.** (*protrusion*) protubérance *f;* **speed ~** ralentisseur *m* **3.** *inf* (*blow*) léger coup *m* **4.** (*thud*) bruit *m* sourd **5.** (*collision*) léger accrochage *m* **6.** *Brit* (*belly*) **she has a big ~** elle est enceinte jusqu'aux yeux **II.** *vt* (*car*) tamponner; (*one's head*) se cogner **III.** *vi* **to ~ along** cahoter; **to ~ up and down** être secoué de tous côtés; **to ~ against sth** se cogner contrer qc

◆**bump into** *vt insep* **1.** (*collide with*) rentrer dans **2.** (*meet*) tomber sur

bumper¹ ['bʌmpəʳ, *Am:* -pɚ] *n* AUTO pare-chocs *m;* **back/front ~** parechoc(s) arrière/avant

bumper² ['bʌmpəʳ, *Am:* -pɚ] *adj* (*crowd, crop*) record; (*packet*) géant(e); (*year, issue*) exceptionnel(le)

bumper car *n* auto-tamponneuse *f*

bumph [bʌmpf] *n no pl s.* **bumf**

bumpkin ['bʌmpkɪn] *n pej, inf* paysan(ne) *m(f);* **country ~** péquenaud(e) *m(f)*

bumptious ['bʌmpʃəs] *adj pej* crâneur(-euse); **a ~ attitude** un style prétentieux

bumpy ['bʌmpi] <-ier, iest> *adj* **1.** (*uneven*) inégal(e) **2.** (*jarring*) cahoteux(-euse); (*road*) défoncé(e) **3.** *fig* difficile; (*life*) mouvementé(e); **to have a ~ ride** passer par des moments difficiles

bun [bʌn] *n* **1.** (*pastry*) petit pain *m* au lait **2.** *Am* (*roll*) *petit pain pour hot-dog ou hamburger* **3.** (*knot of hair*) chignon *m*

bunch [bʌntʃ] <-es> **I.** *n* **1.** (*group of similar objects*) ensemble *m;* (*of bananas*) régime *m;* (*of radishes*) botte *f;* (*of flowers*) bouquet *m;* (*of grapes*) grappe *f;* (*of keys*) trousseau *m* **2.** (*group of people*) groupe *m;* (*of idiots, thieves*) bande *f* **3.** *Am* (*lot*) **a ~ of problems** un tas de problèmes; **a ~ of test papers** SCHOOL, UNIV une pile d'interrogations écrites **4.** (*wad*) **in a ~** en liasse **5.** *pl, Brit* (*hair style*) couettes *fpl* ►**the best of the ~** le meilleur de tous; **the best of a bad ~** le(s) moins médiocre(s) **II.** *vt* **to be ~ed up** être serrés comme des sardines

bundle ['bʌndl] **I.** *n* (*pile*) tas *m;* (*wrapped up*) paquet *m;* (*of papers, banknotes*) liasse *f;* **wrapped in a ~** empaqueté ►**a ~ of laughs** une partie de rire; **a ~ of nerves** un paquet de nerfs; **sb goes a ~ on sth** *Brit, inf* qc botte qn; **to make a ~ on sth** faire son beurre sur qc **II.** *vt inf* fourrer **III.** *vi* **to ~ into sth** (*people*) s'entasser dans qc

◆**bundle up** *vt* (*person*) emmitoufler; (*things*) mettre en paquet

bung [bʌŋ] **I.** *n Brit* bouchon *m* (*en bois ou en liège*) **II.** *vt* **1.** *Brit* (*close*) boucher **2.** *Aus, Brit, inf* (*throw carelessly*) balancer

bungalow ['bʌŋgələʊ, *Am:* -oʊ] *n* petit pavillon *m*

bungee jumping ['bʌndʒɪˌdʒʌmpɪŋ] *n no pl* saut *m* à l'élastique

bung hole *n* bonde *f*

bungle ['bʌŋgl] **I.** *vt* bâcler; **a ~ed operation/attempt** une opération/tentative ratée **II.** *n* embrouille *f*

bungler *n pej* propre *m* à rien

bungling **I.** *n no pl* gâchis *m* **II.** *adj* gaffeur(-euse); **~ fool** [*o* **idiot**] idiot(e) *m(f)*

bunk [bʌŋk] *n* **1.** NAUT couchette *f* **2.** *inf* (*rubbish*) bêtises *fpl* ►**to do a ~** *Aus, Brit, inf* mettre les voiles *fpl*

bunk down *vi inf* dormir

bunk off *inf* **I.** *vi* (*from school*) sécher; (*from meeting*) se casser **II.** *vt* **to ~ school** sécher l'école

bunk bed *n* lit *m* superposé; **bottom/top ~** lit supérieur/inférieur

bunker ['bʌŋkəʳ, *Am:* -kɚ] *n* **1.** MIL abri *m* bétoné **2.** SPORT bunker *m*

bunkum ['bʌŋkəm] *n no pl s.* **bunk**

bunny ['bʌni], **bunny rabbit** *n childspeak* Jeannot lapin *m*

bunsen burner [ˌbʌtsən'bɜːnər, *Am:* 'bʌtsɪnˌbɜːrnɚ] *n* bec *m* Bunsen

bunting ['bʌntɪŋ, *Am:* -t̬ɪŋ] *n no pl* drapeaux *mpl*

buoy [bɔɪ] *n* bouée *f*

buoy up *vt* **1.** (*cause to float*) **to buoy sb up** maintenir qn à flot **2.** *fig* épauler; **to ~ sb's spirits** remonter le moral de qn; **to be buoyed up with new hope** être soutenu par un nouvel espoir

buoyancy ['bɔɪənsi, *Am:* -jən-] *n no pl* **1.** NAUT flottabilité *f* **2.** (*capacity for cheerfulness*) entrain *m*

buoyant ['bɔɪənt, *Am:* -jənt] *adj* **1.** (*able to float*) flottable **2.** (*cheerful*) plein d'entrain; **to be in a ~ mood** être d'humeur gaie **3.** FIN **the market is ~** le marché est ferme

bur *n s.* **burr**

burble ['bɜːbl, *Am:* 'bɜːr-] *vi* **1.** (*make noise*) glouglouter **2.** (*babble*) babiller; **to ~ (on) about sth** marmonner à propos de qc

burden ['bɜːdən, *Am:* 'bɜːr-] **I.** *n* **1.** (*load*) charge *f* **2.** *fig* fardeau *m;* **the ~ of debt/taxation** le fardeau de la dette/de l'impôt; **the ~ of proof** la charge de la preuve; **to place a ~ on sb** déposer un fardeau sur qn **II.** *vt* **1.** (*load*) charger **2.** *fig* surcharger; **I won't ~ you with the details** je vous dispense des détails

burdensome ['bɜːdənsəm, *Am:* 'bɜːr-] *adj form* pesant(e)

bureau ['bjʊərəʊ, *Am:* 'bjʊroʊ] <-x *o* -s *Am, Aus*> *n* **1.** *Am* (*government department*) service *m* gouvernemental **2.** (*office*) bureau *m;* **information ~** bureau *m* d'information **3.** *Brit* (*desk*) secrétaire *m* **4.** *Am* (*chest of drawers*) commode *f*

bureaucracy [bjʊə'rɒkrəsi, *Am:* bjʊ'rɑːkrə-] *n pej* bureaucratie *f*

bureaucrat ['bjʊərəkræt, *Am:* 'bjʊrə-] *n* bureaucrate *mf*

B

bureaucratic [ˌbjʊərə'krætɪk, *Am:* ˌbjʊrə'kræt̬-] *adj* bureaucratique; ~ **hassle** tracasseries *fpl* administratives

burgeoning ['bɜːdʒənɪŋ, *Am:* 'bɜːr-] *adj* qui émerge

burger ['bɜːgəʳ, *Am:* 'bɜːrgɚ] *n inf* biftek haché

burglar ['bɜːgləʳ, *Am:* 'bɜːrglɚ] *n* cambrioleur, -euse *m, f*

burglar alarm *n* alarme *f*

burglarize ['bɜːgləraɪz, *Am:* 'bɜːrglə-] *vt Am s.* **burgle**

burglary ['bɜːgləri, *Am:* 'bɜːr-] <-ies> *n* **1.** (*stealing*) cambriolage *m* **2.** *no pl* LAW vol *m* avec effraction

burgle ['bɜːgl, *Am:* 'bɜːr-] *vt* cambrioler

Burgundy ['bɜːgəndi, *Am:* 'bɜːr-] *n* la Bourgogne

burial ['berɪəl] *n* enterrement *m*

Burkinabe ['bɜːkiːneɪb] **I.** *adj* burkinabé(e) **II.** *n* Burkinabé(e) *m(f)*

Burkina Faso [bɜːˌkiːnə'fæsəʊ] *n* le Burkina Faso

burlesque [bɜː'lesk, *Am:* 'bɜːr-] **I.** *n* parodie *f* **II.** *adj* burlesque

burly ['bɜːli, *Am:* 'bɜːr-] <-ier, -iest> *adj* de forte carrure

Burma ['bɜːmə, *Am:* 'bɜr-] *n* la Birmanie

burn¹ [bɜːn, *Am:* bɜːrn] *n Scot* ruisseau *m*

burn² [bɜːn, *Am:* bɜːrn] **I.** *n* brûlure *f* **II.** <-t *o* -ed, -t *o* -ed> *vi* **1.** (*be in flames*) brûler **2.** (*be overheated: meat, pan*) brûler **3.** (*be switched on: light*) être allumé **4.** (*feel very hot: with fever, irritation*) brûler; **I ~ easily** je prends des coups de soleil; **my eyes are ~ing** mes yeux piquent **5.** (*feel an emotion*) **to be ~ing with desire** brûler de désir; **his face was ~ing with shame/anger** son visage était rouge de honte/colère **6.** *fig* **to ~ to** *+infin* se languir de *+infin* ►**my ears are ~ing** mes oreilles sifflent **III.** <-t *o* -ed, -t *o* -ed> *vt* **1.** (*consume*) brûler; **to be ~ed to the ground** être complètement détruit par le feu; **to be burnt at the stake** mourir sur le bûcher **2.** (*overheat: meat, pan*) laisser brûler; **to ~ sth to a crisp** carboniser qc **3.** (*hurt, irritate: skin*) brûler; **to ~ one's tongue** se brûler la langue **4.** (*consume as fuel*) **to ~ gas** se chauffer au gaz ►**to ~ the candle at both ends** brûler la chandelle par les deux bouts; **money ~s a hole in her pocket** l'argent lui brûle les doigts

◆**burn away I.** *vi* brûler; (*forest, house*) être en feu; (*candle*) se consumer **II.** *vt* détruire par le feu

◆**burn down I.** *vt* incendier **II.** *vi* brûler complètement

◆**burn out I.** *vi* (*stop burning*) s'éteindre; (*fire, candle*) se consumer **II.** *vt* **1.** (*stop burning*) **the boat is burning itself out** le bateau achève de brûler **2.** (*be destroyed*) **the factory was burnt out** le feu a détruit l'usine **3.** (*become ill*) **she burnt herself out** elle s'est ruiné la santé

◆**burn up I.** *vt inf* griller **II.** *vi* **1.** (*be consumed*) se consumer **2.** (*feel constantly*) **to be burnt up with sth** être dévoré par qc **3.** *fig* **he is burning up!** il est brûlant (de fièvre)!

burner ['bɜːnəʳ, *Am:* 'bɜːrnɚ] *n* brûleur *m* ►**to put sth on the back ~** laisser qc de côté

burning ['bɜːnɪŋ, *Am:* 'bɜːrnɪŋ] *adj* **1.** (*on fire: candle*) allumé(e); (*building, clothes*) en feu; (*log*) qui brûle **2.** (*hot*) brûlant(e); (*desire*) ardent(e) **3.** (*controversial*) controversé(e) **4.** (*stinging*) cuisant(e); **a ~ sensation** une sensation de brûlure

> La **Burns Night**, le 25 janvier, jour anniversaire du poète écossais Robert Burns (1759-96), est célébrée dans le monde entier par les Écossais et autres admirateurs du poète. A l'occasion de cette fête, il existe un repas spécial, le "Burns Supper", constitué d'un "Haggis" (une sorte de rôti de viande hâchée épicée à base de tripes de mouton, mélangée avec de l'avoine et des oignons, qui est cuite dans l'estomac du mouton, puis rôtie au four), de "neeps" (navets) et de "mashed tatties" (purée de pommes de terre).

burnt [bɜːnt, *Am:* 'bɜːrnt] *adj* **1.** (*scorched*) roussi(e) **2.** (*consumed*) calciné(e); ~ **beyond recognition** carbonisé

burnt out *adj* (*building*) entièrement brûlé(e); (*executive*) usé(e)

burp [bɜːp, *Am:* bɜːrp] **I.** *n* renvoi *m;* (*from baby*) rot *m* **II.** *vi* rôter; (*baby*) faire un rot **III.** *vt* **to ~ a baby** faire faire son rot à un bébé

burr [bɜːʳ, *Am:* bɜːr] *n* **1.** BOT bardane *f* **2.** (*noise*) bourdonnement *m* **3.** LING grasseyement *m;* **to speak with a ~** rouler les r

burrow ['bʌrəʊ, *Am:* 'bɜːroʊ] **I.** *n* terrier *m* **II.** *vt* creuser **III.** *vi* **1.** ZOOL se terrer **2.** (*dig*) **to ~ through sth** creuser un tunnel à travers qc

bursar ['bɜːsəʳ, *Am:* 'bɜːrsɚ] *n* intendant(e) *m(f);* UNIV administrateur, -trice *m, f*

bursary ['bɜːsəri, *Am:* 'bɜːr-] *n Brit* bourse *f* d'étude

burst [bɜːst, *Am:* bɜːrst] **I.** *n* **1.** (*hole in pipe*) tuyau *m* éclaté **2.** (*brief period*) **a ~ of laughter** un éclat de rire; **a ~ of activity** un regain d'activité; **a ~ of applause** une salve d'applaudissement; **a ~ of gunfire** une rafale de coups de feu; **to put on a ~ of speed** s'emballer **II.** <-, – *o* -ed, -ed *Am*> *vi* **1.** (*explode*) exploser; (*bag, balloon*) éclater; **I'm ~ing** *inf* (*after meal*) je vais éclater; (*cannot wait*) j'en peux plus **2.** (*be eager*) **to be ~ing to** *+infin* mourir d'envie de *+infin;* **he is ~ing with happiness/confidence/pride** il déborde de santé/de confiance en lui/ de fierté **3.** (*showing movement*) **the door ~ open** la porte s'est ouverte brusquement; **she ~ through the window** elle a fait irruption à travers la fenêtre ►**to be ~ing at the seams** *inf* être plein à craquer, être paqueté *Québec;* (*room, cinema*) être bondé III. <-, – *o* -ed, -ed *Am*> *vt* faire éclater; **a river ~s its banks** une rivière sort de son lit

◆**burst in** *vi* faire irruption; **to ~ on sb** faire irruption chez qn

◆**burst out** *vi* 1. (*speak*) s'écrier 2. (*suddenly begin*) **to ~ laughing** éclater de rire

Burundi [bʊ'rʊndi] I. *n* le Burundi II. *adj* burundais(e)

Burundian *n* Burundais(e) *m(f)*

bury ['beri] <-ie-> *vt* 1. (*put underground*) enterrer; **to be buried alive** être enterré vivant; **buried under the snow** enseveli sous la neige 2. (*attend a burial*) **to ~ sb** assister à l'enterrement de qn 3. (*hide*) dissimuler; **to ~ oneself in one's work** fuir dans le travail; **to ~ one's pain** cacher sa douleur ►**to ~ the hatchet** enterrer la hache de guerre

bus [bʌs] I. <-es *o* -ses *Am*> *n* 1. (*vehicle*) autobus *m*; **school ~** car *m* de ramassage scolaire, autobus *m* scolaire *Québec* 2. INFOR bus *m* II. <-ss- *o* -s- *Am*> *vt* transporter en car III. <-ss- *o* -s- *Am*> *vi* voyager en car

bus driver *n* conducteur, -trice *m, f* de bus

bush [bʊʃ] *n* 1. <-es> BOT buisson *m* 2. (*great amount*) **a ~ of hair** une tignasse 3. *no pl* (*land*) **the ~** la brousse ►**to beat about** [*o* **around** *Am*] **the ~** tourner autour du pot

bushel ['bʊʃl] *n* (*unit of volume*) boisseau *m*

bushy ['bʊʃi] <-ier, -iest> *adj* broussailleux(-euse)

busily *adv* activement; **to be ~ doing sth** être très occupé à qc

business ['bɪznɪs] *n* 1. *no pl* (*trade*) affaires *fpl*; **to be good for ~** être bon pour les affaires; **I'm here on ~** je suis ici pour affaires; **to do ~ with sb** faire des affaires avec qn 2. *no pl* (*commerce*) commerce *m*; (*turnover*) chiffre *m* d'affaires 3. *no pl* (*activity*) **to be in ~** avoir une activité commerciale; *inf* être fin prêt; **to put sb out of ~** faire fermer boutique à qn; **to set up in ~ as a baker** s'établir boulanger 4. <-es> (*profession*) métier *m*; **what line of ~ are you in?** que faites-vous/fais-tu dans la vie? 5. <-es> (*firm*) société *f*; **to start up a ~** créer une entreprise; **small ~es** les petites entreprises 6. *no pl* (*matter, task*) affaire *f*; **it's a time-consuming ~** c'est un travail qui prend du temps; **unfinished ~** affaire pendante; **it's none of your ~** *inf* ça ne te/vous regarde pas; **he has no ~ doing this** il n'a aucun droit de faire cela 7. *no pl* (*process*) **to get on with the ~ of sth** s'occuper de qc ►**to mind one's own ~** *inf* se mêler de ses affaires; **to be able to do ~ with sb** pouvoir travailler avec qn; **to mean ~** ne pas plaisanter; **to get down to ~** passer aux choses sérieuses; **like nobody's ~** *inf* extrêmement vite

business address *n* adresse *f* du bureau **business card** *n* carte *f* de visite **business end** *n inf* (*of gun*) gueule *f*; (*of knife*) côté *m* tranchant **business hours** *n* heures *fpl* de bureau **business letter** *n* lettre *f* d'affaires **businesslike** *adj* méthodique **businessman** <-men> *n* homme *m* d'affaires; (*entrepreneur*) entrepreneur *m* **business park** *n* parc *m* commercial **business people** *n pl* gens *mpl* d'affaires **business transaction** *n* transaction *f* commerciale **business trip** *n* voyage *m* d'affaires **businesswoman** <-women> *n* femme *f* d'affaires; (*entrepreneur*) entrepreneuse *f*

busker ['bʌskəʳ, *Am:* -ɚ] *n Aus, Brit* musicien(ne) *m(f)* des rues

bus lane *n* couloir *m* d'autobus **busload** *n* **~s of tourists** des cars entiers de touristes **bus service** *n* réseau *m* d'autobus **bus station** *n* gare *f* routière **bus stop** *n* arrêt *m* d'autobus

bust[1] [bʌst] *n* 1. (*statue*) buste *m* 2. (*bosom*) poitrine *f* (de femme); **a small ~** de petits seins *mpl*; **~ size** tour *m* de poitrine

bust[2] [bʌst] I. *adj inf* 1. (*broken*) cassé(e) 2. (*bankrupt*) **to go ~** faire faillite II. <-, – *o* -ed, -ed *Am*> *vt inf* 1. (*break*) casser 2. (*arrest*) choper

bustle ['bʌsl] I. *vi* **to ~ about** s'activer; **to ~ with activity** grouiller d'activités II. *n no pl* tourbillon *m* d'activité; **hustle and ~** remue-ménage *m*

bust-up ['bʌstʌp] *n Aus, Brit, inf* engueulade *f*; **to have a** (**big**) **~ with sb** s'engueuler avec qn

busy[1] ['bɪzi] <-ier, -iest> *adj* 1. (*occupied*) occupé(e); **I'm very ~ this week** je suis très pris cette semaine; **to be ~ with sth** être occupé à faire qc; **to get ~** se mettre au travail 2. (*full of activity: period, week, shop*) très actif(-ive); (*street*) animé(e); **it's our busiest day** c'est notre journée la plus chargée 3. (*hectic*) **a ~ time** une période mouvementée 4. (*exhausting*) fatigant(e) 5. *pej* (*overly decorated*) trop bariolé(e) 6. *Am* TEL occupé(e) ►**she is as ~ as a bee** elle déborde d'activité

busy[2] ['bɪzi] <-ie-> *vt* **to ~ oneself** s'occuper; **to ~ oneself with sth** s'appliquer à faire qc

busybody ['bɪzɪˌbɒdi, *Am:* -ˌbɑːdi] <-ies> *n pej, inf* mouche *f* du coche; **he is a ~** il se mêle de ce qui ne le regarde pas; **to be an interfering ~** mettre son grain de sel

but [bʌt] I. *conj* mais II. *prep* sauf; **he's nothing ~ a liar** il n'est rien d'autre qu'un menteur; **the last house ~ one** l'avant-dernière maison III. *n* mais *m* ►**there are no ~s about it!** il n'y a pas de mais qui tienne! IV. *adv form* 1. (*only*) seulement; **she's ~ a young girl** elle n'est qu'une petite fille 2. (*really*) (mais) vraiment

butane ['bjuːteɪn] *n no pl* butane *m*

butch [bʊtʃ] *adj pej* 1. (*woman*) masculine 2. (*man*) macho

butcher ['bʊtʃəʳ, *Am:* -ɚ] I. *n* boucher *m* II. *vt* 1. (*slaughter: animal*) abattre; **~ed for meat** tué pour la viande 2. (*murder*) massacrer

3. SPORT **they ~ed the other team** ils ont écrasé l'autre équipe 4. (*mangle: language*) estropier

butchery ['bʊtʃəri] *n no pl* 1. GASTR boucherie *f* 2. (*killing*) carnage *m*

butler ['bʌtləʳ, *Am:* -lɚ] *n* majordome *m*

butt [bʌt] I. *n* 1. (*bottom part: of tree*) souche *f*; (*of rifle*) crosse *f* 2. (*cigarette*) mégot *m* 3. (*blow*) coup *m* de tête 4. (*person*) **to be the ~ of sb's jokes** être la risée de qn 5. (*container*) tonneau *m* 6. *inf* (*bottom*) cul *m* II. *vt* donner un coup de tête à

butter ['bʌtəʳ, *Am:* 'bʌt̬ɚ] I. *n no pl* beurre *m* ►**he/she looks as if ~ wouldn't melt in his/her mouth** on lui donnerait le bon Dieu sans confession II. *vt* beurrer

◆**butter up** *vt* passer de la pommade à

buttercup *n* BOT bouton d'or *m* **butter-dish** *n* beurrier *m*

butterfingers ['bʌtəˌfɪŋgəz, *Am:* 'bʌt̬ɚˌfɪŋgɚz] <-> *n iron* maladroit(e) *m(f)*; **~!** empoté!

butterfly ['bʌtəflaɪ, *Am:* 'bʌt̬ɚ-] <-ies> *n* 1. ZOOL *a. fig* papillon *m* 2. TECH écrou *m* à oreilles 3. SPORT nage *f* papillon ►**to have butterflies in one's stomach** avoir l'estomac noué

buttermilk ['bʌtəmɪlk, *Am:* 'bʌt̬ɚ-] *n no pl* babeurre *m*

buttery ['bʌtəri, *Am:* 'bʌt̬-] <-ier, -iest> *adj* au beurre

buttock ['bʌtək, *Am:* 'bʌt̬-] *n pl* fesses *fpl*

button ['bʌtən] I. *n* 1. FASHION, INFOR bouton *m*, piton *m Québec*; **to do up one's ~s** se boutonner 2. TECH sonnette *f* ►**to be right on the ~** *Am* mettre dans le mille II. *vt* boutonner ►**~ it!** *Am, inf* la ferme!

buttonhole ['bʌtənhəʊl, *Am:* -hoʊl] I. *n* 1. FASHION boutonnière *f* 2. *Brit* (*flower*) (*fleur portée à la*) *boutonnière* II. *vt fig* **he ~d me** il m'a pris au passage

buttress ['bʌtrɪs] <-es> *n* ARCHIT contrefort *m*; **flying ~** arc-boutant *m*

buxom ['bʌksəm] *adj* bien en chair

buy [baɪ] I. *n* achat *m*; **it's quite a ~** c'est plûtot une affaire II. <bought, bought> *vt* 1. acheter; **to ~ a plane ticket** prendre un billet d'avion; **to ~ sb a present** acheter un cadeau à qn 2. *inf* (*believe*) **I don't ~ that** je ne marche pas ►**to ~ the farm** *Am, inf* partir les pieds devant; **to ~ sb's silence** corrompre qn; **to ~ time** gagner du temps

◆**buy in** *vt Brit* s'approvisionner en

◆**buy off** *vt* acheter

◆**buy out** *vt* 1. COM désintéresser; **to buy sb out** racheter les parts de qn 2. *Brit* MIL **to buy oneself out** se racheter

◆**buy up** *vt* **to ~ houses/shares** acheter toutes les maisons/toutes les parts; **to ~ the whole store** *fig* dévaliser tout le magasin

buyer ['baɪəʳ, *Am:* -ɚ] *n* acheteur, -euse *m, f*

buyout ['baɪaʊt] *n* rachat *m*

buzz [bʌz] I. *vi* 1. (*make a low sound*) vrombir; (*buzzer*) sonner; (*bee*) bourdonner 2. *Am, inf* (*be tipsy*) être éméché 3. *fig* **the room ~ed with conversation** la salle résonnait de brouhaha II. *vt* 1. *inf* TEL appeler 2. AVIAT raser III. *n* 1. (*humming noise*) bourdonnement *m*; (*low noise*) vrombissement *m*; (*of doorbell*) sonnerie *f*; **the ~ of conversation** le brouhaha 2. *inf* TEL coup *m* de fil; **to give sb a ~** passer un coup de fil à qn 3. *inf* (*feeling*) **to get a ~ out of sth** prendre son pied avec qc

buzzard ['bʌzəd, *Am:* -ɚd] *n* 1. *Brit* (*hawk*) busard *m*, buse *f* 2. *Am* (*turkey vulture*) urubu *m*

buzzer ['bʌzəʳ, *Am:* -ɚ] *n* avertisseur *m* sonore; **door ~** sonnette *f*

buzz word *n* mot *m* à la mode

by [baɪ] I. *prep* 1. (*near*) **to stand/lie/be ~ sth/sb** être près [*o* à côté] de qc/qn; **close** [*o* **near**] **~ sb/sth** tout près de qn/qc; **~ the sea** au bord de la mer 2. (*during*) **~ day/night** le [*o* de] jour/la [*o* de] nuit; **~ moonlight** au clair de lune; **~ the way** en cours de route 3. (*at latest time*) **~ tomorrow/midnight** d'ici demain; **~ midnight** avant minuit; **by now** à l'heure qu'il est; **~ then** à ce moment-là; **~ the time sb saw him ...** le temps [*o* avant] que qn le voie (*subj*) ... 4. (*showing agent, cause*) **a novel ~ Joyce** un roman de Joyce; **killed ~ sth/sb** tué par qc/qn; **surrounded ~ dogs** entouré de chiens; **made ~ hand** fait (à la) main 5. (*using*) **~ rail/plane/tram** en train/par avion/avec le tram; **~ means of sth** au moyen de qc; **~ doing sth** en faisant qc; **to hold sb ~ the arm** tenir qn par le bras; **to go in ~ the door** entrer par la porte; **to call sb/sth ~ name** appeler qn/qc par son nom 6. (*through*) **~ chance/mistake** par hasard/erreur; **what does he mean ~ that?** que veut-il dire par là? 7. (*past*) **to go ~ Paris** y aller en passant par Paris; **to walk ~ the post-office** passer devant la poste; **to run ~ sb** passer à côté de qn en courant 8. (*alone*) **to do sth/to be ~ oneself** faire qc/être tout seul 9. (*in measurement*) **paid ~ the hour** payé à l'heure; **~ the day** par jour; **to buy ~ the kilo/dozen** acheter au kilo/à la douzaine; **to multiply/divide ~ 4** multiplier/diviser par 4; **to increase ~ 10%** augmenter de 10%; **4 metres ~ 6** de 4 à 6 mètres 10. (*from perspective of*) **to judge ~ appearances** juger d'après les apparences; **it's all right ~ me** *inf* moi, je suis d'accord II. *adv* 1. (*in reserve*) **to put/lay sth ~** mettre qc de côté 2. (*gradually*) **~ and ~** peu à peu 3. (*past*) **to go/pass ~** passer ►**~ and large** d'une façon générale

bye [baɪ] *interj inf* salut

bye-bye [ˌbaɪ'baɪ] *interj inf* au revoir; **to go ~** *Am, childspeak* s'en aller; **to go ~s** *Brit, childspeak* aller faire dodo

by(e)-law *n Brit* 1. (*regional law*) arrêté *m* municipal 2. (*organization's rule*) règlement *m* intérieur

by-election ['baɪɪəlekʃən] *n Brit* élection *f*

partielle
bygone ['baɪgɒn, *Am:* -gɑːn] **I.** *adj* passé(e); **in a ~ age** [*o* **era**] autrefois; **in ~ days** dans l'ancien temps; **a ~ world** *fig* un monde révolu **II.** *n* **to let ~s be ~s** oublier le passé
byline ['baɪlaɪn] *n* (*in press*) signature *f*

> Un **BYO-restaurant** ("Bring Your Own") est en Australie un restaurant ne possèdant pas de licence l'autorisant à vendre de l'alcool et où, de ce fait, les clients peuvent apporter leurs propres boissons alcoolisés.

bypass ['baɪpɑːs, *Am:* -pæs] **I.** *n* **1.** AUTO route *f* de contournement **2.** MED pontage *m* **II.** *vt* **1.** (*make a detour*) contourner **2.** (*ignore*) **to ~ sb** agir sans informer qn **3.** (*avoid*) laisser de côté
bypass operation *n* pontage *m*
bypath ['baɪpɑːθ, *Am:* -pæθ] *n* **1.** sentier *m* détourné **2.** *fig* voie *f* détournée
by-product ['baɪprɒdʌkt, *Am:* -prɑːdəkt] *n* sous-produit *m; fig* effet *m* secondaire
by-road ['bəɪrəʊd, *Am:* -roʊd] *n* route *f* secondaire
bystander ['baɪstændəʳ, *Am:* -dɚ] *n* spectateur, -trice *m, f*
byte [baɪt] *n* INFOR octet *m*
byway ['baɪweɪ] *n* petite *f* route
byword ['baɪwɜːd, *Am:* -wɜːrd] *n* **1.** (*notable example*) **to be a ~ for sth** être l'exemple même de qc **2.** (*saying*) proverbe *m* **3.** (*cliché*) dicton *m*

C

C, c [siː] *n* **1.** (*letter*) C *m*, c *m*; **~ as in Charlie, ~ for Charlie** (*on telephone*) c comme Célestin **2.** MUS do *m* **3.** SCHOOL assez bien *m*; *s.* **cent, century**
C *abbr of* **Celsius 30°~** 30°C *m*
c., ca *prep abbr of* **circa** vers
cab [kæb] *n* taxi *m*; **by ~** en taxi
CAB [ˌsiːeɪ'biː] *n abbr of* **Citizens' Advice Bureau** *Brit* service *m* gratuit d'aide juridique
cabaret ['kæbəreɪ, *Am:* ˌkæbə'reɪ] *n* cabaret *m*
cabbage ['kæbɪdʒ] *n* chou *m*
cabbie *n*, **cabby** *n*, **cabdriver** *n Am* chauffeur *m* de taxi
cabin ['kæbɪn] *n* **1.** (*area on a vehicle*) cabine *f* **2.** (*simple wooden house*) cabane *f*
cabin class *n* deuxième classe *f* **cabin crew** *n* équipage *m* **cabin cruiser** *n* yacht *m* de croisière
cabinet ['kæbɪnɪt] *n* **1.** (*storage place*) meuble *m*; **filing ~** classeur *m*; **medicine ~** armoire *f* à pharmacie **2.** (*glass-fronted*) vitrine *f* **3.** + *sing/pl vb* (*group of advisers*) cabinet *m*
cabinet maker *n* ébéniste *m*
cable ['keɪbl] **I.** *n a.* TEL câble *m*; **to subscribe to ~** (**channels**) s'abonner au câble **II.** *vt* câbler
cable car *n* **1.** (*suspended transport system*) téléphérique *m* **2.** (*carriage on railway*) funiculaire *m* **cablegram** *n* HIST câble *m* **cable television, cable TV** *n no pl* télévision *f* par câble
caboodle [kə'buːdl] *n Am, inf* **the whole** (**kit and**) **~** tout le bataclan
cab rank *n s.* **taxi rank** **cab release** *n* déclencheur *m*
cabriolet ['kæbriəʊleɪ, *Am:* ˌkæbriə'leɪ] *n* décapotable *f*
cab stand *n Am* (*taxi rank*) station *f* de taxis
cacao [kə'kɑːəʊ, *Am:* -oʊ] *n no pl* cacao *m*
cache [kæʃ] *n* **1.** (*storage place*) cachette *f*; (*of weapons*) cache *f* **2.** INFOR cache *f*
cache memory *n* INFOR mémoire *f* cache, antémémoire *f*
cachet ['kæʃeɪ, *Am:* kæʃ'eɪ] *n no pl* cachet *m*
cackle ['kækl] **I.** *vi a. fig* glousser **II.** *n a. pej* gloussement *m*; **to give a ~** glousser
cacophonous *adj* cacophonique
cacophony [kæ'kɒfəni, *Am:* kə'kɑːfə-] *n no pl* cacophonie *f*
cactus ['kæktəs] <-es *o* cacti> *n* cactus *m*
CAD [kæd] *n no pl* INFOR *abbr of* **computer-aided design** PAO *f*
cadaver [kə'deɪvəʳ, *Am:* -'dævɚ] *n* cadavre *m*
CAD/CAM ['kædkæm] *n abbr of* **computer-aided design and manufacture** CFAO *f*
caddie, caddy ['kædi] **I.** *n* SPORT caddie® *m* **II.** <caddied, caddied, caddying> *vi* **to ~ for sb** être le caddie de qn
cadence ['keɪdns] *n* **1.** (*rising and falling sound*) cadence *f* **2.** MUS, LING (*concluding sound*) rythme *m*
cadet [kə'det] *n* **1.** (*military*) élève *mf* d'une école militaire **2.** (*police*) élève *mf* policier
cadge [kædʒ] **I.** *vt pej, inf* taxer **II.** *vi pej, inf* taxer
cadger *n pej* taxeur, -euse *m, f inf*
cadre ['kɑːdəʳ, *Am:* 'kædriː] *n* cadre *m*
Caesar ['siːzəʳ, *Am:* -zɚ] *n* **Julius ~** Jules César *m*
Caesarean (section) *n* césarienne *f*
cafe, café ['kæfeɪ, *Am:* kæf'eɪ] *n* café *m*, estaminet *m Nord, Belgique*, pinte *f Suisse*
cafeteria [ˌkæfɪ'tɪəriə, *Am:* -'tɪri-] *n* cafétéria *f*
caffeine ['kæfiːn, *Am:* kæf'iːn] *n no pl* caféine *f*
cage [keɪdʒ] **I.** *n a. fig* cage *f* **II.** *vt* enfermer dans une cage
cage bird *n* oiseau *m* de volière
caged *adj* (*animal*) en cage
cagey ['keɪdʒi] <-ier, -iest> *adj inf* cachottier(-ère); **to be ~ about sth** être cachottier à propos de qc

cahoots [kə'hu:ts] *npl inf* **to be in ~ with sb** être de mèche avec qn

cairn [keən, *Am:* kern] *n* cairn *m*

Cairo ['keərəʊ, *Am:* 'keroʊ] *n* Le Caire

cajole [kə'dʒəʊl, *Am:* -'dʒoʊl] I. *vt* cajoler; **to ~ sb out of/into doing sth** persuader qn de ne pas faire/de faire qc II. *vi* faire des cajoleries

Cajun ['keɪdʒən] I. *n* Cajun *m* II. *adj* cajun *inv*

cake [keɪk] I. *n* 1. (*sweet*) gâteau *m;* **chocolate ~** gâteau au chocolat; **a piece of ~** un morceau de gâteau; **sponge ~** gâteau *m* mousseline 2. (*savoury: of fish, potato, soap*) pain *m* ►**a piece of ~** *inf* une part du gâteau; **to have one's ~ and eat it (too)** avoir le beurre et l'argent du beurre; **to sell like hot ~** se vendre comme des petits pains II. *vt* (*blood*) coaguler **to be ~d with sth** être couvert de qc III. *vi* 1. (*dry*) sécher 2. (*harden*) durcir; (*blood*) se coaguler

cal. *n abbr of* **calorie** cal *m*

calamity [kə'læməti, *Am:* -ət̬i] <-ties> *n* calamité *f*

calcify ['kælsɪfaɪ] <-ie-> I. *vt* calcifier II. *vi* se calcifier

calcium ['kælsɪəm] *n no pl* calcium *m*

calculable *adj* calculable

calculate ['kælkjʊleɪt, *Am:* -kjə-] I. *vt* calculer; **to ~ sth at sth** estimer qc à qc II. *vi* calculer; **to ~ on sth** compter sur qc

calculated *adj* calculé(e); (*crime*) prémédité(e)

calculating *adj* calculateur(-trice)

calculation *n* calcul *m;* **to make ~s** effectuer des calculs

calculator *n* calculatrice *f*

calculus ['kælkjʊləs, *Am:* -kjə-] *n no pl* calcul *m*

calendar ['kælɪndə^r, *Am:* -dɚ] *n* calendrier *m*

calf[1] [kɑ:f, *Am:* kæf] <calves> *n* ZOOL veau *m*

calf[2] [kɑ:f, *Am:* kæf] <calves> *n* ANAT mollet *m*

calf love *n no pl* amour *m* de jeunesse

caliber ['kæləbɚ] *n no pl, Am s.* **calibre**

calibrate ['kælɪbreɪt] *vt* calibrer

calibre ['kælɪbə^r, *Am:* -əbɚ] *n a. fig* calibre *m*

calico ['kælɪkəʊ, *Am:* -koʊ] *n no pl* calicot *m*

California [ˌkælɪ'fɔ:niə, *Am:* -ə'fɔrnjə] *n* la Californie

Californian I. *n* Californien(ne) *m(f)* II. *adj* californien(ne)

call [kɔ:l] I. *n* 1. TEL appel *m;* **a telephone ~** un appel téléphonique; **to receive a ~** recevoir un coup de fil; **to return a ~** rappeler 2. (*visit*) visite *f;* **to pay a ~ on sb** rendre visite à qn 3. (*shout*) cri *m;* **a ~ for help** un appel au secours; **to give a ~** pousser un cri 4. (*summons*) convocation *f* 5. REL vocation *f* 6. POL appel *m;* **a ~ for sth** un appel à qc 7. *no pl* ECON demande *f* 8. *form* (*need*) *a. iron* besoin *m;* **to have no ~ for sth** ne pas avoir besoin de qc 9. INFOR appel *m* ►**a ~ of nature** un besoin pressant II. *vt* 1. (*address as*) appeler; **to be ~ed sth** s'appeler qc; **to ~ sb names** injurier qn; **to ~ sb after sb** appeler qn comme qn 2. (*telephone*) appeler 3. (*say out loud*) appeler 4. (*make noise to attract*) crier 5. (*summon*) appeler; **to ~ sb to order** rappeler qn à l'ordre; **to ~ sb as a witness** appeler qn à témoin; **to ~ sth to mind** rappeler qc 6. (*regard as*) trouver; **to ~ sb/sth a liar** considérer qn/qc comme menteur; **to ~ sth difficult** trouver qc difficile 7. (*wake by telephoning*) réveiller 8. (*decide to have*) appeler; **to ~ a strike** lancer un appel à la grève ►**to ~ sb's bluff** mettre qn au pied du mur; **to ~ it a day** *inf* s'en tenir là; **to ~ it quits** en rester là; **to ~ (all) the shots** mener la barque; **to ~ a spade a spade** *iron, inf* appeler un chat un chat; **to ~ sth one's own** avoir qc à soi III. *vi* 1. (*telephone*) téléphoner; **to ~ collect** appeler en PCV 2. (*drop by*) passer; **to ~ at sb's place** passer chez qn 3. (*shout*) crier 4. (*summon*) appeler

◆**call away** *vt* **to call sb away** appeler qn

◆**call back** I. *vt* rappeler II. *vi* 1. (*phone again*) rappeler 2. (*return*) repasser

◆**call for** *vt* 1. (*make necessary*) appeler à; **to be called for** être nécessaire 2. (*come to get: person*) appeler; (*object, doctor*) faire venir 3. (*ask*) appeler; **to ~ help** appeler à l'aide 4. (*demand, require: food, attention*) demander

◆**call forth** *vt* provoquer

◆**call in** I. *vt* 1. (*ask to come*) faire venir; **to call sb in to** +*infin* faire venir qn pour +*infin* 2. (*withdraw: money, book*) retirer de la circulation; (*car*) rappeler; (*a loan*) exiger le remboursement de II. *vi* 1. (*pay a visit*) rendre visite; **to ~ on sb** passer chez qn 2. (*phone*) appeler

◆**call off** *vt* 1. (*cancel*) annuler 2. (*order back*) rappeler

◆**call on** *vt insep* 1. (*appeal to*) demander à 2. (*pay a short visit*) rendre visite à 3. *fig* (*appeal to*) avoir recours à

◆**call out** I. *vt* 1. (*shout*) appeler; **to ~ names at sb** injurier qn 2. (*yell*) crier II. *vi* 1. (*shout*) appeler 2. (*yell*) crier 3. *fig* (*demand*) **to ~ for sth** exiger qc

◆**call up** *vt* 1. *Am* (*telephone*) appeler 2. INFOR (*find and display*) appeler 3. (*ordered to join the military*) appeler 4. (*conjure up: memories*) évoquer

call box *n* cabine *f* téléphonique

caller *n* 1. (*person on the telephone*) correspondant(e) *m(f)* 2. (*visitor*) visiteur, -euse *m, f*

call girl *n* call-girl *f*

calligraphy [kə'lɪgrəfi] *n no pl* calligraphie *f*

calling *n form* vocation *f*

calling card *n Am* 1. (*telephone card*) carte *f* de téléphone 2. HIST (*card with one's name*) carte *f* de visite

callous ['kæləs] *adj* cruel(le)

call sign *n* indicatif *m* **call-up** *n* MIL convocation *f*

callus ['kæləs] <-es> *n* durillon *m*

calm [kɑːm] **I.** *adj* calme; **to keep** ~ rester tranquille **II.** *vt* calmer; **to** ~ **oneself** se calmer ◆**calm down I.** *vi* se calmer **II.** *vt* calmer

calmly *adv* calmement

calmness *n no pl* calme *m*

caloric ['kælərɪk, *Am:* kə'lɔːr-] *adj* calorique

calorie ['kæləri] *n* calorie *f;* **to be high/low in** ~**s** être élevé/faible en calories

calorific [ˌkælər'ɪfək] *adj* calorifique

calumny ['kæləmni] *n form* calomnie *f*

calvary ['kælvəri] *n a. fig* calvaire *m*

calve [kɑːv, *Am:* kæv] *vi* vêler

Calvinism ['kælvɪnɪzəm] *n no pl, no art* REL calvinisme *m*

Calvinist REL **I.** *n* calviniste *mf* **II.** *adj* calviniste

CAM [kæm] *n* INFOR, TECH *abbr of* **computer assisted manufacture** FAO *f*

cam [kæm] *n* TECH came *f*

camaraderie [ˌkæmə'rɑːdəri, *Am:* -'rædər-] *n no pl* camaraderie *f*

camber ['kæmbəʳ, *Am:* -bɚ] *n* bombement *m*

Cambodia [kæm'bəʊdɪə, *Am:* -'boʊ-] *n* le Cambodge

Cambodian I. *adj* cambodgien(ne) **II.** *n* Cambodgien(ne) *m(f)*

camcorder ['kæmkɔːdəʳ] *n* caméscope *m*

came [keɪm] *pt of* **come**

camel ['kæml] **I.** *n* **1.** (*animal*) chameau *m;* **she-**~ chamelle *f* **2.** (*colour*) camel *m* **II.** *adj* **1.** (*camelhair*) en poil de chameau **2.** (*colour*) camel *inv*

camel hair, **camel-hair** *n no pl* poil *m* de chameau; **a** ~ **coat** un manteau en poil de chameau

cameo ['kæmɪəʊ, *Am:* -oʊ] *n* **1.** (*carved stone*) camée *m* **2.** THEAT, CINE figurant(e) *m(f)*

camera^{1} ['kæmərə] *n* **1.** (*photography*) appareil *m* photo **2.** (*television*) caméra *f;* **a** ~ **operator** un cadreur; **to be on** ~ être filmé

camera^{2} ['kæmərə] *n no pl a. fig* **in** ~ LAW à huis clos

camera angle *n* angle *m* de prise de vue **cameraman** <-men> *n* CINE cadreur *m* **camera-ready** *adj* TYP prêt(e) à la reproduction **camera shot** *n* CINE prise *f* de vue **camera-shy** *adj* timide face à la caméra

Cameroon [ˌkæmə'ruːn] *n* le Cameroun

Cameroonian I. *adj* camerounais(e) **II.** *n* Camerounais(e) *m(f)*

camomile ['kæməmaɪl, *Am:* -miːl] *n* BOT camomille *f;* ~ **tea** infusion *f* à la camomille

camouflage ['kæməˌflɑːʒ] **I.** *n no pl* camouflage *m* **II.** *vt* camoufler; **to** ~ **oneself** se camoufler

camp^{1} [kæmp] **I.** *n a. fig a.* MIL camp *m;* **holiday** [*o* **summer**] ~ camp de vacances; **refugee** ~ camp de réfugiés; **to pitch** ~ établir un camp; **to be/go on** ~ *Brit* faire du camping; **to break** ~ lever le camp; **to go over to the other** ~ changer de camp **II.** *vi* camper; **to** ~ **out** camper; **to go** ~**ing** faire du camping

camp^{2} [kæmp] THEAT, SOCIOL **I.** *n no pl, no art* (*theatrical style*) manières *fpl* **II.** *adj* **1.** (*theatrical*) affecté(e) **2.** (*effeminate*) efféminé(e)

campaign [kæm'peɪn] **I.** *n* campagne *f;* **a** ~ **for/against sth** une campagne en faveur/contre qc; **advertising** ~ ECON campagne de publicité **II.** *vi* faire campagne; **to** ~ **for sb/sth** faire campagne en faveur de qn/qc; **to** ~ **against sb/sth** faire campagne contre qn/qc

campaigner *n* militant(e) *m(f)*

camp bed *n Brit, Aus* lit *m* de camp **camp chair** *n Brit, Aus* chaise *f* pliante

camper *n* **1.** (*person*) campeur, -euse *m, f* **2.** (*vehicle*) camping-car *m*

camp fever *n no pl s.* **typhus campfire** *n* feu *m* de camp **camp follower** *n* (*group supporter*) sympathisant(e) *m(f)*

camphor ['kæmfəʳ, *Am:* -fɚ] *n no pl* MED camphre *m*

camping *n no pl* camping *m;* **to go** ~ faire du camping; ~ **equipment** équipement *m* de camping; ~ **holiday** vacances *fpl* en camping

camping ground *n Aus,* **camping site** *n Brit* camping *m* **camping van** *n* camping-car *m*

camp site *n* **1.** (*place to camp*) terrain *m* de camping **2.** *Am* (*place for a tent*) place *f* pour camper

campus ['kæmpəs] *n* campus *m;* **to be on** ~ être sur le campus; ~ **life** vie *f* sur le campus

can^{1} [kæn] **I.** *n* **1.** (*metal container*) boîte *f* de conserve; **food** ~ nourriture *f* en boîte; **a beer** ~ une bière en boîte **2.** (*container's contents*) bidon *m;* (*of beer, paint*) boîte *f* **3.** *Am, inf* **the** ~ (*prison*) la taule **4.** *Am, inf* (*toilet*) **the** ~ les chiottes *fpl* ►**a** ~ **of worms** un véritable guêpier; **to be in the** ~ CINE être dans la boîte; *fig* être dans la poche **II.** *vt* **1.** (*put in cans*) mettre en boîte, canner *Québec* **2.** *Am, inf* (*dismiss*) jeter

can^{2} [kən] <could, could> *aux* **1.** (*be able to*) pouvoir; **sb** ~ +*infin* qn peut +*infin;* **I will do all I** ~ je ferais de mon mieux **2.** (*have knowledge*) savoir; **I** ~ **swim/cook** je sais nager/cuisiner; **I** ~ **speak French** je parle le français **3.** (*be permitted to*) pouvoir; ~ **do** aucun problème; *s.* **may 4.** (*offering assistance*) pouvoir; ~ **I help you?** puis-je vous aider?; *s.* **may 5.** (*making a request*) pouvoir; ~ **I come?** est-ce que je peux venir? **6.** (*be possible*) **sb** ~ **do sth** qn fait peut-être qc; **sb** ~ **be wrong** qn a peut-être tort **7.** (*said to show disbelief*) ~ **it be true?** est-ce que c'est possible?; **how** ~ **you?** comment peux-tu faire une chose pareille?; **that** ~ **not be true** ce n'est pas possible

Canada ['kænədə] *n* le Canada

Canada Day *n, jour de la fête nationale canadienne, le 1er juillet*

Canadian I. *adj* canadien(ne) **II.** *n* Canadien(ne) *m(f)*

canal [kə'næl] *n* canal *m*

canalization *n no pl* canalisation *f*

canalize ['kænəlaɪz] *vt* canaliser

canary [kə'neəri, *Am:* -'neri] *n* ZOOL canari *m*

cancel ['kænsl] <-ll- *o Am* -l-> **I.** *vt* **1.** (*annul*) annuler; (*order*) décommander; (*contract*) résilier; (*cheque*) faire opposition à; **to ~ a booking** se décommander; **to ~ each other** s'annuler **2.** (*mark as being used: a stamp*) oblitérer; (*ticket*) composter **II.** *vi* se décommander

cancellation [ˌkænsə'leɪʃən] *n* annulation *f;* (*of a contract*) résiliation *f*

cancer ['kænsəʳ, *Am:* -sɚ] *n* MED cancer *m;* **~ of the throat** cancer de la gorge

Cancer ['kænsəʳ, *Am:* -sɚ] *n* Cancer *m; s. a.* **Aquarius**

cancer cell *n* cellule *f* cancéreuse

cancerous ['kænsərəs] *adj* cancéreux(-euse)

cancer patient *n* cancéreux, -euse *m, f* **cancer research** *n* recherche *f* contre le cancer **cancer specialist** *n* cancérologue *mf*

candelabra [ˌkændəl'ɑːbrə] <-(s)> *n* candélabre *m*

candid ['kændɪd] *adj* franc(he); **~ camera** caméra *f* invisible; **a ~ picture** une photo instantanée

candidacy ['kændɪdəsi] *n no pl* candidature *f*

candidate ['kændɪdət] *n* candidat(e) *m(f);* **to stand as ~ for sth** se porter candidat à qc

candidature ['kændɪdətʃəʳ, *Am:* -dədətʃʊr] *n no pl, Brit s.* **candidacy**

candied ['kændɪd] *adj* glacé(e); **~ fruit** fruits *mpl* confits

candle ['kændl] *n* bougie *f;* **~ grease** suif *m* ▶**to burn one's ~ at both ends** brûler la chandelle par les deux bouts; **to not hold a ~ to sb/sth** ne pas arriver à la cheville de qn/qc

candleholder *n* bougeoir *m* **candlelight** *n no pl* lueur *f* d'une bougie; **to do sth by ~** faire qc à la lueur de la bougie; **a ~ dinner** un dîner aux chandelles **candlelit** *adj* éclairé(e) à la bougie; (*meal*) aux chandelles **Candlemas** *n* REL Chandeleur *f* **candlestick** *n* bougeoir *m*

candor *n Am, Aus,* **candour** ['kændəʳ, *Am:* -ɚ] *n no pl, Brit, Aus, form* franchise *f*

candy ['kændi] **I.** *n* **1.** (*crystallized sugar*) sucre *m* candi **2.** *Am* (*sweets*) bonbon *m;* **~ stick** sucette *f* **II.** *vt* glacer

candy apple *n* pomme *f* d'amour **candyfloss** *n no pl, Brit* barbe *f* à papa **candy store** *n Am* confiserie *f*

cane [keɪn] **I.** *n* **1.** *no pl* (*dried plant stem*) canne *f* **2.** (*stick*) canne *f;* (*for punishment*) fouet *m;* **to get the ~** recevoir un coup de fouet **II.** *vt* **1.** (*weave of cane*) canner **2.** (*hit with a stick*) fouetter

cane chair *n* chaise *f* en rotin **cane sugar** *n no pl* sucre *m* de canne

canine ['keɪnaɪn] **I.** *n* canine *f* **II.** *adj* canin(e)

canine tooth *n* canine *f*

canister ['kænɪstəʳ, *Am:* -əstɚ] *n* boîte *f* en fer

cannabis ['kænəbɪs] *n no pl* cannabis *m*

canned [kænd] *adj* **1.** (*preserved in metal containers: food*) en conserve; (*beer*) en boîte **2.** TV, MUS *pej* (*pre-recorded*) en boîte **3.** *inf* (*drunk*) plein(e); **to get ~** se saouler

cannery ['kænəri] *n* conserverie *f*

cannibal ['kænɪbl] *n* cannibale *mf*

cannibalism ['kænɪbəlɪzəm] *n no pl* cannibalisme *m*

cannibalize ['kænɪbəlaɪz] *vt* récupérer les pièces de

canning *n* mise *f* en conserve

canning factory *n* conserverie *f*

cannon ['kænən] **I.** *n* MIL (*weapon*) canon *m;* **~ fire** tir *m* de canon **II.** *vi* **to ~ into sb/sth** percuter qn/qc

cannonball *n* MIL boulet *m* de canon **cannon fodder** *n* MIL chair *f* à canon

cannot ['kænɒt, *Am:* -ɑːt] *aux* (*can not*) *s.* **can**

canny ['kæni] <-ier, -iest> *adj* (*clever*) rusé(e)

canoe [kə'nuː] *n* **1.** NAUT (*boat*) canot *m* **2.** *Brit* (*kayak*) canoë *m,* canot *m Québec*

canoeing *n no pl* **to go ~** faire du canoë, canoter *Québec*

canoeist *n* canoéiste *mf*

canon ['kænən] *n* canon *m*

canonization *n* canonisation *f*

canonize ['kænənaɪz] *vt* canoniser

can opener *n* ouvre-boîtes *m*

canopy ['kænəpi] *n* **1.** (*cloth*) auvent *m;* (*of bed*) baldaquin *m* **2.** ARCHIT *a. fig* voûte *f*

can't [kɑːnt, *Am:* kænt] = **can + not** *s.* **can**

cant¹ [kænt] *n no pl* **1.** (*insincerely pious talk*) hypocrisie *f;* **a ~ phrase** un cliché **2.** LING (*words specific to a group*) jargon *m*

cant² [kænt] **I.** *n* (*tilt*) inclinaison *f* **II.** *vt* (*tilt*) incliner **III.** *vi* (*lean*) s'incliner

cantankerous [kæn'tæŋkərəs] *adj* acariâtre

cantata [kæn'tɑːtə, *Am:* kən'tɑːt̬ə] *n* MUS cantate *f*

canteen¹ [kæn'tiːn] *n* cantine *f*

canteen² [kæn'tiːn] *n* **1.** *Brit, Aus* (*cutlery container*) ménagère *f* **2.** MIL gourde *f* **3.** (*restaurant*) cantine *f*

canter ['kæntəʳ, *Am:* -t̬ɚ] SPORT **I.** *n* petit galop *m* **II.** *vi* aller au petit galop

canton ['kæntɒn, *Am:* -tɑːn] *n* (*Suiss* state) canton *m*

cantor ['kæntɔːʳ, *Am:* -tɚ] *n* chantre *m*

canvas ['kænvəs] *n* **1.** *no pl* (*type of cloth*) toile *f* **2.** (*embroidery*) canevas *m*

canvass ['kænvəs] **I.** *vt* **1.** (*gather opinion*) sonder; (*customers*) prospecter; **to ~ opinions** sonder l'opinion **2.** ECON (*solicit*) solliciter **3.** POL **to ~ sb** solliciter la voix de qn **4.** *Brit, Aus, inf* (*propose for discussion*) discuter **II.** *vi* **1.** POL faire campagne **2.** ECON faire du démarchage **III.** <-es> *n* POL démarchage *m*

canvassing *n* **1.** ECON démarchage *m* **2.** POL démarchage *m* électoral

canyon ['kænjən] *n* canyon *m*

canyoning *n* canyoning *m*

cap[1] [kæp] **I.** *n* **1.** (*hat*) casquette *f;* **shower** ~ bonnet *m* de douche; **swimming** [*o* **bathing**] ~ bonnet *m* de bain **2.** UNIV ~ **and gown** costume *m* académique; *iron* tenue *f* d'apparat **3.** (*cover*) couvercle *m;* (*of a bottle*) bouchon *m;* (*of a pen, lens*) capuchon *m;* (*of a mushroom*) chapeau *m;* (*of a tooth*) émail *m* **4.** (*limit*) plafond *m* **5.** MED (*contraceptive*) diaphragme *m* ▶ ~ **in hand** chapeau bas; **to put on one's thinking** ~ *inf* cogiter; **if the** ~ **fits, wear it** *Brit, prov* qui se sent morveux se mouche; **to set one's** ~ **at** [*o Am* **for**] **sb** jeter son dévolu sur qn **II.** <-pp-> *vt* **1.** (*limit*) limiter **2.** *Brit* SPORT (*select for national team*) sélectionner pour l'équipe nationale **3.** (*cover*) *a. fig* coiffer; (*bottle*) capsuler; (*a tooth*) recouvrir d'émail; **to** ~ **a pen** remettre le capuchon d'un stylo **4.** (*outdo*) surpasser; **to** ~ **it all** pour couronner le tout

cap[2] [kæp] *n* TYP, PUBL *abbr of* **capital** (**letter**) capitale *f;* **in** ~**s** en capitales

CAP [ˌsiːeiˈpiː] *n* EU *abbr of* **Common Agricultural Policy** PAC *f*

capability [ˌkeɪpəˈbɪləti, *Am:* -t̬i] *n* capacité *f*

capable ['keɪpəbl] *adj* **1.** (*competent*) compétent(e) **2.** (*able*) capable; **to be** ~ **of doing sth** être capable de faire qc

capacity [kəˈpæsəti, *Am:* -t̬i] *n* **1.** <-ties> (*amount*) capacité *f;* (*of container*) contenance *f;* **seating** ~ nombre *m* de places assises; **filled to** ~ comble; **to play to** ~ **audiences** THEAT jouer à guichets fermés **2.** *no pl* (*ability*) aptitude *f;* **to have a** ~ **for sth** avoir une aptitude à faire qc; **to have a** ~ **for alcohol** tenir l'alcool **3.** (*output*) rendement *m;* **at full** ~ à plein rendement **4.** (*position*) fonction *f;* **in the** ~ **of sth** en qualité de qc

cape[1] [keɪp] *n* GEO cap *m*

cape[2] [keɪp] *n* FASHION cape *f*

Cape Canaveral *n* Cap Canaveral *m*

caper[1] **I.** *n* **1.** (*skip*) cabriole *f* **2.** *pej* (*dubious activity*) arnaque *f* **II.** *vi* (*leap about*) gambader

caper[2] *n* GASTR câpre *f*

Cape Town ['keɪptaʊn] *n* le Cap

capillary [kəˈpɪləri, *Am:* ˈkæpəler-] <-ries> **I.** *n* capillaire *f* **II.** *adj* capillaire

capital[1] ['kæpɪtl, *Am:* -ət̬l] **I.** *n* **1.** (*principal city*) *a. fig* capitale *f* **2.** (*letter form*) lettre *f* capitale; **in** (**large**) ~**s** en capitales **II.** *adj* **1.** (*principal: error, city*) principal(e) **2.** (*letter form: letter*) capital(e) **3.** LAW (*punishable by death*) capital(e) **4.** *Brit* (*very good*) excellent(e)

capital[2] ['kæpɪtl, *Am:* -ət̬l] *n* FIN capital *m;* **to put** ~ **into sth** investir dans qc; **to make** ~ (**out**) **of sth** tirer profit de qc

capital assets *n* FIN actif *m* immobilisé **capital gain** *n* LAW plus-value *f* **capital gains tax** *n* impôt *m* sur la plus-value **capital investment** *n* FIN investissement *m* de capitaux

capitalism ['kæpɪtəlɪzəm, *Am:* ˈkæpət̬-] *n no pl* capitalisme *m*

capitalist I. *n a. pej* capitaliste *mf* **II.** *adj* capitaliste

capitalistic *adj* POL, ECON *s.* **capitalist**

capitalization[1] *n no pl* TYP mise *f* en majuscules

capitalization[2] *n* FIN, ECON capitalisation *f*

capitalize[1] ['kæpɪtəlaɪz, *Am:* -pət̬əlaɪz] *vt* TYP mettre en capitales

capitalize[2] ['kæpɪtəlaɪz, *Am:* -pət̬əlaɪz] *vt* FIN capitaliser

capital letter *n* lettre *f* capitale; **in** ~**s** en lettres capitales **capital levy** *n* impôt *m* sur capital **capital market** *n* marché *m* des capitaux **capital punishment** *n no pl* peine *f* capitale

capitulate [kəˈpɪtʃʊleɪt, *Am:* -ˈpɪtʃə-] *vi a. fig* MIL capituler; **to** ~ **to sb/sth** capituler face à qn/qc

capitulation *n* capitulation *f*

cappuccino [ˌkæpʊˈtʃiːnəʊ, *Am:* ˌkæpəˈtʃiːnoʊ] *n* cappuccino *m*

Capricorn ['kæprɪkɔːn, *Am:* -rəkɔːrn] *n* Capricorne *m; s. a.* **Aquarius**

Caps. *n abbr of* **capitals** capitales *fpl*

capsize [kæpˈsaɪz, *Am:* ˈkæpsaɪz] NAUT **I.** *vt* **1.** (*make turn over*) faire chavirer **2.** *fig* (*ruin*) faire échouer **II.** *vi* (*turn over*) chavirer

capstan ['kæpstən] *n* NAUT cabestan *m*

capsule ['kæpsjuːl, *Am:* -sl] *n* capsule *f*

captain ['kæptɪn] **I.** *n a. fig* capitaine *m* **II.** *vt* **1.** (*be in charge of*) mener **2.** (*be officer*) être capitaine de

captaincy ['kæptɪnsi] *no pl n* grade *m* de capitaine

caption ['kæpʃən] *n* **1.** TYP, PUBL légende *f* **2.** CINE, TV sous-titres *mpl*

captivate ['kæptɪveɪt, *Am:* -tə-] *vt* captiver

captive ['kæptɪv] **I.** *n* captif, -ive *m, f* **II.** *adj* captif(-ive); **to take sb** ~ capturer qn; **to hold sb** ~ maintenir qn captif

captivity [kæpˈtɪvəti, *Am:* -t̬i] *n no pl* captivité *f*

captor *n* ravisseur, -euse *m, f*

capture ['kæptʃəʳ, *Am:* -tʃɚ] **I.** *vt* **1.** (*take prisoner*) capturer **2.** (*take possession of: city, control*) prendre; **to** ~ **sth** s'emparer de qc **3.** (*gain*) gagner **4.** ECON (*the market*) s'accaparer **5.** ART, CINE (*atmosphere*) rendre; (*on film*) immortaliser; **to** ~ **the moment** saisir l'instant **6.** *fig* (*attention*) captiver; (*moment, moods*) saisir **7.** INFOR saisir **II.** *n* **1.** (*act of capturing*) capture *f* **2.** (*captured person, thing*) prise *f* **3.** INFOR saisie *f*

car [kɑːʳ, *Am:* kɑːr] *n* voiture *f;* **by** ~ en voiture; ~ **accident** accident *m* de voiture; **res-**

taurant ~ voiture-restaurant *f*
car aerial *n Brit* antenne *f* de voiture
carafe ['kærəf] *n* carafe *f*
caramel ['kærəmel, *Am:* 'kɑːrml] *n* caramel *m*
carapace ['kærəpeɪs, *Am:* 'ker-] *n* carapace *f*
carat ['kærət, *Am:* 'ker-] <-(s)> *n* carat *m*
caravan ['kærəvæn, *Am:* 'ker-] *n* caravane *f*
caraway ['kærəweɪ, *Am:* 'ker-] *n no pl* carvi *m*
carbide ['kɑːbaɪd, *Am:* 'kɑːr-] *n* CHEM carbure *m*
carbine ['kɑːbaɪn, *Am:* 'kɑːrbiːn] *n* carabine *f*
carbohydrate [ˌkɑːbəʊ'haɪdreɪt, *Am:* ˌkɑːrboʊ-] *n* CHEM hydrate *m* de carbone
car bomb *n* voiture *f* piégée
carbon ['kɑːbən, *Am:* 'kɑːr-] *n* **1.** *no pl* CHEM (*element*) carbone *m* **2.** (*carbon paper*) papier *m* carbone
carbon copy *n* **1.** (*copy using special paper*) carbone *m* **2.** *fig* (*very similar*) réplique *f* **carbon dating** *n no pl* datation *f* au carbone **carbon dioxide** *n no pl* CHEM gaz *m* carbonique
carbonic *adj* CHEM carbonique
carbonize ['kɑːbənaɪz, *Am:* 'kɑːr-] CHEM **I.** *vt* carboniser **II.** *vi* se carboniser
carbon monoxide *n no pl* CHEM oxyde *m* de carbone **carbon paper** *n* papier *m* carbone
car boot sale *n Brit* ≈ braderie *f*
carbuncle ['kɑːbʌŋkl, *Am:* 'kɑːr-] *n* **1.** MED (*swelling*) furoncle *m* **2.** (*gem*) escarboucle *f*
carburetor *n Am* TECH carburateur *m*
carburetted *adj* à carburateur
carburettor [ˌkɑːbjə'retəʳ, *Am:* 'kɑːrbəreɪt̬ɚ] *n Brit s.* **carburetor**
carcase, **carcass** ['kɑːkəs, *Am:* 'kɑːr-] <-es> *n a. inf* carcasse *f*
carcinogen ['kɑːsɪnəˌdʒen, *Am:* kɑːr'sɪn-] *n* MED substance *f* cancérigène
carcinogenic *adj* MED cancérigène
carcinoma [ˌkɑːsɪ'nəʊmə, *Am:* kɑːrsn'oʊ-] *n* MED carcinome *m*
card[1] [kɑːd, *Am:* kɑːrd] **I.** *n* **1.** *no pl* (*cardboard*) carton *m* **2.** GAMES carte *f;* **to play ~s** jouer aux cartes **3.** (*piece of stiff paper*) carte *f;* **birthday** ~ carte d'anniversaire; **business** ~ carte de visite; **invitation** ~ carton *m* d'invitation; **index** ~ fiche *f* **4.** (*means of payment*) carte *f;* **cheque** ~ carte bancaire; **credit** ~ carte de crédit; **charge** ~ carte de paiement **5.** (*proof of identity*) pièce *f* d'identité; **identity** ~ carte *f* d'identité; **membership** ~ carte *f* de membre **6.** INFOR carte *f* **7.** *Brit, inf* (*employment papers*) **to give sb his/her ~s** renvoyer qn; **to get one's ~s** être mis à la porte; **to ask for one's ~s** quitter son travail ►**to hold one's ~s close to one's <u>chest</u>** cacher son jeu; **to have a ~ up one's <u>sleeve</u>** avoir une carte dans sa manche; **to put one's ~s on the <u>table</u>** mettre cartes sur table; **to have <u>all</u> the ~s** avoir tous les atouts en main; **to play one's <u>best</u>** ~ jouer son atout; **to <u>throw</u> in one's ~s** abandonner; **to be <u>on</u>** [*o Am* **in**] **the ~s** être très vraisemblable **II.** *vt* **1.** (*write an account*) ficher **2.** *Am* (*demand identification*) demander les papiers d'identité à
card[2] [kɑːd, *Am:* kɑːrd] **I.** *n* (*in mechanics*) peigne *m* **II.** *vt* peigner
cardamom ['kɑːdəmən, *Am:* 'kɑːr-] *n* cardamome *f*
cardboard ['kɑːdbɔːd, *Am:* 'kɑːrdbɔːrd] *n no pl* **1.** (*thick card*) carton *m;* ~ **box** boîte *f* en carton **2.** *fig, pej* **a ~ character** un personnage plat
card catalogue *n* fichier *m*
cardiac ['kɑːdɪæk, *Am:* 'kɑːr-] *adj* MED cardiaque
cardigan ['kɑːdɪgən, *Am:* 'kɑːr-] *n* cardigan *m*
cardinal ['kɑːdɪnl, *Am:* 'kɑːr-] **I.** *n* cardinal *m* **II.** *adj* capital(e)
cardinal number *n* nombre *m* cardinal **cardinal points** *npl* points *mpl* cardinaux
card index *n* fichier *m*
cardiogram ['kɑːdɪəʊgræm, *Am:* 'kɑːrdɪoʊ-] *n* MED cardiogramme *m*
cardphone *n* publiphone *m* **cardpunch** *n* INFOR perforatrice *f* de cartes **card reader** *n* lecteur *m* **card table** *n* table *f* de jeux
care [keəʳ, *Am:* ker] **I.** *n* **1.** (*looking after*) soin *m;* **hair** ~ soin capillaire; **to take good ~ of sb/sth** prendre bien soin de qn/qc; **to be in sb's** ~ être sous la responsabilité de qn; **to be under a doctor's** ~ être suivi par un docteur; **to take ~ of oneself** s'occuper de ses affaires; **to take ~ of sth** s'occuper de qc; **to be in** ~ être à l'Assistance publique; **to be taken into** ~ être confié à l'Assistance publique; (**in**) ~ **of sb** aux bons soins de qn; **take ~!** fais attention (à toi)!; (*goodbye*) salut! **2.** (*carefulness*) prudence *f;* **to do sth with** ~ faire qc avec prudence; **to take ~ with sth/to** +*infin* prendre soin de qc/de +*infin;* **to take ~ that** veiller à ce que +*subj;* **take ~ that you don't fall!** fais attention de ne pas tomber! **3.** (*worry*) souci *m;* **to not have a ~ in the world** ne pas avoir le moindre souci; **to be free from** ~ être insouciant **II.** *vi* **1.** (*be concerned*) se faire du souci; **to ~ about sb/sth** se soucier de qn/qc; **not to ~ about sb/sth** se moquer de qn/qc; **I don't** ~ ça m'est égal; **I couldn't ~ less** je m'en fiche; **she doesn't appear to ~ how she dresses** elle se moque de son apparence; **for all I** ~ pour ce que cela me fait; **who ~s?** qu'est-ce que ça fait? **2.** (*feel affection*) aimer; **to ~ about sb** aimer qn **3.** (*want*) vouloir; **to ~ to** +*infin* vouloir +*infin;* **to ~ for sth** vouloir qc
◆**care for** *vi* **1.** (*like*) aimer **2.** (*look after*) soigner
CARE [keəʳ, *Am:* ker] *n abbr of* **Cooperative for American Relief Everywhere** *Association de Solidarité Internationale au statut de*

bienfaisance

career [kə'rɪəʳ, *Am:* -'rɪr] **I.** *n* carrière *f;* **a ~ politician** un homme politique de carrière **II.** *vi* aller à toute vitesse; **to ~ somewhere** aller quelque part à toute vitesse; **to ~ down a slope** dévaler une pente

careerist *n pej* carriériste *mf*

carefree ['keəfriː, *Am:* 'ker-] *adj* insouciant(e)

careful *adj* **1.** (*cautious*) prudent(e); **to be ~ doing sth** être prudent en faisant qc; **to be ~ with money** être regardant; (**be**) **~!** attention! **2.** (*showing attention*) attentif(-ive); **to be ~ with/of/about sth** faire attention à qc; **to be ~ (that)** veiller à ce que *+subj;* **to be ~ to** *+infin* veiller à *+infin* **3.** (*painstaking: worker*) soigneux(-euse); (*work*) soigné(e); **to make a ~ choice** faire un choix méticuleux; **after ~ consideration** après mûre réflexion; **a ~ examination** un examen attentif; **to pay ~ attention to sth** prêter une attention particulière à qc

carefulness *n no pl* **1.** (*caution*) prudence *f* **2.** (*meticulousness*) soin *m*

caregiver *n Am s.* **carer**

careless *adj* **1.** (*lacking wisdom: driver*) imprudent(e) **2.** (*inattentive*) inattentif(-ive); **a ~ error** une erreur d'inattention; **to be ~ with money** ne pas être regardant **3.** (*not worried*) insouciant(e); **to be ~ of sth** négliger qc **4.** (*unthinking: remark*) irréfléchi(e) **5.** (*lacking care: work*) négligé(e); **to be ~** manquer de soin

carelessness *n no pl* négligence *f*

carer *n* aide *f* à domicile

caress [kə'res] <-es> **I.** *n* caresse *f* **II.** *vt* caresser **III.** *vi* **1.** (*touch*) caresser **2.** (*kiss*) embrasser

caretaker *n* **1.** *Brit* (*janitor*) concierge *mf* **2.** POL **a ~ government** un gouvernement intérimaire

careworn ['keəwɔːn, *Am:* 'kerwɔːrn] *adj* rongé(e) par les soucis

car ferry *n* NAUT ferry *m*

cargo ['kɑːgəʊ, *Am:* 'kɑːrgoʊ] *n* cargaison *f*

cargo aircraft *n* AVIAT avion-cargo *m* **cargo boat** *n* NAUT cargo *m* **cargo plane** *s.* **cargo aircraft** **cargo vessel** *n* bateau *m* de marchandise

car hire *n Brit* location *f* de voitures; **~ company** société *f* de location de voitures

Carib ['kærɪb, *Am:* 'ker-] **I.** *n* **1.** (*person*) Caraïbe *mf* **2.** LING caraïbe *m; s. a.* **English** **II.** *adj* caraïbe

Caribbean **I.** *n no pl* **the ~** les Caraïbes **II.** *adj* **1.** (*pertaining to the Caribbean*) des Caraïbes **2.** (*from the Caribbean*) caribéen(ne)

Caribbean Sea *n* mer *f* des Caraïbes

caribou ['kærɪbuː, *Am:* 'ker-] *n* ZOOL caribou *m*

caricature ['kærɪkətjʊəʳ, *Am:* 'kerəkətjʊr] **I.** *n a. pej* caricature *f;* **to become a ~ of oneself** n'être plus que la caricature **II.** *vt* LIT caricaturer

caricaturist *n* ART caricaturiste *mf*

caries ['keəriːz, *Am:* 'keriːz] *n no pl* MED carie *f;* **dental ~** carie dentaire

caring **I.** *adj* (*person*) généreux(-euse); (*society*) humain(e) **II.** *n no pl* travail *m* social; **the ~ professions** les professions *fpl* paramédicales

car insurance *n no pl* assurance *f* automobile

carjacking *n no pl, Am: vol à main armée d'un véhicule*

carnage ['kɑːnɪdʒ, *Am:* 'kɑːr-] *n no pl* carnage *m*

carnal ['kɑːnl, *Am:* 'kɑːr-] *adj form* charnel(le)

carnation [kɑː'neɪʃən, *Am:* kɑːr-] **I.** *n* **1.** BOT (*plant*) œillet *m* **2.** (*colour*) couleur *f* incarnate **II.** *adj* incarnat(e)

carnival ['kɑːnɪvl, *Am:* 'kɑːrnə-] *n* carnaval *m*

carnivore ['kɑːnɪvɔːʳ, *Am:* 'kɑːrnəvɔːr] *n a. iron* carnivore *m*

carnivorous [kɑː'nɪvərəs, *Am:* kɑːr-] *adj* carnivore

carol ['kærəl, *Am:* 'ker-] **I.** *n* chant *m* **II.** <-ll- *o Am* -l-> *vi* chanter joyeusement

carol-singer *n chanteur de chants de Noël*

carotene ['kærətiːn] *n no pl* carotène *m*

carousel [ˌkærə'sel] *n* **1.** (*merry-go-round*) manège *m* **2.** (*rotating machine*) carrousel *m*

carp¹ [kɑːp, *Am:* kɑːrp] *n* <-(s)> ZOOL, GASTR carpe *f*

carp² [kɑːp, *Am:* kɑːrp] *vi* (*nag about trivial things*) se plaindre; **to ~ about sb/sth** se plaindre de qn/qc; **to ~ at sb** critiquer qn

car park *n Brit, Aus* parking *m,* stationnement *m Québec;* **underground ~** parking souterrain

carpenter ['kɑːpəntəʳ, *Am:* 'kɑːrpnt̬ɚ] *n* menuisier *m*

carpentry ['kɑːpəntri, *Am:* 'kɑːrpn-] *n no pl* menuiserie *f*

carpet ['kɑːpɪt, *Am:* 'kɑːrpət] **I.** *n* **1.** (*floor covering*) *a. fig* tapis *m;* **a ~ of flowers** un tapis de fleurs **2.** *no pl* (*fitted ~*) moquette *f,* tapis *m* plain *Belgique;* **fitted** [*o* **wall-to-wall** *Am*] **~** moquette *f;* **to fit a ~** poser de la moquette ►**to be on the ~** (*be in trouble*) être sur la sellette; **to sweep sth under the ~** essayer de dissimuler qc **II.** *vt* **1.** (*cover a floor*) **to ~ sth** recouvrir qc d'un tapis; (*with fitted carpet*) moquetter qc **2.** *fig, inf* (*severely reprimand*) réprimander

carpetbagger *n Am, pej* (*politician*) profiteur, -euse *m, f*

carpeting *n no pl* tapis *m;* (*of fitted carpet*) moquette *f*

carpet sweeper *n* balai *m* mécanique

carpool *n Am* ≈ covoiturage *m* **car radio** *n* auto-radio *m*

carriage ['kærɪdʒ, *Am:* 'ker-] *n* **1.** (*horse-drawn vehicle*) voiture *f* **2.** *Brit* (*train wagon*) voiture *f* **3.** (*posture*) port *m* **4.** (*part of a type-*

writer) chariot *m* **5.** *no pl, Brit* (*transport costs*) port *m;* ~ **free** franco de port

carriage return *n* TECH retour *m* chariot

carriageway *n Brit* chaussée *f*

carrier ['kærɪəʳ] *n* **1.** (*person*) porteur *m* **2.** MIL véhicule *m* blindé **3.** AVIAT transporteur *m;* (**troop**) ~ avion *m* de transport de troupes **4.** NAUT transport *m;* (**aircraft**) ~ porte-avions *m* **5.** *inf* (*aircraft carrier*) gros porteur *m* **6.** (*disease transmitter*) porteur *m* **7.** (*baby seat*) porte-bébé *m* **8.** (*transport company*) compagnie *f* de transport **9.** *Brit, inf s.* **carrier bag 10.** RADIO ~ (**wave**) onde *f* porteuse

carrier bag *n Brit* **1.** (*plastic*) grand sac *m* en plastique **2.** (*paper*) grand sac *m* en papier

carrion ['kærɪən, *Am:* 'ker-] *n no pl* charogne *f;* ~ **eater** charognard *m*

carrion crow *n* corneille *f* noire

carrot ['kærət, *Am:* 'ker-] *n* **1.** (*vegetable*) carotte *f* **2.** *inf* (*reward*) carotte *f;* **to dangle a ~ for sb** agiter une carotte devant qn

carroty ['kærəti, *Am:* 'kerət̬i] <-ier, -iest> *adj* roux(rousse)

carry ['kæri, *Am:* 'ker-] <-ies, -ied> **I.** *vt* **1.** (*transport*) porter **2.** (*transport*) transporter **3.** (*have on one's person*) avoir sur soi **4.** (*remember: a tune*) se rappeler; **to ~ a memory of sth** se souvenir de qc; **to ~ sth in one's head** retenir qc dans sa tête **5.** MED transmettre **6.** (*have*) **to ~ insurance** être assuré; **to ~ conviction** être convaincant **7.** (*support*) supporter **8.** (*keep going*) continuer **9.** *Am* (*sell*) vendre **10.** (*win support*) gagner à sa cause **11.** (*approve a bill*) voter **12.** PUBL rapporter; **to ~ a headline** faire la une **13.** (*develop: argument*) développer; (*too far*) pousser **14.** MAT (*put into next column: a number*) retenir **15.** (*stand*) **to ~ oneself** se comporter **16.** (*be pregnant: child*) attendre ►**to ~ the <u>can</u>** *Brit, inf* (devoir) payer les pots cassés; **to ~ a <u>torch</u> for sb** *Brit, inf* avoir le béguin pour qn **II.** *vi* **1.** (*be audible*) porter **2.** (*fly*) voler

◆**carry away** *vt* **1.** (*remove*) enlever **2.** (*make excited*) **to get carried away** se laisser emporter; **to be carried away by sth** s'emballer pour qc; (*be enchanted*) s'enthousiasmer pour qc; **don't get carried away!** reste calme!

◆**carry forward** *vt* ECON reporter

◆**carry off** *vt* **1.** (*take away*) enlever **2.** (*succeed*) réussir **3.** (*win*) remporter

◆**carry on I.** *vt* soutenir **II.** *vi* **1.** (*continue*) poursuivre; **to ~ doing sth** continuer à faire qc, perdurer à faire qc *Belgique;* **to ~ as if nothing has happened** faire comme si rien ne s'était passé **2.** *inf* (*make a fuss*) faire des histoires **3.** (*complain*) **to ~ at sb** se plaindre à bâtons rompus

◆**carry out** *vt* réaliser; (*threat, plan*) mettre à exécution; (*attack*) conduire; (*reform, test*) effectuer; (*orders*) exécuter; **to ~ sth to the letter** suivre les ordres à la lettre

◆**carry over I.** *vt* **1.** ECON (*bring forward*) apporter **2.** FIN reporter **3.** (*postpone*) retarder; (*holiday*) reporter **II.** *vi* **to ~ into sth** avoir des répercussions sur qc

◆**carry through** *vt* **1.** (*support*) soutenir **2.** (*complete*) mener à bien

carryall *n* fourre-tout *m inv* **carrycot** *n* porte-bébé *m* **carry-forward** *n* FIN report *m* **carrying agent** *n* agent *m* de transport **carrying capacity** *n* charge *f* utile **carrying-on** <carryings-on> *n inf* **1.** *no pl* (*affair*) affaires *fpl* louches **2.** (*activity*) activité *f* désordonnée **carry-over I.** *n* FIN report *m* **II.** *vt* reporter

cart [kɑːt, *Am:* kɑːrt] **I.** *n* **1.** (*vehicle*) voiture *f* à bras; **horse ~** charrette *f* **2.** *Am* (*supermarket trolley*) chariot *m* ►**to <u>put</u> the ~ before the horse** mettre la charrue devant les bœufs **II.** *vt* **1.** (*transport*) charrier **2.** (*carry*) transporter par camion **3.** (*carry around*) trimballer

carte blanche [ˌkɑːt'blɑ̃ːntʃ, *Am:* ˌkɑːrt'blɑːnʃ] *n no pl* carte *f* blanche; **to be given ~** avoir carte blanche

cartel [kɑː'tel, *Am:* kɑːr-] *n* cartel *m*

carter ['kɑːtəʳ, *Am:* 'kɑːrt̬ɚ] *n* charretier *m*

carthorse ['kɑːtˌhɔːs, *Am:* 'kɑːrthɔːrs] *n* cheval *m* de trait

cartilage ['kɑːtɪlɪdʒ, *Am:* 'kɑːrt̬lɪdʒ] *n* MED *no pl* cartilage *m*

cartload ['kɑːtˌləʊd, *Am:* 'kɑːrtloʊd] *n* charretée *f*

cartographer *n* cartographe *mf*

cartography [kɑː'tɒgrəfi, *Am:* kɑːr'tɑːgrə-] *n no pl* cartographie *f*

carton ['kɑːtn, *Am:* 'kɑːr-] *n* **1.** (*box*) carton *m* **2.** (*packaging*) boîte *f;* (*of milk, juice*) brique *f;* (*of cigarettes*) cartouche *f;* (*of yoghurt, cream*) pot *m*

cartoon [kɑː'tuːn, *Am:* kɑːr-] *n* **1.** (*critical*) dessin *m* satirique **2.** ART (*preparatory*) carton *m* **3.** CINE dessin *m* animé

cartoonist *n* **1.** ART caricaturiste *mf* **2.** CINE dessinateur, -trice *m, f* de dessins animés

cartridge ['kɑːtrɪdʒ, *Am:* 'kɑːr-] *n* **1.** (*ink, ammunition*) cartouche *f* **2.** (*cassette*) cassette *f* **3.** (*pick-up head*) cellule *f* de lecture

cartridge case *n* douille *f* **cartridge paper** *n* papier *m* (à) cartouche

cartwheel ['kɑːthwiːl, *Am:* 'kɑːrt-] **I.** *n* **1.** (*wheel*) roue *f* de charrette **2.** (*sport*) **to do a ~** faire une roue **II.** *vi* faire la roue

carve [kɑːv, *Am:* kɑːrv] **I.** *vt* **1.** (*cut a figure*) sculpter; (*with a chisel*) ciseler; **to be ~d out of stone** être taillé dans la pierre **2.** (*cut*) tailler; (*meat*) découper; **to ~ sth out from sth** tailler qc dans qc **3.** *fig* (*establish*) **to ~ a name for oneself** se faire un nom; **to ~ a niche for oneself** se tailler une place dans qc **II.** *vi* sculpter

◆**carve out** *vt fig* se tailler; **to ~ a career for oneself** faire carrière

carver *n* **1.** ART sculpteur *m* **2.** *Brit* **electric ~**

couteau *m* à découper électrique

carving *n* **1.** *no pl* (*art*) sculpture *f* **2.** (*figure*) sculpture *f;* (*of wood*) figurine *f* en bois

carving knife *n* couteau *m* à découper

car wash *n* lavage *m* de voitures

cascade [kæ'skeɪd] **I.** *n* cascade *f* **II.** *vi* tomber en cascade

case[1] [keɪs] *n* **1.** *a.* MED cas *m;* **in any ~** en tout cas; **in ~ it rains** au cas où il pleuvrait; **as the ~ stands** les choses étant ce qu'elles sont; **a ~ in point** un exemple typique **2.** LING cas *m;* **in the genitive ~** au génitif **3.** LAW affaire *f;* **to lose one's ~** perdre son procès; **to close the ~** clore un dossier; **to make out a ~ for sth** exposer ses arguments en faveur de qc

case[2] [keɪs] *n* **1.** *Brit* (*suitcase*) valise *f* **2.** (*chest*) coffre *m* **3.** (*container*) boîte *f;* (*bottles*) caisse *f;* (*vegetables*) cageot *m;* (*silverware, jewels*) écrin *m;* (*spectacles, cigarettes, flute*) étui *m;* **glass ~** vitrine *f* **4.** TYP *s.* **lower, upper**

casebook *n* **1.** (*book containing extracts*) recueil *m* **2.** MED dossier *m* médical **case law** *n* LAW droit *m* jurisprudentiel **case study** *n* étude *f* de cas

cash [kæʃ] **I.** *n no pl* liquide *m;* **to pay in ~** payer comptant; **~ payment in advance** paiement *m* liquide d'avance; **to be strapped for ~** *inf* être à court d'argent **II.** *vt* (*exchange for money*) toucher; (*cheque*) encaisser

◆**cash in I.** *vt* se faire rembourser ►**to ~ (one's chips)** *inf* casser sa pipe **II.** *vi* **to ~ on sth** tirer profit de qc

cash-and-carry I. *n* magasin *m* de demi-gros **II.** *adj* de demi-gros; ECON **III.** *adv* en demi-gros **cash balance** *n* solde *m* actif **cash box** *n* caisse *f* **cash card** *n Brit* carte *f* de retrait **cash cow** *n inf* vache *f* à lait **cash crop** *n Am* récolte *f* destinée à la vente **cash dispenser** *n Brit* distributeur *m* automatique de billets

cashew ['kæʃu:], **cashew nut** *n* noix *f* de cajou

cash flow *n* cash-flow *m*

cashier[1] [kæ'ʃɪəʳ, *Am:* kæʃ'ɪr] *n* caissier, -ière *m, f*

cashier[2] [kæ'ʃɪəʳ, *Am:* kæʃ'ɪr] *vt* MIL réformer

cash machine *n* distributeur *m* automatique

cashmere ['kæʃmɪə, *Am:* 'kæʒmɪr] *n* cachemire *m*

cash payment *n* paiement *m* (au) comptant **cashpoint** *n Brit* distributeur *m* automatique de billets **cash register** *n* caisse *f* enregistreuse **cash sale** *n* vente *f* au comptant

casing ['keɪsɪŋ] *n* enveloppe *f;* (*of a machine*) coquille *f;* (*of a cable*) gaine *f;* (*of a sausage*) peau *f*

casino [kə'si:nəʊ, *Am:* -noʊ] *n* casino *m*

cask [kɑ:sk, *Am:* kæsk] *n* barrique *f;* (*of wine*) fût *m*

casket ['kɑ:skɪt, *Am:* 'kæskɪt] *n* **1.** (*box*) coffret *m* **2.** *Am* (*coffin*) cercueil *m*

Caspian Sea ['kæspiən] *n* la mer Caspienne

casserole ['kæsərəʊl, *Am:* -əroʊl] **I.** *n* **1.** (*cooking pot*) cocotte *f;* **iron ~** cocotte en fer **2.** (*stew*) ragoût *m* (en cocotte) **II.** *vt* cuire à la cocotte

cassette [kə'set] *n* cassette *f;* **audio ~** cassette audio; **video ~** cassette vidéo

cassette deck *n* platine *f* à cassettes **cassette player** *n* lecteur *m* de cassettes **cassette recorder** *n* magnétophone *m* à cassettes

cast [kɑst, *Am:* kæst] **I.** *n* **1.** THEAT, CINE acteurs *mpl;* (*list*) distribution *f* **2.** (*moulded object*) moule *m* **3.** MED plâtre *m* **4.** (*act of throwing: spear, line*) lancer *m* **5.** *fig* (*of mind*) tournure *f* **6.** (*squint*) **to have a ~ in one's eye** avoir une coquetterie dans l'œil **II.** <cast, cast> *vt* **1.** (*throw*) jeter; (*a line, spear*) lancer **2.** *fig* (*direct: doubt, a shadow*) jeter; **to ~ light on sth** éclaircir qc; **to ~ aspersions on sb** dénigrer qn; **to ~ an eye over sth** balayer qc du regard; **to ~ a slur on sb** porter atteinte à qn **3.** (*allocate roles: play*) distribuer les rôles de; **to ~ sb a part** attribuer un rôle à qn; **to be ~ in the role of sb** jouer le rôle de qn; **to ~ sb to/against type** attribuer un rôle à/de contre-emploi à qn; **to ~ sb as sb** donner le rôle de qn à qn **4.** (*give*) **to ~ one's vote** voter **5.** ART (*make in a mould*) fondre ►**to be ~ in the same mould** être fait sur le même moule; **to ~ one's net wide** étendre la couverture; **to ~ pearls before swine** jeter des perles aux pourceaux

◆**cast about** *vi,* **cast around** *vi* **to ~ for sth** chercher qc

◆**cast aside** *vt* **1.** (*rid oneself of*) se débarrasser de **2.** (*free oneself of*) se défaire de

◆**cast away** *vt* **to be ~** faire naufrage

◆**cast down** *vt* **to be ~** être découragé

◆**cast off I.** *vt* **1.** *s.* **cast aside 2.** (*drop stitches*) **to ~ stitches** arrêter les mailles **3.** (*reject*) rejeter **II.** *vi* NAUT larguer les amarres

◆**cast on I.** *vt* (*stitches*) monter **II.** *vi* monter les mailles

◆**cast out** *vt* **1.** (*reject*) rejeter **2.** (*exorcise: demons, ideas*) chasser

◆**cast up** *vt* rejeter

castanets [kæstə'nets] *npl* castagnettes *fpl*

castaway ['kɑ:stəweɪ, *Am:* 'kæstə-] *n* **1.** (*ship survivor*) naufragé(e) *m(f)* **2.** (*discarded object*) rebut *m*

caste [kɑ:st, *Am:* kæst] *n no pl* caste *f*

caster ['kɑ:stəʳ, *Am:* 'kæstɚ] *n* saupoudroir *m*

caster sugar *n Brit, Aus* sucre *f* en poudre

castigate ['kæstɪgeɪt, *Am:* -tə-] *vt form* **1.** (*criticize*) critiquer sévèrement **2.** (*punish*) châtier

castigation *n* **1.** (*criticism*) critique *f* sévère **2.** (*rebuke*) châtiment *m*

casting ['kɑ:stɪŋ, *Am:* 'kæstɪŋ] *n* **1.** (*moulding*) moulage *m* **2.** THEAT (*role allocation*) distribution *f* des rôles

C

casting vote *n* voix *f* prépondérante
cast iron I. *n no pl* fonte *f* II. *adj* 1. (*made of cast iron*) en fonte 2. *fig* (*very strong*) en béton; **a ~ will** une volonté de fer 3. (*incontestible*) incontestable; (*alibi*) irréfutable 4. (*definite*) certain(e)
castle ['kɑ:sl, *Am:* 'kæsl] I. *n* 1. (*building*) château *m* 2. (*fortress*) château fort 3. *inf* (*chess piece*) tour *f* ►**to build ~s in the air** bâtir des châteaux en Espagne; **an English man's home is his ~** charbonnier est maître dans sa maison II. *vi* GAMES roquer
cast-off [ˌkɑ:st'ɒf, *Am:* 'kæstɑ:f] I. *n pl* ~s 1. (*sth no longer wanted*) rebuts *mpl* 2. (*garment*) nippes *fpl* 3. (*person*) laissés *mpl* pour compte II. *adj* (*clothes*) d'occasion
castor ['kɑ:stəʳ, *Am:* 'kæstɚ] *n* roulette *f*
castor oil *n no pl* huile *f* de ricin **castor stand** *n Am* support *m* à roulettes **castor sugar** *n Brit* sucre *m* en poudre
castrate [kæ'streɪt] *vt* châtrer
casual ['kæʒʊəl, *Am:* 'kæʒu:-] I. *adj* 1. (*relaxed*) décontracté(e) 2. (*not permanent*) occasionnel(le); (*work, worker*) temporaire; (*relation*) de passage; (*sex*) sans lendemain 3. (*careless, not serious*) désinvolte; (*attitude*) insouciant(e); (*glance*) superficiel(le); (*chance*) fortuit(e) 4. FASHION (*clothes*) sport *inv* II. *n* 1. (*worker*) travailleur, -euse *m, f* temporaire 2. *pl* FASHION vêtements *mpl* de sport
casual labour *n* main-d'œuvre *f* temporaire **casual labourer** *n* ouvrier, -ère *m, f* temporaire
casually *adv* 1. (*without premeditation: glance, remark*) en passant; (*meet*) par hasard 2. (*informally: walk*) avec décontraction; (*dressed*) sport 3. (*carelessly: treat*) avec désinvolture
casualty ['kæʒʊəlti, *Am:* 'kæʒu:-] <-ies> *n* 1. (*accident victim*) victime *f* d'un accident; (*injured person*) blessé(e) *m(f)*; (*dead person*) perte *f* humaine 2. *pl* (*victims*) victimes *fpl;* MIL pertes *fpl* 3. *fig* (*negative result*) conséquence *f* néfaste 4. *no pl, no art* (*hospital department*) service *m* des urgences
casual wear *n* vêtements *mpl* sport
cat [kæt] *n* 1. (*feline*) chat(te) *m(f)*; **a she-~** une chatte; **a stray ~** un chat errant 2. (*class of animal*) félin *m* 3. *fig, inf* (*spiteful female*) vache *f* ►**to fight like ~ and dog** se quereller comme chien et chat; **to have a ~ in hell's chance** *Brit* ne pas avoir l'ombre d'une chance; **to play (a game of) ~ and mouse** jouer au chat et à la souris; **the ~'s got sb's tongue** avoir perdu sa langue; **to let the ~ out of the bag** vendre la mèche; **to look like something the ~ brought in** être dégoûtant; **to put the ~ among the pigeons** mettre le loup dans la bergerie; **to rain ~s and dogs** pleuvoir à torrent
CAT [kæt] *n abbr of* **Computer-Assisted Testing** EAO *m*
cataclysmic [ˌkætə'klɪzmɪk, *Am:* ˌkæt̬ə'-] *adj* cataclysmique
catacombs ['kætəku:mz, *Am:* 'kæt̬əkoʊm] *n pl, a. fig* catacombes *fpl*
catalog, catalogue ['kætəlɒg, *Am:* 'kæt̬əlɑ:g] I. *n* 1. (*book*) catalogue *m;* **mail order ~** catalogue de vente par correspondance 2. (*repeated events: of mistakes*) suite *f* II. *vt* cataloguer
catalysis [kə'tæləsɪs] *n no pl* CHEM catalyse *f*
catalyst ['kætəlɪst, *Am:* 'kæt̬-] *n* CHEM *a. fig* catalyseur *m*
catalytic [kætə'lɪtɪk] *adj* catalytique
catamaran [ˌkætəmə'ræn, *Am:* ˌkæt̬-] *n* catamaran *m*
catapult ['kætəpʌlt, *Am:* 'kæt̬-] I. *n* 1. (*device*) catapulte *f* 2. *Brit* GAMES fronde *f* II. *vt* catapulter
cataract ['kætərækt, *Am:* 'kæt̬ərækt] *n* 1. MED cataracte *f* 2. (*waterfall*) cascade *f*
catarrh [kə'tɑ:ʳ, *Am:* kə'tɑ:r] *n no pl* MED catarrhe *m*
catastrophe [kə'tæstrəfi] *n* 1. (*terrible thing*) catastrophe *f* 2. *fig* fléau *m*
catastrophic *adj* catastrophique
catcall ['kætkɔ:l] *n* 1. (*whistle*) sifflet *m* désapprobateur 2. (*call*) coup *m* de sifflet; **to make a ~** siffler
catch [kætʃ] <-es> I. *n* 1. SPORT prise *f* au vol 2. (*fishing*) prise *f*; **to have a good ~** faire une bonne prise 3. (*device*) loquet *m;* (*of window*) loqueteau *m;* (*of jewel*) fermoir *m* 4. *inf* (*suitable partner*) (bon) parti *m* 5. (*trick*) truc *m;* **~-22 (situation)** cercle *m* vicieux II. <*pp, pt* caught> *vt* 1. (*intercept and hold*) attraper; **I have to ~ him before he leaves** je dois le voir avant qu'il parte 2. (*grasp*) saisir 3. (*capture*) attraper; *fig* (*atmosphere*) rendre 4. (*attract*) attirer; (*attention*) retenir 5. *fig* (*captivate*) captiver 6. (*get*) prendre; **to ~ the sun** prendre des couleurs; **to ~ a few rays** prendre un peu le soleil 7. (*not miss: train, bus*) attraper; (*be on time: train, bus*) prendre 8. (*perceive, understand: sounds*) saisir; (*radio*) écouter; (*film*) voir; **to ~ sight of sb/sth** apercevoir qn/qc 9. (*take by surprise*) surprendre; **to get caught** se faire prendre; **to ~ sb doing sth** surprendre qn en train de faire qc; **to ~ sb red handed** prendre qn en flagrant délit; **to ~ sb with their trousers** [*o Am, Aus* **pants**] **down** prendre qn sur le fait accompli; **be caught in the crossfire** être pris dans le feu croisé; *fig* se retrouver entre deux feux 10. (*become entangled*) **to get caught (up) in sth** être pris dans qc; **to ~ one's feet** se prendre les pieds; **to ~ one's dress** faire un accroc à sa robe 11. (*contract: habit*) prendre 12. MED (*be infected*) attraper; **to ~ one's death** attraper la crève 13. (*hit: missile, blow*) atteindre 14. (*start burning*) **to ~ fire** prendre feu 15. *inf* (*fool*) avoir ►**to ~ one's breath** reprendre son souffle; (*stop breathing*) retenir son souffle; **to ~ hell** se faire engueuler; **to be caught short** être à court d'argent; *fig* (*need a*

toilet) être pris d'un besoin pressant **III.** *vi* **1.**(*start: fire*) prendre **2.**(*be stuck*) **to ~ on sth** s'accrocher à qc
◆**catch on** *vi* **1.**(*be popular*) avoir du succès **2.** *inf*(*understand*) piger
◆**catch out** *vt* **1.**(*take by surprise*) surprendre; **to be caught out by sth** être surpris par qc **2.**(*trick*) piéger
◆**catch up I.** *vt* rattraper; **to be/get caught up in sth** être entraîné/se laisser entraîner dans qc **II.** *vi* rattraper son retard; **to ~ with sb/sth** rattraper qn/qc; **to ~ on work** rattraper son travail
catch-all, **catchall** *adj* fourre-tout *inv*
catcher *n* SPORT (*baseball player*) receveur *m*
catching *adj a. fig, inf* contagieux(-euse)
catchment *n* captage *m*
catchphrase *n* rengaine *f* **catch question** *n* colle *f* **catchword** *n* slogan *m*
catchy ['kætʃi] <-ier, -iest> *adj* facile à retenir; (*tune*) entraînant(e)
catechism ['kætɪkɪzəm, *Am:* 'kæt̬-] *n* **1.** REL catéchisme *m* **2.** *fig* doctrine *f*
categorical *adj* catégorique
categorize ['kætəgəraɪz, *Am:* 'kæt̬əgəraɪz] *vt* classer
category ['kætəgəri, *Am:* 'kæt̬əgɔːr-] <-ies> *n* catégorie *f*
cater ['keɪtəʳ, *Am:* -t̬ɚ] **I.** *vi* s'occuper de la restauration; **to ~ for ten on Sunday** recevoir dix personnes dimanche **II.** *vt* **to ~ a party** s'occuper de la restauration d'une soirée
◆**cater for** *vt* (*audience*) s'adresser à; (*children*) proposer des activités pour
caterer *n* traiteur *m*
catering *n no pl* **1.**(*providing of food and drink*) restauration *f* **2.**(*service*) (service) *m* traiteur *m*
caterpillar ['kætəpɪləʳ, *Am:* 'kæt̬ɚpɪlɚ] *n* **1.** ZOOL chenille *f* **2.**(*vehicle*) véhicule *m* à chenilles
caterpillar tractor *n* tracteur *m* à chenilles
caterwaul ['kætəwɔːl, *Am:* 'kæt̬ɚ-] **I.** *n* miaulement *m* **II.** *vi* miauler
catgut ['kætgʌt] *n no pl* **1.** MUS corde *f* de boyau **2.** MED catgut
cathartic [kə'θɑːtɪk, *Am:* kə'θɑːrt̬ɪk] *adj* cathartique
cathedral [kə'θiːdrəl] *n* cathédrale *f*
catherine wheel ['kæθərɪnˌhwiːl] *n* (*fireworks*) soleil *m*
catheter ['kæθɪtəʳ, *Am:* -ət̬ɚ] *n* cathéter *m*
cathode ['kæθəʊd, *Am:* -oʊd] *n* ELEC cathode *f*
cathode ray *n* rayon *m* cathodique
catholic ['kæθəlɪk] **I.** *n* **Catholic** catholique *mf* **II.** *adj* (*roman catholic*) catholique
Catholicism [kə'θɒləsɪzəm, *Am:* -'θɑːlə-] *n no pl* catholicisme *m*
catkin *n* BOT chaton *m* **cat litter** *n* litière *f* de chat
catnap ['kætˌnæp] **I.** *n inf* sieste *f;* **to have a ~** faire un somme **II.** <-pp-> *vi inf* faire la sieste
cat's cradle [ˌkæts'kreɪdl] *n* GAMES jeu *m* de ficelles (*consistant à faire des figures*)
cat's eye *n* **1.**(*stone*) œil *m* de chat **2.** **catseye®** cataphote® *m*
catsuit *n* combinaison *f* moulante
catsup ['kætsəp] *n no pl* ketchup *m*
cattle ['kætl, *Am:* 'kæt̬-] *npl* bétail *m inv;* **dairy ~** vaches *fpl* laitières; **to breed ~** élever des bovins *mpl*
cattle-breeder *n* éleveur *m* de bovins **cattle-breeding** *n no pl* élevage *m* de bovins **cattle-car** *n Am* **1.** AUTO bétaillère *f* **2.** RAIL fourgon *m* à bestiaux **3.**(*group*) troupeau *m* de vaches
catty ['kæti, *Am:* 'kæt̬-] <-ier, -iest> *adj* (*hurtful: of words*) méchant(e); (*remark*) piquant(e)
catwalk *n* **1.**(*narrow walkway*) passerelle *f* **2.** FASHION podium *m*
Caucasian [kɔː'keɪzɪən, *Am:* kɑː'keɪʒən] *form* **I.** *n* **1.**(*white person*) blanc, -che *f* **2.**(*of white decent*) caucasien(ne) *m(f)* **3.**(*the languages of the Caucasus*) langues *fpl* caucasiennes **II.** *adj* **1.**(*light-skinned*) blanc(he) **2.**(*of white decent*) caucasien(ne) **3.**(*pertaining to the Caucasus*) caucasien(ne); **~ countries** pays *mpl* du Caucase
caucus ['kɔːkəs, *Am:* 'kɑː-] *n* <-es> **1.** *Am, NZ* (*political meeting*) comité *m* électoral **2.** *Brit* (*controlling group*) comité *m*
caught [kɔːt, *Am:* kɑːt] *pt, pp of* **catch**
cauldron ['kɔːldrən, *Am:* 'kɑːl-] *n* chaudron *m;* **her heart was a ~ of emotions** *fig* son cœur bouillait d'émotions
cauliflower ['kɒlɪflaʊəʳ, *Am:* 'kɑːlɪˌflaʊɚ] *n* chou-fleur *m*
causal ['kɔːzl, *Am:* 'kɑː-] *adj* causal(e); **the ~ phenomenon of this war** le phénomène à l'origine de cette guerre
causality [kɔː'zæləti, *Am:* kɑː'zælət̬i] *n form* causalité *f*
causative ['kɔːzətɪv, *Am:* 'kɑːzət̬ɪv] **I.** *n* LING causatif *m* **II.** *adj form* **1.**(*showing a cause*) causal(e) **2.** LING causatif(-ive)
cause [kɔːz] **I.** *n* **1.**(*origin*) cause *f;* **he is the ~ of all her woes** il est à l'origine de tous ses malheurs **2.** *no pl* (*motive*) raison *f* **3.** *no pl* (*objective*) cause *f* **4.**(*movement*) cause *f;* **to act for the ~ of democracy** agir pour la démocratie **5.**(*court case*) affaire *f* **II.** *vt* provoquer; (*trouble, delay*) causer; **to ~ sb harm** faire du tort à qn; **the teacher's remarks ~d the child to cry** les remarques du maître ont fait pleurer l'enfant
causeway ['kɔːzˌweɪ, *Am:* 'kɑːz-] *n* chaussée *f;* **The Giant's Causeway** La Chaussée des géants
caustic ['kɔːstɪk, *Am:* 'kɑː-] *adj a. fig* caustique; (*humour*) décapant(e)
cauterise *vt Brit, Aus,* **cauterize** ['kɔːtəraɪz, *Am:* 'kɑːt̬ə-] *vt* cautériser
caution ['kɔːʃən, *Am:* 'kɑː-] **I.** *n no pl*

1. (*carefulness*) prudence *f* 2. (*warning*) avertissement *m;* ~! attention!; **proceed with** ~! roulez au pas!; **to sound a note of** ~ mettre en garde 3. *Brit* (*legal warning*) réprimande *f;* **to let sb off with a** ~ relâcher qn après avertissement ▶**to treat sb/sth with** ~ prendre qn/qc avec des pincettes **II.** *vt form* 1. (*warn*) mettre en garde; **to** ~ **sb against a danger** prévenir qn d'un danger; **to** ~ **sb against doing sth** déconseiller qn de faire qc; **to** ~ **to** +*infin* exhorter qn à +*infin* 2. *Brit* (*warn officially*) **to** ~ **sb** donner un avertissement à qn

cautious ['kɔːʃəs, *Am:* 'kɑː-] *adj* prudent(e); **to be** ~ se montrer prévoyant

cavalcade [ˌkævl'keɪd] *n* 1. (*procession*) cortège *m;* (*on horse*) cavalcade *f* 2. (*succession*) cavalcade *f*

cavalier [ˌkævəl'ɪəʳ, *Am:* -əlɪr] **I.** *n* **Cavalier** cavalier *m* **II.** *adj* cavalier(-ère)

cavalry ['kævəlri] *n no pl + pl vb* cavalerie *f*

cavalryman <-men> *n* 1. HIST cavalier *m* 2. (*in armoured vehicle*) blindé *m*

cave [keɪv] **I.** *n* 1. (*hole*) grotte *f* 2. MIN affaissement *m* **II.** *vi* faire de la spéléologie

◆**cave in** *vi a. fig* céder

caveat ['kæviæt] *n* mise *f* en garde

cavedweller *n* troglodyte *mf* **cave-in** *n* affaissement *m* **caveman** <-men> *n* 1. (*prehistoric man*) homme *m* des cavernes 2. *pej* (*socially underdeveloped*) sauvage *m* **cave painting** *n* peinture *f* rupestre

caver *n Brit, Aus* spéléologue *mf*

cavern ['kævən, *Am:* -ɚn] *n* caverne *f*

cavernous ['kævənəs, *Am:* -ɚn-] *adj* 1. *fig* (*cavern-like*) caverneux(-euse) 2. (*huge*) immense

caviar(e) ['kævɪɑːʳ, *Am:* -ɑːr] *n no pl* œufs *mpl* de lump; (*of sturgeon*) caviar *m* ▶**to be** ~ **to the general** être trop bien pour le peuple

caving *n no pl* spéléologie *f*

cavity ['kævɪti, *Am:* -t̬i] <-ties> *n* 1. ANAT cavité *f* 2. (*hollow space*) creux *m* 3. (*in a tooth*) carie *f*

caw [kɔː, *Am:* kɑː] **I.** *n* croassement *m* **II.** *vi* croasser

cayenne [keɪ'en, *Am:* kaɪ-], **cayenne pepper** *n no pl* poivre *m* de Cayenne

Cayman Islands ['keɪmən,aɪləndz] *n* les îles *fpl* Caïmans

CB [ˌsiː'biː] *n no pl abbr of* **Citizen's Band** CB *f*

CBI [ˌsiːbiː'aɪ] *n Brit abbr of* **Confederation of British Industry** ≈ CNPF *m*

cc [ˌsiː'siː] *n abbr of* **cubic centimetres** cm^3 *m*

CCTV [ˌsiːsiːtiː'viː] *n abbr of* **closed-circuit television** télévision *f* en circuit fermé

ccw. *adj, adv abbr of* **counterclockwise** dans le sens inverse des aiguilles d'une montre

CD [ˌsiː'diː] *n abbr of* **compact disc** CD *m*

CD-player *n abbr of* **compact disc player** lecteur *m* de CD **CD-R** *n abbr of* **Compact Disc Recordable** CD-R *m* (enregistrable)

CD-ROM *n abbr of* **compact disc read-only memory** INFOR CD-ROM *m*, cédérom *m*

CD-ROM drive *n* INFOR lecteur *m* de CD-ROM **CD-ROM writer** *n* graveur *m* de CD-ROM

CD-RW *n abbr of* **Compact Disc Rewritable Unit** CD-RW *m* (réenregistrable)

cease [siːs] *form* **I.** *n no pl* **without** ~ sans cesse **II.** *vi* cesser **III.** *vt* (*aid*) couper; (*fire*) cesser; (*payment*) interrompre

cease-fire *n* cessez-le-feu *m inv*

ceaseless *adj* incessant(e); (*effort*) soutenu(e)

cedar ['siːdəʳ, *Am:* -dɚ] **I.** *n* 1. (*tree*) cèdre *m* 2. *no pl* (*wood*) bois *m* de cèdre **II.** *adj* en cèdre

cede [siːd] *vt form* (*relinquish*) céder

ceiling ['siːlɪŋ] *n* 1. (*opposite floor, upper limit*) plafond *m;* **to impose a** ~ **on prices** plafonner les prix 2. METEO **cloud** ~ couverture *f* nuageuse 3. AVIAT plafond *m* ▶**he hit the** ~ *inf* il explosa de colère

celebrate ['selɪbreɪt] **I.** *vi* faire la fête; **we** ~**d in style** nous avons fêté ça en grande pompe **II.** *vt* 1. (*mark an event with festivities*) célébrer; (*anniversary of death*) commémorer; (*a deal*) fêter 2. REL (*Eucharist*) célébrer 3. (*revere publicly*) **to** ~ **sb as a hero** élever qn au rang de héros

celebrated *adj* (*famous*) célèbre

celebration *n* 1. (*party*) fête *f; inf;* **this calls for a** ~! il faut marquer ça ! 2. (*of an occasion*) cérémonie *f* 3. (*of a death*) commémoration *f* 4. (*religious ceremony*) célébration *f*

celebratory [ˌselə'breɪtəri, *Am:* 'seləbrətɔːri] *adj* de célébration

celebrity [sɪ'lebrəti, *Am:* sə'lebrət̬i] *n* 1. <-ties> (*famous person*) célébrité *f* 2. (*of the entertainment industry*) star *f* 3. *no pl* (*fame*) célébrité *f*

celeriac [sə'lerɪæk] *n no pl* céleri-rave *m*

celery ['seləri] *n no pl* céleri *m*

celestial [sɪ'lestɪəl, *Am:* -tʃl] *adj* céleste

celestial body *n* ASTR corps *m* céleste

celibacy ['selɪbəsi] *n no pl* REL célibat *m*

celibate ['selɪbət] **I.** *n* célibataire *mf* **II.** *adj* célibataire

cell [sel] *n* 1. (*small room*) cellule *f* 2. (*compartments*) case *f* 3. (*part of honeycomb*) alvéole *m o f* 4. BIO, POL cellule *f;* **to use one's grey** ~**s** faire travailler sa matière grise 5. ELEC **battery** ~ élément *m* de pile

cellar ['seləʳ, *Am:* -ɚ] *n* cave *f;* **to keep a** ~ avoir une cave à vin

cellist *n* violoncelliste *mf;* **principal** ~ premier violoncelle *m*

cell nucleus <-clei *o* -es> *n* BIO noyau *m* de cellule

cello ['tʃeləʊ, *Am:* -oʊ] <-s *o* -li> *n* violoncelle *m*

cellophane® ['seləfeɪn] *n* cellophane® *f*

cellphone ['selfəʊn, *Am:* foʊn] *n Am* téléphone *m* portable, cellulaire *m Québec*, natel *m Suisse*

cellular ['seljʊləʳ, *Am:* -lɚ] *adj* 1. (*porous*) *a.*

cellulaire 2. TECH alvéolaire 3. TEL ~ (**tele**)**phone** téléphone *m* portable, cellulaire *m Québec*, natel *m Suisse*

cellulite ['seljəlaɪt] *n no pl* cellulite *f*

celluloid ['seljʊlɔɪd] I. *n no pl* (*multi-purpose plastic*) celluloïd *m* II. *adj* en celluloïd

cellulose ['seljʊləʊs, *Am:* -loʊs] *n no pl* cellulose *f*

Celsius ['selsiəs] *adj* (*thermometer*) de Celsius; **twenty degrees** ~ vingt degrés Celsius

Celt [kelt] *n* Celte *mf*

Celtic ['keltik] I. *adj* celte, celtique II. *n* celtique *m; s. a.* **English**

cement [sɪ'ment] I. *n no pl* 1. (*used in construction*) ciment *m;* **quick-setting** ~ ciment à prise rapide 2. (*concrete*) béton *m* 3. (*binding material*) mastic *m* 4. (*uniting idea*) ciment *m;* **the** ~ **for their future relations** le ciment de leurs relations futures II. *vt* cimenter ►**to** ~ **a friendship** sceller une amitié

cement mixer *n* bétonnière *f*

cemetery ['semətri, *Am:* -teri] <-ries> *n* cimetière *m*

censer ['sensəʳ, *Am:* -sɚ] *n* REL encensoir *m*

censor ['sensəʳ, *Am:* -sɚ] I. *n* censeur *m* II. *vt* censurer

censorious [sen'sɔːrɪəs, *Am:* -'sɔːrɪ-] *adj* sévère

censorship ['sentsəʃɪp, *Am:* -sɚ-] *n no pl* censure *f*

censure ['sentʃɚ] I. *n* critiques *fpl* II. *vt* blâmer

census ['sensəs] *n* 1. (*population count*) recensement *m* 2. (*counting*) décompte *m;* (*of traffic*) comptage *m*

cent [sent] *n* cent *m* ►**I don't care a** ~ je m'en moque éperdument

centenarian [ˌsentɪ'neərɪən, *Am:* -tnerɪ-] *n* centenaire *mf*

centenary[1] [sen'tiːnəri, *Am:* 'sentner-] <-ries> *n* 1. *Brit* siècle *m* d'existence 2. *Am, Aus* centième anniversaire *m*

centenary[2] [sen'tiːnəri, *Am:* 'sentner-] *adj* 1. centenaire; ~ **celebrations** fêtes *fpl* du centenaire 2. (*every hundred years*) séculaire *m*

centennial [sen'tenɪəl] I. *adj* centenaire II. *n* centenaire *m*

center *s.* **centre**

centerpiece *n* 1. (*ornament*) milieu *m* de table 2. *fig* pièce *f* de résistance

centigrade I. *n* 1. (*one hundredth of a unit*) centigrade *m* 2. *no pl* METEO **ten degrees** ~ dix degrés (Celsius) II. *adj* centigrade; **a** ~ **scale** une échelle en centigrades **centigram**(**me**) *n* centigramme *m* **centilitre** *n* centilitre *m* **centimeter** *n Am,* **centimetre** *n Brit, Aus* centimètre *m* **centipede** *n* mille-pattes *m*

central ['sentrəl] *adj* 1. (*close to the middle*) central(e) 2. (*paramount*) primordial(e); (*issue*) essentiel(le) 3. (*national: bank*) central(e)

Central African I. *adj* centrafricain(e) II. *n* Centrafricain(e) *m(f)* **Central African Republic** *n* la République centrafricaine **Central America** *n* l'Amérique *f* centrale **Central Bank** *n* Banque *f* centrale **Central France** *n* le Centre

centralization *n no pl* POL, INFOR centralisation *f*

centralize ['sentrəlaɪz] *vt* POL, INFOR centraliser

central processing unit *n* INFOR unité *f* centrale

centre ['sentəʳ, *Am:* -t̬ɚ] I. *n* centre *m;* **test** ~ centre d'essai II. *vt* centrer

◆**centre on** *vt* se concentrer sur; **she spoke about her travels, centering on India** elle parla de ses voyages en s'attachant surtout à l'Inde

centrepiece *n s.* **centerpiece**

centrifugal *adj inv* PHYS centrifuge

centrifuge ['sentrɪfjuːdʒ, *Am:* -trə-] *n* MED, TECH centrifugeur *m* [*o* centrifugeuse] *f*

centripetal [sen'trɪpɪtl, *Am:* -pət̬l] *adj inv* PHYS centripète

century ['sentʃəri] <-ies> *n* 1. (*100 year period*) siècle *m;* **to be centuries old** avoir plusieurs siècles 2. (*score in cricket*) cent points *mpl*

CEO [ˌsiːiː'əʊ, *Am:* -'oʊ] *n abbr of* **chief executive officer**

ceramic [sɪ'ræmɪk, *Am:* sə-] *adj inv* céramique

ceramics *n + sing vb* céramique *f*

cereal ['sɪərɪəl, *Am:* 'sɪrɪ-] I. *n* céréale *f* II. *adj inv* 1. (*pertaining to grain*) céréalier(-ère) 2. (*made of grain*) de céréale(s)

cerebellum [ˌserɪ'beləm, *Am:* ˌserə-] <- *o* -la> *n* ANAT cervelet *m*

cerebral ['serɪbrəl, *Am:* ˌserə-] *adj* cérébral(e)

cerebrum ['serɪbrəm, *Am:* ˌserə-] <- *o* -bra> *n* ANAT cerveau *m*

ceremonial [ˌserɪ'məʊnɪəl, *Am:* -ə'moʊ-] I. *n form* cérémonial *m; s. a.* **ceremony** II. *adj* cérémonial(e)

ceremonious [ˌserɪ'məʊnɪəs, *Am:* -ə'moʊ-] *adj* cérémonieux(-euse)

ceremony ['serɪməni, *Am:* -əmoʊ-] <-nies> *n* 1. (*celebration*) cérémonie *f* 2. *no pl* (*required behavior*) cérémonial *m;* **to stand on** ~ faire des politesses

cert [sɜːt, *Am:* sɜːrt] *n sing, Brit, inf, abbr of* **certainty: this horse is a dead** ~ **for the 1st race** ce cheval est un coup sûr dans la première course

certain ['sɜːtn, *Am:* 'sɜːr-] I. *adj* certain(e); **to be** ~ **about sth** être certain de qc; **please be** ~ **to turn out the lights** assurez-vous que vous avez éteint les lumières; **he no longer was** ~ **where they lived** il ne savait plus exactement où ils habitaient II. *pron* ~ **of her students** certain(e)s de ses étudiant(e)s

certainly *adv* 1. (*surely*) certainement; **she** ~

is right! elle a raison, c'est sûr ! **2.** (*gladly*) bien sûr; **"do you want to come along?" – "~!"** "tu veux venir aussi ?" – "avec plaisir !"

certainty ['sɜːtənti, *Am:* 'sɜːr-] *n* certitude *f*

certifiable *adj inv* **1.** (*declared*) à déclarer **2.** (*crazy*) **to be ~** être bon pour l'internement

certificate [sə'tɪfɪkət, *Am:* sɚ-] *n* **1.** (*document*) certificat *m;* **birth ~** extrait *m* de naissance; **death/marriage ~** acte *m* de décès/mariage; **doctor's ~** certificat médical; **~ of ownership** titre *m* de propriété **2.** SCHOOL diplôme *m*

certification *n no pl* **1.** (*state or process*) authentification *f* **2.** (*document*) certificat *m*

certify ['sɜːtɪfaɪ, *Am:* -t̬ə-] <-ie-> *vt* certifier; **to ~ sb as insane** déclarer qn fou

certitude ['sɜːtɪtjuːd, *Am:* 'sɜːrt̬ətuːd] *n no pl* certitude *f*

cervical ['sɜːvɪkl, sɜː'vaɪkl, *Am:* 'sɜːrvɪ-] *adj inv* ANAT **1.** (*of the neck*) cervical(e) **2.** (*of the cervix: cancer*) du col (de l'utérus)

cervix ['sɜːvɪks, *Am:* 'sɜːr-] <-es *o* -vices> *n* ANAT col *m* de l'utérus

Cesarean *n s.* **Caesarean**

cessation [se'seɪʃən] *n no pl, form* **1.** (*end*) cessation *f* **2.** (*pause*) interruption *f;* (*of hostilities*) trêve *f*

cesspit ['sespɪt], **cesspool** *n* fosse *f* d'aisances

CET *n abbr of* **Central European Time** heure *f* de l'Europe centrale

Ceylon [sɪ'lɒn, *Am:* -'lɑːn] **I.** *n no pl* **1.** HIST Ceylan *m* **2.** (*Ceylon tea*) thé *m* de Ceylan **II.** *adj inv* cingalais(e); *s. a.* **Sri Lanka**

Ceylonese <-> HIST **I.** *n* Cingalais(e) *m(f)* **II.** *adj* cingalais(e); *s. a.* **Sri Lankan**

cf. *abbr of* **confer** cf.

CFC [ˌsiːef'siː] *n abbr of* **chlorofluorocarbon** CFC *m*

c/h *n abbr of* **central heating** ch. c.

Chad [tschæd] *n* le Tchad; **Lake ~** le lac Tchad

Chadian **I.** *adj* tchadien(ne) **II.** *n* (*person*) Tchadien(ne) *m(f)*

chafe [tʃeɪf] **I.** *vi* **1.** (*become sore*) être à vif **2.** (*become irritated*) **to ~ at sth** enrager contre qc **3.** (*be impatient*) **to ~ to** *+infin* brûler d'envie de *+infin* **II.** *vt* **1.** (*rub sore*) frotter; **the wind ~d her cheeks** le vent l'a mis les joues en feu **2.** (*rub warm*) **to ~ sth in one's hands** réchauffer qc entre ses mains

chafer *n s.* **cock~**, **rose~**

chaff[1] [tʃɑːf, *Am:* tʃæf] *n no pl* **1.** (*husks*) balle *f* **2.** (*cut grass*) *foin haché destiné au bétail* **3.** (*material to be discarded*) broutilles *fpl* ►**to separate the wheat from the ~** séparer le bon grain de l'ivraie

chaff[2] [tʃɑːf, *Am:* tʃæf] **I.** *n no pl* taquinerie *f* **II.** *vt* taquiner

chaffinch ['tʃæfɪntʃ] <-es> *n* pinson *m*

chagrin ['ʃægrɪn, *Am:* ʃə'grɪn] *n* dépit *m*

chain [tʃeɪn] **I.** *n* **1.** (*set of related things*) chaîne *f;* **gold/silver ~** chaîne en or/en argent; **fast food ~** chaîne de fast-food; **~ of mishaps** série *f* de malheurs **2.** (*rings to hold captive*) entraves *fpl;* **ball and ~** boulet *m;* **~ gang** chaîne de forçats; **to be in ~s** être enchaîné **3.** (*restrictions*) joug *m* **II.** *vt* enchaîner ►**to be ~ed to a desk** être rivé à son bureau

chain reaction *n* réaction *f* en chaîne

chain saw *n* tronçonneuse *f* **chain-smoke** *vi* fumer cigarette sur cigarette **chain smoker** *n personne qui fume cigarette sur cigarette* **chain store** *n* succursale *f*

chair [tʃeəʳ, *Am:* tʃer] **I.** *n* **1.** (*seat*) chaise *f* **2.** (*head of an academic department*) chaire *f* **3.** (*head*) présidence *f* **4.** (*place in an official body*) **to have a ~ on a board** être membre d'un comité **5.** *Am* **the ~** (*the electric chair*) chaise *f* électrique **II.** *vt* présider

chair lift *n* télésiège *m* **chairman** <-men> *n* président *m* **chairmanship** *n* présidence *f* **chairperson** *n* président(e) *m(f)* **chairwoman** <-women> *n* présidente *f*

chalet ['ʃæleɪ, *Am:* ʃæl'eɪ] *n* chalet *m*

chalk [tʃɔːk] **I.** *n no pl* craie *f* ►**to be (as different as) ~ and/from cheese** être le jour et la nuit **II.** *vt* écrire à la craie

◆**chalk up** *vt* inscrire

chalkboard *n* tableau *m*

chalky ['tʃɔːki] <-ier, -iest> *adj* **1.** (*made of chalk*) calcaire **2.** (*dusty*) **to be all ~** être plein de craie **3.** (*having a chalk-like quality*) crayeux(-euse) **4.** (*pale*) blafard(e)

challenge ['tʃælɪndʒ] **I.** *n* **1.** (*test, difficulty*) défi *m* **2.** MIL sommation *f* **3.** JUR récusation *f* **II.** *vt* **1.** (*ask to compete*) défier; **to ~ sb to** *+infin* défier qn de *+infin* **2.** (*question*) contester **3.** (*stimulate*) stimuler **4.** MIL **to ~ sb** sommer qn d'indiquer son nom et le motif de sa présence **5.** JUR récuser

challenger *n* concurrent(e) *m(f)*

challenging *adj* stimulant(e)

chamber ['tʃeɪmbəʳ, *Am:* -bɚ] *n* chambre *f;* (*of the heart*) cavité *f;* **Upper/Lower ~** Chambre haute/basse; **combustion ~** chambre à combustion

chamberlain *n* **1.** HIST chambellan *m* **2.** FIN *Brit* trésorier, -ière *m, f* **chambermaid** *n* femme *f* de chambre **chamber music** *n no pl* musique *f* de chambre **chamber pot** *n* HIST pot *m* de chambre

chameleon [kə'miːlɪən] *n* caméléon *m*

chamois ['ʃæmwɑ, *Am:* 'ʃæmi] <-> *n* chamois *m*

chamomile *n s.* **camomile**

champ [tʃæmp] *vi s.* **chomp to ~ (down) on sth, to ~ into sth** mâchonner qc ►**to ~ at the bit** ronger son frein

champagne [ʃæm'peɪn] **I.** *n no pl* champagne **II.** *adj* **1.** (*with ~: brunch*) au champagne **2.** (*colored: dress*) (couleur) champagne *inv*

champion ['tʃæmpiən] **I.** *n* **1.** SPORT champion *m;* **defending ~** champion en titre

2. (*supporter or defender*) défenseur *m* **II.** *vt* défendre **III.** *adj Brit, inf* super *inv*

championship *n* **1.** (*competition*) championnat *m;* **to hold a ~** tenir la tête d'un championnat **2.** *no pl* (*supporting*) défense *f*

chance [tʃɑːns, *Am:* tʃæns] **I.** *n* **1.** *no pl* (*random*) hasard *m;* **by any ~** à tout hasard **2.** *no pl* (*likelihood*) chance *f;* **he didn't give half a ~** il ne m'a pas laissé l'ombre d'une chance; **to do sth on the off ~ that** faire qc dans l'espoir que +*subj* **3.** (*opportunity*) occasion *f;* **to miss one's ~** laisser passer sa chance **4.** (*hazard*) risque *m;* **to take a ~** tenter le coup **II.** *vi* **they ~ed to be there** il se trouve qu'ils étaient là **III.** *vt* tenter; **to ~ one's arm** *Brit tenter le coup*

chancellery *n* chancellerie *f*

chancellor ['tʃɑːnsələʳ, *Am:* 'tʃæn-] *n* **1.** POL chancelier *m;* **Chancellor of the Exchequer** ministre *mf* des Finances britannique **2.** (*university head*) recteur *m*

chancy ['tʃɑːnsi, *Am:* 'tʃæn-] <-ier, -iest> *adj* risqué(e)

chandelier [ˌʃændə'lɪəʳ, *Am:* -'lɪr] *n* lustre *m*

change ['tʃeɪndʒ] **I.** *n* **1.** (*alteration*) changement *m;* **it's a ~ for the worse** c'est changer pour le pire; **to have to make four ~s** devoir changer quatre fois; *iron;* **for a ~** pour changer; **why don't you stop for a ~?** tu ne peux pas t'arrêter un peu, pour changer? **2.** *no pl* (*fluctuation*) évolution *f;* **there's no ~ in his condition** son état n'a pas évolué **3.** (*extra outfit: of clothes*) rechange *m* **4.** *no pl* (*coins*) monnaie *f;* **small ~** petite monnaie; **to have the correct ~** avoir l'appoint; **to give ~** rendre la monnaie, remettre *Belgique* **II.** *vi* **1.** (*alter*) passer; **the traffic light ~d back to red** le feu est repassé au rouge; **the wind ~d to west** le vent a tourné à l'ouest **2.** (*swap trains*) changer; **to ~ in Paris for Marseilles** changer à Paris pour Marseille **3.** (*put on different clothes*) se changer; **I'll ~ into a dress** je me change pour mettre une robe; **the baby needs changing** le bébé a besoin d'être changé **4.** (*change speed*) **to ~ into third gear** passer en troisième **III.** *vt* **1.** (*alter*) changer **2.** (*give coins for*) faire la monnaie de **3.** (*exchange currencies*) **to ~ money** changer de l'argent **4.** (*to swap*) échanger

◆**change down** *vi* rétrograder

◆**change up** *vi* passer à la vitesse supérieure

changeable *adj* instable

change machine *n* monnayeur *m*

changeover *n sing* passage *m*

channel ['tʃænl] **I.** *n* **1.** RADIO fréquence *f;* **I like this ~** j'aime bien cette station **2.** TV chaîne *f;* **cable ~** chaîne cablée; **to turn to another ~** passer sur une autre chaîne; **on ~ one/five** sur la une/cinq **3.** (*waterway*) canal *m;* **The (English) Channel** la Manche **4.** (*means*) moyen *m* de canaliser **II.** <*Brit* -ll- *o Am* -l-> *vt* canaliser

Channel Islands *n* les îles *fpl* Anglo-Normandes **Channel Tunnel** *n no pl* tunnel *m* sous la Manche

chant [tʃɑːnt, *Am:* tʃænt] **I.** *n* **1.** REL incantation *f* **2.** (*utterance*) chant *m* **II.** *vt* **1.** REL psalmodier **2.** (*repeat without pause*) scander **3.** (*sing*) chanter a cappella

chanterelle [ˌtʃæntə'rel, *Am:* ˌtʃænţə-] *n* chanterelle *f*, girolle *f*

Chanukkah *n s.* **Hanukkah**

chaos ['keɪɒs, *Am:* -ɑːs] *n no pl* **1.** (*confusion*) chaos *m* **2.** *fig* pagaille *f;* **to cause ~** semer la pagaille; **the room was in a total ~** la pièce était sens dessus dessous

Chaos Theory *n no pl* théorie *f* du chaos

chaotic [keɪ'ɒtɪk, *Am:* -'ɑːţɪk] *adj* chaotique

chap¹ [tʃæp] <-pp-> **I.** *vi* se gercer **II.** *vt* gercer; **the wind ~ped my lips** le vent m'a gercé les lèvres **III.** *n* gerçure *f*

chap² [tʃæp] *n inf, Brit* (*man*) type *m*

chap. *n abbr of* **chapter** chap. *m*

chapel ['tʃæpl] *n* chapelle *f*

chaperone ['ʃæpərəʊn, *Am:* -əroʊn] **I.** *n* chaperon *m* **II.** *vt* chaperonner

chapter ['tʃæptəʳ, *Am:* -tɚ] *n* **1.** (*section of a book*) chapitre *m* **2.** (*episode*) épisode *m* **3.** *Am* (*branch of a religious organization*) chapitre *m* **4.** *Brit, Aus, form* (*disasters: of accidents*) avalanche *f*

chapter house *n Am* (*meeting place of a religious organization*) maison *f* capitulaire

char [tʃɑːʳ, *Am:* tʃɑːr] <-rr-> *vt* carboniser

character ['kærəktəʳ, *Am:* 'kerəkţɚ] *n* **1.** *no pl* (*set of qualities*) *a.* INFOR, TYP caractère *m* **2.** (*decidedly different person*) personnage *m*

characteristic [ˌkærəktə'rɪstɪk, *Am:* ˌker-] **I.** *n* caractéristique *f* **II.** *adj* caractéristique

characteristically *adv* de manière caractéristique

characterization *n* caractérisation *f*

characterize ['kærəktəraɪz, *Am:* 'kerək-] *vt* caractériser

charade [ʃə'rɑːd, *Am:* -'reɪd] *n* **1.** (*farce*) mascarade *f* **2.** *pl* (*game*) charades *fpl* mimées

charcoal ['tʃɑːkəʊl, *Am:* 'tʃɑːrkoʊl] **I.** *n no pl* **1.** (*hard black fuel*) charbon *m* de bois **2.** ART fusain *m* **II.** *adj* **1.** (*of charcoal*) **~ fire** feu au charbon de bois; **~ drawing** dessin au fusain **2.** (*dark grey*) **~ grey** gris-noir

charcoal-burner *n* charbonnier *m*

charge [tʃɑːdʒ, *Am:* tʃɑːrdʒ] **I.** *n* **1.** (*cost*) frais *mpl;* **free of ~** gratuit; **is there a ~ for kids?** faut il payer pour les enfants? **2.** JUR accusation *f;* **to be arrested on a ~ of murder** être arrêté pour meurtre; **to bring ~s against sb** porter des accusations contre qn; **to drop ~s against sb** retirer sa plainte contre qn **3.** MIL charge *f* **4.** *no pl* (*authority*) **to be in ~** être responsable; **to take ~ of sth** prendre qc en charge; **to have ~ of sb** avoir qn à charge; **I'm in ~ here** c'est moi le chef ici **5.** *no pl* ELEC **to put a battery on ~** recharger une batterie **II.** *vi* **1.** FIN faire payer; **to ~ for admission** faire payer l'entrée; **how much do you ~ for**

a rental car? combien prenez-vous pour la location d'une voiture ? **2.** (*lunge, attack*) charger; **to ~ at sb** charger qn **3.** ELEC (*battery*) se (re)charger **III.** *vt* **1.** FIN faire payer; (*interests, commission*) prélever; **to ~ sth to sb's account** mettre qc sur le compte de qn **2.** (*accuse*) accuser; **to be ~d with sth** être accusé de qc **3.** (*order*) ordonner; **to ~ sb with sth** confier qc à qn **4.** ELEC, MIL (re)charger **5.** (*attack*) charger

chargeable *adj* FIN **to be ~ to tax** être soumis à taxation/imposition

charge account *n Am* (*credit account*) compte *m* courant **charge card** *n* carte *f* de crédit

charged *adj a. fig* chargé(e); (*atmosphere*) tendu(e)

chargé d'affaires [ʃɑːʒeɪdæ'feəʳ, *Am:* ʃɑːrʒeɪdə'fer] <chargés d'affaires> *n* chargé(e) *m(f)* d'affaires

chariot ['tʃæriət] *n* char *m*

charisma [kə'rɪzmə] *n* charisme *m*

charitable ['tʃærɪtəbl, *Am:* 'tʃer-] *adj* **1.** (*with money*) généreux(-euse); (*with kindness*) altruiste **2.** (*concerning charity*) charitable; (*foundation*) caritatif(-ive); (*donations*) généreux(-euse)

charity ['tʃærəti, *Am:* 'tʃerət̬i] *n* **1.** *no pl* (*generosity*) générosité *f;* **Christian ~** charité *f* chrétienne; **human ~** don *m* de soi **2.** (*organisation*) association *f* caritative; **~ work** bonnes œuvres *fpl;* **to accept ~** accepter l'aumône; **to depend on ~** vivre d'aumônes; **to give sth to ~** donner qc aux œuvres *fpl* de charité **3.** <-ties> (*organization*) bonnes œuvres *fpl*

charity shop *n magasin dont les profits vont à un organisme caritatif*

charlatan ['ʃɑːlətən, *Am:* 'ʃɑːrlətən] *n* charlatan *m*

Charles [tʃɑːlz, *Am:* tʃɑːrlz] *n* Charles *m;* **~ the Fifth** (**of Spain**) Charles-Quint *m;* **~ the Bold** Charles le Téméraire

Charlie [tʃɑːli, *Am:* tʃɑːrli] *n inf* Charlot *m*

charm [tʃɑːm, *Am:* tʃɑːrm] **I.** *n* **1.** *no pl* (*quality*) charme *m* **2.** (*characteristic*) attraits *mpl* **3.** (*pendant*) amulette *f* **4.** (*talisman*) talisman *m;* **lucky ~** porte-bonheur *m* **II.** *vt* séduire; **to ~ sb into doing sth** obtenir qc de qn par le charme

charmed *adj* **to have a ~ life** être né sous une bonne étoile

charmer *n* **1.** (*likeable person*) charmeur, -euse *m, f* **2.** *pej* (*trickster*) enjôleur, -euse *m, f* **3.** *pej, iron* (*one with unappealing behaviour*) séducteur, -trice *m, f*

charming *adj* **1.** (*likeable*) *a. pej* charmant(e) **2.** *pej, iron* (*inconsiderate*) odieux(-euse)

chart [tʃɑːt, *Am:* tʃɑːrt] **I.** *n* **1.** (*table*) graphique *m;* **medical ~** courbe *f;* **weather ~** carte *f* **2.** *pl* (*weekly list*) hit-parade *m;* **to drop off the ~s** quitter le hit-parade; **to hit the ~s** entrer au hit-parade **II.** *vt* **1.** (*represent*) représenter; (*progress*) observer; **the map ~s the course of the river** la carte montre le cours de la rivière **2.** (*examine*) examiner **3.** *Am* (*plan*) planifier

charter **I.** *n* **1.** (*written document*) charte *f* **2.** *no pl* AVIAT, NAUT affrètement *m;* **place that has boats for ~** un endroit où des bateaux sont à affréter **3.** AVIAT (*special service*) charter *m* **II.** *vt* affréter; **the club was ~ed ten years ago** le club a été fondé il y a dix ans

charter company <-nies> *n* compagnie *f* charter

chartered *adj* **1.** AUTO, NAUT affrété(e) **2.** *Brit, Aus* (*qualified*) professionnel(le)

charterer ['tʃɑːtərəʳ, *Am:* 'tʃɑːrt̬ɚɚ] *n* affréteur *m*

charter flight *n* vol *m* charter

chase [tʃeɪs] **I.** *n* **1.** (*pursuit*) poursuite *f;* **to give ~ to sb** chasser qn **2.** (*hunt*) chasse *f* **II.** *vi* **to ~ around** [*o* **about**] courir dans tout les sens; (*rollick about*) jouer de façon turbulente **III.** *vt* poursuivre ►**to ~ one's tail trying to get sth** s'évertuer à obtenir qc de qn; **to ~ after women** courir après les femmes

◆**chase after** *vt* courir après

◆**chase off** *vt* faire partir

◆**chase up** *vt Brit, inf* (*data*) retrouver; (*customer*) relancer

chasm ['kæzəm] *n* **1.** (*deep cleft*) gouffre *m* **2.** (*omission*) lacune *f* **3.** (*discrepancy*) disparité *f;* (*of ideologies*) désaccord *m;* **to bridge a ~** combler une différence

chassis ['ʃæsi] <-> *n* châssis *m*

chaste [tʃeɪst] *adj form* **1.** (*pure*) chaste **2.** (*virtuous*) vertueux(-euse) **3.** (*innocent*) innocent(e) **4.** (*simple*) pure

chasten ['tʃeɪsn] *vt* **1.** (*admonish*) réprimander **2.** (*humble*) discipliner

chastise [tʃæ'staɪz, *Am:* 'tʃæstaɪz] *vt* réprimander

chastity ['tʃæstəti, *Am:* -tət̬i] *n no pl* **1.** (*virginity*) vertue *f* **2.** (*abstinence*) chasteté *f*

chat [tʃæt] **I.** *n* **1.** (*conversation*) conversation *f;* **to have a ~ with sb about sth** discuter avec qn au sujet de qc **2.** *no pl* (*inconsequential talk*) bavardage *m* **3.** INFOR chat *m* **II.** *vi* <-tt-> bavarder; **to ~ with** [*o* **to**] **sb about sb/sth** discuter avec qn de qn/qc

chat room *n* chat-room *m* **chat show** *n Brit* talk-show *m*

chatter **I.** *n* conversation *f;* (*of birds*) pépiements *mpl;* **to break out in ~** bavarder **II.** *vi* **1.** (*converse*) **to ~ about sth** converser à propos de qc; **to ~ about everything and nothing** parler de tout et de rien; **to ~ away** parler sans cesse **2.** (*make clacking noises*) claquer; (*machines*) cliqueter; (*birds*) pépier **3.** INFOR chatter ►**the ~ing classes** *Brit, inf, pej* les intellos *mpl*

chatty ['tʃæti, *Am:* 'tʃæt̬-] <-ier, -iest> *adj inf* **1.** (*person*) causant(e) **2.** LIT courant(e)

chauffeur ['ʃəʊfəʳ, *Am:* 'ʃɑːfɚ] **I.** *n* chauffeur *m* **II.** *vt* conduire

chauvinism [ˈʃəʊvɪnɪzəm, *Am:* ˈʃoʊ-] *n no pl* chauvinisme *m*
chauvinist I. *n* chauvin(e); **male** ~ macho *m* II. *adj* chauvin(e); (*man*) macho
chauvinistic *adj* 1. (*patriot*) chauvin(e) 2. (*macho*) machiste
cheap [tʃiːp] *adj* 1. (*inexpensive*) bon marché *inv;* (*ticket*) économique; **dirt** ~ très bon marché; ~ **labour** *pej* main-d'œuvre *f* sous-payée; **to be** ~ **to operate** être peu coûteux à l'utilisation 2. *fig* (*worthless: joke, success*) facile; **to make oneself** ~ être facile; **to feel** ~ avoir honte; **to look** ~ avoir l'air vulgaire 3. *pej* (*shoddy: goods*) de pacotille 4. *pej, inf* (*miserly*) radin(e) 5. *pej* (*mean: trick, liar*) sale ▶**a** ~ **shot** un mauvais coup; ~ **and cheerful** *Brit, Aus, inf* bon et pas cher; **to be** ~ **and nasty** être de la camelote; **to buy something on the** ~ acheter à prix réduit; **to get sth on the** ~ obtenir qc au rabais
cheapen [ˈtʃiːpən] *vt* 1. (*lower price*) déprécier 2. (*reduce morally*) rabaisser
cheaply *adv* (à) bon marché; (*to live, travel*) à peu de frais
cheapness *n no pl* 1. (*price*) bas prix *m* 2. (*morality*) vulgarité *f*
cheapskate I. *n pej, inf* avare *mf* II. *adj pej, inf* radin(e)
cheat [tʃiːt] I. *n* 1. (*trickster*) tricheur, -euse *m, f* 2. (*deception*) tromperie *f* II. *vi* tricher; **to be caught** ~**ing** se faire surprendre en train de tricher III. *vt* tromper; **to** ~ **sb out of sth** escroquer qn de qc; **to** ~ **the taxman** voler le percepteur des impôts; **to feel** ~**ed** se sentir dupé
◆**cheat on** *vt* **to** ~ **sb with sb** tromper qn avec qn
check [tʃek] I. *n* 1. (*inspection*) vérification *f;* **security** ~ inspection *f* de sécurité; **spot** ~**s** inspections *fpl* ponctuelles; **to have a** ~ **in** [*o* **through**] **sth** passer qc en revue; **to take a quick** ~ jeter un coup d'œil 2. (*search for information*) enquête *f;* **background** ~ investigation *f* de fond; **to run a** ~ **on sb** vérifier les antécédents de qn 3. *Am* (*money order*) chèque *m;* **a** ~ **for ...** un chèque pour la somme de ...; **to make a** ~ **out to sb** écrire un chèque à l'ordre de qn; **to pay by** [*o* **with a**] ~ payer par chèque; *s. a.* **cheque** 4. *Am* (*ticket for deposit*) reçu *m* 5. (*pattern*) carreaux *mpl* 6. *Am* (*intersection*) intersection *f* 7. *Am, Scot* (*bill*) addition *f* 8. GAMES échec *m;* **to be in** ~ être (en) échec II. *adj* (*shirt*) à carreaux III. *vt* 1. (*inspect*) vérifier; **to** ~ **through** [*o* **over**] **sth** passer qc en revue; **to double-**~ **sth** revérifier qc 2. (*control: person, ticket, work*) contrôler 3. (*halt*) faire échec à; (*crisis*) enrayer; (*tears*) refouler 4. (*deposit*) mettre en consigne 5. AVIAT enregistrer 6. GAMES **to** ~ **sb's king** mettre le roi en échec IV. *vi* 1. (*examine*) vérifier; **to** ~ **on sth** vérifier qc; **to** ~ **on sb** examiner qn; **to** ~ **with sb/sth** vérifier auprès de qn/qc 2. (*ask*) demander; **to** ~ **with sb** demander à qn 3. (*halt*) s'arrêter 4. *Am* (*be in accordance with*) **to** ~ **with sth** être en harmonie avec qc
◆**check in** I. *vi* (*at airport*) se présenter à l'enregistrement; (*at hotel*) signer le registre II. *vt* enregistrer
◆**check off** *vt* cocher (sur une liste)
◆**check on** *vt* vérifier
◆**check out** I. *vi* quitter l'hôtel; **to** ~ **of a room** payer la facture d'une chambre d'hôtel II. *vt* 1. (*investigate*) enquêter sur 2. (*verify*) vérifier
◆**check through** *vt* contrôler
◆**check up** *vi* vérifier
checkbook *n Am* carnet *m* de chèques
checked *adj* FASHION à carreaux
checkerboard *n Am* échiquier *m*
checkered *adj Am* 1. (*patterned*) à carreaux 2. (*inconsistent*) irrégulier(-ère)
checkers *n* GAMES jeu *m* de dames
check-in *n* enregistrement *m*
check-in counter, **check-in desk** *n* bureau *m* d'enregistrement
checking *n no pl, Am* vérification *f*
checking account *n Am* compte *m* courant
check-in time *n* heure *f* d'enregistrement
checklist *n* liste *f* de contrôle **checkmate** I. *n no pl* 1. (*in chess*) échec *m* et mat 2. (*defeat*) défaite *f* II. *vt* 1. (*in chess*) mettre en échec 2. (*defeat*) vaincre
checkout *n* caisse *f*
checkout counter *n* caisse *f*
checkpoint *n* point *m* de contrôle **check room** *n Am* 1. (*cloakroom*) vestiaire *m* 2. (*luggage deposit*) consigne *f* **check-up** *n* bilan *m* de santé
Cheddar [ˈtʃedəʳ, *Am:* -ɚ] *n* cheddar *m* (*fromage*)
cheek [tʃiːk] *n* 1. (*face*) joue *f* 2. *no pl* (*impertinence*) culot *m;* **to give sb** ~ être impertinent envers qn ▶**to be** ~ **by jowl with sth** être joue contre joue avec qc; **of all the** ~! quel culot!
cheekbone *n* pommette *f*
cheeky [ˈtʃiːki] <-ier, -iest> *adj* effronté(e)
cheep [tʃiːp] I. *n* 1. (*bird's call*) pépiement *m* 2. (*small noise*) couinement *m;* **to not get a** ~ **out of sb** n'obtenir aucun son de qn II. *vi* pépier
cheer [tʃɪəʳ, *Am:* tʃɪr] I. *n* 1. (*shout*) acclamation *f;* **to give a** ~ acclamer; **three** ~**s for the champion!** trois hourras pour le champion! 2. *no pl* (*joy*) gaieté *f;* **to be of good** ~ être joyeux II. *vi* pousser des acclamations III. *vt* 1. (*applaud*) acclamer 2. (~ *up*) remonter le moral à
◆**cheer on** *vt* encourager
◆**cheer up** I. *vt* (*person*) remonter le moral à; (*room*) égayer II. *vi* reprendre courage; ~! courage!
cheerful *adj* 1. (*happy*) joyeux(-euse); **to be** ~

about sth être gai à propos de qc **2.** (*positive attitude*) optimiste **3.** (*bright*) lumineux(-euse); (*colour*) vif(vive); (*tune*) gai(e) **4.** (*willing*) de bonne grâce

cheerfulness *n no pl* gaieté *f*

cheeriness *n no pl* **1.** (*happiness*) joie *f* **2.** (*brightness*) luminosité *f*

cheering *adj* réjouissant(e)

cheerio [ˌtʃɪərɪ'əʊ, *Am:* ˌtʃɪrɪ'oʊ] *interj Brit, inf* salut!

> Les **Cheerleaders** sont aux USA des jeunes filles qui supportent leur équipe sportive. Elles orchestrent le cri des supporters et divertissent le public par des intermèdes pendant lesquels elles utilisent souvent des "pompons". L'uniforme des "Cheerleaders" se compose le plus souvent d'une robe courte ou d'une jupette avec un chemisier, de soquettes et de chaussures de cuir, le tout aux couleurs de l'école ou de l'équipe.

cheery ['tʃɪəri, *Am:* 'tʃɪr-] <-ier, -iest> *adj* gai(e)

cheese [tʃi:z] *n no pl* fromage *m;* **goat's** ~ fromage de chèvre; **hard** ~ fromage à pâte dure ►**the big** ~ *Am, inf* grand chef *m;* **hard/tough/stiff** ~! *inf* pas de chance!; **say** ~ souriez, le petit oiseau va sortir

cheeseburger *n* hamburger *m* au fromage

cheesecake *n* gâteau *m* au fromage

cheesecloth *n no pl* étamine *f*

cheesed off *adj Brit, Aus, inf* **to be** ~ **with sb** en avoir marre de qn

cheese-paring **I.** *adj* pingre **II.** *n no pl, pej* économies *fpl* de bouts de chandelles

cheesy ['tʃi:zi] *adj* **1.** GASTR (*taste*) qui a un goût de fromage; (*smell*) qui sent le fromage **2.** *inf* (*cheap, inauthentic*) ringard(e); **a** ~ **smile** un large sourire

cheetah ['tʃɪ:tə, *Am:* -t̬ə] *n* guépard *m*

chef [ʃef] *n* chef *m;* **head-**~ chef principal; **pastry** ~ chef pâtissier

chemical ['kemɪkl] **I.** *n* **1.** (*atom*) atome *m* **2.** (*additive*) produit *m* chimique **II.** *adj* chimique

chemist ['kemɪst] *n* **1.** (*pharmacist*) chimiste *mf* **2.** *Brit, Aus* (*pharmacist*) pharmacien(ne) *m(f)*

chemistry ['kemɪstri] *n no pl* **1.** (*study of chemicals*) chimie *f;* **the** ~ **of sth** composition *f* chimique de qc; ~ **laboratory** laboratoire *m* de chimie **2.** *inf* (*attraction*) osmose *f*

chemotherapy [ˌki:mə'θerəpi, *Am:* ˌki:moʊ-] *n no pl* chimiothérapie *f*

cheque [tʃek] *n Brit, Aus s.* **check**

cheque book *n Brit, Aus s.* **checkbook**

cheque guarantee card *n Brit, Aus: carte obligatoire lorsque le paiement s'effectue par chèque*

chequered ['tʃekəd, *Am:* -ɚd] *adj Brit, Aus s.* **checkered**

cherish ['tʃerɪʃ] *vt* **1.** (*protect*) aimer **2.** (*remember fondly*) chérir

cheroot [ʃə'ru:t] *n* cigarillo *m*

cherry ['tʃeri] **I.** <-ries> *n* **1.** (*fruit*) cerise *f* **2.** (*tree*) cerisier *m* ►**life is just a bowl of cherries!** *prov* la vie est belle! **II.** *n* **1.** (*of cherry*) à la cerise **2.** (*made of wood*) en cerisier **3.** (*flavoured*) parfumé(e) à la cerise **4.** (*red*) rouge cerise *inv*

cherry-blossom *n* fleur *f* de cerisier **cherry brandy** *n no pl* liqueur *f* de cerise

cherub ['tʃerəb] <-s *o form* -im> *n* chérubin *m*

chervil ['tʃɜ:vɪl, *Am:* 'tʃɜ:r-] *n no pl* cerfeuil *m*

chess [tʃes] *n no pl* échecs *mpl*

chessboard *n* échiquier *m* **chessman** <-men> *n* pièce *f* d'échiquier

chest [tʃest] *n* **1.** (*part of the torso*) poitrine *f;* **hairy** ~ torse *m* velu **2.** (*breasts*) poitrine *f* **3.** (*trunk*) armoire *f;* **medicine** ~ pharmacie *f* ►**to get sth off one's** ~ se soulager le cœur

chestnut **I.** *n* **1.** (*brown nut*) marron *m;* **horse** ~ châtaigne *f;* **hot** ~ marrons chauds **2.** (*old joke*) *vieille plaisanterie qui a perdu son effet* **3.** (*horse*) alezan *m* **II.** *n* **1.** (*with ~s*) aux marrons **2.** (*colour: eyes*) marron; (*hair*) châtain ►**to pull sb's ~s out of the fire** risquer qc pour qn

chesty ['tʃesti] <-ier, -iest> *adj* de poitrine; **to get** ~ *Brit* souffrir de la poitrine

chew [tʃu:] **I.** *n* **1.** (*bite*) bout *m;* **to have a** ~ **on sth** mordre dans qc **2.** (*candy*) bonbon *m* mou **II.** *vt* mâcher ►**to** ~ **the fat with sb** *inf* bavarder avec qn **III.** *vi* **to** ~ **through sth** arriver à bout de qc

chewing gum ['tʃu:ɪŋgʌm] *n no pl* (*gum*) chewing-gum *m*

chewy ['tʃu:i] *adj* caoutchouteux(-euse)

chic [ʃi:k] **I.** *n* élégance *f* **II.** *adj* élégant(e)

chicane [ʃɪ'kein] *n* route *f* en zigzag

chicanery [ʃɪ'keɪnəri] *n no pl* chicanes *fpl*

chick [tʃɪk] *n* **1.** (*chicken*) poussin *m* **2.** (*bird*) oiselet *m*

chicken ['tʃɪkɪn] *n* poulet *m* ►~ **and egg problem** [*o* **situation**] éternel dilemme de la poule ou l'œuf; **to be a spring** ~ être de première jeunesse

chicken broth *n no pl* bouillon *m* de poule

chicken farm *n* ferme *f* de volaille

chickenfeed *n no pl* **1.** (*what chickens eat*) nourriture *f* pour volailles **2.** (*small amount of money*) broutille *f* **chicken-hearted** *adj* lâche **chickenpox** *n* varicelle *f* **chicken-run** *n* poulailler *m*

chickpea ['tʃɪkpi:] *n* pois *m* chiche

chicory ['tʃɪkəri] *n no pl* **1.** (*vegetable*) endive *f,* chicon *m Belgique* **2.** (*powder*) chicorée *f*

chief [tʃi:f] **I.** *n* chef *m;* **to be** ~ **of sth** être à la tête de qc ►**too many ~s and not enough Indians** *prov* trop de dirigeants et pas assez d'exécutants **II.** *adj* **1.** (*top*) premier(-ère) **2.** (*major*) principal(e)

chief clerk *n* employé *m* de bureau en chef **chief editor** *n* éditeur *m* en chef **chief executive officer** *n* président-directeur *m* général **chief justice** *n Am* ~ **of the Supreme Court** Président *m* de la Cour Suprême

chiefly *adv* principalement

chieftain ['tʃiːftən] *n* chef *mf*

chiffon ['ʃɪfɒn, *Am:* ʃɪ'fɑːn] *n* mousseline *f*

chilblain ['tʃɪlbleɪn] *n* engelure *f*

child [tʃaɪld] <children> *n* enfant *m;* **unborn** ~ enfant à naître; **two-year-old** ~ enfant de deux ans ▸**a flower** ~ hippie *mf;* **you are your mother's/father's** ~ tu tiens de ta mère/de ton père; **children should be seen and not heard** *prov* on devrait pouvoir profiter des enfants sans les désagréments

child abuse *n no pl* mauvais *mpl* traitements à enfants; (*sexual*) sévices *mpl* sexuels **childbearing** *n no pl* grossesse *f* **child benefit** *n* ≈ allocations *fpl* familiales **childbirth** *n no pl* accouchement *m* **childhood** *n no pl* enfance *f*

childish *adj pej* immature

childless *adj* sans enfant

childlike *adj* enfantin(e) **childminder** *n Brit* nourrice *f* **childproof** *adj* sans risque pour les enfants; (*cap*) de sécurité

children ['tʃɪldrən] *n pl of* **child**

child-resistant *adj form* résistant(e) aux enfants **child's play** *n* jeu *m* d'enfant

Chile ['tʃɪli] *n* le Chili

Chilean I. *adj* chilien(ne) II. *n* Chilien(ne) *m(f)*

chili ['tʃɪli] <-es> *n Am s.* **chilli**

chill [tʃɪl] I. *n* 1. (*coldness*) fraîcheur *f;* **to catch a** ~ attraper froid; **to take the** ~ **off of sth** réchauffer qc 2. (*shivering*) frisson *m;* **to send a** ~ **down someone's spine** faire frissonner qn de peur *f* 3. (*cold*) coup *m* de froid 4. *fig* froideur *f;* **to cast a** ~ **over sth** jeter un froid sur qc II. *adj* 1. (*cold*) frais(fraîche) 2. *fig* froid(e); *s. a.* **chilly** III. *vt* 1. (*make cold*) refroidir 2. GASTR mettre au frais 3. *fig* refroidir; **to** ~ **sb to the bone** glacer qn jusqu'au sang 4. (*frighten*) faire frissonner; **to be ~ed by the violence** être horrifié par la violence; **to** ~ **the marrow of sb** paralyser qn de peur IV. *vi* refroidir

chilli ['tʃɪli] <-es> *n* piment *m*

chill(i)ness *n no pl* 1. (*coolness*) fraîcheur *f* 2. *fig* froideur *f*

chilling *adj* 1. (*cold*) *a. fig* glacial(e) 2. (*frightening*) à vous donner la chair de poule

chilly ['tʃɪli] <-ier, -iest> *adj* 1. frais(fraîche); **to feel** ~ avoir froid; **if you feel** ~ **...** si vous avez froid ...; **it's a bit** ~ **out today** il fait un peu froid aujourd'hui 2. (*unwelcoming: relationship*) froid(e)

chime [tʃaɪm] I. *n* carillon *m;* **wind ~s** clochettes *fpl* II. *vt, vi* sonner

chimney ['tʃɪmni] *n* 1. (*pipe*) cheminée *f;* (*of stove*) tuyau *m* 2. (*fire-place*) âtre *m* de cheminée

chimney pot *n* conduit *m* de cheminée **chimney stack** *n Brit* tuyau *m* de cheminée **chimney sweep**, **chimneysweeper** *n* ramoneur *m*

chimpanzee [ˌtʃɪmpæn'ziː, *Am:* tʃɪm'pænziː] *n* chimpanzé *m*

chin ['tʃɪn] *n* menton *m* ▸**to keep one's** ~ **up** garder la tête haute; **to take it on the** ~ accepter sans se plaindre

china ['tʃaɪnə] *n no pl* porcelaine *f*

China ['tʃaɪnə] *n* la Chine

chinchilla [tʃɪn'tʃɪlə] *n* chinchilla *m*

Chinese I. *adj* chinois(e) II. *n* 1. (*person*) Chinois(e) *m(f)* 2. LING chinois *m; s. a.* **English**

Chinese cabbage *n* chou *m* chinois **Chinese lantern** *n* lanterne *f* chinoise **Chinese mushroom** *n* champignon *m* chinois **Chinese restaurant** *n* restaurant *m* chinois

chink [tʃɪŋk] I. *n* 1. (*opening*) déchirure *f* 2. (*noise*) tintement *m* 3. *fig* **a** ~ **in sb's armour** faiblesse *f* dans la carapace de qn II. *vi* tinter

chintz [tʃɪnts] *n no pl* chintz *m*

chip [tʃɪp] I. *n* 1. (*flake*) fragment *m* 2. (*place where piece is missing*) ébréchure *f;* **the cup has got a** ~ **in it** la tasse est ébréchée 3. *pl, Brit* (*deep-fried potato*) pommes frites *fpl,* patates frites *fpl Québec* 4. *pl, Am* (*potato snack*) chips *fpl* 5. INFOR puce *f* électronique; **single** ~ **computer** ordinateur *m* à puce unique 6. (*money token*) jeton *m* ▸**to be a** ~ **off the old block** *inf* tenir de ses ancêtres; **to have a** ~ **on one's shoulder** *inf* être aigri; **when the ~s are down** *Brit, inf* lorsque les ennuis arrivent; **to have had one's ~s** *inf* ne plus valoir grand-chose II. *vt* <-pp-> fragmenter III. *vi* <-pp-> s'ébrécher

chip basket *n Brit* panier *m* de frites **chippan** *n Brit* friteuse *f* **chip stand** *n* baraque *f* à frites, friterie *f,* friture *f Belgique*

chipped ['tʃɪpt] *adj* fragmenté(e); (*tooth*) cassé(e); (*plate*) ébréché(e)

chippings *n Brit* gravillons *mpl*

chippy ['tʃɪpi] *n Brit, inf* (*shop*) friterie *f*

chiropodist [kɪ'rɒpədɪst, *Am:* kɪ'rɑːpə-] *n* podologue *mf*

chiropody [kɪ'rɒpədi, *Am:* kɪ'rɑːpə-] *n no pl* podologie *f*

chiropractic ['kaɪrəpræktɪk, *Am:* ˌkaɪroʊpræktɚ] *n no pl* chiropractie *f*

chiropractor *n* chiropracticien(ne) *m(f)*

chirp [tʃɜːp, *Am:* tʃɜːrp] I. *n* pépiement *m* II. *vi* pépier III. *vt* babiller

chirpy <-ier, -iest> *adj* enthousiaste

chirrup *s.* **chirp**

chisel ['tʃɪzl] I. *n* ciseau *m* II. <-ll- *o Am* -l-> *vt* 1. (*cut*) découper 2. *Am, pej, inf* (*get by trickery*) rouler; **to** ~ **sth out of sb** rouler qn de qc

chit [tʃɪt] *n Brit* 1. (*document*) bulletin *m* 2. (*receipt*) reçu *m*

chit-chat [ˈtʃɪtˌtʃæt] I. *n no pl, inf* bavardage *m* II. *vi inf* bavarder
chivalrous [ˈʃɪvlrəs] *adj* galant(e)
chivalry [ˈʃɪvlri] *n no pl* 1. (*behavior*) galanterie *f* 2. (*knights' code*) chevalerie *f*
chives [tʃaɪvz] *npl* ciboulette *f inv*
chloride [ˈklɔːraɪd] *n no pl* chlorure *m inv*
chlorinate [ˈklɔːrɪneɪt] *vt* chlorer
chlorine [ˈklɔːriːn] *n no pl* chlore *m inv*
chlorofluorocarbon [ˈklɔrəˌfluːərəˌkɑː-bən, *Am:* ˌklɔːroʊˌflɔːroʊˌkɑːr-] *n s.* **CFC**
chloroform [ˈklɒrəfɔːm, *Am:* ˈklɔːrəfɔːrm] I. *n no pl* chloroforme *m inv* II. *vt* chloroformer
chlorophyll [ˈklɒrəfɪl, *Am:* ˈklɔːrə-] *n no pl* chlorophylle *f*
chlorous [ˈklɔːrəs] *adj* chloré(e)
choc ice *n glace enrobée de chocolat*
chock [tʃɒk, *Am:* ˈtʃɑːk] *n* cale *f*
chock-a-block *adj* plein(e) à craquer
chock-full *adj* rempli(e); (*of calories*) plein(e); ~ **of people** bondé
chocolate [ˈtʃɒklət, *Am:* ˈtʃɑːk-] *n* chocolat *m;* **bar of** ~ tablette *f* de chocolat
choice [ˈtʃɔɪs] I. *n* 1. *no pl* (*selection*) choix *m;* **to be of sb's** ~ être choisi par qn; **he has no** ~ **but to ...** il n'a pas d'autre moyen que de... 2. *no pl* (*range*) **a wide** ~ une large sélection 3. (*selection*) option *f* II. *adj* 1. (*top quality*) de choix 2. (*angry*) cinglant(e)
choir [ˈkwaɪəʳ, *Am:* ˈkwaɪɚ] *n* chorale *f;* **church** ~ chœurs *mpl*
choirmaster *n* maître *m* de la chorale **choir stalls** *npl* stalles *fpl* des chœurs
choke [tʃəʊk, *Am:* tʃoʊk] I. *n no pl* starter *m* II. *vi* étouffer; **to** ~ **on sth** s'étouffer avec qc; **to** ~ **to death** mourir étouffé; **to** ~ **with laughter** suffoquer de rire III. *vt* 1. (*deprive of air*) étouffer; **to be ~d with anger** suffoquer de colère 2. (*block*) boucher; (*with leaves*) bloquer
◆**choke back** *vt* retenir; (*tears*) ravaler
◆**choke down** *vt* avaler
◆**choke off** *vt* étouffer
◆**choke up** *vt* 1. (*block*) boucher 2. *fig* **to be choked up** être bouleversé
choked *adj* 1. (*upset*) bouleversé(e); **in a** ~ **voice** d'une voix étouffée 2. (*unhappy*) déçu(e)
choker *n* ras *m* du cou; (*for dogs*) collier *m* de chien
cholera [ˈkɒlərə, *Am:* ˈkɑːlɚ-] *n no pl* choléra *m*
choleric [ˈkɒlərɪk, *Am:* ˈkɑːlɚ-] *adj* coléreux(-euse)
cholesterol [kəˈlestərɒl, *Am:* kəˈlestərɑːl] *n no pl* cholestérol *m*
choose [tʃuːz] <chose, chosen> I. *vt* choisir II. *vi* choisir; **to do as one ~s** faire comme on l'entend ►**little** [*o* **not much**] **to** ~ **between ...** pas beaucoup de choix entre ...
choos(e)y [ˈtʃuːzi] <-ier, -iest> *adj* **to be** ~ **about sth** être difficile quant à qc
chop [tʃɒp, *Am:* tʃɑːp] I. *vt* <-pp-> 1. (*cut*) couper; (*herbs*) hacher; **to** ~ **into pieces** couper en morceaux 2. (*reduce*) réduire II. *vi* <-pp-> **to** ~ **and change** *Brit, Aus* (*change opinion*) être versatile; (*switch jobs*) être instable dans sa vie professionnelle III. *n* 1. (*meat*) côtelette *f* 2. (*blow*) coup *m* 3. *Brit, Aus* **to get the** ~ se faire virer; **to be for the** ~ être bon pour le licenciement
◆**chop down** *vt* abattre
◆**chop off** *vt* trancher
chop-chop *interj inf* vite!
chopper *n* (*tool*) hachette *f*
chopping *n no pl* (*wood*) découpage *m*
choppy [ˈtʃɒpi, *Am:* ˈtʃɑːpi] <-ier, -iest> *adj* NAUT agité(e)
chopsticks *npl* baguettes *fpl*
chop suey [ˌtʃɒpˈsuːi, *Am:* ˌtʃɑːp-] *n* chop suey *m* (*râgout à la chinoise*)
choral [ˈkɔːrəl] *adj* choral(e); ~ **society** chorale *f*
chorale *n* 1. (*composition*) choral *m* 2. (*choir*) chorale *f*
chord [ˈkɔːd, *Am:* ˈkɔːrd] *n* accord *m* ►**it strikes a** ~ **with me** ça me rappelle qc
chore [tʃɔːʳ, *Am:* tʃɔːr] *n* 1. (*task*) travail *m* de routine; **household** ~ tâche *f* ménagère 2. (*tedious task*) corvée *f*
choreograph [ˈkɒriəgrɑːf, *Am:* ˈkɔːriəgræf] *vt* faire la chorégraphie de
choreographer *n* chorégraphe *mf*
choreography [ˌkɒrɪˈɒgrəfi, *Am:* ˌkɔːrɪˈɑːgrə-] *n no pl* chorégraphie *f*
chorister [ˈkɒrɪstəʳ, *Am:* ˈkɔːrɪstɚ] *n* choriste *m*
chorus [ˈkɔːrəs, *Am:* ˈkɔːrəs] I. *n* 1. (*refrain*) refrain *m;* **the dawn** ~ le chant matinal des oiseaux 2. + *sing/pl vb* (*singers*) chœur *m* 3. *sing* (*utterance*) chœur *m* II. *vt* chanter en chœur
chose [tʃəʊz, *Am:* tʃoʊz] *pt of* **choose**
chosen *pp of* **choose**
chow [tʃaʊ] *n* 1. *inf* (*food*) bouffe *f* 2. (*dog*) chow-chow *m*
chowder [ˈtʃaʊdəʳ, *Am:* -dɚ] *n no pl* soupe *f*
Christ [kraɪst] I. *n* Jésus Christ *m* II. *interj inf* bon Dieu!; **for ~'s sake** pour l'amour de Dieu
christen [ˈkrɪsən] *vt* 1. (*baptise*) baptiser 2. (*name*) **to be ~ed after sb** recevoir le nom de qn 3. (*nickname*) surnommer 4. (*use for first time*) étrenner
Christendom *n no pl* HIST chrétienté *f*
christening (**ceremony**) *n* (cérémonie *f* du) baptême *m*
Christian [ˈkrɪstʃən] I. *n* chrétien(ne) *m(f)* II. *adj* chrétien(ne)
Christian burial *n* sépulture *f* en terre sainte
Christian era *n* ère *f* chrétienne
Christianity [ˌkrɪstɪˈænəti, *Am:* -tʃɪˈænət̬i] *n no pl* christianisme *m*
Christianize [ˈkrɪstʃənaɪz] *vt* (*person*) con-

vertir au christianisme; (*area*) christianiser
Christian name *n Brit* nom *m* de baptême
Christmas ['krɪstməs, *Am:* 'krɪs-] <-es *o* -ses> *n no pl, no art* Noël *m;* **at** ~ à (la) Noël; **Happy** [*o* **Merry**] ~ Joyeux Noël

> En Grande-Bretagne et aux Etats-Unis, on envoie dès le début du mois de décembre des **Christmas cards** (des cartes de Noël). Cette tradition date du 19ème siècle.

Christmas carol *n* chant *m* de Noël

> Les **Christmas crackers** (invention britannique datant du milieu du 19ème siècle) sont des rouleaux de papier finement décorés qui contiennent un petit cadeau, une blague et une couronne de papier; le plus souvent, au cours du déjeuner, deux personnes tirent en même temps sur chaque rouleau pour en faire éclater le pétard.

Christmas Day *n* Noël *m*

> Pour le **Christmas Day**, on mange dans la plupart des familles une dinde farcie de chair à saucisse et des pommes de terres sautées accompagnées d'un coulis d'airelles. Le repas se termine par le "Christmas pudding" ou "plum pudding", un gâteau cuit à l'étouffée, garni de raisins de Corinthe, de raisins secs et de raisins de Smyrne.

Christmas Eve *n* soir *m* de Noël

> A **Christmas Eve**, qui n'est pas en Grande-Bretagne un jour férié, avant d'aller au lit, les enfants suspendent des "Christmas stockings" (de grandes chaussettes) ou bien des taies d'oreillers, afin qu'on les remplisse de cadeaux pendant la nuit.

Christmas pudding *n* pudding *m* de Noël
Christmas tree *n* sapin *m* de Noël
Christopher ['krɪstəfəʳ, *Am:* -fɚ] *n* Christophe *m;* ~ **Columbus** Christophe Colomb
chromatic [krəʊ'mætɪk, *Am:* kroʊ'mæt̬ɪk] *adj* chromatique
chrome [krəʊm, *Am:* kroʊm] *adj* chromé(e); ~-**plated** recouvert de chrome
chromosome ['krəʊməsəʊm, *Am:* 'kroʊməsoʊm] *n* chromosome *m*
chronic ['krɒnɪk, *Am:* 'krɑːnɪk] *adj* **1.** (*long-lasting*) chronique **2.** (*having a chronic complaint: alcoholic*) invétéré(e) **3.** (*bad*) insupportable **4.** (*habitual*) **to be** ~ **liars** avoir pour habitude de mentir **5.** *Brit, Aus, inf* (*terrible*) atroce
chronicle ['krɒnɪkl, *Am:* 'krɑːnɪ-] **I.** *vt* faire la chronique de **II.** *n* **1.** (*recording*) chronique *f* **2.** *inf* (*story*) histoire *f* **3.** (*title*) chronique *f*
chronicler *n* chroniqueur, -euse *m, f*
chronological *adj* chronologique
chronology [krə'nɒlədʒi, *Am:* krə'nɑːlə-] *n* **1.** *no pl, no art* (*arrangement*) chronologie *f* **2.** *no pl* (*account*) historique *m*
chrysalis ['krɪsəlɪs] <-es> *n* chrysalide *f*
chrysanthemum [krɪ'sænθəməm] *n* chrysanthème *m*
chubby ['tʃʌbi] <-ier, -iest> *adj* potelé(e); (*child*) dodu(e); (*legs*) grassouillet(te); (*face*) joufflu(e)
chuck [tʃʌk] **I.** *n* **1.** (*touch*) petite tape *f;* **to give sb a** ~ **under the chin** donner une tape amicale sous le menton de qn **2.** (*beef cut*) paleron *m* **II.** *vt* **1.** *inf* (*throw*) jeter **2.** *inf* (*end relationship*) plaquer **3.** (*touch*) **to** ~ **sb under the chin** caresser le menton de qn **4.** *inf* (*stop*) abandonner
◆**chuck away** *vt inf* balancer, foutre bas *Suisse* ▶**to chuck money away** jeter l'argent par les fenêtres
◆**chuck out** *vt* **1.** (*throw away*) jeter **2.** (*make leave*) flanquer à la porte
◆**chuck up** *vi inf* lâcher
chucker-out <chuckers-out> *n Brit, inf* videur, -euse *m, f*
chuckle ['tʃʌkl] **I.** *n* gloussement *m;* **to give a** ~ lâcher un petit rire **II.** *vi* glousser; **I** ~ **at myself** je ris de moi-même
chug [tʃʌg] **I.** <-gg-> *vi* souffler **II.** *n* souffle *m; childspeak* (*of a train*) tchou-tchou *m*
chum [tʃʌm] *n inf* copain *m,* copine *f*
chum around, **chum up** <-mm-> *vi Brit, inf* sympathiser
chummy ['tʃʌmi] <-ier, -iest> *adj* **1.** *inf* (*friendly*) amical(e); **to get** ~ **with sb** devenir bon copain avec qn **2.** *pej, inf* (*intimate*) intime
chump [tʃʌmp] *n Brit, inf* cinglé(e) *m(f)* ▶**to go off one's** ~ être maboul
chunk [tʃʌŋk] *n* **1.** (*piece: of food*) gros morceau *m;* (*of stone*) bloc *m* **2.** *inf* (*large part*) grosse partie *f*
chunky ['tʃʌŋki] <-ier, -iest> *adj* **1.** (*thick*) épais(se); ~ **clothes** gros lainage *m,* grosse laine *f* **2.** (*thick-cut: jam*) avec des gros morceaux de fruits **3.** (*stocky*) massif(-ive); **to be** ~ être trapu
Chunnel ['tʃʌnl] *n inf* **the** ~ le tunnel sous la Manche
church [tʃɜːtʃ, *Am:* tʃɜːrtʃ] **I.** *n* **1.** (*building*) église *f;* (*for protestants*) temple *m* **2.** *no pl* (*organization*) Église *f;* **the Anglican Church** l'Eglise *f* anglicane; **to enter the** ~ entrer dans les ordres **3.** *no pl* (*service*) office *m* **II.** *adj* **as poor as a** ~ **mouse** pauvre comme Job
churchgoer *n* pratiquant(e) *m(f)* **churchwarden** *n* **1.** *Brit* (*official*) marguillier *m;* *Am* (*administrator*) fabricien *m* **2.** *Brit* (*clay pipe*) longue pipe en terre blanche **churchyard** *n* cimetière *m* situé autour d'une église
churlish ['tʃɜːlɪʃ, *Am:* 'tʃɜːr-] *adj pej* grossier(-ère)

churn [tʃɜːn, *Am:* tʃɜːrn] **I.** *n* (*for milk*) bidon *m;* (*for butter*) baratte *f* **II.** *vt* **1.** (*stir: butter, cream*) battre **2.** (*agitate*) agiter **III.** *vi* **1.** (*move vigorously*) s'agiter **2.** *fig* (*stomach*) se nouer

◆**churn up** *vt a. fig* retourner; **my emotions are churning up** je suis en effervescence

chute [ʃuːt] *n* **1.** (*tube*) glissière *f;* **rubbish** *Brit* [*o Am* **garbage**] ~ vide-ordures *m* **2.** AVIAT **emergency** ~ toboggan *m* d'évacuation **3.** *s.* **parachute**

chutney ['tʃʌtni] *n condiment en sauce fait à partir de fruits*

CIA [ˌsiːaɪ'eɪ] *n Am abbr of* **Central Intelligence Agency** CIA *f*

Cid *n* **El** ~ Le Cid

CID [ˌsiːaɪ'diː] *n Brit abbr of* **Criminal Investigation Department** police *f* criminelle

cider ['saɪdəʳ, *Am:* -dɚ] *n no pl, no art* **1.** (*alcoholic drink*) cidre *m* **2.** *Am* jus *m* de pommes

cider press *n* pressoir *m* à cidre **cider vinegar** *n* vinaigre *m* de cidre

cigar [sɪ'gɑːʳ, *Am:* -gɑːr] *n* cigare *m*

cigarbox *n* boîte *f* à cigares **cigarcase** *n* étui *m* à cigares **cigar cutter** *n* coupe-cigares *m*

cigarette [ˌsɪgə'ret] *n* cigarette *f;* **to drag on/at a** ~ tirer des bouffées d'une cigarette

cigarette case *n* porte-cigarettes *m* **cigarette end** *n* mégot *m* **cigarette holder** *n* fume-cigarette *m* **cigarette paper** *n* papier *m* à cigarettes

cigarillo [sɪgə'rɪləʊ, *Am:* -oʊ] *n* cigarillo *m*

cinch [sɪntʃ] *n inf* jeu *m* d'enfant

cinder ['sɪndəʳ, *Am:* -dɚ] *n* cendre *f*

Cinderella [ˌsɪndə'relə] *n* Cendrillon *f*

cine-camera ['sɪniˌkæmərə] *n* caméra *f*

cine film *n* film *m*

cinema ['sɪnəmə] *n* cinéma *m;* **a** ~ **ticket/seat** un ticket/siège de cinéma

cinema-goer *n* cinéphile *mf*

Cinemascope® *n* cinémascope® *m*

cinematic [ˌsɪnə'mætɪk, *Am:* -'mæt̬-] *adj* cinématique

cine-projector *n* projecteur *m* de cinéma

cinnamon ['sɪnəmən] *n no pl, no art* cannelle *f;* **a** ~ **stick** un bâton de cannelle

cipher *n* **1.** (*code*) chiffre *m;* **in** ~ codé(e) **2.** (*message*) message *m* codé **3.** *fig* nullité *f;* **to be a mere** ~ être un zéro; **this gadget is a** ~ ce gadget est nul

cipher code *n no pl, no art* code *m* secret

circa ['sɜːkə, *Am:* 'sɜːr-] *prep* environ; (*date*) vers

circle ['sɜːkl, *Am:* 'sɜːr-] **I.** *n* **1.** (*round*) cercle *m;* **to go round in ~s** faire des cercles **2.** (*group*) cercle *m* **3.** (*professionals*) milieu *m;* **to move in exalted ~s** fréquenter la haute société **4.** *no pl* (*in auditorium*) balcon *m;* **in the** ~ au balcon **5.** (*under eyes*) cernes *fpl;* **to come full** ~ revenir au point de départ; **to run/go round in ~s** tourner en rond; **to square the** ~ arrondir les angles; **a vicious** ~ un cercle vicieux **II.** *vt* **1.** (*move round*) tourner autour de **2.** (*surround*) entourer **III.** *vi* tourner

circuit ['sɜːkɪt, *Am:* 'sɜːr-] *n* circuit *m*

circuit breaker *n* disjoncteur *m* **circuit diagram** *n* ELEC schéma *m* d'un circuit électrique ou électronique

circuitous [sɜː'kjuːɪtəs, *Am:* sɚ'kjuːət̬əs] *adj* détourné(e) ►**he always uses** ~ **explanations** ses explications ne vont jamais droit au but; **by** ~ **means** par des moyens détournés

circular ['sɜːkjʊləʳ, *Am:* 'sɜːrkjəlɚ] **I.** *adj* circulaire **II.** *n* circulaire *f;* (*for advertisement*) prospectus *m*

circular letter *n* circulaire *f* **circular saw** *n* scie *f* circulaire **circular ticket** *n* billet *m* circulaire **circular tour**, **circular trip** *n* circuit *m*

circulate ['sɜːkjʊleɪt, *Am:* 'sɜːrkjə-] **I.** *vt* faire circuler; (*card*) mettre en circulation **II.** *vi* circuler

circulating library *n* bibliothèque *f* ambulante

circulation *n no pl* **1.** (*bloodflow*) circulation *f* sanguine **2.** (*copies sold*) tirage *m* **3.** (*currency*) circulation *f;* **to be out of** ~ *inf* ne plus être en circulation

circulatory [ˌsɜːkjʊ'leɪtəri, *Am:* 'sɜːrkjələtɔːri] *adj* circulatoire

circumcise ['sɜːkəmsaɪz, *Am:* 'sɜːr-] *vt* circoncire

circumcision *n* circoncision *f*

circumference [sə'kʌmfərəns, *Am:* sɚ-] *n* circonférence *f;* **in** ~ de circonférence

circumlocution [ˌsɜːkəmlə'kjuːʃən, *Am:* ˌsɜːr-] *n form no pl* circonlocution *f;* **he always speaks with** ~ il tourne toujours autour du pot quand il parle; **let me tell you without** ~ **that ...** permettez-moi de vous dire sans détours que ...

circumnavigate [ˌsɜːkəm'nævɪgeɪt, *Am:* ˌsɜːr-] *vt* **1.** *form* (*sail around*) naviguer autour de; (*by yacht*) contourner **2.** (*move around*) faire le tour de **3.** (*avoid*) éviter

circumnavigation *n form* circumnavigation *f*

circumscribe ['sɜːkəmskraɪb, *Am:* 'sɜːr-] *vt form* circonscrire

circumscription [ˌsɜːkəm'skrɪpʃən, *Am:* ˌsɜːr-] *n no pl* circonscription *f*

circumspect ['sɜːkəmspekt, *Am:* 'sɜːr-] *adj form* circonspect(e)

circumstance ['sɜːkəmstəns, *Am:* 'sɜːrkəmstæns] *n* **1.** (*situation*) circonstance *f;* **in any ~s** en toutes circonstances; **in no ~s** en aucun cas; **due to ~s beyond our control** dû à des circonstances indépendantes de notre volonté; **in the ~s** dans ces conditions **2.** (*fact*) **by force of** ~ par la force des choses; **regardless of** ~ sans tenir compte de la situation; **nothing of** ~ sans aucune importance; **to live in straitened ~s** vivre dans la gêne

circumstantial *adj* circonstanciel(le)
circumvent [ˌsɜːkəm'vent, *Am:* ˌsɜːr-] *vt form* circonvenir; (*regulations*) contourner
circus ['sɜːkəs, *Am:* 'sɜːr-] *n* **1.** (*show*) cirque *m;* **the travelling** ~ le cirque forain; **a ~ ring** une piste de cirque **2.** *pej* cirque *m;* **it's a ~ here!** c'est le cirque ici! **3.** *Brit* (*roundabout*) rond-point *m*
cirrhosis [sɪ'rəʊsɪs, *Am:* sə'roʊ-] *n* cirrhose *f*
cirrus ['sɪrəs] *n* cirrus *m*
CIS [ˌsiːaɪ'es] *n abbr of* **Commonwealth of Independent States** CEI *f*
cissy ['sɪsi] *n inf s.* **sissy**
cistern ['sɪstən, *Am:* -tɚn] *n* citerne *f;* (*of toilet*) chasse d'eau *f*
citadel ['sɪtədəl, *Am:* 'sɪţ-] *n* **1.** (*fortress*) citadelle *f* **2.** (*organization*) empire *m*
citation [saɪ'teɪʃən] *n* citation *f*
cite [saɪt] *vt* citer
citizen ['sɪtɪzn, *Am:* 'sɪţ-] *n* **1.** (*national*) citoyen(ne) *m(f);* **British** ~ sujet *m* britannique **2.** (*resident*) habitant(e) *m(f)*
Citizens' Band *n s.* **CB** CB *f* (*fréquences d'onde radio autorisées pour la communication radio aux Etats-Unis*)
citizenship *n no pl* citoyenneté *f;* **to apply for ~ of a country** demander la nationalité d'un pays; **joint** ~ double nationalité *m;* **good** ~ civisme
citric ['sɪtrɪk] *adj* citrique
citrus ['sɪtrəs] <citrus *o* citruses> *n* agrume *m*
citrus fruit *n* agrume *m*
city ['sɪti, *Am:* 'sɪţ-] <-ies> **I.** *n* **1.** (*town*) ville *f;* **capital** ~ capitale *f* **2.** *Aus* (*centre of capital*) **the** ~ le centre **II.** *adj* urbain(e); (*life*) citadin(e)

> De nombreuses **cities** américaines ont des surnoms. "New York" s'appelle "Gotham" ou "The Big Apple". Par analogie à ce dernier surnom, certains appellent "Los Angeles" "The Big Orange", mais d'autres lui préfèrent le surnom de "The City of the Angels". "Chicago", elle, est dénommée "The Windy City". "The City of Brotherly Love" désigne la ville de "Philadelphia". "Denver" porte le surnom de "The Mile-High city" à cause de son altitude et "Detroit" est dénommée "Motor City" à cause de son industrie automobile.

city father *n* élu *m* local **city hall** *n Am* municipalité *f;* **City Hall** *Am* Hôtel *m* de Ville **city planner** *n* urbaniste *mf*
civic ['sɪvɪk] <inv> *adj* civique; (*building, authorities*) municipal(e); (*centre*) administratif(-ive)
civies ['sɪviz] *n pl s.* **civvies**
civil ['sɪvl] *adj* **1.** <inv> (*of citizens*) civil(e) **2.** (*courteous*) poli(e)
civil action *n* action *f* civile **civil court** *n* tribunal *m* civil **civil defence** *n* protection *f* civile **civil disobedience** *n* désobéissance *f* civile **civil engineer** *n* ingénieur *m* des travaux publics
civilian [sɪ'vɪliən, *Am:* -jən] <inv> **I.** *n* civil *m* **II.** *adj* civil(e); **in ~ life** dans le civil
civility [sɪ'vɪləti, *Am:* -ţi] <-ies> *n* **1.** *no pl* (*politeness*) courtoisie *f* **2.** (*remarks*) politesse *f*
civilization *n* civilisation *f*
civilize ['sɪvəlaɪz] *vt* civiliser
civilized *adj* civilisé(e)
civil law *n* droit *m* civil; **this question is about** ~ cette question concerne le code civil **civil liberties** *n* libertés *fpl* civiques **civil marriage** *n* mariage *m* civil **civil population** *n* population *f* civile **civil rights** *npl* droits *mpl* civils **civil rights movement** *n* mouvement *m* des droits civils **civil servant** *n* fonctionnaire *mf* **civil service** *n* fonction *f* publique

> Le **civil service** en Grande Bretagne est rattaché au centre administratif du pays; il est constitué du service diplomatique, du "Inland Revenue" (service de perception des impôts), du service social et de la santé ainsi que de nombreux établissements publics de formation. Les "civil servants" (fonctionnaires) ont des emplois fixes et ne sont pas touchés par les changements de gouvernement.

civil war *n* guerre *f* civile
civvies ['sɪvɪz] *npl inf* vêtements *mpl* civils; **in** ~ en civil
ckw. *adj, adv abbr of* **clockwise** dans le sens des aiguilles d'une montre
clack [klæk] **I.** *vi* claquer **II.** *n* claquement *m*
claim [kleɪm] **I.** *n* **1.** (*demand*) revendication *f;* **to substantiate a** ~ prouver le bien-fondé d'une affirmation; **to make wild ~s about sth** faire des revendications extravagantes à propos de qc; **to make no ~ to be sth** n'avoir aucune prétention à être qc; **a ~ to fame** une chose notable **2.** (*money demand*) réclamation *f;* (*for welfare benefit*) demande *f* d'allocation; (*for refund*) demande *f* de remboursement; **to make a ~ on one's insurance** réclamer des dommages à son assurance; **to put in a** ~ faire valoir ses droits **3.** (*assertion*) déclaration *f;* **his ~ to have sth** sa déclaration selon laquelle il possède qc **4.** (*right*) droit *m;* **to have no ~s on sb** ne pas avoir prise sur qn; **to lay ~ to sth** prétendre à qc **II.** *vt* **1.** (*demand*) revendiquer; **to ~ that ...** déclarer que ...; **to ~ responsibility for an explosion** revendiquer un attentat **2.** (*assert*) prétendre; **to ~ to be sth** prétendre être qc **3.** (*declare: immunity*) réclamer; (*title, throne*) revendiquer; **to ~ ownership of a property** se déclarer propriétaire d'un bien **4.** (*require*) demander; (*time*) prendre **5.** (*collect: luggage*) récupérer **6.** (*cause sb's death*) **to ~ sb's life** causer la mort de qn ►**to ~ the moral high ground** prétendre être d'une moralité irréprochable

III. *vi* **to ~ for sth** faire une demande de qc; **to ~ for welfare benefit** faire une demande d'allocation; **to ~ for damages** faire une demande de dommages et intérêts; **to ~ on the insurance** demander à être indemnisé

claimant ['kleɪmənt] *n* (*for unemployment benefit*) demandeur, -resse *m, f;* (*to a title, throne*) prétendant(e) *m(f)*

clairvoyance *n no art, no pl* voyance *f*

clairvoyant [ˌkleə'vɔɪən, *Am:* ˌkler-] **I.** *n* voyant(e) *m(f)* **II.** *adj* clairvoyant(e)

clam [klæm] *n* palourde *f,* clam *m;* **~ chowder** soupe *f* aux praires ►**to shut up like a ~** refuser de dire quoi que ce soit (*subj*)

◆**clam up** <-mm-> *vi* se taire

clamber ['klæmbəʳ, *Am:* -bɚ] **I.** *vi* grimper; **to ~ over sth** escalader qc; **to ~ up sth** gravir qc **II.** *n* grimpette *f*

clammy ['klæmi] <-ier, -iest> *adj* froid(e) et moite

clamor ['klæmɚ] *n Am s.* **clamour**

clamorous *adj* **1.** (*vociferous*) vociférant(e) **2.** (*loud*) bruyant(e)

clamour ['klæməʳ, *Am:* -ɚ] **I.** *vi* **1.** (*demand*) **to ~ for sth** réclamer qc à grands cris; **to ~ to do sth** réclamer à faire qc à cor et à cri **2.** (*protest*) vociférer; **to ~ against sth** vociférer contre qc **II.** *n* **1.** (*demands*) revendications *fpl* **2.** (*complaint*) tollé *m;* **to let out a ~ about injustice** hurler à l'injustice **3.** (*noise*) clameur *f*

clamp [klæmp] **I.** *n* **1.** (*fastener*) agrafe *f;* ELEC attache *f* **2.** AUTO sabot *m* de Denver **II.** *vt* **1.** (*fasten*) fixer **2.** (*clench*) serrer; (*handcuffs*) resserrer **3.** AUTO mettre un sabot à

◆**clamp down I.** *vi* **to ~ on sth** sévir contre qc **II.** *vt* fixer

clan [klæn] *n + sing/pl vb, Scot* clan *m*

clandestine [klæn'destɪn] *adj form* clandestin(e); (*affair*) secret(-ète)

clang [klæŋ] **I.** *vi* émettre un bruit **II.** *vt* **1.** (*ring: bell*) faire résonner **2.** (*close*) fermer en faisant du bruit **III.** *n sing* bruit *m* retentissant

clanger *n Brit, inf* **to drop a ~** faire une bourde

clangor *n Am,* **clangour** ['klæŋəʳ, *Am:* -ɚ] *n no pl* bruit *m* métallique

clank [klæŋk] **I.** *vi* cliqueter **II.** *vt* faire cliqueter **III.** *n sing* cliquetis *m*

clap [klæp] **I.** <-pp-> *vt* **1.** (*hit*) taper; **to ~ one's hands** (**together**) frapper dans ses mains; (*applaud*) applaudir **2.** (*applaud*) applaudir **3.** (*place*) jeter; (*a lid*) remettre **II.** <-pp-> *vi* **1.** (*slap palms together*) frapper des mains **2.** (*applaud*) applaudir **III.** *n* **1.** (*act of clapping*) claquement *m;* **to give sb a ~** donner une tape amicale à qn **2.** (*noise: of thunder*) coup *m*

clapped-out *adj Brit, Aus, inf* (*old*) crevé(e)

clapper *n* battant *m*

claptrap *n no pl, pej, inf* baratin *m*

claret ['klærət, *Am:* 'kler-] *n* **1.** (*wine*) bordeaux *m* rouge **2.** (*colour*) bordeaux *m*

clarification *n no pl* (*explanation*) éclaircissement *m*

clarify ['klærɪfaɪ, *Am:* 'kler-] <-ie-> **I.** *vt* **1.** (*make clearer*) clarifier **2.** (*explain: sb's mind, opinion*) éclaircir; (*question*) élucider **3.** (*skim*) clarifier **II.** *vi* se clarifier

clarinet [ˌklærɪ'net, *Am:* ˌkler-] *n* clarinette *f*

clarity ['klærəti, *Am:* 'klerət̬i] *n no pl* clarté *f;* (*of a photo*) netteté *f;* **~ of thought** lucidité *f*

clash [klæʃ] **I.** *vi* **1.** (*fight, argue*) s'affronter; **to ~ over sth** se disputer pour qc; **to ~ with sb/sth** se heurter à qn/qc **2.** (*compete*) s'opposer **3.** (*contradict*) être incompatible; **to ~ with sth** être en contradiction avec qc **4.** (*not match*) être opposé; **this color ~es with the rest of the painting** cette couleur ne va pas très bien avec le reste du tableau **5.** *Brit, Aus* (*coincide*) tomber en même temps **6.** (*make harsh noise*) résonner bruyamment **II.** *vt* **to ~ sth together** faire résonner qc **III.** *n* **1.** (*hostile encounter*) affrontement *m* **2.** (*argument*) querelle *f* **3.** (*contest*) opposition *f* **4.** (*conflict*) conflit *m* **5.** (*incompatibility*) incompatibilité *f* **6.** (*harsh noise*) fracas *m*

clasp [klɑːsp, *Am:* klæsp] **I.** *n* **1.** (*grip*) serrement *m* **2.** (*device*) agrafe *f;* **~ of sth** fermeture *f* de qc **II.** *vt* étreindre; **to ~ one's hands** joindre les mains; **to ~ sb/sth in one's arms** serrer qn/qc dans ses bras

clasp knife *n* canif *m*

class [klɑːs, *Am:* klæs] **I.** *n* **1.** (*student group*) classe *f* **2.** (*lesson*) cours *m* **3.** *Am* UNIV (*graduates*) promotion *f* **4.** (*quality*) **the middle/working ~** la classe moyenne/ouvrière; **the upper ~** la haute société **5.** (*grade*) classe *f;* **to send sth first/second ~** envoyer qc en première/seconde classe **6.** *Brit, Aus* (*type of degree*) mention *f;* **a first ~ honours degree** une licence avec mention très bien ►**to be in a ~ of one's own** être le meilleur dans sa catégorie; **to be out of sb's ~** ne pas être aussi bon que qn **II.** <inv> *adj* de classe; **a world-~ champion** un champion hors pair **III.** *vt* classer; **to ~ sb as sth** considérer qn à qc

class-conscious *adj* conscient(e) des distinctions sociales **class distinctions** *npl* distinction *f* entre les classes

classic ['klæsɪk] **I.** *adj* **1.** (*of excellence*) classique; **his novel is ~ now** son roman est un classique **2.** (*traditional*) traditionnel(le) **3.** (*typical*) typique **4.** *inf* (*foolish*) **how ~!** que c'est stupide! **II.** *n* classique *m*

classical *adj* classique

classically *adv* classiquement

Classicism *n no pl* classicisme *m*

classicist ['klæsɪsɪst] *n* **1.** (*follower of Classicism*) partisan(ne) *m(f)* de la tradition classique **2.** (*expert*) spécialiste *mf* de l'Antiquité

classics *n* **1.** *pl* (*great literature*) grands classiques *mpl* **2.** *no pl* (*Greek and Roman*

studies) lettres *fpl* classiques
classification [ˌklæsɪfɪ'keɪʃən, *Am:* ˌklæsə-] *n* **1.** *no pl, no art* (*categorisation*) classification *f* **2.** (*group*) classe *f*
classified <inv> *adj* classé(e); **the ~ advertisements** les petites annonces
classify ['klæsɪfaɪ] <-ie-> *vt* classer
classless *adj* sans classe
classmate *n* camarade *mf* de classe **classroom** *n* salle *f* de classe **class struggle**, **class war** *n Brit* lutte *f* des classes
classy ['klɑːsi, *Am:* 'klæsi] <-ier, -iest> *adj* qui a de la classe
clatter ['klætəʳ, *Am:* 'klæt̬ɚ] **I.** *vt* entrechoquer bruyamment **II.** *vi* **1.** (*rattle*) cliqueter **2.** (*walk*) marcher bruyamment **III.** *n* fracas *m*
clause [klɔːz, *Am:* klɑːz] *n* **1.** (*part of sentence*) proposition *f* **2.** (*statement in law*) clause *f*
claustrophobia [ˌklɔːstrə'fəʊbɪə, *Am:* ˌklɑːstrə'foʊ-] *n* claustrophobie *f*
claustrophobic *adj* claustrophobe
clavicle ['klævɪkl] *n* clavicule *f*
claw [klɔː, *Am:* klɑː] **I.** *n* **1.** (*nail*) griffe *f*; **to sharpen one's ~s** faire ses griffes **2.** (*pincer*) pince *f* ▶**to get one's ~s into sb/sth** *inf* tenir qn entre ses griffes **II.** *vt* griffer
clay [kleɪ] **I.** *n no pl* **1.** (*earth*) terre *f* glaise; (*for pottery*) argile *f*; **modelling ~** pâte *f* à modeler **2.** SPORT terre *f* battue **II.** *adj* **1.** (*of earth*) d'argile **2.** SPORT en terre battue
clay pigeon *n* pigeon *m* d'argile
clean [kliːn] **I.** *adj* **1.** (*free of dirt*) *a. fig* propre; **spotlessly ~** impeccable; (**as**) **~ as a new pin** propre comme un sou neuf; **to keep one's house ~** tenir sa maison propre **2.** (*with no pollution: fuel*) propre; (*air*) pur(e) **3.** (*fair: fight*) dans les règles **4.** (*moral: life*) sain(e); (*joke*) décent(e) **5.** (*clear, sharp*) net(te); **a ~ design** une belle coupe **6.** *inf* (*straight*) clean *inv* **7.** (*blank: sheet of paper, record*) vierge **8.** (*complete*) définitif(-ive); **to make a ~ sweep of sth** remporter qc; **to make a ~ break** rompre une bonne fois pour toute ▶**to make a ~ breast of sth** dire ce qu'on a sur sa conscience à propos de qc; **to show a ~ pair of heels** *inf* prendre ses jambes à son coup **II.** *n* nettoyage *m*, appropriation *f Belgique*; **to give sth a ~** nettoyer qc, approprier qc *Belgique*, poutser qc *Suisse* **III.** *adv* <inv> complètement; **to ~ forget that ...** bel et bien oublier que ... ▶**a new broom sweeps ~** tout nouveau tout beau **IV.** *vt* **1.** (*remove dirt*) nettoyer, approprier *Belgique*, poutser *Suisse*; **to ~ sth from** [*o* **off**] **sth** enlever qc de qc; **to ~ one's teeth** se brosser les dents; **to ~ one's hands** se laver les mains **2.** (*wash and gut: fish*) vider **V.** *vi* **1.** (*wash*) nettoyer **2.** (*can be washed*) se nettoyer **3.** (*do the cleaning*) faire le ménage
◆**clean out** *vt* **1.** (*clean*) nettoyer à fond **2.** *inf* (*leave penniless: person*) faucher **3.** *inf* (*take all: house*) dévaliser
◆**clean up** **I.** *vt* **1.** (*make clean*) *a. fig* nettoyer; **to clean oneself up** se laver **2.** (*tidy up*) *a. fig* mettre de l'ordre dans **II.** *vi* **1.** (*make clean*) *a. fig* nettoyer **2.** (*tidy*) remettre tout en ordre **3.** (*remove dirt from oneself*) se laver **4.** *Am, inf* (*make profit*) rapporter gros **5.** SPORT raffler tous les prix
clean-cut *adj* **1.** (*sharply outlined*) net(te) **2.** (*neat*) à l'allure soignée
cleaner *n* **1.** (*person*) agent *m* de service; (*woman*) femme *f* de ménage **2.** *no pl* (*substance*) produit *m* d'entretien
cleaning **I.** *n no pl* nettoyage *m*, appropriation *f Belgique*; **to do the ~** faire le ménage **II.** *adj* de ménage
cleaning lady, **cleaning woman** <women> *n* femme *f* de ménage
cleanliness *n no pl* propreté *f*
cleanly *adv* **1.** (*neatly*) de façon bien nette **2.** (*honestly*) dans les règles
cleanse ['klenz] *vt* **1.** (*clean*) nettoyer, approprier *Belgique*, poutser *Suisse* **2.** (*lawful*) purifier
cleanser *n* **1.** (*substance*) détergent *m* **2.** *no pl* (*make-up remover*) démaquillant *m*
clean-shaven *adj* rasé(e) de près
cleansing cream *n no pl, no art* lotion *f* démaquillante
clean-up *n* **1.** (*clean*) nettoyage *m*, appropriation *f Belgique* **2.** (*making legal*) épuration *f* **3.** *no pl, Am* (*profit*) **he made a good ~ from that business** cette affaire lui a rapporté gros
clear [klɪəʳ, *Am:* klɪr] **I.** *adj* **1.** (*understandable*) clair(e); **to make oneself ~** bien se faire comprendre; **to make sth ~ to sb** bien faire comprendre qc à qn; **do I make myself ~?** me suis-je bien fait comprendre?; **as ~ as a bell** parfaitement clair; **let's get this ~** que les choses soient claires *subj*; **as ~ as day** clair comme de l'eau de roche **2.** (*sure, obvious*) clair(e); (*lead, majority, advantage*) net(te); **to be ~ about sth** être sûr de qc **3.** (*free from confusion*) clair(e); (*person*) lucide; **to have a ~ head** avoir les idées claires **4.** (*free from guilt*) **to have a ~ conscience** avoir la conscience tranquille **5.** (*empty*) dégagé(e); **on a ~ day** par temps clair **6.** (*transparent*) transparent(e) **7.** (*pure: skin*) net(te); (*sound*) cristallin(e); (*water*) limpide **8.** (*cloudless*) dégagé(e) **9.** <inv> (*distinct*) net(te); (*voice*) clair(e) **10.** (*free*) libre; **to be ~ of sth** être débarrassé de qc **11.** (*net: profit*) net(te) **12.** <inv> (*not touching*) **to be ~ of sth** ne pas toucher à qc; **to keep ~ of sb/sth** rester à l'écart de qn/qc **II.** *n* **to be in the ~** être au-dessus de tout soupçon **III.** *adv* **to move/get ~ of sth** s'éloigner de qc; **to stand ~ of sth** s'éloigner de qc; **stand ~ of sth!** attention à qc! **IV.** *vt* **1.** (*remove blockage: road, area*) dégager; **to ~ one's throat** s'éclaircir la voix; **to ~ the way to sth** *fig* ouvrir la voie à qc **2.** (*remove doubts*) clarifier; **to ~ one's head** s'éclaircir les idées **3.** (*acquit*) disculper; **to ~ one's**

C

name blanchir son nom; **to ~ a debt** s'acquitter d'une dette **4.** (*empty: drawer, building*) vider; (*table, room*) débarrasser **5.** (*disperse: crowd*) disperser; (*fog, smoke*) dissiper **6.** (*clean*) nettoyer; **to ~ the air** aérer; *fig* détendre l'atmosphère **7.** (*give permission*) approuver; **to ~ sth with sb** avoir l'accord de qn; **to ~ sb to do sth** donner le feu vert à qn; **to ~ customs** dédouaner **8.** SPORT (*ball*) dégager **9.** (*jump over*) franchir **10.** INFOR effacer ►**to ~ the decks** déblayer le terrain **V.** *vi* **1.** (*become transparent*) *a. fig* (*weather, face*) s'éclaircir **2.** (*disappear: fog, smoke*) se dissiper **3.** FIN être viré

◆**clear away** **I.** *vt* débarrasser **II.** *vi* se dissiper

◆**clear off** **I.** *vi inf* filer **II.** *vt* retirer

◆**clear out** **I.** *vt* **1.** (*empty*) vider **2.** (*tidy*) ranger **II.** *vi inf* filer; **to ~ of somewhere** évacuer les lieux

◆**clear up** **I.** *vt* **1.** (*tidy*) ranger **2.** (*resolve*) dissiper **II.** *vi* **1.** (*tidy*) ranger; **to ~ after sb** passer derrière qn **2.** (*go away*) disparaître **3.** (*stop raining*) s'éclaircir

clearance ['klɪərəns, *Am:* 'klɪr-] *n no pl* **1.** (*act of clearing*) dégagement *m* **2.** (*space*) espace *m* libre **3.** (*approval of bank cheque*) compensation *f* **4.** (*permission*) autorisation *f*

clearance sale *n* liquidation *f*

◆**clear-cut** *vt*, **clear-fell** *vt* couper net

clear-headed *adj* **to be ~** avoir les idées claires

clearing *n* clairière *f*

clearing bank *n Brit* banque *f* de compensation **clearing house** *n Brit* maison *f* de compensation **clearing office** *n Brit* bureau *m* de compensation

clearly *adv* **1.** (*distinctly*) clairement **2.** (*well*) distinctement **3.** (*obviously*) manifestement **4.** (*unambiguously*) explicitement

clearness *n* clarté *f*

clear-sighted *adj* lucide

cleavage ['kli:vɪdʒ] *n* **1.** *no pl* (*between breasts*) décolleté *m* **2.** *form* (*split*) division *f*

cleave [kli:v] <*pt, pp* -ed, -ed *o* cleft, cleft *o Am* clove, cloven> *vt* fendre

cleaver *n* hachoir *m*

clef [klef] *n* clé *f*

cleft [kleft] **I.** <inv> *adj* fendu(e) ►**to be caught in a ~ stick** être dans une impasse **II.** *n* fissure *f*

clematis ['klemətɪs, *Am:* 'klemət̬əs] <clematis> *n* clématite *f*

clemency ['klemənsi] *n no pl, form* clémence *f*

clement ['klemənt] *adj form* clément(e)

clench [klentʃ] *vt* serrer dans les mains; **to ~ one's fist** serrer les poings

Cleopatra [ˌkliə'pætrə, *Am:* ˌklioʊpætrə] *n* Cléopâtre *f*

clergy ['klɜ:dʒi, *Am:* 'klɜ:r-] *n + pl vb* clergé *m*

clergyman <-men> *n* ecclésiastique *m*

clergywoman <-women> *n* femme *f* pasteur

cleric ['klerɪk] *n* ecclésiastique *m*

clerical <inv> *adj* **1.** (*clergy*) clérical(e) **2.** (*offices*) administratif(-ive)

clerical error *n* erreur *f* d'écriture **clerical staff** *n* personnel *m* de bureau **clerical work** *n* travail *m* administratif

clerk [klɑ:k, *Am:* klɜ:rk] **I.** *n Am* (*receptionist*) réceptionniste *mf;* **sales ~** vendeur, -euse *m, f* **II.** *vi* travailler comme employé(e) de bureau

clever ['klevəʳ, *Am:* -ɚ] *adj* **1.** (*intelligent*) intelligent(e) **2.** (*skilful*) habile; (*trick*) astucieux(-euse); (*gadget*) ingénieux(-euse); **to be ~ with one's hands** être adroit avec ses mains **3.** *pej* (*quick-witted*) futé(e); **too ~ by half** un petit malin

clever clogs, **clever dick** *n Brit, pej* petit malin, petite maligne *m, f*

cleverness *n no pl* **1.** (*quick-wittedness*) intelligence *f* **2.** (*skill*) habileté *f* **3.** (*intelligent design*) ingéniosité *f*

cliché ['kli:ʃeɪ, *Am:* kli:'ʃeɪ] *n* **1.** (*platitude*) cliché *m* **2.** *no pl, no art* (*worn-out phrase*) phrase *f* toute faite

click [klɪk] **I.** *n* **1.** déclic *m;* (*of heels*) claquement *m* **2.** INFOR clic *m;* **mouse ~** clic sur la souris **II.** *vi* **1.** (*make short sound*) cliqueter **2.** (*friendly*) **to ~ with sb** se découvrir des atomes crochus avec qn **3.** (*clear*) faire un déclic **4.** INFOR cliquer; **to double-~ on the icon** cliquer deux fois de suite sur l'icône **III.** *vt* **1.** (*make short sound: one's fingers*) claquer **2.** INFOR cliquer sur

client ['klaɪənt] *n* client(e) *m(f)*

clientele [ˌkli:ɒn'tel, *Am:* ˌklaɪən-] *n + sing/pl vb* clientèle *f*

cliff [klɪf] *n* falaise *f*

cliffhanger ['klɪfˌhæŋəʳ, *Am:* -ɚ] *n* (*situation*) moment *m* de suspense; (*film*) film *m* à suspense; (*novel*) roman *m* à supense

climactic [ˌklaɪ'mæktɪk] *adj* à son point culminant; (*point*) culminant(e)

climate ['klaɪmɪt] *n* climat *m* ►**the ~ of opinion** les courants *mpl* de l'opinion

climatic [klaɪ'mætɪk] *adj* climatique

climatologist *n* climatologue *mf*

climatology [ˌklaɪmə'tɒlədʒi, *Am:* -'tɑ:lə-] *n no pl* climatologie *f*

climax ['klaɪmæks] **I.** *n* **1.** (*highest point*) apogée *f;* **to reach a ~** atteindre son paroxysme **2.** (*orgasm*) orgasme *m;* **to reach a ~** jouir **II.** *vi* **1.** (*reach high point*) atteindre son paroxysme **2.** (*orgasm*) jouir

climb [klaɪm] **I.** *n* **1.** (*ascent*) montée *f;* (*of mountain*) ascension *f;* **a ~ up/down** une montée/descente **2.** (*steep part*) côte *f* **3.** *fig* ascension *f;* **~ to power** ascension au pouvoir **II.** *vt* grimper; (*mountain*) faire l'ascension de; (*wall*) escalader; (*tree*) grimper à; (*stairs*) monter ►**to ~ the walls** être dingue **III.** *vi* **1.** (*ascend*) grimper; **to ~ over a wall** escalader un mur **2.** (*increase*) augmenter **3.** (*rise*) monter **4.** (*get into*) **to ~ into sth** monter dans qc **5.** (*get out*) **to ~ out of sth** se hisser hors de qc ►**to ~ on the bandwagon** *inf* prendre le train en marche; **to ~ to power** s'élever au pouvoir

◆**climb down** **I.** *vi* **1.** (*go down*) descendre **2.** *fig* revenir sur sa position **II.** *vt* descendre

◆**climb up** **I.** *vi* grimper **II.** *vt* (*tree*) grimper à; (*stairs*) monter

climbdown *n* recul *m*

climber *n* **1.** (*mountains*) alpiniste *mf* **2.** (*rock faces*) varappeur, -euse *m, f* **3.** (*plant*) plante *f* grimpante **4.** *inf* (*striver*) **a social ~** arriviste *mf* **5.** *Am* (*climbing frame*) cage *f* à poules

climbing **I.** *n* **1.** (*mountains*) alpinisme *m*; **to go ~** faire de l'alpinisme **2.** (*rock faces*) varappe *f* **II.** <inv> *adj* **1.** (*of plants*) grimpant(e) **2.** (*for going up mountains*) de montagne

climbing irons *npl* crampons *mpl*

clinch [klɪntʃ] **I.** *n* **1.** (*embrace*) étreinte *f* **2.** (*grasp*) corps *m* à corps; **to get into a ~** s'accrocher; **to get out of a ~** se décrocher **II.** *vt* **1.** (*fix firmly*) conclure **2.** *inf* (*embrace*) étreindre **3.** (*hold in wrestling*) combattre corps à corps **4.** (*secure a nail*) river

clincher *n inf* argument *m* décisif

cling [klɪŋ] <clung, clung> *vi* **1.** (*hold tightly*) **to ~ (together)** être collé l'un à l'autre; **to ~ (on) to sth** se cramponner à qc; (*be dependent on*); **to ~ to sb** s'accrocher à qn **2.** (*persist*) être tenace

cling film *n no pl, no art, Brit* film *m* alimentaire

clinging *adj* collant(e); (*dress*) moulant(e) ►**to be ~** être un pot de colle *inf*

clingy ['klɪŋi] *adj* collant(e)

clinic ['klɪnɪk] *n* **1.** (*hospital*) clinique *f* **2.** (*hospital department*) service *m* **3.** *Brit* (*consultation*) consultation *f*; **to hold a ~** tenir un service de consultation externe

clinical *adj* **1.** MED clinique **2.** (*hospital-like*) austère **3.** *pej* (*emotionless*) froid(e); **to be ~** être froidement objectif

clinician [klɪ'nɪʃən] *n* clinicien(ne) *m(f)*

clink [klɪŋk] **I.** *vt* faire tinter; **to ~ glasses** trinquer **II.** *vi* tinter **III.** *n no pl* **1.** (*ringing*) tintement *m* **2.** *inf* (*prison*) taule *f*

clinker *n no pl, no art* mâchefer *m*

clip¹ [klɪp] **I.** *n* **1.** (*fastener*) trombone *m*; **hair/bicycle ~** pince *f* à cheveux/vélo **2.** (*jewelry*) clip *m* **3.** (*gun part*) chargeur *m* **II.** <-pp-> *vt* **to ~ sth together** attacher qc **III.** *vi* **to ~ on** s'attacher

clip² [klɪp] <-pp-> **I.** *vt* **1.** (*trim*) couper; (*hedge*) tailler; (*sheep*) tondre **2.** (*make hole in*) poinçonner **3.** (*reduce*) diminuer; **to ~ a tenth of a second off the record** améliorer un record d'un dixième de seconde **4.** (*omit syllables*) **to ~ one's words** manger ses mots **5.** (*attach*) attacher **6.** (*hit: the kerb*) accrocher ►**to ~ sb's wings** rogner les ailes à qn **II.** *n* **1.** (*trim*) coupe *f* d'entretien; **to give sth a ~** donner un coup de ciseaux à qn; **to give a hedge a ~** tailler légèrement une haie **2.** (*extract*) clip *m* **3.** (*sharp hit*) claque *f* **4.** *no pl, inf* (*fast speed*) **at a (fair/fast/good) ~** à toute vitesse

clipboard *n* INFOR presse-papiers *m*

clipped *adj* saccadé(e)

clipper *n* NAUT clipper *m*

clipping *n* coupure *f* de presse; **nail ~s** coupe-ongles *m*; **newspaper ~** coupure *f* de journal

clique [kli:k] *n + sing/pl vb, pej* clique *f*

cliquish, cliquey <cliquier, cliquiest> *adj pej* qui a l'esprit de groupe

clitoris ['klɪtərəs, *Am:* 'klɪt̬ɚəs] *n* clitoris *m*

cloak [kləʊk, *Am:* kloʊk] **I.** *n* **1.** (*outer garment*) grande cape *f* **2.** *no pl* (*covering*) manteau *m*; (*of mist*) nappe *f* **II.** *vt* masquer

cloakroom *n* **1.** (*coat deposit*) vestiaire *m* **2.** *Brit* (*toilet*) toilettes *fpl*

clobber ['klɒbəʳ, *Am:* 'klɑ:bɚ] **I.** *vt* **1.** *inf* (*harm*) tabasser **2.** *inf* (*defeat*) écraser; **to ~ sb one** en mettre plein la tête à qn **II.** *n no pl, no art, Brit, Aus, inf* frusques *fpl*

clock [klɒk, *Am:* klɑ:k] **I.** *n* **1.** pendule *f*; **alarm ~** réveil *m*; **to put a ~ back** retarder l'horloge; **to put the ~s forward** [*o Brit* **on**] avancer l'horloge; **round the ~** 24 heures sur 24; **to work against the ~** travailler contre la montre; **to work according to the ~** faire qc en respectant l'horaire; **to have one's eye on the ~** surveiller l'heure **2.** (*speedometer*) compteur *m* **3.** (*mileometer*) compteur *m* kilométrique **II.** *vt* **1.** (*measure time or speed*) chronométrer **2.** *inf* (*hit*) coller un pain

◆**clock in** *vi* pointer

◆**clock out** *vi* pointer (à la sortie)

◆**clock up** *vt insep* **he clocked up 300 miles** il a fait 300 miles au compteur

clockface *n* cadran *m* **clock radio** *n s.* **radio alarm** **clock timer** *n* minuteur *m* **clock-watcher** *n pej* qui ne fait que guetter l'heure de la sortie **clockwise** *adj* dans le sens des aiguilles d'une montre **clockwork** **I.** *n no pl* mécanisme *m* ►**to go like ~** aller comme sur des roulettes **II.** *adj* d'une horloge

clod [klɒd, *Am:* klɑ:d] *n* **1.** (*lump of earth*) motte *f* de terre **2.** (*idiot*) balourd(e) *m(f)*

clog [klɒg, *Am:* klɑ:g] **I.** *n* sabot *m* **II.** <-gg-> *vi* se boucher **III.** <-gg-> *vt* boucher

cloister ['klɔɪstəʳ, *Am:* -stɚ] *n* cloître *m*

clone [kləʊn, *Am:* kloʊn] **I.** *n* clone *m* **II.** *vt* cloner

cloning *n* clonage *m*

close¹ [kləʊs, *Am:* kloʊs] **I.** *adj* **1.** (*near*) proche; **at ~ quarters** de très près; **at ~ range** à bout portant; **~ combat** corps *m* à corps **2.** (*intimate*) proche; **to be ~ to sb** être proche de qn; (*ties*) étroit(e) **3.** (*similar: resemblance*) fort(e); **to be ~ in sth** se ressembler dans qc **4.** (*careful*) minutieux(-euse); (*attention*) soutenu(e); **after ~ consideration** après mûre réflexion **5.** (*airless*) étouffant(e); (*weather*) lourd(e) 6.(*almost equal: contest*) serré(e) 7.(*dense*) serré(e) ►**to keep a ~ eye on sb/sth** surveiller qn/qc de très près II. *adv* 1.(*near in location*) près 2.(*near in time*) proche; **to get ~** (s')approcher 3. *fig* proche ►**to sail ~ to the wind** jouer un jeu dangereux III. *n* impasse *f;* (*of cathedral*) enceinte *f*

close[2] [kləʊz, *Am:* kloʊz] I. *n no pl* fin *f;* **to bring sth to a ~** conclure qc; **to come to a ~** prendre fin II. *vt* 1.(*shut*) fermer 2.(*end*) mettre fin à; (*bank account*) fermer; (*deal*) conclure ►**to ~ the stable door after the horse has bolted** prendre des précautions après coup; **to ~ one's eyes to sth** fermer les yeux sur qc III. *vi* 1.(*shut*) fermer; (*eyes, door*) se fermer 2.(*end*) prendre fin

◆**close down** *vt, vi* fermer définitivement

◆**close in** *vi* 1.(*surround*) **to ~ on sth** se rapprocher de qc 2.(*get shorter*) se raccourcir

◆**close off** *vt* condamner

◆**close up** *vi, vt* fermer

closed *adj* fermé(e) ►**behind ~ doors** à l'abri des regards indiscrets; **a ~ book** ne rien comprendre

close-down *n* fermeture *f* (définitive)

closed season *n* fermeture *f* de la chasse

close-knit *adj* très uni(e)

closely *adv* 1.(*intimately*) étroitement; **to be ~ linked** être très proche 2.(*carefully*) **a ~ guarded secret** un secret bien gardé

closeness *n* 1. *no pl, no art* (*nearness*) proximité *f* 2. *no pl* (*intimacy*) intimité *f* 3.(*airlessness*) lourdeur *f*

closet ['klɒzɪt, *Am:* 'klɑːzɪt] I. *n Am* 1.(*cupboard*) placard *m* 2.(*for food*) garde-manger *m* ►**to come out of the ~** se montrer au grand jour II. *adj* caché(e) III. *vt* enfermer; **to ~ oneself somewhere** s'enfermer quelque part

close to *prep, adv* 1.(*near*) près de; **to be ~ the beginning/end of sth** en être au début/à la fin de qc; **to live ~ work** habiter près de son lieu de travail 2.(*almost*) presque; (*tears*) au bord de; (*death*) au seuil de; **~ doing sth** sur le point de faire qc 3. *fig* **to be/to get ~ sb** être proche/se rapprocher de qn

close-up *n* gros plan *m*

closing I. <inv> *adj* final(e); (*speech*) de clôture II. *n* 1.(*ending*) clôture *f* 2.(*end of business hours*) heure *f* de fermeture; **early ~** fermeture *f* l'après-midi

closing date *n* date *f* limite **closing down** *n* fermeture *f* **closing-down sale** *n* liquidation *f* **closing hour** *n* heure *f* de fermeture **closing price** *n* cours *m* en clôture **closing time** *n Brit s.* **closing hour**

closure ['kləʊʒə^r, *Am:* 'kloʊʒɚ] *n* fermeture *f*

clot [klɒt, *Am:* klɑːt] I. *n* 1.(*lump*) caillot *m* 2. *Brit, iron, inf* (*idiot*) imbécile *mf* II. <-tt-> *vi* coaguler; **an anti-(blood) ~ting agent** un agent anticoagulant

cloth [klɒθ, *Am:* klɑːθ] I. *n* 1. *no pl, no art* (*material*) tissu *m;* **table~** nappe *f* 2.(*duster*) chiffon *m* 3.(*clergy*) clergé *m* ►**to cut one's coat according to one's ~** vivre selon ses moyens II. <inv> *adj* en tissu

clothe [kləʊð, *Am:* kloʊð] *vt* vêtir

clothes *npl* vêtements *mpl,* hardes *fpl Québec;* **to put one's ~ on** s'habiller; **~ designer** styliste *mf*

clothes hanger *n* cintre *m* **clothes horse** *n* séchoir *m* à linge **clothes line** *n* corde *f* à linge **clothes-moth** *n* mite *f* **clothes peg** *n Brit,* **clothes pin** *n Am* pince *f* à linge **clothes rack** *n Am* portant *m*

clothing *n form* vêtements *mpl*

clothing industry *n* industrie *f* du vêtement

cloud [klaʊd] I. *n a. fig* nuage *m* ►**to be on ~ nine** être au septième ciel; **to be under a ~** être l'objet de soupçons II. *vt* 1.(*darken*) *a. fig* obscurcir 2.(*make less clear*) rendre trouble III. *vi* 1.(*become overcast*) se couvrir 2. *fig* s'assombrir

◆**cloud over** *vi* 1.(*become covered with clouds*) se couvrir 2.(*become gloomy*) s'assombrir

cloudburst *n* averse *f* **cloud cover** *n* couche *f* de nuages **cloud cuckoo land** *n pej* **to live in ~** ne pas avoir les pieds sur terre

clouded *adj* 1.(*cloudy*) nuageux(-euse) 2.(*not transparent: liquid*) trouble 3.(*confused: mind*) troublé(e)

cloudless *adj* sans nuages

cloudy <-ier, -iest> *adj* 1.(*overcast*) nuageux(-euse); **partly ~ skies** ciel partiellement couvert 2.(*not transparent: liquid*) trouble 3.(*unclear*) nébuleux(-euse) 4. *fig* **~ eyes** regard *m* embué

clout [klaʊt] I. *n* 1. *inf* (*hit*) taloche *f* 2. *no pl* (*power*) poids *m;* **to have ~** avoir de l'influence II. *vt inf* (*person*) flanquer une taloche à; (*object*) donner un coup à

clove[1] [kləʊv, *Am:* kloʊv] *n* (*plant part*) gousse *f*

clove[2] [kləʊv, *Am:* kloʊv] *n* (*spice*) clou *m* de girofle

clove[3] [kləʊv, *Am:* kloʊv] *pt of* **cleave**

cloven ['kləʊvn, *Am:* 'kloʊ-] I. *pp of* **cleave** II. *adj* fourchu(e)

clover *n no pl* trèfle *m;* **four-leaf ~** trèfle à quatre feuilles ►**to be in ~** être comme un coq en pâte

cloverleaf *n* (*road junction*) croisement *m* en trèfle

clown [klaʊn] I. *n a. fig* clown *m* II. *vi* **to ~ around** faire le clown

clownish ['klaʊnɪʃ] *adj* clownesque

cloying [klɔɪɪŋ] *adj* écœurant(e)

club [klʌb] I. *n* 1.(*group*) club *m;* **to join a ~** adhérer à un club; **tennis ~** club de tennis; **join the ~!** bienvenue au club! 2. *Am* SPORT (*team*) club *m;* **volleyball ~** club de volley-ball 3. SPORT (*stick*) club *m;* **golf ~** club de golf 4.(*weapon*) gourdin *m* 5. GAMES (*playing card*) trèfle *m;* **the queen of ~s** la reine de trèfle 6.(*disco*) boîte *f* II. <-bb-> *vt* frapper avec un gourdin; **to ~ sb/an animal to death** frapper qn/un animal à mort

◆**club together** *vi* se cotiser

clubbing *vi* **to go ~** aller en boîte

club class *n* classe *f* affaires **club foot** *n* MED pied *m* bot **club member** *n* membre *mf* du club **club sandwich** *n* sandwich *m* mixte **club soda** *n Am* eau *f* de Seltz

cluck [klʌk] **I.** *n a. fig* gloussement *m* **II.** *vi a. fig* glousser

clue [klu:] *n* **1.** (*hint*) indice *m* **2.** *fig* (*secret*) secret *m* **3.** (*idea*) idée *f;* **to have a ~ about sth** avoir une idée sur qc; **to not have a ~** ne pas avoir la moindre idée

clued-up *adj Aus, Brit, inf* **to be ~ on sth** être calé en qc

clueless *adj inf* largué(e)

clump¹ [klʌmp] **I.** *vi* (*walk noisily*) marcher d'un pas lourd **II.** *n no pl* (*heavy sound*) bruit *m* de pas lourd

clump² [klʌmp] **I.** *vt* (*group*) **to ~ sth together** rassembler qc **II.** *vi* **to ~ together** se rassembler **III.** *n* (*thick group: of bushes, trees*) massif *m;* (*of persons*) groupe *m;* (*of herbs*) touffe *f;* (*of earth*) motte *f*

clumsiness *n* maladresse *f*

clumsy ['klʌmzi] <-ier, -iest> *adj a. fig* maladroit(e)

clung [klʌŋ] *pp, pt of* **cling**

clunk [klʌŋk] *n* bruit *m* sourd

cluster ['klʌstəʳ, *Am:* -tɚ] **I.** *n* **1.** (*group*) groupe *m;* (*of fruit*) grappe *f;* (*of flowers, trees*) bouquet *m;* (*of persons*) groupe *m;* (*of bees*) essaim *m;* (*of stars*) amas *m* **2.** LING groupe *m* **II.** *vi* **to ~ together** se regrouper

◆**cluster round** *vt* se grouper autour de

cluster bomb *n* bombe *f* à fragmentation

clutch [klʌtʃ] **I.** *vi* **to ~ at sth** se cramponner à qc **II.** *vt* saisir **III.** *n* **1.** *sing* AUTO (*transmission device*) embrayage *m* **2.** (*set: of eggs*) couvée *f* **3.** *fig* (*group*) groupe *m* **4.** (*claw*) *a. fig* griffe *f*

clutch bag *n* pochette *f*

clutter ['klʌtəʳ, *Am:* 'klʌt̬ɚ] **I.** *n no pl* encombrement *m* **II.** *vt* encombrer

cluttered *adj* encombré(e); **to be ~ with sth** être encombré de qc

cm *inv n abbr of* **centimetre** cm *m*

c'mon *inf* = **come on**

CND [ˌsi:en'di:] *n abbr of* **Campaign for Nuclear Disarmament** mouvement *m* pour le désarmement nucléaire

CO [ˌsi:'əʊ, *Am:* -'oʊ] *n* MIL *abbr of* **Commanding Officer** officier *m* commandant

Co. *n* **1.** *no pl abbr of* **company** Cie *f;* **... and ~ ...** et Cie **2.** *Am, Brit* GEO *abbr of* **county** conté *m*

c/o *abbr of* **care of** chez

coach [kəʊtʃ, *Am:* koʊtʃ] **I.** *n* **1.** (*private bus*) car *m* **2.** (*horse-drawn carriage*) carrosse *m* **3.** (*railway carriage*) voiture *f* **4.** (*teacher*) professeur *m* particulier **5.** SPORT (*professional coach*) entraîneur *m* **II.** *vt* **1.** (*give private teaching*) donner des cours de soutien à **2.** SPORT entraîner **3.** (*support professionally*) coacher

coachbuilder *n Brit* AUTO carrossier *m*

coaching *n no pl* **1.** (*support*) soutien *m* **2.** SPORT entraînement *m* **3.** (*professional support*) coaching *m*

coaching staff *n* SPORT équipe *f* d'entraînement

coachman *n* cocher *m*

coach station *n Brit* gare *f* routière **coachwork** *n Brit no pl* AUTO carrosserie *f*

coagulate [kəʊ'ægjʊleɪt, *Am:* koʊ'ægjə-] **I.** *vi* se coaguler **II.** *vt* coaguler

coagulation *n no pl* coagulation *f*

coal [kəʊl, *Am:* koʊl] *n* charbon *m* ►**to carry ~s to Newcastle** porter de l'eau à la rivière; **to drag sb over the ~s** réprimander qn sévèrement

coal-black *adj* noir(e) comme du charbon **coal bunker** *n* coffre *m* à charbon

coalesce [kəʊə'les, *Am:* koʊə-] *vi form* **to ~ into sth** fusionner en qc

coalescence [kəʊə'lesnts, *Am:* koʊə-] *n no pl, form* fusion *f*

coalface *n* front *m* de taille **coalfield** *n* bassin *m* houiller **coal-fired** *adj* (alimenté) au charbon; **~ central-heating** centrale *f* thermique au charbon

coalition [ˌkəʊə'lɪʃən, *Am:* ˌkoʊə-] *n* POL coalition *f*

coal mine *n* mine *f* de charbon **coal miner** *n* mineur *m* **coal mining** *n* charbonnage *m* **coal scuttle** *n* seau *m* à charbon **coal tar** *n* goudron *m* de houille

coarse [kɔ:s, *Am:* kɔ:rs] <-r, -st> *adj a. fig* grossier(-ère); (*salt, sand*) gros(se); (*skin, surface*) rugueux(-euse); (*features*) rude

coarsely *adv* grossièrement

coarsen ['kɔ:sn, *Am:* 'kɔ:r-] **I.** *vt* rendre grossier **II.** *vi* devenir grossier

coarseness *n no pl, a. fig* grossièreté *f*

coast [kəʊst, *Am:* koʊst] **I.** *n* côte *f;* **three miles off the ~** à trois miles de la côte; **from ~ to ~** d'un bout à l'autre du pays ►**the ~ is clear** la voie est libre **II.** *vi* **1.** (*move easily*) avancer en roue libre **2.** (*make progress*) avancer sans difficulté

coastal *adj* côtier(-ère)

coaster *n* **1.** (*boat*) caboteur *m* **2.** (*protector*) dessous *m* de verre

coastguard *n* garde-côte *m;* **the ~** les garde-côtes **coastline** *n no pl* littoral *m* **coast to coast** *adv* d'un bout à l'autre du pays

coat [kəʊt, *Am:* koʊt] **I.** *n* **1.** (*outer garment*) manteau *m;* **leather ~** manteau en cuir **2.** (*animal's outer covering*) pelage *m* **3.** (*layer*) couche *f;* **to give sth a ~** passer une couche sur qc **II.** *vt* couvrir; **to ~ sth with sth** couvrir qc de qc

coated *adj* **to be ~ in sth** être recouvert de qc

coat hanger *n* cintre *m* **coat hook** *n* patère *f*

coating *n s.* **coat**
coat of arms <coats of arms> *n* armoiries *fpl* **coat peg** *n Brit s.* coat hook **coat-tails** *npl* queue *f* de pie ►on **sb's** ~ dans le sillage de qn
co-author [kəʊ'ɔːθəʳ, *Am:* koʊ'ɑːθɚ] **I.** *n* (*not only author*) coauteur *m* **II.** *vt* être le coauteur de
coax [kəʊks, *Am:* koʊks] *vt* enjôler; **to** ~ **sb to do sth** enjôler qn pour qu'il fasse qc (*subj*); **to** ~ **sth out of sb** soutirer qc à qn
coaxing **I.** *n no pl* cajoleries *fpl* **II.** *adj* cajôleur(-euse)
coaxingly *adv* d'un air enjôleur
cobalt ['kəʊbɔːlt, *Am:* 'koʊbɔːlt] *n no pl* cobalt *m*
cobalt blue *n no pl* bleu *m* cobalt
cobble¹ ['kɒbl, *Am:* 'kɑːbl] **I.** *n* (*stone*) pavé *m* **II.** *vt* paver
cobble² ['kɒbl, *Am:* 'kɑːbl] *vt* (*repair*) réparer
◆**cobble together** *vt* bricoler
cobbled *adj* pavé(e)
cobbler *n* cordonnier, -ière *m, f*
cobblestone *n* pavé *m*
cobol, **COBOL** ['kəʊbɒl, *Am:* 'koʊbɔːl] *n* INFOR COBOL *m;* **to programme in** ~ progammer en COBOL
cobra ['kəʊbrə, *Am:* 'koʊbrə] *n* cobra *m*
cobweb ['kɒbweb, *Am:* 'kɑːb-] *n* **1.** (*web made by spider*) toile *f* d'araignée **2.** (*single threads*) fil *m* d'araignée
coca ['kəʊkə, *Am:* 'koʊ-] *n* coca *f*
Coca Cola® *n* coca-cola *m inv*
cocaine [kəʊ'keɪn, *Am:* koʊ-] *n no pl* cocaïne *f* **cocaine addict** *n* cocaïnomane *mf*
coccyx ['kɒksɪks, *Am:* 'kɑːk-] <-es *o* coccyges> *n* coccyx *m*
cochineal [ˌkɒtʃɪ'niːl, *Am:* 'kɑːtʃəniːl] *n no pl* cochenille *f*
cochlea ['ɒkliə, *Am:* 'kɑːk-] <-e *o* -s> *n* ANAT limaçon *m*
cochleae *n pl of* **cochlea**
cock [kɒk, *Am:* kɑːk] **I.** *n* **1.** (*male chicken*) coq *m* **2.** *Brit, inf* (*form of address*) mon vieux **II.** *vt* **1.** (*turn*) pencher; **to** ~ **sth** (**up**) dresser qc **2.** (*ready gun*) armer ►**to** ~ **a snook at sth** faire un pied de nez à qc; **to** ~ **one's eye at sb/sth** donner un coup d'œil à qn/qc
cockade [kɒ'keɪd, *Am:* kɑː'keɪd] *n* cocarde *f*
cock-a-doodle-doo **I.** *interj childspeak* cocorico! **II.** *n* cocorico *m;* **to make a** ~ faire cocorico **III.** *vi* faire cocorico **cock-a-hoop** *adj Brit, inf* **to be** ~ être fier comme Artaban **cock-a-leekie** *n Scot: bouillon de volaille et de poireaux* **cock and bull story** *n* histoire *f* à dormir debout
cockatoo [ˌkɒkə'tuː, *Am:* 'kɑːkə-] <-(s)> *n* cacatoès *m*
cockchafer ['kɒktʃeɪfəʳ, *Am:* 'kɑːktʃeɪfɚ] *n* hanneton *m*
cockcrow ['kɒkkrəʊ, *Am:* 'kɑːkkroʊ] *n* chant *m* du coq; **at** ~ au chant du coq
cocked hat *n* chapeau *m* à cornes
cocker ['kɒkəʳ, *Am:* 'kɑːkɚ] *n* cocker *m*
cockerel ['kɒkərəl, *Am:* 'kɑːkɚ-] *n* coquelet *m*
cocker spaniel *s.* **cocker**
cock-eyed *adj* **1.** *inf* (*not straight*) de traviole **2.** (*ridiculous: idea, plan*) absurde **cock fight** *n* combat *m* de poulets
cockiness *n* suffisance *f*
cockle ['kɒkl, *Am:* 'kɑːkl] *n* coque *f*
cockney ['kɒkni, *Am:* 'kɑːk-] **I.** *n* (*dialect*) cockney *m* **II.** *adj* cockney *inv*
cockpit ['kɒkpɪt, *Am:* 'kɑːk-] *n* **1.** (*pilot's area*) cockpit *m* **2.** *sing* (*area of fighting*) arène *f*
cockroach ['kɒkrəʊtʃ, *Am:* 'kɑːkroʊtʃ] *n* cafard *m*
cockscomb ['kɒkskəʊm, *Am:* 'kɑːkskoʊm] *n* ZOOL crête *f* de coq
cocksure [ˌkɒk'ʃʊəʳ, *Am:* ˌkɑːk'ʃʊr] *adj pej, inf* trop sûr de soi
cocktail ['kɒkteɪl, *Am:* 'kɑːk-] *n* cocktail *m;* **champagne** ~ cocktail au champagne; **shrimp** ~ cocktail de crevettes
cocktail cabinet *n* bar *m* **cocktail dress** *n* robe *f* de cocktail **cocktail lounge** *n* bar *m*
cock-up *n inf* bordel *m;* **to make a** ~ **of sth** faire foirer qc
cocky ['kɒki, *Am:* 'kɑːki] <-ier, -iest> *adj inf* culotté(e)
cocoa ['kəʊkəʊ, *Am:* 'koʊkoʊ] *n no pl* cacao *m*
cocoa butter *n* beurre *m* de cacao
coconut ['kəʊkənʌt, *Am:* 'koʊ-] *n* noix *f* de coco; **grated** ~ noix de coco râpée
coconut butter *n* beurre *m* de coco **coconut matting** *n* natte *f* en fibres de coco **coconut milk** *n* lait *m* de coco **coconut oil** *n* huile *f* de coco **coconut palm** *n* cocotier *m*
cocoon [kə'kuːn] **I.** *n* cocon *m* **II.** *vt* protéger
cod [kɒd, *Am:* kɑːd] <-(s)> *n* **1.** (*fish*) morue *f* **2.** (*fresh fish*) cabillaud *m*
COD [ˌsiːəʊ'diː, *Am:* -oʊ'-] *n abbr of* **cash on delivery** livraison *f* contre remboursement
coda ['kəʊdə, *Am:* 'koʊ-] *n* coda *f*
coddle ['kɒdl, *Am:* 'kɑːdl] *vt* **1.** (*cook gently*) cuire à feu doux **2.** (*treat tenderly*) dorloter
code [kəʊd, *Am:* koʊd] **I.** *n* code *m;* **to write sth in** ~ coder qc; **to decipher a** ~ déchiffrer un code; ~ **of conduct** déontologie *f* **II.** *vt* coder
coded *adj* codé(e)
codeine [kəʊdiːn, *Am:* koʊ-] *n no pl* codéine *f*
code name *n* nom *m* de code
code-named *adj* qui a pour nom de code
co-determination [ˌkəʊdɪtɜːmɪ'neɪʃən, *Am:* ˌkoʊdɪtɜːr-] *n* codétermination *f*
code word *n* mot *m* de passe
codex ['kəʊdeks, *Am:* 'koʊ-] <codices> *n*

manuscrit *m*

codger ['kɒdʒəʳ] *n iron, pej, inf* **an old ~** un vieux type

codices ['kəʊdɪsiːz, *Am:* 'koʊdəsiːz] *n pl of* **codex**

codicil ['kəʊdɪsɪl] *n* LAW codicille *m*

codify ['kəʊdɪfaɪ, *Am:* 'kɑː-] *vt* codifier

cod liver oil *n* huile *f* de foie de morue

codpiece ['kɒdpiːs, *Am:* 'kaːd-] *n* braguette *f*

codswallop ['kɒdzˌwɒləp, *Am:* 'kɑːzˌwɑːləp] *n no pl, Aus, Brit, inf* foutaises *fpl*

coed *adj inf* SCHOOL, UNIV (*school*) mixte; **to go ~** devenir mixte

co-education *n no pl* enseignement *m* mixte **co-educational** *adj* mixte **coefficient** *n* MAT coefficient *m* **coequal** **I.** *n form* égal(e) *m(f)* **II.** *adj form* égale(e)

coerce [kəʊ'ɜːs, *Am:* koʊ'ɜːrs] *vt form* contraindre

coercion [kəʊ'ɜːʃən, *Am:* koʊ'ɜːrʒən] *n no pl, form* coercition *f*

coercive [kəʊ'ɜːsɪv, *Am:* koʊ'ɜːr-] *adj* coercitif(-ive)

coexist *vi* coexister **coexistence** *n no pl* coexistence *f*

coffee ['kɒfi, *Am:* 'kɑːfi] *n* **1.** (*hot drink*) café *m;* **instant ~** café instantané; **a cup of ~** une tasse de café; **a black ~** un café **2.** *s.* **coffee-coloured**

coffee bar *n s.* coffee shop **coffee bean** *n* grain *m* de café **coffee break** *n* pause *f* café; **to have a ~** faire une pause-café **coffee cake** *n* **1.** (*mocha cake*) moka *m* **2.** (*cake served with coffee*) gâteau *m* **coffee-coloured** *adj* couleur café **coffee cup** *n* tasse *f* à café **coffee grinder** *n* moulin *m* à café **coffee grounds** *n* marc *m* de café **coffee house** *n* café *m* **coffee machine** *n* machine *f* à café **coffee mill** *n s.* coffee grinder **coffee pot** *n* cafetière *f* **coffee shop** *n* café *m* **coffee table** *n* table *f* basse

coffer ['kɒfəʳ, *Am:* 'kɑːfɚ] *n* **1.** (*storage place*) coffre *m* **2.** **the ~s** *pl* (*money reserves*) les caisses *fpl*

coffin ['kɒfɪn, *Am:* 'kɔːfɪn] *n Aus, Brit* cercueil *m*

cog [kɒg, *Am:* kɑːg] *n* **1.** (*tooth-like part of wheel*) dent *f* **2.** (*wheel*) roue *f* **3.** *pej* (*minor, yet necessary part*) rouage *m;* **to be a ~ in a machine** n'être qu'un rouage de la machine

cogency ['kəʊdʒəntsi, *Am:* 'koʊ-] *n no pl, form* puissance *f*

cogent ['kəʊdʒənt, *Am:* 'koʊ-] *adj form* convaincant(e)

cogently *adv form* avec force

cogitate ['kɒdʒɪteɪt, *Am:* 'kɑːdʒə-] *vi iron, a. form* cogiter

cogitation *n a. iron* cogitation *f*

cognac ['kɒnjæk, *Am:* 'koʊnjæk] *n* cognac *m*

cognate ['kɒgneɪt, *Am:* 'kɑːg-] *adj* LING apparenté(e); **to be ~ with sth** être apparenté à qc

cognition [kɒg'nɪʃən, *Am:* kɑːg-] *n form* cognition *f*

cognitive ['kɒgnɪtɪv, *Am:* 'kɑːgnət̬ɪv] *adj form* cognitif(-ive)

cognitive psychology *n* psychologie *f* cognitive **cognitive therapy** *n* thérapie *f* cognitive

cognizance *n no pl, form* LAW connaissance *f*

cognizant ['kɒgnɪznt, *Am:* 'kɑːgnə-] *adj form* **to be ~ of the facts** avoir connaissance des faits

cognomen [kɒg'nəʊmən, *Am:* kɑːg'noʊ-] *n* **1.** (*nickname*) surnom *m* **2.** (*ancient Roman's family name*) nom *m* de famille

cogwheel ['kɒgwiːl, *Am:* 'kɑːg-] *n s.* **cog**

cohabit [kəʊ'hæbɪt, *Am:* koʊ-] *vi form* cohabiter

cohabitant *n form* compagnon *m,* compagne *f*

cohabitation *n no pl* cohabitation *f*

cohabitee [ˌkəʊhæbɪ'tiː, *Am:* ˌkoʊ-] *n form s.* **cohabitant**

cohere [kəʊ'hɪəʳ, *Am:* koʊ'hɪr] *vi form* être cohérent

coherence *n no pl* cohérence *f*

coherent ['kəʊ'hɪərənt, *Am:* 'koʊ'hɪr-] *adj* cohérent(e)

coherently *adv* de manière cohérente

cohesion [kəʊ'hiːʒən, *Am:* koʊ-] *n no pl* cohésion *f*

cohesive [kəʊ'hiːsɪv, *Am:* koʊ-] *adj* cohésif(-ive)

cohesiveness *n no pl* cohésion *f*

cohort ['kəʊhɔːt, *Am:* 'koʊhɔːrt] *n a. pej* cohorte *f*

COI *n Brit abbr of* **Central Office of Information** *service d'information gouvernemental*

coiffed *adj iron* coiffé(e)

coiffeur [kwaː'fɜːr] *n* coiffeur *m*

coiffure [kwɒː'fjʊəʳ, *Am:* kwɑː'fjʊr] *n form* coiffure *f*

coil [kɔɪl] **I.** *n* **1.** (*wound spiral*) rouleau *m;* (*of rope*) pli *m* **2.** *inf* MED *s.* **IUD** **II.** *vi* (*snake*) **to ~ around sth** s'enrouler autour de qc **III.** *vt* enrouler; **to ~ oneself around sth** s'enrouler autour de qc

coin [kɔɪn] **I.** *n* pièce *f;* **gold ~** pièce en or **II.** *vt* inventer ►**to ~ it** (**in**) *Brit, inf,* **to ~ money** *Am* faire des affaires en or; **to ~ a phrase ...** pour ainsi dire ...

coinage ['kɔɪnɪdʒ] *n* **1.** *no pl* (*set of coins*) monnaie *f* **2.** (*producing of coins*) frappe *f* **3.** (*system*) système *m* monétaire **4.** (*invented word*) néologisme *m*

coin-box telephone *n* téléphone *m* à pièces

coincide [ˌkəʊɪn'saɪd, *Am:* ˌkoʊ-] *vi* coïncider

coincidence *n* coïncidence *f*

coincident [kəʊ'ɪnsɪdənt, *Am:* koʊ-] *adj* **1.** (*occupying same space or time*) coïncident(e); **to be ~ with sth** coïncider avec qc

2. (*in harmony with*) **to be ~ with sth** concorder avec qc
coincidental *adj* fortuit(e)
coincidentally *adv* par coïncidence
coitus ['kəʊɪtəs, *Am:* 'koʊəţəs] *n no pl, form* coït *m*
coke [kəʊk, *Am:* koʊk] *n no pl* **1.** (*fuel*) coke *m* **2.** *inf* (*cocaine*) coke *f*
Coke® *n* coca *m*
col [kɒl, *Am:* kɑ:l] *n abbr of* **column**
Col *n abbr of* **colonel**
cola ['kəʊlə, *Am:* 'koʊ-] *n* **1.** BOT cola *f* **2.** (*coke*) coca *m*
colander ['kɒləndəʳ, *Am:* 'kʌləndɚ] *n* passoire *f*
cold [kəʊld, *Am:* koʊld] **I.** *adj* <-er, -est> (*not warm*) *a. fig* froid(e); **to be as ~ as ice** être glacé; **a ~ beer** une bière fraîche; **to be ~** (*weather*) faire froid; (*person*) avoir froid; **to go ~** (*soup, coffee*) se refroidir; **to get ~** (*person*) avoir froid; **to be ~ comfort** ne pas être très rassurant ►**to have/get ~ feet** perdre son sang froid; **to pour ~ water on sth** démolir qc **II.** *n* **1.** (*low temperature*) froid *m* **2.** MED (*illness*) rhume *m;* **to catch a ~** attraper froid
cold-blooded *adj* **1.** ZOOL (*ectothermic: animal*) à sang froid **2.** (*extremely evil: murderer*) sans pitié **cold call** *n* visite *f* à froid; (*on the phone*) appel *m* à froid **cold cream** *n* cold-cream *m* **cold cuts** *npl* assiette *f* anglaise **cold front** *n* front *m* froid **cold-hearted** *adj* sans cœur
coldly *adv* froidement; (*to look at*) avec froideur
coldness *n no pl* froideur *f*
cold snap *n* refroidissement *m* **cold sore** *n* MED herpès *m* **cold start** *n* démarrage *m* à froid **cold storage** *n* conservation *f* par le froid; **to put sth in ~** mettre qc en chambre froide **cold store** *n* chambre *f* froide **cold sweat** *n* sueur *f* froide; **to put sb in a ~** donner des sueurs froides à qn **cold turkey** *n Am, Aus, inf* manque *m;* **to quit smoking ~** arrêter de fumer tout à coup **cold war** *n* guerre *f* froide **cold wave** *n* METEO vague *f* de froid
coleslaw ['kəʊlslɔ:, *Am:* 'koʊlslɑ:] *n no pl* salade *f* de chou
coley ['kəʊli, *Am:* 'koʊ-] <-(s)> *n* colin *m*
colic ['kɒlɪk, *Am:* 'kɑ:lɪk] *n no pl* colique *f*
colitis [kɒl'aɪtɪs, *Am:* koʊ'laɪţəs] *n no pl* colite *f*
collaborate [kə'læbəreɪt] *vi a. pej* collaborer; **to ~ on sth** collaborer à qc
collaboration *n* collaboration *f*
collaborationist *adj pej* collaborationniste *mf*
collaborative [kə'æbərətɪv] *adj* fait(e) en commun
collaborator *n a. pej* collaborateur, -trice *m, f,* incivique *mf Belgique*
collage ['kɒlɑ:ʒ, *Am:* kəlɑ:ʒ] *n* collage *m*
collagen ['kɒlədʒən, *Am:* 'kɑ:lə-] *n no pl* collagène *m*
collagen implant, **collagen injection** *n* injection *f* au collagène
collapse [kə'læps] **I.** *vi a. fig* s'effondrer; (*government*) tomber; **to ~ with laughter** s'effondrer de rire **II.** *n a. fig* effondrement *m;* (*of government*) chute *f*
collapsed *adj* MED **a ~ lung** un collapsus pulmonaire
collapsible *adj* pliant(e)
collar ['kɒləʳ, *Am:* 'kɑ:lɚ] **I.** *n* **1.** (*piece around neck*) col *m* **2.** (*band*) collier *m* **II.** *vt* **1.** *inf* saisir au collet **2.** *fig* retenir
collar bone *n* clavicule *f*
collate [kə'leɪt] *vt* collationner
collateral [kə'lætərəl, *Am:* -'læţ-] **I.** *n* FIN nantissement *m* **II.** *adj* collatéral(e)
collateral damage *n* dommages *mpl* collatéraux
colleague ['kɒli:g, *Am:* 'kɑ:li:g] *n* collègue *mf*
collect [kə'lekt, *Am:* 'kɑ:l-] **I.** *vi* **1.** (*gather*) **to ~ (together)** (*crowd*) se rassembler; (*dust, dirt*) s'amasser **2.** (*gather money*) faire la quête **II.** *vt* **1.** (*gather*) rassembler; (*money, taxes*) percevoir; (*water, news*) recueillir **2.** (*gather things as hobby: stamps, antiques*) collectionner **3.** (*pick up*) aller chercher **4.** *form* (*regain control*) reprendre; **to ~ oneself** se reprendre; **to ~ one's thoughts** rassembler ses idées **5.** (*receive*) recevoir **III.** *n* REL collecte *f*
◆**collect up** *vt* rassembler
collectable **I.** *adj* **1.** (*worth collecting*) prisé(e) par les collectionneurs **2.** (*can be collected*) disponible **II.** *n* pièce *f* de collection
collect call *n Am* appel *m* en PCV
collected *adj* (*people*) serein(e)
collectible *s.* **collectable**
collection [kə'lekʃən] *n* **1.** (*money gathered*) collecte *f;* **to have a ~ for sth** faire une collecte pour qc **2.** (*object collected*) collection *f* **3.** *fig* (*large number*) collection *f* **4.** (*range of designed clothes*) collection *f;* **winter/spring ~** collection d'hiver/de printemps **5.** (*act of getting: of rubbish*) ramassage *m*
collective [kə'lektɪv] **I.** *adj* collectif(-ive) **II.** *n* coopérative *f*
collective farm *n* ferme *f* collective
collectively *adv* collectivement
collective noun *n* LING collectif *m*
collectivism [kə'lektɪvɪzm, *Am:* -tə-] *n no pl* collectivisme *m*
collector *n* **1.** (*one who gathers objects*) collectionneur, -euse *m, f;* **a stamp ~** un(e) philatéliste **2.** (*one who collects payments*) collecteur, -trice *m, f;* **a tax ~** un percepteur
collector's item, **collector's piece** *n* pièce *f* de collection
colleen ['kɒli:n, *Am:* 'kɑli:n] *n Irish* jeune fille *f*
college ['kɒlɪdʒ, *Am:* 'kɑ:lɪdʒ] *n* **1.** *Brit* (*private school*) établissement *m* d'enseignement

secondaire privé **2.** (*university*) université *f;* **to go to ~** aller à l'université; **~ of Art** école *f* des beaux-arts; **~ education** études *fpl* supérieures **3.** *Brit* (*collegiate group*) collège *m*

> **College** est le mot qui désigne le temps passé à l'université jusqu'au diplôme du "bachelor's degree", c'est-à-dire 4 ou 5 ans. Les universités, dans lesquelles les étudiants ne peuvent obtenir qu'un "bachelor's degree", sont souvent appelées "colleges"; ainsi que certaines écoles de formation professionnelle. Les vraies "universities", elles, offrent la possibilité de passer des "higher degrees" (des diplômes d'études supérieures), tels que des "master's degrees" ou des "doctorates". Dans les "junior colleges" on peut effectuer les deux premières années du "college" ou apprendre un métier technique.

college graduate *n Am* diplômé(e) *m(f)* d'université

collegiate [kə'liːdʒɪət, *Am:* -dʒɪt] *adj* universitaire

collide [kə'laɪd] *vi* **to ~ with sb/sth** se heurter à qn/qc; **to ~ into sth** heurter qc

collie ['kɒli, *Am:* 'kɑːli] *n* colley *m*

collier ['kɒlɪəʳ, *Am:* 'kɑːljɚ] *n form* **1.** MIN *s.* **coal miner 2.** (*ship*) charbonnier *m*

colliery ['kɒlɪəri, *Am:* 'kɑːljɚ] *n* houillère *f*

collision [kə'lɪʒən] *n* **1.** (*hit*) collision *f;* **to come into ~** entrer en collision **2.** *fig* **a ~ of interests** un conflit d'intérêts

collocate ['kɒləʊkeɪt, *Am:* 'kɑːlə-] **I.** *vi* LING **to ~ with sth** être cooccurrent de qc **II.** *n s.* **collocation**

collocation *n* LING collocation *f*

colloquial [kə'ləʊkwɪəl, *Am:* -'loʊ-] *adj* familier(-ère)

colloquialism *n* expression *f* familière

colloquially *adv* familièrement

colloquy ['kɒləkwi, *Am:* 'kɑːlə-] *n a. form* colloque *m*

collude [kə'luːd] *vi* **to ~ with sb** être de connivence avec qn

collusion [kə'luːʒən] *n no pl* collusion *f*

collywobbles ['kɒlɪˌwɒblz, *Am:* 'kɑːliˌwɑː-] *npl iron, inf* **the ~** la colique

cologne [kə'ləʊn, *Am:* -loʊn] *n no pl, Am* (*aftershave*) eau *f* de cologne

Colombia [kə'lʌmbɪə] *n* la Colombie

Colombian I. *adj* colombien(ne) **II.** *n* Colombien(ne) *m(f)*

> Le **Colombus Day** commémore la découverte du nouveau monde par Christophe Colomb, le 12 octobre 1492. Depuis 1971, le "Colombus Day" est célébré le deuxième lundi d'octobre.

colon ['kəʊlən, *Am:* 'koʊ-] *n* **1.** ANAT colon *m* **2.** LING deux-points *mpl*

colon cancer *n* MED cancer *m* du colon

colonel ['kɜːnl, *Am:* 'kɜːr-] *n* MIL colonel *m*

colonial [kə'ləʊniəl, *Am:* -'loʊ-] **I.** *adj* colonial(e) **II.** *n* colonial(e) *m(f)*

colonialism [kə'ləʊniəlɪzəm, *Am:* -'loʊ-] *n no pl* colonialisme *m*

colonialist I. *n* colonialiste *mf* **II.** *adj* colonialiste

colonisation *n Aus, Brit s.* **colonization**

colonise ['kɒlənaɪz, *Am:* 'kɑːlənaɪz] *vt Aus, Brit s.* **colonize**

colonist *n* colon *m*

colonization *n no pl, Am* colonisation *f*

colonize ['kɒlənaɪz, *Am:* 'kɑːlə-] *vt* coloniser

colonizer *n* colonisateur, -trice *m, f*

colonnade [ˌkɒlə'neɪd, *Am:* ˌkɑːlə'-] *n* ARCHIT colonnade *f*

colony ['kɒləni, *Am:* 'kɑːlə-] *n* colonie *f*

color ['kʌləʳ, *Am:* -ɚ] *Am, Aus* **I.** *n* **1.** (*appearance*) *a. fig* couleur *f;* **to give sth ~, to give ~ to sth** colorer qc **2.** (*dye*) colorant *m;* (*for hair*) coloration *f* **3.** (*ruddiness*) teint *m;* **to put some ~ in one's cheeks** se mettre du fond de teint **4.** *pl* POL, GAMES couleurs *fpl;* **to display one's ~s** montrer son pavillon; **to be awarded one's ~s for a sport** être récompensé pour sa sélection dans une équipe; **to gain one's ~s for a sport** être sélectionné pour faire partie d'une équipe **5.** (*character*) **to show one's true ~s** se montrer tel que l'on est ▶**to pass with flying ~s** être reçu avec mention **II.** *vt* **1.** (*change colour*) colorer; **to ~ one's hair** se teindre les cheveux; **to ~ a room blue** peindre une pièce en bleu **2.** (*distort*) déformer **III.** *vi* rougir

Colorado [ˌkɒlə'rɑːdəʊ, *Am:* ˌkɑːlə'rædoʊ] *n* le Colorado

Colorado (potato) beetle *n* doryphore *m*

coloration [ˌkʌlə'reɪʃən] *n no pl* coloration *f*

colossal [kə'lɒsl, *Am:* -'lɑːsl] *adj* colossal(e)

colossi *n pl of* **colussus**

colossus [kə'lɒsəs] *n* <-es *o* colossi> *a. fig* colosse *m*

colossuses *n pl of* **colossus**

colour ['kʌləʳ, *Am:* -ɚ] *Brit, Aus s.* **color**

colo(u)r bar *n* discrimination *f* raciale

colo(u)r blind *adj* daltonien(ne) **colo(u)r blindness** *n* daltonisme *m*

colo(u)red I. *adj* coloré(e); (*pencil, people*) de couleur **II.** *n* **Colo(u)red** gens *mpl* de couleur

colo(u)r fast *adj* **this shirt is ~ (when washed)** les couleurs de cette chemise résistent au lavage **colo(u)r filter** *n* PHOT filtre *m* de couleur

colo(u)rful *adj* **1.** (*full of colour*) coloré(e) **2.** (*lively*) gai(e); (*part of town*) pittoresque; (*description*) intéressant(e)

colo(u)ring *n no pl* **1.** (*complexion*) complexion *f* **2.** (*chemical*) **artificial ~s** couleurs *fpl* artificielles

colo(u)rless *adj* **1.** (*having no colour*) incolore **2.** (*bland*) fade; (*city*) ennuyeux(-euse)

colo(u)r line *n Am* ségrégation *f* raciale
colo(u)r scheme *n* combinaison *f* de couleurs **colo(u)r slide** *n* diapositive *f* couleur
colo(u)r television *n* télévision *f* (en) couleur

cols *n abbr of* **columns** colonnes *fpl*

colt [kəʊlt, *Am:* koʊlt] *n* **1.** (*young horse*) poulain *m* **2.** (*weapon*) revolver *m*

Columbia [kəˈlʌmbiə] *n* Columbia *f;* **the District of ~** le district fédéral de Columbia

column [ˈkɒləm, *Am:* ˈkɑːləm] *n* **1.** (*pillar*) *a. fig* colonne *f;* **Nelson's Column** le monument de Nelson; **spinal ~** colonne vertébrale **2.** (*article*) rubrique *f*

columnist *n* chroniqueur, -euse *m, f*

coma [ˈkəʊmə, *Am:* ˈkoʊ-] *n* coma *m*

comatose [ˈkəʊmətəʊs, *Am:* ˈkoʊmətoʊs] *adj* **1.** (*in a coma*) comateux(-euse) **2.** *inf* (*coma-like*) **he is always in a ~ state!** il est toujours amorphe!

comb [kəʊm, *Am:* koʊm] **I.** *n* **1.** (*hair device*) peigne *m* **2.** ZOOL *s.* **cockscomb II.** *vt* **1.** (*tidy with a comb*) **to ~ one's hair** se peigner **2.** (*search*) chercher minutieusement; (*book*) décortiquer; **to ~ an apartment for clues** passer l'appartement au peigne fin

combat [ˈkɒmbæt, *Am:* ˈkɑːm-] **I.** *n* combat *m;* **hand-to-hand ~** corps-à-corps *m;* **the ~ between good and evil** la lutte entre le bien et le mal **II.** *vt* combattre; (*desire*) lutter contre

combat aircraft *n* avion *m* de combat

combatant [ˈkɒmbətənt, *Am:* kəmˈbæt-] *n* combattant(e) *m(f)*

combative [ˈkɒmbətɪv, *Am:* kəmˈbæt̬ɪv] *adj* combatif(-ive)

combination [ˌkɒmbɪˈneɪʃən, *Am:* ˌkɑːmbə-] *n* **1.** (*mixture of things*) mélange *m* **2.** (*arrangement*) arrangement *m;* (*of circumstances*) concours *m* **3.** (*sequence of numbers*) combinaison *f* de nombres ►**in ~** en association

combine [kəmˈbaɪn, *Am:* ˈkɑːmbaɪn] **I.** *vt* mélanger; **to ~ business with pleasure** joindre l'utile à l'agréable; **to ~ family life with a career** jongler avec la vie de famille et la carrière; **to ~ money** réunir de l'argent **II.** *vi* s'unir; **to ~ against sb** se liguer contre qn

combined *adj* mélangé(e); (*efforts*) conjugué(e)

combustible [kəmˈbʌstəbl] *adj form* **1.** (*highly flammable*) combustible; (*material*) inflammable **2.** (*excitable*) nerveux(-euse)

combustion [kəmˈbʌstʃən] *n no pl* combustion *f*

combustion chamber *n* chambre *f* de combustion

come [kʌm] <came, come, coming> *vi* **1.** (*arrive*) arriver; **to ~ towards sb** venir vers qn; **the year to ~** l'année à venir; **to ~ to sb's rescue** venir au secours de qn; **to ~ from a place** venir d'un endroit; **to ~ from a rich family** être issu d'une famille riche **2.** (*happen*) arriver; **how ~?** comment ça se fait ? **3.** (*exist*) **to ~ in a size/colour** être disponible en une taille/une couleur; **this shirt ~s with the pants** cette chemise est vendue avec le pantalon; **to ~ cheap(er)** coûter moins cher; **as it ~s** comme ça vient **4.** (*behave like*) **to ~ the poor little innocent with sb** se comporter comme un pauvre petit innocent avec qn **5.** (*become*) **to ~ loose** se desserrer; **to ~ open** s'ouvrir **6.** *inf* (*have an orgasm*) jouir ►**to ~ <u>clean</u> about sth** révéler qc; **to <u>have</u> it coming** n'avoir que ce que l'on mérite; **to ~ <u>unstuck</u>** *Aus, Brit* se décoller; **~ <u>again</u>?** comment?; **<u>don't</u> ~ it (with me)!** ne me le fait pas!; **~ <u>to</u> that!** au fait!

◆**come about** *vi* arriver

◆**come across I.** *vt* (*photos*) tomber sur; (*problem, obstacle*) rencontrer **II.** *vi* faire une impression; **to ~ well/badly** bien/mal passer; **to ~ as sth** donner l'impression d'être qc

◆**come along** *vi* arriver; **~!** allez, viens!; **are you coming along?** tu viens?, tu viens avec? *Belgique*

◆**come apart** *vi* **1.** (*fall to pieces*) tomber en morceaux **2.** (*detach*) se défaire **3.** *fig* (*person*) craquer

◆**come around** *vi s.* **come round**

◆**come at** *vt* **1.** (*attack*) attaquer **2.** (*arrive*) parvenir à

◆**come away** *vi* partir; **to ~ from sth** se détacher de qc

◆**come back** *vi* revenir; **it'll ~ to me** ça me reviendra; **she came back from love/forty and won** elle est revenue de zéro/quarante et a gagné

◆**come by I.** *vt insep* **1.** *s.* **come across 2.** (*obtain by chance*) trouver **II.** *vi* passer

◆**come down** *vi* **1.** (*move down*) descendre; (*curtain*) baisser **2.** (*in rank: people*) descendre d'un rang **3.** (*land*) atterrir **4.** (*fall: rain, snow*) tomber **5.** (*visit southern place*) descendre; **he came down from Paris** il est descendu de Paris **6.** (*become less: prices, cost, inflation*) baisser **7.** (*be detached*) se décrocher **8.** *fig* (*to be a matter*) **to ~ to sth** se ramener à qc; **to ~ to the fact that …** le fait est que …

◆**come forward** *vi* **1.** (*advance*) **to ~ to sb** s'avancer vers qn **2.** (*offer assistance*) se présenter; **to ~ with sth** présenter qc; **to ~ with a suggestion** faire une suggestion

◆**come in** *vi* **1.** (*enter*) entrer; **~!** entrez! **2.** (*arrive*) arriver; (*tide, sea*) monter; (*news, results, call*) s'annoncer; (*money*) rentrer; **to ~ first** arriver premier; **when do grapes ~?** quand commence la saison du raisin? **3.** (*become fashionable*) faire son apparition **4.** (*be*) **to ~ handy/useful** être utile **5.** (*participate in*) intervenir **6.** (*receive*) **to ~ for criticism** faire l'objet de critiques

◆**come into** *vt* **1.** (*enter*) entrer dans; **to ~ office** entrer en fonction; **to ~ fashion** devenir à la mode; **to ~ power** arriver au pouvoir; **to ~ the world** venir au monde **2.** (*get* *involved in*) **to ~ sb's life** s'ingérer dans la vie de qn **3.** (*be relevant*) **to ~ it** entrer en ligne de compte; **anger doesn't ~ it** la colère n'a rien à voir là-dedans **4.** (*inherit*) hériter de

◆come of *vi* arriver; **that's what comes of being too naive** voilà ce qui arrive quand on est trop naïf

◆come off **I.** *vi* **1.** *inf* (*succeed*) réussir **2.** (*end up*) **to ~ well/badly** s'en tirer bien/mal **3.** (*become detached*) se détacher **4.** (*rub off: stain*) partir; (*ink*) s'effacer **5.** (*take place*) avoir lieu; **the film didn't come off** le film n'a pas été projeté **II.** *vt* **1.** (*fall*) tomber de **2.** (*climb down*) descendre de **3.** (*detach*) se détacher de **4.** MED **to ~ of one's injuries** guérir de ses blessures **5.** *Brit* (*stop: alcohol*) arrêter **6.** *inf* (*expression of annoyance*) **~ it!** arrêtes ton char!

◆come on **I.** *vi* **1.** (*exhortation*) **~! you can do it!** allez! tu peux le faire!; **~! will you stop bothering me!** ça suffit! arrête un peu de m'ennuyer! **2.** (*improve*) faire des progrès; **he really came on with his tennis** il a fait de gros progrès au tennis **3.** (*start*) commencer; **to have a headache coming on** sentir venir un mal de tête **4.** (*start to work*) se mettre en route; (*lights*) s'allumer **5.** THEAT, CINE entrer en scène **6.** *Am, inf* (*express sexual interest*) **to ~ to sb** draguer qn **II.** *vt s.* **come upon**

◆come out *vi* **1.** (*appear, go out*) sortir; (*sun, star*) apparaître; (*flowers*) éclore **2.** (*express opinion*) se prononcer; **to ~ in favour of/against sth** se prononcer en faveur/contre qc **3.** (*emerge, result*) sortir; **to ~ of sth** se sortir de qc; **to ~ first** sortir premier **4.** (*become known*) être révélé; **to ~ that ...** s'avérer que ... **5.** (*say*) **to ~ with sth** sortir qc **6.** (*reveal one's homosexuality*) révéler son homosexualité **7.** *Brit* (*strike*) **to ~ on strike** faire la grève **8.** (*be removed*) partir; (*cork*) retirer; (*tooth, hair*) tomber **9.** (*fade: shirt*) déteindre **10.** (*be published: book, film*) sortir **11.** PHOT **the pictures came out pretty nice** les photos ont été réussies; **to not ~** ne rien donner **12.** (*end up*) **to ~ at a price** s'élever à un prix ►**it will all ~ in the wash** *prov* on le saura tôt ou tard

◆come over **I.** *vi* **1.** (*come nearer*) se rapprocher **2.** (*visit*) passer; **why don't you ~ tomorrow?** pourquoi ne viens-tu pas me voir demain? **3.** (*come, travel*) venir; **to ~ from France** venir de France **4.** *Aus, Brit* (*feel*) se sentir **5.** (*make impression*) **to ~ as sth** avoir l'air d'être qc; **to ~ well** bien passer **II.** *vt* (*person*) gagner; **what has ~ you?** qu'est-ce qui te prend?

◆come round *vi* **1.** (*change one's mind*) changer d'avis; **to ~ sb's way of thinking** se rallier à l'opinion de qn **2.** (*regain consciousness*) revenir à soi **3.** (*visit*) passer **4.** (*recur*) arriver

◆come through **I.** *vi* **1.** *Aus, Brit* (*arrive*) arriver **2.** (*survive*) survivre **3.** (*penetrate*) percer; **your love came through my heart** ton amour m'a traversé le cœur **II.** *vt* (*war, injuries*) survivre à

◆come to **I.** *vt* **1.** (*reach*) atteindre; (*decision*) en venir à; (*conclusion*) arriver à; **this road comes to an end** cette route est sans issue; **to ~ rest** s'arrêter; **she will ~ no harm** il ne lui arrivera pas de mal; **to ~ nothing** aboutir à rien; **I can't ~ terms with his illness** je n'arrive pas à me faire à sa maladie **2.** (*amount to*) s'élever à **II.** *vi* revenir à soi

◆come under *vt* **1.** (*be listed under*) être classé sous; **the case came under his care** l'affaire lui incombait **2.** (*be subjected to*) subir; **to ~ criticism** être sujet aux critiques; **to ~ suspicion** commencer à être soupçonné

◆come up **I.** *vi* **1.** (*go up*) monter; **to ~ for tea** monter prendre le thé **2.** (*arise, be mentioned: problem, situation*) se présenter; **to ~ against a problem** se heurter à un problème; **he came up in the speech** il a été cité dans le discours **3.** (*appear*) apparaître; (*sun*) se lever; (*plant*) sortir; (*tide*) monter; **the accident came up at the corner of the street** l'accident est survenu au coin de la rue **4.** (*approach*) (s')approcher; **the flood came up to the city** l'inondation est arrivée jusqu'à la ville **5.** LAW (*case*) passer au tribunal **6.** (*shine*) retrouver de sa brillance **7.** (*produce*) **to ~ with sth** (*solution*) trouver qc; (*idea*) proposer qc **II.** *vt* monter

◆come upon *vt* (*find*) tomber sur

comeback ['kʌmbæk] *n* **1.** (*return*) retour *m;* **to make a ~** faire son retour; *fig* faire une rentrée (théâtrale) **2.** (*retort*) réplique *f*

Comecon ['kɒmɪkɒn, *Am:* 'kɑːmɪkɑːn] *n abbr of* **Council for Mutual Economic Assistance** COMECON *m*

comedian [kə'miːdɪən] *n* comique *mf;* **you are such a ~!** quel comédien!

comedienne [kəˌmiːdi'ən] *n* comique *f*

comedown *n no pl, inf* **1.** (*anticlimax*) déception *f* **2.** (*decline in status*) déclin *m*

comedy ['kɒmədi, *Am:* 'kɑːmə-] *n* **1.** CINE, THEAT, LIT comédie *f* **2.** (*funny situation*) farce *f*

comely ['kʌmli] <-ier, -iest> *adj* beau(belle)

come-on *n Am, inf* **1.** (*expression of sexual interest*) drague *f;* **to give sb the ~** draguer qn **2.** (*enticement*) attrait *m*

comer *n* arrivant(e) *m(f)*

comestible [kə'mestɪbl] **I.** *adj* comestible **II.** *n pl* denrées *fpl* alimentaires

comet ['kɒmɪt, *Am:* 'kɑːmɪt] *n* comète *f*

comeuppance [kʌm'ʌpənts] *n inf* **to get one's ~** avoir ce qu'on mérite

comfort ['kʌmfət, *Am:* -fɚt] **I.** *n* **1.** (*ease*) confort *m;* **for ~** pour le confort **2.** (*consolation*) réconfort *m* **3.** *pl* (*pleasurable things*) commodités *fpl* **II.** *vt* réconforter

comfortable *adj* **1.** (*offering comfort*) confortable **2.** (*pleasant: sensation*) agréable **3.** (*at ease*) à l'aise; **to make oneself ~** se mettre à l'aise; **to not feel ~** se sentir mal à l'aise

C

4. (*having money*) aisé(e) 5. MED **to be ~** ne pas souffrir 6. (*substantial*) confortable; **to be in ~ circumstances** mener une vie aisée; **he has a ~ lead over his opponent** il a une avance confortable sur son adversaire

comfortably *adv* 1. (*in a comfortable manner: sit, lie*) confortablement 2. (*in a pleasant way*) agréablement 3. (*financially stable*) **to live ~** mener une vie aisée; **to be ~ off** être à l'aise financièrement 4. (*easily*) facilement 5. (*substantially*) **to lead ~** avoir une avance confortable

comforter *n Am* (*duvet*) édredon *m*

comforting *adj* consolant(e)

comfortless *adj form* 1. (*without comfort: room*) sans confort 2. *fig* peu rassurant(e); (*prospect*) démoralisant(e)

comfort station *n Am* (*public toilet*) toilettes *fpl*

comfy ['kʌmfi] <-ier, -iest> *adj inf* confortable

comic ['kɒmɪk, *Am:* 'kɑːmɪk] I. *n* 1. (*comedian*) comique *mf* 2. (*cartoon*) bande *f* dessinée II. *adj* comique

comical *adj* comique; **what a ~ idea you had!** quelle drôle d'idée tu as eue!

comic book *n Am* bande *f* dessinée **comic strip** *n* bande *f* dessinée

coming I. *adj* 1. (*next: year*) prochain(e); (*generation*) futur(e) 2. (*approaching*) à venir; (*hurricane*) qui approche; (*difficulties*) qui s'annonce; **in the ~ weeks** dans les semaines à venir; **this ~ Sunday** ce dimanche II. *n* 1. (*arrival*) venue *f* 2. REL **the ~ of the Messiah** l'avènement *m* du Messie ►**~s and goings** les allées et venues *fpl*

comma ['kɒmə, *Am:* 'kɑːmə] *n* virgule *f*

command [kə'mɑːnd, *Am:* -'mænd] I. *vt* 1. (*order*) **to ~ sb** ordonner à qn; **I ~ that** j'ordonne que +*subj* 2. (*have command over: regiment, ship*) commander 3. (*have at one's disposal*) avoir à sa disposition 4. *form* (*inspire: respect*) imposer 5. *form* (*give*) **his house ~s a view on the beach** sa maison donne sur la plage II. *vi* commander III. *n* 1. (*order*) ordre *m;* **he was at John's ~** il était aux ordres de John; **to have sth at one's ~** avoir la responsabilité de qc 2. (*control*) maîtrise *f;* **to be in ~ of oneself** rester maître de soi; **to be in ~ of sth** avoir le contrôle de qc 3. MIL commandement *m;* **to take ~ of a force** prendre le commandement d'une troupe 4. INFOR commande *f* 5. *no pl* (*knowledge: of a language*) maîtrise *f* 6. *no pl, form* (*view*) vue *f*

commandant [ˌkɒmən'dænt, *Am:* 'kɑːməndænt] *n* MIL commandant *m*

commandeer [ˌkɒmən'dɪəʳ, *Am:* ˌkɑːmən'dɪr] *vt* réquisitionner

commander *n* 1. MIL chef *m* 2. *Brit* MIL, NAUT capitaine *m*

commanding *adj* 1. (*authoritative*) autoritaire 2. (*dominant: position*) dominant(e) 3. (*considerable*) considérable

command key *n* INFOR touche *f* de commande **command line** *n* INFOR ligne *f* de commande

commandment *n* commandement *m;* **the Ten Commandments** REL les dix commandements

command module *n* AVIAT module *m* de commande

commando [kə'mɑːndəʊ, *Am:* -'mændoʊ] <-s *o* -es> *n* MIL commando *m*

command post *n* MIL poste *m* de commandement **command prompt** *n* INFOR invite *f* de commande

commemorate [kə'meməreɪt] *vt* commémorer

commemoration *n no pl* commémoration *f;* **in ~ of sb/sth** en commémoration de qn/qc

commemorative [kə'memərətɪv, *Am:* -t̬ɪv] *adj* commémoratif(-ive)

commence [kə'ments] *vi form* commencer

commencement [kə'mentsmənt] *n form* 1. (*beginning*) commencement *m;* (*of a journey, flight*) début *m* 2. *Am* (*graduation ceremony*) remise *f* des diplômes

commend [kə'mend] *vt* 1. (*praise*) louer; **this film was highly ~ed** ce film a été comblé de louanges 2. (*recommend*) recommander

commendable *adj* louable

commendation *n* 1. (*praise*) éloge *m* 2. (*honour*) honneur *m*

commendatory [kə'mendətəri, *Am:* -tɔːri] *adj* (*remark*) élogieux(-euse)

commensurable *adj* 1. MAT (*having common measure*) commensurable 2. *s.* **commensurate**

commensurate [kə'menʃərət, *Am:* -sɚ-] *adj form* **to be ~ with sth** être proportionnel à qc

comment ['kɒment, *Am:* 'kɑːment] I. *n* commentaire *m;* **to make a ~ about sth** faire une observation à propos de qc; **no ~** sans commentaire II. *vi* faire un commentaire; **to ~ on sth** faire des commentaires sur qc; **to refuse to ~ on sth** refuser de commenter qc III. *vt* **to ~ that ...** remarquer que ...

commentary ['kɒməntəri, *Am:* 'kɑːmənter-] *n* commentaire *m*

commentate ['kɒmənteɪt, *Am:* 'kɑːmən-] *vi* TV, RADIO faire le commentaire; **to ~ on sth** commenter qc

commentator *n* TV, RADIO commentateur, -trice *m, f*

comment line *n* INFOR ligne *f* de commentaires

commerce ['kɒmɜːs, *Am:* 'kɑːmɜːrs] *n* commerce *m;* **to be in ~** être dans les affaires

commercial I. *adj* 1. (*relating to commerce*) commercial(e) 2. *pej* (*profit-orientated: production, movie*) mercantile 3. (*available to public*) commercial(e) II. *n* publicité *f*

commercialism [kə'mɜːʃəlɪzəm, *Am:* -'mɜːr-] *n* mercantilisme *m*

commercialization *n no pl, Am* commer-

cialisation *f*
commercialize [kə'mɜːʃəlaɪz, *Am:* -'mɜːr-] *vt Am* commercialiser
commercialized *adj* commercial(e)
commiserate [kə'mɪzəreɪt] *vi* **to ~ with sb** témoigner de la sympathie à qn
commiseration *n* **1.** *no pl* (*sympathy*) commisération *f* **2.** *pl* (*expression of sympathy*) compassion *f*
commission [kə'mɪʃən] **I.** *vt* **1.** (*order*) commander; **to ~ sb to** +*infin* charger qn de +*infin* **2.** MIL mettre en service; **to ~ sb as sth** nommer qn à qc **II.** *n* **1.** (*order*) commission *f;* **to carry out a ~** s'acquitter d'une commission **2.** (*system of payment*) commission *f;* **to be on ~** travailler à la commission **3.** (*investigative body*) commission *f;* **fact-finding ~** commission d'enquête **4.** MIL affectation *f;* **to get one's ~** être nommé officier; **to resign one's ~** donner sa démission **5.** *no pl, form* (*perpetration: of a crime, murder*) perpétration *f* ►**in/out of ~** NAUT, AVIAT en/hors de service
commissionaire [kəˌmɪʃə'neəʳ, *Am:* -'er] *n Brit* commissionnaire *m*
commissioned officer *n* officier *m*
commissioner *n* commissaire *m*
commit [kə'mɪt] <-tt-> *vt* **1.** (*carry out*) commettre; **to ~ suicide** se suicider **2.** (*bind*) engager; **to ~ oneself to a relationship** s'engager dans une relation; **to ~ money to a project** mettre de l'argent dans un projet; **to ~ soldiers to the defence of a region** confier la défense d'une région à des soldats **3.** (*institutionalize: prisoner*) incarcérer; (*patient*) interner; **to ~ sb to prison/a hospital** envoyer qn en prison/à l'hôpital **4.** (*entrust*) confier; **to ~ sth to sb** confier qc à qn; **to ~ to memory** apprendre par cœur; **to ~ to paper** rapporter sur papier
commitment *n* engagement *m;* **he made a ~ to nuclear disarmament** il s'est engagé dans le désarmement nucléaire; **he asked for lighter teaching ~s** il a réclamé un enseignement moins chargé
committed *adj* engagé(e); (*socialist, Christian*) convaincu(e)
committee [kə'mɪti, *Am:* -'mɪt̬-] *n* comité *m;* **to be on a ~** être membre d'un comité; **to be** [*o* **sit**] **on a ~** siéger à une commission
Committee of the Regions *n* Comité *m* des régions
commode [kə'məʊd, *Am:* -'moʊd] *n* chaise *f* percée
commodious *adj form* spacieux(-euse)
commodity [kə'mɒdəti, *Am:* -'mɑːdət̬i] <-ties> *n* **1.** (*product*) denrée *f* **2.** (*raw material*) matière *f* première
commodore ['kɒmədɔːʳ, *Am:* 'kɑːmədɔːr] *n* **1.** MIL (*high-ranking naval officer*) contre-amiral *m* **2.** (*yacht club president*) président(e) *m(f)* de yacht-club
common ['kɒmən, *Am:* 'kɑːmən] **I.** <-er, -est *o* more ~, most ~> *adj* **1.** (*ordinary: name*) courant(e); **in ~ use** d'un usage courant **2.** (*widespread*) notoire; (*disease*) répandu(e); **it is ~ knowledge that...** il est de notoriété publique que...; **to be ~ practice** être d'usage **3.** *inv* (*shared*) commun(e); **the ~ good** le bien commun; **by ~ assent** d'un commun accord; **to make ~ cause with sb** faire cause commune avec qn; **to have sth in ~ with sb/sth** avoir qc en commun avec qn/qc **4.** <-er, -est> *pej* (*low-class*) commun(e); (*criminal, thief*) de bas étage **5.** (*average*) ordinaire; **the ~ people** les gens ordinaires; (*man*) du peuple; (*accent*) populaire **II.** *n* terrain *m* communal
common denominator *n a.* MAT dénominateur *m* commun
commoner *n* roturier, -ière *m, f*
common land *n* territoire *m* commun **common law** *n no pl* droit *m* commun
commonly *adv* communément
commonplace **I.** *adj* banal(e) **II.** *n* lieu *m* commun **common room** *n Brit* salle *f* de détente; **junior/senior ~** salle *f* d'étude **common sense** *n no pl* bon sens *m* **common stock** *n Am* FIN action *f* ordinaire
commonwealth *n* communauté *f* d'États Indépendants **Commonwealth** *n* HIST **the ~** le Commonwealth

> Le **Commonwealth of Nations**, (auparavant "British Commonwealth"), est une organisation bénévole d'États indépendants qui s'est petit à petit développée à partir de l'ancien "British Empire". En 1931, elle fut officiellement fondée avec le "Statute of Westminster". A cette époque, le Canada, l'Australie, l'Afrique du Sud et la Nouvelle-Zélande, qui jouissaient déjà d'une autogestion, furent les premiers États membres avec le Royaume-Uni. La plupart des pays qui étaient auparavant sous le joug britannique décidèrent lors de leur indépendance d'entrer dans le "Commonwealth". Actuellement, l'organisation repose essentiellement sur la coopération culturelle et économique. Les chefs d'États des pays membres du "Commonwealth" se réunissent deux fois par an.

commotion [kə'məʊʃən, *Am:* -'moʊ-] *n* agitation *f*
communal *adj* commun(e); (*facilities*) à usage collectif; (*living, life*) communautaire; **~ ownership** copropriété *f*
commune [kə'mjuːn] *n* + *pl/sing vb* **1.** (*kibbutz-like settlement*) communauté *f* **2.** (*smallest unit of local government*) commune *f*
communicable *adj form* (*emotion, thoughts, information*) communicable; (*disease*) contagieux(-euse) *f*
communicate [kə'mjuːnɪkeɪt] **I.** *vt* communiquer; (*illness*) transmettre **II.** *vi* communiquer; **to ~ with one's hands** communiquer

par gestes; **I'm afraid we just don't** ~ je crains que nous manquions simplement de communication *subj*

communication *n a. form* communication *f;* **means of** ~ moyens *mpl* de communication

communicative [kə'mjuːnɪkətɪv, *Am:* -nəkeɪt̬ɪv] *adj* communicatif(-ive)

communion [kə'mjuːnɪən, *Am:* -njən] *n no pl* **1.** (*intimate communication*) communion *f* **2.** (*religious community*) congrégation *f* (religieuse) **3.** REL Communion *f; s. a.* **Holy Communion**

communiqué [kə'mjuːnɪkeɪ, *Am:* kə,mjuːnɪ'keɪ] *n* communiqué *m*

communism ['kɒmjʊnɪzəm, *Am:* 'kaːmjə-] *n no pl* communisme *m*

communist **I.** *n* communiste *mf* **II.** *adj* communiste; **Communist Party** Parti *m* Communiste

community [kə'mjuːnəti, *Am:* -nət̬i] <-ties> *n* **1.** (*group living in one area*) communauté *f* **2.** (*animals*) faune *f* **3.** (*plants*) flore *f* **4.** (*togetherness*) communauté *f;* **a sense of** ~ un sentiment communautaire; REL, LIT un sentiment de communion; (*mil, pol*) l'esprit *m* de corps **5.** (*public*) **the** ~ l'assistance *f;* **a** ~ **hospital/organization** un hôpital/organisme public

community centre *n* centre *m* culturel

community service *n* LAW travail *m* d'intérêt général **community singing** *n no pl* hymne *m* **community worker** *n* animateur, -trice *m, f* socioculturel(le)

commutable *adj* **1.** (*within commuting distance*) faisable au quotidien **2.** (*able to be converted*) FIN convertible **3.** MAT, TECH permutable **4.** LAW commuable

commutation *n* **1.** (*act of commuting*) *a.* TECH, LAW commutation *f* **2.** MAT, TECH (*changing the order of sth*) permutation *f*

commute [kə'mjuːt] **I.** *vi* **to** ~ **to work** faire la navette entre son domicile et son travail; **to** ~ **from** [*o* **between**] **Brighton to London** faire la navette entre Brighton et Londres; **to** ~ **by train** faire le trajet en train **II.** *vt form* **1.** (*change*) échanger; **to** ~ **sth for** [*o* **into**] **sth** changer qc en qc **2.** LAW commuer **III.** *n* trajet *m*

commuter **I.** *n* banlieusard(e) *m(f),* navetteur, -euse *m, f Belgique* (*personne qui fait la navette entre deux lieux*) **II.** *adj inv* (*traffic*) de pointe; (*train*) de banlieue

commuter belt *n* grande banlieue *f*

Comoran ['kɒmərən, *Am:* 'kaːm-] **I.** *adj* comorien(ne) **II.** *n* Comorien(ne) *m(f)*

Comoros ['kɒmərəʊz, *Am:* 'kaːməroʊz] *npl* **the** ~ [*o* **Comoro Islands**] les Comores *fpl*

compact¹ ['kɒmpækt, *Am:* 'kaːm-] **I.** *adj* compact(e) **II.** *vt form* compacter **III.** *n Am, Aus* AUTO voiture *f* de petit modèle

compact² ['kɒmpækt, *Am:* 'kaːm-] *n* boite *f* à poudre (de riz)

compact³ ['kɒmpækt, *Am:* 'kaːm-] *n form* pacte *m*

compactness *n no pl* compacité *f*

companion [kəm'pænjən] *n* **1.** (*accompanying person or animal*) compagnon *m,* compagne *f;* **travelling** ~ compagnon de voyage **2.** (*reference book*) vademecum *m* **3.** (*churchmen book*) bréviaire *m*

companionable [kəm'pænjənəbl] *adj* de bonne compagnie

companionship *n no pl* compagnie *f*

companionway [kəm'pænjənweɪ] *n* NAUT escalier *m* entre ponts

company ['kʌmpəni] <-ies> *n* compagnie *f;* **Duggan and Company** Duggan et Compagnie; **to be in good/interesting/dull/poor** ~ être en bonne/intéressante/triste/médiocre compagnie; **to keep** ~ **with sb** rester en compagnie de qn; **in** (**the**) ~ **of sb** en compagnie de qn

comparable ['kɒmpərəbl, *Am:* 'kaːm-] *adj* comparable; ~ **to** [*o* **with**] **sth** comparable à qc

comparative [kəm'pærətɪv, *Am:* -'perət̬ɪv] **I.** *n* comparatif *m* **II.** *adj inv* comparatif(-ive)

comparatively *adv* **1.** (*by comparison*) en comparaison **2.** (*relatively*) relativement; ~ **speaking** toutes proportions gardées

compare [kəm'peəʳ, *Am:* -'per] **I.** *vt* comparer **II.** *vi* être comparable ►**to** ~ **favourably with sth** faire le poids avec qc

comparison [kəm'pærɪsn, *Am:* -'per-] *n* comparaison *f;* **by** [*o* **in**] ~ **with sb/sth** en comparaison avec qn/qc; **for** ~ en comparaison; **to bear** ~ **with sb/sth** supporter la comparaison avec qn/qc

compartment [kəm'paːtmənt, *Am:* -'paːrt-] *n a.* RAIL compartiment *m*

compass ['kʌmpəs] <-es> *n* **1.** (*direction-finding device*) boussole *f;* NAUT, TECH compas *m* **2.** *no pl, form* (*range*) portée *f;* **to be beyond the** ~ **of sb's brain/knowledge** être hors du champ de compréhension/connaissance de qn; **to be beyond the** ~ **of sb's powers** être en dehors du pouvoir de qn **3.** MUS registre *m*

compassion [kəm'pæʃən] *n no pl* compassion *f*

compassionate [kəm'pæʃənət] *adj* compatissant(e); ~ **leave** congé *m* exceptionnel

compatibility [kəm,pætə'bɪləti, *Am:* -,pæt̬ə'bɪlət̬i] *n no pl a.* MED, INFOR compatibilité *f*

compatible [kəm'pætəbl, *Am:* -'pæt̬-] *adj* **1.** (*able to co-exist*) *a.* INFOR, MED compatible; **to be** ~ **with sb/sth** être compatible avec qn/qc; (*suited for*); **to be** ~ **with sb/sth** être bien assorti avec qn/qc **2.** (*consistent*) cohérent(e)

compatriot [kəm'pætrɪət, *Am:* -'peɪtrɪ-] *n* **1.** *form* ((*fellow*) *countryman*) compatriote *mf* **2.** *Am* (*companion, work colleague*) collègue *mf*

compel [kəm'pel] <-ll-> *vt* **1.** *form* (*force*) contraindre **2.** *form* (*bring out*) produire

compelling *adj* (*speech*) convaincant(e);

(*film, painting, performance*) fascinant(e)
compendium [kəm'pendɪəm] <-diums *o* -dia> *n* condensé *m*
compensate ['kɒmpənseɪt, *Am:* 'kɑːm-] **I.** *vt* dédommager **II.** *vi* **to ~ for sth** compenser qc
compensation *n no pl* **1.** (*monetary amends*) dédommagement *m;* **~ claim** demande *f* d'indemnisation **2.** (*recompense*) compensation *f;* **in ~** en compensation
compere ['kɒmpeə^r, *Am:* 'kɑːmper] *Brit, inf* **I.** *n* animateur, -trice *m, f* **II.** *vt* (*a show*) animer
compete [kəm'piːt] *vi* **1.** (*strive*) rivaliser; **to ~ for sth** se disputer qc; **to ~ in an event** participer à un évènement; **to ~ with sb** être en compétition avec qn **2.** SPORT être en compétition
competence, **competency** *n no pl* compétence *f*
competent ['kɒmpɪtənt, *Am:* 'kɑːmpɪt̬ənt] *adj* **1.** (*capable*) compétent(e) **2.** LAW (*witness*) autorisé(e)
competition [ˌkɒmpə'tɪʃən, *Am:* ˌkɑːm-] *n* **1.** (*state of competing*) compétition *f;* **to be in ~ with sb** être en compétition avec qn **2.** (*rivalry*) **I'm sure she's no ~** je suis sûr qu'elle n'est pas une adversaire redoutable **3.** (*contest*) **beauty/swimming/diving ~** concours *m* de beauté/de natation/de plongée
competitive [kəm'petətɪv, *Am:* -'pet̬ət̬ɪv] *adj* compétitif(-ive); (*spirit, sports*) de compétition; (*person*) qui a l'esprit de compétition
competitiveness *n no pl* compétitivité *f*
competitor *n* compétiteur, -trice *m, f*
compilation *n* compilation *f*
compile [kəm'paɪl] *vt a.* INFOR compiler
compiler *n* **1.** (*person*) compilateur, -trice *m, f* **2.** INFOR compilateur *m*
complacence, **complacency** *n no pl, pej* suffisance *f*
complacent [kəm'pleɪsənt] *adj pej* suffisant(e)
complain [kəm'pleɪn] *vi* se plaindre; **to ~ about/of sth** se plaindre de qc
complainant [kəm'pleɪnənt] *n* LAW plaignant(e) *m(f)*
complaint [kəm'pleɪnt] *n* **1.** (*expression of displeasure*) *a.* ECON réclamation *f;* **to have/make a ~ about sb/sth** avoir/faire une réclamation à propos de qn/qc; **to make a ~ to sb** faire une réclamation auprès de qn **2.** (*accusation, charge*) plainte *f* **3.** (*illness*) souffrance *f*
complaisance [kəm'pleɪzəns, *Am:* -səns] *n no pl, form* complaisance *f*
complaisant [kəm'pleɪzənt, *Am:* -sənt] *adj form* complaisant(e)
complement ['kɒmplɪmənt, *Am:* 'kɑːm-] *vt* compléter; **to ~ each other** se compléter
complementary [ˌkɒmplɪ'mentəri, *Am:* ˌkɑːmplə'ment̬ɚi] *adj* complémentaire
complete [kəm'pliːt] **I.** *vt* **1.** (*add what is missing*) compléter **2.** (*finish*) achever **3.** (*fill out entirely*) remplir **II.** *adj* **1.** (*whole*) complet(-ète) **2.** (*total*) total(e); **the man's a ~ fool!** l'homme est un parfait idiot!; **~ stranger/mastery** un parfait étranger/une parfaite maîtrise
completely *adv* complètement
completeness *n no pl* intégralité *f*
completion [kəm'pliːʃən] *n no pl* achèvement *m;* **to near ~** être presque à l'état final
complex ['kɒmpleks, *Am:* 'kɑːm-] **I.** *adj* complexe **II.** <-xes> *n* complexe *m*
complexion [kəm'plekʃən] *n* **1.** (*natural appearance of facial skin*) teint *m* **2.** (*character*) complexion *f* ►**to put a different/new ~ on sth** apporter un éclairage différent/nouveau à qc
complexity [kəm'pleksəti, *Am:* -sət̬i] *n* complexité *f*
compliance *n no pl, form* conformité *f;* **in ~ with the law/regulations** conformément à la loi/aux dispositions (réglementaires); **to act** [*o* **be**] **in ~ with sth** se conformer à qc
compliant [kəm'plaɪənt] *adj form* **1.** (*obedient*) docile **2.** (*overly obedient*) maniable
complicate ['kɒmplɪkeɪt, *Am:* 'kɑːmplə-] *vt* compliquer
complicated *adj* compliqué(e)
complication *n a.* MED complication *f*
complicity [kəm'plɪsəti, *Am:* -ət̬i] *n* LAW *no pl, form* complicité *f*
compliment ['kɒmplɪmənt, *Am:* 'kɑːmplə-] **I.** *n* compliment *m;* **to pay sb a ~** adresser un compliment à qn; **with ~s** avec tous nos compliments ►**to be fishing for ~s** mendier les éloges **II.** *vt* **to ~ sb on sth** complimenter qn pour qc
complimentary [ˌkɒmplɪ'mentəri, *Am:* ˌkɑːmplə'ment̬ɚi] *adj* **1.** (*characterized by compliment*) élogieux(-euse); **to be ~ about sth** être élogieux à l'égard de qc **2.** (*free, without charge*) gratuit(e)
comply [kəm'plaɪ] *vi form* **to ~ with sth** se conformer à qc; **to refuse to ~** refuser de se plier
component [kəm'pəʊnənt, *Am:* -'poʊ-] *n* **1.** (*part*) constituant *m;* (*of a system*) élément *m;* **key ~** élément-clé *m* **2.** TECH composant *m*
component part *n* **1.** (*part*) élément *m* constitutif **2.** (*spare part*) pièce *f* détachée
compose [kəm'pəʊz, *Am:* -'poʊz] **I.** *vi* composer **II.** *vt* **1.** (*produce, make up*) composer; **to be ~d of sth** être composé de qc **2.** (*write*) rédiger **3.** (*calm, collect*) calmer; (*one's thoughts*) rassembler; **to ~ oneself** se ressaisir; **to ~ differences** *form* dépasser les différences
composed *adj* **1.** (*collected*) rassemblé(e) **2.** (*calm*) imperturbable
composer *n* compositeur, -trice *m, f*
composite ['kɒmpəzɪt, *Am:* kəm'pɑː-] **I.** *n* **1.** (*mixture*) mélange *m* **2.** PHOT montage *m* **3.** (*mixture of building materials*) agrégat *m*

C

II. *adj* hétéroclite; (*photograph, picture*) composite

composition [ˌkɒmpəˈzɪʃən, *Am:* ˌkɑːm-] *n* composition *f*

compositor *n* compositeur, -trice *m, f*

compost [ˈkɒmpɒst, *Am:* ˈkɑːmpoʊst] **I.** *n no pl* **1.** (*naturally produced*) terreau *m* **2.** (*artificially mixed*) compost *m* **II.** *vt* composter **III.** *vi* fabriquer du compost

composure [kəmˈpəʊʒəʳ, *Am:* -ˈpoʊʒɚ] *n no pl* calme; **to lose/to regain one's ~** perdre/retrouver son sang froid

compound [ˈkɒmpaʊnd, *Am:* ˈkɑːm-] **I.** *vt* **1.** (*make worse: a problem*) aggraver **2.** (*mix*) **to ~ sth with sth** mélanger qc avec qc **3.** (*make up*) constituer **II.** *n* **1.** (*enclosed area*) enceinte *f;* **family ~** domaine *m* familial; **embassy ~** territoire *m* de l'ambassade **2.** CHEM (*mixture*) composé *m;* **nitrogen ~** composé azoté **3.** LING mot *m* composé **4.** (*combination: of feelings, thoughts*) composition *f* **III.** *adj* composé(e)

compound fracture *n* MED fracture *f* ouverte **compound interest** *n* FIN intérêt *m* composé

comprehend [ˌkɒmprɪˈhend, *Am:* ˌkɑːm-] *vi, vt a. form* comprendre

comprehensible [ˌkɒmprɪˈhensəbl, *Am:* ˌkɑːm-] *adj* compréhensible

comprehension [ˌkɒmprɪˈhenʃən, *Am:* ˌkɑːm-] *n no pl* compréhension *f;* **listening ~ test** test d'intégration auditive; **reading ~ test** test de compréhension du langage écrit; **beyond ~** au-delà de tout entendement; **he has no ~ of the size of the problem** il n'a aucune idée de l'ampleur du problème

comprehensive [ˌkɒmprɪˈhensɪv, *Am:* ˌkɑːmprə-] **I.** *adj* intégral(e); (*global: coverage*) total(e); (*list*) complet(-ète); **fully ~** tout compris **II.** *n Brit* école *f* publique du secondaire

> Une **comprehensive school** est un lycée regroupant le premier et le second cycle pour des élèves de 11 à 18 ans. Dans les années 60-70, les "comprehensive schools" remplacèrent dans de nombreuses régions les "grammar schools" (pour des élèves ayant obtenu le "eleven-plus examination") et les "secondary modern schools".

compress¹ [kəmˈpres] *vt* **1.** (*press into small(er) space: air, gas*) comprimer **2.** (*condense*) condenser **3.** INFOR comprimer

compress² <-es> *n* compresse *f*

compressed *adj* (*air*) comprimé(e)

compression [kəmˈpreʃən] *n a.* INFOR compression *f*

compressor *n* compresseur *m* (d'air)

comprise [kəmˈpraɪz] *vt form* **1.** (*consist of*) consister en **2.** (*make up*) constituer

compromise [ˈkɒmprəmaɪz, *Am:* ˈkɑːm-] **I.** *n* compromis *m* **II.** *vi* transiger; **to ~ at** [*o* **on**] **sth** accepter une concession; **after long negotiations they ~d at $3500** après de longs pourparlers ils tranchèrent à 3500 $ **III.** *vt pej* compromettre

compromising *adj* compromettant(e)

comptroller [kənˈtrəʊləʳ, *Am:* -ˈtroʊlɚ] *n* **1.** (*management assistant*) contrôleur, -euse *m, f* de gestion **2.** (*financial inspector*) contrôleur, -euse *m, f* général des finances

compulsion [kəmˈpʌlʃən] *n no pl* **1.** (*irresistible desire/urge*) compulsion *f;* **to have a ~ to** +*infin* avoir un besoin compulsif de +*infin;* **he seems to have a constant ~ to eat** il semble avoir un besoin de manger permanent et irrépressible **2.** (*force*) contrainte *f;* **to be under ~ to** +*infin* être dans l'obligation de +*infin*

compulsive [kəmˈpʌlsɪv] *adj* compulsif(-ive); (*liar*) incorrigible; (*smoker*) invétéré(e); **~ reading/viewing** lecture/spectacle captivant(e); **utterly ~** complètement obsessionnel; **her latest book is a ~ read** son dernier livre est passionnant

compulsory [kəmˈpʌlsəri] *adj* (*attendance, education*) obligatoire; **~ by law** obligé(e) par la loi

compunction [kəmˈpʌŋkʃən] *n no pl* **to have (a) ~ about sth** avoir des scrupules pour qc

computation *n* calcul *m*

compute [kəmˈpjuːt] *vt* calculer ▶**it doesn't ~** *Am* cela ne cadre pas

computer *n* INFOR ordinateur *m*

computer centre *n* centre *m* informatique **computer crime** *n* délinquance *f* informatique **computer freak** *n* crack *inf* en informatique *mf* **computer game** *n* jeu *m* informatique; (*on games console*) jeu *m* vidéo **computer graphics** *n* + *sing/pl vb* infographie *f*

computerization *n no pl* **1.** (*computer storage*) stockage *m* informatique; **the ~ of the company's records** l'informatisation *f* des archives de la société **2.** (*equipping with computers*) informatisation *f*

computerize [kəmˈpjuːtəraɪz, *Am:* -t̬əraɪz] **I.** *vt* **1.** (*store on computer*) stocker sur ordinateur **2.** (*equip with computers*) informatiser **II.** *vi* s'informatiser

computer network *n* réseau *m* informatique **computer programmer** *n* (analyste-)programmeur *mf* (en informatique) **computer science** *n* informatique *f;* **~ course** cours *m* d'informatique **computer scientist** *n* informaticien(ne) *m(f)* **computer search** *n* recherche *f* informatique **computer tomography** *n* MED tomographie *f* **computer virus** <-es> *n* virus *m* informatique

computing *n* informatique *f*

comrade [ˈkɒmreɪd, *Am:* ˈkɑːmræd] *n* camarade *mf*

comradeship *n no pl* camaraderie *f*

COMSAT ['kɒmsæt, *Am:* 'kɑːm-] *n Am abbr of* **communications satellite** satellite *m* de communication

con [kɒn, *Am:* kɑːn] <-nn-> **I.** *vt* **to ~ sb into believing that …** tromper qn en lui faisant croire que …; **to ~ sb out of £10** escroquer qn de £10; **to ~ sth out of sb** escroquer qc de qn **II.** *n inf* arnaque *f*

con artist *n* escroc *m*

concatenation [kɒnˌkætɪ'neɪʃən, *Am:* kənˌkæt̬ə-] *n* INFOR concaténation *f*

concave ['kɒnkeɪv, *Am:* kɑːn-] *adj* concave

concavity [kən'kævɪti, *Am:* kɑːn'kævət̬i] *n* concavité *f*

conceal [kən'siːl] *vt* cacher; (*evidence, surprise*) dissimuler; **to ~ sth from sb** cacher qc à qn; **to ~ the truth** cacher la vérité

concealer *n* correcteur *m* de teint

concealment *n no pl* cachette *f;* (*of information, evidence, feelings*) dissimulation *f*

concede [kən'siːd] **I.** *vt* concéder; **to ~ that …** admettre que …; **to ~ independence to a country** accorder son indépendance à un pays **II.** *vi* céder

conceit [kən'siːt] *n no pl* (*vanity*) suffisance *f*

conceited *adj pej* suffisant(e); **without wishing to sound ~** sans vouloir être prétentieux

conceivable *adj* concevable; **by every ~ means** par tous les moyens possibles et imaginables; **in every ~ place** dans tous les endroits possibles

conceive [kən'siːv] **I.** *vt* **1.** (*imagine, produce: idea, plan, baby*) concevoir **2.** (*arrange: food, exhibition*) élaborer **II.** *vi* concevoir; **to ~ of sb/sth as sth** percevoir qn/qc comme qc

concentrate ['kɒnsəntreɪt, *Am:* 'kɑːn-] **I.** *vi* **1.** (*focus one's thoughts*) se concentrer; **to ~ on sth** se concentrer sur qc **2.** (*gather, come together*) se rassembler **II.** *vt* concentrer; **to ~ one's thoughts** se concentrer **III.** *n* (*not diluted liquid*) concentré *m;* **tomato ~** concentré de tomate; **fruit juice ~** jus *m* de fruit concentré

concentrated *adj* **1.** (*focused*) concentré(e); (*effort*) résolu(e) **2.** (*not diluted: juice, solution*) concentré(e)

concentration *n no pl* concentration *f;* **~ on sth** concentration *f* sur qc; **powers of ~** capacité *f* de concentration; **~ span** temps *m* de concentration; **to lose (one's) ~** se déconcentrer

concentration camp *n* camp *m* de concentration

concentric [kən'sentrɪk] *adj* concentrique

concept ['kɒnsept, *Am:* 'kɑːn-] *n* (*idea, project*) concept *m;* **do you have any ~ of what it will involve?** est-ce que tu te rends compte de ce que cela va impliquer?

conception [kən'sepʃən] *n* conception *f*

conceptual [kən'septʃuəl] *adj* conceptuel(le); **the problem of the policy is ~** la mesure a été mal pensée au niveau du concept

conceptualise *Aus, Brit,* **conceptualize** *Am* **I.** *vi* penser **II.** *vt* conceptualiser

concern [kən'sɜːn, *Am:* -'sɜːrn] **I.** *vt* **1.** (*apply to, involve, affect*) concerner; **to ~ oneself about sth** s'occuper de qc; **to be ~ed with sth** être concerné par qc **2.** (*worry*) inquiéter; **to ~ oneself** s'inquiéter ▸**to whom it may ~** ADMIN à qui de droit **II.** *n* **1.** (*interest*) intérêt *m;* **it was no ~ of hers!** ça ne la regardait absolument pas!; **to be of ~ to sb** intéresser qn **2.** (*care*) souci *m* **3.** (*worry*) inquiétude *f;* **~ for sth** inquiétude à propos de qc; **the subject is of some ~ to her** ce sujet l'inquiète un peu; **his ~ is that …** ce qui l'inquiète c'est que … **4.** (*company, business*) entreprise *f;* **a going ~** une entreprise qui marche bien

concerned *adj* **1.** (*involved*) concerné(e); **as far as I'm ~** en ce qui me concerne; **to be clumsy where romance is ~** être maladroit en matière de romantisme; **the conference is something ~ with linguistics** la conférence a à voir avec la linguistique **2.** (*worried*) inquiet(-ète); **isn't he ~ that she finds out?** il n'a pas peur qu'elle l'apprenne?; **to be ~ to hear sth** être préoccupé d'apprendre qc; **to be ~ about sth** se faire du souci pour qc

concerning *prep* en ce qui concerne

concert ['kɒnsət, *Am:* 'kɑːnsɚt] *n* concert *m;* **~ hall** salle *f* de concert; **~ tour** tournée *f* de concerts; **in ~** *fig* de concert; **in ~ with sb** *fig* en accord avec qn

concerted *adj* **1.** (*joint: action, attack, exercise*) concerté(e) **2.** (*resolute: effort, attempt*) résolu(e)

concert grand *n* piano *m* de concert

concertina [ˌkɒnsə'tiːnə, *Am:* ˌkɑːnsɚ-] **I.** *n* MUS concertina *m* **II.** *vi Aus, Brit* se plier en accordéon

concertmaster *n Am* MUS premier violon *m*

concerto [kən'tʃeətəʊ, *Am:* -'tʃert̬oʊ] <-s *o* -ti> *n* MUS concerto *m*

concert pitch *n* MUS diapason *m* ▸**to be at ~** être au diapason

concession [kən'seʃən] *n* **1.** (*sth granted*) concession *f;* **as a ~** en concession; **to make a ~ to sb** faire une concession à qn; **to make a ~ to sth** tenir compte de qc **2.** (*reduction*) tarif *m* réduit

conciliate [kən'sɪlɪeɪt] **I.** *vi* apporter la réconciliation; **to ~ between two people** réconcilier deux personnes **II.** *vt* **1.** (*gain support of, placate*) apaiser **2.** (*reconcile*) réconcilier

conciliation *n no pl, form* conciliation *f*

conciliation board *n* ≈ conseil *m* des prud'hommes

conciliatory [kən'sɪlɪətəri, *Am:* -tɔːri] *adj* conciliant(e)

concise [kən'saɪs] *adj* (*answer, letter*) concis(e); (*edition, dictionary*) abrégé(e)

conciseness, concision *n no pl* concision *f*

conclave ['kɒnkleɪv, *Am:* 'kɑːn-] *n form* **1.** (*private meeting*) conseil *m* **2.** REL conclave *m*

conclude [kən'klu:d] **I.** *vi* conclure; **to ~ with a remark** conclure en faisant une remarque; **to ~ from sth that ...** conclure à partir de qc que ... **II.** *vt* conclure
concluding *adj* (*chapter, episode*) dernier(-ère); (*remark, word*) de conclusion
conclusion [kən'klu:ʒən] *n* conclusion *f;* **in ~** en conclusion; **to come to a ~** parvenir à une conclusion; **to draw the ~ that ...** tirer la conclusion selon laquelle ...; **don't jump to ~s!** ne va pas te faire de film!
conclusive [kən'klu:sɪv] *adj* concluant(e)
concoct [kən'kɒkt, *Am:* -'kɑ:kt] *vt* concocter
concoction *n* (*dish, drink*) mixture *f; iron;* **a recipe of his ~** une recette de son cru
concourse ['kɒŋkɔ:s, *Am:* 'kɑ:nkɔ:rs] *n* (*of station, airport*) hall *m*
concrete ['kɒnkri:t, *Am:* 'kɑ:n-] **I.** *n no pl* **1.** béton *m;* **reinforced ~** béton armé **2.** *fig* **to be cast in ~** être fixe **II.** *adj* en béton **III.** *vt* **to ~ sth (over)** bétonner qc
concrete mixer *n s.* **cement mixer**
concubine ['kɒŋkjʊbaɪn, *Am:* 'kɑ:ŋ-] *n* HIST concubine *f*
concur [kən'kɜ:ʳ, *Am:* -'kɜ:r] <-rr-> *vi form* (*agree*) **to ~ with sb in sth** être d'accord avec qn sur qc; **to ~ with sb's opinion/view** partager l'opinion/le point de vue de qn
concurrence *n no pl, form* **1.** (*agreement*) accord *m* **2.** (*simultaneous occurrence*) coïncidence *f*
concurrent [kən'kʌrənt] *adj* simultané(e)
concuss [kən'kʌs] *vt* **to be ~ed** être commotionné
concussed *adj* commotionné(e)
concussion [kən'kʌʃən] *n no pl* commotion *f;* **brain ~** commotion cérébrale
condemn [kən'dem] *vt* **1.** (*reprove, denounce, sentence*) condamner; **the book was ~ed as fascist** le livre a été condamné comme étant fasciste; **to be ~ed to death** être condamné à mort **2.** (*formally pronounce unsafe*) **to ~ a building** déclarer un bâtiment insalubre **3.** (*pronounce unsafe for consumption*) déclarer impropre à la consommation
condemnation *n* condamnation *f*
condensation *n no pl* **1.** (*process, on window*) condensation *f* **2.** (*reducing in size*) réduction *f*
condense [kɒn'dens] **I.** *vt* condenser; **to ~ sth into sth** condenser qc en qc **II.** *vi* se condenser
condenser *n* CHEM condenseur *m*
condescend [ˌkɒndɪ'send, *Am:* ˌkɑ:n-] *vi iron* **to ~ to** +*infin* condescendre à +*infin*
condescending *adj* condescendant(e)
condescension [ˌkɒdɪ'senʃən, *Am:* ˌkɑ:n-] *n* condescendance *f*
condiment ['kɒndɪmənt, *Am:* 'kɑ:ndə-] *n form* condiment *m*
condition [kən'dɪʃən] **I.** *n* **1.** (*state*) état *m;* **in mint ~** en parfait état; **in a terrible ~** dans un état lamentable **2.** (*circumstance*) condition *f;* **weather ~s** conditions météorologiques; **working ~s** conditions de travail; **in certain ~s** à certaines conditions **3.** (*term, stipulation*) condition *f;* **on the ~ that ...** à condition que ...; **under the ~s of sth** selon les conditions de qc **4.** (*physical state*) forme *f;* **in peak ~** au meilleur de sa forme; **to be out of ~** ne pas être en forme; **to be in no ~ to** +*infin* ne pas être en état de +*infin* **5.** (*disease*) maladie *f;* **heart ~** maladie cardiaque; **if the patient's ~ worsens ...** si l'état de santé du patient se détériore ... ►**to be in a certain ~** être enceinte, être dans une position intéressante *Belgique* **II.** *vt* conditionner; **to ~ sb to sth/to** +*infin* habituer qn à qc/à +*infin;* **to ~ one's hair** utiliser de l'après-shampooing
conditional **I.** *adj* conditionnel(le); **to be ~ on sth** dépendre de qc **II.** *n* LING **the ~** le conditionnel
conditionally *adv* à titre conditionnel
conditioned *adj* **1.** (*trained*) conditionné(e) **2.** (*accustomed*) habitué(e)
conditioner *n no pl* **1.** (*for hair*) après-shampooing *m* **2.** (*for clothes*) adoucissant *m*
conditioning *n* conditionnement *m*
condo [ˌkɒndəʊ, *Am:* ˌkɑ:ndoʊ] *n Am, inf abbr of* **condominium**
condolence(s) *n* condoléances *fpl;* **to offer one's ~s to sb** *form* présenter ses condoléances à qn
condom ['kɒndəm, *Am:* 'kɑ:n-] *n* préservatif *m*
condominium [ˌkɒndə'mɪnɪəm, *Am:* ˌkɑ:n-] *n* **1.** *Am* (*apartment building with shared areas*) appartement *m* en copropriété **2.** *Am* (*unit of apartment building*) immeuble *m* en copropriété **3.** POL (*jointly governed state*) condominium *m*
condone [kən'dəʊn, *Am:* -'doʊn] *vt* (*violence*) tolérer
conducive [kən'dju:sɪv, *Am:* -'du:-] *adj* propice; **to be ~ to sth** être propice à qc
conduct [kən'dʌkt, *Am:* 'kɑ:n-] **I.** *vt* **1.** (*carry out: negotiations, meeting, experiment*) mener; **to ~ the religious service** célébrer l'office **2.** (*direct: business, orchestra*) diriger; **to ~ one's life** mener sa vie; **to ~ the traffic** faire la circulation **3.** (*guide, lead*) conduire; **to ~ sb round a place** faire visiter un endroit à qn; **a ~ed tour** une visite guidée **4.** (*behave*) **to ~ oneself** se comporter **5.** ELEC, PHYS (*transmit*) être conducteur de **II.** *vi* MUS diriger **III.** *n no pl* **1.** (*management*) gestion *f* **2.** (*behaviour*) comportement *m*
conductive [kən'dʌktɪv] *adj* ELEC, PHYS conducteur(-trice)
conductor *n* **1.** (*director of musical performance*) chef *m* d'orchestre **2.** PHYS, ELEC conducteur *m* **3.** (*fare collector: of bus*) receveur *m;* (*of train*) chef *m* de train
conductress *n* receveuse *f*
conduit ['kɒndjuɪt, *Am:* 'kɑ:nduɪt] *n* conduit *m*

cone [kəʊn, *Am:* koʊn] *n* **1.** MAT cône *m;* **traffic** ~ balise *f* de signalisation **2.** (*cornet for ice cream*) cornet *m;* **ice-cream** ~ cornet de glace **3.** (*oval shaped fruit of a conifer*) pomme *f* de pin

confection [kən'fekʃən] *n form* **1.** (*sweet*) confiserie *f* **2.** (*dish made of sweet ingredients*) pâtisserie *f*

confectioner *n* **1.** (*maker of cakes*) pâtissier, -ière *m, f* **2.** (*seller of confections*) confiseur, -euse *m, f*

confectionery *n no pl* **1.** (*sweets*) confiserie *f* **2.** (*cakes and pastries*) pâtisserie *f*

confederacy [kən'fedərəsi] *n* confédération *f*

Confederacy *n Am* HIST **the** ~ les États confédérés

confederate [kən'fedərət] **I.** *n* confédéré(e) *m(f)* **II.** *adj* HIST confédéré(e)

confederation [kənˌfedə'reɪʃən] *n* confédération *f*

Confederation *n* ECON ~ **of British Industry** ≈ Conseil national du patronat français

> Le **Confederation Day** ou "Canada Day" est le jour de la fête nationale canadienne, fêtée le 1er juillet.

confer [kən'fɜːʳ, *Am:* -'fɜːr] <-rr-> **I.** *vi* se consulter **II.** *vt* **to** ~ **sth on sb** conférer qc à qn

conference ['kɒnfərəns, *Am:* 'kɑːnfɚ-] *n* (*long meeting*) conférence *f* ▶ **to be in** ~ **with sb** être en réunion avec qn

confess [kən'fes] **I.** *vi* **1.** (*admit*) **to** ~ **to sth** avouer qc; **to** ~ **to having done sth** avouer avoir fait qc **2.** REL **to** ~ **to a priest** se confesser à un prêtre **II.** *vt* **1.** (*admit*) avouer; **to** ~ **oneself sth** s'avouer qc **2.** REL (*sins*) confesser

confession [kən'feʃən] *n* **1.** (*admission*) aveu *m;* **to have a** ~ **to make** avoir un aveu à faire **2.** (*admission of a crime*) aveux *mpl;* **to give a** ~ faire des aveux **3.** (*admission of sin*) confession *f;* **to go to** ~ aller se confesser

confessional *n* confessionnal *m*

confessor *n* confesseur *m*

confetti [kən'feti, *Am:* -'fet̬-] *n no pl* confetti *m;* **to shower sb in** ~ couvrir qn de confettis

confidant [ˌkɒnfɪ'dænt, *Am:* ˌkɑːnfə-] *n* confident *m*

confidante [ˌkɒnfɪ'dænt, *Am:* ˌkɑːnfə-] *n* confidente *f*

confide [kən'faɪd] *vt* confier; **to** ~ **sth to sb's care** confier qc au soin de qn; **to** ~ **to sb that ...** confier à qn que ...

confidence ['kɒnfɪdəns, *Am:* 'kɑːnfə-] *n* **1.** *no pl* (*secrecy*) confidence *f;* **in** ~ en confidence **2.** (*complete trust*) confiance *f;* **to place one's** ~ **in sb/sth** faire confiance à qn/qc; **to take sb into one's** ~ faire confiance à qn **3.** *pl* (*secrets*) confidences *fpl;* **to exchange** ~**s** se faire des confidences **4.** *no pl* (*self assurance*) confiance *f* en soi; **to lack** ~ manquer de confiance en soi

confident ['kɒnfɪdənt, *Am:* 'kɑːnfə-] *adj* **1.** (*sure*) sûr(e); **to be** ~ **in oneself** être sûr de soi; **to be** ~ **about sth** être sûr de qc **2.** (*self-assured*) sûr(e) de soi; **she's a very** ~ **person** elle est très sûre d'elle

confidential *adj* confidentiel(le)

confidentially *adv* confidentiellement

confiding [kən'faɪdɪŋ] *adj* confiant(e)

configuration [kənˌfɪgə'reɪʃən, *Am:* kənˌfɪgjə'-] *n* configuration *f*

confine ['kɒnfaɪn, *Am:* 'kɑːn-] **I.** *vt* **1.** (*limit*) limiter; **to be** ~**d to bed** être cloué au lit **2.** (*imprison, keep indoors*) enfermer **3.** MIL **to be** ~**d to quarters** être consigné **II.** *n* **the** ~**s** les limites *fpl;* **to be beyond the** ~**s of sb's understanding** dépasser la compréhension de qn

confined *adj* (*space*) restreint(e)

confinement *n no pl* **1.** (*act of being confined*) internement *m;* ~ **to bed** alitement *m* **2.** (*imprisonment*) détention *f;* **solitary** ~ isolement *m* cellulaire

confirm [kən'fɜːm, *Am:* -'fɜːrm] **I.** *vt* **1.** (*verify*) confirmer **2.** REL **to be** ~**ed** recevoir la confirmation **II.** *vi* confirmer

confirmation [ˌkɒnfə'meɪʃən, *Am:* ˌkɑːnfɚ-] *n a.* REL confirmation *f*

confirmed *adj* **1.** (*firmly established: champion*) confirmé(e); (*bachelor*) endurci(e) **2.** (*permanent, chronic: alcoholic*) invétéré(e)

confiscate ['kɒnfɪskeɪt, *Am:* 'kɑːnfə-] *vt* **to** ~ **sth from sb** confisquer qc à qn

conflict ['kɒnflɪkt, *Am:* 'kɑːn-] **I.** *n* conflit *m;* ~ **of interests** conflit d'intérêts; **to bring sb into** ~ **with sb** amener qn à être en opposition avec qn; **to come into** ~ **with sb** entrer en conflit avec qn **II.** *vi* (*do battle, be opposed to*) **to** ~ **with sb/sth** être en conflit avec qn/qc

conflicting *adj* (*ideas, claim, evidence*) contradictoire; (*interest, advice*) contraire

confluence ['kɒnfluːəns, *Am:* 'kɑːn-] *n* confluence *f*

conform [kən'fɔːm, *Am:* -'fɔːrm] *vi* **to** ~ **to sth** être conforme à qc

conformist **I.** *n* conformiste *mf* **II.** *adj* conformiste

conformity [kən'fɔːmɪti, *Am:* -'fɔːrmət̬i] *n no pl* conformité *f; form;* **in** ~ **with your request** conformément à votre demande

confound [kən'faʊnd] *vt* déconcerter

confront [kən'frʌnt] *vt* (*danger, enemy*) affronter; **to** ~ **sb by sb/sth** confronter qn à qn/qc; **to be** ~**d by a crowd of journalists** se retrouver face à une armée de journalistes

confrontation *n* **1.** *no pl* (*encounter*) confrontation *f* **2.** (*direct clash*) affrontement *m*

confrontational *adj* (*policy, attitude*) d'affrontement; **to be** ~ aimer les conflits

confuse [kən'fjuːz] *vt* **1.** (*perplex: person*) troubler; **you're** ~**ing me!** tu m'embrouilles! **2.** (*put into disarray: matters*) compliquer **3.** (*mix up*) confondre

confused *adj* **1.** (*perplexed*) embrouillé(e); **to**

get ~ in one's notes s'embrouiller dans ses notes; **to be a bit ~ about what to do** ne plus savoir trop quoi faire **2.** (*mixed up*) confus(e)

confusing *adj* confus(e)

confusion [kən'fjuːʒən] *n* **1.** *no pl* (*mix up*) confusion *f* **2.** (*disorder*) désordre *m*

congeal [kən'dʒiːl] *vi* (*grease*) se figer; (*blood*) coaguler

congenial [kən'dʒiːnɪəl, *Am:* -njəl] *adj* agréable

congenital [kən'dʒenɪtəl, *Am:* -ət̬əl] *adj* congénital(e)

congested *adj* **1.** (*overcrowded: street, town*) encombré(e) **2.** MED (*arteries*) congestionné(e); **to have ~ lungs** avoir les poumons pris

congestion [kən'dʒestʃən] *n no pl* **1.** (*overcrowding*) encombrement *m* **2.** (*blockage*) congestion *f*

conglomerate [kən'glɒmərət, *Am:* -'glɑːmɚ-] *n* ECON, GEO conglomérat *m*

conglomeration *n* conglomération *f*

Congo ['kɒŋgəʊ, *Am:* 'kɑːŋgoʊ] **I.** *n* le Congo **II.** *adj* congolais(e)

Congolese **I.** *adj* congolais(e) **II.** *n* Congolais(e) *m(f)*

congratulate [kən'grætʃʊleɪt, *Am:* -'grætʃə-] *vt* féliciter; **to ~ sb on sth** féliciter qn de qc

congratulations *n* félicitations *fpl*

congregate ['kɒŋgrɪgeɪt, *Am:* 'kɑːŋ-] *vi* s'assembler; **to ~ around the entrance** se rassembler devant l'entrée

congregation *n* congrégation *f*

congregational *adj* en assemblée

congress ['kɒŋgres, *Am:* 'kɑːŋ-] *n* congrès *m*; **medical/musical ~** congrès de médecins/de musiciens

congressional *adj* du Congrès

congressman <-men> *n Am* membre *m* masculin du Congrès **congresswoman** <-women> *n Am* membre *f* féminin du Congrès

congruence *n no pl* **1.** MAT congruence *f* **2.** (*agreement*) conformité *f*

congruent ['kɒŋgrʊənt, *Am:* 'kɑːŋ-] *adj* **1.** MAT congru(e) **2.** (*suitable*) **to be ~ with sth** être conforme à qc

conical ['kɒnɪkl, *Am:* 'kɑːnɪ-] *adj* conique

conifer ['kɒnɪfə^r, *Am:* 'kɑːnəfɚ] *n* conifère *m*

coniferous *adj* de conifères

conjectural *adj* conjectural(e)

conjecture [kən'dʒektʃə^r, *Am:* -tʃɚ] **I.** *n* conjecture *f*; **a ~ about sth** une prévision de qc **II.** *vt* conjecturer; **to ~ that ...** supposer que ...

conjugal ['kɒndʒʊgl, *Am:* 'kɑːndʒə-] *adj form* conjugal(e)

conjugate ['kɒndʒʊgeɪt, *Am:* 'kɑːndʒə-] **I.** *vi* se conjuguer **II.** *vt* conjuguer

conjugation *n* conjugaison *f*

conjunction [kən'dʒʌŋkʃən] *n* **1.** LING conjonction *f* **2.** (*combination of events: of circumstances*) concours *m*; **in ~ with sb/sth** conjointement avec qn/qc

conjunctivitis [kənˌdʒʌŋktɪ'vaɪtɪs, *Am:* -tə'vaɪt̬ɪs] *n* conjonctivite *f*

conjure ['kʌndʒə^r, *Am:* -dʒɚ] **I.** *vi* faire des tours de passe-passe **II.** *vt* faire apparaître; (*spirits*) conjurer

◆**conjure up** *vt* évoquer; **to ~ the spirits of the dead** invoquer les esprits

conjurer *n* prestidigitateur, -trice *m, f*

conjuring *n* prestidigitation *f*

conjuring trick *n* tour *m* de prestidigitation

conjuror *n s.* **conjurer**

conk [kɒŋk, *Am:* kɑːŋk] **I.** *n Brit, Aus, iron* tarin *m* **II.** *vt iron, inf* **to ~ one's head on sth** flanquer un gnon à qn

◆**conk out** *vi inf* **1.** (*break down: machine, vehicle*) tomber en panne **2.** (*become exhausted*) s'écrouler

conker *n Brit* marron *m*

con man *n abbr of* **confidence man** escroc *m*

connect [kə'nekt] **I.** *vi* être relié; (*cables, wires*) être connecté; (*rooms*) communiquer; (*train, plane*) assurer la correspondance; **to ~ to the Internet** se connecter sur Internet **II.** *vt* **1.** (*join*) relier; **to ~ sth to sth** relier qc à qc; **to be ~ed** être joint **2.** ELEC brancher; **to ~ sth to the mains** brancher qc sur secteur **3.** (*attach*) raccorder; (*train, wagon*) accrocher **4.** *fig* (*link*) lier; **to be ~ed to sb/with sth** être lié à qn/qc; **to be well ~ed** avoir des relations; **to be ~ed** (*related*) être apparenté **5.** (*associate*) **to ~ sb/sth with sth** associer qn/qc à qc **6.** (*join by telephone*) mettre en communication; **to ~ sb with sb/sth** relier qn par téléphone avec qn/qc **7.** (*in tourism*) **to ~ with sth** assurer la correspondance avec qc **8.** INFOR connecter; **to ~ sb to the Internet** connecter qn sur Internet

Connecticut [kə'netɪkət, *Am:* -'net̬-] *n* le Connecticut

connecting *adj* de connexion; (*room*) communiquant(e); (*time*) de correspondance; **a ~ flight** une correspondance

connection *n* **1.** (*association, logical link*) rapport *f*; **in ~ with sth** au sujet de qc; **to have no ~ with sth** n'avoir aucun rapport avec qc; **to make the ~ between two things** faire le rapprochement entre les deux choses **2.** (*personal link*) lien *m*; **there is no ~ with the Dixons** in n'y a pas de lien *m* de parenté avec les Dixon **3.** *pl* (*contacts*) relations *fpl*; **to have useful ~s** avoir des relations; **to have ~s with the music business** avoir des relations dans l'industrie musicale **4.** ELEC branchement *m* **5.** TEL communication *f* **6.** INFOR (*to the Internet*) connexion *f* **7.** TECH (*of pipes*) raccordement *m* **8.** (*in travel*) correspondance *f* ►**in ~ with ...** à propos de ...; **in this ~ I think that ...** à ce propos, je pense que ...

connector *n* ELEC, INFOR connecteur *m*

connexion *s.* **connection**

connivance [kə'naɪvənts] *n* connivence *f;* ~ **at a crime** complicité *f* dans un crime

connive [kə'naɪv] *vi* **to ~ with sb** être de connivence avec qn

connoisseur [ˌkɒnə'sɜːʳ, *Am:* ˌkɑːnə'sɜːr] *n* connaisseur, -euse *m, f;* **art/wine ~** fin connaisseur en art/vins; **food ~** expert(e) *m(f)* en gastronomie

connotation [ˌkɒnə'teɪʃən, *Am:* ˌkɑːnə-] *n* connotation *f*

conquer ['kɒŋkəʳ, *Am:* 'kɑːŋkɚ] *vt* conquérir; (*Mount Everest*) faire l'ascension de; (*problem*) surmonter

conqueror *n* conquérant(e) *m(f);* **to be the first ~s of Mount Everest** être le premier à avoir fait l'ascension du Mont Everest

conquest ['kɒŋkwəst, *Am:* 'kɑːn-] *n no pl* **1.** MIL conquête *f;* (*of the Anapurna*) ascension *f* **2.** *iron* (*sexual adventure*) conquête *f* amoureuse

conscience ['kɒnʃəns, *Am:* 'kɑːn-] *n* conscience *f;* **a matter of ~** un cas de conscience; **a clear ~** une conscience tranquille; **a guilty ~** une mauvaise conscience; **sth is on one's ~** avoir qc sur la conscience; **sth preys on sb's ~** avoir la conscience tourmentée par qc; **to salve one's ~** avoir la conscience en paix

conscientious *adj* consciencieux(-euse)

conscientiousness *n no pl* conscience *f*

conscientious objector *n* objecteur *m* de conscience

conscious ['kɒnʃəs, *Am:* 'kɑːn-] *adj* **1.** (*deliberate*) conscient(e); (*decision*) délibéré(e) **2.** (*aware*) conscient(e); **fashion ~** qui suit la mode; **to be money ~** avoir la valeur de l'argent; **to be health ~** faire attention à sa santé; **to be ~ of sth** être conscient de qc; **to be/become ~ of the fact that ...** être/devenir conscient du fait que ...

consciousness *n no pl* **1.** MED connaissance *f;* **to lose ~** perdre connaissance; **to recover ~** revenir à soi **2.** (*awareness*) conscience *f;* **to raise one's ~** prendre conscience de qc

conscript [kən'skrɪpt, *Am:* 'kɑːn-] **I.** *n* conscrit *m,* milicien *m Belgique* **II.** *adj* conscrit(e) **III.** *vt* enrôler

conscription [kən'skrɪpʃən] *n no pl* conscription *f*

consecrate ['kɒnsɪkreɪt, *Am:* 'kɑːnsə-] *vt* **1.** REL consacrer **2.** (*dedicate oneself to religious aims: life*) vouer

consecration *n no pl* consécration *f*

consecutive [kən'sekjʊtɪv, *Am:* -jət̬ɪv] *adj* consécutif(-ive)

consecutively *adv* consécutivement

consensus [kən'sensəs] *n no pl* consensus *m;* **to reach a ~ on sth** atteindre l'unanimité sur qc

consent [kən'sent] **I.** *n form* permission *f;* **to give one's ~** accorder son consentement; **by common ~** de l'opinion de tous **II.** *vi* **to ~ to** *+infin* consentir à *+infin*

consequence ['kɒntsɪkwənts, *Am:* 'kɑːnt-] *n* conséquence *f;* **to suffer the ~s** subir les conséquences; **nothing of ~** aucune importance; **as a ~** par conséquent

consequent, **consequential** *adj* résultant; **to be ~ upon the fire** être causé par le feu

consequently *adv* par conséquent

conservation [ˌkɒntsə'veɪʃən, *Am:* ˌkɑːntsɚ-] *n* conservation *f;* **wildlife ~** protection *f* de la vie sauvage

conservationist *n* défenseur, -euse *m, f* de l'environnement

conservation technology *n* technique *f* de conservation

conservatism [kən'sɜːvətɪzəm, *Am:* -'sɜːr-] *n no pl* conservatisme *m*

conservative [kən'sɜːvətɪv, *Am:* -'sɜːrvət̬ɪv] *adj* conservateur(-trice); **to be a ~ dresser** s'habiller de façon traditionnelle; **at a ~ estimate** au minimum

conservatoire [kən'sɜːvətwɑːʳ, *Am:* -'sɜːrvətwɑːr], **conservatory** *n mus* conservatoire *m*

conserve [kən'sɜːv, *Am:* -sɜːrv] *vt* conserver; (*one's strength*) économiser; **to ~ energy** faire des économies d'énergie

consider [kən'sɪdəʳ, *Am:* -ɚ] *vt* **1.** (*think about*) considérer; **to ~ taking a trip** envisager de faire un voyage **2.** (*look attentively at*) examiner **3.** (*show regard for*) prendre en considération **4.** (*regard as*) considérer; **to ~ sb as sth** considérer qn comme qc; **to ~ that ...** penser que ...

considerable *adj* considérable

considerate [kən'sɪdərət] *adj* prévenant(e)

consideration *n no pl* **1.** (*careful thought*) considération *f;* **to take sth into ~** prendre qc en considération **2.** (*thoughtfulness*) égard *m;* **to show ~ for sb** montrer de la considération à qn; **for a small ~** *iron* moyennant finance

considered *adj* **1.** (*carefully thought out*) bien pensé(e) **2.** (*respected*) **well/highly ~** très estimé(e)

considering **I.** *prep* étant donné; **~ the weather** vu le temps **II.** *adv inf* tout compte fait **III.** *conj* ~ (**that**) étant donné que

consign [kən'saɪn] *vt* consigner; **to ~ sth to sb's care** confier qc à qn

consignment *n* **1.** (*instance of consigning*) envoi *m* **2.** ECON arrivage *m* de marchandises; **on ~** en consignation; **goods on ~** marchandises en dépôt permanent

consist [kən'sɪst] *vi* **to ~ of sth** consister en qc

consistency *n no pl* **1.** (*degree of firmness*) consistance *f* **2.** (*being consistent*) cohérence *f*

consistent [kən'sɪstənt] *adj* cohérent(e)

consolation [ˌkɒnsə'leɪʃən, *Am:* ˌkɑːn-] *n no pl* consolation *f;* **words of ~** paroles *fpl* consolatrices; **if it's of any ~ ...** si c'est d'un quelconque réconfort ...

consolation prize *n* prix *m* de consolation

consolatory [kən'sɒlətəri, *Am:* -'sɑːlətɔːri] *adj* réconfortant(e); (*words*) consolateur(-trice)

C

console¹ ['kɒnsəʊl, *Am:* 'kɑːnsɔʊl] *vt* consoler

console² [kən'səʊl, *Am:* -'sɔʊl] *n* (*switch panel*) console *f*

consolidate [kən'sɒlɪdeɪt, *Am:* -'sɑːlə-] **I.** *vi* **1.**(*become stronger*) se consolider **2.**(*unite*) s'unir **II.** *vt* consolider; **to ~ sb's relationship** renforcer les liens avec qn

consolidated *adj* consolidé(e)

consolidation *n no pl* **1.**(*act or condition of becoming stronger*) consolidation *f* **2.** ECON unification *f*

consommé [kən'sɒmeɪ, *Am:* ˌkɑːn'sə'meɪ] *n no pl* bouillon *m*

consonance ['kɒnsənəns, *Am:* 'kɑːn-] *n* MUS consonance *f*

consonant **I.** *n* consonne *f* **II.** *adj* **to be ~ with sth** être en accord avec qc

consort [kən'sɔːt, *Am:* -'sɔːrt] **I.** *vi* s'associer **II.** *n* époux, -ouse *m, f;* **prince ~** prince *m* consort

consortium [kən'sɔːtɪəm, *Am:* -'sɔːrt̬-] <-s *o* -tia> *n* consortium *m*

conspicuous [kən'spɪkjʊəs] *adj* voyant(e); (*beauty*) remarquable; **to be ~ by one's absence** *iron* briller par son absence

conspicuous consumption *n* consommation *f* ostentatoire

conspiracy [kən'spɪrəsi] *n no pl* **1.**(*secret plan*) conspiration *f;* **~ to murder** conspiration de meurtre **2.** *fig* **a ~ against sb** un complot contre qn

conspirator [kən'spɪrətəʳ, *Am:* -t̬ɚ] *n* conspirateur, -trice *m, f*

conspire [kən'spaɪəʳ, *Am:* -'spaɪɚ] *vi* conspirer; **to ~ to** *+infin* comploter pour *+infin*

constable ['kʌnstəbl, *Am:* 'kɑːn-] *n Brit* agent *m* de la police

constabulary [kən'stæbjʊləri, *Am:* -jəler-] *n Brit* la police

constancy *n no pl, form* constance *f*

constant ['kɒnstənt, *Am:* 'kɑːn-] **I.** *n* constante *f* **II.** *adj* **1.**(*continuous*) constant(e); (*chatter*) ininterrompu(e); (*noise*) persistant(e); (*shelling*) permanent(e) **2.**(*unchanging: love*) durable; (*support*) inébranlable; (*temperature*) constante **3.**(*frequent: use*) fréquent(e); **to be in ~ trouble with sb** avoir fréquemment des ennuis avec qn

constantly *adv* constamment; (*bicker*) continuellement; (*complain*) tout le temps

constellation [ˌkɒnstə'leɪʃən, *Am:* ˌkɑːn-] *n* **1.** ASTR constellation *f* **2.**(*group of famous people gathered together*) pléiade *f*

consternation [ˌkɒnstə'neɪʃən, *Am:* ˌkɑːnstɚ-] *n no pl* consternation *f;* **to sb's ~** à la consternation de qn; **this report fills us with ~** ce rapport nous consterne tous

constipate ['kɒnstɪpeɪt, *Am:* 'kɑːnstə-] *vt* constiper

constipated *adj* constipé(e)

constipation *n* constipation *f*

constituency *n* **1.**(*electoral district*) circonscription *f* électorale **2.**(*body of voters in this area*) électeurs, -trices *mpl, fpl* de la circonscription

constituent [kən'stɪtjuənt, *Am:* -'stɪtʃu-] **I.** *n* **1.**(*voter in constituency*) électeur, -trice *m, f* **2.** CHEM, PHYS composant *m* **II.** *adj* constituant(e); **the council's ~ members** les membres constitutifs du conseil

constitute ['kɒnstɪtjuːt, *Am:* 'kɑːnstətuːt] *vt* constituer

constitution *n* **1.** CHEM composition *f* **2.** POL, MED constitution *f;* **to have a strong/weak ~** avoir une bonne/mauvaise constitution

constitutional **I.** *adj* **1.** POL constitutionnel(le); (*amendment*) de la constitution **2.**(*relating to physical state*) diathésique **II.** *n iron* promenade *f*

constrain [kən'streɪn] *vt* **1.**(*restrict*) contraindre **2.** LAW retenir de force

constraint *n* **1.**(*restriction*) contrainte *f;* **under ~** sous la contrainte **2.**(*restraint or holding back of feelings*) retenue *f*

constrict [kən'strɪkt] *vt* étrangler

constriction *n* **1.**(*tightness*) rétrécissement *m* **2.**(*limitation*) restriction *f*

constrictor *n* constricteur *m*

construct [kən'strʌkt] **I.** *n* construction *f* **II.** *vt* construire

construction *n* **1.**(*act of building, word arrangement*) construction *f;* **to work at a ~ site** travailler sur un chantier de construction **2.**(*building*) bâtiment *m* **3.**(*interpretation*) interprétation *f;* **to put a ~ on sth** interpréter qc d'une façon différente

constructional *adj* de construction

constructive [kən'strʌktɪv] *adj* constructif(-ive)

constructor *n* constructeur, -trice *m, f*

construe [kən'struː] *vt* **to ~ sth as sth** interpréter qc comme étant qc

consul ['kɒnsl, *Am:* 'kɑːn-] *n* consul *m*

consular ['kɒnsjʊləʳ, *Am:* 'kɑːn-] *adj* consulaire

consulate ['kɒnsjʊlət, *Am:* 'kɑːn-] *n* consulat *m*

consulate general *n* consulat *m* général

consul general *n* consul *m* général

consult [kən'sʌlt] **I.** *vi* consulter; **to ~ with sb** être en consultation avec qn **II.** *vt* **1.**(*seek information*) consulter **2.**(*examine*) examiner; (*one's feelings*) s'en référer à

consultancy *n* consultation *f*

consultant [kən'sʌltənt] *n* **1.** ECON expert *m* conseil; **computer ~** expert conseil en informatique; **a management ~** un conseiller en organisation; **a public relations ~** un conseiller en relations publiques; **a tax ~** un conseiller fiscal **2.** *Brit* MED spécialiste *mf*

consultation *n* consultation *f;* **to decide sth in ~ with sb** prendre une décision en commun à propos de qc

consultative [kən'sʌltətɪv, *Am:* -t̬ət̬ɪv] *adj* consultatif(-ive)

consulting *adj* consultant(e)

consume [kən'sjuːm, *Am:* -'suːm] *vt* **1.** (*eat or drink*) consommer **2.** (*use up: fuel, energy*) consommer; (*money*) dilapider **3.** (*destroy*) consumer **4.** (*fill with*) **to be ~d** (*by anger, greed, hatred*) être dévoré; (*by envy*) être miné; (*by jealousy*) être rongé; **to be ~d by passion for sb** brûler de passion pour qn

consumer *n* consommateur, -trice *m, f;* ~ **advice/credit** conseils/crédit au consommateur; ~ **rights** droits *mpl* du consommateur; ~ **durables** biens de la consommation durable

consumerism [kən'sjuːmərɪzəm, *Am:* -'suːmɚɪ-] *n* **1.** (*protection of consumers' interests*) défense *f* du consommateur **2.** *pej* (*exaggerated buying emphasis*) consommation *f* excessive

consummate ['kɒnsəmeɪt, *Am:* 'kɑːn-] *adj form* consommé(e); (*athlete*) accompli(e); (*happiness*) total(e); (*liar, thief*) achevé(e)

consummation *n form* **1.** (*completion*) achèvement *m* **2.** (*sexual intercourse*) consommation *f*

consumption [kən'sʌmpʃən] *n* **1.** (*consuming*) consommation *f* **2.** *fig* **to be for the company** ~ s'adresser à la société

contact ['kɒntækt, *Am:* 'kɑːn-] **I.** *n* **1.** (*state of communication*) contact *m;* **to have ~ with the (outside) world** être en contact avec le monde; **to lose ~ with sb** perdre le contact avec qn; **to make ~ with sb** prendre contact avec qn **2.** (*connection*) rapport *m;* **business ~s** relations *fpl* d'affaires **3.** (*act of touching*) **physical ~** contact *m* physique; **to come into ~ with sth** entrer en contact avec qc **4.** ELEC contact *m* électrique ►**they made eye ~** leurs regards se sont croisés **II.** *vt* contacter

contact-breaker *n* disjoncteur *m* **contact lens** *n* lentille *f* de contact **contact man** *n* agent *m* de liaison **contact print** *n* épreuve *f* par contact

contagion [kən'teɪdʒən] *n* contagion *f*

contagious *adj* **1.** contagieux(-euse) **2.** *fig* (*enthusiasm, laugh*) communicatif(-ive)

contain [kən'teɪn] *vt* contenir; (*anger*) retenir; (*examples*) renfermer; **to ~ one's laugh** s'empêcher de rire

container *n* **1.** (*box*) récipient *m* **2.** (*for transport*) conteneur *m*

containerize [kən'teɪnəraɪz] *vt* mettre en conteneur

container ship *n* navire *m* porte-conteneurs

containment *n no pl* action *f* de circonscrire

contaminate [kən'tæmɪneɪt] *vt* contaminer

contamination *n no pl* contamination *f*

contemplate ['kɒntempleɪt, *Am:* 'kɑːnt̬em-] **I.** *vi* méditer **II.** *vt* **1.** (*gaze at*) contempler **2.** (*consider*) considérer; **to ~ suicide** songer au suicide **3.** (*intend*) **to ~ doing sth** penser faire qc; **suicide was never ~d** il n'a jamais été question de suicide

contemplation *n no pl* **1.** (*act of looking*) contemplation *f* **2.** (*deep thought*) recueillement *m;* **to be lost in ~** être perdu dans ses pensées **3.** (*expectation*) prévision *f;* **in ~ of their departure** en prévision de leur départ

contemplative [kən'templətɪv, *Am:* -t̬ɪv] *adj* **1.** (*reflective*) contemplatif(-ive) **2.** (*meditative*) méditatif(-ive)

contemporary [kən'tempərəri, *Am:* -pərer-] **I.** *n* contemporain(e) *m(f)* **II.** *adj* contemporain(e)

contempt [kən'tempt] *n no pl* mépris *m;* **to be beneath ~** être au-dessous de tout; **to have ~ for sb/sth** avoir du mépris pour qn/qc; **to hold sb/sth in ~** mépriser qn/qc; **to treat sb/sth with ~** traiter qn/qc avec dédain

contemptible *adj* méprisable

contemptuous [kən'temptʃuəs] *adj* méprisant(e); (*look*) hautain(e); (*remark*) arrogant(e); **to be very ~ of sb** être très dédaigneux de qn

contend [kən'tend] **I.** *vi* **1.** (*compete*) être en compétition; **to ~ for sth** lutter pour qc; **to ~ for a title** disputer un titre; **to ~ against sb/sth** combattre qn/qc **2.** (*combat or cope with*) **to ~ with sth** affronter qc; **to have sb/sth to ~ with** devoir faire face à qn/qc **3.** (*argue*) **to ~ with sb** se disputer avec qn **II.** *vt* soutenir

contender *n* concurrent(e) *m(f);* (*election, job*) candidat(e) *m(f)*

content[1] ['kɒntent, *Am:* 'kɑːn-] *n* **1.** (*all things inside*) contenu *m;* **to have a high/low fat ~** avoir une riche/pauvre teneur en matières grasses **2.** (*substance*) substance *f*

content[2] [kən'tent] **I.** *vt* satisfaire **to ~ oneself with sth** se contenter de qc **II.** *adj* satisfait(e); **to one's heart's ~** à souhait; **to be ~ with sth** se satisfaire de qc; **to be ~ to** +*infin* ne pas demander mieux que de +*infin*

contented *adj* satisfait(e)

contention [kən'tenʃən] *n no pl* **1.** (*disagreement*) contestation *f;* **in ~** à débattre **2.** (*opinion expressed*) affirmation *f* **3.** (*competition*) compétition *f;* **out of ~** hors compétition

contentious *adj* contesté(e)

contentment *n no pl* contentement *m*

contents *n pl* **1.** (*things held in sth*) contenu *m* **2.** PUBL (**table of**) ~ table *f* des matières

contest [kən'test, *Am:* 'kɑːn-] **I.** *n* **1.** (*competition*) concours *m;* **beauty ~** concours de beauté **2.** SPORT compétition *f* **3.** (*dispute*) combat *m* **II.** *vt* **1.** (*challenge*) contester **2.** (*compete for*) disputer

contestant [kən'testənt] *n* concurrent(e) *m(f)*

context ['kɒntekst, *Am:* 'kɑːn-] *n* contexte *m*

contextual *adj form* contextuel(le)

contextualize [kən'tekstjuəlaɪz, *Am:* kən'tekstʃu-] *vt* contextualiser

continent[1] ['kɒntɪnənt, *Am:* 'kɑːntnənt] *n* continent *m*

continent[2] ['kɒntɪnənt, *Am:* 'kɑːntnənt]

C

adj continent(e)
continental *adj* continental(e)
continental breakfast *n* petit déjeuner *m* continental (*comprenant café, pain et confiture*)
contingency *n form* contingence *f*
contingent [kən'tɪndʒənt] **I.** *n* contingent *m* **II.** *adj* **to be ~ on sth** dépendre de qc
continual [kən'tɪnjuəl] *adj* continuel(le)
continually *adv* continuellement
continuation *n no pl* **1.** (*continuing, next stage*) continuation *f* **2.** (*extension*) prolongement *m*
continue [kən'tɪnju:] **I.** *vi* continuer; **to ~ doing sth** continuer à faire qc; **to ~ as sth** poursuivre en tant que qc; **to ~ on the next page** continuer à la page suivante; **to ~ one's way** poursuivre son chemin **II.** *vt* continuer; (*work*) poursuivre
continued *adj* soutenu(e)
continuity [ˌkɒntɪ'nju:əti, *Am:* ˌkɑ:ntən'u:əṱi] *n no pl* **1.** (*continuous period*) continuité *f* **2.** CINE, TV script *m;* **~ girl** scripte *f;* **~ boy** scripte *m*
continuous *adj* continu(e)
contort [kən'tɔ:t, *Am:* -'tɔ:rt] **I.** *vi* se contorsionner **II.** *vt* **1.** contorsionner **2.** *fig* **to ~ sb's words** déformer les dires de qn
contortion [kən'tɔ:ʃən, *Am:* -'tɔ:r-] *n* contorsion *f*
contortionist *n* contorsionniste *mf*
contour ['kɒntʊə^r, *Am:* 'kɑ:ntʊr] *n* contour *m*
contraband ['kɒntrəbænd, *Am:* 'kɑ:n-] **I.** *n no pl* contrebande *f* **II.** *adj* de contrebande
contraception [ˌkɒntrə'sepʃən, *Am:* ˌkɑ:n-] *n no pl* contraception *f*
contraceptive [ˌkɒntrə'septɪv, *Am:* ˌkɑ:n-] *n* contraceptif *m;* **~ pill** pilule *f* contraceptive
contract[1] ['kɒntrækt] **I.** *n* contrat *m;* **to break/to draw up a ~** rompre/établir un contrat; **to enter into a ~** passer un contrat **II.** *vi* **to ~ to** *+infin* s'engager à *+infin;* **to ~ with sb** passer un contrat avec qn
contract[2] [kən'trækt, *Am:* 'kɑ:n-] **I.** *vi* se contracter **II.** *vt* contracter
◆**contract in** *vi* s'engager
◆**contract out** *vt* **to ~ of sth** se retirer de qc; **to ~ sth to sb** déléguer qc à qn
contraction *n* contraction *f*
contractor *n* entrepreneur *m;* **building ~** entrepreneur de construction
contractual *adj* contractuel(le); (*conditions*) du contrat
contradict [ˌkɒntrə'dɪkt, *Am:* ˌkɑ:n-] *vt, vi* contredire
contradiction *n* contradiction *f*
contradictory [ˌkɒntrə'dɪktəri, *Am:* ˌkɑ:n-] *adj* contradictoire
contralto [kən'træltəʊ, *Am:* -'trælṱoʊ] *n no pl* contralto *mf*
contraption [kən'træpʃən] *n inf* truc *m*
contrary ['kɒntrəri, *Am:* 'kɑ:ntrɚ-] **I.** *n no pl* contraire *m;* **on the ~** au contraire; **to get proof to the ~** avoir la preuve du contraire **II.** *adj* contrariant(e)
contrary to *prep* contrairement à; **~ what sb says** à l'encontre de ce que qn dit; **~ all expectations** contre toute attente; **~ nature** contre nature
contrast [kən'trɑ:st, *Am:* -'træst] **I.** *n* contraste *m;* **in ~ to sth** en contraste avec qc **II.** *vt* comparer **III.** *vi* contraster
contrasting *adj* contrasté(e)
contravene [ˌkɒntrə'vi:n, *Am:* ˌkɑ:n-] *vt* contrevenir à
contravention [ˌkɒntrə'venʃən, *Am:* ˌkɑ:n-] *n* infraction *f;* **to act in ~ of the regulations** être en infraction avec le règlement
contribute [kən'trɪbju:t] **I.** *vi* **to ~ towards/to sth** contribuer à qc **II.** *vt* **1.** (*give towards an aim*) **to ~ sth to/towards sth** offrir qc à qc **2.** (*submit for publication*) **to ~ sth to sth** écrire qc pour qc
contribution *n* **1.** (*something contributed*) contribution *f* **2.** (*text for publication*) article *m*
contributor *n* collaborateur, -trice *m, f;* **to be a ~ to sth** collaborer à qc
contrivance [kən'traɪvəns] *n pej* **1.** (*act of contriving*) invention *f* **2.** (*device*) dispositif *m* **3.** (*inventive capacity*) inventivité *f*
contrive [kən'traɪv] *vt* **1.** (*plan with cleverness*) inventer **2.** (*manage*) parvenir
contrived *adj* forcé(e)
control [kən'trəʊl, *Am:* -'troʊl] <-ll-> **I.** *n* **1.** (*power of command*) contrôle *m;* **to be in ~ of sth** contrôler qc; **to be under ~** être maîtrisé; **to go out of ~** perdre le contrôle; **to lose ~ over sth** perdre le contrôle de qc; **to have ~ over sb** avoir de l'autorité sur qn; **beyond ~** incontrôlable **2.** (*self-restraint*) maîtrise *f* **3.** ECON, FIN contrôle *m* **4.** (*place for checking*) **to go through customs ~** passer à la douane **5.** MED, PHYS (*person*) sujet *m* témoin; **~ group** groupe *m* témoin **6.** (*switches*) commandes *fpl;* **~ board/panel** tableau *m* de bord/commande **II.** *vt* <-ll-> **1.** (*restrain, curb*) maîtriser **2.** (*run*) contrôler ►**to ~ the purse strings** tenir les cordons de la bourse
controlled *adj fig* contenu(e)
controller *n* **1.** (*person*) contrôleur, -euse *m, f* **2.** TECH, INFOR contrôleur *m*
control tower *n* tour *f* de contrôle
controversial [ˌkɒntrə'vɜ:ʃəl, *Am:* ˌkɑ:ntrə'vɜ:r-] *adj* controversé(e)
controversy ['kɒntrəvɜ:si, *Am:* 'kɑ:ntrəvɜ:r-] <-sies> *n* controverse *f*
contusion [kən'tju:ʒən, *Am:* -'tu:-] *n* contusion *f*
conundrum [kə'nʌndrəm] *n* énigme *f*
convalesce [ˌkɒnvə'les, *Am:* ˌkɑ:n-] *vi* **to ~ from sth** se remettre de qc
convalescence *n* convalescence *f*
convalescent [ˌkɒnvə'lesnt, *Am:* ˌkɑ:n-] **I.** *adj* convalescent(e); **to have a long ~**

period avoir une longue période de convalescence **II.** *n* convalescent(e) *m(f)*
convection [kən'vekʃən] *n* convection *f*
convector [kən'vektəʳ, *Am:* -tɚ], **convector heater** *n* convecteur *m*
convene [kən'viːn] **I.** *vi form* se réunir **II.** *vt form* convoquer
convenience [kən'viːnɪəns, *Am:* -'viːnjəns] *n no pl* commodité *f;* **for ~('s sake)** par commodité; **at your ~** comme cela te/vous convient
convenience food *n no pl* aliments *mpl* tout prêts **convenience store** *n Am* épicerie *f* de quartier
convenient [kən'viːnɪənt, *Am:* -'viːnjənt] *adj* commode; (*moment*) opportun(e); **to be ~ for sth** (*within easy reach*) être bien situé pour qc
convent ['kɒnvənt, *Am:* 'kɑːn-] *n* couvent *m;* **to enter a ~** entrer au couvent
convention [kən'venʃən] *n* convention *f*
conventional *adj* conventionnel(le)
conventionally *adv* d'une manière conventionnelle
converge [kən'vɜːdʒ, *Am:* -'vɜːrdʒ] *vi* converger
convergence *n* convergence *f*
convergent [kən'vɜːdʒent, *Am:* -'vɜːr-] *adj* convergent(e)
conversant [kən'vɜːsnt, *Am:* -'vɜːr-] *adj* **to be ~ with sth** être familiarisé avec qc
conversation [ˌkɒnvə'seɪʃən, *Am:* ˌkɑːnvɚ-] *n* conversation *f;* **to hold a ~** tenir une conversation; **to run out of ~** être à court de conversation ▸**to strike up a ~ with sb** entamer une conversation avec qn
conversational *adj* de conversation; **to have ~ skills** être éloquent; **in a ~ tone/style** d'un ton/style léger
conversationally *adv* sur le ton de la conversation; **to be ~ gifted** être éloquent
converse[1] [kən'vɜːs, *Am:* -'vɜːrs] *vi form* converser
converse[2] ['kɒnvɜːs, *Am:* 'kɑːnvɜːrs] **I.** *n* inverse *m* **II.** *adj form* inverse
conversely *adv* inversement
conversion [kən'vɜːʃən, *Am:* -'vɜːrʒən] *n* **1.**(*changing opinions*) conversion *f;* **~ to sth** conversion à qc **2.**(*changing opinions*) **to undergo a ~** changer d'opinion **3.**(*adoption for other purposes*) conversion *f;* (*of house, city*) aménagement *m* **4.** FIN conversion *f;* **~ rate** taux *mpl* de conversion
convert [kən'vɜːt, *Am:* -'vɜːrt] **I.** *n* converti(e) *m(f);* **to become a ~ to sth** se convertir à qc **II.** *vi* **to ~ to sth** se convertir à qc **III.** *vt* **to ~ sth into sth** convertir qc en qc
converter *n* convertisseur *m*
convertible **I.** *n* décapotable *f* **II.** *adj* convertible
convex ['kɒnveks, *Am:* 'kɑːn-] *adj* convexe
convey [kən'veɪ] *vt* **1.**(*transport*) transporter **2.**(*communicate*) transmettre; (*a feeling, idea*) évoquer; **to ~ sth to sb** faire comprendre qc à qn
conveyance *n* **1.**(*act of carrying, vehicle*) transport *m* **2.**(*communication*) transmission *f* **3.** LAW (*property transfer*) cession *f* **4.**(*document showing a transfer*) acte *m* de cession
conveyancing *n no pl* cession *f*
conveyor *n* **1.**(*person/thing that transports*) transporteur *m* **2.** *s. a.* **conveyor belt**
conveyor belt *n* tapis *m* roulant
convict ['kɒnvɪkt, *Am:* 'kɑːn-] **I.** *n* détenu(e) *m(f)* **II.** *vi* rendre un verdict de culpabilité **III.** *vt* **to ~ sb of sth** reconnaître qn coupable de qc
conviction [kən'vɪkʃən] *n* **1.**(*act of finding guilty*) condamnation *f;* **~ for sth** condamnation pour qc **2.**(*firm belief*) conviction *f;* **to have a deep ~ that...** avoir la conviction profonde que...; **to have a ~ about sth** avoir une idée là-dessus
convince [kən'vɪnts] *vt* convaincre
convincing *adj* convaincant(e)
convoluted *adj* compliqué(e)
convoy ['kɒnvɔɪ, *Am:* 'kɑːn-] **I.** *n* convoi *m;* **in ~** en convoi **II.** *vt* convoyer
convulse [kən'vʌls] **I.** *vi* avoir des convulsions; **to ~ in laughter/pain** se tordre de rire/de douleur **II.** *vt* secouer; **to be ~d with laughter** se tordre de rire
convulsion [kən'vʌlʃən] *n* convulsion *f;* **to go into ~s** être pris de convulsions; *iron* se tordre de rire
convulsive [kən'vʌlsɪv] *adj* convulsif(-ive)
coo [kuː] *vi* (*bird*) roucouler; (*person*) murmurer; (*baby*) gazouiller; **to ~ sweet nothings in sb's ear** susurer des mots doux à l'oreille de qn
cook [kʊk] **I.** *n* cuisinier, -ière *m, f* ▸**too many ~s spoil the broth** *prov* trop de cuisiniers gâtent la sauce **II.** *vi* **1.**(*prepare food*) cuisiner **2.**(*be cooked*) cuire **3.** *Am, inf* (*do well*) se débrouiller pas mal **4.** *Am, inf* (*ready to go*) y aller ▸**what's ~ing?** qu'est-ce qui se mijote là? **III.** *vt* **1.**(*prepare food*) cuisiner **2.**(*prepare food using heat*) cuire ▸**to ~ the books** brouiller les comptes; **to ~ sb's goose** mettre qn dans le pétrin
cookbook *n* livre *m* de cuisine
cooker *n Brit* cuisinière *f*
cookery *n no pl* cuisine *f*
cookie ['kʊki] *n Am* **1.**(*sweet biscuit*) biscuit *m;* **chocolate-chip ~** cookie *m* aux pépites de chocolat **2.** *inf* (*person*) type *m,* nana *f;* **a tough ~** un dur à cuire **3.** INFOR cookie *m* ▸**that's the way the ~ crumbles!** c'est la vie!
cooking *n no pl* cuisine *f;* **~ chocolate** chocolat *m* à pâtisserie; **~ oil** huile *f* de cuisson
cool [kuːl] **I.** *adj* **1.**(*slightly cold*) frais(fraîche) **2.**(*calm*) tranquille; *inf* cool; **to keep a ~ head** garder la tête froide **3.**(*unfriendly, cold*) froid(e); (*welcome*) glacial(e) **4.**(*fresh: color*) froid(e) **5.** *inf* (*fashionable*) cool ▸**~ as a cucumber** tranquille **II.** *interj inf* cool! **III.** *n*

no pl **1.** (*coolness*) fraîcheur *f* **2.** (*calm*) sang-froid *m;* **to keep one's ~** garder son calme **IV.** *vi* se refroidir **V.** *vt* **1.** (*make cold*) refroidir **2.** *inf* ~ **it!** reste cool!

cooler *n* **1.** (*box*) glacière *f* **2.** (*cool drink*) rafraîchissement *m*

coolheaded *adj* **to remain ~** garder la tête froide

cooling *adj* rafraîchissant(e)

cooling tower *n* refroidisseur *m*

coolly ['ku:li] *adv* **1.** (*calmly*) avec calme **2.** (*coldly*) froidement

coolness *n no pl* **1.** (*coldness*) fraîcheur *f* **2.** *fig* froideur *f* **3.** (*calmness*) sang-froid *m*

coop [ku:p] **I.** *n* poulailler *m* **II.** *vt* encager

co-op ['kəʊɒp, *Am:* 'koʊɑ:p] *n* coopérative *f*

cooperate [kəʊ'ɒpəreɪt, *Am:* koʊ'ɑ:pəreɪt] *vi* **to ~ in sth** coopérer à qc

cooperation *n* coopération *f;* **~ in sth** coopération à qc

cooperative [kəʊ'ɒpərətɪv, *Am:* koʊ'ɑ:pɚət̬ɪv] **I.** *n* coopérative *f* **II.** *adj* coopératif(-ive)

coordinate [ˌkəʊ'ɔ:dɪneɪt, *Am:* ˌkoʊ'ɔ:r-] **I.** *n* coordonnée *f* **II.** *vi* **to ~ with sth** aller avec qc **III.** *vt* coordonner **IV.** *adj* coordonné(e)

coordination *n no pl* coordination *f*

coordinator *n* coordinateur, -trice *m, f*

coot [ku:t] *n inf* **1.** (*rather dim person*) idiot(e) *m(f)* **2.** (*completely bald*) **as bald as a ~** chauve comme un œuf

cop [kɒp, *Am:* kɑ:p] **I.** *n inf* flic *m;* **to play ~s and robbers** jouer aux gendarmes et aux voleurs ►**it's a <u>fair</u> ~** *Brit* je suis pris sur le fait; **it's not <u>much</u> ~** *Brit, inf* ça ne vaut pas la peine **II.** <-pp-> *vt* **1.** *Brit, Aus, inf* (*be scolded*) **to ~ a load of trouble** avoir un tas de problèmes **2.** (*grab*) saisir; **to ~ a** (**quick**) **look at sth** regarder furtivement qc **3.** *Am* LAW **to ~ a plea** plaider coupable

co-partner *n* coassocié(e) *m(f)* **copartnership** *n* coassociation *f*

cope [kəʊp, *Am:* koʊp] *vi* **1.** (*master a situation*) **to ~ with sth** faire face à qc; **to ~ with a task** affronter une tâche **2.** (*deal with*) **to ~ with sth** supporter qc

Copenhagen [ˌkəʊpən'heɪgən, *Am:* 'koʊpənˌheɪ-] *n* Copenhague

copier ['kɒpɪəʳ, *Am:* 'kɑ:pɪɚ] *n* photocopieuse *f*

co-pilot *n* copilote *mf*

copious ['kəʊpɪəs, *Am:* 'koʊ-] *adj* copieux(-euse); (*notes*) abondant(e); (*amounts*) considérable

copper ['kɒpəʳ, *Am:* 'kɑ:pɚ] **I.** *n* **1.** *no pl* (*metal*) cuivre *m* **2.** *Brit, inf* (*police officer*) flic *mf* **3.** *Brit, inf* (*coin*) petite monnaie *f* **II.** *adj* (*colour*) cuivre; **~-coloured** cuivré(e)

copper beech *n* hêtre *m* rouge **copper-ore** *n* minerai *m* de cuivre **copperplate I.** *n* **1.** *no pl* (*style of handwriting*) gravure *f* sur cuivre au burin **2.** (*metal plaque*) planche *f* de cuivre **II.** *adj* **~ writing** écriture *f* moulée

copper-smith *n* chaudronnier *m* en cuivre

coppice ['kɒpɪs, *Am:* 'kɑ:pɪs] *n* taillis *m*

copulate ['kɒpjʊleɪt, *Am:* 'kɑ:pjə-] *vi* copuler; **to ~ with sb** *inf* s'accoupler avec qn

copulation *n no pl* copulation *f*

copy ['kɒpi, *Am:* 'kɑ:pi] **I.** <-pies> *n* **1.** (*facsimile*) copie *f;* **to make a ~ of sth** photocopier qc **2.** PHOT épreuve *f* **3.** ART reproduction *f* **4.** PUBL (*of a book*) exemplaire *m;* **carbon ~** carbone *m;* **a true ~** une copie conforme **5.** (*text to be published*) article *m* **6.** (*topic for an article*) sujet *m* d'article **7.** INFOR copie *f;* **hard ~** INFOR impression d'un fichier informatique ►**to be a <u>carbon</u> ~ of sb** être le sosie de qn **II.** <-ie-> *vt a. fig* copier; **to ~ a file onto a disk** copier un fichier sur une disquette **III.** *vi pej* (*cheat*) copier; **to ~ from sb** copier sur qn

◆**copy down** *vt* recopier

copybook **I.** *adj* **1.** (*exemplary*) modèle **2.** (*unoriginal*) banal(e) **II.** *n* cahier *m* d'écriture ►**to <u>blot</u> one's ~** ternir sa réputation

copycat **I.** *n pej, childspeak, inf* copieur, -euse *m, f* **II.** *adj* d'imitation **copydesk** *n Am* bureau *m* de rédaction **copy editor** *n* secrétaire *mf* de rédaction

copying ink *n no pl* encre *f* à copier **copying paper** *n* papier *m* à photocopier

copy protection *n* **1.** LAW protection *f* contre la copie frauduleuse **2.** INFOR protection *f* contre le piratage informatique **copyright** **I.** *n* droits *mpl* d'auteur; **to hold the ~ of sth** avoir les droits d'auteur sur qc; **protected under ~** tous droits de reproduction réservés; **out of ~** dans le domaine public **II.** *vt* déposer

copywriter *n* rédacteur, -trice *m, f* publicitaire

coral ['kɒrəl, *Am:* 'kɔ:r-] **I.** *n no pl* corail *m* **II.** *adj* **1.** (*of reddish colour*) corail *inv* **2.** (*of ~*) de corail

coral island *n* île *f* corallienne **coral reef** *n* récif *m* corallien

cord [kɔ:d, *Am:* kɔ:rd] *n* **1.** (*rope*) corde *f;* **umbilical ~** cordon *m* ombilical **2.** (*string*) ficelle *f* **3.** ELEC fil *m* électrique

cordial ['kɔ:dɪəl, *Am:* 'kɔ:rdʒəl] **I.** *adj* **1.** (*friendly*) chaleureux(-euse); (*relations*) cordial(e) **2.** *form* (*strong*) fort(e); (*dislike*) profond(e) **II.** *n no pl* **1.** *Brit, Aus* cordial *m* **2.** *Am* liqueur *f*

cordiality <-ties> *n form* cordialité *f;* **to exchange cordialities** échanger des politesses

cordless *adj* sans fil

cordon ['kɔ:dn, *Am:* 'kɔ:r-] *n* cordon *m*

cords *n pl* pantalon *m* en velours côtelé

corduroy ['kɔ:dərɔɪ, *Am:* 'kɔ:r-] *n* **1.** *no pl* (*material*) velours *m* côtelé **2.** *pl* (*pants*) pantalon *m* en velours côtelé

core [kɔ:ʳ, *Am:* kɔ:r] **I.** *n* **1.** (*centre*) partie *f* centrale **2.** (*centre with seeds*) noyau *m;* **an apple/pear ~** un trognon de pomme/poire **3.** PHYS nucléon *m;* **the ~ of a nuclear reactor** le cœur d'un réacteur nucléaire **4.** (*most* *important part*) essentiel *m;* **to be at the ~ of a problem** être au centre du problème; **to get to the ~ of sth** aller à l'essentiel de qc **5.** ELEC mèche *f* **6.** INFOR mise *f* en mémoire des bits ►**to the ~** au cœur; **to be rotten to the ~** être pourri jusqu'à la moelle **II.** *adj* (*issue*) central(e) **III.** *vt* évider

CORE [kɔːʳ, *Am:* kɔːr] *n Am abbr of* **Congress of Racial Equality** *organisation pour la défense des droits des minorités ethniques*

core memory, **core store** *n* INFOR mémoire *f* à tores **core subject** *n* matière *f* principale

coriander [ˌkɒri'ændəʳ, *Am:* 'kɔːriædɚ] *n* coriandre *f*

cork [kɔːk, *Am:* kɔːrk] **I.** *n* **1.** *no pl* liège *m* **2.** (*stopper*) bouchon *m* **II.** *vt* **1.** (*put stopper in: bottle*) boucher **2.** (*blacken*) **to ~ one's face** se grimer avec un bouchon brûlé

corkage ['kɔkədʒ, *Am:* 'kɔːr-] *n no pl*, **cork charge** *n* droit *m* de bouchon

corkscrew ['kɔːkskruː, *Am:* 'kɔːrk-] **I.** *n* tire-bouchon *m* **II.** *adj* en tire-bouchon

corn¹ [kɔːn, *Am:* kɔːrn] *n* **1.** *Brit* (*cereal*) blé *m* **2.** *Am* (*maize*) maïs *m* **3.** *Am, inf* (*something trite*) banalité *f*

corn² [kɔːn, *Am:* kɔːrn] *n* MED cor *m* ►**to tread on sb's ~s** toucher la corde sensible de qn

corncob *n* épi *m* de maïs

cornea ['kɔːnɪə, *Am:* 'kɔːr-] *n* cornée *f*

corner ['kɔːnəʳ, *Am:* 'kɔːrnɚ] **I.** *n* **1.** (*junction of two roads*) coin *m;* **just around the ~** à deux pas d'ici; **to cut ~s** prendre des raccourcis **2.** (*place*) coin *m;* **to search every ~ of the house** chercher dans les coins et recoins de la maison **3.** SPORT corner *m* **4.** (*difficult position*) **to be in a tight ~** être dans le pétrin; **to drive sb into a (tight) ~** mettre qn au pied du mur; **to get oneself into a (tight) ~** se mettre dans une situation difficile **5.** (*domination*) **to have a ~ of the market** avoir le monopole du marché **6.** (*periphery*) commissure *f;* **out of the ~ of one's eye** du coin de l'œil **7.** *fig* **to be round the ~** être sur le point de; **to have turned the ~** avoir surmonté la crise **II.** *vt* **1.** (*hinder escape*) attraper; *iron* coincer **2.** ECON (*market*) accaparer **III.** *vi* (*auto*) virer; **to ~ well** prendre bien les virages

cornered *adj* acculé(e)

corner house *n* maison *f* faisant l'angle **corner seat** *n* siège *m* en coin **corner shop** *n* magasin *m* du quartier

cornerstone *n* pierre *f* angulaire

cornet ['kɔːnɪt, *Am:* kɔːr'net] *n* **1.** (*brass instrument*) cornet *m* à piston **2.** (*wafer cone*) cornet *m*

cornflakes *npl* cornflakes *mpl* **cornflour** *n no pl, Brit, Aus* farine *f* de maïs **cornflower** **I.** *n* bleuet *m* **II.** *adj* (*blue*) vif(vive)

cornice ['kɔːnɪs, *Am:* 'kɔːr-] *n* ARCHIT corniche *f*

corn poppy <-ppies> *n* coquelicot *m*

Cornwall ['kɔːrnwɔːl] *n* la Cornouailles

corny ['kɔːni, *Am:* 'kɔːr-] <-ier, -iest> *adj inf* banal(e)

corollary [kər'ɒləri, *Am:* 'kɔːrəler-] <-ries> *n form* corollaire *m*

coronary ['kɒrənəri, *Am:* 'kɔːrəner-] **I.** *n inf* infarctus *m* **II.** *adj* coronaire

coronation [ˌkɒrə'neɪʃən, *Am:* ˌkɔːr-] *n* couronnement *m*

coroner ['kɒrənəʳ, *Am:* 'kɔːrənɚ] *n* coroner *m*

corporal ['kɔːpərəl, *Am:* 'kɔːr-] **I.** *n* MIL caporal *m* **II.** *adj form* corporel(le)

corporate ['kɔːpərət, *Am:* 'kɔːr-] **I.** *n* société *f* **II.** *adj* **1.** (*shared by group*) de l'entreprise; (*clients, workers*) de la société; **~ identity** image *f* de marque de l'entreprise **2.** (*collective*) commun(e)

corporation *n* **1.** (*business*) société *f;* **multinational ~** multinationale *f;* **public ~** *Brit* entreprise *f* publique **2.** *Brit* (*local council*) municipalité *f;* **municipal ~** conseil *m* municipal

corporation tax *n* impôt *m* sur les sociétés

corps [kɔːʳ, *Am:* kɔːr] *n* corps *m*

corps de ballet [ˌkɔːdə'bæleɪ, *Am:* ˌkɔːr-] *n* corps *m* de ballet

corpse [kɔːps, *Am:* kɔːrps] *n* cadavre *m*

corpus ['kɔːpəs, *Am:* 'kɔːr-] <-pora *o* -es> *n* **1.** *form* (*collection*) recueil *m* **2.** LING (*collection of texts*) corpus *m*

Corpus Christi [ˌkɔːpəs'krɪsti, *Am:* ˌkɔːr-] REL la Fête-Dieu

corral [kə'rɑːl, *Am:* -'ræl] **I.** *n Am* corral *m* **II.** <-ll-> *vt* enfermer dans un corral

correct [kə'rekt] **I.** *vt* (*put right*) corriger; (*watch*) régler; **I stand ~ed** *form, iron* je reconnais mon erreur **II.** *adj* **1.** (*accurate*) juste; **that is ~** *form* c'est exact **2.** (*proper*) correct; **he's a very ~ gentleman** c'est un monsieur comme il faut

correction [kə'rekʃən] *n* **1.** (*change*) rectification *f;* **subject to ~** sous toutes réserves; **to be subject to ~** être sujet à des modifications **2.** *no pl* (*improvement*) correction *f* **3.** *no pl* (*improvement through punishment*) punition *f*

correction fluid *n* correcteur *m* liquide

corrective [kə'rektɪv] **I.** *adj* correcteur(-trice) **II.** *n* rectificatif *m*

correctly *adv* correctement

correctness *n no pl* exactitude *f*

correlate ['kɒrəleɪt, *Am:* 'kɔːrə-] **I.** *vt* corréler **II.** *vi* (*relate*) **to ~ with sth** être en corrélation avec qc

correlation *n* **1.** (*connection*) corrélation *f* **2.** (*relationship*) lien *m*

correspond [ˌkɒrɪ'spɒnd, *Am:* ˌkɔːrə-] *vi* **1.** (*be equal to*) correspondre; **to ~ with [*o* to] sth** correspondre à qc; **to ~ closely/roughly to sth** être très/peu conforme à qc **2.** (*write*) correspondre; **to ~ with sb** correspondre avec qn

correspondence [ˌkɒrɪ'spɒndəns, *Am:*

ˌkɔːrəˈspɑːn-] *n no pl* correspondance *f;* **business ~** courrier *m* d'affaires; **to enter into ~ with sb** *form* entretenir une correspondance avec qn

correspondent *n* (*writer of letters, journalist*) correspondant(e) *m(f);* **special ~** envoyé(e) *m(f)* spécial; **parliamentary ~** rédacteur, -trice *m, f* parlementaire

corresponding *adj* **1.** (*same*) semblable; **in the ~ period last year** à la même époque l'année dernière **2.** (*accompanying*) correspondant(e)

corridor [ˈkɒrɪdɔːʳ, *Am:* ˈkɔːrədɚ] *n* **1.** (*passage*) corridor *m* **2.** RAIL, AUTO, AVIAT couloir *m*

corrie [ˈkɒri, *Am:* ˈkɔːr-] *n* cirque *m*

corroborate [kəˈrɒbəreɪt, *Am:* -ˈrɑːbə-] *vt* confirmer

corroboration *n* corroboration *f;* **in ~ of sth** à l'appui de qc

corroborative [kəˈrɒbərətɪv, *Am:* -ˈrɑːbɚəṱɪv] *adj* qui confirme

corrode [kəˈrəʊd, *Am:* -ˈroʊd] **I.** *vi* se corroder **II.** *vt* **1.** (*damage*) corroder **2.** *fig* entamer

corrosion [kəˈrəʊʒən, *Am:* -ˈroʊ-] *n no pl* **1.** (*deterioration*) corrosion *f* **2.** *fig* désagrégation *f*

corrosive [kəˈrəʊsɪv, *Am:* -ˈroʊ-] **I.** *adj* destructif(-ive); (*acid*) corrosif(-ive); (*attack*) virulent(e) **II.** *n* produit *m* corrosif

corrugated [ˈkɒrəgeɪtɪd, *Am:* -ṱɪd] *adj* **1.** (*furrowed*) ridé(e) **2.** (*rutted: road*) *iron* ondulé(e)

corrupt [kəˈrʌpt] **I.** *vt* **1.** (*debase*) dépraver **2.** (*influence by bribes*) corrompre **3.** INFOR (*file*) altérer **II.** *vi* se corrompre **III.** *adj* (*influenced by bribes*) corrompu(e); (*practice*) malhonnête; **~ morals** moralité *f* douteuse

corruption *n* **1.** *no pl* (*debasement*) dépravation *f* **2.** (*bribery*) corruption *f* **3.** LING altération *f*

corset [ˈkɔːsɪt, *Am:* ˈkɔːr-] *n* corset *m*

Corsica [ˈkɔːsɪkə, *Am:* ˈkɔːr-] *n* la Corse

Corsican **I.** *adj* corse **II.** *n* **1.** (*person*) Corse *mf* **2.** LING corse *m; s. a.* **English**

cos [kɒs, *Am:* kɑːs] *n* MAT *abbr of* **cosine** cos *m*

cosec [ˈkəʊsek, *Am:* ˈkoʊ-] *n* MAT *abbr of* **cosecant** cosec *f*

cosignatory [ˌkəʊˈsɪgnətəri, *Am:* ˌkoʊˈsɪgnətɔːri] <-ries> *n* cosignataire *mf*

cosine [ˈkəʊsaɪn, *Am:* ˈkoʊ-] *n* cosinus *m*

cosiness *n no pl* confort *m*

cos lettuce [ˈkɒsˌletɪs, *Am:* ˈkɑːsˌleṱ-] *n Brit, Aus* laitue *f* romaine

cosmetic [kɒzˈmetɪk, *Am:* kɑːzˈmeṱ-] **I.** *n* cosmétique *m;* **~s** produits *mpl* de beauté **II.** *adj* **1.** (*related to beauty*) cosmétique; (*surgery*) esthétique **2.** *pej* (*superficial*) superficiel(le); (*change, improvement*) de forme

cosmetician *n* esthéticien(ne) *m(f)*

cosmic [ˈkɒzmɪk, *Am:* ˈkɑːz-] *adj fig* cosmique; (*proportion*) incommensurable

cosmology [kɒzˈmɒlədʒi, *Am:* kɑːzˈmɑːlə-] *n* cosmologie *f*

cosmonaut [ˈkɒzmənɔːt, *Am:* ˈkɑːzmənɑːt] *n* spationaute *mf*

cosmopolitan [ˌkɒzməˈpɒlɪtən, *Am:* ˌkɑːzməˈpɑːlɪ-] **I.** *adj* cosmopolite **II.** *n* cosmopolite *mf*

cosmos [ˈkɒzmɒs, *Am:* ˈkɑːzmoʊs] *n no pl* cosmos *m*

cost [kɒst, *Am:* kɑːst] **I.** *vt* **1.** <cost, cost> (*amount to*) coûter; **to ~ £40** coûter 40 livres; **it ~s him dear** ça lui revient cher **2.** <cost, cost> (*cause the loss of*) coûter; **to ~ sb dear** coûter cher à qn **3.** <costed, costed> (*calculate price*) évaluer le coût de **II.** *n* **1.** (*price*) prix; **at no extra ~** sans dépense supplémentaire; **at huge ~** à grands frais **2.** (*sacrifice*) renoncement *m;* **at great personal ~** en faisant de gros sacrifices; **to learn sth to one's ~** apprendre qc aux dépens de qn; **at all ~(s)** à n'importe quel prix **3.** *pl* LAW frais *mpl* d'instance et dépens

co-star **I.** *n* covedette *f;* **to be sb's ~** avoir la vedette avec qn **II.** <-rr-> *vi* **to ~ with sb** partager la vedette avec qn

costly [ˈkɒstli, *Am:* ˈkɑːst-] <-ier, -iest> *adj* cher(chère); (*mistake*) qui coûte cher; **to prove ~** s'avérer coûteux

cost price *n* prix *m* coûtant; **at ~** au prix de revient

costume [ˈkɒstjuːm, *Am:* ˈkɑːstuːm] *n* costume *m;* **to wear a clown ~** porter un déguisement de clown

cosy [ˈkəʊzi, *Am:* ˈkoʊ-] **I.** <-ier, -iest> *adj* **1.** (*comfortable*) *a. fig* douillet(te); **to feel ~** être confortablement installé **2.** *pej* (*convenient*) pépère **3.** (*intimate*) intime **II.** <-sies> *n* **tea ~** couvre-théière *m;* **egg ~** couvre-œuf *m*

cot [kɒt, *Am:* kɑːt] *n* **1.** (*baby's bed*) lit *m* d'enfant **2.** *Am* (*camp bed*) lit *m* de camp

cot(an), **cotangent** *n* cotangente *f*

cot death *n* mort *f* subite du nourrisson

cottage *n* cottage *m;* **a country ~** une petite maison à la campagne; **thatched ~** chaumière *f*

cottage cheese *n no pl* cottage *m* (*fromage blanc à gros caillots, légèrement salé*) **cottage industry** <-tries> *n* industrie *f* à domicile

cotton [ˈkɒtn, *Am:* ˈkɑːtn] **I.** *n* **1.** coton *m* **2.** fil *m* **II.** *adj* en coton

◆**cotton on** *vi Brit, Aus* **to ~ to sth** piger qc

◆**cotton to** *vt* **to ~ sb** se prendre d'amitié pour qn

cotton bud *n* coton-tige *m* **cotton bush** *n* cotonnier *m* **cotton candy** *n s.* **candyfloss** **cotton-grower** *n* cultivateur, -trice de coton *m* **cotton mill** *n* filature *f* de coton **cottonseed** *n* graine *f* de coton **cotton wool** *n* coton *m* hydrophile ►**to wrap sb in ~** mettre qn dans du coton

couch [kaʊtʃ] **I.** *n* canapé *m;* **psychoanalyst's ~** le divan du psychanalyste **II.** *vt* for-

muler
couchette [kuːˈʃet] *n* couchette *f*
couch potato *n inf* **to be a ~** passer sa vie devant la télé
cough [kɒf, *Am:* kɑːf] **I.** *n* (*loud expulsion of air*) toux *f;* **to give a ~** tousser **II.** *vi* **1.** (*expel air loudly through lungs*) tousser **2.** AUTO avoir des ratés **III.** *vt* tousser en crachant; **to ~ blood** cracher du sang
◆**cough up I.** *vt* **1.** (*bring up*) cracher **2.** *inf* (*pay reluctantly: money*) cracher **II.** *vi inf* **1.** (*pay*) casquer **2.** (*admit*) cracher le morceau
cough drop *n* pastille *f* contre/pour la toux **cough medicine**, **cough mixture** *n* médicament *m* contre la toux
could [kʊd] *pt, subj of* **can**
council [ˈkaʊntsəl] *n* ADMIN conseil *m*
council estate *n Brit* cité *f* de logements sociaux **council flat**, **council house** *n Brit* appartement *m* à loyer modéré **council housing** *n Brit* logements *mpl* sociaux
councillor *n Brit, Aus* conseiller, -ère *m, f;* **a town ~** un conseiller municipal
Council of Economic and Finance Ministers *n* Conseil *m* des ministres de l'Économie et des Finances **Council of Europe** *n* Conseil *m* de l'Europe **Council of Ministers** *n* Conseil *m* des Ministres **Council of the European Union** *n* Conseil *m* de l'Union européenne
councilor *n Am* conseiller *m* juridique; *s. a.* councillor
council tax *n Brit* impôts *mpl* municipaux
counsel [ˈkaʊntsəl] **I.** <*Brit* -ll- *o Am* -l-> *vt* (*advise*) conseiller **II.** *n* **1.** *no pl, form* (*advice*) conseil *m;* **a ~ of perfection** un idéal difficile à atteindre **2.** (*lawyer*) avocat(e) *m(f)* ►**to keep one's own ~** garder ses intentions pour soi
counsel(l)ing *n no pl* assistance *f*
counsel(l)or *n* **1.** (*trained psychological helper*) conseiller, -ère *m, f* **2.** *Am* (*lawyer*) avocat(e) *m(f)*
count¹ [kaʊnt] *n* (*aristocrat*) conte *m*
count² [kaʊnt] **I.** *n* **1.** (*totaling up*) compte *m;* **final ~** décompte *m* définitif; **at the last ~** au dernier comptage **2.** (*measured amount*) dénombrement *m* **3.** (*number*) **to keep/to lose ~ of sth** tenir/perdre le compte de qc **4.** LAW chef *m* d'accusation **5.** (*opinion*) **to agree/disagree with sb on several ~s** être d'accord/en désaccord avec qn à plusieurs égards **6.** (*reason*) **to fail on a number of ~s** échouer pour un certain nombre de raisons ►**to be out for the ~** être K.O. **II.** *vt* **1.** (*number*) compter; **to ~ heads** faire le compte des présents **2.** (*consider*) **to ~ sb as a friend** considérer qn comme un ami ►**to ~ one's blessings** s'estimer heureux; **don't ~ your chickens before they're hatched!** *prov* il ne faut pas vendre la peau de l'ours avant de l'avoir tué; **to ~ the cost(s)** calculer les dépenses **III.** *vi* **1.** (*number*) compter **2.** (*be considered*) **to ~ as sth** être considéré comme qc **3.** (*be of value*) compter; **that's what ~s** c'est ce qui compte; **sth doesn't ~ for anything** ça ne sert à rien; **it ~s towards sth** ça compte pour qc
◆**count down** *vi* faire le compte à rebours
◆**count out I.** *vi* **1.** (*number off aloud*) compter pièce par pièce **2.** SPORT (*defeat*) mettre qn K.O. **II.** *vt always sep, inf* **"count me out of this trip"** "ne comptez pas sur moi pour ce voyage"
countable noun [ˌkaʊntəblˈnaʊn] *n* nom *m* dénombrable
countenance [ˈkaʊntɪnəns, *Am:* -tənəns] **I.** *n no pl* **1.** *form* (*facial expression*) expression *f* du visage **2.** (*approval*) accord *m;* **to give ~ to sth** appuyer qc **3.** (*composure*) maîtrise *f* de soi; **to keep one's ~** *form* garder son sang-froid **II.** *vt form* (*approve*) approuver
counter [ˈkaʊntəʳ, *Am:* -t̬ɚ] **I.** *n* **1.** (*service point*) comptoir *m* **2.** (*machine*) compteur *m* **3.** (*disc*) jeton *m;* **bargaining ~** monnaie *f* d'échange **4.** *fig* **under the ~** sous le manteau **II.** *vt* contrer **III.** *vi* **1.** (*oppose*) riposter; **to ~ with sth** riposter par qc **2.** (*react by scoring*) parer un coup **IV.** *adv* **to run ~ to sth** aller à l'encontre de qc; **to act ~ to sth** agir de façon contraire à qc
counteract [ˌkaʊntərˈækt, *Am:* -t̬ɚ-] *vt* contrarier; (*effect*) contrer
counteractive *adj* **1.** (*working against*) qui agit de façon inefficace **2.** (*neutralizing*) neutralisant(e) **counterattack I.** *n* contre-attaque *f* **II.** *vt* contre-attaquer **III.** *vi* **1.** (*attack in return*) riposter **2.** SPORT contre-attaquer **counterbalance I.** *n* contrepoids *m* **II.** *vt* **1.** (*balance out*) faire contrepoids à **2.** *fig* égaler **countercharge I.** *n* LAW contre-accusation *f* **II.** *vt* LAW faire une contre-accusation **countercheck I.** *n* **1.** (*restraint*) entrave *f* **2.** (*second check*) vérification *f* **3.** *fig* **to put a ~ on sth** mettre un frein à qc **II.** *vt* (*check again*) revérifier **counterclockwise** *adj Am* (*anti-clockwise*) dans le sens inverse des aiguilles d'une montre **counter-espionage** *n* contre-espionnage *m* **counter-espionage service** *n* service *m* de contre-espionnage **counterfeit I.** *adj* faux(fausse) **II.** *vt* contrefaire **III.** *n* contrefaçon *f* **counterfoil** *n* FIN *Brit* talon *m* de chèque **counter-intelligence** *n* contre-espionnage *m* **countermand** *vt* annuler **countermeasure** *n* mesure *f* défensive **counterpart** *n* **1.** (*system*) équivalent *m* **2.** (*person*) homologue *mf* **counterpoint** *n* MUS contrepoint *m* **counterpoise** *form* **I.** *n* **1.** (*force*) contrepoids *m* **2.** *fig* **to be in ~** être en équilibre **II.** *vt* **1.** (*balance out*) faire contrepoids à **2.** *fig* contrebalancer **counterproductive** *adj* qui entrave la productivité; **to prove ~** se révéler inefficace **counter-revolution** *n* contre-révolution *f* **countersign** *vt* contresigner **countersink** *vt* fraiser **counter-terrorism** *n no pl* contre-terrorisme *m*

countess ['kaʊntɪs, *Am:* -t̬ɪs] *n* comtesse *f*
countless *adj* innombrable
country ['kʌntri] **I.** *n* **1.** *no pl* (*rural area*) campagne *f;* **in the ~** dans la campagne **2.** <-ies> (*political unit*) pays *m;* **native ~** patrie *f;* **the whole ~** l'ensemble du pays; **to go to the ~** *Brit, form* appeler le pays à voter **3.** (*area of land*) région *f;* **marshy ~** région *f* marécageuse; **open ~** rase campagne *f;* **rough ~** région *f* sauvage **4.** (*music style*) country *f* **II.** *adj* **1.** (*rural*) campagnard(e) **2.** (*in the countryside: people, manners*) de la campagne; (*road*) de campagne; (*life*) à la campagne **3.** (*relating to music style*) country *inv;* (*singer*) de country
country bumpkin *n* péquenaud(de) *m(f)* **country club** *n* club *m* de loisirs **country dance** *n* danse *f* folklorique **country folk** *n + pl vb* gens *mpl* de la campagne **country house** *n* maison *f* de campagne **countryman** <-men> *n* **1.** (*same nationality*) (**fellow**) ~ compatriote *m;* **countrymen and women** citoyens et citoyennes **2.** (*from rural area*) homme *m* de la campagne **country music** *n* musique *f* country **country road** *n* route *f* de campagne **countryside** *n no pl* campagne *f* **countrywide I.** *adj* qui touche l'ensemble du pays **II.** *adv* dans l'ensemble du pays **countrywoman** <-women> *n* **1.** (*same nationality*) (**fellow**) ~ compatriote *f* **2.** (*from rural area*) femme *f* de la campagne
county ['kaʊnti, *Am:* -t̬i] <-ies> *n* comté *m*
county borough *n Brit* HIST municipalité *f* d'un comté **county council** *n Brit* conseil (régional) *m* du comté **county court** *n Brit* tribunal *m* de grande instance **county seat** *n Am,* **county town** *n Brit* chef-lieu *m* du comté
coup [ku:] <coups> *n* **1.** (*unexpected achievement*) coup *m* inespéré **2.** POL *s.* **coup d'état**
coup de grâce *n* coup *m* de grâce **coup d'état** <coups d'état> *n* coup *m* d'état
coupé ['ku:peɪ] *n* coupé *m*
couple ['kʌpl] **I.** *n* **1.** *no pl* (*a few*) quelque; **a ~ of ...** quelques ..., une couple de ... *Québec;* **another ~ of ...** encore un peu de ...; **every ~ of days** tous les deux jours; **the first ~ of weeks** les deux premières semaines; **over the past ~ of months** dans les deux derniers mois **2.** + *sing/pl vb* (*two people*) couple *m* **II.** *vt* joindre; **sth ~d with sth** (*in conjunction with*) qc en supplément de qc; **sth is ~d to sth** (*linked*) qc est associé à qc **III.** *vi* s'accoupler
couplet ['kʌplɪt] *n* distique *m*
coupling *n* **1.** RAIL, AUTO (*linking device*) attelage *m* **2.** (*linking*) association *f* **3.** (*sexual intercourse: of people*) rapport *m* sexuel; (*of animals*) accouplement *m*
coupon ['ku:pɒn, *Am:* -pɑ:n] *n* **1.** (*voucher*) bon *m* **2.** (*return-slip*) bulletin-réponse *m* **3.** *Brit* (*voucher for basic items*) coupon *m*
courage ['kʌrɪdʒ] *n* (*bravery*) courage *m;* **to show great ~** être très courageux; **to have the ~ of one's convictions** avoir le courage de ses opinions; **to take one's ~ in both hands** prendre son courage à deux mains ►**Dutch** ~ courage *m* pris dans l'alcool
courageous [kə'reɪdʒəs] *adj* courageux(-euse)
courgette [kʊə'ʒet, *Am:* kʊr-] *n* courgette *f*
courier ['kʊrɪəʳ, *Am:* 'kʊrɪɚ] *n* **1.** (*tour guide*) guide *mf* touristique **2.** (*delivers post*) messager *m;* **motorcycle/bike ~** coursier, -ière *m, f*
course [kɔ:s, *Am:* kɔ:rs] **I.** *n* **1.** (*direction*) cours *m;* **to adopt a ~** prendre une direction; **to adopt a middle ~** *fig* opter pour une solution intermédiaire; **to be on ~ for sth** être en route pour qc; *fig* être sur la voie de qc; **to be off ~** dévier du chemin; *fig* faire fausse route; **to change ~** changer de direction; *fig* prendre une autre voie; **to keep one's ~** poursuivre son chemin; *fig* poursuivre sa voie; **to attempt to pervert the ~ of justice** essayer d'entraver le cours de la justice **2.** (*development: of time, event*) cours *m;* **in due ~** dans les temps voulus; **during the ~ of sth** au cours de qc; **sth runs/takes its ~** qc suit/prends son cours; **of ~** bien sûr, sans autre *Suisse;* **of ~ not** bien sûr que non **3.** (*series of classes*) cours *m;* **cooking ~** cours de cuisine; **to do/take/follow a ~ in sth** prendre/suivre un cours de qc **4.** (*treatment*) traitement *m;* **to put sb on a ~ of sth** mettre qn sous traitement de qc **5.** SPORT (*area*) parcours *m;* **golf ~** parcours *m* de golf; **obstacle ~** parcours *m* d'obstacles **6.** (*part of meal*) plat *m* **7.** CONSTR (*layer*) couche *f;* **a damp-proof ~** une couche étanche **II.** *vi* (*river, blood*) couler; **to ~ through sth** couler dans qc
coursebook *n Brit* manuel *m* scolaire **courseware** *n* INFOR didacticiel *m* **coursework** *n no pl* UNIV travail *m*
court [kɔ:t, *Am:* kɔ:rt] **I.** *n* **1.** (*room for trials*) tribunal *m;* **in ~** au tribunal; **to appear in ~** être convoqué au tribunal **2.** (*judicial body*) tribunal *m;* ~ **of law** cour *f* de justice; **to go to ~** aller en justice; **to be a matter for the ~** être à la justice de décider; **to settle out of ~** s'arranger à l'amiable; **to take sb to ~** poursuivre qn en justice; **a sale by order of the ~** une vente judiciaire **3.** (*marked out area for playing*) terrain *m;* (*tennis*) court *m;* **grass ~** court sur gazon **4.** (*yard*) cour *f* **5.** *Brit* (*apartment buildings*) résidence *f* **6.** (*building for royalty*) cour *f* **7.** *no pl, no indef art* (*ruling sovereign*) cour *f;* **at ~** à la cour ►**to pay ~ to sb** faire la cour à qn **II.** *vt* **1.** (*try to attract*) courtiser; (*a woman*) faire la cour à **2.** (*have a relationship*) fréquenter **3.** (*seek*) rechercher; **to ~ danger** aller au-devant du danger **III.** *vi* se fréquenter
court card *n* GAMES figure *f* **court case** *n* affaire *f* **court circular** *n Brit:* *bulletin*

quotidien de la cour royale **court correspondent** *n* correspondant(e) *m(f)* à la cour
courteous ['kɜːtɪəs, *Am:* 'kɜːrt̬ɪ-] *adj* courtois(e)
courtesy ['kɜːtəsi, *Am:* 'kɜːrt̬ə-] <-ies> *n* **1.** (*politeness*) politesse *f* **2.** *no pl* (*decency*) courtoisie *f;* **to have the (common) ~ to** *+infin pej* avoir la courtoisie de *+infin;* **to show sb (some) ~** faire preuve de courtoisie envers qn **3.** (*permission*) autorisation; **(by) ~ of sth** avec l'autorisation de qc; (*because of*) grâce à qc
courtesy bus *n* bus *m* mis à la disposition des clients **courtesy light** *n* AUTO plafonnier *m* **courtesy title** *n* titre *m* de courtoisie
court hearing *n* session *f* au tribunal
courthouse ['kɔːthaʊs, *Am:* 'kɔːrt-] <courthouses> *n Am* palais *m* de justice
courtier ['kɔːtɪəʳ, *Am:* 'kɔːrt̬ɪɚ] *n* courtisan(ne) *m(f)*
court jester *n* HIST bouffon *m* de cour **court martial** *n* cour *f* martiale **court-martial** *vt* traduire en cour martiale
court of appeal *n Brit,* **court of appeals** *n Am* cour *f* d'appel **Court of Auditors** *n* Cour *f* des Comptes **court of inquiry** *n* commission *f* d'enquête **Court of Justice** *n* Cour *f* de Justice **court of law** *n* tribunal *m* **court of session** *n* cour *f* de cassation **court order** *n* décision *f* judiciaire **court record** *n* compte *m* rendu d'audience **courtroom** *n* salle *f* d'audience **courtship** *n* cour *f* **court shoe** *n Brit* escarpin *m* **court tennis** *n* jeu *m* de paume **courtyard** *n* cour *f* intérieure
cousin ['kʌzn] *n* cousin(e) *m(f)*
couture [kuː'tjʊəʳ, *Am:* kuː'tʊr] *n* couture *f*
cove [kəʊv, *Am:* koʊv] *n* (*small bay*) crique *f*
covenant ['kʌvənənt, *Am:* -ænt] **I.** *n* **1.** (*legal agreement*) convention *f* **2.** *Brit* (*charity donation*) don *m* à une œuvre de charité **II.** *vt* convenir de
Coventry ['kɒvntri, *Am:* 'kʌv-] *n* Coventry ►**to send sb to ~** mettre qn en quarantaine
cover ['kʌvəʳ, *Am:* -ɚ] **I.** *n* **1.** (*top*) couverture *f;* (*on pot*) couvercle *m;* (*on furniture*) housse *f* **2.** PUBL couverture *f;* **hard-~ edition** édition *f* reliée; **soft-~ edition** édition *f* de poche; **to read sth from ~ to ~** lire qc de la première à la dernière page **3.** *pl* (*sheets*) **the ~s** les draps *mpl* **4.** (*envelope*) enveloppe *f;* **under plain ~** sous pli simple; **under separate ~** sous pli séparé **5.** (*means of concealing*) couverture *f;* **under ~ of darkness** sous le couvert de la nuit; **to blow sb's ~** révéler l'identité de qn; **to go under ~** prendre une identité d'emprunt; **to use sth as a ~ for sth** utiliser qc comme couverture pour qc **6.** (*shelter*) abri *m;* **to break ~** sortir de l'abri; **to run for ~** se mettre à l'abri **7.** FIN couverture *f* **8.** (*insurance*) couverture *f;* **full ~** garantie *f* totale **9.** GASTR couvert *m* **10.** MUS (*recording*) reprise *f* ►**never judge a book by its ~** il ne faut jamais juger des apparences **II.** *vt* **1.** (*put over*) couvrir; (*surface, wall, sofa*) recouvrir; **to ~ sth with sth** recouvrir qc de qc; **to ~ sth with sth** (re)couvrir qc de qc **2.** (*hide*) dissimuler; **to ~ one's eyes with one's hands** se couvrir les yeux avec les mains; *fig* se voiler la face **3.** (*pay: one's costs*) couvrir **4.** (*extend over*) s'étendre sur **5.** (*travel*) parcourir **6.** (*deal with*) traiter de; **to ~ a lot of ground** *fig* traiter beaucoup de sujets **7.** (*include*) inclure **8.** (*be enough for*) couvrir **9.** (*report on*) couvrir **10.** (*insure*) *a. fig* couvrir; **to ~ sb for/against sth** couvrir qn contre qc **11.** MIL, SPORT couvrir **12.** (*do sb's job*) remplacer **13.** (*adopt song*) reprendre ►**to ~ your ass** [*o* **back**] *inf* se couvrir; **to ~ oneself with glory** se couvrir de gloire; **to ~ a multitude of sins** cacher une multitude de péchés; **to ~ one's tracks** brouiller ses pistes
◆**cover over** *vt* (*obscured*) **to be covered over with sth** être recouvert de qc
◆**cover up I.** *vt* **1.** (*conceal*) dissimuler **2.** (*protect*) recouvrir; **to cover oneself up (warm)** s'emmitoufler; **to keep sth covered up** *fig* garder qc au chaud **II.** *vi* **1.** (*wear sth*) se couvrir **2.** (*protect*) **to ~ for sb** couvrir qn
coverage ['kʌvərɪdʒ] *n a. fig* couverture *f;* **to receive a lot of media ~** recevoir beaucoup d'attention de la presse; **to give comprehensive ~ of sth** traiter de qc de manière complète
coveralls *n pl* bleu *m* de travail
cover charge *n* taxe *f* sur le couvert
covered *adj* **1.** (*roofed over*) couvert(e) **2.** (*insured*) couvert(e)
cover girl *n* cover-girl *f*
covering I. *n* couverture *f;* **floor ~** revêtement *m* de sol **II.** *adj* MIL de couverture
covering letter *n* lettre *f* de présentation
cover note *n Am, Aus* (*covering note*) note *f* explicative **cover story** *n* une *f*
covert ['kʌvət, *Am:* 'koʊvɜːrt] **I.** *adj* caché(e); (*glance*) dérobé(e); **to be ~** être couvert **II.** *n* couvert *m*
cover-up *n* couverture *f*
cover version *n* MUS reprise *f*
covet ['kʌvɪt] *vt* convoiter
cow¹ [kaʊ] *n* **1.** (*female ox*) vache *f* **2.** (*female mammal*) femelle *f;* **elephant ~** femelle éléphant **3.** *pej, inf* vache *f;* **stupid ~** conne *f* **4.** *Aus, pej, inf* (*unpleasant thing*) **a ~ of a ...** un/une ... de merde ►**until/till the ~s come home** quand les poules auront des dents
cow² [kaʊ] *vt* intimider
coward ['kaʊəd, *Am:* 'kaʊɚd] *n pej* lâche *mf*
cowardice ['kaʊədɪs, *Am:* 'kaʊɚ-] *n pej* lâcheté *f*
cowardly *adj* **1.** (*fearful*) peureux(-euse) **2.** (*mean: attack*) lâche
cowboy ['kaʊbɔɪ] **I.** *n* **1.** (*cattle hand*) cowboy *m;* **Cowboys and Indians** les Cow-boys et les Indiens **2.** *inf* (*dishonest tradesperson*)

arnaqueur *m* **II.** *adj* (*typical of western cattle hand*) de cow-boy

cowdung *n no pl* bouse *f* de vache

cower *vi* se cacher

cowherd ['kaʊhɜːd, *Am:* -hɜːrd] *n* berger *m* de vaches

cowhide **I.** *n no pl* peau *f* de vache **II.** *adj* en cuir de vache

cowl [kaʊl] *n* **1.** (*hood*) capuche *f* **2.** (*on chimney*) capuchon *m*

cowling *n* AVIAT capotage *m*

cowman ['kaʊmən] <-men> *n* **1.** (*male cowherd*) *s.* **cowherd** **2.** *Aus* (*cattle farm manager*) vacher, -ère *m, f*

co-worker *n* collègue *mf*

cowshed ['kaʊʃed] *n* étable *f*

cowslip ['kaʊslɪp] *n* primevère *f*

cox ['kɒks, *Am:* 'kɑːks], **coxswain** *n form* barreur *m*

coy [kɔɪ, *Am:* -ɚ] <-er, -est> *adj* **1.** (*secretive*) évasif(-ive) **2.** (*flirtatiously shy*) faussement timide

coyote [kɔɪ'əʊt, *Am:* kaɪ'oʊt̬i] *n* coyote *m*

cozy ['kəʊzi, *Am:* 'koʊ-] *adj Am s.* **cosy**

CP *n abbr of* **Communist Party** PC *m*

CPU [ˌsiːpiː'juː] *n* INFOR *abbr of* **Central Processing Unit** UCT *f*

crab[1] [kræb] *n* **1.** (*sea animal*) crabe *m* **2.** *no pl, no indef art* (*flesh of sea animal*) crabe *m;* ~ **meat** chair *f* de crabe; **dressed** ~ crabe *m* garni **3.** (*in astrology*) Cancer *m* ►**to catch a** ~ SPORT plonger la rame trop profondément

crab[2] [kræb] *vi* gâcher

crab (apple) *n* **1.** (*tree*) pommier *f* sauvage **2.** (*fruit*) pomme *f* aigre

crabbed *adj* **1.** (*too close together*) serré(e); (*writing*) en pattes de mouche **2.** (*bad-tempered*) grognon(ne)

crabby <-ier, -iest> *adj inf* grognon(ne)

crab louse *n* morpion *m*

crack [kræk] **I.** *n* **1.** (*fissure*) fissure *f;* (*on skin*) gerçure *f* **2.** (*opening: of door*) entrebâillement *m;* **to open a door/window (just) a** ~ entrouvrir une porte/fenêtre **3.** (*sharp sound*) craquement *m;* (*of a rifle, whip*) claquement *m* **4.** *inf* (*form of cocaine*) crack *m* **5.** *inf* (*joke*) plaisanterie *f* **6.** *inf* (*attempt*) essai *m;* **to have a** ~ **at sth** tenter qc ►**at the** ~ **of dawn** aux aurores; **the** ~ **of doom** le glas du Jugement dernier **II.** *adj* <inv> d'élite **III.** *vt* **1.** (*make a* ~ *in*) fêler; (*nuts*) casser; **to** ~ **sth open** ouvrir qc **2.** (*solve: a problem*) résoudre; (*a code*) déchiffrer **3.** (*make sound with*) faire claquer; **to** ~ **the whip** faire claquer le fouet; *fig* agir avec autorité **4.** (*hit*) frapper; (*one's knuckles*) craquer; **to** ~ **one's head on sth** se cogner la tête sur qc ►**to** ~ **a joke** dire une plaisanterie **IV.** *vi* **1.** (*have a* ~) se fêler; (*skin, lips*) se gercer; (*paint*) se craqueler; (*facade*) se fissurer **2.** *inf* (*fail: relationship*) casser **3.** (*break down*) craquer **4.** (*make a sharp noise*) craquer; (*whip*) claquer; (*voice*) se casser ►**to get** ~**ing on/with sth** se mettre à faire qc

◆**crack down** *vi* sévir; **to** ~ **on sb/sth** sévir contre qn/qc

◆**crack up** **I.** *vi* **1.** (*break*) se briser **2.** (*have a breakdown*) craquer **3.** *inf* (*laugh*) mourir de rire **II.** *vt* **1.** (*make laugh*) **to crack sb up** faire éclater qn de rire **2.** (*make claims about*) **sth is not all it's cracked up to be** *inf* qc n'est pas aussi fantastique qu'il n'y parait

crackdown *n* mesure *f;* **to habe a** ~ **on** sévir contre

cracked *adj* **1.** (*having fissures*) fissuré(e); (*lips*) gercé(e) **2.** (*crazy*) fêlé(e)

cracker *n* **1.** (*dry biscuit*) biscuit *m* sec **2.** (*device*) pétard *m;* **a Christmas** ~ *Brit: objet cylindrique contenant un pétard et dont il faut tirer les deux bouts pour obtenir le cadeau à l'intérieur* **3.** *inf* (*excellent thing*) **it's a** ~ c'est génial **4.** (*attractive woman*) bombe *f*

crackers *adj* fou(folle)

crackle ['krækl] **I.** *vi* **1.** (*make sharp sounds*) craquer; (*fire, radio*) crépiter **2.** (*be tense*) se tendre **II.** *n* craquement *m;* (*of fire, radio*) crépitement *m*

crackling *n* **1.** (*sound: of a fire*) crépitement *m;* (*of a radio*) friture *f* **2.** (*pork skin*) couenne *f* grillée

crackpot ['krækpɒt, *Am:* -pɑːt] **I.** *n inf* dingue *mf* **II.** *adj inf* fêlé(e)

crack-up *n* **1.** *inf* (*mental breakdown*) dépression *f* **2.** *inf* (*car crash*) accident *m*

cradle ['kreɪdl] **I.** *n* **1.** (*baby's bed*) berceau *m,* berce *f Belgique* **2.** (*framework*) structure *f; Brit* échafaudage *m* ►**the hand that rocks the** ~ **rules the world** le monde est dirigé par les mères **II.** *vt* (*hold in one's arms*) bercer

craft [krɑːft, *Am:* kræft] *inv* **I.** *n* **1.** (*means of transport*) embarcation *f* **2.** *no pl* (*skill*) métier *m* **3.** (*trade*) artisanat *m;* (*of glass-blowing, acting*) art *m;* (*of management*) *iron* finesse *f* **4.** (*ability*) capacité *f* **II.** *vt* créer; (*a poem*) écrire

craftiness *n pej* finesse *f*

craft shop *n* magasin *m* d'artisanat

craftsman <-men> *n* artisan *m*

crafty ['krɑːfti, *Am:* 'kræf-] <-ier, -iest> *adj* rusé(e)

crag [kræg] *n* rocher *m* à pic

craggy <-ier, -iest> *adj* abrupt(e); (*features*) *fig* anguleux(-euse)

cram [kræm] <-mm-> **I.** *vt inf* fourrer; **to** ~ **sb's head with sth** *pej* bourrer la tête de qn de qc **II.** *vi* bûcher

cramfull *adj* bourré(e)

cramp [kræmp] **I.** *vt* gêner ►**to (rather)** ~ **sb's style** *iron, inf* faire perdre les moyens à qn **II.** *n Brit, Aus* crampe *f*

cramped *adj* exigu(ë)

crampon ['kræmpɒn, *Am:* -pɑːn] *n* crampon *m*

cranberry ['krænbəri, *Am:* -ˌber-] <-ies> *n* canneberge *f*

crane [kreɪn] **I.** *n* **1.** (*vehicle for lifting*) grue *f*

2. (*Gruidae bird*) grue *f* **II.** *vt* **to ~ one's neck** tendre le cou **III.** *vi* **to ~ forward** se pencher en avant; **to ~ over sth** se pencher sur qc

crane fly *n* tipule *f*

cranium ['kreɪnɪəm] <craniums *o* crania> *n* crâne *m*

crank[1] ['kræŋk] **I.** *n* **1.** *pej, inf* farfelu(e) *m(f)* **2.** *Am, pej, inf* (*crazy*) dingue *mf;* **a religious ~** un fanatique religieux **II.** *adj inf* dingue

crank[2] [kræŋk] *n* manivelle *f*

crankcase ['kræŋkkeɪs] *n* carter *m*

crankshaft ['kræŋkʃɑːft, *Am:* -ʃæft] *n* vilebrequin *m*

cranky <-ier, -iest> *adj Am, Aus, inf* grincheux(se)

cranny ['kræni] <-ies> *n* fente *f;* **nooks and crannies** coins et recoins *mpl*

crap [kræp] *vulg* **I.** <-pp-> *vi* chier **II.** *n sing,* merde *f;* **to have** [*o Am* **take**] **a ~** chier; **a load of ~** (*nonsense*) un tas de conneries **III.** *adj* merdique

crape [kreɪp] *n s.* **crêpe**

crappy <-ier, -iest> *adj* merdique

crash [kræʃ] **I.** *n* **1.** (*accident*) accident *m;* **a train/plane ~** une catastrophe ferroviaire/aérienne **2.** (*noise*) fracas *m* **3.** ECON (*collapse*) krach *m* **4.** INFOR plantage *m* **II.** *vi* **1.** (*have an accident*) avoir un accident; (*plane*) s'écraser; **to ~ into sb/sth** rentrer dans qn/qc **2.** (*make loud noise*) faire du fracas; **to ~ down** tomber avec fracas; **to ~ to the ground** se fracasser au sol; **the door ~ed open** la porte s'ouvrit avec fracas **3.** ECON (*collapse*) s'effondrer **4.** INFOR se planter **5.** *inf* (*go to sleep*) **to ~ out** s'écrouler **III.** *vt* **1.** (*damage in accident*) **to ~ the car** avoir un accident de voiture; **to ~ one's car into a lorry** entrer en collision avec un camion **2.** (*make noise*) **to ~ sth down** faire tomber qc avec fracas; (*the gears*) faire grincer ►**to ~ a <u>party</u>** s'incruster dans une fête

crash barrier *n Brit, Aus* barrière *f* de sécurité **crash course** *n* cours *m* intensif **crash diet** *n* régime *m* draconien **crash helmet** *n* casque *m* de protection

crashing *adj* <inv> terrible

crash-land *vi* atterrir d'urgence; **to prepare to ~** se préparer à atterrir d'urgence **crash-landing** *n* atterrissage *m* d'urgence **crash programme** *n* SCHOOL *s.* **crash course**

crass [kræs] *adj* **1.** (*gross*) évident(e) **2.** (*coarse*) grossier(-ère)

crate [kreɪt] **I.** *n* **1.** (*open box*) caisse *f* **2.** *iron, inf* (*old car*) tacot *m* **II.** *vt* mettre en caisse

crater ['kreɪtəʳ, *Am:* -t̬ɚ] *n* cratère *m;* **a bomb ~** entonnoir *m*

cravat [krə'væt] *n* foulard *m*

crave [kreɪv] *vt* avoir des envies de; **to be craving for sth** avoir très envie de qc

craving *n* envie *f*

crawfish *n Am* écrevisse *f*

crawl [krɔːl, *Am:* krɑːl] **I.** *vi* **1.** (*move slowly*) ramper; (*car*) rouler au pas; (*baby*) marcher à quatre pattes; **time ~s by** le temps passe lentement **2.** *inf* (*be obsequious*) fayoter; **to ~ (up) to sb** lécher les bottes de qn **3.** *inf* (*to be full of*) **to ~ with sth** grouiller de qc ►**to make sb's <u>flesh</u> ~** donner la chair de poule à qn **II.** *n no pl* **1.** (*movement*) **to go for a ~** ramper **2.** (*slow pace*) **to move at a ~** aller très lentement; **to go at a ~** rouler au pas **3.** SPORT crawl *m*

crawler *n pej, inf* (*obsequious person*) lèche-botte *mf*

crawler lane *n inf* voie *f* pour véhicule lent

crayon ['kreɪən, *Am:* -ɑːn] **I.** *n* crayon *m;* **wax ~s** crayons gras **II.** *vt* crayonner

craze [kreɪz] *n* engouement *m;* **the latest ~** la dernière folie

crazed *adj* halluciné(e); **to be/become ~ with sth** être/devenir enthousiaste pour qc

craziness *n no pl* folie *f*

crazy <-ier, -iest> *adj* fou(folle); **to be ~ about sb/sth** être dingue de qn/qc *inf;* **to do sth like ~** *inf* faire qc comme un dératé

creak [kriːk] **I.** *vi* grincer; (*bones, floor*) craquer; **to ~ into action** *fig* s'activer **II.** *n* grincement *m;* (*of floor, bones*) craquement *m*

creaky <-ier, -iest> *adj* **1.** (*squeaky*) grinçant(e) **2.** (*badly made*) bâclé(e) **3.** (*unsafe*) dangereux(-euse)

cream [kriːm] **I.** *n a.* GASTR crème *f;* **single ~** *Brit* crème liquide; **double ~** *Brit* crème épaisse; **clotted ~** *Brit* crème fraîche épaisse; **salad ~** assaisonnement *m* à salade; **anti-wrinkle ~** crème antirides **II.** *adj* **1.** (*containing cream*) à la crème **2.** (*off-white colour*) crème *inv* **3.** (*silky skin*) **a peaches and ~ complexion** un teint de pêche **III.** *vt* **1.** (*beat*) battre en crème; **~ed potatoes** purée *f* de pommes de terre **2.** (*remove cream*) **to ~ (off)** écrémer **3.** (*add cream*) ajouter de la crème à **4.** (*apply lotion*) se mettre de la crème

cream cheese *n* crème *f* de fromage à tartiner **cream-colo(u)red** *adj* crème

creamer *n* **1.** (*milk substitute*) lait *m* en poudre **2.** (*jug*) pot *m* à crème

creamery ['kriːməri] *n* crémerie *f*

creamy <-ier, -iest> *adj* **1.** (*smooth, rich*) crémeux(-euse) **2.** (*off-white*) crème *inv*

crease [kriːs] **I.** *n* **1.** (*fold*) pli *m;* (*of a book*) pliure *f* **2.** (*cricket*) ligne *f* de tir **II.** *vt* (*wrinkle*) froisser **III.** *vi* se froisser

create [kriː'eɪt] **I.** *vt* **1.** (*produce, invent*) créer; **to ~ sth from sth** produire qc à partir de qc **2.** (*cause: problem, precedent, nuisance*) créer; (*a desire, a scandal, tension*) provoquer; (*a sensation, impression*) faire; **to ~ a disturbance** LAW troubler l'ordre public **3.** (*appoint*) nommer **II.** *vi* **1.** (*be creative*) créer **2.** *Brit, Aus, inf* faire une scène

creation *n a. fig* création *f;* **~ of wealth** enrichissement *m*

creative [kriː'eɪtɪv, *Am:* -t̬ɪv] *adj* **1.** (*inventive: person, activity*) créatif(-ive) **2.** (*which creates: power, artist*) créateur(-trice)

C

creator *n* créateur, -trice *m, f;* **the Creator** le Créateur
creature ['kri:tʃəʳ, *Am:* -tʃɚ] *n a. pej, a. fig* créature *f;* **a weak** ~ *inf* une pauvre créature
creature comforts *npl inf* confort *m* matériel
creche [kreɪʃ] *n Brit, Aus* crèche *f*
credence ['kri:dns] *no pl n form* foi *f*
credentials [krɪ'denʃlz] *npl* références *fpl*
credibility [ˌkredɪ'bɪləti, *Am:* -ə'bɪləţi] *n no pl* crédibilité *f*
credible ['kredəbl] *adj* crédible
credit ['kredɪt] **I.** *n* **1.** (*praise*) mérite *m;* **to sb's** ~ à l'honneur de qn; **to do sb** ~ faire honneur à qn; **to take (the)** ~ **for sth** s'attribuer le mérite de qc **2.** (*recognition*) reconnaissance *f;* **to give sb** ~ **for sth** reconnaître que qn a fait qc **3.** FIN crédit *m;* **to be in** ~ avoir un compte créditeur; **to buy/sell sth on** ~ acheter/vendre qc à crédit **4.** (*completed unit of student's work*) unité *f* de valeur **5.** *pl* (*list of participants*) générique *m* **6.** UNIV unité *f* de valeur **II.** *vt* **1.** FIN (*money*) virer; **to** ~ **sb/an account with a sum** créditer qn/un compte d'une somme **2.** (*believe*) croire **3.** (*give credit to*) attribuer
creditable *adj* estimable
credit agency *n* établissement *m* de crédit **credit card** *n* carte *f* de crédit **credit facilities** *npl* facilités *fpl* de paiement **credit note** *n Aus, Brit* avoir *m*
creditor *n* créancier *m*
credit rating *n* degré *m* de solvabilité
creditworthy *adj* solvable
credulity [krɪ'dju:ləti, *Am:* krə'du:lə-] *n no pl, form* crédulité *f*
credulous ['kredjʊləs, *Am:* 'kredjə-] *adj form* crédule
creed [kri:d] *n form* **1.** (*set of beliefs*) principes *mpl* **2.** (*set of religious beliefs*) croyance *f*
creek [kri:k] *n* **1.** *Brit* (*narrow bay*) crique *f* **2.** *Am, Aus* (*stream*) ruisseau *m* ►**to be up the** ~ **(without a paddle)** *inf* être dans le pétrin
creep [kri:p] **I.** *n* **1.** *inf* (*unpleasant person*) saligaud *m,* sale bête *f* **2.** *inf* (*crawler*) lèche-botte *mf* **3.** *pl* (*goose-flesh*) chair *f* de poule; **to give sb the** ~**s** donner la chair de poule à qn **II.** <crept, crept> *vi* ramper; **to** ~ **in/out** entrer/sortir à pas de loup; **to** ~ **into bed** se glisser sous les draps; **to** ~ **through sth** s'insinuer dans qc; **it makes my flesh** ~ cela me hérisse les cheveux
◆**creep up** *vi* grimper; **to** ~ **on sb** prendre qn par surprise
creeper [-pɚ] *n* plante *f* grimpante
creepy <-ier, -iest> *adj inf* qui donne la chair de poule
creepy-crawly <-ties> *n* bestiole *f*
cremate [krɪ'meɪt, *Am:* kri:'meɪt] *vt* incinérer
cremation *n* incinération *f*
crematorium [ˌkremə'tɔ:rɪəm, *Am:* ˌkri:mə'tɔ:ri-] <-s *o* -ria> *n* crématorium *m*
crème de la crème [ˌkremdəlɑ:'krem] *n no pl* crème *f* de la crème
Creole ['kri:əʊl, *Am:* 'kri:oʊl] **I.** *adj* créole **II.** *n* **1.** (*person*) Créole *mf* **2.** LING créole *m; s. a.* **English**
crêpe [kreɪp] *n* **1.** GASTR crêpe *f* **2.** (*fabric*) crêpe *m*
crept [krept] *pp, pt of* **creep**
crescendo [krɪ'ʃendəʊ, *Am:* -doʊ] **I.** *n* crescendo *m inv* **II.** *adv* crescendo
crescent ['kresnt] **I.** *n* croissant *m* **II.** *adj* en croissant
cress [kres] *n no pl* cresson *m*
crest [krest] **I.** *n* **1.** ZOOL crête *f* **2.** (*top*) *a. fig* crête *f* **3.** (*insignia*) armoiries *fpl* **II.** *vt* atteindre le sommet de
crestfallen ['krestˌfɔ:lən] *adj* découragé(e)
Cretan **I.** *adj* crétois(e) **II.** *n* **1.** (*person*) Crétois *m* **2.** LING crétois *m; s. a.* **English**
Crete [kri:t] *n* Crète *f*
Creutzfeldt-Jacob disease *n* maladie *f* de Creutzfeldt-Jacob
crevasse ['krɪvæs, *Am:* krə'væs] *n* crevasse *f*
crevice ['krevɪs] *n* fissure *f*
crew [kru:] **I.** *n* + *pl/sing vb* **1.** (*working team*) NAUT, AVIAT équipage *m;* RAIL équipe *f* **2.** *pej, inf* (*gang*) bande *f* **II.** *vt* être membre de l'équipage de **III.** *vi* **1.** (*act as crewmember*) **to** ~ **for sb** être l'équipier de qn **2.** *Brit pp, pt of* **crow**
crew cut *n* coupe *f* en brosse
crewman *n* équipier *m* **crewmember** *n* membre *mf* d'équipage
crib [krɪb] **I.** *n* **1.** (*baby's bed*) lit *m* d'enfant **2.** (*model of the nativity scene*) crèche *f* **3.** *inf* (*plagiarized work*) plagiat *m* **II.** <-bb-> *vt pej, inf* plagier **III.** <-bb-> *vi pej, inf* **to** ~ **from sb** copier sur qn
crick [krɪk] **I.** *n* foulure *f;* **to get a** ~ **in one's neck/back** attraper un torticolis/se faire un tour de reins **II.** *vt* se fouler
cricket[1] ['krɪkɪt] *n no pl, n* SPORT cricket *m*
cricket[2] ['krɪkɪt] *n* (*jumping insect*) criquet *m*
crikey ['kraɪki] *interj Brit, inf* mince alors!
crime [kraɪm] *n* **1.** (*illegal act*) crime *m* **2.** (*shameful act*) délit *m*
crime prevention *n* lutte *f* contre le crime **crime wave** *n* vague *f* de criminalité
criminal ['krɪmɪnl] **I.** *n* criminel(le) *m(f)* **II.** *adj* criminel(le)
criminal court *n* tribunal *m* criminel
criminality [ˌkrɪmɪ'næləti, *Am:* -ə'næləţi] *n no pl* criminalité *f*
criminal record *n* casier *m* judiciaire
crimp [krɪmp] *vt* crêper
crimson ['krɪmzn] **I.** *n no pl* cramoisi *m* **II.** *adj* cramoisi(e)
cringe [krɪndʒ] *vi* **1.** (*physically*) avoir un mouvement de recul **2.** *inf* (*embarrassment*) avoir envie de rentrer sous terre

crinkle ['krɪŋkl] I. *vt* froisser II. *vi* (*skin*) se rider; (*paper*) se froisser III. *n* (*in face*) ride *f;* (*in hair*) pli *m*
cripple ['krɪpl] I. *n pej* infirme *mf* II. *vt* 1. (*leave physically disabled*) estropier 2. *fig* (*seriously disable*) endommager 3. (*paralyze*) paralyser
crippling *adj a. fig* paralysant(e)
crisis ['kraɪsɪs] <-ses> *n* crise *f*
crisp [krɪsp] I. <-er, -est> *adj* 1. (*hard and brittle*) croustillant(e); (*snow*) craquant(e) 2. (*firm and fresh*) croquant(e) 3. (*bracing: air*) vif(vive) 4. (*sharp*) tranchant(e) 5. (*quick and precise*) nerveux(-euse) II. *n pl, Brit* chips *fpl*
crispy <-ier, -iest> *adj* croustillant(e)
criss-cross ['krɪskrɒs, *Am:* -krɑːs] I. *vt* entrecroiser II. *vi* s'entrecroiser III. *adj* entrecroisé(e)
criterion [kraɪ'tɪərɪən, *Am:* -'tɪrɪ-] <-ria> *n* critère *m*
critic ['krɪtɪk, *Am:* 'krɪt̬-] *n* 1. (*reviewer*) critique *m* 2. (*censurer*) détracteur *m*
critical *adj* critique
criticism ['krɪtɪsɪzəm, *Am:* 'krɪt̬-] *n* critique *f*
criticize ['krɪtɪsaɪz, *Am:* 'krɪt̬-] *vt, vi* critiquer
critique [krɪ'tiːk] *n* critique *f*
croak [krəʊk, *Am:* kroʊk] I. *vi* 1. (*make deep, rough sound*) croasser 2. *inf* (*die*) crever II. *vt* (*speak with rough voice*) dire d'une voix rauque III. *n* (*crow, person*) croassement *m;* (*frog*) coassement *m*
Croat ['krəʊæt, *Am:* 'kroʊ-] I. *adj* croate II. *n* (*person*) Croate *mf*
Croatia [krəʊ'eɪʃɪə, *Am:* kroʊ-] *n* la Croatie
Croatian *s.* **Croat**
crochet ['krəʊʃeɪ, *Am:* kroʊ'ʃeɪ] I. *n no pl* 1. (*act*) crochet *m* 2. (*work*) ouvrage *m* au crochet II. *vi* faire du crochet III. *vt* faire au crochet
crochet hook, **crochet needle** *n* crochet *m*
crockery ['krɒkəri, *Am:* 'krɑːkɚ-] *n no pl* vaisselle *f*
crocodile ['krɒkədaɪl, *Am:* 'krɑːkə-] <-(s)> *n* crocodile *m*
crocodile tears *npl* **to shed** ~ verser des larmes de crocodile
crocus ['krəʊkəs, *Am:* 'kroʊ-] *n* crocus *m*
croft [krɒft, *Am:* krɑːft] *n Scot* petite ferme *f*
croissant ['krwɑːsɒŋ, *Am:* kwɑː'sã] *n* croissant *m*
crony ['krəʊni, *Am:* 'kroʊ-] *n inf, pej* pote *m*
crook [krʊk] I. *n* 1. *inf* (*rogue*) escroc *m* 2. (*curve*) courbe *f* II. *adj Aus, inf* 1. (*ill*) mal fichu(e) 2. (*be furious*) furieux(euse) 3. (*unsatisfactory*) mauvais(e) III. *vt* plier
crooked *adj* 1. *inf* (*dishonest*) malhonnête 2. (*not straight*) courbé(e); (*nose*) crochu(e)
crooner ['kruːnə^r, *Am:* -ɚ] *n* chanteur *m* de charme
crop [krɒp, *Am:* krɑːp] I. *n* 1. (*plant*) culture *f;* (*cereal*) moisson *f;* (*harvest*) récolte *f* 2. *fig* (*group*) foule *f* 3. (*very short hair cut*) coupe *f* de cheveux ras 4. (*throat pouch*) jabot *m* 5. (*whip*) cravache *f* II. <-pp-> *vt* 1. (*plant land with crops*) cultiver 2. (*cut short*) couper ras 3. (*eat top part of: cow*) brouter III. *vi* produire
◆**crop up** *vi inf* survenir
croquet ['krəʊkeɪ, *Am:* kroʊ'keɪ] *n no pl* croquet *m*
cross [krɒs, *Am:* krɑːs] I. *n* 1. (*gen*) croix *f* 2. (*mixture*) croisement *m* 3. *fig* compromis *m* II. <-er, -est> *adj* maussade; **to get** ~ **with sb** se fâcher contre qn III. *vt* 1. (*go across*) traverser 2. (*lie across each other: one's arms, legs*) croiser 3. (*make sign of cross*) **to** ~ **oneself** se signer 4. (*oppose*) contrecarrer 5. (*crossbreed*) croiser ►**to** ~ **a cheque** *Aus, Brit* barrer un chèque; **to** ~ **sb's mind** venir à l'esprit de qn; **to** ~ **sb's path** se trouver sur le chemin de qn; **to** ~ **swords with sb** croiser le fer avec qn IV. *vi* 1. (*intersect*) se croiser 2. (*go across*) passer
◆**cross off** *vt,* **cross out** *vt* rayer
◆**cross over** I. *vi* faire une traversée II. *vt* 1. (*go across to opposite side*) traverser 2. (*change sides in disagreement*) **to** ~ **to sth** passer à qc
cross-border *adj* transfrontalier(-ère) **crossbow** *n* arbalète *f* **crossbreed** *n* 1. ZOOL, BOT hybride *m* 2. (*half-breed*) métis, -isse *m, f* **cross-check** *vt* vérifier par recoupement **cross-country** I. *adj* 1. (*across countryside*) à travers champs 2. (*across a country*) à travers le pays 3. SPORT (*race*) de cross; (*skier*) de fond; ~ **run** cross *m;* ~ **skiing** ski *m* de fond II. *adv* 1. (*across a country*) à travers le pays 2. (*across countryside*) à travers champs III. *n* 1. (*running*) cross *m* 2. (*ski*) ski *m* de fond **cross-eyed** *adj* qui louche
crossing *n* 1. (*place to cross*) passage *m;* **pedestrian** ~ passage clouté; (*intersection of road and railway*) passage *m* à niveau 2. (*journey across area*) traversée *f*
cross-legged I. *adj* **to be in a** ~ **position** avoir les jambes croisées II. *adv* les jambes croisées; **to sit** ~ être assis en tailleur **cross purposes** *npl* **to be** (**talking**) **at** ~ mal se comprendre **cross reference** *n* renvoi *m* **crossroads** *n* carrefour *m* **cross-section** *n* 1. (*transverse cut*) coupe *f* transversale 2. (*representative mixture*) échantillon *m* **crosswalk** *n Am* (*pedestrian crossing*) passage *m* clouté **crossways** *adv s.* **crosswise** **crosswise** I. *adj* (*transverse*) en travers II. *adv* (*transversely*) transversalement **crossword** (**puzzle**) *n* mots *mpl* croisés
crotch [krɒtʃ, *Am:* krɑːtʃ] *n* entrejambe *m*
crotchet ['krɒtʃɪt, *Am:* 'krɑːtʃət] *n* noire *f*
crotchety ['krɒtʃɪti, *Am:* 'krɑːtʃət̬i] *adj inf* (*child*) grognon(ne)
crouch [kraʊtʃ] *vi* s'accroupir
croup [kruːp] *n no pl* croupe *f*
croupier ['kruːpɪeɪ, *Am:* -eɪ] *n* croupier *m*

C

crow¹ [krəʊ, *Am:* kroʊ] *n* corneille *f* ►**as the ~ flies** à vol d'oiseau

crow² [krəʊ, *Am:* kroʊ] <crowed, crowed *o Brit* crew, crew> *vi* **1.** (*sound a cock-a-doodle-doo*) faire cocorico **2.** (*cry out happily: a baby*) gazouiller

crowd [kraʊd] **I.** *n + pl, sing vb* **1.** (*throng*) foule *f* **2.** *inf* (*particular group of people*) clique *f* ►**to follow the ~** *pej* suivre le troupeau; **to stand out from the ~** sortir du commun **II.** *vt* **1.** (*fill: a stadium*) remplir **2.** *inf* (*pressure*) pousser

crowded *adj* bondé(e)

crowd-puller *n* vedette *f*

crown [kraʊn] **I.** *n* **1.** (*round ornament*) couronne *f* **2.** (*top part*) sommet *m* **II.** *vt* couronner ►**to ~ it all** *Aus, Brit* pour couronner le tout

crown court *n Brit* ≈ cour *f* d'assises

crowning *adj* couronnement *m*

crown jewels *n* joyaux *mpl* de la Couronne

crown prince *n* prince *m* héritier

crow's feet *npl* pattes *fpl* d'oie **crow's nest** *n* nid *m* de pie

CRT [ˌsiːɑːˈtiː, *Am:* -ɑːrˈ-] *n abbr of* **cathode ray tube** tube *m* cathodique

crucial [ˈkruʃl] *adj* crucial(e)

crucible [ˈkruːsɪbl] *n* creuset *m*

crucifix [ˌkruːsɪˈfɪks] *n* crucifix *m*

crucifixion *n* crucifixion *f*

crucify [ˈkruːsɪfaɪ] *vt* crucifier

crude [kruːd] **I.** <-r, -st> *adj* **1.** (*rudimentary*) rudimentaire; (*unsophisticated*) grossier(-ère) **2.** (*vulgar*) vulgaire **II.** *n* pétrole *m* brut

crudeness, crudity *n no pl* **1.** (*lack of refinement*) caractère *m* grossier **2.** (*vulgarity*) grossièreté *f*

cruel [krʊəl] <-(l)ler, -(l)lest> *adj* cruel(le); **to be ~ to sb** être cruel envers qn ►**to be ~ to be kind** *prov* qui aime bien châtie bien

cruelty *n* cruauté *f*

cruise [kruːz] **I.** *n* croisière *f* **II.** *vi* **1.** (*ship*) croiser **2.** (*travel at constant speed: airplane*) planer; (*car*) rouler

cruiser *n* **1.** (*warship*) croiseur *m* **2.** (*pleasure boat*) yacht *m* de croisière

cruise ship *n* bateau *m* de croisière

cruising *n Am* croisière *f*

crumb [krʌm] *n* GASTR **1.** (*very small piece*) miette *f* **2.** (*opposed to crust: bread*) mie *f* **3.** *fig* (*small amount*) miettes *fpl;* (*of comfort*) brin *m*

crumble [ˈkrʌmbl] **I.** *vt* **1.** (*break into crumbs*) émietter **2.** (*break into bits: stone*) effriter **II.** *vi* **1.** (*break into crumbs*) s'émietter **2.** *fig* s'effriter **III.** *n Brit* crumble *m* (*dessert aux fruits recouvert de pâte émiettée et servi tiède*)

crumbly <-ier, -iest> *adj* friable

crummy [ˈkrʌmi] <-ier, -iest> *adj inf* minable; **to feel ~** se sentir mal

crumpet [ˈkrʌmpɪt] *n Brit* crumpet *m* (*petit pain rond spongieux à toaster*)

crumple [ˈkrʌmpl] **I.** *vt* froisser **II.** *vi* **1.** (*dented: mudguard*) se plier **2.** (*wrinkled*) se friper; (*face*) se décomposer **3.** (*collapse*) s'effondrer

crunch [krʌntʃ] **I.** *vt* GASTR croquer **II.** *vi* **1.** (*make crushing sound: gravel, snow*) craquer **2.** GASTR (*crush with the teeth*) **to ~ on sth** croquer dans qc **III.** *n* **1.** (*crushing sound: feet, gravel, snow*) craquement *m* **2.** *no pl, inf* (*difficult situation*) situation *f* critique ►**when it comes to the ~** *inf* au moment critique

crunchy *adj* (*food*) croustillant(e); (*snow*) qui craque sous les pas

crusade [kruːˈseɪd] **I.** *n* croisade *f;* **to start a ~ against sth** partir en croisade contre qc **II.** *vi* **to ~ for/against sth** partir en croisade pour/contre qc

crusader *n* croisé *m*

crush [krʌʃ] **I.** *vt* **1.** (*compress*) écraser; **to be ~ed to death** être mort écrasé **2.** (*cram*) entasser **3.** (*grind*) broyer **4.** (*wrinkle: papers, dress*) froisser **5.** (*shock severely*) anéantir **6.** *fig* (*suppress: a rebellion, an opposition*) écraser **7.** *fig* (*ruin: hopes*) détruire **II.** *vi* **1.** (*compress*) s'écraser **2.** (*cram into*) s'entasser **3.** (*hurry: crowd*) se presser **4.** (*wrinkle*) se froisser **III.** *n* **1.** *no pl* (*crowd of people*) cohue *f* **2.** *inf* (*temporary infatuation*) béguin *m;* **to have a ~ on sb** avoir le béguin pour qn **3.** (*crushed ice drink*) granité *m*

crushing *adj* écrasant(e); (*news, remark*) percutant(e)

crust [krʌst] *n a.* GEO croûte *f*

crustacean [krʌˈsteɪʃən] *n* crustacé *m*

crusty [ˈkrʌsti] <-ier, -iest> *adj* **1.** (*crunchy: bread*) croustillant(e) **2.** (*grumpy, surly*) hargneux(-euse)

crutch [krʌtʃ] *n* **1.** MED (*walking support*) béquille *f;* **to be on ~es** avoir des béquilles **2.** (*source of support*) soutien *m* **3.** ANAT, FASHION *s.* **crotch**

crux [krʌks] *n no pl* cœur *m;* **to be at the ~ of sth** être au cœur de qc

cry [kraɪ] **I.** *n* **1.** *no pl* (*act of shedding tears*) pleurs *mpl;* **to have a ~** pleurer un coup **2.** (*loud utterance*) cri *m;* **to give a ~** pousser un cri **3.** (*appeal*) appel *m;* **a ~ for help** un appel au secours **4.** ZOOL (*yelp*) cri *m* **II.** *vi* pleurer; **to ~ for joy** pleurer de joie ►**it is no good ~ing over spilt** [*o Am* **spilled**] **milk** ce qui est fait est fait **III.** *vt* **1.** (*shed tears*) pleurer; **to ~ oneself to sleep** s'endormir à force de larmes **2.** (*exclaim*) crier ►**to ~ one's eyes out** pleurer à chaudes larmes; **to ~ wolf** crier au loup; **to ~ for the moon** demander la lune

◆**cry off** *vi inf* se décommander

◆**cry out I.** *vi* **1.** (*let out a shout*) pousser des cris **2.** (*say crying*) s'écrier; **to ~ for sth** réclamer qc à grands cris ►**for crying out loud!** *inf* nom de dieu! **II.** *vt* crier

crybaby *n inf* pleurnichard(e) *m(f)*

crying **I.** *n no pl* **1.** (*weeping*) pleurs *mpl*

2. (*yelling*) cris *mpl* **II.** *adj* (*need*) urgent(e) ►**it is a ~ shame that** c'est scandaleux que +*subj*

crypt ['krɪpt] *n* crypte *f*

cryptic ['krɪptɪk] *adj* mystérieux(-euse)

crystal ['krɪstl] **I.** *n* cristal *m* **II.** *adj* **1.** (*crystalline*) *a. fig* cristallin(e) **2.** (*made of crystal*) en cristal

crystal ball *n* boule *f* de cristal **crystal clear** *adj* **1.** (*transparent*) cristallin(e) **2.** (*obvious*) clair(e)

crystalline ['krɪstəlaɪn] *adj* cristallin(e)

crystallization *n no pl* cristallisation *f*

crystallize ['krɪstəlaɪz] **I.** *vi* se cristalliser **II.** *vt* cristalliser; **~d fruits** fruits *mpl* confits

CSE [ˌsiːes'iː] *n Brit* HIST *abbr of* **Certificate of Secondary Education** certificat *m* d'études secondaires (*passé à 16 ans*)

CTC *n Brit abbr of* **city technology college** ≈ collège *m* technique

cub [kʌb] *n* ZOOL petit *m;* **a bear ~** un ourson; **a lion ~** un lionceau

Cuba ['kjuːbə] *n* (l'île *f* de) Cuba

Cuban **I.** *adj* cubain(e) **II.** *n* Cubain(e) *m(f)*

cubbyhole *n* cagibi *m*

cube [kjuːb] **I.** *n* cube *m;* **ice ~** glaçon *m;* **~ root** racine *f* cubique **II.** *vt* GASTR couper en dés

cubic ['kjuːbɪk] *adj* cubique; **a ~ centimetre** un centimètre cube; **~ capacity** volume *m*

cubicle ['kjuːbɪkl] *n* **1.** (*changing room*) cabine *f* **2.** (*sleeping compartment*) box *m*

cuckoo ['kʊkuː, *Am:* 'kuːkuː] **I.** *n* ZOOL coucou *m* **II.** *adj inf* cinglé(e); **to go ~** devenir cinglé(e)

cuckoo clock *n* coucou *m*

cucumber ['kjuːkʌmbəʳ, *Am:* -bɚ] *n* GASTR concombre *m* ►**to be cool as a ~** *inf* être d'un calme imperturbable

cud [kʌd] *n no pl* bol *m* alimentaire; **to chew the ~** *a. inf* ruminer

cuddle ['kʌdl] **I.** *vt* câliner **II.** *vi* se câliner **III.** *n* câlin *m;* **to give sb a ~** câliner qn

cuddly *adj* mignon(ne)

cudgel ['kʌdʒəl] **I.** *n* trique *f* ►**to take up (the) ~s for sb/sth** *Aus, Brit* prendre fait et cause pour qn/qc **II.** <-(l)l-> *vt* frapper à coups de trique; **to ~ sb into doing sth** *fig* faire faire qc à qn à coup de triques ►**to ~ one's brains** se creuser la cervelle

cue [kjuː] *n* **1.** (*signal for an actor*) réplique *f;* **to give sb their ~** donner la réplique à qn **2.** SPORT (*stick used in billiards*) queue *f* ►**to take one's ~ from sb/sth** prendre exemple sur qn/qc; **(right) on ~** au bon moment

cuff [kʌf] **I.** *n* **1.** (*end of sleeve*) poignet *m;* (*for cuff links*) manchette *f* **2.** *Am, Aus* (*turned-up trouser*) revers *m* **3.** (*slap*) gifle *f* **4.** *pl, inf* (*handcuffs*) menottes *fpl* ►**off the ~** à l'improviste; **to speak off the ~** parler au pied levé **II.** *vt* **1.** (*slap playfully*) gifler **2.** *inf* LAW (*handcuff*) menotter

cufflink *n* bouton *m* de manchette

cuisine [kwɪ'ziːn] *n no pl* cuisine *f*

cul-de-sac ['kʌldəsæk] <-s *o* culs-de-sac> *n a. fig* impasse *f*

culinary ['kʌlɪneri, *Am:* -əner-] *adj* culinaire; **~ implements** ustensiles *mpl* de cuisine

cull [kʌl] **I.** *vt* **1.** ZOOL (*limit population by killing*) abattre **2.** (*choose from various sources*) **to ~ sth from sth** choisir qc parmi qc **II.** *n* ZOOL abattage *m*

culminate ['kʌlmɪneɪt] *vi* **to ~ in sth** se terminer par qc

culmination *n no pl* point *m* culminant

culottes [kjuː'lɒts, *Am:* 'kuːlɑːts] *npl* jupe-culotte *f;* **a pair of ~** une jupe-culotte

culpable ['kʌlpəbl] *adj form* coupable; **to hold sb ~ for sth** tenir qn pour coupable de qc

culprit ['kʌlprɪt] *n* coupable *mf*

cult [kʌlt] *n a. fig, pej* REL culte *m*

cultivate ['kʌltɪveɪt, *Am:* -t̬ə-] *vt a. fig* cultiver

cultivated *adj a. fig* cultivé(e)

cultivation *n no pl* AGR culture *f;* **to bring sth under ~** cultiver qc; **to be under ~** être cultivé

cultivator *n* AGR **1.** (*tool or machine*) cultivateur *m* **2.** (*one who cultivates*) cultivateur, -trice *m, f*

cultural *adj* culturel(le)

cultural attaché *n* attaché *m* culturel, attachée *f* culturelle

culture ['kʌltʃəʳ, *Am:* -tʃɚ] **I.** *n a.* BIO culture *f;* **to grow a ~** faire une culture **II.** *vt* BIO faire une culture de

cultured *adj* cultivé(e); **a ~ pearl** une perle de culture

culture shock *n* choc *m* culturel

cum *prep* **a study-~-bedroom** une chambre-bureau

cumbersome ['kʌmbəsəm, *Am:* -bɚ], **cumbrous** *adj* **1.** (*unwieldly*) encombrant(e) **2.** (*awkward: style of writing*) maladroit(e)

cumin ['kʌmɪn] *n no pl* BOT cumin *m*

cumulative ['kjuːmjʊlətɪv, *Am:* -mjələt̬ɪv] *adj* **1.** (*increasing*) cumulatif(-ive) **2.** (*increased*) cumulé(e)

cumulus ['kjumjʊləs, *Am:* -mjə-] <-li> *n* cumulus *m*

cunning ['kʌnɪŋ] **I.** *adj* **1.** (*ingenious: person*) rusé(e); (*plan, device, idea*) astucieux(-euse); **to be ~ of sb to** +*infin* être astucieux de la part de qn de +*infin* **2.** *Am* (*cute: baby, little child*) mignon(ne) ►**as ~ as a fox** rusé(e) comme un renard **II.** *n no pl* ingéniosité *f;* **to show ~** faire preuve d'ingéniosité

cup [kʌp] **I.** *n* **1.** (*drinking container*) tasse *f;* **coffee ~** tasse de café; **a plastic ~** un gobelet; **a ~ of tea** une tasse de thé **2.** *Am* GASTR (*half-pint*) tasse *f* (≈ *230 millilitres ou grammes*)*;* **a ~ of flour** 230 grammes de farine **3.** SPORT (*trophy*) coupe *f;* **world ~** coupe *f* du monde **4.** (*bowl-shaped container*) coupe *f;* **egg ~** coquetier *m* **5.** (*part of bra*) bonnet *m* **6.** GASTR (*punch*) punch *m* **7.** SPORT (*protection*) coque *f* ►**not to be one's ~ of tea** *inf* ne pas être sa tasse de thé **II.** <-pp-> *vt* **1.** (*make bowl-shaped*) **to ~ one's hands** mettre ses mains en coupe **2.** (*put curved hand around*) **to ~ sth in one's hands** entourer qc de ses mains

cupboard ['kʌbəd, *Am:* -ɚd] *n* placard *m*

cup final *n Brit* finale *f*

cupful <-s *o Am* cupsful> *n* tasse *f*

cupola ['kju:pələ] *n* ARCHIT coupole *f*

cuppa ['kʌpə] *n Brit, inf* tasse *f* de thé

cup tie *n* match *m* éliminatoire

curability *n no pl* chances *fpl* de guérison

curable ['kjʊərəbl, *Am:* 'kjʊr-] *adj* guérissable

curate ['kjʊərət, *Am:* 'kjʊrət] *n* vicaire *m*

curator *n* conservateur *m*

curb [kɜ:b, *Am:* kɜ:rb] **I.** *vt* **1.** (*control: emotion, appetite*) refréner; (*inflation, expenses*) limiter **2.** (*hinder*) freiner **II.** *n* **1.** (*control*) frein *m;* **to put a ~ on sth** mettre un frein à qc **2.** *Am s.* **kerb**

curbstone ['kɜ:bstəʊn, *Am:* 'kɜ:rbstoʊn] *n Am s.* **kerbstone**

curd [kɜ:d, *Am:* kɜ:rd] *n no pl* GASTR lait *m* caillé; **lemon ~** ≈ crème *f* de citron

curdle [kɜ:dl, *Am:* kɜ:r-] **I.** *vi* GASTR (se) cailler ►**to make sb's blood ~** glacer le sang de qn **II.** *vt* GASTR cailler ►**to ~ sb's blood** glacer le sang de qn

cure ['kjʊəʳ, *Am:* 'kjʊr] **I.** *vt* **1.** MED (*heal*) *a. fig* guérir; **to ~ sb of sth** guérir qn de qc **2.** (*eradicate*) *a. fig* éradiquer **3.** GASTR (*smoke*) fumer; (*salt*) saler; (*dry*) sécher ►**what can't be ~d must be endured** il faut savoir prendre son mal en patience **II.** *n a. fig* remède *m*

cure-all *n* panacée *f*

curfew *n* LAW couvre-feu *m*

curiosity [ˌkjʊərɪ'ɒsəti, *Am:* ˌkjʊrɪ'ɑ:sət̬i] *n* **1.** *no pl* (*thirst for knowledge*) curiosité *f;* **to burn with ~** brûler de curiosité; **out of ~** par curiosité; **to arouse sb's ~** éveiller la curiosité de qn **2.** (*highly unusual object*) curiosité *f* ►**~ killed the cat** *prov* la curiosité est un vilain défaut

curious ['kjʊərɪəs] *adj* curieux(-euse)

curl [kɜ:l, *Am:* kɜ:rl] **I.** *n* **1.** (*loop of hair*) boucle *f;* (*tight*) frisette *f;* **to fall in ~s** tomber en boucles **2.** (*spiral: of smoke*) volute *f* **II.** *vi* **1.** (*wave*) boucler; (*in tight curls*) friser **2.** (*wind itself*) se recroqueviller; **to ~ round sth** s'enrouler autour de qc **III.** *vt* **1.** (*make curly*) **to ~ one's hair** boucler ses cheveux; (*tightly*) friser ses cheveux **2.** (*wrap*) enrouler **3.** (*roll into ball*) **to ~ oneself** se recroqueviller ►**to ~ one's lip** faire la moue

curler *n* bigoudi *m*

curling iron, **curling tongs** *n* fer *m* à friser

curly ['kɜ:li, *Am:* 'kɜ:r-] <-ier, -iest> *adj* bouclé(e); (*tightly*) frisé(e)

currant ['kʌrənt, *Am:* 'kɜ:r-] *n* **1.** (*dried grapes*) raisin *m* de Corinthe **2.** (*fruit shrub*) groseillier *f* **3.** (*small fruit*) groseille *f*

currency ['kʌrənsi, *Am:* 'kɜ:r-] *n* **1.** (*money used in a country*) devise *f* **2.** *no pl* (*acceptance*) circulation *f;* **to enjoy wide ~** jouir d'une grande diffusion; **to gain ~** se répandre; **to have ~** avoir cours

current ['kʌrənt, *Am:* 'kɜ:r-] **I.** *adj* **1.** (*present*) actuel(le); (*year, research, development*) en cours **2.** (*common*) courant(e); **in ~ use** d'usage courant **3.** FIN (*income, expenditure*) courant(e) **4.** (*latest: craze, fashion, issue*) dernier(-ère) **II.** *n a. fig* courant *m;* **to swim against/with the ~** nager à contre-courant/avec le courant ►**to drift with the ~** se laisser porter au gré des courants

current account *n Brit* compte *m* courant

current affairs, **current events** *n* POL actualité *f* **current expenses** *npl* dépenses *fpl* courantes

currently *adv* actuellement

curriculum vitae [kəˌrɪkjələm'vi:taɪ] <-s *o* curricula vitae> *n* ECON curriculum vitae *m*

curry[1] ['kʌri, *Am:* 'kɜ:r-] **I.** *n* curry *m;* **chicken ~** poulet *m* au curry **II.** *vt* cuisiner au curry; **curried chicken** poulet *m* au curry

curry[2] ['kʌri, *Am:* 'kɜ:r-] *vt* **to ~ favour with sb** *pej* s'insinuer auprès de qn

curse [kɜ:s, *Am:* kɜ:rs] **I.** *vi* jurer **II.** *vt* maudire; **to ~ sb for doing sth** maudire qn d'avoir fait qc **III.** *n* **1.** (*act of swearing*) juron *m;* **to let out a ~** lâcher un juron **2.** (*magic spell*) sort *m;* **to put a ~ on sb** jeter un sort sur qn **3.** *fig* (*very unpleasant thing*) malédiction *f* **4.** (*cause of evil*) fléau *m*

cursed *adj* maudit(e)

cursor *n* INFOR curseur *m;* **to move the ~** déplacer le curseur

cursory ['kɜ:səri, *Am:* 'kɜ:r-] *adj* superficiel(le)

curt [kɜ:t, *Am:* kɜ:rt] <-er, -est> *adj pej* sec(sèche)

curtail [kɜ:'teɪl, *Am:* kɚ-] *vt* **1.** (*limit*) diminuer **2.** (*shorten*) raccourcir; (*stay*) écourter

curtailment *n* réduction *f*

curtain ['kɜ:tn, *Am:* 'kɜ:rtn] *n* **1.** (*material hung at windows*) rideau *m;* **to draw the ~s** tirer les rideaux **2.** *fig* (*screen*) écran *m;* **a ~ of rain** un écran de pluie **3.** THEAT (*stage screen*) rideau *m;* **to raise/lower the ~** lever/baisser le rideau ►**the final ~** le dernier rappel; **to be ~s for sb** *inf* être fini pour qn

curtain call *n* THEAT rappel *m;* **to take a ~** être rappelé **curtain-raiser** *n a. fig* THEAT lever *m* du rideau

curts(e)y ['kə:tsi, *Am:* 'kɜ:rt-] **I.** *vi* **to ~ to sb** faire une révérence à qn **II.** *n* révérence *f;* **to make a ~ to sb** faire une révérence à qn

curvature ['kɜ:vətʃəʳ, *Am:* 'kɜ:rvətʃɚ] *n no pl* courbure *f*

curve [kɜ:v, *Am:* kɜ:rv] **I.** *n* courbe *f;* (*on road*) virage *m;* **to make a ~** (*road*) faire un virage **II.** *vi* se courber; **to ~ round sth** (*path, road*) faire le tour de qc; **to ~ downwards/upwards** (*path*) descendre/monter en courbe

cushion ['kʊʃən] **I.** *n* coussin *m;* **to act as a ~** *a. fig* amortir les chocs **II.** *vt a. fig* amortir; **to ~ sb/sth from sth** protéger qn/qc de qc

cushy ['kʊʃi] <-ier, -iest> *adj pej, inf* (*very easy*) pépère; **a ~ job** une planque; **to have a ~ time** se la couler douce ►**to have a ~ number** *Brit* avoir un boulot pépère

cuss [kʌs] **I.** *vi* jurer **II.** *n* **1.** (*odd person*) individu *m* **2.** (*curse*) juron *m*

custard ['kʌstəd, *Am:* -tɚd] *n no pl* crème *f* anglaise

custard pie *n* tarte *f* à la crème

custodial *adj* (*sentence*) de prison

custodian [kʌ'stəʊdɪən, *Am:* kʌs'toʊ-] *n a. fig* gardien(ne) *m(f)*

custody ['kʌstədi] *n no pl* **1.** LAW (*guardianship*) garde *f;* **to award ~ of sb to sb** accorder la garde de qn à qn **2.** LAW (*detention*) garde *f* à vue; **to take sb into ~** mettre qn en garde à vue

custom ['kʌstəm] *n* **1.** SOCIOL (*tradition*) coutume *f;* **according to ~** selon l'usage; **to be sb's ~ to** *+infin* c'est la coutume de qn de *+infin;* **as is sb's ~** selon la coutume de qn **2.** ECON (*clientele*) clientèle *f*

customary ['kʌstəməri, *Am:* -mer-] *adj* **1.** (*traditional*) coutumier(-ère); **as is ~** comme de coutume **2.** (*usual: hour*) habituel(le)

custom-built *adj* fait(e) sur commande

customer *n* ECON **1.** (*buyer*) client(e) *m(f)* **2.** *pej, inf* (*person*) type *m* ►**the ~ is always right, the ~ is king** *prov* le client est roi

customer number *n* numéro *m* de client **customer service** *n* ECON service *m* clientèle

customise ['kʌstəmaɪz], **customize** *vt Am* personnaliser

custom-made *adj* fait(e) sur commande; (*clothes*) fait(e) sur mesure

customs *n pl* ECON, FIN douane *f;* **to pay ~** payer un droit de douane; **to get through ~** passer la douane

customs barrier *n* barrière *f* douanière **customs clearance** *n* dédouanement *m* **customs declaration** *n* déclaration *f* de douane **customs dues**, **customs duties** *npl* droits *mpl* de douane **customs examination** *n* contrôle *m* douanier **custom(s) house** *n* bureau *m* de douane **customs investigation** *n* contrôle *m* douanier **customs officer**, **customs official** *n* douanier *m* **customs union** *n* union *f* douanière

cut [kʌt] **I.** *n* **1.** (*cutting*) coupure *f;* (*on object, wood*) entaille *f* **2.** (*slice*) tranche *f;* (*of meat*) morceau *m* **3.** (*wound*) coupure *f;* **deep ~** plaie *f* profonde **4.** MED incision *f* **5.** (*style: of clothes, hair*) coupe *f;* **a ~ and blow-dry** une coupe-brushing; **to give a ~** couper **6.** (*share*) part *f* **7.** (*decrease*) réduction *f;* (*in interest, production*) baisse *f;* (*in staff*) compression *f;* **to take a ~ in sth** subir une diminution de qc **8.** *pl* (*decrease in government spending*) compressions *fpl* budgétaires **9.** ELEC (*interruption*) coupure *f* **10.** CINE, LIT coupure *f* **11.** (*blow*) coup *m* **12.** GAMES (*cards*) coupe *f* ►**the ~ and thrust of sth** les estocades *fpl* de qc; **to be a ~ above sb/sth** être un cran au-dessus de qn/qc **II.** *adj* **1.** (*sliced, incised*) coupé(e) **2.** (*shaped*) taillé(e) **3.** (*reduced*) réduit(e) **III.** <cut, cut, -tt-> *vt* **1.** (*make an opening, incision*) couper; **to ~ open a face** ouvrir un visage; **to ~ sth out of sth** découper qc dans qc; **to ~ sb/sth free** délivrer qn/qc (en coupant ses liens) **2.** (*slice*) couper; **to ~ in pieces** couper en morceaux **3.** (*shape*) tailler; (*fingernails, hair, a flower*) couper; (*grass*) tondre; (*initials*) graver **4.** MED inciser **5.** *fig* (*ties*) rompre; **to ~ sb loose** libérer qn **6.** FIN, ECON réduire; (*costs, prices*) diminuer **7.** CINE (*a film*) monter **8.** (*remove*) couper **9.** *Am, inf* SCHOOL, UNIV (*a lesson*) sécher; (*school*) manquer **10.** TECH (*motor*) couper **11.** (*have a tooth emerge*) **to ~ one's teeth** avoir une dent qui sort; **to cut one's teeth on sth** se faire les dents sur qc **12.** (*split card deck: cards*) couper **13.** (*record: CD*) graver **14.** *fig* (*stop: sarcasm*) arrêter ►**to ~ the cackle** *Brit, Aus, inf* arrêter de jacasser; **to ~ capers** arrêter la rigolade; **to ~ a corner** (**too sharply**) prendre un virage à la corde; **to ~ corners** rogner sur les coûts; **to ~ a fine figure, to ~ quite a figure** [*o Brit* **dash**] avoir beaucoup d'allure; **to ~ no ice with sb** ne faire aucun effet à qn; **to ~ it** *Am, inf* le faire; **to ~ one's losses** sauver les meubles; **to ~ one's nose off to spite one's face** scier la branche sur laquelle on est assis; **to ~ sb to the quick** piquer qn au vif; **to ~ sb some slack** faciliter les choses à qn; **to ~ a long story short** en bref; **to ~ sb dead** faire semblant de ne pas reconnaître qn; **to ~ sth** (**a bit**) **fine** ne pas se laisser de marge **IV.** <cut, cut, -tt-> *vi* **1.** (*make an incision*) couper; (*in slice*) trancher **2.** MED inciser **3.** GAMES couper; **to ~ for dealer** tirer pour la donne ►**to ~ to the chase** aller à l'essentiel; **to ~ loose** couper les ponts; **to ~ both ways** à double tranchant; **to ~ and run** filer

◆**cut across** *vt* **1.** (*cut*) couper à travers **2.** *fig* transcender

◆**cut away** *vt* (*slice off*) enlever (en coupant)

◆**cut back** **I.** *vt* **1.** (*trim down*) tailler; (*tree*) élaguer **2.** FIN, ECON réduire; (*costs*) diminuer **II.** *vi* **1.** (*turn around*) revenir en arrière **2.** (*save money*) faire des économies

◆**cut down** *vt* **1.** BOT (*a tree*) abattre **2.** (*do less: wastage*) réduire **3.** (*take out part: a film*) couper **4.** FASHION raccourcir ►**to cut sb down to size** *inf* remettre qn à sa place

◆**cut in** **I.** *vi* **1.** (*interrupt*) intervenir; **to ~ on sb** couper la parole à qn **2.** AUTO se rabattre; **to ~ in front of sb** faire une queue de poisson à qn **II.** *vt* **1.** (*divide profits with*) partager les parts avec **2.** *inf* (*include when playing*) **to cut sb in on the deal** donner sa part à qn

◆**cut into** *vt* **1.** (*start cutting*) couper dans **2.** (*hurt*) blesser **3.** (*start using*) entamer; **to ~ one's free time** empiéter sur son temps libre

4. (*interrupt*) interrompre

◆**cut off** *vt* 1. (*slice away*) couper 2. (*stop talking*) **to cut sb off** interrompre qn 3. TEL, ELEC couper 4. (*isolate*) isoler; **to cut oneself off from sb** couper les liens avec qn; **to be ~ from sth** être coupé de qc 5. *Am* AUTO faire une queue de poisson ►**to cut sb off without a penny** déshériter qn

◆**cut out** I. *vt* 1. (*slice out of*) découper; **to ~ dead wood from a bush** tailler du bois mort d'un buisson; **to cut the soft spots out of the vegetables** enlever les parties abîmées des légumes 2. (*remove from: a book*) découper; **to cut a scene out of a film** couper une séquence dans un film; **to cut sugar out** supprimer le sucre 3. (*stop*) supprimer; **to ~ smoking** arrêter de fumer 4. *Am, inf* (*desist*) **cut it out!** ça suffit ! 5. (*block light*) **to ~ the light** empêcher la lumière de passer 6. (*not include in plans*) **to cut sb out of sth** mettre qn à l'écart de qc; **you can cut me out!** *Brit* tu peux m'oublier! 7. (*exclude*) **to cut sb out of one's will** déshériter qn ►**to have one's work ~ for oneself** avoir du pain sur la planche; **to be ~ for sth** être fait pour qc II. *vi* 1. (*stop*) s'arrêter; (*car*) caler 2. *Am* (*pull away quickly*) faire une queue de poisson; **to ~ of traffic** couper à travers la circulation 3. (*leave quickly*) filer

◆**cut up** I. *vt* 1. (*slice into pieces*) couper; (*herbs*) hacher 2. *Brit* (*cause to suffer*) démoraliser; **to be ~ about sth** être affecté par qc 3. *Brit* AUTO **to cut sb up** faire une queue de poisson à qn II. *vi* **to ~ rough** *Brit* se mettre en rogne

cut-and-dried *adj* 1. (*decided*) déjà décidé(e) 2. (*easy*) très clair(e) **cut and paste** I. *n* couper-coller *m inv* II. *vt* couper-coller III. *vi* faire un couper-coller

cutaway *adj* écorché(e)

cutback *n* réduction *f*

cute [kju:t] <-r, -st> *adj* mignon(ne)

cut flowers *npl* fleurs *fpl* coupées

cuticle ['kju:tɪkl, *Am:* -t̬ə-] *n* ANAT cuticule *f*

cutie ['kju:ti, *Am:* -t̬i], **cutiepie** *n Am, inf* 1. (*woman*) jolie fille *f* 2. (*man*) beau gars *m* 3. (*child*) **to be a real/such a ~** être tout mignon

cutlass ['kʌtləs] <-es> *n* MIL, NAUT coutelas *m*

cutlery ['kʌtləri] *n no pl* couverts *mpl*

cutlet ['kʌtlɪt] *n* 1. (*cut of meat*) côtelette *f* 2. (*patty*) croquette *f*

cut-off I. *n* embargo *m* II. *adj* 1. (*with a limit*) limite; **a ~ point** une limite 2. (*isolated*) isolé(e) 3. FASHION (*short*) raccourci(e) 4. ELEC **a ~ switch/button** un interrupteur *m* **cut-out** I. *n* 1. (*shape*) découpage *m* 2. (*safety device*) disjoncteur *m* II. *adj* découpé(e) **cut-price, cut-rate** *adj* à prix réduit **cut-sheet feed** *n* INFOR chargeur *m*

cutter ['kʌtəʳ, *Am:* 'kʌt̬ɚ] *n* 1. (*tool*) couteau *m;* (*for paper*) cutter *m;* **a pizza ~** un couteau à pizza; (**a pair of**) **~s** une pince coupante 2. (*person*) coupeur, -euse *m, f* 3. (*boat*) vedette *f*

cut-throat *adj* acharné(e)

cutting I. *n* 1. (*article*) coupure *f* 2. BOT bouture *f* II. *adj* 1. (*that cuts: blade, edge*) tranchant(e) 2. *fig* (*remark*) blessant(e); (*wind*) cinglant(e)

cutting edge *n* tranchant *m*

cuttlefish ['kʌtlfɪʃ, *Am:* 'kʌt̬-] <-(es)> *n* ZOOL seiche *f*

CV [ˌsi:'vi:] *n abbr of* **curriculum vitae** CV *m*

cwt. *n abbr of* **hundredweight** ≈ 50 kilos *mpl*

cyanide ['saɪənaɪd] *n no pl* CHEM cyanure *m*

cybercafé ['saɪbəˌkæfeɪ] *n* INFOR cybercafé *m*

cybernaut *n* INFOR cybernaute *mf,* internaute *mf* **cybernetics** *n no pl* INFOR, MED cybernétique *f* **cyberpunk** *n* INFOR cyberpunk *m* **cybersex** *n* INFOR cybersexe *m* **cyberspace** *n* INFOR cyberespace *m*

cyclamen ['sɪkləmən, *Am:* 'saɪklə-] *n* BOT cyclamen *m*

cycle¹ ['saɪkl] SPORT I. *n abbr of* **bicycle** vélo *m* II. *vi abbr of* **bicycle** faire du vélo

cycle² ['saɪkl] *n* cycle *m;* **to do sth on a ... ~** faire qc régulièrement

cycle way *n* piste *f* cyclable

cyclic(al) *adj* cyclique

cycling *n no pl* cyclisme *m;* **~ shorts** short *m* de cycliste, cuissettes *fpl Suisse*

cyclist *n* cycliste *mf*

cyclone ['saɪkləʊn, *Am:* -kloʊn] *n* METEO cyclone *m*

cygnet ['sɪgnɪt] *n* ZOOL jeune cygne *m*

cylinder ['sɪlɪndəʳ, *Am:* -dɚ] *n* 1. MAT cylindre *m* 2. TECH joint *m* de culasse; **to be firing on all four ~s** marcher à pleins gaz

cylinder block *n* TECH bloc-cylindres *m* **cylinder capacity** *n no pl* TECH cylindrée *f* **cylinder head** *n* TECH culasse *f*

cylindrical [sɪ'lɪndrɪkl] *adj* cylindrique

cymbal ['sɪmbl] *n* MUS cymbale *f*

cynic ['sɪnɪk] *n pej* cynique *mf*

cynical *adj pej* cynique

cynicism ['sɪnɪsɪzəm] *n no pl* cynisme *m*

cypher ['saɪfəʳ, *Am:* -fɚ] *n s.* **cipher**

cypress ['saɪprəs] *n* BOT cyprès *m*

Cypriot ['sɪprɪət] I. *adj* c(h)ypriote II. *n* C(h)ypriote *mf*

Cyprus ['saɪprəs] *n* (l'île *f* de) Chypre *f*

Cyrillic [sə'rɪlɪk] I. *adj* cyrillique II. *n* alphabet *m* cyrillique

cyst [sɪst] *n* MED kyste *m*

cystic fibrosis *n* mucoviscidose *f*

cystitis [sɪs'taɪtɪs, *Am:* -t̬ɪs] *n no pl* MED cystite *f*

czar [zɑ:ʳ, *Am:* zɑ:r] *n Am s.* **tsar**

czarina ['zɑ:'ri:nə] *n Am s.* **tsarina**

Czech [tʃek] I. *adj* tchèque II. *n* 1. (*person*) Tchèque *mf* 2. LING tchèque *m; s. a.* **English**

Czechoslovak [ˌtʃekəʊ'sləʊvæk, *Am:* -oʊ'sloʊvɑ:k] I. *n* Tchécoslovaque *mf* II. *adj* tchécoslovaque

Czechoslovakia *n* Tchécoslovaquie *f*
Czechoslovakian *s.* **Czechoslovak**
Czech Republic *n* la République tchèque

D

D, d [diː] <-'s> *n* **1.** LING D *m*, d *m*; **D day** jour *m* J; ~ **as in David** *Brit*, ~ **as in Dog** *Am*, ~ **for David** *Brit*, ~ **for Dog** *Am* (*on telephone*) d comme Désiré **2.** MUS ré *m*
d. **I.** *n* **1.** *abbr of* **day** jour *m* **2.** *abbr of* **diameter** diamètre *m* **II.** *adj abbr of* **died** décédé(e)
DA [ˌdiː'eɪ] *n Am abbr of* **district attorney** ≈ procureur *m* de la République
dab¹ [dæb] **I.** <-bb-> *vt* tamponner; (*eyes*) se tamponner; **to ~ a bit of powder on sth** donner un petit coup de poudre sur qc **II.** <-bb-> *vi* **to ~ at sth** tamponner qc; (*eyes*) se tamponner qc **III.** *n* **a ~ of sth** un petit peu de qc; (*of chocolate*) un petit morceau de qc; (*of paint*) une touche de qc
dab² [dæb] *n* (*fish*) limande *f*
dabble ['dæbl] **I.** <-ling> *vi* **to ~ in** [*o* **with**] **sth** tâter de qc **II.** <-ling> *vt* tremper
dad ['dæd] *n inf* papa *m*; **mum** [*o Am* **mom**] **and ~** papa et maman
daddy ['dædi] *n childspeak, inf* (*father*) papa *m*; **mummy** [*o Am* **mommy**] **and ~** papa et maman *f*
daddy-longlegs *n* ZOOL **1.** *Brit, inf* (*crane fly*) cousin *m* **2.** *Am s.* **harvestman**
daemon ['diːmən] *n s.* **demon**
daffodil ['dæfədɪl] *n* BOT jonquille *f*
daft [dɑːft, *Am:* dæft] *adj Brit, inf* (*idiotic*) bête ▸**to be as ~ as a brush** être con comme un balai
dagger ['dægəʳ, *Am:* -ɚ] *n* dague *f* ▸**to be at ~s drawn with sb** être à couteaux tirés avec qn; **to look ~s at sb** lancer des regards furieux à qn
dahlia ['deɪliə, *Am:* 'dæljə] *n* BOT dahlia *m*

> Le **Dáil** est la Chambre basse de l'"Oireactas", le parlement de l'"Irish Rebublic" (république d'Irlande). Elle comprend 166 députés qui sont élus démocratiquement pour cinq ans. La Chambre haute, le "Seanad" (Sénat) a 60 sénateurs, dont 11 sont désignés par le "taoiseach" (premier ministre), 6 sont choisis par les universités irlandaises, et 43 sont élus pour représenter et défendre des intérêts économiques, culturels et professionnels.

daily ['deɪli] **I.** *adj* quotidien(ne); (*rate, wage, allowance*) journalier(-ère); ~ **routine** train-train *m* quotidien; **on a ~ basis** tous les jours; **one's ~ bread** *inf* pain *m* quotidien **II.** *adv* quotidiennement **III.** <-ies> *n* **1.** PUBL quotidien *m* **2.** *Brit, inf* (*maid*) femme *f* de ménage
daintiness *n no pl* délicatesse *f*
dainty ['deɪnti, *Am:* -t̬i] <-ier, -iest> *adj* délicat(e)
dairy ['deəri, *Am:* 'deri] **I.** *n* **1.** (*building for milk production*) crémerie *f* **2.** (*shop*) laiterie *f* **II.** *adj* laitier(-ère); ~ **herd** troupeau *m* de vaches laitières
dairyman *n* laitier *m* **dairy produce** *n* produits *mpl* laitiers
dais ['deɪɪs] *n* ARCHIT estrade *f*
daisy ['deɪzi] <-sies> *n* BOT marguerite *f*; (*smaller*) pâquerette *f*
daisy wheel *n* marguerite *f* **daisy-wheel typewriter** *n* machine *f* à écrire à marguerite
dally ['dæli] <-ie-> *vi* **1.** (*dawdle*) lambiner; **to ~ over sth** s'attarder à qc **2.** (*have a liaison*) badiner
◆**dally with** *vi* effleurer; (*an idea*) caresser
dam [dæm] **I.** *n* barrage *m* **II.** <-mm-> *vt* **1.** (*block a river*) **to ~ sth** (**up**) [*o* **to ~** (**up**) **sth**] endiguer qc **2.** (*hold back*) **to ~ up** (*emotions*) contenir
damage ['dæmɪdʒ] **I.** *vt* causer des dégâts; **to be badly ~d** subir des dégâts considérables **II.** *n no pl* **1.** (*physical harm*) dégâts *mpl*; ~ **to property** dégâts matériels **2.** (*harm*) préjudice *m*; **to cause sb ~** porter préjudice à qn; **to do ~ to sb/sth** causer du tort à qn/qc **3.** *pl* LAW dommages *mpl* et intérêts **4.** MED lésion *f*; **to suffer brain ~** avoir des lésions cérébrales ▸**the ~ is done** le mal est fait; **what's the ~?** *iron, inf* à combien s'élève la note?
damage limitation *n no pl* **to do ~** limiter les dégâts
Damascus [də'mæskəs] *n* Damas
damask ['dæməsk] **I.** *n no pl* FASHION damas *m* **II.** *adj* damassé(e)
dame [deɪm] *n* **1.** *Am, inf* (*woman*) dame *f* **2.** *Brit* (*title of honor*) *titre d'une femme décorée d'un ordre de chevalerie*
damn [dæm] **I.** *interj inf* zut!; ~ **you!** tu m'emmerdes!; ~ **it!** merde! **II.** *adj* (*irritating*) fichu(e); ~ **fool** crétin *m* ▸ ~ **all** *Brit* que dalle **III.** *vt* **1.** (*lay the guilt for*) condamner **2.** (*curse*) maudire **3.** REL damner ▸**to ~ sb with faint praise** se montrer peu élogieux envers qn; **to be ~ed if you do and ~ed if you don't** je veux bien être pendu si **IV.** *adv inf* vachement; **to know ~ well** savoir très bien; **to be ~ silly** être si stupide **V.** *n no pl, inf* **to not give a ~ about sb/sth** ne rien avoir à foutre de qn/qc
damnable *adj inf* foutu(e)
damnation *n no pl* damnation *f*
damned **I.** *adj* **1.** *inf* (*cursed*) foutu(e) **2.** REL damné(e) **II.** *npl* **the ~** les damnés *mpl* **III.** *adv inf* sacrément
damning *adj* accablant(e)
damp [dæmp] METEO **I.** *adj* humide **II.** *n no pl, Brit, Aus* humidité *f* **III.** *vt* (*wet*) humecter
◆**damp down** *vt a. fig* étouffer; **to ~ sb's spirits** décourager qn

damp course *n* couche *f* d'étanchéité

dampen ['dæmpən] *vt* 1. (*make wet*) humecter 2. (*make a good feeling less: enthusiasm*) étouffer 3. (*make a noise softer*) amortir

damper *n inf* amortisseur *m*

dampness *n no pl* humidité *f*

dance [dɑ:nts, *Am:* dænts] DANCE I. <-cing> *vi* danser ▶**to ~ to sb's tune** faire les quatre volontés de qn II. <-cing> *vt* danser ▶**to ~ attendance on sb** être aux petits soins de qn III. *n* 1. (*instance of dancing*) danse *f*; **to have a ~ with sb** danser avec qn 2. (*set of steps*) pas *mpl*; **slow ~** slow *m* 3. (*social function*) soirée *f* dansante 4. *no pl* (*art form*) danse *f*; **classical/modern ~** danse classique/moderne

dance band *n* orchestre *m* (de danse) **dance music** *n no pl* musique *f* de danse

dancer *n* danseur, -euse *m, f*

dancing *n no pl* danse *f*

dancing master *n* professeur *m* de danse **dancing partner** *n* cavalier *m* **dancing shoes** *npl* chaussons *mpl* de danse

dandelion ['dændɪlaɪən, *Am:* -də-] *n* BOT pissenlit *m*

dandruff ['dændrʌf, *Am:* -drəf] *n no pl* MED pellicule *f*

dandy ['dændi] I. <-ies> *n pej* dandy *m* II. <-ier, -iest> *adj* 1. (*related to a dandy*) dandy 2. *Am, inf* (*excellent*) épatant(e)

Dane [deɪn] *n* Danois(e) *m(f)*

danger ['deɪndʒəʳ, *Am:* -dʒɚ] *n* 1. (*dangerous situation*) danger *m*; **to be in ~** être en danger; **to be out of ~** être hors de danger 2. *no pl, iron* (*chance*) risque *m*

danger area *n* zone *f* de danger **danger money** *n Brit, Aus* FIN prime *f* de risque

dangerous ['deɪndʒərəs] *adj* dangereux(-euse)

dangle ['dæŋgl] I. <-ling> *vi* 1. (*hang*) pendiller; **to ~ from/off sth** pendre à qc 2. (*swing*) balancer II. <-ling> *vt* 1. (*let hang*) laisser pendre 2. (*swing*) balancer 3. (*tempt with*) **to ~ sth before sb** faire miroiter qc à qn

Danish ['deɪnɪʃ] I. *adj* danois(e) II. *n* danois *m*; *s. a.* **English**

dank [dæŋk] *adj* froid(e) et humide

Danube ['dænju:b] *n* GEO Danube *m*

dapper ['dæpəʳ, *Am:* -ɚ] *adj* alerte

dapple ['dæpl] *vt* tacheter

dare [deəʳ, *Am:* der] I. <daring> *vt* 1. (*risk doing*) oser 2. (*face the risk: danger, death*) braver 3. (*challenge*) défier ▶**don't you ~!** tu n'as pas intérêt à faire ça!; **how ~ you do this** comment osez-vous faire cela II. <daring> *vi* (*risk doing*) braver III. *n* (*challenge*) défi *m*; **to do sth as** [*o Am* **on**] **a ~** faire qc pour relever un défi; **it's a ~!** je relève le défi!

daredevil *inf* I. *n* casse-cou *m* II. *adj* audacieux(-euse)

daring I. *adj* 1. (*courageous*) audacieux(-euse) 2. (*revealing*) osé(e) II. *n no pl* audace *f*; **to show ~** se montrer audacieux

dark [dɑ:k, *Am:* dɑ:rk] I. *adj* 1. (*black*) noir(e) 2. (*not light-coloured*) foncé(e); **tall, ~ and handsome** beau, grand et mat 3. *fig* (*tragic*) sombre; (*prediction*) pessimiste; **to have a ~ side** avoir une face cachée; **to look on the ~ side of things** voir la vie en noir 4. (*evil*) méchant(e) 5. (*secret*) secret(-ète) II. *n no pl* **the ~** le noir *f*; **to be afraid of the ~** avoir peur du noir; **to do sth before/after ~** faire qc avant que la nuit tombe *subj*; **a leap in the ~** un saut dans l'inconnu ▶**to be (completely) in the ~** ignorer tout de qc; **to keep sb in the ~** laisser qn dans l'ignorance

Dark Ages *npl* HIST **the ~** l'âge *m* des ténèbres **Dark Continent** *n* **the ~** le continent noir

darken ['dɑ:kən, *Am:* 'dɑ:r-] I. *vi* 1. (*have less light*) s'assombrir 2. (*get darker*) se foncer 3. *fig* s'assombrir II. *vt* 1. (*reduce light*) assombrir 2. (*give a dark colour*) foncer 3. *fig* assombrir

dark horse *n* 1. *Brit, Aus* (*person with hidden qualities*) **to be a ~** avoir des talents cachés 2. *Am* SPORT, POL candidat *m* inattendu

darkly *adv* sinistrement

darkness *n no pl* pénombre *f*; **to plunge sth into ~** plonger qc dans l'obscurité

dark-room *n* PHOT chambre *f* noire **dark-skinned** *adj* à la peau matte

darling ['dɑ:lɪŋ, *Am:* 'dɑ:r-] I. *n* 1. (*beloved*) amour *mf*; **to be a/the ~ of sth** être la coqueluche de qc 2. (*form of address*) chéri(e) *m(f)* II. *adj* adorable

darn[1] [dɑ:n, *Am:* dɑ:rn] I. *vt* repriser II. *n* reprise *f*

darn[2] [dɑ:n, *Am:* dɑ:rn] *interj inf* **~ it!** merde!

darning *n no pl* raccommodage *m*

darning-needle *n* aiguille *f* à repriser

dart [dɑ:t, *Am:* dɑ:rt] I. *n* 1. (*type of weapon*) flèche *f* 2. *pl* (*pub game*) fléchettes *fpl* 3. (*quick run*) se précipiter 4. FASHION pince *f* II. *vi* se précipiter; **to ~ away** s'élancer; **to ~ at sb** se précipiter sur qn III. *vt* 1. (*send*) **to ~ sth at sb** lancer qc à qn; **to ~ an angry look at sb** décocher un regard furieux à qn 2. (*stick out*) **to ~ sth out** darder qc

dartboard *n* cible *f* (de jeu de fléchettes)

dash [dæʃ] I. <-es> *n* 1. (*rush*) précipitation *f*; **a mad ~** une course folle; **to make a ~ for it** prendre ses jambes à son cou; **to make a ~ for sth** se précipiter vers qc 2. *Am* (*short fast race*) sprint *m* 3. (*pinch: salt, pepper*) pincée *f*; (*lemon, oil*) filet *m*; (*drink*) doigt *m* 4. (*punctuation*) tiret *m* 5. (*flair*) brio *m* 6. (*morse signal*) trait *m* 7. *fig* pointe *f* II. *vi* 1. (*hurry*) se précipiter; **to ~ around** courir; **to ~ along sth** courir le long de qc; **to ~ out of sth** sortir en courant de qc; **I must ~** je dois filer 2. (*strike against*) se projeter; (*waves*) se briser III. *vt* 1. (*hit*) heurter; **to be ~ed against sth** être projeté sur qc 2. (*throw with force*) projeter

3. (*destroy, discourage*) anéantir **4.** (*bring*) emmener d'urgence

dashboard *n* tableau *m* de bord

dashing *adj* fringant(e)

DAT [dæt] *n abbr of* **digital audio tape** cassette *f* numérique

data ['deɪtə, *Am:* 'deɪt̬ə] *npl* donnée *f*

data bank *n* INFOR banque *f* de données **database** *n* INFOR base *f* de données **database administrator** *n* INFOR administrateur *m* de base de données **data cartridge** *n* cartouche *f* de données **dataglove** *n* INFOR gant *m* de données **data input** *n* INFOR saisie *f* de données **data processing** *n no pl* traitement *m* de données

date[1] [deɪt] **I.** *n* **1.** (*calendar day*) date *f;* **closing** ~ date de clôture; **out of** ~ dépassé; **in/out of** ~ consommable/périmé; **to** ~ jusqu'à présent; **to be up to** ~ être actuel **2.** (*calendar year*) année *f* **3.** (*appointment*) rendez-vous *m;* **to make a** ~ fixer un rendez-vous; **to make it a** ~ prendre date; **to go out on a** ~ sortir avec qn; **to have a** ~ **with sb** avoir un rencard avec qn *inf* **4.** *Am* (*person*) copain, copine *m, f;* **to find a** ~ se trouver un copain **II.** *vt* **1.** (*have a relationship*) sortir avec **2.** (*give a date*) dater; **your letter** ~**d December 20th** la lettre datée du 20 décembre **3.** (*reveal the age*) **that** ~**s her** ça ne la rajeunit pas **III.** *vi* **1.** (*have a relationship*) sortir avec qn **2.** (*go back to: event*) **to** ~ **from** remonter à **3.** (*show time period*) dater **4.** (*go out of fashion*) être dépassé

date[2] [deɪt] *n* datte *f*

dated *adj* dépassé(e)

date stamp *n* cachet *m* (de la poste)

dative ['deɪtɪv, *Am:* -t̬ɪv] **I.** *n no pl* datif *m;* **to be in the** ~ être au datif **II.** *adj* **the** ~ **case** le datif

daub [dɔːb, *Am:* dɑːb] **I.** *vt* **to** ~ **sth with sth** barbouiller qc de qc **II.** *n* **1.** (*viscous liquid*) enduit *m* **2.** (*bad painting*) barbouillage *m*

daughter ['dɔːtəʳ, *Am:* 'dɑːt̬ɚ] *n* fille *f*

daughter-in-law <daughters-in-law> *n* belle-fille *f*

daunt [dɔːnt, *Am:* dɑːnt] *vt* démonter; **nothing** ~**ed** *Brit* sans se démonter

daunting *adj* intimidant(e)

dawdle ['dɔːdl, *Am:* 'dɑː-] *vi* traîner

dawdler *n* traînard(e) *m(f)*

dawn [dɔːn, *Am:* dɑːn] *n* **1.** *a. fig* aube *f;* **to go back to the** ~ **of time** remonter à la nuit des temps **2.** (*daybreak*) aurore *f;* **at** ~ à l'aube; **from** ~ **to dusk** du matin au soir

day [deɪ] *n* **1.** (*24 hours*) jour *m,* journée *f;* **4 times a** ~ 4 fois par jour; **every** ~ tous les jours; **have a nice** ~**!** bonne journée!, bonjour! *Québec;* **during the** ~ (dans) la journée; **to sleep during the** ~ dormir le jour **2.** (*particular day*) **that** ~ ce jour-là; (**on**) **the following** ~ le lendemain; **from that** ~ **onwards** dès lors; **D-**~ le jour J; **Christmas Day** le jour de Noël; **Boxing Day** *Brit* le lendemain de Noël; **market** ~**s** les jours de marché; **three years ago to the** ~ il y a 3 ans jour pour jour **3.** (*imprecise time*) **one of these** ~**s** un de ces jours; **some** ~ un jour ou l'autre; **every other** ~ tous les deux jours; ~ **in** ~ **out** tous les jours que (le bon) Dieu fait **4.** (*period of time*) journée *f;* **during the** ~ pendant la journée; ~ **of strike action** journée de grève **5.** (*working hours*) journée *f;* **8-hour** ~ journée de 8 heures; **to remain open all** ~ faire la journée continue; ~ **off** jour de congé [*o* repos] **6.** (*salary*) journée *f;* **to work/to be paid by the** ~ travailler/être payé à la journée **7.** (*distance*) **a** ~**'s walk away** à une journée de marche; **it's three** ~**s' journey away by train** c'est à trois journées de train **8.** *pl, form* (*life*) **his/her** ~**s are numbered** ses jours sont comptés; **to end one's** ~**s in a home** finir ses jours à l'hospice ►~ **by** ~ jour après jour

daybreak *n* aube *f; s. a.* **dawn daycare** *n* (*for children*) garderie *f;* (*for the elderly, handicapped*) centre *m* d'accueil de jour; ~ **center** garderie *f* **day center** *n* centre *m* d'accueil de jour **daydream I.** *vi* rêvasser **II.** *n* rêverie *f* **daylight** *n no pl* (lumière *f* du) jour *m;* **in broad** ~ au grand jour ►**to knock the living** ~**s out of sb** *inf* tabasser qn; **to scare the living** ~**s out of sb** *inf* flanquer la frousse à qn **day nursery** <-ries> *n* garderie *f* **day return** *n Brit: billet aller-retour valable une journée* **day shift** *n* **1.** (*period of time*) poste *m* de jour **2.** (*workers*) équipe *f* de jour **daytime** *n* journée *f* **daytime cream** *n* crème *f* de jour **day-to-day** *adj* quotidien(ne) **day trip** *n* excursion *f*

daze [deɪz] **I.** *n no pl* **to be in a** ~ être abasourdi **II.** *vt* **to be** ~**d** être abasourdi

dazed *adj* abasourdi(e)

dazzle ['dæzl] **I.** *vt* éblouir **II.** *n no pl* éblouissement *m*

dazzling *adj* éblouissant(e)

dB *n abbr of* **decibel** dB *m*

DC [ˌdiː'siː] *n* **1.** *abbr of* **direct current** courant *m* continu **2.** *abbr of* **District of Columbia** DC *m*

DD [ˌdiː'diː] *n abbr of* **Doctor of Divinity** docteur *m* en théologie

DDT [ˌdiːdiː'tiː] *n abbr of* **Dichlorodiphenyltrichloroethane** DDT *m*

deacon ['diːkən] *n* diacre *m*

deaconess *n* diaconesse *f*

dead [ded] **I.** *adj* **1.** (*no longer alive*) *a. fig* mort(e); **to be shot** ~ être abattu; **to be** ~ **on arrival at the hospital** être décédé lors du transport à l'hôpital **2.** (*broken*) mort(e); **to go** ~ ne plus fonctionner **3.** (*numb*) engourdi(e) **4.** (*dull*) monotone; (*eyes*) éteint(e) **5.** (*lacking power, energy*) mort(e) **6.** (*out of bounds: ball*) sorti(e) **7.** (*total*) complètement; (*stop*) complet(-ète); **to be** ~ **loss** être du temps perdu ►**over my** ~ **body** il faudra me passer sur le corps; **to be** (**as**) ~ **as a doornail** être tout ce qu'il y a de plus mort; **to be a** ~ **duck**

être foutu d'avance; **to be ~ on one's feet** ne plus tenir sur ses jambes; **~ men tell no tales** *Am, prov* les morts ne parlent pas; **to catch sb ~ to rights** prendre qn en flagrant délit; **to be a ~ ringer for sb** être le sosie de qn; **to be ~ to the world** être presque endormi; **sb would not be seen ~ in sth** (*wear*) qn ne porterait jamais (de son vivant) qc; (*go out*) qn n'irait jamais (de son vivant) dans qc **II.** *n* **1.** *pl* (*dead people*) **the ~** les morts *mpl* **2.** *no pl* (*realm of those who have died*) (royaume *m* des) morts *mpl;* **to rise from the ~** ressusciter; **to come back from the ~** (*come back to life*) revenir à la vie; (*recover form an illness*) recouvrer la santé **3.** SPORT sortie *f* (de balle) ►**to do sth in the ~ of night/winter** faire qc au cœur de la nuit/de l'hiver; **to make enough noise to wake the ~** faire du bruit à réveiller les morts **III.** *adv* **1.** *inf* (*totally*) complètement; **~ certain** sûr et certain; **~ ahead** tout droit; **~ easy** super facile **2.** *Brit, inf* **~ good** super bon; **~ straight** tout droit; **to be ~ set against sth** être complètement opposé à qc; **to be ~ set on sth** vouloir qc à tout prix ►**to stop ~ in one's tracks** stopper net l'avancée de qn

deadbeat [ˌdedˈbiːt] *n Am, Aus, pej, inf* glandeur, -euse *m, f*

deaden [ˈdedən] *vt* **1.** (*numb*) diminuer **2.** (*diminish*) amortir

dead end **I.** *n* impasse *f;* **to reach a ~** être dans une impasse **II.** *adj* **~ street** impasse *f;* **~ job** activité *f* sans débouchés; **a ~ situation** une impasse **III.** *vi* déboucher sur une impasse **dead heat** *n* **to be/to end in a ~** être/arriver ex-æquo **deadline** *n* date *f* limite; **to meet/to miss a ~** respecter/dépasser la date limite **deadlock** *n no pl* impasse *f*

deadly **I.** <-ier, -iest> *adj* mortel(le); (*look*) tueur(-euse) **II.** <-ier, -iest> *adv* **1.** (*in a fatal way*) mortellement **2.** (*absolutely*) terriblement

deadpan *adj* impassible; **~ wit** humour *m* pince-sans-rire **Dead Sea** *n* mer *f* Morte **deadwood** *n no pl* **1.** (*dead branches*) bois *m* mort **2.** *inf* (*useless*) **to cut out the ~ from the staff** dégraisser les effectifs du personnel

deaf [def] **I.** *adj* **1.** (*unable to hear anything*) sourd(e); **to be ~ in one ear** être sourd d'une oreille; **to go ~** devenir sourd **2.** (*hard of hearing*) malentendant(e) ►**to turn a ~ ear** faire la sourde oreille; **to fall on ~ ears** tomber dans l'oreille d'un sourd; **to be (as) ~ as a post** être sourd comme un pot; **to be ~ to sth** rester sourd à qc **II.** *npl* **the ~** les malentendants *mpl*

deafen [ˈdefən] *vt* **1.** (*to lose the power of hearing*) rendre sourd; **to be ~ed** être assourdi **2.** (*overwhelm*) casser les oreilles à **3.** *fig* assourdir

deafening *adj* assourdissant(e)

deaf-mute *n* sourd-muet *m,* sourde-muette *f*

deafness *n no pl* surdité *f*

deal¹ [diːl] *n no pl* **a (great) ~** beaucoup; **a great ~ of work** beaucoup de travail; **a good ~ of money/stress** pas mal d'argent/de stress

deal² [diːl] <dealt, dealt> **I.** *n* **1.** (*agreement*) marché *m* **2.** (*bargain*) affaire *f;* **to make sb a ~** faire faire une affaire à qn **3.** (*pass out cards*) donne *f* ►**what's the big ~?** *Am, inf* où est le problème?; **to get a raw ~** se faire avoir; **what's the ~ with sth?** *Am, inf* qu'est-ce qui ne va pas avec qc?; **what's your ~?** *inf* qu'est-ce que tu proposes? **II.** *vi* **1.** (*make business*) faire des affaires; **to ~ in sth** faire du commerce de qc **2.** (*sell drugs*) dealer **3.** (*pass out cards*) distribuer **III.** *vt* **1.** (*pass out: cards*) distribuer **2.** (*give*) donner; **to ~ sb a blow** porter un coup à qn **3.** (*sell: drugs*) revendre

dealership [ˈdiːləʃɪp, *Am:* -lɚ-] *n* concession *f*

◆**deal out** *vt* distribuer

◆**deal with** *vi* **1.** (*handle: problem*) se charger de **2.** (*discuss: subject*) traiter de **3.** (*do business: partner*) traiter avec

dealer *n* **1.** (*one who sells*) marchand(e) *m(f);* **antique ~** brocanteur *m* **2.** (*drug ~*) dealer *m* **3.** (*one who deals cards*) donneur *m*

dealing *n* transactions *fpl;* (*of drugs*) trafic *m*

dealings *n pl* **1.** (*manner of doing business*) relations *fpl;* **to have ~ with sb** traiter avec qn **2.** (*way of behaving*) façon *f* d'être **3.** (*passing out cards*) distribution *f*

dealt [delt] *pt, pp of* **deal**

dean [diːn] *n* doyen(ne) *m(f)*

dear [dɪəʳ, *Am:* dɪr] **I.** *adj* cher(chère); **to be ~ to sb** être cher à qn; **to do sth for ~ life** faire qc désespérément **II.** *adv* (*cost*) cher **III.** *interj inf* **~ me!, oh ~!** mon Dieu! **IV.** *n* **1.** (*sweet person*) amour *m;* **my ~** mon chéri/ma chérie; *form* mon cher/ma chère; **to be (such) a ~** être gentil; **my ~est** *iron* mon cheri/ma chérie **2.** *no pl, inf* (*friendly address*) mon chou

dearie [ˈdɪəri, *Am:* ˈdɪri] *n* chéri(e) *m(f);* **~ me** mon chéri

dearly *adv* cher

dearth [dɜːθ, *Am:* dɜːrθ] *n no pl, form* pénurie *f*

deary *s.* **dearie**

death [deθ] *n* mort *f;* **to die a natural ~** décéder d'une mort naturelle; **to be put to ~** être mis à mort; **frightened to ~** mort de peur ►**to be at ~'s door** être à l'article de la mort; **to be the ~ of sb** être la fin de qn; *fig* vouloir la mort de qn; **to catch one's ~ (of cold)** attraper la mort; **to feel like ~ warmed up** [*o Am* **warmed over**] se sentir mal; **to ~** (*until one dies*) à mort; (*very much*) à mourir; **to have sb worried to ~** se faire un sang d'encre

deathbed *n* lit *m* de mort **death blow** *n* coup *m* fatal; **to deal sb a ~** porter un coup fatal à qn **death duties** *n Brit, inf* droits *mpl* de succession

deathly **I.** *adv* comme la mort; **~ pale** d'une pâleur cadavérique **II.** *adj* de mort

death penalty *n* **the ~** la peine de mort

death rate *n* taux *m* de mortalité **death row** *n Am* quartier *m* des condamnés à mort; **to be on** ~ attendre d'être exécuté **death sentence** *n* condamnation *f* à mort; **to receive the** ~ être condamné à mort **death squad** *n pej* escadron *m* de la mort **death tax** *Am s.* **death duties** **death toll** *n* victimes *fpl* **death trap** *n* danger *m* mortel

debacle [deɪˈbɑːkl, *Am:* dɪ-] *n* fiasco *m*

debar [dɪˈbɑːʳ, *Am:* -ˈbɑːr] <-rr-> *vt* exclure; **to be ~red from doing sth** ne plus avoir le droit de faire qc; **to be ~red from sth for sth** être interdit par qc de qc

debase [dɪˈbeɪs] *vt* **1.** (*degrade: person*) avilir **2.** ECON *a. fig* dévaloriser

debatable *adj* discutable; **it's ~ whether ...** on peut se demander si ...

debate [dɪˈbeɪt] **I.** *n no pl* débat *m* **II.** *vt* débattre **III.** *vi* **to ~ about sth** débattre de qc; **to ~ whether ...** s'interroger si ...

debater *n* orateur, -trice *m, f*

debauchery [dɪˈbɔːtʃəri, *Am:* ˈbɑː-] *n pej no pl* débauche *f*

debilitate [dɪˈbɪlɪteɪt] *vt* affaiblir

debilitating *adj* débilitant(e)

debility [dɪˈbɪləti, *Am:* dɪˈbɪləṭi] *n no pl* faiblesse *f*

debit [ˈdebɪt] **I.** *n* débit *m;* **to be in ~** avoir un solde débiteur **II.** *vt* **to ~ sth from sth** porter qc au débit de qc

debit card *n* carte *f* de débit

debris [ˈdeɪbriː, *Am:* dəˈbriː] *n no pl* débris *m*

debt [det] *n* dette *f,* pouf *m Belgique;* **to pay back ~s** rembourser des dettes; **to run up a (huge) ~** s'endetter lourdement; **to be out of ~** être acquitté de ses dettes; **to go heavily into ~** s'endetter lourdement ►**to be in ~ to sb** être redevable de qc à qn

debtor *n* débiteur, -trice *m, f*

debug [ˌdiːˈbʌɡ] <-gg-> *vt* INFOR déboguer

debunk [diːˈbʌŋk] *vt* démythifier; (*a myth*) détruire

debut [ˈdeɪbjuː, *Am:* -ˈ-] **I.** *n* (*first performance*) débuts *mpl;* ~ **album** premier album *m* **II.** *vi* faire ses débuts

debutante [ˈdebjuːtɑːnt] *n* débutante *f*

decade [ˈdekeɪd] *n* décennie *f*

decadence [ˈdekədəns] *n no pl* décadence *f*

decadent *adj* décadent(e)

decaf [ˈdiːkæf] **I.** *adj inf abbr of* **decaffeinated** **II.** *n inf* déca *m*

decaffeinated [ˌdiːˈkæfɪneɪtɪd] **I.** *adj* décaféiné(e) **II.** *n inf* décaféiné *m*

decamp [dɪˈkæmp] *vi inf* décamper

decant [dɪˈkænt] *vt* **1.** (*transfer liquid*) décanter **2.** *Brit, fig, inf* **to ~ oneself from sth into sth** se faire transférer de qc à qc

decanter *n* décanteur *m*

decapitate [dɪˈkæpɪteɪt] *vt* décapiter

decapitation *n no pl* décapitation *f*

decathlon [dɪˈkæθlən, *Am:* -lɑːn] *n* décathlon *m*

decay [dɪˈkeɪ] **I.** *n no pl* **1.** (*deterioration*) délabrement *m;* **environmental ~** dégradation *m* de l'environnement; **to fall into ~** se délabrer **2.** (*decline*) *a. fig* déclin *m;* (*of civilization*) décadence *f;* **moral ~** déchéance *f* morale **3.** (*rotting*) décomposition *f* **4.** MED (*dental ~*) carie *f* **5.** PHYS désintégration *f* **II.** *vi* **1.** (*deteriorate*) se détériorer; (*tooth*) se carier; (*food*) pourrir **2.** BIO se décomposer **3.** PHYS se désintégrer **III.** *vt* (*food*) décomposer; (*tooth*) carier

decease [dɪˈsiːs] **I.** *n no pl, form* décès *m;* **upon sb's ~** au décès de qn **II.** *vi* décéder

deceased **I.** *n form* **the ~** (*used for one person*) le défunt, la défunte; (*several persons*) les défunt(e)s **II.** *adj form* décédé(e)

deceit [dɪˈsiːt] *n* tromperie *f*

deceitful *adj* trompeur(-euse)

deceive [dɪˈsiːv] *vt* tromper; **to ~ oneself** se tromper; **to ~ sb into doing sth** tromper qn en faisant qc ►**do my eyes ~ me?** est-ce que mon regard me trahit?

deceiver *n pej* trompeur, -euse *m, f*

decelerate [diːˈseləreɪt] *vt, vi* ralentir

December [dɪˈsembəʳ, *Am:* -bɚ] *n* décembre *m; s. a.* **April**

decency [ˈdiːsəntsi] *n* **1.** *no pl* (*social respectability*) décence *f* **2.** (*goodness*) bonté *f* **3.** *pl* (*approved behavior*) convenances *fpl* **4.** *pl, Am* (*basic comforts*) commodités *fpl*

decent [ˈdiːsənt] *adj* **1.** (*socially acceptable*) décent(e) **2.** (*good*) gentil(le) **3.** (*appropriate*) convenable

decentralization *n no pl* décentralisation *f*

decentralize [diːˈsentrəlaɪz] **I.** *vt* décentraliser **II.** *vi* se décentraliser

decentralized *adj* décentralisé(e)

deception [dɪˈsepʃən] *n* tromperie *f*

deceptive [dɪˈseptɪv] *adj* trompeur(-euse) ►**appearances can be ~** *prov* les apparences peuvent être trompeuses

decibel [ˈdesɪbel] *n* décibel *m*

decide [dɪˈsaɪd] **I.** *vi* (*make a choice*) décider; **to ~ for oneself** se décider **II.** *vt* décider

◆**decide on** *vi* se décider pour

decided *adj* **1.** (*definite*) incontestable **2.** (*clear*) résolu(e) **3.** (*pronounced*) marqué(e)

deciduous [dɪˈsɪdjʊəs, *Am:* -ˈsɪdʒʊ-] *adj* caduc(-uque)

decimal [ˈdesɪml] *n* décimale *f*

decimate [ˈdesɪmeɪt] *vt* décimer

decipher [dɪˈsaɪfəʳ, *Am:* -fɚ] *vt* **1.** (*be able to read*) déchiffrer **2.** (*decode*) décoder

decision [dɪˈsɪʒən] *n* **1.** (*choice*) décision *f;* **a ~ about sth** une décision sur qc; **to make a ~** prendre une décision **2.** LAW décision *f;* **to hand down a ~** rendre une décision de justice **3.** *no pl* (*clearness*) résolution *f*

decision maker *n* décideur *m* **decision-making** *n no pl* prise *f* de décision

decisive [dɪˈsaɪsɪv] *adj* décisif(-ive); (*person, tone, manner*) décidé(e)

deck [dek] **I.** *n* **1.** (*walking surface of a ship*) pont *m;* **to go up on** ~ monter sur le pont **2.** (*level on a bus*) étage *m* **3.** *Am, Aus* (*roofless raised wooden porch*) terrasse *f* **4.** *Am* (*complete set*) ~ **of cards** jeu *m* de cartes; *s. a.* **pack** **5.** ELEC lecteur *m* **6.** MUS platine *f* ►**to clear the** ~**s** tout déblayer **II.** *vt* (*adorn*) orner; **to be** ~**ed with flowers** être orné de fleurs

deckchair ['dektʃeəʳ, *Am:* -tʃer] *n* chaise *f* longue

declaim [dɪ'kleɪm] **I.** *vt form* déclamer **II.** *vi form* s'indigner

declamation [ˌdeklə'meɪʃən] *n form* déclamation *f*

declamatory [dɪ'klæmətəri, *Am:* dɪ'klæmətɔːri] *adj form* déclamatoire

declaration *n* déclaration *f*

declare [dɪ'kleəʳ, *Am:* dɪ'kler] **I.** *vt* déclarer **II.** *vi* **1.** (*announce*) **to** ~ **oneself** (**to be**) **bankrupt** se déclarer en faillite **2.** (*announce a public stance on*) **to** ~ **against/for sth** se déclarer contre/en faveur de qc

decline [dɪ'klaɪn] **I.** *n no pl* **1.** (*deterioration*) déclin *m* **2.** (*decrease*) baisse *f;* **to be on/in the** ~ être en baisse **II.** *vi* **1.** (*diminish*) baisser **2.** (*refuse*) refuser **3.** (*deteriorate*) être sur le déclin **III.** *vt* décliner; **to** ~ **to** +*infin* refuser de +*infin*

declutch [ˌdiː'klʌtʃ] *vi* débrayer

decode [ˌdiː'kəʊd, *Am:* -'koʊd] *vt* **1.** (*decipher a code*) décoder **2.** (*understand*) déchiffrer

decoder *n* décodeur *m*

decolonization [ˌdiːˌkɒlɪnaɪ'zeɪʃən, *Am:* -ˌkɑːlənɪ'-] *n no pl* décolonisation *f*

decommission [ˌdiːkəmɪʃən] *vt* **1.** (*relieve someone*) lever de ses fonctions **2.** (*remove from use*) retirer **3.** (*shut down*) fermer

decompose [ˌdiːkəm'pəʊz, *Am:* -'poʊz] **I.** *vi* se décomposer **II.** *vt* décomposer

decomposition *n no pl* décomposition *f*

decompress [ˌdiːkəm'pres] *vt, vi* décompresser

decompression *n no pl* décompression *f*

decompression chamber *n* chambre *f* de décompression

decontaminate [ˌdiːkən'tæmɪneɪt] *vt* ECOL, CHEM décontaminer

decontamination *n no pl* ECOL, CHEM décontamination *f*

decontrol [ˌdiːkən'trəʊl, *Am:* -'troʊl] <-ll-> *vt* ECON (*trade*) dérégler

decor ['deɪkɔːʳ, *Am:* 'deɪkɔːr] *n* décor *m*

decorate ['dekəreɪt] **I.** *vt* **1.** (*adorn*) décorer **2.** (*add new paint*) peindre **3.** (*add wallpaper*) tapisser **4.** (*give a medal*) décorer **II.** *vi* **1.** (*add new paint*) faire les peintures **2.** (*add wallpaper*) tapisser

decoration *n* **1.** (*sth that adorns*) décoration *f* **2.** (*with paint*) peinture *f* **3.** (*with wallpaper*) tapisserie *f*

decorative ['dekərətɪv, *Am:* -t̬ɪv] *adj* décoratif(-ive); **to look** ~ *iron* faire la potiche

decorator *n Brit* peintre *m* décorateur

decorous ['dekərəs, *Am:* -ɚəs] *adj form* convenable

decorum [dɪ'kɔːrəm] *n no pl, form* bienséance *f*

decoy ['diːkɔɪ] **I.** *n* leurre *m;* **to use sb as a** ~ utiliser qn comme appât **II.** *vt* **to** ~ **sb into doing sth** leurrer qn pour qu'il fasse qc

decrease [dɪ'kriːs, *Am:* 'diːkriːs] **I.** *vi, vt* baisser **II.** *n* baisse *f;* **to be on the** ~ être en baisse

decree [dɪ'kriː] **I.** *n form* **1.** POL décret *m* **2.** LAW jugement *m* **II.** *vt* **1.** (*order by decree*) décréter **2.** LAW ordonner

decree absolute *n* LAW jugement *m* définitif

decree nisi *n* LAW jugement *m* provisoire

decrepit [dɪ'krepɪt] *adj* (*economy*) mal en point; (*building*) délabré(e); (*person*) décrépit(e)

decrepitude [dɪ'krepitjuːd, *Am:* -tuːd] *n no pl, form* décrépitude *f*

decriminalize [ˌdiː'krɪmɪnəlaɪz] *vt* dépénaliser

decry [dɪ'kraɪ] *vt form* décrier

dedicate ['dedɪkeɪt] *vt* **1.** (*devote: life, time*) consacrer; **to** ~ **oneself to sth** se consacrer à qc **2.** (*do in sb's honour*) dédier; **to** ~ **sth to sb** dédier qc à qn **3.** (*sign on: book, record*) dédicacer

dedicated *adj* **1.** (*devoted*) dévoué(e); (*worker*) zélé(e); (*fan*) enthousiaste **2.** (*made for*) spécial(e)

dedication *n* **1.** (*devotion*) dévouement *m;* **to show** ~ **to sth** montrer du dévouement vis-à-vis de qc **2.** (*statement in sb's honour*) dédicace *f* **3.** (*official opening*) consécration *f*

deduce [dɪ'djuːs, *Am:* dɪ'duːs] *vt* déduire

deducible [dɪ'djuːsəbl, *Am:* dɪ'duː-] *adj form* que l'on peut déduire

deduct [dɪ'dʌkt] *vt* déduire

deductible **I.** *adj* déductible **II.** *n Am* franchise *f*

deduction *n* déduction *f;* **to make a** ~ tirer une conclusion

deductive [dɪ'dʌktɪv] *adj* par déduction

deed [diːd] *n* acte *m;* ~ **of a house** acte de propriété; **to do a good** ~ faire une bonne action

deed poll *n* LAW **to do sth by** ~ faire qc légalement

deejay ['diːdʒeɪ] *n* DJ *m*

deem [diːm] *vt form* juger; **to be** ~**ed sth** être jugé qc; **to** ~ **sb to have done sth** considérer qn comme ayant fait qc

deep [diːp] **I.** *adj* **1.** (*not shallow*) profond(e); **how** ~ **is the sea?** quelle est la profondeur de la mer?; **it is 30-metres** ~ elle a 30 mètres de profondeur **2.** (*extending back: stage*) profond(e); (*shelf, strip*) large; (*carpet, snow*) épais(se); **to be 15 cm** ~ faire 15 cm de profondeur/largeur/épaisseur **3.** *fig* (*full, intense*) profond(e); (*need, desire*) grand(e); **to let out a** ~ **sigh** pousser un grand soupir; **to take a** ~

breath respirer profondément; **to be in ~ trouble** avoir de gros ennuis; **to be a ~ disappointment to sb** être très décevant pour qn **4.** *fig* (*profound: aversion, feeling, regret*) profond(e); **to be in ~ concentration** être très concentré; **to be ~ in despair** être au plus profond du désespoir; **to be in ~ thought** être très absorbé; **to have a ~ understanding of sth** avoir une grande compréhension de qc **5.** (*absorbed by*) **to be ~ in sth** être très absorbé dans qc; **to be ~ in debt** être très endetté **6.** (*far back*) **the Deep South** le Sud profond; **~ in the forest** loin dans la forêt; **in the ~ past** il y a très longtemps **7.** *inf* (*hard to understand*) profond(e); (*knowledge*) approfondi(e) **8.** (*low in pitch: voice*) grave **9.** (*dark: colour*) intense; **~ red** rouge foncé; **~ blue eyes** des yeux d'un bleu profond ►**to go off the ~ end about sth** sortir de ses gonds à propos de qc; **to jump in at the ~ end** se jeter à l'eau; **to be in/get into ~ water over sth** être/se mettre dans le pétrin à cause de qc **II.** *adv a. fig* profondément; **to run ~** être profond; **~ inside** dans mon for intérieur; **~ in my heart** tout au fond de moi; **to walk ~ into the night** se promener tard dans la nuit; **to travel ~ inside the countryside** voyager au cœur de la campagne ►**still waters run ~** *prov* il faut se méfier de l'eau qui dort

deepen ['di:pən] **I.** *vt* **1.** (*make deeper*) creuser **2.** (*increase*) augmenter; (*knowledge*) approfondir; (*feeling*) accroître; (*crisis*) aggraver **3.** (*make darker*) foncer **II.** *vi* **1.** (*become deeper*) devenir plus profond **2.** (*increase*) augmenter; (*crisis*) s'aggraver; (*split*) accentuer **3.** (*become lower in pitch*) devenir plus grave **4.** (*become darker*) foncer

deep freeze I. *n* congélateur *m* **II.** *vt* **to deep-freeze** congeler **deep-frozen** *adj* surgelé(e) **deep-fry** *vt* faire cuire dans la friture

deeply *adv* profondément; **to ~ regret sth** regretter beaucoup qc; **to be ~ grateful/interested in sth** être très reconnaissant/intéressé par qc

deepness *n* profondeur *f*

deep-rooted *adj* **1.** (*well established: prejudice*) profond(e) **2.** BOT aux racines profondes **deep-sea animal** *n* animal *m* pélagique **deep-seated** *adj* (*faith*) inébranlable; (*hatred*) profond(e) **deep space** *n* AVIAT espace *m* lointain

deer [dɪəʳ, *Am:* dɪr] *n* chevreuil *m*

deerstalker ['dɪəˌstɔ:kəʳ, *Am:* 'dɪrˌstɔ:kɚ] *n* **1.** (*cap*) casquette *f* de chasse **2.** (*hunter*) chasseur *m* de cerf

deface [dɪ'feɪs] *vt* (*building, wall*) dégrader; (*poster*) gribouiller

defamation *n no pl, form* diffamation *f*

defamatory [dɪ'fæmətəri, *Am:* -tɔ:ri] *adj form* diffamatoire

defame [dɪ'feɪm] *vt form* diffamer

default [dɪ'fɔ:lt, *Am:* dɪ'fɑ:lt] **I.** *n* défaut *m;* **in ~ of sth** faute de qc **II.** *vi* **1.** LAW ne pas comparaître **2.** FIN **to ~ on one's payments** être en défaut de paiement; **she ~ed on her mortgage repayments** elle n'a pas payé ses remboursements de prêt immobilier **3.** INFOR **to ~ to sth** sélectionner qc par défaut

default value *n* INFOR valeur *f* par défaut

defeat [dɪ'fi:t] **I.** *vt* (*person*) battre; (*hopes*) anéantir; **maths ~ him** les maths le dépassent **II.** *n* défaite *f*

defeatism [dɪ'fi:tɪzəm, *Am:* dɪ'fi:t̬ɪ-] *n* défaitisme *m*

defeatist I. *adj* défaitiste **II.** *n* défaitiste *mf*

defecate ['defəkeɪt] *vi form* MED déféquer

defecation *n no pl, form* MED défécation *f*

defect ['di:fekt] **I.** *n* **1.** (*imperfection*) défaut *m* **2.** TECH vice *m* **3.** MED problème *m;* **heart ~** problème au cœur **II.** *vi* POL **to ~ from/to a country** s'enfuir de/vers un pays; **to ~ from the army** quitter l'armée

defection *n* défection *f;* **there were a lot of ~s from the USSR** beaucoup de gens d'URSS sont passés à l'ouest

defective [dɪ'fektɪv] *adj* (*brakes, appliance*) défectueux(-euse); (*hearing, eye-sight*) mauvais(e)

defence [dɪ'fents] *n Aus, Brit* défense *f;* **~ mechanism** réflexe *m* de défense; **to put up a ~** se défendre; **to play in** [*o Am* **on**] **~** jouer en défense

defenceless *adj* sans défense

defence minister *n* ministre *mf* de la Défense

defend [dɪ'fend] *vt, vi* défendre

defendant [dɪ'fendənt] *n* LAW défendeur, -deresse *m, f*

defense [dɪ'fents] *n Am s.* **defence**

defenseless *adj* sans défense

defensible [dɪ'fentsəbl] *adj* **1.** (*capable of being defended*) défendable **2.** (*justifiable*) justifiable

defensive [dɪ'fentsɪv] **I.** *adj* **1.** (*intended for defence*) défensif(-ive) **2.** (*quick to challenge*) sur la défensive **II.** *n* défensive *f;* **to be/go on the ~** être/se mettre sur la défensive

defer [dɪ'fɜ:ʳ, *Am:* dɪ'fɜ:r] <-rr-> **I.** *vi* **to ~ to sb's judgement** s'en remettre au jugement de qn **II.** *vt* FIN, LAW différer

deference ['defərənts] *n no pl, form* déférence *f;* **to pay ~ to sb** avoir des égards pour qn

deferential [ˌdefə'rentʃəl] *adj* respectueux(-euse); **to be ~ to sb** avoir des égards pour qn

deferred payment *n* paiement *m* différé

defiance [dɪ'faɪənts] *n no pl* provocation *f;* **in ~ of sth** au mépris de qc

defiant *adj* provocateur(-trice); (*stand*) de défi; **to remain ~** faire preuve de provocation; **to be in a ~ mood** être d'humeur provocatrice

deficiency [dɪ'fɪʃəntsi] *n* **1.** (*shortage*) manque *m* **2.** (*weakness*) faiblesse *f* **3.** MED carence *f;* **~ disease** maladie par carence

deficient [dɪ'fɪʃənt] *adj* incomplet(-ète); **to**

D

be ~ in sth manquer de qc
deficit ['defɪsɪt] *n* déficit *m,* mali *m Belgique;* **a ~ in sth** un déficit en qc
defile [dɪ'faɪl] *vt form* (*spoil, make dirty*) défigurer
define [dɪ'faɪn] *vt* définir; (*limit, extent*) déterminer; (*eyes, outlines*) dessiner
definite ['defɪnət] **I.** *adj* **1.** (*clearly stated*) défini(e); (*plan, amount*) précis(e); (*opinion, taste*) bien arrêté(e) **2.** (*clear, unambiguous*) net(te); (*reply*) clair(e) et net(te); (*evidence*) évident(e) **3.** (*firm*) ferme; (*refusal*) catégorique **4.** (*sure*) sûr(sure); **to be ~ about sth** être sûr de qc **5.** (*undeniable: asset, advantage*) évident(e) **II.** *n inf* **the date is not yet a ~** la date n'est pas encore sûre; **they are ~s for the party** ils sont sûrs d'être invités à la soirée
definite article *n* article *m* défini
definitely *adv* **1.** (*without doubt*) sans aucun doute; **I will ~ be there** je serai là à coup sûr; **I will ~ do it** je le ferai sans faute; **is she coming? ? – yes,** ~ est-ce qu'elle va venir? – oui, c'est sûr; **it was ~ him in the car** c'est sûr que c'était lui dans la voiture; **it was ~ the best option** c'était sans aucun doute la meilleure solution **2.** (*distinctly: superior, better*) nettement; (*tell*) clairement **3.** (*categorically: decided, sure*) absolument
definition [ˌdefɪ'nɪʃən] *n* définition *f;* **to lack ~** ne pas être net
definitive [dɪ'fɪnətɪv, *Am:* -t̬ɪv] *adj* **1.** (*final*) définitif(-ive); (*proof*) irréfutable **2.** (*best: book*) de référence
deflate [dɪ'fleɪt] **I.** *vt* **1.** (*let air out of*) dégonfler **2.** *fig* (*person*) remettre à sa place; (*hopes*) décevoir; (*reputation*) ternir **3.** ECON, FIN provoquer la déflation de **II.** *vi* se dégonfler
deflated *adj* déçu(e)
deflation *n no pl* ECON, FIN déflation *f*
deflationary *adj* déflationniste
deflect [dɪ'flekt] **I.** *vt* (*ball, blow, shot*) faire dévier; **to ~ sb from doing sth** empêcher qn de faire qc **II.** *vi* **1.** (*change direction of*) dévier **2.** PHYS défléchir
deflection *n* **1.** (*ricochet*) déflexion *f* **2.** (*avoidance*) détournement *m* **3.** SPORT **they scored thanks to a ~ off one of the players** ils ont marqué grâce au fait que le ballon a rebondi sur l'un des joueurs
defoliant *n* défoliant *m*
defoliate [ˌdiː'fəʊlieɪt, *Am:* -'foʊ-] *vt* défolier
deforest [ˌdiː'fɒrɪst, *Am:* -'fɔːr-] *vt* déboiser
deforestation *n no pl* déforestation *f*
deform [dɪ'fɔːm, *Am:* dɪ'fɔːrm] *vt, vi* déformer
deformation *n no pl* déformation *f*
deformed *adj* malformé(e); **to be born ~** naître avec une malformation
deformity [dɪ'fɔːməti, *Am:* dɪ'fɔːrmət̬i] *n* ANAT difformité *f*
defraud [dɪ'frɔːd, *Am:* dɪ'frɑːd] *vt* (*person, company*) escroquer; (*tax office, authority*) frauder
defray [dɪ'freɪ] *vt form* défrayer
defrost [ˌdiː'frɒst, *Am:* -'frɑːst] *vt, vi* (*food*) décongeler; (*fridge, windscreen*) dégivrer
deft [deft] *adj* adroit(e)
defunct [dɪ'fʌŋkt] *adj form* (*person, party*) défunt(e)
defuse [ˌdiː'fjuːz] *vt* désamorcer
defy [dɪ'faɪ] *vt* défier
deg. *n abbr of* **degree** degré *m*
degenerate [dɪ'dʒenəreɪt] **I.** *vi* dégénérer; **to ~ into qc** dégénérer en qc **II.** *adj* dégénéré(e) **III.** *n form* dégénéré(e) *m(f)*
degeneration *n no pl* dégénérescence *f*
degrade [dɪ'greɪd] **I.** *vt* dégrader; **pornography ~s women** la pornographie est dégradante pour les femmes **II.** *vi* se dégrader
degree [dɪ'griː] *n* **1.** (*amount*) *a.* MAT, METEO degré *m* **2.** (*extent*) mesure *f;* **to a certain ~** dans une certaine mesure; **by ~s** par étapes; **to the last ~** sur toute la ligne **3.** (*course of study*) diplôme *m* universitaire; **master's ~** maîtrise *f*
dehumanise *vt Brit, Aus,* **dehumanize** [ˌdiː'hjuːmənaɪz] *vt* déshumaniser
dehydrate [ˌdiːhaɪ'dreɪt] **I.** *vt* (*food, body*) déshydrater **II.** *vi* MED se déshydrater
dehydrated *adj* (*food*) déshydraté(e)
dehydration *n no pl* MED déshydratation *f*
de-ice [ˌdiː'aɪs] *vt* dégeler
deign [deɪn] *vi pej* **to ~ to** *+infin* daigner *+infin*
deism ['deɪɪzəm, *Am:* 'diː-] *n no pl* déisme *m*
deity ['deɪɪti, *Am:* 'diːət̬i] *n* déité *f*
deject [dɪ'dʒekt] *vt* abattre
dejected *adj* abattu(e)
dejection *n no pl* déprime *f*
Delaware ['deləweəʳ, *Am:* -wer] *n* le Delaware
delay [dɪ'leɪ] **I.** *vt* retarder **II.** *vi* tarder **III.** *n* retard *m*
delayed-action *adj* (*fuse*) à retardement
delaying *adj* (*tactics*) dilatoire
delectable [dɪ'lektəbl] *adj* délicieux(-euse); (*person*) excellent(e)
delectation [ˌdiːlek'teɪʃən] *n no pl, iron, form* délice *m;* **for sb's ~** au délice de qn
delegate ['delɪgət] **I.** *n* délégué(e) *m(f)* **II.** *vt* déléguer; **to ~ sb to** *+infin* déléguer qn pour *+infin* **III.** *vi* déléguer
delegation *n* délégation *f*
delete [dɪ'liːt] **I.** *vt* **1.** (*cross out*) rayer; **~ as appropriate** rayer la mention inutile **2.** INFOR (*file, letter*) effacer **II.** *vi* INFOR effacer **III.** *n* INFOR (*~ key*) touche *f* d'effacement
deletion *n* **1.** (*act of erasing*) *a.* INFOR suppression *f* **2.** (*removal*) rature *f*
deli ['deli] *n inf abbr of* **delicatessen**
deliberate [dɪ'lɪbərət] **I.** *adj* (*act, movement*) délibéré(e); (*decision*) voulu(e); **it was ~** cela a été fait exprès **II.** *vi form* délibérer **III.** *vt form* délibérer de
deliberately *adv* intentionnellement

deliberation *n no pl* délibération *f;* **to do sth with ~** faire qc délibérément
delicacy ['delɪkəsi] *n* **1.** (*fine food*) mets *m* raffiné **2.** *no pl* (*fragility*) délicatesse *f;* **to behave with ~** faire preuve de délicatesse **3.** (*sensitivity*) sensibilité *f*
delicate ['delɪkət] *adj* **1.** (*fragile*) délicat(e) **2.** (*highly sensitive: instrument*) fragile **3.** (*fine: balance*) précaire
delicatessen [ˌdelɪkə'tesən] *n* épicerie *f* fine
delicious [dɪ'lɪʃəs] *adj* délicieux(-euse)
delight [dɪ'laɪt] **I.** *n* délice *m;* **to do sth with ~** faire qc avec plaisir; **to take ~ in sth** prendre plaisir à qc **II.** *vt* enchanter
delighted *adj* ravi(e)
◆**delight in** *vi* se délecter à faire
delightful *adj* (*people*) charmant(e); (*evening, place*) délicieux(-euse)
delimit [dɪ'lɪmɪt] *vt form* délimiter
delineate [dɪ'lɪnieɪt] *vt* déterminer; (*boundary*) délimiter
delinquency [dɪ'lɪŋkwəntsi] *n* LAW délinquance *f*
delinquent [dɪ'lɪŋkwənt] **I.** *n* LAW délinquant(e) *m(f);* **a juvenile ~** un jeune délinquant **II.** *adj* **1.** (*related to unlawful behaviour*) délinquant(e) **2.** *Am, form* (*late*) **to be ~ in paying sth** être en défaut de paiement de qc
delirious [dɪ'lɪriəs] *adj* **1.** MED (*affected by delirium*) **to be ~** délirer **2.** (*ecstatic*) délirant(e); **to be ~ with joy** être délirant de joie
deliriously *adv* **1.** (*incoherently*) **to rave ~** délirer **2.** (*extremely*) incroyablement
delirium [dɪ'lɪriəm] *n no pl* délire *m*
deliver [dɪ'lɪvəʳ, *Am:* dɪ'lɪvɚ] **I.** *vt* **1.** (*distribute to addressee: goods*) livrer; (*newspaper, mail*) distribuer **2.** (*recite: lecture, speech*) faire; (*verdict*) prononcer; **to ~ oneself of one's opinion** émettre son opinion **3.** (*direct: a blow*) porter; (*a ball*) lancer **4.** (*give birth to*) **to ~ a baby** mettre un enfant au monde; **she was ~ed by the midwife** c'est la sage-femme qui l'a accouchée; **to be ~ed of a baby** accoucher d'un bébé **5.** (*produce: promise*) tenir **6.** (*hand over*) remettre **7.** (*rescue*) délivrer **8.** *Am* POL (*a vote*) obtenir ►**to ~ the goods** *inf* tenir ses promesses **II.** *vi* **1.** (*make a delivery*) livrer; (*postman*) distribuer le courrier **2.** *fig* tenir ses promesses
delivery [dɪ'lɪvəri] *n* **1.** (*act of distributing goods*) livraison *f;* (*of newspaper, mail*) distribution *f;* **on ~** à la livraison; **to be for ~** être à livrer; **to take ~ of sth** se faire livrer qc **2.** (*manner of speaking*) élocution *f* **3.** (*birth*) accouchement *m* **4.** SPORT lancer *m*
delivery note *n* bon *m* de livraison
delivery room, **delivery suite**, **delivery unit** *n* salle *f* d'accouchement
delivery van *n* camionnette *f* de livraison
delta ['deltə, *Am:* -t̬ə] *n* GEO delta *m*
delta wing *n* AVIAT aile *f* delta
delude [dɪ'lu:d] *vt* tromper; **to ~ oneself** se leurrer
deluge ['delju:dʒ] **I.** *n* déluge *m* **II.** *vt* inonder
delusion [dɪ'lu:ʒən] *n* illusion *f;* **to suffer from the ~ that ...** s'imaginer que ...; **~s of grandeur** folie *f* des grandeurs
de luxe [də'lʌks, *Am:* dɪ'lʌks] *adj* de luxe
delve [delv] *vi* fouiller
demagog ['deməgɑ:g] *n Am s.* **demagogue**
demagogic [ˌdemə'gɒgɪk, *Am:* -'gɑ:dʒɪk] *adj* démagogique
demagogue ['deməgɒg, *Am:* -gɑ:g] *n pej* démagogue *mf*
demagoguery [ˌdemə'gɒgəri, *Am:* -'gɑ:dʒɚ-], **demagogy** *n no pl* démagogie *f*
demand [dɪ'mɑ:nd, *Am:* dɪ'mænd] **I.** *vt* **1.** (*request, require*) demander **2.** (*request forcefully*) exiger; (*payment*) réclamer **3.** (*require*) exiger; (*time, skills*) demander **II.** *n* **1.** (*request*) demande *f* **2.** (*pressured request*) exigence *f;* **her job makes a ~ on her time** son travail est très prenant **3.** ECON (*desire for sth*) demande *f;* **to be in ~** être demandé; **to do sth on ~** faire qc à la demande; **to make a ~ that ...** exiger que +*subj;* **to meet a ~ for sth** satisfaire le besoin de qc **4.** *Brit* (*request for payment*) réclamation *f;* **to receive a ~ for payment** recevoir un avis de paiement
demanding *adj* exigeant(e); (*task, job*) astreignant(e)
demand note *n* demande *f* de paiement
demarcate ['di:mɑ:keɪt, *Am:* di:'mɑ:r-] *vt* délimiter
demarcation *n* démarcation *f*
demarcation line *n* **1.** MIL, POL ligne *f* de démarcation **2.** *fig* distinction *f*
demean [dɪ'mi:n] *vt* **to ~ oneself** s'abaisser
demeaning *adj* avilissant(e)
demeanor *n Am, Aus,* **demeanour** *n Brit, Aus no pl, form* attitude *f*
demented [dɪ'mentɪd, *Am:* -'ment̬ɪd] *adj inf* **1.** (*crazy*) dément(e) **2.** *fig* **to drive sb ~** rendre qn fou
dementia *n* démence *f*
demerit [ˌdi:'merɪt, *Am:* dɪ'mer-] *n* **1.** (*fault*) défaut *m* **2.** *Am* SCHOOL blâme *m*
demesne [dɪ'meɪn] *n* **1.** (*possession*) possession *f* **2.** (*domain*) domaine *m*
demigod ['demigɒd, *Am:* -gɑ:d] *n* demi-dieu *m*
demilitarize [ˌdi:'mɪlɪtəraɪz, *Am:* -t̬əraɪz] *vt* démilitariser
demise [dɪ'maɪz] *n no pl, form* **1.** (*death*) décès *m* **2.** *fig* (*of a company*) fin *f*
demist [ˌdi:'mɪst] *vt Brit* désembuer
demister *n Brit* AUTO dispositif *m* antibuée
demo ['deməʊ, *Am:* -oʊ] *n abbr of* **demonstration** **1.** (*uprising*) manif *f* **2.** (*tape*) maquette *f*
demobilize [ˌdi:'məʊbəlaɪz, *Am:* -'moʊbəlaɪz] **I.** *vt* (*discharge*) démobiliser **II.** *vi* être

D

démobilisé

democracy [dɪ'mɒkrəsi, *Am:* dɪ'mɑː-] *n* démocratie *f*

democrat ['deməkræt] *n* démocrate *mf*

democratic *adj* démocratique

democratisation *n Brit, Aus,* **democratization** *n no pl* démocratisation *f*

democratize [dɪ'mɒkrətaɪz, *Am:* dɪ'mɑːkrə-] *vt Am* démocratiser

demographic [ˌdeməʊ'græfɪk, *Am:* ˌdemə'-] *adj* démographique

demographics *n* statistiques *fpl* démographiques

demography [dɪ'mɒgrəfi, *Am:* dɪ'mɑː-] *n* démographie *f*

demolish [dɪ'mɒlɪʃ, *Am:* dɪ'mɑːlɪʃ] *vt* démolir

demolition [ˌdemə'lɪʃən] *n* démolition *f*

demon ['diːmən] **I.** *n* (*evil spirit*) démon *m* ►**to work like a ~, to be a ~ for work, to be a ~ worker** *inf* travailler comme un fou **II.** *adj inf* démoniaque

demoniac [dɪ'məʊniæk, *Am:* dɪ'moʊ-], **demonic** *adj* démoniaque

demonstrable [dɪ'mɒntstrəbl, *Am:* dɪ'mɑːnt-] *adj* démontrable

demonstrate ['demənstreɪt] **I.** *vt* (*show clearly*) démontrer; (*authority, bravery*) faire preuve de; (*enthusiasm, knowledge*) montrer **II.** *vi* **to ~ against/in support of sth** manifester contre/en faveur de qc

demonstration *n* **1.** (*act of showing*) démonstration *f;* **as a ~ of sth** en signe de qc; **to give sb a ~ of sth** faire la démonstration de qc à qn **2.** (*march or parade*) manifestation *f;* **to hold a ~** faire une manifestation

demonstration model *n* modèle *m* de démonstration

demonstrative [dɪ'mɒntstrətɪv, *Am:* dɪ'mɑːnstrət̬ɪv] *adj* démonstratif(-ive); **to be ~ of sth** démontrer qc

demonstrator *n* **1.** (*person who demonstrates a product*) démonstrateur, -trice *m, f* **2.** (*person who takes part in protest*) manifestant(e) *m(f)*

demoralize [dɪ'mɒrəlaɪz, *Am:* -'mɔːr-] *vt Am* démoraliser

demote [dɪ'məʊt, *Am:* -'moʊt] *vt* MIL rétrograder

demure [dɪ'mjʊəʳ, *Am:* -'mjʊr] *adj* modeste

den [den] *n* **1.** (*lair*) tanière *f* **2.** (*children's playhouse*) cabane *f* **3.** *Am* (*small room*) atelier *m* **4.** *iron* (*place for committing crime*) repaire *m*

denationalize [ˌdiː'næʃənəlaɪz] *vt* (*an industry*) dénationaliser

denial [dɪ'naɪəl] *n* **1.** (*act of refuting*) déni *m* **2.** *no pl* (*refusal*) dénégation *f*

denigrate ['denɪgreɪt] *vt* dénigrer

denim ['denɪm] *n* **1.** *no pl* (*thick cotton cloth*) denim *m;* **a ~ jacket/shirt** une veste/chemise en denim **2.** *pl, inf* (*clothes made of denim*) jean *m;* **to wear ~s** porter un jean

denizen ['denɪzən] *n liter* habitant(e) *m(f)*

Denmark ['denmɑːk, *Am:* 'denmɑːrk] *n* le Danemark

denomination [dɪˌnɒmɪ'neɪʃən, *Am:* -ˌnɑːmə-] *n* **1.** (*religious group*) confession *f* **2.** (*unit of value*) classe *f;* **he collects coins of all ~s** il collectionne les pièces de monnaie de toutes les valeurs

denominational *adj* confessionnel(le)

denominator [dɪ'nɒmɪneɪtəʳ, *Am:* -'nɑːməneɪt̬ɚ] *n* dénominateur *m*

denotation *n* dénotation *f;* **to make a ~ of one's displeasure** dénoter le mécontentement de qn

denote [dɪ'nəʊt, *Am:* -'noʊt] *vt* dénoter

denouement [deɪ'nuːmɑ̃ːŋ] *n* dénouement *m*

denounce [dɪ'naʊnts] *vt* (*an act, an agreement, a treaty*) dénoncer; **to ~ sb as sth** dénoncer qn comme qc; **to ~ sb to the police** dénoncer qn à la police

dense [dents] <-r, -st> *adj* **1.** (*thick, compact: book, crowd, fog*) dense **2.** *fig, inf* (*stupid*) limité(e)

densely *adv* densément

density ['dentsɪti, *Am:* -sət̬i] *n* densité *f*

dent [dent] **I.** *n* **1.** (*a hollow made by pressure*) bosse *f* **2.** *fig* (*adverse effect*) blessure *f* **II.** *vt* **1.** (*put a dent in*) cabosser **2.** *fig* (*have adverse effect on*) **to ~ sb's confidence** entacher la confiance de qn

dental ['dentəl] *adj* dentaire

dental practitioner, **dental surgeon**, **dentist** *n* dentiste *mf*

dentistry ['dentɪstri, *Am:* -t̬ɪ-] *n no pl* médecine *f* dentaire

dentition [den'tɪʃən] *n* ANAT dentition *f*

dentures ['dentʃəz, *Am:* 'dentʃɚz] *npl* denture *f;* **to wear ~** porter un dentier

denude [dɪ'njuːd, *Am:* -'nuːd] *vt a. fig* dépouiller

denunciation [dɪˌnʌntsi'eɪʃən] *n* dénonciation *f*

deny [dɪ'naɪ] *vt* (*accusation*) dénier; (*family*) renier; **to ~ that ...** renier que ...; **to ~ doing sth** dénier avoir fait qc; **to ~ sth to sb** dénier qc à qn; **to ~ oneself** se renier (soi-même)

deodorant [di'əʊdərənt, *Am:* -'oʊ-] *n* déodorant *m*

deodorise *vt Aus, Brit,* **deodorize** [di'əʊdəraɪz, *Am:* -'oʊ-] *vt Am* désodoriser

dep. *n abbr of* **department** département *m*

depart [dɪ'pɑːt, *Am:* dɪ'pɑːrt] **I.** *vi* (*person, train, ship*) partir; (*plane*) décoller; **to ~ from sth** partir de qc; *fig* s'écarter de qc **II.** *vt* quitter

departed **I.** *adj* défunt(e); **~ triumphs** les succès passés **II.** *n pl* **the ~** le/la défunt(e)

department *n* **1.** (*section*) département *m;* (*of an organization*) service *m* **2.** ADMIN, POL département *m* ministériel; **~ of Transport** ministère *m* des Transports **3.** *fig, inf* (*domain*) domaine *m*

departmental *adj* de service; **~ head** chef *m*

de service
department store *n* grand magasin *m*
departure [dɪ'pɑːtʃəʳ, *Am:* dɪ'pɑːrtʃɚ] *n* **1.** (*act of vehicle leaving*) départ *m* **2.** (*deviation*) déviation *f* **3.** (*new undertaking*) changement *m*
departure gate *n* porte *f* d'embarquement
departure lounge *n* salle *f* d'embarquement **departure time** *n* heure *f* de départ
depend [dɪ'pend] *vi* **1.** (*rely on*) **to ~ on** dépendre de; **to ~ on sb/sth doing sth** dépendre de ce que qn/qc fait **2.** (*rely* (*on*)) **to ~ on sb/sth** compter sur qn/qc; **you can ~ on her to be late** *iron* tu peux compter sur elle pour être en retard
dependability [dɪˌpendə'bɪləti, *Am:* dɪˌpendə'bɪləţi] *n no pl* fiabilité *f*
dependable *adj* fiable
dependant *n* (membres *mpl* de la) famille *f*
dependence [dɪ'pendənts] *n no pl* confiance *f*
dependency *n* **1.** *no pl* dépendance *f; s. a.* **dependence** **2.** (*dependent state*) État *m* dépendant
dependent **I.** *adj* **1.** (*contingent*) **to be ~ on sth** dépendre de qc **2.** (*in need of*) dépendant(e); **to be ~ on sth** être dépendant de qc; **to be ~ on drugs** être accro à la drogue **II.** *n Am s.* **dependant**
depending on *prep* **~ sb's mood** selon l'humeur de qn; **~ the weather** en fonction du temps
depict [dɪ'pɪkt] *vt form* **to ~ sth as sth** représenter qc comme qc
depiction *n* représentation *f*
depilatory [dɪ'pɪlətəri, *Am:* -tɔːri] **I.** *n* dépilatoire *m* **II.** *adj* dépilatoire
depilatory cream *n* crème *f* dépilatoire
deplete [dɪ'pliːt] *vt* vider; **to ~ one's bank account** *iron* épuiser son compte en banque
depleted *adj* épuisé(e)
depletion *n* réduction *f*
deplorable *adj* déplorable
deplore [dɪ'plɔːʳ, *Am:* -'plɔːr] *vt* déplorer
deploy [dɪ'plɔɪ] *vt* (*one's resources, troops*) déployer; (*an argument*) exposer
deployment *n no pl* déploiement *m*
depopulate [ˌdiː'pɒpjəleɪt, *Am:* -'pɑːpjə-] *vt pass* dépeupler
deport [dɪ'pɔːt, *Am:* dɪ'pɔːrt] *vt* déporter
deportation [ˌdiːpɔː'teɪʃən, *Am:* -pɔːr'-] *n* déportation *f*
deportee [ˌdiːpɔː'tiː, *Am:* -pɔːr'-] *n* déporté(e) *m(f)*
deportment *n no pl, form* conduite *f*
depose [dɪ'pəʊz, *Am:* dɪ'poʊz] *vt* déposer; (*from a throne*) détrôner
deposit [dɪ'pɒzɪt, *Am:* dɪ'pɑːzɪt] **I.** *vt* **1.** (*put*) déposer; **to ~ money in one's account** déposer de l'argent sur un compte **2.** (*pay as security*) **to ~ sth with sb** verser qc à qn **II.** *n* **1.** (*sediment*) dépôt *m* **2.** (*payment made as first instalment*) provision *f;* **to leave sth as a ~** laisser qc comme provision **3.** (*security*) caution *f;* (*on a bottle*) consigne *f*
deposit account *n Brit* compte *m* de dépôt
deposition [ˌdepə'zɪʃən] *n a. form a.* POL déposition *f;* **to file a ~** remplir une déposition
depositor [dɪ'pɒzɪtəʳ, *Am:* dɪ'pɑːzəţɚ] *n* déposant(e) *m(f)*
depot ['depəʊ, *Am:* 'diːpoʊ] *n* dépôt *m*
deprave [dɪ'preɪv] *vt form* dépraver
depraved *adj* dépravé(e)
depravity [dɪ'prævəti, *Am:* dɪ'prævəţi] *n no pl* dépravation *f*
deprecate ['deprəkeɪt] *vt* **1.** (*disapprove*) désapprouver **2.** (*depreciate*) dévaloriser
deprecating *adj* réprobateur(-trice); **~ stare** regard *m* de réprobation
deprecation *n no pl, a. form* dépréciation *f*
deprecatory ['deprəkətəri, *Am:* 'deprəkətɔːri] *adj s.* **deprecating**
depreciate [dɪ'priːʃieɪt] **I.** *vi* se déprécier **II.** *vt* déprécier
depreciation *n no pl* dépréciation *f*
depredation [ˌdeprə'deɪʃən] *n pl* déprédation *f*
depress [dɪ'pres] *vt* **1.** (*sadden*) désoler **2.** (*reduce or lower in amount: prices*) déprécier; (*the economy*) décourager **3.** *form* (*press down: a button, a pedal*) appuyer sur
depressant **I.** *n* calmant *m* **II.** *adj* calmant(e)
depressed *adj* **1.** (*sad*) déprimé(e); **to be ~ about** [*o Brit* **at**] **sth** être déprimé par qc; **to feel ~** se sentir déprimé **2.** (*affected by depression: market*) dépressionnaire *m*
depressing *adj* déprimant(e)
depression *n* dépression *f*
depressive [dɪ'presɪv] **I.** *n* dépressif, -ive *m, f* **II.** *adj* dépressif(-ive)
deprivation [ˌdeprɪ'veɪʃən] *n* manque *m*
deprive [dɪ'praɪv] *vt* priver; **to ~ sb of sth** priver qn de qc; **to ~ sb of sleep** empêcher qn de dormir
deprived *adj* défavorisé(e)
depth [depθ] *n a. fig* profondeur *f;* **in ~** en profondeur; **in the ~ of winter** en plein hiver; **in the ~s of despair** dans le plus grand désespoir; **with great ~ of feeling** avec une grande sensibilité ►**to get out of one's ~** perdre pied
depth charge *n* bombe *f* d'eau
deputation [ˌdepjə'teɪʃən] *n + pl/sing vb* députation *f*
depute [dɪ'pjuːt] *vt form* **1.** (*appoint*) députer **2.** (*delegate*) déléguer
deputise *vi Aus, Brit,* **deputize** ['depjətaɪz] *vi* **to ~ for sb** représenter qn
deputy ['depjəti, *Am:* -ţi] **I.** *n* député(e) *m(f);* **to act as ~ for sb** agir en tant que représentant de qn **II.** *adj inv* suppléant(e); **~ manager** vice-président(e) *m(f)*
derail [dɪ'reɪl] **I.** *vt* **1.** (*cause to leave tracks*) faire dérailler **2.** *fig* (*negotiation*) faire déraper **II.** *vi* dérailler
derailment *n* **1.** (*accident*) déraillement *m*

2. *fig* dérapage *m*

derange [dɪ'reɪndʒ] *vt* déranger

deranged *adj* dérangé(e)

derangement *n no pl* dérangement *m*

Derby ['dɑ:bi, *Am:* 'dɑ:rb-] *n no pl* derby *m*

deregulate [ˌdi:'regjəleɪt] *vt* déréglementer

deregulation *n no pl* dérégulation *f*

derelict ['derəlɪkt] **I.** *adj* (*building*) délabré(e); (*site*) en ruine; ~ **car** épave *f* **II.** *n form* épave *f*

dereliction *n* **1.** *no pl* (*dilapidation*) délabrement *m* **2.** (*failure*) omission *f*

deride [dɪ'raɪd] *vt form* se moquer de

derision [dɪ'rɪʒən] *n no pl* dérision *f;* **to meet sth with** ~ tourner qc en dérision

derisive [dɪ'raɪsɪv] *adj* dérisoire

derisory [dɪ'raɪsəri] *adj* dérisoire

derivation [ˌderɪ'veɪʃən] *n* **1.** (*origin*) origine *f* **2.** (*process of evolving*) dérivation *f*

derivative [dɪ'rɪvətɪv, *Am:* dɪ'rɪvət̬ɪv] **I.** *adj pej* dérivatif(-ive) **II.** *n* dérivé *m*

derive [dɪ'raɪv] **I.** *vt* **to** ~ **sth from sth** tirer qc de qc **II.** *vi* **to** ~ **from sth** (*a word*) dériver de qc; (*custom*) venir de qc

dermatitis [ˌdɜ:mə'taɪtɪs, *Am:* ˌdɜ:rmə'taɪt̬əs] *n no pl* dermatose *f*

dermatologist *n* dermatologue *mf*

dermatology [ˌdɜ:mə'tɒlədʒi, *Am:* ˌdɜ:rmə'tɑ:lə-] *n no pl* dermatologie *f*

derogate ['derəʊgeɪt, *Am:* 'derə-] *vi form* **to** ~ **from sth** déroger à qc

derogation *n no pl* dérogation *f*

derogatory [dɪ'rɒgətəri, *Am:* dɪ'rɑ:gətɔ:ri] *adj* dédaigneux(-euse)

derrick ['derɪk] *n* **1.** (*crane*) grue *f* **2.** (*tower over an oil well*) derrick *m*

DES [ˌdi:i:'es] *n Brit abbr of* **Department of Education and Science** ministère *m* de l'Éducation

desalinate [ˌdi:'sælɪneɪt] *vt* dessaler

desalination *n no pl* dessalement *m*

desalination plant *n* dispositif *m* de dessalement

descale [ˌdi:'skeɪl] *vt* détartrer

descant ['deskænt, *Am:* 'deskænt] *n* MUS soprano *mf*

descend [dɪ'send] **I.** *vi* **1.** (*go down*) descendre **2.** (*fall: darkness*) tomber **3.** (*deteriorate*) **to** ~ **into sth** tomber en qc **4.** (*lower oneself*) s'abaisser **5. to** ~ **from sb/sth** provenir de qn/qc **II.** *vt* descendre

descendant [dɪ'sendənt] *n* descendant(e) *m(f)*

descent [dɪ'sent] *n* **1.** (*movement*) descente *f* **2.** *fig* (*decline*) déclin *m* **3.** *no pl* (*ancestry*) descendance *f*

describe [dɪ'skraɪb] *vt* décrire; **to** ~ **sb as sth** qualifier qn de qc

description [dɪ'skrɪpʃən] *n* description *f;* **of every** ~ en tout genre; **to answer a** ~ **of sb/sth** correspondre à la description de qn/qc

descriptive [dɪ'skrɪptɪv] *adj* descriptif(-ive); (*statistics*) parlant(e)

desecrate ['desɪkreɪt] *vt* profaner

desecration *n no pl* profanation *f*

desegregate [ˌdi:'segrɪgeɪt] *vt* **to** ~ **schools** mettre fin à la ségrégation raciale dans les écoles

desegregation *n no pl* déségrégation *f*

desensitize [ˌdi:'sensɪtaɪz] *vt Am a.* MED désensibiliser

desert[1] [dɪ'zɜ:t, *Am:* -'zɜ:rt] **I.** *vi* déserter; **to** ~ **to the enemy** passer dans le camp ennemi **II.** *vt* **1.** (*run away from duty: the army, one's post*) déserter **2.** (*abandon*) abandonner

desert[2] ['dezət, *Am:* -ɚt] *n a. fig* désert *m*

deserted *adj* désert(e)

deserter *n* déserteur *m*

desertification [dɪˌzɜ:tɪfɪ'keɪʃən, *Am:* dɪˌzɜ:rt̬ə-] *n no pl* désertification *f*

desertion [dɪ'zɜ:ʃən, *Am:* dɪ'zɜ:r-] *n a. fig* désertion *f*

desert island *n* île *f* déserte

deserts [dɪ'zɜ:ts, *Am:* dɪ'zɜ:rts] *npl* mérites *mpl;* **to get one's** (**just**) ~ recevoir ce que l'on mérite

deserve [dɪ'zɜ:v, *Am:* dɪ'zɜ:rv] *vt* mériter

deservedly *adv* de façon méritée

deserving *adj* **1.** (*meritorious*) méritoire **2.** *form* (*worthy*) **to be** ~ **of sth** être digne de qc

design [dɪ'zaɪn] **I.** *vt* **1.** (*conceive*) concevoir **2.** (*draw*) dessiner **II.** *n* **1.** (*plan or drawing*) concept *m* **2.** (*art of creating designs*) design *m* **3.** (*pattern*) motif *m* **4.** *no pl* (*intention*) intention *f;* **to do sth by** ~ faire qc exprès **III.** *adj inv* (*fault, feature*) de style; (*chair, table*) de design

designate ['dezɪgneɪt] **I.** *vt* désigner; **to** ~ **sth for sb/sth** destiner qc à qn/qc **II.** *adj after n* désigné(e)

designation *n* désignation *f*

designedly *adv* intentionnellement

designer **I.** *n* **1.** (*creator*) désigner *mf* **2.** FASHION styliste *mf* **3.** THEAT décorateur, -trice *m, f* **II.** *adj* (*furniture*) de créateur; (*clothing*) de marque

designer drug *n* drogue *f* de synthèse

designing **I.** *n* conception *f* **II.** *adj pej* sournois(e)

desirable *adj* **1.** (*sought-after*) souhaitable **2.** (*sexually attractive*) désirable

desire [dɪ'zaɪəʳ, *Am:* dɪ'zaɪɚ] **I.** *vt* désirer; **to** ~ **that** désirer que *+subj* **II.** *n* désir *m;* **to express the** ~ **to** *+infin* exprimer le désir de *+infin;* **to be the object of sb's** ~ être l'objet de désir de qn

desirous [dɪ'zaɪərəs, *Am:* dɪ'zaɪrəs] *adj form* **to be** ~ **of doing sth** être désireux de faire qc

desist [dɪ'sɪst] *vi form* renoncer; **to** ~ **from doing sth** renoncer à faire qc

desk [desk] *n* **1.** (*table for writing on, etc*) bureau *m;* **to arrive on sb's** ~ arriver sur le bureau de qn **2.** (*service counter*) caisse *f;* **to work on the** ~ travailler à la caisse **3.** (*news-

paper office or section) rédaction *f*
desktop ['desktɒp, *Am:* -tɑːp -] *n* INFOR ~ (**computer**) ordinateur *m* de table
desktop publishing *n* éditique *f*
desolate ['desələt] *adj* désolé(e)
desolation [ˌdesə'leɪʃən] *n no pl* désolation *f*
despair [dɪ'speəʳ, *Am:* dɪ'sper] **I.** *n no pl* (*feeling of hopelessness*) désespoir *m;* **to be in ~ about sth** être désespéré par qc; **to drive sb to ~** conduire qn au désespoir; **to the ~ of sb** au désespoir de qn ►**to be the ~ of sb** être le désespoir de qn **II.** *vi* désespérer; **to ~ of sb/sth** s'affliger de qn/qc
despairing *adj pej* désespéré(e)
despatch [dɪ'spætʃ] *s.* **dispatch**
desperado [ˌdespə'rɑːdəʊ, *Am:* -doʊ] <-s *o* -es> *n* desperado *m*
desperate ['despərət] *adj* **1.** (*risking all on a small chance: attempt, measure, solution*) désespéré(e) **2.** (*serious: situation*) désespéré(e) **3.** (*great*) extrême; **to be in ~ straits** être dans une grande détresse **4.** (*having great need or desire*) **to be ~ for sth** être prêt à tout pour qc
desperation *n no pl* désespoir *m;* **to drive sb to ~** conduire qn au désespoir
despicable [dɪ'spɪkəbl] *adj* méprisable
despise [dɪ'spaɪz] *vt* mépriser
despite [dɪ'spaɪt] *prep* malgré; **~ having done sth** bien qu'ayant fait qc
despoil [dɪ'spɔɪl] *vt* dévaliser
despondent [dɪ'spɒndənt, *Am:* -'spɑːn-] *adj* découragé(e); **to become ~** se décourager
despot ['despɒt, *Am:* -pət] *n a. iron* despote *m*
despotic *adj* despotique
despotism ['despətɪzəm] *n no pl* despotisme *m*
dessert [dɪ'zɜːt, *Am:* -'zɜːrt] *n* dessert *m*
dessertspoon *n* cuillère *f* à dessert
destabilization *n no pl* déstabilisation *f*
destabilize [ˌdiː'steɪbəlaɪz] *vt* déstabiliser
destination [ˌdestɪ'neɪʃən] *n* destination *f*
destiny ['destɪni] *n* destin *m;* **to be a victim of ~** être une victime du destin; **to escape one's ~** échapper à son destin; **to fight against ~** lutter contre le destin
destitute ['destɪtjuːt, *Am:* -tuːt] **I.** *adj* sans ressources; **~ people** gens *mpl* dans le besoin **II.** *n* manque *m;* **the ~** *pl* la misère
destitution *n no pl* misère *f*
destroy [dɪ'strɔɪ] *vt* **1.** (*demolish: evidence*) démolir **2.** (*kill*) abattre; (*kill humanely: a dog, horse*) endormir **3.** (*ruin*) détruire
destroyer *n* **1.** (*fast military ship*) destroyer *m* **2.** (*person*) destructeur, -trice *m, f*
destructible [dɪ'strʌktəbl] *adj* destructible
destruction [dɪ'strʌkʃən] *n no pl* destruction *f;* **to leave a trail of ~** faire des ravages derrière soi
destructive [dɪ'strʌktɪv] *adj* destructeur(-trice)
destructiveness *n no pl* **1.** (*tendancy: of person*) penchant *m* destructeur **2.** (*effect: of an explosive, war*) effet *m* destructeur
desulphurization [diːˌsʌlfəraɪ'zeɪʃən] *n no pl* CHEM désulfuration *f*
desultory ['desəltəri, *Am:* -tɔːri] *adj form, liter* timide
Det *n abbr of* **Detective** détective *m*
detach [dɪ'tætʃ] *vt* détacher
detachable *adj* détachable; (*collar*) amovible
detached *adj* **1.** (*separated*) séparé(e) **2.** (*disinterested*) détaché(e); (*impartial*) neutre
detachment *n a.* MIL détachement *m*
detail ['diːteɪl, *Am:* dɪ'teɪl] **I.** *n* détail *m;* **in ~** en détail; **to give ~s about sth** donner des renseignements sur qc; **to go into ~** entrer dans les détails; **to take down ~s** prendre des coordonnées *fpl* **II.** *vt* **1.** (*explain fully*) détailler **2.** (*tell*) mentionner **3.** (*assign a duty to sb*) **to ~ sb to** +*infin* affecter qn à +*infin*
detailed *adj* détaillé(e)
detain [dɪ'teɪn] **I.** *vi* retenir **II.** *vt* **1.** (*hold as prisoner*) détenir; **to ~ sb without trial** être emprisonné sans jugement **2.** *form* (*delay*) retarder **3.** *form* (*keep waiting*) faire patienter
detainee [ˌdiːteɪ'niː] *n* détenu(e) *m(f)*
detect [dɪ'tekt] *vt* **1.** (*discover*) découvrir **2.** (*discover presence of*) détecter la présence de **3.** (*sense presence of*) percevoir la présence de
detectable *adj* **1.** (*able to be found*) détectable **2.** (*discernible*) palpable
detection *n no pl* détection *f*
detective [dɪ'tektɪv] *n* **1.** (*police*) inspecteur *m* de police **2.** (*private*) détective *m* privé
detective inspector *n* inspecteur *m* de police judiciaire **detective novel** *n* roman *m* policier **detective story** *n* histoire *f* policière **detective superintendent** *n* commissaire *m* de police judiciaire
detector *n* détecteur *m*
detention [dɪ'tenʃən] *n* **1.** (*being held in custody*) garde *f* à vue **2.** (*act*) détention *f* **3.** (*school punishment*) retenue *f*
detention centre *n* **1.** (*for youths*) centre *m* de détention pour mineurs **2.** (*for refugees*) centre *m* de détention pour réfugiés politiques
deter [dɪ'tɜːʳ, *Am:* -'tɜːr] <-rr-> *vt* **to ~ sb from doing sth** décourager qn de faire qc
detergent [dɪ'tɜːdʒənt, *Am:* -'tɜːr] *n* détergent *m;* (*for clothes*) lessive *f*
deteriorate [dɪ'tɪərɪəreɪt, *Am:* -'tɪrɪ-] *vi* se détériorer
deterioration *n no pl* détérioration *f*
determinable *adj* déterminable
determinant [dɪ'tɜːmɪnənt, *Am:* -'tɜːr-] **I.** *n* déterminant *m* **II.** *adj* déterminant(e)
determinate [dɪ'tɜːmɪnət, *Am:* -'tɜːr-] *adj* **1.** (*limited*) limité(e) **2.** (*of specific scope*) déterminé(e)
determination *n no pl* **1.** (*resolution*) résolution *f* **2.** (*direction towards an aim*) détermination *f*
determine [dɪ'tɜːmɪn, *Am:* -'tɜːr-] **I.** *vi*

D

1. (*decide*) décider 2. (*come to an end*) conclure II. *vt* 1. (*decide*) déterminer 2. (*settle*) régler 3. (*find out*) établir 4. (*influence*) dépendre de 5. (*terminate*) conclure

determined *adj* déterminé(e); **to be ~ to** +*infin* être décidé à +*infin*

deterrence [dɪ'terəns] *n no pl* dissuasion *f*

deterrent [dɪ'terənt] I. *n* dissuasion *f*; **to act as a ~ to sb** dissuader qn II. *adj* dissuasif(-ive)

detest [dɪ'test] *vt* détester

detestable *adj form* détestable

detestation *n no pl, form* haine *f*

dethrone [ˌdiː'θrəʊn, *Am:* dɪ'θroʊn] *vt* détrôner

detonate ['detəneɪt] I. *vi* détoner II. *vt* faire détoner

detonation *n* détonation *f*

detonator *n* détonateur *m*

detour ['diːtʊəʳ, *Am:* 'diːtʊr] *n* détour *m*; **to make** [*o* **take**] **a ~** faire un détour

detoxify [dɪ'tɒksɪfaɪ, *Am:* diː'tɑːk-] *vt* désintoxiquer

detract [dɪ'trækt] I. *vi* (*devalue*) **to ~ from sth** diminuer qc; **to ~ from sb's achievements** minimaliser les performances de qn II. *vt* (*take away*) enlever; **to ~ public attention from sth** détourner l'attention du public de qc

detractor *n* détracteur *m*

detriment ['detrɪmənt] *n no pl* détriment *m*; **to the ~ of sth** au détriment de qc

detrimental *adj* néfaste

detritus [dɪ'traɪtəs, *Am:* -t̬əs] *n no pl* 1. (*small fragments*) détritus *m* 2. (*debris*) ordures *fpl*

deuce[1] [djuːs, *Am:* duːs] *n* 1. (*two on cards or die*) deux 2. (*score in tennis*) égalité *f*; **to be at ~** être à égalité

deuce[2] [djuːs, *Am:* duːs] *n* (*devil*) **what the ~ are you doing?** que diable fais-tu?; **how the ~ are we going to make it?** comment diable allons-nous y arriver?

devaluate [ˌdiː'væljueɪt] *vt s.* **devalue**

devaluation *n* dévaluation *f*

devalue [ˌdiː'væljuː] *vt* 1. (*reduce value of*) déprécier 2. (*reduce relative value of currency*) dévaluer

devastate ['devəsteɪt] *vt* dévaster; (*person*) bouleverser; (*hopes*) anéantir

devastating *adj* 1. (*causing destruction*) dévastateur(-trice) 2. (*powerful*) puissant(e) 3. (*with great effect*) ravageur(-euse)

devastation *n no pl* 1. (*destruction*) dévastation *f* 2. (*being devastated*) désespoir *m*

develop [dɪ'veləp] I. *vi* 1. (*grow, evolve*) *a. fig* se développer; **to ~ into sth** devenir qc; **to ~ out of sth** croître de qc 2. (*become apparent*) se manifester; (*event*) se produire; (*illness*) se déclarer; (*feeling*) naître; (*hole*) se former II. *vt* 1. (*grow, expand*) *a. fig* développer 2. (*acquire*) acquérir; (*infection, habit*) contracter; (*flu, cold*) attraper; (*cancer*) développer 3. (*improve*) développer; (*city*) aménager; (*region*) mettre en valeur; (*symptoms*) présenter; **to ~ sth into sth** transformer qc en qc 4. (*create*) créer 5. (*catch*) attraper; **to ~ an allergy to sth** devenir allergique à qc 6. (*build*) construire 7. PHOT, MAT développer 8. MUS élaborer

developed *adj* développé(e)

developer *n* 1. (*sb who develops*) adolescent(e) *m(f)* 2. (*person that develops land*) promoteur, -trice *m, f* 3. (*company*) compagnie *f* de construction 4. PHOT révélateur *m*

developing *adj* croissant(e)

developing country *n* pays *m* en voie de développement

development *n* 1. (*process*) développement *m* 2. (*growth*) croissance *f* économique 3. (*growth stage*) élaboration *f* 4. (*new event*) développement *m* 5. (*progress*) progrès *m*; (*of a product*) élaboration *f* 6. (*building of*) construction *f* 7. (*building on: of land*) développement *m* 8. (*industrialization*) développement *m* industriel 9. MUS élaboration *f* 10. GAMES mouvement *m*

deviant ['diːviənt] *adj* déviant(e)

deviate ['diːvieɪt] I. *n* déviation *f* II. *vi* **to ~ from sth** 1. (*depart from norm*) s'écarter de qc 2. (*go in another direction*) dévier de qc

deviation *n* 1. (*divergence*) déviation *f*; (*from the mean*) divergence *f* 2. (*compass difference*) différence *f*

device [dɪ'vaɪs] *n* 1. (*mechanism*) machine *f* 2. (*method*) moyen *m*; **a literary/rhetorical ~** un outil littéraire/rhétorique 3. (*bomb*) bombe *f* 4. INFOR périphérique *m* ►**to leave sb to their own ~s** laisser qn se débrouiller seul

devil ['devəl] *n* 1. *no pl* (*Satan*) **the Devil** le Diable; **to be possessed by the Devil** être possédé par le Démon 2. (*evil spirit*) diable *m* 3. *inf* (*wicked person*) démon *m* 4. (*mischevious person*) diable, -esse *m, f*; **be a ~** *inf* être malin; **cheeky ~** malin singe *m*; **lucky ~** veinard *m* 5. (*difficult thing*) **to have a ~ of a job doing sth** avoir de la peine à faire qc 6. (*feisty energy*) énergie *f* débordante; **like the ~** comme un possédé 7. (*indicating surprise*) que diable!; **who/what/where/how the ~...?** qui/que/où/comment diable...? 8. *Am* (*exploited hack*) nègre *m* ►**give the ~ his <u>due</u>** il faut admettre que...; **~ take the <u>hindmost</u>** sauve qui peut!; **between the ~ and the deep blue <u>sea</u>** entre Charybde et Scylla; **<u>there'll</u> be the ~ to pay** les retombées seront rudes; **to <u>go</u> to the ~** aller au diable; **to <u>play</u> the ~ with sth** jouer avec le feu; **<u>speak</u> of the ~** en parlant du loup

devilish *adj* 1. (*evil*) mauvais(e) 2. (*mischievous*) malin(e) 3. (*very difficult*) fastidieux(-euse) 4. (*terrible*) horrible 5. (*very clever*) démoniaque

devil-may-care *adj* insouciant(e)

devilment, devilry *n no pl* diablerie *f*; **to be up to ~** méditer un mauvais coup

devious ['diːviəs] *adj* 1. (*dishonest*) malhon-

nête **2.** (*winding*) détourné(e)
devise [dɪ'vaɪz] **I.** *n* legs *m* **II.** *vt* **1.** (*plan*) élaborer **2.** (*leave property via a will*) léguer
devoid [dɪ'vɔɪd] *adj* **to be ~ of sth** être dénué de qc
devolution [ˌdiːvə'luːʃən, *Am:* ˌdevə'luː-] *n no pl* **1.** (*decentralisation of power*) délégation *f* **2.** POL décentralisation *f* **3.** (*transference of wealth*) dévolution *f*
devolve [dɪ'vɒlv, *Am:* dɪ'vɑːlv] **I.** *vi* **1.** (*transfer*) transférer **2.** (*descend*) déléguer **II.** *vt* déléguer; **to ~ sth on sb** donner la responsabilité de qc à qn
devote [dɪ'vəʊt, *Am:* -'voʊt] *vt* consacrer; **to ~ sth to sb/sth** consacrer qc à qn/qc; **to ~ oneself to sth** se vouer à qc
devoted *adj* dévoué(e)
devotee [ˌdevə'tiː, *Am:* -ə'tiː] *n* **1.** (*supporter*) partisan *m* **2.** (*admirer*) admirateur *m* **3.** (*advocate*) défenseur *m*
devotion [dɪ'vəʊʃən, *Am:* dɪ'voʊ-] *n no pl* **1.** (*loyalty*) fidélité *f* **2.** (*affection*) tendresse *f* **3.** (*admiration*) admiration *f* **4.** (*great attachment*) dévouement *m* **5.** (*religious attachment*) dévotion *f*
devotional *adj* (*book*) de prière
devour [dɪ'vaʊəʳ, *Am:* dɪ'vaʊɚ] *vt* **1.** (*eat eagerly*) dévorer **2.** (*engulf*) ravager **3.** (*consume quickly*) engloutir **4.** *fig* dévorer; **to be ~ed by sth** être dévoré par qc
devouring *adj* dévorant(e)
devout [dɪ'vaʊt] *adj* **1.** (*strongly religious*) dévot(e) **2.** (*compulsive*) fervent(e)
dew [djuː, *Am:* duː] *n no pl* rosée *f*
DEW *n Am* MIL *abbr of* **distant early warning ~ line** couverture *f* radar (*de l'Arctique*)
dewdrop *n* goutte *f* de rosée
dewy *adj* couvert(e) de rosée
dexterity [ˌdek'sterəti, *Am:* -əṱi] *n no pl* **1.** (*skillful handling*) habileté *f* **2.** (*right-handedness*) dextérité *f*
dexterous ['dekstərəs] *adj* habile
dextrose ['dekstrəʊs, *Am:* -stroʊs] *n no pl* dextrose *f*
dextrous ['dekstrəs] *adj s.* **dexterous**
diabetes [ˌdaɪə'biːtiːz, *Am:* -ṱəs] *n no pl* diabète *m*
diabetic [ˌdaɪə'betɪk, *Am:* -'beṱ-] **I.** *n* diabétique *m* **II.** *adj* **1.** (*who has diabetes*) diabétique **2.** (*for diabetics*) pour diabétiques
diabolic [ˌdaɪə'bɒlɪk, *Am:* -'bɑːlɪk], **diabolical** *adj Am* **1.** (*of Devil*) diabolique **2.** (*evil*) démoniaque **3.** *inf* (*very bad*) infernal(e)
diadem ['daɪədem] *n* **1.** (*crown*) diadème *m* **2.** (*wreath*) couronne *f*
diagnose ['daɪəgnəʊz, *Am:* ˌdaɪəg'noʊs] *vt* diagnostiquer
diagnosis [ˌdaɪəg'nəʊsɪs, *Am:* -'noʊ-] <-ses> *n* **1.** (*identification*) diagnostic *m* **2.** (*separation into species*) diagnose *f*
diagnostic [ˌdaɪəg'nɒstɪk, *Am:* -'nɑːstɪk] **I.** *n* diagnostic *m* **II.** *adj* diagnostique
diagonal [daɪ'ægənl] **I.** *n* diagonale *f* **II.** *adj* diagonal(e)
diagram ['daɪəgræm] **I.** *n* **1.** (*drawing*) schéma *m* **2.** (*plan*) carte *f* **3.** (*chart*) diagramme *m* **4.** MAT, PHYS figure *f* **II.** <-mm-> *vt* dessiner
dial ['daɪəl] **I.** *n* **1.** (*clock face*) cadran *m* **2.** (*disc on a telephone*) cadran *m* téléphonique **3.** (*movable plate*) boussole *f* **4.** *Brit, inf* (*face*) visage *m* **II.** <*Brit* -ll- *o Am* -l-> *vi* faire le numéro; **to ~ direct** appeler directement **III.** *vt* (*a number*) composer; (*a country, a person*) avoir
dialect ['daɪəlekt] *n* dialecte *m*
dialectal *adj* dialectal(e)
dialectical [ˌdaɪə'lektɪkəl] *adj* dialectique
dialog *n Am*, **dialogue** ['daɪəlɒg, *Am:* -lɑːg] *n* **1.** (*conversation*) discussion *f* **2.** LIT, THEAT, POL dialogue *m*; **to engage in ~** s'engager dans un dialogue
dialogue box *n* INFOR boîte *f* de dialogue
dial-up service *n* INFOR service *m* d'appels
dialysis [daɪ'æləsɪs] *n no pl* dialyse *f*
diameter [daɪ'æmɪtəʳ, *Am:* -əṱɚ] *n* **1.** (*line*) diamètre *m* **2.** (*magnifying measurement*) grossissement *m*
diametrically [ˌdaɪə'metrɪkəli] *adv* diamétralement
diamond ['daɪəmənd] *n* **1.** (*precious stone*) diamant *m* **2.** (*rhombus*) losange *m* **3.** (*card with diamond symbol*) carreau *m* **4.** (*glittering particle*) poussière *f* de diamant **5.** (*tool for cutting glass*) machine *f* à tailler le diamant **6.** (*baseball field*) terrain *m* de base-ball
diamond anniversary *n* noces *fpl* de diamant **diamond cutting** *n* taille *f* de diamant
diaper ['daɪəpəʳ, *Am:* -pɚ] *n Am* (*nappy*) couche *f*
diaphragm ['daɪəfræm] *n* diaphragme *m*
diarist ['daɪərɪst] *n* auteur *m* de journal intime
diarrhea, **diarrhoea** [ˌdaɪə'rɪə, *Am:* -'riːə] *n no pl* diarrhée *f*
diary ['daɪəri] *n* **1.** (*journal*) journal *m* intime; **to keep a ~** avoir un journal intime **2.** (*planner*) agenda *m*
diatonic [ˌdaɪə'tɒnɪk, *Am:* -'tɑːnɪk] *adj* MUS diatonique
dice [daɪs] **I.** *n* **1.** (*cubes with spots*) dé *m*; **to roll the ~** faire rouler le dé **2.** (*game with dice*) dés *mpl* **3.** (*food in small cubes*) cube *m* ►**no ~!** *Am, inf* c'est hors de question! **II.** *vi* risquer ►**to ~ with death** risquer la mort **III.** *vt* **1.** (*cut into cubes*) couper en dés **2.** *Aus* (*reject*) rejeter
dicey ['daɪsi] <-ier, -iest> *adj Brit, Aus, inf* risqué(e)
dichotomy [daɪ'kɒtəmi, *Am:* -'kɑːṱə-] *n form* dichotomie *f*
dick [dɪk] *n vulg* **1.** (*penis*) bite *f* **2.** (*stupid person*) connard *m*
dickens ['dɪkɪnz] *npl inf* diable *m*; **what the ~...?** que diable...?

D

dickey, **dicky** *adj inf* fragile
Dictaphone® ['dɪktəfəʊn, *Am:* -foʊn] *n* dictaphone *m*
dictate ['dɪkteɪt] **I.** *vi* **1.** (*command*) dicter; **to ~ to sb** imposer à qn **2.** (*say sth to be written down*) dicter **II.** *vt* **1.** (*give order*) dicter **2.** (*make necessary*) imposer **3.** (*say sth to be written down*) dicter
dictation *n* dictée *f*
dictator *n* **1.** (*sb who dictates a text*) *a.* POL dictateur *m* **2.** (*bossy person*) despote *m*
dictatorial *adj pej* dictatorial(e)
dictatorship *n* dictature *f*
diction ['dɪkʃən] *n no pl* diction *f*
dictionary ['dɪkʃənəri, *Am:* -eri] *n* dictionnaire *m*
did [dɪd] *pt of* **do**
didactic [dɪ'dæktɪk, *Am:* daɪ-] *adj* **1.** (*to instruct*) didactique **2.** (*to teach a moral*) moral(e)
diddle ['dɪdl] **I.** *vi inf* **to ~ around** traînasser **II.** *vt inf* **1.** (*cheat*) rouler; **to be ~d out of sth** se faire rouler de qc **2.** (*falsify*) trafiquer
didn't [dɪdənt] = **did not** *s.* **do**
die¹ [daɪ] *n* **1.** (*one of a set of dice*) dé *m* **2.** TECH matrice *f* ►**as straight as ~** honnête; **the ~ is cast** les dés sont jetés
die² [daɪ] <dying, died> **I.** *vi* **1.** (*cease to be*) *a. fig, a. iron* mourir; **to ~ of cancer** mourir du cancer; **to ~ of starvation** mourir de faim; **to be dying to** +*infin* mourir d'envie de +*infin;* **to ~ for a drink** mourir de soif; **to ~ by one's own hand** se suicider **2.** (*go out*) disparaître; (*light*) s'éteindre **3.** *fig* (*fade: hope, feelings*) mourir **4.** (*end*) finir **5.** (*stop functioning*) s'arrêter ►**to ~ hard** disparaître avec difficulté; **never say ~** il ne faut jamais désespérer; **to do or ~** passer ou casser; **to ~ to do sth** mourir d'envie de faire qc; **to be dying for sth** avoir très envie de qc; **to ~ of boredom** mourir d'ennui; **something to ~ for** quelque chose qui fait mourir d'envie **II.** *vt* **to ~ a natural/violent death** mourir d'une mort naturelle/violente; **to ~ a hero's death** mourir en héros **2.** *Brit* **to ~ a/the death** faire un flop
◆**die away** *vi* disparaître; (*sobs*) cesser; (*sound*) s'éteindre; (*wind, anger*) s'estomper
◆**die down** *vi* baisser; (*sound*) s'éteindre; (*wind, emotion*) se calmer
◆**die off** *vi* mourir; (*species*) s'éteindre; (*customs*) se perdre
◆**die out** *vt* s'éteindre
diehard ['daɪhɑːd, *Am:* -hɑːrd] *n pej* invétéré(e)
diesel ['diːzəl, *Am:* -səl] *n no pl* diesel *m*
diesel engine *n* moteur *m* diesel **diesel oil** *n* essence *f* diesel
diet¹ ['daɪət] **I.** *n* **1.** (*what one eats and drinks*) alimentation *f* **2.** (*for medical reasons*) diète *f* **3.** (*to lose weight*) régime *m* **4.** *no pl* (*limited range*) pénurie *f* **II.** *vi* être au régime/à la diète **III.** *vt* mettre au régime
diet² ['daɪət] *n* HIST diète *f*
dietary *adj* alimentaire
dietary fibre *n* fibre *f* diététique
dietetic [ˌdaɪə'tetɪk, *Am:* -'ţeţ-] *adj* diététique
dietetics *n no pl* diététique *f*
dietician, **dietitian** *n* diététicien(ne) *m(f)*, diététiste *mf Québec*
differ ['dɪfəʳ, *Am:* -ɚ] *vi* **1.** (*be unlike*) **to ~ from sth** différer de qc **2.** (*disagree*) **to ~ with sb** être en désaccord avec qn
difference ['dɪfərənts] *n* **1.** (*state of being different*) différence *f;* **to make a big ~** faire une différence considérable; **not to make any ~** ne rien changer; **with a ~** qui sort de l'ordinaire **2.** (*disagreement*) différend *m;* (*of opinion*) divergence *f;* **to put aside ~s** mettre de côté les différends; **to settle ~s** aplanir les différends
different *adj* **1.** (*not the same*) différent(e) **2.** (*distinct*) distinct(e) **3.** (*unusual*) hors du commun ►**they're as ~ as chalk and cheese** *Brit, Aus* ils sont très différents l'un de l'autre; **to be as ~ as night and day** *Am* être le jour et la nuit
differential **I.** *n* **1.** (*difference*) *a.* MAT, TECH différentielle *f* **2.** (*difference in pay*) disparité *f;* **pay ~s** disparités salariales **II.** *adj* différentiel(le)
differentiate [ˌdɪfə'rentʃieɪt] **I.** *vi* faire la différence **II.** *vt* différencier
differentiation *n* **1.** (*distinguishing*) distinction *f* **2.** (*becoming different*) différenciation *f* **3.** (*specializing*) spécialisation *f*
difficult ['dɪfɪkəlt] *adj* difficile
difficulty <-ties> *n* **1.** *no pl* (*being difficult*) difficulté *f* **2.** (*much effort*) peine *f;* **with ~** avec peine **3.** (*problem*) problème *m;* **to encounter ~ties** faire face à des problèmes; **to be fraught with ~ties** être plein de difficultés; **to have ~ doing sth** *no pl* avoir de la peine à faire qc
diffident ['dɪfɪdənt] *adj* **1.** (*shy*) timide **2.** (*modest*) modeste
diffract [dɪ'frækt] *vt* diffracter
diffuse [dɪ'fjuːz] **I.** *vt, vi* **1.** (*disperse*) *a.* PHYS diffuser **2.** (*spread*) répandre **II.** *adj* **1.** (*spread out*) répandu(e) **2.** (*imprecise*) diffus(e) **3.** (*verbose*) verbeux(-euse)
diffusion *n no pl* diffusion *f*
dig [dɪg] **I.** *n* **1.** (*act of digging: in garden*) coup *m* de bêche **2.** (*poke*) coup *m* (de coude) **3.** (*excavation*) fouilles *fpl* **4.** *inf* (*critical, sarcastic remark*) pique *f;* **to have ~s at sb** lancer des piques à qn **5.** *pl, Brit, inf* (*lodgings*) chambre *f* meublée **II.** <-gg-, dug, dug> *vi* **1.** (*turn over ground*) creuser; (*in garden*) bêcher; **to ~ through sth** creuser qc; **to ~ for a bone** creuser pour chercher un os **2.** (*excavate: on a site*) faire des fouilles; **to ~ for sth** chercher qc **3.** (*search*) *a. fig* fouiller; **to ~ into the past** fouiller dans le passé ►**to ~ in one's heels** s'entêter **III.** *vt* **1.** (*move ground: hole,*

tunnel) creuser; (*garden*) bêcher **2.** (*excavate: site*) fouiller **3.** (*thrust*) enfoncer; **to ~ one's hands in(to) one's pockets** enfoncer ses mains dans les poches; **to ~ deep into one's pockets** gratter le fond de ses poches **4.** *inf* (*like*) **I ~ sth** qc me botte ►**to ~ one's own grave** creuser sa propre tombe; **to ~ oneself into a hole** se creuser un trou

◆**dig in** *vi* **1.** MIL se retrancher **2.** *inf* (*eat*) manger

◆**dig into** *vt always sep* (*search*) fouiller dans

◆**dig out** *vt a. fig* déterrer

◆**dig up** *vt a. fig* déterrer ►**to ~ the dirt on sb** déterrer des informations compromettantes sur qn

digest ['daɪdʒest] **I.** *n* condensé *m* **II.** *vi* digérer **III.** *vt* **1.** (*break down*) *a. fig* digérer **2.** (*assimilate*) assimiler

digestible *adj* digeste

digestion *n* digestion *f*

digestive **I.** *adj* digestif(-ive) **II.** *n* gâteau *m* sablé

digger ['dɪgəʳ, *Am:* -ɚ] *n* **1.** (*machine*) excavatrice *f;* (*for the garden*) bêche *f* **2.** (*person*) mineur *m* **3.** *Aus* (*gold miner*) chercheur *m* d'or **4.** *Aus, inf* (*soldier*) soldat *m*

digit ['dɪdʒɪt] *n* **1.** (*number from 0 to 9*) chiffre *m* **2.** (*finger*) doigt *m* **3.** (*toe*) orteil *m*

digital *adj* numérique

digitally *adv* INFOR **to encode ~** utiliser un codage numérique

digital mobile telephony *n* téléphonie *f* numérique mobile **Digital Versatile Disk** *n* disque *m* numérique polyvalent

digitize ['dɪdʒɪtaɪz] *vt* numériser

digitizer *n* INFOR numériseur *m*

dignified *adj* digne

dignify ['dɪgnɪfaɪ] <-ie-> *vt* honorer

dignitary ['dɪgnɪtəri, *Am:* -nəter-] <-ries> *n* dignitaire *m*

dignity ['dɪgnəti, *Am:* -t̬i] *n no pl* **1.** (*respect*) dignité *f* **2.** (*state worthy of respect*) honneur *f*

digress [daɪ'gres] *vi* **to ~ from sth** s'écarter de qc

digressive *adj* disgressif(-ive)

dike [daɪk] *n* fossé *m*

dilapidated [dɪ'læpɪdeɪtɪd, *Am:* -t̬ɪd] *adj* délabré(e)

dilate [daɪ'leɪt, *Am:* 'daɪleɪt] **I.** *vi* se dilater **II.** *vt* dilater

dilation *n no pl* dilatation *f*

dilatory ['dɪlətəri, *Am:* -tɔːri] *adj form* dilatoire; **to be ~ in doing sth** prendre son temps pour faire qc

dilemma [dɪ'lemə] *n* dilemme *m;* **he is in a ~ about** cela lui pose un dilemme

dilettante [ˌdɪlɪ'tænti, *Am:* -ə'tɑːnt] *n* <-s *o* -ti> *pej* dilettante *mf*

diligence ['dɪlɪdʒəns] *n no pl* diligence

diligent *adj* (*using a lot of effort*) appliqué(e)

dill [dɪl] *n no pl* aneth *m*

dilly-dally *vi* **1.** *inf* (*dawdle*) lambiner **2.** *inf* (*vacillate*) hésiter

dilute [daɪ'ljuːt, *Am:* -'luːt] **I.** *vt* **1.** (*add liquid*) diluer **2.** *fig* (*reduce*) édulcorer **II.** *adj* dilué(e)

dilution *n no pl* **1.** (*diluting*) dilution *f* **2.** *fig* (*weakening*) baisse *f*

dim [dɪm] **I.** <-mm-> *vi* (*lights*) baisser **II.** *vt* baisser; **to ~ the headlights** se mettre en code **III.** <-mm-> *adj* **1.** (*not bright*) sombre; (*light*) faible; (*colour*) terne **2.** (*unclear: view*) faible; (*memory*) vague **3.** *fig* (*stupid*) borné(e) ►**to take a ~ view of sth** ne pas apprécier qc

dime [daɪm] *n* pièce *f* de dix cents ►**a ~ a dozen** *Am* treize à la douzaine

dimension [ˌdaɪ'mentʃən, *Am:* dɪ'mentʃən] **I.** *n a. fig* dimension *f* **II.** *vt* mesurer

dimensional *in compounds* **two/three-~** à deux/trois dimensions

diminish [dɪ'mɪnɪʃ] **I.** *vi* diminuer; (*influence*) baisser; **to ~ greatly in value** perdre beaucoup de sa valeur **II.** *vt* diminuer; (*influence*) affaiblir

diminished responsibility *n* responsabilité *f* diminuée

diminution [ˌdɪmɪ'njuːʃən, *Am:* -ə'nuː-] *n* diminution *f*

diminutive [dɪ'mɪnjʊtɪv, *Am:* -jət̬ɪv] **I.** *n* diminutif *m* **II.** *adj* (*small*) minuscule

dimmer ['dɪməʳ, *Am:* -ɚ], **dimmer switch** *n* variateur *m* (d'intensité)

dimness *n no pl* obscurité *f*

dimple ['dɪmpl] **I.** *n* **1.** (*dent in skin*) fossette *f* **2.** (*dent*) ride *f* **II.** *vt* rider

din [dɪn] **I.** *n no pl* vacarme *m* **II.** *vt* **to ~ sth into sb** faire rentrer qc dans la tête de qn

dine [daɪn] *vi form* dîner

◆**dine on** *vi* manger au dîner

diner ['daɪnəʳ, *Am:* -nɚ] *n* **1.** (*person*) dîneur, -euse *m, f* **2.** *Am* (*restaurant*) petit restaurant *m*

dinghy ['dɪŋgi, *Am:* 'dɪŋi] *n* <-ghies> canot *m* pneumatique

dingo ['dɪŋgəʊ, *Am:* -goʊ] *n* <-es> dingo *m*

dingy ['dɪndʒi] <-ier, -iest> *adj* miteux(-euse)

dining room *n* salle *f* à manger

dinky[1] ['dɪŋki] <-kies> *n abbr of* **double income no kids** *personne issue d'un ménage à deux revenus et sans enfant*

dinky[2] ['dɪŋki] *adj* **1.** (*dainty*) mignon(ne) **2.** *Am* (*insignificant*) de rien du tout

dinner ['dɪnəʳ, *Am:* -ɚ] *n* **1.** (*evening meal*) dîner *m,* café *m* complet *Suisse,* souper *m Belgique, Québec, Suisse* **2.** (*lunch*) déjeuner *m*

dinner jacket *n* smoking *m* **dinner party** *n* dîner *m* **dinner service**, **dinner set** *n* service *m* (de table) **dinner table** *n* table *f* (de salle à manger) **dinner time** *n no pl* heure *f* du dîner; **at ~** à l'heure du dîner

dinosaur ['daɪnəsɔːʳ, *Am:* -sɔːr] *n* **1.** (*extinct reptile*) dinosaure *m* **2.** *fig* (*old-fashioned*) fossile *m*

dint [dɪnt] I. *n* marque *f;* **by ~ of sth** à force de qc II. *vt* cabosser

diocese ['daɪəsɪs] *n* diocèse *m*

dioxide [daɪ'ɒksaɪd, *Am:* -'ɑːk-] *n no pl* dioxide *m*

dioxin [daɪ'ɒksɪn, *Am:* -'ɑːk-] *n* dioxine *f*

dip [dɪp] I. *n* 1. (*instance of dipping*) trempage *m* 2. (*sudden drop*) chute *f;* (*of a road*) déclivité *f* 3. (*liquid*) bain *m* 4. (*brief swim*) plongeon *m* 5. (*cleaning liquid*) solution *f* nettoyante 6. (*brief study*) survol *m* rapide 7. (*angle made by magnetic field*) inclinaison *f* magnétique 8. (*angle of stratum*) pendage *m* 9. GASTR dip *m* II. *vi* 1. (*drop down: road*) descendre 2. (*decline: rates*) baisser 3. (*submerge and re-emerge*) plonger 4. (*lower: plane*) piquer III. *vt* 1. (*immerse*) tremper 2. (*put into*) **to ~ sth in sth** plonger qc dans qc 3. (*lower*) baisser 4. (*dim*) **to ~ one's headlights** se mettre en code 5. (*dye*) teindre 6. (*wash: sheep*) laver

◆**dip into** *vt always sep* puiser dans; **to ~ one's pocket** mettre la main à la poche

Dip. *n abbr of* **Diploma** diplôme *m*

diphtheria [dɪf'θɪəriə, *Am:* -'θɪri-] *n* diphtérie *f*

diphthong ['dɪfθɒŋ, *Am:* -θɑːŋ] *n* LING diphtongue *f*

diploma [dɪ'pləʊmə, *Am:* -'ploʊ-] *n* (*certificate*) diplôme

diplomacy *n no pl* diplomatie *f*

diplomat ['dɪpləmæt] *n* diplomate *mf*

diplomatic *adj* diplomatique

diplomatist *n s.* **diplomat**

dipper ['dɪpəʳ, *Am:* -ɚ] *n* ZOOL cincle *m*

dipsomania [ˌdɪpsəʊ'meɪniə, *Am:* -sə'-] *n no pl* MED dipsomanie *f*

dipsomaniac *n* MED dipsomane *mf*

dipstick ['dɪpstɪk] *n* 1. (*measuring rod*) jauge *f* 2. *inf* (*idiot*) imbécile *mf*

dip switch *n* AUTO basculeur *m* de phares

dire ['daɪəʳ, *Am:* 'daɪɚ] *adj* 1. (*terrible*) horrible 2. (*very bad*) mauvais(e) 3. (*serious*) sérieux(-euse) ►**to be in ~ straits** être dans une mauvaise passe

direct [dɪ'rekt] I. *vi* 1. THEAT faire de la mise en scène 2. CINE faire de la réalisation 3. MUS diriger II. *vt* 1. (*control: company*) diriger; (*traffic*) régler 2. (*command*) ordonner; **to ~ sb to** +*infin* ordonner à qn de +*infin;* **as ~ed** selon les instructions 3. (*aim in a direction*) diriger; **to ~ sth towards sth** diriger qc vers qc; **to ~ sb the way to sth** indiquer le chemin de qc à qn 4. (*address*) adresser; **to ~ a remark against sb** faire une remarque à l'intention de qn 5. CINE réaliser 6. THEAT mettre en scène 7. MUS diriger III. *adj* 1. (*straight, immediate*) direct(e); (*danger, cause*) immédiat(e); **in ~ sunlight** en plein soleil 2. (*clear*) direct(e); (*refusal*) catégorique; **the ~ opposite of sth** tout le contraire de qc 3. (*frank*) direct(e); (*person*) franc(he); (*refusal*) net(te) 4. (*without intermediary*) direct(e) IV. *adv* directement; (*broadcast*) en direct

direct action *n* action *f* directe **direct current** *n no pl* courant *m* continu **direct debit** *n* prélèvement *m* automatique **direct dial phone** *n* ligne *f* directe **direct discourse** *n Am* discours *m* direct **direct hit** *n* coup *m* au but

direction [dɪ'rekʃən] *n no pl* 1. (*supervision*) direction *f;* **under the ~ of** sous la direction de 2. CINE, THEAT mise *f* en scène 3. (*course*) orientation *f* 4. (*where sb is going to or from*) direction *f* 5. (*tendency*) sens *m*

directional *adj* directionnel(le)

directive [dɪ'rektɪv] *n form* directive *f*

directly I. *adv* 1. (*immediately*) immédiatement 2. (*shortly*) tout de suite 3. (*right after*) tout de suite après 4. (*frankly*) franchement II. *conj* aussitôt que

direct object *n* objet *m* direct

director *n* 1. ECON (*manager*) directeur, -trice *m, f* 2. CINE, THEAT metteur *mf* en scène 3. (*board member*) administrateur, -trice *m, f;* **board of ~s** conseil *m* d'administration

directorate [dɪ'rektərət] *n* 1. (*responsible department*) direction *f* 2. (*board of directors*) conseil *m* d'administration

directorship *n* direction *f*

directory [dɪ'rektəri] *n* 1. (*book*) annuaire *m;* **address ~** répertoire *m* d'adresses 2. INFOR répertoire *m;* **main ~** répertoire principal; **~ structure** arborescence *f*

directory enquiries *n Brit* (service *m* des) renseignements *mpl*

dirt [dɜːt, *Am:* dɜːrt] *n no pl* 1. (*unclean substance*) saleté; **white shows the ~** le blanc est salissant 2. (*earth*) terre *f* 3. (*bad language*) obscénité *f* 4. (*scandal*) ragots *mpl* 5. (*excrement*) excréments *mpl* 6. (*unclean condition*) crasse *f;* **to treat sb like ~** traiter qn comme un chien ►**to eat ~** ramper

dirt cheap *adj inf* vraiment pas cher(chère) **dirt road** *n Brit, Aus,* **dirt track** *n* chemin *m* de terre battue

dirty ['dɜːti, *Am:* 'dɜːrt̬i] I. *n Brit, Aus no pl* **to do the ~ on sb** faire une vacherie à qn II. *vt* salir III. <-ier, -iest> *adj* 1. (*unclean*) sale 2. (*causing to be dirty*) salissant(e); **to do the ~ work** *fig* faire le sale boulot 3. (*mean*) sale; **~ tricks campaign** une campagne pleine de coups bas 4. (*lewd: movie, book*) cochon(ne); (*look*) noir(e); (*old man*) lubrique; (*weekend*) coquin(e); **~ words** obscénités *fpl;* **~ talk** grossièretés *fpl* 5. (*not pure: colour*) sale; **a ~ grey colour** une couleur grisâtre IV. *adv Brit, inf* **a ~ great car** une super grosse voiture; **to play ~** donner des coups bas; **to talk ~** dire des gros mots; (*make explicit comments*) dire des cochonneries

disability [ˌdɪsə'bɪləti, *Am:* -ət̬i] *n* 1. (*incapacity*) handicap *m* 2. *no pl* (*condition of incapacity*) incapacité *f*

disable [dɪ'seɪbl] *vt* 1. (*make incapable of*

functioning) mettre hors service **2.** MED rendre infirme

disabled **I.** *npl* **the** ~ les handicapés **II.** *adj* handicapé(e)

disablement *n no pl* infirmité *f*

disabuse [ˌdɪsəˈbjuːz] *vt form* détromper

disadvantage [ˌdɪsədˈvɑːntɪdʒ, *Am:* -ˈvæntɪdʒ] **I.** *n* inconvénient *m;* **a social/educational** ~ un handicap social/scolaire; **to be at a** ~ être dans une position désavantageuse; **to be put at a** ~ être désavantagé; **to work to the** ~ **of sth** aller à l'encontre des intérêts de qc **II.** *vt* désavantager

disadvantaged *adj* défavorisé(e)

disadvantageous *adj* désavantageux(-euse)

disaffected [ˌdɪsəˈfektɪd] *adj* **1.** (*disloyal*) révolté(e) **2.** (*estranged*) mécontent(e)

disaffection [ˌdɪsəˈfekʃən] *n no pl* désaffection *f*

disagree [ˌdɪsəˈgriː] *vi* **1.** (*not agree*) ne pas être d'accord **2.** (*argue*) être en désaccord **3.** (*be different*) ne pas concorder **4.** (*have bad effect*) ne pas réussir

disagreeable *adj* désagréable

disagreement *n no pl* **1.** (*lack of agreement*) désaccord *m* **2.** (*argument*) différend *m;* **a** ~ **over sth** ils se sont disputés à propos de qc **3.** (*discrepancy*) divergence *f*

disallow [ˌdɪsəˈlaʊ] *vt* **1.** *a.* LAW rejeter **2.** SPORT refuser

disappear [ˌdɪsəˈpɪəʳ, *Am:* -ˈpɪr] *vi* **1.** (*vanish*) disparaître; **to** ~ **from sight** être perdu de vue **2.** (*become extinct*) disparaître; **to have all but ~ed** *fig* avoir quasiment disparu

disappearance *n no pl* disparition *f*

disappoint [ˌdɪsəˈpɔɪnt] *vt* décevoir; **to** ~ **sb's hopes** ne pas avoir été à la hauteur des espérances de qn

disappointed *adj* déçu(e); **to be** ~ **in sb/sth** être déçu par qn /qc

disappointing *adj* décevant(e)

disappointment *n* **1.** *no pl* (*dissatisfaction*) déception *f* **2.** (*sth or sb that disappoints*) **to be a** ~ **to sb** décevoir qn

disapprobation [ˌdɪsæprəʊˈbeɪʃən, *Am:* ˌdɪsˌæprəˈ-] *n no pl* désapprobation

disapproval *n* désapprobation *f*

disapprove [ˌdɪsəˈpruːv] *vi* ne pas être d'accord; **to** ~ **of sth** désapprouver qc

disarm [dɪsˈɑːm, *Am:* -ɑːrm] **I.** *vi* désarmer **II.** *vt* **1.** (*take weapons away*) désarmer **2.** (*remove fuse*) désamorcer **3.** (*placate*) calmer **4.** (*charm*) désarmer

disarmament *n no pl* désarmement *m*

disarming *adj* désarmant(e)

disarrange [ˌdɪsəˈreɪndʒ] *vt* mettre en désordre

disarray [ˌdɪsəˈreɪ] *n no pl* **1.** (*disorder*) désordre *m* **2.** (*confusion*) confusion *f;* **in a state of** ~ en plein désarroi

disaster [dɪˈzɑːstəʳ, *Am:* dɪˈzæstɚ] *n* **1.** (*huge misfortune*) désastre *m;* ~ **area** région *f* sinistrée; **natural/global** ~ catastrophe *f* naturelle/mondiale; **rail** ~ catastrophe *f* ferroviaire; **to avert** ~ prévenir les catastrophes **2.** (*failure*) désastre *m;* **to spell** ~ **for sth** signifier le désastre pour qn

disastrous [dɪˈzɑːstrəs, *Am:* dɪˈzæstrəs] *adj* **1.** (*causing disaster*) désastreux(-euse) **2.** (*very unsuccessful*) catastrophique

disband [dɪsˈbænd] **I.** *vt* dissoudre **II.** *vi* se dissoudre

disbelief [ˌdɪsbɪˈliːf] *n no pl* incrédulité *f*

disbelieve [ˌdɪsbɪˈliːv] *vt* ne pas croire

disbeliever *n* incrédule *mf*

disburse [dɪsˈbɜːs, *Am:* -ˈbɜːrs] *vt* débourser

disbursement *n* déboursement *m*

disc [dɪsk] *n a.* MED disque *m*

discard **I.** *n* GAMES défausse *f* **II.** *vt* **1.** (*reject*) se débarrasser de **2.** (*reject card*) défausser

disc brake *n* frein *m* à disque

discern [dɪˈsɜːn, *Am:* dɪˈsɜːrn] *vt form* **1.** (*perceive*) discerner **2.** (*distinguish*) distinguer **3.** (*make out*) percevoir

discernable, discernible *adj form* **1.** (*with senses*) visible **2.** (*mentally*) perceptible

discerning *adj form* **1.** (*discriminating*) judicieux(-euse) **2.** (*acute*) perspicace

discernment *n no pl, form* **1.** (*judgement*) perspicacité *f* **2.** (*perception*) discernement *m*

discharge [ˈdɪstʃɑːdʒ, *Am:* ˈdɪstʃɑːrdʒ] **I.** *n no pl* **1.** (*release*) renvoi *m* au foyer **2.** (*release papers*) autorisation *f* (de sortie) **3.** (*firing off*) décharge *f* **4.** (*emission*) émission *f* **5.** (*liquid discharged*) écoulement *m* **6.** (*debt payment*) règlement *m* **7.** (*performing of a duty*) exécution *f;* ~ **of one's duty** accomplissement de sa tâche *m* **8.** (*energy release*) décharge *f* **9.** (*unloading*) déchargement *m* **II.** *vi* **1.** (*unload*) se décharger **2.** MED (*wound*) suinter **3.** (*flow, pour into*) se déverser **III.** *vt* **1.** (*release: a patient*) renvoyer; LAW libérer; (*accused*) acquitter **2.** (*dismiss*) congédier; MIL démobiliser **3.** (*let out, emit*) dégager; (*water*) déverser **4.** *fig* (*utter*) déverser **5.** (*fulfil: one's duty*) accomplir; (*debt*) régler **6.** (*release charge*) décharger **7.** (*unload*) décharger

disciple [dɪˈsaɪpl] *n* disciple *mf*

disciplinary [ˌdɪsəˈplɪnəri, *Am:* ˈdɪsəplɪner-] *adj* disciplinaire; (*problem*) de discipline

discipline [ˈdɪsəplɪn] **I.** *n* discipline *f* **II.** *vt* **1.** (*control*) discipliner **2.** (*punish*) **to** ~ **sb for sth** punir qn pour qc

disciplined *adj* discipliné(e)

disc jockey *n* disc-jockey *m*

disclaim [dɪsˈkleɪm] *vt* **1.** *form* (*deny*) démentir **2.** (*give up right to*) renoncer à

disclaimer *n* **1.** *form* (*denial*) démenti *m* **2.** (*renouncing one's own*) désistement *m*

disclose [dɪsˈkləʊz, *Am:* -ˈkloʊz] *vt* **1.** (*make public*) divulguer; **to** ~ **that ...** révéler que ... **2.** (*uncover*) montrer

disclosure [dɪsˈkləʊʒəʳ, *Am:* -ˈkloʊʒɚ] *n form* **1.** (*act of disclosing*) divulgation *f* **2.** (*revelation*) révélation *f*

D

disco ['dɪskəʊ, *Am:* -koʊ] I. *n* 1. (*event*) discothèque *f* 2. *no pl* (*music*) musique *f* disco 3. (*place*) discothèque *f* 4. (*equipment*) matériel *m* (de disco) II. *vi* 1. (*attend a disco*) aller en boîte 2. (*dance disco*) danser le disco

discolor *Am, Aus,* **discolour** [dɪ'skʌləʳ, *Am:* -lɚ] I. *vi* se décolorer II. *vt* décolorer

discomfiture [dɪ'skʌmpfɪtʃəʳ, *Am:* -tʃɚ] *n no pl, form* embarras *m*

discomfort [dɪ'skʌmpfət, *Am:* -fɚt] *n* 1. *no pl* (*slight pain*) gêne *f* 2. *no pl* (*uneasiness*) malaise *m;* ~ **at sth** sentiment *m* de malaise face à qc 3. (*inconvenience*) inconfort *m*

disconcert [ˌdɪskən'sɜːt, *Am:* -'sɜːrt] *vt* déconcerter; **to be ~ed at sth** être déconcerté par qc

disconnect [ˌdɪskə'nekt] *vt* 1. (*put out of action: electricity, gas, telephone*) couper 2. (*break connection of*) débrancher 3. INFOR *a. fig* déconnecter 4. (*separate*) détacher

disconnected *adj* 1. (*cut off*) déconnecté(e); (*from reality*) coupé(e) 2. (*incoherent*) décousu(e)

disconsolate [dɪ'skɒntsələt, *Am:* -skɑːnt-] *adj* inconsolable

discontent [ˌdɪskən'tent] I. *n no pl* mécontentement *m* II. *adj* mécontent(e)

discontented *adj* mécontent(e)

discontentment *n no pl s.* **discontent**

discontinue [ˌdɪskən'tɪnjuː] *vt form* 1. (*cease*) cesser 2. (*give up*) interrompre 3. (*stop receiving*) suspendre

discontinuity <-ties> *n form* (*lack of continuity*) discontinuité *f*

discontinuous *adj* (*without continuity*) discontinu(e)

discord ['dɪskɔːd, *Am:* -kɔːrd] *n no pl, form* 1. (*disagreement*) désaccord *m;* **to sound a note of** ~ marquer un désaccord 2. (*clashing noise*) son *m* discordant 3. (*lack of harmony*) dissonance *f*

discordant [dɪ'skɔːdənt, *Am:* -'skɔːr-] *adj* 1. (*disagreeing*) opposé(e) 2. (*not in harmony*) discordant(e) ►**to strike a** ~ **note** produire une fausse note

discotheque ['dɪskətek] *n* discothèque *f*

discount ['dɪskaʊnt] I. *n* remise *f;* **to give a** ~ faire une remise; **at a** ~ à prix réduit II. *vt* 1. (*disregard*) ne pas tenir compte de; (*a possibility*) écarter 2. (*reduce: a price*) faire baisser

discount store *n* solderie *f*

discourage [dɪ'skʌrɪdʒ, *Am:* -'skɜːr-] *vt* 1. (*dishearten*) décourager 2. (*dissuade*) dissuader; **to** ~ **sb from doing sth** dissuader qn de faire qc 3. (*oppose*) déconseiller

discouragement *n* découragement *m;* **it should be a** ~ **to thieves** cela devrait dissuader les voleurs

discouraging *adj* décourageant(e)

discourteous [dɪs'kɜːtiəs, *Am:* -kɜːrt̬i-] *adj form* discourtois(e)

discourtesy [dɪs'kɜːtəsi, *Am:* -kɜːrt̬ə-] <-sies> *n form* manque *m* de courtoisie

discover [dɪ'skʌvəʳ, *Am:* -ɚ] *vt* découvrir; **to** ~ **sb doing sth** attraper qn en train de faire qc

discoverer *n* découvreur, -euse *m, f*

discovery [dɪ'skʌvəri] <-ries> *n* découverte *f*

discredit [dɪ'skredɪt] I. *n no pl, form* discrédit *m;* **to bring** ~ **on sth** jeter le discrédit sur qch; **to be to sb's** ~ ne pas être en l'honneur de qn; **he is a** ~ **to his parents** il fait honte à ses parents II. *vt* discréditer

discreditable *adj form* indigne

discreet [dɪ'skriːt] *adj* discret(-ète)

discrepancy [dɪ'skrepəntsi] <-cies> *n form* contradiction *f*

discrete [dɪ'skriːt] *adj* discret(-ète)

discretion [dɪ'skreʃən] *n no pl* 1. (*tact*) discrétion *f;* **to be the** (**very**) **soul of** ~ être la discrétion même 2. (*good judgement*) jugement *m;* **the age of** ~ LAW l'âge de raison 3. (*freedom to do sth*) discrétion *f;* **at the** ~ **of sb** à la discrétion de qn; **to leave sth to sb's** ~ laisser qc à la discrétion de qn; **to have the** ~ **to** +*infin* LAW avoir la possibilité de +*infin* ►~ **is the better part of valour** prudence est mère de sûreté

discretionary *adj* discrétionnaire

discriminate [dɪ'skrɪmɪneɪt] I. *vi* 1. (*see a difference*) distinguer; **to** ~ **between sth and sth** faire la distinction entre qc et qc 2. (*make judgement*) faire de la discrimination; **to** ~ **against sb** faire de la discrimination envers qn; ~ **in favor of sb** favoriser qn; **to be sexually ~d** être victime de discrimination sexuelle II. *vt* distinguer

discriminating *adj form* (*discerning: person*) averti(e); (*palate, taste*) fin(e)

discrimination *n no pl* 1. (*unfair treatment*) discrimination *f* 2. (*discernment*) discernement *m*

discriminatory [dɪ'skrɪmɪnətəri, *Am:* -tɔːri] *adj* discriminatoire

discursive [dɪ'skɜːsɪv, *Am:* -'skɜːr-] *adj pej, form* discursif(-ive)

discus ['dɪskəs] *n* 1. (*object which is thrown*) disque *m* 2. *no pl* (*event or sport*) **the** ~ le lancer du disque

discuss [dɪ'skʌs] *vt* discuter de; **to** ~ **how ...** discuter comment ...; **to** ~ **doing sth** parler de faire qc

discussion *n* discussion *f;* **a** ~ **group** un groupe de discussion; **to be under** ~ être discuté; **to hold** ~ tenir une discussion

discus thrower *n* lanceur, -euse *m, f* de disque

disdain [dɪs'deɪn] I. *n no pl* dédain *m;* ~ **for sb** mépris pour qn II. *vt* dédaigner

disdainful *adj form* dédaigneux(-euse)

disease [dɪ'ziːz] *n a. fig* maladie *f;* **a symptom of a** ~ un symptôme d'une maladie; **to catch a** ~ attraper une maladie; **to die from a** ~ mourir d'une maladie

diseased *adj a. fig* malade

disembark [ˌdɪsɪm'bɑːk, *Am:* -'bɑːrk] *vi*

débarquer

disembarkation *n* débarquement *m*

disembodied [ˌdɪsɪm'bɒdid, *Am:* -bɑːdid] *adj* désincarné(e)

disenchant [ˌdɪsɪn'tʃɑːnt, *Am:* -'tʃænt] *vt* faire perdre ses illusions à

disenchanted *adj* désabusé(e); **to become ~** perdre ses illusions

disenfranchise [ˌdɪsɪn'fræntʃaɪz] *vt* **1.** (*deprive of vote*) priver du droit de vote **2.** (*deprive of rights*) priver de droits

disengage [ˌdɪsɪn'geɪdʒ] **I.** *vi* **1.** (*become detached*) se détacher **2.** (*make a fencing move*) dégager (le fer) **II.** *vt* **1.** (*detach*) dégager; **to ~ a clutch** débrayer; **to ~ oneself from sth** se libérer de qc **2.** (*withdraw*) **to ~ troops** cesser le combat

disengagement *n no pl* désengagement *m*

disentangle [ˌdɪsɪn'tæŋgl] **I.** *vi* se démêler **II.** *vt* **1.** (*untangle*) démêler **2.** *fig* (*unravel*) dégager; **to ~ oneself from sth** se dégager de qc

disfavor *Am, Aus,* **disfavour** [dɪs'feɪvəʳ, *Am:* -vɚ] **I.** *n no pl* désapprobation *f;* **to be in ~** tomber en défaveur; **with ~** avec désapprobation **II.** *vt* défavoriser

disfigure [dɪs'fɪgəʳ, *Am:* -jɚ] *vt* défigurer

disfigurement *n no pl* défigurement *m;* (*of a town*) enlaidissement *m*

disfranchise [dɪs'fræntʃaɪz] *s.* **disenfranchise**

disgorge [dɪs'gɔːdʒ, *Am:* -'gɔːrdʒ] **I.** *vt a. fig* dégorger **II.** *vi* (*river*) se dégorger

disgrace [dɪs'greɪs] **I.** *n no pl* **1.** (*loss of honour*) disgrâce *f;* **to bring ~ on sb** déshonorer qn **2.** (*shameful thing or person*) honte *f* **II.** *vt* déshonorer

disgraceful *adj* honteux(-euse); (*conduct*) scandaleux(-euse); **it is ~ that** c'est une honte que *+subj*

disgruntled [dɪs'grʌntld, *Am:* -t̬ld] *adj* mécontent(e)

disguise [dɪs'gaɪz] **I.** *n* déguisement *m;* **to be in ~** être déguisé **II.** *vt* **1.** (*change appearance*) déguiser; **to ~ oneself** se déguiser **2.** (*hide*) dissimuler

disgust [dɪs'gʌst] **I.** *n no pl* **1.** (*revulsion*) dégoût *m;* **much to sb's ~** au grand dégoût de qn; **to step back in ~ from sth** reculer de dégoût devant qc; **to turn away from sth in ~** s'en aller dégoûté de qc **2.** (*indignation*) écœurement *m* **II.** *vt* **1.** (*sicken*) dégoûter **2.** (*revolt*) écœurer; **to be ~ed at sb/sth** être scandalisé par qn/qc; **to be ~ed with oneself** se dégoûter soi-même

disgusted *adj* dégoûté(e)

disgusting *adj* **1.** (*revolting*) dégoûtant(e) **2.** (*repulsive*) répugnant(e)

dish [dɪʃ] **I.** <-es> *n* **1.** (*container*) plat *m;* **oven-proof ~** plat à four **2.** *pl* **the ~es** la vaisselle *f;* **to do the ~es** faire la vaisselle **3.** *Am* (*plate*) assiette *f* **4.** (*food*) plat *m;* **favorite ~** plat *m* favori; **sweet ~** dessert *m;* **~ of the day** plat du jour **5.** (*equipment*) parabole *f;* **satellite ~** antenne *f* satellite **6.** *inf* (*sexually attractive*) **to be a real ~** (*female*) être un sacré canon; (*male*) être (beau comme) un Apollon **II.** *vt inf* démolir ►**to ~ the dirt on sb/sth** faire éclater un scandale sur qn/qc

◆**dish out** *vt* **1.** (*distribute too liberally*) prodiguer **2.** (*serve*) servir ►**to really be able to dish it out** pouvoir cogner fort

◆**dish up** *vt always sep, inf* **1.** (*serve*) servir **2.** (*offer*) offrir

dish aerial *n Brit* antenne *f* parabolique

disharmonious [ˌdɪshɑː'məʊniəs, *Am:* -hɑːrmoʊ-] *adj form* discordant(e)

disharmony [dɪs'hɑːməni, *Am:* -'hɑːr-] *n no pl, form* dissensions *fpl*

dishcloth ['dɪʃklɒθ, *Am:* -klɑːθ] *n* torchon (à vaisselle) *m*

dishearten [dɪs'hɑːtən, *Am:* -'hɑːr-] *vt* décourager

disheveled *adj Am,* **dishevelled** *adj* négligé(e); (*hair*) en bataille

dishonest [dɪ'sɒnɪst, *Am:* -'sɑːnɪst] *adj* malhonnête; **morally ~** de mauvaise foi

dishonesty *n no pl* **1.** (*lack of honesty*) malhonnêteté *f* **2.** (*dishonest act*) procédé *m* malhonnête

dishonor *Am* **I.** *n no pl, form* déshonneur *m;* **to bring ~ on sb** déshonorer qn; **to face ~** perdre la face **II.** *vt* **1.** (*disgrace*) désavouer **2.** (*not keep: a promise*) faillir

dishonorable *adj Am, form* déshonorant(e)

dishonour [dɪ'sɒnəʳ, *Am:* -'sɑːnɚ] *s.* **dishonor**

dishonourable *s.* **dishonorable**

dishwasher *n* **1.** (*machine*) lave-vaisselle *m* **2.** (*person*) plongeur, -euse *m, f* **dishwater** *n no pl* eau *f* de vaisselle

disillusion [ˌdɪsɪ'luːʒən] **I.** *vt* détromper **II.** *n no pl* désenchantement *m*

disillusioned *adj* désabusé(e); **to be ~ with sb/sth** perdre ses illusions sur qn/qc

disillusionment *n no pl* désillusion *f*

disinclination [ˌdɪsɪnklɪ'neɪʃən] *n no pl* aversion *f*

disinclined [ˌdɪsɪn'klaɪnd] *adj* peu disposé(e)

disinfect [ˌdɪsɪn'fekt] *vt* désinfecter

disinfectant *n no pl* désinfectant *m*

disinfection *n no pl* désinfection *f*

disingenuous [ˌdɪsɪn'dʒenjuəs] *adj form* fallacieux(-euse); (*look*) ambigü(e)

disinherit [ˌdɪsɪn'herɪt] *vt* déshériter

disintegrate [dɪ'sɪntɪgreɪt, *Am:* -t̬ə-] *vi a. fig* désintégrer; (*marriage*) dissoudre; (*into chaos*) dégénérer

disintegration *n no pl* désintégration *f*

disinterested [dɪ'sɪntrəstɪd, *Am:* -'sɪntrɪstɪd] *adj* **1.** (*impartial*) impartial(e); (*advice, observer*) objectif(-ive); (*party*) indépendant(e) **2.** (*uninterested*) indifférent(e)

disjointed [dɪs'dʒɔɪntɪd, *Am:* -t̬ɪd] *adj* décousu(e)

disk [dɪsk] *n* INFOR disque *m;* **hard** ~ disque dur; **floppy** ~ disquette *f;* **formatted 1.44MB floppy** ~ disquette formatée pour lecteurs de 1,44 Mo.; **installation** ~ disquette d'installation; **start-up** ~ disquette de démarrage; **double-sided, high density** ~ disquette double face, haute densité; **compact laser** ~ disque optique compact

disk drive *n* unité *f* de disque(tte); **hard** ~ disque *m* dur; **floppy** ~ lecteur *m* de disquette

diskette [dɪs'kæt] *n* disquette *f*

dislike [dɪs'laɪk] **I.** *vt* ne pas aimer **II.** *n* **1.** *no pl* (*aversion*) aversion *f;* **to take a** ~ **to sb/sth** avoir de l'antipathie *f* pour qn/qc **2.** (*object of aversion*) grief *m*

dislocate ['dɪsləkeɪt, *Am:* dɪ'sloʊ-] *vt* **1.** (*put out of place*) déplacer **2.** MED luxer **3.** (*disturb the working of*) perturber

dislocation *n* **1.** (*displacement*) déplacement *m* **2.** MED luxation *f* **3.** *no pl* (*disturbance*) perturbation *f*

dislodge [dɪ'slɒdʒ, *Am:* -'slɑːdʒ] *vt* **1.** (*extract*) extraire **2.** MIL expulser (manu militari)

disloyal [dɪ'slɔɪəl] *adj* déloyal(e); **to be** ~ **to sb/sth** être déloyal envers qn/qc

dismal ['dɪzməl] *adj* **1.** (*depressing: expression*) lugubre; (*outlook*) sinistre **2.** *inf* (*awful: failure*) terrible; (*truth*) horrible; (*weather*) épouvantable

dismantle [dɪ'smæntl, *Am:* dɪ'smæntl] **I.** *vi* se démonter **II.** *vt* démonter; (*system*) démanteler

dismay [dɪ'smeɪ] **I.** *n no pl* consternation *f;* **to sb's** ~ à la stupeur de qn; **to do sth in** ~ faire qc avec étonnement **II.** *vt* consterner

dismember [dɪ'smembəʳ, *Am:* -bɚ] *vt* démembrer; (*country*) démanteler

dismiss [dɪ'smɪs] *vt* **1.** (*not consider*) déprécier; (*idea, thought*) dénigrer **2.** (*send away*) prendre congé de; **to** ~ **sth from sth** ôter qc de qc; **to** ~ **thoughts from one's mind** chasser des pensées de son esprit **3.** (*fire from work*) licencier; **to be** ~ **from one's job** être démis de ses fonctions **4.** LAW (*appeal*) rejeter; (*court, indictment, charge*) récuser; **to** ~ **a (court) case** aboutir à un non-lieu; **to** ~ **sb from a charge** débouter qn de sa plainte

dismissal *n no pl* **1.** (*disregarding*) dévalorisation *f* **2.** (*firing from a job*) licenciement *m* **3.** (*removal from high position*) destitution *f*

dismissive [dɪ'smɪsɪv] *adj* méprisant(e); **to be** ~ **about sth** mépriser qc

dismount [dɪ'smaʊnt] **I.** *vi* descendre **II.** *vt* (*a horse*) descendre de; (*a rider, machine*) démonter

disobedience [ˌdɪsəʊ'biːdiənts, *Am:* -ə'-] *n no pl* désobéissance *f*

disobedient *adj* désobéissant(e)

disobey [ˌdɪsəʊ'beɪ, *Am:* -ə'-] **I.** *vt* désobéir à **II.** *vi* désobéir

disoblige [ˌdɪsə'blaɪdʒ] *vt form* désobliger

disobliging *adj form* désobligeant(e)

disorder [dɪ'sɔːdəʳ, *Am:* -'sɔːrdɚ] *n* **1.** *no pl* (*lack of order*) désordre *m* **2.** (*disease*) troubles *mpl;* **kidney/mental** ~ troubles rénaux/mentaux **3.** *no pl* (*upheaval*) désordre *m;* **civil** ~ révolte *f;* **public** ~ émeute *f*

disordered *adj* désordonné(e)

disorderly *adj* **1.** (*untidy*) en désordre **2.** (*unruly*) indiscipliné(e); (*conduct*) ivre et incohérent(e)

disorganized [dɪ'sɔːgənaɪzd, *Am:* dɪ'sɔːr-] *adj* désorganisé(e)

disorient [dɪ'sɔːriənt, *Am:* -ent] *vt Am,* **disorientate** *vt* désorienter; **to get** ~**ed** s'égarer

disoriented *adj* désorienté(e)

disown [dɪ'səʊn, *Am:* dɪ'soʊn] *vt* désavouer; (*person, child*) renier

disparage [dɪ'spærɪdʒ, *Am:* -'sper-] *vt* rabaisser

disparagement *n no pl* rabaissement *m*

disparaging *adj* désobligeant(e)

disparate ['dɪspərət] *adj form* disparate

disparity [dɪ'spærəti, *Am:* -'perəti] *n* inégalité *f*

dispassionate [dɪ'spæʃənət] *adj* détaché(e)

dispatch [dɪ'spætʃ] **I.** <-es> *n* **1.** (*something sent*) expédition *f;* (*of clothing*) envoi *m* **2.** (*press report*) dépêche *f* (de l'étranger) ►**to do sth with** ~ *form* faire qc avec diligence; **to be mentioned in** ~**es** être porté aux nues **II.** *vt a. iron* expédier

dispel [dɪ'spel] <-ll-> *vt* chasser; (*fear, rumour*) dissiper; (*myth*) détruire

dispensable [dɪ'spensəbl] *adj* superflu(e)

dispensary [dɪ'spensəri] *n* (*medical store*) pharmacie *f*

dispensation *n form* **1.** (*special permission*) dispense *f;* **a special** ~ une permission exceptionnelle; **a** ~ **by sb/sth** par ordre de qn/qc **2.** (*act of distributing*) distribution *f* **3.** REL dispense *f* **4.** (*ruling system*) exercice *m;* **under the old** ~ sous l'ancien régime

dispense [dɪ'spens] *vt* **1.** (*give out*) distribuer; (*advice, wisdom*) prodiguer; **to** ~ **sth to sb/sth** distribuer qc à qn/qc **2.** (*give out medicine*) préparer

◆**dispense with** *vi* **1.** (*manage without*) se passer de **2.** (*give exemption*) abandonner

dispenser *n* **1.** (*device*) distributeur *m;* **soap/drinks/cash** ~ distributeur de savon/de boissons/de billets **2.** (*organization*) dispensateur *m*

dispersal *n no pl* **1.** (*act of dispersing*) dispersion *f* **2.** (*break up*) effondrement *m*

disperse [dɪ'spɜːs, *Am:* -'spɜːrs] **I.** *vt* disperser **II.** *vi* se disperser

dispersion *n no pl* **1.** *form* (*distribution*) distribution *f* **2.** (*light separation*) dispersion *f* lumineuse

dispirited [dɪ'spɪrɪtɪd, *Am:* -t̬ɪd] *adj* démoralisé(e)

displace [dɪs'pleɪs] *vt* **1.** (*force from place*) déplacer **2.** PHYS dévier **3.** (*take the place of*) remplacer; **to** ~ **sb as sth** supplanter qn en tant que qc

displacement I. *n no pl* 1. (*act of forced moving*) déplacement *m* 2. PSYCH déplacement *m* 3. AUTO cylindrée *f* II. *adj* palliatif(-ive)

display [dɪ'spleɪ] I. *vt* 1. (*arrange*) exposer; (*on a noticeboard*) afficher sur un panneau (d'affichage) 2. (*show*) laisser paraître II. *n* 1. (*arrangement of things*) étalage *m;* **to be on ~** être en vitrine; **firework(s) ~** feu *m* d'artifice 2. *no pl* (*demonstration*) exposition *f;* (*of affection, anger*) démonstration *f;* (*of love*) témoignage *m* 3. INFOR écran *m*

display case *n* vitrine *f* **display window** *n* vitrine *f*

displease [dɪ'spli:z] *vt* mécontenter; **to be ~d by sth** être contrarié par qc

displeasing *adj* contrariant(e); (*sensation*) déplaisant(e)

displeasure [dɪ'spleʒəʳ, *Am:* -ɚ] *n no pl* mécontentement *m;* **much to sb's ~** au grand désappointement de qn

disposable [dɪ'spəʊzəbl, *Am:* -'spoʊ-] I. *adj* 1. (*being thrown away after use*) jetable 2. (*able to be dispensed with: person*) remplaçable 3. ECON (*assets, funds*) disponible II. *n pl, Am* (articles *mpl*) jetables *mpl*

disposable income *n* revenu *m* disponible

disposal *n* 1. *no pl* (*getting rid of*) enlèvement *f* 2. *no pl* (*destruction*) élimination *f* 3. *Am* (*garbage ~ unit*) broyeur *m* d'ordures 4. (*sale*) vente *f;* **for ~** à vendre 5. (*arrangement*) disposition *f* 6. (*avaibility*) **to be at sb's ~** être à la disposition de qn

dispose [dɪ'spəʊz, *Am:* -'spoʊz] *vt form* disposer; **to ~ sb to do sth** disposer qn à (faire) qc ◆**dispose of** *vt* se débarrasser de; (*of evidence*) détruire

disposed *adj form* **to be ~ to** +*infin* être disposé à +*infin*

disposition [ˌdɪspə'zɪʃən] *n* tempérament *m*

dispossess [ˌdɪspə'zes] *vt form* exproprier; **to ~ sb of sth** déposséder qn de qc; **to ~ sb of his home** expulser qn de chez lui

disproportionate [ˌdɪsprə'pɔ:ʃənət, *Am:* -'pɔ:r-] *adj* 1. (*unequal*) démesuré(e); (*number*) disproportionné(e) 2. (*unwarranted*) injustifié(e)

disprove [dɪ'spru:v] *vt* réfuter

disputable *adj* discutable; (*point*) controversé(e)

disputation *n form* débat *m*

disputatious *adj form* contestataire

dispute [dɪ'spju:t] I. *vt* 1. (*argue*) discuter; **to ~ sth hotly** débattre chaudement de qc; **to ~ that ...** opposer un démenti sur le fait que ... 2. (*doubt*) contester II. *vi* se quereller; **to ~ with sb over sth** se quereller avec qn au sujet de qc III. *n* 1. (*argument*) querelle *f;* **to have a ~ with sb** se quereller avec qn 2. POL, ECON conflit *m;* **pay ~** conflit *m* sur le salaire 3. (*debate*) controverse *f;* **to be open to ~** être contestable; **to be beyond ~** être incontestable; **without ~** sans conteste 4. LAW litige *m;* **a ~ over sth** un litige à propos de qc; **to be in ~** être en cause

disqualification *n* 1. *no pl* (*process*) disqualification *f* 2. (*instance*) exclusion *f* 3. LAW suspension *f*

disqualify [dɪ'skwɒlɪfaɪ, *Am:* dɪ'skwɑ:lə-] <-ie-> *vt* 1. (*debar*) rendre inapte; **to ~ sb from sth** rendre qn inapte à qc; **to be ~ied from driving** avoir un retrait de permis 2. SPORT, GAMES disqualifier

disquiet [dɪ'skwaɪət] I. *n no pl, form* appréhension *f;* **growing ~** préoccupation *f* croissante; **~ among sb/sth** inquiétude *f* parmi qn/dans le milieu de qc; **~ over sth** crainte *f* au sujet de qc II. *vt form* préoccuper

disquieting *adj form* troublant(e); **~ way of looking** point *m* de vue inquiétant

disregard [ˌdɪsrɪ'gɑ:d, *Am:* -rɪ'gɑ:rd] I. *vt* 1. (*ignore*) ignorer 2. (*despise*) mépriser II. *n no pl* 1. (*deliberate ignorance*) indifférence *f* 2. (*contempt*) mépris *m*

disrepair [ˌdɪsrɪ'peəʳ, *Am:* -rɪ'per] *n no pl* dégradation *f;* **state of ~** état *m* de délabrement

disreputable *adj* peu recommandable

disrepute [ˌdɪsrɪ'pju:t] *n* discrédit *m;* **to bring sth into ~ with sb** discréditer qc aux yeux de qn

disrespect [ˌdɪsrɪ'spekt] *n no pl* incorrection *f;* **to show ~** manquer de respect; **to show sb ~** faire preuve d'insolence *f* envers qn; **no ~ to sb but ...** malgré tout le respect que l'on doit à qn, ...

disrespectful *adj* irrespectueux(-euse); (*gesture*) insolent(e)

disrupt [dɪs'rʌpt] *vt* 1. (*interrupt and stop*) interrompre; (*career*) briser 2. (*disturb*) perturber

disruption *n* 1. (*interruption*) interruption *f* 2. (*disturbance*) perturbation *f*

disruptive *adj* perturbateur(-trice)

dissatisfaction [dɪsˌsætɪs'fækʃən, *Am:* ˌdɪssæt̬əs'-] *n no pl* mécontentement *m;* **~ with sth** mécontentement de qc

dissatisfied [dɪs'sætɪsfaɪd, *Am:* -'sæt̬əs-] *adj* mécontent(e); **to be ~ with sth** être mécontent de qc

dissect [dɪ'sekt] *vt* 1. (*cut*) disséquer 2. *fig* décortiquer

dissection *n no pl* 1. (*cut*) dissection *f* 2. *fig* épluchage *m*

disseminate [dɪ'semɪneɪt] I. *vt* propager II. *vi* se propager

dissension [dɪ'sentʃən] *n form* dissension *f;* **~ between people** différend *m* entre des personnes

dissent [dɪ'sent] I. *n no pl* désaccord *m* II. *vi* **to ~ from sth** être en désaccord avec qc

dissenter *n* POL opposant(e) *m(f)*

dissenting *adj* dissident(e)

dissertation [ˌdɪsə'teɪʃən, *Am:* -ɚ'-] *n* 1. (*essay*) dissertation *f* 2. UNIV (*degree essay*) mémoire *m;* (*for doctor's degree*) thèse *f* de

doctorat
disservice [ˌdɪsˈsɜːvɪs, *Am:* -ˈsɜːr-] *n no pl* tort *m;* **to do sb/sth a ~** causer tort à qn/qc
dissident [ˈdɪsɪdənt] **I.** *n* dissident(e) *m(f)* **II.** *adj* dissident(e)
dissimilar [ˌdɪsˈsɪmɪləʳ, *Am:* -lɚ] *adj* dissemblable; **to be not ~** ne pas différer
dissimilarity <-ties> *n* dissemblance *f*
dissipate [ˈdɪsɪpeɪt] **I.** *vi* **1.** (*disappear*) se dissiper **2.** *fig* s'évanouir **II.** *vt* **1.** (*cause to disappear*) dissiper **2.** *fig* éclaircir
dissipation *n form* **1.** (*wasting frivously*) gaspillage *m* **2.** (*damaging indulgence*) **a life of ~** une vie de débauche *f*
dissociate [dɪˈsəʊʃieɪt, *Am:* -ˈsoʊ-] *vt* **to ~ sth from sth** dissocier qc de qc
dissociation *n no pl* **1.** (*separation*) dissociation *f* **2.** (*chemical break up*) décomposition *f*
dissolution *n no pl* dissolution *f*
dissolve [dɪˈzɒlv, *Am:* -ˈzɑːlv] **I.** *vi* **1.** (*become part of a liquid*) se dissoudre **2.** (*collapse*) **to ~ into giggles/laughter** être pris de ricanement/se tordre de rire; **to ~ into tears** fondre en larmes **3.** (*disappear*) disparaître; (*tension*) se relâcher **II.** *vt* **1.** (*make become part of a liquid*) (faire) dissoudre **2.** (*turn to liquid*) fondre **3.** (*break up*) désagréger; (*marriage*) dissoudre
dissonance [ˈdɪsənənts] *n no pl* dissonance *f*
dissonant *adj* **1.** MUS dissonant(e) **2.** *fig* (*opinions*) discordant(e)
dissuade [dɪˈsweɪd] *vt form* dissuader; **to ~ sb from doing sth** dissuader qn de faire qc
distance [ˈdɪstənts] **I.** *n* **1.** (*space*) *a. fig* distance *f;* **within a ~ of ...** dans un rayon de ...; **within walking/driving ~** on peut y aller à pied/en voiture **2.** (*space far away*) lointain *m;* **at a ~** avec du recul; **in the ~** au loin ▸**to go the ~** tenir la distance; *fig* aller (jusqu')au bout; **to keep one's ~** garder ses distances; **to keep one's ~ from sb/sth** se tenir à distance de qn/qc **II.** *vt* distancer; **to ~ oneself from sb/sth** se distancer de qn/qc; *fig* prendre ses distances par rapport à qn/qc
distant [ˈdɪstənt] *adj* **1.** (*far away*) éloigné(e); (*shore*) lointain(e); **in the not-too-~ future** dans un proche avenir; **the dim and ~ past** les temps anciens; **at some ~ point in the future** à (long/court) terme **2.** (*not closely related: relative*) éloigné(e) **3.** (*cool: person*) distant(e) **4.** (*faint: memory*) lointain(e)
distantly *adv* **1.** (*in the distance*) de loin **2.** (*in an unfriendly manner*) d'une manière distante **3.** (*not closely*) de loin
distaste [dɪˈsteɪst] *n no pl* répugnance *f;* **~ for sth** aversion *f* pour qc; **to sb's ~** au dégoût de qn
distasteful *adj* répugnant(e); (*topic*) déplaisant(e)
distemper [dɪˈstempəʳ, *Am:* -pɚ] *n* **1.** (*animal disease*) maladie *f* de Carré **2.** (*type of paint*) détrempe *f*
distend [dɪˈstend] *vi* se distendre
distension [dɪˈstentʃən] *n no pl* distension *f*
distil <-ll-> *vt,* **distill** [dɪˈstɪl] *vt Am, Aus, a. fig* distiller
distillation *n no pl* **1.** (*action fo distilling*) distillation *f* **2.** *fig* condensé *m;* **to be a ~ of sth** être l'incarnation *f* de qc
distiller *n* distillateur, -trice *m, f*
distillery *n* distillerie *f*
distinct [dɪˈstɪŋkt] *adj* **1.** (*obviously separate*) distinct(e); **to be ~ from sth** être distinct de qc; **as ~ from sth** par opposition à qc **2.** (*seen: words*) clair(e) **3.** (*noticeable: lack*) évident(e)
distinction *n* **1.** (*difference*) différence *f* **2.** *no pl* (*eminence*) mérite *m;* **he's a writer of great ~** c'est un éminent écrivain **3.** (*honour*) honneur *m;* **to have the ~ of sth** avoir l'honneur de qc; **to have the ~ of being sth** avoir le privilège d'être qc **4.** (*elegance*) distinction *f* **5.** *Brit* (*extremely good marks*) mention *f* très bien
distinctive *adj* **1.** (*distinguishing: feature*) distinctif(-ive) **2.** (*special: taste*) caractéristique **3.** (*clear*) distinct(e)
distinguish [dɪˈstɪŋgwɪʃ] **I.** *vi* faire la distinction **II.** *vt* distinguer; **to ~ sb/sth from sb/sth** distinguer qn/qc de qn/qc; **to ~ oneself in sth** se distinguer dans qc
distinguishable *adj* **1.** (*different*) distinguable **2.** (*recognizable among many*) **to be ~ from sb/sth** être reconnaissable parmi qn/qc **3.** (*that can be heard: sound*) perceptible
distinguished *adj* **1.** (*celebrated*) éminent(e) **2.** (*stylish*) distingué(e)
distort [dɪˈstɔːt, *Am:* -ˈstɔːrt] *vt* dénaturer; (*facts, truth*) altérer; (*history*) travestir
distortion *n* **1.** *fig* (*of truth, facts*) altération *f* **2.** *no pl* PHYS, MUS distorsion *f*
distract [dɪˈstrækt] *vt* distraire; (*attention*) détourner; **to be easily ~ed** être facilement distrait
distracted *adj* distrait(e)
distraction *n* **1.** (*recreation*) distraction *f* **2.** (*diversion*) **to be a ~ from sth** détourner l'attention de qc ▸**to drive sb to ~** rendre qn fou; **to love sb to ~** aimer qn éperdument
distraught [dɪˈstrɔːt, *Am:* -ˈstrɑːt] *adj* **to be ~ with sth** être bouleversé par qc
distress [dɪˈstres] **I.** *n no pl* **1.** (*extreme pain*) souffrance *f* **2.** (*sorrow*) affliction *f;* **to be a ~ to sb** être un fardeau *m* pour qn **3.** (*state of danger*) détresse *f;* **in ~** en détresse **II.** *vt* faire de la peine à; **to ~ oneself** s'inquiéter; **to be deeply ~ed** être profondément affligé
distressed *adj* **1.** (*unhappy*) affligé(e) **2.** (*in difficulties*) en détresse; **to be in ~ circumstances** être dans la détresse; **to be economically ~** être économiquement faible
distressed area *n* zone *f* sinistrée
distressful *adj Am,* **distressing** *adj* **1.** (*causing great worry*) affligeant(e) **2.** (*pain-

ful) douloureux(-euse)

distribute [dɪ'strɪbju:t] *vt* **1.**(*share*) distribuer; **to ~ sth fairly** partager qc équitablement **2.**(*spread over space*) répartir; **to ~ sth evenly** étaler uniformément; **to be widely ~d** être largement répandu **3.** ECON (*goods, films*) distribuer; **to be ~d throughout** être implanté partout

distribution *n no pl* **1.**(*giving out*) distribution *f* **2.**(*spread*) diffusion *f;* (*of goods*) répartition *f;* **equitable/even ~** partage *m* équitable

distribution area *n* ECON zone *f* de (grande) distribution **distribution channel** *n* ECON circuit *m* de distribution **distribution rights** *npl* droits *mpl* de distribution

distributive [dɪ'strɪbjətɪv, *Am:* -jət̬ɪv] *adj* **1.** LING itératif(-ive) **2.** MAT (*type of property*) distributif(-ive)

distributor [dɪ'strɪbjətəʳ, *Am:* -t̬ɚ] *n* **1.**(*person*) distributeur *m;* (*for cars*) concessionnaire *m* **2.**(*device*) distributeur *m* **3.** AUTO delco *m*

district ['dɪstrɪkt] *n* **1.**(*defined area: in city*) quartier *m;* (*in country*) région *f* **2.**(*administrative sector*) district *m* **3.** *Am* (*Washington, DC*) **the District** Washington *m*

district attorney *n Am* ≈ procureur *m* de la République **district council** *n Brit* conseil *m* général **district court** *n Am* cour *f* fédérale

distrust [dɪ'strʌst] **I.** *vt* se méfier de; **to be deeply ~ful** être très méfiant **II.** *n no pl* méfiance *f*

distrustful *adj* méfiant(e); **to be deeply ~ of sth** être très méfiant envers qc

disturb [dɪ'stɜ:b, *Am:* -'stɜ:rb] *vt* **1.**(*bother*) déranger **2.**(*worry*) ennuyer; **to be ~ed that ...** être ennuyé que *+subj;* **to be ~ed to** *+infin* être agacé de *+infin* **3.**(*move around*) déranger; **to ~ sb's hair** décoiffer qn ▶**to ~ the <u>peace</u>** troubler l'ordre public

disturbance [dɪ'stɜ:bənts, *Am:* -'stɜ:r-] *n* **1.**(*nuisance*) dérangement *m;* **to cause a ~** semer le désordre **2.**(*unorderly public incident*) troubles *mpl;* **to cause a ~** troubler l'ordre public **3.** METEO perturbation *f*

disturbed *adj* **1.**(*not peaceful: water, night, sleep*) agité(e) **2.**(*mentally upset*) perturbé(e); **to have a ~ behavior** avoir des troubles du comportement

disturbing *adj* ennuyeux(-euse); **to be ~ to sb** être gênant pour qn; **it is ~ that** c'est pénible que *+subj*

disunity [dɪ'sju:nəti, *Am:* -t̬i] *n no pl* désunion *f;* (*in a group*) discorde *f*

disuse [dɪ'sju:s] *n no pl* non-utilisation *f;* **to fall into ~** tomber en désuétude

disused *adj* non utilisé(e); (*railway lines*) désaffecté(e)

ditch [dɪtʃ] **I.** <-es> *n* fossé *m* **II.** *vt* **1.**(*discard: stolen car*) abandonner; (*proposal*) laisser tomber **2.** *inf* (*stop dating*) laisser tomber **3.**(*land on the sea*) **to ~ a plane** faire un amérrissage forcé **III.** *vi* **1.**(*dig*) creuser un fossé **2.**(*land on the sea*) faire un amérrissage forcé

dither ['dɪðəʳ, *Am:* -ɚ] **I.** *n no pl* excitation *f;* **don't get into such a ~!** *pej* ne te mets pas dans un tel état ! **II.** *vi pej* tergiverser

ditto ['dɪtəʊ, *Am:* 'dɪt̬oʊ] *adv* idem; **~ for me** *Am* idem pour moi

ditty ['dɪti, *Am:* 'dɪt̬-] <-ties> *n* chansonnette *f*

diurnal [daɪ'ɜ:nəl, *Am:* -'ɜ:r-] *adj* **1.**(*daily*) quotidien(ne) **2.**(*active in daylight*) diurne

divan [dɪ'væn] *n* divan *m*

divan bed *n* canapé-lit *m*

dive [daɪv] **I.** *n* **1.**(*plunge*) *a. fig* plongeon *m;* **to take a ~** plonger **2.** AVIAT piqué *m* **3.** *inf* (*undesirable establishment*) boui(-)boui *m* **II.** *vi* <dived *o Am* dove, dived *o Am* dove> **1.**(*plunge*) *a. fig* plonger; **shares ~d by 25% to ...** les actions ont plongé de 25% et sont maintenant à ... **2.**(*go sharply downwards: plane*) descendre en piqué **3.**(*move towards quickly*) **to ~ for sth** se ruer vers qc; **to ~ for cover** plonger à l'abri

diver *n* (*person who dives*) plongeur, -euse *m, f*

diverge [daɪ'vɜ:dʒ, *Am:* -'vɜ:rdʒ] *vi a. fig* diverger; (*roads*) se séparer; **to ~ from sth** s'écarter de qc

divergence [daɪ'vɜ:dʒəns, *Am:* dɪ'vɜ:r-] *n* **1.** *no pl* (*difference*) divergence *f* **2.**(*deviation*) dérive *f*

divergent *adj* (*differing*) divergent(e); **to be ~ from sth** diverger par rapport à qc

diverse [daɪ'vɜ:s, *Am:* dɪ'vɜ:rs] *adj* **1.**(*varied*) divers(e) **2.**(*not alike*) différent(e)

diversification [daɪˌvɜ:sɪfɪ'keɪʃən, *Am:* dɪˌvɜ:r-] *n no pl* ECON diversification *f*

diversify [daɪ'vɜ:sɪfaɪ, *Am:* dɪˌvɜ:r-] <-ie-> **I.** *vi* se diversifier **II.** *vt* diversifier

diversion [daɪ'vɜ:ʃən, *Am:* dɪ'vɜ:r-] *n* **1.** *no pl* (*changing of direction*) déviation *f* **2.**(*distraction*) diversion *f* **3.**(*entertainment*) distraction *f*

diversity [daɪ'vɜ:səti, *Am:* dɪ'vɜ:rsət̬i] *n no pl* diversité *f*

divert [daɪ'vɜ:t, *Am:* dɪ'vɜ:rt] *vt* **1.**(*change the direction of*) dévier **2.**(*distract: attention*) détourner **3.**(*amuse*) divertir

divest [daɪ'vest, *Am:* dɪ-] *vt Am* **to ~ sb of sth** **1.**(*take from*) priver qn de qc **2.**(*get rid of*) **to ~** débarrasser qn de qc **3.**(*dispossess*) déposséder qn de qc

divide [dɪ'vaɪd] **I.** *vt* **1.**(*split*) *a. fig* (*cell, people*) diviser **2.**(*share: food, work, time*) partager; **to ~ sth among/with...** partager qc entre/avec... **3.**(*separate: wall, mountain*) séparer **4.** MAT **to ~ six by two** diviser six par deux **II.** *vi* **1.**(*split*) *a. fig* se diviser; (*road*) bifurquer; (*train, group*) se séparer; **to ~ into sth** se diviser en qc; **our paths ~d** nos routes se sont séparées **2.** MAT **to ~ by a number** être

D

divisible par un nombre **3.** *Brit* POL procéder au vote ►**to ~ and rule** diviser pour régner **III.** *n* **1.** (*gulf*) gouffre *m* **2.** *Am* (*watershed*) ligne *f* de partage des eaux; **the Great Divide** ligne de partage des eaux des Rocheuses

◆**divide off** *vt* séparer

◆**divide out** *vt* partager

◆**divide up** *vt always sep* partager

divided *adj* **1.** (*undecided*) partagé(e) **2.** (*in disagreement*) divisé(e)

dividend ['dɪvɪdend] *n* **1.** ECON, MAT dividende *m* **2.** *fig* **your work eventually paid ~s** ton travail a fini par payer

divination [ˌdɪvɪ'neɪʃən] *n no pl* divination *f*; **powers of ~** pouvoirs *mpl* divinatoires

divine [dɪ'vaɪn] **I.** *adj* divin(e) **II.** *vt* **1.** (*guess correctly*) deviner **2.** (*have insight in the future*) présager

diviner *n* devin *m*

diving *n no pl* **1.** (*jumping*) plongeon *m* **2.** (*swimming*) plongée *f*

diving bell *n* cloche *f* à plongeur **diving board** *n* plongeoir *m* **diving suit** *n* scaphandre *m*

divining rod *n* baguette *f* de sourcier

divinity [dɪ'vɪnəti, *Am:* -əṱi] *n* **1.** *no pl* (*godliness*) divinité *f* **2.** *no pl* (*religion*) théologie *f*

divisible [dɪ'vɪzəbl] *adj* divisible

division [dɪ'vɪʒən] *n* **1.** *no pl* (*splitting up*) partage *m* **2.** (*disagreement*) division *f* **3.** (*border*) ligne *f* de séparation **4.** *no pl* ECON, MAT, MIL, SPORT division *f* **5.** *Brit* (*voting*) vote *m*

division of labour *n* POL division *f* du travail

divisive [dɪ'vaɪsɪv] *adj* qui divise

divorce [dɪ'vɔːs, *Am:* -'vɔːrs] **I.** *n* divorce *m* **II.** *vt* divorcer; **to get ~d from sb** divorcer de qn **III.** *vi* divorcer

divorced *adj* divorcé(e)

divorcee, divorcé(e) *n* homme *m* divorcé, femme *f* divorcée

divot ['dɪvət] *n* motte *f* (de gazon)

divulge [daɪ'vʌldʒ, *Am:* dɪ-] *vt* divulguer

DIY [ˌdiːaɪ'waɪ] *n no pl, Brit, Aus abbr of* **do-it-yourself** bricolage *m*

dizziness *n no pl* vertige *m*

dizzy ['dɪzi] <-ier, -iest> *adj* **1.** (*having a spinning sensation*) pris(e) de vertiges **2.** (*causing a spinning sensation*) vertigineux(-euse) **3.** *inf* (*silly*) tête de linotte; **a ~ blonde** une blonde évaporée **4.** *fig* (*progress*) étourdissant(e)

DJ [ˌdiː'dʒeɪ, *Am:* 'diːdʒeɪ] *n abbr of* **disc jockey** DJ *m*

Djibouti [dʒɪ'buːti] *n* Djibouti

Djiboutian **I.** *adj* djiboutien(ne) **II.** *n* Djiboutien(ne) *m(f)*

DNA [ˌdiːen'eɪ] *n no pl abbr of* **deoxyribonucleic acid** ADN *m*

do [duː] **I.** *n Brit, Aus, inf* (*party*) fête *f* **2. it's a poor ~** *Brit, inf* c'est injuste; **the ~s and don'ts** ce qu'il faut faire et ce qu'il ne faut pas faire **II.** <does, did, done> *aux* **1.** (*word used to form questions*) **~ you have a dog?** avez-vous un chien ? **2.** (*to form negatives*) **Freddy doesn't like olives** Freddy n'aime pas les olives **3.** (*to form negative imperatives*) **don't go!** n'y vas pas ! **4.** (*for emphasis*) **I ~ like her** je l'aime vraiment bien; **~ you (now)** ? ah, oui, vraiment?!; **~ come to our party!** venez à notre fête, vraiment!; **did he yell!** qu'est-ce qu'il a pu hurler!; **so you ~ like beer after all** finalement, tu aimes la bière **5.** (*to replace a repeated verb*) **she runs faster than he does** elle court plus vite que lui; **so ~ I** moi aussi; **"I don't smoke." "neither ~ I."** "je ne fume pas." "moi non plus."; **"may I ?" "please ~!"** *form* "Puis-je ?" "je vous en prie, faites !" **6.** (*in tag questions and replies*) **I saw him yesterday – did you?** je l'ai vu hier – vraiment?; **you like beef, don't you?** tu aimes le bœuf, n'est-ce-pas?; **who did that? – I did** qui a fait ça? – moi; **should I come? – no, don't** dois-je venir – non, surtout pas **III.** <does, did, done> *vt* **1.** (*carry out*) faire; **to ~ sth again** refaire qc; **to ~ justice to sb/sth** être juste envers qn; **this photo doesn't ~ her justice** cette photo ne l'avantage pas; **what ~ you ~ for a living?** qu'est-ce que tu fais comme travail?; **to ~ everything possible** faire tout son possible; **what is he ~ing ...?** que fait-il?; **this just can't be done!** ça ne se fait pas, c'est tout!; **what can I ~ for you?** que puis-je (faire) pour vous?; **to ~ nothing but ...** ne faire que ... **2.** (*undertake*) **what I am going to ~ with you/this cake** qu'est-ce que je vais bien pouvoir faire de toi/de ce gâteau **3.** (*place somewhere*) **what have you done with my coat?** qu'est-ce que tu as fait de mon manteau? **4.** (*adjust*) **can you ~ something with my car?** est-ce que tu peux faire qc pour ma voiture? **5.** (*help*) **can you ~ anything for my back?** pouvez-vous faire qc pour mon dos, docteur?; **this medication does nothing** ce médicament ne fait aucun effet **6.** (*act*) **to ~ right** bien faire; **to ~ sb well** bien agir envers qn **7.** (*deal with*) **if you ~ the washing up, I'll ~ the drying** si tu laves la vaisselle, je l'essuie **8.** (*learn*) **to ~ Chinese** faire du chinois **9.** (*solve: sum*) calculer; (*crosswords*) faire **10.** (*make neat*) **to ~ the dishes** faire la vaisselle; **to ~ one's nails** se faire les ongles; **to ~ one's teeth** se laver les dents; **to get one's hair done** se faire coiffer; **to ~ flowers** arranger les fleurs **11.** (*tour*) **did you ~ India?** est-ce que tu as fait l'Inde ? **12.** (*go at a speed of*) **to ~ ... miles/per hour** faire du ... miles à l'heure; **to ~ ... miles to the gallon** faire du ... litres aux cent **13.** (*cover a distance*) **to ~ Paris to Bordeaux in five hours** faire Paris-Bordeaux en cinq heures **14.** (*be satisfactory*) **"I only have bread – will that ~ you?"** "je n'ai que du pain – ça te va ?" **15.** (*sell*) **to ~ food at lunchtime** servir des repas à midi **16.** (*cook*) faire cuire **17.** (*cause*) **to ~ sb credit** avantager qn; **will you ~ me a favour?**

tu veux me faire plaisir ?; **to ~ sb good/harm** faire du bien/du mal à qn; **to ~ sb the honour of ~ing sth** *form* faire l'honneur à qn de faire qc **18.** *inf* (*burglarize*) **we did the bank** on s'est fait la banque **19.** *inf* (*swindle*) arnaquer **20.** *inf* (*serve prison time*) **to ~ one's time** faire son temps **21.** *Brit, inf* (*suffer*) **to get done for sth** se crever pour qc ►**~ as you would be done by** *Brit, prov* ne faites pas à autrui ce que vous ne voudriez pas qu'on vous fît; **don't just stand there, ~ something!** ne reste pas planté là, réagis!; **what's done cannot be undone** *prov* ce qui est fait est fait; **to ~ it with sb** *inf* coucher avec qn **IV.** <does, did, done> *vi* **1.** (*act*) faire; **you did right** tu as bien fait; **~ as you like** fais comme tu veux **2.** (*be satisfactory*) convenir; **that book will ~** ce livre fera l'affaire; **the money will ~** l'argent suffira; **it doesn't ~ to ~ sth** ça ne sert à rien de faire qc; **will it ~ if I come on Friday?** ça te va si je viens vendredi; **this will have to ~ a meal** il faudra bien que ça nous fasse le repas *subj* **3.** (*manage*) **to ~ well** (*person*) s'en tirer bien; (*business*) marcher bien; **how are you ~ing?** bonjour, ça va ?; **to be ~ing well** aller bien; **you did well to come** tu as bien fait de venir; **this really won't ~!** cela ne peux pas continuer ainsi! **4.** (*finish with*) **to be done with sb/sth** en avoir terminé [*o* fini] avec qn/qc **5.** *inf* (*going on*) **there's something ~ing in town** il y a de l'activité en ville **6.** *Brit, Aus* (*treat*) **to ~ badly/well by sb** mal/bien traiter qn [*o* se conduire mal/bien envers qn]; **he's been hard done by** on s'est mal conduit à son égard **7.** *Brit, inf* (*beat up*) **to ~ for sb** tabasser qn ►**~ or die** marche ou crève; **that will never ~** ça ne suffira jamais; **thank you, that will ~** merci, ça me suffit

◆**do away with** *vi inf* **1.** (*dispose of*) se débarrasser de **2.** (*kill*) liquider

◆**do down** *vt always sep* **1.** *Brit, inf* (*con*) rouler **2.** (*criticize*) dire du mal de

◆**do for** *vt* **1.** *inf* (*defeat, ruin*) bousiller; **to be done for** être foutu **2.** *inf* (*kill*) tuer; **to be done for** être un homme mort **3.** *inf* (*exhaust*) achever; **to be done for** être foutu **4.** *Brit, inf* (*clean house*) **to ~ sb** faire le ménage chez qn

◆**do in** *vt always sep* **1.** *inf* (*murder*) liquider; **to do oneself in** se foutre en l'air **2.** (*make exhausted*) **to be done in** être crevé

domesticated *adj* casanier(-ère)

domesticity [ˌdəʊmes'tɪsəti, *Am:* ˌdoʊmes'-] *n* vie *f* de famille

don [dɒn, *Am:* dɑːn] *n* professeur *m* d'université

donut ['dəʊnʌt, *Am:* 'doʊ] *n Am s.* **doughnut**

doomed *adj* voué(e) à l'échec

◆**do out** *vt always sep* **1.** *Brit, inf* (*decorate*) décorer **2.** *Brit, inf* (*tidy up*) nettoyer à fond **3.** *inf* (*deprive*) **to do sb out of sth** rouler qn

◆**do over** *vt always sep* **1.** *Am, inf* (*redo*) refaire **2.** *Am, inf* (*redecorate*) refaire **3.** *Brit, Aus, inf* (*beat up*) tabasser **4.** *inf* (*ransack*) retourner

◆**do up** **I.** *vt* **1.** (*fasten: buttons*) fermer; (*zip*) remonter; (*laces*) nouer; (*hair, shoes*) attacher; **to ~ sb's buttons** boutonner qn **2.** (*restore: house*) retaper; (*room*) refaire **3.** (*wrap*) emballer **4.** (*dress in an impressive way*) **to be done up** être sur son trente et un; **to do oneself up** se faire beau(belle) **II.** *vi* se fermer

◆**do with** *vt* **1.** (*be related to*) **to have to ~ sth** avoir à voir avec qc; **to have to ~ sb** avoir à faire avec qn; **this book has to ~ human behaviour** ce livre parle du comportement humain **2.** (*bear*) supporter **3.** *Brit, inf* (*need*) **I could ~ a holiday** j'aurais bien besoin de vacances; **I could ~ a sleep** un bon somme me ferait du bien **4.** (*finish*) **to be done with** être fini; **to be done with sth** en avoir fini avec qc; **are you done with the book?** as-tu encore besoin du livre?

◆**do without** *vt* se passer de

DOA [ˌdiːəʊ'eɪ, *Am:* -oʊ-] *adj abbr of* **dead on arrival** décédé(e) en cours de transfert à l'hôpital

docile ['dəʊsaɪl, *Am:* 'dɑːsəl] *adj* docile

docility *n no pl* docilité *f*

dock[1] [dɒk, *Am:* dɑːk] **I.** *n* **1.** (*wharf*) dock *m* **2.** (*for receiving ship*) bassin *m*; **dry ~** cale *f* sèche; **in ~** en réparation **3.** *Am* (*pier*) jetée *f* **II.** *vi* se mettre à quai; **the ship is ~ing** le bateau arrive à quai **III.** *vt* **1.** NAUT amarrer **2.** AVIAT arrimer

dock[2] [dɒk, *Am:* dɑːk] *vt* **1.** (*reduce*) diminuer; **the company has ~ed 15% from the wages** la société a fait une retenue de 15% sur les salaires **2.** (*cut off the tail of*) écourter la queue de

dock[3] [dɒk, *Am:* dɑːk] *n* BOT *no pl* patience *f*

docker *n inf* docker *m*

docket ['dɒkɪt, *Am:* 'dɑː-] **I.** *n* **1.** *Brit, Aus* (*document*) certificat *m* de dédouanage **2.** *Am* (*list of cases*) registre *m* du tribunal **3.** *Am* (*business agenda*) ordre *m* du jour **II.** *vt* consigner

docking *n no pl* **1.** (*stopping in a dock*) amarrage *m* **2.** (*joining together of spacecraft*) arrimage *m* **3.** (*cutting*) réduction *f*; (*of wages*) diminution *f*

dockyard *n* chantier *m* naval

doctor ['dɒktəʳ, *Am:* 'dɑːktɚ] **I.** *n* **1.** (*physician*) médecin *m*; **to go to the ~'s** aller chez le médecin **2.** (*person with a doctorate*) docteur *m*; **~ of Law** docteur en droit; **~'s degree** doctorat *m* ►**the ~'s orders** les instructions *fpl*; **to be just what the ~ ordered** *iron* c'est justement ce qu'il fallait; **this hot bath is just what the ~ ordered** ce bain chaud, c'est exactement ce dont j'avais besoin **II.** *vt* **1.** *pej* (*illegally alter a document*) falsifier **2.** *Brit, pej* (*poison*) frelater **3.** *Brit, Aus, inf* (*neuter*) couper

doctorate *n* doctorat *m*

Un **doctorate** ou un "doctor's degree" dans une matière est le grade académique le plus élevé normalement attribué par une université pour la soutenance d'une thèse. Les "doctorates" les plus courants sont un "Ph.D." ou un "D.Phil." ("Doctor of Philosophy") pour une thèse de troisième cycle; il en existe d'autres tels que le "D.Mus." ("Doctor of Music"), le "MD" ("Doctor of Medicine"), le "LL D" ("Doctor of Laws"). Par exemple, un "D.Litt." ("Doctor of Letters") ou un "D.Sc." (Doctor of Science") peuvent être accordés par une université à une personnalité exceptionnelle pour ses publications d'articles ou autres travaux importants.

doctrinaire *adj pej, form* réactionnaire

doctrine ['dɒktrɪn, *Am:* 'dɑ:k-] *n* doctrine *f*

document ['dɒkjəmənt, *Am:* 'dɑ:-] **I.** *n* document; **travel ~s** papiers *mpl* **II.** *vt* **to ~ a file** rassembler de la documentation pour un dossier

documentary [ˌdɒkjə'mentəri, *Am:* ˌdɑ:kjə'ment̬ə˞i] **I.** <-ries> *n* documentaire *m* **II.** *adj* **1.** (*factual*) documenté(e) **2.** (*contained in documents: evidence*) écrit(e)

documentation *n no pl* **1.** (*evidence*) document *m* **2.** (*information*) documentation *f*

doddery ['dɒdəri, *Am:* 'dɑ:də˞i] <-ier, -iest> *adj* branlant(e)

dodge [dɒdʒ, *Am:* dɑ:dʒ] **I.** *vt* esquiver; (*question*) éluder; (*work*) fuir; (*person*) éviter; (*pursuer*) échapper à **II.** *vi* **1.** (*move quickly*) se défiler **2.** SPORT esquiver **III.** *n* **1.** *inf* (*trick*) combine *f;* **tax ~** magouille *f* fiscale **2.** (*quick movement*) esquive *f*

dodger *n pej* filou *m;* **draft ~** tire-au-flanc *m*

dodgy <-ier, -iest> *adj Brit, Aus, inf* **1.** (*unreliable*) douteux(-euse); (*weather*) incertain(e) **2.** (*dangerous*) risqué(e)

doe [dəʊ, *Am:* doʊ] *n* **1.** (*deer*) biche *f* **2.** (*hare*) hase *f* **3.** (*rabbit*) lapine *f*

DoE *n* **1.** *Brit abbr of* **Department of the Environment** ministère *m* de l'Environnement **2.** *Am abbr of* **Department of Energy** ministère *m* de l'énergie

doer ['du:əʳ, *Am:* -ə˞] *n* personne *f* dynamique

does [dʌz] *he does, she does, it does* **do**

doeskin ['dəʊskɪn, *Am:* 'doʊ-] *n* daim *m*

doesn't *s.* **does not** *s.* **do**

dog [dɒg, *Am:* dɑ:g] **I.** *n* **1.** (*animal*) chien *m;* **hunting ~** chien de chasse; **pet ~** chien de compagnie; **police ~ handler** maître-chien *m* **2.** *pej* (*nasty man*) **the** (**dirty**) **~!** quelle peau de vache! **3.** *pej* (*ugly woman*) cageot *m* ►**you do not have a ~'s chance** *inf* tu n'as aucune chance; **every ~ has its day** *prov* à chacun son heure; **to live a ~'s life** mener une vie de chien; **a ~ in the manger** un empêcheur de tourner en rond; **the lucky ~** le petit veinard; **~ eat ~** *prov* les loups ne se font pas de cadeaux; **to go to the ~s** tourner mal; **to put on the ~** *Am* frimer **II.** <-gg-> *vt* suivre à la trace; **to ~ sb with questions** harceler qn de questions; **the police ~ged the murderer** la police filait l'assassin

dog biscuit *n* biscuit *m* pour chiens **dog collar** *n* **1.** (*a collar around a dog's neck*) collier *m* **2.** *inf* (*jewel*) collier *m* de chien **3.** (*clerical collar*) col *m* de prêtre **dog days** *n pl* période *f* de canicule **dog-eared** *adj* corné(e)

dogged *adj* tenace

dogma ['dɒgmə, *Am:* 'dɑ:g] *n* dogme *m*

dogmatic *adj pej* dogmatique

dogmatism *n no pl* dogmatisme *m*

dogsbody *n Brit, Aus, inf* homme *m* à tout faire, boniche *f*

dog-tired *adj inf* vidé(e)

doing *n no pl* action *f;* **to be** (**of**) **sb's ~** être l'œuvre de qn; **is this your ~?** c'est toi qui as fait ça?

doings *n pl* **1.** *Brit, inf* (*thing*) machin *m* **2.** (*event*) événement *m* **3.** (*activity*) faits *mpl* et gestes

do-it-yourself *n no pl* bricolage *m*

doldrums ['dɒldrəmz, *Am:* 'doʊl-] *npl* **to be in the ~** (*feel depressed*) broyer du noir; FIN être dans le marasme

dole [dəʊl, *Am:* doʊl] **I.** *n* allocation *f* chômage; **the ~ number** le nombre de chômeurs; **to be on the ~** être au chômage **II.** *vt* **to ~ sth out** distribuer qc

doleful *adj* triste

doll [dɒl, *Am:* dɑ:l] *n* **1.** (*toy*) poupée *f* **2.** *Am, inf* (*darling*) petite chérie *f*

dollar ['dɒləʳ, *Am:* 'dɑ:lə˞] *n* dollar *m,* piastre *f Québec*

dollop ['dɒləp, *Am:* 'dɑ:-] *n* portion *f*

dolly <-ies> *n* petite poupée *f*

dolly bird *n Brit, inf* poupée *f*

dolphin ['dɒlfɪn, *Am:* 'dɑ:l-] *n* dauphin *m*

dolt [dəʊlt, *Am:* doʊlt] *n pej* empoté(e) *m(f)*

domain [dəʊ'meɪn, *Am:* doʊ-] *n a.* POL, INFOR domaine *m*

dome [dəʊm, *Am:* doʊm] *n* **1.** ARCHIT dôme *m* **2.** *inf* (*bald head*) crâne *m* d'œuf

domestic [də'mestɪk] **I.** *adj* **1.** (*household: appliance, commitments*) ménager(-ère); (*situation, life, bliss*) familial(e); (*violence, dispute*) conjugal(e); (*fuel*) domestique; **a ~ worker** un(e) employé(e) de maison; **to do ~ work** faire les ménages **2.** (*domesticated: animal*) domestique **3.** ECON, FIN (*not foreign: market, flight, affairs, trade*) intérieur(e); (*products, economy, currency*) national(e); (*crisis, issue*) de politique intérieure; (*wines*) du pays; **gross ~ product** produit *m* national brut **II.** *n* domestique *mf*

domesticate [də'mestɪkeɪt] *vt a. iron* domestiquer

domicile ['dɒmɪsaɪl, *Am:* 'dɑ:mə-] *n form* LAW domicile *m*

dominance ['dɒmɪnənts, *Am:* 'dɑ:mə-] *no pl n a.* MIL suprématie *f*

dominant **I.** *adj a.* BIO, MUS (*characteristic, gene, harmony*) dominant(e) **II.** *n* MUS domi-

nante *f*
dominate ['dɒmɪneɪt, *Am:* 'dɑːmə-] **I.** *vt* dominer **II.** *vi* dominer; (*issue, question*) prédominer
domination *no pl n* **1.** (*control*) domination *f* **2.** (*controlling position*) suprématie *f*
domineer [ˌdɒmɪ'nɪəʳ, *Am:* ˌdɑːmə'nɪr] *vi pej* donner le ton; **to ~ over sb** tyranniser qn
domineering *adj pej* autoritaire
Dominica [ˌdɒmɪ'niːkə, *Am:* ˌdɑː-] *n* GEO Dominique *f*
Dominican I. *adj* **1.** (*of Dominica*) dominicais(e), dominiquais(e) **2.** (*of the Dominican Republic*) dominicain(e) **II.** *n* **1.** (*of Dominica*) Dominicais(e) *m(f)*, Dominiquais(e) *m(f)* **2.** (*of the Dominican Republic*) Dominicain(e) *m(f)*
Dominican Republic *n* République *f* dominicaine
dominion [də'mɪnjən] *n a. form* souveraineté *f*
domino ['dɒmɪnəʊ, *Am:* 'dɑːmənoʊ] <-noes> *n* domino *m*
domino effect *no pl n* effet *m* boule de neige
donate [dəʊ'neɪt, *Am:* 'doʊ-] **I.** *vt* donner; (*money*) faire un don de **II.** *vi* ECON, FIN faire un don
donation *n* don *m*
done *pp of* **do**
doner kebab *n* kebab *m*
donkey ['dɒŋki, *Am:* 'dɑːŋ-] *n* âne *m*
donkey jacket *n Brit* pelisse *f* **donkey work** *no pl n inf* sale boulot *m*
donor ['dəʊnəʳ, *Am:* 'doʊnɚ] *n* donateur, -trice *m, f*; **blood/organ ~** donneur, -euse *m, f* de sang/d'organes
don't = **do not** *s.* **do**
donut *n Am s.* **doughnut**
doodle ['duːdl] **I.** *vi* gribouiller **II.** *n* gribouillage *m*
doom [duːm] **I.** *n* (*grim destiny*) fatalité *f* **II.** *vt* condamner
doomsday *no pl n* REL le Jugement dernier
door [dɔːʳ, *Am:* dɔːr] *n* **1.** (*movable barrier*) porte *f*; **front ~** porte d'entrée; **sliding/swing ~** porte coulissante/battante; **revolving ~** porte à tambour; **to knock at/on the ~** frapper à la porte; **to show sb the ~** mettre qn à la porte; **to lay sth at sb's ~** mettre qc sur le dos de qn; **to shut the ~ in sb's face** fermer la porte au nez à qn; **to leave the ~ open to sth** laisser une porte ouverte à qc **2.** (*house*) pas *m* de porte; **~ to ~** porte à porte **3.** (*doorway*) entrée *f*
doorbell *n* sonnette *f* de porte **doorframe** *n* chambranle *m* **doorkeeper** *n s.* **doorman doorknob** *n* bouton *m* de porte **doorman** <-men> *n* portier *m* **doormat** *n a. pej* paillasson *m*
doornail *n inf* **as dead as a ~** être bel et bien mort
door plate *n* plaque *f* **doorstep I.** *n* perron *m* **II.** <-pp-> *vt Brit, inf* PUBL **to be ~ped** être interviewé sur le pas de porte **door-to-door** *adj* à domicile; **~ selling** porte-à-porte *m*
doorway *n* entrée *f*
dope [dəʊp, *Am:* doʊp] **I.** *n* **1.** *no pl, inf* MED dope *f* **2.** *inf* (*stupid person*) gourde *f* **3.** *no pl, inf* (*information*) tuyau *m* **II.** *vt* MED, TECH doper
dope peddler, dope pusher *n inf* dealer *m*
dopey *adj* <-ier, -iest> **1.** (*drowsy*) hébété(e) **2.** (*silly*) débile
dopy *adj s.* **dopey**
dormant ['dɔːmənt, *Am:* 'dɔːr-] *adj* **1.** (*inactive: volcano*) endormi(e) **2.** BOT, BIO (*not growing*) dormant(e)
dormer (**window**) *n* lucarne *f*
dormitory ['dɔːmɪtəri, *Am:* 'dɔːrmətɔːri] <-ries> *n* **1.** (*sleeping quarters*) dortoir *m* **2.** *Am* (*for students*) foyer *m* d'étudiants; **~ town** ville *f* dortoir
Dormobile® ['dɔːməbiːl, *Am:* 'dɔːr-] *n* camping-car *m*
dormouse ['dɔːmaʊs, *Am:* 'dɔːr-] <-mice> *n* muscardin *m*
dorsal ['dɔːsəl, *Am:* 'dɔːr-] *adj* dorsal(e)
DOS [dɒs, *Am:* dɑːs] *n no pl, no art abbr of* **disk operating system** DOS *m*
dosage ['dəʊsɪdʒ, *Am:* 'doʊ-] *n* dosage *m*
dose [dəʊs, *Am:* doʊs] **I.** *n* **1.** (*portion*) dose *f* **2.** *fig* **in small ~s** à petites doses **II.** *vt* MED traiter
doss [dɒs, *Am:* dɑːs] *inf* **I.** *n Brit, Aus* roupillon *m* **II.** *vi Brit, Aus* roupiller
◆**doss down** *vi Brit, inf* se pieuter
dosser *n Brit, pej, inf* clochard(e) *m(f)*
dosshouse *n Brit, inf* bouge *m*
dossier ['dɒsieɪ, *Am:* 'dɑː-] *n* dossier *m*
dot [dɒt, *Am:* dɑːt] **I.** *n a.* TYP point *m*; **to be on the ~** être à la minute près **II.** <-tt-> *vt* **1.** (*mark with a dot*) pointer **2.** (*distribute widely*) parsemer; **to be ~ted with sth** être criblé de qc ►**to ~ one's i's and cross one's t's** être pointilleux
dote [dəʊt, *Am:* dɑːt] *vi* **to ~ on sb/sth** adorer qn/qc
doting *adj* engoué(e)
dot-matrix printer *n* imprimante *f* matricielle
dotty ['dɒti, *Am:* 'dɑːṭi] *adj* <-ier, -iest> lunatique
double ['dʌbl] **I.** *adj* double **II.** *adv* **1.** (*twice*) deux fois **2.** (*in two: to fold, bend*) en deux; **to start seeing ~** commencer à voir (en) double **III.** *vt* **1.** (*make twice as much/many*) doubler **2.** (*fold in two*) plier **IV.** *vi* **1.** (*become twice as much/many*) doubler **2.** (*serve a second purpose*) *a.* THEAT **to ~ as sb/sth** doubler qn/qc **V.** *n* double *m*; **men's/women's/mixed ~** double messieurs/dames/mixte ►**~ or nothing** [*o Brit* **quits**] GAMES quitte ou double
◆**double back** *vi* faire demi-tour; **to ~ on oneself** revenir à soi-même
◆**double up** *vi* **1.** (*bend over*) se plier en deux; **to ~ with laughter/pain** être plié de rire/de douleur **2.** (*share room*) partager la

même chambre

double-barrelled *adj* 1. (*two barrels: shotgun*) à deux canons 2. *Am, Aus* (*two purposes*) à double usage 3. *Brit* (*name*) double **double bass** <-es> *n* contrebasse *f* **double bed** *n* lit *m* à deux places **double-breasted** *adj* FASHION croisé(e) **double-check** *vt* revérifier **double chin** *n* double menton *m* **double-click** *vi* INFOR double-cliquer **double-cross** I. *vt* doubler II. <-es> *n* double jeu *m* **double-crosser** *n pej* faux jeton *m* **double-dealer** *n pej* fraudeur, -euse *m, f* **double-dealing** I. *n no pl, pej* LAW, ECON, POL fraude *f* II. *adj pej* fraudeur(-euse) **double-decker** *n* autobus *m* à impériale **double Dutch** *no pl n* 1. *inf* baragouin *m* 2. GAMES *jeu de saut à la corde* **double-edged** *adj* 1. (*both negative and positive*) à double tranchant 2. (*with two cutting edges*) à lame double **double-entry bookkeeping** *n* comptabilité *f* en partie double **double feature** *SUBST: programme constitué de deux films principaux* **double-glaze** *vt* poser un double vitrage **double glazing** *no pl n* double vitrage *m* **double-jointed** *adj* très souple **double-park** I. *vi* se garer en double file II. *vt* garer en double file **double-quick** I. *adv* (*very quickly*) très rapidement II. *adj* très rapide; **in ~ time** en un rien de temps

doubles *npl* SPORT double *m*

double-sided *adj* bilatéral(e) **doublespeak** *no pl n* discours *m* ambigu **double standard** *n* **to have ~s** faire deux poids deux mesures **double take** *n* **to do a ~** devoir y regarder à deux fois **doubletalk** *no pl n s.* **doublespeak double-think** *no pl n* pensée *f* contradictoire **double time** *no pl n* double paye *f*

doubly ['dʌbli] *adv* deux fois

doubt [daʊt] *no pl* I. *n* doute *m;* **to be in ~** avoir des doutes; **to cast ~ on sb/sth** mettre qn/qc en doute; **not a shadow of ~** pas une ombre de doute; **no ~** incontestablement; **to have one's ~s about sth** avoir ses doutes quant à qc II. *vt* douter de; **to ~ whether** douter que +*subj*

doubtful *adj* douteux(-euse); **to be ~ about sth** avoir des doutes sur qc; **to be ~ whether** être douteux que +*subj*

doubtless *adv* 1. (*without doubt*) sans aucun doute 2. (*presumably*) sans doute

dough [dəʊ, *Am:* doʊ] *n* 1. GASTR (*mixture to be baked*) pâte *f* 2. *Am, inf* (*money*) pognon *m*

doughnut ['dəʊnʌt, *Am:* 'doʊ-] *n Am* beignet *m,* beigne *m Québec*

doughy ['dəʊi, *Am:* 'doʊ-] *adj* 1. (*dough-like*) pâteux(-euse) 2. *fig* (*pale*) blanc(he) comme un linge

dour [dʊəʳ, *Am:* dʊr] *adj* austère

douse [daʊs] *vt* 1. (*drench*) plonger 2. (*extinguish*) éteindre

dove¹ [dʌv] I. *n* colombe *f* II. *adj* (*grey*) grisâtre

dove² [dəʊv, *Am:* doʊv] *Am pt of* **dive**

dovecot(e) ['dʌvkəʊt, *Am:* -kɑːt] *n* pigeonnier *m*

Dover ['dəʊvəʳ, *Am:* 'doʊvɚ] *n* Douvres

dovetail ['dʌvteɪl] *vi, vt* concorder

dowager ['daʊədʒəʳ, *Am:* -dʒɚ] *n* veuve *f* aristocrate

dowdy ['daʊdi] *adj* <-ier, -iest> *pej* débraillé(e)

dowel ['daʊəl] *n* cheville *f*

down¹ [daʊn] *n* duvet *m*

down² [daʊn] *n* collines *fpl*

down³ [daʊn] I. *adv* 1. (*with movement*) en bas, vers le bas; **to come** [*o* **go**] **~** descendre; **to fall ~** tomber; **to lie ~** s'allonger; **on the way ~ from London** en venant de Londres; **to go ~ to Brighton/the sea** descendre à Brighton/aller à la mer 2. (*less intensity*) **the price is ~** le prix a baissé; **to be ~ 12%** être en baisse de 12%; **the wind died ~** le vent s'apaisa; **the fire is burning ~** le feu s'éteint; **the tyres are ~/right ~** les pneus sont dégonflés/à plat; **sb is run ~** *inf* qn est à plat 3. (*position*) en bas; **~ there/here** là-bas/ici; **further ~** plus bas; **~ South** dans le Sud; **to hit sb when he is ~** frapper qn à terre 4. (*temporal*) **~ to here** jusqu'ici; **~ through the ages** de tout temps; **~ to recent times** jusqu'à présent; **from grandfather ~ to granddaughter** du grand-père à la petite-fille 5. (*in writing*) **to write/get sth ~** coucher qc par écrit ▶**head ~** tête baissée; **to be ~ in the mouth** être abattu; **the sun is ~** le soleil s'est couché; **to pay sth ~** verser un acompte; **to be ~ on sb** en vouloir à qn; **~ with sb/sth!** à bas qn/qc!; *s. a.* **up** II. *prep* **to go ~ the stairs** descendre l'escalier; **to run ~ the slope** descendre la pente en courant; **to fall ~ the stairs** dégringoler les escaliers; **to live ~ the street** habiter plus bas dans la rue; **to paddle ~ stream** descendre le courant en pagayant; **to go/drive ~ the street** descendre la rue; **her hair reaches ~ her back** ses cheveux lui tombent dans le dos; **to come ~ (through) the centuries to sb** être transmis à qn au fil des siècles; **once he has got sth ~ him** *inf* après avoir avalé qc; *s. a.* **up** III. *adj* 1. (*depressed*) **to feel ~** être déprimé 2. INFOR, TECH en panne 3. (*arriving: train*) descendant

down and out, **down-and-out** I. *adj* piteux(-euse) II. *n* clochard(e) *m(f)* **downcast** *adj* 1. (*depressed*) abattu(e) 2. (*looking down: eyes*) baissé(e) **downfall** *n* 1. (*fall from power*) effondrement *m* 2. (*cause of sb's fall*) ruine *f;* **sth is sb's ~** qc est la ruine de qn **downgrade** I. *vt* 1. ECON (*reduce in rank*) dégrader 2. (*disparage*) réduire II. *n a.* ECON dégradation *f* **downhearted** *adj* abattu(e) **downhill** I. *adv* (*toward the bottom of a hill*) en descendant II. *adj* descendant(e); **the ~ hike** la descente

Downing Street *n Brit: résidence officielle*

du Premier ministre britannique située au numéro 10.

download [ˌdaʊn'ləʊd, *Am:* 'daʊnloʊd] **I.** *vt* INFOR télécharger (vers l'aval) **II.** *n* INFOR téléchargement *m*

downmarket I. *adj* bon marché **II.** *adv* à bon marché **down payment** *n* acompte *m* **downplay** *vt* minimiser **downpour** *n* averse *f*, drache *f Belgique* **downright I.** *adj* **1.** (*utter*) pur(e); **it is a ~ disgrace** c'est vraiment une honte **2.** (*frank*) franc(he) **II.** *adv* vraiment **downside** *no pl n* revers *m* **downsize I.** *vt* réduire **II.** *vi* réduire ses effectifs **downsizing** *n* ECON suppression *f* d'emplois

Down's Syndrome ['daʊnz'sɪndrəʊm, *Am:* -ˌsɪndroʊm] *no pl n* syndrome *m* de Down

downstairs I. *adv* en bas de l'escalier **II.** *adj* au rez-de-chaussée **III.** *n no pl* rez-de-chaussée *m* **downstream** *adv* dans le sens du courant **downtime** *no pl n* INFOR, TECH temps *m* d'immobilisation **down-to-earth** *adj* cartésien(ne) **downtown I.** *n no pl, no art* centre *m* **II.** *adv Am* dans/vers le centre ville **III.** *adj Am* du centre ville **downtrodden** *adj* réprimé(e) **downturn** *n* fléchissement *m* **downward I.** *adj* **1.** (*going down*) descendant(e) **2.** (*decreasing*) en baisse; **to be on a ~ trend** avoir une tendance à la baisse **II.** *adv Am s.* **downwards downwards** *adv* vers le bas; **from the 19th century ~** à partir du 19ème siècle

downy ['daʊni] *adj* (*soft*) duveteux(-euse)

dowry ['daʊəri] <-ries> *n* trousseau *m*

dowse[1] [daʊs] *vi* faire de la radiesthésie

dowse[2] [daʊs] *vt s.* **douse**

dowser *n* sourcier, -ière *m, f*

dowsing *n no pl* radiesthésie *f*; **~ rod** baguette *f* de sourcier

doyen ['dɔɪən] *n* doyen(ne) *m(f)*

doz. *n abbr of* **dozen** douzaine *f*

doze [dəʊz, *Am:* doʊz] **I.** *vi* somnoler **II.** *n* (*short nap*) roupillon *m*; **to fall into a ~** s'assoupir

dozen ['dʌzn] *n* (*twelve*) douzaine *f* ►**to talk <u>nineteen</u> to the ~** parler à n'en plus finir

dozy ['dəʊzi, *Am:* 'doʊ-] *adj* <-ier, -iest> **1.** (*drowsy*) somnolent(e) **2.** *Brit, inf* (*stupid*) endormi(e)

DP *n* **1.** *abbr of* **data processing** traitement *m* des données **2.** *abbr of* **displaced person** personne *f* déplacée

D.Phil. *n abbr of* **Doctor of Philosophy** docteur *m* en philosophie

Dr *n abbr of* **Doctor** Dr *m*

drab [dræb] *adj* <drabber, drabbest> *pej* (*colours, existence*) grisâtre

drachma ['drækmə] *n* drachme *f*

draconian [drə'kəʊnɪən, *Am:* -'koʊ-] *adj* draconien(ne)

draft [drɑːft, *Am:* dræft] **I.** *n* **1.** (*preliminary version*) ébauche *f* **2.** *no pl, Am* MIL (*military conscription*) **the ~** l'incorporation *f* militaire *m* **3.** *Brit* FIN, ECON (*bank order*) lettre *f* de change **4.** *Am s.* **draught II.** *vt* **1.** (*prepare a preliminary version*) esquisser; (*a plan*) ébaucher **2.** *Am* MIL (*conscript*) recruter **III.** *adj* **1.** (*preliminary*) en préparation **2.** *Am* MIL appelé(e)

draftee ['drɑːftiː, *Am:* 'dræf-] *n Am* appelé(e) *m(f)*

draftsman ['drɑːftsmən, *Am:* 'dræfts-] <-men> *n Am, Aus* TECH *s.* **draughtsman**

drafty ['dræfti] *adj Am s.* **draughty**

drag [dræg] **I.** *n* **1.** *no pl* PHYS (*force*) résistance *f*; AVIAT traînée *f* **2.** *no pl* (*impediment*) obstacle *m* **3.** *no pl, inf* (*a bore*) raseur, -euse *m, f* **4.** *no pl, inf* SOCIOL (*women's clothes worn by a man*) **to be in ~** être en travesti **5.** *inf* (*breath of cigarette smoke*) taffe *f*; **to have a ~** tirer une taffe **6.** (*dredging*) drague *f* **7.** SPORT *s.* **drag race II.** <-gg-> *vt* **1.** (*pull*) *a. fig* traîner; **to ~ one's feet** traîner les pieds; **to ~ sb out of bed** tirer qn de son lit; **to ~ oneself to sth** se traîner jusqu'à qc; **to ~ sb to sth/sb** traîner qn à qc/chez qn; **to ~ sb's name through the mud** traîner le nom de qn dans la boue **2.** (*search: river, lake*) draguer **3.** INFOR (*icon*) faire glisser **III.** *vi* traîner; (*time, speech*) traîner en longueur; **to ~ on a cigarette** *inf* tirer sur une cigarette

◆**drag along** *vi s.* **drag on**

◆**drag down** *vt* entraîner en bas; **to ~ sb to one's level** rabaisser qn à son niveau

◆**drag in** *vt* **1.** (*pull*) traîner **2.** (*refer to*) faire allusion à

◆**drag on** *vi pej* s'éterniser

◆**drag out** <-gg-> *vt* **1.** (*protract*) faire traîner **2.** (*extract*) **to drag sb out of sth** faire sortir qn de qc; **to drag sth out of sb** soutirer qc à qn

◆**drag up** *vt* **1.** (*mention*) ressortir **2.** *pej* (*raise* (*children*) *badly/roughly*) mal élever

drag lift *n Brit* remonte-pente *m*

dragon ['drægən] *n* dragon *m*

dragonfly ['drægənflaɪ] <-flies> *n* libellule *f*

dragoon [drə'guːn] *n* dragon *m*

drag queen *n* drag queen *m* **drag race** *n* course *f* d'accélération

drain [dreɪn] **I.** *vt* **1.** (*remove liquid from*) *a.* BOT, AGR, MED drainer **2.** *form* (*empty by drinking*) vider **3.** (*tire out*) épuiser **II.** *vi* **1.** (*flow away*) s'écouler **2.** BOT, AGR (*permit drainage*) être drainé **3.** (*vanish gradually*) se vider **III.** *n* **1.** TECH (*pipe for removing liquid*) drain *m* **2.** *pl* TECH canalisation *f* **3.** (*constant expenditure*) fuite *f* **4.** *fig* SOCIOL, ECON **the brain ~** la fuite des cerveaux

drainage ['dreɪnɪdʒ] *n no pl* drainage *m*

drainage basin *n* GEO zone *f* d'influence

draining board *n* déversoir *m*

drainpipe ['dreɪnpaɪp] *n* **1.** TECH collecteur *m* **2.** FASHION **~s** *pl s.* **drainpipe trousers**

drainpipe trousers *npl* pantalon-cigarette *m*

D

drake [dreɪk] *n* canard *m* (mâle)

dram [dræm] *n Scot* gorgée *f*

drama ['drɑːmə] **I.** *n* drame *m* **II.** *adj* dramatique

drama school *n* école *f* de théâtre

dramatic [drə'mætɪk, *Am:* -'mæt̬-] *adj* dramatique

dramatics *npl* **1.** + *sing vb* THEAT (*acting or producing plays*) dramaturgie *f* **2.** *pej* (*exaggerated behaviour*) dramatisation *f*

dramatis personae [ˌdræmətɪspɜː'səʊnaɪ, *Am:* ˌdrɑːmət̬ɪspɚ'soʊ-] *npl*, + *sing vb* THEAT personnages *mpl* principaux

dramatist ['dræmətɪst, *Am:* 'drɑːmət̬ɪst] *n* dramaturge *mf*

dramatization *n* **1.** THEAT, CINE, TV (*adaptation for stage, screen*) adaptation *f* dramatique **2.** *no pl, pej* (*exaggeration of importance*) dramatisation *f*

dramatize ['dræmətaɪz, *Am:* 'drɑːmə-] **I.** *vt* **1.** THEAT, CINE, TV (*adapt for stage or screen*) adapter **2.** (*exaggerate the importance*) dramatiser **II.** *vi* dramatiser

drank [dræŋk] *pt of* **drink**

drape [dreɪp] **I.** *vt* draper; **to be ~d in sth** être drapé de qc **II.** *vi* (*hang loosely: fabric*) draper; (*clothes*) tomber; **to ~ around one's shoulders** se couvrir les épaules **III.** *n* **1.** *no pl* FASHION (*fold*) drapé *m* **2.** *pl* (*curtains*) rideaux *mpl*

draper *n Brit* (*haberdasher*) mercier, -ère *m, f*

drapery ['dreɪpəri] <-ries> *n* **1.** *no pl* (*arranged fabric*) drapé *m* **2.** *no pl, Brit* (*fabric goods*) étoffe *f*; (*for men*) chemiserie *f*; (*for women*) bonneterie *f*

drastic ['dræstɪk] *adj* **1.** (*severe*) drastique; (*measure, cuts*) draconien(ne); (*change*) radical(e); (*action*) énergique; (*rise, change*) dramatique **2.** MED drastique

drat [dræt] *interj* zut!

draught [drɑːft, *Am:* dræft] **I.** *n* **1.** (*air current*) courant *m* d'air **2.** *form* (*gulp*) ingestion *f* de liquide **3.** MED dose *f* **4.** GASTR pression *f*; **on ~** à la pression **5.** NAUT (*water depth*) tirant *m* d'eau **6.** *Brit* GAMES dames *fpl*; **to play ~** jouer aux dames **II.** *adj* **1.** GASTR (*in a cask*) (à la) pression **2.** (*used for pulling: animal*) de trait

draughts board *n Brit* damier *m*

draughtsman <-men> *n* **1.** (*mechanical*) dessinateur, -trice *m, f* (technique) **2.** (*skilled*) bon dessinateur *m*

draughty ['drɑːfti, *Am:* 'dræf-] *adj* <-ier, -iest> plein de courants d'air

draw [drɔː, *Am:* drɑː] **I.** *n* **1.** (*sb/sth attractive*) attraction *f* **2.** (*power to attract attention*) séduction *f* **3.** SPORT (*drawn contest*) match *m* nul **4.** (*lottery*) tirage *m* **5.** (*reaction*) **to be quick on the ~** être rapide à dégainer; *fig* saisir au vol **6.** (*inhaling*) **to have a ~ on sth** prendre une bouffée de qc **II.** <drew, drawn> *vt* **1.** (*make picture*) dessiner; (*a line*) tirer **2.** (*portray*) représenter; (*a picture*) faire **3.** (*pull*) tirer; **to ~ sb aside** mettre qn à l'écart **4.** (*attract*) attirer; (*a cheer*) susciter **5.** (*elicit: a confession*) soutirer; (*a criticism*) provoquer **6.** (*formulate*) faire; (*a conclusion*) tirer **7.** (*extract*) extraire; (*a weapon*) sortir; MED (*blood*) prélever; **to ~ blood** *a. fig* faire saigner **8.** GAMES (*a card*) tirer **9.** (*obtain*) obtenir *inf* **10.** FIN, ECON (*earn*) obtenir; (*a salary*) percevoir **11.** (*select in lottery*) tirer au sort **12.** (*obtain water*) puiser; **to ~ sb's bath** tirer un bain pour qn **13.** GASTR (*get from a cask: beer*) tirer **14.** FIN, ECON (*write a bill: cheque*) tirer **15.** (*inhale: a breath*) prendre; **to ~ breath** *fig* souffler (un peu) **16.** NAUT (*displace water*) jauger **17.** SPORT (*stretch a bow*) bander ▶**to ~ a blank** faire chou blanc; **to ~ the line at sth** fixer des limites à qc; **to ~ a veil over sth** tirer un voile sur qc *f* **III.** <drew, drawn> *vi* **1.** ART (*make a picture*) dessiner **2.** (*move*) se diriger; **to ~ near** s'approcher; (*time*) approcher; **to ~ apart** se séparer; **to ~ away** s'éloigner; (*recoil*) avoir un mouvement de recul; **to ~ ahead of sb/sth** prendre de l'avance sur qn/qc; **to ~ to a close** tirer à sa fin; **to ~ level with sb/sth** égaliser avec qn/qc **3.** (*draw lots*) effectuer un tirage au sort **4.** GAMES (*make a tie score*) faire match nul

◆**draw back** **I.** *vi* **1.** (*recoil*) reculer **2.** (*chose not to do sth*) faire marche arrière **II.** *vt* **1.** (*pull: table, chair*) tirer; (*curtains*) ouvrir **2.** (*attract: person*) faire revenir; **my mother drew me back** ma mère m'a poussé à revenir; **to be drawn back to sth** être attiré par qc

◆**draw down** *vt* (a)baisser

◆**draw in** **I.** *vi* **1.** RAIL, AUTO (*pull in*) arriver **2.** (*become darker: days*) raccourcir; (*nights*) rallonger **II.** *vt* **1.** (*involve*) impliquer **2.** (*retract: reins*) tirer; (*claws*) rentrer **3.** (*inhale*) aspirer

◆**draw off** *vt* retirer; (*a beer*) tirer

◆**draw on** **I.** *vt* **1.** (*use*) se servir de **2.** (*inhale smoke: cigarette, pipe*) tirer sur **3.** (*put on*) mettre; (*boots, gloves*) enfiler **II.** *vi* **1.** (*continue*) s'avancer; (*time*) avancer **2.** *form* (*approach* (*in time*)) s'approcher

◆**draw out** **I.** *vt* **1.** (*bring out*) *a. fig* sortir; (*money*) retirer; **to draw sth out of sth** sortir qc de qc; **to draw sth out of sb** faire parler qn; **to draw sb out of oneself** faire sortir qn de sa réserve **2.** (*prolong*) prolonger; (*vowels*) allonger; (*situation, meeting*) faire traîner; (*meal*) prolonger **3.** (*stretch*) étirer **4.** (*elicit: feelings, memories*) faire ressortir **5.** (*make angry*) pousser à bout **II.** *vi* **1.** RAIL, AUTO (*depart*) partir **2.** (*stay light: days*) rallonger

◆**draw up** **I.** *vt* **1.** (*draft: a document, contract, programme*) dresser; (*a plan*) élaborer **2.** (*pull*) tirer; **to draw oneself up** se dresser **II.** *vi* (*a vehicle*) s'arrêter; (*train*) arriver en gare; (*troops*) faire (une) étape

drawback ['drɔːbæk, *Am:* 'drɑː-] *n* inconvénient *m*

drawbridge *n* pont-levis *m*
drawer ['drɔːʳ, *Am:* 'drɔːr] *n* tiroir *m;* **a chest of ~s** une commode
drawing *n* dessin *m*
drawing board *n* planche *f* à dessin **drawing pin** *n Brit, Aus* punaise *f* **drawing room** *n form* salon *m*
drawl [drɔːl, *Am:* drɑːl] **I.** *n* voix *f* traînante **II.** *vi* parler d'une voix traînante **III.** *vt* marmonner
drawn [drɔːn, *Am:* drɑːn] **I.** *pp of* **draw** **II.** *adj* **1.** (*showing tiredness: face*) tiré(e) **2.** GASTR (*melted*) fondu(e)
dread [dred] **I.** *vt* **1.** (*fear*) craindre **2.** (*be apprehensive*) redouter **II.** *n no pl* terreur *f;* **to fill sb with ~** remplir qn d'effroi; **to live/be in ~ of doing sth** vivre/être dans l'angoisse de faire qc
dreadful *adj* **1.** (*terrible: mistake*) terrible; (*accident*) atroce **2.** (*bad quality*) qui ne vaut rien **3.** (*very great: annoyance, bore*) gros(se)
dreadfully *adv* **1.** (*in a terrible manner*) terriblement **2.** (*poorly*) très faiblement **3.** (*extremely*) fortement
dream [driːm] **I.** *n* rêve *m;* **to have a ~** faire un rêve; **to have a ~ about sth** rêver de qc ▸**in your ~s!** tu rêves!; **like a ~** à merveille; **in my wildest ~s** dans mes rêves les plus fous **II.** *adj* de rêve; **to be (living) in a ~ world** vivre dans un monde imaginaire **III.** <dreamt, dreamt *o* dreamed, dreamed> *vi* rêver; **to ~ about [*o* of] sb/sth** rêver de qn/qc; **~ on!** tu peux toujours y compter!; **to ~ of doing sth** s'imaginer faire qc **IV.** <dreamt, dreamt *o* dreamed, dreamed> *vt* **1.** PYSCH (*experience a dream*) rêver **2.** (*imagine*) imaginer; **to never ~ that...** ne pas même imaginer que ...
◆**dream up** *vt* imaginer
dreamer *n* **1.** PSYCH (*person who dreams*) rêveur, -euse *m, f* **2.** (*impractical person*) idéaliste *mf*
dreamland *n inf* pays *m* de cocagne
dreamless *adj* sans rêve
dreamlike *adj* onirique
dreamt [dremt] *pt, pp of* **dream**
dreamy ['driːmi] *adj* **1.** (*dreamlike*) surréaliste **2.** (*fantisizing*) rêveur(-euse) **3.** *inf* (*delightful*) fabuleux(-euse)
dreary ['drɪəri, *Am:* 'drɪr-] *adj* ennuyeux(-euse)
dredge[1] [dredʒ] **I.** *n* dragueur *m* **II.** *vt* draguer
dredge[2] [dredʒ] *vt* GASTR saupoudrer
dredger[1] *n* TECH dragueur *m*
dredger[2] *n* saupoudroir *m*
dregs [dregz] *npl a. fig* lie *f*
drench [drentʃ] *vt* asperger; **to be ~ed in sweat** être en nage
dress [dres] **I.** *n* **1.** <-es> (*woman's garment*) robe *f* **2.** *no pl* (*clothing*) tenue *f;* **to wear traditional ~** porter le costume traditionnel; **in ceremonial ~** en habit *m* de cérémonie **II.** *vi* s'habiller **III.** *vt* **1.** (*put on clothing*) habiller **2.** GASTR (*greens, salad*) assaisonner; (*vegetables, dish*) accommoder; (*poultry*) habiller **3.** MED (*treat a wound*) panser **4.** (*prepare*) apprêter; (*stone*) taillé(e); **to ~ sb's hair** (bien) coiffer qn **5.** (*decorate: shop windows*) décorer
◆**dress down** **I.** *vi* **to ~ in sth** porter simplement qc **II.** *vt inf* **to dress sb down** passer un savon à qn
◆**dress up** **I.** *vi* **1.** FASHION (*wear formal clothing*) (bien) s'habiller **2.** (*disguise*) se déguiser **II.** *vt* **1.** FASHION (*put on clothing*) **to dress oneself up** s'habiller; **to be all dressed up** être sur son trente et un **2.** (*disguise*) déguiser **3.** (*embellish: a pizza*) garnir; (*a story*) enjoliver **4.** (*present in a better way*) améliorer la présentation de
dress circle *n* THEAT premier balcon *m* **dress coat** *n* manteau *m* habillé
dressed *adj* **1.** (*wearing clothes*) habillé(e) **2.** GASTR (*ready for cooking*) prêt(e) à cuire; (*ready for eating*) prêt(e) à servir
dresser *n* **1.** FASHION **a stylish ~** quelqu'un qui s'habille avec élégance **2.** THEAT habilleur, -euse *m, f* **3.** (*sideboard*) buffet *m* (de cuisine)
dressing *n* **1.** *no pl* FASHION (*wearing clothes*) habillement *m* **2.** GASTR (*sauce*) assaisonnement *m;* **French ~** vinaigrette *f* **3.** MED (*covering for an injury*) pansement *m*
dressing-down *n* **to give sb a ~** enguirlander qn; *inf* habiller qn pour l'hiver **dressing gown** *n* robe *f* de chambre **dressing room** *n* dressing(-room) *m* **dressing table** *n* coiffeuse *f*
dressmaker *n* couturière *f* **dressmaking** *no pl n* couture *f* **dress rehearsal** *n* répétition *f* générale **dress shirt** *n* chemise *f* habillée **dress suit** *n* costume *m* habillé **dress uniform** *n* **full-~** uniforme *m* d'apparat
dressy ['dresi] *adj* <-ier, -iest> **1.** (*stylish: clothing*) habillé(e) **2.** (*formal: occasion*) solennel(le)
drew [druː] *pt of* **draw**
dribble ['drɪbl] **I.** *vi* **1.** (*drool*) baver **2.** (*trickle*) dégouliner **3.** SPORT (*tap the ball*) dribbler **II.** *vt* (*cause to flow in drops*) faire (é)goutter **III.** *n* **1.** *no pl* (*saliva*) bave *f* **2.** (*small droplet*) gouttelette *f* **3.** SPORT (*tapping the ball*) drib(b)le *m*
driblet ['drɪblɪt] *n* gouttelette *f;* **in ~s** en fines gouttelettes
dribs [drɪbz] *npl inf* **in ~ and drabs** petit à petit
dried [draɪd] **I.** *pt, pp of* **dry** **II.** *adj* (*having been dried*) séché(e); (*fruit, vegetables*) sec(sèche); (*mushroom*) déshydraté(e); (*milk*) en poudre
dried-up, **dried up** *adj* (*lake*) asséché(e); (*river*) tari(e)
drier *adj comp of* **dry**
drift [drɪft] **I.** *n* **1.** (*slow movement*) mouve-

D

ment *m;* (*of ship*) dérive *f;* (*of current*) sens *m;* (*of events*) cours *m;* **downward** ~ écroulement *m;* (*of prices*) effondrement *m* **2.** METEO (*mass blown together*) amoncellement *m;* (*of sand*) dune *f;* (*of snow*) congère *f;* (*of clouds*) traînée *f* **3.** (*central meaning*) sens *m* général; **to catch sb's** ~ comprendre où qn veut en venir **4.** TECH (*tool*) jet *m* (d'extraction) **II.** *vi* **1.** (*be moved*) *a. fig* dériver; (*smoke, voice*) flotter; (*attention*) se relâcher; **to** ~ **out to sea** dériver sur la mer **2.** (*move aimlessly*) errer; **to** ~ **away** partir nonchalamment; **to** ~ **along** se laisser aller; **to** ~ **into sth** se laisser aller à qc **3.** METEO (*be piled into drifts: sand*) s'entasser; (*of snow*) former des congères

◆**drift apart** *vi* (*friends*) se perdre de vue

◆**drift off** *vi* s'assoupir; **to** ~ **to sleep** se laisser gagner par le sommeil

drifter *n* personne *f* instable

drift ice *no pl n* glaces *fpl* flottantes

drifting *adj* à la dérive; ~ **snow** amoncellement *m* de neige

drift sand *no pl n* sable *m* mouvant **driftwood** *no pl n* bois *m* de flottage

drill[1] [drɪl] **I.** *n* TECH perceuse *f;* **dentist's** ~ roulette *f* de dentiste **II.** *vt* (*a hole*) percer; (*a well*) forer; (*of rock*) perforer **III.** *vi* forer; **to** ~ **for oil** faire des forages pétroliers

drill[2] [drɪl] **I.** *n* **1.** MIL, SCHOOL (*training*) entraînement *m* **2.** *inf* (*procedure*) **what's the** ~**?** quelle est la consigne? **II.** *vt* entraîner; **to** ~ **sth into sb** faire rentrer qc dans la tête de qn **III.** *vi* s'entraîner

drill bit *n* foret *m*

drilling rig *n* plateforme *f* de forage (pétrolier)

drink [drɪŋk] **I.** *n* **1.** GASTR boisson *f;* **soft** ~ boisson sans alcool; **to have no food or** ~ ne pas s'alimenter *f* **2.** *no pl* (*alcoholic beverage*) verre *m;* **to take to** ~ se mettre à boire **II.** <drank, drunk> *vi* boire; **to** ~ **to sb/sth** boire à la santé de qn/à qc; **to** ~ **and drive** conduire sous l'emprise de l'alcool ►**to** ~ **like a fish** boire comme un trou; **I'll** ~ **to that!** et comment! **III.** <drank, drunk> *vt* boire; **to** ~ **one's fill** boire tout son saoul; **to** ~ **a toast** porter un toast; **to** ~ **sb under the table** tenir l'alcool mieux que qn

◆**drink in** *vt* (*words*) boire; (*beauty, moonlight*) se délecter de

drinkable *adj* **1.** (*safe to drink*) potable **2.** (*easy to drink*) buvable

drinker *n* GASTR **1.** (*person who drinks*) buveur, -euse *m, f* **2.** (*alcoholic*) buveur *m* (invétéré)

drinking I. *n no pl* GASTR **1.** (*beverage*) boire *m* **2.** (*alcohol*) alcool *m;* **to do heavy** ~ boire beaucoup; **her** ~ **destroyed their marraige** son alcoolisme a détruit leur mariage **II.** *adj* GASTR à boire; ~ **glass** verre *m;* ~ **water** eau *f* potable; **a** ~ **man** un homme qui boit; **to change one's** ~ **habits** changer ses habitudes quant à la boisson

drinking fountain *n* fontaine *f* à boissons **drinking straw** *n* paille *f* **drinking water** *no pl n* eau *f* potable **drinking-water supply** *n* alimentation *f* en eau potable

drip [drɪp] **I.** <-pp-> *vi* goutter **II.** <-pp-> *vt* faire (s'é)goutter **III.** *n* **1.** (*drop*) goutte *f* **2.** MED (*feeding*) perfusion *f;* **to be on a** ~ être sous perfusion **3.** *inf* (*idiot*) benêt *m*

drip-dry I. <-ie-> *vi* sécher sans essorer; (*on labels*) ne pas repasser **II.** *adj* ne nécessitant aucun repassage

dripping I. *adj* **1.** (*experiencing a drip: tap, faucet*) qui goutte **2.** (*drenched*) trempé(e) **3.** *iron* **to be** ~ **with sth** être plein de qc **II.** *adv* **to be** ~ **wet** être complètement trempé **III.** *n pl, Am* jus *m* de viande

drive [draɪv] **I.** *n* **1.** (*act of driving*) conduite *f;* **to go for a** ~ aller faire un tour en voiture **2.** (*distance driven*) trajet *m;* **it's a 10 km** ~ **from here** c'est à 10 km d'ici; **it's ten minute's** ~ **from here** c'est à dix minutes d'ici en voiture **3.** *no pl* TECH (*transmission*) propulsion *f;* **front-wheel** ~ traction *f* avant; **a four wheel** ~ un véhicule à quatre roues motrices; **right-hand** ~ (véhicule *m* à) conduite *f* à droite **4.** *no pl* PSYCH dynamisme *m;* **to lack** ~ manquer d'ardeur *f*; **sex** ~ appétit *m* sexuel **5.** (*campaign*) campagne *f;* **to be on an economy** ~ concentrer ses efforts sur l'économie; **a fund-raising** ~ une campagne de récolte de fonds **6.** (*small road*) allée *f* **7.** SPORT (*long hit*) dégagement *m* **8.** AGR (*forced march*) conduite *f* **9.** INFOR **hard disk** ~ unité *f* de disque **II.** <drove, driven> *vt* **1.** AUTO conduire; **to** ~ **10 km** rouler 10 km; **to** ~ **the car in the garage** rentrer la voiture dans le garage **2.** (*urge*) conduire; (*a herd, the economy*) mener; **to** ~ **sb/sth out of sth** chasser qn/qc de qc **3.** (*propel*) entraîner **4.** (*impel*) obliger; **to** ~ **sb to drink/to suicide** pousser qn à la boisson/au suicide **5.** (*render*) rendre; **to** ~ **wild** exciter **6.** (*force through blows: nail, wedge*) planter; (*into the ground*) enfoncer; **to** ~ **a wedge between sb/sth** *a. fig* dresser une barrière entre qn/qc **7.** TECH (*provide the power*) fournir l'énergie **8.** SPORT (*hit*) dégager ►**to** ~ **a hard bargain** attendre beaucoup de qn (en retour); **to** ~ **one's message home** bien se faire comprendre **III.** <drove, driven> *vi* AUTO **1.** (*operate*) conduire; **to** ~ **into sth** rentrer dans qc **2.** (*travel*) se rendre; **to** ~ **past** passer en voiture; **to** ~ **away** partir en voiture **3.** TECH (*function*) fonctionner; (*to cause to function*) actionner; (*to control*) commander; (*to drill*) forer

◆**drive at** *vt inf* en venir à

◆**drive off** *vi* (*car*) démarrer; (*person*) s'en aller en voiture

◆**drive on I.** *vi* poursuivre sa route **II.** *vt* **to drive sb on to** +*infin* pousser qn à +*infin*

◆**drive up** *vi* arriver

drive-in I. *n Am, Aus* drive-in *m inv,* ciné-parc

m Québec **II.** *adj Am, Aus* ~ **cinema** cinéma *m* drive-in, ciné-parc *m Québec*

drive-in bank *n Am, Aus: banque à guichet accessible en voiture* **drive-in cinema**, **drive-in movie** *n Am, Aus* drive-in *m*, ciné-parc *m, Québec*

drivel ['drɪvəl] *no pl n* **to talk** ~ dire des bêtises

driven ['drɪvən] **I.** *pp of* **drive** **II.** *adj* **1.** (*impelled*) animé(e) d'un ardent désir **2.** (*propelled*) actionné(e)

driver *n* **1.** AUTO (*person*) conducteur, -trice *m, f*; **bus** ~ conducteur d'autobus; **lorry/truck/taxi** ~ chauffeur *m* de poids lourd/camion/taxi **2.** SPORT (*golf club*) club *m* de départ **3.** INFOR pilote *m* (de périphérique)

driver's license *n Am* permis *m* de conduire

> Les **Drive through bottle shops** se trouvent partout en Australie. Souvent, ils appartiennent à des hôtels et ressemblent à un garage ouvert ou à une grange (on les appelle souvent aussi des "liquor barns"). On peut y entrer en voiture et, sans avoir besoin d'en descendre, on peut y acheter du vin, de la bière et des spiritueux servis directement par la fenêtre du véhicule.

driveway ['draɪvweɪ] *n* allée *f*

driving **I.** *n* conduite *f*; ~ **while intoxicated** conduite en état d'ivresse **II.** *adj* **1.** AUTO, TECH de conduite **2.** (*related to engine*) moteur(-trice) **3.** METEO (*driven by the wind: rain*) battant(e); ~ **snow** tempête *f* de neige **4.** (*powerful*) puissant(e); ~ **force** le moteur

driving ban *n* retrait *m* de permis (de conduire) **driving force** *no pl n* force *f* directrice **driving instructor** *n* moniteur, -trice *m, f* d'auto-école **driving lessons** *npl* leçons *fpl* de conduite **driving licence** *n Brit* permis *m* de conduire **driving pool** *n* équipe *f* dirigeante **driving school** *n* auto-école *f* **driving test** *n* permis *m* de conduire

drizzle ['drɪzl] **I.** *n no pl* **1.** METEO (*light rain*) bruine *f* **2.** GASTR (*small amount of liquid*) pluie *f* **II.** *vi* METEO bruiner **III.** *vt* GASTR asperger

drizzly *adj* METEO (*day*) de bruine

droll [drəʊl, *Am:* droʊl] *adj* drôle; (*expression*) amusé(e)

dromedary ['drɒmədəri, *Am:* 'drɑːmədər-] <-ries> *n* dromadaire *m*

drone [drəʊn, *Am:* droʊn] **I.** *n no pl* **1.** (*humming sound: of engine*) ronronnement *m*; (*of insects*) bourdonnement *m* **2.** ZOOL, BIO (*male bee*) abeille *f* mâle **3.** *fig* (*lazy person*) feignant(e) **4.** MUS (*low tone*) note *f* (grave) tenue **II.** *vi* **1.** (*make a sound: like an engine*) ronronner; (*like an insect*) bourdonner **2.** (*speak monotonously*) parler d'un ton monotone

◆**drone on** *vi* parler d'un ton monotone

drool [druːl] **I.** *vi* (*slobber: dogs, babies*) baver **II.** *n no pl* **1.** (*saliva*) bave *f* **2.** *fig* ineptie *f*

◆**drool over** *vt* s'extasier devant

droop [druːp] **I.** *vi* **1.** (*sag*) s'affaisser **2.** (*feel depressed*) être déprimé **II.** *n* affaissement *m*

drop [drɒp, *Am:* drɑːp] **I.** *n* **1.** (*liquid portion*) *a. fig* goutte *f*; (*of alcohol*) doigt *m*; ~ **by** ~ goutte à goutte; **to not drink a** ~ ne pas boire une goutte d'alcool **2.** (*fall*) *a. fig* chute *f*; (*from aircraft*) parachutage *m* **3.** (*decrease*) baisse *f*; **a** ~ **in sth** une baisse de qc **4.** (*important height/slope*) chute *f* **5.** (*length, vertical distance*) hauteur *f* **6.** (*difference in level*) écart *m* **7.** (*boiled sweet*) bonbon *m* **8.** *inf* (*collection point*) planque *f* ►**at the** ~ **of a hat** sur le champ **II.** <-pp-> *vt* **1.** (*allow to fall*) lâcher; (*bomb*) larguer; (*anchor*) jeter; (*from airplane*) parachuter; (*by accident*) laisser tomber **2.** (*lower*) baisser **3.** (*abandon*) abandonner; (*person*) laisser tomber; **to** ~ **the subject** parler d'autre chose **4.** *inf* (*express*) laisser échapper; **to** ~ **a hint about sth** faire une allusion à qc; **to** ~ **a word in sb's ear** glisser un mot à l'oreille de qn **5.** (*leave out*) laisser; (*scene, word*) sauter; **to** ~ **one's aitches** *Brit, Aus* ne pas aspirer les h **6.** (*dismiss*) renvoyer **7.** (*give a lift*) déposer **8.** *inf* (*send*) envoyer ►**to** ~ **a brick** [*o Brit* **clanger**] faire une gaffe; **to** ~ **one's guard** baisser la garde; **to let it** ~ **that ...** laisser entendre que ...; **to** ~ **sb like a hot brick** laisser tomber qn comme une vieille chaussette **III.** <-pp-> *vi* **1.** (*fall*) tomber; (*deliberately*) se laisser tomber; (*road, plane*) descendre **2.** (*go lower*) baisser **3.** *inf* (*become exhausted, die*) s'écrouler; **to** ~ (**down**) **dead** mourir subitement ►**to** ~ **like flies** tomber comme des mouches; **the penny** ~**ped** ça a fait tilt; ~ **dead!** *inf* va te faire voir (ailleurs)!

◆**drop back** *vi* se laisser distancer

◆**drop in** *vi inf* **to** ~ **on sb** (*briefly*) faire un saut chez qn; (*unexpectedly*) passer voir qn

◆**drop off** **I.** *vt inf* déposer **II.** *vi* **1.** (*descend*) tomber **2.** (*decrease*) baisser **3.** *inf* (*fall asleep*) s'assoupir; **to** ~ **to sleep** s'endormir

◆**drop out** *vi* (*give up membership*) se retirer; (*of school*) abandonner

drop curtain *n* THEAT rideau *m* **drop-down menu** *n* INFOR menu *m* déroulant

droplet ['drɒlət, *Am:* 'drɑːp-] *n* gouttelette *f*

dropout ['drɒpaʊt, *Am:* 'drɑːp-] *n* **1.** (*sb who drops school*) *étudiant(e) qui abandonne ses études* **2.** (*dissenter*) marginal(e) *m(f)*

dropper ['drɒpəʳ, *Am:* 'drɑːpɚ] *n* pipette *f*

droppings ['drɒpɪŋz, *Am:* 'drɑːpɪŋz] *npl* crottes *fpl*

dross [drɒs, *Am:* drɑːs] *n no pl, pej* âneries *fpl*

drought [draʊt] *n* sécheresse *f*

drove¹ [drəʊv, *Am:* droʊv] *n* **1.** ZOOL troupeau *m* **2.** *pl, inf* (*crowd*) horde *f*; **in** [*o Brit* **in their**] ~**s** en troupeau

drove² [drəʊv, *Am:* droʊv] *pt of* **drive**

drover *n* conducteur *m* de bestiaux

drown [draʊn] I. *vt* noyer; **to ~ oneself** se noyer ►**a ~ing man will clutch at a straw** *prov* il ne faut jamais lâcher prise; **like a ~ed rat** *inf* mouillé jusqu'aux os; **to ~ one's sorrows in drink** noyer son chagrin dans l'alcool II. *vi* se noyer

drowning *n* noyade *f*

drowse [draʊz] *vi* somnoler

drowsy <-ier, -iest> *adj* somnolent(e)

drudge [drʌdʒ] I. *n* bête *f* de somme II. *vi* peiner

drudgery ['drʌdʒəri] *n no pl* corvée *f*

drug [drʌg] I. *n* 1. (*medicine*) médicament *m* 2. (*narcotic*) drogue *f* II. <-gg-> *vt* droguer; **to be ~ged to the eyeballs** *inf* être complètement défoncé

drug addict *n* drogué(e) *m(f)* **drug addiction** *n* toxicomanie *f* **drug dealer** *n* dealer *m* **drug pusher** *n pej* revendeur, -euse *m, f* (de drogue) **drug runner** *n* trafiquant *m* de drogue

drugstore ['drʌgstɔːʳ, *Am:* -stɔːr] *n Am* drugstore *m*

druid ['druːɪd] *n* druide *m*

drum [drʌm] I. *n* 1. (*percussion*) tambour *m* 2. *pl* batterie *f* 3. (*object*) bidon *m* 4. (*washing machine part*) tambour *m* ►**to bang the ~ for sb/sth** rebattre les oreilles avec qn/qc II. <-mm-> *vi* 1. (*play percussion*) battre du tambour 2. (*tap*) *a. fig* tambouriner III. *vt* tambouriner; **to ~ one's fingers** tapoter des doigts
◆**drum into** *vt inf* fourrer dans le crâne

drumbeat ['drʌmbiːt] *n* battement *m* de tambour

drummer *n* batteur *m*

drumstick ['drʌmstɪk] *n* baguette *f*

drunk [drʌŋk] I. *pp of* **drink** II. *adj* 1. (*inebriated*) ivre 2. (*affected*) grisé(e) III. *n pej* alcoolo *mf*

drunkard ['drʌŋkəd, *Am:* -kɚd] *n pej* ivrogne *mf*

drunken ['drʌŋkən] *adj pej* 1. (*in drunk state*) ivre 2. (*addicted*) alcoolique 3. (*showing effects of drink*) d'ivrogne

drunkenness *n no pl* 1. (*being drunk*) ébriété *f* 2. (*habit*) alcoolisme *m*

dry [draɪ] I. <-ier, -iest *o* -er, est> *adj* 1. (*not wet*) sec(sèche); **to go/boil ~** s'assécher 2. (*having no butter: toast*) sans beurre 3. (*with soft drinks*) sans alcool; (*bar*) qui ne sert pas d'alcool 4. (*not sweet: sherry, martini*) sec(sèche); (*champagne*) brut 5. *pej* (*uninteresting*) plat(e) 6. (*sarcastic*) caustique ►**to bleed sb ~** saigner qn à blanc; **to be (as) ~ as a bone** *inf* être sec comme les blés; **to be in ~ dock** être à cale sèche; **to run ~** être vidé II. <dries *o* -s> *n Aus* (*dried season*) sécheresse *f* III. <-ie-> *vt* sécher; (*skin*) dessécher; (*the dishes*) essuyer; (*clothes*) faire sécher; **to ~ oneself** se sécher; **to ~ one's hair** se sécher les cheveux IV. <-ie-> *vi* sécher; (*skin*) se dessécher; **to put sth out to ~** mettre qc à sécher
◆**dry out** *vi* 1. (*make dry*) sécher; (*skin*) se dessécher 2. *inf* (*overcome alcoholism*) se faire désintoxiquer
◆**dry up** I. *vi* 1. (*become dry*) s'assécher 2. (*dry the dishes*) essuyer 3. (*run out: source*) s'assécher; (*goods*) s'épuiser 4. *inf* (*become silent*) la fermer II. *vt* assécher

dry-clean *vt* nettoyer à sec **dry cleaner's** *n no pl* teinturier *m* **dry cleaning** *n* nettoyage *m* à sec

dryer *n* séchoir *m;* **hair ~** sèche-cheveux *m;* **tumble ~** sèche-linge *m*

dry goods *npl* 1. *Brit* (*non-liquid food*) mercerie *f* 2. *Am* FASHION textile *m* **dry ice** *n* neige *f* carbonique

dryness *n no pl* 1. (*lack of wetness*) sécheresse *f* 2. (*drought*) aridité *f* 3. (*opposite of sweet* (*alcohol*)) **the wine has enough ~** le vin est assez sec 4. *pej* (*tedium*) monotone

dry-shod *adj, adv* à pied sec

D.Sc. *n abbr of* **Doctor of Science** docteur *m* en sciences

DTP [ˌdiːtiː'piː] *n abbr of* **desktop publishing** PAO *f*

dual ['djuːəl, *Am:* 'duː-] *adj* double

dub¹ [dʌb] <-bb-> *vt* 1. (*confer knighthood*) adouber 2. (*name*) baptiser

dub² [dʌb] <-bb-> *vt* **to be ~bed into French** être postsynchronisé en français

dubbing *n* 1. *no pl* (*synchronization*) postsynchronisation *f* 2. HIST adoubement *m*

dubious ['djuːbɪəs, *Am:* 'duː-] *adj* 1. *pej* (*doubtful*) douteux(-euse) 2. (*ambiguous*) suspect(e) 3. (*hesitating*) hésitant(e)

Dublin ['dʌblɪn] *n* Dublin

Dubliner *n* Dublinois(e) *m(f)*

duchess ['dʌtʃɪs] *n* duchesse *f*

duchy ['dʌtʃi] *n* duché *m*

duck [dʌk] I. *n* canard *m* ►**like a ~ to water** *inf* comme un poisson dans l'eau II. *vi* 1. (*dip head*) baisser la tête subitement; **to ~ under water** plonger subitement sous l'eau 2. (*hide quickly*) s'esquiver III. *vt* 1. (*evasively dip quickly*) **to ~ one's head** baisser la tête subitement; **to ~ one's head under water** plonger sa tête subitement sous l'eau 2. (*avoid*) esquiver
◆**duck out** *vi* se défiler

duckling ['dʌklɪŋ] *n* caneton *m*

ducky *adj inf* mignon(ne)

duct [dʌkt] *n* conduit *m*

dud [dʌd] I. *n* 1. (*useless object*) toc *m* 2. (*bomb*) bombe *f* non éclatée 3. (*person*) nul(le) *m(f)* 4. (*failure*) échec *m* II. *adj* 1. (*bad*) mauvais(e) 2. (*forged*) faux(fausse); (*cheque*) en blanc

dude [djuːd] *n Am, inf* 1. (*smart urbanite*) dandy *m* 2. (*chap*) type *m*

due [djuː, *Am:* duː] I. *adj* 1. (*owing*) dû(due); (*debt, tax*) exigible; **a bill ~ on 1st January** un effet payable le 1er janvier; **to be ~ sth** devoir qc; **to be ~ sth (to) sb** être redevable de qc à qn; **to fall ~** arriver à échéance; **I am ~ money from sb** qn me doit de l'argent

2. (*appropriate*) **at the ~ time** en temps voulu; **with ~ caution** avec la prudence qui convient; **after ~ consideration** après mûre réflexion; **with (all) ~ respect** sauf votre respect; **to treat sb with the respect ~ to him/her** se comporter envers qn avec tout le respect qui lui est dû **3.** (*expected*) **to be ~ to** +*infin* devoir +*infin;* **to be ~ in** devoir arriver; **the video is ~ out soon** la vidéo va bientôt sortir; **the baby is ~ in May** le bébé doit arriver en mai **II.** *n* **1.** (*right, what is owed*) dû *m;* **to give sb his ~** donner à qn ce qui lui revient **2.** (*fair treatment*) **to give sb their ~** rendre justice à qn **3.** *pl* (*obligatory payment*) droits *mpl;* (*of membership*) cotisation *f;* **to pay ~s** payer ses droits; **to pay one's ~s** (*obligations*) remplir ses obligations; (*debts*) payer ses dettes **III.** *adv* **~ north** plein nord; **to go ~ west** aller droit vers l'ouest

due date *n* échéance *f*

duel ['dju:əl, *Am:* 'du:-] **I.** *n* HIST duel *m;* **to challenge sb to a ~** défier qn en duel **II.** *vi* <*Brit* -ll- *o Am* -l-> HIST se battre en duel

duet [dju'et, *Am:* du-] *n* duo *m*

due to *prep* en raison de; **to be ~ sth** être dû à qc

duffel coat *n* duffel-coat *m*

duffer ['dʌfəʳ, *Am:* -ɚ] *n* âne *m* ►**to be a ~ at physics** être nul en physique

dug [dʌg] **I.** *pt, pp of* **dig II.** *n* mamelle *f*

dugout ['dʌgaʊt] *n* **1.** (*trench*) tranchée *f* **2.** (*shelter*) abri *m* **3.** *Aus* (*canoe*) pirogue *f*

duke [dju:k, *Am:* du:k] *n* duc *m*

dull [dʌl] **I.** *adj* **1.** *pej* (*tedious*) monotone; **deadly ~** mortel(le) **2.** (*not bright*) terne; (*sky, light*) sombre **3.** (*muffled*) sourd(e) **4.** *Am* (*blunt*) émoussé(e) ►**as ~ as ditchwater** ennuyeux comme la pluie **II.** *vt* **1.** (*make dull*) ternir **2.** (*alleviate*) soulager **3.** (*blunt*) engourdir **III.** *vi* **1.** (*become dull*) se ternir **2.** (*become less sharp*) s'émousser

dullness *n no pl* **1.** *pej* (*lacking excitement*) ennui *m* **2.** (*overcast*) *a. fig* tristesse *f;* **the ~ of the weather** le temps couvert

duly ['dju:li, *Am:* 'du:-] *adv* **1.** (*appropriately*) dûment **2.** (*punctually*) en temps voulu

dumb [dʌm] *adj* **1.** (*mute*) muet(te); **deaf and ~** sourd(e)-muet(te); **a ~ approval** un silence de consentement; **to act ~** jouer à l'innocent **2.** *pej, inf* (*unintelligent*) con(ne)

dumbbell ['dʌmbel] *n* **1.** (*weight*) haltère *f* **2.** *Am, pej, inf* con(ne) *m(f)*

dumbfound [ˌdʌm'faʊnd, *Am:* 'dʌmfaʊnd] *vt* abasourdir

dumbfounded *adj* abasourdi(e)

dumbstricken ['dʌmˌstrɪkən], **dumbstruck** *adj* stupéfait(e)

dumfound [ˌdʌm'faʊnd, *Am:* 'dʌmfaʊnd] *vt s.* **dumbfound**

dummy ['dʌmi] **I.** <-mmies> *n* **1.** (*mannequin*) mannequin *m* **2.** (*duplicate*) factice *m* **3.** *Brit, Aus* (*artificial teat*) tétine *f* **4.** *pej* (*fool*) idiot(e) *m(f)* **II.** *adj* **1.** (*duplicate*) factice **2.** (*false*) faux(fausse)

dummy run *n Brit* essai *m*

dump [dʌmp] **I.** *n* **1.** (*area*) décharge *f* **2.** (*messy place*) dépotoir *m* **3.** (*storage place*) dépôt *m* **II.** *vt* **1.** (*throw away*) jeter **2.** (*abandon: project*) abandonner **3.** *inf* (*end relationship suddenly*) larguer **4.** (*save new computer data*) vider

dumping *n* décharge *f*

dumping ground *n* dépotoir *m*

dumpling ['dʌmplɪŋ] *n* quenelle *f*

dumpy <-ier, -iest> *adj* boulot(te)

dun [dʌn] *adj* (*greyish-brown colour*) brun(e) grisâtre

dunce [dʌns] *n pej* âne *m* ►**to be a ~ at sth** être nul en qc

dune [dju:n, *Am:* du:n] *n* dune *f*

dung [dʌŋ] *n no pl* bouse *f*

dungarees [ˌdʌŋgə'ri:z] *npl* **1.** *Brit* (*overall*) salopette *f* **2.** *Am* (*denim clothes*) bleu *m* (de travail)

dungeon ['dʌndʒən] *n* donjon *m*

dunghill ['dʌŋhɪl] *n* fumier *m* ►**to be a ~** être pourri

dunk [dʌŋk] *vt* tremper

duo ['dju:əʊ, *Am:* 'du:oʊ] *n* duo *m*

dup. *n abbr of* **duplicate** double *m*

dupe [dju:p, *Am:* du:p] **I.** *n* dupe *f;* **to be a ~** être dupe **II.** *vt* duper

duplex ['dju:pleks, *Am:* 'du:-] **I.** *n* duplex *m* **II.** *adj* en duplex

duplicate ['dju:plɪkət, *Am:* 'du:-] **I.** *vt* **1.** (*copy*) faire un double de; (*of document*) (photo)copier; (*of cassette, object*) copier; LAW faire un duplicata de **2.** (*replicate*) reproduire; **nothing can ~ motherhood** *fig* rien ne peut remplacer la maternité **3.** (*repeat*) refaire **II.** *adj* en double; **a ~ key** un double de clé; **a ~ recepit/document** le duplicata d'une quittance/d'un document **III.** *n* double *m;* (*of cassette, object*) copie *f;* LAW duplicata *m;* **in ~** en double

duplicator *n* duplicateur *m*

duplicity [dju:'plɪsəti, *Am:* du:'plɪsət̬i] *n no pl, pej, form* duplicité *f*

durability [ˌdjʊərə'bɪləti, *Am:* ˌdʊrə'bɪlət̬i] *n no pl* résistance *f*

durable ['djʊərəbl, *Am:* 'dʊrə-] *adj* **1.** (*hard-wearing*) résistant(e) **2.** (*long-lasting*) durable

duration [djʊ'reɪʃən, *Am:* dʊ-] *n no pl* durée *f* ►**for the ~** provisoirement

duress [djʊ'res, *Am:* dʊ-] *n no pl, form* contrainte *f*

during ['djʊərɪŋ, *Am:* 'dʊrɪŋ] *prep* durant; **~ work** pendant le travail; **~ the week** les jours ouvrables; **to work ~ the night** travailler la nuit; **it happened ~ the night** c'est arrivé au cours de la nuit

dusk [dʌsk] *n* **1.** (*gloom*) pénombre *f* **2.** (*twilight*) *a. fig* crépuscule *m,* brunnante *f Québec*

dusky <-ier, iest> *adj* (*dark*) *a. pej* foncé(e)

dust [dʌst] **I.** *n no pl* poussière *f;* **~ cover** (*for furniture*) housse *f;* (*for books*) jaquette *f* ►**to**

bite the ~ mordre la poussière; **to throw** ~ **in the eyes of sb** jeter à qn de la poudre aux yeux; **to wait till the** ~ **has settled, to let the** ~ **settle, to allow the** ~ **to settle** attendre que tout redevienne calme *subj* **II.** *vt* **1.** (*clean dust from*) dépoussiérer **2.** (*spread finely*) **to** ~ **sth with sth** saupoudrer qc de qc; **to** ~ **sth with insecticide** vaporiser qc d'insecticide **III.** *vi* épousseter

dustbin ['dʌstbɪn] *n Brit* poubelle *f*

duster ['dʌstəʳ, *Am:* -tɚ] *n* chiffon *m,* patte *f Suisse*

dustman ['dʌstmən] <-men> *n Brit* éboueur *m*

dustpan *n* pelle *f* à poussière, ramasse-poussière *m Belgique, Nord*

dust-up *n inf* **1.** (*physical*) bagarre *f* **2.** (*noisy*) altercation *f*

dusty <-ier, -ies> *adj* **1.** (*covered in dust*) poussiéreux(-euse) **2.** (*of greyish colour*) cendré(e)

Dutch [dʌtʃ] **I.** *adj* néerlandais(e), hollandais(e) **II.** *n* **1.** (*people*) **the** ~ les Néerlandais [*o* Hollandais] **2.** LING néerlandais *m* ►**it's double** ~ **to me** c'est de l'hébreu pour moi; *s. a.* **English III.** *adv* **to go** ~ partager l'addition

Dutchman <-men> *n* Néerlandais *m,* Hollandais *m* ►**I'm sure of that or I'm a** ~ j'en suis sûr, ma tête à couper **Dutchwoman** <-women> *n* Néerlandaise *f,* Hollandaise *f*

dutiable ['dju:tiəbl, *Am:* 'du:t̬i-] *adj* taxable

dutiful ['dju:tɪfəl, *Am:* 'du:t̬ɪ-] *adj* soumis(e)

duty ['dju:ti, *Am:* 'du:t̬i] <-ties> *n* **1.** (*obligation*) devoir *m;* **a** ~ **call** une visite de courtoisie; **to do sth out of** ~ faire qc par devoir; **to do one's** ~ faire son devoir; **to entrust with a** ~ confier une tâche **2.** (*task*) fonction *f;* **to do** ~ **for sb** remplacer qn; **to report for** ~ travailler; **to be on/off** ~ reprendre/quitter son travail **3.** (*revenue*) taxe *f;* **customs ~ties** taxes douanières

duty-free [ˌdju:ti'fri:, *Am:* ˌdu:t̬i-] **I.** *adj* hors taxe *inv* **II.** *n* achat *m* hors taxe

duvet ['dju:veɪ, *Am:* du:'veɪ] *n Brit* couette *f*

DVD [ˌdi:vi:'di:] *n inv* INFOR *abbr of* **Digital Versatile Disk** DVD *m inv*

DVD drive *n* INFOR lecteur *m* de DVD **DVD writer** *n* INFOR graveur *m* de DVD

dwarf [dwɔ:f, *Am:* dwɔ:rf] **I.** <-s *o* -ves> *n* (*very small person*) nain(e) *m(f)* **II.** *vt* **1.** (*make smaller*) rapetisser **2.** *fig* écraser

dwell [dwel] <dwelt *o* -ed, dwelt *o* -ed> *vi form* résider; **to** ~ **with sb** habiter avec qn

◆**dwell on** *vi* **1.** (*pay attention to*) s'étendre sur **2.** (*do sth at length*) s'attarder sur

dweller *n form* résidant(e) *m(f)*

dwelling *n form* résidence *f*

dwelt [dwelt] *pp, pt of* **dwell**

dwindle ['dwɪndl] *vi* **to** ~ **to sth** diminuer de qc

dye [daɪ] **I.** *vt* teindre **II.** *n* teinture *f;* (*for hair*) coloration *f*

dye-works ['daɪwɜ:ks, *Am:* -wɜ:rks] *n* teinturerie *f*

dying *adj* **1.** (*process of death*) mourant(e); **to my** ~ **day** à ma mort; **sb's** ~ **words** les dernières paroles de qn **2.** (*ceasing*) moribond(e); **the** ~ **moments of sth** les derniers moments de qc

dyke [daɪk] *n* **1.** (*wall*) digue *f* **2.** (*channel*) fossé *m* **3.** *pej, inf* (*lesbian*) gouine *f*

dynamic [daɪ'næmɪk] *adj* dynamique

dynamics *n* dynamique *f*

dynamite ['daɪnəmaɪt] **I.** *n no pl* dynamite *f* **II.** *vt* dynamiter

dynamo ['daɪnəməʊ, *Am:* -moʊ] <-s> *n* **1.** ELEC dynamo *f* **2.** *fig* **to be a** ~ déborder d'énergie

dynasty ['dɪnəsti, *Am:* 'daɪnə-] <-ies> *n* dynastie *f*

dysentery ['dɪsəntəri, *Am:* -teri] *n no pl* dysenterie *f*

dysfunctional [dɪs'fʌŋkʃənəl] *adj* **to be** ~ fonctionner mal; (*person, family*) à problèmes

dyslexia [dɪ'sleksiə] *n no pl* dyslexie *f*

dyslexic [dɪ'sleksɪk] *adj* dyslexique

dyspepsia [dɪ'spepsiə] *n* dyspepsie *f*

E

E, e [i:] <-'s *o* -s> *n* **1.** (*letter*) E *m,* e *m;* ~ **as in Edward,** ~ **for Edward** (*on telephone*) e comme Eugène **2.** MUS mi *m* **3.** SCHOOL mauvaise note

E *n abbr of* **east** E *m*

each [i:tʃ] **I.** *adj* chaque; ~ **one of you** chacun de vous; ~ **month** tous les mois **II.** *pron* **1.** (*every person*) chacun; ~ **of them** chacun d'entre eux; **£70** ~ 70£ par tête; **we all did 3 hours** ~ nous avons tous fait 3 heures chacun **2.** (*every thing*) **£10** ~ 10£ pièce; **one kilo/three of** ~ un kilo/trois de chaque

each other *reciprocal pron, after verb* l'un l'autre; **made for** ~ faits l'un pour l'autre

eager ['i:gəʳ, *Am:* -gɚ] <more ~, most ~> *adj* **1.** (*keen*) avide; **to be** ~ **for sth** être avide de qc **2.** (*enthusiastic*) enthousiaste **3.** (*impatient*) **with** ~ **anticipation** avec beaucoup d'impatience; **to be** ~ **to** *+infin* être impatient de *+infin*

eager beaver *n inf* **to be an** ~ être quelqu'un de zélé

eagerness *n no pl* impatience *f;* ~ **to succeed** ardent désir de réussir; **to show** ~ **for sth** se montrer enthousiaste pour qc

eagle ['i:gl] *n* aigle *m*

eagle-eyed ['i:glaɪd] *adj* qui a des yeux d'aigle

ear[1] [ɪəʳ, *Am:* ɪr] *n* oreille *f;* **to smile from** ~ **to** ~ sourire jusqu'aux oreilles; ~**, nose and throat specialist** oto-rhino-laryngologiste *mf* ►**to be up to one's ~s in debt/work** avoir des dettes/du travail jusqu'au cou; **to have a good ~ for sth** avoir de l'oreille pour qc; **to be all ~s** être tout ouïe; **to be out on one's ~** se faire sortir; **sb's ~s are burning** qn a les oreilles qui sifflent; **sb's ~s are flapping** qn tend l'oreille; **to have sb's ~** avoir de l'influence sur qn; **to go in one ~ and out the other** rentrer par une oreille et sortir par l'autre; **to have an ~ for music** avoir l'oreille musicale

ear² [ɪəʳ, *Am:* ɪr] *n* BOT épi *m*

earache ['ɪəreɪk, *Am:* 'ɪr-] *n* mal *m* d'oreille(s); **to have (an) ~** avoir mal à l'oreille **earbashing** *n inf* **to give sb an ~** passer un savon à qn **eardrum** *n* tympan *m* **ear infection** *n* otite *f*

earl [ɜːl, *Am:* ɜːrl] *n* comte *m*

earlobe ['ɪələʊb] *n* lobe *m* de l'oreille

early ['ɜːlɪ, *Am:* 'ɜːr-] **I.** *adj* **1.** (*at beginning of day*) matinal(e); **the ~ hours** les premières heures; **in the ~ morning** de bon matin; **~ morning call** appel matinal; **~ riser** lève-tôt **2.** (*close to beginning of period*) premier(-ère); **in the ~ afternoon** en début d'après-midi; **in the ~ 15th century** au début du XVème siècle; **in an earlier letter** dans une lettre précédente; **~ Romantic poetry** poésie du début du Romantisme; **the ~ masters** ART les primitifs **3.** *form* (*prompt*) **to give an ~ answer** donner une réponse rapide **4.** (*ahead of expected time*) anticipé(e); **to be ~** être en avance; **to have an ~ night** se coucher tôt; **~ strawberries** fraises précoces **5.** (*first*) **an ~ edition** une des premières éditions **II.** *adv* **1.** (*in day*) de bonne heure; **to get up ~** se lever tôt **2.** (*ahead of time*) en avance **3.** (*close to beginning of period*) au début de; **~ in life** dans la jeunesse; **~ next year** au début de l'année prochaine; **as ~ as 1803** dès 1803; **what I said earlier** ce que j'ai dit avant **4.** (*prematurely*) prématurément; **to die ~** mourir jeune

Early Church *n* **the ~** l'Église *f* primitive

earmark ['ɪəmɑːk, *Am:* 'ɪrmɑːrk] **I.** *vt* assigner; **the money is ~ed for sth** l'argent est affecté à qc **II.** *n* particularité *f*

earmuffs ['ɪəmʌfs, *Am:* 'ɪr-] *npl* protège-oreilles *m inv*

earn [ɜːn, *Am:* ɜːrn] *vt* **1.** (*be paid*) gagner; **to ~ a living/one's daily bread** gagner sa vie/son pain; **to ~ $800 a week** gagner 800$ par semaine; **he ~s a living from his painting** il vit de sa peinture **2.** *fig* **her painting ~ed her success** sa peinture lui a valu le succès; **to ~ sb nothing but criticism** ne rapporter que des critiques à qn **3.** (*deserve*) mériter

earned income ['ɜːnd'ɪnkʌm, *Am:* 'ɜːrnt-] *n* revenu *m* salarial

earnest ['ɜːnɪst, *Am:* 'ɜːr-] **I.** *adj* **1.** (*serious*) consciencieux(-euse) **2.** (*resolute*) décidé(e); (*attempt*) déterminé(e); (*desire*) ardent(e) **II.** *n no pl* **in ~** sérieusement; **to be in ~** être sérieux

earnings ['ɜːnɪŋz, *Am:* 'ɜːr-] *npl* salaire *m;* **immoral ~** *form* proxénétisme *m*

earnings-related *adj* proportionnel au salaire

earphones ['ɪəfəʊnz, *Am:* 'ɪrfoʊnz] *npl* RADIO, TV (*set*) casque *m;* (*separate*) écouteurs *mpl* **earpiece** *n* **1.** (*of phone*) écouteur *m* **2.** (*of glasses*) embout *m* **earplug** *n pl* boule *f* Quiès® **earring** *n* boucle *f* d'oreille **earshot** *n no pl* **to be in/out of ~** être à/hors de portée de voix

earth [ɜːθ, *Am:* ɜːrθ] **I.** *n no pl* **1.** *a.* ELEC terre *f;* **(planet) Earth** la (planète) terre; **the ~'s crust/atmosphere** la croûte/l'atmosphère terrestre; **to look like nothing on ~** être fagoté comme un sac; **who/where/why on ~ ...** *inf* qui/où/pourquoi donc ... **2.** (*animal's hole*) terrier *m* ▶**to bring sb/to come back (down) to ~** ramener qn/revenir sur terre; **to cost the ~** coûter les yeux de la tête; **to go to ~** se terrer; **to promise the earth** promettre la lune **II.** *vt Brit* ELEC mettre à la terre

earthbound ['ɜːθbaʊnd, *Am:* 'ɜːrθ-] *adj fig* terre à terre

earthenware ['ɜːθnweəʳ, *Am:* 'ɜːrθnwer] **I.** *n no pl* poterie *f* **II.** *adj* en faïence

earthling ['ɜːθlɪŋ, *Am:* 'ɜːrθ-] *n* terrien(ne) *m(f)*

earthly ['ɜːθlɪ, *Am:* 'ɜːrθ-] **I.** *adj* **1.** (*concerning life on earth*) terrestre **2.** *inf* (*possible*) **it is of no ~ use to her** ça ne lui est d'aucune utilité; **there is no ~ reason for him to come** il n'y a aucune raison pour qu'il vienne **II.** *n Brit, inf* **not to have an ~** ne pas avoir la moindre chance

earthquake ['ɜːθkweɪk, *Am:* 'ɜːrθ-] *n* **1.** tremblement *m* de terre **2.** *fig* bouleversement *m*

earthquake zone *n* zone *f* sismique

earth-shattering *adj* incroyable **earthwork** *n* **1.** *pl* MIL levée *f* de terre **2.** (*work*) terrassement *m* **earthworm** *n* lombric *m*

earthy ['ɜːθɪ, *Am:* 'ɜːr-] <-ier, -iest> *adj* **1.** (*with earth*) terreux(-euse) **2.** (*vulgar*) cru(e)

earwax ['ɪəwæks, *Am:* 'ɪr-] *n* cérumen *m*

earwig ['ɪəwɪɡ, *Am:* 'ɪr-] *n* perce-oreille *m*

ease [iːz] **I.** *n* **1.** (*opp: effort*) facilité *f;* **for ~ of use** pour un usage facile; **to do sth with ~** faire qc avec aisance **2.** (*comfort*) aisance *f;* **to feel ill at ~** se sentir mal à l'aise **3.** (*relaxed attitude*) aisance *f;* **to put sb at (their) ~** mettre qn à l'aise **4.** MIL **to stand at ~** se tenir au repos **II.** *vt* (*situation*) améliorer; (*crisis, problem*) atténuer; (*mind*) tranquilliser; (*pain*) adoucir; (*strain*) calmer; (*traffic*) alléger; **to ~ sth into/out of sth** aider qc à entrer dans/à sortir de qc **III.** *vi* s'atténuer; (*tension*) se détendre; (*traffic*) s'améliorer

◆**ease off, ease up** *vi* (*trade*) se ralentir; (*crisis*) se calmer; (*activity*) diminuer; (*pain*) s'estomper

easel ['iːzl] *n* chevalet *m*

easily ['iːzəlɪ] *adv* **1.** (*without difficulty*) facilement; **it's ~ done** c'est facile a faire; **to**

win ~ gagner haut la main **2.** (*clearly*) certainement; **to be ~ the best** être de loin le meilleur **3.** (*probably*) probablement; **you could ~ go** tu pourrais y aller sans problème

east ['i:st] **I.** *n* **1.** (*cardinal point*) est *m;* **to lie 5 km to the ~ of sth** être à 5 km à l'est de qc; **an ~-facing window** une fenêtre exposée à l'est; **to go/drive to the ~** aller/rouler vers l'est; **further ~** plus à l'est **2.** GEO est *m;* **in the ~ of France** dans l'est de la France **3.** POL **the East** (les pays de) l'Est **II.** *adj* d'est, oriental, est; **~ wind** vent *m* d'est; **~ coast** côte *f* est [*o* orientale]

eastbound ['i:stbaʊnd] *adj* en direction de l'est

East End *n Brit: quartiers est de Londres*

Easter ['i:stəʳ, *Am:* -stɚ] *n no pl* REL Pâques *fpl;* **at/over ~** à Pâques

Easter Day *n no pl* REL dimanche *m* de Pâques **Easter egg** *n* œuf *m* de Pâques **Easter holidays** *npl* vacances *fpl* de Pâques **Easter Island** *n* l'île *f* de Pâques

easterly ['i:stəlɪ, *Am:* -stɚ-] **I.** *adj* **1.** (*in the east*) à l'est **2.** (*towards east*) vers l'est **3.** (*from east*) de l'est **II.** *n* vent *m* d'est

Easter Monday *n no pl* REL lundi *m* de Pâques

eastern ['i:stən, *Am:* -stɚn] *adj* d'est; **~ Scotland** l'est de l'Écosse; **the ~ part of the country** l'est du pays

Eastern bloc *n* **the ~** les pays *mpl* de l'Est **Eastern Church** *n* **the ~** l'Église *f* orthodoxe

easterner ['i:stənəʳ, *Am:* -tɚnɚ] *n Am* habitant(e) *m(f)* de la côte Est des USA

easternmost ['i:stənməʊst, *Am:* -stɚnmoʊst] *adj* **the ~ zone** la zone le plus à l'est

Easter Sunday *s.* **Easter Day**

eastward ['i:stwəd, *Am:* -wɚd] **I.** *adj* est; **in an ~ direction** en direction de l'est **II.** *adv s.* **eastwards**

eastwards ['i:stwədz, *Am:* -wɚdz] *adv* vers l'est

easy ['i:zɪ] **I.** *adj* **1.** (*simple*) facile; **within ~ reach** à portée de main; **to be far from ~** ne pas être facile; **it's ~ to cook/clean** c'est facile à cuisiner/à nettoyer; **he's ~ to annoy** il est vite contrarié; **it's an ~ mistake to make** c'est une faute qu'on fait facilement; **~ to get on with** facile à vivre; **it's as ~ as anything** c'est un jeu d'enfant; **that's easier said than done** *inf* c'est plus facile à dire qu'à faire; **the ~ way out** la solution de facilité; **~ money** *inf* argent vite gagné; **available on ~ terms** FIN disponible avec facilités de paiement **2.** (*comfortable, carefree*) confortable; (*mind*) tranquille; **to be ~ in one's mind** être sans souci **3.** (*relaxed*) décontracté(e); (*charm*) agréable; **~ on the ear** agréable à l'oreille; **to walk at an ~ pace** marcher d'un pas souple; **to be on ~ terms** être en bons termes **4.** *pej* (*overly simple*) simplet(te) ►**to be on ~ street** *inf* ne pas avoir de problèmes financiers **II.** *adv* avec précaution; **to go ~ on sth** *inf* être prudent avec qc; **go ~ on coffee!** ralentis un peu le café!; **to go ~ on sb** *inf* y aller doucement avec qn ►**take things ~** n'en fais pas trop; **take it ~!** du calme!; **to be an ~ touch** *inf* être un pigeon; **~ come, ~ go** *inf* vite gagné, vite dépensé **III.** *interj inf* **~ does it!** doucement!

easy-care *adj* facile d'entretien **easy chair** *n* fauteuil *m* **easy-going** *adj* (*person*) facile à vivre; (*attitude*) complaisant(e) **easy-peasy** *adj Brit, childspeak, inf* fastoche

eat [i:t] **I.** <ate, eaten> *vt* manger; **to ~ breakfast/a meal** prendre le petit déjeuner/un repas; **to ~ lunch** déjeuner; **to ~ one's fill** manger à sa faim ►**to ~ sb for breakfast** *inf* ne faire qu'une bouchée de qn; **I'll ~ my hat if ...** je veux bien être pendu si ...; **to ~ sb out of house and home** ruiner qn en nourriture; **to ~ humble pie** [*o* **crow** *Am, Aus*] *inf* mettre sa fierté de côté; **what's ~ing him?** *inf* quelle mouche le pique? **II.** *vi* manger; **to ~ for comfort** manger pour se réconforter; **let's ~ out** allons au restaurant ►**to have sb ~ out of one's hand** faire faire à qn tout ce que l'on veut; **to ~ like a horse** manger comme quatre

◆**eat away** *vt* (*metal, wood*) ronger; (*savings*) entamer; (*time*) dévorer

◆**eat up** *vt* (*meal*) finir de manger; (*time, savings*) dévorer; **eaten up with jealousy** *fig* dévoré de jalousie

eatable ['i:təbl, *Am:* -t̬ə-] *adj* comestible; (*meal*) mangeable

eat-by date ['i:tbaɪˌdeɪt] *n* date *f* de péremption

eaten ['i:tn, *Am:* -t̬ən] *pp of* **eat**

eater ['i:təʳ, *Am:* -t̬ɚ] *n* **1.** (*person*) mangeur, -euse *m, f* **2.** *Brit, inf* (*eating apple*) pomme *f* à couteau

eating ['i:tɪŋ, *Am:* -t̬ɪŋ] **I.** *n* manger *m* **II.** *adj* **~ house** restaurant *m;* **~ habits** habitudes *fpl* alimentaires

eaves [i:vz] *npl* avant-toit *m*

eavesdrop ['i:vzdrɒp, *Am:* -drɑ:p] <-pp-> *vi* écouter aux portes; **to ~ on sth/sb** écouter indiscrètement qc/qn **eavesdropper** *n* oreille *f* indiscrète

ebb [eb] **I.** *vi* **1.** (*tide*) baisser **2.** *fig* **to ~ and flow** monter et descendre **II.** *n no pl* **1.** reflux *m;* **the sea is on the ~** la mer se retire **2.** *fig* **the ~ and flow** les hauts et les bas; **to be at a low ~** avoir le moral très bas

ebony ['ebənɪ] **I.** *n* ébène *m* **II.** *adj* en ébène

ebullient [ɪ'bʌlɪənt, *Am:* -'bʊljənt] *adj* exubérant(e)

EC [ˌi:'si:] *n abbr of* **European Community** CE *f*

e-cash *n* INFOR *abbr of* **electronic cash** monnaie *f* électronique

ECB [ˌi:si:'bi:] *n abbr of* **European Central Bank** BCE *f*

eccentric [ɪk'sentrɪk] **I.** *n* excentrique *mf* **II.** *adj* excentrique; (*behaviour*) bizarre; (*clothes*) original(e)

eccentricity [ˌeksen'trɪsəti, *Am:* -əţɪ] *n* **1.** <-ies> (*traits*) originalité *f* **2.** *no pl* (*quality*) excentricité *f*

ecclesiastical [ɪˌkli:zɪ'æstɪkl] *adj form* ecclésiastique

ECG [ˌi:si:'dʒi:] *n abbr of* **electrocardiogram** ECG *m*

echelon ['eʃəlɒn, *Am:* -lɑ:n] *n* **1.** (*strata*) niveau *m* **2.** MIL échelon *m*

echo ['ekəʊ, *Am:* -oʊ] **I.** <-es> *n a. fig* écho *m* ►**to cheer sb to the ~** applaudir qn à tout rompre **II.** <-es, -ing, -ed> *vi* faire écho; **to ~ with sth** retentir de qc **III.** <-es, -ing, -ed> *vt* **1.** répéter **2.** *fig* rappeler

echo chamber *n* chambre *f* sonore **echo sounder** *n* sondeur *m* à ultrasons

eclipse [ɪ'klɪps] **I.** *n* **1.** éclipse *f;* **lunar/solar ~** éclipse de lune/du soleil **2.** *no pl, fig* **to be in ~** se faire rare; **to go into ~** disparaître petit à petit **II.** *vt* **1.** éclipser **2.** *fig* cacher; **to ~ sb** surpasser qn

ECOFIN ['ekəʊfɪn] *n abbr of* **Economic and Finance Ministers Council** ECOFIN *m*

ecological [ˌi:kə'lɒdʒɪkl, *Am:* -'lɑ:dʒɪ-] *adj* écologique

ecologically [ˌɪ:kə'lɒdʒɪklɪ, *Am:* -'lɑ:dʒɪ-] *adv* de façon écologique; **~ friendly** qui respecte l'écologie; **~ harmful** qui nuit à l'écologie

ecologist [i:'kɒlədʒɪst, *Am:* -'kɑ:lə-] *n* écologiste *mf*

ecology [i:'kɒlədʒɪ, *Am:* -'kɑ:lə-] *n no pl* écologie *f*

ecology movement *n* écologisme *m*

e-commerce ['i:kɒmɜ:s, *Am:* -kɑ:mɜ:rs] *n* commerce *m* électronique

economic [ˌi:kə'nɒmɪk, *Am:* -'nɑ:mɪk] *adj* économique

economical [ˌi:kə'nɒmɪkl, *Am:* -'nɑ:mɪ-] *adj* économe; *pej* avare; **it's not ~** ce n'est pas économique; **to be ~ with the truth** *iron* ne pas dire toute la vérité

Economic and Finance Ministers Council *n* Conseil *m* des ministres de l'Économie et des Finances **Economic and Monetary Union** *n* Union *f* économique et monétaire **Economic and Social Committee** *n* Comité *m* économique et social

economics [ˌi:kə'nɒmɪks, *Am:* -'nɑ:mɪks] *npl* **1.** + *sing vb* (*discipline*) économie *f;* **School of Economics** faculté *f* de sciences économiques **2.** + *pl vb* (*matter*) aspects *mpl* économiques

economist [ɪ'kɒnəmɪst, *Am:* -'kɑ:nə-] *n* économiste *mf*

economize [ɪ'kɒnəmaɪz, *Am:* -'kɑ:nə-] *vi* économiser

economy [ɪ'kɒnəmɪ, *Am:* -'kɑ:nə-] <-ies> *n* économie *f;* **the state of the ~** la situation économique

economy class *n* AVIAT classe *f* économique **economy size** *n* COM paquet *m* familial

ecosystem ['i:kəʊsɪstəm, *Am:* 'ekoʊ-] *n* écosystème *m*

ecotourism ['i:kəʊtʊərɪzəm, *Am:* 'ekoʊ-] *n* écotourisme *m*

ecstasy ['ekstəsɪ] <-ies> *n* **1.** *a.* REL extase *f;* **to be in/go into ecstasies over sth** être/tomber en extase devant qc **2.** *no pl, inf* (*drug*) ecstasy *f*

ecstatic [ɪk'stætɪk, *Am:* ek'stæţ-] *adj* extatique; **to be not exactly ~ about sth** *iron, inf* ne pas être vraiment enchanté de qc

ECU ['eɪkju:, 'i:kju:, *Am:* 'eɪku:] *n abbr of* **European Currency Unit** ECU *m*

Ecuador ['ekwədɔ:ʳ, *Am:* -dɔ:r] *n* l'Équateur *m*

Ecuadorian [ˌekwə'dɔ:rɪən] **I.** *adj* équatorien(ne) **II.** *n* Équatorien(ne) *m(f)*

ecumenical [ˌi:kju:'menɪkl, *Am:* ˌekjʊ'-] *adj form* œcuménique

eczema ['eksɪmə, *Am:* -sə-] *n no pl* eczéma *m*

ed. **I.** *n* **1.** *abbr of* **editor** ed. **2.** *abbr of* **edition** ed. **II.** *adj abbr of* **edited** ed.

eddy ['edɪ] **I.** <-ie-> *vi* **1.** (*smoke, wind*) tourbillonner **2.** (*water*) faire des remous **II.** <-ies> *n* tourbillon *m;* (*of water*) remous *m*

Eden ['i:dn] *n no pl* l'Eden *m;* **the garden of ~** le Paradis terrestre

edge [edʒ] **I.** *n* **1.** (*limit*) *a. fig* bord *m;* (*of road*) bordure *f;* (*of woods*) lisière *f;* (*of table*) rebord *m* **2.** (*cutting part of blade*) tranchant *m;* **a stone with a sharp ~** une pierre à arête vive; **to put an ~ on a knife** aiguiser un couteau; **to take the ~ off sth** émousser qc; *fig* adoucir qc **3.** *no pl* (*sharpness*) acuité *f* ►**to be on ~** être nerveux; **to be on the ~ of one's seat** être tenu en haleine; **it sets my teeth on ~** ça me fait grincer des dents; **to have the ~ over sb/sth** avoir un léger avantage *m* sur qn/qc **II.** <-ging> *vt* **1.** (*border*) border **2.** (*move*) **to ~ one's way into sth** se faufiler dans qc **III.** <-ging> *vi* **to ~ closer** s'approcher lentement; **to ~ away** s'éloigner lentement; **to ~ forward** s'avancer doucement

◆**edge out** *vt* (*opponent*) éliminer

edgeways ['edʒweɪz], **edgewise** *adv* **1.** (*sideways*) latéralement; (*place, push*) de côté **2.** (*with edge foremost*) de chant ►**not to get a word in ~** ne pas pouvoir placer un mot

edgy ['edʒɪ] <-ier, -iest> *adj inf* énervé(e)

edible ['edɪbl] *adj* comestible

edict ['i:dɪkt] *n form* édit *m*

edification [ˌedɪfɪ'keɪʃn] *n no pl, form* instruction *f*

edifice ['edɪfɪs] *n* **1.** *form* (*building*) édifice *m* **2.** *fig* (*of ideas*) structure *f*

edify ['edɪfaɪ] <-ie-> *vt a. iron* édifier

edifying *adj iron* instructif(-ive); *form* édifiant(e)

Edinburgh ['edɪnbrə, *Am:* -bʌrə] *n* Edimbourg

Depuis 1947 à Edimbourg, la capitale de l'Écosse, l'**Edinburgh International Festival** est organisé tous les ans à partir de la mi-août et dure trois semaines. Il présente de nombreuses représentations théâtrales, des concerts, des opéras et des ballets. Parallèlement se déroulent aussi un grand "Film Festival", un "Jazz Festival" et un "Book Festival". En marge du "Festival" officiel s'est développé un très grand "festival fringe", vivant et innovatif, qui propose plus de 1000 manifestations différentes.

edit ['edɪt] *vt* **1.** (*correct*) réviser **2.** (*be responsible for publications*) diriger **3.** CINE (*film*) monter **4.** INFOR (*file*) éditer
◆**edit out** *vt* couper

edition [ɪ'dɪʃn] *n* **1.** TYP édition *f;* **hardback/paperback** ~ édition cartonnée/de poche; **first** ~**s** éditions *fpl* originales; **limited** ~ édition à tirage limité **2.** RADIO, TV diffusion *f* **3.** *Am* (*repetition*) **it's the 11th** ~ **of this tournament** ce tournoi se joue pour la onzième fois **4.** (*copy*) reproduction *f*

editor ['edɪtəʳ, *Am:* -tɚ] *n* **1.** TYP (*of newspaper, magazine*) rédacteur, -trice *m, f* en chef; **sports** ~ rédacteur *m* sportif; (*of publishing department*) éditeur, -trice *m, f* **2.** (*person editing texts: classic texts*) éditeur, -trice *m, f;* (*article*) assistant(e) *m(f)* de rédaction **3.** CINE monteur, -euse *m, f* **4.** INFOR éditeur *m*

editorial [ˌedɪ'tɔːrɪəl, *Am:* -ə'-] **I.** *n* éditorial *m* **II.** *adj* de la rédaction; ~ **staff** rédaction *f*

EDP [ˌiːdiː'piː] *n abbr of* **electronic data processing** informatique *f*

educate ['edʒʊkeɪt] *vt* **1.** (*bring up*) éduquer **2.** (*teach*) instruire; ~**d in Canada** qui a fait ses études au Canada **3.** (*train*) former; (*animal*) dresser **4.** (*inform*) **to** ~ **sb in** [*o* **about**] **sth** informer qn sur qc

educated ['edʒʊkeɪtɪd, *Am:* -t̬ɪd] *adj* instruit(e); **highly** ~ cultivé(e); **to be Oxford** ~ avoir étudié à Oxford

education [ˌedʒʊ'keɪʃn] *n no pl* **1.** (*system*) enseignement *m;* **the Department of** ~ POL le ministère de l'éducation **2.** (*training*) formation *f;* **I had little** ~ j'ai peu d'instruction; **literary** ~ études *fpl* littéraires **3.** UNIV sciences *fpl* de l'éducation

educational [ˌedʒʊ'keɪʃənl] *adj* **1.** SCHOOL scolaire; (*film*) éducatif(-ive); (*software*) pédagogique; (*system*) d'enseignement; **his** ~ **background** son cursus scolaire; ~ **psychology** psychopédagogie *f* **2.** (*instructive*) instructif(-ive); **for** ~ **purposes** dans un but pédagogique **3.** (*raising awareness*) d'information

educationalist [ˌedʒʊ'keɪʃənəlɪst] *n,* **educationist** [ˌedʒʊ'keɪʃənɪst] *n* éducateur, -trice *m, f*

educator ['edʒʊkeɪtəʳ, *Am:* -t̬ɚ] *n Am* éducateur, -trice *m, f*

EEC [ˌiːiː'siː] *n no pl* HIST *abbr of* **European Economic Community** CEE *f*

EEG [ˌiːiː'dʒiː] *n abbr of* **electroencephalogram**

eel [iːl] *n* anguille *f* ▶**to be slippery as an** ~ glisser entre les doigts

eerie ['ɪərɪ, *Am:* 'ɪrɪ] <-r, -st>, **eery** <-ier, -iest> *adj* **1.** (*strange*) sinistre **2.** (*mysterious*) surnaturel(le) **3.** (*frightening*) inquiétant(e)

efface [ɪ'feɪs] *vt* **1.** effacer **2.** *fig* **to** ~ **oneself** s'effacer

effect [ɪ'fekt] **I.** *n* **1.** (*consequence*) effet *m;* **the** ~ **was to make things worse** ça a eu pour effet de faire empirer les choses; **the** ~ **this had on the children** l'effet que cela a eu sur les enfants; **to come into in** ~ (*changes*) prendre effet; (*law*) entrer en vigueur; **to take** ~ (*change*) entrer en vigueur; (*drug*) commencer à agir; **with immediate** ~ avec effet immédiat; **did it have any** ~**?** est-ce que cela eu un effet?; **to great** ~ avec beaucoup d'impact; **to no** ~ en vain; **he uses his contacts to good** ~ il utilise ses connaissances à son avantage **2.** *no pl* (*impression*) effet *m;* **for artistic** ~ pour faire un effet artistique; **the overall** ~ l'effet général; **for** ~ *pej* pour faire de l'effet **3.** *pl* (*artist's tricks*) effets *mpl;* **sound** ~**s** bruitage *m* **4.** (*meaning*) **a letter to the** ~ **that ...** une lettre selon laquelle ...; **in** ~ en effet **5.** *pl* (*belongings*) **personal** ~**s** effets *mpl* personnels **II.** *vt* effectuer; (*merger*) réaliser; (*change*) provoquer

effective [ɪ'fektɪv] *adj* **1.** (*achieving result: measures, medicine*) efficace; (*person*) compétent(e) **2.** (*operative: law*) en vigueur **3.** (*impressive: demonstration, lighting*) impressionnant(e) **4.** (*real: leader*) véritable; (*cost*) effectif

effectiveness *n no pl* efficacité *f*

effeminate [ɪ'femɪnət] *adj pej* efféminé(e)

effervesce [ˌefə'ves, *Am:* -ɚ'-] *vi* pétiller

effervescence [ˌefə'vesns, *Am:* -ɚ'-] *n no pl* effervescence *f*

effervescent [ˌefə'vesnt, *Am:* -ɚ'-] *adj* **1.** effervescent(e); (*drink*) gazeux(-euse) **2.** *fig* exubérant(e)

efficacious [ˌefɪ'keɪʃəs] *adj form* efficace

efficacy ['efɪkəsɪ] *n form* efficacité *f*

efficiency [ɪ'fɪʃnsɪ] *n no pl* **1.** (*competence*) bon fonctionnement *m;* (*of a method*) efficacité *f;* (*of a person*) compétence *f* **2.** TECH rendement *m*

efficient [ɪ'fɪʃnt] *adj* efficace; (*person*) compétent(e)

effigy ['efɪdʒi] *n* effigie *f*

effluent ['eflʊənt] *n* effluent *m*

effort ['efət, *Am:* -ɚt] *n* **1.** (*work*) effort *m;* **to be worth the** ~ valoir la peine; **it's an** ~ **for him to breathe** ça lui demande un effort de respirer; **please make the** ~ **to come** je t'en prie fais l'effort de venir; **she just won't make the** ~ elle ne veut pas faire l'effort; **I'll make every** ~ **to be there** je ferai tout mon possible pour être là **2.** (*attempt*) tentative *f;* **my** ~**s to**

communicate mes efforts pour communiquer
effortless ['efətləs, *Am:* -ət-] *adj* **1.** (*easy*) facile **2.** (*painless*) sans effort; **an ~ gesture** un geste naturel
effrontery [ɪ'frʌntərɪ, *Am:* e'frʌn-] *n no pl, form* effronterie *f;* **to have the ~ to** +*infin* avoir l'audace *f* de +*infin*
effusive [ɪ'fju:sɪv] *adj form* exubérant(e); (*welcome*) chaleureux(-euse)
EFTA ['eftə], **Efta** *n abbr of* **European Free Trade Association** AELE *f*
e.g. [ˌi:'dʒi:] *abbr of* (**exempli gratia**) **for example** par ex.
egg [eg] *n* **1.** œuf *m;* **to lay an ~** pondre un œuf; **beaten/scrambled/fried ~s** œufs battus/brouillés/sur le plat; **hard-boiled/soft-boiled ~** œufs durs/mollets **2.** (*female reproductive cells*) ovule *m* ▶**to have ~ on one's face** *inf* avoir l'air fin; **to put all one's ~s in one basket** mettre tous ses œufs dans le même panier
egg on *vt* bousculer
egg cup, **eggcup** *n* coquetier *m* **egghead** *n pej* intellectuel(le) *m(f)* **eggplant** *n Am, Aus s.* **aubergine** **eggshell** *n* coquille *f* d'œuf **egg spoon** *n* cuillère *f* à œufs **egg timer** *n* sablier *m* **egg yolk** *n* jaune *m* d'œuf
ego ['egəʊ, *Am:* 'i:goʊ] *n* <-s> **1.** PSYCH ego *m* **2.** (*self-esteem*) vanité *f;* **to bolster sb's ~** donner de l'assurance à qn
egocentric [ˌegəʊ'sentrɪk, *Am:* ˌi:goʊ-] *adj pej* égocentrique
egoism ['egəʊɪzəm, *Am:* 'i:goʊ-] *n no pl, pej* égoïsme *m*
egoist ['egəʊɪst, *Am:* 'i:goʊ-] *n pej* égoïste *mf*
egoistic [ˌegəʊ'ɪstɪk, *Am:* ˌi:goʊ-], **egoistical** *adj* égoïste
egotism ['egəʊtɪzəm, *Am:* 'i:goʊ-] *n no pl, pej s.* **egoism**
egotist ['egəʊtɪst, *Am:* 'i:goʊ-] *n pej s.* **egoist**
egotistic [ˌegə'tɪstɪk, *Am:* ˌi:goʊ'-], **egotistical** *adj pej* égotiste
ego trip ['egəʊtrɪp, *Am:* 'i:goʊ-] *n pej* **to be on an ~** faire son mégalo
Egypt ['i:dʒɪpt] *n* l'Égypte *f*
Egyptian [ɪ'dʒɪpʃn] **I.** *adj* égyptien(ne) **II.** *n* Égyptien(ne) *m(f)*
eh [eɪ] *interj inf* **~?** **1.** (*expressing surprise*) quoi! **2.** (*asking for repetition*) hein? **3.** (*inviting response to statement*) non?
eider ['aɪdəʳ, *Am:* -dɚ] *n* eider *m*
eiderdown ['aɪdədaʊn, *Am:* -dɚ-] *n* édredon *m,* fourre *f Suisse*
Eiffel tower [ˌaɪfl'taʊər, *Am:* -'taʊɚ] *n* **the ~** la tour Eiffel
eight [eɪt] **I.** *adj* huit; **he is ~** il a huit ans **II.** *n* **1.** (*number*) huit *m;* **~ o'clock** huit heures; **it's ~** il est huit heures; **~ twenty hours** huit heures vingt **2.** (*boat*) canot *m* à huit rameurs ▶**to have had one over the ~** *Brit, inf* avoir un verre dans le nez
eighteen [ˌeɪ'ti:n] *adj* dix-huit; *s. a.* **eight**
eighteenth [ˌeɪ'ti:nθ] *adj* dix-huitième; *s. a.* **eighth**
eighth [eɪtθ] **I.** *adj* huitième; **~ note** *Am* croche *f* **II.** *n no pl* **1.** (*order*) **the ~** le(la) huitième **2.** (*date*) **the ~ of June, June the ~** le huit juin **3.** (*equal parts*) **to cut a cake into ~s** couper un gâteau en huit **III.** *adv* (*in lists*) huitièmement
eight-hour day *n* journée *f* de huit heures
eightieth ['eɪtɪəθ, *Am:* -t̬ɪəθ] *adj* quatre-vingtième; *s. a.* **eighth**
eighty ['eɪtɪ, *Am:* -t̬ɪ] **I.** *adj* quatre-vingts, huitante *Suisse,* octante *Belgique, Suisse* **II.** *n* **1.** (*number*) quatre-vingts *m* **2.** (*age*) **to be in one's eighties** avoir quatre-vingts ans passés **3.** (*decade*) **the eighties** les années quatre-vingts; *s. a.* **eight**
Eire ['æərə, *Am:* 'erə] *n* République *f* d'Irlande
either ['aɪðəʳ, *Am:* 'i:ðɚ] **I.** *adj* **1.** (*one of two*) **~ method will work** n'importe laquelle des deux méthodes marchera; **I didn't see either film** je n'ai vu ni l'un ni l'autre film; **~ way it's expensive** dans les deux cas, c'est cher **2.** (*both*) **on ~ foot** sur chaque pied **II.** *pron* **which one? – ~** lequel? – n'importe lequel; **~ of you can go** l'un ou l'autre peut y aller **III.** *adv* (*in alternatives*) **~ … or** soit … soit; **it's good with ~ meat or fish** c'est bon avec de la viande ou du poisson; *after neg* non plus; **if he doesn't go, I won't go ~** s'il ne part pas, moi non plus **IV.** *conj* **~ … or …** soit … soit …; **~ buy it or rent it** achetez-le ou (bien) louez-le; **I can ~ stay or leave** je peux ou rester ou partir
ejaculate [ɪ'dʒækjʊleɪt] *vt* **1.** ANAT éjaculer **2.** (*suddenly blurt out*) s'écrier
ejaculation [ɪˌdʒækjʊ'leɪʃn] *n* **1.** ANAT éjaculation *f* **2.** (*sudden outburst*) exclamation *f*
eject [ɪ'dʒekt] **I.** *vt* éjecter; (*coin*) rejeter **II.** *vi* AVIAT s'éjecter
ejection *n* (*of unwanted person*) expulsion *f;* (*of pilot, cassette*) éjection *f*
ejector *n* éjecteur *m*
ejector seat [ɪ'dʒektəʳ si:t, *Am:* -tɚ] *n* siège *m* éjectable
eke out [i:k aʊt] *vt* (*money, food*) faire durer; **to ~ a living** avoir du mal à joindre les deux bouts
elaborate [ɪ'læbərət] **I.** *adj* **1.** (*complicated*) compliqué(e) **2.** (*detailed: plan*) minutieux (-euse); (*meal*) soigné(e); (*style*) travaillé(e); (*excuse*) alambiqué(e) **II.** *vi* donner plus de détails; **to ~ on sth** s'étendre sur qc **III.** *vt* élaborer
elaboration [ɪˌlæbə'reɪʃn] <-(s)> *n* développement *m;* (*of theory*) élaboration *f*
elapse [ɪ'læps] *vi* s'écouler
elastic [ɪ'læstɪk] **I.** *adj a. fig* élastique **II.** *n* (*band*) élastique *m*
elasticity [ˌelæ'stɪsətɪ, *Am:* -t̬ɪ] *n no pl, a. fig* élasticité *f*

E

elated *adj* au comble de la joie
elation [ɪ'leɪʃn] *n no pl* allégresse *f*
Elba ['elbə] *n* l'île *f* d'Elbe
elbow ['elbəʊ, *Am:* -boʊ] **I.** *n a. fig* coude *m* ▶**to give sb the ~** se débarrasser de qn; **to be at sb's ~** être à portée de main **II.** *vt* **to ~ sb out of the way** écarter qn de son chemin
elbow grease *n inf* huile *f* de coude **elbow room** *n* **1.** (*space to move*) espace *m* **2.** (*freedom of action*) marge *f* de manœuvre
elder[1] ['eldəʳ, *Am:* -dɚ] **I.** *n* **1.** (*older person*) aîné(e) *m(f)* **2.** HIST, REL ancien(ne) *m(f)*; **village ~** doyen(ne) *m(f)* du village; **Pliny the Elder** Pline l'Ancien **II.** *adj* aîné(e); **~ statesman** vétéran *m* de la politique
elder[2] ['eldəʳ, *Am:* -dɚ] *n* BOT sureau *m*
elderberry ['eldəberɪ, *Am:* -dɚ-] <-ies> *n* **1.** (*berry*) baie *f* de sureau **2.** *s.* **elder**
elderberry wine *n* vin *m* de sureau
elderly ['eldəlɪ, *Am:* -dɚ-] **I.** *adj* assez âgé **II.** *n no pl* **the ~** les personnes âgées
eldest ['eldɪst] **I.** *adj* aîné(e) **II.** *n no pl* **my ~** mon aîné(e)
elect [ɪ'lekt] **I.** *vt* **1.** (*by voting*) élire; **to ~ sb as president/to sth** élire qn président/à qc **2.** (*decide*) **to ~ to** *+infin* choisir de *+infin* **II.** *n no pl* REL **the ~** les élus *mpl* **III.** *adj* **the archbishop/president ~** le futur archevêque/président
election [ɪ'lekʃn] *n* élection *f*; **to call an ~** appeler aux urnes
election address *n* discours *m* électoral **election booth** *n s.* **polling booth election campaign** *n* campagne *f* électorale **election commission**, **election committee** *n* comité *m* électoral **election day**, **Election Day** *n* journée *f* électorale **election defeat** *n* défaite *f* électorale
electioneering [ɪ,lekʃə'nɪərɪŋ, *Am:* -'nɪr-] *n no pl* campagne *f* électorale
election meeting *n* meeting *m* électoral **election platform** *n* programme *m* électoral **election results** *npl*, **election returns** *npl* résultats *mpl* des élections **election speech** *s.* **election address**
elective [ɪ'lektɪv] **I.** *adj* **1.** *form* (*appointed by election*) élu(e); (*based on voting*) électoral(e) **2.** (*optional: subject*) facultatif(-ive); (*affinity*) électif(-ive); **~ surgery** chirurgie de confort **II.** *n Am* SCHOOL, UNIV cours *m* facultatif
elector [ɪ'lektəʳ, *Am:* -t̬ɚ] *n* **1.** (*person with voting rights*) électeur, -trice *m, f* **2.** *Am* POL membre *m* du collège électoral
electoral [ɪ'lektərəl] *adj* électoral(e)
electorate [ɪ'lektərət] *n* électorat *m*
electric [ɪ'lektrɪk] *adj* électrique; (*fence*) électrifié(e); (*atmosphere*) chargé(e) d'électricité; **~ blanket** couverture *f* chauffante; **~ shock** MED électrochoc *m*
electrical [ɪ'lektrɪkl] *adj* électrique; **~ failure** panne *f* d'électricité; **~ engineer** électrotechnicien(ne) *m(f)*
electrician [ɪ,lek'trɪʃn] *n* électricien(ne) *m(f)*
electricity [ɪ,lek'trɪsətɪ] *n no pl* électricité *f*; **powered by ~** électrique
electrification [ɪ,lektrɪfɪ'keɪʃn] *n no pl* électrification *f*
electrify [ɪ'lektrɪfaɪ] *vt* **1.** ELEC électrifier **2.** *fig* électriser
electroanalysis [ɪ,lektrəʊə'nælɪsɪs] *n* électroanalyse *f*
electrocardiogram [ɪ,lektrəʊ'kɑːdɪəʊgræm, *Am:* -troʊ'kɑːrdɪə-] *n* électrocardiogramme *m*
electrocute [ɪ'lektrəkjuːt] *vt* électrocuter
electrocution [ɪ,lektrə'kjuːʃn] *n* électrocution *f*
electrode [ɪ'lektrəʊd, *Am:* -troʊd] *n* électrode *f*
electroencephalogram [ɪ,lektrəʊen'sefələ,græm, *Am:* -troʊen'sefəloʊ-] *n* électroencéphalogramme *m*
electrolysis [ɪ,lek'trɒləsɪs, *Am:* -'trɑːlə-] *n no pl* électrolyse *f*
electromagnet [ɪ'lektrəʊ'mægnɪt, *Am:* -troʊ'-] *n* électro-aimant *m*
electromagnetic [ɪ,lektrəʊmæg'netɪk, *Am:* -troʊmæg'net̬-] *adj* électromagnétique
electron [ɪ'lektrɒn, *Am:* -trɑːn] *n* électron *m*
electronic [,ɪlek'trɒnɪk, *Am:* ɪ,lek'trɑːnɪk] *adj* électronique
electronics [,ɪlek'trɒniks, *Am:* ɪ,lek'trɑːnɪks] *npl* **1.** + *sing vb* (*science*) électronique *f* **2.** + *pl vb* (*electronic circuits*) circuits *mpl* électroniques
electron microscope *n* microscope *m* électronique
electroplate [ɪ'lektrəʊpleɪt, *Am:* ɪ'lektroʊpleɪt] **I.** *vt* galvaniser; **~ed cutlery** couverts argentés **II.** *n articles plaqués par galvano-plastie*
electroscope [ɪ'lektrəʊ,skəʊp, *Am:* -troʊ,skoʊp] *n* électroscope *m*
electrotherapy [ɪ,lektrəʊ'θerəpɪ, *Am:* -troʊ'-] *n* électrothérapie *f*
elegance ['elɪgəns, *Am:* '-ə-] *n no pl* élégance *f*
elegant ['elɪgənt, *Am:* '-ə-] *adj* élégant(e)
elegy ['elədʒɪ] *n* élégie *f*
element ['elɪmənt, *Am:* '-ə-] *n* **1.** *a.* CHEM, MAT élément *m* **2.** ELEC résistance *f* **3.** (*amount*) **an ~ of luck** une part de chance; **to lose the ~ of surprise** perdre l'effet de surprise **4.** *pl* (*rudiments*) rudiments *mpl* **5.** *pl* METEO **the ~s** les éléments
elemental [,elɪ'mentl, *Am:* -ə'ment̬l] *adj* **1.** (*primitive*) élémentaire; (*feelings, needs*) primaire; **~ forces** puissances naturelles **2.** (*basic*) essentiel(le)
elementary [,elɪ'mentərɪ, *Am:* -ə'ment̬ɚ-] *adj* élémentaire; **~ science** les rudiments de la science; **~ education** *Am* enseignement primaire
elephant ['elɪfənt] *n* éléphant
elephantine [,elɪ'fæntaɪn] *adj* éléphantesque; (*humour*) lourd(e)

elevate ['elɪveɪt] *vt a. fig, form* élever; **to ~ the mind** être édifiant

elevated ['elɪveɪtɪd, *Am:* -t̬ɪd] *adj* **1.** (*raised*) élevé(e); (*railway*) surélevé(e); **~ railroad** *Am* métro *m* aérien **2.** (*important: position*) important(e); **to have an ~ idea of oneself** se faire une haute idée de soi-même **3.** LIT (*style*) soutenu(e); (*thoughts*) sublime

elevation [ˌelɪ'veɪʃn] *n form* **1.** (*height, hill*) hauteur *f;* **an ~ of 1000 m** une altitude de 1000 m **2.** ARCHIT élévation *f* **3.** (*rise*) ascension *f*

elevator ['elɪveɪtəʳ, *Am:* -t̬ɚ] *n Am* **1.** (*lift*) ascenseur *m* **2.** (*for goods*) monte-charge *m*

eleven [ɪ'levn] **I.** *adj* onze **II.** *n* **1.** (*number*) onze *m* **2.** (*team*) **the French ~** le onze de France; **the second ~** la deuxième équipe; *s. a.* **eight**

elevenses [ɪ'levnzɪz] *npl Brit, inf: pause-café vers 11 heures*

eleventh [ɪ'levnθ] *adj* onzième; *s. a.* **eighth**

elf [elf] <elves> *n* elfe *m*

elicit [ɪ'lɪsɪt] *vt form* **1.** (*obtain: information*) obtenir; (*truth*) découvrir; SCHOOL (*answers*) susciter **2.** (*provoke: criticism*) susciter

eligibility [ˌelɪdʒə'bɪləti, *Am:* -t̬ɪ] *n no pl* LAW droit *m*

eligible ['elɪdʒəbl] *adj* éligible; **to be ~ for sth** avoir droit à qc; **to be ~ for promotion** remplir les conditions pour être promu; **to be ~ to vote** être en droit de voter; **an ~ bachelor** un bon parti

eliminate [ɪ'lɪmɪneɪt] *vt* **1.** *a.* ANAT éliminer **2.** (*exclude*) écarter **3.** *inf* (*murder*) supprimer

elimination [ɪˌlɪmɪ'neɪʃn] *n no pl* élimination *f;* (*of diseases*) éradication *f;* **by a process of ~** en procédant par élimination

elimination contest *n* compétition *f* éliminatoire

elite [eɪ'liːt] **I.** *n* élite *f* **II.** *adj* d'élite; (*club*) réservé(e) à l'élite

elitism [ei'liːtɪsm] *n no pl, pej* élitisme *m*

elitist [ei'liːtɪst] *adj pej* élitiste

elixir [ɪ'lɪksəʳ, *Am:* -sɚ] *n* élixir *m*

elk [elk] <-(s)> *n* **1.** (*in Europe*) élan *m* **2.** (*in America*) wapiti *m*

ellipse [ɪ'lɪps] *n* ellipse *f*

elliptic [ɪ'lɪptɪk], **elliptical** *adj* elliptique

elm [elm] *n* orme *m*

elocution [ˌelə'kjuːʃn] *n no pl* élocution *f;* **~ lesson** cours de diction

elongate ['iːlɒŋgeɪt, *Am:* ɪ'lɑːŋ-] **I.** *vt* allonger **II.** *vi* s'allonger

elope [ɪ'ləʊp, *Am:* -'loʊp] *vi* faire une fugue amoureuse; **to ~ with one's beloved** s'enfuir avec son(sa) bien-aimé(e)

eloquent ['eləkwənt] *adj* éloquent(e)

El Salvador [el'sælvəˌdɔːr, *Am:* -dɔːr] *n* Salvador *m*

else [els] *adv* **1.** (*in addition*) **everybody ~** tous les autres; **everything ~** tout le reste; **someone ~** quelqu'un d'autre; **anyone ~** toute autre personne; **why ~?** pour quelle autre raison?; **what/who ~?** quoi/qui d'autre? **2.** (*different*) **something ~** autre chose **3.** (*otherwise*) **or ~ we could see a film** ou bien nous pourrions voir un film; **go now or ~ you'll miss him** vas-y maintenant ou bien tu vas le rater; **do that or ~!** fais ça, sinon tu vas voir!

elsewhere [ˌels'weəʳ, *Am:* 'elswer] *adv* ailleurs

ELT [ˌiːel'tiː] *n abbr of* **English language teaching**

elucidate [ɪ'luːsɪdeɪt] *form* **I.** *vt* élucider; (*mystery*) éclaircir **II.** *vi* s'expliquer

elusive [ɪ'luːsɪv] *adj* **1.** (*evasive: answer*) évasif(-ive) **2.** (*difficult to obtain*) insaisissable; (*memory*) fugace

emaciated [ɪ'meɪʃɪeɪtɪd, *Am:* -t̬ɪd] *adj form* **1.** (*face*) émacié(e) **2.** (*body*) décharné(e)

e-mail, email, E-mail ['iːmeɪl] *n* INFOR *abbr of* **electronic mail** courrier *m* électronique; (*as an abbreviation*) Mél. *m;* **to collect one's ~** relever sa boîte aux lettres électronique

e-mail address *n* adresse *f* électronique

emanate ['eməneɪt] **I.** *vi form* **1.** (*originate*) provenir **2.** (*radiate*) émaner **II.** *vt* émettre; (*gas*) dégager; (*joy*) rayonner de

emancipate [ɪ'mænsɪpeɪt] *vt a.* POL émanciper; (*slave*) affranchir

emancipated *adj a.* POL émancipé(e); (*ideas*) libéral(e)

emancipation [ɪˌmænsɪ'peɪʃn] *n no pl* émancipation *f*

embalm [ɪm'bɑːm, *Am:* em-] *vt* embaumer

embankment [ɪm'bæŋkmənt, *Am:* em-] *n* (*of road*) talus *m;* (*of river*) berge *f;* (*of canal*) digue *f;* **railway ~** remblai *m*

embargo [ɪm'bɑːgəʊ, *Am:* em'bɑːrgoʊ] **I.** <-goes> *n* embargo *m* **II.** *vt* mettre un embargo sur

embark [ɪm'bɑːk, *Am:* em'bɑːrk] **I.** *vi* s'embarquer **II.** *vt* embarquer

embarkation [ˌembɑː'keɪʃn, *Am:* -bɑːr'-] *n* embarquement *m*

embarrass [ɪm'bærəs, *Am:* em'ber-] *vt* embarrasser

embarrassed *adj* embarrassé(e); **I was ~ to ask her** j'étais gêné de lui demander; **to be financially ~** avoir des ennuis d'argent

embarrassing *adj* embarrassant(e); **in an ~ situation** dans une situation embarrassante

embarrassment *n* gêne *f;* **to be an ~ to sb** être une source d'embarras pour qn

embassy ['embəsɪ] <-assies> *n* ambassade *f*

embed [ɪm'bed, *Am:* em-] <-dd-> *vt* **1.** (*fix*) insérer; (*nail*) enfoncer; (*in wall*) encastrer; (*in gold*) incruster; (*in memory*) graver **2.** LING enchâsser **3.** INFOR incorporer

embellish [ɪm'belɪʃ, *Am:* em-] *vt* embellir; (*story*) enjoliver

ember ['embəʳ, *Am:* -bɚ] *n* braise *f*

embezzle [ɪm'bezl] <-ling> *vt* (*funds*) détourner

embezzlement *n no pl* détournement *m* de

E

fonds

embezzler [ɪm'bezləʳ, *Am:* em'bezlɚ] *n* escroc *m*

embitter [ɪm'bɪtəʳ, *Am:* em'bɪt̬ɚ] *vt* aigrir; (*dispute*) envenimer; **an ~ed old man** un vieillard amer

emblem ['embləm] *n* emblème *m*

embodiment *n no pl* incarnation *f*; **the ~ of virtue** la vertu personnifiée

embody [ɪm'bɒdɪ, *Am:* em'bɑːdɪ-] *vt* **1.** (*convey: idea*) incarner **2.** (*personify*) personnifier **3.** (*include*) incorporer

embolism ['embəlɪsm] *n* embolie *f*

emboss [ɪm'bɒs, *Am:* em'bɑːs] *vt* (*metal*) travailler en relief; (*leather*) repousser; **~ed paper** papier gaufré

embrace [ɪm'breɪs, *Am:* em-] **I.** *vt* **1.** embrasser **2.** *fig* (*idea*) adopter; (*offer*) accepter; (*opportunity*) saisir; (*religion*) embrasser **II.** *n* embrassade *f*; **in your ~** dans te bras

embrocation [ˌembrə'keɪʃn, *Am:* -broʊ'-] *n* embrocation *f*

embroider [ɪm'brɔɪdəʳ, *Am:* em'brɔɪdɚ] **I.** *vi* broder **II.** *vt* **1.** broder **2.** *fig* enjoliver

embroidery [ɪm'brɔɪdərɪ, *Am:* em-] *n* **1.** broderie *f* **2.** *no pl, fig* fioritures *fpl*

embryo ['embrɪəʊ, *Am:* -oʊ] *n* embryon *m*

embryonic [ˌembrɪ'ɒnɪk, *Am:* -'ɑːnɪk] *adj* **1.** embryonnaire **2.** *fig* à un stade embryonnaire

emend [ɪ'mend] *vt form* corriger

emerald ['emərəld] **I.** *n* **1.** (*stone*) émeraude *f* **2.** (*colour*) vert *m* émeraude **II.** *adj* vert émeraude

emerge [ɪ'mɜːdʒ, *Am:* -'mɜːrdʒ] *vi* **1.** (*come out*) surgir; (*from the sea*) émerger **2.** (*become known: problem*) se faire jour; (*ideas*) ressortir; (*facts, leader*) apparaître; (*theory*) naître

emergence [ɪ'mɜːdʒəns, *Am:* -'mɜːr-] *n no pl* émergence *f*; (*of ideas*) apparition *f*; (*of circumstances*) révélation *f*; (*of theory*) naissance *f*

emergency [ɪ'mɜːdʒənsɪ, *Am:* -'mɜːr-] **I.** <-ies> *n a.* MED urgence *f*; **state of ~** POL état *m* d'urgence; **to be used only in emergencies** à n'utiliser qu'en cas d'urgence **II.** *adj* (*landing*) forcé(e); (*measures*) d'exception; (*exit, brake*) de secours; (*situation*) d'urgence

emergency lights *n pl* feux *mpl* de détresse **emergency room** *n Am* salle *f* des urgences **emergency services** *n pl: services d'urgence, regroupant les pompiers, la police et les ambulances*

emergent [ɪ'mɜːdʒənt, *Am:* -'mɜːr-] *adj* (*democracy, nation*) jeune; (*talent*) naissant(e)

emery ['emərɪ] *n no pl* émeri *m*

emery board *n* lime *f* à ongles **emery paper** *n* papier *m* (d')émeri

emetic [ɪ'metɪk, *Am:* -'met̬-] **I.** *adj* vomitif(-ive); MED émétique **II.** *n* émétique *m*

EMI [ˌiːem'aɪ] *n abbr of* **European Monetary Institute** IME *m*

emigrant ['emɪgrənt] *n* émigrant(e) *m(f)*

emigrate ['emɪgreɪt] *vi* émigrer

emigration [ˌemɪ'greɪʃn] *n* émigration *f*

eminence ['emɪnəns] *n no pl* **1.** (*honour*) distinction *f*; **to achieve ~** parvenir à une position éminente **2.** (*fame*) renommée *f*

eminent ['emɪnənt] *adj* éminent(e)

eminently *adv* éminemment; (*memorable*) parfaitement; (*forgettable*) tout à fait

emissary ['emɪsərɪ, *Am:* -ser-] <-ies> *n* émissaire *m*

emission [mɪʃn] *n* émission *f*; (*of smoke*) dégagement *m*

emit [ɪ'mɪt] <-tt-> *vt* (*radiation, groan*) émettre; (*odour*) répandre; (*rays*) diffuser; (*smoke*) dégager; (*sparks*) lancer; (*heat, light*) emettre; (*lava*) cracher; (*squeal*) laisser échapper

emoluments [ɪ'mɒljʊməntz, *Am:* -'mɑːl-] *n pl, Brit, form* émoluments *mpl*

emoticon *n* INFOR emoticon *m*

emotion [ɪ'məʊʃn, *Am:* -'moʊ-] *n* **1.** (*affective state*) émotion *f* **2.** (*feeling*) sentiment *m*

emotional [ɪ'məʊʃənl, *Am:* -'moʊ-] *adj* émotionnel(le); (*ceremony*) émouvant(e); (*decision*) impulsif(-ive); (*reaction*) émotif(-ive); **an ~ person** une personne sensible; **don't let's get ~** ne soyons pas trop sensibles; **~ blackmail** chantage au sentiment; **to make an ~ appeal to sb** faire appel aux bons sentiments de qn

emotionally *adv* (*react, behave*) avec émotion; **physically and ~** physiquement et mentalement; **to be ~ involved with sb** avoir une liaison (amoureuse) avec qn

emotionless *adj* impassible

emotive [ɪ'məʊtɪv, *Am:* -'moʊt̬ɪv] *adj* (*issue*) qui déchaîne les passions; (*term*) chargé(e) de connotations

empathy ['empəθɪ] *n no pl* empathie *f*

emperor ['empərəʳ, *Am:* -ɚɚ] *n* empereur *m*

emphasis ['emfəsɪs] <emphases> *n* **1.** (*when explaining*) insistance *f*; **to lay** [*o* **place**] [*o* **put**] **great ~ on sth** mettre l'accent sur qc; **the ~ is on ...** l'accent est mis sur... **2.** LING accentuation *f*; **the ~ is on the first syllable** l'accentuation est sur la première syllabe

emphasize ['emfəsaɪz] *vt* **1.** (*insist on*) souligner; (*fact*) insister sur **2.** LING accentuer

emphatic [ɪm'fætɪk, *Am:* em'fæt̬-] *adj* **1.** (*forcibly expressive*) emphatique; (*assertion*) catégorique; **she's ~ that she can do it** elle est formelle sur le fait qu'elle peut le faire **2.** (*strong*) énergique; (*victory*) écrasant(e); (*answer*) net(te); (*refusal*) formel(le)

empire ['empaɪəʳ, *Am:* -paɪɚ] *n a. fig* empire *m*

empirical [ɪm'pɪrɪkl, *Am:* em-] *adj* empirique

employ [ɪm'plɔɪ, *Am:* em-] *vt* **1.** (*pay to do work*) employer; **he is ~ed in the travel industry** il travaille dans l'industrie du tourisme **2.** (*use*) utiliser

employee [ˌɪmplɔɪ'iː, *Am:* 'em-] *n* employé(e) *m(f)*

employer [ɪm'plɔɪəʳ, *Am:* em'plɔɪɚ] *n* employeur, -euse *m, f;* **~s and employees** la direction et le personnel; **~s' organization** organisation patronale

employment *n no pl* **1.** (*state of having work*) emploi *m;* **~ agency** agence *f* de placement; **to be in ~** *Brit, form* avoir un emploi; **to be in sb's ~** être employé par qn **2.** (*use*) emploi *m*

emporium [ɪm'pɔːrɪəm, *Am:* em-] <-s *o* -ia> *n* grand magasin *m*

empower [ɪm'paʊəʳ, *Am:* em'paʊɚ] *vt* **1.** (*authorize*) autoriser **2.** LAW donner procuration [*o* pleins pouvoirs] à **3.** POL donner du pouvoir à **4.** (*give power to: employees*) responsabiliser; (*disabled*) rendre plus fort

empowerment [im'paʊəmənt, *Am:* em'paʊɚ-] *n no pl* **1.** autorisation *f* **2.** (*of employees*) responsabilisation *f;* (*of the disabled*) l'accès *m* à l'auto-prise en charge

empress ['emprɪs] *n* impératrice *f*

emptiness ['emptɪnɪs] *n no pl* vide *m;* (*of speech*) vacuité *f*

empty ['emptɪ] **I.** <-ier, -iest> *adj* **1.** (*with nothing inside*) vide; (*stomach*) creux(-euse); **on an ~ stomach** à jeun **2.** AUTO à vide **3.** (*without inhabitants*) inoccupé(e) **4.** GASTR (*calories*) non calorique **5.** (*pointless: gesture*) futile; (*words*) vain(e); (*threat*) en l'air **II.** <-ies> *n pl* bouteilles *fpl* vides, vidanges *fpl Belgique* **III.** <-ie-> *vt* vider; **to ~ one's bladder** uriner **IV.** <-ie-> *vi* **1.** se vider **2.** GEO (*river*) **to ~ into sth** se déverser dans qc

◆**empty out** *vt* vider

empty-handed *adj* **1.** les mains vides **2.** *fig* bredouille **empty-headed** *adj* sans cervelle **empty weight** *n* poids *m* à vide

EMS *n abbr of* **European Monetary System** SME *m*

EMU *n abbr of* **Economic and Monetary Union** UEM *f*

emulate ['emjʊleɪt] *vt* **1.** imiter **2.** INFOR émuler

emulation [ˌemjʊ'leɪʃn] *n no pl* **1.** concurrence *f* **2.** INFOR émulation *f*

emulsifier [ɪ'mʌlsifaɪəʳ, *Am:* -ɚ] *n* émulsifiant *m*

emulsify [ɪ'mʌlsɪfaɪ] <-ie-> *vt* émulsifier

emulsion [ɪ'mʌlʃn] *n* **1.** *a.* PHOT émulsion *f* **2.** (*paint*) peinture *f* mate

enable [ɪ'neɪbl] *vt* **1.** (*give the ability, make possible*) **to ~ sb to** +*infin* donner à qn la possibilité de +*infin* **2.** INFOR permettre

enact [ɪ'nækt] *vt* **1.** (*carry out*) effectuer **2.** (*act out*) représenter **3.** POL décréter; (*law*) promulguer; **to ~ that** ordonner que +*subj*

enactment *n* **1.** *no pl* (*carrying out*) exécution *f;* (*of a law*) promulgation *f;* (*of a legislation*) établissement *m* **2.** (*acting out*) représentation *f*

enamel [ɪ'næml] **I.** *n* émail *m* **II.** <-ll- *o* -l- *Am*> *vt* émailler

enamour [ɪ'næməʳ, *Am:* -ɚ] *vt* **to be ~ed of sb** être amoureux de qn; **I'm not very ~ed of the idea** *iron* je ne suis pas vraiment fou de l'idée

encamp [ɪn'kæmp, *Am:* en-] *vi Brit* MIL camper

encampment *n* campement *m*

encase [ɪn'keɪs, *Am:* en-] *vt* **to ~ sth in sth** recouvrir qc de qc

encephalitis [ˌensefə'laɪtɪs, *Am:* enˌsefə'laɪt̬ɪs] *n* encéphalite *f*

enchant [ɪn'tʃɑːnt, *Am:* en'tʃænt] *vt* **1.** (*charm*) enchanter **2.** (*bewitch*) ensorceler

enchanted *adj* enchanté(e)

enchanter *n* enchanteur *m*

enchanting *adj* charmant(e)

enchantment *n* enchantement *m*

enchantress *n* enchanteresse *f*

encircle [ɪn'sɜːkl, *Am:* en'sɜːr-] *vt* **1.** encercler **2.** MIL cerner

encirclement *n* ARCHIT encerclement *m*

enc(l). *n abbr of* **enclosure** PJ *f*

enclose [ɪn'kləʊz, *Am:* en'kloʊz] *vt* **1.** (*surround*) cerner; **to ~ sth in brackets** mettre qc entre parenthèses; **to ~ sth with sth** entourer qc de qc **2.** (*include in same envelope*) joindre

enclosed *adj* **1.** (*document*) joint(e) **2.** (*space*) clos(e) **3.** REL (*order*) cloîtré(e)

enclosure [ɪn'kləʊʒəʳ, *Am:* en'kloʊʒɚ] *n* **1.** (*area*) enceinte *f* **2.** (*for animals*) enclos *m* **3.** (*act of enclosing*) clôture *f* **4.** *Brit* HIST **Royal Enclosure** *enceinte réservée à la famille royale* **5.** (*enclosed item*) pièce *f* jointe

encode [ɪn'kəʊd, *Am:* en'koʊd] *vt* **1.** (*code*) coder **2.** LING encoder **3.** INFOR **to ~ sth digitally** coder qc numériquement

encompass [ɪn'kʌmpəs, *Am:* en-] *vt* **1.** (*surround*) entourer **2.** (*include*) englober

encore ['ɒŋkɔːʳ, *Am:* 'ɑːnkɔːr] *n* **1.** bis *m* **2.** *fig, pej* **as** [*o* **for**] **an ~** comme si cela ne suffisait pas

encounter [ɪn'kaʊntəʳ, *Am:* en'kaʊnt̬ɚ] **I.** *vt* **1.** (*experience*) rencontrer; **to ~ resistance** trouver de la résistance **2.** (*meet*) rencontrer à l'improviste **II.** *n* **1.** rencontre *f;* (*with enemy*) affrontement *m;* **her ~ with the boss** sa collision avec le patron **2.** SPORT confrontation *f*

encourage [ɪn'kʌrɪdʒ, *Am:* en'kɜːr-] *vt* **1.** (*give confidence to*) encourager; **to ~ sb to** +*infin* encourager qn à +*infin* **2.** (*support*) favoriser

encouragement *n no pl* encouragement *m;* **to give ~ to sth** encourager qn

encouraging *adj* stimulant(e); (*sign*) encourageant(e)

encroach [ɪn'krəʊtʃ, *Am:* en'kroʊtʃ] *vi* **1.** (*advance*) gagner du terrain **2.** (*intrude*) **to ~ on** [*o* **upon**] empiéter sur

encroachment *n* **1.** (*intrusion*) intrusion *f;* **~ on human rights** atteinte *f* aux droits de

E

l'homme **2.** (*gradual approach*) empiètement *m*

encryption [ɪn'krɪpʃən] *n* INFOR cryptage *m*

encumber [ɪn'kʌmbəʳ, *Am:* en'kʌmbɚ] *vt* encombrer; **to be ~ed with sth** être gêné par qc

encyclop(a)edia [ɪnˌsaɪklə'piːdɪə, *Am:* en-] *n* encyclopédie *f*

encyclop(a)edic [ɪnˌsaɪklə'piːdɪk, *Am:* en-] *adj* encyclopédique

end [end] **I.** *n* **1.** (*finish*) fin *f;* **to come to an end** se terminer; **to put an ~ to sth** mettre fin à qc **2.** (*last point physically*) bout *m;* SPORT côté *m;* **at the ~ of the corridor** au bout du couloir; **to place sth ~ on against a wall** placer le bout de qc contre un mur **3.** (*last point of a range*) extrémité *f;* **at the other ~ of the scale** à l'autre extrême **4.** (*involving communication, exchange*) **how are things at your ~?** et pour toi, comment ça se passe?; **to keep one's ~ of the bargain** tenir sa part du marché; **I could hear music at the other ~** j'entendais de la musique au bout du fil; **his uncle will be waiting for him at the other ~** son oncle l'attendra là-bas **5.** (*purpose*) objectif *m;* **to this ~** dans cette intention; **to achieve one's ~s** arriver à ses fins; **for commercial ~s** à des fins commerciales **6.** (*death*) **sudden/untimely ~** mort soudaine/précoce; **to meet one's ~** trouver la mort; **to be nearing one's ~** sentir sa fin proche **7.** (*small left over piece*) bout *m;* (*of cigarette*) mégot *m* ►**to burn the candle at both ~s** brûler la chandelle par les deux bouts; **in the ~** [*o* **at the ~ of the day** *Aus, Brit*] au bout du compte; **to reach the ~ of the line** [*o* **road**] arriver en fin de course; **~ of story** un point, c'est tout; **and that's the ~ of the story** et je ne veux plus en entendre parler; **to be at the ~ of one's tether** [*o* **rope** *Am*] être au bout du rouleau; **to come to a bad** [*o* **sticky**] **~** mal finir; **to hold** [*o* **keep**] **one's ~ up** ne pas se laisser démonter; **to make ~s meet** joindre les deux bouts; **to put an ~ to oneself** [*o* **it all**] mettre fin à ses jours **II.** *vt* **1.** (*finish*) finir **2.** (*bring to a stop*) mettre un terme à **III.** *vi* **1.** (*result in*) **to ~ in sth** se terminer en qc **2.** (*finish*) finir; **to ~ with sth** s'achever par qc ◆**end up** *vi* **to ~ in love with sb** finir par tomber amoureux de qn; **to ~ a rich man** finir par devenir riche; **to ~ homeless** se retrouver à la rue; **to ~ a prostitute/in prison** finir prostituée/en prison; **to ~ doing sth** finir par faire qc

endanger [ɪn'deɪndʒəʳ, *Am:* en'deɪndʒɚ] *vt* mettre en danger

endangered species *n* espèce *f* menacée

endearing *adj* inspirant la sympathie; (*smile*) engageant(e)

endearment *n* **to whisper ~s to each other** se murmurer des mots tendres; **terms of ~** paroles *fpl* de tendresse

endeavor *Am,* **endeavour** [ɪn'devəʳ, *Am:* en'devɚ] *Brit* **I.** *vi* essayer; **to ~ to** +*infin* tenter tout son possible pour +*infin* **II.** *n* tentative *f;* **to make every ~ to** +*infin* faire tout son possible pour +*infin*

endemic [en'demɪk] *adj* endémique

ending ['endɪŋ] *n* **1.** (*last part*) fin *f* **2.** LING terminaison *f*

endive ['endɪv, *Am:* 'endaɪv] *n* **1.** *Am* (*chicory*) endive *f,* chicon *m Belgique* **2.** *Brit* (*lettuce*) chicorée *f*

endless ['endlɪs] *adj* **1.** TECH sans fin **2.** (*infinite*) infini(e) **3.** (*going on too long*) interminable

endorse [ɪn'dɔːs, *Am:* en'dɔːrs] *vt* **1.** (*declare approval for*) appuyer **2.** (*promote: product*) approuver **3.** FIN (*cheque*) endosser **4.** *Brit* LAW *décompter des points sur le permis de conduire*

endorsee [ɪnˌdɔː'siː, *Am:* -dɔːr-] *n* endossataire *mf*

endorsement *n* **1.** (*support: of plan*) appui *m* **2.** (*recommendation*) approbation *f* **3.** FIN endossement *m* **4.** (*clause in insurance policy*) avenant *m* **5.** *Brit* LAW sanction *f* portée sur le permis de conduire

endow [ɪn'daʊ, *Am:* en-] *vt* doter; **to be ~ed with sth** être doté de qc

endowment *n* **1.** (*insurance*) pension *f* **2.** (*talent*) talent *m* **3.** *form* BIO **genetic ~** héritage *m* génétique

endpaper *n* page *f* de garde **end product** *n* produit *m* fini **end result** *n* résultat *m* définitif

endurable [ɪn'djʊərəbl, *Am:* en'dʊrə-] *adj* supportable

endurance [ɪn'djʊərəns, *Am:* en'dʊrəns] *n no pl* endurance *f;* **an ~ record** un record d'endurance; **to irritate sb beyond ~** agacer qn au plus haut point

endure [ɪn'djʊəʳ, *Am:* en'dʊr] **I.** *vt* **1.** (*tolerate*) tolérer **2.** (*suffer*) endurer **II.** *vi form* durer

end user *n* utilisateur *m* final

ENE *n abbr of* **east-northeast**

enema ['enɪmə, *Am:* -ə-] <-s *o* -ta> *n* MED lavement *m*

enemy ['enəmɪ] **I.** *n* ennemi(e) *m(f)* **II.** *adj* MIL ennemi(e)

energetic [ˌenə'dʒetɪk, *Am:* -ɚ'dʒeṭ-] *adj* **1.** (*opp: weak*) énergique **2.** (*active*) actif(-ive)

energize ['enədʒaɪz, *Am:* -ɚ-] *vt* **1.** ELEC alimenter (en courant) **2.** *fig* stimuler

energy ['enədʒɪ, *Am:* -ɚ-] <-ies> *n a.* PHYS énergie *f;* **to be bursting with ~** déborder d'énergie; **to conserve one's ~** économiser ses forces; **to channel all one's energies into sth** concentrer tous ses efforts sur qc

energy-saving *adj* **an ~ campaign** une campagne pour les économies d'énergie

enfeeble [ɪn'fiːbl, *Am:* en-] *vt form* affaiblir

enforce [ɪn'fɔːs, *Am:* en'fɔːrs] *vt* mettre en application; (*law*) faire respecter; (*regulation*) faire observer; **~d idleness** oisiveté forcée

enforcement *n no pl* exécution *f;* (*of regu-*

lation) observation *f;* (*of law*) application *f*

enfranchise [ɪn'fræntʃaɪz, *Am:* en-] *vt form* **1.** POL admettre au suffrage **2.** (*free*) affranchir

engage [ɪn'geɪdʒ, *Am:* en-] **I.** *vt* **1.** *form* (*hold interest of*) attirer; (*sb's attention*) éveiller; **to ~ sb in conversation** engager la conversation avec qn **2.** *Brit, form* (*employ*) engager; (*services*) employer **3.** MIL attaquer **4.** TECH activer; (*automatic pilot*) mettre; (*gear*) passer; **to ~ the clutch** embrayer **II.** *vi* **1.** (*interact*) **to ~ with sb** communiquer avec qn; **to ~ with the enemy** MIL attaquer l'ennemi **2.** TECH (*cogs*) s'engrener

◆**engage in** *vt* (*discussion, activity*) prendre part à

engaged *adj* **1.** (*occupied*) occupé(e); **to be otherwise ~** être occupé à qc d'autre; **to be ~ in doing sth** être en train de faire qc; **to be ~ in discussions** être en discussion **2.** (*before wedding*) **~ to be married** fiancé(e); **to get ~ to sb** se fiancer à qn

engagement *n* **1.** (*appointment*) rendez-vous *m* **2.** MIL combat *m* **3.** (*agreement to marry*) fiançailles *fpl*

engagement book, **engagement diary** *n* agenda *m* **engagement ring** *n* bague *f* de fiançailles

engaging *adj* engageant(e)

engender [ɪn'dʒendəʳ, *Am:* en'dʒendɚ] *vt form* engendrer

engine ['endʒɪn] *n* **1.** (*motor*) moteur *m;* **diesel/petrol ~** moteur diesel/à essence **2.** AVIAT réacteur *m;* **jet ~** moteur à réaction **3.** RAIL locomotive *f*

engineer [ˌendʒɪ'nɪəʳ, *Am:* -'nɪr] **I.** *n* **1.** (*person qualified in engineering*) ingénieur *m* **2.** *a.* RAIL mécanicien *m* **3.** TECH technicien *m* **4.** *pej, fig* instigateur, -trice *m, f* **5.** *Am* RAIL conducteur *m* de locomotive **II.** *vt* **1.** construire **2.** *pej* manigancer

engineering [ˌendʒɪ'nɪərɪŋ, *Am:* -'nɪr-] *n no pl* ingénierie *f*

engineering works *n* atelier *m* de constructions mécaniques

England ['ɪŋglənd] *n* l'Angleterre *f*

English ['ɪŋglɪʃ] **I.** *adj* anglais(e); **~ people** les Anglais; **an ~ national** un ressortissant anglais; **an ~ film** un film en anglais; **an ~ class** un cours d'anglais; **the ~ team** l'équipe d'Angleterre; **~ speaker** anglophone *mf* **II.** *n* **1.** *pl* (*people*) **the ~** les Anglais **2.** LING anglais *m;* **to speak ~ fluently** parler couramment (l')anglais; **to write in ~** écrire en anglais; **to translate into ~** traduire en anglais

English Channel *n* **the ~** la Manche **Englishman** <-men> *n* Anglais *m* ►**an ~'s home is his castle** *prov* charbonnier est maître chez lui *prov* **Englishwoman** <-women> *n* Anglaise *f*

engrave [ɪn'greɪv, *Am:* en-] *vt* graver

engraver [en'greɪvɚ] *n* graveur *m*

engraving *n* **1.** (*print*) estampe *f* **2.** (*process*) gravure *f*

engross [ɪn'grəʊs, *Am:* en'groʊs] *vt* **1.** (*interest*) absorber **2.** LAW rédiger

engulf [ɪn'gʌlf, *Am:* en-] *vt* engloutir; **to be ~ed by sth** sombrer dans qc

enhance [ɪn'hɑːns, *Am:* -'hæns] *vt* **1.** (*in appearance*) rehausser; (*eyes*) mettre en valeur **2.** (*improve or intensify*) augmenter; (*chances*) améliorer; **to give ~d performance** être plus performant

enigma [ɪ'nɪgmə] *n* énigme *f*

enigmatic [ˌenɪg'mætɪk, *Am:* -'mæt̬-], **enigmatical** *adj* énigmatique

enjoy [ɪn'dʒɔɪ, *Am:* en-] *vt* **1.** (*get pleasure from*) prendre plaisir à; **I ~ed the meal/coffee** j'ai bien aimé le repas/le café; **to ~ doing sth** aimer faire qc; **to ~ oneself** s'amuser **2.** (*have as advantage*) jouir de; **to ~ sb's confidence** avoir la confiance de qn

enjoyable *adj* (*evening*) agréable; (*film, book*) excellent(e)

enjoyment *n no pl* plaisir *m;* **to get real ~ out of sth** prendre un véritable plaisir à qc

enlarge [ɪn'lɑːdʒ, *Am:* en'lɑːrdʒ] **I.** *vt* **1.** *a.* PHOT agrandir **2.** (*expand: territory*) étendre; (*building, room*) agrandir; (*vocabulary*) accroître **II.** *vi* s'agrandir

◆**enlarge on** *vt* développer

enlargement *n* agrandissement *m*

enlighten [ɪn'laɪtn, *Am:* en-] *vt* éclairer; **to ~ the public about sth** informer le public sur qc

enlightened *adj* éclairé(e)

enlightenment *n no pl* **1.** REL révélation *f* **2.** (*information*) éclaircissement *m;* **it brought us no ~** cela ne nous a apporté aucun éclaircissement **3.** PHILOS **the Enlightenment** le Siècle des lumières

enlist [ɪn'lɪst, *Am:* en-] **I.** *vi* MIL **to ~ in the army** s'engager dans l'armée **II.** *vt* **1.** MIL recruter; **enlisted men** *Am* simples soldats **2. to ~ sb's support/help** s'assurer le soutien/l'aide de qn

enliven [ɪn'laɪvn, *Am:* en-] *vt* animer

enmesh [ɪn'meʃ, *Am:* en-] *vt* **1. to become ~ed in sth** s'empêtrer dans qc **2.** *fig* **to be ~ in sth** être mêlé à qc

enmity ['enmətɪ] <-ies> *n* inimitié *f;* **sb's ~ towards sb** l'hostilité *f* de qn envers qn

ennoble [ɪ'nəʊbl, *Am:* e'noʊbl] *vt* **1.** anoblir **2.** *fig* ennoblir

enormity [ɪ'nɔːmətɪ, *Am:* -'nɔːrmət̬ɪ] <-ies> *n* **1.** *no pl* (*magnitude: of damage*) ampleur *f;* (*of task, mistake*) énormité *f* **2.** *form* (*evil: of a crime*) atrocité *f*

enormous [ɪ'nɔːməs, *Am:* -'nɔːr-] *adj* énorme

enough [ɪ'nʌf] **I.** *adv* suffisamment; **is this hot ~?** est-ce assez chaud?; **it's true ~** ce n'est que trop vrai; **funnily/curiously ~, I …** le plus drôle/curieux, c'est que … **II.** *adj* suffisant; **~ eggs/water** assez d'œufs/d'eau; **that's ~ crying** ça suffit de pleurer **III.** *pron* **I know ~ about it** j'en sais assez; **I've had ~** (*to eat*) ça me suffit; (*when angry*) j'en ai marre; **that should be** ~ cela suffira; **that's ~!** ça suffit!

enquire [ɪn'kwaɪəʳ, *Am:* en'kwaɪɚ] **I.** *vi* **1.** (*ask for information*) **to ~ about sth** se renseigner sur qc; **to ~ after sb** demander des nouvelles de qn; **to ~ after sb's health** s'enquérir de la santé de qn **2.** (*investigate*) **to ~ into a matter** faire des recherches sur un sujet **II.** *vt* demander; **to ~ whether/when ...** demander si/quand ...

enquiry [ɪn'kwaɪərɪ, *Am:* en'kwaɪrɪ] <-ies> *n* **1.** (*investigation of facts*) recherches *fpl;* **to make an ~ into sth** faire une enquête sur qc **2.** LAW investigation *f;* **to hold an ~** faire une enquête; **a public ~** une enquête publique

enrage [ɪn'reɪdʒ, *Am:* en-] *vt* rendre furieux(-euse)

enraged *adj* furieux(-euse)

enrapture [ɪn'ræptʃəʳ, *Am:* en'ræptʃɚ] *vt* ravir

enrich [ɪn'rɪtʃ, *Am:* en-] *vt a.* PHYS enrichir; (*soil*) fertiliser

enrol, enroll *Am, Aus* **I.** *vi* **1.** MIL s'engager **2.** (*register*) **to ~ at the university** s'inscrire à l'université; **to ~ on a course** s'inscrire à un cours **II.** *vt* immatriculer

enrollment *n Am,* **enrolment** *n* enrôlement *m*

en route [ˌɒn'ru:t, *Am:* ˌɑ:n-] *adv* en route

ensemble [ɒn'sɒmbl, *Am:* ɑ:n'sɑ:m-] *n* ensemble *m*

ensign ['ensən] *n* **1.** (*military flag*) drapeau *m* **2.** (*naval flag*) pavillon *m* **3.** (*standard-bearer*) porte-étendard *m*

enslave [ɪn'sleɪv, *Am:* en-] *vt* **1.** asservir **2.** *fig* **to become ~d by sth** devenir l'esclave de qc

ensue [ɪn'sju:, *Am:* en'su:] *vi form* s'ensuivre; **to ~ from sth** résulter de qc

ensuing *adj* suivant(e)

en suite bathroom [ɑ̃:nswi:t'bɑ:θrʊm, *Am:* ˌɑ:nswi:t'bæθru:m] *n* salle *f* de bains attenante

ensure [ɪn'ʃʊəʳ, *Am:* en'ʃʊr] *vt* garantir; (*security*) assurer; **to ~ everything is ready** s'assurer que tout est prêt

ENT *n abbr of* **ear, nose and throat** ORL *f*

entail [ɪn'teɪl, *Am:* en-] *vt* **1.** (*involve*) impliquer; (*risk*) entraîner **2.** (*necessitate*) **to ~ sb doing sth** nécessiter que qn fasse qc

entangle [ɪn'tæŋgl, *Am:* en-] *vt* **1. to ~ oneself** s'emmêler; **to get ~d in sth** s'empêtrer dans qc **2.** *fig* **to get ~d in sth** être mêlé à qc

entanglement *n* **1.** embrouillement *m* **2.** (*situation*) imbroglio *m;* **emotional ~s** aventures *fpl* sentimentales

enter ['entəʳ, *Am:* -t̬ɚ] **I.** *vt* **1.** (*go into: room, phase*) entrer dans; **it never ~ed my mind** *fig* ça ne m'a jamais traversé l'esprit **2.** (*insert*) introduire **3.** (*write down*) inscrire; (*payment*) noter; INFOR (*data*) entrer **4.** (*join: college, school*) entrer à; (*navy, firm*) rejoindre; **to ~ the priesthood** entrer dans les ordres **5.** (*make known: bid*) engager; (*claim, counterclaim*) faire; (*plea*) interjeter; **to ~ a protest** protester formellement ►**to ~ the fray** descendre dans l'arène; (*join a quarrel*) intervenir dans une querelle **II.** *vi* THEAT entrer

◆**enter for** *vt* (*competition, exam*) s'inscrire à; (*race*) s'inscrire pour

◆**enter into** *vt* **1.** (*bind oneself to: alliance, treaty, contract*) conclure; **to ~ a marriage** se marier **2.** (*engage in: conversation*) engager; (*negotations*) entamer; (*explanations*) se lancer dans **3.** (*form part of*) faire partie de ►**to ~ the spirit of things** entrer dans l'ambiance

◆**enter up** *vt* inscrire

◆**enter upon** *vi* débuter dans

enter key *n* INFOR touche *f* entrée

enterprise ['entəpraɪz, *Am:* -t̬ɚ-] *n* **1.** (*undertaking*) entreprise *f* **2.** *no pl* (*initiative*) esprit *m* d'initiative; **to show ~** se montrer entreprenant **3.** (*firm*) entreprise *f*

enterprise culture *n* esprit *m* d'entreprise

enterprising *adj* entreprenant(e)

entertain [ˌentə'teɪn, *Am:* -t̬ɚ-] **I.** *vt* **1.** (*amuse*) amuser; (*with music, stories*) divertir; (*with activity*) occuper **2.** (*offer hospitality to guests*) recevoir **3.** (*consider: doubts*) concevoir; (*suspicion*) éprouver; (*hope*) nourrir; (*idea*) prendre en considération **II.** *vi* recevoir

entertainer [ˌentə'teɪnəʳ, *Am:* -t̬ɚ'teɪnɚ] *n* artiste *mf*

entertaining *adj* divertissant(e)

entertainment *n* divertissement *m,* fun *m* *Québec;* **to provide some ~** offrir des distractions; **the ~ business** l'industrie du spectacle

enthral <-ll-> *vt,* **enthrall** [ɪn'θrɔ:l] *vt Am* captiver

enthrone [ɪn'θrəʊn, *Am:* en'θroʊn] *vt form* **1.** (*install on throne*) placer sur le trône; (*bishop*) introniser **2.** (*sitting*) **to sit ~ed** trôner

enthuse [ɪn'θju:z, *Am:* en'θu:z] **I.** <-sing> *vi* **to ~ about** [*o* **over**] **sth** s'extasier sur qc **II.** <-sing> *vt* **to ~ sb with sth** provoquer l'enthousiasme de qn pour qc

enthusiasm [ɪn'θju:zɪæzəm, *Am:* en'θu:-] *n* enthousiasme *m*

enthusiast [ɪn'θju:zɪæst] *n* enthousiaste; **a chess ~** un(e) passionné(e) d'échecs

enthusiastic [ɪnˌθju:zɪ'æstɪk, *Am:* enˌθu:-] *adj* enthousiaste; **to be ~ about sth** s'enthousiasmer pour qc

entice [ɪn'taɪs, *Am:* en-] *vt* attirer; **to ~ sb away from sth** détourner qn de qc; **to ~ sb to** *+infin* persuader qn de *+infin*

enticement *n* attrait *m;* **to offer ~s** offrir des avantages

enticing *adj* attrayant(e); (*smile*) séduisant(e)

entire [ɪn'taɪəʳ, *Am:* en'taɪɚ] *adj* **1.** (*whole*) tout(e); **an ~ country** un pays entier; **the ~ two hours** les deux heures en entier **2.** (*complete*) complet(-ète)

entirely *adv* entièrement; (*agree*) complète-

ment; ~ **for sb's benefit** uniquement pour qn
entirety [ɪn'taɪəʳətɪ, *Am:* en'taɪrət̬ɪ] *n no pl, form* intégralité *f*
entitle [ɪn'taɪtl, *Am:* en'taɪt̬l] *vt* **1.** LAW **to ~ sb to sth** donner à qn le droit à qc; **to be ~ed to** +*infin* avoir le droit de +*infin* **2.** (*give a title to*) intituler
entitled *adj* autorisé(e)
entitlement *n no pl* **1.** (*authorization*) droit *m* **2.** FIN allocation *f*
entity ['entətɪ, *Am:* -t̬ət̬ɪ] <-ies> *n form* entité *f*
entomology [ˌentə'mɒlədʒɪ, *Am:* -t̬ə'mɑːlə-] *n no pl* entomologie *f*
entrails ['entreɪlz] *npl* entrailles *fpl*
entrain **I.** *vt Am* **1.** (*carry along*) transporter **2.** (*put on board a train*) faire embarquer **II.** *vi* s'embarquer
entrance¹ ['entrəns] *n* **1.** *a.* THEAT entrée *f* **2.** (*right to enter*) admission *f*; **to grant/refuse ~** accorder/refuser l'accès
entrance² [ɪn'trɑːns, *Am:* en'træns] *vt* ravir
entrance examination *n* examen *m* d'entrée **entrance fee** *n* droit *m* d'entrée [*o* d'inscription] **entrance form** *n* fiche *f* d'inscription **entrance hall** *n* hall *m* d'entrée **entrance requirement** *n* conditions *fpl* d'admission **entrance visa** *n s.* **visa**
entrant ['entrənt] *n* participant(e) *m(f)*
entreat [ɪn'triːt, *Am:* en-] *vt* (*implore*) **to ~ sb to** +*infin* supplier qn de +*infin*
entreaty [ɪn'triːtɪ, *Am:* en'triːt̬ɪ] <-ies> *n* supplication *f*
entrench [ɪn'trentʃ, *Am:* en-] *vt* **1.** MIL **to ~ oneself** se retrancher **2.** *fig* **to become ~ed** (*idea, prejudice*) s'être implanté; **to take an ~ed position** prendre une position retranchée
entrepreneur [ˌɒntrəprə'nɜːʳ, *Am:* ˌɑːntrəprə'nɜːr] *n* entrepreneur *m*
entrepreneurial spirit [ˌɒntrəprə'nɜːriəl 'spɪrɪt, *Am:* ˌɑːn-] *n* esprit *m* d'entreprise
entrust [ɪn'trʌst, *Am:* en-] *vt* **to ~ sth to sb** confier qc à qn; **to ~ sb with sth** charger qn de qc; **to ~ sth to sb's care** remettre qc aux soins de qn
entry ['entrɪ] <-ies> *n* **1.** (*act of entering*) entrée *f*; ~ **to Britain** l'entrée en Grande-Bretagne; **to be refused** ~ se faire refuser l'entrée **2.** (*joining an organization*) adhésion *f* **3.** (*recorded item: in dictionary*) entrée *f*; (*in accounts*) écriture *f*; (*in diary*) note *f* **4.** (*application, entrant: exam, competition*) inscription *f*; (*race*) inscrit *m*; **the winning** ~ le candidat gagnant
entry fee *n s.* **entrance fee** **entry form** *n s.* **entrance form** **entry permit** *n* visa *m* d'entrée **entryphone** *n Brit* interphone *m* **entry regulations** *n* règlement *m* d'entrée **entry test** *n* examen *m* d'entrée
entwine [ɪn'twaɪn, *Am:* en-] *vt* entrelacer; **bindweed ~s itself around other plants** le liseron s'enroule autour d'autres plantes; **the two lovers were ~d in each others arms** les deux amoureux étaient enlacés
enumerate [ɪ'njuːməreɪt, *Am:* -'nuː-] *vt* énumérer
enumeration [ɪˌnjuːmə'reɪʃn, *Am:* -ˌnuː-] *n* énumération *f*
enunciate [ɪ'nʌnsɪeɪt] **I.** *vi* articuler **II.** *vt* (*word*) articuler; (*theory*) énoncer; (*sound*) émettre
envelop [ɪn'veləp, *Am:* en-] *vt* envelopper; **~ed in mist** enveloppé de brume
envelope ['envələʊp, *Am:* -loʊp] *n* enveloppe *f*
enviable ['envɪəbl] *adj* enviable
envious ['envɪəs] *adj* envieux(-euse); **to be ~ of sb/sth** envier qn/qc
environment [ɪn'vaɪərənmənt, *Am:* en'vaɪ-] *n* environnement *m*; **home ~** environnement familial; **~-friendly** qui respecte l'environnement
environmental [ɪnˌvaɪərən'mentl, *Am:* enˌvaɪrən'ment̬l] *adj* environnemental(e); ~ **damage** dégâts écologiques; ~ **impact** effets sur l'environnement; ~ **studies** études sur l'environnement
environmentalist [ɪnˌvaɪərən'mentəlɪst, *Am:* enˌvaɪrən'ment̬əl-] *n* environnementaliste *mf*
environs [ɪn'vaɪərənz, *Am:* en'vaɪ-] *npl form* environs *mpl*
envisage [ɪn'vɪzɪdʒ, *Am:* en-] *vt*, **envision** *vt Am* envisager; **to ~ doing sth** envisager de faire qc; **to ~ sb doing sth** envisager que qn fasse qc
envoy ['envɔɪ, *Am:* 'ɑːn-] *n* envoyé(e) *m(f)*
envy ['envɪ] **I.** *n no pl* envie *f*; **to feel ~ towards sb** envier qn; **to be the ~ of sb** faire l'envie de qn ►**to be green with** ~ être vert de jalousie **II.** <-ie-> *vt* envier; **to ~ sb sth** envier qc chez qn
enzyme ['enzaɪm] *n* enzyme *m o f*
EOC *n Brit abbr of* **Equal Opportunities Commission**
EOF *n* INFOR *abbr of* **end of file**
EP [ˌiː'piː] *n abbr of* **extended play**
ephemeral [ɪ'femərəl, *Am:* -ɚ-] *adj* éphémère
epic ['epɪk] **I.** *n* LIT épopée *f* **II.** *adj* **1.** LIT *a. fig* épique **2.** (*large: proportions*) gigantesque
epicenter *n Am*, **epicentre** ['epɪsentəʳ, *Am:* -t̬ɚ] *n* épicentre *m*
epicycle ['epɪsaɪkl, *Am:* '-ə-] *n* MAT, ASTR épicycle *m*
epidemic [ˌepɪ'demɪk, *Am:* -ə'-] **I.** *n* épidémie *f* **II.** *adj* épidémique
epidermis [ˌepɪ'dɜːmɪs, *Am:* -ə'dɜːr-] <-mes> *n* épiderme *m*
epidural [ˌepɪ'djʊərəl, *Am:* -ə'dʊ-] *n* péridurale *f*
epigram ['epɪgræm, *Am:* '-ə-] *n* épigramme *m*
epilepsy ['epɪlepsɪ] *n no pl* épilepsie *f*
epileptic [ˌepɪ'leptɪk] **I.** *n* épileptique *mf* **II.** *adj* épileptique; ~ **fit** crise *f* d'épilepsie

E

epilog *n Am,* **epilogue** ['epɪlɒg, *Am:* -əlɑ:g] *n Brit* épilogue *m*
Epiphany [ɪ'pɪfənɪ] *n no pl* REL l'Épiphanie *f*
episcopal [ɪ'pɪskəpl] *adj* épiscopal(e)
Episcopalian [ɪˌpɪskə'peɪlɪən] **I.** *adj* épiscopalien(ne) **II.** *n* épiscopalien(ne) *m(f)*
episode ['epɪsəʊd, *Am:* -əsoʊd] *n* épisode *m*
episodic [ˌepɪ'sɒdɪk, *Am:* -ə'sɑ:dɪk] *adj* **1.** (*occasional*) épisodique **2.** (*consisting of episodes*) par épisodes
epistle [ɪ'pɪsl] *n* **1.** *iron* (*letter*) missive *f* **2.** LIT épître *m*
epitaph ['epɪtɑ:f, *Am:* -ətæf] *n* épitaphe *f*
epithet ['epɪθet] *n* épithète *f*
epitome [ɪ'pɪtəmɪ, *Am:* -'pɪt̬-] *n sing* comble *m;* **the ~ of beauty** la beauté incarnée [*o* même]; **he is the ~ of Englishness** il représente l'Anglais type; **the ~ of ridiculousness** le comble du ridicule
epitomise *vt Aus, Brit,* **epitomize** [ɪ'pɪtəmaɪz, *Am:* ɪ'pɪt̬-] *vt* incarner
EPNS *n abbr of* **electroplated nickel silver** ruolz *m*
epoch ['i:pɒk, *Am:* 'epək] *n* époque *f;* **glacial ~** période *f* glaciaire
epoch-making *adj* marquant(e)
equable ['ekwəbl] *adj* (*temperament*) égal(e); (*climate*) tempéré(e)
equal ['i:kwəl] **I.** *adj* **1.** (*the same, same in amount: time, terms, share*) égal(e); (*reason, status*) même; **to be ~ to sth** être égal à qc; **~ in volume** de volume égal; **on an ~ footing** sur un pied d'égalité; **~ pay for ~ work** à travail égal, salaire égal **2.** (*able to do*) **to be ~ to a task** être à la hauteur d'une tâche ►**all things being ~** toutes choses égales par ailleurs **II.** *n* égal(e) *m(f);* **to have no ~** ne pas avoir son pareil **III.** <-ll- *Brit o* -l- *Am*> *vt* **1.** MAT être égal à **2.** (*match: amount, record*) égaler
equality [ɪ'kwɒlətɪ, *Am:* -'kwɑ:lət̬ɪ] *n no pl* égalité *f;* **~ between the sexes** égalité des sexes
equalization [ˌi:kwəlaɪ'zeɪʃn, *Am:* -ɪ'-] *n* égalisation *f*
equalize ['i:kwəlaɪz] **I.** *vt* égaliser **II.** *vi Aus, Brit* SPORT égaliser
equalizer ['i:kwəlaɪzəʳ, *Am:* -zɚ] *n Aus, Brit* SPORT but *m* égalisateur; **to score an ~** égaliser
equally ['i:kwəlɪ] *adv* **~ good** aussi bien; **to contribute ~ to sth** contribuer à qc à part égale; **to divide sth ~** diviser qc en parts égales; **but ~, we know that …** mais de même, nous savons que …
equal opportunities *npl Brit,* **equal opportunity** *n Am* égalité *f* des chances
equal(s) sign *n* MAT signe *m* égal
equanimity [ˌekwə'nɪmətɪ, *Am:* -ət̬ɪ] *n no pl* sérénité *f*
equate [ɪ'kweɪt] **I.** *vt* **he ~s sth with sth** pour lui, qc équivaut à qc **II.** *vi* **to ~ to sth** être égal à qc
equation [ɪ'kweɪʒn] *n* équation *f* ►**the other side of the ~** l'autre membre/partie de l'équation
equator [ɪ'kweɪtəʳ, *Am:* -t̬ɚ] *n no pl* **the ~** l'équateur
equatorial [ˌekwə'tɔ:rɪəl] *adj* équatorial(e)
equestrian [ɪ'kwestrɪən] **I.** *adj* (*event, statue*) équestre **II.** *n* cavalier, -ère *m, f*
equidistant [ˌi:kwɪ'dɪstənt] *adj* équidistant(e); **~ from two points** à égale distance de deux points
equilateral [ˌi:kwɪ'lætərəl, *Am:* -'læt̬-] *adj* équilatéral(e)
equilibrium [ˌi:kwɪ'lɪbrɪəm] *n no pl* équilibre *m;* **to lose/maintain one's ~** perdre/garder l'équilibre
equinox ['i:kwɪnɒks, *Am:* -nɑ:ks] <-es> *n* équinoxe *m*
equip [ɪ'kwɪp] <-pp-> *vt* **1.** (*fit out*) équiper; **to ~ oneself with sth** s'équiper de qc **2.** (*prepare*) **to ~ sb for sth** préparer qn à qc
equipment *n no pl* équipement *m;* **camping ~** matériel *m* de camping
equitable ['ekwɪtəbl, *Am:* -t̬ə-] *adj* équitable
equity¹ ['ekwətɪ, *Am:* -t̬ɪ] *n* <-ies> FIN **1.** *pl* (*shares*) actions *fpl* ordinaires; **~ market** marché des actions **2.** *no pl* (*block of stock*) fonds *mpl* propres
equity² *n no pl, form* (*fairness*) équité *f*
equivalence [ɪ'kwɪvələns] *n no pl* équivalence *f*
equivalent [ɪ'kwɪvələnt] **I.** *adj* **~ to sth** équivalent(e) à qc; **to be ~ to doing sth** revenir à faire qc **II.** *n* équivalent *m*
equivocal [ɪ'kwɪvəkl] *adj* **1.** (*ambiguous*) équivoque **2.** (*suspicious*) douteux(-euse); **an ~ position** une situation ambiguë
equivocate [ɪ'kwɪvəkeɪt] *vi form* se dérober
equivocation [ɪˌkwɪvə'keɪʃn] *n no pl, form* dérobades *fpl*
era ['ɪərə, *Am:* 'ɪrə] *n* ère *f;* **communist ~** époque *f* communiste; **post-war ~** après-guerre *m;* **bygone ~** époque révolue; **to usher in an ~** introduire une nouvelle époque
eradicate [ɪ'rædɪkeɪt] *vt* (*disease*) éradiquer; (*crime, corruption*) éliminer
erase [ɪ'reɪz, *Am:* -'reɪs] *vt* **1.** *a.* INFOR, FIN effacer; (*deficit*) éliminer **2.** *Am* (*rub out: blackboard*) effacer
eraser [ɪ'reɪzəʳ, *Am:* -'reɪsɚ] *n Am* gomme *f,* efface *f Québec; s. a.* **rubber**
erasure [ɪ'reɪʒəʳ, *Am:* -ʃɚ] *n Am* effacement *m*
erect [ɪ'rekt] **I.** *adj* **1.** (*upright*) droit(e); **to stand ~** se tenir debout **2.** ANAT (*penis*) en érection **II.** *vt* **1.** (*build*) construire **2.** (*put up*) installer
erectile [ɪ'rektaɪl, *Am:* -təl] *adj* érectile
erection [ɪ'rekʃn] *n a.* ANAT érection *f*
ergonomic [ˌɜgə'nɒmɪk, *Am:* ˌɜ:rgə'nɑ:mɪk] *adj* ergonomique
ergonomics [ˌɜ:gə'nɒmɪks, *Am:* ˌɜ:rgə'nɑ:mɪks] *n no pl, + sing vb* ergonomie *f*

ermine ['ɜːmɪn, *Am:* 'ɜːr-] *n* hermine *f*
erode [ɪ'rəʊd, *Am:* -'roʊd] **I.** *vt* éroder; **to ~ sb's authority** *fig* saper l'autorité de qn **II.** *vi* s'éroder
erogenous [ɪ'rɒdʒənəs, *Am:* -'rɑːdʒɪ-] *adj* érogène
erosion [ɪ'rəʊʒn, *Am:* -'roʊ-] *n no pl* érosion *f*
erotic [ɪ'rɒtɪk, *Am:* -'rɑːt̬ɪk] *adj* érotique
eroticism [ɪ'rɒtɪsɪzəm, *Am:* -'rɑːt̬ə-] *n no pl* érotisme *m*
err [ɜːʳ, *Am:* ɜːr] *vi form* commettre une erreur; **to ~ on the side of caution** pêcher par excès de prudence ►**to ~ is human** *prov* l'erreur est humaine *prov*
errand ['erənd] *n* **1.** course *f;* **to run an ~** faire une course **2.** (*help*) **an ~ of mercy** une mission humanitaire
errand boy *n* garçon *m* de courses
errant ['erənt] *adj* **1.** *form* dévoyé(e) **2.** *iron* (*unfaithful*) infidèle
erratic [ɪ'rætɪk, *Am:* -'ræt̬-] *adj* (*quality, performance*) inégal; (*pulse*) irrégulier(-ère); (*personality, behaviour*) imprévisible
erroneous [ɪ'rəʊnɪəs, *Am:* ə'roʊ-] *adj* (*assumption, conclusion*) erroné(e)
error ['erəʳ, *Am:* -ɚ] *n* **1.** (*mistake*) erreur *f;* **to do sth in ~** faire qc par erreur; **typing ~** faute de frappe; **the margin for ~** la marge d'erreur **2.** *Am* SPORT faute *f* ►**to see the ~ of one's ways** prendre conscience de ses erreurs
error message *n* INFOR message *m* d'erreur
error-prone *adj* qui a tendance à faire des erreurs
error rate *n* taux *m* d'erreur
erudite ['eruːdaɪt, *Am:* -jə-] *adj* érudit(e)
erudition [ˌeruː'dɪʃn, *Am:* -juː'-] *n no pl* érudition *f*
erupt [ɪ'rʌpt] *vi* **1.** (*explode: volcano*) entrer en éruption **2.** MED (*teeth*) sortir; (*rash*) apparaître; **his arms ~ed in a rash** ses bras se sont couverts de boutons
eruption [ɪ'rʌpʃn] *n* éruption *f*
escalate ['eskəleɪt] **I.** *vi* (*increase*) s'intensifier; (*incidents, problem*) s'aggraver; **to ~ into sth** se transformer en qc **II.** *vt* intensifier
escalation [ˌeskə'leɪʃn] *n* (*of fighting*) intensification *f;* (*of crime*) augmentation *f;* **~ of tension** montée *f* de la tension
escalator ['eskəleɪtəʳ, *Am:* -t̬ɚ] *n* **1.** (*stairs*) escalier *m* mécanique; **the down/up ~** l'escalator pour descendre/monter **2.** LAW **~ clause** clause d'indexation
escalope ['eskələp, *Am:* ˌeskə'loʊp] *n* escalope *f;* **turkey ~** escalope de dinde
escapade [ˌeskə'peɪd] *n* escapade *f*
escape [ɪ'skeɪp] **I.** *vi* **1.** (*flee: prisoner*) s'évader; (*animal*) s'échapper **2.** (*leak: gas*) s'échapper; (*liquid*) fuir **3.** INFOR **to ~ from a program** quitter une application ►**to ~ with one's life** s'en sortir vivant **II.** *vt* **1.** (*avoid*) **to ~ sth** échapper à qc; **there's no escaping the fact that ...** on ne peut pas ignorer le fait que ... **2.** (*fail to be noticed or remembered*) **to ~ sb's attention** échapper à l'attention de qn; **her name ~s me** son nom m'échappe **3.** (*not suppressed*) **a cry ~d them** ils ont laissé échapper un cri **III.** *n* **1.** (*act of fleeing*) évasion *f;* **to make (good) one's ~** réussir à s'échapper **2.** (*avoidance*) **to have a narrow ~** l'échapper belle **3.** (*accidental outflow*) fuite *f* **4.** LAW **~ clause** clause *f* dérogatoire
escapee [ɪˌskeɪ'piː] *n* fugitif, -ive *m, f*
escape key *n* touche *f* d'échappement
escapism [ɪ'skeɪpɪzəm] *n no pl, pej* évasion *f*
escapist **I.** *n pej* **to be an ~** fuire la réalité **II.** *adj* (*literature*) d'évasion
escarpment [ɪ'skɑːpmənt, *Am:* e'skɑːrp-] *n* escarpement *m*
ESCB *n abbr of* **European System of Central Banks** SEBC *m*
eschew [ɪ'stʃuː, *Am:* es-] *vt form* **1.** (*renounce*) renoncer à **2.** (*avoid*) refuser
escort ['eskɔːt, *Am:* -kɔːrt] **I.** *vt* **to ~ sb to safety** escorter qn en lieu sûr **II.** *n* **1.** *no pl* (*guard*) escorte *f;* **under police ~** sous escorte policière **2.** (*social companion*) compagnon *m,* hôtesse *f*
ESE *n abbr of* **east-southeast**
Eskimo ['eskɪməʊ, *Am:* -kəmoʊ] <-s> *n* **1.** (*person*) Esquimau(de) *m(f)* **2.** *no pl* LING eskimo *m; s. a.* **English**
ESL [ˌiːes'el] *n abbr of* **English as a second language**
ESN [ˌiːes'en] *n abbr of* **educationally subnormal**
esophagus [iː'sɒfəgəs, *Am:* ɪ'sɑːfə-] *n Am* ANAT *s.* **oesophagus**
esoteric [ˌesəʊ'terɪk, *Am:* ˌesə'-] *adj* ésotérique
ESP [ˌiːes'piː] *n abbr of* **extrasensory perception**
especial [ɪ'speʃl] *adj form* particulier(-ère)
especially [ɪ'speʃəlɪ] *adv* surtout; **he's brought this ~ for you** il a apporté cela exprès pour toi; **I was ~ happy to meet them** j'étais particulièrement content de les rencontrer
espionage ['espɪənɑːʒ] *n no pl* espionage *m*
esplanade [ˌesplə'neɪd, *Am:* 'esplənɑːd] *n* esplanade *f*
espousal [ɪ'spaʊzl] *n no pl, form* **the ~ of an idea** l'adhésion *f* à une idée
espouse [ɪ'spaʊz] *vt form* (*support*) adhérer à; (*belief*) embrasser
espresso [e'spresəʊ, *Am:* -oʊ] <-s> *n* express *m;* **two ~s** deux express
Esq. *n Brit abbr of* **Esquire** (*on letter*) **Robert Richard ~** M. Robert Richard
Esquire [ɪ'skwaɪəʳ, *Am:* 'eskwaɪɚ] *n* **1.** *Brit* (*special title*) Monsieur *m* **2.** *Am* LAW maître *m*
essay[1] [e'seɪ] *n* **1.** SCHOOL rédaction *f* **2.** UNIV dissertation *f* **3.** LIT essai *m*
essay[2] ['eseɪ] *vt* LIT essayer
essayist *n* essayiste *mf*
essence[1] ['esns] *n no pl* (*central point*)

E

essence *f;* **to be of the** ~ être très important; **in** ~ en gros

essence² ['esns] *n* (*fragrance, in food*) essence *f*

essential [ɪ'senʃl] **I.** *adj* (*component, difference*) essentiel(le); ~ **goods** produits *mpl* de première nécessité **II.** *n pl* **the** ~**s** l'essentiel; **to be reduced to its** ~**s** être réduit à l'essentiel

essentially [ɪ'senʃəlɪ] *adv* **1.** (*basically*) en gros **2.** (*mostly*) essentiellement; **to be** ~ **correct** être correct pour l'essentiel

est. *adj* **1.** *abbr of* **estimated 2.** *abbr of* **established**

establish [ɪ'stæblɪʃ] *vt* **1.** (*set up*) établir; (*fellowship, hospital*) fonder **2.** (*find out: facts*) établir **3.** (*demonstrate*) **to** ~ **one's authority over sb** affirmer son autorité sur qn; **to** ~ **sb as** faire reconnaître qn en tant que **4.** ADMIN **to** ~ **residence** élire domicile

established *adj* établi(e)

establishment *n* **1.** (*business*) établissement *m;* **business** ~ maison *f* de commerce; **family** ~ entreprise *f* familiale **2.** *no pl* (*group*) **the** ~ la classe dominante **3.** (*setting up*) création *f* **4.** (*discovery: of facts*) établissement *m*

estate [ɪ'steɪt] *n* **1.** (*land*) propriété *f;* **country** ~ domaine *m* **2.** LAW biens *mpl* **3.** *Brit* ARCHIT **a council** ~ un lotissement HLM; **housing** ~ lotissement *m;* **industrial** ~ zone *f* industrielle **4.** (*the press*) **the fourth** ~ le quatrième pouvoir **5.** (*state*) état *m;* **the holy** ~ **of matrimony** les liens sacrés du mariage **6.** *Brit* (*car*) break *m*

estate agent *n Brit* agent *m* immobilier **estate car** *n Brit* break *m* **estate duty** <-ies>, **estate tax** *n* droits *mpl* de succession

esteem [ɪ'stiːm] **I.** *n no pl* (*respect*) estime *f;* **to fall/rise in sb's** ~ tomber/monter dans l'estime de qn; **to hold sb in high** ~ tenir qn en haute estime **II.** *vt* estimer; **highly** ~**ed** très estimé

estimable ['estɪməbl] *adj form* digne d'estime

estimate ['estɪmeɪt, *Am:* -mɪt] **I.** *vt* (*cost, increase*) estimer **II.** *n* **1.** (*assessment*) estimation *f;* **at a conservative** ~ au bas mot; **at a rough** ~ à vue de nez **2.** (*quote*) devis *m*

estimated ['estɪmeɪtɪd, *Am:* -t̬ɪd] *adj* estimé(e); **estimated time of arrival** heure prévue d'arrivée; **it will cost an** ~ **£1000** le coût est estimé à 1000£

estimation [ˌestɪ'meɪʃn] *n no pl* estimation *f;* **in my** ~ d'après moi

Estonia [es'təʊniə, *Am:* es'toʊ-] *n* l'Estonie *f*

Estonian [es'təʊniən, *Am:* es'toʊ-] **I.** *adj* estonien(ne) **II.** *n* **1.** (*person*) Estonien(ne) *m(f)* **2.** LING estonien *m; s. a.* **English**

estrange [ɪ'streɪndʒ] *vt* **to** ~ **sb from sb/sth** éloigner qn de qn/qc; **her** ~**d partner** son ex-compagnon

estrangement *n* brouille *f*

estrogen ['iːstrəʊdʒən, *Am:* 'estrədʒən] *n Am s.* **oestrogen**

estuary ['estʃʊərɪ, *Am:* 'estʃuːerɪ] <-ies> *n* estuaire *m*

ETA [ˌiːtiː'eɪ] *n abbr of* **estimated time of arrival**

et al. [et'æl] *adv abbr of* **et alii** et autres

etc. *adv abbr of* **et cetera** etc.

et cetera [ɪt'setərə, *Am:* -'set̬ɚ-] *adv* et cætera

etch [etʃ] *vt* **1.** graver à l'eau-forte **2.** *fig* **to be** ~**ed on sb's memory** être gravé dans la mémoire de qn

etcher *n* graveur, -euse *m, f* à l'eau-forte

etching *n* gravure *f* à l'eau-forte

eternal [ɪ'tɜːnl, *Am:* -'tɜːr-] *adj* **1.** (*lasting forever*) éternel(le); ~ **student** *iron* étudiant(e) *m(f)* à vie **2.** *pej* (*incessant*) constant(e) ▶ **hope springs** ~ *prov* l'espoir fait vivre *prov;* ~ **triangle** ménage à trois

eternally [ɪ'tɜːnəlɪ, *Am:* -'tɜːr-] *adv* **1.** (*forever*) éternellement **2.** (*incessantly*) constamment

eternity [ɪ'tɜːnətɪ, *Am:* -'tɜːrnət̬ɪ] *n no pl* éternité *f;* **for all** ~ pour l'éternité; **to wait an** ~ **for sb** attendre qn pendant une éternité

ether ['iːθəʳ, *Am:* -θɚ] *n no pl* **1.** éther *m* **2.** *a.* LIT, RADIO **across the** ~ sur les ondes

ethereal [ɪ'θɪərɪəl, *Am:* -'θɪrɪ-] *adj* éthéré(e)

ethical ['eθɪkl] *adj* éthique

ethics ['eθɪks] *n pl + sing vb* éthique *f;* **code of** ~ code *m* de déontologie

Ethiopia [ˌiːθɪ'əʊpɪə, *Am:* -'oʊ-] *n no pl* l'Éthiopie *f*

Ethiopian [ˌiːθɪ'əʊpɪən, *Am:* -'oʊ-] **I.** *adj* éthiopien(ne) **II.** *n* Éthiopien(ne) *m(f)*

ethnic ['eθnɪk] **I.** *adj* ethnique; ~ **cleansing** purification *f* ethnique **II.** *n Am, Aus* membre *m* d'une minorité ethnique

ethnology [eθ'nɒlədʒɪ, *Am:* -'nɑːlə-] *n no pl* ethnologie *f*

ethos ['iːθɒs, *Am:* -θɑːs] *n no pl* esprit *m;* **working-class** ~ culture *f* prolétaire

ethyl alcohol ['eθɪl 'ælkəhɒl, *Am:* 'eθəl 'ælkəhɑːl] *n* alcool *m* éthylique

etiquette ['etɪket, *Am:* 'et̬ɪkɪt] *n no pl* étiquette *f;* **diplomatic/court** ~ protocole *m* diplomatique/judiciaire

etymological [ˌetɪmə'lɒdʒɪkl, *Am:* ˌet̬ɪmə'lɑːdʒɪkl] *adj* étymologique

etymology [ˌetɪ'mɒlədʒɪ, *Am:* ˌet̬ɪ'mɑːlə-] <-ies> *n* étymologie *f*

EU [ˌiː'juː] *n abbr of* **European Union** UE *f;* ~ **countries** pays *mpl* membres de l'UE

eucalyptus [ˌjuːkə'lɪptəs] <-es *o* -ti> *n* eucalyptus *m*

eucalyptus oil *n no pl* huile *f* d'eucalyptus

Eucharist ['juːkərɪst] *n no pl* REL **the** ~ l'Eucharistie *f*

eulogize ['juːlədʒaɪz] **I.** *vt form* faire le panégyrique de **II.** *vi form* **to** ~ **over sth/sb** faire le panégyrique de qc/qn

eulogy ['juːlədʒɪ] <-ies> *n* (*high praise*)

éloge *m;* (*at funeral*) éloge *m* (funèbre)
eunuch ['ju:nək] *n* eunuque *m*
euphemism ['ju:fəmɪzəm] *n* euphémisme *m*
euphemistic [ˌju:fə'mɪstɪk] *adj* euphémique
euphony ['ju:fənɪ] *n no pl, form* euphonie *f*
euphoria [ju:'fɔ:rɪə] *n no pl* euphorie *f*
euphoric [ju:'fɒrɪk, *Am:* -'fɔ:rɪk] *adj* euphorique
EUR *n abbr of* **Euro** EUR
Eurasia [jʊə'reɪʒə, *Am:* jʊ'-] *n no pl* Eurasie *f*
Eurasian [jʊə'reɪʒn, *Am:* jʊ'-] **I.** *adj* eurasien(ne) **II.** *n* Eurasien(ne) *m(f)*
Euratom [jʊə'rætəm, *Am:* jʊ'ræt̬-] *n no pl, no art abbr of* **European Atomic Energy Community** EURATOM *f*
eurhythmics [ju:'rɪðmɪks, *Am:* jʊ'-] *n Brit + sing vb* gymnastique *f* rythmique
euro ['jʊərəʊ, *Am:* 'jʊroʊ] *n* euro *m;* **changeover to the ~** [*o* **~ changeover**] passage *m* à l'euro; **denominated in ~s** libellé en euros; **to link a currency to the ~** rattacher une monnaie à l'euro
euro area *n* zone *f* euro **euro cent** *n* euro centime *m* **euro coins** *n* pièces *fpl* (en) euro **Eurocrat** *n pej* eurocrate *mf* **eurocurrency** *n* eurodevise *f* **Eurodollar** *n* eurodollar *m* **Euro MP** *n* député(e) *m(f)* européen(ne) **euro notes** *n* billets *mpl* (en) euro
Europe ['jʊərəp, *Am:* 'jʊrəp] *n no pl* l'Europe *m;* **Eastern ~** l'Europe de l'Est
European [ˌjʊərə'pɪən, *Am:* ˌjʊrə-] **I.** *adj* européen(ne) **II.** *n* Européen(ne) *m(f)*
European Central Bank *n* Banque *f* centrale européenne **European Commission** *n* Commission *f* européenne **European Community** *n* Communauté *f* européenne **European Court of Justice** *n* Cour *f* européenne de justice **European Investment Bank** *n* Banque *f* européenne d'investissement **European Monetary Institute** *n* Institut *m* monétaire européen **European Monetary System** *n* Système *m* monétaire européen **European Ombudsman** *n* Médiateur *m* européen **European Parliament** *n* Parlement *m* européen **European System of Central Banks** *n* Système *m* européen de banques centrales **European Union** *n* Union *f* européenne **European Union Treaty** *n* traité *m* sur l'Union européenne
euro zone *n s.* **euro area**
eurythmics *n Am s.* **eurhythmics**
euthanasia [ˌju:θə'neɪzɪə, *Am:* -ʒə] *n no pl* euthanasie *f*
evacuate [ɪ'vækjʊeɪt] *vt* évacuer
evacuation [ɪˌvækjʊ'eɪʃn] *n* évacuation *f*
evacuee [ɪˌvækju:'i:] *n* personne *f* évacuée
evade [ɪ'veɪd] *vt* (*question*) esquiver; (*police*) échapper à; (*tax*) eviter; **to ~ capture** éviter d'être pris
evaluate [ɪ'væljʊeɪt] *vt* (*calculate value*) évaluer
evaluation [ɪˌvæljʊ'eɪʃn] *n* évaluation
evangelical [ˌi:væn'dʒelɪkl] **I.** *n* évangéliste *mf* **II.** *adj* évangélique; *fig* évangélisateur(-trice)
evangelist [ɪ'vændʒəlɪst] *n* évangéliste *mf*
evangelize [ɪ'vændʒəlaɪz] **I.** *vt* évangéliser **II.** *vi* prêcher l'Évangile; **to ~ about sth** *fig* prêcher qc
evaporate [ɪ'væpəreɪt] **I.** *vt* faire évaporer **II.** *vi* s'évaporer; *fig* se volatiliser
evasion [ɪ'veɪʒn] *n* **1.** *no pl* (*avoidance: of responsibility*) fuite *f;* (*of question*) dérobade *f;* **fare ~** resquille *f;* **tax ~** fraude fiscale **2.** (*false answer*) faux-fuyant *m*
evasive [ɪ'veɪsɪv] *adj* évasif(-ive); **an ~ answer** une réponse équivoque; **to take ~ action** effectuer une manœuvre d'évitement; *fig* esquiver la difficulté
eve [i:v] *n no pl* veille *f*
Eve [i:v] *n no art* Eve *f*
even ['i:vn] **I.** *adv* **1.** (*used to intensify*) même; **that's good, ~ better than ...** c'est bien, voire mieux que ...; **not ~** même pas; **~ as a child, she ...** même lorsqu'elle était enfant, elle ...; **~ you have to admit that ...** même toi, tu dois admettre que ... **2.** (*despite*) **~ if ...** même si ...; **~ so ...** tout de même ...; **~ then he ...** et alors, il ...; **~ though he** bien qu'il *+subj* **3.** *with comparative* **~ more/less/better/worse** encore plus/moins/mieux/pire **II.** *adj* **1.** (*level*) nivelé(e); (*temperature*) constant; **~ rows** rangs équilibrés; **an ~ surface** une surface plane **2.** (*equal*) égal(e); **an ~ contest** une compétition équilibrée; **they're ~ on six points each** ils sont à égalité avec six points chacun; **there is an ~ chance that sb wins** qn a autant de chances de gagner que de perdre; **to get ~ with sb** se venger de qn; **now you're ~** maintenant vous êtes quittes **3.** (*constant, regular*) régulier(-ère); **to have an ~ temper** être d'une humeur toujours égale **4.** (*fair, of same amount*) équitable; **an ~ distribution of wealth** une distribution équitable des richesses **5.** MAT pair(e); **an ~ page** une page paire **III.** *vt* **1.** (*make level*) aplanir **2.** (*equalize*) égaliser; **to ~ the score** égaliser la marque
◆**even out** **I.** *vi* (*prices*) s'équilibrer **II.** *vt* égaliser; (*differences*) réduire; **taxes have been evened out** les impôts ont été répartis plus équitablement
◆**even up** *vt* rééquilibrer
evening ['i:vnɪŋ] *n* soir *m;* (*as period, event*) soirée *f;* **good ~!** bonsoir!; **in the ~** le soir; **that ~** ce soir-là; **the previous ~** la veille au soir; **every Monday ~** tous les lundis soir(s); **on Monday ~** lundi dans la soirée, dans la soirée de lundi; **during the ~** dans la soirée; **one July ~** un soir de juillet; **8 o'clock in the ~** 8 heures du soir; **at the end of the ~** en fin de soirée; **all ~** toute la soirée; **we've had a lovely ~** nous avons passé une très bonne soirée
evening class *n* cours *m* du soir **evening**

E

dress *n* tenue *f* de soirée **evening gown** *n* robe *f* du soir **evening meal** *n* dîner *m* **evening (news)paper** *n* journal *m* du soir **evening performance** *n* représentation *f* en soirée **evening star** *n* étoile *f* du berger

evenly ['iːvənlɪ] *adv* **1.** (*calmly*) calmement; **to state sth** ~ déclarer qc posément **2.** (*equally*) équitablement; **to divide sth** ~ partager qc à parts égales; **to be ~ spaced** être espacé de manière régulière

evenness ['iːvnnɪs] *n* régularité *f*

evens *adj Brit* **there's an ~ chance he'll do it** il y a une chance sur deux qu'il le fasse

event [ɪ'vent] *n* **1.** (*happening*) événement *m*; **a social** ~ rencontre *f*; **a sports** ~ un événement sportif; **the athletics ~s** les épreuves d'athlétisme; **after the** ~ après coup **2.** (*case*) cas *m*; **in the** ~ en l'occurrence; **in the ~ (that) it rains** au cas où il pleuvrait; **in either** ~ dans un cas comme dans l'autre

even-tempered ['iːvən'tempəd] *adj* d'humeur égale

eventful [ɪ'ventfl] *adj* plein(e) d'événements

eventual [ɪ'ventʃʊəl] *adj* (*final*) final(e); **the ~ cost will be ...** finalement, le coût total sera de ...

eventuality [ɪˌventʃʊ'æləti, *Am:* -t̬ɪ] <-ies> *n* éventualité *f*

eventually *adv* **1.** (*finally*) finalement **2.** (*some day*) un de ces jours; **he'll do it** ~ il finira bien par le faire

ever ['evəʳ, *Am:* -ɚ] *adv* **1.** (*on any occasion*) **never** ~ jamais; *inf* jamais de la vie; **if you ever meet her** si jamais tu la rencontres; **have you ~ met her?** est-ce que tu l'as déjà rencontrée?; **did he ~ call you?** est-ce qu'il t'a appelé en fait?; **his fastest ~ race** sa course la plus rapide de toutes; **the biggest ship ever** le plus grand bâteau jamis construit **2.** (*always*) toujours; **as** ~ comme toujours; **as good as** ~ aussi bon que d'habitude; **harder than ever** plus difficile que jamais; ~ **since ...** depuis que ...; ~**-smaller computers** des ordinateurs encore plus petits; ~**-vigilant/-popular** toujours vigilant/populaire **3.** (*for emphasis*) **I'm ~ so pleased** je suis si contente; **why ~ did he leave?** pourquoi donc est-il parti?

everglade ['evəgleɪd, *Am:* -ɚ-] *n Am* marais *m*; **the Everglades** les Everglades

evergreen ['evəgriːn, *Am:* -ɚ-] **I.** *n* (*tree*) arbre *m* à feuilles persistantes **II.** *adj* à feuilles persistantes; *fig* éternel(le); ~ **forest** forêt de conifères

everlasting [ˌevə'lɑːstɪŋ, *Am:* -ɚ'læstɪŋ] *adj* **1.** (*undying*) éternel(le) **2.** (*incessant*) perpétuel(le) **3.** *pej* sempiternel(le); (*lectures*) interminable

every ['evrɪ] *adj* **1.** (*each*) ~ **child/cat/pencil/call** chaque enfant/chat/crayon/appel; ~ **time** (à) chaque fois; **not ~ book can be borrowed** les livres ne peuvent pas tous être empruntés; ~ **one of them** tous sans exception; ~ **second counts** chaque seconde compte; ~ **Sunday** chaque dimanche; **in ~ way** à tous points de vue **2.** (*repeated*) ~ **other day** un jour sur deux; ~ **now and then** [*o* **again**] de temps en temps **3.** (*used for emphasis*) ~ **single page** chaque page; **you had ~ chance to go** tu as eu toutes les possibilités d'y aller; **her ~ wish** son moindre désir ►~ <u>**little**</u> **helps** *prov* les petits ruisseaux font les grandes rivières *prov*

everybody ['evriˌbɒdi, *Am:* -ˌbɑːdi] *indef pron, sing* tout le monde; ~ **but Paul** tous sauf Paul; ~ **who agrees** tous ceux qui sont d'accord; **where's ~ going?** où est-ce que tout le monde va?; ~ **else** tous les autres

everyday ['evrɪdeɪ] *adj* quotidien(ne); ~ **language** langage courant; **to write sth in ~ language** écrire en langage parlé; ~ **life** la vie quotidienne; ~ **topic** sujet banal

everyone ['evrɪwʌn] *pron s.* **everybody**

everything ['evrɪθɪŋ] *indef pron, sing* **1.** (*all things*) tout; **is ~ all right?** tout va bien?; ~ **is OK** ça va bien, c'est correct *Québec;* ~ **they drink** tout ce qu'ils boivent; **to do ~ necessary/one can** faire tout le nécessaire/ce qu'on peut; **because of the weather and** ~ à cause du temps et tout ça **2.** (*the most important thing*) **to be ~ to sb** être tout pour qn; **money isn't** ~ ce n'est pas tout d'être riche; **time is** ~ c'est le temps qui compte; *s. a.* **anything**

everywhere ['evrɪweəʳ, *Am:* -wer] *adv* partout; ~ **else** partout ailleurs; **to look ~ for sth** chercher qc partout; ~ **I've looked** partout où j'ai cherché; **people arrived from** ~ les gens arrivaient de toutes parts

evict [ɪ'vɪkt] *vt* **to ~ sb from their home** expulser qn de chez lui

evidence ['evɪdəns] **I.** *n no pl* **1.** LAW (*from witness*) témoignage *m*; (*physical proof*) preuve *f*; **to give** ~ témoigner; **circumstantial** ~ preuve indirecte; **documentary** [*o* **written**] ~ preuve écrite; **forensic** ~ preuve légale; **fresh** ~ nouvelle preuve; **to be used in** ~ être utilisé en témoignage **2.** (*indications*) évidence *f*; **to be much in** ~ être bien en évidence; **to believe only the ~ of one's eyes** ne croire que ce que l'on voit; **on the ~ of recent events** sur la base des récents événements; **to bear ~ of sth** porter la marque de qc **II.** *vt form* **to ~ interest in sth** montrer de l'intérêt pour qc

evident ['evɪdənt] *adj* évident(e)

evil ['iːvl] **I.** *adj* mauvais(e); **the ~ eye** le mauvais œil; ~ **odour** odeur fétide; ~ **spirit(s)** mauvais esprits; **to have an ~ tongue** avoir une langue de vipère **II.** *n pej* mal *m*; **social** ~ fléau *m* social; **the ~s of the past** les erreurs du passé; **good and** ~ le bien et le mal; **it's the lesser of two ~s** c'est un moindre mal

evil-doer *n* malfaiteur *m* **evil-minded** *adj pej* malveillant(e) **evil-tempered** *adj pej* coléreux(-euse); **to be evil-tempered** avoir mauvais caractère

evince [ɪ'vɪns] *vt form* démontrer; **to ~ will-**

ingness to +*infin* manifester la volonté de +*infin;* **to ~ interest** faire preuve d'intérêt
evocation [ˌevəˈkeɪʃn] *n form* évocation *f*
evocative [ɪˈvɒkətɪv, *Am:* -ˈvɑːkət̬ɪv] *adj* évocateur(-trice)
evoke [ɪˈvəʊk, *Am:* -ˈvoʊk] *vt* évoquer; **to ~ a smile** susciter un sourire
evolution [ˌiːvəˈluːʃn, *Am:* ˌevə-] *n no pl* évolution *f*
evolve [ɪˈvɒlv, *Am:* -ˈvɑːlv] **I.** *vi* évoluer **II.** *vt* développer; **to ~ new forms of life** développer de nouvelles formes de vie
ewe [juː] *n* brebis *f*
ewer [ˈjuːəʳ, *Am:* -ɚ] *n* aiguière *f*
ex [eks] <-es> *n inf* (*former spouse*) ex *mf*
ex- *adj* ancien(ne)
exacerbate [ɪgˈzæsəbeɪt, *Am:* -ɚ-] *vt* exacerber
exact [ɪgˈzækt] **I.** *adj* exact(e); **to have the ~ change** avoir l'appoint; **the ~ opposite** tout le contraire; **~ copy** reproduction fidèle **II.** *vt* **1.** exiger; **to ~ revenge on sb** prendre sa revanche sur qn **2.** *pej* extorquer
exacting *adj* (*teacher*) exigeant(e); (*job*) astreignant(e)
exactitude [ɪgˈzæktɪtjuːd, *Am:* -tətuːd] *n no pl* exactitude *f*
exactly *adv* (*precisely*) exactement; **how ~ did he do that?** comment a-t-il fait au juste?; **when ~ did it happen?** quand est-ce que c'est arrivé exactement?; **I don't ~ agree** je ne suis pas tout à fait d'accord; **not ~** pas vraiment
exactness *n* exactitude *f*
exaggerate [ɪgˈzædʒəreɪt] **I.** *vt* exagérer; (*situation*) grossir **II.** *vi* exagérer; **let's not ~!** n'exagérons pas!
exaggerated [ɪgˈzædʒəreɪtɪd, *Am:* -t̬ɪd] *adj* exagéré(e)
exaggeration [ɪgˌzædʒəˈreɪʃn] *n* exagération *f;* **to be prone to ~** avoir tendance à exagérer; **it's no ~ to say that ...** on peut dire sans exagérer que ...
exalt [ɪgˈzɔːlt] *vt* **1.** (*praise*) exalter **2.** (*honour*) **to ~ sth as a virtue** élever qc au rang de vertu
exaltation [ˌegzɔːlˈteɪʃn] *n no pl* exaltation *f*
exalted [ɪgˈzɔːltɪd, *Am:* -t̬ɪd] *adj* **1.** (*elevated*) élevé(e); **~ rank** haut rang; **~ post** poste haut placé **2.** (*jubilant*) exalté(e)
exam [ɪgˈzæm] *n* examen *m;* **to take/pass an ~** passer/réussir un examen
examination [ɪgˌzæmɪˈneɪʃn] *n* examen *m;* **on closer ~** après un examen plus approfondi
examination paper *n* sujet *m* d'examen
examine [ɪgˈzæmɪn] *vt* **1.** (*test*) examiner; **to ~ sb on sth** interroger qn sur qc **2.** (*study, scan*) étudier **3.** LAW interroger
examinee [ɪgˌzæmɪˈniː] *n* candidat(e) *m(f)*
examiner [ɪgˈzæmɪnəʳ, *Am:* -ɚ] *n* examinateur, -trice *m, f*
example [ɪgˈzɑːmpl, *Am:* ɪgˈzæm-] *n* exemple *m;* **for ~** par exemple; **to give sb an ~ of sth** donner à qn un exemple de qc; **to set an ~** donner l'exemple; **to make an ~ of sb** donner qn en exemple
exasperate [ɪgˈzɑːspəreɪt] *vt* exaspérer
exasperating *adj* exaspérant(e)
exasperation [ɪgˌzɑːspəˈreɪʃn] *n no pl* exaspération *f*
excavate [ˈekskəveɪt] **I.** *vt* **1.** (*expose by digging*) déterrer; (*site*) fouiller; **~d site** fouilles *fpl* **2.** (*hollow by digging*) creuser **II.** *vi* faire des fouilles
excavation [ˌekskəˈveɪʃn] *n* **1.** (*digging in ground*) excavation *f;* (*of tumulus*) dégagement *m;* (*of tunnel*) percée *f* **2.** *pl* (*by archeologists*) fouilles *fpl*
excavator [ˈekskəveɪtəʳ, *Am:* -t̬ɚ] *n Aus, Brit* (*machine*) pelleteuse *f*
exceed [ɪkˈsiːd] *vt* dépasser
exceedingly *adv form* excessivement
excel [ɪkˈsel] <-ll-> **I.** *vi* exceller; **to ~ at chess** exceller aux échecs; **to ~ in French** être excellent en français **II.** *vt* **to ~ oneself** se surpasser
excellence [ˈeksələns] *n no pl* excellence *f*
Excellency [ˈeksələnsɪ] *n* Excellence *f;* **Your ~** Votre Excellence
excellent [ˈeksələnt] *adj* **1.** excellent(e); **to have ~ taste** avoir un très bon goût **2.** **~!** parfait!
except [ɪkˈsept] **I.** *prep* sauf; **~ for sb/sth** à l'exception de qn/qc; **why would he do it ~ to annoy me?** pourquoi est-ce qu'il le ferait à moins que ce ne soit pour m'embêter? **II.** *conj* **~ that** sauf que; **to do nothing ~ wait** ne rien faire si ce n'est attendre
excepting *prep, conj* excepté
exception [ɪkˈsepʃn] *n* **1.** (*special case*) exception *f;* **with the ~ of ...** à l'exception de ...; **with a few ~s** à part quelques exceptions **2.** (*objection*) **to take ~ to sth** s'élever contre ▸**the ~ proves the rule** *prov* l'exception confirme la règle *prov*
exceptional [ɪkˈsepʃənl] *adj* exceptionnel(le)
exceptionally [ɪkˈsepʃnəlɪ] *adv* exceptionnellement; **to be ~ clever** être particulièrement intelligent
excerpt [ˈeksɜːpt, *Am:* -sɜːrpt] **I.** *n* extrait *m* **II.** *vt* **to be ~ed from sth** être extrait de qc
excess [ɪkˈses] **I.** <-es> *n* **1.** *no pl* (*overindulgence*) excès *m;* **to do sth to ~** faire qc avec excès **2.** (*surplus amount*) excédent *m;* **in ~ of £500** qui dépasse £500 **3.** *Brit* (*on insurance claim*) franchise *f* **II.** *adj* excédentaire; **~ production** excédent de production
excess baggage *n* excédent *m* de bagage
excessive [ɪkˈsesɪv] *adj* excessif(-ive); **~ zeal** excès *m* de zèle
excess production *n* excédents *mpl*
excess supply *n* stock *m* excédentaire
exchange [ɪksˈtʃeɪndʒ] **I.** *vt* **1.** (*trade for the equivalent*) **to ~ sth for sth** échanger qc contre qc; **to ~ addresses** échanger des adresses **2.** (*interchange*) interchanger **3.** ECON

E

vendre **II.** *n* **1.** (*interchange, trade*) échange *m;* **in ~ for sth** en échange de qc **2.** FIN, ECON change *m;* **foreign ~** devises *fpl* **3.** (*discussion*) échange *m* verbal **4.** TEL (**telephone**) ~ central *m* téléphonique

exchangeable *adj* échangeable; **to be ~ for sth** être échangeable contre qc

exchange broker *n* ECON, FIN courtier *m* en devises **exchange control** *n* ECON, FIN contrôle *m* des changes **exchange dealer** *s.* **exchange broker** **exchange market** *n* ECON, FIN marché *m* des changes **exchange rate** *n* ECON, FIN taux *m* de change; ~ **parity** parité *f* entre devises; ~ **mechanism** mécanisme *m* de change **exchange value** *n* valeur *f* d'échange

exchequer [ɪks'tʃekəʳ, *Am:* -ɚ] *n no pl, Brit* ministère *m* des finances; **Chancellor of the Exchequer** *Brit* ministre *m* des finances

excise[1] ['eksaɪz] *n no pl* taxe *f;* ~ **on alcohol** taxe sur les alcools

excise[2] [ek'saɪz] *vt form* **1.** exciser **2.** *fig* supprimer

excise duty *n* taxe *f*

excitable [ɪk'saɪtəbl, *Am:* -t̬əbl] *adj* **1.** ANAT excitable **2.** (*person*) nerveux(-euse)

excite [ɪk'saɪt] *vt* **1.** (*arouse strong feelings in*) exciter; **to ~ an audience** captiver un public **2.** (*elicit*) susciter; (*curiosity*) piquer; (*passion*) attiser; (*feelings*) provoquer; (*imagination*) stimuler

excited [ɪk'saɪtɪd, *Am:* -t̬ɪd] *adj* **1.** *a.* ANAT, PHYS excité(e) **2.** (*happy*) **~d about an idea** enthousiasmé par une idée; **there is nothing to get ~ about** il n'y a pas de quoi s'exciter; **don't get ~ about it yet** ne te réjouis pas trop vite **3.** (*angry*) **don't get ~!** ne t'énerve pas!

excitement *n* excitation *f;* **to be in a state of ~** être tout excité; **what ~!** quelle émotion!

exciting *adj* (*match, prospect*) passionnant(e); (*discovery*) sensationnel(le)

exclaim [ɪk'skleɪm] **I.** *vi* s'exclamer; **to ~ in delight** pousser un cri de joie **II.** *vt* **to ~ that ...** s'écrier que ...

exclamation [ˌekslə'meɪʃn] *n* exclamation *f*

exclamation mark *n* point *m* d'exclamation

exclude [ɪk'sklu:d] *vt* exclure

excluding *prep* à l'exclusion de; ~ **sb/sth** sans compter qn/qc; ~ **taxes** taxes non comprises

exclusion [ɪk'sklu:ʒn] *n* exclusion *f;* **to the ~ of sth** à l'exclusion de qc

exclusive [ɪks'klu:sɪv] **I.** *adj* **1.** (*debarring*) **two things are mutually ~** deux choses s'excluent mutuellement **2.** (*only, sole, total*) exclusif(-ive); ~ **of tax** taxes non comprises **3.** (*reserved for a few: restaurant*) de luxe; ~ **circles** cercles de la haute société; ~ **to this paper** en exclusivité dans ce journal **II.** *n* (*in media*) exclusivité *f*

excommunicate [ˌekskə'mju:nɪkeɪt] *vt* excommunier

excommunication [ˌekskəˌmju:nɪ'keɪʃn] *n* excommunication *f*

excrement ['ekskrəmənt] *n form* excrément *m*

excrescence [ɪk'skresns] *n* **1.** MED excroissance *f* **2.** *pej* (*ugly object*) protubérance *f*

excreta [ɪk'skri:tə, *Am:* -t̬ə] *n no pl, form* excrétions *fpl*

excrete [ɪk'skri:t] *vt form* excréter

excretion [ɪk'skri:ʃn] *n form* excrétion *f*

excruciating [ɪk'skru:ʃɪeɪtɪŋ, *Am:* -t̬ɪŋ] *adj* atroce; (*pain*) insupportable

excursion [ɪk'skɜ:ʃn, *Am:* -'skɜ:rʒn] *n* excursion *f,* course *f Suisse;* **to go on an ~** partir en excursion

excusable *adj* excusable

excuse [ɪk'skju:z] **I.** *vt* **1.** (*justify*) excuser; **to ~ sb's lateness** excuser le retard de qn; **that does not ~ her lying** ça n'excuse pas ses mensonges **2.** (*allow not to attend*) **he was ~d (from) sport** il a été dispensé de sport; **that does not ~ her from paying her taxes** ça ne la dispense pas de payer ses impôts ►~ <u>**me**</u> (*calling for attention, apologizing*) excuse(z)-moi; (*please repeat*) pardon; (*indignantly*) je m'excuse **II.** *n* excuse *f;* **poor ~** mauvaise excuse; **it's an ~ for missing work** c'est une excuse pour s'absenter du travail; **there's no ~ for it** c'est inexcusable; **an ~ for a film/teacher** *iron* un semblant de film/de prof

ex-directory [ˌeksdɪ'rektərɪ] *adj Aus, Brit* TEL **to be ~** être sur la liste rouge

execrable ['eksɪkrəbl] *adj pej, form* exécrable

execute ['eksɪkju:t] *vt a.* LAW exécuter

execution [ˌeksɪ'kju:ʃn] *n no pl* exécution *f;* **to put a plan into ~** mettre un plan à exécution

executioner [ˌeksɪ'kju:ʃnəʳ, *Am:* -ɚ] *n* bourreau *m*

executive [ɪg'zekjʊtɪv, *Am:* -t̬ɪv] **I.** *n* **1.** (*manager*) cadre *mf;* **junior/senior ~** cadre débutant/supérieur **2.** + *sing/pl vb* POL (pouvoir *m*) exécutif *m;* (*of organization*) comité *m* exécutif **II.** *adj* **1.** POL exécutif(-ive) **2.** ECON (*committee*) de direction; (*post*) de cadre; (*decisions*) de la direction

executor [ɪg'zekjʊtəʳ, *Am:* -t̬ɚ] *n* exécuteur *m* testamentaire

exemplary [ɪg'zemplərɪ] *adj* exemplaire; ~ **damages** dommages et intérêts exemplaires

exemplification [ɪgˌzemplɪfɪ'keɪʃn, *Am:* -plə-] *n* illustration *f*

exemplify [ɪg'zemplɪfaɪ] <-ie-> *vt* illustrer

exempt [ɪg'zempt] **I.** *vt* exempter; **to ~ sb from doing sth** dispenser qn de faire qc **II.** *adj* exempt(e); **to be ~ from tax** être exonéré d'impôt

exemption [ɪg'zempʃn] *n no pl* **1.** (*release*) exemption *f* **2.** MIL, SCHOOL dispense *f* **3.** FIN **tax ~** exonération d'impôt; ~ **from taxes** dégrèvement d'impôts

exercise ['eksəsaɪz, *Am:* -sɚ-] **I.** *vt* **1.** (*giving* *physical exercise to: muscles, body*) exercer; (*dog*) sortir; (*horse*) entraîner; (*one's memory*) entretenir **2.** *form* (*disturb*) **to ~ sb's mind** préoccuper qn **3.** *form* (*apply: authority*) exercer; **to ~ caution** faire preuve de prudence **II.** *vi* faire de l'exercice **III.** *n* **1.** (*training, work-out*) exercice *m;* **to do leg ~s** travailler ses jambes; **written ~s** exercices écrits **2.** MIL manœuvres *fpl* **3.** *sing* (*action, achievement*) exercice *m;* **a marketing ~** une opération de marketing **4.** *no pl* (*use*) usage *m;* **the ~ of tolerance** démonstration *f* de tolérance **5.** *pl, Am* cérémonie *f;* **the graduation ~s** la remise des diplômes

exercise bike *n* vélo *m* d'intérieur **exercise book** *n* cahier *m* d'exercice

exerciser ['eksəsaɪzəʳ, *Am:* -sɚsaɪzɚ] *n* SPORT banc *m* de musculation

exert [ɪg'zɜːt, *Am:* -'zɜːrt] *vt* **1.** (*apply: control, pressure*) exercer; **to ~ (one's) influence** jouer de son influence **2.** (*make an effort*) **to ~ oneself** (*make an effort*) se donner du mal

exertion [ɪg'zɜːʃn, *Am:* -'zɜːr-] *n* effort *m*

exfoliant [ɪks'fəʊlɪənt] *n* exfoliant *m*

exfoliating cream [eksˌfəʊlɪ'eɪtɪŋˌkriːm, *Am:* -ˌfoʊlɪ'eɪt̬ɪŋ-] *n* crème *f* exfoliante

exfoliation [eksˌfəʊlɪ'eɪʃn, *Am:* -ˌfoʊ-] *n no pl* exfoliation *f*

exhalation [ˌekshə'leɪʃn] *n* expiration *f*

exhale [eks'heɪl] **I.** *vt* **1.** (*breathe out*) exhaler **2.** (*give off gases, scents*) dégager **3.** *fig* respirer **II.** *vi* expirer

exhaust [ɪg'zɔːst, *Am:* -'zɑː-] **I.** *vt* épuiser; **to ~ oneself** s'épuiser **II.** *n* **1.** *no pl* (*gas*) gaz *mpl* d'échappement **2.** (*pipe*) pot *m* déchappement

exhausted *adj* épuisé(e)

exhaust fumes *npl* gaz *mpl* d'échappement

exhausting *adj* épuisant(e)

exhaustion [ɪg'zɔːstʃn, *Am:* -'zɑː-] *n no pl* épuisement *m*

exhaustive [ɪg'zɔːstɪv, *Am:* -'zɑː-] *adj* (*comprehensive*) exhaustif(-ive)

exhaust manifold *n* collecteur *m* d'échappement **exhaust pipe** *n* AUTO tuyau *m* d'échappement **exhaust system** *n* AUTO pot *m* d'échappement

exhibit [ɪg'zɪbɪt] **I.** *n* **1.** (*display*) pièce *f* exposée **2.** LAW pièce *f* à conviction **II.** *vt* **1.** (*show*) exposer; **to ~ a parking ticket in the car window** placer un ticket de parking en vue **2.** (*display: character traits*) manifester; **to ~ bias** faire preuve de préjugés **III.** *vi* ART exposer

exhibition [ˌeksɪ'bɪʃn] *n* ART exposition *f;* **~ of paintings** exposition de peinture; **to be on ~** être exposé ▸**to make an ~ of oneself** *pej* se donner en spectacle

exhibitionism [ˌeksɪ'bɪʃnɪzəm] *n no pl* exhibitionisme *m*

exhibitionist [ˌeksɪ'bɪʃnɪst] *n* **1.** MED exhibitioniste *m* **2.** *fig* m'as-tu-vu *m*

exhibitor [ɪg'zɪbɪtəʳ, *Am:* -t̬ɚ] *n* exposant(e) *m(f)*

exhilarating [ɪg'zɪləreɪtɪŋ, *Am:* -t̬ɪŋ] *adj* exaltant(e)

exhilaration [ɪg'zɪləreɪʃn] *n no pl* euphorie *f*

exhort [ɪg'zɔːt, *Am:* -'zɔːrt] *vt form* exhorter

exhortation [ˌeksɔː'teɪʃn, *Am:* ˌegzɔːr-] *n no pl* exhortation *f*

exhumation [ˌekshjuː'meɪʃn] *n no pl* exhumation *f*

exhume [eks'hjuːm, *Am:* egz'uːm] *vt* exhumer

ex-husband *n* ex-mari *m*

exile ['eksaɪl] **I.** *n* **1.** *no pl* (*banishment*) exil *m;* **to go into ~** s'exiler **2.** (*person*) exilé(e) *m(f)* **II.** *vt* **to ~ sb to Siberia/to an island** exiler qn en Sibérie/sur une île

exist [ɪg'zɪst] *vi* **1.** (*be*) exister **2.** (*live*) **to ~ on sth** vivre de qc **3.** (*survive*) subsister

existence [ɪg'zɪstəns] *n* **1.** *no pl* (*being real*) existence *f;* **to be in ~** exister; **to come into ~** naître **2.** (*life*) vie *f*

existent [ˌeg'zɪstent] *adj* existant(e)

existential [ˌegzɪ'stenʃl] *adj* **1.** (*of existence*) existentiel(le) **2.** PHILOS existentialiste

existentialism [ˌegzɪ'stenʃəlɪzəm] *n no pl* existentialisme *m*

existing *adj* actuel(le)

exit ['eksɪt] **I.** *n* sortie *f;* **emergency ~** sortie de secours; **~ visa** visa *m* de sortie **II.** *vi* sortir

exodus ['eksədəs] *n sing* **1.** (*mass departure*) exode *m* **2.** REL **Exodus** l'Exode *m*

exonerate [ɪg'zɒnəreɪt, *Am:* -'zɑːnə-] *vt form* **to ~ sb from sth** disculper qn de qc

exoneration [ɪgˌzɒnə'reɪʃn, *Am:* -ˌzɑːnə-] *n no pl, form* disculpation *f*

exorbitant [ɪg'zɔːbɪtənt, *Am:* -'zɔːrbət̬ənt] *adj* exorbitant(e)

exorcism ['eksɔːsɪzəm, *Am:* -sɔːr-] *n no pl* exorcisme *m*

exorcist ['eksɔːsɪst, *Am:* -sɔːr-] *n* exorciste *mf*

exorcize ['eksɔːsaɪz, *Am:* -sɔːr-] *vt* exorciser

exotic [ɪg'zɒtɪk, *Am:* -'zɑːt̬ɪk] *adj* exotique

expand [ɪk'spænd] **I.** *vi* **1.** (*increase*) augmenter **2.** (*enlarge: city*) s'étendre; PHYS (*metal, gas*) se dilater; (*business, economy*) se développer; **we're ~ing into electronics** nous nous lançons dans l'électronique **II.** *vt* **1.** (*make bigger*) augmenter **2.** (*elaborate*) développer

◆**expand on** *vt* développer

expandable *adj* extensible

expanding *adj* **1.** (*getting bigger*) en pleine croissance **2.** (*adjustable*) extensible

expanse [ɪk'spæns] *n* étendue *f*

expansion [ɪk'spænʃn] *n* **1.** *no pl* (*spreading out*) expansion *f;* (*of gas*) dilatation *f* **2.** *no pl* (*growth: of population*) accroissement *m;* (*of business*) développement *m* **3.** (*elaboration*) développement *m*

expansion card *n* INFOR carte *f* d'extension

expansionism [ɪk'spænʃənɪzəm] *n no pl, pej* expansionnisme *m*

expansive [ɪk'spænsɪv] *adj* expansif(-ive)

expatriate [eks'pætrɪeɪt, *Am:* -'peɪ-] **I.** *n* expatrié(e) *m(f)* **II.** *vt* expatrier

expect [ɪk'spekt] *vt* **1.** (*think likely*) s'attendre à; **to ~ to** +*infin* s'attendre à +*infin;* **to ~ sb to** +*infin* s'attendre à ce que +*subj;* **to ~ sth from sb** s'attendre à qc de la part de qn; **I ~ he'll refuse** je suppose qu'il va refuser **2.** (*require*) attendre; **to ~ sth from sb** attendre qc de qn; **I ~ you to** +*infin* j'attends de vous que vous +*subj;* **is that too much to ~?** est-ce que c'est trop demander? **3.** (*wait for*) attendre; **to be ~ing** (**a baby**) attendre un bébé

expectancy [ɪk'spektəntsi] *n no pl* attente *f;* **look of ~** regard *m* plein d'espoir

expectant [ɪk'spektənt] *adj* qui est dans l'attente

expectation [ˌekspek'teɪʃn] *n* attente *f;* **to live up to sb's ~s** répondre aux attentes de qn

expedience [ɪk'spi:diənts], **expediency** *n no pl* opportunisme *m*

expedient [ɪk'spi:dɪənt] **I.** *adj* opportun(e) **II.** *n* expédient *m*

expedite ['ekspɪdaɪt] *vt form* accélérer

expedition [ˌekspɪ'dɪʃn] *n* expédition *f*

expel [ɪk'spel] <-ll-> *vt* (*pupil*) renvoyer; **to ~ sb from a country** expulser qn d'un pays

expenditure [ɪk'spendɪtʃəʳ, *Am:* -tʃɚ] *n no pl* **1.** (*act of spending*) dépense *f* **2.** (*money*) **~ on sth** les dépenses pour qc

expense [ɪk'spens] *n* **1.** (*cost*) dépense *f;* **at great ~** à grands frais; **to go to the ~ of sth/doing sth** se mettre en frais pour qc/faire qc; **at sb's ~** aux frais de qn **2.** *pl* (*money*) frais *mpl;* **to be on ~s** *Brit* (*meal*) passer dans les frais; (*executive*) avoir ses frais payés **3.** (*disadvantage*) **a joke at my ~** une plaisanterie à mes dépens; **at the ~ of his career** au détriment de sa carrière ►**all ~(s) paid** tous frais payés

expense account *n* note *f* de frais

expensive [ɪk'spensɪv] *adj* cher(chère); **to have ~ tastes** avoir des goûts de luxe

experience [ɪk'spɪərɪəns, *Am:* -'spɪrɪ-] **I.** *n no pl* expérience *f;* **from ~** par expérience ►**to put sth down to ~** considérer qc comme une erreur instructive **II.** *vt* connaître; (*loss*) subir; (*sensation*) ressentir

experienced *adj* expérimenté(e)

experiment [ɪk'sperɪmənt] **I.** *n* expérience *f;* **to conduct an ~** faire une expérience **II.** *vi* **to ~ on animals** faire des expériences sur des animaux; **to ~ with sth on sb/qc** expérimenter qc sur qn/qc; **to ~ with drugs** essayer des drogues

experimental [ɪkˌsperɪ'mentl, *Am:* ekˌsper-] *adj* expérimental(e)

experimentation [ɪkˌsperɪmen'teɪʃn] *n no pl* expérimentation *f*

expert ['ekspɜ:t, *Am:* -spɜ:rt] **I.** *n* expert(e) *m(f);* **gardening ~** expert en jardinage; **an ~ at doing sth** un expert dans l'art de faire qc **II.** *adj* expert(e); **~ at doing sth** expert en qc

expertise [ˌekspɜ:'ti:z, *Am:* -spɜ:r-] *n no pl* **1.** (*knowledge*) compétence *f* **2.** (*skill*) habileté *f*

expiate ['ekspɪeɪt] *vt form* expier

expiation [ˌekspɪ'eɪʃn] *n form* expiation *f*

expiration [ˌekspɪ'reɪʃn, *Am:* -spə-] *n no pl* expiration *f;* **~ date** date *f* d'expiration

expire [ɪk'spaɪəʳ, *Am:* -'spaɪɚ] *vi* **1.** (*terminate*) expirer **2.** *a. fig, form* rendre l'âme

expiry [ɪk'spaɪərɪ, *Am:* -'spaɪ-] *n no pl s.* **expiration**

explain [ɪk'spleɪn] **I.** *vt* expliquer; **to ~ oneself more clearly** s'exprimer plus clairement; **to ~ sth away** trouver des justifications à **II.** *vi* s'expliquer

explanation [ˌeksplə'neɪʃn] *n* explication *f;* **by way of ~ for sth** pour expliquer qc; **to give sb an ~ for why ...** expliquer à qn pourquoi ...

explanatory [ɪk'splænətrɪ, *Am:* -ətɔ:rɪ] *adj* explicatif(-ive)

expletive [ɪk'spli:tɪv, *Am:* 'əkspləṭɪv] *n* juron *m;* **to let out a row of ~s** proférer des injures

explicable [ek'splɪkəbl] *adj* explicable

explicit [ɪk'splɪsɪt] *adj* **1.** (*clear*) **to be ~ about sth** être explicite sur qc **2.** (*showing sexual details*) (à caractère) pornographique

explode [ɪk'spləʊd, *Am:* -'sploʊd] **I.** *vi* **1.** (*blow up*) exploser; (*tyre, ball*) éclater; (*engine, plane*) exploser **2.** (*burst*) exploser; **to ~ into giggles** éclater de rire; **to ~ with** [*o* **in**] **anger** exploser de colère; **to ~ into a riot** dégénérer en révolte **II.** *vt* **1.** (*blow up*) faire exploser; (*tyre, ball*) faire éclater **2.** (*destroy: theory*) démonter; (*myth*) détruire

exploit ['eksplɔɪt] **I.** *vt a. pej* exploiter; (*loophole, change*) profiter de **II.** *n* exploit *m*

exploitation [ˌeksplɔɪ'teɪʃn] *n no pl* exploitation *f*

exploitative [ek'splɔɪtətɪv, *Am:* -ṭəṭɪv] *adj* (*person, behaviour*) profiteur(-euse)

exploration [ˌeksplə'reɪʃn, *Am:* -splɔ:'-] *n* **1.** (*journey*) exploration *f* **2.** (*examination*) examen *m;* **to carry out an ~ of sth** procéder à l'examen de qc **3.** *no pl* (*searching*) **~ for sth** recherche *f* de qc

exploratory [ɪk'splɒrətrɪ, *Am:* -'splɔ:rətɔ:rɪ] *adj* (*voyage*) d'exploration; (*test*) préparatoire; **~ well** sondage *m*

explore [ɪk'splɔ:ʳ, *Am:* -'splɔ:r] **I.** *vt* explorer **II.** *vi* **to ~ for sth** aller à la recherche de qc

explorer [ɪk'splɔ:rəʳ, *Am:* -ɚ] *n* explorateur, -trice *m, f*

explosion [ɪk'spləʊʒn, *Am:* -'sploʊ-] *n* explosion *f*

explosive [ɪk'spləʊsɪv, *Am:* -'sploʊ-] **I.** *adj* explosif(-ive) **II.** *n* explosif *m*

exponent [ɪk'spəʊnənt, *Am:* -'spoʊ-] *n* **1.** (*advocate: of idea*) représentant(e) *m(f)*

2. MAT exposant *m*
export [ɪk'spɔːt, *Am:* -'spɔːrt] I. *vt* exporter; **to ~ sth to Germany** exporter qc en Allemagne II. *vi* exporter III. *n* exportation *f;* **~ goods** biens *mpl* d'exportation; **~ licence** permis *m* d'exporter; **~ business** exportation *f*
exportable *adj* exportable
exportation [ˌekspɔː'teɪʃn, *Am:* -spɔːr-] *n no pl* exportation *f*
exporter [ik'spɔːtəʳ, *Am:* -'spɔːrt̬ɚ] *n* exportateur *m*
expose [ɪk'spəʊz, *Am:* -'spoʊz] *vt* 1. (*uncover*) découvrir; (*part of body*) montrer, révéler; (*scandal, problem, weakness*) révéler; (*person*) dénoncer; **to ~ oneself** s'exhiber 2. (*subject*) **to ~ sb/sth to** (*physical conditions*) soumettre qn/qc à; (*influence, virus*) exposer qn/qc à 3. PHOT exposer; **to over-~ sth** surexposer qc
exposé *n* enquête *f*
exposed *adj* exposé(e)
exposition [ˌekspə'zɪʃn, *Am:* -pə-] *n* exposition *f*
exposure [ɪk'spəʊʒəʳ, *Am:* -'spoʊʒɚ] *n* 1. *a.* PHOT exposition *f* 2. *no pl* MED **to die of ~** mourir de froid 3. *no pl* (*revelation*) révélation *f* 4. *no pl* (*media coverage*) couverture *f* 5. *no pl* (*contact*) **~ to** (*people, influence*) fréquentation *f* de; (*radiation*) exposition *f* à
expound [ɪk'spaʊnd] I. *vi* **to ~ on sth** expliquer qc II. *vt* exposer
express [ɪk'spres] I. *vt* 1. (*convey: thoughts, feelings*) exprimer; **to ~ oneself through music** s'exprimer par la musique 2. (*send*) **to ~ sth to sb** envoyer qc en express à qn II. *adj* 1. RAIL express *inv* 2. LAW exprès(expresse) ►**by ~ delivery** en exprès III. *n* 1. RAIL express *m* 2. *no pl* (*delivery service*) **by ~** en exprès IV. *adv* (*intentional*) exprès
expression [ɪk'spreʃn] *n* expression *f;* **to give ~ to sth** exprimer qc; **to find ~ in sth** se manifester dans qc
expressionless [ɪk'spreʃənlɪs] *adj* inexpressif(-ive)
expressive [ɪk'spresɪv] *adj* expressif(-ive)
expressly *adv* expressément
expressway [ɪk'spresweɪ] *n Am, Aus* autoroute *f*
expropriate [eks'prəʊprɪeɪt, *Am:* -'proʊ-] *vt* exproprier
expropriation [eks'prəʊ prɪeɪʃn, *Am:* -'proʊ-] *n* expropriation *f*
expulsion [ɪk'spʌlʃn] *n no pl* **~ from a country** expulsion *f* d'un pays
exquisite ['ekskwɪzɪt] *adj* 1. (*delicate*) exquis(e) 2. (*intense*) vif(vive)
ex-serviceman [ˌeks'sɜːvɪsmən, *Am:* -'sɜːr-] <-men> *n* ancien combattant *m*
extemporaneous [ekˌstempə'reɪnɪəs] *adj form* impromptu(e)
extempore [ek'stempərɪ] *form* I. *adj* improvisé(e) II. *adv* de manière impromptue
extemporise *vi Aus, Brit, form,* **extemporize** [ɪk'stempəraɪz] *vi* improviser
extend [ɪk'stend] I. *vi* 1. **to ~ for/beyond sth** s'étendre sur/au-delà de qc 2. *fig* **to ~ to sth/doing sth** aller jusqu'à qc/faire qc; **the restrictions ~ to residents** les restrictions s'appliquent aussi aux résidents II. *vt* 1. (*increase*) étendre; **to ~ public awareness of sth** accroître l'intérêt du public pour qc; **to ~ one's house** agrandir sa maison 2. (*prolong*) prolonger 3. (*stretch*) étendre; (*neck*) tendre 4. (*offer*) **to ~ sth to sb** offrir qc à qn; **to ~ one's thanks to sb** présenter ses remerciements à qn; **to ~ a warm welcome to sb** accueillir qn chaleureusement
extension [ɪk'stenʃn] *n* 1. (*increase*) augmentation *f;* (*of scope, role*) extension *f;* (*of opportunities*) augmentation *f* 2. (*continuation*) prolongement *m* 3. (*lengthening of deadline*) prolongation *f* 4. (*added piece*) **~** (**cord**) rallonge *f;* **to build an ~ to a house** agrandir une maison 5. TEL poste *m*
extensive [ɪk'stensɪv] *adj* vaste; (*coverage*) large; (*research*) approfondi(e); (*changes*) profond(e); (*repairs*) important(e); (*damage*) considérable
extent [ɪk'stent] *n no pl* étendue *f;* **to an ~** jusqu'à un point; **to some ~** dans une certaine mesure; **to a greater ~** en grande partie; **to the ~ that** dans la mesure où; **to what ~?** dans quelle mesure?
extenuating *adj form* atténuant(e)
extenuation [ɪkˌstenjʊ'eɪʃn] *n no pl, form* atténuation *f*
exterior [ɪk'stɪərɪəʳ, *Am:* -'stɪrɪɚ] I. *n* extérieur *m;* **on the ~** à l'extérieur II. *adj* extérieur(e)
exterminate [ɪk'stɜːmɪneɪt, *Am:* -'stɜːr-] *vt* exterminer
extermination [ɪkˌstɜːmɪ'neɪʃn, *Am:* -ˌstɜːr-] *n no pl* extermination *f*
external [ɪk'stɜːnl, *Am:* -'stɜːr-] *adj* 1. (*exterior, foreign*) extérieur(e); **~ to sth** étranger à qc 2. (*on surface, skin*) *a.* MED, INFOR externe; **for ~ use only** exclusivement à usage externe
externalize [ɪk'stɜːnəlaɪz, *Am:* -'stɜːr-] *vt* extérioriser
exterritorial [ˌeksˌterɪ'tɔːrɪəl] *adj s.* **extraterritorial**
extinct [ɪk'stɪŋkt] *adj* éteint(e); **to become ~** disparaître
extinction [ɪk'stɪŋkʃn] *n no pl* extinction *f*
extinguish [ɪk'stɪŋgwɪʃ] *vt* éteindre
extinguisher [ɪk'stɪŋgwɪʃəʳ, *Am:* -ɚ] *n* extincteur *m*
extirpate ['ekstəpeɪt, *Am:* -stɚ-] *vt form* extirper
extol [ɪk'stəʊl, *Am:* -'stoʊl] <-ll-> *vt form* louer; **to ~ the virtues of sb/sth** chanter les louanges de qn/qc
extort [ɪk'stɔːt, *Am:* -'stɔːrt] *vt* **to ~ money from sb** extorquer de l'argent à qn; **to ~ a promise from sb** arracher une promesse à qn

E

extortion [ɪk'stɔːʃn, *Am:* -'stɔːr-] *n no pl* extortion *f*
extortionate [ɪk'stɔːʃənət, *Am:* -'stɔːr-] *adj pej* exorbitant(e)
extra ['ekstrə] **I.** *adj* supplémentaire; **to have ~ money** avoir de l'argent en plus; **vegetables are ~** les légumes ne sont pas compris **II.** *adv* **1.**(*more*) en plus **2.**(*very*) **~ thick/strong** super épais/fort **III.** *n* **1.** ECON supplément *m;* **they charge for all sorts of ~s** ils font payer un supplément pour toutes sortes de choses **2.** AUTO option *f* **3.** CINE figurant(e) *m(f)* **IV.** *pron* **to pay ~** payer plus
extract [ɪk'strækt] **I.** *vt* **1.** extraire; **to ~ sth from sth** extraire qc de qc; **to have a tooth ~ed** se faire arracher une dent **2.** *fig* **to ~ a confession from sb** arracher un aveu à qn; **to ~ a piece of information from sb** tirer une information de qn **II.** *n* extrait *m*
extraction [ɪk'strækʃn] *n* **1.**(*removal*) extraction *f* **2.** *no pl* (*origin*) origine *f*
extracurricular [ˌekstrəkə'rɪkjʊlə^r, *Am:* -jələ˞] *adj* parascolaire
extradite ['ekstrədaɪt] *vt* **to ~ sb from Canada to France** extrader qn du Canada vers la France
extradition [ekstrə'dɪʃn] *n no pl* extradition *f*
extramarital [ˌekstrə'mærɪtl, *Am:* -'merət̬l] *adj* extraconjugal(e)
extraneous [ɪk'streɪnɪəs] *adj* sans rapport
extraordinary [ɪk'strɔːdnrɪ, *Am:* -'strɔːr-] *adj* extraordinaire
extrapolate [ek'stræpəleɪt] **I.** *vt* extrapoler **II.** *vi* **to ~ from sth** faire l'extrapolation de qc
extrasensory [ˌekstrə'sensərɪ] *adj* extrasensoriel(le)
extraterrestrial ['ekstrətɪ'restrɪəl, *Am:* -tə'-] **I.** *adj* extraterrestre **II.** *n* extraterrestre *mf*
extraterritorial [ˌekstrəˌterɪ'tɔːrɪəl] *adj* extraterritorial(e)
extraterritoriality *n* LAW extraterritorialité *f*
extra time ['ekstrətaɪm] *n no pl, Aus, Brit* SPORT prolongation *f*
extravagance [ɪk'strævəgəns] *n no pl* extravagance *f*
extravagant [ɪk'strævəgənt] *adj* **1.**(*exaggerated*) extravagant(e); (*claims, demands*) immodéré(e) **2.**(*luxurious*) luxueux(-euse); **~ tastes** des goûts dispendieux
extravaganza [ɪkˌstrævə'gænzə] *n* **1.**(*event*) grand spectacle *m* **2.** MUS fantaisie *f*
extreme [ɪk'striːm] **I.** *adj a.* METEO extrême; (*distress*) profond(e); (*pain*) intense; (*pleasure*) immense; (*happiness*) suprême; **the ~ right** l'extrême droite; **isn't that rather ~?** ce n'est pas un peu excessif? **II.** *n* **1.**(*limit*) extrême *m;* **to go from one ~ to the other** passer d'un extrême à l'autre; **to go to ~s** pousser les choses à l'extrême; **to be driven to ~s** être poussé à bout **2.**(*utmost*) **in the ~** à l'extrême; **to be hospitable in the ~** être des plus accueillant
extremely *adv* extrêmement; (*dull*) horriblement; (*sorry*) infiniment
extremism [ɪk'striːmɪzəm] *n no pl* extrémisme *m*
extremist [ɪk'striːmɪst] *n* extrémiste *mf*
extremity [ɪk'stremətɪ, *Am:* -t̬ɪ] <-ies> *n* **1.**(*end*) extrémité *f* **2.**(*difficulty*) **he helped me in my extremities** il m'a aidé quand j'étais en danger
extricate ['ekstrɪkeɪt] *vt form* dégager; **to ~ oneself from sth** s'extirper de qc; **to ~ oneself from a ticklish situation** *fig* se tirer d'une situation épineuse
extrovert ['ekstrəvɜːt, *Am:* -vɜːrt] **I.** *n* extraverti(e) *m(f)* **II.** *adj* extraverti(e)
exuberance [ɪg'zjuːbərəns, *Am:* -'zuː-] *n no pl* exubérance *f;* **with real ~** avec une joie débordante
exuberant [ɪg'zjuːbərənt, *Am:* -'zuː-] *adj* **1.**(*energetic*) débordant(e) d'énergie; (*style*) exubérant(e) **2.**(*luxuriant*) luxuriant(e)
exude [ɪg'zjuːd, *Am:* -'zuːd] *vt* **to ~ confidence** avoir de la confiance à revendre
exult [ɪg'zʌlt] *vi form* exulter; **to ~ at** [*o* **in**] **sth** se réjouir de qc
exultant [ɪg'zʌltənt] *adj form* joyeux(-euse); **~ cheer** cri *m* de triomphe; **an ~ crowd** une foule qui jubile
exultation [ˌegzʌl'teɪʃn, *Am:* ˌeksʌl'-] *n no pl, form* exultation *f*
ex-wife *n* ex-femme *f*
eye [aɪ] **I.** *n* **1.** ANAT œil *m;* **to blink one's ~s** cligner des yeux; **her ~s flashed with anger** ses yeux jetaient des éclairs de colère **2.**(*hole*) trou *m;* (*of needle*) chas *m* **3.** METEO centre *m* d'une dépression; (*of hurricane*) œil *m* **4.**(*bud on potato*) œil *m* ►**to have an ~ for sth** avoir l'œil pour qc; **to have an ~ for the main chance** *Aus, Brit, inf* ne négliger aucune occasion; **to have ~s in the back of one's head** *inf* avoir des yeux dans le dos; **you're a sight for sore ~s** tu fais plaisir à voir; **to have ~s too big for one's stomach** *iron* avoir les yeux plus gros que le ventre; **to be the ~ of the storm** être au cœur de la tempête; **an ~ for an ~, a tooth for a tooth** *prov* œil pour œil, dent pour dent; **not to be able to take one's ~s off sb/sth** *inf* ne pas lâcher qn/qc du regard; **a black ~** un œil au beurre noir; **to keep one's ~s open** [*o* **skinned** *Brit inf*] ouvrir l'œil; **to do sth with one's ~s open** *inf* faire qc en connaissance de cause; **with one's ~s shut** *inf* les yeux fermés; (**right**) **before sb's very ~s** juste sous les yeux de qn; **as far as the ~ can see** à perte de vue; **not to believe one's ~s** ne pas en croire ses yeux; **to clap ~s on sb/sth** *inf* voir qn/qc; **to keep one's ~s in** *Brit* TENNIS suivre la balle des yeux; **to keep an ~ on sb/sth** *inf* surveiller qn/qc; **to keep an ~ out for sb/sth** *inf* essayer de repérer qn/qc; **to make ~s at sb** *inf* faire de l'œil à qn; **to see ~ to ~ on sth** avoir la même opinion sur qc;

that's one in the ~ for them! *Brit, inf* c'est bien fait pour eux!; **in** [*o* **to**] **sb's ~s** selon qn; **to be up to one's ~s in sth** *inf* en avoir jusqu'au cou **II.** <-d, -d, -ing *o* eying *Am*> *vt* **1.** (*look at carefully*) observer; (*warily*) examiner **2.** *inf* (*look with longing*) reluquer **3. to be brown-/green--d** avoir les yeux bruns/verts

eyeball **I.** *n* globe *m* occulaire ►**to be drugged to the ~s** être complètement défoncé; **to be ~ to ~ with sb** *inf* être face à face avec qn; **to be up to one's ~s in sth** être dans qc jusqu'au cou **II.** *vt Am, inf* observer **eyebrow** *n* sourcil *m;* **to pluck/raise one's ~s** s'épiler/froncer les sourcils **eye-catching** *adj* qui attire l'attention **eye contact** *n* échange *m* de regards; **to make ~ with sb** regarder qn dans les yeux **eyeful** *n* **1. to get an ~ of dirt** recevoir de la saleté dans les yeux **2.** *fig* **to be quite an ~** *inf* valoir le coup d'œil; **to get an ~** *inf* se rincer l'œil **eyelash** <-es> *n* cil *m* **eyelet** *n* œillet *m* **eyelid** *n* paupière *f;* **she didn't bat an ~** elle n'a pas bronché **eyeliner** *n no pl* eye-liner *m* **eye-opener** *n* révélation *f* **eyepiece** *n* oculaire *m* **eye shadow** *n* fard *m* à paupières **eyesight** *n no pl* vue *f* **eyesore** *n* horreur *f* **eyestrain** *n no pl* fatigue *f* oculaire **eye test** *n* examen *m* de la vue **eyetooth** <-teeth> *n* canine *f* supérieure ►**to give one's eyeteeth for sth** donner n'importe quoi pour qc **eyewash** *n* **1.** *no pl* MED collyre *m* **2.** *no pl, inf* (*nonsense*) boniment *m;* **a lot of ~** des foutaises **eyewitness** <-es> *n* témoin *m* oculaire

eyrie ['aɪəri, *Am:* 'eri] *n* aire *m*

e-zine ['i:zi:n] *n* magazine *m* électronique

F

F, f [ef] <-'s *o* -s> *n* **1.** (*letter*) F *m*, f *m;* **~ as in Frederick** *Brit*, **~ as in Fox** *Am*, **~ for Frederick** *Brit*, **~ for Fox** *Am* (*on telephone*) f comme François **2.** MUS fa *m*

f *n abbr of* **feminine** f

F *n abbr of* **Fahrenheit** F

FA [ˌef'eɪ] *n Brit abbr of* **Football Association** *fédération britannique de football*

fable ['feɪbl] *n a. pej* fable *f*

fabled *adj* légendaire

fabric ['fæbrɪk] *n* **1.** *no pl* FASHION tissu *m;* **woollen ~** lainage *m* **2.** *no pl* (*structure*) *a. fig* structure *f;* **the ~ of everyday life** les réalités de la vie

fabricate ['fæbrɪkeɪt] *vt* **1.** (*invent*) inventer **2.** (*manufacture*) fabriquer

fabulous ['fæbjʊləs, *Am:* -jə-] *adj* fabuleux(-euse); (*sum*) astronomique; (*city, character*) légendaire

facade [fə'sɑ:d] *n* **1.** ARCHIT façade *f* **2.** (*appearance*) apparence *f*

face [feɪs] **I.** *n* **1.** ANAT *a. fig* visage *m;* **to lie ~ down** être allongé sur le ventre; **to keep a smile on one's ~** garder le sourire; **to tell sth to sb's ~** dire qc à qn en face **2.** (*expression*) mine *f;* **you should have seen her ~** tu aurais vu sa tête; **to make ~s at sb** [*o* **pull**] faire des grimaces à qn **3.** (*surface*) surface *f;* (*of building*) façade *f;* (*of mountain*) versant *m;* (*of clock*) cadran *m;* **the cards were ~ up** les cartes étaient à l'endroit **4.** (*appearance*) face *f;* **loss of ~** humiliation *f;* **to lose/save ~** perdre/sauver la face **5.** (*image*) image *f* ►**to have a ~ like the back end of a bus** *inf* être laid comme un pou; **to disappear off the ~ of the earth** disparaître de la surface de la terre; **in the ~ of sth** en dépit de qc; **his ~ doesn't fit** *Brit, inf* il n'est pas bien vu; **in the ~ of sth** face à qc; (*despite*) en dépit de qc; **on the ~ of it** à première vue **II.** *vt* **1.** (*turn towards: person, audience*) faire face à; (*room, house*) donner sur; **the house facing ours** la maison en face de la nôtre; **to ~ the front** regarder devant soi **2.** (*confront: problems, danger*) faire face à; (*rival, team*) affronter; **to ~ the facts** regarder les choses en face; **let's face it, it's too big** soyons francs, c'est trop grand; **to be ~d with sth** se trouver confronté à qc; **I can't ~ doing sth** je n'ai pas le courage de faire qc **3.** (*run the risk*) risquer; **to ~ one year in prison** risquer un an de prison **4.** ARCHIT **to ~ sth with sth** revêtir qc de qc ►**to ~ the music** *inf* faire front **III.** *vi* **to ~ towards sth** se tourner vers qc; **to ~ south** (*person*) regarder au sud; (*house*) être exposé au sud; **about ~!** demi-tour!

◆**face up to** *vt* faire face à; **you'll have to ~ your father** il te faudra affronter ton père

facecloth *n* ≈ gant *m* de toilette, ≈ débarbouillette *f Québec*, ≈ lavette *f Suisse* **face cream** *n no pl* crème *f* pour le visage **face-lift** *n* lifting *m;* **to have a ~** se faire faire un lifting **face pack** *n* masque *m* de beauté **face powder** *n no pl* poudre *f* de riz

facet ['fæsɪt] *n* **1.** facette *f* **2.** (*aspect*) aspect *m*

facetious [fə'si:ʃəs] *adj* facétieux(-euse)

face-to-face *adv* face-à-face; **to come ~ with sb/sth** se retrouver face à qn/qc; **to discuss sth ~** parler en tête-à-tête de qc **face value** *n* ECON valeur *f* nominale ►**to take sth at ~** (*uncritically*) prendre qc pour argent comptant; (*literally*) prendre qc au premier degré

facial ['feɪʃl] **I.** *adj* facial(e); (*care, expression*) du visage **II.** *n* soin *m* du visage

facile ['fæsaɪl, *Am:* -ɪl] *adj pej* facile

facilitate [fə'sɪlɪteɪt] *vt* faciliter

facility [fə'sɪləti, *Am:* -t̬i] <-ies> *n* **1.** (*skill*) facilité *f;* **to have a ~ for sth** avoir un don pour qc **2.** (*building*) établissement *m;* **research ~** établissement *m* de recherche; **a training/recycling ~** un centre de formation/recyclage; **a manufacturing ~** une

F

usine **3.** (*feature*) **the computer has a fax** ~ l'ordinateur a un fax; **to have an overdraft** ~ avoir une possibilité de découvert **4.** *pl* (*equipment*) équipement *m;* **the kitchen facilities** l'équipement de la cuisine **5.** *pl* (*amenities*) installations *fpl;* **the washing facilities** les bains-douches *mpl;* **transport facilities** les transports

facing ['feɪsɪŋ] *n* **1.** ARCHIT revêtement *m* **2.** *no pl* FASHION revers *m*

facsimile [fæk'sɪməli] *n* **1.** (*duplicate*) fac-similé *m* **2.** TEL télécopie *f*

fact [fækt] *n* fait *m;* **hard** ~**s** des faits; **in view of the** ~ **that ...** en tenant compte du fait que ...; **a statement of** ~ une constatation; ~ **and fiction** le réel et l'imaginaire; **the** ~ **is, you miss her** le fait est qu'elle te manque ►**the** ~**s of life** *inf* les choses *fpl* de la vie; **in** ~ [*o* **as a matter of** ~] en fait

fact-finding *adj* d'enquête; (*study*) d'information

faction ['fækʃən] *n pej* faction *f*

factor ['fæktəʳ, *Am:* -tɚ] *n* facteur *m;* **the human** ~ le facteur humain

factory ['fæktəri] <-ies> *n* usine *f;* **shoe** ~ fabrique *f* de chaussures; ~ **worker** ouvrier *m* en usine

factory farming *n* élevage *m* industriel **factory ship** *n* navire-usine *m* **factory shop** *n* magasin *m* d'usine

factotum [fæk'təʊtəm, *Am:* -'toʊţəm] *n form* factotum *m;* **a general** ~ *iron* un homme/une femme à tout faire

fact sheet *n* fiche *f* d'informations

factual ['fæktʃʊəl, *Am:* -tʃuːəl] *adj* factuel(le); (*account, information*) basé(e) sur les faits

faculty ['fæklti, *Am:* -ţi] <-ies> *n* **1.** UNIV faculté *f;* **the Faculty of Arts** la faculté des lettres **2.** *no pl, Am* (*staff*) corps *m* enseignant **3.** (*ability*) faculté *f;* **mental faculties** capacités *fpl* intellectuelles

fad [fæd] *n pej, inf* folie *f;* **it's her latest** ~ c'est sa dernière lubie; **a** ~ **for sth** un engouement pour qc

faddish ['fædɪʃ], **faddy** *adj pej, inf* capricieux(-euse); **to be** ~ **about sth** être difficile sur qc

fade [feɪd] **I.** *n* CINE fondu *m* **II.** *vi* **1.** (*wither: flower*) se faner **2.** (*lose colour*) se décolorer; (*colour*) se ternir; (*inscription*) s'effacer **3.** (*disappear*) *a. fig* disparaître; (*light*) baisser; (*echo*) s'évanouir; (*popularity*) baisser; (*hope*) s'amenuiser; (*smile, memory*) s'effacer; **to** ~ **from sight** s'estomper **III.** *vt* **1.** (*wither: flower*) faner **2.** (*cause to lose colour*) décolorer **3.** CINE fondre; **to** ~ **one scene into another** enchaîner deux scènes

◆**fade away** *vi* (*sound, light*) s'affaiblir; (*person*) dépérir

◆**fade in I.** *vi* faire une ouverture en fondu **II.** *vt* faire apparaître en fondu

◆**fade out I.** *vi* faire une fermeture en fondu **II.** *vt* faire disparaître en fondu

faded *adj* (*fabric*) décoloré(e); (*colour*) terni(e); (*incription*) à-demi effacé(e)

faeces ['fiːsiːz] *npl form* fèces *fpl*

faff about, **faff around** *vi Brit, inf* déconner

fag¹ [fæg] *n Aus, Brit, inf* **1.** (*cigarette*) clope *f* **2.** *no pl* (*bother*) corvée *f*

fag² [fæg] *n Am, pej, vulg* (*male homosexual*) pédé *m*

fag end *n* **1.** (*cigarette*) mégot *m* **2.** (*end*) bout *m*

faggot ['fægət] *n* **1.** *Am, pej, vulg* (*homosexual*) pédé *m* **2.** (*bundle*) fagot *m* **3.** *pl, Brit* GASTR *boulettes de viande en sauce*

fail [feɪl] **I.** *vi* **1.** (*not succeed: person, plan*) échouer; **to** ~ **in sth** échouer à qc; **he** ~**ed to beat the record** il n'a pas réussi à battre le record; **he** ~**ed in his attempt to get the contract** il n'a pas réussi à obtenir le contrat; **to be doomed to** ~ être voué à l'échec; **he** ~**ed in his efforts to reconcile them** sa tentative de réconciliation a échoué **2.** (*not to do sth one should do*) **to** ~ **to** +*infin* (*by neglect*) négliger de +*infin;* **to** ~ **to appreciate sth** ne pas être capable de comprendre qc; **to** ~ **in one's duty to sb** manquer à son devoir envers qn; **the parcel** ~**ed to arrive** le paquet n'est pas arrivé **3.** *a.* SCHOOL, UNIV (*not pass a test*) être recalé; **to** ~ **in a subject** être recalé dans une matière; **to** ~ **in a paper/literature/a question** sécher à un examen/en littérature/sur une question **4.** TECH, AUTO (*brakes*) lâcher; (*engine, power steering*) ne pas répondre; (*power*) être coupé **5.** MED (*kidneys, heart*) lâcher; (*health*) se détériorer; **to be** ~**ing fast** (*person*) faiblir de jour en jour **6.** FIN, COM (*go bankrupt*) faire faillite **7.** AGR, BOT (*not grow*) ne rien donner ►**if all else** ~**s** en dernier recours **II.** *vt* **1.** (*not pass: exam, interview*) être recalé à; (*driving test*) rater; **to** ~ **geography** être recalé en géographie **2.** (*not let pass: student, candidate*) recaler **3.** (*not help sb when needed*) faire défaut à; **your courage** ~**s you** le courage te manque; **his nerve** ~**ed him** ses nerfs ont lâché; **you've never** ~**ed me** tu ne m'as jamais déçu **III.** *n* (*unsuccessful result*) échec *m* ►**without** ~ (*definitely*) sans faute; (*always, without exception*) immanquablement

failed *adj* (*attempt,artist*) raté(e); (*company*) qui a fait faillite

failing I. *adj* défaillant(e); **he is in** ~ **health** sa santé se détériore; **to have a** ~ **eyesight** avoir la vue qui baisse; **in the** ~ **light** dans la faible lumière **II.** *n* faiblesse *f;* **the play has one big** ~ la pièce pèche sur un point **III.** *prep* à défaut de; ~ **that** à défaut

fail-safe *adj* (*system, device*) de sécurité

failure ['feɪljəʳ, *Am:* 'feɪljɚ] *n* **1.** *no pl* (*being unsuccessful*) échec *m;* **to end in** ~ se solder par un échec; **to be doomed to** ~ être voué à l'échec **2.** (*unsuccessful person*) raté(e) *m(f);*

to feel a ~ se sentir raté; **he was a ~ as a leader** en tant que leader, il était décevant **3.** *no pl* (*not doing sth*) **his ~ to inform us** le fait qu'il ne nous a pas informés; **their ~ to solve the problem** leur incapacité à résoudre le problème; **~ to follow the instructions will result ...** le non-respect des instructions entraînera ...; **~ to render assistance** non-assistance à personne en danger **4.** (*breakdown*) TECH, ELEC défaillance *f;* **electrical ~** panne *f* de courant; **~ of brake/engine/system** défaillance des freins/du moteur/du système **5.** *no pl* MED, PHYSIOL insuffisance *f;* **heart/liver/kidney ~** insuffisance cardiaque/hépatique/rénale **6.** COM **business ~s** les faillites d'entreprise

faint [feɪnt] **I.** *adj* **1.** (*not strong or clear: sound, murmur*) faible; (*light, odour, mark, smile*) léger(-ère); (*memory, idea*) vague; **~ smile** léger sourire **2.** (*slight: resemblance, possibility, suspicion*) léger(-ère); (*chance*) minime; **he did not make the ~est attempt to apologize** il n'a même pas essayé de s'excuser; **there's not the ~est hope of** il n'y a pas le moindre espoir que +*subj;* **not to have the ~est (idea) ...** *inf* ne pas avoir la moindre idée ... **3.** (*weak*) faible; **he was ~ with hunger** il avait tellement faim qu'il était au bord de l'évanouissement; **to feel ~** se sentir défaillir **II.** *vi* s'évanouir **III.** *n* évanouissement *m;* **to fall (down) in a (dead) ~** *Brit* s'évanouir

faint-hearted I. *adj* craintif(-ive) **II.** *n pl* **the ~** les âmes sensibles; **not for the ~** déconseillé aux âmes sensibles

fair¹ [feəʳ, *Am:* fer] **I.** *adj* **1.** (*just and equal for all: price, society, trial, wage*) juste; (*deal*) équitable; (*competition*) loyal(e); **he had his ~ share** il a eu sa part **2.** (*reasonable: comment, point, question*) légitime; (*in accordance with rules: fight, contest*) en règle; **to be ~ with sb** être juste avec qn; **it's not ~ that** ce n'est pas juste que +*subj;* **~ enough** (*OK*) d'accord; **that was ~ enough** c'était légitime; **it's only ~ to tell her** il faut lui dire; **it's only ~ that** c'est normal que +*subj;* **I think it's ~ to say that ...** je crois qu'il convient de dire que ...; **to be ~, ...** il faut être juste, ... **3.** (*quite large: amount, number, size*) assez grand(e); **it cost a ~ bit** ça a coûté pas mal **4.** (*reasonably good: chance, possibility, prospect*) bon(ne); **to have a ~ idea of sth** savoir à peu près qc **5.** (*average*) **~ (to middling)** moyen(ne) **6.** (*light or blond in colour: hair*) blond(e); (*skin, complexion*) clair(e) **7.** METEO (*pleasant and dry: weather*) agréable; **to be set ~** *Brit* être au beau fixe ►**to give sb a ~ crack of the whip** [*o* **a ~ shake** *Am inf*] donner toutes ses chances à qn; **~ dinkum** *Aus, inf* (*honest, real*) honnête; (*honestly, really*) comme il faut; **by ~ means or foul** par tous les moyens; **~'s ~** *inf* sois juste **II.** *adv* (*in an honest way*) **to play ~** jouer franc jeu ►**~ and square** dans les règles; (*in the centre of the target*) en plein dans le mille

fair² [feəʳ, *Am:* fer] *n* **1.** (*funfair*) fête *f* foraine **2.** ECON salon *m;* **the Frankfurt (book) ~** le salon du livre de Francfort; **trade ~** salon professionnel; **a local craft ~** une exposition-vente artisanale **3.** AGR foire *f*

fair copy <-pies> *n* copie *f* au propre; **to make a ~ of sth** mettre qc au propre **fair game** *n no pl* **to be ~** être une cible autorisée **fairground** *n* champ *m* de foire

fairly *adv* **1.** (*quite, rather*) relativement **2.** (*in a fair way: treat, deal with, share out*) équitablement; **win, fight** honorablement; **~ traded goods** produits du commerce équitable ►**~ and squarely** *Brit, Aus* complètement; (*precisely*) en plein

fair-minded *adj* (*person*) juste

fairness *n no pl* **1.** (*fair treatment, justice*) équité *f;* (*of decision, election, treatment*) impartialité *f;* **lack of ~** manque de justice; **in (all) ~ ...** (*in order to be fair to*) pour être juste; **in ~ to sb** pour rendre justice à qn **2.** (*lightness: of hair*) blondeur *f;* (*of skin*) pâleur *f*

fair play *n no pl* fair-play *m inv;* **to see ~** contrôler que tout se passe bien *subj;* **~!** soyons justes! **fair-sized** *adj* assez grand(e) **fair-skinned** *adj* au teint clair **fair trade** *n no pl* commerce *m* équitable; **~ coffee** café *m* du commerce équitable **fairway** *n* (*in golf*) fairway *m*

fairy ['feəri, *Am:* 'feri] <-ries> *n* (*imaginary creature*) fée *f;* **a good/wicked ~** une bonne/méchante fée

fairyland *n* **1.** *no pl* (*home of fairies*) pays *m* des fées **2.** *no pl, pej* (*realm of fantasy*) monde *m* imaginaire **3.** (*place of magical beauty*) endroit *m* féerique **fairy lights** *npl* guirlande *f* électrique **fairy tale I.** *n* **1.** (*for children*) conte *m* de fée **2.** *pej* histoires *fpl* **II.** *adj* **fairy-tale** de conte de fée; **a ~ wedding** un mariage comme dans un conte de fée

faith [feɪθ] *n* **1.** *no pl* (*confidence, trust*) confiance *f;* **to have ~ in sb/sth** avoir confiance en qn/qc; **to break ~ with sb** ne pas tenir sa promesse envers qn **2.** (*belief*) foi *f;* **to keep the ~** garder la foi; **to lose one's ~** perdre la foi ►**in good ~** de bonne foi

faithful I. *adj* fidèle; (*service, support*) loyal(e); **to be ~ to sb/sth** être fidèle à qn/qc **II.** *n pl* **the ~** les fidèles *mpl*

faithfully *adv* fidèlement; **Yours ~** *Brit, Aus* veuillez agréer, Madame/Monsieur mes sentiments distingués

faith healer *n* guérisseur, -euse *m, f*

faithless *adj* **1.** (*unfaithful*) infidèle **2.** (*disloyal*) déloyal(e) **3.** REL sans foi

fake [feɪk] **I.** *n* **1.** (*counterfeit object*) faux *m* **2.** (*impostor*) imposteur *m* **II.** *adj* faux(fausse); **~ leather** cuir synthétique **III.** *vt* **1.** (*make a counterfeit copy: signature*) contrefaire; (*calculations*) falsifier; **to ~ a painting** faire un

F

faux tableau **2.** (*pretend to feel or experience*) feindre; **to ~ surprise/grief** feindre la surprise/le chagrin; **to ~ a headache/a heart attack** faire semblant d'avoir mal à la tête/une crise cardiaque; **to ~ it** faire semblant **IV.** *vi* faire semblant

fakir ['feɪkɪəʳ, *Am:* fɑː'kɪr] *n* fakir *m*

falcon ['fɔːlkən, *Am:* 'fæl-] *n* faucon *m*

Falkland Islands ['fɔːklædˌaɪləndz], **Falklands** *npl* **the ~** les (îles) Malouines *fpl*

Falklands War *n* guerre *f* des Malouines

fall [fɔːl] <fell, fallen> **I.** *vi* **1.** (*drop down from a height*) tomber; **to ~ to the ground** tomber par terre; **to ~ to one's death** faire une chute mortelle; **to ~ to one's knees** tomber à genoux; **to ~ downstairs** tomber dans les escaliers; **to ~ from a roof/balcony** tomber du toit/balcon; **to ~ from a window** tomber d'une fenêtre; **to ~ (down) dead** tomber raide mort; **to ~ flat** s'étaler; *fig* tomber à plat; **to ~ flat on one's face** s'étaler de tout son long; (*be unsuccessful*) se planter complètement; (*thing, scheme*) rater complètement **2.** (*land: a bomb, missile*) tomber; **the keys fell in the gutter** les clefs sont tombées dans le caniveau; **the blame fell on me** *fig* la faute est tombée sur moi; **his eye fell on me sur moi** *fig* son regard s'est posé sur moi; **the stress ~s on the first syllable** LING l'accent est sur la première syllabe **3.** (*become lower, decrease: demand, numbers, prices*) baisser; (*dramatically*) chuter; **to ~ by 10%** chuter de 10%; **to ~ below a figure/level/standard** tomber en dessous d'un chiffre/niveau; **to ~ to a level/figure** tomber à un niveau/chiffre; **to ~ in sb's estimation** baisser dans l'estime de qn **4.** (*be defeated or overthrown: city, government, dictator*) tomber; **to ~ from power** être déchu; **to ~ to sb** tomber aux mains de qn; (*in an election*) passer aux mains de qn **5.** SPORT (*in cricket: wicket*) tomber **6.** REL (*do wrong, sin*) pécher **7.** (*happen at a particular time*) tomber; **to ~ on a Monday/Wednesday** tomber un lundi/mercredi **8.** (*happen: night, darkness*) tomber **9.** (*belong*) rentrer; **to ~ into a category/class** rentrer dans une catégorie/classe; **to ~ within sth** rentrer dans qc; **to ~ outside sth** tomber en dehors de qc **10.** (*hang down: hair, cloth, fabric*) tomber **11.** (*become*) **to ~ asleep** s'endormir; **to ~ due** arriver à échéance; **to ~ ill** tomber malade; **to ~ silent** devenir silencieux; **to ~ vacant** (*a room*) se libérer; (*a position, post*) être vacant; **to ~ prey to sb/sth** devenir la proie de qn/qc **12.** (*enter a particular state*) **to ~ in love with sb/sth** tomber amoureux de qn/qc; **to ~ out of love with sb/sth** cesser d'être amoureux de qn/qc; **to ~ out of favour with sb** tomber en disgrâce auprès de qn; **to ~ under the influence of sb/sth** tomber sous l'influence de qn/qc; **to ~ under the spell of sb/sth** tomber sous le charme de qn/qc ▶**to ~ on deaf ears** (*cries, pleas, shouts*) ne pas être entendu; **to ~ foul of sb** (*s'attirer les foudres de qn*), **to ~ on stony ground** (*an appeal, message*) tomber dans le vide; **to ~ into the hands of sb** tomber aux mains de qn; **to ~ in line with sth** suivre qc; **to ~ into place** (*fit together*) concorder; (*become clear*) devenir clair; **to ~ short** ne pas être tout à fait à la hauteur; **to ~ short of a record** ne pas réussir à battre un record **II.** *n* **1.** (*act of falling*) chute *f;* **a ~ from a third-storey window** une chute d'une fenêtre du troisième étage; **to break sb's ~** amortir la chute de qn; **to have a ~** tomber; **to have a nasty ~** faire une mauvaise chute; **to take a ~** faire une chute **2.** (*downward movement: of a leaf, of the curtain*) chute *f;* (*of a level, popularity*) baisse *f;* (*of the tide*) descente *f;* **heavy ~s of rain** d'importantes chutes de pluie **3.** (*defeat: of a government, city*) chute *f;* (*of a castle*) prise *f* **4.** *Am* (*autumn*) automne *m* **5.** *pl* (*waterfall*) chutes *fpl* ▶**to take a ~ for sb** *Am* porter le chapeau à la place de qn **III.** *adj Am* (*of autumn*) d'automne

◆**fall about** *vi Brit, Aus, inf* **to ~ (laughing)** se tordre de rire

fall apart *vi a. fig* se désintégrer; (*building*) tomber en ruine; (*person*) s'effondrer

◆**fall away** *vi* **1.** (*become detached: plaster, rock*) tomber **2.** (*slope downward: land, ground*) descendre **3.** *Brit, Aus* (*decrease: attendance, support*) diminuer **4.** (*disappear: negative factor, feeling*) disparaître; (*supporters*) partir

◆**fall back** *vi* **1.** (*move backwards: crowd*) reculer **2.** MIL (*retreat: army*) se replier **3.** *Brit, Aus* (*decrease*) reculer

◆**fall back on** *vt*, **fall back upon** *vt a. fig* se rabattre sur

◆**fall behind I.** *vi* (*become slower, achieve less: child, company, country*) prendre du retard; (*fail to do sth on time*) avoir du retard; **to ~ with** (*work*) prendre du retard dans; (*rent*) prendre du retard dans le paiement de **II.** *vt* **1.** (*become slower than*) prendre du retard sur **2.** (*fail to keep to sth*) **to ~ schedule** prendre du retard **3.** SPORT (*have fewer points than*) passer derrière

◆**fall down I.** *vi* **1.** (*from upright position: person, object*) tomber **2.** (*collapse: a building, structure*) s'effondrer **3.** (*be unsatisfactory: plan, policy*) ne plus tenir; **that's where it falls down** c'est le point faible; **to ~ on the job** *inf* ne pas faire du bon boulot **II.** *vt* (*hole, stairs*) tomber dans; **to ~ a cliff** tomber d'une falaise

◆**fall for** *vt inf* **1.** (*be attracted to*) tomber amoureux de **2.** (*be deceived by*) se laisser prendre à; **and I fell for it!** et je suis tombé dans le panneau!

◆**fall in** *vi* **1.** (*drop in the water*) tomber **2.** (*collapse: the roof, ceiling*) s'effondrer **3.** MIL (*form a line: soldiers, squad, company*)

former les rangs; **to ~ behind sb** se mettre en rang derrière qn

◆**fall in with** *vt* 1. (*agree to: an idea, a suggestion, proposal*) accepter; (*regulations*) suivre 2. (*become friendly with*) fréquenter; **she started to ~ bad company** elle a commencé d'avoir de mauvaises fréquentations

◆**fall off** I. *vi* 1. (*become detached*) tomber 2. (*decrease*) baisser II. *vt* (*of table, roof*) tomber de; **to ~ a horse/bicycle** faire une chute de cheval/de vélo

◆**fall on** *vt*, **fall upon** *vt* 1. (*descend onto*) tomber sur 2. (*attack*) se jeter sur 3. (*eat or seize greedily*) **to ~ food** se jeter sur la nourriture

◆**fall out** *vi* 1. (*drop out*) tomber; **to ~ of a window/vehicle** tomber d'une fenêtre/d'un véhicule; **her hair started to ~** elle a commencé à perdre ses cheveux 2. *inf* (*quarrel*) se brouiller; **to ~ with sb over sth** se brouiller avec qn à propos de qc; **we have fallen out** nous sommes brouillés 3. MIL (*move out of line: soldiers, squad, company*) rompre les rangs 4. (*happen, turn out: things, events*) se passer

◆**fall over** I. *vi* 1. (*drop to the ground*) tomber par terre 2. (*drop on its side*) se renverser II. *vt* 1. (*trip*) trébucher sur; **to ~ one's own feet** trébucher 2. *inf* (*be very eager*) **to ~ oneself to** +*infin* se démener pour +*infin*

◆**fall through** I. *vi* (*plan*) tomber à l'eau; (*sale, agreement*) échouer II. *vt* (*gap, hole*) tomber dans

◆**fall to** *vt* 1. *form* (*be responsible*) incomber à; **it falls to me to tell you ...** il m'incombe de vous dire ... 2. (*fail*) **to ~ pieces** se désintégrer; (*person*) s'effondrer; (*building*) tomber en ruine

fallacious [fə'leɪʃəs] *adj form* fallacieux(-euse)

fallacy ['fæləsi] *n* 1. <-cies> (*false belief or argument*) erreur *f*; **it is a ~ to suppose that ...** il est faux de supposer que ... 2. *no pl, form* (*false reasoning*) sophisme *m*; **a complete ~** une illusion totale

fallen ['fɔːlən] *adj* 1. (*lying on the ground: apple, leaf*) tombé(e); (*tree*) abattu(e); **~ leaves** feuilles mortes 2. (*overthrown: politician, dictator*) déchu(e) 3. REL (*angel*) déchu(e)

fall guy *n inf* bouc *m* émissaire

fallible ['fæləbl] *adj* faillible

falling star *n* ASTR *s.* **meteor**

fall-off *n* baisse *f*; **a ~ in sth** une baisse de qc

fallopian tube *n* ANAT, MED trompe *f* de Fallope

fallout *n no pl* 1. PHYS (*radioactive dust*) retombées *fpl* radioactives 2. (*unpleasant consequences*) retombées *fpl* négatives

fallout shelter *n* abri *m* antiatomique

fallow ['fæləʊ, *Am:* -oʊ] I. *n* jachère *f* II. *adj* 1. AGR (*not planted*) en jachère; **to leave land ~** laisser un terrain en jachère 2. (*when not much happens: period, time*) creux(creuse)

fallow deer *inv n* daim *m*

false [fɔːls] I. *adj a. fig* faux(fausse); **a ~ alarm** une fausse alerte; **a ~ imprisonment** une détention arbitraire; **a ~ bottom** un double fond II. *adv* **to play sb ~** trahir qn

falsehood *n* mensonge *m*; **to see the difference between truth and ~** distinguer le vrai du faux

false move *n* (*clumsy*) un faux pas; (*misguided*) erreur *f*; **one ~ and you're dead** si tu bouges, tu meurs

falseness *n no pl* fausseté *f*

false note *n* fausse note *f* **false start** *n* faux départ *m* **false teeth** *n pl* fausses dents *fpl*

falsification *n no pl* falsification *f*

falsify ['fɔːlsɪfaɪ] *vt* falsifier

falsity ['fɔːlsəti, *Am:* -t̬i] *n no pl s.* **falseness**

falter ['fɔːltəʳ, *Am:* -t̬ɚ] *vi* (*person, voice*) hésiter; (*voice*) trembler; (*conversation*) se tarir; (*courage, negotiations*) fléchir; **to walk without ~ing** marcher sans hésiter

faltering *adj* 1. (*hesitant: voice, words, steps*) hésitant(e) 2. (*seeming about to fail: courage, resolve*) chancelant(e); (*memory*) défaillant(e)

fame [feɪm] *n no pl* 1. (*being famous*) célébrité *f*; **to win ~** devenir célèbre; **her claim to ~** son titre de gloire 2. (*reputation*) renommée *f*

famed *adj* célèbre

familiar [fə'mɪliəʳ, *Am:* -jɚ] I. *adj* 1. (*well-known to oneself*) familier(-ère) 2. (*acquainted*) **to be ~ with sb/sth** connaître qn/qc; **are you ~ with this software?** est-ce que vous connaissez ce logiciel?; **his face is ~** son visage ne m'est pas inconnu; **is the name ~?** ce nom vous dit quelque chose? 3. (*friendly and informal*) familier(-ère); **to be on ~ terms with sb** bien s'entendre avec qn; **he's a bit too ~ with me** il est un peu trop familier avec moi II. *n* démon *m* familier

familiarity [fə,mɪli'ærəti, *Am:* -'erət̬i] *n no pl* 1. (*informal manner*) familiarité *f* 2. (*knowledge*) connaissance *f*; **her ~ with sb/sth** sa connaissance de qn/qc ► **~ breeds contempt** *prov* à trop connaître quelqu'un on risque le mépris

familiarize [fə'mɪliəraɪz, *Am:* -jəraɪz] *vt* familiariser; **to ~ oneself with sth** se familiariser avec qc

family ['fæməli] *n* 1. <-lies> + *sing/pl vb* (*group*) famille *f*; **a ~ of four/six** une famille de quatre/six personnes 2. *no pl* (*relations, family members*) famille *f*; **to be ~** être de la famille; **to be (like) one of the ~** faire partie de la famille; **to run in the ~** être de famille; **to start a ~** avoir des enfants; **do you have ~?** (*children*) vous avez des enfants?; (*relatives*) vous avez de la famille?; (*for families with children: show*) familial(e); **~ viewing** des émissions pour toute la famille; **a ~ fare** un billet famille; **a ~ hotel** un hôtel pour familles

F

family allowance *n Brit s.* **child benefit**
family doctor *n Brit* médecin *m* de famille
family man *n* **1.** (*man enjoying family life*) homme *m* proche de sa famille **2.** (*man with wife and family*) père *m* de famille **family name** *n* nom *m* de famille **family planning** *n no pl* planning *m* familial **family tree** *n* arbre *m* généalogique

famine ['fæmɪn] *n* famine *f*

famished ['fæmɪʃt] *adj inf* **to be ~** être affamé

famous ['feɪməs] *adj* célèbre ►~ **last words!** *inf* tu parles!

famously *adv* **1.** (*as is well-known*) **he ~ replied...** sa réponse, restée célèbre, a été ... **2.** *inf* (*excellently*) à merveille

fan¹ [fæn] **I.** *n* **1.** (*hand-held cooling device*) éventail *m* **2.** (*electrical cooling device*) ventilateur *m* **II.** <-nn-> *vt* **1.** (*cool with a fan*) éventer; **to ~ one's face** s'éventer le visage **2.** (*cause to burn better: amber, flame*) attiser **3.** *fig* (*fears, passions*) attiser

fan² [fæn] *n* (*admirer*) fan *mf;* **to be a ~ of sb/sth** être un fan de qn/qc; (*like very much*) adorer qn/qc

◆**fan out** *vi* (*crowd, roads*) partir dans différentes directions

fan-assisted oven *n* four *m* à chaleur tournante

fanatic [fə'nætɪk, *Am:* -'næt̬ɪk] *n* **1.** *pej* (*obsessed believer*) fanatique *mf* **2.** (*enthusiast*) mordu(e) *m(f);* **a fitness/film/sports ~** un mordu de culture physique/cinéma/sport

fanatical *adj pej* (*follower, supporter*) fanatique; (*devotion, support*) inconditionnel(le); **to be ~ about sth** être inconditionnel de qc

fanaticism [fə'nætɪsɪzəm, *Am:* -'næt̬-] *n no pl* fanatisme *m*

fan belt *n* AUTO courroie *f* de ventilateur

fancied *adj* **1.** (*imaginary*) imaginaire **2.** (*tipped to win: team, horse, candidate*) pressenti(e)

fancier *n* amateur, -trice *m, f*

fanciful *adj* **1.** (*unrealistic: idea, notion*) fantaisiste **2.** (*elaborate: design, style*) fantaisie **3.** (*indulging in fancies: person*) fantasque

fan club *n* fan-club *m*

fancy ['fæntsi] **I.** <-ie-> *vt* **1.** *Brit* (*want, like*) avoir envie de; **I quite ~ the idea** l'idée ne me déplaît pas; **does anyone ~ coming with me?** quelqu'un aurait envie de venir avec moi?; **I didn't ~ walking home** ça ne me disait rien de rentrer à pied **2.** *Brit* (*be attracted to*) être attiré par; **he fancies you** tu lui plais **3.** (*imagine as winner: horse, candidate*) pressentir; **I don't ~ your chances of doing sth** je ne pense pas que tu arriveras à faire qc; **to ~ oneself** être prétentieux; **to ~ oneself as sb** se prendre pour qn **4.** (*imagine*) s'imaginer; **to ~ that ...** croire que ...; **~ (that)!** tu t'imagines!; **I ~ I have seen her before** j'ai l'impression de l'avoir déjà vue; **~ meeting you here!** quelle surprise de te voir ici! **II.** *n* **1.** *no pl* (*liking*) **to take a ~ to sb/sth** s'enticher de qn/qc; **if it takes your ~** si ça vous plaît **2.** *no pl* (*imagination*) imagination *f* **3.** <-cies> (*whimsical idea*) fantaisie *f;* **an idle ~** une lubie; **whenever the ~ takes you** quand ça vous chante **III.** *adj* <-ier, -iest> **1.** (*elaborate: decoration, frills*) fantaisie *inv;* (*sauce, cocktail, camera*) sophistiqué(e); **we'll prepare the dinner, nothing ~** nous préparerons le repas, rien de compliqué **2.** *fig* (*phrases, talk*) recherché(e); **~ footwork** *inf* manœuvres habiles **3.** (*whimsical: ideas, notions*) fantaisiste **4.** *inf* (*expensive: hotel, place, shop*) chic *inv;* **~ car** voiture de luxe; **~ prices** prix astronomiques

fancy dress *n no pl, Brit, Aus* déguisement *m;* **a ~ party** une soirée déguisée; **to come in ~** venir déguisé(e) **fancy-free** *adj* **to be footloose and ~** être libre comme l'air **fancy goods** *npl* articles *mpl* cadeaux **fancy man** *n pej, inf* amant *m*

fanfare ['fænfeəʳ, *Am:* -fer] *n* fanfare *f*

fang [fæŋ] *n* (*long sharp upper teeth: of dog, lion*) croc *m;* (*of snake*) crochet *m;* **~s of a vampire** dents *fpl* d'un vampire

fan heater *n* soufflerie *f* **fan mail** *n no pl* courrier *m* des fans

fantasia *n* fantaisie *f*

fantastic [fæn'tæstɪk] *adj* **1.** (*unreal, magical: animal, figure*) fantastique **2.** *inf* (*wonderful: offer, opportunity, time*) fantastique **3.** (*extremely large: amount, size, sum*) colossal(e) **4.** (*unbelievable, bizarre: coincidence*) incroyable

fantasy ['fæntəsi, *Am:* -t̬ə-] <-ies> *n* **1.** (*wild, pleasant fancy*) fantasme *m;* **a sexual ~** un fantasme sexuel; **to have fantasies about sth** fantasmer sur qc **2.** *pej* (*unreal, imagined thing*) chimère *f;* **a world of ~** un monde imaginaire; **the idea is pure ~** l'idée est du pur délire **3.** *no pl* (*literary genre*) fantastique *m;* **a ~ film** un film fantastique **4.** <-sies> MUS *s.* **fantasia**

fanzine ['fænzi:n] *n* fanzine *m*

fao *abbr of* **for the attention of** à l'attention de

FAQ *n* INFOR *abbr of* **frequently asked question** FAQ *f*

far [fɑ:ʳ, *Am:* fɑ:r] <farther, farthest *o* further, furthest> **I.** *adv* **1.** (*a long distance*) *a. fig* loin; **how ~ is London from here?** Londres est à quelle distance d'ici?; **as ~ as the bridge** jusqu'au pont; **~ from somewhere** loin de quelque part; **~ and wide** partout; **~ away** loin; **~ from sth** loin de qc; **not ~ off** non loin; **£800 would not be ~ off** [*o* **out**] 800£ n'est pas loin; **how ~ would you agree with that?** jusqu'où es-tu d'accord avec ça?; **you can only go so ~** il y a forcément une limite; **~ from it** au contraire; **~ from rich/empty** loin d'être riche/vide; **as ~ as the eye can see** à perte de vue; **~ be it from me to**

+*infin* loin de moi l'idée de +*infin* **2.** (*distant in time*) ~ **away** loin dans le passé; **sth is not ~ off** qc n'est pas loin; **it goes as ~ back as ...** cela remonte jusqu'à ...; **so ~** jusqu'à présent **3.** (*in progress, degree*) **to get as ~ as doing sth** arriver à faire qc; **to not get very ~ with sth** ne pas aller très loin dans qc; **not to get very ~ with sb** ne pas parvenir à grand-chose avec qn **4.** (*much*) ~ **better/nicer/warmer** bien mieux/plus joli/plus chaud; **I would ~ rather walk** je préférerais de loin y aller à pied; **to be ~ too sth** être beaucoup trop qc; **to ~ prefer sth** *Brit* préférer de loin qc **5.** (*connecting adverbial phrase*) **as ~ as** autant que; **as ~ as I can see** d'après ce que je peux en juger; **as ~ as I know** pour autant que je sache *subj;* **as ~ as she/it is concerned** en ce qui la/le concerne; **as ~ as it goes** sans plus ►**by ~** de loin; **~ and away** de loin; **he will go ~** il ira loin; **sth won't go very ~** on n'ira pas loin avec qc; **so ~ so good** jusqu'à présent c'est bien; **to go too ~** aller trop loin; **worse by ~** bien pire **II.** *adj* **1.** (*at great distance*) lointain(e); **in the ~ distance** au loin **2.** (*more distant*) **in the ~ end/side** à l'autre bout/de l'autre côté; **the ~ wall of the room** le mur du fond **3.** (*extreme*) **the ~ left/right of a party** l'extrême gauche/droite d'un parti ►**to be a ~ cry from sb/sth** n'avoir rien à voir avec qn/qc

faraway ['fɑːrəweɪ] *adj* lointain(e); **to have a ~ look in one's eyes** avoir le regard perdu dans le vague

farce [fɑːs, *Am:* fɑːrs] *n* farce *f*

farcical ['fɑːsɪkl, *Am:* 'fɑːr-] *adj* **1.** THEAT (*like a farce: comedy, humour*) burlesque **2.** (*ridiculous: idea, situation*) absurde

fare [feəʳ, *Am:* fer] **I.** *n* **1.** (*price for journey*) tarif *m;* (*bus*) prix *m* du ticket; (*train, plane*) prix *m* du billet; **single/return ~** tarif aller/aller retour; **have you got your ~?** as-tu l'argent pour le trajet?; **~s, please!** paiement des tickets s'il vous plaît **2.** (*traveller in a taxi*) client(e) *m(f)* **3.** *no pl* (*food of a specified type*) cuisine *f* **II.** *vi* (*get on*) **to ~ well/badly** bien/mal s'en sortir; **how did they ~?** comment s'en sont ils sortis?

Far East *n* **the ~** l'Extrême-Orient *m*

farewell [ˌfeə'wel, *Am:* ˌfer-] **I.** *interj form* adieu! **II.** *n* adieu *m;* **to say one's ~s to sb** dire adieu à qn; **to bid sb a last ~** faire un dernier adieu à qn **III.** *adj* d'adieu

fare zone *n* zone *f* de tarif

far-fetched *adj fig* tiré(e) par les cheveux

farm [fɑːm, *Am:* fɑːrm] **I.** *n* ferme *f;* **cattle ~** ferme d'élevage de bétail **II.** *adj* de ferme **III.** *vt* exploiter; **to ~ beef cattle** faire de l'élevage **IV.** *vi* être agriculteur

◆**farm out** *vt* **to ~ work to sb** sous-traiter du travail à qn; **to ~ children to sb** faire garder des enfants par qn

farmer *n* agriculteur, -trice *m, f,* habitant(e) *m(f) Québec;* **cattle ~** éleveur de bétail

farmhand *n s.* **farm worker** **farmhouse** **I.** <-s> *n* ferme *f* **II.** *adj* de ferme

farming *n no pl* agriculture *f;* **cattle ~** élevage *m* de bétail

farmstead *n Am* ferme *f* **farm vehicle** *n* tracteur *m* **farm worker** *n* ouvrier *m* agricole **farmyard** *n* cour *f* de ferme

Far North *n* **the ~** le Grand Nord **far-off** *adj* (*place,*) éloigné(e); (*country, time*) lointain(e) **far-reaching** *adj* (*consequences*) d'un impact considérable; (*reform*) radical(e) **far-seeing** *adj s.* **far-sighted** **far-sighted** *adj* **1.** *Brit, Aus* (*shrewdly anticipating the future: person*) prévoyant(e); (*decision*) avisé(e); (*policy*) à long terme **2.** *Am, Aus* (*long-sighted: person*) hypermétrope

fart [fɑːt, *Am:* fɑːrt] **I.** *n inf* (*gas from bowels*) pet *m;* **to do a ~** faire un pet **II.** *vi inf* péter

farther ['fɑːðəʳ, *Am:* 'fɑːrðɚ] **I.** *adv comp of* **far** **1.** (*at/to a greater distance*) ~ **away from sth** plus loin que qc; ~ **down/up sth** plus bas/haut que qc; ~ **east/west** plus à l'est/l'ouest; ~ **on** plus loin; ~ **on along the road** plus loin sur cette route **2.** (*at/to more advanced point*) ~ **back** plus loin en arrière; ~ **back in time** plus loin dans le passé **3.** (*additional*) *s.* **further** **II.** *adj comp of* **far** (*more distant*) plus éloigné(e); **the ~ end** le côté le plus éloigné

farthest ['fɑːðɪst, *Am:* 'fɑːr-] **I.** *adv superl of* **far** **1.** (*to/at greatest distance: go, come*) **the ~ along/away** le plus loin; **the ~ east/west** le plus à l'est/ouest **2.** (*at/to most advanced point*) **the ~ advanced of the pupils** l'élève le plus avancé **II.** *adj superl of* **far** (*most distant*) le/la plus éloigné(e)

farthing *n* HIST quart *m* de penny

Far West *n* Far West *m*

fascia ['feɪʃə] *n* **1.** *Brit* tableau *m* de bord **2.** (*board above shop window*) enseigne *f*

fascinate ['fæsɪneɪt, *Am:* -əneɪt] *vt* fasciner

fascinating *adj* fascinant(e)

fascination *n no pl* fascination *f;* **a ~ with sth** une fascination pour qc; **to listen/watch in ~** écouter/regarder avec fascination; **sth holds a ~ for sb** qn est fasciné par qc

fascism, **Fascism** ['fæʃɪzəm] *n no pl* fascisme *m*

fascist, **Fascist** **I.** *n* fasciste *mf* **II.** *adj* fasciste

fashion ['fæʃən] **I.** *n* **1.** (*popular style*) mode *f;* **the ~ for sth** la mode de qc; **to be in ~** être à la mode; **to be out of ~** être démodé; **to go out of ~** se démoder; **the latest ~** la dernière mode **2.** *pl* (*newly designed clothes*) créations *fpl* de mode; **the spring ~s** les créations de printemps **3.** *no pl* (*industry*) mode *f;* **Italian ~** la mode italienne **4.** (*manner: friendly, peculiar, stupid*) manière *f;* **after a ~** si on peut dire **II.** *adj* de mode **III.** *vt form* **1.** (*make using hands*) **to ~ sth out of sth** fabriquer qc en qc **2.** *fig* (*create*) créer

fashionable *adj* à la mode; (*area, night-club, restaurant*) branché(e)

F

fashion designer *n* dessinateur , -trice de mode *m* **fashion show** *n* défilé *m* de mode **fashion victim** *n* victime *f* de la mode

fast[1] [fɑːst, *Am:* fæst] **I.** <-er, -est> *adj* **1.** (*opp: slow*) rapide; **to be a ~ runner** courir vite **2.** (*ahead of the time: clock*) en avance; **to be ten minutes ~** avancer de dix minutes **3.** (*firmly fixed*) ferme; **to make sth ~** attacher qc; (*boat*) arrimer qc **4.** (*withstanding washing: colour*) résistant(e) **5.** (*immoral*) frivole **6.** PHOT (*film*) très sensible **II.** *adv* **1.** (*quickly*) vite; **how ~ is that car?** quelle est la vitesse de cette voiture? **2.** (*firmly*) ferme; **stuck ~** bel et bien coincé; **to hold ~ to sth** s'accrocher à qc; **to stand ~** rester ferme **3.** (*deeply: asleep*) profondément

fast[2] [fɑːst, *Am:* fæst] **I.** *vi* jeûner **II.** *n* jeûne *m*

fast and furious I. *adv* (*heart*) **to beat ~** battre la chamade **II.** *adj* effréné(e)

fasten ['fɑːsən, *Am:* 'fæsən] **I.** *vt* **1.** (*attach*) attacher **2.** (*fix*) fixer; (*coat*) boutonner; **to ~ one's eyes on sb/sth** fixer son regard sur qn/qc **3.** (*close*) (bien) fermer **II.** *vi* **1.** (*do up*) s'attacher **2.** (*close*) se fermer

◆**fasten down** *vt* fixer

◆**fasten in** *vt* attacher

◆**fasten on I.** *vt a. fig* s'accrocher à **II.** *vi a. fig* **to ~ to sth/sb** s'accrocher à qn/qc

◆**fasten up I.** *vt* fermer **II.** *vi* se fermer

fastener *n* fermeture *f;* **a snap ~** un bouton-pression; **a zip ~** une fermeture éclair

fast food *n no pl* fast-food *m* **fast forward I.** *n no pl* avance *f* rapide **II.** *vt* **to fast-forward** faire avancer **III.** *vi* **to fast-forward** avancer

fastidious [fə'stɪdɪəs] *adj* (*person*) méticuleux(-euse); (*work*) minutieux(-euse); (*manners, taste, speech*) pointilleux(-euse); **to pay ~ attention to detail** être pointilleux sur les détails

fast lane *n* voie *f* de gauche; (*in UK and Ireland*) voie *f* de droite; **to live life in the ~** *fig* vivre la grande vie

fastness *n no pl* résistance *f*

fat [fæt] **I.** <fatter, fattest> *adj* **1.** (*fleshy*) gros(se); **to get ~** grossir **2.** (*containing fat*) gras(se) **3.** (*thick*) épais(se) **4.** (*large: cheque, fee, profits*) gros(se) **5.** *iron* sacré(e) **II.** *n* **1.** *no pl* (*body tissue*) graisse *f* **2.** *no pl* (*meat tissue*) gras *m* **3.** (*for cooking, in food*) matière *f* grasse ►**to live off the ~ of the land** vivre comme un coq en pâte

fatal ['feɪtəl, *Am:* -t̬əl] *adj* fatal(e); **it would be ~ to stop now** ça serait catastrophique de s'arrêter maintenant

fatalism ['feɪtəlɪzəm, *Am:* -t̬əl-] *n no pl* fatalisme *m*

fatalist *n* fataliste *mf*

fatality [fə'tæləti, *Am:* -t̬i] <-ties> *n* fatalité *f*

fatally *adv* fatalement

fat cat *n pej, inf* profiteur , -euse du système *m*

fate [feɪt] *n sing* destin *m;* **to leave sb to their ~** abandonner qn à son sort; **to meet one's ~** être rattrapé par son destin

fated *adj* destiné(e); **to be ~ to** +*infin* être destiné à +*infin;* **it was ~ that ...** il était écrit que ...

fateful *adj* fatal(e)

fat-free *adj* sans matière graisse **fathead** *n inf* imbécile *mf*

father ['fɑːðə^r, *Am:* -ðɚ] **I.** *n* père *m;* **from ~ to son** de père en fils; **Father Eric** Père Eric **II.** *vt* (*child*) engendrer

Father Christmas *n* le père Noël **father figure** *n* modèle *m* paternel **fatherhood** *n no pl* paternité *f* **father-in-law** <fathers-in-law *o* father-in-laws> *n* beau-père *m,* beaux-pères *mpl* **fatherland** *n* patrie *f*

fatherless *adj* orphelin(e) de père

fatherly *adj* paternel(le)

Father's Day *n no pl* (*end of June*) fête *f* des Pères

fathom ['fæðəm] **I.** *n* NAUT brasse *f* **II.** *vt* saisir

fatigue [fə'tiːg] **I.** *n* **1.** *no pl* épuisement *m* **2.** *no pl* TECH usure *f* **3.** (*soldier's domestic chore*) corvée *f* **4.** *pl* (*soldier's work clothes*) treillis *m* **II.** *vt* **1.** *form* épuiser **2.** TECH user

fat stock *n* bétail *m* engraissé

fatten ['fætən] *vt* engraisser

fattening *adj* **to be ~** faire grossir

fatty ['fæti, *Am:* 'fæt̬-] **I.** *adj* gras(se); (*tissue*) graisseux(-euse) **II.** <fatties> *n pej, inf* petit gros *m,* petite grosse *f*

fatuous ['fætʃʊəs, *Am:* 'fætʃu-] *adj* stupide

faucet ['fɔːsɪt, *Am:* 'fɑː-] *n Am* robinet *m*

fault [fɔːlt] **I.** *n* **1.** *no pl* (*guilt, mistake*) faute *f;* **to be sb's ~ that ...** être de la faute de qn si ...; **the ~ lies with sb/sth** la responsabilité incombe à qn/qc; **through no ~ of sb's own** sans être de la faute de qn; **to be at ~** être dans son tort; **to find ~ with sb/sth** avoir qc à redire à qn/qc **2.** (*character weakness, defect*) défaut *m* **3.** (*crack in earth's surface*) faille *f* **4.** SPORT faute *f* **II.** *vt* avoir qc à redire à; **you can't ~ his argument/pronunciation** tu ne peux rien trouver à redire à son argument/sa prononciation

fault-finder *n pej* râleur, -euse *m, f* **fault-finding I.** *n no pl, pej* critiques *fpl* **II.** *adj pej* râleur(-euse)

faultless *adj* impeccable

faulty *adj* **1.** (*having a defect: product*) défectueux(-euse) **2.** (*mistaken, misleading*) incorrect(e)

faun [fɔːn, *Am:* fɑːn] *n* faune *m*

fauna ['fɔːnə, *Am:* 'fɑː-] *n no pl, + sing/pl vb* faune *f*

favor ['feɪvə^r, *Am:* -vɚ] *Am, Aus s.* **favour**

favorable *adj Am, Aus s.* **favourable**

favored *adj Am, Aus s.* **favoured**

favorite ['feɪvərɪt] *Am, Aus s.* **favourite**

favoritism *n Am, Aus s.* **favouritism**

favour ['feɪvə^r, *Am:* -vɚ] *Brit, Aus* **I.** *n* **1.** *no pl* (*approval*) faveur *f;* **to be in ~ of sth** être en faveur de [*o* pour] qc; **to be in ~** avoir du succès; **to decide in ~ of sth** décider en la faveur de qc; **to be in ~ with sb** être bien vu de qn; **to be/fall out of ~ with sb** être/tomber en disgrâce auprès de qn; **to find ~ with sb** avoir du succès auprès de qn; **to win sb's ~** gagner la faveur de qn; **to have sth in one's ~** sth est en sa faveur **2.** (*helpful act*) service *m;* **to do sb a ~** rendre un service à qn; **do yourself a ~** fais quelque chose de bien **II.** *vt* **1.** (*prefer*) préférer; (*method, solution*) être pour; **to ~ doing sth** préférer faire qc **2.** (*give advantage or benefit to*) favoriser **3.** (*show partiality towards*) favoriser **4.** *Am, inf* (*look like*) ressembler à

favourable *adj* favorable; **to take a ~ view of sth** voir qc sous un jour favorable

favourably *adv* (*review*) favorablement; **to look ~ on an application** donner une opinion favorable à une candidature; **it compares ~ with the other one** il/elle est pratiquement aussi bien que l'autre

favourite ['feɪvərɪt] **I.** *adj* préféré(e) **II.** *n* préféré(e) *mf;* SPORT favori(te) *m(f)*

favouritism *n no pl, pej* favoritisme *m*

fawn¹ [fɔːn, *Am:* fɑːn] **I.** *n* **1.** (*young deer*) faon *m* **2.** (*colour*) beige *m* **II.** *adj* beige

fawn² [fɔːn, *Am:* fɑːn] *vi pej* **to ~ on sb** flagorner qn; **to ~ over sb/sth** ramper devant qn/qc

fawning *adj pej* servile

fax [fæks] **I.** *n* (*message*) fax *m;* **a ~ (machine)** un télécopieur **II.** *vt* faxer *m*

FBI [ˌefbiː'aɪ] *n Am abbr of* **Federal Bureau of Investigation** police *f* judiciaire fédérale

FCO [ˌefsiː'əʊ, *Am:* -'oʊ] *n Brit abbr of* **Foreign and Commonwealth Office** ministère *m* des Affaires étrangères et du Commonwealth

fear [fɪəʳ, *Am:* fɪr] **I.** *n* **1.** *no pl* (*state of being afraid*) peur *f;* **to live in ~** vivre dans la peur; **for ~ of doing sth** par crainte de faire qc; **for ~ that** par crainte que *+subj;* **to be in ~ of sth** craindre qc; **to go in ~ of sth** avoir peur de qc; **to strike ~ into sb** terrifier qn; **without ~ or favour** équitablement **2.** (*worry*) inquiétude *f;* **no ~!** pas question!; **there's no ~ of that happening** il n'y a pas de risque que ça arrive **II.** *vt* avoir peur de; **I ~ you are wrong** j'ai bien peur que tu te trompes *subj*

◆**fear for** *vt* (*person in trouble, one's job*) avoir peur pour; **to ~ the future** craindre l'avenir; **to ~ one's life** craindre pour sa vie

fearful *adj* **1.** (*anxious*) craintif(-ive); **to be ~ of sth** avoir peur de qc; **to be ~ that** être inquiet que *+subj;* **to be ~ of doing sth** avoir peur de faire qc **2.** (*terrible*) affreux(-euse)

fearless *adj* hardi(e)

fearsome *adj* effrayant(e)

feasibility [ˌfiːzə'bɪləti, *Am:* -ṭi] *n no pl* faisabilité *f*

feasibility study *n* étude *f* de faisabilité

feasible ['fiːzəbl] *adj* **1.** (*achievable*) réalisable **2.** *inf* (*plausible*) plausible

feast [fiːst] **I.** *n* **1.** (*meal*) *a. fig* festin *m* **2.** (*holiday*) jour *m* férié **3.** REL fête *f* **II.** *vi* **to ~ on sth** se délecter de qc **III.** *vt* régaler ►**to ~ one's eyes on sth** se délecter à la vue de qc

feat [fiːt] *n* exploit *m;* **~ of skill** tour *m* d'adresse; **~ of engineering** performance *f* technique

feather ['feðəʳ, *Am:* -ɚ] *n* plume *f* ►**to be a ~ in sb's cap** être quelque chose dont qn peut être fier; **as light as a ~** aussi léger qu'une plume

feather bed **I.** *n* lit *m* de plumes **II.** *vt pej* **to feather-bed** choyer

feather-brained *adj* bête

featherweight SPORT **I.** *n* poids *m* plume **II.** *adj* (*boxer*) poids plume

feathery ['feðəri] *adj* léger(-ère)

feature ['fiːtʃəʳ, *Am:* -tʃɚ] **I.** *n* **1.** (*distinguishing attribute*) particularité *f;* **a distinguishing ~** un signe particulier; **a useful ~ of the new software/model** une caractéristique utile du nouveau logiciel/modèle; **to make a ~ of sth** souligner qc particulièrement **2.** *pl* (*facial attributes*) traits *mpl* (du visage) **3.** PUBL article *m;* **a ~ on sth** un document exclusif sur qc **4.** RADIO, TV reportage *m* **5.** CINE **~ (film)** long métrage *m* **II.** *vt* **1.** (*have as aspect, attribute: magazine*) présenter; (*hotel*) offrir; **she's ~d in the programme** on parle d'elle dans l'émission **2.** (*have as performer, star*) avoir pour vedette **III.** *vi* figurer; **to ~ in sth** apparaître dans qc

featureless *adj* sans caractère

feature story *n* reportage *m* exclusif

February ['februəri, *Am:* -eri] *n* février *m;* *s. a.* **April**

feces ['fiːsiːz] *adj Am s.* **faeces**

feckless ['feklɪs] *adj* (*youth, husband*) irresponsable

Fed. *adj abbr of* **federal** fédéral(e)

federal ['fedərəl] *adj* **1.** (*republic, state*) fédéral(e) **2.** *Am* (*of the federation of states*) fédéré(e)

federalism ['fedərəlɪzəm] *n no pl* fédéralisme *m*

federalist *n* fédéraliste *mf*

federate ['fedəreɪt] **I.** *vt* fédérer **II.** *vi* se fédérer

federation *n* fédération *f*

fed up *adj inf* **to be ~ with sb/sth** en avoir marre de qn/qc

fee [fiː] *n* (*of doctor, lawyer, artist*) honoraires *mpl;* **school ~s** frais *mpl* de scolarité; **membership ~** cotisation *f;* **admission ~** droit *m* d'entrée

feeble ['fiːbl] *adj* faible; (*excuse*) faible; (*joke*) mauvais(e)

feeble-minded *adj* faible d'esprit

feebleness *n no pl* faiblesse *f*

feed [fiːd] <fed> **I.** *n* **1.** (*food*) nourriture *f;* **cattle ~** aliments *mpl* pour bétail **2.** *inf* (*meal*) repas *m* **3.** TECH approvisionnement *m* **II.** *vt* **1.** (*give food to, provide food for*) nourrir; **to ~**

the cat donner à manger au chat; **to ~ sth to sb** donner qc à manger à qn; **to ~ sb on sth** nourrir qn de qc **2.**(*supply: machine*) alimenter; (*fire, meter, someone*) approvisionner; **to ~ sth into the computer** entrer qc dans l'ordinateur **3.**(*give*) fournir; **to ~ sth to sb** fournir qc à qn **III.** *vi* manger

◆**feed on** *vt* **1.**(*eat*) se nourrir de **2.**(*exploit*) **they ~ people's fears** ils tirent profit des peurs des gens

◆**feed up** *vt* (*animals*) engraisser; **you need feeding up** tu as besoin de manger

feedback ['fi:dbæk] *n no pl, a. fig* réaction *f;* (*in sound system*) retour *m*

feeder *n* **1.**(*eater*) **a messy ~** un petit cochon **2.**(*baby's bib*) bavoir *m* **3.** TECH système *m* d'approvisionnement

feeder road *n* bretelle *f* d'accès

feeding bottle *n* biberon *m*

feel [fi:l] **I.** *n* **1.** *no pl* (*texture, act of touching*) toucher *m* **2.** *no pl* (*impression*) impression *f;* **a ~ of mystery** un parfum de mystère **3.** *no pl* (*natural talent*) sens *m* inné **II.** <felt> *vi* **1.**(*have a sensation or emotion*) se sentir; **to ~ well/stupid/important** se sentir bien/stupide/important; **to ~ hot/cold** avoir chaud/froid; **to ~ hungry/thirsty** avoir faim/soif; **I ~ unhappy about the idea** l'idée ne m'enchante pas; **to ~ as if ...** se sentir comme si ...; **to ~ like sth/doing sth** avoir envie de qc/faire qc; **how do you ~ about sth?** qu'est-ce que vous pensez de qc? **2.**(*seem*) paraître; **everything ~s different** tout semble différent; **it ~s as if I'd never been away** c'est comme si je n'étais jamais parti **3.**(*use hands to search*) **to ~ around** [*o* **about**] **somewhere** tâter autour de soi quelque part **III.** <felt> *vt* **1.**(*be physically aware of: pain, pressure, touch*) sentir **2.**(*experience*) ressentir; **she ~s the loneliness/shame of her position** elle resent la solitude/la honte de sa situation **3.**(*touch*) toucher; **to ~ your way somewhere** avancer à tâtons quelque part **4.**(*think, believe*) penser; **she ~s nobody listens to her** elle a l'impression que personne ne l'écoute; **what do you ~ about sth?** qu'est-ce que tu penses de qc?

◆**feel for** *vt* avoir de la compassion pour

feeler *n* ZOOL antenne *f* ►**to put out ~s** lancer un ballon d'essai

feel-good *adj* de bien-être

feeling *n* **1.**(*emotion, sensation*) sentiment *m;* **to hurt sb's ~s** blesser qn dans ses sentiments; **a dizzy ~** un vertige; **to play with ~** jouer avec émotion **2.**(*impression, air*) impression *f;* **to get the ~ that ...** avoir l'impression que ...; **I had a ~ he'd win** j'avais une petite idée qu'il gagnerait **3.**(*opinion*) opinion *f* **4.** *no pl* (*physical sensation*) sensation *f* **5.**(*natural talent*) sens *m* inné

feet [fi:t] *n pl of* **foot**

feign [feɪn] *vt* (*ignorance, emotion*) feindre; **to ~ illness/sleep** faire semblant d'être malade/de dormir

feint [feɪnt] **I.** *vi* feinter **II.** *n* feinte *f*

feline ['fi:laɪn] **I.** *adj* félin(e) **II.** *n* félin *m*

fell[1] [fel] *pt of* **fall**

fell[2] [fel] *vt* (*tree*) abattre; (*person*) assommer

fellow ['feləʊ, *Am:* -oʊ] **I.** *n* **1.** *inf* (*guy*) type *m* **2.** *inf* (*boyfriend*) mec *m* **3.**(*comrade*) camarade *mf* **4.** UNIV (*research ~*) assistant(e) *m(f)* de recherche **5.** UNIV (*professor*) professeur *mf* **6.**(*member*) membre *mf* **II.** *adj* **~ sufferer** compagnon *m* d'infortune; **~ student** camarade *mf;* **my ~ passengers** les autres passagers

fellow being *n* semblable *mf* **fellow citizen** *n* concitoyen(ne) *m(f)* **fellow countryman** <-men> *n* compatriote *mf* **fellow feeling** *n* sympathie *f*

fellowship *n* **1.** *no pl* (*comradely feeling*) camaraderie *f* **2.**(*association*) association *f* **3.** UNIV bourse *f;* **research ~** bourse *f* de recherche

fellow-traveller *n a. fig* compagnon *m* de route **fellow worker** *n* collègue *mf*

felon ['felən] *n* criminel(le) *m(f)*

felonious [fɪ'ləʊnɪəs, *Am:* fə'loʊ-] *adj* criminel(le)

felony ['feləni] <-nies> *n Am* crime *m*

felt[1] [felt] *pt, pp of* **feel**

felt[2] [felt] **I.** *n no pl* feutre *f* **II.** *adj* en feutre

felt-tip (**pen**) [ˌfelt'tɪp (pen)] *n* feutre *m*

female ['fi:meɪl] **I.** *adj* **1.**(*related to females*) féminin(e); **~ teachers** enseignantes **2.** TECH femelle **II.** *n a. pej* femelle *f*

feminine ['femənɪn] **I.** *adj a.* LING féminin(e) **II.** *n* LING **the ~** le féminin

femininity [ˌfemə'nɪnəti, *Am:* -t̬i] *n no pl* féminité *f*

feminism ['femɪnɪzəm] *n no pl* féminisme *m*

feminist **I.** *n* féministe *mf* **II.** *adj* féministe

femur ['fi:məʳ, *Am:* -mɚ] <-s *o* -mora> *n form* ANAT fémur *m*

fen [fen] *n* tourbière *f*

fence [fens] **I.** *n* **1.**(*barrier*) barrière *f* **2.** SPORT obstacle *m* **3.** *inf* (*receiver of stolen goods*) receleur, -euse *m, f* ►**to sit on the ~** ne pas se mouiller **II.** *vi* **1.** SPORT faire de l'escrime **2.** *form* se dérober; **to ~ with sb** esquiver qn **III.** *vt* **1.**(*close off*) clôturer **2.**(*sell: stolen goods*) écouler

◆**fence in** *vt* (*garden*) clôturer; *fig* (*person*) coincer

◆**fence off** *vt* clôturer

fencer *n* escrimeur, -euse *m, f*

fencing *n no pl* **1.** SPORT escrime *f* **2.**(*barrier*) clôture *f*

◆**fend for** *vt* **to ~ oneself** se débrouiller tout seul

◆**fend off** *vt* repousser; (*question*) écarter

fender ['fendəʳ, *Am:* -dɚ] *n* **1.**(*frame of fireplace*) pare-feu *m* **2.** *Am* AUTO *s.* **wing**

fennel ['fenl] *n no pl* BOT fenouil *m*

ferment [fə'ment, *Am:* fɚ-] **I.** *vt* **1.**(*change

chemically) laisser fermenter **2.** *fig* attiser **II.** *vi* **1.** (*change chemically*) fermenter **2.** *fig* s'agiter **III.** *n* **1.** *no pl, form* (*state of agitated excitement*) agitation *f* **2.** *no pl s.* **fermentation**

fermentation [ˌfɜːmenˈteɪʃən, *Am:* ˌfɜːr-] *n no pl* fermentation *f*

fern [fɜːn, *Am:* fɜːrn] *n* BOT fougère *f*

ferocious [fəˈrəʊʃəs, *Am:* -ˈroʊ-] *adj* **1.** (*cruel*) féroce **2.** (*extreme: heat, temper*) terrible

ferocity [fəˈrɒsəti, *Am:* -ˈrɑːsət̬i] *n no pl* violence *f*

ferret [ˈferɪt] **I.** *n* ZOOL furet *m* **II.** *vi* **to ~ about in sth** fureter dans qc

◆**ferret out** *vt* dénicher

ferroconcrete [ˌferəʊˈkɒŋkriːt, *Am:* -oʊˈkɑːkriːt] *n no pl* béton *m* armé

ferrous [ˈferəs] *adj* ferreux(-euse)

ferry [ˈferi] <-ies> **I.** *n* ferry *m;* (*smaller*) bac *m,* traversier *m Québec* **II.** *vt* **to ~ sb somewhere** transporter qn quelque part

ferryman <-men> *n* passeur *m*

fertile [ˈfɜːtaɪl, *Am:* ˈfɜːrt̬l] *adj* fertile

fertility [fəˈtɪləti, *Am:* fɚˈtɪlət̬i] *n no pl* fertilité *f*

fertilization *n no pl* fertilisation *f*

fertilize [ˈfɜːtəlaɪz, *Am:* ˈfɜːrt̬ə-] *vt* **1.** (*make able to produce much*) fertiliser **2.** (*impregnate*) féconder

fertilizer *n* engrais *m*

fervent [ˈfɜːvənt, *Am:* ˈfɜːr-] *adj* **1.** (*intensely felt*) intense **2.** (*devoted and enthusiastic*) fervent(e)

fervor *Am, Aus,* **fervour** [ˈfɜːvəʳ, *Am:* ˈfɜːrvɚ] *n no pl* ardeur *f*

fester [ˈfestəʳ, *Am:* -tɚ] *vi* **1.** MED suppurer **2.** (*become rotten and smell*) se putréfier **3.** *fig* (*become worse*) s'envenimer

festival [ˈfestɪvəl] *n* **1.** (*special event*) festival *m* **2.** (*religious day or period*) fête *f*

festive [ˈfestɪv] *adj* festif(-ive); **the ~ season** les fêtes de fin d'année

festivity [feˈstɪvəti, *Am:* -t̬i] <-ies> *n* **1.** *pl* festivités *fpl* **2.** *no pl* (*festiveness*) fête *f*

festoon [feˈstuːn] **I.** *n* feston *m* **II.** *vt* **~ed with sth** orné(e) de

fetal [ˈfiːtl, *Am:* -t̬l] *adj Am s.* **foetal**

fetch [fetʃ] *vt* **1.** (*bring back*) aller chercher; **to ~ sb/sth from somewhere** ramener qn/qc de quelque part; **to ~ sb sth from somewhere** rapporter qc à qn de quelque part; **~ me a glass of water** apporte-moi un verre d'eau; **to ~ and carry for sb** être la bonne à tout faire de qn **2.** (*be sold for*) rapporter; (*a price*) remporter

fetching *adj iron* charmant(e)

fête [feɪt] **I.** *n Brit, Aus* kermesse *f,* ducasse *f Nord, Belgique* **II.** *vt* fêter

fetid [ˈfetɪd, *Am:* ˈfet̬-] *adj form* fétide

fetish [ˈfetɪʃ, *Am:* ˈfet̬-] *n a.* PSYCH fétiche *m*

fetishism [ˈfetɪʃɪzəm, *Am:* ˈfet̬-] *n no pl* fétichisme *m*

fetishist *n* fétichiste *mf*

fetter [ˈfetəʳ, *Am:* ˈfet̬ɚ] **I.** *vt* **to ~ sb to sb/sth** enchaîner qn à qn/qc **II.** *n pl* fers; *fig* joug *m*

fettle [ˈfetl, *Am:* ˈfet̬-] *n no pl, inf* **to be in fine ~** être en bonne forme

fetus [ˈfiːtəs, *Am:* -t̬əs] *n Am s.* **foetus**

feud [fjuːd] **I.** *n* querelle *f* **II.** *vi* **to ~ with sb over sth** se quereller avec qn à cause de qc

feudal [ˈfjuːdəl] *adj* féodal(e)

feudalism [ˈfjuːdəlɪzəm] *n no pl* féodalisme *m*

fever [ˈfiːvəʳ, *Am:* -vɚ] *n* fièvre *f*

feverish *adj a.* MED fébrile

few [fjuː] **I.** <fewer, fewest> *adj* peu de; **there are ~ things that please him** il y a peu de choses qui lui font plaisir; **one of the ~ friends** l'un des rares amis; **there are two too ~** il en manque deux; **not ~er than 100 people** pas moins de 100 personnes; **to be ~ and far between** être rare **II.** *pron* peu; **~ of us** peu d'entre nous **III.** *n* **a ~** quelques un(e)s; **a ~ of us** certains d'entre nous; **I'd like a ~ more** j'en voudrais quelques-uns de plus; **quite a ~ people** pas mal de gens; **they left quite a ~ boxes** ils ont laissé pas mal de boîtes; **the ~** la minorité; **the happy ~** les heureux élus; **the ~ who have the book** les rares à avoir le livre

fewer [ˈfjuːəʳ, *Am:* -ɚ] *adj, pron* moins de; **no ~er than** pas moins que

fewest [ˈfjuːɪst] **I.** *adj* le moins de **II.** *pron* le moins

ff *n abbr of* **following pages** pages *fpl* suivantes

fiancé [fɪˈɒnseɪ, *Am:* ˌfiːɑːnˈseɪ] *n* fiancé *m*

fiancée [fɪˈɒnseɪ, *Am:* ˌfiːɑːnˈseɪ] *n* fiancée *f*

fiasco [fɪˈæskəʊ, *Am:* -koʊ] <-cos *o* -coes> *n* fiasco *m*

fib [fɪb] <-bb-> *inf* **I.** *vi* raconter des boniments **II.** *n* boniments *mpl;* **to tell a ~** raconter des boniments

fibber [ˈfɪbəʳ, *Am:* -ɚ] *n inf* menteur, -euse *m, f;* **you ~!** tu mens!

fiber [ˈfɪbəʳ, *Am:* -ɚ] *n Am,* **fibre** *n* fibre *f;* **moral ~** qualités *fpl* morales

fibreglass *n* fibre *f* de verre **fibre optic cable** *n* câble *m* en fibres optiques **fibre optics** **I.** *n sing* fibre *f* optique **II.** *adj* en fibres optiques

fibula [ˈfɪbjʊlə, *Am:* -jə-] <-s *o* -ae> *n* ANAT péroné *m*

fickle [ˈfɪkl] *adj pej* inconstant(e); (*opinion*) changeant(e); (*weather*) capricieux(-euse)

fiction [ˈfɪkʃən] *n no pl* fiction *f*

fictional *adj* fictif(-ive)

fictitious [fɪkˈtɪʃəs] *adj* **1.** (*fictional*) fictif(-ive) **2.** (*imaginary*) imaginaire

fiddle [ˈfɪdl] **I.** *vt Brit, inf* truquer **II.** *vi* **1.** *inf* (*play the violin*) jouer du violon **2.** (*fidget with/finger aimlessly*) **to ~ with sth** tripoter qc **III.** *n* **1.** *Brit, inf* (*fraud, racket*) combine *f;* **tax ~** fraude *f* fiscale **2.** *inf* (*violin*) violon *m*

fiddler *n* **1.** *inf* MUS joueur, -euse *m, f* de violon

2. *Brit, inf* (*fraudster, swindler*) combinard(e) *m(f)*
fiddly *adj inf* compliqué(e)
fidelity [fɪ'deləti, *Am:* -ṱi] *n no pl* fidélité *f*
fidget ['fɪdʒɪt] **I.** *vi* **1.** (*be impatient*) s'agiter **2.** (*be nervous*) s'énerver **II.** *n* **to be a ~** ne pas tenir en place
fidgety *adj* agité(e)
fief [fi:f] *n* fief *m*
field [fi:ld] **I.** *n* **1.** (*open land*) *a.* MIL, ELEC, INFOR champ *m* **2.** (*sphere of activity*) domaine *m* **3.** SPORT (*ground*) terrain *m* **4.** + *sing/pl vb* (*contestants in competition*) concurrents *mpl;* **she beat off a large ~ to get the job** elle a battu de nombreux candidats pour avoir le job **II.** *vt* SPORT **1.** (*return: ball*) attraper et relancer; *fig* (*questions*) répondre à **2.** (*send: team*) faire jouer
field day *n* **1.** *Am, Aus* (*day outside classroom*) sortie *f* **2.** (*sporting event*) grand jour *m* **3.** *inf* to have a ~, bien s'amuser
fielder *n* chasseur *m*
field glasses *n* jumelles *fpl* **field marshal** *n* maréchal *m* **field mouse** *n* mulot *m* **field sports** *n* activités *fpl* de plein air **fieldwork** *n* travaux *mpl* sur le terrain **fieldworker** *n* homme , femme de terrain *m*
fiend [fi:nd] *n* **1.** (*devil*) démon *m* **2.** *pej* (*brute*) monstre *m* **3.** *inf* (*fan*) mordu(e) *m(f)*
fiendish *adj a. pej* diabolique
fierce [fɪəs, *Am:* fɪrs] *adj* <-er, -est> **1.** (*untamed: animal*) féroce **2.** (*powerful, extreme, violent: love, discussion*) véhément(e); (*expression, competition, combat*) féroce
fiery ['faɪəri, *Am:* 'faɪri] <-ier, -iest> *adj* **1.** (*with fire in it*) brûlant(e); (*red*) vif(vive) **2.** (*passionate*) fougueux(-euse); (*speech*) enflammé(e) **3.** (*intensely spiced*) fortement épicé(e)
FIFA ['fi:fə] *n abbr of* **Federation of International Football Association** FIFA *f*
fife [faɪf] *n* (*instrument or player*) fifre *m*
fifteen [ˌfɪf'ti:n] *adj* quinze; *s. a.* **eight**
fifteenth *adj* quinzième; *s. a.* **eighth**
fifth [fɪfθ] *adj* cinquième; *s. a.* **eighth**
fiftieth ['fɪftiəθ] *adj* cinquantième; *s. a.* **eighth**
fifty ['fɪfti] *adj* cinquante; *s. a.* **eight, eighty**
fifty-fifty *adj* **a ~ chance** cinquante pour cent de chances
fig [fɪg] *n* figue *f*
fig. **I.** *n abbr of* **figure** fig *f* **II.** *adj abbr of* **figurative** fig
fight [faɪt] **I.** <fought, fought> *vi* **1.** (*exchange blows*) se battre **2.** (*wage war, do battle*) combattre; **to ~ with/against sb** se battre avec/contre qn **3.** (*dispute, quarrel bitterly*) **to ~ over sth** se disputer pour qc **4.** (*struggle to overcome sth*) **to ~ for sth** se battre pour qc; **to ~ against sth** lutter contre qc **II.** *vt* (*enemy, crime*) combattre; (*person*) se battre contre; (*a case, an action*) défendre; **to ~ an election** POL mener une campagne électorale ►**to ~ shy of sth/doing sth** être frileux pour qc/pour faire qc **III.** *n* **1.** (*violent confrontation*) bagarre *f;* **to get into a ~ with sb** se bagarrer avec qn **2.** (*quarrel*) dispute *f* **3.** (*battle*) combat *m* **4.** (*struggle, campaign*) lutte *f;* **to show some ~** ne pas se laisser faire; **there's no ~ left in him** il n'a plus de combativité; **to put up a good ~** bien se défendre **5.** SPORT combat *m*
◆**fight back** **I.** *vi* se défendre; **to ~ against cancer** se battre contre le cancer **II.** *vt* **1.** (*fight*) combattre **2.** *fig* (*tears*) refouler
◆**fight off** *vt* **1.** (*repel, repulse*) repousser **2.** (*resist*) battre
◆**fight on** *vi* continuer à se battre
fighter *n* **1.** (*person withstanding problems*) battant(e) *m(f)* **2.** (*person who fights*) combattant(e) *m(f)* **3.** (*military plane*) chasseur *m*
fighting **I.** *n no pl* combats *mpl* **II.** *adj* combatif(-ive)
figment ['fɪgmənt] *n* **a ~ of sb's imagination** le fruit de l'imagination de qn
figurative ['fɪgjərətɪv, *Am:* -jɚəṱɪv] *adj* **1.** (*metaphorical language*) figuré(e) **2.** ART figuratif *m*
figuratively *adv* au figuré; **~ speaking** au sens figuré
figure ['fɪgəʳ, *Am:* -jɚ] **I.** *n* **1.** (*outline of body*) silhouette *f;* **a ~ in the distance** une silhouette au loin; **to have a good ~** avoir un beau corps; **to keep one's ~** garder la ligne **2.** (*personality*) personnalité *f;* **a leading ~ in the movement** un personnage important dans le mouvement; **a ~ of fun** un personnage dont on se moque **3.** (*digit*) chiffre *m;* **to be good at ~s** être bon en calcul **4.** *pl* (*bookkeeping, economic data*) chiffres *mpl* **5.** (*diagram, representation*) figure *f* **II.** *vt* penser **III.** *vi* (*appear*) figurer
◆**figure out** *vt* **1.** (*understand*) (arriver à) comprendre **2.** (*work out*) calculer
figurehead *n a. fig* figure *f* de proue **figure skater** *n* patineur, -euse *m, f* artistique **figure skating** *n* patinage *m* artistique
Fiji ['fi:dʒi:] *n* **~ Islands** îles *fpl* Fidji
Fijian **I.** *adj* fidjien(ne) **II.** *n* Fidjien(ne) *m(f)*
filament ['fɪləmənt] *n* filament *m*
filch [fɪltʃ] *vt inf* chiper
file¹ [faɪl] **I.** *n* **1.** (*binder for ordering documents*) classeur *m* **2.** (*dossier*) dossier *m,* farde *f Belgique,* fiche *f Suisse* **3.** INFOR fichier *m;* **text ~** fichier-texte; **backup ~** fichier de sauvegarde **4.** (*column, queue, row*) file *f;* **in (single) ~** en file indienne **II.** *vt* **1.** (*arrange: data*) classer **2.** LAW (*petition*) déposer **3.** PUBL (*report*) envoyer **III.** *vi* **1.** (*officially register request*) **to ~ for sth** faire une demande de qc; **to ~ for bankruptcy** faire un dépôt de bilan **2.** (*move in line*) marcher en rang; **to ~ in/out** entrer/sortir en rang
◆**file away** *vt* classer
file² [faɪl] **I.** *n* lime *f* **II.** *vt* limer; **to ~ (one's)**

nails se limer les ongles
file manager *n* INFOR gestionnaire *m* de fichiers **file name** *n* INFOR nom *m* de fichier
filibuster ['fɪlɪbʌstəʳ, *Am:* -tɚ] **I.** *n* obstruction *f* **II.** *vi Am* faire de l'obstruction
filigree ['fɪlɪgriː] *n no pl* filigrane *m*
filing ['faɪlɪŋ] *n* **1.** *no pl* (*archiving of documents*) classement *m* **2.** (*official registration of application*) enregistrement *m*
filing cabinet *n* armoire *f* de classement
filings *npl* limaille *f*
Filipino [fɪlɪ'piːnəʊ, *Am:* -noʊ] *n* Philippin(ne) *m(f)*
fill [fɪl] **I.** *vt* **1.** (*make full*) remplir **2.** (*appoint to: post*) pourvoir **3.** (*occupy: post*) occuper **4.** (*seal: a hole*) boucher; (*a tooth*) plomber **5.** (*make person feel*) **to ~ sb with** (*joy, excitement, disgust, anger*) remplir de **6.** (*fulfil: prescription, order*) remplir **II.** *vi* se remplir
◆**fill in I.** *vt* **1.** (*seal opening: a hole*) boucher **2.** (*complete: form*) remplir; **~ your name and address** notez votre nom et votre adresse **3.** (*inform, give the facts*) **to fill sb in on the details, to ~ sb on the details** mettre qn au courant des détails **II.** *vi* **to ~ for sb** remplacer qn
◆**fill out I.** *vt* remplir **II.** *vi* prendre du poids
◆**fill up I.** *vt* remplir; **I need to ~ my car** *Am* j'ai besoin de faire le plein d'essence **II.** *vi* **to ~ with sth** se remplir de qc
filler *n* **1.** (*sealing material*) mastic *m* **2.** (*item space in media*) remplissage *m*
fillet ['fɪlɪt] **I.** *n* filet *m* **II.** *vt* (*meat*) désosser; (*fish*) découper en filets
filling I. *n* **1.** (*for cushion, toy*) rembourrage *m* **2.** (*for tooth*) plombage *m* **3.** GASTR farce *f*; (*for sandwich*) garniture *f* **II.** *adj* (*food*) nourrissant(e); **it's very ~** ça cale bien
filling station *n* station-service *f*
fillip ['fɪlɪp] *n sing* coup *m* de fouet
film [fɪlm] **I.** *n* film *m*; (*for camera*) pellicule *f* **II.** *vt, vi* filmer
film buff *n* cinéphile *mf* **film star** *n* vedette *f* de cinéma **film studio** *n* studio *m* de cinéma
filter ['fɪltəʳ, *Am:* -t̬ɚ] **I.** *n* filtre *m* **II.** *vt* filtrer; (*coffee*) faire passer **III.** *vi* **1.** (*pass*) filtrer **2.** AUTO **to ~ left/right** passer sur la file de gauche/droite
◆**filter out** *vt a. fig* filtrer
◆**filter through** *vi* (*light*) passer à travers; (*news, reports*) filtrer
filter lane *n* voie *f* de dégagement **filter paper** *n* papier *m* filtre **filter tip** *n* cigarette *f* filtre
filth [fɪlθ] *n no pl* **1.** (*dirt*) saleté *f* **2.** (*excrement*) ordure *f* **3.** *pej* (*obscenity*) obscénités *fpl*
filthy I. *adj* sale **II.** *adv inf* **to be ~ rich** être bourré de fric
filtration [fɪl'treɪʃən] *n no pl* filtrage *m*
fin [fɪn] *n* **1.** ZOOL nageoire *f* **2.** TECH aileron *m*
final ['faɪnl] **I.** *adj* **1.** (*last*) final(e) **2.** (*decisive*) définitif(-ive) **3.** (*irrevocable*) irrévocable; **and that's ~!** c'est mon dernier mot! **II.** *n* **1.** SPORT finale *f* **2.** *pl, Brit* UNIV les examens de dernière année **3.** *pl, Am* SCHOOL les examens de fin d'année scolaire
finale [fɪ'nɑːli, *Am:* -'næli] *n sing* finale *m*
finalist ['faɪnəlɪst] *n* finaliste *mf*
finality [faɪ'næləti, *Am:* -t̬i] *n no pl* **1.** (*quality of irreversible conclusion*) irrévocabilité *f* **2.** (*determination*) détermination *f*
finalize ['faɪnəlaɪz] *vt* mettre au point; (*deal*) conclure
finally ['faɪnəli] *adv* **1.** (*at long last, eventually*) finalement **2.** (*expressing relief or impatience*) enfin **3.** (*in conclusion, to conclude*) pour finir **4.** (*conclusively, irrevocably*) définitivement
finance ['faɪnænts] **I.** *vt* financer **II.** *n* **1.** (*cash flow*) finance *f* **2.** *pl* (*capital, funds*) finances *fpl*
finance company, **finance house** *n* société *f* de financement
financial *adj* financier(-ère)
financier [faɪ'næntsiəʳ, *Am:* fɪ'næntsiɚ] *n* financier *m*
finch [fɪntʃ] *n* pinson *m*
find [faɪnd] **I.** <found, found> *vt* trouver; **to ~ sb/sth (to be) sth** trouver que qn/qc est qc; **I ~ it's best to go early** je trouve qu'il vaut mieux y aller tôt; **I ~ it strange to see them again** je trouve étrange de les revoir; **to ~ oneself alone/somewhere** se retrouver seul/quelque part; **to ~ sb guilty/innocent** déclarer qn coupable/innocent; **to be nowhere to be found** être introuvable ►**to ~ fault with sb/sth** trouver qc à redire à qn/qc; **to ~ one's tongue** retrouver sa langue **II.** *vi* LAW **to ~ for/against sb** se prononcer en faveur de/contre qn **III.** *n* trouvaille *f*; **~ function** INFOR fonction *f* recherche
◆**find out I.** *vt* **1.** (*uncover, detect, discover*) découvrir **2.** (*enquire*) essayer de savoir **3.** (*show to be guilty*) **to find sb out** attraper qn; **don't get found out** ne te fais pas prendre **II.** *vi* apprendre; **to ~ about sth** apprendre à propos de qc
finder *n* personne *f* qui trouve
finding *n* **1.** (*discovery*) découverte *f* **2.** *pl* (*conclusion*) conclusions *fpl*
fine¹ [faɪn] **I.** *adj* **1.** (*admirable, excellent: example, food*) excellent(e); (*wine, dish*) fin(e) **2.** (*acceptable, satisfactory*) bien *inv*; **(that's) ~!** c'est bien!; **that's just ~!** *iron* merci beaucoup!; **everything's ~** tout va bien **3.** (*thin, light*) fin(e) **4.** (*cloudless: weather*) beau(belle) **5.** (*distinguished*) raffiné(e) **6.** (*subtle: distinction, nuance*) subtil(e); **there's a ~ line between sth and sth** il n'y a qu'un pas de qc à qc **II.** *adv* **1.** (*acceptable, satisfactorily*) bien; **to feel ~** se sentir bien; **to suit sb ~** convenir parfaitement à qn **2.** (*in fine parts*) finement ►**that's cutting it a bit ~** c'est un peu juste

fine² [faɪn] **I.** *n* amende *f* **II.** *vt* **to ~ sb for sth** LAW condamner qn à une amende pour qc; (*for breaking rule*) faire payer une amende à qn pour qc
◆**fine down** *vt* limer
fine art *n* beaux-arts *mpl*
fineness *n no pl* finesse *f*
finery ['faɪnəri] *n no pl* parure *f*
finesse [fɪ'nes] *n no pl* finesse *f*
fine-tooth comb *n* **to go through sth with a ~** passer qc au peigne fin
finger ['fɪŋgəʳ, *Am:* -gɚ] **I.** *n a. fig* doigt *m;* **one ~ of vodka** un doigt de vodka; **to point a ~ at sb/sth** *a. fig* montrer qn/qc du doigt ►**not to lay a ~ on sb** ne pas toucher qn; **not to lift a ~** ne pas lever le petit doigt **II.** *vt* **1.** (*handle, touch*) toucher **2.** (*play with*) tripoter **3.** *inf* (*reveal to police*) balancer
fingering *n no pl* doigté *m*
fingermark *n* trace *f* de doigt **fingernail** *n* ongle *m* **fingerprint I.** *n* **1.** ANAT, LAW empreinte *f* digitale **2.** *Am s.* **fingermark II.** *vt* prendre les empreintes digitales de **fingertip** *n* bout *m* du doigt
finicky ['fɪnɪki] *adj pej* tatillon(ne)
finish ['fɪnɪʃ] **I.** *vi* **1.** (*cease, conclude*) se terminer **2.** (*go on talking*) finir (de parler) **3.** SPORT finir **II.** *vt* finir; **to ~ doing sth** finir de faire qc **III.** *n* **1.** SPORT arrivée *f* **2.** (*conclusion of process*) fin *f;* **from start to ~** du début jusqu'à la fin **3.** (*quality*) fini *m;* (*on furniture*) finition *f*
◆**finish off I.** *vt* **1.** (*conclude*) finir **2.** (*eat/drink*) finir **3.** *inf* (*beat or make somebody fatigued*) achever **4.** *inf* (*kill*) achever **II.** *vi* finir
◆**finish up** *vi, vt* finir; **to ~ doing sth** se retrouver à faire qc
◆**finish with** *vt* en finir avec; **I haven't finished with that yet** j'ai encore besoin de ça
finished *adj* **1.** (*through, used up*) fini(e); **to be ~ with sth** en avoir fini avec qc **2.** (*final, accomplished*) final(e)
finishing line, **finishing post** *n* ligne *f* d'arrivée **finishing touch** *n* touche *f* finale
finite ['faɪnaɪt] *adj* fini(e); **a ~ number of possibilities** un nombre limité de possibilités; **a ~ verb** un verbe conjugué
Finland ['fɪnlənd] *n* la Finlande
Finn [fɪn] *n* Finlandais(e) *m(f)*
Finnish ['fɪnɪʃ] **I.** *adj* **1.** (*of Finnish descent*) finnois(e) **2.** (*from Finland*) finlandais(e) **II.** *n* **1.** (*person of Finnish descent*) Finnois(e) *m(f)* **2.** (*person from Finland*) Finlandais(e) *m(f)* **3.** (*language*) finnois *m*
fiord [fɪ'ɔːd, *Am:* fjɔːrd] *n s.* **fjord**
fir [fɜːʳ, *Am:* fɜːr] *n* sapin *m*
fir cone *n Brit* cône *m* de sapin
fire ['faɪəʳ, *Am:* 'faɪɚ] **I.** *n* **1.** (*element*) feu *m;* **~!** au feu!; **to catch ~** prendre feu; **to cease ~** cesser le feu; **to open ~ on sb** ouvrir le feu sur qn; **to come under ~ for sth** *fig* être attaqué pour qc **2.** (*burning*) incendie *m;* **to be on ~** être en feu; **to set sth on ~** mettre le feu à qc **3.** (*shots*) coups *mpl* de feu; **~!** feu! ►**there's no smoke without a ~** *prov* il n'y a pas de fumée sans feu; **to play with ~** jouer avec le feu **II.** *vt* **1.** (*set off: rocket*) lancer; (*shot*) tirer; **to ~ a gun at sb/sth** décharger une arme sur qn/qc **2.** (*dismiss: worker*) licencier **3.** (*excite*) **to ~ sb's imagination** stimuler l'imagination de qn; **~d with enthusiasm/new hope** plein d'enthousiasme/de nouvel espoir **4.** (*bake: pot*) cuire **III.** *vi* tirer; **to ~ at sb/sth** tirer sur qn/qc
◆**fire away** *vi* **1.** (*shoot*) tirer **2.** *inf* **~!** vas-y!
◆**fire off** *vt* **1.** (*shoot*) tirer **2.** (*send*) envoyer
fire alarm *n* alerte *f* au feu **firearm** *n* arme *f* à feu **fireball** *n* boule *f* de feu **firebreak** *n* coupe-feu *m* **fire brigade** *n Brit* (sapeurs-)pompiers *mpl,* service *m* du feu *Suisse* **firecracker** *n* pétard *m* **firedamp** *n inf* grisou *m* **fire department** *n Am* (sapeurs-)pompiers *mpl,* service *m* du feu *Suisse* **fire door** *n* porte *f* coupe-feu **fire drill** *n* exercice *m* d'évacuation en cas d'incendie **fire-eater** *n* cracheur *m* de feu **fire engine** *n* voiture *f* de pompiers **fire escape** *n* escalier *m* de secours **fire extinguisher** *n* extincteur *m* **firefighter** *n* (sapeur-)pompier *m*
firefly *n* luciole *f*
fireguard *n* pare-feu *m* **fire hazard** *n* danger *m* d'incendie **fire house** *n Am* caserne *f* de pompiers **fire hydrant** *n* borne *f* d'incendie, hydrant *m Suisse,* hydrante *f Suisse* **fire insurance** *n* assurance *f* incendie **fireman** <-men> *n* pompier *m* **fireplace** *n* cheminée *f* **fireplug** *n Am* bouche *f* d'incendie **fireproof** *adj* résistant(e) aux températures élevées **fireside** *n* cheminée *f;* **by the ~** autour du feu **firewater** *n no pl, iron, inf* gnôle *f* **firewoman** <-women> *n* femme *f* pompier **firewood** *n no pl* bois *m* de chauffage **fireworks** *n pl* feu *m* d'artifice; **there will be ~!** *inf* il y aura du grabuge!
firing ['faɪərɪŋ, *Am:* 'faɪɚ-] *n* **1.** (*action of setting fire*) tir *m* **2.** (*starting: engine*) allumage *m* **3.** (*dismissal*) licenciement *m*
firing line *n* ligne *f* de tir; **to be in the ~** *fig* être dans le collimateur **firing squad** *n* peloton *m* d'exécution
firm¹ [fɜːm, *Am:* fɜːrm] **I.** *adj* **1.** (*hard*) ferme **2.** (*steady*) *a. fig* (*table, basis*) solide **3.** (*resolute*) ferme **II.** *adv* ferme; **to stand ~** *a. fig* rester ferme **III.** *vt* **to ~ (up) sth** raffermir qc **IV.** *vi* **to ~ (up)** se raffermir
firm² [fɜːm, *Am:* fɜːrm] *n* entreprise *f;* **~ of lawyers** cabinet *m* d'avocats
firmly *adv* **1.** (*with authority: state*) d'un ton ferme; (*deal*) avec fermeté **2.** (*strongly, tightly: hold, tie*) fermement
firmness *n no pl* fermeté *f*
first [fɜːst, *Am:* fɜːrst] **I.** *adj* premier(-ère); **for the ~ time** pour la première fois; **the ~ few**

visitors les premiers visiteurs; **the ~ thing that comes into sb's head** la première chose qui vient à l'esprit de qn; **in the ~ flush of success** dans l'ivresse du succès; **to do sth ~ thing** faire qc en premier ►**in the ~ place** *Brit* d'abord; *inf* (*at beginning, most importantly*) primo; **not to know the ~ thing about sth** ne pas avoir la moindre idée de qc; **~ things ~** une chose après l'autre; **~ and foremost** tout d'abord **II.** *adv* en premier; **it ~ happened on Sunday** c'est arrivé la première fois dimanche; **~ of all** *inf* tout d'abord; **at ~** d'abord; **I have to wash ~** je dois d'abord me laver; **~ come ~ served** *inf* les premiers arrivés sont les premiers servis **III.** *n* **1.** (*coming before*) premier, -ère *m, f;* **that's the ~ I've heard of that** c'est la première fois que j'en entends parler; **a ~ for sb** une première pour qn **2.** (*beginning*) commencement *m;* **from the very ~** au tout début **3.** (*date*) **the ~ of June** le premier juin **4.** AUTO première *f* **5.** UNIV ≈ une mention très bien **IV.** *pron* le premier/la première; *s. a.* **eighth**

first aid *n* premiers secours *mpl* **first aid box** *n* trousse *f* de secours **first aid kit** *n Brit* kit *m* de secours **first class I.** *n* première classe *f* **II.** *adj* **first-class** (*hotel, ticket*) de première classe; (*merchandise*) de première qualité; (*restaurant*) excellent(e); (*mail*) (au tarif) rapide **III.** *adv* (*travel*) en première classe; (*send*) au tarif rapide **first cousin** *n* cousin(e) *m(f)* **first-hand** *adj, adv* de première main **first lady** *n Am* **the ~** *femme du président des États-Unis*

firstly *adv* premièrement

first name *n* prénom *m* **first night** *n* première *f* **first offender** *n* criminel(le) *m(f)* sans casier judiciaire **first-rate** *adj* de première classe **first-year student** *n* étudiant(e) *m(f)* de première année

firth [fɜːθ, *Am:* fɜːrθ] *n Scot* bras *m* de mer

fiscal ['fɪskl] *adj* fiscal(e)

fish [fɪʃ] **I.** <-(es)> *n* **1.** ZOOL poisson *m* **2.** *no pl* GASTR poisson *m;* **~ and chips** *poisson frites* ►**(like) a ~ out of water** complètement perdu; **to have bigger ~ to fry** avoir d'autres chats à fouetter **II.** *vi* (*catch fish*) pêcher **III.** *vt* pêcher; (*body*) repêcher; **to ~ the sea/a lake** pêcher en mer/dans un lac; **to ~ sb/sth (out) from sth** sortir qn/qc de qc

◆**fish for** *vt* (*trout, cod*) pêcher; (*compliments, information*) chercher

fishbone *n* arrête *f* **fishcake** *n* ≈ boulette *f* de poisson **fisherman** <-men> *n* pêcheur *m*

fishery ['fɪʃəri] *n* pêche *f*

fish farm *n* établissement *m* de pisciculture **fish finger** *n* bâtonnet *m* de poisson pané **fish hook** *n* hameçon *m*

fishing I. *n no pl* pêche *f* **II.** *adj* de pêche **fishing rod** *n Brit, Aus* canne *f* à pêche **fishing tackle** *n* attirail *m* de pêche

fishmonger *n Brit* poissonnier, -ière *m, f*

fishy ['fɪʃi] <-ier, -iest> *adj* **1.** (*tasting of fish*) qui a un goût de poisson **2.** *inf* (*dubious*) louche

fission ['fɪʃən] *n no pl* fission *f*

fissionable *adj* fissible

fissure ['fɪʃəʳ, *Am:* -ɚ] *n a. fig* fissure *f*

fist [fɪst] *n* poing *m*

fit¹ [fɪt] **I.** <-tter, -ttest> *adj* **1.** (*suitable*) bon(ne); **~ to eat** mangeable; **a meal ~ for a king** un repas digne d'un roi; **~ for human consumption** consommable; **~ for human habitation** habitable; **to see ~ to** +*infin* juger nécessaire de +*infin;* **as you see fit** comme bon vous semble **2.** (*having skills*) capable; **to be not ~ to** +*infin* ne pas être capable de +*infin* **3.** (*ready, prepared*) prêt(e) **4.** (*healthy through physical training*) en forme; **to keep ~** rester en forme ►**to be (as) ~ as a fiddle** *inf* être en pleine forme **II.** <fitting, -tt- *o Am* -> *vt* **1.** (*be correct size for*) aller à **2.** (*position/shape as required*) adapter; **to ~ a new handle on a saucepan** ajuster un nouveau manche sur une casserole **3.** (*match: description*) correspondre à; **music to ~ the occasion** de la musique qui convient à l'occasion; **the theory doesn't ~ the facts** la théorie ne colle pas aux faits **III.** *vi* <fitting, -tt- *o Am* -> **1.** (*be correct size*) aller **2.** (*be appropriate*) s'adapter **IV.** *n no pl* coupe *f;* **the dress is a perfect ~** la robe est à la bonne taille

◆**fit in I.** *vi* **1.** (*fit*) aller; **we will all ~** il y aura de la place pour tout le monde **2.** (*match*) **to ~ with sth** correspondre à qc **3.** (*with group, background*) s'intégrer **II.** *vt* **to fit sb/sth in somewhere** caser qn/qc quelque part

◆**fit out** *vt* équiper; **to fit sb out with sth** éqiper qn de qc

◆**fit together** *vi* s'adapter

◆**fit up** *vt* **1.** (*fit out*) équiper **2.** *inf* monter un coup contre

fit² [fɪt] *n a. fig* crise *f;* (*of anger*) accès *m;* **coughing ~** quinte *f* de toux; **in ~s of laughter** dans un fou rire; **in ~s and starts** par crises; **he'll have a ~** il va faire une crise

fitful *adj* irrégulier(-ère)

fitment *n Brit* élément *m*

fitness *n no pl* **1.** (*competence, suitability*) aptitude *f* **2.** (*good condition, health*) forme *f*

fitted ['fɪtɪd, *Am:* 'fɪt̬-] *adj* **1.** (*adapted, suitable*) **to be ~ for sth** être fait pour qc **2.** (*tailor-made: garment*) ajusté(e); (*wardrobe*) encastré(e); **~ carpet** moquette *f;* **~ kitchen** cuisine équipée; **~ sheet** drap *m* housse

fitter ['fɪtəʳ, *Am:* 'fɪt̬ɚ] *n* **1.** (*tailor's aid*) apprenti*e m* tailleur **2.** (*person maintaining machinery*) technicien(ne) *m(f)* de maintenance

fitting I. *n* **1.** *pl* (*fixtures*) installations *fpl* **2.** *pl, Brit, Aus* (*movable furnishing items*) accessoires *mpl* **3.** (*for clothes*) essayage *m* **II.** *adj* approprié(e)

five [faɪv] *adj* cinq; *s. a.* **eight**

fivefold *adj* cinq fois

fiver *n Am, Brit, inf* billet *m* de cinq

fix [fɪks] **I.** *vt* **1.** (*decide, arrange: colour, date, price*) fixer; **to ~ it for sb to do sth** tout arranger pour que qn fasse qc *subj* **2.** (*repair: bicycle, roof, leak*) réparer; **that's ~ed the problem** ça résoud le problème; **to ~ one's hair** arranger ses cheveux **3.** *Am, inf* (*prepare: food, meal*) préparer **4.** (*arrange dishonestly: race, election*) truquer **5.** (*place*) poser; **to ~ sth on sth** fixer qc à qc; **to ~ sth in one's mind** *fig* bien retenir qc dans sa mémoire; **to ~ the blame on sb** repousser la faute sur qn; **to ~ one's attention/eyes on sth** fixer son attention/les yeux sur qc; **to ~ sb with a stare** fixer qn du regard **6.** *Am, inf* (*sterilize: animal*) couper **7.** TECH fixer **II.** *n* **1.** *sing, inf* (*dilemma, embarrassment*) pépin *m;* **to be in a ~** être dans le pétrin **2.** *inf* (*dosage of narcotics*) dose *f*

◆**fix down** *vt* fixer

◆**fix on** *vt a. inf* fixer

◆**fix up** *vt* **1.** (*supply with*) **to fix sb up, trouver ce qu'il faut à qn, to fix sb up with sth** trouver qc pour qn **2.** (*arrange, organize*) arranger **3.** (*repair, make*) rafistoler

fixation [fɪk'seɪʃən] *n* fixation *f;* **~ with sb/sth** une fixation sur qn/qc

fixed *adj* fixe; (*expression, smile, stare*) figé(e); (*appointment*) fixé(e); **~ term contract** contrat à durée déterminée

fixedly *adv* fixement

fixer *n* **1.** *inf* magouilleur, -euse *m, f* **2.** PHOT fixateur *m*

fixture ['fɪkstʃə^r, *Am:* -tʃɚ] *n* **1.** (*immovable object*) équipement *m* **2.** *Brit, Aus* SPORT rencontre *f* ►**to be a permanent ~** faire partie des meubles

fizz [fɪz] **I.** *vi* pétiller **II.** *n no pl* **1.** (*bubble, frothiness*) pétillement *m* **2.** *inf* (*bubbly wine*) mousseux *m* **3.** *inf* (*lemonade*) limonade *f*

fizzle ['fɪzl] *vi* pétiller

◆**fizzle out** *vi* (*plan, film, match*) partir en eau de boudin

fizzy ['fɪzi] <-ier, -iest> *adj* **1.** (*bubbly*) pétillant(e) **2.** (*carbonated*) gazeux(-euse)

fjord [fɪ'ɔːd, *Am:* fjɔːrd] *n* fjord *m*

flabbergast ['flæbəgɑːst, *Am:* -ɚgæst] *vt inf* souffler

flabby ['flæbi] <-ier, -iest> *adj pej* mou(molle)

flaccid ['flæksɪd] *adj a. fig, form* mou(molle)

flag¹ [flæg] **I.** *n* **1.** (*national symbol*) *a.* INFOR drapeau *m* **2.** NAUT pavillon *m* **II.** <-gg-> *vt* **1.** (*mark*) marquer **2.** *fig* signaler **III.** <-gg-> *vi* faiblir; (*conversation*) languir; (*party, film, player*) faiblir

◆**flag down** *vt* (*taxi*) héler; (*driver, car*) arrêter

flag² [flæg] **I.** *n* dalle *f* **II.** *vt* daller

flag day *n* **1.** *Brit: jour d'action pour des œuvres caritatives* **2.** *Am* **Flag Day** *le 14 juin, jour commémoratif de l'introduction du drapeau national*

flagon ['flægən] *n* pichet *m*

flagpole *n* hampe *f*

flagrant ['fleɪgrənt] *adj* flagrant(e)

flagship **I.** *n* NAUT vaisseau *m* **II.** *adj* (*product, store*) vedette

flagstaff *n s.* **flagpole**

flail [fleɪl] **I.** *n* fléau *m* **II.** *vi* **to ~ (about)** gigoter **III.** *vt* **to ~ one's arms about** agiter ses bras dans tous les sens

flair [fleə^r, *Am:* fler] *n no pl* flair *m;* **to have a ~ for sth** avoir du flair pour qc

flak [flæk] *n inf* (*criticism*) critiques *fpl*

flake [fleɪk] **I.** *vi* (*skin*) peler; (*paint, wood*) s'écailler **II.** *n* **1.** (*peeling*) pellicule *f;* (*of paint, metal*) écaille *f;* (*of chocolate, wood*) copeau *m;* (*of snow, cereal*) flocon *m* **2.** *Am, inf* (*freak, unusual person*) fou, folle *m, f*

◆**flake out** *vi inf* s'endormir d'épuisement

flaky ['fleɪki] <-ier, -iest> *adj* **1.** (*with brittle layers*) écaillé(e); **~ pastry** pâte *f* feuilletée **2.** *Am, inf* (*eccentric*) fou(folle)

flamboyant [flæm'bɔɪənt] *adj* (*style, personality*) haut(e) en couleur; (*gesture*) qui a du panache; (*clothes*) voyant(e)

flame [fleɪm] **I.** *n a. fig* flamme *f;* **to be/go up in ~s** être/monter en flammes **II.** *vi* **1.** (*blaze, burn*) *a. fig* flamber **2.** (*glare*) flamboyer

flaming *adj* **1.** *fig* (*angry, raging, vivid*) enflammé(e) **2.** *Brit, inf* sacré(e)

flamingo [flə'mɪŋgəʊ, *Am:* -goʊ] <-s *o* -es> *n* flamant *m*

flammable ['flæməbl] *adj* inflammable

flan [flæn] *n* tarte *f* aux fruits

Flanders ['flɑːndəz] *n* la(les) Flandre(s)

flange [flændʒ] *n* collet *m*

flank [flæŋk] **I.** *n a.* MIL flanc *m* **II.** *vt* encadrer

flannel ['flænl] *n* **1.** (*woollen material*) flanelle *f;* **~s** pantalon *m* de flanelle **2.** (*facecloth*) ≈ gant *m* de toilette, ≈ débarbouillette *f Québec,* ≈ lavette *f Suisse*

flannelette *n no pl* flanelle *f* de coton

flap [flæp] **I.** <-pp-> *vt* **to ~ sth** agiter qc; **to ~ one's wings** battre des ailes **II.** <-pp-> *vi* **1.** (*fly by waving wings*) battre des ailes **2.** (*vibrate, flutter*) battre **3.** *inf* (*become excited*) s'affoler **III.** *n* **1.** (*flutter*) battement *m* **2.** (*fold*) rabat *m* **3.** (*hinged part*) rabat *m;* (*on wing*) volet *m* de freinage; **a cat ~** une chatière **4.** *inf* (*fluster, panic*) affolement *m;* **to be in a ~** s'affoler

flapjack *n* **1.** *Am* (*pancake*) crêpe *f* **2.** *Brit* (*biscuit*) *biscuit aux flocons d'avoine*

flare [fleə^r, *Am:* fler] **I.** *n* **1.** (*blaze, burst of flame*) flamme *f* **2.** (*signal*) signal *m* (lumineux) **3.** (*widening*) évasement *m* **4.** *pl* FASHION pantalon *m* à pattes d'éléphant **II.** *vi* **1.** (*burn up*) *a. fig* s'enflammer; **tempers ~d** le ton est monté **2.** (*widen, broaden*) s'évaser; (*nostrils*) se dilater **III.** *vt* évaser; (*nostrils*) dilater; **a ~d skirt** une jupe évasée

◆**flare up** *vi* **1.** (*burn up*) s'enflammer **2.** *fig* (*dispute, anger*) éclater **3.** MED se déclencher

flare-up *n* crise *f*

flash [flæʃ] **I.** *vt* **1.** (*shine briefly*) *a. fig* (*smile,* *look*) lancer; (*signal*) envoyer; **to ~ one's headlights** faire un appel de phares; **to ~ a mirror at sb** faire miroiter un miroir en direction de qn **2.** (*show quickly*) montrer rapidement **3.** (*communicate*) **to ~ news** faire un flash d'informations **II.** *vi* **1.** (*shine briefly*) *a. fig* briller; (*headlights*) clignoter; (*eyes*) jeter des éclairs **2.** (*move swiftly*) **to ~ by/past** filer/passer comme un éclair **3.** *inf* (*expose oneself*) s'exhiber; **to ~ at sb** s'exhiber devant qn **III.** *n* **1.** (*burst of light*) éclair *m;* **a ~ of lightning** un éclair; **a ~ of wit** un trait d'esprit; **in a ~** en un rien de temps **2.** PHOT *a. fig* flash *m* **3.** RADIO, TV, PUBL flash *m* **4.** *Brit* (*military insignia or badge*) insigne *m* **IV.** <-er, -est> *adj pej, inf* tape-à-l'œil *inv*

flashback *n* CINE, LIT, THEAT flash-back *m,* rétrospective *f Québec* **flashbulb** *n* PHOT ampoule *f* de flash

flasher *n inf* exhibitionniste *m*

flash flood *n* crue *f* soudaine **flashgun** *n* appareil *m* à flash **flashlight** *n Am* lampe *f* torche **flashpoint** *n* **1.** (*critical/explosive place*) point *m* chaud **2.** CHEM (*ignition temperature of a liquid*) point *m* d'ignition

flashy <-ier, -iest> *adj pej, inf* tape-à-l'œil

flask [flɑːsk, *Am:* flæsk] *n* **1.** (*bottle*) flacon *m* **2.** (*vacuum ~*) thermos® *m o f*

flat¹ [flæt] **I.** *adj* **1.** <-ter, -test> (*smooth and level*) *a.* ANAT, MED plat(e) **2.** <-ter, -test> (*boring*) plat(e) **3.** (*stale: beer, lemonade*) qui n'a plus de bulles **4.** AUTO (*tyre, battery*) à plat **5.** (*absolute: refusal*) clair(e) et net(te) **6.** COM (*rate*) forfaitaire; (*fee*) fixe **7.** MUS bémol; *pej* faux(fausse); **A ~** la bémol ►**and that's ~** un point c'est tout **II.** *adv* **1.** (*in a position*) à plat; **to fall ~ on one's face** tomber à plat sur le visage; **to lie ~ out** être allongé à l'horizontale **2.** (*badly: sing*) faux **3.** *inf* (*absolutely*) **he turned me down ~** il m'a repoussé nettement; **to work ~ out** travailler d'arrache-pied **4.** *inf* (*exactly*) exactement; **in five minutes ~** dans exactement cinq minutes ►**to fall ~** (*joke*) faire un bide; (*plan, attempt*) échouer; (*performance*) manquer ses effets **III.** *n* **1.** (*level surface: of a sword, a knife*) côté *m* plat; **on the ~** à l'horizontale **2.** *Aus, Brit* (*deflated tyre*) pneu *m* à plat **3.** MUS bémol *m*

flat² [flæt] *n Aus, Brit* appartement *m* **flatfish** <-(es)> *n* poisson *m* plat

flatten ['flætn] *vt* aplatir

flatter *vt* flatter

flatterer *n* flatteur, -euse *m, f*

flattering *adj* flatteur(-euse)

flattery ['flætəri, *Am:* 'flæt̬-] *n no pl* flatterie *f*

flatulence ['flætjʊləns, *Am:* 'flætʃə-] *n no pl, form* flatulence *f*

flaunt [flɔːnt, *Am:* flɑːnt] *vt pej* **1.** (*show off*) fanfaronner **2.** (*flout*) défier

flautist ['flɔːtɪst, *Am:* 'flɑːt̬ɪst] *n* flûtiste *mf*

flavo(u)r ['fleɪvəʳ, *Am:* -vɚ] **I.** *n* **1.** GASTR (*taste*) goût *m;* (*of ice cream*) parfum *m;* (*of tea*) arôme *m* **2.** (*characteristic, quality*) note *m* **II.** *vt* GASTR assaisonner; (*sweet dish*) parfumer

flavo(u)ring *n* arôme *m*

flaw [flɔː, *Am:* flɑː] **I.** *n* défaut *m* **II.** *vt* abîmer; **~ed reasoning** un raisonnement fallacieux

flawless *adj* parfait(e)

flax [flæks] *n no pl* lin *m*

flay [fleɪ] *vt* (*animal*) dépecer; **to ~ sb** (**alive**) *fig, inf* écorcher qn à vif

flea [fliː] *n* puce *f*

fleabite ['fliːbaɪt] *n* **1.** (*bite*) piqûre *f* de puce **2.** *fig, inf* broutille *f*

flea-bitten *adj Brit, inf* pourri(e) **flea market** *n* marché *m* aux puces

fleck [flek] *n* **1.** (*speck*) petite tâche *f* **2.** (*particle*) particule *f*

fled [fled] *pp of* **flee**

fledgeling, fledgling ['fledʒlɪŋ] **I.** *n* oisillon *m* **II.** *adj* (*business, industry, state*) qui débute

flee [fliː] <fled> *vt, vi* fuir

fleece [fliːs] **I.** *n* **1.** (*woolly covering*) toison *f* **2.** (*material*) molleton *m* **3.** (*fabric*) laine *f* polaire **4.** (*jacket*) polaire *m* **II.** *vt* **1.** (*cut fur off from: sheep*) tondre **2.** *inf* (*cheat*) plumer

fleet¹ [fliːt] *n* flotte *f;* (*of planes*) escadron *m;* **the firm's car ~** le parc automobile de la compagnie

fleet² [fliːt] <-er, -est> *adj* **to be ~ of foot** avoir le pied léger

fleeting *adj* fugitif(-ive)

Flemish ['flemɪʃ] **I.** *adj* flamand(e) **II.** *n* **1.** (*people*) **the ~** les Flamands *mpl* **2.** LING flamand *m; s. a.* **English**

flesh [fleʃ] *n no pl* chair *f* ►**to want one's pound of ~** exiger son dû; **in the ~** en chair et en os

flesh-coloured *adj Aus, Brit* (de) couleur chair **flesh wound** *n* écorchure *f*

fleshy <-ier, -iest> *adj* (*person, limb*) dodu(e); (*fruit*) charnu(e)

flew [fluː] *pp, pt of* **fly**

flex [fleks] **I.** *vt, vi* fléchir **II.** *n* (*electrical cord*) câble *m*

flexibility [ˌfleksə'bɪləti, *Am:* -t̬i] *n no pl* flexibilité *f*

flexible ['fleksəbl] *adj* flexible

flexitime ['fleksɪtaɪm] *n no pl* horaire *m* à la carte

flick [flɪk] **I.** *vt* (*jerk*) **to ~ sth** donner une tape à qc; **to ~ a switch** pousser un bouton; **I ~ed off my shoes** j'ai ôté mes chaussures; **to ~ one's hair back** secouer ses cheveux en arrière **II.** *vi* **I ~ed through the book** j'ai feuilleté le livre; **my eyes ~ed over to the door** j'ai jeté un coup d'œil vers la porte **III.** *n* **1.** (*hit*) petit coup *m;* **at the ~ of a switch** par une simple pression sur un bouton; **with a ~ of the wrist** d'un mouvement du poignet **2.** **the ~s** *pl, inf* (*cinema*) cinoche *m*

flicker **I.** *vi* (*candle*) vaciller; (*eyes*) cligner; (*lights*) clignoter **II.** *n* **1.** (*unsteady move-*

F

ment) vacillement *m;* (*of eyes*) clignement *m* **2.** (*wavering instant: of hope*) lueur *f*

flick knife *n Aus, Brit* couteau *m* à cran d'arrêt

flier ['flaɪəʳ, *Am:* -ɚ] *n* **1.** (*air traveller*) voyageur *m* (par avion) **2.** (*leaflet*) flyer *m*

flight [flaɪt] *n* **1.** (*act of flying*) vol *m* **2.** (*escape*) *a. fig a.* ECON fuite *f;* **to take ~** prendre la fuite; **the ~ of time** la fuite du temps **3.** (*series*) ~ (**of stairs**) escalier *m;* **we climbed six ~s of stairs** on a grimpé les escaliers de six étages ►**a ~ of fancy** un rêve

flight attendant *n* (*woman*) hôtesse *f* de l'air; (*man*) steward *m* **flight controller** *n* contrôleur, -euse *m, f* de la navigation aérienne **flight deck** *n* poste *m* de pilotage

flightless *adj* (*bird*) coureur

flighty <-ier, -iest> *adj* inconstant(e); (*woman*) volage

flimsy ['flɪmzi] <-ier, -iest> *adj* **1.** (*light and thin: dress, blouse*) léger(-ère) **2.** (*easily broken: construction, structure*) peu solide **3.** (*lacking seriousness: excuse*) faible

flinch [flɪntʃ] *vi* tressaillir; **without ~ing** sans frémir; **to ~ from doing sth** hésiter à faire qc

fling [flɪŋ] <flung> **I.** *vt a. fig* jeter; (*ball*) lancer; **I flung the money back at them** je leur ai renvoyé l'argent à la figure; **to be flung into jail** être jeté en prison **II.** *n* **1.** (*good time*) bon temps *m* **2.** (*affair*) aventure *m*

◆**fling away** *vt* jeter

◆**fling off** *vt* se défaire de

◆**fling on** *vt fam* enfiler

◆**fling open** *vt* ouvrir brusquement

◆**fling out I.** *vt* jeter **II.** *vi* **to ~ of the room** sortir brusquement de la pièce

flint [flɪnt] *n* MIN silex *m*

flip [flɪp] <-pp-> **I.** *vt* (*turn over*) **to ~ sth** (**over**) retourner qc; **to ~ over a pancake** faire sauter une crêpe; **to ~ a coin** lancer une pièce; **to ~ a switch** pousser un bouton **II.** *vi* **1.** (*turn quickly*) **to ~ over** tourner **2.** *inf* (*go mad*) péter les plombs **III.** *n* salto *m*

flip chart *n* paperboard *m*

flip-flop ['flɪpflɒp, *Am:* -flɑːp] *n* **1.** FASHION ~s tongs *fpl* **2.** SPORT saut *m* périlleux

flippancy ['flɪpəntsi] *n no pl* désinvolture *f*

flippant *adj* désinvolte

flipper *n* **1.** ZOOL aileron *m* **2.** (*swimming aid*) palme *f*

flip side *n* **1.** MUS face *f* B **2.** *fig* verso *m*

flirt [flɜːt, *Am:* flɜːrt] **I.** *n* dragueur, -euse *m, f* **II.** *vi* flirter; **to ~ with sb** flirter avec qn; **to ~ with the idea of doing sth** *fig* flirter avec l'idée de faire qc

flirtation [flɜː'teɪʃən, *Am:* flɜːr'-] *n a. fig* flirt *m*

flirtatious *adj* flirteur(-euse)

flit [flɪt] <-tt-> *vi* **1.** (*fly*) voleter **2.** (*move*) aller d'un pas léger **3.** (*pass*) **an idea ~ed through her mind** une idée lui traversa l'esprit

float [fləʊt, *Am:* floʊt] **I.** *vi* **1.** (*on water, air*) *a. fig* flotter; (*boat*) être à flot; **to ~ to the surface** remonter à la surface; **to ~ down the stream** flotter dans le ruisseau (dans le sens du courant); **balloons ~ed by** des ballons flottaient en l'air; **music/the smell of cooking ~ed through the window** de la musique/une odeur de cuisine sortait de la fenêtre **2.** (*move aimlessly*) errer **3.** ECON (*fluctuate in exchange rate*) flotter **II.** *vt* **1.** (*keep afloat*) faire flotter; (*boat*) mettre à flot **2.** ECON, FIN (*offer on the stock market*) introduire en bourse **3.** (*put forward: idea, plan*) lancer **4.** FIN (*currency*) laisser flotter **III.** *n* **1.** (*buoyant device*) flotteur *m;* (*on fishing line*) bouchon *m* **2.** (*decorated parade vehicle*) char *m* **3.** *Aus, Brit* (*cash*) fonds *m* de caisse

◆**float about** *vi,* **float around** *vi fig, inf* (*people, rumour*) circuler

◆**float off** *vi* dériver

floatation [fləʊ'teɪʃən, *Am:* floʊ-] *n s.* **flotation**

floating *adj a. fig* flottant(e)

floating capital *n* FIN fonds *m* de roulement **floating voter** *n* voteur *m* indécis

flock [flɒk, *Am:* flɑːk] **I.** *n* **1.** (*group*) troupeau *m;* (*of birds*) volée *f;* (*of people*) foule *f* **2.** REL ouailles *fpl* **II.** *vi* s'attrouper; **people ~ed to hear him** les gens s'attroupaient pour l'entendre

floe [fləʊ, *Am:* floʊ] *n* bloc *m* de glace; (**ice**) **~s** glaces *fpl* flottantes

flog [flɒg, *Am:* flɑːg] <-gg-> *vt* **1.** (*punish*) fouetter **2.** *Brit, inf* (*sell*) fourguer **3.** *inf* **to be ~ging a dead horse** être en train de perdre son temps

flogging *n* raclée *f*

flood [flʌd] **I.** *vt* **1.** (*overflow*) *a. fig* inonder; (*person*) submerger; **a river ~s its banks** une rivière sort de son lit; **we've been ~ed with protests** nous avons été inondés de protestations **2.** AGR, ECOL (*valley*) irriguer **3.** AUTO (*engine*) noyer **II.** *vi* être inondé; (*river*) déborder; (*people*) affluer **III.** *n* **1.** (*overflow*) inondation *f;* **in ~** en décrue; **the ~s of a river** les crues d'une rivière; **~s of light** des flots de lumière **2.** (*outpouring*) flot *m;* (*of mail, calls*) déluge *m;* (*of products*) invasion *f;* **~s of tears** des torrents de larmes **3.** REL **the Flood** le Déluge

◆**flood back** *vi* remonter à la surface

◆**flood in** *vi* (*water, light*) couler à flots; (*people, mail*) affluer

◆**flood out** *vi* sortir à flots

floodgates *n pl* **to open the ~** ouvrir les vannes **floodlight I.** *n* projecteur *m* **II.** <irr> *vt* éclairer aux projecteurs **flood plain** *n* plaine *f* inondable **flood tide** *n* marée *f* haute **flood waters** *n* crues *fpl;* **the ~ of the Nile** les crues du Nil

floor [flɔːʳ, *Am:* flɔːr] **I.** *n* **1.** (*surface*) sol *m;* (*wooden*) plancher *m* **2.** (*level of a building*) étage *m;* **ground ~ apartment** appartement *m* de plein pied; **first** ~ *Brit* premier étage *m; Am* rez-de-chaussée *m* **3.** GEO (*bottom: of ocean*) fond *m;* (*of forest*) sol *m* **4.** ECON, POL (*place of formal discussion*) **the** ~ le parquet; **to have the** ~ avoir la parole ►**to go through the** ~ (*prices*) toucher le plancher; **to take the** ~ prendre la parole; (*stand up and start dancing*) aller sur la piste de danse **II.** *vt* **1.** (*make floor out of sth*) **to** ~ **a room** poser un revêtement de sol dans une pièce; (*with wood*) parqueter une pièce **2.** (*knock down*) terrasser **3.** (*shock*) désarçonner

floorboard *n* lame *f* de parquet **floorcloth** *n* serpillière *f,* panosse *f Suisse,* wassingue *f Nord*

flooring *n no pl* revêtement *m* de sol

floor lamp *n Am* lampadaire *m* **floor show** *n* animation *f* **floorwalker** *n Am* surveillant(e) *m(f)* dans un magasin

flop [flɒp, *Am:* flɑːp] <-pp-> **I.** *vi* **1.** (*fall*) tomber; (*on seat*) s'affaler **2.** (*fail*) faire un bide **II.** *n inf* flop *m;* **to be a** ~ être un bide

floppy <-ier, -iest> *adj* (*hat, hair*) mou(molle); (*ears*) pendant(e)

floppy (disk) *n* disquette *f*

flora ['flɔːrə] *n no pl* flore *f*

floral *adj* **1.** (*of flowers*) floral(e) **2.** (*depicting flowers*) fleuri(e)

florid ['flɒrɪd, *Am:* 'flɔːr-] *adj* **1.** (*excessively ornamented: style*) ampoulé(e); (*architectural style*) surchargé(e) **2.** *form* (*ruddy*) ~ **complexion** teint *m* rose

Florida ['flɒrɪdə, *Am:* 'flɔːr-] *n* Floride *f*

florist ['flɒrɪst, *Am:* 'flɔːr-] *n* fleuriste *mf*

floss [flɒs, *Am:* flɑːs] **I.** *n* (**dental**) ~ fil *m* dentaire **II.** *vt, vi* **to** ~ (**one's teeth**) se passer du fil dentaire

flotation [fləʊ'teɪʃən, *Am:* floʊ-] *n* FIN introduction *f* en bourse

flotilla [flə'tɪlə, *Am:* floʊ-] *n* flottille *f*

flotsam (**and jetsam**) *n no pl, a. fig* épave *f*

flounce[1] [flaʊnts] *vi* **to** ~ **in/out** entrer/sortir dans un mouvement d'humeur

flounce[2] [flaʊnts] *n* volant *m*

flounder[1] ['flaʊndəʳ, *Am:* -dɚ] *vi* patauger

flounder[2] ['flaʊndəʳ, *Am:* -dɚ] *n* flet *m*

flour ['flaʊəʳ, *Am:* -ɚ] **I.** *n no pl* farine *f* **II.** *vt* **to** ~ **sth** saupoudrer qc de farine

flourish ['flʌrɪʃ, *Am:* 'flɜːr-] **I.** *vi* (*children*) s'épanouir; (*company, school*) prospérer **II.** *vt* brandir **III.** *n* geste *m* théâtral; **with a** ~ d'un geste théâtral

flourishing *adj* florissant(e)

floury ['flaʊəri] <-ier, -iest> *adj* farineux(-euse)

flout [flaʊt] *vt* dédaigner

flow [fləʊ, *Am:* floʊ] **I.** *vi a. fig* couler; (*stream, blood*) circuler; (*air*) passer; (*drinks*) couler à flots; **to** ~ **from sth** découler de qc; **the river ~s through the town** la rivière traverse la ville **II.** *n sing* écoulement *m;* (*of people, words*) flot *m;* (*of capital, tide*) flux *m;* (*of traffic*) affluence *f;* (*of data*) flux *m* ►**to go with the** ~ suivre le courant; **to go against the** ~ aller à contre-courant; **in full** ~ en plein discours

flow chart, **flow diagram** *n* organigramme *m*

flower ['flaʊəʳ, *Am:* 'flaʊɚ] **I.** *n* fleur *f;* **to be in** ~ être en fleur **II.** *vi a. fig* fleurir

flower arrangement *n* composition *f* florale **flower bed** *n* parterre *m* de fleurs

flowered *adj* fleuri(e)

flower pot *n* pot *m* de fleurs

flowery <-ier, -iest> *adj a. pej* fleuri(e)

flown [fləʊn, *Am:* floʊn] *pp of* **fly**

flu [fluː] *n no pl* grippe *f*

fluctuate ['flʌktʃʊeɪt] *vi* fluctuer

fluctuation *n* fluctuation *f*

flue [fluː] *n* hotte *f*

fluency ['fluːəntsi] *n no pl* aisance *f*

fluent *adj* éloquent(e); **to be** ~ **in Portuguese** parler couramment le portugais; **a** ~ **German speaker** une personne qui parle couramment l'allemand

fluently *adv* couramment

fluff [flʌf] **I.** *n no pl* **1.** (*on clothes*) peluches *fpl* **2.** (*down*) duvet *m* **3.** (*dust*) moutons *mpl* de poussière **4.** (*mistake*) raté *m* **II.** *vt inf* rater

fluffy <-ier, -iest> *adj* **1.** (*of or like fluff*) duveteux(-euse); (*clothes*) moelleux(-euse) **2.** GASTR mousseux(-euse)

fluid ['fluːɪd] **I.** *n* fluide *m* **II.** *adj* fluide

flung [flʌŋ] *pp/pt of* **fling**

flunk [flʌŋk] *Am* **I.** *vt inf* se faire recaler en **II.** *vi inf* se faire recaler

fluorescence [flʊə'resns, *Am:* flɔː-] *n no pl* fluorescence *f*

fluorescent *adj* fluorescent(e)

fluoridation *n no pl* fluoration *f*

fluoride ['flʊəraɪd, *Am:* 'flɔːraɪd] *n no pl* CHEM fluor *m*

fluorine ['flʊəriːn, *Am:* 'flɔːriːn] *n no pl* CHEM fluorine *f*

fluorocarbon [ˌflʊərə'kɑːbən, *Am:* ˌflɔːrə'kɑːr-] *n* CHEM chlorofluorocarbone *m*

flurry ['flʌri, *Am:* 'flɜːr-] <-ies> *n a. fig* bourrasque *f;* ~ **of excitement** agitation *f* soudaine

flush[1] [flʌʃ] **I.** *vi* **1.** (*blush*) rougir **2.** (*operate toilet*) tirer la chasse d'eau; **the lavatory didn't** ~ la chasse d'eau n'a pas fonctionné **II.** *vt* **1.** (*cleanse*) **to** ~ **the toilet** tirer la chasse; **to** ~ **sth down the toilet** jeter qc dans les toilettes **2.** (*redden*) faire rougir **III.** *n* **1.** (*reddening*) rougeur *m* **2.** (*rush: of anger, emotion*) accès *m;* (*of pleasure, enthusiasm*) élan *m;* **in the first** ~ **of youth** dans tout l'éclat de sa jeunesse **3.** (*cleansing device*) chasse *f* d'eau; **to pull the** ~ tirer la chasse d'eau

◆**flush out** *vt* (*traitors, spies*) débusquer

flush[2] *adj* **1.** (*level or flat*) de niveau **2.** *inf* (*rich*) qui a des sous

flushed *adj* rouge; ~ **with anger** rouge de colère

fluster ['flʌstəʳ, *Am:* -tɚ] **I.** *vt* **to** ~ **sb** rendre qn nerveux **II.** *n no pl* nervosité *f;* **to be in a** ~ être agité

flute [flu:t] *n* MUS flûte *f*

flutist *n Am s.* **flautist**

flutter ['flʌtəʳ, *Am:* 'flʌt̬ɚ] **I.** *n* **1.** (*act of fluttering: of wings, lashes*) battement *m;* (*of leave, papers*) voltigement *m;* (*of heart*) palpitation *f* **2.** *fig* (*nervousness*) agitation *f;* **to put in/to be all of a** ~ rendre/être nerveux **3.** *sing, Aus, Brit, inf* (*bet*) pari *m;* **to have a** ~ faire un pari **II.** *vi* **1.** (*fly*) voleter; (*bird*) battre des ailes **2.** (*move*) s'agiter; (*heart*) palpiter; (*leaves, papers*) voltiger; (*lashes*) battre; (*flag*) flotter **III.** *vt* **to** ~ **its wings** battre des ailes; **to** ~ **one's eyelashes** battre des cils

fluvial ['flu:vɪəl] *adj* fluvial(e)

flux [flʌks] *n no pl* flux *m;* **to be in a state of** ~ être en mouvement perpétuel

fly¹ [flaɪ] *n* (*trouser zip*) **flies** *Brit* braguette *f*

fly² [flaɪ] <flew, flown> **I.** *vi* **1.** (*travel in air*) voler; **to** ~ **over the Pacific** voler au-dessus du Pacifique **2.** (*travel by plane*) voyager par avion; **to** ~ **first class/in Concorde** voyager par avion en première classe/sur Concorde; **to** ~ **to Canada** aller au Canada par avion; **to** ~ **into/out of Dublin** aller à/partir de Dublin par avion **3.** (*move quickly: arrows, glass, stones*) voler; **he sent me ~ing** il m'a fait faire un vol plané; **he sent the vase ~ing** il a envoyé le vase en l'air **4.** (*hurry*) foncer; **he flew downstairs** il a foncé en bas; **he saw me and flew** dès qu'il m'a vu il a filé; **to** ~ **into a temper** piquer une colère; **the weeks flew by** *fig* les semaines sont passées comme un souffle **5.** (*wave: flag, hair*) voler ▶**to** ~ **in the face of logic/reason** dépasser toute logique/l'entendement; **sb ~s off the handle** la moutarde monte au nez de qn; **to let** ~ **at sb** voler dans les plumes de qn **II.** *vt* **1.** (*pilot: plane*) piloter; **to** ~ **passengers/supplies to a country** transporter des passagers/des approvisionnements par avion vers un pays **2.** (*make move through air: kite*) faire voler; **to** ~ **the UN flag** faire flotter le drapeau des Nations Unies

fly³ *n* (*small winged insect*) mouche *f* ▶**sb wouldn't harm a** ~ qn ne ferait pas de mal à une mouche; **to drop like flies** *inf* tomber comme des mouches; ~ **in the ointment** un cheveu dans la soupe; **on the** ~ *Am* en vitesse

◆**fly away** *vi* s'envoler

◆**fly in** **I.** *vi* arriver en avion **II.** *vt* (*aid, troops*) acheminer par avion

◆**fly off** *vi* s'envoler

◆**fly out** *vi* **to** ~ **to somewhere** s'envoler quelque part

flyaway *adj* (*hair*) indiscipliné(e) **fly-by-night** *adj pej, inf* fantôme **flycatcher** *n* ZOOL colibri *m*

flyer *s.* **flier**

flying **I.** *n no pl* vol *m;* **to be afraid of** ~ avoir peur de l'avion **II.** *adj* **1.** (*able to move: insect*) volant(e) **2.** (*moving in the air: glass, object*) qui vole **3.** (*hurried: visit*) éclair *inv* **4.** (*related to flight: accident*) d'avion; (*lesson*) de pilotage; (*jacket*) de pilote

flying boat *n* hydravion *m* **flying buttress** *n* ARCHIT arc-boutant *m* **flying doctor** *n* médecin *m* volant **flying fish** *n* poisson *m* volant **flying fox** *n* ZOOL macroscélide *m* **flying saucer** *n* soucoupe *f* volante **flying start** *n* SPORT départ *m* en flèche ▶**get off to a** ~ avoir un très bon départ

flyleaf <flyleaves> *n* page *f* de garde **flyover** *n* **1.** *Brit* (*elevated road*) pont *m* routier **2.** *Am s.* **flypast** **flypaper** *n* papier *m* tue-mouche **fly-past** *n* MIL défilé *m* aérien **fly-sheet** *n Brit* double-toit *m* **flytrap** *n* piège *m* à mouches **flyweight** *n* SPORT poids *m* mouche **flywheel** *n* TECH volant *m*

FM [ˌef'em] *n abbr of* **frequency modulation** FM *f*

FO [ˌef'əʊ, *Am:* -oʊ] *n Brit abbr of* **Foreign Office** ministère *m* des affaires étrangères

foal [fəʊl, *Am:* foʊl] *n* poulain *m* ▶**to be in** ~ être pleine

foam [fəʊm, *Am:* foʊm] **I.** *n no pl* mousse *f;* **shaving** ~ mousse à raser **II.** *vi* écumer; (*soap, beer*) mousser; **to** ~ **at the mouth** (*horse*) avoir de l'écume aux lèvres; (*person*) écumer de rage

foam bath *n* bain *m* moussant **foam rubber** *n* caoutchouc *m* mousse

foamy <-ier, -iest> *adj* moussant(e)

fob [fɒb, *Am:* fɑ:b] *n* chaîne *f*

focal ['fəʊkl, *Am:* 'foʊ-] *adj* focal(e)

focal point *n* **1.** (*focus*) foyer *m* **2.** (*central point*) point *m* central

focus ['fəʊkəs, *Am:* 'foʊ-] <-es *o* foci> **I.** *n* **1.** (*centre: of interest, attention*) centre *m;* (*of unrest, discontent*) foyer *m;* **to be the** ~ **of attention** être le centre d'attention **2.** PHYS (*converging point*) *a. fig* foyer *m;* **to be in** ~ être net; **to be out of** ~ être flou; **to bring sth into** ~ mettre qc au point; **to bring sth in(to)** ~ mettre qc au clair **3.** MED foyer *m* **II.** <-s- *o* -ss-> *vi* **1.** (*see clearly*) régler; **to** ~ **on sth** regarder fixement qc **2.** (*concentrate*) **to** ~ **on sth** focaliser sur qc; **try and** ~ **on the exam/the details** essaie de te concentrer sur l'examen/les détails **III.** *vt* **1.** (*concentrate*) concentrer; **to** ~ **one's attention on sth** focaliser son attention sur qc **2.** (*bring into focus*) focaliser; (*lens*) mettre au point; **to** ~ **a camera** faire la mise au point

focus group *n* groupe *m* témoin

fodder ['fɒdəʳ, *Am:* 'fɑ:dɚ] *n no pl* fourrage *m*

foe [fəʊ, *Am:* foʊ] *n form* ennemi(e) *m(f)*

foetal ['fi:təl, *Am:* -t̬əl] *adj* BIO fœtal(e)

foetus ['fi:təs, *Am:* -t̬əs] *n* fœtus *m*

fog [fɒg, *Am:* fɑ:g] **I.** *n a. fig* brouillard *m;* **to be in a** ~ être dans le brouillard **II.** <-gg-> *vt* **1.** (*cover with fog*) embuer **2.** *fig* (*obscure*) brouiller; **the photo is ~ged** la photo est voilée

fog bank *n* banc *m* de brouillard **fogbound** *adj* bloqué(e) par le brouillard
fogey ['fəʊgi, *Am:* 'foʊ-] *n pej, inf* hurluberlu *m;* **old** ~ vieil hurluberlu
foggy ['fɒgi, *Am:* 'fɑːgi] <-ier, -iest> *adj* brumeux(-euse) ►**not to have the foggiest (idea)** *impers* ne pas (en) avoir la moindre idée
foghorn *n* corne *f* de brume **fog lamp, fog light** *n* phare *m* antibrouillard
fogy ['fɒgi, *Am:* 'fɑːgi] <-ies> *n inf s.* **fogey**
foible ['fɔɪbl] *n* particularité *f*
foil[1] [fɔɪl] *n* **1.** (*wrap*) papier *m* d'aluminium **2.** *fig* repoussoir *m*
foil[2] [fɔɪl] *vt* faire échouer; (*plan*) contrecarrer
foil[3] [fɔɪl] *n* SPORT fleuret *m*
◆**foist on, foist upon** *vt* **to foist sth (up)on sb** imposer qc à qn
fold[1] [fəʊld, *Am:* foʊld] *n* **1.** (*sheep pen*) parc *m* à moutons **2.** *fig* (*home*) **the** ~ le bercail
fold[2] [fəʊld, *Am:* foʊld] **I.** *vt* **1.** (*bend over upon self*) plier; (*wings*) replier **2.** (*wrap*) envelopper; **to** ~ **one's arms** croiser les bras; **to** ~ **one's hands** joindre les mains; **with** ~**ed arms** les bras croisés **3.** GASTR **to** ~ **sth into sth** incorporer peu à peu qc dans qc **II.** *vi* **1.** (*bend over upon self*) se plier **2.** (*fail or go bankrupt: business*) mettre la clé sous le paillasson; (*play*) quitter l'affiche **III.** *n* pli *m*
◆**fold up I.** *vt* plier **II.** *vi* se plier
folder *n* **1.** (*cover, holder*) chemise *f* **2.** INFOR classeur *m* **3.** *Am* (*leaflet*) prospectus *m*
folding *adj* pliant(e)
foliage ['fəʊlɪɪdʒ, *Am:* 'foʊ-] *n no pl* feuillage *m*
folio ['fəʊliəʊ, *Am:* 'foʊlioʊ] *n* folio *m*
folk [fəʊk, *Am:* foʊk] **I.** *n* **1.** *pl* (*specific class/group of people*) gens *mpl;* **farming** ~ agriculteurs *mpl;* **old** ~ personnes *fpl* âgées; **ordinary** ~ gens *mpl* ordinaires **2.** *pl, inf* (*parents*) vieux *mpl* **3.** *no pl* MUS folk *m* **II.** *adj* MUS folklorique; (*music*) folk *inv;* (*hero, tale*) populaire; (*medicine*) traditionnel(le)
folk dance *n* danse *f* folklorique
folklore ['fəʊklɔːʳ, *Am:* 'foʊklɔːr] *n no pl* folklore *m*
folk song *n* chanson *f* folk
folksy ['fəʊksi, *Am:* 'foʊk-] <-ier, -iest> *adj* **1.** (*folk*) traditionnel(le) **2.** (*informal*) sans façon
foll. *adj abbr of* **followed or following** suiv
follow ['fɒləʊ, *Am:* 'fɑːloʊ] **I.** *vt* **1.** (*come, go after*) *a. fig* suivre; **to be** ~**ed by sth** être suivi de qc **2.** (*adhere to: instructions, example*) suivre; (*leader*) être le disciple de; (*team*) être supporter de **3.** (*practise, carry out: diet*) suivre; (*career*) poursuivre; (*profession*) exercer **4.** (*understand, watch closely*) suivre ►**to** ~ **one's nose** *inf* y aller au pif; **to** ~ **suit** faire de même **II.** *vi* **1.** (*take same route*) suivre **2.** (*come/happen next*) suivre; **what's to** ~**?** qu'est-ce qu'il y a après? **3.** (*result*) s'ensuivre; **that doesn't** ~ ce n'est pas logique
◆**follow on** *vi* suivre; **to** ~ **from sth** résulter de qc
◆**follow out** *vt* poursuivre; (*orders*) exécuter; (*instructions*) suivre
◆**follow through I.** *vt* mener à terme **II.** *vi* aller jusqu'au bout
◆**follow up I.** *vt* (*lead, suggestion*) donner suite à; (*patient*) suivre; **they followed up their success with a new record** après leur succès ils ont battu un nouveau record **II.** *vi* **to** ~ **on a question** ajouter quelque chose sur un point
follower *n* **1.** (*supporter*) disciple *mf* **2.** POL partisan(e) *m(f)* **3.** SPORT supporter *mf*
following I. *n* **1.** (*explanation*) **the** ~ ce qui suit; **I'd say the** ~ je dirais ceci; **my idea was the** ~ mon idée était la suivante **2.** *pl* (*listed things or people*) **the** ~ les choses/personnes suivantes **3.** *sing* (*group of supporters: of an idea*) partisans *mpl;* (*of a doctrine*) disciples *mpl;* (*of a shop*) clientèle *f;* **the programme has quite a** ~ l'émission a beaucoup de fidèles **II.** *adj inv* **1.** (*next or listed*) suivant(e); **the** ~ **ideas** les idées que voici **2.** (*from behind: wind*) arrière *inv* **III.** *prep* après; ~ **this consultation** après cette consultation
follow-up I. *n* **1.** (*continuation*) suite *f* **2.** MED suivi *m* **II.** *adj* (*work*) de suivi; MED (*visit*) de contrôle; (*letter*) de rappel; (*article*) complémentaire
folly ['fɒli, *Am:* 'fɑːli] *n* folie *f;* **to be a** [*o* **an act of**] ~ être de la folie
fond [fɒnd, *Am:* fɑːnd] <-er, -est> *adj* **1.** (*liking*) **to be** ~ **of sb/sth** aimer beaucoup qn/qc **2.** (*loving, tender: memories, gesture*) bon; (*gesture*) tendre **3.** (*foolish: hope*) naïf(naïve)
fondle ['fɒndl, *Am:* 'fɑːn-] <-ling> *vt* caresser
fondness *n no pl* penchant *m;* **a** ~ **for sth** un penchant pour qc
font [fɒnt, *Am:* fɑːnt] *n* TYP, INFOR police *f* de caractères
food [fuːd] *n* nourriture *f;* **have we got enough** ~**?** est-ce qu'il a assez à manger?; **he loves his** ~ il aime bien manger; **dairy** ~**s** produits *mpl* laitiers; **Italian** ~ la cuisine italienne ►~ **for thought** matière *f* à penser
food chain *n* chaîne *f* alimentaire **food poisoning** *n no pl* intoxication *f* alimentaire **food processor** *n* robot *m* **foodstuff** *n* produit *m* alimentaire
fool [fuːl] **I.** *n* **1.** (*silly person*) idiot(e) *m(f);* **to act the** ~ faire l'idiot; **to be** ~ **enough to** +*infin* être assez stupide pour +*infin;* **to make a** ~ **of sb** tourner qn en ridicule; **to make a** ~ **of oneself** se ridiculiser **2.** (*jester*) fou *m* **3.** (*dessert*) ≈ crème *f* de fruits **II.** *vt* duper; **you can't** ~ **me!** tu ne peux rien me cacher!; **you could have** ~**ed me!** tu plaisantes! **III.** *vi* **to** ~ **about** [*o* **around**] faire l'imbécile **IV.** *adj* stupide
foolhardy *adj* audacieux(-euse)

F

foolish *adj* bête
foolproof *adj* (*machine*) très simple à utiliser; (*idea*) très simple (à mettre en pratique) **foolscap** *n no pl* papier *m* ministre
foot [fʊt] **I.** <feet> *n* **1.** (*of person, object*) pied *m;* (*of animal*) patte *f;* **on ~** à pied; **to get to one's feet** se lever **2.** (*unit*) pied *m* **3.** (*lower part*) pied *m;* **at the ~ of the bed** au pied du lit; **at the ~ of the page** au bas de la page ►**to be back on one's feet** être de nouveau sur pieds; **to have a ~ in both camps** avoir un pied dans chaque camp; **to have one ~ in the grave** avoir un pied dans la tombe; **to have both feet on the ground** avoir les deux pieds sur terre; **to get off on the right/wrong ~** bien/mal commencer; **to fall on your feet** retomber sur ses pieds; **to put your ~ in it** [*o* **one's ~ in one's mouth**] mettre les pieds dans le plat; **to set ~ in sth** mettre les pieds dans qc **II.** *vt* **to ~ the bill** payer la facture
footage ['fʊtɪdʒ, *Am:* 'fʊt̬-] *n no pl* **1.** (*length*) métrage *m* **2.** (*sequence*) séquences *fpl*
foot-and-mouth disease *n* fièvre *f* aphteuse
football ['fʊtbɔːl] *n no pl* **1.** (*soccer*) football *m* **2.** *Am* (**American**) ~ football *m* américain **3.** (*ball*) ballon *f* de football
footballer *n* footballeur, -euse *m, f*
football hooligan *n* hooligan *mf*
foot brake *n* pédale de frein **footbridge** *n* passerelle *f*
footer *n* INFOR pied *m* de page
foothills *n* contreforts *mpl* **foothold** *n* prise *f;* **to gain a ~** *fig* prendre pied
footing *n no pl* **1.** (*grip*) **to lose one's ~** perdre pied **2.** (*basis*) pied *m;* **on a war ~** sur le pied de guerre; **on an equal ~** sur un pied d'égalité
footlights *npl* rampe *f* **footling** *adj* ridicule **footloose** *adj* libre ►**~ and fancy-free** libre comme l'air **footman** <-men> *n* laquais *m* **footnote** *n* note *f* (de bas de page) **footpath** *n* sentier *m* **footprint** *n* empreinte *f* de pied **footrest** *n* repose-pied *m*
footsie ['fʊtsi] *n no pl, inf* **to play ~ with sb** faire du pied à qn
footslog ['fʊtslɒg] <-gg-> *vi inf* marcher
footstep *n* pas *m* ►**to follow in sb's ~s** suivre les traces de qn **footstool** *n* repose-pied *m* **footwear** *n no pl* chaussures *fpl* **footwork** *n no pl* jeu *m* de jambes
for [fɔːʳ, *Am:* fɔːr] **I.** *prep* **1.** pour **2.** (*to give to*) pour; **to do sth ~ sb/sth** faire qc pour qn/qc; **open the door for me, ouvre-moi la porte, to ask/look ~ oneself** demander/regarder (par) soi-même **3.** (*as purpose*) **~ sale/rent** à vendre/louer; **something ~ a headache** quelque chose contre la migraine; **it's time ~ lunch/bed** c'est l'heure du déjeuner/de se coucher; **to invite sb ~ lunch** inviter qn à déjeuner; **to go ~ a walk** aller se promener; **fit ~ nothing** bon à rien; **what ~?** pour quoi faire?; **what's that ~?** à quoi ça sert?; **it's ~ cutting cheese** c'est pour couper le fromage; **to use sth ~ a wedge** utiliser qc comme cale; **~ this to be possible** pour que cela soit possible *subj;* **to look ~ a way to** *+infin* chercher un moyen de *+infin* **4.** (*to acquire*) **eager ~ power/affection** avide de pouvoir/assoiffé d'affection; **to search ~ sth** chercher qc; **to go ~ sb** aller chercher qn; **to ask/hope ~ news** demander/espérer des nouvelles; **to apply ~ a job** faire une demande d'emploi; **to shout ~ help** appeler à l'aide; **to give sth ~ sth else** échanger qc contre qc d'autre; **oh ~ a glass of water!** si seulement j'avais un verre d'eau! **5.** (*towards*) **the train ~ Glasgow** le train pour Glasgow; **to make ~ home** s'apprêter à rentrer chez soi; **to run ~ safety** se sauver en courant; **to reach ~ sc** rattraper qc **6.** (*distance of*) **to walk ~ 8 km** marcher pendant 8 km **7.** (*amount of time*) **~ now** pour l'instant; **~ a while/a time** pendant un moment/un certain temps; **to last ~ hours** durer des heures; **I'm going to be here ~ three weeks** je suis ici pour trois semaines; **I haven't been there ~ three years** je n'y ai pas été depuis trois ans; **I have known her ~ years** je la connais depuis des années; **not ~ another 3 months** pas avant 3 mois **8.** (*on date of*) **to plan sth/have sth finished ~ Sunday** organiser/avoir fini qc pour dimanche; **to set the wedding ~ May 4** fixer le mariage au 4 mai **9.** (*in support of*) **is he ~ or against it?** est-il pour ou contre?; **to fight ~ sth** lutter en faveur de qc **10.** (*employed by*) **to work ~ sb/a company** travailler chez qn/pour une firme **11.** (*the task of*) **it's ~ him to** *+infin* c'est à lui de *+infin* **12.** (*in substitution*) **the substitute ~ the teacher** le remplaçant du professeur; **say hello ~ me** dis/dites bonjour de ma part; **to work/feel ~ sb** travailler à la place de/compatir avec qn **13.** (*as price of*) **a check ~ £100** un chèque de 100£; **I paid £10 ~ it** je l'ai payé 10£ **14.** (*concerning*) **as ~ me/that** quant à moi/cela; **two are enough ~ me** deux me suffiront; **too hard ~ me** trop dur pour moi; **sorry ~ doing sth** désolé d'avoir fait qc; **the best would be ~ me to go** il vaudrait mieux que je parte *subj* **15.** (*in reference to*) **I ~ Italy** I comme Italie; **what's the Chinese ~ "book"?** comment dit-on "livre" en chinois?; **to make it easy/hard ~ sb** (**to do sth**) faciliter/compliquer la tâche à qn **16.** (*as cause*) **excuse me ~ being late** excuse-/excusez-moi d'être en retard; **as the reason ~ one's behaviour** comme raison de son comportement; **in prison for fraud** en prison pour fraude; **~ lack of sth** à cause d'un manque de qc **17.** (*as reason*) **to do sth ~ love** faire qc par amour; **~ fear of doing sth** de peur de faire qc; **to cry ~ joy** pleurer de joie; **he can't talk ~ laughing** le fou rire l'empêche de parler **18.** (*despite*) **~ all that/her money** malgré tout/tout son argent; **~ all I**

know autant que je sache *subj* **19.** (*as*) ~ **example** par exemple; **he** ~ **one** lui par exemple ►**he's** <u>**in**</u> ~ **it!** ça va être sa fête!; **that's kids** ~ <u>**you**</u>**!** c'est typique des gosses! **II.** *conj form* car

forage ['fɒrɪdʒ, *Am:* 'fɔːr-] **I.** *vi* fourrager; **to** ~ **for food** fourrager à la recherche de la nourriture **II.** *n no pl* fourrage *m*

foray ['fɒreɪ, *Am:* 'fɔːr-] *n a. fig* incursion *f*

forbad(**e**) [fə'bæd, *Am:* fɚ-] *pt of* **forbid**

forbear [fɔː'beəʳ, *Am:* fɔːr'ber] <forbore, forborne> *form* **I.** *vi* s'abstenir; **to** ~ **from doing sth** se garder de faire qc **II.** *vi* s'abstenir de **III.** *n s.* **forebear**

forbearance *n no pl, form* indulgence *f*

forbid [fə'bɪd, *Am:* fɚ-] <forbade, forbidden> *vt* interdire; **to** ~ **sb sth** interdire qc à qn; **to** ~ **sb from doing sth** interdire à qn de faire qc ►<u>**God**</u> ~ jamais de la vie!

forbidden **I.** *adj* interdit(e) **II.** *pp of* **forbid**

forbidding *adj* sinistre

forbore [fɔː'bɔːʳ, *Am:* fɔːr'bɔːr] *pt of* **forbear**

forborne [fɔː'bɔːn, *Am:* fɔːr'bɔːrn] *pp of* **forbear**

force [fɔːs, *Am:* fɔːrs] **I.** *n a.* PHYS force *f;* **to be in** ~ être en vigueur; **to come in** ~ arriver en masse; **by sheer** ~ **of numbers** par la force du nombre; **by** ~ **of habit** par habitude; **the** ~ **of sb's personality** le force de caractère de qn; **the** (**Police**) **Force** la police **II.** *vt* forcer; **to** ~ **sb/oneself to** *+infin* forcer qn/se forcer à *+infin;* **to** ~ **one's way** se frayer un chemin; **to** ~ **sth into a suitcase** tasser qc dans une valise; **to** ~ **sb out of the way** forcer qn hors de son chemin; **to** ~ **a smile** faire un sourire forcé; **to** ~ **oneself on sb** s'imposer à qn; **to** ~ **sb into doing sth** forcer qn à faire qc; **the changes were** ~**d on us** on nous a imposé les changements; **to** ~ **a confession out of sb** obtenir une confession par la force ►**to** ~ **sb's** <u>**hand**</u> forcer la main de qn; **to** ~ **an** <u>**issue**</u> forcer une décision

◆**force down** *vt* **1.** (*swallow*) avaler de force **2.** AVIAT faire atterrir de force

◆**force open** *vt* forcer

◆**force out** *vt* **to force sb out** pousser qn dehors

◆**force through** *vt* (*law*) paire passer; (*changes*) précipiter

forced *adj* forcé(e)

force-feed *vt* nourrir de force

forceful *adj* énergique

forceps ['fɔːseps, *Am:* 'fɔːr-] *npl* MED forceps *mpl*

forcible ['fɔːsəbl, *Am:* 'fɔːr-] *adj* **1.** (*involving the use of force*) de force; (*entry*) par effraction **2.** (*effective*) convaincant(e)

forcibly *adv* de force

ford [fɔːd, *Am:* fɔːrd] **I.** *n* gué *m* **II.** *vt* **to** ~ **sth** traverser qc à gué

fore [fɔːʳ, *Am:* fɔːr] **I.** *adj, adv* à l'avant; ~ **and aft** de l'avant à l'arrière **II.** *n no pl* avant *m;* **to bring sb/sth to the** ~ mettre qn/qc en avant; **to come to the** ~ se mettre en avant

forearm *n* avant-bras *m* **forebear** *n* ancêtre *m* **forecast** <forecast *o* forecasted> **I.** *n* **1.** (*prediction*) pronostics *mpl* **2.** (*weather prediction*) prévisions *fpl* météo **II.** *vt* prévoir **forecaster** *n* **1.** ECON prévisionniste *mf* **2.** METEO présentateur, -trice *m, f* météo

foreclose [fɔː'kləʊz, *Am:* fɔːr'kloʊz] **I.** *vt* **1.** (*prevent redemption of*) saisir; **to** ~ **a mortgage** saisir un bien hypothéqué **2.** *form* (*rule out*) écarter; **to** ~ **any chance** écarter toute chance **II.** *vi* FIN saisir; **to** ~ **on sb** saisir qn; **to** ~ **on a mortgage** saisir un bien hypothéqué

forecourt *n* avant-cour *f;* (*of church*) parvis *m;* (*for car sales*) aire *f* d'exposition **forefinger** *n* index *m* **forefoot** <-feet> *n* patte *f* antérieure **forefront** *n no pl* premier rang *m;* **at the** ~ **of sth** au premier rang de qc

forego [fɔː'gəʊ, *Am:* fɔːr'goʊ] <forewent, foregone> *vt s.* **forgo**

foregoing **I.** *adj form* précédent(e) **II.** *n no pl* **the** ~ *form* ce qui précède

foregone **I.** *pp of* **forego** **II.** *adj* **it's a** ~ **conclusion** c'est inévitable

foreground **I.** *n no pl* premier plan *m;* **in the** ~ au premier plan; **to put oneself in the** ~ se mettre en avant **II.** *vt* **to** ~ **sth** mettre qc en avant **forehand** **I.** *n* coup *m* droit **II.** *adj* SPORT ~ **shot** coup *m* droit **forehead** *n* front *m*

foreign ['fɒrɪn, *Am:* 'fɔːr-] *adj* **1.** (*from another country*) étranger(-ère); ~ **exchange** change *m;* **a** ~ **national** un ressortissant étranger **2.** (*involving other countries: trade, policy*) extérieur(e); (*travel, correspondent*) à l'étranger; ~ **relations** relations *fpl* avec l'étranger **3.** *fig* (*not known*) étranger(-ère); **to be** ~ **to sb** être étranger à qn; **to be** ~ **to one's nature** ne pas être dans la nature de qn **4.** (*not belonging: body*) étranger(-ère)

foreign affairs *npl* Affaires *fpl* étrangères; **Ministry of Foreign Affairs** ministère *m* des Affaires étrangères

foreigner *n* étranger, -ère *m, f*

Foreign Office *n no pl, Brit* ministère *m* des Affaires étrangères **Foreign Secretary** *n Brit* ministre *mf* des Affaires étrangères

foreknowledge *n no pl* connaissance *f* préalable; **to have** ~ **of sth** avoir déjà pris connaissance de qc **foreman** <-men> *n* **1.** (*head workman*) contremaître *m* **2.** LAW (*head of jury*) président *m* **foremost** **I.** *adj* plus important(e); **to be one of the** ~ **authorities on** être l'une des autorités les plus en vue **II.** *adv* de loin; **first and** ~ avant tout **forename** *n* prénom *m*

forensic [fə'rensɪk] *adj* légal(e)

forensic medicine *n* médecine *f* légale

foreplay *n no pl* préliminaires *mpl* **forerunner** *n* **1.** (*earlier version*) précurseur *m* **2.** (*warning sign*) signe *m* avant-coureur **foresee** *irr vt* prévoir

foreseeable *adj* prévisible; **in the ~ future** dans un avenir immédiat

foreshadow *vt* annoncer **foresight** *n* prévoyance *f;* **to have the ~ to do sth** faire preuve de la prévoyance en faisant qc **foreskin** *n* prépuce *m*

forest ['fɒrɪst, *Am:* 'fɔːr-] *n a. fig* forêt *f*

forestall *vt* anticiper; (*person*) devancer

forester *n* garde *m* forestier

forest ranger *n Am* garde forestier *m*

forestry ['fɒrɪstri, *Am:* 'fɔːr-] *n no pl* sylviculture *f*

foretaste *n sing* avant-goût *m* **foretell** <foretold> *vt* prédire

forever, for ever [fə'revəʳ, *Am:* fɔːr'evɚ] *adv Brit* toujours; **to take ~ to** +*infin inf* prendre des heures pour +*infin;* **to be ~ doing sth** être toujours en train de faire qc

forewarn *vt* prévenir ►**~ed is forearmed** *prov* un homme averti en vaut deux *prov*

forewent *past of* **forego**

forewoman <-women> *n* **1.** (*head worker*) contremaîtresse *f* **2.** LAW (*head of jury*) présidente *f*

foreword *n* avant-propos *m*

forfeit ['fɔːfɪt, *Am:* 'fɔːr-] **I.** *vt* **1.** (*lose*) perdre **2.** (*give up*) renoncer à **II.** *n* (*in game*) gage *m* **III.** *adj form* LAW déchu(e); **someone's life is ~** quelqu'un paye de sa vie

forfeiture ['fɔːfɪtʃəʳ, *Am:* 'fɔːrfə-] *n* LAW **1.** *no pl* (*loss*) perte *f* **2.** (*penalty involving loss: of property*) saisie *f;* (*of right*) déchéance *f*

forgather [fɔː'gæðəʳ, *Am:* fɔːr'gæðɚ] *vi form* se réunir

forgave [fə'geɪv, *Am:* fɚ-] *pt of* **forgive**

forge [fɔːdʒ, *Am:* fɔːrdʒ] **I.** *vt* **1.** (*make illegal copy: document*) falsifier; (*painting*) contrefaire; **~d documents** des faux **2.** (*heat and shape: metal*) forger **3.** *fig* (*form with effort*) forger; (*career*) se forger **II.** *vi* foncer; **to ~ into the lead** prendre la tête **III.** *n* forge *f*

◆**forge ahead** *vi* **1.** (*take the lead*) prendre de l'avance **2.** (*progress*) aller de l'avant

forger *n* faussaire *mf*

forgery ['fɔːdʒəri, *Am:* 'fɔːr-] <-ies> *n* contrefaçon *f*

forget [fə'get, *Am:* fɚ-] <forgot, forgotten> **I.** *vt* oublier; **to ~ to** +*infin* oublier de +*infin;* **to ~ doing sth** oublier avoir fait qc; **not ~ting ...** sans oublier; **~ it!** laisse tomber!; **to ~ oneself** *form* se laisser aller; **and don't you ~ it!** et tâche de ne pas l'oublier! **II.** *vi* oublier; **to ~ about sb/sth** oublier qn/qc; **to ~ about doing sth** oublier de faire qc; **you can ~ about that holiday** ne compte plus sur les vacances

forgetful *adj* **1.** (*unable to remember things*) distrait(e) **2.** *form* (*oblivious*) oublieux(-euse); **to be ~ of sth** négliger qc

forget-me-not *n* BOT myosotis *m*

forgive [fə'gɪv, *Am:* fɚ-] <forgave, forgiven> **I.** *vt* **1.** (*cease to blame*) pardonner; **to ~ sb (for) sth** pardonner qc à qn; **to ~ sb/oneself for doing sth** pardonner qn/se pardonner d'avoir fait qc; **~ me if I interrupt** excusez-moi de vous interrompre; **~ my ignorance/language** excuse mon ignorance/mon langage **2.** *form* (*not ask for payment*) **to ~ sb sth** faire grâce à qn de qc **II.** *vi* pardonner

forgiven *pp of* **forgive**

forgiving *adj* indulgent(e)

forgo [fɔː'gəʊ, *Am:* fɔːr'goʊ] *irr vt iron, form* renoncer à

forgot [fə'gɒt, *Am:* fɚ'gɑːt] *pt of* **forget**

forgotten *pt of* **forget**

forint ['fɒrɪnt, *Am:* 'fɔːr-] *n* forint *m*

fork [fɔːk, *Am:* fɔːrk] **I.** *n* **1.** (*eating tool*) fourchette *f* **2.** (*garden tool*) fourche *f* **3.** (*Y-shaped division*) embranchement *m;* **take the left/right ~** prendre à gauche/droite à l'embranchement **4.** *pl* (*support of bicycle*) fourche *f* **II.** *vt* (*till: garden*) fourcher **III.** *vi* bifurquer; **to ~ left/right** bifurquer à gauche/droite

◆**fork out** *vt, vi* payer

forked *adj* fourchu(e) ►**to speak with a ~ tongue** mentir

fork-lift (truck) *n* chariot *m* élévateur

forlorn [fə'lɔːn, *Am:* fɔːr'lɔːrn] *adj* **1.** (*sad and alone*) délaissé(e) **2.** (*desolate: place*) abandonné(e) **3.** (*vain*) désespéré(e); **a ~ hope** un mince espoir

form [fɔːm, *Am:* fɔːrm] **I.** *n* **1.** (*type, variety*) forme *f;* **in the ~ of sth** dans la forme de qc; **to take the ~ of sth** être sous la forme de qc **2.** (*outward shape*) *a.* LING forme *f;* **in the ~ of sth** dans la forme de qc; **to take ~** prendre forme **3.** CHEM (*physical state*) forme *f;* **in liquid/solid ~** dans la forme liquide/solide **4.** (*document*) formulaire *m;* **an application ~** (*for a job*) un formulaire de candidature; (*for loan, brochure*) un formulaire de demande **5.** *no pl* (*condition*) forme *f;* **to be in** [*o Brit* **on**] **good/excellent ~** être en bonne/excellente forme; **to be out of ~** ne pas avoir la forme; **on present ~** *Brit* vu l'état des choses actuelles **6.** *no pl* (*correct procedure*) forme *f;* **in due ~** en bonne et due forme; **as a matter of ~, for ~** pour la forme; **what's the ~?** quelle est la marche à suivre? **7.** *Brit* (*class*) classe *f;* **first ~** sixième *f;* **sixth ~** première *f* **8.** *Brit* (*bench*) banc *m* **9.** (*mould*) forme *f* ►**in any (way,) shape or ~** en aucune façon; **true to ~** comme d'habitude **II.** *vt* **1.** (*make the shape of*) former; **to ~ sth into an object** modeler un objet en qc; **I ~ed the ideas into a book** j'ai transformé les idées en un livre **2.** (*develop in the mind: opinion*) former; **to ~ the impression** donner l'impression **3.** (*set up: committee, group*) former; (*friendship*) nouer **4.** LING (*use*) former **5.** *form* (*influence*) former; **to ~ sb/sb's character** former qn/le caractère de qn **6.** (*constitute*) constituer; **to ~ part of sth** faire partie de qc **III.** *vi* se former; **to ~ into groups of six** se regrouper par six

formal ['fɔːməl, *Am:* 'fɔːr-] *adj* **1.** (*proper,*

well-organised) formel(le); **he had no ~ training** il n'a pas eu de formation professionnelle; **~ agreement** accord *m* formel **2.** (*special, ceremonious: occasion, address, behaviour*) formel(le); (*language*) soutenu(e) **3.** (*official*) officiel(le) **4.** (*connected with artistic form*) formel(le)

formaldehyde [fɔːˈmældɪhaɪd, *Am:* fɔːr-] *n no pl* formaldéhyde *m*

formality [fɔːˈmæləti, *Am:* -t̬i] <-ties> *n* formalité *f*

formalize [ˈfɔːməlaɪz, *Am:* ˈfɔːr-] *vt* formaliser

format [ˈfɔːmæt, *Am:* ˈfɔːr-] **I.** *n* format *m* **II.** <-tt-> *vt* INFOR formater

formation [fɔːˈmeɪʃən, *Am:* fɔːr-] *n* formation *f;* **in** (**close**) **~** en rang serré

formative [ˈfɔːmətɪv, *Am:* ˈfɔːrmət̬ɪv] *adj* formateur(-trice)

formatting *n* INFOR formatage *m*

former *adj* **1.** (*first*) premier(-ère); **I prefer the ~** je préfère le premier **2.** (*earlier, older*) ancien(ne); (*existence, era*) antérieur(e)

formerly *adv* avant; (*long ago*) anciennement; **~ known as sb** (*in former times*) auparavant connu sous le nom de qn

formic acid *n* acide *m* formique

formidable [ˈfɔːmɪdəbl, *Am:* ˈfɔːrmə-] *adj* redoutable

formless *adj* informe

formula [ˈfɔːmjʊlə] <-s *o* -lae> *n* **1.** (*mathematical rule*) formule *f;* **a chemical/mathematical ~** une formule chimique/mathématique **2.** COM (*recipe for product*) formule *f* **3.** (*plan*) formule *f;* **~ for success** formule du succès; **a ~ for doing sth** une formule pour faire qc **4.** (*form of words*) tournure *f* **5.** *no pl, Am* (*baby food*) lait *m* en poudre

formulate [ˈfɔːmjʊleɪt, *Am:* ˈfɔːr-] *vt* formuler

formulation *n* formulation *f*

forsake [fəˈseɪk, *Am:* fɔːr-] *vt* <forsook, forsaken> abandonner

forswear [fɔːˈsweəʳ, *Am:* fɔːrˈswer] <forswore, forsworn> *vt* renoncer à

forsythia *n* forsythia *m*

fort [fɔːt, *Am:* fɔːrt] *n* fort *m* ►**to hold the fort** s'occuper de tout

forte[1] [ˈfɔːteɪ, *Am:* fɔːrt] *n sing* fort *m;* **not to be sb's ~** ne pas être le fort de qn

forte[2] [ˈfɔːteɪ, *Am:* fɔːrt-] *adv, adj* MUS forte

forth [fɔːθ, *Am:* fɔːrθ] *adv form* en avant; **go/set ~** se mettre en route; **back and ~** d'avant en arrière; **to pace back and ~** aller et venir; **from that day ~** dorénavant

forthcoming *adj* **1.** (*happening soon*) prochain(e) **2.** (*coming out soon: film, book*) qui va sortir **3.** (*ready, available*) disponible; **no money was ~** l'argent n'arrivait pas **4.** (*ready to give information*) expansif(-ive); **to not be ~ about sth** ne pas être très expansif à propos de qc

forthright *adj* franc(he)

forthwith *adv form* sur-le-champ

fortieth [ˈfɔːtɪəθ, *Am:* ˈfɔːrt̬ɪ-] *adj* quarantième; *s. a.* **eighth**

fortification [ˌfɔːtɪfɪˈkeɪʃən, *Am:* ˌfɔːrt̬ə-] *n* fortification *f*

fortified *adj* **1.** (*with fortification*) fortifié(e) **2.** (*with more energy*) **~ with vitamins** renforcé(e) en teneur en vitamines

fortify [ˈfɔːtɪfaɪ, *Am:* ˈfɔːrt̬ə-] <-ie-> *vt* **1.** (*equip with defences*) fortifier **2.** (*give more strength*) **to ~ oneself with sth** se redonner des forces avec qc **3.** (*recomfort*) **to ~ oneself** se réconforter; **to be fortified with the thought ...** être réconforté à l'idée que ...

fortitude [ˈfɔːtɪtjuːd, *Am:* ˈfɔːrt̬ətuːd] *n no pl, form* force *f* morale

fortnight [ˈfɔːtnaɪt, *Am:* ˈfɔːrt-] *n sing, Brit, Aus* quinzaine *f;* **a ~'s holiday/stay** des vacances/un séjour de quinze jours; **in a ~** dans une quinzaine; **once a ~** une fois tous les quinze jours; **a ~ on Monday** lundi dans quinze jours

fortnightly **I.** *adj* bimensuel(le) **II.** *adv* tous les quinze jours

fortress [ˈfɔːtrɪs, *Am:* ˈfɔːr-] *n* forteresse *f*

fortuitous [fɔːˈtjuːɪtəs, *Am:* fɔːrˈtuːət̬əs] *adj form* fortuite(e)

fortunate [ˈfɔːtʃənət, *Am:* ˈfɔːr-] *adj* chanceux(-euse); **to be ~ to do** [*o* **doing**] **sth** avoir la chance de faire qc; **to be ~ in sth** avoir de la chance dans qc; **it is ~** (**for him**) **that** il a de la chance que +*subj*

fortunately *adv* heureusement

fortune [ˈfɔːtʃuːn, *Am:* ˈfɔːrtʃən] *n* **1.** (*a lot of money*) fortune *f;* **to be worth a ~** valoir une fortune; **to cost a ~** coûter une forture; **to make a/one's ~** faire fortune; **to seek one's ~** chercher fortune **2.** *no pl, form* (*luck*) chance *f;* **to have the good ~ to** +*infin* avoir la chance de +*infin;* **to read/tell sb's ~** dire la bonne aventure à qn **3.** *pl* (*what happens to sb*) destin *m*

fortune cookie *n petit gâteau surprise servi en fin de repas* **fortune hunter** *n* homme *m* interessé, femme *f* interessée **fortune teller** *n* diseur , -euse *m, f* de bonne aventure

forty [ˈfɔːti, *Am:* ˈfɔːrt̬i] *adj* quarante ►**to have ~ winks** *inf* piquer un somme; *s. a.* **eight, eighty**

forum [ˈfɔːrəm] *n* forum *m;* **a ~ for debate** un forum de discussions

forward [ˈfɔːwəd, *Am:* ˈfɔːrwərd] **I.** *adv* **1.** *a. fig* (*towards the front*) en avant; (*position*) à l'avant; **to lean ~** se pencher en avant; **to go ~** avancer; **to run ~** avancer en courant; **to put sth ~** mettre qc en avant; **to push oneself ~** se mettre en avant; **the way ~** la voie à suivre **2.** *form* (*onwards in time*) **to put one's watch ~** avancer sa montre; **from that day ~** à compter de ce jour **II.** *adj* **1.** (*front: position*) avant *inv* **2.** (*towards the front*) en avant; **~ step** pas *m* en avant **3.** (*advanced*) avancé(e); **~ planning** la planification **4.** FIN à terme **5.** *pej* (*too bold and self-confident*) effronté(e) **III.** *n* SPORT avant *m;* **centre** ~ avant-centre *m* **IV.** *vt* **1.** (*send to new address: mail*) faire suivre; **please** ~ faire suivre S.V.P. **2.** *form* COM (*send*) expédier; **to** ~ **sb sth** expédier qc à qn **3.** *form* (*help to progress*) encourager

forwarding address *n* adresse *f* de réexpédition **forward-looking** *adj* tourné(e) vers l'avenir

forwardness *n no pl, pej* précocité *f*

forwards *adv s.* **forward**

forwent [fɔː'went, *Am:* fɔːr-] *pt of* **forgo**

fossil ['fɒsəl, *Am:* 'fɑːsəl] **I.** *n a. pej* fossile *m* **II.** *adj* fossile

fossilized ['fɒsəlaɪzd, *Am:* 'fɑːsə-] *adj* fossilisé(e)

foster ['fɒstəʳ, *Am:* 'fɑːstɚ] **I.** *vt* **1.** (*look after: children*) garder **2.** (*place with a new family*) placer **3.** (*encourage*) encourager; **to** ~ **sth in sb** stimuler qc chez qn **II.** *adj* adoptif(-ive)

fought [fɔːt, *Am:* fɑːt] *pt,pp of* **fight**

foul [faʊl] **I.** *adj* **1.** (*dirty and disgusting*) infect(e); (*air*) vicié(e); (*taste, smell*) infect(e) **2.** (*highly unpleasant: mood*) infâme; **to be** ~ **to sb** être infâme avec qn; **the weather was** ~ il faisait un temps horrible **II.** *n* SPORT coup *m* bas; (*in football*) faute *f* **III.** *vt* **1.** (*pollute*) polluer **2.** (*make dirty*) souiller **3.** SPORT (*player*) commettre une faute contre **4.** (*jam*) **to** ~ **a propeller** se prendre dans une hélice **5.** NAUT (*collide with*) entrer en collision avec

foul-mouthed *adj* grossier(-ère)

foul play *n no pl* LAW acte *m* cirminel; SPORT jeu *m* irrégulier

found¹ [faʊnd] *pt, pp of* **find**

found² [faʊnd] *vt* (*create*) fonder

found³ [faʊnd] *vt* (*melt*) fondre

foundation [faʊn'deɪʃən] *n* **1.** *pl* (*base of a building*) fondation *f;* ~ **stone** première pierre *f;* **to lay the** ~(**s**) **of sth** poser les fondations de qc **2.** *fig* (*basis*) base *f;* **to lay the** ~(**s**) **of sth** poser les bases de qc **3.** *no pl* (*evidence to support sth*) fondement *m;* **to have no** ~ n'avoir aucun fondement **4.** (*organization, establishment*) fondation *f* **5.** *no pl* (*base make-up*) fond *m* de teint; ~ **cream** crème *f* teintée

founder¹ *n* fondateur, -trice *m, f*

founder² *vi* **1.** (*sink*) sombrer **2.** *fig* (*fail*) échouer

founding father *n* père *m* fondateur

foundry ['faʊndri] <-dries> *n* fonderie *f*

fountain ['faʊntɪn, *Am:* -tən] *n* **1.** (*man-made water jet*) fontaine *f* **2.** (*spray*) *a. fig* jet *m*

fountain pen *n* stylo *m* à encre

four [fɔːʳ, *Am:* fɔːr] **I.** *adj* quatre **II.** *n* quatre *m* ▸**to be on all** ~**s** être à quatre pattes; *s. a.* **eight**

four-by-four *n* AUTO quatre-quatre *m* **four-door** (**car**) *n* voiture *f* quatre portes **fourfold I.** *adj* quadruple **II.** *adv* (*to increase*) au quadruple **four-footed** *adj* quadrupède **four-handed** *adj* **1.** (*involving four people*) à quatre **2.** (*for two pianists*) à quatre mains **four-leaf clover**, **four-leaved clover** *n* trèfle *m* à quatre feuilles **four-letter word** *n* **1.** (*swearword*) gros mot *m* **2.** *iron* (*taboo word*) mot *m* obscène **foursome** *n* groupe *m* de quatre personnes; **to be/make up a** ~ être/y aller à quatre **four-square I.** *adj* **1.** (*square and solid: building*) solide; (*person*) carré(e) **2.** (*resolute and immovable*) ferme **II.** *adv* **1.** (*solidly*) solidement **2.** (*firmly*) fermement; **to be** ~ **behind sb** soutenir qc à fond

fourteen [ˌfɔː'tiːn, *Am:* ˌfɔːr-] *adj* quatorze; *s. a.* **eight**

fourteenth *adj* quatorzième; *s. a.* **eighth**

fourth [fɔːθ, *Am:* fɔːrθ] **I.** *adj* quatrième **II.** *n* (*quarter*) quart *m; s. a.* **eighth**

> Le **Fourth of July** ou "Independence Day" est en Amérique le jour férié laïque le plus important. Il commémore la "Declaration of Independence" (déclaration d'indépendance), dans laquelle les colonies américaines, le 4 juillet 1776, ont déclaré leur indépendance vis-à-vis de la Grande-Bretagne. On se rencontre pour pique-niquer, se retrouver en famille ou assister à des matchs de baseball professionnels. Pour couronner cette journée, on organise de grands feux d'artifice dans tout le pays.

four-wheel drive *n* quatre roues motrices *m*

fowl [faʊl] <-(s)> *n* volaille *f*

fox [fɒks, *Am:* fɑːks] **I.** *n* **1.** (*animal*) renard *m;* **a red/silver** ~ un renard roux/argenté **2.** *inf* (*cunning person*) **an old** ~ un vieux renard rusé **3.** *Am, inf* (*sexy woman*) fille *f* sexy **II.** *vt* **1.** (*mystify*) laisser perplexe **2.** (*trick*) **to** ~ **sb into doing sth** berner qn en faisant qc

foxglove *n* BOT digitale *f* **foxhunt** *n* chasse *f* au renard **fox terrier** *n* fox-terrier *m*

foxtrot ['fɒkstrɒt, *Am:* 'fɑːkstrɑːt] <-tt-> *n* fox-trot *m inv*

foxy ['fɒksi, *Am:* 'fɑːk-] <-ier, -iest> *adj* **1.** (*crafty*) rusé(e) (comme un renard) **2.** *Am, inf* (*sexy*) sexy

foyer ['fɔɪeɪ, *Am:* -ɚ] *n* hall *m* d'entrée; (*in theater*) foyer *m*

fracas ['frækɑː, *Am:* 'freɪkəs] <-(ses)> *n Am* **1.** (*noisy fight*) fracas *m* **2.** (*heated dispute*) remue-ménage *m*

fraction ['frækʃən] *n* fraction *f;* **by a** ~ d'une fraction; **a** ~ **of a second** une fraction de seconde

fractional *adj* **1.** MAT fractionnaire **2.** (*tiny*) infime

fractious ['frækʃəs] *adj* grincheux(-euse)

fracture ['fræktʃəʳ, *Am:* -tʃɚ] **I.** *vt* **1.** MED (*break*) fracturer; **to** ~ **one's leg** se fracturer la jambe **2.** (*cause a crack in*) fissurer **3.** *fig* (*destroy: accord*) rompre **II.** *vi* se fracturer **III.** *n a. fig* MED fracture *f;* **a skull** ~ une fracture du crâne

fragile ['frædʒaɪl, *Am:* -əl] *adj* fragile; **to feel ~** se sentir faible

fragility [frə'dʒɪləti, *Am:* -t̬i] *n no pl* fragilité *f*

fragment ['frægmənt, *Am:* 'frægment] **I.** *n a. fig* fragment *m* **II.** *vi a. fig* se fragmenter **III.** *vt a. fig* fragmenter

fragmentary ['frægməntri] *adj* fragmentaire

fragrance ['freɪgrəns] *n* parfum *m*

fragrant *adj* parfumé(e)

frail [freɪl] *adj* **1.** (*weak in body*) frêle **2.** *a. fig* (*not strong*) fragile

frailty <-ties> *n* **1.** *no pl* (*bodily weakness*) fragilité *f* **2.** *no pl* (*moral weakness*) faiblesse *f*

frame [freɪm] **I.** *n* **1.** (*for picture*) *a.* INFOR cadre *m* **2.** (*enclosure: of door, window*) châssis *m* **3.** *pl* (*rim surrounding spectacles*) monture *f* **4.** (*structure*) charpente *f;* (*for tent*) armature *f;* (*for cycle*) cadre *m* **5.** (*body*) ossature *f* **6.** (*section of film strip*) image *f* **7.** (*for plants*) châssis *m* **8.** *fig* **~ of mind** état *m* d'esprit; **~ of reference** système *m* de référence **II.** *vt* **1.** (*put in a frame*) encadrer; **to ~ the face** mettre le visage en valeur **2.** (*put into words*) formuler; (*regulations*) concevoir **3.** *inf* (*falsely incriminate*) monter un coup contre; **to be ~d** être victime d'un coup monté

frames *n* INFOR multifenêtrage *m*

frame-up *n inf* coup *m* monté

framework *n fig* cadre *m*

franc [fræn] *n* franc *m*

France [frɑːns, *Am:* fræns] *n* la France

franchise ['fræntʃaɪz] **I.** *n* COM franchise *f* **II.** *vt* franchiser

Franciscan [fræn'sɪskən] REL **I.** *n* Franciscain *m* **II.** *adj* franciscain(e)

Franco- ['fræŋkəʊ, *Am:* -koʊ] *in compounds* franco-

frank¹ [fræŋk] **I.** *adj* franc(he); **to be ~ with sb about sth** être franc avec qn à propos de qc **II.** *vt* affranchir

frank² [fræŋk] *n Am, inf abbr of* **frankfurter** saucisse *f* de Francfort

frankfurter ['fræŋkfɜːtəʳ, *Am:* -fɜːrt̬ɚ] *n* saucisse *f* de Francfort

frankincense ['fræŋkɪnsents] *n no pl* encens *m*

franking machine *n* machine *f* à affranchir

frantic ['fræntɪk, *Am:* -t̬ɪk] *adj* **1.** (*wild and desperate*) fou(folle); **to drive sb ~** rendre qn fou **2.** (*hurried and confused*) effréné(e)

fraternal [frə'tɜːnl, *Am:* -'tɜːr-] *adj a. fig* fraternel(le)

fraternity [frə'tɜːnəti, *Am:* -'tɜːrnət̬i] <-ties> *n a. fig* fraternité *f*

fraternization *n no pl* fraternisation *f*

fraternize ['frætənaɪz, *Am:* '-ɚ-] *vi* fraterniser

fraud [frɔːd, *Am:* frɑːd] *n* **1.** *no pl* LAW (*obtaining money by deceit*) fraude *f* **2.** (*thing intended to deceive*) imposture *f* **3.** (*deceiver*) imposteur *m*

fraudulence ['frɔːdjʊləns, *Am:* 'frɑːdʒə-] *n no pl* caractère *m* frauduleux

fraudulent *adj* frauduleux(-euse)

fraught [frɔːt, *Am:* frɑːt] *adj* **1.** (*full*) chargé(e); **to be ~ with hatred** être chargé de haine; **to be ~ with problems** être plein de problèmes **2.** (*tense*) tendu(e)

fray¹ [freɪ] *vi* **1.** (*become worn*) s'effilocher **2.** *fig* **tempers ~** les gens s'énervent

fray² [freɪ] *n* **to enter the ~** entrer dans l'arène; **to be ready for the ~** être prêt au combat

freak [friːk] **I.** *n* **1.** (*abnormal thing*) phénomène *m* **2.** (*abnormal person, animal*) monstre *m; fig* phénomène *m* de foire **3.** (*fanatical enthusiast*) fana *mf* **II.** *adj* anormal(e) **III.** *vi* **to ~ (out)** devenir fou(folle)

freckle ['frekl] *n pl* tache *f* de rousseur

freckled *adj* avec des taches de rousseur

free [friː] **I.** <-r, -est> *adj* **1.** (*not tied up or restricted*) *a. fig* (*person, country, elections*) libre; **to set sb/sth ~** libérer qn/qc; **to break ~ of sth** se libérer de qc; **to be ~ from sth** être libéré de qc; **to be ~ to** +*infin* être libre de +*infin;* **feel ~ to** +*infin* n'hésite pas à +*infin;* **to leave sb ~ to** +*infin* laisser qn libre de +*infin;* **to be ~ of sb** être débarrassé de qn; **to go into ~ fall** FIN partir en chute libre; **to get one's arm free of sth** libérer son bras de qc **2.** (*costing nothing: sample*) gratuit(e); **to be ~ of tax** être exonéré de taxes **3.** (*not occupied: seat*) libre; **I'm leaving Monday ~** je laisse mon lundi libre **4.** (*without*) **~ of** [*o* **from**] **sth** sans; **~ of disease/prejudice** dépourvu(e) de toute maladie/de tout préjugé; **~ of commitments** libéré(e) de tout engagement; **~ of additives** sans additifs; **sugar-~** sans sucre **5.** (*giving in large amounts*) généreux(-euse); **to be ~ with one's advice** être prodigue en conseils; **to make ~ with sth** *pej* ne pas se gêner avec qc **6.** (*not strict: translation*) libre ►**to be as ~ as a <u>bird</u>** être libre comme le vent; **there's no such thing as a ~ <u>lunch</u>** c'est ce qui s'appelle renvoyer l'ascenseur; **~ and <u>easy</u>** décontracté(e) **II.** *adv* **1.** (*in freedom*) en (toute) liberté **2.** (*costing nothing*) gratuitement; **~ of charge** gratuit; **for ~** *inf* gratuitement **III.** *vt* **1.** (*release*) **to ~ sb/sth from sth** libérer qn/qc de qc **2.** (*relieve*) **to ~ sb/sth from sth** soulager qn/qc de qc; **to ~ sb from a contract** dégager qn d'un contrat **3.** (*make available*) **to ~ sth for sth** libérer qc pour qc; **to ~ (up) a week to** +*infin* prendre une semaine (de libre) pour +*infin;* **to ~ sb to** +*infin* laisser du temps à qn pour +*infin*

freebie ['friːbiː] *n inf* cadeau *m;* **a ~ pen** un stylo offert

freedom ['friːdəm] *n* liberté *f;* **to have the ~ to** +*infin* avoir la liberté de +*infin;* **~ of action/movement/speech** liberté d'action/de mouvement/d'expression; **~ of information** libre accès *m* à l'information; ~

from hunger/oppression absence *f* de famine/d'oppression; **to give sb the ~ of sth** donner carte blanche à qn pour qc

free enterprise *n* libre entreprise *f* **free-for-all** *n* mêlée *f* générale **freehold I.** *n* LAW propriété *f* foncière **II.** *adj, adv* LAW en propriété **freeholder** *n* propriétaire *m* foncier **free kick** *n* SPORT coup *m* franc **freelance I.** *n* free-lance *mf,* travailleur *m* autonome *Québec* **II.** *adj* free-lance *inv,* autonome *Québec* **III.** *adv* en free-lance **IV.** *vi* travailler en free-lance **freeload** *vi Am, Aus, pej* grapiller; **to ~ off sb** grapiller sur qn **freeloader** *vi Am, Aus, pej* parasite *m*

freely *adv* **1.**(*unrestrictedly*) librement; **I ~ admit that** je l'admets volontiers **2.**(*without obstruction*) sans contrainte **3.**(*frankly*) franchement **4.**(*generously*) généreusement

freeman <-men> *n* (*honorary citizen of city*) citoyen *m* d'honneur **free-market economy** *n* économie *f* de marché

Freemason ['friː,meɪsən] *n* franc-maçon(ne) *m(f)*

freemasonry *n* franc-maçonnerie *f*

free port *n* franc port *m* **free-range** *adj* fermier(-ère) **free speech** *n no pl* liberté *f* d'expression **free-standing** *adj* **1.**(*not fixed*) non-encastré(e); (*lamp*) sur pied **2.**(*not part of group*) indépendant(e); (*organisation*) autonome **freestyle I.** *n no pl* SPORT nage *f* libre **II.** *adj* libre **freethinker** *n* libre penseur, -euse *m, f* **freethinking I.** *n* libre pensée *f* **II.** *adj* libre penseur(-euse) **free trade** *n no pl* libre-échange *f* **freeware** *n* INFOR logiciel *m* gratuit, gratuiciel *m Québec* **freeway** *n Am, Aus* autoroute *f* **freewheel** *vi* être en roue libre **free will** *n no pl* libre arbitre *m;* **to do sth of one's own ~** faire qc de son propre chef

freeze [friːz] <froze, frozen> **I.** *vi* **1.**(*become solid*) geler; **to ~ solid** durcir sous l'action du gel **2.**(*get cold*) geler; **to ~ to death** mourir de froid; **the lake's frozen over** le lac est complètement gelé **3.** *impers* (*be below freezing point*) **it ~s** il gèle **4.** *fig* se figer; **~!** ne bougez plus! **II.** *vt* **1.**(*turn to ice*) geler; (*food*) congeler **2.** *fig* glacer; **to ~ sb with a look** glacer qn sur place d'un regard **3.** CINE **to ~ an image** faire un arrêt sur image **4.** FIN (*pay*) geler; (*account*) bloquer **5.**(*anaesthetize*) insensibiliser **6.** INFOR figer ▸**to make sb's <u>blood</u> ~** glacer le sang de qn **III.** *n* **1.** METEO gel *m;* **big ~** fortes gelées *fpl* **2.** ECON (*stoppage: of price, wage*) gel *m*

◆**freeze out** *vt* (*member of group*) tenir à l'écart

freeze-dried *adj* lyophylisé(e) **freeze-frame** *n* arrêt *m* sur image

freezer *n* congélateur *m;* **chest ~** congélateur bahut; **~ compartment** freezer *m*

freeze-up *n* gelée *f*

freezing I. *adj* glacial(e); (*person*) gelé(e); **it's ~ out** il gèle dehors **II.** *n no pl* congélation *f;* **to be above/below ~** être au-dessus/au-dessous de zéro

freezing fog *n* brouillard *m* givrant **freezing point** *n* point *m* de congélation

freight [freɪt] **I.** *n inv* **1.**(*goods*) fret *m* **2.**(*transportation*) transport *m;* **to send sth by ~** expédier qc en petite vitesse; **air/rail ~** transport aérien/ferroviaire **3.**(*charge*) fret *m* **4.** *Am* RAIL train *m* de marchandises **II.** *adj* (*price*) de marchandises; (*charges*) de fret; (*company, service*) de transport **III.** *adv* (*by freight system*) **to send sth ~** expédier qc en régime ordinaire **IV.** *vt* **1.**(*transport*) affréter **2.**(*load*) *a. fig* charger; **to be ~ed with sth** être chargé de qc

freight car *n Am* RAIL wagon *m* de marchandises

freighter *n* **1.**(*ship*) cargo *m* **2.**(*plane*) avion-cargo *m*

freight train *n Am* RAIL train *m* de marchandises

French [frentʃ] **I.** *adj* français(e); **~ team** équipe de France; **~ speaker** francophone *mf* **II.** *n* **1.**(*people*) **the ~** les Français **2.** LING français *m;* **excuse my ~!** passez-moi l'expression!; *s. a.* **English**

French bean *n Brit s.* **green bean French chalk** *n no pl* craie *f* de tailleur **French dressing** *n no pl* **1.**(*salad dressing*) vinaigrette *f* **2.** *Am* (*American salad dressing*) crème *f* à salade **French fried potatoes, French fries** *npl* (pommes) frites *fpl,* patates *fpl* frites *Québec* **French horn** *n* MUS cor *m* d'harmonie **French kiss** *n* patin *m inf* **French leave** *n no pl* **to take ~** filer à l'anglaise **French letter** *n Aus, Brit, inf* (*condom*) capote *f* anglaise **Frenchman** <-men> *n* Français *m* **French Revolution** *n* **the ~** la Révolution Française **French window** *n* porte-fenêtre *f* **Frenchwoman** <-women> *n* Française *f*

frenetic [frə'netɪk, *Am:* -'neţ-] *adj* frénétique; (*activity*) fébrile

frenzied *adj* frénétique; (*crowd*) en délire; (*bark*) déchaîné(e); (*yell*) de rage; (*effort*) désespéré(e)

frenzy ['frenzi] *n no pl* frénésie *f;* **jealous ~** jalousie *f* aveugle; **a ~ of activity** une activité débordante; **a ~ of excitement** une excitation folle

frequency ['friːkwəntsi] <-ies> *n* fréquence *f;* **low/high ~** basse/haute fréquence; **to happen with increasing ~** arriver de plus en plus fréquemment

frequency band *n* RADIO bande *f* de fréquence **frequency modulation** *n* modulation *f* de fréquence

frequent ['friːkwənt] **I.** *adj* **1.**(*happening often*) fréquent(e); (*expression*) courant(e) **2.**(*regular*) habituel(le); **a ~ visitor** un habitué; **a ~ flyer** un passager fidélisé **II.** *vt* fréquenter

frequently asked questions *n* foire *f* aux questions

fresco ['freskəʊ, *Am:* -koʊ] <-s *o* -es> *n* fresque *f*

fresh [freʃ] *adj* **1.** (*new*) frais(fraîche); **to make a ~ start** repartir à zéro; **~ in sb's mind** tout frais dans la mémoire de qc **2.** (*unused*) nouveau(-elle); (*shirt*) propre **3.** (*recently made*) frais(fraîche); **~ from university** frais émoulu de l'université; **~ from New York** nouvellement arrivé de New York; **~ from the oven/factory** qui sort du four/de l'usine; **~ from the suppliers** qui vient d'être livré; **~ off the presses** qui vient de paraître **4.** (*clean, cool, not stale*) frais(fraîche); (*air*) pur(e); **in the ~ air** au grand air; **to get a breath of ~ air** s'oxygéner **5.** METEO frais(fraîche) **6.** (*not tired*) frais(fraîche) et net(te) **7.** *Am, inf* (*disrespectful*) effronté(e); **to get ~ with** (*teacher*) être insolent avec; (*woman*) prendre des libertés avec ►**to be as ~ as a daisy** être frais comme une rose; **to be ~ out of sth** *Am* être en panne de qc

freshen ['freʃən] **I.** *vt* **1.** (*make newer*) rafraîchir **2.** *Am* (*top up*) **to ~ sb's drink** remplir à nouveau le verre de qn **II.** *vi* METEO se rafraîchir
◆**freshen up I.** *vi* faire un brin de toilette **II.** *vt* rafraîchir

fresher *n Brit, inf s.* **freshman**

freshman <-men> *n* **1.** *Am* (*newcomer*) nouveau venu, nouvelle venue *m, f* **2.** UNIV étudiant(e) *m(f)* de première année

> Un **Freshman** est aux USA un élève en classe de troisième, un "Sophomore" est un élève en classe de seconde, un "Junior", un élève de première et un "Senior" un élève de terminale. Ce sont les termes en usage au cours des années de "High School", même si celle-ci ne débute dans beaucoup de régions qu'à partir de la classe de seconde. Ces notions sont aussi utilisées pour désigner les étudiants des quatre premières années du "College".

freshness *n no pl* fraîcheur *f*

fresh water *n* eau *f* douce **freshwater** *adj* d'eau douce

fret[1] [fret] **I.** <-tt-> *vi* s'inquiéter; (*child*) pleurnicher **II.** *n Brit* **to be in a ~** se faire du mauvais sang; **to get into a ~** se mettre dans tous ses états

fret[2] [fret] *n* MUS sillet *m*

fretful *adj* **1.** (*complaining*) grognon(ne) **2.** (*anxious*) agité(e); (*voice*) inquiet(-ète)

fretsaw ['fretsɔː, *Am:* -sɑː] *n* scie *f* à découper

friar ['fraɪəʳ, *Am:* -ɚ] *n* REL frère *m*

fricative ['frɪkətɪv, *Am:* -t̬ɪv] **I.** *n* LING fricative *f* **II.** *adj* LING fricatif(-ive)

friction ['frɪkʃən] *n no pl* friction *f;* (*between two things*) frottement *m;* (*between two people*) désaccord *m*

Friday ['fraɪdi] *n* vendredi *m;* **on ~s** le vendredi; **every ~** tous les vendredis; **this (coming) ~** ce vendredi; **that ~** ce vendredi-là; **on ~ mornings** le vendredi matin; **on ~ night** vendredi dans la nuit; **a week/fortnight on ~** vendredi en huit/quinze; **every other ~** un vendredi sur deux; **on ~ we are going on holiday** vendredi, on part en vacances

fridge [frɪdʒ] *n* frigo *m*

fridge-freezer *n* réfigérateur-congélateur *m*

fried chicken *n* poulet *m* frit **fried egg** *n* œuf *m* au plat

friend [frend] *n* **1.** (*person*) ami(e) *m(f);* **childhood ~** ami d'enfance; **the best of ~s** les meilleurs amis du monde; **my old ~ the taxman** *iron* mon cher ami le fisc; **a ~ of mine/theirs** l'un de mes/leurs amis; **to be ~s with sb** être ami avec qn; **to be just good ~s** être bons amis, sans plus; **to be a (good) ~ to sb** être un véritable ami pour qn; **to make ~s with sb** se lier d'amitié avec qn; **~s at court** des amis influents **2.** *Brit* (*as form of address*) **my learned ~** LAW mon cher confrère; **my honourable ~** POL mon distingué collègue **3.** (*supporter*) ami *m;* **the ~s of a society** les amis d'une société ►**with ~s like him/her, who needs enemies?** Dieu me garde de mes amis; mes ennemis, je m'en charge!; **a ~ in need is a ~ indeed** *prov* c'est dans le besoin qu'on connaît ses vrais amis; **what are ~s for?** c'est à ça que servent les amis!

friendless *adj* sans amis; **to be ~** ne pas avoir d'ami

friendly I. <-ier, -iest> *adj* **1.** (*showing friendship*) amical(e); (*attitude*) aimable; (*pet*) affectueux(-euse); **not very ~** pas très gentil; **they became ~ on holiday** ils sont devenus amis en vacances; **to be on ~ terms with sb** être en bons termes avec qn; **to get too ~ with sb** se montrer trop familier avec qn **2.** (*pleasant*) **neigbourhood, school** sympathique; (*reception*) accueillant(e) **3.** (*not competitive: match*) amical(e); **un ~ nation** un pays ami **II.** *n* SPORT match *m* amical

friendly society *n Brit* (société) mutuelle *f*

friendship *n* amitié *f;* **to form a ~ with sb** se lier d'amitié avec qn; **to strike up a ~ with sb** se prendre d'amitié pour qn; **the ties of ~** les liens de l'amitié; **to hold out the hand of ~ to sb** tendre la main à qn

frieze [friːz] *n* ARCHIT frise *f*

frigate ['frɪgət] *n* frégate *f*

fright [fraɪt] *n* **1.** *sing* (*feeling*) peur *f;* **to take ~ at sth** s'effrayer de qc **2.** (*awful experience*) frayeur *f;* **to get a ~** avoir peur; **to give sb a ~** effrayer qn ►**to get the ~ of one's life** avoir une peur bleue; **to look a ~** être à faire peur

frighten ['fraɪtən] **I.** *vt* effrayer; **to ~ sb to death** [*o* **to ~ the life out of sb**] faire mourir qn de peur **II.** *vi* prendre peur; **to ~ easily** s'effrayer pour un rien
◆**frighten away, frighten off** *vt* faire fuir

frightful *adj* épouvantable

frigid ['frɪdʒɪd] *adj* **1.** MED frigide **2.** GEO gla-

F

cial(e) **3.** (*unfriendly*) froid(e)

frigidity [frɪ'dʒɪdəti, *Am:* -t̬i] *n* **1.** MED frigidité *f* **2.** *fig* froideur *f*

frill [frɪl] *n* **1.** FASHION volant *m;* (*of shirt*) jabot *m* **2.** (*strip of paper*) papillote *f* **3.** *pl, fig, inf* petits luxes *mpl;* **with no ~s** sans options; **a no-~s airline** une compagnie aérienne sans repas sans service

fringe [frɪndʒ] **I.** *n* **1.** *Aus, Brit* (*hair*) frange *f* **2.** (*edging*) bordure *f* **3.** *fig* (*outer edge*) périphérie *f;* (*of society*) marge *f;* (*of bushes*) lisière *f;* **~ groups** groupes politiques en marge **4.** ART **the ~, ~ theatre** le théâtre d'avant-garde **II.** *vt* franger **III.** *adj no pl* alternatif(-ive)

fringe benefits *n pl* avantages *mpl* sociaux

frippery ['frɪpəri] <-ies> *n pej* colifichet *m*

frisk [frɪsk] **I.** *vi* gambader **II.** *vt* fouiller

frisky ['frɪski] *-ier, -iest adj* **1.** (*lively*) sémillant(e); (*horse*) fringant(e) **2.** *inf* (*sexually playful*) chaud(e)

fritter ['frɪtə^r, *Am:* 'frɪt̬ɚ] *n* beignet *m;* **apple ~s** beignets aux pommes

◆**fritter away** *vt* gaspiller

frivolity [frɪ'vɒləti, *Am:* -'vɑːlət̬i] <-ies> *n* frivolité *f*

frivolous ['frɪvələs] *adj pej* (*person*) frivole; (*thing*) futile

frizzy ['frɪzi] *adj* crépu(e)

fro [frəʊ, *Am:* froʊ] *adv* **to go to and ~** faire des va-et-vient

frock [frɒk, *Am:* frɑːk] *n* robe *f;* (*of monk*) froc *m*

frog [frɒg, *Am:* frɑːg] *n* grenouille *f* ►**to have a ~ in one's throat** avoir un chat dans la gorge

frogman <-men> *n* homme-grenouille *m*

frogmarch *vt* **to ~ sb** emmener qn de force

frogspawn *n no pl* œufs *mpl* de grenouille

frolic ['frɒlɪk, *Am:* 'frɑːlɪk] **I.** <-ck-> *vi* s'ébattre **II.** *n* **~s** ébats *mpl*

frolicsome ['frɒlɪksəm, *Am:* 'frɑːlɪk-] *adj* folâtre

from [frɒm, *Am:* frɑːm] *prep* **1.** de **2.** (*as starting point*) **where is he ~?** d'où est-il?; **the flight ~ London** le vol (en provenance) de Londres; **to fly ~ New York to Tokyo** aller de New York à Tokyo (en avion); **to go ~ door to door** aller de porte en porte; **shirts ~ £5** des chemises à partir de 5£; **~ inside** de l'intérieur **3.** (*temporal*) **~ day to day** de jour en jour; **~ time to time** de temps en temps; **~ his childhood** depuis son enfance; **~ the age of 7 upwards** dès l'âge de 7 ans; **~ that date on(wards)** à partir de cette date **4.** (*at distance to*) **100 metres ~ the river** à 100 mètres du fleuve; **far ~ doing sth** loin de faire qc **5.** (*source, origin*) **a card ~ Dad/Corsica** une carte de papa/Corse; **toys ~ China** jouets venant de Chine; **to drink ~ a cup/the bottle** boire dans une tasse/à la bouteille; **to appear ~ among the trees/beneath sth** surgir d'entre les arbres/de dessous qc; **painted ~ life** peint d'après nature; **translated ~ the English** traduit de l'anglais; **quotations ~ Joyce** citations de Joyce; **~ "War and Peace"** extrait [*o* tiré] de "Guerre et Paix"; **there have been complaints ~ the neighbours** il y a eu des plaints de la part des voisins; **tell her ~ me** dites-lui de ma part **6.** (*in reference to*) **~ what I heard** d'après ce que j'ai entendu (dire); **~ my point of view** *a. fig* de mon point de vue; **to judge ~ appearances** juger selon les apparences; **different ~ the others** différent des autres **7.** (*caused by*) **~ experience** par expérience; **weak ~ hunger** affaibli par la faim; **to die ~ thirst** mourir de soif **8.** (*expressing removal, separation*) **to steal/take sth ~ sb** voler/prendre qc à qn; **to tell good ~ evil** distinguer le bien du mal; **to keep sth ~ sb** cacher qc à qn; **to shade sth ~ the sun** protéger qc du soleil; **4 (subtracted) ~ 7 equals 3** MAT 4 ôté de 7 égale 3 ►**~ <u>bad</u> to worse** de mal en pis

front [frʌnt] **I.** *n* **1.** *sing* (*side: of machine*) avant *m;* (*of building*) façade *f;* (*of shop*) devanture *f;* (*of document*) recto *m;* **lying on his ~** allongé(e) sur le ventre; **the soup's gone all down your ~** tu as fait couler de la soupe sur toi **2.** (*area: of building, vehicle*) devant *m;* (*of crowd, audience*) premiers rangs *m;* **in the ~ of a car** à l'avant d'une voiture; **at the ~ of the procession** en tête du cortège **3.** PUBL (*outside cover: of magazine, book*) couverture *f;* (*of paper*) recto *m* **4.** (*ahead of sb/sth*) **to send sb on in ~** envoyer qn devant; **to be two points in ~** mener par deux points **5.** (*facing*) **in ~ of sb/sth** en face de qn/qc; **in ~ of witnesses** en présence de témoins **6.** THEAT **out ~** dans la salle **7.** (*appearance*) façade *f;* **to put on a bold ~** faire bonne contenance; **to be a ~ for sth** n'être qu'une couverture pour qc **8.** (*area of activity*) côté *m;* **on the work ~** sur le plan du travail **9.** MIL, POL, METEO front *m;* **at the ~** MIL sur le front **10.** *sing* (*promenade beside sea*) front *m* de mer; **on the lake ~** au bord du lac **11.** *no pl, inf* (*impudence*) effronterie *f* ►**to <u>pay</u> up ~** payer d'avance **II.** *adj* **1.** (*in front*) de devant; (*leg, teeth*) de devant; (*wheel*) avant; (*view*) de face; (*seat*) au premier rang; (*in car*) à l'avant; **~ office** réception *f;* **on the ~ cover** en couverture **2.** *fig* de façade **III.** *vt* **1.** *passive* (*put a facade on*) **to be ~ed with timber** avoir une façade en bois **2.** (*be head of*) diriger; (*group*) être à la tête de **3.** TV présenter **IV.** *vi* **1.** (*face*) **to ~ south** être exposé au sud; **to ~ onto** *Am* [*o* **on** *Brit*] **sth** donner sur qc **2.** *fig* **to ~ for sb/sth** servir de couverture à qn/qc

frontage ['frʌntɪdʒ, *Am:* -t̬ɪdʒ] *n* façade *f;* (*of shop*) devanture *f;* **with lake ~** donnant sur le lac

frontal ['frʌntəl, *Am:* -t̬əl] *adj* frontal(e); (*view*) de face; (*attack*) de front

front bench *n Brit* POL (*seats*) *banc des ministres ou des leaders de l'opposition;* **the government ~** les ministres; **the opposition ~**

les membres du cabinet de l'opposition **front door** *n* porte *f* d'entrée **front-end** *n* INFOR interface *f* utilisateur **front garden** *n* jardin *m* de devant

frontier [frʌn'tɪəʳ, *Am:* frʌn'tɪr] *n* **1.** (*limit*) frontière *f* **2.** *Am* (*outlying areas*) **the** ~ *les confins des terres colonisées*

frontier district *n* région *f* frontalière **frontier police** *n* gardes-frontière *mpl* **frontiersman** *-men n Am* HIST *habitant des confins des terres colonisées* **frontier station** *n* poste *m* frontière

front line *n* **1.** MIL front *m* **2.** *fig* première ligne *f* **front page** *n* première page *f* **front-page** *adj* à la une **front runner** *n* favori *m* **front-wheel drive** *n* traction *f* avant

frost [frɒst, *Am:* frɑːst] **I.** *n* **1.** (*period*) gelée *f* **2.** *no pl* (*temperature*) gel *m;* **15 degrees of** ~ 15 degrés au-dessous de zéro **3.** (*hoarfrost*) givre *m;* **ground** ~ gelée blanche **II.** *vt* **1.** (*cover with frost*) givrer **2.** *Am* GASTR glacer **3.** *passive* (*damage*) **to be ~ed** avoir gelé

frostbite ['frɒstbaɪt, *Am:* 'frɑːst-] *n no pl* gelure *f*

frostbitten *adj* gelé(e)

frostbound *adj* durci(e) par le gel

frosted *adj* **1.** (*covered with frost*) gelé(e) **2.** *Am* GASTR glacé(e) **3.** (*opaque: glass*) dépoli(e)

frosting *n no pl, Am* (*icing*) glaçage *m*

frosty ['frɒsti, *Am:* 'frɑːsti] <-ier, -iest> *adj* **1.** (*cold: air*) glacial(e); (*earth*) gelé(e); (*window*) couvert(e) de givre **2.** *fig* glacial(e)

froth [frɒθ, *Am:* frɑːθ] **I.** *n inv* écume *f;* (*of beer*) mousse *f* **II.** *vi* écumer; (*beer*) mousser; **to** ~ **at the mouth** *fig, inf* écumer de rage **III.** *vt* **to** ~ **sth** (**up**) faire mousser qc

frothy <-ier, -iest> *adj* mousseux(-euse); (*sea*) écumeux(-euse)

frown [fraʊn] **I.** *vi* froncer les sourcils; **to** ~ **at sb/sth** regarder qn/qc en fronçant les sourcils; **to** ~ **on sth** *fig* voir qc d'un mauvais œil **II.** *n* froncement *m* de sourcils

froze [frəʊz, *Am:* froʊz] *pt of* **freeze**

frozen **I.** *pp of* **freeze** **II.** *adj* **1.** (*covered with ice*) gelé(e) **2.** (*deep-frozen*) congelé(e); ~ **foods** les surgelés **3.** (*cold*) glacé(e) **4.** FIN bloqué(e)

frugal ['fruːgl] *adj* frugal(e); (*person*) sobre; **to be** ~ **with sth** économiser qc

fruit [fruːt] **I.** *n* **1.** *no pl* BOT fruit *m;* **to be in** ~ porter des fruits **2.** *fig* (*results*) fruits *mpl;* **to bear** ~ porter ses fruits **II.** *vi* porter des fruits

fruitcake *n* **1.** *no pl* GASTR cake *m* **2.** *Aus, Brit, inf* (*person*) cinglé(e) *m(f)*

fruiterer *n Brit* marchand(e) *m(f)* de fruits

fruitful *adj* fructueux(-euse)

fruition [fruː'ɪʃən] *n no pl* **to come to** ~ se réaliser

fruitless *adj* stérile

fruit machine *n* machine *f* à sous **fruit salad** *n no pl* salade *f* de fruits

fruity ['fruːti, *Am:* -t̬i] <-ier, -iest> *adj* **1.** (*tasting of fruit*) fruité(e); (*taste*) de fruit **2.** (*rich: voice*) timbré(e); (*laugh*) généreux(-euse) **3.** *inf* (*suggestive: joke*) salé(e)

frump *n pej: femme mal fagotée*

frustrate [frʌs'treɪt, *Am:* 'frʌstreɪt] <-ting> *vt* **1.** (*annoy*) énerver **2.** (*foil*) contrecarrer

frustrated *adj* frustré(e); (*effort*) vain(e)

frustrating *adj* (*behaviour, child*) énervant(e); (*period, experience*) frustrant(e)

frustration *n* frustration *f*

fry[1] [fraɪ] <-ie-> **I.** *vt* faire frire **II.** *vi* **1.** (*be cooked*) frire **2.** *inf* (*get burnt*) griller

fry[2] [fraɪ] *n* fretin *m*

frying pan *n* poêle *f* (à frire) ►**to jump out of the** ~ **into the fire** tomber de Charybde en Scylla

ft *n abbr of* **foot or feet** pd

fuchsia ['fjuːʃə] **I.** *n* fuchsia *m* **II.** *adj* fuchsia

fuck [fʌk] *vulg* **I.** *vt* **1.** (*have sex with*) baiser **2.** *impers* (*damn*) ~ **it!** merde!; ~ **me!** putain!; ~ **you!** je t'emmerde!; ~ **off!** va te faire foutre! **II.** *vi* baiser **III.** *n no pl,* **1.** (*act*) baise; **to have a fuck** tirer un coup *f* **2.** (*person*) **a good/bad** ~ un bon/mauvais coup **3.** (*used as an expletive*) **for ~'s sake!** bordel!; **what the** ~ **are you doing?** qu'est-ce que tu fous, bordel de merde? **4.** (*intensifier*) **will you go there? – like** ~ **I will!** tu iras? – tu déconnes ou quoi!; ~ **all** que dalle; **not to give a** ~ n'en avoir rien à foutre **IV.** *interj* ~**!** bordel de merde!

fucker *n vulg* (*stupid person*) connard, -asse *m, f*

fuddled ['fʌdld] *adj* **1.** (*confused*) embrouillé(e) **2.** (*drunk*) éméché(e)

fuddy-duddy ['fʌdiˌdʌdi] **I.** <-ies> *n pej, inf* (*old-fashioned person*) vieux schnock *m* **II.** *adj pej, inf* ringard(e)

fudge [fʌdʒ] **I.** *n* **1.** *no pl* (*sweet*) caramel *m* **2.** *sing, pej* (*compromise*) faux-fuyant *m* **II.** <-ging> *vt* **1.** *pej* (*dodge*) esquiver **2.** *pej* (*falsify*) truquer

fuel ['fjuːəl] **I.** *n* **1.** *no pl* (*power source*) combustible *m* **2.** (*petrol*) carburant *m;* **unleaded** ~ essence *f* sans plomb ►**to add** ~ **to the fire** jeter de l'huile sur le feu **II.** <-ll- *o* -l- *Am*> *vt a. fig* alimenter; (*hatred*) attiser; (*doubts*) nourrir; **to be ~led by sth** marcher à qc

fuel consumption *n no pl* consommation *f* d'énergie; (*cars*) consommation *f* de carburant **fuel gauge** *n* jauge *f* de carburant **fuel-injection engine** *n* moteur *m* à injection **fuel oil** *n no pl* mazout *m* **fuel pump** *n* pompe *f* d'alimentation

fug [fʌg] *n no pl* odeur *f* de renfermé

fuggy <-ier, -iest> *adj* (*room*) mal aéré(e); (*air*) vicié(e)

fugitive ['fjuːdʒətɪv, *Am:* -t̬ɪv] **I.** *n* fugitif, -ive *m, f;* (*from war*) réfugié(e) *m(f)* **II.** *adj* fugitif(-ive)

fugue [fjuːg] *n* MUS fugue *f*

fulfil <-ll-> *vt Brit,* **fulfill** [fʊl'fɪl] *vt Am, Aus* **1.** (*satisfy*) accomplir; (*ambition, one's poten-*

tial) réaliser; (*person*) combler; **to ~ oneself** s'épanouir **2.** (*carry out: prophecy*) réaliser; (*contract, function*) remplir; (*promise, role*) tenir

fulfillment *n,* **fulfilment** *n Brit no pl, Am, Aus* (*of task*) accomplissement *m;* (*of ambition*) réalisation *f;* **personal ~** épanouissement *m* personnel

full [fʊl] **I.** <-er, -est> *adj* **1.** (*opp: empty*) plein(e); (*person*) rassasié(e); (*room*) comble; (*disk*) saturé(e); **~ to the brim** rempli à ras bord; **~ to bursting** plein à craquer, paqueté *Québec;* **~ of hate** plein de haine; **to be ~ of praise for sb/sth** ne pas tarir d'éloges sur qn/qc; **to talk with one's mouth ~** parler la bouche pleine; **to do sth on a ~ stomach** faire qc le ventre plein **2.** (*no spaces left: list, hotel*) complet(-ète); **everywhere was ~** tout était complet **3.** (*complete*) complet(-ète); (*text*) intégral(e); (*day*) bien rempli(e); (*explanation*) détaillé(e); (*member*) à part entière; (*professor*) titulaire; **I have a very ~ week ahead** je vais avoir une semaine très chargée; **~ details of the offer** toutes les précisions sur la promotion; **the ~ form of a word** un mot écrit en toutes lettres; **on ~ pay** sans réduction de paye; **~ employment** le plein-emploi; **the ~ horror of sth** toute l'horreur de qc; **to be in ~ swing** battre son plein; **we waited a ~ hour** on a attendu toute une heure; **in ~ view of sb** sous les yeux de qn; **to be ~ of sth** ne parler que de qc; **to be ~ of oneself** être très satisfait de soi; **to be under ~ sail** NAUT avoir toutes voiles dehors **4.** (*maximum*) plein(e); **at ~ volume** à plein volume; **at ~ blast** à fond; **at ~ stretch** tendu au maximum; *fig* à plein régime; **at ~ speed** à toute vitesse; **to get ~ marks** avoir la note maximale; **~ steam ahead!** NAUT en avant toutes!; **to be on ~ beam** être en pleins phares; **to be in ~ cry after sb/sth** se déchaîner après qn/qc **5.** (*rounded: face, cheeks*) rond(e); (*lips*) charnu(e); (*figure*) fort(e); (*skirt*) ample ►**to be ~ of** <u>**beans**</u> *Am* se gourer en plein; *Brit* être en pleine forme; **things have come ~** <u>**circle**</u> la boucle est bouclée; **to be ~ of the** <u>**joys**</u> **of spring** être en pleine forme **II.** *adv* complètement; **~ in the facee** en plein visage; **to be ~ on** être à fond; **to do sth ~ out** faire qc à toute vitesse; **I know ~ well that ...** je sais parfaitement que ... **III.** *n* **in ~** intégralement; **to the ~** à fond; **name in ~** nom et prénoms

fullback *n* SPORT arrière *m* **full-blooded** *adj* (*vigorous*) vigoureux(-euse) **full-blown** *adj* **1.** BOT épanoui(e) **2.** *fig* (*doctor*) diplômé(e); (*aids*) avéré(e); (*war*) qui fait rage **full board** *n* pension *f* complète **full-bodied** *adj* (*wine*) qui a du corps **full-cream milk** *n* lait *m* entier **full-dress** *adj* **1.** MIL de cérémonie; (*parade*) en grande tenue **2.** *fig* (*formal*) officiel(le); (*debate*) dans les règles **full-faced** *adj* au visage rond **full-fledged** *adj Am* **1.** ZOOL qui a toutes ses plumes **2.** (*qualified*) diplômé(e); (*member*) à part entière **full-frontal I.** *adj* vu(e) de face **II.** *n* nu *m* de face **full-grown** *adj* adulte **full-length I.** *adj* **1.** (*for entire body: mirror*) en pied; (*gown*) long(ue) **2.** (*not short: novel*) grand(e); **a ~ film** un long métrage **II.** *adv* de tout son long **full moon** *n* pleine lune *f*

fullness *n no pl* **1.** (*feeling*) plénitude *f;* **to speak out of the ~ of one's heart** parler le cœur débordant de joie **2.** (*shape: of figure*) rondeur *f;* (*of dress, voice*) ampleur *f* **3.** *fig* (*of speech, flavour*) richesse *f* ►**in the ~ of** <u>**time**</u> avec le temps

full-page *adj* (*advertisement*) pleine page **full-scale** *adj* **1.** (*at the same size*) grandeur nature **2.** (*total*) général(e); (*war*) généralisé(e) **3.** (*extensive: action*) de grande envergure; (*study*) approfondi(e) **full score** *n* MUS partition *f* intégrale **full stop** *n* **1.** *Aus, Brit* (*punctuation mark*) point *m* **2.** (*halt*) arrêt *m* définitif; **to come to a ~** aboutir à une impasse **full time** *n* SPORT fin *f* de match **full-time I.** *adj* **1.** (*opp: part-time*) à plein temps; **it's a ~ job doing that** *fig* ça occupe du matin au soir **2.** SPORT (*score*) final(e) **II.** *adv* à plein temps

fully ['fʊli] *adv* **1.** (*completely*) entièrement; (*open*) complètement; (*appreciate*) pleinement; (*understand*) parfaitement; (*study*) à fond; (*explain*) en détail; (*load*) au maximum; **I ~ intended to go** je voulais absolument y aller; **the flight's ~ booked** le vol est complet **2.** (*at least*) au moins; **~ three hours** trois bonnes heures; **~ five years** au moins cinq ans

fully-fledged *adj Brit s.* **full-fledged**

fulminate ['fʌlmɪneɪt] *vi* fulminer

fulsome ['fʊlsəm] *adj* **1.** (*praising*) enthousiaste **2.** (*abundant*) excessif(-ive); **~ compliments** effusions *fpl*

fumble ['fʌmbl] **I.** *vi* **1.** (*look for something*) **to ~ around** fouiller **2.** (*feel for something*) **to ~ around** tâtonner **3.** (*try to say something*) **to ~ for words** chercher ses mots **4.** SPORT laisser tomber le ballon **II.** *vt* **1.** SPORT **to ~ the ball** mal attraper le ballon; (*American football*) perdre le ballon dans la course **2.** (*be awkward with*) manier maladroitement; **to ~ an answer** bredouiller une réponse **III.** *n* maladresse *f*

fume [fjuːm] *vi a. fig* fulminer; **to ~ at sth** fulminer contre qc

fumes *n pl* émanations *fpl;* (*from cars*) vapeurs *fpl* d'essence

fumigate ['fjuːmɪgeɪt] *vt* fumiger

fun [fʌn] **I.** *n* amusement *m;* **for ~** pour s'amuser; **to be ~** être amusant; **have ~!** amusez-vous bien!; **we had a lot of ~ painting it** on s'est bien amusés à le peindre; **he's a lot of ~** il est très marrant; **you're no ~!** tu n'es pas marrant!; **to make ~ of sb** se moquer de qn; **it's raining today, what ~!** il pleut aujourd'hui, comme c'est amusant! **II.** *adj Am, Aus* drôle

function ['fʌŋkʃən] **I.** *n* **1.** (*purpose*) *a.* MAT fonction *f;* **in my ~ as mayor ...** en tant que maire ...; **to fulfil a ~** remplir un rôle; **to be a ~ of sth** être en fonction de qc **2.** (*formal ceremony*) cérémonie *f* **3.** (*formal social event*) réception *f* **II.** *vi* fonctionner; **to ~ as sth** faire fonction de qc

functional *adj* **1.** (*serving a function*) *a.* MED fonctionnel(le) **2.** (*operational, working*) operationnel(le)

functionary ['fʌŋkʃənəri, *Am:* -eri] <-ries> *n* fonctionnaire *mf*

function key *n* INFOR touche *f* de fonction

fund [fʌnd] **I.** *n* fonds *m;* **pension ~** caisse *f* de retraite; **to be short of ~** être à court de capitaux ►**to be a ~ of knowledge** être une mine d'érudition; **to have a ~ of sth** connaître des quantités de choses **II.** *vt* financer

fundamental [ˌfʌndə'mentəl, *Am:* -t̬əl] *adj* fondamental(e); (*need*) vital(e); (*principle*) premier(-ère); (*question, concern*) principal(e); (*importance, error*) capital(e); **to learn the ~s** apprendre les principes de base

fundamentalism [ˌfʌndə'mentəlɪzəm, *Am:* -t̬əl-] *n no pl* fondamentalisme *m*

fundamentalist **I.** *n* fondamentaliste *mf* **II.** *adj* fondamentaliste

fundamentally *adv* **1.** (*basically*) fondamentalement; **~ honest** foncièrement honnête **2.** (*in the most important sense*) **~, ...** au fond, ...

funeral ['fju:nərəl] *n* funérailles *fpl;* **to attend a ~** assister à un enterrement ►**that's his ~** *inf* tant pis pour lui

funeral director *n* entrepreneur *m* des pompes funèbres **funeral march** <-es> *n* marche *f* funèbre **funeral parlo(u)r** *n* entreprise *f* des pompes funèbres, salon *m* funéraire [*o* mortuaire] *Québec*

funereal [fju:'nɪəriəl, *Am:* -'nɪri-] *adj* **1.** (*appropriate to a funeral*) funèbre **2.** (*slow and sad*) lugubre

funfair ['fʌnfeəʳ, *Am:* -fer] *n Brit* fête *f* foraine

fungus ['fʌŋgəs] *n* <fungi> **1.** GASTR champignon *m* **2.** MED mycose *f* **3.** (*mould*) moisissure *f*

funicular [fju:'nɪkjələʳ, *Am:* -ju:lɚ], **funicular railway** *n* funiculaire *m*

funk [fʌŋk] *n no pl* **1.** *Am, Aus* (*depression*) déprime *f;* **to be in a ~** avoir le cafard **2.** *Brit, inf* (*panic*) trouille *f;* **to be in a blue ~** avoir la frousse **3.** MUS funk *m*

funky <-ier, -iest> *adj inf* **1.** MUS funky *inv* **2.** (*unconventionally fashionable*) funky *inv* **3.** (*smelly*) puant(e)

fun-lover *n* personne *f* frivole, amusette *f Belgique* **fun-loving** *adj* qui aime s'amuser

funnel ['fʌnəl] **I.** *n* **1.** (*implement*) entonnoir *m* **2.** (*chimney*) cheminée *f* **II.** <*Brit* -ll- *o Am* -l-> *vt a. fig* verser; (*attention*) canaliser; (*goods, information*) faire passer **III.** *vi* (*people*) s'engouffrer; (*liquid, gases*) passer

funnies *npl Am* bandes *fpl* dessinées

funny ['fʌni] <-ier, -iest> *adj* **1.** (*amusing*) drôle; (*joke*) bon(ne) **2.** (*odd, peculiar*) curieux(-euse); (*thing*) bizarre; (*feeling*) étrange; (*idea*) drôle; **to look ~** être bizarre; **it feels ~ being back here** ça fait bizarre d'être de retour ici **3.** (*dishonest*) malhonnête; (*business*) louche **4.** (*not working or feeling well*) **to feel ~** ne pas se sentir bien; **sth goes ~** qc se met à ne plus bien marcher; **to be (a bit) ~ in the head** être un peu fou **5.** *Brit, inf* **don't try anything funny ~** ne fais pas le malin; **don't you try to be ~ with your mother** *inf* ne fais pas le malin avec ta mère

funny bone *n inf: fourmillement ressenti quand on se cogne le coude* **funny business** *n inf* magouilles *fpl*

fur [fɜ:ʳ, *Am:* fɜ:r] **I.** *n* **1.** *no pl* (*animal hair*) poils *m* **2.** (*clothing*) fourrure *f* **3.** *pl* (*in hunting*) peaux *f* **4.** *no pl* (*hard water deposit*) dépôt *m* calcaire ►**the ~ flies** il y a du grabuge **II.** <-rr-> *vi* **to ~ up** s'entartrer

furious ['fjʊərɪəs, *Am:* 'fjʊrɪ-] *adj* **1.** (*very angry*) furieux(-euse); **to be ~ with sb** être en colère contre qn **2.** (*intense, violent: argument, storm*) violent(e); **at a ~ pace** au pas de charge

furl [fɜ:l, *Am:* fɜ:rl] *vt* rouler; (*sail*) ferler

furlong ['fɜ:lɒŋ, *Am:* 'fɜ:rlɑ:ŋ] *n* furlong *m* (≈ *201 mètres*)

furlough ['fɜ:ləʊ, *Am:* 'fɜ:rloʊ] *n* MIL permission *f*

furnace ['fɜ:nɪs, *Am:* 'fɜ:r-] *n* **1.** (*container for heating*) fourneau *m* **2.** (*central heating unit*) chaudière *f* **3.** (*very hot place*) fournaise *f*

furnish ['fɜ:nɪʃ, *Am:* 'fɜ:r-] *vt* **1.** (*supply*) fournir; **to ~ sb with sth** fournir qc à qn **2.** (*provide furniture*) meubler; **to be ~ed with sth** être équipé de qc

furnishings *npl* ameublement *m*

furniture ['fɜ:nɪtʃəʳ, *Am:* 'fɜ:rnɪtʃɚ] *n no pl* meubles *mpl;* **piece of ~** meuble *m* ►**to be part of the ~** faire partie des meubles

furniture store *n* magasin *m* d'ameublement **furniture van** *n* camion *m* de déménagement

furore [fjʊə'rɔ:ri, *Am:* 'fjʊrɔ:r-] *n* (*outcry*) colère *f;* **to cause a ~** déclencher la fureur

furrier ['fʌriəʳ, *Am:* 'fɜ:riɚ] *n* fourreur *m*

furrow ['fʌrəʊ, *Am:* 'fɜ:roʊ] **I.** *n* **1.** (*groove*) sillon *m* **2.** (*wrinkle*) ride *f* **II.** *vt* **1.** (*make a groove*) labourer **2.** (*make a wrinkle*) rider; **to ~ one's brow** plisser le front

furry ['fɜ:ri] <-ier, -iest> *adj* **1.** (*covered with fur*) à poil **2.** (*looking like fur: toy*) en peluche

further ['fɜ:ðəʳ, *Am:* 'fɜ:rðɚ] **I.** *adj comp of* **far** **1.** (*greater distance*) *a. fig* plus éloigné(e); **at the ~ end of sth** à l'autre bout de qc **2.** (*additional*) supplémentaire; **if you have any ~ problems, ...** si vous avez d'autres problèmes, ...; **on ~ examination** après examen ultérieur; **until ~ notice** jusqu'à nouvel ordre **II.** *adv comp of* **far** **1.** (*greater distance*) *a. fig* plus loin; **~ away** plus loin; ~

back plus loin en arrière; **we didn't get much ~** nous ne sommes pas allés plus loin; **~ and ~** de plus en plus loin; **to go ~ with sth** aller plus avant dans qc; **he wouldn't go any ~** il refusait aller plus loin; **to look ~ ahead** regarder vers l'avenir **2.** (*more*) de plus; **I have nothing ~ to say on this matter** je n'ai rien à ajouter à ce sujet; **~ to your letter** *Brit, Aus, form* par suite à votre lettre ►**this musn't go any ~** ça ne doit pas aller plus loin; **to make sth go ~** faire durer qc **III.** *vt* faire avancer; (*cause, interest*) servir; **training, research** poursuivre; (*career*) faire avancer

furtherance ['fɜːðərəns, *Am:* 'fɜːr-] *n no pl, form* avancement *m;* **in the ~ of sth** pour servir qc

further education *n enseignement appliqué après le collège, souvent destiné aux adultes*

furthermore *adv* en outre

furthermost *adj* le(la) plus reculé(e)

furthest ['fɜːðɪst, *Am:* 'fɜːr-] **I.** *adj superl of* **far** *a. fig* le(la) plus éloigné(e); **the ~ island from the mainland** l'île la plus éloignée du continent **II.** *adv superl of* **far** *a. fig* le plus loin; **to be ~ north** être plus au nord; **£500 is the ~ I can go** 500£ est mon dernier prix

furtive ['fɜːtɪv, *Am:* 'fɜːrt̬ɪv] *adj* (*glance, look*) furtif(-ive); (*air, manner, person*) sournois(e)

fury ['fjʊəri, *Am:* 'fjʊri] *n no pl* fureur *f;* **in a ~** dans un accès de colère; **in a cold ~** dans une rage froide ►**to work like ~** travailler d'arrache-pied

fuse [fjuːz] **I.** *n* **1.** (*electrical safety device*) fusible *m;* **to blow a ~** faire sauter un plomb; **the ~ has gone** le plomb a sauté **2.** (*ignition device, detonator*) détonateur *m* **3.** (*string*) mèche *f* ►**to have a short ~** ne pas avoir de patience; **to blow one's ~** péter les plombs **II.** *vi* **1.** (*melt*) fondre; **to ~ together** s'unifier **2.** (*blow a fuse*) faire sauter les plombs **3.** (*join*) *a. fig* fusionner **III.** *vt* **1.** ELEC faire sauter; **to ~ the lights** faire sauter les plombs **2.** (*melt*) fondre **3.** (*join together*) faire fusionner

fuse box <-xes> *n* boîte *f* à fusibles

fuselage ['fjuːzəlɑːʒ, *Am:* -səlɑːʒ] *n* fuselage *m*

fusion ['fjuːʒən] *n a. fig* fusion *f*

fusion bomb *n* bombe *f* thermonucléaire

fuss [fʌs] **I.** *n no pl* **1.** (*trouble*) histoires *f;* **to make a ~ about sth** faire des histoires pour qc; **I had to make a big ~ to get a refund** j'ai du faire tout un scandale pour me faire rembourser; **it's a lot of ~ about nothing** c'est beaucoup de bruit pour pas grand chose **2. attentiveness** attentions *fpl;* **to make a ~ of** [*o Am* **over**] **sb** être aux petits soins pour qn **II.** *vi* **1.** (*make a fuss*) faire des histoires **2.** (*worry*) **to ~ over sb/sth** s'en faire énormément au sujet de qn/qc **3.** (*be agitated*) s'agiter **4.** (*show attention*) **to ~ over sb** être aux petits soins pour qn **III.** *vt* **I'm not ~ed** ça m'est égal

fusspot ['fʌspɒt, *Am:* -pɑːt] *n inf* enquiquineur, -euse *m, f;* **to be a ~** faire des histoires

fussy ['fʌsi] <-ier, -iest> *adj* **1.** *pej* (*over-particular*) méticuleux(-euse); **to be a ~ eater** être difficile sur la nourriture; **I'm not ~** *Brit, inf* cela m'est égal **2.** *pej* (*overdecorated*) surchargé(e) **3.** (*needing much care: job*) minutieux(-euse)

futile ['fjuːtaɪl, *Am:* -t̬əl] *adj* **1.** (*vain*) vain(e) **2.** (*unimportant*) futile; **to prove ~** se révéler dérisoire

futility [fjuː'tɪləti, *Am:* -t̬i] *n no pl* inutilité *f*

future ['fjuːtʃəʳ, *Am:* -tʃɚ] **I.** *n* **1.** (*the time to come*) avenir *m;* **to have plans for the ~** avoir des projets pour l'avenir; **what the ~ will bring** ce que l'avenir nous réserve; **in (the) ~** à l'avenir **2.** (*prospects*) avenir *m;* **she has a great ~ ahead of her** elle a un bel avenir devant elle; **to face an uncertain ~** affronter des lendemains incertains; **the school of the ~** l'école du futur **3.** LING futur *m;* **to be in the ~ (tense)** être au futur **II.** *adj* futur(e); (*events*) à venir; **at some ~ date** à une date ultérieure

futures market *n* marché *m* à terme

futurism *n no pl* futurisme *m*

futuristic [ˌfjuːtʃə'rɪstɪk] *adj* futuriste

fuze [fjuːz] *s.* **fuse**

fuzz [fʌz] *n no pl* **1.** (*fluff*) peluches *fpl* **2.** (*hair*) touffe *f;* (*on face*) duvet *m* **3.** *Brit, Am, Aus, inf* (*police*) **the ~** les flics

fuzzy *adj* **1.** (*unclear: image*) flou(e); (*sound, reception*) brouillé(e) **2.** *fig* (*confused*) confus(e); **to have a ~ head** avoir l'esprit confus **3.** (*frizzy: hair*) crépu(e); **peaches have ~ skins** les pêches ont des peaux duveteuses

G

G *n,* **g** [dʒiː] <-'s *o* -s> *n* G *m,* g *m;* **~ as in George, ~ for George** (*on telephone*) g comme Gaston

g *n* **1.** <-> *abbr of* **gram** g *m* **2.** <-'s> PHYS *abbr of* **gravity** g *m*

G *n no pl* MUS sol *m*

G I. <-'s> *n Am, Aus, inf* (*$1000*) mille dollars *mpl* **II.** *adj inv, Am abbr of* **General-Audience** (*movie*) tout public; **rated ~** classé tout public

G7 *n abbr of* **Group of 7: the ~** le G7

G8 *n abbr of* **Group of 8: the ~** le G8

gab [gæb] **I.** <-bb-> *vi pej, inf* papoter **II.** *n pej* bagout *m;* **to have the gift of the ~** avoir du bagout

gabardine [ˌgæbə'diːn, *Am:* 'gæbɚdiːn] *n* **1.** *no pl* (*cloth*) gabardine *f* **2.** (*coat*) gabardine *f*

gabble ['gæbl] **I.** *vi* bredouiller; **to ~ away**

pej baragouiner **II.** *vt* bredouiller **III.** *n no pl* bredouillement *m*

gabby <-ier, -iest> *adj inf* jacasseur(-euse)

gaberdine *n s.* **gabardine**

gable ['geɪbl] *n* ARCHIT pignon *m*

gabled *adj* à pignon(s)

gadfly ['gædflaɪ] <-ies> *n* **1.** (*insect*) taon *m* **2.** (*person*) casse-pieds *mf*

gadget ['gædʒɪt] *n* gadget *m*

gadgetry ['gædʒɪtri] *n no pl* gadgets *mpl*

Gaelic ['geɪlɪk] **I.** *adj* gaélique **II.** *n* Gaélique *m; s. a.* **English**

gaff [gæf] *n* gaffe *f* ►**to blow the ~** *Brit, inf* vendre la mèche; **to blow the ~ on sb/sth** dénoncer qn/qc

gaffe [gæf] *n* gaffe *f*

gaffer *n* **1.** *Brit, inf* (*boss*) chef *m* **2.** *Brit, inf* (*old man*) vieux *m*

gag[1] [gæg] **I.** *n* (*cloth*) bâillon *m* **II.** <-gg-> *vt a. fig* bâillonner **III.** <-gg-> *vi* avoir des haut-le-cœur

gag[2] **I.** *n* (*joke*) gag *m;* **to do sth for a ~** *Am, Aus* faire qc pour rire **II.** <-gg-> *vi* plaisanter

gaga ['gɑːgɑː] *adj inf* gaga *inv;* **to go ~** devenir gaga; **to be ~ about** [*o* **over**] **sb** être gaga de qn

gage [geɪdʒ] *Am s.* **gauge**

gaggle ['gægl] *n* (*group*) *a. pej* troupeau *m*

gaiety ['geɪəti, *Am:* -t̬i] <-ies> *n no pl* gaieté *f*

gaily ['geɪli] *adv* **1.** (*happily*) joyeusement; (*laugh*) de bon cœur **2.** (*without thinking*) allègrement **3.** (*brightly*) **~ coloured** aux couleurs gaies

gain [geɪn] **I.** *n* **1.** (*profit*) gain *m,* profit *m;* **to do sth for ~** faire qc par intérêt **2.** (*increase*) augmentation *f;* **a ~ in sth** une augmentation de qc; **weight ~** prise *f* de poids **3.** FIN hausse *f;* **to make ~s** être en hausse **4.** (*advantage*) gain *m* **II.** *vt* **1.** (*obtain*) obtenir; (*confidence, respect, sympathy*) gagner; (*experience, knowledge, reputation*) acquérir; (*victory, success*) remporter; **to ~ time/money** gagner du temps/de l'argent; **to ~ freedom/independence** conquérir sa liberté/son indépendance; **to ~ access to sth** accéder à qc; **to ~ acceptance** être accepté; **to ~ control of sth** prendre le contrôle de qc; **to ~ an impression** avoir une impression; **to ~ insight into sth** avoir un aperçu de qc **2.** (*increase*) gagner; **to ~ altitude** gagner de l'altitude; **to ~ weight/velocity** prendre du poids/de la vitesse; **to ~ popularity/prestige** gagner en popularité/en prestige; **to ~ impetus** [*o* **momentum**] prendre de l'ampleur; **to ~ strength** prendre des forces; **to ~ two minutes** (*clock*), **to ~ ground** gagner du terrain; (*progress*) progresser; **to ~ ground on sb** (*catch up*) rattraper qn, avancer de deux minutes **3.** (*reach: destination*) atteindre ►**to ~ a foothold** prendre pied; **to ~ the upper hand** prendre le dessus; **nothing ventured, nothing ~ed** *prov* qui ne risque rien n'a rien **III.** *vi* **1.** (*benefit*) **to ~ by sth** bénéficier de qc **2.** (*increase: prices, numbers*) augmenter; (*clock, watch*) avancer; **to ~ in popularity** gagner en popularité; **to ~ in confidence** prendre de l'assurance; **to ~ in numbers/height** devenir plus nombreux/plus grand; **to ~ in weight** prendre du poids **3.** (*catch up*) **to ~ on sb/sth** rattraper qn/qc

gainer *n* gagnant(e) *m(f)*

gainful *adj inv* lucratif(-ive); (*employment*) rémunéré(e)

gainfully *adv inv* **to be ~ employed** avoir un emploi rémunéré; **to keep sb ~ employed** employer qn utilement

gainsay <-said, -said> *vt form* contredire

gait [geɪt] *n* démarche *f;* **to walk with a slow/clumsy ~** marcher d'un pas nonchalant/mal assuré

gaiter *n* guêtre *f*

gal[1] [gæl] *n Am, iron, inf* (*girl*) fille *f*

gal[2] ['gælən] <- *o* -s> *n abbr of* **gallon**

gala ['gɑːlə, *Am:* 'geɪ-] *n* **1.** (*social event*) gala *m;* **a ~ night** une nuit de gala **2.** *Brit* (*competition*) compétition *f*

galactic [gə'læktɪk] *adj inv* galactique

galaxy ['gæləksi] <-ies> *n* **1.** (*star system*) galaxie *f* **2.** (*Milky Way*) **the ~** la Voie Lactée **3.** (*group*) pléiade *f*

gale [geɪl] *n* **1.** (*wind*) vent *m* violent; **~-force winds** vents *mpl* forts **2.** *fig* éclat *m;* **~s of laughter** éclats de rire

gale warning *n* avis *m* de tempête

gall[1] [gɔːl] **I.** *n* **1.** (*bile*) bile *f* **2.** (*bold behavior*) toupet *m* **II.** *vt* irriter

gall[2] *n Brit abbr of* **gallon** gallon *m*

gallant ['gælənt] *adj* **1.** (*chivalrous*) galant(e) **2.** (*brave*) vaillant(e)

gallantly *adv* **1.** (*with charm*) galamment **2.** (*bravely*) vaillamment

gallantry ['gæləntri] *n* **1.** *no pl* (*chivalry*) galanterie *f* **2.** *no pl* (*courage*) vaillance *f*

gall bladder *n* vésicule *f* biliaire

gallery ['gæləri] <-ies> *n* galerie *f* ►**to play to the ~** épater la galerie

galley ['gæli] *n* **1.** (*boat*) galère *f* **2.** (*kitchen*) cuisine *f*

galley slave *n* galérien *m*

Gallic ['gælɪk] *adj* **1.** (*of Gaul*) gaulois(e); **the ~ Wars** les guerres des Gaules **2.** (*typically French*) français(e)

galling *adj* humiliant(e)

gallivant [ˌgælɪ'vænt, *Am:* -ə'-] *vi inf* **to ~ about** [*o* **around**] être en vadrouille

gallon ['gælən] *n* **1.** (*unit*) gallon *m* (*≈ 4,55 litres en Grande-Bretagne et ≈ 3,79 litres aux Etats-Unis*) **2.** (*lots*) **~s of sth** litres *mpl* de qc

gallop ['gæləp] **I.** *vi a. fig* (*horse*) galoper; (*rider*) aller au galop; **to ~ away** partir au galop; **to ~ down the street** descendre la rue au galop; (*to be in a hurry*) descendre la rue à toute allure; **to ~ through one's work** expédier son travail **II.** *vt* (*cause to gallop: a horse*) faire galoper **III.** *n sing* galop *m;* **at a ~** *fig* au galop; **to break into a ~** se mettre au

galop
gallows ['gæləʊz, *Am:* -oʊz] *n + sing vb* **the** ~ la potence
gallows humour *n no pl* humour *m* noir
gallstone ['gɔːlstəʊn, *Am:* -stoʊn] *n* calcul *m* biliaire
Gallup poll® ['gæləp pəʊl, *Am:* -poʊl] *n Am, Can* sondage *m* Gallup
galop(p)ing *adj inv* galopant(e)
galore [gə'lɔːʳ, *Am:* -'lɔːr] *adj inv* à profusion
galvanise *vt Brit, Aus s.* **galvanize**
galvanised *adj Brit, Aus s.* **galvanized**
galvanize ['gælvənaɪz] *vt a. fig* galvaniser; **to ~ sb into action** pousser qn à agir
galvanized *adj inv* galvanisé(e)
Gambia ['gæmbɪə] *n* (**the**) ~ la Gambie
Gambian **I.** *adj inv* gambien(ne) **II.** *n* Gambien(ne) *m(f)*
gambit ['gæmbɪt] *n* **1.** (*in chess*) gambit *m* **2.** (*tactic*) tactique *f;* **opening** ~ manœuvre *f* d'approche
gamble ['gæmbl] **I.** *n* risque *m* **II.** *vi* **1.** (*bet*) jouer (de l'argent); **to ~ at cards/on horses** jouer aux cartes/aux courses; **to ~ on the stock market** jouer à la bourse **2.** (*take a risk hoping*) **to ~ on sb/sth** compter sur qn/qc; **to ~ on doing sth** compter faire qc **III.** *vt* jouer; **to ~ everything on sth** *fig* tout miser sur qc
◆**gamble away** *vt* perdre au jeu
gambler *n* joueur, -euse *m, f*
gambling *n no pl* jeu *m*
gambling debts *n* dettes *fpl* de jeu **gambling den** *n pej* tripot *m* **gambling house** *n* salle *f* de jeu **gambling joint** *n s.* **gambling den**
game¹ [geɪm] **I.** *n* **1.** (*play, amusement*) jeu *m;* **computer** ~ jeu pour ordinateur; ~ **of chance/skill** jeu de chance/d'adresse; **to be just a ~ to sb** *a. fig* n'être qu'un jeu pour qn **2.** (*contest: board game, chess*) partie *f;* (*football, rugby*) match *m;* (*tennis*) jeu *m;* ~ **over** fin *f* de partie; **to play a good** ~ faire un bon match **3.** SPORT (*skill level*) jeu *m;* **to be off one's** ~ ne pas être en forme; **to be on one's** ~ bien jouer **4.** *pej* (*dishonest plan*) jeu *m;* **the ~ is up** l'affaire est à l'eau; **to be up to one's old ~s** refaire des siennes; **to play ~s with sb** jouer avec qn; **to beat sb at their own** ~ battre qn à son propre jeu **5.** *pl* (*organized*) jeux *mpl;* **the Olympic ~s** les Jeux olympiques ►**to give the ~ away** vendre la mèche; **the ~ is worth the candle** le jeu n'en vaut pas la chandelle; **to be on the** ~ *Brit, inf* faire le tapin; ~ **over** c'est fini; **to play the** ~ jouer le jeu; **what's your ~?** où veux-tu en venir? **II.** *adj inf* (*willing*) partant(e); **to be ~ to** *+infin* être partant pour *+infin*
game² [geɪm] *n no pl* **1.** (*animal*) gibier *m* **2.** (*meat*) gibier *m*
game birds *n pl* gibier *m* à plumes **Gameboy®** *n* Gameboy *f* **gamecock** *n* coq *m* de combat **gamekeeper** *n* garde-chasse *m*
game laws *npl* règles *fpl* du jeu **game licence** *n* permis *m* de chasse
gamely *adv* courageusement
game plan *n* stratégie *f* **gameplay** *n no pl* gameplay *m* **game point** *n* (*in tennis, handball*) balle *f* de jeu **game reserve** *n* réserve *f* naturelle **game room** *n* salle *f* de jeux **game show** *n* jeu *m* télévisé
gamesmanship *n no pl* astuce *f*
game theory *n* théorie *f* des jeux
gaming *n no pl* jeu *m;* ~ **house** maison *f* de jeu
gaming table *n* table *f* de jeu
gamma radiation *no pl,* **gamma rays** *npl* rayons *mpl* gamma
gammon ['gæmən] *n no pl, Brit* (*ham*) jambon *m*
gammy ['gæmi] <-ier, -iest> *adj Brit, inf* ~ **leg** patte *f* folle
gamut ['gæmət] *n* gamme *f;* **to run the ~ of sth** passer par toute la gamme de qc
gander ['gændəʳ, *Am:* -dɚ] *n* **1.** (*male goose*) jars *m* **2.** *inf* (*look*) **to take a ~ at sth** jeter un coup d'œil à qc ►**what's sauce for the goose is sauce for the** ~ *prov* ce qui vaut pour l'un vaut pour l'autre
gang [gæŋ] **I.** *n* **1.** (*organized group*) bande *f;* (*of workers*) équipe *f;* **chain** ~ chaîne *f* de forçats **2.** *pej* (*criminal group*) gang *m* **3.** *inf* (*group of friends*) bande *f* **II.** *vi pej* **to ~ up on sb** se liguer contre qn; **to ~ up with sb** s'allier à qn
gang bang *n inf* **1.** (*rape*) viol *m* collectif **2.** (*orgy*) gang bang *m*
ganger *n Brit* chef *m* d'équipe
Ganges ['gændʒiːz] *n* **the** ~ le Gange
gangling ['gæŋglɪŋ] *adj* dégingandé(e)
ganglion ['gæŋglɪən] <-lions *o* -glia> *n* MED ganglion *m*
gangly ['gæŋgli] *adv* dégingandé(e)
gangplank ['gæŋplæŋk] *n* passerelle *f*
gangrene ['gæŋgriːn] *n no pl* gangrène *f*
gangrenous ['gæŋgrɪnəs, *Am:* -grə-] *adj* **1.** (*suffering from gangrene*) gangreneux(-euse) **2.** (*corrupt*) gangrené(e)
gangster ['gæŋstəʳ, *Am:* -stɚ] *n* gangster *m*
gang warfare *n no pl* guerre *f* des gangs
gangway ['gæŋweɪ] **I.** *n* **1.** NAUT, AVIAT passerelle *f* **2.** *Brit* (*aisle*) allée *f* **II.** *interj inf* ~! laissez passer!
gantry ['gæntri] <-tries> *n* portique *m*
gaol [dʒeɪl] *n s.* **jail**
gap [gæp] *n* **1.** (*opening*) trou *m;* (*in text*) blanc *m;* (*in teeth*) écart *m;* (*in trees, clouds*) trouée *f;* (*in knowledge*) lacune *f* **2.** (*space*) espace *m* **3.** *fig* créneau *m;* (*emotional*) vide *m;* **market** ~ créneau sur le marché; **to fill a** ~ combler un vide **4.** (*break in time*) intervalle *m* **5.** (*difference*) écart *m;* **the generation** ~ le fossé des générations; **to bridge/close the ~ between sth** réduire l'écart entre qc
gape [geɪp] *vi* **1.** (*stare open-mouthed*) être bouche bée; **to ~ at sb/sth** regarder qn/qc

bouche bée **2.** (*hang open*) s'ouvrir; (*door*) bâiller; **to ~ open** être grand ouvert
gaping *adj* (*wound, hole*) béant(e)
garage ['gærɑːʒ, *Am:* gə'rɑːʒ] **I.** *n* **1.** (*place to house a vehicle*) garage *m;* **one-car ~** garage à une place **2.** *Brit, Aus* (*petrol station*) station-service *f* **3.** (*auto repair shop, dealer*) garage *m* **II.** *vt* rentrer (dans le garage)
garbage ['gɑːbɪdʒ, *Am:* 'gɑːr-] *n no pl* **1.** *Am, Aus, Can* (*household rubbish*) ordures *fpl;* **to take the ~ out** sortir les poubelles **2.** *pej* (*nonsense, useless ideas*) âneries *fpl;* **to talk ~** dire des âneries ►**~ in, ~ out** INFOR qualité des entrées = qualité des sorties
garbage can *n Am, Can* poubelle *f* **garbage chute** *n Am, Can* vide-ordures *m,* dévaloir *m Suisse* **garbage collector** *n Am, Can* éboueur *m* **garbage disposal, garbage disposer** *n Am, Can* broyeur *m* à ordures **garbage dump** *n Am, Can* dépôt *m* d'ordures **garbage truck** *n Am, Aus, Can* benne *f* à ordures
garble ['gɑːbl, *Am:* 'gɑːr-] *vt* déformer
garbled *adj* confus(e)
garden ['gɑːdn, *Am:* 'gɑːr-] **I.** *n* **1.** *Brit* (*piece of land next to a house*) jardin *m;* **~ furniture** meubles *mpl* de jardin; **~ hose** tuyau *m* d'arrosage **2.** *Am, Aus, Can* (*area planted to a specific purpose*) jardin *m;* **flower ~** jardin d'agrément; **vegetable ~** jardin potager ►**to lead sb up the ~ path** mener qn en bateau **II.** *vi* jardiner
garden apartment *n Am* rez-de-jardin *m* **garden centre** *n* jardinerie *f* **garden city** <-ties> *n Brit* cité-jardin *f*
gardener *n* jardinier, -ière *m, f*
gardening *n no pl* jardinage *m*
garden party <-ties> *n* garden-party *f*
gargle ['gɑːgl, *Am:* 'gɑːr-] **I.** *vi* se gargariser **II.** *n* gargarisme *m;* **to have a ~ with sth** faire un gargarisme de qc
gargoyle ['gɑːgɔɪl, *Am:* 'gɑːr-] *n* gargouille *f*
garish ['geərɪʃ, *Am:* 'ger-] *adj pej* (*colours*) criard(e); (*taste, appearance*) vulgaire
garland ['gɑːlənd, *Am:* 'gɑːr-] **I.** *n* guirlande *f* **II.** *vt* orner de guirlandes
garlic ['gɑːlɪk, *Am:* 'gɑːr-] **I.** *n no pl* ail *m* **II.** *adj* (*sauce, bread*) à l'ail; (*smell, breath*) d'ail
garlic press <-es> *n* presse-ail *m*
garment ['gɑːmənt, *Am:* 'gɑːr-] *n form* vêtement *m;* **~ industry** industrie *f* du vêtement
garnet ['gɑːnɪt, *Am:* 'gɑːr-] *n* grenat *m*
garnish ['gɑːnɪʃ, *Am:* 'gɑːr-] **I.** *vt* garnir **II.** <-shes> *n* garniture *f*
garret ['gærət, *Am:* 'ger-] *n* **1.** ARCHIT combles *fpl* **2.** (*attic room*) mansarde *f*
garrison ['gærɪsn, *Am:* 'gerə-] **I.** *n* garnison *f* **II.** *vt* **to be ~ed** être en garnison; **to ~ a place** mettre une garnison dans un endroit
garrulous ['gærələs, *Am:* 'ger-] *adj* bavard(e)
garter ['gɑːtəʳ, *Am:* 'gɑːrt̬ɚ] **I.** *n* **1.** (*band for stockings, socks*) jarretière *f* **2.** *Am* (*suspender*) jarretelle *f* ►**the order of the ~** *Brit* l'ordre de la Jarretière **II.** *vt* **to be ~ed** porter une jarretière
garter belt *n Am* porte-jarretelles *m* **garter stitch** *n* point *m* mousse
gas [gæs] **I.** <-es *o* -sses> *n* **1.** (*not a liquid or solid, fuel*) gaz *m;* **a ~ grill/stove/oven** un grill/four à gaz **2.** *no pl, inf* MED anesthésie *f* **3.** *no pl* MIL gaz *m* de combat; **~ mask** masque à gaz; **poison ~** gaz asphyxiant **4.** *no pl, Am, Can, inf* (*petrol*) essence *f;* **to get ~** prendre de l'essence; **to step on the ~** appuyer sur l'accélérateur **5.** *Am, inf* **a ~** une bonne rigolade **II.** <-ss-> *vt* (*by accident*) asphyxier; (*deliberately*) gazer
gasbag *n pej, inf* bavard(e) *m(f)* **gas chamber** *n* chambre *f* à gaz **gas cooker** *n* **1.** (*stove*) cuisinière *f* à gaz **2.** (*small device*) réchaud *m* à gaz
gaseous ['gæsɪəs] *adj* gazeux(-euse)
gas fire *n Brit* chauffage *m* au gaz **gas-fitter** *n Brit* chauffagiste *m* **gas gauge** *n Am, Can* jauge *f* d'essence
gash [gæʃ] **I.** <-shes> *n* (*deep cut, wound*) entaille *f;* (*on face*) balafre *f* **II.** *vt* entailler; (*face*) balafrer
gasholder *n* réservoir *m* à gaz
gasket ['gæskɪt] *n* joint *m* de culasse ►**to blow a ~** péter les plombs
gas lighter *n* **1.** (*igniting device*) allume-gaz *m* **2.** (*cigarette lighter*) briquet *m* à gaz **gas main** *n* conduite *f* de gaz **gasman** <-men> *n Brit, inf* employé(e) *m(f)* du gaz **gas mask** *n* masque *m* à gaz **gas meter** *n* compteur *m* de gaz
gasolene ['gæsəliːn], **gasoline** *n Am, Can* (*petrol*) essence *f*
gasometer *n* gazomètre *m*
gasp [gɑːsp, *Am:* gæsp] **I.** *vi* **1.** (*catch one's breath*) haleter; **to ~ for air** haleter **2.** *Brit, inf* (*be eager*) **to be ~ing for sth** mourir d'envie de qc; **to be ~ing for a drink** mourir de soif; **to be ~ing for a cigarette** mourir d'envie de fumer une cigarette **II.** *vt* **to ~** (**out**) **sth** dire qc d'une voix haletante **III.** *n* sursaut *m;* **to give a ~ of surprise/fear** rester bouche bée ►**to be at one's last ~** rendre le dernier soupir; **to do sth to the last ~** faire qc jusqu'au bout
gas pedal *n* pédale *f* d'accélération **gas pipe** *n* conduite *f* de gaz **gas pump** *n Am, Can* pompe *f* à essence **gas ring** *n Brit* brûleur *m* **gas station** *n Am, Can* station-service *f* **gas station operator** *n Am, Can* pompiste *m* **gas stove** *n* réchaud *m* à gaz
gassy ['gæsi] <-ier, -iest> *adj* très gazeux(-euse)
gastric ['gæstrɪk] *adj* MED gastrique
gastric flu *n* MED grippe *f* intestinale **gastric juices** *n pl* MED sucs *mpl* gastriques
gastritis [gæ'straɪtɪs, *Am:* -t̬əs] *n no pl* MED gastrite *f*
gastroenteritis [ˌgæstrəʊˌentə'raɪtɪs, *Am:* -troʊˌent̬ə'raɪt̬əs] *n no pl* MED gastroentérite *f*

gastronomic [ˌgæstrəˈnɒmɪk, *Am:* -ˈnɑːmɪk] *adj* gastronomique

gastronomy [gæˈstrɒnəmi, *Am:* -ˈstrɑːnə-] *n no pl* gastronomie *f*

gastroscopy [ˌgæsˈtrəʊskɒpi] *n* MED gastroscopie *f*

gasworks *n + sing vb* usine *f* à gaz

gate [geɪt] *n* **1.** (*entrance barrier: of field*) barrière *f;* (*of garden, property*) portail *m;* **safety ~** portail de sécurité; RAIL barrière *f* automatique **2.** (*for horses*) **starting ~** starting-gate **3.** (*number of paying customers*) entrées *fpl* **4.** AVIAT porte *f* **5.** NAUT vanne *f*

gatecrash I. *vt* (*attend sth uninvited*) **to ~ a party** aller à une soirée sans y être invité; (*attend without paying*) resquiller **II.** *vi* **1.** (*attend uninvited*) s'inviter **2.** (*attend without paying*) resquiller **gatecrasher** *n* resquilleur, -euse *m, f* **gatehouse** *n* loge *f* **gatekeeper** *n* gardien(ne) *m(f);* RAIL garde-barrière *mf* **gate-legged table, gate-leg table** *n* table *f* à abattants **gate money** *n Brit, Aus* entrées *fpl* **gatepost** *n* poteau *m* de barrière ►**between you and me and the ~** entre nous **gateway** *n* **1.** (*entrance*) entrée *f* **2.** (*means of access*) porte *f* **3.** INFOR passerelle *f*

gather [ˈgæðəʳ, *Am:* -ɚ] **I.** *vt* **1.** (*collect together: things, information*) rassembler; (*berries, herbs, flowers*) cueillir; (*by asking: intelligence*) recueillir; **to ~ one's thoughts** rassembler ses idées **2.** (*pull nearer*) **to ~ sb in one's arms** serrer qn dans ses bras; **to ~ a sheet around oneself** s'enrouler dans un drap **3.** FASHION (*fabric*) froncer **4.** (*increase*) **to ~ speed** prendre de la vitesse **5.** (*accumulate*) **to ~ courage** rassembler son courage; **to ~ dust** ramasser la poussière; **to ~ one's strength** reprendre des forces **6.** (*infer*) conclure; (*from other people*) comprendre **II.** *vi* (*people*) se rassembler; (*clouds*) s'amasser; (*storm*) se préparer

gathering I. *n* rassemblement *m;* **a social/family ~** une réunion informelle/de famille **II.** *adj* (*darkness, speed*) croissant(e); (*storm*) menaçant(e)

GATT [gæt] *n no pl, no art abbr of* **General Agreement on Tariffs and Trade** GATT *m*

gauche [gəʊʃ, *Am:* goʊʃ] *adj* gauche

gaudy [ˈgɔːdi, *Am:* ˈgɑː-] <-ier, -iest> *adj* (*colours*) tape-à-l'œil; (*display*) de mauvais goût

gauge [geɪdʒ] **I.** *n* **1.** (*size*) calibre *m* **2.** RAIL écartement *m* **3.** (*instrument*) jauge *f* **II.** *vt* évaluer

gaunt [gɔːnt, *Am:* gɑːnt] *adj* **1.** (*very thin: face*) décharné(e) **2.** (*desolate: landscape*) désolé(e)

gauntlet [ˈgɔːntlɪt, *Am:* ˈgɑːnt-] *n* gantelet *m* ►**to take up/throw down the ~** relever/jeter le gant; **to run the ~ of sth** subir qc; **they ran the ~ of a lot of criticism** ils ont été sévèrement critiqués

gauze [gɔːz, *Am:* gɑːz] *n no pl* gaze *f*

gauzy <-ier, -iest> *adj* (*very thin*) transparent(e)

gave [geɪv] *pt of* **give**

gavel [ˈgævl] *n* **1.** (*small hammer of judge etc*) marteau *m* **2.** (*of auctioneer*) maillet *m*

gawk [gɔːk, *Am:* gɑːk] *vi inf* rester la bouche ouverte; **to ~ at sb/sth** regarder qn/qc la bouche ouverte

gawky *adj* dégingandé(e)

gay [geɪ] **I.** *adj* **1.** (*homosexual*) gay *inv,* homo *inf* **2.** (*cheerful, lighthearted*) gai(e) **II.** *n* gay *m,* homo *m inf*

gaze [geɪz] **I.** *vi* regarder fixement; **to ~ around oneself** regarder autour de soi **II.** *n* regard *m;* **to be exposed to the public ~** être exposé au regard du public

gazelle [gəˈzel] *n* gazelle *f*

gazette [gəˈzet] *n* **1.** *Am* (*newspaper*) gazette *f* **2.** (*official newspaper*) journal *m* officiel

gazetteer [ˌgæzəˈtɪəʳ, *Am:* -ˈtɪr] *n* index *m* géographique

GB [ˌdʒiːˈbiː] *n no pl* **1.** *abbr of* **Great Britain** GB *f* **2.** INFOR *abbr of* **gigabyte** Go *m*

GBH [ˌdʒiːbiːˈeɪtʃ] *n Brit* LAW *abbr of* **grievous bodily harm** coups *mpl* et blessures

GCE [ˌdʒiːsiːˈiː] *n abbr of* **General Certificate of Education** diplôme *m* de fin d'études secondaires

GCHQ [ˌdʒiːsiːeɪtʃˈkjuː] *n Brit abbr of* **Government Communications Headquarters** *centre d'interception des télécommunications étrangères*

GCSE [ˌdʒiːsiːesˈiː] *n Brit abbr of* **General Certificate of Secondary Education** certificat *m* d'études secondaires (*passé à 16 ans*)

> Le **GCSE**, autrefois appelé le "O-Level" ("Ordinary level"), est le premier examen que passent les élèves de 16 ans en Angleterre, au pays de Galles et en Irlande du Nord. Il est possible de prendre une seule matière mais la plupart des élèves essaient de passer cet examen dans sept ou huit matières différentes. En Écosse, ce premier examen s'appelle "Standard Grade".

Gdns *n abbr of* **Gardens** *jardins* (*dans les adresses*)

GDP [ˌdʒiːdiːˈpiː] *n abbr of* **gross domestic product** PIB *m*

GDR *n no pl* HIST *abbr of* **German Democratic Republic** RDA *f*

gear [gɪəʳ, *Am:* gɪr] **I.** *n* **1.** AUTO (*speed*) vitesse *f;* **in first/second/third ~** en première/seconde/troisième; **to be in neutral** [*o* **out of**] **~** être au point mort; **to change** [*o Am* **shift**] **~** changer de vitesse; **to shift into top** [*o Am* **high**] **~** passer à la vitesse maximale **2.** (*mechanism*) mécanisme *m* **3.** TECH (*set of ~s*) **~(s)** engrenage *m* **4.** (*toothed wheel*) roue *f* dentée **5.** *no pl, inf* (*equipment*) attirail *m;*

(*clothes*) tenue *f* **6.** *no pl, inf* (*belongings*) affaires *fpl* **7.** *no pl, inf* (*trendy clothes*) fringues *fpl* ►**to move up a ~** passer à la vitesse supérieure; **to be out of ~** être au point mort; **to shift into high ~** passer à plein régime **II.** *vi* s'engrener **III.** *vt* **1.** TECH engrener **2.** *fig* **to ~ sth to sth** adapter qc à qc; **to be ~ed for sth** être préparé pour qc

◆**gear down** *vt* démultiplier

◆**gear up I.** *vi* se préparer; **to ~ for sth** se préparer pour qc **II.** *vt* **1.** TECH multiplier **2.** *fig* préparer; **to be geared up to sth** être préparé à qc; **to get geared up for sth** se préparer pour qc

gearbox <-xes>, **gearcase** *n* boîte *f* de vitesses

geared *adj* (*with gears*) à vitesses

gearing *n no pl* **1.** AUTO embrayage *m* **2.** (*set of gears*) engrenage *m* **3.** *Brit* FIN, ECON taux *m* d'endettement

gear lever *n Brit, Aus,* **gearshift** *n Am,* **gear stick** *n Brit* **1.** (*lever*) levier *m* de vitesses **2.** (*action*) changement *m* de vitesses

gearwheel *n* **1.** (*toothed wheel*) (roue *f* d') engrenage *m* **2.** (*cogwheel on bike*) pignon *m*

gee ['dʒiː] *interj Am, Can, inf* ouah

geese *n pl of* **goose**

geezer ['giːzəʳ, *Am:* -zɚ] *n inf* **old ~** vieux schnock *m;* **funny old ~** drôle de bonhomme *m*

geisha, **geisha girl** *n* geisha *f*

gel [dʒel] *n* gel *m*

gelatin *n Am, Aus,* **gelatine** [dʒə'lətiːn] *n no pl* gélatine *f*

gelatinous *adj* gélatineux(-euse)

geld [geld] *vt* (*animal*) castrer

gelding *n* **1.** (*gelded horse*) hongre *m;* (*gelded animal*) animal *m* castré **2.** (*castrated man*) castrat *m*

gem [dʒem] *n* **1.** (*jewel*) pierre *f* précieuse **2.** (*precious, helpful person*) perle *f*

Gemini ['dʒemɪni] *n* Gémeaux *mpl; s. a.* **Aquarius**

gen [dʒen] **I.** *n no pl, Brit, inf* tuyaux *mpl* **II.** <-nn-> *vi Brit, inf* **to ~ up on sth** se renseigner sur qc

gender ['dʒendəʳ, *Am:* -dɚ] *n* **1.** (*sexual identity*) sexe *m* **2.** LING genre *m*

gene [dʒiːn] *n* gène *m*

genealogical [ˌdʒiːnɪə'lɒdʒɪkl, *Am:* -'lɑːdʒɪ-] *adj* (*tree*) généalogique

genealogist *n* généalogiste *mf*

genealogy [ˌdʒiːnɪ'ælədʒi] *n* généalogie *f*

gene pool *n* patrimoine *m* génétique

general ['dʒenrəl] **I.** *adj* général(e); **rain will become ~ in the north** les pluies vont se généraliser au nord; **in ~** en général; **~ American** LING américain *m* standard **II.** *n* MIL général *m;* **~ lieutenant** général de corps d'armée

general anaesthetic *n* anesthésie *f* générale **general assembly** *n* assemblée *f* générale **general delivery** *n no pl, Am* poste *f* restante **general director** *n* directeur *m* général **general editor** *n* rédacteur, -trice *m, f* en chef **general election** *n* élections *fpl* législatives **general headquarters** *n* quartier *m* général

generality [ˌdʒenə'ræləti, *Am:* -t̬i] <-ties> *n* généralité *f;* **the ~ of ...** la plupart de ...

generalization *n* généralisation *f*

generalize ['dʒenərəlaɪz] *vt, vi* généraliser

generally ['dʒenrəli] *adv* **1.** (*usually*) généralement **2.** (*mostly*) dans l'ensemble **3.** (*in a general sense*) **~ speaking ...** d'une manière générale ... **4.** (*widely, extensively*) généralement; **to be ~ available** être disponible pour tout le monde; **it is ~ believed that ...** il est courant de croire que ...; **to be ~ reputed to be sth** avoir la réputation générale d'être qc

general management *n no pl* direction *f* générale **general manager** *n* directeur *m* général **General Post Office** *n* la Poste **general practitioner** *n Brit, Aus, Can* médecin *m* généraliste **general staff** *n* MIL état-major *m* **general store** *n Am, Can* magasin *m* d'alimentation générale **general strike** *n* grève *f* générale **general view** *n no pl* avis *m* général; **in the ~ ...** de l'avis général ...

generate ['dʒenəreɪt] *vt* **1.** (*produce: energy*) produire **2.** *fig* (*cause to arise*) engendrer; (*reaction, feeling*) susciter; (*ideas, interest*) faire naître **3.** LING générer **4.** ECON générer **5.** MAT engendrer

generating station *n* centrale *f* électrique

generation [ˌdʒenə'reɪʃən] **I.** *n* **1.** (*set of people born in the same time span*) *a. fig* génération *f;* **for ~s** pendant des générations et des générations **2.** (*production*) production *f* **II.** *in compounds* **first- and second-~ immigrants** immigrés de première et seconde génération

generative ['dʒenərətɪv, *Am:* -t̬ɪv] *adj* **1.** *form* BIO reproducteur(-trice) **2.** LING génératif(-ive)

generator *n* **1.** (*dynamo*) dynamo *f;* (*bigger*) groupe *m* électrogène **2.** *form* (*producer*) générateur, -trice *m, f*

generic [dʒɪ'nerɪk] **I.** *adj* (*term, brand*) générique **II.** *n* **1.** *Aus* COM produit *m* générique **2.** MED médicament *m* générique

generosity [ˌdʒenə'rɒsəti, *Am:* -'rɑːsət̬i] *n no pl* générosité *f*

generous ['dʒenərəs] *adj* généreux(-euse); **a ~ helping** une part généreuse; **a ~ tip** un gros pourboire; **to be ~ in defeat** ne pas être mauvais perdant; **to be ~ with sth** ne pas être avare de qc

genesis ['dʒenəsɪs] *n no pl, form* (*origin*) genèse *f*

gene therapy *n sing* thérapie *f* génique

genetic [dʒɪ'netɪk, *Am:* -'net̬ɪk] *adj* génétique

geneticist [dʒɪ'netɪsɪst, *Am:* -'net̬ə-] *n* généticien(ne) *m(f)*

genetics *n + sing vb* génétique *f*

G

Geneva [dʒəˈniːvə] *n* Genève
Genevan I. *adj* genevois(e) II. *n* Genevois(e) *m(f)*
genial [ˈdʒiːnɪəl] *adj* cordial(e)
geniality [ˌdʒiːnɪˈæləti, *Am:* -t̬i] *n no pl* affabilité *f*
genie [ˈdʒiːni] <-nii *o* -nies> *n* génie *m* ►**to let the ~ of change out of the bottle** précipiter le changement
genitalia [dʒenɪˈteɪliə] *npl form,* **genitals** *npl* parties *fpl* génitales
genitive [ˈdʒenətɪv, *Am:* -ət̬ɪv] *adj* génitif *m*
genius [ˈdʒiːnɪəs] *n* génie *m;* **a stroke of ~** un coup de génie; **to show ~** faire preuve de génie; **evil ~** mauvais génie
genned up *pt of* **gen**
genocide [ˈdʒenəsaɪd] *n no pl* génocide *m*
genre [ˈʒɑ̃ːnrə] *n* genre *m*
gent [dʒent] *n Brit, Aus, inf, iron* 1.(*gentleman*) gentleman *m* 2.*pl* **Gents** toilettes *fpl* pour hommes
genteel [dʒenˈtiːl] *adj* distingué(e); *pej* maniéré(e)
gentian [ˈdʒenʃən] *n* gentiane *f*
gentian violet *n* bleu *m* de méthylène
gentle [ˈdʒentl] *adj* 1.(*kind, calm*) doux(douce); **to be as ~ as a lamb** être doux comme un agneau 2.(*subtle: hint, persuasion, reminder*) discret(-ète) 3.(*moderate: breeze, exercise*) doux(douce) 4.(*high-born*) **to be of ~ birth** être bien né
gentlefolk *npl* gens *mpl* de bonne famille
gentleman <-men> *n* 1.(*polite, well-behaved man*) gentleman *m* 2.(*polite term of reference*) monsieur *m;* **a ~'s club** un club pour messieurs 3.(*male audience members*) **ladies and ~** mesdames et messieurs 4.(*man of high social class*) gentilhomme *m* **gentlemanly** *adj* en gentleman **gentleness** *n no pl* douceur *f*
gentry [ˈdʒentri] *n no pl, Brit* **the ~** la petite noblesse; **landed ~** aristocratie *f* terrienne
gents *n pl* toilettes *fpl* pour hommes
genuine [ˈdʒenjʊɪn] *adj* 1.(*not fake*) authentique; **the ~ article** *inf* le vrai de vrai 2.(*real, sincere*) sincère; **in ~ surprise** avec un air de surprise réelle
genus [ˈdʒiːnəs] <-nera> *n* BIO genre *m*
geographer [dʒɪˈɒgrəfəʳ, *Am:* -ˈɑːgrəfɚ] *n* géographe *mf*
geographic(al) *adj* géographique
geography [dʒɪˈɒgrəfi, *Am:* -ˈɑːgrə-] *n no pl* géographie *f*
geological *adj* géologique
geologist *n* géologue *mf*
geology [dʒɪˈɒlədʒi, *Am:* -ˈɑːlə-] *n no pl* géologie *f*
geometric(al) *adj* géométrique
geometric *adj* géométrique
geometry [dʒɪˈɒmətri, *Am:* -ˈɑːmətri] *n no pl* géométrie *f*
geophysics [ˌdʒiːəʊˈfɪzɪks, *Am:* -oʊˈ-] *n no pl* géophysique *f*

> En Grande-Bretagne, les **George Cross** et **George Medal** sont des distinctions honorifiques qui furent introduites en 1910 et doivent leur nom au roi George VI. Ces deux décorations sont attribuées à des civils pour leur courage exceptionnel.

Georgia [ˈdʒɔːdʒə, *Am:* ˈdʒɔːr-] *n* la Géorgie
geranium [dʒəˈreɪnɪəm] *n* géranium *m*
geriatric [ˌdʒeriˈætrɪk] *adj* gériatrique
germ [dʒɜːm, *Am:* dʒɜːrm] *n* 1.(*embryo*) *a. fig* germe *m* 2. MED microbe *m*
German [ˈdʒɜːmən, *Am:* ˈdʒɜːr-] I. *adj* allemand(e); **~ speaker** germanophone *mf* II. *n* 1.(*person*) Allemand(e) *m(f)* 2. LING allemand *m; s. a.* **English**
germane [dʒəˈmeɪn, *Am:* dʒɚ-] *adj form* **to be ~ to sth** être apparenté à qc
Germanic *adj* germanique
German measles *n* rubéole *f* **German shepherd** *n* berger *m* allemand
Germany [ˈdʒɜːməni, *Am:* ˈdʒɜːr-] *n* l'Allemagne *f;* **East/West ~** Allemagne de l'Est/de l'Ouest; **Federal Republic of ~** République *f* fédérale d'Allemagne
germ cell *n* gamète *m* **germ-free** *adj* stérile
germicidal *adj* antiseptique
germicide [ˈdʒɜːmɪsaɪd, *Am:* ˈdʒɜːrmə-] *n* antiseptique *m*
germinal [ˈdʒɜːmɪnəl, *Am:* ˈdʒɜːrmə-] *adj* embryonnaire
germinate [ˈdʒɜːmɪneɪt, *Am:* ˈdʒɜːrmə-] I. *vi* germer II. *vt* faire germer
germination *n no pl* germination *f*
germ warfare *n* guerre *f* bactériologique
gerund [ˈdʒerənd] *n* gérondif *m*
gesticulate [dʒeˈstɪkjʊleɪt, *Am:* -jə-] *vi form* gesticuler
gesticulation *n form* gesticulation
gesture [ˈdʒestʃəʳ, *Am:* -tʃɚ] I. *n* geste *m;* **welcoming ~** geste de bienvenue II. *vi* exprimer par gestes III. *vt* **to ~ sb to** +*infin* faire un geste à qn de +*infin*
get [get] I. <got, got *o Am, Aus* gotten> *vt inf* 1.(*obtain*) obtenir; **to ~ sb for sth** obtenir qc pour qn; **to ~ sb sth** (*offer*) offrir qc à qn; **to ~ food/money** se procurer de la nourriture/l'argent; **to ~ a moment** avoir un moment; **to ~ a glimpse of sb/sth** apercevoir qn/qc; **to ~ the impression that ...** avoir l'impression que ...; **to ~ time off** prendre du temps libre; **to ~ pleasure out of sth** tirer du plaisir de qc 2.(*receive*) recevoir; **to ~ a surprise** avoir une surprise; **to ~ a radio station** capter une station de radio 3.(*find: idea, job*) trouver 4.(*catch*) attraper; **to ~ measles** attraper la rougeole; **to ~ one's plane/bus** avoir son avion/bus 5.(*fetch*) aller chercher 6.(*buy*) acheter; **to ~ sth for sb** acheter qc à qn 7. *inf* (*hear, understand*) piger; **to ~ it** piger; **to ~ sb/sth wrong** mal capter qn/qc 8.(*prepare*) préparer 9. *inf* (*confuse*) embrouiller 10. *inf*

(*irk*) ennuyer **11.** *inf* (*make emotional*) **to ~ to sb** remuer les tripes de qn **12.** (*strike*) toucher **13.** *inf* (*notice*) remarquer **14.** *Am, inf* (*deal with*) **to ~ the door** aller à la porte; **to ~ the telephone** répondre au téléphone; **to ~ a meal** se charger du repas **15.** (*cause to be*) **to ~ sb to do sth** faire faire qc à qn; **to ~ sb/sth doing sth** faire faire qc à qn/qc; **to ~ sb ready** préparer qn; **to ~ sth finished/typed** finir/taper qc; **to ~ sth delivered** faire livrer qc; **to ~ sth somewhere** faire passer qc quelque part ►**to ~ cracking** *inf* s'y mettre; **to ~ going** *inf* y aller **II.** *vi* **1.** (*become*) devenir; **to ~ upset** se fâcher; **to ~ used to sth** s'habituer à qc; **to ~ to be sth** devenir qc; **to ~ to like sth** commencer à aimer qc; **to ~ married** se marier **2.** (*have opportunity*) **to ~ to** +*infin* avoir l'occasion de +*infin* **3.** (*travel*) prendre; **to ~ home** rentrer chez soi

◆**get about** *vi* se déplacer

◆**get across I.** *vt* faire traverser; (*a message*) faire passer **II.** *vi* **1.** (*go across*) traverser **2.** (*communicate*) **to ~ to sb/sth** communiquer avec qn/qc

◆**get ahead** *vi* **1.** (*go ahead*) avancer; **to ~ in sth** prendre de l'avance dans qc **2.** (*lead*) prendre la tête

◆**get along** *vi* **1.** (*progress*) avancer; **how are you getting along?** comment ça va? **2.** (*be on good terms*) s'entendre bien; **to ~ with sb** s'entendre avec qn **3.** (*go*) s'en aller

◆**get around** *vt, vi s.* **get round**

◆**get at** *vt insep, inf* **1.** (*suggest*) **to ~ sth** en venir à qc **2.** *Aus, Brit* (*criticize*) s'en prendre à **3.** (*influence illegally*) suborner **4.** (*reach*) atteindre

◆**get away** *vi* s'en aller

◆**get back I.** *vt* récupérer **II.** *vi* **1.** (*come back*) revenir **2.** (*step back*) reculer

◆**get by** *vi* **1.** (*manage*) se débrouiller; **to ~ on sth** s'en sortir avec qc **2.** (*pass*) passer

◆**get down I.** *vt* **1.** (*fetch down*) descendre **2.** (*reduce*) faire baisser; **to ~ weight** perdre du poids **3.** (*disturb*) **to get sb down** déprimer qn, déforcer qn *Belgique* **4.** (*write down*) noter **5.** (*swallow*) avaler **II.** *vi* **1.** (*go down*) descendre **2.** (*bend down*) se baisser; **to ~ on one's knees** s'agenouiller; **to ~ on the ground** se mettre par terre **3.** (*begin to do sth*) **to ~ to sth** se mettre à qc

◆**get in I.** *vt* **1.** (*bring inside*) rentrer **2.** *inf* (*find time for*) **to get sb in** caser qn **3.** (*say*) placer; **to get a word in** placer un mot **4.** (*stock up*) faire provision de **5.** (*ask to come help*) faire venir **6.** (*send*) envoyer **II.** *vi* **1.** (*become elected*) se faire élire **2.** (*enter*) entrer **3.** (*find time for*) **to ~ doing sth** trouver du temps pour faire qc **4.** (*arrive*) arriver; **to ~ from work** rentrer du travail

◆**get into** *vt* **1.** (*involve, become interested in*) se mettre à; **to get sb into the habit of doing sth** habituer qn à faire qc; **to ~ the habit of doing sth** prendre l'habitude de faire qc; **to get sb into trouble** mettre qn dans le pétrin **2.** (*enter*) entrer dans; **to ~ a school** rentrer dans une école; **to ~ a car** monter dans une voiture, embarquer dans une voiture *Québec*

◆**get off I.** *vi* **1.** (*exit*) descendre **2.** (*depart*) partir **3.** (*start sleeping*) **to ~ (to sleep)** s'endormir **II.** *vt* **1.** (*exit*) descendre de **2.** (*remove from*) **to get sth off sth** enlever qc de qc **3.** (*help start sleeping*) **to get a baby off (to sleep)** endormir un bébé **4.** (*send*) envoyer **5.** (*avoid punishment*) **to get sb off sth** dispenser qn de qc; **to ~ military service** échapper au service militaire

◆**get on** *vi* **1.** (*experience good relationship*) s'entendre **2.** (*manage*) s'en sortir **3.** (*continue*) continuer **4.** (*get older*) se faire vieux **5.** (*get late*) se faire tard

◆**get out I.** *vt* **1.** (*exit*) sortir **2.** (*remove*) retirer **II.** *vi* **1.** (*leave*) sortir **2.** (*stop*) **to ~ of sth** arrêter qc **3.** (*avoid*) **to ~ of doing sth** éviter de faire qc

◆**get over** *vt* **1.** (*recover from*) **to ~ sth** (*illness, shock*) se remettre de qc; (*difficulty*) surmonter qc **2.** (*forget about*) oublier **3.** (*to go across*) franchir

◆**get round I.** *vt* **1.** (*avoid*) contourner **2.** *Brit* (*persuade*) **to ~ sb to** +*infin* convaincre qn de +*infin* **II.** *vi* circuler

◆**get through I.** *vi* **1.** (*make understand*) **to ~ to sb** faire comprendre à qn **2.** (*succeed in contacting*) avoir la communication; **to ~ to sb/sth** avoir qn/qc (en ligne) **II.** *vt* **1.** (*make understood*) faire comprendre **2.** (*survive*) surmonter **3.** (*finish*) finir **4.** (*succeed*) réussir **5.** (*get communication*) communiquer; **to get a message through** communiquer un message; **to get sb through to sb** passer qn à qn

◆**get together I.** *vi* se rassembler **II.** *vt* rassembler

◆**get up I.** *vt* **1.** (*organize*) organiser **2.** (*cause*) **to ~ speed** prendre de la vitesse; **to ~ one's strength/courage to** +*infin* rassembler ses forces/son courage pour +*infin* **3.** (*wake up*) **to get sb up** faire lever qn **4.** (*move up*) monter **5.** (*climb*) **to ~ the ladder/a tree** monter à l'échelle/sur un arbre **6.** *inf* (*dress*) **to get sb/oneself up like sth** déguiser/se déguiser comme qc **II.** *vi* **1.** (*wake up, stand up*) se lever **2.** (*climb*) monter

◆**get up to** *vt* fabriquer *inf*

get-at-able *adj inf* accessible

getaway ['getəweɪ, *Am:* 'geţ-] *n inf* fuite *f*; **to make a ~** filer; **~ car** voiture *f* en fuite

get-together *n inf* réunion *f*; **a family ~** une réunion de famille **get-up** *n inf* accoutrement *m*

geyser ['gi:zəʳ, *Am:* -zɚ] *n* **1.** (*hot spring*) geyser *m* **2.** *Brit* (*water heater*) chauffe-eau *m*

Ghana ['gɑ:nə] *n* le Ghana

Ghanaian I. *adj* ghanéen(ne) **II.** *n* Ghanéen(ne) *m(f)*

ghastly ['gɑ:stli, *Am:* 'gæst-] <-ier, -iest>

G

adj inf horrible

ghee [giː] *n* beurre *m* clarifié

Ghent [gent] *n* Gand

gherkin ['gɜːkɪn, *Am:* 'gɜːr-] *n* cornichon *m*

ghetto ['getəʊ, *Am:* 'geţoʊ] <-s *o* -es> *n* ghetto *m*

ghetto blaster *n inf* poste *m* radio-cassette

ghost [gəʊst, *Am:* goʊst] **I.** *n* **1.** (*spirit*) fantôme *m* **2.** (*memory*) ombre *f* ►**to <u>give</u> up the** ~ rendre l'âme **II.** *vt* écrire; **to** ~ **a book** servir de nègre à l'auteur d'un livre **III.** *vi* servir de nègre

ghostly <-ier, -iest> *adj* spectral(e)

ghost town *n* ville *f* fantôme **ghostwriter** *n* nègre *m*

ghoul [guːl] *n* goule *f*

GI [ˌdʒiː'aɪ] *n Am* MIL GI *m* (*soldat américain*)

giant ['dʒaɪənt] **I.** *n* géant *m* **II.** *adj* de géant

giantess *n* géante *f*

gibber ['dʒɪbəʳ, *Am:* -ɚ] *vi pej* baragouiner

gibberish *n no pl, pej* charabia *m*

gibbet ['dʒɪbɪt] *n* gibet *m*

gibbon ['gɪbən] *n* gibbon *m*

gibe [dʒaɪb] *n, vi s.* **jibe**

giblets ['dʒɪblɪts] *npl* abats *mpl*

Gibraltar [dʒɪ'brɔːltəʳ, *Am:* -'brɑːltɚ] *n* Gibraltar

giddy ['gɪdi] <-ier, -iest> *adj s.* **dizzy**

gift [gɪft] *n* **1.** (*present*) cadeau *m;* **to be a** ~ **from the Gods** être un don des dieux **2.** *inf* (*sth easily obtained*) gâteau *m* **3.** (*talent*) don *m;* **to have the** ~ **of (the) gab** *inf* avoir la langue bien pendue

gift certificate *n Am s.* **gift token**

gifted *adj* doué(e); (*child*) surdoué(e)

gift horse *n* **never look a** ~ **in the mouth** *prov* à cheval donné on ne regarde pas la bride **gift shop** *n* boutique *f* de cadeaux **gift token, gift voucher** *n* chèque-cadeau *m*

gig¹ [gɪg] **I.** *n inf* concert *m;* **to have a** ~ jouer sur scène **II.** *vi* <-gg-> donner un concert

gig² [gɪg] *n* cabriolet *m*

gigabyte ['gɪgəbaɪt] *n* INFOR gigaoctet *m*

gigantic [dʒaɪ'gæntɪk, *Am:* -ţɪk] *adj* gigantesque

giggle ['gɪgl] **I.** *vi* rire bêtement **II.** *n* **1.** (*laugh*) petit rire *m* nerveux; **to have a** ~ **over sth** avoir un fou rire à cause de qc **2.** *no pl, Aus, Brit, inf* (*joke*) blague *f;* **to do sth for a** ~ faire qc pour rire **3.** *pl* (*laugh attack*) fou rire *m;* **to get (a fit of) the ~s** avoir le fou rire

gild [gɪld] *vt* dorer ►**to** ~ **the <u>lily</u>** *pej* renchérir sur la perfection

gilded *adj* doré(e)

gill [gɪl] *n* (*0.142 litres*) quart *m* de pinte

gills *n pl* branchies *fpl* ►**to be <u>stuffed</u> to the** ~ *inf* être rempli à ras bord; **to be <u>green</u> about the** ~ devenir vert

gilt [gɪlt] **I.** *adj* doré(e) **II.** *n* dorure *f* ►**to take the** ~ **off the <u>gingerbread</u>** *Brit, inf* gâter le plaisir

gilt-edged *adj* **1.** (*with a gilded edge: book*) doré(e) sur tranche **2.** FIN (*securities, stocks*) d'Etat **3.** (*of high quality*) de tout premier ordre

gimcrack ['dʒɪmkræk] *adj pej* ringard(e)

gimlet ['gɪmlɪt] *n* vrille *f*

gimlet-eyed *adj* **to be** ~ avoir des yeux perçants

gimmick ['gɪmɪk] *n pej* **1.** (*trick*) truc *m* **2.** (*attention-getter*) astuce *f*

gimmicky *adj pej* qui relève du gadget

gin¹ [dʒɪn] *n* gin *m;* ~ **and tonic** gin-tonic

gin² [dʒɪn] *n* (*trap*) piège *m*

ginger ['dʒɪndʒəʳ, *Am:* -dʒɚ] **I.** *n* **1.** *no pl* (*root spice*) gingembre *m* **2.** (*reddish-yellow*) roux *m* **3.** *s.* **ginger ale II.** *adj* roux(rousse)

ginger ale *n limonade au gingembre* **ginger beer** *n bière à base de gingembre* **gingerbread** *n no pl* ≈ pain *m* d'épice, ≈ couque *f Belgique* **ginger group** *n Aus, Brit* POL groupe *m* de pression **ginger-haired** *adj* roux(rousse)

gingerly *adv* doux(douce)

ginger nut *n Aus, Brit,* **ginger snap** *n Am* gâteau *m* sec au gingembre

gingivitis [ˌdʒɪndʒɪ'vaɪtɪs, *Am:* -dʒə'vaɪţəs] *n no pl* gingivite *f*

ginseng ['dʒɪnseŋ] *n no pl* ginseng *m*

gipsy ['dʒɪpsi] *n Brit s.* **gypsy**

giraffe [dʒɪ'rɑːf, *Am:* dʒə'ræf] <-(s)> *n* girafe *f*

girder ['gɜːdəʳ, *Am:* 'gɜːrdɚ] *n* poutre *f*

girdle ['gɜːdl, *Am:* 'gɜːr-] **I.** *n* **1.** (*belt*) ceinture *f* **2.** (*corset*) gaine *f* **II.** *vt* ceindre

girl [gɜːl, *Am:* gɜːrl] *n* fille *f*

girl Friday *n* aide *f* de bureau **girlfriend** *n* petite amie *f,* blonde *f Québec* **Girl Guide** *n Brit s.* **guide**

girlhood *n no pl* enfance *f*

girlie ['gɜːli, *Am:* 'gɜːr-] **I.** <-r, -st> *adj* de fillette; **a** ~ **magazine** un magazine érotique **II.** *n inf* fillette *f*

girlish *adj* de jeune fille

giro ['dʒaɪrəʊ, *Am:* -roʊ] *n Brit* **1.** *no pl* (*credit transfer system*) virement *m* bancaire **2.** (*cheque*) mandat *m* postal

giro transfer *n Brit* virement *m* bancaire; (*at post-office*) virement *m* postal

girth [gɜːθ, *Am:* gɜːrθ] *n* **1.** (*circumference*) circonférence *f* **2.** *iron* (*obesity*) tour *m* de taille **3.** (*strap around horse*) sangle *f;* **to loosen a** ~ dessangler

gist [dʒɪst] *n* substance *f;* **to give sb the** ~ **of sth** résumer qc pour qn; **to get the** ~ **of sth** comprendre l'essentiel

give [gɪv] **I.** *vt* <gave, given> **1.** (*hand over, offer, provide*) *a. fig* donner; **to** ~ **sth to sb** [*o* **to** ~ **sb sth**] donner qc à qn; **to** ~ **sb the creeps** donner la chair de poule à qn; **to** ~ **sb an injection** faire une piqûre à qn; **to** ~ **sb one's due** rendre son dû à qn; **to** ~ **one's life to sth** sacrifier sa vie pour qc; **to** ~ **sb a smile** faire un sourire à qn; **to** ~ **sb a strange look** jeter un regard étrange à qn; **to** ~ **sb trouble** créer des problèmes à qn; **to** ~ **sth a push**

pousser qn; **to ~ sb a call** passer un coup de fil à qn; **to ~ sth a go** essayer qc; **to ~ sb pleasure** procurer de la joie à qn; **to ~ sb/sth a bad name** faire une mauvaise réputation à qn/qc; **to ~ (it) one's all** [*o Am* **best**] donner de son mieux; **to ~ sb to understand sth** laisser entendre qc à qn; **don't ~ me that!** ne me raconte pas d'histoires!; **~ me a break!** laisse-moi tranquille!; **to not ~ a damn** *inf* s'en foutre complètement **2.** (*pass on*) *a.* TEL **to ~ sb sth** passer qc à qn ►**to ~ a dog a bad name** *Brit, prov* qui veut noyer son chien l'accuse de la rage; **to not ~ much for sth** ne pas donner cher pour qc; **to ~ sb what for** *inf* passer un savon à qn **II.** *vi* <gave, given> **1.** (*offer*) donner; **to ~ as good as one gets** rendre coup pour coup; **to ~ of one's best** donner de son mieux **2.** (*alter in shape*) se détendre ►**it is better to ~ than to receive** *prov* il y a plus de bonheur à donner qu'à recevoir

◆**give away** *vt* **1.** (*reveal*) révéler; **to give the game away** vendre la mèche; **to give sb away** dénoncer qn **2.** (*offer for free*) distribuer **3.** *form* (*bring to altar*) conduire à l'autel

◆**give back** *vt* rendre

◆**give in I.** *vi* **1.** (*cease fighting*) céder; **to ~ to sth** céder à qc **2.** (*surrender*) se rendre **II.** *vt* donner; (*homework, papers*) remettre

◆**give off** *vt* émettre; (*smell, heat*) dégager

◆**give out I.** *vi* **1.** (*run out*) s'épuiser **2.** (*stop working*) lâcher **II.** *vt* **1.** (*distribute*) distribuer **2.** (*announce*) annoncer **3.** (*produce: noise*) émettre

◆**give over** *vi Brit, inf* **1.** (*cease*) **to ~ doing sth** arrêter de faire qc **2. ~!** ça suffit!

◆**give up I.** *vt* **1.** (*resign*) abandonner **2.** (*quit*) **to ~ doing sth** arrêter de faire qc **3.** (*stop being friendly towards*) cesser de voir qn; **to ~ one's friends** ne plus voir ses amis **4.** (*hand over*) **to ~ sth to sb** remettre qc à qn; **to give oneself up to the police** se rendre à la police **II.** *vi* **1.** (*quit*) abandonner **2.** (*cease trying to guess*) donner sa langue au chat *inf*

give-and-take *n* concessions *fpl*

giveaway I. *n* **1.** *no pl, inf* (*that which exposes sth*) **to be a ~ when sb says sth** se trahir quand qn se dit qc; **to be a dead ~** en dire long **2.** (*free gift*) cadeau *m* (promotionnel) **II.** *adj* gratuit(e); **to be a ~ price** être donné

given ['gɪvn] **I.** *n* **to take it as a ~ that ...** être sûr que ... **II.** *adj* (*time, place*) donné(e); **to be ~ to doing sth** être enclin à faire qc **III.** *prep* étant donné **IV.** *pp of* **give**

given name *n Am* nom *m* de baptême

giver ['gɪvəʳ, *Am:* -ɚ] *n* donneur, -euse *m, f*

glacé ['glæseɪ, *Am:* glæs'eɪ], **glacéed** *adj Am* glacé(e); (*fruit*) confit(e)

glacial ['gleɪsiəl, *Am:* 'gleɪʃəl] *adj* **1.** (*related to glacier*) glaciaire **2.** (*extremely cold*) glacial(e)

glacier ['glæsiəʳ, *Am:* 'gleɪʃɚ] *n* glacier *m*

glad [glæd] <gladder, gladdest> *adj* content(e)

gladden ['glædn] *vt* réjouir

gladiator ['glædɪeɪtəʳ, *Am:* -t̬ɚ] *n* gladiateur *m*

gladiolus [ˌglædɪ'əʊləs, *Am:* -'oʊ-] <-es *o* -li> *n* glaïeul *m*

gladly *adv* avec plaisir

gladness *n no pl* contentement *m*

glad rags *n no pl, iron* **to put on one's ~** mettre ses plus belles fringues

glamor ['glæməʳ, *Am:* -ɚ] *n no pl, Am, Aus s.* **glamour**

glamorise *vt Aus, Brit,* **glamorize** *vt* rendre attrayant

glamorous *adj Am s.* **glamourous**

glamour ['glæməʳ, *Am:* -ɚ] *n no pl, Aus, Brit* glamour *m*

glamour boy *n* beau garçon *m* **glamour girl** *n* belle fille *f*

glance [glɑːns, *Am:* glæns] **I.** *n* coup *m* d'œil; **to take a ~ at sth** jeter un coup d'œil; **at a ~** d'un coup d'œil; **at first ~** au premier coup d'œil **II.** *vi* **1.** (*look cursorily*) **to ~ at sb/sth** jeter un coup d'œil sur qn/qc; **to ~ up** lever les yeux; **to ~ around** jeter un coup d'œil autour de soi; **to ~ through/over sth** parcourir qc (du regard) **2.** (*shine*) étinceler

◆**glance off I.** *vi* ricocher **II.** *vt* ricocher sur

gland [glænd] *n* glande *f*

glandular ['glændjʊləʳ, *Am:* -dʒəlɚ] *adj* glandulaire

glandular fever *n* mononucléose *f*

glare [gleəʳ, *Am:* gler] **I.** *n* **1.** (*mean look*) regard *m* furieux **2.** *no pl* (*bright reflection*) éclat *m* de lumière **3.** *fig* **to be in the (full)/in a ~ of publicity** être dans les feux des projecteurs **II.** *vi* **1.** (*look*) **to ~ at sb** lancer un regard furieux à qn **2.** (*shine overly brightly*) briller avec éclat

glaring *adj* **1.** (*that which blinds*) éblouissant(e) **2.** (*obvious*) flagrant(e); (*weakness*) manifeste

Glasgow ['glɑːzgəʊ, *Am:* 'glæskoʊ] *n* Glasgow

glass [glɑːs, *Am:* glæs] *n* **1.** (*hard transparent material*) verre *m;* **pane of ~** vitre *f* **2.** (*mirror*) miroir *m* **3.** (*glassware*) verrerie *f* **4.** (*holder for drinks, drink in a glass*) verre *m*

glass-blower *n* souffleur *m* de verre **glass-cutter** *n* vitrier *m*

glasses *n* **1.** *pl* (*device to improve vision*) lunettes *fpl* **2.** *pl* (*binoculars*) jumelles *fpl*

glass fibre *n s.* **fibreglass**

glassful *n* verre *m*

glasshouse *n* serre *f* **glassware** *n no pl* objets *mpl* de verre **glassworks** *npl* verrerie *f*

glassy ['glɑːsi, *Am:* 'glæsi] <-ier, -iest> *adj* vitreux(-euse)

Glaswegian [glæz'wiːdʒən, *Am:* glæs-] *n* habitant(e) *m(f)* de Glasgow

glaucoma [glɔː'kəʊmə, *Am:* glɑː'koʊ-] *n* glaucome *m*

glaucous ['glɔːkəs, *Am:* 'glɑː-] *adj* glauque

glaze [gleɪz] **I.** *n* vernis *m* **II.** *vt* **1.** (*make shiny*) lustrer; (*paper*) glacer **2.** (*fit with glass*) vitrer

glaz(i)er *n* vitrier *m*

gleam [gliːm] **I.** *n* lueur *f* **II.** *vi* briller

glean [gliːn] *vt* glaner

gleanings *npl* glanure *f*

glee [gliː] *n no pl* jubilation *f*

gleeful *adj* jubilant(e)

glen [glen] *n* vallée *f*

glib [glɪb] <glibber, glibbest> *adj* désinvolte

glide [glaɪd] **I.** *vi* **1.** (*move smoothly*) glisser **2.** (*fly*) planer **II.** *n* (*sliding movement*) glissé *m*

glider *n* planeur *m*

glider pilot *n* pilote *m* de planeur

gliding *n* vol *m*

gliding club *n* club *m* de glisse

glimmer ['glɪməʳ, *Am:* -ɚ] *n* lueur *f*

glimpse [glɪmps] **I.** *vt* apercevoir **II.** *n* aperçu *m;* **to catch a ~ of sb** entrevoir qc

glint [glɪnt] **I.** *vi* luire **II.** *n* trait *m* de lumière

glisten ['glɪsn] *vi* scintiller

glitch [glɪtʃ] *n inf* pépin *m*

glitter ['glɪtəʳ, *Am:* 'glɪt̬ɚ] **I.** *vi* scintiller ►**all that ~s is not gold** *prov* tout ce qui brille n'est pas or **II.** *n no pl* **1.** (*sparkling*) scintillement *m* **2.** (*shiny material*) paillette *f*

glittering *adj* **1.** (*sparkling*) scintillant(e) **2.** (*impressive*) somptueux(-euse)

glitz [glɪts] *n no pl* faste *m*

glitzy <-ier, -iest> *adj* fastueux(-euse)

gloat [gləʊt, *Am:* gloʊt] *vi* exulter; **to ~ over sth** jubiler à l'idée de qc

global ['gləʊbl, *Am:* 'gloʊ-] *adj* (*worldwide*) mondial(e); **~ warming** réchauffement *m* de la planète

globe [gləʊb, *Am:* gloʊb] *n* **1.** (*round map of world*) globe *m* **2.** (*ball-shaped object*) sphère *f*

globetrotter ['gləʊbˌtrɒtəʳ, *Am:* 'gloʊbˌtrɑːt̬ɚ] *n* globe-trotter *mf*

globule ['glɒbjuːl, *Am:* 'glɑːbjuːl] *n* gouttelette *f*

gloom [gluːm] *n no pl* **1.** (*depression, hopelessness*) morosité *f;* **~ and doom** tout va mal **2.** (*darkness*) obscurité *f* **3.** LIT ténèbres *fpl*

gloominess ['gluːmɪnəs] *n no pl* **1.** (*hopelessness*) morosité *f* **2.** (*darkness*) obscurité *f*

gloomy ['gluːmi] <-ier, -iest> *adj* **1.** (*dismal*) lugubre **2.** (*dark*) sombre

glorification [ˌglɔːrɪfɪ'keɪʃən, *Am:* ˌglɔːrəfə'-] *n no pl* exaltation *f*

glorify ['glɔːrɪfaɪ, *Am:* ˌglɔːrə-] <-ie-> *vt a.* REL glorifier

glorious ['glɔːrɪəs] *adj* **1.** (*honourable, illustrious*) *a. iron* glorieux(-euse) **2.** (*splendid*) splendide

glory ['glɔːri] **I.** *n no pl a.* REL gloire *f* **II.** <-ie-> *vi* exulter de joie

glory hole *n inf* débarras *m*

gloss¹ [glɒs, *Am:* glɑːs] *n no pl* **1.** (*shine or shiny substance*) vernis *m* **2.** (*lip moisturizer*) brillant *m* à lèvres

gloss² [glɒs, *Am:* glɑːs] **I.** <-es> *n* PUBL, LIT glose *f* **II.** *vt* gloser

glossary ['glɒsəri, *Am:* 'glɑːsər-] <-ries> *n* glossaire *m*

gloss paint *n no pl* laque *f*

glossy ['glɒsi, *Am:* 'glɑːsi] **I.** <-ier, -iest> *adj* **1.** (*shiny*) *a.* TYP brillant(e); **~ magazine** *Brit* magazine *m* en papier glacé **2.** (*only superficially attractive*) *a. pej* miroitant(e) **II.** <-ssies> *n* **1.** *Am, Aus* PHOT (*shiny picture*) cliché *m* sur papier glacé **2.** PUBL (*woman's magazine*) magazine *m* féminin

glottal stop *n* LING, LING coup *m* de glotte

glottis ['glɒtɪs, *Am:* 'glɑːt̬əs] <-es> *n* MED pharyngite *f*

glove [glʌv] **I.** *n* FASHION gant *m* ►**to <u>fit</u> like a ~** aller comme un gant; **to do sth with the ~s <u>off</u>** faire qc sans prendre de gants **II.** *vt Am* ganter

glovebox, **glove compartment** *n* AUTO boîte *f* à gants

glover *n* gantier, -ière *m, f*

glow [gləʊ, *Am:* gloʊ] **I.** *n* **1.** (*radiance of light*) lueur *f;* (*of colours*) éclat *m* **2.** (*radiance of heat*) rougeoiement *m* **3.** (*feeling of warmth*) couleurs *fpl;* **to have a ~** avoir des couleurs; **to give sb a ~** donner à qn des couleurs **4.** *fig* (*of pride*) élan *m* **II.** *vi* **1.** (*illuminate or look radiant*) rayonner; **to ~ with pride/pleasure** rayonner de fierté/de plaisir **2.** (*be red and hot*) rougeoyer

glower *vi* regarder d'un air méchant; **to ~ at sb** regarder qn de travers

glowing *adj* **1.** (*burning*) incandescent(e) **2.** *fig* chaleureux(-euse); (*report, reviews*) élogieux(-euse)

glow lamp, **glowlight** *n* ELEC veilleuse *f*

glow-worm *n* ZOOL ver *m* luisant

glucose ['gluːkəʊs, *Am:* -koʊs] *n no pl* CHEM, GASTR, MED glucose *m*

glue [gluː] **I.** *n* **1.** *no pl* colle *f;* **to stick to sb like ~** coller qn **2.** (*binding element*) pot *m* de colle **II.** *vt* coller; **to be ~d to sth** *fig* être collé à qc; **to keep one's eyes ~d to sb/sth** rester les yeux fixés sur qn/qc

glue-sniffing *n action de sniffer de la colle*

glue stick *n* bâtonnet *m* de colle

glum [glʌm] <glummer, glummest> *adj* contrarié(e)

glut [glʌt] **I.** *n* ECON excédent *m* **II.** <-tt-> *vt* **1.** ECON **to ~ sth with sth** saturer qc de qc; **to be ~ted** être saturé **2.** (*to drink, eat in excess*) gaver; **to ~ oneself on sth** se gaver de qc

gluten ['gluːtən] *n no pl* GASTR gluten *m*

glutinous ['gluːtɪnəs, *Am:* -tnəs] *adj* GASTR glutineux(-euse)

glutton [glʌtn] *n* **1.** *pej* (*overeater*) glouton(ne) *m(f)* **2.** *fig* (*enthusiast*) enthousiaste *mf*

gluttonous ['glʌtənəs] *adj* **1.** (*eating excess-*

ively) glouton(ne) **2.** (*excessively greedy*) insatiable

gluttony ['glʌtəni] *n no pl* gloutonnerie *f*

glycerin ['glɪsərɪn] *n Am*, **glycerine** *n Brit, Aus*, **glycerol** *n no pl* CHEM, MED glycérine *f*

glycol ['glaɪkɒl, *Am:* -kɑːl] *n no pl* CHEM glycine *f*

GMT [ˌdʒiːem'tiː] *n abbr of* **Greenwich Mean Time** TU *m*

gnarled [nɑːld, *Am:* nɑːrld] *adj* noueux(-euse)

gnash [næʃ] *vt* **to ~ one's teeth** *a. fig* grincer des dents

gnat [næt] *n* (*tiny fly*) moucheron *m* ►**to strain at a/every ~** ergoter sur des vétilles

gnaw [nɔː, *Am:* nɑː] **I.** *vi a. fig* ronger; **to ~ on sth/at sb** ronger qc/qn **II.** *vt a. fig* ronger; **to be ~ed by fear/doubt** être rongé par la peur/le doute

gnawing **I.** *adj* (*pain*) lancinant(e) **II.** *n no pl* obsession *f*

gneiss [naɪs] *n no pl* GEO gneiss *m*

gnome [nəʊm, *Am:* noʊm] *n* LIT (*elf*) gnome *m*; **garden ~** nain *m* de jardin

GNP [ˌdʒiːen'piː] *n no pl* FIN *abbr of* **Gross National Product** PNB *m*

gnu [nuː] <-(s)> *n* ZOOL gnou *m*

go [gəʊ, *Am:* goʊ] **I.** <went, gone> *vi* **1.** *a.* TECH aller; **to ~ home** aller à la maison; **to ~ to a concert/party** aller à un concert/une fête; **to ~ badly/well** aller mal/bien; **to ~ from bad to worse** aller de mal en pis **2.** (*travel, leave*) partir; **to ~ on a cruise/holiday/a trip** partir en croisière/vacances/voyage **3.** (*do*) **to ~ doing sth** aller faire qc; **to ~ biking/jogging** aller faire du vélo/du jogging **4.** (*become*) devenir; **to ~ public/bald/haywire** devenir célèbre/chauve/fou; **to ~ red** rougir; **to ~ wrong** se tromper **5.** (*exist*) être; **to ~ hungry/thirsty** avoir faim/soif; **as sth ~es** tel que qc est **6.** (*pass*) passer **7.** (*begin*) commencer; **ready, steady** [*o Am* **set**], **~** attention, prêts, partez **8.** (*fail*) péricliter; MED (*die*) mourir **9.** ECON (*be sold*) être vendu; **to ~ like hot cakes** partir comme des petits pains; **to ~ for sth** coûter qc **10.** (*contribute*) contribuer **11.** (*be told/sung*) **the story ~es that ...** on dit que ... **II.** <went, gone> *vt* faire ►**to ~ a long way** faire un long chemin; **to ~ it alone** le faire tout seul **III.** <-es> *n* **1.** (*turn*) élan *m* **2.** (*attempt*) essai *m*; **all in one ~** tout d'un seul coup **3.** (*a success*) succès *m*; **to be no ~** ne pas être un succès **4.** (*energy*) énergie *f* ►**to be on the ~** être à la bourre; **to have a ~ at sb about sth** en avoir après qn à cause de qc; **from the word ~** depuis le début

◆**go about** **I.** *vi* circuler **II.** *vt* **1.** (*travel, walk around*) parcourir; **to ~ the streets** faire un tour dans les rues **2.** (*undertake*) se mettre à; **to ~ it/this** s'y prendre **3.** (*be busy: one's business, work*) vaquer à **4.** (*be in circulation*) *s.* **do around**

◆**go abroad** *vi* **1.** (*be current: rumour*) courir **2.** (*travel*) partir à l'étranger

◆**go after** *vi* **to ~ sb/sth** courir après qn/qc

◆**go against** *vi* **to ~ sb/sth** aller à l'encontre de qn/qc

◆**go ahead** *vi* avancer; (*begin*) commencer

◆**go along** *vi* avancer

◆**go around** *vi* **1. to ~ sth** faire le tour de qc **2.** (*visit*) **to ~ to sb's** faire un tour chez qn **3.** (*rotate*) **to ~** tourner **4.** (*be in circulation*) circuler; **to ~ that ...** le bruit court que ... **5.** (*suffice for all*) (**not**) **enough to ~** ne pas être suffisant

◆**go at** *vi* **to ~ sb/sth** s'attaquer à qn/qc

◆**go away** *vi* partir; **to ~ from sth** s'éloigner de qc

◆**go back** *vi* **1.** (*move backwards*) reculer **2.** (*return, date back*) revenir en arrière

◆**go between** *vi* faire l'intermédiaire

◆**go beyond** *vi* aller au-delà

◆**go by** *vi* **1.** (*pass by*) passer; **to ~ sb** passer chez qn; **to let sth ~** laisser passer qc **2.** (*be guided by*) **to ~ sth** être conduit par qc **3.** (*be known by*) **to ~ the name of sb** être inscrit sous le nom de qn

◆**go down** *vi* **1.** (*get down*) descendre; ASTR (*set*) se coucher; NAUT (*sink*) sombrer **2.** (*collapse*) *a.* INFOR s'effondrer; TECH tomber en panne **3.** (*decrease*) *a.* FIN baisser; (*in size*) *a.* MED diminuer **4.** (*lose, be defeated*) perdre **5.** *Brit* (*visit quickly*) passer **6.** (*be received*) **to ~ well/badly with sb** être bien/mal reçu par qn

◆**go far** *vi* **1.** (*have success*) aller loin **2.** (*make a significant contribution*) **to ~ towards sth** faire un grand pas dans qc

◆**go for** *vi* **1.** (*fetch*) **to ~ sth** aller chercher qc **2.** (*try to achieve*) **to ~ sth** essayer d'avoir qc **3.** (*attack*) **to ~ sb** s'en prendre à qn **4.** (*be true for*) **to ~ sb/sth** être valable pour qn/qc **5.** (*sell for*) **to ~** être vendu pour **6.** *inf* (*like*) **to ~ sb/sth** avoir le béguin pour qn/qc

◆**go in** *vi* **1.** (*enter*) entrer **2.** TECH (*be installed*) rentrer **3.** (*go behind a cloud*) se cacher **4.** *inf* (*be understood*) rentrer

◆**go into** *vi* **1.** (*enter*) entrer dans; **to ~ action/effect** entrer en action/vigueur; **to ~ detail** entrer dans les détails **2.** (*begin*) MED **to ~ a coma/trance** tomber dans le coma/en transe **3.** (*begin career in: business, production*) se lancer dans **4.** (*crash into*) rentrer dans

◆**go off** *vi* **1.** (*leave*) partir; **to ~ sth** partir de qc **2.** TECH, ELEC (*stop working*) s'éteindre **3.** (*explode*) exploser **4.** *Brit, Aus* (*decrease in quality*) se délabrer; GASTR (*rot*) pourrir **5.** (*stop liking*) **to ~ sb/sth** se détacher de qn/qc **6.** (*happen*) arriver; **to ~ badly/well/smoothly** rencontrer un refus/une approbation **7.** (*digress*) **to ~ the subject** s'écarter du sujet **8.** (*fall asleep*) s'endormir

◆**go on** *vi* **1.** (*go further, continue*) continuer **2.** (*pass*) passer **3.** (*happen*) se passer **4.** (*move on, proceed*) avancer **5.** (*start, embark on*) *a.*

G

MED, THEAT, MUS commencer; ELEC, TECH se mettre en marche **6.** (*base conclusions on*) **to ~ sth** s'appuyer sur qc **7.** (*fit*) aller

◆**go out** *vi* **1.** *a. Brit a.* SPORT sortir **2.** (*travel*) partir **3.** ELEC, TECH (*stop working*) s'éteindre **4.** (*be sent out*) RADIO, TV être diffusé **5.** (*recede*) démissionner **6.** (*become unfashionable*) se démoder

◆**go over** *vi* **1.** (*go up and down: a border, river, street*) traverser **2.** (*exceed: a budget, limit*) dépasser **3.** (*be received*) **to ~ badly/well** être mal/bien accueilli **4.** (*examine*) vérifier

◆**go through** *vi* **1.** (*pass in and out of*) *a.* MED, PSYCH **~ sth** passer par qc **2.** (*be routed through*) **to ~ sb/sth** passer par chez qn/qc **3.** POL, ADMIN passer **4.** (*look through*) **to ~ sth** examiner qc

◆**go to** *vi* **to ~ sb** incomber à qn; **to ~ court** aller devant les tribunaux; **to ~ expense** se mettre en frais

◆**go together** *vi* **1.** (*harmonize*) **to ~ with sth** aller ensemble avec qn **2.** (*date*) sortir ensemble

◆**go under** *vi* **1.** NAUT (*sink*) sombrer **2.** (*move below*) **to ~ sth** aller sous qc **3.** ECON (*fail*) chuter **4.** (*be known by*) **to ~ sth** être inscrit sous qc

◆**go up** *vi* **1.** (*move higher, travel northwards*) monter **2.** (*increase*) *a.* FIN, ECON augmenter **3.** (*approach*) **to ~ to sb/sth** s'approcher de qn/qc **4.** (*burn up*) *a. fig* s'enflammer **5.** *Brit* UNI **to ~** (*return to university*) reprendre la fac

◆**go with** *vi* **1.** (*accompany, harmonize*) **to ~ sb** aller avec qn **2.** (*be associated with*) **to ~ sth** être associé à qn **3.** (*agree with*) **to ~ sb/sth on sth** être d'accord avec qn/qc sur qc **4.** **to ~ sb** (*date*) sortir avec qn

◆**go without** *vt, vi* **to ~ (sth)** faire (qc) sans

goad [gəʊd] **I.** *vt* **1.** (*spur*) **to ~ sb/sth to sth** inciter qn/qc à qc **2.** (*tease*) exciter **II.** *n* motivation *f*

go-ahead I. *n no pl* carte *f* blanche **II.** *adj Aus, Brit* plein(e) d'allant

goal [gəʊl] *n a.* SPORT but *m*

goalie *inf*, **goalkeeper** *n* SPORT gardien *m* de but **goal line** *n* SPORT ligne *f* de but **goalpost** *n* SPORT poteau *m*

goat [gəʊt, *Am:* goʊt] *n* **1.** ZOOL, BIO chèvre *f* **2.** *pej, inf* (*old sexually active man*) vieux cochon *m*

Goat *n* Capricorne *m; s. a.* **Aquarius**

goatee [gəʊ'tiː, *Am:* goʊt-] *n* bouc *m*

gobble ['gɒbl, *Am:* 'gɑː-] **I.** *vi* **1.** *inf* (*eat quickly*) bouffer **2.** (*make turkey noise*) glouglouter **II.** *vt inf* bouffer **III.** *n* (*turkey noise*) glouglou *m*

gobbledegook, **gobbledygook** *n no pl, pej, inf* charabia *m*

go-between *n* intermédiaire *m;* **to act as a ~** faire l'intermédiaire

goblet ['gɒblət, *Am:* 'gɑː-] *n* coupe *f*

goblin ['gɒblɪn, *Am:* 'gɑː-] *n* LIT lutin *m*

go-cart *n Am s.* **go-kart**

god [gɒd, *Am:* gɑːd] *n* REL *a. fig* dieu *m*

god-awful *adj inf* merdique **godchild** *n* filleul(e) *m(f)* **goddaughter** *n* filleule *f* **goddess** <-es> *n* REL *a. fig* déesse *f* **godfather** *n* REL *a. fig* parrain *m* **god-fearing** *adj* REL pieux(-euse) **god-forsaken** *adj pej* perdu(e) **godhead**, **Godhead** *n no pl* REL divinité *f* **godless** *adj* **1.** REL athée **2.** *pej* (*evil*) mauvais(e) **godlike** *adj a.* REL divin(e) **godly** *adj* REL pieux(-euse) **godmother** *n* REL marraine *f* **godparent** *n* REL parrain *m* et marraine *f* **godsend** *n inf* cadeau *m* du ciel **godson** *n* REL filleul *m*

goer *n* **1.** (*person*) **a cinema-~** un cinéphile; **a church~** un pratiquant **2.** (*viable project*) bon coup *m* **3.** *inf* (*girl*) bon coup *m vulg*

goes *3rd pers sing of* **go**

go-getter *n* homme, femme *m, f* d'action **go-getting** *adj* dynamique

goggle ['gɒgl, *Am:* 'gɑː-] **I.** *vi inf* **to ~ at sb/sth** reluquer qn/qc **II.** *n* regard *m* fixe

goggle-box <-es> *n Brit, inf* téloche *f* **goggle-eyed** *adj inf* avec des yeux en boules de loto

goggles *npl* lunettes *fpl* protectrices

go-go dancer *n* go-go dancer *m*

going I. *n* **1.** (*act of leaving*) départ *m* **2.** (*conditions*) conditions *fpl;* **while the ~ is good** tant que les conditions sont bonnes **3.** (*progress*) progression *f* **4.** *no pl* (*attendance*) fréquentation *f* **II.** *adj* **1.** (*available*) disponible **2.** (*in action*) en marche; **to get sth ~** mettre qc en marche **3.** (*current*) qui marche; **a ~ concern** une entreprise florissante **III.** *vi aux* **to be ~ to** *+infin* être sur le point de *+infin*

going price *n* **1.** (*market price*) prix *m* du marché **2.** (*current price*) cours *m* du jour **goings-on** *npl* **1.** (*unusual events*) choses *fpl* extraordinaires **2.** (*activities*) affaires *fpl*

goiter *n Am*, **goitre** ['gɔɪtəʳ, *Am:* -t̬ɚ] *n Brit, Aus no pl* MED goitre *m*

go-kart *n* karting *m*

gold [gəʊld, *Am:* goʊld] **I.** *n* **1.** *no pl, no indef art* (*metal or colour*) or *m* **2.** *no pl, no indef art* (*golden object*) objet *m* en or ►**to have a heart of ~** avoir un cœur en or **II.** *adj* **1.** (*made of gold: ring, tooth, watch*) en or; (*medal, record, coin*) d'or **2.** <more ~, most ~> (*colour*) doré(e), or *inv* ►**not all that glitters is ~** *prov* tout ce qui brille n'est pas d'or

gold bullion *n* lingot *m* d'or **gold coin** *n* pièce *f* en or **gold content** *n no pl* teneur *f* en or **gold-digger** *n* **1.** MIN (*gold miner*) chercheur, -euse *m, f* d'or **2.** *fig, pej* (*money-seeker*) personne *f* vénale **gold disc** *n* disque *m* en or **gold dust** *n no pl* poudre *f* d'or

golden *adj* **1.** (*made of gold*) en or **2.** (*concerning gold*) d'or **3.** <more ~, most ~> (*colour of gold*) doré(e) **4.** (*very good: mem-

ory) en or ►silence **is** ~ *prov* le silence est d'or

golden age *n* âge *m* d'or **golden goose** *n* poule *f* aux œufs d'or **golden mean** *n no pl* juste *m* milieu **golden triangle** *n no pl, no indef art* GEO **the** ~ le triangle d'or **golden wedding** *n* noces *fpl* d'or

goldfinch <-es> *n* ZOOL chardonneret *m* **goldfish** <-(es)> *n* BIO poisson *m* rouge

gold foil *n no pl, no indef art* papier *m* doré **gold leaf** *n no pl, no indef art* feuille *f* d'or **gold medal** *n* SPORT médaille *f* d'or **goldmine** *n* mine *f* d'or **gold nugget** *n* pépite *f* d'or **gold plating** *n no pl, no indef art* MIN dorure *f* **gold reserves** *npl* FIN, ECON réserves *fpl* en or **gold-rimmed** *adj* à monture en or **goldsmith** *n* orfèvre *mf* **gold standard** *n* FIN étalon *m* or

golf [gɒlf, *Am:* gɑːlf] **I.** *n no pl* golf *m* **II.** *vi* jouer au golf

golf ball *n* SPORT balle *f* de golf **golf club** *n* SPORT club *m* de golf **golf course** *n* SPORT terrain *m* de golf

golfer *n* SPORT golfeur, -euse *m, f*

golf links *npl* SPORT *s.* **golf course**

Goliath [gəʊ'laɪəθ] *n a. fig* Goliath *m*

golliwog ['gɒlɪwɒg, *Am:* 'gɑːlɪwɔːg] *n poupée noire de chiffon*

golly ['gɒli, *Am:* 'gɑː-] *interj inf* sapristi

gollywog *n Brit, Aus s.* **golliwog**

goloshes [gə'lɒʃɪz] *npl* galoches *fpl*

gondola ['gɒndələ, *Am:* 'gɑː-] *n* gondole *f*

gondolier *n* gondolier, -ère *m, f*

gone [gɒn, *Am:* gɑːn] **I.** *pp of* **go** **II.** *adj* **1.** (*no longer there*) parti(e) **2.** (*dead*) disparu(e) **3.** *inf* (*pregnant*) en cloque **4.** *inf* (*drunk*) bourré(e) **5.** *inf* (*infatuated*) **to be** ~ **on sb** être toqué de qn

goner *n sing, no def art* **to be a** ~ (*be bound to die*) être mourant; (*be irreparable*) être un cas désespéré; (*sb in trouble*) être en difficulté

gong [gɒŋ, *Am:* gɑːŋ] *n* **1.** (*flat bell*) gong *m* **2.** *Brit, Aus, inf* (*an award*) décoration *f*

goo [guː] *n no pl, a. fig, inf* guimauve *f*

good [gʊd] **I.** <better, best> *adj* bon(ne); **to be a** ~ **catch** être une bonne affaire; **to have** ~ **eyes/ears** avoir de bons yeux/bonnes oreilles; **to be** ~ **with one's hands** être adroit de ses mains; **to have** (**got**) **it** ~ *inf* avoir (eu) de la chance; **to be/sound too** ~ **to be true** être/paraître trop beau pour être vrai; **to be** ~ **for business** ECON être bon pour les affaires; **all in** ~ **time** chaque chose en son temps; **to make sth** ~ (*pay for*) payer qc; (*do successfully*) faire qc avec succès; **to be as** ~ **as new** être comme neuf; **to be** ~ **and ready** être fin prêt; **the** ~ **old days** le bon vieux temps **II.** *n no pl* bien *m;* **to be up to no** ~ n'avoir rien de bon en tête; **to do sb** ~ **to** *+infin* faire du bien à qn de *+infin;* **for one's own** ~ pour son bien ►for ~ définitivement; for ~ (**and all**) une fois pour toute **III.** *interj* **1.** (*said to express approval*) bien **2.** (*said to express surprise or shock*) ~ **God!** mon Dieu!; ~ **gracious!** c'est pas vrai! **3.** (*said as greeting*) ~ **evening!** bonsoir!; ~ **morning!** bonjour! **4.** *Brit* (*said to accept order*) **very** ~**!** d'accord!

good afternoon *interj* (*meeting*) bonjour!; (*parting*) au revoir! **Good Book** *n* **the** ~ la Bible **goodbye** **I.** *interj* au revoir! **II.** *n* au revoir *m;* **to say** ~ **to sb** dire au revoir à qn; **to say** ~ **to sth** dire adieu à qc **good-for-nothing** **I.** *n pej* bon(ne) *m(f)* à rien **II.** *adj pej* bon(ne) à rien **Good Friday** *n no pl* REL Vendredi *m* saint **good-humored** *adj Am,* **good-humoured** *adj* de bonne humeur **good-looking** **I.** <more ~, most ~ *o* better-looking, best-looking> *adj* beau(belle) **II.** *n* belle allure *f* **good looks** *n no pl* belle allure *f*

goodly *adj* considérable

good-natured *adj* **1.** (*having pleasant character*) d'un bon naturel **2.** (*not malicious*) bienveillant(e)

goodness **I.** *n no pl* **1.** (*moral virtue or kindness*) bonté *f* **2.** GASTR (*healthful qualities*) qualités *fpl* nutritives **3.** (*said for emphasis*) **for** ~**' sake** pour l'amour de Dieu; ~ **knows ...** Dieu sait ...; **honest to** ~ vrai de vrai **II.** *interj* (**my**) ~ (**me**)! mon Dieu!

goodnight *interj* bonne nuit!

goods *npl* **1.** (*freight*) marchandises *fpl* **2.** ECON, LAW (*wares, personal belongings*) biens *mpl* ►**to** deliver **the** ~ y arriver

good-sized *adj* assez grand(e)

goods station *n Brit* RAIL gare *f* de marchandises **goods traffic** *n no pl, Brit* trafic *m* de marchandises **goods train** *n Brit* RAIL train *m* de marchandises

good-tempered *adj irr* aimable **goodwill** *n no pl* **1.** (*willingness*) bonne volonté *f* **2.** ECON goodwill *m*

goody **I.** <-dies> *n* **1.** GASTR friandise *f* **2.** *pl* THEAT, CINE **the goodies** les bons *mpl* **II.** *interj childspeak* bien

gooey ['guːi] <gooier, gooiest> *adj* **1.** (*sticky*) collant(e) **2.** *fig* (*overly sentimental*) à la guimauve

goof [guːf] *Am* **I.** *vi inf* faire des conneries **II.** *n inf* **1.** (*mistake*) connerie *f* **2.** (*silly person*) imbécile *mf*

◆**goof up** *vt Am, inf* foutre

goofy <goofier, goofiest> *adj Am, inf* bête comme ses pieds

goolies ['guːliz] *npl Brit, inf* couilles *fpl*

goon [guːn] *n pej, inf* tocard(e) *m(f)*

goose [guːs] *n* oie *f*

gooseberry ['gʊzbəri, *Am:* 'guːsberi] <-ries> *n* groseille *f* ►**to** play ~ *Brit, inf* jouer les chaperons

goosebumps *n Am,* **gooseflesh** *n no pl,* **goose pimples** *npl* chair *f* de poule **goose-pimply** *adj inf* **to go/get** (**all**) ~ en avoir la chair de poule **goosestep** **I.** <-pp-> *vi* MIL marcher au pas de l'oie **II.** *n no pl* pas *m* de l'oie

goos(e)y ['gu:si] <-sier, -siest> *adj Aus s.* **goose-pimply**

gore¹ [gɔ:ʳ, *Am:* gɔ:r] **I.** *n* MED sang *m* **II.** *vt* transpercer

gore² [gɔ:ʳ, *Am:* gɔ:r] FASHION **I.** *n* soufflet *m* **II.** *vt* gonfler

gorge [gɔ:dʒ, *Am:* gɔ:rdʒ] **I.** *n* **1.** GEO (*wide ravine*) gorge *f* **2.** (*contents of stomach*) bile *f;* **sb's ~ rises** *a. fig* avoir envie de vomir **3.** *inf* (*large feast*) gueuleton *m* **II.** *vi* **to ~ on sth** se gaver de qc **III.** *vt* **to ~ oneself on sth** se gaver de qc

gorgeous I. *adj a. fig* merveilleux(-euse) **II.** *n* merveille *f*

gorilla [gə'rɪlə] *n* ZOOL, BIO *a. fig* gorille *m*

gormless ['gɔ:mlɪs, *Am:* 'gɔ:rm-] *adj Brit, inf* stupide

gorse [gɔ:s, *Am:* gɔ:rs] *n no pl* BOT, BIO genêt *m*

gory ['gɔ:ri] <-rier, -riest> *adj a. fig, iron* sanglant(e)

gosh [gɒʃ, *Am:* gɑ:ʃ] *interj inf* zut alors

gosling ['gɒzlɪŋ, *Am:* 'gɑ:z-] *n* ZOOL oison *m*

go-slow *n Brit* ECON grève *f* du zèle

gospel ['gɒspl, *Am:* 'gɑ:s-] *n* **1.** REL **Gospel** Évangile *m* **2.** MUS gospel *m* **3.** *fig* (*principle*) évangile *m*

gossamer ['gɒsəməʳ, *Am:* 'gɑ:səmɚ] *n* BIO gaze *f*

gossip ['gɒsɪp, *Am:* 'gɑ:səp] **I.** *n* **1.** *no pl* (*rumour*) potins *mpl;* **to have a ~ about sb** raconter des potins sur qn **2.** *pej* (*person who gossips*) commère *f* **II.** *vi* cancaner; **to ~ about sb** faire des commérages sur qn

gossip column *n* PUBL échos *mpl*

gossipy *adj* cancanier(-ère)

got [gɒt, *Am:* gɑ:t] *Brit pt, pp of* **get**

Gothic ['gɒθɪk, *Am:* 'gɑ:θɪk] **I.** *adj* gothique **II.** *n no pl* LING, TYP, PUBL gothique *m*

gotten ['gɒtən, *Am:* 'gɑ:tən] *Am, Aus pp of* **got**

gouge [gaʊdʒ] **I.** *vt* **1.** (*pierce*) **to ~ sth in(to) sth** percer qc à travers qc **2.** *Am, inf* (*overcharge*) surcharger **II.** *n* ciseau *m*

goulash ['gu:læʃ, *Am:* -lɑ:ʃ] *n no pl* GASTR goulache *m o f*

gourd [gʊəd, *Am:* gɔ:rd] *n* BOT, BIO cucurbitacée *f*

gourmand ['gʊəmənd, *Am:* 'gʊrmɑ:nd] *n* gourmand(e) *m(f)*

gourmet ['gʊəmeɪ, *Am:* 'gʊr-] GASTR **I.** *n* gourmet *m* **II.** *adj* (*restaurant*) gastronome

gourmet shop *n* GASTR épicerie *f* fine

gout [gaʊt] *n no pl* MED goutte *f*

Gov. *n* **1.** *abbr of* **governor** gouverneur *m* **2.** *abbr of* **government** gouvernement *m*

govern ['gʌvn, *Am:* -ɚn] **I.** *vt* **1.** (*rule, control*) gouverner **2.** *fig* (*feelings*) maîtriser **3.** LAW (*regulate*) régir **4.** LING régir **II.** *vi* POL, ADMIN gouverner

governess ['gʌvənɪs, *Am:* -ɚnəs] <-es> *n* gouvernante *f*

governing *adj* gouvernant(e); (*coalition*) au pouvoir; **a ~ body** un conseil d'administration

government ['gʌvənmənt, *Am:* -ɚn-] *n* POL, ADMIN gouvernement *m;* **~ policy** police *f* d'État

governmental *adj* POL, ADMIN gouvernemental(e)

Government House *n Brit* parlement *m*

government paper *n* emprunt *m* d'État

governor ['gʌvənəʳ, *Am:* -ɚnɚ] *n* **1.** POL, ADMIN (*leader of area*) gouverneur *m* **2.** (*leader of state*) chef *m* d'État **3.** *Brit* (*leader of organization*) président *m* **4.** *Brit, inf* (*boss*) chef *m* **5.** AUTO, TECH (*speed controller*) régulateur *m*

gown [gaʊn] *n* **1.** (*dress*) robe *f* **2.** MED (*short medical robe*) blouse *f*

GP [ˌdʒi:'pi:] *n Brit, Aus* MED *abbr of* **general practitioner** généraliste *mf*

GPO [ˌdʒi:pi:'əʊ, *Am:* -'oʊ] *n Brit* ADMIN *abbr of* **General Post Office** service *m* postal

grab [græb] **I.** *n* **to make a ~ for/at sth** essayer de saisir qc ►**to be up for ~s** être à prendre **II.** <-bb-> *vt* **1.** (*snatch, take hold of*) *a.* LAW saisir; **to ~ sth out of sb's hands** prendre qc des mains de qn **2.** *inf* (*get, acquire: a meal*) prendre **3.** (*take advantage of: a chance*) saisir **4.** *inf* **how does sth ~ you?** comment tu trouves/vous trouvez qc?; **it doesn't ~ me** ça ne me dit rien **III.** <-bb-> *vi* **to ~ at sth** se saisir de qc; **to ~ at sb** s'agripper à qn

grace [greɪs] **I.** *n a.* REL grâce *f;* **to do sth with (a) good/bad ~** faire qc de bonne/mauvaise grâce **II.** *vt form* **1.** (*honour*) honorer **2.** (*make beautiful*) rendre grâce à

grace(ful) *adj* gracieux(-euse)

graceless *adj* disgracieux(-euse)

Graces *n pl* **the ~** les trois Grâces

gracious ['greɪʃəs] **I.** *adj* **1.** (*courteous*) affable **2.** (*elegant*) gracieux(-euse) **3.** REL plein(e) de grâce **II.** *interj* (**good**) **~** (**me**)! mon Dieu!

gradation [grə'deɪʃən, *Am:* grəɪ'-] *n* **1.** (*measured step in a range*) étagement *m* **2.** ART, MUS (*gradual transition*) transition *f*

grade [greɪd] **I.** *n* **1.** (*rank*) rang *m;* (*on scale*) échelon *m* **2.** (*type, quality*) qualité *f* **3.** *Am* SCHOOL (*level in school*) classe *f* **4.** *Am* SCHOOL, UNI (*marks in school*) note *f* **5.** (*level*) niveau *m* **6.** *Am* GEO (*gradient, slope*) pente *f* ►**to make the ~** se montrer à la hauteur **II.** *vt* **1.** SCHOOL, UNI (*evaluate*) noter **2.** (*categorize*) classer **3.** *Am* (*reduce slope*) niveler

grade crossing *n Am* RAIL passage *m* à niveau; *s.* **level crossing**

grade school *n Am* SCHOOL école *f* primaire

gradient ['greɪdɪənt] *n* GEO, AUTO pente *f*

grading *n* **1.** (*gradation*) classification *f* **2.** (*classification*) catégorie *f*

Le système d'attribution des notes en usage aux USA, le **grading system**, utilise les lettres de l'alphabet A, B, C, D, E et F, bien que la lettre E soit très rare. A est la meilleure note et F ("Fail") signifie très insuffisant. Les lettres peuvent être accompagnées du signe plus ou moins. Celui qui obtient un A+ a vraiment réalisé une bonne performance.

gradual ['grædʒʊəl] *adj* **1.** (*not sudden*) graduel(le) **2.** (*not steep*) doux(douce)
gradually *adv* graduellement
graduate ['grædʒʊət] **I.** *n* **1.** UNI diplômé(e) *m(f)* **2.** *Am* SCHOOL bachelier, -ière *m, f* **II.** *vi* UNIV obtenir son diplôme; SCHOOL avoir son bac; **to ~ from sth to sth** passer de qc à qc **III.** *vt* **1.** *Am* SCHOOL, UNI (*award degree*) remettre un diplôme à **2.** (*arrange in a series, mark out*) graduer **3.** (*change gradually*) graduer
graduated *adj* graduel(le)
graduate school *n* UNIV ≈ troisième *m* cycle **graduate studies** *n* UNIV ≈ études *fpl* de troisième cycle
graduation [ˌgrædʒʊ'eɪʃən, *Am:* ˌgrædʒu'-] *n* **1.** SCHOOL, UNI (*completion of schooling*) remise *f* des diplômes; **~ ceremony** cérémonie *f* de remise des diplômes **2.** (*promotion*) promotion *f* **3.** (*marks of calibration*) graduation *f*
graffiti [grə'fiːti, *Am:* -ţi] **I.** *n no pl* ART graffiti *m* **II.** *vi* faire des graffiti **III.** *vt* graffiter
graft[1] [grɑːft, *Am:* græft] **I.** *n* greffe *f* **II.** *vt a. fig* greffer
graft[2] [grɑːft, *Am:* græft] **I.** *n Brit, inf* boulot *m* de forçat **II.** *vi Brit, inf* bosser dur
graft[3] [grɑːft, *Am:* græft] POL **I.** *n* corruption *f* **II.** *vi* (*receive*) recevoir des pots de vin; (*give*) verser des pots de vin
grafter *n Brit, inf* bosseur *m*
Grail [greɪl] *n* REL, HIST **the ~** *s.* **Holy Grail**
grain [greɪn] **I.** *n* **1.** *a.* AGR, GASTR, PHOT *a. fig* grain *m;* **a ~ of truth** un brin de vérité **2.** (*direction of fibres: of wood*) veinure *f;* (*of meat*) fibre *f* **3.** (*.0648 grams*) once *f* ►**to go against the ~ for sb** aller à l'encontre de la nature de qn **II.** *vt* **1.** (*granulate*) grener **2.** (*texturize*) greneler
grain elevator *n* AGR silo *m* à céréales **grain export** *n* exportations *fpl* de céréales **grain market** *n* marché *m* céréalier
grammar ['græməʳ, *Am:* -ɚ] *n* grammaire *f*
grammar book *n* grammaire *f*
grammarian *n* grammairien(ne) *m(f)*
grammar school *n Brit* ≈ lycée *m; Am* ≈ école *f* primaire

Les **grammar schools** les plus anciennes en Grande-Bretagne ont été fondées il y a plusieurs siècles pour l'apprentissage du latin. Vers 1950, les élèves qui avaient réussi à l'examen de l'"eleven-plus examination" étaient admis dans les "grammar schools". Environ 20% des élèves seulement réussissaient à cet examen et les autres allaient dans une "secondary modern school" (correspondant au collège). Ces deux écoles furent réorganisées dans les années 60-70 en "comprehensive schools" (lycée de premier et second cycle).

grammatical [grə'mætɪkl, *Am:* -'mæţɪ-] *adj* LING grammatical(e)
gram(me) [græm] *n* gramme *m*
gramophone ['græməfəʊn, *Am:* -foʊn] *n* gramophone *m*
grampus ['græmpəs] <-es> *n* ZOOL, BIO épaulard *m*
gran [græn] *n inf abbr of* **grandmother** mamie *f*
granary ['grænəri] AGR **I.** <-ries> *n* grenier *m* **II.** *adj fig* céréalier(-ère)
granary bread *no pl,* **granary loaf** <-loaves> *n Brit* GASTR pain *m* complet
grand [grænd] **I.** *adj a. inf* grand(e); **in ~ style** en grandes pompes; **the Grand Canyon** le Grand Canyon; **to make a ~ entrance** faire une grande entrée; **~ old age** *a. iron* grand âge *m* **II.** *n* **1.** *inv, inf* FIN (*one thousand dollars/pounds*) brique *f* **2.** MUS *s.* **grand piano**
grandad *n inf* papi *m* **grandchild** <-children> *n* petit-fils *m,* petite-fille *f* **granddad** *s.* **grandad granddaughter** *n* petite-fille *f*
grandee [græn'diː] *n* grande *f*
grandeur ['grændʒəʳ, *Am:* -dʒɚ] *n no pl* grandeur *f;* **delusions of ~** mégalomanie *f*
grandfather *n* grand-père *m*
grandiloquent [græn'dɪləkwənt] *adj pej, form* grandiloquent(e)
grandiose ['grændɪəʊs, *Am:* -oʊs] *adj* grandiose
grand jury <-ries> *n Am* LAW grand jury *m* **grand larceny** *n no pl* LAW vol *m* qualifié
grandly *adv* grandement
grandma *n inf* mamie *f* **grand master, grandmaster** *n* **1.** GAMES (*chess pro*) professionnel(le) *m(f)* des échecs **2.** (*head of order*) grand maître *m* **grandmother** *n* grand-mère *f* **grandpa** *n inf* papi *m* **grandparent** *n* grands-parents *mpl* **grand piano** *n* MUS piano *m* à queue **grand slam** *n* grand chelem *m* **grandson** *n* petit-fils *m* **grandstand** *n* SPORT premières tribunes *fpl* **grand sum, grand total** *n* FIN somme *f* totale
grange [greɪndʒ] *n Brit* ferme *f*
granite ['grænɪt] *n no pl* MIN granit *m*
grannie, granny ['græni] <-nies> *n inf* mamie *f*
grant [grɑːnt, *Am:* grænt] **I.** *n* **1.** (*money for education*) bourse *f;* **to apply for a ~** demander une bourse **2.** (*from authority*) subvention *f* **II.** *vt* **1.** (*allow*) **to ~ sb sth** accorder qc à qn **2.** (*transfer legally*) **to ~ sb sth** céder qc à qn **3.** *form* (*consent to fulfil*) **to ~ sb sth** concéder qc à qn; **to ~ sb a request** accéder à la demande de qn **4.** (*admit to*) reconnaître; **to ~ that ...** admettre que ... ►**to take sth for ~ed** considérer qc comme allant de soi

G

granulated ['grænjʊleɪtɪd, *Am:* -jəleɪt̬ɪd] *adj* (*sugar*) cristallisé(e)

granule ['grænju:l] *n* grain *m*

grape [greɪp] *n* raisin *m*

grapefruit <-s> *n* pamplemousse *m* **grapevine** *n* vigne *f* ►**sb heard on the ~ that ...** qn a entendu dire que ...

graph [grɑ:f, *Am:* græf] **I.** *n* graphique *m* **II.** *vt* tracer sous forme graphique

graphic *adj* **1.** (*using a graph*) graphique **2.** (*vividly descriptive*) vivant(e)

graphic design *n no pl* conception *f* graphique

graphics *npl* **1.** (*drawings*) graphique *m* **2.** (*presentation*) art *m* graphique

graphics card *n* INFOR carte *f* graphique

graphite ['græfaɪt] *n* graphite *m*

graphology [græ'fɒlədʒi, *Am:* grə'fɑ:lə-] *n no pl* graphologie *f*

grapple ['græpl] *vi* **1.** (*fight*) lutter **2.** *fig* **to ~ with sth** se débattre avec qc

grasp [grɑ:sp, *Am:* græsp] **I.** *n no pl* **1.** (*grip*) prise *f* **2.** (*attainability*) portée *f;* **to be within sb's ~** être à la portée de qn **3.** (*understanding*) compréhension *f;* **to have a good ~ of a subject** bien maîtriser un sujet; **to lose one's ~** (*person*) perdre son emprise **II.** *vt* **1.** (*take firm hold*) empoigner; **to ~ sb by the arm/hand** saisir qn par le bras/la main **2.** (*understand*) saisir **III.** *vi* **to ~ at sth** essayer de saisir qc; **to ~ at the chance** saisir l'occasion

grasping *adj pej* cupide

grass [grɑ:s, *Am:* græs] **I.** *n* **1.** <-es> (*genus of plant*) herbe *f* **2.** *no pl* (*green plant*) herbe *f;* **a blade/tuft of ~** un brin/une touffe d'herbe **3.** (*lawn*) gazon *m;* **to cut the ~** tondre le gazon **4.** (*pasture*) pâture *f;* **to be at ~** (*cattle*) être au vert *m* **5.** *no pl, inf* (*marijuana*) herbe *f* **6.** *Brit, inf* (*informer*) balance *f* ►**to let the ~ grow under one's feet** perdre son temps; **the ~ is (always) greener on the other side (of the fence)** *prov* on n'est jamais content de son sort **II.** *vt* mettre en herbe **III.** *vi Aus, Brit, inf* **to ~ on sb to sb** dénoncer qn à qn

grasshopper *n* sauterelle *f* ►**to be knee-high to a ~** être haut comme trois pommes **grassland** *n no pl* prairie *f* **grass roots** *npl* **1.** (*ordinary people*) peuple *m* **2.** (*basic level: of a party, organization*) base *f* **grass snake** *n* couleuvre *f*

grassy <-ier, -iest> *adj* herbeux(-euse)

grate[1] [greɪt] *n* **1.** (*grid in fireplace*) grille *f* de foyer **2.** (*fireplace*) foyer *m*

grate[2] [greɪt] **I.** *vi* **1.** (*annoy: noise*) agacer; **to ~ on sb** taper sur les nerfs de qn **2.** (*rub together*) grincer **II.** *vt* (*shred*) râper

grateful *adj* reconnaissant(e); **to be ~ to sb for sth** être reconnaissant envers qn de qc

grater *n* râpe *f*

gratification [ˌgrætɪfɪ'keɪʃən, *Am:* ˌgræt̬ə-] *n* satisfaction *f*

gratify ['grætɪfaɪ, *Am:* 'græt̬ə-] <-ie-> *vt* **1.** (*please*) **to be ~ied at sth** être content de qc **2.** (*satisfy*) satisfaire

gratifying *adj* agréable

grating **I.** *n* grille *f* **II.** *adj* grinçant(e)

gratis ['greɪtɪs, *Am:* 'græt̬əs] **I.** *adj* gratuit(e) **II.** *adv* gratuitement

gratitude ['grætɪtju:d, *Am:* 'græt̬ətu:d] *n no pl, form* gratitude *f*

gratuitous [grə'tju:ɪtəs, *Am:* -'tu:ət̬əs] *adj* gratuit(e)

gratuity [grə'tju:əti, *Am:* -'tu:ət̬i] <-ties> *n* **1.** *form* (*tip*) pourboire *m* **2.** *Brit* MIL prime *f* de démobilisation

grave[1] [greɪv] *n* (*burial place*) tombe *f*

grave[2] [greɪv] *adj* **1.** (*seriously bad*) grave **2.** (*serious*) sérieux(-euse) **3.** (*worrying*) inquiétant(e) **4.** (*momentous*) capital(e) **5.** (*solemn: music*) solennel(le)

grave-digger, **gravedigger** *n* fossoyeur *m*

gravel ['grævəl] **I.** *n* **1.** (*small stones*) gravier *m;* **a ~ path/driveway** une allée de gravier **2.** MED calcul *m* **II.** *vt* gravillonner

gravestone *n* pierre *f* tombale **graveyard** *n* cimetière *m*

gravitate ['grævɪteɪt] *vi* **to ~ towards sb/sth** être attiré par qn/qc

gravitation [ˌgrævɪ'teɪʃən] *n no pl* **1.** (*movement*) mouvement *m* **2.** (*attracting force*) gravitation *f*

gravitational *adj* de gravitation

gravity ['grævəti, *Am:* -t̬i] *n no pl* gravité *f*

gravy ['greɪvi] *n no pl* **1.** (*meat juices*) jus *m* de viande **2.** *Am, inf* (*easy money*) bénef *m*

gravy boat *n* saucière *f*

gray [greɪ] *adj Am s.* **grey**

grayish ['greɪɪʃ] *adj Am* grisâtre *péj;* (*hair*) grisonnant(e)

graze[1] [greɪz] **I.** *n* égratignure *f* **II.** *vt* **1.** (*injure surface skin*) écorcher; **to ~ one's knee/elbow** s'égratigner le genou/coude **2.** (*touch lightly*) effleurer

graze[2] [greɪz] **I.** *vi* **1.** (*eat grass: cattle, sheep*) paître **2.** *inf* (*eat frequent small meals*) grignoter **II.** *vt* (*cattle, sheep, herds*) faire paître

grease [gri:s] **I.** *n* graisse *f* **II.** *vt* graisser ►**like ~ed lightning** en quatrième vitesse; **to ~ sb's palm** graisser la patte à qn

greasepaint *n* fard *m* gras **greaseproof paper** *n* papier *m* sulfurisé

greasy ['gri:si] *n* gras(se)

great [greɪt] **I.** *n* grand(e) **II.** *adj* **1.** (*very big, famous and important*) grand(e); **a ~ deal of time/money** beaucoup de temps/d'argent; **a ~ many people** beaucoup de gens **2.** (*wonderful*) merveilleux(-euse); **to be a ~ one for doing sth** ne pas avoir son pareil pour faire qc; **the ~ thing about sb/sth is that ...** le grand avantage de qn/qc est que ...; **to be ~ at doing sth** *inf* être doué pour faire qc; **~!** *iron, inf* génial! **3.** (*very healthy*) en pleine forme **4.** (*for emphasis*) **~ big** énorme **5.** (*good*) excellent(e); (*organizer*) de première ►**to be no ~ shakes at doing sth** ne pas être très

doué pour faire qc
great-aunt *n* grand-tante *f* **Great Bear** *n* ASTR Grande Ourse *f* **Great Britain** *n* la Grande-Bretagne

Great Britain est constituée du royaume d'Angleterre, du royaume d'Écosse et de la principauté du pays de Galles. Le roi Edward Ier d'Angleterre annexa en 1282 le pays de Galles et le donna en 1301 à son propre fils, le "Prince of Wales". Le roi James VI d'Écosse hérita en 1603 de la couronne d'Angleterre sous le titre de James Ier et en 1707 les parlements des deux royaumes furent réunis. Avec l'Irlande du Nord, ces deux pays constituent le "United Kingdom" (Royaume-Uni). Le terme géographique de "British Isles" (îles Britanniques) comprend l'île principale de la Grande-Bretagne, l'Irlande, l'Isle of Man, les Hébrides, Orkney, Shetland, les îles Scilly et les "Channel Islands" (îles Anglo-Normandes).

greatcoat *n* pardessus *m*
Greater *n* agglomération *f;* ~ **Manchester/Los Angeles** l'agglomération de Manchester/de Los Angeles
Greater London *n* le Grand Londres
great-grandchild *n* arrière-petit-fils *m,* arrière-petite-fille *f* **great-grandparents** *n pl* arrière-grands-parents *mpl* **Great Lakes** *n* les Grands Lacs
greatly *adv form* très
great-nephew *n* arrière-neveu *m*
greatness *n no pl* grandeur *f*
great-niece *n* petite-nièce *f* **great-uncle** *n* grand-oncle *m* **Great Wall** *n* **the ~ of China** la grande Muraille de Chine
Grecian *adj* (*Greek*) grec(que)
Greece [gri:s] *n* la Grèce
greed [gri:d] *n no pl* (*desire for more*) avidité *f;* ~ **for food** gloutonnerie *f*
greediness *n no pl s.* **greed**
greedy *adj* **1.** (*wanting food*) gourmand(e); **a ~ pig** *inf* un goinfre **2.** (*wanting too much*) avide; ~ **for money/power** avide d'argent/de pouvoir; ~ **for water** (*plant*) gourmand en eau
Greek [gri:k] **I.** *adj* grec(que) **II.** *n* **1.** (*person*) Grec, que *m, f* **2.** LING grec *m;* **ancient ~** grec ancien ►**it's all ~ to me** pour moi c'est du chinois; *s. a.* **English**
green [gri:n] **I.** *adj* **1.** (*color*) vert(e); **greyish-~ eyes** des yeux gris-vert **2.** (*ecological: product, policies, issues*) écologique; (*person, vote, party*) écologiste ►**to have ~ fingers** *Brit, Aus* avoir la main verte; **it makes him ~ with envy** ça le fait pâlir d'envie **II.** *n* **1.** *no pl* (*colour*) vert *m* **2.** *pl* (*green vegetables*) légumes *mpl* verts **3.** (*member of Green Party*) écologiste *mf;* **the Greens** les Verts *mpl* **4.** (*area of grass*) espace *m* vert **5.** SPORT green *m; s. a.* **blue**
greenback *n Am, inf* billet *m* vert **green belt** *n* zone *f* verte **green card** *n* **1.** *Brit* (*car insurance document*) carte *f* verte **2.** *Am* (*residence and work permit*) carte *f* de séjour
greenery ['gri:nəri] *n no pl* verdure *f*
green fingers *n pl, inf* **to have ~** avoir la main verte **greenfly** *n* puceron *m* **greengage** *n* reine-claude *f* **greengrocer** *n Brit* marchand(e) *m(f)* de fruits et légumes, légumier, -ère *m, f Belgique* **greenhorn** *n* débutant(e) *m(f)* **greenhouse** *n* serre *f*
greenish ['gri:nɪʃ] *adj* tirant sur le vert, verdâtre *péj*
greenish-blue *adj* vert-bleu *inv*
Greenland ['gri:nlənd] *n* le Groenland
Greenlander *n* Groenlandais(e) *m(f)*
greenness *n* couleur *f* verte; (*of a fruit*) verdeur *f*
green pepper *n* poivron *m* vert **green thumb** *n Am, fig* **to have a ~** avoir la main verte
Greenwich ['grɪnɪtʃ, *Am:* 'gren-] *n* Greenwich
Greenwich Mean Time *n* temps *m* universel
greeny *s.* **greenisch**
greet [gri:t] *vt* **1.** (*welcome by word or gesture*) saluer **2.** (*receive*) accueillir **3.** (*make itself noticeable*) attendre
greeting *n* **1.** (*welcome*) salut *m;* **to send ~s to sb** envoyer ses salutations à qn; **in ~** en signe de salut **2.** *pl* (*goodwill*) vœux *mpl;* **to exchange ~s** échanger des vœux **3.** (*receiving*) accueil *m*
greeting(s) card *n* carte *f* de vœux
gregarious [grɪ'geərɪəs, *Am:* -'gerɪ-] *adj* **1.** (*liking company*) sociable **2.** ZOOL grégaire
Grenada [grə'neɪdə] *n* Grenade *f*
Grenadan **I.** *adj* grenadien(ne) **II.** *n* Grenadien(ne) *m(f)*
grenade [grɪ'neɪd] *n* grenade *f*
grew [gru:] *pt of* **grow**
grey [greɪ] *adj* **1.** (*colored*) gris(e); **~ matter** matière *f* grise; **to go** [*o* **turn**] **~** grisonner **2.** *fig* **she went** [*o* **turned**] **~ on hearing that** elle a blêmi en entendant ça; *s. a.* **blue**
greyhound *n* lévrier *m*
greying *adj* grisonnant(e)
greyish ['greɪɪʃ] *adj Am s.* **grayish**
grey matter *n inf* matière *f* grise
grid [grɪd] *n* **1.** (*a grating*) grille *f* **2.** (*pattern*) quadrillage *m* **3.** SPORT ligne *f* de départ **4.** (*electricity network*) **the ~** le réseau électrique national
griddle ['grɪdl] **I.** *n* plaque *f* en fonte **II.** *vt* faire cuire sur une plaque en fonte
gridiron ['grɪdaɪən, *Am:* -aɪɚn] *n* **1.** (*metal grid*) gril *m* **2.** *Am* (*American football field*) terrain *m* de football américain
gridlock *n* embouteillage *m*
grief [gri:f] *n no pl* **1.** (*extreme sadness*) chagrin *m;* **to cause sb ~** causer du chagrin à qn **2.** (*pain*) douleur *f* ►**to come to ~** échouer; (*have an accident*) avoir un accident

G

grievance ['gri:vns] *n* **1.** (*complaint*) doléance *f* **2.** (*sense of injustice*) grief *m*

grieve [gri:v] **I.** *vi* **1.** (*be sad*) être peiné; **to ~ over sth** se désoler de qc **2.** (*mourn*) être en deuil *m;* **to ~ for sb/sth** pleurer qn/qc **II.** *vt* **1.** (*distress*) affliger **2.** (*make sad*) chagriner **3.** (*annoy*) contrarier

grievous ['gri:vəs] *adj form* **1.** (*error*) grave; (*news*) douloureux(-euse) **2.** JUR **~ bodily harm** coups et blessures *mpl*

grievous bodily harm *n no pl* LAW coups *mpl* et blessures

grill [grɪl] **I.** *n* **1.** (*part of cooker*) gril *m* **2.** (*food*) grillade *f* **3.** *Am* (*informal restaurant*) restaurant grill *m* **II.** *vt* **1.** (*cook*) faire griller **2.** *inf* (*interrogate*) cuisiner; **to ~ sb about sth** cuisiner qn au sujet de qc

grille [grɪl] *n* grille *f*

grilling *n inf* cuisson *f* sur le gril

grim [grɪm] *adj* **1.** (*very serious*) grave; **to be ~-faced** avoir une mine sévère **2.** (*unpleasant*) désagréable **3.** (*horrible*) terrible; **~ outlook** perspective effroyable ►**to hang on like ~ death** (*person*) se cramponner de toutes ses forces; **to feel ~** *inf* ne pas avoir le moral

grimace [grɪ'meɪs, *Am:* 'grɪməs] **I.** *n* grimace *f* **II.** *vi* **1.** (*negatively*) faire la grimace; **to ~ with pain** grimacer de douleur **2.** (*for fun*) faire des grimaces

grime [graɪm] **I.** *n* **1.** (*ingrained dirt*) saleté *f* **2.** (*soot*) suie *f* **II.** *vt* **to be ~d** être encrassé

grimy ['graɪmi] <-ier, -iest> *adj* **1.** (*filthy*) crasseux(-euse) **2.** (*sooty*) noir(e) de suie

grin [grɪn] **I.** *n* sourire *m* **II.** *vi* faire un large sourire ►**to ~ and bear it** garder le sourire

grind [graɪnd] **I.** *n inf* **1.** (*tiring work*) corvée *f;* **the daily ~** le train-train quotidien **2.** (*sound*) grincement *m* **3.** (*dance*) déhanchement *m* **II.** <ground, ground> *vt* **1.** (*mill: corn, pepper, coffee*) moudre; (*meat*) hacher **2.** (*crush*) écraser **3.** (*make noise*) grincer; **to ~ one's teeth** grincer des dents **4.** (*sharpen*) aiguiser **5.** (*polish*) polir **III.** *vi* **1.** (*move noisily*) grincer; **to ~ to a halt** s'immobiliser; **to ~ up the hill** monter la colline en crissant **2.** *inf* (*dance*) se déhancher

◆**grind down** *vt* **1.** (*file*) polir **2.** (*mill*) moudre **3.** (*wear*) user ►**to ~ sb down** avoir qn à l'usure; (*oppress*) accabler qn

◆**grind out** *vt* **1.** (*produce continuously*) produire régulièrement **2.** (*produce in a boring manner*) rabâcher **3.** (*extinguish: cigarette*) écraser

grinder *n* **1.** (*crushing machine*) moulin *m;* **coffee-~** moulin à café **2.** (*sharpener*) meule *f* **3.** (*man who sharpens things*) rémouleur *m*

grindstone *n* pierre *f* à aiguiser ►**to keep one's nose to the ~** travailler sans relâche

gringo ['grɪŋgəʊ, *Am:* -goʊ] *n pej* gringo *m*

grip [grɪp] **I.** *n* **1.** (*hold*) prise *f* **2.** (*way of holding*) adhérence *f* **3.** (*bag*) sac *m* de voyage ►**to come to ~s with sth** s'attaquer à qc; **to get a ~ on oneself** se ressaisir; **to be in the ~ of sth** être en proie à qc **II.** <-pp-> *vt* **1.** (*hold firmly*) empoigner **2.** (*overwhelm*) **to be ~ped by emotion** être saisi par l'émotion **3.** (*interest deeply*) captiver **III.** *vi* adhérer

gripe [graɪp] **I.** *n inf* plainte *f* **II.** *vi inf* ronchonner

gripping *adj* **1.** (*exciting*) passionnant(e) **2.** (*stabbing*) lancinant(e)

grisly ['grɪzli] *adj* **1.** (*repellant*) repoussant(e) **2.** *fig, inf* macabre

gristle ['grɪsl] *n no pl* nerfs *mpl*

grit [grɪt] **I.** *n* **1.** *no pl* (*small stones*) gravillon *m* **2.** *no pl* (*courage*) cran *m* **II.** <-tt-> *vt* **1.** (*scatter*) sabler **2.** (*press together*) *a. fig* **to ~ one's teeth** serrer les dents

gritty *adj* **1.** (*covered with grits*) couvert(e) de gravillons **2.** (*courageous*) courageux(-euse)

grizzle ['grɪzl] *vi pej, inf* **1.** (*cry continually: baby, small child*) pleurnicher **2.** (*complain*) ronchonner

grizzly **I.** <-ier, iest> *adj* grisonnant(e) **II.** <-zzlies> *n* grizzli *m*

groan [grəʊn, *Am:* groʊn] **I.** *n* gémissement *m* **II.** *vi* **1.** (*make a noise: floorboards, hinges*) grincer; (*people*) gémir; **~ in pain** gémir de douleur **2.** *inf* (*complain*) grogner

groats [grəʊts, *Am:* groʊts] *n pl* gruau *m*

grocer ['grəʊsəʳ, *Am:* 'groʊsɚ] *n* **1.** (*shopkeeper*) épicier, -ière *m, f* **2.** (*food shop*) épicerie *f*

grocery ['grəʊsəri, *Am:* 'groʊ-] <-ies> *n* épicerie *f*

grog [grɒg, *Am:* grɑ:g] *n* grog *m*

groggy ['grɒgi, *Am:* 'grɑ:gi] <-ier -iest> *adj* groggy *inv*

groin [grɔɪn] *n* **1.** ANAT aine *f* **2.** (*male sex organs*) testicules *fpl*

groom [gru:m] **I.** *n* **1.** (*person caring for horses*) palefrenier *m* **2.** (*bridegroom*) marié *m* **II.** *vt* **1.** (*clean: animal*) faire la toilette de; (*horse*) panser **2.** (*prepare*) préparer; **to ~ sb for sth** préparer qn à qc

groove [gru:v] *n* **1.** (*long narrow indentation*) rainure *f* **2.** MUS sillon *m* ►**to get into a ~** devenir routinier; **get into the ~!** allez, vas-y!

groovy <-ier, -iest> *adj inf* épatant(e)

grope [grəʊp, *Am:* groʊp] **I.** *n* **1.** (*touch with hands*) tâtonnement *m* **2.** *inf* (*unwelcome sexual touch*) pelotage *m* **II.** *vi* **1. to ~ for sth** chercher qc à tâtons **2.** *fig* tâtonner **III.** *vt* **1. to ~ one's way** avancer à tâtons **2.** *inf* (*touch sexually*) peloter

gropingly ['grəʊpɪŋli, *Am:* 'groʊp-] *adv* à tâtons

gross [grəʊs, *Am:* groʊs] **I.** *adj* **1.** *form* JUR grave; **~ negligence** faute *f* lourde **2.** (*very fat*) obèse **3.** *Am* (*extremely offensive*) vulgaire **4.** *Am* (*revolting*) dégueulasse **5.** (*total*) total(e) **6.** FIN (*pay, amount, income*) brut(e) **II.** *vt* FIN gagner brut

gross domestic product *n* produit *m* intérieur brut

grossly *adv* **1.**(*extremely: unfair*) profondément **2.**(*in a gross manner*) grossièrement

gross national product *n* produit *m* national brut

grotesque [grəʊ'tesk, *Am:* groʊ-] **I.** *n* ART, LIT grotesque *m* **II.** *adj* grotesque

grotto ['grɒtəʊ, *Am:* 'grɑːt̬oʊ] <-tto(e)s> *n* grotte *f*

grotty ['grɒti, *Am:*'grɑːt̬i] *adj inf* minable; **to feel ~** se sentir vaseux

grouch [graʊtʃ] **I.** *n* **1.**(*grudge*) rouspéteur, -euse *m, f;* **to have a ~ against sb** en vouloir à qn **2.**(*grumpy person*) grincheux, -euse *m, f* **II.** *vi* ronchonner

grouchy <-ier, -iest> *adj* grognon

ground¹ [graʊnd] **I.** *n no pl* **1.**(*the Earth's surface*) terre *f;* **burnt to the ~** brûlé de fond en comble; **above ~** en surface; MIN à la surface; **below ~** sous terre; MIN au jour **2.**(*soil*) sol *m* **3.**(*large area of land*) domaine *m;* **waste ~** terres *fpl* incultes **4.**(*facilities for outdoor sports*) terrain *m* **5.**(*specific place for animals*) **fishing ~s** lieux *mpl* de pêche **6.**(*bottom of the sea*) fond *m* de la mer **7.** *Am* ELEC prise *f* de terre; **~ wire** fil *m* neutre; *s. a.* **earth 8.**(*area of knowledge*) domaine *m;* **we found some common ~** nous avons trouvé un terrain d'entente; **to be on safe ~** reposer sur des bases solides **9.**(*reason*) raison *f;* **~s for divorce** motifs *mpl* de divorce; **on the ~s that ...** à cause de ...; **on what ~s ?** à quel titre ? **II.** *vt* **1.**(*base*) baser; **to be ~ed in sth** être basé sur qc; **to ~ sb in Latin** former qn en latin **2.** AVIAT (*unable to fly*) empêcher de voler; (*forbid*) interdire de vol; **to be ~ed** rester au sol **3.**(*run aground: ship*) échouer **4.**(*unable to move*) **to be ~ed** être incapable de bouger; *inf* (*teenager*) être consigné **5.** *Am* ELEC mettre à la masse **III.** *vi* (*ship*) échouer

ground² [graʊnd] **I.** *pt of* **grind II.** *adj* moulu(e); (*meat*) haché(e) **III.** *n pl* sédiment *m;* **coffee ~s** marc *m* de café

ground beef *n no pl* hachis *m* de bœuf **ground control** *n* contrôle *m* au sol **ground crew** *n* équipage *m* non navigant **ground floor** *n* rez-de-chaussée *m* ►**to go in on the ~** être là depuis le début **ground frost** *n* gelée blanche

grounding *n no pl* rudiments *mpl*

groundless *adj* sans fondement

groundnut *n* **1.**(*plant, oil*) arachide *f* **2.**(*peanut*) cacahouète *f* **ground-breaking** *adj* novateur(-trice) **ground rules** *n pl* règles *fpl* de base **groundsheet** *n* tapis *m* de sol **groundskeeper** *n Am,* **groundsman** *n Brit, Aus* gardien *m* de parc **ground staff** *n no pl* **1.**(*maintenance at sports ground*) équipe *f* d'entretien des terrains de sport **2.**(*non-flying staff at airport*) personnel *m* non navigant **ground station** *n* RADIO, TV station *f* terrestre **groundswell** *n no pl* **1.**(*heavy sea*) lame *f* de fond **2.**(*increase*) hausse *f;* **a ~ of public opinion** un grand mouvement d'opinion publique **ground-to-air missile** *n* missile *m* sol-air **ground-to-ground missile** *n* missile *m* sol-sol **groundwork** *n no pl* travail *m* préparatoire; **to lay the ~ for sth** préparer le terrain pour qc

group [gruːp] **I.** *n* **1.**(*several together*) groupe *m* **2.**(*specially assembled*) réunion *f* **3.**(*category*) classe *f* **4.**(*business association*) groupement *m* **5.**(*musicians*) formation *f* **II.** *vt* grouper **III.** *vi* se grouper; **to ~ together round sb** se rassembler autour de qn

group captain *n Brit* MIL colonel *m* (de l'armée de l'air) **group dynamics** *npl* dynamique *f* de groupe

groupie ['gruːpi] *n inf* groupie *f*

grouping *n* groupement *m;* **age ~ of the population** répartition *f* de la population par groupes d'âge

group practice *n* cabinet *m* de groupe **group therapy** *n* psychothérapie *f* de groupe **group ticket** *n* **1.** AUTO titre *m* de transport **2.**(*in tourism*) billet *m* de groupe

grouse¹ [graʊs] *n* (*bird*) tétras *m* ►**to go ~-beating** faire le rabatteur

grouse² [graʊs] **I.** *n* **1.**(*complaint*) grief *m* **2.**(*complaining person*) râleur, -euse *m, f* **II.** *vi* ronchonner; **to ~ at sb** grogner contre qn

grove [grəʊv, *Am:* groʊv] *n* **1.**(*group of trees*) bocage *m* **2.**(*orchard*) verger *m;* **orange ~** orangeraie *f;* **olive ~** oliveraie *f*

grovel ['grɒvl, *Am:* 'grɑːvl] <*Brit* -ll- *o Am* -l-> *vi* **1.**(*behave obsequiously*) **to ~ before sb** se prosterner devant qn **2.**(*crawl*) ramper; **to ~ on one's knees** se mettre à genoux; **to ~ about in the dirt** se traîner dans la boue

grow [grəʊ, *Am:* groʊ] <grew, grown> **I.** *vi* **1.** BIO, AGR (*increase in size: trees, plants, hair*) pousser; (*child, animal*) grandir; **to ~ taller** grandir **2.**(*increase*) croître; **to ~ by 2%** augmenter de 2% **3.**(*flourish*) se développer **4.**(*develop*) développer **5.**(*become, get*) devenir; **to ~ wiser** s'assagir; **to ~ worse** s'empirer; **to ~ to like sth** finir par aimer qc **II.** *vt* **1.**(*cultivate: tomatoes, maize*) cultiver; (*flowers*) faire pousser **2.**(*let grow: a beard, moustache*) se laisser pousser; **to ~ one's hair** se laisser pousser les cheveux **3.** ECON (*develop*) développer ►**money doesn't ~ on trees** l'argent ne pousse pas sur les arbres

◆**grow into** *vt* devenir; **to ~ a man** devenir un homme; **to ~ a shirt** pouvoir porter à présent une chemise

◆**grow out of** *vt* **to ~ one's shoes** ne plus pouvoir porter ses chaussures; **to ~ doing sth** passer l'âge de faire qc

◆**grow up** *vi* **1.**(*become adult*) devenir adulte; **when I ~ I'm going to ...** quand je serai grand, je serai ...; **I grew up on candies** j'ai grandi en me nourrissant de bonbons **2.**(*develop*) développer ►**~, will you!** grandi, veux-tu!

grower *n* **1.**(*plant growing a certain way*) **a fast/slow ~** qui pousse vite/lentement

2. (*market gardener*) cultivateur, -trice *m, f;* **coffee-/tobacco-~** producteur, -trice *m, f* de café/de tabac; **rose-~** rosiériste *mf;* **fruit-/vegetable-~** maraîcher, -ère *m, f*

growing **I.** *n no pl* **1.** (*developing*) croissance *f* **2.** AGR culture *f* **II.** *adj* **1.** (*developing: boy, girl*) en pleine croissance **2.** ECON en pleine expansion **3.** (*increasing*) qui augmente

growing pains *npl* **1.** (*pains in the joints*) douleurs *fpl* de croissance **2.** (*adolescent problems*) problèmes *mpl* affectifs de l'adolescent **3.** (*initial difficulties*) premières difficultés *fpl*

growl [graʊl] **I.** *n* **1.** (*low throaty sound: of a dog*) grognement *m* **2.** (*rumble: of stomach*) gargouillement *m* **3.** *fig* grondement *m* **II.** *vi* (*dog*) grogner; (*person*) gronder; **to ~ out sth** grommeler qc

grown [grəʊn, *Am:* groʊn] **I.** *pp of* **grow** **II.** *adj* grand(e); **a ~ man** un homme adulte; **to be fully ~** avoir fini de grandir

grown-up **I.** *n* adulte *mf* **II.** *adj* adulte

growth [grəʊθ, *Am:* groʊθ] *n* **1.** *no pl* (*increase in size*) croissance *f* **2.** (*stage of growing*) développement *m;* **this plant has reached full ~** cette plante est arrivée à maturité **3.** *no pl* (*increase*) essor *m;* **rate of ~** taux *m* d'expansion **4.** ECON (*development*) croissance *f;* **~ area** secteur *m* de croissance **5.** (*increase in importance*) expansion *f* **6.** (*growing part of plant*) pousse *f* **7.** (*whiskers*) **to have a three days' ~ on one's chin** avoir une barbe de trois jours **8.** (*caused by disease*) tumeur *f*

growth industry *n* ECON industrie *f* en expansion **growth rate** *n* ECON taux *m* de croissance

groyne [grɔɪn] *n Brit* brise-lames *m*

grub [grʌb] **I.** *n* **1.** (*larva*) larve *f* **2.** *inf* (*food*) bouffe *f;* **~('s) up!** à la soupe!; **pub-~** *nourriture servie dans un pub* **II.** <-bb-> *vi* fouiner; **to ~ about for sth** fouiller qc **III.** *vt* **to ~ up** fouir; **to ~ up roots/tree stumps** extirper des racines/souches d'arbres

grubby <-ier, -iest> *adj inf* **1.** (*filthy*) crasseux(-euse) **2.** *fig* véreux(-euse)

grudge [grʌdʒ] **I.** *n* rancune *f;* **to have a ~ against sb** avoir une dent contre qn **II.** *vt* **to ~ sb sth** donner qc à qn à contrecœur

grudging *adj* fait(e) à contrecœur

grudgingly *adv* de mauvaise grâce

gruel ['gruːəl] *n* gruau *m*

gruelling *adj* épuisant(e)

gruesome ['gruːsəm] *adj* horrible

gruff [grʌf] *adj* bourru(e); (*voice*) gros(se)

grumble ['grʌmbl] **I.** *n* (*complaint*) grognement *m* **II.** *vi* grommeler; **mustn't ~** il ne faut pas se plaindre; **to ~ about sb/sth** trouver à redire à qn/qc

grumbling *adj* grognon; **~ appendix** appendicite *f* chronique

grumpy ['grʌmpi] *adj inf* **1.** (*bad tempered*) grincheux(-euse), gringe *Suisse* **2.** (*temporarily annoyed*) grognon

grunt [grʌnt] **I.** *n* grognement *m* **II.** *vi* grogner

G-string ['dʒiːstrɪŋ] *n* FASHION string *m*

Guadeloupe [ˌgwɑːdə'luːp] *n* la Guadeloupe

guarantee [ˌgærən'tiː, *Am:* ˌger-] **I.** *n* **1.** (*promise*) promesse *f* **2.** (*promise of repair, replacement*) garantie *f* **3.** (*document*) contrat *m* de garantie **4.** (*certainty*) sûreté *f* **5.** (*person, institution*) garant(e) *m(f)* **6.** (*responsibility for sb's debt*) caution *f* **7.** (*item given as security*) gage *m;* **to leave sth as a ~** laisser qc en gage **II.** *vt* **1.** (*promise*) **to ~ sb sth** garantir qc à qn **2.** (*promise to correct faults*) protéger; **to be ~d for three years** être assuré pendant trois ans **3.** (*make certain*) **to ~ that ...** garantir que ... **4.** (*take responsibility for sb's debt*) se porter garant de

guaranteed *adj* garanti(e)

guarantor [ˌgærən'tɔːʳ, *Am:* 'gerən'tɔːr] *n* **1.** (*one who guarantees*) garant(e) *m(f)* **2.** (*person responsible for a person, thing*) caution *f*

guaranty ['gærənti, *Am:* 'gerənṱi] *n* **1.** (*acceptance of debt*) garantie *f* **2.** (*thing offered as security*) gage *m*

guard [gɑːd, *Am:* gɑːrd] **I.** *n* **1.** (*person*) garde *m;* **prison ~** *Am* gardien(ne) *m(f)* de prison; **security ~** garde chargé de la sécurité; **to be on ~** être de faction; **to be under ~** être sous surveillance; **to keep ~ over sb/sth** surveiller qn/qc **2.** (*defensive stance*) position *f* de défense; **to be on one's ~** être sur ses gardes; **to be caught off one's ~** tromper la vigilance de qn; *fig* être pris au dépourvu; **to drop one's ~** ne plus être méfiant **3.** (*protective device*) dispositif *m* de sécurité; **face~** masque *m* protecteur; **fire~** garde-feu *m* **4.** *Brit* (*railway official*) garde-corps *m;* **chief ~** chef *m* de train **II.** *vt* garder; **to ~ sb from danger** protéger qn d'un danger; **to ~ sb/sth against sb/sth** protéger qn/qc de qn/qc

◆**guard against** *vt* se protéger contre; **to ~ doing sth** se garder de faire qc

guard dog *n* chien *m* de garde **guard duty** *n* garde *f;* **to be on ~** être de faction

guarded *adj* protégé(e)

guardhouse *n* MIL corps *m* de garde

guardian ['gɑːdɪən, *Am:* 'gɑːr-] *n* **1.** (*responsible person*) tuteur, -trice *m, f* **2.** *form* (*protector*) protecteur, -trice *m, f;* **to be ~ of sth** être le gardien de qc

guardian angel *n a. fig* ange *m* gardien **guardianship** *n no pl* **1.** (*being a guardian*) garde *f* **2.** *form* (*care*) tutelle *f*

guard rail *n* barrière *f* de sécurité **guardroom** *n* MIL corps *m* de garde **Guards** *n Brit* MIL **the ~** (*important army regiment*) les régiments de la garde royale

> Il y a sept régiments de la **Guards** appartenant aux "Household Troops" du monarque

britannique: deux régiments de cavalerie "Household Cavalry": les "Life Guards" et les "Blues and Royals" et cinq régiments d'infanterie: les "Grenadier Guards", les "Coldstream Guards", les "Scots Guards", les "Irish Guards" et les "Welsh Guards". La cérémonie de la relève de la garde ("changing the guard") a lieu tous les deux jours à 11 h 30 devant "Buckingham Palace".

guardsman <-men> *n* **1.** *Brit* garde *m* **2.** *Am* soldat *m* de la garde nationale

Guatemala [ˌgwɑːtɪˈmɑːlə, *Am:* -t̬əˈ-] *n* le Guatemala

Guatemalan **I.** *adj* guatémaltèque **II.** *n* Guatémaltèque *mf*

Guernsey [ˈgɜːnzi, *Am:* ˈɜːrn-] *n* (**the island of**) ~ (l'île *f* de) Guernesey

guer(r)illa [gəˈrɪlə] *n* guérillero *m;* ~ **group** guérilla *f;* ~ **leader** chef *m* de guérilla; ~ **warfare** guérilla *f*

guess [ges] **I.** *n* supposition *f;* **a lucky** ~ un coup de chance; **Mike's ~ is that ...** d'après Mike ...; **to have** [*o Am* **take**] **a** ~ deviner; **to make a wild** ~ risquer une hypothèse; **at a** ~ au jugé; **at a rough** ~ approximativement ►**it's anybody's** [*o* **anyone's**] ~ Dieu seul le sait **II.** *vi* **1.** (*conjecture*) deviner, taper à pouf *Belgique* **2.** *Am* (*believe, suppose*) supposer ►**to keep sb ~ing** laisser qn dans l'ignorance **III.** *vt* **1.** (*conjecture*) deviner **2.** (*estimate*) évaluer **3.** (*suppose*) supposer ►~ **what?** tu sais quoi?

guessing game *n a. fig* devinettes *fpl*

gues(s)timate *n inf* calcul *m* au pifomètre

guesswork *n no pl* estimation *f;* **it's a matter of** ~ c'est une question de conjecture

guest [gest] **I.** *n* **1.** (*invited or paid for person*) invité *m;* **special** ~ invité de marque; **paying** ~ (*renter*) hôte *mf* payant; (*lodger*) pensionnaire *mf* **2.** (*in tourism/hotel customer*) client(e) *m(f)* **3.** (*guesthouse customer*) invité(e) *m(f)* ►**be my** ~ fais/faites comme chez toi/vous **II.** *vi* **to ~ on a show/an album** être invité à une émission/sur un album

guest house *n* pension *f* de famille **guest room** *n* chambre *f* d'amis **guest worker** *n* travailleur, -euse *m, f* immigré(e)

guffaw [gəˈfɔː, *Am:* -ˈfɑː] **I.** *n* gros éclat *m* de rire **II.** *vi* rire bruyamment

guidance [ˈgaɪdns] *n no pl* **1.** (*help and advice*) conseil *m* **2.** (*direction*) direction *f* **3.** (*steering system: system*) guidage *m*

guide [gaɪd] **I.** *n* **1.** (*person, book*) *a. fig* guide *m* **2.** (*indication*) indication *f;* **as a** ~ à titre indicatif; **as a rough** ~ à peu près **3.** (*girl* ~) éclaireuse *f* **II.** *vt a. fig* guider; **to be ~d by sb/sth** se laisser guider par qn/qc; **to be ~d by one's emotions** suivre son instinct

guidebook *n* guide *m*

guided *adj* **1.** (*led by a guide*) guidé(e) **2.** (*automatically steered*) téléguidé(e)

guide dog *n* chien *m* d'aveugle **guideline** *n* directive *f*

guiding hand *n fig* soutien *m* **guiding principle** *n* principe *m* directeur

guild [gɪld] *n* guilde *f*

guilder *n* florin *m*

guile [gaɪl] *n no pl, form* ruse *f*

guileful *adj form* fourbe

guileless *adj* sincère

guillotine [ˈgɪlətiːn] *n* **1.** HIST guillotine *f* **2.** *Aus, Brit* (*paper cutter*) massicot *m*

guilt [gɪlt] *n no pl* **1.** (*shame for wrongdoing*) mauvaise conscience *f;* **feelings of** ~ sentiments *mpl* de culpabilité **2.** (*responsibility for crime*) culpabilité *f*

guiltless *adj* innocent(e)

guilty [ˈgɪlti, *Am:* -t̬i] <-ier, -iest> *adj* coupable; (*secret*) inavouable; **to have a ~ conscience** avoir mauvaise conscience; **to find sb not** ~ déclarer qn non coupable; **to give a not ~ verdict** donner un verdict d'acquittement; **until proven** ~ jusqu'à ce que la preuve de culpabilité soit faite *subj*

guinea [ˈgɪni] *n Brit* guinée *f*

Guinea [ˈgɪni] *n* la Guinée

guinea fowl *n* pintade *f*

Guinean **I.** *adj* guinéen(ne) **II.** *n* Guinéen(ne) *m(f)*

guinea pig *n* **1.** ZOOL cochon *m* d'Inde **2.** *fig* cobaye *m*

guise [gaɪz] *n no pl* **1.** (*style of dress*) paraître *m;* **to be in the ~ of sb/sth** être sous l'aspect de qn/qc **2.** (*appearance*) apparence *f* **3.** (*pretence*) simulation *f;* **under the ~ of seeing me ...** sous le prétexte de me voir ...

guitar [gɪˈtɑːʳ, *Am:* -ˈtɑːr] *n* guitare *f*

guitarist *n* guitariste *mf*

gulch [gʌltʃ] *n Am* (*gully*) ravin *m*

gulf [gʌlf] *n* **1.** (*area of sea*) golfe *m* **2.** (*chasm*) *a. fig* gouffre *m;* **there is a ~ between us** il y a un gouffre qui nous sépare; **we have to bridge the** ~ nous devons calmer notre différend

Gulf of Lions *n* le Golfe du Lion **Gulf Stream** *n* **the** ~ le Gulf Stream

gull[1] [gʌl] *n* mouette *f; s. a.* **seagull**

gull[2] [gʌl] *vt* duper

gullet [ˈgʌlɪt] *n* **1.** (*food pipe*) œsophage *m* **2.** (*throat*) gosier *m* ►**to stick in sb's** ~ rester en travers de la gorge

gullible [ˈgʌləbl] *adj* crédule

gully <-llies> *n* **1.** (*narrow gorge*) petit ravin **2.** (*channel*) couloir *m*

gulp [gʌlp] **I.** *n* **1.** (*large swallow*) bouchée *f;* (*of a drink*) gorgée *f* **2.** *fig* (*of air*) bouffée *f* **II.** *vt* engloutir **III.** *vi* avoir la gorge nouée; **to ~ for air** respirer à pleins poumons

gum[1] [gʌm] **I.** *n* ANAT gencive *f;* ~ **shield** protection *f* dentaire **II.** <-mm-> *vi Am* mâchonner

gum[2] [gʌm] **I.** *n* **1.** (*soft sticky substance*) gomme *f* **2.** (*glue*) colle *f* **3.** (*sweet*) bonbon *m* gélifié **4.** (*chewing* ~) chewing-gum *m* **5.** BOT gommier *m* **II.** *vt* coller; **to ~ down an envelop** cacheter une enveloppe

◆**gum up** *vt* **to ~ the works** bousiller le travail

gumboil ['gʌmbɔɪl] *n* MED inflammation *f* des gencives

gumdrop ['gʌmdrɒp, *Am:* -drɑːp] *n* boule *f* de gomme

gummy ['gʌmi] *adj* **1.** (*sticky*) gluant(e) **2.** (*with glue on*) collant(e) **3.** <-ier, -iest> **a ~ grin** (*showing gums*) un large sourire

gumption ['gʌmpʃən] *n no pl, inf* **1.** (*courage*) cran *m* **2.** (*intelligence*) jugeote *f;* **to have the ~ to** +*infin* avoir la présence d'esprit de +*infin*

gumshield ['gʌmʃiːld] *n* protection *f* dentaire

gumshoe *n* **1.** (*waterproof overshoe*) caoutchouc *m* **2.** *Am, inf* (*detective*) privé *m* **gum tree** *n* gommier *m* ►**to be up a ~** *inf* être dans le pétrin

gun [gʌn] **I.** *n* **1.** (*weapon*) arme *f* à feu **2.** (*handgun*) revolver *m* **3.** SPORT pistolet *m;* **to wait for the starting ~** attendre le signal de départ; **at the ~** au signal **4.** (*device*) pistolet *m* **5.** *Am* (*person*) bandit *m* armé ►**to do sth with ~s blazing** faire qc avec détermination; **to jump the ~** SPORT partir avant le départ; **to stick to one's ~s** ne pas en démordre **II.** <-nn-> *vt inf* accélérer

◆**gun down** *vt* **to gun sb down** abattre qn

◆**gun for** *vt* **1.** (*pursue*) en avoir après **2.** (*strive for*) vouloir à tout prix

gun barrel *n* (*of a rifle, pistol*) canon *m* **gunfight** *n* affrontement *m* de coups de feu **gunfire** *n* **1.** (*gunfight*) fusillade *f* **2.** (*shots*) coups *m* de feu **3.** MIL canonnade *f* **gun licence** *n* permis *m* de port d'armes **gunman** <-men> *n* malfaiteur *m* armé

gunner *n* artilleur *m*

gunpoint *n* **at ~** sous la menace d'une arme **gunpowder** *n no pl* poudre *f* à canon **gunrunner** *n* contrebandier *m* d'armes **gunrunning** *n no pl* contrebande *f* d'armes **gunshot** *n no pl* coup *m* de feu **gunshot wound** *n* blessure *f* par balle **gunslinger** *n* **1.** HIST bandit *m* armé **2.** *Brit, fig* homme *m* de caractère

gurgle ['gɜːgl, *Am:* 'gɜːr-] **I.** *n* **1.** (*happy noise*) gargouillis *m* **2.** (*noise of water*) gargouillement *m* **II.** *vi* **1.** (*make happy, bubbling noise: baby*) babiller; **to ~ with pleasure/with delight** gazouiller de plaisir/de joie **2.** (*make pleasant noise: water*) gargouiller

guru ['gʊru, *Am:* 'guːruː] *n* **1.** (*religious leader*) gourou *m* **2.** (*expert advisor*) mentor *m*

gush [gʌʃ] **I.** *n* **1.** (*burst*) bouillonnement *m;* (*of water*) jaillissement *m* **2.** *fig* effusion *f* **II.** *vi* **1.** (*any liquid*) jaillir **2.** *pej* (*praise excessively*) se répandre en compliments **III.** *vt* faire jaillir

gusher *n* puits *m* jaillissant

gushing *adj pej* (*person*) trop exubérant(e); (*water*) jaillissant(e)

gushy *adj pej* vif(vive)

gusset ['gʌsɪt] *n* pièce *f* d'étoffe

gust [gʌst] **I.** *n* (*of wind*) rafale *f;* **a ~ of laughter** un éclat de rire **II.** *vi* souffler par rafales

gusto ['gʌstəʊ, *Am:* -toʊ] *n no pl* **with ~** avec plaisir

gusty <-ier -iest> *adj* de grand vent

gut [gʌt] **I.** *n* **1.** (*intestine*) intestin *m;* **a ~ feeling** une intuition; **a ~ reaction** une réaction viscérale **2.** (*animal intestine*) boyau *m* **3.** *pl* (*bowels*) entrailles *fpl* **4.** (*belly*) ~(**s**) ventre *m;* **my ~s hurt** j'ai mal au ventre **5.** *pl* (*courage*) cran *m;* **to have ~s** avoir du cran; (*strength of character*) avoir une force de caractère; **it takes ~s** il faut du cran ►**to have sb's ~s for garters** *Brit, iron, inf* punir qn **II.** <-tt-> *vt* **1.** (*remove the innards*) vider **2.** (*destroy*) ravager

gutless *adj inf* **1.** (*lacking courage*) lâche **2.** (*lacking enthusiasm*) **to be ~** manquer de punch

gutsy ['gʌtsi] <-ier, -iest> *adj* **1.** (*brave*) courageux(-euse) **2.** (*adventurous*) casse-cou **3.** (*powerful*) vaillant(e)

gutter ['gʌtəʳ, *Am:* 'gʌt̬ɚ] *n* **1.** (*drainage channel: at the roadside*) caniveau *m;* (*on the roof*) gouttière *f* **2.** *fig* **to be in the ~** être à la rue; **to end up in the ~** finir sous les ponts; **the language of the ~** la langue de la rue

gutter press *n no pl, Brit, pej* **the ~** la presse à sensation

guttural ['gʌtərəl, *Am:* 'gʌt̬-] **I.** *adj* **1.** (*throaty*) rauque **2.** LING guttural(e) **II.** *n* LING gutturale *f*

guy [gaɪ] *n inf* **1.** (*man*) type *m* **2.** *pl, Aus, Am* (*people*) ami(e)s *pl;* **hi ~s!** salut les gars! **3.** (*sb with a strange appearance*) épouvantail *m* **4.** (*rope to fix a tent, guy rope*) corde *f* de tente

Guyana [gaɪ'ænə] *n* Guyana *m*

Guyanese [ˌgaɪə'niːz] **I.** *adj* guyanais(e) **II.** *n* Guyanais(e) *m(f)*

Guy Fawkes' Day, **Guy Fawkes' Night** *n en Grande-Bretagne, le 5 novembre, on commémore le jour où Guy Fawkes a tenté d'incendier le Parlement en 1605*

guzzle ['gʌzl] *inf* **I.** *vt* **1.** (*eat*) *a. fig* bouffer **2.** (*drink*) siffler **II.** *vi* (*food*) s'empiffrer; (*drink*) se pinter

gym [dʒɪm] *n* **1.** *abbr of* **gymnastics** **2.** *abbr of* **gymnasium** **3.** *Am abbr of* **physical education**

gymkhana [dʒɪm'kɑːnə] *n* SPORT gymkhana *m*

gymnasium [dʒɪm'neɪzɪəm] *n* gymnase *m,* halle *f* de gymnastique *Suisse*

gymnast ['dʒɪmnæst] *n* gymnaste *mf*

gymnastic *adj* gymnastique

gymnastics *npl* (*physical exercises*) gymnas-

tique *f*
gym shoes *n* chaussures *fpl* de sport **gym shorts** *n* shorts *m* (de sport)
gynaecological *adj* gynécologique
gynaecologist *n* gynécologue *mf*
gynaecology *n no pl* gynécologie *f*
gynecological *adj Am, Aus s. a.* **gynaecological**
gynecologist *n Am, Aus s. a.* **gynaecologist**
gynecology [ˌgaɪnə'kɒlədʒi, *Am:* -'kɑːlə-] *n Am, Aus s. a.* **gynaecology**
gyp [dʒɪp] *n* **1.** *Aus, Brit, inf* **to give sb ~** (*pain*) flanquer une raclée à qn; (*bad behaviour*) mal se comporter **2.** (*bad deal*) escroquerie *f*
gypsum ['dʒɪpsəm] *n no pl* gypse *m*
gypsy ['dʒɪpsi] <-sies> *n* (*from Spain*) gitan(e) *m(f)*; (*from Eastern Europe*) tzigane *mf*
gyrate [ˌdʒaɪ'reɪt] *vi* **1.** (*revolve*) tourner **2.** (*dance suggestively*) se trémousser **3.** (*dance whirling round*) tournoyer
gyration *n* **1.** (*movement*) giration *f* **2.** *fig* fluctuation *f* boursière
gyrocompass ['dʒaɪrəʊ'kɒmpəs, *Am:* -roʊˌkʌm-] *n* compas *m* gyroscopique
gyroscope ['dʒaɪrəskəʊp, *Am:* -skoʊp] *n* NAUT, AVIAT gyroscope *m*

H

H, h [eɪtʃ] <-'s> *n* H *m*, h *m*; **~ as in Harry, ~ for Harry** (*on telephone*) h comme Henri
ha [hɑː] *interj iron* ah!
habeas corpus [ˌheɪbɪəs'kɔːpəs, *Am:* -'kɔːr-] *n no pl* LAW habeas corpus *m*
haberdasher ['hæbədæʃəʳ, *Am:* -ɚdæʃɚ] *n* **1.** *Brit* (*seller of sewing goods*) mercier, -ière *m, f* **2.** *Am* (*dealer in men's clothing*) chemisier, -ière *m, f*
haberdashery *n* **1.** *Brit* mercerie *f* **2.** *Am* chemiserie *f*
habit ['hæbɪt] *n* **1.** (*repeated action*) habitude *f*; **eating ~s** habitudes alimentaires; **from force of ~** par habitude; **to break a ~** changer une habitude; **to be in the ~ of doing sth** avoir l'habitude de faire qc; **to do sth out of ~** faire qc par habitude; **to do sth by sheer force of ~** faire qc par pure habitude; **to get into the ~ of doing sth** prendre l'habitude de faire qc; **to make a ~ of sth** prendre l'habitude de qc; **to pick up a ~** prendre une habitude **2.** *inf* (*drug addiction*) accoutumance *f*; **to have a heroin ~** *péj* être accro à l'héroïne **3.** (*special clothing*) habit *m*; **riding ~** tenue *f* d'équitation
habitable *adj* habitable
habitat ['hæbɪtæt, *Am:* '-ə-] *n* habitat *m*
habitation [ˌhæbɪ'teɪʃən] *n no pl* habitation *f*; **fit/unfit for human ~** habitable/inhabitable
habitual [hə'bɪtʃuəl] *adj* **1.** (*occurring often, as a habit*) habituel(le); **to become ~** devenir une habitude **2.** (*usual*) d'usage **3.** (*act by force of habit*) *a. pej* invétéré(e)
habituate [hə'bɪtʃueɪt] *vt* habituer; **to be ~d to sb/sth** être habitué à qn/qc; **to become ~d to sth** s'habituer à qc; **to be ~d to** *+infin* être habitué à *+infin*
hack¹ [hæk] **I.** *n* **1.** (*cut*) entaille *f* **2.** (*blow*) coup *m* **II.** *vt* **1.** (*chop wildly/violently*) tailler; **to ~ sb to death** lacérer qn à mort **2.** (*kick opponent in sport*) donner un coup de pied à **3.** *Am, Aus, inf* (*cope with difficult situation*) **not to be able to ~ it** ne pas pouvoir s'en sortir **III.** *vi* **to ~ at sth** taillader qc; **to ~ off sth** trancher qc
◆**hack around** *vi* traînailler
◆**hack off** *vt inf* **to be hacked off** en avoir marre
hack² [hæk] INFOR **I.** *vt* pirater **II.** *n* piratage *m* (informatique)
hack³ [hæk] **I.** *vi* se promener à cheval; **to go ~ing** se promener à cheval **II.** *n* **1.** (*horse*) cheval *m* **2.** (*rural horse-ride*) promenade *f* à cheval **3.** *Am, inf* (*taxi car*) taxi *m* **4.** *pej* (*bad journalist*) gratte-papier *m*
hacker [hækəʳ, *Am:* -ɚ] *n Am* INFOR pirate *m* (informatique)
hackles *npl* **1.** (*hairs on a dog's neck*) poils *mpl* du cou **2.** (*feathers on a bird's neck*) plumes *fpl* du cou ►**to make sb's ~ rise** hérisser qn; **to get one's ~ up** se hérisser; **sth raises ~** qc hérisse
hackney carriage *n Brit* fiacre *m*
hackneyed *adj pej* rebattu(e)
hacksaw ['hæksɔː, *Am:* -sɑː] *n* scie *f* à métaux
had [həd, *stressed:* hæd] *pt, pp of* **have**
haddock ['hædək] *inv n* aiglefin *m*
hadn't ['hædnt] = **had not** *s.* **have**
haematite ['hemətaɪt] *n Brit, Aus* hématite *f*
haemoglobin [ˌhiːmə'gləʊbɪn, *Am:* 'hiːməgloʊ-] *n no pl, Brit, Aus* hémoglobine *f*
haemophilia [ˌhiːmə'fɪlɪə, *Am:* ˌhiːmoʊ'-] *n no pl, Brit, Aus* hémophilie *f*
haemophiliac *n Brit, Aus* hémophile *mf*
haemorrhage ['hemərɪdʒ, *Am:* -ɚɪdʒ] *Brit, Aus* **I.** *n* **1.** MED hémorragie *f* **2.** *fig* pénurie *f*; **a ~ of esteem** un manque d'estime **II.** *vi* faire une hémorragie
haemorrhoids ['hemərɔɪdz] *npl* hémorroïdes *fpl*
haft [hɑːft, *Am:* hæft] *n* manche *m*
hag [hæg] *n pej* sorcière *f*
haggard ['hægəd, *Am:* -ɚd] *adj* égaré(e); (*look*) hagard(e)
haggis ['hægɪs] *n no pl, Scot* GASTR *panse de brebis farcie*
haggle ['hægl] **I.** *vi* chicaner **II.** *vt* **to ~ sth down** marchander qc
Hague [heɪg] *n* **the ~** La Haye
haha, ha-ha, ha ha [hɑː'hɑː] *interj iron* ha,

ha!

hail¹ [heɪl] I. *n* grêle *f;* **a ~ of abuse** une flopée d'injures; **a ~ of insults/stones** une volée d'insultes/de pierres II. *vi* grêler

hail² [heɪl] *vt* saluer; (*a taxi*) héler

hair [heəʳ, *Am:* her] *n* **1.** (*~ of head, locks*) cheveux *mpl;* **a tuft of ~** une touffe de cheveux; **to wash/have one's ~ cut** se laver/se faire couper les cheveux **2.** *no pl* (*single ~*) cheveu *m* **3.** (*single locks on head and body*) poil *m* **4.** (*furry covering on plant*) duvet *m* ►**that'll put ~s on your chest** *iron, inf* ça te rendra plus viril; **the ~ of the dog** l'antidote contre la gueule de bois; **to get in sb's ~** taper sur les nerfs de qn; **if sb harms a ~ on sb's head** si qn touche à un cheveu de qn; **keep your ~ on!** *Brit, Aus, iron, inf* calmez-vous!; **to make sb's ~ stand on end** *inf* faire dresser les cheveux sur la tête de qn; **to not turn a ~** ne pas montrer ses sentiments

hairbrush *n* brosse *f* à cheveux **hair conditioner** *n* après-shampoing *m* **hair curler** *n* bigoudi *m* **haircut** *n* **1.** (*cut*) coupe *f* de cheveux; **to get a ~** se faire couper les cheveux **2.** (*hairstyle*) coiffure *f* **hairdo** <-s> *n iron, inf* coiffure *f* **hairdresser** *n* coiffeur, -euse *m, f;* **to go to the ~'s** aller chez le coiffeur **hairdressing** *n* coiffure *f* **hairdressing salon** *n* salon *m* de coiffure **hair drier, hair dryer** *n* sèche-cheveux *m,* foehn *m Suisse* **hairgrip** *n* pince *f* à cheveux

hairless *adj* chauve

hairline *n* racine *f* des cheveux **hairnet** *n* filet *m* **hairpiece** *n* mèche *f* postiche **hairpin** *n* épingle *f* à cheveux **hair-raising** *adj inf* effrayant(e) **hair remover** *n* crème *f* épilatoire **hair restorer** *n* régénérateur *m* capillaire **hair roller** *n* rouleau *m* **hair slide** *n* barrette *f* **hair-splitting** I. *n* ergoterie *f* II. *adj pej* subtil(e) **hairspray** *n* laque *f;* **a can of ~** une bombe de laque **hairstyle** *n* coiffure *f*

hairy ['heəri, *Am:* 'heri] *adj* **1.** (*having much hair*) poilu(e) **2.** *inf* (*desperate, alarmingly dangerous*) périlleux(-euse) **3.** (*pleasantly risky/scaring*) effrayant(e)

Haiti ['heɪti, *Am:* -t̬i] *n* Haïti *m sans art*

Haitian I. *adj* haïtien(ne) II. *n* Haïtien(ne) *m(f)*

hake [heɪk] <-(s)> *n* colin *m*

hale [heɪl] *adj* vigoureux(-euse); **~ and hearty** frais et gaillard

half [hɑːf, *Am:* hæf] I. <-halves> *n* **1.** (*equal part, fifty per cent*) moitié *f;* **in ~** en deux; **to cut sth into halves** couper qc en deux; **a pound and a ~** une livre et demie; **~ an hour/a dozen** une demi-heure/demi-douzaine; **~ the audience** la moitié du public; **~ (of) the time** la moitié du temps; **the first ~ of a century** la première moitié du siècle; **at ~ past nine** à neuf heures et demie **2.** SPORT **first/second ~** première/deuxième mi-temps **3.** *Brit, inf* (*half pint of beer*) demi *m* **4.** *Brit* (*child's ticket for public transport*) **~ (fare)** tarif *m* enfant ►**~ and ~** moitié-moitié; **too clever by ~** trop malin(-igne); **to go halves on sth** partager qc; **to not do things by halves** ne pas faire les choses à moitié; **other ~** autre moitié; **in ~ a second** [*o* **tick** *Brit*] en moins d'une seconde II. *adj* demi(e); **a ~ glass** un demi-verre; **two and a ~ cups** deux tasses et demie; **~ man, ~ beast** mi-homme, mi-animal; **the second ~ century** la seconde moitié du siècle III. *adv* à moitié; **~ asleep/naked** à moitié endormi/nu; **to be ~ right** ne pas avoir tout à fait tort; **to be not ~ bad** ne pas être si mauvais que ça; **~ as tall again** moitié moins grand; **not ~!** et comment!

halfback *n* SPORT demi-arrière *m* **half-baked** *adj pej, inf* qui ne tient pas debout **half board** *n no pl* demi-pension *f* **half-breed** *n pej* métis(se) *m(f)* **half-brother** *n* demi-frère *m* **half-caste** *s.* half-breed **half cock** *n* **to go off at ~** *Am* mal partir **half-crown** *n* HIST demi-couronne *f* **half-dozen** *n* demi-douzaine *f* **half-empty** *adj* à moitié vide **half-fare** *n* demi-tarif *m* **half-full** *adj* à moitié plein **half-hearted** *adj* sans enthousiasme; (*attempt*) hésitant(e) **half-mast** *n* **at ~** à mi-mât; **to fly a flag at ~** monter son pavillon en berne; **to lower to ~** descendre à mi-mollet **half-moon** *n* demi-lune *f;* **~ shaped** en forme de demi-lune **half note** *n Am* MUS blanche *f* **halfpence** *inv,* **halfpenny** <-pennies> *n* HIST demi-penny *m* **half-price** I. *n* demi-tarif *m;* **at ~** à demi-tarif II. *adj, adv* demi-tarif **half rest** *n Am* MUS pause *f* **half-sister** *n* demi-sœur *f* **half-timbered** *adj* à colombage **half-time** *n* SPORT mi-temps *f;* **at ~** à la mi-temps; **~ score** score *m* à la mi-temps **half-title** *n* PUBL avant-titre *m* **half tone** *n* **1.** (*semitone*) demi-ton *m* **2.** (*printing method for pictures*) demi-teinte *f;* **in ~** à demi-teinte **halfway** I. *adj* milieu *m;* **~ point** point *m* à mi-chemin; **~ line** SPORT ligne *f* des cinquante mètres II. *adv* **1.** (*in the middle of a point*) à mi-chemin; **~ down** à mi-hauteur; **~ through** à mi-terme; **~ through the year** au milieu de l'année; **~ up** à mi-côté; **to meet sb ~** rencontrer qn à mi-distance; *fig* trouver un compromis **2.** (*partly*) à peu près **half-wit** *n pej* simple *mf* d'esprit **half-yearly** I. *adj* semestriel(le) II. *adv* tous les six mois

halibut ['hælɪbət] <-(s)> *n* flétan *m,* elbot *m Belgique*

halitosis [ˌhælɪ'təʊsɪs, *Am:* -'toʊ-] *n no pl* mauvaise haleine *f*

hall [hɔːl] *n* **1.** (*room by front door*) entrée *f;* (*of public building, hotel*) hall *m,* allée *f Suisse* **2.** (*corridor*) couloir *m* **3.** (*large public room*) salle *f,* aula *f Suisse;* **church/concert ~** salle paroissiale/de concert **4.** UNIV, SCHOOL réfectoire *m;* **to dine in ~** manger au réfectoire; **~ of residence** résidence *f* universitaire **5.** (*large country house*) manoir *m*

hallelujah [ˌhælɪ'luːjə] I. *interj* alléluia! II. *n*

alléluia *m*

hallmark ['hɔːlmɑːk, *Am:* -mɑːrk] **I.** *n* **1.** *Brit* (*engraved identifying mark*) cachet *m* de contrôle **2.** ECON (*identifying symbol*) empreinte *f;* **to bear all the ~s of sb/sth** porter toutes les marques de qn/qc **II.** *vt* contrôler; **to ~ gold** poinçonner de l'or

hallo [hə'ləʊ, *Am:* -'loʊ] <-s> *interj Brit s.* **hello**

hallow ['hæləʊ, *Am:* -oʊ] *vt* sanctifier

hallowed *adj* saint(e)

Halloween, **Hallowe'en** *n no pl* Halloween *m*

> **Halloween** est le 31 octobre, la veille du "All Saint's Day" ou "All Hallows" (la Toussaint). Depuis la nuit des temps, on l'associe aux esprits et aux sorcières. Les enfants fabriquent des "jack-o-lanterns" (des lanternes avec des citrouilles) et en Écosse ils s'en vont "disguising", c'est-à-dire qu'ils se déguisent et vont de maison en maison pour collecter de l'argent de poche en chantant et en récitant des poèmes. Aux USA, les enfants se déguisent le soir et ils font du porte-à-porte, un sac à la main. Quant les habitants ouvrent leur porte, les enfants crient "Trick or Treat!": on doit leur donner une sucrerie ("treat") ou bien on reçoit un gage ("trick"). De nos jours, les gages ou mauvaises farces se font rares car les enfants ne vont que dans les maisons dont l'éclairage extérieur est allumé en signe de bienvenue.

hallucinate [hə'luːsɪneɪt] *vi* avoir des hallucinations

hallucination *n no pl* hallucination *f*

hallucinogenic [həˌluːsɪnə'dʒenɪk, *Am:* -noʊ'-] *adj* hallucinogène

halo ['heɪləʊ, *Am:* -loʊ] <-s *o* -es> *n* **1.** (*light*) auréole *f* **2.** *fig* nimbe *m* **3.** (*light circle on moon*) halo *m*

halogen ['hælədʒen, *Am:* 'hæloʊ-] *n* halogène *m*

halogen bulb *n* ampoule *f* halogène

halogen lamp *n* lampe *f* halogène

halt [hɒlt, *Am:* hɔːlt] **I.** *n no pl* **1.** (*standstill, stoppage*) arrêt *m;* **production ~** arrêt de production; **to bring sth to a ~** faire marquer un temps d'arrêt; **to call a ~** arrêter; **to come to a ~** s'interrompre momentanément; **to screech to a ~** s'arrêter avec un crissement de pneus **2.** (*interruption*) interruption *f;* **to have a ~** faire une pause **II.** *vt* arrêter **III.** *vi* faire halte

halter ['hɔːltəʳ, *Am:* -t̬ɚ] *n* licou *m*

halter-neck **I.** *n* dos *m* nu **II.** *adj* dos nu *inv*

halting *adj* hésitant(e)

halve [hɑːv, *Am:* hæv] *vt* **1.** (*lessen by 50 per cent*) diminuer de moitié **2.** (*cut in two equal pieces*) diviser en deux

halyard ['hæljəd, *Am:* -jɚd] *n* NAUT drisse *f*

ham [hæm] *n* **1.** (*cured pork meat*) jambon *m* **2.** *pej* (*incompetent actor*) **~ actor** cabotin *m* **3.** (*non-professional radio operator*) **radio ~** radio-amateur *m*

hamburger ['hæmbɜːgəʳ, *Am:* -bɜːrgɚ] *n* GASTR hamburger *m*

ham-fisted *adj Brit, Aus,* **ham-handed** *adj Am, pej* maladroit(e)

hamlet ['hæmlət] *n* hameau *m*

hammer ['hæməʳ, *Am:* -ɚ] **I.** *n* **1.** (*tool*) marteau *m;* **the ~ and sickle** la faucille et le marteau; **to come under the ~** être mis aux enchères **2.** (*part of modern gun*) chien *m* **II.** *vt* **1.** (*hit with tool*) marteler; **to ~ a nail into sth** enfoncer un clou dans qc **2.** *inf* (*beat easily in sports*) **to ~ sb** battre qn à plates coutures; **to ~ sb to a pulp** réduire qn en bouillie **3.** FIN, ECON écraser **4.** (*condemn, disapprove of*) massacrer **III.** *vi* marteler; **to ~ on a door** frapper à la porte

◆**hammer away** *vi* travailler d'arrache-pied

◆**hammer in** *vt* enfoncer à coups de marteau

◆**hammer out** *vt* **1.** (*shape by beating*) étendre sous le marteau **2.** (*find solution after difficulties*) élaborer; (*a settlement*) mettre au point

hammerhead *n* requin *m* marteau

hammock ['hæmək] *n* hamac *m*

hamper[1] ['hæmpəʳ, *Am:* -pɚ] *vt* **1.** (*restrict ability to achieve*) **to ~ sth** gêner qc; **to ~ sb** empêtrer qn **2.** (*disturb*) embarrasser **3.** (*limit extent of activity*) entraver

hamper[2] ['hæmpəʳ, *Am:* -pɚ] *n* **1.** (*large picnic basket*) panier *m* **2.** *Am* (*basket for dirty linen*) manne *f*

hamster ['hæmstəʳ, *Am:* -stɚ] *n* hamster *m*

hamstring ['hæmstrɪŋ] **I.** *n* tendon *m* du jarret; **strained ~** tendon *m* foulé; **to pull a ~** déchirer un tendon **II.** <irr> *vt* couper les jarrets à

hand [hænd] **I.** *n* **1.** (*limb joined to arm*) main *f;* **to do sth by ~** faire qc à la main; **to be good with one's ~s** être adroit de ses mains; **to shake ~s with sb** serrer la main de qn; **to take sb by the ~** prendre qn par la main; **to deliver a letter by ~** distribuer une lettre par porteur; **get your ~s off!** ne me touche pas!; **to keep one's ~s off sb** ne pas toucher qn; **to tie ~ and foot** lier pieds et poings; **~ in ~** main dans la main; **Hands up!** Hauts les mains! **2.** (*responsibility, control*) **to have sth in ~** avoir qc sous contrôle; **to have sth well in ~** avoir qc bien en main; **to take sb in ~** prendre qn en main; **to get out of ~** échapper au contrôle; **to have a ~ in sth** être impliqué dans qc; **to be out of one's ~** ne rien pouvoir y faire; **to be in good ~s** être en de bonnes mains; **to eat in/out of sb's ~s** manger dans la main de qn; **to fall into the wrong ~s** tomber entre de mauvaises mains; **to put sth into the ~s of sb/sth** confier qc à qn; **to put a matter into the ~s of a solicitor** confier une affaire à un avocat; **to get sb/sth off one's ~s** se débarrasser de qn/qc **3.** (*reach*) **to be at ~** être à portée de la main; **to have sth to ~** avoir quelque chose sous la main; **to keep sth close at ~** garder qc à portée de main; **in** [*o* **on**] ~ (*available to use*) à disposition **4. in** [*o Am* **at**] ~ (*in progress*) en cours; **the job at ~** le travail en cours; **the problem in ~** le problème en question **5.** (*pointer on clock/watch*) aiguille *f;* **the big/little ~** la grande/petite aiguille **6.** GAMES (*assortment of cards*) jeu *m;* (*section/round of card game*) partie *f* **7.** (*manual worker*) ouvrier, -ère *m, f* **8.** *pl* (*sailor*) équipage *m* **9.** (*skillful person*) personne *f* habile; **to be an old ~ at sth** être un expert en qc **10.** (*assistance with work*) aide *f;* **to give sb a ~** donner un coup de main à qn **11. to keep one's ~ in** (*stay in practise*) garder la main **12. to give sb a big ~** (*clap performer enthusiastically*) applaudir qn vivement **13.** (*measurement of horse's height*) paume *f* **14.** (*handwriting, penmanship*) signature *f* ►**a bird in the ~** (**is worth two in the bush**) un tiens vaut mieux que deux tu l'auras; **to be ~ in glove** être de mèche; **to make/lose money ~ over fist** s'enrichir/perdre de l'argent rapidement; **I only have one pair of ~s** je n'ai que deux mains; **to put one's ~ in the till** puiser dans la caisse; **to keep a firm ~ on sth** garder une main ferme sur qc; **at first ~** à première vue; **to have one's ~s full** avoir du pain sur la planche; **on the one ~ ... on the other** (~) ... d'une part ... d'autre part ...; **at second ~** par ouï-dire; **I could beat you with one ~ tied** Je pourrais te battre avec une main dans le dos; **to ask for sb's ~ in marriage** *form* demander la main de qn; **to go ~ in ~ with sth** aller de pair avec qc; **to have got sb on one's ~s** avoir qn à sa charge; **to lay one's ~s on sth** s'emparer de qc **II.** *vt* **to ~ sb sth** passer qc à qn ►**to ~ sb a line, to ~ a line to sb** *pej, inf* donner un tuyau à qn

◆**hand around** *vt* faire passer

◆**hand back** *vt* (*give back, return to*) repasser; **to hand sb sth back** [*o* **to hand sth back to sb**] rendre qc à qn

◆**hand down** *vt* **1.** (*pass on within family*) transmettre; **to hand sth down from one generation to another** transmettre qc de génération en génération **2.** (*drink*) descendre **3.** *Am* LAW (*make decision public*) prononcer; **to ~ judgement on sb** prononcer un jugement sur qn

◆**hand in** *vt* remettre

◆**hand on** *vt* **1.** (*pass through family*) transmettre **2.** (*pass on*) passer

◆**hand out** *vt* **1.** (*distribute to group equally: roles, samples*) distribuer **2.** (*give, distribute*) donner; **to ~ advice to sb** donner des conseils à qn

◆**hand over** *vt* **to ~ sth to sb** (*cheque*) remettre qc à qn

◆**hand round** *vt* faire passer; **to ~ papers** faire circuler des documents

handbag *n* sac *m* à main, sacoche *f Belgique* **handball** *n* hand-ball *m* **handbill** *n* prospectus *m* **handbook** *n* guide *m;* **student ~** manuel *m* de l'étudiant **handbrake** *n* frein *m* à main

h & c *n abbr of* **hot and cold** (**water**) eau *f* chaude

handcart *n* charrette *f* à bras **handcuff** *vt* passer les menottes à; **to ~ sb to sb/sth** attacher qn à qn/qc avec des menottes **handful** *n no pl* **1.** (*quantity holdable in hand*) poignée *f* **2.** (*small number, small quantity*) petit nombre *m;* **the ~ of sb**(**s**)**/sth**(**s**), **who ...** les quelques personnes/choses qui ... **3.** (*person hard to manage*) **a bit of a ~** un peu de fil à retordre **4.** *iron* (*a lot*) **quite a ~** presque une poignée **hand grenade** *n* grenade *f* à main **handgun** *n* revolver *m*

handicap ['hædɪkæp] **I.** *n a. fig* handicap *m* **II.** <-pp-> *vt* handicaper

handicapped *adj* handicapé(e)

handicraft ['hændɪkrɑ:ft, *Am:* -kræft] **I.** *adj* artisanal(e) **II.** *n Am* artisanat *m*

handiwork ['hændɪwɜ:k, *Am:* -wɜ:rk] *n no pl* **1.** (*work*) travail *m* manuel **2.** *fig, iron* faute *f*

handkerchief <-s> *n* mouchoir *m*

handle ['hændl] **I.** *n* **1.** (*handgrip to move objects*) manche *m;* **pot ~** manche de casserole; **door ~** poignée *f* de la porte, clenche *f Belgique;* **to turn a ~** tourner une clef **2.** *inf* (*name with highborn connotations*) titre *m* **3.** INFOR poignée *f* **II.** *vt* **1.** (*feel/grasp an object*) toucher **2.** (*move/transport sth*) manipuler **3.** (*deal with, direct, manage*) prendre en main; **to ~ a job** s'occuper d'un travail **4.** (*discuss, write about, portray*) traiter **5.** (*operate dangerous/difficult object*) manœuvrer **6.** *Brit* (*deal in, trade in*) négocier **III.** *vi + adv/prep* **to ~ well** être (facilement) maniable; **~ with care, glass!** fragile!

handlebar, handlebar moustache *n* moustache *f* en guidon **handlebars** *npl* guidon *m*

handler *n* **1.** (*person who carries*) porteur *m;* **a baggage ~** un porteur de valises **2.** (*dog trainer*) maître-chien *m*

handling *n no pl* manipulation *f;* (*of tool*) maniement *m;* (*of car*) maniabilité *f*

handling charge, handling fee *n* frais *mpl* de manutention

hand luggage *n* bagage *m* à main **handmade** *adj* fait(e) à la main **hand-me-downs** *n pl* vêtements *mpl* usagés **hand-operated** *adj* manuel(le)

handout *n* **1.** (*leaflet*) prospectus *m* **2.** *pej* (*goods/money for needy*) aumône *f* **3.** UNIV polycopié *m*

hand-picked *adj* trié(e) sur le volet **handrail** *n* main *f* courante **handshake** *n* poignée *f* de main

handsome *adj* **1.** (*traditionally attractive looking*) beau(belle); **~ face** un beau visage; **the most ~ man** le plus bel homme **2.** (*impressive/majestic looking*) imposant(e) **3.** (*larger* *than expected*) considérable **4.** (*well-meaning/gracious*) bon(ne); **a ~ apology** une bonne excuse

hands-on *adj* (*experience, training*) pratique

handspring *n* saut *m* de mains **handstand** *n* poirier *m* **hand-to-mouth I.** *adj* au jour le jour; **to lead a ~ existence** vivre au jour le jour **II.** *adv* **to live** (**from**) ~ *a. fig* vivre au jour le jour **handwork** *n* travail *m* manuel **handwriting** *n no pl* écriture *f* **handwritten** *adj* écrit(e) à la main

handy *adj* **1.** (*user-friendly, practical*) maniable; **a ~ form** une forme pratique **2.** (*nearby*) à portée de main **3.** (*manually clever/skilful*) habile **4.** (*convenient*) pratique; **to come in ~** être utile

handyman <-men> *n* homme *m* à tout faire

hang [hæŋ] **I.** <hung, hung> *vi* **1.** (*be suspended: from hook*) être accroché; (*from above*) être suspendu **2.** (*droop, fall: clothes, curtain, hair*) tomber; (*arm*) pendre **3.** (*bend over*) se pencher; **to ~ out of the window** se pencher par la fenêtre **4.** (*die by execution*) être pendu **5.** (*float: smoke, smell*) flotter ►**to ~ by a <u>hair</u>** ne tenir qu'à un cheveu **II.** *vt* **1.** <hung, hung> (*attach: from hook*) accrocher; (*from above*) suspendre; (*washing*) étendre; (*wallpaper*) poser; (*picture*) exposer; **to ~ sth on/from sth** accrocher qc à qc **2.** <hung, hung> *passive* (*ornate*) **to be hung with sth** être orné de qc **3.** <hung, hung> (*droop*) **to ~ one's head** baisser la tête **4.** <hung, hung *o* -ed, -ed> (*execute through suspension*) pendre; **to ~ oneself** se pendre **5.** <hung, hung> **to ~ a left/right** (*do a left/right turn*) faire un virage à gauche/droite **III.** *n no pl* (*clothes' hanging*) tombé *m* ►**to <u>get</u> the ~ of sth** *fig, inf* piger qc; **to not <u>give</u> a ~** *inf* s'en foutre

hang about, hang around I. *vi* **1.** (*waste time*) traîner **2.** *inf* (*wait*) poireauter **II.** *vt* **to ~ the bars** traîner dans les bars; **to ~ sb** traîner avec qn

◆**hang back** *vi* **1.** (*remain behind*) rester en arrière **2.** (*hesitate*) hésiter

◆**hang in** *vi Am, inf* tenir bon

◆**hang on I.** *vi* **1.** (*wait briefly*) patienter; **~!** TEL ne quittez pas! **2.** (*hold on to*) *a. fig* se cramponner; **to ~ to sth** ne pas lâcher qc **3.** *inf* (*remain firm*) tenir bon **II.** *vt* **1.** (*fasten onto*) se cramponner à **2.** (*rely on, depend on*) dépendre de **3. to ~ sb's word** (*listen very carefully*) être pendu aux lèvres de qn

◆**hang out I.** *vt* pendre (au dehors); (*the washing*) étendre; (*a flag*) sortir **II.** *vi* **1.** *inf* (*hang loosely*) pendre (dehors) **2.** *inf* (*spend time*) traîner

◆**hang over** *vt* planer sur

◆**hang round** *vi, vt Brit s.* **hang around**

◆**hang together** *vi* se tenir

◆**hang up I.** *vi* raccrocher; **to ~ on sb** raccrocher au nez de qn **II.** *vt a. fig* accrocher

hangar ['hæŋgəʳ, *Am:* -ɚ] *n* hangar *m*

hangdog *adj* déconfit(e)

hanger *n* cintre *m*

hanger-on <hangers-on> *n pej* parasite *m*

hang-glider *n* deltaplane *m* **hang-gliding** *n* deltaplane *m*

hanging I. *n* pendaison *f* **II.** *adj* suspendu(e)

hangman <-men> *n* bourreau *m*

hangnail *n* MED ongle *m* incarné

hangout *n* **1.** *inf* (*favourite bar or cafe*) bar *m* habituel **2.** *inf* (*place sb lives*) crèche *f*

hangover *n* **1.** (*sickness after excessive alcohol*) gueule *f* de bois **2.** *pej* (*things from the past*) débris *mpl*

hang-up *n inf* complexe *m*; **to have a ~ about sth** être complexé par qc

hank [hæŋk] *n* mèche *f*

hanker after *vt*, **hanker for** *vt* se languir de

hankering *n* nostalgie *f*; **to have a ~ for sb/sth** aspirer à revoir qn/qc

hankie, hanky *n inf abbr of* **handkerchief** mouchoir *m*

hanky-panky *n no pl, iron, inf* **1.** (*dubious behavior*) entourloupettes *fpl* **2.** (*sexual*) galipettes *fpl*

Hanukkah ['hɑːnəkə] *n no pl* Hanouka *f*

haphazard [ˌhæp'hæzəd] *adj pej* **1.** (*badly planned, aimless, disorganized*) désordonné(e) **2.** (*chance, random, arbitrary*) au petit bonheur (la chance)

hapless *adj* infortuné(e)

happen ['hæpən] **I.** *vi* arriver; **to ~ to sb** arriver à qn; **whatever ~s** quoi qu'il arrive; **to ~ again** se reproduire **II.** *vt* **it ~s that ...** il se trouve que ...; **to ~ to do sth** faire qc par hasard; **I ~ to do sth** il se trouve que je fais qc

happening *n* **1.** (*events, circumstances, matters*) événement *m* **2.** (*performance*) happening *m*

happily *adv* **1.** (*contentedly, willingly*) heureux(-euse); **~ married** être heureux en ménage **2.** (*fortunately, luckily*) par chance

happiness *n no pl* bonheur *m*

happy ['hæpi] <-ier, -iest *o* more ~, most ~> *adj* heureux(-euse); **in happier times** dans des temps meilleurs; **to be ~ about sb/sth** être content de qn/qc; **a ~ accident** un heureux hasard; **a ~ birthday** un joyeux anniversaire

happy-go-lucky *adj* insouciant(e) **happy medium** *n* meilleur compromis *m*

harass [hə'ræs] *vt* harceler

harassed *adj* harcelé(e)

harassment *n* harcèlement *m*

harbor *Am, Aus,* **harbour** ['hɑːbəʳ, *Am:* 'hɑːrbɚ] **I.** *n* port *m*; **fishing ~** un port de pêche **II.** *vt* **1.** (*cling to negative ideas: resentments, suspicions*) nourrir **2.** (*keep in hiding*) donner asile à

hard [hɑːd, *Am:* hɑːrd] **I.** *adj* **1.** (*firm, rigid*) *a. fig* dur(e); **~ left/right** extrême gauche/droite *f* **2.** (*difficult, complex*) difficile; **to be ~ of hearing** être dur d'oreille; **to give sb a ~ time** donner du fil à retordre à qn; **to learn**

the ~ way apprendre à ses dépens; **to do sth the ~ way** ne pas prendre le plus court chemin **3.** (*harsh, intense: fight, winter, work*) rude; **to be a ~ worker** travailler dur; **to have a ~ time** en baver; **to give sb a ~ time** mener la vie dure à qn; **to be ~ on sb/sth** malmener qn/qc **4.** (*strong*) *a. fig* (*drinking, person*) fort(e); (*drugs*) dur(e) **5.** (*reliable: facts, evidence*) tangible **6.** (*~ core*) hard *inv inf* **7.** (*containing much lime: water*) calcaire ▸**no ~ feelings!** sans rancune!; **~ luck!** pas de chance!; **to drive a ~ bargain** en demander beaucoup; **to be as ~ as nails** être un dur; **to play ~ to get** faire languir **II.** *adv* **1.** (*solid, rigid*) dur; **~ boiled** dur(e) **2.** (*energetically, vigorously: play, study, try, work*) sérieusement; (*press, pull*) fort **3.** (*painfully, severely*) durement **4.** (*closely*) **to follow ~ (up)on sb/sth** suivre qn/qc de près

hardback **I.** *n* édition *f* reliée **II.** *adj* (*edition*) relié(e) **hard-bitten** *adj* impudent(e) **hardboard** *n no pl* contreplaqué *m* **hard-boiled** *adj* **1.** (*cooked*) **~ egg** œuf *m* dur **2.** *fig, inf* dur(e) à cuire **hard by** *prep form* tout à côté de **hard cash** *n* argent *m* liquide **hard copy** *n* INFOR copie *f* sur papier **hard core** **I.** *n* **1.** (*dedicated inner circle within group*) noyau *m* dur **2.** *Brit* (*road foundation mixture*) gravier *m* **3.** ART, MUS hardcore *m* **II.** *adj* ART, MUS **hardcore** hardcore *inv* **hard court** *n* SPORT, TENNIS terrain *m* à revêtement dur **hard currency** *n* devise *f* forte **hard disk** *n* INFOR disque *m* dur **hard drink** *n* boisson *f* forte **hard drinker** *n* buveur *m* invétéré **hard drug** *n* drogue *f* dure **hard-earned** *adj* bien mérité(e); **~ money** argent *m* gagné à la sueur de son front

harden **I.** *vt* **1.** (*make more solid/firmer*) durcir **2.** (*make tougher*) endurcir **II.** *vi* **1.** (*become more solid/firmer*) durcir **2.** (*become less flexible/conciliatory*) s'endurcir

hard feelings *n* mauvais sentiment *m* **hard-fought** *adj* **1.** (*achieved after much effort*) bien mérité(e) **2.** (*relentless*) acharné(e) **hard hat** *n* **1.** (*hat*) casque *m* **2.** (*worker*) ouvrier *m* du bâtiment **hard-headed** *adj* réaliste **hard-hearted** *adj pej* insensible **hard-hit** *adj* (*in very bad position*) mal placé(e) **hard-hitting** *adj* sans indulgence **hard labour** *n no pl* travaux *mpl* forcés **hard line** *n* POL ligne *f* dure **hardliner** *n* POL pur *m* et dur **hard liquor** *s.* **hard drink**

hardly *adv* **1.** (*barely, only a little*) presque pas; **~ anything** presque rien; **~ ever** presque jamais **2.** (*certainly not*) sûrement pas

hardness *n no pl a.* CHEM dureté *f*

hard-nosed *adj inf* dur(e) **hard on** *prep* juste derrière **hard-pressed** *adj* en difficulté **hard sell** *n* commercialisation *f* agressive **hardship** *n* détresse *f* **hard shoulder** *n Brit* bande *f* d'arrêt d'urgence **hardtop** *n* AUTO capote *f* rigide **hardware** *n no pl* **1.** (*things for house/garden*) articles *mpl* de quincaillerie **2.** INFOR hardware *m*, matériel *m* **hard-wearing** *adj* résistant(e) **hardwood** *n* bois *m* dur **hard-working** *adj* travailleur(-euse)

hardy *adj a.* BOT résistant(e)

hare [heəʳ, *Am:* her] <-(s)> *n* lièvre *m*

harebrained *adj* fou(folle)

harelip *n* bec-de-lièvre *m*

harem ['hɑːriːm, *Am:* 'herəm] *n a. fig, iron* harem *m*

harm [hɑːm, *Am:* hɑːrm] **I.** *n* dommage *m*; **there's no ~ in asking** il n'y a pas de mal à demander; **sb meant no ~** qn ne pensait pas à mal; **to do sb/sth ~** nuire à qn/qc; **to do more ~ than good** faire plus de mal que de bien **II.** *vt* nuire à; **it wouldn't ~ sb to** *+infin iron* ça ne ferait pas de mal à qn de *+infin*

harmful *adj* nuisible

harmless *adj* **1.** (*causing no harm*) inoffensif(-ive) **2.** (*banal*) anodin(e)

harmonic [hɑː'mɒnɪk, *Am:* hɑːr'mɑː-] *adj* harmonique

harmonica *n* harmonica *m*

harmonious *adj* harmonieux(-euse)

harmonium [hɑː'məʊniəm, *Am:* hɑːr'moʊ-] *n* harmonium *m*

harmonization *n no pl* harmonisation *f*

harmonize ['hɑːmənaɪz, *Am:* 'hɑːr-] **I.** *vt a.* MUS harmoniser **II.** *vi* s'harmoniser

harmony ['hɑːməni, *Am:* 'hɑːr-] *n* harmonie *f*; **in ~** en harmonie

harness ['hɑːnɪs, *Am:* 'hɑːr-] **I.** *n* harnais *m* ▸**work in ~ with sb** travailler en tandem avec qn **II.** *vt* **1.** (*secure*) **to ~ sb/sth to sth** harnacher qn/qc à qc **2.** *fig* (*make productive, exploit*) **to ~ sth** mettre qc à profit

harp [hɑːp, *Am:* hɑːrp] *n* harpe *f*

harpoon [ˌhɑː'puːn, *Am:* ˌhɑːr-] **I.** *n* harpon *m* **II.** *vt* harponner

harpsichord ['hɑːpsɪkɔːd, *Am:* 'hɑːrpsɪkɔːrd] *n* clavecin *m*

harrow ['hærəʊ, *Am:* 'heroʊ] **I.** *n* herse *f* **II.** *vt* **1.** (*plough earth using harrow*) herser **2.** (*disturb, frighten, scare*) tourmenter

harrowing *adj* terrible

harsh [hɑːʃ, *Am:* hɑːrʃ] *adj* rude; (*colours*) cru(e); (*voice*) perçant(e)

hart [hɑːt, *Am:* hɑːrt] *n* cerf *m*

harum-scarum [ˌheərəm'skeərəm, *Am:* ˌherəm'skerəm] **I.** *adv* en quatrième vitesse **II.** *adj* distrait(e)

harvest ['hɑːvɪst, *Am:* 'hɑːr-] **I.** *n a. fig* récolte *f* **II.** *vt* récolter **III.** *vi* faire la récolte

harvester *n* **1.** (*machine*) moissonneuse *f*; **combined ~** moissonneuse-batteuse *f* **2.** (*sb who harvests*) moissonneur, -euse *m, f*

harvest festival *n* fête *f* des moissons **harvest moon** *n* pleine lune *f*

has [hæz] *3rd pers. sing of* **have**

has-been *n pej, inf* has been *m*

hash[1] [hæʃ] *n* **1.** (*chopped meat, vegetable dish*) hachis *m* **2.** *no pl, inf* (*messed up try,* *shambles*) pagaille *f;* **to make a ~ of sth** foutre qc en l'air

hash[2] [hæʃ] *n inf abbr of* **hashish** hasch *m*

hash browns *npl* pommes *fpl* de terre sautées

hashish ['hæʃɪʃ] *n no pl* haschisch *m*

hasn't = has not *s.* **have**

hassle ['hæsl] **I.** *n inf* **1.** (*bother*) emmerdement *m;* **to give sb ~** emmerder qn; **to be such a ~** être tellement emmerdant **2.** (*argument, dispute*) engueulade *f* **II.** *vt inf* emmerder

hassock ['hæsək] *n* **1.** (*tuft of grass*) touffe *f* d'herbe **2.** (*cushion*) genouillère *f*

haste [heɪst] *n no pl* **1.** (*sth done hurriedly*) hâte *f;* **to make ~** se hâter **2.** *pej* (*doing sth too quickly*) précipitation *f*

hasten **I.** *vt form* hâter **II.** *vi* se hâter

hasty *adj* **1.** (*fast, quick, hurried*) rapide **2.** (*rashly, badly thought out: decisions, conclusions*) précipité(e)

hat [hæt] *n* chapeau *m*

hatch[1] [hætʃ] **I.** *vi* couver **II.** *vt* **1.** (*cause egg split allowing birth*) couver **2.** (*devise in secret: plan*) mijoter **III.** *n* **1.** (*eggs*) couvée *f* **2.** (*to pass food in kitchen*) passe-plat *m*

hatch[2] [hætʃ] *vt* hachurer

hatchback *n* porte *f* arrière

hatchet ['hætʃɪt] *n* hachette *f*

hatchet-faced *adj inf* **to be ~** avoir le visage taillé à la serpe **hatchet man** *n* **1.** *inf* (*worker*) sbire *m* **2.** *inf* (*thug*) homme *m* de main **3.** *inf* PUBL gratte-papier *m*

hatching *n no pl* **1.** BIO (*being born*) éclosion *f* **2.** (*parallel marks*) hachures *fpl*

hate [heɪt] **I.** *n* haine *f;* **to feel ~ for sb** éprouver de la haine pour qn; **to give sb a look of ~** regarder qn avec des yeux pleins de haine **II.** *vt* haïr; **to ~ doing sth/to do sth** détester faire qc

hateful *adj* haineux(-euse)

hatred *n no pl* haine *f;* **to nurse an irrational ~ of sb/sth** nourrir une haine inexplicable pour qn/qc

hatstand *n* porte-manteau *m*

hatter ['hætəʳ, *Am:* -t̬ɚ] *n* **as mad as a ~** complètement fou(folle)

hat-trick *n* triple victoire *f*

haughty ['hɔːti, *Am:* 'hɑːt̬i] <-ier, iest> *adj pej* hautain(e)

haul [hɔːl] **I.** *vt* **1.** (*pull with effort*) tirer, haler *Québec* **2.** (*tow*) remorquer **3.** (*transport goods*) transporter par camion **II.** *n* **1.** (*distance*) trajet *m* **2.** (*quantity caught*) prise *f;* (*of stolen goods*) butin *m;* (*of drugs*) saisie *f* **3.** *sing* (*pull*) **to give a ~ on sth** tirer sur qc

◆**haul away** *vt* tirer fort

◆**haul down** *vt* descendre

◆**haul off** *vi Am, inf* se tirer

◆**haul up** *vt* **1.** (*bring up*) monter; (*flag*) hisser **2.** (*bring*) **to haul sb up in court** traîner qn devant la cour de justice

haulage ['hɔːlɪdʒ] *n no pl* **1.** (*transportation*) transport *m* **2.** (*transportation costs*) coûts *mpl* de transport

haulage business, haulage company *n* entreprise *f* de transport **haulage contractor** *n* entrepreneur *m* de transport **haulage firm** *n s.* **haulage company**

hauler *n Am,* **haulier** *n Brit, Aus* **1.** (*transporter*) transporteur *m* **2.** (*driver*) chauffeur *m*

haunch [hɔːntʃ] <-es> *n* **1.** ANAT (*upper leg and buttock*) hanche *f* **2.** (*cut of meat*) morceau *m* d'aloyau

haunt [hɔːnt] **I.** *vt* hanter **II.** *n* repaire *m*

haunted *adj* **1.** (*frequented by ghosts*) hanté(e) **2.** (*troubled, suffering: look, eyes*) tourmenté(e)

haunting **I.** *n no pl* harcèlement *m* **II.** *adj* **1.** (*persistently disturbing: fear/memory*) harcelant(e) **2.** (*memorably stirring: beauty, melody*) marquant(e)

Havana [hə'vænə] *n* La Havane

have [hæv] **I.** <has, had, had> *aux, vt* avoir; **to ~ to** +*infin* avoir à +*infin;* **to ~ got sth** *Brit, Aus* avoir qc; **has he/~ you ...?** est-ce qu'il a/tu as ...?; **to ~ sth to do** avoir qc à faire; **to ~ the honesty/patience to** +*infin* avoir l'honnêteté/la patience de +*infin;* **to ~ news of sb** avoir des nouvelles de qn; **to ~ visitors** avoir de la visite; **to ~ sth ready** avoir qc de prêt; **to ~ a swim** nager; **to ~ a walk** se promener; **to ~ a talk with sb** avoir une discussion avec qn; **to ~ a bath/shower** prendre un bain/une douche; **to ~ a try** essayer; **to be had** (*to get*) à avoir; **the apples to be had** les pommes qu'il y a ►**to ~ the time** avoir le temps; **to ~ it in for sb** *inf* avoir qn dans le collimateur; **to ~ had it** *inf* (*be broken*) être foutu; **to ~ had it with sb/sth** *inf* en avoir marre de qn/qc; **to ~ sb** *inf* avoir qn; **to be had** *inf* se faire avoir **II.** *n pl, inf* **the ~s** les richards *mpl*

◆**have around** *vt* (*invite*) recevoir

◆**have back** *vt* recevoir en retour

◆**have in** *vt* **to have sb in** avoir qn à la maison

◆**have off** *vt* **1.** *Brit, Aus, inf* (*have sexual intercourse*) **to have it off with sb** coucher avec qn **2.** (*remove*) **to have sth off** (*clothes*) enlever qc

◆**have on** *vt* **1.** (*wear: clothes*) porter **2.** (*carry*) porter; **to have sth on oneself** porter qc sur soi **3.** (*possess information*) **to have sth on sb/sth** avoir qc sur qn/qc **4.** *Brit, inf* (*fool sb to believe*) **to have sb on** rouler qn **5.** (*plan*) avoir en tête

◆**have out** *vt* **1.** *inf* (*remove*) retirer; (*tooth*) extraire; **to have one's appendix out** se faire enlever l'appendice; **to have a tooth out** se faire arracher une dent **2.** *inf* (*argue, discuss strongly*) **to have it out with sb** s'expliquer avec qn **3.** (*take out*) **to have sth out** sortir qc

◆**have over** *vi* recevoir

◆**have up** *vt Brit, inf* **to be had up for sth** passer devant le tribunal pour qc

haven ['heɪvən] *n* refuge *m*

have-not *n* sans-le-sou *mf*
haven't ['hævənt] = **have + not** *s.* **have**
haves *npl inf* richards *mpl*
havoc ['hævək] *n no pl* ravages *mpl;* **to play ~ with sth** déranger qc; **to wreak ~** faire des ravages
haw [hɔː] **I.** *interj* hum! **II.** *vi* **to hum and ~** *Brit, Aus,* **to hem and ~** *Am* tourner autour du pot
Hawaii [hə'waɪiː] *n* Hawaï *m*
Hawaiian I. *adj* hawaïen(ne) **II.** *n* **1.** (*person*) Hawaïen(ne) *m(f)* **2.** LING hawaïen *m; s.a.* **English**
hawk [hɔːk] **I.** *n a. fig a.* POL faucon *m* **II.** *vt* colporter **III.** *vi* faire du colportage
hawker *n* colporteur, -euse *m, f*
hawk-eyed *adj* au regard perçant
hawk moth *n* ZOOL sphinx *m*
hawser ['hɔːzəʳ, *Am:* 'hɑːzɚ] *n* NAUT cordage *m*
hawthorn ['hɔːθɔːn, *Am:* 'hɑːθɔːrn] *n no pl* aubépine *f,* cenellier *m Québec*
hay [heɪ] *n no pl* foin *m* ►**to make ~ while the sun shines** battre le fer pendant qu'il est chaud; **to hit the ~** *inf* se mettre au pieu
haycock *n* botte *f* de foin **hay fever** *n* rhume *m* des foins **hay rack** *n* râtelier *m* **hayrick** *n s.* **haystack haystack** *n* tas *m* de foin ►**a needle in a ~** une aiguille dans une motte de foin
haywire *adj inf* **to go/be ~** être perturbé/s'emballer
hazard ['hæzəd, *Am:* -ɚd] **I.** *n* **1.** (*danger*) danger *m;* **to be one of the known ~s of a job** c'est le risque du métier **2.** *no pl* (*risk*) risque *m;* **to be a ~ to sb/sth** être un risque pour qn/qc; **fire ~** risque *m* d'incendie **II.** *vt* risquer; **to ~ a try** se risquer
hazardous *adj* **1.** (*uncertain*) hasardeux(-euse) **2.** (*risky*) risqué(e) **3.** (*dangerous*) dangereux(-euse)
hazard (warning) lights *npl* AUTO warnings *mpl*
haze [heɪz] **I.** *n a. fig* brume *f* **II.** *vt* **to ~ sb/sth** éreinter qn/qc à la tâche
hazel ['heɪzəl] **I.** *n* noisetier *m* **II.** *adj* (*eyes*) noisette *inv*
hazelnut I. *n* noisette *f* **II.** *adj* noisette *inv*
hazy <-ier, -iest> *adj a. fig* brumeux(-euse)
he [hiː] *pers pron* **1.** (*male person or animal*) il; **~'s** [*o* **~ is**] **my father** c'est mon père; **~'s gone away but ~'ll be back soon** il est parti mais il va revenir; **here ~ comes** le voilà; **her baby is a ~** son bébé est un garçon **2.** (*unspecified sex*) **if somebody comes, ~ will buy it** si quelqu'un vient, il l'achètera; **~ who ...** *form* celui qui ... **3.** REL (*God*) **He answered my prayer** Il a exaucé ma prière
head [hed] **I.** *n* **1.** *a. fig* tête *f;* **a hundred ~ of cattle** cent têtes de bétail; **to win by a ~** gagner d'une tête d'avance; **to need a clear ~ to** *+infin* avoir besoin d'être à tête reposée pour *+infin;* **to put ideas into sb's ~** mettre des idées dans la tête de qn; **to use one's ~** se creuser la tête; **at the ~ of the table** en tête de table **2.** *no pl* (*letter top*) en-tête *m* **3.** (*coin face*) côté *m* pile **4.** (*person in charge*) chef *m; Brit* SCHOOL directeur, -trice *m, f* **5.** (*water source*) source *f* **6.** (*beer foam*) mousse *f* ►**to have one's ~ buried in a book** avoir la tête plongée dans un livre; **to have one's ~ in the clouds** avoir la tête dans les nuages; **to have a good ~ for figures** avoir la bosse des maths; **to be ~ over heels in love** être fou amoureux; **to have a ~ for heights** *Brit* ne pas avoir le vertige; **to have a good ~ on one's shoulders** avoir la tête bien posée sur ses épaules; **to be ~ and shoulders above sb** avoir plus d'une tête d'avance sur qn; **~s or tails?** pile ou face?; **to keep one's ~ above water** garder la tête hors de l'eau; **to keep a cool ~** garder la tête froide; **to go straight to sb's ~** (*alcohol, wine*) monter à la tête de qn; **to go to sb's ~** (*fame, success*) monter à la tête de qn; **to have taken sth into one's ~** s'être mis qc dans la tête; **to be off one's ~** *inf* délirer; **~ on** de front **II.** *vt* **1.** (*lead*) être à la tête de **2.** SPORT **to ~ the ball** faire une tête **III.** *vi* aller; **to ~ home** aller à la maison **IV.** *adj* principal(e)
◆**head back** *vi* retourner; **to ~ home/to the camp** retourner à la maison/au camp
◆**head for** *vt* **1.** (*go towards*) se diriger vers; **to ~ the exit** aller vers la sortie **2.** *fig* **to ~ disaster** aller au désastre
◆**head off I.** *vt* **1.** (*get in front of sb*) aller au devant de qn; (*turn sb aside*) se détourner de qn **2.** *fig* (*avoid*) éviter **II.** *vi* **to ~ towards/to sth** garder le cap sur qc
◆**head up** *vt* diriger
headache ['hedeɪk] *n a. fig* maux *mpl* de tête
headband *n* bandeau *m* **headbanger** *n inf* MUS hard rocker *m* **head-butt I.** *n* SPORT coup *m* de tête **II.** *vt* donner un coup de tête à **head cold** *n* rhume *m* de cerveau **headdress** <-es> *n* coiffure *f*
header *n* **1.** SPORT tête *f* **2.** (*headfirst jump*) plongeon *m* **3.** INFOR haut *m* de page
headfirst I. *adv a. fig* la tête la première **II.** *adj* **~ dive/jump** tête *f* **headhunt** *vt inf* débaucher **headhunter** *n a. inf a.* ECON chasseur *m* de tête
heading *n* en-tête *m*
headlamp *n* phare *m* **headland** *n* langue *f* de terre
headless *adj* affolé(e)
headlight *s.* **headlamp headline I.** *n* gros titre *m;* **the ~s** la une des journaux; **to make the ~s** faire la une des journaux **II.** *vt* **to ~ sth** mettre qc à la une **headline inflation** *n Brit: système de calcul des taux d'inflation* **headlong** *Am, Aus* **I.** *adv* la tête la première; *fig* précipitamment **II.** *adj* direct(e) **headmaster** *n* directeur *m* **headmistress** <-es> *n* directrice *f* **head office** *n* centrale

f **head of state** <heads of state> *n* chef *m* d'État **head-on** I. *adj* de front; (*collision*) frontal(e) II. *adv* de plein front **headphones** *npl* écouteurs *mpl* **headquarters** *npl, + sing, pl vb* MIL quartier *m* général; (*of firms, companies*) maison *f* mère; (*of the police*) direction *f* **headrest** *n* appuie-tête *m* **head restraint** *n* appuie-tête *m* **headroom** *n no pl* hauteur *f* sous plafond **headscarf** <-scarves> *n* foulard *m* **headset** *n* écouteurs *mpl* **headship** *n* 1. ADMIN (*position of authority*) chef *m* de service 2. *Brit* SCHOOL (*position of authority*) chef *m* d'établissement **headshrinker** *n* 1. (*tribesman*) chef *m* de tribu 2. *inf* (*psychiatrist*) psy *m* **head start** *n* avance *f*; **to give sb a ~** donner de l'avance à qn **headstone** *n* pierre *f* tombale **headstrong** *adj* qui a la tête dure **head teacher** *n* directeur, -trice *m, f* **head waiter** *n* maître *m* d'hôtel **headwater** *n* eau *f* de source **headway** *n no pl* **to make ~** faire des progrès **headwind** *n* vent *m* de face **headword** *n* entrée *f*

heady ['hedi] <-ier, -iest> *adj* enivrant(e)

heal [hiːl] I. *vt* 1. (*give treatment*) guérir 2. *fig* **to ~ differences** régler des différends II. *vi* guérir; (*wound, injury*) passer

health [helθ] *n no pl, a. fig a.* ECON santé *f*; **for ~ reasons** pour des raisons de santé; **to be in good/bad ~** être en bonne/mauvaise santé; **to drink to sb's ~** boire à la santé de qn; **to restore sb to ~** redonner la santé à qn

healthcare *n no pl* soins *mpl* **health care** *n no pl* soins *mpl* médicaux **health centre** *n* centre *m* médical **health certificate** *n* certificat *m* médical **health farm** *n* institut *m* de remise en forme **health food** *n* alimentation *f* diététique **health food shop, health food store** *n* magasin *m* d'alimentation diététique **health hazard** *n* risque *m* pour la santé **health insurance** *n* assurance-maladie *f* **health resort** *n Am* (*health farm*) station *f* thermale **Health Service** *n Brit* santé *f* (publique) **health visitor** *n Brit* MED visiteur *m* médical

healthy <-ier, -iest> *adj a.* FIN sain(e)

heap [hiːp] I. *n* tas *m*; **to pile sth into ~s** entasser qc ►**a** (**whole**) **~ of work** beaucoup de travail II. *vt* entasser

hear [hɪəʳ, *Am:* hɪr] <heard, heard> *vt, vi* 1. (*perceive with ears*) entendre 2. (*be told about*) entendre dire

heard [hɜːd, *Am:* hɜːrd] *pt, pp of* **hear**

hearing *n* 1. *no pl* (*ability to hear*) ouïe *f*; **to be hard of ~** être dur d'oreille 2. LAW (*official examination*) audition *f*

hearing aid *n* appareil *m* auditif

hearsay ['hɪəseɪ, *Am:* 'hɪr-] *n no pl* on-dit *m*

hearse [hɜːs, *Am:* hɜːrs] *n* corbillard *m*

heart [hɑːt, *Am:* hɑːrt] *n a. fig* cœur *m*; **to have a weak** [*o* **bad**] **~** être cardiaque; **to have a hard ~** avoir un cœur de pierre; **to have a good ~** avoir bon cœur; **to break sb's ~** briser le cœur de qn; **to be at the ~ of sth** être au cœur de qc; **to get to the ~ of the matter** aller au cœur des choses ►**one's ~ is in one's boots** *Brit, inf* se dégonfler; **from the bottom of the/one's ~** de tout cœur; **to one's ~'s content** à cœur joie; **to have one's ~ in the right place** avoir le cœur à droite; **to put one's ~ and soul into sth** mettre tout son cœur et toute son âme dans qc; **to be all ~** être entier; **with all one's ~** de tout cœur; **to die of a broken ~** mourir d'amour; **to know by ~** savoir par cœur; **after one's own ~** à cœur joie; **to not have the ~ to** *+infin* ne pas avoir le cœur à *+infin*; **to set one's ~ on sth** se consacrer à qc de tout cœur

heartache ['hɑːteɪk, *Am:* 'hɑːrt-] *n no pl* peine *f* de cœur

heart attack *n* crise *f* cardiaque **heartbeat** *n* battement *m* du cœur **heartbreak** *n no pl* 1. (*distress*) déchirement *m* 2. (*romantic distress*) chagrin *m* d'amour **heartbreaking** *adj* déchirant(e) **heartbroken** *adj* **to be ~** avoir le cœur brisé **heartburn** *n* brûlures *fpl* d'estomac **heart disease** *n* maladie *f* cardiovasculaire

heartening ['hɑːtənɪŋ, *Am:* 'hɑːrt-] *adj* réconfortant(e)

heart failure *n* arrêt *m* cardiaque

heartfelt ['hɑːtfelt, *Am:* 'hɑːrt-] *adj* sincère

hearth [hɑːθ, *Am:* hɑːrθ] *n* âtre *m*

hearthrug *n* tapis *m* de cheminée

heartily *adv* (*to applaud*) chaleureusement; (*to laugh*) de bon cœur; (*to dislike*) profondément; (*to eat*) de bon appétit

heartland *n* centre *m*

heartless *adj* sans cœur

heart murmur *n* souffle *m* au cœur **heart-rending** *adj* déchirant(e) **heart-searching** I. *n* réflexion *f* II. *adj* réfléchi(e) **heartstrings** *npl* **to pull at sb's ~** toucher la corde sensible de qn **heart-throb** *n inf* idole *f* **heart-to-heart** I. *n* tête-à-tête *m* II. *adj* **to have a ~ conversation** se parler franchement **heart transplant** *n* greffe *f* du cœur **heartwarming** *adj* encourageant(e)

hearty ['hɑːti, *Am:* 'hɑːrṭi] <-ier, -iest> *adj* 1. (*enthusiastic: congratulations, welcome*) chaleureux(-euse) 2. (*large, strong: appetite, breakfast*) gros(se); **to have a ~ dislike for sth** détester profondément qc; **to be hale and ~** avoir bon pied bon œil

heat [hiːt] I. *n no pl* 1. (*warmth, high temperature*) chaleur *f*; (*of the day*) moment *m* le plus chaud; **to turn down the ~** baisser le chauffage; **to cook sth on a high/low ~** faire cuire qc à feu vif/doux 2. (*emotional state*) feu *m*; **with ~** avec vivacité; **in the ~ of the moment/argument** dans le feu de l'action/la discussion 3. (*sports race*) éliminatoire *f* 4. *no pl* (*ready to breed*) chaleur *f*; **to be in ~** être en chaleur ►**the ~ is on** la machine est lancée; **to put the ~ on sb** faire pression sur qn; **to take the ~ off sb** servir de bouclier à qn II. *vt,*

vi chauffer
◆**heat up** *vt* chauffer
heated *adj* **1.** (*made warm: pool*) chauffé(e); (*blanket*) chauffant(e) **2.** (*emotional: debate*) passionné(e)
heatedly *adv* vigoureusement
heater *n* radiateur *m;* **water ~** chauffe-eau *m*
heat exchanger *n* échangeur *m* de chaleur
heath [hi:θ] *n* lande *f*
heathen ['hi:ðn] **I.** *n pej* (*not religious*) païen(ne) *m(f)* **II.** *adj* païen(ne)
heathenish *adj* païen(ne)
heather ['heðəʳ, *Am:* -ɚ] *n* bruyère *f*
heating *n* chauffage *m*
heating engineer *n* chauffagiste *m* **heating system** *n* chauffage *m* **heat pump** *n* pompe *f* à chaleur **heat rash** *n* boutons *mpl* de chaleur **heat-resistant, heat-resisting** *adj* thermorésistant(e) **heat-seeking** *adj* MIL (*missile*) à tête chercheuse aux infrarouges **heat shield** *n* TECH bouclier *m* thermique **heat stroke** *n* coup *m* de chaleur **heat treatment** *n* **1.** (*treatment to eliminate diseases: of milk*) stérilisation *f* par ultra-haute température **2.** (*relaxing method*) thermothérapie *f* **heatwave** *n* vague *f* de chaleur
heave [hi:v] **I.** *vi* **1.** (*pull*) tirer **2.** (*push*) pousser **3.** (*move up and down*) se soulever **4.** NAUT virer de bord **5.** (*vomit*) vomir **II.** *vt* **1.** (*lift, haul: object, anchor*) jeter **2.** *fig* **to ~ a sigh of relief** pousser un soupir de soulagement **III.** *n* gros effort *m*
◆**heave to** *vi* <hove to, hoved to> NAUT se mettre en panne
heaven ['hevən] *n* ciel *m;* **to go to ~** aller au ciel; **it's ~** *inf* c'est le paradis; **to be ~ on earth** être merveilleux; **to be in ~** être aux anges ►**to move ~ and earth to** *+infin* remuer ciel et terre pour *+infin;* **what/where/when/who/why in ~'s name** que/où/quand/qui/pourquoi diable; **the ~ opens** il se met à pleuvoir; **for ~s sake!** bon sang!; **good ~s!** bonté divine!; **it stinks to high ~** ça schlingue; **~s above!** juste ciel!; **~ only knows** Dieu seul le sait; **~ forbid** Dieu m'en/nous en garde; **thank ~s** Dieu merci
heavenly <-ier, -iest> *adj* **1.** (*of heaven: body*) céleste **2.** (*pleasure-giving*) divin(e)
heaven-sent *n* manne *f*
heavily *adv* **1.** (*in a heavy way: to walk, fall*) lourdement; (*to sleep*) profondément **2.** (*considerably*) fortement; **to drink/smoke ~** boire/fumer beaucoup; **it's raining ~** il pleut à verse
heavy ['hevi] **I.** *adj* <-ier, -iest> **1.** (*weighing a lot: object, food*) lourd(e); **to do ~ lifting/carrying** porter des choses lourdes; **how ~ is it?** combien ça pèse? **2.** (*hard, difficult: work, breathing*) pénible; (*schedule, day*) chargé(e); (*book, film*) difficile; (*pitch*) lourd(e) **3.** (*intense, strong: rainfall, accent*) fort(e); (*blow*) violent(e); (*cold*) gros(se); (*sleep*) profond(e) **4.** (*abundant: applause, frost, gale*) fort(e); (*crop, investment*) gros(se); (*period*) abondant(e); **to be ~ on fuel** consommer beaucoup; **to be ~ with sth** être rempli de qc **5.** (*not delicate, coarse: features*) grossier(-ère); (*step, style*) lourd(e) **6.** (*severe: fine, sea*) gros(se); (*casualties, losses*) lourd(e) **7.** (*oppressive: responsibility, sky, perfume*) lourd(e); (*smell*) fort(e) **8.** (*excessive: drinker, smoker*) gros(se); **to be a ~ sleeper** avoir le sommeil lourd **9.** (*large, thick: beard, clouds, shoes*) gros(se) **10.** *vulg* (*threatening*) difficile; **to get ~ with sb** devenir agressif avec qn ►**to do sth with a ~ hand** faire qc en utilisant la manière forte; **things got really ~** les choses se sont gâtées; **to make ~ weather of sth** faire tout un plat de qc; **to be ~ on sb** être dur avec qn **II.** *adv* **to weigh ~** peser lourd; **to be ~-going** être ardu **III.** *n* <-ies> *inf* dur *m*
heavy-duty *adj* (*boots*) solide; (*tyre, machine*) robuste; (*clothes*) de travail; (*gardening*) gros(se); (*vehicle*) utilitaire lourd **heavy-going** *adj* ardu(e) **heavy goods vehicle** *n* poids *m* lourd **heavy-handed** *adj* (*style, reaction*) musclé(e) **heavy-hearted** *adj* **to be ~** avoir le cœur gros **heavy industry** *n* industrie *f* lourde **heavy metal** *n* **1.** (*lead, cadmium*) métal *m* lourd **2.** (*rock 'n roll*) heavy metal *m* **heavy water** *n* eau *f* lourde **heavyweight I.** *adj* **1.** (*in boxing*) poids lourd **2.** (*particularly heavy cloth*) lourd(e) **II.** *n* poids *m* lourd
Hebrew [hi:'bru:] **I.** *n* hébreu *m; s. a.* **English II.** *adj* hébreu
Hebrides ['hebrɪdi:z] *n* **the ~** les Hébrides
heck [hek] *interj inf* flûte!; **what the ~!** oh, et puis flûte!
heckle ['hekl] *vt* apostropher
heckler *n* perturbateur, -trice *m, f*
hectare ['hekteəʳ, *Am:* -ter] *n* hectare *m*
hectic ['hektɪk] *adj* (*week*) mouvementé(e); (*pace*) effréné(e)
hectic fever *n* fièvre *f* hectique
hectoliter *n Am,* **hectolitre** ['hektəʊˌli:təʳ, *Am:* -toʊˌli:t̬ɚ] *n* hectolitre *m*
he'd [hi:d] = **he had/he would** *s.* **have/will**
hedge [hedʒ] **I.** *n* **1.** (*line of bushes*) haie *f* **2.** (*protection*) barrière *f* **II.** *vi* se réserver **III.** *vt passive* **to be ~d with sth** être entouré de qc ►**to ~ one's bets** se couvrir
◆**hedge about** *vt,* **hedge around** *vt* **1.** (*surround with a hedge*) entourer d'une haie **2.** (*hinder, hamper*) **to be ~ around with sth** être rempli de qc
◆**hedge in** *vt* entourer d'une haie; **to be hedged in with sth** être entouré de qc
hedgehog *n* hérisson *m* **hedgerow** *n* haie *f*
hedging *n* FIN opération *f* de couverture
heebie-jeebies ['hi:bɪ'dʒi:bɪz] *npl* **the ~** la trouille
heed [hi:d] **I.** *vt form* (*advice, warning*) tenir compte de **II.** *n* **to pay ~ to sth** tenir compte

de qc

heedful *adj form* **to be ~ of sb's advice** tenir compte du conseil de qn

heedless *adj* inattentif(-ive); **~ of the risk** sans se soucier des risques

hee-haw ['hi:hɔ:, *Am:* -hɑ:] **I.** *n* hi-han *m* **II.** *vi* faire hi-han

heel [hi:l] **I.** *n* **1.** (*back of foot, sock, shoe*) talon *m* **2.** (*back of the hand*) paume *f* **3.** *pej, inf* (*unfair person*) peau *f* de vache ►**to be down at the ~** être en mauvais état; **to be hard on sb's ~s** être sur les talons de qn; **to bring sb to ~** rappeler qn à l'ordre; **to bring a dog to ~** rappeler un chien; **to come to ~** (*dog*) venir aux pieds; **to take to one's ~s** prendre ses jambes à son cou; **to turn on one's ~** tourner les talons; **to be at sb's ~s** être sur les talons de qn; **under the ~ of sb/sth** sous la botte de qn/qc **II.** *interj* au pied! **III.** *vt* SPORT (*ball*) talonner

heel bar *n* cordonnerie-minute *f*

hefty ['hefti] <-ier, -iest> *adj* **1.** (*big and strong: person*) corpulent(e) **2.** (*considerably large: hardback, price rise*) énorme; **~ push** gros effort *m*

heifer ['hefəʳ, *Am:* -ɚ] *n* génisse *f*

height [haɪt] *n* **1.** (*top to bottom: of a person*) taille *f;* (*of a thing*) hauteur *f* **2.** *pl* (*high places*) **to be afraid of ~s** avoir le vertige; **to rise to giddy ~s** *iron, inf* atteindre des sphères vertigineuses; **to scale (new) ~s** atteindre un nouveau record **3.** (*hill*) **~s** les hauteurs *fpl* **4.** *fig* (*strongest point*) sommet *m;* (*of career, glory*) apogée *m;* (*of folly, stupidity, kindness*) comble *m;* **to be at the ~ of one's career** être au sommet de sa carrière; **to be at the ~ of fashion** être du dernier cri; **to attain great ~s** atteindre les hautes sphères

heighten ['haɪtn] *vt* **1.** (*elevate*) rehausser **2.** (*increase*) augmenter

heinous ['heɪnəs] *adj form* abominable

heir [eəʳ, *Am:* er] *n* héritier; **~ to the throne** héritier du trône *m;* **to be (the) ~ to sth** hériter de qc

heir apparent *n* héritier *m* présomptif

heiress ['eərɪs, *Am:* 'erɪs] *n* héritière *f;* **to be (the) ~ to sth** hériter de qc

heirloom ['eəlu:m, *Am:* 'er-] *n* héritage *m;* **the table is a family ~** la table est un meuble de famille

heist [haɪst] *n inf* casse *m;* **jewelry ~** le casse d'une bijouterie

held [held] **I.** *adj* **hand-~** portable; **a firmly-~ opinion** une opinion tenace; **a long-~ view** un point de vue de longue date **II.** *pt, pp of* **hold**

helicopter ['helɪkɒptəʳ, *Am:* -kɑ:ptɚ] *n* hélicoptère *m*

helipad ['helɪpæd] *n* aire *f* d'atterrissage d'hélicoptères

heliport ['helɪpɔ:t, *Am:* -pɔ:rt] *n* héliport *m*

helium ['hi:lɪəm] *n no pl* hélium *m*

hell [hel] **I.** *n no pl* **1.** (*Devil's residence*) *a. fig* enfer *m;* **to go to ~** aller en enfer; **~ on earth** l'enfer; **to go through ~** vivre l'horreur; **to make sb's life ~** *inf* rendre la vie impossible à qn **2.** *inf* (*very much*) **it's as cold as ~** il fait un froid de canard; **it's as hot as ~** il fait une chaleur d'enfer; **as hard as ~** horriblement dur; **I suffered like ~** j'ai souffert comme c'est pas permis; **a ~ of a decision/performance** une sacrée décision/performance ►**not to have a chance in ~** n'avoir aucune chance; **to go ~ for leather** *inf* aller à toute pompe; **come ~ or high water** *inf* quoi qu'il arrive; **to have been to ~ and back** avoir vécu l'enfer; **all ~ breaks loose** la panique éclate; **to annoy the ~ out of sb** *inf* énerver qn au plus haut point; **to be ~** être atroce; **to beat the ~ out of sb** passer qn à tabac; **to do sth for the ~ of it** faire qc pour le plaisir; **to frighten the ~ out of sb** *inf* ficher la trouille de sa vie à qn; **to give sb ~ for sth** engueuler qn comme du poisson pourri à cause de qc; **go to ~!** *vulg* va te faire voir!; **there will be ~ to pay** *inf* ça va barder **II.** *interj* **what the ~ are you doing?** mais qu'est-ce que tu fous? ►**~'s bells** bon sang; **to work like ~** *vulg* travailler comme un dingue; **the ~ you do!** *Am, inf* c'est ça!; **to hope to ~** *inf* espérer vraiment; **what the ~!** *vulg* et puis merde!

he'll [hi:l] = **he will** *s.* **will**

hell-bent [ˌhel'bent, *Am:* '-ˌ-] *adj* acharné(e)

hellfire *n no pl* feux *mpl* de l'enfer

hellish *adj* (*day*) infernal(e); (*experience, weather*) atroce

hellishly *adv* atrocement

hello [hə'ləʊ, *Am:* -'loʊ] **I.** <-s> *n* bonjour *m;* **to give sb a ~** donner le bonjour à qn **II.** *interj* **1.** (*said in greeting*) bonjour!; **to say ~ to sb** dire bonjour à qn **2.** (*beginning of phone call*) allo! **3.** (*attract attention*) il y a quelqu'un? **4.** (*surprise*) tiens!

helm [helm] *n* barre *f*

helmet ['helmɪt] *n* casque *m*

helmsman ['helmzmən] *n* <-men> barreur, -euse *m, f*

help [help] **I.** *vi* aider; **that doesn't ~** cela n'avance à rien **II.** *vt* **1.** (*assist*) aider; **to ~ sb with his homework** aider qn à faire ses devoirs **2.** (*contribute to*) faciliter; **to ~ the pain** soulager la douleur **3.** (*prevent*) **I can't ~ it** je n'y peux rien; **it can't be ~ed** on n'y peut rien; **she can't ~ being famous** ce n'est pas de sa faute si elle est célèbre; **to not be able to ~ (doing) sth** ne pas pouvoir s'empêcher de faire qc; **she couldn't ~ but see the letter** elle n'a pas pu s'empêcher de voir la lettre **4.** (*serve*) servir; **to ~ oneself to sth** se servir de qc **5.** *inf* (*steal*) se servir **III.** *n no pl* **1.** (*assistance*) aide *f;* **to be a ~** (*things*) servir; (*people*) aider **2.** (*sb employed for small jobs*) aide *f;* **to have ~** [*o Am* **hired ~**] **come in** avoir une femme de ménage ►**there'll be no ~ for it but to** +*infin* il n'y a pas d'autre choix que de +*infin;* **every little bit ~s** les petits ruisseaux font les grandes rivières **IV.** *interj* ~! au secours!; **so ~ me God** je jure que c'est la vérité

◆**help out** *vt* aider

helper *n* assistant(e) *m(f)*

helpful *adj* **1.** (*willing to help*) serviable **2.** (*useful*) utile

helping I. *n* **1.** (*portion: food*) portion *f* **2.** *fig* part *f* **II.** *adj* **to give sb a ~ hand** donner un coup de main

helpless *adj* démuni(e); **to be ~ against sb** être impuissant face à qn

helpline ['helplaɪn] *n* assistance *f* téléphonique

helter-skelter [ˌheltə'skeltəʳ, *Am:* -t̬ɚ'skelt̬ɚ] **I.** *adj* désordonné(e) **II.** *adv* dans tous les sens

hem [hem] **I.** *n* ourlet *m;* **to take the ~ up of a skirt** raccourcir une jupe **II.** <-mm-> *vt* faire un ourlet à **III.** *interj* hum!

◆**hem about** *vt*, **hem in** *vt* (*surround*) entourer

he-man ['hi:mæn] <-men> *n inf* homme *m* viril

hematite *Am s.* **haematite**

hemisphere ['hemɪsfɪəʳ, *Am:* -sfɪr] *n* hémisphère *m*

hemline ['hemlaɪn] *n* ourlet *m;* **the ~s are going up** la mode raccourcit

hemlock ['hemlɒk, *Am:* -lɑ:k] *n no pl* (*poison plant*) ciguë *f*

hemoglobin *Am s.* **haemoglobin**

hemophilia *Am s.* **haemophilia**

hemophiliac *Am s.* **haemophiliac**

hemorrhage *Am s.* **haemorrhage**

hemorrhoids *Am s.* **haemorrhoids**

hemp [hemp] *n no pl* chanvre *m*

hen [hen] *n* **1.** (*female bird*) poule *f* **2.** *Scot* (*addressing a woman*) ma chérie

hence [hens] *adv* **1.** (*therefore*) de là; **~ his bruises** c'est pour ça qu'il a des bleus **2.** (*from now*) d'ici; **two years ~** d'ici deux ans

henceforth [ˌhens'fɔ:θ, *Am:* -'fɔ:rθ], **henceforward** *adv* dorénavant

henchman ['hentʃmən] <-men> *n* sbire *m*

hencoop ['henku:p], **henhouse** *n* poulailler *m*

henna ['henə] **I.** *n* (*tropical shrub, dye*) henné *m* **II.** *vt* teindre au henné

hen night, **hen party** *n soirée entre femmes où l'une d'entre elles enterre sa vie de jeune fille*

henpecked ['henpekt] *adj* dominé(e) par sa femme

hepatitis [ˌhepə'taɪtɪs, *Am:* -t̬ɪs] *n no pl* hépatite *f*

heptathlon [hep'tæθlɒn, *Am:* -lɑ:n] *n* heptathlon *m*

her [hɜ:ʳ, *Am:* hɜ:r] **I.** *poss adj* (*of a she*) son, sa *m, f,* ses *pl; s. a.* **my II.** *pers pron* **1.** (*she*) elle; **it's ~** c'est elle; **older than ~** plus vieux qu'elle; **if I were ~** si j'étais elle **2.** *objective pron direct* la, l' + *vowel; indirect* lui; *after prep* elle; **look at ~** regarde/regardez-la; **I saw ~** je l'ai vue; **he told ~ that ...** il lui a dit que ...; **he'll give sth to ~** il va lui donner qc; **it's for/from ~** c'est pour/d' elle

herald ['herəld] **I.** *vt* annoncer **II.** *n* **1.** (*sign*) annonce *f;* **to be a ~ of sth** annoncer qc **2.** (*bringer of news*) héraut *m*

heraldic *adj* héraldique

heraldry ['herəldri] *n no pl* héraldique *f*

herb [hɜ:b] *n* herbe *f* aromatique; **dried/fresh ~s** fines herbes sèches/fraîches

herbaceous [hɜ:'beɪʃəs, *Am:* hɚ'-] *adj* herbacé(e); **~ border** massif d'herbacées

herbalism ['hɜ:bəlɪzəm, *Am:* 'hɜ:r-] *n no pl* herboristerie *f*

herbalist *n* herboriste *mf*

herbicide ['hɜ:bɪsaɪd, *Am:* 'hɜ:r-] *n* herbicide *m*

herbivorous [hɜ:'bɪvərəs, *Am:* hɜ:r-] *adj* herbivore

herculean [ˌhɜ:kjʊ'li:ən, *Am:* ˌhɜ:rkju:'-] *adj* herculéen(ne)

Hercules ['hɛ:kjəli:z, *Am:* 'hɛrkjə-] *n* Hercule *m;* **to be a ~** être fort comme Hercule

herd [hɜ:d, *Am:* hɜ:rd] **I.** *n* **1.** (*large group of animals*) troupeau *m;* (*of deer*) harde *f;* (*of whales*) banc *m* **2.** *pej* (*group of people*) troupeau *m* **II.** *vt* (*animals*) garder **III.** *vi* vivre en troupeau

◆**herd together I.** *vt* (*animals*) rassembler en troupeau **II.** *vi* se regrouper

herd instinct *n pej* instinct *m* grégaire

herdsman *n* gardien(ne) *m(f)* de troupeau

here [hɪəʳ, *Am:* hɪr] **I.** *adv* **1.** (*in, at, to this place*) ici; **over ~** ici; **give it ~** *inf* donne-le/-la moi; **~ and there** ça et là **2.** (*indicating presence*) **Paul is ~** Paul est là; **~ you are** te voilà; **~ is sb/sth** voici qn/qc; **my colleague ~** mon/ma collègue que voici **3.** (*now*) **~, I am referring to sth** là, je veux parler de qc; **we can stop ~** on peut s'arrêter là; **where do we go from ~?** qu'est-ce qu'on fait maintenant?; **~ goes** *inf* allons-y; **~ we go** (*cheer*) nous voilà; (*annoyance*) c'est reparti ►**~ and now** immédiatement; **~ today and gone tomorrow** c'est un vrai courant d'air **II.** *interj* hé!; **~, take it!** viens, prends-le!; (*at roll-call*) présent!

hereabouts *adv* par ici **hereafter I.** *adv form* (*in text*) ci-après; (*in time*) désormais **II.** *n* **the ~** l'au-delà *m* **hereby** *adv form* par la présente; **the undersigned ~ declare ...** le soussigné déclare ...

hereditary [hɪ'redɪtri, *Am:* hə'redɪter-] *adj* héréditaire

heredity [hɪ'redəti, *Am:* hə'redɪ-] *n no pl* hérédité *f*

herein [ˌhɪər'ɪn, *Am:* ˌhɪr-] *adv* **1.** (*in this document*) dans ce document; **the letter enclosed ~** la lettre ci-incluse **2.** (*in this matter*) en cela

hereof *adv* de la présente

heresy ['herəsi] *n* hérésie *f*

heretic ['herətɪk] *n* hérétique *mf*

heretical *adj* hérétique

hereupon [ˌhɪərəˈpɒn, *Am:* ˌhɪrəˈpɑːn] *adv form* sur quoi

herewith *adv form* ci-inclus; **enclosed ~ a copy** ci-joint une copie

heritage [ˈherɪtɪdʒ, *Am:* -t̬ɪdʒ] *n no pl* patrimoine *m*

hermaphrodite [hɜːˈmæfrədaɪt, *Am:* hɚˈmæfroʊ-] **I.** *n* hermaphrodite *m* **II.** *adj* hermaphrodite

hermetic [hɜːˈmetɪk, *Am:* hɚˈmet̬-] *adj* **1.** (*air-tight, protected: seal*) hermétique **2.** *fig* (*existence*) renfermé(e)

hermit [ˈhɜːmɪt, *Am:* ˈhɜːr-] *n* ermite *m*

hermitage [ˈhɜːmɪtɪdʒ, *Am:* ˈhɜːrmɪt̬ɪdʒ] *n* ermitage *m*

hermit crab *n* bernard-l'(h)ermite *m*

hernia [ˈhɜːnɪə, *Am:* ˈhɜːr-] *n* hernie *f*

hero [ˈhɪərəʊ, *Am:* ˈhɪroʊ] <-es> *n* **1.** (*brave man, main character*) héros *m* **2.** (*sb greatly admired*) idole *f* **3.** (*sandwich*) gros sandwich *m*

heroic [hɪˈrəʊɪk, *Am:* hɪˈroʊ-] **I.** *adj* héroïque **II.** *n pl* **1.** (*high-flown language*) discours *m* mélodramatique **2.** *pej* (*risky action*) coup *m* d'éclat

heroin [ˈherəʊɪn, *Am:* -oʊ-] *n no pl* héroïne *f*

heroin addict *n* héroïnomane *mf*

heroine [ˈherəʊɪn, *Am:* -oʊ-] *n* héroïne *f*

heroism [ˈherəʊɪzəm, *Am:* -oʊ-] *n* héroïsme *m;* **act of ~** acte *m* héroïque

heron [ˈherən] <-(s)> *n* héron *m*

herpes [ˈhɜːpiːz] *n* herpès *m*

herring [ˈherɪŋ] <-(s)> *n* hareng *m*

herringbone [ˈherɪŋbəʊn, *Am:* -boʊn] **I.** *n no pl* **1.** (*pattern*) chevron *m* **2.** SPORT montée *f* en ciseau **II.** *adj* en chevrons

herring gull *n* goéland *m* argenté

hers [hɜːz, *Am:* hɜːrz] *poss pron* (*belonging to her*) le sien, la sienne, les sien(ne)s; **it's not my bag, it's ~** ce n'est pas mon sac, c'est le sien; **this house is ~** cette maison est la sienne; **this glass is ~** ce verre est à elle; **a book of ~** (l')un de ses livres

herself [hɜːˈself, *Am:* hɚ-] *pers pron* **1.** *reflexive* se, s' + *vowel;* **she hurt ~** elle s'est blessée **2.** *emphatic* elle-même **3.** *after prep* elle(-même); **she's proud of ~** elle est fière d'elle; **she lives by ~** elle vit seule; **she told ~ that ...** elle s'est dit que ...; *s. a.* **myself**

hertz [hɜːts, *Am:* hɜːrts] *n* hertz *m*

he's [hiːz] **1.** = **he is** *s.* **he** **2.** = **he has** *s.* **have**

hesitant [ˈhezɪtənt] *adj* hésitant(e); **to be ~ about doing sth** hésiter à faire qc

hesitantly *adv* avec hésitation

hesitate [ˈhezɪteɪt] *vi* hésiter

hesitation *n* hésitation *f;* **to have no ~ in doing sth** *form* ne pas hésiter à faire qc

hessian [ˈhesɪən, *Am:* ˈheʃən] *n no pl, Brit* toile *f* de jute

heterogeneous [ˌhetərəˈdʒiːnɪəs, *Am:* ˌhet̬əroʊˈ-] *adj* hétérogène

heterosexual [ˌhetərəˈsekʃʊəl, *Am:* ˌhet̬əroʊˈ-] **I.** *n* hétérosexuel(le) *m(f)* **II.** *adj* hétérosexuel(le)

het up *adj inf* dans tous ses états

hew [hjuː] <hewed, hewed *o* hewn> *vt passive* (*stone*) tailler; (*wood*) couper; **roughly-~n timber** du bois équarri

hewer *n* tailleur *m* de pierres

hewn [ˈhjuːn] *pp of* **hew**

hex [heks] *n Am, Aus, inf* sort *m;* **to put a ~ on sb/sth** jeter un sort sur qn/qc

hexagon [ˈheksəgən, *Am:* -gɑːn] *n* hexagone *m*

hexagonal *adv* hexagonal(e)

hexameter [heksˈæmɪtəʳ, *Am:* -ət̬ɚ] *n* hexamètre *m*

hey [heɪ] *interj inf* **1.** (*said to attract attention*) hep! **2.** (*expressing surprise*) oh!

heyday [ˈheɪdeɪ] *n* âge *m* d'or; **in sb's ~** dans ses beaux jours

hey presto [ˈheɪˈprestəʊ, *Am:* -toʊ] *interj Brit, Aus, inf* et hop!

HGV [ˌeɪtʃdʒiːˈviː] *n Brit abbr of* **heavy goods vehicle** PL *m*

hi [haɪ] *interj* salut!

hiatus [haɪˈeɪtəs, *Am:* haɪˈeɪt̬əs] <-uses> *n* LING hiatus *m*

hibernate [ˈhaɪbəneɪt, *Am:* -bɚ-] *vi* hiberner

hibernation *n no pl* hibernation *f;* **to go into ~** hiberner

hibiscus [hɪˈbɪskəs] <-es> *n* hibiscus *m*

hiccough [ˈhɪkʌp], **hiccup** **I.** *n* hoquet *m;* **to have the ~s** avoir le hoquet **II.** *vi* <-pp- *o* -p-> avoir le hoquet

hid [hɪd] *vt, vi s.* **hide**

hidden [ˈhɪdn] **I.** *pp of* **hide** **II.** *adj* **1.** (*out of sight: feelings, talent*) caché(e); **~ agenda** programme *m* secret **2.** ECON (*assets, reserves*) latent(e)

hide[1] [haɪd] *n* peau *f;* **calf ~** veau *m* ►**neither ~ nor hair of sb/sth** aucune trace de qn/qc; **to save one's ~** sauver sa peau

hide[2] [haɪd] <hid, hidden> **I.** *vi* se cacher **II.** *vt* cacher; **to ~ sth from sb** cacher qc à qn ►**to not ~ one's light under a bushel** *prov* ne pas se mettre en valeur **III.** *n Brit, Aus* cachette *f*

◆**hide away** **I.** *vt* **to hide sth away** cacher qc **II.** *vi* se cacher

◆**hide out** *vi,* **hide up** *vi* se cacher

hide-and-seek [ˌhaɪdnˈsiːk] *n* cache-cache *m;* **to play ~** jouer à cache-cache **hideaway** *n* cachette *f*

hideous [ˈhɪdɪəs] *adj* **1.** (*ugly*) hideux(-euse) **2.** (*unpleasant*) horrible

hideout *n* cachette *f*

hiding[1] [ˈhaɪdɪŋ] *n inf, a. fig* raclée *f;* **to get a real ~** prendre une bonne raclée ►**to be on a ~ to nothing** c'est peine perdue

hiding[2] [ˈhaɪdɪŋ] *n no pl* **to be in ~** se tenir caché; **to go into ~** se cacher

hierarchic(al) [ˌhaɪəˈrɑːkɪk(l), *Am:*

ˌhaɪ'rɑːr-] *adj* hiérarchique

hierarchy ['haɪərɑːki, *Am:* 'haɪrɑːr-] *n* hiérarchie *f*

hieroglyph [ˌhaɪərəʊ'glɪf, *Am:* ˌhaɪroʊ'-] *n* hiéroglyphe *m*

hieroglyphics *n + sing vb* hiéroglyphes *mpl*

hi-fi ['haɪfaɪ] **I.** *n abbr of* **high-fidelity** hi-fi *f inv* **II.** *adj abbr of* **high-fidelity** hi-fi *inv*

higgledy-piggledy [ˌhɪgldɪ'pɪgldi] *adj, adv* pêle-mêle *inv*

high [haɪ] **I.** *adj* **1.** (*elevated*) haut(e); (*forehead*) large; **thirty meters ~ and three meters wide** trente mètres de haut et trois mètres de large; **shoulder/waist-~** à hauteur d'épaule/à la taille; **a ~ jump** un saut en hauteur; **to do a ~ dive** faire un grand plongeon **2.** (*above average*) élevé(e); (*technology, opinion, quality*) haut(e); (*secretary*) de haut niveau; (*hopes*) grand(e); (*calibre*) gros(se); (*explosive*) de forte puissance; (*colour*) vif(vive); **of the ~est calibre** du meilleur calibre; **a ~ definition television** une télévision à haute définition; **to be full of ~ praise for sb/sth** ne pas tarir d'éloges sur qn/qc **3.** MED élevé(e); (*fever*) fort(e); **to suffer from ~ blood-pressure** avoir de la tension **4.** (*important, eminent: priest*) grand(e); (*treason, rank*) haut(e); **to have friends in ~ places** avoir des amis bien placés; **an order from on ~** un ordre venant de haut; **to be ~ and mighty** *pej* prendre des grands airs **5.** (*noble: ideal, character*) noble; **to have ~ principles** avoir des principes **6.** (*intoxicated by drugs*) shooté(e); **to be (as) ~ as a kite** être complètement défoncé **7.** (*euphoric*) **to be ~** être sur un petit nuage **8.** (*of high frequency, shrill*) haut(e) **9.** (*beginning to go bad: food*) avancé(e) ►**a ~ drama** un grand drame; **the ~ summer** le cœur de l'été; **to be in ~ spirits** être de bonne humeur; **with one's head held ~** (avec) la tête haute; **to leave sb ~ and dry** planter qn là *inf;* **to stink to ~ heaven** (*stink*) sentir la mort; (*be very suspicious*) sentir le soufre; **come hell or ~ water** qu'il vente ou qu'il pleuve; **~ days and holidays** grandes occasions *fpl;* **sb's stock is ~** la popularité de qn est en hausse; **to be ~ time to** *+infin* être grand temps de *+infin;* **to have a ~ old time** *inf* passer du bon temps; **to be for the ~ jump** *Brit* aller se faire engueuler **II.** *adv a. fig* haut; **the sea/tide runs ~** la mer/la marée monte vite ►**to hold one's head ~** tenir la tête haute; **to live ~ on the hog** vivre comme un pacha; **to search for sth ~ and low** chercher qc dans chaque recoin **III.** *n* **1.** (*high(est) point/level/amount*) sommet *m;* **an all-time ~** un niveau jamais atteint; **~s and lows** des hausses *fpl* et des baisses; *fig* des hauts *mpl* et des bas; **to reach a ~** atteindre un plafond **2.** (*euphoria caused by drugs*) **to be on a ~** planer **3.** (*heaven*) **from on/on ~** du/au ciel

highbrow *pej* **I.** *adj* intello *inf* **II.** *n* intello *mf inf*

highchair *n* chaise *f* haute **high-class** *adj* de grande classe **high court** *n Brit* LAW tribunal *m* civil; **the High Court** la Haute cour; *Am* Cour *f* suprême

higher education *n* études *fpl* supérieures

> En Écosse, **le Higher Grade** est un examen que les élèves passent à la fin de leur cinquième année scolaire (un an après le "GCSE"). Il est possible d'être examiné dans une seule matière, mais la plupart des élèves essaient de passer environ cinq "Highers".

higher mathematics *n* mathématiques *fpl* supérieures **higher-up** *n inf* supérieur(e) *m(f)*

high-fibre *adj* riche en fibres **high fidelity** *n* haute fidélité *f* **highflier** *n* ambitieux, -euse *m, f* **high-flown** *adj* pompeux(-euse) **high-handed** *adj* tyrannique **high-handedness** *n no pl* caractère *m* tyrannique **high heels** *n* talons *mpl* aiguilles **highjack** *vt s.* **hijack** **high-level** *adj* de haut niveau **highlight** **I.** *n* **1.** (*most interesting part*) meilleur moment *m* **2.** *pl* (*bright tint in hair*) mèches *fpl* **II.** *vt* **1.** (*draw attention*) souligner **2.** (*mark with pen*) surligner **highlighter** *n* surligneur *m*

highly *adv* hautement; **~-educated** très instruit(e); **~-skilled** très doué(e); **to speak ~ of someone** dire beaucoup de bien de qn

highness *n* **1.** (*title*) altesse *f;* **His/Her Highness** Son Altesse **2.** (*level*) hauteur *f*

high noon *n* plein midi *m*

high-performance *adj* de haute performance **high-pitched** *adj* **1.** (*high: tone*) aigu(ë) **2.** (*steep*) abrupt(e) **high point** *n* point *m* culminant **high-powered** *adj* très puissant(e) **high-pressure** **I.** *n* haute pression *f* **II.** *adj* **1.** TECH à haute pression **2.** ECON **~ sales techniques** techniques *fpl* de vente à l'arrachée **III.** *vt Am* mettre la pression sur **high-ranking** *adj* de haut rang **high-resolution** *n* INFOR haute résolution *f* **high-rise** **I.** *n* tour *f* **II.** *adj* **a ~ block/building** une tour **high-risk** *adj* à haut risque **high school** *n* **1.** *Brit, Aus* établissement *m* d'enseignement secondaire **2.** *Am* lycée *m*

> En Grande-Bretagne, le nom de **high school** était autrefois employé pour désigner une "grammar school" (≈ lycée), mais de nos jours il désigne une "secondary school" (≈ collège).

high seas *n pl* haute mer *f;* **on the ~** en haute mer **high season** *n* haute saison *f;* **at ~** à haute saison **high society** *n* haute société *f* **high-speed train** *n* train *m* à grande vitesse **high-spirited** *adj* **1.** (*cheerful, lively*) vif(vive) **2.** (*fiery*) fougueux(-euse) **high spot** *n inf* clou *m*

higher education *n no pl* études *fpl* universitaires

high-flyer *n* ambitieux, -euse *m, f* **highland** *n* région *f* montagneuse; **the Highlands** les Highlands

highness *n* **1.** *no pl* (*state of being high*) hauteur *f* **2. His/Her Highness** Son Altesse *f*

high-profile *adj* (*person*) très en vue; (*action, issue*) très discuté(e) **high-rise I.** *n* tour *f* **II.** *adj* ~ **building/block** tour *f* **high street** *n no pl* grand-rue *f;* **high-street shop** petit commerce *m* **hightail** *Am* **I.** *vi inf* se magner **II.** *vt inf* **to ~ it out of sth** se tirer de qc **high tea** *n Brit* repas *m* du soir **high-tech** *adj* high-tech *inv* **high-tension I.** *n* haute tension *f* **II.** *adj* (*cable*) à haute tension **high tide** *n* **1.** GEO marée *f* haute **2.** *fig* point *m* culminant **highway** *n Am* autoroute *f* **Highway Code** *n* code *m* de la route **high wire** *n* corde *f* raide

hijack ['haɪdʒæk] **I.** *vt* détourner **II.** *n* détournement *m*

hijacker *n* terroriste *mf;* **plane ~** pirate *mf* (de l'air)

hijacking *n no pl* détournement *m*

hike [haɪk] **I.** *n* **1.** (*long walk with backpack*) randonnée *f;* **to go on a ~** faire une randonnée **2.** *Am, inf* (*increase*) augmentation *f* **II.** *vi, vt* augmenter

hiker *n* randonneur, -euse *m, f*

hiking *n* randonnée *f*

hilarious [hɪ'leərɪəs, *Am:* -'lerɪ-] *adj* **1.** (*very amusing*) hilarant(e) **2.** (*noisy and amusing*) délirant(e)

hilarity [hɪ'lærəti, *Am:* -'lerət̬i] *n no pl* hilarité *f*

hill [hɪl] *n* **1.** (*small mountain*) *a. fig* colline *f* **2.** (*hillside*) coteau *m;* **the ~s** (*grapevine*) les coteaux **3.** (*steep slope*) côte *f* ►**to be over the ~** *inf* se faire vieux; **sth ain't worth a ~ of beans** *Am, inf* ne pas valoir un haricot; **as old as the ~s** vieux comme le monde

hillbilly ['hɪlbɪli] <-lies> *n Am, pej* péquenaud(e)

hillock *n* butte *f* **hillside** *n* flanc *m* de la colline; **on the ~** à flanc de colline **hilltop I.** *n* sommet *m* de la colline **II.** *adj* au sommet d'une colline

hilly <-ier, -iest> *adj* vallonné(e)

hilt [hɪlt] *n* (*handle of a weapon: of a gun*) crosse *f;* (*of a dagger, knife*) manche *m;* (*of a sword*) poignée *f* ►**to be in debt to the ~** être endetté jusqu'au cou; **to support sb to the ~** soutenir qn à fond

him [hɪm] *pers pron* **1.** (*he*) lui; **it's ~** c'est lui; **older than ~** plus vieux que lui; **if I were ~** si j'étais lui **2.** *objective pron direct* le, l' + *vowel; indirect, after prep* lui; **look at ~** regarde/regardez-le; **I saw ~** je l'ai vu; **she told ~ that ...** elle lui a dit que ...; **he'll give sth to ~** il va lui donner qc; **it's for/from ~** c'est pour/de lui ►**everything comes to ~ who waits** *prov* tout vient à point à qui sait attendre

Himalayas [ˌhɪmə'leɪəz] *npl* **the ~** l'Himalaya *m*

himself [hɪm'self] *pers pron* **1.** *reflexive* se, s' + *vowel;* **he hurt ~** il s'est blessé **2.** (*emphatic*) lui-même **3.** *after prep* lui(-même); **he's proud of ~** il est fier de lui; **he lives by ~** il vit seul; **he told ~ that ..** il s'est dit que ...; *s. a.* **myself**

hind¹ [haɪnd] *adj* de derrière ►**to talk the ~ legs off a donkey** *inf* être un véritable moulin à paroles

hind² [haɪnd] <-(s)> *n* ZOOL biche *f*

hinder ['hɪndəʳ, *Am:* -dɚ] *vt* faire obstacle à; **to ~ progress** freiner les progrès; **to ~ sb in their efforts** entraver les efforts de qn; **to ~ sb from doing sth** empêcher qn de faire qc

Hindi ['hɪndiː] **I.** *n* hindi *m; s. a.* **English II.** *adj* hindi

hindmost ['haɪndməʊst, *Am:* -moʊst] *adj* dernier(-ère) ►**(let the) devil take the ~** sauve qui peut

hindquarters [ˌhaɪnd'kwɔːtəz, *Am:* 'haɪndˌkwɔːrt̬ɚz] *npl* ZOOL arrière-train *m*

hindrance ['hɪndrəns] *n* obstacle *m*

hindsight ['haɪndsaɪt] *n* recul *m;* **in ~, with (the benefit of) ~** avec du recul

Hindu ['hɪnduː] **I.** *n* REL hindou(e) *m(f)* **II.** *adj* REL hindou(e)

Hinduism ['hɪnduːɪzəm] *n no pl* REL hindouisme *m*

hinge [hɪndʒ] **I.** *n* charnière *f* **II.** *vi* **1.** (*revolve*) *a. fig* tourner; **to ~ (up)on sb/sth** tourner autour de qn/qc **2.** (*depend on*) **to ~ (up)on sb/sth** dépendre de qn/qc

hint [hɪnt] **I.** *n* **1.** (*slight amount*) soupçon *m* **2.** (*allusion*) allusion *f;* **to drop a ~** faire une allusion; **to be unable to take a ~** ne pas comprendre vite **3.** (*practical tip*) conseil *m;* **a handy ~** un truc **II.** *vt* **to ~ sth to sb** insinuer qc à qn **III.** *vi* **to ~ at sth** faire une allusion à qc

hip¹ [hɪp] *n* hanche *f* ►**to shoot from the ~** *inf* dégainer en tirant

hip² [hɪp] *n* (*rose hip*) églantine *f*

hip³ [hɪp] **I.** *adj inf* branché(e) **II.** *interj* **~ ~ hooray!** hip hip hourra!

hip hop I. *n* hip-hop *m* **II.** *adj* hip-hop *inv*

hippie ['hɪpi] **I.** *n* hippie *mf* **II.** *adj* hippie

hippo ['hɪpəʊ, *Am:* -oʊ] *n inf* hippopotame *m*

hippopotamus [ˌhɪpə'pɒtəməs, *Am:* -'pɑːt̬ə-] <-es *o* -mi> *n* hippopotame *m*

hippy ['hɪpi] <-pies> *s.* **hippie**

hire ['haɪəʳ, *Am:* 'haɪr] **I.** *n no pl* location *f;* **to be on ~** être à louer; **"for ~"** "à louer"; **a car ~ business** une location de voiture; **a ~ purchase** un achat à crédit; **to buy sth on ~** acheter qc à crédit; **a ~ purchase agreement** un contrat de crédit **II.** *vt* **1.** (*rent*) louer; **to ~ sth by the hour/day** louer qc à l'heure/la journée **2.** *Am* (*employ*) engager

◆**hire out** *vt* louer; **to ~ sth by the hour** louer qc à l'heure; **to hire oneself out as sth** offrir ses services en tant que qc

his [hɪz] **I.** *poss adj* (*of a he*) son, sa, ses *pl;* **he lost ~ head** il a perdu la tête; *s. a.* **my II.** *poss pron* (*belonging to him*) le sien, la sienne, les sien(ne)s; **a friend of** ~ un ami à lui; **this glass is** ~ ce verre est à lui; *s. a.* **hers**

Hispanic [hɪs'pænɪk] **I.** *adj* **1.** (*related to Spanish-speaking countries*) latino-américain(e) **2.** (*related to Spain*) hispanique **II.** *n* latino-américain(e) *m(f)*

hiss [hɪs] **I.** *vi, vt* siffler **II.** *n* sifflement *m*

historian [hɪ'stɔːriən] *n* historien(ne) *m(f)*

historic(al) *adj* historique

history ['hɪstəri] *n* histoire *f;* **to make** ~ faire l'histoire

hit [hɪt] **I.** *n* **1.** (*blow, stroke*) *a. fig* coup *m;* **to make a** ~ **at sb/sth** attaquer qn/qc; **to take a direct** ~ (*be bombed*) être frappé **2.** SPORT coup *m;* (*in fencing*) touche *f;* **to score a** ~ toucher; **to score a direct** ~ taper dans le mille **3.** (*success*) succès *m;* **a smash** ~ un grand succès; ~ **film** un film à succès **4.** (*successful song*) tube *m* **5.** *Am, inf* (*murder*) meurtre *m* **II.** <-tt-, hit, hit> *vt* **1.** (*strike*) *a. fig* frapper; **to** ~ **one's head** se cogner la tête; **I don't know what** ~ **him** je ne sais pas ce qu'il lui est arrivé **2.** (*crash into: tree, car*) percuter **3.** (*reach*) *a. fig* atteindre; **to** ~ **rock bottom** avoir le moral au plus bas; **to be** ~ (*be shot*) être touché **4.** SPORT (*a ball*) frapper; (*person*) toucher **5.** (*affect negatively*) toucher **6.** (*arrive at*) arriver à **7.** (*encounter, come up against: iceberg*) heurter; **to** ~ **a bad patch** prendre un mauvais tour; **to** ~ **a lot of resistance** rencontrer beaucoup de résistance; **to** ~ **a traffic jam** tomber sur un bouchon **8.** *Am, inf* (*attack, kill*) buter **9.** (*press: key, button*) appuyer sur ►**to** ~ **the bottle** picoler; **to** ~ **the ceiling** sortir de ses gonds; **to** ~ **the deck** s'aplatir au sol; **to** ~ **the hay** *inf* aller au pieu; **to** ~ **the headlines** faire les gros titres; **to** ~ **home** frapper les esprits; **to** ~ **the jackpot** toucher le jackpot; **to** ~ **the nail on the head** tomber juste; **to** ~ **the road** s'en aller; **to** ~ **the roof** être furieux; **sth really** ~**s the spot** qc est juste ce qu'il faut; **to** ~ **one's stride** trouver son rythme **III.** *vi* **1.** (*strike*) frapper **2.** (*collide*) **to** ~ **at sb/sth** se heurter à qn/qc **3.** (*attack*) **to** ~ **at sth** attaquer qc

◆**hit back** *vi* riposter

◆**hit off** *vt always sep* **to hit it off with sb** bien s'entendre avec qn

◆**hit out** *vi* **to** ~ **at sb** (*physically*) frapper qn; (*verbally*) s'en prendre à qn

◆**hit on** *vi* **1.** (*think of*) trouver **2.** *Am, inf* (*show sexual interest*) allumer

hit-and-run [ˌhɪtən'rʌn] **I.** *n* **1.** (*accident*) délit *m* de fuite **2.** MIL ~ **warfare** guerre *f* éclair **II.** *adj* ~ **accident** délit *m* de fuite; ~ **driver** chauffard *m* en délit de fuite; ~ **attack** MIL attaque *f* éclair

hitch [hɪtʃ] **I.** *n* **1.** (*temporary difficulty or obstacle*) anicroche *f;* **technical** ~ incident *m* technique; **without a** ~ sans accroc **2.** (*knot*) nœud *m* **II.** *vt* **1.** (*fasten*) **to** ~ **sth to sth** attacher qc à qc **2.** *inf* (*hitchhike*) **to** ~ **a lift** faire du stop **III.** *vi inf* faire du stop

◆**hitch up** *vt* remonter

hitcher *n s.* **hitch-hiker**

hitch-hike *vi* faire de l'auto-stop, faire du pouce *Québec* **hitch-hiker** *n* auto-stoppeur, -euse *m, f* **hitch-hiking** *n* auto-stop *m*

hi-tech [ˌhaɪ'tek] *adj* hi-tech *inv*

hitherto [ˌhɪðə'tuː, *Am:* -ɚ'-] *adv form* jusqu'ici

hitman ['hɪtmæn] <-men> *n* tueur *m*

hit-or-miss *adj* au petit bonheur la chance

hit parade *n* hit-parade *m*

HIV [ˌeɪtʃaɪ'viː] *n no pl abbr of* **human immunodeficiency virus** HIV *m*

hive [haɪv] *n* ruche *f*

hive off I. *vi* se retirer **II.** *vt Brit, Aus* décentraliser

hives *n + sing vb* urticaire *f*

hl *n abbr of* **hectolitre** hl. *m*

HMG [ˌeɪtʃem'dʒiː] *n Brit abbr of* **Her/His Majesty's Government** le gouvernement de Sa Majesté

HMI [ˌeɪtʃem'aɪ] *n Brit abbr of* **Her/His Majesty's Inspector (of schools)** inspecteur *m* de l'éducation nationale

HMS [ˌeɪtʃem'es] *n abbr of* **Her/His Majesty's Ship** bâtiment *m* de Sa Majesté

HMSO [ˌeɪtʃemes'əʊ, *Am:* -'oʊ] *n abbr of* **Her/His Majesty's Stationery Office** *service gouvernemental de publication*

HNC [ˌeɪtʃen'siː] *n Brit abbr of* **Higher National Certificate** ≈ BTS *m*

HND [ˌeɪtʃen'diː] *n Brit abbr of* **Higher National Diploma** *diplôme supérieur d'aptitudes techniques*

ho [həʊ, *Am:* hoʊ] *interj inf* **1.** (*to express scorn, surprise*) ha ha! **2.** (*to attract attention*) hé ho!

HO [ˌeɪtʃ'əʊ, *Am:* -'oʊ] *n abbr of* **Home Office** ministère *m* de l'Intérieur

hoard [hɔːd, *Am:* hɔːrd] **I.** *n* réserves *fpl* **II.** *vt* amasser

hoarding *n* **1.** *Brit, Aus* (*advertising board*) panneau *m* d'affichage; **an advertising** ~ un panneau de publicité **2.** (*temporary fence around building*) clôture *f* de chantier

hoar frost *n* givre *m*

hoarse [hɔːs, *Am:* hɔːrs] *adj* enroué(e)

hoarseness *n no pl* enrouement *m*

hoax [həʊks, *Am:* hoʊks] **I.** *n* canular *m;* **a bomb** ~ une fausse alerte à la bombe **II.** *vt* faire un canular à; **to** ~ **sb into thinking sth** faire croire à qn qc

hoaxer *n personne qui fait des canulars téléphoniques*

hob [hɒb, *Am:* hɑːb] *n Brit* **1.** (*stove*) foyer *m* **2.** (*electric stove*) plaque *f* chauffante

hobble ['hɒbl, *Am:* 'hɑːbl] **I.** *vi* boiter **II.** *vt* entraver

hobby ['hɒbi, *Am:* 'hɑːbi] <-bies> *n* passe-temps *m inv*

hobby-horse *n* **1.** (*stick with horse's head*) cheval *m* à bascule **2.** (*favourite topic*) dada *m*

hobnailed ['hɒbneɪld, *Am:* 'hɑːb-] *adj* à

clous
hobnob ['hɒbnɒb, *Am:* 'hɑːbnɑːb] <-bb-> *vi pej, inf* traîner
hock[1] [hɒk, *Am:* hɑːk] **I.** *n inf* **to be in ~** être au clou; **to be in ~ to sb/sth** être endetté auprès de qn/qc **II.** *vt inf* mettre au clou
hock[2] [hɒk, *Am:* hɑːk] *n* jarret *m*
hockey ['hɒki, *Am:* 'hɑːki] *n* hockey *m;* **ice ~** hockey *m* sur glace; **~ stick** crosse *f* de hockey
hocus-pocus [ˌhəʊkəs'pəʊkəs, *Am:* ˌhoʊkəs'poʊ-] *n* **1.** (*meaningless talk*) blabla *m* **2.** (*formula for tricks*) abracadabra
hodgepodge ['hɒdʒpɒdʒ, *Am:* 'hɑːdʒpɑːdʒ] *n s.* **hotchpotch**
hoe [həʊ, *Am:* hoʊ] *n* houe *f*
hog [hɒg, *Am:* hɑːg] **I.** *n* porc *m* châtré **II.** <-gg-> *vt inf* s'accaparer
Hogmanay ['hɒgməneɪ, *Am:* 'hɑːg-] *n no pl, Scot s.* **New Year's Eve**
hogshead ['hɒgzhed, *Am:* 'hɑːgz-] *n* barrique *f*
hogwash ['hɒgwɒʃ, *Am:* 'hɑːgwɑːʃ] *n pej, inf* conneries *fpl*
hoi polloi [ˌhɔɪpə'lɔɪ] *npl pej, iron, inf* **the ~** la populace
hoist [hɔɪst] *vt* **1.** (*raise or haul up*) remonter; (*a flag*) hisser **2.** (*be present*) rester ▶**to ~ a few** *Am* se descendre quelques verres; **to be ~(ed) with one's own petard** être pris à son propre piège
hold [həʊld, *Am:* hoʊld] **I.** *n* **1.** (*grasp, grip*) *a.* SPORT prise *f;* **to catch ~ of sb/sth** saisir qn/qc; **to get ~ of sb/sth** (*find*) trouver qn/qc; **to have a strong ~** serrer avec force; **to keep ~ of sth** maintenir qc; **to lose ~ of sth** lâcher prise qc; **to take ~ of sb/sth** saisir qn/qc **2.** (*intentional delay*) suspens *m;* **to be on ~** TEL être en attente; **to put sth on ~** mettre qc en suspens; **to put sb on ~** faire attendre qn **3.** (*control, controlling force*) emprise *f;* **to have a ~ on sb** avoir une emprise sur qn **4.** NAUT, AVIAT soute *f* **5.** (*understanding*) **to get ~ of sth** saisir qc; **to have a ~ of sth** comprendre qc ▶**no ~s barred** sans retenue **II.** <held, held> *vt* **1.** (*grasp*) tenir; **to ~ hands** se tenir la main; **to ~ sb in one's arms** prendre qn dans ses bras; **to ~ sb/sth tight** serrer qn/qc (dans ses bras) **2.** (*keep*) maintenir; **to ~ one's head high** garder sa tête haute; **to ~ one's stomach in** rentrer son ventre; **to ~ oneself straight** se tenir droit; **to ~ (on to) the lead** maintenir la tête; **to be able to ~ one's drink** tenir l'alcool; **to ~ sb to his/her word** obliger qn à tenir sa promesse **3.** (*retain: interest, attention*) retenir; (*room*) réserver; LAW détenir; **to ~ sb in custody** maintenir qn en détention préventive; **to be held** être en garde à vue; **to ~ sb prisoner/hostage** maintenir qn prisonnier/en otage **4.** (*maintain*) maintenir; **to ~ oneself badly** se comporter mal; **to ~ oneself in readiness** se maintenir prêt; **to ~ the road** tenir la route **5.** (*delay, stop*) retarder; **~ it!** arrête(z) tout!; **to ~ one's fire** MIL *a. fig* arrêter les hostilités; **to ~ sb's phone calls** suspendre les appels **6.** (*hold back*) retenir; **to ~ one's breath** retenir sa respiration; *fig* mettre sa main au feu **7.** (*contain*) contenir; **to ~ no interest** ne présenter aucun intérêt; **what the future ~s** ce que réserve l'avenir; **sth ~s many surprises** qc réserve bien des surprises **8.** (*possess, own*) avoir; (*majority, shares, record*) détenir **9.** (*conduct: negotiations*) mener; (*conversation, conference*) tenir; (*party, tournament*) organiser; **the election is held on monday** l'élection a lieu lundi; **to ~ a surgery** MED faire une intervention chirurgicale **10.** (*believe*) considérer; **sb is held in great respect** qn est tenu en grand respect; **to ~ sb responsible for sth** tenir qn pour responsable de qc ▶**to ~ sb at bay** tenir qn à distance; **to ~ all the cards** avoir toutes les cartes en main; **to ~ the fort** monter la garde; **to ~ the key to sth** avoir la clé de qc; **~ the line!** ne quittez pas!, gardez la ligne! *Québec;* **to ~ one's own** tenir bon; **to ~ the purse strings** tenir les ficelles de la bourse; **to ~ the reins** tenir les rênes; **to ~ the stage** [*o Brit, Aus* **floor**] tenir le devant de la scène; **to ~ sway over sth** faire la pluie et le beau temps dans qc; **~ your tongue!** tais-toi!; **sth ~s water** qc se tient; **there's no ~ing her/him (back)** rien ne peut la/le retenir **III.** *vi* **1.** (*remain*) *a. fig* tenir; **~ tight** tenez bon!; **to ~ still** ne pas bouger; **to ~ true** être vrai **2.** (*continue*) durer; (*weather*) se maintenir **3.** (*believe*) croire **4.** (*contain, promise*) **... what the future ~s ...** ce que le futur réserve
◆**hold against** *vt* **to hold it against sb** en vouloir à qn
◆**hold back I.** *vt* retenir; (*tears, anger*) contenir; **to ~ information** ne pas dévoiler des informations ▶**there's no holding me (back)** rien ne peut me retenir **II.** *vi* se retenir; **to ~ from doing sth** se retenir de faire qc
◆**hold down** *vt* maintenir; (*person*) maîtriser; (*job*) garder
◆**hold forth** *vi pej* **to ~ about sth** disserter sur qc
◆**hold in** *vt* retenir; **to hold one's stomach in** rentrer son ventre
◆**hold off I.** *vt* **1.** (*keep distant*) tenir à distance **2.** (*postpone, delay*) remettre à plus tard **II.** *vi* **1.** (*postpone, delay*) différer; **the rain has held off** il n'a pas plu **2.** (*keep distant*) se tenir à distance
◆**hold on** *vi* **1.** (*affix, attach*) maintenir **2.** (*keep going*) **to ~ (tight)** tenir bon **3.** (*wait*) attendre
◆**hold out I.** *vt* **1.** (*stretch out*) tendre **2.** (*offer*) offrir **II.** *vi* **1.** (*resist*) tenir bon **2.** (*continue: supplies*) durer **3.** (*not do/tell*) **to ~ on sb** cacher qc à qn **4.** (*hope*) **to ~ for sth** espérer qc
◆**hold over** *vt* **1.** *Am* (*extend*) prolonger **2.** (*defer*) **to hold sth over until monday** remettre qc à lundi

◆**hold onto** *vt* **1.** (*grasp*) *a. fig* s'accrocher à **2.** (*keep, not throw away*) garder
◆**hold to** *vt* s'en tenir à
◆**hold together** **I.** *vi* tenir ensemble **II.** *vt* maintenir ensemble
◆**hold under** *vt* opprimer
◆**hold up** **I.** *vt* **1.** (*support*) soutenir **2.** (*put in the air, raise*) lever; **to be held up by** (**means of**)/**with sth** être maintenu par qc; **to ~ one's head high** *fig* garder la tête haute **3.** (*delay*) retarder **4.** (*rob*) attaquer **5.** (*offer as example*) **to hold sb up as sth** présenter qn comme qc; **to hold sth up to ridicule** considérer comme ridicule **II.** *vi* **1.** (*exist as true*) (se) tenir **2.** (*get along*) s'entendre
◆**hold with** *vi* être d'accord avec

holdall ['həʊldɔːl, *Am:* 'hoʊld-] *n* fourre-tout *m inv*

holder *n* **1.** (*device for holding objects*) support *m* **2.** (*owner*) détenteur, -trice *m, f;* **office-~** propriétaire *mf;* **~ of shares** actionnaire *mf*

holding *n* **1.** (*tenure of land or property*) propriété *f* **2.** *pl* (*property in stocks or bonds*) fonds *mpl*

holding company *n* holding *m*

holdover *n Am* reste *m*

hold-up *n* **1.** (*act of robbing*) hold-up *m* **2.** (*delay*) suspension *f*

hole [həʊl, *Am:* hoʊl] **I.** *n* **1.** (*hollow space, cavity*) trou *m* **2.** (*animal's burrow: of fox, rabbit*) terrier *m* **3.** SPORT trou *m* **4.** *inf* (*unpleasant place*) trou *m* **5.** *inf* (*difficult situation*) **to be in the ~** *Am* être dans la mouise **II.** *vt* **1.** (*make holes, perforate*) trouer **2.** SPORT (*hit a ball into a hole in golf*) **to ~ a ball** lancer une balle dans le trou
◆**hole up** *vi inf* se terrer

holiday ['hɒlədeɪ, *Am:* 'hɑːlə-] **I.** *n* **1.** *Brit, Aus* (*vacation*) vacances *fpl;* **to be** (**away**) **on ~** être en vacances; **to take ~** prendre des vacances **2.** (*public day off*) jour *m* férié **II.** *vi* être en vacances

holiday address *n* adresse *f* de vacances **holiday camp** *n* camp *m* de vacances **holiday course** *n* cours *m* de vacances **holiday destination** *n* destination *f* **holiday entitlement** *n* jours *mpl* de congés légaux **holiday flat** *n* appartement *m* de vacances **holiday house** *n* maison *f* de vacances **holidaymaker** *n* vacancier, -ière *m, f* **holiday mood** *n* ambiance *f* de vacances **holiday resort** *n* lieu *m* de vacances

holiness ['həʊlɪnɪs, *Am:* 'hoʊ] *n* **1.** (*sanctity*) sainteté *f* **2.** **His/Your Holiness** (*title used in speaking to or of the Pope*) Sa/votre Sainteté

holism ['həʊlɪzəm, *Am:* 'hoʊ-] *n* PHILOS holisme *m*

Holland ['hɒlənd, *Am:* 'hɑːlənd] *n* la Hollande

holler ['hɒləʳ, *Am:* 'hɑːlɚ] **I.** *vi Am, inf* gueuler **II.** *n Am, inf* gueulante *f*

hollow ['hɒləʊ, *Am:* 'hɑːloʊ] **I.** *adj a. fig, pej* creux(-euse); (*promise*) vain(e); (*laughter*) faux(fausse) ►**to beat sb ~** battre qn haut la main **II.** *n* creux *m* **III.** *vt* GEO **to ~** (**out**) **sth, to ~ sth** (**out**) creuser qc **IV.** *adv* creux; **to feel ~** avoir un creux

holly ['hɒli, *Am:* 'hɑːli] *n* houx *m*

hollyhock ['hɒlɪhɒk, *Am:* 'hɑːlɪhɑːk] *n* mauve *f*

holm [həʊm, *Am:* hoʊm] *n Brit* îlot *m*

holm oak *n* chêne *m* vert

holocaust ['hɒləkɔːst, *Am:* 'hɑːləkɑːst] *n* holocauste *m;* **the Holocaust** l'holocauste

hologram ['hɒləgræm, *Am:* 'hɑːlə-] *n* hologramme *m*

holster ['həʊlstəʳ, *Am:* 'hoʊlstɚ] *n* étui *m* (de revolver)

holy ['həʊli, *Am:* 'hoʊ-] <-ier, -iest> *adj a. fig* saint(e); **to be a ~ terror** être une sacrée terreur

Holy Communion *n* sainte communion *f* **Holy Father** *n* Saint-Père *m* **Holy Scripture** *n* Saintes Écritures *fpl* **Holy See** *n* Saint-Siège *m* **Holy Spirit** *n* Saint-Esprit *m* **holy war** *n* **the ~** la guerre sainte **Holy Week** *n no art* semaine *f* sainte

homage ['hɒmɪdʒ, *Am:* 'hɑːmɪdʒ] *n* hommage *m;* **to pay ~ to sb** rendre hommage à qn

home [həʊm, *Am:* hoʊm] **I.** *n* foyer *m;* **at ~** *no pl* à la maison; **to leave ~** *no pl* quitter la maison; **to make oneself at ~** *no pl* se mettre à l'aise **II.** *adv* **1.** (*at or to one's place*) à la maison **2.** (*one's country*) au pays **3.** (*understanding*) **to bring sth ~ to sb** faire comprendre qc à qn ►**until the cows come ~** jusqu'à la saint-glinglin; **sth is nothing to write ~ about** qc n'est rien d'important **III.** *adj a.* SPORT local(e)

home in on *vi* viser

home address *n* adresse *f* (à la maison) **home affairs** *npl Brit* POL affaires *fpl* intérieures **home-baked** *adj* fait(e) maison **home banking** *n* home banking *m,* banque *f* à domicile **home birth** *n* accouchement *m* à domicile **home brew** *n* bière *f* maison **homecoming** *n* retour *m* au foyer

> **Homecoming** aux USA est une fête importante dans les "High Schools" et dans les universités. Ce jour-là, l'équipe de football vient "à la maison" pour un match à domicile. Il y a une grande fête et une élève – ou une étudiante – très appréciée est élue "homecoming queen".

home computer *n* ordinateur *m* familial **home cooking** *n* cuisine *f* maison **Home Counties** *n Brit: comtés en bordure de Londres* **home economics** *n no pl* arts *mpl* ménagers **home exercise machine** *n* home-trainer *m* **home-grown** *adj* cultivé(e) soi-même **home help** *n* aide *f* familiale **homeland** *n* pays *m* natal

homeless I. *adj* sans abri II. *n + pl vb* **the ~** les sans-abri *inv*

homelike *adj* douillet(te)

home loan *n* FIN hypothèque *f*

homely <-ier, -iest> *adj* 1. *Brit, Aus* (*plain*) simple 2. *Am, Aus, pej* (*ugly, not good looking*) laid(e)

home-made *adj* fait(e) maison **home-maker** *n* femme *f* au foyer **home market** *n* marché *m* intérieur **Home Office** *n Brit* ministère *m* de l'Intérieur

homeopath ['həʊmiəʊpæθ, *Am:* 'hoʊmioʊ-] *n* homéopathe *mf*

homeopathy [ˌhəʊmi'ɒpəθi, *Am:* ˌhoʊmi'ɒpə-] *n* homéopathie *f*

homeowner *n* propriétaire *mf* **homepage** *n* INFOR page *f* d'accueil **home plate** *n Am* SPORT coup *m* **home rule** *n* POL autogestion *f* **Home Secretary** *n Brit* ministre *mf* de l'Intérieur **homesick** *adj* **to feel ~** avoir le mal du pays **homesickness** *n no pl* mal *m* du pays

homespun *adj* simple

homestead *n Am, Aus: terre agraire assignée de 160 acres*

home straight, **home stretch** *n Am, a. fig* dernière ligne *f* droite **home team** *n* équipe *f* autochtone **home town** *n* ville *f* natale **home truth** *n* quatre vérités *fpl;* **to tell sb a few ~s** dire à qn ses quatre vérités **homeward** I. *adv* vers sa maison II. *adj* (*journey*) de retour **homeward-bound** *adj* **to be ~** être sur le chemin du retour; **~ bound journey** voyage *m* de retour **homewards** *adv s.* **homeward** **homework** *n* 1. (*work after school*) devoirs *mpl* 2. (*paid work done at home*) travail *m* à domicile **homeworker** *n* travailleur, -euse *m, f* à domicile

homey ['həʊmi, *Am:* 'hoʊ-] *adj s.* **homely**

homicidal *adj Am, Aus* LAW homicide; **~ maniac** un criminel très dangereux

homicide ['hɒmɪsaɪd, *Am:* 'hɑːmə-] *n Am, Aus, form* LAW homicide *m*

homing pigeon *n* pigeon *m* voyageur

homoeopath *n* MED *s.* **homeopath**

homoeopathic *adj* MED *s.* **homeopathic**

homoeopathy *n* MED *s.* **homeopathy**

homogeneous *adj* homogène

homogenize [hə'mɒdʒənaɪz, *Am:* hə'mɑːdʒə-] *vt* homogénéiser

homogenous *s.* **homogeneous**

homograph ['hɒməgrɑːf, *Am:* 'hɑːməgræf] *n* LING homographe *m*

homonym ['hɒmənɪm, *Am:* 'hɑːmə-] *n* LING homonyme *m*

homophobia [ˌhɒmə'fəʊbiə, *Am:* ˌhoʊmə'foʊ-] *n no pl* homophobie *f*

homophone ['hɒməfəʊn, *Am:* 'hɑːməfoʊn] *n* LING homophone *m*

homosexual [ˌhɒmə'sekʃʊəl, *Am:* ˌhoʊmoʊ-] *adj* homosexuel(le)

homosexuality *n no pl* homosexualité *f*

Hon. *n abbr of* **Honorary** honoraire

Honduran I. *adj* hondurien(ne) II. *n* Hondurien(ne) *m(f)*

Honduras [hɒn'djʊərəs, *Am:* hɑːn'dʊr-] *n* le Honduras

hone [həʊn, *Am:* hoʊn] I. *vt a. fig* aiguiser II. *n* meule *f*

honest ['ɒnɪst, *Am:* 'ɑːnɪst] *adj* honnête

honestly I. *adv* 1. (*truthfully, with honesty*) honnêtement 2. (*with certainty*) franchement II. *interj* vraiment!

honest-to-goodness *adj* vrai(e)

honesty ['ɒnɪsti, *Am:* 'ɑːnɪ-] *n* honnêteté *f;* **in all ~** en toute honnêteté

honey ['hʌni] *n* 1. (*sweet liquid from bees*) miel *m* 2. *Am* (*pleasant person*) personne *f* délicieuse; (*excellent or good thing*) délice *m* 3. (*darling, dear*) chéri(e) *m(f)*

honeybee *n* abeille *f* **honeycomb** I. *n* rayon *m* (de miel) II. *adj* en nid-d'abeilles **honeydew** *n* melon *m* **honeymoon** I. *n* (*post-marriage holiday*) lune *f* de miel II. *vi* être en lune de miel

honeysuckle *n* chèvrefeuille *m*

honk [hɒŋk, *Am:* hɑːŋk] I. *vi, vt* 1. (*make the sound of wild goose*) cacarder 2. (*make a sound with a car horn*) klaxonner II. *n* 1. (*sound made by wild goose*) criaillement *m* 2. (*sound made by car horn*) coup *m* de klaxon

honor ['ɑːnɚ] *n Am, Aus s.* **honour**

honorary ['ɒnərəri, *Am:* 'ɑːnərer-] *adj a.* UNIV honorifique

honour ['ɒnə^r] I. *n Brit, Aus* honneur *m;* **in ~ of** en l'honneur de; **His/Your Honour** LAW Son/Votre Honneur II. *vt* honorer

hono(u)rable I. *adj a.* POL honorable II. *n* (*aristocrat*) noble *mf*

hono(u)rs degree *n* UNIV *diplôme universitaire d'Etat correspondant à une maîtrise*

hono(u)rs list *n liste sur laquelle est affiché le nom des diplômés*

hons *n abbr of* **honours** honneurs *mpl*

hood[1] [hʊd] *n* 1. (*covering for head*) capuche *f;* **cooker ~** toque *f;* **pram ~** capote *f* 2. *Am* AUTO *s.* **bonnet**

hood[2] [hʊd] *n Am, inf* gangster *m*

hood[3] [hʊd] *n Am, inf abbr of* **neighborhood** quartier *m*

hoodlum ['huːdləm] *n* truand *m*

hoodwink ['hʊdwɪŋk] *vt* truander

hoof [huːf, *Am:* hʊf] I. <hooves *o* hoofs> *n* (*hard covering on animal's foot*) sabot *m;* **on the ~** vivant(e) II. *vi* **to ~ it** traîner ses savates

hoo-ha ['huːhɑː] *n no pl, inf* ramdam *m*

hook [hʊk] I. *n* (*curved device*) *a.* SPORT crochet *m;* (*for coats*) patère *f;* (*for fish*) hameçon *m* ►**by ~ or by <u>crook</u>** par tous les moyens; **~, <u>line</u> and sinker** complètement II. *vt* accrocher; (*a fish*) hameçonner; **to ~ sth to sth** accrocher qc à qc III. *vi* s'agrafer

◆**hook on** I. *vi* 1. (*attach*) s'accrocher à 2. ELEC être raccordé à II. *vt* accrocher

◆**hook up** I. *vt* 1. (*hang, fix*) accrocher;

(*dress, bra*) agrafer **2.** (*connect, link up*) raccorder; (*computers*) connecter **II.** *vi* **1.** (*fasten: dress*) s'agrafer **2.** (*connect*) se raccorder

hooked *adj* **1.** (*curved like a hook*) crochu(e) **2.** (*addicted to, dependent on*) accroché(e)

hooker[1] *n Am, Aus, inf* pute *f*

hooker[2] *n* SPORT crochet *m*

hook-up *n* groupe *m* émetteur

hooky *n Am, Aus, inf* **to play ~** sécher

hooligan ['huːlɪgən] *n* hooligan *m*

hooliganism *n no pl* hooliganisme *m*

hoop [huːp] *n* (*ring*) anneau *m* ►**to put sb through the ~(s)** cuisiner qn

hoop earring *n* créole *f*

hoopoe ['huːpuː] *n* huppe *f*

hoot [huːt] **I.** *vi* **1.** (*make an owl's sound*) hululer **2.** (*make a sound*) mugir; (*train*) siffler; (*with horn*) klaxonner **3.** (*shout in disapproval*) huer; **to ~ with laughter** se tordre de rire **II.** *vt* **1.** (*make a sound*) **to ~ one's horn** klaxonner **2.** (*boo*) huer **III.** *n* **1.** (*owl's sound*) hululement *m* **2.** (*whistle*) mugissement *m;* (*of train*) sifflement *m;* (*of horn*) coup *m* de klaxon **3.** (*shout*) huée *f;* **~s of laughter** hurlements *mpl* de rire

◆**hoot down** *vt* huer

hooter *n* **1.** (*siren, steam whistle*) klaxon *m* **2.** *Am, Aus, inf* (*big nose*) tarin *m*

Hoover® ['huːvəʳ, *Am:* -vɚ] **I.** *n Brit, Aus* aspirateur *m* **II.** *vt* aspirer **III.** *vi* passer l'aspirateur

hop[1] [hɒp, *Am:* hɑːp] <-pp-> **I.** *vi* sauter; **to ~ in a car** grimper dans une voiture; **to ~ out of sth** sauter de qc **II.** *vt* **~ it!** *Brit, inf* dégage! **III.** *n* **1.** (*hopping movement*) saut *m* **2.** *inf* (*informal dance*) sauterie *f* **3.** (*short journey*) saut *m* ►**to catch sb on the ~** *Brit, inf* attraper qn à l'improviste

hop[2] [hɒp, *Am:* hɑːp] *n* **1.** (*vine with flower clusters*) houblon *m;* **~s** le houblon **2.** *pl, Aus, NZ, inf* (*beer*) mousse *f*

hope [həʊp, *Am:* hoʊp] **I.** *n* espoir *m;* **beyond ~** sans espoir **II.** *vi* espérer; **to ~ for sth** espérer qc **III.** *vt* espérer; **I ~ not** j'espère que non; **to ~ to** +*infin* espérer +*infin*

hopeful I. *adj* plein d'espoir **II.** *n* espoir *m*

hopefully *adv* plein d'espoir

hopeless *adj* désespéré(e)

hopelessly *adv* désespérément

hopper ['hɒpəʳ, *Am:* 'hɑːpɚ] *n* entonnoir *m*

hop-picker *n* houblonnier, -ière *m, f*

hopping mad *adj inf* furax

hoppole I. *vt* houblonner **II.** *n* perche *f* à houblon

hopscotch *n no pl* marelle *f*

horde [hɔːd, *Am:* hɔːrd] *n* horde *f*

horizon [hə'raɪzn] *n a. fig* horizon *m*

horizontal I. *adj* horizontal(e) **II.** *n no pl* MAT horizontale *f*

hormone ['hɔːməʊn, *Am:* 'hɔːrmoʊn] *n* hormone *f*

horn [hɔːn, *Am:* hɔːrn] *n* **1.** ZOOL corne *f* **2.** *no pl* (*material*) corne *f* **3.** (*receptacle, shape*) corne *f* **4.** (*honk*) klaxon *m* **5.** MUS cor *m* ►**to be on the ~s of a dilemma** être assis entre deux chaises; **to take the bull by the ~s** prendre le taureau par les cornes

◆**horn in** *vi Am, inf* **to ~ on sth** fourrer son nez dans qc

horned *adj* à cornes

hornet ['hɔːnɪt, *Am:* 'hɔːr-] *n* frelon *m*

hornless *adj* sans corne

horn-rimmed ['hɔːnrɪmt, *Am:* 'hɔːrn-] *adj* (*glasses*) à monture d'écaille

horny <-ier, -iest> *adj* **1.** (*made of horn*) en corne **2.** *inf* (*sexually excited, lustful*) chaud(e)

horoscope ['hɒrəskəʊp, *Am:* 'hɔːrəskoʊp] *n* horoscope *m*

horrendous [hɒ'rendəs, *Am:* hɔː'ren-] *adj* **1.** (*awful, horrible*) épouvantable **2.** (*exaggerated*) monstrueux(-euse)

horrible ['hɒrəbl, *Am:* 'hɔːr-] *adj* horrible

horrid ['hɒrɪd, *Am:* 'hɔːr-] *adj* atroce

horrific [hə'rɪfɪk, *Am:* hɔː'rɪf-] *adj* horrifiant(e)

horrify ['hɒrɪfaɪ, *Am:* 'hɔːr-] <-ied> *vt* horrifier

horror ['hɒrəʳ, *Am:* 'hɔːrɚ] *n* horreur *f;* **to one's ~** à sa grande horreur; **to be paralyzed with ~** être saisi d'horreur; **the ~s of famine/war** les horreurs de la famine/guerre; **a ~ film** un film d'horreur

horror-stricken, **horror-struck** *adj* frappé(e) d'horreur

hors d'œuvre [ɔː'dɜːv, *Am:* ɔːr'dɜːrv] <-s> *n Brit, Aus* hors-d'œuvre *m inv*

horse [hɔːs, *Am:* hɔːrs] *n* **1.** ZOOL cheval *m;* **~ and carriage** attelage *m* **2.** SPORT cheval *m* d'arçons ►**to eat like a ~** manger comme quatre; **to put the cart before the ~** mettre la charrue avant les bœufs; **to flog a dead ~** perdre son temps; **to get on one's high ~** monter sur ses grands chevaux; **to be on one's high ~** prendre des grands airs; **to hear sth straight from the ~'s mouth** apprendre qc de source sûre; **to back the wrong ~** miser sur le mauvais cheval

◆**horse about** *vi*, **horse around** *vi* faire le pitre

horseback I. *n* **on ~** à cheval; **police on ~** police *f* montée **II.** *adj* **~ riding** équitation *f;* **a ~ rider** un cavalier **III.** *adv* à cheval **horsebox**, **horse car** *n* van *m* **horse chestnut** *n* marron *m* d'Inde **horse-drawn** *adj* attelé(e) **horsefly** <-ies> *n* frein *m* à cheval **horsehair I.** *n no pl* crin *m* de cheval **II.** *adj* en crin de cheval **horse-laugh** *n* rire *m* de cheval **horseman** <-men> *n* cavalier *m* **horsemanship** *n no pl* équitation *f*

horseplay *n no pl* tohu-bohu *m*

horsepower *inv n* cheval-vapeur *m* **horse-race** *n* course *f* de chevaux **horse racing** *n* hippisme *m* **horseradish** *n* raifort *m* **horse riding** *n* équitation *f* **horse sense** *n inf* jugeote *f* **horseshoe** *n* fer *m* à cheval **horsetrading** *n no pl, pej* marchandage *m*

horsewhip <-pp-> *vt* cravacher **horsewoman** <-women> *n* cavalière *f*

hors(e)y ['hɔːsi, *Am:* 'hɔːr-] <-ier, -iest> *adj* **1.** (*of or resembling a horse*) chevalin(e) **2.** (*devoted to horses*) fou(folle) de cheval

horticultural *adj no pl* horticole

horticulture ['hɔːtɪkʌltʃəʳ, *Am:* 'hɔːrt̬əkʌltʃɚ] *n* horticulture *f*

hose¹ [həʊz, *Am:* hoʊz] *n* tuyau *m;* **a garden** ~ un tuyau d'arrosage

hose² [həʊz, *Am:* hoʊz] *n no pl s.* **hosiery**

hosepipe [həʊzpaɪp, *Am:* hoʊz-] *n Brit s.* **hose**

hosier *n form* marchand(e) *m(f)* de bas

hosiery ['həʊziəri, *Am:* 'hoʊʒɚi] *n no pl* bas *mpl*

hospice ['hɒspɪs, *Am:* 'hɑːspɪs] *n* MED hospice *m*

hospitable *adj* hospitalier(-ère)

hospital ['hɒspɪtəl, *Am:* 'hɑːspɪt̬əl] *n* hôpital *m;* ~ **staff/bill** le personnel/tarif hospitalier; **to go to the** ~ *no pl, Am* aller à l'hôpital; **to be admitted to** ~ rentrer à l'hôpital; **to be discharged from** ~ sortir de l'hôpital; **to spend time in** [*o Am* **in the**] ~ *no pl* être hospitalisé

hospitality [ˌhɒspɪ'tæləti, *Am:* ˌhɑːspɪ'tælət̬i] *n no pl* hospitalité *f*

hospitalization *n* hospitalisation *f*

hospitalize ['hɒspɪtəlaɪz, *Am:* 'hɑːspɪt̬əl-] *vt* hospitaliser

host¹ [həʊst, *Am:* hoʊst] **I.** *n* **1.** (*organizer of an event*) hôte, -esse *m, f;* (*in hotel*) hôtelier *m;* **to play** ~ **to sth** accueillir qc **2.** TV animateur, -trice *m, f* **3.** BIO, INFOR hôte *m* **4.** INFOR serveur *m* **II.** *adj* **1.** (*hosting: family, city*) d'accueil **2.** INFOR serveur **III.** *vt* **1.** (*act as a host to: party*) donner **2.** TV animer

host² [həʊst, *Am:* hoʊst] *n sing* multitude *f*

host³ [həʊst, *Am:* hoʊst] *n* REL hostie *f*

hostage ['hɒstɪdʒ, *Am:* 'hɑːstɪdʒ] *n* otage *m;* **take sb (as a)** ~ prendre qn en otage

host country *n* pays *m* d'accueil

hostel ['hɒstl, *Am:* 'hɑːstl] *n* **1.** (*cheap hotel*) pension *f;* **youth** ~ auberge *f* de jeunesse **2.** *Brit* (*housing for homeless*) foyer *m*

hosteller *n* hôte, -esse *m, f*

hostess ['həʊstɪs, *Am:* 'hoʊ-] *n* hôtesse *f*

hostile ['hɒstaɪl, *Am:* 'hɑːstl] *adj* (*climate*) hostile; (*aircraft*) ennemi(e); **to be** ~ **to sth** être hostile à qc

hostility [hɒ'stɪləti, *Am:* hɑː'stɪlət̬i] <-ies> *n* **1.** *no pl* (*unfriendliness*) hostilité *f;* **to show** ~ **to sb** montrer de l'hostilité envers qn **2.** *pl, form* (*fighting*) hostilités *fpl*

hot [hɒt, *Am:* hɑːt] <-ter, -test> *adj* **1.** (*very warm*) chaud(e) **2.** (*spicy*) fort(e) **3.** (*fiery*) brûlant(e) **4.** *inf* (*skilful*) super doué(e); **to be** ~ **at sth** être super doué en qc **5.** *inf* (*demanding*) **to be** ~ **on sth** être dingue de qc **6.** (*dangerous*) brûlant(e); **to be too** ~ **to handle** être un sujet brûlant **7.** *inf* (*sexually attractive*) chaud(e) **8.** (*exciting: music, news, party*) chaud(e) ►**to be (just) so much** ~ **air** n'être que du vent; **to get (all)** ~ **under the collar** s'échauffer; **to get into** ~ **water** se fourrer dans le pétrin

◆**hot up I.** *vt* chauffer; **to** ~ **a car's engine** trafiquer le moteur d'une voiture **II.** *vi* s'échauffer; (*situation*) s'intensifier

hot air *n pej* fanfaronnade *f*

hot-air balloon *n* montgolfière *f*

hotbed ['hɒtbed, *Am:* 'hɑːt-] *n* couche *f*

hot-blooded *n* fougueux(-euse)

hotchpotch ['hɒtʃpɒtʃ, *Am:* 'hɑːtʃpɑːtʃ] *n* potée *f*

hot dog *n* **1.** (*sausage in a roll*) hot-dog *m* **2.** *Am, Aus, inf* (*show-off*) frimeur, -euse *m, f* **hot dogging** *n inf* frime *f*

hotel [həʊ'tel, *Am:* hoʊ-] *n* hôtel *m*

hotel accommodation *n* hébergement *m* à l'hôtel **hotel bill** *n* note *f* d'hôtel

hotelier [həʊ'telieɪ, *Am:* ˌhoʊtel'jeɪ] *n* hôtelier, -ière *m, f*

hotel industry *n* industrie *f* hôtelière **hotelkeeper** *n* directeur, -trice *m, f* d'hôtel **hotel register** *n* registre *m* de l'hôtel **hotel staff** *n* personnel *m* hôtelier

hotfoot I. *adv* à la hâte **II.** *vt* **to** ~ **it somewhere** *inf* aller quelque part à toute vitesse **hothead** *n* coléreux, -euse *m, f* **hotheaded** *adj* irascible **hothouse** *n* serre *f* **hotline** *n* **1.** POL téléphone *m* rouge **2.** TEL hotline *f*

hotly *adv* ardemment

hot metal *n* plomb *m* **hotplate** *n* plaque *f* chauffante **hot potato** *n inf* sujet *m* brûlant **hotrod** *n inf* AUTO bagnole *f* trafiquée **hot seat** *n* **1.** *fig* (*difficult position*) position *f* difficile **2.** (*electric chair*) chaise *f* électrique **hotshot** *n Am, Aus, inf* as *m* **hot spot** *n inf* boîte *f* de nuit **hot stuff** *n* (*sexy woman, man*) canon *m* **hot-tempered** *adj* irascible **hot-water bottle** *n* bouillotte *f*

hound [haʊnd] **I.** *n* chien *m* de chasse **II.** *vt* pourchasser

◆**hound down** *vt* pourchasser

hour ['aʊəʳ, *Am:* 'aʊr] *n* heure *f;* **to be paid by the** ~ être payé à l'heure; **at any** ~ à toute heure; **to keep irregular/regular** ~**s** ne pas avoir/avoir des heures fixes; **to keep late** ~**s** se coucher à pas d'heure; **for** ~**s** pendant des heures; **at all** ~**s of the day and night** *pej* à n'importe quelle heure du jour ou de la nuit; **every** ~ **on the** ~ toutes les heures; **opening** ~**s** heures *fpl* d'ouverture; **an** ~ **away** à une heure de distance ►**sb's** ~ **has come** l'heure de qn est venue

hour hand *n* grande aiguille *f*

hourly *adv* toutes les heures

house [haʊs] **I.** *n* **1.** (*building*) maison *f* **2.** POL chambre *f* **3.** THEAT salle *f;* **to play to a full** ~ jouer devant une salle pleine **4.** MUS house *f* ►**you should set your own** ~ **in order before** tu devrais d'abord mettre de l'ordre dans vos propres affaires **II.** *vt* **1.** (*give place to*

H

live) héberger **2.** (*contain*) contenir
house arrest *n* maison *f* d'arrêt **houseboat** *n* péniche *f* **housebreaker** *n* cambrioleur, -euse *m, f* **housebreaking** *n no pl* cambriolage *m* **housecoat** *n* robe *f* de chambre **housefly** *n* mouche *f* domestique **household** **I.** *n* ménage *m* **II.** *adj* ménager(-ère) **householder** *n* **1.** (*owner*) propriétaire *mf* de maison **2.** (*tenant*) locataire, -trice *m, f* **household waste** *n* ordures *fpl* ménagères **house-hunt** *vi* être à la recherche d'un logement **house husband** *n* homme *m* au foyer **housekeeper** *n* intendant(e) *m(f)* **housekeeping** *n no pl* **1.** (*management*) ménage *m* **2.** (*money*) argent *m* du ménage **housekeeping money** *n no pl* argent *m* du ménage **housemaid** *n* employée *f* de maison **houseman** *n Brit* assistant *m* médical **house martin** *n* hirondelle *f* de fenêtre **house music** *n* house *f* music **house physician** *n* médecin *mf* de l'établissement **houseplant** *n* plante *f* d'appartement **house-proud** *adj Brit, Aus* ordonné(e) **houseroom** *n* **I wouldn't give sth** ~ je n'aimerais pas avoir cela même en cadeau **house rules** *npl* règlement *m* intérieur **Houses of Parliament** *n Brit* Parlement *m* **house starts** *npl* commencement *m* des travaux de construction **house surgeon** *n Brit* chirurgien *m* hospitalier, chirurgienne *f* hospitalière **house-to-house** *adj* de porte en porte **housetop** *n* toiture *f* **housetrained** *adj* propre **house-warming** *n no pl* crémaillère *f;* ~ **party** pendaison *f* de la crémaillère; **to have a** ~ pendre la crémaillère **housewife** <-wives> *n* femme *f* au foyer **housework** *n* travaux *mpl* ménagers

housing *n* logement *m*

housing association *n* entreprise *f* de construction de logements **housing benefit** *n Brit* aide *f* au logement **housing conditions** *npl* conditions *fpl* d'habitat **housing development** *n Am* (*housing estate*) lotissement *m* **housing estate** *n Brit* lotissement *m* **housing problem** *n* problème *m* de logement **housing programme** *n* programme *m* de création de logements **housing scheme** *n* **1.** (*estate*) lotissement *m* **2.** (*project*) projet *m* de construction de lotissement **housing shortage** *n* manque *m* de logements

hovel ['hɒvl, *Am:* 'hʌv-] *n pej* taudis *m*

hover ['hɒvəʳ, *Am:* 'hʌvɚ] *vi* **1.** (*stay in air*) planer; (*helicopter*) effectuer un vol stationnaire **2.** (*wait near*) guetter; **to** ~ **around sb** rôder autour de qn **3.** *fig* (*hesitate*) hésiter; **to** ~ **between sth and sth** osciller entre qc et qc

hovercraft <– *o* -s> *n* aéroglisseur *m* **hoverport** *n* port *m* pour aéroglisseurs **hovertrain** *n* chemin *m* de fer suspendu

how [haʊ] **I.** *adv* **1.** (*in what way*) comment; **to know** ~ **to** +*infin* savoir +*infin;* ~ **is it that he is here?** comment se fait-il qu'il soit là? *subj;* ~**?** *inf* quoi?; ~ **come** [*o* **so**]**?** comment ça? **2.** (*asking about condition*) comment; ~ **are you?** comment vas-tu/allez-vous?; ~ **was the film?** comment était le film? **3.** (*exclamation*) comme, que; ~ **nice!** comme c'est gentil; ~ **kind she is!** comme elle est gentille! **4.** (*that*) que; **he told me** ~ **he had seen her there** il m'a dit qu'il l'avait vue là-bas ▸ ~ **do you do?** bonjour!, enchanté! *form; s. a.* **many, much, long, old, far** **II.** *n* comment *m;* **to know the** ~(**s**) **and why**(**s**) **of sth** savoir le pourquoi et le comment de qc

how-do-you-do [ˌhaʊdjʊ'duː, *Am:* 'haʊdəjuːduː] *n inf* cinéma *m*

however [haʊ'evəʳ, *Am:* -ɚ] **I.** *adv* **1.** (*in whatever way*) de quelque manière que +*subj;* ~ **you look at it** de quelque manière qu'on envisage la chose **2.** (*to whatever extent*) si … que +*subj;* ~ **small** si petit qu'il/que ce soit; ~ **intelligent she is** si intelligente qu'elle soit; ~ **hard I try** j'ai beau essayer; ~ **much it rains** même s'il pleut des cordes **II.** *conj* **1.** (*in whichever way*) cependant **2.** (*nevertheless*) néanmoins

howl [haʊl] **I.** *vi* **1.** (*cry*) hurler **2.** *inf* (*laugh*) hurler de rire **II.** *n* hurlements *mpl*

◆**howl down** *vt* huer

howler *n inf* gaffe *f*

howling *adj inf* (*party, success*) d'enfer

HP, hp [ˌeɪtʃ'piː] *n* **1.** *Brit, inf abbr of* **hire purchase** achat *m* à crédit **2.** *abbr of* **Houses of Parliament** Parlement *m* **3.** *abbr of* **horsepower** CV *m*

HQ [ˌeɪtʃ'kjuː] *n abbr of* **headquarters** QG *m*

HRH [ˌeɪtʃɑːʳ'eɪtʃ, *Am:* -ɑːr'-] *n abbr of* **Her/His Royal Highness** Son Altesse Royale

HST *n abbr of* **high-speed train** ≈ TGV *m*

ht *n abbr of* **height** hauteur *f*

HTML [ˌeɪtʃtiːem'el] *n abbr of* **Hypertext Markup Language** INFOR HTML *m*

http *n no pl* http *m*

hub [hʌb] *n* **1.** (*middle part of a wheel*) moyeu *m* **2.** *fig* milieu *m*

hubbub ['hʌbʌb] *n no pl, a. fig* brouhaha *m*

hubcap ['hʌbkæp] *n* enjoliveur *m*

huckleberry ['hʌklbəri, *Am:* -'ber-] *n Am* airelle *f*

huckster ['hʌkstəʳ, *Am:* -stɚ] *n pej* **1.** (*noisy salesman*) camelot *m* **2.** *Am* (*advertisement writer*) rédacteur, -trice *m, f* publicitaire

huddle ['hʌdl] **I.** *vi* se blottir dans un coin **II.** *n* (*muddle*) fouillis *m;* **to go into a** ~ faire des messes basses

◆**huddle down** *vi* se blottir

◆**huddle together** *vi* se serrer l'un contre l'autre/les uns contre les autres

◆**huddle up** *vi* se blottir l'un contre l'autre; **to** ~ **against sb/sth** se blottir contre qn/qc

hue [hjuː] *n no pl a. fig* couleur *f* ▸ ~ **and cry** *pej* hauts cris *mpl*

huff [hʌf] **I.** *vi* souffler ▸**to** ~ **and puff** haleter; (*express annoyance*) rouspéter **II.** *vt* souffler sur **III.** *n inf* mauvaise tête *f;* **to be in a ~** ronchonner; **to get into a ~** devenir grognon; **to go off in ~** arrêter de ronchonner

huffy <-ier, -iest> *adj* **1.** (*touchy*) susceptible **2.** (*annoyed*) fâché(e)

hug [hʌg] **I.** <-gg-> *vt* **1.** (*hold close to body*) embrasser **2.** *fig* (*cling firmly to*) se tenir à **II.** *vi* s'embrasser **III.** *n* embrassement *m;* **to give sb a ~** embrasser qn

huge [hjuːdʒ] *adj* énorme

hugely *adv* énormément

hugeness *n* immensité *f*

hulk [hʌlk] *n* **1.** (*large person*) colosse *m* **2.** (*disused ship*) ponton *m*

hulking *adj* colossal(e)

hull¹ [hʌl] *n* NAUT coque *f*

hull² [hʌl] **I.** *n* (*covering of seed*) cosse *f* **II.** *vt* éplucher; (*beans, peas*) écosser

hullabaloo [ˌhʌləbəˈluː] *n* fracas *m;* **to make a ~** faire du vacarme

hullo [həˈləʊ, *Am:* -ˈloʊ] *interj Brit s.* **hello**

hum¹ [hʌm] <-mm-> **I.** *vi* **1.** (*make a low continuous sound*) *a. fig* (*bee*) bourdonner; (*machine*) vrombir; (*person*) fredonner **2.** (*be full of activity*) bourdonner d'activité; **to make things ~** faire tourner les affaires **3.** *Brit, inf* (*stink*) chlinguer ►**to ~ and haw** *Brit, Aus* tourner autour du pot **II.** *vt* fredonner **III.** *n* (*of insect*) bourdonnement *m;* (*of machinery, plane*) vrombissement *m;* (*of voices*) bruit *m* sourd; (*of melody*) fredonnement *m*

hum² [hʌm] *interj* hmm!

human [ˈhjuːmən] *adj* humain(e)

humane [hjuːˈmeɪn] *adj* humain(e)

humanism [ˈhjuːmənɪzəm] *n* humanisme *m*

humanistic [ˌhjuːməˈnɪstɪk] *adj* humaniste

humanitarian [hjuːˌmænɪˈteəriən, *Am:* hjuːˌmænəˈteri-] **I.** *n* philanthrope *mf* **II.** *adj* humanitaire

humanities *n pl* sciences *fpl* humaines

humanity [hjuːˈmænəti, *Am:* -t̬i] *n* humanité *f*

humanize [ˈhjuːmənaɪz] *vt* humaniser

humanly *adv* humainement; **everything ~ possible** tout ce qui est humainement possible

human nature *n* nature *f* humaine **human race** *n* espèce *f* humaine **human resources** *n* ressources *fpl* humaines **human rights** *npl* droits *mpl* de l'homme

humble [ˈhʌmbl] **I.** *adj* humble; **welcome to my ~ abode** *iron* bienvenue de mon humble antre; **~ beginnings** balbutiements *mpl;* **of ~ birth** de basse naissance; **in my ~ opinion, ...** à mon humble avis, ... **II.** *vt* **to be ~d by sb/sth** être humilié par qn/qc

humbleness *n* humilité *f*

humbug [ˈhʌmbʌg] *n* **1.** *no pl* (*nonsense*) ineptie *f* **2.** (*fraud*) escroquerie *f* **3.** *Brit* bonbon *m* à la menthe

humdrum [ˈhʌmdrʌm] **I.** *adj* monotone **II.** *n* monotonie *f*

humid [ˈhjuːmɪd] *adj* humide

humidifier *n* humidificateur *m*

humidify [hjuːˈmɪdɪfaɪ] *vt* humidifier

humidity [hjuːˈmɪdəti, *Am:* -t̬i] *n no pl* humidité *f*

humiliate [hjuːˈmɪlieɪt] *vt* humilier

humiliating *adj* humiliant(e)

humiliation *n* humiliation *f*

humility [hjuːˈmɪləti, *Am:* -t̬i] *n no pl* humilité *f*

hummingbird [ˈhʌmɪŋbɜːd, *Am:* -bɜːrd] *n* colibri *m*

humor *n Am, Aus,* **humour** [ˈhjuːməʳ, *Am:* -mɚ] *n no pl* **1.** (*capacity for amusement*) humour *m;* **sense of ~** sens *m* de l'humour; **to have a/no sense of ~** avoir/ne pas avoir le sens de l'humour **2.** (*something amusing*) humour *m* **3.** (*mood*) humeur *f;* **in (a) good/bad ~** de bonne/mauvaise humeur

humo(u)rist *n* **1.** (*writer*) humouriste *mf* **2.** (*funny person*) comique *mf*

humo(u)rless *adj* dépourvu(e) d'humour

humo(u)rous *adj* humoristique

hump [hʌmp] **I.** *n* bosse *f* ►**to be over the ~** avoir passé le cap **II.** *vt inf* traîner

humpback [ˈhʌmpbæk] *n* **1.** (*round back*) bosse *f* **2.** ZOOL baleine *f* à bosse

humpbacked *adj* bossu(e); **~ bridge** pont *m* à arcades

humph [hʌmpf, mm] *interj* mmmh!

Hun [hʌn] *n* **1.** HIST Hun *m* **2.** *pej* (*German*) boche *mf*

hunch [hʌntʃ] **I.** *n* intuition *f;* **to have a ~ that ...** avoir le présentiment que ... **II.** *vi* faire le dos rond **III.** *vt* bomber; **to ~ one's back** faire le dos rond

hunchback [ˈhʌntʃbæk] *n* **1.** (*rounded back*) dos *m* rond **2.** (*person*) bossu(e) *m(f)*

hundred [ˈhʌndrəd] <-(s)> *adj* cent; *s. a.* **eight, eighty**

hundredfold [ˈhʌndrədfəʊld, *Am:* -foʊld] *n* centième *mf*

hundredth *adj* centième; *s. a.* **eighth**

hundredweight <-> *n* demi-quintal *m*

hung [hʌŋ] **I.** *pt, pp of* **hang II.** *adj* suspendu(e)

Hungarian I. *adj* hongrois(e) **II.** *n* **1.** (*person*) Hongrois(e) *m(f)* **2.** LING hongrois *m; s. a.* **English**

Hungary [ˈhʌŋgəri] *n* la Hongrie

hunger [ˈhʌŋgəʳ, *Am:* -gɚ] *n no pl* **1.** (*pain from lack of food*) faim *f;* **a ~ strike** une grève de la faim **2.** (*desire*) soif *f;* **~ for knowledge** soif *f* de savoir; **to have no ~ for sth** ne pas avoir envie de qc

hung parliament *n parlement qui n'a pas de majorité nette*

hungry [ˈhʌŋgri] <-ier, -iest> *adj* **1.** (*desiring food*) affamé(e); **to go ~** être affamé **2.** (*want badly*) assoiffé(e); **to be ~ for sth** être assoiffé de qc; **~ for success** assoiffé de succès

hunk [hʌŋk] *n* **1.** (*large, thick piece*) gros morceau *m;* **~ of bread** une grosse tranche de pain **2.** *inf* (*attractive man*) canon *m*

H

hunky-dory *adj inf* au poil; **to be all ~** marcher comme sur des roulettes

hunt [hʌnt] **I.** *vt* **1.** (*chase to kill*) chasser **2.** (*search for*) rechercher **II.** *vi* **1.** (*chase to kill*) chasser **2.** (*search*) rechercher; **to ~ through sth** fouiller dans qc; **to ~ high and low for sth** remuer ciel et terre pour trouver qc **III.** *n* **1.** (*hunting action, place*) chasse *f;* **to go on a ~** partir pour la chasse **2.** (*search*) recherche *f;* **to be on the ~ for sb** rechercher qn; **to be on the ~ for sth** être en quête de qc **3.** (*association of hunters*) amicale *f* de chasseurs

◆**hunt down** *vt* **1.** (*for catching: animal*) traquer **2.** (*to find out following the tracks: animal*) dépister

hunt out, **hunt up** *vt* dénicher

hunter *n* **1.** (*one that hunts*) chasseur, -euse *m, f* **2.** (*hunting dog*) chien *m* de chasse

hunting *n no pl* chasse *f;* **to go ~** partir chasser

hunting ground *n* terrain *m* de chasse

hunting licence *n* permis *m* de chasse

hunting season *n* saison *f* de chasse

huntress ['hʌntrɪs] *n* chasseuse *f*

huntsman ['hʌntsmən] <-men> *n* chasseur *m*

hurdle ['hɜːdl, *Am:* 'hɜːr-] **I.** *n* **1.** (*fence*) haie *f;* **to take a ~** aborder une haie **2.** *pl* (*hurdle race*) course *f* de haies **3.** (*obstacle, impediment*) obstacle *m* **II.** *vi* courir une course de haies **III.** *vt* **1.** (*jump over*) sauter **2.** *fig* franchir

hurdler *n* coureur *m* de haies

hurdle race *n* course *f* de haies

hurdy gurdy ['hɜːdiˌgɜːdi, *Am:* ˌhɜːrdi'gɜːrdi] *n* orgue *m* de barbarie

hurl [hɜːl, *Am:* hɜːrl] *vt* **1.** (*throw violently*) lancer (violemment) **2.** *fig* (*abuse, insults*) balancer; **to ~ oneself at sb** se jeter sur qn; **to ~ oneself into one's work** s'absorber dans son travail

hurly-burly ['hɜːliˌbɜːli, *Am:* 'hɜːrlɪbɜːr-] *n* tohu-bohu *m*

hurrah [hə'rɑː], **hurray** *interj* hourra!

hurricane ['hʌrɪkən, *Am:* 'hɜːrɪkeɪn] *n* ouragan *m;* **~ force wind** cyclone *m*

hurricane lamp *n* lampe *f* tempête **hurricane warning** *n* avis *m* de tempête

hurried *adj* **1.** (*fast*) rapide **2.** (*neglected, dashed off*) bâclé(e) **3.** (*sooner or faster than intended*) précipité(e)

hurry ['hʌri, *Am:* 'hɜːr-] <-ied> **I.** *vi* se dépêcher **II.** *vt* presser **III.** *n* précipitation *f;* **it's no great ~** ce n'est pas très pressé; **to do sth in a ~** faire qc à toute allure; **to not forget sth in a ~** ne pas oublier qc dans sa hâte; **to leave in a ~** partir précipitamment

◆**hurry along I.** *vi* se dépêcher **II.** *vt* presser

◆**hurry away**, **hurry off I.** *vi* filer **II.** *vt* emmener en toute hâte

◆**hurry on I.** *vi* s'empresser **II.** *vt* presser

◆**hurry up I.** *vi* se dépêcher **II.** *vt* **to hurry sb up** faire presser qn; **to hurry sth up** activer qc

hurt [hɜːt, *Am:* hɜːrt] **I.** <hurt, hurt> *vi* faire mal; **my knee/stomach ~s** mon genou me fait mal/j'ai mal à l'estomac **II.** *vt* **1.** (*cause pain: person, animal*) blesser **2.** (*harm, damage: sb's feelings, pride*) heurter; **to ~ sb** blesser qn; **to ~ sth** abîmer qc **III.** *adj* blessé(e) **IV.** *n* **1.** (*pain*) douleur *f* **2.** (*injury*) blessure *f* **3.** (*offence*) offense *f*

hurtful *adj* blessant(e)

hurtle ['hɜːtl, *Am:* 'hɜːrt-] **I.** *vi* foncer; **to ~ down** dévaler **II.** *vt* précipiter

husband ['hʌzbənd] **I.** *n* mari *m* **II.** *vt* (*money*) bien gérer; **to ~ sb** être aux petits soins pour qn

husbandry ['hʌzbəndri] *n no pl* **1.** (*care, management*) **bad ~** mauvais traitements *mpl;* **good ~** bons soins *mpl* **2.** AGR **animal ~** élevage *m* (d'animaux)

hush [hʌʃ] **I.** *n no pl* silence *m;* **deathly ~** silence de mort; **a ~ fell** un silence glacial s'abattit **II.** *interj* chut! **III.** *vi* se taire **IV.** *vt* **1.** (*make quiet*) faire taire **2.** (*soothe*) calmer

◆**hush up** *vt pej* étouffer

hush-hush [ˌhʌʃ'hʌʃ] *adj inf* top secret(-ète)

hush money *n inf* prix *m* du silence

husk [hʌsk] **I.** *n* **1.** (*outside covering*) enveloppe *f* externe **2.** *Am* (*outside covering of maize*) son *m* du maïs **II.** *vt* décortiquer

husky¹ ['hʌski] <-ier, -iest> *adj* **1.** (*low, rough*) rauque; (*voice*) enroué(e) **2.** *Am* (*big, strong*) robuste

husky² ['hʌski] *n* husky *m* (sibérien)

hussy ['hʌsi] *n pej* fille *f* de joie

hustings ['hʌstɪŋz] *npl* propagande *f* préélectorale

hustle ['hʌsl] **I.** *vt* **1.** (*push*) pousser; **to ~ sb away** emmener qn de force; **to ~ sb into sth** pousser qn dans qc **2.** (*hurry*) presser **3.** (*jostle*) bousculer **4.** *inf* (*urge*) pousser; **to ~ sb into doing sth** pousser qn à faire qc **II.** *vi* **1.** (*hurry*) se presser **2.** *inf* (*practice prostitution*) faire le trottoir **3.** *Am, inf* (*swindle*) arnaquer **III.** *n* **1.** (*activity*) **~ (and bustle)** effervescence *f* **2.** *Am, inf* (*swindle*) arnaque *f*

hustler *n inf* **1.** *Am* (*swindler*) escroc *mf* **2.** (*prostitute*) tapineuse *f*

hut [hʌt] *n* **1.** (*small dwelling place*) cabane *f* **2.** (*garden shelter*) abri *m* de jardin **3.** (*temporary building*) baraque *f* **4.** (*mountain shelter*) refuge *m*

hutch [hʌtʃ] *n* **1.** (*box for animals*) cage *f;* (*for rabbits*) clapier *m* **2.** *pej* (*hut*) bicoque *f* **3.** (*cabinet, for dishes*) dressoir *m*

hyacinth ['haɪəsɪnθ] *n* jacinthe *f*

hyaena [haɪ'iːnə] *n s.* **hyena**

hybrid ['haɪbrɪd] *n* **1.** BOT, ZOOL hybride *m* **2.** (*something mixed*) croisement *m*

hydrangea [haɪ'dreɪndʒə] *n* hortensia *m*

hydrant ['haɪdrənt] *n* bouche *f* d'incendie

hydrate ['haɪdreɪt] *n* hydrate *m*

hydraulic [haɪ'drɒlɪk, *Am:* -'drɑːlɪk] *adj*

hydraulique **hydraulics** *n + sing vb* hydraulique *f*
hydrocarbon [ˌhaɪdrə'kɑːbən, *Am:* -droʊ-'kɑːr-] **I.** *n* hydrocarbure *m* **II.** *adj* d'hydrocarbure
hydrochloric acid [ˌhaɪdrəʊklɒrɪk'æsɪd, *Am:* -droʊklɔːrɪk'æsɪd] *n no pl* acide *m* chlorhydrique
hydroelectric [ˌhaɪdrəʊɪ'lektrɪk, *Am:* -droʊ-] *adj* hydroélectrique
hydrofoil ['haɪdrəfɔɪl, *Am:* -droʊ-] *n* hydroptère *m*
hydrogen ['haɪdrədʒən] *n no pl* hydrogène *m*
hydrogen bomb *n* bombe *f* à hydrogène **hydrogen peroxide** *n* eau *f* oxygénée **hydrogen sulphide** *n* hydrogène *m* sulfuré
hydrophobia [ˌhaɪdrə'fəʊbɪə, *Am:* -droʊ-'foʊ-] *n* **1.** *no pl* (*fear of water*) hydrophobie *f* **2.** (*rabies*) rage *f*
hyena [haɪ'iːnə] *n* hyène *f*
hygiene ['haɪdʒiːn] *n no pl* hygiène *f;* **personal** ~ hygiène corporelle
hygienic [haɪ'dʒiːnɪk, *Am:* ˌhaɪdʒi'enɪk] *adj* hygiénique
hygrometer ['haɪgrɒmətəʳ, *Am:* -grɑːmətɚ] *n* hygromètre *m*
hygroscope ['haɪgrəskəʊp, *Am:* -groʊs-koʊp] *n* hygroscope *m*
hymn [hɪm] *n* hymne *m*
hymnal, hymnbook *n* livre *m* de cantiques
hype [haɪp] **I.** *n no pl* battage *m* publicitaire **II.** *vt* faire du battage publicitaire pour
hyperactive *adj* hyperactif(-ive)
hyperbola [haɪ'pɜːbələ, *Am:* -'pɜːr-] *n* MAT hyperbole *f*
hyperbole [haɪ'pɜːbəli, *Am:* -'pɜːr-] *n no pl* LIT hyperbole *f*
hyperbolic *adj* hyperbolique
hypercritical *adj* exagérément *m* critique **hyperlink** *n* INFOR hyperlien *m* **hypermarket** *n* hypermarché *m* **hypersensitive** *adj* **1.** (*sensitive*) hypersensible; **to be ~ to sth** être hypersensible à qc **2.** (*touchy*) susceptible; **to be ~ about sth** être (très) susceptible au sujet de qc **hypertext I.** *n* INFOR hypertexte *m* **II.** *adj* INFOR hypertextuel(le)
hyphen ['haɪfn] *n* **1.** (*short line between two words*) trait *m* d'union **2.** (*short line at the end of a line*) tiret *m*
hyphenate ['haɪfəneɪt] *vt* lier
hypnosis [hɪp'nəʊsɪs, *Am:* -'noʊ-] *n no pl* hypnose *f*
hypnotherapy [ˌhɪpnə'θerəpi, *Am:* -noʊ'-] *n no pl* hypnothérapie *f*
hypnotic [hɪp'nɒtɪk, *Am:* -'nɑːt̬ɪk] *adj* hypnotique
hypnotist *n* hypnotiseur *m*
hypnotize ['hɪpnətaɪz] *vt* hypnotiser
hypochondria [ˌhaɪpə'kɒndrɪə, *Am:* -poʊ'kɑːn-] *n no pl* hypocondrie *f*
hypochondriac I. *n* hypocondriaque *mf* **II.** *adj* hypocondriaque
hypocrisy [hɪ'pɒkrəsi, *Am:* -'pɑːkrə-] *n no pl* hypocrisie *f*
hypocrite ['hɪpəkrɪt] *n* hypocrite *mf*
hypocritical *adj* hypocrite
hypodermic [ˌhaɪpə'dɜːmɪk, *Am:* -poʊ-'dɜːr-] *adj* hypodermique
hypotenuse [ˌhaɪ'pɒtənjuːz, *Am:* -'pɑː-tənuːs] *n* MAT hypoténuse *f*
hypothermia [ˌhaɪpə'θɜːmɪə, *Am:* -poʊ-'θɜːr-] *n no pl* hypothermie *f*
hypothesis [haɪ'pɒθəsɪs, *Am:* -'pɑːθə-] <-ses> *n* hypothèse *f*
hypothetical [ˌhaɪpə'θetɪkl, *Am:* -poʊ-'θet̬-] *adj* hypothétique; (*question*) théorique
hysteria [hɪ'stɪərɪə, *Am:* -'sterɪ-] *n no pl* hystérie *f*
hysteric [hɪ'sterɪk] **I.** *adj* hystérique **II.** *n* hystérique *mf*
hysterical *adj* surexcité(e)
Hz *n abbr of* **hertz** Hz *m*

I

I, i [aɪ] <-'s> *n* I *m,* i *m;* ~ **as in Isaac** *Brit,* ~ **as in Item** *Am,* ~ **for Isaac** *Brit,* ~ **for Item** *Am* (*on telephone*) i comme Irma
I *pers pron* (*1st person sing*) je, j' + *vowel;* **she and ~** elle et moi; **it was ~ who did that** c'est moi qui ai fait ça
IAEA *n abbr of* **International Atomic Energy Agency** AIEA *f*
IATA [aɪ'ɑːtə, *Am:* ˌaɪˌeɪˌtiː'eɪ] *n abbr of* **International Air Transport Association** IATA *f*
ibex ['aɪbeks] *n* bouquetin *m*
ibid. [ɪ'bɪd] *adv abbr of* **ibidem** (**in the same place**) ibid.
IC [ˌaɪ'siː] *n abbr of* **integrated circuit** circuit *m* intégré
i/c *abbr of* **in charge** (**of**) responsable (de)
ICBM [ˌaɪsiːbiː'em] *n abbr of* **intercontinental ballistic missile** missile *m* balistique intercontinental
ice [aɪs] **I.** *n* **1.** (*frozen water*) glace *f;* (*on road*) verglas *m;* **to put sth on ~** (*food, drink*) mettre qc à rafraîchir **2.** (*~ cube*) glaçons *mpl* **3.** (*~ cream*) glace *f* ►**to put sth on ~** geler qc; **to break the ~** rompre la glace; **to be skating on thin ~** avancer sur un terrain glissant **II.** *vt* glacer
ice age *n* période *f* glaciaire **ice axe** *n* piolet *m* **iceberg** *n* iceberg *m* **icebound** *adj* (*ship*) pris(e) par les glaces **icebox** *n* **1.** (*chilled box*) glacière *f* **2.** *Brit* (*freezer in fridge*) freezer *m* **ice-breaker** *n* brise-glace *m* **ice cap** *n* calotte *f* glaciaire **ice-cold** *adj* glacé(e) **ice cream** *n* crème *f* glacée **ice-cream maker** *n* sorbetière *f* **ice-cream**

parlour *n* glacier *m* **ice cube** *n* glaçon *m*
iced *adj* **1.** (*frozen*) gelé(e) **2.** (*cold: coffee, tea*) glacé(e); (*water*) avec des glaçons **3.** (*covered with icing*) glacé(e)
ice floe *n* banquise *f* **ice hockey** *n* hockey *m* sur glace
Iceland ['aɪslənd] *n* l'Islande *f*
Icelander *n* Islandais(e) *m(f)*
Icelandic **I.** *adj* islandais(e) **II.** *n* islandais *m; s. a.* **English**
ice lolly *n Brit* esquimau *m* (glacé) **ice pack** *n* **1.** (*cold pack for swelling*) vessie *f* de glace **2.** (*sea ice*) mer *f* de glace **ice pick** *n* pic *m* à glace **ice rink** *n* patinoire *f* **ice skate** **I.** *n* patin *m* à glace **II.** *vi* **ice-skate** patiner (sur la glace) **ice skating** *n* patinage *m* sur glace **ice tea** *n* thé *m* glacé **ice water** *n* eau *f* glacée
icicle ['aɪsɪkl] *n* **1.** (*directed upwards*) stalagmite *f* **2.** (*directed downwards*) stalactite *f*
icing *n* glaçage *m* ►**to be the ~ on the cake** *pej* être la cinquième roue du carrosse; (*unexpected extra*) être la cerise sur le gâteau
icing sugar *n* sucre *m* glace
icon ['aɪkɒn, *Am:* -kɑːn] *n* **1.** (*religious painting*) *a.* INFOR icône *f* **2.** (*sth famous or admired*) idole *f*
ICU [ˌaɪsiː'juː] *n abbr of* **intensive care unit** service *m* de soins intensifs
icy ['aɪsi] *adj* **1.** (*of ice, covered with ice*) glacé(e); (*road*) verglacé(e); (*ground*) gelé(e); **~ patches** plaques *fpl* de verglas **2.** (*very cold: wind*) glacial(e); (*feet, water*) glacé(e) **3.** *fig* (*unfriendly*) glacial(e)
I'd [aɪd] = **I would** *s.* **would**
ID *n* pièce *f* d'identité
Idaho ['aɪdəhəʊ, *Am:* -hoʊ] *n* l'Idaho *m*
ID card [aɪ'diːˌkɑːd] *n* carte *f* d'identité
idea [aɪ'dɪə, *Am:* -'diːə] *n* **1.** (*notion, opinion, suggestion, plan*) idée *f* **2.** (*conception*) conception *f;* **to not be sb's ~ of sth** ne pas être ce que qn appelle qc **3.** (*impression*) impression *f;* **to have an ~ that …** avoir l'impression que … **4.** (*purpose*) **the ~ behind sth** le but de qc; **with the ~ of doing sth** dans le but de faire qc ►**what an ~!** bonne idée!; **to not have the slightest ~** ne pas avoir la moindre idée; **the very ~!** quelle idée!
ideal [aɪ'dɪəl, *Am:* -'diː-] **I.** *adj* idéal(e) **II.** *n no pl* idéal *m*
idealise [aɪ'dɪəlaɪz, *Am:* -'diːə] *vt* idéaliser
idealism [aɪ'dɪəlɪzəm, *Am:* aɪ'diːə-] *n no pl* idéalisme *m*
idealist *n* idéaliste *mf*
idealistic *adj* idéaliste
idealize *vt Am s.* **idealise**
ideally [aɪ'dɪəli, *Am:* 'diːli] *adv* idéalement
identical [aɪ'dentɪkl, *Am:* -t̬ə-] *adj* identique; **~ twins** vrais jumeaux *mpl*
identifiable *adj* identifiable
identification [aɪˌdentɪfɪ'keɪʃən, *Am:* -t̬ə-] *n no pl* **1.** (*determination*) identification *f* **2.** (*ID*) pièce *f* d'identité
identification papers *npl* papiers *mpl* d'identité **identification parade** *n* séance *f* d'identification
identifier *n* INFOR identifiant *m*
identify [aɪ'dentɪfaɪ, *Am:* -t̬ə-] <-ied> **I.** *vt* identifier; (*car, house*) reconnaître; **to ~ oneself** décliner son identité; **to ~ oneself with sth** se reconnaître dans qc **II.** *vi* s'identifier; **to ~ with sb** s'identifier à qn; **to be ~ied with sth** être assimilé à qc
identikit® [aɪ'dentɪkɪt, *Am:* -t̬ə] *n Brit, Aus* **~ (picture)** portrait-robot *m*
identity [aɪ'dentəti, *Am:* -t̬ət̬i] *n* identité *f*
identity card *n* carte *f* d'identité
ideological *adj* idéologique
ideologist *n* idéaliste *mf*
ideology [ˌaɪdɪ'ɒlədʒi, *Am:* -'ɑːlə-] <-ies> *n* idéologie *f*
idiocy ['ɪdɪəsi] *n* idiotie *f*
idiom ['ɪdɪəm] *n* LING **1.** (*phrase with fixed meaning*) forme *f* idiomatique **2.** (*language*) idiome *m*
idiomatic [ˌɪdɪə'mætɪk, *Am:* -'mæt̬-] *adj* idiomatique
idiosyncratic [ˌɪdɪəʊsɪŋ'krætɪk, *Am:* -oʊsɪn'kræt̬-] *adj* particulier(-ère)
idiot ['ɪdɪət] *n* idiot(e) *m(f)*
idiotic *adj* bête
idle ['aɪdl] **I.** *adj* **1.** (*lazy, doing nothing*) oisif(-ive); **to lie ~** rester inactif **2.** (*not working, without action: person*) inactif(-ive); (*period*) d'inactivité; **in my ~ moments** à mes moments de loisir **3.** (*with nothing to do: person*) désœuvré(e); (*factory, machine*) à l'arrêt **4.** (*pointless, without purpose*) inutile; (*threat, talk*) en l'air; (*rumours, fear*) sans fondement; (*curiosity*) simple; **~ boast** bluff *m* **5.** FIN (*capital*) improductif(-ive) **II.** *vi* **1.** (*willingly do nothing*) paresser **2.** (*having nothing to do*) être inactif **3.** (*operate at slow speed: engine, machine*) tourner au ralenti; (*computer, disk drive, screen*) être en veille
idleness *n no pl* **1.** (*not acting, not operating*) inactivité *f* **2.** (*laziness*) oisiveté *f*
idler *n* paresseux, -euse *m, f*
idol ['aɪdl] *n* idole *f*
idolatrous [aɪ'dɒlətrəs, *Am:* -'dɑːlə-] *adj* REL idolâtre
idolatry [aɪ'dɒlətri, *Am:* -'dɑːlə-] *n* idolâtrie *f*
idolise *vt,* **idolize** ['aɪdəlaɪz] *vt Am* idolâtrer
IDP *n abbr of* **International Driving Permit** permis *m* de conduire international
idyll ['ɪdɪl, *Am:* 'aɪdəl] *n a. fig* idylle *f*
idyllic *adj* idyllique
i.e. [ˌaɪ'iː] *abbr of* **id est** c-à-d.
if [ɪf] **I.** *conj* **1.** si **2.** (*supposing that*) **~ it snows** s'il neige; **~ not** sinon; **as ~ it were true** comme si c'était vrai; **~ they exist at all** si tant est qu'ils existent; **~ A is right, then B is wrong** si A est juste, B est faux; **I'll stay, ~ only for a day** je reste, ne serait-ce qu'un jour **3.** (*every time that*) **~ he needs me, I'll help**

him s'il a besoin de moi, je l'aide **4.** (*whether*) **I wonder ~ he'll come** je me demande s'il viendra **5.** (*although*) **even ~** même si; **cold ~ sunny weather** un temps froid quoiqu'ensoleillé **II.** *n* si *m inv;* **no ~s and buts!** pas de si et de mais!

iffy ['ɪfi] <-ier, -iest> *adj inf* hasardeux(-euse)

igloo ['ɪglu:] *n* igloo *m*

igneous ['ɪgnɪəs] *adj* igné(e)

ignite [ɪg'naɪt] **I.** *vi a. fig* s'enflammer **II.** *vt form* **1.** (*cause to burn*) *a. fig* enflammer **2.** (*cause to break out*) provoquer

ignition [ɪg'nɪʃən] *n no pl* **1.** AUTO allumage *m;* **to switch the ~ on** démarrer **2.** AVIAT mise à feu *f* **3.** *form* (*causing to burn*) embrasement *m*

ignition coil *n* bobine *f* d'allumage **ignition key** *n* clé *f* de contact **ignition switch** *n* contact *m* de démarrage

ignominious [ˌɪgnə'mɪnɪəs] *adj* ignominieux(-euse)

ignominy ['ɪgnəmɪni] *n no pl* ignominie *f*

ignorance ['ɪgnərəns] *n no pl* ignorance *f*

ignorant *adj* ignorant(e)

ignore [ɪg'nɔ:ʳ, *Am:* -'nɔ:r] *vt* ignorer

iguana [ɪ'gwa:nə] *n* iguane *m*

ill [ɪl] **I.** *adj* **1.** (*sick*) malade; **to fall ~** tomber malade; **to feel ~** ne pas se sentir bien **2.** (*bad, harmful*) mauvais(e); (*effects*) néfaste; **~ fortune** malchance *f;* **~ will** malveillance *f* **II.** *adv* mal; **to be ~-chosen/-prepared** être mal choisi/préparé; **to speak/think ~ of sb** dire/penser du mal de qn; **to feel ~ at ease** se sentir mal à l'aise; **I can ~ afford sth** je peux difficilement me permettre qc; **it ~ behoves sb to** *+infin* cela va mal à qn de *+infin* **III.** *n* **1.** (*problem*) mal *m;* **the ~s of society** les maux de la société **2.** *pl* (*sick people*) **the ~** les malades *mpl* **3.** *no pl* (*evil*) mal *m;* **to wish sb ~** souhaiter du mal à qn

I'll [aɪl] = **I will** *s.* **will**

ill-advised *adj* malavisé(e); **to be ~ to** *+infin* ne pas avoir intérêt à *+infin* **ill-assorted** *adj Brit, Aus* mal assorti(e) **ill at ease** *adj* mal à l'aise **ill-bred** *adj* mal élevé(e) **ill-breeding** *n* mauvaise éducation *f*

illegal [ɪ'li:gəl] *adj* **1.** (*forbidden by the law*) illégal(e) **2.** (*forbidden by the law or moral rules*) illicite

illegality [ˌɪlɪ'gæləti, *Am:* -t̬i] *n* illégalité *f*

illegible [ɪ'ledʒəbl] *adj* illisible

illegitimate [ˌɪlɪ'dʒɪtɪmət, *Am:* -'dʒɪt̬ə-] *adj* **1.** (*not permitted according to law*) illégitime **2.** (*unauthorized*) illicite

ill-fated *adj* **1.** (*having bad luck*) malchanceux(-euse) **2.** (*bringing bad luck*) maléfique **ill-favoured** *adj* (*person*) tombé en disgrâce; (*object*) passé(e) de mode **ill-gotten gains** *npl* POL, ECON argent *m* sale

illiberal [ɪ'lɪbərəl] *adj form* **1.** *Am* (*unaccepting of new ideas*) intolérant(e) **2.** POL (*power*) totalitaire

illicit [ɪ'lɪsɪt] *adj* illicite

illimitable [ɪ'lɪmɪtəbl, *Am:* -t̬ə-] *adj* sans limites

ill-informed *adj* **1.** (*wrongly informed*) mal informé(e) **2.** (*not much informed*) peu informé(e)

Illinois [ˌɪlɪ'nɔɪ] *n* l'Illinois *m*

illiteracy [ɪ'lɪtərəsi, *Am:* -'lɪt̬-] *n no pl* illettrisme *m*

illiteracy rate *n* taux *m* d'illettrisme

illiterate [ɪ'lɪtərət, *Am:* -'lɪt̬-] **I.** *adj* **1.** (*unable to read or write*) analphabète **2.** (*uncultured, uneducated: person*) inculte; (*style*) incorrect(e) **3.** *pej* (*ignorant*) ignorant(e) **II.** *n* analphabète *mf*

ill-mannered *adj* (*person*) mal élevé(e); (*behavior*) grossier(-ère) **ill-natured** *adj* (*person*) qui a mauvais caractère; (*work*) ingrat(e)

illness *n* maladie *f*

illogical [ɪ'lɒdʒɪkl, *Am:* -'la:dʒɪ-] *adj* illogique

illogicality *n no pl* illogisme *m*

ill-omened *adj* **1.** (*bad boding*) de mauvais augure **2.** (*badly boded*) infortuné(e) **ill-starred** *adj* sous une mauvaise étoile **ill-tempered** *adj* **1.** (*by nature*) **to be ~** avoir mauvais caractère **2.** (*occasionally*) de mauvaise humeur **ill-timed** *adj* inopportun(e) **ill-treat** *vt* maltraiter **ill-treatment** *n* **1.** (*act of ill-treating*) maltraitance *f* **2.** (*result of ill-treating*) mauvais traitements *mpl*

illuminate [ɪ'lu:mɪneɪt, *Am:* -mə-] *vt* **1.** (*light up*) *a. fig* éclairer **2.** (*decorate with light*) illuminer **3.** ART (*manuscript*) enluminer

illuminating *adj a. fig* éclairant(e)

illumination *n* **1.** *no pl, form* (*light*) éclairage *m;* (*of building*) illumination *f* **2.** *pl* (*light decoration*) illuminations *fpl* **3.** *no pl* (*decoration of books with gold*) enluminure *f* **4.** *no pl, fig* (*clarification*) éclaircissement *m*

illusion [ɪ'lu:ʒən, *Am:* -'lu:-] *n* illusion *f;* **to have no ~s about sth** ne pas se faire d'illusions sur qc; **to labor under the ~ that ...** s'imaginer que ...

illusionist *n* illusionniste *mf*

illusive [ɪ'lu:sɪv], **illusory** *adj* illusoire

illustrate ['ɪləstreɪt] *vt* illustrer

illustration *n* **1.** (*drawing*) illustration *f* **2.** (*example*) exemple *m*

illustrative ['ɪləstrətɪv, *Am:* ɪ'lʌstrət̬ɪv] *adj form* caractéristique

illustrator *n* illustrateur, -trice *m, f*

illustrious [ɪ'lʌstrɪəs] *adj* illustre

ill-conceived *adj* mal préparé(e)

illegal immigrant *n* immigré *m* clandestin

ill-equipped *adj* mal équipé(e) **ill-fitting** *adj* mal ajusté(e) **ill-gotten** *adj* mal acquis(e) **ill will** *n* malveillance *f*

ILO *n abbr of* **International Labour Organisation** OIT *f*

I'm [aɪm] = **I am** *s.* **am**

image ['ɪmɪdʒ] *n* **1.** (*likeness*) ressemblance *f;* **to be the living ~ of sb** être le portrait vivant de qn; **it is the spitting ~ of him** c'est lui tout craché **2.** (*picture*) image *f* **3.** (*reputation*) image *f* de marque

imagery ['ɪmɪdʒəri] *n no pl* LIT imagerie *f*

imaginable *adj* imaginable

imaginary [ɪ'mædʒɪnəri, *Am:* -əner-] *adj* imaginaire

imagination [ɪˌmædʒɪ'neɪʃən] *n* imagination *f;* **not by any stretch of the** ~ pas même en rêve; **to capture sb's** ~ passionner qc; **to leave nothing to the** ~ ne rien laisser deviner

imaginative [ɪ'mædʒɪnətɪv, *Am:* -t̬ɪv] *adj* ingénieux(-euse)

imagine [ɪ'mædʒɪn] *vt* imaginer; **to be ~ing things** s'imaginer des choses; ~ **that!** tu penses!

imbalance [ˌɪm'bæləns] *n* déséquilibre *m*

imbecile ['ɪmbəsiːl, *Am:* -sɪl] *n* **1.** (*stupid person*) imbécile *mf* **2.** (*sb born with a weak mind*) crétin(e) *m(f)*

imbecility [ˌɪmbə'sɪləti, *Am:* -t̬i] *n* imbécillité *f*

imbibe [ɪm'baɪb] *vt* **1.** *form* (*absorb*) absorber **2.** *iron* (*drink*) boire **3.** *fig* (*take in: ideas*) assimiler

imbue [ɪm'bjuː] *vt form* **to** ~ **with sth** imprégner de qc

IMF [ˌaɪem'ef] *n no pl abbr of* **International Monetary Fund** FMI *m*

imitate ['ɪmɪtəɪt] *vt* imiter

imitation **I.** *n* **1.** *no pl* (*mimicry*) mimique *f;* (*of voices*) imitation *f;* **in** ~ **of sb/sth** en imitant qn/qc **2.** (*copy*) copie *f* **II.** *adj* faux(fausse); ~ **leather** skaï *m*

imitative ['ɪmɪtətɪv, *Am:* -teɪt̬ɪv] *adj* imitatif(-ive)

imitator ['ɪmɪtətəʳ, *Am:* -t̬ɚ] *n* imitateur, -trice *m, f*

immaculate [ɪ'mækjʊlət] *adj* **1.** REL, LIT immaculé(e) **2.** (*flawless*) impeccable

immanence ['ɪmənəns] *n no pl* immanence *f*

immanent *adj* immanent(e); **to be** ~ **in sth** être immanent à qc

immaterial [ˌɪmə'tɪərɪəl, *Am:* -'tɪrɪ-] *adj* **1.** (*unimportant*) insignifiant(e); **it's** ~ c'est sans aucune importance **2.** *a.* PHILOS immatériel(le)

immature [ˌɪmə'tjʊəʳ, *Am:* -'tʊr] *adj* **1.** (*not developed: people, animals*) immature; (*sexually*) sans expérience; (*fruit*) vert(e) **2.** *pej* (*childish*) immature

immaturity *n no pl* immaturité *f*

immeasurable [ɪ'meʒərəbl] *adj* **1.** (*too large to measure*) incommensurable; (*time*) infini(e) **2.** *fig* énorme; (*effect*) incalculable

immediacy [ɪ'miːdɪəsi] *n no pl* caractère *m* immédiat; (*of problem*) imminence *f*

immediate [ɪ'miːdɪət, *Am:* -diɪt] *adj* **1.** (*instant*) immédiat(e); (*danger*) imminent(e); **to take** ~ **effect/action** prendre effet/agir immédiatement **2.** (*nearest*) proche; (*area, vicinity*) immédiat(e); **the** ~ **family** les proches parents **3.** (*direct: cause*) direct(e)

immediately **I.** *adv* **1.** (*at once*) immédiatement; ~ **after** aussitôt après **2.** (*closely*) ~ **after sth** juste après qc **II.** *conj Brit* dès que

immense [ɪ'mens] *adj* immense; (*importance*) considérable

immensely *adv* énormément

immensity [ɪ'mensəti, *Am:* -t̬i] *n no pl* immensité *f;* (*of task*) énormité *f*

immerse [ɪ'mɜːs, *Am:* -'mɜːrs] *vt* **1.** PHYS immerger **2.** *fig* **to be ~d in sth** être absorbé dans qc

immersion [ɪ'mɜːʃən, *Am:* -'mɜːr-] *n no pl* **1.** PHYS immersion *f* **2.** *fig* absorption *f*

immersion heater *n* chauffe-eau *m* électrique

immigrant ['ɪmɪgrənt] *n* immigrant(e) *m(f);* ~ **family** famille *f* immigrée

immigrate ['ɪmɪgreɪt] *vi* immigrer

immigration *n no pl* immigration *f;* ~ **control** services *mpl* de l'immigration

imminence ['ɪmɪnəns] *n no pl* imminence *f*

imminent *adj* imminent(e)

immobile [ɪ'məʊbaɪl, *Am:* -'moʊbl] *adj* **1.** (*not moving*) immobile **2.** (*fixed*) fixe

immobilise [ɪ'məʊbəlaɪz, *Am:* -'moʊ-] *vt* immobiliser

immobility [ˌɪmə'bɪləti, *Am:* -moʊ'bɪlət̬i] *n no pl* immobilité *f*

immobilize *vt Am s.* **immobilise**

immoderate [ɪ'mɒdərət, *Am:* -'mɑːdɚ-] *adj* immodéré(e); (*demand*) excessif(-ive); ~ **drinking** abus *m* d'alcool

immodest [ɪ'mɒdɪst, *Am:* -'mɑːdɪst] *adj pej* **1.** (*conceited*) prétentieux(-euse) **2.** (*indecent*) impudique

immolate ['ɪməleɪt] *vt form* immoler

immoral [ɪ'mɒrəl, *Am:* -'mɔːr-] *adj* immoral(e)

immortal [ɪ'mɔːtl, *Am:* -'mɔːrt̬l] **I.** *adj* **1.** (*undying*) immortel(le) **2.** (*unforgettable*) éternel(le) **II.** *n* immortel(le) *m(f)*

immortalise [ɪ'mɔːtəlaɪz, *Am:* -'mɔːrt̬ə-] *vt* immortaliser

immortality [ˌɪmɔː'tæləti, *Am:* -ɔːr'tælət̬i] *n no pl* immortalité *f*

immortalize *vt Am s.* **immortalise**

immovable [ɪ'muːvəbl] **I.** *adj* **1.** (*immobile*) fixe **2.** *fig* (*invariable*) inébranlable; (*person*) inflexible **3.** LAW (*property*) immobilier(-ère) **II.** *n* biens *mpl* immobiliers

immune [ɪ'mjuːn] *adj* **1.** MED (*person*) immunisé(e); (*system, deficiency, reaction*) immunitaire; **to be** ~ **to sth** être immunisé contre qc **2.** (*not vulnerable*) insensible; ~ **to nasty remarks** imperméable aux méchancetés **3.** (*protected, exempt*) **to be** ~ **from sth** être à l'abri de qc; (*taxation*) être exonéré de qc

immune system *n* système *m* immunitaire

immunise ['ɪmjənaɪz] *vt* immuniser

immunity [ɪ'mjuːnəti, *Am:* -t̬i] *n no pl* MED, LAW immunité *f*

immunize *vt Am s.* **immunise**

immunological [ˌɪmjʊnəʊ'lɒdʒɪkl, *Am:*

-jənoʊ'lɑːdʒɪ-] *adj* immunologique
immunologist *n* immunologiste *mf*
immure [ɪ'mjʊəʳ, *Am:* -'mjʊr] *vt fig* enfermer
immutable [ɪ'mjuːtəbl, *Am:* -t̬ə-] *adj* immuable
imp [ɪmp] *n a. pej* diablotin *m*
impact ['ɪmpækt] **I.** *n no pl, a. fig* impact *m;* **on** ~ à l'arrivée **II.** *vt Am, Aus* **1.** (*hit*) heurter **2.** *fig* avoir un impact sur **III.** *vi Am, Aus* **to** ~ **on sb/sth** avoir un impact sur qn/qc
impacted *adj* MED avec impaction
impair [ɪm'peəʳ, *Am:* -'per] *vt* (*chance, relations*) compromettre; (*health, abilities*) détériorer; (*hearing*) affaiblir; (*mind, strength*) diminuer
impaired *adj* (*vision, mobility*) réduit(e); **hearing-~ person** personne *f* malentendante
impale [ɪm'peɪl] *vt* empaler
impalpable [ɪm'pælpəbl] *adj* impalpable
impart [ɪm'pɑːt, *Am:* -'pɑːrt] *vt* donner; (*knowledge*) transmettre
impartial [ɪm'pɑːʃl, *Am:* -'pɑːr-] *adj* impartial(e)
impartiality *n no pl* impartialité *f*
impassable *adj a. fig* infranchissable
impasse ['æmpɑːs, *Am:* 'ɪmpæs] *n no pl, a. fig* impasse *f*
impassioned [ɪm'pæʃnd] *adj* passionné(e)
impassive [ɪm'pæsɪv] *adj* impassible
impatience [ɪm'peɪʃns] *n no pl* impatience *f*
impatient *adj* impatient(e)
impeach [ɪm'piːtʃ] *vt Am* POL, LAW mettre en accusation; **to ~ sb for sth** limoger qn pour qc
impeachment *n* **1.** LAW mise *f* en accusation **2.** *Am* POL impeachment *m*
impeccable [ɪm'pekəbl] *adj* impeccable; (*manners*) irréprochable
impecunious [ˌɪmpɪ'kjuːnɪəs] *adj form* impécunieux(-euse)
impede [ɪm'piːd] *vt* gêner
impediment [ɪm'pedɪmənt] *n* **1.** (*hindrance*) entrave *f;* **an ~ to success** un obstacle à la réussite **2.** MED dysfonctionnement *m;* **speech** ~ troubles *mpl* de l'élocution
impel [ɪm'pel] <-ll-> *vt* **1.** (*drive*) **to ~ sb to** +*infin* pousser qn à +*infin* **2.** (*force*) forcer; **to feel ~led to** +*infin* se sentir obligé de +*infin*
impending [ɪm'pendɪŋ] *adj* imminent(e)
impenetrable [ɪm'penɪtrəbl] *adj* **1.** (*impossible to pass through*) impénétrable; (*fog*) à couper au couteau **2.** *fig* (*impossible to understand*) incompréhensible
impenitent [ɪm'penɪtənt, *Am:* -ətənt] *adj form* impénitent(e); **to be ~ about sth** ne pas se repentir du tout de qc
imperative [ɪm'perətɪv, *Am:* -t̬ɪv] **I.** *adj a.* LING impératif(-ive); **it is ~ that** il est indispensable que +*subj* **II.** *n* **1.** (*essential thing*) impératif *m* **2.** *no pl* LING **the** ~ l'impératif *m*
imperceptible [ˌɪmpə'septəbl, *Am:* -pɚ'septə-] *adj* imperceptible
imperfect [ɪm'pɜːfɪkt, *Am:* -'pɜːr-] **I.** *adj* **1.** (*not perfect*) imparfait(e) **2.** (*flawed*) défectueux(-euse) **3.** (*not sufficient*) insuffisant(e) **4.** (*not finished*) inachevé(e) **II.** *n no pl* LING **the** ~ l'imparfait *m*
imperfection *n* **1.** (*flaw*) défaut *m* **2.** *no pl* (*lack of perfection*) imperfection *f*
imperial [ɪm'pɪəriəl, *Am:* -'pɪr-] *adj* **1.** HIST impérial(e); **Imperial Rome/China** Rome/la Chine impériale **2.** (*British*) de l'Empire (britannique); (*measure*) ayant cours au Royaume-Uni
imperialism [ɪm'pɪəriəlɪzəm, *Am:* -'pɪrɪ-] *n no pl, pej* impérialisme *m*
imperialist **I.** *n pej* impérialiste *mf* **II.** *adj* impérialiste
imperialistic *adj* impérialiste
imperil [ɪm'perəl] <-ll- *Aus, Brit,* -l- *Am*> *vt form* mettre en péril
imperious [ɪm'pɪərɪəs, *Am:* -'pɪrɪ-] *adj* **1.** (*bossy*) tyrannique **2.** (*arrogant*) impérieux(-euse)
imperishable [ɪm'perɪʃəbl] *adj* impérissable
impermanent [ɪm'pɜːmənənt, *Am:* -'pɜːr-] *adj* temporaire
impermeable [ɪm'pɜːmɪəbl, *Am:* -'pɜːr-] *adj a. fig* (*cloth, material*) imperméable; (*wall*) étanche; ~ **to sth** étanche à qc
impersonal [ˌɪm'pɜːsənl, *Am:* -'pɜːr-] *adj* **1.** PSYCH détaché(e) **2.** LING impersonnel(le)
impersonate [ɪm'pɜːsəneɪt, *Am:* -'pɜːr-] *vt* **1.** (*imitate*) imiter **2.** (*pretend to be*) se faire passer pour
impersonator *n* **1.** THEAT imitateur *m* **2.** LAW imposteur *m*
impertinent [ɪm'pɜːtɪnənt, *Am:* -'pɜːrt̬n-] *adj* impertinent(e)
imperturbable [ˌɪmpə'tɜːbəbl, *Am:* -pɚ'tɜːr-] *adj form* imperturbable
impervious [ɪm'pɜːvɪəs, *Am:* -'pɜːr-] *adj* **1.** PHYS imperméable; ~ **to fire/water** résistant au feu/à l'eau **2.** PSYCH indifférent(e)
impetuous [ɪm'petʃʊəs, *Am:* -'petʃu-] *adj* impétueux(-euse); (*action*) impulsif(-ive)
impetus ['ɪmpɪtəs, *Am:* -t̬əs] *n no pl* élan *m;* **commercial** ~ essor *m* commercial
impiety [ɪm'paɪəti, *Am:* -t̬i] *n no pl, a. fig* sacrilège *m*
impinge [ɪm'pɪndʒ] *vi* **1.** (*restrict*) empiéter **2.** (*affect*) **to ~ on sb** affecter qn
impious ['ɪmpɪəs] *adj* impie
impish ['ɪmpɪʃ] *adj* espiègle
implacable [ɪm'plækəbl] *adj form* implacable; (*thirst*) insatiable
implacably *adv form* implacablement
implant [ɪm'plɑːnt, *Am:* -'plænt] **I.** *n* implant *m* **II.** *vt* **1.** MED greffer **2.** PSYCH inculquer
implausible [ɪm'plɔːzɪbl, *Am:* -'plɑː-] *adj* peu plausible
implement¹ ['ɪmplɪmənt] *n* **1.** (*tool*) instrument *m;* **farming ~s** outillage *m* agricole **2.** (*small tool*) ustensile *m*
implement² ['ɪmplɪment] *vt* **1.** (*put into effect*) exécuter; (*plan, law, agreement*)

I

mettre en application **2.** INFOR implémenter

implementation *n* **1.** *no pl* (*executing*) exécution *f* **2.** INFOR implémentation *f*

implicate ['ɪmplɪkeɪt] *vt* impliquer

implication *n* implication *f;* **by ~** implicitement

implicit [ɪm'plɪsɪt] *adj* **1.** (*suggested*) implicite; (*agreement*) tacite **2.** (*total*) absolu(e)

implied [ɪm'plaɪd] *adj* implicite

implode [ɪm'pləʊd, *Am:* -'ploʊd] *vi* **1.** (*collapse*) imploser **2.** *fig* s'écrouler

implore [ɪm'plɔːʳ, *Am:* -'plɔːr] *vt* implorer; **to ~ sb to** *+infin* supplier qn de *+infin*

imploring *adj* implorant(e)

implosion [ɪm'pləʊʒən, *Am:* -'ploʊ-] *n no pl, a. fig* implosion *f*

imply [ɪm'plaɪ] <-ie-> *vt* **1.** (*suggest*) sous-entendre **2.** (*mean*) impliquer

impolite [ˌɪmpə'laɪt] *adj* impoli(e)

impoliteness *n no pl* **1.** (*lack of good manners*) impolitesse *f* **2.** (*rudeness*) grossièreté *f*

impolitic [ɪm'pɒlətɪk, *Am:* -'pɑːlə-] *adj* imprudent(e)

imponderable [ɪm'pɒndərəbl, *Am:* -'pɑːn-] **I.** *adj* impondérable **II.** *n* impondérable *m*

import [ɪm'pɔːt, *Am:* -'pɔːrt] **I.** *vt* importer **II.** *n* **1.** (*good*) importation *f* **2.** *no pl* (*significance*) importance *f*

importance [ɪm'pɔːtənts, *Am:* -'pɔːr-] *n no pl* importance *f*

important *adj* **1.** (*significant*) important(e); (*event*) capital(e); **it is ~ that** il est important que *+subj* **2.** (*influential: person*) influent(e)

importantly *adv* d'un air important

importation [ˌɪmpɔː'teɪʃən, *Am:* -pɔːr'-] *n no pl* ECON importation *f*

import duty <-ies> *n* taxe *f* à l'importation

importunate [ɪm'pɔːtʃʊnət, *Am:* -'pɔːrtʃənɪt] *adj form* importun(e)

importune [ˌɪmpə'tjuːn, *Am:* ˌɪmpɔːr'tuːn] *vt form* **1.** (*ask persistently*) importuner **2.** LAW racoler

impose [ɪm'pəʊz, *Am:* -'poʊz] **I.** *vt* imposer; **to ~ sth on sb** infliger qc à qn; **to ~ a tax on sth** taxer qc **II.** *vi* s'imposer; **to ~ on sb's patience** abuser de la patience de qn

imposing *adj* imposant(e)

imposition [ˌɪmpə'zɪʃən] *n* **1.** *no pl* (*of sanctions*) application *f* **2.** *fig* dérangement *m*

impossibility [ɪmˌpɒsə'bɪləti, *Am:* -ˌpɑːsə'bɪləṭi] *n* impossibilité *f*

impossible [ɪm'pɒsəbl, *Am:* -'pɑːsə-] **I.** *adj a. fig* impossible; (*problem*) insoluble; **it is ~ that** il est impossible que *+subj* **II.** *n no pl* **the ~** l'impossible *m*

impossibly *adv* incroyablement

imposter, **impostor** [ɪm'pɒstəʳ, *Am:* -'pɑːstɚ] *n* imposteur *m*

impotence ['ɪmpətəns, *Am:* -ṭəns] *n no pl* **1.** MED impuissance *f* **2.** *fig* faiblesse *f*

impotent *adj* **1.** MED impuissant **2.** *fig* faible

impound [ɪm'paʊnd] *vt* confisquer

impoverish [ɪm'pɒvərɪʃ, *Am:* -'pɑːvɚ-] *vt* appauvrir

impoverished *adj* appauvri(e)

impracticable *adj* impraticable

impractical [ɪm'præktɪkl] *adj* **1.** (*not skilled: person*) qui manque d'esprit pratique **2.** (*not adapted for use or action*) pas pratique; (*high heels*) importable **3.** (*not sensible, unrealistic: plan*) irréalisable; (*idea*) peu réaliste **4.** *Am* (*impracticable*) impraticable

imprecation [ˌɪmprɪ'keɪʃən] *n form* imprécation *f*

imprecise [ˌɪmprɪ'saɪs] *adj* imprécis(e)

impregnable [ɪm'pregnəbl] *adj* **1.** MIL imprenable **2.** *Aus, Brit, fig* inattaquable

impregnate ['ɪmpregneɪt, *Am:* ɪm'preg-] *vt* **1.** BIO féconder **2.** (*make absorb*) imbiber

impresario [ˌɪmprɪ'sɑːrɪəʊ, *Am:* -prə'sɑːrɪoʊ] *n* impresario *m*

impress [ɪm'pres] **I.** *vt* **1.** (*stamp*) imprimer **2.** (*affect*) impressionner; **I'm not ~ed by that** ça me laisse froid; **sth is ~ed on sb's memory** qc est gravé dans la mémoire de qn **3.** (*make realize*) **to ~ sth on sb** faire comprendre qc à qn **II.** *vi* faire impression

impression [ɪm'preʃən] *n* **1.** (*idea*) impression *f* **2.** (*effect*) impression *f;* **to create a good ~** faire une bonne impression; **to make an ~ on sb** faire de l'effet à qn **3.** (*imitation*) imitation *f* **4.** (*imprint*) empreinte *f* **5.** TYP tirage *m*

impressionable *adj pej* influençable; **~ age** âge où l'on se laisse influencer

impressionism [ɪm'preʃnɪzəm] *n no pl* impressionnisme *m*

impressionist **I.** *n* **1.** MUS, ART impressionniste *mf* **2.** (*imitator*) imitateur, -trice *m, f* **II.** *adj* impressionniste

impressionistic *adj* impressionniste

impressive [ɪm'presɪv] *adj* impressionnant(e); (*spectacle*) saisissant(e)

imprint[1] [ɪm'prɪnt] *vt* **1.** (*stamp*) imprimer; (*coins*) graver; **to ~ a seal** marquer d'un sceau **2.** *fig* (*on the memory*) graver

imprint[2] ['ɪmprɪnt] *n* **1.** (*mark*) empreinte *f* **2.** TYP **publisher's ~** marque *f* d'éditeur **3.** *fig* trace *f*

imprison [ɪm'prɪzən] *vt* emprisonner

imprisonment *n no pl* emprisonnement *m,* collocation *f Belgique*

improbability *n no pl* invraisemblance *f*

improbable [ɪm'prɒbəbl, *Am:* -'prɑːbə-] *adj* improbable; **an ~-sounding excuse** une excuse invraisemblable; **it is ~ that he will come** il est peu probable qu'il vienne

impromptu [ɪm'prɒmptjuː, *Am:* -'prɑːmptuː] *adj* impromptu(e); **to make an ~ speech** improviser un discours

improper [ɪm'prɒpəʳ, *Am:* -'prɑːpɚ] *adj* **1.** (*not suitable*) incorrect(e); (*behaviour*) malséant(e); (*use*) abusif(-ive); **to make ~ use of sth** faire mauvais usage de qc **2.** (*indecent*) inconvenant(e); (*suggestion*) indécent(e); (*remark*) déplacé(e)

impropriety [ˌɪmprəˈpraɪəti, *Am:* -t̬i] <-ies> *n* **1.** (*improper doings*) inconvenance *f* **2.** (*indecency*) indécence *f*

improve [ɪmˈpruːv] **I.** *vt* améliorer **II.** *vi* s'améliorer; (*wine*) se bonifier

◆**improve on** *vi* perfectionner

improvement *n* **1.** (*betterment*) amélioration *f;* (*of machine*) perfectionnement *m;* **to be an ~ on sb/sth** être supérieur à qn/qc **2.** *no pl* (*betterment*) progrès *m;* (*of illness*) amélioration *f* **3.** (*increase in value*) revalorisation *f*

improvident [ɪmˈprɒvɪdənt, *Am:* -ˈprɑːvə-] *adj form* **1.** (*not planning*) imprévoyant(e) **2.** (*opp: thrifty*) dépensier(-ère)

improvisation *n* improvisation *f*

improvise [ˈɪmprəvaɪz] **I.** *vt* improviser; **to ~ a speech** faire un discours impromptu **II.** *vi* improviser

imprudent [ɪmˈpruːdnt] *adj* imprudent(e)

impudence [ˈɪmpjʊdəns] *n no pl* impudence *f*

impudent *adj* impertinent(e)

impugn [ɪmˈpjuːn] *vt form* contester

impulse [ˈɪmpʌls] *n* **1.** (*urge*) élan *m;* **an ~ of curiosity** une soudaine curiosité; **to do sth on (an) ~** faire qc sur un coup de tête; **to have a sudden ~ to** +*infin* avoir subitement envie de +*infin* **2.** ELEC, PHYS impulsion *f* **3.** ANAT influx *m* nerveux **4.** (*motive*) **the ~ behind sth** la raison qui se cache derrière qc

impulsion *n s.* **impulse**

impulsive [ɪmˈpʌlsɪv] *adj* impulsif(-ive)

impunity [ɪmˈpjuːnəti, *Am:* -t̬i] *n no pl* impunité *f*

impure [ɪmˈpjʊəʳ, *Am:* -ˈpjʊr] *adj* impur(e)

impurity <-ies> *n* impureté *f*

imputation *n form* imputation *f*

impute [ɪmˈpjuːt] *vt* **to ~ sth to sb** imputer qc à qn

in [ɪn] **I.** *prep* **1.** (*inside, into*) dans; **to be ~ bed** être au lit; **sitting ~ the window** assis devant la fenêtre; **gun ~ hand** revolver au poing; **to put sth ~ sb's hands** remettre qc entre les mains de qn; **~ town/jail** en ville/prison; **~ the country/hospital** à la campagne/l'hôpital; **~ France/Burgundy/Tokyo/Cyprus** en France/Bourgogne/à Tokyo/Chypre; **~ Peru/the West Indies/the Loiret** au Pérou/aux Antilles/dans le Loiret **2.** (*within*) **~ sb's face/the picture** sur le visage de qn/l'image; **~ the snow/sun** sous la neige/au soleil; **the best ~ France/town** le meilleur de France/la ville; **to find sth ~ Joyce** trouver qc chez Joyce; **to find a friend ~ sb** trouver un ami en qn **3.** (*position of*) **~ the beginning/end** au début/à la fin; **right ~ the middle** en plein milieu **4.** (*during*) **~ the twenties** dans les années vingt; **to be ~ one's thirties** avoir la trentaine; **~ the reign of Caesar** sous le règne de César; **~ those days** à cette époque-là; **~ May/spring** en mai/au printemps; **~ the afternoon** (dans) l'après-midi; **at 11 ~ the morning** à 11 h du matin; **see you ~ the morning** à demain matin **5.** (*at later time*) **~ a week/three hours** dans une semaine/trois heures; **~ (the) future** à l'avenir **6.** (*within a period*) **to do sth ~ 4 hours** faire qc en 4 heures **7.** (*for*) **he hasn't done that ~ years/a week** il n'a pas fait ça depuis des années/de toute une semaine **8.** (*in situation, state, manner of*) **~ fashion** à la mode; **~ search of sb/sth** à la recherche de qn/qc; **~ this way** de cette manière; **~ anger** sous l'effet de la colère; **~ fun/earnest** pour rire/de bon; **to be ~ a hurry** être pressé; **to be/fall ~ love with sb** être/tomber amoureux de qn; **~ alphabetical order** par ordre alphabétique; **to write ~ ink/pencil** écrire à l'encre/au crayon; **written ~ black and white** écrit noir sur blanc; **dressed ~ red** vêtu de rouge **9.** (*concerning*) **deaf ~ one ear** sourd d'une oreille; **to be interested ~ sth** s'intéresser à qc; **to have faith ~ God** croire en Dieu; **to have confidence ~ sb** avoir confiance en qn; **to have a say ~ the matter** avoir voix au chapitre; **a change ~ attitude** un changement d'attitude; **a rise ~ prices** une augmentation des prix; **it's rare ~ apes** c'est rare chez les singes **10.** (*by*) **~ saying sth** en disant qc; **to spend one's time ~ doing sth** passer son temps à faire qc **11.** (*taking the form of*) **to speak ~ French** parler (en) français; **~ the form of a request** sous forme de demande **12.** (*made of*) **~ wood/stone** en bois/pierre **13.** (*sound of*) **~ a whisper** en chuchotant; **to speak ~ a loud/low voice** parler à voix haute/basse; **to answer ~ a soft voice/a pedantic tone** répondre d'une voix douce/sur un ton pédant **14.** (*aspect of*) **2 metres ~ length/height** 2 mètres de long/haut; **~ every respect** à tous points de vue **15.** (*ratio*) **two ~ six** deux sur six; **to buy sth ~ twos** acheter qc par deux; **once ~ ten years** une fois tous les dix ans; **10 ~ number** au nombre de 10; **~ part** en partie; **~ tens** par dizaines **16.** (*substitution of*) **~ sb's place** à la place de qn; **~ lieu of sth** en guise de qc **17.** (*as consequence of*) **~ return/reply** en échange/réponse ►**~ heaven's name!** au nom du Ciel!; **~ all** (*all together*) en tout; **all ~ all** en général; **to be ~ and out of sth** ne cesser d'entrer et de sortir de qc **II.** *adv* (*to a place*) **to be ~** être là; (*at home*) être à la maison; (*in jail*) être en prison ►**to be ~ for sth** *inf* être bon pour qc; **~ on sth** au courant de qc; *s. a.* **in between III.** *adj* (*popular*) dans le vent; **to be ~** être à la mode; *s. a.* **out IV.** *n* **the ~s and outs** les tenants et les aboutissants

in [ɪn] *n abbr of* **inch** pouce *m*

inability [ˌɪnəˈbɪləti, *Am:* -t̬i] *n no pl* incapacité *f*

inaccessible [ˌɪnækˈsesəbl] *adj* inaccessible

inaccuracy [ɪnˈækjʊrəsi, *Am:* -jɚə-] <-ies>

I

n inexactitude *f*

inaccurate [ɪn'ækjərət, *Am:* -jɚət] *adj* inexact(e)

inaction [ɪn'ækʃən] *n no pl* inaction *f;* (*of person*) passivité *f*

inactive [ɪn'æktɪv] *adj* inactif(-ive)

inactivity [ˌɪnæk'tɪvəti, *Am:* -t̬i] *n no pl* inactivité *f*

inadequacy [ɪn'ædɪkwəsi] <-ies> *n* **1.** (*insufficiency*) insuffisance *f* **2.** (*defect*) imperfection *f*

inadequate [ɪn'ædɪkwət] *adj* inadéquat(e); **woefully ~** tristement inapte; **to feel ~** ne pas se sentir à la hauteur

inadmissible [ˌɪnəd'mɪsəbl] *adj* inadmissible; **~ evidence** preuves *fpl* irrecevables

inadvertent [ˌɪnəd'vɜːtənt, *Am:* -əd'vɜːr-] *adj* commis(e) par inadvertance

inadvisable [ˌɪnəd'vaɪzəbl] *adj* inopportun(e); **it is ~ to** *+infin* il est déconseillé de *+infin*

inalienable [ɪn'eɪlɪənəbl] *adj form* inaliénable

inane [ɪ'neɪn] *adj* bête

inanimate [ɪn'ænɪmət] *adj* inanimé(e)

inanity [ɪ'nænəti, *Am:* -t̬i] <-ies> *n* ineptie *f*

inapplicable [ɪn'æplɪkəbl] *adj* inapplicable

inappropriate [ˌɪnə'prəʊprɪət, *Am:* -'proʊ-] *adj* inapproprié(e)

inapt [ɪn'æpt] *adj* inapte

inaptitude [ɪn'æptɪtjuːd, *Am:* -tətuːd] *n no pl* inaptitude *f*

inarticulate [ˌɪnɑː'tɪkjʊlət, *Am:* -ɑːr'-] *adj* **1.** (*unable to express oneself*) **to be ~** être incapable de s'exprimer **2.** (*unclear*) incompréhensible

inartistic [ˌɪnɑː'tɪstɪk, *Am:* -ɑːr'-] *adj* **to be ~** n'avoir aucun sens artistique

inasmuch as [ˌɪnəz'mʌtʃ əz] *conj form* **1.** (*because*) puisque **2.** (*to the extent that*) étant donné que; *s. a.* **insofar as**

inattention [ˌɪnə'tenʃən] *n no pl* manque *m* d'attention

inattentive [ˌɪnə'tentɪv, *Am:* -t̬ɪv] *adj* inattentif(-ive)

inaudible [ɪn'ɔːdəbl, *Am:* -'ɑː-] *adj* inaudible

inaugural [ɪ'nɔːgjʊrəl, *Am:* -'nɑːg-] *adj* inaugural(e)

inaugurate [ɪ'nɔːgjʊreɪt, *Am:* -'nɑːg-] *vt* **1.** (*open*) inaugurer **2.** *Am* (*induct into office*) investir de ses fonctions

inauguration *n* **1.** *no pl* (*opening*) inauguration *f* **2.** (*induction*) investiture *f*

inauspicious [ˌɪnɔː'spɪʃəs, *Am:* -ɑː'spɪʃ-] *adj form* peu propice

in between **I.** *prep* entre **II.** *adv* entre les deux

in-between **I.** *adj* intermédiaire **II.** *n* **the ~s** ceux qui sont entre les deux

inboard ['ɪnbɔːd, *Am:* 'ɪnbɔːrd] **I.** *adj* **1.** (*within a ship, vehicle, plane*) à bord **2.** NAUT (*engine*) in-bord *inv* **II.** *adv* à bord **III.** *n* **1.** (*engine*) moteur *m* in-bord **2.** (*boat*) in-bord *m inv*

inborn [ˌɪn'bɔːn, *Am:* 'ɪnbɔːrn] *adj* inné(e)

in-box ['ɪnbɒks, *Am:* -bɑːks] *n* INFOR boîte *f* de réception

inbred [ˌɪn'bred, *Am:* 'ɪnbred] *adj* **1.** (*closely related: animal*) issu(e) de croisements consanguins; (*person*) ayant un fort degré de consanguinité **2.** (*inherent*) inné(e)

inbreeding [ˌɪn'briːdɪŋ, *Am:* 'ɪnbriːdɪŋ] *n no pl* consanguinité *f*

in-built ['ɪnbɪlt] *s.* **built-in**

Inc. [ɪŋk] *adj abbr of* **Incorporated** SA

Inca ['ɪŋkə] **I.** *n* Inca *mf* **II.** *adj* inca *inv*

incalculable [ɪn'kælkjʊləbl] *adj* incalculable; (*value*) inestimable

incandescent [ˌɪnkæn'desnt, *Am:* -ken'-] *adj* incandescent(e); **~ with anger** rouge de colère

incantation [ˌɪnkæn'teɪʃən] *n* incantation *f*

incapability *n no pl* incapacité *f*

incapable [ɪn'keɪpəbl] *adj* incapable

incapacitate [ˌɪnkə'pæsɪteɪt] *vt* **1.** (*prevent from functioning*) rendre incapable; (*machine*) rendre hors d'état de marche; **to ~ sb from doing sth** mettre qn dans l'incapacité de faire qc **2.** LAW invalider

incapacity [ˌɪnkə'pæsəti, *Am:* -t̬i] *n no pl* incapacité *f*

incarcerate [ɪn'kɑːsəreɪt, *Am:* -'kɑːr-] *vt* **1.** *form* incarcérer **2.** *fig* **to be ~d in sth** être emprisonné dans qc

incarnate [ɪn'kɑːneɪt, *Am:* -'kɑːr-] *adj* incarné(e)

incarnation *n* incarnation *f*

incautious [ɪn'kɔːʃəs, *Am:* -'kɑː-] *adj form* imprudent(e)

incendiary [ɪn'sendɪəri, *Am:* -eri] *adj* incendiaire

incense ['ɪnsents] **I.** *n no pl* encens *m* **II.** *vt* encenser

incensed *adj* furieux(-euse); **to get ~ with sth** être furieux contre qc

incentive [ɪn'sentɪv, *Am:* -t̬ɪv] *n* **1.** FIN, ECON prime *f* **2.** *no pl* (*cause for action*) motivation *f;* **to give an ~** motiver

inception [ɪn'sepʃən] *n no pl* commencement *m*

incertitude [ɪn'sɜːtɪtjuːd, *Am:* -'sɜːrt̬ɪtuːd] *n* incertitude *f*

incessant [ɪn'sesnt] *adj pej* incessant(e)

incest ['ɪnsest] *n no pl* inceste *m*

incestuous *adj* incestueux(-euse)

inch [ɪntʃ] **I.** <-es> *n* pouce *m;* **every ~** chaque centimètre ►**give her/him an ~ and she/he'll take a mile** *prov* si on lui tend le petit doigt, il/elle prend tout le bras; **to look every ~ sth** ressembler en tout point à qc; **to avoid** [*o* **miss**] **sb/sth by an ~** manquer qn de peu/qc d'un doigt; **not to budge** [*o* **give**] [*o* **move**] **an ~** ne pas bouger d'un pouce; **~ by ~** petit à petit **II.** *vi + directional adv* **to ~ along** [*o* **forward**] avancer à petits pas **III.** *vt* **to ~ oneself/sth** s'avancer/avancer qc d'un pouce

incidence ['ɪntsɪdənts] *n* taux *m*
incident *n* incident *m*
incidental *adj* **1.** (*minor*) secondaire; ~ **expenses** faux frais *mpl;* ~ **music** musique *f* de fond **2.** (*occurring by chance*) accidentel(le) **3.** (*that happens as a consequence*) **to be ~ to sth** accompagner qc
incidentally *adv* **1.** (*by the way*) à propos **2.** (*accidentally*) incidemment
incinerate [ɪn'sɪnəreɪt] *vt* incinérer
incinerator *n* incinérateur *m*
incipient [ɪn'sɪpɪənt] *adj form* naissant(e); **at an ~ stage** à un stade précoce
incise [ɪn'saɪz] *vt form* **1.** MED inciser **2.** (*engrave*) **to ~ sth into sth** graver qc sur qc
incision [ɪn'sɪʒən] *n* MED incision *f*
incisive [ɪn'saɪsɪv] *adj* incisif(-ive)
incisor *n* incisive *f*
incite [ɪn'saɪt] *vt* inciter, instiguer *Belgique*
incitement *n no pl* incitation *f*
incivility [ˌɪnsɪ'vɪləti, *Am:* -t̬i] *n no pl, form* impolitesse *f*
inclement [ɪn'klemənt] *adj form* inclément(e)
inclination [ˌɪnklɪ'neɪʃən] *n* **1.** (*tendency*) tendance *f* **2.** (*liking*) penchant *m* **3.** (*slope*) inclinaison *f*
incline[1] [ɪn'klaɪn] **I.** *vi* **1.** *form* (*tend*) **to ~ to(wards) sth** tendre vers qc **2.** (*lean*) pencher **II.** *vt* **1.** *form* (*encourage*) **to ~ sb to** +*infin* porter qn à +*infin* **2.** (*make lean*) incliner; **to ~ one's head** baisser la tête
incline[2] ['ɪnklaɪn] *n* pente *f*
inclined *adj* enclin(e)
inclose [ɪn'kləʊz, *Am:* -'kloʊz] *vt s.* **enclose**
include [ɪn'klu:d] *vt* comprendre
including *prep* (y) compris; **not ~ tax** taxe non comprise; **ten books ~ two novels** dix livres dont deux romans; **up to and ~ 6th June** jusqu'au 6 juin inclus
inclusion [ɪn'klu:ʒən] *n no pl* inclusion *f*
inclusive [ɪn'klu:sɪv] *adj* compris(e); **all-~** tout compris; **from Monday to Thursday ~** du lundi au jeudi inclus
incognito [ˌɪnkɒg'ni:təʊ, *Am:* ˌɪnkɑ:g'ni:toʊ] *adv* incognito
incoherent [ˌɪnkəʊ'hɪərənt, *Am:* -koʊ'hɪrənt] *adj* incohérent(e)
income ['ɪŋkʌm, *Am:* 'ɪn-] *n* revenu *m*
income tax *n* impôt *m* sur le revenu
incoming *adj* **1.** (*arriving*) qui arrive; (*call*) de l'extérieur **2.** (*new*) nouveau(-elle) **3.** (*recently elected*) entrant(e)
incomings *npl* rentrées *fpl*
incommensurable *adj* **1.** (*incommensurate*) incommensurable **2.** MAT (*number*) irrationnel
incommensurate [ˌɪnkə'menʃərət, *Am:* -sɚ-] *adj* **1.** (*out of proportion*) **to be ~ with sth** être sans rapport avec qc **2.** (*incommensurable*) incommensurable
incommunicado [ˌɪnkəˌmju:nɪ'kɑ:dəʊ, *Am:* -doʊ] **I.** *adj iron, form* injoignable **II.** *adv iron, form* **to be held ~** être tenu au secret
incomparable [ɪn'kɒmprəbl, *Am:* -'kɑ:m-] *adj* incomparable
incompatibility *n no pl* incompatibilité *f;* ~ **of blood groups** incompatibilité sanguine
incompatible [ˌɪnkəm'pætəbl, *Am:* -'pæt̬-] *adj* incompatible
incompetence [ɪn'kɒmpɪtənts, *Am:* -'kɑ:mpət̬ənts], **incompetency** *n no pl, pej* incompétence *f*
incompetent **I.** *adj pej* incompétent(e) **II.** *n pej* incapable *mf*
incomplete [ˌɪnkəm'pli:t] *adj* **1.** (*not complete*) incomplet(-ète) **2.** (*not finished*) inachevé(e)
incomprehensible [ˌɪnˌkɒmprɪ'hensəbl, *Am:* ˌɪnkɑ:m-] *adj* incompréhensible
inconceivable [ˌɪnkən'si:vəbl] *adj* inconcevable
inconclusive [ˌɪnkən'klu:sɪv] *adj* peu concluant(e)
incongruous [ɪn'kɒŋgrʊəs, *Am:* -'kɑ:ŋ-] *adj* incongru(e)
inconsequent [ɪn'kɒnsɪkwənt, *Am:* -'kɑ:n-] *adj* inconséquent(e)
inconsequential *adj* sans conséquence
inconsiderable [ˌɪnkən'sɪdrəbl] *adj* insignifiant(e)
inconsiderate [ˌɪnkən'sɪdərət] *adj pej* **to be ~ to sb** manquer d'égards envers qn
inconsistency [ˌɪnkən'sɪstəntsi] <-ies> *n* inconsistance *f*
inconsistent *adj* inconsistant(e)
inconsolable [ˌɪnkən'səʊləbl, *Am:* -'soʊ-] *adj* inconsolable
inconspicuous [ˌɪnkən'spɪkjʊəs] *adj* discret(-ète); **to try to look ~** essayer de passer inaperçu
incontestable [ˌɪnkən'testəbl] *adj form* incontestable
incontinent [ɪn'kɒntɪnənt, *Am:* -'kɑ:ntən-] *adj* incontinent(e)
incontrovertible [ɪnˌkɒntrə'vɜ:təbl, *Am:* -ˌkɑ:ntrə'vɜ:rt̬ə-] *adj form* irréfutable
inconvenience [ˌɪnkən'vi:nɪəns] **I.** *n* désagrément *m* **II.** *vt* déranger
inconvenient *adj* inopportun(e)
incorporate [ɪn'kɔ:pəreɪt, *Am:* -'kɔ:r-] *vt* **1.** (*integrate*) incorporer **2.** (*include*) comprendre **3.** *Am* LAW, ECON **to ~ a company** constituer en société
incorporation *n no pl* **1.** (*integration*) incorporation *f* **2.** LAW, ECON constitution *f* en société
incorporeal [ˌɪnkɔ:'pɔ:rɪəl, *Am:* -kɔ:r'-] *adj* incorporel(le)
incorrect [ˌɪnkə'rekt] *adj* **1.** (*not correct*) incorrect(e); **to prove ~** s'avérer inexact **2.** *fig* déplacé(e)
incorrigible [ɪŋ'kɒrɪdʒəbl, *Am:* ɪn'kɔ:rə-] *adj* incorrigible
incorruptible [ˌɪnkə'rʌptəbl] *adj* incorruptible

increase[1] [ɪn'kriːs] *vi, vt* augmenter; **to ~ tenfold/threefold** décupler/tripler

increase[2] ['ɪnkriːs] *n* **1.**(*quantitative*) augmentation *f;* **~ in sth** augmentation de qc; **tax ~** hausse *f* de l'impôt; **to be on the ~** être en augmentation **2.**(*qualitative*) intensification *f*

increasing *adj* croissant(e)

increasingly *adv* de plus en plus

incredible [ɪn'kredɪbl] *adj* incroyable

incredibly *adv* incroyablement

incredulity [ˌɪnkrɪ'djuːləti, *Am:* -'duːləṱi] *n no pl* incrédulité *f*

incredulous [ɪn'kredjʊləs, *Am:* -'kredʒʊ-] *adj* incrédule

increment ['ɪŋkrəmənt] *n* **1.**(*increase*) augmentation *f* **2.** MAT, INFOR incrément *m*

incremental *adj* incrémentiel(le)

incriminate [ɪn'krɪmɪneɪt] *vt* incriminer

incriminating *adj* compromettant(e)

incubate ['ɪnkjʊbeɪt] **I.** *vt* **1.** MED incuber **2.** *a.* ZOOL couver **II.** *vi* **1.** MED être en incubation **2.** *a. fig* couver

incubation *n no pl* incubation *f*

incubator *n* **1.** MED couveuse *f* **2.** BIO incubateur *m*

inculcate ['ɪnkʌlkeɪt] *vt form* **to ~ sth in sb** inculquer qc à qn

incumbent [ɪŋ'kʌmbənt] **I.** *adj* **1.**(*office-bearing*) en exercice **2.** *form* (*obliged*) **it is ~ on sb to** *+infin* il incombe à qn de *+infin* **II.** *n* (*of post*) titulaire *mf*

incur [ɪn'kɜːʳ, *Am:* -'kɜːr] <-rr-> *vt* encourir; (*losses*) subir; (*debt*) contracter; (*sb's anger*) s'attirer

incurable [ɪn'kjʊərəbl, *Am:* -'kjʊrə-] *adj* incurable

incursion [ɪn'kɜːʃən, *Am:* -'kɜːr-] *n* incursion *f*

indebted [ɪn'detɪd, *Am:* -'deṱ-] *adj* **1.**(*obliged*) **~ to sb for sth** redevable à qn de qc **2.** FIN endetté(e)

indebtedness *n no pl* **1.**(*state of obligation*) dette *f* **2.** FIN endettement *m*

indecency [ɪn'diːsəntsi] *n no pl* **1.**(*impropriety*) inconvenance *f* **2.**(*lewdness*) obscénité *f* **3.**(*immorality*) indécence *f* **4.** LAW outrage *m* public à la pudeur

indecent *adj* indécent(e)

indecent assault *n* LAW attentat *m* à la pudeur **indecent exposure** *n* LAW outrage *m* public à la pudeur

indecipherable [ˌɪndɪ'saɪfrəbl] *adj* **1.**(*opp: legible*) indéchiffrable **2.**(*incomprehensible*) inintelligible

indecision [ˌɪndɪ'sɪʒən] *n no pl* indécision *f*

indecisive [ˌɪndɪ'saɪsɪv] *adj* indécis(e)

indeclinable [ɪndɪ'klaɪnəbl] *adj* LING indéclinable

indecorous [ɪn'dekərəs] *adj form* inconvenant(e)

indeed [ɪn'diːd] *adv* **1.**(*as was suspected*) en effet **2.**(*emphasizing*) vraiment; **it's very sad ~** c'est vraiment triste **3.** *Brit* (*really?*) **~?** vraiment?

indefatigable [ˌɪndɪ'fætɪgəbl, *Am:* -'fæṱ-] *adj form* infatigable

indefensible [ˌɪndɪ'fensəbl] *adj* indéfendable

indefinable [ˌɪndɪ'faɪnəbl] *adj* indéfinissable

indefinite [ɪn'defɪnət, *Am:* -ənət] *adj* indéfini(e)

indefinite article *n* article *m* indéfini

indefinitely *adv* indéfiniment

indelible [ɪn'deləbl] *adj* indélébile

indemnify [ɪn'demnɪfaɪ] <-ie-> *vt* **1.**(*compensate*) indemniser **2.**(*insure*) assurer

indemnity [ɪn'demnəti, *Am:* -ṱi] *n form* **1.**(*compensation*) indemnité *f;* **to pay ~** verser des indemnités **2.** *no pl* (*insurance*) assurance *f*

indent [ɪn'dent] **I.** *vi* **1.** TYP faire un alinéa **2.** *Aus, Brit* COM **to ~ on sb for sth** commander qc à qn **II.** *vt* **1.**(*notch*) denteler **2.** TYP mettre en retrait **III.** *n* **1.** *Aus, Brit* COM commande *f;* **to place an ~ for sth** passer une commande de qc **2.** TYP alinéa *m*

indentation [ˌɪnden'teɪʃən] *n* **1.** TYP alinéa *m* **2.**(*notch*) entaille *f;* (*of coast*) découpage *m;* (*in metal*) bosse *f* **3.**(*notched edge*) dentelure *f*

independence [ˌɪndɪ'pendəns] *n no pl* indépendance *f*

Independence Day *n aux États-Unis, le 4 juillet est célébré en souvenir du jour de 1776 où les 13 colonies ont déclaré leur indépendance vis-à-vis de l'Angleterre.*

independent **I.** *adj a.* LING indépendant(e) **II.** *n* POL **an Independent** un(e) non-inscrit(e)

in-depth ['ɪndepθ] *adj* approfondi(e)

indescribable [ˌɪndɪ'skraɪbəbl] *adj* indescriptible

indestructible [ˌɪndɪ'strʌktəbl] *adj* indestructible; (*toy*) incassable

indeterminable [ˌɪndɪ'tɜːmɪnəbl, *Am:* -'tɜːr-] *adj* indéterminable

indeterminate [ˌɪndɪ'tɜːmɪnət, *Am:* -'tɜːr-] *adj* indéterminé(e)

index ['ɪndeks] **I.** *n* **1.** <-es> (*alphabetical list*) index *m* **2.** <-ices *o* -es> ECON, MAT (*figure*) indice *m;* **the cost-of-living ~** l'indice officiel du coût de la vie **3.** <-ices *o* -es> (*indication*) indice *m* **4.** *no pl* REL **the Index** l'Index *m* **II.** *vt a.* ECON indexer

indexation [ˌindek'seɪʃən] *n no pl* ECON indexation *f*

index card *n* fiche *f*

indexer *n* index *m*

index finger *n* index *m* **index-linked** *adj Brit* ECON (*pension*) indexé(e)

India ['ɪndɪə] *n* l'Inde *f*

Indian **I.** *adj* **1.** GEO indien(ne), de l'Inde **2.** HIST des Indes **II.** *n* (*person*) Indien(ne) *m(f)*

Indiana [ˌɪndi'ænə] *n* l'Indiana *m*

Indian club *n* SPORT mil *m* **Indian corn** *n no pl, Am* maïs *m* **Indian file** *n s.* **single file** **Indian hemp** *n* chanvre *m* indien **Indian**

ink *n* encre *f* de Chine **Indian Ocean** *n* l'océan *m* Indien **Indian summer** *n* **1.** (*warm autumn weather*) été *m* indien **2.** (*pleasant period in late life*) deuxième printemps *m*

India paper *n no pl* papier *m* bible **India rubber** *n s.* **rubber**

indicate ['ɪndɪkeɪt] **I.** *vt* indiquer **II.** *vi Brit* AUTO **to ~ left/right** mettre son clignotant à gauche/droite

indication *n a.* MED indication *f;* **there is every/no ~ that ...** tout/rien ne porte à croire que ...

indicative [ɪn'dɪkətɪv, *Am:* -t̬ɪv] **I.** *adj a.* LING indicatif(-ive); **~ sentence** une phrase à l'indicatif **II.** *n* LING indicatif *m*

indicator *n a.* TECH indicateur *m*

indices ['ɪndɪsi:z] *n pl of* **index**

indict [ɪn'daɪt] *vt* LAW **to ~ sb on sth** inculper qn de qc

indictable *adj* LAW passible d'une condamnation

indictment *n* LAW acte *m* d'accusation

indie ['ɪndi] *adj* indépendant(e)

Indies ['ɪndiz] *npl* les Indes *fpl;* **the West ~** les Antilles *fpl*

indifference [ɪn'dɪfrəns] *n no pl* indifférence *f;* **~ to sb/sth** indifférence envers qn/qc

indifferent *adj* **1.** (*not interested*) indifférent(e) **2.** (*not of good quality*) médiocre

indigenous [ɪn'dɪdʒɪnəs] *adj* indigène

indigestible [ˌɪndɪ'dʒəstəbl] *adj* inassimilable

indigestion [ˌɪndɪ'dʒəstʃən] *n no pl* indigestion *f*

indignant [ɪn'dɪgnənt] *adj* indigné(e)

indignation *n no pl, no indef art* indignation *f*

indignity [ɪn'dɪgnɪti, *Am:* -nət̬i] *n* humiliation *f*

indirect [ˌɪndɪ'rekt] *adj a.* LING indirect(e); **by ~ means** de manière détournée

indirect object *n* objet *m* indirect **indirect tax** *n* FIN impôts *mpl* indirects

indiscernible [ˌɪndɪ'sɜ:nəbl, *Am:* -'sɜ:r-] *adj* insaisissable; **~ to the naked eye** invisible à l'œil nu

indiscipline [ɪn'dɪsɪplɪn] *n no pl, form* indiscipline *f*

indiscreet [ˌɪndɪ'skri:t] *adj* indiscret(-ète)

indiscretion [ˌɪndɪ'skreʃən] *n no pl* indiscrétion *f*

indiscriminate [ˌɪndɪ'skrɪmɪnət] *adj* **1.** (*unthinking*) sans arrière-pensée; (*uncritical*) dépourvu(e) d'esprit critique **2.** (*random*) gratuit(e)

indispensable [ˌɪndɪ'spensəbl] *adj* indispensable

indisposed [ˌɪndɪ'spəʊzd, *Am:* -'spoʊzd] *adj* **1.** (*slightly ill*) indisposé(e) **2.** *form* (*averse, unwilling*) réticent(e)

indisposition [ˌɪndɪspə'zɪʃən] *n form* **1.** *sing* (*illness*) indisposition *f* **2.** *no pl, no indef art* (*disinclination*) réticence *f*

indisputable [ˌɪndɪ'spju:təbl, *Am:* -t̬ə-] *adj* indéniable

indistinct [ˌɪndɪ'stɪŋkt] *adj* indistinct(e)

indistinguishable [ˌɪndɪ'stɪŋgwɪʃ əbl] *adj* indiscernable

individual [ˌɪndɪ'vɪdʒuəl] **I.** *n* individu *m* **II.** *adj* (*case*) individuel(le); (*attention*) particulier(-ère); (*needs, style*) personnel(le)

individual case *n* cas *m* isolé

individualise [ˌɪndɪ'vɪdʒuəlaɪz] *vt* individualiser

individualism [ˌɪndɪ'vɪdʒuəlɪzəm] *n no pl, no indef art a.* PHILOS individualisme *m*

individualist *n a.* PHILOS individualiste *mf*

individualistic *adj* individualiste

individuality [ˌɪndɪˌvɪdʒu'æləti, *Am:* -ˌvɪdʒu'ælət̬i] *n* individualité *f*

individualize *vt Am s.* **individualise**

individually *adv* individuellement

indivisible [ˌɪndɪ'vɪzəbl] *adj* indivisible

Indochina [ˌɪdəʊ'tʃaɪnə] *n* l'Indochine *f*

indoctrinate [ɪn'dɒktrɪneɪt, *Am:* -'dɑ:k-] *vt pej* endoctriner

indoctrination *n no pl, no indef art, pej* endoctrinement *m*

indolent ['ɪndələnt] *adj pej* indolent(e)

indomitable [ɪn'dɒmɪtəbl, *Am:* -'dɑ:mət̬ə-] *adj* indomptable

Indonesia [ˌɪndəʊ'ni:zɪə, *Am:* -də'ni:ʒə] *n* l'Indonésie *f*

Indonesian **I.** *adj* indonésien(ne) **II.** *n* **1.** (*person*) Indonésien(ne) *m(f)* **2.** LING indonésien *m; s. a.* **English**

indoor ['ɪndɔ:ʳ, *Am:* ˌɪn'dɔ:r] *adj* d'intérieur; (*sports*) en salle; (*pool, court*) couvert(e); **~ activities** activités *fpl* qui se pratiquent en intérieur

indoors *adv* à l'intérieur

indubitable [ɪn'dju:bɪtəbl, *Am:* -'du:bɪt̬ə-] *adj form* indubitable

indubitably *adv form* indubitablement

induce [ɪn'dju:s, *Am:* -'du:s] *vt* **1.** (*persuade*) *a.* ELEC, PHYS induire **2.** (*cause*) *a.* MED provoquer; **to ~ a pregnant woman** provoquer un accouchement

inducement *n* instigation *f*

induct [ɪn'dʌkt] *vt* instituer

induction *n* **1.** (*installation in office*) installation *f* **2.** *Am* MIL (*the army, the military*) incorporation *f* **3.** (*initiation*) initiation *f* **4.** *no pl, no indef art* PHILOS, PSYCH, ELEC, PHYS induction *f* **5.** MED provocation *f*

induction coil *n* ELEC bobine *f* d'induction

induction course *n* cours *m* d'initiation

inductive [ɪn'dʌktɪv] *adj* ELEC, MAT, PHILOS inductif(-ive)

indulge [ɪn'dʌldʒ] **I.** *vt* **1.** (*allow oneself to enjoy: one's passion, desire*) céder à; **to ~ oneself in sth** s'accorder qc **2.** (*spoil*) gâter; **to ~ oneself** se faire plaisir **II.** *vi* se laisser tenter; **to ~ in sth** (*allow oneself*) s'offrir qc; (*to become involved in*) se livrer à qc

indulgence [ɪn'dʌldʒəns] *n* **1.** (*treat*) gâte-

I

rie *f* **2.** *no pl, no indef art* (*leniency*) indulgence *f* **3.** *no pl* (*instance of indulging in sth: in a passion, hobby*) abandon *m;* (*in food*) gourmandise *f;* **to be one's ~** être son péché mignon **4.** REL (*Catholic doctrine*) indulgence *f*

indulgent *adj* **to be ~ towards sb/sth** être indulgent envers qn/qc

industrial [ɪn'dʌstriəl] *adj* industriel(le)

industrial dispute *n* conflit *m* social

industrialise [ɪn'dʌstriəlaɪz] **I.** *vi* s'industrialiser **II.** *vt* industrialiser

industrialism [ɪn'dʌstriəlɪzəm] *n no pl, no indef art* industrialisme *m*

industrialist *n* **1.** (*person with high position in industry*) industriel(le) *m(f)* **2.** (*person employed in industry*) ouvrier, -ière *m, f*

industrialization *n no pl, no indef art* industrialisation *f*

industrialize *Am s.* **industrialise**

industrial park *n* zone *f* industrielle **Industrial Revolution** *n* Révolution *f* Industrielle **industrial tribunal** *n* conseil *m* des prud'hommes

industrious [ɪn'dʌstrɪəs] *adj* actif(-ive)

industry ['ɪndəstri] *n a. form* industrie *f;* **heavy/light ~** l'industrie lourde/légère; **the computer/electricity ~** les industries électroniques/électriques; **the tourist ~** l'industrie du tourisme

inebriate [ɪ'ni:brɪeɪt] *vt form* enivrer

inedible [ɪn'edəbl] *adj* **1.** (*unsuitable as food*) immangeable **2.** *pej* (*extremely unpalatable*) invivable

ineducable [ɪn'edʒʊkəbl] *adj* inéducable

ineffable [ɪn'efəbl] *adj form* ineffable

ineffective [ˌɪnɪ'fektɪv] *adj* inefficace

ineffectual [ˌɪnɪ'fektʃʊəl] *adj form* inefficace; (*efforts*) vain(e); **to be ~ at doing sth** ne pas être capable de faire qc

inefficiency [ˌɪnɪ'fɪʃənsi] *n no pl, no indef art* inefficacité *f*

inefficient *adj* non rentable; (*person, organization*) incompétent(e)

inelegant [ˌɪn'elɪgənt] *adj* inélégant(e)

ineligible [ɪn'elɪdʒəbl] *adj* inéligible; **to be ~ to** *+infin* ne pas avoir le droit de *+infin;* **to be ~ for sth** ne pas avoir droit à qc

inept [ɪ'nept] *adj* **1.** (*clumsy*) inepte **2.** (*unskilled*) inapte; **to be ~ at doing sth** être inapte à faire qc; **to be socially ~** être socialement inadapté

inequality [ˌɪnɪ'kwɒləti, *Am:* -'kwɑ:ləṱi] *n* inégalité *f*

inequitable [ɪn'ekwɪtəbl, *Am:* -wəṱə-] *adj form* inéquitable

inequity [ɪn'ekwəti, *Am:* -ṱi] *n form* iniquité *f*

ineradicable [ˌɪnɪ'rædɪkəbl] *adj form* (*impression*) indéracinable; (*disease*) incurable

inert [ɪ'nɜ:t, *Am:* -'nɜ:rt] *adj a. fig, pej* inerte

inertia [ɪ'nɜ:ʃə, *Am:* ˌɪn'ɜ:r-] *n no pl, no indef art a.* PHYS inertie *f*

inertia reel seat belt *n* ceinture *f* automatique

inescapable [ˌɪnɪ'skeɪpəbl] *adj* inéluctable

inessential [ˌɪnɪ'senʃl] **I.** *adj* insignifiant(e) **II.** *n pl* insignifiance *f*

inestimable [ɪn'estɪməbl] *adj form* inestimable

inevitable [ɪn'evɪtəbl, *Am:* -ṱə-] **I.** *adj* inévitable **II.** *n no pl, no indef art* **the ~** l'inévitable *m*

inexact [ˌɪnɪg'zækt] *adj* inexact(e)

inexcusable [ˌɪnɪk'skju:zəbl] *adj pej* inexcusable

inexhaustible [ˌɪnɪg'zɔ:stəbl, *Am:* -'zɔ:stəbl] *adj* inexhaustible

inexorable [ˌɪn'eksərəbl] *adj form* inexorable

inexpediency *n no pl, no indef art, form* caractère *m* inapproprié

inexpedient [ˌɪnɪk'spi:dɪənt] *adj form* inapproprié(e)

inexpensive [ˌɪnɪk'spensɪv] *adj* bon marché

inexperience [ˌɪnɪk'spɪəriənts] *n no pl* inexpérience *f*

inexperienced *adj* inexpérimenté(e)

inexpert [ɪn'ekspɜ:t, *Am:* -spɜ:rt] *adj* inexpert(e)

inexplicable [ˌɪnɪk'splɪkəbl, *Am:* ˌɪn'ək-] **I.** *adj* inexplicable **II.** *n no pl, no indef art* **the ~** l'inexplicable *m*

inextricable [ˌɪnɪk'strɪkəbl] *adj* inextricable

infallible [ɪn'fæləbl] *adj* infaillible

infamous ['ɪnfəməs] *adj* **1.** (*notorious*) infamant(e) **2.** (*abominable*) infâme

infamy ['ɪnfəmi] *n* infamie *f*

infancy ['ɪnfəntsi] *n a. fig* enfance *f*

infant *n* enfant *m;* **a newborn ~** un nouveau-né

infanticide [ɪn'fæntɪsaɪd, *Am:* -ṱə-] *n no pl, no indef art, form* infanticide *m*

infantile ['ɪnfəntaɪl] *adj pej* infantile

infant mortality *n* mortalité *f* infantile

infantry ['ɪnfəntri] *n no pl, no indef art* MIL **the ~** *+ sing/pl vb* infanterie *f*

infantryman <-men> *n* MIL fantassin *m*

infant school *n* école *f* maternelle

infatuated [ɪn'fætʃʊeɪtɪd, *Am:* -ueɪṱɪd] *adj* **to be ~ with sb/sth** être entiché de qn/qc; **to become ~ with sb/sth** s'enticher de qn/qc

infatuation *n* toquade *f*

infect [ɪn'fekt] *vt* **1.** (*contaminate*) *a. fig, pej* contaminer; **to ~ sb with sth** transmettre qc à qn; **to become ~ed** s'infecter **2.** (*pass on sth desirable: one's laugh, good humour*) communiquer; **to ~ sb with sth** communiquer qc à qn

infection *n* MED infection *f*

infectious *adj a.* MED contagieux(-euse)

infelicitous [ˌɪnfɪ'lɪsɪtəs, *Am:* -əṱəs] *adj pej, form* malheureux(-euse)

infer [ɪn'fɜ:ʳ, *Am:* -'fɜ:r] <-rr-> *vt* **to ~ sth from sth** inférer qc de qc

inference ['ɪnfərəns] *n form* inférence *f*

inferior [ɪnˈfɪərɪəʳ, *Am:* -ˈfɪrɪɚ] **I.** *adj* inférieur(e) **II.** *n* inférieur(e) *m(f)*; (*in rank*) subalterne *mf;* **social ~s** classes *fpl* inférieures
inferiority [ɪnˌfɪəriˈɒrəti, *Am:* -ˌfɪriˈɔːrət̬i] *n no pl, no indef art* infériorité *f*
inferiority complex *n* complexe *m* d'infériorité
infernal [ɪnˈfɜːnəl, *Am:* -ˈfɜːr-] *adj* infernal(e)
inferno [ɪnˈfɜːnəʊ, *Am:* -ˈfɜːrnoʊ] *n* incendie *m*
infertile [ɪnˈfɜːtaɪl, *Am:* -ˈfɜːrt̬l] *adj* **1.** MED (*sterile*) stérile **2.** AGR (*unable to produce good crops*) infertile
infertility [ˌɪnfəˈtɪləti, *Am:* -fɚˈtɪlət̬i] *n no pl, no indef art* **1.** MED stérilité *f* **2.** AGR infertilité *f*
infest [ɪnˈfest] *vt a. pej, fig* infester
infestation *n pej* **1.** (*instance of infesting*) infestation *f;* (*of pests*) épidémie *f;* (*of rats*) envahissement *m* **2.** *no pl, no indef art* (*state of being infested*) contamination *f*
infidel [ˈɪnfɪdəl, *Am:* -fədel] *n no pl, pej* REL, HIST **the ~** les infidèles *mpl*
infidelity [ˌɪnfɪˈdeləti, *Am:* -fəˈdelət̬i] <-ies> *n* infidélité *f*
infighting [ˈɪnfaɪtɪŋ] *n no pl, no indef art* conflit *m* interne
infiltrate [ˈɪnfɪltreɪt, *Am:* ɪnˈfɪl-] **I.** *vt* **1.** *a.* CHEM, PHYS infiltrer **2.** *fig* (*idea, theory*) faire passer **II.** *vi* CHEM, PHYS s'infiltrer
infiltration *n no pl a.* MIL, CHEM, PHYS infiltration *f*
infiltrator *n* MIL espion(ne) *m(f)*
infinite [ˈɪnfɪnət, *Am:* -fənɪt] **I.** *adj a.* MAT infini(e) **II.** *n* **the Infinite** l'infini *m*
infinitely *adv* infiniment
infinitesimal [ˌɪnfɪnɪˈtesɪml] *adj form a.* MAT infinitésimal(e)
infinitive [ɪnˈfɪnətɪv, *Am:* -t̬ɪv] LING **I.** *n* infinitif *m;* **to be in the ~** être à l'infinitif **II.** *adj* infinitif(-ive)
infinity [ɪnˈfɪnəti, *Am:* -t̬i] *n* **1.** *no pl, no indef art* (*infinite distance/extent*) *a.* MAT infini *m* **2.** *no pl, no indef art* (*state of being infinite, huge amount*) infinitude *f*
infirm [ɪnˈfɜːm, *Am:* -ˈfɜːrm] *adj* infirme
infirmary [ɪnˈfɜːməri, *Am:* -ˈfɜːr-] *n* MED **1.** (*hospital*) hôpital *m* **2.** *Am* (*sick room*) infirmerie *f*
infirmity [ɪnˈfɜːməti, *Am:* -ˈfɜːrmət̬i] *n a. form* infirmité *f*
inflame [ɪnˈfleɪm] *vt* **1.** (*provoke and intensify: emotions, feelings*) enflammer; **~d with passion** être pris d'une passion ardente **2.** (*stir up*) **to ~ sb** mettre qn en colère; **to ~ sb with anger/desire** exciter la colère/le désir de qn
inflammable [ɪnˈflæməbl] *adj* **1.** (*burning easily*) inflammable **2.** *fig* explosif(-ive)
inflammation [ˌɪnfləˈmeɪʃən] *n* MED inflammation *f*
inflammatory [ɪnˈflæmətəri, *Am:* -tɔːr-] *adj* **1.** MED (*tending to cause inflammation*) inflammatoire **2.** (*intentionally exacerbating*) exacerbé(e)
inflatable [ɪnˈfleitəbl, *Am:* -t̬ə-] **I.** *adj* gonflable **II.** *n* pneumatique *m*
inflate [ɪnˈfleɪt] **I.** *vt a. pej a.* ECON gonfler **II.** *vi* se gonfler
inflated *adj* **1.** *a. pej a.* ECON gonflé(e) **2.** *pej, form* LING enflé(e)
inflation [ɪnˈfleɪʃən] *n no pl, no indef art* **1.** FIN (*general price rise*) inflation *f* **2.** (*act of filling with air*) gonflage *m*
inflationary *adj* FIN inflationniste
inflect [ɪnˈflekt] *vt* **1.** LING décliner; (*verb*) conjuguer **2.** (*change: voice*) moduler
inflection *n* **1.** (*change*) *a.* MAT inflexion *f* **2.** LING déclinaison *f;* (*verb*) conjugaison *f*
inflexibility *n no pl, no indef art, pej* inflexibilité *f*
inflexible [ɪnˈfleksəbl] *adj pej* inflexible; **to be ~ in one's opinion** demeurer inflexible dans ses opinions
inflexion *n s.* **inflection**
inflict [ɪnˈflɪkt] *vt* **to ~ sth on sb** infliger qc à qn; **to ~ sth on oneself** s'infliger qc; **to ~ one's opinion/views on sb** imposer son opinion/son point de vue à qn
infliction *n no pl, no indef art* châtiment *m*
influence [ˈɪnflʊəns] **I.** *n* influence *f;* **to be an ~ on sb/sth** avoir de l'influence sur qn/qc; **to enjoy ~** avoir de l'influence; **to be/fall under sb's ~** *pej* être/tomber sous l'influence de qn ►**to be under the ~** *iron, inf* (*drunk*) être sous l'effet de l'alcool; **driving under the ~** conduire en état d'ivresse **II.** *vt* influencer
influential *adj* influent(e)
influenza [ˌɪnflʊˈenzə] *n no pl, form* MED grippe *f*
influx [ˈɪnflʌks] *n no pl* influx *m*
inform [ɪnˈfɔːm, *Am:* -ˈfɔːrm] *vt* informer; **to ~ sb about sth** informer qn de qc; **to ~ the police** alerter la police; **to ~ sb what/when/where/whether ...** dire à qn ce que/quand/où/si ...
informal *adj* informel(le); (*meeting, invitation*) non-officiel(le); (*manner, style, person*) simple; (*mood, clothes*) décontracté(e); (*party, dinner*) sans cérémonie; (*announcement, talks*) officieux(-euse); **dress ~** tenue *f* de ville
informality [ˌɪnfɔːˈmæləti, *Am:* -fɔːrˈmælət̬i] *n no pl, no indef art* **1.** (*lack of formality*) simplicité *f* **2.** (*lack of officiality*) caractère *m* officieux
informant [ɪnˈfɔːmənt, *Am:* -ˈfɔːr-] *n* informateur, -trice *m, f*
information [ˌɪnfəˈmeɪʃən, *Am:* -fɚˈ-] *n* information *f*
information content *n no pl* INFOR listage *m* de données informatiques **information retrieval** *n no pl, no indef art* INFOR consultation *f* de données informatiques **information science(s)** *npl* informatique *f* **information storage** *n no pl* INFOR sauvegarde *f* **information superhighway** *n* autoroute *f* de l'information **information**

I

technology *n no pl* technologie *f* de l'information
informative [ɪn'fɔːmətɪv, *Am:* -'fɔːrmət̬ɪv] *adj* informatif(-ive)
informed *adj* informé(e)
informer *n* délateur, -trice *m, f*
infraction [ɪn'frækʃən] *n* infraction *f*
infradig [ˌɪnfrə'dɪg] *adj Brit, iron* **to be ~ for sb** être au-dessous de tout pour qn
infrared ['ɪnfrə'red] *adj* infrarouge
infrastructure ['ɪnfrəˌstrʌktʃəʳ, *Am:* -tʃɚ] *n* infrastructure *f*
infrequent [ɪn'friːkwənt] *adj* rare
infringe [ɪn'frɪndʒ] *vt* LAW (*a law*) enfreindre; (*sb's right*) violer
infringement *n* **1.** LAW violation *f* **2.** SPORT infraction *f*
infuriate [ɪn'fjʊərɪeɪt, *Am:* -'fjʊrɪ-] *vt* **to ~ sb** rendre qn furieux
infuse [ɪn'fjuːz] **I.** *vt* **1.** (*fill*) **to ~ sb with courage/energy** donner du courage/de l'énergie à qn; **to ~ sth into sb** inspirer qc à qn **2.** *form* (*steep in liquid: tea, herbs*) laisser infuser **II.** *vi* infuser
infusion *n* **1.** (*input*) ECON investissement *m* **2.** MED (*of blood, plasma*) perfusion *f* **3.** (*brew*) infusion *f*
ingenious [ɪn'dʒiːnɪəs, *Am:* -njəs] *adj* ingénieux(-euse)
ingenuity [ˌɪndʒɪ'njuːəti, *Am:* -t̬i] *n no pl, no indef art* ingéniosité *f*
ingenuous [ɪn'dʒenjʊəs] *adj form* ingénu(e)
ingest [in'dʒest] *vt* ingérer
inglenook ['ɪŋglnʊk] *n* ARCHIT coin *m* cheminée
inglorious [ɪn'glɔːrɪəs, *Am:* -'glɔːrɪ-] *adj pej* ignominieux(-euse)
ingoing ['ɪngəʊɪŋ, *Am:* -goʊ-] *adj* entrant(e)
ingot ['ɪŋgət] *n* (*of gold, silver*) lingot *m*
ingrained [ˌɪn'greɪnd] *adj* incrusté(e)
ingratiate [ɪn'greɪʃɪeɪt] *vt pej* **to ~ oneself with sb** s'insinuer dans les bonnes grâces de qn
ingratitude [ɪn'grætɪtjuːd, *Am:* -'græt̬ətuːd] *n no pl, no indef art* ingratitude *f*
ingredient [ɪn'griːdɪənt] *n* **1.** (*food item in recipe*) ingrédient *m* **2.** (*component*) composant *m*
in-group ['ɪngruːp] *n pej, inf* masse *f* (populaire); **to be in with the ~** faire partie de la masse
ingrowing, **ingrown** [ɪn'grəʊn, *Am:* 'ɪngroʊn] *adj Am* incarné(e)
inhabit [ɪn'hæbɪt] *vt* habiter (dans)
inhabitable *adj* habitable
inhabitant [ɪn'hæbɪtənt] *n* habitant *m*
inhale [ɪn'heɪl] *vt, vi* inhaler
inhaler *n* MED inhalateur *m*
inharmonious [ˌɪnhɑː'məʊnɪəs, *Am:* -hɑːr'moʊ-] *adj pej a.* MUS discordant(e)
inherent [ɪn'hɪərənt, *Am:* -'hɪr-] *adj a.* PHILOS inhérent(e); **to be ~ in sth** être inhérent à qc
inherit [ɪn'herɪt] **I.** *vt a. fig* **to ~ sth from sb** hériter (de) qc de qn **II.** *vi* hériter
inheritable *adj* LAW, MED héréditaire
inheritance [ɪn'herɪtəns] *n a.* LAW héritage *m*
inhibit [ɪn'hɪbɪt] *vt* **1.** (*prevent*) empêcher; **to ~ sb/sth from doing sth** empêcher qn/qc de faire qc **2.** (*hinder, impair*) inhiber
inhibition *n a.* PSYCH inhibition *f*
inhospitable [ˌɪnhɒ'spɪtəbl, *Am:* ɪn'hɑːspɪt̬ə-] *adj pej* inhospitalier(-ère)
in-house ['ɪnhaʊs] COM **I.** *adj* interne **II.** *adv* sur place
inhuman [ɪn'hjuːmən] *adj a. pej* inhumain(e)
inhumane [ˌɪnhjuː'meɪn] *adj a. pej* inhumain(e)
inhumanity [ˌɪnhjuː'mænəti, *Am:* -t̬i] *n no pl, no indef art, pej* inhumanité *f*
inimical [ɪ'nɪmɪkl] *adj form* hostile; **to be ~ to sth** être défavorable à qc
inimitable [ɪ'nɪmɪtəbl, *Am:* -t̬ə-] *adj* inimitable
iniquitous [ɪ'nɪkwɪtəs, *Am:* -t̬əs] *adj* inique
iniquity [ɪ'nɪkwəti, *Am:* -t̬i] *n* iniquité *f*
initial [ɪ'nɪʃəl] **I.** *n* initiale *f* **II.** *adj* initial(e) **III.** <*Brit* -ll- *o Am, Aus* -l-> *vt* signer
initialise *vt*, **initialize** [ɪ'nɪʃəlaɪz] *vt Am* INFOR initialiser
initially [ɪ'nɪʃəli] *adv* initialement
initiate[1] [ɪ'nɪʃɪeɪt] *vt a.* LAW initier; **to ~ sb into sth** initier qn à qc
initiate[2] [ɪ'nɪʃiət] *n* (*in a club, organization*) membre *mf;* (*in a spiritual community*) initié(e) *m(f)*
initiation [ɪˌnɪʃɪ'eɪʃən] *n* initiation *f*
initiative [ɪ'nɪʃətɪv, *Am:* -t̬ɪv] *n* initiative *f;* **to have/lose the ~ in sth** avoir/perdre l'initiative de qc; to show ~ montrer de l'initiative
inject [ɪn'dʒekt] *vt* MED, ECON injecter
injection *n* ECON, MED injection *f*
injection moulding *n* moulage *m* par injection
injudicious [ˌɪndʒuː'dɪʃəs] *adj* peu judicieux(-euse)
injunction [ɪn'dʒʌŋkʃən] *n* disposition *f;* **to issue an ~ to** +*infin* donner l'ordre de +*infin*
injure ['ɪndʒəʳ, *Am:* -dʒɚ] *vt* **1.** (*wound*) blesser; **to ~ oneself** se blesser **2.** (*damage*) endommager; **to ~ one's health** détruire sa santé **3.** *form* (*do wrong to*) causer du tort à
injured *adj* blessé(e)
injury ['ɪndʒəri] <-ries> *n* blessure *f* ►**to add <u>insult</u> to ~** faire de mal en pis
injustice [ɪn'dʒʌstɪs] *n* injustice *f*
ink [ɪŋk] **I.** *n* ART, BIO, TYP encre *f;* **to write in ~** écrire à l'encre **II.** *vt* TYP (*cover with printing fluid*) encrer
ink bottle *n* encrier *m* **ink-jet printer** *n* imprimante *f* à jet d'encre
inkling ['ɪŋklɪŋ] *n* **1.** (*slight knowledge, suspicion*) vague idée *f;* **to have an ~ that ...** avoir idée que ... **2.** (*hint*) signe *m*
ink pad *n* tampon *m* encreur **inkstain** *n*

tâche *f* d'encre

inky <-ier, -iest> *adj* **1.** (*covered with ink*) couvert(e) d'encre **2.** (*very dark*) noir(e)

inlaid [ˌɪnˈleɪd, *Am:* ˈɪnleɪd] **I.** *adj* incrusté(e); ~ **work** marqueterie *f* **II.** *pt, pp of* **inlay**

inland [ˈɪnlənd] **I.** *adj* intérieur(e) **II.** *adv* (*to go*) vers l'intérieur; (*to live*) dans les terres

Inland Revenue *n Brit, NZ* fisc *m* **inland trade** *n Brit* marché *m* intérieur

in-laws [ˈɪnlɔːz, *Am:* -lɑːz] *npl* belle-famille *f*

inlay [ˌɪnˈleɪ] **I.** *n* **1.** *no pl* (*embedded pattern*) marqueterie *f* **2.** MED (*filling for tooth*) plomb *m* **II.** <inlaid, inlaid> *vt* **to ~ sth with sth** incruster qc de qc

inlet [ˈɪnlet] *n* **1.** GEO bras *m* de rivière **2.** *Brit* TECH tuyau *m* d'alimentation

in-line skate *n* patin *m* en ligne **in-line skating** *n no pl* patin *m* en ligne

inmate [ˈɪnmeɪt] *n* pensionnaire *mf*

inn [ɪn] *n* auberge *f*

innards [ˈɪnədz, *Am:* -ɚdz] *npl inf* **1.** (*entrails*) ANAT entrailles *fpl* **2.** GASTR abats *mpl* **3.** TECH (*internal workings of machinery*) système *m* interne

innate [ɪˈneɪt] *adj* inné(e)

inner [ˈɪnəʳ, *Am:* -ɚ] *adj* **1.** (*inside, internal*) *a.* PSYCH intérieur(e); **in the ~ London area** dans le centre de Londres **2.** (*private*) intime

inner circle *n* cercle *m* fermé **inner city** **I.** *n* quartiers *mpl* défavorisés **II.** *adj* **inner-city** des quartiers défavorisés; ~ **areas** quartiers *mpl* défavorisés **inner ear** *n* oreille *f* interne **inner man** *n* moi *m* profond **innermost** *adj* le/la/les plus intime(s); **the ~ feelings/thoughts** les sentiments/les pensées les plus intimes; **in sb's ~ being** dans le for intérieur de qn; **the ~ circle** le cœur **inner tube** *n* chambre *f* à air

innings [ˈɪnɪŋz] *n Brit* **to have a good ~** (*live a long life*) avoir une vie bien remplie

innocence [ˈɪnəsns] *n no pl* innocence *f;* **sb's ~ of sth** l'innocence de qn pour qc; **in all ~** en toute innocence

innocent **I.** *adj* innocent(e); (*substance*) inoffensif(-ive) **II.** *n* innocent(e) *m(f)*

innocuous [ɪˈnɒkjʊəs, *Am:* -ˈnɑːk-] *adj* inoffensif(-ive)

innovate [ˈɪnəveɪt] *vi* innover

innovation *n* innovation *f*

innovative [ˈɪnəvətɪv, *Am:* -veɪt̬ɪv] *adj* innovateur(-trice)

innovator *n* innovateur, -trice *m, f*

innuendo [ˌɪnjuːˈendəʊ, *Am:* -doʊ] <-s *o* -es> *n* insinuation *f;* **to make an ~ about sth** faire des insinuations sur qc; **sexual ~** avances *fpl* sexuelles

innumerable [ɪˈnjuːmərəbl, *Am:* -ˈnuː-] *adj* innombrable

innumerate [ɪˈnjuːmərət, *Am:* -ˈnuːmɚ-] *adj* **to be ~** ne pas savoir calculer

inoculate [ɪˈnɒkjʊleɪt, *Am:* -ˈnɑːkjə-] *vt* inoculer

inoculation *n* inoculation *f*

inoffensive [ˌɪnəˈfensɪv] *adj* inoffensif(-ive)

inoperable [ˌɪnˈɒpərəbl, *Am:* -ˈɑːpɚ-] *adj* **1.** MED (*not treatable*) inopérable **2.** (*unable to function*) inopérant(e)

inoperative [ˌɪnˈɒpərətɪv, *Am:* -ˈɑːpɚət̬ɪv] *adj form* **1.** (*not in effect*) *a.* LAW périmé(e) **2.** (*not able to function*) **to be ~** être en panne

inopportune [ˌɪnˈɒpətjuːn, *Am:* -ˌɑːpɚˈtuːn] *adj form* inopportun(e)

inordinate [ɪˈnɔːdɪnət, *Am:* -ˈnɔːr-] *adj pej, form* immodéré(e)

inorganic [ˌɪnɔːˈgænɪk, *Am:* -ɔːrˈ-] *adj* CHEM inorganique

in-patient [ˈɪnpeɪʃnt] *n* patient *m* hospitalisé, patiente *f* hospitalisée

input [ˈɪnpʊt] **I.** *n* **1.** *no pl, no indef art* (*sth put into a system*) apport *m* **2.** (*contribution*) contribution *f* **3.** ELEC (*place, device*) entrée *f;* (*supply of power*) puissance *f* d'alimentation **4.** INFOR saisie *f* (de données) **II.** <-tt-> *vt* INFOR entrer

input data *npl* INFOR données *fpl* entrées **input device** *n* INFOR périphérique *m* d'entrée

inquest [ˈɪnkwest] *n a.* COM *a. fig* enquête *f*

inquire [ɪnˈkwaɪəʳ, *Am:* -ˈkwaɪr] *vt, vi s.* **enquire**

inquiry *n Brit, Am s.* **enquiry**

inquisition [ˌɪnkwɪˈzɪʃən] *n pej* inquisition *f;* **the Inquisition** l'Inquisition

inquisitive [ɪnˈkwɪzətɪv, *Am:* -t̬ɪv] *adj* curieux(-euse); **to be ~ about sb/sth** être curieux au sujet de qn/qc

inroad [ˈɪnrəʊd, *Am:* -roʊd] *n pl* **1.** MIL (*penetration*) invasion *f;* **to make ~s into sth** *a. iron* envahir qc **2.** (*reduce noticeably*) **to make ~s into sth** (*money, savings*) faire un grand trou dans qc

inroads *n pl* **to make ~s into sth** pénétrer qc

inrush [ˈɪnrʌʃ] *n sing* afflux *m*

insalubrious [ˌɪnsəˈluːbrɪəs] *adj form* insalubre

ins and outs *n pl* tenants *mpl* et aboutissants

insane [ɪnˈseɪn] *adj* **1.** *inf* MED malsain(e) **2.** *inf* (*crazy*) fou(folle)

insanitary [ɪnˈsænɪtri, *Am:* -teri] *adj pej* malsain(e)

insanity [ɪnˈsænəti, *Am:* -t̬i] *n no pl, no indef art* **1.** MED (*mental illness*) insanité *f;* **to plead ~** plaider une irresponsabilité **2.** *inf* (*craziness*) folie *f*

insatiable [ɪnˈseɪʃəbl] *adj* insatiable

inscribe [ɪnˈskraɪb] *vt* **1.** (*engrave*) inscrire **2.** (*write*) écrire

inscription [ɪnˈskrɪpʃən] *n* **1.** (*handwritten dedication in book*) dédicace *f* **2.** (*inscribed words*) inscription *f*

inscrutable [ɪnˈskruːtəbl, *Am:* -t̬ə-] *adj* insondable

insect [ˈɪnsekt] *n* insecte *m*

insecticide [ɪnˈsektɪsaɪd] *n* insecticide *m*

insecure [ˌɪnsɪˈkjʊəʳ, *Am:* -ˈkjʊr] *adj* **1.** (*lacking confidence*) **to be ~** manquer d'assurance

2. (*unstable*) instable; (*job, future*) précaire **3.** (*not firm or fixed*) peu solide **4.** (*unsafe: computer system*) vulnérable

insecurity [ˌɪnsɪˈkjʊərəti, *Am:* -ˈkjʊrət̬i] *n no pl* **1.** (*unsafeness*) insécurité *f* **2.** (*lack of self-confidence*) manque *m* d'assurance **3.** (*precariousness*) précarité *f*

inseminate [ɪnˈsemɪneɪt] *vt* inséminer; **to ~ a woman** inséminer une femme artificiellement

insemination *n no pl, no indef art* insémination *f*

insensible [ɪnˈsensəbl] *adj form* insensible; **to be ~ to/of sth** être insensible à qc

insensitive [ɪnˈsensətɪv, *Am:* -t̬ɪv] *adj a. pej* insensible; **to be ~ to sth** être insensible à qc

inseparable [ɪnˈseprəbl] *adj* **1.** (*emotionally very close*) stoïque **2.** (*inextricably connected*) *a.* LING inséparable

insert [ɪnˈsɜːt, *Am:* -ˈsɜːrt] **I.** *vt* insérer **II.** *n* **1.** (*extra loose pages*) insertion *f* **2.** (*extra piece in shoe, clothing*) incrustation *f*

insertion *n* insertion *f*

in-service [ˈɪnsɜvɪs, *Am:* -sɜːr-] *adj* à l'intérieur de l'entreprise

inshore [ˌɪnˈʃɔːʳ, *Am:* -ˈʃɔːr] **I.** *adj* (*near coast*) côtier(-ère) **II.** *adv* (*towards coast*) vers la côte

inside [ɪnˈsaɪd] **I.** *adj inv* **1.** (*internal*) *a. fig* intérieur(e); **~ information** informations *fpl* de première main; **~ joke** plaisanterie *f* maison; **~ job** coup *m* monté de l'intérieur; **~ story** vérité *f* **2.** AUTO **~ lane** *Brit, Aus* voie *f* de gauche; **~ lane** *Am* voie *f* de droite **3.** SPORT **to be on the ~ track** être sur le couloir intérieur; **~ left/right** intérieur *m* gauche/droit **4.** (*inseam*) **~ leg** *Brit, Aus* entre-jambes *m* **II.** *n* **1.** *no pl* (*internal part or side*) intérieur *m;* **to turn sth ~ out** retourner qc; *fig* mettre qc sens dessus dessous; **to know a place ~ out** connaître un endroit comme sa poche; **to know the ~ of sth** connaître les dessous de qc **2.** *pl* (*entrails*) entrailles *fpl* **3.** AUTO **to overtake on the ~** *Brit, Aus* dépasser à gauche; **to pass on the ~** *Am* dépasser à droite **III.** *prep* **1.** (*within*) à l'intérieur de; **from ~ sth** de l'intérieur de qc; **~ oneself** en soi-même; **~ of sth** *Am, inf* à l'intérieur de qc; **to play/go ~ the house** jouer/entrer dans la maison **2.** (*within time of*) en moins de; **~ of sth** *Am, inf* en moins de qc **IV.** *adv* **1.** (*within something*) à l'intérieur; **to go ~** entrer **2.** *inf* (*in jail*) en taule **3.** (*internally*) intérieurement; *s. a.* **outside**

inside of *prep Am, inf s.* **inside**

insider *n* initié(e) *m(f)*

insider dealing, **insider trading** *n* délit *m* d'initié

insidious [ɪnˈsɪdɪəs] *adj pej* insidieux(-euse)

insight [ˈɪnsaɪt] *n* **1.** *no pl, no indef art* (*capacity for deep understanding*) perspicacité *f;* **to have ~ into sth** avoir connaissance de qc **2.** (*instance of deep understanding*) aperçu *m;* **to gain ~ into sb/sth** pouvoir se faire une idée de qn/qc; **to give sb ~ into sb/sth** éclairer qn sur qn/qc

insignia [ɪnˈsɪgnɪə] *n* insignes *mpl*

insignificance [ˌɪnsɪgˈnɪfɪkəns] *n no pl, no indef art* insignifiance *f;* **to fade into ~** paraître insignifiant

insignificant *adj* insignifiant(e)

insincere [ˌɪnsɪnˈsɪəʳ, *Am:* -ˈsɪr] *adj pej* insincère; (*artificial*) faux(fausse)

insinuate [ɪnˈsɪnjʊeɪt] *vt* insinuer; **to ~ oneself into sth** s'insinuer dans qc

insinuation *n* insinuation *f*

insipid [ɪnˈsɪpɪd] *adj a. pej* insipide

insist [ɪnˈsɪst] *vi, vt* insister

insistence [ɪnˈsɪstəns] *n no pl, no indef art* insistance *f*

insistent *adj* insistant(e); **to be ~ that ...** insister sur le fait que ...

insofar as [ˌɪnsəʊˈfɑːr əz, *Am:* -soʊˈfɑːr əz] *adv* dans la mesure où

insole [ˈɪnsəʊl, *Am:* -soʊl] *n* semelle *f* (intérieure)

insolence [ˈɪnsələns] *n* insolence *f*

insolent *adj* insolent(e)

insoluble [ɪnˈsɒljʊbl, *Am:* -ˈsɑːljə-] *adj* CHEM insoluble

insolvency *n no pl* insolvabilité *f*

insolvent [ɪnˈsɒlvənt, *Am:* -ˈsɑːl-] **I.** *adj* insolvable **II.** *n* débiteur, -trice *m, f* insolvable

insomnia [ɪnˈsɒmnɪə, *Am:* -ˈsɑːm-] *n no pl, no indef art* insomnie *f*

insomniac **I.** *n* insomniaque *mf* **II.** *adj* insomniaque

insomuch as *adv s.* **inasmuch as**

inspect [ɪnˈspekt] *vt* **1.** (*examine carefully*) *a.* MIL inspecter **2.** (*examine officially*) contrôler

inspection *n* inspection *f;* **on closer ~** vu de plus près

inspector *n* inspecteur, -trice *m, f;* **school ~** inspecteur, -trice *m, f* pédagogique; **tax ~** inspecteur, -trice *m, f* des Contributions; **ticket ~** contrôleur, -euse *m, f*

inspiration [ˌɪnspəˈreɪʃən] *n* inspiration *f*

inspire [ɪnˈspaɪəʳ, *Am:* -ˈspaɪr] *vt a. form a.* MED inspirer; **to ~ sth in sb** inspirer qc à qn

inspired *adj* inspiré(e)

in spite of *prep* en dépit de; **~ oneself** malgré soi; **~ everyone** envers et contre tous; **~ the fact that he is rich** bien qu'il soit riche

instability [ˌɪnstəˈbɪləti, *Am:* -t̬i] *n no pl, no indef art, a. pej a.* PSYCH instabilité *f*

instal(l) [ɪnˈstɔːl] *vt a.* CONSTR, INFOR, TECH installer; **to ~ the carpets** *Am, Aus* poser la moquette; **to ~ oneself** s'installer; **to ~ sb in an old people's home** placer qn dans un centre pour personnes du troisième âge

installation [ˌɪnstəˈleɪʃən] *n* **1.** *no pl, no indef art* CONSTR installation *f* **2.** MIL (*place, facility*) site *m* **3.** (*officially putting in office*) institution *f* **4.** ART forme *f*

instal(l)ment *n* **1.** RADIO, TV (*part*) suite *f* **2.** COM traite *f;* **to be payable in monthly ~s**

être payable par mensualités; **to pay for sth by ~s** payer qc par traites

instal(l)ment plan *n* COM *s.* **hire purchase**

instance [ˈɪnstəns] **I.** *n* **1.** (*particular case*) cas *m;* **in this ~** dans ce cas présent **2. for ~** (*for example*) par exemple **3.** *form* **in the first ~** (*at first*) en premier lieu; **in the second ~** (*later*) en second lieu **4.** *form* (*urging, request, order*) instance *f;* **to do sth at sb's ~** faire qc à l'instance de qn **II.** *vt form* **to ~ sth** statuer qc en exemple

instant **I.** *n* instant *m;* **at the same ~** au même instant; **for an ~** pour un instant; **in an ~** en un instant; **to do sth this ~** faire qc tout de suite; **the next ~** l'instant suivant; **not for an ~** pas une seule fois **II.** *adj a.* GASTR instantané(e); **~ replay** *Brit* répétition *f* immédiate

instantaneous [ˌɪnstənˈteɪnɪəs] *adj* instantané(e)

instantaneously *adv* instantanément

instantly *adv* immédiatement

instant replay *n* ralenti *m*

instead of [ɪnˈsted ɒv, *Am:* -ɑːv] *prep* **~ sb/sth** à la place de qn/qc; **~ doing sth** au lieu de faire qc

instep [ˈɪnstep] *n* ANAT coup-de-pied *m*

instigate [ˈɪnstɪgeɪt] *vt form* **1.** (*initiate, cause to happen*) promouvoir **2.** (*incite*) inciter, instiguer *Belgique*

instigation *n no pl, no indef art, form* instigation *f;* **to do sth at the ~ of sb** faire qc à l'instigation de qn

instil <-ll-> *vt,* **instill** [ɪnˈstɪl] *vt Am* **to ~ sth into sb** apprendre qc à qn

instinct [ˈɪnstɪŋkt] *n* instinct *m;* **to do sth by ~** faire qc d'instinct; **a business/political ~** un sens des affaires/pour la politique; **to have an ~ for sth** avoir de l'instinct pour qc

instinctive *adj* instinctif(-ive)

institute [ˈɪntstɪtjuːt, *Am:* -tuːt] **I.** *n* institut *m* **II.** *vt* instituer

institution *n a. inf* institution *f*

institutional *adj* **1.** (*organizational*) *a.* COM institutionnel(le) **2.** (*established: religion*) institué(e)

institutionalise *vt,* **institutionalize** [ˌɪntstɪˈtjuːʃəəlaɪz] *vt Am* **1.** (*place in organization for care*) instituer **2.** (*make into custom*) institutionnaliser

in-store [ˌɪnˈstɔːʳ] *adj, adv* à l'intérieur du magasin

in-store detective *n* surveillant *m* de grande surface

instruct [ɪnˈstrʌkt] *vt* **1.** (*teach*) **to ~ sb in sth** instruire qn dans qc; **to ~ the jury** LAW instruire la cour d'assises **2.** (*direct, order formally*) **to ~ sb to** *+infin* donner une instruction à qn de *+infin* **3.** *Brit, Aus* LAW instruire

instruction *n* instruction *f;* **to give sb ~s** donner des instructions à qn; **to act on ~s** agir conformément aux instructions; **to carry out ~s** suivre les instructions; **sb's ~s are to** *+infin* qn a pour instruction de *+infin;* **to give sb ~ in sth** instruire qn dans qc

instruction book *n s.* **instruction manual**

instruction leaflet *n* notice *f* **instruction manual** *n* livret *m* d'instruction **instruction repertoire** *n* INFOR jeu *m* d'instructions

instructive *adj* instructif(-ive)

instructor *n* **1.** (*teacher of particular skill*) moniteur, -trice *m, f;* **driving/ski ~** moniteur, -trice *m, f* de conduite/ski **2.** *Am* UNIV (*teacher*) professeur *m*

instructress *n* professeur *m*

instrument [ˈɪnstrʊmənt, *Am:* -strə-] *n a. fig* instrument *m;* **to be the ~ of sb** être l'instrument de qn

instrumental **I.** *adj* **1.** (*relating to tools*) *a.* MUS instrumental(e) **2.** (*greatly influential*) **to be ~ to sth** aider à qc; **to be ~ in doing sth** aider à faire qc **II.** *n* instrumental *m*

instrumentation [ˌɪnstrʊmenˈteɪʃən, *Am:* -strə-] *n no pl* MUS, TECH instrumentation *f*

instrument board, **instrument panel** *n* tableau *m* de bord

insubordinate [ˌɪnsəˈbɔːdɪnət, *Am:* -ˈbɔːrdənɪt] *adj pej* insubordonné(e); **~ behaviour** insubordination *f*

insubstantial [ˌɪnsəbˈstænʃl] *adj* **1.** (*lacking substance*) formel(le) **2.** (*lacking significance*) négligeable **3.** *form* (*not real*) imaginaire

insufferable [ɪnˈsʌfrəbl] *adj pej* insupportable; **to be ~** être insupportable

insufficiency [ˌɪnsəˈfɪʃəntsi] *n a.* MED insuffisance *f*

insufficient *adj* insuffisant(e); **to release sb for ~ evidence** relaxer qn pour manque de preuves; **to be ~ for sth** être insuffisant pour qc

insular [ˈɪntsjələʳ, *Am:* -sələ˞] *adj* **1.** GEO (*relating to an island*) insulaire **2.** *pej* (*parochial, narrow-minded*) borné(e)

insularity [ˌɪntsjəˈlærəti, *Am:* -səˈlerəṱi] *n no pl* **1.** GEO insularité *f* **2.** *pej* étroitesse *f* d'esprit

insulate [ˈɪntsjəleɪt, *Am:* -sə-] *vt* isoler

insulating *adj* isolant(e)

insulating tape *n* chatterton *m*

insulation *n no pl* **1.** (*protective covering*) isolant *m* **2.** (*protection from outside influences*) isolation *f*

insulin [ˈɪntsjʊlɪn, *Am:* -sə-] *n no pl, no indef art* insuline *f*

insult[1] [ɪnˈsʌlt] *vt* insulter

insult[2] [ˈɪnsʌlt] *n a. fig* insulte *f* ►**to add ~ to injury** et pour comble

insuperable [ɪnˈsjuːprəbl, *Am:* -ˈsuː-] *adj form* insurmontable

insupportable [ˌɪnsəˈpɔːtəbl, *Am:* -ˈpɔːrṱə-] *adj* insupportable

insurance [ɪnˈʃʊərəns, *Am:* -ˈʃʊrəns] *n* **1.** *no pl, no indef art* (*financial protection*) assurance *f;* **life ~** assurance vie **2.** *no pl, no indef art* (*payment by insurance company*) montant *m* de l'assurance **3.** *no pl, no indef art* (*premium*) prime *f* d'assurance **4.** *no pl, no indef art* (*profession*) assurances *fpl* **5.** (*measure taken for protection*) mesure *f* de protection

insurance agent *n* agent *m* d'assurances **insurance broker** *n* courtier *m* d'assurances **insurance company** <-ies> *n* compagnie *f* d'assurances **insurance cover** *n* couverture *f* (d'assurance) **insurance policy** <-ies> *n* police *f* d'assurance **insurance premium** *n* prime *f* d'assurance

insure [ɪn'ʃʊəʳ, *Am:* -'ʃʊr] *vt* assurer

insured I. *adj* assuré(e) **II.** *n form* LAW **the** ~ l'assuré(e) *m(f)*

insurer *n* **1.** (*insurance agent*) assureur *m* **2.** *pl* (*insurance company*) assurance *f*

insurmountable [ˌɪnsə'maʊntəbl, *Am:* -sɚ'maʊnt̬ə-] *adj* insurmontable

insurrection [ˌɪnsə'rekʃən, *Am:* -sə'rek-] *n* insurrection *f;* **to crush the** ~ écraser la révolte

intact [ɪn'tækt] *adj a. fig* intact(e)

intake ['ɪnteɪk] *n* **1.** (*action of taking in*) prise *f;* (*of food, drink*) consommation *f;* (*air*) admission *f* **2.** (*amount taken in*) apport *m;* **daily** ~ ration *f* journalière; ~ **of calories** apport *m* calorique **3.** (*quantity of people*) admissions *fpl;* MIL contingent *m* **4.** TECH (*mechanical aperture*) admission *f*

intangible [ɪn'tændʒəbl] *adj* impalpable

integer ['ɪntɪdʒəʳ, *Am:* -dʒɚ] *n* MAT entier *m*

integral ['ɪntɪgrəl, *Am:* -t̬ə-] *adj* **1.** (*central, essential*) indispensable; **to be an** ~ **part** faire partie intégrante; **to be** ~ **to sb/sth** être indispensable à qn/qc **2.** (*built-in*) incorporé(e) **3.** (*complete*) intégral(e)

integral calculus *n* MAT calcul *m* intégral

integrate ['ɪntɪgreɪt, *Am:* -t̬ə-] **I.** *vt* **1.** (*cause to merge socially*) intégrer **2.** (*incorporate, unite*) compléter **II.** *vi* s'intégrer

integrated *adj* **1.** (*included*) intégré(e) **2.** (*desegregated: school, education*) de déségrégation raciale

integrated circuit *n* circuit *m* intégré

integration *n no pl* **1.** (*social/cultural assimilation*) intégration *f;* **racial** ~ déségrégation *f* raciale **2.** (*unification, fusion*) unification *f*

integrity [ɪn'tegrəti, *Am:* -t̬i] *n no pl* **1.** (*incorruptibility, uprightness*) intégrité *f;* **a man/a woman of** ~ un homme/une femme intègre **2.** (*high ethical standards*) honnêteté *f* **3.** *form* (*unity, wholeness*) totalité *f*

intellect ['ɪntəlekt, *Am:* -t̬ə-] *n no pl* **1.** (*faculty*) intelligence *f;* **man/woman of** ~ homme/femme intelligent(e) **2.** (*thinker, intellectual*) intellectuel(le) *m(f)*

intellectual [ˌɪntə'lektʃʊəl, *Am:* -t̬ə-] **I.** *n* intellectuel(le) *m(f)* **II.** *adj* intellectuel(le)

intelligence [ɪn'telɪdʒəns] *n no pl* **1.** (*alertness, brain power*) *a.* INFOR intelligence *f* **2.** + *sing/pl vb* (*inside information, low-down*) entendement *m* **3.** (*department gathering inside knowledge*) service *m* de renseignements

intelligence quotient *n* quotient *m* intellectuel **intelligence service** *n* service *m* de renseignements **intelligence test** *n* test *m* d'intelligence

intelligent *adj* intelligent(e)

intelligentsia [ɪnˌtelɪ'dʒentsɪə] *n sing/pl vb* **the** ~ l'intelligentsia *f*

intelligible [ɪn'telɪdʒəbl] *adj* intelligible; **hardly** ~ à peine compréhensible; **he was so drunk that he was hardly** ~ il était si ivre qu'on le comprenait à peine

intend [ɪn'tend] *vt* **1.** (*aim for, plan*) avoir l'intention; **to** ~ **doing/to** +*infin* avoir l'intention de +*infin;* **to** ~ **sb to do sth** avoir l'intention que qn fasse qc *(subj);* **it was not ~ed that** l'intention n'était pas que +*subj;* **what I** ~ **is ...** mon intention est ...; **to be ~ed as sth** être censé être qc **2.** (*earmark, destine*) **to be ~ed for sb/sth** être destiné à qn/qc; **to be ~ed to** +*infin* être destiné à +*infin*

intended I. *n sing, iron* fiancé(e) *m(f)* **II.** *adj* **1.** (*intentional*) intentionnel(le) **2.** (*planned*) prévu(e); (*mistake, effect*) voulu(e)

intense [ɪn'tents] *adj* **1.** (*extreme, strong*) intense; (*pain, excitement*) vif(vive); (*feeling, interest*) profond(e) **2.** (*passionate: person*) véhément(e)

intensify [ɪn'tentsɪfaɪ] **I.** *vt* intensifier; (*the pressure*) augmenter **II.** *vi* s'accroître

intensity [ɪn'tentsəti, *Am:* -t̬i] *n no pl* intensité *f*

intensive *adj* intensif(-ive); (*analysis*) serré(e)

intent [ɪn'tent] **I.** *n* **1.** (*intention*) intention *f;* **to all ~s and purposes** virtuellement **2.** *form* LAW **to loiter with** ~ faire un délit d'intention **II.** *adj* **1.** (*absorbed, concentrated, occupied*) absorbé(e); **to be** ~ **on sb/sth** être tout entier à qn/qc **2.** (*hell-bent, set*) **to be/seem** ~ **on sth** être enclin à qc

intention [ɪn'tentʃən] *n* intention *f;* **I still don't know what his ~s are** je ne sais toujours pas quelles sont ses intentions; **it wasn't my** ~ **to exclude you** je n'avais nullement l'intention de t'exclure; **to have no** ~ **of doing sth** n'avoir nullement l'intention de faire qc

intentional *adj* intentionnel(le)

interact [ˌɪntər'ækt, *Am:* ɪnt̬ɚ'ækt] *vi* interagir

interaction *n* interaction *f*

interactive *adj* interactif(-ive)

interactive TV *n* TV *f* interactive

interbreed [ˌɪntə'briːd, *Am:* -t̬ɚ'-] **I.** *vt irr* entrecroiser **II.** *vi irr* se reproduire par croisement; **to** ~ **with sth** se croiser avec qc

intercede [ˌɪntə'siːd, *Am:* -t̬ɚ'-] *vi* intercéder; **to** ~ **with sb for/on behalf of sb** plaider auprès de qn pour/en faveur de qn

intercept [ˌɪntə'sept, *Am:* -t̬ɚ'-] *vt* intercepter

interception *n* interception *f*

interceptor *n* **1.** (*person*) *personne qui intercepte* **2.** (*aircraft*) intercepteur *m*

intercession [ˌɪntəˈseʃən, *Am:* -t̬ɚ-] *n* intercession *f;* **through the ~ of sb/sth** par l'intercession de qn/qc

interchange [ˌɪntəˈtʃeɪndʒ, *Am:* -t̬ɚ-] **I.** *n* **1.** *form* échange *m* **2.** échangeur *m* (d'autoroute) **II.** *vt* échanger **III.** *vi* s'interchanger

interchangeable *adj* interchangeable

intercity [ˌɪntəˈsɪti] *Brit* **I.** *n* service *m* interurbain **II.** *adj* interurbain(e)

intercom [ˈɪntəkɒm, *Am:* -t̬ɚkɑːm] *n* interphone *m;* **through (an) ~** par interphone; **to speak over the ~** parler par l'interphone

intercommunicate [ˌɪntəkəˈmjuːnɪkeɪt, *Am:* -t̬ɚ-] *vi* communiquer

intercontinental [ˌɪntəˌkɒntɪˈnentl, *Am:* -t̬ɚˌkɑːntəˈnent̬l] *adj* intercontinental(e)

intercourse [ˈɪntəkɔːs, *Am:* -t̬ɚkɔːrs] *n no pl* **1.** (*relationship*) rapports *mpl;* **sexual ~** relations *fpl* sexuelles **2.** *form* fréquentation *f;* **social ~** fréquentation du monde

interdenominational [ˌɪntə dɪˌnɒmɪˈneɪʃənl, *Am:* -t̬ɚdɪˌnɑːməˈ-] *adj* interconfessionnel(le)

interdepartmental [ˈɪntəˌdiːpɑːtˈ mentl, *Am:* -t̬ɚˌdiːpɑːrtˈment̬l] *adj* interdépartemental(e); **~ work** travail entre services

interdependence [ˌɪntədɪˈpendəns, *Am:* -t̬ɚdiːˈ-] *n no pl* interdépendance *f*

interdependent *adj* interdépendant(e)

interdict [ˌɪntəˈdɪkt, *Am:* -t̬ɚ-] *form* **I.** *vt* **1.** LAW **to ~ sth to sb** interdire qc à qn **2.** *Am* MIL prohiber **II.** *n* LAW défense *f*

interest [ˈɪntrəst, *Am:* -trɪst] **I.** *n* **1.** *no pl* (*curiousity*) intérêt *m;* **to take an ~ in sth** s'intéresser à qc; **to lose ~ in sb/sth** se désintéresser de qn/qc; **to be of ~** être intéressant; **just out of ~** juste par curiosité **2.** (*hobby*) centre *m* d'intérêt; **to pursue one's own ~s** poursuivre ses propres buts **3.** (*profit, advantage*) intérêt *m;* **to be in sb's ~** être dans l'intérêt de qn; **in the ~s of humanity** dans l'intérêt de l'humanité **4.** *no pl* (*cost of borrowing money*) intérêt *m;* **at 5 % ~** à un intérêt de 5 %; **rate of ~** taux *m* d'intérêts; **~ on a loan** intérêts *mpl* sur un prêt; **to earn/pay ~** gagner/payer des intérêts **5.** FIN (*stake*) intérêt *m;* **to have an ~ in sb/sth** être intéressé par qn/qc **II.** *vt* intéresser; **to ~ sb in sth** éveiller l'intérêt de qn pour qc

interested *adj* **1.** (*arousing interest*) intéressé(e); **to be ~ in sb/sth** être intéressé par qn/qc; **to be ~ in doing sth** être intéressé de faire qc; **I am ~ to know more about it** cela m'intéresse d'en savoir plus **2.** (*concerned, involved*) intéressé(e); **the ~ parties** les parties concernées

interesting *adj a. iron* intéressant(e); **to have ~ things to say** avoir qc d'intéressant à dire; **that's an ~-looking hat** c'est un chapeau intéressant

interface [ˈɪntəfeɪs, *Am:* -t̬ɚ-] **I.** *n a.* INFOR interface *f;* **his job is to be an ~ between the departments** son travail est de jouer l'intermédiaire entre les départements; **graphic/parallel/serial ~** interface graphique/parallèle/série **II.** *vi* avoir une interface **III.** *vt* **to ~ sth** mettre qc en interface

interfere [ˌɪntəˈfɪəʳ, *Am:* -t̬ɚˈfɪr] *vi* **1.** (*become involved*) **to ~ in sth** se mêler de qc; (*sb's private life, a relationship*) s'immiscer dans qc; **she is always ~ing** elle se mêle toujours de ce qui ne la regarde pas **2.** (*hinder*) **to ~ with sth** gêner qc **3.** (*disturb*) **to ~ with sb/sth** contrarier qn/qc **4.** (*handle without permission*) **to ~ in/with sth** toucher à qc **5.** RADIO, TECH (*hamper signals*) **to ~ with sth** perturber qc **6.** *Brit* (*molest children*) **to ~ with sb** abuser de qn

interference [ˌɪntəˈfɪərəns, *Am:* -t̬ɚˈfɪr-] *n no pl* **1.** (*interfering*) ingérence *f;* (*in sb's privacy*) intrusion *f* **2.** RADIO, TECH interférences *fpl*

interfering *adj* importun(e)

interim [ˈɪntərɪm, *Am:* -t̬ɚ-] **I.** *n no pl* intérim *m;* **in the ~** dans l'intérim **II.** *adj inv* intérimaire

interior [ɪnˈtɪərɪəʳ, *Am:* -ˈtɪrɪɚ] **I.** *adj inv* intérieur(e); (*decorator, scene*) d'intérieur; **I visited only the ~ regions of the country** je n'ai visité que les régions de l'intérieur du pays **II.** *n* **1.** (*inside*) intérieur *m* **2.** POL (*home affairs*) **the Interior** les affaires *fpl* intérieures; **the Ministry of the Interior** le ministère de l'Intérieur; **the U.S. Department of the Interior** *ministère chargé de l'aménagment du territoire et de la gestion des parcs nationaux*

interior decoration *n* décoration *f* d'intérieur **interior design** *n* architecture *f* d'intérieur **interior designer** *n* architecte *mf* d'intérieur

interject [ˌɪntəˈdʒekt, *Am:* -t̬ɚ-] **I.** *vt form* (*remark, words*) lancer **II.** *vi* intervenir

interjection *n* interjection *f*

interlace [ˌɪntəˈleɪs, *Am:* -t̬ɚ-] *vt* entrelacer

inter-library loan [ɪntəˈlaɪbrərɪˌləʊn] *n* prêt *m* inter-bibliothèque

interlocutor [ˌɪntəˈlɒkjʊtəʳ, *Am:* -t̬ɚˈlɑːkjət̬ɚ] *n form* interlocuteur, -trice *m, f*

interloper [ˈɪntələʊpəʳ, *Am:* -t̬ɚloʊpɚ] *n pej* intrus(e) *m(f)*

interlude [ˈɪntəluːd, *Am:* -t̬ɚluːd] *n* intermède *m;* **musical ~** interlude *m* musical

intermarry [ˌɪntəˈmæri, *Am:* ˈɪnt̬ɚˌmer-] <-ie-> *vi* **1.** (*marry with a different group*) **to ~ with sth** se marier avec qc **2.** (*marry within a family*) se marier au sein de la même famille

intermediary [ˌɪntəˈmiːdɪəri, *Am:* -t̬ɚˈmiːdɪer-] <-ries-> **I.** *n* intermédiaire *mf;* **through an ~** par un intermédiaire **II.** *adj* intermédiaire

intermediate [ˌɪntəˈmiːdɪət, *Am:* -t̬ɚ-] *adj* intermédiaire; **~ course** cours *m* de niveau moyen; **to be ~ between sth** être l'intermediaire entre qc

intermezzo [ˌɪntəˈmetsəʊ, *Am:* -t̬ɚˈmet-soʊ] <-s *o* -zi> *n* intermezzo *m*

interminable [ɪnˈtɜːmɪnəbl, *Am:* -ˈtɜːr-] *adj* interminable

intermission [ˌɪntəˈmɪʃən, *Am:* -t̬ɚ-] *n* interruption *f;* **without ~** sans arrêt; **after/during ~** *Am* après/pendant la pause

intermittent [ˌɪntəˈmɪtnt, *Am:* -t̬ɚ-] *adj* intermittent(e); **she made ~ movie appearances** elle a fait quelques apparitions ponctuelles dans des films

intern [ɪnˈtɜːn, *Am:* -ˈtɜːrn] **I.** *vt* interner **II.** *vi* UNIV, SCHOOL **to ~ in a company** faire un stage dans une entreprise **III.** *n Am* **1.** MED interne *mf* **2.** (*trainee*) stagiaire *mf*

internal *adj* intérieur(e); (*affairs, bleeding, investigation*) interne; **for ~ use only** à usage interne uniquement

international [ˌɪntəˈnæʃənəl, *Am:* -t̬ɚ-] **I.** *adj* international(e); **on the/an ~ level** au/à un niveau international **II.** *n* **1.** *Brit* SPORT (*player*) international(e) *m(f)* **2.** (*sports match*) match *m* international **3.** (*communist organisation*) **International** l'Internationale *f*

internationalise *vt,* **internationalize** [ˌɪntəˈnæʃənəlaɪz, *Am:* -t̬ɚ-] *vt Am* internationaliser

internaut *n* internaute *mf*

internecine war [ɪntəˈniːsaɪnˌwɔːʳ, *Am:* -t̬ɚˈniːsɪn-] *n* guerre *f* de destruction réciproque

internee [ˌɪntɜːˈniː, *Am:* -tɜːrˈ-] *n* interné(e) *m(f)*

internet [ˈɪntənet, *Am:* -t̬ɚ-] **I.** *adj* Internet *inv* **II.** *n* Internet *m;* **the ~** le réseau Internet; **to access the ~** accéder à Internet

internet access *n* branchement *m* Internet **internet-based learning** *n* apprentissage *m* par Internet **internet café** *n* cybercafé *m* **internet search engine** *n* chercheur *m* web

internist [ɪnˈtɜːnɪst, *Am:* -ˈtɜːr-] *n* **1.** *Am* (*general practitioner*) médecin *m* généraliste **2.** (*specialist in inner medicine*) spécialiste *mf* des maladies organiques

internment [ɪnˈtɜːnmənt, *Am:* -ˈtɜːrn-] *n no pl* internement *m*

internment camp *n* camp *m* d'internement

internship *n Am* **1.** MED internat *m* **2.** (*traineeship*) stage *m*

interpellation [ɪnˌtɜːpəˈleɪʃən, *Am:* -ˌtɜːr-] *n* POL interpellation *f*

interphone [ˈɪntəfəʊn] *n Am s.* **intercom**

interplanetary [ˌɪntəˈplænɪtəri, *Am:* -t̬ɚˈplænəter-] *adj inv* interplanétaire

interplay [ˈɪntəpleɪ, *Am:* -t̬ɚ-] *n no pl* interaction *f*

Interpol [ˈɪntəpɒl, *Am:* -t̬ɚpaːl] *n no art abbr of* **International Criminal Police Commission** Interpol *m*

interpolate [ɪnˈtɜːpəleɪt, *Am:* -ˈtɜːr-] *vt form* interpoler; **to ~ sth into sth** intercaler qc dans qc; **to ~ a text** altérer un texte par interpolation

interpolation *n* interpolation *f*

interpret [ɪnˈtɜːprɪt, *Am:* -ˈtɜːrprət] **I.** *vt* interpréter; **to ~ sth as sth** interpréter qc comme qc **II.** *vi* faire l'interprète

interpretation *n a.* THEAT, LIT interprétation *f;* **to be open to ~** être sujet à interprétation; **to put an ~ on sth** donner une interprétation à qc

interpreter *n* **1.** LIT, THEAT interprète *mf* **2.** (*oral translator*) interprète *mf* **3.** (*type of computer program*) interprète *m*

interrelated *adj* en corrélation

interrogate [ɪnˈterəgeɪt] *vt* **1.** (*cross-question*) questionner **2.** (*get data from computer*) consulter

interrogation *n* interrogation *f;* **to take sb for ~** emmener qn pour un interrogatoire; **under ~** en train de subir un interrogatoire

interrogation mark, **interrogation point** *n* point *m* d'interrogation

interrogative [ˌɪntəˈrɒgətɪv, *Am:* -t̬ɚˈraːgət̬ɪv] **I.** *n* LING interrogatif *m* **II.** *adj* **1.** (*having questioning form*) interrogateur(-trice) **2.** (*of word type asking question: pronoun*) interrogatif(-ive)

interrogator *n* interrogateur, -trice *m, f*

interrogatory [ˌɪntəˈrɒgətəri, *Am:* -t̬ɚˈraːgətɔːr-] *adj* interrogateur(-trice)

interrupt [ˌɪntəˈrʌpt, *Am:* -t̬ɚ-] *vt* interrompre; **will you stop ~ing me!** arrête de me couper la parole

interrupter *n* interrupteur *m*

interruption *n* interruption *f;* **~ in the flow of food** rupture dans la chaîne alimentaire; **without ~** sans arrêt

intersect [ˌɪntəˈsekt] **I.** *vt* **1.** (*cross at a junction*) entrecouper **2.** (*divide with criss-crossing lines*) couper **II.** *vi* se couper; **the highway ~s the expressway near the hotel** l'autoroute croise la voie rapide près de l'hôtel; **~ing roads** carrefour

intersection *n* **1.** (*crossing of lines*) intersection *f* **2.** *Am, Aus* (*junction*) croisement *m*

intersperse [ˌɪntəˈspɜːs, *Am:* -t̬ɚˈspɜːrs] *vt* entremêler; **to be ~d throughout the text** être éparpillé dans tout le texte

interstate [ˌɪntəˈsteɪt, *Am:* ˈɪnt̬ɚ-] **I.** *adj inv, Am* entre États **II.** *n Am* autoroute *f*

interstellar [ˌɪntəˈsteləʳ, *Am:* -t̬ɚˈstelɚ] *adj inv, form* interstellaire

interstice [ɪnˈtɜːstɪs, *Am:* -ˈtɜːr-] *n form* interstice *m*

intertwine [ˌɪntəˈtwaɪn, *Am:* -t̬ɚ-] **I.** *vt* entrelacer **II.** *vi* s'accoler

interurban [ˌɪntəˈɜːbən, *Am:* -t̬ɚˈɜːr-] *adj Am* interurbain(e)

interval [ˈɪntəvl, *Am:* -t̬ɚ-] *n* **1.** (*period*) intervalle *m;* **at five minutes ~s** à cinq minutes d'intervalle; **at regular ~s** à intervalles réguliers **2.** METEO période *f;* **sunny ~s** éclaircies *fpl* ensoleillées **3.** THEAT, MUS entracte *m*

4. (*gap between notes*) intervalle *m*
intervene [ˌɪntəˈviːn, *Am:* -t̬ɚ-] *vi* **1.** (*involve oneself to help*) intervenir; **to ~ on sb's behalf** intervenir au nom de qn **2.** *pej* (*meddle unhelpfully*) interférer **3.** (*come to pass between*) s'écouler
intervening *adj inv* intervenant(e); **in the ~ period** pendant la période qui s'écoula
intervention [ˌɪntəˈvenʃən, *Am:* -t̬ɚ-] *n* intervention *f*
interventionist *adj* interventionniste
interview [ˈɪntəvjuː, *Am:* -t̬ɚ-] **I.** *n* **1.** (*formal talk for job*) entretien *m;* **to have a job ~** avoir un entretien pour un emploi; **a telephone ~** un entretien téléphonique **2.** PUBL, RADIO, TV interview *f* **II.** *vt* **1.** (*question for a job*) faire passer un entretien à **2.** (*question for the police: suspect*) interroger **3.** (*ask celebrity*) interviewer **III.** *vi* **1.** (*question for a job*) faire passer des entretiens **2.** PUBL, RADIO, TV faire une interview
interviewee [ˌɪntəvjuːˈiː, *Am:* -t̬ɚ-] *n* interviewé(e) *m(f)*
interviewer *n* interviewer *m;* **market research ~** enquêteur, -teuse *m, f*
interweave [ˌɪntəˈwiːv, *Am:* -t̬ɚ-] **I.** *vt irr* **1.** (*weave together*) entrelacer; (*threads*) tisser ensemble **2.** *fig* mêler; **to be interwoven with sth** être étroitement lié à qc **II.** *vi* **1.** (*weave together*) s'entrelacer **2.** *fig* s'entremêler
intestate [ɪnˈtesteɪt] *adj inv* LAW intestat
intestinal flora *n* flore *f* intestinale
intestine [ɪnˈtestɪn] *n pl* MED intestin *m*
intimacy [ˈɪntɪməsi, *Am:* -t̬ə-] <-cies> *n* **1.** *no pl* (*closeness*) intimité *f* **2.** *pl* (*intimate relations*) relations *fpl* intimes **3.** *pl* (*intimate remarks*) familiarités *fpl*
intimate[1] [ˈɪntɪmət, *Am:* -t̬ə-] **I.** *adj* **1.** (*close*) intime; **~ circle** cercle *m* d'intimes; **to be on ~ terms with sb** être intime avec qn **2.** (*very detailed*) approfondi(e) **II.** *n* intime *mf*
intimate[2] [ˈɪntɪmeɪt, *Am:* -t̬ə-] *vt* signifier
intimation [ˌɪntɪˈmeɪʃən, *Am:* -t̬ə-] *n* (*hint*) signe *m*
intimidate [ɪnˈtɪmɪdeɪt] *vt* intimider; **to ~ sb into doing sth** décourager qn de faire qc; **I felt somewhat ~d by the amount of work** *fig* j'ai été quelque peu impressionné par la somme de travail
intimidating *adj* intimidant(e)
intimidation *n no pl* intimidation *f*
into [ˈɪntʊ, *Am:* -tə] *prep* **1.** dans **2.** (*movement to inside*) **to come/go ~ a place** entrer dans un lieu; **to put sth ~ it/place** mettre qc dedans/en place; **to get/let sb ~ a car** monter/faire monter qn en voiture; **to get ~ a shirt** enfiler une chemise; **to retreat ~ one's self** se replier sur soi-même **3.** (*movement towards*) **to walk** [*o* **drive**] **~ a tree** percuter un arbre; **to run** [*o* **bump**] **~ sb/sth** tomber sur qn/qc **4.** (*through time of*) **to work late ~ the night** travailler tard dans la nuit **5.** (*change to*) **to put sth ~ English** traduire qc en anglais; **to change notes ~ coins** changer des billets contre des pièces; **to force sb ~ doing sth** forcer qn à faire qc **6.** (*begin*) **to burst ~ tears/laughter** éclater en sanglots/de rire; **to get ~ the habit of doing sth** prendre l'habitude de faire qc **7.** (*make smaller*) **3 ~ 6 goes twice** 6 divisé par 3 donne 2; **to cut sth ~ two/slices** couper qc en deux/tranches **8.** *inf* (*interested in*) **to be ~ sb/sth** être un dingue de qn/qc
intolerable *adj* intolérable; **an ~ place to live in** un lieu où il est insupportable de vivre
intolerance [ɪnˈtɒlərəns, *Am:* -ˈtɑːlɚ-] *n no pl* intolérance *f;* **~ of alcohol** intolérance à l'alcool
intolerant *adj* intolérant(e); **to be ~ of alcohol** ne pas supporter l'alcool; **to be ~ of different opinions** ne pas tolérer des opinions différentes
intonation [ˌɪntəˈneɪʃən, *Am:* -toʊˈ-] *n sing* **1.** LING (*cadence/modulation of voice*) intonation *f;* **to speak with a French ~** parler avec un accent français **2.** MUS intonation *f*
intone [ɪnˈtəʊn, *Am:* -ˈtoʊn] *vt form* **1.** (*say, recite*) entonner **2.** REL psalmodier
intoxicate [ɪnˈtɒksɪkeɪt, *Am:* -ˈtɑːk-] *vt, vi* **1.** (*cause drunkenness*) enivrer **2.** *fig* (*excite*) griser
intoxicating *adj a. fig* enivrant(e); **an ~ drink** une boisson alcoolisée
intoxication *n no pl* **1.** MED intoxication *f* **2.** (*drunkenness*) ivresse *f* **3.** *fig* ivresse *f*
intractable [ˌɪnˈtræktəbl] *adj* intraitable
intracutaneous [ɪntrækjuːˈteɪnəs] *adj* MED intracutané(e)
intramural [ˌɪntrəˈmjʊərəl, *Am:* -ˈmjʊrəl] *adj* intra-muros
intranet *n* intranet *m*
intransigence [ɪnˈtrænsɪdʒəns, *Am:* -sə-] *n no pl, form* intransigeance *f*
intransigent *adj form* intransigeant(e)
intransitive [ɪnˈtrænsətɪv, *Am:* -t̬ɪv] LING **I.** *adj* intransitif(-ive) **II.** *n* intransitif *m*
intrauterine [ˌɪntraˈjuːtəraɪn, *Am:* -t̬ɚɪn] *adj* intra-utérin(e)
intravenous [ˌɪntrəˈviːnəs] *adj* intraveineux(-euse)
in-tray [ˈɪntreɪ] *n* boîte *f* de réception
intrepid [ɪnˈtrepɪd] *adj* intrépide
intricacy [ˈɪntrɪkəsi] <-cies> *n* complexité *f*
intricate [ˈɪntrɪkət] *adj* **1.** (*complicated*) compliqué(e) **2.** (*complex*) complexe
intrigue[1] [ɪnˈtriːg] **I.** *vt* éveiller la curiosité de; **to be ~d by sth** être intrigué par qc **II.** *vi* intriguer
intrigue[2] [ˈɪntriːg] *n* intrigue *f;* **an ~ against sb/sth** une machination contre qn/qc
intriguing *adj* mystérieux(-euse)
intrinsic [ɪnˈtrɪnsɪk] *adj* intrinsèque
introduce [ˌɪntrəˈdjuːs, *Am:* -ˈduːs] *vt* **1.** (*acquaint*) **to ~ sb to sb** présenter qn à qn; **to ~ oneself** se présenter **2.** (*raise interest in*

I

subject) **to ~ sb to sth** faire connaître qc à qn **3.** (*bring in*) introduire; (*law, controls*) établir; (*products*) lancer; **to ~ sth into a country** introduire qc dans un pays **4.** (*insert*) introduire **5.** (*announce*) présenter

introduction [ˌɪntrəˈdʌkʃən] *n* **1.** (*making first acquaintance*) présentation *f;* **she performed the ~s** elle a fait les présentations; **my next guest needs no ~** mon prochain invité n'a pas besoin d'être présenté; **a letter of ~** une lettre de recommandation; **to serve as an ~ to sth** servir d'introduction à qc **2.** (*establishment*) introduction *f;* **~ into the market** lancement *m* sur le marché **3.** MED (*insertion*) introduction *f* **4.** (*preliminary section*) introduction *f*

introductory [ˌɪntrəˈdʌktəri] *adj* d'introduction; (*price*) de lancement

introspection [ˌɪntrəˈspekʃən, *Am:* -troʊˈ-] *n no pl* introspection *f*

introspective [ˌɪntrəˈspektɪv, *Am:* -troʊˈ-] *adj* introspectif(-ive)

introvert [ˌɪntrəˈvɜːt, *Am:* -troʊˈvɜːrt] *n* introverti(e) *m(f)*

introverted *adj* recueilli(e)

intrude [ɪnˈtruːd] **I.** *vi* **1.** (*meddle*) s'immiscer; **to ~ into sth** s'immiscer dans qc **2.** (*go where shouldn't be*) s'ingérer; **to ~ on sb** faire intrusion auprès de qn **II.** *vt* **1.** (*force*) imposer **2.** (*meddle*) immiscer

intruder *n* **1.** (*unwelcome visitor*) importun *m* **2.** LAW (*burglar, thief*) intrus(e) *m(f)*

intrusion [ɪnˈtruːʒən] *n* intrusion *f*

intrusive [ɪnˈtruːsɪv] *adj* importun(e)

intuition [ˌɪntjuːˈɪʃən, *Am:* -tuːˈ-] *n no pl* intuition *f;* **to base one's judgement on ~** baser son jugement sur une intuition; **to have an ~ that ...** avoir le sentiment que ...; **my own ~ is that we should continue with it** mon sentiment est que nous devrions continuer cela

intuitive [ɪnˈtjuːɪtɪv] *adj* intuitif(-ive)

Inuit [ˈɪnuɪt] **I.** *adj* inuit *inv* **II.** *n* **1.** *pl* (*people*) Inuits *mfpl* **2.** LING inuktitut *m; s. a.* **English**

Inuk *n no pl* Inuk *mf*

inundate [ˈɪnʌndeɪt, *Am:* -ən-] *vt* **1.** (*flood*) inonder **2.** *fig* **to be ~d with sth** être débordé par qc

inundation *n no pl* **1.** (*flooding*) inondation *f* **2.** *fig* invasion *f*

inure [ɪˈnjʊəʳ, *Am:* -ˈnjʊr] *form* **I.** *vi* s'endurcir **II.** *vt* habituer; **to ~ sb against sth** endurcir qn contre qc

invade [ɪnˈveɪd] *vt a. fig* envahir; **to ~ the peace** *fig* violer la paix; **to ~ sb's privacy** porter atteinte à la vie privée de qn; **to ~ quiet** violer la tranquillité

invader *n* **1.** (*aggressive trespasser*) envahisseur *m* **2.** *fig* (*unwelcome presence*) intrus(e) *m(f)*

invalid[1] [ˈɪnvəlɪd] **I.** *n* invalide *mf* **II.** *adj* invalide; **an ~ chair** un fauteuil roulant **III.** *vt* réformer; **to be ~ed out of sth** être réformé de qc

invalid[2] [ɪnˈvælɪd] *adj* **1.** (*not legally binding*) non valide **2.** (*unsound*) nul(le) et non avenu(e)

invalidate [ɪnˈvælɪdeɪt] *vt* **1.** (*make erroneous*) invalider **2.** LAW **to ~ sth** rendre qc nul; (*a ballot*) vicier; (*a decision*) casser; (*a judgement*) infirmer

invalidism [ˌɪnvəˈlɪdɪzəm] *n Am,* **invalidity** *n no pl, a. fig* invalidité *f;* **~ of an evidence** nullité *f* d'une preuve

invaluable [ɪnˈvæljʊəbl, *Am:* -juə-] *adj* inestimable

invariable [ɪnˈveəriəbl, *Am:* -ˈverɪ-] *adj form* invariable; **the menu is ~** le menu ne varie pas

invariably *adj* invariablement

invasion [ɪnˈveɪʒən] *n* **1.** MIL invasion *f;* **~ by enemy forces** invasion par les forces ennemies **2.** *no pl* (*interference: of privacy*) intrusion *f*

invective [ɪnˈvektɪv] *n no pl, form* invective *f*

inveigle [ɪnˈveɪgl] *vt form* inciter, instiguer *Belgique;* **to ~ sb into sth** inciter qn à faire qc

invent [ɪnˈvent] *vt* inventer

invention *n* invention *f;* **power(s) of ~** force *f* d'imagination

inventive *adj* inventif(-ive)

inventiveness *n no pl* inventivité *f*

inventor *n* TECH inventeur, -trice *m, f*

inventory [ˈɪnvəntri, *Am:* -tɔːr-] <-ies> **I.** *n a. Am* inventaire *m;* **to take ~** faire l'inventaire **II.** *adj* inventorié(e)

inverse [ɪnˈvɜːs, *Am:* -ˈvɜːrs] **I.** *adj* inverse; **to be in ~ proportion to sth** être en disproportion avec qc **II.** *n no pl, inf* inverse *m*

inversion *n no pl, form* inversion *f*

invert [ɪnˈvɜːt, *Am:* -ˈvɜːrt] *vt* **1.** (*turn over, upturn, reverse*) inverser **2.** (*reverse decision*) renverser

invertebrate [ɪnˈvɜːtɪbrət, *Am:* -ˈvɜːrt̬əbrɪt] **I.** *n* BIO invertébré *m* **II.** *adj* invertébré(e)

invest [ɪnˈvest] **I.** *vt* investir; **to ~ time and effort in sth** investir du temps et des efforts dans qc; **to ~ sth on sb** investir qn de qc; **to ~ sb with full authority** investir qn d'une pleine autorité; **to ~ capital in a company** investir des capitaux dans une entreprise **II.** *vi* investir; **to ~ in sth** investir dans qc

investigate [ɪnˈvestɪgeɪt] *vt* (*a case, crime*) enquêter sur; **to ~ how/whether/why ...** rechercher comment/si/pourquoi ...

investigation *n* enquête *f*

investigative *adj* investigateur(-trice); **~ journalism** journalisme *m* d'investigation

investigator *n* enquêteur, -trice *m, f*

investment [ɪnˈvestmənt] *n* investissement *m*

investment fund *n* fonds *mpl* d'investissements **investment trust** *n* société *f* d'in-

vestissements
investor *n* investisseur *m*
inveterate [ɪn'vetərət, *Am:* -'veṱ-] *adj pej* (*liar, smoker*) invétéré(e); ~ **criminal** récidiviste *mf;* ~ **prejudice** récidive *f*
invidious [ɪn'vɪdɪəs] *adj* **1.** (*arousing resentment: position, task*) peu enviable **2.** (*unjust: comparison, choice*) inéquitable
invigilate [ɪn'vɪdʒɪleɪt] *vt Brit, Aus* surveiller
invigilator *n Brit, Aus* SCHOOL, UNIV (*exam supervisor*) surveillant(e) *m(f)*
invigorate [ɪn'vɪgəreɪt] *vt* **1.** (*fortify, rejuvenate*) revigorer **2.** *fig* réveiller; (*the economy*) relancer
invigorating *adj* **1.** (*physically fortifying, rejuvenating*) revigorant(e) **2.** *fig* (*stimulating, heartening*) stimulant(e)
invincible [ɪn'vɪnsəbl] *adj* **1.** (*invulnerable, unalterable*) invincible; **an** ~ **will** une volonté de fer **2.** (*unchangeable unawareness*) insurmontable
invisible [ɪn'vɪzəbl] *adj a.* ECON invisible; ~ **to the naked eye** invisible à l'œil nu; ~ **ink** encre *f* sympathique
invitation [ˌɪnvɪ'teɪʃən] *n* invitation *f;* **by** ~ sur invitation; **an** ~ **to sth** une invitation à qc
invite [ɪn'vaɪt] **I.** *vt* **1.** (*request to attend*) inviter; **to** ~ **sb for/to sth** inviter qn à qc; **to** ~ **oneself** s'inviter soi-même; **to** ~ **sb to** +*infin* inviter qn à +*infin* **2.** (*formally request*) solliciter **3.** (*provoke, tempt reaction*) encourager; **to** ~ **criticism** encourager la critique; **to** ~ **sb to** +*infin* encourager qn à +*infin* **II.** *n inf* invitation *f*
inviting *adj* **1.** (*alluring, attractive: look, prospect, smile*) aguichant(e) **2.** (*tempting and provoking negativeness*) incitatif(-ive)
in vitro [ɪn'viːtrəʊ, *Am:* -troʊ] *adj, adv* in vitro
in vitro fertilization *n* fécondation *f* in vitro
invocation [ˌɪnvə'keɪʃən] *n* **1.** *form* (*prayers to spirits/Gods*) invocation *f* **2.** *no pl* (*use as resort*) appel *m* **3.** *no pl* (*trigger off memories*) évocation *f*
invoice ['ɪnvɔɪs] **I.** *vt* (*goods*) facturer; (*a client*) envoyer une facture à **II.** *n* facture *f;* ~ **for sth** facture de qc; **to make out an** ~ **of sth** dresser la facture de qc
invoke [ɪn'vəʊk, *Am:* -'voʊk] *vt* **1.** (*cite*) évoquer **2.** (*call on*) invoquer
involuntary [ɪn'vɒləntəri, *Am:* -'vɑːlənter-] *adj* involontaire
involve [ɪn'vɒlv, *Am:* -'vɑːlv] *vt* **1.** (*concern, affect*) impliquer **2.** (*include, number among*) inclure **3.** (*entail, necessitate*) nécessiter
involved *adj* **1.** (*knotty, tangled: story*) embrouillé(e) **2.** (*implicated, mixed up in*) impliqué(e); **to be** ~ **in sth** être mêlé à qc
involvement *n* **1.** (*commitment*) engagement *m* **2.** (*participation*) participation *f*
invulnerable [ɪn'vʌlnərəbl, *Am:* -nɚ-] *adj a. fig* invulnérable; **to be** ~ **to sth** être invulnérable à qc
inward ['ɪnwəd, *Am:* -wɚd] **I.** *adj* **1.** (*ingoing, towards centre*) intérieur(e) **2.** ECON (*investment, trade*) interne **3.** (*inmost, personal, private: life*) intime **II.** *adv* **1.** (*in direction of centre*) vers l'intérieur **2.** (*towards personal centre*) à l'intérieur
inwardly *adv* intérieurement
inwardness *n no pl* intériorité *f*
inwards *adv* **1.** (*towards centre spatially*) vers l'intérieur **2.** (*movement to personal centre*) sur soi
in-word *n* mot *m* à la mode
I/O *n* INFOR *abbr of* **input/output** E/S *f*
IOC *n abbr of* **International Olympic Committee** COI *m*
iodine ['aɪədiːn, *Am:* -daɪn] *n no pl* iode *f*
IOM *n abbr of* **Isle of Man** île *f* de Man
ion ['aɪən] *n* ion *m*
Ionic [aɪ'ɒnɪk, *Am:* -'ɑːnɪk] *adj* ionique
iota [aɪ'əʊtə, *Am:* -'oʊṱə] *n no pl* iota *m;* **there is not one** ~ **of truth in that** il n'y a pas un brin de vérité dans cela
IOU [ˌaɪəʊ'juː, *Am:* -oʊ'-] *n abbr of* **I owe you** *inf* (*document specifying debts*) *a. fig* reconnaissance *f* de dette
IOW *n abbr of* **Isle of Wight** île *f* de Wight
Iowa ['aɪəwə] *n* l'Iowa *m*
IPA [ˌaɪpiː'eɪ] *n abbr of* **International Phonetic Alphabet** API *m*
IQ [ˌaɪ'kjuː] *n abbr of* **intelligence quotient** QI *m*
IRA [ˌaɪɑːr'eɪ, *Am:* -ɑːr'-] *n no pl abbr of* **Irish Republican Army** IRA *f*
Iran [ɪ'rɑːn, *Am:* -'ræn] *n* l'Iran *m*
Iranian [ɪ'reɪnjən] **I.** *adj* iranien(ne) **II.** *n* Iranien(ne) *m(f)*
Iraq [ɪ'rɑːk] *n* l'Irak *m*
Iraqi **I.** *adj* irakien(ne) **II.** *n* Irakien(ne) *m(f)*
irascible [ɪ'ræsəbl] *adj form* irascible
irate [aɪ'reɪt] *adj* furieux(-euse)
IRBM *n abbr of* **intermediate-range ballistic missile** IRBM *m*
Ireland ['aɪələnd, *Am:* 'aɪr-] *n* l'Irlande *f;* **Republic of** ~ République *f* d'Irlande
iridescent [ˌɪrɪ'desnt] *adj* chatoyant(e)
iris ['aɪərɪs, *Am:* 'aɪ-] <-es> *n a.* BOT iris *m*
Irish ['aɪərɪʃ, *Am:* 'aɪ-] **I.** *adj* irlandais(e) **II.** *n* **1.** (*people*) **the** ~ les Irlandais **2.** LING irlandais *m;* ~ **Gaelic** irlandais gaélique; *s. a.* **English**
Irishman *n* Irlandais *m* **Irishwoman** *n* Irlandaise *f*
irk [ɜːk, *Am:* ɜːrk] *vt* irriter
irksome ['ɜːksəm, *Am:* 'ɜːrk-] *adj* irritant(e)
iron ['aɪən, *Am:* 'aɪɚn] **I.** *n* **1.** *no pl* (*metal*) fer *m;* **a man of** ~ un homme de fer **2.** (*device for pressing clothes*) fer *m* à repasser; **steam** ~ fer *m* à vapeur **3.** SPORT (*golf club*) fer *m* ►**to have several** (**many**) ~**s in the fire** avoir plusieurs cordes à son arc; **an** ~ **fist in a velvet glove** une main de fer dans un gant de velours **II.** *vt* (*the laundry*) repasser; **to** ~ **sth out** arranger qc **III.** *vi* repasser

I

Iron Age *n* l'âge *m* de fer **iron constitution** *n* santé *f* de fer **Iron Curtain** *n* rideau *m* de fer **iron discipline** *n* discipline *f* de fer **iron grip** *n* poignée *f* de fer **iron hand** *n* main *f* de fer; **to rule with an ~** gouverner qc d'une main de fer

ironic, ironical *adj* ironique

ironing *n no pl* repassage *m*

ironing board *n* table *f* à repasser

iron lung *n* PHYSIOL, MED poumon *m* d'acier **ironmonger** *n Brit* quincaillier, -ière *m, f;* **~'s** quincaillerie *f* **ironmongery** *n no pl, Brit* quincaillerie *f* **iron ore** *n* minerai *m* de fer **iron ration** *n* ration *f* de survie **iron will** *n* volonté *f* de fer **ironwork** *n no pl* ferrure *f* **ironworks** *npl + sing vb* sidérurgie *f*

irony ['aɪərəni, *Am:* 'aɪ-] *n no pl* ironie *f*

irradiate [ɪ'reɪdɪeɪt, *Am:* ɪr'-] *vt* irradier

irrational [ɪ'ræʃənəl] *adj* irrationnel(le)

irrational number *n* MAT nombre *m* irrationnel

irreconcilable [ɪˌrekən'saɪləbl] *adj* inconciliable

irrecoverable [ˌɪrɪ'kʌvərəbl] *adj* irrécouvrable; **an ~ financial loss** une perte financière irrécupérable

irredeemable [ˌɪrɪ'di:məbl] *adj* **1.** (*not able to be saved, corrected*) irrémédiable; (*mistake, error*) irréparable; (*person, stupidity*) incurable; (*sinner*) irrémissible **2.** ECON non remboursable

irrefutable [ˌɪrɪ'fju:təbl, *Am:* ɪ'refjət̬ə-] *adj form* irréfutable

irregular [ɪ'regjələ^r, *Am:* -lɚ] **I.** *adj* **1.** *a.* LING, MIL irrégulier(-ère) **2.** *form* (*abnormal, peculiar: behaviour, habits, private life*) désordonné(e) **II.** *n* MIL (*unofficial soldier*) soldat *m* irrégulier

irregularity <-ies> *n* irrégularité *f*

irrelevance [ɪ'reləvənts, *Am:* ɪr'-], **irrelevancy** *n form* insignifiance *f;* **to be an ~** être insignifiant

irrelevant *adj* insignifiant(e)

irremediable [ˌɪrɪ'mi:dɪəbl] *adj form* irrémédiable

irreparable [ɪ'repərəbl] *adj* irréparable

irreplaceable [ˌɪrɪ'pleɪsəbl] *adj* irremplaçable

irrepressible [ˌɪrɪ'presəbl] *adj* irrépressible

irreproachable [ˌɪrɪ'prəʊtʃəbl, *Am:* -'proʊ-] *adj form* irréprochable

irresistible [ˌɪrɪ'zɪstəbl] *adj* irrésistible

irresolute [ɪ'rezəlu:t] *adj pej, form* irrésolu(e)

irrespective [ˌɪrɪ'spektɪv] *adj* **~ of sth** indépendamment de qc

irrespective of *prep* sans tenir compte de; **~ whether he agrees** qu'il soit d'accord ou non

irresponsible [ˌɪrɪ'spɒnsəbl, *Am:* -'spɑ:n-] *adj pej* irresponsable

irretrievable [ˌɪrɪ'tri:vəbl] *adj* (*situation*) irréversible; (*mistake*) irrattrapable

irreverence [ɪ'revərəns] *n no pl* irrévérence *f*

irreverent [ɪ'revərənt] *adj* irrévérencieux(-euse)

irreversible [ˌɪrɪ'vɜ:səbl, *Am:* -'vɜ:r-] *adj* irréversible; (*decision*) irrévocable

irrevocable [ɪ'revəkəbl] *adj* irrévocable

irrigate ['ɪrɪgeɪt] *vt* **1.** (*supply water to*) irriguer **2.** MED (*wash*) laver

irrigation **I.** *n no pl* **1.** (*water supply to land*) irrigation *f* **2.** (*washing*) lavage *m* **II.** *adj* d'irrigation

irrigation plant *n* dispositif *m* d'irrigation

irritable ['ɪrɪtəbl, *Am:* -t̬ə-] *adj pej* irritable

irritant ['ɪrɪtənt, *Am:* -t̬ənt] *n* **1.** (*source of problems*) tracas *m* **2.** (*sth inflaming body part*) substance *f* irritante

irritate ['ɪrɪteɪt] *vt a.* MED irriter

irritated *adj* irrité(e); **to feel ~ at sth** s'irriter de qc

irritating *adj a.* MED irritant(e)

irritation *n a.* MED irritation *f;* **to be an ~ to sb** être une source d'énervement pour qn

is [ɪz] *3rd pers sing of* **to be**

ISBN [ˌaɪesbi:'en] *n abbr of* **International Standard Book Number** ISBN *m*

ISDN *n* TEL *abbr of* **integrated services digital network** réseau *m* Numeris

Islam [ɪz'lɑ:m] *n no art, no pl* l'Islam *m*

Islamic [ɪz'læmɪk, *Am:* -'lɑ:-] *adj* REL, HIST islamique

island ['aɪlənd] *n a. fig* île *f*

islander *n* insulaire *mf*

Isle of Man *n* l'île *f* de Man **Isle of Wight** *n* l'île *f* de Wight

isn't ['ɪznt] = **is not**

isobar ['aɪsəbɑ:^{r}, *Am:* -soʊbɑ:r] *n* METEO isobare *f*

isolate ['aɪsəleɪt] *vt* isoler; **to ~ oneself** s'isoler

isolated *adj* isolé(e)

isolation *n no pl* isolement *m*

isolation hospital *n* hôpital *m* de mise en quarantaine

isolationism [ˌaɪsə'leɪʃnɪzəm] *n no pl, pej* isolationnisme *m*

isolation ward *n* salle *f* de quarantaine

isosceles triangle [aɪ'sɒsli:zˌtraɪæŋgl, *Am:* -'sɑ:sl-] *n* MAT triangle *m* isocèle

isotherm ['aɪsəθɜ:m, *Am:* -soʊθɜ:rm] *n* METEO, PHYS isotherme *f*

isotope ['aɪsətəʊp, *Am:* -toʊp] *n* PHYS, ELEC isotope *m*

Israel ['ɪzreɪl, *Am:* -riəl] *n* Israël *m sans art*

Israeli **I.** *adj* israélien(ne) **II.** *n* Israélien(ne) *m(f)*

Israelite ['ɪzrɪəlaɪt] *n* Israélite *mf*

issue ['ɪʃu:] **I.** *n* **1.** (*problem, topic*) question *f;* **at ~** (*in discussion/controversial*) controversé(e); **to make an ~ of sth** (*make fuss/dispute*) faire tout un problème de qc; **to take ~ with sb over sth** *form* (*dispute sth clearly/markedly*) prendre le contre-pied de qn sur qc **2.** (*single publication*) numéro *m* **3.** FIN, ECON (*distribution of shares, stamps*) émission *f* **II.** *vt* **1.** (*put out*) délivrer; **to ~ sb with sth** délivrer qc à qn; **to ~ an arrest warrant** *Am* diffuser un avis de recherche **2.** (*make public: a bank notes, statement*) émettre; (*a communiqué, newsletter*) rendre public **III.** *vi* **to ~ from sth** *form* sortir de qc

isthmus ['ɪsməs] *n* isthme *m*

it [ɪt] **I.** *dem pron* ce, c' + *vowel;* **who was ~?** qui était-ce?; **~ is ...** c'est ..., ça est... *Belgique;* **~ all** tout cela; **~'s Paul who did that** c'est Paul qui a fait ça **II.** *pers pron* il, elle; **your pen/card? ~ is on my desk** ton stylo/ta carte? il/elle est sur mon bureau **III.** *impers pron* il; **what time is ~?** quelle heure est-il?; **~'s cold, ~'s snowing** il fait froid, il neige; **~'s 10 km to the town** il y a 10 km jusqu'à la ville; **~ seems that ...** il semble que ...; **~ is said that ...** on dit que ... **IV.** *objective pron* **1.** (*direct object*) le, la, l' + *vowel;* **your card? I took ~?** ta carte? je l'ai prise; **I can do ~** je peux le/la faire **2.** (*indirect object*) lui; **give ~ something to eat** donne-lui à manger **3.** (*prepositional object*) **I heard of/about ~** j'en ai entendu parler; **I'm just coming back from ~** j'en reviens; **I'm afraid of ~** j'en ai peur; **I fell into ~** j'y suis tombé; **I went to ~** j'y suis allé; **think of ~** pensez-y; **put the glass on/beside ~** mets le verre dessus/à côté **4.** (*non-specific object*) en; **to have ~ in for sb** en avoir après qn ►**that's ~!** ça y est!; (*in anger*) ça suffit!; **this is ~!** nous y sommes!

IT [ˌaɪ'tiː] *n no pl* INFOR *abbr of* **Information Technology** informatique *f*

Italian [ɪ'tæljən] **I.** *adj* italien(ne) **II.** *n* **1.** (*person*) Italien(ne) *m(f)* **2.** LING italien *m; s. a.* **English**

italic [ɪ'tælɪk] **I.** *adj* italique; **~ type** caractère *m* en italique **II.** *n pl* INFOR, TYP italiques *mpl;* **in ~s** en italique

italicise *vt,* **italicize** [ɪ'tælɪsaɪz] *vt Am* TYP **to ~ sth** mettre qc en italique

Italy ['ɪtəli, *Am:* 'ɪt̬-] *n* l'Italie *f*

itch [ɪtʃ] **I.** *vi a. inf* démanger **II.** *n* démangeaison *f*

itchy <-ier, -iest> *adj* irritant(e)

item ['aɪtəm, *Am:* -t̬əm] *n* **1.** (*point, thing*) *a.* INFOR article *m;* **~ of clothing** article *m* de vêtement; **~ by ~** point par point; **luxury ~** article *m* de luxe; **~ of news** nouvelle *f* **2.** *inf* (*couple in relationship*) couple *m*

itemize ['aɪtəmaɪz] *vt* **to ~ sth** présenter qc point par point

itinerant [aɪ'tɪnərənt] **I.** *n* itinérant(e) *m(f)* **II.** *adj* itinérant(e)

itinerary [aɪ'tɪnərəri, *Am:* -ərer-] <-ies> *n* itinéraire *m*

it'll ['ɪtl, *Am:* 'ɪt̬l] = **it will**

its [ɪts] *poss adj* (*of sth*) son, sa, ses *pl;* **~ colour/weight** sa couleur/son poids; **the cat hurt ~ head** le chat s'est blessé à la tête

it's [ɪts] = **it is**

itself [ɪt'self] *reflex pron* **1.** *after verbs* se, s' + *vowel* **2.** (*specifically*) lui-même, elle-même; **the place ~** la place elle-même; **the plan in ~** le plan en soi; **to do sth by ~** faire qc tout(e) seul(e); *s. a.* **myself**

ITV ['aɪtiː'viː] *n no pl, no art, Brit abbr of* **Independent Television** *chaîne de télévision privée britannique*

IUD [ˌaɪjuː'diː] *n* MED *abbr of* **intra-uterine device** stérilet *m*

IV *adj abbr of* **intravenous** iv

I've [aɪv] = **I have**

IVF [ˌaɪviː'ef] *n* MED *abbr of* **in vitro fertilisation** fécondation *f* in vitro

ivory ['aɪvəri] <-ies> **I.** *n* **1.** (*from elephants' tusks*) ivoire *m* **2.** *pl* (*set of ivory goods*) ivoirerie *f* **3.** *pl, iron, inf* (*keys of piano*) touches *fpl* de piano **II.** *n* **1.** (*of substance from tusks*) en ivoire **2.** (*cream, not white*) ivoire *inv*

Ivory Coast *n* la Côte d'Ivoire **ivory tower** *n fig* tour *f* d'ivoire

ivy ['aɪvi] <-ies> *n* lierre *m*

J

J

J, j [dʒeɪ] <-'s *o* -s> *n* J, j *m;* **~ as in Jack** *Brit,* **~ as in Jig** *Am,* **~ for Jack** *Brit,* **~ for Jig** *Am* (*on telephone*) j comme Joseph

jab [dʒæb] **I.** *n* **1.** (*shove*) coup *m* **2.** SPORT direct *m* **3.** *Aus, Brit, inf* MED piqûre *f;* **a flu ~** un vaccin contre la grippe **II.** <-bb-> *vt* **1.** (*poke or prick*) planter **2.** (*push*) **to ~ sth in(to) sth** donner des coups de qc dans qc **III.** <-bb-> *vi* **1.** SPORT **to ~ at sb** lancer un direct à qn **2.** (*thrust at*) **to ~ at sb/sth with sth** donner un coup de qc à qn/qc

jabber ['dʒæbəʳ, *Am:* -ɚ] *pej* **I.** *n* baragouin *m* **II.** *vi* baragouiner; (*chatter*) jacasser **III.** *vt* **to ~ (out) sth** bredouiller qc

jabbering *n s.* **jabber**

jack [dʒæk] *n* **1.** TECH vérin *m* **2.** AUTO cric *m* **3.** (*card*) valet *m* **4.** (*plug*) prise *f* **5.** (*small ball*) cochonnet *m*

◆**jack in** *vt Brit, inf* plaquer

◆**jack up** *vt* **1.** (*raise*) soulever; **to jack a car up** soulever une voiture à l'aide d'un cric **2.** *fig, inf* (*prices, rent*) faire grimper

Jack [dʒæk] *n inf* **every man ~ of them** absolument tout le monde; **before you can say ~ Robinson** en moins de temps qu'il n'en faut pour le dire; **I'm all right ~** *inf* ça roule pour moi

jackal ['dʒækɔːl, *Am:* -əl] *n* chacal *m*

jackass ['dʒækæs] *n* **1.** ZOOL âne *m* **2.** *inf* (*idiot*) idiot(e) *m(f)*

jackboot ['dʒækbuːt] *n* MIL botte *f* à l'écuyère ►**under the ~** sous la dictature

jackdaw ['dʒækdɔː, *Am:* -dɑː] *n* choucas *m*

jacket ['dʒækɪt] *n* **1.** veste *f* **2.** (*of book*) cou-

verture *f* **3.** *Am, Aus* MUS pochette *f*
jacket potato *n* pomme de terre *f* en robe des champs
jack-in-the-box ['dʒækɪnðəbɒks, *Am:* -bɑːks] <-es> *n* diable *m* à ressort; **he jumps up and down like a** ~ il ne tient plus en place
jackknife ['dʒæknaɪf] **I.** *n* **1.** (*large folding knife*) couteau *m* de poche **2.** (*type of dive*) saut *m* carpé **II.** *vi* AUTO se mettre en portefeuille
jackpot ['dʒækpɒt, *Am:* -pɑːt] *n* jackpot *m;* **to hit the** ~ ramasser le gros lot; *fig, inf* décrocher la timbale
jacuzzi® [dʒə'kuːzi] *n* jacuzzi® *m*
jade [dʒeɪd] *no pl n* jade *m*
jaded ['dʒeɪdɪd] *adj* **to be** ~ **with sth** être las de qc
jag [dʒæg] *n Am* soûlerie *f;* **she went on a crying** ~ elle a eu une crise de larmes
jagged ['dʒægɪd] *adj* déchiqueté(e); (*coastline*) découpé(e); (*rock*) pointu(e); (*speech, cut*) irrégulier(-ère)
jaggy ['dʒægi] <-ier, -iest> *adj* entaillé(e)
jaguar ['dʒægjʊəʳ, *Am:* 'dʒægwɑːr] *n* jaguar *m*
jail [dʒeɪl] **I.** *n* prison *f;* **to be in** ~ faire de la prison; **to put sb in** ~ incarcérer qn; **to be released from** ~ être libéré (de prison) **II.** *vt* emprisonner; **to** ~ **sb for three months** condamner qn à trois mois de prison
jailbird ['dʒeɪlbɜːd, *Am:* -bɜːrd] *n* récidiviste *mf*
jailbreak ['dʒeɪlbreɪk] *n* évasion *f* (de prison); **to attempt a** ~ faire une tentative d'évasion
jailer ['dʒeɪləʳ, *Am:* -lɚ] *n* gardien(ne) *m(f)* de prison
jailor ['dʒeɪləʳ, *Am:* -lɚ] *n s.* **jailer**
jalopy [dʒə'lɒpɪ, *Am:* -'lɑːpɪ] *n inf* bagnole *f*
jam¹ [dʒæm] *n* confiture *f* ►~ tomorrow demain, on rase gratis
jam² [dʒæm] **I.** *n* **1.** *inf* (*awkward situation*) pétrin *m* **2.** *no pl* (*crowd*) cohue *f;* AUTO embouteillage *m* **3.** (*in machine*) bourrage *m* **4.** MUS bœuf *m* **II.** <-mm-> *vt* **1.** (*cause to become stuck*) coincer; (*machine, mechanism*) bloquer; **to** ~ **sth open** maintenir qc ouvert **2.** (*cram*) **to** ~ **sth into sth** fourrer qc dans qc **3.** RADIO brouiller **III.** <-mm-> *vi* **1.** (*become stuck*) se coincer; (*brakes, photocopier*) se bloquer **2.** (*play music*) *faire des improvisations collectives de jazz*
Jamaica [dʒə'meɪkə] *n* la Jamaïque
Jamaican **I.** *adj* jamaïquain(e) **II.** *n* Jamaïquain(e) *m(f)*
jamboree [ˌdʒæmbə'riː] *n* **1.** (*celebration*) festivités *fpl;* **a political/marketing** ~ un rassemblement politique/publicitaire **2.** (*scouts' meeting*) jamboree *m*
jam jar ['dʒæmdʒɑːr] *n* pot *m* à confiture
jammy ['dʒæmɪ] <-ier, -iest> *adj* **1.** couvert(e) de confiture **2.** *Brit, fig, inf* verni(e); ~ **beggar** [*o* **devil**] veinard(e)
jam-packed [ˌdʒæm'pækt] *adj inf* bondé(e); **to be** ~ (**with people**) être plein à craquer
jam session *n inf* **to have a** ~ faire un bœuf
jangle ['dʒæŋgl] **I.** *vt* **1.** (*cause to make metallic noise: keys*) faire cliqueter; (*bells*) agiter **2.** (*upset*) troubler; (*sb's nerves*) ébranler **II.** *vi* tinter **III.** *n* (*of keys*) cliquetis *m;* (*of bell*) tintement *m*
janitor ['dʒænɪtəʳ, *Am:* -ət̬ɚ] *n Am, Scot* concierge *mf*
January ['dʒænjʊərɪ, *Am:* -juerɪ] *n* janvier *m; s. a.* **April**
Jap [dʒæp] **I.** *n pej, inf abbr of* **Japanese: the ~s** les Japs **II.** *adj* japonais(e)
Japan [dʒə'pæn] *n* le Japon
Japanese [ˌdʒæpə'niːz] **I.** *adj* japonais(e) **II.** *n* **1.** (*person*) Japonais(e) *m(f)* **2.** LING japonais *m; s. a.* **English**
jar¹ [dʒɑːʳ, *Am:* dʒɑːr] *n* **1.** (*container*) jarre *f;* (*of jam*) pot *m* **2.** (*drink*) **to have a** ~ prendre un pot
jar² [dʒɑːʳ, *Am:* dʒɑːr] **I.** <-rr-> *vt* ébranler; (*person*) choquer; **to** ~ **one's elbow** se cogner le coude **II.** <-rr-> *vi* **1.** (*cause feelings*) **to** ~ **on sb** froisser qn **2.** (*make a sound*) rendre un son discordant **3.** (*be unsuitable: effect*) ne pas être à sa place; **to** ~ **with sth** jurer avec qc **III.** *n* secousse *f*
jargon ['dʒɑːgən, *Am:* 'dʒɑːr-] *n no pl* jargon *m*
jasmine ['dʒæsmɪn] *n no pl* jasmin *m*
jaundice ['dʒɔːndɪs, *Am:* 'dʒɑːn-] *n no pl* MED jaunisse *f*
jaundiced ['dʒɔːndɪst, *Am:* 'dʒɑːn-] *adj* **1.** MED qui a la jaunisse **2.** *fig, form* amer(-ère); **to take a** ~ **view of sth** regarder qc d'un mauvais œil
jaunt [dʒɔːnt, *Am:* dʒɑːnt] *n* excursion *f;* **to go on a** ~ faire une balade
jaunty ['dʒɔːntɪ, *Am:* 'dʒɑːnt̬ɪ] <-ier, -iest> *adj* enjoué(e); (*step*) vif(vive)
javelin ['dʒævlɪn] *n* javelot *m*
jaw [dʒɔː, *Am:* dʒɑː] **I.** *n* **1.** ANAT mâchoire *f* **2.** *pl* (*mouth*) gueule *f* ►**to have a** (**good**) ~ *inf* tailler une bavette **II.** *vi inf* papoter **III.** *vt Am* **he used to** ~ **her all the time** il lui faisait toujours la morale
jawbone ['dʒɔːbəʊn, *Am:* 'dʒɑːboʊn] *n* mâchoire *f*
jawbreaker ['dʒɔːˌbreɪkə, *Am:* 'dʒɑːˌbreɪkɚ] *n* **1.** *Am, Aus* (*sweet*) bonbon *m* dur **2.** *inf* (*tongue twister*) mot *m* imprononçable
jay [dʒeɪ] *n* geai *m*
jaywalk ['dʒeɪwɔːk, *Am:* -wɑːk] *vi Am* **1.** (*dangerously*) traverser dangereusement une rue **2.** (*illegally*) *traverser une rue sans respecter le code de la route*
jaywalker ['dʒeɪwɔːkəʳ, *Am:* -wɑːkɚ] *n* piéton(ne) *m(f)* ne respectant pas le code la route
jaywalking ['dʒeɪ wɔːkɪŋ, *Am:* -wɑːkɪŋ] *n no pl* imprudence *f* des piétons
jazz [dʒæz] *n no pl* **1.** MUS jazz *m* **2.** *Am, pej,*

inf (*nonsense*) baratin *m* ►**and all that** ~ *pej, inf* et tout le tremblement

◆**jazz up** *vt inf* **1.** MUS adapter pour le jazz **2.** (*brighten or enliven*) égayer; **to** ~ **food with spices** relever la nourriture avec des épices

jazzy ['dʒæzɪ] <-ier, -iest> *adj* **1.** MUS qui rappelle le jazz **2.** *inf* (*flashy*) tapageur(-euse)

JCB® [ˌdʒeɪsiː'biː] *n Brit* tractopelle *f*

jealous ['dʒeləs] *adj* **1.** (*envious*) jaloux(-ouse); **to be** ~ **of sb/sth** être jaloux de qn/qc **2.** (*protective*) **to keep a** ~ **watch over sb** surveiller qn d'un œil jaloux

jealousy ['dʒeləsɪ] <-ies> *n* jalousie *f*

jeans [dʒiːnz] *npl* jean(s) *m;* **a pair of** ~ une paire de jeans

jeep® [dʒiːp] *n* jeep *f*

jeer [dʒɪəʳ, *Am:* dʒɪr] **I.** *vt* huer **II.** *vi* railler; **to** ~ **at sb** se moquer de qn **III.** *n* raillerie *f*

Jehovah [dʒɪ'həʊvə, *Am:* -'hoʊ-] *n no art, no pl* Jéhovah *m*

Jehovah's Witness *n* Témoin *m* de Jéhovah

jell [dʒel] *vi s.* **gel**

jellied ['dʒelɪd] *adj* en gelée

jelly ['dʒelɪ] <-ies> *n* **1.** (*substance, spread*) gelée *f* **2.** *Aus, Brit* (*dessert*) *dessert de gélatine au goût et à la couleur de fruit* ►**to beat sb to a** ~ *Brit* mettre qn en bouillie

jellyfish ['dʒelifɪʃ] <-es> *n* **1.** ZOOL méduse *f* **2.** *Am, inf* (*person*) lopette *f*

jemmy ['dʒemɪ] *Aus, Brit* **I.** <-ies> *n* pince-monseigneur *f* **II.** <-ie-> *vt* **to** ~ **open sth** forcer qc à la pince-monseigneur

jeopardise *vt Aus, Brit,* **jeopardize** ['dʒepədaɪz, *Am:* '-ɚ-] *vt* mettre en danger

jeopardy ['dʒepədɪ, *Am:* -ɚ-] *n no pl* **in** ~ en danger; **to put sth in** ~ mettre qc en péril

jerk [dʒɜːk, *Am:* dʒɜːrk] **I.** *n* **1.** (*movement*) secousse *f;* (*pull*) coup *m* sec; **to wake up with a** ~ se réveiller en sursaut **2.** *Am, inf* (*stupid person*) pauvre crétin(e) *m(f)* **3.** SPORT épaulé-jeté *m* **II.** *vi* tressaillir; **to** ~ **to a halt** s'arrêter brusquement **III.** *vt* **1.** (*move*) donner une secousse à; **she** ~**ed me out of the room** elle m'a forcé à sortir de la pièce **2.** SPORT (*weight*) faire un épaulé-jeté

◆**jerk off** *vi Am, vulg* se branler

◆**jerk out** *vi* bafouiller

jerkin ['dʒɜːkɪn, *Am:* 'dʒɜːr-] *n* blouson *m*

jerky ['dʒɜːkɪ, *Am:* 'dʒɜːr-] **I.** <-ier, -iest> *adj* saccadé(e); **a** ~ **style of writing** une écriture irrégulière **II.** *n no pl, Am* **beef** ~ *du bœuf séché en lanières*

jerry-built ['dʒerɪˌbɪlt] *adj pej* fait à la va-vite; (*house*) de mauvaise qualité

jerrycan *n* jerrycan *m*

jersey ['dʒɜːzɪ, *Am:* 'dʒɜːr-] *n* **1.** (*garment*) tricot *m* **2.** SPORT maillot *m* **3.** *no pl* (*cloth*) jersey *m*

Jersey ['dʒɜːzɪ, *Am:* 'dʒɜːr-] *n* (l'île *f* de) Jersey

Jerusalem [dʒə'ruːsələm] *n* Jérusalem

jest [dʒest] **I.** *n form* plaisanterie *f;* **to say sth in** ~ dire qc pour rire ►**many a true word is spoken in** ~ *prov* on dit souvent la vérité sous le couvert d'une plaisanterie **II.** *vi form* **to** ~ **about sth** plaisanter sur qc

jester ['dʒestəʳ, *Am:* -tɚ] *n* HIST bouffon *m;* **court** ~ fou *m* du roi

Jesuit ['dʒezjʊɪt] **I.** *n* jésuite *m* **II.** *adj* jésuite

Jesuitical [ˌdʒezjʊ'ɪtɪkl] *adj* jésuitique

Jesus ['dʒiːzəs] **I.** *n no art, no pl* Jésus *m;* ~ **Christ** Jésus-Christ *m* **II.** *interj vulg* nom de Dieu!

jet¹ [dʒet] **I.** *n* **1.** (*plane*) avion *m* à réaction **2.** (*stream*) jet *m* **3.** (*hole*) gicleur *m* **II.** <-tt-> *vi* **1.** (*fly*) **to be** ~**ing in from Paris** arriver de Paris en avion; **to be** ~**ing off to Canada** s'envoler pour le Canada **2.** (*spurt*) gicler

jet² [dʒet] *n no pl* (*stone*) jais *m*

jet engine *n* moteur *m* à réaction **jet fighter** *n* chasseur *m* à réaction **jetfoil** *n* hydroglisseur *m* **jet lag** *n* décalage *m* horaire

jet-propelled [ˌdʒetprə'peld] *adj* à réaction

jet propulsion *n* propulsion *f* par réaction

jetsam ['dʒetsəm] *n no pl s.* **flotsam**

jet set ['dʒetset] *n inf* **the** ~ le [*o* la] jet-set

jettison ['dʒetɪsn, *Am:* 'dʒet̬ə-] *vt* **1.** (*get rid of*) **to** ~ **sb** se débarrasser de qn; **to** ~ **sth** se délester de qc **2.** (*reject*) abandonner; **to** ~ **sth for sth** renoncer à qc pour qc **3.** (*throw*) jeter par-dessus bord

jetty ['dʒetɪ, *Am:* 'dʒet̬-] *n* **1.** (*pier*) embarcadère *m* **2.** (*breakwater*) jetée *f*

Jew [dʒuː] *n* Juif *m,* Juive *f*

jewel ['dʒuːəl] *n* **1.** (*stone*) pierre *f* précieuse **2.** (*watch part*) rubis *m* **3.** *a. fig* joyau *m* ►**the crown** ~**s** les joyaux de la couronne

jeweler ['dʒuːəlɚ] *n Am,* **jeweller** ['dʒuːələʳ] *n* bijoutier, -ière *m, f;* **a** ~**'s (shop)** une bijouterie

jewellery *n,* **jewelry** ['dʒuːəlrɪ] *n Am no pl* bijouterie *f*

Jewess ['dʒuːes, *Am:* -ɪs] *n* Juive *f*

Jewish ['dʒuːɪʃ] *adj* juif(juive)

Jewry ['dʒuːrɪ] *n no pl, form* communauté *f* juive

Jew's harp *n* guimbarde *f*

jib¹ [dʒɪb] *n* (*sail*) foc *m*

jib² [dʒɪb] *n* (*arm of crane*) flèche *f*

jib³ <-bb-> *vi* **1.** (*be reluctant*) **to** ~ **at doing sth** rechigner à faire qc **2.** (*stop suddenly*) **the horse** ~**bed at the obstacle** le cheval a refusé l'obstacle

jibe [dʒaɪb] **I.** *n* raillerie *f;* **to make a** ~ lancer une moquerie **II.** *vi* **1. to** ~ **at sb** se moquer de qn **2.** *Am, Aus, inf* **to** ~ **with sb/sth** s'accorder avec qn/qc

jiffy ['dʒɪfɪ] *n no pl, inf* **in a** ~ en un clin d'œil; **she'll be back in a** ~ elle revient tout de suite

Jiffy bag® *n* enveloppe *f* matelassée

jig [dʒɪg] **I.** <-gg-> *vt* faire sauter **II.** <-gg-> *vi* (*move around/about*) se trémousser; **to** ~ **up and down** sautiller **III.** *n* gigue *f* **2.** *Am, inf* **the** ~ **is up** tout est fichu

J

jigger ['dʒɪgəʳ, *Am:* -ɚ] **I.** *n mesure de 42 ml* **II.** *vt Am* truquer
jiggered ['dʒɪgəd, *Am:* -ɚd] *adj Aus, Brit, inf* **1.** étonné(e) **2.** (*exhausted*) **to feel completely** ~ être éreinté ▶**well, I'll be** ~! *Brit, inf* zut alors!
jiggery-pokery [ˌdʒɪgərɪ'pəʊkərɪ, *Am:* -'poʊ-] *n no pl, inf* entourloupettes *fpl*
jiggle ['dʒɪgl] **I.** *vt* **to** ~ **about** [*o* **around**] secouer légèrement **II.** *vi* se trémousser
jigsaw (**puzzle**) *n a. fig* puzzle *m*
jilt [dʒɪlt] *vt* plaquer; **to** ~ **sb for sb** laisser tomber qn pour qn d'autre
Jim Crow [ˌdʒɪm'krəʊ, *Am:* -'kroʊ] *n no art, no pl, Am, pej* nègre *m,* négresse *f*
jimjams ['dʒɪmdʒæmz] *npl* **1.** *Brit, childspeak* (*pyjamas*) pyjama *m* **2.** (*nervousness*) **to have the** ~ avoir les nerfs à fleur de peau
jimmy ['dʒɪmɪ] *n, vt Am s.* **jemmy**
jingle ['dʒɪŋgl] **I.** *vi* tinter **II.** *vt* faire tinter **III.** *n* **1.** *no pl* (*noise*) tintement *m* **2.** (*in advertisements*) jingle *m*
jingoism ['dʒɪŋgəʊɪzəm, *Am:* -goʊ-] *n no pl, pej* chauvinisme *m*
jingoist *n pej* chauvin(e) *m(f)*
jingoistic [ˌdʒɪŋgəʊ'ɪstɪk, *Am:* -goʊ'-] *adj pej* chauvin(e)
jinks [dʒɪŋks] *npl* **high** ~ rigolade *f;* **to get up to high** ~ se payer du bon temps
jinx [dʒɪŋks] **I.** *n no pl* porte-malheur *m;* **to break the** ~ échapper à la guigne; **to put a** ~ **on sb/sth** jeter un sort à qn/qc **II.** *vt* porter malheur à; **to be** ~**ed** avoir la guigne
jitters ['dʒɪtəz, *Am:* 'dʒɪt̬ɚz] *npl inf* frousse *f;* **to get the** ~ avoir la trouille; **to give sb the** ~ flanquer la frousse à qn
jittery ['dʒɪtərɪ, *Am:* 'dʒɪt̬-] <-ier, -iest> *adj inf* froussard(e); **to get** ~ avoir la frousse
jiujitsu [ˌdʒuː'dʒɪtsuː] *n no pl, Aus s.* **jujitsu**
jive [dʒaɪv] **I.** *n* swing *m* **II.** *vi* danser le swing
Joan of Arc *n* HIST Jeanne d'Arc *f*
job [dʒɒb, *Am:* dʒɑːb] *n* **1.** (*work*) emploi *m;* **to apply for a** ~ poser sa candidature pour un emploi; **to get a** ~ trouver un travail; **to give up a** ~ démissionner; **his** ~ **at the factory** son boulot à l'usine; **a** ~ **in marketing** un emploi dans le commerce **2.** (*piece of work*) tâche *f;* **to make a good** ~ **of sth** se surpasser dans qc **3.** *no pl* (*duty*) travail *m* ▶**to have a** ~ **doing sth** avoir du mal à faire qc; **to do the** ~ *inf* faire l'affaire; **that's just the** ~ *inf* c'est tout à fait ce qu'il faut
job advertisement *n* offre *f* d'emploi
job analysis *n* analyse *f* des tâches
jobber ['dʒɒbəʳ, *Am:* 'dʒɑːbɚ] *n* **1.** COM négociant(e) *m(f)* en titres **2.** *Am* (*wholesaler*) grossiste *mf*
Job Centre *n Brit* agence *f* pour l'emploi **job counsellor** *n* conseiller, -ère *m, f* de l'emploi **job creation** *n* création *f* d'emplois **job creation scheme** *n Aus, Brit* programme *m* de création d'emplois **job cuts** *npl* réductions *fpl* d'emplois **job description** *n* profil *m* du poste **job evaluation** *n Brit* évaluation *f* des tâches **job hunt** *n inf* chasse *f* à l'emploi; **to be** ~**ing** être à la recherche d'un emploi **job interview** *n* entretien *m* d'embauche
jobless ['dʒɒblɪs, *Am:* 'dʒɑːb-] **I.** *adj* sans emploi **II.** *npl* chômeurs *mpl*
jobless figures *npl* **the** ~ le nombre de demandeurs *mpl* d'emploi
job lot *n* lot *m* **job market** *n* **the** ~ le marché de l'emploi **job offer** *n* offre *f* d'emploi **job security** *n* sécurité *f* de l'emploi **jobseeker** *n Brit* demandeur, euse d*m, f*emploi **job share** *n Brit* partage *m* du travail **job sharing** *n Brit* partage *m* des fonctions **job title** *n* titre *m* (de fonction)
Jock [dʒɒk, *Am:* dʒɑːk] *n Brit, inf* Ecossais(e) *m(f)*
jockey ['dʒɒkɪ, *Am:* 'dʒɑːkɪ] **I.** *n* jockey *m* **II.** *vi* **to** ~ **for sth** intriguer pour obtenir qc; **to** ~ **for position** jouer des coudes
jockstrap ['dʒɒkstræp, *Am:* 'dʒɑːk-] *n* slip *m* à coquille
jocular ['dʒɒkjʊləʳ, *Am:* 'dʒɑːkjəlɚ] *adj* badin(e); **in a** ~ **vein** d'un ton rieur; **to be in a** ~ **mood** être d'une humeur joviale
Joe Bloggs [ˌdʒəʊ'blɒgz, *Am:* ˌdʒoʊ'blɑːgz] *n no art, Brit, inf* Monsieur Tout-le-monde
jog [dʒɒg, *Am:* dʒɑːg] **I.** *n no pl* **1.** (*pace*) petit trot **2.** (*run*) jogging *m;* **to go for a** ~ faire du jogging **3.** (*knock*) poussée *f;* **to give sth a** ~ donner un coup sec à qc **II.** <-gg-> *vi* faire du jogging **III.** <-gg-> *vt* secouer; **to** ~ **sb's elbow** pousser le coude de qn ▶**to** ~ **sb's memory** rafraîchir la mémoire de qn
◆**jog along** *vi* **1.** *inf* (*advance slowly*) aller cahin-caha **2.** *fig* aller tant bien que mal
jogger ['dʒɒgəʳ, *Am:* 'dʒɑːgɚ] *n* joggeur, -euse *m, f*
jogging ['dʒɒgɪŋ, *Am:* 'dʒɑːgɪŋ] *n no pl* jogging *m*
joggle ['dʒɒgl, *Am:* 'dʒɑːgl] **I.** *vt* **to** ~ **sb/sth** (**about/around**) secouer qn/qc **II.** *n* légère secousse *f*
john [dʒɒn, *Am:* dʒɑːn] *n Am, Aus, inf* (*toilet*) cabinets *mpl*
John Bull *n no art, no pl, inf* l'Anglais type
johnny ['dʒɒni, *Am:* 'dʒɑː-] *n Brit, inf* (*condom*) capote *f*
join [dʒɔɪn] **I.** *vt* **1.** (*connect*) joindre; (*using glue, screws*) assembler; (*towns, roads*) relier; **to** ~ **hands** se donner la main; **to** ~ (**together**) **in marriage** unir par le mariage **2.** (*go and be with*) rejoindre; (*in a car, on a walk*) rattraper; **to** ~ **a plane/train** monter dans un avion/train; **to** ~ **the line** *Am,* **to** ~ **the queue** *Brit* prendre la queue; **to** ~ **sb in doing sth** se joindre à qn pour qc **3.** (*reach, touch: river, road*) rejoindre **4.** (*become a member of: club, party*) adhérer à; (*sect, company*) entrer dans; **to** ~ **the army** s'engager dans l'armée; **to** ~

forces with sb s'unir à qn; **to ~ the ranks of the unemployed** compter parmi les chômeurs **5.** (*involved in*) s'inscrire à ►**~ the club!** bienvenue au club! **II.** *vi* **1.** (*connect*) se joindre; **to ~ with sb in doing sth** se joindre à qn pour faire qc **2.** (*become a member*) adhérer **III.** *n* raccord *m*

◆**join in I.** *vi* participer; **to ~ doing sth** prendre part à qc **II.** *vt* se joindre à

◆**join up I.** *vi* **1.** MIL s'engager; (*for activity*) se retrouver **2.** (*converge: roads, rivers*) se rejoindre **II.** *vt* (*link: points*) relier; (*parts*) rattacher

joiner ['dʒɔɪnəʳ, *Am:* -nɚ] *n* menuisier *m*

joinery ['dʒɔɪnərɪ] *n no pl* menuiserie *f*

joint [dʒɔɪnt] **I.** *adj* commun(e); **it was a ~ effort** ce furent des efforts conjugués **II.** *n* **1.** ANAT articulation *f;* (*in wood*) assemblage *m;* (*in pipe*) jointure *f* **2.** (*meat*) rôti *m* **3.** *inf* (*place*) endroit *m* **4.** *inf* (*nightclub*) boîte *f* (de nuit) **5.** *inf* (*of drug*) joint *m* ►**to put sb's nose out of ~** défriser qn

joint account *n* compte *m* joint **joint committee** *n* commission *f* mixte **joint debtor** *n* codébiteur, -trice *m, f*

jointed ['dʒɔɪntəd, *Am:* -t̬ɪd] *adj* articulé(e)

jointly ['dʒɔɪntlɪ] *adv* conjointement

joint owner *n* copropriétaire *mf* **joint property** *n* copropriété *f* **joint-stock company** *n* société *f* par actions **joint venture** *n* coentreprise *f*

joist [dʒɔɪst] *n* solive *f*

jojoba oil [həʊ'həʊbə,ɔɪl, *Am:* hoʊ'hoʊ-] *n* huile *f* de jojoba

joke [dʒəʊk, *Am:* dʒoʊk] **I.** *n* **1.** (*sth funny*) plaisanterie *f;* **to tell a ~** raconter une blague; **to do sth for a ~** faire qc pour rire; **to get beyond a ~** commencer à ne plus être drôle; **she can't take a ~** elle ne comprend pas la plaisanterie; **to play a ~ on sb** jouer un tour à qn; **it's no ~** ce n'est pas une blague; **the ~'s on her** c'est à vous/eux de rire **2.** *inf* (*sth very easy*) **this is a ~** ça, c'est de la tarte; **it's no ~ being a farmer** ce n'est pas drôle d'être fermier **3.** *inf* (*ridiculous thing or person*) risée *f;* **he's a complete ~!** ce qu'il est drôle! **II.** *vi* plaisanter; **to ~ about sth** se moquer de qc; **you must be joking!** tu veux/vous voulez rire!

joker ['dʒəʊkəʳ, *Am:* 'dʒoʊkɚ] *n* **1.** (*one who jokes*) blagueur, -euse *m, f* **2.** *inf* (*foolish person*) imbécile *mf* **3.** (*card*) joker *m* ►**he's the ~ in the pack** avec lui c'est le grand inconnu

joking ['dʒəʊkɪŋ, *Am:* 'dʒoʊkɪŋ] **I.** *adj* de plaisanterie; **it's no ~ matter** il n'y a pas de quoi rire **II.** *n no pl* plaisanterie *f;* **~ apart** blague *f* à part

jokingly *adv* en plaisantant

jollification [,dʒɒlɪfɪ'keɪʃn, *Am:* ,dʒɑːlə-] *n* (*merrymaking*) réjouissances *fpl*

jollity ['dʒɒlətɪ, *Am:* 'dʒɑːlət̬ɪ] *n no pl* gaieté *f*

jolly ['dʒɒlɪ, *Am:* 'dʒɑːlɪ] **I.** <-ier, -iest> *adj* **1.** (*happy*) joyeux(-euse) **2.** (*cheerful*) jovial(e) **II.** *adv Brit, inf* drôlement; **a ~ good teacher** un prof formidable

◆**jolly along** *vt always sep* amadouer

jolt [dʒəʊlt, *Am:* dʒoʊlt] **I.** *n* **1.** (*jerk*) secousse *f* **2.** (*shock*) choc *m* **II.** *vt a. fig* secouer; **to ~ sb into doing sth** inciter qn à faire qc; **to ~ sb into action** pousser qn à l'action; **to ~ sb out of their lethargy** sortir qn de sa léthargie **III.** *vi* (*person*) tressauter; (*vehicle*) cahoter

Jordan ['dʒɔːdn, *Am:* 'dʒɔːr-] *n* **1.** (*country*) la Jordanie **2.** (*river*) le Jourdain

Jordanian [dʒɔː'deɪnɪən, *Am:* dʒɔːr-] **I.** *adj* jordanien(ne) **II.** *n* Jordanien(ne) *m(f)*

josh [dʒɒʃ, *Am:* dʒɑːʃ] *inf* **I.** *vt* taquiner **II.** *vi* blaguer

joss stick ['dʒɒsstɪk, *Am:* 'dʒɑːs-] *n* bâtonnet *m* d'encens

jostle ['dʒɒsl, *Am:* 'dʒɑːsl] **I.** *vt* bousculer **II.** *vi* se bousculer; **to ~ for sth** jouer des coudes pour avoir qc

jot [dʒɒt, *Am:* dʒɑːt] **I.** <-tt-> *vt* **to ~ sth (down)** noter qc **II.** *n no pl* **not a ~ of truth** pas un mot de vrai; **not to give a ~ about sb/sth** se moquer éperdument de qn/qc

jotter ['dʒɒtəʳ, *Am:* 'dʒɑːt̬ɚ] *n Aus, Brit* **~ (pad)** bloc-notes *m*

jottings ['dʒɒtɪŋz, *Am:* 'dʒɑːt̬ɪŋz] *npl* notes *fpl*

joule [dʒuːl] *n* joule *m*

journal ['dʒɜːnl, *Am:* 'dʒɜːr-] *n* **1.** (*periodical*) revue *f;* **quarterly ~** revue trimestrielle **2.** (*newspaper, diary*) journal *m;* **to keep a ~** tenir un journal

journalese [,dʒɜːnə'liːz, *Am:* ,dʒɜːr-] *n no pl, pej* jargon *m* journalistique

journalism ['dʒɜːnlɪzəm, *Am:* 'dʒɜːr-] *n no pl* journalisme *m*

journalist ['dʒɜːnlɪst, *Am:* 'dʒɜːr-] *n* journaliste *mf;* **freelance ~** pigiste *mf*

journalistic [,dʒɜːnə'lɪstɪk, *Am:* ,dʒɜːr-] *adj* journalistique

journey ['dʒɜːnɪ, *Am:* 'dʒɜːr-] **I.** *n* (*travel*) *a. fig* voyage *m;* (*period in movement*) trajet *m;* **a two-hour train ~** un trajet de deux heures en train **II.** *vi* voyager; **to ~ to Rome** faire un voyage à Rome

joust [dʒaʊst] **I.** *vi* jouter **II.** *n* joute *f*

jovial ['dʒəʊvɪəl, *Am:* 'dʒoʊ-] *adj* jovial(e)

joviality [,dʒəʊvɪ'ælətɪ, *Am:* ,dʒoʊvɪ'ælət̬ɪ] *n no pl* jovialité *f*

jowl [dʒaʊl] *n* **~[s]** bajoues *fpl*

joy [dʒɔɪ] *n* **1.** (*gladness*) joie *f;* **to be filled with ~** être comblé de joie; **to jump for ~** sauter de joie; **to shout/weep for ~** crier/pleurer de joie; **to be a ~ to sb** être une joie pour qn; **the ~ of winning/singing** le plaisir de gagner/chanter; **the ~s of teaching** les joies de l'enseignement **2.** *no pl, Brit, inf* **I got no ~ out of him** je n'arriverai à rien avec lui; **any ~?** ça a marché?

joyful ['dʒɔɪfl] *adj* joyeux(-euse)

joyless ['dʒɔɪləs] *adj* (*person, face*) sans joie; (*marriage*) malheureux(-euse)
joyous ['dʒɔɪəs] *adj* joyeux(-euse)
joyride ['dʒɔɪraɪd] *n* virée *f*
joyrider *n chauffard dans une voiture volée*
joystick ['dʒɔɪstɪk] *n* **1.** AVIAT levier *m* de commande **2.** INFOR joystick *m*, manette *f* de jeu
JP [ˌdʒeɪ'piː] *n Brit abbr of* **Justice of the Peace** juge *m* de paix
Jr *n abbr of* **Junior** junior *m*
jt *adj abbr of* **joint** joint(e)
jubilant ['dʒuːbɪlənt] *adj* enchanté(e)
jubilation [ˌdʒuːbɪ'leɪʃn] *n no pl* jubilation *f*
jubilee ['dʒuːbɪliː] *n* jubilé *m*
Judaism ['dʒuːdeɪɪzəm] *n no pl* judaïsme *m*
judder ['dʒʌdəʳ, *Am:* -ɚ] *Aus, Brit* **I.** *vi* trembler; **to ~ to a stop** s'arrêter avec des trépidations **II.** *n no pl* secousse *f*
judge [dʒʌdʒ] **I.** *n* juge *m;* (*in contest*) arbitre *m;* **to be/not be a good ~ of sth** être bon/mauvais juge en qc; **to be a good ~ of character** savoir bien juger les gens; **a ~ of horses/wine** un expert en chevaux/vins; **I'll be the ~ of that!** c'est moi qui en jugerai! **II.** *vi* **1.** (*decide*) juger; **to ~ by** [*o* **from**] **sth** juger d'après qc; **judging by the style** à en juger par le style **2.** LAW rendre un jugement **III.** *vt* **1.** (*decide*) juger; (*contest*) arbitrer **2.** (*estimate*) estimer **3.** (*appreciate*) apprécier ►**you can't ~ a book by its cover** *prov* il ne faut pas se fier aux apparences
judg(e)ment ['dʒʌdʒmənt] *n* **1.** LAW jugement *m* **2.** (*opinion*) avis *m* **3.** (*discernment*) appréciation *f;* **use your ~** c'est à toi/vous de juger
judg(e)mental [dʒʌdʒ'məntəl, *Am:* -t̬əl] *adj* critique
judicial [dʒuː'dɪʃl] *adj* judiciaire
judiciary [dʒuː'dɪʃərɪ, *Am:* -ierɪ] <-ies> *n* **1.** (*system*) système *m* judiciaire **2.** (*judges*) magistrature *f*
judicious [dʒuː'dɪʃəs] *adj* judicieux(-euse)
judo ['dʒuːdəʊ, *Am:* -doʊ] *n no pl* judo *m*
jug [dʒʌg] *n Aus, Brit* (*container*) cruche *f*
juggernaut ['dʒʌgənɔːt, *Am:* -ɚnɑːt] *n* poids *m* lourd
juggle ['dʒʌgl] *vt* **to ~** (**with**) **sth** jongler avec qc
juggler ['dʒʌgləʳ, *Am:* -lɚ] *n* jongleur, -euse *m, f*
juice [dʒuːs] *n* **1.** *a. fig* jus *m;* **grapefruit ~** jus de pamplemousse **2.** (*bodily liquid*) suc *m*
juicy ['dʒuːsɪ] <-ier, -iest> *adj* juteux(-euse)
jujitsu [dʒuː'dʒɪtsuː] *n no pl* jiu-jitsu *m*
jukebox ['dʒuːkbɒks, *Am:* -bɑːks] *n* jukebox *m*
julep ['dʒuːlɪp, *Am:* -ləp] *n* julep *m*
Juliet ['dʒuːliət, *Am:* -liet] *n* **Romeo and ~** Roméo et Juliette
July [dʒuː'laɪ] *n* juillet *m;* **the Fourth of ~** *Am* le quatre juillet; *s. a.* **April**
jumble ['dʒʌmbl] **I.** *n no pl* **1.** *a. fig* fouillis *m* **2.** *Brit* (*unwanted articles*) bric-à-brac *m* **II.** *vt* mélanger
jumbo ['dʒʌmbəʊ, *Am:* -boʊ] **I.** *adj* géant(e) **II.** *n inf* jumbo-jet *m*
jump [dʒʌmp] **I.** *vi* **1.** (*leap*) sauter; **to ~ out of sth** sauter de qc; **to ~ up** se lever d'un bond; **to ~ up and down** sauter en l'air; **to ~ up and down with excitement** sautiller d'excitation; **to ~ forward/across** faire un bond en avant/franchir d'un bond; **to ~ in** (*car*) sauter dans; **to ~ on** (*bus, train*) sauter dans; (*bicycle, horse*) sauter sur **2.** (*jerk*) sursauter; **to make sb ~** faire sursauter qn **3.** *Aus, Brit, inf* (*be annoyed*) **to ~ up and down** être très agacé **4.** (*increase suddenly*) faire un bond; **to ~ by 70%** faire un bond de 70% **5.** (*skip*) sauter; **to ~ from one thing to another** passer d'un seul coup d'une chose à une autre ►**to ~ to conclusions** tirer des conclusions trop hâtives; **to ~ to the conclusion that ...** conclure trop vite que ...; **to ~ for joy** bondir de joie; **to go ~ in the lake** *inf* aller se faire voir; **to ~ out of one's skin** sursauter; **to be really ~ing** *inf* être animé **II.** *vt* **1.** (*leap across or over*) sauter par-dessus **2.** *Am* (*attack*) **to ~ sb** sauter sur qn **3.** (*skip*) sauter **4.** (*disregard*) **to ~ bail** se soustraire à la justice; **to ~ the** (**traffic**) **lights** passer au feu rouge; **to ~ a queue** *Aus, Brit* passer avant son tour ►**to ~ the gun** être prématuré; **and ~ to it** et que ça saute; **to ~ ship** déserter le navire **III.** *n* **1.** (*leap*) saut *m;* **parachute ~** saut en parachute **2.** (*hurdle*) obstacle *m* **3.** (*step*) pas *m;* **to be one ~ ahead of one's competitors** avoir une longueur d'avance sur ses concurrents **4.** (*head-start*) avance *f;* **to get a ~ on sb** devancer qn
◆**jump about** *vi* sautiller
◆**jump at** *vi* **to ~ an opportunity** sauter sur une occasion
◆**jump down** *vi inf* **to ~ sb's throat** remballer qn
◆**jump on** *vt* (*blame*) s'en prendre à
◆**jump out at** *vt* sauter aux yeux de
jumped-up ['dʒʌmptʌp] *adj Brit, pej, inf* prétentieux(-euse)
jumper ['dʒʌmpəʳ, *Am:* -pɚ] *n* **1.** (*person or animal*) sauteur, -euse *m, f* **2.** *Aus, Brit* (*pullover*) pull *m* **3.** *Am* (*pinafore dress*) robe-tablier *f*
jump leads *n pl* câbles *mpl* de démarrage
jump rope *n Am* corde *f* à sauter
jump-start ['dʒʌmpstɑːt, *Am:* -stɑːrt] *vt* (*car*) faire démarrer avec des câbles; (*economy*) relancer
jumpy ['dʒʌmpɪ] <-ier, -iest> *adj inf* nerveux(-euse)
junction ['dʒʌŋkʃn] *n* (*roads*) intersection *f;* (*for trains*) nœud *m* ferroviaire
juncture ['dʒʌŋktʃəʳ, *Am:* -tʃɚ] *n no pl, form* **at this ~** à ce moment précis
June [dʒuːn] *n* juin *m;* *s. a.* **April**
jungle ['dʒʌŋgl] *n* jungle *f* ►**it's a ~ out**

there c'est un panier de crabes là-dedans
junior ['dʒuːnɪəʳ, *Am:* -njɚ] **I.** *adj* **1.** (*younger*) junior **2.** SPORT minime; ~ **tennis team** équipe *f* de tennis des minimes **3.** *Am* (*lower level of education*) ~ **college** université *f* de premier cycle; ~ **high school** collège *m* **4.** *Brit* (*for 7–11 year-olds*) ~ **school** école *f* primaire **5.** (*lower in rank*) subordonné(e); ~ **doctor** *Brit* médecin *m* des hôpitaux **II.** *n* **1.** *no pl, Am* (*son*) junior *m* **2.** (*low-ranking person*) subordonné(e) *m(f)* **3.** *Brit* SCHOOL élève *mf* du primaire; **the** ~**s** les primaires; **to move up to the Juniors** aller dans le primaire **4.** *Am* SCHOOL étudiant(e) *m(f)* de premier cycle
juniper ['dʒuːnɪpəʳ, *Am:* -pɚ] *n* genévrier *m*
junk[1] [dʒʌŋk] **I.** *n* **1.** *no pl* (*jumble*) brocante *f;* ~ **shop** bric-à-brac *m* **2.** (*rubbish*) vieilleries *fpl;* **the** ~ **on TV** les navets à la télé; ~ (**food**) nourriture *f* industrielle; ~ **mail** réclame *f* **3.** *Am, inf* (*narcotic drugs*) came *f* **II.** *vt inf* balancer
junk[2] [dʒʌŋk] *n* (*vessel*) jonque *f*
junket ['dʒʌŋkɪt] *n* voyage *m* aux frais de la princesse
junkie ['dʒʌŋkɪ] *n inf* **1.** (*drug addict*) camé(e) *m(f)* **2.** (*addict*) accro *mf;* **to be a coffee/TV** ~ être un accro du café/de la télévision **junkpile**, **junkyard** *n* décharge *f*
junta ['dʒʌntə, *Am:* 'hʊntə] *n* junte *f*
Jupiter ['dʒuːpɪtəʳ, *Am:* -t̬ɚ] *n* ASTR Jupiter *f*
jurisdiction [ˌdʒʊərɪs'dɪkʃn, *Am:* ˌdʒʊrɪs-] *n no pl* juridiction *f*
jurisprudence [ˌdʒʊərɪs'pruːdns, *Am:* ˌdʒʊrɪs-] *n no pl* jurisprudence *f*
jurist ['dʒʊərɪst, *Am:* 'dʒʊrɪst] *n* juriste *mf*
juror ['dʒʊərəʳ, *Am:* 'dʒʊrɚ] *n* juré(e) *m(f)*
jury ['dʒʊərɪ, *Am:* 'dʒʊrɪ] *n* jury *m;* **the members of the** ~ les membres du jury
just [dʒʌst] **I.** *adv* **1.** (*at that moment*) juste; **to be** ~ **doing sth** être juste en train de faire qc; **to have** ~ **done sth** venir de faire qc; **he** ~ **left** *Am* il vient de partir; ~ **after 10 o'clock** juste après dix heures; **I saw him** ~ **now** je viens juste de le voir; ~ **then** juste à ce moment-là; ~ **last Friday** pas plus tard que vendredi dernier; ~ **as he finished** il venait justement de finir **2.** (*only*) juste; **he** ~ **smiled** il n'a fait que sourire; ~ **sit down** assieds-toi/asseyez-vous donc; ~ **for fun** juste pour s'amuser; (**not**) ~ **anybody** (pas) n'importe qui; ~ **in case it rains** juste au cas où il pleuvrait **3.** (*barely*) tout juste; ~ **in time** juste à temps; ~ **about** tout juste **4.** (*very*) vraiment ►**I'm** ~ <u>**about**</u> **ready** je suis prêt(e) tout de suite; **it's** ~ **my** <u>**luck**</u> c'est bien ma chance; **it's** ~ **one of those** <u>**things**</u> *prov* ce sont des choses qui arrivent; <u>**isn't**</u> **it** ~? *inf* c'est le moins qu'on puisse dire; ~ **as** <u>**well**</u>**!** heureusement! **II.** *adj* (*fair*) juste; (*cause*) légitime; (*reward*) méritée; **the** ~ les justes ►**to get one's** ~ <u>**deserts**</u> avoir ce qu'on méritait
justice ['dʒʌstɪs] *n* **1.** *a.* LAW justice *f;* **to bring sb to** ~ traduire qn en justice **2.** (*judge*) juge *mf;* **Supreme Court** ~ *Am* juge de la Cour suprême ►**to** <u>**do**</u> **sb** ~ mettre qn en valeur
justifiable [ˌdʒʌstɪ'faɪəbl, *Am:* ˌdʒʌstə'-] *adj* justifiable
justifiably *adv* légitimement
justification [ˌdʒʌstɪfɪ'keɪʃn, *Am:* -tə-] *n no pl* justification *f*
justified [ˌdʒʌstɪfaɪd] *adj* justifié(e); **to feel** ~ **in doing sth** se sentir autorisé à faire qc
justify ['dʒʌstɪfaɪ] *vt* justifier; **to** ~ **sb's faith** mériter la confiance de qn; **to** ~ **oneself to sb** se justifier devant qn
justly ['dʒʌstlɪ] *adv* avec raison
jut [dʒʌt] <-tt-> *vi* **to** ~ **out of sth** dépasser de qc
jute [dʒuːt] *n no pl* jute *m*
juvenile ['dʒuːvənaɪl, *Am:* -nl] *adj* **1.** *form* (*young*) juvénile; (*delinquent*) jeune; ~ **court** tribunal *m* pour enfants; **to play the** ~ **lead** jouer un rôle de jeune premier **2.** *pej* (*childish*) puéril(e)
juxtapose [ˌdʒʌkstə'pəʊz, *Am:* 'dʒʌkstəpoʊz] *vt* juxtaposer
juxtaposition [ˌdʒʌkstəpə'zɪʃn] *n no pl* juxtaposition *f;* **to place sth in** ~ **with sth** juxtaposer deux choses

K

K, k [keɪ] <-'s> *n* K, k *m;* ~ **as in King**, ~ **for King** (*on telephone*) k comme Kléber
K *n* INFOR *abbr of* **kilobyte** Ko *m*
kail ['keɪl] *n* chou *m* frisé
kajal (**eyeliner**) **pencil** [kəˌjel('aɪlaɪnə)ˌpensl] *n Am* (crayon) *m* khôl *m*
kale *s.* **kail**
kaleidoscope [kə'laɪdəskəʊp, *Am:* -skoʊp] *n* kaléidoscope *m*
kamikaze [ˌkæmɪ'kɑːzɪ, *Am:* ˌkɑːmə-] *adj* kamikaze *m*
kangaroo [ˌkæŋgə'ruː] <-(s)> *n* kangourou *m*
kangaroo court *n* tribunal *m* irrégulier
Kansas ['kænzəs] **I.** *n* le Kansas **II.** *adj* du Kansas
karaoke [ˌkæri'əʊki, *Am:* ˌkeri'oʊ-] *n* karaoké *m;* ~ **club**/**night** club/soirée de karaoké
karate [kə'rɑːtɪ, *Am:* kæ'rɑːt̬ɪ] *n no pl* karaté *m;* ~ **chop** *coup porté avec le tranchant de la main*
karma ['kɑːmə, *Am:* 'kɑːr-] *n* karma *m*
Kashmir [ˌkæʃ'mɪəʳ, *Am:* ˌkæʃ'mɪr] *n* **1.** (*material*) cachemire *m* **2.** GEO ~ le Cachemire
Kashmiri [ˌkæʃ'mɪəʳi, *Am:* ˌkæʃ'mɪri] **I.** *adj* cachemirien(ne) **II.** *n* **1.** (*person*) Cachemirien(ne) *m(f)* **2.** LING cachemirien *m; s. a.* **Eng-**

K

lish

kayak ['kaɪæk] *n* kayak *m*

kayaking *n* kayak *m*

KB [ˌkeɪ'biː], **kbyte** *n* INFOR *abbr of* **kilobyte** Ko *m*

kc *n abbr of* **kilocycle** kC

KC *n abbr of* **King's Counsel** avocat *m* de la couronne, conseiller *m* du roi *Québec*

kebab [kə'bæb, *Am:* -'bɑːb] *n* kébab *m*

keel [kiːl] *n* NAUT quille *f*

keel over *vi* s'évanouir

keen [kiːn] *adj* **1.** (*eager*) enthousiaste; (*sportswoman*) passionné(e); **to be ~ on** (*project, policy*) tenir à; (*artist, food, boyfriend, sport*) adorer; **to be ~ on doing sth** (*want to do it*) tenir à faire qc; (*do it a lot*) adorer faire qc; **to be ~ to leave** avoir hâte de partir; **I'm not ~ on her/going** *inf* elle ne me plaît pas/ça ne m'emballe pas de partir **2.** (*perceptive: mind, eye*) vif(vive); (*hearing, awareness*) fin(e); (*eyesight*) perçant(e) **3.** (*extreme: interest, desire*) vif(vive); (*competition*) acharné(e) **4.** (*biting*) mordant(e)

keep [kiːp] **I.** *n* **1.** *no pl* (*living costs*) frais *mpl* de logement; **to earn one's ~** gagner sa vie **2.** (*tower*) donjon *m* ►**for ~s** pour de bon **II.** <kept, kept> *vt* **1.** (*not let go of: property*) garder; (*visitor*) retenir; **to ~ the children** (*after divorce*) avoir la garde des enfants; **to ~ information from sb** cacher des informations à qn; **~ this to yourself** garde ça pour toi/gardez ça pour vous **2.** (*store*) ranger; **~ the plant by a window** placer la plante près d'une fenêtre; **I ~ a bottle in the fridge** j'ai une bouteille au frigo **3.** (*maintain in a given state*) **to ~ sb/sth under control** maîtriser qn/qc; **to ~ sb under observation** garder qn en observation; **to ~ one's eyes fixed on sb/sth** garder ses yeux fixés sur qn/qc; **~ one's head up/down** garder la tête levée/baissée; **to ~ sb awake/in suspense** empêcher qn de dormir/laisser qn dans l'expectative; **to ~ food/a child warm** garder un plat/enfant au chaud; **~ this room tidy** garder cette pièce en ordre; **to ~ sb waiting** faire attendre qn **4.** (*look after*) **to ~ house** tenir la maison; **to ~ animals** avoir des animaux; **to ~ a mistress** entretenir une maîtresse **5.** (*respect: rules, conditions*) respecter; (*promise*) tenir; (*appointment*) se rendre à **6.** (*write regularly: record, accounts*) tenir; **to ~ a record of sth** prendre qc en note **7.** (*for security*) **to ~ watch over sth** surveiller qc; **to ~ guard** monter la garde **8.** (*prevent*) **to ~ sb from doing sth** empêcher qn de faire qc **9.** (*help or force to continue*) **to ~ sb doing sth** obliger qn à continuer à faire qc; **to ~ sb talking** retenir qn; **here's an apple/$50 to ~ you going** voilà une pomme pour tenir le coup/50$ pour voir venir; **we have enough oil to ~ us going for a month** on a assez de fioul pour tenir un mois ►**to ~ one's balance** [*o* **feet**] garder son équilibre; **to ~ one's hand in** garder la main; **to ~ oneself to oneself** garder ses distances; **to ~ a secret** garder un secret; **to ~ time** rester en mesure **III.** <kept, kept> *vi* **1.** (*stay fresh*) se conserver **2.** (*stay*) **to ~ calm** garder son calme; **to ~ left** rester sur la gauche; **to ~ warm** se protéger du froid; **to ~ inside** rester à l'intérieur; **to ~ quiet** rester tranquille; **~ down!** ne bouge/bougez pas! **3.** (*continue*) **to ~ doing sth** continuer à faire qc; **I ~ going somehow** je me maintiens; **he ~s pestering me** il n'arrête pas de me harceler ►**how are you ~ing?** *Brit* comment allez-vous/vas-tu?

◆**keep at I.** *vi* **to ~ sth** persévérer dans qc; **~ it!** continue/continuez!; **to ~ sb** *Am* harceler qn **II.** *vt* **to keep sb at sth** faire continuer qc à qn

◆**keep away I.** *vi* **to ~ from sb/sth** ne pas s'approcher de qn/qc **II.** *vt* **to keep sb/sth away from sb/sth** tenir qn/qc à l'écart de qn/qc

◆**keep back I.** *vi* (*stay away*) ne pas s'approcher; **to ~ from sb/sth** garder ses distances de qn/qc **II.** *vt* **1.** (*hold away*) **to keep sb/sth back from sb/sth** empêcher qn/qc de s'approcher de qn/qc **2.** (*retain: money*) retenir; (*information*) cacher

◆**keep down** *vt* **1.** (*repress: costs, speed, level*) empêcher d'augmenter; (*protesters, workers*) contrôler **2.** (*not vomit*) **to keep sth down** se retenir de rendre qc

◆**keep from I.** *vt always sep* **1.** (*prevent*) **to keep sb from doing sth** empêcher qn de faire qc **2.** (*retain information*) **to keep sth from sb** cacher qc à qn **II.** *vi* **to ~ doing sth** s'abstenir de faire qc

◆**keep in** *vt* **to keep sb in** retenir qn; (*pupil*) garder en retenue; **to keep one's emotions in** retenir ses émotions

◆**keep in with** *vi* rester en bons termes avec

◆**keep off** *vt* **1.** (*stay off*) rester à l'écart de; **'~ the grass'** pelouse interdite **2.** *Brit, fig* **to ~ a subject** éviter d'aborder un sujet **3. to keep sb/sth off sth** tenir qn/qc à l'écart de qc

◆**keep on I.** *vi* **1.** (*continue*) **to ~ doing sth** continuer à faire qc **2.** (*pester*) **to ~ at sb about sth** harceler qn au sujet de qc **II.** *vt* (*worker*) garder

◆**keep out I.** *vi* rester (en) dehors; **to ~ of sth** ne pas se mêler de qc **II.** *vt always sep* empêcher d'entrer

◆**keep to** *vi* **1.** (*stay*) **to ~ one's bed** garder le lit; **~ the path** rester sur le chemin **2.** (*respect*) **to ~ sth** suivre scrupuleusement qc

◆**keep up** *vt* **to ~ appearances** garder les apparences

◆**keep up with** *vi* (*runner, driver*) aller à la même vitesse que; (*other pupils*) arriver à suivre ►**to ~ the Joneses** faire aussi bien que les voisins

keeper ['kiːpəʳ, *Am:* -pɚ] *n* (*of animals, in football*) gardien(ne) *m(f)*

keep-fit *n* gymnastique *f* d'entretien
keeping ['ki:pɪŋ] *n* **1.** (*guarding*) garde *mf;* **to leave sb/sth in sb's ~** confier qn/qc à qn **2.** (*respecting*) **to be in/out of ~ with** (*policy, philosophy*) correspondre/ne pas correspondre à; (*aims, principles*) être en accord/désaccord avec; (*period, style*) s'harmoniser/détonner avec
keepsake ['ki:pseɪk] *n* souvenir *m*
keg [keg] *n* baril *m*
kelp [kelp] *n no pl* varech *m*
kennel ['kenl] **I.** *n* **1.** (*dog shelter*) niche *f* **2.** *pl + sing or pl verb, Brit* (*boarding for dogs*) chenil *m* **II.** *vt* **to ~ a dog** mettre un chien dans un chenil
Kentucky [ken'tʌki, *Am:* kən-] **I.** *n* le Kentucky **II.** *adj* du Kentucky
Kenya ['kenjə] *n* le Kenya
Kenyan ['kenjən] **I.** *adj* kényan(ne) **II.** *n* Kényan(ne) *m(f)*
kept [kept] **I.** *pt, pp of* **keep** **II.** *adj* entretenu(e)
kerb [kɜ:b, *Am:* kɜ:rb] *n Aus, Brit* bordure *f* du trottoir
kerb drill *n Brit: consignes pour traverser la rue en toute sécurité*
kernel ['kɜ:nl, *Am:* 'kɜ:r-] *n* **1.** (*centre of fruit*) noyau *m* **2.** (*cereal seed*) grain *m* **3.** *fig* noyau *m;* **a ~ of truth** un fond de vérité
kerosene ['kerəsi:n] *n no pl, Am, Aus* **1.** (*paraffin*) pétrole *m* **2.** (*for jet engines*) kérosène *m; no pl*
kestrel ['kestrəl] *n* crécerelle *f*
ketchup ['ketʃəp] *n no pl* ketchup *m*
kettle ['ketl, *Am:* 'ket̬-] *n* bouilloire *f;* **to put the ~ on** mettre de l'eau à chauffer ►**to be a different ~ of fish** être une autre paire de manches
kettledrum ['ketldrʌm, *Am:* 'ket̬-] *n* timbale *f*
key [ki:] **I.** *n* **1.** (*locking device*) clé [*o* clef] *f* **2.** *no pl* (*essential point*) **the ~ to sth** la clé de qc **3.** (*list: of symbols*) légende *f;* (*of answers*) solutions *fpl* **4.** MUS ton *m;* **in the ~ of C major** en do majeur; **off ~** faux **5.** INFOR touche *f,* piton *m Québec;* **SHIFT ~** touche Majuscule; **FUNCTION ~** touche (de) Fonction; **to twiddle at the ~s** tapoter sur des touches, pitonner *Québec* **II.** *adj* (*factor, question, figure*) clé [*o* clef]; **sth is ~** qc est essentiel **III.** *vt* **1.** (*type*) saisir; **to ~ in a password** taper un code **2.** (*adapt*) **to ~ sth to sb** adapter qc à qn
◆key up *vt* **to be keyed up** être excité
keyboard ['ki:bɔ:d, *Am:* -bɔ:rd] **I.** *n* MUS, INFOR clavier *m;* **to play ~s** jouer du synthétiseur **II.** *vt* saisir
keyboarder *n* claviste *mf*
keyboard operator *n* opérateur, -trice *m, f* de saisie
keyhole ['ki:həʊl, *Am:* -hoʊl] *n* trou *m* de serrure
keyhole surgery *n* chirurgie *f* endoscopique
keynote ['ki:nəʊt, *Am:* -noʊt] *n* tonique *m;* **to be the ~ of sth** être l'idée-force de qc
keynote address, keynote speech *n* discours *m* programme
keypad ['ki:pæd] *n* INFOR pavé *m;* **numeric ~** pavé numérique
key ring *n* porte-clé *m* **key signature** *n* MUS armature *f* **keystone** *n* clé *f* de voute **key stroke** *n* frappe *f* **key word** *n* **1.** (*cipher*) code *m* **2.** (*important word*) mot-clé *m*
kg *n abbr of* **kilogram** kg *m*
khaki ['kɑ:kɪ, *Am:* 'kækɪ] **I.** *n no pl* kaki *m* **II.** *adj* kaki *inv*
kHz *n abbr of* **kilohertz** kHz *m*
kibbutz [kɪ'bʊts] *n* kibboutz *m*
kick [kɪk] **I.** *n* **1.** (*blow with foot*) coup *m* de pied **2.** (*excited feeling*) **to get a ~ out of sth** prendre plaisir à qc; **to do sth for ~s** faire qc pour s'amuser **3.** (*gun jerk*) recul *m* **4.** (*strong effect*) coup *m* ►**to need a ~ in the <u>arse</u>** *vulg* avoir besoin d'un coup de pied au cul; **a ~ in the <u>teeth</u>** un coup vache **II.** *vt* donner un coup de pied dans; **to ~ oneself** s'en vouloir; **to ~ the ball into the net** envoyer le ballon au but; **to ~ a can out of the way** ôter une boîte du milieu d'un coup de pied ►**to ~ the <u>bucket</u>** casser sa pipe; **to ~ one's <u>heels</u>** *Brit* poireauter
◆kick about **I.** *vi inf* traîner **II.** *vt* (*ball*) taper dans; **to kick an idea about** [*o* **around**] *inf* tourner et retourner une idée
◆kick against *vi* résister à ►**to ~ the <u>pricks</u>** se rebiffer
◆kick around *s.* **kick about**
◆kick back *vt* renvoyer (avec le pied)
◆kick in **I.** *vt* enfoncer à coup de pied **II.** *vi* (*system, mechanism*) se déclancher
◆kick off **I.** *vi* donner le coup d'envoi **II.** *vt* **to kick sth off with sth** enlever qc d'un coup de pied
◆kick out **I.** *vt* **to kick sb/sth out** jeter qc/qn dehors; **to be kicked out of school** être renvoyé de l'école **II.** *vi* **to ~ against sb/sth** se révolter contre qn/qc
◆kick over *vt* **to kick sb/sth over** renverser qn/qc
◆kick up *vt* **1.** **to ~ dust** faire voler la poussière **2.** *fig* **to ~ a fuss** faire des histoires
kickback ['kɪkbæk] *n* pot-de-vin *m*
kicker ['kɪkə^r^, *Am:* -ɚ] *n* SPORT botteur *m*
kick-start ['kɪkstɑ:t, *Am:* -stɑ:rt] **I.** *n* démarreur *m* (au pied) **II.** *vt* (*motorcycle*) démarrer au pied; (*process, economy*) relancer
kick turn *n* SPORT conversion *f*
kid [kɪd] **I.** *n* **1.** (*child*) gosse *mf* **2.** *Am, Aus* (*young person*) gamin(e) *m(f);* **~ sister** *Am* petite sœur; **~ brother** *Am* petit frère **3.** (*young goat*) chevreau *m,* chevrette *f* **4.** (*goatskin*) chevreau ►**to treat sb with ~ <u>gloves</u>** prendre des gants avec qn **II.** <-dd-> *vi* raconter des blagues; **no ~ding** sans rire **III.** *vt* faire marcher; **to ~ oneself** se faire des illusions
kidnap ['kɪdnæp] <-pp-> *vt* kidnapper

K

kidnapper [-ɚ] *n* kidnappeur, -euse *m, f*
kidnapping ['kɪdnæpɪŋ] *n* enlèvement *m*
kidney ['kɪdnɪ] *n* 1. ANAT rein *m* 2. (*food*) rognon *m*
kidney bean *n* haricot *m* rouge **kidney donor** *n* donneur *m* de rein **kidney machine** *n* rein *m* artificiel **kidney-shaped** *adj* en forme de haricot **kidney stone** *n* calcul *m* rénal
kill [kɪl] I. *n no pl* mise *f* à mort ►**to be in at the** ~ assister au dénouement; **to go in for the** ~ descendre dans l'arène II. *vi* tuer III. *vt* 1. (*cause to die*) tuer; **to** ~ **oneself** se suicider; **to** ~ **oneself laughing** *inf* être mort de rire; **to** ~ **oneself trying** *inf* se tuer à essayer; **would it** ~ **you to be polite?** ça te défriserait d'être poli?; **my back/knee is** ~**ing me** mon dos/genou me fait atrocement souffrir 2. (*destroy*) supprimer ►**to** ~ **two birds with one stone** *prov* faire d'une pierre deux coups; **to** ~ **the fatted calf** tuer le veau gras; **to** ~ **sb with kindness** nuire à qn par excès d'attentions; **to** ~ **time** tuer le temps
◆**kill off** *vt* 1. exterminer 2. *fig* éliminer
killer ['kɪləʳ, *Am:* -ɚ] *n* 1. (*murderer*) tueur, -euse *m, f;* **to be a** ~ (*disease, drug*) être meurtrier 2. *fig* **to be a** ~ (*joke*) être à mourir de rire; (*ruthless person*) être impitoyable
killer disease *n* maladie *f* mortelle **killer instinct** *n* agressivité *f* **killer whale** *n* orque *f*
killing ['kɪlɪŋ] I. *n* massacre *m* ►**to make a** ~ *inf* réussir un beau coup II. *adj* 1. (*exhausting*) tuant(e) 2. (*funny*) tordant(e)
killjoy ['kɪldʒɔɪ] *n pej* rabat-joie *m inv*
kiln ['kɪln] *n* four *m*
kilo ['ki:ləʊ, *Am:* -oʊ] *n* kilo *m*
kilobyte ['kɪləbaɪt, *Am:* -oʊ-] *n* kilo-octet *m inv*
kilogram(me) ['kɪleʊgræm, *Am:* '-oʊ-, '-ə-] *n* kilogramme *m*
kilometer [kɪ'lɑ:mət̬ɚ] *n Am,* **kilometre** [kɪ'lɒmɪtəʳ] *n* kilomètre *m*
kilowatt ['kɪləwɒt, *Am:* -oʊwɑ:t] *n* kilowatt *m*
kilowatt hour *n* kilowattheure *m*
kilt [kɪlt] *n* kilt *m*

> Le **kilt** ou "Highland dress" d'un Écossais date du 16ème siècle et était autrefois constitué d'une seule pièce d'étoffe. Au 17ème siècle, on en fit deux vêtements séparés: le "kilt" et le "plaid". C'est aussi de cette époque que date le "sporran" (une bourse attachée à la ceinture). Ce n'est qu'au 18ème siècle que les différents "tartans" (motifs écossais) furent créés pour des familles ou des clans spécifiques. Pour des occasions particulières ou des mariages, beaucoup d'hommes portent encore le "kilt" de nos jours.

kimono [kɪ'məʊnəʊ, *Am:* kə'mɔʊnə] *n* kimono *m*
kin [kɪn] *n* parents *mpl;* **his next of** ~ son plus proche parent
kind¹ [kaɪnd] *adj* gentil(le), fin(e) *Québec;* **to be** ~ **to sb** être gentil avec qn; **to be** ~ **to sb** (*photo*) montrer qn à son avantage; **with** ~ **regards** cordialement
kind² [kaɪnd] I. *n* 1. (*group*) genre *m;* **the first of its** ~ le premier de sa catégorie; **I've heard/said nothing of the** ~ je n'ai rien entendu/dit de ce genre; **all** ~**s of** toutes sortes de; **it's some** ~ **of insect/map** c'est une espèce d'instinct/de carte; **what** ~ **of day/book is it?** quel genre de jour/livre est-ce?; **a** ~ **of** une sorte de 2. (*payment*) **to pay sb in** ~ payer qn en nature 3. (*similarly*) **to answer in** ~ renvoyer l'ascenseur II. *adv inf* ~ **of difficult/angry** plutôt difficile/coléreux; **I'd** ~ **of hoped she'd come** en fait, j'espérais qu'elle viendrait
kindergarten ['kɪndəgɑ:tn, *Am:* -dɚgɑ:r-] *n* école *f* maternelle
kind-hearted *adj* ayant bon cœur
kindle ['kɪndl] *vt* 1. (*fire*) allumer 2. (*imagination*) éveiller 3. (*desire*) enflammer
kindling ['kɪndlɪŋ] *n no pl* petit bois *m*
kindly ['kaɪndlɪ] I. *adj* (*person*) aimable; (*smile, voice*) doux(douce); **to be a** ~ **soul** être la gentillesse même II. *adv* gentiment; **not to take** ~ **to sb/sth** ne pas apprécier qn/qc
kindness ['kaɪndnɪs] *n* 1. *no pl* (*manner*) gentillesse *f* 2. <-es> (*kind act*) petite *f* attention
kindred ['kɪndrɪd] I. *n* parents *mpl* II. *adj* 1. (*related by blood*) apparenté(e) 2. (*similar*) semblable
kinetic [kɪ'netɪk, *Am:* -'net̬-] *adj* PHYS cinétique
king [kɪŋ] *n* roi *m*
kingdom ['kɪŋdəm] *n* 1. (*country*) royaume *m* 2. (*domain*) **animal/plant** ~ règne *m* animal/végétal ►**till** ~ **come** jusqu'à la fin des siècles
kingfisher ['kɪŋˌfɪʃəʳ, *Am:* -ɚ] *n* martin-pêcheur *m*
kingly ['kɪŋlɪ] *adj* royal(e)
kingpin ['kɪŋpɪn] *n* **to be the** ~ **of sth** être le cerveau de qc
King's Bench *n Brit* LAW Cour *f* supérieure de justice
king-size ['kɪŋsaɪz] *adj* (*bed, duvet*) très grand(e); (*packet, bottle*) géant(e)
kink [kɪŋk] *n* 1. (*unwanted twist*) mauvais pli *m;* (*in pipe, rope*) nœud *m* 2. *Am, Aus* (*sore muscle*) froissement *m* 3. (*problem*) problème *m;* **to iron out a few** ~**s** résoudre quelques problèmes 4. (*strange habit*) vice *m*
kinky ['kɪŋkɪ] <-ier, -iest> *adj* 1. (*with tight curls*) légèrement frisé(e) 2. (*unusual*) bizarre; ~ **sex** pratiques *fpl* sexuelles un peu spéciales
kinship ['kɪnʃɪp] *n* parenté *f;* **to feel a** ~ **with sb** avoir de nombreuses affinités avec qn
kiosk ['ki:ɒsk, *Am:* -ɑ:sk] *n* 1. (*stand*) kiosque *m* 2. *Brit* (**telephone**) ~ cabine *f* télé-

phonique

kip [kɪp] **I.** *n Aus, Brit no pl, inf* plumard *m;* **to get some ~** aller roupiller **II.** <-pp-> *vi Aus, Brit, inf* pioncer

kipper ['kɪpəʳ, *Am:* -ɚ] *n* hareng *m* fumé

Kiribati [ˌkirə'bæs, *Am:* 'kɪ-] *n* Kiribati *f*

kirk [kɜːk, *Am:* kɜːrk] *n Scot* église *f*

kiss [kɪs] **I.** *n* bise *f,* baise *f Belgique;* **give me a ~** donne/donnez-moi un baiser; **love and ~es** (*in a letter*) grosses bises *fpl;* **to blow sb a ~** envoyer un baiser à qn **II.** *vi* s'embrasser **III.** *vt* donner un baiser à, donner un bec *Belgique, Québec, Suisse;* **to ~ sb goodnight/goodbye** embrasser qn en lui souhaitant bonne nuit/disant au revoir; **to ~ sth goodbye** *inf* pouvoir dire adieu à

kiss of death *n* **to be the ~ to sth** porter le coup fatal à qc

kiss-off ['kɪsɒf, *Am:* -ɑːf] *n Am* **to give sb the ~** plaquer qn

kiss of life *n* bouche-à-bouche *m;* **to give sb the ~** faire du bouche-à-bouche à qn

kit [kɪt] *n* **1.** (*set*) trousse *f;* (*for activity*) nécessaire *m;* **tool ~** kit *m* **2.** (*components*) pièces *fpl* détachées; **in ~ form** en pièces détachées **3.** *Brit* (*clothes: for sport*) tenue *f*

kit out *vt Brit* équiper

kitchen ['kɪtʃɪn] *n* cuisine *f*

kitchenette [ˌkɪtʃɪ'net] *n* kitchenette *f*

kitchen foil *n* papier *m* d'aluminium **kitchen garden** *n* potager *m* **kitchen knife** *n* couteau *m* de cuisine **kitchen range** *n Am* cuisinière *f* **kitchen sink** *n* évier *m* ▶**everything but the ~** tout sauf les murs **kitchen stove** *s.* **kitchen range** **kitchen towel** *n* essuie-tout *m* **kitchen unit** *n* élément *m* de cuisine

kite [kaɪt] *n* cerf-volant *m;* **to fly a ~** faire voler un cerf-volant ▶**go fly a ~!** *inf* laisse-moi tranquille !

kith [kɪθ] *n* **~ and kin** amis et parents *mpl*

kitsch [kɪtʃ] *n no pl, pej* kitsch *inv*

kitten ['kɪtn] *n* chaton *m* ▶**to have ~s about sth** piquer une crise à cause de qc

Kittsian **I.** *adj* kitticien(ne) **II.** *n* Kitticien(ne) *m(f)*

kitty ['kɪtɪ, *Am:* 'kɪt̬-] *n* **1.** *childspeak* (*cat*) minou *m* **2.** (*money*) caisse *f*

kiwi ['kiːwiː] *n* **1.** (*bird*) kiwi *m* **2.** GASTR **~ (fruit)** kiwi *m* **3.** *inf* (*New Zealander*) Néo-Zélandais(e) *m(f)*

kJ *n abbr of* **kilojoule** kJ *m*

KKK [ˌkeɪkeɪ'keɪ] *n abbr of* **Ku Klux Klan**

Kleenex® ['kliːneks] *n* kleenex® *m*

kleptomania [ˌkleptə'meɪnɪə, *Am:* -toʊ'-] *n no pl* kleptomanie *f*

kleptomaniac [ˌkleptə'meɪnɪæk, *Am:* -toʊ'-] *n* kleptomane *mf*

km *n abbr of* **kilometre** km *m*

km/h *n abbr of* **kilometres per hour** km/h *m*

knack [næk] *n no pl* (*skill*) tour *m* de main; **to have the ~ of doing sth** avoir le don de faire qc

knackered ['nækəd, *Am:* -ɚd] *adj Aus, Brit, inf* foutu(e)

knapsack ['næpsæk] *n Am, Brit* sac *m* à dos

knead [niːd] *vt* pétrir; **to ~ sb's muscles** travailler les muscles de qn

knee [niː] **I.** *n* genou *m;* **to get down on one's ~s** se mettre à genoux; **to sit sb on one's ~** mettre qn sur ses genoux; **on your ~s!** à genoux ! ▶**to bring sb to their ~s** forcer qn à capituler **II.** *vt* donner un coup de genou à

knee breeches *npl* culotte *f* courte **kneecap** **I.** *n* rotule *f* **II.** <-pp-> *vt* **to ~ sb** tirer dans le genou de qn **knee-deep** *adj* **to be ~ in water** avoir de l'eau jusqu'aux genoux **knee-high** *n Am* **to be ~ to a grasshopper** *iron, inf* être haut comme trois pommes

knee-jerk reaction *n pej* réaction *f* instinctive

kneel [niːl] <knelt *o* -ed *Am,* knelt *o* -ed *Am*> *vi* **to ~ (down)** s'agenouiller; **she was ~ing** elle était à genoux

knees-up ['niːzʌp] *n Brit, inf* **to have a ~** faire la bringue

knell [nel] *n* glas *m;* **to be [*o* sound] the ~ for sth** sonner le glas de qc

knelt [nelt] *pt of* **kneel**

knew [njuː, *Am:* nuː] *pt of* **know**

knickerbockers ['nɪkəbɒkəz, *Am:* -ɚbɑːkɚz] *npl* **1.** (*trousers*) culotte *f* de golf **2.** *Am* (*knickers*) knickers *mpl*

knickers ['nɪkəz, *Am:* -ɚz] **I.** *npl Brit* slip *m* (de femme) ▶**to get one's ~ in a twist** *Aus, Brit, iron, inf* se mettre dans tous ses états **II.** *interj Brit, inf* **~!** mince!

knick-knack ['nɪknæk] *n usu pl, inf* bibelot *m*

knife [naɪf] <knives> **I.** *n* couteau *m;* **knives and forks** des couverts ▶**sth you could cut with a ~** qc à couper au couteau; **to get [*o* have] one's ~ into sb** en vouloir à qn; **to put [*o* stick] the ~ in** descendre qn en flèche; **to turn [*o* twist] the ~ in the wound** retourner le couteau dans la plaie; **the knives are out for sb** *Aus, Brit* on ne donne pas cher de la peau de qn; **to be under the ~** MED être sur le billard **II.** *vt* poignarder; **to get ~d** recevoir un coup de couteau

knife-edge *n* **to be (balanced) on a ~** (*situation*) ne tenir qu'à un fil; **to be on a financial ~** être financièrement au bord de l'abîme; **a ~ decision** une décision précaire

knife sharpener *n* aiguisoir *m*

knifing ['naɪfɪŋ] *n* attaque *f* au couteau

knight [naɪt] **I.** *n* **1.** (*man*) chevalier *m* **2.** (*chess figure*) cavalier *m* ▶**~ in shining armour** prince *m* charmant **II.** *vt* faire chevalier

knight-errant [ˌnaɪt'erənt] <knights-errant> *n* chevalier *m* errant

knighthood ['naɪthʊd] *n* chevalerie *f;* **to give sb a ~** faire qn chevalier

> En Grande-Bretagne, les gens qui ont rendu de grands services à leur pays sont élevés au rang de **knighthood** et acquièrent le titre de "Sir" précédant leur nom, comme par exemple "Sir John Smith" (on dit: Sir John). La femme d'un "Sir" a le titre de "Lady", tel que "Lady Smith" (et c'est ainsi qu'on s'adresse à elle). Ensemble, il faudrait les appeler "Sir John and Lady Smith". Depuis 1917 il est aussi possible pour une femme d'obtenir le titre de "Dame" pour services rendus à la nation; par exemple, "Dame Mary Smith" (on dit: Dame Mary).

knit [nɪt] **I.** *n* tricot *m* **II.** <-ted *o* knit , -ted *o* knit *Am*> *vi* **1.** (*connect wool*) tricoter **2.** (*mend: bones*) se souder **3.** (*join*) lier **III.** *vt* (*make with wool*) tricoter; **to ~ sb sth** tricoter qc pour qn; **a ~ted skirt** une jupe en tricot ▸**to ~ one's brows** froncer les sourcils

◆**knit together** **I.** *vi* **1.** (*join*) se réunir **2.** (*mend*) se souder **II.** *vt* **1.** (*join by knitting*) **to knit two together** tricoter deux mailles ensemble **2.** (*join*) unir

◆**knit up** **I.** *vt Aus, Brit* tricoter **II.** *vi Aus, Brit* **to ~ easily** (*wool*) se tricoter facilement

knitter ['nɪtəʳ, *Am:* 'nɪt̬ɚ] *n* tricoteur, -euse *m, f*

knitting ['nɪtɪŋ, *Am:* 'nɪt̬ɪŋ] *n* **1.** (*action*) tricotage *m; no pl* **2.** (*material*) tricot *m*

knitting needle *n* aiguille *f* à tricoter

knitwear ['nɪtweəʳ, *Am:* -wer] *n no pl* tricots *mpl*

knob [nɒb, *Am:* nɑːb] *n* **1.** (*round handle: of door, cane, bed, switch*) bouton *m* **2.** (*small amount: of butter*) noix *f*

knobbly ['nɒblɪ, *Am:* 'nɑːbl-] <-ier, -iest> *adj*, **knobby** ['nɒbɪ, *Am:* 'nɑːbɪ] *adj Am* noueux(-euse); (*knees*) bossué(e)

knock [nɒk, *Am:* nɑːk] **I.** *n* coup *m;* **a loud ~** un coup retentissant; **to take a ~** *inf* en prendre un coup; **to be able to take the ~s** être capable d'encaisser les coups **II.** *vi a.* TECH cogner; **to ~ at the door** frapper à la porte; **my knees are ~ing** mes genoux s'entrechoquaient **III.** *vt* **1.** (*hit*) frapper; **to ~ sb/sth to the ground** faire tomber qn/qc par terre; **to ~ sb senseless** [*o* **silly**] sonner qn; **to ~ a nail into wood** enfoncer un clou dans du bois **2.** *inf* (*criticize*) dire du mal de; **I'm not ~ing the idea** je ne rejette pas cette idée ▸**to ~ an idea/a plan on the head** *Brit* laisser tomber une idée/un projet; **to ~ (some) sense into sb** apprendre à vivre à qn; **to ~ spots off sb/sth** *Brit* éclipser qn/qc; **to ~ sb sideways** stupéfier qn

◆**knock about, knock around** **I.** *vi inf* **1.** traîner **2.** *fig* bourlinguer **II.** *vt always sep* **to knock sb/sth about** tabasser qn/malmener qc

◆**knock back** *vt inf* **1.** (*return: ball*) renvoyer **2.** *Brit, inf* (*reject*) refuser **3.** *Aus, Brit, inf* (*cost*) **to knock sb back £5** coûter 5£ à qn **4.** *inf* (*drink*) siffler

◆**knock down** *vt* **1.** (*cause to fall*) renverser **2.** (*hit: object*) abattre; (*person*) jeter à terre **3.** (*demolish: building*) détruire; (*door*) défoncer **4.** (*reduce: seller*) solder; (*buyer*) faire baisser **5.** (*sell at auction*) **to knock sth down to sb** adjuger qc à qn **6.** *fig* **to ~ every argument** démonter tous les arguments

◆**knock off** **I.** *vt* **1.** (*cause to fall off*) **to knock sb/sth off sth** faire tomber qn/qc de qc **2.** *inf* (*reduce*) **to knock 10% off the price** faire un rabais de 10% sur le prix **3.** *inf* (*steal*) piquer **4.** *inf* (*murder*) liquider **5.** (*produce easily: job*) expédier; (*book, article*) bâcler ▸**knock it off!** ça suffit! **II.** *vi* arrêter de travailler

◆**knock out** *vt* **1.** (*stun*) assommer; (*drink, drugs*) endormir **2.** (*remove*) retirer; (*teeth*) casser; (*nail*) faire sortir; (*contents*) vider **3.** (*eliminate*) *a.* SPORT éliminer **4.** *inf* (*produce*) débiter **5.** *inf* (*work hard*) **to knock oneself out doing sth** se tuer à faire qc **6.** *fig* **to knock sb out** couper le sifflet à qn

◆**knock over** *vt* renverser

◆**knock together** *vt* **1.** (*hit together*) entrechoquer **2.** *inf* (*produce quickly*) bricoler en vitesse; (*meal*) improviser **3.** *fig* **to knock heads together** secouer un bon coup

◆**knock up** **I.** *vt* **1.** *Brit* (*make quickly*) *s.* **knock together 2.** *Aus, Brit, inf* (*wake*) réveiller **3.** *Am, inf* (*make pregnant*) **to knock sb up** mettre qn en cloque **II.** *vi* (*in tennis*) faire des balles

knockabout ['nɒkəˌbaʊt, *Am:* 'nɑːk-] *adj* THEAT, CINE burlesque

knockdown ['nɒkdaʊn, *Am:* 'nɑːk-] *adj* **1.** (*cheap: price*) sacrifié(e) **2.** (*easily dismantled*) démontable

knocker ['nɒkəʳ, *Am:* 'nɑːkɚ] *n* heurtoir *m*

knocking copy [ˌnɒkɪŋ'kɒpɪ, *Am:* ˌnɑːkɪŋ'kɑːpɪ] *n no pl, no indef art* ECON publicité *f* comparative dépréciative

knocking-off time *n no pl, no indef art* heure *f* de la sortie

knock-kneed [ˌnɒk'niːd, *Am:* 'nɑːk-] *adj* aux genoux cagneux

knock-on effect *n Brit* répercussions *fpl*

knockout ['nɒkaʊt, *Am:* 'nɑːk-] **I.** *n* **1.** *Aus, Brit* (*tournament*) épreuve *f* éliminatoire **2.** SPORT K.-O. *m;* **to win by a ~** gagner par K.-O. **3.** (*attractive person or thing*) merveille *f* **II.** *adj* **1.** *Aus, Brit* SPORT éliminatoire **2.** (*stunning*) foudroyant(e); (*idea*) époustouflant(e); **~ blow** coup de grâce **3.** (*soothing*) **~ drops** soporifique *m*

knock-up ['nɒkʌp, *Am:* 'nɑːk-] *sing n* échauffement *m*

knoll [nəʊl, *Am:* noʊl] *n* tertre *m*

knot[1] [nɒt, *Am:* nɑːt] **I.** *n* nœud *m;* (*small group*) noyau *m* ▸**sb's stomach is in ~s** qn a l'estomac noué; **to tie oneself up in ~s** s'embrouiller **II.** <-tt> *vt* nouer; **to ~ a tie** faire un nœud de cravate; **to ~ sth together** nouer qc ensemble **III.** <-tt-> *vi* (*muscles, stomach*) se nouer

knot² *n* NAUT nœud *m*

knotty ['nɒtɪ, *Am:* 'nɑːt̬ɪ] *adj* **1.** (*full of knots*) noueux(-euse); (*hair*) emmêlé(e) **2.** (*difficult*) embrouillé(e); (*problem*) épineux(-euse)

know [nəʊ, *Am:* noʊ] **I.** <knew, -n> *vt* **1.** (*have knowledge*) savoir; (*facts*) connaître; **to ~ a bit of English** savoir un peu parler anglais; **she ~s all about them** (*has heard about*) elle sait tout d'eux; **not to ~ the first thing about sth/sb** ne pas savoir la moindre chose sur qc/qn; **if you ~ what I mean** si tu vois/vous voyez ce que je veux dire; **to ~ sth by heart** savoir qc sur par cœur **2.** (*be familiar with: person, date, price, name, details*) connaître; **I ~ the man who lives here** je connais l'homme qui habite ici; **to ~ sb by name/sight** connaître qn de nom/vue; **she ~s all about it** (*is an expert on*) elle sait tout là-dessus; **she didn't want to ~ me!** elle ne voulait pas entendre parler de moi; **~ing her, ...** telle que je la connais, ...; **to get to ~ sb/sth** faire la connaissance de qn/apprendre qc; **to ~ a place like the back of one's hand** connaître un lieu comme le fond de sa poche; **she ~s everything there is to ~ about art** elle sait que tout ce qui compte, c'est de s'y connaître en art **3.** (*experience*) **to have ~n wealth** avoir connu la richesse **4.** (*recognize*) **to ~ sb/sth by sth** reconnaître qn/qc à qc **5.** (*differentiate*) **to ~ sth/sb from sth/sb** distinguer qc/qn de qc/qn ►**you ~ something** [*o* **what**]**?** *inf* tu sais/vous savez quoi? **II.** <knew, -n> *vi* **1.** savoir; **as far as I ~** autant que je sache; **how should I ~?** comment le saurais-je?; **to ~ better than sb** mieux s'y connaître que qn **2.** *inf* (*understand*) comprendre; **you ~** tu vois/vous voyez **III.** *n* **to be in the ~ about sth** être au courant de qc

◆**know of** *vt* avoir entendu parler de; **I ~ a good doctor** je connais un bon docteur

know-all ['nəʊɔːl, *Am:* 'noʊ-, -ɑːl] *n Aus, Brit, pej, inf* je-sais-tout *mf*

know-how ['nəʊhaʊ, *Am:* 'noʊ-] *n no pl, no indef art* savoir-faire *m*

knowing ['nəʊɪŋ, *Am:* 'noʊ-] **I.** *adj* informé(e); (*look, smile*) entendu(e) **II.** *n no pl, no indef art* savoir *m;* **there's no ~** on ne sait jamais

knowingly ['nəʊɪŋli, *Am:* 'noʊ-] *adv* sciemment

know-it-all ['nəʊɪtɔːl, *Am:* 'noʊɪt̬-, -ɑːl] *n Am s.* **know-all**

knowledge ['nɒlɪdʒ, *Am:* 'nɑːlɪdʒ] *n no pl, no indef art* connaissance *f;* **to have no ~ of sth** tout ignorer de qc; **to have some ~ of sth** avoir quelques connaissances sur qc; **sb's ~ of sth** les connaissances de qn sur qc; **a working ~** des connaissances pratiques; **to my ~** à ma connaissance; **not to my ~** pas que je sache; **to do sth without sb's ~/with sb's full ~** faire qc à l'insu de/au vu et au su de qn

knowledgeable ['nɒlɪdʒəbl, *Am:* 'nɑː-] *adj* bien informé(e)

known [nəʊn, *Am:* noʊn] **I.** *pp of* **know** **II.** *adj* (*criminal, admirer*) connu(e); **to make sth ~** faire connaître qc; **he's better ~ as** il est plus connu comme; **to make oneself ~ to sb** se faire connaître de qn

knuckle ['nʌkl] *n* **1.** ANAT articulation *f* **2.** GASTR jarret *m* ►**to be near the ~** *Brit, inf* être limite; **to get a rap over the ~s** se faire taper sur les doigts

◆**knuckle down** *vi inf* s'y mettre sérieusement

◆**knuckle under** *vi inf* céder

knuckle-duster ['nʌkldʌstəʳ, *Am:* -tɚ] *n* coup-de-poing *m* américain

KO [ˌkeɪ'əʊ, *Am:* -'oʊ] **I.** *n abbr of* **knockout** K.-O.; **to win with a ~** gagner par K.-O. **II.** <'d> *vt abbr of* **knock out to ~ sb** *a. fig* mettre qn K.-O.

koala [kəʊ'ɑːlə, *Am:* koʊ-], **koala bear** *n* koala *m*

kohl [kəʊl, *Am:* koʊl] *n no pl* khôl *m*

kooky ['kuːkɪ] *adj Am, inf* dingue

Koran [kə'rɑːn, *Am:* -'ræn] *n no pl, no indef art* **the ~** le Coran

Koranic [kə'rænɪk] *adj* coranique

Korea [kə'rɪə] *n* la Corée; **North/South ~** la Corée du Nord/Sud

Korean [kə'rɪən] **I.** *adj* coréen(ne) **II.** *n* **1.** (*person*) Coréen(ne) *m(f)* **2.** LING coréen *m; s. a.* **English**

kosher ['kəʊʃəʳ, *Am:* 'koʊʃɚ] *adj* **1.** REL casher *inv* **2.** *inf* (*legitimate*) O.-K.; **not quite ~** pas très catholique

kowtow [ˌkaʊ'taʊ] *vi pej, inf* **to ~ to sb** ramper devant qn

Kremlin ['kremlɪn] *n no pl* **the ~** le Kremlin

kudos ['kjuːdɒs, *Am:* 'kuːdoʊz] *npl* prestige *m*

Ku Klux Klan ['kuː'klʌks'klæn] *n no pl, no indef art* **the ~** le Ku Klux Klan

kumquat ['ʌmkwɒt, *Am:* -kwɑːt] *n* kumquat *m*

Kurd [kɜːd, *Am:* kɜːrd] *n* Kurde *mf*

Kurdish [ˌkɜːdɪʃ, *Am:* ˌkɜːr-] **I.** *adj* kurde **II.** *n* kurde *m; s. a.* **English**

Kurdistan [ˌkɜːdɪ'stɑːn, *Am:* ˌkɜːrdɪ'stæn] *n* le Kurdistan

Kuwait [kʊ'wəɪt] *n* le Koweït [*o* Kuwait]

Kuwaiti [kʊ'wəɪti] **I.** *adj* koweïtien(ne) **II.** *n* Koweïtien(ne) *m(f)*

kW *n abbr of* **kilowatt** kW *m*

kWh *n abbr of* **kilowatt hour** kWh *m*

KWIC *n* INFOR *abbr of* **key word in context** mot-clé *m* en contexte

KWOC *n* INFOR *abbr of* **key word out of context** mot-clé *m* hors contexte

L

L, l [el] <-s> *n* L *m*, l *m*; ~ **as in Lucy** *Brit*, ~ **as in Love** *Am*, ~ **for Lucy** *Brit*, ~ **for Love** *Am* (*on telephone*) l comme Louis

l *n abbr of* **litre** l *m*

L I. *n Brit abbr of* **Learner** élève *m* conducteur accompagné **II.** *adj abbr of* **large** L

LA [ˌel'eɪ] *n abbr of* **Los Angeles** LA

lab [læb] *n abbr of* **laboratory** labo *m*

label ['leɪbəl] **I.** *n* **1.** *a.* INFOR étiquette *f* **2.** (*brand name*) marque *f*; **designer** ~ griffe *f* **3.** MUS label *m* **II.** *vt* <-ll *o* -l *Am*>, *vt a. fig* étiqueter

labeling *n Am, Aus*, **labelling** *n Brit no pl, no indef art* étiquetage *m*

labor ['leɪbɚ] *n Am, Aus s.* **labour**

laboratory [lə'bɒrətəri, *Am:* 'læbrəˌtɔːri] <-ies> *n* laboratoire *m*

laboratory assistant *n* laborantin(e) *m(f)* **laboratory findings**, **laboratory results** *npl* résultats *mpl* de laboratoire **laboratory stage** *n* stade *m* expérimental **laboratory test** *n* test *m* en laboratoire

Labor Day *n Am no pl* (*first September Monday*) fête *f* du Travail

laborious [lə'bɔːrɪəs] *adj* laborieux(-euse)

laborer *n* manœuvre *m*

labor union *n* syndicat *m*

labour ['leɪbəʳ, *Am:* -bɚ] **I.** *n* **1.** (*work*) *a.* MED travail *m* **2.** *no pl* (*workers*) main-d'œuvre *f* ►~**s of** <u>**Hercules**</u> travaux *mpl* d'Hercule **II.** *vi* **1.** (*work hard*) travailler dur **2.** (*do with effort*) peiner; **to** ~ **at** [*o* **on**] **sth** peiner sur qc; **to** ~ **for sth** se donner de la peine pour qc **3.** PSYCH **to** ~ **under a delusion/the illusion that ...** se faire des illusions/s'imaginer que ... **III.** *vt* s'étendre sur ►**to** ~ **a** <u>**point**</u> insister lourdement

labour camp *n* camp *m* de travaux forcés **labour costs** *npl* prix *m* de la main-d'œuvre **Labour Day** *n no pl, no indef art* fête *f* du Travail **labour dispute** *n* conflit *m* social

labourer *n* manœuvre *m*; **farm** ~ ouvrier, -ière *m, f* agricole

Labour Exchange *n Brit* ECON agence *f* pour l'emploi **labour force** *n* **1.** (*population*) actifs *mpl* **2.** (*employees*) effectif *m* **labour-intensive** *adj* qui exige un travail intensif

Labourite *n partisan du parti travailliste*

labour market *n* marché *m* de l'emploi **labour movement** *n* POL mouvement *m* ouvrier **labour pains** *npl* MED douleurs *fpl* de l'accouchement **Labour Party** *n no pl, Aus, Brit* POL **the** ~ le parti travailliste **labour relations** *npl* relations *fpl* salariés-patronat **labour-saving** *adj* qui facilite le travail **labour shortage** *n* pénurie *f* de main-d'œuvre **labour troubles** *npl* agitation *f* ouvrière **labour ward** *n* MED salle *f* de travail

Labrador (**retriever**) ['læbrədɔːr (rɪ'triːvəʳ), *Am:* -dɔːr (-ɚ)] *n* ZOOL labrador *m*

laburnum [lə'bɜːnəm, *Am:* -'bɜːr-] *n* BOT cytise *m*

labyrinth ['læbərɪnθ, *Am:* -ɚ-] *n* labyrinthe *m*

lace [leɪs] **I.** *n* **1.** *no pl* (*cloth*) dentelle *f* **2.** (*edging*) bordure *f* **3.** (*cord*) lacet *m* **II.** *vt* **1.** (*fasten*) lacer **2.** (*add*) ajouter; **to** ~ **a drink with alcohol** corser une boisson

◆**lace into** *vt* s'en prendre à

◆**lace up I.** *vt* lacer **II.** *vi* se lacer

lacerate ['læsəreɪt] *vt a. fig* lacérer

laceration *n* lacération *f*

lace-ups *npl* chaussures *fpl* à lacets

lachrymal ['lækrɪməl] *adj* lacrymal(e)

lack [læk] **I.** *n no pl* manque *m* **II.** *vt* manquer de

lackadaisical [ˌlækə'deɪzɪkl] *adj* indolent(e)

lackey ['læki] *n* **1.** HIST laquais *m* **2.** *pej* larbin *m*

lacking *adj inf* (*stupid*) simplet(te)

lackluster *adj Am*, **lacklustre** ['lækˌlʌstəʳ, *Am:* -ɚ] *adj Aus, Brit* terne

laconic [lə'kɒnɪk, *Am:* -'kɑːnɪk] *adj* laconique

lacquer ['lækəʳ, *Am:* -ɚ] **I.** *n* laque *f* **II.** *vt* laquer

lacrosse [lə'krɒs, *Am:* -'krɑːs] *n no pl* SPORT lacrosse *m*

lacuna [lə'kjuːnə] <-s *o* -nae> *n form* ANAT, LING lacune *f*

lad [læd] *n inf* gars *m*; **a bit of a** ~ un gars super

ladder ['lædəʳ, *Am:* -ɚ] **I.** *n* **1.** *a. fig* (*device*) échelle *f* **2.** *Aus, Brit* (*in stocking*) maille *f* filée **II.** *vt, vi* (*stockings*) filer

laddie ['lædi] *n Scot, inf* petit gars *m*

laden ['leɪdn] *adj* chargé(e); **to be** ~ **with sth** être chargé de qc

la-di-da [ˌlɑːdɪ'dɑː, *Am:* -diː-] *adj pej, inf* maniéré(e)

lading ['leɪdɪŋ] *n* NAUT fret *m*

ladle ['leɪdl] **I.** *n* louche *f*, poche *f Suisse* **II.** *vt* **to** ~ (**out**) (*soup*) servir

lady ['leɪdi] <-ies> *n* **1.** (*title*) lady *f*; **the** ~ **of the house** *form* la maîtresse de maison **2.** (*woman*) dame *f*; **ladies and gentlemen!** mesdames et messieurs!

ladybird *n Aus, Brit* **ladybug** *n Am* coccinelle *f* **lady-in-waiting** <-ies> *n* dame *f* d'honneur **lady-killer** *n inf* coureur *m* de jupons **ladylike** *adj* distingué(e) **ladyship** *n* **1.** *form* **Her/Your Ladyship** Madame la Baronne [*o* Comtesse] **2.** *pej, iron* **her** ~ **doesn't want to come** madame ne veut pas venir **lady's man** *n* homme *m* à femmes

lag[1] [læg] **I.** *n* **1.** (*lapse of time*) décalage *m* **2.** (*delay*) retard *m* **II.** <-gg-> *vi* être à la traîne

lag[2] [læg] <-gg-> *vt Brit* isoler

lager ['lɑːgəʳ, *Am:* -gɚ] *n* bière *f* blonde

lager lout *n Brit, inf* voyou *m*

lagging *n* isolation *f* thermique

lagoon [lə'gu:n] *n* lagune *f;* (*of an atoll*) lagon *m*
laid [leɪd] *pt, pp of* **lay**
laid-back [ˌleɪd'bæk] *adj* décontracté(e)
lain [leɪn] *pp of* **lie**
lair [leəʳ, *Am:* ler] *n a. fig* tanière *f*
laird [leəd, *Am:* lerd] *n Scot* propriétaire *mf* d'un domaine
laissez-faire ['leɪseɪ'feəʳ, *Am:* 'leseɪ'fer] *n no pl* POL laisser-faire *m*
laity ['leɪəti] *n no pl* REL **the** ~ le profane
lake [leɪk] *n* lac *m*
Lake Constance *n* le lac de Constance **lake dwelling** *n* HIST habitation *f* lacustre **Lake Erie** *n* le lac Érie **Lake Geneva** *n* le lac Léman **Lake Lucerne** *n* le lac des Quatre-Cantons **Lake Superior** *n* le lac Supérieur
lam [læm] **I.** *n Am, inf* **to be on the** ~ être en cavale; **to take it on the** ~ se barrer **II.** <-mm-> *vt inf* tabasser
lama ['lɑ:mə] *n* REL lama *m*
lamb [læm] **I.** *n a. fig* agneau *m* **II.** *vi* agneler
lambast(e) [læm'bæst, *Am:* -'beɪst] *vt* vilipender
lamb chop *n* côtelette *f* d'agneau **lamblike** *adj* doux(douce) comme un agneau **lambskin** *n no pl* astrakan *m* **lamb's lettuce** *n no pl, no indef art* mâche *f* **lambswool** *n* laine *f* d'agneau
lame [leɪm] *adj* estropié(e); (*argument*) boiteux(-euse)
lameness *n no pl* claudication *f;* (*of excuse*) faiblesse *f*
lament [lə'ment] **I.** *n* MUS, LIT complainte *f* **II.** *vt a. iron* déplorer; **to** ~ **sb's death** pleurer qn **III.** *vi* **to** ~ **over sb** déplorer la mort de qn
lamentable *adj* lamentable
lamentation [ˌlæmen'teɪʃən, *Am:* -ən'-] *n* lamentation *f*
laminate ['læmɪnət] TECH **I.** *n* laminage *m* **II.** *vt* laminer
laminated *adj* **1.** (*bonded in layers*) laminé(e) **2.** (*covered with plastic*) plastifié(e)
lamp [læmp] *n* lampe *f*
lampoon [læm'pu:n] **I.** *n* satire *f* **II.** *vt* railler
lamppost *n* réverbère *m* **lampshade** *n* abat-jour *m*
LAN [læn] *n* INFOR *abbr of* **local area network** réseau *m* local
lance [lɑ:ns, *Am:* læns] **I.** *n* MIL lance *f* **II.** *vt* MED inciser
lancet ['lɑ:nsɪt, *Am:* 'lænsɪt] *n* MED lancette *f*
lancet arch <-es> *n* ARCHIT arc *m* lancéolé **lancet window** *n* fenêtre *f* en ogive
land [lænd] **I.** *n* **1.** *no pl a.* AGR terre *f;* **by** ~ par voie de terre **2.** (*area of ground*) terrain *m* **3.** (*nation*) pays *m* ►**the Land of the Rising Sun** le pays du soleil levant **II.** *vi* **1.** AVIAT atterrir **2.** NAUT débarquer **3.** (*end up*) *a.* SPORT retomber; **to** ~ **on one's feet** retomber sur ses pieds **III.** *vt* **1.** (*bring onto land: plane*) faire atterrir; (*boat*) faire accoster; **to** ~ **a plane on water** faire amerrir un avion **2.** (*unload*) décharger **3.** (*obtain: contract*) décrocher; (*fish*) prendre; (*job*) dégoter
◆**land up** *vi* atterrir
land-based *adj* MIL basé(e) au sol
landed *adj* terrien(ne)
landfall *n* **1.** AVIAT atterrissage *m* **2.** NAUT terre *f;* **to make** ~ toucher terre **landfill** *n* remblai *m* **landfill site** *n* décharge *f* **land forces** *npl* MIL armée *f* de terre **landholder** *n* propriétaire *mf* terrien(ne) **landholding** *n* propriété *f* foncière
landing *n* **1.** ARCHIT cage *f* d'escalier **2.** AVIAT atterrissage *m* **3.** NAUT débarquement *m*
landing card *n* carte *f* de débarquement **landing craft** *n* MIL péniche *f* de débarquement **landing field** *n* terrain *m* d'aviation **landing gear** *n* AVIAT train *m* d'atterrissage **landing net** *n* épuisette *f* **landing stage** *n* débarcadère *m* **landing strip** *n* piste *f* d'atterrissage
landlady *n* propriétaire *f*
landless *adj* sans terre
landlocked *adj* sans accès à la mer **landlord** *n* propriétaire *m* **landlubber** *n inf* marin *m* d'eau douce **landmark** *n* **1.** (*feature of a landscape*) repère *m* **2.** *fig* événement *m* décisif; **to be a** ~ faire date **landmine** *n* mine *f* terrestre **land office** *n Am* HIST cadastre *m* **landowner** *n* propriétaire *mf* foncier(-ère) **land reform** *n* réforme *f* agraire
landscape ['lændskeɪp] **I.** *n* **1.** GEO paysage *m* **2.** INFOR mode *m* de paysage **II.** *vt* (*garden*) aménager
landscape architect *n* paysagiste *mf* **landscape architecture** *n no pl* architecture *f* paysagiste **landscape format** *n* TYP format *m* horizontal **landscape gardener** *s.* **landscape architect** **landscape gardening** *s.* **landscape architecture** **landscape painter** *n* paysagiste *mf*
landslide *n* **1.** GEO glissement *m* de terrain **2.** POL raz-de-marée *m* électoral **landslip** *n Brit* GEO *s.* **landslide** **land tax** <-es> *n* impôt *m* foncier **landward** *adj, adv* vers la terre **landwards** *adv s.* **landward**
lane [leɪn] *n* **1.** (*road*) petite route *f* **2.** (*street*) ruelle *f* **3.** (*marked strip*) AUTO voie *f* **4.** SPORT couloir *m* **5.** (*route*) **air** ~ couloir *f* aérien; **shipping** ~ route *f* de navigation
language ['læŋgwɪdʒ] *n* **1.** *no pl* (*system of communication*) langage *m;* **bad** ~ langage grossier; **foul** ~ grossièretés *fpl* **2.** (*idiom of a cultural community*) langue *f* ►**to speak the same** ~ parler la même langue; *fig* être sur la même longueur d'onde
language acquisition *n no pl* acquisition *f* du langage **language laboratory** *n* laboratoire *m* de langues **language learning** *n* apprentissage *m* des langues
languid ['læŋgwɪd] *n* **1.** (*very slow*) alangui(e) **2.** (*pleasantly slow*) langoureux(-euse)
languish *vi* (se) languir; **to** ~ **in obscurity** rester dans l'obscurité; **to** ~ **for sth** languir

L

après qc

languishing *adj* languissant(e); (*look*) langoureux, -euse

lank [læŋk] *adj* **1.**(*straight, limp and long*) ~ **hair** des cheveux raides et ternes **2.**(*tall and thin*) élancé(e)

lanky *adj* dégingandé(e)

lanolin ['lænəlɪn] *n* lanoline *f*

lantern ['læntən, *Am:* -t̬ɚn] *n* **1.**(*light in a container*) lanterne *f;* **Chinese** ~ lanterne vénitienne; **paper** ~ lampion *m* **2.** ARCHIT lanterneau *m*

lanyard ['lænjəd, *Am:* -jɚd] *n* **1.**(*short rope or cord*) cordon *m* **2.**(*cord on a sailing ship*) ride *f* de hauban

Laos [laʊs] *n* le Laos

lap¹ [læp] *n* giron *m* ►**in the ~ of the gods** *Brit* entre les mains des dieux; **to live in the ~ of luxury** vivre dans le grand luxe

lap² [læp] SPORT **I.** *n* tour *m* de piste **II.** <-pp-> *vt* **to ~ sb** prendre un tour d'avance sur qn **III.** *vi* (*complete one circuit*) boucler un circuit

lap³ [læp] **I.** *vt* **1.**(*drink*) laper **2.**(*wrap*) enrouler **II.** *vi* (*hit gently*) **to ~ against sth** clapoter contre qc

◆**lap up** *vt* **1.**(*drink*) laper **2.** *inf* (*accept eagerly*) s'empresser d'accepter

lapdog ['læp,dɒg, *Am:* -dɑːg] *n* **1.**(*small dog*) chien *m* d'appartement **2.**(*person dominated by another*) béni *m* oui-oui

lapel [lə'pel] *n* revers *m;* **to grab sb by the ~s** attraper qn par le col

lapis lazuli [,læpɪs'læzjʊli, *Am:* -'læzə-] *n* **1.**(*blue gemstone*) lapis *m* (lazuli) **2.**(*blue colour*) bleu *m* lapis

Lapland ['læplænd] *n* Laponie *f*

Laplander *n* lapon(ne) *m(f)*

Lapp [læp] **I.** *adj* lapon(e) **II.** *n* **1.**(*person*) Lapon(e) *m(f)* **2.** LING lapon *m; s. a.* **English**

lapse [læps] **I.** *n* **1.** *no pl* (*period*) intervalle *m;* (*of time*) laps *m* **2.**(*temporary failure*) faute *f;* (*of judgement*) erreur *f;* (*of memory*) trou *m;* (*in behavior*) écart *m;* (*concentration, standards*) baisse *f* **II.** *vi* **1.**(*make worse*) faire une erreur; (*standards, concentration*) baisser **2.**(*end*) se périmer; (*contract*) expirer; (*subscription*) prendre fin **3.**(*revert to*) **to ~ into sth** tomber dans qc; **to ~ into one's native dialect** retomber dans son dialecte d'origine; **to ~ into giggles** se transformer en fou rire; **to ~ into silence** s'enfermer dans son mutisme

lapsed *adj* **1.**(*no longer involved: member*) déchu(e); ~ **Catholic** un catholique qui n'est plus pratiquant **2.**(*discontinued: policy, contract*) caduc(-que); (*passport, ticket*) expiré(e)

laptop ['læptɒp, *Am:* -tɑːp] *n* portable *m*

laptop computer *n* ordinateur *m* portable

lapwing ['læpwɪŋ] *n* vanneau *m*

larceny ['lɑːsəni, *Am:* 'lɑːr-] *n Am no pl* larcin *m*

larch [lɑːtʃ, *Am:* lɑːrtʃ] *n* mélèze *m*

lard [lɑːd, *Am:* lɑːrd] **I.** *n no pl* saindoux *m* **II.** *vt* larder; **to ~ sth with sth** *fig* truffer qc de qc

larder *n* garde-manger *m inv;* **to stock up one's ~** faire ses provisions

large [lɑːdʒ, *Am:* lɑːrdʒ] **I.** *adj* **1.**(*great: number*) grand(e); (*audience*) nombreux(-euse); **to grow ~er** s'agrandir **2.**(*fat*) gros(se); **to get ~er** grossir **3.**(*of wide range*) **a ~ amount of work** beaucoup de travail; **~r-than-expected** plus important que prévu; **~st-ever** le plus grand qu'il soit; **on a ~ scale** sur une grande échelle ►**as ~ as life** en chair et en os; **to be ~er than life** se faire remarquer **II.** *n* **to be at ~** être en liberté **III.** *adv* **by and ~** en gros

large-hearted *adj* au grand cœur

largely *adv* en grande partie

large-minded *adj* aux idées larges

largeness *n* **1.**(*size*) grandeur *f* **2.**(*extensiveness*) étendue *f* **3.**(*generosity*) générosité *f*

large-scale *adj* **1.**(*in large proportions*) à grande échelle **2.**(*extensive*) grand(e); (*emergency aid*) de grande envergure; **in front of the ~ disaster ...** devant l'ampleur du désastre ...

largesse [lɑː'dʒes, *Am:* lɑːr'-] *n* largesse *f*

lariat ['lærɪət, *Am:* 'ler-] *n* **1.** *Am* lasso *m* **2.** *Brit* longe *f*

lark¹ [lɑːk, *Am:* lɑːrk] *n* alouette *f* ►**to get up with the ~** se lever au chant du coq

lark² [lɑːk, *Am:* lɑːrk] **I.** *n Brit, inf* (*joke*) blague *f;* **for a ~** pour rigoler **II.** *vi Brit, inf* **to ~ about** faire des farces

larkspur ['lɑːkspɜːʳ, *Am:* 'lɑːrkspɜːr] *n* pied-d'alouette *m*

larva ['lɑːvə] <-vae> *n* larve *f*

laryngitis [,lærɪn'dʒaɪtɪs, *Am:* ,ler-ɪn'dʒaɪt̬ɪs] *n* laryngite *f*

larynx ['lærɪŋks, *Am:* 'ler-] <-ynxes *o* -ynges> *n* larynx *m*

lasagne [lə'zænjə, *Am:* -'zɑːnjə] *n no pl* lasagne *f*

lascivious [lə'sɪvɪəs] *adj* lascif, -ive

laser ['leɪzəʳ, *Am:* -zɚ] *n* laser *m*

laser beam *n* rayon *m* laser **laser printer** *n* imprimante *f* laser **laser show** *n* spectacle *m* laser **laser surgery** *n* chirurgie *f* au laser

lash¹ [læʃ] <-shes> *n* cil *m; s. a.* **eyelash**

lash² [læʃ] **I.** <-shes> *n* **1.**(*whip*) fouet *m* **2.**(*flexible part of a whip*) lanière *f* **3.**(*stroke of a whip*) coup *m* de fouet **4.** *fig* (*criticism*) **to come under the ~** être sous le feu de la critique; **to feel the full ~ of sb's tongue** ressentir les paroles acerbes de qn **II.** *vt* **1.**(*whip*) fouetter **2.**(*criticize*) s'en prendre à **3.**(*attach*) attacher **III.** *vi* **1.**(*beat*) fouetter; **to ~ at sth** frapper qc d'un grand coup de fouet; **to ~ against the windows** fouetter les vitres **2.**(*move violently*) **to ~ around** se débattre **3.**(*tie*) **to ~ sb/sth to sth** attacher qn/qc à qc; **to ~ sth together** ligoter qc **4.**(*drive*) **to ~ sb into sth** mettre qn dans un état de qc

◆lash down I. *vt* amarrer II. *vi* pleuvoir dru
◆lash out *vi* 1.(*attack physically*) envoyer des coups; **to ~ at sb with sth** donner un grand coup à qn avec qc 2.(*attack verbally*) **to ~ at sb** bombarder qn de paroles blessantes; **to ~ against sb** critiquer qn avec violence; *pej* descendre qn en flammes 3.(*go on a spending spree*) **to ~ on sth** faire des folies 4. *Brit, Aus, inf* **to ~ £500** se permettre de dépenser 500 livres
lashing *n* 1.(*punishment*) flagellation *f;* **to take a ~** prendre un coup de fouet; **to give sb a tongue ~** faire de vertes réprimandes à qn 2. *pl, Brit* (*a lot*) beaucoup; **~s of cream** une tonne de crème
lass [læs] <-sses> *n,* **lassie** *n Brit, Scot* 1. *inf* (*girl or young woman*) fille *f* 2.(*daughter*) gamine *f* 3. *inf* (*form of address*) fillette *f*
lassitude ['læsɪtju:d, *Am:* -tu:d] *n form* lassitude *f*
lasso [læ'su:, *Am:* 'læsoʊ] I. <-os *o* -oes> *n* lasso *m* II. *vt* prendre au lasso
last[1] [lɑ:st, *Am:* læst] I. *n* **the ~** le(la) dernier(-ère); **that's the ~ of sth** voici ce qui reste de qc; **that's the ~ I saw of her** je ne l'ai jamais revue; **to never hear the ~ of it** ne jamais finir d'en entendre parler; **to pour the ~ of the gin** verser ce qui reste de gin; **the ~ but one** [*o Am* **the next to ~**] plus qu'un ►**to the ~** jusqu'au bout II. *adj* dernier(-ère); **~ Monday** lundi dernier; **~ January** en janvier dernier; **at the ~ moment** à la dernière minute; **for the ~ 2 years** depuis 2 ans; **the day before ~** avant-hier; **~ thing at night** avant de se coucher ►**to be on one's ~ legs** être à bout; ECON être au bord de la faillite; **to be the ~ straw** être la goutte d'eau; **it's the ~ straw that breaks the camel's back** c'est la goutte d'eau qui fait déborder le vase III. *adv* 1.(*most recently*) la dernière fois 2.(*coming after everyone/everything*) en dernier; **to arrive ~** arriver dernier(-ère); **second (to) ~** avant-dernier 3.(*finally*) finalement ►**at (long) ~** enfin; **~ but not least** enfin et surtout; **to the ~** *form* (*until the end*) jusqu'à la fin; (*and always will be*) pour l'éternité
last[2] [lɑ:st, *Am:* læst] I. *vi* 1.(*continue*) durer 2.(*remain good*) se maintenir 3.(*be enough*) être suffisant 4.(*to endure*) endurer II. *vt* **to ~ the pace** tenir le rythme; **to ~ (sb) a lifetime** en avoir pour la vie; **it ~s me for one week** cela me fait tenir une semaine
last-ditch *adj,* **last-gasp** *adj* ultime
lasting *adj* continu(e); (*damage*) permanent(e); (*cough*) persistant(e); (*peace*) durable
lastly *adv* en dernier lieu
last-minute *adj* de dernière minute **last name** *n* nom *m* de famille
lat. *n abbr of* **latitude** latitude *f*
latch [lætʃ] I. *n* loquet *m;* **to be on the ~** ne pas être verrouillé II. *vt* 1.(*close*) fermer au loquet 2. TECH verrouiller
◆latch on to *vi Brit, inf* 1.(*attach*) s'accrocher à 2.(*understand*) piger
latchkey ['lætʃki:] *n* clef *f* de la porte d'entrée
latchkey child *n enfant dont les parents travaillent et qui est livré à lui-même*
late [leɪt] I. *adj* 1.(*after appointed time*) en retard; (*arrival, frost*) tardif(-ive); **to be one hour ~** avoir une heure de retard 2.(*delayed*) retardé(e) 3.(*advanced time*) tard; **it's getting ~** il se fait tard; **~ nineteenth-century** à la fin du dix-neuvième siècle; **~ summer** vers la fin de l'été; **to be in one's ~ twenties** avoir la vingtaine bien tassée; **to keep ~ hours** se coucher tard 4.(*deceased*) feu; **my ~ father** feu mon père 5.(*recent*) récent(e) II. *adv* 1.(*after usual time*) en retard; **too little, too ~** trop peu, trop tard 2.(*at an advanced time*) **~ in the day/at night** vers la fin du jour/de la nuit; **~ in life** sur le tard 3.(*recently*) pas plus tard que; **of ~** récemment ►**it's rather ~ in the day** to +*infin* c'est un peu tard pour +*infin*
latecomer ['leɪtˌkʌmə^r^, *Am:* -ɚ] *n* retardataire *mf*
lately *adv* (*recently*) dernièrement; **until ~** jusqu'à récemment
lateness *n* retard *m*
late night show *n* TV programme *m* de fin de soirée
latent ['leɪtnt] *adj* latent(e); (*period*) de latence; (*talent*) prêt(e) à percer
later ['leɪtə^r^] I. *adj comp of* **late** 1.(*at future time*) ultérieur(e) 2.(*not punctual*) plus tard II. *adv comp of* **late** ensuite; **no ~ than nine o'clock** pas plus tard que neuf heures; **~ on** un peu plus tard; **call you ~!** à plus tard
lateral ['lætərəl, *Am:* 'læt̬ɚəl] *adj* latéral(e)
latest ['leɪtɪst] I. *adj superl of* **late** (*most recent*) **the ~ ...** le(la) tout(e) dernier(-ère) ... II. *n* **at the (very) ~** au plus tard; **to know the ~** connaître la dernière; **the ~ we can stay is two o'clock** on peut rester jusqu'à deux heures au plus tard
lath [lɑ:θ, *Am:* læθ] *n* latte *f;* **a ~ and plaster wall** un mur plâtré et latté
lathe [leɪð] *n* tour *m*
lathe operator *n* tourneur *m*
lather I. *n no pl* 1.(*fine bubbles*) mousse *f* de savon 2.(*bubbles of sweat on horses*) écume *f* ►**to be in a ~** être en nage; **to get (oneself) into a ~** s'énerver II. *vi* mousser III. *vt* savonner
Latin ['lætɪn, *Am:* -ən] I. *adj* 1. LING, GEO latin(e) 2. *Am* latino-américain(e) II. *n* 1.(*person*) Latin(e) *m(f)* 2. *Am* Latino-américain(e) *m(f)* 3. LING latin *m; s. a.* **English**
Latin America *n* l'Amérique *f* latine
latino [lə'ti:əʊ, *Am:* -noʊ] *n* latino *mf*
latish ['leɪtɪʃ, *Am:* -t̬ɪʃ] I. *adj* un peu en retard II. *adv* un peu tardivement
latitude ['lætɪtju:d, *Am:* 'læt̬ətu:d] *n* 1.(*geographical position*) latitude *f;* **in these ~s** sous ces latitudes 2. *form* (*freedom*) liberté

f d'action; **to show a degree of** ~ faire preuve d'une marge de manœuvre

latrine [lə'triːn] *n* latrines *fpl*

latter ['lætəʳ, *Am:* 'læt̬ɚ] *adj* **1.** (*second of two*) second(e) **2.** (*near the end*) dernier, -ière

latterly *adv* vers la fin

lattice ['lætɪs, *Am:* 'læt̬-] *n* treillis *m*

Latvia ['lætvɪə] *n* la Lettonie

Latvian **I.** *adj* letton(e) **II.** *n* **1.** (*person*) Letton(e) *m(f)* **2.** LING letton *m; s. a.* **English**

laudable ['lɔːdəbl, *Am:* 'lɑː-] *adj form* louable

laudanum ['lɔːdənəm, *Am:* 'lɑː-] *n no pl* laudanum *m*

laudatory ['lɔːdətəri, *Am:* 'lɑːdətɔːr-] *adj form* flatteur, -euse

laugh [lɑːf] **I.** *n* **1.** (*sound expressing amusement*) rire *m;* **to get a** ~ faire rire **2.** *inf* (*an amusing activity*) blague *f* **3.** *Brit, inf* (*an amusing person*) rigolo, -ote *m, f* ►**to do sth for a** ~ faire qc pour rire **II.** *vi* **1.** (*express amusement*) rire; **to** ~ **aloud** s'esclaffer; **to** ~ **at sb/sth** se moquer de qn/qc; **to** ~ **till one cries** pleurer de rire **2.** *inf* (*scorn*) **to** ~ **at sb/sth** se rire de qn/qc ►**to** ~ **sth out of court** tourner qn en ridicule; **to** ~ **like a drain** rire à gorge déployée; **to** ~ **one's head off** *inf* rire comme une baleine; **he who ~s last ~s longest** *prov* rira bien qui rira le dernier; **to be ~ing** *inf* être soulagé

◆**laugh off** *vt* tourner en plaisanterie ►**to laugh one's head off** être mort de rire

laughable *adj* comique

laughing **I.** *n* rires *mpl* **II.** *adj* rieur(-euse); **this is no** ~ **matter** il n'y a pas de quoi rire

laughing gas *n* gaz *m* hilarant

laughter ['lɑːftəʳ, *Am:* 'læftɚ] *n* rire *m* ►~ **is the best medicine** *prov* le rire est le meilleur des remèdes

launch¹ [lɔːntʃ, *Am:* lɑːntʃ] *n* (*boat*) vedette *f*

launch² **I.** *n a. fig* lancement *m;* ~ **party** réception *f* de lancement **II.** *vt* **1.** (*send out*) lancer; **to** ~ **a boat** mettre un bateau à l'eau **2.** (*begin something: attack*) déclencher; (*campaign*) lancer; (*product*) promouvoir

◆**launch into** *vt* se lancer dans; **to** ~ **a passionate speech** se livrer à un discours passionné

◆**launch out** *vi Brit* se développer

launching *n* **1.** (*sending off*) lancement *m;* (*of ship*) mise *f* à l'eau **2.** (*ceremony to initiate*) lancement *m*

launching pad *n* **1.** (*starting area*) plate-forme *f* de lancement **2.** (*starting point*) point *m* de départ **launching site** *n* base *f* de lancement

launch pad *s.* **launching pad** **launch window** *n* créneau *m* de lancement

launder ['lɔːndəʳ, *Am:* 'lɑːndɚ] *vt* **1.** *form* (*wash*) laver **2.** (*disguise origin: money*) blanchir

launderette *n,* **laundrette** [lɔːn'dret, *Am:* lɑːndə'ret] *n,* **Landromat** *n Am* laverie *f* automatique

laundry ['lɔːndri, *Am:* 'lɑːn-] *n* **1.** (*dirty clothes*) linge *m* (sale); **to do the** ~ faire la lessive **2.** (*freshly washed clothes*) linge *m* propre **3.** (*place for washing clothes*) blanchisserie *f,* buanderie *f Québec*

laundry basket *n* panier *m* à linge **laundry service** *n* service *m* de blanchissage

laureate ['lɒrɪət, *Am:* 'lɔːriɪt] *n form* lauréat(e) *m(f)*

laurel ['lɒrəl, *Am:* 'lɔːr-] *n* laurier *m* ►**to rest on one's ~s** se reposer sur ses lauriers

lava ['lɑːvə] *n* lave *f*

lavatory ['lævətri, *Am:* -tɔːri] *n* toilettes *fpl;* **to go to the** ~ aller aux toilettes

lavatory seat *n* siège *m* des cabinets

lavender ['lævəndəʳ, *Am:* -dɚ] **I.** *n* lavande *f* **II.** *adj* bleu lavande *inv*

lavish ['lævɪʃ] **I.** *adj* **1.** (*luxurious*) somptueux(-euse); (*person*) prodigue; (*reception*) grandiose; (*spending*) considérable; (*praise*) dithyrambique; ~ **banquet** festin *m;* ~ **promises** profusion *f* de promesses **2.** (*generous*) généreux(-euse) **II.** *vt* **to** ~ **sth on sb** couvrir qn de qc

law [lɔː, *Am:* lɑː] *n* **1.** (*rule, set of rules*) loi *f;* **the first** ~ **of sth** la première règle de qc; ~ **and order** ordre *m* public; **to be against the** ~ être réfractaire à la loi; **to break/obey the** ~ enfreindre/respecter la loi; **to take the** ~ **into one's own hands** se faire justice soi-même **2.** (*legislation*) droit *m;* **civil** ~ droit civil **3.** *inf* (*police*) police *f* **4.** (*court*) justice *f;* **to go to** ~ recourir à la justice **5.** (*scientific principle*) loi *f;* ~ **of averages** loi des probabilités ►**the** ~ **of the jungle** la loi de la jungle; **there's one** ~ **for the rich and another for the poor** *prov* avoir deux poids et deux mesures; **he is a** ~ **unto himself** il n'en fait qu'à sa tête

law-abiding *adj* respectueux(-euse) de la loi **lawbreaker** *n* personne *f* qui transgresse la loi **law court** *n* tribunal *m* **law enforcement** *n Am* application *f* de la loi

lawful *adj form* **1.** (*legal*) légal(e); ~ **demands** revendications *fpl* légitimes **2.** (*law-abiding*) qui respecte la loi; ~ **person** partisan(ne) *m(f)* de l'ordre

lawfulness *n form* légitimité *f*

lawless *adj* **1.** (*without laws*) sans loi; (*country*) en proie à l'anarchie **2.** (*illegal*) illégal(e)

lawmaker *n* législateur, -trice *m, f*

lawn¹ [lɔːn, *Am:* lɑːn] *n* (*grass*) pelouse *f*

lawn² [lɔːn, *Am:* lɑːn] *n* (*textile*) linon *m*

lawnmower *n* tondeuse *f* **lawn tennis** *n form* tennis *m* sur gazon

law school *n Am* faculté *f* de droit **law student** *n* étudiant(e) *m(f)* en droit **lawsuit** *n* procès *m;* **to bring** [*o Am* **file**] **a** ~ **against sb** intenter un procès à qn

lawyer ['lɔːjəʳ, *Am:* 'lɑːjɚ] *n* avocat(e) *m(f)*

lax [læks] *adj* **1.** (*lacking care*) négligent(e); **to be ~ in doing sth** faire qc avec insouciance **2.** (*lenient*) indulgent(e)

laxative ['læksətɪv, *Am:* -t̬ɪv] **I.** *n* laxatif *m* **II.** *adj* laxatif(-ive)

laxity ['læksəti, *Am:* -t̬i] *n no pl* relâchement *m*

laxness *n* négligence *f*

lay¹ [leɪ] **I.** <laid, laid> *vt* **1.** (*place, arrange*) poser; **to ~ the table** mettre la table **2.** (*render*) **to ~ sth bare** mettre qc à nu; **to ~ sb/sth open to ridicule** ridiculiser qn/qc **3.** (*hatch: egg*) pondre **4.** FIN (*wager*) parier **5.** (*state*) **to ~ claim to sth** revendiquer qc ►**to ~ sth at sb's door** *Brit, Aus* mettre qc sur le compte de qn; **to ~ sth on the table** (*present for discussion*) mettre qc à l'ordre du jour **II.** <laid, laid> *vi* pondre **III.** *n* configuration *f*

◆**lay about** *vt* attaquer

◆**lay aside** *vt a. fig* mettre de côté

◆**lay back** *vt* reposer

◆**lay before** *vt* **to lay sth before sb** soumettre qc à qn; **to lay one's case before sb** exposer son cas à qn

◆**lay by** *vt* mettre de côté

◆**lay down** *vt* **1.** (*place on a surface*) déposer; **to ~ one's arms** déposer les armes **2.** (*relinquish*) quitter **3.** (*decide on*) convenir; **it's laid down that** il est convenu que +*subj* **4.** (*establish: rule, principle*) établir; **to ~ the law** dicter sa loi

◆**lay in** *vt* stocker

◆**lay into** *vt* **1.** *inf* (*assault*) rosser **2.** *inf* (*attack verbally*) tuer **3.** (*eat heartily*) déglutir

◆**lay off I.** *vt* **1.** (*fire*) licencier; (*temporarily*) mettre au chômage technique **2.** *inf* (*stop*) arrêter **3.** *inf* (*leave alone*) ficher la paix à **II.** *vi* arrêter; **~!** arrête

◆**lay on** *vt* **1.** (*install*) installer **2.** (*organize*) organiser; (*food, drinks*) fournir **3.** (*place*) mettre; **to lay stress on sth** attacher de la valeur à qc; **to lay the blame on sb** donner la faute à qn ►**to lay (so much as) a finger on sb** toucher qn; **to lay hands on sb** REL bénir qn; **to lay one's hands on sth** lever la main sur qc

◆**lay open** *vt* **1.** (*uncover*) découvrir **2.** (*expose*) exposer; **to lay oneself open** se mettre à nu; **to lay one's heart open to sb** mettre son cœur à nu devant qn

◆**lay out** *vt* **1.** (*organize*) planifier **2.** (*spread out*) étaler **3.** (*prepare for burial*) exposer **4.** *inf* (*render unconscious*) liquider; **to lay sb out cold** refroidir qn **5.** *inf* (*spend lots of money*) **to lay money out on sth** mettre beaucoup d'argent dans qc **6.** *Am* (*explain*) **to lay sth out for sb** exposer qc à qn

◆**lay up** *vt* **1.** (*build up a stock*) stocker **2.** NAUT (*ship*) désarmer **3.** *inf* (*be put out of action*) **to be laid up (in bed) with sth** être cloué au lit avec qc

lay² [leɪ] *adj* **1.** (*not professional*) profane **2.** (*not of the clergy*) laïc(laïque)

lay³ [leɪ] *pt of* **lie**

layabout *n inf* flemmard(e) *m(f)* **layaway** *n no pl, Am* (*way of buying*) **to buy/put on ~** acheter à crédit **lay-by** *n* **1.** *Brit* (*stopping place*) aire *f* de repos **2.** *no pl, Aus* (*way of buying*) **to buy/put on ~** acheter à crédit **3.** *Aus* (*purchased item*) article *m* de vente

layer I. *n* **1.** (*uniform level of substance*) couche *f* **2.** *fig* (*level*) niveau *m* **3.** (*laying hen*) pondeuse *f* **II.** *vt* **1.** (*arrange into layers*) **to ~ sth with sth** mettre qc en couches avec qc **2.** (*cut into layers*) dégrader **III.** *vi* faire des couches

layered *adj* en couches

layette [leɪ'et] *n* layette *f*

layman *n* **1.** (*unknowledgeable man*) profane *m* **2.** REL laïc(que) *m(f)*

lay-off *n* licenciement *m*

layout *n* **1.** (*design, plan*) plan *m* **2.** TYP mise *f* en page

layover *n Am s.* **stopover**

laywoman *n* **1.** (*untrained woman*) profane *f* **2.** (*person in a church*) laïque *f*

laze [leɪz] <-zing> *vi* paresser

laziness ['leɪzɪnɪs] *n no pl* paresse *f*

lazy ['leɪzi] <-ier, -iest> *adj* **1.** *pej* (*not showing energy*) paresseux(-euse) **2.** (*tranquil*) tranquil(le)

lb *n abbr of* **pound** livre *f*

L/C *n abbr of* **letter of credit** lettres *fpl* de crédit

LCD [ˌelsiː'diː] **I.** *adj abbr of* **liquid crystal display** à cristaux liquides **II.** *n abbr of* **liquid crystal display** affichage *m* à cristaux liquides

LCD screen *n* écran *m* à cristaux liquides

LCM *n abbr of* **London College of Music** Conservatoire *m* de musique de Londres

lead¹ [liːd] **I.** <led, led> *vt* **1.** (*be in charge of*) diriger; (*a discussion, an inquiry*) mener **2.** (*be the leader of*) mener **3.** (*guide*) mener; **to ~ the way** montrer le chemin **4.** (*cause to have/do sth*) **to ~ sb into/to sth** conduire qn dans qc; **to ~ sb into/to problems** mettre qn dans le pétrin; **to ~ sb to** +*infin* amener qn à +*infin;* **to ~ sb to believe** amener qn à croire; **to ~ sb astray** détourner qn du droit chemin **5.** COM, SPORT (*be ahead of*) **to ~ sb** être en avance sur qn **6.** (*live a particular way*) **to ~ a life of luxury** mener une vie de luxe ►**to ~ sb by the nose** *inf* mener qn par le bout du nez **II.** <led, led> *vi* **1.** (*direct*) mener; **to ~ to/into/onto sth** mener à/à travers/sur qc **2.** (*guide*) guider **3.** (*be ahead*) mener **4.** *fig* (*cause to develop, happen*) **to ~ to sth** aboutir à qc **5.** GAMES jouer le premier **III.** *n* **1.** *no pl* (*front position*) tête *f;* **to take the ~** prendre la tête **2.** (*advantage*) avance *f;* **to have a ~ of two points** avoir une avance de deux points **3.** (*example*) exemple *m* **4.** (*clue*) indice *m* **5.** (*leading role*) rôle *m* principal **6.** (*connecting wire*) câble *m* **7.** *Brit, Aus* (*rope for pet*) laisse *f* **8.** GAMES **to have the ~** jouer le premier

◆**lead along** *vt* conduire

◆**lead aside** *vt* prendre à part

◆**lead away** **I.** *vt* **1.** (*take away: prisoner*) emmener **2.** *fig* éloigner du sujet **II.** *vi fig* s'éloigner du sujet

◆**lead off** **I.** *vt* **1.** (*start*) commencer **2.** (*take away*) emmener **II.** *vi* commencer

◆**lead on** **I.** *vi* avancer **II.** *vt pej* **to lead sb on** tromper qn

◆**lead up to** *vt* **1.** (*slowly introduce*) **to ~ sth** en venir à qc **2.** (*precede*) conduire à

lead² [led] *n* **1.** *no pl* (*metallic substance*) plomb *m* **2.** (*pencil filling*) mine *f* de crayon **3.** *pl, Brit s.* **leading**

leaded ['ledəd] *adj* contenant du plomb

leaden ['ledn] *adj pej, fig* **1.** (*dark and heavy*) chargé(e); **a ~ sky** un ciel de plomb **2.** (*heavy: limbs*) de plomb **3.** (*oppressive*) lourd(e) **4.** (*somber, not vivacious*) plombé(e) **5.** (*unimaginative*) lourd(e)

leader ['li:dəʳ, *Am:* -dɚ] *n* **1.** (*decision maker*) leader *m* **2.** *Brit* (*primary violinist*) premier violon *m* **3.** *Am s.* **conductor** **4.** *Brit s.* **editorial**

leadership *n no pl* **1.** (*leading position, action*) direction *f;* **to be under sb's ~** être sous la direction de qn **2.** (*leaders*) dirigeants *mpl* **3.** ECON leadership *m*

lead-free ['ledfri:] *adj* sans plomb

lead guitar *n* **1.** (*melody guitar*) air *m* de guitare **2.** (*guitar player*) guitariste *mf*

leading ['ledɪŋ] **I.** *adj* leader **II.** *n no pl, Brit* **1.** (*lead roof covering*) ardoise *f* **2.** (*lead strips in windows*) baguettes *fpl* de plombs

leading article *n Brit s.* **editorial** **leading-edge** *adj* (*technology*) de pointe **leading lady** *n* premier rôle *m* féminin **leading light** *n inf* phare *m fig* **leading man** *n* premier rôle *m* masculin **leading question** *n* question *f* insinuante

lead pencil *n s.* **pencil** **lead-poisoning** *n* intoxication *f* par le plomb **lead singer** *n* première voix *f* **lead story** *n* PUBL article *m* leader **lead time** *n* temps *m* de procuration **lead-up** *n* prémisses *fpl*

leaf [li:f] <leaves> *n* **1.** *a.* BOT. TECH feuille *f* **2.** (*table part*) rallonge *f* ►**to take a ~ from sb's book** en prendre de la graine sur qn; **to shake like a ~** trembler comme une feuille

leafless *adj* (*not having leaves*) effeuillé(e)

leaflet ['li:flɪt] **I.** *n* prospectus *m* **II.** <-t- *o a. Brit* -tt-> *vt, vi* distribuer des prospectus

leafy ['li:fi] <-ier, iest> *adj* vert(e)

league [li:g] *n* **1.** *a.* SPORT ligue *f* **2.** *fig* (*group with similar level*) groupe *m* homogène; **to be/not be in the same ~ as sb/sth** être/ne pas être de force égale avec qn/qc ►**to be in ~ with sb** avoir des points communs avec qn

leak [li:k] **I.** *n a. fig* fuite *f* **II.** *vi* **1.** (*let escape*) fuir **2.** (*let enter*) laisser filtrer; **to ~ like a sieve** être une vraie passoire **III.** *vt* **1.** (*let escape*) laisser passer **2.** *fig* **to ~ sth to sb** divulguer qc à qn

leakage ['li:kɪdʒ] *n* fuite *f*

leaky <-ier, -iest> *adj* qui fuit

lean¹ [li:n] <leant, leant *o Am* leaned, leaned> **I.** *vi* **1.** (*be inclined*) pencher; **to ~ against sth** s'appuyer contre qc **2.** *fig* (*tend towards*) avoir des tendances; **to ~ to the left/right** avoir des tendances de gauche/droite **II.** *vt* appuyer; **to ~ oneself** s'appuyer; **to ~ sth against sth** appuyer qc contre qc

◆**lean back** *vi* se pencher en arrière

◆**lean forward** *vi* se pencher en avant

◆**lean on** *vi* **to ~ sb** **1.** (*rely on*) se reposer sur qn **2.** *inf* (*exert pressure*) faire pression sur qn

◆**lean out** *vi* **to ~ of sth** se pencher à l'extérieur de qc

◆**lean over** **I.** *vt* se pencher vers **II.** *vi* **to ~ to sb** se pencher vers qn

lean² [li:n] *adj* maigre

leaning *n* **1.** (*inclination*) penchant *m;* **a ~ for sth** avoir un penchant pour qc; **political ~s** tendances *fpl* politiques **2.** *no pl* (*tilting*) inclinaison *f*

leant [lent] *pt, pp of* **lean**

lean-to ['li:ntu:] *n* annexe *f*

leap [li:p] **I.** <leapt, leapt *o Am* leaped, leaped> *vi* sauter; **to ~ over sb/sth** sauter par-dessus qn/qc; **to ~ with joy** sauter de joie **II.** <leapt, leapt *o Am* leaped, leaped> *vt* sauter par-dessus; (*horse*) faire sauter **III.** *n a. fig* bond *m;* **to take a ~** se jeter ►**to do sth by ~s and bounds** faire qc rapidement; **a ~ in the dark** un pas dans l'inconnu

◆**leap at** *vt a. fig* **to ~ sb/sth** se jeter sur qn/qc

◆**leap out** *vi* sauter à l'œil

◆**leap up** *vi* **1.** (*jump up*) sauter en l'air **2.** (*rise quickly*) faire un bond en avant

leapfrog **I.** *n no pl* saute-mouton *m* **II.** <-gg-> *vt* **1.** (*surpass*) **to ~ sb/sth** aller plus loin que qn/qc **2.** (*skip*) sauter **III.** <-gg-> *vi* **1.** (*surpass*) **to ~ past sb** passer devant qn **2.** (*skip*) **to ~ from sth to sth** passer de qc à qc

leapt [lept] *pt, pp of* **leap**

leap year *n* année *f* bissextile

learn [lɜ:n, *Am:* lɜ:rn] <learnt, learnt *o Am* learned, learned> *vt, vi* apprendre ►**to ~ sth by heart** apprendre qc par cœur

learned *adj* **1.** (*taken from environment*) inculqué(e) **2.** *form* (*very educated, scholarly*) érudit(e)

learner *n* élève *mf*

learning *n no pl* **1.** (*acquisition of knowledge, skill*) formation *f* **2.** (*extensive knowledge, education*) érudition *f*

learning disability *n* <-ies> inadaptation *f* **learning disabled** *adj* inadapté(e)

learnt [lɜ:nt, *Am:* lɜ:rnt] *pt, pp of* **learn**

lease [li:s] **I.** *vt* louer; **to ~ sb sth, to ~ sth from sb** louer qc à qn; **to ~ sth to sb/sth** louer qc à qn/qc **II.** *n* bail *m,* baux *mpl;* **to be on a ~** être affermé

leasehold ['li:shəʊld, *Am:* -hoʊld] **I.** *n*

1. (*contract*) bail *m;* **to have sth on ~** avoir qc en location **2.** (*house*) propriété *f* louée à bail **II.** *adj* loué(e) à bail
leaseholder *n* preneur, -euse *m, f* à bail
leash [liːʃ] *n Am s.* **lead** laisse *f;* **to be on a ~** être tenu en laisse; **to be kept on a ~** être mené à la laisse
leasing ['liːsɪŋ] *n no pl* leasing *m*
leasing company *n* société *f* de leasing
least [liːst] **I.** *adv* moins; **~ of all** moins que tout; **the ~ difficult** le moins difficile **II.** *adj* moindre; **the ~ little thing** la moindre chose **III.** *n* le moins; **at ~** au moins; **not in the ~** pas du tout; **to say the ~** le moins qu'on puisse dire; **it's the ~ I can do** c'est la moindre des choses; **that's the ~ of my worries** c'est le moindre de mes soucis
leather ['leðəʳ] *n no pl* cuir *m*
leathering *n* tannée *f*
leatherneck ['leðənek] *n Am, inf* (*US Marine*) infanterie *f* de marine
leathery ['leðəri] <-ier, -iest> *adj* **1.** (*tough and thick*) coriace **2.** *pej* (*tough and tasteless*) dur(e) comme de la semelle **3.** (*rough and weathered*) tanné(e)
leave[1] [liːv] **I.** <left, left> *vt* **1.** (*let*) laisser; **to ~ sb sth** laisser qc à qn; **to ~ sb/sth doing sth** laisser qn/qc faire qc; **to ~ sb/sth be** laisser qn/qc tranquille; **to ~ sb alone** laisser qn tranquille **2.** (*depart from: home, wife, work*) quitter ►**to ~ a lot to be desired** laisser beaucoup à désirer; **to ~ sb in the lurch** laisser qn dans l'incertitude; **to ~ sb on the sidelines, to ~ sb standing** laisser qn sur la touche; **to ~ sb cold** laisser qn froid; **to ~ it at that** en rester là **II.** <left, left> *vi* partir **III.** *n* départ *m;* **to take (one's) ~ of sb** prendre congé de qn
◆**leave behind** *vt a. fig* laisser (derrière soi)
◆**leave off** **I.** *vt* **1.** (*omit*) **to leave sb/sth off** laisser qn/qc **2.** (*stop*) **to ~ sth** arrêter qc; **to ~ sb** quitter qn **II.** *vi* (*stop*) arrêter
◆**leave on** *vt* **1.** (*keep on*) garder **2.** (*radio*) laisser en marche
◆**leave out** *vt* **1.** (*omit*) omettre **2.** (*leave outside*) laisser dehors
◆**leave over** *vt* **to be left over from sth** être mis sur la touche de qc
leave[2] [liːv] *n* **1.** *no pl* (*permission, consent*) permission *f* **2.** *no pl* (*vacation time*) congé *m;* **to be on ~** être en congé
leaven ['levn] *vt* **1.** (*make rise*) faire lever **2.** *fig* (*make lighter, funnier*) **to be ~ed by sth** être détendu grâce à qc
leave-taking *n* adieu *m*
leaving *n* **1.** *no pl* (*departure*) départ *m* **2.** (*remaining things*) **~s** vestiges *mpl* **3.** *pl* (*leftovers*) restes *mpl*
leaving certificate *n* diplôme *m* de fin d'études **leaving party** *n* fête *f* d'adieu
leavings *npl* restes *mpl*
Lebanese [ˌlebəˈniːz] **I.** *adj* libanais(e) **II.** *n* Libanais(e) *m(f)*
Lebanon ['lebənən, *Am:* -nɑːn] *n* le Liban
lecher ['letʃəʳ, *Am:* -ɚ] *n pej* vicieux *m*
lecherous *adj pej* vicieux(-euse)
lechery ['letʃəri] *n no pl, pej* lubricité *f*
lectern ['lektən, *Am:* -tɚn] *n* pupitre *m*
lecture ['lektʃəʳ, *Am:* -tʃɚ] **I.** *n* **1.** (*formal speech*) discours *m* **2.** (*educational talk*) conférence *f* **3.** UNIV cours *m* magistral **4.** *pej* (*preaching*) sermon *m;* **to give sb a ~ on sth** faire un sermon à qn sur qc **5.** (*advice*) conseil *m;* **to give sb a ~ on sth** donner un conseil à qn pour qc **II.** *vi* tenir une conférence **III.** *vt* **to ~ sb on sth** **1.** (*give a speech*) tenir un discours à qn sur qc **2.** (*reprove*) faire la morale à qn sur qc **3.** (*advise*) donner un bon conseil à qn sur qc
lecture note *n* notes *fpl* de cours
lecturer *n* **1.** (*person giving talks*) conférencier, -ière *m, f* **2.** (*university teacher*) chargé(e) *m(f)* de cours
lecture room *n* UNIV amphithéâtre *m* **lecture theatre** *n* amphithéâtre *m* **lecture tour** *n* voyage *m* de conférence
led [led] *pt, pp of* **lead**
LED [ˌeliːˈdiː] *n s.* **light-emitting diode** diode *f* électroluminescente
LED display *n* affichage *m* à diode électroluminescente
ledge [ledʒ] *n* plinthe *f*
ledger *n* COM grand livre *m*
ledger line *n* MUS ligne *f* de portée
lee [liː] **I.** *adj* à l'abri du vent **II.** *n* côté *m* sous le vent
leech [liːtʃ] <-es> *n a. fig, pej* sangsue *f*
leek [liːk] *n* poireau *m*
leer [lɪəʳ, *Am:* lɪr] **I.** *vi* **to ~ at sb** loucher sur qn **II.** *n* regard *m* équivoque
leeward ['liːwəd, *Am:* -wɚd] METEO **I.** *adj* sous le vent **II.** *adv* au vent
leeway ['liːweɪ] *n no pl* **1.** (*freedom, flexibility*) marge *f* **2.** (*flexible time frame*) temps *m* perdu
left[1] [left] **I.** *n* **1.** *no pl* (*direction opposite right*) gauche *f* **2.** *no pl* (*left side*) côté *m* gauche; **on/to the ~** à gauche **3.** *no pl* (*political grouping*) **the ~** la gauche; **party on the ~** parti *m* de gauche **4.** *inf s.* **left-hander** **II.** *adj* gauche **III.** *adv* à gauche
left[2] [left] *pt, pp of* **leave**
left-hand **I.** *adj* gauche; **~ drive** conduite *f* à gauche **II.** *n* gauche *f* **left-handed** *adj* **1.** (*regularly using left hand*) gaucher(-ère) **2.** (*for left hand use*) pour gaucher(-ère) **left-hander** *n* gaucher, -ère *m, f*
leftist ['leftɪst] **I.** *adj* POL *a. pej* gauchiste **II.** *n* POL *a. pej* gauchiste *mf*
left-luggage office *n Brit* consigne *f*
leftover ['leftˌəʊvə, *Am:* -ˌoʊvɚ] **I.** *adj* **~ food** un reste de nourriture **II.** *n pl* restes *mpl*
left wing *n + sing/pl vb* POL aile *f* gauche **left-wing** *adj* POL gauchiste **left-winger** *n* POL gauchiste *mf*
leg [leg] **I.** *n* **1.** (*bodily limb*) jambe *f* **2.** (*cloth-*

L

ing part) jambe *f* **3.** (*support*) pied *m* **4.** (*segment: of a competition*) manche *f* ►**to give sb a ~ up** *inf* donner un coup de pouce à qn; **to pull sb's ~** faire marcher qn **II.** *vt* <-gg-> *inf* **to ~ it** (*go by foot*) aller à pied; (*walk in a hurry*) presser le pas

legacy ['legəsi] <-ies> *n a.* LAW *a. fig* héritage *m*

legal ['li:gl] *adj* légal(e)

legality [li:'gæləti, *Am:* -t̬i] *n no pl* légalité *f*

legalization *n no pl* légalisation *f*

legalize ['li:gəlaɪz] *vt* légaliser

legally ['li:gəli] *adv* légalement

legate ['legɪt] *n* légat *m*

legation [lɪ'geɪʃən] *n* légation *f*

legend ['ledʒənd] *n* légende *f*

legendary ['ledʒəndri, *Am:* -der-] *adj* légendaire

legerdemain [ˌledʒədə'meɪn, *Am:* -ɚdə'-] *n no pl* tour *m* de passe-passe

leggings ['legɪŋz] *npl* caleçons *mpl* longs

leggy ['legi] <-ier, -iest> *adj* aux longues jambes

legible ['ledʒəbl] *adj* lisible

legion ['li:dʒən] *n a.* HIST *a. fig* légion *f*

legionary ['li:dʒənəri, *Am:* -eri] **I.** *adj* de la légion **II.** *n a.* HIST légionnaire *m*

legislate ['ledʒɪsleɪt] *vi* légiférer; **to ~ for all situations** prendre toutes les possibilités en compte

legislation *n no pl* législation *f*

legislative ['ledʒɪslətɪv, *Am:* -sleɪt̬ɪv] *adj form* législatif(-ive)

legislator *n* législateur, -trice *m, f*

legislature ['ledʒɪsleɪtʃəʳ, *Am:* -sleɪtʃɚ] *n* législature *f*

legitimacy [lɪ'dʒɪtɪməsi, *Am:* lə'dʒɪt̬ə-] *n no pl* légitimité *f*

legitimate [lɪ'dʒɪtɪmət, *Am:* lə'dʒɪt̬ə-] *adj* légitime

legitimise *vt Brit, Aus,* **legitimize** [lɪ'dʒɪtəmətaɪz, *Am:* lə'dʒɪt̬ə-] *vt* légitimer

legless *adj* **1.** (*without legs*) cul-de-jatte **2.** *Brit, inf* (*extremely drunk*) pinté(e)

legroom ['legrʊm, *Am:* -ru:m] *n no pl* espace *m* pour les jambes

legume ['legju:m] *n* légume *m*

leguminous [lɪ'gju:mɪnəs, *Am:* lə'gju:-] *adj* légumineux(-euse)

leisure ['leʒəʳ, *Am:* 'li:ʒɚ] *n no pl* loisir(s) *m(pl)*; **a gentleman of ~** un rentier; **a man/a lady of ~** un homme/une femme sans profession ►**at one's ~** au bon loisir de qn

leisure activities *n* loisirs *mpl*

leisured *adj form* (*activities*) de loisir

leisure hours *n* moments *mpl* de loisir

leisurely **I.** *adj* paisible; **at a ~ pace** tranquillement **II.** *adv* en toute tranquillité

leisure time *n no pl* loisirs *mpl* **leisure wear** *n* tenue *f* décontractée

LEM *n abbr of* **lunar excursion module** lem *m*

lemming ['lemɪŋ] *n* ZOOL lemming *m*

lemon ['lemən] *n* **1.** (*sour fruit*) citron *m* **2.** *no pl* (*hot drink*) thé *m* au citron **3.** *no pl* (*colour*) jaune *m* citron **4.** *Brit, Aus, inf* (*a very foolish person*) minable *mf*

lemonade [ˌlemə'neɪd] *n Brit, Aus, Am* limonade *f*

lemon cheese *n,* **lemon curd** *n no pl* ≈ crème *f* au citron **lemon grass** *n* citronnelle *f* **lemon peel**, **lemon rind** *n* écorce *f* de citron **lemon squash** *n Brit, Aus* limonade *f* **lemon-squeezer** *n* presse-citron *m* **lemon tea** *n* thé *m* au citron **lemon tree** *n* citronnier *m*

lend [lend] <lent, lent> *vt* **1.** (*give for a short time*) prêter; **to ~ sb sth** prêter qc à qn; **to ~ money to sb** prêter de l'argent à qn **2.** (*impart, grant*) **to ~ sb/sth sth** donner qc à qn/qc; **to ~ colour to sth** donner de la couleur à qc; **to ~ weight to an argument** donner du poids à un argument **3.** (*accommodate*) **to ~ oneself to sth** se prêter à qc ►**to ~ an ear** prêter l'oreille; **to ~ a hand to sb** donner un coup de main à qn; **to ~ one's name to sth** donner son nom à qc

lender *n* **1.** (*person*) prêteur, -euse *m, f* **2.** (*organization*) organisme *m* prêteur

lending **I.** *n* prêt *m* **II.** *adj* de prêt

lending library *n s.* **public library**

length [leŋθ] *n* (*measurement*) longueur *f*; **to be x metres in ~** faire x mètres de long; **a ~ of ribbon/string** une longueur de ruban/cordon ►**the ~ and breadth** la longueur et la largeur; **to go to any ~s to** +*infin* ne pas avoir peur de +*infin;* **to go to great ~s to** +*infin* remuer terre et ciel pour +*infin*

lengthen ['leŋθən] **I.** *vt* **1.** (*cause time extension*) prolonger **2.** (*make longer*) rallonger; **to be ~ed** (*vowels*) être allongé **II.** *vi* s'allonger

lengthways, **lengthwise** *adv, adj* dans le sens de la longueur

lengthy <-ier, -iest> *adj* long(ue); (*discussion*) interminable

lenience ['li:niənts] *n,* **leniency** *n no pl* indulgence *f*

lenient *adj* indulgent(e)

lens [lenz] <-ses> *n* lentille *f*; **~es of glasses** lentilles de verre

lent [lent] *pt of* **lend**

Lent [lent] *n no pl, no art* carême *m*

lentil ['lentl, *Am:* -t̬l] *n* BOT lentille *f*

Leo ['li:əʊ, *Am:* -oʊ] *n* Lion *m; s. a.* **Aquarius**

Leonardo da Vinci *n* HIST Léonard de Vinci *m*

leonine ['lɪənaɪn] *adj form* (*hair, head, mane*) de lion

leopard ['lepəd, *Am:* -ɚd] *n* léopard *m*

leotard ['li:ətɑ:d, *Am:* -tɑ:rd] *n* **1.** (*fashion*) maillot *m* **2.** SPORT justaucorps *m*

leper ['lepəʳ, *Am:* -ɚ] *n a. fig* lépreux, -euse *m, f*

leprosy ['leprəsi] *n no pl* lèpre *f*

leprous ['leprəs] *adj* lépreux(-euse)

lesbian ['lezbɪən] **I.** *n* lesbienne *f* **II.** *adj* lesbien(ne)

lesion ['liːʒən] *n* lésion *f*

Lesotho [lə'suːtuː, *Am:* lə'soʊtoʊ] *n* le Lesotho

less [les] **I.** *adj comp of* **little** moins de; ~ **wine/nuts** moins de vin/noix; **sth of ~ value** qc de moindre valeur **II.** *adv* moins; **no more, no ~** ni plus ni moins; ~ **and less** de moins en moins; **to see sb ~** voir qn moins souvent; **to grow ~** diminuer; **not him, much** [*o* **still**] ~ **her** pas lui, encore moins elle **III.** *pron* moins; ~ **and** ~ de moins en moins; ~ **than 10** moins de 10; **to have ~ than sb** en avoir moins que qn; **to cost ~ than sth** coûter moins que qc; **the ~ you eat, the ~ you get fat** moins on mange, moins on grossit ▸**in ~ than no time** en un rien de temps **IV.** *prep* ~ **5%** moins 5%

lessen ['lesn] **I.** *vi* (*fever*) diminuer; (*pain, enthusiasm*) se calmer; (*noise, symptoms*) s'atténuer **II.** *vt* (*risk*) diminuer; (*cost*) réduire; (*importance*) amoindrir; (*noise*) atténuer; (*pain, enthusiasm*) calmer

lesser ['lesəʳ, *Am:* -ɚ] *adj* moindre; **to a ~ extent** dans une moindre mesure; **the ~ drawback** le moindre inconvénient

lesser-known *adj* moins connu(e)

lesson ['lesn] *n* **1.** (*time period for teaching*) cours *m;* **driving ~** cours *m* de conduite **2.** *pl* (*teaching*) cours *mpl* **3.** (*useful experience*) leçon *f;* **to draw a ~ from sth** tirer une leçon de qc; **to teach sb a ~** donner une leçon à qn

let[1] [let] *n* SPORT balle *f* au filet

let[2] [let] **I.** *n Brit* location *f;* **to sign a five-year ~** signer un bail pour cinq ans **II.** <let, let> *vt* **1.** (*give permission*) laisser; **to ~ sb** +*infin* laisser qn +*infin* **2.** (*allow*) laisser; ~ **him be!** laisse-le tranquille!; **to ~ one's hair grow** laisser pousser ses cheveux; **to ~ sb/sth (be) alone** laisser qn/qc tranquille; **to ~ sb know sth** faire savoir à qn; **to ~ sth pass** laisser passer qc **3.** (*in suggestions*) **~'s go** on y va; ~ **us pray** prions **4.** (*filler while thinking*) **~'s see** voyons; ~ **me think** attends (un moment) **5.** (*expressing defiance*) ~ **sb** +*infin* laisser +*infin;* ~ **it rain** laisse faire **6.** (*giving a command*) **to ~ sb do sth** faire que qn fasse qc *subj* **7.** MAT **to ~ sth be sth** supposer que qc est qc ▸**to ~ one's hair down** se laisser aller; ~ **alone** et encore moins; **to ~ fly** balancer

◆**let down I.** *vt* **1.** (*lower: window*) baisser; (*object*) faire descendre; (*hair*) détacher **2.** (*fail, disappoint*) décevoir; (*car*) lâcher **3.** (*leave: person*) laisser tomber **4.** *Brit, Aus* (*deflate: tyres*) dégonfler **5.** FASHION rallonger **II.** *vi* descendre

◆**let in** *vt* laisser entrer; **to let oneself in the house** ouvrir la porte; **to open the windows and ~ some air** ouvrir les fenêtres pour laisser entrer un peu d'air ▸**to let oneself in for sth** mettre les pieds dans qc; **to let sb in on sth** mettre qn au courant de qc

◆**let off** *vt* **1.** (*punish only mildly*) **to let sb off** faire grâce à qn **2.** (*fire: a bomb*) faire exploser; (*fireworks*) tirer; (*a gun*) décharger ▸**to ~ steam** *inf* se défouler

◆**let on** *vi inf* **1.** (*divulge*) dire; **to ~ that ...** laisser comprendre que ...; (*show*) laisser paraître que ... **2.** (*claim, pretend*) prétendre

◆**let out I.** *vi Am* (*end*) finir **II.** *vt* **1.** (*release*) laisser sortir; (*a burp, air, a cry, a chuckle*) laisser échapper; (*secret*) divulguer; **he let the air out of the balloon** il dégonfle le ballon; **he ~ the water from the bathtub** il vide l'eau de la baignoire **2.** FASHION (*make wider: a dress*) élargir **3.** (*rent*) louer

◆**let up I.** *vi* **1.** (*become weaker or stop*) cesser; (*rain*) se calmer; (*the fog*) disparaître **2.** (*go easy on*) **to ~ on sb** pardonner qc à qn **3.** (*release*) **to ~ on sth** relâcher qc **II.** *vt* laisser se relever

lethal ['liːθl] *adj* **1.** (*able to cause death*) létal(e) **2.** (*extremely dangerous*) *a. fig* ~ **weapon** mortel(le)

lethargic [lɪ'θɑːdʒɪk, *Am:* lɪ'θɑːr-] *adj* **1.** (*lacking energy*) léthargique **2.** (*drowsy, unwilling to do anything*) apathique

lethargy ['leθədʒi, *Am:* -ɚ-] *n no pl* léthargie *f*

Lett *adj, n s.* **Latvian**

letter ['letəʳ, *Am:* 'leṭɚ] *n* lettre *f* ▸**to the ~** à la lettre

letter bomb *n* lettre *f* piégée **letterbox** *n Brit, Aus* boîte *f* à lettres **letterhead** *n* **1.** (*top of letter*) en-tête *m* **2.** (*paper with address*) papier *m* à en-tête

lettering *n no pl* inscription *f*

letter-quality *adj* qualité courrier

Lettish *adj, n s.* **Latvian**

lettuce ['letɪs, *Am:* 'leṭ-] *n* laitue *f*

leucocyte ['luːkəʊsaɪt, *Am:* -koʊ-] *n* MED leucocyte *m*

leukaemia *n,* **leukemia** *n Am* leucémie *f*

leukocyte *n s.* **leucocyte**

level ['levəl] **I.** *adj* **1.** (*horizontal, flat*) plat(e); (*spoon*) rase; (*flight*) horizontal(e) **2.** (*having the same height, amount*) **to be ~ with sth** être au niveau de qc **3.** *Brit, Aus* (*having the same position*) à égalité; ~ **in ability** à un même niveau **4.** (*steady*) égal(e); **to keep a ~ head** garder la tête au clair; **in a ~ tone** sur un ton calme; **in a ~ voice** avec une voix calme ▸**to do one's ~ best** faire tout son possible **II.** *adv* droit; **to draw ~ with sth** arriver à la même hauteur que qc **III.** *n* **1.** niveau *m;* **water/oil ~** niveau d'eau/huile; **ground ~** rez-de-chaussée *m;* **above sea ~** au-dessus du niveau de la mer; **at the local/national/regional ~** au niveau local/national/régional; **at a higher ~** à un plus haut niveau; **at the (very) highest ~** au plus haut niveau **2.** (*amount, rate: of alcohol, inflation*) taux *m* **IV.** <*Brit* -ll- *o Am* -l-> *vt* **1.** (*make level*) niveler **2.** (*smoothen and flatten*) aplanir **3.** (*demolish completely: building, town*) raser **4.** (*point*) **to ~ sth at sb** (*a gun, pistol, rifle*) diriger qc sur qn; **to ~ sth against sb** *fig* diriger qc contre qn **V.** *vi* <*Brit* -ll- *o Am* -l->

inf **to ~ with sb** parler franchement avec qn
◆**level down** *vt* niveler par le bas
◆**level off** *vi,* **level out** I. *vi* 1. (*cease to fall or rise*) se stabiliser 2. (*cease to slope*) s'aplanir II. *vt* égaliser
◆**level up** *vt* accroître le niveau moyen

level crossing *n Brit, Aus* passage *m* à niveau **level-headed** *adj* réfléchi(e) **level pegging** *n Brit, Aus* **to be (on) ~** être à égalité

lever ['li:və^r, *Am:* 'levɚ] I. *n* 1. (*bar controlling a machine*) levier *m;* **brake ~** *Brit* frein *m* à main; *s. a.* **handbrake** 2. (*device moving heavy object*) pince-monseigneur *f* 3. *fig* (*use of threat*) moyen *m* de pression II. *vt + adv/ prep* **to ~ sth (up)** soulever qc avec un levier

leverage ['li:vərɪdʒ, *Am:* 'levɚ-] *n no pl* 1. (*action of using lever*) *a.* ECON, FIN effet *m* de levier 2. *fig* influence *f*

leviathan *n,* **Leviathan** [lɪ'vaɪəθən] *n* 1. REL léviathan *m* 2. (*something huge*) monstre *m*

levitate ['levɪteɪt] I. *vt* **to ~ sb/sth** mettre qn/qc en lévitation II. *vi* léviter

levity ['levəti, *Am:* -ţi] *n no pl* légèreté *f*

levy ['levi] I. *n* taxe *f* II. <-ie-> *vt* lever; **to ~ a fine on sb** infliger une amende à qn; **to ~ (a) tax on sth** percevoir une taxe sur qc

lewd [lju:d, *Am:* lu:d] *adj pej* lubrique; (*lecherous*) lascif(-ive); (*behaviour*) grivois(e); (*comments*) désobligeant(e); (*gesture*) obscène; (*joke*) scabreux(-euse); (*speech*) équivoque

lewdness *n no pl* lubricité *f*

lexical ['leksɪkl] *adj* lexical(e)

lexicographer *n* lexicographe *mf*

lexicography [ˌleksɪ'kɒgrəfi, *Am:* -kɑ:'grə-] *n no pl* lexicographie *f*

lexicology [ˌleksɪ'kɒlədʒi, *Am:* -'kɑ:lə-] *n no pl* lexicologie *f*

lexicon ['leksɪkən, *Am:* -kɑ:n] *n* lexique *m*

lexis ['leksɪs] *n no pl* LING lexique *m*

LF *n abbr of* **low frequency** fréquence *f* basse

liability [ˌlaɪə'bɪləti, *Am:* -ţi] *n* 1. *no pl* (*financial responsibility*) responsabilité *f;* **limited ~ company** société *f* à responsabilité limitée 2. (*sb/sth causing trouble*) poids *m*

liable ['laɪəbl] *adj* 1. (*prone*) enclin(e); **to be ~ to sth** être enclin à qc 2. LAW responsable; **to be ~ for sth** être responsable de qc; **to be ~ to sth** *Brit, Aus* être soumis à qc

liaise [lɪ'eɪz] *vi* **to ~ with sb/sth** être en contact avec qn/qc

liaison [li'eɪzn, *Am:* 'li:əzɑ:n] *n no pl* 1. (*contact*) liaison *f* 2. *Am* (*sb who connects groups*) agent *f* de liaison

liaison officer *n* intermédiaire *mf*

liar ['laɪə^r, *Am:* -ɚ] *n* menteur, -euse *m, f*

lib [lɪb] *n no pl, inf abbr of* **liberation** libération *f*

libel ['laɪbl] I. *n* JUR, PUBL diffamation *f;* **~ on sb** calomnie *f* sur qn II. <*Brit* -ll- *o Am* -l-> *vt* JUR, PUBL diffamer

libellous *adj,* **libelous** *adj Am* JUR, PUBL 1. (*sth judged as libel*) diffamatoire 2. (*spreading libel*) calomnieux(-euse); **to have a really ~ tongue** avoir une vraie langue de vipère

liberal ['lɪbərəl] I. *adj* 1. (*tolerating lifestyles or beliefs*) *a.* ECON libéral(e) 2. (*generous*) généreux(-euse) 3. (*not strict: interpretation*) libre II. *n* libéral(e) *m(f)*

liberal arts *n Am* **the ~** les arts *mpl* libéraux

liberalism ['lɪbərəlɪzəm] *n no pl* libéralisme *m*

liberality [ˌlɪbə'ræləti, *Am:* -ţi] *n no pl* 1. (*generosity*) libéralité *f* 2. (*not being prejudiced*) libéralisme *m*

liberalization *n* libéralisation *f*

liberalize ['lɪbərəlaɪz] *vt* libéraliser

liberate ['lɪbəreɪt] *vt* 1. (*free*) libérer 2. *fig, iron, inf* (*steal*) voler

liberation *n no pl* libération *f;* **~ from sb/sth** émancipation *f* de qn/qc

liberation organization *n* organisation *f* de libération

liberator *n* libérateur, -trice *m, f*

Liberia [laɪ'bɪəriə] *n* le Liberia

Liberian I. *adj* libérien(ne) II. *n* Libérien(ne) *m(f)*

libertine ['lɪbəti:n, *Am:* -ɚ-] *n pej, form* libertin(e) *m(f)*

liberty ['lɪbəti, *Am:* -ɚţi] *n no pl, form* liberté *f;* **to be at ~** être libre; **to take liberties with sb/sth** prendre des libertés avec qn/qc

libidinous [lɪ'bɪdɪnəs, *Am:* lə'bɪdnəs] *adj form* libidineux(-euse)

libido [lɪ'bi:dəʊ, *Am:* -doʊ] *n* libido *f*

Libra ['li:brə] *n* Balance *f; s. a.* **Aquarius**

Libran I. *n* **to be a ~** être Balance II. *adj* du signe de la Balance; *s. a.* **Aquarius**

librarian [laɪ'breərɪən, *Am:* -'brer-] *n* bibliothécaire *mf*

library ['laɪbrəri, *Am:* -brer-] <-ies> *n* 1. (*books or media collection*) bibliothèque *f* 2. (*serial publication*) collection *f* ►**a walking ~** une encyclopédie vivante

library book *n* livre *m* de bibliothèque **library film** *n* film *m* d'archives **library ticket** *n* carte *f* de bibliothèque

libretto [lɪ'bretəʊ, *Am:* -'breţoʊ] *n* livret *m*

Libya ['lɪbɪə] *n* la Libye

lice [laɪs] *n pl of* **louse**

licence ['laɪsənts] *n* 1. (*document*) permis *m;* **gun ~** permis *m* de port d'arme; **dog ~** plaque *f* de chien 2. (*maker's permission*) licence *f;* **under ~** sous autorisation 3. *no pl, form* (*freedom*) licence *f;* **to allow sb ~** permettre à qn des licences; **to have ~ to** *+infin* avoir l'autorisation de *+infin*

license ['laɪsənts] I. *vt* **to ~ sb to** *+infin* donner à qn la licence de *+infin* II. *n Am s.* **licence**

licensed *adj* sous licence; (*restaurant*) ayant une licence de débit de boissons; **to be ~ to** *+infin* avoir la licence de *+infin*

licensee [ˌlaɪsənt'si:] *n form* concessionnaire

mf; (*of a pub/bistro/restaurant*) gérant(e) *m(f)*

license plate *n Am* plaque *f* d'immatriculation

licenser *n* titulaire *mf* du droit de licence

licensing *adj* de licence; **vehicle ~ centre** service *m* des cartes grises

licensing hours *n Brit: heures pendant lesquelles les pubs ont le droit de vendre de l'alcool* **licensing laws** *n Brit* loi *f* sur les débits de boissons

licentiate [laɪ'sentʃiət, *Am:* -ʃiɪt] *n* UNIV licencié(e) *m(f)*

licentious [laɪ'senʃəs] *adj pej, form* licencieux(-euse)

lichen ['laɪkən] *n* BIO, BOT lichen *m*

lick [lɪk] **I.** *n* **1.** (*running of tongue over sth*) lèchement *m* **2.** (*small quantity or layer: of colour*) touche *f* **3.** MUS (*brief phrase in music*) **a few ~s** quelques notes ►**a (cat's) ~ and a promise** *Brit, inf* une toilette de chat; **a good ~** *Brit, inf* une vitesse d'enfer **II.** *vt* **1.** (*move tongue across sth*) lécher **2.** *fig* (*lightly touch*) **flames ~ (at) sb/sth** effleurer qn/qc **3.** *Am, inf* (*defeat without difficulty*) écraser **4.** *inf* (*strike sb repeatedly*) tabasser ►**to ~ sb's arse** [*o Am* **ass**] *vulg* lécher le cul de qn; **to ~ sb's boots** lécher les bottes de qn

licking *n a. inf* dérouillée *f*

licorice ['lɪkərɪs, *Am:* -ɚɪʃ] *n no pl, Am s.* **liquorice**

lid [lɪd] *n* **1.** (*removable covering*) couvercle *m* **2.** (*eyelid*) paupière *f* ►**to blow the ~ off sth** lever le secret sur qc; **to keep the ~ on sth** garder le secret sur qc; **to put the ~ on sth** *Brit, Aus* (*be the final misfortune*) être le bouquet; **to put a ~ on sth** *Am* (*stop*) mettre un point final à qc

lido ['li:dəʊ, *Am:* -doʊ] *n Brit* **1.** (*outdoor swimming baths*) piscine *f* en plein air **2.** (*section of a beach*) plage *f*

lie[1] [laɪ] **I.** <-y-> *vi* mentir; **to ~ to sb** mentir à qn ►**to ~ through one's teeth** mentir comme un arracheur de dents **II.** <-y-> *vt* **to ~ one's way somewhere** s'en sortir par un mensonge **III.** <-ie-> *n* mensonge *m;* **to be a pack of ~s** n'être que mensonge; **to give the ~ to sb** convaincre qn d'un mensonge; **to give the ~ to sth** démentir qc

lie[2] [laɪ] **I.** <-y-, lay, lain> *vi* **1.** (*be horizontally positioned*) être couché; **to ~ on one's back/in bed/on the ground** être couché sur le dos/sur son lit/par terre; **to ~ flat** être posé à plat **2.** (*exist, be positioned*) être; **to ~ off the coast** ne pas être loin de la côte; **to ~ on the route to ...** être en route vers ...; **to ~ in ruins** être en ruine; **to ~ fallow** AGR, BOT être en friche **3.** *form* (*be buried somewhere*) reposer **4.** (*be responsibility of*) **to ~ with sb/sth** incomber à qn/qc ►**to see how the land ~s** regarder la situation; **to ~ heavily on one's mind** rester couché sur ses positions **II.** *n no pl, Brit, Aus* configuration *f*

◆**lie about** *vi* traîner

◆**lie back** *vi* se pencher en arrière

◆**lie behind** *vi, vt* être derrière

◆**lie down** *vi* se coucher ►**to ~ on the job** se la couler douce; **to take sth lying down** prendre qc sur soi

◆**lie in** *vi inf* traîner au lit

◆**lie up** *vi Brit* rester à la maison

lie detector *n* détecteur *m* de mensonge

lie-in *n Brit, inf* **to enjoy a ~** faire une grasse matinée

lieu [lu:] *n no pl, form* **in ~ of sth** à la place de qc

Lieut *n abbr of* **Lieutenant** Lt *m*

lieutenant [lef'tenənt, *Am:* lu:-] *n* lieutenant *m*

life [laɪf] <lives> *n* vie *f;* **for ~** pour la vie; **to be full of ~** être plein de vie ►**~ after death** la vie après la mort; **to be a matter of ~ and death** c'est une question de vie ou de mort; **to be the man/woman in sb's ~** *inf* être l'homme/la femme de la vie de qn; **it's a hard ~!** *iron, inf* quelle chienne de vie!; **to be larger than ~** se faire remarquer; **to make a new ~** se refaire une vie; **to bring sth to ~** donner naissance à qc; **to come to ~** reprendre connaissance; *fig* prendre de l'entrain; **to take sb's ~** mettre fin aux jours de qn; **to take one's (own) ~** mettre fin à ses jours; **not on your ~!** *inf* certainement pas!; **that's ~!** c'est la vie!

life-and-death *adj* (*situation*) de vie ou de mort; (*struggle*) à mort **life annuity** <-ties> *n* rente *f* viagère **life assurance** *n no pl s.* **life insurance** **lifebelt** *n* bouée *f* de sauvetage **lifeboat** *n* bateau *m* de sauvetage **lifebuoy** *n s.* **life belt** **life cycle** *n* cycle *m* de vie **life expectancy** <-cies> *n* espérance *f* de vie **life force** *n* force *f* vitale **life form** *n* BIO forme *f* de vie **life-giving** *adj* vivifiant(e) **lifeguard** *n* maître-nageur *m* **life history** *n s.* **life cycle** **life imprisonment** *n no pl* emprisonnement *m* à vie **life instinct** *n* instinct *m* de survie **life insurance** *n* assurance *f* vie **life jacket** *n* gilet *m* de sauvetage

lifeless *adj* **1.** (*dead*) mort(e) **2.** *fig* (*without activity*) qui manque de vie; (*without energy*) dépourvu(e) d'énergie

lifelike *adj* fidèle à la réalité

lifeline *n* **1.** NAUT démarcation *f* du périmètre surveillé **2.** *fig* (*aid for living*) ligne *f* de conduite

lifelong *adj* à vie

life member *n* membre *mf* à vie **life peer** *n Brit* pair *m* à vie **life preserver** *n Am* **1.** (*life belt*) ceinture *f* de sauvetage **2.** (*life buoy*) bouée *f* de sauvetage **3.** (*life jacket*) gilet *m* de sauvetage

lifer ['laɪfəʳ, *Am:* -fɚ] *n inf* **1.** *a. Am* condamné(e) *m(f)* à perpète **2.** *s.* **life sentence**

life raft *n* radeau *m* **lifesaver** *n,* **life-saver** *n* **1.** (*rescuer*) sauveteur, -euse *m, f*

2. *Aus, NZ* (*person watching out for swimmers*) surveillant(e) *m(f)* de baignade 3. (*very good thing*) planche *f* de salut **life sentence** *n* peine *f* d'emprisonnement à vie **life-size** *adj*, **life-sized** *adj* grandeur nature **lifespan** *n* espérance *f* de vie **lifestyle** *n* style *m* de vie **life-support system** *n* respirateur *m* artificiel **life's work** *n no pl* œuvre *f* d'une vie **life-threatening** *adj* potentiellement mortel(le); **it's not ~** ce n'est pas mortel **lifetime** *n* 1. (*time one is alive*) vie *f;* **in sb's ~** de la vie de qn; **~ guarantee** garantie *f* à vie; **to happen once in a ~** n'arriver qu'une seule fois dans la vie; **to seem like a ~** sembler être toute une vie 2. (*time sth exists, functions*) durée *f* de vie **life work** *n no pl s.* **life's work**

lift [lɪft] I. *n Brit* 1. (*elevator*) ascenseur *m;* **a ~ attendant** un garçon d'ascenseur; **a ~ shaft** une cage d'ascenseur 2. (*device for lifting: for goods*) monte-charge *m inv;* (*for skiers*) téléski *m* 3. (*upward motion*) **to give sth a ~** soulever qc 4. (*car ride*) **to give sb a ~** prendre qn en voiture; **to give sb a ~ to a place** déposer qn à un endroit 5. *no pl, fig* (*positive feeling*) **to give sb a ~** donner du courage à qn; (*cheer up*) donner le moral à qn 6. (*rise, increase*) augmentation *f* 7. *no pl* (*upward force*) poussée *f* 8. *no pl* AVIAT portance *f* II. *vi* se lever; (*fog*) se dissiper III. *vt* 1. (*move upwards*) lever; (*weights*) soulever 2. *fig* (*raise*) élever; **to ~ one's eyes** lever les yeux au ciel; **to ~ one's voice** élever la voix 3. *fig* (*make entertaining and interesting*) relever 4. (*make tighter*) lifter; **to ~ one's face** se faire faire un lifting du visage 5. (*unearth*) récolter 6. (*move by air*) soulever en l'air 7. (*stop: a ban, restrictions*) lever 8. *inf* (*steal*) piquer; (*plagiarize*) copier 9. (*remove from*) enlever ►**to not ~ a <u>finger</u>** ne pas lever le petit doigt

◆**lift down** *vt Brit, Aus* descendre

◆**lift off** *vi* décoller

◆**lift up** *vt* soulever ►**to ~ one's <u>head</u>** lever la tête; **to ~ one's <u>voice</u>** élever la voix

lift-off *n* AVIAT, TECH décollage *m*

ligament ['lɪgəmənt] *n* ligament *m*

ligature ['lɪgətʃəʳ, *Am:* -tʃɚ] *n a.* MUS ligature *f*

light¹ [laɪt] I. *adj* 1. *a. fig* GASTR léger(-ère) 2. (*not intense, strong: breeze, rain*) petit(e); **a ~ eater/smoker** un petit mangeur/fumeur; **to be a ~ sleeper** avoir le sommeil léger ►**to be as ~ as a <u>feather</u>** être léger comme une plume II. *adv* légèrement ►**to <u>get off</u> ~** s'enlever facilement; **to <u>travel</u> ~** voyager avec peu de bagages III. *n pl* conclusions *fpl*

light² [laɪt] I. *n* 1. *no pl* (*energy, source of brightness, lamp*) *a. fig* lumière *f;* **artificial/natural ~** lumière artificielle/naturelle; **to cast ~ on sth** jeter la lumière sur qc; **to be the ~ of sb's life** être la lumière de la vie de qn 2. *no pl* (*brightness*) lueur *f;* **to do sth by the ~ of sth** faire qc à la lumière de qc; **by the ~ of a lamp/the moon/stars** à la lueur d'une lampe/de la lune/des étoiles 3. *no pl* (*daytime*) lumière *f* du jour; **first ~** premières lueurs *fpl* 4. *no pl* (*way of perceiving*) jour *m;* **to see/show sb/sth in a bad/good ~** voir/montrer qn sous un bon/mauvais jour 5. *no pl* (*flame for igniting*) feu *m;* **to catch ~** prendre feu 6. *pl* (*person's abilities, standards*) facultés *fpl* ►**to <u>be</u> out like a ~** *inf* s'endormir comme une masse; **to <u>bring</u> sth to ~** faire la lumière sur qc; **to <u>come</u> to ~** éclater au grand jour; **<u>in</u> the ~ of sth,** *Am* **<u>in</u> ~ of sth** sous le jour de qc II. *adj* clair(e) III. *vt* <lit, lit *o a. Am* lighted, lighted> 1. (*illuminate*) *a. fig* éclairer 2. (*start burning: a cigarette, pipe*) allumer IV. *vi* <lit, lit *o a. Am* lighted, lighted> s'allumer

◆**light up** I. *vt* 1. (*make illuminated*) éclairer 2. (*ignite*) allumer II. *vi* 1. (*become bright*) *a. fig* s'éclairer 2. (*start smoking tobacco*) allumer une cigarette

◆**light (up)on** *vi* trouver

light bulb *n* ampoule *f* électrique

lighten¹ I. *vi* s'éclairer; (*sky*) s'éclaircir II. *vt* éclairer; (*colour*) éclaircir

lighten² I. *vt* 1. (*make less heavy*) alléger 2. *fig* (*make more bearable, easier*) soulager 3. (*bleach, make paler*) éclaircir 4. (*make less tense, serious*) **to ~ sth** (*sb's mood*) rendre qc plus léger II. *vi* se relâcher

lighter ['laɪtəʳ, *Am:* -t̬ɚ] *n* allumeur *m*

light-fingered *adj* agile de ses doigts **light-footed** *adj* leste **light-headed** *adj* 1. (*faint*) étourdi(e) 2. (*silly and ebullient*) écervelé(e) **light-hearted** *adj* (*person*) allègre; (*atmosphere*) joyeux(-euse); (*speech, remark*) léger(-ère) **light heavyweight** *n* poids *m* léger

lighthouse *n* phare *m*

lighting *n* éclairage *m*

lightly *adv* légèrement; **to sleep ~** avoir le sommeil léger; **to not take sth ~** ne pas prendre qc à la légère

light meter *n* posemètre *m*

lightness *n no pl* 1. (*opp: heaviness*) *a. fig* légèreté *f* 2. (*brightness*) clarté *f*

lightning ['laɪtnɪŋ] *n no pl* éclair *m;* **a flash of ~** foudre *f;* **to be quick as ~** être aussi rapide que l'éclair; **to be struck by ~** être frappé par la foudre

lightning attack *n* attaque *f* éclair **lightning conductor** *n Brit* paratonnerre *m* **lightning rod** *n Am* 1. (*safety device*) paratonnerre *m* 2. *fig* (*lightning conductor*) souffre-douleur *m inv* **lightning strike** *n Brit, Aus* grève *f* surprise

light opera *n* opérette *f* **light pen** *n* 1. (*reader for bar codes*) stylo *m* optique 2. (*computer input device*) photostyle *m*

lights *npl* poumons *mpl*

lightship *n* bateau-feu *m*

lightweight I. *adj* 1. (*of light weight*) léger(-ère) 2. (*sport*) poids léger *inv* 3. *pej, fig* (*not influential: person*) qui manque d'envergure **II.** *n* **1.** (*class of competitors*) poids *mpl* légers **2.** (*competitor*) poids *m* léger **3.** (*person lacking importance*) personne *f* manquant d'envergure

light year *n* année *f* lumière

ligneous *adj* ligneux(-euse)

lignite ['lɪgnaɪt] *n* lignite *m*

likable ['laɪkəbl] *adj Am, Aus s.* **likeable**

like[1] [laɪk] **I.** *vt* aimer; **to ~ doing sth** aimer faire qc; **sb would ~ sth** qn aimerait qc; **how would you ~ ... ?** comment aimerais-tu/ aimeriez-vous ...?; **I'd ~ to see sb** +*infin* j'aimerais bien voir qn +*infin* **II.** *vi* vouloir; **if you ~** si tu veux/vous voulez **III.** *n pl* préférences *fpl;* **sb's ~s and dislikes** ce que qn aime et n'aime pas

like[2] [laɪk] **I.** *adj inv* semblable; **to be of ~ mind** être du même avis **II.** *prep* **1.** (*similar to*) **to be ~ sb/sth** être semblable à qn/qc; **to look ~ sth** ressembler à qc; **what was it ~?** comment était-ce? **2.** (*in the manner of*) comme; **just ~ anybody else** comme tout le monde; **to work ~ crazy** travailler comme un fou **3.** (*such as*) tel(le) que; **there is nothing ~ sth** il n'y a rien de tel que qc ►**~ father, ~ son** tel père, tel fils **III.** *conj* comme; **he speaks ~ he was drunk** il parle comme s'il était ivre; **he doesn't do it ~ I do** il ne le fait pas comme moi **IV.** *n* semblable *mf;* **he and his ~** lui et ses semblables; **I've never heard the ~** je n'ai jamais entendu une chose pareille

likeable ['laɪkəbl] *adj* sympathique

likelihood ['laɪklɪhʊd] *n no pl* probabilité *f*

likely ['laɪkli] **I.** <-ier, -iest *o* more ~, most ~> *adj* **1.** probable; **to be ~ that** être probable que +*subj* **2.** (*promising*) prometteur(-euse) ►**a ~ story!** *iron* qu'est-ce que c'est que cette salade? **II.** <more ~, most ~> *adv* probablement ►**as ~ as not** selon toute vraisemblance; **not ~!** jamais de la vie!

like-minded *adj* sympathisant(e)

liken ['laɪkən] *vt* **to ~ sb/sth to sb/sth** comparer qn/qc à qn/qc

likeness <-es> *n* **1.** (*looking similar*) ressemblance *f;* **a family ~** un air de famille **2.** (*representation*) représentation *f* **3.** (*portrait*) portrait *m*

likewise ['laɪkwaɪz] *adv* **1.** (*in a similar way*) pareillement **2.** *inf* (*me too*) moi aussi **3.** (*introducing similar point*) de même

liking ['laɪkɪŋ] *n no pl* penchant *m;* **to be to sb's ~** *form* être au goût de qn

lilac ['laɪlək] **I.** *n* lilas *m* **II.** *adj* lilas

lilliputian [ˌlɪlɪ'pju:ʃən, *Am:* -ə'-] *adj iron* lilliputien(ne)

lilo® ['laɪləʊ, *Am:* -loʊ] *n Brit* matelas *m* pneumatique

lilt [lɪlt] *n no pl* air *m* entraînant

lily ['lɪli] <-lies> *n* lys *m*

limb [lɪm] *n* **1.** (*tree extension*) branche *f* **2.** (*body extension*) membre *m* ►**to be/go out on a ~ to** +*infin* être dans une situation difficile pour +*infin*

limber ['lɪmbəʳ, *Am:* -bɚ] *adj* souple

limber up *vi* **1.** *fig* (*get prepared*) se préparer **2.** SPORT (*get flexible, supple*) faire des assouplissements; (*do warm-up exercises*) s'échauffer

limbo ['lɪmbəʊ, *Am:* -boʊ] *n no pl* **1.** (*place in afterlife*) limbes *fpl* **2.** *fig* (*waiting state*) stade *m* transitoire; **to be in ~** être en suspens

lime[1] [laɪm] **I.** *n* **1.** (*green citrus fruit*) citron *m* vert **2.** *no pl* (*juice from lime fruit*) citronnade *f* **3.** (*citrus fruit tree*) limettier *m* **II.** *adj* **1.** (*light yellowish-green*) citron vert *inv* **2.** GASTR au citron vert

lime[2] [laɪm] **I.** *n no pl* (*white deposit*) chaux *f* **II.** *vt* chauler

lime[3] [laɪm] *n* (*linden tree*) tilleul *m*

limelight ['laɪmlaɪt] *n no pl* **the ~** les projecteurs *mpl;* **to be in the ~** être sous les projecteurs

limerick ['lɪmərɪk, *Am:* -ɚ-] *n* épigramme *m*

limestone ['laɪmstəʊn, *Am:* -stoʊn] *n no pl* pierre *f* à chaux

limit ['lɪmɪt] **I.** *n* limite *f;* **to put a ~ on sth** limiter qc; **to drive above the ~** conduire en dépassant la limite de vitesse; **to know no ~s** ne pas connaître de limite; **to do sth within ~s** faire qc à l'intérieur des limites **II.** *vt* limiter; **to ~ oneself to sth** se limiter à qc

limitation [ˌlɪmɪ'teɪʃən] *n* **1.** *no pl* (*keeping under control, lessening*) limitation *f* **2.** *pej* **~s** (*shortcomings*) limites *fpl;* **to have/know one's ~s** avoir des/connaître ses limites **3.** (*legal time limit*) délais *mpl*

limited *adj* **1.** limité(e); **to be ~ to sth** être limité à qc **2. Limited** (*being a type of company*) à responsabilité limitée

limited company *n* société *f* à responsabilité limitée **limited edition** *n* édition *f* à tirage limité **limited liability** *n no pl* responsabilité *f* limitée

limitless *adj* illimité(e)

limousine ['lɪməzi:n] *n* limousine *f*

limp[1] [lɪmp] **I.** *vi* boîter **II.** *n no pl* boitement *m*

limp[2] [lɪmp] *adj* **1.** (*floppy, loose*) mou(molle) **2.** *fig* (*exhausted*) crevé(e) **3.** *fig* (*lacking forcefulness*) faible

limpet ['lɪmpɪt] *n* (*type of mollusc*) patelle *f* ►**to cling to sb like a ~** être pendu à qn comme un pot de colle

limpid ['lɪmpɪd] *adj a. fig* limpide

limy ['laɪmi] *adj* calcaire

linac *n abbr of* **linear accelerator**

linchpin ['lɪntʃpɪn] *n* goupille *f*

linden ['lɪndən] *n Am* (*lime tree*) tilleul *m*

line[1] [laɪn] <-ning> *vt* (*cover*) doubler ►**to ~ one's pockets with sth** se mettre de l'argent plein les poches avec qc

line[2] [laɪn] **I.** *n* **1.** (*mark*) *a.* TYP, INFOR, TEL ligne *f;* (*of poem*) vers *m;* **hold the ~!** ne quittez pas!, gardez la ligne! *Québec* **2.** (*drawn line*) trait *m* **3.** (*row*) file *f;* (*of trees*) rangée *f;* **front**

L

~ ligne *f* de front; **to be in a** ~ être aligné; **to be/stay on the** ~ être/rester en ligne; **to go on** ~ se mettre en ligne; **to stand in** ~ faire la queue **4.** *Am* (*path without curves, arcs*) ligne *f* droite **5.** (*chronological succession: of disasters*) succession *f;* (*of family*) lignée *f* **6.** (*cord*) corde *f;* (*for fishing*) ligne *f* **7.** *pl* (*general idea*) fil *m* rouge; **along the ~s of sth** sur toute la ligne de qc; **along the same ~s as sth** sur une même ligne que qc ►**to be first in** ~ être le premier en tête; **to be out of** ~ ne pas être en accord; **to drop sb a** ~ *inf* écrire une petite bafouille à qn; **in** ~ **with sb/sth** en accord avec qn/qc **II.** <-ning> *vt* **to** ~ **sth** faire des lignes sur qc; **to** ~ **the route** border la route; **to become ~d** se rider

◆**line up I.** *vt* **1.** (*put in a row facing*) aligner **2.** (*plan, organize*) planifier; **to line sth up with sb for ...** planifier qc avec qn pour ... **3.** (*rally, organize against*) **to line sb/sth up against sb/sth** dresser qn/qc contre qn/qc **II.** *vi* **1.** (*stand in a row*) se mettre en ligne **2.** *Am* (*wait one behind another*) faire la queue **3.** (*rally, organize against*) **to** ~ **against/behind sb/sth** se mettre contre/derrière qn/qc

lineage ['lɪnɪɪdʒ] *n* lignée *f;* **to be of royal** ~ descendre d'une lignée royale; **to trace sb's** ~ remonter l'arbre *m* généalogique de qn

lineal ['lɪnɪəl] *adj* en ligne directe; **he claimed** ~ **descent from Henry VIII** il a prétendu descendre directement d'Henry VIII

linear ['lɪnɪəʳ, *Am:* -ɚ] *adj* **1.** (*relating to lines or length*) linéaire **2.** (*direct*) direct(e)

linen ['lɪnɪn] *n no pl* **1.** (*cloth*) linge *m;* **bed** ~ draps *mpl* **2.** (*flax*) lin *m* ►**to wash one's dirty** ~ **in public** laver son linge sale en famille

liner ['laɪnəʳ, *Am:* -nɚ] *n* **1.** (*removable lining*) fond *m;* **dustbin** ~ *Brit* sac *m* à poubelle **2.** (*material used for lining a cloth*) doublure *f* **3.** (*passenger ship*) paquebot *m;* **ocean** ~ transatlantique *m*

linesman ['laɪnzmən] <-men> *n* arbitre *m* de touche

line-up *n* **1.** (*selection*) sélection *f;* **we've got a** ~ **of guests on our show** notre programme aligne de nombreux invités **2.** (*row*) file *f* **3.** *Am* (*identity parade*) alignement *m* pour la revue; **police** ~ séance *f* d'identification

linger ['lɪŋgəʳ, *Am:* -gɚ] *vi* **1.** (*hang around*) traîner **2.** (*be slow to do*) s'attarder; **to** ~ **on sb/sth** [*o* **over**] s'attarder sur qn/qc **3.** (*be slow to die*) **to** ~ **on** subsister

lingerie ['lænʒəri:, *Am:* ˌlɑ:nʒə'reɪ] *n* lingerie *f*

lingering ['lɪŋgərɪŋ] *adj* **1.** (*remaining*) persistant(e); (*fears*) tenace; (*effect*) à long terme; **I have** ~ **doubts on sth** mes doutes sur qc subsistent encore **2.** (*long: death*) lent(e); (*illness*) chronique; (*kiss*) langoureux(-euse)

lingo ['lɪŋgəʊ, *Am:* -goʊ] <-goes> *n pej, inf* charabia *m*

linguist ['lɪŋgwɪst] *n* **1.** LING linguiste *mf* **2.** (*person skilled in languages*) **I'm no** ~ je ne suis pas doué pour les langues

linguistic *adj* linguistique

linguistics *n + sing vb* linguistique *f*

lining ['laɪnɪŋ] *n* doublure *f*

link [lɪŋk] **I.** *n* **1.** (*ring in a chain*) maillon *m* **2.** (*connection between two units*) *a.* INFOR lien *m;* **a** ~ **to the outside world** un lien avec le monde extérieur; **rail** ~ liaison *f* ferroviaire; **radio/satellite/telephone** ~ liaison *f* radio/par satellite/téléphonique; **to sever ~s with sb** rompre toute relation avec qn ►**to be the weak** ~ **in a chain** être le maillon faible de la chaîne **II.** *vt* **1.** (*connect*) **to** ~ **things together** relier des choses entre elles **2.** (*associate*) **to** ~ **sth to sth** associer qc à qc **3.** (*clasp*) **to** ~ **hands** se donner la main **III.** *vi* coïncider

linkman <-men> *n Brit* présentateur *m*

links [lɪŋks] *n + sing vb* **1.** (*golf course*) parcours *m* de golf **2.** *Scot* (*hilly ground near a seashore*) dunes *fpl*

link-up *n* **1.** (*connection between systems*) connexion *f* **2.** (*establishment of such a connection: of a spacecraft*) arrimage *m*

linkwoman <-women> *n Brit* (*broadcasting job*) présentatrice *f*

linnet ['lɪnɪt] *n* linotte *f*

linoleum [lɪ'nəʊlɪəm, *Am:* -'noʊ-] *n no pl* linoléum *m*

linseed ['lɪnsi:d] *n no pl* graine *f* de lin

linseed oil *no pl n* huile *f* de lin

lint [lɪnt] *n no pl* **1.** *Brit* MED compresse *f* **2.** *Am* fibres *fpl* de coton

lintel ['lɪntl, *Am:* -t̬l] *n* linteau *m*

lion ['laɪən] *n* **1.** ZOOL lion *m* **2.** (*celebrated person*) monstre *m* ►**the ~'s share** la part du lion

lioness [laɪə'nes] <-sses> *n* lionne *f*

lion-hearted *adj* extrêmement courageux(-euse); **to be a** ~ **man/woman** avoir un courage à toute épreuve

lionize ['laɪənaɪz] *vt* **to** ~ **sb** faire de qn une célébrité

lion-tamer *n* dompteur, -euse *m, f* de lions

lip [lɪp] *n* **1.** lèvre *f;* **to curl one's** ~ faire la moue; **to lick one's ~s** se lécher les lèvres **2.** (*rim*) bord *m* **3.** *no pl, inf* (*impudent speech*) **any more of your** ~ **and ...** si tu fais encore l'insolent, ... ►**the question is on everyone's ~s** la question est sur toutes les lèvres; **to bite one's** ~ se retenir; **to hang on sb's lips** être suspendu aux lèvres de qn; **to smack one's ~s** se lécher les babines

lip gloss *n* brillant *m* à lèvres

liposuction ['laɪpəʊˌsʌkʃən, *Am:* 'lɪpoʊ-] *n* liposuccion *f*

lip-read *vt, vi* lire sur les lèvres **lip salve** *n no pl* baume *m* pour les lèvres **lip service** *no pl n pej* **to give** ~ **to sb** faire du lèche-botte à qn **lipstick** *n no pl* tube *m* de rouge à lèvres; **to wear** ~ mettre du rouge à lèvres

liquefy ['lɪkwəfaɪ] <-ie-> I. *vt* 1. CHEM liquéfier 2. FIN devenir plus liquide II. *vi* se liquéfier
liqueur [lɪ'kjʊəʳ, *Am:* -'kɜːr] *n* liqueur *f*
liquid ['lɪkwɪd] I. *n* liquide *m* II. *adj a.* FIN liquide ▶**to have a ~ lunch** *iron* prendre un déjeuner bien arrosé
liquid assets *n* liquidités *fpl*
liquidate ['lɪkwɪdeɪt] *vt* liquider
liquidation *n* 1. ECON, FIN liquidation *f* 2. (*killing*) assassinat *m*
liquidity [lɪ'kwɪdəti, *Am:* -t̬i] *n no pl* CHEM, ECON liquidité *f;* **to have a ~ problem** avoir un problème de trésorerie
liquidize ['lɪkwɪdaɪz] *vt* fluidifier
liquidizer *n Aus, Brit* centrifugeuse *f*
liquor ['lɪkəʳ, *Am:* -ɚ] *n no pl, Am, Aus* spiritueux *m;* **he cannot hold his ~** il ne tient pas l'alcool
liquorice ['lɪkərɪs, *Am:* -ɚ-] *n no pl* réglisse *f*
lira ['lɪərə, *Am:* 'lɪrə] *n* lire *f*
Lisbon ['lɪzbən] *n* Lisbonne
lisp [lɪsp] I. *n no pl* zézaiement *m;* **to have a ~** zozoter II. *vi* avoir un cheveu sur la langue III. *vt* dire en zozotant
list[1] [lɪst] I. *n* (*itemized record*) liste *f;* **~ of prices** tarifs *mpl;* **shopping ~** liste des courses; **~ of stocks** FIN cote *f;* **to make a ~ of sth** dresser la liste de qc II. *vt* 1. (*make a list*) répertorier; **to ~ sth in alphabetical order** classer qc par ordre alphabétique 2. (*enumerate*) énumérer 3. FIN coter; **shares ~ed on Paris market** actions cotées à la Bourse de Paris
list[2] [lɪst] I. *vi* NAUT **to ~ to port/starboard** prendre de la gîte à bâbord/tribord II. *n* NAUT gîte *f*
listen ['lɪsən] I. *n inf* **to have a ~ to sth** prêter l'oreille à qc; **John, have a ~ to this!** Jean, écoute ça un peu ! II. *vi* **to ~ to sb/sth** écouter qn/qc; **to ~ with half an ear** écouter d'une oreille distraite; **to ~ to reason** écouter la voix de la raison; **to ~ to sb playing music** écouter qn jouer de la musique; **to ~ (out) for sth** tendre l'oreille pour entendre qc; **will you ~ out for the phone ?** peux-tu surveiller le téléphone ?
◆**listen in** *vi* 1. RADIO écouter 2. (*listen to private conversation*) **to ~ to** [*o* **on**] **sth** écouter qc discrètement
listener ['lɪsnəʳ, *Am:* -ɚ] *n* auditeur, -trice *m, f*
listening *n no pl* écoute *f*
listing ['lɪstɪŋ] *n* 1. (*list*) liste *f* 2. INFOR listing *m* 3. *pl, Brit* (*in media*) programmes *mpl*
listless *adj* 1. (*lacking energy: person*) mou(molle) 2. (*lacking enthusiasm*) amorphe 3. *fig* (*economy*) ralenti(e)
lists *npl* HIST, SPORT **the ~** la lice
lit [lɪt] *pt, pp of* **light**
litany ['lɪtəni] <-nies> *n* litanie *f*
litchi ['laɪtʃiː, *Am:* 'liː-] *n s.* **lychee**
liter ['liːtəʳ, *Am:* -t̬ɚ] *n Am s.* **litre**
literacy ['lɪtərəsi, *Am:* 'lɪt̬ɚ-] *n no pl* 1. (*ability to read and write*) degré *m* d'alphabétisation 2. (*ability to understand*) **computer ~** compréhension *f* de l'informatique
literal ['lɪtərəl, *Am:* 'lɪt̬ɚ-] *adj* 1. (*original meaning*) littéral(e) 2. (*not figurative: sense*) propre; (*interpretation*) littéral(e); (*translation*) mot à mot 3. (*not exaggerated*) réaliste
literally *adv* littéralement; **to take sth ~** prendre qc au pied de la lettre
literary ['lɪtərəri, *Am:* 'lɪt̬ərer-] *adj* 1. (*relating to literature*) littéraire 2. (*well-informed about literature: man, woman*) de lettres; **his speech really sounds ~** il parle vraiment comme un livre
literate ['lɪtərət, *Am:* 'lɪt̬ɚ-] I. *adj* 1. (*able to read and write*) alphabétisé(e); **to be ~** savoir lire et écrire 2. (*able to function in a particular area*) **to be computer ~** s'y connaître en informatique; **a financially ~ partner** un associé calé en finance 3. (*well-educated*) cultivé(e) II. *n* personne *f* cultivée
literature ['lɪtrətʃəʳ, *Am:* 'lɪt̬ɚətʃɚ] *n no pl* 1. (*written artistic works*) littérature *f;* **nineteenth-century ~** littérature du XIXème siècle 2. (*specialist texts, promotional material*) documentation *f*
lithe [laɪð] *adj* 1. (*supple*) agile 2. (*slim*) svelte
lithograph ['lɪθəgrɑːf, *Am:* -græf] I. *n* lithographie *f* II. *vt* lithographier
lithography [lɪ'θɒgrəfi, *Am:* -'θɑːgrə-] *n no pl* lithographie *f*
Lithuania [ˌlɪθjʊ'eɪnɪə, *Am:* ˌlɪθʊ-] *n* la Lituanie
Lithuanian I. *adj* lituanien(ne) II. *n* 1. (*person*) Lituanien(ne) *m(f)* 2. LING lituanien *m; s. a.* **English**
litigant ['lɪtɪgənt, *Am:* 'lɪt̬-] *n* LAW plaideur, -euse *m, f*
litigate ['lɪtɪgeɪt, *Am:* 'lɪt̬-] LAW I. *vi* aller en justice II. *vt* contester en justice
litigation *n no pl* LAW 1. (*dispute*) litige *m* 2. (*trial*) **to go to ~** intenter un procès
litigious [lɪ'tɪdʒəs] *adj pej* LAW procédurier(-ère)
litmus ['lɪtməs] *n no pl* 1. CHEM tournesol *m* 2. *fig* **~ test** test *m* décisif
litmus paper *no pl n* papier *m* de tournesol
litre ['liːtəʳ, *Am:* -t̬ɚ] *n* litre *m;* **per ~** par litre; **6-~ engine** moteur de 6 litres
litter ['lɪtəʳ, *Am:* 'lɪt̬ɚ] I. *n* 1. *no pl* (*refuse*) détritus *mpl;* **a ~ bin** une poubelle 2. *no pl* (*domestic disorder*) bazar *m* 3. ZOOL portée *f* 4. *no pl* (*bedding for cats*) litière *f* 5. MED civière *f* II. *vt* **to be ~ed with sth** être recouvert de qc; **to ~ a place with sth** recouvrir un endroit de détritus; **his dirty clothes ~ed the floor** ses vêtements sales jonchaient le sol
litter bug *n Am, Aus,* **litter lout** *n Brit, inf* porc *m*
little ['lɪtl] I. *adj* <less, least> 1. (*small*) petit(e); **a ~ house** une maisonnette 2. (*young*) **the ~ ones** les petits 3. (*brief*) **for a**

L

~ **while** pendant un court instant; **to have a ~ word with sb** échanger deux mots avec qn **4.** (*not enough*) peu de; **too ~ time** trop peu de temps; **he works ~** il ne travaille guère **5.** (*unimportant: problem*) léger(-ère) **6.** (*weak: smile*) pauvre **II.** *pron* peu; **a ~ more** encore un peu; **as ~ as possible** le moins possible; **to know ~** ne pas savoir grand-chose; **we see ~ of him** on ne le voit guère; **to have ~ to say** n'avoir presque rien à dire **III.** *adv* peu; **~ by ~** peu à peu; **a ~ more/less than ...** un peu plus/moins que ...; **to be ~ better** être à peine meilleur; **a ~ more than a minute ago** il y a peine une minute; **as ~ as possible** le moins possible; **to be ~ short of sth** friser qc; **a ~-known place** un endroit méconnu; **~ did I think that ...** j'étais loin de penser que ...

littleness *n no pl* petitesse *f*

liturgical *adj* liturgique

liturgy ['lɪtədʒi, *Am:* 'lɪt̬ɚ-] <-gies> *n* liturgie *f*

livable *adj* **1.** (*fit to live in*) habitable **2.** *inf* supportable **3.** (*companionable*) **to be ~ with** être facile à vivre

live¹ [laɪv] **I.** *adj* **1.** (*living*) vivant(e); **real ~** en chair et en os **2.** RADIO, TV en direct; **to give a ~ performance** jouer en public **3.** (*carrying electrical power*) conducteur **4.** MIL amorcé(e) **5.** (*burning*) ardent(e) **II.** *adv* **1.** RADIO, TV en direct **2.** MUS en public

live bait *n* appât *m* vivant

live² [lɪv] **I.** *vi* **1.** (*be alive*) vivre; **the right to ~** le droit à la vie; **as long as sb ~s** tant qu'il y aura de la vie; **to only ~ for sb/sth** ne vivre que pour qn/qc **2.** (*reside*) habiter; **to ~ together/apart** vivre ensemble/séparés ►**to ~ under a cloud** être né sous une mauvaise étoile; **long ~ the king/queen!** longue vie au roi/à la reine!; **we ~ and learn** on apprend à tout âge; **to ~ and let ~** faire preuve de tolérance; **to ~ to regret sth** passer sa vie à regretter qc; **to ~ by one's wits** se débrouiller pour vivre **II.** *vt* vivre; **to ~ a life of luxury** mener un grand train de vie; **to ~ life to the full** profiter pleinement de la vie; **to ~ one's own life** vivre sa vie; **to make life worth living** faire en sorte que la vie vaille la peine d'être vécue *subj* ►**to ~ a lie** vivre dans le mensonge; **to ~ and breathe sth** ne vivre que pour qc

◆**live down** *vt* (*one's past*) faire oublier; (*failure, mistake*) chercher à effacer

◆**live in** *vi* habiter sur place; (*student*) être interne

◆**live off**, **live on** *vt* **to ~ sth** vivre de qc; **to ~ sb** vivre aux crochets de qn; **his brother lives off his inheritance** son frère vit de son héritage ►**to ~ the fat of the land** vivre comme un coq en pâte

◆**live out** *vi* **1.** (*live*) **to ~ one's life** passer sa vie **2.** (*fulfil: one's destiny*) décider de; (*one's dreams, fantasies*) réaliser

◆**live through** *vt* survivre à

◆**live up to** *vt* (*expectations*) répondre à; (*promises*) tenir; (*reputation*) faire honneur à; (*principles*) vivre selon; **to ~ a standard** être à la hauteur

liveable *adj s.* **livable**

livelihood ['laɪvlɪhʊd] *n* moyens *mpl* d'existence; **to earn one's ~** gagner sa vie; **to lose one's ~** perdre son gagne-pain

liveliness *n no pl* entrain *m*

lively ['laɪvli] *adj* **1.** (*full of life and energy*) vif(vive); (*person*) plein(e) d'entrain; (*manner, nature*) pétulant(e); (*party, conversation*) animé(e); (*imagination*) fertile; (*example, expression*) percutant(e); (*business, trade*) en pleine activité; **to take a ~ interest in sth** avoir un vif intérêt pour qc **2.** (*lifelike*) vivant(e) **3.** (*bright*) éclatant(e) **4.** *Brit* (*difficult or exciting*) **to make sth ~ for sb** rendre la vie difficile à qn

liven up **I.** *vt* animer; (*person, food*) égayer **II.** *vi* s'animer; (*person*) s'égayer

liver¹ ['lɪvəʳ, *Am:* -ɚ] *n* foie *m*; **~ transplant** greffe *f* de foie; **~ scan** échographie *f* du foie

liver² ['lɪvəʳ, *Am:* -ɚ] *n* **clean ~** vertueux, -euse *m, f*; **fast ~** noceur, -euse *m, f*; **loose ~** débauché(e) *m(f)*

liver complaint *no pl n* maladie *f* du foie

liverish ['lɪvərɪʃ] *adj* **1.** (*suffering from liver problems*) **to be ~** avoir mal au foie; **to get ~** avoir une crise de foie **2.** (*peevish*) de mauvaise humeur

Liverpudlian [ˌlɪvə'pʌdliən, *Am:* -ɚ'-] *n* habitant *m* de Liverpool

liver sausage *n*, **liverwurst** *n no pl, Am, Aus* saucisse *f* de foie

livery ['lɪvəri] *n* livrée *f*

livestock ['laɪvstɒk, *Am:* -stɑːk] **I.** *n + sing vb* bétail *m* **II.** *adj* (*breeder, breeding*) de cheptel; (*fair*) aux bestiaux

livid ['lɪvɪd] *adj* **1.** (*discoloured*) livide; **a ~ bruise** un bleu enluminé **2.** (*furious*) furieux(-euse); **to be ~ with anger** être blême de colère; **absolutely ~** être furibond

living ['lɪvɪŋ] **I.** *n* **1.** *no pl* (*livelihood*) vie *f*; **I paint for a ~** je vis de ma peinture; **to work for one's ~** travailler pour gagner sa vie; **to make one's ~ as a sth/in sth** gagner sa vie en faisant qc **2.** *no pl* (*way of life*) vie *f*; **standard of ~** niveau *m* de vie; **a fast ~** vie *f* de plaisirs; **to make a good ~** bien gagner sa vie **3.** *no pl* (*people who are still alive*) **the ~** les vivants *mpl* **II.** *adj* **1.** (*alive*) vivant(e); **does he have any ~ grandparents?** ses grands-parents sont-ils toujours en vie?; **I don't think there will be a ~ soul down here** je ne pense pas qu'il y ait âme qui vive par ici **2.** (*existent: language, legend*) vivant(e); (*tradition*) vivace **3.** (*exact: image*) exact(e); **to be the ~ image of sb** être le portrait tout craché de qn; **to be the ~ embodiment of sb/sth** être la personnification même de qn/qc ►**to scare the ~ daylights out of sb** faire une peur bleue à qn

living conditions *npl* conditions *fpl* de vie **living death** *n* to be ~ être l'enfer **living quarters** *npl* **1.** (*housing*) logements *mpl* **2.** MIL quartier *m* **living room** *n* séjour *m,* vivoir *m Québec* **living salary** *n* salaire *m* de subsistance **living space** *no pl n* espace *m* vital **living wage** *no pl n s.* **living salary**

lizard ['lɪzəd, *Am:* -ɚd] *n* lézard *m;* ~ **jacket/pocketbook** pochette/sac à main en lézard

llama ['lɑːmə] *n* lama *m*

load [ləʊd, *Am:* loʊd] **I.** *n* **1.** (*amount carried*) charge *f;* **to take a ~ of sth** prendre beaucoup de qc; **a ship with a full ~ of passengers** un paquebot rempli de passagers **2.** (*burden*) poids *m;* **that's a ~ off sb's mind** avoir l'esprit soulagé **3.** (*amount of work*) **a heavy/light ~ of work** beaucoup/peu de travail; **to lighten the ~** rendre la vie plus facile; **to share the ~** partager la besogne **4.** *inf* (*lots*) **a ~ of sth** un tas de qc; **what a ~ of rubbish!** que de sornettes! ►**get a ~ of this!** *inf* regarde/écoute un peu ça! **II.** *vt* **1.** AUTO, INFOR, MIL charger **2.** (*burden*) **to ~ sb with sth** accabler qn de qc **3.** TECH (*film , software*) charger; (*camera*) armer; (*cassette*) insérer ►**to ~ the dice** piper les dés; **to ~ the dice in favour of/against sb/sth** tricher dans le but de favoriser/desservir qn/qc **III.** *vi* se charger; (*lorry*) prendre un chargement

◆**load down** *vt* **1.** (*load*) **to load sb/sth down with sth** charger qn/qc de qc **2.** (*overload*) surcharger; **to be loaded down with presents** crouler sous les cadeaux

◆**load up** **I.** *vt* charger **II.** *vi* faire le chargement

loaded *adj* **1.** (*filled with live ammunition*) chargé(e) **2.** (*not objective: question*) insidieux(-euse); **to be ~ in favour of sb/sth** avoir un parti pris pour qn/qc **3.** GAMES ~ **dice** dés pipés **4.** *inf* cousu(e) d'or **5.** *Am, inf* (*drunk*) **to be ~** être plein

load line *n* NAUT ligne *f* de charge

loadstar *n s.* **lodestar**

loadstone *n s.* **lodestone**

loaf [ləʊf, *Am:* loʊf] <loaves> *n* pain *m;* **fruit/nut ~** pain aux raisins/noix ►**half a ~ is better than none** *prov* faute de grives on mange des merles *prov;* **use your ~!** *Brit* fais travailler tes neurones!

loaf about, **loaf around** *vi* traînasser

loafer *n* **1.** (*person who avoids work*) fainéant(e) *m(f)* **2.** FASHION mocassin *m*

loam [ləʊm, *Am:* loʊm] *n no pl* **1.** (*fertile soil*) terreau *m* **2.** (*raw material for bricks*) terre *f* de moulage

loamy *adj* riche en terreau

loan [ləʊn, *Am:* loʊn] **I.** *vt* prêter; **to ~ sth to sb, to ~ sb sth** prêter qc à qn **II.** *n* **1.** (*borrowed money*) emprunt *m;* **a $50,000 ~** un emprunt de 50,000 dollars; **to apply for/take out a ~** faire un emprunt **2.** (*act of lending*) prêt *m;* **to be on long-term/short-term ~** avoir un prêt à long/court terme; **the book I want is out on ~** le livre que je veux est emprunté

loanword *n* LING mot *m* d'emprunt

loath [ləʊθ, *Am:* loʊθ] *adj form* **to be ~ to** +*infin* répugner à +*infin*

loathe [ləʊð, *Am:* loʊð] *vt* détester

loathing *n no pl* répugnance *f;* **with ~** avec révulsion; **deep ~** dégoût *m* profond; **to fill sb with ~** dégoûter qn; **to have a ~ for sb/sth** avoir qn/qc en horreur

loathsome *adj* répugnant(e)

lob [lɒb, *Am:* lɑːb] **I.** <-bb-> *vt* **1.** jeter; **to ~ sth over sb/sth** envoyer qc par dessus qn/qc **2.** (*in tennis*) lober **II.** *n* **1.** (*a ball projected in this way*) chandelle *f* **2.** (*act of hitting a ball in this way*) lob *m*

lobby ['lɒbi, *Am:* 'lɑːbi] **I.** <-bbies> *n* **1.** ARCHIT entrée *f;* (*of hotel*) hall *m;* (*of theater*) foyer *m* **2.** (*influential group*) lobby *m* **II.** <-ie-> *vi* exercer une pression; **to ~ to have sth done** faire pression pour obtenir qc; **to ~ against/for sth** exercer une pression contre/en vue de qc **III.** <-ie-> *vt* faire pression sur

lobbyist *n* membre *m* d'un groupe de pression

lobe [ləʊb, *Am:* loʊb] *n* lobe *m*

lobster ['lɒbstə^r, *Am:* 'lɑːbstɚ] *n* homard *m*

local ['ləʊkəl, *Am:* 'loʊ-] **I.** *adj* local(e); (*accent, dialect, councillor*) régional(e); (*hero*) du pays; (*police*) municipal(e) **II.** *n* **1.** *pl* (*inhabitant of a place*) habitants *mpl* de la région **2.** *Am* (*bus*) bus *m* urbain **3.** *Brit* (*neighborhood pub*) bistro *m* du coin **4.** *Am* (*local branch of a trade union*) branche *f* syndicale locale

local aneasthetic *n* anesthésie *f* locale **local area network** *n inf* réseau *m* local **local authorities** *n* autorités *fpl* locales **local branch** <-nches> *n* branche *f* régionale; (*of a bank, agency*) succursale *f* régionale; (*of a shop, building society*) filiale *f* régionale **local call** *n* communication *f* locale **local charge** *n* tarif *m* local **local colour** *no pl n* couleur *f* locale

locale [ləʊ'kɑːl, *Am:* loʊ'kæl] *n* **1.** (*scene where sth happens*) scène *f* **2.** (*literary setting*) théâtre *m*

local government *n no pl* **1.** (*government of towns*) administration *f* communale **2.** (*government of counties*) administration *f* départementale

locality [ləʊ'kæləti, *Am:* loʊ'kælət̬i] <-ties> *n* localité *f*

localization *n no pl* localisation *f*

localize ['ləʊkəlaɪz, *Am:* 'loʊ-] *vt* localiser

local news *n + vb sing* informations *fpl* locales **local paper** *n* journal *m* local **local time** *no pl n* heure *f* locale **local traffic** *no pl n* trafic *m* local **local train** *n* omnibus *m*

locate [ləʊ'keɪt, *Am:* 'loʊ-] **I.** *vi* s'installer **II.** *vt* **1.** (*situate*) situer; **to be ~d at/in/near/on sth** être situé à/dans/à côté de/sur qc **2.** (*find*) localiser
location *n* **1.** (*particular place*) emplacement *m* **2.** (*positioning*) localisation *f* **3.** CINE **on ~** en extérieur
loc. cit. [ˌlɒk'sɪt, *Am:* ˌlɑːk'sɪt] *abbr of* **loco citato** loc. cit.
loch [lɒk, *Am:* lɑːk] *n Scot* **1.** (*lake*) lac *m* **2.** (*fjord*) fjord *m*
lock¹ [lɒk, *Am:* lɑːk] *n* mèche *f* de cheveux
lock² [lɒk, *Am:* lɑːk] **I.** *n* **1.** (*fastening device*) serrure *f;* **combination ~** serrure à combinaison **2.** (*unit of a canal*) écluse *f* **3.** (*wrestling hold*) clef *f;* **to hold sb in a body ~** immobiliser qn avec son corps **4.** *Aus, Brit* AUTO antivol *m* ►**~, stock and barrel** dans sa totalité; **to be under ~ and key** être enfermé à clef **II.** *vt* **1.** (*fasten with a lock*) fermer à clef, barrer *Québec* **2.** (*confine safely*) enfermer **3.** (*be held fast*) **to be ~ed** être bloqué; (*be jammed*) être coincé; **to be ~ed in ice** être pris dans les glaces ►**to ~ horns over sth** se disputer pour qc **III.** *vi* se bloquer
◆**lock away** *vt* **1.** (*secure behind a lock*) mettre en sécurité **2.** (*confine in prison or hospital*) enfermer **3.** (*confine somewhere free of disruption*) **to lock oneself away** s'isoler
◆**lock in** *vt* enfermer à clef
◆**lock on** *vi,* **lock onto** *vi* MIL accrocher
◆**lock out** *vt* **1.** (*prevent entrance by locking all doors*) enfermer dehors; **she locked herself out of the car** elle a laissé les clefs de sa voiture à l'intérieur **2.** ECON priver de travail
◆**lock up** **I.** *vt* **1.** (*lock away*) mettre sous clef; (*documents*) mettre en sûreté **2.** (*confine in prison or mental hospital*) enfermer **II.** *vi* fermer
locker ['lɒkəʳ, *Am:* 'lɑːkɚ] *n* casier *m*
locker room *n* vestiaire *m*
locket ['lɒkɪt, *Am:* 'lɑːkɪt] *n* médaillon *m*
lockjaw ['lɒkdʒɔː, *Am:* 'lɑːkdʒɑː] *n no pl* tétanos *m*
lock-keeper *n* éclusier *m*
lockout *n* **1.** (*management tactic in labour disputes*) riposte *f* patronale à un mouvement de grève **2.** *no pl* (*tactic of locking out employees*) privation *f* de travail des grévistes
locksmith ['lɒksmɪθ, *Am:* 'lɑːk-] *n* serrurier *m*
lockup *n inf* violon *m*
loco ['ləʊkəʊ, *Am:* 'loʊkoʊ] *adj inf* dingue
locomotion [ˌləʊkə'məʊʃən, *Am:* ˌloʊkə'moʊ-] *n no pl* locomotion *f*
locomotive [ˌləʊkə'məʊtɪv, *Am:* ˌloʊkə'moʊt̬ɪv] **I.** *n* locomotive *f* **II.** *adj* locomotif(-ive)
locution [lə'kjuːʃən, *Am:* loʊ'-] *n* locution *f*
lode [ləʊd, *Am:* loʊd] *n* MIN filon *m*
lodestar ['ləʊdstɑːʳ, *Am:* 'loʊdstɑːr] *n* **1.** (*star*) étoile *f* polaire **2.** (*guide*) guide *m*
lodge [lɒdʒ, *Am:* lɑːdʒ] **I.** *vi* **1.** (*stay in a rented lodging*) loger; **to ~ with sb** loger chez qn **2.** (*become fixed*) se loger **II.** *vt* **1.** (*accommodate*) lofer **2.** LAW **to ~ an appeal/objection** faire appel/objection; **to ~ a complaint** porter plainte; **to ~ a protest** protester **3.** *Brit* (*deposit for security*) **to ~ sth with sb** déposer qc chez qn **4.** (*make become fixed*) loger **III.** *n* **1.** (*small house*) pavillon *m;* **hunting/ski ~** gîte *m;* (*for porter, caretaker*) loge *f* **2.** *Brit* (*entrance room*) loge *f* **3.** (*beaver's lair*) hutte *f*
lodger *n* locataire *mf;* **to take in ~s** louer des chambres
lodging *n* **~(s)** logement *m;* **board and ~** pension *f* complète; **to find a night's ~** trouver une chambre pour la nuit; **to take ~s with sb** prendre une chambre chez qn
lodging house *n* pension *f*
loft [lɒft, *Am:* lɑːft] **I.** *n* **1.** (*space under a roof*) grenier *m* **2.** (*living space*) loft *m* **II.** *vt* lancer haut
lofty ['lɒfti, *Am:* 'lɑːf-] *adj* **1.** (*noble, exalted*) noble **2.** *pej* (*haughty, supercilious*) hautain(e)
log¹ [lɒg, *Am:* lɑːg] **I.** *n* (*piece of wood*) rondin *m;* (*for fire*) bûche *f;* **a ~ fire** un feu de bois ►**to sleep like a ~** dormir comme une souche **II.** <-gg-> *vt* (*tree*) débiter; (*forest*) décimer
log² [lɒg, *Am:* lɑːg] **I.** *n* registre *m;* **~ (book)** NAUT journal *m* de bord; AUTO carnet *m* de route; AVIAT carnet *m* de vol **II.** *vt* enregistrer **III.** *vi* INFOR **to ~ into sth** se connecter à qc
◆**log in** **I.** *vi* **1.** (*record one's arrival*) s'enregistrer; **to ~ to work** pointer **2.** INFOR (*log on*) se connecter **II.** *vt* connecter; **to log oneself in sth** se connecter à qc
log³ *n abbr of* **logarithm** logarithme *m*
logbook *n s.* **log**
logger ['lɒgəʳ, *Am:* 'lɑːgɚ] *n* bûcheron *m*
loggerheads *npl* **to be at ~ with sb/over sth** être en désaccord avec qn/concernant qc
logic ['lɒdʒɪk, *Am:* 'lɑːdʒɪk] *n no pl* logique *f*
logical *adj* logique
login **I.** *n* INFOR ouverture *f* d'une session, connexion *f* **II.** *vt* INFOR ouvrir une session
logistics [lə'dʒɪstɪks, *Am:* loʊ'-] *n + sing vb* logistique *f*
logo ['lɒgəʊ, *Am:* 'loʊgoʊ] *n* logo *m*
logoff **I.** *n* INFOR clôture *f* de session **II.** *vt* INFOR clore une session
logon *s.* **login**
loin [lɔɪn] **I.** *n* filet *m* **II.** *adj* **~ steak** filet *m*
loincloth ['lɔɪnklɒθ, *Am:* '-klɑːθ] *n* pagne *m*
loiter ['lɔɪtəʳ, *Am:* -t̬ɚ] *vi* **1.** (*linger*) flâner **2.** (*hang about idly*) **to ~ about** traîner
loiterer *n pej* glandeur, -euse *m, f inf*
loll [lɒl, *Am:* lɑːl] *vi* **1.** (*hang around lazily*) flâner **2.** (*sit, lie lazily*) se prélasser **3.** (*stand lazily, loaf about*) fainéanter **4.** (*hang loosely*) **to ~ out** pendre
lollipop ['lɒlipɒp, *Am:* 'lɑːlipɑːp] *n* sucette *f,* suçon *m Québec*
lollop ['lɒləp, *Am:* 'lɑːləp] *vi* galoper
lolly ['lɒli, *Am:* 'lɑːli] <-lies> *n* **1.** *Aus, Brit*

(*lollipop*) sucette *f* **2.** *no pl, Brit, inf* (*money*) fric *m*

London ['lʌndən] *n* Londres

Londoner I. *adj* londonien(ne) **II.** *n* Londonien(ne) *m(f)*

lone [ləʊn, *Am:* loʊn] *adj* **1.** (*solitary*) solitaire **2.** (*single*) seul(e); (*father, parent*) célibataire ►**to play a ~ hand** faire cavalier seul

loneliness ['ləʊnlɪnɪs, *Am:* 'loʊn-] *n no pl* solitude *f*

lonely ['ləʊnli, *Am:* 'loʊn-] <-ier, -iest *o* more ~, most ~> *adj* **1.** (*unhappy because alone*) seul(e) **2.** (*solitary*) solitaire **3.** (*isolated*) isolé(e); (*street*) peu fréquenté(e)

lonely hearts club *n* club *m* de rencontres

loner ['ləʊnəʳ, *Am:* 'loʊnɚ] *n* solitaire *mf*

lonesome ['ləʊnsəm, *Am:* 'loʊn-] *adj* **1.** (*lonely*) seule(e) **2.** (*isolated*) isolé(e)

long¹ [lɒŋ, *Am:* lɑːŋ] **I.** *adj* long(ue); **to be a ~ way from sth** être loin de qc; **to have come a ~ way** revenir de loin; **to have a ~ way to go** avoir du chemin à faire; **to have a ~ memory for sth** avoir de la mémoire pour qc ►**to have a ~ arm** avoir le bras long; **to make a ~ face** faire la tête; **in the ~ run** à la longue; **to be a ~ shot** être un coup à tenter; **not by a ~ shot** loin de là; **the ~ and the short of it is that ...** le fin mot de l'histoire c'est que ...; **~ time no see** *inf* voilà un revenant; **to be ~ in the tooth** ne plus être de la première jeunesse **II.** *adv* **1.** (*a long time*) depuis longtemps; **~ ago** il y a longtemps; **~ after/before** bien après/avant; **not ~ after sth** pas bien longtemps après qc; **before ~** avant bien longtemps; **to take ~ to** +*infin* prendre du temps pour +*infin;* **at ~ last** enfin; **~ live the king!** longue vie au roi! **2.** (*for the whole duration*) **all day/night ~** toute la journée/nuit; **as ~ as sb lives** aussi longtemps que qn est en vie **3.** ((*but*) *only if*) **as ~ as ...** seulement si ... **4.** (*no more*) **to no ~er** +*infin* ne plus +*infin* **5.** (*goodbye*) **so ~** à bientôt

long² [lɒŋ, *Am:* lɑːŋ] *vi* avoir envie; **to ~ for sb/sth** désirer qn/qc; **to ~ to** +*infin* avoir envie de +*infin*

long. *n abbr of* **longitude** longitude *f*

longboat *n* chaloupe *f* **long-distance I.** *adj* **1.** (*going a long way: flight*) long-courrier; (*train*) grande ligne **2.** (*separated by a great distance*) à distance; (*call*) longue distance **3.** SPORT (*race, runner*) de fond **II.** *adv* **to phone ~** faire un appel longue distance; **to travel ~** faire un long voyage **long drink** *n* long drink *m*

longevity [lɒn'dʒevəti, *Am:* lɑːn'dʒevəṱi] *n no pl* longévité *f*

long-haired *adj pej* aux cheveux longs; (*animals*) aux poils longs

longing *n* envie *f;* **a ~ for sb/sth** une envie de qn/qc

longish *adj inf* assez long(ue); **to take a ~ time** prendre assez de temps

longitude ['lɒŋgɪtjuːd, *Am:* 'lɑːndʒətuːd] *n* longitude *f*

longitudinal *adj* longitudinal(e) ►**to take ~ readings** lire en diagonale

long jump *n* SPORT **the ~** le saut en longueur **long-life** *adj* (*food, milk*) longue conservation; (*battery*) longue durée **long-lived** *adj* **1.** (*living long*) d'une grande longévité **2.** (*lasting long*) de longue durée; (*feud, friendship*) de longue date **long-lost** *adj* perdu(e) depuis longtemps **long-playing record** *n* 33 tours *m* **long-range** *adj* **1.** (*across a long distance*) longue portée **2.** (*long-term*) à long terme **long-range aircraft** *n* long-courrier *m* **long-sighted** *adj* **1.** (*having long sight*) hypermétrope **2.** *Am* (*having foresight*) prévoyant(e) **long-standing** *adj* de longue date **long-suffering** *adj* d'une patience à toute épreuve **long-term** *adj* **1.** (*effective on a longer period*) à long terme **2.** (*lasting long*) de longue durée **long vacation** *n Brit* grandes vacances *fpl* **long wave I.** *n* grandes ondes *fpl* **II.** *adj* **long-wave** longues ondes **longways** *adv* en longueur **long-winded** *adj* prolixe **longwise** *s.* **longways**

loo [luː] *n Aus, Brit, inf* chiottes *fpl*

look [lʊk] **I.** *n* **1.** (*act of looking, examining*) regard *m;* **to give sb a ~** jeter un regard à qn; **to have a ~ at sth** jeter un coup d'œil à qc; **to take a (good) hard ~ at sb/sth** regarder qn/qc de près **2.** (*appearance, expression*) air *m;* **to have the ~ of sb/sth** avoir l'air de qn/qc; **by the ~ of things** selon toute apparence; **sb's ~s** l'allure *f* de qn; **sb's good ~s** le physique de qn **3.** (*act of searching*) **to have a ~ for sb/sth** chercher qn/qc **4.** (*specified style*) look *m* ►**if ~s could kill** si les yeux pouvaient tuer **II.** *interj* regarde(z)! **III.** *vi* **1.** (*use one's sight*) **to ~ at sb/sth** regarder qn/qc; **to ~ sb up and down** regarder qn de haut en bas; **to ~ out (of) the window** regarder par la fenêtre; **to be not much to ~ at** ne pas en valoir la peine; **to ~ the other way** regarder dans l'autre direction; **to ~ askance at sb** regarder qn d'un air soupçonneux **2.** + *adj or n* (*appear, seem, resemble*) avoir l'air; **to ~ one's age** faire son âge; **to ~ one's best** être à son avantage; **to ~ as if sb is doing sth** avoir l'air de faire qc; **to ~ like sb/sth** ressembler à qn/qc **3.** (*hope*) **to ~ to do sth** espérer faire qc; **to ~ ahead** se tourner vers l'avenir **4.** (*pay attention*) faire attention **5.** (*regard, consider*) **to ~ at sth** considérer qc **6.** (*examine, study, evaluate*) **to ~ at sth** examiner qc **7.** (*face a particular direction*) **to ~ north** faire face au nord ►**to ~ daggers at sb** foudroyer du regard; **don't ~ a gift-horse in the mouth** *prov* à cheval donné on ne regarde pas à la bride *prov;* **to make sb ~ small** remettre qn à sa place; **~ before you leap** *prov* il ne faut pas sauter les yeux fermés

◆**look about** *vi* regarder

◆**look after** *vt* s'occuper de; **to ~ oneself** prendre soin de soi; **to ~ one's interests** veil-

ler sur ses propres intérêts; **to ~ number one** *pej* ne penser qu'à ses propres intérêts
◆**look ahead** *vi* regarder devant soi
◆**look around** *vi Am s.* **look round**
◆**look away** *vi* regarder ailleurs; **to ~ from sth** détourner les yeux de qc
◆**look back** *vi* regarder derrière soi; **to ~ on sth** revenir sur qc; **to never ~** ne jamais regarder en arrière
◆**look down** *vi* **1.** (*from above*) regarder en bas **2.** (*lower one's eyes*) baisser les yeux **3.** (*hate*) **to ~ on sb/sth** mépriser qn/qc
◆**look for** *vt* **1.** (*seek*) chercher **2.** (*expect*) s'attendre à
◆**look forward** *vi* **1.** (*anticipate pleasurably*) **to ~ to sth** attendre qc avec impatience; **to ~ to seeing sb** être impatient de revoir qn **2.** *form* (*anticipate with specified feelings*) **to ~ to sth** espérer qc; **looking forward to hearing from you** en attendant une réponse de votre part
◆**look in** *vi Brit, Aus* regarder à l'intérieur; **to ~ on sb** passer voir qn; **to ~ at the office** passer au bureau
◆**look into** *vi* **1.** (*investigate*) examiner; (*reasons*) étudier **2.** (*predict*) envisager
◆**look on** *vt*, **look upon** *vt* considérer
◆**look out I.** *vt Brit* trouver **II.** *vi* **1.** (*face a particular direction*) **to ~ on sth** regarder qc **2.** (*watch out, be careful*) **to ~ for sb/sth** se méfier de qn/qc **3.** (*look for*) **to ~ for sb/sth** rechercher qn/qc; **to ~ for oneself** chercher le meilleur pour soi; **to ~ for number one** penser à ses propres intérêts
◆**look over** *vt* jeter un coup d'œil à
◆**look round I.** *vi* **1.** (*turn around to look*) se retourner **2.** (*look in all directions*) regarder autour de soi **3.** (*search*) **to ~ for sb/sth** chercher qn/qc **II.** *vt* (*inspect*) faire le tour de; (*house*) visiter
◆**look through** *vt* **1.** (*look*) regarder; **to ~ the window** regarder par la fenêtre **2.** (*examine*) examiner **3.** (*peruse*) parcourir **4.** (*not acknowledge sb*) **to look** (**straight**) **through sb** ne pas reconnaître qn
◆**look to** *vt* **1.** (*take care*) faire attention à; **to ~ it that ...** faire en sorte que ... **2.** (*expect*) **to ~ sb/sth for sth** se tourner vers qn/qc pour qc **3.** (*count on*) compter sur
◆**look up I.** *vt* **1.** (*consult a reference work*) chercher **2.** (*look for and visit*) aller voir **II.** *vi* **1.** *a. fig* (*raise one's eyes upward*) **to ~ from sth** lever les yeux de qc; **to ~ at sb/sth** lever les yeux vers qn/qc **2.** (*improve*) s'améliorer **3.** (*see as role model*) **to ~ to sb** avoir de l'admiration pour qn
lookalike *n* double *m*
looker *n inf* jolie fille *f*
looker-on <lookers-on> *n* spectateur, -trice *m, f*
look-in *n Aus, Brit, inf* visite *f;* **to not get a ~** ne pas avoir la moindre chance
looking glass <-es> *n form* glace *f*
lookout *n* **1.** (*observation post*) guet *m* **2.** (*person set as a guard*) guetteur *m* **3.** (*act of keeping watch*) **to be on the ~ for sb/sth** être à la recherche de qn/qc; **to keep a ~ for sth** guetter qc ►**to be a good/bad ~ for sb** être de bonne/mauvaise augure pour qn; **to be sb's ~** être l'affaire de qn
look-over *n* coup *m* d'œil
loom¹ [lu:m] *n* métier *m* à tisser
loom² [lu:m] *vi* **1.** (*come threateningly into view*) apparaître **2.** (*be ominously near*) surgir; **to ~ on the horizon** se dessiner sur l'horizon
loony ['lu:ni] **I.** <-ier, -iest> *adj inf* cinglé(e) **II.** <-nies> *n pej, inf* cinglé(e) *m(f)*
loop [lu:p] **I.** *n* **1.** (*curve*) *a.* INFOR boucle *f* **2.** ELEC circuit *m* fermé **3.** (*contraceptive coil*) stérilet *m* **II.** *vi* former une boucle **III.** *vt* **to ~ sth** faire une boucle avec qc ►**to ~ the loop** faire un looping
loophole ['lu:phəʊl, *Am:* -hoʊl] *n* lacune *f*
loose [lu:s] **I.** *adj* **1.** (*not tight: knot, rope, screw*) desserré(e); (*clothing*) ample; (*skin*) relâché(e); **~ connection** mauvais contact *m* **2.** (*partly detached, not confined*) détaché(e); **to get ~** se détacher; **to let a dog ~ on sb** lâcher un chien sur qn; **~ sheet of paper** feuille *f* de papier libre **3.** (*release*) **to let sth ~** lâcher qc **4.** (*not exact*) vague; (*translation*) approximatif(-ive) **5.** (*not strict or controlled: discipline, style*) relâché(e) **6.** (*sexually immoral*) amoral(e); **~ living** vie *f* dissolue; **~ morals** mœurs *fpl* relâchées **II.** *adv* **to hang ~** pendre ►**hang ~!** reste calme! **III.** *n* **to be on the ~** être en cavale **IV.** *vt form* lâcher
loose-leaf *adj* à feuilles mobiles; **~ book** classeur *m*
loosely *adv* **1.** (*not fixed*) lâchement; **to hang ~** pendre **2.** (*not tightly*) sans serrer; (*tied, wrapped*) mal; **to be ~ dressed** porter des vêtements amples **3.** (*not exactly*) approximativement **4.** (*not strictly*) de façon relâchée; **~ organized society** société *f* désorganisée
loosen ['lu:sn] **I.** *vt* **1.** (*untie*) défaire **2.** (*unfasten*) desserrer **3.** (*weaken*) relâcher; **to ~ sb's tongue** délayer sa langue; **to ~ ties with sb/sth** distendre ses liens avec qn/qc **II.** *vi* **1.** *a. fig* (*unfasten*) se desserrer **2.** (*relax*) se détendre
loot [lu:t] **I.** *n no pl* butin *m* **II.** *vt* piller **III.** *vi* se livrer au pillage
looting *n no pl* pillage *m*
lop [lɒp, *Am:* lɑ:p] <-pp-> *vt* **to ~ (off)** élaguer
lope [ləʊp, *Am:* loʊp] *vi* **to ~ across sth** gambader à travers qc
lopsided [ˌlɒp'saɪdɪd, *Am:* ˌlɑ:p-] *adj* asymétrique; (*picture*) de travers; (*grin*) en coin
loquacious [lə'kweɪʃəs, *Am:* loʊ'-] *adj* loquace
lord [lɔ:d, *Am:* lɔ:rd] *n* **1.** *Brit* (*British peer*) lord *m;* **~ of the manor** châtelain *m;* **to live like a ~** vivre comme un seigneur; **to act like the ~ of the manor** se prendre pour un grand

seigneur **2.** (*powerful man*) seigneur *m;* **drug** ~ parrain *m* de la drogue **3.** (*god*) **the Lord** le Seigneur

lordly <-ier, -iest> *adj* **1.** (*superior, beautiful*) majestueux(-euse) **2.** (*arrogant*) hautain(e); **to give oneself** ~ **airs** se donner des grands airs

lordship *n* **1.** *no pl, form* (*dominion, authority*) autorité *f* **2.** *Brit* (*used to refer to a British peer*) Majesté *f;* **his/your** ~ Sa/Votre Majesté

lore [lɔːʳ, *Am:* lɔːr] *n no pl* **1.** (*traditional knowledge*) tradition *f;* **common** ~ usage *m* commun **2.** (*legends*) légende *f*

lorry ['lɒri, *Am:* 'lɔːr-] <-ies> *n Brit* camion *m;* ~ **driver** camionneur *m*

lose [luːz] <lost, lost> **I.** *vt* perdre; **to** ~ **one's life** perdre la vie; **to** ~ **one's breath** perdre son souffle; **to** ~ **no time in doing sth** ne pas perdre de temps à faire qc; **to** ~ **one's control of sb/sth** perdre le contrôle de qn/qc; **to** ~ **one's head/nerve** perdre la tête/son sang froid ►**to** ~ **face** perdre face; **to** ~ **heart** perdre courage; **to** ~ **one's heart to sb/sth** tomber amoureux de qn/qc; **to have lost one's marbles** *iron* perdre la tête; **to have nothing to** ~ n'avoir rien à perdre; **to** ~ **one's shirt** perdre sa chemise; **to** ~ **sight of sth** perdre de vue qc; **to** ~ **sleep over sth** s'en faire pour qc; **to** ~ **touch with sb** rester en contact avec qn; **to** ~ **touch with reality** perdre tout sens de la réalité; **to** ~ **track of sb/sth** perdre la trace de qn/qc; **to** ~ **one's way** s'égarer **II.** *vi* perdre; **to** ~ **to sb/sth** se faire battre par qn/qc

loser *n* **1.** (*defeated person, group*) perdant(e) *m(f)* **2.** *pej* (*habitually unsuccessful person*) loser *m*

losing *adj* perdant(e); (*battle*) perdu(e) d'avance

loss [lɒs, *Am:* lɑːs] <-es> *n* perte *f;* **to be at a** ~ **to** *+infin* être embarrassé pour *+infin;* **to sell at a** ~ ECON vendre à perte

loss-making *adj* à perte

lost [lɒst, *Am:* lɑːst] **I.** *pt, pp of* lose **II.** *adj* (*soul*) en peine; (*opportunity*) manqué(e); **to be** ~ être perdu; **to get** ~ s'égarer; **lost property (office)** objets *mpl* trouvés ►**a** ~ **cause** une cause perdue

lot [lɒt, *Am:* lɑːt] *n* **1.** (*much/many*) **a** ~**/**~**s** beaucoup; **a** ~ **of people/rain** beaucoup de gens/pluie; **to do a** ~ **of travelling** voyager beaucoup; ~**s of children** beaucoup d'enfants; **to feel a** ~ **better** se sentir beaucoup mieux; **to be a** ~ **on the road** être souvent sur la route **2.** (*group of people*) groupe *m;* **my** ~ les miens **3.** (*everything*) **the** ~ le tout **4.** (*fate*) sort *m;* **to cast in one's** ~ **with sb** partager le sort de qn; **it falls to sb's** ~ **to do sth** *form* le sort a voulu que qn fasse qc *+subj* **5.** (*share in a lottery*) sort *m;* **to draw** ~**s** tirer au sort; **to choose sb/sth by** ~ choisir qn/qc au sort **6.** *Am, Aus* (*plot of land*) terrain *m;* **building** ~ lotissement *m;* **parking** ~ parking *m* **7.** (*unit in an auction*) lot *m* ►**to be a bad** ~ ne pas valoir cher

loth [ləʊθ, *Am:* loʊθ] *adj s.* **loath**

lotion ['ləʊʃən, *Am:* 'loʊ-] *n no pl* lotion *f*

lottery ['lɒtəri, *Am:* 'lɑːt̬ɚ-] <-ies> *n* loterie *f;* ~ **ticket** billet *m* de loterie

lotus ['ləʊtəs, *Am:* 'loʊt̬əs] <-es> *n* **1.** (*flower*) fleur *f* de lotus **2.** *no pl* (*plant*) lotus *m*

loud [laʊd] **I.** *adj* **1.** (*very audible*) fort(e); ~ **and clear** clair et précis **2.** *pej* (*garish*) criard(e) **3.** *pej* (*aggressively noisy*) bruyant(e); ~ **mouth** *inf* grande gueule *f* **II.** *adv* bruyamment; (*to laugh out, to speak*) fort

loudhailer [ˌlaʊd'heɪləʳ, *Am:* -lɚ] *n Brit, Aus* porte-voix *m*

loudness *n no pl* bruit *m*

loudspeaker *n* **1.** (*megaphone*) haut-parleur *m* **2.** (*radio, hi-fi speaker*) enceinte *f*

Louisiana [luˌiːzi'ænə] *n* la Louisiane

lounge [laʊndʒ] **I.** *n* salon *m* **II.** *vi* **1.** (*recline in a relaxed way*) se prélasser **2.** (*be, stand idly*) paresser

lounge suit *n* complet *m*

louse [laʊs] **I.** *n* **1.** <lice> (*insect*) pou *m* **2.** <-es> *inf* (*contemptible person*) salaud, salope *m, f* **II.** *vt inf* **to** ~ **sth up, to** ~ **up sth** foutre qc en l'air

lousy <-ier, -iest> *adj pej, inf* **1.** (*of poor quality*) nul(le); **to feel** ~ se sentir mal foutu **2.** (*meagre*) **a** ~ **£5** 5 malheureuses livres **3.** (*infested with lice*) pouilleux(-euse) ►**to be** ~ **with sth** être bourré de qc

lout [laʊt] *n inf* brute *f*

loutish ['laʊtɪʃ, *Am:* -t̬ɪʃ] *adj pej* grossier(-ère)

louver *n Am,* **louvre** ['luːvəʳ, *Am:* -ɚ] *n* persienne *f*

lovable *adj* adorable

love [lʌv] **I.** *vt* **1.** aimer; **to feel** ~**d** se sentir aimé **2.** (*greatly like*) **to** ~ **to** *+infin* adorer *+infin;* **I'd** ~ **you to come** ça me ferait vraiment plaisir que tu viennes *subj* ►~ **me,** ~ **my dog** *prov* il faut me prendre comme je suis **II.** *n* **1.** *no pl* (*strong affection or passion*) amour *m;* ~ **at first sight** coup *m* de foudre; **to be in** ~ **with sb** être amoureux de qn; **to make** ~ **to sb** faire l'amour à qn; **to be head over heels in** ~ **with each other** être fous amoureux l'un de l'autre; **to fall in** ~ **with sb** tomber amoureux de qn; **to give sb one's** ~ (*on letter*) transmettre ses amitiés à qn **2.** *no pl, Brit* (*endearing form of address*) mon chéri, ma chérie **3.** *no pl* SPORT zéro *m;* **forty-**~ quarante zéro ►**you wouldn't find one not for** ~ **(n)or money** c'est impossible d'en trouver; **there is no** ~ **lost between the two** ils ne peuvent pas s'encadrer

love affair *n* liaison *f;* **to have a** ~ **with sth** *fig* avoir une passion pour qc **lovebird** *n fig* ~**s** tourtereaux *mpl* **love child** *n* enfant *m* de l'amour **love game** *n* SPORT jeu *m* blanc **love handles** *n pl, inf* poignées *fpl* d'amour **love-hate relationship** *n* relation *f* hou-

leuse
loveless *adj* sans amour
love letter *n* lettre *f* d'amour **love life** *n inf* vie *f* amoureuse
loveliness *n no pl* charme *m;* **to have a radiant** ~ avoir un charme fou
lovely ['lʌvli] <-ier, -iest> *adj* beau(belle)
love-making *n* amour *m* (physique); **to be good at** ~ bien savoir faire l'amour **love nest** *n* nid *m* d'amour
lover *n* **1.** (*for a woman*) amant *m;* (*for a man*) maîtresse *f;* **to be/become ~s** être/devenir amants; **her live-in** ~ le partenaire avec qui elle vit **2.** (*sb who loves sth*) amoureux, -euse *m, f;* **nature/opera** ~ un amoureux de la nature/l'opéra
lovesick *adj* **to be** ~ avoir un chagrin d'amour
love song *n* chanson *f* d'amour **love story** *n* histoire *f* d'amour
lovey [lʌvi] *n Brit, inf* mignon(ne) *m(f)*
loving *adj* tendre; ~ **care** affection
low [ləʊ, *Am:* loʊ] **I.** *adj* <-er, -est> **1.** (*not high or tall, not great: altitude, wall*) bas(se); (*neckline*) plongeant(e); ~ **heels** petits talons **2.** (*small in number*) faible; **to be ~ in cholesterol** être peu riche en cholestérol; **to be ~ in calories** être hypocalorique; ~ **alcohol drink** boisson peu alcoolisée; **to be ~ in funds** avoir peu de réserves **3.** (*reduced in quantity: level*) bas(se); **to be ~ on sth** n'avoir presque plus de qc **4.** (*intensity: frequency, sound, voice*) bas(se); (*light*) faible; **to keep one's voice** ~ parler tout bas **5.** (*poor, not of high quality*) mauvais(e); **to hold sth in ~ regard** mésestimer qc **6.** (*lowly, not important*) **to be a ~ priority** ne pas être une priorité **7.** (*unfair, mean*) **a ~ trick** un coup bas; **to get** ~ être malhonnête **8.** (*sad, dejected*) **in ~ spirits** abattu(e); **to feel** ~ ne pas avoir le moral **II.** <-er, -est> *adv* bas; **to fly** ~ voler bas; **to be cut** ~ (*dress, blouse*) être très décolleté; **to drop** ~ chuter; **to turn the music ~er** baisser la musique **III.** *n* **1.** (*low level*) **record** ~ baisse *f* record; **to hit a** ~ chuter; **to reach an all-time** ~ atteindre son niveau le plus bas **2.** (*difficult moment*) **the highs and ~s** les hauts et les bas **3.** METEO zone *f* de basse pression
lowborn *adj* de basse extraction **lowbrow** *pej* **I.** *adj* peu intellectuel(le) **II.** *n* personne *f* peu intellectuelle **low-calorie** *adj* hypocalorique **low comedy** *n* farce *f* **low-cut** *adj* décolleté(e) **low-down** *adj inf* (*people*) abject(e)
lower[1] ['ləʊəʳ, *Am:* 'loʊɚ] *vt* **1.** (*let down, haul down*) baisser; (*landing gear, lifeboat*) descendre; (*sails, mast*) amener; **to ~ a flag** baisser pavillon; **to ~ oneself to** +*infin* s'abaisser pour +*infin* **2.** (*reduce, decrease*) *a. fig* baisser; **to ~ one's voice** baisser le ton; **to ~ one's expectations** ne pas attendre trop **3.** (*diminish*) rabaisser **4.** (*demean, degrade*) **to ~ oneself to** +*infin* s'abaisser à +*infin*
lower[2] [laʊəʳ, *Am:* laʊr] *vi* se couvrir; **~ing sky** ciel *m* menaçant; **to ~ at sb** jeter un regard menaçant à qn
lower[3] ['ləʊəʳ, *Am:* 'loʊɚ] *adj* inférieur(e); **in the ~ back** dans le bas du dos
lower case, **lower-case letter** *n* TYP minuscule *f*
low-fat *adj* allégé(e) **low-key** *adj* (*debate, speech*) modéré(e); **a ~ affair** un événement discret; **to take a ~ approach to sth** aborder qc en toute discrétion **lowland** *n* plaine *f*
low level *n* de bas niveau; **on a** ~ à un bas niveau **low-level radiation** *n* PHYS radiation *f* de faible niveau
lowly ['ləʊli, *Am:* 'loʊ-] <-ier, -iest> *adj* modeste
Low Mass *n* REL messe *f* basse **low-necked** *adj* décolleté(e)
lowness *n no pl* **1.** (*state of being low*) faible hauteur *f* **2.** MUS gravité *f* **3.** (*baseness*) bassesse *f*
low-noise *adj* AUTO peu bruyant(e) **low-pitched** *adj* grave **low-pollution** *adj* AUTO à faible taux de pollution **low pressure** *adj* de basse pression **low profile** *n* profil *m* bas **low season** *n* basse saison *f* **low-spirited** *adj* **to be** ~ ne pas avoir le moral **Low Sunday** *n* premier dimanche *m* après Pâques **low tide**, **low water** *n* marée *f* basse
loyal ['lɔɪəl] *adj* (*support*) loyal(e); **to remain ~ to sb/sth** demeurer loyal envers qn/qc; **to be ~ to one's beliefs** être fidèle à ses convictions
loyalist **I.** *n* loyaliste *mf* **II.** *adj* loyaliste
loyalty ['lɔɪəlti, *Am:* -t̬i] <-ties> *n* loyauté *f;* **sb's ~ to sth** la loyauté de qn envers qc; **to have divided ~ties** être partagé
lozenge ['lɒzɪndʒ, *Am:* 'lɑːzəndʒ] *n* losange *m;* **fruit** ~ bonbon *m* aux fruits; **throat/cough ~s** pastille *f* pour la gorge/toux
LP [ˌel'piː] *n abbr of* **long-playing record** 33 tours *m*
LSD [ˌeles'diː] **I.** *n no pl abbr of* **lysergic acid diethylamide** LSD *m* **II.** *adj* (*trip*) au LSD
Ltd ['lɪmɪtɪd, *Am:* -ət̬ɪd] *n abbr of* **limited** ≈ SARL *f*
lubricant ['luːbrɪkənt] *n no pl* lubrifiant *m*
lubricate ['luːbrɪkeɪt] *vt* **1.** (*apply grease to reduce friction*) graisser **2.** (*make slippery/smooth*) lubrifier ►**to ~ sb's tongue** délier la langue à qn
lubrication **I.** *n no pl* graissage *m* **II.** *adj* (*system*) de graissage
lubricator *n* lubrifiant *m*
lucerne [luː'sɜːn, *Am:* -'sɜːrn] *n* luzerne *f*
lucid ['luːsɪd] *adj* lucide; (*moment*) de lucidité
luck [lʌk] *n no pl* **1.** ((*good*) *fortune*) chance *f;* **a stroke of** ~ un coup de chance; **to not believe one's** ~ ne pas croire à sa chance; **to bring sb** ~ porter chance à qn; **to be in/out of** ~ avoir/ne pas avoir de la chance; **to be down on one's** ~ avoir la guigne; **to be the ~ of the draw** être une question de chance;

with (any) ~ avec un peu de chance; my ~ is in *Brit* c'est mon jour de chance; as ~ would have it ... le hasard a voulu que ...; bad ~! pas de chance!; no such ~! *inf* tu parles!; don't do that, it's bad ~ ne fais pas ça, ça porte malheur 2.(*success*) chance *f;* with no ~ sans succès; to wish sb good ~ in sth souhaiter bonne chance à qn pour qc; did you have any ~ opening that bottle? est-ce que tu as réussi à ouvrir cette bouteille?

luckless *adj form* malchanceux(-euse)

lucky <-ier, -iest> *adj* 1.(*have luck: person*) chanceux(-euse); **to be ~ at games/in love** avoir de la chance au jeu/en amour; **it is ~ that ...** heureusement que ...; **to count oneself ~** s'estimer heureux; **you ~ thing!** *inf* tu as de la chance!; **he'll be ~!** il peut toujours courir!; **to make a ~ guess** deviner au hasard 2.(*bringing good fortune: number*) porte-bonheur *inv;* ~ **day** jour *m* de chance ►~ **devil!** veinard!

lucky dip *n* GAMES ≈ jeu *m* de pêche

lucrative ['lu:krətɪv, *Am:* -t̬ɪv] *adj* lucratif(-ive)

lucre ['lu:kəʳ, *Am:* -kɚ] *n no pl, iron, pej* lucre *m;* **to do sth for (filthy) ~** faire qc pour l'appât du gain

ludicrous ['lu:dɪkrəs] *adj* (*idea*) ridicule; **to look ~** avoir l'air ridicule

ludo ['lu:dəʊ, *Am:* -doʊ] *n Brit* ≈ jeu *m* des petits chevaux

lug [lʌg] I. *vt* <-gg-> *inf* **to ~ sth (around)** trimbaler qc; **to ~ sth away** emporter qc II. *n Aus, Brit s.* **lughole**

luggage ['lʌgɪdʒ] *n no pl* bagages *mpl;* **two items of ~** deux bagages; **hand ~** bagage à main

luggage rack *n* 1.(*on train, bus, bicycle*) porte-bagages *m* 2.(*made of elastic strings*) filet *m* à bagages 3.(*on car roof*) galerie *f* **luggage van** *n Aus, Brit* compartiment *m* à bagages

lughole *n Brit, inf* esgourde *f*

lugubrious [lə'gu:brɪəs] *adj* lugubre

lukewarm [ˌlu:k'wɔ:m, *Am:* -'wɔ:rm] *adj a. fig* tiède; **to be ~ about an idea** ne pas être très chaud pour une idée

lull [lʌl] I. *vt a. fig* endormir; **to ~ sb into believing that ...** arriver à faire croire à qn que ...; **to ~ sb into a false sense of security** donner une fausse impression de sécurité à qn II. *n* pause *f;* (*in fighting*) accalmie *f;* **a ~ in consumer demand** une période de creux dans la demande des consommateurs; **a ~ in the conversation** un blanc dans la conversation; **a ~ in fighting** un répit dans les combats; **the ~ before the storm** le calme avant l'orage

lullaby ['lʌləbaɪ] *n* berceuse *f*

lumbago [lʌm'beɪgəʊ, *Am:* -goʊ] *n no pl* lumbago *m*

lumbar puncture *n* MED ponction *f* lombaire

lumber¹ ['lʌmbəʳ, *Am:* -bɚ] *vi* (*person, animal*) avancer à pas lourds; (*tanks, cart, wagon*) rouler lourdement

lumber² ['lʌmbəʳ, *Am:* -bɚ] *vt Aus, Brit, inf* **to get ~ed with sth** se coltiner qc

lumber³ ['lʌmbəʳ, *Am:* -bɚ] *n no pl, Am, Aus* 1.(*unuseful items*) bric-à-brac *m* 2.(*wood*) bois *m* de construction

lumberjack *n* bûcheron(ne) *m(f)* **lumberman** *n* 1. *s.* **lumberjack** 2.(*person who deals in timber*) négociant(e) *m(f)* en bois **lumber room** *n* débarras *m* **lumber trade** *n Am* commerce *m* du bois **lumberyard** *n* dépôt *m* de bois

luminary ['lu:mɪnəri, *Am:* 'lu:məner-] *n* 1.(*prominent person*) sommité *f* 2. CINE, THEAT star *f*

luminosity [ˌlu:mɪ'nɒsəti, *Am:* ˌlu:mə'nɑ:sət̬i] *n no pl* 1.(*brightness, quality*) luminosité *f* 2.(*brilliance*) virtuosité *f*

luminous ['lu:mɪnəs, *Am:* 'lu:mə-] *adj* 1.(*visible in darkness*) fluorescent(e) 2.(*brilliant*) sensationnel(le)

lump [lʌmp] I. *n* 1.(*solid mass of a substance: of coal, sugar*) morceau *m;* (*of clay*) motte *f;* (*in cooking*) grumeau *m* 2.(*abnormal growth*) grosseur *f* 3. *inf* (*oaf*) empoté(e) *m(f);* **fat ~** gros tas *m* ►**to have a ~ in one's throat** avoir la gorge nouée II. *vt* 1.(*combine*) regrouper; **to ~ all the people in the same group** mettre tout le monde dans le même groupe; *fig* mettre tout le monde dans le même panier 2.(*endure*) **if you don't like it, you can ~ it** si ça ne te plaît pas c'est pareil

lump payment *n* versement *m* unique **lump sugar** *n* sucre *m* en morceaux **lump sum** *n* somme *f* forfaitaire; ~ **payment** versement *m* unique; **to pay in a ~** payer en une fois

lumpy <-ier, -iest> *adj* (*custard, sauce*) grumeleux(-euse); (*surface*) irrégulier(-ère)

lunacy ['lu:nəsi, *Am:* 'lu:-] *n no pl* 1.(*craziness*) folie *f;* **it's sheer ~** c'est de la folie douce 2. *vulg* (*mental illness, insanity*) démence *f*

lunar ['lu:nəʳ, *Am:* 'lu:nɚ] *adj* lunaire; (*eclipse*) de lune

lunatic ['lu:nətɪk] I. *n* 1.(*crazy person*) dingue *mf* 2. POL **the ~ fringe** les extrémistes 3. *vulg* (*mentally ill person*) fou, folle *m, f* II. *adj* dingue

lunatic asylum *n pej* asile *m* de fous

lunch [lʌntʃ] I. *n* déjeuner *m,* dîner *m Belgique, Québec;* **buffet ~** buffet *m;* **business ~** déjeuner d'affaires; **to be out to ~** être parti déjeuner; **to have ~** déjeuner, dîner *Belgique, Québec* ►**to <u>be</u> out to ~** être dérangé II. *vi* déjeuner, dîner *Belgique, Québec;* **to ~ on sandwiches** manger des sandwichs au déjeuner

lunch break *n* pause *f* de midi

luncheon ['lʌntʃən] *n form* déjeuner *m*

luncheon meat *n* pâté *m* de viande **luncheon voucher** *n Brit* ticket-repas *m*

lunch hour *n s.* **lunch break** **lunchtime**

I. *n* heure *f* du déjeuner; **yesterday** ~ hier midi; **to do sth at** ~ faire qc pendant l'heure du déjeuner; **to do sth by** ~ faire qc d'ici midi II. *adj* (*concert*) de midi
lung [lʌŋ] *n* poumon *m* ►**to have good ~s** *iron* avoir du coffre; **to shout at the top of one's ~s** crier à pleins poumons
lung cancer *n* cancer *m* du poumon
lunge [lʌndʒ] I. *vi* **to ~ at sb** se précipiter sur qn II. *n* **to make a ~ at sb/sth** se précipiter sur qn/qc
lupin *n*, **lupine** ['lu:pɪn] *n Am* lupin *m*
lurch [lɜ:tʃ, *Am:* lɜ:rtʃ] I. *vi* (*crowd, person*) tituber; (*train, ship*) tanguer; (*car*) faire une embardée II. *n* embardée *f;* **to give a ~** tituber ►**to leave sb in the lurch** laisser qn en plan
lure [lʊəʳ, *Am:* lʊr] I. *n* 1. (*attraction*) attrait *m* 2. (*bait, decoy*) leurre *m* II. *vt* appâter; **to ~ sb away from sth** entraîner qn loin de qc; **to ~ sb/sth into a trap** attirer qn/qc dans un piège
lurid ['lʊərɪd, *Am:* 'lʊrɪd] *adj pej* 1. (*ghastly, terrible: accounts*) atroce; (*detail*) sordide 2. (*vivid or glowing in colour: sunset, carpet*) flamboyant(e)
lurk [lɜ:k, *Am:* lɜ:rk] *vi* 1. (*hide*) **to ~ (about)** se tapir 2. *fig* **to ~ beneath the surface** traîner à la surface; **fears ~ beneath the apparent calm** la peur rôde malgré le calme apparent; **old prejudices were ~ing behind what he said** de vieux préjugés ressortaient derrière ce qu'il disait
lurker *n* INFOR rôdeur, -euse *m, f*
luscious ['lʌʃəs] *adj* 1. (*richly sweet: fruit, wine*) gorgé(e) de sucre 2. (*delicious*) succulent(e) 3. *inf* (*voluptuous: girl, lips*) pulpeux(-euse); (*curves*) généreux(-euse) 4. (*fertile: landscape, land*) riche
lush [lʌʃ] I. *adj* <-er, -est> 1. (*luxuriant*) luxuriant(e); (*grass*) gras(se) 2. (*luxurious*) luxueux(-euse) II. *n Am, inf* alcoolo *mf*
lust [lʌst] *n* 1. (*biblical sin*) luxure *f* 2. (*modern sense*) désir *m* sexuel; **to satisfy one's ~** satisfaire son appétit sexuel 3. (*greed*) soif *f;* **~ for money/power/revenge** soif d'argent/de pouvoir/de revanche; **~ for life** fureur *f* de vivre
luster *n no pl, Am s.* **lustre**
lustful *adj* lascif(-ive)
lustre ['lʌstə, *Am:* -tɚ] *n Aus, Brit* 1. (*glow*) éclat *m;* **a car with a rich ~** une voiture d'un lustre éclatant 2. *fig* brio *m*
lustreless *adj Aus, Brit* (*hair*) terne
lusty ['lʌsti] <-ier, -iest> *adj* (*children*) plein(e) d'énergie; (*cry*) énergique; (*voice*) puissant(e)
lute [lu:t] *n* luth *m*
Lutheran ['lu:θərən] I. *adj* luthérien(ne) II. *n* luthérien(ne) *m(f)*
Luxembourg ['lʌksəmbɜ:g, *Am:* -bɜ:rg] *n* 1. (*province*) (la province de) Luxembourg 2. (*country*) le Luxembourg; **the Grand Duchy of ~** le Grand-Duché du Luxembourg 3. (*capital*) Luxembourg(-ville) *m*
Luxembourger *n* Luxembourgeois(e) *m(f)*
Luxembourg(ian) *adj* luxembourgeois(e)
Luxemburgish *n* luxembourgeois *m; s. a.* **English**
luxuriant [lʌg'ʒʊərɪənt, *Am:* -'ʒʊrɪ-] *adj* luxuriant(e); (*carpet*) épais(se); (*writing*) très riche; **~ hair** chevelure fournie
luxuriate [lʌg'ʒʊərɪeɪt, *Am:* -'ʒʊrɪ-] *vi* se prélasser
luxurious [lʌg'ʒʊərɪəs, *Am:* -'ʒʊrɪ-] *adj* luxueux(-euse); (*tastes*) de luxe; **to take a ~ bath** se prélasser dans un bain
luxury ['lʌkʃəri, *Am:* -ʃɚ-] I. <-ies> *n pl* luxe *m;* **to live a life of ~** vivre dans le luxe; **to buy oneself little luxuries** s'acheter des petits plaisirs II. *adj* (*goods*) de luxe
LV *n abbr of* **luncheon voucher** ticket-repas *m*
LW *n abbr of* **long wave** GO *fpl*
lychee ['laɪtʃi:, *Am:* 'li:tʃi:] *n* litchi *m*
lying ['laɪɪŋ] I. *present participle of* **lie** II. *n* (*place to lie*) couche *f* III. *adj* menteur(-euse)
lymph [lɪmpf] *n no pl* lymphe *f*
lymphatic [lɪm'fætɪk, *Am:* -'fæt̬-] *adj* lymphatique
lymph gland, lymph node *n* ganglion *m* lymphatique
lynch [lɪntʃ] *vt* lyncher
lynx [lɪŋks] <-(es)> *n* lynx *m*
lynx-eyed *adj* **to be ~** avoir un œil de lynx
lyre ['laɪəʳ, *Am:* 'laɪr] *n* lyre *f*
lyric ['lɪrɪk] I. *adj* (*poet, poetry*) lyrique II. *n* 1. (*short poem*) petit poème *m* lyrique 2. *pl* (*words for song*) paroles *fpl*
lyrical *adj* lyrique; **to wax ~ about sth** s'emballer à propos de qc
lyricism ['lɪrɪˌsɪzəm] *n no pl* lyrisme *m*
lyricist *n* parolier, -ière *m, f*

M

M, m [em] <-'s> *n* M *m*, m *m;* **~ as in Mary** *Brit,* **~ as in Mike** *Am,* **~ for Mary** *Brit,* **~ for Mike** *Am* (*on telephone*) m comme Marcel
M I. *n abbr of* **male** homme *m* II. *adj abbr of* **medium** M
m I. *n* 1. *abbr of* **metre** m *m* 2. *abbr of* **mile** mile *m* 3. *abbr of* **million** million *m* 4. *abbr of* **minute(s)** min *f* 5. *abbr of* **masculine** masculin *m* II. *adj abbr of* **married** marié(e)
ma [mɑ:] *n inf* 1. (*mother*) maman *f* 2. (*old woman*) madame *f* 3. *Am* (*title*) madame *f*
MA [ˌem'eɪ] *n abbr of* **Master of Arts** ≈ maîtrise *f* de lettres
mA *n abbr of* **milliampere** mA *m*
ma'am [mæm] *n* 1. *Am* = **madam** madame *f* 2. *Brit* (*to royalty*) votre majesté
mac¹ [mæk] *n Brit, inf* imper *m*
mac² [mæk] *n Am, inf* m'sieur *m*

Mac [mæk] *n* INFOR *abbr of* **Macintosh** Mac *m*

macabre [mə'kɑːbrə] *adj* macabre

macadam [mə'kædəm] *n* macadam *m*

macaroni [ˌmækə'rəʊni, *Am:* -ə'roʊ-] *n no pl* macaroni *m*

macaroni cheese *n* macaronis *mpl* au fromage

mace¹ [meɪs] *n no pl* (*ornamental rod*) masse *f*

mace² [meɪs] *n Brit* (*spice*) macis *m*

Mace® [meɪs] **I.** *n no pl* gaz *m* lacrymogène **II.** *vt* **to ~ sb** asperger qn de gaz lacrymogène

Macedonia [ˌmæsɪ'dəʊniə, *Am:* -ə'doʊni-] *n* la Macédoine

Macedonian **I.** *adj* macédonien(ne) **II.** *n* **1.** (*person*) Macédonien(ne) *m(f)* **2.** LING macédonien *m; s. a.* **English**

Mach [mɑːk] *n no pl* PHYS Mach; **at ~ 1** à Mach 1

machete [mə'ʃeti, *Am:* -'ʃeṭ-] *n* machette *f*

machine [mə'ʃiːn] **I.** *n* **1.** (*mechanical device*) *a. pej* machine *f* **2.** (*washing ~*) machine *f* (à laver) **3.** (*vending ~*) distributeur *m* **4.** *inf* (*automobile, motorcycle*) engin *m* **5.** (*controlling system*) appareil *m;* **the party ~** la machine du parti **II.** *vt* **1.** (*operate on a machine: tool, part*) usiner **2.** (*saw: hem*) coudre

machine gun *n* mitrailleuse *f* **machine-made** *adj* fabriqué(e) à la machine **machine operator** *n* opérateur, -trice *m, f* **machine-readable** *adj* INFOR lisible par ordinateur

machinery [mə'ʃiːnəri] *n no pl* **1.** (*machines*) machines *fpl* **2.** (*working parts of machine*) mécanisme *m* **3.** (*working parts of organization*) rouages *mpl*

machine tool *n* machine-outil *f* **machine-washable** *adj* lavable en machine

machinist *n* **1.** (*operator of a machine*) opérateur, -trice *m, f* **2.** *Brit* (*operator of a sewing machine*) piqueur, -euse *m, f* **3.** (*person working on a machine*) mécanicien(ne) *m(f)*

macho ['mætʃəʊ, *Am:* 'mɑːtʃoʊ] **I.** *n* macho *m* **II.** *adj pej, inf* macho

mackerel ['mækrəl] <-(s)> *n* maquereau *m*

mackintosh ['mækɪntɒʃ, *Am:* -tɑːʃ] *n Brit* imperméable *m*

macro ['mækrəʊ, *Am:* -roʊ] *n* INFOR macro *f*

macrobiotic [ˌmækrəʊbaɪ'ɒtɪk, *Am:* -roʊbaɪ'ɑːṭɪk] *adj* macrobiotique

macrocosm ['mækrəʊkɒzəm, *Am:* -roʊkɑːzəm] *n* macrocosme *m*

macroeconomics [ˌmækrəʊiːkə'nɒmɪks, *Am:* -roʊˌekə'nɑːmɪks] *n* macroéconomie *f*

mad [mæd] *adj* **1.** <-er, -est> *a. inf* (*insane, frantic*) fou(folle); (*animal*) enragé(e); **to go ~** devenir fou; **we went ~ and bought a new car** on a fait une folie: on s'est acheté une nouvelle voiture; **to drive sb ~** rendre qn fou; **to be in a ~ rush** être extrêmement pressé; **to get into a ~ panic** paniquer complètement; **I ran/searched like ~** j'ai couru/cherché comme un fou **2.** <-er, -est> *inf* (*angry*) furieux(-euse); **to be/get ~ at sb** être/devenir furieux contre qn; **don't get ~ at me** ne te fâche pas contre moi **3.** <-er, -est> *inf* (*enthusiastic*) dingue; **to be ~ about sb/sth** être dingue de qn/qc; **the fans went ~** c'était la folie parmi les fans ►**to be (as) ~ as a <u>hatter</u>** être fou à lier

Madagascan **I.** *n* **1.** (*people*) Malgache *mf* **2.** (*language*) malgache *m* **II.** *adj* malgache

Madagascar [ˌmædə'gæskəʳ, *Am:* -kɚ] *n* Madagascar *f;* **in ~** à Madagascar

madam ['mædəm] *n* **1.** *no pl* (*polite form of address*) madame *f* **2.** (*head of brothel*) mère *f* maquerelle

madden ['mædən] *vt* exaspérer

maddening *adj* exaspérant(e)

made [meɪd] **I.** *pp, pt of* **make II.** *adj* **~ in ...** fabriqué à ...; **well-~** bien fait(e); **a strongly-~ house** une maison solide; **to have (got) it ~** *inf* c'est du tout cuit

Madeira [mə'dɪərə, *Am:* -'dɪrə] *n* (*wine*) madère *m*

made to measure *adj* (*suit*) sur mesure

made-up *adj* **1.** (*wearing make-up*) maquillé(e) **2.** (*untrue*) faux(fausse) **3.** (*invented*) inventé(e) **4.** (*made in advance*) tout(e) fait(e)

madhouse *n pej, inf* maison *f* de fous

madly *adv* **1.** (*frantically*) comme un(e) fou(folle); **to behave ~** avoir un comportement de fou **2.** (*very much, intensely*) follement

madman *n* fou *m*

madness *n no pl* folie *f*

madwoman *n* folle *f*

maelstrom ['meɪlstrəm] *n a. fig* tourbillon *m*

maestro ['maɪstrəʊ, *Am:* -stroʊ] *n* maestro *m*

Mafia, mafia ['mæfiə, *Am:* 'mɑː-] *n* Maf(f)ia *f,* maf(f)ia *f*

mag [mæg] *n inf abbr of* **magazine** magazine *m*

magazine [ˌmægə'ziːn, *Am:* 'mægəziːn] *n* **1.** (*publication*) magazine *m;* **women's ~s** les magazines féminins **2.** MIL magasin *m*

maggot ['mægət] *n* asticot *m*

Magi ['meɪdʒaɪ] *npl* **the ~** les Mages *mpl*

magic ['mædʒɪk] **I.** *n no pl* magie *f;* **(as if) by ~** comme par magie **II.** *adj* magique; (*show*) de magie; **that's ~** *Brit, inf* c'est génial

magical *adj* magique; (*evening, surroundings*) fabuleux(se)

magically *adv* comme par magie

magic carpet *n* tapis *m* volant

magician [mə'dʒɪʃən] *n* magicien(ne) *m(f)*

magisterial [ˌmædʒɪ'stɪərɪəl, *Am:* -'stɪrɪ-] *adj form* magistral(e)

magistrate ['mædʒɪstreɪt] *n* magistrat(e) *m(f)*

magistrate's court *n* tribunal *m* d'instance

magnanimity [ˌmægnə'nɪməti, *Am:* -ṭi] *n no pl, form* magnanimité *f*

magnanimous [mæg'nænɪməs, *Am:*

-əməs] *adj form* magnanime

magnate ['mægneɪt] *n* magnat *m*

magnesia [mæg'niːʃə, *Am:* -ʒə] *n no pl* magnésie *f*

magnesium [mæg'niːzɪəm] *n no pl* magnésium *m*

magnet ['mægnɪt] *n* (*metal*) aimant *m;* **to be a ~ for sb/sth** *fig* exercer une attraction sur qn/qc

magnetic *adj a. fig* magnétique; **~ person** personne *f* qui a du magnétisme; **~ north** pôle *m* magnétique

magnetism ['mægnətɪzəm, *Am:* -t̬ɪ-] *n no pl* magnétisme *m*

magnetize ['mægnətaɪz] *vt, vi Am* magnétiser

magnification [ˌmægnɪfɪ'keɪʃən] *n no pl* grossissement *m*

magnificence [mæg'nɪfɪsəns] *n no pl* magnificence *f*

magnificent *adj* magnifique

magnify ['mægnɪfaɪ] *vt* **1.** (*make bigger*) grossir **2.** (*make worse*) aggraver

magnifying glass *n* loupe *f*

magnitude ['mægnɪtjuːd, *Am:* -tuːd] *n no pl* **1.** (*great size*) *a. fig* ampleur *f* **2.** ASTR magnitude *f*

magnolia [mæg'nəʊlɪə, *Am:* -'noʊljə] **I.** *n* **1.** BOT magnolia *m* **2.** (*colour*) blanc *m* cassé **II.** *adj* blanc cassé *inv*

magnum opus [ˌmægnəm'əʊpəs, *Am:* -'oʊpəs] *n no pl, form* œuvre *f* maîtresse

magpie ['mægpaɪ] *n* **1.** (*bird*) pie *f* **2.** *pej* (*collector*) *quelqu'un qui ne jette rien*

maharaja(h) [ˌmɑːhə'rɑːdʒə] *n* HIST maharajah *m*

maharani [ˌmɑːhə'rɑːni] *n* HIST maharani *f*

mahogany [mə'hɒgəni, *Am:* -'hɑːgən-] *n no pl* acajou *m;* **a ~ table** une table en acajou

maid [meɪd] *n* domestique *f*

maiden ['meɪdən] **I.** *n* jeune *f* fille **II.** *adj* premier(-ère)

maiden flight *n* baptême *m* de l'air **maiden name** *n* nom *m* de jeune fille

mail[1] [meɪl] **I.** *n no pl a.* INFOR courrier *m;* **by ~** par la poste **II.** *vt Am* expédier

mail[2] [meɪl] *n no pl* (*armour*) maille *f*

mailbag *n* sac *m* postal **mailbox** *n Am* boîte *f* aux lettres; INFOR boîte *f* (aux lettres) électronique

mailing *n* mailing *m*

mailing list *n* fichier *m* d'adresses

mailman *n Am* (*postman*) facteur *m* **mail order** *n* vente *f* par correspondance **mailshot** *n Brit* mailing *m*

maim [meɪm] *vt* mutiler

main [meɪn] **I.** *adj* principal(e); **that's the ~ thing** c'est l'essentiel; **he has an eye for the ~ chance** il ne laisse pas passer une occasion **II.** *n* **1.** TECH conduite *f* **2.** *Brit* (*supply network: sewage*) égout *m;* (*water*) canalisation *f;* (*electricity*) secteur *m;* **to be on the ~s** être sur secteur; **turn the electricity off at the ~s** coupez le courant au compteur

Maine [meɪn] **I.** *n* le Maine **II.** *adj* du Maine

mainframe ['meɪnfreɪm] *n* INFOR **1.** (*computer*) macroordinateur *m* **2.** (*central unit*) unité *f* centrale

mainland ['meɪnlənd] *n no pl* **the ~** le continent; **~ Europe** l'Europe *f* continentale

mainline ['meɪnlaɪn] **I.** *n* les grandes lignes *fpl* **II.** *vt, vi inf* se shooter; **~ heroin** se shooter à l'héroïne

mainly *adv* **1.** (*primarily*) principalement **2.** (*mostly*) surtout

main road *n* route *f* principale **mainspring** *n* **1.** (*spring*) ressort *m* **2.** *fig* mobile *m* **mainstay** *n* pilier *m* **mainstream I.** *n no pl* courant *m* dominant **II.** *adj* dominant(e); (*film, product*) grand public

maintain [meɪn'teɪn] *vt* **1.** (*keep: order*) maintenir; **to ~ contact/silence** garder contact/le silence; **to ~ one's cool** *Am, inf* garder son calme **2.** (*preserve: machine*) entretenir **3.** (*provide for*) entretenir; **to ~ oneself** s'entretenir **4.** (*assert*) soutenir; (*one's innocence*) clamer

maintenance ['meɪntənəns] *n no pl* **1.** (*keeping*) maintien *m* **2.** (*preservation: of buildings, machines*) entretien *m* **3.** (*alimony*) pension *f* alimentaire

maintenance costs *n* frais *mpl* d'entretien

maisonette [ˌmeɪzə'net] *n Brit* duplex *m*

maize [meɪz] *n no pl* maïs *m*

Maj. *n abbr of* **Major** major *m*

majestic *adj* majestueux(-euse)

majesty ['mædʒəsti] *n* **1.** *no pl* (*tremendous beauty*) splendeur *f* **2.** (*title for royalty*) majesté *f;* **Her/His/Your Majesty** Sa/Votre Majesté

major ['meɪdʒəʳ, *Am:* -dʒɚ] **I.** *adj* majeur(e); **A ~** MUS la majeur **II.** *n* **1.** MIL major *m* **2.** *Am, Aus* (*primary subject*) matière *f* principale; **to be a history ~** faire histoire comme matière principale **III.** *vi Am, Aus* **to ~ in history** faire histoire comme matière principale

Majorca [mə'jɔːkə, *Am:* -jɔːr-] *n* Majorque *f*

majority [mə'dʒɒrəti, *Am:* -'dʒɔːrət̬i] *n* majorité *f;* **the great ~ of children** la grande majorité des enfants; **an overall ~** une majorité absolue

make [meɪk] **I.** <made, made> *vt* **1.** (*do*) faire; **to ~ coffee/soup/dinner** faire du café/de la soupe/le dîner; **I'll ~ you some tea** je te fais du thé; **to ~ time** trouver du temps; **to ~ sth (out) of sth** faire qc à partir de qc; **made of plastic/paper** en plastic/papier; **to show what one's (really) made of** *fig* montrer de quoi qn est fait; **to ~ a call** passer un coup de fil; **to ~ a decision** prendre une décision; **to ~ a start on sth** commencer qc **2.** (*create, change*) **to ~ sb curious/ill** rendre qn curieux/malade; **they made her vice-president** ils l'ont nommée vice-présidente; **to ~ sth easy/public** rendre qc facile/public; **that made the situation worse** ça a fait empirer les choses; **to ~ oneself useful/look ridiculous** se rendre utile/ridicule; **to ~ oneself heard/understood** se faire entendre/comprendre; **to ~ oneself known to sb** se présenter à qn **3.** (*earn, get: money, enemies*) se faire; **to ~ friends** se faire des ami(e)s; **to ~ profits/losses** faire des bénéfices/des pertes; **to ~ a living** gagner sa vie **4.** (*force, cause*) **to ~ sb/sth do sth** faire faire qc à qn; **to ~ sb change their mind** faire changer d'avis qn; **it ~s me feel sick** ça me rend malade **5.** *inf* (*get to, reach*) **to ~ it** y arriver; **I can't ~ it tomorrow** demain je ne peux pas; **to ~ it to sth** arriver à qc; **I made the team** j'ai été accepté dans l'équipe; **we made the final** on est arrivés en finale **6.** (*calculate, decide*) **I ~ it 5000** je trouve 5000; **we'll ~ it Friday/$30** disons vendredi/30$ ▸**to ~ sb's day** faire plaisir à qn; **to ~ the grade** y arriver; **to ~ sense** avoir du sens; **to ~ sense of sth** arriver à comprendre qc; **to ~ or break sb/sth** décider du sort de qn/qc; **to be made of money** rouler sur l'or **II.** *vi* aller; **to ~ towards sth** se diriger vers qc ▸**to ~ do with sth** faire avec qc; **to ~ as if to** *+infin form* sembler vouloir *+infin;* **to ~ like** *Am* faire comme si **III.** *n* marque *f* ▸**to be on the ~** *pej* en vouloir

◆**make believe** *vt* faire semblant

◆**make for** *vt* **1.** (*head for*) se diriger vers **2.** (*result in*) conduire à

◆**make of** *vt* **1.** (*understand, think of*) **to make sth of sb/sth** penser qc de qn/qc; **what do you ~ it?** qu'est-ce que tu en penses?; **can you make anything of it?** tu y comprends quelque chose? **2.** (*consider important*) **to make too much of sb/sth** accorder trop d'importance à qn/qc ▸**do you want to make something of it?** *inf* tu as quelque chose à redire?

◆**make off** *vi inf* se tirer; **to ~ with sth** partir avec qc

◆**make out I.** *vi inf* **1.** (*succeed, cope*) s'en sortir; **how are you making out?** tu t'en sors? **2.** (*have sex*) **to ~ with sb** se faire qn **II.** *vt* **1.** *inf* (*claim*) prétendre; **to make sb/sth out to be sth** faire passer qn/qc pour qc; **she makes herself out to be a genius** elle se fait passer pour un génie **2.** (*understand with difficulty*) distinguer; (*writing*) déchiffrer; *fig* discerner; **to make sb out** comprendre qn **3.** (*write: a cheque*) faire; **the cheque's made out to me** le chèque est à mon nom ▸**to ~ a case for sth** *Aus, Brit* présenter des arguments pour qc

◆**make over** *vt* **1.** LAW (*transfer ownership*) céder **2.** *Am* (*alter, convert*) **to ~ sth into sth** transformer qc en qc **3.** (*re-do, alter*) reprendre

◆**make up I.** *vt* **1.** (*compensate*) compenser; (*a deficit, loss*) combler; (*the time, ground*) rattraper; **I'll make it up to you** je tâcherai de me rattraper **2.** (*complete: a sum, team*) compléter; **to ~ the difference** payer la différence **3.** (*settle*) arranger; (*a dispute*) régler; **to make it up** se réconcilier **4.** (*comprise*) composer; **to ~ the majority of sth** former la majorité de qc; **to be made up of** (*people*) être composé de; (*things*) contenir **5.** (*put make-up on*) maquiller **6.** (*invent*) inventer **7.** (*prepare*) préparer **8.** PUBL mettre en pages **9.** (*decide*) **to ~ one's mind** se décider **II.** *vi* **1.** (*be friends again*) se réconcilier **2.** (*put on make-up*) se maquiller

◆**make up for** *vt* compenser; (*disappointment*) rattraper; **to ~ lost time** rattraper le temps perdu

◆**make up to** *vt Aus, Brit, pej* (*flatter*) flatter

make-believe *n no pl* illusion *f* **make-over** *n* **1.** (*beauty treatment*) soin *m* de beauté **2.** (*redecoration*) transformation *f*

maker *n* **1.** (*manufacturer*) fabricant(e) *m(f);* (*of a film*) réalisateur, -trice *m, f* **2.** (*God*) **to meet one's Maker** rencontrer son Créateur

makeshift I. *adj* de fortune **II.** *n* solution *f* provisoire

make-up *n* **1.** (*constitution*) constitution *f* **2.** (*character*) caractère *m* **3.** *no pl* (*cosmetics*) maquillage *m;* **to put on ~** se maquiller

make-up artist *n* maquilleur, -euse *m, f* **make-up remover** *n* démaquillant *m*

making *n* **1.** *no pl* (*production*) fabrication *f;* (*of a film*) tournage *m;* **to be in the ~** être en cours de fabrication **2.** *pl, fig* (*essential qualities*) étoffe *f* ▸**this is history in the ~** (*crisis, success*) c'est un moment d'histoire; **this is a disaster in the ~** il y a un désastre qui se prépare; **she is a star in the ~** c'est une vedette de demain; **to be the ~ of sb** former le caractère de qn; **to be of one's own ~** être de sa faute; **to have all the ~s of sth** avoir tous les ingrédients pour qc

maladjusted [ˌmæləˈdʒʌstɪd] *adj* PSYCH inadapté(e)

maladministration [ˈmælədˌmɪnɪˈstreɪʃən] *n no pl, form* mauvaise gestion *f*

maladroit [ˈmælədrɔɪt] *adj form* maladroit(e)

Malagasy [ˌmæləˈgæsi] **I.** *adj* malgache **II.** *n* **1.** (*person*) Malgache *mf* **2.** LING malgache *m;* *s. a.* **English**

malaise [mæˈleɪz] *n no pl* malaise *m*

malapropism [ˈmæləprɒpɪzəm, *Am:* -prɑːpɪ-] *n* LING *mot employé à la place d'un autre qui produit un effet comique involontaire*

malaria [məˈleərɪə, *Am:* -ˈlerɪ-] *n no pl* malaria *f*

Malawi [məˈlɑːwi] *n* Malawi *m*

Malawian I. *adj* malawite **II.** *n* Malawite *mf*

Malay [məˈleɪ, *Am:* ˈmeɪleɪ], **Malayan I.** *n* **1.** (*people*) Malais(e) *m(f)* **2.** LING malais *m;* *s. a.* **English II.** *adj* malais(e)

Malaysia [məˈleɪzɪə, *Am:* -ʒə] *n* la Malaisie

Malaysian I. *n* Malaisien(ne) *m(f)* **II.** *adj* malaisien(ne)

M

malcontent ['mælkəntənt] *n pej, form* mécontent(e)
Maldives ['mɔldi:vz, *Am:* 'mældaɪvz] *npl* les Maldives *fpl*
male [meɪl] **I.** *adj* (*animal*) mâle; (*person*) masculin(e); ~ **teachers** les profs hommes; **the** ~ **lead** l'acteur principal **II.** *n* **1.** (*person*) homme *m; pej* mâle *m;* ~**-dominated** (*society*) dominé(e) par les hommes; (*profession*) essentiellement masculin **2.** (*animal*) mâle *m*
male chauvinism *n* machisme *m* **male chauvinist pig** *n pej, inf* macho *m*
malediction [,mælɪ'dɪkʃən, *Am:* -ə'-] *n* malédiction *f*
male menopause *n* andropause *f*
malformation [,mælfɔ:'meɪʃən] *n* MED malformation *f*
malfunction [,mæl'fʌŋkʃən] **I.** *vi form* mal fonctionner **II.** *n* défaillance *f*
Mali ['mɑ:li] *n* le Mali
Malian **I.** *adj* malien(ne) **II.** *n* Malien(ne) *m(f)*
malice ['mælɪs] *n no pl* malveillance *f;* **to bear** ~ **to sb** vouloir du mal à qn
malicious *adj* **1.** (*bad: person*) malveillant(e) **2.** LAW délictueux(-euse); ~ **wounding** blessures *fpl* volontaires
malign [mə'laɪn] **I.** *adj form* pernicieux(-euse); (*spirits*) malin(-igne) **II.** *vt* calomnier
malignancy [mə'lɪgnənsi] *n* **1.** MED malignité *f* **2.** *fig* malveillance *f*
malignant *adj* **1.** MED malin(-igne) **2.** *fig* malveillant(e)
malinger [mə'lɪŋgə^r, *Am:* -gɚ] *vi pej* jouer aux malades
malingerer *n pej* faux malade *m,* fausse malade *f*
mall [mɔ:l] *n* centre *m* commercial
mallard ['mælɑ:d, *Am:* -ɚd] <-(s)> *n* colvert *m*
malleable ['mælɪəbl] *adj* malléable
mallet ['mælɪt] *n a.* SPORT maillet *m*
mallow ['mæləʊ, *Am:* -oʊ] *n* mauve *f*
malnutrition [,mælnju:'trɪʃən, *Am:* -nu:'-] *n no pl* malnutrition *f*
malodorous [,mæl'əʊdərəs, *Am:* -'oʊ-] *adj form* malodorant(e)
malpractice [,mæl'præktɪs] *n* faute *f* professionnelle; **medical** ~ faute *f* médicale
malt [mɔ:lt] **I.** *n no pl* **1.** (*grain*) malt *m* **2.** *s.* **malt whisky** **II.** *vt* malter
Malta ['mɔ:ltə, *Am:* -t̬ə] *n* Malte *f*

La **Republic of Malta**, qui fut de 1814 à 1947 une colonie britannique et une base navale, s'est fait connaître ces dernières années pour son "English language learning center" (centre linguistique de l'anglais). Ce sont avant tout des jeunes venus de toutes parts de l'Europe qui se rendent sur l'île, afin de prendre part à des cours d'anglais de grande renommée. Le plus souvent, les élèves en linguistique sont logés chez l'habitant. En été, ils peuvent participer à de nombreuses activités de plage. Dans la ville de Paceville, le soir, il y a un programme d'animation très varié spécialement organisé pour les jeunes gens.

Maltese [,mɔ:l'ti:z] **I.** *adj* maltais(e) **II.** *n* Maltais(e) *m(f)*
maltreat [,mæl'tri:t] *vt form* maltraiter
maltreatment *n no pl* mauvais traitement *m*
malt vinegar *n* vinaigre *m* de malt **malt whisky** *n* (whisky *m*) pur malt *m*
mama [mə'mɑ:, *Am:* 'mɑ:mə] *n* maman *f*
mammal ['mæməl] *n* mammifère *m*
mammalian *adj* mammifère
mammary *adj* mammaire
mammography [mæ'mɒgrəfi, *Am:* mə'mɑ:grə-] *n no pl* mammographie *f*
mammoth ['mæməθ] **I.** *adj* (*corporation*) monstre; (*undertaking*) gigantesque **II.** *n* mammouth *m*
man [mæn] <men> **I.** *n* **1.** (*male human*) homme *m;* **she married a Greek** ~ elle a éousé un Grec; **a lazy/rich** ~ un homme paresseux/riche **2.** *no pl* (*human race*) l'homme *m* **3.** (*object in games*) pion *m* ►**to talk (as)** ~ **to** ~ parler d'homme à homme; **a** ~ **to** ~ **talk** une discussion entre hommes; **as one** ~ comme un seul homme; **to a** ~ tous; **the** ~ **in the street** l'homme de la rue **II.** *vt* <-nn-> prendre la responsabilité de; **to** ~ **a ship** être membre de l'équipage d'un navire
manacle ['mænəkl] **I.** *n pl* menottes *fpl* **II.** *vt* (*chain*) passer les menottes à; **to** ~ **sb/sth to sth** menotter qn/qc à qc
manage ['mænɪdʒ] **I.** *vt* **1.** (*accomplish*) **to** ~ **to** *+infin* arriver à *+infin;* **I** ~**d to miss the plane** je me suis débrouillé pour rater l'avion; **how did you** ~ **that?** comment tu as fait?; **can you** ~ **six o'clock/the cooking?** six heures, ça vous va?; **can you** ~ **the cooking?** tu pourras t'occuper du repas? **2.** (*deal with*) *a.* ECON gérer **II.** *vi* (*cope*) s'en tirer; (*achieve aim*) réussir
manageable *adj* (*task*) faisable; (*vehicle*) manœuvrable; (*person*) docile
management *n* ECON gestion *f;* (*managers*) la direction; ~ **skills** compétences *fpl* de gestion
management accounting *n* comptabilité *f* de gestion
management buyout *n* rachat *m* d'entreprise (*par ses cadres*) **management consultant** *n* conseiller, -ère *m, f* en gestion d'entreprise **management studies** *n* études *fpl* en gestion d'entreprise
manager *n* **1.** (*person with control function*) manager *mf* **2.** (*of shop, project*) gérant(e) *m(f)* **3.** (*of artist*) manager *mf* **4.** SPORT entraîneur *mf*
manageress *n* gérante *f*
managerial *adj* directorial(e); ~ **position**

poste *m* de cadre; ~ **skills** qualités *fpl* de gestionnaire
managing director *n Brit* directeur *m* général
Mancunian [mæŋ'kju:niən, *Am:* mæn-] *n* habitant *m* de Manchester
mandarin[1] ['mændərɪn, *Am:* -dɚ-] *n* (*fruit*) mandarine *f*
mandarin[2], **Mandarin** ['mændərɪn, *Am:* -dɚ-] **I.** *n* mandarin *m* **II.** *adj* mandarin
mandate ['mændeɪt] **I.** *n* mandat *m* **II.** *vt* mandater
mandatory ['mændətri, *Am:* -tɔ:ri] *adj* obligatoire
mandible ['mændɪbl] *n* mandibule *f*
mandolin(e) ['mændəlɪn] *n* mandoline *f*
mane [meɪn] *n* crinière *f*
maneater *n* **1.** ZOOL mangeur *m* d'hommes **2.** *fig, inf* mangeuse *f* d'hommes
maneuver [mə'nu:vəʳ, *Am:* -vɚ] *n, vt, vi Am s.* **manoeuvre**
maneuverable [mə'nu:vərəbl] *adj Am s.* **manoeuvrable**
manganese ['mæŋgəni:z] *n no pl* manganèse *m*
mange [meɪndʒ] *n no pl* gale *f*
mangel ['mæŋgl], **mangel-wurzel** *n* betterave *f* fourragère
manger ['meɪndʒəʳ, *Am:* -dʒɚ] *n* mangeoire *f*
mangetout [mɑ̃:ʒ'tu:] *n Brit* mange-tout *m inv*
mangle[1] ['mæŋgl] *vt* **1.** (*ruin: person, limb*) mutiler; (*meat*) charcuter; (*clothes*) déchirer **2.** *fig* massacrer
mangle[2] ['mæŋgl] *n Brit* **1.** (*for clothes*) essoreuse *f* (à rouleaux) **2.** *Am* (*ironing machine*) repasseuse *f*
mango ['mæŋgəʊ, *Am:* -goʊ] *n* <-go(e)s> mangue *f*
mangrove ['mæŋgrəʊv, *Am:* 'mæŋgroʊv] *n* **1.** (*tree*) palétuvier *m* **2.** (*swamp*) mangrove *f*
mangy ['meɪndʒi] <-ier, -iest> *adj* **1.** (*suffering from mange*) galeux(-euse) **2.** *inf* (*overused, not clean*) miteux(-euse)
manhandle ['mænhændl] *vt* **1.** (*handle roughly*) brutaliser; **they ~d him into the car** ils l'ont forcé à entrer dans la voiture **2.** (*lift*) **to ~ sth somewhere** transporter qc quelque part à la force des bras
manhole ['mænhəʊl, *Am:* -hoʊl] *n* regard *m*
manhood ['mænhʊd] *n no pl* (*age*) l'âge *m* d'homme; (*manliness*) virilité *f*
man-hour ['mænaʊəʳ] *n* heure *f* de main-d'œuvre
manhunt ['mænhʌnt] *n* chasse *f* à l'homme
mania ['meɪnɪə] *n* **1.** PSYCH manie *f;* **persecution ~** délire *m* de persécution **2.** *pej* (*obsession*) manie *f;* **to have a ~ for buying shoes** avoir la folie des chaussures
maniac *n* **1.** *inf* (*fan*) fou *m*, folle *f;* **football ~** fou de football **2.** (*obsessive*) maniaque *mf;* **a ~ when it comes to punctuality** un maniaque de la ponctualité **3.** (*dangerous person*) fou *m*, folle *f*
maniacal *adj* **1.** (*maniac behaviour*) PSYCH maniaque **2.** *inf* (*crazy*) fou(folle)
manic ['mænɪk] *adj* **1.** PSYCH maniaque **2.** *inf* (*activity, laughter*) fou(folle)
manic depression *n* psychose *f* maniaco-dépressive **manic-depressive** *adj* maniaco-dépressif(-ive)
manicure ['mænɪkjʊəʳ, *Am:* -kjʊr] **I.** *n* manucure *f* **II.** *vt* manucurer; **to ~ one's nails** se faire les ongles
manicurist *n* manucure *mf*
manifest ['mænɪfest] **I.** *adj* manifeste **II.** *vt* révéler; **his cancer ~ed itself too rapidly** son cancer s'est manifesté trop rapidement
manifestation *n form* manifestation *f*
manifestly *adv* manifestement
manifesto [ˌmænɪ'festəʊ, *Am:* -toʊ] <-sto(e)s> *n* manifeste *m*
manifold ['mænɪfəʊld, *Am:* -foʊld] **I.** *n* TECH, AUTO tubulure *f* **II.** *adj* multiple
manipulate [mə'nɪpjʊleɪt, *Am:* -jə-] *vt* **1.** *pej* (*influence unfairly*) manipuler; (*statistics, figures*) trafiquer **2.** (*control with hands*) manœuvrer **3.** (*treat body with hands*) manipuler
manipulation *n* **1.** *pej* (*unfair influence*) manipulation *f;* **~s** manœuvres *f* **2.** *no pl* (*therapy*) manipulation *f*
manipulative *adj pej* manipulateur(-trice)
manipulator *n* manipulateur, -trice *m, f*
mankind [ˌmæn'kaɪnd] *n no pl* humanité *f*
manly <-ier, -iest> *adj* viril(e)
man-made *adj* artificiel(le); (*fibres*) synthétique
manned [mænd] *adj* AVIAT habité(e)
mannequin ['mænɪkɪn] *n* mannequin *m*
manner ['mænəʳ, *Am:* -ɚ] *n no pl* **1.** (*style*) manière *f* **the ~ in which she spoke/painted** sa manière de parler/peindre; **in a ~ of speaking** en quelque sorte **2.** *pl* (*social behaviour*) manières *fpl;* **to teach sb ~s** apprendre les bonnes manières à qn; **that's bad ~s** ce n'est pas des manières **3.** (*way of behaving*) façon *f* d'être **4.** *form* (*kind, type*) sorte *f;* **all ~ of ...** toutes sortes de ... ►**she does things as if to the ~ born** elle fait les choses comme si c'était naturel; **not by any ~ of means** *Brit* absolument pas
mannerism ['mænərɪzəm] *n* **1.** (*behaviour*) particularité *f* **2.** ART maniérisme *m*
manoeuvrable [mə'nu:vrəbl] *adj* manœuvrable
manoeuvre [mə'nu:vəʳ, *Am:* -vɚ] **I.** *n pl* (*military exercises*) manœuvres *fpl;* **on ~s** en manœuvres ►**to have room for ~** avoir de la marge (de manœuvre) **II.** *vt* **1.** (*move: vehicle*) manœuvrer; (*furniture*) déplacer; **to ~ sth through a door** faire passer qc par une porte **2.** (*pressure*) **to ~ sb into doing sth** forcer qn à faire qc; **to ~ sb into a compromise** amener

M

qn vers un compromis **III.** *vi* manœuvrer

manor ['mænəʳ, *Am:* -ɚ], **manor house** *n* **1.** (*house in country*) manoir *m* **2.** *Brit* HIST domaine *m* seigneurial; **lord of the ~** châtelain *m*

manpower ['mænpaʊəʳ, *Am:* -ɚ] *n no pl* main-d'œuvre *f*

manse [mæns] *n Scot* maison *f* du pasteur

manservant ['mænsɜːvənt, *Am:* -sɜːr-] *n* domestique *mf*

mansion ['mænʃən] *n* manoir *m*; **you live in a ~!** quel palace!

manslaughter ['mænslɔːtəʳ, *Am:* -slɑːt̬ɚ] *n no pl* homicide *m* involontaire

mantelpiece ['mæntlpiːs] *n* dessus *m* de cheminée

mantra ['mæntrə] *n* mantra *m*

manual ['mænjuəl] **I.** *adj* manuel(le) **II.** *n* **1.** (*book*) manuel *m* **2.** (*car*) voiture *f* à vitesses manuelles

manufacture [ˌmænjʊ'fæktʃəʳ, *Am:* -tʃɚ] **I.** *vt* **1.** (*produce*) manufacturer; **to ~ novels** *pej* fabriquer des romans **2.** (*fabricate: excuse, story*) fabriquer **II.** *n no pl* fabrication *f*

manufactured goods *n* produits *mpl* manufacturés

manufacturer *n* fabricant *m*; (*of cars*) constructeur *m*

manufacturing *adj* industriel(le); (*industry*) de fabrication

manure [mə'njʊəʳ, *Am:* -'nʊr] *n no pl* engrais *m*

manuscript ['mænjʊskrɪpt] *n* manuscrit *m*

Manx [mæŋks] **I.** *n* **1.** *pl* (*people*) habitants *mpl* de l'île de Man **2.** (*language*) mannois **II.** *adj* mannois(e)

many ['meni] <more, most> **I.** *adj* beaucoup de; **very ~ flowers** un très grand nombre de fleurs; **his ~ books** ses nombreux livres; **how ~ glasses?** combien de verres?; **too/so ~ people** trop/tellement de gens; **one chair too ~** une chaise en trop; **as ~ words/letters as** autant de mots/lettres que; **~ times** [*o* **a time**] souvent ►**~ happy returns!** joyeux anniversaire! **II.** *pron* beaucoup; **~ are here** un grand nombre sont ici; **I've read so/too ~** j'en ai tant/trop lu; **not ~ like it** peu l'apprécient; **one too ~** un de trop; **I saw ~ more** j'en ai vu un autre; *s. a.* **much III.** *n* **the ~** la masse

many-sided *adj* à plusieurs facettes

Maori ['maʊri] **I.** *n* **1.** (*people*) Maori *mf* **2.** LING maori *m*; *s. a.* **English II.** *adj* maori

map [mæp] **I.** *n* **1.** (*representation: of a country*) carte *f*; (*of a town, building, subway*) plan *m*; **a route ~** une carte routière **2.** RAIL carte *f* du réseau **3.** (*outline*) schéma *m* **4.** (*stars*) planisphère *m* ►**to blow sth off the ~** faire disparaître qc de la surface de la terre; **to put sth on the ~** faire connaître qc **II.** <-pp-> *vt* (*region*) dresser une carte de

◆**map out** *vt* (*process, policy*) faire le plan de; (*future, career*) prévoir; **his life was all mapped out** sa vie était toute tracée devant lui

maple ['meɪpl] *n* **1.** (*tree*) érable *m* **2.** *no pl* (*wood*) (bois *m* d')érable *m*

maple leaf *n* feuille *f* d'érable **maple sugar** *n no pl, Am* sucre *m* d'érable **maple syrup** *n no pl* sirop *m* d'érable

mar [mɑːʳ, *Am:* mɑːr] <-rr-> *vt* troubler; (*sb's enjoyment, day*) gâcher

marathon ['mærəθən, *Am:* 'merəθɑːn] **I.** *n* marathon *m* **II.** *adj* **1.** (*related to a marathon: race*) de marathon **2.** *fig* marathon *inv*; **~ negotiations** négociations-marathon *fpl*

marauding *adj* rôdeur(-euse)

marauder [mə'rɔːdəʳ, *Am:* -ɚ] *n* **1.** (*travelling criminal*) maraudeur, -euse *m, f* **2.** (*roving animal*) maraudeur *m*

marble ['mɑːbl, *Am:* 'mɑːr-] **I.** *n* **1.** *no pl* (*stone*) marbre *m*; **a ~ table** une table en marbre **2.** (*for games*) bille *f*; **~s** (*game*) billes ►**to lose one's ~s** *inf* perdre la boule **II.** *vt* marbrer

march [mɑːtʃ, *Am:* mɑːrtʃ] **I.** <-ches> *n* **1.** MIL, MUS marche *f*; **to be on the ~** être en marche; **to be within a day's ~** être à un jour de marche **2.** (*political action*) manifestation *f* **II.** *vi* **1.** MIL marcher en rang; **quick ~!** en marche! **2.** (*walk with determination*) marcher d'un pas décidé; **he ~ed up to me** il a marché sur moi **3.** (*to express opinions*) manifester; **to ~ against animal cruelty** défiler contre la cruauté envers les animaux **III.** *vt* **to ~ sb off** emmener qn

March [mɑːtʃ, *Am:* mɑːrtʃ] *n* mars *m*; *s. a.* **April**

marching orders *n* feuille *f* de route ►**to get one's ~** *Brit, inf* se faire mettre à la porte; **to give sb his ~** *Brit, inf* mettre qn à la porte

> **Mardi Gras** est l'équivalent américain de carnaval. Cette fête trouve son origine chez les colons français de New Orleans (dans l'État nommé plus tard Louisiane). Bien que la plupart des gens aujourd'hui fassent un parallèle entre "Mardi Gras" et New Orleans, cette fête est aussi célébrée à Biloxi/Mississippi et Mobile/Alabama. A New Orleans les "krewes" (sociétés carnevalesques) organisent pendant la saison de nombreuses fêtes et de nombreux bals ainsi qu'un très beau défilé pour mardi gras.

mare [meəʳ] *n* jument *f*

margarine [ˌmɑːdʒəriːn, *Am:* ˌmɑːrdʒɚɪn] *n no pl* margarine *f*

marge [mɑːdʒ, *Am:* mɑːrdʒ] *n Brit, inf abbr of* **margarine** margarine *f*

margin ['mɑːdʒɪn, *Am:* 'mɑːr-] *n* **1.** TYP marge *f* **2.** (*periphery of an area*) bord *m* **3.** *a.* SOCIOL, ECON marge *f*; **there's no ~ for error** nous n'avons pas de marge d'erreur; **to win by a narrow ~** gagner de justesse

marginal **I.** *adj* **1.** (*insignificant, very little*) marginal(e); (*interest, element, artist*)

mineur(e) **2.** (*written in margin: notes*) en marge **II.** *n Brit, Aus* siège *m* disputé
marginal constituency *n Brit, Aus* localité *f* disputée
marginalise *vt Brit, Aus,* **marginalize** ['mɑːdʒɪnəlaɪz, *Am:* 'mɑːr-] *vt* marginaliser
marginally *adv* légèrement
marguerite [ˌmɑːgər'iːt] *n* marguerite *f*
marigold ['mærɪgəʊld, *Am:* 'merɪgoʊld] *n* souci *m*
marihuana, **marijuana** [ˌmærɪ'wɑːnə, *Am:* ˌmerɪ'-] *n no pl* marihuana *f,* marijuana *f*
marina [mə'riːnə] *n* port *m* de plaisance
marinade [ˌmærɪ'neɪd, *Am:* ˌmer-] *n* GASTR marinade *f*
marinate ['mærɪneɪt, *Am:* 'mer-] *vt* mariner
marine [mə'riːn] **I.** *adj* **1.** (*concerning sea life*) marin(e) **2.** (*concerning shipping matters*) maritime **3.** (*concerning naval operations*) naval(e) **II.** *n* **1.** MIL marine *m* **2.** (*navy*) marine *f*
marionette [ˌmærɪə'net, *Am:* ˌmer-] *n* marionnette *f*
marital ['mærɪtəl, *Am:* 'merɪt̬əl] *adj* matrimonial(e); (*infidelity*) conjugal(e)
marital status *n form* situation *f* de famille
maritime ['mærɪtaɪm, *Am:* 'mer-] *adj form* maritime
marjoram ['mɑːdʒərəm, *Am:* 'mɑːrdʒɚəm] *n no pl* marjolaine *f*
mark¹ [mɑːk, *Am:* mɑːrk] *n* (*currency*) mark *m*
mark² [mɑːk, *Am:* mɑːrk] **I.** *n* **1.** (*spot, stain*) tache *f;* **finger ~** trace *f* de doigt **2.** (*scratch*) marque *f* **3.** (*feature*) trait *m;* **the ~ of genius** le signe du génie; **as a ~ of sth** en signe de qc **4.** (*written sign, signal*) marque *f;* **punctuation ~** signe *m* de ponctuation; **question ~** point *m* d'interrogation **5.** SCHOOL note *f* **6.** (*specified point*) **it costs around the $50 ~** ça coûte autour de 50$; **under the 5% ~** en-dessous de 5%; **it's over the 25 kilo ~** ça pèse plus que 25 kilos **7.** (*target*) cible *f;* **to hit the ~** toucher le but **8.** SPORT ligne *f* de départ; (*on your ~s*) à vos marques ►**to make one's ~ on sb/sth** laisser son empreinte sur qn/qc; **there are no ~s for guessing sth** il n'y a pas besoin d'être un génie pour deviner qc; **to be quick/slow off the ~** avoir l'esprit vif/lent; **to be up to the ~** être à la hauteur **II.** *vt* **1.** (*stain, spoil: clothes*) tacher; (*body*) faire des marques sur; (*wood, glass*) marquer **2.** (*show by sign or writing: name, price*) indiquer; (*distance, direction*) marquer; **to ~ one's name on one's clothing, to ~ one's clothing with one's name** marquer ses vêtements avec son nom; **the site is ~ed by a plaque** une plaque signale le site; **this sign ~s a danger** ce signe signale un danger **3.** (*constitute*) caractériser; (*beginning, end*) indiquer; (*time, a turning point*) marquer **4.** (*celebrate: occasion*) marquer; **they marked the anniversary with demonstrations** l'anniversaire a été commémoré par des manifestations **5.** *Am* (*clearly identify*) **to ~ sb as sth** repérer qn comme étant qc **6.** (*assess: homework*) noter **7.** SPORT marquer **8.** INFOR surligner ►**to ~ time** marquer le pas; (**you**) **~ my words!** faites bien attention à ce que je vous dis! **III.** *vi* (*stain*) tacher
◆**mark down** *vt* **1.** (*reduce: prices*) baisser; **to be marked down** (*shares*) s'inscrire à la baisse **2.** *Brit* SCHOOL **to mark sb down for spelling mistakes** baisser la note de qn à cause de l'orthographe
◆**mark off** *vt* **1.** (*divide: land*) délimiter; (*intervals*) marquer **2.** (*cross off*) rayer
◆**mark out** *vt* **1.** (*distinguish*) distinguer **2.** *Brit* (*indicate a boundary*) délimiter **3.** *Brit, Aus* (*clearly identify*) **to mark sb out as sth** souligner que qn est qc; **to mark sb out from sth** distinguer qn de qc
◆**mark up** *vt* (*increase*) augmenter
marked *adj* **1.** (*apparent, clear*) marqué(e) **2.** (*striking*) frappant(e); (*improvement*) sensible; (*accent*) prononcé(e); **to walk with a ~ limp** boîter de façon prononcée **3.** (*with distinguishing marks*) marqué(e); **to be a ~ man** être condamné
markedly *adv* d'une façon marquée; **to be ~ different** être nettement différent
marker *n* **1.** (*sign, symbol*) *a. fig* marque *f* **2.** (*sign to indicate position*) balise *f* **3.** (*examiner*) correcteur, -trice *m, f* **4.** INFOR marqueur *m* **5.** (*pen*) marqueur *m* **6.** SPORT marqueur, -euse *m, f* **7.** *fig* **to put down a ~** signaler ses intentions
marker pen *n* marqueur *m*
market ['mɑːkɪt, *Am:* 'mɑːr-] **I.** *n* marché *m;* **at the ~** au marché; **job ~** marché du travail; **to be in the ~ for sth** être acheteur de qc; **to put sth on the ~** mettre qc sur le marché; **to put a house on the ~** mettre une maison en vente; **there's a good ~ for sth** il y a une grosse demande pour qc; **the female ~** les consommatrices **II.** *vt* commercialiser; **you need to ~ yourself better** il faut que tu saches te vendre *subj*
marketable *adj* vendable; (*commodities*) commercialisable
market analyst *n* analyste *mf* de marché **market day** *n* jour *m* du marché **market economy** *n* économie *f* de marché **market forces** *n pl* les forces *fpl* du marché
marketing *n no pl* **1.** (*selling operations*) marketing *m* **2.** *Am* (*grocery shopping*) courses *fpl*
market leader *n* entreprise *f* en tête de marché **marketplace** *n* **1.** (*place for market*) place *f* du marché **2.** (*commercial arena*) arène *f* commerciale **market price** *n* prix *m* du marché **market research** *n* étude *f* de marché **market share** *n* part *f* de marché **market value** *n* valeur *f* marchande
markings *n pl* **1.** (*identifying marks*) marques *fpl;* (*on animals*) taches *fpl* **2.** (*on vehicle*)

M

insignes *mpl;* (*on roads*) signalisation *f*

marksman <-men> *n* tireur *m* d'élite **marksmanship** *n no pl* adresse *f* au tir

mark-up *n* (*profit*) marge *f* bénéficiaire; (*increase*) majoration *f*

marmalade ['mɑːməleɪd, *Am:* 'mɑːr-] *n no pl* confiture *f* d'oranges

marmot *n* marmotte *f,* siffleux *m Québec*

maroon[1] [mə'ruːn] **I.** *n* **1.** *no pl* (*colour*) bordeaux *m* **2.** (*firework*) fusée *f* de détresse **II.** *adj* bordeaux *inv*

maroon[2] [mə'ruːn] *vt* abandonner

marquee [mɑː'kiː, *Am:* mɑːr-] *n Brit, Aus* **1.** (*tent*) grande tente *f* **2.** *Am* (*canopy*) auvent *m*

marriage ['mærɪdʒ, *Am:* 'mer-] *n a. fig* mariage *m;* **related by** ~ parents par alliance

marriageable *adj* mariable; **to be of ~ age** être en âge de se marier

marriage bureau *n Brit* agence *f* matrimoniale **marriage ceremony** *n* cérémonie *f* du mariage **marriage certificate** *n* acte *m* de mariage **marriage guidance counsellor** *n Brit, Aus* conseiller, -ère *m, f* conjugal(e)

married **I.** *n pl* marié(e); **the young/ newly-~s** les jeunes/nouveaux mariés **II.** *adj* **1.** (*concerning marriage: couple*) marié(e); (*life*) conjugal(e) **2.** (*very involved*) **to be ~ to sth** être marié avec qc

marrow ['mærəʊ, *Am:* 'meroʊ] *n* **1.** *Brit, Aus* (*vegetable*) courge *f* **2.** MED moelle *f* ►**to be chilled to the ~** être gelé jusqu'à la moelle; **to be frightened to the ~** être mort de peur

marrowbone *n* os *m* à moelle

marry ['mæri, *Am:* 'mer-] **I.** *vt* **1.** (*wed officially*) épouser, marier *Belgique, Nord, Québec* **2.** (*officiate at ceremony*) marier **3.** (*organize wedding of*) marier **4.** *fig* (*associate*) marier ►**to ~ money** faire un mariage d'argent **II.** *vi* se marier; **to get married to sb** se marier avec qn

marsh [mɑːʃ, *Am:* mɑːrʃ] <-shes> *n* marais *m*

marshal ['mɑːʃl, *Am:* 'mɑːr-] **I.** <*Brit* -ll- *o Am* -l-> *vt* **1.** (*assemble: data*) rassembler; (*resources*) assembler **2.** (*control: demonstrators, soldiers*) rassembler; **to ~ one's forces** MIL rassembler les troupes; *fig* mobiliser ses troupes **II.** *n* **1.** (*at demonstration*) membre *m* du service d'ordre **2.** *Am* (*person heading parade*) chef *m* de file **3.** *Am* (*police officer*) officier *m* de la police fédérale **4.** MIL ~ **of the Royal Air Force** *Brit* Commandant *m* en Chef des Forces Aériennes **5.** *Am* (*police officer*) ≈ capitaine *m* de gendarmerie; (*fire officer*) ≈ capitaine *m* des pompiers

marshalling yard *n* gare *f* de triage

marshland ['mɑːʃlænd, *Am:* 'mɑːrʃ-] *n* région *f* marécageuse

marshmallow, marsh mallow ['mɑːʃmæləʊ, *Am:* 'mɑːrʃ-] *n* guimauve *f*

marshy ['mɑːʃi, *Am:* 'mɑːr-] <-ier, -iest> *adj* marécageux(-euse)

marsupial [mɑː'suːpɪəl, *Am:* mɑːr'-] *n* marsupial *m*

marten ['mɑːtɪn, *Am:* 'mɑːrtn] *n* mart(r)e *f*

martial ['mɑːʃəl, *Am:* 'mɑːr-] *adj* martial(e)

martial law *n* loi *f* martiale

Martian ['mɑːʃən, *Am:* 'mɑːr-] **I.** *adj* martien(ne) **II.** *n* (*being from Mars*) *a. pej* martien(ne) *m(f)*

martin ['mɑːtɪn, *Am:* 'mɑːrtn] *n* ZOOL martinet *m*

martinet [ˌmɑːtɪ'net, *Am:* ˌmɑːrtə'-] *n* **to be a ~** être intraitable sur la discipline

martini [mɑː'tiːni, *Am:* mɑːr-] *n* martini *m*

Martin Luther King's Birthday *n no pl, Am* HIST (*Jan 15*) anniversaire *m* de Martin Luther King

martyr ['mɑːtəʳ, *Am:* 'mɑːrt̬ɚ] **I.** *n* martyr(e) *m(f)* ►**to make a ~ of oneself** jouer au souffre-douleur; **to be a ~ to sth** souffrir cruellement de qc **II.** *vt* martyriser

martyrdom ['mɑːtədəm, *Am:* 'mɑːrt̬ɚ-] *n no pl* martyre *m*

marvel ['mɑːvl, *Am:* 'mɑːr-] **I.** *n* merveille *f;* **your're a ~** tu es formidable; **it's a ~ to me how ...** je ne sais vraiment pas comment ...; **it's a ~ to me that** je n'en reviens pas que *+subj;* **it's a ~ that** c'est un miracle que *+subj* **II.** <*Brit* -ll- *o Am* -l-> *vi* s'émerveiller; **to ~ at sb/sth** s'étonner de qn/qc **III.** *vt* **to ~ that** s'émerveiller que *+subj*

marvellous, **marvelous** *adj Am* merveilleux(-euse); **to feel ~** se sentir extraordinairement bien

Marxism ['mɑːksizm, *Am:* 'mɑːrk-] *n no pl* marxisme *m*

Marxist **I.** *n* marxiste *mf* **II.** *adj* marxiste

Maryland ['meərilænd, *Am:* 'merələnd] **I.** *n* le Maryland **II.** *adj* du Maryland

marzipan ['mɑːzɪpæn, *Am:* 'mɑːr-] *n no pl* pâte *f* d'amandes

mascara [mæ'skɑːrə, *Am:* -'skerə] *n no pl* mascara *m*

mascot ['mæskət, *Am:* -kɑːt] *n* mascotte *f;* **lucky ~** porte-bonheur *m*

masculine ['mæskjəlɪn] **I.** *adj* masculin(e); LING masculin **II.** *n* masculin *m*

masculinity *n no pl* masculinité *f*

mash [mæʃ] **I.** *n Brit, inf* purée *f* de pommes de terre **II.** *vt* écraser (en purée); **to ~ potatoes** passer les pommes de terre

MASH *n Am abbr of* **Mobile Army Surgical Hospital** unité *f* médicale de campagne

mashed potato *n* purée *f* de pommes de terre

mask [mɑːsk, *Am:* mæsk] **I.** *n a. fig* masque *m;* **as a ~ for sth** pour dissimuler qc **II.** *vt* masquer

masked *adj* masqué(e)

masochism ['mæsəkɪzəm] *n no pl* masochisme *m*

masochist *n* masochiste *mf*

mason ['meɪsn] *n* **1.** (*stoneworker*) tailleur *m* de pierre **2.** (*Freemason*) franc-maçon *m*

3. *Am* (*bricklayer*) maçon *m*
masonic [mə'sɒnɪk, *Am:* -'sɑːnɪk] *adj* maçonnique
masonry *n no pl* **1.** (*trade, stones*) maçonnerie *f* **2.** (*Freemasonry*) franc-maçonnerie *f*
masquerade [ˌmɑːskə'reɪd] **I.** *n* mascarade *f* **II.** *vi* **to** ~ **as sth** se déguiser en qc
mass [mæs] **I.** *n no pl* **1.** (*formless quantity, quantity of matter*) *a.* PHYS masse *f;* (*of persons*) foule *f* **2.** (*large quantity*) grande quantité *f;* (*of contradictions*) multitude *f;* (*of the people, population*) majorité *f;* ~**es of sth** des tonnes de qc; ~**es of people** des tas de gens **II.** *vi* s'amonceler; (*troops, demonstrators*) se masser **III.** *adj* (*large*) massif(-ive); (*widespread*) de masse
Massachusetts [ˌmæsə'tʃuːsɪts] **I.** *n* le Massachusetts **II.** *adj* du Massachusetts
massacre ['mæsəkə^r, *Am:* -kɚ] **I.** *n* **1.** (*killing of many people*) massacre *m* **2.** (*loss or defeat*) hécatombe *f* **II.** *vt a. fig* massacrer
massage ['mæsɑːdʒ, *Am:* mə'-] **I.** *n* massage *m;* **to give sb a** ~ masser qn **II.** *vt* **1.** (*rub*) masser **2.** (*modify: figures*) fignoler
massage parlour *n* salon *m* de massage
mass circulation *n* diffusion *f* de masse
masseur [mæ'sɜː^r, *Am:* -'sɜːr] *n* masseur, -euse *m, f*
masseuse [mæ'sɜːz] *n* masseuse *f*
massive ['mæsɪv] *adj* **1.** (*heavy, solid: rock*) massif(-ive) **2.** (*huge: amount*) énorme **3.** (*severe: attack, stroke*) foudroyant(e)
mass market **I.** *n* marché *m* de (la) grande consommation **II.** *vt* **to mass-market sth** commercialiser qc à grande échelle **mass media** *n* + *sing o. pl vb* **the** ~ les mass-médias *mpl* **mass meeting** *n* assemblée *f* **mass murder** *n* tuerie *f* **mass murderer** *n* tueur *m* fou **mass-produce** *vt* produire en série **mass production** *n* production *f* en série **mass psychology** *n* psychologie *f* de masse
mast¹ [mɑːst, *Am:* mæst] *n* **1.** NAUT mât *m* **2.** (*flag pole*) **at half-**~ ≈ en berne **3.** RADIO, TV pylône *m*
mast² [mɑːst, *Am:* mæst] *n* **1.** (*fruit of oak tree*) gland *m* **2.** (*fruit of beech tree*) faîne *f*
master **I.** *n* **1.** (*person in control*) maître(sse) *m(f);* **the** ~ (**of the house**) le maître de maison **2.** (*competent person*) maître *m;* **to be a** ~ **of sth** être un maître de qc; **dancing/singing** ~ professeur *m* de danse/de chant **3.** *Brit* (*schoolteacher: in primary school*) instituteur *m;* (*in secondary school*) professeur *m* **4.** (*manager of a college*) principal *m* **5.** (*title for a young man*) Monsieur *m* **6.** UNIV maître *m* ►**no man can serve two** ~**s** *prov* nul ne peut servir deux maîtres; **to be one's own** ~ être son propre maître **II.** *vt* **1.** (*have knowledge, control of*) maîtriser **2.** (*overcome*) surmonter
master-at-arms *n* maître *m* d'armes **master bedroom** *n* chambre *f* principale **master builder** *n* maître *m* maçon **master copy** <-pies> *n* original *m* **master disk** *n* disque *m* maître **master file** *n* fichier *m* principal
masterful *adj* **1.** (*authoritative*) magistral(e) **2.** (*skilful*) compétent(e) **3.** (*dominating*) plein(e) d'autorité
master key *n* passe-partout *m*
masterly *adj* magistral(e)
mastermind **I.** *n* **1.** (*expert*) spécialiste *mf* **2.** (*planner, organizer*) cerveau *m* **II.** *vt* orchestrer **Master of Arts** *n* **1.** (*university degree*) ≈ maîtrise *f* de lettres **2.** (*person*) ≈ maître *m* ès lettres **master of ceremonies** *n* maître *m* de cérémonie **Master of Science** **1.** (*university degree*) ≈ maîtrise *f* de sciences **2.** (*person*) ≈ maître *m* ès sciences
masterpiece *n* chef-d'œuvre *m*

> En Grande-Bretagne, **un Master's degree** est le plus souvent un grade académique que l'on obtient à la fin de ses études pour un travail de recherche scientifique ("dissertation"). Quelques uns de ses Master's degree sont: "MA" ("Master of Arts"), "MSc" ("Master of Science"), "MLitt" ("Master of Letters") et "MPhil" ("Master of Philosophy"). En Écosse cependant un "MA" est un premier diplôme académique.

masterstroke *n* tour *m* de main
master tape *n* bande *f* originale
mastery ['mɑːstəri, *Am:* 'mæstɚ-] *n no pl* maîtrise *f*
masticate ['mæstɪkeɪt] *vt* (*person*) mâcher; (*animal*) ruminer
mastication *n no pl* (*person*) mastication *f;* (*animal*) rumination *f*
masturbate ['mæstəbeɪt, *Am:* -tɚ-] **I.** *vi* se masturber **II.** *vt* masturber
masturbation *n no pl* masturbation *f*
mat [mæt] *n* **1.** (*floor protection*) tapis *m;* **bath** ~ tapis de bain; **beach** ~ natte *f* **2.** (*doormat*) paillasson *m* **3.** (*protection for furniture*) housse *f;* (*decorative*) napperon *m;* (**place**) ~ set *m* de table; (**table**) ~ dessous *m* de plat; (**beer**) ~ dessous *m* de verre **4.** (*covering*) revêtement *m*
match¹ [mætʃ] <-tches> *n* allumette *f;* **to put a** ~ **to sth** mettre le feu à qc
match² [mætʃ] **I.** *n* **1.** (*one of a pair*) pendant *m* **2.** (*partner*) **to be a good** ~ **for sb** bien aller avec qn; **to make a good** ~ être un bon parti **3.** (*competitor*) adversaire *mf* (valable); **to be a** ~ **for sb** être au niveau de qn; **to be no** ~ **for sb** ne pas faire le poids avec qn **4.** (*same colour*) quelque chose d'assorti; **to be a good** ~ **for sth** être bien coordonné avec qc **5.** SPORT match *m* ►**to have a slanging** ~ avoir une prise de bec **II.** *vi* (*clothes, colours*) être assortis; (*blood types*) correspondre; (*pieces of evidence*) être pareil; **two socks that** ~ deux chaussettes qui vont ensemble

M

III. *vt* 1.(*be a match for: clothes*) être assorti à; (*blood type, piece of evidence, specification, need*) correspondre à 2.(*find a match for: clothes*) trouver quelque chose d'assorti à; (*blood type, piece of evidence*) faire correspondre à; (*specification, need*) satisfaire; **to ~ skills to jobs** adapter les compétences aux métiers 3.(*equal: rival*) être à la hauteur de; (*achievement*) égaler; **we'll ~ your salary** vous recevrez le même salaire; **I can't ~ his experience** je n'ai pas son expérience

matchbox <-xes> *n* boîte *f* d'allumettes

matching *adj* correspondant(e); FASHION assorti(e)

matchless *adv* incomparable

matchmaker *n* entremetteur, -euse *m, f*

match point *n* SPORT balle *f* de match

matchstick *n* allumette *f*

mate¹ [meɪt] I. *n* 1. *Brit, Aus, inf* (*friend*) copain, -ine *m, f;* (*school*) camarade *mf;* (*at work*) collègue *mf* 2.(*sexual partner*) compagnon *m,* compagne *f* 3. BIO partenaire *mf* 4. *Brit, Aus, inf* (*form of address*) mon pote 5.(*assistant*) aide *mf;* **driver's ~** coéquipier, -ière *m, f* II. *vi* s'accoupler III. *vt* **to ~ sth with sth** accoupler qc avec qc

mate² [meɪt] I. *n* GAMES mat *m* II. *vt* faire échec et mat à

material [mə'tɪəriəl, *Am:* -'tɪri-] I. *n* 1.(*for making things, doing jobs*) *a. fig* matériau *m;* **raw ~s** matières *fpl* premières; (*building ~s*) matériaux de construction; **he's promotion ~** *fig* il a l'étoffe pour la promotion 2.(*cloth*) tissu *m* 3.(*documentation, sources*) matière *f* 4. *pl* (*equipment*) matériel *m;* **writing ~s** fournitures *fpl* de bureau; **teaching ~s** matériel *m* pédagogique II. *adj* 1.(*relating to the physical*) matériel(le) 2.(*important*) essentiel(le)

materialism *n no pl* matérialisme *m*

materialist *n* matérialiste *mf*

materialistic *adj* matérialiste

materialize *vi* 1.(*become fact*) se matérialiser; (*hope, dream*) se réaliser 2.(*take physical form*) se concrétiser 3.(*appear suddenly*) surgir; **he's not going to ~** il ne va pas venir

maternal [mə'tɜːnəl, *Am:* -'tɜːr-] *adj* maternel(le); **to be ~ towards sb** materner qn

maternity *n no pl* maternité *f*

maternity benefit *n* allocation *f* (de) maternité **maternity clinic** *n* maternité *f* **maternity dress** <-sses> *n* robe *f* de grossesse **maternity hospital** *n* maternité *f* **maternity leave** *n* congé *m* (de) maternité **maternity ward** *n* service *m* de maternité

matey ['meɪti, *Am:* -ṭi] I.<-ier, -iest> *adj Brit, Aus, inf* 1.(*sociable*) amical(e) 2.(*close*) copain(-ine) II.<-s> *n inf* mec *m*

math [mæθ] *n Am, inf abbr of* **mathematics** maths *fpl*

mathematical *adj* mathématique

mathematician *n* mathématicien(ne) *m(f)*

mathematics [ˌmæθə'mætɪks, *Am:* -'mæṭ-] *n + sing vb* mathématiques *fpl*

maths *n + sing vb, Brit, Aus, inf abbr of* **mathematics** maths *fpl*

matinee ['mætɪneɪ, *Am:* ˌmætən'eɪ] *n* matinée *f;* (*in the afternoon*) séance *f;* **a ~ performance** une matinée

mating *n* ZOOL accouplement *m*

mating season *n* ZOOL la saison des amours

matriarch ['meɪtrɪɑːk, *Am:* -ɑːrk] *n* matrone *f*

matriarchy *n* <-rchies> matriarcat *m*

matriculate [mə'trɪkjʊleɪt, *Am:* -jə-] *vi* (*enter university*) être admis à l'université

matriculation *n* UNIV inscription *f*

matrimony ['mætrɪməni, *Am:* -rəmoʊ-] *n no pl* mariage *m*

matrix ['meɪtrɪks] <-ixes *o* -ices> *n* (*mould*) *a.* MAT matrice *f*

matron ['meɪtrən] *n* 1.(*at boarding school*) intendante *f* 2.(*nurse*) infirmière *f* en chef 3. *Am* (*employee in prison*) gardienne *f* 4. *iron* (*middle-aged woman*) matrone *f*

matronly *adj iron* **a ~ figure** une vraie matrone

matt [mæt], **matte** *adj Am* mat(e)

matted *adj* enchevêtré(e); (*hair*) emmêlé(e); (*wool*) feutré(e)

matter ['mætəʳ, *Am:* 'mæṭɚ] I. *n* 1. *no pl, a. fig* (*substance*) matière *f* 2.(*subject*) sujet *m;* **the ~ in hand** le sujet en question 3.(*affair*) affaire *f;* **as a ~ of fact** en fait; **for that ~** d'ailleurs; **in this ~** à cet égard; **business ~s** affaires *fpl;* **a ~ of taste/opinion** une question de goût/point de vue; **a ~ for your parents** quelque chose qui concerne vos parents; **a ~ of minutes** une affaire de quelques minutes; **in a ~ of seconds** dans une poignée de secondes; **the truth of the ~** le fin mot de l'histoire 4. *pl* (*the situation*) choses *fpl;* **as ~s stand** au point où en sont les choses; **to make ~s worse** pour arranger les choses; **to take ~s into one's own hands** prendre les choses en mains 5.(*problème*) **the ~** le problème; **what's the ~ (with you)?** qu'y a t-il? 6.(*importance*) **no ~!** peu importe!; **no ~ what** peu importe ce que *+subj;* **no ~ who/what/where** qui/quoi/où que ce soit *subj;* **no ~ how** de n'importe quelle manière II. *vi* importer; **it doesn't ~ if ...** cela n'a pas d'importance si ...; **it ~s that** il importe que *+subj*

matter-of-fact *adj* 1.(*straightforward*) terre-à-terre 2.(*emotionless: style*) prosaïque

mattress ['mætrɪs] *n* matelas *m*

mature [mə'tjʊəʳ, *Am:* -'tʊr] I. *adj* 1.(*adult or full grown*) mûr(e); (*animal*) adulte; (*tree*) adulte 2.(*experienced: person, attitude*) mûr(e); (*work*) de maturité 3. *form* (*very thoughtful*) réfléchi(e); **after ~ consideration** après mûre réflexion 4.(*payable*) arrivé(e) à terme II. *vi* 1.(*become physically adult*) devenir adulte 2.(*develop fully*) mûrir; (*wine*) vieillir 3.(*become payable*) arriver à terme III. *vt*

1. GASTR affiner 2. (*make more adult*) faire mûrir
mature student *n Brit* étudiant(e) *m(f)* plus âgé(e)
maturity *n no pl* 1. (*result of becoming mature*) maturité *f* 2. FIN échéance *f*
maudlin ['mɔːdlɪn, *Am:* 'mɑːd-] *adj* 1. (*melancholic*) mélancolique 2. (*drunken*) ivre aux larmes
maul [mɔːl, *Am:* mɑːl] *vt* 1. (*beat*) blesser grièvement; (*animal*) maltraiter 2. (*criticize: person*) éreinter; (*thing*) démolir

> **Maundy Thursday** est le jeudi saint lors de la "Holy week" (semaine sainte). Ce jour là, le monarque distribue le "Maundy money" à des personnes âgéees élus. Le nombre de personnes choisies est celui de l'âge du monarque et chacun acquiert un lot de pièces d'argent gravées spécialement pour cette occasion.

Mauritania [ˌmɒrɪ'teɪniə, *Am:* ˌmɔːrɪ'-] *n* la Mauritanie
Mauritian I. *adj* mauricien(ne) II. *n* Mauricien(ne) *m(f)*
Mauritius [mə'rɪʃəs, *Am:* mɔː'rɪʃiəs] *n* (l'île *f*) Maurice
mausoleum [ˌmɔːsə'liːəm, *Am:* ˌmɑː-] *n* mausolée *m*
mauve [məʊv, *Am:* moʊv] *adj* mauve
maverick ['mævərɪk, *Am:* 'mævɚ-] *n* 1. (*unorthodox person*) non-conformiste *mf* 2. *Am* ZOOL **male ~** bouvillon *m;* **female ~** génisse *f*
mawkish ['mɔːkɪʃ, *Am:* 'mɑː-] *adj* extravagant(e)
max [mæks] *n abbr of* **maximum** max *m*
maxi *n inf* (*dress*) robe *f* longue
maxim ['mæksɪm] *n* maxime *f*
maximize *vt* 1. (*extend*) maximiser 2. INFOR (*window*) agrandir
maximum ['mæksɪməm] I. <-ima *o* -imums> *n* maximum *m;* **up to a ~ of 500** jusqu'à un maximum de 500 II. *adj* maximum; **~ temperatures** températures maximales
may [meɪ] *<3rd pers. sing* may, might, might> *aux* 1. *form* (*be allowed*) **~ I come in ?** puis-je entrer ?; **if I ~ just say this** si je peux me permettre de dire ceci 2. (*possibility*) **I may go/finish** je pourrais partir/finir; **she ~ well return** il se pourrait bien qu'elle revienne ▸**that's as ~ be** cela se peut (bien); **be that as it ~** quoi qu'il en soit
may [meɪ] *n* aubépine *f*
May [meɪ] *n* (*month*) mai *m; s. a.* **April**
maybe *adv* 1. (*perhaps*) peut-être; **~ he'll stop** il va peut-être s'arrêter 2. (*approximately*) environ 3. (*suggestion*) **~ we should stop** on devrait peut-être s'arrêter
Mayday *n* mayday *m*
May Day *n no pl* (*May 1*) 1er mai *m*

> **May Day** n'est jamais férié, mais le lundi qui suit le premier dimanche de mai.

mayfly ['meɪflaɪ] *n* éphémère *f*
mayhem ['meɪhem] *n no pl* désordre *m;* **to create ~** semer la pagaille
mayonnaise [ˌmeɪə'neɪz] *n* mayonnaise *f*
mayor [meə^r, *Am:* meɪɚ] *n* maire *m,* maïeur *m Belgique,* président *m Suisse* (*dans les cantons de Valais et de Neuchâtel*)
mayoress [meə'res, *Am:* 'meɪɚɪs] <-sses> *n* mairesse *f*
maypole ['meɪpəʊl, *Am:* -poʊl] *n mât de fête du 1er Mai*
maze [meɪz] *n* dédale *m*
mb *n abbr of* **millibar** mbar. *m*
Mb *n abbr of* **megabyte** Mo *m*
MBA [ˌembiː'eɪ] *n abbr of* **Master of Business Administration** MBA *m*
MC [ˌem'siː] *n* 1. *abbr of* **Master of Ceremonies** maître *m* de cérémonie 2. *abbr of* **Medical Corps** corps *m* médical 3. *Am abbr of* **Member of Congress** membre *mf* du congrès 4. *abbr of* **Military Cross** croix *f* militaire
MD [ˌem'diː] *n* 1. *abbr of* **managing director** directeur *m* général 2. *Am, Aus abbr of* **Doctor of Medicine** Docteur *m* en Médecine
me [miː] *objective pron* me, m' + *vowel,* moi *tonic form;* **it's ~** c'est moi; **look at ~** regarde/regardez-moi; **she saw ~** elle m'a vu; **he told ~ that ...** il m'a dit que ...; **he'll give sth to ~** il va me donner qc; **older than ~** plus vieux que moi
meadow ['medəʊ, *Am:* -oʊ] *n* pré *m*
meadowland *n* prairie *f*
meager *adj Am,* **meagre** ['miːgə^r, *Am:* -gɚ] *adj* maigre
meal^1^ [miːl] *n* repas *m;* **come for a ~** viens dîner ▸**to make a ~ of sth** faire un plat de qc
meal^2^ [miːl] *n* 1. (*coarsely ground grain*) semoule *f* 2. (*flour*) farine *f*
mealtime *n* heure *f* du repas
mealy *adj* farineux(-euse)
mealy-mouthed *adj* mielleux(-euse)
mean^1^ [miːn] *adj* 1. (*miserly*) avare; **to be ~ with sth** être avare de qc 2. (*unkind, aggressive*) méchant(e); **to be ~ to sb** être méchant envers qn; **to have a ~ streak** avoir un côté mauvais; **to play a ~ trick on sb** jouer un sale tour à qn 3. (*wretched*) misérable; **the ~ streets** les bas quartiers 4. *fig* (*poor*) pauvre 5. *inf* (*excellent*) excellent(e) ▸**to be no ~ feat** ne pas être une mince affaire
mean^2^ [miːn] <meant, meant> *vt* 1. (*express meaning*) signifier; **it ~s "hello" in Arabic** ça veut dire "salut" en arabe; **what do you ~ by that?** qu'est-ce que tu veux dire?; **I ~ that** je suis sérieux; **I ~ (to say)** vraiment 2. (*refer to*) parler de; **do you ~ me?** tu veux dire moi? 3. (*result in*) impliquer; **that ~s we'll have to start again** ce qui veut dire

qu'il faut recommencer; **this ~s war** c'est la guerre **4.** (*have significance*) **it ~s a lot to me** c'est important pour moi **5.** (*intend, suppose*) **to ~ to** +*infin* avoir l'intention de +*infin;* **I didn't ~ to upset you** je ne voulais pas te faire de peine; **to be ~t to be sth** être destiné à qc; **to be ~t for sb** (*money, letter*) être destiné à qn; (*person*) être fait pour qn; **you were ~ to be here** tu étais supposé être là; **to ~ well** avoir de bonnes intentions

mean³ [mi:n] **I.** *n* **1.** (*middle*) milieu *m* **2.** MAT moyenne *f* **II.** *adj* moyen(ne)

meander [mɪ'ændəʳ, *Am:* -dɚ] **I.** *n* méandre *m* **II.** *vi* **1.** (*wander*) flâner **2.** (*digress: speaker*) faire une digression **3.** (*flow in curves*) serpenter

meanie [mi:ni] *n inf* **to be a ~ 1.** (*miserly person*) être mesquin **2.** (*unkind person*) être vache

meaning *n* **1.** (*signification*) signification *f;* **do you get my ~?** tu vois ce que je veux dire? **2.** (*interpretation*) interprétation *f* **3.** (*significance, value*) sens *m;* **to have a special ~ for sb** être particulièrement important pour qn ►**what is the ~ of this?** qu'est-ce que cela veut dire?

meaningful *adj* **1.** (*important or serious*) pertinent(e); (*relationship*) sérieux(-euse) **2.** (*implying something*) entendu(e) **3.** (*worthwhile*) sérieux(-euse)

meaningless *adj* **1.** (*without sense*) dépourvu(e) de sens **2.** (*with little importance*) insignifiant(e) **3.** (*vague*) vague

meanness *n no pl* **1.** (*lack of generosity*) avarice *f* **2.** (*unkindness*) méchanceté *f*

means *n* **1.** (*method*) moyen *m;* **a ~ of persuading people** un moyen de persuader les gens **2.** *pl* (*income*) moyens *mpl;* **a person of ~** une personne qui a les moyens ►**a ~ to an end** un moyen de parvenir à ses fins; **the end justifies the ~** *prov* la fin justifie les moyens; **not to be sth by any ~** être loin d'être qc; **by all ~** certainement; **by no ~** en aucun cas

means test *n* évaluation *f* des ressources **means-test** *vt* (*person*) évaluer les ressources de

meant [ment] *pt, pp of* **mean**

meantime *n* **for the ~** pour l'instant; **in the ~** pendant ce temps(-là) **meanwhile** *adv* entre-temps

measles ['mi:zlz] *n + sing vb* rougeole *f*

measly ['mi:zli] *adj pej* minable

measurable *adj* mesurable; (*great*) remarquable

measure ['meʒəʳ, *Am:* -ɚ] **I.** *n* **1.** (*measurement, unit, system*) mesure *f* **2.** (*set amount, portion*) mesure *f;* (*alcohol*) dose *f;* **half ~** demi-mesure *f* **3.** (*instrument*) mètre *m;* (*ruler*) règle *f;* (*container*) verre *m* doseur **4.** (*degree*) part *f;* **in great ~** en grande partie; **a ~ of success** un certain succès **5.** (*proof, indication*) preuve *f* **6.** *fig* (*plan, action*) mesure *f;* **to take ~s** prendre des mesures ►**for good ~** en plus; **to get the ~ of sb** jauger qn **II.** *vt* **1.** (*judge size*) mesurer; **to ~ sb** prendre les mesures de qn **2.** (*stating size*) mesurer; **to ~ six metres by two metres** mesurer six mètres sur deux **3.** *fig* (*consider: one's strength*) mesurer; (*one's words*) peser **4.** (*judge*) juger **III.** *vi* mesurer

◆**measure out** *vt* mesurer

◆**measure up I.** *vt* **1.** (*measure*) mesurer; (*person*) prendre les mesures de **2.** *fig* jauger **II.** *vi* être à la hauteur; **to ~ to sb/sth** être à la hauteur de qn/qc; **how does it ~ to her last book?** est-ce aussi bon que son dernier livre?

measured *adj* (*voice, tone*) mesuré(e); (*step*) compté(e); (*response*) contrôlé(e)

measurement *n* **1.** *no pl* (*measuring*) mesure *f* **2.** *pl* (*size details*) mensurations *fpl;* **to take sb's ~s** prendre les mesures de qn

measuring jug *n* verre *m* gradué

meat [mi:t] *n* **1.** *no pl* (*flesh of animals*) viande *f* **2.** *pl* (*flesh of person*) chair *f* **3.** *no pl* (*edible parts: of fish*) chair *f; Am* (*of fruit*) chair *f* **4.** *no pl* (*subject matter*) substance *f* ►**to be ~ and drink to sb** être du pain béni pour qn; **one man's ~ is another man's poison** *prov* le malheur des uns fait le bonheur des autres

meatball *n* boulette *f* de viande **meatloaf** *n* gâteau *m* de viande **meat pie** *n* tourte *f* à la viande **meat products** *n* produits *mpl* carnés

meaty *adj* **1.** (*consisting of meat: taste, smell*) de viande **2.** (*large, strong: person*) charnu(e) **3.** (*full of substance*) *a. fig* substantiel(le)

Mecca ['mekə] *n* la Mecque; **a ~ for sb/sth** *fig* un paradis pour qn/qc

mechanic [mɪ'kænɪk] *n* mécanicien(ne) *m(f)*

mechanical *adj* **1.** (*relating to machines: failure, problem, reliability*) mécanique; **~ engineer/engineering** ingénieur en mécanique *mf;* **~ engineering** la mécanique **2.** (*technical*) technique **3.** (*by machine*) mécanisé(e) **4.** (*machine-like*) machinal(e)

mechanics *n + sing v, a. fig* rouages *fpl*

mechanism ['mekənɪzəm] *n* **1.** (*working parts*) mécanisme *m* **2.** (*method*) procédé *m;* **defence ~** système *m* de défense

mechanize ['mekənaɪz] *vt* mécaniser; (*troops*) motoriser

medal ['medl] *n* médaille *f*

medalist *n Brit,* **medallist** *n Am* médaillé(e) *m(f)*

medallion [mɪ'dælɪən, *Am:* mə'dæljən] *n* médaillon *m*

meddle ['medl] *vi* intervenir; **to ~ in sth** se mêler de qc; **to ~ with sth** fourrer son nez dans qc

meddlesome ['medlsəm] *adj* indiscret(-ète)

media ['mi:diə] **I.** *n* **the ~** les médias *mpl* **II.** *adj* des médias; (*coverage*) médiatique; **~ studies** études *fpl* de communication

media coverage *n* couverture *f* médiatique
mediaeval [ˌmedi'iːvəl] *adj s.* **medieval**
media event *n* événement *m* médiatique
media magnate *n* magnat *m* de la presse
median ['miːdiən] *adj* **1.** (*average*) moyen(ne) **2.** MAT, TECH médian(e)
mediate ['miːdɪeɪt] **I.** *vi* **to ~ between sb and sb** servir de médiateur entre qn et qn **II.** *vt* arbitrer; (*settlement*) négocier
mediation [ˌmiːdɪ'eɪʃən] *n no pl* médiation *f*
mediator *n* médiateur, -trice *m, f*
medic ['medɪk] *n inf* **1.** (*doctor*) toubib *m* **2.** (*medical student*) étudiant(e) *m(f)* en médecine
Medicaid ['medɪkeɪd] *n no pl, Am: organisme prenant en charge les dépenses de santé des personnes de moins de 65 ans vivant en-dessous du seuil de pauvreté*
medical ['medɪkəl] **I.** *adj* médical(e); **to take ~ advice** demander conseil à un médecin **II.** *n inf* visite *f* médicale
medical examination *n* visite *f* médicale
Medicare ['medɪkeəʳ, *Am:* -ker] *n Am: régime d'assurance maladie*
medication [ˌmedɪ'keɪʃən] <-(s)> *n* médication *f;* **to be taking ~ for sth** suivre un traitement pour qc
medicinal *adj* médicinal(e); (*properties*) thérapeutique; **~ drug** médicament *m*
medicine ['medsən, *Am:* 'medɪsən] *n* **1.** (*drug*) médicament *m;* **cough ~** médicament contre la toux **2.** *no pl* (*science, practice*) médecine *f;* **herbal ~** phytothérapie *f* ►**to give sb a dose of their own ~** rendre la monnaie de sa pièce à qn; **to take one's ~** avaler la pilule
medicine cabinet *n* armoire *f* à pharmacie
medicine man <-men> *n* guérisseur, -euse *m, f*
medieval [ˌmedɪ'iːvl, *Am:* ˌmiːdɪ-] *adj a. pej* moyenâgeux(-euse); (*literature*) du Moyen-Âge
mediocre [ˌmiːdɪ'əʊkəʳ, *Am:* -'oʊkɚ] *adj* médiocre
mediocrity [ˌmiːdɪ'ɒkrəti, *Am:* -'ɑːkrət̬i] *n no pl* médiocrité *f*
meditate ['medɪteɪt] *vi* méditer
meditation *n no pl* méditation *f*
Mediterranean [ˌmedɪtə'reɪniən] **I.** *adj* méditerranéen(ne) **II.** *n* **1. the ~** la Méditerranée **2.** (*person*) méditerranéen(ne) *m(f)*
Mediterranean Sea *n* mer *f* Méditerranée
medium ['miːdiəm] **I.** *adj* **1.** (*average*) moyen(ne) **2.** GASTR (*steak*) à point **3.** (*size*) medium *inv* **II.** *n* **1.** <-s *o* media> (*a means*) moyen *m;* **through the ~ of dance/radio** par l'intermédiaire de la danse et de la radio **2.** (*middle state, midpoint*) milieu *m;* **to find a happy ~** trouver le juste milieu **3.** (*art material, form*) matériau *m* **4.** PUBL, TV média *m;* **advertising ~** organe *m* de publicité; **print ~** presse *f* écrite **5.** <-s> (*spiritualist*) médium *m* **6.** (*environment*) milieu *m* **7.** INFOR support *m*
medium-dry *adj* demi-sec *inv* **medium-length** *adj* FASHION (qui arrive) au genou **medium-range** *adj* MIL de moyenne portée **medium-rare** *adj* GASTR à point **medium-sized** *adj* de taille moyenne **medium-term** *adj* à moyen terme **medium wave** *n Brit* RADIO onde *f* moyenne
medley ['medli] *n* **1.** (*mixture*) mélange *m* **2.** (*mixture of tunes*) pot-pourri *m*
meek [miːk] **I.** *adj* doux(douce) **II.** *n* REL **the ~** les humbles
meet [miːt] <met, met> **I.** *vt* **1.** (*encounter*) rencontrer; (*an enemy*) affronter; **to ~ sb face to face** se trouver nez à nez avec qn; **to ~ sb's glance** croiser le regard de qn **2.** (*by arrangement*) retrouver **3.** (*make the acquaintance of*) faire la connaissance de **4.** (*fulfil: standard, need*) répondre à; (*costs*) prendre en charge; (*deadline*) respecter; (*obligation*) remplir; (*challenge*) relever **5.** (*counter: accusation*) recevoir ►**to ~ one's death** trouver la mort; **there's more to this than ~s the eye** c'est moins simple que ça en a l'air; **to make ends ~** joindre les deux bouts; **to ~ one's Waterloo** essuyer une défaite irréversible; **to ~ sb halfway** couper la poire en deux **II.** *vi* **1.** (*encounter*) se rencontrer **2.** (*assemble*) se réunir **3.** SPORT, MIL s'affronter **4.** (*get acquainted*) faire connaissance **5.** (*join*) se rejoindre; (*eyes*) se rencontrer; **we met in Paris** on s'est connus à Paris **III.** *n* **1.** *Am* (*sporting event*) rencontre *f* **2.** *Brit* (*fox hunt*) rendez-vous *m* de chasse
◆**meet up** *vi* **we met up in Paris, I met up with him in Paris** je l'ai retrouvé à Paris
◆**meet with** *vt* rencontrer; (*failure*) essuyer; (*success*) remporter; (*reaction*) être reçu avec
meeting *n* **1.** (*organized gathering*) réunion *f,* épluchette *f Québec;* **to have a ~ with sb** avoir une réunion avec qn **2.** *Brit* (*sporting event*) rencontre *f* **3.** (*act of coming together*) rencontre *f;* **a ~ of minds** une entente profonde
meeting place *n* lieu *m* de rencontre **meeting point** *n* point *m* de rendez-vous
megabyte ['megəbaɪt] *n* INFOR méga-octet *m*
megahertz ['megəhɜːts, *Am:* -hɜːrts] *n* mégahertz *m*
megalomania [ˌmegələ'meɪnɪə, *Am:* -oʊ'-] *n no pl* mégalomanie *f*
megalomaniac **I.** *n* mégalomane *mf* **II.** *adj* mégalomane
megaphone ['megəfəʊn, *Am:* -foʊn] *n* mégaphone *m*
megastore ['megəstɔːʳ, *Am:* -stɔːr] *n* grande surface *f*
megawatt ['megəwɒt, *Am:* -wɑːt] *n* mégawatt *m*
melancholic *adj form* mélancolique
melancholy ['melənkɒli, *Am:* -kɑːli] **I.** *n* <-lies> mélancolie *f* **II.** *adj* mélancolique

M

La **Melbourne Cup** (coupe), qui a toujours lieu le premier mardi de novembre, est la course hippique australienne la plus appréciée. Ce jour de course, on observe pendant trois minutes un arrêt total de toutes les activités dans toute l'Australie, car tous les travailleurs suivent la course soit à la télévision, soit à la radio. Des millions de dollars sont pariés; et dans tout le pays, on s'habille comme pour une fête et on déguste à midi du poulet au champagne.

melee ['meleɪ, *Am:* 'meɪleɪ] *n* mêlée *f*
mellow ['meləʊ, *Am:* -loʊ] **I.** <-er, -est *o* more ~, most ~> *adj* **1.** (*not harsh*) *a. fig* doux(douce) **2.** (*matured: character*) mûri(e) **II.** *vi a. fig* s'adoucir **III.** *vt a. fig* adoucir
melodic [mə'lɒdɪk, *Am:* mə'lɑːdɪk] *adj* mélodique
melodious [mɪ'ləʊdiəs, *Am:* mə'loʊ-] *adj* mélodieux(-euse)
melodrama ['melədrɑːmə, *Am:* -oʊ-] *n* mélodrame *m*
melodramatic [ˌmelədrə'mætɪk, *Am:* -oʊdrə'mæt̬-] *adj* mélodramatique
melody ['melədi] <-odies> *n* mélodie *f*
melon ['melən] *n* melon *m*
melt [melt] **I.** *vi* fondre **II.** *vt a. fig* fondre
◆melt away *vi* (*snow*) fondre; (*worries, people*) disparaître
meltdown ['meltdaʊn] *n* fusion *f*
melting point *n* point *m* de fusion **melting pot** *n fig* melting-pot *m;* **cultural** ~ creuset *m* culturel
member ['membəʳ, *Am:* -bɚ] *n* membre *m;* ~ **of Parliament/Congress** membre du Parlement/du Congrès; ~**s of the public** membres du public
membership I. *n* **1.** + *sing or pl vb* (*people*) membres *mpl* **2.** (*state of belonging*) adhésion *f;* **to enlarge** ~ **of the EU** agrandir l'UE **II.** *adj* d'adhésion; **annual** ~ **fee** cotisations *fpl* annuelles **membership card** *n* carte *f* d'adhérent
membrane ['membreɪn] *n* membrane *f*
memento [mɪ'mentəʊ, *Am:* mə'mentoʊ] <-s *o* -es> *n* mémento *m*
memo ['meməʊ, *Am:* -oʊ] *n abbr of* **memorandum** mémo *m;* **to send** (**out**) **a** ~ **to sb** faire passer une note à qn
memoir ['memwɑːʳ, *Am:* -wɑːr] *n* **1.** (*essay*) mémoire *m;* (*of the town*) histoire *f* **2.** (*autobiography*) ~(**s**) mémoires *fpl*
memo pad *n* bloc-notes *m*
memorabilia [ˌmemərə'bɪlia] *n pl* souvenirs *mpl*
memorable ['memərəbl] *adj* mémorable
memorandum [ˌmemə'rændəm] <-s *o* -anda> *n* **1.** *form* (*message*) note *f* **2.** (*document*) mémorandum *m* **3.** LAW protocole *m*
memorial [mə'mɔːriəl] *n* mémorial *m;* **as a** ~ **to sb** à la mémoire de qn
Memorial Day *n no pl* journée *f* du souvenir (*fin mai aux USA et début juillet au Canada*) **memorial service** *n* office *m* commémoratif
memorize ['meməraɪz] *vt* **1.** (*commit to memory*) mémoriser **2.** (*learn by heart*) apprendre par cœur
memory ['meməri] *n* **1.** (*ability to remember*) mémoire *f;* **a** ~ **for names/numbers** une mémoire des noms/chiffres; **from** ~ de mémoire; **to have a** ~ **like an elephant** avoir une mémoire d'éléphant; **to commit sth to** ~ apprendre qc par cœur; **in** ~ **of sb/sth** en souvenir de qn/qc; **if my** ~ **serves me right** si ma mémoire est bonne **2.** (*remembered event*) souvenir *m* **3.** INFOR mémoire *f*
memory bank *n* INFOR bloc *m* de mémoire **memory capacity** *n* INFOR capacité *f* de mémoire **memory chip** *n* INFOR puce *f* mémoire **memory dump** *n* INFOR vidage *m* de mémoire **memory expansion card** *n* INFOR carte *f* d'extension de mémoire **memory management** *n* INFOR gestion *f* de mémoire **memory protection** *n* INFOR protection *f* de mémoire
men [men] *n pl of* **man**
menace ['menəs] **I.** *n* **1.** (*threat*) menace *f;* **to demand money with** ~**s** extorquer de l'argent sous la menace **2.** (*danger*) menace *f* **II.** *vt form* menacer
menacing *adj* menaçant(e)
mend [mend] **I.** *n* raccommodage *m* **2.** *inf* **to be on the** ~ aller mieux **II.** *vt* **1.** (*repair*) réparer; (*socks*) repriser **2.** (*improve*) corriger ►**to** ~ **ones fences with sb** *prov* se réconcilier avec qn; **to** ~ **one's ways** s'amender **III.** *vi a. fig* se remettre; (*wound*) guérir
menial ['miːnɪəl] *adj* servile
meningitis [ˌmenɪn'dʒaɪtɪs, *Am:* -t̬ɪs] *n no pl* méningite *f*
menopause ['menəpɔːz, *Am:* -pɑːz] *n no pl* ménopause *f*
men's room ['menzˌruːm] *n Am* toilettes *fpl* pour hommes
menstrual ['menstrʊəl, *Am:* -strəl] *adj form* menstruel(le)
menstruate ['menstrʊeɪt, *Am:* -stru-] *vi form* avoir ses règles
menstruation *n no pl, form* menstruation *f*
mental ['mentəl, *Am:* -t̬əl] *adj* **1.** (*related to the mind: age, health*) mental(e) **2.** *Brit, inf* (*crazy*) fou(folle); **to be** ~ **about sth** être complètement fou de qc
mental block *n* blocage *m* **mental hospital** *n* hôpital *m* psychiatrique
mentality [men'tæləti, *Am:* -t̬i] *n* mentalité *f*
mentally *adv* mentalement; ~ **stable** équilibré(e); ~ **deranged** déséquilibré(e)
mentally handicapped *adj* handicapé(e) mental(e)
mention ['menʃən] **I.** *n* mention *f;* **no** ~ **was**

made of sb/sth il n'a pas été fait mention de qn/qc; **to receive a (special) ~** être reconnu **II.** *vt* mentionner; **you never ~ed having a brother!** tu ne m'avais pas dit que tu avais un frère!; **to ~ sth in passing** signaler qc en passant; **don't ~ it!** il n'y a pas de quoi!; **not to ~ ...** sans parler de ...

mentor ['mentɔːʳ, *Am:* -tɚ] *n* mentor *m*

menu ['menjuː] *n* GASTR, INFOR menu *m;* **context/pull-down ~** menu contextuel/déroulant; **~-bar** barre *f* de menu; **what's on the ~ today?** *fig* qu'est-ce qui est au programme aujourd'hui?

menu-driven *adj* INFOR piloté(e) par menu

MEP [ˌemiːˈpiː] *n abbr of* **Member of the European Parliament** député(e) *m(f)* au Parlement européen

mercenary ['mɜːsɪnəri, *Am:* 'mɜːrsəner-] **I.** *n* <-aries> mercenaire *m* **II.** *adj pej* mercenaire

merchandise ['mɜːtʃəndaɪz, *Am:* 'mɜːr-] *n no pl, form* marchandises *fpl*

merchandizing *n* merchandising *m*

merchant ['mɜːtʃənt, *Am:* 'mɜːr-] **I.** *n* **1.** (*trader*) négociant(e) *m(f)* **2.** (*retailer*) commerçant(e) *m(f)* **II.** *adj* marchand(e)

merchant bank *n* banque *f* d'affaires **merchant navy** *n* marine *f* marchande **merchant ship** *n* navire *m* marchand

merciful ['mɜːsɪfəl, *Am:* 'mɜːr-] *adj* (*God*) miséricordieux(-euse); (*sentence*) clément(e)

merciless ['mɜːsɪlɪs, *Am:* 'mɜːr-] *adj pej* impitoyable

mercury ['mɜːkjʊri, *Am:* 'mɜːrkjəri] *n no pl* (*metal*) mercure *m*

Mercury ['mɜːkjʊri, *Am:* 'mɜːrkjəri] *n no art, no pl* Mercure *m*

mercy ['mɜːsi, *Am:* 'mɜːr-] *n no pl* pitié *f;* REL miséricorde *f;* **to have ~ on sb** avoir pitié de qn; **to show no ~** ne montrer aucune compassion; **to be at the ~ of sb** être à la merci de qn; **to throw oneself upon sb's ~** s'en remettre à la merci de qn; **to plead for ~** demander grâce

mere [mɪəʳ, *Am:* mɪr] *adj* simple; **it costs a ~ $500** ça ne coûte que 500$

merely ['mɪəli, *Am:* 'mɪr-] *adv* simplement; **she ~ smiled at me** elle s'est contentée de me sourire

merge [mɜːdʒ, *Am:* mɜːrdʒ] **I.** *vi* **1.** (*join*) se (re)joindre **2.** ECON fusionner **3.** (*fade*) **to ~ into sth** se fondre dans qc **4.** (*blend*) **to ~ into/with sth** se mêler à qc **II.** *vt* **1.** (*unify*) unifier **2.** ECON fusionner

merger *n* ECON fusion *f*

meridian [məˈrɪdɪən] *n* méridien *m*

meringue [məˈræŋ] *n* meringue *f*

merit ['merɪt] **I.** *n* **1.** (*virtue*) valeur *f* **2.** (*advantage*) mérite *m;* **to judge sb on his own ~s** juger qn en fonction de ses mérites; **to consider each case on its own ~s** juger au cas par cas **II.** *vt form* mériter

meritocracy [ˌmerɪˈtɒkrəsi, *Am:* -əˈtɑːkrə-] <-acies> *n* méritocratie *f*

mermaid ['mɜːmeɪd, *Am:* 'mɜːr-] *n* sirène *f*

merriment ['merɪmənt] *n no pl* gaieté *f*

merry ['meri] *adj* **1.** (*happy*) joyeux(-euse); **Merry Christmas** Joyeux Noël **2.** *Brit, inf* (*slightly drunk*) pompette

merry-go-round *n* manège *m*

mesh [meʃ] **I.** *n no pl* **1.** (*net*) maille *f;* **wire ~** treillis *m* **2.** *fig* réseau *m* **II.** *vi* **1.** (*join: gears*) s'engrener **2.** (*be in harmony*) concorder **III.** *vt* (*gears*) engrener

mesmerize ['mezməraɪz] *vt* hypnotiser

mess [mes] **I.** *n* **1.** (*not tidy*) bazar *m,* margaille *f Belgique;* **to be in a ~** être en fouillis; **to make a ~** faire un chantier; **your work is a real ~** ton travail est fait n'importe comment **2.** (*dirty*) **to make a ~ on sth** salir qc **3.** (*trouble*) **to get oneself into a (bit of a) ~** se mettre dans de beaux draps; **to make a ~ of sth** massacrer qc **4.** (*animal excrement*) crotte *f* **5.** *Brit* (*officer's eating hall*) mess *m* **II.** *vt inf* **1.** (*make untidy*) **to ~ sth (up)** mettre du désordre dans qc **2.** (*botch up*) **to ~ sth (up)** gâcher qc **III.** *vi* **1.** (*be silly*) faire l'imbécile **2.** manger au mess

◆**mess about, mess around** *vi* (*have fun*) s'amuser; **to ~ with sth** faire l'imbécile avec qc; **it saves us messing about with buses** ça nous évite les embêtements des bus

◆**mess with** *vt* (*tools, machinery*) faire l'imbécile avec; (*drugs*) toucher à; **don't ~ me** ne me provoque pas

message ['mesɪdʒ] *n a.* INFOR message *m*

messenger ['mesɪndʒəʳ, *Am:* -dʒɚ] *n* messager, -ère *m, f;* (*in offices*) coursier, -ière *m, f*

messiah [məˈsaɪə] *n* messie *m;* **the Messiah** le Messie

messy ['mesi] <-ier, -iest> *adj* **1.** (*untidy: room*) désordonné(e); (*presentation*) brouillon(ne); (*clothes*) débraillé(e) **2.** (*dirty*) sale **3.** *fig* **it's a ~ business** c'est une sale embrouille

met [met] **I.** *pt of* **meet II.** *adj Brit, inf s.* **meterological**

met. *adj abbr of* **meteorological** météo *inv*

metabolic *adj* métabolique

metabolism [mɪˈtæbəlɪzəm] *n* métabolisme *m*

metal ['metl, *Am:* 'meṭ-] *n* métal *m*

metal detector *n* détecteur *m* de métaux

metallic [mɪˈtælɪk, *Am:* məˈ-] *adj* **1.** (*metal like*) métallique; (*paint*) métallisé(e); *fig* (*sound*) métallique **2.** (*consisting of metal*) en métal; **~ alloy** métal *m* allié

metallurgy [mətˈælədʒi, *Am:* 'məṭəlɜːr-] *n no pl* métallurgie *f*

metalwork *n* travail *m* des métaux **metalworker** *n* ferronnier, -ère *m, f*

metamorphosis [ˌmetəˈmɔːfəsɪs, *Am:* ˌmeṭəˈmɔːrfə-] <-oses> *n* métamorphose *f*

metaphor ['metəfəʳ, *Am:* 'meṭəfɔːr] *n* métaphore *f*

metaphorical *adj* métaphorique

M

metaphysical *adj* métaphysique
metaphysics [ˌmetəˈfɪzɪks, *Am:* ˌmeţ-] *n no pl* métaphysique *f*
mete out *vt* infliger
meteor [ˈmiːtiəʳ, *Am:* -ţiɚ] *n* météore *f;* ~ **shower** averse *f* météorique
meteoric *adj* **1.** (*pertaining to meteors*) météorique **2.** (*extremely rapid*) fulgurant(e)
meteorite [ˈmiːtiəraɪt, *Am:* -ţi-] *n* météorite *m o f*
meteorological *adj* météorologique
meteorologist *n* météorologiste [*o* météorologue] *mf*
meteorology [ˌmiːtiəˈrɒlədʒi, *Am:* -əˈrɑːlə-] *n no pl* météorologie *f*
meter¹ [ˈmiːtəʳ, *Am:* -ţɚ] **I.** *n* compteur *m;* (**parking**) ~ parcmètre *m* **II.** *vt* (*gas, water*) mesurer au compteur
meter² [ˈmiːtəʳ, *Am:* -ţɚ] *Am s.* **metre**
methane [ˈmiːθeɪn, *Am:* ˈmeθeɪn] *n* méthane *m*
method [ˈmeθəd] *n* méthode *f;* ~ **of payment** méthode de paiement ▶**there's** ~ **in his madness** ce n'est pas aussi fou que ça en a l'air
method acting *n* THEAT méthode *f* de Stanislavski
methodical *adj* méthodique
Methodist **I.** *n* méthodiste *mf* **II.** *adj* méthodiste
methodology [ˌmeθəˈdɒlədʒi, *Am:* -ˈdɑːlə-] *n* méthodologie *f*
methylated spirits *n no pl, Aus, Brit* alcool *m* à brûler
meticulous [mɪˈtɪkjʊləs] *adj* méticuleux(-euse); **to be** ~ **about sth** être très méticuleux avec qc
metre [ˈmiːtəʳ, *Am:* -ţɚ] *n* **1.** (*unit of measurement*) mètre *m;* **cubic/square** ~ mètre *m* cube/carré **2.** (*poetic rhythm*) mesure *f*
metric [ˈmetrɪk], **metrical** *adj* métrique
metro [ˈmetrəʊ, *Am:* -roʊ] *n* métro *m*
metronome [ˈmetrənəʊm, *Am:* -noʊm] *n* métronome *m*
metropolis [məˈtrɒpəlɪs, *Am:* -ˈtrɑːpəl-] *n form* métropole *f*
metropolitan [ˌmetrəˈpɒlɪtən, *Am:* -ˈpɑːlə-] *adj* métropolitain(e); **the** ~ **police** *Brit* la police de Londres
mettle [ˈmetl, *Am:* ˈmeţ-] *n no pl, form* courage *m;* **to show one's** ~ montrer de quoi on est capable; **to be on one's** ~ être au meilleur de sa forme
mew [mjuː] **I.** *n* miaulement *m* **II.** *vi* miauler
Mexican **I.** *adj* mexicain(e) **II.** *n* Mexicain(e) *m(f)*
Mexico [ˈmeksɪkəʊ, *Am:* -koʊ] *n* le Mexique
Mexico City *n* Mexico
mezzanine [ˈmetsəniːn, *Am:* ˈmez-] *n* ~ (**floor**) mezzanine *f*
Mg *n abbr of* **magnesium** Mg *m*
MHR *n Am abbr of* **Member of the House of Representatives** membre *mf* de la Chambre des représentants
MHz *n abbr of* **megahertz** MHz. *m*
miaow [miːˈaʊ] **I.** *n* miaulement *m* **II.** *vi* miauler
mica [ˈmaɪkə] *n no pl* mica *m*
mice [maɪs] *n pl of* **mouse**
mickey [ˈmɪki] *n Aus, Brit, inf* **to take the** ~ **out of sb** se payer la tête de qn
Mickey Mouse [ˌmɪkiˈmaʊs] *n* Mickey *m*
Michigan [ˈmɪʃɪgən] **I.** *n* le Michigan **II.** *adj* du Michigan
microbe [ˈmaɪkrəʊb, *Am:* -kroʊb] *n* microbe *m*
microbiology *n no pl* microbiologie *f* **microchip** *n* puce *f* (électronique) **micro climate** *n* microclimat *m* **microcomputer** *n* INFOR micro-ordinateur *m* **microcosm** *n* microcosme *m* **microelectronics** *n no pl* microélectronique *f* **microfiche** *n* microfiche *f* **microfilm** *n* microfilm *m* **micrometer** *n* **1.** (*measuring device*) micromètre *m* **2.** *Am s.* **micrometre**
micron *n s.* **micrometre**
Micronesia [ˌmaɪkrəʊˈniːziə, *Am:* -kroʊˈniʒə] *n* la Micronésie
Micronesian **I.** *adj* micronésien(ne) **II.** *n* Micronésien(ne) *m(f)*
micro-organism *n* micro-organisme *m*
microphone [ˈmaɪkrəfəʊn, *Am:* -foʊn] *n* microphone *m*
microprocessor *n* INFOR microprocesseur *m*
microscope [ˈmaɪkrəskəʊp, *Am:* -skoʊp] *n* microscope *m*
microscopic *adj* microscopique
microwave [ˈmaɪkrəʊweɪv, *Am:* -kroʊ-] **I.** *n* **1.** (*oven*) micro-ondes *m* **2.** (*short wave*) micro-onde *f* **II.** *vt* faire cuire au micro-ondes
microwave oven *n* four *m* à micro-ondes
mid [mɪd] **in** ~-**spring** au milieu de l'été; **she's in her** ~ **sixties** elle a autour de soixante-cinq ans
midair *n* **in** ~ en l'air; **a** ~ **collision** une collision aérienne
mid-air **I.** *n* **in** ~ en plein air **II.** *adj* en plein air
midday [ˌmɪdˈdeɪ] *n* midi *m inv, no art;* **at** ~ à midi, entre l'heure de midi *Belgique;* **for my** ~ **meal** pour mon repas de midi
middle [mɪdl] **I.** *n sing* **1.** *a. fig* (*centre*) milieu *m;* **in the** ~ **of sth** au milieu de qc; **in the** ~ **of 2002** au milieu de l'année 2002; **to be in the** ~ **of doing sth** être en train de faire qc; **in the** ~ **of nowhere** *pej* en pleine pampa **2.** *inf* (*waist*) taille *f* **II.** *adj* **1.** (*in the middle*) du milieu; **in my** ~ **forties** quand j'avais autour de quarante-cinq ans **2.** (*intermediate*) moyen(ne)
middle age *n* ≈ cinquantaine *f* **middle-aged** *adj* d'une cinquantaine d'années **Middle Ages** *n* **the** ~ le Moyen-Âge **Middle America** *n* l'Amérique moyenne **middlebrow** *adj* (*programme, muis*) accessible; (*viewers*) moyen(ne) **middle-class**

adj de classe moyenne; *pej* bourgeois(e) **middle class, middle classes** *npl* **the** ~ classe *f* moyenne; *pej* la bourgeoisie; **the upper/lower** ~ la haute bourgeoisie/bourgeoisie **Middle East** *n* **the** ~ le Moyen-Orient **middleman** <-men> *n* intermédiaire *m* **middle management** *n* les cadres *mpl* moyens **middle name** *n* deuxième prénom *m;* **reliable is my** ~ fiable, c'est moi **middle-of-the-road** *adj* **1.**(*moderate*) modéré(e) **2.** *pej* (*boring*) moyen(ne) **middleweight** *n* SPORT poids *m* moyen

middling ['mɪdlɪŋ] *adj inf* **1.**(*average, not very good*) moyen(ne) **2.**(*moderate*) modéré(e)

Mideast *s.* **Middle East**

midge [mɪdʒ] *n pl, a. fig* moustique *m*

midget ['mɪdʒɪt] **I.** *adj* miniature **II.** *n* nain(e) *m(f)*

midlife crisis *n* crise *f* aux alentours de la cinquantaine

midnight I. *n no pl* minuit *m;* **at** ~ à minuit **II.** *adj* de minuit ▸**to burn the** ~ **oil** travailler jusqu'au beau milieu de la nuit **midpoint** *n sing a.* MAT centre *m* **midriff** *n* taille *f* **midshipman** <-men> *n Brit, Am* enseigne *m* de vaisseau

midst [mɪdst] *n no pl* **in the** ~ **of** au milieu de qc

midsummer *n* **1.** *no pl* (*middle part of summer*) cœur *m* de l'été; **in** ~ en plein été **2.**(*solstice*) solstice *m* d'été **Midsummer('s) Day** *n* solstice *m* d'été **midterm** *n no pl* **1.** POL (*middle of period of office*) milieu *m* de mandat; ~ **election/poll** élection/sondage en cours de mandat **2.**(*middle of a term*) UNIV, SCHOOL milieu *m* de trimestre; ~ **tests** examens de mi-trimestre **midway I.** *adv* à mi-chemin **II.** *n Am* champ *m* de foire **midweek** *n no pl* milieu *m* de la semaine **midwife** <-wives> *n* sage-femme *f* **midwifery** *n no pl* obstétrique *f* **midwinter** *n no pl* **1.**(*middle of winter*) milieu *m* de l'hiver **2.**(*solstice*) solstice *m* d'hiver

miffed [mɪft] *adj inf* vexé(e)

might[1] [maɪt] **I.** *pt of* **may II.** *aux* **1.**(*expressing possibility*) **sb/sth** ~ *+infin* qn/qc pourrait *+infin;* **sb/sth** ~ **have done sth** qn/qc aurait pu faire qc; **she** ~ **not win** elle pourrait ne pas gagner; **it** ~ **have been ...** ça aurait pu être ...; **are you coming? – I** ~ est-ce que tu viens? – Peut-être **2.** *Brit, form* (*polite form of may*) ~ **I ...?** pourrais-je ...? **3.**(*reproachfully*) ~ **I ask/know** est-ce que je pourrais demander/savoir; **you** ~ **have called** tu aurais pu appleler; **you** ~ **have known that ...** tu aurais dû te douter que ... **4.** *form* (*politely make suggestion*) ~ **I suggest ...?** pourrais-je suggérer ...?; ~ **I make a suggestion?** pourrais-je me permettre de faire une suggestion? ▸**you** ~ **as well do sth** tant qu'à faire, tu devrais faire qc

might[2] [maɪt] *n no pl* **1.**(*authority*) pouvoir *m* **2.**(*strength*) MIL force *f* ▸**with all one's** ~ de toutes ses forces

mighty I. <-ier, -iest> *adj* puissant(e) **II.** *adv Am, inf* sacrément

migraine ['mi:greɪn, *Am:* 'maɪ-] <-(s)> *n* migraine *f*

migrant ['maɪgrənt] **I.** *n* migrant(e) *m(f);* ZOOL oiseau *m* migrateur **II.** *adj* (*worker*) migrant(e)

migrate [maɪ'greɪt, *Am:* '-] *vi* (*animals, things*) migrer; (*persons*) émigrer; **to** ~ **to sth** (é)migrer vers qc

migration <-(s)> *n* migration *f*

migratory ['maɪgrətri, *Am:* -tɔ:r-] *adj* **1.**(*related to migration: phenomenon, movement*) migratoire **2.**(*migrating: bird, people*) migrateur(-trice)

mike [maɪk] *n inf abbr of* **microphone** micro *m*

mild [maɪld] **I.** <-er, -est> *adj* **1.**(*not severe or intense: annoyance, shock*) petit(e); (*climate, day*) modéré(e); (*day*) tempéré(e); (*asthma, infection*) sans gravité; (*cigarette, criticism, increase*) léger(-ère); (*curry, flavour*) doux(douce) **2.**(*in character*) doux(douce); **to be of a** ~ **disposition** avoir bon caractère **II.** *n no pl, Brit* bière *f* douce

mildew ['mɪldju:, *Am:* -du:] *n no pl* mildiou *m*

mildly *adv* **1.**(*gently*) gentiment **2.**(*slightly*) légèrement ▸**to put it** ~ c'est le moins qu'on puisse dire

mild-mannered *adj* calme

mildness *n no pl* douceur *f*

mile [maɪl] *n* mile *m;* **for** ~**s and** ~**s** sur des kilomètres ▸**to be better by** ~**s** être mille fois mieux; **to be** ~**s away** être à des lieues; (*lost in thought*) j'étais dans la lune; **to stick** [*o* **stand**] **out a** ~ crever les yeux

mileage ['maɪlɪdʒ] *n no pl* **1.**(*travelling expenses*) frais *fpl* de déplacement **2.**(*distance traveled*) distance *f* parcourue en miles; **it gives good** ~ elle ne consomme pas beaucoup ▸**to get** ~ **out of sth** tirer bon profit de qc

mileometer [maɪ'lɒmɪtəʳ, *Am:* -'lɑ:məţɚ] *n Aus, Brit* compteur *m* de miles

milestone ['maɪlstəʊn, *Am:* -stoʊn] *n* **1.**(*roadside distance marker*) borne *f* kilométrique **2.** *fig* (*significant event*) événement *m* marquant

militant ['mɪlɪtənt] **I.** *adj* militant(e) **II.** *n a.* POL militant(e) *m(f)*

militarism ['mɪlɪtərɪzəm, *Am:* -tɚ-] *n no pl* militarisme *m*

militarist *n* militariste *mf*

militaristic *adj* militariste

militarize ['mɪlɪtəraɪz] *vt* militariser

military ['mɪlɪtri, *Am:* -ter-] **I.** *n* **the** ~ l'armée *f* **II.** *adj* militaire

military academy *n* école *f* militaire

militate *vi* **to** ~ **against sth** devenir un

M

obstacle à

militia [mɪ'lɪʃə] *n* milice *f*

milk [mɪlk] **I.** *n no pl* lait *m;* **full fat** ~ lait entier; **long-life** ~ lait longue conservation; **semi-skimmed/skimmed** ~ lait demi-écrémé/écrémé ▶**it's no use crying over spilt** ~ ce qui est arrivé est arrivé **II.** *vt* **1.**(*extract milk*) traire **2.**(*take money from*) soutirer de l'argent à **3.**(*exploit: story, situation*) tirer avantage de

milk bar *n* **1.**(*snack bar*) milk-bar *m* **2.** *Aus* (*shop*) crémerie *f* **milk chocolate** *n* chocolat *m* au lait **milk float** *n Brit* véhicule *m* de laitier **milking machine** *n* trayeuse *f* **milkman** <-men> *n Brit* laitier *m* **milk powder** *n* lait *m* en poudre **milk product** *n* produit *m* laitier **milk run** *n* vol *m* de routine **milkshake** *n* milk-shake *m;* **strawberry** ~ un milk-shake à la fraise **milk tooth** *n* dent *f* de lait

milky <-ier, -iest> *adj* laiteux(-euse)

Milky Way *n no pl* **the** ~ la voie lactée

mill [mɪl] **I.** *n* **1.**(*building or machine*) moulin *m;* **coffee/pepper** ~ moulin à café/à poivre **2.**(*factory*) usine *f* ▶**to put sb through the** ~ en faire baver à qn **II.** *vt* **1.**(*grind*) mouliner **2.**(*shape: metal*) travailler **III.** *vi* **to** ~ (**about** [*o* **around**]) fourmiller

millennium [mɪ'lenɪəm] <-s *o* -ennia> *n* millénaire *m*

millennium bug *n* INFOR bogue *m* de l'an 2000

miller *n* meunier, -ière *m, f*

millet ['mɪlət] *n no pl* millet *m*

millibar *n* millibar *m* **milligram(me)** *n* milligramme *m* **milliliter** *n Am,* **millilitre** *n* millilitre *m* **millimeter** *n Am,* **millimetre** *n* millimètre *m*

million ['mɪlɪən, *Am:* '-jən] <-(s)> *n* **1.**(*a thousand thousand*) million *m;* **eight** ~ **people** huit millions de personnes; ~**s of people/things** des millions de gens/de choses **2.** *inf*(*countless number*) millier *m;* ~**s of things** des milliers de choses; **a** ~ **times** des milliers de fois; **to be one in a** ~ être unique **3.**(*money*) million *m;* **to make** ~**s** faire des millions ▶**to feel like a** ~ **dollars** [*o Am* **bucks**] se sentir merveilleusement bien

millionaire [ˌmɪlɪə'neəʳ, *Am:* -'ner] *n* millionnaire *mf*

millipede ['mɪlɪpiːd] *n* mille-pattes *m*

millpond *n* réservoir *m* de moulin; **the sea was like a** ~ c'était une mer d'huile **millstone** *n* meule *f* ▶**to be a** ~ **around sb's neck** être un fardeau pour qn **mill wheel** *n* roue *f* de moulin

mime [maɪm] **I.** *n* **1.**(*silent body movements*) mime *m* **2.**(*play without speech*) pantomime *f* **3.**(*artist*) mime *mf* **II.** *vi* faire des mimiques; **to** ~ **to a song** chanter en play-back **III.** *vt* mimer

mimic ['mɪmɪk] <-ck-> **I.** *vt* imiter **II.** *n* imitateur, -trice *m, f*

mimicry ['mɪmɪkri] *n no pl* imitation *f;* BIO mimétisme *m*

mimosa [mɪ'məʊzə, *Am:* -'moʊsə] *n* mimosa *m*

min. *n* **1.** *abbr of* **minute** min. *f* **2.** *abbr of* **minimum** min. *m*

minaret [ˌmɪnə'ret] *n* minaret *m*

mince [mɪns] **I.** *vt* hacher ▶**not to** ~ **one's words** ne pas mâcher ses mots **II.** *vi* marcher à petits pas **III.** *n no pl, Aus, Brit* viande *f* hachée

mincemeat *n no pl* **1.** *Brit: hachis de fruits secs en compote* **2.** *inf* **to make** ~ **of sb** faire de qn de la chair à saucisses **mince pie** *n tartelette farcie de mincemeat, consommée à Noël*

mincer *n* hachoir *m*

mincing *adj* (*tone*) affecté(e); (*behaviour, gesture*) maniéré(e)

mind [maɪnd] **I.** *n* **1.**(*brain*) esprit *m;* **to have a good** ~ être intelligent **2.**(*thought, memory*) esprit *m;* **to bring sth to** ~ rappeler qc; **bear in** ~ **that ...** n'oubliez pas que ...; **I'll bear you in** ~ je penserai à vous; **it slipped my** ~ ça m'a sorti de l'esprit **3.**(*intention*) esprit *m;* **to have sth in** ~ avoir qc en tête; **I have half a** ~ **to** +*infin* ça me démange de +*infin;* **to know one's** (**own**) ~ savoir ce que l'on veut **4.**(*consciousness*) esprits *mpl;* **to be out of one's** ~ avoir perdu la raison; **there's something on my** ~ je suis préoccupé; **to take one's** ~ **off sth** se distraire de qc; **keep your** ~ **on the problem** concentre-toi sur le problème; **I can't keep my** ~ **off food/her** je n'arrête pas de penser à la nourriture/à elle **5.** *sing* (*opinion*) avis *m;* **to change one's** ~ changer d'avis; **to sb's** ~ d'après qn **6.**(*intelligent person*) esprit *m* ▶**to be in the back of sb's** ~ être dans l'arrière-pensée de qn; **in one's** ~**'s eye** dans son esprit; **to be in two** ~**s about sth** être partagé au sujet de qc **II.** *vt* **1.**(*be careful of*) faire attention à; **don't** ~ **me** ne fais pas attention à moi; ~ **the step** prenez garde à la marche; ~ **what you're doing** fais attention à ce que tu fais; ~ **you do sth** n'oublie pas de faire qc; ~ **you don't do sth** prends garde de ne pas faire qc; ~ **you, it's not easy, it's not easy,** ~ ce n'est pas évident, remarque **2.**(*look after*) garder **3.**(*concern oneself*) s'occuper de; **to** ~ **one's business** s'occuper de ses affaires; **don't** ~ **sb/sth** ne fais pas attention à qn/qc **4.**(*object*) **to** ~ **sb/sth** être gêné par qn/qc; **I don't** ~ **sb/sth** qn/qc ne me gêne pas; **hot or cold? – I don't** ~ chaud ou froid? – c'est pareil; **I don't** ~ **if I do** je veux bien; **I wouldn't mind a coffee/having a shower** ça me dirait bien de prendre un café/une douche; **what I** ~ **is ...** ce qui m'ennuie c'est ...; **I wouldn't** ~ **sth** j'aimerais bien qc; **I don't** ~ **doing sth** ça ne me dérange pas de faire qc; **I don't** ~ **his doing sth** cela ne me dérange pas qu'il fasse qc; **if you don't** ~ **me saying so, ...** si je peux me permettre de le dire, ...; **would you** ~ **doing sth?** pourriez-vous faire qc? **5.** *Scot* (*remember*) se souvenir **6.** *Am, Scot* (*obey*) obéir à ►**to ~ one's P's and Q's** se tenir **III.** *vi* **to ~ about sth** se soucier de qc; **do you ~ if ...?** est-ce que cela vous ennuie si ...?; **if you don't ~** si cela ne vous ennuie ne pas; **I don't ~!** ça m'est égal!; **do you ~!** je vous demande pardon!; **never ~!** ça ne fait rien!; **never you ~!** *inf* cela ne te/vous regarde pas!

◆**mind out** *vi Brit* **~!** fais attention!; **to ~ for sb/sth** faire attention à qn/qc

mind-bending *adj inf* hallucinogène **mind-blowing** *adj inf* hallucinant(e) **mind-boggling** *adj inf* époustouflant(e)

minded *adj* **1.** (*inclined to think in specific way*) disposé(e); **he's ~ to leave** il est incliné à partir; **liberal-~** libéral(e); **to be commercially ~** être bon commerçant **2.** (*enthusiastic*) intéressé(e); **to be wine-~** s'intéresser au vin; **to be politically ~** s'intéresser à la politique

minder *n* **1.** (*bodyguard*) garde du corps *m* **2.** (*helper*) aide *mf*

mindful *adj form* **1.** (*careful*) attentif(-ive); **to be ~ of sth** être attentif à qc **2.** (*aware*) conscient(e); **to be ~ of sth** avoir pleine conscience de qc **3.** *form* (*willing*) **to be ~ to** *+infin* être disposé à *+infin*

mindless *adj* **1.** (*unaware*) inconscient(e); (*violence*) gratuit(e) **2.** (*stupid, simple*) stupide; (*activity*) abrutissant(e)

mind-reader *n fig* voyant(e) *m(f)*

mine[1] [maɪn] *poss pron* (*belonging to me*) le mien, la mienne; **they're not his glasses, they're ~** ce ne sont pas ses lunettes, ce sont les miennes; **this glass is ~** ce verre est à moi; **a colleague of ~** un de mes collègues; *s. a.* **hers**

mine[2] [maɪn] **I.** *n* MIN *a. fig* mine *f;* **a ~ of information** une mine d'informations **II.** *vt* MIN (*coal, iron*) extraire; (*area*) exploiter ►**to ~ a rich seam of sth** exploiter le filon de qc

mine[3] [maɪn] **I.** *n* MIL mine *f;* **to clear an area of ~s** déminer une zone **II.** *vt* miner

mine-detector *n* détecteur *m* de mines **minefield** *n a. fig* champ *m* de mines **mine-layer** *n* poseur *m* de mines

miner *n* mineur *m*

mineral ['mɪnərəl] **I.** *n* **1.** CHEM minéral *m;* (*ore*) **2.** *pl, Brit* (*soft drinks*) boissons *fpl* gazeuses **II.** *adj* minéral(e); **~ ore** minérai *m*

mineralogical *adj* minéralogique

mineralogist *n* minéralogiste *mf*

mineralogy [,mɪnə'rælədʒi, *Am:* -'rɑːlə-] *n no pl* minéralogie *f*

mineral oil *n* huiles *fpl* minérales **mineral water** *n* eau *f* minérale

minesweeper *n inf* démineur *m*

mingle ['mɪŋgl] **I.** *vt* **1.** (*mix*) mélanger; **to be ~d with sth** être mélangé avec qc **2.** *fig* mêler; **to be ~d with sadness/a noise** être mêlé de tristesse/à un bruit **II.** *vi* **1.** (*mix*) se mélanger; **to ~ with sth** se mélanger à qc **2.** (*in group*) se mêler; **to ~ with the guests/crowd** se mêler aux invités/à la foule

mini ['mɪni] **I.** *adj* mini *inv* **II.** *n* **1.** (*skirt*) mini-jupe *f* **2.** (*dress*) robe *f* mini

miniature ['mɪnɪtʃəʳ, *Am:* -iətʃɚ] **I.** *adj* miniature **II.** *n* miniature *f*

miniature camera *n* appareil *m* 24 x 36 **miniature railway** *n* train *m* miniature

minibus ['mɪnɪbʌs] *n* minibus *m*

minicab ['mɪnɪkæb] *n Brit* radio-taxi *m*

minim ['mɪnɪm] *n Aus, Brit* MUS blanche *f*

minimal ['mɪnɪml] *adj* minimal(e)

minimize ['mɪnɪmaɪz] *vt* minimiser

minimum ['mɪnɪməm] **I.** <-s *o* minima> *n* minimum *m;* **to/at a ~** au minimum **II.** *adj* minimum

mining *n no pl* exploitation *f* minière

mining engineer *n* ingénieur *m* des mines **mining industry** *n* industrie *f* minière

minion ['mɪnjən] *n pej* larbin *m*

miniskirt ['mɪnɪskɜːt, *Am:* -skɜːrt] *n* mini-jupe *f*

minister ['mɪnɪstəʳ, *Am:* stɚ] **I.** *n* **1.** POL ministre *mf* **2.** REL pasteur *m* **II.** *vi* **to ~ to sb** servir qn

ministerial [,mɪnɪ'stɪəriəl, *Am:* -'stɪri-] *adj* ministériel(le)

ministry ['mɪnɪstri] <-ies> *n a.* POL, REL ministère *m;* **~ of agriculture** ministère de l'Agriculture

mink [mɪŋk] *n no pl* vison *m*

minor ['maɪnəʳ, *Am:* -nɚ] **I.** *adj* mineur(e) **II.** *n* mineur(e) *m(f)*

Minorca [mɪ'nɔːka, *Am:* -'nɔːr-] *n* Minorque *f*

minority [maɪ'nɒrəti, *Am:* -'nɔːrət̬i] **I.** <-ties> *n* minorité *f;* **to be in a ~** être minoritaire; **ethnic minorities** minorités ethniques **II.** *adj* minoritaire

minstrel ['mɪnstrəl] *n* HIST ménestrel *m*

mint[1] [mɪnt] *n* **1.** *a.* BOT menthe *f* **2.** (*confectionery*) bonbon *m* à la menthe; **a chocolate ~** un chocolat à la menthe

mint[2] [mɪnt] **I.** *n* **1.** (*coin factory*) Hôtel *m* de la Monnaie **2.** *inf* (*sum of money*) fortune *f* **II.** *vt* (*coin*) frapper; (*stamp*) estamper; (*usage*) lancer **III.** *adj* neuf(neuve) ►**to be in ~ condition** être comme neuf

mint tea *n* thé *m* à la menthe

minuet [,mɪnju'et] *n* menuet *m*

minus ['maɪnəs] **I.** *prep a.* MAT moins; **5 ~ 2 equals 3** 5 moins 2 font 3; **he left ~ his coat/wallet** *inf* il est parti sans son manteau/son portefeuille **II.** *adj* **1.** MAT négatif(-ive) **2.** *fig* (*quantity*) négligeable **III.** *n* moins *m; s. a.* **plus**

minuscule ['mɪnəskjuːl, *Am:* -ɪ-] *adj* minuscule

minute[1] ['mɪnɪt] **I.** *n* **1.** (*sixty seconds*) minute *f;* **just a ~** une minute; **the ~ I arrived** dès que je suis arrivé; **to leave sth to the last ~** laisser qc jusqu'à la dernière minute **2.** *pl* (*record*) procès-verbal *m;* **to take the ~s** faire le

M

procès-verbal **II.** *vt* noter dans le procès-verbal

minute² [maɪ'nju:t, *Am:* -'nu:t] *adj* minuscule; **in ~ detail** dans le moindre détail

minute hand *n* petite aiguille *f*

minutely *adv* minutieusement

minx [mɪŋks] *n* petite peste *f*

miracle ['mɪrəkl] *n* miracle *m;* **it's a ~ I'm here** c'est un miracle que je sois là *subj;* **a ~ of technology** un miracle de la technologie; **a ~ drug/cure** un médicament/traitement miracle

miraculous [mɪ'rækjʊləs, *Am:* -jə-] *adj* miraculeux(-euse)

mirage ['mɪrɑ:ʒ] *n a. fig* mirage *m*

mire ['maɪəʳ, *Am:* maɪr] *sing* **I.** *n* **1.** (*swamp*) boue *f* **2.** *fig* (*confusing situation*) labyrinthe *m;* (*unpleasant situation*) pétrin *m* **II.** *vt* **~d in detail/bureaucracy** noyé(e) dans les détails/la paperasserie

mirror ['mɪrəʳ, *Am:* -ɚ] **I.** *n a. fig* miroir *m;* (**rear-view**) ~ rétroviseur *m;* (**wing**) ~ rétroviseur *m* extérieur ►**to hold a ~ to society** refléter la société **II.** *vt* refléter

mirror image *n* reflet *m*

mirth [mɜ:θ, *Am:* mɜ:rθ] *n no pl* gaieté *f*

misadventure *n* mésaventure *f;* **death by ~** mort *f* accidntelle **misapprehension** *n* malentendu *m;* **to be under a ~** avoir une fausse impression **misappropriate** *vt* détourner **misappropriation** *n no pl* détournement *m* **misbehave** *vi a. fig* mal se comporter, se méconduire *Belgique* **misbehavior** *n Am, Aus,* **misbehaviour** *n no pl, Brit* mauvais comportement *m*

misc [ˌmɪsə'leɪnɪəs] *abbr of* miscellaneous divers(e)

miscalculate *vt* mal calculer **miscalculation** *n a. fig* mauvais calcul *m* **miscarriage** *n* **1.** MED fausse couche *f* **2.** LAW **~ of justice** erreur *f* judiciaire **miscarry** <-ied, -ying> *vi* **1.** MED avoir une fausse couche **2.** (*go wrong*) échouer

miscellaneous [ˌmɪsə'leɪnɪəs] *adj* divers(e)

miscellany [mɪ'seləni, *Am:* 'mɪsəleɪ-] <-anies> *n* **1.** (*mixture*) mélange *f* **2.** (*book*) recueil *m*

mischief *n* bêtises *fpl;* **to get up to ~** faire des bêtises; **to be full of ~** avoir toujours des bêtises en tête; **to make ~** semer la zizanie

mischievous ['mɪstʃɪvəs, *Am:* -tʃə-] *adj* **1.** (*mocking: child, grin*) malicieux(-euse) **2.** (*mean: person, remark*) malveillant(e); (*antics*) mauvais(e); (*rumours*) vilain(e)

misconceived *adj* (*plan, idea*) mal conçu(e) **misconception** *n* idée *f* fausse **misconduct** *n no pl* (*bad behaviour*) mauvaise conduite *f;* **professional ~** faute *f* professionnelle; **sexual ~** outrage *m* à la pudeur **misconstruction** *n form* mauvaise interprétation *f;* **to be open to ~** prêter à confusion **misconstrue** *vt* mal comprendre **miscount** **I.** *n* erreur *f* de calcul **II.** *vt* mal compter **misdeal** **I.** *n* fausse *f* donne **II.** *vt* **to ~ cards** faire une fausse donne **III.** *vi* faire une fausse donne

misdeed *n form* méfait *m*

misdemeanor [ˌmɪsdɪ'mi:nəʳ, *Am:* -nɚ] *n Am,* **misdemeanour** *n* délit *m*

misdirect *vt* **1.** (*give wrong directions*) envoyer à la mauvaise adresse **2.** (*instruct wrongly*) mal orienter; LAW (*jury*) mal instruire **3.** *fig* (*emotions*) mal orienté(e)

miser ['maɪzəʳ, *Am:* -zɚ] *n* avare *mf*

miserable ['mɪzrəbl] *adj* **1.** (*unhappy*) malheureux(-euse); **to feel ~** avoir le cafard; **to make life ~ for sb** rendre la vie dure à qn **2.** (*poor, wretched*) misérable **3.** (*unpleasant: day, weather, conditions*) épouvantable; (*performance, failure*) lamentable **4.** *Aus, NZ* (*stingy*) radin(e) **5.** (*small: pay*) misérable; **a ~ £20** la somme misérable de 20£

miserably *adv* **1.** (*unhappily*) avec un air malheureux **2.** (*extremely: cold*) horriblement **3.** (*badly: fail*) lamentablement

miserly *adj* (*attitude*) mesquin(e)

misery ['mɪzəri] *n* **1.** (*suffering*) souffrance *f;* **to bring ~ to sb** faire le malheur de qn; **to put sb out of their ~** abréger les souffrances de qn **2.** (*distress: of war*) misère *f* **3.** (*sadness*) tristesse *f;* **to make sb's life a ~** empoisonner la vie de qn **4.** (*person*) grincheux, -euse *m, f*

misfire *vi* **1.** (*fail to fire: weapon*) faire long feu; (*engine*) avoir des ratées **2.** *fig* (*plan*) échouer

misfit ['mɪsfɪt] *n* marginal(e) *m(f)*

misfortune *n* **1.** *no pl* (*bad luck*) malchance *f;* **to have the ~ to** *+infin* avoir la malchance de *+infin* **2.** (*mishap*) malheur *m* **misgiving** *n* doute *m* **misguided** *adj* (*idea*) mal avisé(e) **mishandle** *vt* **1.** (*handle without care*) manipuler sans précaution **2.** (*organize badly*) mal organiser **3.** (*deal badly with: situation*) mal gérer; (*child*) être maladroit avec **mishap** *n form* incident *m* **mishear** *vt irr* **to have ~d sth** avoir mal entendu qc

mishmash ['mɪʃmæʃ] *n* méli-mélo *m inv*

misinform *vt* **to ~ sb about sth** mal informer qn sur qc **misinterpret** *vt* mal interpréter **misinterpretation** *n* mauvaise interprétation *f;* **open to ~** qui prête à confusion **misjudge** *vt* se tromper sur **misjudgement** *n* erreur *f* de jugement

mislay [ˌmɪs'leɪ] *vt irr, form* égarer

mislead *vt irr* **1.** (*by accident*) induire en erreur **2.** (*persuade*) tromper; **to ~ sb into believing sth** faire croire qc à qn à tort; **to let oneself be misled** se laisser tromper **misleading** *adj* trompeur(-euse) **mismanage** *vt* mal gérer **mismanagement** *n* mauvaise gestion *f* **mismatch** *n* décalage *m* **misname** *vt* appeler à tort **misnomer** *n* terme *m* inapproprié

misogynist **I.** *n* misogyne *mf* **II.** *adj* misogyne

misogyny [mɪ'sɒdʒɪni, *Am:* -'sɑ:dʒ-] *n* misogynie *f*

misplace *vt form* égarer **misplaced** *adj* mal placé(e); (*fear*) mal fondé(e) **misprint** *n* coquille *f* **mispronounce** *vt* mal prononcer **mispronunciation** *n* **1.** *no pl* (*poor pronunciation*) mauvaise prononciation *f* **2.** (*wrong pronunciation*) faute *f* de prononciation **misread** *vt irr* **1.** (*read badly*) mal lire **2.** *fig* mal interpréter **misrepresent** *vt* (*facts*) déformer; **to ~ sb as sth** faire passer à tort qn pour qc **misrepresentation** *n* **1.** (*false reporting*) déformation *f* **2.** *no pl* (*false representation*) représentation *f* erronée

miss[1] [mɪs] *n* (*form of address*) mademoiselle *f;* **Miss Italy** Miss Italie

miss[2] [mɪs] **I.** <-sses> *n* **1.** (*not hit*) coup *m* manqué **2.** (*failure: film, record*) flop *m* ►**to give sth a ~** *Brit, Aus, inf* faire l'impasse sur qc **II.** *vi* **1.** (*not hit sth*) *a.* SPORT rater **2.** (*misfire*) avoir des ratés **III.** *vt* **1.** (*not hit, not catch: target, bus, train*) rater; **the bullet just ~ed me** la balle m'a manqué de peu **2.** (*not meet: deadline*) dépasser **3.** (*avoid*) échapper à; **I just ~ed being shot** j'ai échappé à un coup de feu de justesse **4.** (*not see: page*) sauter; (*stop*) rater; **don't ~ her new play** ne rate pas sa nouvelle pièce **5.** (*not hear*) ne pas entendre; **sorry I ~ed that ...** excuse-moi je n'ai pas compris ... **6.** (*be absent: school, class*) manquer **7.** (*not take advantage: opportunity, offer*) laisser passer **8.** (*regret absence*) **she ~es them** ils lui manquent; **did you ~ me?** est-ce que je t'ai manqué?; **I ~ driving** ça me manque de conduire **9.** (*notice loss*) **I'm ~ing my wedding ring** mon alliance a disparu ►**to ~ the boat** rater le coche; **to ~ the point** n'avoir pas compris; **she completely ~ed the point** elle est passée complètement à côté

◆**miss out I.** *vt* **1.** (*omit*) omettre **2.** (*overlook*) oublier **II.** *vi* rater quelque chose; **to be missing out on sth** ne pas profiter de qc

misshapen [ˌmɪsˈʃeɪpən] *adj* **1.** (*out of shape*) déformé(e) **2.** (*malformed*) difforme

missile [ˈmɪsaɪl, *Am:* ˈmɪsəl] *n* **1.** (*weapon*) missile *m* **2.** (*object thrown*) projectile *m*

missile defence system *n* système *m* de défense antimissile

missing [ˈmɪsɪŋ] *adj* **1.** (*lost or stolen*) disparu(e); **to go ~** disparaître; **to report sb ~** signaler la disparition de qn **2.** (*not confirmed as alive*) disparu(e); **to be ~ in action** être porté disparu **3.** (*absent, not present*) *a. fig* absent(e) **4.** (*left out*) manquant(e)

missing link *n* chaînon *m* manquant

mission [ˈmɪʃən] *n* mission *f*

missionary [ˈmɪʃənəri, *Am:* -əner-] <-ries> *n* missionnaire *m*

mission control *n* centre *m* de contrôle

misspell *vt irr* mal orthographier **misspelling** *n* faute *f* d'orthographe **misspent** *adj* gaspillé(e)

mist [mɪst] *n* **1.** (*light fog*) brume *f* **2.** *Brit* (*condensation*) buée *f;* (*of tears*) voile *m*

◆**mist up** *vi* (*valley*) s'embrumer; (*window*) s'embuer

mistake [mɪˈsteɪk] **I.** *n* erreur *f;* **careless ~** faute d'étourderie; **my ~** je me suis trompé; **there's some ~** il y a erreur; **spelling/typing ~** faute d'orthographe/de frappe; **by ~** par erreur ►**make no ~ about it** tu peux être sûr **II.** *vt irr* **you can't ~ it, there's not mistaking it** tu ne peux pas le rater; **I mistook you for your brother** je t'ai pris pour ton frère

mistaken I. *pp of* **mistake II.** *adj* **to be ~ about sb/sth** se tromper à propos de qn/qc; **in the ~ belief that ...** croyant à tort que ...; **if I'm not much ~** si je ne m'abuse; **it was a case of ~ identity** il y avait erreur sur la personne

mister [ˈmɪstəʳ, *Am:* -tɚ] *n* monsieur *m*

mistime *vt* **1.** (*misjudge timing*) mal calculer **2.** SPORT rater

mistletoe [ˈmɪsltəʊ, *Am:* -toʊ] *n* gui *m*

mistook [mɪˈstʊk] *pt of* **mistake**

mistranslate *vt* mal traduire **mistranslation** *n* erreur *f* de traduction **mistreat** *vt* maltraiter

mistress [ˈmɪstrɪs] *n a. pej* maîtresse *f*

mistrial [ˌmɪsˈtraɪəl, *Am:* ˈmɪsˌ-] *n* **1.** (*wrongly conducted trial*) *jugement entaché d'un vice de procédure* **2.** *Am* (*trial without decision*) *procès lors duquel le jury ne parvient pas à prendre une décision*

mistrust [ˌmɪsˈtrʌst] **I.** *n no pl* méfiance *f* **II.** *vt* se méfier de

mistrustful *adj* méfiant(e); **to be ~ of sb/sth** se méfier de qn/qc

misty [ˈmɪsti] <-ier, -iest> *adj* **1.** (*slightly foggy*) brumeux(-euse) **2.** (*unclear: eyes*) embué(e); **to be ~-eyed** être tout ému **3.** (*vague*) vague

misunderstand I. *vt irr* mal comprendre; **to be misunderstood** être incompris; **to ~ each other** mal se comprendre; **don't ~ me!** comprenez-moi bien! **II.** *vi irr* mal comprendre **misunderstanding** *n* **1.** (*misinterpretation*) erreur *f* d'interprétation **2.** (*quarrel*) malentendu *m* **3.** *no pl* (*difficulty in communication*) quiproquo *m*

misuse[1] [ˌmɪsˈjuːs] *n* **1.** (*wrong use*) mauvais emploi *m;* (*of word*) emploi *m* abusif **2.** (*excess use*) abus *m*

misuse[2] [ˌmɪsˈjuːz] *vt* (*tool, product*) mal employer; (*power, position*) abuser de

mite[1] [maɪt] *n* mite *f;* **dust ~s** acariens *mpl*

mite[2] **I.** *n* **1.** (*small child, thing*) petite chose *f* **2.** (*small amount*) **a ~ of sth** un peu de qc **II.** *adv inf* **a ~ ...** un tantinet ...

mitigate [ˈmɪtɪgeɪt, *Am:* -ˈmɪt̬-] *vt form* (*effect, cruelty*) atténuer

mitigating circumstances *n* LAW circonstances *fpl* atténuantes

mitigation *n no pl* LAW atténuation *f;* **to use sth in ~ of sth** utiliser qc à la décharge de qc

mitten [ˈmɪtn] *n* **1.** (*with bare fingers*) moufle *f* **2.** (*fingerless*) mitaine *f*

mix [mɪks] **I.** *n* **1.** (*combination*) mélange *m* **2.** (*pre-mixed ingredients*) préparation *f;* **bread ~** préparation pour faire du pain **3.** MUS

M

mixage *m* **II.** *vi* **1.** (*combine*) se mélanger **2.** (*make contact with people*) être sociable; **to ~ easily** se lier facilement; **the people you ~ with** les gens que tu fréquentes **III.** *vt* **1.** (*put ingredients together: dough, drink, paint*) mélanger; **to ~ sth into sth** mélanger qc à qc; **to ~ sth with sth** mélanger qc et qc; **you shouldn't ~ your drinks** tu devrais éviter de faire des mélanges **2.** MUS mixer

◆**mix in** *vt* incorporer

◆**mix up** *vt* **1.** (*confuse*) confondre; **I mix you up with your brother** je te confonds avec ton frère **2.** (*put in wrong order*) mélanger **3.** (*combine ingredients: dough*) mélanger **4.** (*associate*) **to get mixed up in sth** se mêler à qc

mixed *adj* **1.** (*assorted: vegetables, flavours*) assorti(e) **2.** (*involving opposites: marriage*) mixte; (*bathing*) mixte; **a person of ~ race** un(e) métis(se) **3.** (*positive and negative: reactions, reviews*) mitigé(e); **to be a ~ blessing** avoir du bon et du mauvais; **to have ~ feelings about sth** être partagé à propos de qc

mixed bag, mixed bunch *n* assortiment *m;* **it's a ~** il y a de tout **mixed doubles** *n pl* double *m* mixte **mixed farming** *n* polyculture *f* **mixed metaphor** *n* métaphore *f* incohérente

mixer *n* **1.** (*machine*) mixeur *m;* (*for cement*) bétonnière *f;* **hand ~** fouet *m* **2.** (*friendly person*) **to be a ~** être sociable **3.** (*drink*) *jus de fruit ou boisson gazeuse à mélanger à un alcool*

mixer tap *n* mélangeur *m*

mixture ['mɪkstʃəʳ, *Am:* -tʃɚ] *n* **1.** (*combination*) mélange *m* **2.** (*combined substances*) préparation *f*

mix-up *n* **1.** (*confusion*) confusion *f* **2.** (*misunderstanding*) malentendu *m*

MLR *n abbr of* **minimum lending rate** taux *m* de crédit minimum

mm *n abbr of* **millimetre** mm *m*

mnemonic [nɪ'mɒnɪk, *Am:* nɪ'mɑːnɪk] *n* moyen *m* mnémotechnique

mo [moʊ] *n Am abbr of* **month** mois *m*

moan [məʊn, *Am:* moʊn] **I.** *n* **1.** (*sound of pain*) gémissement *m* **2.** (*complaint*) plainte *f* **II.** *vi* **1.** (*make a sound: person, wind*) gémir; **to ~ with pain** gémir de douleur **2.** (*complain*) se plaindre; **to ~ about sth** se plaindre de qc

moat [məʊt, *Am:* moʊt] *n* (*of castle, town*) douve *f;* (*for animals*) fossé *m*

mob [mɒb, *Am:* mɑːb] **I.** *n* **1.** (*crowd*) foule *f;* **~ psychology/violence** psychologie/violence des masses **2.** (*criminal organization*) maf(f)ia *f* **3.** *Brit, inf* (*gang*) clique *f* **4.** (*ordinary people*) **the ~** la populace **5.** *Aus* (*herd*) troupeau *m* **II.** <-bb-> *vt* assaillir

mobile ['məʊbaɪl, *Am:* 'moʊbəl] **I.** *n* **1.** (*telephone*) portable *m,* cellulaire *m Québec,* natel *m Suisse* **2.** (*work of art*) mobile *m* **II.** *adj* mobile; (*shop, library*) ambulant(e); **to be ~** (*own a car*) être motorisé

mobile home *n* mobile home *m* **mobile phone** *n* téléphone *m* portable, cellulaire *m Québec,* natel *m Suisse*

mobility [məʊ'bɪləti, *Am:* moʊ'bɪləţi] *n no pl* mobilité *f;* **social ~** *Brit* mobilité *f* sociale

mobilization *n* mobilisation *f*

mobilize ['məʊbɪlaɪz, *Am:* -bə-] *vt* mobiliser

mob rule *n* loi *f* de la jungle

moccasin ['mɒkəsɪn, *Am:* 'mɑːkəsən] *n* mocassin *m*

mocha ['mɒkə, *Am:* 'moʊkə] *n no pl* moka *m*

mock [mɒk, *Am:* mɑːk] **I.** *n Brit, inf* (*exam*) examen *m* blanc **II.** *adj* **1.** (*not real*) faux(fausse); **~ leather** similicuir *m* **2.** (*imitated: emotion*) simulé(e) **3.** (*practice: exam*) blanc(he) **III.** *vi* **to ~ at sb** se moquer de qn **IV.** *vt* **1.** (*ridicule*) se moquer de **2.** (*ridicule by imitation*) **to ~ sb/sth** imiter qn/qc en se moquant

mocker *n* moqueur, -euse *m, f*

mockery *n* **1.** (*ridicule*) moquerie *f* **2.** (*subject of derision*) sujet *m* de moquerie; **to make a ~ of sb/sth** tourner qc/qc en dérision **3.** (*insulting failure*) parodie *f*

mocking *n* moquerie *f*

mockingbird *n* ZOOL moqueur *m*

mock turtle soup *n* consommé *m* de veau

MOD *n Brit abbr of* **Ministry of Defense** ministère *m* de la Défense

mod. *adj abbr of* **modern** moderne

modal ['məʊdəl, *Am:* 'moʊ-] *adj* (*verb*) modal(e)

modality *n* modalité *f*

modal verb *n* verbe *m* modal

mod cons *n* confort *m* moderne

mode ['məʊd, *Am:* 'moʊd] *n* **1.** (*style, state*) mode *m;* **~ of transport** moyen de transport; **~ of expression/existence** mode d'expression/d'existence; **in stopwatch ~** en mode chronomètre **2.** *no pl, form* (*fashion*) mode *f*

model ['mɒdəl, *Am:* 'mɑːdəl] **I.** *n* **1.** (*representation*) maquette *f* **2.** (*example, creation, version*) *a.* ART modèle *m* **3.** (*mannequin*) mannequin *m* **II.** *adj* **1.** (*ideal*) modèle **2.** (*small: car, aircraft, figures*) miniature **III.** <-ll-> *vt* **1.** (*produce*) *a. fig* modeler; **to ~ sth in clay** modeler qc en argile; **to ~ sth on sth** modeler qc sur qc; **to ~ oneself on sb** prendre qn pour modèle **2.** (*show: clothes*) présenter **IV.** *vi* **1.** (*show clothes*) être mannequin **2.** (*pose*) poser (comme modèle)

modem ['məʊdem, *Am:* 'moʊdəm] *n* INFOR *abbr of* **MODulator DEModulator** modem *m*

moderate ['mɒdərət, *Am:* 'mɑːdɚ-] **I.** *n* POL modéré(e) *m(f)* **II.** *adj* **1.** (*neither great nor small: size, ability*) moyen(ne) **2.** (*avoiding extremes*) *a.* POL modéré(e); (*climate*) tempéré(e) **III.** *vt* **1.** (*make less extreme*) modérer **2.** (*control: examination, debate*) être le mod-

érateur pour **IV.** *vi* se modérer
moderately *adv* (*good, big*) raisonnablement; (*reply, react*) avec modération
moderation *n* modération *f*; **in** ~ avec modération
moderator *n* **1.** (*chairman*) président(e) *m(f)* **2.** (*mediator*) médiateur, -trice *m, f* **3.** UNIV examinateur, -trice *m, f*
modern ['mɒdən, *Am:* 'mɑːdɚn] *adj* moderne; ~ **children** les enfants d'aujourd'hui; ~ **languages** les langues modernes
modernity *n* modernité *f*
modernize ['mɒdənaɪz, *Am:* 'mɑːdɚ-] **I.** *vt* moderniser **II.** *vi* se moderniser
modest ['mɒdɪst, *Am:* 'mɑːdɪst] *adj* **1.** (*not boastful, not large*) modeste **2.** (*not provocative: person*) pudique; (*garment*) convenable
modesty *n* **1.** (*without boastfulness*) modestie *f* **2.** (*without sexual provocation*) pudeur *f*
modicum ['mɒdɪkəm, *Am:* 'mɑːdɪ-] *n no pl* minimum *m*
modifiable *adj* modifiable
modification [ˌmɒdɪfɪ'keɪʃən, *Am:* ˌmɑːdɪ-] *n* modification *f*
modifier *n* LING modificateur *m*
modify ['mɒdɪfaɪ, *Am:* 'mɑːdɪ-] <-ie-> *vt* modifier
modish ['məʊdɪʃ, *Am:* 'moʊ-] *adj form* à la mode
modular ['mɒdjʊləʳ, *Am:* 'mɑːdʒəlɚ] *adj* modulaire
modulate ['mɒdjʊleɪt, *Am:* 'mɑːdʒə-] *vt* moduler
modulation *n* modulation *f*
module ['mɒdjuːl, *Am:* 'mɑːdʒuːl] *n* module *m*
mogul ['məʊgəl, *Am:* 'moʊ-] *n* magnat *m*
mohair ['məʊheəʳ, *Am:* 'moʊher] *n* mohair *m*
Mohammed [məʊ'hæmɪd, *Am:* moʊ-] *n no pl* Mahomet *m*
moist [mɔɪst] *adj* humide; (*cake*) moelleux(-euse)
moisten ['mɔɪsn] **I.** *vt* (*cloth*) humidifier; (*skin*) hydrater **II.** *vi* (*eyes*) s'embuer
moisture ['mɔɪstʃəʳ, *Am:* -tʃɚ] *n* humidité *f*
moisturize ['mɔɪstʃəraɪz] *vt* hydrater; **to** ~ **one's skin** s'hydrater la peau
moisturizer *n* crème *f* hydratante
molar ['məʊləʳ, *Am:* 'moʊlɚ] **I.** *n* molaire *f* **II.** *adj* molaire
molasses [məʊ'læsɪz, *Am:* moʊ-] *n no pl* mélasse *f*
mold [məʊld, *Am:* moʊld] *vi Am s.* **mould**
Moldavia [mɒl'deɪviə, *Am:* mɑːl-] *n* la Moldavie
Moldavian **I.** *adj* moldave **II.** *n* **1.** (*person*) Moldave *mf* **2.** LING moldave *m*; *s. a.* **English**
molder ['moʊldɚ] *vi Am s.* **moulder**
molding *n Am s.* **moulding**
Moldova [mɒl'dəʊvə, *Am:* mɑːl'doʊ-] *n s.* **Moldavia**
Moldovan *s.* **Moldavian**
moldy ['moʊldi] *adj Am s.* **mouldy**
mole¹ [məʊl, *Am:* moʊl] *n* (*animal, spy*) taupe *f*
mole² [məʊl, *Am:* moʊl] *n* ANAT grain *m* de beauté
molecular [mə'lekjʊləʳ, *Am:* -jəlɚ] *adj* moléculaire
molecule ['mɒlɪkjuːl, *Am:* 'mɑːlɪ-] *n* molécule *f*
molehill ['məʊlhɪl, *Am:* 'moʊl-] *n* taupinière *f*
moleskin *n* (*fabric*) moleskine *f*
molest [mə'lest] *vt* **1.** (*attack*) agresser **2.** (*attack sexually*) agresser sexuellement
molestation *n* **1.** (*physical attack*) agression *f* **2.** (*sexual attack*) agression *f* sexuelle
moll [mɒl, *Am:* mɑːl] *n Am, Aus, inf* compagne *f*
mollify ['mɒlɪfaɪ, *Am:* 'mɑːlə-] <-ie-> *vt* **1.** (*pacify*) calmer **2.** (*reduce effect*) apaiser
mollusc *n,* **mollusk** ['mɒləsk, *Am:* 'mɑːləsk] *n Am* mollusque *m*
mollycoddle ['mɒlɪkɒdl, *Am:* 'mɑːlɪkɑːdl] *vt pej, inf* couver
molt [məʊlt, *Am:* moʊlt] *n, vt, vi Am s.* **moult**
molten ['məʊltən, *Am:* 'moʊl-] *adj* (*metal*) en fusion
mom [mɒm, *Am:* mɑːm] *n* maman *f*
moment ['məʊmənt, *Am:* 'moʊ-] *n* **1.** (*time*) moment *m*; **it'll just take a few** ~**s** ca ne sera pas long; **not for a** ~ pas un instant; **at any** ~ d'un moment à l'autre; **in a** ~ dans un moment; **at the** ~ en ce moment; **the** ~ **I arrive/arrived** dès que j'arriverai/je suis arrivé; **the play had its** ~**s** il y a eu de bons moments dans la pièce; **she has her** ~**s** elle a des moments d'inspiration **2.** *form* (*importance*) importance *f*
momentarily ['məʊməntrəli, *Am:* ˌmoʊmən'ter-] *adv* **1.** (*very briefly*) momentanément **2.** *Am* (*very soon*) dans une minute
momentary ['məʊməntri, *Am:* 'moʊmənter-] *adj* momentané(e)
momentous [mə'mentəs, *Am:* moʊ'mentəs] *adj* capital(e)
momentum [mə'mentəm, *Am:* moʊ'mentəm] *n no pl, a. fig* élan *m*; **to gain** ~ prendre de l'élan; **to lose** ~ être en perte de vitesse
momma ['mɒmə, *Am:* 'mɑːmə] *n Am s.* **mama**
mommy *n Am s.* **mummy**
Mona Lisa *n* **the** ~ La Joconde
monarch ['mɒnək, *Am:* 'mɑːnɚk] *n* monarque *mf*
monarchist *n* monarchiste *mf*
monarchy <-chies> *n* monarchie *f*
monastery ['mɒnəstri, *Am:* 'mɑːnəster-] <-ries> *n* monastère *m*
monastic [mə'næstɪk] *adj* **1.** REL monastique

M

2. (*ascetic*) monacal(e)

Monday ['mʌndi] *n* lundi *m; s. a.* **Friday**

monetary ['mʌnɪtəri, *Am:* 'mɑːnəteri] *adj* monétaire

Monetary Union *n* Union *f* monétaire

money ['mʌni] *n no pl* argent *m;* **I paid good ~ for this** j'ai payé pour ça; **it's ~ well spent** c'est de l'argent bien dépensé; **the ~'s good** c'est bien payé; **there's ~ in sth** il y a de l'argent à se faire dans qc; **to get one's ~'s worth** en avoir pour son argent; **to make ~** faire de l'argent; **to put ~ into sth** investir dans qc; **to put ~ on sth** parier sur qc; **to put ~ on sb/sth doing sth** parier que qn/qc fera qc ▶**you pays your ~ and you takes your choice** *prov* la décision n'appartient qu'à toi/vous; **to be ~ for jam** *Brit* être de l'argent facile; **put your ~ where your mouth is** passez à la caisse; **~ doesn't grow on trees** *prov* l'argent ne tombe pas du ciel *prov;* **to be made of ~, to be in the ~** être plein aux as *inf;* **for my ~** pour moi; **to have ~ to burn** avoir de l'argent à jeter par la fenêtre; **~ talks** *prov* l'argent est roi *prov*

moneybelt *n* ceinture-portefeuille *f* **money box** <-es> *n Brit* tirelire *f*

moneyed *adj form* cossu(e)

money-grubbing *adj pej* cupide **moneymaker** *n* affaire *f* lucrative **moneymaking** *adj* lucratif(-ive) **money market** *n* marché *m* monétaire **money order** *n Am, Aus* mandat *m* postal **money-spinner** *n* mine *f* d'or

Mongol ['mɒŋgl, *Am:* 'mɑːŋgəl] **I.** *adj* mongol(e) **II.** *n* **1.** (*person*) Mongol(e) *m(f)* **2.** LING mongol *m; s. a.* **English**

Mongolia [mɒŋ'gəʊlɪə, *Am:* mɑːŋ'goʊ-] *n* la Mongolie

Mongolian I. *adj* mongolien(ne) **II.** *n* mongolien(ne) *m(f)*

mongrel ['mʌŋgrəl, *Am:* 'mɑːŋ-] *inf* **I.** *n* bâtard(e) *m(f)* **II.** *adj* bâtard(e)

monitor ['mɒnɪtə^r, *Am:* 'mɑːnɪt̬ɚ] **I.** *n* **1.** (*screen*) moniteur *m;* **15-inch ~** moniteur de 15 pouces **2.** (*apparatus*) appareil *m* de contrôle **3.** (*observer*) observateur, -trice *m, f* **II.** *vt* **1.** (*check, observe*) contrôler **2.** (*watch*) surveiller **3.** (*listen to*) écouter; (*a conversation*) suivre

monk [mʌŋk] *n* moine *m*

monkey ['mʌŋki] **I.** *n* singe *m* ▶**to make a ~ out of sb** tourner qn en ridicule **II.** *vi* **to ~ about/around** faire des singeries

monkey business *n inf* (*trickery*) magouilles *fpl;* (*games*) bêtises *fpl* **monkey wrench** *n Am* clé *f* anglaise **2.** *Am* **to throw a ~ into sth** mettre la pagaille dans qc

monochrome ['mɒnəʊkrəʊm, *Am:* 'mɑːnoʊlroʊm] **I.** *adj* **1.** (*using black and white*) noir et blanc *inv* **2.** (*only one colour*) monochrome **3.** (*tedious, unexciting*) monotone **II.** *n* monochrome *m*

monocle ['mɒnəkl, *Am:* 'mɑːnə-] *n* monocle *m*

monogamy [mə'nɒgəmi, *Am:* mə'nɑːgə-] *n no pl* **1.** (*state of being married*) *a.* ZOOL monogamie *f* **2.** (*faithfulness*) fidélité *f*

monogram ['mɒnəgræm, *Am:* 'mɑːnə-] *n* monogramme *m*

monolingual [ˌmɒnəʊ'lɪŋgwəl, *Am:* ˌmɑːnə-] *adj* monolingue

monolithic [ˌmɒnə'lɪθɪk, *Am:* ˌmɑːnə-] *adj pej* monolithique

monologue ['mɒnəlɒg, *Am:* 'mɑːnəlɑːg] *n* monologue *m*

monopolize [mə'nɒpəlaɪz, *Am:* -'nɑːpəlaɪz] *vt* monopoliser

monopoly [mə'nɒpəli, *Am:* -'nɑːpəl-] <-lies> *n* monopole *m*

monosyllabic [ˌmɒnəsɪ'læbɪk, *Am:* ˌmɑːnə-] *adj* **1.** LING (*having only one syllable*) monosyllabique **2.** *pej* (*taciturn, uncommunicative*) peu bavard(e); **to give a ~ reply** répondre par monosyllabes

monotone ['mɒnətəʊn, *Am:* 'mɑːnətoʊn] *n no pl* ton *m* monocorde

monotonous *adj* monotone

monotony [mə'nɒtəni, *Am:* -'nɑːtən-] *n no pl* monotonie *f*

monoxide [mɒ'nɒksaɪd, *Am:* mə'nɑːk-] *n* monoxyde *m*

monsoon [mɒn'suːn, *Am:* mɑːn-] *n* mousson *f*

monster ['mɒnstə^r, *Am:* 'mɑːnstɚ] **I.** *n* monstre *m* **II.** *adj inf* monstre

monstrosity [mɒn'strɒsəti, *Am:* mɑːn'strɑːsət̬i] <-ties> *n* monstruosité *f*

monstrous ['mɒnstrəs, *Am:* 'mɑːn-] *adj* monstrueux(-euse)

montage [mɒnt'ɑːʒ, *Am:* 'mɑːntɑːʒ] *n* montage *m*

month [mʌnθ] *n* mois *m;* **the sixth of the ~** le six du mois; **to be three ~s old** avoir trois mois; **a six-~-old baby** un bébé de six mois; **a two ~s' holiday** des vacances de deux mois; **a ~s' notice/salary** un mois de préavis/de salaire

monthly I. *adj* mensuel(le) **II.** *adv* mensuellement **III.** *n* mensuel *m*

Montreal [ˌmɒntri'ɔːl, *Am:* ˌmɑːn-] *n* Montréal

monument ['mɒnjʊmənt, *Am:* 'mɑːnjə-] *n* monument *m;* **a ~ to their perseverance** *fig* un témoignage de leur persévérance

monumental *adj* monumental(e)

moo [muː] **I.** <-s> *n* meuglement *m* **II.** *vi* meugler **III.** *interj* meuh

mood¹ [muːd] *n* **1.** (*feeling*) humeur *m;* **in a good/bad ~** de bonne/mauvaise humeur; **to be in a talkative ~** être loquace; **sb is in one of his/her ~s** qn est encore mal luné(e); **as the ~ takes him** selon son humeur; **to be in the ~ for celebrating** être d'humeur à faire la fête; **to be in no ~ to** +*infin form* ne pas être d'humeur à +*infin* **2.** (*atmosphere*) ambiance; **to lighten the ~** détendre l'atmosphère

mood² [muːd] *n* LING mode *m*

moodiness *n no pl* **1.** (*liability to depression*) humeur *f* maussade **2.** (*fluctuating feelings*) humeur *f* changeante

moody [ˈmuːdi] <-dier, -diest> *adj* **1.** (*having fluctuating feelings*) lunatique **2.** (*depressive*) mal luné(e)

moon [muːn] **I.** *n no pl* lune *f;* **full/new ~** pleine/nouvelle lune; **half ~** demi-lune *f* ►**to be over the ~ about sth** être au ciel avec qc; **to promise sb the ~** promettre la lune à qn **II.** *vi* **1.** (*hang about*) **to ~ about/around** traînasser **2.** *inf* (*exhibit*) montrer son derrière

moonbeam *n* rayon *m* de lune **moon boot** *n* après-ski *m* **moonlight I.** *n no pl* clair *m* de lune **II.** *vi* <-ghted> *inf* travailler au noir **moonlit** *adj* éclairé(e) par la lune **moonshine** *n no pl* **1.** (*moonlight*) clair *m* de lune **2.** *inf* (*illegal alcoholic drink*) alcool *m* de contrebande **3.** *inf* (*nonsense*) balivernes *fpl* **moonstone** *n* pierre *f* de lune **moonstruck** *adj* dans la lune

moor¹ [mɔːʳ, *Am:* mʊr] *n* (*open area*) lande *f*

moor² [mɔːʳ, *Am:* mʊr] *vt* NAUT amarrer

mooring [ˈmʊərɪŋ, *Am:* ˈmʊrɪŋ] *n* NAUT mouillage *m;* **~s** amarres *fpl*

moose [muːs] *n* élan *m*

moot point *n* **it's a ~** ça se discute

mop [mɒp, *Am:* mɑːp] **I.** *n* **1.** ((*floor*) ~) balai *m* à laver; (**sponge**) ~ balai-éponge *m;* (**dish**) ~ brosse à vaisselle *f;* **to need a ~** avoir besoin d'un coup de serpillière **2.** (~ *of hair*) tignasse *f* **II.** <-pp-> *vt* **1.** (*clean with mop*) essuyer; **to ~ the floor** passer la serpillière **2.** (*wipe sweat from*) s'essuyer; **to ~ one's forehead** s'éponger le front

◆**mop up I.** *vt* **1.** (*clean*) essuyer **2.** (*absorb*) éponger **II.** *vi* passer un coup de serpillière

mope [məʊp, *Am:* moʊp] *vi* se morfondre

moped *n* mobylette® *f*

moral [ˈmɒrəl, *Am:* ˈmɔːr-] **I.** *adj* moral(e); **he has no ~ fibre** il n'a pas de force de caractère **II.** *n* **1.** (*moral message*) morale *f* **2.** *pl* (*standards*) moralité *f*

morale [məˈrɑːl, *Am:* -ˈræl] *n no pl* moral *m*

moralist [ˈmɒrəlɪst, *Am:* ˈmɔːr-] *n* moraliste *mf*

morality [məˈræləti, *Am:* mɔːˈræləṭi] <-ties> *n* moralité *f*

moralize [ˈmɒrəlaɪz, *Am:* ˈmɔːr-] *vi* faire la morale

moral support *n no pl* soutien *m* moral

morass [məˈræs] *n* **1.** (*boggy area*) marais *m* **2.** *fig* bourbier *m*

moratorium [ˌmɒrəˈtɔːrɪəm, *Am:* ˌmɔːr-] <-s *o* -ria> *n* moratoire *m;* **to propose a ~ on sth** propose un moratoire pour qc

morbid [ˈmɔːbɪd, *Am:* ˈmɔːr-] *adj* morbide

more [mɔːʳ, *Am:* mɔːr] **I.** *adj comp of* **much, many** plus de; **~ wine/nuts** davantage de vin/noix; **to have ~ sth than sb** avoir plus de qc que qn; **is there any ~ wine?** y a-t-il encore du vin?; **no ~ wine at all** plus du tout de vin; **some ~ wine** encore un peu de vin; **a few ~ nuts** quelques noix de plus; **~ and ~ questions** de plus en plus de questions **II.** *adv comp of* **much, many** plus; **~ gifted than me** plus doué que moi; **to drink a bit/much ~** boire un peu/beaucoup plus; **once ~** une fois de plus; **never ~** plus jamais; **to see ~ of sb** voir qn plus souvent; **~ than 10** plus de 10; **~ than ever** plus que jamais; **the ~ you try** plus tu essaies; **the ~ I ask him** plus je lui demande; **she complains ~ and ~** elle se plaint de plus en plus **III.** *pron comp of* **much, many** plus; **~ and ~** de plus en plus; **to have ~ than sb** en avoir plus que qn; **to cost ~ than sth** coûter plus que qc; **the ~ you eat, the ~ you get fat** plus on mange, plus on grossit; **he eats ~ and ~** il mange de plus en plus; **do you need ~?** en veux-tu encore?; **what ~ does he want?** que veut-il de plus?; **there is nothing ~ to do** il n'y a plus rien à faire; **many do it but ~ don't** beaucoup le font mais plus encore ne le font pas ►**all the ~** d'autant plus; **all the ~ so because** d'autant plus que; **~ or less** plus ou moins

moreover [mɔːˈrəʊvəʳ, *Am:* -ˈroʊvɚ] *adv form* de plus

morgue [mɔːg, *Am:* mɔːrg] *n Am, Aus* **1.** (*place for corpses*) morgue *f* **2.** *fig* (*boring atmosphere*) **to be a ~** être mortel **3.** (*archives*) archives *fpl*

moribund [ˈmɒrɪbʌnd, *Am:* ˈmɔːr-] *adj pej, form* moribond(e)

Mormon [ˈmɔːmən, *Am:* ˈmɔːr-] **I.** *n* mormon(e) *m(f)* **II.** *adj* mormon(e)

morning [ˈmɔːnɪŋ, *Am:* ˈmɔːr-] *n* **1.** (*begin of a day*) matin *m;* **good ~!** bonjour!; **in the ~** le matin; **the ~ after** le lendemain matin; **on Sunday ~** dimanche matin; **every Monday ~** tous les lundis matin(s); **I'll come in the ~** je viendrai dans la matinée; **I'll call this ~** j'appellerai ce matin; **one July ~** un matin de juillet; **early in the ~** de bon matin; **6/11 o'clock in the ~** six/onze heures du matin **2.** (*as unit of time*) matinée *f,* avant-midi *m* (*en Belgique et féminin au Québec*)

morning-after pill *n* pilule *f* du lendemain **morning sickness** *n* nausées *fpl*

Moroccan I. *adj* marocain(e) **II.** *n* Marocain(e) *m(f)*

morocco *n* ~ (**leather**) maroquin *m*

Morocco [məˈrɒkəʊ, *Am:* -ˈrɑːkoʊ] *n* le Maroc

moron [ˈmɔːrɒn, *Am:* ˈmɔːrɑːn] *n pej, inf* débile *mf*

moronic *adj pej, inf* débile

morose [məˈrəʊs, *Am:* -ˈroʊs] *adj* **1.** (*depressed, sullen*) morose **2.** (*dully aggressive*) renfrogné(e)

morphine [ˈmɔːfiːn, *Am:* ˈmɔːr-] *n* morphine *f*

morphological *adj* morphologique

morphology [mɔːˈfɒlədʒi, *Am:* mɔːrˈfɑːlə-] *n* morphologie *f*

> **Morris dancing** existe depuis très longtemps, mais les origines de cette tradition demeurent inconnues; le nom viendrait de "Moorish" (mauresque). Cette danse a surtout une signification à "Whitsuntide" (Pentecôte). Les "Morris dancers" sont le plus souvent des groupes d'hommes habillés en blanc, et certains d'entre eux portent des carillons autour de leurs mollets. Chacun porte soit un bâton, un mouchoir ou une couronne dans la main. La danse est pleine d'élan et les danseurs tapent des pieds, sautillent et sautent en l'air.

Morse [mɔːs, *Am:* mɔːrs], **Morse code** *n no pl* morse *m*

morsel ['mɔːsl, *Am:* 'mɔːr-] *n* **1.** (*tiny amount of food*) bouchée *f* **2.** (*tiny amount*) brin *m*

mortadella [ˌmɔːtə'delə, *Am:* ˌmɔːr-] *n* mortadelle *f*

mortal ['mɔːtl, *Am:* 'mɔːrt̬l] **I.** *adj* mortel(le) **II.** *n* mortel, -le *m, f*

mortality [mɔː'tæləti, *Am:* mɔːr'tælət̬i] *n no pl* mortalité *f*

mortar ['mɔːtəʳ, *Am:* 'mɔːrtɚ] *n* mortier *m*

mortgage ['mɔːgɪdʒ, *Am:* 'mɔːr-] **I.** *n* crédit *m* immobilier **II.** *vt* hypothéquer ►**to be ~d up to the hilt** être hypothéqué au maximum

mortician [mɔː'tɪʃən, *Am:* mɔːr-] *n Am* entrepreneur *m* de pompes funèbres

mortification [ˌmɔːtɪfɪ'keɪʃən, *Am:* ˌmɔːrt̬ə-] *n no pl* mortification *f*

mortify ['mɔːtɪfaɪ, *Am:* 'mɔːrt̬ə-] *vt* mortifier; **I was mortified!** j'étais humilié

mortuary ['mɔːtʃəri, *Am:* 'mɔːrtʃuer-] *n* mortuaire *m*

mosaic [məʊ'zeɪɪk, *Am:* moʊ-] *n* mosaïque *f*

Moscow ['mɒskəʊ, *Am:* 'mɑːkaʊ] *n* Moscou

Moses ['məʊzɪz, *Am:* 'moʊ-] *n* Moïse *m*

Moslem ['mɒzləm, *Am:* 'mɑːzlem] *adj, n s.* **Muslim**

mosque [mɒsk, *Am:* mɑːsk] *n* mosquée *f*

mosquito [mə'skiːtəʊ, *Am:* -t̬oʊ] <-es *o* -s> *n* moustique *m*, brûlot *m Québec*

mosquito net *n* moustiquaire *f*

moss [mɒs, *Am:* mɑːs] <-es> *n* mousse *f*

mossy <-ier, -iest> *adj* moussu(e)

most [məʊst, *Am:* moʊst] **I.** *adj superl of* **many, much** le plus de; **to have the ~ nuts/wine** avoir le plus de noix/vin; **for the ~ part** en majeure partie; **~ people** la plupart des gens **II.** *adv superl of* **many, much** le plus; **the ~ beautiful dog** le chien le plus beau; **the ~ incredible story** l'histoire la plus incroyable; **a ~ beautiful evening** une merveilleuse soirée; **what I want ~** ce que je désire le plus; **~ of all** par-dessus tout; **~ likely** très probablement; **I cried ~** j'ai pleuré le plus **III.** *pron superl of* **many, much ~ were good** la plupart étaient bons; **~ was wasted** la plus grande partie était gâchée; **~ of them/the time** la plupart d'entre eux/du temps; **~ of the wine** la majorité du vin; **at the very ~** au grand maximum; **to make the ~ of sth/oneself** tirer le meilleur parti de qc/soi-même; **the ~ you can have is ...** on peut avoir tout au plus ...; **I won ~** j'ai gagné le plus

mostly *adv* **1.** (*usually*) la plupart du temps **2.** (*nearly all*) pour la plupart **3.** (*in the majority*) principalement

MOT [ˌeməʊ'tiː, *Am:* -oʊ'-] *n Brit abbr of* **Ministry of Transport** contrôle *m* technique

motel [məʊ'tel, *Am:* moʊ-] *n* motel *m*

moth [mɒθ, *Am:* mɑːθ] *n* mite *f*

mothball **I.** *n* boule *f* de naphtaline **II.** *vt* **1.** (*store*) mettre en réserve **2.** (*stop*) geler

moth-eaten *adj* mité(e)

mother ['mʌðəʳ, *Am:* -ɚ] **I.** *n* **1.** (*female parent*) mère *f* **2.** *Am s.* **motherfucker** ►**the ~ of all ... the ~ of all storms** la tempête des tempêtes **II.** *vt* materner **III.** *adj* mère

motherboard *n* INFOR carte *f* mère **mother country** *n* mère *f* patrie **motherfucker** *n vulg* (*man*) connard *m;* (*woman*) salope *f;* (*thing*) saloperie *f* **motherhood** *n* maternité *f*

Mothering Sunday *n no pl, Brit s.* **Mother's Day**

mother-in-law <mothers- *o* -laws> *n Brit* belle-mère *f*

motherly *adj* maternel(le)

mother-of-pearl *n* nacre *f* **Mother's Day** *n Brit, Am* fête *f* des Mères **mother tongue** *n* langue *f* maternelle

mothproof *adj* traité(e) à l'antimite

motif [məʊ'tiːf, *Am:* moʊ-] *n* motif *m*

motion ['məʊʃən, *Am:* 'moʊ-] **I.** *n* **1.** (*movement*) mouvement *m;* **in slow ~** au ralenti; **to put sth in ~** mettre qc en marche **2.** *Brit, Aus* MED selles *fpl* **3.** (*formal suggestion at meeting*) motion *f* ►**to set the wheels in ~** lancer le processus; **to go through the ~s** faire semblant **II.** *vt* **to ~ sb to** +*infin* faire signe à qn de +*infin;* **to ~ sb in** faire signe à qn d'entrer **III.** *vi* **to ~ to sb** faire signe à qn

motionless *adj* immobile

motion picture *n Am, form* film *m*

motivate ['məʊtɪveɪt, *Am:* 'moʊt̬ə-] *vt* motiver; **to ~ sb to** +*infin* motiver qn à +*infin;* **racially ~d crime** les crimes racistes

motivation *n* motivation *f*

motive ['məʊtɪv, *Am:* 'moʊt̬ɪv] **I.** *n* motif *m;* (*for the murder*) mobile *m* **II.** *adj* moteur(-trice)

motley ['mɒtli, *Am:* 'mɑːt-] <-ier, -iest> *adj* (*crowd*) bigarré(e); (*collection*) hétéroclite

motor ['məʊtəʳ, *Am:* 'moʊt̬ɚ] **I.** *n* **1.** (*engine*) *a. fig* moteur *m* **2.** *Brit, inf* (*car*) bagnole *f* **II.** *adj* **1.** *Brit, Aus* (*referring to vehicles*) automobile; (*accident*) de voiture **2.** (*related to body movement*) moteur(-trice) **III.** *vi* **1.** (*drive*) rouler **2.** (*drive fast*) *a. fig* foncer

motorbike *n inf* moto *f* **motorboat** *n* bateau *m* à moteur **motor car** *n Brit* auto *f* **motorcycle** *n form* motocyclette *f* **motorcycling** *n* motocyclisme *m* **motorcyclist** *n* motocycliste *mf* **motor-driven** *adj* à moteur

motoring *adj Brit* automobile; (*costs*) de voiture

motorist *n* automobiliste *mf*

motorization *n* motorisation *f*

motorize ['məʊtəraɪz, *Am:* 'moʊt̬ə-] *vt* motoriser

motor vehicle *n* véhicule *m* motorisé **motorway** *n Brit* autoroute *f*

mottled ['mɒtld, *Am:* 'mɑːt̬ld] *adj* tacheté(e); (*skin*) marbré(e)

motto ['mɒtəʊ, *Am:* 'mɑːt̬oʊ] *n* <-s *o* -es> devise *f*

mould[1] [məʊld, *Am:* moʊld] *n no pl* BIO moisissure *f*

mould[2] [məʊld, *Am:* moʊld] **I.** *n* moule *m* **II.** *vt* (*clay*) mouler; (*character*) former

moulder *vi* **1.** (*decay*) moisir **2.** *fig* pourrir

moulding *n* **1.** (*ornament*) moulure *f* **2.** (*stucco*) stuc *m* **3.** ART moulage *m*

mouldy <-ier, -iest> *adj* **1.** (*covered in mould*) moisi(e) **2.** *inf* (*shabby*) minable

moult [məʊlt, *Am:* moʊlt] *vi* ZOOL (*birds*) perdre ses plumes; (*snakes, insects, crustaceans*) muer

mound [maʊnd] *n* (*of objects*) tas *m;* **a burial ~** un monticule funéraire

mount[1] [maʊnt] *n* mont *m*

mount[2] [maʊnt] **I.** *n* **1.** (*backing, setting frame*) marie-louise *f;* (*of a gem*) monture *f* **2.** (*support*) support *m* **3.** (*horse*) monture *f* **II.** *vt* **1.** (*get on: bicycle*) monter sur; (*ladder*) grimper à; (*stairs*) monter; **to ~ a bicycle/horse** monter à bicyclette/cheval; **to ~ sb on a horse** hisser qn sur un cheval **2.** (*organize: an attack, a campaign*) lancer; (*an operation, a squadron*) monter **3.** (*fix for display: a gem, painting*) monter **4.** (*set*) **to ~ guard over sth** monter la garde sur qc **III.** *vi* **1.** (*climb*) *a. fig* monter **2.** SPORT se mettre en selle **3.** (*increase*) augmenter

◆**mount up** *vi* augmenter

mountain ['maʊntɪn, *Am:* -t̬ən] *n* montagne *f* ►**to make a ~ out of a molehill** faire tout un plat de pas grand chose; **~s of sth** *inf* des tas de qc

mountain bike *n* vélo *m* tout terrain

mountaineer *n* **1.** (*climber*) alpiniste *mf* **2.** *Am* montagnard *m*

mountaineering *n no pl* alpinisme *m*

mountainous *adj* **1.** (*rocky*) montagneux(-euse) **2.** NAUT (*wave*) immense

mountain range *n* GEO chaîne *f* de montagnes **Mountain time** *n* heure *f* des Montagnes Rocheuses

mounted ['maʊntɪd, *Am:* -t̬ɪd] *adj* (*police*) monté(e); **to be ~ on a horse** être en selle

mourn [mɔːn, *Am:* mɔːrn] **I.** *vi* **to ~ for sb/sth** pleurer qn/qc **II.** *vt* pleurer

mourner *n* proche *mf* du défunt; **the ~s** le cortège funèbre

mournful *adj* **1.** (*melancholic*) mélancolique **2.** (*gloomy*) sinistre

mourning *n no pl* **1.** (*grieving*) deuil *m;* **in ~** en deuil **2.** (*wailing*) gémissement *m*

mouse [maʊs] <mice> *n* **1.** (*small rodent*) *a. pej* souris *f* **2.** (*shy person*) timide *mf* **3.** INFOR souris *f*

mouse button *n* INFOR **right/left ~** bouton *m* droit/gauche de la souris **mouse hole** *n* trou *m* de souris **mouse mat** *n* tapis *m* de souris **mouse pad** *n* tapis *m* pour souris **mouse pointer** *n* pointeur *m* de la souris **mousetrap** *n* piège *m* à souris

mousse [muːs] *n* mousse *f*

moustache [mə'stɑːʃ, *Am:* 'mʌstæʃ] *n* moustache *f*

mousy ['maʊsi] *adj* **1.** (*shy*) timide **2.** (*plain, unprepossessing*) fade **3.** (*dull: colour*) terne

mouth[1] [maʊθ] *n* **1.** ANAT bouche *f;* (*of an animal*) gueule *f;* **to keep one's ~ shut** se taire; **to shut one's ~** *inf* la fermer; **to make sb's ~ water** faire saliver qn **2.** (*opening*) ouverture *f;* (*of a bottle*) goulot *m;* (*of a cave, volcano*) bouche *f;* (*of a river*) embouchure *f* ►**to be all ~** *inf* n'avoir que de la gueule; **to be down in the ~** être déprimé; **to shoot off one's ~ about sth** *inf* crier qc sur les toits

mouth[2] [maʊð] *vt* **1.** (*utter*) proférer **2.** (*mime*) articuler sans son

mouthful *n* **1.** (*amount of food*) bouchée *f* **2.** (*amount of drink*) gorgée *f* **3.** *inf* (*unpronounceable word*) **to be a ~** être difficile à prononcer

mouth organ *n* harmonica *m* **mouthpiece** *n* **1.** TEL, MUS (*of a telephone*) microphone *m;* (*of a musical instrument, pipe*) embout *m* **2.** SPORT protège-dents *m* **3.** POL porte-parole *m* **mouth-to-mouth** **I.** *adj* bouche à bouche *inv;* **~ resuscitation** bouche à bouche *m* **II.** *n* bouche *m* à bouche **mouthwash** *n* bain *m* de bouche **mouthwatering** *adj* appétissant(e)

movable *adj* mobile; (*heavy object, article*) transportable

move [muːv] **I.** *n* **1.** (*movement*) mouvement *m;* **to be on the ~** (*travelling*) être parti; (*working*) être en déplacement; **they're watching our every ~** ils surveillent tous nos mouvements **2.** (*act*) action *f;* (*in game*) coup *m;* **a good/bad ~** une bonne/mauvaise décision; **a good career ~** une décision profitable à la carrière **3.** (*change: of home, premises*) déménagement *m;* (*of job*) changement *m* ►**to get a ~ on** se grouiller **II.** *vi* **1.** (*position*) bouger; (*on wheels*) rouler; **to ~ out of the way** s'écarter du chemin **2.** (*walk, run*) se déplacer **3.** *inf* (*intensive use*) **he can really ~!** (*runner*) il court bien!; (*dancer*) il bouge bien! **4.** (*act*) agir; (*in games*) avancer **5.** (*develop*) bouger; **things are moving at**

M

last les choses bougent enfin **6.** (*change: to new home, premises*) déménager; (*to new job*) bouger; **we're moving to Ireland** nous déménageons en Irlande; **we're moving into e-commerce** nous nous lançons dans le commerce électronique **7.** (*change attitude*) faire des concessions; **they won't ~ on working hours** ils ne feront pas la moindre concession sur les heures de travail **8.** *inf* (*leave*) partir **9.** (*be bought*) se vendre **10.** (*frequent*) **to ~ in exalted circles** fréquenter les gens bien placés **11.** *form* (*suggest*) **to ~ for an adjournment** proposer l'ajournement **III.** *vt* **1.** (*to new position: object*) bouger; (*passengers, troops*) transporter; **~ that bag** bouge ce sac; **~ the vase to the right/over there** mets le vase à droite/là-bas **2.** (*to new time: meeting*) déplacer; (*patient*) déplacer le rendez-vous de **3.** (*to new address*) déménager; (*to new job*) muter; **to ~ house** déménager; **we ~d her to sales** nous l'avons transférée à la vente; **we ~d the factory to Ireland** nous avons transféré l'usine en Irlande **4.** (*cause movements in: arms, legs*) bouger; (*branches*) agiter; (*machinery*) faire bouger **5.** (*cause emotions*) toucher; **to be ~d to tears** être ému aux larmes **6.** (*persuade*) persuader; **what ~d you to write the book?** qu'est-ce qui vous a poussé à écrire le livre? **7.** (*suggest at meeting*) proposer ►**to ~ the goalposts** *inf* changer les règles du jeu; **to ~ heaven and earth** remuer ciel et terre; **to ~ mountains** soulever des montagnes

◆**move about** **I.** *vi* **1.** (*not stay still*) bouger **2.** (*go around*) circuler **3.** (*travel*) voyager **4.** (*change address*) déménager **5.** (*change jobs*) changer d'emploi **II.** *vt* changer de place

◆**move along** **I.** *vt* faire circuler **II.** *vi* **1.** (*walk further on*) avancer **2.** (*run further on*) courir **3.** (*drive further on*) continuer à rouler **4.** (*make room*) faire de la place **5.** (*develop*) avancer

◆**move aside** *vi s.* **move over**

◆**move away** **I.** *vi* **1.** (*move house*) déménager; **to ~ from one city to another** déménager d'une ville à l'autre **2.** (*change*) **to ~ from a market/field** quitter un marché/un domaine **II.** *vt always sep* **to move a chair/sb's arm away** déplacer une chaise/pousser le bras de qn

◆**move back** **I.** *vt* faire revenir **II.** *vi* emménager à nouveau

◆**move down** **I.** *vi* baisser **II.** *vt* SCHOOL **to move sb down** rétrograder qn; **to move sb down a grade** *Am* descendre d'une classe

◆**move forward** **I.** *vt* faire avancer **II.** *vi* avancer

◆**move in** **I.** *vi* **1.** (*into a house, an office*) emménager; **to ~ with a friend** emménager avec un ami **2.** (*intervene: police, troops*) intervenir **3.** (*advance to attack*) **to ~ on sb** avancer sur qn **II.** *vt* faire entrer

◆**move off** *vi* **1.** (*walk*) partir; (*parade, protesters*) se mettre en mouvement **2.** (*run*) s'élancer **3.** (*drive*) démarrer **4.** (*fly*) décoller

◆**move on** **I.** *vi* **1.** (*continue a journey*) reprendre la route; (*traffic*) se remettre en mouvement **2.** (*walk*) avancer **3.** (*be ordered away*) circuler **4.** (*to new stage*) passer à autre chose; (*in career*) monter dans la hiérarchie; **to ~ to higher things** passer à quelque chose de mieux **5.** (*develop*) changer **6.** (*pass: time*) passer **7.** (*change subject*) continuer; **to ~ to sth** passer à qc **II.** *vt* **1.** (*ask to leave*) faire circuler **2.** (*force to leave*) faire partir **3.** *Brit* (*help progress*) faire avancer

◆**move out** **I.** *vi* **1.** (*to new home, office*) déménager; (*leave home*) quitter la maison; **to ~ of sth** quitter qc **2.** (*to retreat*) se retirer **II.** *vt* sortir; (*person*) faire partir; (*furniture*) déménager

◆**move over** **I.** *vi* **1.** (*make room*) se pousser **2.** (*switch to*) **to ~ to sth** passer à qc **3.** (*leave position*) laisser sa place **II.** *vt* (*move aside*) mettre de côté

◆**move up** **I.** *vi* **1.** (*go up, rise*) monter **2.** SCHOOL passer (dans une classe supérieure) **3.** (*make room*) faire de la place **4.** (*have promotion*) avoir de l'avancement **5.** (*increase*) augmenter **II.** *vt* **1.** (*go upward*) monter **2.** SCHOOL passer **3.** (*give promotion*) promouvoir

movement ['mu:vmənt] *n* **1.** (*motion, group*) *a.* MED, MUS mouvement *m;* **a ~ with his left hand** un mouvement de sa main gauche **2.** *no pl* FIN fluctuation *f;* **an upaward ~ in share prices** une tendance à la hausse des actions **3.** *no pl* (*tendency*) tendance *f;* **a ~ towards/against sth** un mouvement vers/contre qc **4.** *pl, Brit, Aus* (*activities*) mouvements *mpl*

movie ['mu:vi] *n Am, Aus* (*film*) film *m;* **the ~s** le cinéma

movie camera *n* caméra *f* **moviegoer** *n Am, Aus* cinéphile *mf* **movie star** *n* vedette *f* de cinéma **movie theater** *n Am* cinéma *m*

moving **I.** *adj* **1.** (*that moves: vehicle*) en mouvement; (*part*) mobile **2.** (*motivating*) moteur(-trice); **the ~ drive** l'énergie **3.** (*touching*) émouvant(e) **II.** *n no pl* déménagement *m;* **~ expenses** frais *mpl* de déménagement

moving pavement *n* trottoir *m* roulant **moving staircase** *n* escalier *m* mécanique

mow [məʊ, *Am:* moʊ] <mowed, mown *o* mowed> **I.** *vi* (*cut grass, grain*) tondre **II.** *vt* tondre; (*a field*) faucher

◆**mow down** *vt* faucher

mower *n* **1.** (*lawn cutter*) tondeuse *f* à gazon **2.** (*on a farm*) faucheuse *f*

mown [məʊn, *Am:* moʊn] *pp of* **mow**

MP [ˌem'pi:] *n* **1.** *Brit, Can abbr of* **Member of Parliament** député(e) *m(f)* **2.** *abbr of* **Metropolitain Police** police *f* municipale **3.** *abbr of* **Military Police** police *f* militaire

mpg *n abbr of* **miles per gallon** miles *mpl* au gallon

mph [ˌempiːˈeɪtʃ] *abbr of* **miles per hour** miles par heure *mpl*
Mr [ˈmɪstəʳ, *Am:* -tɚ] *n abbr of* Mister (*title for man*) M.; ~ **Big** le grand chef; ~ **Right** l'homme *m* idéal ▸**no more** ~ **Nice Guy** finies les politesses
Mrs [ˈmɪsɪz] *n abbr of* Mistress **1.** (*woman*) Mme **2.** (*representative*) Madame *f;* **to be** ~ **Average** être Madame Tout-le-Monde
ms [ˌemˈes] *n abbr of* **manuscript** manuscrit *m*
Ms [mɪz] *n abbr of* Miss *terme d'adresse pour une femme qui évite la distinction entre Miss et Mrs*
MSc [ˌemesˈsiː] *n abbr of* Master of Science ≈ maîtrise *f* de sciences
Mt *n abbr of* Mountain Mt. *m*
MT *n Am abbr of* Mountain time heure *f* des Montagnes Rocheuses
much [mʌtʃ] <more, most> **I.** *adj* beaucoup de; ~ **criticism is justified** de nombreuses critiques sont justifiées; **you don't need** ~ **water** il ne faut pas beaucoup d'eau; **how** ~ **milk?** combien de lait?; **too/so** ~ **water** trop/tellement d'eau; **as** ~ **water as** autant d'eau que; **three times as** ~ **water** trois fois plus d'eau **II.** *adv* très; ~ **better** beaucoup mieux; **thank you very** ~ merci beaucoup; **I don't use it** ~ je ne m'en sers pas beaucoup; **he's** ~ **like his father** il est tout à fait comme son père; **to be** ~ **surprised** être fort surpris; **a** ~ **praised/criticized building** un bâtiment très apprécié/critiqué; **a** ~ **deserved rest/shower** un repos/une douche bien mérité(e); ~ **to my astonishment** à mon grand étonnement; **I like you as** ~ **as her** je vous aime autant qu'elle; ~ **the best** de loin le meilleur; **not him,** ~ **less her** pas lui, encore moins elle; *s. a.* **many III.** *pron* beaucoup; ~ **of the criticism** beaucoup de critiques; **not** ~ **of the money is left** il ne reste pas grand-chose de l'argent; ~ **of the day** une bonne partie de la journée; **too** ~ trop; **you earn twice as** ~ **as me** tu gagnes deux fois plus que moi; **I don't think** ~ **of it** je n'en pense pas grand bien; **to make** ~ **of sb/sth** faire grand cas de qn/qc
muchness *n no pl, inf* **to be much of a** ~ être pareils
muck [mʌk] *n Brit* **1.** *no pl, inf* (*dirt*) saleté *f* **2.** *no pl, inf* (*waste*) ordures *fpl* **3.** *no pl, inf* (*excrement*) crotte *f* **4.** *no pl, inf* BOT, AGR fumier *m* **5.** *no pl, inf* (*bad quality*) merde *f* ▸**to make a** ~ **of sth** gâcher qc
◆**muck about I.** *vi inf* **1.** (*have fun*) s'amuser **2.** (*be silly*) faire l'imbécile; **to muck about with sth** faire l'imbécile avec **II.** *vt inf* **to muck sb about** se moquer de qn
◆**muck in** *vi* (*help*) y mettre du sien
◆**muck out I.** *vt* nettoyer **II.** *vi* nettoyer les écuries
◆**muck up** *vt Brit, inf* **1.** (*spoil*) foutre en l'air **2.** (*dirty*) salir
muckheap *n* tas *m* de fumier **muckraker** *n* fouille-merde *mf* **muckraking** *n* étalage *m* de scandales **muck-up** *n inf* gâchis *m*
mucky <-ier, -iest> *adj* **1.** (*dirty*) sale **2.** (*obscene*) cochon(ne)
mucus [ˈmjuːkəs] *n* mucus *m*
mud [mʌd] *n no pl* boue *f* ▸**to drag sb's name through the** ~ traîner le nom de qn dans la boue; **to hurl** ~ **at sb** crier des injures à qn
muddle [ˈmʌdl] *n* **1.** (*confused situation*) embrouille *f;* **we're in a** ~ on est dans le pétrin; **to get in a** ~ s'embrouiller; **to get sth in(to) a** ~ embrouiller qc **2.** (*untidy state*) désordre *m* **3.** (*mental confusion*) **to be in a** ~ être perdu
◆**muddle along** *vi* survivre
◆**muddle through** *vi* se débrouiller
◆**muddle up** *vt* **1.** (*make sb confused*) embrouiller; **to get (all) muddled up** s'embrouiller **2.** (*disorganize*) embrouiller **3.** (*confuse sth with sth*) confondre; **to muddle sb up with sb** confondre qn avec qn
muddle-headed *adj* confus(e)
muddy I. *vt* **1.** (*make dirty*) salir **2.** (*confuse*) embrouiller ▸**to** ~ **the waters** brouiller les pistes **II.** <-ier, -iest> *adj* sale; (*ground*) boueux(-euse)
mudguard *n* (*of a car*) pare-boue *m;* (*of a bicycle*) garde-boue *m* **mudpack** *n* masque *m* à l'argile **mudslinger** *n inf* diffamateur, -trice *m, f* **mudslinging** *n inf* diffamation *f*
muff [mʌf] **I.** *n* FASHION manchon *m* **II.** *vt* (*mess up*) rater; **to** ~ **one's lines** oublier son texte
muffin [ˈmʌfɪn] *n* **1.** *Am* GASTR muffin *m* (*petit gâteau*) **2.** *Brit* muffin *m* (*petit pain rond*)
muffle [ˈmʌfl] *vt* **1.** (*make quieter*) étouffer **2.** *fig* emmitoufler
muffler *n* **1.** *Am* AUTO silencieux *m* **2.** (*scarf*) écharpe *f*
mug [mʌg] **I.** *n* **1.** (*drinking vessel*) grande tasse *f* **2.** *Brit, inf* (*foolish person*) idiot(e) *m(f)* **3.** *pej* (*face*) tronche *f* **II.** <-gg-> *vt* agresser
◆**mug up on** *vt inf* potasser
mugger *n* agresseur, -euse *m, f*
mugging *n* agression *f*
muggins *n no pl* idiot(e) *m(f)*
muggy <-ier, -iest> *adv* lourd, fade *Belgique;* **it's** ~ il fait lourd
mugwump [ˈmʌgwʌmp] *n Am* **1.** (*boss, chief*) patron(ne) *m(f)* **2.** (*stubborn person*) entêté(e) *m(f)*
Muhammad *n s.* **Mohammed**
mulatto [mjuːˈlætəʊ, *Am:* məˈlæt̬oʊ] <-s *o* -oes> *n* mulâtre, -tresse *m, f*
mulberry [ˈmʌlbri, *Am:* -ber-] *n* **1.** (*fruit*) mûre *f* **2.** (*tree*) mûrier *m*
mule¹ [mjuːl] *n* (*donkey*) *a. pej* mule *f*
mule² [mjuːl] *n* **1.** (*woman's shoe*) mule *f* **2.** (*house shoe*) pantoufle *f*
mulish *adj* têtu(e)
mull [mʌl] *vt* aromatiser; ~**ed wine** vin chaud

M

et épicé

◆**mull over** *vt* retourner dans sa tête

mullah ['mʌlə] *n* mollah *m*

multicolo(u)red *adj* multicolore **multicultural** *adj* multiculturel(le) **muiltidisciplinary** *adj* multidisciplinaire **multifunctional** *adj* polyvalent(e) **multigrade oil** *n* huile *f* multigrade **multilateral** *adj* POL multilatéral(e) **multimedia** I. *adj* multimédia II. *n* multimédia *m* **multimillionaire** *n* multimillionnaire *mf* **multinational** I. *adj* multinational(e) II. *n* multinationale *f*

multiple ['mʌltɪpl, *Am:* -t̬ə-] *adj* multiple

multiple-choice *adj* à choix multiple

multiple sclerosis *n* sclérose *f* en plaques

multiplex ['mʌltɪpleks, *Am:* -t̬ə-] *n* complexe *m* multisalles, multiplexe *m*

multiplication [ˌmʌltɪplɪ'keɪʃən, *Am:* -t̬ə-] *n* multiplication *f*

multiplicity [ˌmʌltɪ'plɪsəti, *Am:* -t̬ə'plɪsət̬i] *n no pl, form* multiplicité *f*

multiplier *n* MAT multiplicateur, -trice *m, f*

multiply ['mʌltɪplaɪ, *Am:* -t̬ə-] I. *vt* multiplier; **to ~ (out) sth and sth** multiplier qc avec qc II. *vi* se multiplier

multipurpose *adj* (*tool*) à utilisation multiple; (*building*) polyvalent(e) **multiracial** *adj* multiracial(e) **multistage** *adj* de plusieurs étapes **multistor(e)y** *adj* à plusieurs étages; (*car park*) à plusieurs niveaux **multitasking** *n* INFOR traitement *m* multitâche

multitude ['mʌltɪtjuːd, *Am:* -t̬ətuːd] *n* 1. (*large number*) multitude *f;* **a ~ of sth** un tas de qc 2. *pl* (*many people*) multitudes *fpl*

multi-user system *n* INFOR configuration *f* multiposte

mum¹ [mʌm] *n* (*mother*) maman *f*

mum² [mʌm] *adj* **to keep ~** *inf* se taire

mumble ['mʌmbl] *vt, vi* marmonner

mumbo jumbo [ˌmʌmbəʊ'dʒʌmbəʊ, *Am:* -boʊ'dʒʌmboʊ] *n no pl, inf* charabia *m*

mummy¹ ['mʌmi] <-mies> *n* (*mother*) maman *f*

mummy² ['mʌmi] <-mies> *n* (*body*) momie *f*

mumps [mʌmps] *n + sing v* MED oreillons *mpl*

munch [mʌntʃ] *vt, vi* mastiquer

mundane [mʌn'deɪn] *adj* 1. (*ordinary*) banal(e) 2. (*worldly*) terrestre

municipal [mjuː'nɪsɪpl, *Am:* -əpl] *adj* municipal(e)

municipality *n* municipalité *f*

munitions [mjuː'nɪʃənz] *n* munitions *fpl*

mural ['mjʊərəl, *Am:* 'mjʊrəl] *n* fresque *f*

murder ['mɜːdəʳ, *Am:* 'mɜːrdɚ] I. *n* (*killing*) meurtre *m;* (*emphasizing premeditation*) assassinat *m;* **attempted ~** tentative *f* de meurtre ►**to be ~** être tuant; **to get away with ~** tout se permettre; **to scream blue ~** crier comme un forcené II. *vt* 1. (*kill*) assassiner 2. *fig* massacrer

murderer *n* meurtrier *m*

murderess *n* meurtrière *f*

murderous *adj a. fig* meurtrier(-ère); (*heat*) tuant(e)

murky ['mɜːki, *Am:* 'mɜːr-] <-ier, -iest> *adj a. fig* obscur(e); (*water*) trouble; (*day, weather*) couvert; **it's a ~ business** c'est louche

murmur ['mɜːməʳ, *Am:* 'mɜːrmɚ] I. *vi* murmurer; **to ~ to oneself** marmonner dans sa barbe II. *vt* murmurer III. *n* murmure *m;* **without a ~** sans broncher

muscle ['mʌsl] *n* 1. ANAT muscle *m;* **not to move a ~** ne pas bouger d'un poil 2. *fig* (*influence*) pouvoir *m;* **to flex one's ~s** se faire les muscles

◆**muscle in** *vi* s'imposer; **to ~ on sth** s'imposer dans qc

muscle-bound *adj* très musclé(e) **muscleman** <-men> *n* Monsieur *m* Muscle

Muscovite ['mʌskəvaɪt] *n* moscovite *mf*

muscular ['mʌskjʊləʳ, *Am:* -kjələɚ] *adj* 1. (*relating to muscles*) musculaire 2. (*strong*) musclé(e)

muscular dystrophy *n* myopathie *f*

muse¹ [mjuːz] *n* muse *f*

muse² [mjuːz] *vi* songer; **to ~ on sth** méditer sur qc

museum [mjuː'zɪəm] *n* musée *m*

museum piece *n* pièce *f* de musée

mush [mʌʃ] *n no pl, a. fig, inf* bouillie *f;* **to be ~** (*film, book*) être à l'eau de rose

mushroom ['mʌʃrʊm, *Am:* -ruːm] I. *n a. fig* champignon *m;* **cultivated ~s** champignons *mpl* de culture; **poisonous/edible ~** champignon vénéneux/comestible II. *vi* pousser comme des champignons

mushroom cloud *n* champignon *m* nucléaire

mushy ['mʌʃi] *adj* <-ier, -iest> *a. fig* en bouillie; (*film, story*) à l'eau de rose

music ['mjuːzɪk] *n inv* musique *f;* **classical/pop ~** musique classique/pop; **rock'n'roll ~** rock'n'roll *m;* **that's ~ to my ears** ça fait plaisir à entendre

musical ['mjuːzɪkəl] I. *adj* musical(e); **to be ~** être musicien; **a ~ instrument** un instrument de musique; **a ~ genius** un génie de la musique II. *n* comédie *f* musicale

music(al) box *n* boîte *f* à musique **music hall** *n* music-hall *m*

musician [mjuː'zɪʃən] *n* musicien(ne) *m(f)*

music lover *n* mélomane *mf* **music stand** *n* pupitre *m*

musk [mʌsk] *n no pl* musc *m*

muskrat ['mʌskræt] *n* rat *m* musqué

Muslim ['mʊzlɪm, *Am:* 'mʌzləm] I. *n* musulman(ne) *m(f)* II. *adj* musulman(ne)

muslin ['mʌzlɪn] *n* mousseline *f;* **a ~ dress** une robe en mousseline

muss [mʌs] I. *vt Am* (*cloth*) froisser; (*hair*) ébouriffer II. *n no pl, Am* cirque *m*

mussel ['mʌsl] *n* moule *f*

must [mʌst] **I.** *aux* devoir; **you ~ go now** il faut que tu partes maintenant *subj;* **you ~n't be late** tu ne dois pas arriver en retard; **he ~ be late** il doit être en retard; **you simply ~ come** tu dois venir absolument; **I ~ thank you** il faut que je vous remercie *subj;* **~ you whistle like that?** tu as vraiment besoin de siffler comme ça? **II.** *n inf* must *m*

mustache [ˈmʌstæʃ] *n Am* moustache *f*

mustang [ˈmʌstæŋ] *n* mustang *m*

mustard [ˈmʌstəd, *Am:* -tɚd] *n inv* **1.** (*plant, paste*) moutarde *f* **2.** (*colour*) moutarde *m* ▸**to cut the ~** faire le poids

muster [ˈmʌstəʳ, *Am:* -tɚ] **I.** *vt* rassembler; **to ~ one's courage** rassembler son courage **II.** *vi* (*come together*) se rassembler **III.** *n* rassemblement *m;* MIL revue *f* ▸**to pass ~** faire l'affaire

mustn't [ˈmʌsnt] = **must not** *s.* **must**

musty [ˈmʌsti] <-ier, -iest> *adj* (*smell, taste*) de moisi; (*room, book*) qui sent le moisi; **to taste ~** avoir un goût de moisi; **to smell ~** sentir le renfermé

mutant [ˈmjuːtənt] **I.** *n* mutant(e) *m(f)* **II.** *adj* mutant(e)

mutation [mjuːˈteɪʃən] *n* mutation

mute [mjuːt] **I.** *n* **1.** (*person*) muet(te) *m(f)* **2.** MUS sourdine *f* **II.** *vt* **1.** (*soften*) assourdir; *fig* atténuer **2.** MUS mettre la sourdine à **III.** *adj* muet(te)

muted *adj* (*reaction, support*) tiède; (*criticism*) voilé(e); (*occasion*) discret(-ète); (*colour*) sourd(e); (*sound*) assourdi(e)

mutilate [ˈmjuːtɪleɪt, *Am:* -t̬əl-] *vt a. fig* mutiler

mutilation *n* mutilation *f*

mutineer [ˌmjuːtɪˈnɪəʳ, *Am:* -tnˈɪr] *n* mutin *m*

mutinous [ˈmjuːtɪnəs, *Am:* -t̬n-] *adj* mutin(e)

mutiny [ˈmjuːtɪni] **I.** *n no pl* mutinerie *f* **II.** *vi* se mutiner

mutter [ˈmʌtəʳ, *Am:* ˈmʌt̬ɚ] **I.** *vi* **to ~ about sth** marmonner qc; **to ~ (away) to oneself** marmonner dans sa barbe **II.** *vt* marmonner; **to ~ sth to sb under one's breath** marmonner qc dans sa barbe

mutton [ˈmʌtən] *n inv* mouton *m* **2.** *inf* **~ dressed up as lamb** une vieille bique

mutton chop, mutton chop whiskers *n pl* rouflaquettes *fpl*

mutual [ˈmjuːtʃuəl] *adj* mutuel(le); (*friend*) commun(e); (*feeling*) réciproque

mutual fund *n* fonds *m* commun de placement **mutual insurance** *n* FIN mutuelle *f*

mutually *adv* mutuellement

Muzak® [ˈmjuːzæk] *n* musique *f* d'ambiance

muzzle [ˈmʌzl] **I.** *n* **1.** (*animal mouth*) museau *m* **2.** (*mouth covering*) muselière *f;* **to put a ~ on the dog** museler un chien **II.** *vt a. fig* museler

muzzy [ˈmʌzi] <-ier, -iest> *adj* **1.** (*hazy, confused*) confus(e) **2.** (*unclear, blurred*) flou(e)

MW *n abbr of* **medium wave** ondes *fpl* moyennes

my [maɪ] *poss adj* mon *m,* ma *f;* **~ dog/house/children** mon chien/ma maison/mes enfants; **this car is ~ own** cette voiture est à moi; **I hurt ~ foot/head** je me suis blessé le pied/à la tête

myopic [maɪˈɒpɪk, *Am:* -ˈɑːpɪk] *adj a. fig, form* myope

myriad [ˈmɪrɪəd] *n form* myriade *f*

myrrh [mɜːʳ, *Am:* mɜːr] *inv n* myrrhe *f*

myrtle [ˈmɜːtl, *Am:* ˈmɜːrt̬l] *n* myrte *m*

myself [maɪˈself] *reflex pron* **1.** *after verbs* me, m' + *vowel;* **I injured/corrected ~** je me suis blessé/corrigé; **I always enjoy ~** je m'amuse toujours; **when I express/exert ~** quand je m'exprime/m'exerce; **I've bought ~ a bag** je me suis acheté un sac **2.** (*I or me*) moi-même; **my brother and ~** mon frère et moi-même; **I'll do it ~** je le ferai moi-même; **I did it all by ~** je l'ai fait tout seul; **I prefer Mozart ~** personnellement je préfère Mozart **3.** *after prep* **I said to ~ ...** je me suis dit ...; **I am ashamed at ~** j'ai honte; **I live by ~** je vis seul

mysterious [mɪˈstɪərɪəs, *Am:* -ˈstɪrɪ-] *adj* mystérieux(-euse)

mystery [ˈmɪstəri] <-ies> *n* mystère *m;* **to be a ~ to sb** être un mystère pour qn

mystic [ˈmɪstɪk] **I.** *n* mystique *mf* **II.** *adj* mystique

mystical *adj* mystique

mysticism [ˈmɪstɪsɪzəm] *inv n a. pej* mysticisme *m*

mystification [ˌmɪstɪfɪˈkeɪʃən] *inv n* mystification *f*

mystify [ˈmɪstɪfaɪ] *vt* **to ~ sb** laisser qn perplexe

mystique [mɪsˈtiːk] *inv n form* mystique *f*

myth [mɪθ] *n a. pej* mythe *m*

mythical [ˈmɪθɪkl] *adj a. pej* mythique

mythological *adj* mythologique; **a ~ hero** un héros de la mythologie

mythology [mɪˈθɒlədʒi, *Am:* -ˈθɑːlə-] *n* mythologie *f*

N

N, n [en] <-'s> *n* N *m,* n *m;* **~ as in Nelly** *Brit,* **~ as in Nan** *Am* (*on telephone*), **~ for Nelly** *Brit,* **~ for Nan** *Am* n comme Nicolas

N *n* **1.** *abbr of* **north** N *m* **2.** *abbr of* **Newton** N *m*

n *n* **1.** MAT *abbr of* **n** n *m* **2.** *abbr of* **noun** n *m* **3.** *abbr of* **neuter** N *m*

'n(') *conj abbr of* **and** et

NA, N/A *abbr of* **not applicable** sans rapport

NAACP [ˌendʌbleɪsiːˈpiː] *n Am abbr of* **National Association for the advancement**

of Colored People *association de défense des droits civiques des Afro-Américains*

nab [næb] <-bb-> *vt inf* choper; **to ~ sb doing sth** choper qn en train de faire qc

nadir ['neɪdɪəʳ, *Am:* -dɚ] *n form* nadir *m;* **to reach its ~** *fig* atteindre son point le plus bas

naff [næf] <-er, -est> *adj Brit, inf* ringard(e)

nag[1] [næg] *n* bourrin *m*

nag[2] [næg] **I.** <-gg-> *vi* faire des remarques incessantes; **to ~ at sb** harceler qn **II.** <-gg-> *vt* harceler; **to ~ sb to do/about doing sth** harceler qn pour qu'il(elle) fasse qc *+subj* **III.** *n inf (person)* râleur, -euse *m, f*

nagger *n* râleur, -euse *m, f*

nagging I. *n* remarques *fpl* **II.** *adj* **1.** *(criticizing: person)* râleur(-euse); **his ~ wife** sa mégère de femme **2.** *(continuous)* tenace

nail [neɪl] **I.** *n* **1.** *(metal fastener)* clou *m* **2.** *(finger/toe end)* ongle *m;* **to bite/paint one's ~s** se ronger/se vernir les ongles ▶**to be a ~ in sb's/sth's coffin** être un autre coup funeste à qn/qc **II.** *vt* **1.** *(fasten)* **to ~ sth to sth** clouer qc à qc **2.** *inf (catch)* épingler ▶**to ~ one's colours to the mast** proclamer haut et fort ses positions

◆**nail down** *vt* **1.** *(nail)* clouer **2.** *(identify, find out)* définir; **I can't nail it down** je n'arrive pas dire ce que c'est **3.** *(get clear answer from)* obtenir une réponse de; **to nail sb down to a specific date** obtenir de qn qu'il fixe une date précise

nail-biting *adj* à suspense **nail brush** *n* brosse *f* à ongles **nail clippers** *npl* coupe-ongles *m* **nail file** *n* lime *f* à ongles **nail polish** *n Am* vernis *m* à ongles **nail scissors** *n* ciseaux *mpl* à ongles **nail varnish** *n* vernis *m* à ongles

naive, naïve [naɪ'iːv, *Am:* nɑː'-] *adj pej* naïf(-ive); **to make the ~ assumption that...** avoir la naïveté de supposer que ...

naïveté [naɪ'iːvəteɪ, *Am:* ˌnɑːiːv'teɪ], **naivety** [naɪ'iːvəti, *Am:* nɑː'iːvət̬i] *n inv* naïveté *f*

naked ['neɪkɪd] *adj* **1.** *(uncovered) a. fig* nu(e); **stark ~** *inf* nu comme un verre; **half ~** à moitié nu; **to strip ~** se mettre nu; **to the ~ eye** à l'œil nu **2.** *(not hidden)* flagrant(e); *(ambition)* non-dissimulé(e)

nakedness *n* nudité *f*

NALGO ['nælgəʊ, *Am:* -goʊ] *n Brit abbr of* **National and Local Government Officers Association** *syndicat des fonctionnaires de l'administration*

namby-pamby [ˌnæmbɪ'pæmbi] *adj inf* gnangnan *inv*

name [neɪm] **I.** *n* **1.** *(what one is called)* nom *m;* **full ~** nom et prénom; **first ~** prénom *m;* **last ~** nom de famille; **what's your ~?** comment t'appelles-tu?; **by ~** de nom; **someone by the ~ of** quelqu'un sous le nom de; **to call sb ~s** injurier qn; **to be sth in ~ only** n'avoir de qc que le nom; **in the ~ of sb/sth** au nom de qn/qc; **under the ~ of** sous le nom de **2.** *(reputation)* réputation *f;* **to have a ~ for sth** avoir une réputation de qc; **to make a ~ for oneself** se faire une réputation ▶**to be the ~ of the game** être tout ce qui compte; **to take sb's ~ in vain** parler de qn; **a ~ to conjure with** un nom prestigieux **II.** *vt* **1.** *(call)* nommer; *(child, file, product)* appeler; **to be ~d after/for sb** recevoir le nom de qn; **someone ~d Jones** un nommé Jones **2.** *(appoint)* nommer **3.** *(list)* citer **4.** *(specify)* désigner; *(time, conditions, price)* fixer; **to be ~d as the boss** être désigné comme patron

name-calling *npl* injures *fpl* **name-dropping** *n no pl* name-dropping *m (fait de citer des noms de personnalités pour impressionner ses interlocuteurs)*

nameless *adj* **1.** *(not named)* inconnu(e) **2.** *(anonymous)* anonyme **3.** *(indefinable)* sans nom

namely *adv* à savoir

nameplate *n* médaillon *m* **namesake** *n* homonyme *m*

Namibia [næ'mɪbɪə, *Am:* nə'-] *n* la Namibie

Namibian I. *adj* namibien(ne) **II.** *n* Namibien(ne) *m(f)*

nan [nɑːn] *n Brit, inf* mamie *f*

nanny ['næni] *n* **1.** *(grandmother)* mamie *f* **2.** *(babysitter)* nurse *f*

nanny goat *n* bique *f*

nanosecond ['nɑːnəʊ'sekənd, *Am:* -oʊˌ-] *n* nanoseconde *f*

nap[1] [næp] **I.** *n* sieste *f;* **to have a ~** faire une sieste **II.** <-pp-> *vi* faire une sieste; **to be caught ~ping** être pris au dépourvu

nap[2] [næp] *inv n* poil *m*

napalm ['neɪpɑːm] *inv n* napalm *m*

nape [neɪp] *n* nuque *f*

napkin ['næpkɪn] *n* serviette *f*

Napoleon [nə'pəʊlɪən, *Am:* -'poʊ-] *n* Napoléon *m*

nappy ['næpi] <-ies> *n* couche *f*

nappy liner *n* couche *f* **nappy rash** *n no pl* rougeurs *fpl* aux fesses

narcissism ['nɑːsɪsɪzəm, *Am:* 'nɑːrsəsɪ-] *n no pl* narcissisme *m*

narcissus [nɑː'sɪsəs, *Am:* nɑːr'-] <narcissuses *o* -(narcissi)> *n* narcisse *m*

narcotic [nɑː'kɒtɪk, *Am:* nɑːr'kɑːt̬-] **I.** *n* **1.** *Am* LAW *(illegal drug)* stupéfiant *m* **2.** MED *(drug causing sleepiness)* narcotique *m* **II.** *adj* **1.** LAW *(illegal)* de stupéfiant **2.** MED *(sleep-inducing)* narcotique

nark [nɑːk, *Am:* nɑːrk] **I.** *vt inf* énerver **II.** *n Brit, inf* mouchard(e) *m(f)*

narrate [nə'reɪt, *Am:* 'nereɪt] *vt* raconter

narration [nə'reɪʃən, *Am:* ner'eɪʃən] *n no pl* narration *f*

narrative ['nærətɪv, *Am:* 'nerət̬ɪv] **I.** *n* récit *m* **II.** *adj* narratif(-ive)

narrator [nə'reɪtəʳ, *Am:* 'nereɪt̬ɚ] *n* narrateur, -trice *m, f*

narrow ['nærəʊ, *Am:* 'neroʊ] **I.** <-er, -est>

adj a. fig étroit(e); (*victory*) de justesse; **to have a ~ escape** l'échapper belle; **to have a ~ mind** avoir l'esprit étroit **II.** *vi* **1.** (*become narrow*) se rétrécir **2.** *fig* (*gap*) se réduire **III.** *vt* **1.** (*make ~*) rétrécir **2.** *fig* (*gap*) réduire; (*possibilities*) limiter

◆narrow down I. *vt* (*activities*) limiter; (*choices, possibilities*) restreindre; (*candidates*) réduire le nombre de **II.** *vi* se réduire; **to ~ to sth** se limiter à qc

narrowboat *n* NAUT *s.* **canal boat**

narrowly *adv* **1.** (*just*) de peu **2.** (*closely*) de près **3.** (*in a limited way*) étroitement

narrow-minded *adj* (*person*) à l'esprit étroit; (*opinions, views*) étroit(e)

NASA ['næsə] *n no pl, no art, Am abbr of* **National Aeronautics and Space Administration** NASA *f*

nasal ['neɪzl] *adj* **1.** (*concerning nose*) nasal(e) **2.** (*squeaky: voice*) nasillard(e)

nascent ['næsənt] *adj* naissant(e)

nastiness ['nɑːstɪnəs, *Am:* 'næstɪ-] *inv n* **1.** (*being unpleasant*) caractère *m* désagréable; (*of a smell*) mauvaise odeur *f;* (*of a taste*) mauvais goût *m* **2.** (*being bad*) méchanceté *f* **3.** (*amorality*) caractère *m* ignoble

nasturtium [nə'stɜːʃəm, *Am:* -'stɜːr-] *n* capucine *f*

nasty ['nɑːsti, *Am:* 'næsti] <-ier, -iest> *adj* **1.** (*unpleasant*) désagréable **2.** (*spiteful*) méchant(e); **to turn ~** devenir méchant **3.** (*bad, serious: accident, habit*) vilain(e) **4.** (*morally bad*) ignoble; **to have a ~ mind** avoir l'esprit mal tourné

natal ['neɪtl, *Am:* -t̬l] *adj* natal(e)

nation ['neɪʃən] *n* **1.** (*country, state*) nation *f;* **to serve the ~** servir l'État *m* **2.** (*people living in a state*) peuple *m;* **the whole ~** le pays entier **3.** *Am* (*ethnic group or tribe*) nation *f*

national ['næʃənəl] **I.** *adj* national(e) **II.** *n pl* ressortissant(e) *m(f)*

national anthem *n* hymne *m* national **national debt** *n* dette *f* publique

> Le **national emblem** (emblème national) de l'Angleterre est la "Tudor rose", la rose blanche de la maison royale de York posée à plat sur la rose rouge de la maison des Lancaster. L'emblème national de l'Irlande est le "shamrock", une sorte de trèfle que son patron Saint Patrick aurait utilisé pour symboliser la Sainte Trinité. Le "thistle" (chardon) de l'Écosse a été choisi comme emblème national par le roi James III au 15ème siècle. Le "dragon" du pays de Galles fut utilisé jadis comme emblème sur les bannières. Les Gallois ont aussi le "leek" (poireau) comme symbole qui, selon Shakespeare, fut porté lors de la bataille de Poitiers contre les Français en 1356; la "daffodil" (jonquille), bien plus poétique, remplace ce premier symbole depuis le 20ème siècle.

National Front *n* Front *m* national **National Health Service** *n Brit* Sécurité *f* sociale **national income** *n* revenu *m* national **National Insurance** *n Brit* cotisation *f* à la Sécurité sociale

nationalism ['næʃnəlɪzəm] *n no pl, pej* nationalisme *m*

nationalist ['næʃnəlɪst] **I.** *adj* nationaliste **II.** *n* nationaliste *mf*

nationalistic *adj pej* nationaliste

nationality [ˌnæʃə'næləti] <-ties> *n* nationalité *f;* **to have British ~** être de nationalité anglaise

nationalization [ˌnæʃənəlaɪ'zeɪʃən, *Am:* -ɪ'-] *n* nationalisation *f*

nationalize ['næʃənəlaɪz] *vt* nationaliser

national park *n* parc *m* national **National Socialism** *n* national-socialisme *m*

nation state *n* état-nation *m* **nationwide** **I.** *adv* à l'échelle nationale; (*opinion*) national(e) **II.** *adj* au niveau national; (*be known*) dans tout le pays

native ['neɪtɪv, *Am:* -t̬ɪv] **I.** *adj* **1.** (*born in or local to place*) natif(-ive); (*plant*) aborigène **2.** (*of place of origin*) de naissance; (*country*) d'origine **3.** (*indigenous, primitive*) indigène; (*village*) primitif(-ive) **4.** (*local, traditional*) du pays **5.** (*original*) natif(-ive); (*language*) maternel(le) **6.** (*innate aptitude*) naturel(le); (*talent*) inné(e) **II.** *n* **1.** (*born, living in a place*) autochtone *mf;* **to be a ~ of Monaco** être originaire de Monaco; **to speak English like a ~** parler l'anglais comme un natif **2.** *pej* (*indigene*) indigène *mf*

Native American **I.** *n* Amérindien(ne) *m(f)* **II.** *adj* amérindien(ne) **native speaker** *n* locuteur, -trice *m, f* natif(-ive); **to be an English ~** être de langue maternelle anglaise

Nativity [nə'tɪvəti, *Am:* -ət̬i] *n no pl* la Nativité

NATO, Nato ['neɪtəʊ, *Am:* -t̬oʊ] *n no pl, no art abbr of* **North Atlantic Treaty Organisation** OTAN *f;* **~ troops** les troupes de l'OTAN

natter ['nætəʳ, *Am:* 'næt̬ɚ] *inf* **I.** *vi inf* bavarder; **to ~ away for hours** bavarder pendant des heures **II.** *n* causerie *f;* **to have a ~ with sb** bavarder avec qn

natty <-ier, -iest> *adj inf* **1.** (*spruce, smart: dress*) chic *inv* **2.** (*well-designed*) bien imaginé(e); (*car*) bien conçu(e) **3.** (*handy*) astucieux(-euse)

natural ['nætʃərəl, *Am:* -ɚəl] **I.** *adj* naturel(le); (*state*) primitif(-ive); (*parents*) biologique; **it's ~** c'est normal; **it's only ~ that** il est tout à fait naturel que *+subj;* **to be a ~ leader** être né pour être un meneur **II.** *n inf* talent *m;* **to be a ~ for sth** être doué pour qc; **as a singer, she's a ~** c'est une chanteuse née

natural-born *adj* né(e) **natural childbirth** *n no pl* accouchement *m* naturel **natural classification** *n* classification *f* naturelle **natural food** *n* alimentation *f* naturelle

N

natural gas *n* gaz *m* naturel **natural history** *n* histoire *f* naturelle
naturalism ['nætʃərəlɪzəm, *Am:* -ɚəl-] *n no pl* naturalisme *m*
naturalist I. *n* naturaliste *mf* II. *adj* naturaliste
naturalistic [ˌnætʃərəl'ɪstɪk, *Am:* -ɚəl-] *adj* naturaliste
naturalization [ˌnætʃərəlaɪ'zeɪʃən, *Am:* -ɚəlɪ'-] *n* naturalisation *f*
naturalize ['nætʃərəlaɪz, *Am:* -ɚəl-] I. *vt* naturaliser II. *vi* BOT s'acclimater
natural language *n* langage *m* naturel **natural law** *n* loi *f* de la nature **natural life** *n* espérance *f* de vie
naturally *adv* naturellement; **it comes ~ to her** c'est inné chez elle; **she's ~ generous** elle est d'un naturel généreux
natural numbers *npl* nombres *mpl* naturels **natural resources** *npl* ressources *fpl* naturelles **natural science**, **natural sciences** *npl* sciences *fpl* naturelles **natural selection** *n* sélection *f* naturelle **natural wastage** *n Brit* départs *mpl* volontaires
nature ['neɪtʃəʳ, *Am:* -tʃɚ] *n* 1. *no pl, no art* (*environment, natural forces*) nature *f* 2. (*essential qualities, temperament*) nature *f*; **things of this ~** les choses de ce genre; **in the ~ of things** dans la nature des choses; **by ~** de nature; **it's in her ~ to do that** c'est dans son tempérament de faire ça
nature conservancy *n no pl* protection *f* de la nature **nature lover** *n* amoureux, -euse *m, f* de la nature **nature reserve** *n* réserve *f* naturelle **nature study** *n no pl* histoire *f* naturelle **nature trail** *n* sentier *m* (aménagé) **nature worship** *n no pl* (*worshipping nature*) adoration *f* de la nature
naturism ['neɪtʃərɪzəm] *n* naturisme *m*
naturist ['neɪtʃərɪst] *n* naturiste *mf*
naught [nɔːt, *Am:* nɑːt] *n* zéro *m* ►**to come to ~** n'aboutir à rien
naughty ['nɔːti, *Am:* 'nɑːţi] <-ier, -iest> *adj* 1. (*badly behaved, mischievous*) *a. iron* vilain(e) 2. (*wicked*) méchant(e) 3. *iron, inf* (*sexually stimulating*) cochon(ne)
Nauru [nɑː'uːruː] *n* Nauru *f*
nausea ['nɔːsɪə, *Am:* 'nɑːzɪə] *n no pl* nausée *f*; **a feeling of ~** une envie de vomir; **to suffer from ~** avoir mal au cœur
nauseate ['nɔːsɪeɪt, *Am:* 'nɑːzɪ-] *vt a. fig, pej, form* écœurer; **to be ~d by sth** être dégoûté par qc
nauseating *adj* 1. (*making feel sick*) nauséabond(e) 2. *fig, pej* dégoûtant(e)
nauseous ['nɔːsɪəs, *Am:* 'nɑːʃəs] *adj* nauséeux(-euse); **to be** [*o* **feel**] **~** avoir des nausées
nautical ['nɔːtɪkəl, *Am:* 'nɑːţɪ-] *adj* nautique
nautical mile *n* mil(l)e *m* nautique
naval ['neɪvəl] *adj* naval(e); (*officer*) de marine
naval academy *n* école *f* navale **naval base** *n* base *f* navale **naval power** *n* puissance *f* maritime **naval repair yard** *n* chantier *m* naval **naval warfare** *n no pl* 1. (*military fighting*) guerre *f* maritime 2. (*act of fighting*) combat *m* naval
nave [neɪv] *n* nef *f*
navel ['neɪvl] *n* nombril *m* ►**to contemplate one's ~** se regarder le nombril
navigable *adj* navigable; (*balloon*) dirigeable
navigate ['nævɪgeɪt] I. *vt* 1. NAUT naviguer; **to ~ the ocean/a river** naviguer sur l'océan/une rivière 2. (*steer, pilot*) gouverner 3. (*manage to get through*) **to ~ one's way to the door** se frayer un chemin jusqu'à la porte 4. (*overcome*) surmonter II. *vi* 1. NAUT, AVIAT naviguer 2. AUTO diriger
navigation [ˌnævɪ'geɪʃən] *n no pl* navigation *f*
navigator ['nævɪgeɪtəʳ, *Am:* -ţɚ] *n* 1. NAUT navigateur, -trice *m, f* 2. AUTO assistant(e) *m(f)* du pilote
navvy ['nævi] <-vvies> *n Brit, inf* terrassier *m*
navy ['neɪvi] I. <-vies> *n* 1. (*military fleet*) **the Navy** la Marine; **to serve in the ~** servir dans la marine 2. (*colour*) marine II. *adj* bleu marine *inv*
nay [neɪ] I. *adv form* même II. *n Am* non *m*; **ayes and ~s** voix pour et contre
Nazi ['nɑːtsi] *n a. pej* nazi(e) *m(f)*
Naziism *no pl,* **Nazism** *n no pl* nazisme *m*
NB [ˌen'biː] *adv no pl abbr of* **nota bene** NB
NCO [ˌensiː'əʊ, *Am:* -'oʊ] *n abbr of* **Non-Commissoned Officer** sous-officier *m*
NE [ˌen'iː] *n abbr of* **north-east** N-E *m*
neap tide *n* marée *f* de morte-eau
near [nɪəʳ, *Am:* nɪr] I. *adj* 1. (*over distance*) proche; **the ~est place** l'endroit le plus proche 2. (*in time*) proche; **in the ~ future** dans un proche avenir 3. (*dear*) proche; **a ~ and dear friend** un ami intime 4. (*similar*) proche; (*portrait*) ressemblant(e); **the ~est thing to sth** ce qui se rapproche le plus de qc 5. (*not quite*) **to the ~est pound** à une livre près; **to have a ~ accident** frôler l'accident; **to have a ~ escape** s'échapper de justesse II. *adv* 1. (*in space or time*) près; **to be ~** (*building*) être à proximité; (*event*) être imminent; **to come ~** s'approcher; **how ~ is the post office?** à quelle distance se trouve la poste?; **to live quite ~** habiter tout près; **~ at hand** à portée de (la) main; **to come ~er to sb/sth** se rapprocher de qn/qc; **we're getting ~ Easter** nous nous approchons de Pâques 2. (*almost*) presque; **a ~ perfect murder** un meurtre presque parfait; **as ~ as I can guess** autant que je puisse deviner *subj* 3. **~ to** (*person*) proche de; (*building, town*) près de; **to be ~ to tears** *fig* être au bord des larmes; **to be ~ to doing sth** être sur le point de faire qc; **I came ~ to winning** j'ai presque gagné III. *prep* 1. (*in proximity to*) **~ sb/sth** près de qn/qc; **~ the house** aux abords de la maison; **~ the end/top of the page** vers la fin/le haut de la page; **to be nowhere ~ sth** être loin de qc;

we're nowhere ~ an agreement nous sommes loin de trouver un accord; **to be ~ the end of the month** être vers la fin du mois **2.** (*almost*) **it's ~/nowhere ~ midnight** il est presque/loin d'être minuit; **it's ~ Christmas** Noël approche; **it's nowhere ~ enough** c'est loin de suffire **3.** (*like*) **it's the same story or ~ it** c'est la même histoire ou presque; **nowhere ~ the truth** à mille lieues de la vérité **IV.** *vt* s'approcher de; **it's ~ing completion** c'est presque achevé; **to be ~ing one's goal** toucher au but

nearby ['nɪəbaɪ, *Am:* ˌnɪr'-] **I.** *adj* proche; **there are a few shops ~** il y a quelques magasins tout près d'ici **II.** *adv* à proximité; **is it ~?** est-ce que c'est tout près d'ici?

Near East *n* **the ~** le Proche-Orient

nearly ['nɪəli, *Am:* 'nɪr-] *adv* presque; **~ certain** à peu près certain; **not ~ enough** loin d'être suffisant; **to be not ~ as bad as sth** être loin d'être aussi mauvais que qc; **to be ~ there** être presque arrivé; **to be ~ screaming** être sur le point de crier; **he very ~ lost his life** il a failli perdre la vie

near miss <-es> *n* **1.** (*attack*) coup *m* raté de peu; **it was a ~** cela a raté de peu **2.** (*accident*) accident *m* évité de justesse; **to have a ~** y échapper de justesse; **that was a ~** il s'en est fallu de peu **3.** *fig* **the lottery was a ~ for him** il a raté la loterie de peu **nearside** *Brit, Aus* **I.** *n* côté *m* gauche **II.** *adj* (*lane*) de gauche **near-sighted** *adj Am* myope **near-sightedness** *n no pl* myopie *f*

neat [ni:t] *adj* **1.** (*orderly, well-ordered*) ordonné(e); (*room*) bien rangé(e); (*handwriting, appearance*) soigné(e); (*beard*) bien soigné(e); **to be ~ in one's dress** s'habiller de façon soignée; **~ and tidy** propre et bien rangé **2.** (*skilful*) adroit(e); (*answer*) bien formulé(e) **3.** (*undiluted, pure*) sec(sèche) **4.** *Am, Aus, inf* (*good: bike*) super *inv;* (*guy*) formidable

neatly *adj* **1.** (*carefully*) soigneusement **2.** (*cleverly*) adroitement

neatness *n no pl* (*of person*) apparence *f* soignée; (*of house, dress*) netteté *f*

Nebraska [nɪ'bræskə, *Am:* nə-] **I.** *n* le Nebraska **II.** *adj* du Nebraska

nebulous ['nebjʊləs] *adj* nébuleux(-euse); (*promise*) vague

necessarily ['nesəsərəli] *adv* **1.** (*as a necessary result*) nécessairement **2.** (*inevitably, therefore*) inévitablement **3.** (*perforce*) forcément; **I don't ~ have to believe him** je ne suis pas forcé de le croire

necessary ['nesəsəri, *Am:* -ser-] **I.** *adj* nécessaire; **to make the ~ arrangements** prendre les dispositions utiles; **the restructuring is ~** la reconstruction est indispensable; **it is ~ that** il faut que *+subj;* **it is ~ for him to do it** il faut qu'il le fasse *+subj;* **it is not ~ to** *+infin* ce n'est pas la peine de *+infin;* **to do what is ~** faire ce qu'il faut; **if ~** au besoin **II.** *n* **1.** (*requirements*) **the ~** le nécessaire **2.** *inf* (*money*) **the ~** le fric

necessitate [nɪ'sesɪteɪt, *Am:* nə'-] *vt form* nécessiter; **to ~ sb's doing sth** obliger qn à faire qc

necessity [nɪ'sesəti, *Am:* nə'sesət̬i] <-ties> *n* **1.** *no pl* (*the fact of being necessary*) nécessité *f;* **a case of absolute ~** un cas de force majeure **2.** (*need*) besoin *m;* **in case of ~** en cas de besoin; **when the ~ arises** quand le besoin se fait sentir; **~ for sb to** *+infin* besoin pour qn de *+infin* **3.** (*basic need*) besoin *m;* **to be a ~** être indispensable; **the bare necessities** le strict nécessaire ▶ **~ is the mother of invention** *prov* la nécessité rend ingénieux

neck [nek] **I.** *n* **1.** (*body part*) cou *m* **2.** (*nape*) nuque *f* **3.** (*area below head*) encolure *f* **4.** (*cleavage*) décolleté *m* **5.** (*cut of meat*) collier *m* **6.** (*long thin object part: of a bottle*) goulot *m;* (*of a vase*) col *m;* (*of a violin*) manche *m* **7.** (*distance in horse racing*) **by a ~** d'une encolure ▶ **in this ~ of the woods** *inf* dans le coin; **to be up to one's ~ in sth** *inf* être complètement impliqué dans qc; **to be breathing down sb's ~** être tout près de qn; **to fling one's arms round sb's ~** se jeter au cou de qn; **to get it in the ~** avoir des ennuis; **to have sb around one's ~** avoir qn sur le dos; **to finish ~ and ~** arriver au coude à coude; **to stick one's ~ out** prendre des risques **II.** *vi inf* **1.** (*kiss*) se bécoter **2.** (*caress*) se peloter

necklace *n* collier *m* **neckline** *n* encolure *f;* **low ~** décolleté *m* **necktie** *n Am* cravate *f*

nectar ['nektə^r, *Am:* -tɚ] *n* nectar *m*

nectarine ['nektərɪn, *Am:* ˌnetə'ri:n] *n* nectarine *f*

née [neɪ] *adj* née

need [ni:d] **I.** *n* **1.** (*want, requirement, lack*) besoin *m;* **his ~ is greater than yours** il est plus dans le besoin que toi; **to be badly in ~ of sth** avoir grandement besoin de qc; **the ~ for vigilance** la nécessité d'être vigilant; **to meet sb's ~s** subvenir aux besoins de qn; **as the ~ arises** quand la nécessité se fera ressentir; **if ~ be** en cas de besoin; **there's no ~ to buy it** il n'est pas nécessaire de l'acheter; **there's no ~ to shout!** tu n'as pas besoin de crier!; **no ~ for tears** pas besoin de pleurer **2.** *no pl* (*emergency, crisis*) difficulté *f;* **in his hour of ~ his friend was there** dans les moments difficiles, son ami était là **II.** *vt* **1.** (*require*) avoir besoin de; **all you ~ is a pen** tu n'as besoin que d'un stylo; **I ~ time to think** il me faut du temps pour réfléchir; **you'll be ~ing your sunglasses today!** tu devras porter tes lunettes aujourd'hui!; **I ~ someone to help me** j'ai besoin que l'on m'aide; **teaching ~s patience** l'enseignement requiert de la patience; **some changes are sorely ~ed** on a grandement besoin de quelques changements; **your dogs ~ brushing** vos chiens auraient besoin d'être brossés **2.** (*must,*

N

have to) **to ~ to** *+infin* être obligé de *+infin;* **he ~s to improve** il faut qu'il s'améliore; **they didn't ~ to wait long** ils n'ont pas eu à attendre longtemps; **you ~ to read these books** il est nécessaire que tu lises ces livres; **they ~ to be tested** ils doivent être testés ►**that's all we ~!** *iron* il ne manquait plus que ça! **III.** *aux* **~ I attend the conference?** faut-il vraiment que j'assiste à la conférence?; **his death ~ never have happened so soon** sa mort n'aurait jamais dû arriver si tôt; **you ~n't worry** *inf* tu n'as pas à t'inquiéter; **to ~ not** *+infin* ne pas avoir à *+infin;* **you ~n't have done all this work** *Brit* il n'était pas nécessaire que vous fassiez tout ce travail; **you ~n't take your car** ce n'est pas la peine que vous preniez votre voiture

needle ['ni:dl] **I.** *n* aiguille *f* ►**to look** [*o* **search**] **for a ~ in a haystack** chercher une aiguille dans une botte de foin; **to be on the ~** se piquer **II.** *vt* **1.** *inf* (*annoy*) agacer **2.** (*prick*) piquer

needle match *n* match *m* acharné

needless *adj* superflu(e); **~ to say ...** inutile de dire ...

needlework *n no pl* couture *f*

needs [ni:dz] *adv* nécessairement; **~ must, must ~** *form* il le faut bien

needy ['ni:di] **I.** <-ier, -iest> *adj* nécessiteux(-euse) **II.** *npl* **the ~** les nécessiteux

ne'er-do-well *n* vaurien(ne) *m(f)*

nefarious [nɪ'feərɪəs, *Am:* nə'ferɪ-] *adj pej, form* infâme

negate [nɪ'geɪt] *vt* **1.** *form* (*nullify*) annuler **2.** (*deny existence of*) nier l'existence de **3.** LING mettre au négatif

negation [nɪ'geɪʃən] *n no pl, form* négation *f;* **to be the ~ of sth** être l'antithèse de qc

negative ['negətɪv, *Am:* -t̬ɪv] **I.** *adj* **1.** (*denoting denial, refusal*) *a.* ELEC négatif(-ive) **2.** (*expressing negation: clause*) de nullité **3.** (*pessimistic*) négatif(-ive); **to be ~ about sb/sth** se montrer négatif au sujet de qn/qc **II.** *n* **1.** (*rejection, refusal*) négative *f;* **in the ~** par la négative **2.** (*photographic image*) négatif *m* **III.** *vt* **1.** (*say no to*) dire non à **2.** (*reject, decline*) rejeter **3.** (*contradict*) contredire **IV.** *interj* négatif!

negatively *adv* négativement

negative sign *n* signe *m* moins

negativity [ˌnegə'tɪvəti, *Am:* -ət̬i] *n* négativité *f*

neglect [nɪ'glekt] **I.** *vt* négliger; (*garden, building*) laisser à l'abandon; (*duties*) oublier; (*opportunity*) laisser échapper; **to ~ to** *+infin* omettre de *+infin* **II.** *n* **1.** (*not caring*) négligence *f;* **to happen through ~** être dû à la négligence **2.** (*poor state*) manque *m* d'entretien; **to be in a state of ~** être à l'abandon

neglected *adv* négligé(e); (*building*) mal entretenu(e); (*family*) délaissé(e); **to feel ~** se sentir délaissé

neglectful *adj* négligent(e); **to be ~ of sb/sth** négliger qn/qc; **to be ~ of one's duties** être oublieux de son devoir

negligence ['neglɪdʒənts] *n no pl* négligence *f*

negligent *adj* négligent(e); (*attitude, air*) nonchalant(e); **to be ~ of sth** négliger qc

negligible ['neglɪdʒəbl] *adj* négligeable

negotiable *adj* **1.** (*can be negotiated*) négociable **2.** (*able to be traversed*) franchissable; (*road*) praticable **3.** (*transferable*) transférable; **~ securities** fonds *mpl* négociables

negotiate [nɪ'gəʊʃieɪt, *Am:* -'goʊ-] **I.** *vt* **1.** (*discuss, bargain*) négocier; **to be ~d** à débattre **2.** (*travel through: obstacle*) franchir; (*bend*) négocier **3.** (*surmount or solve: problems, difficulties*) surmonter **II.** *vi* négocier; **to ~ for peace with sb** entreprendre des pourparlers de paix avec qn; **to ~ with sb** être en pourparlers avec qn

negotiation [nɪˌgəʊʃi'eɪʃən, *Am:* -ˌgoʊ-] *n* négociation *f;* **to be in ~ with sb** être en pourparlers avec qn

negotiator *n* négociateur, -trice *m, f*

Negress ['ni:gres, *Am:* -grɪs] *n pej* négresse *f*

Negro ['ni:grəʊ, *Am:* -groʊ] <-es> **I.** *n pej* nègre *m* **II.** *adj pej* nègre

neigh [neɪ] **I.** *n* hennissement *m* **II.** *vi* hennir

neighbor ['neɪbɚ] *Am, Aus* **I.** *n* **1.** (*person living next-door*) voisin(e) *m(f)* **2.** (*adjacent country*) pays *m* limitrophe **3.** (*fellow-citizen*) prochain *m* ►**love your ~ as you love yourself** aime ton prochain comme toi-même **II.** *vi Am* **to ~ with sb** se montrer bon voisin avec qn

neighborhood ['neɪbɚhʊd] *n Am, Aus* **1.** (*quarter*) quartier *m;* **the library is in my ~** la bibliothèque est près de chez moi; **~ shops** commerces *mpl* de proximité **2.** (*people of the quarter*) voisinage *m* **3.** (*vicinity*) environs *mpl;* **in the ~ of sth** *fig* aux alentours de qc

neighboring *adj Am, Aus* **1.** (*nearby, not far away*) avoisinant(e) **2.** (*bordering*) limitrophe; (*country*) frontalier(-ère)

neighborliness *n Am, Aus no pl* bon voisinage *m;* **good ~** bons rapports *mpl* entre voisins

neighborly ['neɪbɚli] *adj Am, Aus* (*relations, visit*) de bon voisinage; (*person*) amical(e); **to be ~ people** être de bons voisins

neighbour *Brit, Aus s.* **neighbor**

neighbourhood *n Brit, Aus s.* **neighborhood**

neighbouring *adj Brit, Aus s.* **neighboring**

neighbourliness *n Brit, Aus s.* **neighborliness**

neighbourly *adj Brit, Aus s.* **neighborly**

neither ['naɪðər, *Am:* 'ni:ðɚ] **I.** *pron* aucun (des deux); **which one? – ~** (**of them**) lequel? – ni l'un ni l'autre **II.** *adv* ni; **~ ... nor ...** ni ... ni ...; **he is ~ hurt nor dead** il n'est ni blessé ni mort ►**sth is ~ here nor there** qc importe peu **III.** *conj* non plus; **if he won't eat, ~ will I** s'il ne mange pas, moi non plus **IV.** *adj* aucun des deux; **in ~ case** ni dans un cas ni dans l'autre; **~ book is good** ces deux livres ne sont bons ni l'un ni l'autre

neoclassical [ˌniːəʊ'klæsɪkəl, *Am:* -oʊ'-] *adj* néo-classique

Neolithic [ˌniːəʊ'lɪθɪk, *Am:* -oʊ'-] *adj* néolithique ►**to live in the ~ age** vivre à l'âge de pierre

neologism [niː'ɒlədʒɪzəm, *Am:* -'ɑːlə-] *n form* néologisme *m*

neon ['niːɒn, *Am:* -ɑːn] *n* néon *m*

neo-Nazi I. *n* néonazi(e) *m(f)* II. *adj* néonazi(e) **neo-Nazism** *n* néonazisme *m*

neon lamp, **neon light** *n* éclairage *m* au néon **neon sign** *n* enseigne *f* au néon **neon tube** *n* néon *m*

Nepal [nə'pɔːl] *n* le Népal

Nepalese [ˌnepəl'iːz], **Nepali** [nɪ'pɔːli] I. *adj* népalais(e) II. *n* 1. (*person*) Népalais(e) *m(f)* 2. LING népalais *m; s. a.* **English**

nephew ['nevjuː, *Am:* 'nef-] *n* neveu *m*

nephritis [nɪ'fraɪtɪs, *Am:* -t̬əs] *n no pl* néphrite *f*

nepotism ['nepətɪzəm] *n no pl, pej* népotisme *m*

Neptune ['neptjuːn] *n no pl* Neptune *f*

nerd [nɜːd, *Am:* nɜːrd] *n inf* nul(le) *m(f)*

nerve [nɜːv, *Am:* nɜːrv] I. *n* 1. ANAT nerf *m;* **~ ending** terminaison *f* nerveuse; **~ disease** maladie *f* des nerfs 2. *pl* (*worry*) nerfs *mpl;* **to be a bundle of ~s** être un paquet de nerfs; **to calm one's ~s** se calmer; **to get on sb's ~s** *inf* agacer qn; **to live on one's ~s** *Brit* vivre sur les nerfs 3. *no pl, inf* (*audacity*) culot *m;* **to have the ~ to** +*infin* avoir le culot de +*infin* 4. *no pl* (*courage*) courage *m;* **to keep/lose one's ~** avoir/perdre son sang-froid ►**~s of iron** [*o* **steel**] des nerfs très solides; **to hit a (raw) ~** toucher le nerf sensible II. *vt* donner du courage à; **to ~ oneself (up) to** +*infin Brit* s'armer de courage pour +*infin*

nerveless *adj* 1. (*without nerves, calm*) imperturbable 2. (*lacking courage, coolness*) inerte 3. (*diffuse, insipid*) insipide; **to be ~** manquer de vigueur 4. ANAT, BIO sans nerfs; (*plants*) sans nervures

nerve-racking, **nerve-wrecking** *adj* éprouvant(e)

nervous ['nɜːvəs, *Am:* 'nɜːr-] *adj* 1. (*agitated, excited*) nerveux(-euse); **to be a ~ wreck** être à bout de nerfs; **to be ~ about doing sth** être nerveux à l'idée de faire qc 2. (*tense, anxious*) angoissé(e); **to make sb ~** rendre qn nerveux; **to feel ~** avoir les nerfs en boule; **to be ~ about doing sth** avoir peur de faire qc; **to be ~ in sb's presence** ne pas être à son aise devant qn 3. (*timid*) timide; **to make sb ~** mettre qn mal à l'aise; **to be ~** (*for performance, test*) avoir le trac 4. MED nerveux(-euse)

nervous breakdown *n* dépression *f* nerveuse

nervously *adv* nerveusement

nervousness *n no pl* 1. (*nervous condition*) nervosité *f* 2. (*fearfulness, anxiety*) trac *m*

nervous system *n* système *m* nerveux

nervy ['nɜːvi, *Am:* 'nɜːr-] <-ier, -iest> *adj* 1. *Am, pej* (*rude and bold*) **to be ~** avoir du toupet 2. *Brit* (*nervous*) nerveux(-euse)

nest [nest] I. *n* 1. (*animal's home*) nid *m* 2. (*set*) jeu *m* II. *vi* se nicher

nest egg *n* pécule *m*

nesting box *n* nichoir *m*

nestle ['nesl] I. *vt* blottir; **to ~ sth on sb/sth** blottir qc dans qc/contre qn II. *vi* (*child*) se blottir; **to ~ down in bed** se pelotonner dans son lit; **to ~ amongst sth** se nicher parmi qc; **to ~ up to sb** se nicher contre qc; **a village nestling in the hills** un village niché sur la colline

nestling ['nestlɪŋ] *n* oisillon *m*

net[1] [net] I. *n* 1. *a. fig* filet *m* 2. *no pl* (*material*) tulle *f;* **~ stockings** bas *mpl* résilles ►**to slip through the ~** passer à travers les mailles du filet II. <-tt-> *vt* 1. (*catch: fish*) attraper; (*criminals*) arrêter 2. (*hit into a net*) **to ~ sth** envoyer qc dans le filet

net[2] [net] I. *adj* 1. (*after deduction*) net(te) 2. (*final*) final(e) II. *vt* (*profit*) rapporter net; (*of person*) gagner net

Net [net] *n* INFOR **the ~** le Net; **a ~ surfer** un(e) infonaute, un(e) internaute

netball ['netbɔːl] *n Brit no pl* netball *m*

net curtain *n* voilage *m*

Netherlands ['neðələndz, *Am:* -ɚləndz] *n* **the ~** les Pays-Bas *mpl*

netiquette ['netɪket] *n* INFOR étiquette *f* de réseau, nétiquette *f*

Netspeak ['netspiːk] *adj* INFOR internetais(e)

netting ['netɪŋ, *Am:* 'net̬ɪŋ] *n no pl* 1. (*material*) filets *mpl* 2. SPORT (*netted structure*) treillis *m* métallique

nettle ['netl, *Am:* 'net̬-] I. *n* ortie *f* ►**to grasp the ~** prendre le taureau par les cornes II. *vt* agacer

nettlerash *n* urticaire *f*

network ['netwɜːk, *Am:* -wɜːrk] I. *n* 1. (*system*) réseau *m;* **~ card** INFOR carte *f* réseau 2. (*number, variety*) ensemble *m* 3. (*group of broadcasting stations*) chaînes *fpl;* **~ television** chaîne *f* de télévision nationale II. *vt* 1. (*link together*) relier; INFOR, TECH connecter 2. (*broadcast*) diffuser III. *vi* tisser un réseau de relations

networking *n no pl* 1. INFOR (*work*) travail *m* en réseau 2. INFOR (*connecting*) mise *f* en réseau 3. (*making contacts*) établissement *m* d'un réseau de contacts

neural ['njʊərəl, *Am:* 'nʊrəl] *adj* nerveux(-euse)

neuralgia [njʊə'rældʒə, *Am:* nʊ'-] *n no pl* névralgie *f*

neuralgic [njuː'rældʒɪk, *Am:* nʊ'-] *adj* névralgique

neurasthenia [ˌnjʊərəs'θiːnɪə, *Am:* ˌnʊræs'-] *n* neurasthénie *f*

neuritis [njʊə'raɪtɪs, *Am:* nʊ'raɪt̬əs] *n* né-

vrite *f*
neurological *adj* neurologique
neurologist *n* neurologue *mf*
neurology [njʊəˈrɒlədʒi, *Am:* nʊˈrɑːlə-] *n no pl* neurologie *f*
neuron [ˈnjʊərɒn, *Am:* ˈnʊrɑːn], **neurone** *n* neurone *m*
neurosis [njʊəˈrəʊsɪs, *Am:* nʊˈroʊ-] <neuroses> *n* névrose *f*
neurosurgeon *n* neurochirurgien(ne) *m(f)*
neurosurgery *n no pl* neurochirurgie *f*
neurotic [njʊəˈrɒtɪk, *Am:* nʊˈrɑːt̬ɪk] **I.** *n* névrosé(e) *m(f)* **II.** *adj* névrosé(e)
neuter [ˈnjuːtəʳ, *Am:* ˈnuːt̬ɚ] **I.** *adj* neutre **II.** *vt* **1.** *(castrate: males)* castrer **2.** *(sterilize)* châtrer **3.** *(weaken, neutralize)* neutraliser
neutral [ˈnjuːtrəl, *Am:* ˈnuː-] **I.** *adj* **1.** *(impartial)* neutre **2.** *(unemotional)* de marbre **II.** *n* **1.** *(non-combatant)* neutre *m* **2.** AUTO point *m* mort
neutrality [njuːˈtræləti, *Am:* nuːˈtræləṭi] *n no pl* neutralité *f*
neutralization [ˌnjuːtrəlaɪˈzeɪʃən, *Am:* ˌnuːtrəlɪˈ-] *n no pl* neutralisation *f*
neutralize [ˈnjuːtrəlaɪz, *Am:* ˈnuː-] *vt* neutraliser
neutron [ˈnjuːtrɒn, *Am:* ˈnuːtrɑːn] *n* neutron *m*
neutron bomb *n* bombe *f* à neutrons
Nevada [nəˈvɑːdə, *Am:* -væ-] **I.** *n* le Nevada **II.** *adj* du Nevada
never [ˈnevəʳ, *Am:* -ɚ] *adv* jamais; **I ~ eat meat** je ne mange jamais de viande; **~ in all my life** jamais de la vie; **~ again!** plus jamais!; **~ ever** plus jamais; **he ~ told me that!** *inf* elle ne m'a pas dit ça! ►**~ <u>mind</u>** ça ne fait rien; **~ <u>mind</u> that/him** ne fais pas attention à ça/lui
never-ending *adj* interminable
nevermore *adv* ne … plus jamais
nevertheless [ˌnevəðəˈles, *Am:* ˌnevɚ-] *adv* néanmoins
Nevisian **I.** *adj* névicien(ne) **II.** *n* Névicien(ne) *m(f)*
new [njuː, *Am:* nuː] **I.** *adj* **1.** *(just made)* neuf(neuve); **brand ~** tout neuf **2.** *(latest, replacing former one)* nouveau(-elle); **a ~ summer** un nouvel été; **~ blood** *fig* sang *m* nouveau; **a ~ boy/girl** *Brit* un nouveau/une nouvelle; **to feel like a ~ man/woman** se sentir revivre; **I'm ~ around here** je suis nouveau ici; **I'm ~ to the Internet/this job** je ne suis pas habitué à Internet/à ce boulot; **this place is ~ to me** je ne connais pas cet endroit; **everything is so ~ to me** je ne suis pas encore habitué; **we're ~ to London** nous venons d'arriver à Londres ►**a ~ <u>broom</u> sweeps clean** *prov* tout nouveau, tout beau; **<u>what's</u> ~?** quoi de neuf? **II.** *adv* récemment
New Age *adj* new age *inv* **newbie** *n* INFOR internaute *mf* novice **newborn** **I.** *adj* **1.** *(just born)* nouveau-né(e); **~ baby** nouveau-né(e) *m(f)* **2.** *(freshly formed: democracy, science)* tout(e) jeune **II.** *n pl* les nouveau-nés **New Brunswick** *n* le Nouveau-Brunswick **new-built** *adv* nouvellement construit **New Caledonia** *n* la Nouvelle-Calédonie **newcomer** *n* **1.** *(freshly arrived person)* nouveau venu *m*, nouvelle venue *f* **2.** *(beginner)* débutant(e) *m(f)*
newel [ˈnjuːəl, *Am:* ˈnuː-] *n* noyau *m*
New England *n* la Nouvelle-Angleterre **newfangled** *adj pej* dernier cri *inv* **new-fashioned** *adj* à la dernière mode **new-found** *adv* tout(e) nouveau(-elle) **Newfoundland**[1] *n* Terre-Neuve *f* **Newfoundland**[2], **Newfoundland dog** *n* ZOOL terre-neuve *m* **New Hampshire** *n* le New Hampshire
newish [ˈnjuːɪʃ, *Am:* ˈnuː-] *adj inf* assez neuf(neuve)
new-laid *adj* tout frais; **~ egg** œuf fraîchement pondu **new-look** *adj* new-look *inv*
newly *adv* **1.** *(recently)* nouvellement; **~-discovered documents** documents découverts récemment; **~ married** jeune marié(e) **2.** *(freshly, once again)* de frais; **~ painted** fraîchement peint(e)
newly-wed *n* jeune marié(e) *m(f)*
New Man *n Brit* homme *m* moderne **New Mexico** **I.** *n* le Nouveau-Mexique **II.** *adj* du Nouveau-Mexique **new-mown** *adv* fraîchement tondu **New Orleans** *n* la Nouvelle-Orléans
news [njuːz, *Am:* nuːz] *n no pl* **1.** *(fresh information)* nouvelle(s) *fpl;* **a piece of ~** une nouvelle; **the latest ~** les dernières nouvelles; **to be in the ~** faire parler de soi; **financial/sports ~** chronique *f* sportive/financière; **to break the ~ to sb** annoncer la nouvelle à qc; **when the ~ broke** quand on a su la nouvelle; **to have got ~ for sb** avoir du nouveau à annoncer à qc; **that's ~ to me** je ne savais pas **2.** TV, RADIO *(programme)* **the ~** informations *fpl;* **on the ~** aux informations ►**no ~ is <u>good</u> ~** *prov* pas de nouvelles, bonnes nouvelles
news agency *n* agence *f* de presse **newsagent** *n Brit, Aus* **1.** *(newspaper shop)* maison *f* de la presse **2.** *(person selling newspapers)* marchand(e) *m(f)* de journaux **news bulletin** *n Brit* bulletin *m* d'informations **newscast** *n* informations *fpl* **newscaster** *n* présentateur, -trice *m, f* **news channel** *n* chaîne *f* d'informations **news conference** *n* conférence *f* de presse **newsflash** *n* flash *m* d'information **newsgroup** *n* INFOR infogroupe *m*, forum *m* **news item** *n* **1.** point *m* d'information **2.** INFOR article *m* de forum **newsletter** *n* bulletin *m* **news magazine** *n* magazine *m* d'actualités **news media** *n* médias *mpl* **newsmonger** *n* commère *f inf*
New South Wales *n* les Nouvelles-Galles du Sud
newspaper *n* journal *m;* **daily ~** quotidien *m* **newspaper advertising** *n* publicité *f* dans la presse **newspaper editor** *n* rédacteur, -trice *m, f* **newspaperman** *n* journal-

iste *m* **newspaper report** *n* reportage *m* **newspaper reporter** *n* reporter *mf* **newspaperwoman** *n* journaliste *f*

newsprint *n no pl* **1.**(*paper*) papier *m* journal **2.**(*ink*) encre *f* **news program(me)** *n no pl* informations *fpl* télévisées **newsreader** *n Brit, Aus* présentateur, -trice *m, f* (de journal télévisé) **newsreel** *n* actualités *fpl* (filmées) **news release** *n Am* communiqué *m* de presse **newsroom** *n* salle *f* de rédaction **news-stand** *n* kiosque *m* **newsworthy** *adj* d'un intérêt médiatique; **a ~ event** un événement qui vaut la peine d'être publié

newsy ['nju:zi, *Am:* 'nu:-] <-ier, -iest> *adj* plein(e) de nouvelles

newt [nju:t, *Am:* nu:t] *n* triton *m*

New Testament *n no pl* Nouveau Testament *m* **new year** *n* nouvel an *m;* **~'s card** carte *f* de nouvel an; **Happy New Year!** bonne année! **New Year's Day** *n no pl* le jour de l'an **New Year's Eve** *n no pl* la Saint-Sylvestre **New York I.** *n* New York **II.** *adj* new-yorkais(e) **New Yorker** *n* New-yorkais(e) *m(f)* **New Zealand I.** *n* la Nouvelle-Zélande **II.** *adj* néo-zélandais(e) **New Zealander** *n* Néo-Zélandais(e) *m(f)*

next [nekst] **I.** *adj* **1.**(*after this one*) prochain(e); **~ month** le mois prochain; **you're ~** c'est votre tour; **she's** (**the**) **~ to** *+infin* c'est à son tour de *+infin;* **to be the ~ sth but one** être celui d'après; **who's ~?** à qui le tour? **2.**(*following*) suivant(e); **the ~ day** le lendemain; **in the ~ two days/ten minutes** d'ici deux jours/dix minutes **3.**(*in series, space: house*) voisin(e); **on the ~ floor up/down** à l'étage plus haut/bas; **at the ~ table** à la table d'à-côté; **I need the ~ size** il me faut une taille au-dessus **II.** *adv* **1.**(*afterwards*) ensuite; **David left ~** David est ensuite parti **2.**(*in a moment*) maintenant; **~, add the eggs** maintenant, incorporer les œufs **3.**(*second*) après; **the ~ oldest is John** c'est John qui est ensuite le plus âgé **4.**(*again*) la prochaine fois; **when I ~ come** quand je reviendrai **III.** *pron* **the ~** le(la) prochain(e); **after this bus, the ~ is in one hour** le prochain bus est dans une heure; **the ~ to leave was David** ensuite, c'est David qui est parti; **from one minute to the ~** d'une minute à l'autre; **I'm in London one day, Paris the ~** je suis à Londres un jour, à Paris le lendemain

next door I. *adv* à côté **II.** *adj* **1.**(*in or at the next place*) d'à-côté; **to be the boy/girl ~ type** être quelqu'un de très simple **2.** *Brit, fig* **to be ~ to sth** il s'en faut de peu pour qu'il soit ... **III.** *n* maison *f* d'à-côté; **the woman/man ~** la dame/le monsieur d'à-côté **next-door neighbour** *n* voisin(e) *m(f)* d'à-côté **next of kin** *n* plus proche parent *m*

next to *adv* **1.**(*beside*) à côté de; **~ the skin** à même la peau **2.**(*almost*) presque; **to cost ~ nothing** coûter trois fois rien; **it takes ~ no time** c'est très rapide **3.**(*second to*) **~ last** avant-dernier; **~ Bach, I like Mozart best** après Bach, c'est Mozart que je préfère

nexus ['neksəs] *n* lien *m*

NF [ˌen'ef] *n Brit abbr of* **National Front** FN *m*

NHS [ˌenəɪtʃ'es] *n Brit abbr of* **National Health Service** *services de santé britanniques*

NI [ˌen'aɪ] **1.** *Brit abbr of* **National Insurance** Sécurité *f* Sociale **2.** *abbr of* **Northern Ireland** Irlande *f* du Nord

Niagara Falls [naɪˌægərə'fɔ:lz] *n* **the ~** les chutes *fpl* du Niagara

nib [nɪb] *n* plume *f*

nibble ['nɪbl] **I.** *n* **1.**(*small bite*) morceau *m* **2.** *pl, Brit, inf* (*snack*) amuse-gueule *m* **II.** *vt* **1.**(*eat with small bites*) grignoter, gruger *Québec* **2.**(*peck at sensually*) mordiller **III.** *vi* **1.**(*snack lightly*) grignoter **2.**(*show interest in*) **to ~ at sth** se montrer tenté par qc **3.**(*deplete slowly*) **to ~ away at sth** grignoter doucement qc

Nicaragua [ˌnɪkə'rægjʊə, *Am:* -ə'rɑ:gwə] *n* le Nicaragua

Nicaraguan I. *n* Nicaraguayen(ne) *m(f)* **II.** *adj* nicaraguayen(ne)

nice [naɪs] *adj* **1.**(*pleasant, agreeable*) agréable; **~ weather** beau temps; **far ~r** beaucoup plus beau; **~ to meet you!** enchanté de faire votre connaissance!; **it's ~ doing sth** c'est agréable de faire qc **2.**(*kind, friendly*) gentil(le); **a ~ chap/guy** un bon gars; **be ~ to your sister!** sois gentil avec ta sœur!; **it was ~ of you to call** c'est gentil que tu aies appelé **3.**(*beautiful*) joli(e) **4.**(*socially approved: person, accent*) sympathique **5.** *iron* (*unpleasant, bad, awkward*) joli(e) **6.**(*fine, subtle*) subtil(e) ►**~ work if you can get it!** il y en a qui ont de la chance!

nicely *adv* **1.**(*well*) bien **2.**(*politely*) poliment

nicety ['naɪsəti, *Am:* -ṭi] <-ties> *n* **1.** *no pl* (*subtle, finer point*) subtilité *f* **2.** *pl* (*precise distinctions*) subtilités *fpl* **3.**(*social conventions*) convenances *fpl;* **social ~ties** mondanités *fpl*

niche [ni:ʃ, *Am:* nɪtʃ] *n* **1.**(*in wall*) niche *f* **2.**(*suitable position*) créneau *m* ►**to find one's ~** trouver sa voie

nick [nɪk] **I.** *n* **1.**(*cut*) entaille *f* **2.**(*chip, dent*) ébréchure *f* **3.** *no pl, Brit, inf* (*prison*) taule *f* **4.** *no pl, Brit, inf* (*police station*) poste *m* ►**in the ~ of time** juste à temps **II.** *vt* **1.**(*cut*) entailler; **to ~ oneself** se couper **2.**(*chip, dent*) ébrécher **3.** *Brit, Aus, inf* (*steal*) piquer **4.** *Brit, inf* (*arrest, catch*) pincer **5.** *Am, inf* (*charge unfairly, trick*) rouler

nickel ['nɪkl] *n* **1.** *no pl* (*metallic element*) nickel *m* **2.** *Am* (*coin*) pièce *f* de cinq cents

nickname ['nɪkneɪm] **I.** *n* surnom *m* **II.** *vt* surnommer

Nicosia [ˌnɪkəʊ'si:ə] *n* Nicosie

nicotine ['nɪkəti:n] *n no pl* nicotine *f*

nicotine patch *n* patch *m* de nicotine

N

Nidwald *n no pl* **the half-canton of** ~ le demi-canton de Nidwald Unterwald
niece [ni:s] *n* nièce *f*
nifty ['nɪfti] <-ier, -iest> *adj inf* **1.** (*stylish, smart*) chouette **2.** (*skilful, effective*) habile
Niger ['naɪdʒəʳ, *Am:* -dʒɚ] *n* le Niger
Nigeria [naɪ'dʒɪəriə, *Am:* -'dʒɪri-] *n* le Nigeria
Nigerian **I.** *adj* nigérian(e) **II.** *n* Nigérian(e) *m(f)*
Nigerien **I.** *adj* nigérien(e) **II.** *n* Nigérien(e) *m(f)*
niggardly ['nɪgədli, *Am:* -ɚd-] *adj pej* **1.** (*stingy, miserly*) mesquin(e) **2.** (*meagre*) piètre
nigger ['nɪgəʳ, *Am:* -ɚ] *n pej* négro *m*, négresse *f*
niggle ['nɪgl] **I.** *vi* pinailler; **to** ~ **over sth** trouver à redire au sujet de qc **II.** *vt* **there's something niggling me** il y a quelque chose qui me travaille **III.** *n* remarque *f*
niggling *adj* tatillon(ne); (*doubt*) obsédant(e)
nigh [naɪ] *adv* proche
night [naɪt] **I.** *n* **1.** (*end of day*) soir *m;* **last** ~ hier soir; **10** (**o'clock**) **at** ~ 10 heures du soir; **the** ~ **before** la veille au soir **2.** (*opp: day*) nuit *f;* **good** ~**!** bonne nuit!; **last** ~ cette nuit; **open at** ~ ouvert la nuit; ~ **and day** nuit et jour; **during the** ~ au cours de la nuit; **during Tuesday** ~ mardi, dans la nuit; **far into the** ~ tard dans la nuit; **at dead of** ~ en pleine nuit; **the Arabian Nights** les Mille et Une Nuits; **to work** ~**s** être de nuit **3.** (*evening spent for activity*) soirée *f;* **a girls'** ~ **out** une soirée entre filles; **Wagner** ~ soirée Wagner **II.** *adj* de nuit
nightbird *n* oiseau *m* de nuit **nightcap** *n* **1.** (*cap*) bonnet *m* de nuit **2.** (*drink*) *boisson généralement alcoolisée prise avant de se coucher* **nightclothes** *npl* vêtements *mpl* de nuit **nightclub** *n* boîte *f* de nuit **night-clubbing** *n* **to go** ~ sortir en boîte **night doctor** *n* médecin *m* de nuit **nightdress** *n* chemise *f* de nuit **nightfall** *n no pl* tombée *f* du jour [*o* de la nuit], brunante *f Québec* **nightgown** *n* chemise *f* de nuit **nightie** *n inf* chemise *f* de nuit
nightingale ['naɪtɪŋgeɪl, *Am:* -tən-] *n* rossignol *m*
nightlife *n no pl* vie *f* nocturne **night light** *n* veilleuse *f*
nightly **I.** *adj* **1.** (*done each night*) de tous les soirs **2.** (*nocturnal*) nocturne **II.** *adv* tous les soirs
nightmare *n* cauchemar *m;* **the worst** ~ la pire hantise; ~ **scenario** scénario *m* catastrophe; ~ **visions** visions *fpl* cauchemardesques
nightmarish *adj* cauchemardesque
night nurse *n* infirmier, -ère *m, f* de nuit **night owl** *n inf* oiseau *m* de nuit **night porter** *n* gardien *m* de nuit **night safe** *n Brit* coffre *m* de nuit **night school** *n* cours *mpl* du soir **night shift** *n* équipe *f* de nuit; **to work on the** ~ être de nuit **nightshirt** *n* chemise *f* de nuit **nightspot** *n inf* boîte *f* de nuit
nightstick *n Am* matraque *f*
night storage heater *n* chauffage *m* par accumulation **night table** *n* table *f* de nuit **night-time** *n* nuit *f* **nightwatchman** *n* veilleur *m* de nuit
nihilism ['naɪɪlɪzəm, *Am:* 'naɪə-] *n no pl* nihilisme *m*
nihilist ['naɪɪlɪst, *Am:* 'naɪə-] *n* nihiliste *mf*
nihilistic *adj* nihiliste
nil [nɪl] *n no pl* **1.** (*nothing*) néant *m* **2.** *Brit* (*no score*) zéro *m*
Nile [naɪl] *n* **the** ~ le Nil
nimble ['nɪmbl] <-r, -est> *adj* **1.** (*agile*) agile **2.** (*quick-witted*) vif(vive)
NIMBY, **nimby** ['nɪmbi] *n pej abbr of* **not in my back yard** riverain *m* contestataire
nincompoop ['nɪŋkəmpu:p, *Am:* 'nɪn-] *n pej, inf* gourde *f*
nine [naɪn] **I.** *adj* neuf *inv* ►**a** ~ **day wonder** une merveille d'un jour; *s. a.* **eight II.** *n* neuf *m inv* ►**be done** (**up**) **to the** ~**s** *inf* être sur son trente et un
ninepins ['naɪnpɪnz] *npl Brit* quilles *fpl* ►**to be going down like** ~ tomber comme des mouches
nineteen [ˌnaɪn'ti:n] *adj* dix-neuf *inv; s. a.* **eight**
nineteenth *adj* dix-neuvième; *s. a.* **eighth**
ninetieth *adj* quatre-vingt-dixième; *s. a.* **eighth**
ninety ['naɪnti, *Am:* -t̬i] *adj* quatre-vingt-dix *inv*, nonante *Belgique, Suisse; s. a.* **eight, eighty**
ninny ['nɪni] *n inf* gourde *f*
ninth [naɪnθ] **I.** *adj* neuvième **II.** *n* **1.** (*position*) neuvième *mf* **2.** (*fraction*) neuvième *m* **3.** (*date*) **the** ~ **of July** le neuf juillet; *s. a.* **eighth**
nip[1] [nɪp] **I.** <-pp-> *vt* **1.** (*bite*) mordre; **to** ~ **sth off** couper qc avec les dents **2.** (*pinch*) pincer ►**to** ~ **sth in the bud** étouffer qc dans l'œuf **II.** <-pp-> *vi* **1.** (*bite*) mordre **2.** *Brit, Aus, inf* (*move quickly*) filer; **to** ~ **across to sth** aller vite en face; **to** ~ **off** se sauver; **to** ~ **into a shop** faire un saut dans un magasin **III.** *n* **1.** (*pinch*) pincement *m* **2.** (*bite*) morsure *f* **3.** (*feeling of cold*) **there's a** ~ **in the air** il fait frisquet
nip[2] [nɪp] *n Brit, inf* goutte *f*
nipple ['nɪpl] *n* **1.** (*part of breast*) mamelon *m* **2.** (*teat for bottle*) tétine *f*
nippy ['nɪpi] <-ier, -iest> *adj* **1.** *Brit, Aus, inf* (*quick*) rapide **2.** *inf* (*chilly*) frisquet(te)
Nissen hut *n* hutte *f* préfabriquée
nit [nɪt] *n* **1.** *Brit, Aus, pej, inf* (*stupid person*) crétin(e) *m(f)* **2.** (*insect egg*) lente *f*
niter ['naɪtəʳ, *Am:* -t̬ɚ] *n Am s.* **nitre**
nit-picking **I.** *adj pej, inf* tatillon(ne) **II.** *n pej, inf* chipotage *m*

nitrate ['naɪtreɪt] *n* nitrate *m*
nitre ['naɪtəʳ, *Am:* -t̬ɚ] *n* nitre *m*
nitric ['naɪtrɪk] *adj* nitrique
nitrite ['naɪtraɪt] *n* nitrite *m*
nitrogen ['naɪtrədʒən] *n no pl* azote *m*
nitroglycerin(e) [ˌnaɪtrəʊ'glɪsəriːn, *Am:* -troʊ'-] *n no pl, Am* nitroglycérine *f*
nitrous ['naɪtrəs] *adj* **1.** (*of or containing nitrogen*) d'azote **2.** (*of nitre*) nitreux(-euse)
nitty-gritty [ˌnɪti'grɪti, *Am:* ˌnɪt̬ɪ'grɪt̬-] *n no pl, inf* **the ~** la dure réalité; **to get down to the ~** passer aux choses sérieuses
nitwit ['nɪtwɪt] *n inf* idiot(e) *m(f)*
NNE [ˌnɔːθnɔːθ'iːst, *Am:* ˌnɔːrθnɔːrθ'-] *n abbr of* **north-north-east** N-N-E *m*
NNW [ˌnɔːθnɔːθ'west, *Am:* ˌnɔːrθnɔːrθ'-] *n abbr of* **north-north-west** N-N-O *m*
no [nəʊ, *Am:* noʊ] **I.** *adj* **1.** (*not any*) **to have ~ time/money/pen** ne pas avoir le temps/d'argent/de stylo; **to be ~ friend/genius** ne pas être un ami/génie; **to be of ~ importance/interest** n'avoir aucune importance/aucun intérêt; **to have ~ more ideas** ne plus avoir d'idées; **~ one/man can do it** personne ne peut le faire; **~ doctor would do it** aucun médecin ne le ferait; **there is ~ way of getting out** il est impossible de sortir; **I'm in ~ mood for excuses** je ne suis pas d'humeur à écouter vos excuses; **there's ~ hurry** ça ne presse pas **2.** (*prohibition*) **~ smoking/entry** défense de fumer/d'entrer; **~ parking** stationnement interdit ►**by ~ means** aucunement; **in ~ time** en un rien de temps; **in ~ way** aucunement; **~ way!** pas question! **II.** *adv* **I'm ~ great singer** je ne suis pas un grand chanteur; **I ~ longer work** je ne travaille plus; **it was ~ easy task** ce n'était pas une chose facile; **to be ~ better** (*patient*) ne pas aller mieux; **~ more than 30** pas plus de 30 ►**~ less** rien que ça *inf;* **to be ~ more** n'être plus **III.** <-es *o* -s> *n* non *m inv;* **to not take ~ for an answer** insister **IV.** *interj* non!; **oh ~!** oh non!
No., no. <Nos. *o* nos.> *n abbr of* **number** n° *m*
nobble ['nɒbl] *vt Brit, Aus, inf* **1.** (*influence*) soudoyer **2.** (*seize*) attraper **3.** (*steal*) faucher
Nobel prize [ˌnəʊbel'praɪz, *Am:* ˌnoʊbel-'praɪz] *n* prix *m* Nobel
Nobel prize winner *n* lauréat(e) *m(f)* du prix Nobel
nobility [nəʊ'bɪləti, *Am:* noʊ'bɪlət̬i] *n no pl* noblesse *f*
noble ['nəʊbl, *Am:* 'noʊ-] **I.** *adj* **1.** (*aristocratic, honourable*) noble **2.** (*exalted: ideas*) grand(e) **II.** *n* noble *mf*
nobleman <-men> *n* noble *m*
noble-minded *adj* généreux(-euse)
nobly *adv* noblement
nobody ['nəʊbədi, *Am:* 'noʊbaːdi] **I.** *pron indef pron, sing* personne; **~ spoke** personne n'a parlé; **~ but me** personne sauf moi; **we saw ~ else** nous n'avons vu personne d'autre; **he told ~** il ne l'a dit à personne **II.** *n inf* zéro *m;* **those people are nobodies** ces gens sont des moins que rien
no-claim(s) bonus *n Brit, Aus* bonus *m*
nocturnal [nɒk'tɜːnəl, *Am:* naːk'tɜːr-] *adj form* nocturne
nod [nɒd, *Am:* naːd] **I.** *n* signe *m* de la tête; **to give sb a ~** faire un signe de la tête à qn ►**a ~'s as good as a wink to a blind horse** *inf* l'allusion est claire; **to give sb the ~** donner le feu vert à qn; **on the ~** *Brit, inf* sans discussion **II.** <-dd-> *vt* **to ~ one's head** dire oui d'un signe de la tête; **to ~ (one's) agreement** donner son accord d'un signe de tête **III.** <-dd-> *vi* **to ~ to sb** saluer qn d'un signe de tête
◆**nod off** <-dd-> *vi inf* s'endormir
nodding *adj* **to have a ~ acquaintance with sth** connaître vaguement qc
node [nəʊd, *Am:* noʊd] *n* nœud *m*
no-go area *n* MIL zone *f* interdite
nohow ['nəʊhaʊ, *Am:* 'noʊ-] *adv Am* en aucun cas
noise [nɔɪz] *n* **1.** *no pl* (*unpleasant sounds*) bruit *m;* **to make ~** faire du bruit **2.** (*sound*) bruit *m;* **a clinking/rattling ~** un tintement/cliquetis **3.** *no pl* ELEC interférence *f* ►**to make a ~ about sth** *inf* faire du tapage autour de qc; **to make a ~ about doing sth** *inf* laisser entendre qu'il/elle fasse qc *+subj;* **to make ~s** *inf* faire beaucoup de bruit; (*make trouble*) faire des histoires; **to make (all) the right ~s** dire ce qui convient
noiseless *adj* silencieux(-euse)
noise level *n* niveau *m* sonore **noise pollution** *n* nuisances *fpl* sonores **noise prevention** *n* mesures *fpl* antibruit
noisily *adv* bruyamment
noisy ['nɔɪzi] <-ier, -iest> *adj* bruyant(e); **to be ~** (*person*) faire du bruit
nomad ['nəʊmæd, *Am:* 'noʊ-] *n* nomade *mf*
nomadic [nəʊ'mædɪk, *Am:* noʊ-] *adj* nomade; (*existence*) de nomade
no-man's-land *n fig* no man's land *m inv*
nominal ['nɒmɪnl, *Am:* 'naːmə-] *adj* **1.** (*in name*) de nom **2.** (*small*) nominal(e)
nominally ['nɒmɪnəli, *Am:* 'naːmə-] *adv* nominalement
nominate ['nɒmɪneɪt, *Am:* 'naːmə-] *vt* **1.** (*propose*) proposer; (*for award*) sélectionner; **to ~ sb for a post** désigner qn à un poste **2.** (*appoint*) nommer
nomination [ˌnɒmɪ'neɪʃən, *Am:* ˌnaːmə-] *n* **1.** (*proposal*) proposition *f;* **an Oscar ~** une nomination pour l'oscar **2.** (*appointment*) nomination *f*
nominative ['nɒmɪnətɪv, *Am:* 'naːmənət̬ɪv] **I.** *n* nominatif *m* **II.** *adj* nominatif(-ive)
nominee [ˌnɒmɪ'niː, *Am:* ˌnaːmə-] *n* nominé *m;* **an Oscar ~** un nominé pour l'oscar
non-aggression *n no pl* non-agression *f;* **~ pact** pacte *m* de non-agression **non-alco-**

N

holic *adj* non alcoolisé(e) **non-aligned** *adj* non-aligné(e) **non-believer** *n* non-croyant(e) *m(f)*

nonchalant ['nɒnʃələnt, *Am:* ˌnɑːnʃə'lɑːnt] *adj* nonchalant(e)

non-combatant *adj* non-combattant(e) **non-combustible** *adj* non combustible **non-commissioned officer** *n* sous-officier *m* **non-committal** *adj* qui n'engage à rien; **to be** ~ ne pas s'engager **nonconformist** I. *n* non-conformiste *mf* II. *adj* non-conformiste **nonconformity** *n no pl* non-conformité *f* **non-cooperation** *n* non coopération *f* **nondescript** *adj* (*colour*) indéfinissable; (*person*) quelconque

none [nʌn] I. *pron* 1. (*nobody*) personne; ~ **but sb** seulement qn; ~ **other than sb** nul autre que qn 2. (*not any*) aucun; ~ **of the wine** pas une goutte de vin; ~ **of the cake** pas un morceau du gâteau; **I have some money but she has** ~ j'ai de l'argent, mais elle n'en a pas; ~ **of that!** ça suffit! 3. *pl* (*not any*) ~ (**at all**) pas un seul; ~ **of them** aucun d'entre eux; ~ **of my letters arrived** aucune de mes lettres n'est arrivée; ~ **of your speeches!** pas de discours! ►**it's** ~ **of your business** ce ne sont pas tes affaires II. *adv* 1. (*not*) ~ **the less** néanmoins; **to feel** ~ **the worse** ne se sentir pas plus mal 2. (*not very*) **it's** ~ **too soon/sure** ce n'est pas trop tôt/si sûr; **it's** ~ **too warm** il ne fait pas si chaud que ça ►**to be** ~ **the wiser** ne pas être plus avancé

nonentity [nɒ'nentəti, *Am:* nɑː'nent̬ət̬i] *n* (*person*) personne *f* insignifiante; (*thing*) chose *f* insignifiante

non-essential I. *adj* non essentiel(le) II. *n pl* ~**s** accessoires *mpl*

nonetheless *adv* néanmoins

non-event *n* ratage *m* **non-existence** *n no pl* non-existence *f* **non-existent** *adj* inexistant(e) **non-fiction** *n* ouvrages *mpl* généraux **non-flammable** *adj* ininflammable **non-infectious** *adj* non contagieux(-euse) **non-iron** *adj* infroissable **non-negotiable** *adj* non négociable

no-no *n inf* **that's a** (**definite**) ~ ça ne se fait pas

nonplus <-ss-> *vt* dérouter

non-polluting *adj* non polluant(e) **non-productive** *adj* non productif(-ive) **non-profit**, **non-profit-making** *adj Am* à but non lucratif **non-proliferation** I. *n no pl* POL non-prolifération *f* II. *adj* POL de non-prolifération **non-refundable** *adj* non remboursable **non-resident** *n* non-résident(e) *m(f)* **non-returnable** *adj* non consigné(e) **non-scheduled** *adj* spécial(e)

nonsense *n no pl* absurdité *f;* ~! quelle bêtise!; **to talk** ~ dire des absurdités; **it is** ~ **to say that ...** il est absurde de dire que ...; **what's all this** ~? qu'est-ce que c'est que ces bêtises?; **to make** (**a**) ~ **of sth** *Brit, Aus* saboter qc; **not to stand any** ~ *Brit* ne pas aimer les plaisanteries

nonsensical *adj* absurde

non-shrink *adj* irrétrécissable **non-skid** *adj* antidérapant(e) **non-smoker** *n* non-fumeur, -euse *m, f* **non-smoking** *adj* non-fumeurs **non-starter** *n inf* **to be a** ~ être voué à l'échec **non-stick** *adj* anti-adhérent(e); ~ **pan** poêle *f* antiadhésive **non-stop** I. *adj* 1. (*without stopping*) sans arrêt; (*flight*) sans escale; (*train*) direct(e) 2. (*uninterrupted*) ininterrompu(e) II. *adv* non-stop **non-taxable** *adj* non imposable **non-toxic** *adj* non toxique **non-verbal** *adj* non verbal(e) **non-violent** *adj* non-violent(e)

noodle¹ ['nuːdl] *n pl* nouilles *fpl;* ~ **soup** soupe *f* au vermicelle

noodle² ['nuːdl] *n Am, inf* 1. (*idiot*) nouille *f* 2. (*head*) caboche *f*

noodle³ ['nuːdl] *vi Am, inf* MUS jouer quelques notes

nook [nʊk] *n* coin *m*

noon [nuːn] *n* midi *m;* **at/about** ~ à/vers midi

no one ['nəʊwʌn, *Am:* 'noʊ-] *pron s.* **nobody**

noose [nuːs] *n* nœud *m* ►**to have a** ~ **around one's neck** être pris au collet

nope [nəʊp, *Am:* noʊp] *adv inf* non

nor [nɔːʳ, *Am:* nɔːr] *conj* 1. (*and also not*) ~ **do I/we** moi/nous non plus; **it's not funny,** ~ (**is it**) **clever** c'est ni drôle, ni intelligent; **I can not speak German,** ~ **can I write it** je ne parle pas l'allemand et je ne l'écris pas non plus 2. (*not either*) ni; *s. a.* **neither**

Nordic ['nɔːdɪk, *Am:* 'nɔːr-] *adj* nordique

norm [nɔːm, *Am:* nɔːrm] *n* norme *f;* **safety** ~**s** normes de sécurité

normal ['nɔːml, *Am:* 'nɔːr-] I. *adj* 1. (*conforming standards*) normal(e); **in the** ~ **way** normalement 2. (*usual: doctor*) habituel(le); **as** (**is**) ~ comme d'habitude; **in** ~ **circumstances** en temps normal II. *n no pl* normale *f;* **to return to** ~ retourner à la normale

normalcy ['nɔːməlsi, *Am:* 'nɔːr-] *n Am,* **normality** *n Brit no pl* normalité *f*

normalize ['nɔːməlaɪz, *Am:* 'nɔːr-] I. *vt* régulariser II. *vi* se régulariser

normally ['nɔːməli, *Am:* 'nɔːr-] *adv* normalement

Normandy ['nɔːməndi, *Am:* 'nɔːr-] *n* la Normandie

north [nɔːθ, *Am:* nɔːrθ] I. *n* 1. (*cardinal point*) nord *m;* **to lie 5 km to the** ~ **of sth** être à 5 km au nord de qc; **a** ~**-facing window** une fenêtre exposée au nord; **to go/drive to the** ~ aller/rouler vers le nord; **further** ~ plus au nord 2. GEO nord *m;* **in the** ~ **of France** dans le nord de la France II. *adj* nord *inv;* ~ **wind** vent *m* du nord; ~ **coast** côte *f* nord; **a** ~ **wall** un mur exposé au nord; **in** ~ **Paris** dans le nord de Paris III. *adv* au nord; (*travel*) vers le nord

North Africa *n* l'Afrique *f* du Nord **North**

African I. *adj* nord-africain(e) II. *n* Nord-africain(e) *m(f)* **North America** *n* l'Amérique *f* du Nord **North American** I. *n* Nord-américain(e) *m(f)* II. *adj* nord-américain(e) **North Carolina** I. *n* la Caroline-du-Nord II. *adj* de Caroline-du-Nord **North Dakota** I. *n* le Dakota-du-Nord II. *adj* du Dakota-du-Nord **north-east** I. *n* nord-est *m; s. a.* **north** II. *adj* nord-est *inv; s. a.* **north** III. *adv* au nord-est; (*travel*) vers le nord-est; *s. a.* **north** **north-easterly** *adj* nord-est; *s. a.* **northerly** **north-eastern** *adj* du nord-est

northerly *adj* 1. (*of or in the northern part*) au nord; ~ **part/coast** partie *f*/côte *f* nord 2. (*towards the north*) vers le nord; **in a ~ direction** vers le nord 3. (*from the north*) du nord; ~ **wind** vent *m* de nord

northern ['nɔːðən, *Am:* 'nɔːrðɚn] *adj* du nord, septentrional; ~ **hemisphere** hémisphère *m* nord; ~ **Scotland** le nord de l'Écosse; **the ~ part of the country** le nord du pays

northerner *n* nordiste *mf*

Northern Ireland *n* Irlande *f* du Nord **Northern Lights** *n* l'aurore *f* boréale

northernmost *adj* le plus au nord

Northern Territory *n* Territoire-du-Nord *m* **North Korea** *n* la Corée du Nord **North Pole** *n* **the** ~ le pôle Nord **North Sea** I. *n* **the** ~ la mer du Nord II. *adj* de la mer du Nord **North Star** *n* **the** ~ l'étoile *f* polaire **North Tipperary** *n* la Tipperary du Nord **North Vietnamese** *n* Nord-vietnamien(ne) *m(f)* **North Wales** *n* le Nord du pays de Galles

northward I. *adj* au nord II. *adv* vers le nord **northwards** *adv* vers le nord

north-west I. *n* nord-ouest *m inv; s. a.* **north** II. *adj* nord-ouest; *s. a.* **north** III. *adv* au nord-ouest; (*travel*) vers le nord-ouest; *s. a.* **north** **north-westerly** *adj* nord-ouest *inv; s. a.* **northerly** **north-western** *adj* du nord-ouest *inv* **Northwest Territories** *n pl* les Territoires du Nord-Ouest

Norway ['nɔːweɪ, *Am:* 'nɔːr-] *n* la Norvège

Norwegian [nɔː'wiːdʒən, *Am:* nɔːr'-] I. *adj* norvégien(ne) II. *n* 1. (*person*) Norvégien(ne) *m(f)* 2. LING norvégien *m; s. a.* **English**

nose [nəʊz, *Am:* noʊz] I. *n* nez *m;* **to have a runny ~** avoir le nez qui coule; **to blow one's ~** se moucher le nez; **to have a ~ job** se faire refaire le nez; ~ **to tail** AUTO pare-chocs contre pare-chocs ►**with one's ~ in the air** d'un air hautain; **to put one's ~ to the grindstone** *inf* travailler sans relâche; **to put sb's ~ out of joint** *inf* dépiter qn; **to keep one's ~ clean** *inf* se tenir à carreau; **to get up sb's ~** *Brit, Aus, inf* casser les pieds à qn; **to have a (good) ~ for sth** avoir du nez pour qc; **to have one's ~ in sth** avoir le nez dans qc; **to keep one's ~ out of sth** *inf* ne pas se mêler de qc; **to poke one's ~ into sth** *inf* fouiner dans qc; **under sb's ~** sous le nez de qn II. *vi* 1. (*move*) **to ~ forwards** s'avancer 2. *inf* (*search*) **to ~ about** [*o* **around**] fouiner; **to ~ into sth** fouiller dans qc III. *vt* **to ~ one's way forwards/in/out/up** s'avancer/entrer/sortir/monter lentement; **to ~ its way through sth** progresser dans qc

◆**nose out** I. *vt* découvrir II. *vi* avancer prudemment

nosebag *n* musette *f* **nosebleed** *n* saignement *m* de nez; **to have a ~** saigner du nez **nosedive** I. *n* 1. AVIAT piqué *m;* **to go into a ~** descendre en piqué 2. FIN chute *f* libre; **to take a ~** faire une chute libre II. *vi* 1. AVIAT descendre en piqué 2. FIN faire une chute libre **nose ring** *n* anneau *m* de nez

nosey <-ier, -iest> *adj s.* **nosy**

nosh [nɒʃ, *Am:* nɑːʃ] I. *n no pl, Brit, Aus, inf* (*food*) bouffe *f* II. *vi Brit, Aus, inf* (*eat*) bouffer

nosh-up ['nɒʃʌp, *Am:* 'nɑːʃ-] *n Brit, Aus, inf* bouffe *f*

nostalgia [nɒ'stældʒə, *Am:* nɑː'-] *n no pl* nostalgie *f*

nostalgic [nɒ'stældʒɪk, *Am:* nɑː'-] *adj* nostalgique

nostril ['nɒstrəl, *Am:* 'nɑːstrəl] *n* narine *f;* (*of a horse*) naseau *m*

nosy ['nəʊzi, *Am:* 'noʊ-] <-ier, -iest> *adj pej* curieux(-euse)

nosy parker *n Brit, inf* fouineur, -euse *m, f,* mêle-tout *m Belgique*

not [nɒt, *Am:* nɑːt] *adv* 1. (*expressing the opposite*) ne … pas; **he's ~ here** il n'est pas ici; **it's red ~ blue** c'est rouge et pas bleu; **of course ~** bien sûr que non; ~ **so fast** pas si vite; **I hope ~** j'espère que non; **whether it rains or ~** qu'il pleuve ou pas; ~ **even a present** même pas un cadeau; ~ **that I'm interested** ce n'est pas que je sois intéressé; ~ **that I know** pas que je sache; ~ **at all** (pas) du tout; **thanks – ~ at all** merci – de rien; ~ **including sth** sans compter qc; ~ **to mention that …** sans parler de … 2. (*in tags*) **isn't it?, won't they?** n'est-ce pas? 3. (*less than*) ~ **a minute later** à peine une minute plus tard; **to be ~ a mile away** être à à peine un mile 4. (*expressing an opposite*) pas; ~ **always** pas toujours; ~ **much** pas beaucoup; ~ **that …** pas que …; ~ **up to much** pas terrible; ~ **I** pas moi

notable ['nəʊtəbl, *Am:* 'noʊt̬ə-] *adj* 1. (*eminent*) remarquable; **to be ~ for sth** être connu pour qc 2. (*remarkable*) notable; **with a few ~ exceptions** à part quelques exceptions

notably *adv* 1. (*particularly*) notamment; **most ~** plus particulièrement 2. (*in a noticeable way*) remarquablement

notary ['nəʊtəri, *Am:* 'noʊt̬ɚ-], **notary public** <-ies> *n* notaire *m*

notation [nəʊ'teɪʃən, *Am:* noʊ-] *n* notation *f*

notch [nɒtʃ, *Am:* nɑːtʃ] I. *vt* (*cut*) entailler II. *n* 1. (*V-shaped indentation*) entaille *f* 2. (*degree, hole in a belt*) cran *m;* **to go up a ~** monter d'un cran

◆**notch up** *vt* remporter

note [nəʊt, *Am:* noʊt] I. *n* 1. (*short informal letter*) mot *m;* **to write sb a ~** écrire un mot à

N

qn **2.** (*reminder*) note *f;* **to make/take a ~ of sth** noter qc **3.** LIT commentaire *m* **4.** MUS note *f* **5.** (*mood*) note *f;* **to strike a ~** être bien dans la note; **to strike the right ~** sonner juste **6.** *Brit, Aus* (*piece of paper money*) billet *m* **7.** *form* (*important*) **of ~** d'importance; **nothing of ~** rien d'important **II.** *vt form* **1.** (*write down*) noter **2.** (*mention, observe*) remarquer

◆**note down** *vt* prendre note de

notebook *n* **1.** (*book*) carnet *m* **2.** (*laptop*) notebook *m*

noted *adj* célèbre; **to be ~ for sth** être célèbre pour qc; **to be ~ as an expert** être connu en tant qu'expert

notepad *n* bloc-notes *m* **notepaper** *n no pl* papier *m* à lettres **noteworthy** <-ier, -iest> *adj form* notable; **nothing/something ~** rien/quelque chose de remarquable

nothing ['nʌθɪŋ] **I.** *indef pron, sing* **1.** (*not anything*) rien; **~ happened** rien ne s'est passé; **we saw ~ else/more** nous n'avons rien vu d'autre/de plus; **~ new** rien de neuf; **next to ~** presque rien; **~ came of it** cela n'a rien donné; **~ doing!** rien à faire!; **good for ~** bon à rien; **to make ~ of it** ne rien y comprendre; **there's ~ to laugh at** il n'y a pas de quoi rire; **~ much** pas grand-chose **2.** (*not important*) **that's ~!** ce n'est rien du tout!; **time is ~ to me** le temps ne compte pas pour moi **3.** (*only*) **~ but sth** seulement qc; **he is ~ if not strict** il est strict avant tout ►**to look like ~ on earth** avoir l'air de n'importe quoi; **~ ventured, ~ gained** *prov* qui ne risque rien n'a rien; **it's ~ to do with me** ça ne me regarde pas; **it's (got) ~ to do with sth** ça n'a rien à voir avec qc **II.** *adv* **it's ~ less than sth** être ni plus ni moins qc; **it's ~ less than scandalous** c'est ni plus ni moins un scandale; **it's ~ short of great/madness** c'est génial/de la folie ni plus ni moins; **it's ~ more than a joke** ça n'est rien de plus qu'une plaisanterie; **he's ~ like me** il ne me ressemble pas du tout; **I'm ~ like as good as my brother** je suis loin d'être aussi bon que mon frère; **~ daunted, I went on** nullement découragé, je continuai **III.** *n* **1.** (*non-existence*) rien *m* **2.** MAT, SPORT zéro *m;* **three to ~** *Am* trois à zéro **3.** (*person*) nullité *f; s. a.* **anything, something**

notice ['nəʊtɪs, *Am:* 'noʊt̬ɪs] **I.** *vt, vi* remarquer; **to ~ sb/sth do sth** remarquer que qn/qc fait qc **II.** *n* **1.** (*announcement: in paper*) annonce *f;* (*for birth, marriage*) avis *m;* (*on board*) affiche *f;* (*review*) critique *f* **2.** *no pl* (*attention*) attention *f;* **to escape sb's ~** échapper à l'attention de qn; **to take ~ of sb/sth** faire attention à qn/qc; **take no ~ of sb/sth** ne pas prêter attention à qn/qc **3.** *no pl* (*warning*) avis *m;* **to give sb ~ of sth** prévenir qn de qc; **at short ~** avec peu de préavis; **at a moment's ~** immédiatement; **until further ~** jusqu'à nouvel ordre **4.** *no pl* (*when ending contract*) *a.* LAW avis *m;* **to give (in) one's ~** donner sa démission; **to be given one's ~** être licencié; **to give an employee a month's ~** donner son mois à qn

noticeable *adj* perceptible

notice board *n Aus, Brit* panneau *m* d'affichage, valves *fpl Belgique*

notification [ˌnəʊtɪfɪ'keɪʃən, *Am:* ˌnoʊt̬ə-] *n* notification *f;* **to get ~ of sth** être notifié de qc

notify ['nəʊtɪfaɪ, *Am:* 'noʊt̬ə-] <-ie-> *vt* notifier; **to ~ sb of sth** aviser qn de qc

notion ['nəʊʃən, *Am:* 'noʊ-] *n* idée *f;* **to have no ~ of sth** n'avoir aucune idée de qc

notional *adj form* fantasque; (*payment*) symbolique

notoriety [ˌnəʊtə'raɪəti, *Am:* ˌnoʊt̬ə'raɪət̬i] *n no pl* notoriété *f;* **to achieve ~ for sth** acquérir une notoriété dans qc

notorious [nəʊ'tɔːrɪəs, *Am:* noʊ'tɔːrɪ-] *adj* notoire; **to be ~ for sth** être tristement célèbre pour qc

notwithstanding [ˌnɒtwɪθ'stændɪŋ, *Am:* ˌnɑːt-] *form* **I.** *prep* en dépit de **II.** *adv* néanmoins

nougat ['nuːgɑː, *Am:* 'nuːgət] *n no pl* nougat *m*

nought [nɔːt, *Am:* nɑːt] *n* zéro *m*

noughts and crosses *n Brit* GAMES morpion *m*

noun [naʊn] *n* nom *m*

nourish ['nʌrɪʃ, *Am:* 'nɜːr-] *vt* (*feed*) nourrir

nourishing ['nʌrɪʃɪŋ, *Am:* 'nɜːr-] *adj* nourrissant(e)

nourishment *n no pl* (*food*) nourriture *f*

nous [naʊs, *Am:* nuːs] *n no pl, Aus, Brit, inf* bon sens *m*

Nova Scotia [ˌnəʊvə'skəʊʃə, *Am:* ˌnoʊvə'skoʊ-] *n* la Nouvelle-Ecosse

novel[1] ['nɒvl, *Am:* 'nɑːvl] *n* roman *m*

novel[2] ['nɒvl, *Am:* 'nɑːvl] *adj* nouveau(-elle); (*idea, concept*) original

novelette [ˌnɒvə'let, *Am:* ˌnɑːvə-] *n pej* roman *m* à l'eau de rose

novelist ['nɒvəlɪst, *Am:* ˌnɑːvə-] *n* romancier, -ère *m, f*

novelty ['nɒvəlti, *Am:* 'nɑːvlt̬i] <-ies> *n* **1.** *no pl* (*newness, originality*) nouveauté *f* **2.** (*trinket*) fantaisie *f;* **a ~ bracelet** un bracelet fantaisie

November [nəʊ'vembə^r, *Am:* noʊ'vembɚ] *n* novembre *m; s. a.* **April**

novice ['nɒvɪs, *Am:* 'nɑːvɪs] **I.** *n* **1.** (*inexperienced person*) apprenti(e) *m(f)* **2.** REL novice *mf* **II.** *adj* **1.** (*inexperienced*) débutant(e); (*pilot*) inexpérimenté(e) **2.** REL novice

now [naʊ] **I.** *adv* **1.** (*at the present time, shortly*) maintenant; **she's coming ~** elle vient tout de suite; **~ everyone can vote** de nos jours, tout le monde a le droit de voter; **I'll call her (right) ~** je vais l'appeler immédiatement; **I'm shaving right ~** je suis en train de me raser; **she'll be in Glasgow by ~** elle devrait être à Glasgow; **he'll call any time ~** il doit appeler incessamment sous peu; **and ~ for the question** et maintenant en ce qui concerne la question; **she called just ~** elle vient d'appeler juste à l'instant; **before ~** auparavant; **as of ~** dès à présent **2.** (*in narrative*) **she was an adult ~** elle était alors adulte; **by ~ she was very angry** à ce moment-là, elle était très en colère **3.** (*involving the listener*) **~, you need good equipment** écoute, il te faut un bon équipement; **~ his brother would never do that** son frère, lui, ne ferait jamais ça; **~ don't interrupt me!** ne m'interromps donc pas!; **~ that changes everything!** ah, voilà qui change tout!; **be careful ~!** fais attention!; **come ~!** allons!; **well ~!** eh bien!; **~, ~** voyons, voyons; (*warning*) allons allons; **~ then, who's next?** bon, qui est le prochain?; **~ then, we'll need a screwdriver** bon alors, il nous faut un tourne-vis; **~ then, stop arguing** allons, arrêtez de vous disputer ►(**every**) **~ and then** de temps en temps; (**it's**) **~ or never** c'est maintenant ou jamais; **~ you're/we're talking!** à la bonne heure! **II.** *conj* **~** (**that**) ... maintenant que ... **III.** *adj inf* actuel(le)

nowadays ['naʊədeɪz] *adv* de nos jours

nowhere ['nəʊweəʳ, *Am:* 'noʊwer] **I.** *adv* **a.** *fig* nulle part; **to appear from ~** apparaître de je ne sais où; **I've ~ to put my things** je ne sais pas où mettre mes vêtements; **he is ~ to be found** on ne le trouve nulle part; **to start one's career from ~** commencer au plus bas de l'échelle; **to be getting ~** ne pas y arriver; **to get sb ~** mener qn nulle part; **to finish ~** finir loin derrière; **to be ~ near a place** être loin d'un endroit; **to be ~ near right** être loin d'être juste **II.** *adj inf* qui ne mène à rien

nowt [naʊt] *pron no pl, inf* rien *m;* **there's ~ so queer as folk** il n'y a rien de plus imprévisible que l'être humain

noxious ['nɒkʃəs, *Am:* 'nɑːk-] *adj form* nocif(-ive)

nozzle ['nɒzl, *Am:* 'nɑːzl] *n* embout *m;* (*of hose*) jet *m;* (*of a petrol pump*) pistolet *m;* (*of a vacuum cleaner*) suceur *m*

NSPCC [ˌenesˌpiːsiː'siː] *n Brit abbr of* **National Society for the Prevention of Cruelty to Children** *société pour la protection de l'enfance*

NT *n* **1.** *abbr of* **New Testament** Nouveau Testament *m* **2.** *Brit abbr of* **National Trust** Société *f* pour la conservation des sites et monuments

nuance ['njuːɑːns, *Am:* 'nuː-] *n* nuance *f*

nub [nʌb] *n* **the ~ of the matter** le cœur du sujet

nubile ['njuːbaɪl, *Am:* 'nuːbɪl] *adj* nubile

nuclear ['njuːkliəʳ, *Am:* 'nuːkliɚ] *adj* nucléaire ►**to go ~** *inf* exploser

nuclear-free *adj* (*zone*) antinucléaire

nuclear medicine *n* médecine *f* nucléaire **nuclear non-proliferation treaty** *n* traité *m* de non-prolifération des armes nucléaires **nuclear power station** *n* centrale *f* (d'énergie) nucléaire **nuclear reactor** *n* réacteur *m* nucléaire

nucleus ['njuːklɪəs, *Am:* 'nuː-] <-ei *o* -es> *n* noyau *m*

nude [njuːd, *Am:* nuːd] **I.** *adj* nu(e) **II.** *n* **1.** ART nu *m* **2.** (*naked*) **in the ~** tout nu

nudge [nʌdʒ] **I.** *vt* **1.** (*push with the elbow*) pousser du coude **2.** (*push gently*) pousser **3.** (*persuade sb into sth*) **to ~ sb into sth** pousser qn dans qc; **to ~ sb into doing sth** pousser qn à faire qc **4.** (*approach*) approcher; **to be nudging fifty** approcher les cinquante ans **II.** *n* coup *m* du coude; **to give sb a ~** donner un coup de coude à qn; (*encourage*) pousser qn; **if I forget, give me a ~** si j'oublie, rappelle-le-moi

nudist ['njuːdɪst, *Am:* 'nuː-] *n* nudiste *mf*

nudist beach *n* plage *f* de nudistes **nudist colony** *n* camp *m* de nudistes

nudity ['njuːdəti, *Am:* 'nuːdət̬i] *n no pl* nudité *f*

nugget ['nʌgɪt] *n* **1.** (*formed lump*) pépite *f;* **gold ~** pépite d'or **2.** GASTR nugget *m* (*boulette de viande panée*) **3.** *iron* (*interesting information*) bribe *f*

nuisance ['njuːsns, *Am:* 'nuː-] *n* **1.** (*annoyance*) ennui *m;* **she's a ~** elle est pénible; **that's such a ~** c'est vraiment embêtant; **what a ~!** que c'est embêtant!; **to make a ~ of oneself** embêter le monde **2.** LAW dommage *m;* **public ~** atteinte *f* portée à l'ordre public

nuisance call *n* appel *m* anonyme

nuke [nuːk, njuːk] **I.** *vt inf* **1.** MIL atomiser **2.** *Am, Aus* (*cook in microwave*) passer au four à micro-ondes **II.** *n inf* bombe *f* nucléaire

null [nʌl] *adj* LAW caduque

nullification [ˌnʌlɪfɪ'keɪʃən] *n* LAW annulation *f*

nullify ['nʌlɪfaɪ] <-ie-> *vt* annuler

nullity ['nʌləti, *Am:* -t̬i] *n no pl* LAW invalidité *f*

numb [nʌm] **I.** *adj* **1.** (*deprived of sensation*) engourdi(e); (*nerve*) insensible; **to go ~** s'engourdir **2.** *fig* hébété(e); **I felt ~ after hearing the news** j'étais sous le choc à l'écoute de la nouvelle **II.** *vt* **1.** (*deprive of sensations: limbs*) engourdir **2.** (*desensitize*) désensibiliser **3.** (*lessen: pain*) endormir

number ['nʌmbəʳ, *Am:* -bɚ] **I.** *n* **1.** (*arithmetical unit*) nombre *m* **2.** (*written symbol*) chiffre *m* **3.** (*on numbered item: telephone, page, bus*) numéro *m;* **my mobile ~** mon numéro de mobile; **a wrong ~** un faux numéro **4.** (*individual item: sketch, magazine*) numéro *m;* **he was driving a classy little ~** il conduisait une voiture superbe; **she wore a little red ~** elle portait une petite robe rouge **5.** *no pl* (*amount*) nombre *m;* **a small/large ~ of sth** un petit/grand nombre de qc; **any ~ of friends/books** de nombreux amis/livres; **in large/huge/enormous ~s** en très grand nombre; **by** (**sheer**) **force of ~s** par le

N

nombre; **to be few in** ~ être peu nombreux ►**to look out for** ~ **one** prendre soin de soi; **to be** (**the**) ~ **one** être le meilleur; **there's safety in** ~**s** *prov* plus on est nombreux, moins on court de risques; **to have sb's** ~ connaître qn; **his** ~ **is up** c'est trop tard pour lui **II.** *vt* **1.** (*assign a number to*) numéroter **2.** (*be sth in number*) compter; **to be** ~**ed amongst sth** compter parmi qc

numbering *n no pl* comptage *m*

number plate *n Brit* plaque *f* minéralogique

> Le **Number 10 Downing Street** est la résidence officielle du "prime minister" britannique (premier ministre). La résidence date du 17ème siècle et fut construite par Sir George Downing, un homme politique, spéculateur en immobilier et espion. Le premier ministre habite à un étage supérieur et le reste du bâtiment est occupé par les bureaux du gouvernement ainsi que par les salles de réunion du cabinet. Le "Chancellor of the Exchequer" (ministre des Finances) habite dans la maison d'à côté, au numéro 11.

numbness *n no pl* **1.** (*being numb*) engourdissement *m* **2.** (*lack of emotional feeling*) insensibilité *f*

numeracy ['nju:mərəsi, *Am:* 'nu:-] *n no pl* MAT calcul *m;* ~ **skills** aptitudes *fpl* en calcul

numeral ['nju:mərəl, *Am:* 'nu:-] *n* chiffre *m*

numerate ['nju:mərət, *Am:* 'nu:-] *adj* MAT qui a le sens de l'arithmétique

numerical [nju:'merɪkl, *Am:* nu:-] *adj* numérique

numeric keypad *n* INFOR touches *fpl* numériques

numerous ['nju:mərəs, *Am:* 'nu:-] *adj* nombreux(-euse)

numskull ['nʌmskʌl] *n pej* nigaud(e) *m(f)*

nun [nʌn] *n* religieuse *f*

nuptial ['nʌpʃl] *adj form* nuptial(e)

nurse [nɜ:s, *Am:* nɜ:rs] **I.** *n* **1.** (*health worker*) infirmier, -ère *m, f* **2.** (*nanny*) nurse *f* **II.** *vt* **1.** (*care for*) soigner; **to** ~ **sb back to health** faire recouvrer la santé à qn **2.** (*project*) mijoter **3.** (*nurture*) nourrir **4.** (*harbour: feeling*) nourrir; (*contact*) cultiver; (*fire*) entretenir **5.** (*hold carefully*) bercer **6.** (*breast-feed*) allaiter **7.** (*drink*) siroter **III.** *vi* téter

nursery ['nɜ:səri, *Am:* 'nɜ:r-] <-ies> *n* **1.** ((*day*) ~) crèche *f;* **to go to** (**a**) ~ aller à la crèche **2.** (*bedroom for infants*) chambre *f* d'enfants **3.** BOT pépinière *f*

nursery rhyme *n* comptine *f* **nursery school** *n* maternelle *f,* école *f* gardienne *Belgique* **nursery slopes** *npl Brit* SPORT pentes *fpl* de ski pour débutants

nursing I. *n no pl* **1.** (*profession*) profession *f* d'infirmier(-ère) **2.** (*practice*) soins *mpl* **II.** *adj* **1.** (*concerning nursing: profession*) d'infirmier; (*department*) des soins; (*staff*) soignant **2.** (*breast-feeding*) qui allaite

nursing home *n* clinique *f;* (*for the elderly*) maison *f* de retraite

nurture ['nɜ:tʃəʳ, *Am:* 'nɜ:rtʃɚ] **I.** *vt form* **1.** (*feed*) nourrir **2.** (*encourage, harbour*) nourrir **3.** (*bring up*) éduquer **II.** *n no pl* (*upbringing*) éducation *f*

nut [nʌt] *n* **1.** (*hard edible fruit*) noix *f;* (*of hazel*) noisette *f* **2.** TECH écrou *m* **3.** *inf* (*crazy*) cinglé(e) *m(f)* **4.** (*enthusiast*) dingue *mf* **5.** *inf* (*person's head*) caboche *f* **6.** *Am, inf* (*money*) capital *m* ►**the** ~**s and bolts of sth** les détails *mpl* pratiques de qc; **to be a hard** ~ **to crack** (*person*) être peu commode; (*problem*) être un problème difficile à résoudre; **to be off one's** ~ être cinglé; **to do one's** ~ *Brit, Aus, inf* voir rouge; **to use one's** ~ utiliser ses neurones

nutcracker *n* casse-noix *m* **nuthatch** <-es> *n* sittelle *f* **nuthouse** <-s> *n inf* asile *m* **nutmeg** *n* GASTR **1.** (*hard fruit*) noix *f* muscade **2.** *no pl* (*warm, aromatic spice*) muscade *f*

nutrient ['nju:triənt, *Am:* 'nu:-] **I.** *n* aliment *m* **II.** *adj* nutritif(-ive)

nutrition [nju:'trɪʃən, *Am:* nu:-] *n no pl* nutrition *f*

nutritional *adj* nutritionnel(le); (*value*) nutritif(-ive)

nutritionist *n* nutritionniste *mf*

nutritious [nju:'trɪʃəs, *Am:* nu:-] *adj* nutritif(-ive)

nuts [nʌts] **I.** *npl vulg* (*testicles*) couilles *fpl* **II.** *adj* cinglé(e); **to go** ~ voir rouge; **to be** ~ **about sb/sth** être dingue de qn/qc

nutshell ['nʌtʃel] *n no pl* coquille *f* de noix ►**to put it in a** ~ pour résumer; **in a** ~ en bref

nut tree *n* noyer *m;* (*of hazel*) noisetier *m*

nutty ['nʌti, *Am:* 'nʌţ-] <-ier, -iest> *adj* **1.** (*full of nuts*) aux noix; (*chocolate*) aux noisettes **2.** (*like nuts: taste*) de noix; (*like hazelnut*) de noisette **3.** *inf* (*crazy, eccentric*) dingue; (**as**) ~ **as a fruitcake** complètement ravagé

nuzzle ['nʌzl] **I.** *vt* fourrer son nez dans **II.** *vi* fouiner; **to** ~ (**up**) **against sb/sth** fourrer son nez dans qn/qc; **to** ~ **at sb's shoulder** se blottir contre l'épaule de qn

NW [ˌen'dʌblju:] *n abbr of* **north-west** N-O *m*

NY [ˌen'waɪ] *n abbr of* **New York** New York

nylon ['naɪlɒn, *Am:* -lɑ:n] **I.** *n* nylon *m* **II.** *adj* en nylon; (*thread*) de nylon

nymph [nɪmf] *n* nymphe *f*

nympho ['nɪmpfəʊ, *Am:* -foʊ] *n inf* nympho *f*

nymphomania [ˌnɪmfə'meɪnɪə, *Am:* -foʊ'-] *n no pl* nymphomanie *f*

nymphomaniac [ˌnɪmfə'meɪnɪæk, *Am:* -foʊ'-] **I.** *n* nymphomane *f* **II.** *adj* nymphomane

NZ [ˌen'zed, *Am:* -'zi:] *n abbr of* **New Zealand** NZ *f*

O

O, **o** [əʊ, *Am:* oʊ] <-'s> *n* **1.** (*letter*) O *m*, o *m*; ~ **as in Oliver** *Brit*, ~ **as in Oboe** *Am* (*on telephone*), ~ **for Oliver** *Brit*, ~ **for Oboe** *Am* o comme Oscar **2.** (*zero*) zéro *m*

oaf [əʊf, *Am:* oʊf] *n pej* rustre *m*

oafish ['əʊfɪʃ, *Am:* 'oʊ-] *adj pej* rustre

oak [əʊk, *Am:* oʊk] *n* **1.** (*tree*) chêne *m* **2.** *no pl* (*wood*) chêne *m*; ~ **cupboard** armoire *f* en chêne ▸**tall ~s from little acorns grow** *prov* les petits ruisseaux font des grandes rivières

OAP [ˌəʊeɪ'piː, *Am:* ˌoʊ-] *n Brit abbr of* **old-age pensioner** retraité(e) *m(f)*

oar [ɔːʳ, *Am:* ɔːr] *n* rame *f* ▸**to put one's ~ in** *pej, inf* mettre son grain de sel

oarsman ['ɔːzmən, *Am:* 'ɔːrz-] <-men> *n* SPORT rameur *m*

oarswoman ['ɔːzwʊmən, *Am:* 'ɔːrz-] <-women> *n* SPORT rameuse *f*

OAS [ˌəʊeɪ'es, *Am:* ˌoʊ-] *n Am abbr of* **Organization of American States** Organisation *f* des États américains

oasis [əʊ'eɪsɪs, *Am:* oʊ-] <-ses> *n* oasis *f*

oatcake ['əʊtkeɪk, *Am:* 'oʊt-] *n* galette *f* d'avoine

oath [əʊθ, *Am:* oʊθ] *n* **1.** LAW serment *m*; **under** [*o* **upon** *Brit*] ~ sous serment; **to take the** ~ prêter serment; **to take an** ~ **of sth** faire le serment de qc **2.** (*swear word*) juron *m*

oatmeal ['əʊtmiːl, *Am:* 'oʊt-] **I.** *n no pl* **1.** (*flour*) farine *f* d'avoine; ~ **biscuits** biscuits *mpl* d'avoine **2.** (*porridge*) bouillie *f* d'avoine **3.** (*colour*) gris *m* beige **II.** *adj* gris *inv* beige

oats ['əʊts, *Am:* 'oʊt-] *n pl* avoine *f* ▸**to feel one's** ~ *Am, inf* avoir faim; **to sow one's wild** ~ faire les quatre cent coups

OAU [ˌəʊeɪ'juː, *Am:* ˌoʊ-] *n abbr of* **Organization of African Unity** OUA *f*

obduracy ['ɒbdjʊərəsi, *Am:* 'ɑːbdʊr-] *n no pl, pej, form* entêtement *m*

obdurate ['ɒbdjʊərət, *Am:* 'ɑːbdʊrɪt] *adj pej, form* **1.** (*stubborn*) obstiné(e) **2.** (*difficult to deal with*) inflexible; (*problem*) intraitable

OBE [ˌəʊbiː'iː, *Am:* ˌoʊ-] *n Brit abbr of* **Officer of the Order of the British Empire** officier *m* de l'Ordre de l'Empire britannique

obedience [ə'biːdɪəns, *Am:* oʊ'-] *n no pl* obéissance *f*

obedient [ə'biːdɪənt, *Am:* oʊ'-] *adj* obéissant(e); **to be** ~ **to sb/sth** être obéissant envers qn/qc

obelisk ['ɒbəlɪsk, *Am:* 'ɑːbəl-] *n* ARCHIT obélisque *m*

obese [əʊ'biːs, *Am:* oʊ'-] *adj* obèse

obesity [əʊ'biːsəti, *Am:* oʊ'biːsət̬i] *n no pl* obésité *f*

obey [əʊ'beɪ, *Am:* oʊ'-] **I.** *vt* obéir à; (*law*) se conformer à **II.** *vi* obéir

obituary [əʊ'bɪtʃʊəri, *Am:* oʊ'bɪtʃueri] <-ies>, **obituary notice** *n* nécrologie *f*

object ['ɒbdʒɪkt, *Am:* 'ɑːb-] **I.** *n* **1.** (*thing*) *a. fig* objet *m* **2.** (*purpose, goal*) but *m*; **money is no** ~ peu importe le prix; **with this** ~ à cette fin **3.** *form* (*subject*) objet *m*; **the** ~ **of his desire** l'objet de son désir **4.** (*of verb*) complément *m* d'objet **II.** *vi* faire objection **III.** *vt* objecter; **to** ~ **that ...** faire valoir que ...

◆**object to** *vt* (*plan, policy*) s'opposer à; (*behaviour, mess*) se plaindre de; **to** ~ **sb doing sth** s'opposer à ce que qn fasse qc (*subj*)

objection [əb'dʒekʃən] *n* objection *f*; **to raise ~s to sth** soulever des objections à qc; **have you any** ~ **to my doing sth?** est-ce que tu vois un inconvénient à ce que je fasse qc? (*subj*)

objectionable [əb'dʒekʃənəbl] *adj form* désagréable

objective [əb'dʒektɪv] **I.** *n* objectif *m* **II.** *adj* objectif(-ive)

objectively *adv* objectivement

objectivity [ˌɒbdʒɪk'tɪvəti, *Am:* ˌɑːbdʒek'tɪvət̬i] *n no pl* objectivité *f*

object lesson *n* bon exemple *m*; **an** ~ **in how to** +*infin* un parfait exemple de la manière de +*infin*

objector *n* protestataire *mf*

obligate ['ɒblɪgeɪt, *Am:* 'ɑːblɪ-] *vt* **to** ~ **sb** mettre qn dans l'obligation

obligation [ˌɒblɪ'geɪʃən, *Am:* ˌɑːblə'-] *n no pl* obligation *f*; **to be under an** ~ **to** +*infin* être dans l'obligation de +*infin*; **to have an** ~ **to sb** avoir une dette envers qn; **to meet one's ~s** faire face à ses engagements

obligatory [ə'blɪgətəri, *Am:* -tɔːri] *adj* obligatoire

oblige [ə'blaɪdʒ] **I.** *vt* **1.** (*compel*) obliger; **to** ~ **sb to** +*infin* obliger qn à +*infin* **2.** (*perform a service for*) rendre service à; **would you** ~ **me with your book?** auriez-vous l'amabilité de me prêter votre livre?; ~ **him by shutting the door** faites-lui le plaisir de fermer la porte; **to be ~d to sb** être reconnaissant envers qn; **I'd be ~d if you'd leave now** je vous saurai gré de partir immédiatement; **much ~d** merci beaucoup **II.** *vi* rendre service

obliged *adj* obligé(e)

obliging *adj* obligeant(e)

oblique [ə'bliːk, *Am:* oʊ'-] **I.** <-r, -st> *adj* **1.** (*indirect*) indirect(e); (*road*) détourné(e) **2.** (*slanting: line*) oblique; (*look*) en biais **3.** MAT (*angle*) oblique **II.** *n* oblique *f*

obliterate [ə'blɪtəreɪt, *Am:* -'blɪt̬-] *vt* **1.** (*erase, wipe out*) effacer **2.** (*destroy*) détruire; (*town*) rayer de la carte **3.** (*cancel: stamp*) oblitérer

obliteration [əˌblɪtə'reɪʃən, *Am:* -ˌblɪt̬-] *n no pl* **1.** (*erasing*) *a. fig* effacement *m* **2.** (*destruction*) destruction *f* **3.** (*stamp*) oblitération *f*

oblivion [ə'blɪvɪən] *n no pl* oubli *m*; **to sink into** ~ tomber dans l'oubli; **to drink oneself into** ~ boire jusqu'à l'oubli; **to be bombed into** ~ être rasé par les bombes

oblivious [ə'blɪvɪəs] *adj* (*unaware*) oublieux(-euse); **to be ~ of sth** ne pas être conscient de qc

oblong ['ɒblɒŋ, *Am:* 'ɑːblɑːŋ] **I.** *n* rectangle *m* **II.** *adj* MAT oblong(ue)

obnoxious [əb'nɒkʃəs, *Am:* -'nɑːk-] *adj pej* odieux(-euse)

oboe ['əʊbəʊ, *Am:* 'oʊboʊ] *n* MUS hautbois *m*

oboist *n* MUS hautboïste *mf*

obscene [əb'siːn] *adj* **1.** (*indecent*) obscène **2.** (*shocking*) scandaleux(-euse)

obscenity [əb'senəti, *Am:* -t̬i] <-ties> *n* **1.** *no pl* (*obscene behaviour*) obscénité *f* **2.** (*swear word*) obscénité *f* **3.** (*offensive situation*) infamie *f*

obscure [əb'skjʊəʳ, *Am:* -'skjʊr] **I.** <-r, -st> *adj* **1.** (*not well known*) obscur(e); (*author*) inconnu(e); (*village*) ignoré(e) **2.** (*difficult to understand*) incompréhensible; (*text*) obscur(e) **II.** *vt* **1.** (*make difficult*) obscurcir **2.** *fig* **to ~ sth from sb** cacher qc de qn

obscurity [əb'skjʊərəti, *Am:* -'skjʊrət̬i] *n no pl* obscurité *f*; **to rise from ~** sortir de l'anonymat

obsequious [əb'siːkwɪəs] *adj pej, form* obséquieux(-euse)

observable *adj* observable

observance [əb'zɜːvəns, *Am:* -'zɜːr-] *n form* observance *f*

observant [əb'zɜːvənt, *Am:* -'zɜːr-] *adj* (*alert*) observateur(-trice)

observation [ˌɒbzə'veɪʃən, *Am:* ˌɑːbzɚ'-] *n a.* LAW, MED observation *f*; **to admit sb to hospital for ~** faire entrer qn à l'hôpital en observation; **to keep sb in hospital for ~** garder qn à l'hôpital en observation; **under ~** en observation

observation car, **observation coach** *n Am* véhicule *m* de transport panoramique

observation post *n* poste *m* d'observation

observation tower *n* belvédère *m*

observation ward *n* station *f* d'observation

observatory [əb'zɜːvətri, *Am:* -'zɜːrvətɔːr-] *n* observatoire *m*

observe [əb'zɜːv, *Am:* -'zɜːrv] *vt, vi a. form* observer; **to ~ sb do(ing) sth** observer qn en train de faire qc; **to ~ the speed limit** respecter la limite de vitesse; **to ~ the decencies** observer les règles de bienséance

observer *n* (*watcher*) observateur, -trice *m, f*

obsess [əb'ses] *vt* obséder

obsessed *adj* obsédé(e)

obsession [əb'seʃən] *n a.* MED obsession *f*

obsessive [əb'sesɪv] **I.** *adj* (*secrecy*) obsessionnel(le); (*type*) obsessif(-ive); **to be ~ about sth** être obsédé par qc **II.** *n* obsessionnel(le) *m(f)*

obsolescence [ˌɒbsə'lesənts, *Am:* ˌɑːb-] *n no pl* (*of equipment*) obsolescence *f*

obsolescent [ˌɒbsə'lesnt, *Am:* ˌɑːb-] *adj* obsolète

obsolete ['ɒbsəliːt, *Am:* ˌɑːb-] *adj* désuet(e); (*word, technique*) obsolète; (*design, form*) démodé(e); (*method*) dépassé(e); **to become ~** se démoder

obstacle ['ɒbstəkl, *Am:* 'ɑːbstə-] *n* obstacle *m*

obstacle course *n* **1.** MIL parcours *m* d'obstacles **2.** *fig* parcours *m* du combattant

obstacle race *n* course *f* d'obstacles

obstetrician [ɒbstə'trɪʃən, *Am:* ɑːbstə'trɪʃ-] *n* obstétricien(ne) *m(f)*

obstetrics [ɒb'stetrɪks, *Am:* əb'-] **I.** *n no pl* obstétrique *f* **II.** *adj* obstétrique

obstinacy ['ɒbstɪnəsi, *Am:* 'ɑːbstə-] *n no pl* **1.** (*characteristic*) obstination *f* **2.** (*of a cold, problem*) persistance *f*

obstinate ['ɒbstɪnət, *Am:* 'ɑːbstə-] *adj* (*person, refusal*) obstiné(e); (*weed*) tenace; (*cold, pain, problem*) persistant(e); **to be ~ in doing sth** s'obstiner à faire qc

obstruct [əb'strʌkt] *vt* **1.** *a.* MED (*intestines, path*) obstruer; (*progress, traffic*) bloquer **2.** LAW, SPORT faire obstruction à

obstruction [əb'strʌkʃən] *n a.* LAW, SPORT obstruction *f*; **to cause an ~** faire obstruction

obstructionism *n no pl, pej* obstructionnisme *m*

obstructive [əb'strʌktɪv] *adj pej* (*attitude, tactic*) obstructionniste

obtain [əb'teɪn] **I.** *vt form* obtenir; **to ~ sth from sb** obtenir qc de qn **II.** *vi form* être en vigueur; **~ed rules** les lois en vigueur

obtainable *adj* disponible

obtrude [əb'truːd] **I.** *vt form* imposer; **to ~ one's opinions on sb** imposer ses idées à qn; **to ~ oneself on others** s'imposer **II.** *vi* s'imposer

obtrusive [əb'truːsɪv] *adj* (*question, person*) indiscret(-ète); (*smell*) pénétrant(e)

obtuse [əb'tjuːs, *Am:* ɑːb'tuːs] *adj a. form* obtus(e)

obviate ['ɒbvɪeɪt, *Am:* 'ɑːb-] *vt form* (*eliminate*) obvier à; **to ~ the necessity of sth** prévenir la nécessité de qc

obvious ['ɒbviəs, *Am:* 'ɑːb-] **I.** *adj* évident(e); (*stain*) voyant(e); **to make sth ~ to sb** rendre qc clair et distinct à qn **II.** *n* évidence *f*; **to state the ~** enfoncer les portes ouvertes

obviously **I.** *adv* manifestement **II.** *interj* évidemment!

occasion [ə'keɪʒən] **I.** *n* occasion *f*; **on that ~** en cette occasion; **for the ~** pour l'occasion; **on another ~** à une autre occasion; **on ~** à l'occasion; **on rare ~s** rarement **II.** *vt form* **to ~ sb sth** occasionner qc à qn

occasional *adj* occasionnel(le); **to have an ~ beer** boire une bière de temps en temps; **to pay an ~ visit** faire une visite de temps en temps

occasionally *adv* de temps en temps

occult [ɒ'kʌlt, *Am:* ə'-] **I.** *adj* occulte **II.** *n no pl* **the ~** l'occulte *m*

occupancy ['ɒkjəpəntsi, *Am:* 'ɑːkjə-] *n no pl, form* occupation *f*

occupancy rate *n* taux *m* d'occupation
occupant ['ɒkjəpənt, *Am:* 'ɑːkjə-] *n form* occupant(e) *m(f)*
occupation [ˌɒkjə'peɪʃən, *Am:* 'ɑːkjə'-] *n a. form a.* MIL occupation *f*
occupational *adj* professionnel(le)
occupational pension scheme *n* retraite *f* complémentaire professionnelle **occupational therapy** *n* ergothérapie *f*
occupied *adj* occupé(e)
occupier *n* occupant(e) *m(f)*
occupy ['ɒkjʊpaɪ, *Am:* 'ɑːkjuː-] *vt a. form* occuper; **to ~ oneself** s'occuper; **to ~ one's mind** s'occuper l'esprit; **to ~ one's time** occuper son temps; **to ~ one's time in doing sth** s'occuper à faire qc; **~ing forces** les forces *fpl* occupantes
occur [ə'kɜːʳ, *Am:* -'kɜːr] <-rr-> *vi* **1.**(*take place: event, accident*) avoir lieu; (*change, explosion, mistake*) se produire; (*symptom*) apparaître; (*problem, opportunity*) se présenter **2.**(*be found*) se trouver **3.**(*come to mind*) **it ~s to me that ...** il me semble que ...; **it ~ed to me to** *+infin* il m'est venu à l'idée de *+infin*
occurrence [ə'kʌrəns, *Am:* -'kɜːr-] *n* **1.**(*event*) fait *m;* **an everyday ~** un fait quotidien **2.** *no pl* (*incidence*) incidence *f*
ocean ['əʊʃən, *Am:* 'oʊ-] *n* océan *m* ►**~s <u>of</u> sth** des montagnes de qc
ocean-going *adj* de haute mer
Oceania [ˌəʊʃi'ɑːniə, *Am:* ˌoʊ-] *n* l'Océanie *f*
ocean liner *n* transatlantique *m*
oceanography [ˌəʊʃə'nɒgrəfi, *Am:* ˌoʊʃə'nɑːgrə-] *n no pl* océanographie *f*
ocelot ['əʊsɪlɒt, *Am:* 'ɑːsəlɑːt] *n* ZOOL ocelot *m*
ocher ['əʊkəʳ, *Am:* 'oʊkɚ] *n Am*, **ochre** *n no pl* **1.**(*colour*) ocre *m* **2.**(*earthy substance*) ocre *f*
o'clock [ə'klɒk, *Am:* -'klɑːk] *adv* **it's 2 ~** il est deux heures
OCR [ˌəʊsiː'ɑːʳ, *Am:* ˌoʊ-] *n* INFOR *abbr of* **optical character recognition** ROC *f*
octagon ['ɒktəgən, *Am:* 'ɑktəgɑːn] *n* octogone *m*
octane ['ɒkteɪn, *Am:* 'ɑːk-] *n* octane *m*
octane (**number**), **octane rating** *n* indice *m* d'octane
octave ['ɒktɪv, *Am:* 'ɑːk-] *n* MUS octave *f*
octet [ɒk'tet, *Am:* ɑːk-] *n + pl, sing vb* MUS octuor *m*
October [ɒk'təʊbəʳ, *Am:* ɑːk'toʊbɚ] *n* octobre *m; s. a.* **April**
octogenarian [ˌɒktədʒɪ'neərɪən, *Am:* ˌɑːktoʊdʒɪ'nerɪ-] *n* octogénaire *mf*
octopus ['ɒktəpəs, *Am:* 'ɑːk-] <-es *o* -pi> *n* octopode *m*
oculist ['ɒkjʊlɪst, *Am:* 'ɑːkjə-] *n s.* **ophthalmologist**
OD [ˌəʊ'diː, *Am:* ˌoʊ-] *abbr of* **overdose I.** *n* OD *f* **II.** *vi* <-ing, -ed> **to ~ on sth** *a. fig* prendre une overdose de qc; (*food*) forcer sur qc
odd [ɒd, *Am:* ɑːd] *adj* <-er, -est> **1.**(*strange*) bizarre; **to look ~** avoir l'air bizarre **2.**(*not a pair: socks*) dépareillé(e) **3.**(*not even: number*) impair **4.**(*and more*) et quelques; **50 ~ people** une cinquantaine de personnes **5.**(*occasional*) occasionnel(le); **to have the ~ drink** prendre un verre de temps en temps; **at ~ times** de temps en temps; **~ jobs** petits travaux *mpl* ►**the ~ <u>man</u> out** l'intrus *m;* **to feel the ~ <u>man</u> out** ne pas se sentir à sa place
oddball ['ɒdbɔːl, *Am:* 'ɑːd-] **I.** *n inf* hurluberlu *mf* **II.** *adj inf* farfelu(e)
oddity ['ɒdəti, *Am:* 'ɑːdət̬i] *n* **1.**(*strange person*) hurluberlu *m* **2.**(*strange thing*) bizarrerie *f*
oddly *adv* bizarrement; **~ enough** bizarrement
oddment *n* reste *m*
odds *npl* (*probability*) chances *fpl;* (*for betting*) cote *f;* **to give long ~ on/against sth** donner toutes les chances/aucune chance à qc; **to lengthen/shorten the ~** accroître/amincir les chances; **against all** (**the**) **~** contre toute espérance ►**to be <u>at</u> ~ with sb/sth** être en désaccord avec qn/qc; **~ and <u>ends</u>** *Aus, Brit, inf* bricoles *fpl;* **it <u>makes</u> no ~** cela n'a pas d'importance
odds-on [ˌɒdz'ɒn, *Am:* ˌɑːdz'ɑːn] *adj* **it's ~ that** il y a toutes les chances pour que *+subj;* **it seems ~ that ...** il y a gros à parier que ...; **the ~ favourite** le grand favori
ode [əʊd, *Am:* oʊd] *n* ode *f*
odious ['əʊdɪəs, *Am:* 'oʊ-] *adj form* odieux(-euse)
odometer [ɒ'dɒmɪtəʳ, *Am:* oʊ'dɑːmət̬ɚ] *n* **1.** *Am* (*mileometer*) odomètre *m* **2.** *Aus, Brit s.* **mileometer**
odor ['əʊdəʳ, *Am:* 'oʊdɚ] *n Am, Aus, form*, **odour** *n Aus, Brit, form* odeur *f*
odo(**u**)**rless** *adj form* inodore
odyssey ['ɒdɪsi, *Am:* 'ɑːdɪ-] *n* odyssée *f*
OECD [ˌəʊiːsiː'diː, *Am:* ˌoʊ-] *n abbr of* **Organization for Economic Cooperation and Development** OCDE *f*
oesophagus [iː'sɒfəgəs, *Am:* ɪ'sɑːfə-] <-agi *o* -guses> *n* ANAT œsophage *m*
oestrogen ['iːstrəʊdʒən, *Am:* 'estrə-] *n* oestrogène *m*
of [əv, *stressed:* ɒv] *prep* **1.**(*belonging to*) de; **the end ~ the film/play** la fin du film/de la pièce; **the works ~ Joyce** les œuvres de Joyce; **a friend ~ mine/theirs** un de mes/leurs amis; **a page ~ it is torn** une page en est arrachée; **a drawing ~ Paul's** (*he owns it*) un dessin appartenant à Paul; (*he drew it*) un dessin fait par Paul; **a drawing ~ Paul** (*he is on it*) un portrait de Paul **2.**(*describing*) **a man ~ courage/no importance** un homme courageux/sans importance; **a city ~ wide avenues** une ville aux larges avenues; **80 years ~ age** âgé de 80 ans; **it's kind ~ him**

c'est gentil à lui [*o* de sa part]; **this idiot ~ a plumber** cet imbécile de plombier **3.** (*dates and time*) **the 4th ~ May/in May ~ 2002** le 4 mai/en mai 2002; **ten/a quarter ~ two** *Am* deux heures moins dix/le quart **4.** (*nature, content*) **a ring ~ gold** une bague en or; **to smell/taste ~ cheese** sentir le/avoir un goût de fromage; **~ itself, it's not important** en soi, ce n'est pas important; **it happened ~ itself** c'est arrivé tout seul **5.** (*among*) **one ~ the best** un des meilleurs; **I know two ~ them** j'en connais deux d'entre eux; **he knows the five ~ them** il les connaît tous les cinq; **many ~ them came** beaucoup d'entre eux sont venus; **they are five ~ them** ils sont (à) cinq; **two ~ the five** deux sur les cinq; **you ~ all people** toi entre tous; **he ~ all people should know better** lui, plus que tout le monde, devrait savoir; **today ~ all days** justement aujourd'hui

off [ɒf, *Am:* ɑːf] **I.** *prep* **1.** (*apart from*) **to be one metre ~ sb/sth** être à un mètre de qn/qc; **the top is ~ the jar** le couvercle n'est pas sur le bocal; **~ the point** hors de propos; **~ Dover** au large de Douvres; **the mill is ~ the road** le moulin est à l'écart de la route **2.** (*away from*) **her street is ~ the avenue** sa rue part de l'avenue; **to take sth ~ the shelf/wall** prendre qc sur l'étagère/enlever qc du mur; **keep ~ the grass** pelouse interdite; **to go ~ the air** RADIO quitter l'antenne **3.** (*down from*) **to fall/jump ~ a ladder** tomber/sauter d'une échelle; **to get ~ the train** descendre du train **4.** (*from*) **to eat ~ a plate** manger dans une assiette; **to wipe the water ~ the bench** essuyer l'eau du banc; **to cut a piece ~ this cheese** couper un morceau de ce fromage; **to take £10 ~ the price** faire une réduction de 10£; **to borrow money ~ sb** *inf* emprunter de l'argent à qn **5.** (*stop liking*) **to go ~ sb/sth** cesser d'aimer qn/qc; **to be ~ drugs** être désintoxiqué **II.** *adv* **1.** (*not on*) **to switch/turn sth ~** éteindre/arrêter qc; **it's ~ between them** *fig* c'est fini entre eux **2.** (*away*) **the town is 8 km ~** la ville est à 8 km; **not far/some way ~** pas très loin/à quelque distance; **to go/run ~** partir/partir en courant; **it's time I was ~** il est temps que je m'en aille *subj;* **we're ~ on Tuesday** nous ne sommes pas là jeudi; **to be ~** SPORT avoir pris le départ **3.** (*removed*) **there's a button ~** il manque un bouton; **the lid's ~** le couvercle n'est pas dessus; **with one's coat ~** sans manteau **4.** (*free from work*) **to get ~ at 4:00** sortir du travail à 4 h; **to get a day ~** avoir un jour de congé; **to take time/an afternoon ~** prendre du temps/un après-midi de libre **5.** (*completely*) **to kill ~** anéantir; **to pay sth ~** finir de payer qc **6.** COM **5 % ~** 5 % de rabais **7.** (*until gone*) **to walk ~ the dinner** faire une promenade digestive; **to sleep ~ the wine** cuver son vin; **to work ~ the calories** brûler les calories ►**straight** [*o* **right**] **~** tout de suite; **~ and on** [*o* **on and ~**] de temps en temps; **it rained ~ and on** il pleuvait par intermittence **III.** *adj inv* **1.** (*not on: light*) éteint(e); (*tap*) fermé(e); (*water, electricity*) coupé(e); (*concert*) annulé(e); (*engagement*) rompu(e) **2.** (*bad: day*) mauvais(e); (*milk*) tourné(e); (*food*) avarié(e) **3.** (*free from work*) **to be ~ at 5 o'clock** terminer à 5 h; **I'm ~ on Mondays** je ne suis pas là le lundi **4.** *Aus, Brit* (*provided for*) **to be badly ~** être dans la gêne; **to be well/badly ~ for sth** être bien pourvu en/à court de qc **5.** (*sold out*) **veal is ~ now** il n'y a plus de veau **6.** *Brit* (*rude*) **that's a bit ~!** c'est plutôt dur à avaler!; **to go ~ on sb** *Am, inf* engueuler qn **IV.** *n no pl, Brit* départ *m* **V.** *vt Am, inf* (*kill*) buter

offal [ˈɒfəl, *Am:* ˈɑːfəl] *n no pl* abats *mpl*

offbeat [ˌɒfˈbiːt, *Am:* ˌɑːf-] *adj* hors du commun; (*music*) original(e)

off-center *adj Am,* **off-centre** *adj* **1.** (*not in center*) désaxé(e) **2.** *fig* (*humour*) décalé(e) **off-chance** *n* **on the ~** à tout hasard **off colo(u)r** *adj* **1.** *Brit* (*bad*) **to feel a bit ~** se sentir mal **2.** (*somewhat obscene*) obscène **off day** *n inf* **to have an ~** avoir une sale journée

offence [əˈfents] *n* **1.** LAW (*crime*) délit *m;* **to convict sb of an ~** condamner qn pour un délit **2.** *no pl* (*upset feelings*) offense *f;* **to cause ~ to sb** offenser qn; **to take ~ at sth** s'offenser de qc; **no ~ (intended)** je ne voulais pas t'offenser **3.** *no pl* (*attack*) attaque *f* **4.** *Am* SPORT offensive *f;* **to be on ~** être sur l'offensive

offend [əˈfend] **I.** *vi* LAW commettre un délit **II.** *vt* (*upset sb's feelings*) offenser

offender *n* LAW délinquant(e) *m(f);* **a first ~** un délinquant primaire

offense [əˈfens] *n Am s.* **offence**

offensive [əˈfensɪv] **I.** *adj* **1.** (*causing offense: remark, smell*) offensant(e); (*language*) insultant(e); (*joke*) injurieux(-euse) **2.** (*attack*) offensif(-ive) **II.** *n* MIL offensive *f;* **to go on the ~** passer à l'offensive

offer [ˈɒfəʳ, *Am:* ˈɑːfɚ] **I.** *vt* **1.** (*give*) offrir; **to ~ sb sth** offrir qc à qn **2.** (*give choice of having*) **to ~ sb sth** proposer qc à qn; **to ~ a choice** donner un choix; **to ~ congratulations** adresser des félicitations **3.** (*volunteer*) **to ~ to** +*infin* proposer de +*infin;* **to ~ a suggestion** faire une suggestion **4.** (*provide: information, excuse, reward*) donner; **to have much to ~** avoir beaucoup à donner; **to ~ resistance** offrir de la résistance; **to ~ a glimpse** donner un coup d'œil; **what have you got to ~?** qu'est-ce que vous proposez? **5.** (*bid*) faire une offre de **6.** (*sell*) proposer; **we're ~ing them at £20 each** nous les offrons à 20 livres pièce; **to be ~ed for sale** être mis en vente **II.** *vi* **1.** (*volunteer*) se proposer **2.** (*happen: occasion*) se présenter **III.** *n a.* ECON offre *f;* **on ~** en vente; **to make sb an ~ they can't refuse** faire une offre à qn qui ne se refuse pas; **to be on special ~** *Aus, Brit* être en promotion

offering *n* 1.(*thing offered*) offre *f;* **the ~s on TV** ce que la télé nous propose; **the ~s of thanks** les remerciements *mpl* 2. REL offrande *f;* **sacrificial ~** sacrifice *m*

offhand [ˌɒfˈhænd, *Am:* ˌɑːf-] I. *adj* désinvolte II. *adv* de but en blanc

office [ˈɒfɪs, *Am:* ˈɑːfɪs] *n* 1.(*room for working*) bureau *m;* **to stay at the ~** rester au bureau; **the finance ~** le bureau des finances; **a doctor's ~** *Am* un cabinet de médecin 2.(*authoritative position*) fonction *f;* **to hold ~** être au pouvoir; (*minister, mayor*) être en fonction; **to be out of ~** ne plus être au pouvoir; **to come into ~** arriver au pouvoir

Office *n Brit* (*government department*) ministère *m*

office automation *n* INFOR bureautique *f* **office block** *n Aus, Brit* complexe *m* de bureaux **office building** *n Am s.* **office block** **office equipment** *n* équipement *m* de bureau **office hours** *npl* heures *fpl* de bureau; **to do sth out(side) of ~** faire qc en dehors des heures de bureau **Office of Fair Trading** *n no pl, Brit* service *m* de protection du consommateur

officer *n* 1.(*person in army, police*) officier *m;* **yes ~** oui, monsieur/madame 2.(*civil servant*) fonctionnaire *mf* 3.(*manager*) responsable *mf*

office space *n no pl* bureaux *mpl* **office staff** *n no pl* personnel *m* de bureau **office suite** *n* INFOR suite *f* bureautique **office supplies** *npl* fournitures *fpl* de bureau **office worker** *n* employé(e) *m(f)* de bureau

official [əˈfɪʃl] I. *n* 1.(*responsible person*) officiel(le) *m(f)* 2. *Am* (*referee*) arbitre *mf* II. *adj* officiel(le)

officialdom [əˈfɪʃldəm] *n no pl, pej* bureaucratie *f*

officialese [əˌfɪʃəˈliːz] *n no pl, Am* jargon *m* administratif

officially *adv* officiellement

Official Secrets Act *n* loi *f* sur la défense des secrets d'État

officiate [əˈfɪʃɪeɪt] *vi form* officier; **to ~ at a wedding** officier à un mariage

officious [əˈfɪʃəs] *adj pej* (trop) zélé(e)

offing [ˈɒfɪŋ, *Am:* ˈɑːfɪŋ] *n no pl* **to be in the ~** être en vue

off key I. *adv* MUS faux; **to sing ~** chanter faux II. *adj* 1.(*out of tune*) qui sonne faux 2. *fig* (*inopportune*) qui tombe mal **off-licence** *n Brit* 1.(*licence*) licence *f* pour la vente d'alcool 2.(*shop*) magasin *m* de vins et de spiritueux **off-limits** *adj* interdit d'accès **off-line** *adj* INFOR hors-ligne; **to be ~** être déconnecté; **to go ~** se déconnecter **offload** *vt* 1.(*unload*) décharger; (*passengers*) débarquer 2.(*get rid of*) refourguer 3.(*relieve oneself*) **to ~ sth on to sb** se décharger de qc sur qn; **to ~ responsibility on to sb** rejeter la responsabilité sur qn **off-peak** I. *adv* 1.(*outside peak hours*) aux heures creuses 2.(*off season*) en basse saison; **to go on vacation when it's ~** partir en vacances hors saison II. *adj* en basse saison; (*call*) aux heures creuses; **~ hours** heures *fpl* creuses **off-piste** *n* hors-piste *m inv* **off-putting** *adj* 1.(*disconcerting*) peu engageant(e) 2.(*extremely unpleasant*) désagréable **off season** *n* hors-saison *f* **offset** <offset, offset> I. *vt* 1. FIN (*compensate*) compenser; **to ~ sth by sth** compenser qc par qc 2.(*print using offset*) **to ~ sth** imprimer qc en offset 3.(*place out of line*) désaxer II. *n* 1.(*compensation*) compensation *f* 2. PUBL offset *m* 3. AUTO (*of wheels*) désaxage *m* 4. BOT rejeton *m* **offshore** I. *adj* 1.(*at sea*) au large; (*nearer to coast: fishing, waters*) côtier(-ère) 2.(*blowing towards the sea: wind*) de terre 3.(*related to oil extracting: drilling, company*) offshore *inv* 4. COM, POL (*abroad*) extraterritorial(e) II. *adv* au large **offside** I. *adj* 1. SPORT hors-jeu *inv;* **~ position** position *f* de hors-jeu; **offside rule** règle *f* du hors-jeu 2. AUTO côté conducteur II. *adv* SPORT hors-jeu III. *n* 1. SPORT hors-jeu *m inv* 2. *Brit* **the ~** la place du conducteur **offspring** <offspring> *n* (*young animal, child*) progéniture *f* **offstage** I. *adj* 1.(*behind the stage*) en coulisses 2.(*private: life*) privé(e) II. *adv* 1.(*privately*) dans le privé 2.(*away from the stage*) derrière les coulisses; **to hear sb's voice ~** entendre la voix de qn de derrière les coulisses **off-street parking** *n* parking *m* privé **off-the-cuff** *adj* impromptu(e) **off-the-peg** *adj* (*clothes*) de prêt-à-porter **off-the-wall** (*humour*) loufoque **off-white** *n* blanc *m* cassé

OFT *abbr of* **Office of Fair Trading** *Brit* Service *m* de protection du consommateur

often [ˈɒfən, *Am:* ˈɑːfən] *adv* souvent; **it's not ~ that ...** ce n'est pas souvent que ...; **how ~** combien de fois; **as ~ as not** la plupart du temps

ogle [ˈəʊgl, *Am:* ˈoʊ-] I. *vi* lorgner; **to ~ at sb** lorgner qn II. *vt* lorgner

ogre [ˈəʊgəʳ, *Am:* ˈoʊgɚ] *n* 1.(*monster*) ogre *m* 2. *inf* (*frightening person*) monstre *m*

ogress [ˈəʊgres, *Am:* ˈoʊ-] *n* 1.(*monster*) ogresse *f* 2. *inf* (*frightening woman*) monstre *m*

oh [əʊ, *Am:* oʊ] I. *interj* oh!; **~ dear!** mon dieu!; **~ really?** ah oui? II. *n* oh *m*

Ohio [əʊˈhaɪəʊ, *Am:* oʊˈhaɪoʊ] I. *n* l'Ohio *m* II. *adj* de l'Ohio

OHMS [ˌəʊeɪtʃemˈes, *Am:* ˌoʊ-] *Brit abbr of* **On Her/His Majesty's Service** au service de sa majesté

oik [ɔɪk] *n Brit, pej, inf* plouc *mf*

oil [ɔɪl] I. *n* 1.(*lubricant, for cooking*) huile *f;* **to change the ~** faire la vidange; **to check the ~** contrôler le niveau d'huile; (*corn ~*) huile de maïs; **to cook with ~** cuisiner à l'huile 2. *no pl* (*petroleum*) pétrole *m;* **to drill for ~** chercher du pétrole 3.(*oil-based colours*) **~s** *pl* huiles *fpl* ►**to burn the midnight**

O

~ travailler jusqu'à tard dans la nuit; **to mix like ~ and water** mal se mélanger **II.** *vt* huiler
oilcake *n* tourteau *m* **oilcan** *n* bidon *m* d'huile **oil change** *n* AUTO vidange *f* **oil-cloth** *n* toile *f* cirée **oil company** *n* compagnie *f* pétrolière **oil consumption** *n* consommation *f* de pétrole **oil crisis** *n* crise *f* du pétrole **oil-exporting** *adj* exportateur(-trice) de pétrole **oilfield** *n* champ *m* pétrolifère **oil-fired** *adj* ~ **heating system** chauffage *m* central au mazout **oil lamp** *n* lampe *f* à pétrole **oil level** *n* TECH niveau *m* d'huile **oil painting** *n* peinture *f* à l'huile ▸**to be no ~** *Aus, Brit, fig, iron* ne pas être une huile **oil pipeline** *n* oléoduc *m* **oil-producing** *adj* producteur(-trice) de pétrole **oil production** *n* production *f* pétrolifère **oilrig** *n* plate-forme *f* de forage **oilskin** *n* toile *f* cirée **oil slick** *n* nappe *f* de pétrole **oil tanker** *n* NAUT pétrolier *m* **oil well** *n* puits *m* de pétrole
oily ['ɔɪli] <-ier, -iest> *adj* **1.** (*oil-like*) huileux(-euse) **2.** (*soaked in oil, greasy*) graisseux(-euse) **3.** (*unpleasantly polite*) visqueux(-euse)
ointment ['ɔɪntmənt] *n* MED onguent *m*
OK, okay [ˌəʊ'keɪ, *Am:* ˌoʊ-] *inf* **I.** *adj* **1.** (*fine*) O.K.; **to be ~** aller bien; **that's ~** ça va; **is it ~ to go now?** est-ce que je peux m'en aller maintenant?; **to be an ~ bloke** être un mec bien; **to be ~ about sth** être O.K. pour qc; **to be ~ for money/work** avoir assez d'argent/de travail; **to be ~ for a drink** être d'accord pour boire un verre **2.** (*not bad*) pas mal **II.** *interj* O.K.!, d'accord! **III.** <OKed, okayed> *vt* approuver **IV.** *n* accord *m;* **to get the ~** avoir l'accord; **to give the ~** donner son accord **V.** *adv* bien; **to go ~** aller bien
Oklahoma [ˌəʊklə'həʊmə, *Am:* ˌoʊklə'hoʊ-] **I.** *n* l'Oklahoma **II.** *adj* de l'Oklahoma
okra ['əʊkrə, *Am:* 'oʊ-] *n* okra *m*
old [əʊld, *Am:* oʊld] **I.** *adj* <-er, -est> **1.** (*not young, new*) vieux(vieille); **to grow ~er** vieillir; **to collect ~ clothes** collecter les vieux vêtements **2.** (*denoting an age*) âgé(e); **how ~ is she?** quel âge a-t-elle?; **she is six years ~** elle a six ans; **to be ~ enough to** +*infin* être assez grand pour +*infin* **3.** (*former*) ancien(ne) **4.** (*long known: friend*) de longue date **5.** (*expression of affection*) vieux(vieille) ▸**in the (good) ~ days** dans le bon vieux temps; **to be as ~ as the hills** être aussi vieux que Mathusalem **II.** *n* (*elderly people*) **the ~** *pl* les vieux *mpl*
old age *n* vieillesse *f;* **in one's ~** sur ses vieux jours **old-age pension** *n* retraite *f* **old-age pensioner** *n* retraité(e) *m(f)* **Old Bill** *n no pl, Brit, inf* flics *mpl* **old boy** *n* **1.** *Brit, inf* (*old man*) vieux croûton *m* **2.** *Aus, Brit* (*former pupil*) ancien élève *m* **old-established** *adj* bien établi(e) **old-fashioned** *adj pej* **1.** (*out: clothes, views*) démodé(e) **2.** (*traditional*) d'autrefois **old girl** *n* **1.** *Brit, inf* (*old woman*) vieille *f* **2.** *Aus, Brit* (*former pupil*) ancienne élève *f* **old hand** *n* ancien(ne) *m(f);* **to be an ~ at sth** être un expert dans qc
oldie *n inf* **1.** MUS vieux tube *m* **2.** CINE vieux film *m*
oldish *adj* qui n'est plus tout(e) jeune
old lady *n inf* (*one's wife, mother*) vieille *f* **old maid** *n pej* vieille fille *f* **old-maidish** *adj pej* vieille fille **old man** *n inf* (*husband, father*) vieux *m* **old master** *n* ART tableau *m* de maître **old people's home** *n* maison *f* de retraite **old-style** *adj* à l'ancienne **Old Testament** *n no pl* Ancien Testament *m* **old-timer** *n Am, inf* vieux *m* de la vieille; **well ~, it's getting late** allez mon vieux, il se fait tard **old wives' tale** *n* histoire *f* à dormir debout **Old World** *n no pl* Ancien Monde *m*
oleander [ˌəʊli'ændəʳ, *Am:* ˌoʊli'ændɚ] *n* BOT laurier *m* rose
olive ['ɒlɪv, *Am:* 'ɑːlɪv] **I.** *n* **1.** (*fruit*) olive *f* **2.** (*tree*) olivier *m* **3.** (*wood*) (bois *m* d')olivier *m* **4.** (*colour*) vert *m* olive **II.** *adj* olive *inv;* (*skin*) mat(e)
olive branch *n* rameau *m* d'olivier **olive grove** *n* oliveraie *f* **olive oil** *n* huile *f* d'olive
Olympiad [ə'lɪmpɪæd, *Am:* oʊ'-] *n* olympiades *fpl*
Olympian [ə'lɪmpɪən, *Am:* oʊ'-] **I.** *n Am* SPORT olympien(ne) *m(f)* **II.** *adj* olympien(ne); (*god*) de l'Olympe
Olympic [ə'lɪmpɪk, *Am:* oʊ'-] *adj* (*champion, flame, stadium*) olympique; **International ~ Committee** Comité *m* international des Jeux olympiques
Oman [əʊ'mɑːn, *Am:* oʊ'-] *n* Oman *m*
Omani **I.** *adj* omanais(e) **II.** *n* Omanais(e) *m(f)*
ombudsman ['ɒmbʊdzmən, *Am:* 'ɑːmbədz-] *n* POL médiateur *m*
omelet(te) ['ɒmlɪt, *Am:* 'ɑːmlət] *n* (*egg dish*) omelette *f* ▸**you can't make an ~ without breaking eggs** *prov* on ne fait pas d'omelette sans casser des œufs
omen ['əʊmen, *Am:* 'oʊ-] *n* augure *m;* **to be a good/bad ~ for sth** être de bon/mauvais augure pour qc; **to take sth as a good/bad ~** prendre qc pour un bon/mauvais signe
ominous ['ɒmɪnəs, *Am:* 'ɑːmə-] *adj* **1.** (*announcing sth bad*) de mauvais augure **2.** (*threatening*) menaçant(e)
omission [ə'mɪʃən, *Am:* oʊ'-] *n* omission *f*
omit [ə'mɪt, *Am:* oʊ'-] <-tt-> *vt* omettre
omnibus ['ɒmnɪbəs, *Am:* 'ɑːm-] *n* **1.** (*anthology*) recueil *m* **2.** *form* (*bus*) omnibus *m*
omnipotence [ɒm'nɪpətəns, *Am:* ɑːm'nɪpət̬əns] *n no pl* omnipotence *f*
omnipotent [ɒm'nɪpətənt, *Am:* ɑːm'nɪpət̬ənt] *adj* omnipotent(e)
omnipresent [ˌɒmnɪ'preznt, *Am:* ˌɑːm-] *adj form* omniprésent(e)

omniscient [ɒmˈnɪʃnt, *Am:* ɑːm-] *adj* omniscient(e)

omnivorous [ɒmˈnɪvərəs, *Am:* ɑːm-] *adj* **1.**(*eating plants and meat*) omnivore **2.** *fig* (*voracious*) vorace

on [ɒn, *Am:* ɑːn] **I.** *prep* **1.**(*in contact with top*) sur; ~ **the table** sur la table; **a table with a glass ~ it** une table avec un verre dessus; ~ **the ground** par terre **2.**(*in contact with*) **a fly ~ the wall/ceiling** une mouche sur la table/le mur/au plafond; **a cut ~ one's finger** une coupure au doigt; **a bottle with a label ~ it** une bouteille avec une étiquette dessus; **to hang ~ a branch** pendre à une branche; **to put sth ~ sb's shoulder/finger** mettre qc sur l'épaule/au doigt de qn; **to be ~ the plane** être dans l'avion; **I have the money ~ me** j'ai l'argent sur moi **3.**(*by means of*) **to go there ~ the train/bus** y aller en train/bus; ~ **foot/a bike** à pied/vélo; **to keep a dog ~ a lead** tenir un chien en laisse **4.**(*source of*) **to run ~ gas** fonctionner au gaz; **to live ~ one's income** vivre de ses revenus; **to be ~ £2,000 a month** gagner 2.000£ par mois **5.** MED **to be ~ drugs** se droguer; **to be ~ cortisone** être sous cortisone **6.**(*spatial*) ~ **the right/left** à droite/gauche; ~ **the corner/back of sth** au coin/dos de qc; **a house ~ the river** une maison au bord du fleuve; **a house/to live ~ Baker Street** une maison dans/habiter Baker Street **7.**(*temporal*) ~ **Sunday/Fridays** dimanche/le vendredi; ~ **May the 4th** le 4 mai; ~ **the evening of May the 4th** le soir du 4 mai; ~ **his birthday** le jour de son anniversaire **8.**(*at time of*) **to leave ~ time** partir à l'heure; **to stop ~ the way** s'arrêter en route; ~ **sb's death/arrival** à la mort/l'arrivée de qn; ~ **arriving there** en arrivant là-bas; **to finish ~ schedule** finir selon les prévisions **9.**(*about*) **a lecture ~ Joyce** un cours sur Joyce; **to speak ~ unemployment** parler du chômage; **my views ~ the economy** mon point de vue sur l'économie; **I agree with you ~ this** je suis d'accord avec toi sur ce point; **to compliment sb ~ sth** féliciter qn pour qc; **to be there ~ business** être là pour affaires **10.**(*through medium of*) ~ **TV** à la télé; ~ **video** en vidéo; ~ **CD** sur CD; **to speak ~ the radio/phone** parler à la radio/au téléphone; **to work ~ a computer** travailler sur ordinateur; **to play sth ~ the flute** jouer qc à la flûte **11.**(*involvement*) **to be ~ the committee** faire partie de la commission; **to work ~ a project** travailler à un projet; **two ~ each side** deux de chaque côté **12.**(*against*) **an attack/to turn ~ sb** une attaque/se retourner contre qn **13.**(*payments*) **to buy sth ~ credit** acheter qc à crédit; **this is ~ me** *inf* c'est ma tournée; **I'm ~ £30,000 a year** je gagne 30,000£ par an **14.**(*progress*) **to be ~ page 10** en être à la page 10; **to be ~ 10 points** *Aus, Brit* SPORT avoir 10 points **15.**(*for*) **to spend £10 ~ sth** dépenser 10£ pour qc **16.**(*connected to*) **to be ~ the phone** (*have one*) avoir le téléphone; (*talking*) être au téléphone **II.** *adv* **1.**(*wearing*) **to have nothing ~** être nu; **I put a hat ~** j'ai mis un chapeau; **what he has ~** ce qu'il porte **2.**(*forwards*) **to go/move ~** continuer/avancer; **to talk/work ~** continuer de parler/travailler; **from that day ~** à partir de ce jour-là; **well ~ in the morning** tard dans la matinée **3.**(*aboard*) **to get ~** monter **4.**(*on duty*) de service ►**what's he ~ <u>about</u>?** *Aus, Brit, inf* qu'est-ce qu'il raconte?; **to be always ~ <u>about</u> sth** *inf* ne pas arrêter de déblatérer sur qc; **to be always ~ <u>at</u> sb** *inf* être toujours sur le dos de qn; ~ **<u>and</u>** ~ continuellement **III.** *adj* **1.**(*not off: light*) allumé(e); (*tap*) ouvert(e); (*water, gas*) branché(e); **to be ~** (*machine*) être en marche; **the top is ~** le couvercle est mis; **the concert is still ~** (*not cancelled*) le concert n'est pas annulé; (*not over*) le concert n'est pas fini **2.**(*happening*) **I've got something ~ tonight** j'ai quelque chose de prévu ce soir; **I've got a lot ~ at the moment** j'ai beaucoup à faire en ce moment; **the game/film is ~ tonight** le match a lieu/on joue le film ce soir; **is the wedding still ~?** est-ce que le mariage aura lieu quand même?; **what's ~?** (*films, TV*) qu'est-ce qu'il y a à la télé/au cinéma?; **you're ~** THEAT, TV c'est à toi **3.**(*good*) **one of my ~ days** un de mes bons jours; **it's not ~** c'est inacceptable; *s. a.* **off, onto**

once [wʌnts] **I.** *adv* **1.**(*a single time*) une fois; ~ **a week** une fois par semaine; ~ **and for all** une fois pour toutes; ~ **or twice** une ou deux fois; ~ **upon a time there was …** il était une fois; **he was on time for ~** pour une fois, il était à l'heure **2.**(*formerly*) autrefois ►~ **<u>bitten</u> twice shy** *prov* chat échaudé craint l'eau froide **II.** *conj* (*as soon as*) une fois que; **but ~ I'd arrived, …** mais une fois arrivé, … ►**<u>at</u> ~** (*immediately*) tout de suite; **<u>all</u> at ~** soudain

once-over [ˈwʌntsˌəʊvəʳ, *Am:* ˈwʌntsˌoʊvɚ] *n inf* **1.**(*cursory examination*) coup *m* d'œil; **to give sb/sth a ~** jeter un coup d'œil sur qn/qc **2.**(*cursory cleaning*) petit coup *m;* **to give sth a ~ with sth** donner un petit coup de qc à qc

oncoming [ˈɒnkʌmɪŋ, *Am:* ˈɑːn-] *adj* (*vehicle*) venant en sens inverse

oncosts *n pl, Brit* COM coûts *mpl* fixes

one [wʌn] **I.** *n* un *m* ►**in ~s and <u>twos</u>** un par un ou deux par deux; **to drink sth <u>down</u> in ~** boire qc d'un seul trait; **to be sth and sth (all) <u>in</u> ~** être à la fois qc et qc **II.** *adj* **1.** *numeral* un(e); ~ **hundred** cent; **as ~ man** comme un seul homme; ~ **man out of/in two** un homme sur deux; **a ~-bedroom flat** un deux pièces **2.** *indef* un(e); **we'll meet ~ day** on se verra un de ces jours; ~ **winter night** par une nuit d'hiver **3.**(*sole, single*) seul(e); **her ~ and only hope** son seul et unique espoir **4.**(*same*) même; **to be ~ on sth** être du même avis sur qc; **they're ~ and the same person** c'est une

O

seule et même personne; **all the files on the ~ disk** tous les fichiers sur la même disquette; *s. a.* **eight III.** *pron* **1.** *impers pron* on; **what ~ can do** ce qu'on peut faire; **~'s** son(sa); **to wash ~'s face** se laver le visage **2.** *indef pron* (*particular thing, person*) un(e); **~ Mr Smith** un certain M. Smith; **~ of them** l'un d'entre eux; **have you got ~?** est-ce que tu en as un?; **to be ~ of the members/us** être l'un des membres/nôtres; **not ~** pas un; **~ by ~** un par un; **no ~** personne; **every ~** chacun(e) **3.** *dem pron* **this ~** celui(celle)-là; **which ~?** lequel(laquelle)?; **any ~** n'importe lequel(laquelle); **to be the only ~** être le(la) seul(e); **the thinner ~** le(la) plus mince; **the little ~s** les petits; **the ~ on the table** celui(celle) qui est sur la table; **the ~ who ...** celui(celle) qui ... ►**I for ~** moi, pour ma part

one another *reciprocal pron s.* **each other**
one-armed *adj* manchot(e) **one-armed bandit** *n Am, Aus* GAMES machine *f* à sous **one-eyed** *adj* borgne **one-handed I.** *adv* d'une seule main **II.** *adj* manchot(e) **one-horse town** *n* trou *m* perdu **one-legged** *adj* unijambiste **one-liner** *n* boutade *f*

one-man *adj* **1.** (*of one person*) à un seul homme **2.** (*done by one man*) fait(e) par un seul homme **3.** (*done for one man*) pour un seul homme; (*boat*) une place **one-man band** *n* homme-orchestre *m* **one-man show** *n a. pej* one man show *m*

one-night stand *n* **1.** (*performance*) représentation *f* exceptionnelle **2.** (*sexual relationship*) aventure *f* sans lendemain **one-off I.** *n Aus, Brit* quelque chose d'unique; **to be a ~** être unique **II.** *adj* unique **one-parent** *adj* monoparental(e) **one-piece I.** *n* (maillot *m*) une pièce **II.** *adj* une pièce *inv*

onerous ['ɒnərəs, *Am:* 'ɑːnɚ-] *adj form* onéreux(-euse)

oneself [wʌn'self] *reflex pron* **1.** *after verbs* se, s' + *vowel,* soi *tonic form;* **to deceive/express ~** se tromper/s'exprimer **2.** (*same person*) soi-même; *s. a.* **myself**

one-sided *adj* (*view of things*) partial(e); (*action*) unilatéral(e) **one-time** *adj* **1.** (*former*) ancien(ne) **2.** (*happening only once*) d'une fois **one-track mind** *n* **to have a ~** n'avoir qu'une seule chose en tête

one-way *adj a. fig* à sens unique **one-way street** *n* sens *m* unique **one-way ticket** *n* aller *m* simple

one-woman show *n spectacle solo féminin*

ongoing ['ɒngəʊɪŋ, *Am:* 'ɑːngoʊ-] *adj* **1.** (*happening now*) en cours; **~ state of affairs** l'état actuel des choses **2.** (*continuing*) continuel(le); (*process*) continu(e); **to have an ~ relationship** avoir une relation suivie

onion ['ʌnɪən] *n* oignon *m*

onion skin *n* pelure *f* d'oignon

online *adj, adv* INFOR en ligne; **to go ~** se connecter

online data service *n* serveur *m* **online shop** *n* cyberboutique *f*

onlooker ['ɒnlʊkə^r^, *Am:* 'ɑːnlʊkɚ] *n* spectateur, -trice *m, f*

only ['əʊnli, *Am:* 'oʊn-] **I.** *adj* seul(e); (*son, child*) unique; **the ~ glass he has** le seul verre qu'il a; **the ~ way of doing sth** la seule façon de faire qc; **I'm not the ~ one** il n'y a pas que moi; **the ~ thing is ...** seulement ... **II.** *adv* seulement; **not ~ ... but** non seulement ... mais; **I can ~ say ...** je ne peux que dire ...; **he has ~ two** il n'en a que deux; **it's ~ too true** ce n'est que trop vrai; **he ~ listened** il n'a fait qu'écouter; **~ Paul can do it** seul Paul peut le faire; **I've ~ just eaten** je viens juste de manger **III.** *conj* (*but*) seulement; **it's lovely ~ it's too big** c'est mignon mais un peu trop grand

ono *adv Aus, Brit* COM *abbr of* **or near(est) offer** à débattre

on-off *adj* **1.** (*having two positions: control*) marche-arrêt **2.** (*not continuous: relationship, plan*) en dents de scie

onrush ['ɒnrʌʃ, *Am:* 'ɑːn-] *n* **1.** (*emotional surge*) flot *m* **2.** (*advancing throng*) ruée *f*

onset ['ɒnset, *Am:* 'ɑːn-] *n no pl* début *m*

onshore ['ɒnʃɔː^r^, *Am:* 'ɑːnʃɔːr] **I.** *adj* **1.** (*on land*) à terre **2.** (*from the sea: wind*) du large **II.** *adv* **1.** (*on land*) à terre **2.** (*from the sea*) du large

on-site *adj, adv* sur place

onslaught ['ɒnslɔːt, *Am:* 'ɑːnslɑːt] *n a. fig* attaque *f;* **to withstand an ~** résister à une attaque massive; **to face an ~ of criticism** faire face à un déferlement de critiques

Ontario [ɒn'teəriəʊ, *Am:* ɑːn'terioʊ] *n* l'Ontario *m*

on-the-job training *n* formation *f* en entreprise

onto, on to ['ɒntuː, *Am:* 'ɑːntuː] *prep* **1.** (*in direction of*) sur; **to put sth ~ the chair** poser qc sur la chaise; **to climb ~ a bike** enfourcher un vélo; **to step ~ the pavement** monter sur le trottoir **2.** (*progress to*) **to come ~ a subject** aborder un sujet **3.** (*connection*) **to put sb ~ sb/sth** conseiller qn/qc à qn; **to be ~ sb/sth** soupçonner qn/qc; **to be ~ something** être sur une piste

onus ['əʊnəs, *Am:* 'oʊ-] *n no pl* obligation *f;* **the ~ is on sb to** +*infin* il incombe à qn de +*infin*

onward ['ɒnwəd, *Am:* 'ɑːnwɚd] **I.** *adj* (*connection, flight*) en avant **II.** *adv s.* **onwards**

onwards *adv* en avant; **from tomorrow ~** à partir de demain; **from this time ~** désormais

onyx ['ɒnɪks, *Am:* 'ɑːnɪks] **I.** *n no pl* onyx *m* **II.** *adj* en onyx

oodles ['uːdlz] *npl inf* **~ of sth** un [*o* des] tas de qc

oomph [ʊmf] *n no pl, inf* **1.** (*power*) énergie *f;* (*car*) allure *f* **2.** (*sex appeal*) allure *f*

oops [uːps] *interj* houp-là!

ooze [uːz] **I.** *vi* **1.** (*seep out*) dégouliner; **to ~ from sth** dégouliner de qc; **to ~ down the**

wall dégouliner le long du mur **2.** *fig* (*be full of*) déborder de **II.** *vt* **1.** (*seep out*) suinter **2.** *fig* déborder de **III.** *n no pl* vase *f*

opacity [əʊ'pæsəti, *Am:* oʊ'pæsət̬i] *n no pl, a. fig* opacité *f*

opal ['əʊpl, *Am:* 'oʊ-] **I.** *n* opale *f* **II.** *adj* opalin(e)

opalescent [ˌəʊpə'lesnt, *Am:* ˌoʊ-] *adj* opalescent(e)

opaque [əʊ'peɪk, *Am:* oʊ-] *adj a. fig* opaque

op. cit. *abbr of* **opere citato** op. cit.

OPEC ['əʊpek, *Am:* 'oʊ-] *n abbr of* **Organization of Petroleum Exporting Countries** OPEP *f*

open ['əʊpən, *Am:* 'oʊ-] **I.** *n* **1.** (*outdoors, outside*) (**out**) **in the** ~ dehors; (*in the country*) en plein air; **to sleep out in the** ~ dormir à la belle étoile; **to get sth** (**out**) **in the** ~ *fig* mettre qc au grand jour **2.** SPORT **Open** open *m* **II.** *adj* **1.** (*unclosed, not closed*) *a. fig* (*room, box, arms*) ouvert(e); (*letter*) décacheté(e); (*legs*) écarté(e); **half** ~ entrouvert(e); **to push sth** ~ ouvrir qc; **with eyes wide** ~ les yeux grand ouverts; *fig* en connaissance de cause **2.** (*undecided: problem, question*) non résolu(e); (*result*) indécis(e); **to keep one's options** ~ envisager toutes les possibilités; **to leave the date** ~ ne pas fixer de date **3.** (*available, possible*) ~ **to sb** (*course, club*) ouvert(e) à qn; ~ **to the public** accessible au public **4.** (~*-minded*) ouvert(e); **to be** ~ **to sth** être ouvert à qc; **to have an** ~ **mind** avoir l'esprit large **5.** (*not closed in, unrestricted*) libre; (*view, road*) dégagé(e); (*field*) sans enclos; (*ticket*) open *inv;* **the** ~ **road** la grand-route; **on the** ~ **sea** en haute mer; **in the** ~ **country** en rase campagne; **in** ~ **court** en plein tribunal; ~ **space** espace *m* libre; ~ **spaces** grands espaces *mpl;* **to sleep in the** ~ **air** dormir à la belle étoile; **to be in the** ~ **air** être au grand air **6.** (*uncovered, exposed*) découvert(e); (*drain*) à ciel ouvert; **to be** ~ **to sth** être exposé à qc **7.** (*public: scandal*) public(-que) **8.** (*frank: person*) franc(he); (*conflict*) ouvert(e) **9.** SPORT (*game*) ouvert(e); (*tournament*) open *inv* **10.** (*still available: job*) vacant(e) **11.** (*likely to be affected by*) **to be** ~ **to sth** être exposé à qc; **to be** ~ **to question** être contestable; **to be** ~ **to criticism** s'exposer à la critique **12.** ECON (*cheque*) en blanc ►**it's** ~ **house** c'est une journée portes ouvertes **III.** *vi* **1.** (*change from closed*) s'ouvrir; ~ **wide!** ouvre(z) grand! **2.** (*give access*) **to** ~ **on to/into sth** donner sur qc **3.** (*ready for service*) ouvrir **4.** (*start*) commencer **5.** (*become visible*) éclore **IV.** *vt* **1.** (*change from closed*) ouvrir; (*legs*) écarter; (*pores*) dilater; **to** ~ **again** rouvrir; **to** ~ **wide/slightly** ouvrir grand/entrouvrir; **to** ~ **one's eyes** entrouvrir les yeux; *fig* être vigilant; **to** ~ **the door to sth** *fig* être réceptif à qc **2.** (*remove fastening*) ouvrir; (*bottle*) déboucher **3.** (*start service*) ouvrir **4.** (*inaugurate*) inaugurer **5.** (*start, set up*) commencer; (*negotiations, conservation*) engager; **to** ~ **fire** ouvrir le feu **6.** (*reveal*) révéler; **to** ~ **one's heart to sb** ouvrir son cœur à qn **7.** (*make available to public*) ouvrir (au public)

◆**open out** **I.** *vi* **1.** (*open*) s'ouvrir **2.** (*become more communicative*) s'ouvrir **3.** (*become wider*) s'élargir; **to** ~ **into sth** s'élargir pour devenir qc **4.** (*grow bigger*) se développer **II.** *vt* **1.** (*open*) ouvrir **2.** (*make bigger*) développer **3.** (*widen*) élargir

◆**open up** **I.** *vi* **1.** (*open*) *a. fig* s'ouvrir; **to** ~ **to sb** s'ouvrir à qn **2.** (*start a business*) ouvrir **3.** (*shoot*) ouvrir le feu **II.** *vt a. fig* ouvrir

open-air *adj* (*concert, market*) en plein air; (*swimming pool*) découvert(e) **open-cast mining** *n* MIN exploitation *f* minière à ciel ouvert **open day** *n Brit* journée *f* portes ouvertes **open-ended** *adj* (*question, discussion*) ouvert(e); (*commitment, offer*) flexible; (*contract, credit*) à durée indéterminée; (*period*) indéterminé(e); (*situation*) flou(e)

opener *n* **1.** (*device: for bottles*) décapsuleur *m;* (*for tins*) ouvre-boîtes *m;* **a letter** ~ un coupe-papier **2.** (*event*) premier numéro *m*

open-heart surgery *n* chirurgie *f* à cœur ouvert

opening **I.** *n* **1.** (*gap, hole*) ouverture *f;* (*breach*) brèche *f* **2.** (*opportunity*) occasion *f;* (*of work*) poste *m* **3.** (*beginning, introduction*) début *m* **4.** (*start, first performance*) ouverture *f;* (*ceremony, exhibition*) inauguration *f* **II.** *adj* d'ouverture; (*ceremony*) d'inauguration

opening bid *n* première mise *f* à prix **opening hours** *n* heures *fpl* d'ouverture **opening night** *n* **1.** THEAT première *f* **2.** SPORT première rencontre *f* **opening time** *n* heure *f* d'ouverture

open letter *n* lettre *f* ouverte

openly *adv* **1.** (*frankly, honestly*) franchement **2.** (*publicly*) publiquement

open market *n* marché *m* public **open-minded** *adj* **1.** (*accessible to new ideas*) qui a l'esprit large; **to be** ~ avoir l'esprit large **2.** (*unprejudiced*) sans préjugés **open-mindedness** *n* ouverture *f* d'esprit **open-mouthed** *adj* bouche *f* bée **open-necked** *adj* à col ouvert; (*blouse, dress*) échancré(e)

openness *n no pl* franchise *f*

open-plan *adj* sans cloison **open prison** *n Brit* prison *f* ouverte **open sandwich** *n* canapé *m* **open season** *n* chasse *f* ouverte **open secret** *n* secret *m* de Polichinelle **open ticket** *n* billet *m* ouvert **open-top** *adj* (*car*) décapotable **Open University** *n Brit* Centre *m* de Télé-enseignement Universitaire

opera ['ɒprə, *Am:* 'ɑːpr-] *n* opéra *m*

operable ['ɒpərəbl, *Am:* 'ɑːpər-] *adj* **1.** (*working, functioning*) utilisable **2.** MED opérable

opera glasses *n* lorgnette *f* **opera house** *n* opéra *m*

operate ['ɒpəreɪt, *Am:* 'ɑːpər-] **I.** *vi* **1.** (*work, run: machine, system*) fonctionner **2.** (*be in effect: drug, law, decision*) faire effet **3.** (*perform surgery*) opérer **4.** COM, MIL opérer **II.** *vt* **1.** (*work, run: a machine, system*) faire fonctionner **2.** (*run, manage: store, business*) gérer; (*factory*) diriger; (*farm*) exploiter
◆operate on *vt* **to ~ sb for sth** opérer qn de qc; **to be operated on** (*person*) se faire opérer

operating costs *n pl* frais *mpl* d'exploitation **operating profit** *n* bénéfice *m* d'exploitation **operating room** *n Am s.* **operating theatre operating system** *n* système *m* d'exploitation **operating table** *n* table *f* d'opération **operating theatre** *n* salle *f* d'opération

operation [ˌɒpə'reɪʃən, *Am:* ˌɑːpə-] *n* **1.** (*way of working*) fonctionnement *m* **2.** (*functioning state*) **to be in ~** être en marche; **to come into ~** (*machines*) commencer à fonctionner; (*system, rules*) entrer en application **3.** MIL, MAT, COM opération *f* **4.** (*surgery*) opération *f;* **to have an ~** subir une opération

operational *adj* **1.** (*related to operations*) opérationnel(le); (*costs, profit*) d'exploitation **2.** (*working*) en état de marche

operative ['ɒpərətɪv, *Am:* 'ɑːpɚət̬ɪv] **I.** *n* ouvrier, -ère *m, f* **II.** *adj* **1.** MED opératoire **2.** (*functioning*) **to be ~** fonctionner **3.** (*having effect: rule, system*) en vigueur; **to become ~** entrer en vigueur **4.** LING **the ~ word** le mot-clé

operator ['ɒpəreɪtəʳ, *Am:* 'ɑːpəreɪt̬ɚ] *n* **1.** (*person*) opérateur, -trice *m, f* **2.** TEL standardiste *mf* **3.** (*company*) opérateur *m*

operetta [ˌɒpə'retə, *Am:* ˌɑːpə'ret̬-] *n* MUS opérette *f*

ophthalmic [ɒf'θælmɪk, *Am:* ɑːf-] *adj* ophtalmique; **~ medicine** ophtalmologie *f*

ophthalmologist [ˌɒpθə'mɒlədʒɪst, *Am:* ˌɑːfθæl'mɑːlə-] *n* ophtalmologue *mf*

ophthalmology *n* MED ophtalmologie *f*

opinion [ə'pɪnjən] *n* **1.** (*belief, assessment*) opinion *f;* **public ~** opinion publique; **it is my ~ that ...** je pense que ... **2.** (*view*) avis *m;* **in my ~** à mon avis; **to be of the ~ that ...** estimer que ...; **to have a high/bad ~ of sb/sth** estimer/mésestimer qn/qc; **to have a high ~ of oneself** avoir (une) bonne opinion de soi; **it's just a matter of ~** c'est tout simplement une question de point de vue

opinionated [ə'pɪnjəneɪtɪd, *Am:* -t̬ɪd] *adj* dogmatique

opinion poll *n* sondage *m* d'opinion

opium ['əʊpiəm, *Am:* 'oʊ-] *n no pl* opium *m*

opossum [ə'pɒsəm, *Am:* -'pɑːsəm] *n* opossum *m*

opponent [ə'pəʊnənt, *Am:* -'poʊ-] *n* **1.** POL opposant(e) *m(f);* **~ of sth** opposant à qc **2.** SPORT adversaire *mf*

opportune ['ɒpətjuːn, *Am:* ˌɑːpɚ'tuːn] *adj* opportun(e); **at an ~ moment** au moment voulu

opportunism [ˌɒpə'tjuːnɪzəm, *Am:* ˌɑːpɚ'tuː-] *n no pl* opportunisme *m*

opportunist [ˌɒpə'tjuːnɪst, *Am:* ˌɑːpɚ'tuː-] **I.** *n* opportuniste *mf* **II.** *adj* opportuniste

opportunity [ˌɒpə'tjuːnəti, *Am:* ˌɑːpɚ'tuːnət̬i] <-ties> *n* **1.** (*convenient occasion*) occasion *f;* **a unique ~ to** *+infin* une occasion unique de *+infin;* **an ~ of doing sth** une occasion pour faire qc; **at every ~** aussi souvent que possible; **to take an ~ to** *+infin* saisir l'occasion de *+infin* **2.** (*chance for advancement*) possibilité *f*

oppose [ə'pəʊz, *Am:* -'poʊz] *vt* s'opposer à; **to be ~d to sth** être contre qc

opposed *adj* opposé(e); **to be ~ to sth** être hostile à qc

opposing *adj* opposé(e); (*team*) adverse; (*opinion*) contraire

opposite ['ɒpəzɪt, *Am:* 'ɑːpə-] **I.** *n* contraire *m;* **the ~ of sth** le contraire de qc; **quite the ~!** bien au contraire!; **he did just the ~** il a fait tout le contraire ▶ **~s attract** les contraires s'attirent **II.** *adj* **1.** (*absolutely different: tendency, character*) opposé(e); (*opinion*) contraire; **to be ~ to sth** être contraire à qc **2.** (*on the other side*) opposé(e); **the ~ side of the street** l'autre côté de la rue **3.** (*facing*) d'en face; **~ to [*o* from] sth** face à qc; **see ~ page** voir page ci-contre **III.** *adv* (*facing*) en face de; **to be ~ to sth** être en face de qc; **the building ~** l'immeuble d'en face **IV.** *prep* en face de; **to sit ~ (one another)** être assis face à face

opposition [ˌɒpə'zɪʃən, *Am:* ˌɑːpə-] *n* **1.** *no pl* (*resistance*) opposition *f;* **~ to sth** opposition à qc **2.** POL opposition *f;* **leader of the Opposition** le chef de l'opposition **3.** (*contrast*) contraste *m* **4.** (*opposing team*) adversaire *mf*

oppress [ə'pres] *vt* **1.** (*force into submission*) opprimer **2.** (*overburden*) accabler

oppressed **I.** *adj* opprimé(e) **II.** *n* **the ~** les opprimés *mpl*

oppression [ə'preʃən] *n no pl* oppression *f*

oppressive [ə'presɪv] *adj* **1.** (*burdensome*) oppressif(-ive); (*regime*) tyrannique **2.** (*close, stifling*) suffocant(e); (*heat*) étouffant(e)

oppressor *n* oppresseur *m*

opt [ɒpt, *Am:* ɑːpt] *vi* opter; **to ~ to** *+infin* choisir de *+infin*

opt in *vi* choisir de participer

opt out *vi* choisir de ne pas participer; **to ~ of sth** choisir de ne plus participer à qc

optic ['ɒptɪk, *Am:* 'ɑːp-] **I.** *n* PHOT optique *f* **II.** *adj* optique

optical *adj* optique; (*illusion*) d'optique

optician [ɒp'tɪʃən, *Am:* ɑːp-] *n* opticien(ne) *m(f)*

optics *n* optique *f*

optimal ['ɒptɪml, *Am:* 'ɑːp-] *adj* optimal(e)

optimism ['ɒptɪmɪzəm, *Am:* 'ɑːptə-] *n no pl* optimisme *m*

optimist ['ɒptɪmɪst, *Am:* 'ɑːptə-] *n* optimiste *mf;* **to be a born ~** être un optimiste né
optimistic *adj* optimiste
optimize ['ɒptɪmaɪz, *Am:* 'ɑːptə-] *vt* optimiser
optimum ['ɒptɪməm, *Am:* 'ɑːptə-] **I.** *n* optimum *m* **II.** *adj* (*choice*) optimal(e)
option ['ɒpʃən, *Am:* 'ɑːp-] *n* **1.** (*choice*) option *f* **2.** (*possibility*) choix *m;* **to have the ~ of doing sth** pouvoir choisir de faire qc; **I have no ~ but to pay** je n'ai pas d'autre alternative que de payer **3.** (*right to buy or sell*) option *f;* **to take up an ~** lever une option **4.** INFOR option *f*
optional *adj* facultatif(-ive)
opulence ['ɒpjʊləns, *Am:* 'ɑːpjə-] *n no pl* opulence *f*
opulent ['ɒpjʊlənt, *Am:* 'ɑːpjə-] *adj* opulent(e)
or [ɔːʳ, *Am:* ɔːr] *conj* ou; **either ... ~ ...** ou (bien) ... ou (bien) ...; **to ask whether ~ not sb is coming** demander si oui ou non qn vient; **I can't read ~ write** je ne sais ni lire ni écrire; **a minute ~ so/two** environ une minute/quelques minutes; **someone/something ~ other** je ne sais qui/quoi; **somewhere/sometime ~ other** quelque part/tôt ou tard; **come here ~ else!** viens/venez ici! sinon...; *s. a.* **either**
oracle ['ɒrəkl, *Am:* 'ɔːr-] *n* oracle *m*
oral ['ɔːrəl] *adj* **1.** (*spoken*) oral(e) **2.** (*related to the mouth*) buccal(e); (*contraceptive*) oral(e); (*medication*) par voie orale
orange ['ɒrɪndʒ, *Am:* 'ɔːrɪndʒ] **I.** *adj* orange *inv* **II.** *n* **1.** (*fruit*) orange *f* **2.** (*colour*) orange *m; s. a.* **blue**
orangeade [ˌɒrɪndʒ'eɪd, *Am:* ˌɔːrɪndʒ'-] *n Am* orangeade *f*
orange juice *n* jus *m* d'orange
Orangeman's Day *n no pl, Can, Irish* (*July 12*) *est célébré par les protestants d'Irlande du Nord en commémoration de la défaite de James II en 1690* **orange tree** *n* oranger *m*
orang-(o)utang [ɔːˌræŋuː'tæn, *Am:* ɔː'ræŋətæn] *n* orang-outan *m*
oration [ɔː'reɪʃən] *n* discours *m* solennel; **funeral ~** oraison *f* funèbre
orator ['ɒrətəʳ, *Am:* 'ɔːrət̬ɚ] *n* orateur, -trice *m, f*
oratory ['ɒrətəʳi, *Am:* 'ɔːrətɔːri] *n* oratoire *m*
orbit ['ɔːbɪt, *Am:* 'ɔːr-] **I.** *n* **1.** (*planet course*) orbite *f;* **to be in ~ around sth** être en orbite autour de qc **2.** (*sphere of activity, interest*) domaine *m* **3.** (*very high place*) haute sphère *f;* **taxes go into ~** les impôts atteignent des sommes exorbitantes **4.** ANAT orbite *f* ▶**to go into ~** sortir de ses gonds **II.** *vi* être en orbite **III.** *vt* **1.** (*encircle, travel in circular path*) décrire une orbite autour de **2.** (*put into orbit*) placer en orbite
orbital **I.** *n* périphérique *m* **II.** *adj* orbital(e); (*path, way*) périphérique
orbiter *n* orbiteur *m*
orchard ['ɔːtʃəd, *Am:* 'ɔːrtʃɚd] *n* verger *m*
orchestra ['ɔːkɪstrə, *Am:* 'ɔːrkɪstrə] *n* orchestre *m*
orchestral *adj* orchestral(e)
orchestra pit *n* fosse *f* d'orchestre **orchestra stalls** *n Brit* fauteuils *mpl* d'orchestre
orchestrate ['ɔːkɪstreɪt, *Am:* 'ɔːr-] *vt a. pej* orchestrer
orchestration [ˌɔːkɪ'streɪʃən, *Am:* ˌɔːr-] *n* MUS orchestration *f*
orchid ['ɔːkɪd, *Am:* 'ɔːr-] *n* orchidée *f*
ordain [ɔː'deɪn, *Am:* ɔːr'-] *vt* **1.** REL ordonner; **to be ~ed priest** être ordonné prêtre **2.** (*decree, order*) décréter
ordeal [ɔː'diːl, *Am:* ɔːr'-] *n* épreuve *f*
order ['ɔːdəʳ, *Am:* 'ɔːrdɚ] **I.** *n* **1.** *no pl* (*tidiness*) ordre *m;* **to put sth in ~** ranger qc; **to put one's affairs in ~** mettre ses affaires en ordre **2.** (*particular sequence*) ordre *m;* **in alphabetical/chronological ~** par ordre alphabétique/chronologique; **in reverse ~** à l'envers; **to be out of/in ~** être en désordre/en ordre **3.** (*command*) ordre *m;* **on sb's ~s** sur l'ordre de qn; **to take ~s from sb** être aux ordres de qn **4.** (*working condition*) **in working/running ~** en état de marche; **to be out of ~** être hors service **5.** (*state of peaceful harmony*) ordre *m;* **to keep ~ in the classroom** faire régner la discipline dans la classe; **to restore ~ in a country** faire régner l'ordre dans un pays **6.** (*all right*) **to be in ~** être en règle; **is it in ~ to** +*infin*? est-il permis de +*infin*?; **that is perfectly in ~** aucune objection; **a celebration is in ~** rien ne s'oppose à une fête; **his behaviour is out of ~** son comportement est inapproprié **7.** (*purpose*) **in ~ to** +*infin* afin de +*infin;* **in ~ for you to succeed ...** pour réussir ...; **in ~ that everyone can see** pour que tout le monde puisse voir *subj* **8.** *Brit* (*social class, rank*) classe *f* **9.** (*request to supply goods*) commande *f;* **to put in an ~** passer (une) commande; **done to ~** fait sur commande **10.** (*kind*) genre *m;* **of the highest ~** de premier ordre **11.** (*system, constitution*) ordre *m* **12.** REL (*fraternity, brotherhood*) ordre *m;* **to take holy ~s** entrer dans les ordres **13.** MAT degré *m* **14.** (*procedure rules*) **~ of procedure** règlement *m* intérieur ▶**the ~ of the day** l'ordre du jour **II.** *vi* commander **III.** *vt* **1.** (*command*) ordonner; **to ~ sb to** +*infin* donner l'ordre à qn de +*infin;* **I was ~ed to leave** on m'a ordonné de partir; **to ~ sb out** ordonner à qn de sortir; **to ~ sb about** donner des ordres à qn **2.** (*request goods or a service*) commander **3.** (*arrange*) arranger; **to ~ one's thoughts** reprendre son esprit; **to ~ sth into groups** classer qc en groupes **4.** (*ordain, decide*) **to ~ that ...** décréter que ... **5.** (*arrange according to procedure*) régler
order book *n* carnet *m* de commandes
ordered *adj* ordonné(e); (*life, structure*) régulier(-ère)
order form *n* bon *m* de commande

O

orderly I. *n* 1. (*hospital attendant*) aide-infirmier, -ère *m, f* 2. MIL planton *m* 3. (*person assisting execution process*) auxiliaire *mf* II. *adj* 1. (*methodically arranged*) méthodique 2. (*tidy*) ordonné(e); (*room*) en ordre 3. (*well-behaved, not unruly*) discipliné(e); **in an ~ fashion** dans le calme

order picking *n* triage *m* de commandes

order processing *n* traitement *m* de commandes

ordinal ['ɔːdɪnəl, *Am:* 'ɔːrdənəl] I. *n* ordinal *m* II. *adj* ordinal(e)

ordinance ['ɔːdənənts, *Am:* 'ɔːrdən-] *n* (*decree or law*) ordonnance *f*

ordinarily *adv* normalement

ordinary ['ɔːdənəri, *Am:* 'ɔːrdəner-] I. *n* 1. (*normal state*) ordinaire *m;* **out of the ~** qui sort de l'ordinaire; **nothing out of the ~** rien d'inhabituel 2. *Brit* (*judge*) juge *m* 3. REL ordinaire *m* II. *adj* ordinaire; (*clothes*) de tous les jours; **in the ~ way** en temps normal; **she's no ~ teacher** ce n'est pas un enseignant comme les autres

ordinary seaman <-men> *n* matelot *m*

ordinary share *n* action *f* ordinaire

ordination [ˌɔːdɪ'neɪʃn, *Am:* ˌɔːrdən'eɪ-] *n* REL ordination *f*

ordnance ['ɔːdnənts, *Am:* 'ɔːrd-] *n* MIL ordonnance *f*

ore [ɔːʳ, *Am:* ɔːr] *n* minerai *m;* **iron/copper ~** minerai de fer/cuivre

oregano [ˌɒrɪ'gɑːnəʊ, *Am:* ɔː'regənoʊ] *n* *no pl* origan *m*

Oregon ['ɒrɪgən, *Am:* 'ɔː-] I. *n* l'Oregon II. *adj* de l'Oregon

organ ['ɔːgən, *Am:* 'ɔːr-] *n* 1. MUS orgue *f* 2. (*body part*) organe *m*

organ donor *n* donneur, -euse *m, f* d'organe

organ-grinder *n* 1. (*musician*) joueur, -euse *m, f* d'orgue de Barbarie 2. *fig* responsable *mf*

organic [ɔː'gænɪk, *Am:* ɔːr'-] *adj* 1. (*related to living substance*) organique 2. (*not artificial: fruit, agriculture*) biologique 3. (*fundamental*) fondamental(e) 4. (*systematic*) systématique

organism ['ɔːgənɪzəm, *Am:* 'ɔːr-] *n* organisme *m*

organist ['ɔːgənɪst, *Am:* 'ɔːr-] *n* organiste *mf*

organization [ˌɔːgənaɪ'zeɪʃən, *Am:* ˌɔːrgənɪ'-] *n* 1. *no pl* (*act of organizing*) organisation *f* 2. (*group*) organisation *f* 3. (*association*) association *f* 4. *no pl* (*tidiness*) ordre *m*

organizational *adj* d'organisation

organization chart *n* ECON organigramme *m*

Organization for Economic Cooperation and Development *n* Organisation *f* de coopération et de développement économique

Organization of African Unity *n no pl* Organisation *f* de l'unité africaine

Organization of Petroleum Exporting Countries *n* Organisation *f* des pays exportateurs de pétrole

organize ['ɔːgənaɪz, *Am:* 'ɔːr-] I. *vt* 1. (*arrange*) organiser; (*taxi, snack*) s'occuper de; **to get ~d** s'organiser 2. *Am* (*bring in a trade union*) syndiquer II. *vi* 1. (*arrange*) s'organiser 2. *Am* (*form a trade union*) se syndiquer

organized *adj* organisé(e)

organizer *n* 1. (*book or device to organize*) organisateur *m* 2. INFOR agenda *m* électronique 3. (*person who organizes*) organisateur, -trice *m, f*

orgasm ['ɔːgæzəm, *Am:* 'ɔːr-] I. *n* orgasme *m* II. *vi* avoir un orgasme

orgasmic [ɔː'gæsmɪk, *Am:* ɔːr'-] *adj* 1. (*related to orgasms*) orgasmique 2. *fig, inf* fantastique

orgy ['ɔːdʒi, *Am:* 'ɔːr-] <-gies> *n a. fig* orgie *f;* **an ~ of drinking** une beuverie

Orient ['ɔːriənt] *n* **the ~** l'Orient *m*

orient *vt Am* orienter; **to ~ oneself** s'orienter

oriental [ˌɔːri'entəl] I. *n* Oriental(e) *m(f)* II. *adj* oriental(e); (*carpet*) d'Orient

orientate ['ɔːriənteɪt, *Am:* 'ɔːrien-] *vt* orienter; **to ~ oneself** s'orienter

orientation [ˌɔːriən'teɪʃən, *Am:* ˌɔːrien'-] *n* *no pl* orientation *f*

orientation course *n Am* UNIV cours *m* de présentation

orienteering [ˌɔːriən'tɪərɪŋ, *Am:* ˌɔːrien'tɪr-] *n no pl* exercice *m* d'orientation sur le terrain

orifice ['ɒrɪfɪs, *Am:* 'ɔːrə-] *n form* orifice *m*

origin ['ɒrɪdʒɪn, *Am:* 'ɔːrədʒɪn] *n* origine *f*

original I. *n* 1. (*not a copy or imitation*) original *m* 2. (*unusual person*) original(e) *m(f)* II. *adj* 1. (*initial: sin*) originel(le); **return to the ~ condition** retour à l'état d'origine 2. (*new, novel, unique*) original(e) 3. (*not copied or imitated, firsthand: painting*) authentique; (*manuscript*) original(e)

originality [əˌrɪdʒən'æləti, *Am:* əˌrɪdʒɪ'nælət̬i] *n no pl* originalité *f*

originally *adv* 1. (*first condition*) à l'origine 2. (*at source*) au départ

originate [ə'rɪdʒəneɪt, *Am:* ə'rɪdʒɪ-] I. *vi* 1. (*begin*) voir le jour; (*fire, disease*) se déclarer; **to ~ in sth** (*habit, river*) prendre sa source dans qc 2. (*come from*) **to ~ from sth** provenir de qc; (*person*) être originaire de qc; **the legend ~s with a popular custom** la légende tire son origine d'une coutume populaire II. *vt* être à l'origine de

Orkney Islands ['ɔːkniˌaɪləndz, *Am:* 'ɔːrk-], **Orkneys** *npl* les (îles *fpl*) Orcades *fpl*

Orleans ['ɔːliənz, *Am:* 'ɔrliənz] *n* Orléans

ornament ['ɔːnəmənt, *Am:* 'ɔːr-] I. *n* 1. (*decoration, adornment*) ornement *m* 2. (*small object*) bibelot *m* 3. MUS fioriture *f* II. *vt* ornementer

ornamental *adj* ornemental(e)

ornamentation [ˌɔːnəmen'teɪʃən, *Am:* ˌɔːr-] *n no pl, form* ornementation *f*

ornate [ɔː'neɪt, *Am:* ɔːr'-] *adj* **1.** (*elaborately decorated*) orné(e) richement **2.** (*language*) châtié(e)
ornithologist *n* ornithologiste *mf*
ornithology [ˌɔːnɪ'θɒlədʒi, *Am:* ˌɔːrnə'θɑːlə-] *n no pl* ornithologie *f*
orphan ['ɔːfn, *Am:* 'ɔːr-] **I.** *n* orphelin(e) *m(f)* **II.** *vt* **to be ~ed** devenir orphelin(e)
orphanage ['ɔːfnɪdʒ, *Am:* 'ɔːr-] *n* orphelinat *m*
orthodontist [ˌɔːθəʊ'dɒntɪst, *Am:* ˌɔːrθoʊ'dɑːnt̬ɪst] *n* orthodontiste *mf*
orthodox ['ɔːθədɒks, *Am:* 'ɔːrθədɑːks] *adj* **1.** (*religiously accepted, conventional*) orthodoxe **2.** (*unoriginal, conventional*) conformiste **3.** (*strictly religious*) intégriste
orthodoxy ['ɔːθədɒksi, *Am:* 'ɔːrθədɑːk-] <-xies> *n* (*orthodox practice*) orthodoxie *f*
orthogonal [ɔː'θɒgənl, *Am:* ɔːr'θɑːgən-] *adj* MAT orthogonal(e)
orthographic, **orthographical** *adj* orthographique
orthography [ɔː'θɒgrəfi, *Am:* -'θɑːgrə-] *n no pl* orthographe *f*
orthopaedic [ˌɔːθə'piːdɪk, *Am:* ˌɔːrθoʊ'-] *adj Brit* orthopédique
orthopaedics *npl Brit* orthopédie *f*
orthopaedist *n Brit* orthopédiste *mf*
orthopedic *adj Am s.* **orthopaedic**
orthopedics *npl Am s.* **orthopaedics**
orthopedist *n Am s.* **orthopaedist**
OS [ˌəʊ'es, *Am:* ˌoʊ-] **1.** *abbr of* **ordinary seaman** matelot *m* **2.** *Brit abbr of* **Ordnance Survey** *institut national de cartographie* **3.** *abbr of* **outsize** grande taille *f*
Oscar ['ɒskəʳ, *Am:* 'ɑːskɚ] *n* oscar *m*
oscillate ['ɒsɪleɪt, *Am:* 'ɑːsleɪt] **I.** *vi* **1.** (*swing back and forth*) osciller **2.** (*vary, fluctuate*) fluctuer **II.** *vt* faire osciller
oscillation [ˌɒsɪ'leɪʃən, *Am:* ˌɑːsl'eɪ-] *n form* oscillation *f*
oscilloscope [ə'sɪləskəʊp, *Am:* -skoʊp] *n* oscilloscope *m*
osmosis [ɒz'məʊsɪs, *Am:* ɑːz'moʊ-] *n* osmose *f*
osmotic *adj* osmotique
osprey ['ɒspreɪ, *Am:* 'ɑːspri] *n* balbuzard *m*
ossify ['ɒsɪfaɪ, *Am:* 'ɑːsə-] **I.** *vi* **1.** (*turn into bone*) s'ossifier **2.** *pej, form* (*become fixed or rigid*) se scléroser; (*become conservative*) devenir réactionnaire **II.** *vt* fossiliser
ostensible [ɒ'stensəbl, *Am:* ɑː'sten-] *adj* apparent(e)
ostensibly *adv* soi-disant
ostentation [ˌɒsten'teɪʃən, *Am:* ˌɑːstən'-] *n no pl, pej* ostentation *f*
ostentatious [ˌɒsten'teɪʃəs, *Am:* ˌɑːstən'-] *adj* **1.** (*pretentious*) prétentieux(-euse) **2.** (*done for display*) ostentatoire
osteoarthritis [ˌɒstɪəʊɑː'θraɪtɪs, *Am:* ˌɑːstɪoʊɑːr'θraɪt̬ɪs] *n no pl* arthrose *f*
osteopath ['ɒstɪəʊpɑːθ, *Am:* 'ɑːstɪoʊpæθ] *n* MED ostéopathe *mf*
osteoporosis [ˌɒstɪəʊpə'rəʊsɪs, *Am:* ˌɑːstɪoʊpə'roʊ-] *n no pl* MED ostéoporose *f*
ostracism ['ɒstrəsɪzəm, *Am:* 'ɑːstrə-] *n no pl* ostracisme *m*
ostracize ['ɒstrəsaɪz, *Am:* 'ɑːstrə-] *vt* **1.** (*socially exclude*) frapper d'ostracisme **2.** (*banish*) mettre en quarantaine
ostrich ['ɒstrɪtʃ, *Am:* 'ɑːstrɪtʃ] *n* **1.** (*bird*) autruche *f* **2.** *pej* (*person*) *personne pratiquant la "politique de l'autruche"*
OT *n abbr of* **Old Testament** Ancien Testament *m*
other ['ʌðəʳ, *Am:* -ɚ] **I.** *adj* autre; **some ~ way of doing sth** une autre façon de faire qc; **the ~ one/three** l'autre/les trois autres; **the ~ woman/man** l'autre; **some ~ time** une autre fois; **the ~ day** l'autre jour; **every ~ day/week** un jour/une semaine sur deux; **every ~ week** toutes les deux semaines; **any ~ questions?** encore une question?; **~ people come** d'autres arrivent **II.** *pron* **1.** (*different ones*) autre; **the ~s** les autres; **none ~ than Paul** nul autre que Paul; **each ~** l'un(e) l'autre; **some eat, ~s drink** les uns mangent, d'autres boivent; **there might be ~s** il pourrait y en avoir d'autres **2.** *sing* (*either/or*) **to choose one or the ~** choisir l'un ou l'autre; **not to have one without the ~** ne pas avoir l'un sans l'autre **3.** (*being vague*) **someone/something or ~** quelqu'un/quelque chose **III.** *adv* autrement; **somehow or ~** d'une manière ou d'une autre
other than *prep* (*besides*) **~ sb/sth** à part qn/qc; **he can't do anything ~ pay** il ne peut que payer; **no choice ~ to stay** pas d'autre choix que de rester; **it's anything ~ perfect** c'est tout sauf parfait
otherwise ['ʌðəwaɪz, *Am:* '-ɚ-] **I.** *adj form* autre **II.** *adv* **1.** (*differently*) autrement; **married or ~** marié ou non; **Samantha, ~ known as Sam** Samanatha, que l'on connaît également sous le nom de Sam; **it is forbidden to speak or ~ communicate with them** il est interdit de communiquer avec eux d'une manière ou d'une autre **2.** (*in other respects*) par ailleurs **III.** *conj* sinon
OTT [ˌəʊtiː'tiː, *Am:* ˌoʊ-] *Brit, inf abbr of* **over the top** exagéré(e)
otter ['ɒtəʳ, *Am:* 'ɑːt̬ɚ] *n* loutre *f*
OU [ˌəʊ'juː, *Am:* ˌoʊ-] *n Brit abbr of* **Open University** ≈ CTU *m*
ouch [aʊtʃ] *interj* aïe!
ought [ɔːt, *Am:* ɑːt] *aux* **1.** (*have as a duty, should*) **he ~ to tell her** il devrait lui dire **2.** (*had better*) **we ~ to do something** il vaudrait mieux que nous fassions qc +*subj* **3.** (*be wise or advisable*) **you ~ not to do that** tu ne devrais pas faire cela
ounce [aʊns] *n* once *f* ►**not a ~ of sth** pas du tout de qc, pas une brique de qc *Suisse*
our ['aʊəʳ, *Am:* 'aʊɚ] *poss adj* notre *mf*, nos *pl*; *s. a.* **my**
ours ['aʊəz, *Am:* 'aʊɚz] *poss pron* (*belonging*

O

to us) le , la nôtre; **it's not their bag, it's** ~ ce n'est pas leur sac, c'est le nôtre; **this house is** ~ cette maison est la nôtre; **a book of** ~ (l')un de nos livres; **this table is** ~ cette table est à nous

ourselves [aʊə'selvz, *Am:* aʊɚ-] *poss pron* **1.** *after verbs* nous; **we hurt** ~ nous nous sommes blessés **2.** (*we or us*) nous-mêmes; *s. a.* **myself**

oust [aʊst] *vt* évincer; POL démettre

out [aʊt] **I.** *vt* **1.** (*knock out*) assommer **2.** (*reveal sb's homosexuality*) révéler l'homosexualité de **II.** *prep inf s.* **out of** **III.** *adv* **1.** (*not inside*) dehors; **to go** ~ sortir; **get** ~**!** dehors!; **to find one's way** ~ trouver la sortie **2.** (*outside*) dehors; **it's cold** ~ (**there**) il fait froid dehors; **keep** ~**!** défense d'entrer!; **to eat** ~ aller au restaurant **3.** (*distant, away*) loin; **ten miles** ~ à dix miles; **far/a long way** ~ loin; ~ **at sea** au large; **she's** ~ **in front** être loin devant; ~ **in California/the country** en Californie/à la campagne; **to go** ~ **to India** partir pour l'Inde; **the tide is going** ~ la mer se retire **4.** (*remove*) **to cross** ~ **words** rayer des mots; **to get a stain** ~ enlever une tache; **to put** ~ **a fire** éteindre un feu **5.** (*available*) **the best one** ~ le meilleur sur le marché **6.** (*unconscious*) **to knock** ~ assommer; **to pass** ~ s'évanouir; **to be** ~ **cold** être assommé **7.** (*completely*) **burnt** ~ entièrement brûlé; **to be tired** ~ être épuisé; **to cry** ~ hurler **8.** (*emerge*) **to come** ~ se révéler **9.** (*come to an end, conclude*) **to go** ~ (*fire*) s'éteindre; **to die** ~ s'éteindre progressivement **10.** (*not fashionable*) **to go** ~ passer de mode **11.** (*incorrect*) **to be** ~ se tromper; **to be** ~ **by 5 minutes** avancer de cinq minutes; (*be late*) retarder de cinq minutes ▶ ~ **and** <u>**about**</u> (*on the road*) de sortie; (*healthy*) sur pied; ~ **and** <u>**away**</u> largement; ~ <u>**with**</u> **it!** dis/dites-le donc!; *s. a.* **inside, in** **IV.** *adj* **1.** (*absent, not present*) sorti(e) **2.** (*released, published: film, novel*) sorti(e) **3.** (*revealed: news*) rendu(e) public(-que) **4.** BOT (*flower*) en fleur **5.** (*visible*) **the sun/moon is** ~ le soleil/la lune brille **6.** (*finished*) fini(e); **before the week is** ~ avant la fin de la semaine **7.** (*not working: fire, light*) éteint(e); (*workers*) en grève **8.** *inf* (*in existence*) **to be** ~ être sur le marché **9.** (*unconscious, tired*) K.-O. *inv* **10.** SPORT (*ball*) sortie(e); (*player*) éliminé(e); *fig* sur la touche **11.** (*not possible*) **that's right** ~ c'est hors de question **12.** (*unfashionable*) passé de mode **13.** *Brit* (*drunk*) bourré(e) **14.** (*mistaken*) **to be** ~ se tromper ▶ **to** <u>**be**</u> ~ **for sth/to** +*infin* chercher à qc/à +*infin* **V.** *n* échappatoire *f* **2.** *Am* **to be** <u>**at**</u>**/on the** ~**s with sb** être brouillé avec qn

out and out *adj* complet(-ète); (*liar*) fini(e)

outback *n no pl, Aus* intérieur *m* des terres **outbid** *vt irr* surenchérir sur **outboard (motor)** *n* **1.** (*motor for boat*) moteur *m* hors-bord **2.** (*boat with outboard motor*) hors-bord *m inv* **outbreak** *n* **1.** (*sudden start: of war*) déclenchement *m;* (*of spots, of violence*) éruption *f;* (*of fever*) accès *m;* (*of hives*) crise *f;* **thunderous** ~**s** des coups *mpl* de tonnerre **2.** (*epidemic*) épidémie *f* **outbuilding** *n* dépendance *f* **outburst** *n* accès *m* **outcast** **I.** *n* proscrit(e) *m(f);* **a social** ~ un paria **II.** *adj* proscrit(e) **outclass** *vt* surclasser **outcome** *n* résultat *m;* (*of the election*) issue *f* **outcrop** *n* GEO éminence *f;* **an** ~ **of rocks** une protubérance rocheuse **outcry** <-ries> *n* tollé *m;* **a public** ~ une clameur de protestation **outdated** *adj* **1.** (*old*) désuet(-ète); (*word*) vieilli(e) **2.** (*out of fashion*) démodé(e) **outdistance** *vt* distancer **outdo** *vt irr* surpasser **outdoor** *adj* extérieur(e); (*swimming pool*) découvert(e); (*sports, activity*) de plein air; **to be an** ~ **type** aimer le grand air **outdoors** *n* dehors *m;* **the great** ~ la pleine nature

outer ['aʊtəʳ, *Am:* -t̬ɚ] *adj* extérieur(e); **the** ~ **suburbs** la grande banlieue

Outer Hebrides *n* les îles *fpl* Hébrides **outermost** *n* confins *mpl* **Outer-Rhodes** *n* **the half-canton of Appenzell** ~ le demi-canton d'Appenzell Rhodes-Extérieures **outer space** *n no pl* espace *m*

outfall *n* (*of river*) embouchure *f;* (*of drain, sewer*) écoulement *m* **outfield** *n no pl* touche *f* **outfit** *n* **1.** (*set of clothes*) tenue *f* **2.** *pej* (*firm*) boîte *f* **outflow** *n* sortie *f;* (*of capital*) évasion *f* **outgoing** *adj* **1.** (*sociable*) sociable **2.** (*extrovert*) extraverti(e) **3.** (*leaving*) sortant(e) **outgrow** *vt irr* **1.** (*grow too big for: clothes, cradle*) devenir trop grand pour; **to** ~ **sth** (*a habit, taste, interest*) passer l'âge de faire qc; **to** ~ **one's friends** ne plus à voir grand-chose en commun avec ses amis; **to** ~ **all that** dépasser tout ça **2.** (*grow too fast*) grandir plus vite que **3.** (*become bigger or faster than*) dépasser **outgrowth** *n* **1.** (*growing*) développement *m* **2.** *fig* (*result*) développement *m* **3.** MED, ZOOL, BOT excroissance *f* **outhouse** **I.** *n* **1.** (*small separate building*) dépendance *f* **2.** *Am* (*outdoor toilet*) toilettes *fpl* extérieures **II.** *vt* remiser

outing *n* **1.** (*walk*) sortie *f;* **to go on an** ~ faire une sortie; **family** ~ sortie en famille **2.** (*revealing of homosexuality*) outing *m* (*le fait de révéler l'homosexualité d'une personne*)

outlandish *adj pej* saugrenu(e) **outlast** *vt* survivre à **outlaw** **I.** *n* hors-la-loi *m inv* **II.** *vt* **1.** (*ban*) interdire **2.** (*make illegal*) déclarer illégal **outlay** *n* dépenses *fpl* **outlet** *n* **1.** (*exit*) sortie *f;* (*of a river*) embouchure *f* **2.** (*means of expression*) exutoire *m* **3.** (*store or business*) point *m* de vente **4.** *Am* ELEC prise *f* de courant **outline** **I.** *n* **1.** (*general plan*) plan *m;* **the main** ~ les grandes lignes *fpl* **2.** (*rough plan*) ébauche *f;* **in** ~ en gros **3.** (*description of main points*) synthèse *f* **4.** ART (*contour*) contour *m* **5.** (*summary*) résumé *m* **II.** *vt* **1.** (*draw outer line of*) esquisser; **to be ~d against the horizon** se dessiner à l'horizon **2.** (*summarize*) résumer **outlive** *vt* survivre à **outlook** *n* **1.** (*future prospect*) perspective *f;* **the weather ~** prévisions *fpl* météorologiques **2.** (*general view, attitude*) attitude *f* **outlying** *adj* éloigné(e) **outmaneuver** *vt Am,* **outmanoeuvre** *vt Brit, Aus* déjouer **outmoded** *adj* démodé(e) **outnumber** *vt* être supérieur en nombre à; **to be ~ed** être en minorité

out of *prep* **1.** (*towards outside from*) hors de, en dehors de; **to go ~ the door/room** sortir par la porte/de la pièce; **to jump ~ bed** sauter hors du lit; **to take sth ~ a box** prendre qc dans une boîte; **to look/lean ~ the window** regarder par/se pencher à la fenêtre **2.** (*outside from*) **~ water/sight/reach** hors de l'eau/de vue/d'atteinte; **to drink ~ a glass** boire dans un verre **3.** (*away from*) **to be ~ town/the office** ne pas être en ville/au bureau; **to get ~ the rain** se mettre à l'abri de la pluie; **~ the way!** pousse-toi/poussez-vous! **4.** (*without*) **to be ~ sth** ne plus avoir qc; **to be ~ money/work** être à court d'argent/sans emploi; **~ breath** hors d'haleine; **~ order** en panne **5.** (*from*) **made ~ wood/a blanket** fait en bois/avec une couverture; **to copy sth ~ a file** copier qc dans un fichier; **to get sth ~ sb** soutirer qc à qn; **to read ~ the novel** lire un extrait du roman **6.** (*because of*) **to do sth ~ politeness** faire qc par politesse **7. in 3 cases ~ 10** dans 3 cas sur 10 ►**to be ~ it** être dépassé; **to be ~ one's mind/head** avoir perdu l'esprit/la tête; **~ the frying pan and into the fire** *prov* tomber de Charybde en Scylla; **~ this world** (*excellent*) divin **out of bounds** *adj* **to be ~ to sb** être interdit d'accès à qn **out-of-court** *adj* LAW (*settlement*) à l'amiable **out-of-date** *adj* **1.** (*existing after a fixed date*) périmé(e) **2.** (*worthless*) caduc(-que) **3.** (*no more in use*) obsolète **4.** (*not in use for long time*) désuet(-ète); (*word*) vieilli(e) **5.** (*out of fashion*) démodé(e) **out-of-the-way** *adj* à l'écart **out-of-town** *adj* en dehors du centre-ville **out-of-work** *adj* sans emploi

outpace *vt* dépasser **outpatient** *n* patient(e) *m(f)* en consultation externe; **~s' (department)** service *m* des soins externes **outperform** *vt* être plus performant que **outplay** *vt* SPORT jouer mieux que **outpost** *n* **1.** MIL (*guards to prevent attack*) avant-poste *m* **2.** (*base to prevent attack*) camp *m* volant **3.** (*distant branch or settlement*) bastion *m* **outpouring** *n* **1.** (*uncontrolled expressed feelings*) défoulement *m* **2.** (*sudden flow*) déferlement *m* **3.** (*many things produced in short period*) foisonnement *m* **4.** *pl* (*outburst of emotion*) effusions *fpl*

output *n no pl* **1.** (*amount produced*) ECON rendement *m;* **total ~** productivité *f* globale **2.** (*production*) production *f* **3.** (*power, energy*) puissance *f* **4.** INFOR sortie *f* **output data** *n* **1.** INFOR données *fpl* en sortie **2.** ECON résultats *mpl* fournis **output device** *n* INFOR périphérique *m* de sortie **output unit** *n* INFOR unité *f* de sortie

outrage ['aʊtreɪdʒ] **I.** *n* **1.** (*cruelty*) atrocité *f* **2.** (*shock, indignation*) indignation *f;* **with ~** d'indignation; **to express ~ at sth** exprimer son indignation à propos de qc; **a sense of ~** un sentiment de révolte **3.** (*indecent action*) scandale *m* **II.** *vt* **to be ~d by sth** être indigné par qc

outrageous [aʊt'reɪdʒəs] *adj* **1.** (*cruel*) atroce **2.** (*shocking, exaggerated*) scandaleux(-euse); **it is ~ that** c'est scandaleux que *+subj* **3.** (*bold*) scandaleux(-euse)

outré ['u:treɪ, *Am:* u:'treɪ] *adj* extravagant(e)

outrider *n* escorte *f* à moto

outrigger ['aʊtrɪgə^r, *Am:* -ɚ] *n* (*boat*) outrigger *m*

outright I. *adj* **1.** (*complete, total*) absolu(e) **2.** (*clear, direct: winner*) parfait(e); (*victory*) total(e) **II.** *adv* **1.** (*completely, totally*) à fond; (*to reject, to refuse*) en bloc **2.** (*immediately*) sur le coup **outrun** *vt irr* **1.** (*go faster than*) distancer **2.** *fig* (*escape from*) échapper à **3.** *fig* (*go beyond*) dépasser **outsell** *vt* (*person, shop*) vendre plus que; (*product*) se vendre plus que **outset** *n no pl* commencement *m;* **at the ~** au départ *m;* **from the ~** dès le début **outshine** *vt irr* être plus brillant que

outside I. *adj* **1.** (*external: door*) extérieur(e) **2.** (*not belonging to sth: call, world, help*) extérieur(e); **my ~ interests** mes centres *mpl* d'intérêts **3.** (*not likely: possibility, chance*) faible **4.** (*highest*) maximum; **at an ~ estimate** au maximum **5.** *Brit, Aus* AUTO **~ lane** voie *f* de droite; *Am* voie *f* de gauche **6.** SPORT **~ left/right** ailier *m* gauche/droit **II.** *n* **1.** *no pl* (*external part or side*) *a. fig* extérieur *m;* **on/from the ~** à/vu de l'extérieur **2.** (*at most*) **at the (very) ~** tout au plus **3.** *Brit, Aus* AUTO **to overtake on the ~** dépasser à droite; *Am* dépasser à gauche **III.** *prep* **1.** (*not within*) à l'extérieur de; **from ~ sth** de l'extérieur de qc; **to play/go ~ the house** jouer en dehors de/sortir de la maison; **~ the nature reserve** hors du parc naturel; **experts from ~ the company/school** des experts externes à l'entreprise/l'école **2.** (*next to*) **~ sb's window** sous la fenêtre de qn; **to wait ~ the door** attendre devant la porte **3.** (*not during*) **~ business hours** en dehors des heures de travail **4.** (*besides*) **~ sb/sth** sauf qn/qc **IV.** *adv* **1.** (*outdoors*) dehors, à la porte *Belgique;* **to go ~** sortir **2.** (*not inside*) à l'extérieur **3.** (*beyond*) au-delà **4.** (*except for*) excepté; **~ of us/Paris** à part nous/Paris; *s. a.* **inside**

outside broadcast *n* retransmission *f* en direct **outside line** *n* ligne *f* extérieure **outside of** *prep Am, inf s.* **outside**

outsider *n* **1.** (*stranger*) étranger, -ère *m, f* **2.** (*not belonging to a group, office*) interven-

O

ant extérieur *m,* intervenante extérieure *f* **3.** (*outcast*) exclu(e) *m(f)* **4.** SPORT outsider *m* **outsize I.** *adj a. fig* énorme; (*clothes*) grande taille *inv* **II.** *n* grande taille *f* **outskirts** *npl* périphérie *f* **outsourcing** *n no pl* approvisionnement *m* à l'extérieur **outspoken** *adj* franc(he) **outstanding** *adj* **1.** (*excellent, extraordinary*) exceptionnel(le) **2.** (*of special note, remarkable*) remarquable **3.** (*noticeable: feature, incident*) marquant(e) **4.** (*remaining: debt, amount*) impayé(e); (*holiday*) à prendre; (*work*) inachevé(e); (*issue, business*) en suspens; (*invoice*) en souffrance; (*problems*) non résolu(e) **outstation** *n* avant-poste *m* **outstay** *vt* rester plus longtemps que; **I've ~ my welcome** j'ai abusé de votre hospitalité **outstretched** *adj* **1.** (*extended to the maximum*) tendu(e) **2.** (*lying*) allongé(e) **3.** (*unwrapped*) déployé(e) **outstrip** *vt irr* **1.** (*go faster, leave behind*) devancer **2.** (*be better than, surpass*) surpasser **3.** (*be greater than, exceed*) excéder **out tray** *n* corbeille *f* de départ **out-turn** *n no pl* rendement *m* **outvote** *vt* remporter les suffrages sur; **to be ~d** perdre le vote **outward I.** *n no pl* extérieur *m* **II.** *adj* **1.** (*exterior, external*) extérieur(e); **to all ~ appearances** selon toute apparence **2.** (*going out*) vers l'extérieur; (*boat*) en partance; **the ~ journey** l'aller **3.** (*apparent, superficial*) apparent(e) **III.** *adv s.* **outwards outwardly** *adv* apparemment **outwards** *adv* vers l'extérieur **outweigh** *vt* **1.** (*win*) l'emporter sur **2.** (*exceed*) dépasser **outwit** <-tt-> *vt* se montrer plus malin que **outwork** *n no pl* travail *m* à domicile; MIL bastion *m* **outworker** *n* travailleur, -euse *m, f* à domicile

oval ['əʊvəl, *Am:* 'oʊ-] **I.** *n* ovale *m* **II.** *adj* ovale

Oval Office *n* bureau *m* oval

ovary ['əʊvəri, *Am:* 'oʊ-] <-ries> *n* ovaire *m*

ovation [əʊ'veɪʃən, *Am:* oʊ-] *n* ovation *f;* **thunderous ~** tonnerre *m* d'applaudissements; **to give sb an ~** faire une ovation à qn

oven ['ʌvən] *n* four *m;* **to cook sth in a slow/moderate ~** cuire qc au four à basse température/à température moyenne

oven glove *n* gant *m* isolant **ovenproof** *adj* résistant(e) aux hautes températures **oven-ready** *adj* prêt(e) à enfourner **ovenware** *n* plats *mpl* à four

over ['əʊvəʳ, *Am:* 'oʊvɚ] **I.** *prep* **1.** (*above*) sur; **to hang the picture ~ the desk** accrocher le tableau au-dessus du bureau; **the bridge ~ the motorway** le pont traversant l'autoroute; **to fly ~ the sea** survoler la mer; **4 ~ 12 equals a third** MAT 4 sur 12 équivalent à un tiers **2.** (*on*) **to hit sb ~ the head** frapper qn à la tête; **to drive ~ sth** écraser qc (en voiture); **to spread a cloth ~ it/the table** mettre une nappe dessus/sur la table **3.** (*across*) **view ~ the valley** vue sur la vallée; **to go ~ the bridge** traverser le pont; **to live ~ the road** vivre de l'autre côté de la route; **it rained all ~ England** il a plu sur toute l'Angleterre; **famous all ~ the world** connu dans le monde entier; **to look ~ a house** visiter une maison; **~ the page** sur la page suivante; **to look ~ sb's shoulder** regarder par-dessus l'épaule de qn; **to jump ~ the fence** sauter la barrière; **~ the dune** de l'autre côté de la dune **4.** (*during*) **~ the winter** pendant l'hiver; **~ the years** au fil des années; **~ time** avec le temps; **~ a two-year period** sur une période de deux ans; **to stay ~ the weekend** rester tout le week-end **5.** (*more than*) **~ 40°** au-dessus de 40°; **~ $50** plus de 50$; **to speak for ~ an hour** parler plus d'une heure; **to be ~ an amount/a point** dépasser une somme/un point; **~ and above that** en plus de ça; **children ~ 14** les enfants de plus de 14 ans; **to value sth ~ money** préférer qc à l'argent **6.** (*through*) **I heard it ~ the radio** je l'ai entendu à la radio; **to hear sth ~ the noise** entendre qc par-dessus le bruit; **what came ~ him?** qu'est-ce qui lui a pris? **7.** (*in superiority to*) **he's ~ me** il est mon supérieur; **to rule ~ the Romans** régner sur les Romains; **to have command ~ sth** avoir le commandement de qc; **to have an advantage ~ sb** avoir un avantage sur qn **8.** (*about*) **~ sth** au sujet de qc; **to puzzle ~ this question** tenter de résoudre cette question; **they'll be a long time ~ it** ça va leur prendre longtemps **9.** (*for checking*) **to watch ~ a child** surveiller un enfant; **to look/go ~ a text** jeter un coup d'œil sur/parcourir un texte **10.** (*past*) **to be ~ the worst** avoir le pire derrière soi; *s. a.* **under II.** *adv* **1.** (*at a distance*) **it's ~ here/there** c'est ici/là-bas **2.** (*moving across*) **to come ~ here** venir (par) ici; **to go ~ there** aller là-bas; **to pass/hand sth ~** faire passer/remettre qc; **he has gone ~ to France** il est allé en France; **he swam ~ to me** il a traversé à la nage pour me rejoindre; **call her ~** appelle-la; **he went ~ to the enemy** *fig* il est passé à l'ennemi **3.** (*on a visit*) **come ~ tonight** passe(z) ce soir **4.** (*moving above: go, jump*) par-dessus; **to fly ~** passer dans le ciel **5.** (*downwards*) **to fall ~** tomber; **to knock sth ~** faire tomber qc **6.** (*another way up*) **to turn the page/pancake ~** tourner la page/crêpe **7.** (*completely*) **that's her all ~** c'est bien d'elle; **to look for sb all ~** chercher qn partout; **to turn sth ~ and ~** tourner et retourner qc en tous sens; **to talk/think sth ~** discuter de/bien réfléchir à qc **8.** (*again*) **to count them ~ again** les recompter encore une fois; **I repeated it ~ and ~** je n'ai cessé de le répéter; **to do sth all ~** *Am* refaire qc entièrement **9.** (*more*) **children of 14 and ~** les enfants de 14 ans et plus; **7 into 30 goes 4 and 2 ~** 30 divisé par 7 font 4, reste 2; **there are two (left) ~** il en reste deux de plus; **if there's any ~** s'il en reste **10.** (*too*) trop; **that's a bit ~ optimistic** c'est un peu trop optimiste **11.** (*sb's turn*) **it's ~ to him**

c'est son tour; **"~"** RADIO, AVIAT "à vous"; ~ **and out** terminé **III.** *adj inv* **1.** (*finished*) fini; **it's all** ~ tout est fini; **the snow is** ~ il a cessé de neiger **2.** (*remaining*) de reste; **there are three left** ~ il en reste trois

overabundant *adj* surabondant(e) **overact** *vt, vi* exagérer **overactive** *adj* trop actif(-ive) **overage**[1] *n* surplus *m* **overage**[2] *adj* trop âgé(e) **overall I.** *n* **1.** (*protective clothing*) blouse *f* **2.** *pl* (*one-piece protective suit*) combinaison *f* **3.** *pl Am* (*working trousers*) *s.* **dungarees** salopette *f* **II.** *adj* (*commander, pattern*) général(e); (*results*) global(e); ~ **winner** grand gagnant *m* **III.** *adv* dans l'ensemble **overanxious** *adj* hyperanxieux(-euse)

overawe [ˌəʊvər'ɔː, *Am:* ˌoʊvɚ'ɑː] *vt* intimider

overbalance *vi* se déséquilibrer **overbearing** *adj pej* arrogant(e) **overbid** *irr vt, vi* surenchérir **overblown** *adj* **1.** *fig* ampoulé(e) **2.** BOT (*flower*) trop ouvert(e) **overboard** *adv* par-dessus bord; **to fall** ~ tomber par-dessus bord; **Man ~!** un homme à la mer!; **to go** ~ s'emballer; **to chuck sb/sth** ~ se débarrasser de qn/qc **overbook** *vt* surréserver **overbooking** *n* surréservation *f* **overborrowed** *adj* surendetté(e) **overburden** *vt* surcharger; **to be ~ed with sth** être accablé de qc **overcapacity** *n* surcapacité *f* **overcast** *adj* (*sky*) chargé(e); (*weather*) couvert(e) **overcautious** *adj* exagérément prudent(e) **overcharge I.** *vt* faire payer trop cher à; **they ~d me $20** ils m'ont fait payer 20$ en trop **II.** *vi* demander trop **overcoat** *n* pardessus *m* **overcome** <irr> **I.** *vt* (*enemies*) vaincre; (*obstacle, fear, problems*) surmonter; **to** ~ **temptation** résister à la tentation; **to be** ~ **with sth** (*fear, emotion*) être gagné par qc **II.** *vi* vaincre **overconfident** *adj* trop sûr(e) de soi **overcooked** *adj* trop cuit(e) **overcrowded** *adj* (*room, train*) bondé(e); (*prison, city*) surpeuplé(e); (*class*) surchargé(e) **overcrowding** *n* surpeuplement *m;* (*of classroom*) surchargement *m* **overdeveloped** *adj* très développé(e) **overdo** *vt* **1.** (*exaggerate*) exagérer; **don't** ~ **it!** (*irony, salt*) n'en rajoute pas!; (*work*) n'en fait pas trop! **2.** (*use too much*) exagérer sur **3.** (*cook too long*) cuire trop longtemps **overdone** *adj* **1.** (*exaggerated: make-up*) exagéré(e) **2.** (*cooked too long*) trop cuit(e) **overdose I.** *n* overdose *f;* **to take an** ~ **of sth** faire une overdose de qc; **to die of an** ~ mourir d'une overdose **II.** *vi* **to** ~ **on sth** être en overdose de qc; *fig* avoir une overdose de qc **overdraft** *n* FIN découvert *m* bancaire **overdraft facility** *n* FIN autorisation *f* de découvert **overdraw** *irr* **I.** *vi* mettre son compte à découvert **II.** *vt* **to** ~ **sth** mettre qc à découvert **overdress** *n* blouse *f* **overdressed** *adj* **to be** ~ être habillé trop élégamment **overdrive** *n no pl* **1.** AUTO, TECH surrégime *m* **2.** *fig* **to go into** ~ se jeter dans une activité fiévreuse **overdue** *adj* (*work, book*) en retard; (*bill*) impayé(e) **over easy** *adj Am: œufs au plat grillés des deux côtés* **overeat** *irr vi* se gaver; **to** ~ **on sth** se gaver de qc **over-egg** *vt fig* **to** ~ **the pudding** en rajouter *inf* **overemphasize** *vt* insister trop sur **overestimate I.** *n* surestimation *f* **II.** *vt* surestimer **overexcited** *adj* surexcité(e) **overexert** *vt* **to** ~ **oneself** se surmener **overexpose** *vt* PHOT surexposer **overexposure** *n no pl* PHOT surexposition *f* **overflow I.** *n* **1.** (*of liquid*) débordement *m* **2.** (*pipe*) trop-plein *m* **3.** (*surplus*) surplus *m* **II.** *vi a. fig* déborder; **to** ~ **with sth** déborder de qc; **to be full to ~ing** être plein à craquer; **to** ~ (**full to**) **~ing with emotion** déborder d'émotions **III.** *vt fig* inonder **overfly** *irr vt* AVIAT survoler **overgrown** *adj* **1.** (*too full of plants*) envahi(e); **to be** ~ **with sth** être envahi de qc **2.** *pej* (*immature*) attardé(e) **overhang** *irr* **I.** *n* surplomb *m* **II.** *vt* surplomber; **to be overhung with sth** être surplombé par qc; *fig* être dépassé par qc **overhanging** *adj* en surplomb **overhaul I.** *n* révision *f* **II.** *vt* **1.** (*examine and repair*) réviser **2.** *fig* remanier **overhead I.** *n* **1.** (*running costs of business*) ~(**s**) frais *mpl* généraux **2.** *inf* (*projector*) rétroprojecteur *m* **3.** (*transparency*) transparent *m* **II.** *adj* **1.** (*above head level: railway*) aérien(ne); ~ **cable** ligne *f* à haute tension; ~ **lighting** éclairage *m* au plafond; ~ **volley** balle *f* haute **2.** (*concerning running business: costs*) courant(e) **3.** (*taken from above*) en l'air **III.** *adv* en l'air **overhear** *irr* **I.** *vt* **to** ~ **sth** entendre qc par hasard; **to** ~ **sb** entendre ce que dit qn; **to** ~ **sb saying sth** entendre qn dire qc **II.** *vi* entendre **overheat I.** *vt a. fig* surchauffer; **to get ~ed** s'échauffer **II.** *vi* **1.** (*get too hot*) trop chauffer; (*engine*) chauffer **2.** *fig* s'échauffer **3.** FIN (*economy*) être en surchauffe **overindulge I.** *vt* être trop indulgent avec **II.** *vi* savourer; **to** ~ **in sth** s'adonner à qc **overindulgent** *adj* **to be** ~ être trop indulgent **overjoyed** *adj* fou(folle) de joie **overkill** *n no pl* **it's** ~ c'est exagéré; **a media** ~ un matraquage médiatique **overland** *adj, adv* par route **overlap I.** *n* chevauchement *m* **II.** <irr> *vi* se chevaucher **III.** <irr> *vt* chevaucher **overleaf** *adv* au verso **overload I.** *n* **1.** (*too much demand of electricity*) surtension *f* **2.** *no pl* (*excess*) surcharge *f* **II.** <irr> *vt a. fig* surcharger; (*roads*) encombrer **overlong** *adj* trop long(ue) **overlook I.** *n Am* (*viewpoint*) aperçu *m* **II.** *vt* **1.** (*have a view of*) donner sur **2.** (*not notice, forget*) négliger **3.** (*ignore, disregard*) laisser passer

overly *adv* extrêmement

overmanning *n* sureffectifs *mpl* **overmuch I.** *adv, pron* trop **II.** *adj* trop de **overnight I.** *adj* **1.** (*during the night: journey, convoy*) de nuit **2.** (*for a night: stay*) d'une nuit; SPORT (*leader*) du jour **3.** (*sudden*) du jour au lendemain; **to be an** ~ **celebrity** devenir une célébrité du jour au lendemain II. *adv* 1. (*for a night*) la nuit; **to stay ~** passer la nuit 2. (*during the night*) toute la nuit 3. (*very quickly*) du jour au lendemain III. *n* nuit *f* IV. *vi* passer la nuit **overnight bag** *n* sac *m* de voyage **overpass** *n* CONSTR (*for roads*) autopont *m;* (*for railway line*) pont *m* ferroviaire **overpay** *irr vt* surpayer **overpopulated** *adj* surpeuplé(e) **overpopulation** *n no pl* surpopulation *f* **overpower** *vt* 1. (*overcome*) maîtriser 2. (*defeat*) vaincre 3. *fig* (*by music, fumes*) accabler **overpowering** *adj* bouleversant(e) **overproduction** *n* surproduction *f* **overrated** *adj* surestimé(e) **overreach** *vt* **to ~ oneself** présumer de ses forces **overreact** *vi* **to ~ to sth** réagir à outrance à qc **overreaction** *n* réaction *f* excessive **override** I. *n* 1. (*device for automatic control*) commande *f* d'arrêt du contrôle automatique 2. *Am* POL veto *m* II. *vt* 1. (*not accept*) passer outre à 2. (*be more important*) avoir la priorité sur 3. (*by manual control*) interrompre le contrôle automatique de III. *vi* poser son veto **overriding** *adj* primordial(e) **overrule** *vt a.* LAW rejeter; (*decision*) annuler **overrun** I. *n* 1. (*extension, invasion*) invasion *f* 2. (*exceeding allowed time, cost*) dépassement *m;* (**cost**) ~ dépassement du coût estimé; **~ of a project** dépassement du temps imparti à un projet 3. (*speeding of a vehicle*) dépassement *m* de vitesse II. <overran, overrun> *vt* 1. (*occupy, invade*) envahir; **to be ~ with sth** être envahi de qc; (*be infested*) être infesté de qc; (*be filled*) être inondé de qc 2. (*take, use too much: one's time, budget*) dépasser 3. (*run, extend over*) dépasser III. <overran, overrun> *vi* 1. (*exceed allotted time*) durer plus longtemps que prévu 2. (*exceed allotted money*) dépasser le budget prévu; **to ~ on costs** dépasser les frais **overseas** I. *adj* 1. (*across the sea: colony, person*) d'outre-mer; (*trade, aid*) extérieur(e) 2. (*related to a foreign country: trip*) à l'étranger; (*student*) étranger(-ère) II. *adv* 1. (*to a foreign country*) à l'étranger 2. (*across the sea*) outre-mer **oversee** *vt irr* surveiller **overseer** *n* surveillant(e) *m(f)* **oversell** *irr vt* 1. (*sell more*) vendre trop de 2. (*exaggerate the merits of*) exagérer les mérites de **overshadow** *vt* 1. (*cast a shadow over*) ombrager 2. *fig* **to ~ sb/sth** (*cast gloom over*) jeter une ombre sur qn/qc; (*appear more important*) faire de l'ombre à qn/qc; **to be ~ed by sb** être éclipsé par qn **overshoe** *n* protection *f* de chaussure **overshoot** *irr vt* dépasser ►**to ~ the mark** dépasser les bornes **oversight** *n* 1. (*failure to notice sth*) oubli *m;* **by an ~** par oubli 2. (*surveillance*) surveillance *f* **oversimplify** *vt* **to ~ sth** simplifier qc à l'excès **oversize** *adj,* **oversized** *adj Am* de grande taille **oversleep** *irr vi* se réveiller trop tard **overspend** I. *vi* dépenser trop; **to ~ on a budget** dépasser son budget II. *vt* dépasser III. *n* dépassement *m* budgétaire **overspill** *n* surpopulation *f* **overstaffed** *adj* en sureffectif **overstate** *vt* exagérer **overstay** *vt* **to ~ one's time** rester plus longtemps que prévu; **to ~ a visa** dépasser la durée de péremption d'un visa; **I've ~ed my welcome** j'ai abusé de votre hospitalité **overstep** *vt irr* dépasser ►**to ~ the mark** dépasser les bornes **oversubscribed** *adj* (*share offer*) sursouscrit(e)

overt ['əʊvɜːt, *Am:* 'oʊvɜːrt] *adj* déclaré(e)

overtake *irr* I. *vt* 1. (*go past, become greater: a car, a country, a competitor*) dépasser 2. (*exceed: an amount, a level*) dépasser 3. (*happen*) rattraper; **to be ~n by fate** être frappé par le sort; **to be ~n by events** être rattrapé par les événements; **to be ~n by grief** être pris de chagrin; **to ~ sb** s'emparer de qn II. *vi* dépasser **overtax** *vt* 1. (*tax excessively*) surtaxer 2. *fig* surmener; **to ~ oneself** se surmener **over-the-counter** *adj* FIN, MED en vente libre **over-the-top** *adj Brit* exagéré(e) **overthrow** I. *n* 1. (*removal from power*) renversement *m* 2. SPORT (*ball thrown too far*) hors-jeu *m inv* II. <irr> *vt* renverser **overtime** *n* 1. (*extra work*) heures *fpl* supplémentaires; **to be/do on ~** faire des heures supplémentaires; **to earn ~** être payé pour les heures supplémentaires 2. *Am* SPORT prolongations *fpl* **overtired** *adj* épuisé(e) **overtone** *n* 1. (*implication*) sous-entendu *m;* **an ~ of sth** une pointe de qc 2. MUS *s.* **harmonic**

overture ['əʊvətjʊəʳ, *Am:* 'oʊvɚtʃɚ] *n a. fig* ouverture *f*

overturn I. *vi* basculer; (*car*) se renverser; (*boat*) chavirer II. *vt a. fig* renverser; (*boat*) faire chavirer **overvalue** *vt* 1. (*in money*) surévaluer 2. (*in esteem*) surestimer **overview** *n* vue *f* d'ensemble **overweight** I. *n* excès *m* de poids II. *adj* (*too heavy*) trop lourd(e); (*person*) trop gros(se); **to be 10 kilos ~** peser dix kilos de trop **overweighted** *adj* **to be ~** être surchargé; *Am* (*person*) avoir pris de l'embonpoint **overwhelm** *vt* 1. (*defeat: enemy*) écraser 2. (*bury, inundate*) submerger; **to be ~ed with sth** (*letters*) être submergé de qc; (*work*) être accablé de qc 3. (*have emotional effect*) bouleverser; **to be quite ~ed** être bouleversé; **to be ~ed by grief** être accablé de chagrin; **to be ~ed with joy** être au comble de la joie **overwhelming** *adj* (*majority, argument, victory*) écrasant(e); (*support*) massif(-ive); (*grief, heat*) accablant(e); (*joy*) immense; (*desire, need*) irrésistible; **to feel an ~ urge to** *+infin* éprouver un besoin irrésistible de *+infin* **overwork** I. *n no pl* surmenage *m* II. *vi* se surmener III. *vt* (*person, body*) surmener; (*machine, idea*) utiliser à outrance **overwrought** *adj* surexcité(e)

ovulate ['ɒvjəleɪt, *Am:* 'ɑːvjuː-] *vi* ovuler

ovulation [ˌɒvjə'leɪʃən, *Am:* ˌɑːvjuː'-] *n no pl* ovulation *f*

ovum ['əʊvəm, *Am:* 'oʊ-] <ova> *n* ovule *m*

ow *interj* aïe!
owe [əʊ, *Am:* oʊ] *vt a. fig* devoir; **to ~ sb sth** devoir qc à qn; **to ~ sb thanks/gratitude** *form* devoir à qn de la reconnaissance/gratitude
owing *adj* dû(due)
owing to *prep form* en raison de
owl [aʊl] *n* chouette *f*
owlish ['aʊlɪʃ] *adj* comme un hibou
own [əʊn, *Am:* oʊn] **I.** *pron* **my ~** le(la) mien(ne); **it is my ~** c'est à moi; **to have problems of one's ~** avoir ses propres problèmes; **a room of one's ~** une chambre à soi ►**to come into one's ~** révéler ses qualités; **to get one's ~ back on sb** *inf* prendre sa revanche sur qn; **(all) on one's ~** (tout) seul **II.** *adj* propre; **to use one's ~ car/brush** utiliser sa propre voiture/brosse; **in one's ~ time** (*outside working hours*) en dehors des heures de travail de qn; (*setting one's own speed*) à son propre rythme **III.** *vt* posséder; **as if they ~ed the place** comme s'ils étaient chez eux **IV.** *vi* avouer; **to ~ to sth** *form* reconnaître qc
◆**own up** *vi* avouer; **to ~ to sth** avouer qc
owner *n* propriétaire *mf*
ownership ['əʊnəʃɪp, *Am:* 'oʊnɚ-] *n no pl* propriété *f*
ox [ɒks, *Am:* ɑːks] <oxen> *n* bœuf *m*
OXFAM ['ɒksfæm, *Am:* 'ɑːks-] *n abbr of* **Oxford Commitee for Famine Relief** Oxfam *m*
oxidation [ˌɒksɪ'deɪʃən, *Am:* ˌɑːksɪ'-] *n Am* CHEM *s.* **oxidization**
oxide ['ɒksaɪd, *Am:* 'ɑːk-] *n* oxyde *m*
oxidization *n Am* CHEM oxydation *f*
oxidize ['ɒksɪdaɪz, *Am:* 'ɑːk-] **I.** *vi* s'oxyder **II.** *vt* oxyder
oxtail ['ɒksteɪl, *Am:* 'ɑːks-] *n* queue *f* de bœuf
oxygen ['ɒksɪdʒən, *Am:* 'ɑːksɪ-] *n no pl* oxygène *m*
oxygen mask *n* masque *m* à oxygène
oxygen tent *n* tente *f* à oxygène
oxymoron [ˌɒksɪ'mɔːrɒn, *Am:* ˌɑːksɪ'mɔːrɑːn] *n* oxymore *m*
oyster ['ɔɪstəʳ, *Am:* -stɚ] *n* huître *f;* **~ shell** coquille *f* d'huître
oyster bed *n* banc *m* d'huîtres
oz [aʊnts] *n abbr of* **ounce** once *f*
ozone ['əʊzəʊn, *Am:* 'oʊzoʊn] *n no pl* **1.** CHEM ozone *m* **2.** *inf* (*clean air*) air *m* pur
ozone hole *n* trou *m* dans la couche d'ozone
ozone layer *n* couche *f* d'ozone

P

P, p [piː] <-'s> *n* **1.** P *m*, p *m;* **~ as in Peter, ~ for Peter** (*on telephone*) p comme Pierre **2.** *Brit* (*penny*) pence *inv* ►**to mind one's ~'s and Q's** faire attention à ce que l'on dit
PA [ˌpiː'eɪ] *n* **1.** (*assistant to a superior*) *abbr of* **personal assistant** **2.** (*loudspeaker*) *abbr of* **public address system** **3.** *Am abbr of* **Pennsylvania**
pa[1] *n inf* (*father*) papa *m*
pa[2] *adv abbr of* **per annum** par an
pace [peɪs] **I.** *n* **1.** (*step*) pas *m;* **to take a ~** faire un pas; **a few ~s away from sth** à deux pas de qc **2.** (*speed*) pas *m;* **to force the ~** forcer l'allure; **to gather ~** prendre de la vitesse; **to quicken one's ~** presser le pas; **to set the ~** donner l'allure; **to keep up the ~** maintenir la cadence; **to stand the ~** tenir le rythme; **at sb's own ~** à son (propre) rythme; **the ~ of life** le rythme de la vie; **to keep ~ with sb/sth** *a. fig* suivre qn/qc ►**to spot sth at 20 ~s** flairer qc à cent mètres; **to put sb/sth through their/its ~s** mettre qn/qc à l'épreuve **II.** <pacing> *vt* **to ~ sth (off)** arpenter qc **III.** *vi* marcher; **to ~ up and down** marcher de long en large
pacemaker ['peɪsˌmeɪkəʳ, *Am:* -kɚ] *n* **1.** SPORT (*speed setter*) meneur, -euse *m, f* **2.** (*heart rhythm regulator*) stimulateur *m* cardiaque
pacesetter *n s.* **pacemaker**
pachyderm ['pækɪdɜːm, *Am:* -ədɜːrm] *n* pachyderme *m*
pacific [pə'sɪfɪk] *adj* pacifique
Pacific **I.** *n* **the ~** le Pacifique **II.** *adj* pacifique
pacification *n no pl* pacification *f*
Pacific Ocean *n* océan *m* Pacifique
pacifier ['pæsɪfaɪəʳ, *Am:* -əfaɪɚ] *n* **1.** (*person*) pacificateur, -trice *m, f* **2.** *Am* (*baby's dummy*) tétine *f*
pacifism ['pæsɪfɪzəm, *Am:* 'pæsə-] *n no pl* pacifisme *m*
pacifist **I.** *n* pacifiste *mf* **II.** *adj* pacifiste
pacify ['pæsɪfaɪ, *Am:* 'pæsə-] <-ie-> *vt* **1.** (*establish peace*) pacifier **2.** (*calm*) calmer
pack [pæk] **I.** *n* **1.** *Am* (*box: of cigarettes*) paquet *m;* (*of beer*) pack *m;* **a four-/six-~** un pack de 4/6 **2.** (*rucksack*) sac *m* à dos **3.** (*group*) groupe *m;* (*of wolves, hounds*) meute *f* **4.** SPORT mêlée *f* **5.** MIL patrouille *f* **6.** (*set of cards*) jeu *m* **7.** (*beauty treatment*) masque *m;* **face/clay ~** masque pour le visage/à l'argile **8.** *pej* (*group, set*) tas *m;* **nothing but a ~ of lies** rien qu'un tissu de mensonges **II.** *vi* **1.** (*prepare travel luggage*) faire ses bagages; **to ~ into a case** tenir dans une valise **2.** (*cram*) s'entasser; **to ~ into a room** s'entasser dans une pièce **3.** (*compress*) se tasser ►**to send sb ~ing** envoyer promener qn **III.** *vt* **1.** (*put into*) ranger dans une valise; **to ~ one's bags** *a. fig* faire ses valises; **did you ~ the camera?** ty as pris l'appareil-photo?; **to ~ a lot into a suitcase** mettre plein de choses dans une valise; **to ~ sth tightly** bien emballer qc **2.** (*wrap*) emballer; (*for sale*) conditionner **3.** (*fill*) **to ~ sth with sth** remplir qc de qc; **to be ~ed with tourists** être rempli de touristes

P

4. (*cram*) entasser; **to be ~ed like sardines** être serrés comme des sardines 5. (*compress*) tasser 6. (*have the force*) **to ~ a gun/power** porter une arme/de la force; **to ~ a punch** *a. fig* avoir du punch
◆**pack in** *vt* 1. (*put in*) emballer 2. (*cram in*) entasser 3. *inf* (*stop*) **to pack sb/sth in** plaquer qn/qc; **to pack all in** tout plaquer; **pack it in!** laisse(z) tomber! 4. (*attract an audience*) **they're ~ing them in** ils attirent un monde fou
◆**pack off** *vt inf* expédier
◆**pack up** I. *vt* 1. (*pack: for post, storage*) emballer; (*for travel*) rassembler; **to ~ one's belongings** faire ses valises 2. *inf* (*finish*) laisser tomber; **to pack** (**it**) **up** laisser tomber; **to ~ smoking** arrêter la cigarette II. *vi* 1. (*pack and go*) plier bagage 2. *inf* (*stop: work*) arrêter de bosser; (*smoking*) arrêter de fumer 3. *Brit, inf* (*stop functioning*) lâcher
package ['pækɪdʒ] I. *n* 1. (*packet*) paquet *m* 2. (*set*) ensemble *m;* **the ~ on offer** l'ensemble de propositions II. *vt* 1. (*pack*) emballer; (*for sale*) conditionner 2. *fig* présenter
package deal *n* contrat *m* forfaitaire **package holiday** *n Am* voyage *m* à forfait **package store** *n Am* magasin *m* de vins et de spiritueux **package tour** *s.* **package holiday**
packaging *n no pl* 1. (*wrapping materials*) conditionnement *m* 2. (*the wrapping of goods*) emballage *m* 3. (*presentation*) packaging *m*
packed lunch *n* panier-repas *m*
packer *n* empaqueteur, -euse *m, f*
packet ['pækɪt] *n Brit, Aus, a. inf* paquet *m;* **soup in a ~** soupe en sachet; **to cost a ~** coûter un paquet
pack ice *n* banquise *f*
packing *n no pl* 1. (*putting things into cases*) emballage *m* 2. (*protective wrapping*) conditionnement *m* 3. INFOR compression *f*
pact [pækt] *n* pacte *m*
pad [pæd] I. *n* 1. (*piece of material, rubber*) tampon *m;* **cotton wool ~** coton *m;* **scouring ~** tampon *m* à récurer; **ink ~** tampon *m* encreur; (**sanitary**) **~** serviette *f* périodique 2. (*protection*) coussinet *m;* SPORT protection *f;* **knee ~** genouillère *f* 3. FASHION (*shoulder*) épaulette *f* 4. (*book of blank paper*) bloc *m;* **drawing ~** bloc de papier à dessin 5. (*sole of an animal*) coussinet *m* 6. (*take-off and landing area*) piste *f;* **helicopter ~** piste pour hélicoptère; **launching ~** rampe *f* de lancement 7. *inf* (*house or flat*) piaule *f* 8. (*water-lily leaf*) feuille *f* de nénuphar II. <-dd-> *vt* matelasser
◆**pad out** *vt* (*essay*) délayer
padded *adj* matelassé(e); (*cell*) capitonné(e); (*bra*) rembourré(e); **~ shoulders** épaulettes *fpl*
padding *n no pl* 1. (*material*) rembourrage *m* 2. (*protecting material*) protections *fpl*
3. (*adding information*) remplissage *m*
paddle[1] ['pædl] I. *n* 1. (*oar*) pagaie *f* 2. NAUT pale *f* II. *vt* 1. (*row*) pagayer 2. *Am, inf* (*spank*) donner la fessée à ►**to ~ one's own canoe** diriger seul sa barque III. *vi* (*row*) pagayer
paddle[2] ['pædl] I. *n* promenade *f* dans l'eau; **to go for a ~** aller marcher dans l'eau II. *vi* patauger
paddling pool *n* pataugeoire *f*
paddock ['pædək] *n* (*on farm*) enclos *m;* (*at racecourse*) paddock *m*
paddy ['pædi] *n* 1. (*rice*) riz *m* paddy 2. (*field*) *s.* **paddy field**
paddy field *n* rizière *f* **paddy wagon** *n Am, Aus, inf* panier *m* à salade
padlock ['pædlɒk, *Am:* -lɑːk] I. *n* cadenas *m* II. *vt* cadenasser
paediatric [ˌpiːdɪ'ætrɪk] *adj* pédiatrique
paediatrician *n* MED pédiatre *mf*
paediatrics *n no pl* pédiatrie *f*
paedophile ['piːdəʊfaɪl] *n* pédophile *mf*
pagan ['peɪgən] I. *n* païen(ne) *m(f)* II. *adj* païen(ne)
paganism ['peɪgənɪzəm] *n no pl* paganisme *m*
page[1] [peɪdʒ] *n* 1. (*one sheet of paper*) *a. fig* page *f;* **front ~** première page; **sports ~** page des sports; **a ~ in history** une page de l'histoire 2. INFOR page *f;* **home ~** (*on site*) page *f* d'accueil; (*individual*) page *f* personnelle; **to visit a ~** accéder à une page; **bottom of ~** bas *m* de page
page[2] [peɪdʒ] I. *n* (*attendant*) page *m* II. *vt* 1. (*over loudspeaker*) appeler 2. (*by pager*) envoyer un message à
pageant ['pædʒənt] *n* 1. (*historical show*) reconstitution *f* historique 2. (*show*) spectacle *m* pompeux
pageantry *n no pl* faste *m*
pageboy *n* 1. (*servant in a hotel*) groom *m* 2. (*boy at wedding*) garçon *m* d'honneur 3. (*hairstyle*) carré *m*
page layout *n* mise *f* en page
pager *n* radio-messagerie *f*
pagination [ˌpædʒɪ'neɪʃən, *Am:* -ən'eɪʃən] *n no pl* pagination *f*
pagoda [pə'gəʊdə, *Am:* -'goʊ-] *n* pagode *f*
paid [peɪd] I. *pt, pp of* **pay** II. *adj* **~ holiday** *Am* [*o* **vacation**] congés *mpl* payés
paid-up *adj* 1. (*having paid a subscription*) **~ member** adhérent(e) *m(f);* **a fully ~ supporter** un membre actif 2. (*paid: capital*) versé(e)
pail [peɪl] *n Am* seau *m*
pain [peɪn] I. *n* 1. (*physical suffering*) douleur *f;* **to be in ~** souffrir; **I have a ~ in my leg** j'ai une douleur dans la jambe; **to double up in ~** se tordre de douleur 2. (*mental suffering*) souffrance *f* 3. *pl* (*great care*) peine *f;* **to be at ~s to** +*infin,* **to go to great ~s to** +*infin* se donner beaucoup de peine pour +*infin* ►**to be a ~** (**in the neck**) *inf* être /casse-pieds; **on**/

under ~ **of sth** sous peine de qc **II.** *vt* **it ~s sb to** *+infin* cela fait de la peine à qn de *+infin*
pained *adj* peiné(e)
painful *adj* **1.** (*causing physical pain*) douloureux(-euse); (*death*) pénible **2.** (*upsetting, embarrassing*) pénible
painkiller *n* analgésique *m*
painless *adj* **1.** (*not painful*) indolore **2.** *fig* facile
painstaking ['peɪnzˌteɪkɪŋ] *adj* méticuleux(-euse)
painstakingly *adv* avec soin
paint [peɪnt] **I.** *n a. pej* peinture *f;* **~s** couleurs *fpl;* **oil ~s** couleurs à l'huile; **~ pot** pot *m* de peinture; **~ roller** rouleau *m* à peinture **II.** *vi* peindre; **to ~ in oils/watercolours** peindre à l'huile/l'aquarelle **III.** *vt* **1.** (*put colour on*) peindre **2.** *pej* (*apply make-up*) peinturlurer **3.** (*conceal with paint*) **to ~ sth out** [*o* **to ~ out sth**], **to ~ over sth** couvrir qc de peinture **4.** (*describe*) dépeindre; **to ~ a grim/rosy picture of sth** dresser un portrait sombre/rose de qc ►**to ~ the town red** faire la fête
paintbox *n* boîte *f* de couleurs **paintbrush** *n* pinceau *m*
painted *adj* peint(e)
painter¹ *n* peintre *mf*
painter² *n* amarre *f*
painting *n* **1.** (*activity*) peinture *f* **2.** (*picture*) tableau *m*
paint stripper *n no pl* décapant *m* **paintwork** *n no pl* peintures *fpl*
pair [peəʳ, *Am:* per] *n* **1.** (*two*) paire *f;* **a ~ of trousers** un pantalon; **a ~ of tweezers** une pince à épiler; **in ~s** par deux **2.** (*couple*) couple *m;* **you're a fine ~!** vous faites la paire! ►**I've only got one ~ of hands** je n'ai que deux mains
◆**pair off I.** *vi* former un couple; **to ~ with sb** se mettre avec qn **II.** *vt* **to pair sb off with sb** mettre qn avec qn
◆**pair up I.** *vi* se mettre ensemble; **to ~ with sb** se mettre avec qn **II.** *vt* (*people*) grouper par paires; (*things*) regrouper
pajamas [pə'dʒɑːməz] *npl Am s.* **pyjamas**
Pakistan [ˌpɑːkɪ'stɑːn, *Am:* 'pækɪstæn] *n* le Pakistan
Pakistani I. *adj* pakistanais(e) **II.** *n* Pakistanais(e) *m(f)*
pal [pæl] *n inf* pote *mf*
pal up *vi Brit, Aus, inf* devenir pote(s)
palace ['pælɪs, *Am:* -əs] *n* palais *m*
palaeography [ˌpælɪ'ɒgrəfi, *Am:* ˌpeɪlɪ'ɑːgrə-] *n no pl* paléographie *f*
palaeolithic [ˌpælɪəʊ'lɪθɪk, *Am:* ˌpeɪlɪoʊ'-] *adj* paléolithique
palaeontologist *n* paléontologue *mf*
palaeontology [ˌpælɪɒn'tɒlədʒi, *Am:* ˌpeɪlɪɑːn'tɑːlə-] *n* paléontologie *f*
palatable ['pælətəbl, *Am:* -əţə-] *adj* **1.** (*fit to eat or drink: food*) mangeable; (*drink*) buvable **2.** (*easy to accept*) acceptable
palatal ['pælətəl, *Am:* -ţ-] *adj* palatal(e)
palate ['pælət] *n* palais *m*
palatial [pə'leɪʃl] *adj* somptueux(-euse)
palaver [pə'lɑːvəʳ, *Am:* -'lævɚ] *n inf* histoire *f;* **what a ~!** quelle histoire!
pale [peɪl] **I.** *adj* pâle; **to look ~** être pâle **II.** *vi* blêmir; **to ~ in comparison with sth** ne pas soutenir la comparaison avec qc; **to ~ into insignificance** perdre toute importance
paleface *n pej* visage *m* pâle
paleness *n no pl* pâleur *f*
Palestine ['pælɪstaɪn, *Am:* -ə-] *n* la Palestine
Palestinian I. *adj* palestinien(ne) **II.** *n* Palestinien(ne) *m(f)*
palette ['pælɪt] *n* palette *f*
palisade [ˌpælɪ'seɪd, *Am:* -ə'-] *n* **1.** (*strong protective fence*) palissade *f* **2.** *pl, Am* (*cliffs*) falaises *fpl*
pall¹ [pɔːl] *vi* devenir lassant
pall² [pɔːl] *n* **1.** (*cloth covering a coffin*) drap *m* mortuaire **2.** *Am* (*a coffin* (*at a funeral*)) cercueil *m* **3.** (*covering smoke cloud*) voile *m* **4.** *fig* voile *m;* **to cast a ~ over sth** jeter un voile sombre sur qc
pallbearer ['pɔːlˌbeərəʳ, *Am:* -ˌberɚ] *n* porteur *m* de cercueil
pallet ['pælɪt] *n* palette *f*
palliative ['pælɪətɪv, *Am:* -ţɪv] **I.** *n* palliatif *m* **II.** *adj* palliatif(-ive)
pallid ['pælɪd] *adj* **1.** (*very pale*) blafard(e) **2.** (*lacking verve*) pâle
pallor ['pæləʳ, *Am:* -ɚ] *n* pâleur *f*
pally ['pæli] <-ier, -iest> *adj inf* **to be ~ with sb** être copain avec qn
palm [pɑːm] **I.** *n* paume *f;* **to read sb's ~** lire les lignes de la main ►**to have sb in the ~ of one's hand, to have sb eating out of the ~ of one's hand** faire ce que l'on veut de qn **II.** *vt* dissimuler (dans sa main)
◆**palm off** *vt* **to palm sth off on sb** refiler qc à qn; **to palm sth off as sth** faire passer qc pour qc; **to palm sb off with sth** refiler qc à qn
palmist ['pɑːmɪst] *n* chiromancien(ne) *m(f)*
Palm Sunday *n* Dimanche *m* des Rameaux
palm (**tree**) *n* palmier *m;* **~ leaf** feuille *f* de palmier
palpable ['pælpəbl] *adj* (*feeling*) palpable; (*sincerity*) évident(e); (*change*) tangible; **a ~ reminder of sth** une évocation concrète de qc
palpitate ['pælpɪteɪt, *Am:* -pə-] *vi* palpiter
palpitations [ˌpælpɪ'teɪʃnz, *Am:* -pə'-] *n* MED palpitations *fpl*
paltry ['pɔːltri] <-ier, -iest> *adj* **1.** (*small and worth little*) dérisoire **2.** (*of poor quality*) minable
pampas ['pæmpəs, *Am:* -pəz] *n* pampa *f*
pamper ['pæmpəʳ, *Am:* -pɚ] *vt* dorloter; **to ~ oneself** se dorloter; **to ~ sb/sth with sth** gâter qn/qc avec qc
pamphlet ['pæmflɪt] *n* pamphlet *m*
pan¹ [pæn] **I.** *n* **1.** (*saucepan*) casserole *f;* (*for frying*) poêle *f* **2.** *Am* (*container for oven*) plat *m;* (*for cakes*) moule *m* **3.** (*toilet bowl*)

cuvette (des WC) *f* **II.** *vt Am* faire revenir à la poêle

pan² [pæn] *vi* CINE faire un panoramique

pan³ [pæn] *vt inf* (*criticize*) démolir

◆**pan out** *vi* (*happen*) se passer; **to ~ all right** s'arranger

panacea [ˌpænə'sɪə] *n* panacée *f*

panache [pə'næʃ] *n no pl* panache *m*

Panama Canal *n* Canal *m* de Panama

Pan-American ['pænə'merɪkən] *adj* panaméricain(e)

panatella [ˌpænə'telə] *n* cigarillo *m*

pancake ['pænkeɪk] *n* crêpe *f*

Pancake Day, **Pancake Tuesday** *n Brit, inf* mardi *m* gras

pancreas ['pæŋkriəs] *n* pancréas *m*

panda ['pændə] *n* panda *m*

pandemonium [ˌpændə'məʊniəm, *Am:* -də'moʊ-] *n* charivari *m*

pander *vi pej* **to ~ to sb/sth** céder face à qn/qc; **to ~ sb's whims** se plier aux caprices de qn

p and p [ˌpiːən'piː] *n abbr of* **postage and packing** frais *mpl* d'envoi

pane [peɪn] *n* vitre *f*

panel ['pænəl] **I.** *n* **1.** (*wooden sheet*) panneau *m* **2.** (*formed metal sheet*) tôle *f* **3.** FASHION pan *m* **4.** PUBL tableau *m* **5.** (*team*) panel *m;* **a ~ of experts** un comité d'experts **6.** (*instrument board*) tableau *m* de bord; **control ~** tableau de contrôle **II.** *vt* lambrisser

panel discussion *n* conférence-débat *f*

panel game *n Brit* **1.** (*on television*) jeu *m* télévisé **2.** (*on radio*) jeu *m* radiophonique

paneling *n Am no pl* boiseries *fpl*

panelist *n Am* **1.** (*member of an expert team*) expert(e) *m(f)* **2.** (*member of a team*) participant(e) *m(f)*

panelling *n s.* **paneling**

panellist *n s.* **panelist**

pang [pæŋ] *n* **1.** (*pain*) élancement *m* **2.** *fig* accès *m;* **~s of remorse/guilt** remords *mpl*

panhandle ['pænhændl] *Am* **I.** *n* bande *f* de terre **II.** *vi inf* faire la manche **III.** *vt inf* taxer; **to ~ money** taxer de l'argent

panhandler *n Am, inf* mendiant(e) *m(f)*

panic ['pænɪk] **I.** *n* panique *f;* **to get in/into a ~** paniquer **II.** <-ck-> *vi* **1.** (*lose control*) **to ~ about sth** paniquer à cause de qc **2.** (*cause quick thoughtless action*) s'affoler **III.** *vt* affoler; **to ~ sb into doing sth** précipiter qn à faire qc **IV.** *adj* (*decison, measure*) dicté par la panique; **panic buying** le stockage

panicky <-ier, iest> *adj* affolé(e)

panic-stricken *adj* pris(e) de panique

pannier ['pæniəʳ, *Am:* -jɚ] *n* panier *m*

panorama [ˌpænə'rɑːmə, *Am:* -'ræmə] *n* panorama *m*

panoramic [ˌpænə'ræmɪk] *adj* panoramique; **~ scene** vue *f* panoramique

panpipes ['pænpaɪps] *npl* flûte *f* de Pan

pansy ['pænzi] <-sies> *n* (*small garden flower*) pensée *f*

pant [pænt] **I.** *vi* haleter; **to ~ for breath** chercher son souffle **II.** *vt* dire en haletant **III.** *n* halètement *m*

pantechnicon [pæn'teknɪkən] *n Brit* grand camion *m* de déménagement

pantheism ['pæntθiɪzəm] *n no pl* panthéisme *m*

pantheist **I.** *n* panthéiste *mf* **II.** *adj* panthéiste

pantheistic *adj* panthéiste

panther ['pæntθəʳ, *Am:* -θɚ] *n* **1.** (*black leopard*) panthère *f* **2.** (*cougar*) *a. Am* puma *m*

pantie girdle *n s.* **panty girdle**

panties ['pæntɪz, *Am:* -t̬ɪz] *npl* culotte *f*

pantihose *n s.* **pantyhose**

pantomime ['pæntəmaɪm, *Am:* -t̬ə-] *n* **1.** *Brit* (*Christmas entertainment*) spectacle *m* de Noël **2.** (*mime*) pantomime *f*

pantry ['pæntri] <-tries> *n* placard *m* à provisions

pants *npl* **1.** *Brit* (*underpants*) slip *m* **2.** *Am* (*trousers*) pantalon *m* ►**to be ~** être complètement nul; **to beat the ~ off sb** n'avoir rien à voir avec; **to bore the ~ off sb** emmerder qn à l'extrême; **to scare the ~ off sb** faire une peur bleue à qn; **to be caught with one's ~ down** *inf* être pris au dépourvu

pants suit, **pantsuit** *n Am* tailleur-pantalon *m*

panty girdle *n* gaine-culotte *f* **pantyhose** *npl Am, Aus* (*tights*) collant *m* **panty liner** *n* protège-slip *m*

pap [pæp] *n no pl* **1.** (*soft food for babies*) bouillie *f* **2.** *pej, inf* (*worthless entertainment*) idioties *fpl*

papacy ['peɪpəsi] *n no pl* **1.** (*pope's authority or office*) papauté *f* **2.** (*pope's tenure*) pontificat *m*

papal ['peɪpl] *adj* papal(e); **~ election** élection *f* du pape

papaya [pə'paɪə] *n* papaye *f*

paper ['peɪpəʳ, *Am:* -pɚ] **I.** *n* **1.** *no pl* (*writing material*) papier *m;* **~ hat** chapeau *m* en papier; **to commit sth to ~** coucher qc par écrit; **to get sth down on ~** mettre qc par écrit; **on ~** en théorie **2.** (*newspaper*) journal *m;* **daily ~** quotidien *m* **3.** (*wallpaper*) papier *m* peint **4.** (*official documents in general*) document *m;* **~s** pièces *fpl;* (*for identity*) papiers *mpl* (d'identité) **5.** *no pl* (*set of exam questions*) épreuve *f* **6.** UNIV (*by student*) exposé *m;* (*at conference, in review*) papier *m;* **to give a ~** faire un exposé **II.** *vt* tapisser **III.** *vi* (*hide*) **to ~ over problems** dissimuler les problèmes; **to ~ over the cracks** dissimuler les failles

paperback *n* livre *m* de poche; **~ edition** édition *f* de poche **paper bag** *n* sac *m* en papier **paper boy** *n* livreur *m* de journaux **paper chain** *n* guirlande *f* de papier **paper clip** *n* trombone *m* **paper cup** *n* gobelet *m* en papier **paper feed** *n* avance *f* papier **paper jam** *n* bourrage *m* **paperknife** *n* coupe-papier *m inv* **paper mill** *n* usine *f* à papier

paper money *n no pl* papier-monnaie *m* **paper-thin** *adj* fin(e) comme du papier (à cigarette) **paper tiger** *n pej* tigre *m* de papier **paper tissue** *n* mouchoir *m* en papier **paper tray** *n* bac *m* à feuilles **paperweight** *n* presse-papiers *m* **paperwork** *n no pl* paperasserie *f*

papier-mâché [ˌpæpɪeɪ'mæʃeɪ, *Am:* ˌpeɪpə˞mə'ʃeɪ] *n no pl* carton-pâte *m*

paprika ['pæprɪkə, *Am:* pæp'riː-] *n no pl* paprika *m*

Papua ['pæpuə, *Am:* 'pæpjuə] *n* la Papouasie

Papuan I. *adj* papou(e) II. *n* 1. (*inhabitant*) Papou(e) *m(f)* 2. LING papou *m; s. a.* **English**

Papua New Guinea *n* la Papouasie-Nouvelle-Guinée **Papua New Guinean** I. *adj* papouan(e)-néo-guinéen(ne) II. *n* Papouan(e)-Néo-Guinéen(ne) *m(f)*

papyrus [pə'paɪərəs, *Am:* -'paɪrəs] <-ruses *o* -yri> *n* papyrus *m*

par [pɑːʳ, *Am:* pɑːr] *n no pl* 1. (*equality*) **to be on a ~ with sb** être au même niveau que qn; **below ~** en dessous de la moyenne; **to feel under ~** ne pas se sentir dans son assiette; **at/above/below ~** au niveau/au-dessus/au-dessous du pair 2. FIN **~ value** valeur *f* nominale ▶**that's about ~ for the course** *pej* c'est ce à quoi il faut s'attendre

par. *n abbr of* **paragraph** paragraphe *m*

parable ['pærəbl, *Am:* 'per-] *n* parabole *f*

parabola [pə'ræbələ] *n* MAT parabole *f*

parachute ['pærəʃuːt, *Am:* 'per-] I. *n* parachute *m* II. *vi* descendre en parachute III. *vt* (*person*) parachuter; (*things*) larguer par parachute

parachute jump *n* saut *m* en parachute **parachute jumper** *n* parachutiste *mf*

parachutist *n* parachutiste *mf*

parade [pə'reɪd] I. *n* 1. (*procession*) parade *f* 2. (*military procession*) défilé *m;* **to be on ~** être à l'exercice 3. (*inspection of soldiers*) revue *f* 4. *Brit* (*row of shops*) rangée *f* II. *vi* défiler III. *vt* 1. (*exhibit*) afficher 2. (*show off*) faire étalage de; *pej, fig* étaler; **to ~ one's concern over sth** exhiber son inquiétude au sujet de qc; **to ~ one's knowledge** faire étalage de ses connaissances

paradigm ['pærədaɪm, *Am:* 'per-] *n form* 1. (*model*) modèle *m* 2. (*model of methodology*) paradigme *m* 3. (*example*) exemple *m*

paradise ['pærədaɪs, *Am:* 'per-] *n* paradis *m*

paradox ['pærədɒks, *Am:* 'perədɑːks] <-xes> *n no pl* paradoxe *m;* **it is a ~ that** il est paradoxal que +*subj*

paradoxical *adj* paradoxal(e)

paradoxically *adv* paradoxalement

paraffin ['pærəfɪn, *Am:* 'per-] *n no pl* 1. *Brit* (*fuel*) pétrole *m* 2. (*wax made from petroleum*) paraffine *f* solide

paragliding ['pærəˌglaɪdɪŋ, *Am:* 'per-] *n no pl* parapente *m*

paragon ['pærəgən, *Am:* 'perəgɑːn] *n* (*of virtue*) parangon *m;* (*of democracy, discretion*) modèle *m*

paragraph ['pærəgrɑːf, *Am:* 'perəgræf] *n* paragraphe *m*

Paraguay ['pærəgwaɪ, *Am:* 'perəgweɪ] *n* Paraguay *m*

Paraguayan I. *n* Paraguayen(ne) *m(f)* II. *adj* paraguayen(ne)

parakeet ['pærəkiːt, *Am:* 'per-] *n* perruche *f*

parallel ['pærəlel, *Am:* 'per-] I. *n* 1. GEO (*position of line*) parallèle *m* 2. MAT parallèle *f* 3. *fig* (*comparison*) parallèle *m;* **to draw a ~** établir un parallèle; **without ~** sans pareil; **in ~** en parallèle 4. ELEC **in ~** en dérivation II. *adj a. fig* parallèle; **~ to sth** parallèle à qc III. *vt* 1. (*be ~ to*) *a.* MAT être parallèle à 2. (*be similar to*) être analogue à 3. (*be equal to*) égaler

parallel bars *npl* SPORT barres *f* parallèles

parallelism *n* parallélisme *m*

parallelogram *n* parallélogramme *m*

Paralympic Games *n* Jeux *mpl* Paralympiques

Paralympics [ˌpærə'lɪmpɪks] *n* Paralympiques *mpl*

paralyse ['pærəlaɪz, *Am:* 'per-] *vt Brit, Aus s.* **paralyze**

paralysis [pə'ræləsɪs] <-yses> *n* paralysie *f*

paralytic [ˌpærə'lɪtɪk, *Am:* ˌperə'lɪt̬-] I. *adj* 1. (*with paralysis*) paralytique 2. *inf* (*completely drunk and incapable*) ivre mort(e) II. *n* paralytique *mf*

paralyze ['pærəlaɪz, *Am:* 'per-] *vt* 1. (*render immobile, powerless*) paralyser 2. (*stupefy*) stupéfier; **to feel ~d with fear** être transi de peur

paramedic [ˌpærə'medɪk, *Am:* ˌper-] *n* auxiliaire *mf* médical(e)

parameter [pə'ræmɪtəʳ, *Am:* -ət̬ə˞] *n* 1. *pl* (*determining characteristics*) paramètre *m* 2. *pl* (*set of limits*) limite *f;* **in the ~s of the search** dans les limites de la recherche

parametric *adj* paramétrique

paramilitary [ˌpærə'mɪlɪtri, *Am:* ˌperə'mɪləter-] I. *adj* paramilitaire II. *n* membre *mf* d'un groupe paramilitaire

paramount ['pærəmaʊnt, *Am:* 'per-] *adj form* suprême; (*importance*) crucial(e)

paranoia [ˌpærə'nɔɪə, *Am:* ˌper-] *n* paranoïa *f*

paranoiac I. *adj* paranoïaque II. *n* paranoïaque *mf*

paranoid ['pærənɔɪd, *Am:* 'perənɔɪd] I. *adj* paranoïaque; **don't be so ~!** arrête ta parano! II. *n* paranoïaque *mf*

parapet ['pærəpɪt, *Am:* 'perəpet] *n* parapet *m*

paraphernalia [ˌpærəfə'neɪlɪə, *Am:* ˌperəfə˞'neɪljə] *n + sing vb, a. pej* attirail *m*

paraphrase ['pærəfreɪz, *Am:* 'per-] I. *vt* paraphraser II. *n* paraphrase *f*

paraplegia [ˌpærə'pliːdʒə, *Am:* ˌper-] *n no pl* paraplégie *f*

paraplegic I. *adj* paraplégique II. *n* paraplé-

P

gique *mf*
parapsychology [ˌpærəsaɪˈkɒlədʒi, *Am:* ˌperəsaɪˈkɑːlə-] *n no pl* parapsychologie *f*
parasite [ˈpærəsaɪt, *Am:* ˈper-] *n* parasite *m*
parasitic *adj* **1.** (*behaving like biological parasite*) parasitaire **2.** (*behaving like human parasite*) parasite
parasol [ˈpærəsɒl, *Am:* ˈperəsɔːl] *n* ombrelle *f*
paratrooper *n* parachutiste *mf*
paratroops [ˈpærətruːps, *Am:* ˈper-] *n* parachutistes *mpl*
parboil [ˈpɑːbɔɪl, *Am:* ˈpɑːr-] *vt* faire cuire à demi
parcel [ˈpɑːsəl, *Am:* ˈpɑːr-] **I.** *n* **1.** (*objects sent in paper*) paquet *m* **2.** (*small ~*) colis *m* **3.** *Am* (*area of land*) parcelle *f* **II.** <*Brit* -ll- *o Am* -l-> *vt* empaqueter
◆**parcel out** *vt* partager; (*land*) morceler
◆**parcel up** *vt* empaqueter
parcel bomb *n* colis *m* piégé **parcel post** *n* service *m* des colis postaux
parch [pɑːtʃ, *Am:* pɑːrtʃ] *vt* dessécher; **I'm ~ed** je meurs de soif
parchment *n* parchemin *m*
pardon [ˈpɑːdn, *Am:* ˈpɑːr-] **I.** *vt* **1.** (*excuse*) pardonner; **to ~ sb for sth** pardonner qc à qn **2.** LAW (*prisoner*) grâcier **II.** *interj* **1.** (*said to excuse oneself*) excusez-moi! **2.** (*indignantly*) pardon! **III.** *n* **1.** LAW pardon *m* **2.** *form* (*said to request repetition*) **I beg your ~?** pardon?; **I beg your ~!** je vous demande pardon!
pardonable *adj* pardonnable
pare [peəʳ, *Am:* per] *vt* **1.** (*peel outer layer of a fruit*) éplucher **2.** (*cut*) **to ~ one's nails** rogner les ongles **3.** (*cut back*) réduire; **to ~ (down** [*o* **back**]) **spending** rogner sur les dépenses
pared-down *adj* (*version*) abrégé(e); (*style*) concis(e)
parent [ˈpeərənt, *Am:* ˈperənt] *n* père *m*, mère *f*; **~s** les parents *mpl*; **single ~** parent célibataire
parentage [ˈpeərəntɪdʒ, *Am:* ˈperənt̬ɪdʒ] *n no pl* **1.** (*descent from parents*) origine *f* **2.** (*position of a parent*) lignée *f*
parental *adj* parental(e); (*authority*) des parents
parent company <-nies> *n* société *f* mère
parenthesis [pəˈrentθəsɪs] <-theses> *n pl* parenthèse *f*
parenthood *n no pl* condition *f* des parents
pariah [pəˈraɪə] *n* **1.** (*outcast person*) paria *mf* **2.** *fig* exclu(e) *m(f)*
paring [ˈpeərɪŋ, *Am:* ˈperɪŋ] *n pl* **1.** (*narrow, peeled off strip*) épluchures *fpl* **2.** (*cut off pieces of finger nails*) **nail ~s** rognures *fpl*
parish [ˈpærɪʃ, *Am:* ˈper-] *n* paroisse *f*
parishioner [pəˈrɪʃənəʳ, *Am:* -ɚ] *n* paroissien(ne) *m(f)*
parish-pump politics *n Brit* politique *f* de clocher
Parisian [pəˈrɪziən, *Am:* -ˈrɪʒ-] **I.** *n* Parisien(ne) *m(f)* **II.** *adj* parisien(ne)
parity [ˈpærəti, *Am:* ˈperət̬i] *n no pl* parité *f*; **pay ~** égalité *f* de salaire
park [pɑːk, *Am:* pɑːrk] **I.** *n* parc *m* **II.** *vt* **1.** AUTO garer **2.** *inf* (*deposit*) déposer **3.** *inf* (*sit down*) **to ~ oneself** s'installer **III.** *vi* se garer
parka [ˈpɑːkə, *Am:* ˈpɑːr-] *n* parka *m o f*
park-and-ride *n* parking *m* relais
parking *n no pl* **1.** AUTO stationnement *m* **2.** (*space to park*) la place *f*
parking area *n* aire *f* de stationnement **parking bay** *n* emplacement *m* de parking **parking disc** *n* disque *m* de stationnement **parking lights** *n Am, Aus* (*sidelights*) feux *mpl* de position **parking lot** *n Am* parking *m*, stationnement *m Québec* **parking meter** *n* parcmètre *m* **parking ticket** *n* procès *m* verbal (*pour stationnement illégal*)
park keeper *n* gardien *m* de parc **parkway** *n Am, Aus* grande voie *f* de communication
parky [ˈpɑːki, *Am:* ˈpɑːr-] <-ier, -iest> *adj Brit, inf* (*weather*) frisquet
Parl. *n abbr of* **Parliament** Parlement *m*
parlance [ˈpɑːlənts, *Am:* ˈpɑːr-] *n no pl, form* langage *m*; **in common ~** en langage courant
parley [ˈpɑːli, *Am:* ˈpɑːrleɪ] **I.** *n* pourparlers *mpl* **II.** *vi* parlementer
parliament [ˈpɑːləmənt, *Am:* ˈpɑːrlə-] *n* parlement *m*; **the Parliament** le Parlement

> Le **Parliament** est composé selon la constitution britannique des deux "Houses of Parliament" et de la reine. Les deux "Houses of Parliament" siègent dans le "Palace of Westminster" à Londres. La Chambre basse, élue par le peuple et composée par la plupart des ministres, s'appelle "House of Commons". Ses membres sont les "members of parliament" ou "MPs". La Chambre haute, "House of Lords", peut voter exceptionnellement des lois. Les députés, "peers of the realm", se divisent en trois groupes. Certains ont de par leur fonction, soit en tant que juges, les "law lords", soit en tant qu'évêques de l'église anglicane, la "Church of England", un siège dans la Chambre haute. D'autres sont élus à vie en tant que "life peers" et d'autres encore ont obtenu leur siège de par leur titre de noblesse héréditaire. Une commission de juges de la "House of Lords" intervient dans la plupart des affaires en tant qu'instance juridique suprême du Royaume-Uni.

parliamentarian *n* **1.** (*respected and skilful MP*) parlementaire *mf* **2.** (*Member of Parliament*) membre *m* du Parlement **3.** *Am* (*tactical expert in institution*) parlementaire *m*
parliamentary *adj* parlementaire
parlor *n Am*, **parlour** [ˈpɑːləʳ, *Am:* ˈpɑːrlɚ] *n* **1.** (*room where people can talk*) parloir *m* **2.** (*shop providing specific service, living room*) salon *m*

parlo(u)r game *n* jeu *m* de société
parlo(u)rmaid *n* HIST femme *f* de chambre
parochial [pə'rəʊkiəl, *Am:* -'roʊ-] *adj* 1. (*referring to parish*) paroissial(e) 2. *pej* (*provincial, self-concerned*) nombrilique
parochialism *n pej* esprit *m* de clocher
parochial school *n Am* école *f* religieuse
parodist *n* parodiste *mf*
parody ['pærədi, *Am:* 'per-] I. <-dies> *n* 1. (*imitation*) parodie *f* 2. *pej* (*travesty*) parodie *f* II. <-ie-> *vt* parodier
parole [pə'rəʊl, *Am:* -'roʊl] I. *n no pl* libération *f* conditionnelle; **to be released on ~** être libéré sur parole II. *vt* **to ~ sb** mettre qn en liberté conditionnelle
paroxysm ['pærəksɪzəm, *Am:* 'per-] *n* paroxysme *m;* (*of joy, rage*) accès *m*
parquet ['pɑːkeɪ, *Am:* pɑːr'keɪ] *n no pl* parquet *m*
parrot ['pærət, *Am:* 'per-] I. *n* perroquet *m* II. *vt pej* répéter comme un perroquet; **to ~ sb** répéter ce que dit qn
parry ['pæri, *Am:* 'per-] I. <-ie-> *vt* 1. (*avert/defend against attack*) esquiver; **to ~ a blow** parer un coup 2. (*avert pressure skilfully*) détourner; (*problem*) éluder II. *n* <-rries> 1. (*action of defeating attacks*) riposte *f* 2. (*cleverly defend against attacks*) parade *f*
parse [pɑːz, *Am:* pɑːrs] *vt* analyser; **to ~ a sentence** faire l'analyse grammaticale d'une phrase
parsimonious [ˌpɑːsɪ'məʊniəs, *Am:* ˌpɑːrsə'moʊ-] *adj pej, form* parcimonieux(-euse); **to be ~ with compliments** *fig* être avare de compliments
parsley ['pɑːsli, *Am:* 'pɑːr-] *n no pl* persil *m*
parsnip ['pɑːsnɪp, *Am:* 'pɑːr-] *n* panais *m*
parson ['pɑːsən, *Am:* 'pɑːr-] *n* prêtre *m*
parsonage ['pɑːsənɪdʒ, *Am:* 'pɑːr-] *n* presbytère *m*
parson's nose *n* croupion *m*
part [pɑːt, *Am:* pɑːrt] I. *n* 1. (*not the whole*) partie *f;* **the best ~ of the day** le meilleur moment de la journée; **~ of growing up is ...** grandir ça veut dire aussi ...; **in large ~** en majeure partie; **for the most ~** pour la plupart 2. (*component of machine*) pièce *f;* **spare ~s** pièces de rechange 3. (*area, region*) région *f;* **the best restaurant in these ~s** le meilleur restaurant par ici 4. (*measure*) mesure *f;* **to add one ~ of sugar** ajouter une mesure de sucre 5. (*role, involvement*) participation *f;* **to want no ~ in sth** ne pas vouloir se mêler de qc; **for my ~** pour ce qui me concerne; **on sb's ~** de la part de qn 6. (*episode in media serial*) épisode *m* 7. CINE, THEAT (*character*) rôle *m;* MUS partie *f* 8. *Am* (*parting of hair*) raie *f,* ligne *f* des cheveux *Belgique* ►**to become ~ of the furniture** faire partie du décor; **to be ~ and parcel of sth** faire partie intégrante de qc; **to dress the ~** s'habiller de façon appropriée; **to take sb's ~** prendre parti pour qn II. *adv* en partie; **~ Irish ~ American** un peu irlandais un peu américain III. *vt* 1. (*divide, separate*) séparer; (*curtains*) entrouvrir; **to ~ sth from sth** séparer qc de qc; **to ~ company from sb** se séparer de qn; **to ~ one's hair** se faire une raie 2. (*move apart*) écarter IV. *vi* se diviser; (*curtains*) s'entrouvrir; (*people*) se quitter; **to ~ from sb/sth** quitter qn/qc; **to ~ with sb/sth** se séparer de; **to ~ on good/bad terms** partir en bons/mauvais termes; **to ~ with one's cash** *inf* débourser de l'argent; **his lips ~ed in a smile** ses lèvres s'entrouvrirent dans un sourire
part exchange *n* reprise *f;* **in ~** en reprise
partial ['pɑːʃəl, *Am:* 'pɑːr-] *adj* 1. (*only in part*) partiel(le) 2. (*biassed*) partial(e) 3. (*fond of*) **to be ~ to sth** avoir un faible pour qc
partiality [ˌpɑːʃi'æləti, *Am:* ˌpɑːrʃi'ælət̬i] *n no pl* 1. (*bias*) partialité *f* 2. (*liking*) penchant *m*
partially *adv* partiellement; (*cooked*) en partie; **to be ~ sighted** être malvoyant
participant [pɑː'tɪsɪpənt, *Am:* pɑːr'tɪsə-] *n* participant(e) *m(f)*
participate [pɑː'tɪsɪpeɪt, *Am:* pɑːr'tɪsə-] *vi* participer; **to ~ in sth** prendre part à qc
participation *n no pl* participation *f*
participle ['pɑːtɪsɪpl, *Am:* 'pɑːrtɪsɪ-] *n* participe *m*
particle ['pɑːtɪkl, *Am:* 'pɑːrt̬ə-] *n* 1. (*small amount of matter*) particule *f* 2. (*the tiniest quantity*) quantité *f* infime
particular [pə'tɪkjələʳ, *Am:* pɚ'tɪkjəlɚ] I. *adj* 1. (*indicating sth individual*) particulier(-ère); (*reason*) précis(e); **that ~ day** ce jour-là; **there were no ~ problems** il n'y avait aucun proclème particulier; **pay ~ attention to spelling** fais particulièrement attention à l'orthographe; **this passage is of ~ interest** ce passage est particulièrement intéressant; **in ~** en particulier; **nothing ~** rien de spécial 2. (*demanding, fussy, meticulous*) exigeant(e); **to be very ~ about sth** être très tatillon au sujet de qc; **to be ~ about one's appearance** soigner sa tenue II. *n* 1. *pl, form* (*details*) détails *mpl* 2. *no pl* (*special*) **the ~** le particulier
particularize [pə'tɪkjʊləraɪz, *Am:* pɚ'-] *vt* 1. (*detail each item*) détailler 2. (*limit to special point*) particulariser
particularly *adv* particulièrement
parting ['pɑːtɪŋ, *Am:* 'pɑːrt̬ɪŋ] *n* 1. (*separation, saying goodbye*) séparation *f;* **~ words** mots *mpl* d'adieu 2. *Brit, Aus* (*line in hair*) raie *f,* ligne *f* des cheveux *Belgique;* **centre/side ~** raie *f* médiane/de côté
parting shot *n* pique *f*
partisan [ˌpɑːtɪ'zæn, *Am:* 'pɑːrt̬ɪzən] I. *adj a.* POL partisan(ne) II. *n* partisan(e) *m(f)*
partition [pɑː'tɪʃən, *Am:* pɑːr'-] I. *n* 1. (*structural division in building*) cloison *f* 2. INFOR partition *f* 3. (*division: of country*) partition *f* II. *vt* 1. (*divide buildings, rooms*) cloisonner; **to ~ sth into several parts** diviser qc

P

en plusieurs parties; **to ~ sth off** séparer qc par une cloison **2.** (*divide countries into nations*) diviser

partly ['pɑːtli, *Am:* 'pɑːrt-] *adv* en partie

partner ['pɑːtnəʳ, *Am:* 'pɑːrtnɚ] **I.** *n* **1.** (*part owner of company*) associé(e) *m(f)* **2.** (*accomplice*) complice *mf;* **~ in crime** complice **3.** (*in a couple*) compagnon, compagne *m, f* **4.** (*in game, project*) partenaire *mf* **II.** *vt* (*for game, dance, project*) être le partenaire de

partnership *n* **1.** (*condition of being partner*) association *f* **2.** (*firm owned by partners*) société *f;* (*of lawyers*) étude *f;* **to go into ~ with sb** s'associer avec qn

partnership agreement *n* accord *m* de partenariat

part of speech *n* partie *f* de discours **part owner** *n* copropriétaire *mf* **part ownership** *n* copropriété *f* **part payment** *n* règlement *m* partiel

partridge ['pɑːtrɪdʒ, *Am:* 'pɑːr-] <-(dges)> *n* perdrix *f*

part-time *adj, adv* à temps partiel

party ['pɑːti, *Am:* 'pɑːrt̬i] **I.** *n* <-ties> **1.** (*social gathering*) fête *f* **2.** (*evening gathering*) soirée *f;* **to have a ~** faire une soirée **3.** (*reception*) réception *f* **4.** (*political group*) parti *m* **5.** (*group of visitors*) groupe *m* **6.** (*side in lawsuit, contract*) partie *f;* **the guilty ~ hasn't been found** le coupable en question n'a pas été trouvé; **to be a ~ to sth** être mêlé à qc; **to be ~ to an arrangement** participer à un arrangement/accord; **to be a ~ to a crime** être complice d'un crime **7.** *Am, inf* (*person*) type *m* **II.** <-ie-> *vi* faire la fête

party conference *n Brit* conférence *f* du parti **party congress** *n Am* congrès *m* du parti **partygoer** *n* fêtard(e) *m(f) inf* **party leader** *n* chef *m* de parti **party line** *n* **1.** (*shared phone connection*) ligne *f* téléphonique partagée **2.** (*policy on particular questions*) politique *f* du parti; **to toe the ~** obéir aux directions du parti **party political broadcast** *n Brit, Aus* émission *f* réservée à un parti politique **party politics** *n* politique *f* de parti **party pooper** *n Am, iron, inf* trouble-fête *mf*

parvenu ['pɑːvənjuː, *Am:* 'pɑːrvənuː] *n pej, form* parvenu(e) *m(f)*

pass [pɑːs, *Am:* pæs] **I.** <-es> *n* **1.** (*mountain road*) col *m* **2.** SPORT (*transfer of a ball*) passe *f;* **a ~ to sb** une passe à qn **3.** (*movement*) passage *m* **4.** *no pl* (*sexual advances, overture*) avance *f;* **to make a ~ at sb** faire des avances à qn **5.** *Brit* SCHOOL, UNIV (*successful exam result*) réussite *f;* **to get/obtain a ~ in an exam** être reçu à un examen; **a ~ degree** un diplôme sans mention **6.** (*authorisation permitting entry*) laisser-passer *m inv;* (*for public transport*) titre *m* de transport; **a bus ~** un abonnement **7.** *Am* UNIV, SCHOOL (*permit to leave class*) permission *f* **8.** *no pl* (*predicament, difficult state*) passe *f;* **to reach a ~** arriver à un tel point **II.** *vt* **1.** (*go past*) passer devant; AUTO dépasser **2.** (*exceed: point, level*) dépasser **3.** (*hand to*) **to ~ sth to sb** passer qc à qn; **to ~ sth across/through sth** faire passer qc au-dessus de/à travers qc; **to ~ sth around** faire passer qc **4.** (*accept*) approuver; (*student*) faire passer; **to be ~ed fit** être reconnu apte **5.** SPORT (*transfer to another player*) passer; **to ~ sth to sb** passer qc à qn **6.** (*be successful in: exam, test*) réussir **7.** (*occupy*) passer; **to ~ one's days/time doing sth** passer ses journées/son temps à faire qc; **to ~ the time** passer le temps **8.** POL (*officially approve: bill, law*) adopter **9.** (*utter, pronounce*) émettre; (*a comment, remark*) faire; **to ~ judgement on sb/sth** rendre un jugement sur qn/qc; **to ~ sentence on sb** LAW prononcer une condamnation contre qn **10.** *form* MED (*excrete*) **to ~ urine** [*o* **water**] uriner; **to ~ faeces** aller à la selle ►**to ~ the buck to sb/sth** *pej, inf* rejeter la responsabilité sur qn/qc **III.** *vi* **1.** (*move by, go away*) passer; **to ~ unnoticed** passer inaperçu; **to ~ across sth** traverser qc; **to ~ across sth** descendre qc; **to let sb ~** laisser passer qn **2.** (*enter*) passer; **to let a comment ~** laisser passer un commentaire; **to ~ into sth** passer dans qc **3.** (*overtake*) dépasser **4.** (*transfer*) **to ~ from sth to sth** passer de qc à qc; **to ~ from generation to generation** passer de génération en génération **5.** SPORT (*transfer ball*) faire une passe **6.** SCHOOL (*qualify*) être reçu; **to ~ the driving test** avoir son permis de conduire **7.** (*obtain majority approval: motion, resolution*) passer **8.** (*elapse: hours, evening, day*) passer **9.** (*transfer*) passer; **to ~ from sth to sth** passer de qc à qc; **sth ~es to sb** qc revient à qn **10.** *fig* (*not know the answer*) passer; **to ~ on a question** passer sur une question **11.** (*take place*) se passer **12.** (*disappear*) disparaître

◆**pass away** **I.** *vi* **1.** (*die*) décéder **2.** (*gradually fade*) disparaître **II.** *vt* (*time, hours*) passer

◆**pass by** **I.** *vi* **1.** (*elapse*) passer; **time passes by** le temps s'écoule **2.** (*go past*) passer (à côté) **II.** *vt* passer devant; **life passes sb by** qn passe à côté de la vie

◆**pass down** *vt* passer; (*songs, tradition*) transmettre; **to pass sth down from sb to sb** passer qc de qn à qn

◆**pass for** *vt* **he could ~ for an American** il passerait pour un Américain

◆**pass off** **I.** *vt* **to pass sb/sth off as sb/sth** faire passer qn/qc pour qn/qc; **to pass oneself off as sb/sth** se faire passer pour qn/qc **II.** *vi* **1.** (*take place successfully*) se passer **2.** (*fade away, wear off*) passer

◆**pass on** **I.** *vi* **1.** (*continue moving*) passer son chemin **2.** (*change subject*) **to ~ to sth** passer à qc **3.** (*die of natural cause*) décéder **II.** *vt* **1.** (*give after getting: information, virus, tips*) transmettre; **to pass sth on to sb** transmettre qc à qn **2.** (*hand down: stories, traditions, clothes*) transmettre **3.** ECON (*costs*) répercuter; **to be passed on to sb** se répercuter sur qn **4.** (*give to next person*) faire passer

◆**pass out** **I.** *vi* **1.** (*become unconscious*) perdre connaissance **2.** *Brit, Aus* (*graduate as an officer*) sortir **II.** *vt* (*distribute*) distribuer

◆**pass over** *vt* **to pass sb over** ignorer qn; **to ~ sth** passer qc sous silence; **to be passed over for promotion** ne pas se faire accorder de promotion

◆**pass through** **I.** *vt a. fig* traverser **II.** *vi* passer; (*bullet*) traverser

◆**pass up** *vt* laisser passer

passable ['pɑːsəbl, *Am:* 'pæsə-] *adj* **1.** (*traversable, unobstructed*) franchissable; (*motorway, pass, roads*) praticable **2.** (*average, fair: chess player, pianist*) passable

passage ['pæsɪdʒ] *n* **1.** (*act or process of moving through*) *a. fig* passage *m;* **~ through sth** passage dans qc; **the ~ of time** l'écoulement du temps **2.** (*journey*) voyage *m;* NAUT traversée *f* **3.** (*corridor*) passage *m* **4.** (*path*) corridor *m* **5.** (*duct*) *a.* MED conduit *m* **6.** LIT, MUS (*excerpt*) passage *m* **7.** (*transition*) passage *m;* **~ from sth to sth** passage de qc à qc **8.** POL (*of bill*) adoption *f*

passageway *n* passage *m*

passbook *n* livret *m* de caisse d'épargne

passenger ['pæsəndʒəʳ, *Am:* -əndʒɚ] *n* passager, -ère *m, f;* (*in public transport*) voyageur, -euse *m, f*

passenger aircraft *n* avion *m* de ligne **passenger car** *n* RAIL, AUTO voiture *f* de voyageurs **passenger coach** *n* voiture *f* de voyageurs **passenger list** *n* liste *f* des passagers **passenger mile** *n* kilomètre-passager *m* **passenger service** *n* service *m* voyageurs **passenger train** *n* train *m* de voyageurs

passer-by <passers-by> *n* passant(e) *m(f)*

passing **I.** *adj* **1.** (*going past*) qui passe; **a ~ car** une voiture qui passe; **with each ~ day** à chaque jour qui passe **2.** (*brief, fleeting, short-lived*) passager(-ère); (*glance*) furtif(-ive) **3.** (*unimportant, casual: remark, thought*) en passant **II.** *n no pl* **1.** (*passage*) passage *m;* (*of time*) écoulement *m* **2.** SPORT (*passes*) passe *f* **3.** (*end*) mort *f; fig* fin *f*

passing place *n* voie *f* de dédoublement

passion ['pæʃən] *n* passion *f;* **to have a ~ for sth** avoir la passion de qc; **to have a ~ for sb** aimer qn passionnément; **to have a ~ for doing sth** adorer faire qc; **sb's ~ for gambling** sa passion pour le jeu; **crime of ~** crime *m* passionnel; **to hate sb/sth with a ~** avoir horreur de qn/qc

passionate ['pæʃənət, *Am:* -ənɪt] *adj* passionné(e); (*relation, drama*) passionnel(le); **to be ~ about sth** être passionné au sujet de qc

passionflower *n* passiflore *f* **passion fruit** *n* fruit *m* de la passion

passionless *adj pej* sans passion

passive ['pæsɪv] **I.** *n no pl* LING passif *m;* **to put sth in the ~** mettre qc au passif **II.** *adj a.* LING passif(-ive); **a ~ verb** un verbe au passif; **the ~ voice** la forme passive

passiveness, **passivity** *n no pl* passivité *f*

passkey *n* passe-partout *m inv* **pass mark** *n Brit, Aus* moyenne *f;* **to get the ~** avoir la moyenne

Passover ['pɑːsəʊvəʳ, *Am:* 'pæsˌoʊvɚ] *n no pl, no art* Pâque *f* juive

passport ['pɑːspɔːt, *Am:* 'pæspɔːrt] *n* passeport *m;* **a ~ to sth** *fig* un passeport pour qc

passport control *n* contrôle *m* des passeports **passport holder** *n* détenteur, -trice *m, f* de passeport

password *n a.* INFOR mot *m* de passe; **to enter one's ~** entrer son mot de passe

past [pɑːst, *Am:* pæst] **I.** *n a.* LING passé *m;* **to be a thing of the ~** appartenir au passé; **sb with a ~** qn au passé chargé; **to write in the ~** écrire au passé **II.** *adj* **1.** (*being now over*) passé(e); **his ~ crimes** ses crimes; **the ~ week** la semaine dernière **2.** LING **~ tense** temps *m* du passé; **~ simple** prétérit *m;* **~ perfect** plus-que-parfait *m;* **~ participle** participe *m* passé **3.** (*bygone*) révolu(e); **in times ~** [*o* **~ times**] autrefois **4.** (*former*) ancien(ne); **Eve's ~ husband** l'ex-mari d'Eve **III.** *prep* **1.** (*temporal*) plus de; **ten/quarter ~ two** deux heures dix/et quart; **it's ~ 2 o'clock** il est 2 h passées; **to be ~ thirty** avoir plus de trente ans **2.** (*spatial*) plus loin que; **to go ~ the church** aller plus loin que l'église; **it's just ~ sth** c'est juste un peu plus loin que qc **3.** (*after*) **when we've got ~ the exams** après les examens; **he's ~ it** *pej, iron* il a passé l'âge **4.** (*beyond*) au-delà de; **~ belief/description** incroyable/indescriptible; **to be ~ the due/expiration date** être en souffrance/périmé; **to be ~ work** ne plus être en état de travailler; **I'm ~ caring** ça m'est égal; **I wouldn't put it ~ them** ils en sont bien capables **IV.** *adv* devant; **to run/swim ~** passer en courant/à la nage

pasta ['pæstə, *Am:* 'pɑːstə] *n no pl* pâtes *fpl*

paste [peɪst] **I.** *n no pl* **1.** (*sticky mixture*) pâte *f* **2.** (*adhesive substance*) colle *f* **3.** GASTR (*mixture*) pâte *f;* **anchovy ~** pâte d'anchois; **a beef ~** un pâté de viande; **a fish ~** une mousse de poisson; **a tomato ~** un concentré de tomates **4.** (*glass in jewellery*) pâte *f* de verre **II.** *vt* **1.** (*fasten, fix*) coller; **to ~ glue** appliquer de la colle **2.** INFOR (*insert with computer*) coller **3.** *inf* (*beat easily, thrash*) donner une raclée à

pasteboard ['peɪstbɔːd, *Am:* -bɔːrd] *n no pl* carton *m*

pastel ['pæstəl, *Am:* pæ'stel] **I.** *n* ART pastel *m* **II.** *adj* pastel *inv*

paste-up *n* collage *m*

pasteurization *n no pl* pasteurisation *f*

pasteurize ['pæstʃəraɪz] *vt* pasteuriser

pastime ['pɑːstaɪm, *Am:* 'pæs-] *n* passe-temps *m*

past master *n* **to be a ~ at doing sth** avoir le don de faire qc

pastor ['pɑːstəʳ, *Am:* 'pæstɚ] *n* pasteur *m*

pastoral *adj* pastoral(e); ~ **work** *Brit* travail *m* d'écoute et de soutien

past perfect (**tense**) *n* LING plus-que-parfait *m*

pastry ['peɪstri] <-ries> *n* **1.** *no pl* GASTR (*cake dough*) pâte *f* **2.** GASTR (*cake*) pâtisserie *f*

pastry cook *n* pâtissier, -ière *m, f*

pasture ['pɑːstʃəʳ, *Am:* 'pæstʃɚ] *n* AGR pâture *f;* ~**s new** *Brit,* **new** ~**s** *Am, fig* nouveaux horizons *mpl;* **to put sth out to** ~ mettre qc en pâture; **to put sb out to** ~ *fig, inf* mettre qn à la retraite

pasture land *n* pâturages *mpl*

pasty[1] ['pæsti] *n* pâté *m;* **beef** ~ pâté de viande

pasty[2] ['peɪsti] <-ier, -iest> *adj pej* pâteux(-euse); (*skin, complexion*) terreux(-euse)

pat[1] [pæt] **I.** <-tt-> *vt* (*tap*) tapoter; **to** ~ **sb on the head** tapoter la tête de qn; **to** ~ **sb on the back** *fig* féliciter qn **II.** *n* **1.** (*gentle stroke, tap*) petite tape *f;* **to give sb/sth a** ~ donner une petite tape à qn/qc **2.** (*little quantity: of butter*) rondelle *f*

pat[2] [pæt] *pej* **I.** *adj* facile; **a** ~ **answer** une réponse toute prête **II.** *adv* **to have an answer off** [*o Am* **down**] **down** ~ avoir une réponse toute prête; **to know sth off** ~ connaître qc par cœur

patch [pætʃ] **I.** *n* **1.** (*small area*) pièce *f;* **a fog** ~ une nappe de brouillard; **an ice** ~ une plaque de gel; **a** ~ **of ground** un bout de terrain; **a** ~ **of blue sky** un morceau de ciel bleu **2.** *Brit, inf* (*phase*) période *f;* **to go through a bad** ~ passer par un moment difficile **3.** (*area for work*) secteur *m* **4.** (*repair piece*) pièce *f;* (*for tyre*) rustine *f* **5.** (*cover for eye*) cache *m* **6.** MED (*piece of fabric*) patch *m* ►**to be not a** ~ **on sb/sth else** *Brit, Aus, inf* ne pas arriver à la cheville de qn/qc **II.** *vt* (*cover, reinforce, sew up*) rapiécer; **to** ~ **a tyre** poser une rustine sur une roue

◆**patch up** *vt* **1.** (*renovate, restore, mend*) rafistoler **2.** *fig* (*settle: differences*) régler; **they've patched things up between them** ils se sont racommodés

patchwork ['pætʃwɜːk, *Am:* -wɜːrk] **I.** *n no pl, a. fig* patchwork *m* **II.** *adj* en patchwork

patchy ['pætʃi] <-ier, -iest> *adj* (*quality, performance*) inégal(e)

pâté ['pæteɪ, *Am:* pɑː'teɪ] *n* (*of meat*) pâté *m;* (*of fish*) mousse *f*

patent ['peɪtənt, *Am:* 'pætənt] **I.** *n* LAW brevet *m;* **to take out a** ~ **on sth** faire breveter qc **II.** *adj* **1.** (*protected under a patent*) breveté(e) **2.** *form* (*evident, unmistakable*) manifeste **3.** FASHION (*polished: handbag, jacket, shoes*) verni(e) **III.** *vt* breveter

patented *adj* breveté(e)

patentee [ˌpeɪtən'tiː, *Am:* ˌpætən'tiː] *n* détenteur, -trice *m, f* de brevet

patent leather *n* cuir *m* verni **patent office** *n* institut *m* de la propriété industrielle

paternal [pə'tɜːnəl, *Am:* -'tɜːr-] *adj* paternel(le)

paternalism [pə'tɜːnəlɪzəm, *Am:* -'tɜːr-] *n no pl, pej* paternalisme *m*

paternalistic *adj pej* paternaliste

paternity [pə'tɜːnəti, *Am:* -'tɜːrnəṭi] *n no pl, a. fig, form* paternité *f*

paternity leave *n* congé *m* parental **paternity suit** *n* action *f* en recherche de paternité

path [pɑːθ, *Am:* pæθ] *n* **1.** (*footway, trail*) *a.* INFOR chemin *m;* (*of a garden*) allée *f;* **the** ~ **to sth** le chemin vers qc; **to clear a** ~ dégager une voie **2.** (*direction*) trajet *m;* (*of a bullet, missile*) trajectoire *f;* **of a storm** passage *m;* **to block somebody's** ~ bloquer le passage de qn **3.** *fig* voie *f;* **the** ~ **of his career** son itinéraire de carrière; **to choose the** ~ **of sth** choisir la voie de qc; **the** ~ **to success** le chemin de la gloire

pathetic [pə'θetɪk, *Am:* -'θeṭ-] *adj* **1.** (*sad*) pathétique **2.** (*not good*) lamentable

pathfinder ['pɑːθfaɪndəʳ, *Am:* 'pæθˌfaɪndɚ] *n* éclaireur, -euse *m, f*

pathological *adj* pathologique

pathologist *n* pathologiste *mf;* LAW médecin *m* légiste

pathology [pə'θɒlədʒi, *Am:* -'θɑːlə-] *n a. fig* pathologie *f*

pathos ['peɪθɒs, *Am:* -θɑːs] *n* pathétique *m*

pathway ['pɑːθweɪ, *Am:* 'pæθ-] *n a. fig* sentier *m*

patience ['peɪʃns] *n no pl* **1.** (*tolerance*) patience *f;* **to have** ~ **with sb/sth** faire preuve de patience avec qn/qc; **to have infinite** ~ avoir une patience infinie; **to lose one's** ~ perdre patience; **to try sb's** ~ mettre la patience de qn à l'épreuve **2.** *Brit, Aus* GAMES jeu *m* de patience

patient **I.** *adj* patient(e); **to be** ~ **with sb** être patient avec qn; **just be** ~**!** sois patient! **II.** *n* MED patient(e) *m(f)*

patina ['pætɪnə, *Am:* -ənə] *n no pl, a. fig* patine *f*

patio ['pætɪəʊ, *Am:* 'pæṭɪoʊ] <-s> *n* patio *m*

patio door *n* porte *f* vitrée

patriarch ['peɪtrɪɑːk, *Am:* -ɑːrk] *n a. fig* patriarche *m*

patriarchal *adj* patriarcal(e)

patriarchy <-ies> *n* patriarcat *m*

patrician [pə'trɪʃən] **I.** *n* patricien(ne) *m(f)* **II.** *adj* patricien(ne)

patriot ['peɪtrɪət] *n* patriote *mf*

patriotic *adj* patriotique; (*person*) patriote

patriotism *n no pl* patriotisme *m*

patrol [pə'trəʊl, *Am:* -'troʊl] **I.** <-ll-> *vi* patrouiller **II.** <-ll-> *vt* patrouiller dans **III.** *n* patrouille *f;* **to be on** ~ être de patrouille

patrol car *n* voiture *f* de police **patrolman**

n Am agent *m* de police (en patrouille) **patrol wagon** *n Am* voiture *f* de police

patron ['peɪtrən] *n* **1.** *form* (*customer*) client(e) *m(f)* **2.** (*benefactor of charity*) patron(ne) *m(f)*; ~ **of the arts** mécène *m*

patronage ['pætrənɪdʒ, *Am:* 'peɪtrən-] *n no pl* **1.** (*support of a cause*) patronage *m* **2.** (*sponsorship*) parrainage *m* **3.** *form* ECON (*trade given by customer*) clientèle *f* **4.** *pej* POL népotisme *m*

patronize ['pætrənaɪz, *Am:* 'peɪtrən-] *vt Am* **1.** *form* (*regularly be a customer of*) fréquenter **2.** *pej* (*treat condescendingly, underrate*) **to ~ sb** traiter qn avec condescendance

patronizing *adj pej* condescendant(e)

> L'Angleterre, l'Écosse, le pays de Galles et l'Irelande, ont leurs propres **patron saints** (saints patrons). "St George" d'Angleterre est célébré le 23 avril; "St Patrick" d'Irlande, le 17 mars (jour férié); "St Andrew" d'Écosse, le 30 novembre (l'apôtre André fut crucifié sur une croix en forme d'X, d'où la croix blanche de St Andrew - "St Andrew's cross" ou "saltire" - sur le drapeau bleu écossais) et "St David" du pays de Galles est fêté le 1er mars.

patter[1] ['pætəʳ, *Am:* -t̬ɚ] *n no pl* (*clever, fast talk*) baratin *m*

patter[2] ['pætəʳ, *Am:* -t̬ɚ] **I.** *n no pl* (*sound*) petit bruit *m;* (*of rain*) crépitement *m* ▸**they'll be hearing the ~ of tiny feet** ils attendent un heureux événement **II.** *vi* **1.** (*walk lightly using small steps*) trottiner **2.** (*cause soft sound: rain*) crépiter

pattern **I.** *n* **1.** (*identifiable structure*) schéma *m;* **on the usual ~** selon le schéma habituel; **~s of activity/behaviour** modes d'activité/de comportement; **a ~ of living** un mode de vie **2.** ART (*design, motif*) motif *m;* **a chevron ~** un chevron **3.** FASHION (*paper guide for dressmaking*) patron *m* **4.** (*sample of textiles, paper*) échantillon *m* **5.** *no pl* (*example, model, norm*) modèle *m;* **on the ~ of sb/sth** sur l'exemple de qn/qc **II.** *vt* **1.** (*give form*) modeler **2.** (*decorate*) orner

pattern book *n* catalogue *m* d'échantillons

patterned *adj* à motifs

paunch [pɔːntʃ, *Am:* pɑːntʃ] *n* panse *f*

paunchy <-ier, -iest> *adj* bedonnant(e)

pauper ['pɔːpəʳ, *Am:* 'pɑːpɚ] *n* indigent(e) *m(f);* **~'s grave** fosse *f* commune

pause [pɔːz, *Am:* pɑːz] **I.** *n* pause *f* ▸**to give sb ~** *form* donner à réfléchir à qn **II.** *vi* faire une pause; **to ~ for thought** prendre une pause pour réfléchir

pave [peɪv] *vt a. fig* paver; **to be ~d with sth** être pavé de qc; **to ~ the way for sth** ouvrir la voie à qc

pavement *n* **1.** (*paved footway beside roads*) trottoir *m* **2.** *Am, Aus* (*highway covering*) chaussée *f*

pavement artist *n* artiste *mf* des rues

pavilion [pəˈvɪljən] *n* pavillon *m*

paving *n no pl* **1.** (*paved space*) pavage *m* **2.** (*material used to pave*) dallage *m*

paving stone *n Brit* pavé *m*

paw [pɔː, *Am:* pɑː] **I.** *n a. iron, a. inf* patte *f* **II.** *vt* **1.** (*strike with the paw*) donner un coup de patte à **2.** *pej, inf* (*touch in an offensive way*) tripoter **III.** *vi* donner des coups de pattes

pawn[1] *n* GAMES *a. fig* pion *m;* **to be a ~ in the game** n'être qu'un pion sur l'échiquier

pawn[2] **I.** *vt* **to ~ sth** mettre qc en gage **II.** *n* gage *m;* **to be in ~** être en gage

pawnbroker *n* prêteur, -euse *m, f* sur gages

pawnbroker's shop, **pawn shop** *n* mont-de-piété *m*

pay [peɪ] **I.** *n* paie *f;* **to be in the ~ of sb/sth** être à la solde de qn/qc **II.** <paid, paid> *vt* **1.** (*give money*) payer; **to ~ sb $500** payer qn 500$; **to ~ sb for sth** payer qn pour qc; **to ~ cash/dollars** payer en liquide/en dollars; **to ~ a refund** effectuer un remboursement; **to ~ sth into an account** verser qc sur un compte; **to ~ sb to** +*infin* payer qc pour +*infin;* **to ~ a salary** verser un salaire; **to ~ sb poorly** mal payer qn; **to ~ one's debts** payer ses dettes; **to ~ a loan** rembourser un prêt; **to ~ one's way** payer sa part; **to ~ five dollars an hour** payer cinq dollars de l'heure; **to ~ the price** *fig* payer le prix **2.** (*benefit, be worthwhile, repay*) rapporter; **to ~ sb sth** rapporter qc à qn; **to ~ dividends** *fig* porter ses fruits **3.** (*give*) **to ~ attention to sth** prêter attention à qc; **to ~ a call on sb**, **to ~ sb a call** rendre visite à qn; **to ~ sb a compliment** faire un compliment à qn; **to ~ homage to sb/sth** rendre hommage à qn/qc; **to ~ one's respects to sb** présenter ses respects à qn ▸**he who ~s the piper calls the tune** *prov* quelqu'un qui paye a bien le droit de choisir; **to put paid to sth** *Brit, Aus, fig* mettre qc à terre **III.** <paid, paid> *vi* **1.** (*settle, recompense*) payer; **to ~ by cash** payer en liquide; **to ~ by cheque/credit card** payer par chèque/carte de crédit **2.** (*suffer*) payer; **to ~ with one's life** *fig* payer de sa vie **3.** (*benefit, be worthwhile*) rapporter; **insulation ~s for itself** l'isolation fait économiser ce qu'elle coûte; **it ~s to** +*infin* ça rapporte de +*infin;* **it doesn't ~ to** +*infin* ce n'est pas rentable de +*infin;* **to ~ through the nose for sth** *inf* payer le prix fort pour qc

◆**pay back** *vt* **1.** (*return money*) rembourser; **to pay sb sth back** rembourser qc à qn **2.** (*get revenge*) **to pay sb back for sth** faire payer qc à qn

◆**pay for** *vt* (*goods*) payer; (*crime*) payer pour

◆**pay in** *vt* (*money*) verser

◆**pay off** **I.** *vt* **1.** (*pay: debt, creditor*) rembourser **2.** (*make redundant*) licencier ▸**to ~ old scores** régler un vieux compte **II.** *vi fig* payer

◆**pay out** **I.** *vt* **1.** (*expend, spend money*) payer **2.** (*unwind: rope*) laisser filer **3.** (*retali-*

P

ate against) **to pay sb out** faire payer qn; **to ~ sb for doing sth** faire payer qn d'avoir fait qc **II.** *vi* payer

◆pay up *vi* payer

payable *adj* payable; ~ **to sb/sth** à la charge de qn/qc; **to make a cheque ~ to sb/sth** faire un chèque à l'ordre de qn/qc; ~ **at sight** payable à vue

pay-as-you-earn, Pay As You Earn *n Brit* retenue *f* à la source de l'impôt sur le revenu

paycheck *n Am,* **paycheque** *n Brit* chèque *m* de fin de mois **payday** *n no pl* jour *m* de paie **pay desk** *n* caisse *f*

PAYE [ˌpiːeɪwaɪ'iː] *n no pl, Brit abbr of* **Pay As You Earn** retenue *f* à la source

payee [peɪ'iː] *n* bénéficiaire *mf*

payer *n* payeur, -euse *m, f*

pay freeze *n* gel *m* des salaires **pay hike** *n Am* augmentation *f* des salaires

paying *adj* **1.** (*who pays*) payant(e) **2.** (*profitable*) rentable; **a ~ proposition** une bonne affaire

paying guest *n* pensionnaire *m*

paymaster *n* **1.** MIL trésorier, -ière *m, f* **2.** *pej* (*sponsor*) commanditaire *m*

payment *n* **1.** (*sum paid*) paiement *m* **2.** (*repayment*) remboursement *m;* **30 easy ~s** 30 versements *mpl* par traites **3.** (*reward*) récompense *f*

pay negotiations *n* négociations *fpl* salariales **pay-off** *n* **1.** (*bribe*) pot-de-vin *m;* **to receive a ~ from sb** percevoir un pot-de-vin de qn **2.** *inf* (*positive result*) fruit *m* **3.** (*profit on a bet*) récompense *f* **4.** (*leaving payment*) indemnités *fpl* (de départ) **pay office** *n* bureau *m* de paie **payout** *n* FIN remboursement *m* **pay phone** *n* téléphone *m* à pièces **pay raise, pay rise** *n* augmentation *f* de salaire **payroll** *n* **1.** (*list of wages payable*) traitements et salaires *mpl;* **a monthly ~** une paie mensuelle **2.** (*list of employees*) effectif *m;* **to be on the ~** être employé **pay settlement** *n* accord *m* salarial **payslip** *n* feuille *f* de paie **pay TV** *n* télévision *f* à la carte

PC [ˌpiː'siː] **I.** *n* **1.** *abbr of* **Police Constable** agent *m* de police **2.** INFOR *abbr of* **Personal Computer** PC *m* **II.** *adj Am abbr of* **politically correct** politiquement correct(e)

p. c. *abbr of* **per cent** pour cent

PE [ˌpiː'iː] *no pl n abbr of* **physical education** EPS *f*

pea [piː] *n* petit pois *m* ▸**to be like two ~s in a pod** se ressembler comme deux gouttes d'eau

peace [piːs] *n no pl a. fig* paix *f;* ~ **activist** activiste *mf* pacifiste; ~ **enforcement troops** troupes *fpl* pour le maintien de la paix; ~ **conference/negotiations** conférence *f*/négociations *fpl* pour la paix; **to make ~** faire la paix; **to be at ~** (*countries*) être en paix; (*deceased*) reposer en paix; **to be at ~ with the world** ne pas avoir le moindre souci; **to keep/disturb the ~** veiller à/troubler l'ordre public; **to make one's ~ with sb** faire la paix avec qn; **to leave sb/sth in ~** laisser qn/qc en paix; **I'd like a bit of ~ now** je voudrais un peu de calme maintenant; **to give sb no ~** ne pas laisser de répit à qn ▸**to hold one's ~** garder le silence; **to smoke the ~ pipe** fumer le calumet de la paix

peaceable, peaceful *adj* **1.** (*non-violent*) pacifique **2.** (*quiet*) paisible

peacekeeping **I.** *n no pl* pacification *f* **II.** *adj* de pacification; ~ **force** forces *fpl* de maintien de la paix **peace-loving** *adj* pacifique **peacemaker** *n* pacificateur, -trice *m, f* **peacemaking** *n* pacification *f* **peace movement** *n* mouvement *m* pour la paix **peacetime** *n no pl* temps *m* de paix **peace treaty** *n* traité *m* de paix

peach [piːtʃ] **I.** <-es> *n* **1.** (*sweet, yellow fruit*) pêche *f;* ~ **tree** pêcher *m* **2.** *inf* (*nice*) chou(te) *m(f);* **a ~ of an evening** une super soirée **II.** *adj* (*colour*) pêche *inv*

peacock ['piːkɒk, *Am:* -kɑːk] *n* paon *m*

pea green *n no pl* vert *m* pomme

peak [piːk] **I.** *n* **1.** (*mountain top*) pic *m;* **to reach the ~** atteindre le sommet **2.** (*climax*) sommet *m;* (*in a period*) moment *m* le plus fort; (*of a trend*) apogée *f;* **to be at the ~ of one's career** être au sommet de sa carrière **3.** *Brit* (*hat part*) visière *f* **II.** *vi* (*sb's career*) être à son sommet; (*athletes*) atteindre un record; (*figures, rates, production*) atteindre son niveau maximum **III.** *adj* **1.** (*the busiest*) ~ **hours** heures *fpl* de pointe **2.** (*the best, highest: speed, capacity*) maximal(e); (*demand*) record; (*season*) haut(e); **in ~ condition** dans le meilleur état; **in ~ periods** pendant les périodes de pointe; ~ **time viewing** heures de pointe d'écoute

peaked *adj* **1.** (*pointed, having a peak*) pointu(e) **2.** *Am* (*tired or sick*) souffrant(e)

peak hours *npl* heures *fpl* de pointe

peaky *adj Brit* fatigué(e); **to feel/look ~** se sentir/avoir l'air fatigué

peal [piːl] **I.** *n* (*of bells*) carillon *m;* (*of thunder*) grondement *m;* **~s of laughter** éclats *mpl* de rire **II.** *vi* (*thunderstorm*) gronder; (*bells*) carillonner; **to ~ with laughter** éclater de rire

peanut ['piːnʌt] *n* cacahuète *f,* pinotte *f Québec;* ~ **oil/butter** huile *f*/beurre *m* de cacahuètes ▸**to pay ~s** payer des clopinettes

pear [peəʳ, *Am:* per] *n* poire *f;* ~ **tree** poirier *m*

pearl [pɜːl, *Am:* pɜːrl] *n a. fig* perle *f;* **to be a ~** être une perle; ~ **necklace** collier *m* de perles; **cultured ~s** perles de culture; ~ **button** bouton *m* de nacre; ~ **of dew** perle de rosée; **~s of wisdom** *fig* propos édifiants; ~ **grey** gris *m* perle ▸**to be a ~ of great price** *prov* ne pas avoir de prix; **to cast one's ~s before swine** *prov* jeter des perles aux cochons *prov*

pearly <-ier, -iest> *adj* **1.** (*made of pearl*) de

perles **2.** (*pearl-colored*) nacré(e)
peasant ['pezənt] *n* paysan(ne) *m(f)*
peat [pi:t] *n no pl* tourbe *f*
pebble ['pebl] *n* galet *m*
pebbly ['pebli] *adj* caillouteux(-euse)
pecan [pɪ'kæn, *Am:* pɪ'kɑ:n] *n* pécan *m;* ~ **nut** noix *f* de pécan; ~ **tree** pacanier *m*
peccadillo [ˌpekə'dɪləʊ, *Am:* -oʊ] <-s *o* -oes> *n* peccadille *f*
peck [pek] **I.** *n* **1.** (*bite made by a beak*) coup *m* de bec **2.** (*quick kiss*) bécot *n;* **to give sb a** ~ faire un bécot à qn **II.** *vt* **1.** (*bite with a beak*) becqueter **2.** (*strike with beak*) donner un coup de bec à; **to** ~ **holes in sth** faire un trou à coups de bec dans qc; **to** ~ **sth out** arracher qc avec le bec **3.** (*eat*) becqueter; (*food*) picorer **4.** (*kiss quickly*) bécoter **III.** *vi* **1.** (*bite with one's beak*) becqueter; **to** ~ **at sth** becqueter qc **2.** (*nibble at*) picorer; **to** ~ **at one's food** *inf* picorer sa nourriture **3.** (*kiss*) se bécoter
pecking order *n* ordre *m* hiérarchique
peckish ['pekɪʃ] *adj* **1.** *Brit, Aus* (*slightly hungry*) **to feel rather** ~ avoir une petite faim **2.** *Am* (*irritable*) irascible
pectin ['pektɪn] *n no pl* pectine *f*
peculiar [pɪ'kju:lɪər, *Am:* -'kju:ljɚ] *adj* **1.** (*strange, unusual*) étrange; **to be/seem a little** ~ **to sb** être/paraître un peu étrange à qn **2.** (*sick, nauseous*) bizarre; **to feel a little** ~ se sentir un peu bizarre **3.** (*belonging to, special*) particulier(-ère); **to be** ~ **to sb** être particulier à qn; **of** ~ **interest** d'un intérêt particulier
peculiarity [pɪˌkju:lɪ'ærəti, *Am:* -'erət̬i] <-ties> *n* **1.** (*strangeness*) étrangeté *f* **2.** (*strange habit*) bizarrerie *f* **3.** (*idiosyncrasy*) particularité *f*
peculiarly *adv* **1.** (*strangely*) étrangement **2.** (*belonging to, especially*) particulièrement
pecuniary [pɪ'kju:nɪəri, *Am:* -eri] *adj form* pécuniaire
pedagogic(al) *adj* pédagogique
pedagogue ['pedəgɒg, *Am:* -gɑ:g] *n* pédagogue *mf*
pedagogy ['pedəgɒdʒi, *Am:* -gɑ:dʒi] *n no pl* pédagogie *f*
pedal ['pedəl] **I.** *n* pédale *f* **II.** <*Brit, Aus* -ll- *o Am* -l-> *vi* pédaler **III.** *vt* **to** ~ **a bike** faire du vélo
pedal boat *n* pédalo *m*
pedalo® ['pedələʊ, *Am:* -oʊ] *n* pédalo *m*
pedant ['pedənt] *n pej* pédant(e) *m(f)*
pedantic *adj pej* pédant(e)
pedantry <-tries> *n pej* pédanterie *f*
peddle ['pedl] *vt pej* colporter; **to** ~ **drugs** faire du trafic de drogue
peddler *n Am s.* **pedlar**
pederast ['pedəræst] *n Am* pédéraste *m*
pederasty *n no pl* pédérastie *f*
pedestal ['pedɪstəl] *n* piédestal *m* ►**to knock sb off their** ~ faire tomber qn de son piédestal; **to put sb on a** ~ mettre qn sur un piédestal
pedestrian **I.** *n* piéton(ne) *m(f)* **II.** *adj* **1.** (*for walkers*) piéton(ne) **2.** *form* (*uninteresting, dull*) prosaïque **pedestrian crossing** *n* passage *m* piéton
pedestrianise *vt Aus, Brit,* **pedestrianize** *vt* transformer en zone piétonne
pedestrian precinct *n* zone *f* piétonne
pediatrician *n Am s.* **paediatrician**
pediatrics *n Am s.* **paediatrics**
pedicure ['pedɪkjʊər, *Am:* -kjʊr] *n* pédicure *f*
pedicurist *n* pédicure *mf*
pedigree ['pedɪgri:] *n* **1.** (*genealogy: of an animal*) pedigree *m;* (*of a person*) ascendance *f;* ~ **dog** chien *m* de race **2.** (*educational, professional background*) antécédents *mpl* **3.** (*history, background*) histoire *f*
pedlar ['pedlər, *Am:* -lɚ] *n Brit, Aus* **1.** *pej* (*spreader of ideas*) colporteur, -euse *m, f* **2.** *Brit, Aus* (*drug dealer*) revendeur, -euse *m, f* **3.** (*travelling salesman*) colporteur, -euse *m, f*
pedophile ['pi:dəʊfaɪl] *n Am s.* **paedophile**
pee [pi:] *inf* **I.** *n no pl* pipi *m;* **to have** [*o* **do**] **a** ~ faire pipi; **to go** ~ *Am, childspeak* aller faire pipi **II.** *vi* faire pipi **III.** *vt* (*one's pants*) mouiller; **to** ~ **oneself** se mouiller
peek [pi:k] **I.** *n* coup *m* d'œil; **to take a** ~ **at sb/sth** jeter un coup d'œil sur qn/qc **II.** *vi* jeter un coup d'œil furtif; **to** ~ **in/over sth** jeter un coup d'œil dans/par-dessus qc
peel [pi:l] **I.** *n* pelure *f* **II.** *vt* peler; (*fruit, vegetables*) éplucher; **to** ~ **off wallpaper** décoller le papier peint; **to** ~ **the wrapping from sth** enlever l'emballage de qc; ~**ed prawns** crevettes décortiquées ►**to keep one's eyes** ~**ed for sth** *inf* faire gaffe à qc **III.** *vi* (*skin*) peler; (*paint*) s'écailler; (*wallpaper*) se décoller
◆**peel away** *vt* décoller; (*fruit, skin*) peler
◆**peel off** **I.** *vt* enlever; **to** ~ **an adhesive strip** décoller un ruban adhésif; **to peel the paper off sth** enlever le papier de qc; **to peel wallpaper off** décoller le papier peint **II.** *vi* **1.** (*come off*) se décoller **2.** (*veer away: car, motorbike*) s'écarter
peeler *n* éplucheur *m*
peelings *npl* épluchures *fpl*
peep¹ [pi:p] **I.** *n* **1.** (*answer, utterance*) bruit *m;* **not to raise a** ~ ne pas souffler mot; **to not give a** ~ ne pas broncher *inf;* **one more** ~ **out of you** encore un mot; **we didn't hear a** ~ **from him** il n'a pas émis le moindre son **2.** (*tiny bird sound*) pépiement *m;* **to make a** ~ pépier **II.** *vi* pépier
peep² [pi:p] **I.** *n* coup *m* d'œil; **to have a** ~ **at sth** regarder furtivement qc; **to get a** ~ **at sth** voir qc rapidement; **a** ~ **of light** un rayon de lumière; **with the first** ~ **of spring** avec les premiers signes du printemps **II.** *vi* **1.** (*look quickly, look secretly*) **to** ~ **at sb/sth** jeter un coup d'œil sur qn/qc; **to** ~ **into/through sth** jeter un coup d'œil à l'intérieur de/à travers qc **2.** (*appear, come partly out*) sortir
peephole ['pi:phəʊl, *Am:* -hoʊl] *n* judas *m*

peer¹ [pɪəʳ, *Am:* pɪr] *vi* regarder; **to ~ into the distance** scruter au loin

peer² [pɪəʳ, *Am:* pɪr] *n* pair *m;* ~ **group** pairs *mpl;* **to have no ~s** être hors pair; **to be liked by one's ~s** être aimé de ses pairs

peerage ['pɪərɪdʒ, *Am:* 'pɪrɪdʒ] *n no pl, Brit* noblesse *f;* **to be given a ~** recevoir le titre de pair

peerless *adj form* hors pair

peeved [pi:vd] *adj inf* **to be ~ at sb for sth** être en rogne envers qn à cause de qc

peevish ['pi:vɪʃ] *adj* grincheux(-euse)

peewit ['pi:wɪt] *n s.* **pewit**

peg [peg] **I.** *n* (*small hook*) piquet *m;* (*for clothes*) pince *f* à linge; (*of a violin, guitar*) cheville *f* ▶**to buy off the ~** acheter du prêt-à-porter; **to take sb down a ~ or two** remettre qn à sa place; **to use sth as a ~ to hang sth on** prendre qc comme prétexte à qc **II.** <-gg-> *vt* **1.** (*fix*) fixer (avec des piquets) **2.** (*hold at certain level*) maintenir **3.** (*guess correctly*) deviner

◆**peg out I.** *vt* **1.** (*hang out: laundry*) étendre **2.** (*mark*) délimiter **II.** *vi Aus, Brit* **1.** *inf* (*die*) crever **2.** (*stop working: car, machine*) lâcher

peg-leg *n inf* jambe *f* de bois

pejorative [pɪ'dʒɒrətɪv, *Am:* -'dʒɔ:rət̬ɪv] *adj form* péjoratif(-ive)

peke *inf,* **pekin(g)ese** [ˌpi:kɪŋ'i:z] **I.** <-(s)> *n Brit* pékinois *m* **II.** *adj* **a ~ dog** un chien pékinois

pelican ['pelɪkən] *n* pélican *m*

pellet ['pelɪt] *n* **1.** (*small, hard ball*) boulette *f;* (*of animal feed*) granulé *m* **2.** (*animal excrement*) crotte *f* **3.** (*gunshot*) plomb *m*

pelt¹ [pelt] *n* **1.** (*animal skin*) peau *f* **2.** (*fur*) fourrure *f*

pelt² [pelt] **I.** *n no pl* **at full ~** à toute vitesse **II.** *vt* **to ~ sb with sth** bombarder qn de qc; **to ~ sb with insults** couvrir qn d'insultes **III.** *vi* **1.** *impers* (*rain heavily*) **it's ~ing down** il pleut des cordes **2.** (*run, hurry*) courir à toutes jambes; **to ~ across the yard** traverser la cour à toutes jambes

pen¹ [pen] **I.** *n* **1.** (*writing instrument*) stylo *m;* **to live by one's ~** vivre de sa plume; **to put ~ to paper** écrire; **to write in ~** écrire au stylo **2.** (*quill*) plume *f* ▶**the ~ is mightier than the sword** *prov* la plume est plus tranchante que l'épée **II.** <-nn-> *vt* (*letter*) écrire

pen² [pen] **I.** *n* parc *m;* **pig ~** porcherie *f* **II.** <-nn-> *vt* parquer

penal ['pi:nəl] *adj* (*code*) pénal(e); (*institution*) pénitentiaire

penalize ['pi:nəlaɪz] *vt* sanctionner

penalty ['penəlti, *Am:* -t̬i] <-ties> *n* **1.** LAW peine *f* **2.** (*punishment*) pénalité *f* **3.** (*disadvantage*) inconvénient *m* **4.** (*fine, extra charge*) amende *f* **5.** SPORT penalty *m*

penance ['penəns] *n no pl* pénitence *f;* **to do ~ for sth** faire pénitence de qc

pence [pens] *n pl of* **penny**

penchant ['pɑ:nʃɑ:n, *Am:* 'pentʃənt] *n pej* penchant *m;* **his ~ for smoking cigars** son faible pour les cigares

pencil ['pentsəl] **I.** *n* **1.** (*writing instrument*) crayon *m;* ~ **drawing** dessin *m* au crayon; **coloured ~** crayon *m* de couleur; **in ~** au crayon **2.** (*thin line: of light*) trait *m;* **~-thin** mince comme un fil **II.** <*Brit* -ll- *o Am* -l-> *vt* écrire au crayon

◆**pencil in** *vt* (*date, appointment*) noter comme possible

pencil box *n* plumier *m* **pencil case** *n* trousse *f* **pencil sharpener** *n* taille-crayon *m*

pendant ['pendənt] *n* pendentif *m*

pending ['pendɪŋ] **I.** *adj* **1.** (*awaiting*) en suspens **2.** LAW en instance **II.** *prep form* en attendant

pendulum ['pendjələm, *Am:* -dʒələm] *n* pendule *m*

penetrate ['penɪtreɪt] *vt* pénétrer

penetrating *adj* pénétrant(e); (*analysis, mind, person*) perspicace

penetration *n* pénétration *f*

penfriend *n* correspondant(e) *m(f)*

penguin ['peŋgwɪn] *n* pingouin *m*

penholder ['penˌhəʊldəʳ, *Am:* -ˌhoʊldɚ] *n* porte-plume *m*

penicillin [ˌpenɪ'sɪlɪn] *n* pénicilline *f*

peninsula [pə'nɪnsjʊlə, *Am:* -sələ] *n* péninsule *f*

peninsular *adj* péninsulaire

penis ['pi:nɪs] <-nises *o* -nes> *n* pénis *m*

penitence ['penɪtəns] *n no pl* **1.** (*repentant feelings, repentance*) repentir *m* **2.** REL pénitence *f*

penitent I. *n* pénitent(e) *m(f)* **II.** *adj form* pénitent(e)

penitential *adj* pénitentiel(le)

penitentiary [ˌpenɪ'tentʃəri] *n Am* pénitencier *m*

penknife ['pennaɪf] <-knives> *n* canif *m*

pen name *n* nom *m* de plume

pennant ['penənt] *n* fanion *m*

penniless *adj* sans le sou

Pennsylvania [pensɪl'veɪniə] **I.** *n* la Pennsylvanie **II.** *adj inv* de Pennsylvanie

penny ['peni] <-ies *o Brit* pence> *n* **1.** <pence> (*value*) penny *m;* **I don't get a ~ in royalties** je ne reçois pas un sou de droits d'auteur **2.** <-ies> (*coin*) penny *m* ▶**the ~ (has) dropped!** ça a fait tilt!; **a ~ for your thoughts** à quoi penses-tu?; **two** [*o* **ten**] **a ~** treize à la douzaine

penny-pinching *adj* grippe-sou

pen pal *n s.* **penfriend**

pension ['pentʃən] **I.** *n* **1.** (*payment*) pension *f* **2.** (*retirement money*) retraite *f;* **to draw a ~** toucher une retraite; **to live on a ~** vivre de sa retraite; **to retire on a ~** percevoir une pension **3.** (*boarding house*) pension *f* **II.** *vt* **to ~ sb off, to ~ off sb** mettre qn à la retraite

pensionable *adj Brit* **to be of ~ age** avoir l'âge de la retraite

pensioner *n Brit* retraité(e) *m(f)*, bénéficiaire *mf* d'une retraite *Suisse;* **activities for ~s** activités pour le troisième âge

pension fund *n* assurance *f* vieillesse **pension scheme** *n* plan *m* de retraite

pensive ['pentsɪv] *adj* pensif(-ive); (*silence*) méditatif(-ive)

pentagon ['pentəgən, *Am:* -t̬əgɑːn] *n* pentagone *m;* **the Pentagon** le Pentagone

Pentecost ['pentəkɒst, *Am:* -t̬ɪkɑːst] *n no pl* Pentecôte *f*

penthouse ['penthaʊs] *n appartement luxueux au dernier étage d'un imeuble*

pent-up *adj* refoulé(e)

penury ['penjʊəri, *Am:* -jʊri] *n no pl, form* pénurie *f*

peony ['piːəni] <-nies> *n* pivoine *f*

people ['piːpl] **I.** *npl* **1.** (*persons*) gens *fpl;* **country/city ~** les gens de la campagne/ville; **married ~** les gens mariés; **divorced ~** les divorcés; **homeless ~** les sans-abris **2.** (*persons comprising a nation*) peuple *m* **3.** *pl* (*ordinary citizens*) **the ~** le peuple; **a ~'s park** un parc public **4.** *pl inf* (*family*) famille *f;* (*associates*) collaborateurs *mpl* **II.** *vt* **to be ~d by sth** être peuplé de qc

People's Republic *n* République *f* populaire

pep [pep] *n no pl, inf* punch *m;* **to be full of ~** avoir du punch

pep up <-pp-> *vt* remonter le moral de qn; **to pep sb up with sth** donner du tonus à qn avec qc; **to pep sth up with sth** donner du piquant à qc avec qc

pepper ['pepəʳ, *Am:* -ɚ] **I.** *n* **1.** *no pl* (*hot spice*) poivre *m;* **a ~ sauce/steak** une sauce/un steak au poivre **2.** (*vegetable*) poivron *m* **II.** *vt* **1.** (*add pepper to*) poivrer **2.** (*pelt*) **to ~ sb/sth with sth** assaillir qn/qc de qc; **to ~ sb with bullets** cribler qn de balles; **to be ~ed with sth** être émaillé de qc; **to be ~ed with mistakes** être truffé de fautes

pepper-and-salt *adj* (*hair*) poivre et sel *inv* **peppercorn** *n* grain *m* de poivre **pepper mill** *n* moulin *m* à poivre **peppermint** *n* **1.** *no pl* (*mint plant*) menthe *f* (poivrée); **~ tea** thé *m* à la menthe **2.** (*candy*) bonbon *m* à la menthe

peppery ['pepəri] *adj* **1.** (*full of pepper*) poivré(e) **2.** (*irritable, bad-tempered*) irascible

pep pill *n inf* excitant *m*

peptic ['peptɪk] *adj* digestif(-ive)

peptic ulcer *n* ulcère *m* à l'estomac

per [pɜːʳ, *Am:* pɜːr] *prep* par; **~ mail/annum** par tête/courrier/an; **£5 ~ kilo/hour** 5£ le kilo/l'heure; **100 km ~ hour** 100 km à l'heure; **~ cent** pour cent; (**as**) **~ account** suivant facture; **as ~ usual** *inf* comme d'habitude

per capita *adj, adv* (*income*) par habitant

perceivable *adj* perceptible

perceive [pə'siːv, *Am:* pɚ'-] *vt* **1.** (*see, sense, regard*) percevoir; **to ~ that ...** s'apercevoir que ...; **to ~ sb/sth to be sth** percevoir qn/qc comme qc **2.** (*believe*) penser

per cent *Brit,* **percent** [pə'sent, *Am:* pɚ-] *Am* **I.** *n* pour cent *m* **II.** *adv* pour cent; **25/50 ~ of sth** 25/50 pour cent de qc

percentage [pə'sentɪdʒ, *Am:* pɚ'sent̬ɪdʒ] *n* **1.** (*rate or proportion*) pourcentage *m;* **a ~ discount/increase** une ristourne/augmentation en pourcentage; **to express sth as a ~** exprimer qc en pourcentage **2.** *Am, Aus* (*advantage*) avantage *m*

perceptible *adj* perceptible; **~ to the ear/eye** perceptible à l'oreille/à l'œil

perception [pə'sepʃən, *Am:* pɚ'-] *n* perception *f*

perceptive [pə'septɪv, *Am:* pɚ'-] *adj* **1.** (*related to perception*) de la perception; (*faculties*) percepteur(-trice) **2.** (*attentive: analysis, remark*) pertinent(e); (*observer*) perspicace

perch[1] [pɜːtʃ, *Am:* pɜːrtʃ] **I.** <-es> *n* perchoir *m* ►**to knock sb off his ~** faire tomber qn de son piédestal **II.** *vi* se percher **III.** *vt* percher; **to be ~ed somewhere** être perché quelque part; **to ~ oneself on sth** se jucher sur qc

perch[2] [pɜːtʃ, *Am:* pɜːrtʃ] <-(es)> *n* (*fish*) perche *f*

percolate ['pɜːkəleɪt, *Am:* 'pɜːr-] **I.** *vt* filtrer; **to ~ coffee** faire passer le café **II.** *vi* **1.** (*filter through*) passer **2.** (*spread*) filtrer

percolator *n* percolateur *m*

percussion [pə'kʌʃən, *Am:* pɚ'-] **I.** *n no pl* percussion *f;* **to be on ~** être aux percussions; **to play ~** jouer des percussions **II.** *adj* (*instrument*) à percussion; (*player, solo*) de percussion

percussionist *n* percussionniste *mf*

perdition [pə'dɪʃən, *Am:* pɚ'-] *n no pl* perdition *f*

peregrine ['perɪgrɪn], **peregrine falcon** *n* faucon *m* pèlerin

peremptorily *adv* péremptoirement

peremptory [pə'remptəri] *adj* péremptoire

perennial [pər'eniəl, *Am:* pə'ren-] **I.** *n* vivace *f* **II.** *adj* **1.** (*living several years, not annual*) vivace **2.** (*happening repeatedly, constantly*) perpétuel(le); (*beauty, hope*) éternel(le)

perfect[1] ['pɜːfɪkt, *Am:* 'pɜːr-] **I.** *adj* **1.** (*ideal*) parfait(e); **to have a ~ right to** *+infin* avoir parfaitement le droit de *+infin;* **~ in every way** parfait sous tout rapport **2.** (*absolute*) véritable; (*silence*) complet(-ète) **II.** *n no pl* parfait *m*

perfect[2] [pə'fekt, *Am:* pɜːr-] *vt* perfectionner

perfectible *adj* perfectible

perfection [pə'fekʃən, *Am:* pɚ'-] *n no pl* perfection *f;* **to do sth to ~** faire qc à la perfection

perfectionist *n* perfectionniste *mf*

perfectly *adv* **1.** (*very well*) parfaitement **2.** (*completely*) complètement **3.** (*extremely*)

P

extrêmement
perforate ['pɜːfəreɪt, *Am:* 'pɜːr-] *vt* perforer
perforation *n* **1.** (*hole in sth*) trou *m* **2.** (*set of holes*) pointillés *mpl* **3.** *no pl* (*act of perforating*) perforation *f*
perform [pə'fɔːm, *Am:* pɚ'fɔːrm] **I.** *vt* **1.** (*act, sing or play in public*) interpréter; (*a play*) jouer; (*a trick, dance*) exécuter **2.** (*do, accomplish*) accomplir; (*function, task*) remplir; (*operation*) procéder à **II.** *vi* **1.** (*give an artistic performance*) jouer **2.** (*operate, give results: system, machine*) fonctionner; **to ~ well/badly** (*car, camera, worker*) faire une bonne/mauvaise performance; (*player*) bien/mal jouer; (*company*) avoir de bons/mauvais résultats; **how did she ~ under pressure?** comment a été son travail sous la pression?
performance [pə'fɔːmənts, *Am:* pɚ'fɔːr-] *n* **1.** (*execution on stage, staging*) représentation *f;* (*of an artist, actor*) interprétation *f;* **to give a ~ of a play** donner une représentation d'une pièce; **to give a ~ of a symphony** interpréter une symphonie **2.** (*show of ability, quality*) *a.* SPORT performance *f;* **her ~ in exams** ses résultats aux examens; **a better ~ by the company** de meilleurs résultats pour la société; **getting them ready for school is quite a ~!** les préparer pour l'école est une sacrée performance!; **we're paid on ~** nous sommes payés au résultat **3.** (*accomplishing*) exécution *f;* **~ test** test *m* de qualité **4.** *inf* (*fuss*) cirque *m*
performance level *n* **1.** (*degree of success*) degré *m* de réussite **2.** (*output*) *a.* ECON rendement *m*
performer *n* interprète *mf*
perfume ['pɜːfjuːm, *Am:* 'pɜːr-] **I.** *n* parfum *m;* **to put on ~** mettre du parfum **II.** *vt* parfumer
perfunctory [pə'fʌŋktəri, *Am:* pɚ'-] *adj* rapide; **he made a ~ enquiry about my health** il m'a posé des questions sommaires sur ma santé
pergola ['pɜːgələ, *Am:* 'pɜːr-] *n* pergola *f*
perhaps [pə'hæps, *Am:* pɚ'-] *adv* peut-être
peril ['perəl] **I.** *n form* péril *m;* **to be full of ~s and pitfalls** être semé d'embûches; **to be in ~** être en danger; **at one's ~** à ses risques et périls; **at ~ of sth** au péril de qc **II.** <*Brit* -ll- *o Am* -l-> *vt* **to ~ sb/sth** mettre qn/qc en péril
perilous ['perələs] *adj form* périlleux(-euse)
perimeter [pə'rɪmɪtəʳ, *Am:* pə'rɪmət̬ɚ] *n* **1.** (*edge, border*) bordure *f* **2.** (*length of edge*) périmètre *m*
perimeter fence *n* clôture *f*
period ['pɪəriəd, *Am:* 'pɪri-] **I.** *n* **1.** (*length of time*) *a.* GEO, ECON période *f;* **in/over a ~ of six months** sur une période de six mois **2.** (*interval of time*) intervalle *m;* **he's had ~s of unemployment** il a eu des périodes de chômage; **~s of sun** intervalles ensoleillés **3.** (*lesson, class session*) classe *f* **4.** (*distinct stage*) époque *f* **5.** (*menstruation*) règles *fpl;* **to get/have one's ~** avoir ses règles; **~ pain** douleur *f* menstruelle **6.** *Am* LING point *m* **II.** *adj* (*furniture, instruments, drama*) d'époque
periodic *adj* périodique
periodical I. *adj* périodique **II.** *n* périodique *m*
peripheral *adj a.* INFOR périphérique; **to be ~ to sth** être accessoire à qc; **~ (unit)** INFOR périphérique *m*
periphery [pə'rɪfəri] <-ries> *n* périphérie *f;* **to remain on the ~** rester en marge
periscope ['perɪskəʊp, *Am:* -skoʊp] *n* périscope *m*
perish ['perɪʃ] **I.** *vi* **1.** (*die*) périr **2.** *Aus, Brit* (*deteriorate, spoil*) se détériorer; (*rubber, leather*) s'abîmer; (*vegetables*) se gâter ►**~ the thought!** ne parle pas de malheur **II.** *vt* détériorer; (*rubber, leather*) abîmer; (*food*) avarier
perishable *adj* périssable
perishing *adj* **1.** (*spoiling*) abîmé(e) **2.** *Aus, Brit, inf* (*extremely cold, freezing cold*) glacial(e); **it's ~!** on gèle! **3.** *Aus, Brit* (*damn, darn*) sacré(e)
peristyle ['erɪstaɪl] *n* péristyle *m*
peritonitis [ˌperɪtə'naɪtɪs, *Am:* -toʊ'naɪt̬ɪs] *n no pl* péritonite *f*
perjure ['pɜːdʒəʳ, *Am:* 'pɜːrdʒɚ] *vt* **to ~ oneself** se parjurer
perjured *adj* faux(fausse)
perjurer *n* parjure *mf*
perjury ['pɜːdʒəri, *Am:* 'pɜːr-] *n* faux serment *m;* **to commit ~** faire un faux serment
perk¹ [pɜːk, *Am:* pɜːrk] *n* (*advantage*) avantage *m*
perk² [pɜːk, *Am:* pɜːrk] *Am* **I.** *vt inf* (*make in percolator, percolate*) passer; **to ~ coffee** faire passer le café **II.** *n* percolateur *m*
◆**perk up I.** *vi* **1.** (*become more lively*) s'animer **2.** (*cheer up*) se ragaillardir **3.** (*increase, recover*) augmenter **4.** (*twitch: ears*) se dresser **II.** *vt* **1.** (*cheer up*) ranimer **2.** (*make more interesting*) relever **3.** (*cause increase in*) augmenter **4.** (*raise*) *a. fig* relever; **to ~ one's ears** dresser l'oreille
perky *adj* gai(e)
perm [pɜːm, *Am:* pɜːrm] **I.** *n* **1.** (*permanent wave*) permanente *f* **2.** *Brit, inf abbr of* **permutation II.** *vt* **to ~ sb's hair** faire une permanente à qn; **to get one's hair ~ed** se faire faire une permanente; **~ed hair** cheveux permanentés
permanence ['pɜːmənənts, *Am:* 'pɜːr-], **permanency** *n no pl* permanence *f;* **sense of ~** sentiment *m* de durée
permanent I. *adj* permanent(e); (*change, closure*) définitif(-ive); (*position*) fixe; (*ink*) indélébile; **to keep a ~ inventory** faire un inventaire journalier **II.** *n* permanente *f*
permanent way *n no pl, Brit* voie *f* ferrée
permeable ['pɜːmɪəbl, *Am:* 'pɜːr-] *adj* **1.** (*letting liquid, gas go through*) perméable; **~ to water** perméable à l'eau **2.** (*penetrable*)

pénétrable

permeate ['pɜːmɪeɪt, *Am:* 'pɜːr-] **I.** *vt form* pénétrer **II.** *vi form* **to ~ into sth** pénétrer qc; **to ~ through sth** s'infiltrer dans qc

permissible [pə'mɪsəbl, *Am:* pɚ'-] *adj* acceptable

permission [pə'mɪʃən, *Am:* pɚ'-] *n no pl* permission *f;* **to ask for ~** demander la permission; **to give ~** donner la permission; **to need ~ from sb to** *+infin* avoir besoin de l'autorisation de qn pour *+infin;* **with your ~** avec votre autorisation

permissive *adj* permissif(ive)

permissiveness *n no pl* permissivité *f;* **sexual ~** libération *f* sexuelle

permit ['pɜːmɪt, *Am:* 'pɜːr-] **I.** *n* permis *m* **II.** <-tt-> *vt* permettre; **to ~ sb to** *+infin* autoriser qn à *+infin;* **to ~ oneself sth** se permettre qc **III.** *vi* permettre; **to ~ of sth** *form* permettre qc; **weather ~ing** si le temps le permet; **if time ~s …** s'il y a le temps …

permitted *adj* permis(e); (*hours*) autorisé(e)

permutation [ˌpɜːmjuː'teɪʃən, *Am:* ˌpɜːr-] *n a.* MAT permutation *f*

permute [pə'mjuːt, *Am:* pɚ-] *vt* permuter

pernicious [pə'nɪʃəs, *Am:* pɚ'-] *adj* **1.** *form* (*harmful*) nocif(-ive) **2.** MED pernicieux(-euse)

pernickety [pə'nɪkəti, *Am:* pɚ'nɪkəṱi] *adj Brit, pej* **1.** (*overly exact or fussy*) **to be ~ about sth** être pointilleux à propos de qc **2.** (*needing extra care*) minutieux(-euse)

peroxide [pə'rɒksaɪd, *Am:* -'rɑːk-] *n no pl* peroxyde *m*

peroxide blonde *pej* **I.** *n* blond *m* décoloré, blonde *f* décolorée **II.** *adj* blond(e) décoloré(e)

perpendicular [ˌpɜːpən'dɪkjʊləʳ, *Am:* ˌpɜːrpən'dɪkjuːlɚ] **I.** *adj* **1.** (*very steep*) abrupt(e) **2.** (*at an angle of 90°*) **to be ~ to sth** être perpendiculaire à qc **II.** *n* perpendiculaire *f*

perpetrate ['pɜːpɪtreɪt, *Am:* 'pɜːrpə-] *vt form* (*crime*) perpétrer; (*error*) commettre; **to ~ a hoax on sb** jouer un tour à qn

perpetration *n form* LAW **the ~ of sth against sb** la perpétration de qc contre qn

perpetrator *n form* auteur *mf*

perpetual [pə'petʃʊəl, *Am:* pɚ'petʃu-] *adj* (*lasting forever, continuous*) perpétuel(le); (*check, inventory*) continuel(le); (*student, trust*) éternel(le)

perpetuate [pə'petʃʊeɪt, *Am:* pɚ'petʃu-] *vt* perpétuer; (*species*) faire reproduire; (*stereotype*) reproduire

perpetuity [ˌpɜːpɪ'tjuːəti, *Am:* ˌpɜːrpə'tuːəṱi] *n no pl, form* perpétuité *f;* **for ~** à perpétuité

perplex [pə'pleks, *Am:* pɚ'-] *vt* **1.** (*confuse and worry*) laisser perplexe **2.** (*puzzle*) intriguer **3.** (*complicate*) compliquer

perplexed *adj* perplexe; **to be ~ by sth** être intrigué par qc

perplexity [pə'pleksəti, *Am:* pɚ'pleksəṱi] <-ties> *n* (*bewilderment*) perplexité *f;* **to look/stare at sth in ~** regarder/fixer qc de manière abasourdie

per pro. *abbr of* **per procurationem** (**by proxy**) p.p.

perquisite ['pɜːkwɪzɪt, *Am:* 'pɜːr-] *n form s.* **perk**

per se [ˌpɜː'seɪ, *Am:* ˌpɜːr-] *adv* en soi

persecute ['pɜːsɪkjuːt, *Am:* 'pɜːrsɪ-] *vt* **1.** (*subject to hostility*) persécuter **2.** (*harass*) harceler

persecution *n* persécution *f*

persecution complex *n no pl* complexe *m* de persécution

persecutor *n* persécuteur, -trice *m, f*

perseverance *n no pl* persévérance *f*

persevere [ˌpɜːsɪ'vɪəʳ, *Am:* ˌpɜːrsə'vɪr] *vi* **to ~ in** (**doing**) **sth** persévérer à faire qc

persevering **I.** *n no pl* persévérance *f;* **~ with sth** persévérance dans qc **II.** *adj* persévérant(e); (*worker*) acharné(e)

Persia ['pɜːʃə, *Am:* 'pɜːrʒə] *n* la Perse

Persian **I.** *adj* persan(e), perse **II.** *n* **1.** (*person*) Persan(e) *m(f),* Perse *mf* **2.** LING persan *m,* perse *m; s. a.* **English**

persist [pə'sɪst, *Am:* pɚ'-] *vi* **1.** (*continue*) continuer; (*cold, heat, rain*) persister; (*habit, tradition*) perdurer **2.** (*continue despite difficulty*) persister; **to ~ with one's effort** persister dans ses efforts; **to ~ in doing sth** persister à faire qc

persistence [pə'sɪstəns, *Am:* pɚ'-] *n no pl* **1.** (*continuation*) continuation *f* **2.** (*determination, perserverance*) obstination *f;* **sb's ~ with sth** l'obstination de qn pour qc

persistent *adj* **1.** (*long lasting*) persistant(e); (*difficulties*) perpétuel(le); (*rumour*) ancré(e) **2.** (*continuous, constant*) continuel(le); (*demand, rain*) constant(e) **3.** (*determined, perservering*) déterminé(e); **~ offender** criminel *m* récidiviste; **to be ~ in sth** être persévérant dans qc

person ['pɜːsən, *Am:* 'pɜːr-] <-s *o* people> *n* personne *f;* **~ of great ability** individu *m* d'une grande capacité; **book ~** bibliophile *mf;* **cat/dog ~** amateur *m* de chien/chat; **people ~** personne *f* sociable; **~ of principle** individu *m* à principe; **homeless ~** sans-abri *mf;* **to have sth about** (**one's**) **~** avoir qc sur soi; **an ordinary ~** une personne ordinaire; **in ~** en personne; **in the ~ of sb** en la personne de qn; **per ~** par personne **2.** LING personne

personable ['pɜːsənəbl, *Am:* 'pɜːr-] *adj* agréable

personage ['pɜːsənɪdʒ, *Am:* 'pɜːr-] *n form* personnage *m*

personal *adj* **1.** (*of a particular person, individual*) personnel(le); (*estate, property*) privé(e); **~ data** coordonnées *fpl* **2.** (*direct, done in person: service*) personnel(le); **to give sth ~ attention** s'occuper personnellement de qc; **I like the ~ touch** j'aime bien le côté humain **3.** (*private*) privé(e); (*letter*) personnel(le); **~ diary** journal *m* intime **4.** (*offensive*) offensant(e); **to get ~** devenir offensant;

nothing ~! rien de personnel! **5.** (*bodily, physical*) physique; (*hygiene*) intime; **his ~ appearance** son apparence **6.** (*human*) humain(e)

personal assistant *n* assistant(e) *m(f)* **personal computer** *n* ordinateur *m* personnel

personality <-ties> *n* personnalité *f;* ~ **test** test *m* psychologique

personalize ['pɜːsənəlaɪz, *Am:* 'pɜːr-] *vt* (*gift, approach*) personnaliser

personally *adv* personnellement; **she came ~** elle est venue en personne; **I didn't mean that ~** je ne visais personne

personal organizer *n* agenda *m* **personal stereo** *n* baladeur *m*

personalty ['pɜːsənəlti, *Am:* 'pɜːrsənəlţi] <-ties> *n Am* biens *mpl* personnels

personification [pəˌsɒnɪfɪ'keɪʃən, *Am:* pɚˌsɑːnɪ-] *n* **1.** (*perfect example, embodiment*) incarnation *f* **2.** LIT personnification *f*

personify [pə'sɒnɪfaɪ, *Am:* pɚ'sɑːnɪ-] *vt* **1.** (*be perfect example, embody*) incarner **2.** (*represent in human form*) personnifier

personnel [ˌpɜːsən'el, *Am:* ˌpɜːr-] *n* **1.** *pl* (*staff, employees*) personnel *m* **2.** *no pl* (*human resources department*) ressources *fpl* humaines

personnel department *n* département *m* du personnel **personnel director** *n* directeur, -trice *m, f* du personnel **personnel management** *n no pl* **1.** (*human resources directors*) direction *f* du département du personnel **2.** (*study of human resources*) étude *f* des ressources humaines **personnel manager** *n* gérant(e) *m(f)* du personnel **personnel turnover** *n no pl* renouvellement *m* du personnel

perspective [pə'spektɪv, *Am:* pɚ'-] *n* **1.** (*viewpoint*) perspective *f;* **to get sth in ~** placer qc dans son contexte; **from a historical ~** d'un point de vue historique; **a ~ on sth** un point de vue sur qc **2.** (*method of representation*) perspective *f;* **in ~** en perspective; **out of ~** hors de la perspective

perspicacious [ˌpɜːspɪ'keɪʃəs, *Am:* ˌpɜːr-] *adj form* perspicace; (*analysis*) profond(e)

perspicacity [ˌpɜːspɪ'kæsəti, *Am:* ˌpɜːrspɪ'kæsəţi] *n no pl, form* perspicacité *f*

perspicuity [ˌpɜːspɪ'kjuːəti, *Am:* ˌpɜːrspɪ'kjuːəţi] *n no pl, form* clairvoyance *f*

perspicuous [pə'spɪkjʊəs, *Am:* pɚ'-] *adj form* clair(e)

perspiration [ˌpɜːspə'reɪʃən, *Am:* ˌpɜːr-] *n no pl* transpiration *f;* **dripping with ~** en nage

perspire [pə'spaɪəʳ, *Am:* pɚ'spaɪɚ] *vi* transpirer

persuade [pə'sweɪd, *Am:* pɚ'-] *vt* persuader; **to ~ sb into sth** persuader qn de qc; **to ~ sb to** +*infin* convaincre qn de +*infin*

persuasion *n* **1.** (*convincing*) persuasion *f* **2.** (*conviction*) croyance *f;* **to be of the Catholic/Protestant ~** être de croyance catholique/protestante; **parties of every ~** des partis de toutes tendances

persuasive *adj* persuasif(-ive); **he was very ~** il était très persuasif; ~ **powers** pouvoir *m* de persuasion

pert [pɜːt, *Am:* pɜːrt] *adj* **1.** (*sexually attractive, cheeky*) coquin(e) **2.** (*impudent*) effronté(e) **3.** (*attractive, neat*) mignon(ne) **4.** (*small and firm*) petit(e) et ferme

◆**pertain to** *vt form* se rapporter à

pertinent ['pɜːtɪnənt, *Am:* 'pɜːrtnənt] *adj form* pertinent(e); **to be ~ to sth** avoir un rapport avec qc

perturb [pə'tɜːb, *Am:* pɚ'tɜːrb] *vt* perturber; **I'm very ~ed** je suis très troublé

Peru [pə'ruː] *n* le Pérou

perusal *n no pl, form* lecture *f;* **for one's ~** pour sa lecture (personnelle)

peruse [pə'ruːz] *vt form* lire; (*document*) étudier

Peruvian **I.** *adj* péruvien(ne) **II.** *n* Péruvien(ne) *m(f)*

pervade [pə'veɪd, *Am:* pɚ'-] *vt form* (*morally*) pénétrer; (*physically*) envahir

pervasive *adj form* étendu(e); (*smell*) envahissant(e)

perverse [pə'vɜːs, *Am:* pɚ'vɜːrs] *adj pej* **1.** (*deliberately unreasonable, harmful*) pervers(e); (*interest*) malsain(e); (*pride*) mal placé(e) **2.** (*sexually deviant*) pervers(e)

perversion *n pej* **1.** (*abnormal behavior*) perversion *f* **2.** (*corruption*) corruption *f;* (*of the truth*) déformation *f*

perversity [pə'vɜːsəti, *Am:* pɚ'vɜːrsəţi] <-ties> *n pej* **1.** (*unreasonable behavior*) attitude *f* déraisonnable **2.** (*abnormal behaviour*) perversité *f*

pervert ['pɜːvɜːt, *Am:* 'pɜːrvɜːrt] **I.** *n pej* **1.** (*extreme sexual deviant*) pervers(e) *m(f)* **2.** (*creepy person*) sale type *m* **II.** *vt* **to ~ sb** pervertir qn; **to ~ sth** déformer qc; **to ~ the course of justice** entraver l'action de la justice

peseta [pə'seɪtə] *n* peseta *f*

peso ['peɪsəʊ, *Am:* -soʊ] *n* peso *m*

pessimism ['pesɪmɪzəm, *Am:* 'pesə-] *n no pl* pessimisme *m*

pessimist *n* pessimiste *mf*

pessimistic *adj* pessimiste

pest [pest] *n* **1.** (*animal*) animal *m* nuisible; (*insect*) insecte *m* nuisible **2.** *inf* (*annoying person*) casse-pieds *mf inv*

pest control *n* **1.** (*removal*) lutte *f* contre la vermine **2.** (*service*) service *m* de lutte contre les infestations

pester *vt* **to ~ sb for sth** harceler qn pour obtenir qc

pesticide ['pestɪsaɪd, *Am:* 'pestə-] *n* pesticide *m*

pestilent ['pestɪlənt, *Am:* 'pestlənt], **pestilential** *adj* **1.** (*insalubrious*) pestilentiel(le) **2.** (*troublesome*) pénible

pestle ['pesl] *n* pilon *m*

pesto ['pestəʊ, *Am:* -toʊ] *n* pistou *m*

pet [pet] **I.** *n* **1.** (*house animal*) animal *m* domestique **2.** *pej* (*favorite person*) chouchou(te) *m(f)* **3.** *inf* (*nice or thoughtful person*) ange *m* **4.** *Aus, Brit, inf* (*love, darling*) chéri(e) *m(f)* **II.** *adj* **1.** (*concerning domestic animals: cat*) domestique **2.** (*favorite*) favori(te); ~ **peeve** bête *f* noire; **to be sb's ~ hate** être la bête noire de qn **III.** *vt* **1.** (*treat well*) chouchouter **2.** (*cuddle*) peloter

petal ['petl, *Am:* 'pet̬l] *n* **1.** (*flower part*) pétale *m* **2.** *Brit, inf* (*love, darling*) chéri(e) *m(f)*

peter ['pi:təʳ, *Am:* -t̬ɚ] *vi* **to ~ out** (*food*) s'épuiser; (*trail, track, path*) disparaître; (*conversation, interest*) tarir

Peter ['pi:təʳ, *Am:* -t̬ɚ] **to rob ~ to pay Paul** déshabiller Pierre pour habiller Paul

petite [pə'ti:t] *adj* menu(e); ~ **clothing** vêtement *m* pour femmes menues

petition [pɪ'tɪʃən, *Am:* pə'-] **I.** *n* **1.** (*signed document*) pétition *f* **2.** LAW demande *f*; **to file a ~ for divorce** faire une demande de divorce **II.** *vi* **1.** (*start a petition*) **to ~ about sth** pétitionner pour qc **2.** (*request formally*) **to ~ for sth** faire une requête de qc; **to ~ for divorce** demander le divorce **III.** *vt* adresser une pétition à

petitioner *n* pétitionnaire *mf*

petrifaction [ˌpetrɪ'fækʃən], **petrification** *n* pétrification *f*

petrify ['petrɪfaɪ] **I.** *vi* se pétrifier **II.** *vt* pétrifier

petrifying *adj* terrifiant(e)

petrochemical [ˌpetrəʊ'kemɪkəl, *Am:* -roʊ'-] **I.** *n pl* produits *mpl* pétrochimiques *f* **II.** *adj* pétrochimique

petrodollar ['petrəʊˌdɒləʳ, *Am:* -roʊˌdɑ:lɚ] *n* pétrodollar *m*

petrol ['petrəl] *n Aus, Brit no pl* essence *f*; **unleaded ~** essence sans plomb

petrol can *n Aus, Brit* bidon *m* d'essence **petrol company** *n* compagnie *f* pétrolière **petrol consumption** *n no pl, Aus, Brit* consommation *f* d'essence **petrol engine** *n Aus, Brit* moteur *m* à essence

petroleum [pɪ'trəʊliəm, *Am:* pə'troʊ-] *n* pétrole *m*

petrol gauge *n Aus, Brit* jauge *f* d'essence **petrol pump** *n Aus, Brit* pompe *f* à essence **petrol station** *n Aus, Brit* station-service *f* **petrol tank** *n Aus, Brit* réservoir *m* d'essence

petticoat ['petɪkəʊt, *Am:* 'pet̬ɪkoʊt] *n* jupon *m*

pettifogging ['petɪfɒgɪŋ, *Am:* 'pet̬ɪfɑ:gɪŋ] *adj pej* tatillon(ne)

pettiness *n no pl* **1.** (*triviality, insignificance*) insignifiance *f* **2.** (*small-mindedness*) étroitesse *f* d'esprit

petting *n* **1.** (*stroking*) caresses *fpl* **2.** (*sexual fondling and touching*) attouchements *mpl*

pettish *adj* maussade

petty ['peti, *Am:* 'pet̬-] <-ier, -iest> *adj pej* **1.** (*narrow-minded*) mesquin(e) **2.** (*trivial*) insignifiant(e) **3.** (*minor*) mineur(e)

petty cash *n* petite caisse *f* **petty crime** *n no pl* petite délinquance *f*

petulant ['petjələnt, *Am:* 'petʃə-] *adj* irrité(e)

petunia [pɪ'tju:niə, *Am:* pə'tu:njə] *n* pétunia *m*

pew [pju:] *n* banc *m* (d'église) ►**take a ~!** asseyez-vous!

pewit *n* **1.** (*lapwing*) vanneau *m* **2.** (*black-headed sea gull*) mouette *f* **3.** (*lapwing's call*) cri *m* du vanneau

pewter ['pju:təʳ, *Am:* -t̬ɚ] *n no pl* étain *m*; **a ~ plate** une assiette en étain

PGCE *n Brit abbr of* **Postgraduate Certificate of Education** diplôme *m* de spécialisation dans l'enseignement

pH [ˌpi:'eɪtʃ] *n* pH *m*

phalanx ['fælæŋks, *Am:* 'feɪlæŋks] <-es *o* phalanges> *n form* phalange *f*

phallic ['fælɪk] *adj* phallique

phallus ['fæləs] <-es *o* phalli> *n* phallus *m*

phantom ['fæntəm, *Am:* -t̬əm] **I.** *n* fantôme *m* **II.** *adj* fantôme

pharaoh ['feərəʊ, *Am:* 'feroʊ] *n* pharaon *m*

pharisaic [ˌfærɪ'seɪɪk], **pharisaical** *adj* **1.** (*of Jewish sect*) pharisaïque **2.** *fig, pej* hypocrite

Pharisee ['færɪsi:, *Am:* 'ferɪ-] *n a. pej* pharisien(ne) *m(f)*

pharmaceutical *adj* pharmaceutique

pharmaceuticals *n pl* produits *mpl* pharmaceutiques

pharmaceutics [ˌfɑ:mə'sju:tɪks, *Am:* ˌfɑ:rmə'su:t̬-] *n + sing v* pharmacie *f*

pharmaceutics industry *n no pl* industrie *f* pharmaceutique

pharmacist *n* pharmacien(ne) *m(f)*

pharmacology [ˌfɑ:mə'kɒlədʒi, *Am:* ˌfɑ:rmə'kɑ:lə-] *n no pl* pharmacologie *f*

pharmacy ['fɑ:məsi, *Am:* 'fɑ:r-] <-cies> *n* pharmacie *f*

pharyngitis [ˌfærɪn'dʒaɪtɪs, *Am:* ˌferɪn'dʒaɪt̬ɪs] *n no pl* pharyngite *f*

phase [feɪz] **I.** *n* phase *f*; **moon ~** phase *f* lunaire; **to go through a ~** faire sa crise; **in a ~** dans une phase; **in ~** en phase; **out of ~** déphasé **II.** *vt* échelonner; **to ~ machines into a technology** introduire progressivement des machines à une technologie; **to be ~d** être échelonné

◆**phase in** *vt* introduire progressivement

◆**phase out** *vt* retirer progressivement; (*production*) stopper progressivement; **to phase sb out** se débarrasser de qn

PhD [ˌpi:eɪtʃ'di:] *n abbr of* **Doctor of Philosophy** doctorat *m*; **a ~ in sth** un doctorat en qc; **to do/work on a ~** être/étudier en doctorat; **to be a ~** être titulaire d'un doctorat

pheasant ['fezənt] <-(s)> *n* faisant *m*

phenomenal *adj* phénoménal(e)

phenomenon [fɪ'nɒmɪnən, *Am:*

fə'nɑːmənɑːn] <phenomena *o* -s> *n* phénomène *m*

phew [fjuː] *interj inf* ouf!

phial ['faɪəl] *n Brit* fiole *f*

Philadelphia [ˌfɪlə'delfiə] *n* Philadelphie

Philadelphian *n* habitant(e) *m(f)* de Philadelphie

philander [fɪ'lændəʳ, *Am:* -dɚ] *vi* **to ~ with sb** draguer qn

philanderer *n* dragueur, -euse *m, f*

philanthropic *adj* philanthrope

philanthropist *n* philanthrope *mf*

philanthropy [fɪ'lænθrəpi, *Am:* fə'-] *n no pl* philanthropie *f*

philatelic *adj* philatélique

philatelist *n* philatéliste *mf*

philately [fɪ'lætəli, *Am:* -'læt̬-] *n no pl* philatélie *f*

philharmonic [ˌfɪlɑː'mɒnɪk, *Am:* ˌfɪlhɑːr'mɑːnɪk] *adj* philharmonique

Philippine *adj* philippin(ne)

Philippines ['fɪlɪpiːnz, *Am:* 'fɪlə-] *npl* **the ~** les Philippines

philistine ['fɪlɪstaɪn, *Am:* -stiːn] *n pej* Philistin *m*

philological *adj* philologique

philologist *n* philologue *mf*

philology [fɪ'lɒlədʒi, *Am:* fɪ'lɑːlə-] *n no pl* philologie *f*

philosopher *n* philosophe *mf*

philosophic, **philosophical** *adj* **1.** (*concerning philosophy*) philosophique **2.** (*calm*) philosophe

philosophize [fɪ'lɒsəfaɪz, *Am:* -'lɑːsə-] *vi* philosopher

philosophy [fɪ'lɒsəfi, *Am:* -'lɑːsə-] *n no pl* philosophie *f*

philter *n Am*, **philtre** ['fɪltəʳ, *Am:* -t̬ɚ] *n Brit* filtre *m*

phlebitis [flɪ'baɪtɪs, *Am:* fliː'baɪt̬ɪs] *n* MED phlébite *f*

phlegm [flem] *n no pl* **1.** (*mucus*) glaire *f* **2.** (*calmness, calm temperament*) flegme *m*

phlegmatic [fleg'mætɪk, *Am:* -'mæt̬-] *adj* flegmatique

phobia ['fəʊbiə, *Am:* 'foʊ-] *n* phobie *f;* **~ about sth** phobie de qc

phoenix ['fiːnɪks] *n* phénix *m;* **to rise from the ashes like a ~** renaître de ses cendres tel un phénix

phone [fəʊn, *Am:* foʊn] **I.** *n* téléphone *m;* **to answer the ~** répondre au téléphone; **to hang up the ~** raccrocher; **to hang the ~ up on sb** raccrocher au nez de qn; **to pick up the ~** prendre le téléphone; **by ~** par téléphone; **on the ~** au téléphone; **~ call/line** appel *m*/ligne *f* téléphonique; **to be on the ~** *Brit* être au téléphone **II.** *vi* téléphoner; **he ~d for a pizza** il a commandé une pizza par téléphone **III.** *vt* téléphoner à

◆**phone back** *vi, vt* rappeler

◆**phone in** *vi* téléphoner; **to ~ sick** téléphoner pour prévenir qu'on est malade

◆**phone up** *vt* téléphoner à

phone booth, **phone box** *n* cabine *f* téléphonique **phonecard** *n* carte *f* téléphonique **phone-in I.** *n* émission *f* de radio interactive **II.** *adj* interactif(-ive)

phoneme ['fəʊniːm, *Am:* 'foʊ-] *n* LING phonème *m*

phonetic [fə'netɪk, *Am:* foʊ'net̬-] *adj* phonétique

phonetician *n* phonéticien(ne) *m(f)*

phonetics *n + sing v* phonétique *f*

phoney ['fəʊni, *Am:* 'foʊ-] **I.** <-ier, -iest> *adj inf* **1.** (*fake*) faux(fausse) **2.** (*bogus: story*) bidon *inv* ►**to be as ~ as a two-dollar bill** *Am* (*person*) être un faux jeton; (*story, tears*) être du bidon **II.** *n pej, inf* **1.** (*impostor*) imposteur *m* **2.** (*insincere person*) faux jeton *m* **3.** (*fake*) faux *m*

phonic ['fɒnɪk, *Am:* 'fɑːnɪk] *adj* phonique

phonology [fə'nɒlədʒi, *Am:* -'nɑːlə-] *n no pl* phonologie *f*

phony ['fəʊni, *Am:* 'foʊ-] *adj Am s.* **phoney**

phooey ['fuːi] *interj iron, inf* pfft!

phosphate ['fɒsfeɪt, *Am:* 'fɑːs-] *n* phosphate *m*

phosphorescence [ˌfɒsfə'resns, *Am:* ˌfɑːs-] *n no pl* phosphorescence *f*

phosphorescent *adj* phosphorescent(e)

phosphoric [fɒs'fɒrɪk, *Am:* fɑːs'fɔːr-], **phosphorous** *adj* CHEM phosphorique

phosphorus ['fɒsfərəs, *Am:* 'fɑːs-] *n no pl* phosphore *m*

photo ['fəʊtəʊ, *Am:* 'foʊt̬oʊ] <-s> *n inf abbr of* **photograph** photo *f*

photo album *n* album *m* photos **photocall** *n Brit* séance *f* de photos **photocell** *n* photocellule *f*

photocopier *n* photocopieur *m*

photocopy ['fəʊtəʊˌkɒpi, *Am:* 'foʊt̬oʊˌkɑː-pi] **I.** <-ies> *n* photocopie *f* **II.** *vt* photocopier

photoelectric *adj* photoélectrique **photo finish** *n* SPORT photo-finish *f* **Photofit®** *n Brit* portrait *m* robot **photoflash** *n* flash *m*

photogenic [ˌfəʊtəʊ'dʒenɪk, *Am:* ˌfoʊt̬oʊ'-] *adj* photogénique

photograph ['fəʊtəgrɑːf, *Am:* 'foʊt̬oʊgræf] **I.** *n* photo(graphie) *f;* **colour/black-and-white ~** photo couleur/noir et blanc; **to take of ~ of sb/sth** prendre une photo de qn/qc **II.** *vt* photographier **III.** *vi* **to ~ well** être bien en photo

photograph album *n form* PHOT *s.* **photo album**

photographer *n* photographe *mf*

photographic *adj* photographique

photography [fə'tɒgrəfi, *Am:* -'tɑːgrə-] *n no pl* photographie *f*

photojournalism *n no pl* photojournalisme *m* **photo library** *n* photothèque *f* **photometer** *n* photomètre *m* **photomontage** *n* photomontage *m*

photon ['fəʊtɒn, *Am:* 'foʊtɑːn] *n* photon *m*

photo opportunity *n s.* photocall **photo**

reporter *n* reporter *mf* photographe **photosensitive** *adj* photosensible **photosetting** *n* ART photocomposition *f* **photostat** <-tt-> *vt* photocopier **photosynthesis** *n no pl* photosynthèse *f*

phrasal verb [ˌfreɪzəl'vɜːb, *Am:* ˌfreɪzəl'vɜːrb] *n* LING verbe *m* composé

phrase [freɪz] **I.** *n* **1.** (*words not forming sentence*) locution *f;* **verb/noun** ~ syntagme *m* verbal/nominal **2.** (*idiomatic expression*) expression *f;* **in sb's** ~ comme dit qn **3.** MUS phrase *f* **II.** *vt* formuler

phrase book *n* guide *m* de conversation

phraseology [ˌfreɪzi'ɒlədʒi, *Am:* -'ɑːlə-] *n no pl* LING phraséologie *f*

phrenetic [frə'netɪk, *Am:* frɪ'net̬-] *adj s.* **frenetic**

phut [fʌt] *adv* **to go** ~ *Brit, Aus, inf* tomber à l'eau; (*of a person, an object*) claquer

physical **I.** *adj* physique **II.** *n* MED visite *f* médicale

physical education *n* éducation *f* physique **physical examination** *n* visite *f* médicale

physically *adv* physiquement

physical sciences *n pl* sciences *fpl* physiques **physical therapy** *n Am s.* **physiotherapy** **physical training** *n* éducation *f* physique

physician [fɪ'zɪʃən] *n* (*doctor*) médecin *m*

physicist ['fɪzɪsɪst] *n* **1.** (*scientist*) physicien(ne) *m(f)* **2.** (*student*) étudiant(e) *m(f)* en sciences physiques

physics ['fɪzɪks] *n + sing v* physique *f*

physio ['fɪziəʊ, *Am:* -oʊ] *n* <-s> *Brit, inf* **1.** (*physiotherapist*) kiné *mf* **2.** *no pl* (*physiotherapy*) kinésithérapie *f*

physiognomy [ˌfɪzi'ɒnəmi, *Am:* -'ɑːgnə-] *n no pl, form* ANAT physionomie *f*

physiologist *n* physiologiste *mf*

physiology [ˌfɪzi'ɒlədʒi, *Am:* -'ɑːlə-] *n no pl* physiologie *f*

physiotherapist *n* kinésithérapeute *mf*

physiotherapy [ˌfɪziəʊ'θerəpi, *Am:* -oʊ'-] *n no pl* kinésithérapie *f*

physique [fɪ'ziːk] *n* physique *m*

pianist ['pɪənɪst, *Am:* 'piːnɪst] *n* pianiste *mf*

piano ['pjɑːnəʊ, *Am:* pi'ænoʊ] <-s> **I.** *n* piano *m;* **to play the** ~ [*o Am* **to play** ~] jouer du piano **II.** *adv* piano

piazza [pɪ'ætsə, *Am:* -'ɑːt-] *n* place *f*

pic *n inf* **1.** (*film*) film *m* **2.** (*picture*) image *f* **3.** (*photo*) photo *f*

piccalilli [ˌpɪkə'lɪli] *n no pl* pickles *mpl*

piccolo ['pɪkələʊ, *Am:* -loʊ] <-s> *n* MUS piccolo *m*

pick¹ [pɪk] *n* (*tool*) pioche *f;* **ice** ~ pic *m* à glace

pick² [pɪk] **I.** *vt* **1.** (*select*) choisir; (*team*) sélectionner; (*winner*) désigner **2.** (*harvest*) cueillir; (*mushrooms*) ramasser; **to** ~ **grapes** cueillir du raisin; (*for wine*) faire les vendanges **3.** (*remove: spot*) gratter; **to** ~ **one's nose/teeth** se curer le nez/les dents; **to** ~ **sth from/out of sth** retirer qc de qc; **to** ~ **sth clean** décortiquer qc **4.** (*steal*) voler; **to** ~ **a lock** crocheter une serrure; **to** ~ **sb's pocket** voler qc dans la poche de qn ▶**to** ~ **sb's brains** *inf* demander conseil à qn; **to** ~ **holes in sth** relever les défauts de qc; **to** ~ **a fight with sb** chercher la bagarre avec qn **II.** *vi* choisir; **to** ~ **and choose among sb/sth** faire son choix parmi qn/qc **III.** *n* **1.** (*selection*) **to take one's** ~ faire son choix **2.** *inf* (*the best*) **the** ~ (*person*) la crème; (*of thing*) le meilleur; **to have one's** ~ **of sth** avoir le choix de qc

◆**pick at** *vt* **1.** (*nibble: food*) picorer **2.** (*pull at: sore*) gratter

◆**pick off** *vt* **1.** (*shoot*) abattre **2.** (*remove*) enlever

◆**pick on** *vt* **1.** (*bully*) embêter **2.** (*criticize*) s'en prendre à **3.** (*select*) choisir

◆**pick out** *vt* **1.** (*select*) choisir **2.** (*recognize*) reconnaître **3.** (*manage to see*) distinguer **4.** (*highlight*) **to be picked out** être mis en évidence **5.** (*play*) **to** ~ **a tune on an instrument** pianoter un air sur un instrument

◆**pick over** *vt* trier

◆**pick up** **I.** *vt* **1.** (*detect: broadcast, signal*) capter **2.** (*learn*) apprendre; **to** ~ **a little French** apprendre quelques mots de français; **to** ~ **the tune** trouver l'air **3.** (*stop for, collect: thing, person*) aller chercher; **to** ~ **passengers** prendre des passagers; (*survivor*) recueillir **4.** (*catch: illness*) attraper **5.** (*tidy: books, toys*) ranger **6.** (*acquire*) acheter **7.** *inf* (*make acquaintance for sex*) emballer **8.** (*detect*) relever; (*radio signal*) intercepter; (*scent*) détecter; (*plane, ship*) repérer **9.** (*continue, resume*) reprendre **10.** *inf* (*arrest*) arrêter **11.** (*react to a point*) reprendre; (*a mistake*) relever; **can I pick you up on that** est-ce que je peux vois reprendre là-dessus? **12.** (*lift*) prendre; (*from the ground*) ramasser **13.** (*lift up*) relever; (*weight*) soulever; (*pen*) prendre; **to** ~ **the phone** prendre le téléphone; **to pick oneself up** *a. fig* se relever **14.** (*collect: news*) relever; (*idea*) chercher; (*a prize*) récolter **15.** (*pay*) **to** ~ **the bill** [*o Am* **check**] *inf* casquer **16.** *inf* (*earn*) ramasser **17.** (*accentuate a colour, shape*) relever **18.** (*find and take*) choisir **II.** *vi* **1.** (*improve: condition*) s'améliorer; (*business*) reprendre; (*person*) se rétablir **2.** (*continue, increase*) reprendre

pickaback ['pɪkəbæk] *n inf s.* **piggyback**

pickax *n Am,* **pickaxe** *n* pioche *f*

picker *n* cueilleur, -euse *m, f*

picket ['pɪkɪt] **I.** *n* **1.** (*striker*) gréviste *mf* en faction; (*demonstrator*) manifestant(e) *m* **2.** (*strike action*) piquet *m* de grève; (*at demonstration*) cordon de manifestants **3.** (*pointed stake for fence*) piquet *m* **II.** *vt* **1.** (*demonstrate: factory*) former un piquet de grève face à; (*parliament*) former un cordon de protestation face à **2.** (*blockade*) clôturer de piquets **III.** *vi* faire le piquet de grève

picket fence *n* palissade *f* **picket line** *n*

P

piquet *m* de grève
picking *n* cueillette *m*
pickings *npl* **1.**(*gains*) bénéfices *mpl* **2.**(*left-overs*) restes *mpl*
pickle ['pɪkl] **I.** *n* **1.**(*relish*) pickle *m* (*condiment de légumes conservés dans du vinaigre*) **2.** *Am* (*gherkin*) ≈ cornichon *m* ►**to be in a** (**pretty**) ~ *inf* être dans le pétrin **II.** *vt* **to ~ sth** conserver qc dans le vinaigre
pickled *adj* **1.**(*conserved in vinegar*) au vinaigre **2.** *fig, inf* (*drunk*) bourré(e); **to get ~** se pinter
picklock ['pɪklɒk, *Am:* -lɑːk] *n* **1.**(*burglar*) crocheteur *m* **2.**(*instrument*) crochet *m*
pick-me-up *n* remontant *m*
pickpocket ['pɪkpɒkɪt, *Am:* -ˌpɑːkɪt] *n* pickpocket *m*
pickup *n* **1.**(*part of gramophone*) lecteur *m* **2.** *inf* (*collection*) ramassage *m* **3.**(*collection point*) point *m* de ramassage **4.**(*collection stop*) arrêt *m* **5.** *inf*(*casual partner*) partenaire *mf* de rencontre **6.**(*improvement*) amélioration *f* **7.** *s.* **pickup truck**
pickup truck *n* camionnette *f*
picky <-ier, -iest> *adj pej, inf* difficile
picnic ['pɪknɪk] **I.** *n* pique-nique *m;* **to go on a ~** faire un pique-nique ►**to be no ~** *inf* ne pas être une partie de plaisir **II.** <-ck-> *vi* pique-niquer
picnicker *n* pique-niqueur, -euse *m, f*
pictogram ['pɪktəgræm] *n* pictogramme *m*
pictorial [pɪk'tɔːriəl] **I.** *adj* **1.**(*done as picture*) pictural(e) **2.**(*with pictures: story, representation*) en images **II.** *n* magazine *m* illustré
picture ['pɪktʃəʳ, *Am:* -tʃɚ] **I.** *n* **1.**(*visual image*) image *f* **2.**(*photos*) photo *f;* **to take a ~ of sth** prendre une photo de qc; **wedding ~** photo de mariage **3.**(*film*) film *m;* **to go to the ~s** aller au cinéma **4.**(*painting*) tableau *m;* (*drawing*) dessin *m;* **to draw a ~** faire un dessin **5.**(*mental image, image on TV*) image *f* **6.**(*account, depiction*) tableau *m;* **to paint a ~ of sth** peindre le portrait de qc **7.**(*current situation*) **to be in the ~** être au courant; **to get the ~** *inf* piger; **to put/keep sb in the ~** mettre/tenir qn au courant; **to leave sb out of the ~** laisser qn sur la touche ►**sb's face is a ~** *Brit* la tête de qn est à mourir de rire **II.** *vt* **1.**(*represent*) représenter **2.**(*imagine*) **to ~ oneself** s'imaginer; **to ~ sb doing sth** s'imaginer qn en train de faire qc; **to ~ sth to oneself** s'imaginer qc **3.**(*describe*) dépeindre
picture book *n* livre *m* illustré **picture frame**, **picture-frame** *n* cadre *m* **picture gallery** *n* galerie *f* de photos **picture-goer**, **picturegoer** *n* cinéphile *mf* **picture library** *n* photothèque *f* **picture postcard** *n* carte *f* postale, carte-vue *f Belgique*
picturesque [ˌpɪktʃə'resk] *adj* pittoresque
picture window *n* fenêtre *f* panoramique
piddle ['pɪdl] *inf* **I.** *n* pipi *m* **II.** *vi* faire pipi
piddling *adj pej, inf* insignifiant(e)
pidgin ['pɪdʒɪn] *n* pidgin *m*
pie [paɪ] *n* GASTR (*savoury*) tourte *f;* (*sweet*) tarte *f* (recouverte de pâte) ►**~ in the sky** *inf* des châteaux en Espagne; **easy as ~** *inf* simple comme bonjour
piece [piːs] *n* **1.**(*bit*) morceau *m;* (*land*) parcelle *f;* (*glass, pottery*) fragment *m;* **in ~s** en morceaux; **to tear sth into ~s** déchirer qc en morceaux; **to fall to ~s** s'effondrer; **in one ~** en un seul morceau; *fig* (*person*) intact(e); **to come to ~s** partir en morceaux; (*kit furniture*) se démonter; **to take to ~s** *Brit* démonter; **to go** (**all**) **to ~s** *fig* s'effondrer **2.**(*item, one of set*) **a ~ of baggage** une valise; **~ of clothing** un vêtement; **a ~ of paper** une feuille de papier; **a ~ of furniture** un meuble; **a ~ of advice** un conseil; **a ~ of evidence** une preuve; **a ~ of information** une information; **a ~ of news** une nouvelle **3.**(*unit in game: chess*) pièce *f* **4.**(*work: written, musical*) morceau *m;* (*painted, drawn, sculpted*) pièce *f;* **a good ~ of work** du bon travail; **a lovely ~ of dancing** un beau morceau de danse **5.**(*coin*) pièce *f;* **a 50p ~** une pièce de 50 pence **6.** *vulg* (*woman*) meuf *f* ►**to be a ~ of cake** *inf* être du gâteau; **to want a ~ of the cake** vouloir une part du gâteau; **to give sb a ~ of sb's mind** *inf* dire ses quatre vérités à qn; **to pick up the ~s** recoller les morceaux; **to say one's ~** dire ce qu'on a à dire
piece together *vt* **1.**(*assemble*) rassembler **2.**(*reconstruct*) reconstituer
piecemeal **I.** *adv* petit à petit **II.** *adj* (*approach, reforms, construction*) par étapes succesives; *pej* peu méthodique **piece rate** *n* salaire *m* à la tâche **piecework** *n no pl* travail *m* à la pièce; **to do ~** travailler à la tâche **piece-worker** *n* ouvrier, -ière *m, f* payé à la tâche
pie chart *n* camembert *m*
pied *adj* ZOOL bigarré(e)
pie-eyed *adj inf* bourré(e)
pier [pɪəʳ, *Am:* pɪr] *n* **1.**(*boardwalk*) jetée *f* **2.** ARCHIT (*pillar: in church*) pilier *m;* (*in foundations*) pile *f*
pierce [pɪəs, *Am:* pɪrs] **I.** *vt* **1.**(*make a hole in*) *a. fig* percer; **to have one's ears ~d** se faire percer les oreilles **2.**(*go through*) transpercer **II.** *vi a. fig* **to ~ into sth** percer qc; **to ~ through sth** transpercer qc
piercing **I.** *adj* **1.**(*biting: cold, rain, wind*) glacial(e) **2.**(*sharp, penetrating: eyes, look*) perçant(e); (*reply, wit*) mordant(e) **3.**(*loud*) perçant(e) **II.** *n* piercing *m*
piety ['paɪəti, *Am:* -t̬i] *n no pl, form* piété *f*
piffle ['pɪfl] *n no pl, pej, inf* foutaises *fpl*
piffling ['pɪflɪŋ] *adj pej, inf* insignifiant(e)
pig [pɪg] **I.** *n* **1.**(*animal*) cochon *m;* **a wild ~** sanglier **2.** *pej, inf* (*swinish person*) porc *m;* **to be a ~ to sb** être un salaud avec qn **3.** *inf* (*police man, woman*) poulet *m* **4.** *inf* (*overeater*) **to make a** (**real**) **~ of oneself** se goinfrer; **a greedy ~** un goinfreur ►**to buy a ~ in a poke** acheter les yeux fermés; **to make a**

~'s **ear of sth** *Brit, inf* saloper qc; **and ~s might fly** *Brit* quand les poules auront des dents **II.** *vt* **to ~ oneself on sth** se goinfrer de qc

◆**pig out** *vi inf* se goinfrer; **to ~ on sth** se goinfrer de qc; **to be pigged out** être goinfré

pigeon ['pɪdʒən] *n* pigeon *m*

pigeon fancier *n Brit, Aus* colombophile *mf*

pigeon-hole I. *n* **1.** (*box*) casier *m* **2.** *fig* **to put in** [*o* **in ~s**] **a ~** (*person*) cataloguer; (*thing*) étiqueter **II.** *vt* **1.** (*classify*) classer **2.** (*label*) étiqueter **3.** (*put off*) remettre à plus tard **pigeon-toed** *adj* **to be ~** avoir les pieds tournés en dedans

piggery ['pɪgəri] <-ies> *n* **1.** AGR *a. pej* porcherie *f* **2.** (*character*) gloutonnerie *f*

piggish ['pɪgɪʃ] *adj pej* **to be ~** être un porc

piggy ['pɪgi] **I.** *adj* <-ier, -iest> *pej, inf* **1.** (*selfish*) égoïste **2.** (*small and pink*) **~ eyes** avec de petits yeux de cochon **II.** <-ies> *n childspeak, inf* cochon *m* ►**to be ~ in the middle** être entre l'écorce et l'arbre

piggyback I. *n* **to give sb a ~** (**ride**) porter qn sur le dos **II.** *adv* sur le dos **piggy bank** *n* tirelire *f* (*en forme de cochon*) **pig-headed** *adj pej* têtu(e) comme une mule

piglet ['pɪglət, *Am:* -lɪt] *n* porcelet *m*

pigment ['pɪgmənt] *n* pigment *m*

pigmentation [ˌpɪgmen'teɪʃən] *n no pl* pigmentation *f*

pigskin *n* peau *f* de porc **pigsty** *n a. fig, pej* porcherie *f*, boiton *m Suisse* **pigswill** *n no pl, a. pej* pâtée *f*

pigtail ['pɪgteɪl] *n* natte *f*

pike¹ [paɪk] *n* ZOOL brochet *m*

pike² [paɪk] *n Am* **to be the best thing to come down the ~** être génial

pike³ [paɪk] *n* (*weapon*) pique *m*

pikestaff ['paɪkstɑːf, *Am:* -stæf] *n no pl* **as plain as a ~** *Brit* clair(e) comme le jour

pilchard ['pɪltʃəd, *Am:* -tʃɚd] *n* pilchard *m*

pile¹ [paɪl] **I.** *n* **1.** (*heap*) pile *f*; **a ~ of letters** une pile de lettres; **to have** (**got**) **~s of sth** *inf* avoir un tas de qc **2.** *inf* (*fortune*) fric *m*; **to make a ~** *inf* faire un tas de fric **3.** (*big building*) édifice *m* **II.** *vt* entasser; (*objects*) empiler; **to ~ sth** (**high**) empiler qc; **to be ~d high with sth** être couvert de piles de qc

◆**pile in** *vi* s'entasser

◆**pile off** *vi* sortir en masse

◆**pile on** *vt* **1.** (*heap*) amonceler **2.** (*exaggerate*) exagérer; **to pile it on** *inf* exagérer; **to ~ the agony** *Brit, inf* dramatiser

◆**pile up I.** *vi* s'accumuler **II.** *vt* **1.** (*increase*) accumuler **2.** (*pile*) entasser

pile² [paɪl] *n* ARCHIT pieu *m*

pile³ [paɪl] *n no pl* poil *m*

piles *npl inf* hémorroïdes *fpl*

pile-up *n* **1.** *inf* (*car crash*) carambolage *m* **2.** (*accumulation*) accumulation *f*

pilfer ['pɪlfəʳ, *Am:* -fɚ] **I.** *vt* piquer **II.** *vi* voler; **to ~ from sb** voler à qn

pilferer *n* voleur, -euse *m, f*

pilfering *n* larcins *mpl*

pilgrim ['pɪlgrɪm] *n* pèlerin(e) *m(f)*

pilgrimage *n a. fig* pèlerinage *m*

pill [pɪl] *n* **1.** (*medicinal tablet*) pilule *f* **2.** (*contraceptive tablet*) **the ~** la pilule; **to be on the ~** prendre la pilule ►**to be a hard ~ to swallow** être dur à avaler; **to sweeten the ~** dorer la pilule

pillage ['pɪlɪdʒ] **I.** *vt, vi form* piller **II.** *n no pl, form* pillage *m*

pillar ['pɪləʳ, *Am:* -ɚ] *n a. fig* pilier *m*; **a ~ of flame/smoke** une colonne de feu/fumée

pillar box *n Brit* boîte *f* aux lettres

pillbox ['pɪlbɒks, *Am:* -bɑːks] *n* **1.** (*small container for tablets*) boîte *f* à pilules **2.** MIL blockhaus *m*

pillion ['pɪlɪən, *Am:* 'pɪljən] **I.** *n Brit, Aus* (*motorbike's seat*) siège *m* arrière **II.** *adv Brit, Aus* **to ride/sit ~** monter/être assis derrière; **to travel ~** voyager à l'arrière

pillory ['pɪləri] **I.** <-ie-> *vt* **to ~ sb/sth** mettre qn/qc au pilori **II.** *n* pilori *m*

pillow ['pɪləʊ, *Am:* -oʊ] *n* oreiller *m*, coussin *m Belgique*

pillowcase, **pillow cover**, **pillowslip** *n* taie *f* d'oreiller

pilot ['paɪlət] **I.** *n a.* TEL pilote *m* **II.** *vt* **1.** (*guide*) piloter; (*person*) guider **2.** (*make trial product*) tester

pilot boat *n* bateau-pilote *m* **pilot fish** *n* poisson *m* pilote **pilot lamp** *n* témoin *m*

pilotless *adj* sans pilote

pilot light *n* **1.** (*monitoring light*) témoin *m* **2.** (*small flame igniting heating*) veilleuse *f* **pilot program** *n Am*, **pilot scheme** *n Brit, Aus* projet *m* pilote **pilot's licence** *n* permis *m* de pilotage **pilot's licence** *n* brevet *m* de pilote **pilot study** *n* enquête *f* pilote

pimento [pɪ'mentəʊ, *Am:* -toʊ] <-s> *n* piment *m*

pimp [pɪmp] **I.** *n* maquereau *m* **II.** *vi* être proxénète

pimple ['pɪmpl] *n* bouton *m*

pimply <-ier, -iest> *adj* boutonneux(-euse)

PIN [pɪn] *n abbr of* **Personal Identification Number** code *m* confidentiel

pin [pɪn] **I.** *n* **1.** (*needle*) épingle *f*; **a safety ~** une épingle de nourrice; **a hat ~** une épingle à chapeau **2.** MIL (*safety device on grenade*) goupille *f* **3.** (*ornamental object for clothing*) épingle *f* **4.** *Am* (*brooch*) broche *f* **5.** *pl* gambettes *fpl* **6.** SPORT (**bowling**) **~** quille *f* ►**as clean as a new ~** propre comme un sou neuf; **you could hear a ~ drop** *fig* on entendait les mouches voler; **to have ~s and needles in sth** avoir des fourmis à qc; **to be on ~s and needles** *Am* être tout excité **II.** <-nn-> *vt* **1.** (*fix with pin*) épingler; **to ~ a medal on sb** accrocher une médaille sur qn; **to ~ a hem** épingler un ourlet **2.** (*immobilize*) bloquer; **~ned to the floor** coincé(e) contre le sol **3.** *inf* (*accuse*) **to ~ the blame on sb** attribuer la

P

responsabilité à qn; **they'll ~ it on me** ils vont me coller ça sur le dos ►**to ~ back one's ears** [*o* **one's ears back**] *inf* tendre l'oreille
◆**pin down** *vt* **1.** (*define exactly*) identifier; **it's hard to ~ what I felt** c'est difficile de définir exactement ce que j'ai ressenti **2.** (*pressure sb to decide*) coincer; **to ~ sb to sth** coincer qn sur qc **3.** (*restrict sb's movement*) coincer **4.** (*fix with pin*) accrocher
◆**pin together** *vt* épingler ensemble
◆**pin up** *vt* (*on wall*) punaiser; **~ one's hair** attacher ses cheveux

pinafore ['pɪnəfɔːʳ, *Am:* -fɔːr] *n* **1.** (*apron*) tablier *m* **2.** *Brit, Aus s.* **pinafore dress**

pinafore dress *n* robe-chasuble *f*

pinball ['pɪnbɔːl] *n* flipper *m*

pincer *n* **1.** *pl* ZOOL (*finger-like parts*) pince *f* **2.** **~s** *pl* (*tool extracting nails*) pinces *fpl*

pinch [pɪntʃ] **I.** *vt* **1.** (*nip, tweak*) pincer; **to ~ oneself** *fig* se pincer **2.** (*grip hard*) serrer; **the shoes ~ my feet** les chaussures me font mal aux pieds **3.** *inf* (*steal*) piquer **II.** *vi* serrer; (*boots, shoes, slippers*) blesser **III.** *n* **1.** (*nip*) pincement *m;* **to give sb a ~** pincer qn **2.** (*minute/small quantity*) pincée *f* ►**at/in a ~** si besoin est; **to feel the ~** être en difficultés; **to take sth with a ~ of salt** ne pas prendre qc au pied de la lettre

pinched *adj* (*face, features*) tiré(e)

pincushion ['pɪnˌkʊʃən] *n* pelote *f* à épingles

pine¹ [paɪn] *n* **1.** (*tree*) pin *m* **2.** (*wood*) (bois *m* de) pin *m;* **a stripped ~ wardrobe** une armoire en pin décapé

pine² [paɪn] *vi* se languir; **to ~ for sb/sth** languir après qn/qc

pineapple ['paɪnæpl] *n* ananas *m;* **tinned** [*o* **canned** *Am*] **~s** ananas *m* en conserve

pine cone *n* pomme *f* de pin, pive *f Suisse* **pine grove** *n* pinède *f* **pine needle** *n* aiguille *f* de pin **pine wood** *n no pl* (bois *m* de) pin *m*

ping [pɪŋ] **I.** *n* tintement *m* **II.** *vi* tinter

Ping-Pong® *n no pl, inf* ping-pong *m*

pinhead ['pɪnhed] *n* **1.** (*part of pin*) tête *f* d'épingle **2.** *pej, inf* (*simpleton*) crétin *m*

pinion ['pɪnjən] *n* TECH pinion *m*

pink¹ [pɪŋk] **I.** *n* **1.** (*colour*) rose *m* **2.** BOT œillet *m* ►**to be in the ~** *iron* se porter comme un charme; **in the ~ of condition** en pleine forme **II.** *adj* rose; **to turn ~** rosir; (*person, face*) rougir ►**to see ~ elephants** *iron* avoir des hallucinations; *s. a.* **blue**

pink² [pɪŋk] *vt* denteler

pinkie *n inf* petit doigt *m*

pinking shears *npl* ciseaux *mpl* à cranter

pinko ['pɪŋkəʊ, *Am:* -koʊ] <-s *o* -es> *n pej* gauchiste *mf*

pinky *adj inf* rosé(e)

pinnace ['pɪnɪs] *n* pinasse *f*

pinnacle ['pɪnəkl] *n* sommet *m*

pinpoint ['pɪnpɔɪnt] **I.** *vt* **1.** (*give exactly: place*) localiser; (*time*) déterminer **2.** *fig* (*identify*) mettre le doigt sur **II.** *adj* **with ~ accuracy** avec extrême précision **III.** *n* point *m*

pinprick ['pɪnprɪk] *n* **1.** (*making hole*) coup *m* d'épingle; (*pain*) sensation *f* de piqure **2.** (*irritation*) égratignure *f*

pinstripe ['pɪnstraɪp] *n no pl* petite rayure *f;* **to wear ~s** porter un costume à fines rayures; **a ~(d) shirt** une chemise à fines rayures

pint [paɪnt] *n a. inf* pinte *f;* **do you fancy a ~?** ça te dire de boire une bière?

pint-size, **pint-sized** *adj inf* petit format

pin-up *n* pin up *f inv;* (*male*) star *f* (masculine)

pinwheel *n Am* petit moulin *m* à vent

pioneer [ˌpaɪə'nɪəʳ, *Am:* -'nɪr] **I.** *n* pionnier, -ière *m, f* **II.** *adj* pionnier(-ère) **III.** *vt* être le pionnier pour

pioneering *adj* de pionnier

pious ['paɪəs] *adj* REL *a. iron* pieux(-euse)

pip¹ [pɪp] *n* BOT noyau *m* de fruit

pip² [pɪp] *n pl, Brit* bip *m*

pip³ [pɪp] <-pp-> *vt Brit, inf* battre ►**to ~ sb at the post** battre qn sur le poteau

pipe [paɪp] **I.** *n* **1.** *a.* TECH (*industrial tube*) tuyau *m* **2.** (*for smoking*) pipe *f* **3.** MUS (*wind instrument*) pipeau *m;* (*in organ*) tuyau *m;* **the ~s** la cornemuse **4.** (*sound: of bird*) chant *m* ►**put that in your ~ and smoke it** *inf* mets-toi ça bien dans le crâne **II.** *vt* **1.** (*transport using cylinders*) **to ~ sth** acheminer qc par canalisation **2.** (*sing, speak shrilly: bird*) pépier; (*of person*) dire d'une voix aiguë **3.** MUS jouer (du pipeau/de la cornemuse)
◆**pipe down** *vi inf* **1.** (*be quiet*) fermer sa gueule **2.** (*be quieter*) baisser le ton
◆**pipe up** *vi* se faire entendre

pipe cleaner *n* cure-pipe *m* **pipe dream**, **pipedream** *n* château *m* en Espagne **pipe fitter** *n* plombier *m*

pipeline ['paɪplaɪn] *n* pipeline *m;* **in the ~** *fig* en préparation

piper ['paɪpəʳ, *Am:* -pɚ] *n* flûtiste *mf*

piping **I.** *n no pl* **1.** (*pipes*) tuyauterie *f* **2.** GASTR glaçage *m* **3.** (*sewing material*) ganse *f* **4.** (*sound of bagpipes*) cornemuse *f* **II.** *adj* aigu(ë)

piping hot *adj* (*drink*) bouillant(e); (*food*) brûlant(e)

pipsqueak ['pɪpskwiːk] *n pej, inf* demi-portion *f*

pique [piːk] **I.** *n no pl* ressentiment *m;* **a fit of ~** une crise de colère **II.** *vt* lancer des piques à; **to ~ sb's curiosity/interest** piquer la curiosité/l'intérêt de qn

piracy ['paɪərəsi, *Am:* 'paɪrə-] *n no pl* piraterie *f;* COM piratage

pirate ['paɪərət, *Am:* 'paɪrət] **I.** *n* pirate *mf* **II.** *adj* (*copy, video*) pirate **III.** *vt* pirater

pirouette [ˌpɪrʊ'et, *Am:* -u'et] **I.** *n* pirouette *f* **II.** *vi* faire une pirouette

Pisces ['paɪsiːz] *n* Poissons *mpl; s. a.* **Aquarius**

piss [pɪs] *vulg* **I.** *n no pl* pisse *f;* **to have a ~**

aller pisser; **to need a** ~ avoir envie de pisser ►**to take the** ~ **out of sb** *Brit* se foutre de la gueule de qn **II.** *vi* **1.** (*urinate*) pisser **2.** *Brit, Aus, inf* (*rain*) pleuvoir comme vache qui pisse **III.** *vt* **to** ~ **oneself** se pisser dessus

♦**piss about, piss around** *vi Brit, Aus, inf* faire n'importe quoi

piss artist *n Brit, inf* **1.** (*glib, unconvincing person*) charlot *m* **2.** (*alcoholic*) alcoolo *mf*

pissed *adj* **1.** *Brit, Aus, inf* bourré(e); **to be** ~ **as a newt** être rond comme une queue de pelle **2.** *Am, inf* furax

piss-up *n Brit, Aus, inf* beuverie *f*

pistachio [pɪ'stɑːʃiəʊ, *Am:* -'stæʃioʊ] <-s> *n* pistache *f*

pistil ['pɪstɪl] *n* BOT pistil *m*

pistol ['pɪstəl] *n* pistolet *m;* **to hold a** ~ **to sb's head** *fig* mettre à qn le couteau sous la gorge

pistol shot *n* coup *m* de pistolet

piston ['pɪstən] *n* TECH piston *m*

piston engine *n* moteur *m* à pistons **piston ring** *n* segment *m* **piston stroke** *n* course *f*

pit[1] [pɪt] **I.** *n* **1.** (*in ground*) fosse *f* **2.** (*mark*) *a.* MED marque *f;* **in the** ~ **of the stomach** dans le creux de l'estomac **3.** INFOR, TECH (*hollow, depression*) creux *m* **4.** (*mine*) mine *f* **5.** THEAT, MUS (*area of seating*) parterre *m;* **orchestra** ~ fosse *f* d'orchestre **6.** (*in motor racing*) stand *m* ►**to be the** ~**s** *inf* être nul **II.** *vt* **1.** (*make holes in*) creuser un trou; ~**ted by small pox** grêlé par la petit vérole **2.** (*place in opposition*) **to** ~ **sb against sb** opposer qn contre qn

pit[2] [pɪt] <-tt-> *Am* **I.** *n* noyau *m* **II.** *vt* dénoyauter

pit-a-pat [ˌpɪtə'pæt, *Am:* 'pɪt̬əpæt] **I.** *adv* **to go** ~ (*toddler*) aller à petits pas; (*rain*) faire des tapotements; (*heart*) battre **II.** *n* (*of feet*) petits pas *mpl;* (*of heart, rain*) battement rapide *m*

pit bull *n* pitbull *m*

pitch[1] [pɪtʃ] **I.** *n* **1.** *Brit, Aus* SPORT (*playing field*) terrain *m* de jeu; **football** ~ terrain *m* de foot **2.** *Brit* (*place for camping*) emplacement (*m* pour la tente) **3.** *Am* SPORT (*baseball*) centre *m* du terrain **4.** MUS, LING (*tone depth, height*) tonalité *f;* **perfect** ~ oreille *f* absolue **5.** (*sales talk*) baratin *m* **6.** *Brit* stand *m* **7.** (*slope in roofs*) pente *f* ►**to be at fever** ~ être très excité **II.** *vt* **1.** (*throw*) faire tomber **2.** (*force sb into situation*) **to** ~ **sb/sth into sth** plonger qn/qc dans qc **3.** SPORT lancer **4.** (*fix level of sound: note*) donner; **to** ~ **the voice high/low** hausser/baisser le ton **5.** (*put up*) tent, planter; **to** ~ **camp** établir un camp **6.** (*aim*) **to** ~ **sth at** (*consumers, market*) s'adresser à; (*audience*) adapter qc pour **III.** *vi* **1.** (*suddenly thrust*) tomber; **to** ~ **forward** tomber en avant **2.** (*slope*) être en pente **3.** SPORT lancer

♦**pitch in** *vi inf* s'y mettre

♦**pitch into** *vt* **1.** (*attack verbally*) **to** ~ **sb** agresser qn **2.** (*begin task enthusiastically*) se jeter sur

♦**pitch out** *vt* jeter

pitch[2] [pɪtʃ] *n no pl* (*bitumen*) brai *m*

pitch-black, pitch-dark *adj* (*dark*) noir comme dans un four

pitched battle *n* bataille *f* rangée

pitcher[1] *n Am* (*jug*) cruche *f;* **tea** ~ théière *f*

pitcher[2] *n* SPORT lanceur *m*

pitchfork ['pɪtʃfɔːk, *Am:* -fɔːrk] *n* fourche *f* à fumier

piteous ['pɪtiəs, *Am:* 'pɪt̬-] *adj* **1.** (*arousing pity*) pitoyable **2.** (*heartbreaking*) déchirant(e); **to be a** ~ **sight** être un spectacle déchirant

pitfall ['pɪtfɔːl] *n* écueil *m*

pith [pɪθ] *n no pl* **1.** BOT (*white substance in citrus*) pulpe *f;* (*part of plants*) moelle *f* **2.** *fig* (*main point*) quintessence *f*

pithead ['pɪtˌhed] *n sing, Brit, Aus* MIN entrée *f* d'une mine

pith helmet *n* HIST casque *m* colonial

pithy ['pɪθi] <-ier, -iest> *adj* **1.** (*succinct, concise*) succinct(e) **2.** (*containing much pith: fruit*) pulpeux(-euse); (*plant*) médulleux(-euse)

pitiable *form,* **pitiful** *adj* (*conditions, excuse, sight*) lamentable

pitiless *adj* impitoyable

piton ['piːtɒn, *Am:* -tɑːn] *n* SPORT piton *m*

pitta ['pɪtə, *Am:* 'pɪt̬ə], **pitta bread** *n* pitta *f*

pittance ['pɪtənts] *n sing, pej* salaire *m* de misère

pituitary [pɪ'tjuːɪtəri, *Am:* -'tuːəteri], **pituitary gland** *n* hypophyse *f*

pity ['pɪti, *Am:* 'pɪt̬-] **I.** *n no pl* **1.** (*compassion*) pitié *f;* **in** ~ par pitié; **to feel** ~ **for sb/sth** avoir de la pitié pour qn/qc; **to take** ~ **on sb/sth** prendre qn/qc en pitié; **for** ~**'s sake** par pitié **2.** (*unfortunate matter*) **it's a** ~**!** c'est dommage!; **more's the** ~ malheureusement; **what a** ~ quel dommage **II.** <-ies, -ied> *vt* avoir de la peine pour; **I** ~ **his parents** j'ai de la peine pour ses parents

pitying *adj* compatissant(e); (*deriding*) dédaigneux(-euse)

pivot ['pɪvət] **I.** *n* **1.** TECH (*axis holding sth up*) pivot *m* **2.** *fig* (*focal point, hub*) point *m* d'axe; **to be the** ~ **of sth** être le point d'axe de qc **3.** (*key person*) personne *f* clef **II.** *vi* pivoter; **to** ~ **around sth** *a. fig* pivoter autour de qc; **to** ~ **round** pivoter; **to** ~ **through ninety degrees** virer à 90 degrés

pix *inf pl of* **pic**

pixel [pɪksəl] *n* INFOR pixel *m*

pixie *n* lutin *m*

pixy ['pɪksi] *n* <-ies> *s.* **pixie**

pizza ['piːtsə] *n* pizza *f*

pizzazz [pɪ'zæz] *n no pl, inf* panache *m*

pizzeria *n* pizzeria *f*

placard ['plækɑːd, *Am:* -ɑːrd] *n* pancarte *f;* (*on wall*) affiche *f*

placate [plə'keɪt, *Am:* 'pleɪkeɪt] *vt* apaiser

P

placatory [plə'keɪtəri, *Am:* 'pleɪkətɔːr-] *adj form* apaisant(e)

place [pleɪs] **I.** *n* **1.** (*location, area*) endroit *m;* (*of birth, death, work*) *form* lieu *m;* ~ **of refuge** refuge *m;* **in ~s** par endroits; **to be in two ~s at once** être en deux endroits à la fois **2.** (*residence, commercial location*) adresse *f;* (*dwelling*) résidence *f;* (*house*) maison *f;* (*flat*) appartement *m;* **at Paul's ~** chez Paul; **a little ~ in Corsica** un petit village en Corse; ~ **of residence** domicile *m* **3.** *no pl* (*appropriate setting*) endroit *m;* **it's not a ~ for sb** ce n'est pas la place de qn; **it's not the ~/no ~ to** *+infin* ce n'est pas l'endroit/un endroit pour *+infin* **4.** (*position*) place *f;* **to be in one's/its ~** être à sa place; **to lose one's ~** perdre sa place; **the ~ where he gets shot** le moment où on lui tire dessus; **in ~ of sb/sth** à la place de qn/qc; **to give sb sth in ~** donner à qn qc à la place; **out of ~** déplacé(e); **to be in ~** être en place; **in the first/second ~** en premier/second lieu; **to take first/second ~** se placer premier/second; **to take second ~ to sth** *fig* passer après qc; **people in high ~s** des gens haut placés **5.** (*square*) place *f;* **market ~** place du marché **6.** MAT **to three decimal ~s** avec trois décimales **7.** (*seat*) place *f;* **is this ~ taken?** cette place est-elle libre?; **to lay a ~ at the table** mettre un couvert sur la table; **to change ~s with sb** changer de place avec qn; **to keep sb a ~** garder une place à qn; **to have a ~ on** *Aus, Brit* [*o* **in** *Am*] **a course** être admis à suivre un cours **8.** *Am, inf* (*indefinite location*) **any ~** n'importe où; **some ~** quelque part; **every ~** partout; **no ~** nulle part ►**all over the ~** partout; **the files were all over the place** les dossiers étaient sens dessus dessous; **the film was all over the place** le film était complètement incohérent; **to go ~s** *inf* (*become successful*) faire son chemin **II.** *vt* **1.** (*position, put*) placer; **to ~ an advertisement in the newspaper** mettre une annonce dans le journal; **to ~ a comma** mettre une virgule; **to ~ sth on the agenda** mettre qc à l'ordre du jour **2.** (*situate*) situer; **to be well ~d** être bien situé; **to be well/badly ~d to** *+infin fig* être bien/mal placé pour *+infin* **3.** (*impose*) **to ~ an embargo on sb/sth** frapper qn/qc d'embargo; **to ~ a limit on sth** fixer une limite à qc **4.** (*ascribe*) **to ~ the blame on sb** jeter le blâme sur qn; **to ~ one's hopes on sb/sth** mettre tous ses espoirs en qn/qc; **to ~ emphasis on sth** *a. fig* mettre l'accent sur qc; **to ~ one's faith** [*o* **trust**] **in sb/sth** faire confiance à qn/qc **5.** (*arrange for*) **to ~ an order for sth** passer une commande de qc; **to ~ a bet** faire un pari; **to ~ sth at sb's disposal** mettre qc à la disposition de qn **6.** (*appoint to a position*) **to ~ sb in charge of sth** charger qn de qc; **to ~ sb under arrest** arrêter qn **7.** (*classify*) placer; **~d first/second** classé premier/second; **to ~ sth above** [*o* **before**] [*o* **over**] **sth** faire passer qc avant qc; **to ~ sb's face** se souvenir de qn

placebo [plə'siːbəʊ, *Am:* -boʊ] <-s> *n* MED placebo *m*

place card *n* carte *f* de table **place kick** *n* SPORT remise *f* en jeu **place mat** *n* set *m* de table

placement *n* placement *m*

placement examination *n* test *m* d'embauche **placement service** *n* service *m* de placement

place name *n* nom *m* de lieu

placenta [plə'sentə, *Am:* -t̬ə] <-s *o* -ae> *n* MED placenta *m*

placid ['plæsɪd] *adj* placide

placing *n* **1.** (*place in exam, race*) place *f* **2.** (*layout*) positionnement *m*

plagiarism ['pleɪdʒərɪzəm, *Am:* -dʒɚɪ-] *n no pl* plagiat *m*

plagiarist *n* plagiaire *mf*

plagiarize ['pleɪdʒəraɪz] *vt, vi* plagier

plague [pleɪg] **I.** *n* **1.** (*disease*) épidémie *f* **2. the ~** (*bubonic plague*) la peste **3.** (*infesting of animals*) fléau *m* **4.** (*source of annoyance*) plaie *f* ►**to avoid sb like the ~** éviter qc comme la peste **II.** *vt* tourmenter

plaice [pleɪs] *inv n* carrelet *m*

plaid [plæd] **I.** *n no pl, Am* FASHION plaid *m; s. a.* **tartan II.** *adj* en plaid; *s. a.* **tartan**

plain [pleɪn] **I.** *adj* **1.** (*one colour*) uni(e) **2.** (*unflavoured: yoghurt*) nature; ~ **chocolate** chocolat *m* noir **3.** (*uncomplicated: clothes, cookery*) très simple; **a ~ wooden table** une table en bois toute simple; ~ **and simple** pur(e) et simple **4.** (*clear, obvious*) clair(e); **in ~ language** en langage clair; **it's ~ that …** il est clair que …; **to be ~ enough** être assez clair; **to make sth ~** ne pas faire mystère de qc; **to make oneself ~ to sb** se rendre clair à qn; **to be ~ with sb** être clair avec qn **5.** (*mere, pure: truth, torture*) pur(e); **it's ~ selfishness** c'est de l'égoïsme pur **6.** (*unattractive*) sans attraits ►**to be as ~ as the nose on your face** se voir comme le nez au milieu de la figure **II.** *adv* **1.** (*done in unadorned style*) clairement **2.** *inf* (*downright*) vraiment **III.** *n* **1.** GEO plaine *f;* **the ~s** la prairie **2.** (*knitting stitch*) maille *f*

plain clothes LAW **I.** *n* vêtements *mpl* de civil; **in ~** en civil **II.** *adj* (*of non-uniformed police*) en civil

plainly *adv* **1.** (*simply*) simplement **2.** (*clearly*) clairement **3.** (*obviously*) franchement **4.** (*undeniably*) indéniablement

plainness *n no pl* **1.** (*simplicity*) simplicité **2.** (*obviousness*) évidence *f* **3.** (*unattractiveness*) apparence *f* quelconque

plain sailing *n fig* **to be ~** être simple comme bonjour **plain-spoken** *adj* **to be ~** être franc

plaintiff ['pleɪntɪf, *Am:* -t̬ɪf] *n* plaignant(e) *m(f)*

plaintive ['pleɪntɪv, *Am:* -t̬ɪv] *adj* (*cry, voice*) plaintif(-ive)

plait [plæt] *Brit* **I.** *n* tresse *f* **II.** *vt* tresser

plan [plæn] **I.** *n* **1.** (*detailed scheme, programme*) plan *m;* **the ~ is to surprise them** l'idée est de les surprendre; **four-point ~** plan en quatre étapes; **to go according to ~** se dérouler comme prévu; **to make ~s for sth** planifier qc **2.** (*vaguer intention, aim*) projet *m;* **to have ~s** avoir des projets; **I have other ~s** je suis occupé; **to change ~s** changer ses projets **3.** FIN, ECON (*insurance scheme*) plan *m* **4.** (*diagram, drawing*) plan *m* **II.** <-nn-> *vt* **1.** (*work out in detail*) planifier; **to ~ to do/on doing sth** projeter de faire qc; **~ned economy** ECON économie *f* planifiée; **to ~ things to so as to see everybody** organiser les chose de façon à voir tout le monde **2.** (*design, make a plan*) faire le plan de **III.** *vi* faire des projets; **we need to ~ ahead** nous devons prévoir à l'avance; **to ~ for retirement** prévoir sa retraite; **to ~ on doing sth** avoir le projet de faire qc

plane¹ [pleɪn] **I.** *n* **1.** (*level surface*) niveau *m* **2.** MAT plan *m* **3.** (*level of thought, intellect*) niveau *m;* **to be on a certain ~** être à un certain niveau; (*be superior*) avoir un certain niveau **II.** *adj a.* MAT plat(e)

plane² [pleɪn] **I.** *n* (*tool*) rabot *m* **II.** *vt* raboter

plane³ [pleɪn] *n* (*aircraft*) avion *m;* **to board the ~** monter dans l'avion

plane⁴ [pleɪn] *n* BOT **~** (**tree**) platane *m*

plane crash *n* catastrophe *f* aérienne

planet ['plænɪt] *n* planète *f;* **~ Earth** planète *f* Terre

planetarium [ˌplænɪ'teərɪəm, *Am:* -'terɪ-] <-s *o* -ria> *n* planétarium *m*

planetary ['plænɪtəri, *Am:* -teri] *adj* planétaire

plank [plæŋk] *n* **1.** (*long board*) planche *f* **2.** (*important element*) point *m*

planking *n no pl* plancher *m*

plankton ['plæŋktən] *n no pl* plancton *m*

planner *n* planificateur, -trice *m, f;* **a city ~** un(e) urbaniste

planning *n no pl* planification *f;* **city ~** urbanisme *m*

planning permission *n* permis *m* de construire

plant [plɑːnt, *Am:* plænt] **I.** *n* **1.** BIO plante *f;* **indoor ~** plante *f* d'intérieur **2.** (*factory*) usine *f* **3.** *no pl* (*machinery for companies*) équipement *m* **4.** (*informer*) taupe *f* **5.** *sing* (*object placed to mislead*) *objet destiné à faire prendre quelqu'un* **II.** *vt a. fig* planter; (*a bomb*) poser; (*spy*) infiltrer; (*colony, idea*) implanter; **to ~ drugs on sb** placer de la drogue pour faire prendre qn; **to ~ oneself somewhere** *inf* se planter quelque part; **to ~ doubts about sth** semer des doutes sur qc

plantain ['plæntɪn] *n* **1.** (*fruit*) banane *f* plantain **2.** (*plant*) plantain *m*

plantation [plæn'teɪʃən] *n* plantation *f*

planter *n* **1.** (*owner of plantation*) planteur, -euse *m, f* **2.** (*supporting structure for plant holder*) cache-pot *m* **3.** (*device for planting seeds*) plantoir *m*

plaque [plɑːk, plæk, *Am:* plæk] *n* **1.** (*plate identifying building*) plaque *f;* **brass/stone ~** plaque en laiton/pierre **2.** *no pl* MED plaque *f* dentaire

plash [plæʃ] **I.** *n* clapotis *m* **II.** *vi* **1.** (*make a splashing sound*) clapoter **2.** (*play in the water*) barboter

plasma ['plæzmə] **I.** *n* plasma *m* **II.** *adj* plasmagène

plaster ['plɑːstəʳ, *Am:* 'plæstɚ] **I.** *n* **1.** (*substance used in building*) *a.* MED plâtre *m;* **in ~** dans le plâtre **2.** *Brit* (*tape for wound*) sparadrap *m* **II.** *vt a. inf* plâtrer; **~ed with slogans/posters** couvert(e) de slogans/d'affiches

plasterboard *n no pl* CONSTR placoplâtre® *m*

plaster cast *n a.* ART plâtre *m*

plastered *adj inf* bourré(e)

plasterer *n* plâtrier *m*

plastic ['plæstɪk] **I.** *n* plastique *m;* **to pay with ~** *inf* payer par carte de crédit **II.** *adj* **1.** (*made from plastic*) en plastique **2.** *pej* (*artificial: food*) synthétique; (*smile*) artificiel(le) **3.** ART (*malleable*) plastique

plastic arts *n pl* arts *mpl* plastiques **plastic bag** *n* sac *m* en plastique **plastic bomb** *n* bombe *f* au plastic **plastic bullet** *n* projectile *m* plastic **plastic explosive** *n* explosif *m* au plastic

Plasticine® ['plæstəsiːn, *Am:* -tɪ-] *n Brit no pl* pâte *f* à modeler

plasticity [plæ'stɪsəti, *Am:* -ţi] *n no pl* plasticité *f*

plastic money *n no pl* cartes *fpl* de crédit **plastics industry** *n* industrie *f* des matières plastiques **plastic surgery** *n* chirurgie *f* plastique

plate [pleɪt] **I.** *n* **1.** (*dish, dinner plate*) assiette *f;* **a ~ of pasta** une assiette de pâtes **2.** (*panel, sheet*) plaque *f* **3.** (*on earths's crust*) plaque *f* **4.** (*sign*) *a.* AUTO, TYP plaque *f;* **brass ~** plaque en laiton **5.** TYP (*picture in book*) planche *f* **6.** (*cutlery*) (**silver**) ~ argenterie *f* ▶**to have a lot on one's ~** *Brit* en avoir pardessus la tête; **to give sth to sb on a ~** *inf* servir qc à qn sur un plateau doré **II.** *vt* (*with gold, silver*) plaquer; **silver-plated** plaqué(e) argent

plateau ['plætəʊ, *Am:* plæt'oʊ] <-x *Brit o Am, Aus* -s> *n* **1.** GEO (*elevated plain*) plateau *m* **2.** (*flat period*) plateau *m;* **to reach a ~** se stabiliser

plated *adj* (*coated in metal*) métallisé(e); (*of jewellery*) plaqué(e); **~ with chrome** chromé(e); **~ with gold** plaqué(e) or; **~ with silver** plaqué(e) argent

plateful *n* assiette *f*

plate glass *n* verre *m* pour vitrage

platelet ['pleɪlət] *n* PHYS plaquette *f*

plate rack *n* égouttoir *m* à vaisselle **plate-warmer** *n* chauffe-assiettes *m*

platform ['plætfɔːm, *Am:* -fɔːrm] *n*

P

1. (*raised surface*) plateforme *f* 2. *Brit, Aus* RAIL quai *m* 3. (*stage*) estrade *f;* **to share a ~ with sb** partager la tribune avec qn; **to be a ~ for sth** *fig* être une tribune pour qc 4. *pl s.* **platform shoes**

platform shoes *npl* chaussures *fpl* à semelles compensées

plating *n* placage *m*

platinum ['plætɪnəm, *Am:* 'plætnəm] *n no pl* platine *m*

platitude ['plætɪtjuːd, *Am:* 'plæţətuːd] *n pej* lieu *m* commun

platitudinous *adj pej, form* banal(e)

platonic [plə'tɒnɪk, *Am:* -'tɑːnɪk] *adj* platonique

platoon [plə'tuːn] *n + sing/pl vb* MIL section *f*

platter ['plætəʳ, *Am:* 'plæţɚ] *n Brit* plateau *m*

platypus ['plætɪpəs, *Am:* 'plæţ-] <-es> *n* ornithorynque *m*

plausibility [ˌplɔːzə'bɪlɪti, *Am:* ˌplɑːzə'bɪləţi] *n no pl* plausibilité *f*

plausible ['plɔːzəbl, *Am:* 'plɑː-] *adj* plausible

play [pleɪ] I. *n* 1. *no pl* (*games*) jeu *m;* **to be at ~** être en train de jouer; **to do sth in ~** faire qc par jeu; **to be in/out of ~** être en/hors-jeu; **to make a bad/good ~** bien/mal jouer 2. (*theatrical piece*) pièce *f* de théâtre; **one-act ~** pièce en un acte 3. *no pl* (*freedom to move*) jeu *m* ►**to make a ~ for sb** draguer qn; **to bring sth into ~** faire rentrer qc en jeu; **to come into ~** rentrer en jeu; **to allow sb full ~** laisser entière liberté à qn II. *vi* jouer; (*radio*) marcher; **to ~ on the piano** jouer du piano; **to ~ in attack** jouer attaquant; **to ~ to a full house** jouer à guichets fermés ►**to ~ fast and loose with sb/sth** traiter qn/qc à la légère; **to ~ to the gallery** amuser la galerie; **to ~ into sb's hands** faire le jeu de qn; **to ~ for time** essayer de gagner du temps III. *vt* 1. GAMES jouer; **to ~ bridge/cards/golf** jouer au bridge/aux cartes/au golf; **to ~ house** jouer au papa et à la maman; **to ~ host to sb** accueillir qn; **to ~ Germany** SPORT jouer contre l'Allemagne; **to ~ the horses** jouer aux courses; **to ~ a slot machine** jouer à la machine à sous; **to ~ the stock market** jouer en Bourse; **to ~ a joke on sb** faire une blague à qn; **to ~ a trick on sb** jouer un tour à qn 2. (*perform: symphony, role*) interpréter; (*flute, guitar*) jouer de; **they were ~ing Mozart** (*orchestra*) ils jouaient Mozart; (*radio station*) ils faisaient passer du Mozart; **to ~ a CD** mettre un CD; **to ~ a concert** donner un concert; **we're ~ing the New Theatre** on passe au New Theatre; **to ~ a vital role in sth** *fig* jouer un rôle fondamental dans qc ►**to ~ ball with sb** *inf* coopérer avec qn; **to ~ ducks and drakes with money** jeter l'argent par les fenêtres; **to ~ both ends against the middle** semer la zizanie; **to ~ second fiddle to sb** être dans l'ombre de qn; **to ~ the field** avoir plusieurs amants; **to ~ footsie with sb** *inf* faire du pied à qn; **to ~ gooseberry** *Brit* tenir la chandelle; **to ~ it cool** rester calme; **to ~ it safe** rester prudent(e); **to ~ hard to get** se laisser désirer; **to ~ hardball** *Am* ne pas être tendre; **to ~ havoc with sth** chambouler qc; **to ~ (merry) hell with sth** ficher qc en l'air; **to ~ hook(e)y** *Am, Aus* faire l'école buissonnière; **to ~ a hunch** agir par intuition; **to ~ possum** (*pretend to be asleep*) faire semblant de dormir; (*pretend to be ignorant or unaware*) faire l'innocent(e); **to ~ truant (from school)** *Brit* faire l'école buissonnière; **to ~ dumb** faire le con; **to ~ sb false** *form* tromper qn

◆**play about** *vi* s'amuser

◆**play along** I. *vi* **to ~ with sb** MUS accompagner qn; (*accept plans*) marcher avec qn II. *vt always sep, pej* **to play sb along** faire marcher qn

◆**play around** *vi* 1. (*play*) jouer 2. *pej* (*be unfaithful*) coucher à droite et à gauche; **to ~ with sb** avoir une aventure avec qn 3. (*imagine*) **to ~ with** (*ideas, possibilities*) imaginer 4. *pej* (*tamper*) **to ~ with sth** tripoter qc

◆**play at** *vt* 1. jouer à 2. *pej* **what are you ~ing at?** à quoi tu joues?; **he's playing at being in charge** il fait son numéro de personne responsable

◆**play down** *vt* minimiser

◆**play off** I. *vi* SPORT **to ~ for third place** jouer pour connaître le gagnant de la troisième place II. *vt* **to play sb off against sb** monter qn contre qn

◆**play on** I. *vt* (*exploit*) **to ~ sb's feelings/weakness** exploiter les sentiments/la faiblesse de qn II. *vi* (*keep playing*) continuer de jouer

◆**play out** *vt* 1. (*enact: fantasies*) réaliser; (*scene, scenario*) jouer 2. (*follow assigned or fated role: destiny*) suivre; **the tragedy played out in New York** la tragédie qui s'est déroulée à New York

◆**play up** I. *vt* 1. (*exaggerate*) exagérer 2. *Brit* (*cause pain to*) taquiner; **my leg is playing me up** ma jambe me taquine II. *vi* 1. **to ~ to sb** flatter qn 2. *Brit* (*cause trouble*) faire des siennes; **my leg is playing up** ma jambe me taquine

playable *adj* jouable

play-act *vi* jouer la comédie

playback *n no pl* play-back *m*

playbill *n* affiche *f*

playboy *n pej* play-boy *m*

player *n* 1. (*participant, performer*) joueur, -euse *m, f;* **football ~** footballeur, -euse *m, f;* **tennis player** joueur de tennis, -euse *m, f;* **a cello ~** un(e) violoncelliste; **a flute ~** un(e) flûtiste 2. (*stage actor*) acteur, -trice *m, f* 3. (*device*) lecteur *m;* (*for CDs*) platine *f;* **a DVD ~** un lecteur de DVD

playful *adj* (*person, animal*) joueur(-euse), jouette *Belgique;* (*mood, nature, remark*) enjoué(e)

playground *n* (*for children*) cour *f* de récréation **playgroup** *n* jardin *m* d'enfants **playhouse** *n* **1.** (*theatre*) théâtre *m* **2.** (*miniature house*) maison *f* pour jouer

playing card *n* carte *f* à jouer **playing field** *n* terrain *m* de sports

playmate ['pleɪmeɪt] *n* (*childhood playfellow*) copain, copine *m, f*

play-off *n* match *m* pour départager deux équipes

playpen ['pleɪpen] *n* parc *m* (pour bébé)

playroom *n* salle *f* de jeu **playschool** *n Brit* jardin *m* d'enfants **playsuit** *n* barboteuse *f* **plaything** *n fig, pej* jouet *m* **playtime** *n* récréation *f* **playwright** *n* dramaturge *mf*

plaza ['plɑːzə] *n* place *f*

plc [ˌpiːel'siː] *n Brit abbr of* **public limited company** ≈ SARL *f*

plea [pliː] *n* **1.** (*entreaty, appeal*) appel *m;* **to make a ~ for help/mercy** appeler à l'aide/la clémence **2.** (*formal statement by a defendant*) défense *f;* **to enter a ~ of guilty/not guilty** plaider coupable/non coupable **3.** *form* (*pretext, excuse*) excuse *f*

plead [pliːd] <pleaded, pleaded> **I.** *vi* **1.** (*implore, beg*) implorer; **to ~ for forgiveness/mercy** implorer le pardon/la grâce; **to ~ with sb to** *+infin* implorer qn de *+infin* **2.** + *adj* (*answer to a charge in court*) plaider; **to ~ guilty** plaider coupable **II.** *vt* **1.** (*argue or represent in court: insanity*) plaider; **to ~ sb's case** plaider la cause de qn **2.** (*claim as a pretext: ignorance*) invoquer **3.** (*argue for: a cause*) défendre

pleading *adj* (*look*) suppliant(e)

pleasant ['plezənt] *adj* (*weather, person*) agréable; **to be ~ to sb** être agréable avec qn

pleasantry ['plezəntri] <-tries> *n* plaisanterie *f;* **polite pleasantries** amabilités *fpl*

please [pliːz] **I.** *vt* faire plaisir à; **to be hard to ~** être difficile (à contenter); **~ yourself** *inf* fais comme tu voudras **II.** *vi* **1.** (*be agreeable*) faire plaisir; **eager to ~** désireux(-euse) de plaire **2.** (*think fit, wish*) **if you ~** s'il te/vous plaît; **to do as one ~s** faire à sa guise; **do whatever you ~** fais comme tu veux ►**~ God!** si Dieu le veut! **III.** *interj* **1.** (*with a request*) s'il te/vous plaît; **if you ~** *form* s'il vous plaît; **~ close the gate** merci de fermer la porte **2.** (*said to accept sth politely*) **yes ~** oui je veux bien **3.** *Brit* (*said to attract attention*) pardon

pleased *adj* content(e); **to be ~ with oneself** être content de soi; **I am ~ to inform you that …** j'ai le plaisir de vous informer que …; **~ to meet you** enchanté ►**to be as ~ as Punch about sth** être content comme tout à propos de qc

pleasing *adj* (*agreeable: manner*) agréable; (*news*) qui fait plaisir

pleasurable *adj* agréable

pleasure ['pleʒəʳ, *Am:* -ɚ] *n no pl* plaisir *m;* **at sb's ~** au gré de qn; **it's a ~** je vous en prie; **to take ~ in sth/in doing sth** prendre plaisir à qc/faire qc; **is it for business or ~?** est-ce que c'est pour le travail ou pour les vacances?

pleasure boat *n* bateau *m* de plaisance

pleat [pliːt] *n* pli *m*

pleb [pleb] *n Brit, pej, inf abbr of* **plebeian** prolo *mf*

plebeian [plɪ'biːən] **I.** *adj pej, form* prolétaire **II.** *n* prolétaire *mf*

plebiscite ['plebɪsɪt, *Am:* -əsaɪt] *n* plébiscite *m*

pledge [pledʒ] **I.** *n* **1.** (*solemn promise*) promesse *f;* **to fulfil a ~** tenir une promesse; **to give a ~ to** *+infin* promettre de *+infin;* **to sign the ~** faire vœu d'abstinence **2.** (*pawned object, token*) gage *m* **3.** (*promised charitable donation*) promesse *f* de don **II.** *vt* promettre; **to ~ to** *+infin* promettre de *+infin;* **to ~ money** faire une promesse de don; **they're ~d to cut taxes** il promettent de diminuer les impôts

plenary ['pliːnəri] **I.** *adj* **1.** *form* (*total, full, unqualified: indulgence*) entier(-ère); (*power*) plein(e) **2.** (*be attended by all members: assembly, session*) plénier(-ère) **II.** *n* assemblée *f* plénière

plentiful *adj* (*supply*) abondant(e); **the cherries are ~ this year** il y a des quantités de cerises cette année

plenty ['plenti, *Am:* -t̬i] **I.** *n* (*abundance*) abondance *f* **II.** *adv* bien assez; **it's ~ big enough** c'est bien assez grand; **~ good/bad** *Am, inf* très bon/mauvais **III.** *pron* **~ of money/time** beaucoup d'argent/de temps; **there was ~ of room** il y avait plein de place; **to have ~** en avoir bien assez; **that's ~** c'est largement assez

pleonasm ['pliːəʊnæzəm, *Am:* -oʊ-] *n* LING pléonasme *m*

pleurisy ['plʊərəsi, *Am:* 'plʊrə-] *n no pl* MED pleurésie *f*

plexus ['pleksəs] <-(es)> *n* **1.** ANAT plexus *m* **2.** (*network*) réseau *m*

pliable ['plaɪəbl] *adj* **1.** (*supple, easily bendable*) souple **2.** (*easily influenced and led*) influençable

pliers ['plaɪəz, *Am:* 'plaɪɚz] *npl* pince *f;* **a pair of ~** une pince

plight [plaɪt] *n* détresse *f;* **to be in a dreadful ~** être dans une situation désespérée

plimsoll ['plɪmpsəl] *n Brit* tennis *f,* espadrille *f Québec*

PLO [ˌpiːel'əʊ, *Am:* -'oʊ] *n no pl s.* **Palestine Liberation Organization the ~** l'OLP *f*

plod [plɒd, *Am:* plɑːd] <-dd-> *vi* **1.** (*walk slowly and heavily*) marcher péniblement **2.** (*work without enthusiasm, slowly*) **to ~ along** trimer; **to ~ through sth** avancer laborieusement dans qc

plodder ['plɒdəʳ, *Am:* 'plɑːdɚ] *n* bûcheur, -euse *m, f*

plodding *adj* laborieux(-euse)

P

plonk[1] [plɒŋk, *Am:* plʌŋk] *n Brit, Aus, inf* (*wine*) piquette *f*

plonk[2] [plɒŋk, *Am:* plʌŋk] **I.** *n inf* bruit *m* sourd **II.** *vt inf* poser bruyamment; **to ~ oneself down on sth** s'affaler sur qc

plonker *n Brit, inf* andouille *f*

plop [plɒp, *Am:* plɑːp] **I.** *n* (*on hard surface*) pouf *m;* (*on water*) plouf *m* **II.** *adv* (*on hard surface*) en faisant pouf; (*on water*) en faisant plouf **III.** <-pp-> *vi* **1.** (*fall with this sound: on hard surface*) tomber en faisant pouf; (*on water*) faire plouf **2.** (*fall heavily*) tomber lourdement

plot [plɒt, *Am:* plɑːt] **I.** *n* **1.** (*conspiracy, secret plan*) complot *m;* **the Gunpowder Plot** la Conspiration des Poudres **2.** (*story line*) intrigue *f* **3.** (*small piece of land*) parcelle *f;* **building ~** parcelle à bâtir; **garden ~** jardin *m;* **vegetable ~** potager *m* ►**the ~ thickens** *iron* les choses se compliquent **II.** <-tt-> *vt* **1.** (*conspire*) comploter **2.** (*create: story line*) écrire **3.** (*present or represent graphically: curve*) tracer **4.** MIL (*position*) pointer **III.** <-tt-> *vi* comploter

plotter ['plɒtəʳ, *Am:* 'plɑːt̬ɚ] *n* **1.** (*person*) conspirateur, -trice *m, f* **2.** INFOR traceur *m*

plough [plaʊ] **I.** *n* charrue *f;* **to be under the ~** être cultivé ►**put one's hand to the ~** se mettre à la tâche **II.** *vt* **1.** (*till*) labourer **2.** *fig* **to ~ one's way through sth** (*move through*) avancer péniblement dans qc; (*finish off*) réussir à finir qc **III.** *vi* **1.** (*till ground*) labourer **2.** (*advance*) **to ~ into a wall** entrer en plein dans un mur; **to ~ through a crowd** foncer à travers une foule; **to ~ through a book/job** peiner sur un livre/une tâche

◆**plough back** *vt* (*profits*) réinvestir

◆**plough in** *vt* enfouir en labourant

◆**plough up** *vt* labourer

ploughman's *n Brit, Aus,* **ploughman's lunch** <-es> *n Brit, Aus: assiette de crudités avec du pain et du fromage ou du jambon*

ploughshare *n* soc *m* de charrue

plow [plaʊ] *n Am s.* **plough**

ploy [plɔɪ] *n* ruse *f*

pluck [plʌk] **I.** *n* cran *m;* **to have ~** avoir du cran **II.** *vt* **1.** (*remove by picking away*) cueillir **2.** (*remove quickly*) arracher **3.** (*remove hair, feathers*) arracher; (*chicken*) plumer; **to ~ one's eyebrows** s'épiler les sourcils **4.** (*sound: strings of instrument*) pincer **5.** (*pull at*) tirer sur **6.** (*remove from a situation*) **to ~ sb from sth** sortir qn de qc ►**to ~ sth out of the air** inventer qc

◆**pluck at** *vt* **1.** (*pick at*) cueillir qc **2.** (*pull at*) arracher qc

◆**pluck out** *vt* arracher

plucky <-ier, -iest> *adj* courageux(-euse)

plug [plʌg] **I.** *n* **1.** (*connector, socket*) prise *f* de courant; (*for peripheral, phone*) fiche *f;* **to pull the ~ on sth** débrancher qc; *fig* stopper qc **2.** (*stopper*) bonde *f* **3.** *inf* (*publicity*) pub *f;* **to give a book a ~** faire la promotion d'un livre **4.** (*spark plug*) bougie *f* **5.** (*wall plug*) cheville *f* **6.** (*chunk: of tobacco*) chique *f* **II.** <-gg-> *vt* **1.** (*stop up, close: hole*) boucher; (*leak*) arrêter **2.** *inf* (*publicize*) faire du battage pour **3.** *Am, inf* (*shoot*) flinguer **III.** <-gg-> *vi* faire de la pub

◆**plug in I.** *vt* brancher **II.** *vi* se brancher

plughole ['plʌghəʊl, *Am:* -hoʊl] *n* trou *m* d'écoulement

plug-in *n* INFOR module *m* d'extension, plugiciel *m* **plug-in card** *n* INFOR carte *f* enfichable **plug-ugly** <-lies> *n Am, inf* (*thug*) voyou *m*

plum [plʌm] **I.** *n* **1.** (*fruit*) prune *f* **2.** (*exceptionally good opportunity*) affaire *f* **II.** *adj* **1.** (*purplish-red colour*) prune *inv* **2.** (*exceptionally good or favourable: job, part*) en or

plumage ['pluːmɪdʒ] *n no pl* plumage *m*

plumb [plʌm] **I.** *vt* sonder **II.** *adj* d'aplomb; **to be out of ~** ne pas être d'aplomb **III.** *adv* **1.** *inf* (*exactly*) en plein **2.** *Am, inf* (*completely*) complètement **IV.** *n* aplomb *m*

◆**plumb in** *vt* (*washing machine*) raccorder

plumber *n* plombier *m*

plumbing *n no pl* plomberie *f;* **~ contractor** plombier *m;* **a ~ fixture** installation *f* de plomberie; **the ~ work** la plomberie

plumb line *n* fil *m* à plomb

plume [pluːm] *n* **1.** (*large feather*) plume *f* **2.** (*ornament of feathers*) plumet *m* **3.** (*cloud*) nuage *m*

plumed *adj* à plumes

plummet ['plʌmɪt] *vi* tomber à la verticale; (*prices, profits*) s'effondrer; (*confidence*) tomber à zéro

plummy ['plʌmi] <-ier, -iest> *adj* **1.** (*having a plum colour*) prune **2.** (*sounding deep or rich in tone: voice*) d'aristocrate

plump [plʌmp] **I.** *adj* **1.** (*rounded, slightly fat: chicken*) dodu(e); **~ and juicy grapes** de gros raisins juteux **2.** (*fat*) potelé(e); **pleasingly ~** aux formes généreuses **II.** *vt* **to ~ (up)** (*cushions*) remettre en forme **III.** *vi* **to ~ for sb/sth** opter pour qn/qc

plumpness *n no pl* embonpoint *m*

plunder ['plʌndəʳ, *Am:* -dɚ] **I.** *vt* piller **II.** *vi* se livrer au pillage **III.** *n no pl* **1.** (*stolen goods, booty*) butin *m* **2.** (*act of plundering*) pillage *m*

plunderer *n* pilleur, -euse *m, f*

plunge [plʌndʒ] **I.** *n* **1.** (*sharp decline*) chute *f* **2.** (*swim*) plongeon *m* ►**to take the ~** se jeter à l'eau **II.** *vi* **1.** (*fall suddenly or dramatically*) plonger; *fig* (*prices, profits*) s'effondrer; **to ~ to one's death** faire une chute mortelle; **to ~ over/into sth** plonger sur/dans qc **2.** (*leap*) **to ~ into sth** plonger dans qc **3.** (*enter suddenly, dash*) **to ~ into** se précipiter dans **4.** (*begin abruptly*) **to ~ in** se lancer; **to ~ into sth** se lancer dans qc **III.** *vt* **1.** (*immerse*) **to ~ sth into sth** plonger qc dans qc; **to ~ a knife into sb/sth** planter un couteau dans qn/qc **2.** (*cause to experience abruptly*) **to ~ sb/sth into sth** plonger qn/qc dans qc

plunger *n* ventouse *f*

plunk [plʌŋk] *n, adv, vt Am s.* **plonk**

pluperfect ['plu:ˌpɜ:fɪkt, *Am:* -ˌpɜ:r-] **I.** *adj* LING plus-que-parfait; **the ~ tense** le plus-que-parfait **II.** *n* LING **the ~** le plus-que-parfait

plural ['plʊərəl, *Am:* 'plʊrəl] **I.** *n* **the ~** le pluriel; **in the ~** au pluriel; **first person ~** première personne du pluriel **II.** *adj* **1.** LING pluriel(le) **2.** (*pluralistic*) pluraliste

pluralism ['plʊərəlɪzəm, *Am:* 'plʊrəl-] *n no pl* pluralisme *m*

pluralistic *adj* pluraliste

plurality [plʊə'rælǝti, *Am:* plʊ'rælǝt̬i] <-ties> *n* **1.** *no pl* (*variety*) pluralité *f* **2.** (*largest single share of votes*) majorité *f* simple; **to have a ~** avoir la majorité

plus [plʌs] **I.** *prep* (*and*) *a.* MAT plus; **5 ~ 2 equals 7** 5 plus 2 égale 7 **II.** *adj* **1.** (*more*) plus; **to have 200 ~** en avoir plus de 200 **2.** (*having a positive charge*) positif(-ive) **III.** *n* **1.** (*sign*) plus *m* **2.** *fig* atout *m; s. a.* **minus**

plus fours *npl* pantalon *m* de golf

plush [plʌʃ] **I.** *adj* **1.** (*luxurious, expensive: restaurant*) de luxe **2.** (*made of plush: upholstery*) en peluche **II.** *n* peluche *f*

plutocracy [plu:'tɒkrəsi, *Am:* -'tɑ:krə-] <-cies> *n* **1.** *no pl* (*system of government, country*) ploutocratie *f* **2.** (*the wealthy elite*) **the ~** les nantis

plutonium [plu:'təʊniəm, *Am:* -'toʊ-] *n no pl* plutonium *m*

ply¹ [plaɪ] *n no pl* **1.** (*thickness of cloth or wood*) épaisseur *f* **2.** (*strand of rope*) brin *m;* (*of wool*) fil *m;* **two-~ rope** corde *f* à deux brins **3.** (*~wood*) contre-plaqué *m*

ply² [plaɪ] <-ie-> **I.** *vt* **1.** (*work at steadily: a tool*) manier; **to ~ one's trade** faire son travail **2.** (*supply continuously*) **to ~ sb with food** ne pas cesser de servir à manger à qn; **to ~ sb with questions** presser qn de questions **II.** *vi* (*travel*) faire la navette

plywood ['plaɪwʊd] *n no pl* contre-plaqué *m*

pm, p.m. *adv abbr of* **post meridiem 1.** (*in the afternoon*) de l'après-midi **2.** (*in the evening*) du soir

PM [ˌpi:'em] *n* **1.** *Brit abbr of* **Prime Minister** premier ministre *m* **2.** *abbr of* **post-mortem** autopsie *f*

PMT *n abbr of* **pre-menstrual tension** syndrome *m* prémenstruel

pneumatic [nju:'mætɪk, *Am:* nu:'mæt̬-] *adj* pneumatique

pneumatic drill *n* marteau-piqueur *m*

pneumonia [nju:'məʊnɪə, *Am:* nu:'moʊnjə] *n no pl* MED pneumonie *f*

PO [ˌpi:'əʊ, *Am:* -'oʊ] *n* **1.** *abbr of* **postal order** mandat *m* postal **2.** *abbr of* **post office** bureau *m* de poste **3.** *Am abbr of* **pilot officer** sous-lieutenant *m*

poach¹ [pəʊtʃ] *vt* pocher

poach² [pəʊtʃ] **I.** *vt* **1.** (*catch illegally*) **to ~ animals/game** braconner **2.** (*appropriate unfairly or dishonestly: ideas*) s'approprier **3.** (*lure away*) débaucher **II.** *vi* **1.** (*catch illegally*) braconner **2.** (*encroach*) empiéter

poacher *n* braconnier, -ière *m, f*

poaching *n no pl* braconnage *m*

PO Box <-es> *n abbr of* **Post Office Box** BP *f*

pocket ['pɒkɪt, *Am:* 'pɑ:kɪt] **I.** *n* poche *f;* **back ~** poche arrière; **from one's ~** de sa poche; **air ~** trou *m* d'air; **out-of-~ expenses** frais *mpl* ▶**to have deep ~s** avoir beaucoup d'argent; **to pay for sth out of one's own ~** payer qc de sa poche; **to be in ~** rentrer dans ses frais; **to be out of ~** ne pas rentrer dans ses frais; **to put pride in one's ~** mettre sa fierté dans sa poche; **to have sb in one's ~** avoir qn dans sa poche; **to have sth in one's ~** avoir qc dans la poche; **to line one's ~s** se remplir les poches; **to live in each other's ~s** *pej* être tout le temps les uns sur les autres **II.** *adj* de poche **III.** *vt* empocher; **to ~ one's change** prendre la monnaie ▶**to ~ one's pride** ravaler sa fierté

pocketbook *n* **1.** *Am* (*woman's handbag*) sac *m* à main **2.** *Am* (*paperback book*) livre *m* de poche **3.** (*wallet, ability to pay*) portefeuille *m* **pocket calculator** *n* calculatrice *f* de poche **pocket camera** *n* appareil *m* photo compact

pocketful *n* **a ~ of sth 1.** (*pocket full of*) une pleine poche de qc **2.** (*a lot*) plein de qc

pocket handkerchief *n* mouchoir *m* de poche **pocketknife** <-knives> *n* couteau *m* de poche **pocket money** *n no pl* argent *m* de poche **pocket-size(d)** *adj* (*television*) de poche; (*kid*) haut(e) comme trois pommes

pockmarked *adj* (*face*) avec des marques; (*surface*) creusé(e) de trous

pod [pɒd, *Am:* pɑ:d] *n* **1.** (*seed container*) gousse *f;* **pea ~** cosse *f* de pois **2.** (*container under an aircraft*) nacelle *f*

POD *abbr of* **pay on delivery** payable à la livraison

podgy ['pɒdʒi, *Am:* 'pɑ:dʒi] *adj pej* grassouillet(te)

podium ['pəʊdiəm, *Am:* 'poʊ-] <-dia> *n* podium *m;* **to knock sb off his ~** *fig* prendre la place de qn

poem ['pəʊɪm, *Am:* poʊəm] *n* poème *m*

poet ['pəʊɪt, *Am:* poʊət] *n* poète *m*

poetic [pəʊ'etɪk, *Am:* poʊ'et̬-] *adj* poétique; **it's ~ justice** c'est un juste retour des choses

poetry ['pəʊɪtri, *Am:* 'poʊə-] *n no pl* poésie *f;* **to have ~** être plein de poésie; **~ in motion** la grâce personnifiée

po-faced *adj Brit, Aus* **1.** *pej* (*humorlessly solemn*) avec une tête d'enterrement **2.** (*expressionless*) impassible

poignant ['pɔɪnjənt] *adj* (*sight*) poignant(e)

point [pɔɪnt] **I.** *n* **1.** (*sharp end*) pointe *f;* **knife ~** pointe d'un couteau; **pencil ~** pointe d'un crayon **2.** (*promontory*) promontoire *m;* **rocky ~** promontoire rocheux **3.** (*particular place*) endroit *m;* **at the ~ where ...** à l'endroit où … **4.** (*intersection*) point *m* **5.** (*particular time*) moment *m;* (*in a process*) point *m;* **to be at the ~ of death** être à l'article de la mort; **at this ~ in time** à ce stade; **at the ~ where she leaves the house** au moment où elle quitte la maison; **they'd reached a ~ where war was inevitable** ils avaient atteint un seuil à partir duquel la guerre était inévitable; **the ~ of no return** le point de non-retour; **saturation/boiling ~** point de saturation/d'ébullition; **starting ~** point de départ; **to do sth up to a ~** faire qc jusqu'à un certain point **6.** (*sth expressed, main idea*) point *m;* **that's a good ~** ça, c'st un point intéressant; **to come to the ~** en venir au fait; **to make a ~ in favour of/against sth** faire une remarque en faveur de/contre qc; **to drive home a ~** insister sur un point; **to be beside the ~** être hors sujet; **to get to the ~** aller à l'essentiel; **to get the ~ of sth** saisir qc; **to miss the ~ of sth** ne pas comprendre qc; **to make one's ~** dire ce qu'on a à dire; **to prove one's ~** démontrer qu'on a raison; **to see sb's ~** voir ce que qn veut dire **7.** (*purpose*) intérêt *m;* **no/little ~ (in) doing sth** pas/peu d'intérêt à faire qc; **what's the ~ of sth/ of doing sth?** quel est l'intérêt de qc/de faire qc? **8.** (*aspect*) **a weak/strong ~** un point faible/fort **9.** (*unit of counting or scoring*) point *m* **10.** MAT virgule *f;* **two ~ three** deux virgule trois **11.** (*dot*) point *m* **12.** *Brit, Aus* (*socket*) (**power**) ~ prise *f* de courant **13.** *pl, Brit* (*rail switch or junction*) aiguillage *m* **14.** *pl* (*toes of ballet shoes*) pointes *f* ►**a case in ~** un bon exemple; **to make a ~ of doing sth** tenir absolument à faire qc; **you should make a ~ of checking the oil regularly** vous devriez vous astreindre à vérifier l'huile régulièrement **II.** *vi* **1.** (*show with one's finger*) **to ~ at sb/sth** montrer du doigt qn/qc **2.** (*use as evidence or proof*) **to ~ to sth** attirer l'attention sur qc **3.** (*indicate*) **to ~ to sth** indiquer qc; **everything ~s to you as the murderer** tout vous désigne comme le meurtrier **4.** INFOR **to ~ to an icon** pointer sur une icône **III.** *vt* **1.** (*aim*) **to ~ sth at sb/sth** diriger qc sur qn/qc; **to ~ a finger at sb** pointer le doigt sur qc; **to ~ the finger at sb** montrer qn du doigt **2.** (*direct, show position or direction*) **to ~ sb in the right direction** montrer le chemin à qn; **to ~ sb/sth towards sb/sth** diriger qn/qc vers qn/qc; **to ~ the way to sth** indiquer la direction de qc; *fig* montrer la voie à suivre pour qc

◆**point out** *vt* **1.** (*show*) montrer **2.** (*say*) **to ~ that …** faire remarquer que …

◆**point up** *vi form* souligner

point-blank I. *adv* **1.** (*at very close range*) à bout portant; **to fire (a weapon) ~** tirer à bout portant **2.** (*bluntly, directly*) de but en blanc **II.** *adj* **1.** (*very close, not far away*) **to shoot sb/sth at ~ range** tirer à bout portant **2.** (*blunt, direct*) de but en blanc; **~ question** question *f* à brûle-pourpoint **point duty** *n Brit* **to be on ~** (*policeman*) diriger la circulation

pointed *adj* **1.** (*tapering to a point, having a point*) pointu(e) **2.** (*penetrating*) lourd(e) de sous-entendus

pointer *n* **1.** (*long piece of metal, rod*) règle *f* **2.** *pl, inf* (*advice, tip*) tuyau *m* **3.** (*indicator*) *a.* INFOR pointeur *m;* **a laser ~** un pointeur *m* laser

pointless *adj* **it's ~** ça n'a pas de sens; **it's ~ to go now** ça ne sert à rien d'y aller maintenant

point of order *n* question *f* relative à la procédure **point of sale** *n* point *m* de vente **point of view** *n* point *m* de vue **pointsman** <-men> *n Brit* aiguilleur *m* **point system** *n* système *m* des points

poise [pɔɪz] **I.** *n no pl* aisance *f;* **to lose/regain one's ~** perdre/retrouver son sang-froid **II.** *vt* **to ~ sth** mettre qc en équilibre; **to be ~d to** +*infin* se tenir prêt à +*infin;* **~d in the air** suspendu(e) en l'air; **~d on the brink of action** prêt(e) à agir

poised *adj* (*calm*) **person** calme; (*behaviour*) plein d'assurance

poison ['pɔɪzən] **I.** *n* poison *m;* **to lace sth with ~** arroser qc de poison; **to take ~** s'empoisonner ►**one man's meat is another man's ~** *prov* le malheur des uns fait le bonheur des autres; **what's your ~?** *iron* à quoi tu carbures? **II.** *vt* **1.** (*give poison to*) *a. fig* empoisonner; (*mind*) corrompre; **to ~ sb's mind against sb/sth** monter qn contre qn/qc **2.** (*put poison in: water, drink*) empoisonner

poisoner *n* empoisonneur, -euse *m, f*

poison gas *n no pl* gaz *m* toxique

poisoning *n no pl* empoisonnement *m*

poisonous *adj* **1.** (*containing poison: mushroom, plant*) vénéneux(-euse); (*snake*) venimeux(-euse); (*gas*) toxique **2.** (*excessively malicious, malignant*) pernicieux(-euse); (*atmosphere*) nocif(-ive)

poke¹ [pəʊk, *Am:* poʊk] *n* **to buy a pig in a ~** *pej* acheter chat en poche

poke² [pəʊk, *Am:* poʊk] **I.** *n* **1.** (*jab*) petit coup *m;* **to give sb a ~** donner un petit coup à qn **2.** (*push*) poussée *f;* **to give sb a ~** pousser qn **II.** *vt* **1.** (*prod*) pousser avec le doigt; **to ~ one's finger in sb's eye** mettre le doigt dans l'œil de qn **2.** (*extend, make a thrust*) enfoncer; **to ~ sth out of sth** sortir qc de qc; **to ~ one's tongue out** tirer la langue; **to ~ a hole in sth** faire un trou dans qc (avec le doigt) ►**to ~ fun at sb** se moquer de qn; **to ~ one's nose into sb's business** *inf* fourrer son nez dans les affaires de qn; **to ~ (up) a fire** tisonner le feu **III.** *vi* sortir; **to ~ out from sth** dépasser de qc; **to ~ at sb/sth** tâter qn/qc

poker¹ *n* (*card game*) poker *m;* **a game of ~** un jeu de poker

poker² *n* (*tool*) tisonnier *m*

pokey ['pəʊki, *Am:* 'poʊ-] *n* **the ~** la tôle

pok(e)y *adj* **1.** (*small*) exigu(e) **2.** *Am* (*annoy-*

ing slow) lent(e) **3.** *inf* (*powerful: car*) puissant(e)

Poland ['pəʊlənd, *Am:* 'poʊ-] *n* la Pologne

polar ['pəʊlə^r, *Am:* 'poʊlɚ] *adj* **1.** GEO polaire **2.** (*complete*) ~ **opposites** opposé(e)s complets(-ètes)

polar bear *n* ours *m* blanc **polar cap** *n* calotte *f* glaciaire **polar circle** *n* cercle *m* polaire **polar front** *n* front *m* polaire **polar ice** *n no pl* glace *f* polaire

polarity [pəʊ'lærəti, *Am:* poʊ'lerəṱi] *n no pl* polarité *f*

polarization *n no pl* polarisation *f*

polarize ['pəʊləraɪz, *Am:* 'poʊ-] *vt, vi* polariser

polar lights *npl* aurore *f* boréale; *s. a.* **northern lights**

Pole [pəʊl, *Am:* poʊl] *n* (*person*) Polonais(e) *m(f)*

pole[1] [pəʊl, *Am:* poʊl] *n* poteau *m;* (*for tent*) mât *m;* (*for skiing*) bâton *m;* **electricity/telegraph** ~ poteau électrique/télégraphique; **fishing** ~ *Am* canne *f* à pêche ►**to be up the** ~ *Brit* (*wrong*) se planter; (*mad*) être complètement fou

pole[2] [pəʊl, *Am:* poʊl] *n* **1.** (*axis of rotation*) pôle *m;* **the minus/positive** ~ pôle négatif/positif **2.** (*one of two opposed positions*) antipode *m;* **to be ~s apart** être aux antipodes l'un de l'autre

poleaxe ['pəʊlæks, *Am:* 'poʊl-] *vt* **to ~ sth** abattre qc; **to ~ sb** terrasser qn

polecat *n* putois *m*

polemic [pə'lemɪk] **I.** *n* **1.** (*attack*) polémique *f* **2.** *pl* (*controversial debate*) la polémique *f* **II.** *adj* polémique

pole position *n no pl* pole position *f;* **to be in** ~ être en pole position **Pole Star** *n* étoile *f* polaire **pole vault** *n* saut *m* à la perche **pole vaulter** *n* perchiste *mf*

police [pə'li:s] **I.** *n pl* **the** ~ (*in town*) la police; (*outside towns*) la gendarmerie; ~ **department** *Am,* ~ **service** *Brit* service *m* de police; ~ **inspector/commissioner** inspecteur/préfet de police *m;* ~ **intervention** intervention *f* de police **II.** *vt* **1.** (*officially control and guard*) maintenir l'ordre dans **2.** (*control and regulate*) contrôler; **to ~ oneself** se faire la police **3.** MIL contrôler

police car *n* voiture *f* de police **police court** *n* tribunal *m* de police **police dog** *n* chien *m* policier **police escort** *n* escorte *f* policière **police force** *n* **1.** *no pl* (*body of police*) forces *fpl* de l'ordre **2.** (*administrative unit*) **the** ~ la police **policeman** <-men> *n* policier *m* **police officer** *n* agent *mf* de police **police patrol** *n* patrouille *f* de police **police presence** *n no pl* présence *f* de la police **police raid** *n* raid *m* **police record** *n* casier *m* judiciaire; **to have a long** ~ avoir un casier judiciaire chargé **police state** *n pej* état *m* policier **police station** *n* poste *m* de police **policewoman** <-women> *n* femme *f* policier

policy[1] ['pɒləsi, *Am:* 'pɑ:lə-] <-cies> *n a.* POL politique *f;* **it's company** ~ c'est la politique de la société

policy[2] ['pɒləsi, *Am:* 'pɑ:lə-] <-cies> *n* (*insurance*) police *f* d'assurance; **to take out a** ~ souscrire une police d'assurance

policyholder *n* assuré(e) *m(f)* **policy maker** *n* décideur *m* **policy number** *n* numéro *m* d'assurance **policy owner** *n* propriétaire *m* d'une assurance **policy statement** *n* déclaration *f* de principe

polio [ˌpəʊliəʊ, *Am:* ˌpoʊlioʊ] *n* polio *f*

poliomyelitis [ˌpəʊliəʊmaɪə'laɪtɪs, *Am:* ˌpoʊlioʊˌmaɪə'laɪṱəs] *n* poliomyélite *f*

polish ['pɒlɪʃ, *Am:* 'pɑ:lɪʃ] **I.** *n* **1.** (*substance to polish things*) cirage *m;* **furniture** ~ cire *f;* **shoe** ~ cirage à chaussures; **silver** ~ produit *m* d'entretien pour les métaux **2.** (*act of polishing sth*) **to give sth a** ~ faire briller qc; **to give one's shoes a** ~ cirer ses chaussures **3.** (*sophisticated or refined style*) raffinement *m* **II.** *vt a. fig* polir; (*shoes, floor, furniture*) cirer; (*silver, brass*) astiquer; **to ~ one's English** perfectionner son anglais

◆**polish off** *vt* **1.** (*finish completely*) finir **2.** (*defeat easily*) achever

◆**polish up** *vt* **1.** (*polish to a shine*) faire briller **2.** (*improve, brush up*) perfectionner

Polish ['pəʊlɪʃ, *Am:* 'pou-] **I.** *adj* polonais(e) **II.** *n* LING polonais *m; s. a.* **English**

polished *adj* **1.** (*rubbed to a shine*) lustré(e) **2.** (*showing sophisticated style*) raffiné(e); ~ **manner(s)** gestes *m* raffinés **3.** (*showing great skill*) accompli(e); **a ~ performance of the sonata** une interprétation *f* parfaite de la sonate

polisher *n* **1.** (*person who polishes sth*) cireur, -euse *m, f;* **silver** ~ polisseur *m* de métaux **2.** (*tool or device to polish*) (**floor**) ~ cireuse *f*

polite [pə'laɪt] *adj* **1.** (*courteous*) poli(e); **to make ~ conversation** bavarder poliment **2.** (*refined, cultured*) raffiné(e); ~ **society** bonne société *f*

politely *adv* poliment

politeness *n no pl* politesse *f*

politic ['pɒlɪtɪk, *Am:* 'pɑ:lə-] *adj* **to think it ~ to** +*infin* trouver plus adroit de +*infin*

political *adj* politique

politically *adv* **to resolve sth** ~ résoudre qc politiquement; ~ **correct** politiquement correct

political prisoner *n* prisonnier *m* politique

politician *n* politicien(ne) *m(f)*

politicize [pe'lɪtɪsaɪz, *Am:* -'lɪṱə-] *vt* politiser

politics *n + sing vb* **1.** (*activities*) politique *f;* **to talk** ~ parler politique; **to be into** ~ faire de la politique; **to go into** ~ se lancer dans la politique; **office** ~ politique de bureau; **what are your ~?** vous êtes de quel parti? **2.** *Brit* (*political science*) science *f* politique

P

polka ['pɒlkə, *Am:* 'poʊl-] *n* polka *f*
polka dot *n* pois *m*
poll [pəʊl, *Am:* poʊl] **I.** *n* **1.** (*public survey*) sondage *m;* **a public opinion** ~ un sondage d'opinion **2.** **the** ~**s** *pl* (*voting places*) urnes *fpl;* **to go to the** ~**s** aller aux urnes **3.** (*results of a vote*) scrutin *m* **4.** (*number of votes cast*) voix *fpl* **II.** *vt* **1.** (*record the opinion*) interroger; **half the people** ~**ed** la moitié des personnes interrogées **2.** (*receive*) **to** ~ **votes** obtenir des voix
pollard ['pɒləd, *Am:* 'pɑːlɚd] **I.** *n* **1.** (*tree shorn of branches*) arbre *m* écimé **2.** (*animal that has lost its horns*) animal *m* décorné **II.** *vt* (*animal*) décorner; (*tree*) étêter
pollen ['pɒlən, *Am:* 'pɑːlən] *n no pl* pollen *m*
pollen count *n* taux *m* de pollen
pollinate ['pɒlɪneɪt, *Am:* 'pɑːlə-] *vt* **to** ~ **sth** féconder qc avec du pollen
polling booth *n Brit, Aus* isoloir *m* **polling card** *n Brit, Aus* carte *f* de vote **polling day** *n Brit, Aus* jour *m* des élections **polling place** *n Am,* **polling station** *n Brit, Aus* bureau *m* de vote
pollster ['pəʊlstəʳ, *Am:* 'poʊlstɚ] *n* sondeur, -euse *m, f*
pollutant [pəl'uːtənt] *n* polluant *m*
pollute [pə'luːt] *vt* **1.** (*contaminate, make impure*) polluer **2.** *fig* (*destroy the purity, wholesomeness*) corrompre
polluter *n* pollueur, -euse *m, f*
pollution *n no pl* pollution *f;* **air/water** ~ pollution de l'air/de l'eau
polo ['pəʊləʊ, *Am:* 'poʊloʊ] *n* SPORT, FASHION polo *m*
polo neck *n* col *m* roulé **polo shirt** *n* polo *m*
poly ['pɒli, *Am:* 'pɑːli] *n Brit, inf abbr of* **polytechnic** ≈ IUT *m*
polyamide ['pɒli'æmaɪd, *Am:* ˌpɑːli-] *n* CHEM polyamide *m*
polyclinic ['pɒlɪklɪnɪk, *Am:* ˌpɑːlɪ'-] *n* polyclinique *f*
polycotton *n* coton *m* mélangé
polyester [ˌpɒli'estəʳ, *Am:* ˌpɑːli'estɚ] *n no pl* CHEM polyester *m;* ~ **shirt/trousers** chemise/pantalon en polyester
polygamist *n* polygame *mf*
polygamous *adj* polygame
polygamy [pə'lɪgəmi] *n no pl* polygamie *f*
polyglot ['pɒlɪglɒt, *Am:* 'pɑːlɪglɑːt] **I.** *adj* polyglotte **II.** *n* polyglotte *mf*
polygon ['pɒlɪgən, *Am:* 'pɑːlɪgɑːn] *n* polygone *m*
polygonal *adj* polygonal(e)
Polynesia [ˌpɒlɪ'niːʒə, *Am:* ˌpɑːlə'niːʒə] *n* la Polynésie
polyp ['pɒlɪp, *Am:* 'pɑːlɪp] *n* polype *m*
polyphonic *adj* MUS polyphonique
polyphony [pə'lɪfəni] *n no pl* MUS polyphonie *f*
polystyrene [ˌpɒlɪ'staɪəriːn, *Am:* ˌpɑːlɪ-] *n no pl, Brit, Aus* polystyrène *m*
polytechnic [ˌpɒlɪ'teknɪk, *Am:* ˌpɑːlɪ-] *n Brit* ≈ Institut *m* universitaire de technologie
polythene ['pɒlɪθiːn, *Am:* 'pɑːlɪ-] *n no pl, Brit* polyéthylène *m*
polythene bag *n Brit, Aus* sachet *m* en matière plastique
pomade [pəʊ'məɪd, *Am:* pɑː'meɪd] *n no pl* pommade *f*
pomander *n* diffuseur *m*
pomegranate ['pɒmɪgrænɪt, *Am:* 'pɑːmˌgræn-] *n* grenade *f*
pomp [pɒmp, *Am:* pɑːmp] *n no pl* pompe *f;* ~ **and circumstance** grand apparat *m*
pomposity [pɒm'pɒsəti, *Am:* pɑːm'pɑːsəţi] *n no pl, pej* air *m* pompeux
pompous ['pɒmpəs, *Am:* 'pɑːm-] *adj pej* pompeux(-euse)
poncho ['pɒntʃəʊ, *Am:* 'pɑːntʃoʊ] *n* poncho *m*
pond [pɒnd, *Am:* pɑːnd] *n* **1.** (*still water*) mare *f;* (*larger*) étang *m;* **duck** ~ mare à canards; **fish** ~ étang *m* à poisson **2.** *iron* (*ocean, Atlantic ocean*) **the** ~ l'Océan *m*
ponder **I.** *vt* réfléchir à **II.** *vi* méditer
ponderous *adj pej* **1.** (*heavy and awkward*) lourd(e) **2.** (*tediously laborious or dull*) pesant(e)
pone [pəʊn] *n Am* **corn** ~ pain *m* de maïs
pong [pɒŋ, *Am:* pɑːŋ] **I.** *n Brit, Aus, pej, inf* puanteur *f* **II.** *vi Brit, Aus, pej, inf* **to** ~ **of sth** (s)chlinguer qc
pontiff ['pɒntɪf, *Am:* 'pɑːnţɪf] *n form* **the** ~ pontife *m;* **the sovereign** ~ le souverain pontife
pontifical *adj* pontifical(e)
pontificate[1] [pɒn'tɪfɪkeɪt, *Am:* pɑːn-] *vi pej* **to** ~ **about sth** pontifier au sujet de qc
pontificate[2] [pɒn'tɪfɪkət, *Am:* pɑːn-] *n form* pontificat *m*
pontoon [pɒn'tuːn, *Am:* pɑːn-] *n* **1.** (*floating device*) flotteur *m* **2.** *no pl, Brit* (*blackjack*) vingt-et-un *m*
pontoon bridge *n* pont *m* flottant
pony ['pəʊni, *Am:* 'poʊ-] *n* poney *m*
ponytail *n* queue *f* de cheval **pony-trekking** *n Brit* randonnée *f* à dos de poney
poodle ['puːdl] *n* **1.** ZOOL caniche *m* **2.** *Brit, pej, iron* **to be sb's** ~ être le chien de qn
pooh [puː] **I.** *n pl, Brit, Aus, childspeak, inf* caca *m;* **to do a** ~ faire caca **II.** *vi Brit, Aus, childspeak, inf* faire caca **III.** *interj inf* berk !
pooh-pooh [ˌpuː'puː] *vt inf* faire fi de
pool[1] [puːl] **I.** *n* **1.** (*body of any liquid*) mare *f;* (*of water, rain, blood, light*) flaque *f* **2.** (*construction built to hold water*) bassin *m* **3.** (*swimming* ~) piscine *f* **II.** *vt* mettre en commun
pool[2] [puːl] **I.** *n* **1.** (*common fund*) fonds *f* commun **2.** (*common supply*) réservoir *m;* (*for cars*) parc *m;* (*of contacts*) réseau *m;* **a** ~ **of talent** un vivier de talents **3.** SPORT billard *m* américain; **to shoot** ~ *Am, inf* jouer au billard américain **4.** *Am* (*total money staked in gamb-*

ling) cagnotte *f* **5. the ~s** *Brit* ≈ loto sportif; **to do the ~s** jouer au loto *m* sportif **II.** *vt* **1.** (*combine in a common fund*) **to ~ sth** mettre qc en commun **2.** (*share*) partager

poolroom *n Am* salle *f* de billard

poop[1] [puːp] *n* (*stern of a ship*) poupe *f*

poop[2] [puːp] *n no pl, Am, inf* (*information*) **to get the ~ on sb/sth** trouver un tuyau sur qn/qc

poop[3] [puːp] **I.** *n Am no pl, inf* crotte *f;* **dog ~** crotte de chien **II.** *vi inf* crotter

pooper scooper [ˈpuːpəˌskuːpəʳ, *Am:* -pɚˌskuːpɚ], **poop scoop** *n* ramasse-crottes *m*

poor [pʊəʳ, *Am:* pʊr] **I.** *adj* **1.** (*lacking money*) pauvre **2.** (*of inadequate quality*) mauvais(e); **to be ~ at sth** être mauvais à qc; **to be ~ in sth** être médiocre en qc; **to give a ~ account of oneself** faire mauvaise impression; **~ attendance at lectures** faible présence *f* aux cours; **to be a ~ excuse for sth** être une mauvaise excuse pour qc; **to have a ~ eyesight** avoir une mauvaise vue; **a ~ harvest** une mauvaise récolte; **to be in ~ health** être en mauvaise santé; **a ~ memory** une mauvaise mémoire; **to be a ~ sailor** ne pas avoir le pied marin **3.** (*deserving of pity*) pauvre **4.** *iron* (*humble*) humble; **in my ~ opinion** à mon humble avis ►**to take a ~ view of sb/sth** avoir une mauvaise opinion de qn/qc **II.** *n* **the ~** *pl* les pauvres *mpl*

poorly **I.** *adv* **1.** (*in a manner resulting from poverty*) pauvrement; **to be ~ off** être pauvre **2.** (*inadequately, badly*) mal; **~ dressed** mal habillé(e); **to think ~ of sb/sth** avoir une mauvaise opinion de qn/qc **II.** *adj* souffrant(e); **to feel ~** être malade

poorness *n no pl* **1.** (*inadequacy*) médiocrité *f* **2.** (*poverty*) pauvreté *f*

poor relation *n* cousin pauvre(e) *m(f)*

pop[1] [pɒp, *Am:* pɑːp] **I.** *n* **1.** *inf* boisson *f* gazeuse **2.** (*noise*) pan *m* **II.** *vi* **1.** (*make a sound: cork*) sauter; (*balloon, corn*) éclater; (*ears*) se déboucher **2.** (*go*) **to ~ over/across to sth** faire un saut à qc; **to ~ into sth** entrer rapidement dans qc **III.** *vt* **1.** (*make a sound: cork*) faire sauter; (*balloon*) faire éclater **2.** (*put*) mettre; **~ it on the table** pose le sur la table **3.** *inf* (*take: drugs*) prendre **IV.** *adv* **to go ~** exploser

◆**pop in** *vi* (*to shop*) entrer rapidement; (*to friend's house*) passer

◆**pop off** *vi* **1.** *inf* (*die*) claquer **2.** *inf* (*leave*) filer; **to ~** filer à la maison

◆**pop out** *vi* sortir

◆**pop up** *vi* surgir

pop[2] [pɒp, *Am:* pɑːp] **I.** *adj* **1.** (*popular*) pop *inv* **2.** *pej* de quatre sous; **~ psychology** psychologie *f* à bon marché **II.** *n no pl* (*pop music*) pop *f*

pop art *n no pl* pop art *m* **pop concert** *n* concert *m* pop **pop culture** *n* culture *f* pop **pop group** *n* groupe *m* pop **pop music** *n no pl* musique *f* pop **pop singer** *n* chanteur, -euse *m, f* pop **pop song** *n* chanson *f* pop **pop star** *n* vedette *f* de la chanson

pop[3] [pɒp, *Am:* pɑːp] *n Am* (*father*) papa *m*

popcorn [ˈpɒpkɔːn, *Am:* ˈpɑːpkɔːrn] *n no pl* pop-corn *m*

pope [pəʊp, *Am:* poʊp] *n* **1.** (*Bishop of Rome*) pape *m* **2.** (*Orthodox priest*) pope *m*

popery *n no pl, pej* papisme *m*

popgun *n* pistolet *m* à bouchon

poplar [ˈpɒpləʳ, *Am:* ˈpɑːplɚ] *n* peuplier *m*

poplin [ˈpɒplɪn, *Am:* ˈpɑːplɪn] *n no pl* popeline *f;* **a ~ dress** une robe en popeline

popper [ˈpɒpəʳ, *Am:* ˈpɑːpɚ] *n Brit, inf* bouton-pression *m*

poppet [ˈpɒpɪt, *Am:* ˈpɑːpɪt] *n Aus, Brit, inf* mon chou

poppy [ˈpɒpi, *Am:* ˈpɑːpi] <-ppies> *n* coquelicot *m;* (*for drugs*) pavot *m*

poppycock [ˈpɒpɪkɒk, *Am:* ˈpɑːpɪkɑːk] *n no pl, pej, inf* sornettes *fpl*

Poppy Day *n Brit* jour *m* anniversaire de l'armistice

poppy seeds *npl* graines *fpl* de pavot

populace [ˈpɒpjʊləs, *Am:* ˈpɑːpjəlɪs] *n no pl* **the ~** le peuple

popular [ˈpɒpjʊləʳ, *Am:* ˈpɑːpjəlɚ] *adj* **1.** (*liked, understood by many people*) populaire; (*brand*) courant(e); **to be ~** être apprécié de tous; **to be ~ with the students** être populaire auprès des étudiants; **you won't be ~ if you say that** ça na va pas te rendre populaire de dire ça **2.** (*widespread*) étendu(e); **a ~ misconception** une idée fausse largement répandue **3.** (*of or by the people: culture, tradition*) populaire; (*feeling*) du peuple

popularity [ˌpɒpjʊˈlærəti, *Am:* ˌpɑːpjəˈlerət̬i] *n no pl* popularité *f*

popularize [ˈpɒpjʊləraɪz, *Am:* ˈpɑːpjə-] *vt* **1.** (*make known or liked*) rendre populaire **2.** (*make understood by many*) populariser

popularly *adv* **1.** (*commonly*) communément; **as is ~ believed** comme on le pense généralement; **it is ~ known as ...** c'est familièrement appelé ...; **to be ~ thought of as sth** passer aux yeux de tous comme qc **2.** (*in an accessible style*) populairement

populate [ˈpɒpjəleɪt, *Am:* ˈpɑːpjə-] *vt* peupler

population *n* population *f;* **~ explosion** explosion *f* démographique

population density *n* densité *f* de la population

populous [ˈpɒpjʊləs, *Am:* ˈpɑːpjə-] *adj form* populeux(-euse)

pop-up book *n* livre *m* avec découpes en relief **pop-up window** *n* INFOR incrustation *f*

porcelain [ˈpɔːsəlɪn, *Am:* ˈpɔːr-] *n no pl* porcelaine *f;* **~ plate** assiette *f* en porcelaine

porch [pɔːtʃ, *Am:* pɔːrtʃ] *n* **1.** (*roofed part: of a house, church*) porche *m;* (*of a hotel*) marquise *f* **2.** *Am* (*veranda*) véranda *f* **3.** *Am* (*awning*) auvent *m;* (*of a hotel, store*) marquise *f*

porcupine ['pɔːkjʊpaɪn, *Am:* 'pɔːr-] *n* porc-épic *m*

pore [pɔːʳ, *Am:* pɔːr] *n* pore *m* ►**happiness oozing from every** ~ joie qui émane de toute sa personne
◆**pore over** *vi* (*letter, map*) étudier de près; (*text*) étudier de façon très approfondie; **to** ~ **books** se plonger dans les livres

pork [pɔːk, *Am:* pɔːrk] *n no pl* porc *m;* ~ **meat** viande *f* de porc

pork chop *n* côtelette *f* de porc

porker *n* goret *m*

pork pie *n Brit* pâté *m* en croûte

porky **I.** <-ier, -iest> *adj pej, inf* gras(se) comme un porc **II.** <-kies> *n Am, inf* porc-épic *m*

porn [pɔːn, *Am:* pɔːrn] *n inf no pl* porno *m*

pornographic *adj* **1.** (*containing pornography*) pornographique **2.** (*obscene*) obscène

pornography [pɔː'nɒgrəfi, *Am:* pɔːr'nɑːgrə-] *n* pornographie *f*

porous ['pɔːrəs] *adj* (*permeable*) poreux(-euse); (*skin*) perméable

porpoise ['pɔːpəs, *Am:* 'pɔːr-] *n* marsouin *m*

porridge ['pɒrɪdʒ, *Am:* 'pɔːr-] *n no pl* bouillie *f* d'avoine

porridge oats *npl* flocons *mpl* d'avoine

port[1] [pɔːt, *Am:* pɔːrt] *n* **1.** (*harbour*) port *m;* **in** ~ au port; ~ **of call** NAUT escale *f; fig* halte *f;* **to come into** ~ entrer dans le port; **to leave** ~ lever l'encre **2.** INFOR port *m* **3.** *Aus* (*travelling case, bag*) sac *m* de voyage ►**any** ~ **in a storm** nécessité n'a pas de loi

port[2] [pɔːt, *Am:* pɔːrt] **I.** *n no pl* AVIAT, NAUT bâbord *m;* **to turn to** ~ virer à bâbord **II.** *adj* NAUT, AVIAT **the** ~ **side** à bâbord

port[3] [pɔːt, *Am:* pɔːrt] *n no pl* (*wine*) porto *m*

port[4] [pɔːt, *Am:* pɔːrt] *vt* INFOR transférer

portable ['pɔːtəbl, *Am:* 'pɔːrt̬ə-] *adj* portatif(-ive); **a** ~ **radio** un poste portatif; **a** ~ **computer** un ordinateur portable; **a** ~ **telephone** un téléphone portable, un cellulaire *Québec,* un natel *Suisse*

portage ['pɔːtɪdʒ, *Am:* 'pɔːrt̬ɪdʒ] *n no pl* transport *m*

port authority *n* autorité *f* portuaire **port charges** *npl* droits *mpl* de port

portcullis [ˌpɔːt'kʌlɪs, *Am:* ˌpɔːrt-] <-es> *n* herse *f*

portentous [pɔː'tentəs, *Am:* pɔːr'tent̬əs] *adj* **1.** *form* (*signifying something to come*) de mauvais présage; (*expression*) grave; (*event*) funeste **2.** *pej* (*pompous*) pompeux(-euse)

porter ['pɔːtəʳ, *Am:* 'pɔːrt̬ɚ] *n* **1.** (*person who carries*) porteur *m;* (*in hopsital*) brancardier *m* **2.** *Brit* (*doorkeeper*) concierge *mf;* **night** ~ gardien(ne) *m(f)* de nuit; **hall/hotel** ~ portier *m* **3.** *Am* (*train attendant*) employé(e) *m(f)* des wagons-lits

portfolio [pɔːt'fəʊlɪəʊ, *Am:* pɔːrt'foʊlɪoʊ] *n* **1.** (*case*) serviette *f* **2.** (*examples of drawings, designs*) portfolio *m* **3.** FIN, POL portefeuille *m*

porthole ['pɔːthəʊl, *Am:* 'pɔːrthoʊl] *n* hublot *m*

portico ['pɔːtɪkəʊ, *Am:* 'pɔːrt̬ɪkoʊ] <-es *o* -s> *n* portique *m*

portion ['pɔːʃən, *Am:* 'pɔːr-] **I.** *n* **1.** (*part*) partie *f;* **to accept one's** ~ **of the blame** accepter sa part de responsabilité **2.** GASTR portion *f* **II.** *vt* **to** ~ (**out**) **sth** [*o* **to** ~ **sth** (**out**)] partager qc; **to** ~ (**out**) **sth among sb** répartir qc entre plusieurs personnes

portly ['pɔːtli, *Am:* 'pɔːrt-] <-ier, -iest> *adj* corpulent(e)

portrait ['pɔːtrɪt, *Am:* 'pɔːrtrɪt] *n a. fig* portrait *m*

portrait format *n* format *m* portrait

portraitist, **portrait painter** *n* portraitiste *mf*

portraiture *n no pl* le portrait

portray [pɔː'treɪ, *Am:* pɔːr'-] *vt* dépeindre; **he's ~ed as a monster** il est présenté comme un monstre; **the actor ~ing the king** l'acteur qui incarne le roi

portrayal *n* (*by painter, journalist*) portrait *m;* (*of a situation*) description *f*

Portugal ['pɔːtjʊgəl, *Am:* 'pɔːrtʃəgəl] *n* le Portugal

Portuguese [ˌpɔːtjʊ'giːz, *Am:* ˌpɔːrtʃə'-] **I.** *adj* portugais(e) **II.** *n* **1.** (*person*) Portugais(e) *m(f)* **2.** LING portugais *m; s. a.* **English**

port wine *n s.* **port**

POS [ˌpiːəʊ'es] *abbr of* **point of sale**

pose[1] [pəʊz, *Am:* poʊz] *vt* **1.** (*cause*) poser; (*difficulty*) soulever; (*threat*) présenter **2.** (*ask: question*) poser; **to** ~ **questions** questionner

pose[2] [pəʊz, *Am:* poʊz] **I.** *vi* **1.** (*assume a position: person*) poser **2.** (*behave in an affected manner*) se donner des airs **3.** (*pretend to be*) **to** ~ **as sb/sth** se faire passer pour qn/qc **II.** *n* **1.** (*bodily position*) pose *f* **2.** (*pretence*) affectation *f*

poser *n* **1.** *inf* (*problem*) question *f* difficile; **it's a bit of a ~!** c'est plutôt un casse-tête! **2.** *pej* (*person*) poseur, -euse *m, f*

posh [pɒʃ, *Am:* pɑːʃ] *inf* **I.** *adj* **1.** (*stylish*) chic *inv* **2.** *Brit* (*upper-class: woman, accent*) B.C.B.G. **II.** *adv Brit* **to talk** ~ parler comme un(e) snob

posit ['pɒzɪt, *Am:* 'pɑːzɪt] *vt form* avancer; (*theory*) proposer; **to** ~ **that** suggérer que +*subj*

position [pə'zɪʃən] **I.** *n* **1.** (*place*) place *f;* **to be in a different** ~ être dans une position différente **2.** (*location*) situation *f;* **in/into** ~ en place; **to get in** ~ être en place; **to put sb/sth into** ~ mettre qn/qc en place **3.** SPORT, MIL position *f* **4.** *Brit, Aus* (*rank*) place *f;* **the horse arrived in second** ~ le cheval est arrivé second **5.** (*job*) emploi *m;* **a** ~ **of responsibility/of trust** un poste à responsabilité/de confiance; **to apply for a** ~ poser sa candidature pour un emploi **6.** (*situation*) situation *f;* **to be**

in the ~ of having to *+infin* se trouver dans la situation de devoir *+infin;* **to be in no ~ to help/criticize** être mal palcé pour aider/critiquer; **from a ~ of strength** dans une position de force **7.** *form* (*opinion*) position *f;* **John's ~ is that ...** d'après Jean, ...; **to take the ~ that ...** adopter le point de vue que ...; **to take a hardline ~** adopter une position dure **II.** *vt* **1.** (*arrange, adjust*) mettre en position; (*troops*) poster **2.** (*put in place: object*) mettre en place; (*village*) situer; **to ~ the car to turn right** placer la voiture en position pour tourner à droite; **to ~ oneself on sth** se mettre sur qc **3.** (*promote*) positionner

positive ['pɒzətɪv, *Am:* 'pɑːzəṱɪv] *adj* **1.** (*certain*) certain(e); (*evidence*) concret(-ète); **are you quite ~?** êtes-vous sûr?; **to be ~ about sth** être sûr de qc **2.** (*giving cause for hope: attitude, response*) positif(-ive); (*criticism*) constructif(-ive); **to think ~** voir les choses de façon positive; **they were ~ about the idea** ils étaient enthousiastes pour l'idée **3.** MED, MAT, ELEC positif(-ive) **4.** (*complete: miracle, outrage*) véritable

positive discrimination *n* discrimination *f* positive

positively *adv* **1.** (*in the affirmative: reply*) positivement **2.** (*in a good way: react*) positivement; **more ~** de façon plus positive **3.** *inf* (*completely*) absolument; **you're ~ certain?** tu es absolument certain?; **they ~ hate him** ils le détestent franchement

poss. *adj abbr of* **possessive** possessif(-ive)

posse ['pɒsi, *Am:* 'pɑːsi] *n* troupe *f;* (*of reporters, armed policemen*) détachement *m*

possess [pə'zes] *vt a. fig* posséder; **what ~ed you?** qu'est-ce qui vous a pris?; **to be ~ed by anger/ambition** être possédé par la colère/l'ambition

possessed *adj* possédé(e); **to behave like sb ~** sembler être sous l'emprise d'une puissance occulte

possession *n* **1.** *no pl* (*having*) possession *f;* **it's** [*o* **I have it**] **in my ~** c'est en ma possession; **to come into ~ of sth** *form* acquérir qc; **the ball is in my ~** SPORT j'ai le ballon **2.** *pl* (*something owned*) biens *mpl* **3.** POL colonie *f*

possessive *adj* possessif(-ive)

possessor *n iron, form* possesseur *m*

possibility [ˌpɒsə'bɪləti, *Am:* ˌpɑːsə'bɪləṱi] *n* **1.** <-ties> (*feasible circumstance or action*) possibilité *f;* **it's a ~** c'est une possibilité **2.** *pl* (*potential*) potentiel *m* **3.** *no pl* (*likelihood*) éventualité *f;* **there is every ~ that** il est fort possible que *+subj;* **is there any ~ that ...?** *form* y a-t-il une possibilité pour que *+subj?*

possible ['pɒsəbl, *Am:* 'pɑːsə-] *adj* **1.** (*that can be done*) possible; **we did everything ~ to help** nous avons fait tout notre possible pour aider; **there is no ~ excuse for this** il n'y a aucune excuse pour ça; **as clean/good as ~** aussi propre/bon que possible; **as soon as/if ~** dès que/si possible **2.** (*that could happen*) éventuel(le)

possibly *adv* **1.** (*by any means*) **he did all he ~ could to land the plane** il a fait tout ce qui était dans son possible pour atterrir **2.** (*adding emphasis*) **how can you ~ say that?** comment peux-tu dire une chose pareille?; **could you ~ lend me your car?** vous serait-il possible de me prêter votre voiture?; **he said he could not ~ go to the reception** il a dit qu'il lui était impossible d'aller à la réception; **I can't ~ accept it** je ne peux vraiment pas accepter **3.** (*perhaps*) peut-être; **very ~** très probablement

possum ['pɒsəm, *Am:* 'pɑːsəm] <-(s)> *n* opossum *m*

post¹ [pəʊst, *Am:* poʊst] **I.** *n no pl, Brit* **1.** (*mail*) courrier *m;* **the second ~** la seconde livraison (de courrier) **2.** (*postal system*) poste *f;* **by ~** par la poste; **the cheque's in the ~** le chèque vient de partir **II.** *vt Brit, Aus* poster

post² [pəʊst, *Am:* poʊst] **I.** *n* **1.** (*job/place where someone works*) poste *m;* **to take up a ~** entrer en fonction **2.** MIL poste *m* **II.** *vt* poster; **to ~ oneself somewhere** se poster quelque part; **to be ~ed somewhere** être affecté quelque part ►**to ~ bail for sb** *Am* payer la caution de qn

post³ [pəʊst, *Am:* poʊst] **I.** *n* **1.** (*pole*) poteau *m* **2.** (*stake*) pieu *m* **3.** SPORT poteau *m* **II.** *vt Brit, Aus* annoncer ►**to keep sb ~ed** tenir qn au courant

post *prep* post; **~-communism** post-communisme; **~-communist Russia** la Russie de l'après-communisme; **a ~-concert dinner** un dîner après le concert

postage ['pəʊstɪdʒ, *Am:* 'poʊ-] *n no pl* affranchissement *m*

postage meter *n Am* machine *f* à affranchir **postage paid** *adj* port *m* payé; **~ reply card** carte-réponse *f* affranchie **postage stamp** *n form* timbre *m* poste

postal ['pəʊstəl, *Am:* 'poʊ-] **I.** *adj* postal(e); **~ vote** vote *m* postal **II.** *n* carte *f* postale

postal code *n* code *m* postal

postbag *n Brit* sac *m* postal; **to have a heavy ~ on a subject** avoir une avalanche de lettres sur un sujet **postbox** <-es> *n Brit, Aus* boîte *f* aux lettres **postcard** *n* carte *f* postale **postcode** *n Brit* code *m* postal **postdate** *vt* postdater; **his marriage ~d the revelation** son mariage était postérieur à la révélation

posted *adj* posté(e); **to keep sb ~** tenir qn au courant

poster *n* (*announcement*) affiche *f;* (*in home*) poster *m*

poste restante ['pəʊst'restɑːnt, *Am:* ˌpoʊstres'tɑːnt] *Brit* **I.** *n* poste *f* restante **II.** *adv* en poste restante

posterior [pɒ'stɪərɪəʳ, *Am:* pɑː'stɪrɪɚ] **I.** *adj form* **1.** (*later in time*) postérieur(e) **2.** (*towards the back*) derrière **II.** *n* postérieur *m*

posterity [pɒ'sterəti, *Am:* pɑː'-] *n no pl* postérité *f*

post-free *Brit* I. *adj* port payé *inv;* (*envelope, reply card*) affranchi(e) II. *adv* en port payé **postgraduate** I. *n* étudiant(e) *m(f)* de troisième cycle II. *adj* de troisième cycle **posthaste** *adv form* en toute hâte **posthumous** *adj form* posthume

posting[1] *n* (*mailing*) envoi *m* par la poste

posting[2] *n Brit* (*appointment to a job*) affectation *f*

Post-it® *n* post-it *m* **postman** <-men> *n* facteur, -trice *m, f* **postmark** I. *n* cachet *m* de la poste II. *vt* oblitérer **postmaster** *n* receveur, -euse *m, f* des postes **post meridiem** *adv s.* p.m. **post-modern** *adj* postmoderne **post-modernism** *n no pl* postmodernisme *m* **post-mortem** I. *n* 1. MED ~ (**examination**) autopsie *f;* **to carry out a** ~ faire une autopsie 2. *inf* (*discussion*) synthèse *f* rétrospective II. *adj* 1. (*related to a post-mortem*) d'autopsie 2. (*after death*) post-mortem *inv* **post-natal** *adj* post-natal(e) **Post Office** *n* **the** ~ la Poste **post office** *n* bureau *m* de poste **post-operative** *adj* postopératoire **post-paid** I. *adj* port payé II. *adv* en port payé

postpone [pəʊst'pəʊn, *Am:* poʊst'poʊn] *vt* (*delay*) différer, postposer *Belgique;* **to ~ sth till a certain time** renvoyer qc à une date ultérieure; **I've ~d travelling** j'ai retardé mon voyage

postponement *n* 1. (*delaying*) délai *m* 2. *no pl* (*deferment*) renvoi *m* à une date ultérieure; (*of payment*) retard *m;* (*of a court case*) ajournement *m*

postroom *n Brit* bureau *m* de poste

postscript ['pəʊstskrɪp, *Am:* 'poʊs-] *n* 1. (*at the end of a letter*) post-scriptum *m* 2. (*at the end of a story, article*) postface *f* 3. *fig* **to add a ~ to sth** dire un mot de plus

postulate[1] ['pɒstjəleɪt, *Am:* 'pɑːstʃə-] *vt form* postuler; (*theory*) suggérer

postulate[2] ['pɒstjələt, *Am:* 'pɑːstʃəlɪt] *n form* postulat *m*

posture ['pɒstʃəʳ, *Am:* 'pɑːstʃɚ] I. *n* 1. *no pl* (*habitual position of the body*) posture *f;* **to have a good/bad ~** bien/mal se tenir 2. (*pose*) pose *f;* **in a very awkward ~** dans une très fâcheuse posture; **in a kneeling/an upright ~** (en position) agenouillée/debout; **to adopt a ~** prendre une pose 3. *no pl* (*attitude*) attitude *f* II. *vi pej* se donner des airs

post-war *adj* d'après-guerre; ~ **era** après-guerre *f*

posy ['pəʊzi, *Am:* 'poʊ-] <-sies> *n* petit bouquet *m*

pot[1] [pɒt, *Am:* pɑːt] *n no pl, inf* herbe *f*

pot[2] [pɒt, *Am:* pɑːt] I. *n* 1. (*container*) pot *m;* (*for cooking*) marmite *f;* **~s and pans** casseroles *fpl;* **coffee ~** cafetière *f* 2. (*amount contained in a pot: of paint*) pot *m;* **a ~ of tea** une théière 3. *inf* (*trophy given as a prize*) coupe *f* 4. *inf* (*a lot*) **~s of sth** des tas de qc; **~s of money** beaucoup d'argent; **to have ~s of money** rouler sur l'or 5. *inf* (*potbelly*) gros ventre *m* 6. *Brit* (*shot*) **to take a ~ at sb/sth** tirer à l'aveuglette sur qn/qc ▸**it's (a case of) the ~ calling the kettle black** c'est l'hôpital qui se moque de la charité *prov;* **to go to ~** *inf* (*country, economy, business*) aller à la ruine; (*hopes, plan*) tomber à l'eau II. <-tt-> *vt* 1. (*put in a pot*) **to ~ sth (up)** [*o* **to ~ (up) sth**] (*plants*) mettre en pot qc; (*food*) mettre qc en conserve 2. (*put in billiard pocket*) faire rentrer dans le trou 3. *inf* (*shoot*) buter III. *vi* (*make pottery*) faire de la poterie

potable *adj form* potable

potash ['pɒtæʃ, *Am:* 'pɑːt-] *n* potasse *f*

potassium [pə'tæsiəm] *n no pl* potassium *m*

potassium chloride *n no pl* chlorure *m* de potassium

potato [pə'teɪtəʊ, *Am:* -ţoʊ] <-es> *n* pomme *f* de terre; **mashed ~es** purée *f* (de pommes de terre)

potato beetle, **potato bug** *n Am* doryphore *m* **potato chips** *npl Am, Aus,* **potato crisps** *npl Brit* chips *fpl* **potato masher** *n* presse-purée *m* **potato peeler** *n* économe *m*

potbellied *adj* bedonnant(e)

potbelly [pɒt'beli, *Am:* 'pɑːtˌbel-] <-llies> *n* gros ventre *m*

potboiler ['pɒtˌbɔɪləʳ, *Am:* 'pɑːtˌbɔɪlɚ] *n pej* œuvre *f* alimentaire

poteen [pɒ'tiːn, pɒ'tʃiːn, *Am:* poʊ'tiːn] *n Irish: whisky distillé illégalement*

potency ['pəʊtənsi, *Am:* 'poʊ-] *n no pl* 1. (*strength*) force *f;* (*of temptation, spell*) pouvoir *m;* (*of a drug, fertilizer*) efficacité *f;* (*of a weapon*) puissance *f* 2. MED puissance *f* sexuelle

potent *adj* puissant(e); (*motive, argument*) convaincant(e); (*drink*) très fort(e); (*force, spell, temptation*) profond(e); MED viril

potential I. *adj* potentiel(le) II. *n no pl* potentiel *m;* **the growth ~ of the company** le potentiel de croissance d'une société; **to achieve one's ~** atteindre son maximum; **to have considerable ~** offrir des possibilités *fpl* considérables

potentiality *n form* 1. *no pl* (*ability*) potentialité *f* 2. <-ties> (*capacity*) possibilité *f*

potentially *adv* potentiellement

pot-herb *n* herbe *f* potagère

pothole ['pɒtˌhəʊl, *Am:* 'pɑːtˌhoʊl] *n* 1. (*hole in road surface*) nid *m* de poule 2. (*underground hole*) caverne *f* 3. (*problem*) problème *m*

potholer *n Brit* spéléologue *mf*

pot-hook *n* crémaillère *f* **pot-hunter** *n inf* chasseur *m* de trophées

potion ['pəʊʃən, *Am:* 'poʊ-] *n* 1. (*drink*) breuvage *m;* **love/magic ~** philtre *m* d'amour/magique 2. *pej* (*medicine*) potion *f*

pot luck *n no pl* **to take ~** (*choose at random*) choisir au hasard; (*take what is available*) prendre ce qu'il y a **pot plant** *n* plante *f* d'appartement

potpourri [ˌpəʊ'pʊəri:, *Am:* ˌpoʊpʊ'ri:] *n no pl* pot-pourri *m*

pot roast *n* rôti *m* à la cocotte

potshot ['pɒtʃɒt, *Am:* 'pɑ:tʃɑ:t] *n* **1.** (*not carefully aimed shot*) tir *m* à l'aveuglette; **to take a ~ at sb/sth** tirer à l'aveuglette sur qn/qc **2.** (*spoken or written attacks*) attaque *f*

potted ['pɒtɪd, *Am:* 'pɑ:t̬ɪd] *adj* **1.** (*in a pot: plant*) en pot; (*food*) en conserve; **~ meat** terrine *f* **2.** *Brit, inf* (*shorter*) condensé(e); (*biography, story*) abrégé(e)

potter¹ ['pɒtəʳ, *Am:* 'pɑ:t̬ɚ] *n* (*pottery artist*) potier *m*

potter² ['pɒtəʳ, *Am:* 'pɑ:t̬ɚ] **I.** *n no pl, Brit* (*stroll*) petite promenade *f* **II.** *vi Brit* **1.** (*go along in an unhurried manner*) suivre tranquillement sa route; **to ~ around the village** faire le tour du village sans se presser; **to ~ in** entrer en traînassant **2.** (*pass time*) traîner

pottery ['pɒtəri, *Am:* 'pɑ:t̬ɚ-] *n* poterie *f*

potty ['pɒti, *Am:* 'pɑ:t̬i] **I.** <-ier, -iest> *adj Brit, inf* farfelu(e); **to be ~ about sb/sth** être fou de qn/qc; **it's ~ to do that!** c'est idiot de faire ça! ►**to go ~** devenir dingue; **to drive sb ~** rendre qn dingue **II.** <-ties> *n* pot *m* de bébé

pouch [paʊtʃ] *n* **1.** (*a small bag*) petit sac *m;* **a tobacco ~** une blague à tabac **2.** (*purse*) bourse *f* **3.** (*animal's pocket*) poche *f*

pouf(fe) [pu:f] *n* pouf *m*

poulterer ['pəʊltərəʳ, *Am:* 'poʊlt̬ɚɚ] *n Brit* marchand(e) *m(f)* de volailles

poultice ['pəʊltɪs, *Am:* 'poʊlt̬ɪs] *n* cataplasme *m*

poultry ['pəʊltri, *Am:* 'poʊl-] *n* **1.** *pl* (*birds*) volaille *f* **2.** *no pl* (*meat*) volaille *f*

poultry farm *n* lieu *m* d'élevage de volailles **poultry farming** *n no pl* élevage *m* de volaille

pounce [paʊns] **I.** *vi* **1.** (*jump*) sauter; (*attacker, animal*) bondir **2.** (*seize: police*) bondir **II.** *n* (*claw*) serre *f*

◆**pounce on** *vt* (*prey*) bondir sur; (*victim, suspect*) se jeter sur; (*opportunity, mistake*) sauter sur

pound¹ [paʊnd] *n* (*unit of weight, currency*) livre *f;* **ten ~s sterling** dix livres sterling; **a ~ coin** une pièce d'une livre; **100-~ note** [*o Am* **bill**] billet *m* de 100 livres ►**to demand one's ~ of flesh from sb** exiger réparation sans faire de concession

pound² [paʊnd] *n* (*place for stray animals, cars*) fourrière *f*

pound³ [paʊnd] **I.** *vt* **1.** (*hit repeatedly*) frapper; **to ~ the table** *fig* frapper du poing sur la table; **the waves ~ed the ship** les vagues fouettaient le navire **2.** (*walk heavily and noisily*) marcher d'un pas pesant; **to ~ in** entrer en martelant le pavé **3.** (*walk along*) **to ~ the pavement** battre le trottoir; **to ~ the beat** patrouiller **4.** (*crush: spices*) piler; **to ~ into pieces** réduire en miettes **5.** (*beat*) battre **6.** (*bombard*) pilonner **II.** *vi* **1.** (*beat on noisily*) frapper; **to ~ on a locked door** marteler une porte fermée à clef à grands coups de poings; **to ~ on a table** frapper fort sur une table; **to ~ on a wall** cogner sur un mur; **to ~ away at sth** taper sur qc à tours de bras; **to ~ away at the keyboard** taper sur le clavier comme un forcené **2.** (*walk/run noisily*) marcher/courir d'un pas pesant **3.** (*beat*) battre fort; (*heart*) battre vite; **my head is ~ing** j'ai des élancements dans la tête

pounder *n* **a two-pounder** (*fish*) un poisson de deux livres

pounding *n no pl* battement *m;* (*of guns*) pilonnage *m;* **there's a ~ in my head** ma tête résonne comme un tambour; **to take a ~** être pilonné; (*defeat*) essuyer une défaite; (*be criticized*) être descendu en flammes

pour [pɔ:ʳ, *Am:* pɔ:r] **I.** *vt* **1.** (*cause to flow*) verser **2.** (*serve*) servir; **to ~ coffee** servir du café; **to ~ sb sth** servir qc à qn **3.** *fig* déverser; **the company ~ed a lot of money into the project** la société a investi beaucoup d'argent dans le projet ►**to ~ oil on troubled waters** calmer la tempête; **to ~ scorn on sb/sth** rejeter qn/qc avec dédain; **to ~ money down the drain** jeter l'argent par la fenêtre; **to ~ cold water on sth** se montrer peu enthousiaste pour qc **II.** *vi* **1.** (*fill a glass or cup*) verser **2.** (*flow in large amounts*) couler à flots; (*fumes*) s'échapper; **water ~ed through the hole** l'eau coulait à travers le trou; **the crowd ~ed into the theatre** la foule entrait en masse dans le théâtre; **to be ~ing with sweat** ruisseler de sueur **3.** (*rain*) **it's ~ing (with rain)** il pleut à verse

◆**pour in** **I.** *vi* se déverser; (*letters, messages, reports*) arriver par milliers **II.** *vt* verser; (*money*) investir

◆**pour out** **I.** *vt* **1.** (*serve from a container: liquids*) verser **2.** (*recount*) déverser; **to ~ one's problems/thoughts to sb** déballer ses problèmes/pensées à qn **3.** (*cause to flow quickly*) répandre **II.** *vi* se déverser

pout [paʊt] **I.** *vi* faire la moue **II.** *vt* **to ~ one's lips** faire la moue **III.** *n* moue *f*

poverty ['pɒvəti, *Am:* 'pɑ:vɚt̬i] *n no pl* pauvreté *f;* **to live in (abject) ~** vivre dans le besoin; **grinding ~** la misère; **a ~ of sth** *form* une pénurie de qc; **he has such a ~ of intelligence** il est dénué d'intelligence

poverty line *n* seuil *m* de pauvreté; **to live below the ~** vivre en dessous du seuil de pauvreté **poverty-stricken** *adj* frappé(e) par la misère

POW [ˌpi:əʊ'dʌblju:, *Am:* -oʊ'-] *n* **1.** *abbr of* **Prince of Wales** Prince *m* de Galles **2.** *abbr of* **prisoner of war** prisonnier, -ère *m, f* de guerre

powder ['paʊdəʳ, *Am:* -dɚ] **I.** *n* **1.** *no pl* poudre *f;* **curry ~** curry en poudre; **to reduce sth to a ~** réduire qc en poudre **2.** *no pl* (*make-up*) poudre *f;* **to cover oneself with**

P

talcum ~ se mettre du talc **3.** *no pl* (*snow*) poudreuse *f* **4.** *Brit* (*washing powder*) détergent *m* **II.** *vt* saupoudrer; **to ~ one's nose** *a. iron* se poudrer le nez; **to be ~ed with sth** être saupoudré de qc; **to ~ oneself** se poudrer

powdered *adj* **1.** (*in powder form*) en poudre; (*coffee*) instantané(e) **2.** (*covered with powder*) poudré(e)

powder keg *n* (*situation*) poudrière *f* **powder puff** *n* houppette *f* **powder room** *n* toilettes *fpl* pour dames **powder snow** *n no pl* poudreuse *f*

powdery ['paʊdəri] *adj* poudreux(-euse); (*chalk*) friable

power ['paʊəʳ, *Am:* 'paʊɚ] **I.** *n* **1.** *no pl* (*ability to control*) pouvoir *m;* **to be in sb's ~** être à la merci de qn; **to have sb in one's ~** tenir qn en son pouvoir **2.** *no pl* (*political control*) pouvoir *m;* **the party in ~** le parti au pouvoir; **to seize ~** prendre le pouvoir; **~ block** majorité *f* **3.** (*country, organization, person*) puissance *f* **4.** (*right*) pouvoir *m;* **to be in one's ~ to** +*infin* être en son pouvoir de +*infin;* **it is within sb's ~ to** +*infin* c'est dans les compétences *fpl* de qn de +*infin* **5.** *no pl* (*ability: of concentration, persuasion*) pouvoir *m;* **to loose the ~ of speech** perdre l'usage *m* de la parole; **to do everything in one's ~** faire tout ce qui est en son pouvoir **6.** *no pl* (*strength*) puissance *f;* **~ walking** marche *f* en force **7.** *no pl* (*electricity*) énergie *f;* **~ failure** panne *f* d'alimentation; **~ switch** interrupteur *m* général; **~ system** dispositif *m* d'alimentation; **~ drill** perceuse *f* électrique; **~ hammer** marteau-pilon *m* **8.** *no pl* (*magnifying strength*) agrandissement *m* **9.** (*value of magnifying strength*) grossissement *m* **10.** *no pl* MAT puissance *f;* **three to the ~ two** trois puissance deux ▸**more ~ to your elbow** [*o Am* **to you**]! tant mieux pour vous!; **to do sb a ~ of good** faire un bien fou à qn; **the ~ behind the throne** celui qui tire les ficelles; **the ~s that be** les autorités *fpl* **II.** *vi* (*move*) **to ~ along the track** foncer sur la piste; **to ~ up** s'entraîner **III.** *vt* (*engine, rocket*) propulser; **nuclear-~ed** nucléaire

◆**power down** *vi* s'arrêter

◆**power up** **I.** *vi* se mettre en route **II.** *vt* allumer

power-assisted steering *n* AUTO direction *f* assistée **powerboat** *n* hors-bord *m* **power brakes** *npl* AUTO servofreins *mpl* **power cable** *n* câble *m* d'alimentation **power cut** *n Brit, Aus* coupure *f* de courant **power-driven** *adj* motorisé(e)

powerful *adj* **1.** (*influential, mighty*) puissant(e) **2.** (*having great physical strength*) vigoureux(-euse); (*arms, legs, muscles, swimmer*) puissant(e) **3.** (*having a great effect: wind, storm*) violent(e); (*bite, ideas*) profond(e); (*drug, voice*) fort(e); (*explosion, medicine, incentive*) puissant(e); (*evidence, argument*) solide **4.** (*affecting the emotions: drama, literature, music*) puissant(e); (*language, painting, emotions*) fort(e) **5.** (*able to perform very well: car, computer, motor*) performant(e); (*light*) intense; (*memory*) puissant(e)

powerfully *adv* **1.** (*effectively*) efficacement **2.** (*using great force*) puissamment **3.** (*greatly: influenced*) fortement

powerhouse *n* (*for creativity, talent*) atelier *m*

powerless *adj* impuissant(e); **to be ~ to** +*infin* ne pas pouvoir +*infin;* **to be ~ against sb/sth** être impuissant face à qn/qc

power line *n* **1.** ELEC ligne *f* électrique **2.** (*high voltage electrical line*) ligne *f* (à) haute tension **power mower** *n* tondeuse *f* à gazon **power of attorney** *n* procuration *f* **power pack** *n* ELEC **1.** (*assemblage of electrical units*) montage *m* en kit **2.** (*converting current*) convertisseur *m* **power plant** *n s. a.* **power station** **power point** *n Brit, Aus* prise *f* de courant **power sequence** *n Am,* **power set** *n* MAT suite *f* exponentielle **power sharing** *n* POL partage *m* du pouvoir **power station** *n* centrale *f* électrique; **coal-fired/nuclear ~** centrale thermique/nucléaire **power steering** *n* AUTO direction *f* assistée **power tool** *n* outil *m* électrique

powwow ['paʊwaʊ] *n* **1.** (*North American Indian assembly*) assemblée *f* **2.** *fig, inf* discussion *f*

pox [pɒks, *Am:* pɑːks] *n no pl, inf* **the ~** la variole

poxy ['pɒksi, *Am:* 'pɑːk-] <-ier, -iest> *adj Brit, inf* pauvre

pp *n abbr of* **pages** pp. *fpl*

PR [piː'ɑːʳ, *Am:* -'ɑːr] *n no pl* **1.** *abbr of* **proportional representation** représentation *f* proportionnelle **2.** *abbr of* **public relations** relations *fpl* publiques; **a ~ man** un responsable des relations publiques

practicable *adj form* faisable; (*idea*) réalisable; **it is not ~ to** +*infin* il n'est pas envisageable de +*infin*

practical ['præktɪkl] **I.** *adj* **1.** (*not theoretical*) pratique; **for all ~ purposes** à toutes fins utiles **2.** (*realistic: person, solution*) pratique; **it is ~ to do sth** qc est faisable **3.** (*suitable*) fonctionnel(le) **4.** (*who can do jobs*) bricoleur(euse) **5.** (*virtual*) potentiel(le) **II.** *n* épreuve *f* pratique; **biology/chemistry ~** travaux *mpl* pratiques de biologie/de chimie

practicality *n no pl* **1.** (*suitability*) fonctionnalité *f* **2.** (*effectiveness*) efficacité *f* **3.** (*usefulness*) utilité *f* pratique **4.** (*attitude*) pragmatisme *m*

practically *adv* pratiquement; **to be ~ minded** avoir l'esprit pratique; **~ speaking** concrètement (parlant)

practice ['præktɪs] **I.** *n* **1.** *no pl* (*action, performance*) pratique; **I've had a lot of ~** j'ai eu beaucoup d'entraînement; **in ~** en pratique; **to put sth into ~** mettre qc en pratique **2.** (*nor-*

mal procedure) pratique *f;* it's common ~ to +*infin* c'est une pratique courante de +*infin;* to make a ~ of sth prendre l'habitude de qc 3. (*training session*) entraînement *m;* ballet/music ~ exercices *mpl* de danse/de musique; to be out of/in ~ être rouillé/entraîné 4. (*business: of a doctor*) cabinet *m;* legal ~ cabinet *m* juridique *f* 5. *no pl* (*work*) exercice *m* ►~ makes perfect c'est en forgeant qu'on devient forgeron *prov* II. *vt Am s.* practise

practiced *adj Am s.* practised

practise ['præktɪs] *Brit, Aus* I. *vt* 1. (*do, carry out*) pratiquer; (*good hygiene*) avoir 2. (*improve skill*) s'exercer à; (*backhand*) améliorer; (*flute, one's English*) travailler; to ~ doing sth s'entraîner à faire qc 3. (*work in: dentistry, law, medicine*) exercer ►to ~ what one preaches mettre en pratique ses propres préceptes II. *vi* 1. (*train*) s'exercer 2. SPORT s'entraîner 3. (*work in a profession*) exercer

practised *adj Brit, Aus* (*experienced, skilled*) expérimenté(e); (*pianist*) chevronné(e); (*liar*) invétéré(e); to be ~ at doing sth être expert dans l'art de qc

practising *adj Brit, Aus* (*catholic*) pratiquant; (*doctor*) en exercice

practitioner [præk'tɪʃənə^r, *Am:* -ɚ] *n form* praticien(ne) *m(f);* legal ~ juriste *mf;* medical ~ médecin *m*

pragmatic [præg'mætɪk, *Am:* -'mæt̬-] *adj* pragmatique

prairie ['preəri, *Am:* 'preri] *n* (*area of flat land*) plaine *f*

Prairie *n no pl* the ~(s) la Grande Prairie

praise [preɪz] I. *vt* 1. (*express approval*) faire l'éloge de; (*child*) féliciter; he ~d the work of the firefighters il a rendu hommage au travail des pompiers; to ~ sb for sth féliciter qn pour qc; a much-~d documentary un documentaire qui a reçu des critiques très élogieuses; to ~ sb/sth to the skies porter qn/qc aux nues 2. (*worship*) exalter; (*God*) louer II. *n no pl* 1. (*expression of approval*) éloge *m;* to sing the ~s of sb/sth chanter les louanges *fpl* de qn/qc; in ~ of sb/sth en l'honneur de qn/qc 2. *form* (*worship*) louange *f;* ~ be (to God)! Dieu soit loué!; to give ~ to God/the Lord glorifier Dieu/le Seigneur

praiseworthy ['preɪzˌwɜːði, *Am:* -ˌwɜːr-] *adj* digne d'éloges

pram [præm] *n Brit, Aus* landau *m*

prance [prɑːns, *Am:* præns] *vi* 1. (*move with exaggerated movements*) faire des entrechats; to ~ around/about virevolter; (*children*) gambader 2. (*move with high steps: horse*) caracoler

prang [præŋ] I. *vt Brit, Aus, inf* bousiller II. *n Brit, Aus, inf* accrochage *m*

prank [præŋk] *n* canular; to play a ~ on sb jouer un tour à qn

prat [præt] *inf* I. *n* con(ne) *m(f);* to make a ~ of oneself *Brit, inf* faire le con II. <-tt-> *vi Brit, inf* to ~ about déconner

prattle ['prætl, *Am:* 'præt̬-] I. *vi pej* bavasser; (*child*) babiller; to ~ on for hours parler pendant des heures II. *n no pl* verbiage *m;* (*of children*) babillage *m*

prawn [prɔːn, *Am:* prɑːn] *n* crevette *f* rose

prawn cocktail *n* cocktail *m* de crevettes

pray [preɪ] I. *vt, vi* prier II. *adv form* ~, do come in! veuillez entrer, je vous (en) prie!

prayer [preə^r, *Am:* prer] *n* prière *f;* in ~ en prière; to answer sb's ~ exaucer la prière de qn; not to have a ~ of doing sth n'avoir que de maigres espoirs de faire qc

prayer book *n* livre *m* de prières **prayer mat** *n* tapis *m* de prière **prayer meeting** *n* prières *fpl* en groupe **prayer wheel** *n* moulin *m* à prières

praying mantis ['preɪɪŋ'mæntɪs, *Am:* -t̬ɪs] *n* mante *f* religieuse

pre *prep* pré; ~-revolutionary France la France d'avant la révolution; a ~-term meeting une réunion avant le début du trimestre

preach [priːtʃ] I. *vi* 1. (*give a sermon*) faire un sermon; to ~ to sb prêcher qn 2. *pej* (*lecture*) to ~ to sb sermonner qn; to ~ at sb about sth faire la leçon à qn sur qc ►to ~ to the converted prêcher un converti II. *vt* prêcher; to ~ a sermon faire un sermon; to ~ patience/restraint exhorter à la patience/à la modération

preacher *n* pasteur *m*

preachify <-ie-> *vi pej, inf* (*priest*) faire du prêchi-prêcha; (*teacher*) sermonner

preamble [priː'æmbl] *n form* 1. (*introduction*) préambule *m* 2. (*to an essay, a statute*) introduction *f* 3. (*to a lecture*) prologue *m* 4. *no pl* (*introductory remarks or activity*) préliminaires *mpl*

prearrange [ˌpriːə'reɪndʒ] *vt* préprogrammer

prebend ['prebənd] *n Brit* (*salary given to a clergyman*) rétribution *f* canonique

prebendary <-ries> *n* ecclésiastique *m* chargé d'offices

precarious [prɪ'keərɪəs, *Am:* -'kerɪ-] *adj* précaire

precast [ˌpriː'kɑːst, *Am:* 'priːkæst] *adj* ARCHIT précoulé(e)

precaution [prɪ'kɔːʃən, *Am:* -'kɑː-] *n* précaution *f;* to take ~(s) against sth prendre des mesures *fpl* contre qc

precautionary *adj* préventif(-ive)

precede [prɪ'siːd] *vt* précéder

precedence ['presɪdəns, *Am:* 'presə-] *n no pl* 1. (*priority*) priorité *f;* to give ~ to sb/sth laisser la priorité à qn/qc 2. *form* (*order of priority*) préséance *f;* to take ~ over sb prendre le pas sur qn

precedent *n* précédent *m;* to break with ~ couper d'avec le passé; to set a ~ créer un précédent

preceding *adj* précédent(e); (*decade*) dernier(-ère); (*year*) d'avant; the ~ day la veille

precept ['priːsept] *n form* 1. (*rule*) précepte

m **2.** (*principle*) principe *m*

precinct ['pri:sɪŋkt] *n* **1.** (*enclosed area*) enceinte *f;* **within the ~s of sth** dans l'enceinte de qc; **the ~s of sth** les environs *mpl* de qc; ~(**s**) (*of church, college*) pourtour *m* **2.** *Brit* (*shopping area*) (**shopping**) ~ zone *f* commerçante; (**pedestrian**) ~ zone *f* piétonne **3.** *Am* (*police or fire service district*) quartier *m* de sécurité **4.** *Am* (*electoral district*) circonscription *f* électorale

precious ['preʃəs] **I.** *adj* **1.** (*of great value*) précieux(-euse); **to be ~ to sb** être cher à qn **2.** *pej* (*affected*) affecté(e); (*person*) compassé(e) **II.** *adv inf* ~ **few** très peu; **to be ~ little help** n'être d'aucun secours

precipice ['presɪpɪs, *Am:* 'presə-] *n* **1.** (*steep side*) précipice *m* **2.** *fig* (*dangerous situation*) gouffre *m;* **to stand at the edge of the ~** être au bord du précipice

precipitate[1] [prɪ'sɪpɪteɪt] **I.** *vt form* **1.** (*throw down from a height*) précipiter **2.** (*cause suddenly*) *a.* CHEM précipiter **3.** (*make happen*) déclencher **II.** *vi* CHEM **to ~** (**out**) précipiter **III.** *n* CHEM *no pl* précipité *m*

precipitate[2] [prɪ'sɪpɪtət, *Am:* -tɪt] *adj form* (*marriage*) hâtif(-ive); (*involvement*) prématuré(e); (*return*) précipité(e); (*person*) impétueux(-euse); **to act with ~ haste** agir précipitamment; **to be ~ in doing sth** être prompt à faire qc

precipitation *n no pl* précipitation *f*

precipitous [prɪ'sɪpɪtəs, *Am:* -t̬əs] *adj* **1.** (*very steep*) abrupt(e); (*slope*) escarpé(e) **2.** (*rapid: decline*) soudain(e) **3.** *form* (*precipitate*) précipité(e)

précis ['preɪsi:, *Am:* preɪ'si:] **I.** *n* résumé *m* **II.** *vt form* faire un condensé de

precise [prɪ'saɪs] *adj* **1.** (*accurate, exact*) précis(e); (*pronunciation*) clair(e); (*observation*) détaillé(e); (*tone of voice*) juste; (*work*) soigné(e) **2.** (*careful: movement*) précis(e); **to be ~ about doing sth** être minutieux en faisant qc

precisely *adv* **1.** (*exactly*) précisément; **at ~ midnight** à minuit précis **2.** (*just*) juste; **to do ~ the opposite** faire tout le contraire; **to do ~ that** faire précisément cela; ~ **because of** justement à cause de **3.** (*carefully: work*) avec rigueur

precision [prɪ'sɪʒən] *n no pl* précision *f;* **with mathematical ~** avec une rigueur mathématique; **with great ~** avec (un) grand soin; ~ **timing** chronométrage *m* de précision

preclude [prɪ'klu:d] *vt form* empêcher; (*possibility*) exclure; **to ~ sb from doing sth** empêcher qn de faire qc

precocious [prɪ'kəʊʃəs, *Am:* -'koʊ-] *adj* **1.** (*developing early: maturity, talent, skill*) précoce **2.** *pej* (*maturing too early*) prématuré(e)

precociousness, **precocity** *n no pl, form* **1.** (*early development*) précocité *f* **2.** *pej* (*maturing too early*) prématurité *f*

preconceived [ˌpri:kən'si:vd] *adj pej* préconçu(e)

preconception [ˌpri:kən'sepʃən] *n pej* idée *f* préconçue

precondition [ˌpri:kən'dɪʃən] *n* condition *f* préalable

precook ['pri:kʊk] *vt* précuire

precursor [ˌpri:'kɜ:səʳ, *Am:* prɪ'kɜ:rsɚ] *n form* **1.** (*forerunner*) précurseur *m* **2.** (*harbinger*) annonciateur, -trice *m, f*

predate [pri:'deɪt] *vt form* **1.** (*to write an earlier date*) antidater **2.** (*to exist before*) être antérieur à

predator ['predətəʳ, *Am:* -t̬ɚ] *n* (*animal*) prédateur *m;* (*bird*) rapace *m*

predatory *adj* **1.** (*preying*) prédateur(-trice); (*robber*) sans scrupule; ~ **bird** oiseau *m* de proie **2.** (*exploitative*) exploiteur(-euse)

predecessor ['pri:dɪsesəʳ, *Am:* 'predəsesɚ] *n* prédécesseur *m*

predestination [ˌpri:destɪ'neɪʃən] *n no pl* prédestination *f*

predestine [ˌpri:'destɪn] *vt* prédestiner

predetermine [ˌpri:dɪ'tɜ:mɪn, *Am:* -'tɜ:rmən] *vt form* déterminer à l'avance; (*signal, time*) convenir de

predicament [prɪ'dɪkəmənt] *n form* situation *f* difficile; **financial ~** difficulté *f* financière; **to be in a ~** être dans une impasse; **to find oneself in a ~** se trouver en difficulté; **to get oneself into a ~** se mettre dans l'embarras

predicate[1] ['predɪkət, *Am:* 'predɪkɪt] *n* prédicat *m*

predicate[2] ['predɪkeɪt] *vt* **1.** (*assert*) **to ~ that ...** partir du principe que ... **2.** *form* (*base*) **to be ~d on sth** être fondé sur qc

predicative *adj* LING prédicatif(-ive)

predict [prɪ'dɪkt] *vt* prédire; **the volcano is ~ed to erupt soon** on prévoit que le volcan entrera en éruption bientôt

predictable *adj* **1.** (*able to be predicted*) prévisible **2.** *pej* (*not very original*) banal(e)

prediction *n* prédiction *f*

predilection [ˌpri:dɪ'lekʃən, *Am:* ˌpredəl'ek-] *n form* prédilection *f;* **to have a ~ for sth** avoir un faible pour qc

predispose [ˌpri:dɪ'spəʊz, *Am:* -'spoʊz] *vt* **1.** *form* (*influence*) **to ~ sb to** *+infin* prédisposer qn à *+infin;* **to ~ to support sb** prédisposer en faveur de qn **2.** MED **to ~ sb to sth** prédisposer qn à qc

predisposition [ˌpri:dɪspə'zɪʃən] *n* prédisposition *f;* **a ~ to sth** une prédisposition pour qc; MED une prédisposition à qc

predominance [prɪ'dɒmɪnəns, *Am:* -'dɑ:mə-] *n no pl* prédominance *f*

predominant *adj* prédominant(e); (*characteristic, feature, smell*) dominant(e); (*role*) prépondérant(e)

predominantly *adv* (*European, hostile*) majoritairement; **horses figure ~ in his paintings** il a peint surtout des chevaux

predominate [prɪ'dɒmɪneɪt, *Am:*

-'dɑːmə-] *vi* **1.** (*be the most important*) prédominer **2.** (*be more numerous*) être majoritaire

pre-eminence *n no pl, form* prééminence *f;* **Canada's ~ in this sport** la primauté du Canada dans ce sport; **sb's intellectual ~** la supériorité intellectuelle de qn **pre-eminent** *adj form* prééminent(e); (*artist, scientist, sportsman*) éminent(e) **pre-empt** *vt form* **1.** (*act before: person*) devancer; (*action, choice*) anticiper **2.** (*to have a legal right*) avoir une priorité légale sur **3.** (*to use one's legal right*) exercer son droit de préemption sur **pre-emption** *n* **1.** (*prior action*) action *f* préventive; **war of ~** MIL guerre *f* d'assaut **2.** *Am, Aus* (*right of appropriation before others*) droit *m* de préemption **3.** ECON marché *m* préférentiel **pre-emptive** *adj* préventif(-ive)

preen [priːn] **I.** *vi* **1.** (*tidy its feathers: birds*) se lisser les plumes **2.** *pej* (*tidy oneself up*) se pomponner **II.** *vt* **1.** (*tidy: feathers*) lisser **2.** *pej* (*groom*) **to ~ oneself** se pomponner **3.** *pej* (*congratulate*) **to ~ oneself on sth** s'enorgueillir de qc

pre-exist *vt* préexister à **pre-existing** *adj* pre-existant(e)

prefab ['priːfæb] *inf* **I.** *n* préfabriqué *m* **II.** *adj* en préfabriqué

prefabricate [ˌpriː'fæbrɪkeɪt] *vt* préfabriquer

preface ['prefɪs] **I.** *n* (*introduction*) préface *f;* (*of a report*) préliminaire *m;* (*of a speech*) introduction *f;* **the ~ to this disaster** le prélude à ce désastre **II.** *vt form* **1.** (*write a preface to*) préfacer **2.** (*introduce*) **to ~ sth with sth** faire précéder qc de qc

prefatory ['prefətri, *Am:* -tɔːri] *adj form* préliminaire

prefect ['priːfekt] *n* **1.** (*official*) préfet *m* **2.** *Brit, Aus* SCHOOL *élève plus âgé chargé de la discipline*

prefer [prɪ'fɜːʳ, *Am:* priː'fɜːr] <-rr-> *vt* **1.** (*like better*) préférer; **to ~ sth to sth** préférer qc à qc; **I would ~ you to do sth** je préférerais que tu fasses qc *subj;* **sb would ~ that** qn aimerait mieux que *+subj* **2.** *Brit* LAW **to ~ charges against sb** porter plainte contre qn

preferable ['prefrəbl] *adj* préférable

preferably *adv* de préférence

preference ['prefrəns] *n no pl* (*liking better, preferred thing*) préférence *f;* **for ~** de préférence; **in ~ to doing sth** plutôt que de faire qc

preferential *adj* préférentiel(le)

preferred *adj* préféré(e); **my ~ solution** la solution que je préfère

prefigure [ˌpriː'fɪgəʳ, *Am:* -'fɪgjɚ] *vt form* préfigurer; (*change*) annoncer

prefix ['priːfɪks, *Am:* 'priːfɪks] <-es> *n* **1.** LING préfixe *m* **2.** *Brit* (*dialling code*) indicatif *m* (téléphonique)

pregnancy ['pregnəntsi] *n no pl* grossesse *f;* (*in animals*) gestation *f*

pregnancy test *n* test *m* de grossesse

pregnant *adj* **1.** MED (*woman*) enceinte; **to be ~ by sb** être enceinte de qn; **to become ~ by sb** tomber enceinte de qn; **to get sb ~** mettre qn enceinte **2.** (*meaningful*) lourd(e) de sens

preheat [ˌpriː'hiːt] *vt* préchauffer

prehistoric *adj a. pej* préhistorique; (*views*) archaïque

prehistory [ˌpriː'hɪstri] *n no pl* préhistoire *f*

prejudge [ˌpriː'dʒʌdʒ] *vt pej* **to ~ sb** avoir des préjugés sur qn; **to ~ sth** préjuger de qc

prejudice ['predʒʊdɪs] **I.** *n* **1.** (*preconceived opinion*) préjugé *m* **2.** *no pl* (*bias*) parti *m* pris; **without ~ to sth** sans porter atteinte à qc **II.** *vt* porter atteinte à; (*chances*) compromettre; (*cause, outcome, result*) préjuger de; LAW (*case*) entraver le déroulement de; (*witness, jury*) influencer

prejudiced *adj pej* (*attitude, judgement, opinion*) préconçu(e); (*witness*) partial(e)

prejudicial *adj form* (*effect*) néfaste; **~ to our safety** préjudiciable à notre sécurité

preliminary [prɪ'lɪmɪnəri, *Am:* prɪ-'lɪməner-] **I.** *adj* (*selection, stage, study, talk*) préliminaire; SPORT (*heat*) éliminatoire **II.** <-ries> *n* **1.** (*introduction*) préliminaire *m;* **as a ~** en (guise d')introduction **2.** SPORT épreuve *f* éliminatoire **3.** *form* (*preliminary exam: with mark selection*) examen *m* préparatoire; (*with quota selection*) concours *m* d'entrée **4.** *pl* PUBL sélection *f*

prelude ['preljuːd] *n* **1.** (*preliminary*) prélude *f;* **a ~ to peace** un préliminaire de paix **2.** MUS prélude *m*

premarital [ˌpriː'mærɪtl, *Am:* -'merəţl] *adj* avant le mariage

premature ['premətʃəʳ, *Am:* ˌpriːmə'tʊr] *adj* prématuré(e)

premeditated [ˌpriː'medɪteɪtɪd, *Am:* -teɪţɪd] *adj* prémédité(e)

premeditation [ˌpriːmedɪ'teɪʃən] *n no pl, form* préméditation *f*

premier ['premiəʳ, *Am:* prɪ'mɪr] **I.** *n Can, Aus* premier ministre *m* **II.** *adj* le(la) plus important(e)

première ['premieəʳ, *Am:* prɪ'mɪr] **I.** *n* première *f* **II.** *vt* donner la première de **III.** *vi* faire la première

premise ['premɪs] **I.** *n* prémisse *f;* **on the ~ that** en supposant que *+subj* **II.** *vt form* **1.** (*base*) fonder; **to ~ one's argument on sth** appuyer son raisonnement sur qc **2.** *Am* (*preface*) faire une introduction à

premises *n pl* locaux *mpl;* **on the premises** sur place

premium ['priːmiəm] **I.** *n* **1.** (*sum, amount*) prime *f* **2.** (*extra amount*) supplément *m;* **at a 5% ~** moyennant un supplément de 5%; **to be sold at a ~** être vendu à prix fort **3.** (*prize*) prix *m* **4.** *Am* (*petrol*) super *m* ▸**to be at a ~** valoir cher **II.** *adj* **1.** (*high*) élevé(e); (*price*) fort(e) **2.** (*top-quality*) de première qualité

premium bond *n Brit* obligation *f* d'État

premium offer *n* offre *f* exceptionnelle

premium quality *n* qualité *f* supérieure

premonition [ˌpriːməˈnɪʃən] *n* prémonition *f*

prenatal [ˌpriːˈneɪtl, *Am:* -t̬l] *adj Am, Aus* prénatal(e)

preoccupation [ˌpriːɒkjʊˈpeɪʃən, *Am:* priːˌɑːkjuːˈ-] *n* préoccupation *f*

preoccupied *adj* **to be ~** être préoccupé; **a ~ frown** un froncement de sourcils inquiet; **to be ~ with sb/sth** se faire du souci pour qn/qc

preoccupy [priːˈɒkjʊpaɪ, *Am:* priːˈɑːkjuː-] <-ie-> *vt* préoccuper

preordain [ˌpriːɔːˈdeɪn, *Am:* -ɔːrˈ-] *vt form* prédestiner; **a ~ed path** une voie toute tracée; **to be ~ed to** *+infin* être prédestiné à *+infin;* **it is ~ed that ...** il est écrit que ...

prepack(age) [ˌpriːˈpæk(ɪdʒ)] *vt Brit* préemballer

prepaid [ˌpriːˈpeɪd] *adj* prépayé(e); (*envelope, postcard*) préaffranchi(e); (*charge*) réglé(e) d'avance

prepaid reply *n* réponse *f* (en) port payé

preparation [ˌprepəˈreɪʃən] **I.** *n* **1.** *no pl* (*getting ready*) préparation *f;* **in ~ for sth** en préparation de qc **2.** (*substance*) préparation *f;* **beauty ~** produit *m* de beauté **3.** *pl* (*measures*) préparatifs *mpl;* **to make (one's) ~s for sth/to** *+infin* se préparer à qc/à *+infin* **II.** *adj* (*stage*) préparatoire; (*time*) de préparation

preparatory [prɪˈpærətəri, *Am:* -ˈperətɔːr-] *adj* préparatoire; (*sketch, report*) préliminaire; **~ to doing sth** en vue de faire qc

preparatory school *n Brit* école *f* primaire privée; *Am* lycée *m* privé

prepare [prɪˈpeəʳ, *Am:* -ˈper] **I.** *vt* préparer; **to ~ the way** ouvrir la voie; **to ~ to** *+infin* s'apprêter à *+infin;* **to ~ sb for sth/to** *+infin* préparer qn à qc/à *+infin* **II.** *vi* **to ~ for sth** se préparer à qc

prepared *adj* **1.** (*ready, willing*) prêt(e); **to be ~ for sth** être prêt à affronter qc; **to be ~ to** *+infin* être prêt à *+infin;* **to be ~ to make a concession** accepter de faire une concession; **I'm not ~ to let you do this** je ne suis pas disposé à te laisser faire ça **2.** (*made*) préparé(e) ►**"Be Prepared"** "(Scout) toujours prêt"

preparedness *n no pl, form* **military ~** la préparation militaire; **state of ~** état *m* d'alerte préventive

prepay [ˌpriːˈpeɪ] *vt irr* payer d'avance

prepayment *n* paiement *m* par anticipation

preponderance [prɪˈpɒndərənts, *Am:* -ˈpɑːn-] *n no pl, form* prépondérance *f*

preponderant *adj form* prépondérant(e)

preposition [ˌprepəˈzɪʃən] *n* préposition *f*

prepossessing [ˌpriːpəˈzesɪŋ] *adj* remarquable; **not ~** sans intérêt; (*person*) peu brillant(e)

preposterous [prɪˈpɒstərəs, *Am:* -ˈpɑːstɚ-] *adj* extravagant(e); (*accusation*) absurde; (*idea*) farfelu(e)

preppie, preppy [ˈprepi] <-ies> *Am* **I.** *n* **to be a ~** être BCBG **II.** *adj* <-ier, -iest> BCBG *inv*

prerequisite [ˌpriːˈrekwɪzɪt] *n form* condition *f* préalable

prerogative [prɪˈrɒgətɪv, *Am:* -ˈrɑːgət̬ɪv] *n form* **1.** (*right*) prérogative *f* **2.** (*privilege*) privilège *m* **3.** (*responsibility*) responsabilité *f*

presage [ˈpresɪdʒ] *vt form* présager

Presbyterian **I.** *n* presbytérien(ne) *m(f)* **II.** *adj* presbytérien(ne)

presbytery [ˈprezbɪtri, *Am:* -teri] *n* REL presbytère *m*

preschool **I.** *n Am, Aus* maternelle *f* **II.** *adj* préscolaire

prescribe [prɪˈskraɪb] *vt* **1.** (*give as treatment*) **to ~ sth for sb** prescrire qc à qn; **to be ~d sth** se faire prescrire qc **2.** (*recommend*) **to ~ sth to sb** recommander qc à qn **3.** *form* (*allocate*) allouer **4.** (*order*) dicter; **as ~d by law** comme dicté par la loi; **internationally ~d standards** normes *fpl* internationales

prescription [prɪˈskrɪpʃən] *n* **1.** (*doctor's order*) ordonnance *f* **2.** *form* (*rule*) prescription *f*

prescriptive *adj pej, form* normatif(-ive)

presence [ˈprezənts] *n* présence *f;* **in sb's ~** en la présence de qn ►**to make one's ~ felt** se faire remarquer

presence of mind *n* présence *f* d'esprit

present¹ [ˈprezənt] **I.** *n no pl* **the ~** le présent; **at ~** à présent, à cette heure *Belgique* ►**there's no time like the ~** *prov* il ne faut jamais remettre au lendemain ce que l'on peut faire le jour même *prov* **II.** *adj* **1.** (*current*) actuel(le); **at the ~ moment/time** en ce moment **2.** LING **~ tense** (temps *m*) présent *m* **3.** (*in attendance, existing*) présent(e); **all those ~** tous ceux qui sont présents; **~ company excepted** à l'exception des personnes ici présentes

present² [ˈprezənt] **I.** *n* (*gift*) cadeau *m;* **birthday/wedding ~** cadeau d'anniversaire/de mariage; **to get sth as a ~** avoir qc en cadeau; **to give sth to sb as a ~** offrir qc à qn; **to make sb a ~ of sth** faire cadeau à qn de qc **II.** *vt* **1.** (*give*) présenter; **to ~ sb with a challenge** mettre qn à défi; **to ~ sb with (the) facts** exposer les faits à qn; **to ~ sb with an ultimatum/a petition** soumettre un ultimatum/une pétition à qn; **to ~ sth to sb, to ~ sb with sth** (*gift*) offrir qc à qn; (*award, report*) remettre qc à qn; **to ~ sb with a diploma/medal** remettre un diplôme/une médaille à qn **2.** (*offer*) offrir; **to ~ a cheerful atmosphere** offrir un cadre attrayant; **to ~ a contrast to sth** offrir un contraste avec qc **3.** (*exhibit*) exposer; (*paper, report*) présenter **4.** (*introduce*) présenter **5.** *Aus, Brit* (*host*) présenter **6.** (*perform: concert, show*) donner **7.** (*deliver: bill*) remettre **8.** (*bring before court*) exposer ►**to ~ arms** MIL présenter les armes; **to ~ one's compliments** *a. iron* présenter ses compliments; **to ~ oneself** se présenter

presentable [prɪ'zentəbl, *Am:* prɪ'zenṱə-] *adj* présentable; **to look ~** avoir l'air présentable; **to make oneself ~** s'arranger

presentation [ˌprezən'teɪʃən] *n* **1.** (*act of presenting*) présentation *f;* (*of a theory*) exposition *f;* (*of a dissertation, thesis*) soutenance *f;* **to give a ~ on sth** faire un exposé sur qc **2.** (*act of giving: of a medal, gift*) remise *f;* **to make a ~ of sth** remettre qc

present-day *adj* actuel(le); **~ London** le Londres d'aujourd'hui

presentiment [prɪ'zentɪmənt] *n form* pressentiment *m;* **to have a ~ of danger** pressentir un danger

presently ['prezəntli] *adv* **1.** (*soon*) bientôt **2.** (*now*) à présent

present participle *n* participe *m* présent

preservation [ˌprezə'veɪʃən, *Am:* -ɚ'-] *n no pl* **1.** (*upkeep*) conservation *f;* **to be in a poor/an excellent state of ~** être dans un mauvais/excellent état de conservation **2.** (*maintenance: wood, leather, garden*) entretien *m;* **~ of order** maintien *m* de l'ordre **3.** (*protection*) préservation *f*

preservative *n* conservateur *m;* **free from artificial ~s** sans conservateurs

preserve [prɪ'zɜːv, *Am:* -'zɜːrv] **I.** *vt* **1.** (*maintain, keep*) conserver; (*peace, status quo*) maintenir **2.** (*protect*) préserver; **to ~ sb from insanity** préserver qn de la folie **II.** *n* **1.** (*specially conserved fruit*) conserve *f;* **apricot/strawberry ~** conserve d'abricots/de fraises **2.** (*domain, responsibility*) domaine *m;* **to be the ~ of the rich** être le domaine des riches; **to regard sth as one's ~** considérer qc à soi **3.** *Am* (*reserve*) réserve *f;* **game ~** réserve de gibier; **nature/wildlife ~** réserve naturelle/sauvage

preserved *adj* **1.** (*maintained*) bien conservé(e); (*building*) en bon état; **to be badly ~** être mal entretenu **2.** GASTR en conserve; **~ food** conserves *fpl*

preshrunk [ˌpriː'ʃrʌŋk] *adj* prélavé(e)

preside [prɪ'zaɪd] *vi* **to ~ at sth** présider à qc

presidency *n* présidence *f;* **to run for the ~ of the US** se présenter à la présidence des États-Unis; **during his/her ~** au cours de sa présidence

president ['prezɪdənt] *n* président(e) *m(f);* **the ~ of the United States** le président des États-Unis; **Mr President** M. le Président; **Madam President** Madame la Présidente

presidential *adj* (*of president*) présidentiel(le)

President's Day *n no pl, Am: fêté le troisième lundi de février aux États-Unis et remplace les deux anciens jours fériés, Lincoln Day et Washington Day*

press [pres] **I.** *n* **1.** (*push*) pression *f;* **to give sth a ~** appuyer sur qc **2.** (*ironing action*) repassage *m;* **to give sth a ~** donner un coup de fer (à repasser) à qc **3.** (*instrument for pressing*) presse *f;* **garlic ~** presse-ail *m* **4.** *pl* (*media*) presse *f;* **a ~ campaign/conference** une campagne/conférence de presse; **a ~ agency/card** une agence/carte de presse; **~ reports** reportages *mpl;* **to have a bad/good ~** avoir bonne/mauvaise presse; **to leak sth to the ~** divulguer qc à la presse **5.** (*crowd*) foule *f* ▶**freedom of the ~** liberté *f* de la presse; **to be in** [*o Am* **on**] **~** être sous presse; **to go to ~** aller sous presse **II.** *vt* **1.** (*push*) appuyer sur; **to ~ sth open** ouvrir qc en appuyant dessus; **to ~ sth into a hole** pousser qc dans un trou; **he ~ed his leg against mine** il a pressé sa jambe contre la mienne **2.** (*squeeze*) serrer **3.** (*extract juice from*) presser **4.** (*iron*) repasser **5.** (*force, insist*) faire pression sur; **to ~ sb to** +*infin* presser qn de +*infin;* **to ~ sb for an answer/decision** presser qn de répondre/prendre une décision **6.** LAW **to ~ charges against sb/sth** engager des poursuites contre qn/qc ▶**to ~ home one's advantage** profiter de l'avantage; **to ~ one's luck** forcer la chance **III.** *vi* **1.** (*push*) appuyer; **to ~ against sth** presser contre qc **2.** (*be urgent*) presser; **time is ~ing** le temps presse

◆**press ahead** *vt* continuer

◆**press down I.** *vt* **to press sth down** [*o* **to ~ sth**] appuyer sur qc **II.** *vi* appuyer; **to ~ on sth** appuyer sur qc

◆**press for** *vt* faire pression pour obtenir

◆**press forward**, **press on** *vi* continuer; **to ~ with** continuer avec

press clipping, **press cutting** *n* coupure *f* de journaux

pressed *adj* pressé(e); **to be ~ for time** manquer de temps **press gallery** *n* tribune *f* de la presse **press-gang** *vt* **to ~ sb into doing sth** faire pression sur qn pour qu'il fasse qc

pressing *adj* pressant(e); (*issue, matter*) urgent(e)

pressman *n* journaliste *m* **press photographer** *n* photographe *mf* de presse **press release** *n* communiqué *m* de presse **press stud** *n Aus, Brit* bouton-pression *m* **press-up** *n Brit* traction *f*

pressure ['preʃəʳ, *Am:* -ɚ] **I.** *n* **1.** (*force*) pression *f;* **to apply ~** faire pression; **to put ~ on sth** exercer une pression sur qc; **to be under ~** être sous pression; **at ~** à pression; **a ~ cabin** une cabine de pressurisation **2.** *no pl* (*stress*) pression *f;* **to have ~** être sous pression **3.** (*demands*) pression *f;* **to be under ~ to** +*infin* être contraint de +*infin;* **to do sth under ~ from sb** faire qc sous la pression de qn; **to bring ~ to bear on sb to do sth** faire pression sur qn pour qu'il fasse qc *subj* **4.** *pl* (*pressure*) pression *f* **II.** *vt* **to ~ sb to** +*infin* contraindre qn à +*infin*

pressure cooker *n* autocuiseur *m* **pressure groupe** *n* groupe *m* de pression

pressurize ['preʃəraɪz] *vt Am* **1.** (*control air pressure*) pressuriser **2.** (*persuade by force*) **to**

P

~ **sb to do sth** faire pression sur qn pour qu'il fasse qc *subj*
prestige [pre'sti:ʒ] *n no pl* prestige *m;* ~ **hotel** hôtel *m* de prestige
prestigious [pre'stɪdʒəs] *adj* prestigieux(-euse)
presumably [prɪ'zju:məbli, *Am:* prɪ'zu:mə-] *adv* sans doute
presume [prɪ'zju:m, *Am:* prɪ'zu:m] **I.** *vt* présumer; ~**d dead** présumé mort **II.** *vi* être importun; **to ~ to** *+infin* se permettre de *+infin;* **to ~ on sb/sth** abuser de qn/qc
presumption [prɪ'zʌmpʃən] *n* présomption *f;* **the ~ is that ...** il est à présumer que ...
presumptive [prɪ'zʌmptɪv] *adj* par présomption
presumptuous *adj* présomptueux(-euse)
presuppose [ˌpri:sə'pəʊz, *Am:* -'poʊz] *vt form* présupposer
presupposition [ˌpri:sʌpə'zɪʃən] *n* présupposition *f*
pre-tax *adj* avant impôt
pretence [prɪ'tents, *Am:* 'pri:tents] *n no pl* comédie *f;* **to keep up a ~ of sth** continuer de feindre qc; **to make no ~ of sth/doing sth** ne pas feindre qc/de faire qc; **to make no ~ to being/having sth** ne pas avoir la prétention d'être/de faire qc; **under the ~ of sth/of doing sth** sous prétexte de qc/de faire qc
pretend [prɪ'tend] **I.** *vt* **1.** (*claim*) prétendre **2.** (*feign*) faire semblant; **to ~ that one is asleep** faire semblant de dormir **II.** *vi* **1.** (*feign*) faire semblant; **to ~ to** *+infin* faire semblant de *+infin;* **to ~ to be sb** se faire passer pour qn **2.** (*claim*) **to ~ to sth** prétendre à qc; **to ~ to** *+infin* prétendre *+infin;* **I don't ~ to be an expert** je ne prétends pas être un expert
pretended *adj* prétendu(e)
pretender *n* prétendant(e) *m(f)*
pretense [prɪ'tents, *Am:* 'pri:tents] *n no pl, Am s.* **pretence**
pretension [prɪ'tentʃən] *n* prétention *f;* **to have ~s to doing sth** avoir la prétention de faire qc
pretentious [prɪ'tentʃəs] *adj pej* prétentieux(-euse)
pretentiousness *n no pl, pej* prétention *f*
preterit(e) ['pretərɪt, *Am:* 'preţ̬ɚɪt] *n* LING **1.** (*in English*) prétérit *m* **2.** (*in French*) passé *m* simple
preternatural [ˌpri:tə'nætʃərəl, *Am:* -ţ̬ɚ'nætʃɚəl] *adj form* surnaturel(le)
pretext ['pri:tekst] *n* prétexte *m;* **on the ~ of doing sth** sous prétexte de faire qc; **to give sth as a ~** donner qc comme prétexte
pretty ['prɪti, *Am:* 'prɪţ̬-] **I.** *adj* <-ier, -iest> joli(e) ►**to be not just a ~ face** en avoir dans le crâne; **a ~ penny** une coquette somme; **it's not a ~ sight** ce n'est pas beau à voir **II.** *adv* assez; **to be ~ certain** être presque certain; **~ nearly finished** presque terminé; **~ well everything** bien des choses; **~ much** à peu près ►**to be sitting ~** avoir le bon filon
pretzel ['pretsl] *n* bretzel *m*
prevail [prɪ'veɪl] *vi* **1.** (*triumph*) l'emporter **2.** (*be widespread*) prédominer
◆**prevail (up)on** *vt* **to ~ sb to** *+infin* persuader qn de *+infin*
prevailing *adj* actuel(le); **under ~ law** dans le cadre de la loi en vigueur
prevailing wind *n* vent *m* dominant
prevalence ['prevələnts] *n no pl* **1.** (*common occurrence*) prédominance *f* **2.** (*frequency*) fréquence *f*
prevalent *adj* **1.** (*common*) courant(e); (*disease*) répandu(e); (*opinion*) général(e) **2.** (*frequent*) fréquent(e)
prevaricate [prɪ'værɪkeɪt, *Am:* prɪ'verɪ-] *vi form* **to ~ over sth** tergiverser au sujet de
prevarication *n no pl, form* faux-fuyant *m*
prevent [prɪ'vent] *vt* **1.** (*keep from happening*) empêcher; (*disaster*) éviter; **to ~ sb/sth (from** *Am*) **doing sth** empêcher qn/qc de faire qc; **to ~ a disease from spreading/a bomb from exploding** éviter que la maladie ne se propage/qu'une bombe n'explose (*subj*) **2.** MED prévenir
prevention *n no pl* prévention *f;* **society for the ~ of cruelty to animals** société *f* protectrice des animaux ►**~ is better than cure, an ounce of ~ is worth a pound of cure** *Am, prov* mieux vaut prévenir que guérir *prov*
preventive *adj* préventif(-ive)
preview ['pri:vju:] **I.** *n* **1.** (*show*) avant-première *f* **2.** (*exhibition*) vernissage *m* **3.** (*trailer*) bande-annonce *f* **II.** *vt* visionner **III.** *vi* être présenté en avant-première
previous ['pri:viəs] *adj* précédent(e); **on the ~ day** la veille; **the ~ evening** la veille au soir; **no ~ experience required** aucune expérience exigée; **the ~ summer** l'été dernier; **on my ~ visit to Florida** lors de mon dernier voyage en Floride; **to have (no) ~ convictions** avoir un casier vierge
previously *adv* **1.** (*beforehand*) avant **2.** (*formerly*) par le passé
prewar [ˌpri:'wɔ:ʳ, *Am:* -'wɔ:r] *adj* d'avant-guerre
prey [preɪ] *n no pl* proie *f;* **to be easy ~ for sb** être une proie facile pour qn ►**to be/fall ~ to sb/sth** être/devenir la proie de qn/qc; **to be ~ to all sorts of fears** être en proie à toutes les peurs
◆**prey on** *vt* **1.** (*attack: animals*) chasser; (*old people*) s'attaquer à **2.** (*worry*) **to ~ sb's mind** préoccuper qn
price [praɪs] **I.** *n* prix *m;* **computer ~s** le prix des ordinateurs; **a ~ fall/rise** une baisse/augmentation des prix; **a ~ range** une gamme de prix; **a ~ tag** une étiquette; **to ask a high ~** demander un prix élevé; **to make/name a ~** fixer/donner un prix; **to fetch a ~** atteindre une somme; **the ~ one has to pay for fame** le prix à payer pour la célébrité; **to put a ~ on sth** évaluer qc ►**to set a ~ on sb's head**

mettre la tête de qn à prix; **to pay a heavy ~, to pay the ~** payer le prix; **at a ~** à un prix fort; **at any ~** à n'importe quel prix; **what ~ sth?** que devient qc? **II.** *vt* **1.** (*mark with price tag*) mettre le prix sur; **to be ~d at one franc** coûter un franc **2.** (*set value*) fixer le prix de; **to be reasonably ~** avoir un prix raisonnable; (*restaurant*) être abordable **3.** (*inquire about cost*) demander le prix de ►**to ~ oneself out of the market** ne plus pouvoir suivre la concurrence du marché

priceless *adj* inestimable

price stability *n* stabilité *f* des prix

pricey ['praɪsi] <pricier, priciest> *adj inf* chérot

pricing ['praɪsɪŋ] *n* fixation *f* du prix

prick [prɪk] *vt* piquer; (*balloon*) crever; **to ~ (one's) sth** (se) piquer qc ►**to ~ the balloon** tout gâcher; **to ~ sb's conscience** réveiller la conscience de qn

◆**prick up** *vt* (*ears*) dresser

prickle ['prɪkl] **I.** *n* **1.** (*thorn*) épine *f* **2.** (*tingle*) picotement *m;* (*of pleasure*) frisson *m* **II.** *vi* picoter **III.** *vt* piquer

prickly <-ier, -iest> *adj* **1.** (*thorny*) épineux(-euse) **2.** (*tingling: cloth*) qui gratte; **to feel ~** avoir des fourmillements **3.** *inf* (*easily offended*) irritable

prickly pear *n* figue *f* de Barbarie

pride [praɪd] **I.** *n* **1.** *no pl* (*proud feeling*) fierté *f;* **to feel great ~** être très fier; **to take ~ in sb/sth** être fier de qn/qc; **to take ~ in one's appearance** être soucieux de son apparence **2.** (*self-respect*) orgueil *m;* **to have too much ~ to** +*infin* être trop orgueilleux pour +*infin;* **to hurt sb's ~** blesser qn dans son orgueil; **to swallow one's ~** ravaler son orgueil **3.** (*animal group*) bande *f* ►**to be one's ~ and joy** être la fierté de qn; **to have ~ of place** avoir la place d'honneur **II.** *vt* **to ~ oneself on doing sth** être fier de faire qc; **to ~ oneself on being sth** ne pas cacher son orgueil d'être qc

priest [priːst] *n* prêtre *m*

priestess ['priːstes, *Am:* -stɪs] *n* prêtresse *f*

priesthood *n no pl* (*position, office*) sacerdoce *m;* **to enter the ~** entrer dans les ordres

priestly *adj* sacerdotal(e)

prig [prɪg] *n pej* **to be a ~** se prendre pour un saint

priggish *adj pej* hautain(e)

prim [prɪm] <-mer, -mest> *adj pej* prude; **to be ~ (and proper)** être très convenable

primacy ['praɪməsi] *n no pl, form* primauté *f*

prima donna [priːmə'dɒnə, *Am:* -'dɑːnə] *n* **1.** (*number one singer*) prima donna *f inv* **2.** *pej* **to behave like a ~** se prendre pour une star

primaeval [praɪ'miːvəl] *adj Brit s.* **primeval**

primal ['praɪməl] *adj* primitif(-ive)

primarily *adv* essentiellement

primary ['praɪməri, *Am:* -mer-] **I.** *adj* principal(e); (*colour, election, school*) primaire; (*meaning, importance*) premier **II.** <-ies> *n* **1.** *Brit* (*school*) école *f* primaire **2.** *Am* POL primaire *f*

primate ['praɪmeɪt, *Am:* -mɪt] *n* **1.** ZOOL primate *m* **2.** REL primat *m*

prime [praɪm] **I.** *adj* **1.** (*main*) premier(-ère); **~ suspect** suspect *m* numéro un **2.** (*best*) de premier ordre; (*food*) de premier choix; (*example*) parfait(e); (*quality*) premier(-ère) **II.** *n* **1.** *no pl* apogée *m;* **to be in one's ~** être à son apogée; **to be past one's ~** être sur son déclin; **in the ~ of life** dans la fleur de l'âge **2.** MAT nombre *m* premier **III.** *vt* **1.** (*prepare*) préparer; (*bomb, gun, pump*) amorcer; (*wood, surface*) apprêter; **to ~ oneself to** +*infin* se préparer à +*infin* **2.** (*inform*) informer

prime minister *n* premier ministre *m*

prime number *n* nombre *m* premier

primer ['praɪmər, *Am:* -mɚ] *n* base *f*

prime time *n* heures *fpl* de grande écoute

primeval [praɪ'miːvəl] *adj* ASTR primitif(-ive)

primitive ['prɪmɪtɪv, *Am:* -t̬ɪv] *adj* primitif(-ive)

primordial [praɪ'mɔːdiəl, *Am:* -'mɔːr-] *adj form* primordial(e)

primrose ['prɪmrəʊz, *Am:* -roʊz], **primula** *n* primevère *f*

primus® ['praɪməs] *n* réchaud *m* de camping

prince [prɪnts] *n* prince *m*

Prince Edward Island *n* l'île *f* du Prince-Edouard

princely *adj* princier(-ère)

princess [prɪn'ses, *Am:* 'prɪntsɪs] *n* princesse *f*

principal ['prɪntsəpl] **I.** *adj* (*main*) principal(e) **II.** *n* **1.** (*director of college*) directeur, -trice *m, f,* préfet, -ète *m, f Belgique* **2.** (*sum of money*) capital *m*

principality [ˌprɪntsɪ'pæləti, *Am:* -sə'pælət̬i] *n* principauté *f*

principally *adv* principalement

principle ['prɪntsəpl] **I.** *n* principe *m;* **on ~** par principe **II.** *adj* (*person*) qui a des principes

print [prɪnt] **I.** *n* **1.** (*printed lettering or writing*) caractères *mpl;* **bold ~** caractères gras **2.** (*printed text*) texte *m* **3.** (*photo*) épreuve *f* **4.** (*fingerprint*) empreinte *f* **5.** (*pattern on fabric*) imprimé *m* **6.** (*engraving*) gravure *f* ►**to appear in ~** être publié; **to go out of ~** être épuisé; **to be in/out of ~** être en stock/épuisé **II.** *vt* **1.** (*produce, reproduce*) imprimer; (*special issue, copies*) tirer; **to be ~ed in hardback** être édité en version reliée **2.** (*write*) écrire en lettres d'imprimerie **3.** PHOT tirer **III.** *vi* **1.** (*produce*) imprimer; **to be ~ing** être sous presse **2.** (*write in unjoined letters*) écrire en lettres d'imprimerie

◆**print out** *vt* imprimer

printable *adj* imprimable

printed circuit board *n* ELEC carte *f* de circuits imprimés

printer *n* **1.** (*person*) imprimeur *m* **2.** INFOR imprimante *f;* **ink-jet/laser/thermal** ~ imprimante à jet d'encre/à laser/thermique; ~ **driver** gestionnaire *m* d'imprimante

printing *n* **1.** *no pl* (*act*) impression *f* **2.** (*business*) imprimerie *f* **3.** (*print run*) tirage *m*

printing ink *n* encre *f* d'imprimerie **printing press** *n* presse *f* d'imprimerie **printing works** *n* imprimerie *f*

printout *n* INFOR sortie *f* d'imprimante **print run** *n* tirage *m* **print shop** *n* imprimerie *f*

prior ['praɪəʳ, *Am:* 'praɪɚ] **I.** *adv form* ~ **to sth** avant qc; ~ **to doing sth** avant de faire qc **II.** *adj form* précédent(e); (*approval*) préalable; (*arrest, conviction*) antérieur(e); **to have a** ~ **engagement** avoir d'autres engagements; **without** ~ **notice** sans préavis **III.** *n* prieur *m*

priority [praɪ'ɒrəti, *Am:* -'ɔːrəṯi] **I.** *n* priorité *f;* **top** ~ priorité absolue; **to have a high** ~ être d'une grande importance; **to give** ~ **to sb/sth** donner la priorité à qn/qc; **to have** ~ **over sb** avoir la préséance sur qn; **to get one's priorities right** savoir ce qui est important **II.** *adj* prioritaire; (*task*) prioritaire; **to get** ~ **treatment** être traité en priorité

priory ['praɪəri] *n* prieuré *m*

prise [praɪz] *vt Brit, Aus* **to** ~ **sth off** [*o* **to** ~ **off sth**] retirer qc à l'aide d'un levier; **to** ~ **sth open** ouvrir qc à l'aide d'un levier; **to** ~ **sth out of sth** extirper qc de qc

prism [prɪzəm] *n* prisme *m*

prismatic *adj* **1.** (*resembling a prism*) prismatique **2.** (*formed by a transparent prism, brilliant*) à prismes

prison ['prɪzən] *n* **1.** (*jail*) prison *f;* **to go to** ~ aller en prison; **to put sb in** ~ emprisonner qn; **to send sb to** ~ envoyer qn en prison; **to throw sb into** ~ jeter qn en prison; **in** ~ en prison; ~ **life** la vie carcérale; ~ **yard** cour de prison **2.** *no pl* (*time in jail*) réclusion *f*

prison camp *n* camp *m* de prisonniers **prison cell** *n* cellule *f* (de prison)

prisoner *n* prisonnier, -ère *m, f;* **political** ~ prisonnier *m* politique; **to hold sb** ~ détenir qn; **to take sb** ~ faire qn prisonnier

prison inmate *n* détenu(e) *m(f)*

pristine ['prɪstiːn] *adj form* virginal(e); **in** ~ **condition** comme neuf

privacy ['prɪvəsi, *Am:* 'praɪ-] *n no pl* intimité *f;* **to disturb sb's** ~ déranger qn dans son intimité; **in the** ~ **of one's home** dans l'intimité de son foyer; **to want some** ~ désirer être seul

private ['praɪvɪt, *Am:* -vət] **I.** *adj* **1.** (*not public*) privé(e) **2.** (*personal: opinion, papers*) personnel(le) **3.** (*confidential*) confidentiel(le); **to keep sth** ~ garder qc confidentiel; **their** ~ **joke** une plaisanterie entre eux **4.** (*not open to the public*) privé(e); (*ceremony, funeral*) célébré(e) dans l'intimité **5.** (*for personal use*) privé(e); (*house, lesson*) particulier(-ère) **6.** (*not state-run*) privé(e) **7.** (*secluded*) retiré(e) **8.** (*not social*) réservé(e) **9.** (*undisturbed*) tranquille **II.** *n* **1.** *no pl* (*privacy*) **in** ~ en privé; **to speak to sb in** ~ parler à qn en particulier **2.** *pl, inf* (*genitals*) parties *fpl* (génitales) **3.** (*lowest-ranking army soldier*) soldat *m* de deuxième classe

private detective *n* détective *m* privé **private enterprise** *n* entreprise *f* privée

privateer [ˌpraɪvə'tɪəʳ, *Am:* -'tɪr] *n* corsaire *m*

private life *n* vie *f* privé

privately *adv* **1.** (*in private, not publicly*) en privé; (*celebrate*) dans l'intimité; **to speak** ~ **with sb** parler à qn en particulier **2.** (*secretly*) en secret **3.** (*personally*) à titre personnel; (*benefit*) personnellement **4.** (*by private individuals, not publicly*) ~**-owned business** commerce *m* qui appartient au secteur privé

private member *n Brit, Can, Aus, NZ* simple député(e) *m(f)* **private parts** *n* parties *fpl* intimes **private school** *n* école *f* privée **private secretary** *n* secrétaire *m* particulier, secrétaire *f* particulière

privation [praɪ'veɪʃən] *n no pl, form* privation *f*

privatization *n no pl* privatisation *f*

privatize ['praɪvɪtaɪz, *Am:* -və-] *vt* privatiser

privet ['prɪvɪt] *n no pl* troène *m*

privilege ['prɪvəlɪdʒ] **I.** *n* **1.** (*special right or advantage*) privilège *m;* **diplomatic** ~ immunité *f* diplomatique; **to have the** ~ **of doing sth** avoir le privilège de faire qc **2.** (*honour*) honneur *m;* **it is a** ~ **to** +*infin* c'est un honneur de +*infin* **II.** *vt* **to be** ~**d to** +*infin* avoir le privilège de +*infin*

privileged *adj* **1.** (*special, having some privileges*) privilégié(e) **2.** (*confidential: communication*) privé(e)

privy ['prɪvi] **I.** *adj form* **to be** ~ **to sth** avoir connaissance de qc; **to be** ~ **to the truth about sth** connaître la vérité sur qc **II.** *n* cabinets *mpl*

prize[1] [praɪz] **I.** *n* **1.** (*thing to be won*) prix *m;* (*in the lottery*) lot *m;* **to carry off a** ~ remporter un prix **2.** (*reward*) récompense *f* ▶**there are no** ~**s for guessing** ce n'est pas difficile de deviner **II.** *adj* **1.** *inf* (*first-rate*) de premier ordre; (*idiot*) fini(e) **2.** (*prize-winning*) primé(e) **III.** *vt* priser; **sb's** ~**d possession** le bien le plus prisé de qn; **to** ~ **sth highly** faire grand cas de qc

prize[2] [praɪz] *vt s.* **prise**

prizefight *n* match *m* de boxe professionnel **prizefighter** *n* boxeur, -euse *m, f* professionnel(le) **prizefighting** *n no pl* boxe *f* professionnelle **prize-giving** *n* distribution *f* des prix **prize list** *n* palmarès *m* **prize money** *n* SPORT argent *m* du prix **prize ring** *n* ring *m* **prizewinner** *n* (*of a game*) gagnant(e) *m(f);* (*of an exam*) lauréat(e) *m(f)* **prizewinning** *adj* primé(e)

pro[1] [prəʊ, *Am:* proʊ] *n inf* pro *mf;* **a tennis** ~ un pro du tennis

pro[2] [prəʊ, *Am:* proʊ] **I.** *n* pour *m;* **the** ~**s of sth** les avantages *m* de qc; **the** ~**s and cons of**

sth le pour et le contre de qc **II.** *prep* pour; **to be ~-European** être pro-européen **III.** *adj, adv* pour; **he has always been ~ sport** il a toujours été pour l'activité sportive

proactive [ˌprəʊ'æktɪv, *Am:* ˌproʊ'-] *adj* qui prend les devants; (*strategy*) anticipé(e)

probability [ˌprɒbə'bɪləti, *Am:* ˌprɑːbə'bɪləṱi] *n* probabilité *f;* **in all ~** selon toute probabilité

probable ['prɒbəbl, *Am:* 'prɑːbə-] *adj* vraisemblable; **it is ~ that** il est probable que +*subj*

probably *adv* probablement

probate ['prəʊbeɪt, *Am:* 'proʊ-] **I.** *n no pl* **1.** LAW homologation *f;* **to grant ~ of a will** (faire) homologuer un testament **2.** *Aus* FIN droit *m* de succession **II.** *vt Am* homologuer

probation *n no pl* **1.** ECON période *f* d'essai; **to be on ~** faire un stage **2.** LAW probation *f;* **to be (out) on ~** être en liberté surveillée; **to get ~** être mis à l'épreuve; **to revoke sb's ~** annuler la mise à l'épreuve de qn **3.** *Am* SCHOOL, UNIV période *f* de mise à l'épreuve; **to place sb on ~** sanctionner qn

probationary *adj* de probation; (*period*) d'essai

probationer [prəʊ'beɪʃənəʳ, *Am:* proʊ-'beɪʃənɚ] *n* **1.** *Am* (*offender on probation*) délinquant *m* en liberté surveillée **2.** (*newly appointed person*) stagiaire *mf*

probe [prəʊb, *Am:* proʊb] **I.** *vi* faire des recherches; **to ~ for sth** rechercher qc; **to ~ into sth** fouiller dans qc **II.** *vt* **1.** (*examine or investigate thoroughly*) explorer; (*past, person, mystery*) sonder; (*murder*) chercher à éclaircir; (*rubble*) chercher dans **2.** MED sonder **III.** *n* **1.** (*thorough examination, investigation*) enquête *f;* **he made a ~ into the wreckage of the car** il a examiné les débris de la voiture **2.** MED, AVIAT sonde *f*

probing *adj* très poussé(e)

probity ['prəʊbəti, *Am:* 'proʊbəṱi] *n no pl, form* probité *f*

problem ['prɒbləm, *Am:* 'prɑːbləm] *n* problème *m;* **weight ~** problème de poids; **to pose a ~ for sb** créer un problème à qn; **to have a drinking ~** avoir un problème d'alcoolisme

problematic(al) *adj* **1.** (*creating difficulty*) problématique **2.** (*questionable, disputable*) discutable

problem child *n* enfant *m* à problèmes

proboscis [prəʊ'bɒsɪs, *Am:* proʊ'bɑːsɪs] *n* **1.** (*snout*) museau *m* **2.** (*mouthpart*) trompe *f*

procedural *adj* **1.** (*related to procedure*) de procédure **2.** LAW procédural(e)

procedure [prə'siːdʒəʳ, *Am:* -dʒɚ] *n* procédure *f*

proceed [prə'siːd, *Am:* proʊ'-] *vi form* **1.** (*progress*) continuer; **to ~ with sth** poursuivre qc; **to ~ with a lawsuit** intenter un procès; **to ~ against sb** poursuivre qn en justice **2.** (*come from*) **to ~ from sth** provenir de qc **3.** (*continue walking, driving*) avancer **4.** (*continue: debate, work*) se poursuivre **5.** (*start, begin*) commencer; **to ~ with sth** commencer (avec) qc; **to ~ to** +*infin* se mettre à +*infin*

proceeding *n* **1.** (*action*) procédé *m* **2.** *pl* (*activities*) activités *fpl* **3.** *pl* LAW poursuites *fpl* judiciaires; **disciplinary ~s** mesures *fpl* disciplinaires; **to institute ~s against sb** intenter un procès à qn **4.** *pl, form* (*record of conference*) actes *mpl* **5.** *pl, form* (*debates*) débats *mpl*

proceeds *n pl* bénéfices *mpl*

process[1] ['prəʊses, *Am:* 'prɑː-] **I.** *n* **1.** (*series of actions, steps*) processus *m;* **a long and painful ~** un travail long et pénible; **the ~ of ageing** le processus de l'âge; **to be in the ~ of doing sth** être en train de faire qc **2.** LAW, ADMIN procédure *f* **3.** (*method*) procédé *m* ►**in the ~** en même temps **II.** *vt* **1.** (*act upon, treat*) traiter; (*raw materials*) transformer **2.** INFOR traiter **3.** PHOT développer

process[2] [prəʊ'ses, *Am:* proʊ-] *vi form* défiler (en procession)

processing *n no pl* **1.** (*treatment*) traitement *m;* (*of food*) préparation *f* industrielle **2.** PHOT développement *m;* **one-hour ~** développement en une heure

procession [prə'seʃən] *n* **1.** *a. fig* cortège *m;* (*of cars*) file *f;* **a non-stop ~ of visitors** un défilé interminable de visiteurs **2.** REL procession *f*

processor *n* INFOR processeur *m*

proclaim [prə'kleɪm, *Am:* proʊ'-] *vt form* proclamer; (*war, one's love*) déclarer

proclamation [ˌprɒklə'meɪʃən, *Am:* ˌprɑːklə-] *n form* déclaration *f;* **to issue a ~** faire une proclamation

proclivity [prə'klɪvəti, *Am:* proʊ'klɪvəṱi] *n form* penchant *m*

procrastinate [prəʊ'kræstɪneɪt, *Am:* proʊ'kræstə-] *vi* atermoyer

procrastination *n no pl* ajournement *m* ►**~ is the thief of time** il ne faut pas remettre au lendemain ce que l'on peut faire le jour même *prov*

procreate ['prəʊkrɪeɪt, *Am:* 'proʊ-] *vi form* procréer

procreation *n no pl, form* procréation *f*

procurable [prə'kjʊərəbl, *Am:* proʊ'-] *adj* que l'on peut se procurer

procurator fiscal *n Scot* LAW ≈ procureur *m* général

procure [prə'kjʊəʳ, *Am:* proʊ'kjʊr] *form* **I.** *vt* (*acquire, obtain*) procurer; **I've ~d a new part** je me suis procuré une pièce de rechange **II.** *vi form* faire du proxénétisme

procurement *n no pl, form* **1.** (*acquisition of supplies*) obtention *f* **2.** (*system of supply*) équipement *m*

procurer *n form* proxénète *m*

prod [prɒd, *Am:* prɑːd] **I.** *n* **1.** (*jab*) petit coup *m* **2.** (*push*) poussée *f;* **to need a ~** avoir besoin d'être poussé; **to give sb a ~** pousser qn **II.** <-dd-> *vt a. fig* pousser; **to ~ sb into**

P

doing sth pousser qn à faire qc **III.** <-dd-> *vi* **to ~ at sb/sth** pousser qn/qc

prodigal ['prɒdɪgl, *Am:* 'prɑːdɪ-] *adj form* prodigue

prodigious *adj form* **1.**(*enormous, immense*) énorme **2.**(*amazing, astonishing*) prodigieux(-euse)

prodigy ['prɒdɪdʒi, *Am:* 'prɑːdə-] *n* prodige *mf*

produce[1] [prə'djuːs, *Am:* -'duːs] *vt* **1.**(*create*) produire; (*effect*) provoquer; (*illusion*) créer; (*meal*) confectionner; (*odour*) dégager; (*report*) rédiger **2.**(*manufacture*) fabriquer **3.**(*give birth to*) donner naissance à **4.**(*bring before the public: film, programme*) produire; (*opera, play*) mettre en scène; (*book*) préparer; **a beautifully ~d biography** une biographie merveilleusement présentée **5.**(*direct a recording*) procéder à l'enregistrement de **6.**(*bring into view, show*) montrer; (*gun, knife, weapon*) sortir; (*ticket, identification*) présenter; (*alibi*) fournir **7.**(*cause, bring about*) entraîner; (*hysteria, uncertainty*) provoquer; (*results*) produire **8.**(*result in, yield*) rapporter **9.** ELEC (*a spark*) faire jaillir

produce[2] ['prɒdjuːs, *Am:* 'prɑːduːs] *n no pl* **1.**(*agricultural products*) produits *mpl;* **dairy/agricultural ~** produits laitiers/agricoles; **~ section** *Am* rayon *m* de produits frais **2.** *fig* produit *m*

producer *n* producteur, -trice *m, f;* (*of a play*) metteur *m* en scène

product ['prɒdʌkt, *Am:* 'prɑːdʌkt] *n a. fig* produit *m*

production *n no pl* **1.**(*manufacturing process*) fabrication *f;* **to go into ~** entrer en production **2.**(*manufacturing yield, quantity produced*) production *f;* **a drop in ~** une baisse de la production **3.** CINE, TV, RADIO (*act of producing*) production *f* **4.** THEAT (*version*) mise *f* en scène; (*show*) production *f* **5.** MUS production *f* **6.** *form* (*presentation*) présentation *f*

production capacity *n* capacité *f* productrice (d'une société) **production costs** *npl* coûts *mpl* de la production **production director** *n* directeur, -trice *m, f* de production **production line** *n* chaîne *f* de fabrication **production manager** *n* directeur, -trice *m, f* de la production **production platform** *n* plate-forme *f* de production **production time** *n* temps *m* de fabrication **production volume** *n* volume *m* de production

productive *adj* **1.**(*producing*) productif(-ive); (*land, soil*) fertile **2.**(*accomplishing much*) fécond(e); (*conversation, meeting*) fructueux(-euse)

productivity *n no pl* **1.**(*productiveness*) productivité *f* **2.**(*effectiveness of production*) rentabilité *f*

productivity bonus *n* prime *f* à la productivité

Prof. [prɒf, *Am:* prɑːf] *n abbr of* Professor Prof. *m*

prof [prɒf, *Am:* prɑːf] *n inf abbr of* **professor** prof *mf*

profanation *n* REL profanation *f*

profane [prə'feɪn, *Am:* proʊ'-] *adj* **1.**(*blasphemous*) blasphématoire; (*language*) grossier(-ère) **2.** *form* (*secular*) profane

profanity [prə'fænəti, *Am:* proʊ'fænət̬i] *n form* **1.**(*blasphemy*) blasphème *m* **2.**(*foul language, swearing, obscene word*) juron *m;* **this film contains ~** ce film contient des propos obscènes

profess [prə'fes] *vt* professer; **to ~ to** +*infin* prétendre +*infin;* **to ~ oneself satisfied with sth** se déclarer satisfait de qc

professed *adj* **1.**(*self-acknowledged, openly declared*) avéré(e); (*Christian, Marxist*) confirmé(e); (*enemy*) déclaré(e) **2.**(*alleged*) présumé(e)

professedly *adv* soi-disant

profession [prə'feʃən] *n* profession *f;* **teaching ~** profession d'enseignant(e); **to enter a ~** entrer dans une profession

professional I. *adj* professionnel(le); **to go ~** passer professionnel; **he looks ~!** il a l'air d'être du métier! **II.** *n* professionnel(le) *m(f)*

professionalism *n no pl* professionnalisme *m*

professor [prə'fesəʳ, *Am:* -ɚ] *n* professeur *mf*

professorial *adj* professoral(e)

professorship *n* UNIV chaire *f*

proffer ['prɒfəʳ, *Am:* 'prɑːfɚ] *vt form* offrir; (*observation*) faire; (*opinion*) donner

proficiency [prə'fɪʃnsi] *n no pl* compétence *f;* **~ in sth** compétence en qc; **to show ~** être compétent

proficient *adj* compétent(e); **to be ~ at/in sth** être compétent dans

profile ['prəʊfaɪl, *Am:* 'proʊ-] **I.** *n* **1.**(*outline*) profil *m;* **in ~** de profil **2.**(*portrayal*) portrait *m* **3.**(*public image*) **to raise sb's/sth's ~** mieux faire connaître qn/qc; **in a high-~ position** dans une position en vue ▸**to keep a low ~** garder un profil bas **II.** *vt* **1.**(*describe*) faire le portrait de **2.**(*draw a profile of*) dessiner le profil de

profit ['prɒfɪt, *Am:* 'prɑːfɪt] **I.** *n* profit *m;* FIN bénéfice *m;* **to sell sth at a ~** vendre qc à profit; **to make a ~** faire un bénéfice **II.** *vi* **to ~ from/by sth** tirer profit de qc **III.** *vt* profiter à

profitability *n no pl* rentabilité *f*

profitable ['prɒfɪtəbl, *Am:* 'prɑːfɪt̬ə-] *adj* **1.**(*producing a profit: business*) rentable; (*investment*) lucratif(-ive) **2.**(*advantageous, beneficial*) avantageux(-euse); **to make ~ use of one's time** bien profiter de son temps

profiteer [ˌprɒfɪ'tɪəʳ, *Am:* ˌprɑːfɪ'tɪr] *n pej* profiteur, -euse *m, f*

profiteering *n no pl, pej* affairisme *m*

profit-making *adj* rentable; (*association*) à but lucratif **profit margin** *n* marge *f* bénéficiaire **profit-sharing** *n* participation *f* aux bénéfices **profit-taking** *n* FIN prise *f* de bénéfices

profligate ['prɒflɪgət, *Am:* 'prɑːflɪgɪt] *adj form* **1.** (*wasteful*) prodigue **2.** (*dissolute*) débauché(e)

profound [prə'faʊnd] *adj* profond(e); (*knowledge*) approfondi(e)

profundity [prə'fʌndəti, *Am:* proʊ'-] *n* profondeur *f*

profuse [prə'fjuːs] *adj* **1.** (*abundant: bleeding, perspiration*) abondant(e) **2.** *fig* (*apologies*) profus(e); **to be ~ in sth** se confondre en qc

profusion *n no pl, form* profusion *f;* **in ~** à profusion

prog *n abbr of* **program** émission *f*

progenitor [prəʊ'dʒenɪtəʳ, *Am:* proʊ'dʒenət̬ɚ] *n form* ancêtre *mf*

progeny ['prəʊdʒəni, *Am:* 'prɑːdʒə-] *n pl, form* progéniture *f*

prognosis [prɒg'nəʊsɪs, *Am:* prɑːg'noʊ-, -] *n form* **1.** MED pronostic *m* **2.** ECON prévision *f*

prognosticate [prɒg'nɒstɪkeɪt, *Am:* prɑːg'nɑːstɪ-] *vt form* pronostiquer; **to ~ that ...** présager que ...

program ['prəʊgræm, *Am:* 'proʊ-] **I.** *n* (*computer instructions*) programme *m;* **to write a ~** faire un programme **II.** <-mm-> *vt* (*make program for*) programmer

programmable *adj* programmable

programme ['prəʊgræm, *Am:* 'proʊ-] *Am, Aus* **I.** *n* **1.** (*broadcast*) émission *f* **2.** (*presentation, guide, list of events*) programme *m;* **fitness ~** programme de mise en forme physique **3.** (*plan*) programme *m;* **modernisation ~** plan *m* de modernisation **II.** <-mm-> *vt* programmer

programmer *n* **1.** INFOR, RADIO, TECH (*person*) programmeur, -euse *m, f* **2.** (*device*) programmateur *m*

programming *n a.* INFOR programmation *f*

programming language *n* langage *m* de programmation

progress ['prəʊgres, *Am:* 'prɑː-] **I.** *n no pl* progrès *mpl;* **to make ~** faire des progrès; **the patient is making ~** l'état du patient s'améliore; **to be in ~** être en cours; **to stop sb's ~** stopper la progression de qn; **to make slow ~** avancer lentement; **the slow ~ of the enquiry** la lenteur de l'enquête; **to make ~ towards sth** avancer vers qc; **to give sb a ~ report** présenter un bilan à qn **II.** *vi* progresser; **to ~ to sth** passer à qc; **to ~ towards sth** s'acheminer vers qc

progression [prə'greʃən] *n no pl a.* MAT progression *f;* **~ of a disease** progression d'une maladie

progressive [prə'gresɪv] **I.** *adj* **1.** *a.* LING progressif(-ive) **2.** (*favouring social progress*) progressiste **II.** *n* **1.** (*advocate of social reform*) progressiste *mf* **2.** LING **the ~** la forme progressive

progressively *adv* progressivement

prohibit [prə'hɪbɪt, *Am:* proʊ'-] *vt* (*forbid*) interdire; **to ~ sb from doing sth** interdire à qn de faire qc; **to be ~ed by law** être prohibé

prohibition [ˌprəʊɪ'bɪʃən, *Am:* ˌproʊ-] *n* **1.** (*ban*) interdiction *f;* **a ~ on meat imports** une interdiction des importations de viande **2.** LAW, HIST prohibition *f*

prohibitive *adj* prohibitif(-ive)

project[1] ['prɒdʒekt, *Am:* 'prɑː-] *n* projet *m;* **the airport ~** le projet d'aéroport

project[2] [prəʊ'dʒekt, *Am:* prə-] **I.** *vt* **1.** (*forecast: cost, timescale*) prévoir; **to be ~ed to** *+infin* être projeté de *+infin;* **the ~ed increase** l'augmentation prévue **2.** (*send out*) projeter; **to ~ one's voice** faire entendre sa voix; **to ~ one's mind into the future** projeter ses pensées dans l'avenir; **to ~ oneself** se mettre en avant **3.** CINE (*show on screen*) **to ~ sth onto sth** projeter qc sur qc **4.** PSYCH **to ~ sth onto sb/sth** projeter qc sur qn/qc; **to ~ oneself onto sb** se projeter sur qn **II.** *vi* (*protrude*) avancer; **~ing teeth** dents en avant

projectile [prəʊ'dʒektaɪl, *Am:* prə'dʒektəl] *n* (*object thrown as weapon*) projectile *m*

projection [prəʊ'dʒekʃən, *Am:* prə-] *n* **1.** (*forecast*) estimation *f* **2.** (*protrusion*) avancée *f* **3.** *no pl* CINE, PSYCH projection *f*

projectionist *n* projectionniste *mf*

projector [prə'dʒektəʳ, *Am:* -'dʒektɚ] *n* projecteur *m*

prolapse ['prəʊlæps, *Am:* 'proʊ-] *n* MED prolapsus *m*

prole [prəʊl, *Am:* proʊl] *pej* **I.** *n abbr of* **proletarian** prolo *mf* **II.** *adj* prolo

proletarian **I.** *n* prolétaire *mf* **II.** *adj* prolétarien(ne)

proletariat [ˌprəʊlɪ'teərɪət, *Am:* ˌproʊlə'terɪ-] *n no pl* prolétariat *m*

proliferate [prə'lɪfəreɪt, *Am:* proʊ'-] *vi* proliférer

proliferation *n no pl* prolifération *f*

prolific [prə'lɪfɪk, *Am:* proʊ'-] *adj* prolifique

prolix ['prəʊlɪks, *Am:* proʊ'lɪks] *adj pej, form* prolixe

prolog *n a. Am,* **prologue** ['prəʊlɒg, *Am:* 'proʊlɑːg] *n Brit, a. fig* prologue *m;* **to be a ~ to sth** être le prologue de qc; *fig* être le prologue à qc

prolong [prə'lɒŋ, *Am:* proʊ'lɑːŋ] *vt* prolonger

prolongation [ˌprəʊlɒŋ'geɪʃən, *Am:* ˌproʊlɑːŋ'-] *n no pl* prolongation *f*

prom [prɒm, *Am:* prɑːm] *n* **1.** *Am* (*formal school dance*) bal *m* des écoliers **2.** *Brit* (*concert*) concert *m* **3.** *Brit* (*seaside walkway*) promenade *f*

PROM *n* INFOR *abbr of* **programmable read-only memory** mémoire *f* morte programmable

promenade [ˌprɒmə'nɑːd, *Am:* ˌprɑːmə'neɪd] **I.** *n Brit, a. form* promenade *f* **II.** *vi* se promener

prominence ['prɒmɪnəns, *Am:* 'prɑːmə-] *n no pl* **1.** (*conspicuousness*) proéminence *f;* **to give ~ to sth** donner la priorité à qc **2.** (*importance*) importance *f;* **to gain ~** gagner en importance *f;* **to occupy a position of ~** occuper un poste important

prominent *adj* **1.** (*conspicuous: chin,*) saillant(e); (*teeth*) en avant; **to put sth in a ~ position** mettre qc au premier plan **2.** (*well-known: musician*) éminent(e); **a ~ figure in the movement** un personnage important dans le mouvement; **to be ~ in sth** être éminent dans qc

promiscuity [ˌprɒmɪ'skjuːəti, *Am:* ˌprɑːmɪ'skjuːət̬i] *n no pl* promiscuité *f* sexuelle

promiscuous [prə'mɪskjuəs] *adj pej* aux nombreux partenaires sexuels

promise ['prɒmɪs, *Am:* 'prɑːmɪs] **I.** *vt* promettre; **to ~ sb sth** promettre qc à qn; **to ~ sb to** +*infin* promettre à qn de +*infin;* **to ~ oneself sth** se promettre qc à soi-même; **we're ~d snow** on nous promet de la neige; **it's true, I ~ you** c'est vrai, je t'assure **II.** *vi* promettre **III.** *n* **1.** (*pledge*) promesse *f;* **to break/keep one's ~ to sb** manquer à/tenir sa promesse à qn; **~s, ~s!** ce ne sont que des promesses de Gascon! **2.** *no pl* (*potential*) espoir *m;* **a young person of ~** un jeune espoir; **to show ~** être très prometteur; **to fulfil one's (early) ~** répondre à tous les espoirs

Promised Land *n* **the ~** la Terre Promise

promising *adj* (*career, work*) prometteur(-euse); **musician** qui promet; **to get off to a ~ start** bien démarrer

promissory note ['prɒmɪsəriˌnəʊt, *Am:* 'prɑːmɪsɔːriˌnoʊt] *n* billet *m* à ordre

promontory ['prɒməntəri, *Am:* 'prɑːməntɔːr-] <-ries> *n* GEO *s.* **headland** promontoire *m*

promote [prə'məʊt, *Am:* -'moʊt] *vt* promouvoir; **to ~ sb to sth** promouvoir qn au rang de qc; **to ~ a new book** faire la promotion d'un nouveau livre

promoter *n* promoteur, -trice *m, f*

promotion *n a.* COM promotion *f;* **sb's ~ to sth** la promotion de qn au rang de qc

promotional material *n* matériel *m* publicitaire

prompt [prɒmpt, *Am:* prɑːmpt] **I.** *vt* **1.** (*spur*) encourager; **what ~ed you to write?** qu'est-ce qui vous a poussé à écrire **2.** THEAT (*remind of lines*) souffler le texte à **II.** *adj* (*quick*) prompt(e); (*action, delivery*) rapide; **to be ~ in doing sth** être prompt à faire qc **III.** *adv* promptement **IV.** *n* **1.** INFOR message *m* **2.** THEAT (*person*) souffleur, -euse *m, f;* (*words*) to give sb a ~, souffler son texte à qn

prompt box <-es> *n* THEAT trou *m* du souffleur

prompter *n* THEAT souffleur, -euse *m, f*

promptly *adv* **1.** (*quickly*) promptement **2.** *inf* (*immediately afterward*) tout de suite

promptness *n no pl* promptitude *f*

prompt note *n* lettre *f* de rappel

promulgate ['prɒmlgeɪt, *Am:* 'prɑːml-] *vt form a.* LAW promulguer

promulgation *n no pl, form a.* LAW promulgation *f*

prone [prəʊn, *Am:* proʊn] *adj* **1.** (*disposed*) **to be ~ to** (*behaviour*) être enclin à qc; (*illness*) être sujet à qc **2.** (*likely, liable*) **to be ~ to** +*infin* avoir tendance à +*infin* **3.** (*lying flat*) sur le ventre

prong [prɒŋ, *Am:* prɑːŋ] *n* (*of fork*) dent *f*

pronominal [prəʊ'nɒmɪnl, *Am:* proʊ'nɑːmə-] *adj* LING pronominal(e)

pronoun ['prəʊnaʊn, *Am:* 'proʊ-] *n* LING pronom *m*

pronounce [prə'naʊnts] *vt* **1.** LING, LING (*speak*) prononcer **2.** (*declare*) déclarer; **to ~ sb/sth guilty** déclarer qn/qc coupable; **to ~ sb man and wife** déclarer qn mari et femme

◆**pronounce on** *vt* se prononcer sur

pronounceable *adj* prononçable

pronounced *adj* prononcé(e)

pronouncement *n* (*declaration*) déclaration *f*

pronto ['prɒntəʊ, *Am:* 'prɑːnt̬oʊ] *adv inf* et que ça saute

pronunciation [prəˌnʌntsɪ'eɪʃən] *n* prononciation *f*

proof [pruːf] **I.** *n* **1.** *no pl* (*facts establishing truth*) *a.* LAW, MAT preuve *f;* **to have ~ of sth** avoir la preuve de qc; **to be ~ of sth** être la preuve de qc **2.** *no pl* (*test*) épreuve *f;* **to put sb/sth to the ~** mettre qn/qc à l'épreuve **3.** TYP, PHOT (*first printing*) épreuve *f* **II.** *adj* **1.** (*impervious*) imperméable; **to be ~ against burglars** être à l'épreuve des cambriolages; **bomb-~** à l'épreuve des bombes; **child-~** qui résiste aux enfants **2.** (*degree of strength*) *indique la proportion d'alcool pur dans les spiritueux* **III.** *vt* imprégner

proofread <proofread> TYP, PUBL **I.** *vt* corriger **II.** *vi* faire des corrections **proofreader** *n* correcteur, -trice *m, f* **proofreading** *n no pl* TYP, PUBL correction *f*

prop¹ [prɒp, *Am:* prɑːp] *n* **1.** (*support*) support *m* **2.** *pl* THEAT, CINE accessoire *m*

prop up *vt* soutenir

prop² [prɒp, *Am:* prɑːp] *n* **1.** ECON *abbr of* **proprietor 2.** *abbr of* **propeller**

propaganda [ˌprɒpə'gændə, *Am:* ˌprɑːpə'-] *n no pl, no indef art, pej* propagande *f;* **a ~ war/film** une guerre/un film de propagande

propagandist *n pej* propagandiste *mf*

propagate ['prɒpəgeɪt, *Am:* 'prɑːpə-] **I.** *vt form a.* BOT propager; **to ~ oneself** se propager **II.** *vi* se propager

propagation *n no pl* propagation *f*

propane ['prəʊpeɪn, *Am:* 'proʊ-] *n no pl, no indef art* CHEM propane *m*

propel [prə'pel] <-ll-> *vt* faire avancer; **to be**

~**led by wind** être entraîné par le vent
propellant [prəˈpelənt] *n* **1.** (*fuel*) carburant *m* **2.** (*gas*) gaz *m* propulseur
propeller *n* hélice *f*
propeller shaft *n* TECH arbre *m* de transmission
propelling pencil *n Brit, Aus* portemine *m*
propensity [prəˈpensəti, *Am:* -t̬i] *n no pl, form* propension *f;* **to have a ~ to do/for sth** avoir une propension à faire/à qc
proper [ˈprɒpəʳ, *Am:* ˈprɑːpɚ] **I.** *adj* **1.** (*real: meal, tool, teacher*) vrai(e); **they haven't got ~ classrooms** ils n'ont pas de véritables salles de classe **2.** (*suitable, correct: method, training, place*) convenable; **to make ~ safety checks** effectuer des contrôles de sécurité convenables; **the ~ time for sth** le moment qui convient pour qc **3.** (*socially respectable*) respectable; **to be ~ to** *+infin* être bien pour *+infin;* **it's right and ~ for him to do that** c'est tout à fait normal qu'il le fasse **4.** *form* (*itself*) **in Paris ~** dans Paris intra-muros; **the teaching ~** l'enseignement à proprement parler **II.** *adv Brit, inf* **1.** (*very*) proprement **2.** *iron* (*genteelly*) correctement
proper fraction *n* MAT fraction *f*
properly *adv* **1.** (*correctly*) correctement; **pronounce the word ~** prononce le mot comme il faut; **~ speaking** à proprement parler **2.** *Brit, inf* (*thoroughly*) parfaitement
proper name, **proper noun** *n* nom *m* propre
property [ˈprɒpəti, *Am:* ˈprɑːpɚt̬i] *n* **1.** *no pl* (*possession*) bien *m;* **personal ~** bien personnel; **is this your ~?** est-ce que cela vous appartient? **2.** *no pl* LAW (*right to possession*) propriété *f* **3.** *no pl* (*buildings and land*) biens *mpl* immobiliers **4.** (*house*) propriété *f* **5.** <-ties> (*attribute*) propriété *f* **6.** <-ties> THEAT (*prop*) accessoire *m*
property developer *n* ECON promoteur, -trice *m, f* immobilier **property market** *n no pl* marché *m* immobilier **property owner** *n* propriétaire *mf* foncier **property room** *n* THEAT salle *f* des accessoires **property speculation** *n no pl* ECON spéculation *f* immobilière **property tax** *n* impôt *m* foncier
prophecy [ˈprɒfəsi, *Am:* ˈprɑːfə-] <-ies> *n* prophétie *f*
prophesy [ˈprɒfɪsaɪ, *Am:* ˈprɑːfə-] <-ie-> **I.** *vt* prophétiser **II.** *vi* faire des prédictions
prophet [ˈprɒfɪt, *Am:* ˈprɑːfɪt] *n a.* REL prophète *m*
prophetess [ˈprɒfɪtes, *Am:* ˈprɑːfɪt̬əs] *n* prophétesse *f*
prophetic [prəˈfetɪk] *adj* prophétique
prophylactic [ˌprɒfɪˈlæktɪk, *Am:* ˌproʊfəˈ-] **I.** *adj* MED prophylactique **II.** *n* **1.** MED (*preventative medicine*) traitement *m* préventif **2.** *Am* (*condom*) préservatif *m*
prophylaxis [prɒfɪˈlæksɪs, *Am:* ˌproʊfəˈ-] *n no pl* MED prophylaxie *f*
propitious [prəˈpɪʃəs] *adj form* propice
proponent [prəˈpəʊnənt, *Am:* -ˈpoʊ-] *n* partisan(e) *m(f)*
proportion [prəˈpɔːʃən, *Am:* -ˈpɔːr-] *n* **1.** (*comparative part*) proportion *f;* **the ~ of sth to sth** la proportion de qc par rapport à qc **2.** (*quantifiable relationship*) **to increase in ~ to sth** augmenter en proportion de qc; **in ~ to sb's income** proportionnellement au revenu de qn; **to be sth in ~ to sth** être qc proportionnellement à qc **3. relative importance, to have/keep a sense of ~** avoir/garder le sens de la mesure; **to keep sth in ~** relativiser qc; **to get things out of ~** perdre le sens de la mesure; **retaliation in ~ to the attack** riposte proportionnelle à l'attaque; **to be in/out of ~ to sth** être proportionné/disproportionné par rapport à qc **4. ~s** *pl* (*size, dimensions*) proportions *fpl;* **a building of gigantic ~s** un bâtiment aux proportions énormes
proportional *adj* proportionnel(le); **to be ~ to sth** être proportionnel à qc
proportionality *n no pl* proportionnalité *f*
proportional representation *n no pl* représentation *f* proportionnelle
proportionate [prəˈpɔːʃənət, *Am:* -ˈpɔːrʃənɪt] *adj s.* **proportional**
proportioned *adj* proportionné(e); **well ~** bien proportionné; **to be generously ~** avoir des formes généreuses
proposal *n* proposition *f;* **a ~ to** *+infin* une proposition pour *+infin;* **a marriage ~** une demande en mariage
propose [prəˈpəʊz, *Am:* -ˈpoʊz] **I.** *vt* **1.** (*suggest*) proposer; **to ~ doing sth** proposer de faire qc; **to ~ a toast** porter un toast **2.** (*intend*) projeter; **to ~ to do/doing sth** projeter de faire qc **II.** *vi* (*offer oneself in marriage*) **to ~ to sb** faire une demande en mariage à qn ►**man ~s, God disposes** *prov* l'homme propose, Dieu dispose *prov*
proposer *n* initiateur, -trice *m, f* d'une proposition
proposition [ˌprɒpəˈzɪʃən, *Am:* ˌprɑːpəˈ-] **I.** *n* proposition *f;* **the business is a worthwhile ~** c'est une affaire rentable **II.** *vt* faire une proposition à
propound [prəˈpaʊnd] *vt form* exposer
proprietary [prəˈpraɪətri, *Am:* -teri] *adj* **1.** (*related to owner, ownership*) de propriété; (*air, behavior*) de propriétaire **2.** (*with registered trade name: product, article*) de marque déposée
proprietary name *n* marque *f* déposée
proprietor *n* propriétaire *m*
proprietorship *n* propriété *f*
proprietress *n* propriétaire *f*
propriety [prəˈpraɪəti, *Am:* -t̬i] <-ties> *n* bienséance *f;* **to observe the proprieties** observer les règles de bienséance
propulsion [prəˈpʌlʃən] *n no pl* propulsion *f*
pro rata [ˌprəʊˈrɑːtə, *Am:* ˌproʊˈreɪt̬ə] **I.** *adj form* proportionnel(le) **II.** *adv form* au prorata

prorate *vt,* **pro-rate** *vt Am* **to ~ sth** partager qc au prorata

prosaic [prə'zeɪɪk, *Am:* proʊ'-] *adj form* prosaïque

proscenium [prə'siːnɪəm, *Am:* proʊ'-] <-s *o* proscenia> *n* THEAT avant-scène *f*

proscribe [prə'skraɪb, *Am:* proʊ'-] *vt form* proscrire

proscription [prə'skrɪpʃən, *Am:* proʊ'-] *n no pl, form* proscription *f*

prose [prəʊz, *Am:* proʊz] *n no pl, no indef art* LIT prose *f;* ~ **poem** poème *m* en prose

prosecute ['prɒsɪkjuːt, *Am:* 'prɑːsɪ-] **I.** *vt a.* LAW poursuivre; **to ~ sb for sth** poursuivre qn pour un délit de qc; **to ~ studies** poursuivre des études **II.** *vi* engager des poursuites judiciaires

prosecuting *adj* de l'accusation; **the ~ attorney** l'accusation *f*

prosecution *n* **1.** *no pl* LAW (*court proceedings*) poursuites *fpl;* **to face ~** s'exposer à des poursuites; **to be liable to ~** être passible de poursuites **2.** *no pl* LAW (*the prosecuting party*) **the ~** l'accusation *f;* **witness for the ~** témoin *m* à charge

prosecutor *n* LAW accusateur, -trice *m, f*

prosody ['prɒsədi, *Am:* 'prɑːsə-] *n no pl, no indef art* prosodie *f*

prospect ['prɒspekt, *Am:* 'prɑːspekt] **I.** *n* **1.** (*likely future*) perspective *f;* **the ~ is for more rain/higher inflation** on nous prédit encore de la pluie/une plus forte inflation; **I find that a worrying ~** je trouve cette éventualité préoccupante; **there are more changes in ~** il y a des changements en perspective **2.** (*chance of sth*) chance *f;* **there is no ~ of that happening** il n'y a aucun risque que ça arrive *subj;* **employment ~s** chances d'emploi **3.** (*potential customer*) client(e) *m(f)* potentiel(le) **4.** (*potential associate*) **the new ~s** (*for team, membership*) membre *m* éventuel, possible candidat(e) *m(f)* **5.** (*view*) vue *f* **II.** *vi* MIN prospecter; **to ~ for gold** prospecter de l'or

prospective *adj* (*member, player*) futur(e); (*employer*) éventuel(le)

prospector *n* MIN prospecteur *m;* **gold ~** chercheur *m* d'or

prospectus [prə'spektəs] *n* prospectus *m*

prosper ['prɒspəʳ, *Am:* 'prɑːspɚ] *vi* prospérer

prosperity [prɒ'sperəti, *Am:* prɑː'sperət̬i] *n no pl* prospérité *f*

prosperous *adj* (*business, economy*) prospère

prostate ['prɒsteɪt, *Am:* 'prɑː-] *n* ANAT prostate *f*

prostitute ['prɒstɪtjuːt, *Am:* 'prɑːstətuːt] **I.** *n* prostitué(e) *m(f)* **II.** *vt* prostituer; **to ~ oneself** se prostituer; **to ~ one's talents** vendre ses talents

prostitution *n no pl* prostitution *f*

prostrate ['prɒstreɪt, *Am:* 'prɑːstreɪt] **I.** *adj* **1.** (*lying face downward*) prosterné(e) **2.** (*overcome*) prostré(e); **to be ~ with grief** être prostré de douleurs **II.** *vt* **to ~ oneself** se prosterner

prostration *n* prostration *f*

protagonist [prə'tægənɪst, *Am:* proʊ'-] *n* protagoniste *mf*

protect [prə'tekt] *vt* protéger; (*interests*) préserver; **to ~ oneself against sth** se protéger de qc

protection *n no pl* protection *f*

protection factor *n* facteur *m* de protection

protectionism *n no pl, pej* protectionnisme *m*

protectionist *adj pej* protectionniste

protective *adj* **1.** (*affording protection*) de protection; ~ **custody** détention *f* préventive **2.** (*wishing to protect*) protecteur(-trice); **to be ~ of sb/sth** être soucieux de qn

protector *n* **1.** (*sb who protects sth*) *a.* HIST protecteur, -trice *m, f* **2.** (*device*) protection *f*

protectorate [prə'tektərət, *Am:* -ɪt] *n* protectorat *m*

protein ['prəʊtiːn, *Am:* 'proʊ-] *n* protéine *f*

protest ['prəʊtest, *Am:* 'proʊtest] **I.** *n* protestation *f;* **to make/register a ~** émettre/enregistrer une protestation; **to do sth under ~** faire qc en protestant; **to do sth in ~ at sth** faire qc pour protester contre qc **II.** *vi* protester; **to ~ about sb/sth** émettre une objection sur qn/qc; (*demonstrators*) manifester contre qn/qc **III.** *vt* **1.** (*solemnly affirm*) assurer; **to ~ one's innocence** protester de son innocence **2.** *Am* (*show dissent*) protester contre

Protestant ['prɒtɪstənt, *Am:* 'prɑːt̬ə-] *n* REL protestant(e) *m(f);* **the ~ church** l'église protestante

Protestantism *n no pl, no indef art* protestantisme *m*

protestation [ˌprɒtes'teɪʃən, *Am:* ˌprɑːt̬es'teɪ-] *n pl* **1.** (*strong objection*) protestations *fpl* **2.** (*strong affirmation*) assurance *f*

protester *n* protestataire *mf*

protest march *n* marche *f* de protestation

protest vote *n* vote *m* protestataire

protocol ['prəʊtəkɒl, *Am:* 'proʊt̬əkɔːl] *n* **1.** *no pl* (*system of rules*) protocole *m* **2.** POL (*formal international agreement*) protocole *m* d'accord; **Geneva ~s** les accords *mpl* de Genève

proton ['prəʊtɒn, *Am:* 'proʊtɑːn] *n* proton *m*

prototype ['prəʊtətaɪp, *Am:* 'proʊt̬ə-] *n* prototype *m*

protract [prə'trækt, *Am:* proʊ'-] *vt form* prolonger

protracted *adj* prolongé(e)

protraction *n* **1.** *no pl* (*prolonging*) prolongation *f* **2.** ANAT (*muscle action*) extension *f*

protractor *n* **1.** (*angle measuring device*) rapporteur *m* **2.** ANAT (*muscle*) extenseur *m*

protrude [prə'tru:d, *Am:* proʊ'-] *vi* saillir; **to ~ from sth** saillir de qc

protruding *adj* protrubérant(e)

protrusion [prə'tru:ʒən, *Am:* proʊ'-] *n* protubérance *f*

protuberance [prə'tju:bərəns, *Am:* proʊ'tu:-] *n form* protubérance *f*

proud [praʊd] **I.** *adj* **1.** (*pleased and satisfied*) fier(fière); **to be ~ to** +*infin* être fier de +*infin;* **as ~ as a peacock** fier comme un coq **2.** (*forward*) **to stand ~ of sth** dépasser légèrement qc **II.** *adv* **to do sb ~** faire honneur à qn

provable ['pru:vəbl] *adj* prouvable

prove [pru:v] <proved *o Am* proven> **I.** *vt* prouver; **to ~ a point** démontrer qu'on a raison; **to ~ oneself (to be) sth** montrer qu'on est qc **II.** *vi* s'avérer; **to ~ (to be) impossible** s'avérer impossible

proven ['pru:vən] **I.** *Am pp of* **prove II.** *adj* (*remedy*) efficace; **a ~ impossibility** une imposibilité prouvée

provenance ['prɒvənənts, *Am:* 'pra:vən-] *n no pl, form* provenance *f*

proverb ['prɒvɜ:b, *Am:* 'pra:vɜ:rb] *n* proverbe *m*

proverbial *adj* proverbial(e)

provide [prəʊ'vaɪd, *Am:* prə-] *vt* **1.** (*supply, make available: food, clothing, money, answers, instructions*) fournir; (*security, access*) offrir; (*education*) assurer; **to ~ sth for sb/sth, to ~ sb/sth with sth** apporter qc à qn/qc; **to ~ oneself with sth** (*equip*) se procurer qc **2.** *form* LAW prévoir

◆provide for *vt* (*emergency, possibility*) prévoir; (*one's family*) subvenir aux besoins de

provided (that) *conj* pourvu que +*subj;* **he'll get it ~ he pays for it** il l'aura à condition de le payer

providence ['prɒvɪdənts, *Am:* 'pra:və-] *n no pl* providence *f*

providential *adj form* providentiel(le)

provider *n a.* INFOR fournisseur *m*

providing *conj* pourvu que +*subj*

province ['prɒvɪnts, *Am:* 'pra:vɪnts] *n* **1.** (*area*) province *f;* **the ~s** la province **2.** *no pl* (*branch of a subject*) matière *f*

provincial I. *adj a. pej* provincial(e); (*city*) de province **II.** *n a. pej* provincial(e) *m(f)*

proving flight *n* MIL, AVIAT *s.* **test flight proving ground** *n* terrain *m* d'essai

provision [prəʊ'vɪʒən, *Am:* prə-] *n* **1.** (*act of providing*) **to be responsible for the ~ of food/bedding** assurer l'approvisionnement de nourriture/l'équipement en literie *m;* **the ~ of education** les services de l'éducation **2.** *pl* (*food*) provisions *fpl* **3.** (*preparation, prior arrangement*) disposition *fpl;* **to make ~ for sb/sth** prendre des dispositions pour qn/qc **4.** (*stipulation in a document*) disposition *f*

provisional *adj* provisoire

proviso [prə'vaɪzəʊ, *Am:* prə'vaɪzoʊ] <-s> *n* clause *f;* **with/on the ~ that** sous condition que +*subj*

provocation [ˌprɒvə'keɪʃən, *Am:* ˌpra:və'-] *n* provocation *f*

provocative [prə'vɒkətɪv, *Am:* -'va:kəţɪv] *adj* provocant(e); **you're being ~** tu fais de la provocation

provoke [prə'vəʊk, *Am:* -'voʊk] *vt* provoquer; **to ~ sb/sth into doing sth** pousser par la provocation qn/qc à faire qc

provoking *adj* provocant(e)

provost ['prɒvəst, *Am:* 'proʊvoʊst] *n* **1.** *Brit, Am* UNIV recteur, -trice *m, f* **2.** *Scot* (*mayor*) maire *m*

prow [praʊ] *n* NAUT proue *f*

prowess ['praʊɪs] *n no pl, form* prouesse *f*

prowl [praʊl] **I.** *n* tournée *f* à la recherche d'une proie; **to be on the ~** rôder **II.** *vt* rôder dans **III.** *vi* rôder

prowl car *n Am s.* **patrol car**

prowler *n* rôdeur, -euse *m, f*

proximity [prɒk'sɪməti, *Am:* pra:k'sɪməţi] *n no pl, form* proximité *f;* **to be in (close) ~ to sb/sth** être très proche de qn/qc

proxy ['prɒksi, *Am:* 'pra:k-] <-ies> *n* **1.** (*authority*) procuration *f* **2.** (*person*) mandataire *mf*

prude [pru:d] *n pej* prude

prudence ['prudns] *n no pl* prudence *f*

prudent ['pru:dnt] *adj* prudent(e)

prudery ['pru:dəri] <-ies> *n pej* pruderie *f*

prudish ['pru:dɪʃ] *adj pej* prude

prune[1] [pru:n] *vt* **1.** BOT (*trim: tree, shrub*) **to ~ sth (down)** tailler qc **2.** (*make smaller: article*) raccourcir; (*costs, budget*) tailler dans

prune[2] [pru:n] *n* (*dried plum*) prune *f*

pruning *n* taillage *m*

pruning hook *n* BOT taille-haie *m* **pruning knife** *n* BOT sécateur *m*

prurience ['prʊərɪəns, *Am:* 'prʊrɪ-] *n no pl, pej, form* lubricité *f*

prurient *adj pej, form* lubrique

Prussia ['prʌʃə] *n* HIST, POL, GEO Prusse *f*

Prussian I. *n* HIST Prussien(ne) *m(f)* **II.** *adj* prussien(ne)

prussic acid [ˌprʌsɪk'æsɪd] *n no pl* acide *m* prussique

pry[1] [praɪ] <pries, pried> *vi* être indiscret; **to ~ into sth** fouiner dans qc

pry[2] [praɪ] *vt Am s.* **prise**

prying *adj* (*eyes, neighbours*) curieux(-euse)

PS [ˌpi:'es] *n abbr of* **postscript** PS *m*

psalm [sa:m] *n* REL psaume *m*

psalmody *n* REL psalmodie *f*

pseud [sju:d, *Am:* su:d] *n Brit, pej, inf* frimeur, -euse *m, f*

pseudo ['sju:dəʊ, *Am:* 'su:doʊ] **I.** *adj* (*false*) pseudo *inv;* **~-intellectual** pseudo-intellectuel(le) **II.** *n* (*pretentious or insincere person*) faux-cul *m*

pseudonym ['sju:dənɪm, *Am:* 'su:-] *n* pseudonyme *m*

pseudonymous *adj* pseudonyme

psittacosis [ˌsɪtə'kəʊsɪs, *Am:* -'koʊ-] *n* ZOOL, MED psittacose *f*

P

PSV *n abbr of* **public service vehicle** véhicule *m* de transports en commun
psych *vt inf* **1.** (*subject to psychotherapy*) faire une analyse à **2.** (*prepare mentally*) préparer mentalement; **to ~ oneself up** se préparer mentalement
psyche ['saɪki] *n* psyché *m*
psychedelic [ˌsaɪkɪ'delɪk, *Am:* -kə'-] *adj* psychédélique
psychiatric *adj* psychiatrique
psychiatrist *n* psychiatre *mf*
psychiatry [saɪ'kaɪətri] *n no pl* psychiatrie *f*
psychic ['saɪkɪk] **I.** *n* voyant(e) *m(f)* **II.** *adj* **1.** (*concerning occult powers*) parapsychologique **2.** (*of the mind*) psychique; **to be ~** avoir des dons de voyance
psychical *adj s.* **psychic**
psychoanalyse [ˌsaɪkəʊ'ænəlaɪz, *Am:* -koʊ'-] *vt Aus, Brit* psychoanalyser
psychoanalysis [ˌsaɪkəʊə'næləsɪs, *Am:* -koʊə'-] *n no pl* psychanalyse *f*
psychoanalyze [ˌsaɪkəʊ'ænəlaɪz, *Am:* -koʊ'ænəlaɪz] *vt Am* psychanalyser
psychological *adj* psychologique
psychologist *n* psychologue *mf*
psychology [saɪ'kɒlədʒi, *Am:* -'kɑːlə-] <-ies> *n* psychologie *f*
psychopath ['saɪkəʊpæθ, *Am:* -kəpæθ] *n* psychopathe *mf*
psychopathy *n* psychopathie *f*
psychosis [saɪ'kəʊsɪs, *Am:* -'koʊ-] <-ses> *n* psychose *f*
psychotic [saɪ'kɒtɪk, *Am:* -'kɑːt̬ɪk] **I.** *adj* psychotique **II.** *n* psychotique *mf*
PT [ˌpiː'tiː] *n no pl* SCHOOL *abbr of* **physical training** EPS *f*
pt *n* **1.** *abbr of* **pint** pinte *f* **2.** *abbr of* **point** point *m* **3.** *abbr of* **part** partie *f*
PTA *n abbr of* **parent teacher association** association *f* de parents d'élèves
ptarmigan ['tɑːmɪgən, *Am:* 'tɑːrmɪ-] *n* ZOOL perdrix *f* blanche
PTO [ˌpiːtiː'əʊ, *Am:* -'oʊ] *abbr of* **please turn over** TSVP
pub¹ [pʌb] *n Aus, Brit, inf abbr of* **public-house** pub *m*
pub crawl *n Brit, inf* tournée *f* des bistros
pub² [pʌb] **I.** *n abbr of* **publication II.** *vt abbr of* **publish**
puberty ['pjuːbəti, *Am:* -bɚt̬i] *n no pl* puberté *f*
pubic ['pjuːbɪk] *adj* pubien(ne)
public ['pʌblɪk] **I.** *adj* public(-que); **~ opinion** opinion *f* publique; **in the ~ interest** dans l'intérêt général; **at ~ expense** aux frais du contribuable; **to go ~ with sth** rendre qc public **II.** *n no pl, + sing/pl vb* public *m;* **sb's ~** le public de qn; **in ~** en public
public accountant *n Am* ADMIN, ECON expert-comptable *m,* experte-comptable *f* **public address**, **public address system** *n* système *m* de haut-parleurs **public affairs** *npl* affaires *fpl* publiques
publican *n Aus, Brit* patron (ne) *m(f)* d'un pub
public appearance *n* apparition *f* en public **public appointment** *n* position *f* de l'État **public assistance** *n Am* ADMIN, POL aide *f* sociale
publication [ˌpʌblɪ'keɪʃən] *n* publication *f*
public authority *n* **1.** (*authority of the state*) autorité *f* de l'État **2.** (*department, authority*) service *m* public **public bar** *n Brit* bar *m* **public company** *n Brit* FIN, ECON société *f* anonyme **public convenience** *n Aus, Brit, form* toilettes *fpl* publiques **public debt** *n s.* **national debt public domain** *n* domaine *m* public **public enemy** *n* ennemi *m* public; **~ number one** ennemi public numéro un **public expenditure**, **public expense** *n* ADMIN, POL, ECON dépenses *fpl* publiques **public funds** *npl* Trésor *m* public **public health** *n no pl* MED, ADMIN santé *f* publique **public health service** *n* service *m* de la santé publique **public holiday** *n* jour *m* férié **public house** *n Brit, form s.* **pub public interest** *n* intérêt *m* public
publicist ['pʌblɪsɪst] *n* publiciste *mf*
publicity [pʌb'lɪsəti, *Am:* -t̬i] **I.** *n no pl* publicité *f;* **to get a lot of ~** attirer beaucoup de publicité; **it's good/bad ~** c'est de la bonne/mauvaise publicité **II.** *adj* publicitaire
publicity agent *n* agent *m* publicitaire **publicity campaign** *n* ECON campagne *f* publicitaire **publicity department** *n* ECON service *m* de la publicité **publicity material** *n* matériel *m* publicitaire **publicity stunt** *n* coup *m* publicitaire
publicize ['pʌblɪsaɪz] *vt* (*event*) annoncer; **don't ~ it** ne le crie pas sur les toits; **her much-~d divorce** son divorce dont les médias ont beaucoup parlé
public law *n* LAW droit *m* public **public limited company** *n s.* **public company public loan** *n* ADMIN, POL emprunt *m* d'État
publicly *adv* publiquement; **a ~ funded project** un projet subventionné par les fonds publics
public-minded *adj* social(e) **public nuisance** *n* LAW danger *m* public **public opinion** *n* opinion *f* publique **public opinion poll** *n s.* **opinion poll public property** *n* propriété *f* de l'État; **her life is ~** *fig* sa vie intéresse tout le monde **public prosecutor** *n* avocat(e) *m(f)* général(e) **public records** *npl* archives *fpl* publiques **public relations** *npl* relations *fpl* publiques **public relations officer** *n* attaché(e) *m(f)* de presse **public school** *n* **1.** *Brit* SCHOOL (*private school*) école *f* privée **2.** *Am, Aus* (*state funded school*) école *f* publique **public sector** *n* secteur *m* public **public servant** *n* ADMIN, POL **1.** (*State employee*) employé(e) *m(f)* de l'État **2.** *Aus, NZ* AMIN, POL (*administrative employee of State*) employé(e) *m(f)* du service public; *s. a.* **civil servant public ser-**

vice *n* 1. ADMIN, POL (*service for community*) service *m* public 2. (*State administrative service*) fonction *f* publique; **in ~** au service de l'État; *s. a.* **civil service** **public-spirited** *s.* **public-minded** **public telephone** *n* téléphone *m* public **public transport** *n,* **public transportation** *n Am* transports *mpl* public **public utility** *n* FIN, ECON *entreprise publique de production et de distribution en eau, gaz et électricité* **public works** *npl* ADMIN, POL travaux *mpl* publics

publish ['pʌblɪʃ] *vt* publier; **to have sth ~ed** faire publier qc

publisher *n* 1. (*publishing company*) maison *f* d'édition 2. (*position in publishing*) éditeur, -trice *m, f*

publishing *n no pl, no art* l'édition *f*

puck [pʌk] *n* SPORT palet *m*

pucker I. *vt* **to ~ sth** (**up**) froncer de qc II. *vi* **to ~** (**up**) (*face, lips*) se plisser

pudding ['pʊdɪŋ] *n* 1. (*steamed dish*) pudding *m* 2. *Brit* (*sweet course*) dessert *m*

pudding-head *n inf* imbécile *mf*

puddle ['pʌdl] *n* flaque *f* d'eau

pudgy ['pʊdʒi] <pudgier, pudgiest> *adj Am* trapu(e)

puerile ['pjʊəraɪl, *Am:* 'pju:ərɪl] *adj form* puéril(e)

Puerto Rican I. *adj* portoricain(e) II. *n* Portoricain(e) *m(f)*

Puerto Rico ['pwɜ:təʊ'ri:kəʊ, *Am:* ˌpwerṭə'ri:koʊ] *n* Porto Rico

puff [pʌf] I. *vi* 1. (*blow*) souffler; (*steam engine*) lancer des bouffées de vapeur; **to ~ at/on a cigarette** tirer sur une cigarette 2. (*be out of breath*) haleter; **I came ~ up the hill** j'ai monté la colline en haletant 3. (*smoke*) **to ~ at** [*o* **on**] **a cigar** tirer sur un cigare II. *vt* 1. (*smoke: a cigar, cigarette*) tirer sur 2. (*blow*) souffler 3. *pej* (*over-enthusiastically praise*) faire l'éloge de III. *n* 1. *inf* (*blast: of air, smoke*) bouffée *f;* **to vanish in a ~ of smoke** s'évanouir dans un nuage de fumée 2. *Am, Can* (*stuffed quilt*) édredon *m; s. a.* **eiderdown** 3. *no pl, Brit, inf* (*breath*) souffle *m;* **to be out of ~** être à bout de souffle 4. (*light pastry*) chou *m* à la crème 5. *pej, inf* (*praising writing, speech*) pub *f*

◆**puff out** I. *vt* 1. (*cause to swell*) gonfler 2. (*emit*) **to ~ smoke** envoyer des bouffées de fumée 3. *inf* (*exhaust*) crever II. *vi* 1. (*swell*) se gonfler 2. (*move in short bursts*) sortir par bouffées

◆**puff up** I. *vt* gonfler; **to puffed up with pride** être bouffi d'orgueil II. *vi* gonfler; (*eyes*) enfler

puff adder *n* céraste *m*

puffball *n* BOT, BIO vesse-de-loup *f*

puffin ['pʌfɪn] *n* ZOOL macareux *m*

puff pastry *n* pâte *f* feuilletée

puffy <-ier, -iest> *adj* bouffi(e)

pug [pʌg] *n* ZOOL carlin *m*

pugnacious [pʌg'neɪʃəs] *adj form* pugnace

pugnacity [pʌg'næsəti, *Am:* -ṭi] *n no pl, form* pugnacité *f*

pug nose *n pej* nez *m* en patate

puke [pju:k] *inf* I. *vt* **to ~ sth** (**up**) [*o* **to ~** (**up**) **sth**] vomir qc II. *vi* **to ~** (**up**) vomir; **to make sb** (**want to**) **~** donner à qn envie de vomir

pukka ['pʌkə] *adj* (*genuine*) vrai(e); (*of good quality*) bon(ne)

pull [pʊl] I. *vt* 1. (*exert force, tug, draw*) tirer; (*rope*) tirer sur; **to ~ sth open** ouvrir qc; **to ~ a chair closer to sb/sth** rapprocher une chaise de qn/qc; **to ~ sth across a river** faire traverser la rivière à qc en tirant; **to ~ sth through a tube** tirer qc à travers un tube; **to ~ sb to one side** tirer qn sur le côté; **to ~ a toy along** tirer un jouet; **to ~ sth to pieces** mettre qc en morceaux; **to ~ the trigger** appuyer sur la gâchette; **he ~ed the bottle off the table** il a fait tomber la bouteille de la table 2. (*extract*) extraire; (*tooth, plant*) arracher; (*cork*) enlever; (*gun, knife*) sortir; **to ~ sth out of sth** sortir qc de qc; **to ~ sb out of sth** extraire qn de qc; **to ~ a gun/knife on sb** tire une arme/un couteau pour attaquer qn; **to ~ a beer** tirer une bière (à la) pression 3. MED (*strain: muscle, tendon*) se déchirer 4. (*attract*) attirer; **to ~ sb towards sb** attirer qn vers qn 5. *Aus, Brit, inf* (*pick up: boyfriend, girlfriend*) emballer ►**to ~ a face at sb** faire une grimace à qn; **to ~ sb's leg** *inf* faire marcher qn; **not to ~ one's punches** *inf* ne pas mâcher se mots; **to ~ strings** faire marcher ses relations; **to ~ one's weight** *inf* mettre les bouchées doubles II. *vi* 1. (*exert a pulling force*) tirer; **to ~ at the handle** tirer la poignée 2. (*row*) ramer III. *n* 1. (*act of pulling*) coup *m;* **to give sth a ~** tirer sur qc; **winning the election will be a long ~** *fig* remporter l'élection sera un travail de longue haleine 2. *no pl, inf* (*influence*) influence *f* 3. (*knob, handle*) poignée *f* 4. (*attraction*) attrait *m* 5. (*deep inhale or swig*) **to take a ~ on a cigarette** tirer une bouffée sur une cigarette; **to take a ~ on a bottle** prendre une goulée a la bouteille 6. SPORT (*a mishit*) essai *m* manqué

◆**pull about** *vt* **to pull sb/sth about** tirer qn/qc dans tous les sens

◆**pull ahead** *vi* prendre la tête; **to ~ of sb** prendre de l'avance sur qn

◆**pull apart** *vt* 1. (*break into pieces, dismantle*) **to pull sth apart** démonter qc 2. (*separate using force*) **to pull sb/sth apart** séparer qn/qc avec force 3. (*severely criticise*) **to pull sb/sth apart** descendre qn/qc en flammes

◆**pull away** I. *vi* (*train*) partir; (*car*) démarrer II. *vt* (*letter, hand*) retirer; **to pull a child away from the road** écarter un enfant de la chaussée

◆**pull back** I. *vi* 1. (*troops*) **to ~ from sth** se retirer de qc 2. (*change mind*) changer d'avis II. *vt* retirer

◆**pull down** *vt* 1. (*move from higher to*

P

lower position) *a. fig* (*blind*) baisser **2.** (*demolish*) démolir **3.** (*weaken*) affaiblir **4.** *inf* (*earn wages*) se faire

◆**pull in** I. *vi* **1.** (*arrive in station*) arriver **2.** AUTO (*after overtaking*) se rabattre; (*to park*) s'arrêter II. *vt* **1.** (*attract in large numbers: fans, a crowd*) attirer **2.** *Brit* LAW arrêter **3.** *Brit, inf* (*earn wages*) se faire **4.** (*by breathing in*) **to pull one's stomach in** rentrer son ventre

◆**pull off** I. *vt* **1.** (*take off: lid, sweater*) enlever **2.** *inf* (*succeed in difficult task*) réussir; **to pull it off** réussir **3.** (*leave: road*) quitter II. *vi* se retirer

◆**pull out** I. *vi* **1.** (*take out*) sortir **2.** (*drive onto a road*) déboîter **3.** (*leave station*) partir **4.** (*withdraw*) se retirer; **to ~ of sth** se retirer de qc II. *vt* **1.** (*leave*) retirer **2.** (*take out*) sortir **3.** (*remove: tooth, troops*) retirer; (*plug*) enlever; (*plant*) déraciner **4.** (*select*) choisir

◆**pull over** I. *vt* **1.** (*order to stop: car, driver*) faire s'arrêter (sur le côté) **2.** (*put on or take off garment*) **to pull sth over one's head** passer qc par la tête II. *vi* s'arrêter

◆**pull round** *vi Brit* se rétablir

◆**pull through** I. *vi* s'en sortir II. *vt* **to pull sb/sth through** tirer qn/qc d'affaire

◆**pull together** I. *vt* **1.** (*regain composure*) **to pull oneself together** se ressaisir **2.** (*organise, set up*) **to pull sth together** rassembler qc II. *vi* coopérer

◆**pull up** I. *vt* **1.** (*raise*) *a. fig* remonter; (*blind*) lever; **to ~ a chair** prendre une chaise **2.** (*uproot*) arracher **3.** (*stop*) arrêter **4.** *inf* (*reprimand*) rembarrer II. *vi* s'arrêter

pull-down menu *n* INFOR menu *m* déroulant

pullet ['pʊlɪt] *n* poulet *m*

pulley ['pʊli] <-eys> *n* TECH poulie *f*

pull-in *n Brit* **1.** (*parking area*) aire *f* de repos **2.** (*café*) café *m* sur le bord de la route

pull-out I. *n* **1.** MIL (*withdrawal of soldiers*) retrait *m* **2.** PUBL (*part of magazine*) encart *m* publicitaire II. *adj* (*able to be folded away: bed, table*) dépliable

pullover ['pʊləʊvəʳ, *Am:* -oʊvɚ] *n Brit* pullover *m*

pull-up *n* **1.** (*exercise*) traction *f* **2.** (*place by roadside for stopping*) aire *f* de repos

pulmonary ['pʌlmənəri, *Am:* -ner-] *adj* pulmonaire

pulp [pʌlp] I. *n* **1.** (*soft wet mass*) pulpe *f;* **to reduce sth to (a) ~** réduire qc en pâte **2.** TECH pâte *f* à papier **3.** (*fleshy part of fruit*) pulpe *f;* **to reduce sth to (a) ~** réduire qc en purée **4.** (*popular and sensational, trashy*) **~ novel** roman *f* à sensation **5.** *fig, inf* **to beat sb to a ~** faire de qn de la bouillie II. *vt* **to ~ sth** **1.** (*reduce to a pulp*) écraser qc en pâte; (*fruit*) écraser qc en purée **2.** (*withdraw from market*) envoyer au pilon

pulpit ['pʊlpɪt] *n* REL chaire *f*

pulsar ['pʌlsɑːʳ, *Am:* -sɑːr] *n* ASTR pulsar *m*

pulsate [pʌl'seɪt, *Am:* 'pʌlseɪt] *vi* (*move rhythmically*) battre; (*music*) vibrer ►**the ~ing heart of sth** *fig* le pouls de qc

pulsation *n* pulsation *f*

pulse[1] [pʌls] I. *n* **1.** (*heartbeat*) pouls *m;* **to take sb's ~** prendre le pouls de qn **2.** (*single vibration*) pulsation *f* **3.** (*rhythm*) rythme *m* ►**to have one's finger on the ~ of sth** être tout à fait au courant de qc II. *vi* battre

pulse[2] [pʌls] *n* GASTR légume *m* sec

pummel ['pʌml] *vt* **1.** (*beat*) **to ~ sb** rouer qn de coups **2.** *Am, inf* (*criticize, defeat*) descendre

pump[1] [pʌmp] *n* **1.** *Aus, Brit* (*low heeled slip on shoe*) semelle *f* plate **2.** *Am, Aus* (*high-heeled shoe*) escarpin *m* **3.** (*plimsoll*) espadrille *f*

pump[2] I. *n* pompe *f;* **water/fuel ~** pompe à eau/essence II. *vt* **1.** (*use pump on*) pomper; **to ~ water out of a boat** pomper l'eau pour l'évacuer d'un bateau; **to ~ oil through a pipeline** pomper du pétrole dans un pipeline; **to ~ into a tyre** pomper de l'air dans une roue; **to ~ money into a industry** injecter de l'argent dans une industrie; **~ed full of heroin** plein d'héroïne; **to ~ sb's stomach** MED faire un lavage d'estomac à qn **2.** (*interrogate*) tirer les vers du nez à

◆**pump out** *vt* **1.** (*clear: water*) pomper; **to ~ flooded houses** pomper l'eau des maisons inondées **2.** (*produce: students, novels*) débiter; (*music, information*) débiter

pumpernickel ['pʌmpənɪkl, *Am:* -pɚ-] *n no pl* pumpernickel *m* (*pain de seigle noir*)

pumping *n* pompage *m*

pumpkin ['pʌmpkɪn] *n* citrouille *f*

pun [pʌn] I. *n* calembour *m* II. <-nn-> *vi* faire un jeu de mots

punch[1] [pʌntʃ] I. *vt* **1.** (*hit*) **to ~ sb** donner un coup de poing à qn; **to ~ sth** frapper qc d'un coup de poing; **she ~ed me in the nose/stomach** elle m'a donné un coup de poing sur le nez/dans le ventre; **to ~ sb unconscious** assommer qn **2.** *Am* (*press: key, button*) appuyer sur; (*a number*) composer **3.** *Am, Can* AGR (*drive*) **to ~ cattle/a herd** conduire le bétail/un troupeau II. <-ches> *n* **1.** (*hit*) coup *m* de poing; **to give sb a ~** donner un coup de poing à qn; **she gave me a ~ on the nose/in the stomach** elle m'a donné un coup de poing sur le nez/dans le ventre **2.** *inf* (*strong effect*) punch *m;* **with ~** avec du punch

punch[2] [pʌntʃ] I. *vt* **1.** (*pierce*) percer; (*paper*) perforer; **to ~ holes in sth** faire des trous dans qc **2.** (*stamp*) poinçonner; (*a ticket*) composter II. <-ches> *n* **1.** (*piercing*) poinçon *m* **2.** (*tool for puncturing*) poinçonneuse *f;* (*for paper*) perforeuse *f*

◆**punch in** *vi* pointer (en entrant)

◆**punch out** *vi* pointer (en sortant)

punch[3] [pʌntʃ] *n* (*drink*) punch *m*

Punch (and Judy) *n* Guignol *m*

punchbag *n Brit* sac *m* de sable **punch card** *n* carte *f* perforée **punch-drunk** *adj a.*

fig sonné(e)

punching bag *n* SPORT punching-bag *m* **punching ball** *n* punching-ball *m*

punch line *n* chute *f* (*d'une histoire drôle*) **punch tape** *n* INFOR ruban *m* perforé **punch-up** *n Brit* bagarre *f;* **to have a ~** se bagarrer

punctilious [pʌŋk'tɪliəs] *adj form* pointilleux(-euse)

punctual ['pʌŋktʃuəl] *adj* à l'heure; (*person*) ponctuel(le)

punctuality *n no pl* ponctualité *f*

punctuate ['pʌŋktʃueɪt] *vt a.* LING ponctuer

punctuation *n no pl* ponctuation *f*

punctuation mark *n* signe *m* de ponctuation

puncture ['pʌŋktʃəʳ, *Am:* -tʃɚ] **I.** *vt* **1.** (*pierce*) perforer; (*tyre*) crever; **to ~ a hole in sth** percer un trou dans qc **2.** MED ponctionner; **a ~d lung** un poumon perforé **3.** *fig* (*deflate*) **to ~ sb's arrogance** clouer le bec à qn **II.** *vi* (*burst: tyre, tire*) crever **III.** *n* **1.** (*hole*) perforation *f;* (*tyre*) crevaison *f;* **to have a ~** crever **2.** MED ponction *f;* (*of bite, injection*) piqûre *f;* **a ~ wound** une marque de piqûre

pundit ['pʌndɪt] *n* POL *a. pej* expert(e) *m(f)*

pungent ['pʌndʒənt] *adj* **1.** (*strong, unpleasant*) fort(e) **2.** (*critical*) mordant(e)

punish ['pʌnɪʃ] *vt* **1.** (*penalize*) punir; **to ~ sb with a fine** frapper qn d'une amende; **to ~ sb with imprisonment** punir qn d'une peine d'emprisonnement **2.** (*treat badly*) malmener; **to ~ oneself** se malmener

punishable *adj* punissable

punishing **I.** *adj* **1.** (*difficult*) dur(e) **2.** (*trying*) épuisant(e) **II.** *n* punition *f*

punishment *n* **1.** (*punishing*) punition *f* **2.** (*penalty*) sanction *f;* LAW peine *f* **3.** *inf* (*severe treatment*) **to take a lot of ~** *inf* (*person*) encaisser; (*furniture*) en voir de toutes les couleurs

punitive ['pju:nɪtɪv, *Am:* -t̬ɪv] *adj form* **1.** (*penalizing*) punitif(-ive) **2.** (*severe*) sévère

punitive damages *n pl* dommages et intérêts exemplaires *mpl*

punk [pʌŋk] **I.** *n* **1.** *Am, inf* (*worthless person*) vaurien *m* **2.** *inf* (*inexperienced person*) branleur *m* **3.** (*anarchist*) punk *m* **4.** (*~ fan*) punk *mf* **II.** *adj* punk *inv*

punnet ['pʌnɪt] *n Aus, Brit* barquette *f*

punt¹ [pʌnt] SPORT **I.** *vt* **to ~ the ball** envoyer la balle d'un coup de volée **II.** *vi* envoyer un coup de volée **III.** *n* coup *m* de volée

punt² [pʌnt] *n* (*Irish currency*) livre *f* irlandaise

punter *n Brit, inf* **1.** (*gambler*) parieur, -euse *m, f* **2.** (*customer*) client(e) *m(f)*; **the ~s** (*the public*) le public **3.** (*prostitute's customer*) micheton *m*

puny ['pju:ni] <-nier, -niest> *adj* **1.** (*thin and weak: person*) chétif(-ive); (*hand, arm*) frêle **2.** (*with little power*) *a. fig* faible

pup [pʌp] **I.** *n* (*baby animal: dog*) chiot *m* ►**to buy a ~** se faire rouler **II.** *vi* <-pp-> mettre bas

pupa ['pju:pə] <pupas *o* pupae> *n* ZOOL chrysalide *f*

pupil¹ ['pju:pl] *n* (*school child*) élève *mf*

pupil² ['pju:pl] *n* ANAT pupille *f*

puppet ['pʌpɪt] *n* **1.** (*doll*) poupée *f;* (*on strings*) marionnette *f* **2.** *pej* (*one controlled by another*) marionnette *f*

puppeteer [pʌpɪ'tɪəʳ, *Am:* -ə'tɪr] *n* **1.** THEAT marionnettiste *mf* **2.** *pej* manipulateur, -trice *m, f*

puppet governement *n* gouvernement *m* fantoche **puppet show** *n* spectacle *m* de marionnettes

puppy ['pʌpi] <-ppies> *n* chiot *m*

purchase ['pɜ:tʃəs, *Am:* 'pɜ:rtʃəs] **I.** *vt* **1.** *form* (*buy*) acheter **2.** *form* FIN (*acquire*) acquérir **II.** *n form* **1.** (*item*) achat *m* **2.** (*act of buying*) achat *m* **3.** FIN (*acquiring*) acquisition *f* **4.** (*hold, grip*) prise *f*

purchase invoice *n* facture *f* d'achat **purchase order** *n* bon *m* de commande **purchase price** *n* prix *m* d'achat

purchaser *n* **1.** (*buyer*) acheteur, -euse *m, f* **2.** (*purchasing agent*) acquéreur *m*

purchasing **I.** *n form* achat *m* **II.** *adj* d'achat

purchasing department *n* service *m* des achats **purchasing power** *n* pouvoir *m* d'achat

pure [pjʊəʳ, *Am:* pjʊr] *adj* pur(e)

purebred ['pjʊəbred, *Am:* 'pjʊr-] **I.** *n* animal *m* de race **II.** *adj* de race

purée ['pjʊəreɪ, *Am:* pjʊ'reɪ] **I.** *vt* **to ~ sth** mettre qc en purée **II.** *n* purée *f*

purely *adv* purement; **~ by chance** tout à fait par hasard

purgative ['pɜ:gətɪv, *Am:* 'pɜ:rgət̬ɪv] **I.** *n* purgatif *m* **II.** *adj* purgatif(-ive)

purgatory ['pɜ:gətri, *Am:* 'pɜ:rgətɔ:ri] *n no pl* **1.** REL purgatoire *m* **2.** *fig* (*unpleasant experience*) supplice *m*

purge ['pɜ:dʒ, *Am:* 'pɜ:rdʒ] **I.** *vt a. fig* purger; **to ~ opponents** éliminer des adversaires **II.** *n a. fig* purge *f*

purification [ˌpjʊərɪfɪ'keɪʃən, *Am:* ˌpjʊrə-] *n no pl* purification *f*

purify ['pjʊərɪfaɪ, *Am:* 'pjʊrə-] *vt a. fig* purifier

purism *n no pl* purisme *m*

purist *n* puriste

puritan ['pjʊərɪtən, *Am:* 'pjʊrɪ-] **I.** *n* puritain(e) *m(f)* **II.** *adj* puritain(e)

puritanical *adj pej* puritain(e)

Puritanism *n no pl* puritanisme *m*

purity ['pjʊərəti, *Am:* 'pjʊrɪt̬i] *no pl n* pureté *f*

purl [pɜ:l, *Am:* pɜ:rl] **I.** *n* maille *f* à l'envers **II.** *adj* **~ stitch** maille *f* à l'envers **III.** *vt, vi* tricoter à l'envers

purloin [pɜ:'lɔɪn, *Am:* pɚ-] *vt iron, form* dérober

purple ['pɜ:pl, *Am:* 'pɜ:r-] **I.** *adj* **1.** (*blue and red mixed*) violet(te) **2.** (*red*) pourpre; **to**

P

become ~ (**in the face**) rougir ►**to be** ~ **with rage** être cramoisi de colère **II.** *n no pl* **1.** (*blue and red mixed*) violet *m* **2.** (*crimson*) pourpre *m; s. a.* **blue**

purplish *adj* violacé(e)

purport ['pɜ:pət, *Am:* pɜ:r'pɔ:rt] **I.** *vi form* **to** ~ **to** +*infin* prétendre +*infin;* **to** ~ **to be sth** prétendre être qc; (*thing*) être censé être qc **II.** *n* **1.** (*substance: of document, speech*) teneur *f* **2.** (*purpose*) but *m*

purpose ['pɜ:pəs, *Am:* 'pɜ:rpəs] **I.** *n* but *m;* **for financial/humanitarian ~s** dans un but financier/humanitaire; **to have a strength of** ~ être très résolu; **to serve a** ~ faire l'affaire; **for that very** ~ à cette fin; (*for this reason*) pour cette raison; **for all practical ~s** en fait; **to be to no** ~ être inutile; **on** ~ exprès **II.** *vi form* **to** ~ **to** +*infin* se proposer de +*infin*

purpose-built *adj* construit(e) spécialement

purposeful *adj* (*determined*) résolu(e)

purposeless *adj* **1.** (*pointless: act*) inutile; (*crime, violence*) gratuit(e) **2.** (*having no aim: life*) sans but **3.** (*without determination: person*) sans conviction

purposely *adv* exprès

purr [pɜ:r, *Am:* pɜ:r] **I.** *vi* ronronner **II.** *n* ronronnement *m*

purse [pɜ:s, *Am:* pɜ:rs] **I.** *n* **1.** *Am* (*handbag*) sac *m* (à main) **2.** *Brit* (*wallet*) porte-monnaie *m inv,* bourse *f Belgique* **3.** (*money: of a person*) moyens *mpl;* **public** ~ trésor *m* public **4.** SPORT (*prize*) prix *m* ►**to hold the** ~ **strings** tenir les cordons de la bourse **II.** *vt* **to** ~ **one's lips** pincer les lèvres **III.** *vi* (*lips*) se pincer

pursuance [pə'sju:ənts, *Am:* pɚ'su:-] *n no pl, form* exécution *f*

pursuant *adv form* LAW ~ **to sth** conformément à qc

pursue [pə'sju:, *Am:* pɚ'su:] *vt* **1.** (*follow*) *a. fig* poursuivre **2.** (*seek to find: dreams, happiness*) rechercher; (*one's aims*) poursuivre **3.** (*continue*) *a. fig* poursuivre; (*way, line*) suivre; **we won't** ~ **the matter any further** nous n'allons pas nous étendre sur ce sujet **4.** (*engage in: career, studies*) poursuivre

pursuer *n* **1.** (*chaser*) poursuivant(e) *m(f)* **2.** *Scot* LAW plaignant(e) *m(f)*

pursuit [pə'sju:t, *Am:* pɚ'su:t] *n* **1.** (*action of pursuing*) poursuite *f;* **to be in** ~ **of sb/sth** être à la poursuite de qn/qc; **in** ~ **of happiness** à la recherche du bonheur **2.** (*activity*) activité *f*

purulent ['pjʊərələnt, *Am:* 'pjʊrə-] *adj* purulent(e)

purvey [pə'veɪ, *Am:* pɚ'-] *vt form* ECON fournir; (*a service*) offrir

purveyance *n no pl, form* approvisionnement *m*

purveyor *n form* ECON fournisseur *m*

pus [pʌs] *n no pl* pus *m*

push [pʊʃ] **I.** *vt* **1.** (*shove, give a push, forcefully move*) *a. fig* pousser; **to** ~ **a door open** ouvrir une porte en la poussant; **to** ~ **sth into sth** fourrer qc dans qc; **to** ~ **sb down the stairs** pousser qn dans les escaliers; **to** ~ **sb in/out of sth** pousser qn à l'intérieur/hors de qc; **to** ~ **one's head through the window** passer sa tête par la fenêtre; **to** ~ **sth to the back of one's mind** *fig* refouler qc; **to** ~ **one's way through sth** se frayer un chemin à travers qc; **to** ~ **sb out of the way** écarter qn; **to be ~ed** être bousculé **2.** (*persuade*) pousser; **to** ~ **sb into doing sth** pousser qn à faire qc; **don't** ~ **me too far** ne me pousse pas à bout **3.** (*force, be demanding: students, workers*) pousser; **to** ~ **oneself** se forcer; **to** ~ **sb for an answer/a date** pousser qn à donner une réponse/une date; **to** ~ **one's luck** y aller un peu fort; **to** ~ **sb too hard** exiger trop de qn; **that's ~ing it a bit** c'est un peu fort **4.** (*press: button, bell*) appuyer sur; **to** ~ **sth into sth** enfoncer qc dans qc **5.** *inf* (*be short of*) **to be ~ed** (**for time**) être très pressé; **to be ~ed for money** être à court d'argent **6.** *inf* (*promote*) faire la pub de; (*plan, system*) préconiser; (*person, candidate, idea*) soutenir; **to** ~ **oneself** se mettre en avant **7.** (*approach age*) **to be ~ing 30** approcher de la trentaine **8.** *inf* (*sell: drugs*) revendre **II.** *vi* **1.** (*force movement*) pousser; ~ (*on door*) poussez; **to** ~ **past sb** bousculer qn **2.** (*apply pressure*) *a. fig* faire pression; ~ (*on bell*) appuyez **3.** (*pass through*) *a.* MIL avancer; **to** ~ **into/out of sth** entrer/sortir de qc en se frayant un chemin **III.** <-shes> *n* **1.** (*shove*) *a. fig* poussée *f;* **to give sb/sth a** ~ *a. fig* pousser qn/qc; **to give a car a** ~ **start** faire démarrer la voiture en la poussant; **sth needs a** ~ il faut pousser qc; **I need a** ~ il faut me pousser **2.** (*act of pressing*) pression *f;* **at the** ~ **of a button** à la pression du bouton **3.** (*strong action*) effort *m;* **to make a** ~ **for sth** faire un effort pour qc; **the final** ~ **for victory** le dernier effort avant la victoire **4.** (*help, persuasion*) encouragement *m;* **he needs a bit of a** ~ il a besoin d'un petit coup de pouce **5.** (*ad, campaign*) campagne *f;* **to have a** ~ mener une campagne ►**to get the** ~ *inf* se faire plaquer; (*be fired*) se faire virer; **to give sb the** ~ *inf* (*break up with*) plaquer qn; (*fire*) flanquer qn à la porte; **when** ~ **comes to shove** s'il le faut; **at a** ~ *Brit, inf* au besoin

◆**push ahead** *vi* persévérer; **to** ~ **with sth** aller de l'avant avec qc

◆**push along I.** *vi inf* s'en aller **II.** *vt* **to push sth along** pousser qc

◆**push about, push around** *vt inf* **to push sb around** marcher sur les pieds à qn

◆**push away** *vt* repousser

◆**push back** *vt a. fig* **to push sb/sth back** repousser qn/qc

◆**push down** *vt* **1.** (*knock down*) renverser **2.** (*press down*) appuyer sur; **to push sth down sth** enfoncer qc dans qc **3.** (*lower down*) *a.* ECON faire baisse

◆**push for** *vt* faire pression pour

◆**push forward** **I.** *vt* **1.** (*advance*) pousser en avant **2.** (*promote*) **to push sth forward** faire avancer qc **3.** (*call attention to oneself*) **to push oneself forward** se mettre en avant **II.** *vi* avancer

◆**push in** **I.** *vt* **1.** (*insert, break*) enfoncer; **to push one's way in** se frayer un passage **2.** (*force in*) **to push sb in** pousser qn dedans **II.** *vi* **1.** (*force way in*) s'introduire de force **2.** (*interfere*) intervenir **3.** (*cut in line*) resquiller

◆**push off** **I.** *vi* **1.** *inf* (*leave*) se casser; **~!** dégage! **2.** NAUT (*set sail*) pousser au large **II.** *vt* NAUT **to push sth off** pousser qc au large

◆**push on** **I.** *vi* continuer; **to ~ with sth** continuer qc **II.** *vt* pousser

◆**push out** **I.** *vt* **1.** (*force out*) **to push sb/sth out** pousser qn/qc dehors; **to push sb/sth out of sth** faire sortir qn/qc de qc en le poussant **2.** (*get rid of*) **to push sb out** exclure qn ►**to push the boat out** *Brit, inf* (*spend a lot*) vivre la grande vie **II.** *vi* BOT pousser

◆**push over** *vt* **to push sb/sth over** faire tomber qn/qc

◆**push through** **I.** *vi* se frayer un chemin **II.** *vt* **1.** (*have accepted: proposal, measure*) fairer passer **2.** (*help to pass through*) **to push sb through sth** faire passer qn à travers qc **3.** (*go through*) se frayer un chemin à travers

◆**push up** *vt* **1.** (*move higher*) **to push sb/sth up** relever qn/qc **2.** ECON (*cause increase*) augmenter ►**to ~ the daisies** *iron* manger les pissenlits par la racine

pushbike *n Aus, Brit, inf* bécane *f* **push-button** **I.** *n* bouton *m* **II.** *adj* (*telephone*) à touches; (*controls*) à boutons **pushcart** *n* charrette (à bras) *f* **pushchair** *n Brit* poussette *f*

pusher *n pej* **1.** (*drug ~*) dealer *m* **2.** (*pushy person*) arriviste *mf*

pushing *n no pl* poussée *f*

pushover *n inf* **1.** (*easy success*) **to be a ~** être du gâteau **2.** (*easily influenced*) **to be a ~** être facile à convaincre **3.** (*weak*) **to be a ~ for sth** craquer pour qc

pushpin ['pʊʃpɪn] *n Am* punaise *f*

push-start *vt* **to ~ sth** faire démarrer qc en le/la poussant **push-up** **I.** *n Am* (*press-up*) traction *f;* **to do ~s** faire des pompes **II.** *adj* (*bra*) rembourré(e)

pushy ['pʊʃi] *adj pej* **1.** (*ambitious*) ambitieux(-euse) **2.** (*domineering*) autoritaire **3.** (*careerist*) arriviste *mf*

puss [pʊs] <-sses> *n inf* **1.** (*cat*) minou *m* **2.** (*girl*) minette *f*

pussy ['pʊsi] *n* <-ssies> **1.** *inf* (*cat*) minou *m* **2.** *Brit, vulg* chatte *f*

pussyfoot ['pʊsifʊt] *vi* **to ~ (around)** tergiverser

pussy willow *n* saule *m*

pustule ['pʌstju:l, *Am:* -tʃu:l] *n* MED pustule *f*

put [pʊt] <-tt-, put, put> *vt* **1.** (*place*) mettre; **to ~ sth on/in/around sth** mettre qc sur/dans/autour de qc; **to ~ sth into sth** mettre qc dans qc; (*thrust*) enfoncer qc dans qc; **to ~ some more milk in one's tea** rajouter du lait dans son thé; **to ~ one's head through the window** passer la tête par la fenêtre **2.** (*direct*) mettre; **to ~ the blame for sth on sb** rejeter la responsabilité de qc sur qn; **to ~ the emphasis on sth** mettre l'accent sur qc; **to ~ faith in sth** croire en qc; **to ~ a spell on sb** jeter un sort sur qn; **to ~ a tax on sth** taxer qc; **to ~ sb in their place** remettre qn à sa place; **to ~ oneself in sb's place** se mettre à la place de qn; **to ~ an idea in sb's head** mettre une idée dans la tête de qn; **to ~ pressure on sb** mettre qn sous pression **3.** (*invest*) placer; **to put sth in an account** déposer qc sur un compte; **to ~ money on sth** placer de l'argent sur qc; **to ~ a bet on a race** miser sur une course; **to ~ energy/time/money into sth** investir de l'énergie/du temps/de l'argent dans qc; **I put £500 towards the cost** j'ai contribué de 500£; **I've put £500 towards a new computer** j'ai mis de côté 500£ pour un nouvel ordinateur **4.** GASTR (*add*) **to ~ sth in sth** ajouter qc à qc **5.** (*cause to be*) mettre; **to ~ sb in a good mood/at ease** mettre qn de bonne humeur/à l'heure; **to ~ sb in prison/in a taxi** mettre qn en prison/dans un taxi; **to ~ sb to bed/to death** mettre qn au lit/à mort; **to ~ sb in a rage** mettre qn en colère; **to ~ sb to shame** faire honte à qn; **to ~ sb on trial** faire passer qn en jugement; **to ~ sb to work** faire travailler qn; **to ~ sb under pressure** mettre qn sous pression; **to ~ sb under oath** faire prêter serment à qn; **to ~ sb at risk** faire courir un danger à qn; **to ~ one's affairs in order** mettre ses affaires en ordre; **to ~ sth right** arranger qc; **to ~ one's ideas into practice** mettre ses idées en pratique; **to ~ one's hope in sb/sth** miser ses espoirs sur qn/qc **6.** (*present: point of view*) présenter; (*case, problem*) exposer; (*question*) poser; (*arguments*) proposer; (*proposition*) faire; **to ~ sth to a vote** soumettre qc à un vote; **to ~ it to sb that** suggérer à qn que +*subj* **7.** (*express*) dire; **to ~ it bluntly** pour parler franc; **to ~ sth on paper** mettre qc sur papier; **I coudn't have ~ it better** on ne saurait mieux le formuler; **could you ~ that more tactfully?** pourrais tu dire ça avec un peu plus de tact?; **as sb ~ it** comme qn dit; **how to ~ it** comment dire; **to ~ one's feelings into words** mettre des mots sur ses sentiments **8.** (*value*) **to ~ efficiency before appearance** placer l'efficacité avant l'apparence; **I ~ value for money first** pour moi ce qui compte d'abord c'est le rapport qualité prix; **I'd ~ her right at the top** pour moi, c'est la meilleure **9.** (*estimate*) estimer; **to ~ sb/sth at sth** estimer qn/qc à qc **10.** SPORT **to ~ the shot** lancer le poids

◆**put about** <-tt-> *irr* **I.** *vt* (*spread rumour*) **to put sth about** faire circuler qc; **to put it about that ...** faire circuler le bruit que ...

P

II. *vi* NAUT virer de bord

◆**put across** <-tt-> *vt irr* **to put sth across** faire comprendre qc; (*idea, message*) faire passer qc; **she puts herself across well** elle sait comment se présenter

◆**put aside** <-tt-> *vt irr* **1.** (*leave ignore: work, problem, argument*) mettre de côté **2.** (*save*) mettre de côté; **to put some money aside** mettre de l'argent de côté; **to ~ some time** se réserver du temps

◆**put away** <-tt-> *vt irr* **1.** (*save, set aside*) mettre de côté **2.** *inf* (*eat*) engloutir **3.** (*clean up*) ranger **4.** *inf* (*have institutionalized*) **to be ~** (*in an old people's home*) être mis en maison de retraite; (*in prison*) être emprisonné; (*in hospital*) être interné **5.** *inf* (*kill*) **to put sb away** éliminer **6.** *fig* (*ignore, remove: worries, idea*) écarter **7.** SPORT (*defeat*) battre

◆**put back** <-tt-> *vt irr* **1.** (*return to its place*) **to put sth back** remettre qc (à sa place) **2.** (*postpone*) remettre **3.** (*invest*) remettre **4.** (*delay*) retarder **5.** *inf* (*drink*) siffler

◆**put by** <-tt-> *vt irr* mettre de côté

◆**put down** <-tt-> *irr* **I.** *vt* **1.** (*set down*) poser; **I couldn't put the book down** je ne pouvais pas lâcher le livre **2.** (*put to bed*) **to put a baby down** coucher un bébé **3.** (*lower, decrease*) baisser **4.** (*drop off*) **to put sb down** déposer qn **5.** (*pay, give as deposit*) verser **6.** TEL **to ~ the (tele)phone** raccrocher le téléphone **7.** (*write*) inscrire; **to put sth down on paper** coucher qc sur papier; **to put sb down for sth** inscrire qn sur la liste pour qc; **to put one's name down for sth** s'inscrire pour qc; **I put my name down for the tennis club** je me suis inscrit au tennis club; **put me down for £20** je donnerai 20£; **they put it down on the bill** ils l'ont mis sur la facture; **I'll put it down in my diary** je vais le noter dans mon agenda **8.** (*attribute*) **to ~ sth to sb/sth** mettre qc sur le compte de qn/qc **9.** (*consider*) **to ~ sb as sth** prendre qn pour qc **10.** (*preserve: food, wine*) mettre en réserve **11.** MIL (*suppress: a rebellion*) réprimer **12.** *inf* (*deride*) humilier **13.** (*have killed*) abattre; (*a dog*) faire piquer **14.** AVIAT poser **II.** *vi* AVIAT se poser

◆**put forward** <-tt-> *vt irr* **1.** (*submit, offer*) avancer; (*a candidate, plan*) proposer; **to ~ oneself forward for promotion** demander une promotion **2.** (*advance*) avancer

◆**put in** <-tt-> *irr* **I.** *vt* **1.** (*place inside*) mettre (dedans); (*from outside*) rentrer **2.** (*add, insert: ingredient, paragraph*) ajouter **3.** (*plant*) planter **4.** (*install*) (faire) installer **5.** (*appoint*) désigner; (*at election*) élire **6.** FIN (*deposit*) déposer **7.** (*invest, devote*) investir; **to ~ 8 hours' work** faire 8 heures de travail **8.** (*present*) présenter; (*claim*) déposer; (*protest*) formuler; **to ~ a plea** plaider; **to put one's name in for sth** poser sa candidature à qc; **to put sb in for sth** inscrire qn à qc; (*for exam*) présenter qn à qc **9.** (*make*) **to ~ a (phone) call to sb** passer un coup de fil à qn **II.** *vi* **1.** (*dock*) faire escale **2.** (*apply for*) **to ~ for sth** faire une demande de qc; **to ~ for a job** poser sa candidature pour un travail; **to put sb in for sth** inscrire qn à qc

◆**put off** <-tt-> *vt irr* **1.** (*take off*) enlever **2.** (*turn off: light, tv*) éteindre; (*gas, water*) fermer **3.** (*drop off: passenger*) déposer **4.** (*postpone, delay*) repousser; **to put sth off for a week** remettre qc à une semaine; **to put sb off** décommander qn **5.** (*repel*) dégoûter; **to put sb off their dinner** couper l'appétit à qn; **her voice puts a lot of people off** sa voix rebute pas mal de gens **6.** (*dissuade*) dissuader; **to put sb off doing sth** dissuader qn de faire qc **7.** (*distract*) déconcentrer ▸**never ~ until tomorrow what you can do today** *prov* il ne faut jamais remettre à demain ce que l'on peut faire le jour même *prov*

◆**put on** <-tt-> *vt irr* **1.** (*wear*) porter; **to ~ some make-up** se maquiller; **to put clean things on** mettre des vêtements propres, se rapproprier *Belgique, Nord* **2.** (*turn on*) allumer; **I'll put the kettle on** je vais faire bouillir de l'eau; **to ~ the brakes** freiner **3.** (*play: CD, film*) passer; (*play, concert*) monter **4.** (*assume, pretend*) affecter; (*an air, accent*) prendre; **to put it on** faire semblant; (*show off*) crâner; **to ~ an act** jouer la comédie; **to put sb on** faire marcher qn **5.** (*indicate, inform*) **to put sb on to sth** indiquer qc à qn; **to put sb on to** (*dentist, shop*) indiquer qn à qn; (*culprit*) mettre qn sur la piste de **6.** (*increase, add*) augmenter; **to ~ weight/3 kilos** prendre du poids/3 kilos; **to ~ speed** prendre de la vitesse; **to put 10% on the price of sth** majorer de 10% le prix de qc **7.** (*provide: extra trains, flights*) mettre en service; (*dinner party*) offrir; (*TV programme*) passer **8.** (*begin cooking*) **to put the dinner on** se mettre à cuisiner **9.** (*bet*) **to put sth on sth** miser qc sur qc **10.** (*hand over to*) **to put sb on the (tele)phone** passer qn; **I'll put you on to your mother** je te passe ta mère **11.** (*prescribe*) **to put sb on steroids** prescrire des stéroïdes à qn

◆**put out** <-tt-> *irr* **I.** *vt* **1.** (*take outside*) sortir; **to put sth out of the window** passer qc par la fenêtre **2.** (*extend*) étendre; (*new shoots*) déployer; **to ~ one's hand** tendre la main; **to ~ one's tongue** tirer la langue **3.** (*throw out*) expulser **4.** (*issue: announcement, warning*) faire passer **5.** (*broadcast*) diffuser **6.** (*produce*) produire **7.** (*lay out for ready use: clothes, tools*) préparer; (*cutlery, plates*) placer; **to put sth out for sb/sth** sortir qc à qn/qc **8.** (*contract out, allocate work*) **to put sth out to private contractors** donner qc à des agents privés; **to put sth out to tender** lancer un appel d'offres pour qc **9.** (*bother*) déranger; **she really put herself out for us** elle s'est vraiment donné beaucoup de mal pour nosu **10.** (*disconcert*) contrarier; **to be ~ by sth** être déconcerté par qc **11.** (*extinguish, turn off*) éteindre; (*gas, water*) fermer **12.** (*dislocate*) démettre; **to put one's shoulder out** se démettre l'épaule **13.** (*make unconscious*) endormir **14.** (*spend*) dépenser **15.** (*place: money*) placer **II.** *vi* **1.** NAUT (*set sail*) quitter le port **2.** *Am, inf* (*have sex*) **to ~ for sb** coucher avec qn

◆**put over** <-tt-> *vt irr* **1.** (*make understood*) **to put sth over** faire comprendre qc **2.** *Am* (*postpone*) remettre à plus tard **3.** *inf* **to put one over on sb** avoir qn

◆**put through** <-tt-> *vt irr* **1.** TEL (*connect*) **to put sb through** mettre qn en ligne; **to put sb through to sb** passer qn à qn **2.** (*implement*) **to put sth through** mener qc à bien; (*proposal, deal*) faire accepter qc; (*deal*) conclure qc; **to put a bill through parliament** faire accepter une propositon de loi par le parlement **3.** (*make endure*) **to put sb through sth** faire subir qc à qn; **to put sb through hell** faire souffrir le martyre à qn; **he really put me through it** il m'en a fait baver **4.** (*support financially*) **to put sb through college** payer l'université à qn; **to put oneself through college** se payer l'université

◆**put together** <-tt-> *vt irr* **1.** (*assemble: pieces*) assembler; (*radio, band, model*) monter; (*vase*) recoller; (*facts*) reconstituer **2.** (*place near*) **to put two things together** mettre deux choses côte à côte; *fig* rapprocher deux choses **3.** (*connect*) **to put clues/facts together** rapprocher des indices/des faits; **to put two sets of figures together** comparer deux séries de chiffres **4.** MAT (*add*) **to put 10 and 15 together** additionner 10 et 15 **5.** GASTR (*mix*) mélanger **6.** (*prepare, organize: plan, strategy*) élaborer; (*book, programme*) faire; (*team*) rassembler; (*legal case*) constituer **7.** (*create: dinner*) improviser ►**to put two and two together** *prov* tirer ses conclusions

◆**put up** <-tt-> *irr* **I.** *vt* **1.** (*raise*) lever; **to ~ one's hand** lever la main; (*satellite*) placer en orbite **2.** (*build, install*) ériger; (*tent*) dresser; (*kit furniture*) monter; (*shelves*) poser; (*umbrella*) ouvrir; (*wallpaper*) poser **3.** *Brit* (*increase: price*) augmenter **4.** (*give shelter*) **to put sb up** héberger qn **5.** (*submit, present*) présenter; **to ~ a struggle** opposer une résistance; **to put sb up as sth** proposer qn comme qc; **to put sb up for election** proposer qn à une élection; **to put sth up for sale/rent** mettre qc en vente/location; **to be ~ for sale/auction** être en vente/aux enchères; **to put sb up to doing sth** *inf* pousser qn à faire qc **6.** (*provide: money*) fournir **7.** (*prepare*) préparer **8.** (*display: poster*) accrocher; (*notice*) afficher; (*sign*) mettre **II.** *vi* **1.** (*lodge*) **to ~ at sb's place/in an hotel** loger chez qn/à l'hôtel; **to ~ at sb's place/in an hotel for the night** passer la nuit chez qn/à l'hôtel **2.** (*apply for*) poser sa candidature; **to ~ for election** se porter candidat à l'élection **3.** *inf* (*stand*) **to ~ with sb/sth** supporter qn/qc

putative ['pju:tətɪv, *Am:* -t̬ət̬ɪv] *adj form* putatif(-ive)

put-down *n inf* réplique *f* bien envoyée **put-off** *n inf* excuse *f* **put-on** *n Am, inf* **it's a ~** il/elle fait semblant **put option** *n* ECON option *f* de vente

putrefaction [ˌpju:trɪ'fækʃən, *Am:* -trə'-] *n no pl, form* (*decay*) putréfaction *f*

putrefy ['pju:trɪfaɪ, *Am:* -trə-] <-ie-> *vi form* se putréfier

putrid ['pju:trɪd] *adj form* **1.** (*decayed*) putride **2.** (*worthless*) infâme

putsch [pʊtʃ] <-tsches> *n* putsch *m*

putt [pʌt] SPORT **I.** *vt, vi* putter **II.** *n* putt *m*

putter[1] *n* putter *m;* **to be a good ~** bien putter

putter[2] *vi Am s.* **potter**

putting *n no pl* SPORT putting *m*

putting green *n* SPORT green *m*

putty *n no pl* mastic *m* ►**to be (like) ~ in sb's hands** se laisser mener par le bout du nez

put-up *adj inf* **a ~ job** un coup monté **put-upon** *adj inf* **to feel ~** se sentir exploité

puzzle ['pʌzl] **I.** *vt* intriguer **II.** *vi* **to ~ about [*o* over] sth** chercher à comprendre qc **III.** *n* **1.** (*analytical game*) devinette *f* **2.** (*mechanical game*) casse-tête *m* **3.** (*jigsaw ~*) puzzle *m,* casse-tête *m Québec* **4.** (*mystery*) mystère *m*

◆**puzzle out** *vt* deviner

puzzled *adj* **1.** (*worried*) perplexe; **we are ~ about what to do now** nous ne savons que faire maintenant **2.** (*surprised*) surpris(e)

puzzler *n* mystère *m;* **that question was a real ~** cette question était une sacrée colle

puzzling *adj* déroutant(e)

PVC [ˌpi:vi:'si:] CHEM *abbr of* **polyvinyl chloride** **I.** *n* PVC *m* **II.** *adj* en PVC

PWR *n abbr of* **pressurized water reactor** REP *m*

PX *n Am abbr of* **Post Exchange** coopérative *f* militaire

pygmy ['pɪgmi] **I.** *n pej* pygmée *m* **II.** *adj* ZOOL pygmée

pyjamas [pə'dʒɑ:məz] *npl* pyjama *m;* **a pair of ~** un pyjama

pylon ['paɪlɒn, *Am:* -lɑ:n] *n* pylône *m*

pyramid ['pɪrəmɪd] *n* pyramide *f*

pyramid selling *n no pl* ECON, LAW vente *f* pyramidale

pyre ['paɪəʳ, *Am:* 'paɪɚ] *n* bûcher *m* funéraire

Pyrex® ['paɪəreks] **I.** *n* pyrex® *m* **II.** *adj* en pyrex

pyrites [ˌpaɪə'raɪti:z, *Am:* paɪ'-] <-tae> *n* pyrite *f*

pyromania [ˌpaɪrəʊ'meɪnɪə, *Am:* ˌpaɪroʊ'-] *n no pl* pyromanie *f*

pyromaniac *n* pyromane *mf*

pyrotechnic(al) *adj* **1.** (*relating to fireworks*) pyrotechnique **2.** (*brilliant: wit*) époustouflant(e)

pyrotechnics *n* **1.** + *sing v* (*science*) pyro-

P

technie *f* **2.** *pl* (*fireworks, brilliance*) feu *m* d'artifice

python ['paɪθən, *Am:* -θɑːn] <-(ons)> *n* python *m*

Q

Q, q [kjuː] <-'s> *n* Q *m*, q *m*; ~ **as in Queenie** *Brit*, ~ **as in Queen** *Am*, ~ **for Queenie** *Brit*, ~ **for Queen** *Am* (*on telephone*) q comme Quintal

Q *n abbr of* **Queen** reine *f*

Qatar [kə'tɑː(r), *Am:* 'kɑːtɑːr] *n* le Qatar

Qatari [kə'tɑːrɪ] **I.** *adj* qatari(e) **II.** *n* qatari(e) *m(f)*

QC [ˌkjuː'siː] *n Brit abbr of* **Queens Counsel** *titre donné à un éminent avocat*

QED [ˌkjuːiː'diː] *abbr of* **quod erat demonstrandum** CQFD

qtr *n abbr of* **quarter** quart *m*

qua [kwɑː] *prep form* en tant que

quack¹ [kwæk] **I.** *n* (*duck's sound*) coin-coin *m sans pl* **II.** *interj childspeak* ~-~ coin-coin **III.** *vi* cancaner

quack² [kwæk] *pej* **I.** *n* **1.** (*fake doctor*) charlatan *m* **2.** *Aus, Brit, inf* (*doctor*) toubib *m* **II.** *adj* (*doctor, medicine*) de charlatan

quad [kwɒd, *Am:* kwɑːd] *n* **1.** *inf* (*quadruplet*) quadruplé(e) *m(f)* **2.** *s.* **quadrangle**

quadrangle ['kwɒdræŋgl, *Am:* 'kwɑːdræŋ-] *n* cour *f* intérieure

quadrant ['kwɒdrənt, *Am:* 'kwɑːdrənt] *n* **1.** (*quarter of circle*) quart *m* de cercle **2.** (*quarter*) quart *m*

quadraphonic [ˌkwɒdrə'fɒnɪk, *Am:* ˌkwɑːdrə'fɑːnɪk] *adj* quadriphonique

quadratic [kwɒ'drætɪk, *Am:* kwɑː'dræt̬-] *adj* de second degré

quadrilateral [ˌkwɒdrɪ'lætərəl, *Am:* ˌkwɑːdrɪ'læt̬-] *n* quadrilatère *m*

quadruped ['kwɒdrʊped, *Am:* 'kwɑːdrʊ-] *n* quadrupède *m*

quadruple ['kwɒdruːpl, *Am:* 'kwɑːdruː-] **I.** *vt, vi* quadrupler **II.** *adj* quadruple

quadruplet ['kwɒdruːplət, *Am:* kwɑː'druːplɪt] *n* quadruplé(e) *m(f)*

quaff [kwɒf, *Am:* kwɑːf] *vt* lamper

quagmire ['kwægmaɪə(r), *Am:* -ɚ] *n* bourbier *m*

quail¹ [kweɪl] <-(s)> *n* (*small bird*) caille *f*

quail² [kweɪl] *vi* (*feel fear*) trembler; **to ~ with fear** trembler de peur; **to ~ before sb/sth** trembler devant qn/qc

quaint [kweɪnt] *adj* **1.** (*charming: village, landscape*) pittoresque **2.** *pej* (*old-fashioned*) vieillot(te)

quake [kweɪk] **I.** *n* tremblement *m* de terre **II.** *vi* (*earth, person*) trembler; **to ~ with sth** trembler de qc; **to ~ with laughter** se tordre de rire; **to ~ in one's boots** trembler de peur

Quaker ['kweɪkə(r), *Am:* -kɚ] *n* quaker, -resse *m, f*

qualification [ˌkwɒlɪfɪ'keɪʃn, *Am:* ˌkwɑːlɪ-] *n* **1.** (*credentials, skills*) qualification *f* **2.** (*document, exam*) diplôme *m* **3.** (*the act of qualifying*) obtention *f* d'un diplôme **4.** (*limiting criteria*) réserve *f* **5.** (*condition*) condition *f* **6.** SPORT, LING qualification *f*

qualified *adj* **1.** (*competent*) qualifié(e) **2.** (*trained*) diplômé(e); **I'm not ~ to answer this question** je ne suis pas compétent pour répondre à cette question **3.** (*limited*) mitigé(e)

qualify ['kwɒlɪfaɪ, *Am:* 'kwɑːlɪ-] <-ie-> **I.** *vt* **1.** (*give credentials, make eligible*) qualifier **2.** (*add reservations to*) nuancer **3.** LING qualifier **4.** (*give the right*) donner droit à **5.** (*describe*) **to ~ sb/sth as sth** qualifier qn/qc de qc **II.** *vi* **1.** SPORT se qualifier **2.** (*meet standards*) **to ~ for sth** remplir les conditions requises pour qc; **it hardly qualifies as sth** on ne peut pas appeler ça qc **3.** (*be eligible*) **to ~ for sth** avoir droit à qc **4.** (*have qualifications*) être qualifié **5.** (*complete training*) obtenir son diplôme; **to ~ as an engineer** obtenir son diplôme d'ingénieur

qualifying **I.** *n no pl* **1.** (*meeting standard*) accréditation *f* **2.** SPORT qualification *f* **II.** *adj* **1.** SPORT, UNI, SCHOOL (*round, exam*) éliminatoire; (*candidates*) sélectionné(e) **2.** LING qualificatif(-ive)

qualitative ['kwɒlɪtətɪv, *Am:* 'kwɑːlɪteɪt̬ɪv] *adj* qualitatif(-ive)

quality ['kwɒlətɪ, *Am:* 'kwɑːlət̬ɪ] **I.** <-ies> *n* qualité *f*; **high/low ~** bonne/mauvaise qualité; **she has managerial qualities** c'est une bonne gestionnaire **II.** *adj* de qualité

quality control *n* contrôle *m* qualité

quality time *n no pl: moments privilégiés passés avec quelqu'un*

qualm [kwɑːm] *n* **1.** (*scruple*) scrupule *m*; **to have no ~s about doing sth** ne pas avoir de scrupules à faire qc **2.** (*worry*) réticences *fpl*

quandary ['kwɒndərɪ, *Am:* 'kwɑːn-] *n* dilemme *m*; **to be in a real ~** ne pas savoir du tout quoi faire

quango ['kwæŋgəʊ, *Am:* -goʊ] *n Brit, pej abbr of* **quasi-autonomous non-governmental organization** organisme *m* autonome

quantifiable *adj* quantifiable

quantification [ˌkwɒntɪfɪ'keɪʃn, *Am:* ˌkwɑːnt̬ə-] *n* quantification *f*

quantify [ˌkwɒntɪfaɪ, *Am:* ˌkwɑːnt̬ə-] *vt* quantifier

quantitative ['kwɒntɪtətɪv, *Am:* 'kwɑːnt̬əteɪt̬ɪv] *adj* quantitatif(-ive)

quantity ['kwɒntətɪ, *Am:* 'kwɑːnt̬ət̬ɪ] <-ies> *n* quantité *f*; **to double the ~ of a recipe** doubler les quantités d'une recette; **a ~ of cotton wool** du coton; **in ~** en grande quantité

quantity discount *n* réduction *f* pour achat en gros **quantity surveyor** *n Brit* métreur,

-euse *m, f* **quantity theory** *n* théorie *f* quantitative

quantum ['kwɒntəm, *Am:* 'kwɑːnt̬əm] <quanta> *n* PHYS quantum *m*

quantum mechanics *n* mécanique *f* quantique **quantum leap** *n fig* pas *m* de géant

quarantine ['kwɒrəntiːn, *Am:* 'kwɔːrən-] **I.** *n* quarantaine *f* **II.** *vt* **to ~ sb/an animal** mettre qn/un animal en quarantaine

quark [kwɑːk, *Am:* kwɑːrk] *n* PHYS quark *m*

quarrel ['kwɒrəl, *Am:* 'kwɔːr-] **I.** *n* dispute *f;* **a ~ over sth** une dispute à propos de qc; **to have a ~** se disputer **II.** <-ll-> *vi* se disputer; **to ~ about sth** se disputer à propos de qc

quarrelsome ['kwɒrəlsəm, *Am:* 'kwɔːr-] *adj* querelleur(-euse)

quarry ['kwɒrɪ, *Am:* 'kwɔːr-] **I.** *n* **1.** (*mine*) carrière *f* **2.** *fig* proie *f* **II.** <-ie-> *vt* **1.** (*extract: mineral*) extraire **2.** (*cut into: hillside*) creuser

quart [kwɔːt, *Am:* kwɔːrt] *n* **1.** *Brit: 1,136 litres,* pinte *f Québec* **2.** *Am: 0,946 litres* ►**to be like putting a ~ into a pint pot** *Brit* tenter l'impossible

quarter ['kwɔːtə(r), *Am:* 'kwɔːrt̬ɚ] **I.** *n* **1.** (*one fourth*) quart *m;* **three ~s** trois quarts; **a ~ of an hour** un quart d'heure **2.** (*15 minutes*) **a ~ to three** trois heures moins (le) quart; **a ~ past** [*o Am* **after**] **three** trois heures et quart **3.** (*1/4 of year, school term*) trimestre *m* **4.** *Am* (*25 cents coin*) pièce *f* de 25 cents; (*sum*) 25 cents *m* **5.** (*neighbourhood*) quartier *m;* **at close ~s** de près; **from all ~s** de tous côtés **6.** (*mercy*) quartier *m;* **to give no ~** ne pas faire de quartier **7.** *pl* (*unspecified group or person*) milieu *m;* **there have been protests from some ~s** il y a eu des protestations de la part de certains **8.** (*area of compass*) quart *m;* **from the north ~** du quart nord **II.** *vt* **1.** (*cut into four*) **to ~ sth** couper qc en quatre **2.** *pass* (*give housing*) **to be ~ed** être cantonné **III.** *adj* quart de; **a ~ hour** un quart d'heure; **a ~ pound** ≈ 100 grammes

quarter day *n Brit* terme *m* **quarterdeck** *n* NAUT pont *m* arrière **quarterfinal** *n* quart *m* de finale; **in the ~s** aux quarts de finale

quarterly ['kwɔːtəlɪ, *Am:* 'kwɔːrt̬ɚlɪ] **I.** *adv* par trimestre **II.** *adj* (*magazine*) trimestriel(le)

quartermaster *n* MIL intendant(e) *m(f)*

quarter-tone *n* MUS quart *m* de ton

quartet, **quartette** [kwɔː'tet, *Am:* kwɔːr-] *n* MUS quatuor *m*

quartz [kwɔːts, *Am:* kwɔːrts] *n no pl* quartz *m*

quartz clock *n* pendule *f* à quartz **quartz lamp** *n* lampe *f* à quartz **quartz watch** *n* montre *f* à quartz

quasar ['kweɪzɑː(r), *Am:* -zɑːr] *n* ASTR quasar *m*

quash [kwɒʃ, *Am:* kwɑːʃ] *vt* **1.** (*suppress: rebellion*) écraser; (*suggestion, objection*) balayer; (*rumours*) faire taire; (*dreams, hopes, plans*) anéantir **2.** LAW (*conviction, verdict, sentence*) casser; (*law, bill, writ*) annuler

quasi- ['kwɑːsɪ, *Am:* 'kweɪsaɪ] *in compounds* quasi

quatrain ['kwɒtreɪn, *Am:* 'kwɑːtreɪn] *n* LIT quatrain *m*

quaver ['kweɪvə(r), *Am:* -vɚ] **I.** *vi* chevroter **II.** *n* **1.** (*shake*) tremblement *m;* **a ~ in one's voice** un tremblement dans la voix **2.** *Aus, Brit* MUS croche *f*

quay [kiː] *n* quai *m*

queasy ['kwiːzɪ] *adj* **1.** (*nauseous*) **to feel ~** avoir mal au cœur; **to have a ~ stomach** avoir des haut-le-cœur **2.** (*unsettled*) mal à l'aise; (*conscience*) mauvais(e); **to feel ~ about sth** être mal à l'aise à propos de qc

Quebec [kwɪ'bek, *Am:* kwiː'bek] *n* **1.** (*province*) le Québec **2.** (*town*) Québec

queen [kwiːn] **I.** *n* **1.** (*female monarch*) *a. fig* reine *f* **2.** GAMES dame *f;* **~ of hearts** dame de cœur **3.** *pej* (*gay man*) folle *f* **II.** *vt* GAMES damer ►**to ~ it over sb** faire la grande dame avec qn

queen bee *n* **1.** ZOOL reine *f* des abeilles **2.** *pej* (*bossy woman*) femme *f* autoritaire

queenly <-ier, iest> *adj* de reine

Queen Mother *n* reine *f* mère **Queen's Counsel** *n Brit* LAW *avocat le plus haut placé dans l'échelle hiérarchique* **Queen's English** *n no pl, Brit* anglais *m* correct; **to speak ~** parler un anglais correct

queer [kwɪə(r), *Am:* kwɪr] **I.** <-er, -est> *adj* **1.** (*strange: ideas*) bizarre; **to feel rather ~** ne pas se sentir bien; **to be a ~ fish** être un drôle de numéro; **to be ~ in the head** être toqué **2.** *pej* (*homosexual*) pédé **II.** *n pej* (*a homosexual*) pédé *m* **III.** *vt* **to ~ sb's pitch** *Aus, Brit, inf* gâcher les projets de qn

quell [kwel] *vt* **1.** (*put an end: unrest, rebellion*) réprimer; (*emotions*) apaiser **2.** (*silence, subdue*) faire taire; **to ~ sb with a look** faire taire qn du regard

quench [kwentʃ] *vt* **1.** (*satisfy*) **to ~ sb's thirst** étancher la soif de qn **2.** (*put out: fire*) éteindre **3.** (*suppress: anger, desire, enthusiasm*) réprimer

querulous ['kwerʊləs, *Am:* 'kwerjə-] *adj* geignard(e); **in a ~ voice** d'un ton geignard

query ['kwɪərɪ, *Am:* 'kwɪrɪ] **I.** <-ies> *n* **1.** (*question*) question *f;* **there's a ~ over sth** il y a des doutes sur qc **2.** INFOR requête *f* **II.** <-ie-> *vt* **1.** (*ask*) demander; **to ~ whether ...** (se) demander si ... **2.** (*check: bill*) faire vérifier **III.** *vi* (se) demander

quest [kwest] *n* recherche *f;* **in ~ of sb/sth** à la recherche de qn/qc; **the ~ for truth** la quête de la vérité; **our ~ to save lives** notre mission de sauver des vies

question ['kwestʃən] **I.** *n* **1.** (*inquiry*) *a.* SCHOOL, UNIV question *f;* **to ask sb a ~** poser une question à qn; **frequently asked ~s** INFOR questions *fpl* courantes, foire *f* aux questions **2.** LING interrogation *f* **3.** *no pl* (*doubt*) **without ~** sans aucun doute; **to be beyond ~** ne pas faire de doute; **to come into ~** être mis en

Q

doute; **it's open to** ~ cela se discute; **to call sth into** ~ mettre qc en doute **4.** (*issue*) question *f;* **to be a** ~ **of time/money** être une question de temps/d'argent; **to be out of the** ~ être hors de question; **there's no** ~ **of sb doing sth** il est hors de question que qn fasse qc (*subj*); **the time/place in** ~ le lieu en question **II.** *vt* **1.** (*ask*) questionner **2.** (*interrogate*) *a.* SCHOOL interroger **3.** (*doubt: ability, facts, findings*) mettre en doute; **I'd** ~ **whether that's true** je me pose la question si c'est vrai

questionable *adj* discutable

questioner *n* interrogateur, -trice *m, f*

questioning I. *n no pl* interrogatoire *m;* **to be taken in for** ~ être conduit à un interrogatoire **II.** *adj* (*look*) interrogateur(-trice); (*mind*) curieux(-euse)

question mark *n* point *m* d'interrogation **question master** *n Brit* animateur, -trice *m, f* de jeu

questionnaire [ˌk(w)estʃəˈneə(r), *Am:* ˌkwestʃəˈner] *n* questionnaire *m*

question time *n Brit* POL *séance de questions-réponses entre les députés et les ministres*

queue [kjuː] **I.** *n Aus, Brit* **1.** (*line*) queue *f;* (*in traffic*) file *f;* **to be in a** ~ **for sth** faire la queue pour qc; **to join a** ~ se mettre à la queue; **to jump the** ~ passer devant tout le monde **2.** INFOR file *f* d'attente **II.** *vi* **1.** (*wait*) faire la queue; **to** ~ **for sth/to** +*infin* faire la queue pour qc/pour +*infin* **2.** INFOR être en file d'attente

◆**queue up** *s.* **queue**

quibble [ˈkwɪbl] **I.** *n* chicane *f* **II.** *vi* chicaner

quibbler [ˈkwɪblə(r), *Am:* -lɚ] *n pej* chicanier, -ère *m, f*

quibbling [ˈkwɪblɪŋ] **I.** *n no pl* chicaneries *fpl* **II.** *adj* chicanier(-ère)

quiche [kiːʃ] *n* quiche *f*

quick [kwɪk] **I.** <-er, -est> *adj* **1.** (*fast: answer, succession*) rapide; ~ **as lightning** rapide comme l'éclair; **to have a** ~ **one** (*drink*) s'en jeter un petit; **to have a** ~ **sandwich** manger un sandwich sur le pouce; **to give sb a** ~ **call** passer un petit coup de fil à qn; **to give sb a** ~ **kiss** donner un petit bisou à qn; **the** ~**est way** le chemin le plus rapide; **to have a** ~ **temper** s'emporter facilement; **to be a** ~ **learner** apprendre vite; **he's** ~ **to point out problems** il est rapide quand il s'agit de voir un problème **2.** (*smart*) vif(vive); **to have a** ~ **mind** être vif d'esprit; ~ **thinking** rapidité d'esprit **II.** <-er, -est> *adv* vite; **as** ~ **as possible** aussi vite que possible; **to get rich** ~ s'enrichir rapidement **III.** *interj* vite! **IV.** *n* (*edge of digit*) **to bite/cut nails to the** ~ se ronger les ongles jusqu'au sang; **to cut sb to the** ~ *fig* piquer qn au vif

quick-acting *adj* **to be** ~ agir vite

quicken [ˈkwɪkən] **I.** *vt* **1.** (*make faster: pace*) accélérer **2.** (*awaken: curiosity, interest*) aiguiser; (*imagination*) exciter **II.** *vi* **1.** (*increase speed*) accélérer **2.** (*become alive*) s'éveiller

quick-fire *adj* rapide **quick-frozen** *adj* surgelé(e)

quickie [ˈkwɪkɪ] **I.** *n* **1.** *inf* (*fast thing*) **to make it a** ~ se dépêcher **2.** *inf* **to have a** ~ (*fast drink*) s'en jeter un petit **II.** *adj* (*divorce*) rapide

quicklime *n no pl* chaux *f* vive

quickly *adv* vite; **the report was** ~ **written** le rapport a été écrit rapidement

quickness *n no pl* rapidité *f*

quicksand [ˈkwɪksænd] *n no pl* sables *mpl* mouvants

quicksilver [ˈkwɪksɪlvə(r), *Am:* -vɚ] *n no pl s.* **mercury** vif-argent *m*

quickstep [ˈkwɪkstep] *n no pl* **1.** (*dance*) quickstep *m* **2.** MUS musique *f* rapide

quick-tempered *adj* **to be** ~ s'emporter facilement **quick-witted** *adj* vif(vive)

quid¹ [kwɪd] *n Brit, inf* (*pounds*) livre *f* ►**to be** ~**s** **in** être peinard; **to be not the** **full** ~ *Aus* être un peu toqué

quid² [kwɪd] *n inf* (*chewing tobacco*) chique *f*

quid pro quo [ˈkwɪdprəʊˈkwəʊ, *Am:* -proʊˈkwoʊ] *n* compensation *f*

quiescent [kwɪˈesnt, *Am:* kwaɪˈ-] *adj form* tranquille

quiet [ˈkwaɪət] **I.** *n no pl* **1.** (*silence*) silence *m* **2.** (*unexcitement*) calme *m* ►**on the** ~ en cachette; **to get married on the** ~ se marier en douce **II.** *adj* **1.** (*not loud*) doux(douce); (*voice*) bas(se) **2.** (*silent*) tranquille; **be** ~ tais-toi; **to keep** ~ se tenir tranquille; **to keep sb** ~ (*with activity*) tenir qn tranquille; (*with bribe*) faire taire qn **3.** (*secret: arrangement*) caché(e); **to keep sth** ~**, keep** ~ **about sth** garder qc pour soi; **to have a** ~ **word with sb** glisser discrètement un mot à l'oreille de qn **4.** (*unostentatious*) simple; (*clothes*) sobre; (*wedding*) intime **5.** (*calm*) calme; **they're a** ~ **couple** c'est un couple discret; **to have a** ~ **night in** passer une soirée tranquille à la maison

quieten [ˈkwaɪətn] *vi, vt* **1.** (*calm*) calmer **2.** (*allay*) apaiser

◆**quieten down I.** *vi* **1.** (*become quiet*) se taire **2.** (*calm*) se calmer **II.** *vt* **1.** (*silence*) calmer **2.** (*calm* (*down*)) apaiser

quietly *adv* **1.** (*silently*) silencieusement **2.** (*behaving well: play*) sagement **3.** (*speaking*) doucement **4.** (*peacefully*) paisiblement **5.** (*discreetly*) discrètement; **to be** ~ **confident** être calme et sûr de soi

quietness *n no pl* (*calm*) tranquillité *f*

quiff [kwɪf] *n* toupet *m*

quill [kwɪl] *n* **1.** (*feather*) penne *f* **2.** (*on porcupine*) piquant *m* **3.** (*pen*) plume *f* d'oie

quilt [kwɪlt] **I.** *n* édredon *m;* **continental** ~ couette *f* **II.** *vt* piquer

quin [kwɪn] *n Brit abbr of* **quintuplet**

quince [kwɪns] *n* coing *m*

quinine [kwɪˈniːn, *Am:* ˈkwaɪnaɪn] *n no pl*

quinine *f*
quintessential [ˌkwɪntɪ'sentʃəl, *Am:* -te'sen-] *adj* (*typical*) **the ~ sth** l'archétype de qc
quintet(te) [kwɪn'tet] *n* MUS quintette *m*
quintuple ['kwɪntjʊpl, *Am:* kwɪn'tuː-] **I.** *adj* quintuple **II.** *vt* quintupler **III.** *vi* se quintupler
quintuplet ['kwɪntjuːplet, *Am:* kwɪn'tʌplɪt] *n* quintuplé(e) *m(f)*
quip [kwɪp] *n* bon mot *m*
quirk [kwɜːk, *Am:* kwɜːrk] *n* **1.** (*habit*) excentricité *f* **2.** (*oddity*) bizarrerie *f*
quit [kwɪt] **I.** *vt* **1.** (*leave*) *a.* INFOR quitter; **to ~ one's job** démissionner **2.** (*stop*) abandonner; **~ bothering me** arrête de m'embêter **II.** *vi* **1.** (*give up*) abandonner **2.** (*resign*) démissionner
quite [kwaɪt] **I.** *adv* **1.** (*fairly*) assez; **~ a distance** assez loin; **~ a lot of money/letters** vraiment beaucoup d'argent/de lettres **2.** (*completely*) complètement; (*different*) tout à fait; **it's ~ simple** c'est très simple **3.** (*exactly*) tout à fait; **that's not ~ right** ce n'est pas tout à fait exact; **he didn't ~ succeed** il n'a pas vraiment réussi; **I don't ~ understand** je n'ai pas tout à fait compris; **~ the wrong way to do it** vraiment la mauvaise manière de s'y prendre; **~ the opposite** plutôt le contraire **4.** (*really*) véritable; **it was ~ a struggle** c'était vraiment difficile; **it's been ~ a day!** quelle journée!; **he's ~ the hero, isn't he?** *iron* c'est tout à fait un héros, n'est-ce pas? **II.** *interj* c'est ça!
quits [kwɪts] *adj* **to be ~ with sb** être quitte envers qn; **to call it ~** en rester là
quiver¹ ['kwɪvə(r), *Am:* -ɚ] **I.** *n* (*shiver*) tremblement *m;* (*excitement, fear*) frisson *m* **II.** *vi* frémir; **to ~ with rage** trembler de colère
quiver² ['kwɪvə(r), *Am:* -ɚ] *n* carquois *m*
quiz [kwɪz] **I.** <-es> *n* **1.** (*game*) jeu-concours *m* **2.** *Am* (*short test*) contrôle-surprise *m* **II.** *vt* questionner
quiz show *n* jeu-concours *m* **quizmaster** *n* animateur, -trice *m, f* de jeu
quizzical ['kwɪzɪkl] *adj* **1.** (*questioning*) perplexe **2.** (*teasing*) moqueur(-euse)
quoit [kɔɪt, *Am:* kwɔɪt] *n Am* palet *m*
quorum ['kwɔːrəm] *n* quorum *m*
quota ['kwəʊtə, *Am:* 'kwoʊt̬ə] *n* **1.** (*allowance*) quota *m;* (*export, import*) contingent *m* **2.** (*ration*) dose *f*
quotable *adj* digne d'être cité
quotation [kwəʊ'teɪʃn, *Am:* kwoʊ'-] *n* **1.** (*words*) citation *f* **2.** (*estimate*) devis *m* **3.** FIN cotation *f*
quotation marks *npl* guillemets *mpl*
quote [kwəʊt, *Am:* kwoʊt] **I.** *n* **1.** *inf* (*quotation*) citation *f* **2.** *pl, inf* (*punctuation*) guillemets *mpl* **3.** *inf* (*estimate*) devis *m* ►**~ … unquote** je cite … fin de citation **II.** *vt* **1.** (*repeat*) citer; **the press ~d him as saying sth** selon les journaux, il aurait dit qc **2.** (*give: price*) établir; **we were ~d £650** le devis était de 650£ **3.** FIN **to be ~d on the Stock Exchange** être coté en Bourse **III.** *vi* citer
quotidian [kwəʊ'tɪdɪən, *Am:* kwoʊ'-] *adj form* quotidien(ne)
quotient ['kwəʊʃnt, *Am:* 'kwoʊ-] *n* quotient *m*
qv [ˌkjuː'viː] *abbr of* **quod vide** cf.
qwerty keyboard [ˌkwɜːtɪ'kiːbɔːd, *Am:* ˌkwɜːrt̬ɪ'kiːbɔːrd] *n* clavier *m* qwerty

R

R, r [ɑːʳ, *Am:* ɑːr] <-'s *o* -s> *n* R *m,* r *m;* **~ as in Robert** *Brit,* **~ as in Roger** *Am* (*on telephone*), **~ for Robert** *Brit,* **~ for Roger** *Am* r comme Raoul
r. [ɑːʳ, *Am:* ɑːr] SPORT *abbr of* **run** point *m*
R [ɑːʳ, *Am:* ɑːr] **I.** *n* **1.** *abbr of* **resistance** résistance *f* **2.** *abbr of* **River** rivière *f* **II.** *adj Am abbr of* **restricted** interdit aux moins de dix-sept ans
rabbi ['ræbaɪ] *n* rabbin *m*
rabbit ['ræbɪt] **I.** *n* lapin *m;* **wild ~** lapin de garenne **II.** *vi Brit, Aus, pej, inf* **what are you rabbiting on about?** que nous racontes-tu là?
rabbit burrow *n* terrier *m* (de lapin) **rabbit food** *n iron* crudités *fpl* **rabbit hole** *n s.* **rabbit burrow** **rabbit hutch** *n* clapier *m* **rabbit punch** <-es> *n* coup *m* de lapin **rabbit skin** *n* peau *f* de lapin
rabble ['ræbl] *n no pl* **1.** *pej* (*mob*) cohue *f* **2.** *pej* SOCIOL **the ~** la populace
rabble-rouser *n* agitateur, -trice *m, f* **rabble-rousing** **I.** *n* incitation *f* à la révolte **II.** *adj* qui incite à la révolte
rabid ['ræbɪd] *adj* **1.** *pej* (*fervent*) mordu(e) **2.** (*fanatical*) fanatique **3.** (*suffering from rabies*) enragé(e)
rabies ['reɪbiːz] *n + sing vb* la rage
RAC [ˌɑːreɪ'siː] *n Brit abbr of* **Royal Automobile Club** *organisme britannique d'assistance pour les automobilistes*
raccoon [rə'kuːn, *Am:* ræk'uːn] *n* raton *m* laveur
race¹ [reɪs] **I.** *n* **1.** SPORT **a 100-metre ~** un cent mètres **2.** (*contest*) course *f;* **the ~ for the presidency** la course à la présidence ►**a ~ against time** une course contre la montre **II.** *vi* **1.** (*compete*) courir; **to ~ against sb** faire la course avec qn; **to ~ each other** se faire la course **2.** (*rush*) aller à toute allure; (*heart, engine*) s'emballer; **to ~ along/past** aller/passer à toute vitesse **3.** (*hurry*) se dépêcher; **to ~ for a bus** se dépêcher pour attraper un bus **III.** *vt* **1.** (*compete with*) faire la course avec **2.** (*enter for races*) faire courir **3.** (*rev up*) emballer **4.** (*transport*) emmener à toute vitesse
race² [reɪs] *n no pl* (*grouping*) race *f*
race³ [reɪs] *n* GEO canal *m*

race conflict *n no pl* conflit *m* racial **racecourse** *n* champ *m* de courses **race hatred** *n no pl* haine *f* raciale **racehorse** *n* cheval *m* de course **race meet** *n Am,* **race meeting** *n* courses *fpl*
racer *n* coureur, -euse *m, f*
race relations *npl* relations *fpl* interraciales **race riot** *n* émeute *f* raciale
racial ['reɪʃl] *adj* racial(e)
racialism ['reɪʃəlɪzəm] *n Brit no pl* racisme *m*
racialist I. *n Brit* raciste *mf* II. *adj* raciste
raciness ['reɪsɪnɪs] *n no pl* 1. (*excitement*) verve *f* 2. (*suggestiveness*) grivoiserie *f*
racing *n* 1. (*act of racing*) course *f* 2. (*races: horses*) les courses *fpl;* (*cars, cycles*) la course *f*
racing bicycle, **racing bike** *n inf* vélo *m* de course **racing car** *n* voiture *f* de course **racing driver** *n* pilote *mf* automobile **racing pigeon** *n* pigeon *m* voyageur de compétition **racing stable** *n* écurie *f* de course **racing yacht** *n* yacht *m* de course
racism ['reɪsɪzəm] *n no pl* racisme *m*
racist I. *n* raciste *mf* II. *adj* raciste
rack [ræk] I. *n* 1. (*frame, shelf*) étagère *f;* (*for the oven*) grille *f;* (*for dishes*) égouttoir *m;* (*in dishwasher*) panier *m* 2. (*joint*) ~ **of lamb** carré *m* d'agneau 3. (*torture*) chevalet *m* de torture; **to be on the** ~ *fig* être au supplice 4. *Am, inf* (*bed*) pieu *m* II. *vt* (*hurt*) torturer; **to be ~ed with doubts** être tiraillé par les doutes ▶**to ~ one's brains** se creuser la tête
racket ['rækɪt] *n* 1. SPORT raquette *f* 2. *pl* (*games*) jeu *m* de paume 3. *no pl, inf* (*noise*) vacarme *m* 4. *pej* (*dishonest scheme*) escroquerie *f*
racketeer [,rækɪ'tɪəʳ, *Am:* -ə'tɪr] *n pej* racketteur *m*
racking *adj* épouvantable; (*pain*) atroce
rack-rent *n* loyer *m* exorbitant
racoon *n s.* **raccoon**
racy ['reɪsɪ] <-ier, -iest> *adj* 1. (*lively*) piquant(e); (*person*) plein(e) de vie 2. (*titillating*) émoustillant(e)
radar ['reɪdɑːʳ, *Am:* -dɑːr] *n no pl* radar *m*
radar scanner *n* balayeur *m* radar **radar station** *n* station *f* radar **radar trap** *n* contrôle *m* radar
radial ['reɪdɪəl] *adj* radial(e)
radiant ['reɪdɪənt] *adj* 1. (*shining*) rayonnant(e); (*heat*) radiant(e) 2. (*happy*) radieux(-euse) 3. (*beautiful*) éblouissant(e)
radiate ['reɪdɪeɪt] I. *vi* 1. (*emit rays*) rayonner 2. (*emanate: emotion*) émaner; (*paths*) diverger II. *vt* 1. (*emit*) émettre; **to ~ energy/light** émettre de la lumière/de l'énergie; **to ~ heat** dégager de la chaleur 2. (*display*) répandre
radiation *n no pl* (*waves*) radiation *f;* (*light*) irradiation *f;* (*heat*) rayonnement *m;* ~ **levels** niveaux *mpl* de radiation
radiation therapy *n* radiothérapie *f*
radiator ['reɪdɪeɪtəʳ, *Am:* -t̬ɚ] *n* radiateur *m*
radiator cap *n* bouchon *m* de radiateur **radiator grille** *n* AUTO calandre *f*
radical ['rædɪkl] I. *n* 1. (*person*) radical(e) *m(f)* 2. CHEM radical *m* II. *adj* radical(e)
radicalism ['rædɪkəlɪzəm] *n no pl* radicalisme *m*
radicle ['rædɪkl] *n* (*radical*) radical *m*
radio ['reɪdɪəʊ, *Am:* -oʊ] I. *n* 1. *no pl* (*communication, broadcasting*) radio *f;* **on the** ~ à la radio; **over the** ~ sur les ondes radio 2. (*device*) (poste *m* de) radio *f* II. *vt* (*call*) contacter par radio; (*send*) envoyer par radio III. *vi* envoyer un message par radio
radioactive [,reɪdɪəʊ'æktɪv, *Am:* -oʊ'-] *adj* radioactif(-ive)
radioactivity *n no pl* radioactivité *f*
radio alarm, **radio alarm clock** *n* radio-réveil *m* **radio amateur** *n* radioamateur *m* **radio beacon** *n* radiophare *m* **radio broadcast** *n* émission *f* radiophonique
radiocarbon dating [,reɪdɪəʊkɑːbən'deɪtɪŋ, *Am:* -oʊkɑːrbən'deɪt̬-] *n no pl* datation *f* au carbone 14
radio cassette recorder *n* radiocassette *m* **radio communication** *n no pl* contact *m* radio **radio contact** *n* contact *m* radio **radio-controlled** *adj* télécommandé(e)
radiographer *n* radiologue *mf*
radiography [,reɪdɪ'ɒgrəfɪ, *Am:* -'ɑːgrə-] *n* radiographie *f*
radio ham *n* radioamateur *m*
radiologist *n* radiologue *mf*
radiology [,reɪdɪ'ɒlədʒɪ, *Am:* -'ɑːlə-] *n no pl* radiologie *f*
radio message *n* message *m* radio **radio operator** *n* opérateur-radio, opératrice-radio *m, f* **radiopager** *n* récepteur *m* de radiomessagerie **radio programme** *n* 1. (*broadcast*) émission *f* de radio 2. (*schedule*) programme *m* radio
radioscopy [,reɪdɪ'ɒskəpɪ] *n no pl* MED radioscopie *f*
radio set *n* poste *m* radio **radio station** *n* station *f* de radio; **local** ~ radio *f* locale **radiotelephone** *n* radiotéléphone *m* **radio telescope** *n* radiotélescope *m* **radiotherapy** *n no pl* radiothérapie *f* **radio transmitter** *n* poste *m* émetteur **radio wave** *n* onde *f* hertzienne
radish ['rædɪʃ] <-es> *n* radis *m*
radium ['reɪdɪəm] *n no pl* radium *m*
radium treatment *n* radiumthérapie *f*
radius ['reɪdɪəs] <-dii> *n* 1. (*half of diameter*) rayon *m* 2. ANAT radius *m*
RAF [ɑːʳeɪ'ef, *Am:* ,ɑːr-] *n abbr of* **Royal Air Force** *armée de l'air britannique*
raffia ['ræfɪə] *n no pl* raphia *m*
raffle ['ræfl] I. *n* tombola *f* II. *vt* mettre en tombola
raft [rɑːft, *Am:* ræft] I. *n* 1. (*flat vessel*) radeau *m* 2. *Am* (*a lot*) **a ~ of sth** une montagne de qc II. *vi* **to ~ across/down the river**

traverser/descendre la rivière en radeau **III.** *vt* **to ~ wood** flotter en trains

rafter *n* **1.** ARCHIT chevron *m* **2.** (*raft user*) personne *f* qui fait du radeau

rafting *n* rafting *m*

rag [ræg] **I.** *n* **1.** (*cloth*) lambeau *m* **2.** *pl* (*old clothes*) guenilles *fpl* **3.** *Am* (*duster*) chiffon *m* à épousseter **4.** *Brit* (*student event*) *kermesse d'étudiants* **5.** *pej, inf* (*newspaper*) torchon *m* **6.** (*ragtime music*) ragtime *m* **II.** <-gg-> *vt inf* taquiner

ragbag ['rægbæg] **I.** *n* sac *m* à chiffons **II.** *adj* varié(e)

rage [reɪdʒ] **I.** *n* **1.** (*anger*) colère *f*; **to be in a ~** être furieux **2.** *Aus, inf* (*event*) succès *m* ▶**to be all the ~** faire fureur **II.** *vi* **1.** (*express fury*) **to ~ at sb/sth** fulminer contre qn/qc **2.** (*continue: battle*) faire rage; (*epidemic*) sévir; (*sea*) être démonté **3.** (*blow violently: wind*) souffler en tempête

ragged *adj* **1.** (*torn*) en lambeaux; (*clothes*) en haillons **2.** (*wearing rags: children*) en guenilles; (*appearance*) négligé(e) **3.** (*rough*) dentelé(e); (*coastline*) découpé(e) **4.** (*irregular*) irrégulier(-ère) **5.** (*disorderly*) désordonné(e)

raging *adj* **1.** (*angry*) furieux(-euse) **2.** METEO violent(e); (*sea*) démonté(e) **3.** (*burning fiercely*) ardent(e); **a ~ inferno** un véritable brasier **4.** (*severe*) fort(e); **a ~ toothache** une rage de dents **5.** (*extreme*) **it was a ~ bore** c'était ennuyeux à en mourir

ragout ['rægu:, *Am:* ræg'u:] *n no pl* ragoût *m*

ragtag I. *n* **~ (and bobtail)** racaille *f inf* **II.** *adj* hétéroclite

ragtime *n no pl* ragtime *m*

rag trade *n inf* confection *f*

rai [reɪ] *n* MUS raï *m*

raid [reɪd] **I.** *n* **1.** (*attack*) raid *m* **2.** (*robbery*) hold-up *m inv* **3.** (*search*) descente *f* **II.** *vt* **1.** (*attack*) lancer un raid contre **2.** (*search*) faire une descente dans **3.** (*rob*) attaquer; **to ~ the fridge** *fig* faire une razzia dans le frigidaire; **to ~ sb's handbag** vider le sac de qn

rail [reɪl] **I.** *n* **1.** (*for trains*) rail *m*; **by ~** en train; **~ ticket** billet *m* de train; **to go off the ~s** sortir des rails; *fig* s'écarter du droit chemin **2.** (*fence*) barre *f*; (*on track*) corde *f*; (*for protection*) garde-fou *m* **3.** (*to hang things*) tringle *f* **II.** *vt* transporter par train

◆**rail against** *vt* s'en prendre à

◆**rail off** *vt* fermer à l'aide d'une barrière

railcar *n* autorail *m* **railcard** *n Brit: carte de réduction d'une compagnie ferroviaire* **railhead** *n* tête *f* de ligne

railing *n pl* grille *f*; **a wooden ~** une palissade

railroad I. *n Am* **1.** (*track*) voie *f* ferrée **2.** (*system*) chemin *m* de fer **II.** *vt inf* imposer; **to ~ sb into doing sth** forcer qn à faire qc

railroad crossing *n* passage *m* à niveau **railroad embankment** *n* remblai *m* **railroad schedule** *n* horaire *m* des chemins de fer **railroad strike** *n* grève *f* des employés des chemins de fer **railroad track** *n* voie *f* ferrée

railway *n Brit* **1.** (*train tracks*) voie *f* ferrée **2.** (*rail system*) chemin *m* de fer; **the French ~s** les chemins de fer français

railway bridge *n* pont *m* ferroviaire **railway carriage** *n* voiture *f* wagon **railway crossing** *n* passage *m* à niveau **railway embankment** *n* remblai *m* **railway engine** *n* locomotive *f* **railway guide** *n* indicateur *m* des chemins de fer **railway line** *n* **1.** (*track*) voie *f* ferrée **2.** (*system*) ligne *f* de chemin de fer **railwayman** <-men> *n* cheminot *m* **railway network** *n* réseau *m* ferroviaire **railway station** *n* gare *f* ferroviaire **railway timetable** *n* horaire *m* des chemins de fer **railway track** *n* voie *f* ferrée

rain [reɪn] **I.** *n no pl* **1.** (*precipitation*) pluie *f*; **heavy/gentle ~** pluie battante/fine; **in the ~** sous la pluie; **to be caught in the ~** être surpris par la pluie **2.** *pl* (*season*) saison *f* des pluies ▶**come ~ or shine** qu'il pleuve ou qu'il vente **II.** *vi* pleuvoir **III.** *vt fig* **to ~ blows/questions on sb** faire pleuvoir les coups/les questions sur qn ▶**it's ~ing cats and dogs** il pleut des cordes

rain off, rain out *vt* **to be rained off** être annulé à cause de la pluie

rainbow ['reɪnbəʊ, *Am:* -boʊ] *n a. fig* arc-en-ciel *m*

rainbow coalition *n* POL coalition *f* hétéroclite

raincheck *n* **I'll take a ~** ça sera pour une autre fois

rain cloud *n* nuage *m* de pluie **raincoat** *n* imperméable *m* **raindrop** *n* goutte *f* de pluie **rainfall** *n no pl* **1.** (*period*) chute *f* de pluie **2.** (*quantity*) pluviosité *f* **rainforest** *n* forêt *m* tropicale **rain gauge** *n* pluviomètre *m* **rainproof** *adj* imperméable **rainwater** *n no pl* eau *f* de pluie

rainy <-ier, -iest> *adj* pluvieux(-euse); (*season*) des pluies

raise [reɪz] **I.** *n Am, Aus* augmentation *f* **II.** *vt* **1.** (*lift*) lever; (*blinds, curtain*) monter; (*flag*) hisser; (*eyebrows*) froncer **2.** (*cause to rise*) soulever **3.** (*rouse*) réveiller; **to ~ sb from the dead** relever qn d'entre les morts **4.** (*stir up: dust*) soulever **5.** (*increase*) augmenter; **to ~ one's voice** hausser le ton; **to ~ the tone** *iron* élever la voix **6.** (*bet more than*) **to raise sb $10** faire une relance de 10$ **7.** MAT élever **8.** (*improve*) améliorer; (*standard of living*) augmenter **9.** (*promote*) promouvoir **10.** (*arouse: laugh, murmur, cheer*) provoquer; (*doubts*) semer; (*fears*) engendrer; (*havoc*) causer; (*hopes*) faire naître; (*suspicions*) éveiller; **to ~ a smile** faire sourire **11.** (*introduce: issue, question*) soulever; **I'll ~ this with him** je lui en parlerai **12.** (*collect: funds*) rassembler; (*money*) se procurer **13.** *form* (*build: monument*) ériger **14.** (*bring up: children, family*) élever **15.** (*cultivate*) cultiver; (*cattle*) élever **16.** (*end: embargo, siege*) lever **17.** (*contact*) joindre ►**to ~ eyebrows** faire grincer des dents; **to ~ the roof** faire un bruit de tonnerre

raisin ['reɪzn] *n* raisin *m* sec

rake¹ [reɪk] *n pej* débauché *m*

rake² [reɪk] *n* (*slope*) inclinaison *f*

rake³ [reɪk] **I.** *n* (*tool*) râteau *m* **II.** *vt* ratisser

◆**rake in** *vt* **1.** (*mix*) remuer à la pelle **2.** *inf* (*earn money*) **to rake it in** remuer le fric à la pelle

◆**rake up** *vt* **1.** (*gather: leaves*) ramasser **2.** (*refer to*) remuer

rake-off *n inf* pourcentage *m*

rakish ['reɪkɪʃ] *adj* **1.** (*jaunty*) désinvolte **2.** (*immoral*) débauché(e)

rally¹ ['rælɪ] <-ies> *n* rallye *m*

rally² ['rælɪ] **I.** <-ies> *n* **1.** (*improvement*) amélioration *f;* FIN remontée *f* **2.** (*in tennis*) echange *m* **II.** <-ies, -ied> *vi* **1.** (*improve*) aller mieux; **shares rallied** les cours sont remontés **2.** SPORT faire un rallye

rally³ ['rælɪ] **I.** <-ies> *n* rassemblement *m* **II.** <-ies, -ied> *vt* **to ~ sb against/in favour of sth** rallier qn contre/à la cause de qc

◆**rally round** **I.** *vt* venir à l'aide de **II.** *vi* se rallier

rally driver *n* pilote *mf* de rallye

RAM [ræm] *n* INFOR *abbr of* **Random Access Memory** RAM *f*

ram [ræm] **I.** *n* (*male sheep*) bélier *m* **II.** <-ming, -med> *vt* (*door*) défoncer; (*car*) emboutir

Ramadan [ˌræmə'dæn, *Am:* -dɑːn] *n* Ramadan *m*

ramble ['ræmbl] **I.** *n* randonnée *f* **II.** *vi* **1.** (*hike*) se balader **2.** (*meander*) déambuler **3.** (*talk incoherently*) divaguer

rambler *n* **1.** (*walker*) randonneur, -euse *m, f* **2.** BOT rosier *m* grimpant

rambling **I.** *n pl* divagations *fpl* **II.** *adj* **1.** (*spreading: building, town*) plein(e) de dédales; (*plant*) grimpant(e); (*path*) sinueux(-euse) **2.** (*incoherent*) incohérent(e); (*speech*) décousu(e) **3.** (*wandering*) vagabond(e)

ramekin ['reɪmkɪn, *Am:* 'ræməkɪn] *n* ramequin *m*

ramification [ˌræmɪfɪ'keɪʃn] *n* ramification *f*

ramify ['ræmɪfaɪ] <-fies, -fied> *vi* ramifier

ramp [ræmp] *n* **1.** (*incline*) rampe *f* **2.** AVIAT passerelle *f* **3.** (*speed deterrent*) ralentisseur *m*

rampage [ræm'peɪdʒ, *Am:* 'ræmpeɪdʒ] **I.** *n* **to go on the ~** tout saccager **II.** <-ging> *vi* se déchaîner

rampant ['ræmpənt] *adj* endémique

rampart ['ræmpɑːt, *Am:* -pɑːrt] *n* rempart *m*

ramshackle ['ræmʃækl] *adj* **1.** (*dilapidated*) délabré(e) **2.** *pej* (*disorganized*) branlant(e)

ran [ræn] *pt of* **run**

ranch [rɑːntʃ, *Am:* ræntʃ] <-es> *n* ranch *m*

rancher *n* **1.** (*owner*) propriétaire *m* de ranch **2.** (*worker*) cow-boy *m*

rancid ['rænsɪd] *adj* rance; **to go ~** rancir

rancor *n Am, Aus s.* **rancour**

rancour ['ræŋkəʳ, *Am:* -kɚ] *n no pl* **1.** (*bitterness*) rancœur *f* **2.** (*hate*) rancune *f*

random ['rændəm] **I.** *n no pl* **at ~** au hasard **II.** *adj* fait(e) au hasard; (*sample*) prélevé(e) au hasard; (*attack, crime*) aveugle; (*error*) aléatoire

random access *n* INFOR accès *m* aléatoire

random access memory *n* INFOR mémoire *f* vive

randy ['rændɪ] <-ier, -iest> *adj Brit, inf* en chaleur

rang [ræŋ] *pt of* **ring**

range [reɪndʒ] **I.** *n no pl* **1.** (*distance covered: of a weapon*) portée *f;* (*of a plane*) rayon *m* d'action; (*of action*) champ *m;* **at a ~ of** à une distance de; **at long ~** à longue portée; **within one's ~** à sa portée; **at close ~** à bout portant; **out of ~** hors de portée **2.** (*scope: of vision, hearing*) champ *m;* (*of voice*) étendue *f;* (*of ability*) répertoire *m;* **to be out of ~** être hors d'atteinte **3.** (*spread, selection: of products, colors*) gamme *f;* (*products, sizes, patterns*) choix *m;* (*of temperatures*) écart *m;* (*of prices, jobs, possibilities*) éventail *m;* (*of fashion*) collection *f;* **a wide ~ of products** une grande gamme de produits; **a narrow ~ of products** une gamme limitée de produits; **a full ~ of sth** un assortiment complet de qc; **that is beyond my price ~** cela dépasse ma tranche de prix; **a car at the top of the ~** une voiture huat de gamme **4.** (*sphere, domain: of activity*) champ *m;* (*of knowledge*) étendue *f;* (*of influence, research*) domaine *m;* **beyond sb's ~ of competence** au-delà de la compétence de qn **5.** (*row: of buildings*) rangée *f;* (*of mountains*) chaîne *f* **6.** (*shooting ~*) champ *m* de tir **7.** *Brit* (*large stove*) fourneau *m* **8.** *Am* (*feeding land*) prairie *f* **II.** *vi* **1.** (*vary*) varier; **to ~ between sth and sth** varier entre qc et qc; **to ~ from sth to sth** aller de qc à qc **2.** (*wander*) errer **3.** (*travel*) parcourir **4.** (*be placed in a row*) s'aligner **5.** (*deal with*) **to ~ over sth** couvrir qc **6.** (*cover a distance*) **to ~ over sth** avoir une portée de qc; (*eyes*) parcourir qc **III.** *vt* aligner; **to ~ oneself against sb/sth** s'aligner contre qn/qc

rangefinder *n* télémètre *m*

ranger *n* garde *m* forestier; **park ~** gardien(ne) *m(f)* de parc national

rangy <-ier, -iest> *adj* sans une once de graisse

rank¹ [ræŋk] **I.** *n* **1.** *no pl* (*position*) rang *m;* **the top ~s of government** les hautes sphères du pouvoir; **to pull ~** profiter de son statut **2.** MIL rang *m;* **to close ~s** *a. fig* serrer les rangs; **the ~s** les hommes du rang; **to rise from the ~s** sortir du rang; **to join the ~s** aller à l'armée **3.** (*members of a group*) rang *m;* **the ~s of racing drivers** les rangs de coureurs automobiles **4.** (*row or line*) rangée *f;* (*for taxis*) station *f* **II.** *vi* se classer; **to ~ above sb**

être supérieur à qn; **to ~ as sb/sth** être reconnu comme qn/qc **III.** *vt* classer; **to ~ sb among sb/sth** compter qn parmi qn/qc; **to ~ sth among sth** classer qc comme qc

rank² [ræŋk] *adj* **1.**(*absolute*) parfait(e) **2.**(*growing thickly: plant*) luxuriant(e) **3.**(*overgrown*) envahi(e) **4.**(*smelling unpleasant*) nauséabond(e)

ranking officer *n Am* (*officer in charge*) officier *m* responsable

rankle ['ræŋkl] *vi* rester sur le cœur; **it ~s with me** ça me reste sur le cœur

ransack ['rænsæk] *vt* **1.**(*search*) fouiller **2.**(*plunder*) mettre à sac **3.**(*rob*) piller

ransom ['rænsəm] **I.** *n* rançon *f;* **to hold sb/sth to ~** mettre qn/qc à rançon; *fig* exercer un chantage sur qn/qc; **to be held to ~** *fig* avoir le couteau sous la gorge ►**a king's ~** une somme fabuleuse **II.** *vt* racheter

rant [rænt] **I.** *n* vitupération *f* **II.** *vi* déblatérer; **to ~ and rave** tempêter

rap [ræp] **I.** *n* **1.**(*sharp knock*) coup *m* sec **2.** *no pl* (*music style*) rap *m* **3.** *Am, inf* (*talk*) causette *f* ►**to get a ~ on the knuckles** taper sur les doigts; **to beat the ~** échapper à une condamnation; **to take the ~** payer, (pour le crime d'un autre) **II.** *adj* **1.**(*related to music*) (de) rap; **a ~ artist** un(e) rappeur(-euse) **2.** *Am, inf* (*related to chat*) **to have a ~ session** tailler une bavette **III.** <-ping, -ped> *vt* **1.**(*hit sharply*) frapper à **2.**(*criticize*) réprouver ►**to get one's knuckles ~ped** [*o* **to be ~ped on the knuckles**] se faire taper sur les doigts **IV.** *vi* **1.**(*hit*) frapper **2.**(*sing*) rapper **3.** *Am, inf* (*talk*) tchatcher

rapacious [rə'peɪʃəs] *adj form* rapace

rapacity [rə'pæsətɪ, *Am:* -t̬ɪ] *n no pl* rapacité *f*

rape [reɪp] **I.** *n* **1.** *no pl* (*sexual attack*) viol *m* **2.** BOT colza *m* **II.** *vt* violer

rapid ['ræpɪd] **I.** *adj* rapide **II.** *n pl* rapides *mpl*

rapidity [rə'pɪdətɪ, *Am:* -t̬ɪ] *n no pl* rapidité *f*

Rapid Reaction Force *n* MIL Force *f* d'intervention rapide

rapier ['reɪpɪəʳ, *Am:* -ɚ] *n* rapière *f*

rapist ['reɪpɪst] *n* violeur *m*

rapper ['ræpə(r)] *n* rappeur, -euse *m, f*

rapport [ræ'pɔːʳ, *Am:* -'pɔːr] *n no pl* relation *f*

rapprochement [ræ'prɒʃmɒŋ, *Am:* ˌræprɔːʃ-] *n form no pl* rapprochement *m*

rap sheet *n Am* casier *m* judiciaire

rapt [ræpt] *adj* **1.**(*fascinated: attention*) profond(e); (*look, person*) captivé(e) **2.** *Aus, inf s.* **wrapped**

rapture ['ræptʃəʳ, *Am:* -tʃɚ] *n* **1.** *no pl* (*great pleasure*) ravissement *m* **2.** *pl* (*extase*) extase *f;* **to be in ~s about sth** être ravi de qc; **to go into ~s** s'extasier

rapturous *adj* frénétique; (*reception*) délirant(e)

rare [reəʳ, *Am:* rer] *adj* **1.**(*uncommon*) rare **2.**(*undercooked*) saignant(e) **3.**(*thin*) raréfié(e) ►**to be a ~ bird** être un oiseau rare

rarebit ['reəbɪt, *Am:* 'rer-] *n* **Welsh ~** *toast au fromage*

rarefied ['reərɪfaɪd, *Am:* 'rerə-] *adj* pauvre en oxygène; *fig* loin des réalités

rarely ['reəlɪ, *Am:* 'rer-] *adv* rarement

rarity ['reərətɪ, *Am:* 'rerət̬ɪ] <-ies> *n no pl* rareté *f;* **to be something of a ~** ne pas être fréquent

rascal ['rɑːskl, *Am:* 'ræskl] *n* polisson(ne) *m(f)*

rash [ræʃ] **I.** *n* irritation *f;* **heat ~** irritation due à la chaleur; **to bring sb out in a ~** donner de l'urticaire à qn **II.** *adj* irréfléchi(e); **in a ~ moment** dans un moment d'égarement; **that was ~ of you** c'était risqué de ta part

rasher *n* tranche *f* de bacon

rashness *n no pl* imprudence *f*

rasp [rɑːsp, *Am:* ræsp] **I.** *n* **1.**(*harsh sound*) grincement *m* **2.**(*coarse file*) râpe *f* **II.** *vi* **1.**(*make a harsh sound*) grincer **2.**(*talk roughly*) crier d'une voix grinçante **3.**(*irritate*) **to ~ on sb** porter sur les nerfs de qn **III.** *vt* râper

raspberry ['rɑːzbrɪ, *Am:* 'ræzˌber-] <-ies> *n* **1.**(*fruit*) framboise *f* **2.**(*plant*) framboisier *m*

rasping *adj* râpeux(-euse)

rasta [ˌræstə, *Am:* ˌrɑːstə] **I.** *n inf* rasta *mf* **II.** *adj inf* rasta *inv*

rastafarian [ˌræstə'feərɪən, *Am:* ˌrɑːstə'ferɪ-] **I.** *n* rastafari *mf* **II.** *adj* rastafari *inv*

rat [ræt] *n* **1.**(*rodent*) rat *m* **2.** *inf* (*bad person*) ordure *f*

♦**rat on** *vt* <-tt-> *inf* trahir

ratable *adj s.* **rateable**

ratbag *n Brit, inf* vieille canaille *f*

ratchet ['rætʃɪt] *n* TECH rochet *m*

rate [reɪt] **I.** *n* **1.**(*ratio*) taux *m* **2.**(*speed*) vitesse *f;* **at a ~ of knots** à toute allure; **at a fast ~** à toute vitesse; **at a slow ~** doucement **3.**(*charge*) taux *m;* **the going ~** le taux courant; **mortgage ~s** les taux d'emprunt **4.** *pl, Aus, Brit* (*local tax*) impôts *mpl* locaux ►**at this ~** à ce compte-là; **at any ~** en tout cas **II.** *vt* **1.**(*consider*) considérer; **to ~ sb/sth as sth** considérer qn/qc comme qc; **a highly ~d journalist** un journaliste très estimé; **do you ~ him?** *inf* il est bien? **2.**(*evaluate*) évaluer **3.**(*rank, classify*) classer **4.** *Aus, Brit* FIN évaluer **5.**(*deserve*) mériter **III.** *vi* se classer; **to ~ as sth** être considéré comme qc

rateable *adj Brit* imposable

rather ['rɑːðəʳ, *Am:* 'ræðɚ] **I.** *adv* **1.**(*preferably*) plutôt; **~ than** *+infin* plutôt que de *+infin;* **I would ~ do sth/that you did sth** je préférerais faire qc/que tu fasses qc *subj;* **I'd ~ not** je ne préfère pas **2.**(*more exactly*) plus exactement; **~ … than …** plutôt … que … **3.**(*very*) assez; **he answered the telephone ~ sleepily** il répondit au téléphone quelque peu endormi; **to be ~ more expensive than …** être nettement plus cher que … **II.** *interj Brit* et comment!

ratification [ˌrætɪfɪ'keɪʃn, *Am:* ˌræt̬ə-] *n no*

pl ratification *f*
ratify ['rætɪfaɪ, *Am:* 'ræt̬ə-] <-fies, -fied> *vt* ratifier
rating[1] *n* **1.** *no pl* estimation *f* **2.** *pl* (*number of viewers*) audimat® *m*
rating[2] *n Brit* (*sailor*) matelot *m*
ratio ['reɪʃɪəʊ, *Am:* -oʊ] <-os> *n* proportion *f;* **the ~ of nurses to patients** le nombre d'infirmières par malade
ration ['ræʃn] **I.** *n* ration *f* **II.** *vt* rationner
rational *adj* logique; (*explanation*) rationnel(le)
rationale [ˌræʃə'nɑːl, *Am:* -'næl] *n* raisonnement *m*
rationalism ['ræʃnəlɪzəm] *n no pl* PHILOS rationalisme *m*
rationalist PHILOS **I.** *n* rationaliste *mf* **II.** *adj* rationaliste
rationalistic *adj* PHILOS rationaliste
rationality [ˌræʃə'næləti, *Am:* -t̬ɪ] *n no pl* rationalité *f*
rationalization *n no pl* rationalisation *f*
rationalize ['ræʃnəlaɪz] *vi, vt* rationaliser
rationing ['ræʃnɪŋ] *n no pl* rationnement *m*
rat poison *n* mort-aux-rats *f* **rat race** *n* foire *f* d'empoigne
rattle ['rætl, *Am:* 'ræt̬-] **I.** *n* **1.** *no pl* (*noise*) bruit *m;* (*of fire*) crépitement *m;* (*of keys, coins*) cliquetis *m* **2.** (*toy*) hochet *m* **3.** (*of rattlesnake*) sonnettes *fpl* **II.** <-ling, -led> *vi* (*make noises*) faire du bruit; **to ~ along** rouler dans un bruit de ferraille **III.** *vt* **1.** (*bang together*) agiter **2.** (*make nervous*) déranger; **to get ~d** paniquer
◆**rattle away** *vi* jacasser
◆**rattle off** *vt* débiter
◆**rattle on** *vi* jacasser
rattlebrain ['rætlbreɪn] *n inf* écervelé(e) *m(f)*
rattlesnake ['rætlsneɪk, *Am:* 'ræt̬-] *n* serpent *m* à sonnette
rattletrap ['rætltræp] *n inf* tacot *m*
rattling **I.** *adj* **1.** (*that rattles*) bruyant(e) **2.** (*fast*) à toute allure **II.** *adv* drôlement bon(ne)
rat trap *n* piège *m* à rats
ratty ['rætɪ, *Am:* 'ræt̬-] <-ier, -iest> *adj inf* grincheux(-euse)
raucous ['rɔːkəs, *Am:* 'rɑː-] *adj* **1.** (*loud*) rauque; (*laughter*) bruyant(e) **2.** (*noisy*) bruyant(e)
raunchy ['rɔːntʃɪ, *Am:* 'rɑːn-] <-ier, -iest> *adj* torride
ravage ['rævɪdʒ] *vt* saccager
rave [reɪv] **I.** *n* **1.** *Brit, inf* rave *f* **2.** *no pl* (*music*) ~ (**music**) rave *f* **II.** *adj* élogieux(-euse) **III.** *vi* **1.** (*talk wildly, incoherently*) délirer; **to ~ about sb/sth** divaguer à propos de qn/qc **2.** (*address in an angry way*) tempêter; **to ~ against sb/sth** s'emporter contre qn/qc **3.** (*praise*) s'extasier; **to ~ about sb/sth** faire l'éloge de qn/qc **4.** (*attend a rave party*) être en rave
raven ['reɪvn] *n* (*bird*) corbeau *m*
ravenous *adj* vorace
ravine [rə'viːn] *n* ravin *m*
raving ['reɪvɪŋ] **I.** *n* délire *m* **II.** *adj* **1.** (*angry*) furieux(-euse); ~ **mad** complètement fou(folle) **2.** (*extreme*) délirant(e); (*success*) fou(folle); **to be a ~ beauty** être d'une grande beauté
ravioli [ˌrævi'əʊli, *Am:* -'oʊ-] *n no pl* raviolis *mpl*
ravish ['rævɪʃ] **I.** *vt* (*please greatly*) ravir **II.** *vt* (*rape*) violer
ravishing *adj* **1.** (*beautiful*) ravissant(e) **2.** (*delicious*) délicieux(-euse)
raw [rɔː, *Am:* rɑː] **I.** *n* **in the ~** tel qu'il/telle qu'elle est **II.** *adj* **1.** (*unprocessed*) brut(e); **raw material** *a. fig* matière *f* première **2.** (*uncooked*) cru(e) **3.** (*inexperienced: beginner*) total(e); **a ~ recruit** un bleu **4.** (*unrestrained*) sans frein; (*energy*) sans retenue **5.** (*sore*) à vif **6.** (*chilly*) âpre **7.** (*frank*) cru(e) ►**to get a ~ deal** se faire avoir; **to touch a ~ nerve** piquer au vif
rawboned [ˌrɔː'bəʊnd] *adj* maigre
rawhide ['rɔːhaɪd, *Am:* 'rɑː-] *n* fouet *m* à lanières
Rawlplug® ['rɔːlplʌg, *Am:* 'rɑːl-] *n Brit* cheville *f*
ray [reɪ] *n* **1.** (*light*) rayon *m* **2.** (*radiation*) radiation *f* **3.** (*science fiction*) rayon *m* laser; ~ **gun** fusil *m* à rayons laser **4.** (*trace*) lueur *f* **5.** (*fish*) raie *f* ►**a ~ of sunlight** un rayon de soleil; **a ~ of hope** une lueur d'espoir
rayon® ['reɪɒn, *Am:* -ɑːn] *n* rayonne *f*
raze [reɪz] *vt* raser
razor ['reɪzə^r, *Am:* -zɚ] **I.** *n* rasoir *m* **II.** *vt* raser
razor blade *n* lame *f* de rasoir **razor cut** *n* coupe *f* de cheveux au rasoir **razor-sharp, razor sharp** *adj* **1.** (*very sharp*) tranchant(e) comme un rasoir **2.** (*clear: mind*) acéré(e)
razzle ['ræzl] *n no pl, Brit* **to be/go (out) on the ~** faire la bringue
R & B [ˌɑː^rənd'biː, *Am:* ˌɑːr-] *n abbr of* **rhythm and blues** rhythm and blues *m*
RC [ˌaː'siː, *Am:* ˌɑːr-] **I.** *n abbr of* **Red Cross** Croix-Rouge *f* **II.** *adj abbr of* **Roman Catholic** catholique
RCMP *n abbr of* **Royal Canadian Mounted Police** *police montée canadienne*
Rd *n abbr of* **road** r. *f*
re [reɪ] *prep* concernant
RE [ˌɑː^r'iː] *n Brit abbr of* **religious education** éducation *f* religieuse
reach [riːtʃ] **I.** <-es> *n* **1.** *no pl* (*accessibility*) portée *f;* **within arm's ~** à portée de main; **within easy ~ of schools and shops** avec écoles et boutiques à proximité; **to be beyond sb's ~** être hors de portée de qn; **to be out of ~** (*too far*) être hors de portée; (*too expensive*) être inabordable; (*impossible*) être du domaine du rêve **2.** (*arm length*) rayon *m* d'action; SPORT allonge *f* **3.** *no pl* (*sphere of action*) champ *m* d'action **II.** *vt* **1.** (*arrive at*) atteindre;

(*Italy, London*) arriver à; (*destination*) arriver à; (*person*) parvenir à **2.** (*come to: agreement*) aboutir à; (*conclusion*) arriver à; (*decision*) prendre; (*level, point, situation, stage*) atteindre; **I'd ~ed a state of exhaustion** j'étais maintenant dans un état d'épuisement **3.** (*stretch for*) atteindre; **to ~ one's hand out** tendre sa main; **to ~ sb (down/over/up) sth** passer qc à qn; **to ~ sth down** descendre qc; **to ~ up to sth** monter jusqu'à qc **4.** (*contact: colleague*) joindre; (*market, public*) toucher **5.** (*understand*) comprendre **6.** (*pass*) passer **III.** *vi* s'étendre; **I can't ~** je n'y arrive pas; **to ~ to sth** s'étendre jusqu'à qc; **to ~ for sth** (étendre le bras pour) saisir qc; **to ~ over for sth** tendre le bras pour prendre qc ▶**to ~ for the stars** essayer d'atteindre la lune

◆**reach out** *vi* **1.** (*with arm*) tendre le bras; **to ~ for sth** tendre le bras pour prendre qc **2.** (*communicate*) communiquer; **to ~ to sb** aller vers qn

reaches *n* étendue *f;* **the upper/lower ~ of the Amazon** la haute/basse Amazone; **the farthest ~ of the universe** le fin fond de l'univers; **the upper ~ of government/society** les hautes sphères du gouvernement/de la société

react [rɪ'ækt] *vi a.* MED, CHEM réagir; **to be slow to ~** être long à réagir

reaction [rɪ'ækʃn] *n* **1.** (*response*) *a.* MED, PHYS, CHEM réaction *f;* **a ~ to sb/sth** une réaction à qn/qc; **a ~ against sth** une réaction contre qc; **a chain ~** une réaction en chaîne **2.** *pl* (*physical reflexes*) réflexes *mpl* **3.** *pej, form* POL réaction *f*

reactionary [rɪ'ækʃənrɪ, *Am:* -erɪ] **I.** *adj pej* POL réactionnaire **II.** <-ies> *n pej* POL réactionnaire *mf*

reactivate [riː'æktɪveɪt, *Am:* -tə-] **I.** *vt* réactiver; (*file*) rouvrir; (*memories*) réveiller **II.** *vi* se réactiver

reactive [riː'æktɪv] *adj* réactif(-ive)

reactor [rɪ'æktəʳ, *Am:* -tɚ] *n* PHYS réacteur *m*

reactor core *n* cœur *m* du réacteur

read¹ [red] *adj* lu(e); **little/widely ~** (*magazine*) peu/très lu; (*student*) peu/très cultivé(e) ▶**to take sth as ~** tenir qc pour acquis

read² [riːd] **I.** *n no pl* lecture *f;* **have a ~ of this** lis-moi ça; **it's a good ~** ça se laisse lire **II.** *vt* <read, read> **1.** (*decipher words*) lire; **to ~ sth voraciously** dévorer qc **2.** (*decipher signs: music*) lire; **to ~ sb's lips** lire sur les lèvres de qn **3.** (*speak aloud*) lire à voix haute; **to ~ sb to sleep** faire la lecture à qn jusqu'à ce qu'il s'endorme; **to ~ sth back to sb** relire qc à qn **4.** (*interpret: situation*) analyser; **to ~ too much into sth** aller trop loin dans l'interprétation de qc; **to ~ sth in sb's face** lire qc sur le visage de qn; **to ~ sb's mind, to ~ sb like a book** lire dans les pensées de qn **5.** (*to note information*) relever **6.** (*hear and understand*) recevoir **7.** *Brit, form* UNIV étudier **8.** PUBL corriger **9.** (*show information*) indiquer ▶**to ~ in the cards/tea-leaves that ...** lire dans les cartes/le marc de café que ...; **~ my lips!** écoute bien ce que je te dis!; **to ~ the Riot Act to sb** faire une sommation à qn **III.** *vi* **1.** (*decipher words*) lire; **to ~ about sb/sth** lire des choses sur qn/qc **2.** (*speak aloud*) lire à voix haute **3.** (*have an effect*) **to ~ well** se lire bien ▶**to ~ between the lines** lire entre les lignes

◆**read out** *vt* **1.** (*read aloud*) lire à voix haute **2.** INFOR afficher

◆**read over, read through** *vt* parcourir

◆**read up** *vi* **to ~ on sb/sth** lire sur qn/qc

readability [ˌriːdə'bɪlɪtɪ, *Am:* -ət̬ɪ] *n no pl* lisibilité *f*

readable *adj* **1.** (*capable of being read*) lisible **2.** (*worth reading*) qui mérite d'être lu **3.** (*easy to read*) facile à lire

reader *n* **1.** (*person who reads*) lecteur, -trice *m, f* **2.** (*book of extracts: school*) livre *m* de lecture; (*university*) recueil *m* de textes **3.** (*device*) lecteur *m* **4.** *Brit* UNIV professeur *mf*

readership *n no pl* lectorat *m*

readily ['redɪlɪ] *adv* **1.** (*willingly*) volontiers **2.** (*easily*) facilement

readiness *n no pl* **1.** (*willingness*) bonne volonté *f;* **sb's ~ to** +*infin* le désir de qn de +*infin* **2.** (*quickness*) empressement *m* **3.** (*preparedness*) **to be in ~ for sth** être prêt pour qc

reading **I.** *n* **1.** *no pl* (*activity*) lecture *f* **2.** *no pl* (*material*) lecture *f;* **a little light ~** un peu de lecture légère; **to make good bedtime ~** être un bon livre de chevet **3.** (*recital*) lecture *f;* **poetry ~** lecture de poésie **4.** (*interpretation*) interprétation *f* **5.** TECH relevé *m* **II.** *adj* (*speed*) de lecture; **to have a ~ knowledge of English** savoir lire l'anglais; **to have a ~ age of seven** avoir un niveau de lecture d'un enfant de sept ans

reading list *n* liste *f* des ouvrages à lire **reading material** *n* lecture *f* **reading room** *n* salle *f* de lecture

readjust [ˌriːə'dʒʌst] **I.** *vt a.* TECH régler; (*tie, glasses*) rajuster **II.** *vi* **to ~ to sth** se réadapter à qc

readjustment *n* réajustement *m;* POL réadaptation *f*

read only memory *n* INFOR mémoire *f* morte **read/write head** *n* INFOR tête *f* de lecture-écriture

ready ['redɪ] **I.** <-ier, -iest> *adj* **1.** (*prepared*) prêt(e); **to be ~ for sth** être prêt pour qc; **to get ~ for sth** se préparer à qc; **to get sb/sth ~ for sth** préparer qn/qc à qc; **to be ~ and waiting, to be ~, willing and able** être fin prêt; **to be ~ to** +*infin* être disposé à +*infin;* **to be ~ with an excuse** avoir une excuse toute prête **2.** (*quick*) prêt(e); (*mind*) vif(vive); **~ cash** argent *m* liquide; **~ to hand** à portée de main; **to have a ~ reply to every question** avoir réponse à tout; **to have a ~ tongue** avoir la langue déliée **3.** SPORT **~, steady, go!** *Brit* à vos marques, prêts, partez! **II.** <-ies> *n*

R

1. (*prepared*) **at the ~** prêt(e) 2. *inf* (*money*) **the ~** [*o* **readies**] le cash III. *vt* <-ie-> préparer

ready-made *adj* 1. (*in finished form*) prêt(e) à l'emploi; (*meal*) préparé(e); (*clothing*) de prêt-à-porter 2. (*on hand*) tout(e) prêt(e); (*excuse*) tout(e) fait(e) **ready reckoner** *n* barème *m* **ready-to-wear** I. *adj* de prêt-à-porter II. *n no pl* prêt-à-porter *m*

reaffirm [ˌriːə'fɜːm, *Am:* -'fɜːrm] *vt* réaffirmer

reafforest [ˌriːə'fɒrɪst, *Am:* -'fɔːr-] *vt Brit, Aus* ECOL *s.* **reforest**

real [rɪəl, *Am:* riːl] I. *adj* 1. (*actual*) vrai(e); (*threat*) véritable; (*costs*) réel(le); **in ~ life** dans la vraie vie; **in ~ terms** FIN en valeur absolue 2. (*genuine*) véritable; *Brit* (*food*) traditionnel(le); **a ~ man** *iron* un (vrai) homme 3. (*main*) vrai(e) 4. (*considerable*) véritable; (*gentleman, problem*) vrai(e) ►**to be the ~ McCoy** *inf* être du vrai de vrai II. *adv Am, inf* (*really*) vachement

real estate *n no pl, Am, Aus* (*land and property*) biens *mpl* immobiliers

realignment [ˌriːə'laɪnmənt] *n* réalignement *m;* AUTO équilibrage *m*

realism ['rɪəlɪzəm, *Am:* 'riːlɪ-] *n no pl a.* ART, LIT réalisme *m*

realist I. *n a.* ART, LIT réaliste *mf* II. *adj* ART, LIT réaliste

realistic *adj a.* ART, LIT réaliste

reality [rɪ'ælətɪ, *Am:* -t̬ɪ] *n* 1. *no pl* (*facts*) réalité *f;* **in ~** en réalité; **to come back to ~** revenir à la réalité; **to be out of touch with ~** être déconnecté de la réalité; **to make one's ambition/plan a ~** réaliser son ambition/plan; **to become a ~** se réaliser 2. *no pl* ART, LIT réalisme *m*

realizable *adj* réalisable

realization *n* 1. (*perception*) prise *f* de conscience 2. *no pl* (*fulfillment, acquisition of profit*) réalisation *f*

realize ['rɪəlaɪz, *Am:* 'riːə-] *vt* 1. (*know: fact, situation*) réaliser; **sorry, I never ~d** désolé, je ne me rendais pas compte; **I ~ you're in a hurry** je me rends compte que vous êtes pressé; **do you ~ what this means?** tu te rends compte de ce que ça veut dire? 2. (*achieve*) réaliser 3. FIN (*assets*) réaliser; (*price*) rapporter

really ['rɪəlɪ, *Am:* 'riːə-] I. *adv* vraiment; **did you ~ say that?** tu as vraiment dit ça?; **I ~ can't stand her** vraiment je ne peux pas la voir; **it's easy ~** en fait c'est facile II. *interj* 1. (*surprise*) c'est vrai? 2. (*annoyance*) vraiment!

realm [relm] *n* 1. (*kingdom*) *a. fig* royaume *m* 2. (*area of interest*) domaine *m;* **within the ~(s) of possibility** dans le domaine du possible

realtor ['rɪəltəʳ, *Am:* 'riːəlt̬ɚ] *n Am, Aus* (*estate agent*) agent *m* immobilier

realty ['rɪəltɪ, *Am:* 'riːəlt̬ɪ] *n no pl* biens *mpl* immobiliers

reanimate [riː'ænɪmeɪt] *vt a. fig* ranimer

reap [riːp] I. *vt* 1. (*harvest*) moissonner 2. (*get as reward*) récolter; **to ~ the benefit/profits from sth** tirer profit/des profits de qc; **to ~ what one has sown** récolter ce qu'on a semé ►**he who sows the wind shall ~ the whirlwind** *prov* qui sème le vent récolte la tempête II. *vi* (*harvest*) moissonner

reaper *n* 1. (*harvester*) moissonneur, -euse *m, f* 2. (*machine*) moissonneuse *f*

reappear [ˌriːə'pɪəʳ, *Am:* -'pɪr] *vi* réapparaître; **to ~ from somewhere** ressurgir de quelque part

rear[1] [rɪəʳ, *Am:* rɪr] I. *adj* arrière; **the ~ door/entrance** la porte/l'entrée de derrière II. *n* 1. (*back part*) **the ~** l'arrière; **to bring up the ~** fermer la marche 2. *inf* (*buttocks*) derrière *m;* **to be a pain in the ~** être un enquiquineur

rear[2] [rɪəʳ, *Am:* rɪr] I. *vt* 1. (*bring up*) élever 2. (*raise*) lever; **to ~ one's ugly head again** *pej* poindre de nouveau à l'horizon 3. *form* (*build*) dresser II. *vi* 1. (*raise: horse*) se dresser 2. (*extend high*) s'élever

rear admiral *n* contre-amiral *m*

rear-engined *adj* **to be ~** avoir un moteur à l'arrière

rearguard *n no pl* MIL arrière-garde *f;* **a ~ action** un combat d'arrière-garde

rearm [ˌriː'ɑːm, *Am:* -'ɑːrm] *vi, vt* réarmer

rearmament [riː'ɑːməmənt, *Am:* -'ɑːrmə-] *n no pl* réarmement *m*

rearmost ['rɪəməʊst, *Am:* 'rɪrmoʊst] *adj* **the ~ ...** le(la) tout(e) dernière

rearrange [ˌriːə'reɪndʒ] *vt* réarranger; (*skirt*) réajuster; (*schedule*) modifier; **to ~ the order of sth** remettre de l'ordre dans qc

rear view mirror *n* rétroviseur *m* **rear-wheel drive** *n* roues *fpl* arrières motrices; (*car*) traction *f* arrière

reason ['riːzn] I. *n* 1. (*ground*) raison *f;* **the ~ why ...** la raison pour laquelle ...; **the ~ for sth** la raison de qc; **sb's ~ for doing sth** la raison pour laquelle qn fait qc; **for no particular ~** pour aucune raison particulière; **to have good/no ~ to** +*infin* avoir de bonnes raisons/n'avoir aucune raison de +*infin;* **to have every ~ to** +*infin* avoir toutes les raisons de +*infin;* **by ~ of sth** pour cause de qc 2. (*judgment*) raison *f;* **within ~** tout en restant raisonnable; **to see ~** entendre raison; **to be beyond all ~** dépasser la raison; **it stands to ~ that ...** il va sans dire que ... 3. (*sanity*) raison *f;* **to lose one's ~** perdre la raison II. *vt* **to ~ that ...** calculer que ...; **to ~ sth out** résoudre qc; **to ~ out that ...** déduire que ... III. *vi* raisonner

◆**reason with** *vi* discuter avec

reasonable *adj* raisonnable; **beyond a ~ doubt** sans l'ombre d'un doute

reasonably *adv* 1. (*with reason*) raisonnablement 2. (*acceptably*) assez; **~ priced** à un prix raisonnable

reasoned *adj* raisonné(e)

reasoning *n no pl* raisonnement *m*

reassurance [ˌriːə'ʃʊərəns, *Am:* -'ʃʊrəns] *n* **1.** *no pl* (*relieving of worry*) assurance *f* **2.** (*giving reassurance*) réconfort *m*

reassure [ˌriːə'ʃʊəʳ, *Am:* -'ʃʊr] *vt* rassurer

reassuring *adj* rassurant(e)

rebate ['riːbeɪt] *n* **1.** (*refund*) remboursement *m* **2.** (*discount*) rabais *m*

rebel ['rebl] **I.** *n a. fig* rebelle *mf* **II.** <-ll-> *vi* (*revolt*) *a. fig* se rebeller

rebellion [rɪ'belɪən, *Am:* -'beljən] *n* rébellion *f*

rebellious *adj* rebelle

rebirth [ˌriː'bɜːθ, *Am:* -'bɜːrθ] *n a.* REL renaissance *f*

reboot [ˌriː'buːt] INFOR **I.** *vt, vi* redémarrer **II.** *n* redémarrage *m*

rebound [rɪ'baʊnd, *Am:* riː'-] **I.** *vi* rebondir; **to ~ off sth** rebondir contre qc; **to ~ against sb** *fig* se retourner contre qn **II.** *n* **1.** *no pl* SPORT rebond *m;* **to hit a ball on the ~** frapper une balle après le rebond **2.** *no pl, fig* **to be on the ~** être sous le coup d'une déception

rebuff [rɪ'bʌf] **I.** *vt* rebuter **II.** *n* refus *m;* **to meet with a ~** essuyer une rebuffade

rebuild [ˌriː'bɪld] *vt irr, a. fig* reconstruire; (*engine*) remonter

rebuke [rɪ'bjuːk] **I.** *vt* réprimander **II.** *n* réprimande *f*

rebut [rɪ'bʌt] <-tt-> *vt* réfuter

rebuttal [rɪ'bʌtl, *Am:* -'bʌt̬-] *n* réfutation *f*

recalcitrant [rɪ'kælsɪtrənt] *adj* récalcitrant(e)

recall [rɪ'kɔːl] **I.** *vt* **1.** (*remember*) se rappeler; **I don't ~ seeing anyone** je ne me souviens pas avoir vu qui que ce soit *subj* **2.** (*call back*) rappeler **3.** (*withdraw*) retirer **II.** *vi* se souvenir **III.** *n* **1.** (*memory*) mémoire *f* **2.** (*summoning back*) *a.* POL rappel *m* **3.** (*withdrawal*) retrait *m* ►**to be lost beyond ~** être perdu à jamais

recant [rɪ'kænt] **I.** *vt* rétracter; REL abjurer **II.** *vi* se rétracter; REL abjurer

recap¹ ['riːkæp] **I.** *vi, vt* <-pp-> *abbr of* **recapitulate** récapituler **II.** *n abbr of* **recapitulation** récapitulation *f*

recap² [ˌriː'kæp] *vt* AUTO rechaper

recapitulate [ˌriːkə'pɪtʃʊleɪt, *Am:* -'pɪtʃə-] *vi, vt* récapituler

recapitulation *n* récapitulation *f;* MUS reprise *f*

recapture [ˌriː'kæptʃəʳ, *Am:* -tʃɚ] *vt* **1.** (*capture again*) reprendre **2.** (*reexperience*) retrouver **3.** (*recreate*) recréer

recast [ˌriː'kɑːst, *Am:* -'kæst] *vt* **1.** (*cast again*) THEAT, CINE **to ~ a play** redistribuer les rôles d'une pièce **2.** (*put into new form*) remanier

recede [rɪ'siːd] *vi* **1.** (*move backward: tide*) s'éloigner; (*fog*) s'estomper; **to ~ into the distance** disparaître au lointain **2.** (*diminish*) s'estomper; (*memories*) s'évanouir; (*prices, hopes*) baisser

receding *adj* (*chin*) fuyant(e)

receipt [rɪ'siːt] *n* **1.** (*document*) reçu *m;* (*for rent*) quittance *f* de loyer; (*at checkout*) ticket *m* de caisse **2.** *pl* (*amount of money*) recettes *fpl* **3.** (*act of receiving*) réception *f;* **payable on ~** payable à la réception; **I am in ~ of your letter** *form* j'accuse réception de votre lettre

receive [rɪ'siːv] *vt* **1.** (*get, hear, see*) *a.* TECH recevoir; **to ~ recognition** être reconnu; **to ~ sb loud and clear** recevoir qn cinq sur cinq **2.** (*endure*) subir; (*a rebuke*) essuyer; **to ~ a long sentence** être condamné à une peine de longue durée **3.** (*greet*) accueillir **4.** *form* (*accommodate*) recevoir **5.** (*admit to membership*) admettre **6.** LAW receler; **guilty of receiving** coupable de recel ►**it is more blessed to give than to ~** *prov* donner est plus doux que recevoir

received *adj* reçu(e); **~ pronunciation** *Brit* prononciation standard

receiver *n* **1.** (*on telephone*) combiné *m* **2.** TECH récepteur *m* **3.** (*bankruptcy official*) administrateur *m* judiciaire **4.** LAW receleur, -euse *m, f*

recent ['riːsnt] *adj* récent(e); **in ~ times** ces derniers temps

recently *adv* récemment

receptacle [rɪ'septəkl] *n* **1.** récipient *m* **2.** *fig* réceptacle *m*

reception [rɪ'sepʃn] *n* **1.** *no pl* (*welcome*) accueil *m;* **the idea got a frosty/warm ~** l'idée a été mal/bien accueillie **2.** *no pl* RADIO, TV réception *f* **3.** (*social event*) réception *f* **4.** (*area in a hotel or building*) réception *f;* **in ~** à la réception

reception area *n* réception *f* **reception class** *n Brit* ≈ cours *m* préparatoire **reception desk** *n* réception *f*

receptionist *n* réceptionniste *mf*

reception room *n* salle *f* de réception; (*in a house*) séjour *m*

receptive *adj* réceptif(-ive); **to be ~ to an idea** être ouvert à une idée

receptiveness, **receptivity** *n no pl* réceptivité *f*

recess [rɪ'ses, *Am:* 'riːses] <-es> *n* **1.** POL vacances *fpl* parlementaires **2.** *Am, Aus* SCHOOL récréation *f* **3.** (*alcove*) renfoncement *m* **4.** (*in trial*) suspension *f* de séance **5.** *pl* (*secret places*) recoins *mpl*

recessed *adj* encastré(e)

recession [rɪ'seʃn] *n* ECON récession *f;* **to be in/go into ~** être en/entrer en récession

recessive [rɪ'sesɪv] *adj* BIO récessif(-ive)

recharge [ˌriː'tʃɑːdʒ, *Am:* -'tʃɑːrdʒ] **I.** *vt* recharger ►**to ~ one's batteries** recharger ses accus **II.** *vi* se recharger

rechargeable *adj* rechargeable

rechristen [ˌriː'krɪsən] *vt* rebaptiser

recidivism [rɪ'sɪdɪvɪzəm, *Am:* -'sɪdə-] *n no pl* récidive *f*

recidivist *n* récidiviste *mf*

recipe ['resəpɪ] *n* recette *f;* **the ~ for success** la meilleure formule pour réussir ►**to be a ~**

for __**disaster**__ mener (tout) droit à la catastrophe

recipient [rɪ'sɪpɪənt] *n* (*of a transplant*) receveur, -euse *m, f;* (*of welfare, money*) bénéficiaire *mf;* (*of mail, gift*) destinataire *mf;* (*of an award*) lauréat(e) *m(f)*

reciprocal I. *adj* 1. (*mutual*) réciproque 2. (*reverse*) opposé(e) 3. MAT (*number*) inverse II. *n* MAT réciproque *f*

reciprocate [rɪ'sɪprəkeɪt] I. *vt* (*love*) retourner; (*trust, admiration*) rendre; **to be ~d** être réciproque II. *vi* 1. (*respond*) en faire autant; **to ~ with sth** répliquer avec qc 2. TECH effectuer un mouvement alternatif

reciprocity [ˌresɪ'prɒsətɪ, *Am:* -'prɑːsət̬ɪ] *n no pl* réciprocité *f*

recital [rɪ'saɪtl, *Am:* -t̬l] *n* 1. MUS récital *m* 2. (*description*) énoncé *m*

recitation [ˌresɪ'teɪʃn] *n* LIT récitation *f*

recitative [ˌresɪtə'tiːv] *n* MUS récitatif *m*

recite [rɪ'saɪt] I. *vt* 1. (*repeat*) réciter 2. (*list*) énoncer II. *vi* réciter

reckless ['reklɪs] *adj* 1. (*careless*) imprudent(e) 2. (*rash*) inconscient(e)

recklessness *n no pl* 1. (*carelessness*) imprudence *f* 2. (*rashness*) inconscience *f*

reckon ['rekən] I. *vt* 1. (*calculate*) calculer 2. (*consider*) penser; **to be ~ed (to be) sth** être considéré comme qc II. *vi inf* (*presume*) **could you help me with this? – I ~ not!** pourrais-tu m'aider pour cela? – je ne crois pas!

◆**reckon in** *vt* tenir compte de

◆**reckon on** *vt insep* 1. (*count on*) compter sur 2. (*expect*) s'attendre à; **to ~ doing sth** compter faire qc

◆**reckon up** *vt* calculer

◆**reckon with** *vt insep* 1. (*take account of*) compter avec; **to be sth to be reckoned with** être qc avec lequel il faut compter 2. (*expect*) s'attendre à

◆**reckon without** *vt insep* ne pas prévoir

reckoner *n* MAT *s.* **ready reckoner**

reckoning *n* 1. (*calculating, estimating*) calculs *mpl;* **to be out in one's ~** se tromper dans ses calculs 2. (*avenging, punishing*) règlement *m* de compte

reclaim [rɪ'kleɪm] *vt* 1. (*claim back*) récupérer 2. (*make usable: land*) assainir 3. *form* (*reform*) guérir

reclamation [ˌreklə'meɪʃn] *n no pl* 1. (*reclaiming*) récupération *f* 2. (*getting back*) retour *m;* (*expenses*) remboursement *m* 3. (*making usable*) bonification *f;* (*of land*) amendement *m;* (*from the sea*) assèchement *m* 4. *form* (*reformation*) amendement *m*

recline [rɪ'klaɪn] I. *vi* 1. (*lean back*) s'allonger 2. (*be horizontal*) être étendu II. *vt* (*head, arm*) appuyer; (*seat*) incliner

recliner *n* chaise *f* longue

reclining chair *n* siège *m* inclinable

recluse [rɪ'kluːs, *Am:* 'rekluːs] *n* reclus(e) *m(f)*

recognition [ˌrekəg'nɪʃn] *n no pl* reconnaissance *f;* **to change beyond ~** devenir méconnaissable; **to achieve ~** être (publiquement) reconnu; **in ~ of sth** en reconnaissance de qc; **there's a growing ~ that ...** il est de plus en plus reconnu que ...

recognizable *adj* reconnaissable

recognize ['rekəgnaɪz] *vt* 1. (*know again*) reconnaître 2. (*appreciate*) être reconnaissant pour 3. (*acknowledge*) reconnaître

recognized *adj* reconnu(e)

recoil [rɪ'kɔɪl] I. *vi* 1. (*spring back*) reculer; **to ~ in horror/in disgust** reculer d'horreur/de dégoût; **to ~ from sth** se rétracter devant qc 2. (*rebound: muscle, spring*) se détendre 3. *fig* **to ~ on sb/sth** se retourner contre qn/qc II. *n* recul *m*

recollect [ˌrekə'lekt] I. *vt* se rappeler II. *vi* se souvenir

recollection [ˌrekə'lekʃn] *n* souvenir *m;* **to the best of my ~** (d')aussi loin que je me rappelle *subj*

recommend [ˌrekə'mend] *vt* recommander; **it is not to be ~ed** ce n'est pas conseillé

recommendable *adj* recommandable

recommendation [ˌrekəmen'deɪʃn, *Am:* -mən'-] *n* 1. (*suggestion*) recommandation *f* 2. (*advice*) conseil *m*

recompense ['rekəmpens] I. *n no pl* 1. (*reward*) récompense *f* 2. (*compensation*) indemnité *f* II. *vt* 1. (*reward*) récompenser 2. (*make amends*) dédommager

reconcile ['rekənsaɪl] *vt* 1. (*make friends again*) réconcilier; **to be ~d** être réconcilié(e) 2. (*make compatible*) concilier; **to ~ sth with sth** réconcilier qc avec qc 3. (*accept*) **to ~ oneself to sth** se faire à l'idée de qc

reconciliation [ˌrekənˌsɪlɪ'eɪʃn] *n* 1. (*restoration of good relations*) réconciliation *f* 2. *no pl* (*making compatible*) conciliation *f*

recondition [ˌriːkən'dɪʃn] *vt* rénover; (*machines*) reconstruire; (*buildings*) réhabiliter

reconnaissance [rɪ'kɒnɪsns, *Am:* -'kɑːnə-] I. *n* MIL reconnaissance *f* II. *adj* MIL de reconnaissance

reconnoiter *Am,* **reconnoitre** [ˌrekə'nɔɪtəʳ, *Am:* ˌriːkə'nɔɪt̬ɚ] I. *vt* MIL reconnaître II. *vi* MIL effectuer une reconnaissance

reconsider [ˌriːkən'sɪdəʳ, *Am:* -ɚ] *vt, vi* reconsidérer; **I think you should ~** je crois que vous devriez y repenser

reconstruct [ˌriːkən'strʌkt] *vt* 1. (*build*) reconstruire 2. (*create*) recréer 3. (*reorganize*) restructurer 4. (*assemble evidence*) reconstituer 5. (*simulate a crime*) procéder à une reconstitution de

reconstruction [ˌriːkən'strʌkʃn] *n* 1. (*rebuilding*) reconstruction *f;* (*of a country*) relèvement *m;* (*of economy*) redressement *m* 2. (*imaginary recreation*) reconstitution *f*

record[1] ['rekɔːd, *Am:* -ɚd] I. *n* 1. (*account*) rapport *m;* LAW enregistrement *m;* (*of proceedings*) procès-verbal *m;* **to be on ~** (*statement*) être enregistré; **to be on (the) ~ as saying ...**

avoir dit en public que ...; **to put the ~ straight** mettre les choses au clair; **to say sth on/off the ~** dire qc officiellement/officieusement; **strictly off the ~** en toute confidentialité **2.** (*note*) note *f;* **to keep a ~ of sth** noter qc; **to leave a ~ of sth** laisser une trace de qc; **there is no ~ of your complaint** il n'y a pas de trace de votre réclamation **3.** (*file*) dossier *m;* **medical ~** dossier *m* médical; **public ~s** archives *fpl* **4.** *no pl* (*personal history*) antécédents *mpl;* **criminal ~** casier *m* (judiciaire); **to have a clean ~** avoir un passé sans tache *m;* **to have a good/bad ~** avoir bonne/mauvaise réputation *f* **5.** (*achievements*) résultats *mpl;* **safety ~** résultats en matière de sécurité **6.** (*recording*) enregistrement *m* **7.** (*music disc*) disque *m* **8.** (*achievement*) *a.* SPORT record *m* **9.** INFOR article *m* **II.** *adj* (*unbeaten*) record *inv;* **in ~ time** en un temps record; **to reach a ~ high/low** atteindre son record le plus haut/bas

record² [rɪ'kɔːd, *Am:* -'kɔːrd] **I.** *vt* **1.** (*make a recording of*) enregistrer **2.** (*write about: event*) rapporter; LAW prendre acte de **3.** (*register*) indiquer **II.** *vi* (*person, machine*) enregistrer; (*sound*) s'enregistrer

record-breaker *n* SPORT champion(ne) *m(f)* **record-breaking** *adj* record *inv;* **a ~ $1000** un montant record de 1000$; **a ~ 1000 visitors** un nombre record de mille visiteurs **record changer** *n* chargeur *m* de disques; (*for CDs*) chargeur *m* de CD **record company** *n* maison *f* de disques

recorded *adj* enregistré(e); (*computer file*) sauvegardé(e)

recorded delivery *n Brit* envoi *m* recommandé

recorder *n* **1.** (*tape*) magnétophone *m* **2.** (*video*) magnétoscope *m* **3.** (*instrument*) flûte *f* à bec

record holder *n* détenteur, -trice *m, f* de record

recording *n* (*material or process*) enregistrement *m*

recording session *n* séance *f* d'enregistrement **recording studio** *n* studio *m* d'enregistrement

record label *n* (*brand*) label *m* **record library** *n* (*discs*) discothèque *f* **record player** *n* tourne-disque *m*

recount [rɪ'kaʊnt] **I.** *vt* **1.** (*count again*) recompter **2.** (*narrate*) raconter **II.** *vi* POL recompter **III.** *n* recomptage *m;* POL nouveau dépouillement *m* du scrutin

recoup [rɪ'kuːp] *vt* (*losses*) compenser; (*strength*) récupérer; **to ~ one's costs** rentrer dans ses frais

recourse [rɪ'kɔːs, *Am:* 'riːkɔːrs] *n no pl, form* recours *m;* **to have ~ to sb** avoir recours à qn; **to have ~ to sth** faire appel à qc

recover [rɪ'kʌvəʳ, *Am:* -ɚ] **I.** *vt* **1.** (*get back: property*) récupérer; (*balance, composure*) retrouver; (*consciousness*) reprendre; (*health*) recouvrer; (*strength*) récupérer; **to ~ one's costs** rentrer dans ses frais **2.** LAW se faire attribuer; (*damages, compensation*) obtenir **II.** *vi* **1.** (*regain health*) récupérer **2.** (*return to normal*) se rétablir

re-cover [ˌriː'kʌvəʳ, *Am:* -ɚ] *vt* recouvrir

recoverable *adj* **1.** FIN recouvrable; (*costs*) récupérable; (*damage, loss*) indemnisable **2.** INFOR récupérable

recovery [rɪ'kʌvərɪ, *Am:* -ɚɪ] *n* **1.** *no pl* MED rétablissement *m;* **the rate of ~** le taux de guérison; **to make a full/quick/slow ~ from sth** guérir complètement/rapidement/lentement de qc **2.** ECON (*of a company, market*) reprise *f;* (*of shares, prices*) remontée *f* **3.** <-ies> (*getting back*) récupération *f;* (*of cost*) récupération *f;* (*of damages*) indemnisation *f;* (*of debts*) recouvrement *m*

recovery room *n* salle *f* de réveil **recovery service** *n no pl* service *m* de dépannage **recovery ship** *n* bateau *m* de sauvetage **recovery vehicle** *n* véhicule *m* de dépannage

recreate ['rekrieɪt] *vt* recréer

recreation *n* **1.** (*pleasurable activity*) récréation *f* **2.** *no pl* (*process*) divertissement *m*

recreational *adj* de loisir

recreational drug *n* drogue *f* récréative **recreational vehicle** *n Am* camping-car *m*

recreation centre *n* salle *f* polyvalente **recreation ground** *n Brit* terrain *m* de jeux **recreation room** *n* salle *f* de jeux

recriminate [rɪ'krɪmɪneɪt, *Am:* -əneɪt] *vi* récriminer

recrimination *n pl* récrimination *f*

recruit [rɪ'kruːt] **I.** *vt* (*persuade to join: soldiers*) enrôler; (*members*) recruter; (*employees*) embaucher **II.** *vi* recruter **III.** *n a.* MIL recrue *f*

recruiting **I.** *n no pl* **1.** MIL recrutement *m* **2.** ECON embauchage *m* **II.** *adj* ECON d'embauche **recruiting centre, recruiting office** *n* bureau *m* du personnel

recruitment *n no pl* recrutement *m;* (*of employees*) embauche *f*

recruitment agency *n* agence *f* de recrutement **recruitment drive** *n* campagne *f* de recrutement

rectangle ['rektæŋgl] *n* rectangle *m*

rectangular [rek'tæŋgjʊləʳ, *Am:* -gjəlɚ] *adj* rectangulaire

rectification [ˌrektɪfɪ'keɪʃn, *Am:* ˌrektə-] *n* **1.** *no pl* (*remedying*) rectification *f* **2.** ELEC redressement *m*

rectify ['rektɪfaɪ, *Am:* -tə-] <-ie-> *vt* **1.** (*make right*) rectifier **2.** ELEC (*current*) redresser **3.** CHEM rectifier

rectilinear [ˌrektɪ'lɪnɪəʳ, *Am:* -tə'-] *adj* rectiligne

rectitude ['rektɪtjuːd, *Am:* -tətuːd] *n no pl, form* rectitude *f*

rector ['rektəʳ, *Am:* -tɚ] *n* **1.** *Brit* REL recteur *m* **2.** *Scot* (*university official*) recteur *m* **3.** *Am*

R

(*of primary school*) directeur, -trice *m, f;* (*of secondary school*) proviseur *m;* (*of college*) principal(e) *m(f)*

rectory ['rektəri] <-ies> *n* presbytère *m*

rectum ['rektəm] *n* MED rectum *m*

recuperate [rɪ'ku:pəreɪt] *vi* se remettre

recuperation *n no pl* rétablissement *m*

recur [rɪ'kɜ:ʳ, *Am:* -'kɜ:r] *vi* (*words*) revenir; (*symptoms*) réapparaître; (*event*) se reproduire; (*occasion*) se représenter; (*number*) être récurrent

recurrence [rɪ'kʌrəns, *Am:* -'kɜ:r-] *n* (*of symptoms*) réapparition *f;* (*of event*) récurrence; **if there is any** ~ si cela se reproduit

recurrent *adj* récurrent(e)

recurring *adj* récurrent(e)

recycle [rɪ'saɪkl] *vt* recycler

recycling I. *n no pl* recyclage *m* II. *adj* de recyclage

red [red] I. *adj* rouge; (*hair*) roux(rousse) ▶**not a** ~ **cent** *Am, inf* pas un sou; ~ **as a beetroot** rouge comme un coquelicot II. *n* 1.(*colour*) rouge *m;* (*hair*) roux *m;* **to turn red** (*with dye*) devenir rouge; (*with embarrassment*) rougir 2. POL rouge *mf* ▶**in the** ~ à découvert; *s. a.* **blue**

Red Army *n* POL Armée *f* rouge **red-blooded** *adj* ardent(e) **redcap** *n* 1. *Brit, inf* MIL tunique *f* rouge 2. *Am* (*railway porter*) porteur *m* **red card** *n* carton *m* rouge **red carpet** I. *n no pl* tapis *m* rouge II. *adj* **to be given the** ~ **treatment** être traité en prince **Red China** *n no pl, inf* Chine *f* communiste **Red Crescent** *n no pl* **the** ~ le Croissant-Rouge **Red Cross** *n no pl* **the** ~ la Croix-Rouge

redcurrant ['red,kʌrənt] *n* groseille *f*

red deer *inv n* cerf *m* (commun)

redden ['redn] *vt, vi* rougir

reddish ['redɪʃ] *adj* rougeâtre; (*hair*) tirant sur le roux

redecorate [,ri:'dekəreɪt] I. *vt* redécorer; (*with paint*) repeindre; (*with paper*) retapisser II. *vi* refaire la décoration

redeem [rɪ'di:m] *vt* 1.(*compensate for*) compenser 2. REL racheter 3.(*save: reputation*) sauver; **to** ~ **oneself** se racheter 4.(*convert into money, goods*) convertir; (*wealth*) réaliser 5.(*buy back*) racheter 6.(*pay off*) solder; (*debts*) régler 7.(*fulfill*) satisfaire à; (*promise*) tenir

redeemable *adj* 1.(*able to be redeemed*) rachetable; (*mortgage, loan*) amortissable; (*bill*) remboursable 2.(*convertible*) convertible

Redeemer *n no pl* REL **the** ~ le Rédempteur

redeeming *adj* **the only** ~ **feature of sb/sth** la seule chose qui rattrape qn/qc

redefine [,i:dɪ'faɪn] *vt* redéfinir

redemption [rɪ'dempʃn] *n no pl* 1.(*release from blame*) rachat *m* 2. REL rédemption *f* 3.(*rescue*) **to be beyond** ~ être irrécupérable 4. FIN (*of a coupon, voucher*) compensation *f;* (*of a debt, mortgage*) remboursement *m*

redeploy [,ri:dɪ'plɔɪ] *vt* redéployer

redeployment *n* redéploiement *m*

redesign [,ri:dɪ'zaɪn] *vt* reconcevoir

redevelop [,ri:dɪ'veləp] *vt* réaménager

redevelopment *n* réaménagement *m*

red-faced *adj* embarrassé(e) **red-haired** *adj* roux(rousse) **red-handed** *adj* **to catch sb** ~ (sur)prendre qn la main dans le sac **redhead** *n* roux *m,* rousse *f* **red-headed** *adj* 1.(*with red hair*) *s.* **red-haired** 2. ZOOL à tête rouge **red herring** *n* faux problème *m* **red-hot** *adj* 1.(*heated*) chauffé(e) au rouge 2. *fig* ardent(e) 3.(*extremely hot*) brûlant(e) 4.(*exciting*) chaud(e) 5.(*fresh*) de dernière minute **Red Indian** *n pej* Peau-Rouge *mf*

redirect [,ri:dɪ'rekt] *vt* (*visitor*) réorienter; (*energy*) canaliser; (*letter*) réexpédier; (*mail*) faire suivre; (*on internet*) réorienter

redistribute [,ri:dɪ'strɪbju:t] *vt* redistribuer

redistribution *n no pl* redistribution *f*

red-letter day *n* jour *m* à marquer d'une pierre blanche **red light** *n* feu *m* rouge; **to run a** ~ brûler un feu rouge **red-light district** *n* quartier *m* chaud **red meat** *n no pl* viande *f* rouge

redneck ['rednek] *n Am, pej, inf* (*bumpkin*) péquenaud(e) *m(f)*

redness ['rednɪs] *n no pl* rougeur *f*

redo [,ri:'du:] *vt irr* refaire

redolent ['redələnt] *adj form* 1.(*smelling*) **to be** ~ **of sth** dégager un parfum de qc 2.(*bad smelling*) **to be** ~ **with sth** avoir des relents de qc 3.(*suggestive*) évocateur(-trice); **sth** ~ **of sth** qc qui évoque qc

redouble [rɪ'dʌbl] *vt* redoubler

redoubtable [rɪ'daʊtəbl, *Am:* -t̬ə-] *adj* redoutable

red pepper *n* 1.(*vegetable*) poivron *m* rouge 2. *no pl* (*spice*) paprika *m*

redraft [,ri:'drɑ:ft, *Am:* -'dræft] I. *vt* remanier II. *n* remaniement *m*

redress [rɪ'dres] I. *vt* régulariser; (*imbalance*) redresser II. *n* 1.(*remedy*) régularisation *f;* (*of imbalance*) redressement *m;* (*of grievance*) satisfaction *f* 2. LAW réparation *f*

Red Sea *n no pl* **the** ~ la Mer Rouge **redskin** *n pej* Peau-Rouge *mf* **red tape** *n no pl, pej* paperasserie *f*

reduce [rɪ'dju:s, *Am:* -'du:s] I. *vt* 1.(*make less*) réduire; (*speed*) modérer; (*taxes*) diminuer; **to** ~ **a backlog** rattraper un retard 2.(*make cheaper*) solder; (*price*) baisser 3. MIL dégrader 4.(*cook*) réduire 5.(*force*) réduire; **to** ~ **sb/sth to sth** réduire qc/qn à qc; ~**d to tears** en larmes; **to be reduced to doing sth** être réduit à faire qc II. *vi* 1. *Am* (*diet*) maigrir; **to be reducing** être au régime 2.(*cook: sauce*) réduire

reduced *adj* 1.(*made cheaper*) soldé(e); (*fare, wage*) réduit(e) 2.(*diminished*) réduit(e)

reducer *n* réducteur *m*

reduction [rɪ'dʌkʃn] *n* réduction *f;* (*in traffic*) diminution *f;* (*in wages*) baisse *f*

redundancy [rɪ'dʌndənsɪ] *n* **1.** *no pl, Brit, Aus* (*losing a job*) licenciement *m* **2.** (*not working*) chômage *m* **3.** LING redondance *f*
redundancy payment *n Brit, Aus* indemnité *f* de licenciement
redundant [rɪ'dʌndənt] *adj* **1.** (*superfluous*) excessif(-ive) **2.** LING redondant(e) **3.** *Brit, Aus* (*out of a job*) licencié(e); **to make sb ~** licencier qn **4.** *fig* **to make sb ~** rendre qn inutile
reduplication [rɪˌdju:plɪ'keɪʃn, *Am:* -ˌdu:plə'-] *n* LING réduplication *f*
redwood *n* séquoia *m*
reed [ri:d] *n* **1.** BOT roseau *m* **2.** MUS anche *f*
re-educate [ˌri:'edʒʊkeɪt] *vt* rééduquer
reedy ['ri:dɪ] *adj* **1.** (*full of reeds*) couvert(e) de roseaux **2.** (*sounding thin: voice*) suraigu(ë)
reef¹ [ri:f] *n* GEO récif *m*
reef² [ri:f] **I.** *n* NAUT ris *m* **II.** *vt* **to ~ the sails** aris(s)er les voiles
reefer¹ *n inf* **1.** (*drug cigarette*) joint *m* **2.** (*cannabis*) hasch *m*
reefer² *n* (*jacket*) caban *m*
reef knot *n* (*square knot*) nœud *m* plat
reek [ri:k] **I.** *vi* puer; **to ~ of sth** puer qc **II.** *n* relent *m*
reel [ri:l] **I.** *n* **1.** (*storage*) rouleau *m* **2.** (*winding device*) dévidoir *m* **3.** (*bobbin*) bobine *f;* (*for photos*) pellicule *f* **4.** (*for fishing line*) moulinet *m* **5.** (*dance*) contredanse *f* **II.** *vi* **1.** (*move unsteadily*) tituber; **to ~ back** s'écarter en titubant; **to send sb ~ing** envoyer valser qn; **the news left me ~ing** *fig* la nouvelle m'a abasourdi **2.** (*recoil*) être éjecté **3.** (*whirl*) tourbillonner **4.** (*dance*) danser un quadrille
◆**reel in** *vt* remonter
◆**reel off** *vt* débiter
re-elect [ˌri:ɪ'lekt] *vt* réélire
re-election *n* réélection *f*
reel-to-reel tape recorder *n* magnétophone *m* à bandes magnétiques
re-enter [ˌri:'entəʳ, *Am:* -t̬ɚ] **I.** *vt* **1.** (*go in again*) rentrer dans **2.** (*enter again: politics*) revenir à; (*college*) réintégrer **3.** INFOR retaper; (*data*) saisir de nouveau **II.** *vi* rentrer
re-entry [ˌri:'entrɪ] <-ies> *n* **1.** (*entering again*) rentrée *f* **2.** (*new enrolment*) réinscription *f*
ref [ref] *n* **1.** *inf abbr of* **referee** arbitre *mf* **2.** *abbr of* **reference** (*code*) réf. *f*
refectory [rɪ'fektərɪ] <-ies> *n* (*at school*) cantine *f;* (*at university*) restaurant *m* universitaire
refer [rɪ'fɜ:ʳ, *Am:* -'fɜ:r] <-rr-> *vt* **1.** (*direct*) renvoyer; (*in a hospital, to a doctor*) envoyer; **to ~ sb (back) to sb/sth** (r)envoyer qn à qc/qn **2.** (*pass, send on: a problem, matter*) soumettre; **to ~ sb/sth to sb/sth** soumettre qn/qc à qn/qc; **to ~ sth back to sth** (*a decision, dispute*) remettre qc à qc
◆**refer to** *vt* **1.** (*allude*) faire allusion à; **to ~ sb as sth** appeler qn qc **2.** (*mention*) se référer à; **referring to your letter/phone call** suite à votre lettre/appel téléphonique **3.** (*speak of*) parler de; **to never ~ sth** ne jamais parler de qc **4.** (*concern*) concerner **5.** (*apply to*) s'appliquer à **6.** (*consult, turn to*) consulter; **to refer (back) to sb/sth** consulter qn/qc ►**~ drawer** FIN refusé
referral *n* envoi *m;* **she is a ~ from Dr Jones** elle est envoyée par le Docteur Jones
referee [ˌrefə'ri:] **I.** *n* **1.** (*umpire*) arbitre *mf* **2.** (*for employment*) référence *f* **II.** <-d> *vt, vi* arbitrer
reference ['refrəns] *n* **1.** (*allusion*) référence *f;* **with ~ to ...** à propos de ce que ...; **in ~ to sb/sth** à propos de qn/qc **2.** (*responsibilities*) **terms of ~** mandat *m* **3.** (*consultation*) **without ~ to sb** sans passer par qn **4.** (*in text*) renvoi *m* **5.** (*recommendation*) référence *f;* **to write sb a ~** écrire une lettre de référence à qn
reference book *n* ouvrage *m* de référence
reference mark *n* renvoi *m* **reference number** *n* numéro *m* de référence
referendum [ˌrefə'rendəm] <-s *o* -da> *n form* POL référendum *m*
refill [ˌri:'fɪl] **I.** *n* recharge *f;* **do you want a ~?** tu en veux un autre ? **II.** *vt* recharger **III.** *vi* AUTO faire le plein
refine [rɪ'faɪn] *vt* **1.** (*purify*) raffiner **2.** (*polish*) affiner
refined *adj* **1.** (*purified*) raffiné(e); (*metal*) purifié(e) **2.** (*sophisticated*) sophistiqué(e) **3.** (*very polite*) raffiné(e)
refinement *n* **1.** (*improvement*) raffinement *m* **2.** *no pl* (*purification*) raffinage *m;* (*of metals*) affinage *m* **3.** *no pl* (*polishing of ideas*) peaufinage *m* **4.** *no pl* (*good manners*) raffinement *m*
refinery [rɪ'faɪnərɪ] <-ies> *n* raffinerie *f*
reflate [ri:'fleɪt] *vt* relancer
reflation *n* ECON relance *f*
reflect [rɪ'flekt] **I.** *vt* **1.** (*throw back: heat*) renvoyer; (*light*) réfléchir **2.** (*reveal*) refléter; (*image*) renvoyer **II.** *vi* **1.** (*contemplate*) réfléchir **2.** (*show quality*) **the results ~ well on him** les résultats sont tout à son honneur; **to ~ badly on sb/sth** jeter le discrédit sur qn/qc
reflecting *adj* réfléchissant(e)
reflecting telescope *n* télescope *m* à miroirs
reflection [rɪ'flekʃn] *n* **1.** (*reflecting*) réflexion *f;* **sound ~** retour *m* du son **2.** (*mirror image*) reflet *m* **3.** (*thought*) réflexion *f;* **on ~** à la réflection **4.** (*criticism*) atteinte *f;* **to be no ~ on sth** ne pas porter atteinte à qc; **it's a ~ on all of us** ça se répercute sur nous tous
reflective *adj* **1.** (*reflecting*) réfléchissant(e) **2.** (*thoughtful*) songeur(-euse)
reflector *n* réflecteur *m*
reflex ['ri:fleks] <-es> **I.** *n* réflexe *m* **II.** *adj* réflexe
reflex camera *n* appareil reflex *m*
reflexion [rɪ'flekʃn] *n Brit s.* **reflection**
reflexive [rɪ'fleksɪv] **I.** *adj* **1.** (*independent of*

R

will) réflexe **2.** LING réfléchi(e) **II.** *n* LING **1.** (*pronoun*) pronom *m* réfléchi **2.** (*verb*) verbe *m* réfléchi
refloat [ˌriː'fləʊt, *Am:* -'floʊt] *vt* renflouer
reflux [ˌriː'flʌks] *n* reflux *m*
reforest [ˌriː'fɒrɪst, *Am:* -'fɔːr-] *vt* reboiser
reform [rɪ'fɔːm, *Am:* -'fɔːrm] **I.** *vt* réformer **II.** *vi* se corriger **III.** *n* réforme *f* **IV.** *adj* de réforme
re-form, **reform** [ˌriː'fɔːm, *Am:* -'fɔːrm] **I.** *vt* reformer **II.** *vi* MIL reformer les rangs
reformation [ˌrefə'meɪʃn, *Am:* -ɚ'-] *n* réforme *f*
Reformation *n* REL **the ~** la Réforme
reformatory [rɪ'fɔːmətrɪ, *Am:* -'fɔːrmətɔːrɪ] <-ies> *n Am* (*detention centre*) centre *m* de détention pour mineurs
reformer *n* réformateur *m*
reform school *n* maison *f* de rééducation
refract [rɪ'frækt] *vt* PHYS réfracter
refraction *n* réfraction *f*
refractory [rɪ'fræktərɪ] *adj form* réfractaire
refrain[1] [rɪ'freɪn] *vi form* s'abstenir; **kindly ~ from smoking** prière de s'abstenir de fumer
refrain[2] [rɪ'freɪn] *n* refrain *m*
refresh [rɪ'freʃ] *vt* **1.** (*enliven*) se détendre; (*memory*) rafraîchir **2.** (*cool*) rafraîchir **3.** INFOR (*screen*) réactualiser
refresher course [rɪ'freʃəʳ, *Am:* -ɚ] *n* cours *m* de révision
refreshing *adj* **1.** (*cooling*) rafraîchissant(e) **2.** (*unusual: idea*) vivifiant(e); **it's ~ to** +*infin* ça fait du bien de +*infin;* **it makes a ~ change** ça change
refreshment *n* **1.** *form* (*rest*) repos *m* **2.** *no pl, form* (*eating and drinking*) une collation **3.** *pl* (*food and drink*) un buffet
refrigerant [rɪ'frɪdʒərənt] *n* réfrigérant *m*
refrigerate [rɪ'frɪdʒəreɪt] *vt* réfrigérer
refrigeration *n no pl* réfrigération *f*
refrigerator *n* réfrigérateur *m*
refuel [ˌriː'fjuːəl] <-ll- *o* -l-> **I.** *vi* se ravitailler en carburant **II.** *vt* **1.** (*fill again*) ravitailler en carburant **2.** (*give new arguments*) alimenter
refuge ['refjuːdʒ] *n a. fig* refuge *m;* **to take ~ in sth** chercher refuge dans qc; **to take ~ in drink/drugs** se réfugier dans l'alcool/la drogue
refugee [ˌrefjʊ'dʒiː] *n* réfugié(e) *m(f)*
refugee camp *n* camp *m* de réfugiés
refund [rɪ'fʌnd, *Am:* riː'-] **I.** *vt* rembourser **II.** *n* remboursement *m;* **to get a ~** se faire rembourser
refurbish [ˌriː'fɜːbɪʃ, *Am:* -'fɜːrbɪʃ] *vt form* rénover
refusal [rɪ'fjuːzl] *n* (*rejection*) refus *m;* (*of an application*) rejet *m*
refuse[1] [re'fjuːz, *Am:* rɪ'fjuːz] **I.** *vi* refuser **II.** *vt* refuser; (*consent*) ne pas accorder; (*offer*) rejeter; **to ~ to** +*infin* refuser de +*infin*
refuse[2] ['refjuːs] *n no pl* déchets *mpl;* **kitchen ~** ordures *fpl* ménagères
refuse bin *n* poubelle *f* **refuse collection** *n* ramassage *m* des ordures **refuse collector** *n Brit, form* éboueur *m* **refuse disposal** *n* traitement *m* des ordures ménagères **refuse dump** *n* décharge *f* **refuse incineration** *n* incinération *f* des déchets
refutable *adj* réfutable
refutation [ˌrefjuː'teɪʃn] *n* réfutation *f*
refute [rɪ'fjuːt] *vt* réfuter
regain [rɪ'geɪn] *vt* (*recover*) recouvrer; (*consciousness*) reprendre; (*lost ground, control, territory*) regagner
regal ['riːgl] *adj* royal(e); (*bearing*) altier(-ère)
regale [rɪ'geɪl] *vt* régaler
regalia [rɪ'geɪlɪə, *Am:* -'geɪljə] *n no pl,* + *sing/pl vb* **1.** (*clothes*) tenue *f;* **in full ~** en grande tenue **2.** (*insignia*) insignes *mpl;* **the Queen's ~** les insignes *mpl* de la reine
regard [rɪ'gɑːd, *Am:* -'gɑːrd] **I.** *vt* **1.** (*consider*) considérer; **to be ~ed as the best/a pioneer** être considéré comme le meilleur/un pionnier; **to ~ sb/sth with admiration/mistrust** considérer qn/qc avec admiration/méfiance; **a higly ~ed doctor** un docteur hautement estimé **2.** (*concern*) regarder; **as ~s the house/your son** en ce qui concerne la maison/votre fils **II.** *n form* **1.** (*consideration*) considération *f;* **without ~ for sth** sans tenir compte de qc **2.** (*esteem*) estime *f;* **out of ~ for sb/sth** par estime pour qn/qc; **to hold sb/sth in low ~** ne pas porter qn/qc très haut dans son estime; **to hold sb/sth in high ~** avoir beaucoup d'estime pour qn/qc; (**give my**) **~s to your sister** transmettez mes amitiés à votre sœur **3.** (*gaze*) regard *m* **4.** (*aspect*) **in this ~** à cet égard **5.** (*concerning*) **with ~ to sb/sth, having ~ to sth** en tenant compte de qc
regardful *adj* **to be ~ of sth** être attentif à qc
regarding *prep* concernant
regardless *adv* tout de même
regardless of *prep* (*sex, class*) sans distinction de; (*difficulty, expense*) sans se soucier de
regatta [rɪ'gætə, *Am:* -'gɑːt̬ə] *n* NAUT régate *f*
regency ['riːdʒənsɪ] *n* régence *f*
Regency style *n* style *m* régence
regenerate [rɪ'dʒenəreɪt] **I.** *vt* **1.** BIO, ANAT régénérer **2.** (*revive: cities*) revitaliser **II.** *vi* BIO se régénérer
regeneration *n no pl* **1.** BIO régénération *f* **2.** (*improvement*) renaissance *f;* (*of cities*) revitalisation *f*
regenerative cream *n* crème *f* régénératrice
regent ['riːdʒənt] *n* régent(e) *m(f)*
reggae ['regeɪ] *n no pl* reggae *m*
regicide ['redʒɪsaɪd] *n* régicide *mf*
regime, **régime** [reɪ'ʒiːm, *Am:* rə'-] *n* régime *m*
regimen ['redʒɪmen, *Am:* -əmen] *n form* régime *m*
regiment ['redʒɪmənt, *Am:* -əmənt] **I.** *n* + *sing/pl vb* régiment *m* **II.** *vt pej* réglementer
regimentation [ˌredʒɪmen'teɪʃn, *Am:*

-əmən'-] *n pej* discipline *f* de fer

region ['ri:dʒən] *n* région *f;* **the Birmingham ~** la région de Birmingham ►**in the ~ of** aux environs de

regional *adj* **1.** (*of regions*) régional(e) **2.** (*local*) local(e)

regionalism ['ri:dʒənə,lɪzəm] *n* régionalisme *m*

register ['redʒɪstəʳ, *Am:* -stɚ] **I.** *n* **1.** (*list*) registre *m;* **electoral ~** liste *f* électorale **2.** *Am* (*for money*) *s.* **till** **3.** LING registre *m* **II.** *vt* **1.** (*record*) inscrire; (*birth, death*) déclarer; (*car*) immatriculer; (*trademark, invention*) déposer **2.** *Brit* (*luggage*) faire enregistrer **3.** (*record mail*) envoyer en recommandé **4.** TECH enregistrer **III.** *vi* **1.** (*record officially*) **to ~ as sth** s'inscrire comme qc; **to ~ as unemployed** s'inscrire au chômage; **to ~ for a course** s'inscrire à un cours; **to ~ with sb/sth** s'inscrire auprès de qn/qc **2.** TECH s'enregistrer

registered *adj* **1.** (*recorded*) enregistré(e); (*patent*) déposé(e) **2.** (*qualified: practioner*) agréé(e); (*childminder*) agréé(e); *Am* (*official*) diplômé(e) d'état; (*voter*) inscrit(e) sur les listes

registered letter *n* lettre *f* recommandée

registered nurse *n* infirmière *f* diplômée d'État

register office *n Brit* bureau *m* d'état civil; **a ~ wedding** mariage *m* civil

registered trademark *n* marque *f* déposée

registrar [,redʒɪ'strɑ:ʳ, *Am:* 'redʒɪstrɑ:r] *n* **1.** (*official*) officier *m* d'état civil **2.** *Brit* (*university administrator*) responsable *mf* administratif **3.** *Brit, Aus* (*hospital doctor*) interne *mf*

registration [,redʒɪ'streɪʃn] *n* **1.** (*action of registering*) *a.* SCHOOL, UNIV inscription *f;* (*of births, deaths*) déclaration *f;* (*at airport, hotel*) enregistrement *m* **2.** (*for vehicles*) immatriculation *f*

registration document *n Brit* certificat *m* d'inscription **registration fee** *n* cotisation *f;* (*club*) droit *m* d'inscription **registration number** *n* numéro *m* d'immatriculation

registry office *n s.* **register office**

regress [rɪ'gres] *vi form* MED régresser

regression [rɪ'greʃn] *n no pl, form* MED régression *f*

regressive *adj form* régressif(-ive); (*tax*) dégressif(-ive)

regret [rɪ'gret] **I.** <-tt-> *vt* regretter **II.** <-tt-> *vi* regretter; **I ~ to have to inform you that ...** *form* je suis désolé de devoir vous annoncer que ...; **to ~ having done sth** regretter d'avoir fait qc **III.** *n* regret *m;* **a pang of ~** une crise de remords

regretful *adj* désolé(e); (*feeling*) de regret; (*smile*) navré(e); **to be ~ about sth** avoir des regrets à propos de qc

regretfully *adv* avec regret

regrettable *adj* regrettable

regroup [,ri:'gru:p] **I.** *vt* regrouper **II.** *vi* se regrouper

regular ['regjʊləʳ, *Am:* -jəlɚ] **I.** *adj* **1.** (*harmonious, steady*) régulier(-ère); **on a ~ basis** régulièrement; **a ~ customer** un(e) habitué(e) **2.** (*normal*) normal(e); (*procedure, doctor*) habituel(le); (*size*) standard *inv;* (*gas*) ordinaire; (*reader*) fidèle **3.** MAT symétrique **4.** (*correct*) régulier(-ère) *inf* **5.** LING régulier(-ère) **6.** *inf* (*real*) vrai(e); **a ~ fellow** [*o* **guy** *Am*] un type sympa; **to be a ~ fool** être complètement stupide ►**as ~ as clockwork** réglé comme du papier à musique **II.** *n* **1.** (*visitor*) habitué(e) *m(f)* **2.** MIL **a ~ (soldier)** un soldat de l'armée régulière

regularity [,regjʊ'lærətɪ, *Am:* -'lerəṭɪ] *n no pl* régularité *f*

regularize ['regjʊləraɪz] *vt* régulariser

regularly *adv* régulièrement

regulate ['regjʊleɪt] *vt* **1.** (*administer*) réglementer **2.** (*adjust*) régler

regulation **I.** *n* **1.** (*rule*) règlement *m;* (*health, safety*) norme *f;* **the rules and ~s** le règlement; **in accordance with the ~s** conformément aux règlements en vigueur **2.** *no pl* ADMIN réglementation *m* **3.** *no pl* (*action: of a machine*) réglage **II.** *adj* réglementaire

regulator *n* régulateur, -trice *m, f;* ADMIN contrôleur *m*

regulatory [,regjʊ'leɪtrɪ, *Am:* 'regjəleɪtɔ:rɪ] *adj form* régularisateur(-trice)

regulatory body *n* ADMIN organisme *m* de contrôle

regurgitate [ri:'gɜ:dʒɪteɪt, *Am:* -'gɜ:rdʒə-] *vt* **1.** (*eat: food*) régurgiter **2.** *pej* (*echo*) recracher

rehab ['ri:hæb] **I.** *n inf* désintox *inv;* **to go into ~** faire une cure de désintox **II.** *vt* **1.** (*rehabilitate socially*) réinsérer **2.** (*restore*) réhabiliter

rehabilitate [,ri:ə'bɪlɪteɪt, *Am:* -əteɪt] *vt* **1.** (*restore*) *a. fig* réhabiliter **2.** (*restore reputation*) réhabiliter **3.** (*restore to health*) rééduquer **4.** (*rehabilitate socially*) réinsérer

rehabilitation *n no pl* **1.** (*restoring*) *a. fig* réhabilitation *f* **2.** (*reforming criminals*) réinsertion *f* **3.** (*return to health*) rééducation *f* **4.** (*detoxification*) désintoxication *f*

rehabilitation centre *n* (*for young people*) centre *m* de rééducation; (*for addicts*) centre *m* de désintoxication

rehash [,ri:'hæʃ] **I.** *vt* **1.** *pej, inf* (*recycle ideas*) resservir **2.** (*discuss after event*) ressasser **II.** *n pej, inf* **to be a ~** être du réchauffé

rehearsal [rɪ'hɜ:sl, *Am:* -'hɜ:rsl] *n* **1.** THEAT répétition *f* **2.** MIL exercice *m*

rehearse [rɪ'hɜ:s, *Am:* -'hɜ:rs] *vt* (*a play, scene*) répéter; (*lines*) réciter; (*arguments*) ressasser

reign [reɪn] **I.** *vi* régner; **to ~ supreme** régner en maître absolu **II.** *n* règne *m;* **during the ~ of Queen Victoria** sous le règne de la reine Victoria; **a ~ of terror** un règne de terreur

reimburse [,ri:ɪm'bɜ:s, *Am:* -'bɜ:rs] *vt form* rembourser; **to ~ sb for sth** rembourser qn de qc

reimbursement *n form* remboursement *m*

rein [reɪn] *n* **1.** (*for horse riding*) rêne *f;* (*for horse driving*) guide *f* **2.** *Brit* (*controls for children*) harnais-laisse *m* ►**to give sb a free ~** laisser les rênes libres à qn; **to keep a tight ~ on sb/sth** garder le contrôle sur qn/qc; **to hand over the ~s to sb** passer les rênes à qn ◆**rein in** *vt* (*horse*) tirer les reines de; (*child, ambition*) freiner

reincarnation [ˌriːɪnkɑː'neɪʃn, *Am:* -kɑːr'-] *n* réincarnation *f*

reindeer ['reɪndɪəʳ, *Am:* -dɪr] *n inv* renne *m*

reinforce [ˌriːɪn'fɔːs, *Am:* -'fɔːrs] *vt* **1.** (*strengthen*) renforcer; (*argument, demand*) appuyer **2.** (*increase: troops*) renforcer

reinforced concrete *n* béton *m* armé

reinforcement *n* **1.** *no pl* (*of building*) armature *f* **2.** *pl* (*fresh troops*) *a. fig* renforts *mpl*

reinstate [ˌriːɪn'steɪt] *vt form* **1.** (*return sb to job*) réintégrer **2.** (*restore to former state*) rétablir

reinsure [ˌriːɪn'ʃʊəʳ, *Am:* -'ʃʊr] *vt* réassurer

reintegrate [ˌriː'ɪntəgreɪt] *vt* réintégrer

reintegration *n* réintégration *f;* (*of criminal*) réinsertion *f;* (*of patient*) réadaptation *f*

reinvent [ˌriːɪn'vent] *vt* réinventer

reissue [ˌriː'ɪʃuː, *Am:* -'ɪʃjuː] **I.** *vt* rééditer **II.** *n* réédition *f*

reiterate [riː'ɪtəreɪt, *Am:* ri'ɪt̬-] *vt form* réitérer

reiteration *n form* réitération *f*

reject [rɪ'dʒekt] **I.** *vt* **1.** (*decline*) rejeter; (*application, article*) refuser; **to feel ~ed** se sentir rejeté **2.** LAW (*bill*) rejeter; (*complaint*) débouter; (*claim, authority*) contester **3.** (*resist transplant*) rejeter **4.** TECH (*of products*) mettre au rebut **II.** *n* **1.** (*sub-standard product*) rebut *m* **2.** (*ostracised person*) laissé-pour-compte *mf*

rejection [rɪ'dʒekʃn] *n a.* MED rejet *m;* **a fear of ~** une peur d'être rejeté; **a ~ letter** une lettre de refus

rejoice [rɪ'dʒɔɪs] *vi form* **to ~ at sth** se réjouir de qc; **to ~ in doing sth** se régaler à faire qc

rejoicing *n no pl, form* réjouissance *f;* **~ at sth** réjouissance à propos de qc

rejoin [ˌriː'dʒɔɪn] **I.** *vt* (*friends*) rejoindre; (*club*) se réinscrire à; (*regiment*) rallier; (*motorway*) rattraper **II.** *vi form* se rejoindre

rejoinder *n form* réplique *f;* **amusing/sharp ~** le mot pour rire/qui fait mouche

rejuvenate [riː'dʒuːvəneɪt] *vt* **1.** (*restore youth*) rajeunir; **to feel ~d** se sentir rajeuni **2.** (*invigorate*) revigorer **3.** (*modernize*) rajeunir

rekindle [riː'kɪndl] *vt* attiser; (*interest*) ranimer

relapse [rɪ'læps] **I.** *n form* rechute *f* **II.** *vi* rechuter; **to ~ into alcoholism/drug abuse** retomber dans l'alcoolisme/la toxicomanie

relate [rɪ'leɪt] **I.** *vt* **1.** (*establish connection*) relier; **I couldn't ~ the two cases** je n'arrivais pas à faire le rapprochement entre ces deux cas **2.** *form* (*tell*) relater **II.** *vi* **1.** (*concern*) **to ~ to sb/sth** se rapporter à qn/qc **2.** (*feel sympathy with*) **to ~ to sb** communiquer avec qn **3.** (*identify with*) **to ~ to sb** s'identifier à qn

related *adj* **1.** (*linked*) relié(e) **2.** (*having a link*) lié(e); (*subjects*) connexe **3.** (*same family*) parent(e); **to be ~ by marriage** être parent par alliance **4.** (*from same species*) apparenté(e)

relating to *prep* concernant

relation [rɪ'leɪʃn] *n* **1.** *no pl* (*link*) relation *f;* **in ~ to** en relation avec; **to bear no ~ to sb/sth** n'avoir aucun rapport avec qn/qc **2.** (*relative*) parent(e); **~ by marriage** parent par alliance; **to have ~s in a country** avoir de la famille dans un pays **3.** *pl* (*dealings between people(s)*) relations *fpl;* **have sexual ~s with sb** avoir des rapports sexuels avec qn

relationship *n* **1.** (*link*) relation *f* **2.** (*family connection*) lien *m* de parenté **3.** (*between people*) relation *f;* **~ to sb** relation avec qn; **we have a business ~** nous sommes en relation d'affaires; **to be in a ~ with sb** être avec qn

relative ['relətɪv, *Am:* -t̬ɪv] **I.** *adj form* **1.** (*connected to*) lié(e); **to be ~ to sth** être lié à qc **2.** (*in comparison*) relatif(-ive); **to be ~ to sth** être relatif à qc **II.** *n* parent(e) *m(f)*

relative clause *n* proposition *f* relative

relatively *adv* relativement; **~ speaking** comparativement

relative pronoun *n* pronom *m* relatif

relativity [ˌrelə'tɪvətɪ, *Am:* -t̬ɪ] *n no pl* relativité *f*

relax [rɪ'læks] **I.** *vi* se détendre; **~!** détends-toi! **II.** *vt* relâcher

relaxation [ˌriːlæk'seɪʃn] *n* **1.** (*recreation*) relaxation *f;* **for ~** pour se détendre **2.** (*liberalising*) assouplissement *m*

relaxed *adj* décontracté(e)

relaxing *adj* relaxant(e); (*day*) de détente

relay ['riːleɪ] **I.** *vt* relayer **II.** *n* **1.** (*group*) relais *m* **2.** SPORT (*race*) course *f* de relais

re-lay [ˌriː'leɪ] *vt* (*carpet*) reposer; (*floor*) réaménager

release [rɪ'liːs] **I.** *vt* **1.** (*free*) libérer **2.** LAW libérer; **to ~ on bail** relâcher sous caution; **to ~ on parole** remettre en liberté conditionnelle; **to ~ on probation** remettre en liberté surveillée **3.** (*free from suffering*) délivrer **4.** (*move sth*) dégager; (*brake*) lâcher **5.** PHOT (*shutter*) déclencher **6.** (*detonate*) lâcher **7.** (*allow to escape: gas, steam*) relâcher **8.** (*weaken: grip*) relâcher **9.** (*make public*) publier **10.** (*publish*) sortir **II.** *n no pl* **1.** (*act of freeing*) libération *f;* (*from prison*) sortie *f* **2.** (*handle*) manette *f* de déblocage; (*of brake, clutch*) desserrage *m* **3.** (*act of releasing*) déblocage *m;* (*of handbrake*) desserrage *m* **4.** (*freeing: of funds, goods*) déblocage *m* **5.** (*relaxation*) relâchement *m;* (*of tension*) diminuation *f* **6.** (*freeing *from bad feeling*) délivrance *f* **7.** (*escape of gases*) échappement *m* **8.** *no pl* (*making public*) publication *f* **9.** (*public relations info*) communiqué *m* **10.** (*new CD, film*) sortie *f*; **to be on ~** être sorti

relegate ['relɪgeɪt, *Am:* 'relə-] *vt* **1.** (*demote*) reléguer **2.** *Brit* (*move team down*) descendre dans le classement

relent [rɪ'lent] *vi* (*people*) se radoucir; (*wind, rain*) se calmer

relentless *adj* implacable; (*pressure, criticism*) incessant(e)

relevance ['reləvəns], **relevancy** *n no pl* **1.** (*appropriateness*) pertinence *f*; **to have ~ to sth** avoir un rapport avec qc **2.** (*importance*) importance *f*

relevant *adj* **1.** (*appropriate*) pertinent(e); (*documents*) d'intérêt; (*evidence*) approprié(e) **2.** (*important*) important(e)

reliability [rɪˌlaɪə'bɪlətɪ, *Am:* -t̬ɪ] *n no pl* **1.** (*dependability*) fiabilité *f* **2.** (*trustworthiness*) confiance *f*

reliable [rɪ'laɪəbl] *adj* **1.** (*dependable*) fiable **2.** (*credible*) sûr(e); (*evidence*) solide; (*figures, testimony*) fiable **3.** (*trustworthy*) de confiance

reliance [rɪ'laɪəns] *n no pl* (*dependence*) **~ on sb/sth** dépendance *f* sur qn/de qc

reliant *adj* **to be ~ on sb/sth to** +*infin* dépendre de qn/qc pour +*infin*

relic ['relɪk] *n* **1.** (*from past*) vestige *m* **2.** REL *a. pej* relique *f*

relief [rɪ'li:f] **I.** *n* **1.** (*after sth bad*) soulagement *m*; **much to my ~, to my great ~** à mon grand soulagement; **to feel an incredible sense of ~** se sentir grandement soulagé; **that's a ~** quel soulagement **2.** *no pl* (*help*) aide *f*; **tax ~** un dégrèvement fiscal **3.** (*replacement*) substitut *m* **4.** MIL libération *f* **5.** *fig* **to throw sth into ~** mettre qc en évidence **6.** ART, GEO relief *m* **II.** *adj* (*substitute*) de remplacement

relief map *n* carte *f* topographique **relief train** *n* train *m* supplémentaire **relief worker** *n* **1.** (*substitute*) suppléant(e) *m(f)* **2.** (*worker for third-world*) travailleur, -euse *m,f* humanitaire

relieve [rɪ'li:v] *vt* **1.** (*take worries from*) soulager; **to be ~d about sth/that ...** être soulagé à propos de qc/que... **2.** (*substitute for*) remplacer **3.** MIL (*city*) libérer **4.** (*weaken negative feelings: boredom*) dissiper; (*anxiety*) calmer; (*pressure*) atténuer; (*tension*) diminuer **5.** (*alleviate: famine*) lutter contre; (*symptoms*) soulager **6.** (*take away*) **to ~ sb of sth** débarrasser qn de qc; *iron* délester qn de qc **7.** (*urinate, defecate*) **to ~ oneself** se soulager

relieved *adj* soulagé(e)

religion [rɪ'lɪdʒən] *n a. fig* religion *f*

religious [rɪ'lɪdʒəs] *adj* **1.** (*of religion*) religieux(-euse) **2.** (*meticulous*) scrupuleux(-euse)

religiously *adv* religieusement

relinquish [rɪ'lɪŋkwɪʃ] *vt form* (*give up*) abandonner; (*post*) quitter; (*leadership*) abandonner

relish ['relɪʃ] **I.** *n* **1.** *no pl* (*enjoyment*) plaisir *m* **2.** (*sauce*) condiment *m* **II.** *vt* aimer; **to ~ the thought that ...** se réjouir à la pensée que ...

reload [ˌri:'ləʊd, *Am:* -'loʊd] **I.** *vt* recharger **II.** *vi* se recharger

relocate [ˌri:ləʊ'keɪt, *Am:* -'loʊkeɪt] **I.** *vi* déménager **II.** *vt* (*person*) transférer; (*object*) déplacer; (*company, production*) déménager

relocation *n* (*of a company*) déménagement *m*; (*of a person*) transfert *m*

reluctance [rɪ'lʌktəns] *n no pl* réticence *f*; **with some ~** avec réticence

reluctant *adj* réticent(e); **a ~ hero** un héros malgré lui

rely [rɪ'laɪ] <-ie-> *vi* **1.** (*trust*) **to ~ on sb/sth** compter sur qn/qc; **to ~ on sb for sth** compter sur qn pour qc **2.** (*depend on*) **to ~ (up)on sb/sth** dépendre de qn/qc

REM [ˌɑ:ri:'em] *n abbr of* **Rapid Eye Movement** mouvement *m* rapide des yeux

remain [rɪ'meɪn] *vi* rester; **to ~ in bed** rester au lit; **to ~ anonymous** garder l'anonymat; **to ~ silent** garder le silence; **much ~s to be done** il reste beaucoup à faire; **the fact ~s that ...** il n'empêche que ...; **it (only) ~s for me to ...** il ne me reste plus qu'à ...

remainder **I.** *n no pl* **1.** (*rest*) restant *m*; (*people*) reste *m* **2.** MAT reste *m* **II.** *vt* (*books*) solder

remaining *adj* qui reste; **our only ~ hope** notre seul espoir

remains *npl* **1.** (*leftovers*) restes *mpl* **2.** HIST vestiges *mpl* **3.** *form* (*corpse*) dépouille *f*

remake [ˌri:'meɪk] **I.** <remade> *vt* refaire **II.** *n* (*new version*) remake *m*

remand [rɪ'mɑ:nd, *Am:* -'mænd] **I.** *vt* renvoyer; **to ~ in custody** placer en détention provisoire; **to ~ on bail** mettre en liberté sous caution **II.** *n no pl* renvoi *m*; **to be on ~** être en détention préventive; (*on bail*) être en liberté provisoire

remand centre *n Brit, Aus* centre *m* de détention provisoire

remark [rɪ'mɑ:k, *Am:* -'mɑ:rk] **I.** *vt* faire remarquer **II.** *n* remarque *f*

remarkable *adj* remarquable

remarkably *adv* remarquablement

remarriage [ˌri:'mærɪdʒ, *Am:* -'mer-] *n* remariage *m*

remarry [ˌri:'mærɪ, *Am:* -'mer-] <-ie-> **I.** *vt* remarier **II.** *vi* se remarier

remedial [rɪ'mi:dɪəl] *adj form* (*action*) de correction; (*class*) de rattrapage; MED de rétablissement

remedy ['remədɪ] **I.** <-ies> *n* **1.** (*treatment*) remède *m*; **to be beyond ~** être incurable **2.** (*legal redress*) recours *m* (légal) **II.** *vt form* remédier à

remember [rɪ'membəʳ, *Am:* -bɚ] **I.** *vt* se souvenir de; **I ~ed to see her** je me suis souvenu que je devais la voir; **I ~ed seeing**

R

her je me suis souvenu l'avoir vue; **a night to ~** une nuit inoubliable **II.** *vi* se souvenir ▶**you ~** *inf* vous savez

remembrance [rɪ'membrəns] *n form* souvenir *m;* **in ~ of sb** en souvenir de qn

> Le **Remembrance Day**, "Remembrance Sunday" ou "Poppy Day" est le deuxième dimanche de novembre (en souvenir de l'armistice du 11 novembre 1918), jour au cours duquel tous les soldats tombés pendant les deux guerres mondiales sont honorés par un service religieux et une cérémonie. Les gens portent partout un coquelicot rouge en tissu, symbole des champs de bataille de Flandre qui étaient fleuris de coquelicots après la Première Guerre mondiale. A 11 heures, on observe ce jour-là deux minutes de silence.

remind [rɪ'maɪnd] *vt* rappeler; **~ me to call her** rappelle-moi de l'appeler; **to ~ sb of sb/sth** faire penser qn à qn/qc; **that ~s me!** je me souviens!

reminder *n* **1.** (*making sb remember*) aide-mémoire *m inv* **2.** (*sth awakening memories*) rappel *m*

reminisce [ˌremɪ'nɪs, *Am:* -ə'-] *vi* évoquer le passé; **to ~ about sth** évoquer qc

reminiscence [ˌremɪ'nɪsns, *Am:* -ə'-] *n form* **1.** *no pl* (*reflection of past*) réminiscence *f* **2.** (*memory*) souvenir *m* **3.** *pl, form* mémoires *fpl*

reminiscent *adj* **1.** (*suggestive*) évocateur(-trice); **to be ~ of sth** rappeler qc **2.** (*recalling the past: mood*) nostalgique

remiss [rɪ'mɪs] *adj form* négligent(e)

remission [rɪ'mɪʃn] *n no pl* **1.** *Brit* (*reducing prison sentence*) remise *f* de peine **2.** (*cancellation of debt*) remise *f* **3.** MED rémission *f*

remit [rɪ'mɪt] **I.** <-tt-> *vt form* **1.** *Brit* (*shorten prison sentence*) remettre **2.** (*mail money*) envoyer **3.** (*pass on to different authority*) relayer **II.** *n no pl* attributions *fpl*

remittance [rɪ'mɪtns] *n form* versement *m*

remittent *adj form* MED rémittent(e)

remix ['riːmiks] MUS **I.** *vt* remixer **II.** <-es> *n* remix *m*

remnant ['remnənt] *n* **1.** (*remaining*) reste *m;* (*of cloth*) coupon *m* **2.** *fig* vestige *m*

remnant sale *n* soldes *fpl* de fin de série

remodel [ˌriː'mɒdl, *Am:* -'mɑːdl] <-ll- *o* -l-> *vt* remodeler

remorse [rɪ'mɔːs, *Am:* -'mɔːrs] *n no pl, form* remords *m*

remorseful *adj form* repentant(e)

remorseless *adj form* **1.** (*relentless*) incessant(e) **2.** (*callous*) impitoyable; (*cruelty*) sans pitié **3.** (*severe*) implacable

remote [rɪ'məʊt, *Am:* -'moʊt] <-er, -est *o* more ~, most ~> *adj* **1.** (*distant in place*) lointain(e) **2.** (*far from towns*) isolé(e) **3.** (*distant in time*) éloigné(e) **4.** (*standoffish*) distant(e) **5.** (*unlikely: likelihood*) infime ▶**not to have the ~st idea about sth** ne pas avoir la moindre idée de qc

remote control *n* télécommande *f*

remote-controlled *adj* télécommandé(e); (*television*) avec télécommande

remotely *adv* d'aucune façon

remoteness *n no pl* (*of things*) isolement *m;* (*of people*) distance *f*

remould ['riːməʊld, *Am:* -moʊld] **I.** *vt* **1.** (*design again*) remodeler **2.** *Brit, Aus* (*remake tyre*) rechaper **II.** *n* rechapage *m*

remount [ˌriː'maʊnt] *vt* remonter sur

removable *adj* **1.** (*cleanable*) lavable **2.** (*easy to take off*) amovible

removal [rɪ'muːvl] *n* **1.** *no pl, Brit* (*to new home*) déménagement *m* **2.** *no pl* (*dismissal*) éviction *f* **3.** (*act of removing: of people*) déplacement *m;* (*of objects*) enlèvement *m;* (*of words, entries*) retrait *m*

removal firm *n* compagnie *f* de déménagement **removal man** *n Brit* déménageur *m* **removal van** *n* fourgon *m* de déménagement

remove [rɪ'muːv] *vt* **1.** (*take away*) enlever; (*entry, name*) rayer; (*word, film, handcuffs*) retirer; (*troublemaker, spectators*) faire sortir; (*ban*) lever; (*difficulty*) écarter; (*make-up, stain*) ôter; (*stitches*) enlever **2.** (*take off: clothes*) retirer; (*tie*) enlever **3.** (*dismiss: from job*) renvoyer; (*from office*) destituer **4.** *fig* (*doubts, fears*) effacer

remover *n* **1.** *Brit* (*worker, company*) déménageur *m* **2.** (*liquid*) **stain ~** détachant *m;* **nail-varnish ~** dissolvant *m*

remunerate [rɪ'mjuːnəreɪt] *vt form* rémunérer

remuneration *n form* rémunération *f*

remunerative *adj form* rémunérateur(-trice)

Renaissance [rɪ'neɪsns, *Am:* ˌrenə'sɑːns] *n* **the ~** la Renaissance

renal ['riːnl] *adj* rénal(e); **~ specialist** spécialiste *mf* des reins

renal calculus *n* calculs *mpl* rénaux

rename [ˌriː'neɪm] *vt* renommer

rend [rend] <rent *o Am* rended> *vt form* **1.** (*tear*) déchirer **2.** (*split*) diviser

render *vt form* **1.** (*make*) rendre **2.** (*perform music*) interpréter **3.** (*give*) donner; **~ services to the Crown** servir la Couronne **4.** (*hand in*) soumettre **5.** (*translate*) traduire **6.** (*put plaster on wall*) plâtrer

rendering ['rendərɪŋ] *n* **1.** (*performance of art work*) interprétation *f* **2.** (*translation*) traduction *f*

rendezvous ['rɒndɪvuː, *Am:* 'rɑːndeɪ-] **I.** *n inv* **1.** (*meeting*) rendez-vous *m* **2.** (*meeting place*) lieu *m* de rendez-vous **II.** *vi* se rencontrer; **to ~ with sb** retrouver qn

rendition [ren'dɪʃn] *n* interprétation *f*

renegade ['renɪgeɪd, *Am:* 'renə-] **I.** *n pej, form* renégat(e) *m(f)* **II.** *adj pej, form* rebelle

renege [rɪ'neɪg, *Am:* -'nɪg] *vi form* **to ~ on** (*promise*) manquer à; (*deal*) ne pas honorer

renew [rɪ'nju:, *Am:* -'nu:] *vt* 1. (*begin again: promise, agreement*) renouveler; (*attack*) relancer; (*friendship, relationship*) renouer; (*subscription*) renouveler 2. (*replace*) changer
renewable *adj* renouvelable
renewal *n* 1. (*extension*) renouvellement *m* 2. (*regeneration of area*) rénovation *f*
renewed *adj* renouvelé(e); (*relationship*) renoué(e); **to receive ~ support** recevoir un regain de soutien
rennet ['renɪt], **rennin** *n no pl* présure *f*
renounce [rɪ'naʊns] *vt form* 1. (*relinquish: arms, force, violence*) renoncer a 2. (*deny: authority*) réfuter
renovate ['renəveɪt] *vt* rénover
renovation *n* rénovation *f;* **to be under ~** être en cours de rénovation; **~ work** travaux *mpl* de rénovation
renown [rɪ'naʊn] *n no pl, form* renommée *f;* **to win ~ as sth** gagner une réputation en tant que qc; **of ~** de renom
renowned *adj form* réputé(e)
rent[1] [rent] I. *n* déchirure *f* II. *pt, pp of* **rend**
rent[2] [rent] I. *n* loyer *m;* **to pay a higher ~** payer un loyer plus élevé; **to raise ~s** augmenter les loyers; **to be behind with the ~** avoir des loyers de retard; **for ~** a louer II. *vt* louer
rental I. *n* location *f* II. *adj* de location; *Am* (*library*) payant(e)
rent-a-room *n Am* location *f* de chambres **rent arrears** *n* arriérés *mpl* de loyer **rent boy** *n Brit, inf* jeune prostitué *m* homosexuel **rent control** *n* encadrement *m* des loyers
renter *n* locataire *mf*
rent-free *adj* gratuit(e) **rent rebate** *n* réduction *f* de loyer **rent review** *n* révision *f* des loyers **rent subsidy** *n* subvention *f* de loyer
renunciation [rɪˌnʌnsɪ'eɪʃn] *n no pl* renonciation *f*
reopen [ri:'əʊpən, *Am:* -'oʊ-] I. *vt* (*open*) rouvrir II. *vi* se rouvrir
reopening *n* réouverture *f*
reorder [ˌri:'ɔ:də^r] I. *n* nouvelle commande *f* II. *vt* 1. (*order*) commander a nouveau 2. (*rearrange*) réorganiser
reorganization *n* réorganisation *f*
reorganize [ri:'ɔ:gənaɪz, *Am:* -'ɔ:rgən-] I. *vt* réorganiser II. *vi* se réorganiser
rep [rep] *n* 1. *inf* (*travelling salesperson*) *abbr of* **representative** VRP *mf* 2. *inf abbr of* **repertory company** compagnie *f* théâtrale de répertoire
Rep. [rep] I. *n abbr of* **Republic** République *f* II. *adj abbr of* **Republican** républicain(e)
repaint [ri:'peɪnt] *vt, vi* repeindre
repair [ri:'peə^r, *Am:* -'per] I. *vt* 1. (*restore*) réparer; (*road*) rénover 2. (*set right*) réparer II. *vi* **to ~ somewhere** se rendre quelque part III. *n* 1. (*mending*) réparation *f;* **to be in need of ~** avoir besoin d'une réparation; **beyond ~** irréparable; **to be under ~** être en cours de réparation 2. (*state*) état *m;* **to be in good/bad ~** être en bon/mauvais état
repairable *adj* réparable
repair kit *n* trousse *f* de réparation **repairman** <-men> *n* 1. (*for house*) réparateur *m* 2. (*for cars*) garagiste *m* **repair shop** *n* atelier *m* de réparation
repaper [ri:'peɪpə^r] *vt* retapisser
reparable ['repərəbl] *adj* réparable; (*loss*) compensable
reparation [ˌrepə'reɪʃn] *n form* réparation *f;* **to make ~ for sth** réparer qc
repartee [ˌrepɑ:'ti:, *Am:* -ɑ:r'-] *n no pl* repartie *f*
repatriate [ri:'pætrɪeɪt, *Am:* -'peɪtrɪ-] *vt* rapatrier
repatriation *n no pl* rapatriation *f*
repay [rɪ'peɪ] <repaid> *vt* 1. (*pay back*) repayer; (*debt, loan*) s'acquitter de 2. (*reward for kindness*) récompenser
repayable *adj* remboursable
repayment *n* remboursement *m*
repeal [rɪ'pi:l] I. *vt* (*decree, law*) abroger II. *n no pl* abrogation *f*
repeat [rɪ'pi:t] I. *vt* 1. (*say again*) répéter; **~ after me!** répétez après moi!; **don't ~ this but ...** ne le répète pas mais ... 2. (*recite*) réciter 3. (*do again*) refaire 4. SCHOOL (*class, year*) redoubler, doubler *Belgique* 5. COM, ECON (*order*) renouveler 6. **to ~ itself** (*incident*) se répéter; **to ~ oneself** se répéter II. *vi* 1. (*reoccur*) se répéter 2. *inf* (*give indigestion*) **to ~ on sb** donner des renvois a qn III. *n* 1. (*sth happening again*) répétition *f* 2. TV rediffusion *f* IV. *adj* récurrent(e)
repeated *adj* répété(e); **despite ~ attempts** malgré une succession de tentatives
repeatedly *adv* à plusieurs reprises
repeater *n* fusil *m* a répétition
repeat mark *n* MUS barre *f* de reprise **repeat order** *n* commande *f* renouvelée **repeat performance** *n* 1. (*repetition of show*) deuxième représentation *f* 2. (*same as before*) même prestation *f* 3. LAW récidive *f*
repel [rɪ'pel] <-ll-> *vt* 1. (*ward off*) parer 2. MIL (*attack*) repousser 3. (*force apart*) repousser 4. (*disgust*) dégoûter
repellent [rɪ'pelənt] I. *n* 1. (*lotion for insects*) insecticide *m;* **mosquito ~** lotion *f* antimoustique 2. (*impervious substance*) (**water**) ~ enduit *m* hydrofuge II. *adj* repoussant(e)
repent [rɪ'pent] I. *vi form* se repentir II. *vt* regretter
repentance [rɪ'pentənts] *n no pl* repentir *m*
repentant *adj form* repentant(e); **to feel ~** se repentir
repercussion [ˌri:pə'kʌʃn, *Am:* -pɚ'-] *pl n* répercussion *f*
repertoire ['repətwɑ:^r, *Am:* -ɚtwɑ:r] *n* répertoire *m*
repertory ['repətrɪ, *Am:* -ɚtɔ:rɪ] *n no pl* 1. (*of plays etc*) répertoire *m* 2. (*theatre*) thé-

R

âtre *m* de répertoire

repertory company *n Brit* compagnie *f* théâtrale de répertoire **repertory theatre** *n Brit* (*theatre company*) théâtre *m* de répertoire

repetition [ˌrepɪ'tɪʃn, *Am:* -ə'-] *n* répétition *f*; **this book is full of ~** ce livre se répète sans arrOt

repetitious, **repetitive** *adj pej* répétitif(-ive)

replace [rɪ'pleɪs] *vt* **1.** (*take the place of*) remplacer **2.** (*put back*) replacer; **to ~ the receiver** raccrocher **3.** (*substitute*) remplacer; **to ~ sth with sth** remplacer qc par qc

replaceable *adj* remplatable

replacement **I.** *n* remplacement *m* **II.** *adj* de remplacement

replay [ˌriː'pleɪ] **I.** *vt* **1.** (*play again: melody, match*) rejouer **2.** (*play again: recording*) repasser **II.** *n* **1.** (*replayed match*) nouvelle rencontre *f* **2.** (*replaying a recording*) répétition *f*

replenish [rɪ'plenɪʃ] *vt form* remplir; (*replace*) réapprovisionner

replete [rɪ'pliːt] *adj* rempli(e); (*person*) repu(e)

replica ['replɪkə] *n* réplique *f*; (*of a car, ship*) copie *f*; (*of sb*) sosie *m*

replicate ['replɪkeɪt] *vt* reproduire

reply [rɪ'plaɪ] **I.** <-ied> *vi* **1.** (*respond*) répondre **2.** (*react*) répliquer **II.** <-ies> *n* **1.** (*response*) réponse *f* **2.** (*reaction*) riposte *f*

reply coupon *n* bulletin-réponse *m* **reply-paid envelope** *n* enveloppe *f* pré-affranchie

repoint [riː'pɔɪnt] *vt* ARCHIT rejointoyer

report [rɪ'pɔːt, *Am:* -'pɔːrt] **I.** *n* **1.** (*account*) rapport *m* **2.** (*shorter account*) compte rendu *m* **3.** TV, RADIO reportage *m*; **weather ~** bulletin *m* météorologique **4.** LAW procès-verbal *m* **5.** SCHOOL bulletin *m* **6.** (*unproven claim*) rumeur *f*; **there have been ~s of fighting** on nous a rapporté qu'il y avait des batailles **7.** *form* (*explosion*) détonation *f* **II.** *vt* **1.** (*give an account of: casualties, facts*) rapporter; TV, RADIO faire un reportage sur; **the way the press ~ed the incident** la façon dont la presse a rapporté l'incident; **he is ~ed to be living in Egypt** il paraît qu'il vit en Egypte; **he ~ed that everyone had left the building** il a annoncé que tout le monde avait quitté le bâtiment **2.** (*make public*) annoncer **3.** (*inform*) signaler; **to be ~ed missing** être porté disparu **4.** (*denounce*) dénoncer; **fault** signaler **5.** POL rapporter **III.** *vi* **1.** (*write a report*) faire un rapport; **to ~ on sth to sb** faire un rapport a qn sur qc **2.** (*in journalism*) faire un reportage; **~ing from New York, our correspondent ...** de New York, notre correspondant ... **3.** (*present oneself formally*) se présenter; **to ~ to sb/a place** se présenter a qn/un endroit; **to ~ sick** dire qu'on est malade

◆**report back** **I.** *vt* (*give results*) rapporter **II.** *vi* **1.** (*give a report*) faire un rapport; **to ~ to sb on sth** rendre un rapport a qn sur qc **2.** (*be back*) être de retour

◆**report to** *vt* ADMIN **to ~ sb** travailler sous la direction de qn; **who do you ~?** qui est votre supérieur?

report card *n Am* bulletin *m* scolaire

reported *adj* **1.** (*so-called*) soi-disant(e) **2.** (*known*) connu(e)

reportedly *adv* à ce qu'on dit

reported speech *n* LING discours *m* indirect

reporter *n* journaliste *mf*

repose [rɪ'pəʊz, *Am:* -'poʊz] **I.** *vi form* se reposer **II.** *vt form* remettre; **to ~ hope in sb/sth** mettre son espoir en qn/qc **III.** *n no pl, form* calme *m*

repository [rɪ'pɒzɪtrɪ, *Am:* -'pɑːzɪtɔːrɪ] <-ies> *n form* **1.** (*store*) dépôt *m* **2.** (*store of sth*) réserve *f* **3.** *fig* (*of information*) mine *f*

repossess [ˌriːpə'zes] *vt* saisir

repossession *n* saisie *f*

repost *vt* INFOR réafficher

reprehensible [ˌreprɪ'hensəbl] *adj form* répréhensible

represent [ˌreprɪ'zent] *vt* **1.** (*show, symbolize, be representative of*) représenter; **poorly ~ed** insuffisamment représenté(e) **2.** (*be: progress, loss*) représenter **3.** *form* (*claim as*) **to ~ sth as sth** présenter qc comme qc; **to ~ oneself as sth** se faire passer pour qc

representation *n* représentation *f* ►**to make ~s to sb about sth** *form* exprimer des inquiétudes au sujet de qc auprès de qn

representative **I.** *adj a.* POL représentatif(-ive) **II.** *n* **1.** (*person representing another*) *a.* ECON, POL représentant(e) *m(f)*; **elected ~** élu(e) *m(f)* **2.** *Am* (*member of House of Representatives*) député(e) *m(f)*

repress [rɪ'pres] *vt* réprimer; (*one's tears*) retenir

repressed *adj a.* PSYCH refoulé(e)

repression *n no pl* répression *f*; PSYCH refoulement *m*

repressive *adj* répressif(-ive)

reprieve [rɪ'priːv] **I.** *vt* LAW gracier; (*leave alone*) accorder un sursis à **II.** *n* **1.** LAW grâce *f* **2.** *fig* délai *m*

reprimand ['reprɪmɑːnd, *Am:* -rəmænd] **I.** *vt* réprimander **II.** *n* réprimande *f*

reprint [ˌriː'prɪnt] **I.** *vt* rééditer **II.** *n* réédition *f*

reprisal [rɪ'praɪzl] *n* représailles *fpl*; **to take ~s against sb** exercer des représailles contre qn; **as a ~ for sth** en représailles a qc

reproach [rɪ'prəʊtʃ, *Am:* -'proʊtʃ] **I.** *vt* faire des reproches; **to ~ sb for doing sth** reprocher à qn d'avoir fait qc; **to ~ oneself** se faire des reproches **II.** *n* reproche *m*; **to be above ~** être au-dessus de tout reproche; **to be a ~ to sb/sth** être une honte pour qn/qc

reproachful *adj* réprobateur(-trice)

reprobate ['reprəbeɪt] *n iron, form* honte *f*

reprocess [ˌriː'prəʊses, *Am:* -'prɑːses] *vt* ECOL, TECH retraiter

reprocessing *n no pl* ECOL, TECH retraitement *m*

reprocessing plant *n* ECOL, TECH usine *f* de retraitement

reproduce [ˌriːprəˈdjuːs, *Am:* -ˈduːs] **I.** *vi* se reproduire **II.** *vt* reproduire; **to ~ oneself** se reproduire

reproduction [ˌriːprəˈdʌkʃn] *n* reproduction *f*

reproductive [ˌriːprəˈdʌktɪv] *adj* reproducteur(-trice)

reproof [rɪˈpruːf] *n form* réprimande *f*

re-proof [riːˈpruːf] *vt* réimperméabiliser

reprove [rɪˈpruːv] *vt form* réprimander

reproving *adj form* réprobateur(-trice)

reptile [ˈreptaɪl] *n* reptile *m*

republic [rɪˈpʌblɪk] *n* république *f*

republican **I.** *n* républicain(e) *m(f)* **II.** *adj* républicain(e)

republication [ˌriːˌpʌblɪˈkeɪʃn] *n no pl* republication *f*

repudiate [rɪˈpjuːdɪeɪt] *vt form* (*accusation, claim*) récuser; (*suggestion*) rejeter

repugnance [rɪˈpʌgnəns] *n no pl, form* répugnance *f*

repugnant *adj form* répugnant(e)

repulse [rɪˈpʌls] **I.** *vt a.* MIL repousser **II.** *n form* rejet *m*

repulsion *n no pl a.* PHYS répulsion *f*

repulsive *adj* répulsif(-ive)

repurchase [ˌriːˈpɜːtʃəs] *vt* racheter

repurchase price *n* prix *m* de rachat

reputable *adj* convenable

reputation [ˌrepjʊˈteɪʃn] *n* réputation *f;* **to have a ~ for sth** être connu pour qc; **to have a ~ as sth** avoir une réputation de qc; **to make a ~ for oneself as sth** se faire une réputation en tant que qc; **to know sb/sth by ~** connaître qn/qc de nom

repute [rɪˈpjuːt] *n form no pl* renom *m;* **of ill/good ~** de mauvaise/bonne renommée; **to be held in high ~ by sb** être très estimé par qn

reputed *adj* réputé(e)

reputedly *adv* notoirement

request [rɪˈkwest] **I.** *n* **1.** (*act of asking*) demande *f;* **at sb's ~** a la demande de qn; **on ~** sur demande **2.** (*formally asking*) sollicitation *f* **3.** RADIO demande *f* **II.** *vt* **1.** (*ask for: help, information*) demander; **to ~ sb to** *+infin* prier qn de *+infin* **2.** RADIO demander

request programme, **request show** *n* RADIO programme *m* a la demande **request stop** *n Brit* arrêt *m* facultatif

requiem (**mass**) [ˈrekwɪəm-] *n* requiem *m inv*

require [rɪˈkwaɪəʳ, *Am:* -ˈkwaɪɚ] *vt* **1.** (*need*) nécessiter; **to be ~d for sth** être nécessaire pour qc; **~d reading** ouvrage *m* incontournable **2.** (*demand*) demander; **to be ~d of sb** être requis de qn **3.** (*officially order*) **to be ~d to** *+infin* être prié de *+infin* **4.** *form* (*wish to have*) désirer

requirement *n* exigence *f;* **to meet the ~s of sb/sth** répondre aux besoins de qn/qc

requisite [ˈrekwɪzɪt] **I.** *adj form* requis(e) **II.** *n pl* accessoires *mpl*

requisition **I.** *vt* **to ~ sth from sb** requisitionner qc de qn **II.** *n no pl* requisition *f;* **a ~ order** une requisition

reroute [ˌriːˈruːt] *vt* détourner

rerun [ˌrɪːˈrʌn] **I.** *vt irr* **1.** (*show again: series*) rediffuser **2.** (*hold again: race, election*) recommencer **II.** *n* **1.** CINE, TV rediffusion *f* **2.** (*repeat*) répétition *f*

resale [ˈriːseɪl] *n* ECON revente *f*

resale value *n* valeur *f* de rachat

reschedule [ˌriːˈʃedjuːl, *Am:* -ˈskedʒuːl] *vt* (*meeting, programme*) reprogrammer; (*date*) reporter; (*debt*) rééchelonner

rescind [rɪˈsɪnd] *vt form* LAW abroger; (*contract*) annuler

rescue [ˈreskjuː] **I.** *vt* sauver; (*hostage, prisoner*) libérer **II.** *n* sauvetage *m;* (*of a hostage, prisoner*) libération *f;* **to go to the ~** arriver à la rescousse; **to come to sb's ~** venir à la rescousse de qn

rescue operation *n* opération *f* de sauvetage **rescue party** *n* équipe *f* de sauvetage

rescuer *n* sauveteur *m*

rescue worker *n* sauveteur *m*

research [rɪˈsɜːtʃ, *Am:* -ˈsɜːrtʃ] **I.** *n* **1.** (*investigation*) recherche *f;* **cancer ~** recherche contre le cancer; **~ into sth** recherche *f* en qc; **to carry out ~ into sth** faire de la recherche sur qc **2.** (*texts*) travaux *mpl* **II.** *vi* (*carry out research*) faire de la recherche; **to ~ into sth** faire une étude de qc **III.** *vt* étudier

research and development *n* recherche *f* et développement *m* **research assistant** *n* assistant(e) *m(f)* de recherche

researcher *n* UNIV chercheur *m;* (*for news programmes*) documentaliste *mf*

research work *n* travail *m* de recherche **research worker** *n* chercheur *m*

resemblance [rɪˈzembləns] *n no pl* ressemblance *f;* **family ~** air *m* de famille; **to bear a ~ to sb/sth** avoir des ressemblances avec qn/qc

resemble [rɪˈzembl] *vt* ressembler à, tirer sur *Belgique, Nord;* **there was nothing resembling a post office** il n'y avait pas un bureau de poste à l'horizon

resent [rɪˈzent] *vt* (*person*) en vouloir à; (*situation, attitude*) avoir du ressentiment contre; **to ~ doing sth** être mécontent d'avoir à faire qc; **to ~ sb's doing sth** en vouloir à qn d'avoir fait qc

resentful *adj* mécontent(e)

resentment *n* rancoœur *f;* **to feel** (**a**) **~ against sb** être en colère après qn

reservation [ˌrezəˈveɪʃn, *Am:* -ɚˈ-] *n* **1.** (*hesitation, doubt*) réserve *f;* **~s about sth** des réserves sur qc; **with/without ~**(**s**) sous/sans réserve **2.** (*booking*) réservation *f* **3.** (*area of land*) réserve *f*

reserve [rɪˈzɜːv, *Am:* -ˈzɜːrv] **I.** *n* **1.** *no pl, a. form* réserve *f;* **with/without ~** sous/sans réserve; **to have/keep sth in ~** avoir/mettre

R

qc en réserve; **to put sth on** ~ mettre qc de côté **2.** SPORT remplaçant(e) *m(f)* **II.** *vt* **1.** (*keep: leftovers, rest*) garder **2.** (*save*) **to** ~ **sth for sb/sth** mettre qc de côté pour qn/qc; **to** ~ **the right to** +*infin* se réserver le droit de +*infin* **3.** (*make a reservation: room, seat, ticket*) réserver

reserve currency *n* monnaie *f* de réserve

reserved *adj* réservé(e)

reserve price *n* prix *m* minimal

reservist [rɪˈzɜːvɪst, *Am:* -ˈzɜːr-] *n* MIL réserviste *mf*

reservoir [ˈrezəvwɑːʳ, *Am:* -ɚvwɑːr] *n a. fig* réservoir *m*

reset [ˌriːˈset] *irr vt* **1.** (*to set again: clock, timer*) remettre à l'heure; (*meter*) remettre à zéro **2.** MED (*broken bone*) remboîter **3.** INFOR (*computer, system*) réinitialiser

reset button *n* INFOR, ELEC touche *f* reset

resettle [ˌriːˈsetl] **I.** *vi* aller s'installer; **to** ~ **down south** aller s'installer dans le sud **II.** *vt* (*people*) déplacer; (*land*) repeupler

reshuffle [ˌriːˈʃʌfl] **I.** *vt* POL remanier **II.** *n* POL remaniement *m* ministériel

reside [rɪˈzaɪd] *vi form* résider

residence [ˈrezɪdəns] *n a. form* résidence *f;* **to take up** ~ emménager

residence permit *n* permis *m* de séjour

resident I. *n a.* POL résident(e) *m(f);* **~s' parking** stationnement *m* réservé aux riverains **II.** *adj* **1.** (*stay*) domicilié(e) **2.** (*living where one is employed*) sur place

residential *adj* résidentiel(le); (*staff*) à demeure; ~ **establishment** résidence *f;* ~ **course** stage *m* avec logement sur place

residential school *n* internat *m*

resident permit *n* permis *m* de séjour

residual [rɪˈzɪdjʊəl, *Am:* -ˈzɪdʒu-] **I.** *adj* restant(e); (*income*) net(te); PHYS résiduel(le) **II.** *n* résidu *m;* MAT reste *m*

residuary [rɪˈzɪdjʊərɪ, *Am:* -ˈzɪdʒuerɪ] *adj* restant(e)

residue [ˈrezɪdjuː, *Am:* -əduː] *n* **1.** *a. form* résidu *m* **2.** (*of estate*) reste *m*

resign [rɪˈzaɪn] **I.** *vi* **1.** (*leave one's job*) démissionner **2.** GAMES abandonner **II.** *vt* **1.** (*leave: post*) abandonner **2. to** ~ **oneself to sth/doing sth** se résigner à qc/à faire qc

resignation [ˌrezɪgˈneɪʃn] *n* **1.** (*official letter*) (lettre *f* de) démission *f;* **to hand in one's** ~ remettre sa démission **2.** *no pl* (*act of resigning*) démission *f* **3.** *no pl* (*acceptance*) résignation *f*

resigned *adj* résigné(e); **to be** ~ **to sth/doing sth** s'être résigné à qc/à faire qc

resilience [rɪˈzɪlɪəns, *Am:* ˈzɪljəns] *n no pl* **1.** (*ability to regain shape*) élasticité *f* **2.** (*ability to recover quickly*) résistance *f*

resilient *adj* **1.** (*able to keep shape*) élastique **2.** (*able to survive setbacks*) résistant(e)

resin [ˈrezɪn] *n no pl* résine *f;* **fir/pine** ~ résine de sapin/pin

resinous *adj* résineux(-euse)

resist [rɪˈzɪst] **I.** *vt* **1.** (*withstand*) résister à **2.** (*refuse to accept*) s'opposer à **II.** *vi* résister

resistance [rɪˈzɪstəns] *n* résistance *f;* **to offer no** ~ **to sb/sth** n'opposer aucune résistance à qn/qc; **to put up (a) determined** ~ opposer une résistance déterminée ▶**to take the** <u>**path**</u> [*o* <u>**line**</u> *Brit*] **of least** ~ choisir la solution de facilité

resistance fighter *n* résistant(e) *m(f)*

resistant *adj* résistant(e); **to be** ~ **to sth** être résistant à qc

resistor [rɪˈzɪstəʳ, *Am:* -tɚ] *n* ELEC rhéostat *m*

resit [ˈriːsɪt] **I.** *vt irr, Brit* SCHOOL, UNIV (*examination*) repasser **II.** *n Brit* SCHOOL, UNIV seconde session *f*

resolute [ˈrezəluːt] *adj form* résolu(e); (*belief, character, stand*) décidé(e)

resolution *n* résolution *f*

resolvable *adj* résoluble

resolve [rɪˈzɒlv, *Am:* -ˈzɑːlv] **I.** *vt* **1.** (*decide*) **to** ~ **that ...** décider que ...; **to** ~ **to** +*infin* se résoudre à +*infin* **2.** (*settle*) régler; **to** ~ **one's differences** régler un différend **3.** (*solve*) résoudre; **the problem** ~**d itself** le problème s'est réglé tout seul **II.** *n form* résolution *f*

◆**resolve on** *vt* **to** ~ **sth/doing sth** prendre la décision de qc/de faire qc

resolved *adj* décidé(e); **to be** ~ **to** +*infin* avoir décidé de +*infin*

resonance [ˈrezənəns] *n no pl* (*of an instrument*) résonance *f;* (*of laughter*) retentissement *m;* (*of thunder*) grondement *m*

resonant *adj* résonant(e)

resonate [ˈrezəneɪt] *vi* résonner

resort [rɪˈzɔːt, *Am:* -ˈzɔːrt] *n* **1.** (*place for holidays*) villégiature *f;* **health** ~ station *f* thermale; **holiday** ~ lieu *m* de vacances **2.** *no pl* **without** ~ **to sth** sans recours à qc; **as a last** ~ en dernier recours

◆**resort to** *vt* **to** ~ **sth/doing sth** recourir à qc/à faire qc

resound [rɪˈzaʊnd] *vi* résonner

resounding *adj a. fig* retentissant(e)

resource [rɪˈsɔːs, *Am:* ˈriːsɔːrs] **I.** *n pl* ressources *fpl;* **energy/natural** ~**s** les ressources d'énergie/naturelles **II.** *vt* financer; **to be inadequately** ~**d** manquer de ressources

resource centre *n* centre *m* de documentation

resourceful *adj* (*person*) ingénieux(-euse)

respect [rɪˈspekt] **I.** *n* **1.** *no pl* (*esteem or consideration*) respect *m;* **to have** ~ **for sb/sth** avoir du respect pour qn/qc; **to show** ~ **for sb/sth** montrer du respect à qn/qc; **to command** ~ susciter le respect; **to earn the** ~ **of sb** gagner le respect de qn; **out of** ~ **for sb/sth** par respect pour qn/qc **2.** *pl, form* (*polite greetings*) **to pay one's** ~**s to sb** présenter ses hommages à qn; **to pay one's last** ~**s to sb** rendre un dernier hommage à qn ▶**in** <u>**many**</u>/<u>**some**</u> ~**s** à beaucoup d'égards/à certains égards; **in** <u>**all**</u> ~**s** à tous égards; <u>**in**</u> ~ **of sth** *form* à l'égard de qc; **in** <u>**this**</u> ~ à cet égard **II.** *vt*

respecter; **to ~ oneself** s'estimer
respectable *adj* respectable; (*area, person, behaviour*) décent(e); **to make oneself ~** se rendre présentable
respected *adj* respecté(e)
respectful *adj* respectueux(-euse); **to be ~ of sth** être respectueux envers qc
respectfully *adv* respectueusement; **~ yours ...** respectueusement ...
respecting *prep form* concernant
respective *adj* respectif(-ive)
respectively *adv* respectivement
respiration [ˌrespəˈreɪʃn] *n no pl, form* respiration *f*
respirator [ˈrespəreɪtəʳ, *Am:* -t̬ɚ] *n* MED respirateur *m*
respiratory [rɪˈspaɪərətrɪ, *Am:* ˈrespɚ-ətɔːrɪ] *adj* respiratoire
respite [ˈrespaɪt, *Am:* -pɪt] *n no pl, form* **1.** (*pause*) répit *m;* **a short ~ from sth** un moment de répit dans qc **2.** (*delay*) délai *m*
resplendent [rɪˈsplendənt] *adj form* resplendissant(e)
respond [rɪˈspɒnd, *Am:* -ˈspɑːnd] **I.** *vt* répondre **II.** *vi* **1.** (*answer*) **to ~ to sth** répondre à qc **2.** (*react*) réagir
respondent [rɪˈspɒndənt, *Am:* -ˈspɑːn-] *n* **1.** (*in poll*) personne *f* sondée **2.** (*defendant*) défendeur, -eresse *m, f*
response [rɪˈspɒns, *Am:* -ˈspɑːns] *n* (*reaction, answer*) réponse *f;* **to meet with a bad/good ~** être bien/mal accueilli; **in ~ to sth** en réponse à qc
response time *n* INFOR temps *m* de réponse; (*on phone*) attente *f*
responsibility [rɪˌspɒnsəˈbɪlətɪ, *Am:* -ˌspɑːnsəˈbɪlət̬ɪ] *n* responsabilité *f;* **whose ~ is this?** qui est le responsable pour ceci?; **to claim ~ for sth** revendiquer la responsabilité de qc; **to take full ~ for sth** prendre l'entière responsabilité de qc; **to have a ~ to sb/sth** avoir une responsabilité envers qn/qc
responsible [rɪˈspɒnsəbl, *Am:* -ˈspɑːn-] *adj* responsable; (*job, task*) à responsabilité; **to be ~ for sth/sb** être responsable de qc/qn; **to be ~ for doing sth** avoir la responsabilité de faire qc; **to hold sb/sth ~ for sth** tenir qn/qc responsable de qc
responsibly *adv* de façon responsable
responsive [rɪˈspɒnsɪv, *Am:* -ˈspɑːn-] *adj a.* MED réceptif(-ive)
respray¹ [ˌriːˈspreɪ] *vt* (*car*) repeindre
respray² [ˈriːspreɪ] *n* nouvelle couche *f* de peinture
rest [rest] **I.** *vt* **1.** (*repose*) reposer; **to ~ one's feet** se reposer les pieds **2.** (*support*) reposer; **to ~ sth against/(up)on sth** appuyer qc contre/sur qc **II.** *vi* **1.** (*cease activity*) se reposer **2.** *form* (*be dealt with*) incomber; **the matter ~s with them** la question dépend d'eux **3.** (*be supported*) reposer; **to ~ on sth** s'appuyer sur qc **4.** (*depend*) **to ~ on sb/sth** s'appuyer sur qn/qc ▶**to let sth rest** mettre qc de côté, **let it ~!** laisse faire!; **to ~ on one's laurels** se reposer sur ses lauriers; **~ in peace** reposer en paix; **you can ~ assured that ...** vous pouvez être assuré(s) que ... **III.** *n* **1.** (*repose*) repos *m;* (*at work*) pause *f;* **to have a ~** se reposer; **give it a ~!** *inf* laisse tomber! **2.** MUS pause *f* **3.** (*support*) support *m* **4.** *no pl, + sing/pl verb* (*remainder*) **the ~** le reste; **the ~ of the cake** le reste du livre; **the ~ of the people/books** les autres personnes/livres; **and all the ~** *inf* et tout le reste ▶**to come to ~** s'arrêter; **at ~** (*not moving*) au repos; (*dead*) mort
restart [ˌriːˈstɑːt, *Am:* -ˈstɑːrt] *vt* (*computer*) redémarrer; (*car*) remettre en marche; (*negotiations*) relancer
restate [ˌriːˈsteɪt] *vt* réaffirmer
restaurant [ˈrestrɒnt, *Am:* -tərɑːnt] *n* restaurant *m*
restaurant car *n Brit* wagon-restaurant *m*
restaurateur [ˌrestərəˈtɜːʳ, *Am:* -tɚəˈtɜːr] *n form* restaurateur, -trice *m, f*
rest cure *n* cure *f* de repos **rest-day** *n* jour *m* de congé
restful *adj* tranquille; (*atmosphere*) reposant(e); (*place*) de repos; **to be ~ to the eyes** être reposant pour les yeux
rest home *n* maison *f* de repos
resting place *n* abri *m;* **sb's last ~** la dernière demeure de qn
restitution [ˌrestɪˈtjuːʃn, *Am:* -ˈtuː-] *n no pl* **1.** (*return*) restitution *f* **2.** (*compensation*) compensation *f*
restive [ˈrestɪv] *adj* agité(e); (*horse*) rétif(-ive)
restless *adj* **1.** (*fidgety*) agité(e) **2.** (*impatient*) impatient(e); **to get ~** s'impatienter; (*start making trouble*) s'agiter **3.** (*wakeful*) troublé(e); (*night*) agité(e)
restock [ˌriːˈstɒk, *Am:* -ˈstɑːk] **I.** *vt* réapprovisionner; (*lake*) remplir **II.** *vi* se réapprovisionner
restoration *n* **1.** *no pl* (*act of restoring*) restauration *f* **2.** *no pl* (*reestablishment*) rétablissement *f* **3.** *no pl, form* (*return to owner*) remise *f*
restorative **I.** *n* fortifiant *m* **II.** *adj* reconstituant(e)
restore [rɪˈstɔːʳ, *Am:* -ˈstɔːr] *vt* **1.** (*return to original state*) restaurer **2.** (*reestablish*) rétablir **3.** *form* (*return to owner*) restituer **4.** (*return to former state*) ramener; INFOR réafficher; **to ~ sb to health** rétablir la santé de qn
restorer *n* ARCHIT, ART, CONSTR restaurateur, -trice *m, f*
restrain [rɪˈstreɪn] *vt* **1.** (*physically check: troublemaker*) retenir; **to ~ sb from doing sth** empêcher qn de faire qc; **to ~ oneself from doing sth** se retenir de faire qc **2.** (*keep under control: dog, horse*) maîtriser; (*inflation*) contenir
restrained *adj* **1.** (*calm*) contenu(e) **2.** (*not emotional*) sobre; (*policy*) mesuré(e)
restraint [rɪˈstreɪnt] *n* **1.** *no pl* (*self-control*)

R

mesure *f;* **to exercise** ~ *form* faire preuve de mesure **2.** (*restriction*) contrainte *f;* (*on press*) limitation *f;* (*on imports*) restriction *f*

restrict [rɪ'strɪkt] *vt* **1.** (*limit*) restreindre; **to ~ sth to sth** limiter qc à qc; **to ~ oneself to sth** se limiter à qc **2.** (*confine*) limiter à un endroit

restricted *adj* **1.** (*limited*) restreint(e); (*view*) limité(e) **2.** (*confined*) limité(e)

restricted area *n* zone *f* interdite **restricted document** *n* document *m* secret **restricted entry** *n* entrée *f* réservée **restricted parking** *n* parking *m* réservé

restriction *n* **1.** (*limit*) restriction *f;* (*of speed*) limitation *f* **2.** *no pl* (*limitation*) limitation *f*

restrictive *adj pej* restrictif(-ive)

restring [,riː'strɪŋ] *irr vt* (*beads*) enfiler de nouveau; (*instrument*) remonter; (*tennis racket*) recorder

rest room ['restruːm] *n Am* toilettes *fpl*

restructure [,riː'strʌktʃəʳ, *Am:* -tʃɚ] *vt* restructurer

restructuring *n* restructuration *f*

result [rɪ'zʌlt] **I.** *n* **1.** (*consequence*) résultat *m;* **end ~** résultat final; **the ~s of an accident** les conséquences d'un accident; **as a ~ of sth** par suite de qc; **as a ~** en conséquence **2.** *Brit, inf* SPORT victoire *f* **3.** (*reached by calculation*) résultat *m* ►**with no ~** sans résultat **II.** *vi* résulter; **to ~ in sth** avoir qc pour résultat; **to ~ in sb('s) doing sth** avoir pour résultat que qn fait qc

resultant [rɪ'zʌltənt] *adj form s.* **resulting**

resume [rɪ'zjuːm, *Am:* -'zuːm] **I.** *vt* **1.** (*start again*) recommencer; (*work*) reprendre; (*journey*) poursuivre; **to ~ doing sth** se remettre à faire qc **2.** *form* (*reoccupy*) reprendre **II.** *vi form* continuer

résumé ['rezjuːmeɪ, *Am:* 'rezʊmeɪ] *n* **1.** (*summary*) résumé *m;* **to give sb a ~ of sth** faire à qn le résumé de qc **2.** *Am, Aus* (*curriculum vitae*) *s.* **CV**

resumption [rɪ'zʌmpʃn] *n* reprise *f*

resurface [,riː'sɜːfɪs, *Am:* -'sɜːrfɪs] **I.** *vi* **1.** (*rise to the surface again*) revenir à la surface **2.** (*reappear: problem*) réapparaître; (*friend*) refaire surface **II.** *vt* refaire le revêtement de

resurgence [rɪ'sɜːdʒəns, *Am:* -'sɜːrdʒəns] *n no pl, form* réapparition *f*

resurgent *adj form* renaissant(e)

resurrect [,rezə'rekt] *vt* **1.** (*revive*) ranimer; (*idea*) faire revivre **2.** (*bring back to life*) ressusciter

resurrection *n no pl* résurrection *f*

resuscitate [rɪ'sʌsɪteɪt, *Am:* -əteɪt] *vt* **1.** (*revive from unconsciousness*) ressusciter **2.** (*revive*) ranimer

retail ['riːteɪl] COM **I.** *n no pl* détail *m* **II.** *adj* de détail **III.** *vt* vendre au détail **IV.** *vi* se vendre au détail; **to ~ at £4** être vendu à 4£ **V.** *adv* au détail

retailing *n* vente *f* au détail

retail outlet *n* point *m* de vente

retailer *n* commerçant(e) *m(f);* **book ~s** libraires *mpl*

retail price *n* prix *m* de détail **retail price index** *n* indice *m* des prix de détail

retain [rɪ'teɪn] *vt* **1.** *form* (*keep*) retenir; (*independence, format*) garder; (*right, title*) conserver **2.** *form* (*remember*) retenir **3.** (*hold in place*) maintenir **4.** (*employ*) retenir; **to ~ sb's services** s'assurer les services de qn

retainer *n* **1.** (*fee*) avance *f* **2.** *iron* (*servant*) serviteur *m*

retaining wall *n* mur *m* de soutien

retake [,riː'teɪk] **I.** *vt irr* **1.** (*take again: territory*) reprendre **2.** (*regain: title*) regagner **3.** (*film again*) refaire **4.** (*resit: exam*) repasser **5.** (*capture again: criminal*) rattraper **II.** *n* CINE reprise *f*

retaliate [rɪ'tælɪeɪt] *vi* riposter; **to ~ against sb with sth** user de représailles contre qn avec qc

retaliation *n no pl* riposte *f;* **in ~ for sth** en représailles de qc

retaliatory [rɪ'tælɪətrɪ, *Am:* -tɔːrɪ] *adj* de rétorsion

retard [rɪ'tɑːd, *Am:* -'tɑːrd] **I.** *vt form* retarder; (*development*) ralentir **II.** *n pej* (*retarded person*) demeuré(e) *m(f)*

retardation [,riːtɑː'deɪʃn, *Am:* -tɑːr'-] *n no pl, form* (*slowing down*) retard *m*

retarded *adj* attardé(e)

retch [retʃ] *vi* avoir la nausée

retention [rɪ'tenʃn] *n no pl* **1.** *form* (*keeping*) rétention *f;* (*of heat*) conservation *f* **2.** *form* (*memory*) mémoire *f* **3.** (*securing sb's services*) maintien *m*

retentive [rɪ'tentɪv, *Am:* -t̬ɪv] *adj* (*memory*) bon(ne)

rethink [,riː'θɪŋk] **I.** *vt irr* (*reconsider*) repenser **II.** *vi irr* (*reconsider*) reconsidérer **III.** *n no pl* (*reconsideration*) reconsidération *f;* **to have a ~** repenser

reticent ['retɪsnt, *Am:* 'ret̬əsnt] *adj* réticent(e); **to be ~ about doing sth** avoir des réticences à faire qc

retina ['retɪnə, *Am:* 'retnə] <-s *o* -nae> *n* ANAT rétine *f*

retinue ['retɪnjuː, *Am:* 'retnuː] *n* suite *f*

retire [rɪ'taɪəʳ, *Am:* -'taɪɚ] **I.** *vi* **1.** (*stop working*) prendre sa retraite; **to ~ from business** se retirer des affaires **2.** (*stop competing*) se retirer; **to ~ from sth** abandonner qc **3.** *form* (*withdraw*) se retirer **4.** *form* (*go to bed*) se coucher **II.** *vt* **1.** (*cause to stop working*) **to ~ sb from sth** mettre qn à la retraite de qc **2.** (*pull back*) replier

retired *adj* retraité(e); **a ~ police officer** un officier de police à la retraite

retiree *n Am* retraité(e) *m(f)*

retirement *n* retraite *f;* **to go into ~** partir en retraite; **to come out of ~** reprendre sa carrière; **to be in ~** être à la retraite; **to take**

early ~ prendre une retraite anticipée; ~ **benefits** allocation *f* de retraire; **to live in** ~ *fig* vivre en ermite

retirement age *n* âge *m* de la retraite **retirement home** *n* maison *f* de retraite **retirement pay, retirement pension** *n* pension *f* de retraite

retiring *adj* réservé(e)

retort [rɪ'tɔːt, *Am:* -'tɔːrt] **I.** *vi* répliquer **II.** *n* réplique *f;* **to make a** ~ lancer une réplique

retouch [ˌriː'tʌtʃ] *vt* PHOT retoucher

retouching *n* INFOR retouche *f*

retrace [riː'treɪs] *vt* **1.** (*go back over*) retracer; **to** ~ **one's steps** revenir sur ses pas **2.** (*go over in one's mind*) reconstituer

retract [rɪ'trækt] **I.** *vt* (*withdraw*) rétracter; (*statement*) revenir sur; (*wheels*) rentrer **II.** *vi* **1.** (*withdraw words*) se rétracter **2.** (*be drawn out of sight*) rentrer

retraction *n form* rétraction *f*

retrain [riː'treɪn] **I.** *vt* (*train anew*) recycler; **to** ~ **sb in sth** faire suivre une nouvelle formation en qc à qn **II.** *vi* se recycler; **to** ~ **as sth** suivre une nouvelle formation en qc

retread [ˌriː'tred, *Am:* -'trɑːd] **I.** *vt* AUTO (*tyre*) rechaper **II.** *n* rechapé *m*

retreat [rɪ'triːt] **I.** *vi* **1.** MIL *a. fig* battre en retraite **2.** (*move backwards*) reculer **3.** (*withdraw*) se retirer **II.** *n* **1.** MIL retraite *f;* **to beat a** ~ *a. fig* battre en retraite **2.** (*change of position*) revirement *m* **3.** (*safe place*) abri *m;* **my country** ~ ma maison de campagne **4.** (*period of seclusion*) retraite *f;* **to go on a** ~ faire une retraite

retrench [rɪ'trentʃ] **I.** *vi form* se retrancher **II.** *vt* (*personnel*) restreindre

retrenchment *n* **1.** *form* (*cut in spending*) réduction *f* **2.** *no pl* (*cutting down*) économies *fpl*

retrial [ˌriː'traɪəl, *Am:* 'riːtraɪl] *n* LAW nouveau procès *m*

retribution [ˌretrɪ'bjuːʃn, *Am:* -rə'-] *n no pl, form* châtiment *m*

retributive [rɪ'trɪbjʊtɪv] *adj form* de châtiment; (*justice*) punitif(-ive)

retrieval [rɪ'triːvl] *n no pl* **1.** (*regaining*) recouvrement *m;* (*of stolen goods*) récupération *f* **2.** INFOR extraction *f*

retrieve [rɪ'triːv] *vt* **1.** (*get sth back*) retrouver **2.** INFOR extraire **3.** (*fetch*) rapporter ►**to** ~ **the situation** sauver la situation

retriever *n* chien *m* d'arrêt

retroactive [ˌretrəʊ'æktɪv, *Am:* -roʊ'-] *adj* rétroactif(-ive)

retrograde ['retrəgreɪd] *adj* rétrograde

retrogressive [ˌretrə'gresɪv, *Am:* 'retrəg-res-] *adj* rétrograde

retrorocket [ˌretrəʊ'rɒkɪt, *Am:* 'retroʊˌrɑːkɪt] *n* TECH rétrofusée *f*

retrospect ['retrəspekt] *n no pl* **in** ~ rétrospectivement

retrospective **I.** *adj* **1.** (*looking back*) rétrospectif(-ive) **2.** *Brit, form* LAW *s.* **retroactive** **II.** *n* rétrospective *f*

retrovirus ['retrəʊvaɪərəs, *Am:* 'retroʊˌvaɪ-] *n* retrovirus *m*

retry [ˌriː'traɪ] *vt* **1.** LAW rejuger **2.** INFOR relancer

retune *vt* accorder

return [rɪ'tɜːn, *Am:* -'tɜːrn] **I.** *n* **1.** (*coming, going back*) retour *m;* **on one's** ~ dès son retour, retour *m* au pouvoir; ~ **to work** reprise *f* du travail **2.** (*giving back*) retour *m;* (*of money*) remboursement *m;* (*of stolen goods*) restitution *f* **3.** (*sending back*) renvoi *m* **4.** (*recompense*) récompense *f* **5.** *Brit, Aus* (*ticket, fare*) aller-retour *m;* ~ (**journey**) retour *m* **6.** (*stroke hit*) renvoi *m;* ~ **of serve** retour de service **7.** (*profit*) bénéfice *m* **8.** *pl, Am* POL résultats *mpl* électoraux **9.** *pl* (*returned goods*) rendus *mpl* **10.** *no pl* INFOR touche *f* de retour ►**many** <u>**happy**</u> ~**s** (**of the day**) bon anniversaire; <u>**by**</u> ~ **of post** *Brit, Aus* par retour du courrier; **to do sth by** ~ faire qc en retour; <u>**in**</u> ~ **for sth** en retour de qc **II.** *vi* **1.** (*go back*) retourner **2.** (*come back: person, symptoms*) revenir; **to** ~ **from somewhere/sth** revenir de quelque part/qc; **to** ~ **home** rentrer **III.** *vt* **1.** (*give back*) rendre; **to** ~ **goods** retourner des marchandises; **to** ~ **sb's love** aimer qn en retour; **to** ~ **a call** rappeler **2.** (*place back*) remettre; **to** ~ **sth to its place** remettre qc à sa place **3.** FIN rapporter **4.** *form* LAW déclarer; (*judgement*) prononcer; **to** ~ **a verdict of guilty/not guilty** déclarer l'accusé coupable/non coupable **5.** *Brit* (*elect*) élire **6.** SPORT renvoyer

returnable *adj* consigné(e)

return address *n* adresse *f* de l'expéditeur **return fare** *n* aller-retour *m* **return flight** *n* vol *m* retour

returning officer *n Brit, Can* POL directeur, -trice *m, f* du scrutin

return match *n* match *m* retour **return ticket** *n* **1.** *Aus, Brit* aller-retour *m* **2.** (*ticket for return*) billet *m* de retour

reunification [riːˌjuːnɪfɪ'keɪʃn, *Am:* -nəfɪ'-] *n no pl* réunification *f*

reunion [ˌriː'juːnɪən, *Am:* -'juːnjən] *n* **1.** (*meeting*) réunion *f* **2.** (*meeting of group members*) assemblée *f* **3.** *no pl, form* (*bringing together*) retrouvailles *fpl*

reunite [ˌriːjuː'naɪt] *vt* réunir; (*after quarrel*) réconcilier; **to be** ~**d with sb** retrouver qn

reusable *adj* réutilisable; (*battery*) rechargeable

reuse [ˌriː'juːz] *vt* réutiliser

rev [rev] **I.** *n pl abbr of* **revolution** tour *m* minute **II.** *vt* <-vv-> **to** ~ **sth** (**up**) faire gronder qc **III.** *vi* <-vv-> s'emballer

Rev. *n abbr of* **Reverend** Révérend *m*

revaluation [riːˌvæljʊ'eɪʃn] *n* **1.** (*new estimation*) revalorisation *f* **2.** (*change in value*) réévaluation *f*

revalue [riː'væljuː] *vt* **1.** (*estimate again*) revaloriser **2.** (*change the value of*) réestimer;

to ~ **a currency** réévaluer une devise

revamp [ˌriːˈvæmp] *vt inf* 1. (*reorganize*) remanier; (*department*) restructurer; (*method*) réorganiser; (*play*) modifier 2. (*redecorate*) retaper

rev counter [ˈrevˌkaʊntəʳ, *Am:* -t̬ɚ] *n* compte-tours *m*

Revd *n abbr of* **Reverend** Révérend *m*

reveal [rɪˈviːl] *vt* révéler

revealing *adj* 1. (*interesting*) révélateur(-trice) 2. (*low-cut*) décolleté(e)

reveille [rɪˈvælɪ, *Am:* ˈrevlɪ] *n no pl, no art* MIL réveil *m*

revel [ˈrevəl] I. *vi* se réjouir; **to ~ in sth/doing sth** se délecter de qc/à faire qc II. *n pl* festivités *fpl*

revelation *n* (*revealing*) révélation *f*

Revelation *n no pl* REL l'Apocalypse *f*

reveler *n Brit,* **reveller** *n Am* fêtard(e) *m(f) inf*

revelry [ˈrevlrɪ] <-ies> *n* festivités *fpl*

revenge [rɪˈvendʒ] I. *n no pl* vengeance *f;* **to take (one's) ~ on sb for sth** se venger sur qn pour qc; **to do sth in ~ for sth** faire qc pour se venger de qc ►**~ is sweet** *prov* la vengeance est douce II. *vt* (*avenge*) venger

revenue [ˈrevənjuː, *Am:* -ənuː] *n* 1. *no pl* (*income*) revenu *m* 2. *pl* (*instances of income*) recettes *fpl*

revenue stamp *n Am* timbre *m* fiscal

reverberate [rɪˈvɜːbəreɪt, *Am:* -ˈvɜːrbəreɪt] *vi* 1. (*echo*) résonner; **to ~ through(out) sth** retentir à travers qc; *fig* avoir des répercussions dans qc 2. (*be heard*) faire du bruit

reverberation *n* 1. *no pl* (*echoing*) répercussion *f* 2. (*echo*) réverbération *f*

revere [rɪˈvɪəʳ, *Am:* -ˈvɪr] *vt form* révérer

reverence [ˈrevərəns] *n no pl* révérence *f;* **to have ~ for sb/sth** avoir du respect pour qn/qc

reverend [ˈrevərənd] I. *adj* vénérable II. *n* révérend *m*

reverent *adj* 1. (*showing reverence*) respectueux(-euse) 2. (*feeling reverence*) plein(e) de vénération

reverie [ˈrevəri] *n* rêverie *f*

reversal *n* 1. (*change to opposite*) revirement *m* 2. (*turning other way*) renversement *m;* (*of roles*) inversion *f* 3. (*misfortune*) revers *m* 4. LAW annulation *f*

reverse [rɪˈvɜːs, *Am:* -ˈvɜːrs] I. *vt* 1. *Aus, Brit* (*move backwards*) retourner; **to ~ a vehicle out of somewhere** sortir un véhicule de quelque part; **to ~ a vehicle into sth** reculer un véhicule dans qc 2. (*turn the other way*) retourner 3. (*change to opposite, exchange*) inverser; (*trend, situation*) renverser; **to ~ the charges** *Brit, Can* TEL demander une communication en PCV 4. LAW (*judgement*) annuler II. *vi Aus, Brit* faire marche arrière; **to ~ into/out of the garage** rentrer dans le/sortir du garage en marche arrière; **to ~ into sth** rentrer dans qc en faisant marche arrière III. *n* 1. *no pl* (*opposite*) contraire *m;* **to do sth in ~** faire qc à l'envers 2. (*gear*) marche *f* arrière; **to be in ~** être en marche arrière 3. (*misfortune*) échec *m* 4. (*back*) revers *m;* (*of a coin*) envers *m;* (*of a document*) verso *m* IV. *adj* contraire; (*direction*) opposé(e); (*order*) inverse; **the ~ side** (*of paper*) le verso; (*of garment*) l'envers *m;* **to do sth in ~ order** faire qc à l'envers

reverse-charge *adj Brit* (*call*) en PCV

reverse discrimination *n* discrimination *f* à l'envers **reverse gear** *n* marche *f* arrière

reversible *adj* 1. FASHION réversible 2. (*not permanent: decision*) révocable; (*operation*) réversible

reversion [rɪˈvɜːʃn, *Am:* -ˈvɜːrʒn] *n no pl* 1. *form* (*return to earlier position*) retour *m* 2. LAW réversion *f*

revert [rɪˈvɜːt, *Am:* -ˈvɜːrt] *vi* 1. (*return to former state*) **to ~ to sth** revenir à qc; **to ~ to the question** revenir sur une question; **to ~ to type** (*plant*) retourner à l'état sauvage; *fig* (*person*) reprendre ses mauvaises habitudes 2. LAW **to ~ to sb** revenir à qn

review [rɪˈvjuː] I. *vt* 1. (*consider*) revoir 2. (*reconsider*) reconsidérer 3. (*revise*) réviser; (*notes*) revoir 4. (*write about*) faire la critique de; **favourably ~ed** qui a reçu de bonnes critiques 5. MIL passer en revue 6. *Am* (*study again*) *s.* **revise** II. *n* 1. (*examination*) examen *m;* (*of a situation*) bilan *m;* **to carry out a ~ of sth** revoir qc; **to be under ~** être en cours de révision 2. (*reconsideration*) révision *f;* **to come up for ~** devoir être révisé; **to be subject to ~** faire l'objet d'une révision 3. (*criticism*) critique *f;* **bad ~s** mauvaises critiques *fpl* 4. (*periodical*) revue *f* 5. MIL revue *f* 6. THEAT *s.* **revue** 7. *Am* UNIV révision *f*

reviewer *n* critique *mf*

revise [rɪˈvaɪz] I. *vt* 1. (*reread*) réviser 2. (*reconsider*) revoir; (*opinion*) changer; **to ~ sth downwards/upwards** revoir qc à la baisse/à la hausse 3. *Brit, Aus* (*study again*) réviser II. *vi Aus, Brit* **to ~ for sth** faire des révisions pour qc

revision [rɪˈvɪʒn] *n* révision *f;* **for ~** à revoir

revisionism [rɪˈvɪʒənɪzəm] *n* révisionnisme *m*

revisionist I. *n* révisionniste *mf* II. *adj* révisionniste

revisit [ˌriːˈvɪzɪt] *vt, vi* revisiter

revitalise *vt Aus, Brit,* **revitalize** [riːˈvaɪtəlaɪz, *Am:* -t̬əl-] *vt* ranimer; (*trade*) relancer

revival *n* 1. (*restoration to consciousness*) retour *m* à la vie 2. (*rebirth*) renaissance *f;* (*of custom*) réapparition *f;* (*of a law*) remise en vigueur *f;* (*of interest*) réveil *m;* **an economic ~** une reprise économique 3. THEAT reprise *f*

revive [rɪˈvaɪv] I. *vt* 1. MED (*patient*) réanimer 2. (*give life to: tired person*) ranimer; (*hopes, interest*) faire renaître; (*economy, custom, fashion*) relancer; **to ~ sb's spirits** remonter le moral de qn 3. (*mount a new production*) remonter II. *vi* 1. MED reprendre connaissance

2. (*be restored: tired person*) retrouver ses esprits; (*hopes, interest*) renaître; (*economy, business*) reprendre; (*custom, fashion*) revenir

revocation [ˌrevəˈkeɪʃn] *n* (*of law, decision, order*) annulation *f;* (*of will*) révocation *f*

revoke [rɪˈvəʊk, *Am:* -ˈvoʊk] *vt* LAW révoquer; (*order*) annuler; (*licence*) retirer

revolt [rɪˈvəʊlt, *Am:* -ˈvoʊlt] POL **I.** *vi* se révolter; **to ~ against sb/sth** s'insurger contre qn/qc **II.** *vt* (*disgust*) révolter; **it ~s sb to** *+infin* ça dégoûte qn de *+infin* **III.** *n* révolte *f;* **to be in ~** être en rébellion; **to rise in ~** se soulever

revolting *adj* révoltant(e); **to taste ~** avoir un goût infâme

revolution [ˌrevəˈluːʃn] *n* **1.** (*revolt*) révolution *f* **2.** (*rotation*) tour *m*

revolutionary [ˌrevəˈluːʃənrɪ, *Am:* -ʃenerɪ] **I.** <-ies> *n* révolutionnaire *mf* **II.** *adj* révolutionnaire

revolutionize [ˌrevəˈluːʃnaɪz] *vt* révolutionner

revolve [rɪˈvɒlv, *Am:* -ˈvɑːlv] **I.** *vi* **1.** (*turn*) tourner **2. to ~ around sth** être axé sur **II.** *vt* faire tourner

revolver [rɪˈvɒlvəʳ, *Am:* -ˈvɑːlvɚ] *n* revolver *m*

revolving *adj* en rotation

revolving chair *n* chaise *f* pivotante **revolving door** *n* porte *f* à tambour **revolving fund** *n* fonds *m* de roulement

revue [rɪˈvjuː] *n* revue *f*

revulsion [rɪˈvʌlʃn] *n no pl* dégoût *m;* **~. at sth** dégoût devant qc; **to fill sb with ~** remplir qn de dégoût

reward [rɪˈwɔːd, *Am:* ˈwɔːrd] **I.** *n* récompense *f;* **the ~(s) of sth** les fruits de qc **II.** *vt* **1.** (*give a reward*) récompenser **2.** *form* (*repay*) rémunérer

rewarding *adj* gratifiant(e)

rewind [ˌriːˈwaɪnd] *irr* **I.** *vt* rembobiner; (*watch*) remonter **II.** *vi* (*wind back*) rembobiner **III.** *n* rembobinage *m;* **a ~ button** une touche de rembobinage

rewire [ˌriːˈwaɪəʳ, *Am:* -ˈwaɪɚ] *vt* TECH réinstaller; (*a building*) refaire l'installation électrique de

reword [ˌriːˈwɜːd, *Am:* -ˈwɜːrd] *vt* (*text*) recomposer; (*answer, treaty*) reformuler

rework [ˌriːˈwɜːk] *vt* retravailler

rewrite [ˌriːˈraɪt] *irr* **I.** *vt* LIT réécrire **II.** *n* nouvelle version *f*

RFC *n abbr of* **Rugby Football Club** club *m* de rugby

RGN [ˌɑːʳdʒiːˈen] *n Brit abbr of* **registered general nurse** infirmière *f* diplômée d'Etat

Rh *n abbr of* **rhesus** Rh *m*

rhapsody [ˈræpsədɪ] <-ies> *n* rapsodie *f* ►**to go into rhapsodies about sth** s'extasier sur qc

rhesus factor [ˈriːsəsˌfæktəʳ, *Am:* -tɚ] *n no pl* rhésus *m*

rhesus negative *adj* rhésus négatif *inv* **rhesus positive** *adj* rhésus positif *inv*

rhetoric [ˈretərɪk, *Am:* ˈreţ-] *n no pl* rhétorique *f;* **the ~ of the far right** le discours de l'extrême droite

rhetorical *adj* rhétorique; (*style*) ampoulé(e); **a ~ question** une question de pure forme

rheumatic [ruːˈmætɪk, *Am:* -ˈmæţ-] *adj* rhumatisant(e); (*pain*) rhumatismal(e)

rheumatics *npl + sing vb, inf* rhumatismes *mpl*

rheumatism [ˈruːmətɪzəm] *n no pl* MED rhumatisme *m*

rheumatoid arthritis [ˌruːmətɔɪdˌɑːˈθraɪtɪs, *Am:* -ˌɑːrˈθraɪţɪs] *n no pl* MED polyarthrite *f* rhumatoïde

Rhine [raɪn] *n* **the ~** le Rhin

rhino *inf,* **rhinoceros** [raɪˈnɒsərəs, *Am:* -ˈnɑːsɚ-] <-(es)> *n* rhinocéros *m*

Rhode Island [ˌrəʊdˈaɪlənd] **I.** *n* le Rhode Island **II.** *n* du Rhode Island

rhododendron [ˌrəʊdəˈdendrən, *Am:* ˌroʊ-] *n* rhododendron *m*

rhombus [ˈrɒmbəs, *Am:* ˈrɑːm-] <-es *o* -i> *n* losange *m*

rhubarb [ˈruːbɑːb, *Am:* -bɑːrb] **I.** *n no pl* rhubarbe *f* **II.** *interj mot prononcé par des acteurs pour simuler une conversation*

rhyme [raɪm] **I.** *n* **1.** (*similar sound*) rime *f;* **in ~** en vers **2.** (*ode*) comptine *f* ►**without ~ or reason** sans rime ni raison **II.** *vt* faire rimer **III.** *vi* rimer

rhyming slang *n argot qui substitue à un mot qui rime ou un autre mot qui évoque cette rime, par exemple "mince pies" pour "eyes"*

rhythm [ˈrɪðəm] *n* (*beat*) rythme *m*

rhythm and blues *n* MUS rhythm and blues *m* **rhythm guitar** *n* guitare *f* rythmique

rhythmic(al) *adj* rythmique

RI [ˌɑːʳˈaɪ, *Am:* ˌɑːr-] *n abbr of* **religious instruction** cours *m* d'instruction religieuse

rib [rɪb] **I.** *n* **1.** (*bone*) côte *f* **2.** (*meat joint*) côte *f* **3.** (*in structure*) armature *f;* (*in umbrella*) baleine *f* **4.** *no pl* (*stripe*) côtes *fpl* **II.** <-bb-> *vt inf* taquiner

ribald [ˈrɪbəld] *adj* grivois(e)

ribaldry [ˈrɪbəldri] *n* grivoiserie *f*

ribbon [ˈrɪbən] *n* **1.** (*long strip*) ruban *m* **2.** (*of medal*) galon *m* ►**to be cut to ~s** mettre qc en lambeaux

ribcage *n* cage *f* thoracique

ribonucleic acid [ˌraɪbəʊnjuːkleɪɪkˈæsɪd] *n* BIO, CHEM acide *m* ribonucléique

ribtickling *adj Brit, inf* désopilant(e)

rice [raɪs] *n no pl* riz *m*

ricefield *n* rizière *f* **rice growing** *n no pl* riziculture *f* **ricepaper** *n* papier *m* de riz **rice pudding** *n* gâteau *m* de riz

rich [rɪtʃ] **I.** <-er, -est> *adj* **1.** (*wealthy*) *a.* GEO riche; **to grow ~** s'enrichir **2.** AGR (*harvest*) abondant(e) **3.** (*opulent*) somptueux(-euse) **4.** (*plenty*) **to be ~ in sth** être riche en qc; **vit-**

R

amin-~ vitaminé(e); **wool-/cotton-~** à haut pourcentage de laine/coton **5.** (*intense*) riche; (*colour*) onctueux(-euse) **6.** (*fatty: meal*) riche **7.** *pej, inf* (*laughable*) un peu fort (de café) **II.** *n* **1. the ~** *pl* les riches *mpl* **2.** *pl* les richesses *fpl*

richly *adj* (*dressed, decorated*) richement; **that you so ~ deserve** que vous méritez largement

Richard (the) Lionheart ['rɪtʃəd'laɪən-hɑːt, *Am:* -hɑːrt] *n* HIST Richard Cœur de Lion *m*

richness *n no pl* **1.** (*affluence*) richesse *f* **2.** (*intensity: of a colour, flavour*) intensité *f*

Richter scale *n* échelle *f* de Richter

rick [rɪk] **I.** *n* meule *f* **II.** *vt Brit, Aus* (*part of the body*) se tordre

rickets ['rɪkɪts] *n no pl* rachitisme *m*

rickety ['rɪkətɪ, *Am:* -t̬ɪ] *adj* branlant(e)

rickshaw ['rɪkʃɔː, *Am:* -ʃɑː] *n* rickshaw *m*

ricochet ['rɪkəʃeɪ] **I.** *vi* ricocher **II.** *n* ricochet *m*

rid [rɪd] <rid *o* ridded, rid> *vt* (*free from*) **to rid sb/sth of sth** débarrasser qn/qc de qc/ ►**to get ~ of sb/sth** se débarrasser de qn/qc

riddance ['rɪdns] *n inf* **good ~ (to bad rubbish)** bon débarras

ridden ['rɪdn] **I.** *pp of* **ride II.** *adj* **guilt-~** rongé(e) de culpabilité

riddle¹ ['rɪdl] *n* énigme *f*

riddle² ['rɪdl] **I.** *n* crible *m* **II.** *vt* **1.** (*perforate*) cribler; **to be ~d with** (*holes, mice, mistakes*) être infesté de **2.** (*sieve*) passer au crible

ride [raɪd] **I.** <rode, ridden> *vt* **1.** (*sit on*) **to ~ a bike/horse** monter à vélo/cheval; **to ~ a bike to a place** aller en vélo à un endroit; **to be riding a bike/motorbike** être à vélo/en moto **2.** (*go in vehicle: a bike, roundabout*) monter sur; (*a bus, train, car*) monter dans; **he rode the donkey into the village** il est entré dans le village sur l'âne **3.** (*canoe, raft: rapids*) prendre **4.** (*travel: a distance*) faire **5.** (*surf: waves*) chevaucher **6.** *Am, inf* (*pressure*) être sur le dos de **II.** <rode, ridden> *vi* **1.** (*ride a horse*) monter à cheval **2.** (*travel*) aller à dos d'animal; **he was riding on a donkey** il était sur un âne; **you can ~ across Paris on your bike** tu peux traverser Paris à bicyclette ►**to let sth ~** *inf* laisser faire les choses; **to ~ roughshod over sb** fouler aux pieds qn; **sth is riding on sth** qc dépend de qc **III.** *n* **1.** (*journey*) trajet *m;* (*on a bike*) tour *m;* (*on horse*) promenade *f; Am* **to give sb a ~,** emmener qn (en voiture) **2.** (*fairground trip*) tour *m* **3.** (*attraction*) **a ~ on the roller coaster** un tour sur les montagnes russes ►**to take sb for a ~** *inf* faire marcher qn; **sb has a rough/an easy ~** les choses sont difficiles/ faciles pour qn; **to give sb a rough/an easy ~** rendre les choses difficiles/faciles pour qn

◆**ride out** *vt a. fig* surmonter

◆**ride up** *vi* remonter

rider *n* **1.** (*on horse*) cavalier, -ière *m, f;* (*on bike*) cycliste *mf;* (*on motorbike*) motocycliste *mf* **2.** (*amendment*) annexe *f* **3.** (*addition to statement*) clause *f* additionnelle

ridge [rɪdʒ] *n* **1.** GEO crête *f* **2.** METEO (*of pressure*) ligne *f* **3.** (*joint: of roof*) arête *f* **4.** (*on surface*) nervure *f* **5.** *Aus, pej* **to have been around the ~s** avoir vécu

ridge pole *n* faîtière *f*

ridicule ['rɪdɪkjuːl] **I.** *n no pl* ridicule *m* **II.** *vt* ridiculiser

ridiculous *adj* ridicule; **don't be ~!** ne dis pas n'importe quoi!

riding ['raɪdɪŋ] *n no pl* équitation *f*

riding breeches *n* culotte *f* de cheval **riding crop** *n* cravache *f* **riding school** *n* école *f* d'équitation **riding whip** *s.* **riding crop**

rife [raɪf] *adj form* très répandu(e); **the economy is ~ with corruption** l'économie est dominée par la corruption

riffle ['rɪfl] *vt* (*pages*) feuilleter

riffraff ['rɪfræf] *n pl, pej* racaille *f*

rifle¹ ['raɪfl] *n* fusil *m*

rifle² ['raɪfl] *vt, vi* fouiller

rifle range *n* champ *m* de tir; (*in funfair*) stand *m* de tir

rift [rɪft] *n* **1.** (*fissure*) fissure *f;* GEO rift *m* **2.** (*quarrel*) division *f;* **to heal the ~** régler le différend

rift valley *n* GEO rift *m*

rig [rɪg] <-gg-> **I.** *vt* **1.** *pej* (*falsify result: election*) truquer; (*market*) manipuler **2.** (*equip with mast: yacht*) gréer **II.** *n* **1.** (*oil industry*) derrick *m* **2.** *Am* (*truck*) semi-remorque *m o f* **3.** (*sail assembly*) gréement *m* **4.** *inf* (*clothing*) tenue *f*

rigging *n no pl* **1.** (*manipulation of results*) trucage *m* **2.** (*ropes on ships*) gréement *m*

right [raɪt] **I.** *adj* **1.** (*morally good, justified: policy, attitude*) bon(ne); (*distribution, punishment*) juste; **to do the ~ thing** bien agir; **you did the ~ thing in the circumstances** tu as fait ce qu'il fallait; **it's just not ~** ce n'est pas normal; **to keep on the ~ side of the law** rester dans la légalité **2.** (*true, correct: answer, method, suspicion*) bon(ne); **to be ~ about sth** avoir raison à propos de qc; **42, that can't be ~** 42, ce n'est pas possible; **that's ~, 42** c'est bien ça, 42; **the ~ way round** [*o* **around** *Am*] dans le bon sens; **to be on the ~ side of forty** ne pas avoir encore quarante ans **3.** (*best, appropriate*) bon(ne); **the ~ way to do things** la manière convenable de faire les choses; **is this the ~ way to the post office?** est-ce que c'est le bon chemin pour la poste?; **to be in the ~ place at the ~ time** être là où il faut au bon moment **4.** (*direction*) droit(e); **to make a ~ turn** tourner à droite; **a ~ hook** SPORT un crochet du droit **5.** (*well*) bien; **to be not (quite) ~ in the head** *inf* ne pas avoir toute sa tête; **to be as ~ as rain** *inf* se porter comme un charme **6.** (*in correct state*) **to put sth ~** redresser qc; **to put a clock ~** mettre une pendule à l'heure 7. *inf* (*complete*) vrai(e); (*idiot*) véritable II. *n* 1. (*civil privilege*) droit *m;* **to be within one's ~s to so sth** être dans son droit de faire qc; **you've no ~ to do that** vous n'avez aucun droit de faire ça; **she's a painter/writer in her own ~** elle est peintre/écrivain grâce à ses propres mérites 2. *no pl* (*lawfulness*) bien *m;* **I'm in the ~** j'ai raison 3. *pl* (*copyright*) droits *mpl;* **all ~s reserved** tous droits réservés 4. (*right side*) droite *f;* **on the ~** à droite; **to make a ~** *Am* tourner à droite; **take the next ~** prenez la prochaine à droite 5. SPORT droit *m* 6. *pl* (*orderliness*) **to put sth to ~s** mettre de l'ordre dans qc; **to put the world to ~s** refaire le monde III. *adv* 1. (*correctly: answer*) correctement 2. (*well: work*) bien; **she doesn't dress/talk ~** elle ne sait pas s'habiller/parler; **he'll be ~** *Aus, inf* ça va aller 3. (*in rightward direction*) à droite; **to turn right** tourner à droite 4. (*precisely*) exactement; **to be ~ behind sb** être juste derrière qn; (*encourage*) soutenir qn IV. *vt* 1. (*rectify: mistake*) rectifier; (*situation*) redresser 2. (*set upright*) redresser V. *interj* 1. (*states accord*) d'accord! 2. (*attracts attention*) bon! 3. *inf* (*requests confirmation*) n'est-ce pas? 4. *inf* (*warns*) **be on time, ~?** soyez à l'heure, compris?

Right [raɪt] *n* POL **the ~** la droite; **far ~** extrême droite *f;* **on the ~** à droite

right angle *n* angle *m* droit **right-angled** *adj* à angle droit

righteous ['raɪtʃəs] I. *adj form* 1. (*virtuous*) vertueux(-euse) 2. (*rightful*) justifié(e) II. *n* **the ~** *pl, form* les justes

rightful *adj* (*share, owner*) légitime

right-hand *adj* droit(e); **on the ~ side** du côté droit **right-hand drive** *adj* avec la conduite à droite **right-handed** *adj* droitier(-ère) **right-hand man** *n* bras droit *m*

rightist ['raɪtɪst] I. *n* POL personne *f* de droite II. *adj* (*views*) de droite

rightly *adv* correctement; **quite ~** à juste titre

right-minded *adj* sensé(e) **right of way** <-rights> *n* 1. (*footpath*) passage *m* 2. (*on road*) **to have ~** avoir priorité **rights issue** *n Brit* FIN émission *f* de droits de souscription **right-wing** *adj* POL (*attitudes, party*) de droite

rigid ['rɪdʒɪd] *adj* 1. (*inflexible: material*) rigide; **to be ~ with fear/pain** être paralysé par la peur/douleur; **to be bored ~** *Brit, inf* s'ennuyer à cent sous de l'heure 2. (*unchangeable: censorship, rules*) strict(e) 3. (*intransigent*) inflexible

rigidity [rɪ'dʒɪdətɪ, *Am:* -t̬ɪ] *n no pl* 1. (*hardness*) rigidité *f* 2. (*inflexibility*) inflexibilité *f*

rigmarole ['rɪgmərəʊl, *Am:* -məroʊl] *n no pl, pej* comédie *f*

rigor *n Am, Aus s.* **rigour**

rigor mortis [ˌrɪgə'mɔːtɪs, *Am:* -ɚ'mɔːrt̬ɪs] *n no pl* MED rigidité *f* cadavérique

rigorous ['rɪgərəs] *adj* rigoureux(-euse)

rigour ['rɪgə^r, *Am:* -ɚ] *n Brit, Aus* rigueur *f*

rig-out *n inf* accoutrement *m*

rile [raɪl] *vt inf* énerver

rim [rɪm] I. *n* 1. (*brim*) bord *m;* (*of wheel*) jante *f* 2. (*edge: of crater, lake*) bord *m;* **the Pacific ~** la ceinture du Pacifique II. <-mm-> *vt* 1. (*surround*) border 2. (*frame*) cercler; **gold-~med glasses** des lunettes cerclées d'or

rimless *adj* (*glasses*) non cerclé(e)

rind [raɪnd] *n no pl* (*of lemon*) écorce *f;* (*of bacon*) couenne *f;* (*of cheese*) croûte *f,* couenne *f Suisse*

ring[1] [rɪŋ] I. *n* 1. (*circle*) anneau *m;* (*drawn*) cercle *m* 2. (*stain*) tache *f;* (*under eyes*) cerne *f* 3. (*circle of people*) cercle *m;* (*of spies, criminals*) réseau *m* 4. (*jewellery*) bague *f;* **diamond ~** bague de diamants; (**wedding**) **~** alliance *f* 5. *Brit* (*cooking device*) brûleur *m;* **to put a pan on the ~** mettre une casserole sur le feu 6. *pej* (*clique: of drugs, spies*) cercle *m* 7. (*arena: of boxing*) ring *m;* (*of circus*) arène *f* ►**to run ~s around sb** battre qn à plate(s) couture(s) II. *vt* 1. (*encircle*) encercler 2. *Brit* (*on paper*) entourer 3. (*mark: bird*) baguer

ring[2] [rɪŋ] I. *n* 1. *no pl, Brit* (*telephone call*) coup *m* de fil; **to give sb a ~** passer un coup de fil à qn 2. (*sound*) sonnerie *f* 3. *no pl* (*quality*) accent *m;* **it had the ~ of truth about it** cela avait des accents de vérité II. <rang, rung> *vt* 1. *Brit* (*call on telephone*) appeler 2. (*produce sound: bell*) faire sonner; (*alarm*) déclencher; **to ~ the changes** varier III. <rang, rung> *vi* 1. *Brit* (*call on telephone*) appeler; **your brother rang for you** ton frère t'a appelé 2. (*produce bell sound: telephone, bell*) sonner; (*ears*) tinter; **to ~ at the door** sonner à la porte ►**to ~ true** sonner juste

◆**ring back** *vt* rappeler

◆**ring in** I. *vt* **to ~ the New Year** sonner la nouvelle année II. *vi* appeler

◆**ring off** *vi Brit* raccrocher

◆**ring out** I. *vt* **to ~ the old Year** sonner la fin de l'année II. *vi* retentir 0

◆**ring up** I. *vt* 1. (*telephone*) téléphoner à 2. (*key in sale*) enregistrer II. *vi* téléphoner

ringback service *n* TEL service *m* de rappel automatique **ring binder** *n* classeur *m* à anneaux, cartable *m Québec*

ringer *n* sonneur *m;* **to be a dead ~ for sb** *inf* être le sosie de qn

ring finger *n* annulaire *m*

ringing I. *n no pl* sonnerie *f;* (*in ears*) tintement *m* II. *adj* (*cheer, crash*) retentissant(e)

ringing tone *n* tonalité *f* de sonnerie

ringleader *n pej* meneur, -euse *m, f*

ringlet ['rɪŋlɪt] *n pl* (*in hair*) boucle *f*

ringpull *n* anneau *m*

ring road *n Brit, Aus* boulevard *m* de ceinture

ringside I. *n* premier rang *m* II. *adj* 1. (*seats*) au premier rang 2. *fig* (*view*) de premier plan

rink [rɪŋk] *n* (*for ice skating*) patinoire *f;* (*for* *roller skating*) piste *f*

rinse [rɪns] **I.** *vt, vi* rincer **II.** *n* rinçage *m;* **to give sth a ~** rincer qc

riot ['raɪət] **I.** *n* (*disturbances*) émeute *f* ►**to be a ~** *inf* être tordant; **the garden is a ~ of colour** le jardin est une symphonie de couleurs **II.** *vi* se soulever; *fig* faire un scandale **III.** *adv* **to run ~** *fig* se déchaîner; (*imagination*) s'emballer

rioter *n* **1.** émeutier, -ière *m, f* **2.** *pej* casseur, -euse *m, f*

riot gear *n* tenue *f* anti-émeute

rioting *n no pl* émeutes *fpl*

riotous *adj* **1.** (*rebellious: crowd*) violent(e) **2.** (*boisterous*) déchaîné(e); (*party*) délirant(e)

riot squad *n* ≈ CRS *mpl*

rip [rɪp] **I.** *n* accroc *m* **II.** <-pp-> *vi* se déchirer ►**to let ~** se déchaîner **III.** <-pp-> *vt* déchirer; **to ~ sth apart** mettre qc en pièces; **to ~ sth open** ouvrir qc en le déchirant; **to ~ sth out** arracher qc

◆**rip off** *vt* **1.** (*remove fast: cover*) déchirer; (*clothes*) enlever à toute vitesse **2.** *inf* (*overcharge*) arnaquer **3.** *inf* (*steal*) piquer

◆**rip up** *vt* (*pull apart fast*) déchirer

RIP [ˌɑːʳaɪ'piː, *Am:* ˌɑːr-] *abbr of* **rest in peace** ici repose

ripcord ['rɪpkɔːd, *Am:* -kɔːrd] *n* cordon *m* (de parachute)

ripe [raɪp] *adj* **1.** (*ready to eat: fruit*) mûr(e); (*cheese*) fait(e) **2.** (*all ready*) prêt(e); **a ~ old age** un âge avancé; **at the ~ old age of 16** *iron* au grand âge de 16 ans

ripen ['raɪpən] **I.** *vt* faire mûrir **II.** *vi* mûrir

ripeness *n no pl* maturité *f*

rip-off *n inf* arnaque *f*

riposte [rɪ'pɒst, *Am:* -'poʊst] *vi* riposter

ripple ['rɪpl] **I.** *n* **1.** (*in water*) ride *f;* (*of applause*) vague *f* **2.** (*showing interest*) frémissement *m* **3.** (*ice cream with layers*) **chocolate ~** *glace à la vanille, panachée de chocolat* **II.** *vt* (*produce wave in*) faire ondoyer **III.** *vi* ondoyer

rip-roaring ['rɪprɔːrɪŋ, *Am:* ˌrɪp'-] *adj inf* détonant(e)

rise [raɪz] **I.** *n no pl* **1.** (*in status, power*) montée *f* **2.** (*increase*) hausse *f;* (**pay**) **~** *Brit* augmentation *f* de salaire; **to be on the ~** être en hausse ►**to give ~ to sth** donner lieu à qc; **to give ~ to hopes** faire naître l'espoir; **to get** [*o* **take**] **a ~ out of sb** mettre qn en boîte **II.** <rose, risen> *vi* **1.** (*move upwards: person in chair or bed*) se lever; (*smoke*) s'élever; **to ~ from the table** se lever de table; **to ~ to the bait** mordre à l'hameçon **2.** (*in status*) s'élever; **to ~ to power** arriver au pouvoir; **to ~ to the challenge** relever le défi; **to ~ to the occasion** se montrer à la hauteur de la situation; **to ~ in sb's esteem** monter dans l'estime de qn; **~ to fame** devenir célèbre **3.** (*become higher: road, river*) monter; (*temperature, prices*) augmenter; (*hopes*) grandir; (*dough*) lever **4.** (*be higher: trees, buildings*) s'élever **5.** THEAT (*curtain*) se lever **6.** (*become visible: moon, sun*) se lever; (*river*) monter **7.** REL **to ~ from the dead** ressusciter d'entre les morts **8.** (*rebel*) se soulever

◆**rise above** *vt insep* **1.** (*overcome: difficulties*) surmonter **2.** (*be superior*) s'élever au-dessus de

◆**rise up** *vi* **1.** (*to rebel*) se soulever **2.** (*go up*) se lever; (*smoke*) s'élever

risen ['rɪzn] *pp of* **rise**

riser *n* **1.** (*somebody getting up*) **early ~** lève-tôt *mf;* **late ~** lève-tard *mf* **2.** (*part of step*) contremarche *f* **3.** *pl, Am* (*set of steps*) tribune *f*

rising **I.** *n* soulèvement *m* **II.** *adj* **1.** (*in status: fame*) grandissant(e); (*politician*) qui monte **2.** (*in number: temperature, prices*) en hausse; (*floodwaters*) en crue **III.** *prep Brit* **to be ~ four** aller sur ses quatre ans

risk [rɪsk] **I.** *n* risque *m;* **fire/safety ~** risque d'incendie/pour la sécurité; **there's a ~ of sth/doing sth** il y a un risque de qc/de faire qc; **to run the ~ of doing sth** courir le risque de faire qc; **at the ~ of doing sth** au risque de faire qc; **to be worth the ~** valoir la peine de prendre le risque; **at one's own ~** à ses risques et périls; **to be at ~** être en danger **II.** *vt* risquer ►**to ~ life and limb** risquer sa peau

risk capital *n* capital-risque *m* **risk factor** *n* facteur *m* de risque **risk-free** *adj* sans risque

risky ['rɪskɪ] <-ier, -iest> *adj* risqué(e)

risqué ['riːskeɪ, *Am:* rɪ'skeɪ] *adj* (*joke*) risqué(e)

rissole ['rɪsəʊl, *Am:* -oʊl] *n* croquette *f*

rite [raɪt] *n pl* rite *m;* **last ~s** derniers sacrements *mpl*

ritual ['rɪtʃʊəl, *Am:* -uəl] **I.** *n* rituel *m* **II.** *adj* rituel(le)

ritzy ['rɪtsɪ] <-ier, -iest> *adj inf* sélect(e)

rival ['raɪvl] **I.** *n* rival(e) *m(f)* **II.** *adj* rival(e) **III.** <-ll- *o Am* -l-> *vt* rivaliser avec; **to ~ sb in sth** rivaliser avec en qc

rivalry ['raɪvlrɪ] *n* rivalité *f*

river ['rɪvəʳ, *Am:* -ɚ] **I.** *n* **1.** (*water*) rivière *f;* (*to the sea*) fleuve *m;* **the ~ Mersey** le Mersey **2.** (*quantity*) flot *m* ►**down ~** en aval; **up ~** en amont **II.** *adj* fluvial(e)

river-bed *n* lit *m* de la rivière **riverside** **I.** *n no pl* rive *f* **II.** *adj* (*restaurant*) au bord de l'eau

rivet ['rɪvɪt] **I.** *n* rivet *m* **II.** *vt* **1.** (*joined*) riveter **2.** (*interest*) fasciner; **to be ~ed by a film** être captivé par un film ►**to be ~ed to the spot** être cloué sur place

riveting ['rɪvətɪŋ, *Am:* -t̬ɪŋ] *adj inf* captivant(e)

RN [ˌɑːr'en] *n Brit* MIL *abbr of* **Royal Navy** ≈ marine *f* nationale

RNA [ˌɑːren'eɪ] *n abbr of* **ribonucleic acid** ARN *m*

RNLI [ˌɑːrenel'aɪ] *n Brit* NAUT *abbr of* **Royal National Lifeboat Institution** société *f* nationale de sauvetage en mer

roach [rəʊtʃ, *Am:* roʊtʃ] *n* gardon *m*

road [rəʊd, *Am:* roʊd] *n* **1.** (*linking places*) route *f;* **dirt ~** chemin *m* de terre; **by ~** par la route; **the Brighton ~** la route de Brighton; **on the ~** (*when driving*) sur la route; (*travelling*) sur les routes, on tour, en tournée **2.** (*in residential area*) rue *f;* **down the ~** en bas de la rue ▶**to come to the end of the ~** arriver en fin de parcours; **the ~ to hell is paved with good intentions** *prov* l'enfer est pavé de bonnes intentions; **all ~s lead to Rome** *prov* tous les chemins mènent à Rome; **some years down the ~** d'ici quelques années; **to get sth on the ~** *inf* commencer qc; **let's hit the ~!** *inf* en route!; **to be on the ~ to recovery** être sur la voie de la guérison; **to be on the right ~** *Brit* être sur la bonne voie

road accident *n* accident *m* de la route **roadblock** *n* barrage *m* routier **road construction** *n* construction *f* des routes **road fund licence** *n Brit* ≈ vignette *f* **road haulage** *n no pl* transport *m* routier **road hog** *n pej, inf* chauffard *m* **road holding** *n no pl* tenue *f* de route **roadhouse** <-houses> *n Am* relais *m* **road map** *n* carte *f* routière **road race** *n* course *f* cycliste **road rage** *n* furie *f* au volant, agressivité *f* des automobilistes **road safety** *n no pl* sécurité *f* routière **road sense** *n* sens *m* de la conduite sur route **roadshow** *n* tournée *f* **roadside** **I.** *n* bord *m* de la route **II.** *adj* (situé) au bord de la route; **to make a ~ stop** s'arrêter au bord de la route **road sign** *n* panneau *m* de signalisation

roadster ['rəʊdstə(r), *Am:* 'roʊdstɚ] *n* roadster *m*

road-test *vt* **to ~ a car** tester une voiture sur route **road traffic** *n no pl* circulation *f* (routière) **road transport** *n no pl, Brit* transports *mpl* routiers **road user** *n* usager *m* de la route **roadway** *n no pl* chaussée *f* **roadwork** *Am no pl,* **roadworks** *npl Brit, Aus* travaux *mpl* d'entretien du réseau routier **roadworthy** *adj* en bon état

roam [rəʊm, *Am:* roʊm] **I.** *vi* errer **II.** *vt* errer dans

roar [rɔːʳ, *Am:* rɔːr] **I.** *vi* hurler; (*lion*) rugir; (*motorbike*) gronder; **to ~ with laughter** hurler de rire **II.** *n* **1.** (*growl*) rugissement *m* **2.** *no pl* (*loud noise*) grondement *m*

roaring **I.** *adj* hurlant(e); (*lion*) rugissant(e); (*motorbike*) vrombissant(e); (*thunder*) qui gronde; (*inferno, traffic*) important(e); **a ~ fire** une belle flambée; **to be a ~ success** *inf* avoir un succès fou **II.** *adv* complètement

roast [rəʊst, *Am:* roʊst] **I.** *vt* rôtir; (*coffee*) torréfier **II.** *vi* griller **III.** *n* rôti *m* **IV.** *adj* rôti(e); (*coffee*) torréfié(e); (*potato*) rôti(e)

roast beef *n* rosbif *m*

roasting **I.** *n* **1.** (*action of cooking*) rôtissage *m;* (*coffee*) torréfaction *f* **2.** *inf* (*criticism*) savon *m;* **to give/get a ~** passer/recevoir un savon **II.** *adj* **1.** *inf* (*very hot and dry*) brûlant(e); **to be ~** (*person*) mijoter **2.** (*used to roast: tin, pan*) à rôtir **III.** *adv* **~ hot** brûlant(e)

rob [rɒb, *Am:* rɑːb] <-bb-> *vt* **1.** (*burgle*) voler; (*a bank*) dévaliser **2.** (*defraud*) escroquer **3.** (*deprive*) priver; **~bed of my dignity** privé de ma dignité ▶**to ~ Peter to pay Paul** *prov* déshabiller Saint-Pierre pour habiller Saint-Paul

robber ['rɒbəʳ, *Am:* 'rɑːbɚ] *n* voleur, -euse *m, f*

robbery ['rɒbərɪ, *Am:* 'rɑːbɚɪ] <-ies> *n* **1.** (*burglary*) vol *m* **2.** *no pl* (*burglary*) cambriolage *m*

robe [rəʊb, *Am:* roʊb] *n* **1.** (*formal*) robe *f* de soirée **2.** (*dressing gown*) robe *f* de chambre

robin ['rɒbɪn, *Am:* 'rɑːbɪn] *n* rouge-gorge *m*

robot ['rəʊbɒt, *Am:* 'roʊbɑːt] *n* **1.** (*machine*) robot *m* **2.** *pej* (*person*) automate *m*

robotics [rəʊ'bɒtɪks, *Am:* roʊ'bɑːt̬ɪks] *npl + sing/pl vb* robotique *f*

robust [rəʊ'bʌst, *Am:* roʊ'-] *adj* **1.** (*strong*) robuste **2.** (*finances*) solide **3.** (*defence*) ferme

robustness *n no pl* **1.** (*vitality*) robustesse *f* **2.** (*strength*) solidité *f* **3.** (*frankness*) fermeté *f*

rock¹ [rɒk, *Am:* rɑːk] *n* **1.** (*substance*) roche *f* **2.** (*stone*) rocher *m;* **to be solid as a ~** être solide comme un roc **3.** *Am, Aus* (*lump of stone*) pierre *f* **4.** *no pl* (*solid sweet*) ≈ sucre *m* d'orge ▶**on the ~s** (*experiencing difficulties*) en pleine débâcle; (*with ice*) avec des glaçons

rock² [rɒk, *Am:* rɑːk] **I.** *vt* **1.** (*swing*) balancer; (*a baby*) bercer; **to ~ sb to sleep** bercer qn pour l'endormir **2.** (*shake: person, house*) secouer ▶**to ~ the boat** *inf* faire des vagues **II.** *vi* **1.** (*undulate*) se balancer; **to ~ back and forth** se balancer d'avant en arrière **2.** (*dance*) danser le rock'n'roll **III.** *n* MUS rock *m*

rock-and-roll *n no pl* rock and roll *m* **rock band** *n* groupe *m* de rock **rock bottom** *n* fond *m;* **to be at ~** tomber au plus bas; (*person*) avoir le moral à zéro; **to hit ~** toucher le fond **rock bun, rock cake** *n Brit, Aus* rocher *m* **rock climber** *n* varappeur, -euse *m, f* **rock climbing** *n no pl* varappe *f* **rock-crystal, rock crystal** *n* cristal *m* de roche

rocker ['rɒkəʳ, *Am:* 'rɑːkɚ] *n* **1.** (*chair*) fauteuil *m* à bascule **2.** (*singer*) rocker, -euse *m, f* **3.** *Am* (*rock song*) rock *m* **4.** *Am* (*rock fan*) rocker, -euse *m, f* ▶**to be off one's ~** *inf* être fou

rockery ['rɒkrɪ, *Am:* 'rɑːkɚɪ] <-ies> *n* rocaille *f*

rocket¹ ['rɒkɪt, *Am:* 'rɑːkɪt] **I.** *n* **1.** (*vehicle, firework*) fusée *f* **2.** *no pl, inf* (*reprimand*) **to give sb a ~** engueuler qn **II.** *vi* **to ~ (up)** monter en flèche; **to ~ to sth** atteindre rapidement qc **III.** *vt* attaquer à la roquette

rocket² ['rɒkɪt, *Am:* 'rɑːkɪt] *n* (*herb*) roquette *f*

rocket launcher *n* MIL lance-fusées *m*

rocket science *n inf* **it's not ~** ce n'est pas

R

sorcier

rock face *n* paroi *f* rocheuse **rock festival** *n* festival *m* de rock **rock formation** *n* formation *f* rocheuse

Rockies ['rɒkɪz] *n* **the** ~ les Rocheuses *fpl*

rocking ['rɒkɪŋ, *Am:* 'rɑːk-] *n* balancement *m*

rocking chair *n* fauteuil *m* à bascule, chaise *f* berçante, berçante *f Québec* **rocking horse** *n* cheval *m* à bascule

rock music *n no pl* musique *f* rock **rock'n'roll** *s.* rock-and-roll **rock plant** *n* BOT plante *f* alpestre **rock salt** *n no pl* sel *m* gemme **rock star** *n* star *f* de rock

rocky[1] ['rɒkɪ, *Am:* 'rɑːkɪ] <-ier, -iest> *adj* rocheux(-euse)

rocky[2] ['rɒkɪ, *Am:* 'rɑːkɪ] <-ier, -iest> *adj* **1.** (*weak*) patraque **2.** *inf* (*doomed*) chancelant(e)

Rocky Mountains *n* les Montagnes *fpl* Rocheuses

rococo [rə'kəʊkəʊ, *Am:* -'koʊkoʊ] **I.** *n no pl* rococo *m* **II.** *adj* rococo *inv*

rod [rɒd, *Am:* rɑːd] *n* **1.** (*thin bar: of wood*) baguette *f;* (*of metal*) tige *f;* (*for support*) tringle *f;* (*for punishment*) *a. fig* canne *f* **2.** (*fishing rod*) canne *f* à pêche ►**to rule sth with a** ~ **of iron** gouverner qc avec une main de fer

rode [rəʊd, *Am:* roʊd] *pt of* **ride**

rodent ['rəʊdnt, *Am:* 'roʊ-] *n* rongeur *m*

rodeo ['rəʊdɪəʊ, *Am:* 'roʊdɪoʊ] <-s> *n* rodéo *m*

roe[1] [rəʊ, *Am:* roʊ] *n* (*fish eggs*) œufs *mpl* de poisson

roe[2] [rəʊ, *Am:* roʊ] <-(s)> *n* (*deer*) chevreuil *m*

roe buck, roebuck *n* chevreuil *m* mâle

roger ['rɒdʒəʳ, *Am:* 'rɑːdʒɚ] *interj* compris!

rogue [rəʊg, *Am:* roʊg] **I.** *n* **1.** (*villain*) crapule *f* **2.** (*criminal, lively person*) voyou *m* **II.** *adj* (*animal*) solitaire; (*car, product*) défaillant(e); **a** ~ **state** un état voyou

roguish *adj* espiègle

role, rôle [rəʊl, *Am:* roʊl] *n* rôle *m;* **the leading** ~ le premier rôle; **to take on a** ~ accepter un rôle; **he played a** ~ **in this decision** il a joué un rôle dans cette décision

role model *n* modèle *m* **role play(ing)** *n* jeu *m* de rôle **role reversal** *n* renversement *m* de rôle

roll [rəʊl, *Am:* roʊl] **I.** *vt* **1.** (*push circular object*) faire rouler; (*dice*) jeter **2.** (*move in circles*) rouler; **to** ~ **one's eyes/one's r's** rouler les yeux/les r **3.** (*shape: into cylinder*) enrouler; (*into ball*) rouler en boule; **to** ~ **oneself into a ball** se mettre en boule; **to be many things all** ~**ed into one** être plusieurs choses à la fois **4.** (*make: cigarette*) rouler **5.** (*flatten, compress: grass*) passer au rouleau; (*metal*) laminer **II.** *vi* **1.** (*move around an axis*) rouler; (*car*) faire un tonneau; **eyes** rouler **2.** (*undulate*) onduler; (*ship*) tanguer **3.** (*be in operation*) tourner **4. make noise** (*thunder*) gronder ►**to be** ~**ing in the aisles** se tordre de rire; **to get the ball** ~**ing** mettre les choses en route; **heads will** ~ (**for this**) des têtes vont tomber; **to** ~ **with the punches** *Am, inf* encaisser les coups **III.** *n* **1.** (*movement*) roulement *m;* (*in gymnastics*) roulade *f;* (*by plane*) looping *m;* **to be on a** ~ *fig* être bien parti **2.** (*cylinder*) rouleau *m;* (*of fat*) bourrelet *m;* **a** ~ **of film** une pellicule **3.** (*noise: of drum, thunder*) roulement *m* **4.** (*names*) liste *f;* **to call the** ~ faire l'appel **5.** (*bread*) petit pain *m;* **cheese on a** ~ *Am* sandwich *m* au fromage

◆**roll back I.** *vt* **1.** *Am* ECON (*costs*) baisser **2.** (*return to last state*) faire reculer **II.** *vi* ECON rouler en arrière

◆**roll by** *vi* (*vehicle*) passer; (*time*) s'écouler

◆**roll down I.** *vt* (*sleeve*) baisser; (*window*) descendre **II.** *vi* (*tears*) couler; (*car*) débouler

◆**roll in** *vi* **1.** (*stagger into*) rappliquer **2.** *inf* (*arrive: money, customers*) crouler sous l'argent ►**to be rolling in it** être plein aux as

◆**roll on I.** *vi* continuer; (*time*) s'écouler **II.** *vt* **1.** (*apply with a roller*) appliquer au rouleau **2.** (*put on*) enfiler **3.** *Brit, Aus, inf* (*expresses wish*) vivement; ~ **next year!** vivement l'année prochaine!

◆**roll out I.** *vt* **1.** (*flatten*) aplatir à l'aide d'un rouleau; (*pastry*) étendre au rouleau **2.** *Am* (*make available: product*) sortir **3.** (*unroll*) *a. fig* (*red carpet*) dérouler **II.** *vi Am* sortir; **to** ~ **of bed** sortir du lit

◆**roll over** *vi* se retourner; (*car*) capoter

◆**roll up I.** *vi inf* se pointer **II.** *vt* **1.** (*coil: string*) enrouler **2.** (*fold up*) *a. fig* (*sleeves*) retrousser

roll bar *n* AUTO arceau *m* de sécurité **roll call, roll-call** *n* appel *m* **roll collar** *n* col *m* roulé

roller ['rəʊləʳ, *Am:* 'roʊlɚ] *n* rouleau *m;* (*for roads*) rouleau *m* compresseur; (*for metal*) laminoir *m;* (*for hair*) bigoudi *m*

roller bearing *n* TECH roulement *m* à rouleaux

rollerblade ['rəʊləbleɪd, *Am:* 'roʊlɚ-] *vi* faire du roller

Rollerblade® ['rəʊləbleɪd, *Am:* 'roʊlɚ-] *n* patin *m* en ligne, roller *m*

roller blind *n Brit, Aus* store *m*

roller coaster *n* montagnes *fpl* russes ►**to be on an emotional** ~ passer par des hauts et des bas

roller skate *n* patin *m* à roulettes **roller-skate** *vi* faire du patin à roulettes **roller-skating** *n* patin *m* à roulettes **roller towel** *n* essuie-main(s) *m*

rollicking ['rɒlɪkɪŋ, *Am:* 'rɑːlɪ-] **I.** *adj* joyeux(-euse) **II.** *n Brit, inf* **to give sb a** ~ engueuler qn

rolling mill *n* laminoir *m* **rolling pin** *n* rouleau *m* (à pâtisserie) **rolling stock** *n* matériel *m* roulant **rolling stone** *n* **to be a** ~ rouler sa bosse ►**a** ~ **gathers no moss** *prov* pierre qui roule n'amasse pas mousse

roll-neck ['rəʊlnek, *Am:* 'roʊl-] *n* col *m* roulé

roll-on ['rəʊlɒn, *Am:* 'roʊlɑːn] **I.** *n* **1.** (*garment*) gaine *f* **2.** (*deodorant*) déodorant *m* **II.** *adj* (*deodorant*) à bille

roll-on roll-off *adj* de type roulier

roly-poly (**pudding**) [ˌrəʊlɪ'pəʊlɪ-, *Am:* ˌroʊlɪ'poʊ-] **I.** *n* gâteau *m* roulé à la confiture **II.** *adj inf* grassouillet(te)

ROM [rɒm, *Am:* rɑːm] *n no pl* INFOR *abbr of* **Read Only Memory** ROM *m*

romaine [reʊ'meɪn, *Am:* rə-] *n* salade *f* romaine

Roman ['rəʊmən, *Am:* 'roʊ-] **I.** *adj* romain(e) **II.** *n* Romain, -e *m, f;* **the ~s** les Romains

Roman Catholic **I.** *n* catholique *mf* **II.** *adj* catholique

romance [rəʊ'mæns, *Am:* roʊ'-] *n* **1.** (*love affair*) liaison *f* **2.** (*love story*) roman *m* d'amour; LIT roman *m* de chevalerie **3.** (*glamour*) charme *m*

Romanesque [ˌrəʊmə'nesk, *Am:* ˌroʊ-] **I.** *adj* roman(e) **II.** *n no pl* ARCHIT **the ~** le Roman

Romania [rə'meɪnɪə, *Am:* roʊ'-] *n* la Roumanie

Romanian **I.** *adj* roumain(e) **II.** *n* **1.** (*person*) Roumain(e) *m(f)* **2.** LING roumain *m; s. a.* **English**

romantic [rəʊ'mæntɪk, *Am:* roʊ'mænt̬ɪk] **I.** *adj* **1.** (*concerning love*) *a.* LIT, ART romantique **2.** (*unrealistic*) romanesque **II.** *n* romantique *mf*

romanticism [rəʊ'mæntɪsɪzəm, *Am:* roʊ'mænt̬ə-] *n no pl* romantisme *m*

Romany ['rɒmənɪ, *Am:* 'rɑːmə-] **I.** *n* **1.** (*person*) tzigane *mf* **2.** LING tzigane *m; s. a.* **English** **II.** *adj* tzigane

Rome ['rəʊm, *Am:* 'roʊm] *n* Rome ►**~ was not built in a day** *prov* Paris ne s'est pas fait en un jour; **when in ~ do as the Romans do** *prov* à Rome faites comme les Romains

romp [rɒmp, *Am:* rɑːmp] **I.** *n* **1.** (*erotic activity*) ébats *mpl* **2.** (*diversion*) farce *f* **II.** *vi* s'ébattre; **to ~ home** *Brit* arriver dans un fauteuil

rompers ['rɒmpəʳz, *Am:* 'rɑːmpɚz] *npl Am* (*romper suit*) barboteuse *f*

roof [ruːf] <-s> **I.** *n* toit *m;* (*of a cave, the mouth*) voûte *f;* **in the ~** sous les combles ►**to hit the ~** sortir de ses gonds **II.** *vt* couvrir; **to ~ sth in** recouvrir qc

roofer *n* couvreur *m*

roof garden *n* jardin *m* sur le toit

roofing *n no pl* **1.** (*material*) toiture *f* **2.** (*activity*) pose *f* de la toiture

roof rack *n Brit* galerie *f* (de voiture) **rooftop** *n* toit *m* ►**to shout sth from the ~s** crier qc sur les toits

rook [rʊk] *n* **1.** (*bird*) freux *m* **2.** (*chess piece*) tour *f*

rookery *n* colonie *f* de corneilles

rookie ['rʊkɪ] *n Am, Aus, inf* **1.** (*recruit*) bleu *m;* (*cop*) flic *m* débutant **2.** MIL recrue *f*

room [ruːm] **I.** *n* **1.** (*in house*) pièce *f,* place *f Belgique, Nord;* (*bedroom*) chambre *f;* (*classroom, meeting room*) salle *f;* (*for work*) bureau *m;* **~ and board** chambre et pension **2.** *no pl* (*space*) place *f;* **to take up ~** prendre de la place; **there's not enough ~ to swing a cat** il n'y a pas de place pour se retourner **3.** *no pl* (*possibility*) marge *f;* **to have ~ for sth** avoir une marge de qc; **to have ~ for improvement** pouvoir mieux faire **II.** *vi* **to ~ with sb** *Am* (*share a room*) partager une chambre avec qn

roomed *adj* **two-~ flat** deux-pièces *m*

rooming house ['ruːmɪŋˌhaʊs] *n Am* (*boarding house*) maison *f* de rapport

room-mate *n* **1.** (*sb sharing room*) camarade *mf* de chambre **2.** *Am* (*sb sharing flat*) colocataire, -trice *m, f* **room service** *n* service *m* des chambres

roomy ['ruːmɪ] <-ier, -iest> *adj* spacieux(-euse)

roost [ruːst] **I.** *n* perchoir *m* **II.** *vi* se percher ►**to come home to ~ if you do that it will come home to ~** si tu fais ça, ça se retournera contre toi

rooster *n Am, Aus* (*cockerel*) coq *m*

root [ruːt] **I.** *n a. fig* racine *f;* **to take ~** *a. fig* prendre racine; **to put down** (**new**) **~s** *fig* s'enraciner; **the ~ of all evil** la source de tous les maux; **to lie at the ~ of a problem** être à l'origine d'un problème; **to get to the ~ of a problem** prendre un problème à la racine **II.** *vt* enraciner **III.** *vi* (*establish roots*) s'enraciner

◆**root around** *vi* fouiller; **to ~ for sth** fouiller à la recherche de qc

◆**root for** *vt inf* soutenir

◆**root out** *vt* éliminer

root beer *n Am* (*soft drink*) *boisson gazeuse à base de racines de plantes* **root cause** *n* cause *f* première

rootless *adj* (*lacking base*) sans racines

root sign *n* MAT radical *m* **root vegetable** *n* légume *m* à racine comestible

rope [rəʊp, *Am:* roʊp] **I.** *n* **1.** (*solid cord*) corde *f* **2.** (*of garlic*) tresse *f;* **~ of pearls** sautoir *m* **3.** *pl* (*in boxing ring*) corde *f* ►**it's money for old ~** c'est de l'argent pour pas grand chose; **to know the ~s** connaître son affaire sur le bout des doigts; **to learn the ~s** apprendre les ficelles; **to show sb the ~s** mettre qn au courant **II.** *vt* **1.** (*fasten*) attacher **2.** SPORT **to ~ sb** (**together**) encorder qn

◆**rope in** *vt inf* (*get help from*) forcer un peu

◆**rope off** *vt* séparer à l'aide d'une corde

◆**rope up** *vi* s'encorder

rope dancer *n* THEAT *s.* **rope-walker** **rope ladder** *n* échelle *f* de corde **rope-walker** *n* THEAT funambule *mf*

rop(e)y ['rəʊpɪ, *Am:* 'roʊ-] <-ier, -iest> *adj* **1.** *inf* (*inferior*) minable **2.** *inf* (*sick feeling*) patraque

R

ro-ro ['rəʊrəʊ] *adj abbr of* **roll-on-roll-off** de type roulier

rosary ['rəʊzərɪ, *Am:* 'roʊ-] <-ies> *n* **1.** (*prayer beads*) chapelet *m* **2.** (*prayers*) rosaire *f*

rose¹ [rəʊz, *Am:* roʊz] **I.** *n* **1.** BOT rose *f* **2.** (*colour*) rose *m* **3.** ARCHIT rosace *f* **4.** (*on watering can*) pomme *f* **II.** *adj* rose; *s. a.* **blue**

rose² [rəʊz, *Am:* roʊz] *pt of* **rise**

rosebud *n* bouton *m* de rose **rosebush** *n* rosier *m* **rose garden** *n* roseraie *f* **rose hip** *n* églantine *f*

rosemary ['rəʊzmərɪ, *Am:* 'roʊzmer-] *n no pl* romarin *m*

rosette [rəʊ'zet, *Am:* roʊ'-] *n* **1.** (*rose shape*) rosette *f* **2.** (*for allegiance*) décoration *f* **3.** (*for winner*) cocarde *f*

rose water *n no pl* eau *f* de rose **rose window** *n* ARCHIT rosace *f*

rosin ['rɒzɪn, *Am:* 'rɑːzən] *n no pl* MUS colophane *f*

RoSPA *n Brit abbr of* **Royal Society for the Prevention of Accidents** association *f* pour la prévention des accidents

roster ['rɒstəʳ, *Am:* 'rɑːstɚ] *n no pl, Am, Aus* rota *m*

rostrum ['rɒstrəm, *Am:* 'rɑːs-] <-s *o* rostra> *n* **1.** (*for conductor*) estrade *f* **2.** (*for public speaker*) tribune *f*

rosy ['rəʊzɪ, *Am:* 'roʊ-] <-ier, -iest> *adj* **1.** (*coloured*) rose **2.** *fig* **to look rosy** être prometteur

rot [rɒt, *Am:* rɑːt] **I.** *n* **1.** *no pl* pourriture *f* **2.** *fig* **to stop the ~** arrêter les dégâts **II.** <-tt-> *vi* **1.** (*decay*) pourrir **2.** *fig* **to leave sb to ~** laisser dépérir qn **III.** *vt* décomposer
 ◆**rot away I.** *vt* pourrir **II.** *vi* se décomposer

rota ['rəʊtə, *Am:* 'roʊṱə] *n Brit* rota *m*

rotary ['rəʊtərɪ, *Am:* 'roʊṱɚ-] *adj* rotatif(-ive)

rotate [rəʊ'teɪt, *Am:* 'roʊteɪt] **I.** *vt* **1.** (*turn round*) faire tourner **2.** (*alternate*) alterner; **to ~ duties** remplir des fonctions a tour de rôle **II.** *vi* **to ~ around sth** tourner autour de qc

rotating *adj* (*cylinder*) rotatif(-ive); (*post*) tournant(e)

rotation *n* **1.** (*action of rotating*) rotation *f;* **~s per minute** tours-minutes *mpl* **2.** (*taking turns*) roulement *m;* **in ~** a tour de rôle

rotatory ['rəʊtətərɪ, *Am:* 'roʊtətɔːr-] *adj* rotatoire; (*motion*) de rotation

rote [rəʊt, *Am:* roʊt] *n no pl, pej* **by ~** par cœur; **~ learning** apprentissage *m* par cœur

rotor ['rəʊtəʳ, *Am:* 'roʊṱɚ] *n* rotor *m*

rotten ['rɒtn, *Am:* 'rɑːtn] *adj* **1.** (*putrid*) pourri(e) **2.** (*nasty*) méchant(e) **3.** (*no good*) infect(e); **to feel ~** (*ill*) se sentir mal en point; (*guilty*) se sentir mal

rotund [rəʊ'tʌnd, *Am:* roʊ'-] *adj form* rond(e)

rotunda [rəʊ'tʌndə, *Am:* roʊ'-] *n* ARCHIT rotonde *f*

rouble ['ruːbl] *n* rouble *m*

rouge [ruːʒ] *n no pl* rouge *m* a joues

rough [rʌf] **I.** *adj* **1.** (*uneven: surface, material*) rugueux(-euse); (*ground, road*) raboteux(-euse) **2.** (*poorly made*) brut(e) **3.** (*unmelodic*) rauque; (*accent*) rude **4.** (*imprecise: guess*) approximatif(-ive); (*work*) gros(se); **a ~ drawing** une ébauche **5.** (*harsh*) brutal(e) **6.** (*stormy: sea*) agité(e); (*weather*) mauvais(e) **7.** (*difficult*) difficile; (*justice*) sommaire; **to be ~ on sb** *inf* être dur avec qn **8.** *Brit, inf* (*unwell*) **to feel ~** se sentir mal **II.** *n* **1.** (*sketch*) ébauche *f* **2.** (*in golf*) rough *m* **3.** (*unfinished*) **in ~** au brouillon ►**to take the ~ with the smooth** prendre le bon avec le mauvais **III.** *vt* **to ~ it** *inf* vivre a la dure **IV.** *adv* **1.** (*violently*) brutalement; **to cut up ~** devenir violent(e) **2.** (*in difficulty*) rudement; **to live ~** vivre a la dure

roughage ['rʌfɪdʒ] *n no pl* fibres *fpl* alimentaires

rough-and-ready *adj* **1.** (*primitive*) de faton grossiFre **2.** (*made fast*) fait(e) à la hâte; (*plan*) vite préparé(e) **rough-and-tumble** *n* bousculade *f* **roughcast** *n no pl* TECH crépi *m* **rough diamond** *n Brit, Aus* diamant *m* brut; (*person*) brute *f* au cooer tendre

roughen ['rʌfn] *vt* rendre rugueux

rough-hewn *adj* **1.** (*not smoothed off*) dégrossi(e) **2.** (*impolite*) grossier(-ère) **roughhouse** *Am* **I.** *vi* se taquiner **II.** *vt* malmener **III.** <-s> *n inf* bagarre *f*

roughly *adv* **1.** (*approximately*) grossièrement; (*calculate*) approximativement; **~ speaking** en général **2.** (*aggressively*) rudement

roughneck ['rʌfnek] *n* **1.** *Am, inf* (*oil rig worker*) *personne qui travaille sur une plateforme pétrolifère* **2.** *Am, Aus, inf* (*antisocial man*) voyou *m*

roughness *n no pl* **1.** (*quality of surface*) rugosité *f;* (*of the ground*) inégalité *f* **2.** (*unfairness*) brutalité *f;* (*of a game*) violence *f*

roughshod ['rʌfʃɒd, *Am:* -ʃɑːd] *adj* **to ride ~ over sb** traiter qn avec le plus grand mépris

roulette [ruː'let] *n no pl* roulette *f*

round [raʊnd] **I.** *n* **1.** (*shape*) rond *m* **2.** (*work: of a guard*) ronde *f;* (*of a postman*) tournée *f;* **the daily ~** la routine quotidienne; **to do the ~s** (*illness, story*) circuler **3.** SPORT (*of golf*) partie *f;* (*of championship*) manche *f;* (*in horsejumping*) parcours *m;* **a clear ~** un parcours sans faute **4.** (*unit: of bread*) tranche *f;* (*of ammunition*) cartouche *f;* **two ~s of sandwiches** deux sandwichs; **a ~ of applause** des applaudissements **5.** (*series: of drinks*) tournée *f;* (*of voting*) tour *m;* (*of applications, interviews*) série *f* **6.** MUS canon *m* **II.** *adj* **1.** (*shape*) rond(e) **2.** *fig* (*vowel*) arrondi(e); (*number*) rond(e); (*sum*) rondelette; **a ~ 50** 50 tout rond **III.** *adv* autour; **to go ~ and ~** tourner en rond; **the long way ~** le chemin le plus long; **come ~ tomorrow** passez demain; **all (the) year ~** tout au long de l'année; **taking things** [*o* **taken**] **all ~** tout compte fait

IV. *prep* 1. (*surrounding*) autour de; **all ~ sth** tout autour de qc; **to stand ~ sb** entourer qn; **to put sth ~ sb** envelopper qn de qc 2. (*circling*) **to go ~ sth** faire le tour de qc [*o* contourner]; **the earth goes ~ the sun** la terre tourne autour du soleil; **to swim/run ~ sth** nager/courir autour de qc; **to find a way ~ a problem** *fig* arriver a contourner un problème 3. (*to other side of*) **to go ~ the corner** tourner au coin; **just ~ the corner** *fig* a deux pas d'ici 4. (*visit*) **to go ~ the hotels** faire le tour des hôtels; **to show sb ~ a place** faire visiter un lieu a qn 5. (*here and there*) **to wander ~ the world** errer de par le monde; **to drive ~ France** parcourir la France V. *vt* 1. (*form into a curve*) arrondir 2. (*move*) contourner; (*bend*) prendre; (*cape*) doubler

◆**round down** *vt* arrondir au chiffre inférieur

◆**round off**, **round out** *vt* terminer

◆**round on** *vt* s'en prendre à

◆**round up** *vt* 1. (*increase*) arrondir au chiffre supérieur 2. (*gather*) rassembler

roundabout I. *n Aus, Brit* 1. (*junction*) rond-point *m* 2. *Brit* (*ride*) manège *m* II. *adj* indirect(e); **to take a ~ route** faire un détour; **to ask sb in a ~ way** demander a qn de manière détournée

rounded *adj* (*shape*) arrondi(e)

rounders *n + sing vb Brit: jeu ressemblant au baseball*

roundly *adv form* sévèrement; **to defeat sb ~** infliger une sévère défaite a qn

round-shouldered *adj* vouté(e) **round-table conference**, **round-table discussion**, **round-table meeting** *n* table *f* ronde **round-the-clock** I. *adj* de jour et de nuit II. *adv* vingt-quatre heures sur vingt-quatre

roundup *n* 1. (*of news*) résumé *m* 2. (*of cattle*) regroupement *m;* (*of suspects*) rassemblement *m*

rouse [raʊz] *vt* 1. (*waken*) réveiller; **to ~ oneself from a pleasant daydream** sortir d'un rêve agréable 2. (*activate*) stimuler; (*crowd*) soulever; **to ~ sb to** *+infin* pousser qn à *+infin;* **to ~ to action** pousser a l'action 3. (*cause*) provoquer; (*admiration, ire*) susciter

rousing *adj* (*cheer, welcome*) enthousiaste; (*speech, chant*) vibrant(e)

roustabout ['raʊstəbaʊt] *n* manœuvre *m*

rout [raʊt] I. *vt a. fig* mettre en déroute II. *n* déroute *f*

◆**rout out** *vt* débusquer

route [ruːt, *Am:* raʊt] I. *n* 1. (*way*) itinéraire *m* 2. *Am* (*delivery path*) tournée *f;* **to have a milk ~** livrer le lait; **to have a paper ~** distribuer les journaux 3. *Am* (*road*) route *f* 4. *fig* voie *f;* **the ~ to success** la voie du succès II. *vt* faire passer

routine [ruː'tiːn] I. *n* 1. (*habit*) routine *f;* **to do sth as a matter of ~** faire qc systématiquement; **daily ~** train-train *m* quotidien; **to go into a ~** ressortir la même rengaine; **to give sb a ~** faire son numéro habituel a qn; **cleaning ~** mode *m* de nettoyage 2. THEAT numéro *m* 3. INFOR routine *f* II. *adj* 1. (*regular*) ordinaire; (*medical case*) banal(e); (*check-up*) de routine; (*enquiry, inspection*) d'usage 2. *pej* (*uninspiring*) routinier(-ère)

routinely *adv* systématiquement

rove [rəʊv, *Am:* roʊv] I. *vi* errer II. *vt* (*world*) parcourir; (*the countryside*) errer dans

row[1] [rəʊ, *Am:* roʊ] *n* (*of trees, houses*) rangée *f;* (*of seats, people*) rang *m;* (*of cars*) file *f;* **to move up a few ~s** se déplacer de quelques rangs; **to stand in a ~** être en rang; **in ~s** en rang; **in a ~** d'affilée

row[2] [rəʊ, *Am:* roʊ] I. *n Aus, Brit* 1. (*quarrel*) querelle *f*, bringue *f Suisse;* **to have a ~ with sb** se disputer avec qn 2. (*noise*) vacarme *m;* **to make a ~** faire du vacarme II. *vi Brit, inf* **to ~ about sth** s'engueuler a cause de qc

row[3] [raʊ] I. *vi* ramer; SPORT faire de l'aviron; **to ~ across the lake** traverser le lac a la rame; **to ~ back/away** revenir/partir a la rame II. *vt* **to ~ the boat to sth** ramer vers qc; **to ~ sb/sth** transporter qn/qc en canot; **to ~ the boat back home** ramener le bateau a la rame; **to ~ sb across the lake** ramener qn en canot sur le lac III. *n* rame *f;* **to go for a ~** faire un tour de canot

rowan [rəʊən, *Am:* roʊən] *n* sorbier *m*

rowboat ['rəʊbəʊt, *Am:* 'roʊboʊt] *n Am* canot *m* (a rames)

rowdy ['raʊdɪ] <-ier, -iest> *adj pej* tapageur(-euse); **to be ~** faire du raffut

rower *n* rameur, -euse *m, f*

rowing *n no pl* aviron *m*

rowing boat *n* canot *m*

royal ['rɔɪəl] I. *adj* 1. (*of a monarch*) *a. fig* royal(e); **Your/His/Her ~ Highness** Votre/Son Altesse 2. *Am, inf* (*big*) gros(se) II. *n inf* membre *mf* de la famille royale

royalist I. *n* royaliste *mf* II. *adj* royaliste

R

> Le **Royal Observatory** (observatoire) a été construit en 1675 afin d'obtenir des données très précises sur la position des étoiles pour établir des cartes de routes maritimes. Le "Greenwich meridian" ne fut fixé officiellement qu'en 1884 dans le monde entier comme le degré zéro de longitude. C'est pour cela que l'on calcule actuellement le temps des 24 fuseaux horaires mondiaux sur la base de l'heure à Greenwich, connu communément sous la désignation de "Greenwich Mean time" (GMT) ou "Universal Time".

Royal Navy *n Brit* MIL ≈ marine *f* nationale

royalty ['rɔɪəltɪ, *Am:* -t̬ɪ] *n* 1. *no pl* (*sovereignty*) royauté *f;* **to treat sb like ~** traiter qn comme un roi [*o* une reine] 2. *pl* (*copyrights*) royalties *fpl*

RP [ˌɑːˈpiː, *Am:* ˌɑːr-] *n Brit abbr of* **received**

pronunciation prononciation *f* standard
RPI *n Brit abbr of* **retail price index**
rpm [ˌɑːpiːˈem, *Am:* ˌɑːr-] *n abbr of* **revolutions per minute** tr/min *m*
RR *n Am abbr of* **Railroad** chemin *m* de fer
RRP *n Brit abbr of* **recommended retail price**
RSPCA [ˌɑːrˈesˌpiːsiːˈeɪ, *Am:* ˌɑːr-] *n Brit abbr of* **Royal Society for the Prevention of Cruelty to Animals** ≈ SPA *f*
RSVP *abbr of* **répondez s'il vous plaît** RSVP
Rt Hon. *n abbr of* **Right Honourable** très honorable
rub [rʌb] **I.** *n* frottement *m;* **to give sth a ~** frotter qc **II.** <-bb-> *vt* frotter; (*body*) frictionner; (*blackboard*) essuyer; (*one's eyes, hands*) se frotter; **to ~ sth clean** nettoyer qc (en frottant); **to ~ oneself** (**up**) **against sth** se frotter contre qc; **to ~ up** astiquer ▶**to rub sb's nose in it** mettre le nez de qn dedans; **to ~ shoulders** [*o* **elbows** *Am*] **with sb** *inf* côtoyer qn; **to ~ sb** (**up** *Aus, Brit*) **the wrong way** prendre qn a rebrousse-poil **III.** <-bb-> *vi* se frotter; **the shoes ~ against my heel** les chaussures me serrent au talon
◆**rub along** *vi Brit, inf* **to ~** (**together**) s'entendre plus ou moins bien
◆**rub down** *vt* **1.** (*prepare for decoration*) nettoyer; **to ~ with sandpaper** poncer avec du papier de verre **2.** (*dry*) essuyer (en frottant)
◆**rub in** *vt* **1.** (*spread on skin*) faire pénétrer **2.** *inf* (*keep reminding*) rappeler sans cesse
◆**rub off I.** *vi* **1.** (*become clean*) s'effacer; (*mark*) partir **2.** (*affect*) **~ on sb** déteindre sur qn **II.** *vt* effacer; **to rub dirt off** enlever les saletés
◆**rub out** *vt* **1.** (*erase*) effacer **2.** *Am, inf* (*murder*) éliminer
rubber [ˈrʌbəʳ, *Am:* -ɚ] **I.** *n* **1.** (*elastic substance*) caoutchouc *m* **2.** *Aus, Brit* (*eraser*) gomme *f*, efface *f Québec* **3.** *Am, inf* (*condom*) capote *f* **4.** *pl, Am* (*waterproof shoes*) bottes *fpl* en caoutchouc **5.** (*in bridge*) partie *f* **II.** *adj* en caoutchouc
rubber band *n* élastique *m* **rubber dinghy** *n* bateau *m* pneumatique **rubber plant** *n* caoutchouc *m* **rubber tree** *n* arbre *m* a gomme **rubber stamp I.** *vt pej* approuver **II.** *n* tampon *m;* **to put one's ~ on sth** approuver qc
rubbery [ˈrʌbərɪ] <-ier, -iest> *adj* **1.** (*rubber-like*) caoutchouteux(-euse); **to taste ~** avoir une consistance caoutchouteuse **2.** *inf* (*weak*) mou(molle)
rubbing *n* frottement *m;* (**brass**) **~** frottage *m* (*sur bronze*)
rubbish [ˈrʌbɪʃ] **I.** *n no pl, Brit* **1.** *inf* (*waste*) déchets *mpl;* **to take the ~ out** sortir les poubelles **2.** *inf* (*nonsense*) bêtises *fpl;* **a load of ~** un tas de bêtises; **to talk ~** dire des bêtises **3.** *inf* (*junk, goods on sale*) camelote *f* **II.** *vt Aus, Brit, inf* débiner
rubbish bin *n* poubelle *f* **rubbish chute** *n* vide-ordures *m*, dévaloir *m Suisse* **rubbish dump** *n* décharge *f* publique
rubbishy *adj Aus, Brit, inf* nul(le)
rubble [ˈrʌbl] *n no pl* **1.** (*smashed rock*) gravats *mpl* **2.** (*from demolished building*) décombres *mpl* **3.** *fig* **to reduce sth to ~** réduire qc en poussière
rub-down *n* friction *f;* **to give sb a ~** frictionner qn
rubella [ruːˈbelə] *n no pl, form* MED rubéole *f*
rubric [ˈruːbrɪk] *n form* rubrique *f*
ruby [ˈruːbɪ] **I.** <-ies> *n* rubis *m* **II.** *adj* **1.** (*coloured*) (couleur) rubis *inv* **2.** (*made of stones: necklace, bracelet*) de rubis
RUC [ˌɑːjuːˈsiː, *Am:* ˌɑːr-] *n abbr of* **Royal Ulster Constabulary** Police *f* royale d'Ulster
ruck [rʌk] **I.** *n* **1.** (*average crowd*) foule *f;* **to lift sb out of the ~** distinguer qn de la masse; **to rise above the ~** s'élever au-dessus de la foule **2.** (*in rugby*) mêlée *f* **3.** (*fold*) pli *m* **II.** *vt* froisser **III.** *vi* se froisser
◆**ruck up I.** *vt* froisser **II.** *vi* se froisser
rucksack [ˈrʌksæk] *n Brit* sac *m* a dos
ruckus [ˈrʌkəs] *n Am, inf* grabuge *m*
ructions [ˈrʌkʃnz] *npl Aus, Brit, inf* grabuge *m*
rudder [ˈrʌdəʳ, *Am:* -ɚ] *n* gouvernail *m*
ruddy [ˈrʌdɪ] **I.** <-ier, -iest> *adj* **1.** (*red*) rouge; (*complexion*) rougeaud(e) **2.** *Aus, Brit, inf* (*bloody*) sacré(e) **II.** *adv Aus, Brit, inf* (*bloody*) sacrément
rude [ruːd] *adj* **1.** (*impolite*) impoli(e); **to be ~ to sb** être impoli envers qn **2.** (*coarse*) grossier(-ère) **3.** (*sudden*) soudain(e); (*shock*) rude; **I had a ~ awakening** j'ai perdu mes illusions
rudimentary [ˌruːdɪˈmentrɪ, *Am:* -dəˈ-] *adj form* rudimentaire
rudiments [ˈruːdɪmənts, *Am:* -də-] *npl* rudiments *mpl*
rueful [ˈruːfəl] *adj* attristé(e)
ruffian [ˈrʌfɪən] *n* voyou *m*
ruffle [ˈrʌfl] *vt* **1.** (*agitate*) agiter **2.** (*upset*) troubler ▶**to ~ sb's feathers** hérisser les poils de qn
rug [rʌg] *n* carpette *f* ▶**to pull the ~** (**out**) **from under sb's feet** couper l'herbe sous les pieds de qn
rugby [ˈrʌgbɪ] *n no pl* rugby *m;* **a ~ team/ball** une équipe/balle de rugby
rugby league *n* rugby *m* a treize
rugged [ˈrʌgɪd] *adj* **1.** (*uneven: cliff, mountains*) découpé(e); (*country, coast, bank*) accidenté(e); (*ground*) rocailleux(-euse) **2.** (*tough: individual, face*) rude **3.** (*solid: vehicle, constitution*) robuste
ruin [ˈruːɪn] **I.** *vt* **1.** (*destroy*) *a. fig* (*reputation, country*) ruiner; (*dress*) abemer; **you'll ~ your health/skin** tu vas t'abîmer la santé/la peau **2.** (*spoil: day, plan, house*) gâcher; (*child*) gâter **3.** (*impoverish*) ruiner **II.** *n* ruine *f;* **to be in/fall into ~**(**s**) être/tomber en ruine; **to be on the edge of ~, to face ~** être

au bord de la ruine; **to be on the road to ~** aller a la ruine

ruination [ˌruːɪ'neɪʃn, *Am:* -ə'-] *n no pl* ruine *f*

ruinous ['ruːɪnəs, *Am:* 'ruːə-] *adj* **1.** (*expensive*) ruineux(-euse) **2.** (*destructive*) **in ~ condition** en ruine; **to be ~ to sth** ruiner qc; **a ~ war for the country** une guerre qui a ruiné le pays

rule [ruːl] **I.** *n* **1.** (*instruction*) règle *f;* **to play by the ~s** jouer d'après les règles; **the school ~s** le règlement scolaire; **to make it a ~ to** *+infin* avoir pour règle de *+infin* **2.** *no pl* (*control*) autorité *f;* **under Conservative ~** sous les conservateurs **3.** (*ruler*) règle *f* ►**as a ~ of thumb** en général; **as a general ~** en règle générale; **~s are made to be broken** *prov* les règles sont faites pour être violées; **to be the ~** être la règle **II.** *vt* **1.** (*govern*) gouverner **2.** (*control*) mener **3.** (*draw: line*) tirer; (*paper*) tracer des lignes sur **4.** (*decide*) décider; LAW déclarer ►**to ~ the roost** faire la loi; **to be ~d by sb** écouter les conseils de qn **III.** *vi* (*control*) régner ►**to ~ supreme** régner en maetre absolu

◆**rule off** *vt* tirer

◆**rule out** *vt* exclure; **to ~ doing sth** décider de ne pas faire qc

rule book *n* **the ~** le règlement

ruler *n* **1.** (*controlling person*) dirigeant(e) *m(f)* **2.** (*measuring device*) rFgle *f*

ruling **I.** *adj* **1.** (*governing*) dirigeant(e); (*party*) au pouvoir **2.** (*primary*) premier(-ère) **II.** *n* décision *f;* **to give a ~** rendre une décision

rum [rʌm] *n* rhum *m*

Rumania *n s.* **Romania**

Rumanian *n, adj s.* **Romanian**

rumba ['rʌmbə] *n* rumba *f*

rumble ['rʌmbl] **I.** *n no pl* grondement *m* **II.** *vi* gronder **III.** *vt Brit, inf* (*person*) voir venir; (*trick*) piger

rumbling **I.** *n* **1.** *pl* (*indication*) signes *mpl* **2.** (*sound*) grondement *m;* (*of stomach*) gargouillis *m* **II.** *adj* **a ~ noise** un grondement; **a ~ stomach** un estomac qui gargouille

ruminant ['ruːmɪnənt, *Am:* -mə-] **I.** *n* ruminant *m* **II.** *adj* ruminant(e)

ruminate ['ruːmɪneɪt, *Am:* -mə-] *vi* ruminer

rummage ['rʌmɪdʒ] **I.** *vi* fouiller **II.** *n no pl* bric-a-brac *m;* **to have a ~ around in sth** farfouiller dans qc

rummy ['rʌmɪ] *n no pl* rami *m*

rumor *Am,* **rumour** ['ruːmə^r^, *Am:* -mɚ] *Brit, Aus* **I.** *n* rumeur *f;* **to circulate a ~ that …** faire circuler la rumeur que …; **~ has it that …** le bruit court que … **II.** *vt* **sb is ~ed to be sth/doing sth** la rumeur dit que qn serait qc/ferait qc; **it is ~ed that …** la rumeur dit que …

rump [rʌmp] *n* **1.** (*meat*) ~ (**steak**) rumsteck *m* **2.** (*rear: of animal, person*) croupe *f* **3.** (*faction*) minorité *f*

rumple ['rʌmpl] *vt* froisser; (*hair*) ébouriffer

rumpus ['rʌmpəs] *n no pl, inf* boucan *m* ►**to raise a ~** faire du boucan; (*complain*) faire (tout) un cirque

run [rʌn] **I.** *n* **1.** (*jog*) course *f;* **at a ~** au pas de course; **to break into a ~** se mettre a courir; **to go for a ~** (aller) courir; **to make a ~ for it** foncer **2.** (*excursion*) tour *m;* **to go for a ~ in the car** (aller) faire un tour en voiture **3.** (*journey*) trajet *m;* **he does the London ~** il fait les trajets sur Londres; **the school ~** le ramassage des enfants; **to be a one-hour ~ from sth** être a une heure de qc; (**bombing**) **~** MIL sortie *f* **4.** (*series*) série *f;* (*of cards*) suite *f;* **to have a ~ of good/bad luck** être en veine/dans la déveine **5.** (*period*) période *f;* (*of events*) cours *m;* **in the long ~** a la longue; **in the short ~** a court terme; **to have a long ~** THEAT tenir longtemps l'affiche; (*TV series*) passer pendant longtemps **6.** (*production*) lot *m;* **a** (**print**) **~ of 5000** un tirage de 5000 exemplaires **7.** (*demand*) ruée *f;* **a ~ on sth** une forte demande de qc **8.** (*type*) genre *m;* **the common ~ of films/students** les films/étudiants ordinaires **9.** (*trend*) *a. fig* tendance *f* **10.** (*enclosed area: for animals*) enclos *m;* (*for skiing*) piste *f* **11.** (*freedom*) **to have the ~ of sth** avoir qc a son entière disposition **12.** SPORT point *m* **13.** (*hole*) maille *f* filée; **to have a ~ in tights** avoir les bas filés **14.** (*leak: of ink, paint*) bavure *f* ►**to give sb/sth a ~ for their money** donner du fil a retordre a qn/qc; **to have a** (**good**) **~ for one's money** en avoir pour son argent; **to have the ~s** *inf* avoir la courante; **to be on the ~** être en cavale; (*extremely busy*) être en train de cavaler **II.** *vi* <ran, run> **1.** (*move fast using feet*) courir; **to ~ at sb** foncer sur qn; **to come ~ning towards sb** venir vers qn en courant; **to ~ in/out** entrer/sortir en courant; **to ~ up/down the street** monter/descendre la rue en courant; **to ~ across/into sth** traverser/entrer dans qc en courant; **to ~ along/around sth** passer le long/autour de qc; **to ~ for help/the bus** courir pour chercher de l'aide/attraper le bus; **to ~ on the spot/for cover** courir sur place/a l'abri; **don't come ~ning to me** *fig* ne viens pas pleurer chez moi **2.** (*operate*) fonctionner; (*wheel, engine*) tourner; **to keep the economy ~ning** faire tourner l'économie; **to ~ off the mains** se brancher sur secteur; **to ~ on diesel** rouler au diesel; **we're ~ning on time** nous sommes dans les temps; **is the Brighton train ~ning?** est-ce que le train de Brighton est en service? **3.** (*go*) filer; **I have to ~** je dois filer **4.** (*flee*) fuir **5.** (*last*) durer; **to ~ for two years** (*play*) être a l'affiche pendant deux ans; (*TV series*) passer pendant deux ans; (*contract*) être valable deux ans **6.** (*flow: water, nose*) couler; (*eyes*) pleurer; (*ink, paint*) baver; (*colour*) déteindre; **to ~ into sth** se jeter dans qc; **to ~ high** être houleux **7.** *Am* POL se porter candidat; **to ~ for President** être

R

candidat a la présidence; **to ~ against sb** se présenter contre qn **8.** + *adj* (*be*) être; **to ~ dry** s'assécher; **to ~ short of sth** être a court de qc **9.** (*ladder*) filer **10.** (*follow route*) passer; **the river ~s through Burgundy/by the road** la rivière coule à travers la Bourgogne/le long de la route; **the bus ~s past the church to the city centre** le bus va au centre-ville en passant devant l'église vers l **11.** SPORT faire du jogging ►**to ~ round** [*o* **around** *Am*] **in circles** (*to be busy*) se mettre en quatre; **to ~ in the family** tenir de famille; **to ~ through one's head** trotter dans la tête; **to ~ wild** (*animal*) être en toute liberté; (*person*) courir partout **III.** *vt* <ran, run> **1.** (*by moving feet: race, distance*) courir **2.** (*enter in race*) courir; **to ~ a horse** faire courir un cheval; **to ~ a candidate** présenter un candidat **3.** (*drive*) conduire; **to ~ sb home/to the station** conduire qn a la maison/a la gare; **to ~ a truck into a garage** rentrer un camion dans un garage **4.** (*pass*) faire passer; **to ~ one's hand through one's hair** se passer la main dans les cheveux; **to ~ a comb through one's hair** se passer un coup de peigne; **to ~ a vacuum cleaner over a rug** passer l'aspirateur sur un tapis **5.** (*operate*) faire fonctionner; (*a car*) entretenir; (*train*) faire circuler; (*motor, program*) faire tourner **6.** (*manage, govern*) gérer; (*firm, government, theatre*) diriger; (*household, store, hotel*) tenir; **a well-/badly-~ school** une école bien/mal gérée; **to be too expensive to ~** être trop cher **7.** (*let flow: tap, water*) faire couler; **to ~ a bath** faire couler un bain **8.** (*tell*) **to ~ sth by sb** soumettre qc à qn **9.** (*issue: an article*) publier; (*series, a film*) passer **10.** (*smuggle*) faire passer **11.** (*not heed*) **to ~ a red light** ne pas s'arrêter au feu rouge **12.** (*incur: danger, risk*) courir **13.** (*have: temperature, a deficit*) avoir; (*test*) effectuer ►**to ~ one's eye over sth** parcourir qc du regard; **to ~ oneself into the ground** s'épuiser; **to ~ a mile** *Brit, inf* se tirer; **to ~ the show** faire la loi; **to ~ sb ragged** éreinter qn

◆**run about** *vi s.* **run around**

◆**run across** *vt, vi* traverser

◆**run after** *vt* poursuivre

◆**run along** *vi* (*leave*) partir; **~ now** va maintenant

◆**run around** *vi* **1.** (*bustle*) courir dans tous les sens **2.** (*run freely*) **to ~ in the street** courir dans la rue **3.** *inf* (*have affair*) **to ~ with sb** avoir une liaison avec qn

◆**run away** *vi* s'enfuir; **to ~ with the idea that ...** aller s'imaginer que ...; **you let your imagination ~ with you** ton imagination s'emballe

◆**run down** **I.** *vt inf* **1.** (*criticize*) dénigrer **2.** *Brit* (*reduce: factory*) fermer progressivement; (*production*) réduire progressivement **3.** (*hit: car, person*) renverser; (*boat*) heurter **4.** (*exhaust*) décharger; **to ~ oneself down** se vider **5.** (*find*) découvrir **II.** *vi* **1.** *Brit* (*become lower: output*) baisser **2.** (*lose power: clock*) s'arrOter; (*battery*) se décharger **3.** (*deteriorate*) se détériorer

◆**run in** *vt* **1.** *inf* (*arrest*) arrêter **2.** *Aus, Brit* (*prepare engine: car*) roder

◆**run into** *vt* **1.** (*meet by chance*) rencontrer par hasard **2.** AUTO entrer en collision avec **3.** (*reach: thousands*) atteindre; **to ~ debt** s'endetter

◆**run off** **I.** *vi* **1.** *inf* (*leave*) s'enfuir; **to ~ home** rentrer chez soi **2.** *inf* (*steal*) **to ~ with sth** se tirer avec qc **3.** (*drain*) s'écouler **II.** *vt* **1.** (*reproduce*) tirer des exemplaires de; **to ~ a copy** faire une copie **2.** (*write quickly*) pondre **3.** (*lose through running*) **to ~ one's pounds** [*o* **to run one's pounds off**] perdre des kilos en courant **4.** (*drain*) laisser s'écouler

◆**run on** *vi* **1.** (*continue talking*) parler sans s'arrêter; **to ~ for another hour** ne plus s'arrêter de parler pendant une heure; **to ~ and on for three pages** continuer sur trois pages **2.** (*continue*) se poursuivre **3.** (*be preoccupied by*) tourner autour de

◆**run out** *vi* **1.** (*contract*) expirer **2.** (*be short of*) **to ~ of sth** se trouver à court de qc; **to ~ patience** perdre patience **3.** *inf* (*abandon*) **to ~ on sb** abandonner qn

◆**run over** **I.** *vi* *a. fig* déborder **II.** *vt* **1.** (*injure: person*) renverser **2.** (*read again*) revoir **3.** (*exceed*) excéder

◆**run through** **I.** *vt* **1.** (*rehearse: a speech, an act*) répéter **2.** (*read or repeat quickly*) repasser sur **3.** (*stab*) **to run sb through with sth** transpercer le corps de qn avec qc **4.** (*pervade*) traverser **5.** (*spend*) venir à bout de **II.** *vi* passer en courant

◆**run to** *vt* **1.** (*amount to*) s'élever à; (*include*) comprendre **2.** (*make affordable*) permettre **3.** (*showing a tendency*) être enclin à **4.** (*increase: bill*) laisser accumuler **5.** (*produce: dress*) fabriquer **6.** *Aus, Brit* (*raise: flag*) hisser

◆**run up against** *vt* se heurter à

runabout *n* petite voiture *f*

runaround *n no pl* **to give sb the ~** faire tourner qn en bourrique

runaway **I.** *adj* **1.** (*out of control: train, car*) fou(folle); (*horse*) emballé(e) **2.** (*which has fled: from an institution*) en fuite; (*from home*) fugueur(-euse) **3.** (*enormous: success*) immense; (*inflation*) galopant(e) **II.** *n* fugueur, -euse *m, f*; (*from prison*) fugitif, -ive *m, f*

rundown¹ *n* **1.** (*report, account, summary*) résumé *m* **2.** *no pl* (*reduction, cut*) compression *f*

rundown² *adj* **1.** (*dilapidated*) décrépit(e); (*facilities*) défectueux(-euse) **2.** (*worn out*) à bout

rune [ruːn] *n* (*mysterious mark*) symbole *m*

rung [rʌŋ] **I.** *pp of* **ring** **II.** *n* **1.** (*ladder step*) échelon *m* **2.** (*level*) niveau *m*

run-in *n* **1.** *inf* (*argument, quarrel*) dispute *f* **2.** (*prelude*) prélude *m*

runner ['rʌnəʳ, *Am:* -ɚ] *n* **1.** (*person that runs*) coureur, -euse *m, f* **2.** (*racing horse*) cheval *m* partant **3.** (*messenger*) messager *m* **4.** (*smuggler*) trafiquant(e) *m(f)* **5.** (*blade*) patin *m* **6.** (*rod to slide on*) glissière *f* **7.** (*stem*) tige *f* **8.** (*long rug, strip of carpet*) tapis *m* ▶**to do a ~** *inf* s'échapper

runner bean *n Brit* haricot *m* vert

runner-up *n* second(e) gagnant(e) *m(f)*

running **I.** *n no pl* **1.** (*action of a runner*) course *f* **2.** (*operation*) fonctionnement *m;* **the day-to-day ~ of the business** l'organisation quotidienne d'une compagnie ▶**to be in/out of the ~** être/ne pas être dans la course **II.** *adj* **1.** (*in a row, consecutive*) de suite **2.** (*ongoing*) permanent(e); (*commentary*) simultané(e) **3.** (*operating*) en marche **4.** (*flowing*) courant(e)

running costs *npl* coûts *mpl* d'entretien

runny ['rʌnɪ] <-ier, -iest> *adj* coulant(e); (*nose*) qui coule; (*sauce*) liquide

run-off *n* **1.** (*second election*) deuxième tour *m* **2.** (*extra competition*) *épreuve supplémentaire pour départager des ex-{quo* **3.** (*rainfall*) eaux *fpl* de ruissellement **run-of-the-mill** *adj* courant(e)

runt [rʌnt] *n* avorton *m*

run-through *n* THEAT, MUS répétition *f*

run-up *n* **1.** (*running approach*) course *f* **2.** *Brit* (*prelude, final stage*) dernière étape *f;* **the ~ to sth** le compte à rebours avant qc

runway *n* piste *f*

rupee [ruː'piː] *n* roupie *f*

rupture ['rʌptʃəʳ, *Am:* -tʃɚ] **I.** *vi* se rompre; (*blood vessel*) éclater **II.** *vt* rompre; **to ~ oneself** se faire une hernie **III.** *n* **1.** (*act of bursting*) rupture *f* **2.** (*hernia*) hernie *f*

rural ['rʊərəl, *Am:* 'rʊrəl] *adj* rural(e)

ruse [ruːz] *n* ruse *f*

rush¹ [rʌʃ] *n* (*grass-like plant*) jonc *m*

rush² [rʌʃ] **I.** *n* **1.** (*hurry*) précipitation *f;* **to be in a ~** être pressé; **to leave in a ~** partir précipitamment; **in the ~ to finish on time** dans la hâte de finir à temps **2.** (*charge, attack*) ruée *f;* **there was a ~ to the stairs** il y a eu une ruée vers l'escalier **3.** (*surge*) afflux *m;* (*of air*) bouffée *f;* (*of dizziness*) soudaine vague *f* **4.** (*migration of large numbers*) ruée *f;* **gold ~** ruée *f* vers l'or **5.** SPORT course *f* **II.** *vi* **1.** (*hurry*) se précipiter; **to ~ in/out** se ruer dedans/dehors; **to ~ to talk to/help sb** se précipiter pour parler à/aider qn; **to ~ about** courir dans tous les sens; **to ~ up to sb** arriver en courant vers qn; **to ~ towards sb** se précipiter vers qn; **to ~ at sb/sth** se ruer sur qn/qc **2.** (*hurry into*) **to ~ into sth** se lancer aveuglément dans qc; **to ~ to conclusions** tirer des conclusions trop vite **3.** *Am* SPORT attaquer **III.** *vt* **1.** (*hurry*) faire à la hâte **2.** (*to transport*) emmener d'urgence **3.** (*pressure: person*) bousculer; (*job*) faire très vite; **to ~ dinner** dîner à la hâte; **to ~ sb into doing sth** pousser qn à faire qc **4.** (*attack*) prendre d'assaut; (*person*) attaquer ▶**not to ~ one's fences** *Brit* agir avec méthode

◆**rush through** *vt* (*book*) lire en vitesse; (*bill*) faire voter rapidement; (*order*) traiter d'urgence

rush hour *n* heure *f* de pointe **rush job** *n* travail *m* urgent

rusk [rʌsk] *n* biscotte *f*

Russia ['rʌʃə] *n* la Russie

Russian **I.** *adj* russe **II.** *n* **1.** (*person*) Russe *mf* **2.** LING russe *m; s. a.* **English**

Russian Federation *n* **the ~** la Fédération de Russie **Russian Revolution** *n* **the ~** la Révolution Russe

rust [rʌst] **I.** *n no pl* **1.** (*metallic decay*) rouille *f* **2.** (*colour*) couleur *f* rouille **II.** *vi* **to ~** (**away/through**) se rouiller **III.** *vt* rouiller

rust-coloured *adj* (de couleur) rouille *inv;* (*hair*) roux

rustic ['rʌstɪk] *adj* **1.** (*of the country*) rustique **2.** (*simple, plain*) simple

rustle ['rʌsl] **I.** *vi* se froisser **II.** *vt* **1.** (*cause to move noisily*) froisser **2.** *Am, Aus* (*steal*) voler **III.** *n* froissement *m*

◆**rustle up** *vt* faire rapidement

rustler *n Am, Aus* (*cattle thief*) voleur, -euse *m, f* de bétail

rusty ['rʌstɪ] <-ier, -iest> *adj* rouillé(e); **my ~ German** mon allemand approximatif

rut [rʌt] *n* **1.** (*track*) sillon *m* **2.** *no pl* ZOOL rut *m* ▶**to be (stuck) in/get out of a ~** s'enfoncer dans le/sortir du train-train

rutabaga [ˌruːtə'beɪgə, *Am:* -t̬ə'-] *n Am* rutabaga *m*

ruthless ['ruːθlɪs] *adj* sans pitié; (*ambition*) ravageur(-euse); (*behaviour*) cruel(le); (*decision, dictator, plan*) impitoyable; **to be ~ in doing sth** (*cruel*) faire qc de manière cruelle; (*severe*) être sans pitié pour faire qc; **to be ~ in enforcing the law** appliquer implacablement la loi

ruthlessness *n no pl* caractère *m* impitoyable

RV [ˌɑːʳ'viː, *Am:* ˌɑːr-] *n Am abbr of* **recreational vehicle** camping-car *m*

Rwanda [rʊ'ændə, *Am:* -'ɑːn-] *n* le Ruanda [*o* Rwanda]

Rwandan **I.** *adj* rwandais(e) **II.** *n* Rwandais(e) *m(f)*

rye [raɪ] *n no pl* seigle *m*

rye bread *n no pl* pain *m* de seigle

R

S

S [es] *n*, **s** [es] <-'s> *n* s *m*, S *m inv;* ~ **as in Sugar**, ~ **for Sugar** (*on telephone*) s comme Suzanne

S I. *n no pl* 1. *abbr of* **south** S *m* 2. *Am abbr of* **satisfactory** II. *adj* 1. *abbr of* **south, southern** sud *inv* 2. *abbr of* **small** S

s *inv abbr of* **second** s *f*

SA *n* 1. *abbr of* **South Africa** Afrique *f* du Sud 2. *abbr of* **South America** Amérique *f* du Sud 3. *abbr of* **Salvation Army** Armée *f* du Salut

Sabbath ['sæbəθ] *n* 1. (*Jewish celebration*) sabbat *m* 2. (*Christian Sunday*) dimanche *m*

sabbatical [sə'bætɪkl, *Am:* -'bæt̬-] I. *n* congé *m* sabbatique; **to be on** ~ être en congé sabbatique II. *adj* sabbatique

saber ['seɪbəʳ, *Am:* -bɚ] *n Am s.* **sabre**

sable ['seɪbl] *n no pl* zibeline *f*

sabotage ['sæbətɑːʒ] I. *vt* saboter II. *n* sabotage *m*

saboteur [ˌsæbə'tɜːʳ, *Am:* -'tɜːr] *n* saboteur, -euse *m, f*

sabre ['seɪbəʳ, *Am:* -bɚ] *n Aus, Brit* sabre *m*

sac [sæk] *n* BIO, ANAT sac *m*

saccharin ['sækərɪn] *n no pl* saccharine *f*

saccharine ['sækəriːn, *Am:* -ɚɪn] *adj pej* mielleux(-euse); **with a** ~ **smile** d'un sourire mielleux

sachet ['sæʃeɪ, *Am:* -'-] *n* sachet *m*

sack[1] [sæk] I. *n* 1. (*bag*) sac *m;* **paper/plastic** ~ sac en papier/plastique 2. *no pl, Am, Aus, inf* (*bed*) **to jump into/hit the** ~ se pieuter 3. *no pl, inf* (*dismissal from job*) **to get the** ~ se faire virer; **to give sb the** ~ virer qn II. *vt* virer

sack[2] [sæk] I. *n no pl* (*pillaging*) pillage *m* II. *vt* mettre à sac

sackcloth ['sækklɒːθ, *Am:* -klɑːθ] *n no pl* grosse toile *f* ►**to be in** ~ **and ashes** être contrit

sackful *n* plein sac *m;* **a** ~ **of apples** un plein sac de pommes

sacking *n* 1. (*firing, dismissal*) licenciement *m;* **mass** ~ licenciement massif 2. (*sackcloth*) grosse toile *f* 3. (*plundering and destruction*) pillage *m*

sack race *n* course *f* en sac

sacrament ['sækrəmənt] *n* 1. (*Christian ceremony*) sacrement *m* 2. **the** ~ (*consecrated bread and wine*) la communion; **to take** [*o* **receive**] **the** ~ communier

sacramental *adj* sacramentel(le)

sacred ['seɪkrɪd] *adj* sacré(e); **to be** ~ **to sb** être sacré pour qn

sacrifice ['sækrɪfaɪs, *Am:* -rə-] I. *vt a. fig* sacrifier; **to** ~ **sb to the gods** donner qn en sacrifice aux dieux II. *vi* **to** ~ **to sb** sacrifier à qn III. *n a. fig* sacrifice *m* ►**to make the ultimate** [*o* **supreme**] ~ faire le sacrifice suprême

sacrilege ['sækrɪlɪdʒ, *Am:* -rə-] *n* sacrilège *m*

sacrilegious *adj* sacrilège

sacristy ['sækrɪsti] *n* REL sacristie *f*

sacrosanct ['sækrəʊsæŋkt, *Am:* -roʊ-] *adj iron* sacro-saint(e)

sad [sæd] <-dd-> *adj* 1. (*unhappy, feeling sorrow*) triste; **to look** ~ avoir l'air triste; **to make sb** ~ attrister qn 2. (*deplorable, shameful*) navrant(e) ►**to be** ~**der but wiser** recevoir une leçon dure mais profitable; ~ **to say** malheureusement

sadden ['sædən] *vt* attrister

saddle ['sædl] I. *n a.* GASTR selle *f* ►**to be in the** ~ (*riding*) être en selle; (*in charge*) tenir les rênes II. *vt* 1. (*put a* ~ *on: horse*) seller 2. *inf* (*burden*) **to** ~ **sb with sth** mettre qc sur les bras de qn; **to** ~ **oneself with debts** s'encombrer de dettes

saddlebag ['sædlbæg] *n* sacoche *f*

saddler *n* sellier *m*

saddle-sore ['sædlsɔːʳ] *adj* **to be** ~ avoir mal aux fesses

sadism ['seɪdɪzəm, *Am:* 'sædɪ-] *n no pl* sadisme *m*

sadist *n* sadique *mf*

sadistic *adj* sadique

sadness *n no pl, form* tristesse *f*

sae, **SAE** *n abbr of* **stamped addresssed envelope, self-addressed envelope** enveloppe *f* libellée aux nom et adresse de l'expéditeur

safari [sə'fɑːri] *n* safari *m;* **to go on** (**a**) ~ faire un safari **safari park** *n* réserve *f* d'animaux

safe [seɪf] I. *adj* 1. (*out of danger*) en sécurité; **to be not** ~ être en danger; **to be** ~ **from sth** être à l'abri de qc 2. (*not harmed: person*) hors de danger; (*object*) intact(e); ~ **and sound** sain et sauf 3. (*secure*) sûr(e); **to feel** ~ se sentir en sécurité; **to keep sth in a** ~ **place** conserver qc dans un lieu sûr; **to put sth somewhere** ~ mettre qc en lieu sûr 4. (*not dangerous: streets*) sûr(e); (*roof, building*) solide; (*meat, product*) sans danger; **to be not** ~ être dangereux 5. (*not taking risks, not risky*) sûr(e); (*choice, driver*) prudent(e); (*method, contraceptive*) sans risque; **to be not** ~ être dangereux; **it is** ~ **to say that ...** je peux dire sans prendre de risque que ...; **to be** ~ **with sb** ne rien risquer avec qn; **it is a** ~ **bet that ...** il y a fort à parier que ...; **to be in** ~ **hands** être entre de bonnes mains ►**to be as** ~ **as houses** *Brit* ne présenter aucun risque; **to wish a** ~ **journey to sb** souhaiter un bon voyage à qn; **to be on the** ~ **side** par précaution; **it is better to be** ~ **than sorry** *prov* deux précautions valent mieux qu'une; **to play it** ~ ne pas prendre de risques II. *n* coffre-fort *m*

safe-blower, **safe-breaker** *n Aus, Brit* perceur *m* de coffres-forts **safe deposit** *n* coffre *m* **safe deposit box** *n* coffre *m* **safeguard** I. *vt* protéger II. *n* garantie *f* **safe keeping** *n no pl* sécurité *f;* **in** ~ en lieu sûr; **to give sth to sb** [*o* **leave sth with sb**] **for** ~ confier qc à la garde de qn; **to be in sb's** ~ être sous la garde de qn **safe seat** *n* POL siège *m* assuré **safe sex** *n* rapports *mpl* sexuels protégés

safety ['seɪfti] *n no pl* sécurité *f;* **in** ~ en sécurité; **to be concerned for the** ~ **of sb** s'inquiéter du sort de qn; **to lead sb to a place of** ~ mettre qn en lieu sûr ▶**there's** ~ **in numbers** *prov* plus on est nombreux, moins on court de risques

safety belt *n* ceinture *f* de sécurité **safety catch** *n* cran *m* d'arrêt **safety glass** *n* verre *m* sécurit® **safety helmet** *n* casque *m* de sécurité, chapeau *m* de sécurité *Québec* **safety lamp** *n* lampe *f* de sûreté **safety lock** *n* verrouillage *m* de sécurité **safety measures** *npl* mesures *fpl* de sécurité **safety net** *n* **1.** (*protective net*) filet *m* de sécurité **2.** *fig* (*means of help or protection*) mesure *f* de sûreté **safety pin** *n* épingle *f* de nourrice **safety razor** *n* rasoir *m* de sûreté **safety regulations** *npl* réglementation *f* sur la sécurité **safety valve** *n* **1.** TECH soupape *f* de sûreté **2.** *fig* soupape *f*

saffron ['sæfrən] *n no pl* safran *m*

sag [sæg] **I.** <-gg-> *vi* **1.** (*drop, sink or hang down*) s'affaisser **2.** *fig* (*sink*) baisser **II.** *n no pl* **1.** (*sinking or drooping condition*) affaissement *m* **2.** (*fall*) baisse *f*

saga ['sɑːgə] *n a. pej* saga *f*

sagacious [sə'geɪʃəs] *adj form* sagace

sagacity [sə'gæsəti, *Am:* -t̬i] *n no pl, form* sagacité *f*

sage [seɪdʒ] *n no pl* sauge *f*

Sagittarius [ˌsædʒɪ'teərɪəs, *Am:* -ə'terɪ-] *n no art* Sagittaire *m; s. a.* **Aquarius**

Sahara [sə'hɑːrə, *Am:* -'herə] *n* **the** ~ le Sahara

said [sed] **I.** *pp, pt of* **say II.** *adj inv* cité(e)

sail [seɪl] **I.** *n* **1.** (*material*) voile *f* **2.** *no pl* (*journey over water*) traversée *f;* **to come** [*o* **go**] **for a** ~ faire un tour en bateau; **to set** ~ prendre la mer; **to set** ~ **for/from some place** partir en bateau pour/d'un endroit **3.** (*windmill blade*) aile *f* ▶**to be under** ~ être en mer **II.** *vi* **1.** (*travel on boat with sails*) faire de la voile **2.** (*travel on water: ship, tanker*) naviguer; **to** ~ **away** partir en bateau; **to** ~ **around the world** faire le tour du monde en voile **3.** (*start voyage*) prendre la mer **4.** (*move smoothly*) voler; **to** ~ **by** [*o* **past**] passer; **to** ~ **on to victory** voler vers la victoire **5.** *inf* (*attack*) **to** ~ **into sb** attaquer qn **6.** (*do easily*) **to** ~ **through sth** réussir qc sans problèmes ▶**to** ~ **close to** [*o* **near**] **the wind** jouer avec le feu **III.** *vt* **1.** (*navigate*) manœuvrer; (*ship*) commander **2.** (*travel on a body of water: seas*) parcourir

sailboard *n* planche *f* à voile **sailboarding** *n* planche *f* à voile **sailboat** *n Am* voilier *m*

sailing *n* **1.** (*act of travelling on water*) navigation *f* **2.** (*boat sport*) voile *f* **3.** (*departure by ship/boat*) appareillage *m*

sailing boat *n Aus, Brit* voilier *m* **sailing ship**, **sailing vessel** *n* voilier *m*

sailor *n* marin *m;* **to be a good** ~ avoir le pied marin

sailor suit *n* costume *m* marin

sailplane *n* planeur *m*

saint [seɪnt] *n a. fig* saint(e) *m(f);* **Saint Peter** Saint-Pierre *m;* **to be no** ~ ne pas être un saint

sainted *adj* saint(e)

saintliness *n no pl* sainteté *f*

saintly *adj* de saint

Saint Patrick's Day, le 17 mars, est la fête du saint patron de l'Irlande. Aux USA, cependant, ce n'est pas un jour férié légal. Beaucoup de gens portent ce jour là la couleur verte et organisent des fêtes. Dans certaines villes, il y a aussi des défilés dont le plus connu et le plus important est celui qui a lieu à New York.

sake[1] [seɪk] *n* **1.** (*purpose*) **for the** ~ **of** [*o* **for sth's** ~] **sth** pour qc; **for the** ~ **of art/one's family** pour l'amour de l'art/de sa famille; **for economy's** ~ par économie; **for the** ~ **of peace** pour avoir la paix; **for the** ~ **of principle** pour le principe **2.** (*advantage, benefit*) **for the** ~ **of** [*o* **for sb's** ~] **sb** faire qc pour le bien de qn ▶**for Christ's** [*o* **God's**] [*o* **goodness**] [*o* **heaven's**] ~ *pej, inf* pour l'amour de Dieu

sake[2] [seɪk], **saki** *n* (*Japanese rice drink*) saké *m*

salable ['seɪləbl] *adj Am s.* **saleable**

salacious [sə'leɪʃəs] *adj pej* salace

salad ['sæləd] *n* salade *f*

salad bowl *n* saladier *m* **salad cream** *n Brit* sauce *f* pour salade **salad days** *npl* années *fpl* de jeunesse **salad dressing** *n* vinaigrette *f*

salami [sə'lɑːmi] *n no pl* salami *m*

sal ammoniac *n* sel *m* ammoniac

salaried *adj* salarié(e); (*job*) rémunéré(e); **a** ~ **employee** un salarié; ~ **staff** salariés *mpl*

salary ['sæləri] *n* salaire *m*

salary cut *n* réduction *f* de salaire **salary deduction** *n* retenue *f* sur salaire **salary earner** *n* salarié(e) *m(f)* **salary increase** *n* augmentation *f* de salaire **salary scale** *n* échelle *f* des salaires

sale [seɪl] *n* **1.** (*act of selling*) vente *f;* **to put sth up for** ~ mettre qc en vente; **for** ~ à vendre, à remettre *Belgique;* **on** ~ en vente **2.** *pl* (*amount sold*) chiffre *m* d'affaires **3.** *pl* (*special selling event*) **the** ~**s** les soldes, les aubaines *Québec;* **summer** ~**s** soldes d'été

saleable *adj* vendable

sale price *n* prix *m* de vente **saleroom** *n Brit* salle *f* des ventes **sales analysis** *n* analyse *f* des ventes **sales clerk** *n Am* (*sales assistant*) vendeur, -euse *m, f* **sales department** *n* service *m* des ventes **sales director** *n* directeur , -trice des ventes *m* **sales drive** *n* campagne *f* de vente **sales execu-**

S

tive *n* directeur, -trice *m, f* des ventes **sales figures** *npl* chiffres *mpl* de vente **sales force** *n* force *f* de vente **sales forecast** *n* prévision *f* des ventes **salesgirl** *n* vendeuse *f* **sales invoice** *n* FIN facture *f* **saleslady** *s.* salesgirl **sales ledger** *n* FIN journal *m* des ventes **salesman** *n* **1.** (*in shop*) vendeur *m* **2.** (*representative*) représentant *m* **sales manager** *n* directeur *m* commercial **salesmanship** *n no pl* technique *f* de vente **salesperson** *n* **1.** (*in shop*) vendeur, -euse *m, f* **2.** (*representative*) représentant(e) *m(f)* **sales pitch** *n* **1.** ECON arguments *mpl* de vente **2.** *fig* boniments *mpl* **sales receipt** *n* reçu *m* **sales rep** *n inf,* **sales representative** *n* VRP *mf* **salesroom** *n s.* saleroom **sales tax** *n Am* FIN taxe *f* sur le chiffre d'affaires **saleswoman** *n* **1.** (*in shop*) vendeuse *f* **2.** (*representative*) représentante *f*

salient ['seɪlɪənt, *Am:* 'seɪljənt] *adj* saillant(e)

saline ['seɪlaɪn, *Am:* -li:n] **I.** *adj* salin(e) **II.** *n* solution *f* saline; MED sérum *m* physiologique

saliva [sə'laɪvə] *n no pl* salive *f*

salivary *adj* salivaire

salivate ['sælɪveɪt, *Am:* 'sælə-] *vi* saliver

sallow ['sæləʊ, *Am:* -oʊ] *adj* <-er, -est *o* more ~, most ~> jaunâtre

sally ['sæli] <-lies> *n* **1.** MIL (*sortie*) sortie *f* **2.** *fig* (*excursion, attempt*) excursion *f*

sally forth, **sally out** <-ie-> *vi* **1.** (*go out*) *a. fig* sortir **2.** MIL faire une sortie

salmon ['sæmən] *n* saumon *m;* **smoked** ~ saumon fumé

salmonella [ˌsælmə'nelə] *n no pl* salmonelle *f*

salmonella poisoning *n no pl* salmonellose *f*

salmon trout *n* truite *f* saumonée

salon ['sælɒn, *Am:* se'lɑ:n] *n* salon *m;* **hairdressing** ~ salon de coiffure/beauté; **literary** ~ salon littéraire

saloon [sə'lu:n] *n* **1.** *Brit* (*car*) berline *f* **2.** *Am* (*public bar*) bar *m;* **a billiard** ~ une salle de billard **3.** HIST saloon *m*

salsify ['sælsɪfaɪ, *Am:* -sə-] *n no pl* salsifis *m*

salt [sɔ:lt] **I.** *n a. fig* sel *m;* **a pinch of** ~ une pincée de sel; **sea/celery** ~ sel de mer/céleri; **bath** ~**s** sels de bain ▶**to take sth with a** **pinch** [*o* **grain**] **of** ~ ne pas prendre qc au pied de la lettre; **to rub** ~ **in the/sb's wound** remuer le couteau dans la plaie; **to sit above/below the** ~ être assis au bout de la table; **worth one's** ~ digne de ce nom **II.** *vt* saler **III.** *adj* **1.** (*with salt*) salé(e) **2.** *fig* (*tears*) amère

SALT [sɔ:lt] *n abbr of* **Strategic Arms Limitation Talks** négociations *fpl* SALT

salt cellar *n* salière *f* **salt lake** *n* lac *m* salé **salt mine** *n* mine *f* de sel **saltshaker** *n Am, Aus* salière *f* **salt water** *n no pl* **1.** (*sea water*) eau *f* de mer **2.** (*water with salt*) eau *f* salée **salt-water** *adj* **1.** (*of salted water: lake*) d'eau salée **2.** (*of sea water: fish*) d'eau de mer

salty *adj a. fig* salé(e)

salubrious [sə'lu:briəs] *adj form* salubre

salutary ['sæljətəri, *Am:* -ter-] *adj* salutaire

salutation *n* **1.** *form* (*expression of greeting*) salutation *f* **2.** (*gesture*) salut *m;* **in** ~ en guise de salut

salute [sə'lu:t] **I.** *vt a.* MIL saluer **II.** *vi* MIL faire le salut militaire **III.** *n* MIL salut *m;* **to take the** ~ passer les troupes en revue

Salvadorian [ˌsælvə'dɔ:rɪən] **I.** *adj* salvadorien(ne) **II.** *n* Salvadorien(ne) *m(f)*

salvage ['sælvɪdʒ] **I.** *vt a. fig* sauver **II.** *n no pl* **1.** (*retrieval from destruction*) récupération *f* **2.** (*sth saved/salvaged*) sauvetage *m* **3.** LAW (*payment*) indemnité *f*

salvage operation *n* opération *f* de sauvetage

salvation [sæl'veɪʃən] *n no pl a.* REL salut *m*

Salvation Army *n no pl* Armée *f* du Salut

salve [sælv, *Am:* sæv] **I.** *n* baume *m* **II.** *vt* soulager

salver *n form* plateau *m* d'argent

salvo ['sælvəʊ, *Am:* -voʊ] <-s *o* -es> *n a. fig* salve *f*

SAM [sæm] *n abbr of* **surface-to-air missile** missile *m* sol-air

same [seɪm] **I.** *adj, pron* (*exactly similar*) même; **the** ~ **as sb/sth** le(la) même que qn/qc; **the** ~ **way as sb** de la même manière que qn; ~ **difference** c'est du pareil au même; **the** ~ **again** encore un autre; **at the** ~ **time** au même moment; (**the**) ~ **to you** vous de même ▶**to be one and the** ~ une seule et même chose; **by the** ~ **token** de même **II.** *adv* **to think/do the** ~ penser/faire de même; **the** ~ **as** de la même façon que; ~ **as usual** comme d'habitude

sameness *n no pl* **1.** (*resemblance*) similitude *f* **2.** (*monotony*) monotonie *f*

Samoa Islands [sə'məʊə, *Am:* -moʊ-] *npl* les îles *fpl* Samoa

Samoan **I.** *adj* samoan(ne) **II.** *n* Samoan(ne) *m(f)*

sample ['sɑ:mpl, *Am:* 'sæm-] **I.** *n* **1.** (*small representative unit*) échantillon *m;* MED prélèvement *m* **2.** (*music extract*) sample *m* **II.** *vt* **1.** (*try*) essayer; **to** ~ **the delights of sth** goûter aux délices de qc **2.** (*survey*) sonder **3.** MED prélever **4.** MUS sampler

sampler *n* **1.** *Am* (*collection of items*) échantillonnage *m* **2.** (*person or device*) sondeur *m* **3.** MUS sampler *m*

sampling *n* **1.** (*activity of taking a survey*) prélèvement *m* d'échantillons **2.** (*sample in statistics*) échantillonnage *m* **3.** *no pl* MUS échantillonnage *m*

sanatorium [ˌsænə'tɔ:rɪəm] <-s *o* -ria> *n* sanatorium *m*

sanctify ['sæŋktɪfaɪ] <-ie-> *vt* **1.** REL sanctifier **2.** *form* consacrer

sanctimonious [ˌsæŋktɪ'məʊnɪəs, *Am:* -'moʊ-] *adj pej* moralisateur(-trice)

sanction ['sæŋkʃən] I. *n* sanction *f* II. *vt* sanctionner
sanctity ['sæŋktəti, *Am:* -t̬i] *n no pl* REL 1. (*sacredness*) caractère *m* sacré 2. (*holiness*) sainteté *f*
sanctuary ['sæŋktʃʊəri, *Am:* -tʃueri] *n* <-ries> *a. fig* sanctuaire *m;* (*for animals*) réserve *f;* **to seek/find ~ in sth** chercher/trouver refuge dans qc
sand [sænd] I. *n* 1. *no pl* (*granular substance*) sable *m* 2. *pl* (*large expanse of sand*) banc *m* de sable II. *vt* sabler III. *adj* de sable
sandal ['sændl] *n* sandale *f*
sandbag I. *n* sac *m* de sable II. <-gg-> *vt* renforcer avec des sacs de sable **sandbank**, **sandbar** *n* banc *m* de sable **sandblast** *vt* sabler **sandblasting** *n no pl* sablage *m* **sandboy** *n* **to be as happy as a ~** être heureux comme un poisson dans l'eau **sandcastle** *n* château *m* de sable **sandglass** *n* sablier *m* **sandman** *n no pl, childspeak* **the ~** le marchand de sable **sandpaper** I. *n no pl* papier *m* de verre II. *vt* poncer **sandpit** *n Brit* sablière *f* **sandstone** *n no pl* grès *m* **sandstorm** *n* tempête *f* de sable
sandwich ['sænwɪdʒ, *Am:* 'sændwɪtʃ] I. <-es> *n* sandwich *m;* **a hero/submarine ~** *Am* un sandwich baguette; **a round of ~es** *Brit* un sandwich II. *adj* en sandwich; **a ~ cookie** un biscuit fourré III. *vt* coincer; **to be ~ed** être pris en sandwich
sandwich bar *n* sandwicherie *f* **sandwich board** *n: panneau publicitaire porté en sandwich par une personne* **sandwich course** <-es> *n Brit* UNIV formation *f* alternée **sandwichman** <-men> *n* homme-sandwich *m*
sandy *adj* <-ier, -iest> 1. (*containing sand*) sableux(-euse) 2. (*with sand texture*) de sable 3. (*with sand colour*) sable
sand yacht *n* char *m* à voile
sane [seɪn] *adj* 1. (*of sound mind*) sain(e) 2. (*sensible*) raisonnable
sang [sæŋ] *pt of* **sing**
sanguine ['sæŋgwɪn] *adj form* 1. (*optimistic*) optimiste 2. (*blood-red*) rouge sanguin *inv;* (*complexion*) rubicond(e)
sanitarium [ˌsænɪ'teərɪəm, *Am:* -'terɪ-] <-s *o* -ria> *n Am* MED *s.* **sanatorium**
sanitary ['sænɪtəri, *Am:* -teri] *adj* sanitaire; (*pad, towel*) hygiénique
sanitation [ˌsænɪ'teɪʃən] *n no pl* hygiène *f*
sanity ['sænəti, *Am:* -t̬i] *n no pl* 1. (*mental health*) santé *f* mentale 2. (*sensibleness*) bon sens *m*
sank [sæŋk] *pt of* **sink**
Santa Claus [ˌsæntə'klɔːz, *Am:* 'sænt̬əˌklɑːz] *n* père *m* Noël
Santo Domingue *n* Saint-Domingue
sap¹ [sæp] *n no pl, a. fig* sève *f*
sap² [sæp] <-pp-> *vt* miner
sapling ['sæplɪŋ] *n* jeune arbre *m*
sapphire ['sæfaɪəʳ, *Am:* -aɪɚ] I. *n* saphir *m* II. *adj* 1. (*bright blue*) saphir *inv* 2. (*relating to sapphires*) de saphir
sarcasm ['sɑːkæzəm, *Am:* 'sɑːr-] *n no pl* sarcasme *m*
sarcastic [sɑː'kæstɪk, *Am:* sɑːr'-] *adj* sarcastique
sarcophagus [sɑːr'kɑːfə-] <-es *o* -gi> *n* sarcophage *m*
sardine [sɑː'diːn, *Am:* sɑːr'-] *n* sardine *f* ►**to be packed (in) like ~s** être serrés comme des sardines
Sardinia [sɑː'dɪniə, *Am:* sɑːr-] *n* la Sardaigne
sardonic [sɑː'dɒnɪk, *Am:* sɑːr'dɑːnɪk] *adj* sardonique
sari ['sɑːri] *n* sari *m*
sartorial [sɑː'tɔːriəl, *Am:* sɑːr'-] *adj form* vestimentaire
SAS [ˌeseɪ'es] *n Brit* MIL *abbr of* **Special Air Service** *commandos britanniques aéroportés*
sash¹ [sæʃ] <-es> *n* écharpe *f*
sash² [sæʃ] <-es> *n* ARCHIT châssis *m*
sash window *n* fenêtre *f* à guillotine
sassy *adj inf* effronté(e)
sat [sæt] *pt, pp of* **sit**
Satan ['seɪtən] *n no pl, no art* Satan *m*
satanic [sə'tænɪk] *adj* satanique
satchel ['sætʃəl] *n* sacoche *f*
sate [seɪt] *vt form* rassasier; (*hunger, desire*) assouvir
satellite ['sætəlaɪt, *Am:* 'sæt̬-] I. *n* satellite *m* II. *adj* satellite
satellite broadcasting *n no pl* transmission *f* par satellite **satellite country** *n* POL *s.* **satellite state** **satellite dish** *n* parabole *f* **satellite picture** *n* photo *f* satellite **satellite state** *n* état *m* satellite **satellite television** *n no pl* télévision *f* par satellite
satiate ['seɪʃɪeɪt] *vt* assouvir
satiety [sə'taɪəti, *Am:* -t̬i] *n no pl, form* satiété *f*
satin ['sætɪn, *Am:* 'sætn] I. *n* satin *m* II. *adj* à satiété
satire ['sætaɪəʳ, *Am:* -aɪɚ] *n* satire *f*
satirical [sə'tɪrɪkl] *adj* satirique
satirist *n* satiriste *mf*
satirize ['sætəraɪz, *Am:* 'sæt̬-] *vt* faire la satire de
satisfaction [ˌsætɪs'fækʃən, *Am:* ˌsæt̬-] *n no pl* 1. (*state of being satisfied*) satisfaction *f;* **to give sb ~** donner satisfaction à qn; **to one's ~** à la grande satisfaction de qn; **to be ~ to sb** être une grande satisfaction pour qn 2. (*payment: of a debt*) acquittement *m* 3. (*compensation*) réparation *f*
satisfactory [ˌsætɪs'fæktəri, *Am:* ˌsæt̬-] *adj* satisfaisant(e)
satisfy ['sætɪsfaɪ, *Am:* -əs-] <-ie-> I. *vt* 1. (*meet desires: hunger, curiosity, need*) satisfaire; **to ~ oneself** se satisfaire 2. (*provide sth to fulfil sth: demand, requirements, conditions*) satisfaire à 3. (*convince*) convaincre; **to be satisfied as to sth** être convaincu de qc; **to**

S

~ **oneself of sth** s'assurer de qc **4.** (*pay off: debt*) s'acquitter de; **to ~ sb** s'acquitter auprès de qn ►**to ~ the examiners** *Brit* SCHOOL, UNIV être reçu à l'examen **II.** *vi* donner satisfaction
satisfying *adj* satisfaisant(e)
saturate ['sætʃəreɪt] *vt* **1.** (*make completely wet*) imprégner; **to be ~d with sth** être imprégné de qc **2.** (*fill to capacity*) saturer; **to be ~d with sth** être saturé de qc
saturation *n no pl* CHEM, ECON saturation *f*
saturation point *n* point *m* de saturation
Saturday ['sætədeɪ, *Am:* 'sæt̬ɚ-] *n* samedi *m; s. a.* **Friday**
Saturn ['sætən, *Am:* 'sæt̬ɚn] *n no pl no art* Saturne *m*
satyr ['sætəʳ, *Am:* 'seɪt̬ɚ] *n* satire *f*
sauce [sɔːs, *Am:* sɑːs] *n* **1.** (*liquid*) sauce *f*; **mushroom/tomato ~** sauce tomate/aux champignons **2.** *inf* (*impudence, impertinence*) culot *m* ►**what's ~ for the goose is ~ for the gander** *prov* ce qui est bon pour l'un l'est pour l'autre
sauce boat *n* saucière *f* **saucepan** *n* casserole *f*
saucer ['sɔːsəʳ, *Am:* 'sɑːsɚ] *n* soucoupe *f*, sous-tasse *f Belgique, Suisse*
saucily ['sɔːsɪli, *Am:* 'sɑː-] *adv* avec toupet
sauciness *n no pl* **1.** (*impudence*) toupet *m* **2.** *Brit* (*smuttiness*) coquinerie *f*
saucy ['sɔːsi, *Am:* 'sɑː-] *adj* <-ier, -iest> *inf* **1.** (*impudent*) culotté(e) **2.** *Brit* (*suggestively sexy: underwear*) coquin(e)
Saudi Arabia [ˌsaʊdiə'reɪbiə] *n* l'Arabie *f* saoudite
Saudi (**Arabian**) **I.** *adj* saoudien(ne) **II.** *n* Saoudien(ne) *m(f)*
sauerkraut ['saʊəkraʊt, *Am:* 'saʊɚ-] *n no pl* choucroute *f*
sauna ['sɔːnə, *Am:* 'saʊ-] *n* sauna *m*; **to have a ~** faire un sauna
saunter ['sɔːntəʳ, *Am:* 'sɑːnt̬ɚ] **I.** *vi* flâner **II.** *n sing* flânerie *f*
sausage ['sɒsɪdʒ, *Am:* 'sɑːsɪdʒ] *n* saucisse *f*; (*dried*) saucisson *m* ►**not a ~** *Brit, iron, inf* que dalle
sausage dog *n Brit, inf* teckel *m* **sausage meat** *n no pl* chair *f* à saucisse **sausage roll** *n Brit, Aus* ≈ friand *m*
savage ['sævɪdʒ] **I.** *adj* **1.** (*wild and primitive: animal, landscape*) sauvage **2.** (*fierce*) *a. fig* cruel(le); **to deal a ~ blow to sb/sth** s'attaquer violemment à qn/qc **3.** (*primitive*) barbare **II.** *n pej* sauvage *mf* **III.** *vt* **1.** (*attack*) attaquer sauvagement **2.** *fig* attaquer violemment
savageness, **savagery** *n no pl* férocité *f*
savanna(**h**) [sə'vænə] *n* savane *f*
save [seɪv] **I.** *vt* **1.** (*rescue*) sauver; **to ~ one's own skin** sauver sa peau; **to ~ sb from falling** empêcher qn de tomber; **to ~ sb from sth** protéger qn de qc **2.** (*keep for future use*) mettre de côté; (*money*) épargner **3.** (*collect: coins, stamps*) collectionner **4.** (*avoid wasting*) économiser; **to ~ one's breath** économiser sa salive; **to ~ one's strength** ménager ses forces; **to ~ time** gagner du temps **5.** (*reserve*) réserver **6.** (*prevent from doing*) épargner **7.** INFOR sauvegarder; **to ~ as …** enregistrer sous … **8.** SPORT (*a goal*) arrêter ►**to ~ sb's bacon** sauver la peau de qn; **to ~ oneself the trouble** ne pas se donner la peine **II.** *vi* économiser **III.** *n* SPORT arrêt *m*
save [seɪv] **I.** *prep form* excepté; **all ~ the youngest** tous à l'exception du plus jeune **II.** *conj form* **~ that …** excepté que …
saveloy *n Brit* cervelas *m*
saver *n* épargnant(e) *m(f)*
saving I. *n* **1.** (*economy*) économie *f*; **to live off one's ~s** vivre sur ses économies **2.** (*rescue*) sauvetage *m*; **to be the ~ of sb** être le salut de qn **II.** *prep* sauf
savings account *n* compte *m* d'épargne **savings bank** *n* caisse *f* d'épargne **savings book** *n* livret *m* d'épargne, carnet *m* d'épargne *Suisse*
savior *n Am*, **saviour** ['seɪvjəʳ, *Am:* -ɚ] *n Brit, Aus* sauveur *m*
savor ['seɪvɚ] *Am* **I.** *n* saveur *f* **II.** *vt* savourer
savoriness *n Am no pl* saveur *f*
savory *Am* **I.** *adj* **1.** (*salty*) salé(e) **2.** (*spicy*) épicé(e) **3.** (*appetizing*) savoureux(-euse) **4.** (*socially acceptable*) recommandable **II.** *n Brit* canapé *m*
savour ['seɪvəʳ, *Am:* -vɚ] *n Brit, Aus s.* **savor**
savouriness *n Brit, Aus s.* **savoriness**
savoury *n Brit, Aus s.* **savory**
savoy (**cabbage**) *n* chou *m* frisé
savvy ['sævi] *inf* **I.** *adj* <-ier, -iest> débrouillard(e) **II.** *n no pl* jugeote *f* **III.** *vi* piger
saw[1] [sɔː, *Am:* sɑː] *pt of* **see**
saw[2] [sɔː, *Am:* sɑː] **I.** *n* scie *f* **II.** *vt, vi* <-ed, sawn *o* -ed, -ed> scier
saw[3] [sɔː, *Am:* sɑː] *n* dicton *m*
sawdust ['sɔːdʌst, *Am:* 'sɑː-] *n no pl* sciure *f*
sawmill ['sɔːmɪl, *Am:* 'sɑː-] *n* scierie *f*
sawn [sɔːn, *Am:* sɑːn] *pp of* **saw**
Saxon I. *adj* saxon(ne) **II.** *n* **1.** (*person*) Saxon(ne) *m(f)* **2.** LING saxon *m; s. a.* **English**
Saxony ['sæksəni] *n* la Saxe
saxophone ['sæksəfəʊn, *Am:* -foʊn] *n* saxophone *m*
saxophonist *n* saxophoniste *mf*
say [seɪ] **I.** <said, said> *vt* **1.** (*express*) dire; **to ~ sth about sb/sth** dire qc à propos de qn/qc; **to have nothing to ~ to sb** n'avoir rien à dire à qn; **to ~ goodbye to sb** dire au revoir à qn; **to ~ goodbye to sth** *inf* dire adieu à qc; **it is said that …** on dit que …; **people ~ …** on dit que …; **to ~ a prayer** dire une prière; (**let's**) **~ …** disons que … **2.** (*show: watch, device*) indiquer ►**to ~ amen to sth** dire amen à qc; **to ~ cheese** dire cheese; **before sb could ~ Jack Robinson** avant que qn ait eu le temps de dire ouf *subj*; **to ~ the least** c'est le moins que l'on puisse dire *subj*; **~ no**

more! n'en dites pas davantage!; **to ~ nothing of sth** sans parler de qc; **you can ~ that again!** *inf* tu veux répéter!; **you don't ~!** c'est pas possible!; **you said it!** *inf* tu l'as dit!; **to go without ~ing** aller sans dire **II.** <said, said> *vi* dire; **I must ~** je dois avouer; **what do you ~ to a drink?** qu'est-ce que tu dirais d'un verre? ►**that is to ~** c'est-à-dire; **I can't ~** je ne sais pas; **I must ~!** ça alors!; **not to ~ ...** si ce n'est ...; **I'll ~!** *inf* et comment!; **I ~!** *Brit* ça alors! **III.** *n no pl* parole *f;* **to have one's ~** dire son mot; **to have a ~ in sth** avoir son mot à dire dans qc

SAYE [ˌeseɪwaɪ'iː] *abbr of* **Save As You Earn** *plan d'épargne à contributions mensuelles aux intérêts exonérés d'impôts*

saying *n* **1.** *no pl* (*act of saying*) dire *m;* **there's no ~** il n'y a pas à dire; **it goes without ~** cela va sans dire **2.** (*proverb*) proverbe *m;* **as the ~ goes** comme dit le proverbe; (*what people say*) comme on dit

say-so *n no pl, inf* **1.** (*approval*) autorisation *f;* **to have sb's ~** avoir l'accord de qn **2.** (*unproved assertion*) assentiment *m*

scab [skæb] *n* **1.** (*over a wound*) croûte *f* **2.** *pej, inf* (*strike-breaker*) jaune *mf* **3.** *no pl* BOT teigne *f* **4.** *no pl* ZOOL gale *f*

scabbard ['skæbəd, *Am:* -ɚd] *n* fourreau *m*

scabby ['skæbi] *adj* <-ier, -iest> **1.** (*having scabs*) couvert(e) de croûtes **2.** ZOOL galeux(-euse) **3.** *Irish, Scot, inf* (*loathsome*) méprisable

scabies ['skeɪbiːz] *n no pl* MED gale *f*

scaffold ['skæfə(ʊ)ld, *Am:* 'skæfld] *n* **1.** HIST échafaud *m* **2.** *s.* **scaffolding**

scaffolding *n no pl* échafaudage *m*

scalawag ['skæləwæg] *n Am s.* **scallywag**

scald [skɔːld, *Am:* skɑːld] **I.** *vt* **1.** (*burn*) ébouillanter **2.** (*heat*) faire chauffer (sans bouillir) **II.** *n* MED brûlure *f*

scalding *adj* bouillant(e); **~ hot** brûlant(e)

scale¹ [skeɪl] **I.** *n* **1.** ZOOL écaille *f* **2.** *no pl* (*mineral coating*) calcaire *m;* (*of a boiler, coffee machine, iron*) tartre *m* **3.** MED plaque *f* dentaire **II.** *vt* détartrer

scale² [skeɪl] **I.** *n* **1.** (*system of gradations*) *a.* ECON échelle *f;* (*of thermometer*) graduation *f;* **to be in ~** être à l'échelle; **a sliding ~** une échelle mobile; **on a large/small ~** à grande/petite échelle **2.** ~(**s**) (*weighing device*) balance *f;* **a bathroom ~** un pèse-personne **3.** *no pl* (*great size*) étendue *f;* **advantages of ~** les avantages *mpl* du commerce de grande envergure **4.** MUS gamme *f;* **practice ~s** faire des gammes ►**to tip the ~s** faire pencher la balance **II.** *vt* escalader; **to ~ the heights of a profession** *fig* gravir les échelons d'une profession **III.** *vi* ECON être en (phase d')expansion

◆**scale down I.** *vt* réduire **II.** *vi* ECON être en perte de vitesse

◆**scale up I.** *vt* augmenter **II.** *vi* être en augmentation

scale drawing *n* TECH, ARCHIT dessin *m* à l'échelle **scale model** *n* modèle *m* réduit

Scales *n* (*Libra*) Balance *f*; *s. a.* **Aquarius**

scallion ['skæljən] *n* échalote *f*

scallop ['skɒləp, *Am:* 'skɑːləp] *n* **1.** (*shellfish*) coquille *f* Saint-Jacques **2.** (*escalope*) escalope *f*

scallywag ['skælɪwæg] *n inf* garnement *m*

scalp [skælp] **I.** *n* **1.** (*head skin*) cuir *m* chevelu **2.** HIST scalp *m* **3.** *fig* **to take a ~** remporter une victoire écrasante **II.** *vt* **1.** HIST (*cut off scalp*) scalper **2.** *Am, Aus, inf* (*re-sell at inflated price*) revendre au marché noir **3.** *Am, iron, inf* (*defeat*) filer une déculottée

scalpel ['skælpəl] *n* MED scalpel *m*

scaly ['skeɪli] *adj* <-ier, -iest> **1.** ZOOL écailleux(-euse) **2.** TECH entartré(e)

scam [skæm] *n inf* arnaque *f*

scamp¹ [skæmp] *n inf* coquin(e) *m(f)*

scamp² [skæmp] *vt* bâcler

scamper *vi* trottiner

scan [skæn] **I.** <-nn-> *vt* **1.** (*scrutinize*) scruter **2.** (*read quickly: newspaper, text*) parcourir; (*magazine*) feuilleter **3.** MED passer au scanner; **to ~ the brain** faire à qc un scanner cérébral **4.** INFOR scanner **5.** LIT (*verse*) scander **II.** <-nn-> *vi* **1.** (*read quickly*) parcourir **2.** LIT scander **III.** *n* **1.** (*act of scrutinizing*) scrutation *f* **2.** MED scanner *m;* **brain ~** scanner *m* du cerveau **3.** INFOR scannage *m*

scandal ['skændl] *n* **1.** (*causing outrage*) scandale *m* **2.** *no pl* (*gossip*) ragot *m;* **to spread ~** colporter une rumeur

scandalize ['skændəlaɪz] *vt* scandaliser

scandalmonger ['skændlmʌŋgəʳ, *Am:* -ˌmɑːŋgɚ] *n pej* langue *f* de vipère

scandalous *adv* **1.** (*causing scandal*) scandaleux(-euse) **2.** (*disgraceful*) honteux(-euse)

Scandinavia [ˌskændɪ'neɪviə] *n* la Scandinavie

Scandinavian I. *adj* scandinave **II.** *n* Scandinave *mf*

scanner ['skænəʳ, *Am:* -ɚ] *n* **1.** INFOR scanneur *m;* **hand-held ~** scanneur à main; **flatbed ~** scanneur à plat **2.** MED scanner *m*

scanning *n* INFOR exploration *f*

scant [skænt] **I.** *adj* maigre; **to show ~ attention** avoir peu d'attention **II.** *vt form* répartir de façon inéquitable

scantily *adv* insuffisamment; **~ dressed** légèrement vêtu(e); **~ clad** peu habillé(e)

scanty *adj* **1.** (*very small*) menu(e); (*bathing suit*) minuscule **2.** (*barely sufficient*) à peine suffisant(e); (*information, proof*) maigre

scapegoat ['skeɪpgəʊt, *Am:* -goʊt] *n* bouc *m* émissaire

scapula ['skæpjʊlə] <-s *o* -lae> *pl n* ANAT omoplate *f*

scar [skɑːʳ, *Am:* skɑːr] **I.** *n* **1.** MED (*mark on skin*) cicatrice *f* **2.** (*from a blade*) balafre *f;* **~ tissue** tissu *m* cicatriciel **3.** (*mark of damage*) stigmate *m* **4.** PSYCH (*emotional, psychological*) traumatisme *m* **5.** GEO écueil *m* **II.** <-rr-> *vt*

S

MED **to be ~red by sth** garder les traces de qc; **to be ~red for life** être marqué à vie **III.** *vi* **to ~ (over)** se cicatriser

scarab ['skærəb, *Am:* 'sker-] *n* scarabée *m*

scarce [skeəs, *Am:* skers] *adj* rare; **to make oneself ~** s'éclipser

scarcely *adv* **1.** (*barely*) à peine **2.** (*certainly not*) pas du tout

scarcity ['skeəsəti, *Am:* 'skersəṭi] *n no pl* **1.** (*lack*) pénurie *f* **2.** (*rareness*) **~ value** valeur *f* de rareté

scare [skeəʳ, *Am:* sker] **I.** *vt* effrayer; **to ~ sb into/out of doing sth** forcer qn à faire/à ne pas faire qc sous la menace; **to ~ sb stiff** faire une peur bleue à qn; **to ~ the life out of sb** terroriser qn **II.** *vi* prendre peur **III.** *n* **1.** (*sudden fright*) frayeur *f;* **to give sb a ~** faire une frayeur à qn **2.** (*public panic*) panique *f;* **bomb ~** alerte *f* à la bombe

◆scare away, scare off *vt* **1.** (*frighten into leaving*) effrayer **2.** (*discourage*) décourager

scarecrow ['skeəkrəʊ, *Am:* 'skerkroʊ] *n* épouvantail *m*

scaremonger ['skeəˌmʌŋgəʳ, *Am:* 'skerˌmɑːŋgɚ] *n pej* alarmiste *mf*

scarf[1] [skɑːf, *Am:* skɑːrf] <scarves *o* -s> *n* **1.** (*headscarf*) foulard *m* **2.** (*protecting from cold*) écharpe *f*

scarf[2] [skɑːf, *Am:* skɑːrf] *vt Am, inf* bouffer; **to ~ sth (down/up)** (tout) bouffer qc

scarifying *adj* **1.** (*badly hurtful*) très douloureux(-euse) **2.** (*terrifying*) terrifiant(e)

scarlet ['skɑːlət, *Am:* 'skɑːr-] **I.** *n no pl* écarlate *f* **II.** *adj* écarlate

scarlet fever *n no pl* MED scarlatine *f*

scarp [skɑːp, *Am:* skɑːrp] *n* **1.** MIL escarpe *f* **2.** (*double forewall*) glacis *m*

scarper *vi Brit, Aus, inf* déguerpir

scary ['skeəri, *Am:* 'skeri] *adj* <-ier, -iest> effrayant(e)

scat[1] [skæt] *interj inf* oust(e)

scat[2] [skæt] *n no pl* fiente *f*

scathing ['skeɪðɪŋ] *adj* cinglant(e); **to be ~ about sb/sth** dénigrer qn/qc

scatter ['skætəʳ, *Am:* 'skæṭɚ] **I.** *vt* disperser; (*seeds*) semer ►**to ~ sth to the four winds** semer qc aux quatre vents **II.** *vi* **1.** (*disperse*) se disperser **2.** (*to strew seeds*) semer ►**to ~ to the four winds** *form* semer aux quatre vents

scatterbrain *n pej* écervelé(e) *m(f)* **scatterbrained** *adj* étourdi(e) **scatter cushion** *n Brit, Aus* coussin *m* décoratif

scattered *adj* **1.** (*strewn about*) éparpillé(e) **2.** (*widely separated*) dispersé(e) **3.** (*sporadic*) rare

scattering *n* **1.** (*dispersion*) dispersion *f* **2.** (*sowing*) semailles *fpl* **3.** TECH diffusion *f*

scavenge ['skævɪndʒ] **I.** *vi* **1.** (*collect discarded things*) faire de la récupération **2.** ZOOL être un charognard **II.** *vt* **1.** (*collect*) récupérer **2.** *fig* glaner

scavenger *n* **1.** ZOOL charognard(e) *m(f)* **2.** (*person cleaning the streets*) éboueur *m*

scenario [sɪ'nɑːrɪəʊ, *Am:* sə'nerɪoʊ] *n* scénario *m;* **nightmare ~** vision *f* de cauchemar

scene [siːn] *n* **1.** THEAT, CINE *a. fig* scène *f;* **to appear on the ~** entrer en scène; **the ~ is set in France** l'action se déroule en France **2.** (*place*) lieu *m;* (*of operations*) théâtre *m;* **on the ~** sur les lieux; **at the ~ of the crash** sur les lieux de l'accident **3.** (*view*) vue *f* **4.** (*scenery*) décor *m;* **a change of ~** un changement de décor; *fig* un changement de cadre **5.** (*milieu, area*) scène *f;* **to be/not be sb's ~** *inf* être/ne pas être le genre de qn **6.** (*fuss*) scène *f;* **to make a ~** faire une scène ►**to set the ~** planter le décor; **to be/do sth behind the ~s** être/faire qc dans les/en coulisses

scene change *n* changement *m* de décor

scene painter *n* THEAT décorateur, -trice *m, f*

scenery ['siːnəri] *n no pl* **1.** (*landscape*) paysage *m* **2.** THEAT, CINE décor *m* ►**to blend into the ~** se fondre dans le décor

scene-shifter *n* THEAT machiniste *mf*

scenic ['siːnɪk] *adj* **1.** THEAT de scène **2.** (*picturesque: landscape*) pittoresque; (*railway, route*) panoramique

scent [sent] **I.** *n* **1.** (*aroma*) odeur *f* **2.** *no pl, Brit* (*perfume*) parfum *m* ►**to throw sb off the ~** lancer qn sur une fausse piste; **to be on the ~ of sb/sth** être sur la piste de qn/qc **II.** *vt* **1.** (*person*) sentir **2.** (*animal*) flairer **3.** (*sense*) pressentir **4.** (*apply scent*) parfumer

scent bottle *n* flacon *m* de parfum

scentless *adj* inodore

scepter ['septɚ] *n Am s.* **sceptre**

sceptic ['skeptɪk] *n* sceptique *mf*

sceptical *adj* sceptique

scepticism ['skeptɪsɪzəm] *n no pl* scepticisme *m*

sceptre ['septəʳ, *Am:* -tɚ] *n* sceptre *m*

schedule ['ʃedjuːl, *Am:* 'skedʒuːl] **I.** *n* **1.** (*timetable*) emploi *m* du temps; **to draw up/to stick a ~** préparer/s'en tenir à un planning; (*of a bus, train, aircraft*) horaire *m;* **flight ~** plan *m* de vol **2.** (*plan*) **according to ~** selon les prévisions *fpl* **3.** FIN programme *m* **II.** *vt* **1.** (*plan*) prévoir **2.** (*arrange*) programmer

scheduled *adj* prévu(e); (*building*) classé(e); (*flight, service*) régulier(-ère)

schematic [skɪ'mætɪk, *Am:* skiː'mæṭ-] *adj* schématique; **~ drawing** croquis *m*

scheme [skiːm] **I.** *n* **1.** (*programme*) plan *m* **2.** *pej* (*deceitful plot*) complot *m* **II.** *vi, vt pej* comploter

schemer *n pej* intrigant(e) *m(f)*

scheming *adj pej* intrigant(e)

schilling ['ʃɪlɪŋ] *n* schilling *m*

schism ['sɪzəm] *n* **1.** (*division into two*) scission *f* **2.** (*doctrinal division*) schisme *m*

schismatic [sɪz'mætɪk, *Am:* -'mæṭ-] **I.** *adj* REL schismatique **II.** *n* **1.** REL hétérodoxe *mf*

2. POL séparatiste *mf*
schist [ʃɪst] *n no pl* GEO schiste *m*
schizophrenia [ˌskɪtsəʊ'fri:nɪə, *Am:* -sə'-] *n no pl* schizophrénie *f*
schizophrenic I. *adj* PSYCH, MED 1.(*suffering from schizophrenia*) schizophrène 2.(*behaviour*) schizoïde II. *n* PSYCH, MED schizophrène *mf*
scholar ['skɒləʳ, *Am:* 'skɑ:lɚ] *n* UNIV 1.(*academic*) universitaire *mf* 2.(*educated person*) érudit(e) *m(f)* 3.(*holder of a scholarship*) boursier, -ière *m, f*
scholarly *adj* UNIV 1.(*reflecting study: article*) savant(e) 2.(*erudite*) érudit(e) 3.(*learned*) instruit(e)
scholarship *n* 1. *no pl* (*academic achievement*) érudition *f* 2.(*financial award*) bourse *f*
scholarship holder *n* SCHOOL, UNIV boursier, -ière *m, f*
scholastic [skə'læstɪk] *adj* scolaire
scholasticism *n no pl* scolastique *f*
school[1] [sku:l] I. *n* 1.(*institution*) école *f*; **primary** ~ école primaire; **secondary** ~ collège *m*; **public** ~ *Am*, **state** ~ école publique; **public** ~ *Brit* école privée; **to teach** ~ faire la classe 2.(*premises*) école *f* 3. *no pl* (*school session*) cours *m* 4. + *sing vb/pl vb* (*all students and staff*) école *f*; **the whole** ~ toute l'école 5.(*division of university*) année *f* 6. ART, SOCIOL, PHILOS école *f* ►**to tell tales out of** ~ faire des révélations II. *vt* dresser III. *adj* scolaire
school[2] [sku:l] *n* (*of fish*) banc *m*
school age *n* âge *m* scolaire **school attendance** *n* fréquentation *f* scolaire **schoolbag** *n* cartable *m* **school board** *n Am* ADMIN conseil *m* de classe **school book** *n* livre *m* de classe **schoolboy** *n* élève *m*; (*of primary age*) écolier *m*; (*secondary*) collégien *m*; (*from sixth form to university*) lycéen *m* **schoolchild** <-ren> *n* écolier, -ière *m, f* **schooldays** *npl* période *f* scolaire **school fees** *npl* frais *mpl* de scolarité, minerval *m Belgique*, écolage *m Suisse* **schoolgirl** I. *n* élève *f*; (*of primary age*) écolière *f*; (*secondary*) collégienne *f*; (*from sixth form to university*) lycéenne *f* II. *adj* d'élève **school hall** *n* amphithéâtre *m* **schoolhouse** <-es> *n Am* école *f*
schooling *n no pl* 1.(*for people*) scolarité *f* 2.(*for animals*) dressage *m*
school leaver *n Brit, Aus* élève *mf* ayant terminé sa scolarité **school-leaving certificate** *n Brit* SCHOOL certificat *m* (de fin) d'études **school magazine** *n* journal *m* d'école **schoolmaster** *n* maître *m* d'école **schoolmate** *n* camarade *mf* de classe **schoolmistress** <-es> *n* maîtresse *f* d'école

> **School of the air** est le nom que porte un réseau de radio pour le "outback" d'Australie, et qui émet dans des régions rurales isolées sans écoles afin d'instruire les enfants. Une douzaine de ces "écoles" couvre une région de 2,5 million de km² et concerne des centaines d'enfants. Les enfants reçoivent par courrier du matériel pédagogique et renvoient par courrier les devoirs qu'ils ont écrits. Les élèves communiquent par radio avec leurs professeurs et leurs camarades et sont surveillés le plus souvent par leurs parents ou par une enseignante à domicile.

school report *n* bulletin *m* scolaire **schoolroom** *n* salle *f* de classe

> Le **school system** américain (système scolaire) commence avec l'"elementary school" (du CP jusqu'à la 6ème ou 4ème). Dans certaines régions, après le "sixth grade", la classe de 6ème, les élèves vont dans une autre école, la "junior high school" (de la classe de 5ème à la 3ème). Ensuite, les élèves fréquentent pendant trois ans la "high school". Dans les régions qui ne possèdent pas de "junior high school", les élèves vont après huit années de "elementary school" directement en "high school", qui commence alors avec le "ninth grade", c'est à dire l'équivalent de la classe de troisième. L'école finit uniformément avec le "twelfth grade", l'équivalent de la classe de terminale.

schoolteacher *n* enseignant(e) *m(f)*
schooner ['sku:nəʳ, *Am:* -nɚ] *n* 1. NAUT goélette *f* 2. *Am, Aus* (*beer glass*) grand verre *m* à bière
sciatic [saɪ'ætɪk, *Am:* -'æt̬-] *adj* sciatique
sciatica [saɪ'ætɪkə, *Am:* -'æt̬-] *n no pl* sciatique *f*
science ['saɪənts] I. *n* science *f* II. *adj* scientifique
science fiction I. *n no pl* LIT, CINE science-fiction *f* II. *adj* de science-fiction
scientific [ˌsaɪən'tɪfɪk] *adj* scientifique
scientist ['saɪəntɪst, *Am:* -t̬ɪst] *n* scientifique *mf*
sci-fi ['saɪˌfaɪ] I. *n abbr of* **science fiction** science-fiction *f* II. *adj* de science-fiction
scintillating ['sɪntɪleɪtɪŋ, *Am:* -t̬leɪt̬ɪŋ] *adj a. fig* brillant(e)
scion ['saɪən] *n* 1. BOT greffon *m* 2. *pej* rejeton *m*
scissors ['sɪzəz, *Am:* -ɚz] *npl* 1.(*tool*) ciseaux *mpl*; **a pair of** ~ une paire de ciseaux *mpl* 2. SPORT ~ **kick** ciseau *m*
scissors and paste *n pej* **a** ~ **and paste job** un ramassis d'éléments disparates
sclerosis [sklə'rəʊsɪs, *Am:* sklɪ'roʊ-] *n no pl* MED sclérose *f*
scoff[1] [skɒf, *Am:* skɑ:f] I. *vi* (*mock*) **to** ~ **at sb/sth** se moquer de qn/qc II. *n* dédain *m*
scoff[2] [skɒf, *Am:* skɑ:f] *vt Brit, inf* (*eat*

S

greedily) bouffer

scold [skəʊld, *Am:* skoʊld] *vt* gronder

scolding *n* réprimande *f*

scone [skɒn, *Am:* skoʊn] *n: petit pain sucré servi avec du beurre*

scoop [skuːp] **I.** *n* **1.** (*food utensil*) pelle *f;* (*smaller*) cuillère *f;* **ice-cream** ~ cuillère à glace; **measuring** ~ mesure *f* **2.** (*amount held by a scoop*) mesure *f* **3.** (*ice-cream portion*) boule *f* **4.** (*piece of news*) exclusivité *f* **II.** *vt* **1.** (*pick up*) *a. fig* **to** ~ (**up**) **sth** ramasser qc (à la pelle/à la cuillère) **2.** (*make a hole*) enlever; **to** ~ **sth out** creuser **3.** (*measure*) doser **4.** PUBL, TV, RADIO livrer en exclusivité **5.** (*win*) décrocher; **to** ~ **the pool** *Brit, Aus, inf* rafler tous les prix

scoot [skuːt] *vi inf* mettre les gaz

scooter [ˈskuːtəʳ, *Am:* -t̬ɚ] *n* **1.** (*child's toy*) trottinette *f* **2.** (*motorcycle*) scooter *m*

scope [skəʊp, *Am:* skoʊp] *n no pl* **1.** (*extent of area*) étendue *f;* (*of person*) compétences *fpl;* (*of undertaking, plan*) envergure *f* **2.** (*possibility*) possibilité *f;* **limited/considerable** ~ champ *m* d'action limité/considérable; **to give** ~ **for sth** laisser le champ libre à qc; **to be beyond the** ~ **of sb** dépasser les compétences de qn

scorch [skɔːtʃ, *Am:* skɔːrtʃ] **I.** *vt* **1.** (*burn*) brûler **2.** (*dry*) dessécher **II.** *vi* brûler

Scorpio [ˈskɔːpiəʊ, *Am:* ˈskɔːrpioʊ] *n* Scorpion *m; s. a.* **Aquarius**

scorpion [ˈskɔːpiən, *Am:* ˈskɔːr-] *n* scorpion *m*

Scot [skɒt, *Am:* skɑːt] **I.** *adj* écossais(e); ~**s pine** pin *m* sylvestre **II.** *n* (*person*) Écossais *m*

scotch [skɒtʃ, *Am:* skɑːtʃ] *vt* mettre fin à

Scotch [skɒtʃ, *Am:* skɑːtʃ] **I.** *n no pl* scotch *m* **II.** *adj* écossais(e)

Scotch broth *n no pl: soupe de légumes et d'agneau*

scot-free [ˌskɒtˈfriː, *Am:* ˌskɑːtˈ-] *adv* impunément; **to get away** ~ partir en toute impunité

Scotland [ˈskɒtlənd, *Am:* ˈskɑːt-] *n* l'Écosse *f*

Scotland Yard *n* Scotland Yard *m*

Scotsman <-men> *n* Écossais *m* **Scotswoman** <-women> *n* Écossaise *f*

Scottish [ˈskɒtɪʃ, *Am:* ˈskɑːt̬ɪʃ] **I.** *adj* écossais(e) **II.** *n pl* **the** ~ les Écossais

scoundrel [ˈskaʊndrəl] *n pej* crapule *f*

scour [skaʊəʳ, *Am:* skaʊɚ] **I.** *vt* **1.** (*scrape clean*) récurer **2.** (*search: fields*) ratisser; **to** ~ **sth for sb/sth** fouiller qc pour trouver qn/qc **II.** *n no pl* récurage *m*

scourer *n* éponge *f* métallique

scourge [skɜːdʒ, *Am:* skɜːrdʒ] **I.** *n* **1.** (*affliction*) fléau *m* **2.** (*whip*) fouet *m* **II.** *vt* **1.** (*afflict*) affliger **2.** (*whip*) flageller

Scout, **scout** [skaʊt] *n* **1.** (*boy*) scout *m* **2.** (*girl*) jeannette *f*

Scoutmaster, **scoutmaster** *n* guide *mf* des scouts

scowl [skaʊl] **I.** *n* mine *f* patibulaire **II.** *vi* avoir un air sinistre; **to** ~ **at sb** regarder qn de travers

scrabble [ˈskræbl] *vi* trifouiller

scrag [skræg] <-gg-> *vt* **1.** *inf* engueuler **2.** (*kill*) tordre le cou à

scraggy <-ier, -iest> *adj* maigre

scram [skræm] <-mm-> *vi inf* se casser

scramble [ˈskræmbl] **I.** <-ling> *vi* **1.** (*clamber*) grimper; **to** ~ **through the hedge** grimper par-dessus la haie; **to** ~ **down/up the hillside** descendre/escalader la pente; **to** ~ **through** se frayer un passage **2.** (*rush*) se précipiter; **to** ~ **for sth** se ruer vers qc; **to** ~ **into jeans** enfiler son jeans; **to** ~ **up a ladder** monter une échelle à toute vitesse **3.** (*struggle*) **to** ~ **for sth** se battre pour qc **II.** <-ling> *vt* brouiller **III.** *n* **1.** *no pl* (*clambering*) escalade *f* **2.** *no pl* (*rush, struggle*) bousculade *f;* **the** ~ **for the door** la ruée vers la porte; **the** ~ **for profits** la course aux profits

scrambled eggs *n* œufs *mpl* brouillés

scrap[1] [skræp] **I.** *n* **1.** (*small piece*) morceau *m;* (*of paper, cloth*) bout *m;* (*of information*) bribe *f;* **not a** ~ **of evidence** pas la moindre preuve **2.** *pl* (*leftovers*) restes *mpl* **3.** *no pl* (*metal*) ferraille *f* **II.** <-pp-> *vt* **1.** (*get rid of*) se débarrasser de **2.** *fig* (*plan*) abandonner **3.** (*use for scrap metal*) apporter à la casse

scrap[2] [skræp] **I.** *n inf* empoignade *f* **II.** <-pp-> *vi* s'empoigner; **to** ~ **over sth with sb** s'empoigner pour qc avec qn

scrapbook *n* album *m* de collection **scrap dealer** *n* ferrailleur, -euse *m, f*

scrape [skreɪp] **I.** *vt* gratter; (*one's shoes*) frotter; (*one's knee*) s'écorcher; (*car*) érafler; (*one's hair*) brosser ►**to** ~ (**the bottom of**) **the barrel** racler les fonds de tiroir; **to** ~ **a living** s'en sortir tout juste **II.** *vi* **1.** (*make a scraping sound*) grincer **2.** (*scratch*) gratter **3.** (*rub against*) frotter **4.** (*manage*) **to** ~ **home** réussir de justesse **III.** *n* **1.** *no pl* (*sound*) grincement *m* **2.** (*act of scraping*) grattement *m;* **to give one's boots a** ~ donner un bon coup de brosse à ses bottes **3.** (*graze on skin*) égratignure *f* ►**to be in a** ~ *inf* être dans le pétrin

◆**scrape along** *vi s.* **scrape by**

◆**scrape away** *vt* gratter

◆**scrape by** *vi* s'en sortir

◆**scrape through** *vt, vi* réussir de justesse

scraper *n* racloir *m*

scrap heap *n* tas *m* de ferraille

scrapings *npl* restes *mpl;* (*of wood, metal*) copeaux *mpl;* (*of paint*) raclures *fpl*

scrap iron *n no pl* ferraille *f* **scrap merchant** *n Brit s.* **scrap dealer**

scrappy <-ier, -iest> *adj* **1.** (*badly made: work*) inégal(e); (*film, novel, essay*) décousu(e); (*education*) insuffisant(e) **2.** *Am, inf* (*brawler*) bagarreur(-euse)

scratch [skrætʃ] **I.** *n* **1.** (*small cut on skin*) égratignure *f,* griffe *f Belgique* **2.** *no pl* (*acceptable standard*) bon état *m;* **to come up to** ~

correspondre à une attente; **to bring sb/sth up to** ~ remettre qn à sa place/qc en état **3.** (*beginning state*) début *m;* **to start** (**again**) **from** ~ recommencer depuis le début **II.** *adj* improvisé(e) **III.** *vt* **1.** (*cut slightly*) égratigner **2.** (*relieve an itch*) gratter; **to** ~ **one's arm/head** se gratter le bras/la tête **3.** (*erase, remove*) effacer **4.** (*write hastily*) griffonner ▶**to** ~ **the surface of sth** effleurer qc **IV.** *vi* **1.** (*scraping a surface*) gratter **2.** *Brit* (*scribble*) gribouiller **3.** (*reunite*) **to** ~ **up** réunir

scratch about, **scratch around** *vi Brit* essayer de dénicher; **to** ~ **for sth** fouiller du regard pour trouver qc

◆**scratch out** *vt* gratter; (*line, word*) rayer ▶**to scratch sb's eyes out** arracher les yeux à qn

scratch card *n* carte *f* à gratter **scratch paper** *n no pl, Am* (*rough paper*) (feuille *f* de) brouillon *m*

scratchy <-ier, -iest> *adj* **1.** (*with scratches: record*) rayé(e) **2.** (*irritating to skin*) irritant(e)

scrawl [skrɔːl, *Am:* skrɑːl] **I.** *vt, vi* gribouiller **II.** *n* gribouillage *m*

scrawny [ˈskrɔːni, *Am:* ˈskrɑː-] <-ier, -iest> *adj* sec(sèche)

scream [skriːm] **I.** *n* **1.** (*cry*) hurlement *m* **2.** *no pl* (*of engine*) crissement *m* **3.** *no pl, inf* bouffonnerie *f;* **to be a** ~ être à mourir de rire **II.** *vi* hurler; **to** ~ **in terror** hurler de terreur; **to** ~ **for help** crier à l'aide; **to** ~ **with laughter** hurler de rire; **to** ~ **about sth** se mettre en rage à cause de qc **III.** *vt* hurler; **to** ~ **oneself hoarse** s'égosiller; **to** ~ **one's head off** *inf* s'époumoner

screaming **I.** *adj* hurlant(e) **II.** *n no pl* hurlements *mpl*

scree [skriː] *n no pl* éboulis *m*

screech [skriːtʃ] **I.** *n* cri *m;* **a** ~ **of laughter** un éclat de rire **II.** *vt, vi* **to** ~ **with delight/pain** crier de joie/douleur

screech owl *n* effraie *f*

screed *n* (long) discours *m;* **to write** ~**s and** ~**s** en écrire des lignes et des lignes

screen [skriːn] **I.** *n* **1.** TV, INFOR écran *m;* **15-inch** ~ écran 15 pouces; **split/touch** ~ écran partagé/tactile; **on** ~ à l'écran **2.** (*panel for privacy*) cloison *f;* (*decorative*) paravent *m;* (*for protection*) écran *m* **3.** *no pl, Am, fig* (*of troops*) camouflage *m* **4.** (*sieve*) passoire *f* **II.** *vt* **1.** (*hide*) cacher; **to** ~ **sth from view** dissimuler qc **2.** (*protect*) protéger; **to** ~ **sb/sth from sth** protéger qn/qc de qc **3.** (*examine*) examiner **4.** (*put through a screening device*) passer au scanner *fig* **5.** TV passer à l'écran; CINE projeter **6.** (*put through a sieve*) passer à la passoire

◆**screen off** *vt* cloisonner

screening *n* **1.** CINE projection *f* **2.** TV diffusion *f* **3.** *no pl* (*test*) *a.* MED examen *m*

screenplay *n* scénario *m* **screen refresh rate** *n* fréquence *f* de rafraîchissement d'image **screen saver** *n* économiseur *m* d'écran **screenshot** *n* INFOR saisie *f* de l'écran **screen test** *n* CINE essais *mpl* **screen writer** *n* scénariste *mf*

screw [skruː] **I.** *n* **1.** (*pin*) vis *f* **2.** (*turn*) rotation *f;* **to give sth a** ~ (*with fingers*) tourner qc; (*with screwdriver*) visser qc **3.** (*propeller*) hélice *f* **4.** *Brit, inf* (*prisoner*) maton(ne) *m(f)* ▶**to have a** ~ **loose** *iron, inf* ne pas tourner rond; **to put the** ~**s on sb** *inf* mettre le couteau sous la gorge à qn; **to have one's head screwed on** (**right**) *inf* avoir la tête bien sur les épaules **II.** *vt* **1.** (*fasten*) **to** ~ (**on**) visser **2.** (*fasten by twisting*) serrer **3.** *inf* (*to con*) entuber **4.** (*extort*) **to** ~ **sth out of sb** extorquer qc à qn **5.** *vulg* baiser **III.** *vi* **1.** (*move in a curve*) se visser **2.** *vulg* baiser

◆**screw down** *vt* visser

◆**screw off** **I.** *vt* dévisser **II.** *vi* se dévisser

◆**screw up** **I.** *vt* **1.** (*fasten*) visser; **to** ~ **one's eyes** plisser les yeux **2.** *inf* foutre en l'air **II.** *vi* se visser

screwball *n Am, inf* (*crazy person*) drôle d'oiseau *m* **screwdriver** *n* tournevis *m* **screw top** *n* fermeture *f* à vis

screwy <-ier, iest> *adj inf* taré(e)

scribble [ˈskrɪbl] **I.** *vt* griffonner **II.** *vi* **1.** (*write*) griffonner; (*on a wall*) faire des graffitis **2.** *iron* gribouiller **III.** *n* gribouillage *m*

scribbler *n pej or iron* écrivaillon *m*

scribbling block, **scribbling pad** *n* bloc-notes *m*

scrimmage [ˈskrɪmɪdʒ] *n a.* SPORT mêlée *f*

scrimp [skrɪmp] *vi* économiser

scrip issue *n* FIN *émission d'actions gratuites*

script [skrɪpt] **I.** *n* **1.** (*written text: of film*) script *m;* (*of play*) texte *m* **2.** (*style of writing*) script *m* **3.** *Brit, Aus* (*exam answer paper*) copie *f* **4.** *Aus* directive *f* **II.** *vt* écrire le script de

script girl *n* CINE scripte *f*

scriptural *adj* biblique

scripture [ˈskrɪptʃər, *Am:* -tʃɚ] *n* **1.** *no pl* (*Bible*) ~(**s**) Écritures *fpl* **2.** (*sacred writings*) livre *m* sacré

scriptwriter [ˈskrɪptraɪtə^{r}, *Am:* -t̬ɚ] *n* CINE, TV scénariste *mf*

scroll [skrəʊl, *Am:* skroʊl] **I.** *n* **1.** (*roll of paper*) rouleau *m* **2.** (*scroll-shaped ornament*) volute *f* **II.** *vi* INFOR dérouler; **to** ~ **up/down** faire défiler vers le haut/le bas

scroll bar *n* INFOR barre *f* de défilement

scrooge [skruːdʒ] *n pej* radin(e) *m(f)*

scrotum [ˈskrəʊtəm, *Am:* ˈskroʊt̬əm] <-tums *o* -ta> *n* scrotum *m*

scrounge [skraʊndʒ] **I.** *vt inf* (*to con sth out of sb*) **to** ~ **sth off sb** taper qc à qn **II.** *vi pej, inf* **to** ~ **off sb** taxer qn **III.** *n pej or iron, inf* resquille *f;* **to be on the** ~ être un tapeur

scrounger [ˈskraʊndʒə^{r}, *Am:* -ɚ] *n pej, inf* tapeur, -euse *m, f*

scrub[1] [skrʌb] <-bb-> **I.** *vt* **1.** (*clean by rubbing*) frotter **2.** (*cancel*) rayer **II.** *vi* (*clean by rubbing*) frotter **III.** *n no pl* **to give sth a**

S

(**good**) ~ astiquer qc

scrub² [skrʌb] *n* **1.** *no pl* (*short trees and bushes*) buissons *mpl* **2.** *no pl* (*area covered with bushes*) broussaille *f*

scrubber *n Brit, pej, inf* traînée *f*

scrubbing brush *n a. Am* brosse *f*

scruff [skrʌf] *n* **1.** ANAT nuque *f* **2.** *Brit, inf* (*woman*) truie *f;* (*man*) porc *m*

scruffy <-ier, -iest> *adj* mal entretenu(e)

scrum ['skrʌm] *n* SPORT mêlée *f*

scrummage ['skrʌmɪdʒ] *n s.* **scrum**

scrumptious ['skrʌmpʃəs] *adj Brit, inf* super *inv*

scrumpy ['skrʌmpi] *n no pl, Brit* moût *m*

scrunch [skrʌntʃ] **I.** *vi* crisser **II.** *vt* (*crush*) écraser **III.** *n no pl* crissement *m*

scruple ['skru:pl] **I.** *n* scrupule *m* **II.** *vi* avoir des scrupules

scrupulous ['skru:pjʊləs] *adj* scrupuleux(-euse); **to be ~ about doing sth** avoir scrupule à faire qc

scrutineer [ˌskru:tɪ'nɪəʳ, *Am:* -tn'ɪr] *n Brit, Aus* scrutateur, -trice *m, f*

scrutinise *Brit, Aus,* **scrutinize** ['skru:tɪnaɪz, *Am:* -tə-] *vt* **1.** (*examiner*) scruter **2.** (*inspect closely*) examiner

scrutiny ['skru:tɪni, *Am:* -təni] *n no pl* examen *m* minutieux; **to come under** (**close**) ~ être passé au peigne fin

scuba ['sku:bə] *n* appareil *m* de plongée

scuba diving *n* plongée *f;* **to go ~** faire de la plongée

scud [skʌd] <-dd-> *vi* filer

scuff [skʌf] **I.** *vt* **1.** (*roughen surface of*) élimer **2.** (*drag along the ground*) draguer; **to ~ one's feet** traîner des pieds **II.** *vi* marcher en traînant les pieds

scuffle ['skʌfl] **I.** *n* bagarre *f,* margaille *f Belgique* **II.** *vi* se bagarrer

scull [skʌl] **I.** *vi* ramer **II.** *n* aviron *m*

scullery ['skʌləri] *n* buanderie *f*

sculpt [skʌlpt] *vt, vi* sculpter

sculptor *n* sculpteur *m*

sculptress *n* sculpteuse *f*

sculptural *adj* sculptural(e)

sculpture ['skʌlptʃəʳ, *Am:* -tʃɚ] **I.** *n* sculpture *f* **II.** *vt, vi s.* **sculpt**

scum [skʌm] *n no pl* **1.** (*material floating on liquid*) mousse *f* **2.** *pej* (*worthless people*) rebut *m*

scupper ['skʌpəʳ, *Am:* -ɚ] *vt a. fig* couler

scurf [skɜ:f, *Am:* skɜ:rf] *n no pl* pellicules *fpl*

scurrilous ['skʌrɪləs, *Am:* 'skɜ:rɪ-] *adj pej* calomnieux(-euse)

scurry ['skʌri, *Am:* 'skɜ:ri] <-ie-> **I.** *vi* trottiner **II.** *n no pl* hâte *f*

scurvy ['skɜ:vi, *Am:* 'skɜ:r-] **I.** *n no pl* scorbut *m* **II.** *adj* infâme

scut *n* (*tail of rabbit, deer*) moignon *m*

scuttle¹ ['skʌtl, *Am:* 'skʌt̬-] *vi* courir

scuttle² ['skʌtl, *Am:* 'skʌt̬-] *vt* **1.** (*go down: ship*) couler **2.** (*put an end to*) mettre un terme à

scuttle³ ['skʌtl, *Am:* 'skʌt̬-] *n s.* **coal scuttle**

scythe [saɪð] **I.** *n* faux *f* **II.** *vt* faucher

SDI [ˌesdi:'ɑɪ] *n Am abbr of* **Strategic Defense Initiative** IDS *f*

SDRs *npl abbr of* **special drawing rights** DTS *m*

SE [ˌes'i:] *n abbr of* **southeast** SE *m*

sea [si:] *n no pl, a. fig* mer *f;* **to be at ~** être au large; **beyond the ~** outre-mer; **by ~** par voie maritime; **to put** (**out**) **to ~** appareiller; **the open ~** le large; **to go to ~** partir en mer

sea air *n no pl* air *m* marin **sea anemone** *n* anémone *f* de mer **sea animal** *n* animal *m* marin **sea-based** *adj* MIL basé(e) en mer **sea bathing** *n no pl* bain *m* de mer **sea bed** *n no pl* fond *m* marin **sea bird** *n* oiseau *m* de mer **seaboard** *n sing* côte *f* **seaborne** *adj* transporté(e) par voie maritime **sea breeze** *n* vent *m* du large **sea calf** <calves> *n* phoque *m* **sea coast** *n* côte *f* **sea cow** *n* dugong *m* **sea dog** *n* **an old ~** un vieux loup de mer **sea fish** <-(es)> *n* poisson *m* de mer **seafood** *n* fruits *mpl* de mer **sea front** *n sing* front *m* de mer **seagoing** *adj* en état de naviguer **seagull** *n* mouette *f* **sea horse** *n* hippocampe *m*

seal¹ [si:l] *n* phoque *m*

seal² [si:l] **I.** *n* **1.** (*official wax mark*) sceau *m* **2.** (*stamp*) cachet *m* **3.** (*device to prevent opening*) cachet *m;* (*on door*) fermoir *m* **4.** (*airtight or watertight joint*) joint *m* ►**sb's ~ of approval** l'approbation de qn **II.** *vt* **1.** (*put a seal on*) cacheter **2.** (*make airtight or watertight*) colmater **3.** (*close: frontier, port*) fermer **4.** (*confirm and finalize*) approuver

◆**seal off** *vi* sceller

sea legs *npl* **to get one's ~** s'habituer à la mer

sea level *n no pl* niveau *m* de la mer

sealing *n no pl* cachetage *m*

sealing wax *n no pl* cire *f* à cacheter

sea lion *n* otarie *f*

seal ring *n* bague *f* avec un sceau **sealskin** **I.** *n no pl* peau *f* de phoque **II.** *adj* en peau de phoque

seam [si:m] **I.** *n* **1.** (*in fabric*) couture *f* **2.** (*hem*) ourlet *m* **3.** (*junction*) jointure *f* **4.** NAUT joint *m* **5.** (*welded*) soudure *f* **6.** (*between rocks*) veine *f* **7.** *fig* **to be bursting at the ~s** être plein à craquer **II.** *vt* (*stitch together*) coudre

seaman ['si:mən] <-men> *n* **1.** (*sailor*) marin *m* **2.** (*rank*) matelot *m;* **ordinary ~** *Brit* matelot; **able ~** *Brit* matelot breveté

sea mile *n* mile *m* marin

seamless *adj* **1.** (*without seam*) sans coutures **2.** *fig* continu(e); (*transition*) sans accrocs

seamstress ['sempstrɪs, *Am:* 'si:mstrɪs] *n* couturière *f*

seamy <-ier, -iest> *adj* sordide

seaplane *n* hydravion *m* **seaport** *n* port *m* maritime **sea power** *n no pl* puissance *f* navale

sear [sɪəʳ, *Am:* sɪr] *vt* **1.** (*scorch*) brûler **2.** (*cause pain: in memory*) graver **3.** (*fry quickly*) saisir **4.** (*cauterize*) cautériser

search [sɜːtʃ, *Am:* sɜːrtʃ] **I.** *n* **1.** (*act of searching*) recherches *fpl;* **to go off in ~ of sth** partir à la recherche de qc **2.** (*police ~: of a building*) perquisition *f;* (*of a person*) fouille *f* **3.** INFOR recherche *f* **II.** *vi* **1.** (*make a search*) faire des recherches; **to ~ after sth** rechercher qc; **to ~ for sb/sth** chercher qn/qc; **to ~ through** fouiller **2.** INFOR effectuer une recherche **III.** *vt* **1.** (*seek*) chercher **2.** (*look in*) fouiller; (*place, street*) ratisser **3.** INFOR rechercher; (*directory, file*) rechercher dans **4.** (*examine carefully: conscience, heart*) examiner; (*face, memory*) scruter ►~ **me!** *inf* (je n'en ai) pas la moindre idée!

◆**search out** *vt* chercher

searcher *n* personne *f* en quête

search function *n* INFOR fonction *f* de recherche

searching *adj* **1.** (*penetrating: look*) inquisiteur(-trice) **2.** (*exhaustive: question*) approfondi(e)

searchlight *n* projecteur *m* **search operation** *n* recherches *fpl* **search party** <-ties> *n* expédition *f* de secours **search warrant** *n* mandat *m* de perquisition

searing *adj* **1.** (*scorching*) brûlant(e) **2.** (*painful: pain*) cuisant(e) **3.** (*critical: criticism*) virulent(e)

seascape *n* **1.** (*picture*) marine *f* **2.** (*view*) vue *f* sur la mer **seashell** *n* coquillage *m* **seashore** *n no pl* **1.** (*beach*) plage *f* **2.** (*land near sea*) littoral *m* **seasick** *adj* **to be ~** avoir le mal de mer **seasickness** *n* mal *m* de mer **seaside I.** *n no pl* bord *m* de mer *m* **II.** *adj Brit* (*activity, town*) du bord de mer; (*holiday*) au bord de la mer

season ['siːzən] **I.** *n* **1.** (*period of year*) saison *f;* **the Christmas/Easter ~** la période de Noël/Pâques; **the festive ~** les fêtes de fin d'année; **Season's Greetings** Joyeux Noël et Bonne Année; **the holiday ~** la période des vacances; **the high/low ~** la haute/morte saison; **in/out of ~** pendant/en dehors de la saison touristique **2.** (*fertile period*) chaleur *f* **3.** SPORT saison *f* **4.** (*of concerts, films*) *Brit* festival *m* **II.** *vt* **1.** (*add salt and pepper*) assaisonner **2.** (*dry out: wood*) faire sécher **III.** *vi* (*wood*) sécher

seasonable *adj* de saison

seasonal *adj* **1.** (*of time of year*) saisonnier(-ère) **2.** (*grown in a season*) de saison

seasoned *adj* **1.** (*experienced*) expérimenté(e) **2.** (*dried: wood*) sec(sèche) **3.** (*spiced*) assaisonné(e)

seasoning *n* **1.** *no pl* (*salt and pepper*) assaisonnement *m* **2.** (*herb or spice*) condiment *m* **3.** *no pl* (*drying out*) séchage *m*

season ticket *n* **1.** THEAT, SPORT abonnement *m* **2.** AUTO carte *f* d'abonnement **season ticket holder** *n* **1.** THEAT, SPORT abonné(e) *m(f)* **2.** AUTO détenteur, -trice *m, f* d'une carte d'abonnement

seat [siːt] **I.** *n* **1.** (*furniture*) siège *m;* **back ~** siège arrière; **is this ~ free/taken?** est-ce que cette place est libre/prise?; **to keep a ~ for sb** garder une place à qn **2.** THEAT fauteuil *m* **3.** *sing* (*part: of a chair*) siège *m;* (*of trousers, pants*) fond *m* **4.** (*buttocks*) fesses *fpl* **5.** (*elected position*) siège *m;* **to take one's ~** prendre ses fonctions **6.** (*country residence*) résidence *f;* **a country ~** un château **7.** (*style of riding*) assiette *f* ►**by the ~ of one's pants** par intuition **II.** *vt* **1.** (*sit down*) asseoir **2.** (*offer a seat*) placer **3.** (*have enough seats for*) **the hall ~s 250 guests** le réfectoire peut contenir 250 invités à table

seat belt *n* ceinture *f* de sécurité

seating *n no pl* capacité *f* d'accueil; **a restaurant has ~ for 60** un restaurant a 60 couverts

seating arrangements *npl* plan *m* de table

seating room *n* salon *m*

SEATO ['siːtəʊ, *Am:* -t̬oʊ] *n no pl, no art abbr of* **Southeast Asia Treaty Organization** OTASE *f*

sea urchin *n* oursin *m* **seaward I.** *adv* vers la mer **II.** *adj* **1.** (*facing*) face à la mer **2.** (*moving*) vers le large; (*breeze*) du large **seawater** *n no pl* eau *f* de mer **seaway** *n* chenal *m* **seaweed** *n no pl* algues *fpl* **seaworthy** *adj* (*boat*) en état de naviguer

sec [sek] *n abbr of* **second** seconde *f*

secateurs [ˌsekə'tɜːz, *Am:* 'sekət̬ɚz] *npl* sécateur *m*

secede [sɪ'siːd] *vi* **to ~ from sth** faire sécession de qc

secession [sɪ'seʃən] *n no pl* sécession *f*

secluded [sɪ'kluːdɪd] *adj* retiré(e)

seclusion [sɪ'kluːʒən] *n no pl* **1.** (*privacy: of person, place*) tranquillité *f* **2.** (*separate*) isolement *m*

second¹ ['sekənd] **I.** *adj* **1.** (*after first*) deuxième; **every ~ week/year** tous les quinze jours/deux ans **2.** (*after winner*) second(e) **3.** (*not first in importance, size*) deuxième; **to be ~ only to sb/sth** être juste derrière qn/qc; **to be ~ to none** être le meilleur **4.** (*another: car, chance*) deuxième; **to be a ~ Mozart** être un nouveau Mozart; **to ask for a ~ opinion** demander un deuxième avis; **to have ~ thoughts about sth** ne plus être sûr de qc **II.** *n* **1.** *Brit* (*degree grade*) *licence avec mention bien/assez bien* **2.** *no art, no pl* (*second gear*) seconde *f;* **to change down to ~** rétrograder en seconde **3.** *pl* (*extra helping*) supplément *m;* **anyone for ~s?** est-ce que qn en veut encore? **4.** (*imperfect item*) article *m* de deuxième choix **5.** (*in a duel*) témoin *m* **6.** (*in boxing*) soigneur *m* **III.** *adv* deuxième **IV.** *vt* **1.** (*support*) appuyer; **I'll ~ that** je suis d'accord **2.** *Brit, Aus* MIL détacher; **to be ~ed from sth to sth** être détaché de qc vers qc

second² ['sekənd] *n* seconde *f*

S

secondary ['sekəndəri, *Am:* -deri] **I.** *adj* secondaire **II.** <-ries> *n s.* **secondary school**

secondary industry *n* industrie *f* secondaire **secondary school** *n* **1.** (*school for children over 11*) école *f* secondaire **2.** *no pl* (*education*) enseignement *m* secondaire

second best *adj* **to feel** ~ se sentir relégué en second choix; **to settle for** ~ se rabattre sur un deuxième choix

second chamber *n* POL deuxième chambre *f*

second class **I.** *n* deuxième classe *f* **II.** *adv* **1.** (*in second class: travel*) en deuxième classe **2.** *Brit* (*by second-class mail*) en tarif lent **III.** *adj* **second-class** **1.** (*in second class: ticket, carriage*) de deuxième classe **2.** *pej* (*inferior: service, treatment*) de deuxième rang **second cousin** *n* cousin(e) *m(f)* au second degré **second-degree burn** *n* brulûre *f* au second degré

seconder *n* partisan(e) *m(f)* d'une motion

second floor *n* **1.** *Brit, Aus* (*second floor above ground*) deuxième étage *m* **2.** *Am, Aus* (*floor above ground*) premier étage *m* **second-hand** **I.** *adj* **1.** (*for purchases: clothes, shop*) d'occasion **2.** (*from sb else: news*) de seconde main **II.** *adv* **1.** (*used: buy*) d'occasion **2.** (*from third party: hear*) d'un tiers **second hand** *n* aiguille *f* des secondes **second language** *n* seconde langue *f* **second lieutenant** *n* second lieutenant *m*

secondly *adv* deuxièmement

secondment *n Brit, Aus no pl* (*transfer*) détachement *m*

second nature *n* seconde nature *f* **second-rate** *adj* de deuxième rang **second sight** *n no pl* double vue *f*

secrecy ['si:krəsi] *n no pl* **1.** (*act*) secret *m;* **in** ~ en secret; **to swear sb to** ~ faire jurer le secret à qn **2.** (*ability*) discrétion *f*

secret ['si:krɪt] **I.** *n* secret *m;* **to let sb in on a/the** ~ mettre qn dans le secret; **to make no** ~ **of sth** ne pas cacher qc **II.** *adj* **1.** (*known to few*) secret(-ète); **to keep sth** ~ **from sb** cacher qc à qn **2.** (*hidden: door*) dérobé(e)

secret agent *n* agent *m* secret

secretarial *adj* (*staff, course*) de secrétariat

secretariat [ˌsekrə'teəriət, *Am:* -'teri-] *n* secrétariat *m*

secretary ['sekrətəri, *Am:* -rəteri] <-ries> *n* **1.** (*office assistant*) secrétaire *mf* **2.** (*assistant head*) **company** ~ secrétaire *mf* général **3.** (*assistant ambassador*) secrétaire *mf* d'ambassade

secretary General <secretaries General> *n* secrétaire *m* général, secrétaire *f* générale

secrete [sɪ'kri:t] *vt* **1.** (*have secretion: of gland*) secréter **2.** *form* (*hide*) cacher

secretion *n* sécrétion *f*

secretive ['si:krətɪv, *Am:* -t̬ɪv] *adj* (*behaviour*) secret(-ète); (*person*) cachottier(-ère)

sect [sekt] *n* secte *f*

sectarian [sek'teərɪən, *Am:* -'terɪ-] **I.** *adj* sectaire **II.** *n* sectaire *mf*

section ['sekʃən] **I.** *n* **1.** (*part*) partie *f;* (*of a road, railway*) tronçon *m;* (*of a document*) chapitre *m;* (*of an orange*) quartier *m;* (*of a newspaper*) pages *fpl;* **the sports** ~ les pages sportives **2.** (*department*) service *m* **3.** MUS **the brass** ~ les cuivres **4.** (*military unit*) groupe *m* **5.** (*surgical cut*) section *f* **II.** *vt* **1.** (*divide*) sectionner; **to be ~ed into subject areas** être divisé en domaines **2.** *Brit* MED interner

◆**section off** *vt* séparer

sectional **I.** *adj* **1.** *pej* (*limited to a group*) particulier(-ère); (*championship, conflict*) interne **2.** (*done in section: drawing*) en coupe **3.** *Am* (*made in sections: furniture*) modulaire **II.** *n Am* meuble *m* modulaire

sector ['sektəʳ, *Am:* -tɚ] *n* secteur *m*

secular ['sekjʊləʳ, *Am:* -lɚ] *adj* (*non-religious: education*) laïque

secularize ['sekjʊləraɪz] *vt* laïciser

secure [sɪ'kjʊəʳ, *Am:* -'kjʊr] **I.** *adj* <-rer, -est *o* more ~, most ~> **1.** (*safe: base, ladder*) sûr(e); **financially** ~ sans risques financiers **2.** (*unworried*) en sécurité; ~ **in the knowledge that ...** sûr que ... **3.** (*guarded*) protégé(e) **II.** *vt* **1.** (*obtain: release, loan*) obtenir **2.** (*make safe: doors, windows*) bien fermer; (*position*) assurer; (*house*) protéger **3.** (*fasten: seatbelt*) attacher **4.** (*guarantee: loan*) garantir **5.** *fig* (*protect*) protéger

security [sɪ'kjʊərəti, *Am:* 'kjʊrət̬i] <-ties> *n* **1.** *no art, no pl* (*measures*) sécurité *f* **2.** *no art, no pl* (*personnel*) service *m* de sécurité **3.** *no pl* (*safety*) sécurité *f* **4.** *sing* (*payment guarantee*) garantie *f;* **to stand** ~ **for sb** se porter garant(e) de qn **5.** *pl* (*investments*) valeurs *fpl* (boursières)

security cordon *n* cordon *m* de sécurité **Security Council** *n* Conseil *m* de sécurité **security forces** *npl* forces *fpl* de sécurité **security guard** *n* gardien(ne) *m(f)* **security of employment** *n* sécurité *f* de l'emploi

sedan [sɪ'dæn] *n Am, Aus* berline *f*

sedate [sɪ'deɪt] **I.** *adj* (*pace, person*) calme **II.** *vt* donner un sédatif à

sedation *n no pl* sédation *f*

sedative ['sedətɪv, *Am:* -t̬ɪv] **I.** *adj* sédatif(-ive) **II.** *n* sédatif *m*

sedentary ['sedəntəri, *Am:* -teri] *adj* (*person, lifestyle*) sédentaire

sediment ['sedɪmənt, *Am:* 'sedə-] *n* **1.** *no pl* (*deposit*) dépôt *m* **2.** (*substance*) sédiment *m*

sedimentary [ˌsedɪ'mentri] *adj* sédimentaire

sedition [sɪ'dɪʃən] *n no pl, form* sédition *f*

seduce [sɪ'dju:s, *Am:* -'du:s] *vt* séduire; **to be ~d into doing sth** se laisser convaincre de faire qc

seducer *n* séducteur, -trice *m, f*

seduction [sɪ'dʌkʃən] *n* **1.** *no pl* (*persuasion into sex*) séduction *f* **2.** (*seductive*) ~(**s**) charme *m*

seductive [sɪ'dʌktɪv] *adj* **1.** (*sexy*) séducteur(-trice) **2.** (*attractive: argument*) séduisant(e)

see[1] [si:] *n* diocèse *m;* **the Holy See** le Saint-Siège

see[2] [si:] <saw, seen> **I.** *vt* **1.** (*perceive with eyes*) voir **2.** (*watch: a play, page, sights*) voir **3.** (*view: house for sale*) voir **4.** (*meet socially*) voir; **to ~ a little of sb** ne pas voir qn souvent; **~ you!** *inf* à bientôt **5.** (*accompany*) raccompagner; **I'll ~ you to the door** Je t'accompagne jusqu'à la porte **6.** (*have relationship with*) sortir avec **7.** (*understand*) voir; **to ~ sth in a new light** voir qc sous un autre jour; **to ~ reason** entendre raison **8.** (*envisage: chance, possibility*) voir; **I saw it coming** je m'y attendais **9.** (*ensure*) **to ~ (that)** ... s'assurer que ... ► **~ you around!** à bientôt!; **to ~ the colour of sb's money** voir la couleur de l'argent de qn; **to not ~ sb for dust** ne pas revoir qn de sitôt; **I will ~ him in hell first** plutôt mourir; **to ~ the last** [*o Brit, Aus* **the back**] **of sb/sth** se débarrasser de qn/qc; **to ~ the light** (*understand*) comprendre; (*be converted*) avoir une révélation; **I've got to ~ a man about a dog** (*evasive reply*) j'ai à faire; **to ~ stars** voir des étoiles; **to ~ one's way (clear) to doing sth** être d'accord pour faire qc; **to not ~ the wood** *Brit, Aus* [*o Am* **the forest**] **for the trees** se perdre dans les détails; **he/she wouldn't be seen dead in sth** *inf* il/elle ne le ferait pour rien au monde **II.** *vi a. fig* voir; **as far as the eye can ~** à perte de vue; **~ing is believing** il faut le voir pour le croire; **wait and ~** on verra; **let me ~** voyons voir; **we'll/I'll (have to) ~** nous verrons/je verrai; **as far as I can ~** d'après ce que je comprends ► **not to ~ eye to eye with sb** ne pas être d'accord avec qn; **you must do what you ~ fit** fais ce qu'il te semble le mieux

◆**see about** *vt inf* s'occuper de ► **we'll soon ~ that!** *inf* c'est ce qu'on verra!

◆**see in** **I.** *vi* voir à l'intérieur **II.** *vt* **1.** (*perceive*) trouver **2.** (*welcome*) faire entrer; **to see the New Year in** fêter le Nouvel An

◆**see into** *vt* **1.** (*see*) *a. fig* voir; **to ~ the future** lire dans l'avenir **2.** (*escort*) **to see sb into bed** aider qn à se mettre au lit

◆**see off** *vt* **1.** (*accompany*) **to see sb off** accompagner qn **2.** (*drive away*) faire fuir **3.** (*deal with*) battre

◆**see out** *vt* **1.** (*escort to door*) accompagner; **to see sb out of the house** raccompagner qn à la porte; **I'll see myself out** inutile de me raccompagner **2.** (*last until end of*) **to see the winter out** passer l'hiver

◆**see through** *vt* **1.** (*look through*) voir à travers **2.** (*not be deceived by: lies*) déceler **3.** (*support*) aider **4.** (*continue to end*) faire jusqu'au bout

◆**see to** *vt* **1.** (*attend to*) s'occuper de **2.** *inf* (*mend*) réparer **3.** (*ensure*) **to ~ it that** faire en sorte que +*subj*

seed [si:d] **I.** *n* **1.** (*plant grain*) graine *f;* (*of fruit*) pépin *m;* **to sow ~s** semer des graines **2.** (*beginning*) germe *m;* **it sowed the ~s of doubt in her mind** ça a semé le doute dans son esprit **3.** SPORT tête *f* de série **II.** *vt* **1.** (*sow with seed*) ensemencer **2.** (*start*) germer **3.** (*remove seeds from*) épépiner **4.** SPORT **to be ~ed** être classé

seedbed *n* **1.** (*area of ground*) semoir *m* **2.** (*place in which things develop*) vivier *m*

seed corn *n* graine *f* de semence

seedling *n* plant *m*

seed potato *n* pomme *f* de terre de semence

seedtime *n* AGR semailles *fpl*

seedy ['si:di] <-ier, -iest> *adj* **1.** (*dubious: district, hotel*) sordide **2.** (*unwell*) patraque **3.** (*queasy*) barbouillé(e)

seeing *conj* **~ that ...** sachant que ...

seek [si:k] <sought> **I.** *vt* **1.** *form* (*look for*) chercher **2.** (*strive for: happiness, revenge*) rechercher; (*asylum, one's fortune*) chercher; (*justice, damages*) demander **3.** (*ask for: advice, permission*) demander **II.** *vi* **1.** *form* (*search*) chercher; **~ and ye shall find** quand on cherche on trouve **2.** *form* (*attempt*) **to ~ to** +*infin* essayer de +*infin*

seeker *n* chercheur, -euse *m, f;* **an asylum ~** un demandeur d'asile

seem [si:m] *vi* **1.** (*appear to be*) sembler; **it ~s as if ...** il semble que ... **2.** (*appear*) **it ~s as if ...** on dirait que ...; **so it ~s** on dirait; **it ~s not** il semble que non; **it ~s like months since I started** j'ai l'impression que ça fait des mois que j'ai commencé

seeming *adj form* apparent(e)

seemingly *adv* apparemment

seen [si:n] *pp of* **see**

seep [si:p] *vi* filtrer; **to ~ into sth** s'infiltrer dans qc

seepage ['si:pɪdʒ] *n no pl* infiltration *f*

see-saw **I.** *n* **1.** (*game*) bascule *f* **2.** *fig* va-et-vient *m inv* **II.** *vi* **1.** (*play*) jouer à la bascule **2.** (*move back and forth*) balancer **3.** (*rise and fall*) osciller **4.** *fig* être en dents de scie

seethe [si:ð] *vi* **1.** (*bubble up*) *a. fig* bouillonner; **to ~ with anger** bouillir de colère **2.** (*be crowded*) grouiller; **to be ~ing with sth** grouiller de qc

see-through *adj* transparent(e)

segment ['segmənt] **I.** *n* partie *f;* (*of orange, circle*) quartier *m;* (*of a worm*) segment *m* **II.** *vt* (*market, population*) segmenter **III.** *vi* se segmenter

segmentation [ˌsegmən'teɪʃən] *n no pl* segmentation *f*

segregate ['segrɪgeɪt, *Am:* -rə-] *vt* **1.** (*isolate*) isoler **2.** (*separate*) séparer **3.** (*separate racially*) soumettre à la ségrégation

segregation *n no pl* ségrégation *f*

seismic ['saɪzmɪk] *adj* **1.** GEO (*waves*) sismique **2.** (*damaging*) monumental(e)

seismograph ['saɪzməgrɑ:f, *Am:* -græf] *n* sismographe *m*

seismologist *n* sismologue *mf*

seismology [saɪz'mɒlədʒi, *Am:* -'mɑːlə-] *n no pl* sismologie *f*

seize [siːz] *vt* 1.(*grasp*) saisir; **to ~ hold of sth** saisir qc; **to ~ sb by the arm/throat/wrist** saisir qn par le bras/à la gorge/par le poignet 2.(*capture*) capturer; (*hostage, power*) prendre; (*city, territory*) s'emparer de 3.(*confiscate: drugs*) saisir

◆**seize on** *vt* sauter sur

◆**seize up** *vi* (*machine, programme*) se bloquer; (*engine*) se gripper

seizure ['siːʒəʳ, *Am:* -ʒɚ] *n* 1.*no pl* (*seizing: of power, territory*) prise *f;* (*of drugs, property*) saisie *f* 2.MED crise *f* 3.(*stroke*) attaque *f*

seldom ['seldəm] *adv* rarement

select [sɪ'lekt, *Am:* sə'-] I.*vt* 1.(*choose*) choisir 2.SPORT, INFOR sélectionner II.*vi* choisir III.*adj* 1.(*exclusive*) sélect(e) 2.(*chosen*) choisi(e)

selection *n* 1.*no pl* (*choosing*) choix *m* 2.*sing* (*range*) sélection *f* 3.(*extracts*) morceaux *mpl* choisis

selection committee *n* comité *m* de sélection

selective *adj* sélectif(-ive); **~ breeding** élevage par sélection; **~ entry** sélection à l'entrée

selector *n* 1.SPORT (*team chooser*) sélectionneur, -euse *m, f* 2.(*switch*) sélecteur *m*

self [self] *n* 1.<selves> **to find one's true ~** trouver sa véritable personnalité; **to be (like) one's former/old ~** être de nouveau soi-même 2.*no pl, form* PSYCH **the ~** le moi ▶**unto thine own ~ be** true *prov* sois honnête avec toi-même

self-abasement *n no pl* auto-avilissement *m*

self-abuse *n* 1.(*behavior to cause harm*) auto-mutilation *f* 2.(*masturbation*) *a. fig* masturbation *f* **self-acting** *adj* automatique **self-addressed envelope** *n* enveloppe *f* libellée aux nom et adresse de l'expéditeur **self-adhesive** *adj* autocollant(e) **self-appointed** *adj pej* autoproclamé(e) **self-assertion** *n* autoritarisme *m* **self-assertive** *adj* autoritaire **self-assurance** *n no pl* assurance *f* **self-assured** *adj* sûr(e) de soi **self-aware** *adj* conscient(e) de soi-même; **this child is already ~** cet enfant se connaît déjà bien **self-awareness** *n no pl* connaissance *f* de soi **self-catering** *Aus, Brit* I.*adj* en location II.*n no pl* (*tourism*) location *f* **self-cent(e)red** *adj pej* égocentrique **self-colo(u)red** *adj* uni(e) **self-composed** *adj* calme; **to remain ~** garder son calme **self-conceited** *adj pej* vaniteux(-euse) **self-confessed** *adj* avoué(e) **self-confidence** *n no pl* confiance *f* en soi **self-conscious** *adj* embarrassé(e) **self-contained** *adj* 1.(*self-sufficient*) autosuffisant(e) 2.(*independent: apartment*) indépendant(e) 3.*pej* (*reserved*) indépendant(e) **self-contradictory** *adj form* qui se contredit **self-control** *n no pl* sang-froid *m* **self-critical** *adj* critique à l'égard de soi-même **self-criticism** *n no pl* autocritique *f* **self-deception** *n no pl* illusion *f* **self-defeating** *adj* qui va à l'encontre du but recherché; **~ attempt** tentative *f* échouée d'avance **self-defence** *n no pl, Aus, Brit* 1.(*protection*) légitime défense *f* 2.(*skill*) autodéfense *f* **self-denial** *n no pl* sacrifice *m* de soi **self-destructive** *adj* 1.(*destructive*) autodestructible 2.BIO (*materials*) biodégradable **self-determination** *n no pl* POL autodétermination *f* **self-discipline** *n no pl* autodiscipline *f* **self-drive** *Brit* I.*adj* AUTO sans chauffeur II.*n* voiture *f* sans chauffeur **self-educated** *adj* autodidacte **self-effacing** *adj* discret(-ète) **self-employed** I.*adj* indépendant(e); **a ~ builder** un artisan maçon II.*n pl* **the ~** les libéraux **self-esteem** *n no pl* estime *f* de soi **self-evident** *adj* évident(e) **self-explanatory** *adj* qui s'explique de soi-même **self-expression** *n no pl* expression *f* individuelle **self-fulfilling** *adj* qui se réalise tout seul; **pessimism is ~** le pessimisme engendre le malheur **self-fulfilment** *n* épanouissement *m* de soi **self-governing** *adj* autonome **self-government** *n no pl* POL autonomie *f* **self-help group** *n* groupe *m* de discussion **self-importance** *n no pl, pej* suffisance *f* **self-important** *adj pej* suffisant(e) **self-imposed** *adj* que l'on s'impose soi-même; (*exile*) volontaire; **this is my ~ deadline** je me suis fixé ce délai **self-indulgence** *n no pl* complaisance *f* envers soi-même **self-indulgent** *adj* complaisant(e) **self-inflicted** *adj* volontaire **self-interest** *n no pl* intérêt *m* personnel

selfish ['selfɪʃ] *adj* égoïste

selfishness *n no pl, pej* égoïsme *m*

selfless *adj* altruiste; **in a ~ way** de façon désintéressée

selflessness *n* altruisme *m*

self-made *adj* **a ~ man** un self-made-man; **he is a ~ millionaire** il est devenu millionnaire par ses propres moyens **self-opinionated** *adj pej* borné(e) **self-pity** *n no pl* apitoiement *m* sur son (propre) sort **self-portrait** *n* autoportrait *m* **self-possessed** *adj* posé(e) **self-preservation** *n no pl* survie *f* **self-r(a)ising flour** *n no pl* farine *f* avec levure **self-reliance** *n no pl* indépendance *f* **self-reliant** *adj* indépendant(e) **self-respect** *n no pl* dignité *f;* **to take away sb's ~** avilir qn **self-respecting** *adj* qui se respecte **self-righteous** *adj pej* persuadé(e) d'avoir raison **self-sacrifice** *n no pl* dévouement *m* **self-sacrificing** *adj* **to be ~** avoir l'esprit de sacrifice **self-satisfaction** *n no pl, pej* autosatisfaction *f* **self-satisfied** *adj pej* content(e) de soi; **to look ~** avoir l'air suffisant **self-seeking** *pej* I.*n* égoïsme *m* II.*adj* égoïste **self-service** I.*n* libre-service *m* II.*adj* en libre service; **a ~ laundry** une laverie automatique; **a ~ restaurant** un self-service **self-**

sufficiency *n no pl* 1. (*autarky*) autosuffisance *f* 2. (*feeling of pride*) suffisance *f* **self-sufficient** *adj* autosuffisant(e); **to be ~ in food** subvenir à ses besoins en alimentation; **to be a ~ creature** être du genre indépendant **self-supporting** *adj* financièrement autonome **self-tanner** *n* autobronzant *m* **self-taught** *adj* 1. (*self-educated*) autodidacte; **a ~ person** un autodidacte 2. (*acquired by oneself*) appris(e) en autodidacte **self-willed** *adj pej* volontaire **self-winding watch** *n* montre *f* automatique

sell [sel] I. *n no pl* (*thing to sell*) vente *f*; **hard/soft ~** vente agressive/non agressive II. *vt* <sold, sold> vendre, remettre *Belgique;* **to ~ wholesale/retail** vendre en gros/au détail; **to ~ at a loss/profit** vendre à perte/en réalisant un bénéfice; **to ~ sth on credit** vendre qc à crédit; **to ~ forward** FIN vendre à terme ►**to ~ one's body** vendre son corps; **to ~ one's soul to the devil** vendre son âme au diable; **to ~ sb down the river** lâcher qn; **he sold himself short** il n'a pas su se vendre à sa juste valeur III. *vi* <sold, sold> se vendre ►**to ~ like hot cakes** se vendre comme des petits pains

◆**sell off** *vt* liquider; **to sell sth off at half price** brader qc à moitié prix

◆**sell out** I. *vi* 1. (*sell everything*) vendre jusqu'à épuisement des stocks; **to ~ of goods/a brand** liquider des marchandises/une marque 2. (*betray cause*) **to ~ on sb** vendre qn II. *vt* 1. (*have none left*) **to be sold out** être épuisé; **tickets are sold out for tonight** ce soir, on joue à guichets fermés 2. *pej, inf* (*betray*) vendre 3. (*sell*) vendre

◆**sell up** *Aus, Brit* I. *vi* tout vendre II. *vt* vendre

sell-by date *n Brit* date *f* de péremption

seller *n* 1. (*sb who sells sth*) vendeur, -euse *m, f;* **flower ~** fleuriste *mf* 2. (*product that sells well*) produit *m* qui se vend bien; **~s of the year** meilleures ventes *fpl* de l'année

selling *n* vente *f*

selling point *n* atout *m* **selling price** *n* prix *m* de vente

Sellotape® ['seləʊteɪp, *Am:* -oʊ-] *n no pl, Brit* Scotch® *m*

sell-out *n* 1. (*no tickets left*) **this play was a total ~** cette pièce a joué à guichets fermés 2. (*betrayal*) trahison *f*

selves [selvz] *n pl of* **self**

semantic [sɪ'mæntɪk, *Am:* sə'mæntɪk] *adj* LING sémantique **semantics** *npl* LING sémantique *f*

semaphore ['seməfɔːʳ, *Am:* -fɔːr] *n no pl* sémaphore *m*

semblance ['sembləns] *n no pl, form* semblant *m*

semen ['siːmən] *n no pl* semence *f*

semester [sɪ'mestəʳ, *Am:* sə'mestɚ] *n* semestre *m*

semi ['semi] *n* 1. *Aus, Brit, inf* (*one houses joined to another*) *s.* **semi-detached** 2. *Am, Aus, inf* (*kind of truck*) *s.* **articulated truck** 3. *inf* SPORT *s.* **semi-final**

semibreve *n Aus, Brit* MUS ronde *f* **semicircle** *n* demi-cercle *m* **semicircular** *adj* semi-circulaire **semicolon** *n* point-virgule *m* **semiconductor** *n* ELEC semi-conducteur *m* **semi-conscious** *adj* **to be ~** être à moitié conscient **semi-detached** I. *adj* (*house*) jumelé(e) II. *n* maison *f* jumelée **semi-final** *n* SPORT demi-finale *f* **semi-finalist** *n* SPORT demi-finaliste *mf* **semi-finished** *adj* semi-fini(e)

seminal ['semɪnəl, *Am:* 'semə-] *adj* 1. *form* (*work*) de fond; (*role*) décisif(-ive) 2. (*of semen*) séminal(e)

seminar ['semɪnɑːʳ, *Am:* -ənɑːr] *n* 1. UNIV séminaire *m* 2. (*workshop*) stage *m*

seminary ['semɪnəri, *Am:* -ner-] *n* séminaire *m*

semi-precious *adj* (*stone*) semi-précieux(-euse)

semiquaver ['semɪˌkweɪvəʳ, *Am:* -vɚ] *n Aus, Brit* MUS double croche *f*

semiskilled [ˌsemɪ'skɪld] *adj* spécialisé(e)

Semite ['siːmaɪt, *Am:* 'semaɪt] *n* Sémite *mf*

semitic *adj* sémitique

semitone *n* demi-ton *m* **semi-trailer** *n* semi-remorque *m* **semi-tropical** *adj s.* **subtropical**

semolina [ˌsemə'liːnə] *n no pl* semoule *f*

sempstress *n s.* **seamstress**

Sen. *n Am abbr of* **Senator** sénateur *m*

senate ['senɪt] I. *n no pl* 1. POL sénat *m;* **the ~** le Sénat 2. (*university governing body*) **Senate** conseil *m* d'université II. *adj* POL sénatorial(e)

senator ['senətəʳ, *Am:* -tɚ] *n* sénateur, -trice *m, f*

senatorial [ˌsenə'tɔːriəl] *adj Am, form* sénatorial(e); (*candidate*) au Sénat

send [send] I. *vt* <sent, sent> 1. COM (*despatch*) envoyer; **to ~ sth by post/airmail** envoyer qc par courrier/avion; **to ~ one's regards** envoyer ses amitiés; **to ~ sb to prison** LAW envoyer qn en prison; **to ~ sb after sb** envoyer qn à la recherche de qn 2. (*cause to happen*) envoyer 3. *Brit* (*make*) **to ~ sb crazy** rendre qn fou ►**to ~ sb to Coventry** mettre qn en quarantaine; **to ~ sb packing** *inf* envoyer qn promener II. *vi* <sent, sent> (*send message*) **to ~ to ask for sth** s'enquérir de qc

◆**send away** I. *vi* **to ~ for sth** demander qc par courrier; **I sent away for a brochure** j'ai demandé (par courrier) qu'on m'envoie une brochure II. *vt* 1. (*dismiss*) **to send sb away** renvoyer qn 2. (*make sb go*) **to send sb away to some place** expédier qn quelque part

◆**send back** *vt* renvoyer

◆**send down** I. *vt* 1. *Brit* (*expel*) **to send sb down** expulser qn 2. LAW (*put in prison*) incarcérer II. *vi* (*order*) **to ~ for sth** demander qc

◆**send for** *vt* 1. (*summon*) envoyer

S

chercher; **to ~ help** envoyer chercher de l'aide **2.** (*request*) demander par courrier

◆**send forth** *vt* émettre

◆**send in** *vt* **1.** (*submit*) soumettre **2.** (*send*) envoyer **3.** COM (*order*) placer **4.** (*let in*) faire entrer; **~ him/her in** faites-le/la entrer **5.** MIL (*reinforcements*) envoyer

◆**send off** **I.** *vt* **1.** (*post*) expédier; (*letter*) poster **2.** *Aus, Brit* SPORT expulser; **to get sent off** se faire expulser **II.** *vi s.* **send away**

◆**send on** *vt* renvoyer; (*a letter*) faire suivre

◆**send out** *vt* **1.** (*emit*) émettre **2.** (*mail*) expédier **3.** (*dispatch*) détacher

◆**send up** *vt* **1.** (*to drive up*) faire monter; (*a rocket*) lancer **2.** *Am* (*put in prison*) incarcérer **3.** *inf* (*make a parody of*) caricaturer

sender *n* expéditeur, -trice *m, f;* **'return to ~'** 'retour à l'envoyeur'

send-off *n* **to give sb a ~** dire au revoir à qn

send-up *n inf* caricature *f*

Senegal [ˌsenɪ'gɔːl] *n* le Sénégal

Senegalese [ˌsenɪgə'liːz] **I.** *adj* sénégalais(e) **II.** *n* Sénégalais(e) *m(f)*

senile ['siːnaɪl] *adj* sénile; **to go ~** devenir sénile

senility [sɪ'nɪləti, *Am:* sə'nɪləṭi] *n no pl* sénilité *f*

senior ['siːniəʳ, *Am:* -njɚ] **I.** *adj* **1.** (*older*) aîné(e); **to be three years ~** avoir trois ans de plus que qn; **John B. O'Malley ~** John B. O'Malley père **2.** SCHOOL, UNIV (*pupil*) de terminale; (*student*) de dernière année; **the ~ boys/girls** les grand(e)s; **~ part of a school** classes *fpl* supérieures **3.** (*high-ranking*) supérieur(e); (*employee*) de grade supérieur; **to be ~ to sb** être au-dessus de qn; (*longer in service*) avoir plus d'ancienneté que qn **4.** (*related to the elderly*) du troisième âge **II.** *n* **1.** (*older person*) aîné(e) *m(f);* **to be sb's ~** être l'aîné de qn; **to be two years sb's ~, to be sb's ~ by two years** être l'aîné de qn de deux ans **2.** (*person of higher rank*) supérieur(e) *m(f)* **3.** *Am* (*pupil of a graduating class*) étudiant(e) *m(f)* de dernière année **4.** SPORT, SCHOOL **the ~s** les grand(e)s **5.** (*elderly person*) personne *f* du troisième âge

senior citizen *n* personne *f* du troisième âge

senior high school *n Am* lycée *m*

seniority [ˌsiːni'ɒrəti, *Am:* siː'njɔːrəṭi] *n no pl* **1.** (*older*) âge *m* **2.** (*higher in rank*) ancienneté *f*

sensation [sen'seɪʃən] *n* **1.** PHYSIOL sensation *f* **2.** (*feeling*) impression *f;* **to have the ~ that ...** avoir l'impression que ... **3.** (*strong excitement*) sensation *f*

sensational *adj* **1.** (*excited feeling*) sensationnel(le) **2.** *pej* PUBL (*newspaper*) à sensation; (*disclosure*) qui fait sensation

sense [sents] **I.** *n* **1.** *no pl* (*common sense*) sens *m* **2.** *pl* (*judgement*) raison *f;* **to bring sb to his/her ~s** ramener qn à la raison **3.** MED, PHYSIOL sens *m;* **the ~ of smell** l'odorat *m;* **the ~ of taste** le goût; **the ~ of touch** le toucher; **the ~ of hearing** l'ouïe *f;* **the ~ of sight** la vue **4.** (*meaning*) sens *m* **5.** (*way*) sens *m;* **in every ~** dans tous les sens; **in a ~** dans un certain sens ▶**there's no ~ in doing sth** ça n'a aucun sens de faire qc; **what's the ~ in doing sth?** à quoi cela sert-il de faire qc ?; **sth doesn't make (any) ~** qc ne rime à rien; **to make (good) ~** se tenir; **he talks ~** ce qu'il dit se tient **II.** *vt* sentir

senseless *adj* **1.** (*foolish, pointless*) insensé(e); (*killing*) gratuit(e); **it is ~ to** *+infin* ça n'a aucun sens de *+infin* **2.** MED (*unconscious*) inanimé(e)

sense organ *n* organe *m* sensitif

sensibility [ˌsentsɪ'bɪləti, *Am:* -sə'bɪləṭi] *n no pl* ART, SOCIOL **1.** (*sensitiveness*) sensibilité *f* **2.** *pl* (*feelings*) susceptibilité *f*

sensible ['sentsɪbl, *Am:* -sə-] *adj* raisonnable

sensibly *adv* **1.** (*with rationally*) raisonnablement **2.** (*suitably*) correctement

sensitive ['sentsɪtɪv, *Am:* -səṭɪv] *adj* **1.** (*understanding*) compréhensif(-ive); **to be ~ to sth** être sensible à qc **2.** (*touchy*) sensible

sensitiveness, **sensitivity** *n a. fig* sensibilité *f*

sensitize ['sentsɪtaɪz, *Am:* -sə-] *vt Am* (*make aware of*) sensibiliser

sensor ['sentsəʳ, *Am:* -sɚ] *n* TECH, ELEC capteur *m*

sensory ['sentsəri] *adj* sensoriel(le)

sensual ['sentsjʊəl, *Am:* -ʃuəl] *adj* sensuel(le)

sensualist *n* personne *f* voluptueuse

sensuality [ˌsentsju'æləti, *Am:* -ʃu'æləṭi] *n no pl* sensualité *f*

sensuous ['sentsjʊəs, *Am:* -ʃuəs] *adj* sensuel(le)

sent [sent] *pp, pt of* **send**

sentence ['sentəns, *Am:* -ṭəns] **I.** *n* **1.** (*decision of a court*) condamnation *f;* **jail ~** condamnation à la prison; **life ~** condamnation à perpétuité; **to get a ~** être condamné; **to pronounce (a) ~ on sb** prononcer une condamnation contre qn; **to serve a ~** purger une peine **2.** (*group of words*) phrase *f* **II.** *vt* **to ~ sb to sth** condamner qn à qc

sententious [sen'tenʃəs] *adj pej, form* sentencieux(-euse)

sentient ['senʃnt] *adj form* sensible

sentiment ['sentɪmənt, *Am:* -ṭə-] *n form* **1.** (*feeling*) sentiment *m* **2.** (*opinion*) opinion *f*

sentimental *adj a. pej* sentimental(e)

sentimentalism *n no pl, pej, form* sentimentalisme *m*

sentimentality [ˌsentɪmen'tæləti, *Am:* -ṭəmen'tæləṭi] *n no pl, pej* sentimentalité *f*

sentimentalize [ˌsentɪ'mentəlaɪz, *Am:* -ṭə'menṭəlaɪz] *vt Am, pej* romancer

sentry ['sentri] *n* sentinelle *f;* **to stand ~** être en faction

sentry box *n* guérite *f*

separable ['sepərəbl] *adj form* séparable

separate¹ ['seprət, *Am:* 'sepɚɪt] *adj* **1.** (*not

joined physically) séparé(e); **a ~ piece of paper** une feuille à part **2.** (*distinct*) distinct(e) **3.** (*different*) différent(e); **to go ~ ways** prendre des chemins différents

separate² ['sepəreɪt] **I.** *vt* séparer; **to ~ sb/sth from sb/sth else** séparer qn/qc de qn/qc; **to ~ egg whites from yolks** séparer les blancs des jaunes **II.** *vi* se séparer; **to ~ from sb/sth** se séparer de qn/qc

separated *adj* séparé(e)

separates *n pl* coordonnés *mpl*

separation *n* séparation *f*

separatism ['sepərətɪzm] *n no pl* séparatisme *m*

separatist **I.** *n* séparatiste *mf* **II.** *adj* séparatiste

separator *n* séparateur *m*

sepia ['siːpɪə] **I.** *adj* (couleur) sépia *inv* **II.** *n* sépia *f*

sepsis ['sepsɪs] *n no pl* infection *f*

September [sep'tembəʳ, *Am:* -bɚ] *n* septembre *m; s. a.* **April**

septic ['septɪk] *adj* infecté(e); **to go ~** s'infecter

septuagenarian [ˌseptjʊədʒɪ'neəriən, *Am:* -tuədʒə'neri-] *n* septuagénaire *mf*

sepulcher *n Am,* **sepulchre** ['sepəlkəʳ, *Am:* -ɚ] *n* sépulcre *m*

sequel ['siːkwəl] *n* **1.** (*continued story*) suite *f;* **the ~ to sth** la suite de qc **2.** (*consequence*) conséquence *f*

sequence ['siːkwəns] *n* **1.** (*order*) suite *f* **2.** (*part of film*) séquence *f*

sequential [sɪ'kwenʃl] *adj form* séquentiel(le)

sequester *vt* **1.** LAW (*confiscate*) saisir **2.** *Am* (*isolate*) isoler

sequestrate [sɪ'kwestreɪt] *vt* saisir

sequestration *n no pl* **1.** (*temporary confiscation*) saisie *f* **2.** *Am* (*isolation*) isolation *f*

sequin ['siːkwɪn] *n* paillette *f*

sequoia [sɪ'kwɔɪə] *n* BOT séquoia *m*

Serb [sɜːb, *Am:* sɜːrb] **I.** *adj* serbe **II.** *n* Serbe *mf*

Serbia ['sɜːbɪə, *Am:* 'sɜːr-] *n* la Serbie

Serbian **I.** *adj* serbe **II.** *n* LING serbe *m; s. a.* **English**

Serbo-Croat [ˌsɜːbəʊ'krəʊæt, *Am:* ˌsɜːrboʊkroʊ'-], **Serbo-Croatian** **I.** *n* LING serbo-croate *m; s. a.* **English** **II.** *adj* serbo-croate

serenade [ˌserə'neɪd] **I.** *vt* chanter la sérénade **II.** *n* sérénade *f*

serene [sɪ'riːn, *Am:* sə'-] <-r, -st> *adj* serein(e)

serenity [sɪ'renəti, *Am:* sə'renət̬i] *n no pl* sérénité *f*

serf [sɜːf, *Am:* sɜːrf] *n* HIST serf, -ve *m, f*

serfdom *n no pl* HIST servage *m*

sergeant ['sɑːdʒənt, *Am:* 'sɑːrdʒənt] *n* **1.** (*officer*) sergent *m* **2.** *Brit* (*policeman*) brigadier *m*

sergeant major *n* sergent-major *m*

serial ['sɪəriəl, *Am:* 'sɪri-] **I.** *n* feuilleton *m;* **TV ~** feuilleton télévisé **II.** *adj* en série

serialize ['sɪəriəlaɪz, *Am:* 'sɪri-] *vt* **1.** PUBL publier en feuilleton **2.** RADIO, TV adapter en feuilleton

series ['sɪəriːz, *Am:* 'sɪriːz] *inv n* série *f;* **in ~** en série; **TV ~** série télévisée

serious ['sɪəriəs, *Am:* 'sɪri-] *adj* **1.** (*not funny, sincere*) sérieux(-euse); **to be ~ about sb/sth** être sérieux avec qn/qc; **to be ~ about doing sth** envisager sérieusement de faire qc **2.** (*concerning, solemn*) grave **3.** *inf* (*substantial*) important(e); **to have some ~ difficulty** avoir de grosses difficultés; **~ money** beaucoup d'argent **4.** (*extremely good*) excellent(e)

seriously *adv* **1.** (*sincerely*) sérieusement; (*wounded*) grièvement; **to take sb/sth ~** prendre qn/qc au sérieux **2.** *inf* (*really*) vraiment **3.** *inf* (*very, extremely*) très

seriousness *n no pl* **1.** (*truthfulness*) sérieux *m;* **in all ~** sérieusement **2.** (*serious or grave nature*) gravité *f*

sermon ['sɜːmən, *Am:* 'sɜːr-] *n a. pej* sermon *m*

serpent ['sɜːpənt, *Am:* 'sɜːr-] *n* serpent *m*

serrated [sɪ'reɪtɪd, *Am:* 'sereɪt̬ɪd] *adj* en dents de scie

serum ['sɪərəm, *Am:* 'sɪrəm] <-s *o* sera> *n* sérum *m*

servant ['sɜːvənt, *Am:* 'sɜːr-] *n* **1.** (*household helper*) serviteur *m,* servante *f* **2.** (*person working for public*) employé(e) *m(f);* **a public ~** un(e) employé(e) de la fonction publique

serve [sɜːv, *Am:* sɜːrv] **I.** *vt* **1.** (*help or attend to customer*) servir **2.** (*provide food/drink for guests*) servir; **to ~ alcohol** servir de l'alcool **3.** (*work for, give service to*) être au service de **4.** (*complete a due period*) servir; **to ~ one's time** purger sa peine; **to ~ 10 years** servir 10 ans à l'armée; **to ~ one year as director** exercer sa fonction de directeur pendant un an **5.** (*help achieve, meet needs*) servir à; **to ~ the purpose** faire l'affaire **6.** (*provide with public transportation: region, town*) desservir **7.** (*hit* (*a ball*) *to start a game*) servir **8.** (*formally deliver*) **to ~ sb with sth** délivrer qc à qn ►**to ~ sb <u>right</u>** être bien fait pour qn **II.** *vi a.* SPORT servir; **to ~ in the army/a shop** servir dans l'armée/un magasin; **to ~ to** +*infin* servir à +*infin* **III.** *n* service *m*

◆**serve out** *vt* **1.** GASTR *s.* **serve up** **2.** (*complete a due period*) finir; (*a jail sentence*) purger

◆**serve up** *vt* servir

server ['sɜːvəʳ, *Am:* 'sɜːrvɚ] *n* **1.** (*tableware for serving food*) service *m;* **salad ~s** service à salade **2.** (*waiter*) serveur, -euse *m, f* **3.** INFOR serveur *m* **4.** (*person serving the ball*) serveur, -euse *m, f*

service ['sɜːvɪs, *Am:* 'sɜːr-] **I.** *n* **1.** (*set*) service *m;* **tea ~** service à thé **2.** (*assistance*) service *m;* **bus ~** service des bus; **out of ~** hors service; **to be of ~ to sb** être utile à qn; **to do sb**

S

a ~ rendre service à qn **3.** REL service *m* **4.** TECH entretien *m;* AUTO révision *f;* **the ~s** *(pl)* aire *f* de services **5.** MIL **the ~s** l'armée *f;* ~ **personnel** personnel *m* militaire ►**to be in** ~ être en service; **to be at sb's** ~ *iron* être au service de qn **II.** *vt* entretenir; (*car*) réviser

serviceable *adj* utilisable

service area *n* **1.** (*area for getting petrol*) aire *f* de services **2.** (*area served by broadcasting station*) zone *f* d'émission **service bus, service car** *n Aus, NZ* car *m* de tourisme **service center** *n Am* aire *f* de services **service charge** *n* service *m* **service contract** *n* **1.** (*employment contract*) contrat *m* **2.** (*warranty*) garantie *f* **service elevator** *n Am* ascenseur *m* de service **service entrance** *n* porte *f* de service **service industry** *n* prestataire *m* de service **service lift** *n s.* **service elevator serviceman** *n* militaire *m* **service road** *n* voie *f* d'accès **service sector** *n* secteur *m* tertiaire **service station** *n* station-service *f* **servicewoman** *n* femme *f* militaire

serviette [ˌsɜːvɪ'et, *Am:* ˌsɜːr-] *n Brit* serviette *f*

servile ['sɜːvaɪl, *Am:* 'sɜːrvl] *adj pej* servile

servility [sɜː'vɪləti, *Am:* sɜːr'vɪləṱi] *n no pl, pej, form* servilité *f*

serving ['sɜːvɪŋ, *Am:* 'sɜːr-] **I.** *n* portion *f* **II.** *adj* **1.** (*working*) en fonction **2.** (*incarcerated*) en prison **3.** MIL au service

servitude ['sɜːvɪtjuːd, *Am:* 'sɜːrvətuːd] *n no pl, form* servitude *f*

sesame ['sesəmi] **I.** *n no pl* sésame *m* **II.** *adj* au sésame

session ['seʃən] *n* **1.** (*formal sitting or meeting*) *a.* INFOR session *f;* **parliamentary** ~ session parlementaire; **a recording** ~ une session d'enregistrement **2.** (*period for specific activity*) séance *f;* **training** ~ séance d'entraînement **3.** *Am, Scot* (*period for classes*) cours *m* **4.** UNIV année *f* universitaire

set [set] **I.** *n* **1.** (*prepared scenery on stage, setting*) scène *f;* (*in film, tv*) plateau *m;* **on** ~ sur le plateau **2.** ANAT **the ~ of sb's jaw** la dentition **3.** (*hair arrangement*) mise *f* en plis **4.** (*group or collection*) *a.* INFOR (*of keys, tools, golf clubs*) jeu *m;* (*of stamps, numbers, books*) série *f;* (*of gems, sheets*) parure *f;* **a tea/china** ~ un service à thé/en porcelaine; **a chess** ~ un jeu d'échec; ~ **of furniture** mobilier *m* **5.** (*group of people*) groupe *m;* **literature** ~ groupe littéraire **6.** MAT (*group*) ensemble *m* **7.** (*television apparatus*) poste *m;* **a TV/radio** ~ un poste de télévision/radio **8.** SPORT (*games*) set *m* **9.** (*musical performance*) partie *f* **II.** *adj* **1.** (*ready, prepared*) prêt(e); **to be (all)** ~ **for sth** être prêt pour qc; **to get** ~ se tenir prêt **2.** (*fixed*) fixe; (*expression, face, smile*) figé(e); (*date, opinion, idea*) arrêté(e) **3.** (*resolute*) résolu(e); **to be ~ on doing sth** être résolu à faire qc **4.** (*assigned*) obligatoire; (*book, subject*) au programme; (*task*) assigné(e) ►**to be ~ in one's ways** avoir ses petites habitudes **III.** *vt* <set, set> **1.** (*place, put in some place*) poser **2.** (*situated*) *a.* CINE, LIT, THEAT situer; **a house ~ on a cliff** une maison située sur une falaise; **the scene is ~ in sth** l'action se déroule dans qc **3.** (*cause to be*) mettre; **to ~ a boat afloat** mettre un bateau à l'eau; **to ~ sth on fire** mettre le feu à qc; **to ~ sth in motion** mettre qc en route; **to ~ sth on the road to sth** mettre qc sur la voie de qc; **to ~ sb loose/free** lâcher/libérer qn **4.** (*adjust: clock, timer*) régler; (*trap*) tendre; **to ~ the alarm for 7.00 a.m.** mettre le réveil sur 7 heures **5.** (*prepare: stage*) préparer; **to ~ the table** mettre la table **6.** (*establish, fix: a limit, price, date*) fixer; **to ~ a deadline** fixer une date limite; **to ~ an example to sb** donner un exemple à qn; **to ~ oneself a goal** se fixer un but; **to ~ a record** établir un record; **to ~ a price at £125 000** fixer un prix à 125 000 livres **7.** (*place in normal position*) remettre; **to ~ a broken bone** réduire une fracture **8.** (*arrange*) **to ~ sb's hair** se faire une mise en plis **9.** (*encrust, adorn: jewel*) sertir; **to ~ sth with sth** sertir qc de qc **10.** TYP (*lay out*) composer **11.** *Aus, Brit* (*cause to start*) **to ~ to** *+infin* se mettre à *+infin;* **to ~ sb to do/doing sth** faire faire qc à qn; **to ~ sb to work** mettre qn au travail; **to ~ homework** donner des devoirs **12.** (*provide with music*) **to ~ sth to music** mettre qc en musique ►**to ~ course for sth** mettre le cap sur qc; **to ~ one's heart on doing sth** avoir bon espoir de faire qc; **to ~ one's teeth** serrer les dents; **to ~ foot in sth** mettre les pieds dans qc; **to ~ one's mind at ease** rassurer qn; **to ~ one's mind to sth** (*concentrate on*) s'appliquer à qc; (*approach sth in determined manner*) s'attaquer à qc; **to ~ sail for some place** mettre les voiles pour un endroit; **to ~ the scene for sth** (*conditions are right*) réunir toutes les conditions pour qc; (*make sth likely to happen*) préparer le terrain pour qc; **to ~ the world ablaze** embraser le monde **IV.** *vi* **1.** (*go down, sink*) se coucher **2.** (*become firm*) durcir; (*jelly, cement*) prendre; (*bone*) se ressouder **3.** *fig* se durcir

◆**set about** *vt* **1.** (*begin, start work upon*) **to ~ doing sth** se mettre à faire qc **2.** *inf* (*attack*) attaquer

◆**set against** *vt* **to set sth against sth** **1.** (*offset*) déduire qc de qc **2.** (*compare, weigh up*) comparer qc à qc **3.** (*use as a compensating item, offset*) contrebalancer qc par qc **4.** (*make oppose*) dresser qn contre qn/qc; **to be dead ~ sb/sth** être résolument opposé à qn/qc

◆**set apart** *vt* **1.** (*distinguish*) distinguer **2.** (*reserve*) mettre de côté; **to ~ a day for doing sth** se réserver un jour pour faire qc

◆**set aside** *vt* **1.** (*put aside*) *a. fig* **to set sth aside** mettre qc de côté; (*time*) réserver qc **2.** (*declare invalid*) annuler **3.** (*reject*) rejeter

◆**set back** *vt* **1.** (*delay, hold up*) retarder **2.** (*position or place away from*) mettre en retrait de **3.** *inf* (*cost*) **to set sb back** coûter à qn

◆**set down** *vt* **1.** (*land*) poser; **to set a plane down** poser un avion **2.** (*drop off*) déposer **3.** (*write down*) inscrire; **to set sth down in sth** inscrire qc dans qc; **to ~ one's thoughts** coucher ses pensées par écrit

◆**set forth** *vt form s.* **set out**

◆**set in** *vi* survenir

◆**set off** **I.** *vi* se mettre en route; **to ~ on sth** partir pour qc; **to ~ on a journey** partir en voyage **II.** *vt* **1.** (*detonate*) déclencher **2.** (*cause sb to do or start sth*) **to set sb off doing sth** faire faire qc à qn **3.** (*enhance*) rehausser

◆**set on** *vt* **1.** (*cause sb/sth to attack physically*) **to set sb/an animal on sb** lâcher qn/un animal sur qn **2.** (*attack*) se jeter sur

◆**set out** **I.** *vt a. fig* exposer **II.** *vi* **1.** *s.* **set off** **2.** (*intend/have the intention, aim*) **to ~ to** +*infin* avoir l'intention de +*infin*

◆**set to** *vi* **1.** (*begin to work or deal with sth*) **to ~ work** se mettre au travail **2.** *inf* (*begin fighting*) **to ~ with sth** en venir aux mains avec qn

◆**set up** *vt* **1.** (*place in position or view*) dresser; (*camp*) établir; **to set sth up again** relever qc **2.** (*establish*) créer; **to ~ sb in business** lancer qn dans les affaires **3.** (*organize*) organiser **4.** (*claim to be sth*) **to set oneself up as sth** s'établir comme qc **5.** (*make pretentiou1s*) **to set oneself up as sth** se poser en qc **6.** (*make healthy*) **to set sb up again** remettre qn sur pieds **7.** (*provide*) **to set sb up with sth** approvisionner qn en qc **8.** *inf* (*deceive, frame*) piéger

setback *n* revers *m*

set-in *adj* rapporté(e)

setsquare ['setskweəʳ, *Am:* -skwer] *n Aus, Brit* équerre *f*

settee [se'ti:] *n* canapé *m*

setter ['setəʳ, *Am:* 'set̬ɚ] *n* setter *m*

setting *n* **1.** (*location, scenery*) cadre *m* **2.** (*position*) réglage *m* **3.** (*frame for jewel*) monture *f* **4.** TYP (*layout*) composition *f* **5.** MUS arrangement *m*

setting lotion *n* lotion *f* pour mise en plis

settle ['setl, *Am:* 'set̬-] **I.** *vi* **1.** (*get comfortable*) s'installer **2.** (*calm down*) se calmer **3.** (*end dispute*) se régler **4.** *form* (*pay*) régler; **to ~ with sb** régler qn **5.** (*live permanently*) s'établir **6.** (*accumulate*) se déposer **7.** (*land*) se poser **8.** (*sink down*) s'affaisser **II.** *vt* **1.** (*calm down*) calmer **2.** (*decide*) décider de **3.** (*resolve: details, a crisis*) régler **4.** (*pay*) régler **5.** (*colonize*) coloniser ▶**to ~ an <u>account</u> with sb, to ~ sb's <u>hash</u>** régler son compte à qn

◆**settle down** **I.** *vi* **1.** (*get comfortable*) s'installer **2.** (*adjust* (*to new situation*)) **to ~ in sth** s'adapter à qc **3.** (*calm down*) se calmer **4.** (*start a quiet life*) se ranger **II.** *vt* **to settle oneself down with sth** s'installer dans qc

◆**settle for** *vt* accepter

◆**settle in** *vi* s'installer

◆**settle on** *vt* **1.** (*decide on*) décider de; **to ~ a date** s'entendre sur une date **2.** (*bestow*) **to settle sth on sb** faire don de qc à qn

◆**settle up** *vi* régler

◆**settle upon** *vt form s.* **settle on**

settled *adj* **1.** (*comfortable*) installé(e) **2.** (*calm*) stable **3.** (*established*) rangé(e) **4.** (*fixed: idea*) fixe

settlement *n* **1.** (*agreement*) arrangement *m;* **to reach a ~** trouver un arrangement **2.** FIN, ECON (*payment*) règlement *m* **3.** LAW (*property arrangement*) constitution *f* **4.** (*colony*) colonie *f* **5.** (*colonization*) colonisation *f* **6.** *no pl* (*sinking*) affaissement *m*

settlement house *n* centre *m* d'œuvres sociales

settler *n* colon *m*

set-to *n inf* bagarre *f* **set-up** *n* **1.** (*way things are arranged*) situation *f* **2.** (*arrangement*) arrangement *m* **3.** *inf* (*conspiracy*) coup-monté *m*

seven ['sevn] *adj* sept; *s. a.* **eight**

sevenfold ['sevnfəʊld, *Am:* -foʊld] **I.** *adj* septuple **II.** *adv* sept fois autant; **to increase ~** multiplier par sept

seventeen [ˌsevn'ti:n] *adj* dix-sept; *s. a.* **eight**

seventeenth *adj* dix-septième; *s. a.* **eighth**

seventh *adj* septième ▶**to be in ~ <u>heaven</u>** être au septième ciel; *s. a.* **eighth**

seventieth *adj* soixante-dixième, septantième *Belgique, Suisse; s. a.* **eighth**

seventy ['sevənti, *Am:* -t̬i] *adj* soixante-dix, septante *Belgique, Suisse; s. a.* **eight**

sever ['sevəʳ, *Am:* 'sevɚ] *vt* **1.** (*cut*) *a. fig* **to ~ sth from sth** sectionner qc de qc **2.** (*put an end*) *a. fig* rompre

several ['sevərəl] **I.** *adj* **1.** (*some*) **~ times** plusieurs fois **2.** (*separate*) différent(e); **the ~ interests of each** les divers intérêts de chacun **II.** *pron* **we've got ~** nous en avons plusieurs; **~ of us** plusieurs d'entre nous

severance ['sevərənts] *n no pl, form* séparation *f*

severance pay *n* indemnité *f* de licenciement

severe [sɪ'vɪəʳ, *Am:* sə'vɪr] *adj* <-r, -st> sévère; (*illness, wound*) grave; (*winter, weather, test*) rigoureux(-euse); (*headache, injury, pain*) violent(e)

severity [sɪ'verəti, *Am:* sə'verət̬i] *n no pl* sévérité *f;* (*of illness, wound*) gravité *f;* (*of climate*) rigueur *f;* (*pain*) violence *f*

sew [səʊ, *Am:* soʊ] <sewed, sewn *o* sewed> **I.** *vt* coudre; **hand/machine ~n** cousu main/machine **II.** *vi* coudre

◆**sew up** *vt* **1.** (*repair by sewing*) recoudre **2.** (*stitch*) suturer **3.** *inf* (*arrange*) conclure

sewage ['su:ɪdʒ] *n no pl* eaux *fpl* usées

sewer ['səʊə^r, *Am:* 'soʊɚ] *n* égout *m* ►**to have a mind like a** ~ être dégoûtant

sewerage ['sʊərɪdʒ, *Am:* 'su:ɚɪdʒ] *n no pl* égout *m*

sewing *n no pl* couture *f*

sewing basket *n* boîte *f* à couture **sewing class** *n* classe *f* de couture **sewing machine** *n* machine *f* à coudre

sewn [səʊn, *Am:* soʊn] *pp of* **sew**

sex [seks] **I.** <-es> *n* **1.** (*gender*) sexe *m;* **the weaker/opposite** ~ le sexe faible/opposé; **members of the male/female** ~ membres de la gente masculine/féminine **2.** *no pl* (*erotic stimulation*) sexe *m;* **experience of** ~ expérience *f* sexuelle; ~ **before/outside marriage** rapports sexuels hors mariage/ extraconjugaux; **casual** ~ rapports *mpl* sexuels de rencontre; **group** ~ partouze *f inf;* **to have** ~ avoir des rapports sexuels **3.** *no pl* (*reproduction: persons*) rapports *mpl* sexuels; (*reproduction: animals*) accouplement *m* **II.** *vt* **to** ~ **sb/an animal** déterminer le sexe de qn/d'un animal

sexagenarian [ˌseksədʒɪ'nəriən, *Am:* dʒɪ-'neri-] **I.** *n* sexagénaire *mf* **II.** *adj* sexagénaire

sex education *n* éducation *f* sexuelle

sexism ['seksɪzəm] *n no pl, pej* sexisme *m*

sexist **I.** *adj pej* sexiste **II.** *n* sexiste *mf*

sexless *adj* asexué(e)

sex life *n* vie *f* sexuelle

sextant ['sekstənt] *n* sextant *m*

sextet(te) [sek'stet] *n* sextuor *m*

sexual ['sekʃʊəl, *Am:* -ʃuəl] *adj* sexuel(le)

sexuality [ˌsekʃʊ'æləti, *Am:* -ʃu'ælət̬i] *n no pl* sexualité *f*

sexually *adv* sexuellement

sexy ['seksi] <-ier, -iest> *adj inf* (*person, dress*) sexy; (*book, film*) érotique

Seychelles [seɪ'ʃelz] *n* les Seychelles *fpl*

shabby ['ʃæbi] <-ier, -iest> *adj* miteux(-euse); (*excuse*) minable

shack [ʃæk] **I.** *n* cabane *f* **II.** *vi inf* **to** ~ **up together** vivre ensemble

shackle ['ʃækl] *vt* enchaîner; **to be ~d by sth** être prisonnier de qc

shade [ʃeɪd] **I.** *n* **1.** *no pl* (*protected from sunlight*) *a. fig* ombre *f* **2.** (*covering for light bulb*) abat-jour *m* **3.** *pl, Am* (*blind*) store *m* **4.** (*variation*) *a. fig* nuance *f* **5.** *no pl* (*a little*) soupçon *m;* **a** ~ **under/over sth** un peu plus de/moins de qc **6.** *pl, inf* (*dark glasses*) lunettes *fpl* noires ►**to leave sb/sth in the** ~ laisser qn/ qc dans l'ombre **II.** *vt* **1.** (*protect from brightness*) ombrager; (*eyes*) protéger; **to be ~d by a tree** être à l'ombre d'un arbre **2.** (*darken parts*) ombrer **3.** *inf* (*win*) gagner de justesse **4.** (*decrease*) baisser progressivement **III.** *vi* **1.** (*alter colour*) se dégrader; **to** ~ **from sth into sth** se fondre de qc en qc **2.** (*be indistinguishable*) **to** ~ **into sth** se confondre avec qc **3.** (*decrease*) baisser

◆**shade in** *vt* **1.** (*darken*) ombrer **2.** (*colour*) colorer

shaded *adj* **1.** (*under shade*) ombragé(e) **2.** TYP en grisé

shading *n no pl* **1.** (*shade of colour*) nuances *fpl* **2.** (*darker area*) ombres *fpl*

shadow ['ʃædəʊ, *Am:* -oʊ] **I.** *n* **1.** (*darker space*) *a. fig* ombre *f;* **to be in** ~ être à l'ombre; **to cast a** ~ **on sb/sth** projeter une ombre sur qn/qc; **to follow sb like a** ~ suivre qn comme son ombre **2.** (*darkness*) obscurité *f* **3.** *pl* (*darker area under eye*) cernes *fpl* **4.** (*trace*) ombre *f;* **the** ~ **of doubt** l'ombre d'un doute ►**to be a** ~ **of one's former self** n'être plus que l'ombre de soi-même; **to be afraid of one's own** ~ avoir peur de son ombre; **to be under sb's** ~ vivre dans l'ombre de qn **II.** *vt* **1.** (*create dimmer area*) assombrir **2.** (*bring darkness*) ombrager **3.** (*trail*) filer **4.** (*follow*) suivre **III.** *adj Brit, Aus* fantôme

shadowy <-ier, -iest> *adj* **1.** (*in the shadow*) ombragé(e) **2.** (*darker*) *a. fig* sombre **3.** (*vague*) vague

shady ['ʃeɪdi] <-ier, -iest> *adj* **1.** (*protected from light*) ombragé(e) **2.** *inf* (*dubious*) louche; **a** ~ **character** un drôle de caractère

shaft [ʃɑ:ft, *Am:* ʃæft] **I.** *n* **1.** (*handle*) manche *m* **2.** (*piston*) essieu *m* **3.** (*ray*) trait *m* **4.** MIN puits *m* **5.** (*extended passage*) **lift** [*o Am* **elevator**] ~ cage *f* d'ascenseur; **ventilation** ~ cheminée *f* d'aération ►**to give sb the** ~ *Am, inf* donner une raclée à qn **II.** *vt* arnaquer

shagged (out) *adj Brit, Aus, pej, inf* crevé(e)

shaggy ['ʃægi] <-ier, -iest> *adj* **1.** (*with rough hair*) touffu(e) **2.** (*unkempt*) ébouriffé(e) ►**a** ~ **dog story** une histoire sans queue ni tête

shah [ʃɑ:] *n* schah *m*

shake [ʃeɪk] **I.** *n* **1.** (*wobble*) secousse *f;* ~ **of one's head** hochement *m* de la tête **2.** *pl, inf* tremblote *f;* **to get the ~s** avoir la tremblote **3.** *Am, inf* (*milk shake*) milk-shake *m* ►**in two ~s of a duck's tail** *inf* en moins de deux; **to be no great** ~ **as sth** ne pas casser trois pattes à un canard comme qc **II.** <shook, shaken> *vt* **1.** (*joggle, agitate*) secouer; **to** ~ **oneself** se secouer; **to** ~ **one's head** secouer la tête; **to** ~ **sb awake** secouer qn pour le réveiller; **to** ~ **one's fist at sb** montrer le poing à qn; **to** ~ **hands with sb** serrer la main à qn; **to** ~ **sb by the hand** serrer la main à qn; **to** ~ **one's hips** bouger les hanches **2.** (*unsettle*) secouer ►**to** ~ **a leg** *inf* se secouer; **more than you can** ~ **a stick at** *inf* plus que nécessaire **III.** <shook, shaken> *vi* trembler; **to** ~ **with fear** trembler de peur; ~ **well before using** bien agiter avant emploi ►**to** ~ **in one's boots** en trembler; **to** ~ **like a leaf** *Brit, Aus* trembler comme une feuille

◆**shake down** *inf* **I.** *vt Am* racketter **II.** *vi* **1.** (*achieve harmony: person*) s'accommoder **2.** (*stay overnight*) aller au pieu

◆**shake off** *vt* **1.** (*agitate to remove*) secouer **2.** (*eliminate*) se débarrasser de **3.** *fig* **to** ~ **shackles** se libérer de ses chaînes

◆**shake out** *vt* secouer
◆**shake up** *vt* 1.(*agitate*) secouer 2.(*upset*) bouleverser
shakedown *Am* I.*n inf* 1.(*bringing into order*) rodage *m* 2.(*extortion*) extortion *f* 3.(*search*) fouille *f* II.*adj* 1.(*settling down*) de rodage 2.(*with a trial run*) d'essai
shaken I.*pp of* shake II.*adj* secoué(e)
shaker *n* 1.(*for mixing liquids*) shaker *m* 2.(*for dispensing powder*) **a salt/pepper/sugar** ~ une salière/poivrière/saupoudreuse 3.(*device for dice*) cornet *m* à dés
shake-up *n inf* bouleversement *m*
shakily ['ʃeɪkɪli] *adv* 1.(*not stable*) branlant(e) 2.(*uncertainly*) mal assuré(e); **to walk** ~ marcher d'un pas mal assuré
shaking I.*n* (*shake*) secousse *f* II.*adj* (*disturbed*) tremblant(e)
shaky <-ier, -iest> *adj* 1.(*jerky: voice, writing, hand*) tremblotant(e); **to walk ~ on one's feet** marcher d'un pas mal assuré 2.(*wavering: memory, knowledge*) vacillant(e) 3.(*upset*) secoué(e) 4.(*unstable: chair, building*) branlant(e); (*person*) faible; (*economy*) instable; **to be on ~ ground** être sur un terrain glissant
shall [ʃæl] *aux* 1.(*future*) **I ~ do ...** je ferai ... 2.(*ought to, must*) **you ~ obey** tu devras obéir 3.(*expresses what is mandatory*) **it ~ be unlawful** il est interdit
shallot [ʃə'lɒt, *Am:* -'lɑːt] *n* échalote *f*
shallow ['ʃæləʊ, *Am:* -oʊ] *adj* 1.(*not deep*) peu profond(e) 2.(*superficial*) superficiel(le)
shallowness *n no pl* manque *m* de profondeur
sham [ʃæm] *pej* I.*n* 1.(*fake*) imitation *f* 2.(*imposter*) imposteur *m* 3.(*lie*) imposture *f* 4.(*hypocrisy*) hypocrisie *f* 5.*no pl* (*pretense*) comédie *f* II.*adj* 1.(*false*) faux(fausse); (*marriage*) blanc(he) 2.(*pretending*) simulé(e) III.<-mm-> *vt* simuler IV.*vi* faire semblant
shamble ['ʃæmbl] *vi* traîner les pieds
shambles *n sing vb, inf* pagaille *f*
shambolic [ʃæm'bɒlɪk, *Am:* -'bɑːlɪk] *adj Brit, inf* bordélique
shame [ʃeɪm] I.*n no pl* 1.(*humiliation*) *a. iron* honte *f;* **to hang/bow one's head in** ~ baisser la tête de honte; **to feel a deep (sense of)** ~ éprouver un profond ressentiment; **to die of** ~ mourir de honte; **to feel no** ~ n'éprouver aucune honte; **to put sb to** ~ faire honte à qn; **to my ~ ...** honte à moi ...; **it's a crying ~ that** c'est une honte que +*subj;* **to bring ~ on sb** être une honte pour qn 2.(*pity*) dommage *m;* **what a ~ that** quel dommage que +*subj;* **it's a great ~ that** c'est vraiment dommage que +*subj* II.*interj* quelle honte! III.*vt* (*discredit*) discréditer
◆**shame into** *vt* **to shame sb/sth into doing sth** obliger qn/qc à faire qc
shamefaced *adj* honteux(-euse)
shameful *adj pej* honteux(-euse)
shameless *adj pej* 1.(*unashamed*) éhonté(e) 2.(*insolent*) effronté(e) 3.(*without decency*) sans pudeur
shammy ['ʃæmi] <-mies> *n inf,* **shammy leather** *n no pl, inf* peau *f* de chamois
shampoo [ʃæm'puː] I.*n* shampooing *m;* **~ and set** shampooing *m* mise en plis II.*vt* shampooiner
shamrock ['ʃæmrɒk, *Am:* -rɑːk] *n* trèfle *m*
shandy ['ʃændi] <-dies> *n Brit, Aus* panaché *m*
shank [ʃæŋk] *n* 1.(*shaft of tool*) manche *m* 2.(*leg*) jambe *f*
shanty ['ʃænti, *Am:* -t̬i] <-ties> *n* baraque *f*
shanty town *n* bidonville *m*
shape [ʃeɪp] I.*n* 1.(*outline*) forme *f;* **out of** ~ déformé(e); **to lose** ~ se déformer; **to take** ~ prendre forme; **in the ~ of sth** dans la forme de qc; **in any ~ or form** dans n'importe quelle forme; **to be oval in** ~ être de forme ovale; **to take the ~ of sb/sth** prendre la forme de qn/qc; **in all ~s and sizes** *fig* de toutes sortes 2.*no pl* (*condition*) forme *f;* **in bad/great** ~ en mauvaise/super forme; **to get back into** ~ retrouver la forme; **to be out of** ~ ne pas avoir la forme; **to be in no ~ to** +*infin* ne pas avoir la forme pour +*infin;* **to get into** ~ mettre en forme; **to knock** [*o Am* **lick**] **sb/sth into** ~ remettre qn/qc sur pied II.*vt* 1.(*form*) modeler; (*wood, stone*) tailler; **to ~ sth out of sth** modeler qc à partir de qc 2.*fig* former
SHAPE *n abbr of* **Supreme Headquarters Allied Powers Europe** SHAPE *m* (*quartier général des forces alliées de l'OTAN en Europe*)
shapeless *adj* informe
shapely <-ier, -iest> *adj* bien fait(e)
shard [ʃɑːd, *Am:* ʃɑːrd] *n* débris *m;* (*of metal, glass*) éclat *m;* (*of a bottle*) tesson *m*
share [ʃeəʳ, *Am:* ʃer] I.*n* 1.(*part*) part *f;* **to go ~s on sth** partager les frais pour qc; **to have one's (fair) ~ of sth** *a. iron* avoir sa part de qc; **to have more than one's (fair)** ~ avoir plus que sa part de qc 2.(*partial ownership*) action *f* II.*vi* partager ►**~ and ~ alike** à chacun sa part III.*vt* partager; **to ~ a birthday** avoir son anniversaire le même jour; **to ~ (common) characteristics** avoir des caractéristiques communes; **to want to ~ one's life with sb** vouloir partager la vie de qn
◆**share out** *vt* partager; **to share sth out among people** répartir qc parmi des personnes; **to share sth out between people** partager qc entre des personnes
share capital *n* capital *m* social **share certificate** *n* titre *m* d'action(s)
sharecropper ['ʃeəˌkrɒpəʳ, *Am:* 'ʃerˌkrɑːpɚ] *n* métayer, -ère *m, f*
sharecropping *n* métayage *m*
shareholder *n* actionnaire *mf* **share issue** *n* émission *f* des actions
share-out *n* partage *m* **shareware** *n no pl* INFOR partagiciel *m*
shark [ʃɑːk, *Am:* ʃɑːrk] <-(s)> *n* requin *m*

S

sharp [ʃɑːp, *Am:* ʃɑːrp] I. *adj* 1. (*pointed*) tranchant(e); (*pencil*) bien taillé(e) 2. (*angular: features, corner*) anguleux(-euse); (*nose, teeth*) pointu(e); (*edge, angle*) aigu(ë) 3. (*stabbing*) violent(e) 4. *fig* (*biting: critic, word, attack*) cinglant(e); (*look, eyes*) perçant(e); (*rebuke, reprimand*) sévère; (*tongue*) acéré(e) 5. (*piquant*) épicé(e) 6. ~ **practice** pratique *f* malhonnête 7. (*very cold*) pénétrant(e) 8. (*sudden*) brusque; (*deterioration, drop*) soudain(e) 9. (*abrupt*) abrupt(e) 10. (*marked*) marqué(e); ~ **left/right** virage *m* à gauche/droite 11. (*clear-cut*) net(te); **to bring into ~ focus** mettre au point 12. (*perceptive: mind*) vif(vive); (*question*) perspicace; **to have a ~ eye for sth** avoir l'œil pour qc; **to keep a ~ watch on sb/sth** observer d'un œil attentif qn/qc 13. *inf* (*trendy*) stylé(e) 14. MUS dièse *m;* **C ~** do *m* dièse II. *adv* **at twelve o'clock ~** à midi pile; **to make a ~ left** tourner à gauche toute III. *n* 1. (*tone above expected note*) dièse *m* 2. (*tone higher*) ton *m* au dessus

sharpen *vt* 1. (*make more cutting*) aiguiser; (*pencil*) tailler 2. (*strengthen*) aiguiser; (*debate, pain, fear*) aviver; (*skills*) affiner 3. (*improve distinctness*) rendre plus net(te) 4. (*increase perceptiveness*) affiner 5. MUS (*mark one tone higher*) diéser

sharpener *n* (*for pencil*) taille-crayon *m;* (*for knife*) aiguisoir *m*

sharper *n inf* tricheur, -euse *m, f*

sharp-eyed *adj* perspicace **sharp-featured** *adj* **to be ~** avoir les traits durs

sharpness *n no pl* 1. (*capacity of cutting*) tranchant *m;* (*of a pencil, needle*) pointe *f* 2. (*acutenesss: of a pain*) violence *f* 3. (*bitterness: of a comment*) âpreté *f* 4. (*suddenness*) brusquerie *f;* **the ~ of a curve** un virage brusque 5. (*steepness: of an incline*) escarpement *m* 6. (*intensity*) violence *f* 7. (*clarity*) netteté *f* 8. (*perceptiveness*) acuité *f;* (*of mind*) finesse *f* 9. (*chic*) stylé(e)

sharpshooter *n* tireur *m* d'élite **sharp-sighted** *adj* perspicace **sharp-tempered** *adj* coléreux(-euse) **sharp-tongued** *adj* **to be ~** avoir la langue acérée **sharp-witted** *adj* sagace

shat [ʃæt] *pt, pp of* **shit**

shatter I. *vt* briser en morceaux II. *vi* se briser en morceaux

shattering *adj* épuisant(e)

shatterproof [ˈʃætəpruːf, *Am:* ˈʃæt̬ɚ-] *adj* **~ windscreen** pare-brise *m* en verre sécurit®

shave [ʃeɪv] I. *n* rasage *m;* **to have a ~** se raser ►**to be a <u>close</u> ~** être juste; **to have a <u>close</u> ~** l'échapper de justesse II. *vi* se raser III. *vt* 1. (*remove body hair*) raser; **to ~ one's legs** se raser les jambes 2. (*decrease by stated amount*) réduire

shaven *adj* rasé(e); **~ head** crâne *m* rasé

shaver *n* rasoir *m*

shaving I. *adj* **a ~ cream/foam** une crème/mousse à raser; **~ brush** blaireau *m* II. *n* rasage *m*

shawl [ʃɔːl, *Am:* ʃɑːl] *n* châle *m*

she [ʃiː] I. *pers pron* (*female person or animal*) elle; **~'s my mother** c'est ma mère; **~'s gone away but ~'ll be back soon** elle est partie mais elle va revenir; **here ~ comes** la voilà; **there's a cow and ~'s hungry** voilà une vache et elle a faim; **her baby is a ~** son bébé est une fille; **~ who ...** *form* celle qui ... II. *prefix* **a ~-cat** une chatte; **a ~-devil** une diablesse

s/he *pers pron* (*he or she*) il/elle

sheaf [ʃiːf] <sheaves> *n* (*of corn, wheat*) gerbe *f;* (*of papers*) liasse *f*

shear [ʃɪəʳ, *Am:* ʃɪr] <sheared, sheared *o* shorn> I. *vt* 1. (*cut*) tondre; **to ~ sb's hair** se raser la tête 2. *fig* **to be shorn of sth** être dépouillé de qc II. *vi* TECH tondre

◆**shear off** I. *vt* 1. (*cut off*) tondre 2. (*tear off*) arracher II. *vi* se détacher

shearer *n* 1. (*person*) tondeur, -euse *m, f* 2. TECH tondeuse *f*

shearing *n no pl* tonte *f*

shears [ʃɪəz, *Am:* ʃɪrz] *npl* 1. (*pair of scissors*) cisailles *fpl* 2. (*for sheep*) tondeuse *f*

sheath [ʃiːθ] *n* 1. (*tightly fitting layer*) gaine *f* 2. (*knife covering*) étui *m* 3. *Brit* (*condom*) préservatif *m* 4. (*narrow dress*) fourreau *m*

sheathe [ʃiːð] *vt* 1. (*put in a sheath*) rengainer 2. (*overlay, cover*) recouvrir

sheathing *n* revêtement *m*

shebang [ʃɪˈbæŋ] *n no pl, Am, inf* **the whole ~** tout le fourbi

shed [ʃed] *n* abri *m*

sheet [ʃiːt] *n* INFOR feuille *f*

shelf [ʃelf] <-ves> *n* 1. (*storage*) étagère *f,* tablar(d) *m Suisse* 2. (*rock*) rebord *m* 3. ECON **off the ~** sous forme de stock ►**to be <u>on</u> the ~** *Brit, Aus, inf* (*abandoned*) être laissé pour compte; (*unmarried*) être vieille fille

shelf life *n no pl* durée *f* de conservation avant vente **shelf space** *n* rayonnage *m*

shell [ʃel] I. *n* 1. (*exterior*) coquille *f;* (*crab, tortoise*) carapace *f* 2. *no pl* (*rigid exterior*) caisse *f* 3. (*basic structure*) carcasse *f* 4. (*gun explosives*) cartouche *f;* (*artillery*) obus *m* 5. (*rowing boat*) canot *m* de compétition ►**to <u>bring</u> a child out of his/her ~** faire sortir un enfant de sa réserve; **to <u>come</u> out of one's ~** sortir de sa coquille; **to <u>crawl</u> into one's ~** se glisser à l'intérieur de sa coquille; *fig* se refermer sur soi-même II. *vt* 1. (*remove shell: nuts*) décortiquer; (*peas*) écosser 2. (*fire*) bombarder III. *vi* **to ~ easily** se laisser décortiquer

◆**shell out** *inf* I. *vt* casquer II. *vi* **to ~ for sb/sth** raquer pour qn/qc

shellac [ʃəˈlæk] *n* laque *f*

shell company *n* société *f* écran **shellfish** *n* crustacé *m* **shell hole** *n* trou *m* d'obus

shelling *n no pl* MIL bombardement *m*

shellproof *adj* blindé(e) **shell shock** *n* troubles *mpl* nerveux **shell-shocked** *adj* traumatisé(e)

shelter ['ʃeltəʳ, *Am:* -t̬ɚ] **I.** *n* **1.** (*building*) refuge *m;* (*from rain, bombs*) abri *m* **2.** *no pl* protection, refuge *m;* **to find ~** trouver refuge **3.** *fig* **tax ~** échappatoire *f* fiscale **II.** *vi* **1.** (*find protection*) s'abriter; **to ~ from sth** s'abriter de qc **2.** (*be a refugee*) se réfugier **III.** *vt* **1.** (*protect: from weather*) abriter **2.** (*give refuge: fugitive*) accueillir **3.** *fig* (*from truth*) protéger

sheltered *adj* **1.** (*against weather*) abrité(e) **2.** *fig* (*overprotected*) **to be ~** vivre dans un cocon

shelve¹ [ʃelv] *vt* **1.** (*place on a shelf*) mettre sur les rayons **2.** (*postpone: project*) mettre en suspens; (*elections, meeting*) ajourner

shelve² *vi* GEO descendre en pente douce

shelving *n no pl* rayonnage *m*

shenanigans [ʃɪ'nænɪgənz] *npl* manigances *fpl*

shepherd ['ʃepəd, *Am:* -ɚd] **I.** *n* **1.** (*person who rears sheep*) berger *m* **2.** REL pasteur *m* **II.** *vt* **1.** (*look after: sheep*) garder **2.** (*drive: animal, herd*) mener; (*people*) guider **3.** (*usher*) conduire

shepherdess <-es> *n* bergère *f*

shepherd's pie *n* hachis *m* parmentier

sherbet ['ʃɜ:bət, *Am:* 'ʃɜ:r-] *n* **1.** *no pl, Brit, Aus* (*sweet powder*) *poudre acidulée consommée en confiserie ou en boisson* **2.** *Am* (*sorbet*) sorbet *m*

sheriff ['ʃerɪf] *n* **1.** *Am* (*lawkeeper*) shérif *m* **2.** *Brit* (*county representative*) shérif *m* **3.** *Scot* (*judge*) juge *m* du tribunal de grande instance

sherry ['ʃeri] <-rries> *n* xérès *m*

Shetland Islands, Shetlands ['ʃetləndz] *n* **the ~** les Shetland *fpl;* **South ~** les Shetland du Sud

shield [ʃi:ld] **I.** *n* **1.** (*defence*) bouclier *m;* **protective ~** plaque *f* de protection **2.** (*protective layer*) protection *f* **3.** (*with heraldic arms*) blason *m* **4.** (*with logo*) écusson *m* **5.** (*prize*) plaque *f* **6.** *Am* (*police badge*) plaque *f* **II.** *vt* protéger; **to ~ sb from sth** protéger qn de qc; **to ~ one's hands** se protéger les mains

shift [ʃɪft] **I.** *vt* **1.** (*rearrange*) changer de place; (*blame*) rejeter; **to ~ one's ground** changer d'avis **2.** *Am* (*mechanics: gears/lanes*) changer de **3.** (*hurry*) **to ~ oneself** se dépêcher **4.** *Brit, Aus, inf* (*dispose of*) se débarrasser de; (*stains*) enlever **II.** *vi* **1.** (*rearrange position*) changer de place; (*wind*) tourner; **to ~ into reverse** *Am* passer en marche arrière **2.** *inf* (*move over*) se pousser **3.** *inf* (*move very fast*) aller très vite **III.** *n* **1.** (*alteration*) modification *f* **2.** (*period of work*) poste *m*, durée *f* de travail d'une équipe; **to work in ~s** faire les postes; **night/day ~** poste de jour/de nuit **3.** (*people working a shift*) équipe *f;* **to be on the night/day ~** travailler dans l'équipe de jour/de nuit

shifting *adj* qui se déplace; (*values, belief*) changeant(e); **~ sands** sables *mpl* mouvants; **the ~ sands of sth** la versatilité de qc

shift key *n* touche *f* de majuscule

shiftless *adj pej* (*idle*) fainéant(e)

shift work *n no pl* travail *m* posté **shift worker** *n* travailleur, -euse *m, f* posté(e)

shifty ['ʃɪfti] <-ier, -iest> *adj* fourbe; **~ eyes** regard *m* fuyant; (*look*) sournois(e)

Shiite ['ʃi:aɪt] **I.** *adj* chiite **II.** *n* Chiite *mf*

shilling ['ʃɪlɪŋ] *n* shilling *m; s. a.* **pound**

shilly-shally ['ʃɪliʃæli] *vi pej, inf* se tâter

shimmer ['ʃɪməʳ, *Am:* -ɚ] **I.** *vi* chatoyer **II.** *n no pl* **1.** (*flickering*) scintillement *m* **2.** (*diffused: sound*) sonorité *f* vacillante

shin [ʃɪn] *n* **1.** (*below knee*) tibia *m* **2.** *no pl* (*beef*) jarret *m*

◆**shin down** <-nn-> *vi* dégringoler lestement

◆**shin up** <-nn-> *vi* grimper lestement

shindig ['ʃɪndɪg] *n inf* (*loud party*) fête *f* joyeuse

shine [ʃaɪn] **I.** *n no pl* éclat *m* ►**rain or ~** par tous les temps; **to take a ~ to sb** s'amouracher de qn **II.** <shone *o* shined, shone *o* shined> *vi* **1.** (*emit, reflect light*) briller; (*brightly*) étinceler; (*light*) illuminer **2.** (*excel*) être une lumière; **to ~ at foreign languages** exceller en langues étrangères **3.** (*be obvious*) **to ~ through many actions** se dévoiler par ses actions; **his courage doesn't ~ out of him** il brille par son absence de courage **III.** <shone *o* shined, shone *o* shined> *vt* **1.** (*point light*) braquer une lumière sur **2.** (*polish*) faire reluire; (*shoes*) faire briller

◆**shine out** *vi* (*easily seen*) **to ~ of sb** émaner de qn

shiner *n inf* œil *m* poché

shingle ['ʃɪŋgl] *n* **1.** *no pl* (*pebble*) caillou *m;* (*beach*) plage *f* de galets **2.** (*tiles*) bardeau *m*

shingles *n no pl* MED zona *m*

shining *adj* **1.** (*polished*) reluisant(e) **2.** (*bright: eyes*) brillant(e) **3.** (*outstanding*) resplendissant(e); (*example*) parfait

shiny <-ier, -iest> *adj* brillant(e); (*metal*) luisant(e)

ship [ʃɪp] **I.** *n* bateau *m;* (*merchant*) cargo *m;* (*passenger*) paquebot *m;* (*sailing*) voilier *m;* **a ~'s papers** papiers *mpl* de bord; **to board a ~** embarquer; **by ~** en/par bateau **II.** *vt* <-pp-> **1.** (*send by boat*) expédier par bateau; (*freight*) charger **2.** (*transport*) transporter

◆**ship off** *vt* expédier par bateau

◆**ship out** *vt* envoyer par bateau

shipboard *adj* à bord d'un navire **shipbuilder** *n* constructeur *m* de navires **shipbuilding** *n no pl* construction *f* navale **shipload** *n* cargaison *f* **shipmate** *n* camarade *m* de bord

shipment *n* **1.** (*freight*) chargement *m* **2.** *no pl* (*action*) fret *m*

shipowner *n* propriétaire *mf* de bateau

shipper *n* **1.** (*transportation*) affréteur *m* **2.** (*organisation*) expéditeur, -trice *m, f*

shipping *n no pl* **1.** (*ships*) navires *mpl*

S

2. (*freight*) expédition *f*

shipping agency *n* agence *f* maritime **shipping agent** *n* agent *m* maritime **shipping company** *n* compagnie *f* de navigation **shipping department** *n* service *m* des expéditions **shipping expenses** *n* frais *mpl* d'expédition **shipping lane** *n* voie *f* de navigation **shipping line** *n* compagnie *f* de navigation **shipping note** *n* note *f* de chargement **shipping routes** *npl* routes *fpl* de navigation

ship's chandler *n* fournisseur *m* d'équipement maritime

shipshape ['ʃɪpʃeɪp] *adj inf* bien rangé(e); **to get ~** mettre en ordre

shipway *n* canal *m* maritime **shipwreck** I. *n* 1. (*accident*) naufrage *m* 2. (*remains*) épave *f* II. *vt* 1. (*sink*) faire couler; **to be ~ed** faire naufrage 2. *fig* ruiner **shipwright** *n* constructeur *m* de navires **shipyard** *n* chantier *m* maritime

shire horse *n* cheval *m* de gros trait

shirk [ʃɜːk, *Am:* ʃɜːrk] *pej* I. *vt* (*duty, obligation*) manquer à; **to ~ doing sth** se défiler devant qc II. *vi* **to ~ from sth** se débiner devant qc

shirker *n pej* flemmard(e) *m(f)*

shirt [ʃɜːt, *Am:* ʃɜːrt] *n* chemise *f;* **short-/long-sleeved ~** chemise à manches courtes/longues ►**to give sb the ~ off one's back** donner à qn jusqu'à sa dernière chemise; **he lost his ~ at this game** il a tout perdu à ce jeu; **to put one's ~ on sth** jouer tout ce que l'on possède sur qc

shirt collar *n* col *m* de chemise **shirt front** *n* plastron *m*

shirting *n* toile *f* pour chemise

shirt sleeve *n* manche *f* de chemise; **to be in ~s** être en bras de chemise ►**to roll up one's ~s** remonter ses manches

shirty <-ier, -iest> *adj Brit, Aus, pej, inf* en rogne

shit [ʃɪt] *pej* I. *n no pl, inf* 1. (*faeces*) merde *f;* **to have** [*o Am* **take**] **a ~** chier 2. *pej* (*nonsense*) connerie *f* 3. (*annoyed*) **to get a lot of ~ about sth** être emmerdé à propos de qc 4. (*unfairness*) **don't take** (**any**) **~ from him!** ne te laisse pas faire par lui! 5. (*anything*) **to not give a ~ about anything** se foutre de tout 6. (*things*) saloperies *fpl* 7. (*cannabis*) shit *m* ►**to have ~ for brains** être con comme un balai; **big ~!** quel merdier!; **to be up ~**(**s**) **creek** (**without a paddle**) être dans la merde; **to beat the ~ out of sb** taper qn comme un fou; **when** (**the**) **~ flies** quand la merde nous tombera dessus; **to frighten the ~ out of sb** flanquer la frousse à qn; **no ~!** merde alors! II. *interj* merde! III. <-tt-, shit *o* shitted *o* shat, shit *o* shitted *o* shat> *vi* chier IV. <-tt-, shit *o* shitted *o* shat, shit *o* shitted *o* shat> *vt Am* **to ~ oneself** chier dans son froc; **to ~ bricks** se chier dessus

shite [ʃaɪt] *n Brit, pej, inf* 1. (*person*) chiant(e) *m(f)* 2. *no pl* (*rubbish*) ordures *fpl*

shitty ['ʃɪti, *Am:* 'ʃɪt̬-] <-ier, -iest> *adj pej, inf* 1. (*bad, worthless*) merdique 2. (*contemptible*) dégueulasse 3. (*dirty*) dégueulasse 4. (*sick*) **to feel ~** se sentir mal

shiver ['ʃɪvəʳ, *Am:* -ɚ] I. *n* 1. (*tremble*) frisson *m;* **to feel a ~** frissonner; **a ~ goes** (**up and**) **down sb's spine** avoir froid dans le dos; **to send ~s** (**up and**) **down sb's spine** donner des sueurs froides à qn 2. *pl* (*state*) tremblement *m;* **to give sb the ~s** *inf* faire peur à qn II. *vi* frissonner; **to ~ with cold/like a leaf** trembler de froid/comme une feuille

shivery <-ier, -iest> *adj* frissonnant(e); **to feel ~** se sentir fiévreux

shoal [ʃəʊl, *Am:* ʃoʊl] *n* 1. (*shallow water*) bas-fond *m* 2. (*sand bank*) banc *m* de sable 3. (*fish*) banc *m* de poissons; **in ~s** en bande 4. *fig* (*many*) multitude *f;* (*of people*) foule *f;* **they came in ~s** ils sont venus en masse

shock[1] [ʃɒk, *Am:* ʃɑːk] I. *n* 1. (*unpleasant surprise*) choc *m;* **it was a ~ to the system!** ça m'a secoué!; **to come as a ~ to sb** bouleverser qn; **to get a ~** être surpris 2. *inf* (*electric shock*) décharge *f* 3. *no pl* (*health condition*) état *m* de choc; **to suffer from ~** souffrir d'un traumatisme 4. *no pl* (*jarring*) secousse *f* II. *vt* choquer

shock[2] [ʃɒk, *Am:* ʃɑːk] *n no pl* tignasse *f*

shock absorber *n* amortisseur *m*

shocker *n inf* 1. (*which affronts: film*) film *m* à sensations; (*novel*) roman *m* à sensations; **this song was made to be a ~** cette chanson devait faire sensation 2. (*person*) **to be a ~** être impossible

shock-headed *adj* qui porte une tignasse

shocking *adj* 1. (*scandalous*) choquant(e) 2. (*very bad*) atroce; (*accident*) terrible; (*crime*) odieux(-euse); (*weather, conditions*) épouvantable 3. (*causing distress: news, scene*) bouleversant(e); (*truth*) terrible 4. (*surprising*) étonnant(e)

shocking pink *n* rose *m* bonbon

shockproof *adj* 1. (*undamageable*) résistant(e) aux chocs 2. (*insulated*) isolé(e)

shock therapy, **shock treatment** *n* traitement *m* par électrochoc **shock troops** *npl* troupes *fpl* d'assaut **shock wave** *n* onde *f* de choc

shod [ʃɒd] I. *pt, pp of* **shoe** II. *adj* chaussé(e)

shoddy <-ier, -iest> *adj pej* 1. (*poorly produced*) de mauvaise qualité 2. (*disrespectful*) méprisable

shoe [ʃuː] I. *n* 1. (*foot covering*) chaussure *f,* soulier *m Québec;* **to do up the ~s** lacer ses chaussures; **flat/high-heeled ~s** chaussures plates/à talons hauts; **to put on/take off ~s** se chausser/se déchausser 2. (*horseshoe*) fer *m* ►**if I were in your ~s** *inf* si j'étais à votre place; **to fill sb's ~s** prendre la place de qn; **to shake in one's ~s** avoir une peur bleue II. <shod *o Am* shoed, shod *o Am* shoed> *vt* (*horse*) ferrer

shoeblack *n Brit* cireur *m* de chaussures **shoehorn** I. *n* chausse-pied *m* II. *vt* résumer **shoelace** *n* lacet *m* de chaussure; **to tie one's ~s** lacer ses chaussures **shoemaker** *n* cordonnier *m* **shoe polish** *n* cirage *m* **shoe-repair shop** *n* cordonnerie *f* **shoeshine** *n Am* (*shoe cleaning*) cirage *m* de chaussures **shoeshine boy** *n Am* (*shoe cleaner*) cireur *m* de chaussures **shoeshop** *n* magasin *m* de chaussures **shoe size** *n* pointure *f* **shoestore** *n* magasin *m* de chaussures **shoestring** *n Am* (*shoelaces*) lacet *m* de chaussures ►**to do sth on a ~** *inf* faire qc avec très peu d'argent **shoe tree** *n* forme *f*

shone [ʃɒn, *Am:* ʃoʊn] *pt, pp of* **shine**

shoo [ʃuː] I. *interj inf* ouste! II. *vi inf* (*drive away*) chasser

shook [ʃʊk] *n pt of* **shake**

shoot [ʃuːt] I. *n* 1. (*hunting activity*) partie *f* de chasse 2. CINE tournage *m* 3. PHOT séance *f* photo 4. (*buds*) pousse *f* II. *interj* mince alors! III. <shot, shot> *vi* 1. (*fire a bullet*) tirer; **to ~ at sb/sth** tirer sur qn/qc; **to ~ on sight** tirer à vue 2. CINE tourner 3. PHOT prendre des photos 4. (*move rapidly*) filer; **to ~ in/out of the house** se précipiter dans/hors de la maison; **to ~ to fame** devenir célèbre du jour au lendemain; **to ~ (the) rapids** descendre les rapides; **to ~ ahead** prendre la tête; **to ~ ahead of sb** passer devant qn 5. *Am* (*aim*) **to ~ for sth** viser qc 6. BOT pousser 7. SPORT tirer ►**to ~ from the hip** parler sans réfléchir; **to ~ for the moon** demander la lune; **to be shot through with haste** être bâclé IV. <shot, shot> *vt* 1. (*discharge weapon: person*) tirer sur; (*animal*) chasser; **to ~ sb dead** tuer qn; **he was shot** on lui a tiré dessus 2. (*film*) tourner 3. (*photograph*) photographier 4. *fig* (*direct*) **to ~ questions at sb** mitrailler qn de questions 5. *Am* SPORT (*goal, baskets*) marquer; **to ~ pool** faire une partie de billard 6. *inf* (*inject: heroin*) se piquer à ►**to ~ one's bolt** être épuisé; *fig* jouer sa dernière carte; **to ~ the breeze** *inf* parler de la pluie et du beau temps; **to ~ darts at sb** *inf* mitrailler qn du regard; **to ~ oneself in the foot** *inf* se causer du tort à soi même; **to ~ the works** *Am, inf* tenter le tout pour le tout

◆**shoot away** *vi* 1. (*fire*) continuer à tirer 2. (*say*) **~!** allez, dis-le!

◆**shoot down** *vt* 1. (*kill: person*) descendre 2. (*bring down: airplane*) abattre 3. *inf* (*refute*) descendre; **to be shot down in flames** être descendu en flammes

◆**shoot off** I. *vt* (*gun*) décharger ►**to shoot one's mouth off** *inf* ne pas s'empêcher d'ouvrir son bec II. *vi* partir en trombe

◆**shoot out** I. *vi* (*flame, water*) jaillir; (*person, car*) partir en trombe II. *vt* **to shoot it out** *inf* avoir un règlement de compte; **to ~ one's tongue** tirer la langue

◆**shoot past** I. *vi* passer en trombe II. *vt* passer en trombe devant; **to ~ the traffic lights** griller le feu rouge

◆**shoot up** I. *vi* 1. (*grow rapidly*) pousser vite 2. (*increase rapidly*) monter en flèche; (*rocket, skyscraper*) s'élever 3. *inf* (*inject*) se shooter II. *vt* (*person*) tirer sur; (*building*) mitrailler; **to be shot up** recevoir des balles

shooting I. *n no pl* 1. (*act, killing*) fusillade *f* 2. (*firing*) tirs *mpl* 3. (*hunting*) chasse *f* 4. (*sport*) tir *m* 5. CINE tournage *m* 6. PHOT séance *f* photo II. *adj* (*pain*) lancinant(e)

shooting box *n* pavillon *m* de chasse **shooting gallery** *n* stand *m* de tir **shooting jacket** *n* gilet *m* de chasse **shooting lodge** *n* pavillon *m* de chasse **shooting range** *n* champ *m* de tir **shooting script** *n* scénario *m* **shooting season** *n* saison *f* de la chasse **shooting star** *n a. fig* étoile *f* filante **shooting war** *n* guerre *f* chaude

shop [ʃɒp, *Am:* ʃɑːp] I. *n* 1. (*boutique, emporium*) magasin *m*; **record ~** magasin de disques; **to go to the ~s** aller faire les courses; **to set up ~** ouvrir un magasin; **to set up ~ as a baker** ouvrir une boulangerie; **to set up ~ on one's own** se mettre à son compte 2. *Brit, Aus* (*process of buying goods*) courses *fpl*; **to do the weekly ~** faire les courses de la semaine 3. (*manufacturing area*) atelier *m*; **repair/assembly ~** atelier de réparation/de montage ►**all over the ~** *inf* (*everywhere*) partout; (*in confusion*) en pagaille II. <-pp-> *vi* faire ses courses; **to ~ for sth** aller acheter qc; **to ~ at the market/at Marks and Spencers** faire ses courses au marché/chez Marks and Spencer

shopaholic *n personne qui adore faire du lèche-vitrine* **shop assistant** *n Brit* vendeur, -euse *m, f* **shopbreaking** *n acte de vandalisme commis contre les magasins* **shopfitter** *n* agenceur *m* de magasins **shopfittings** *npl* agencements *mpl* de magasins **shop floor** *n* 1. (*factory*) atelier *m* 2. (*workers*) ouvriers *mpl* **shop front** *n* vitrine *f* de magasin **shop girl** *n Brit* vendeuse *f* **shopkeeper** *n* commerçant(e) *m(f)* **shoplifter** *n* voleur, -euse *m, f* à l'étalage **shoplifting** *n* vol *m* à l'étalage

shopper *n* personne *f* qui fait ses courses

shopping *n no pl* 1. (*purchasing*) courses *fpl*, magasinage *m Québec*; (*Christmas*) achats *mpl*; **to do the ~** faire les courses, magasiner *Québec*; **to go ~** aller faire les courses; **to go on a ~ binge** dévaliser les magasins 2. (*items purchased*) achats *mpl*

shopping arcade *n* galerie *f* marchande **shopping bag** *n* 1. *Brit* (*for goods*) sac *m* à provisions; **string ~** filet *m* à provisions 2. *Am* (*carrier bag*) grand sac *m* **shopping cart** *n Am* (*shopping trolley*) chariot *m* de supermarché **shopping center** *n* centre *m* commercial, centre *m* d'achats *Québec* **shopping list** *n* liste *f* des achats à faire **shopping mall** *n Am, Aus* (*shopping centre*)

grand centre *m* commercial **shopping street** *n* rue *f* commerçante **shopping trolley** *n Brit* chariot *m* de supermarché
shop-soiled *adj Brit, Aus* defraîchi(e) **shop steward** *n* délégué(e) *m(f)* syndical(e) **shop talk** *n no pl* discussion *f* de travail **shopwalker** *n* chef *m* de rayon **shop window** *n* (*display*) vitrine *f* **shopworn** *adj* **1.** *Am* (*shopsoiled*) défraîchi(e) **2.** (*tedious*) rassi(e)
shore [ʃɔːʳ, *Am:* ʃɔːr] **I.** *n* **1.** (*coast*) côte *f* **2.** (*beach*) plage *f*; **from** (**the**) ~ du bord de la mer; **on** ~ sur le rivage **II.** *vt a. fig* ~ (**up**) étayer
shore leave *n* permission *f* à terre **shoreline** *n* littoral *m*
shorn [ʃɔːn, *Am:* ʃɔːrn] *pp of* **shear**
short [ʃɔːt, *Am:* ʃɔːrt] **I.** *adj* **1.** (*not long*) court(e); **to be** ~ **for sth** être à court de qc **2.** (*not tall*) petit(e) **3.** (*not far: distance*) pas très loin; **at** ~ **range** à courte portée **4.** (*brief*) bref(brève); (*memory*) court(e); **at** ~ **notice** dans un bref délai; **in the** ~ **term** à court terme; ~ **and sweet** aussi rapide qu'un éclair **5.** (*not enough*) **to be in** ~ **supply of sth** manquer de qc; **to be** ~ **on brains** ne pas en avoir beaucoup dans la cervelle; **to be** ~ **of breath** être essoufflé; **to be** ~ (**of cash**) *inf* être sur la corde raide; **to be** ~ **of space** être à l'étroit; **to be** ~ **of time** ne pas avoir assez de temps **6. to be** ~ **with sb** manquer de patience avec qn ▶**the** ~ **answer is 'no'** en un mot c'est 'non'; **to have a** ~ **fuse** démarrer au quart de tour; **to get** ~ **shrift from sb** se faire envoyer sur les roses; **to make** ~ **shrift of sth** ne pas traîner avec qc; **to draw the** ~ **straw** tirer à la courte paille; **to make** ~ **work of sb** ne faire qu'une bouchée de qn; **to make** ~ **work of sth** se dépêcher de faire qc **II.** *n* **1.** CINE (*genre*) court métrage *m* **2.** *inf* ELEC court-circuit *m* **3.** *Brit, inf* (*alcohol*) alcool *m* fort **III.** *adv* (*to stop*) net; **to stop** ~ **of doing sth** se retenir de faire qc; **to cut** ~ abréger; **to cut sb** ~ couper la parole à qn; **to go** ~ **of sth** manquer de qc; **to run** ~ **of sth** se trouver à court de qc; **to be caught short** être pris d'un besoin pressant; (*need money*) être à court d'argent ▶**in** ~ en bref
shortage [ˈʃɔːtɪdʒ, *Am:* ˈʃɔːrt̬ɪdʒ] *n* pénurie *f*
shortbread, **shortcake** *n no pl* sablé *m* **short-change** *vt* **1.** (*return insufficient change*) ne pas rendre assez de monnaie à **2.** *inf* **to be** ~**d** être dupé **short circuit I.** *n* court-circuit *m* **II.** *vi* se mettre en court-circuit **III.** *vt* **to short-circuit 1.** (*create wrong current flow*) court-circuiter **2.** (*reduce time*) diminuer **shortcoming** *n* défauts *mpl* **shortcrust**, **shortcrust pastry** *n no pl* pâte *f* brisée **short cut** *n* **1.** INFOR raccourci *m* **2.** *fig* solution *f* de facilité **short-dated** *n* FIN à courte échéance
shorten [ˈʃɔːtən, *Am:* ˈʃɔːr-] **I.** *vt* raccourcir; (*story*) abréger **II.** *vi* **1.** (*make shorter*) raccourcir **2.** (*reduce odds*) s'affaiblir
shortening[1] *n no pl, Am, Aus* raccourcissement *m*
shortening[2] *n* GASTR matière *f* grasse
shortfall *n* FIN déficit *m* **short film** *n* court-métrage *m*
shorthand *n no pl, Brit, Aus, Can* sténo(graphie) *f*; **to do** ~ faire de la sténo; **in** ~ en sténo; ~ **pad** bloc-notes *m* ▶**which is** ~ **for ...** ce qui en gros veut dire ...
short-handed *adj* **to be** ~ être en sous-effectif **shorthand notebook** *n* bloc-notes *m* **shorthand notes** *npl* notes *fpl* en sténo **shorthand typist** *n Aus, Brit* sténo(graphe) *mf*
short-haul *adj* **1.** (*short distance: flight, route*) court-courrier *inv* **2.** (*short-term: effort*) à court terme **short-haul jet** *n* avion *m* court-courrier **short-list** *vt* sélectionner **short-lived** *adj* (*happiness*) de courte durée
shortly *adv* peu de temps
shortness *n no pl* **1.** (*being short*) petite taille *f* **2.** (*brevity*) brièveté *f* **3.** (*insufficiency*) manque *m* **4.** MED (*of breath*) essoufflement *m*
short order *n Am* formule *f* rapide **short-order dish** *n* formule *f* rapide **short pastry** *n* pâte *f* brisée **short-range** *adj* **1.** MIL (*missile*) de courte portée **2.** (*not long-range: estimate, weather forecast*) à court terme
shorts *npl* **1.** (*short trousers*) short *m*; **a pair of** ~ un short **2.** *Am* (*underpants*) caleçon *m*
short-sighted *adj* **1.** (*myopic*) myope **2.** (*not prudent*) imprévoyant(e) **short-sleeved** *adj* à manches courtes **short-staffed** *adj Aus, Brit* **to be** ~ être en sous-effectif **short-stay parking** *n* parking *m* de courte durée **short story** *n* nouvelle *f* **short story writer** *n* nouvelliste *mf* **short-tempered** *adj* coléreux(-euse) **short-term** *adj* (*loan, policy, memory*) à court terme **short time** *n* chômage *m* partiel **short wave** *n* ondes *fpl* courtes; **short-wave signal** signal *m* en ondes courtes; **short-wave radio/receiver** radio *f*/récepteur *m* à ondes courtes **short-winded** *adj* essoufflé(e)
shot[1] [ʃɒt, *Am:* ʃɑːt] **I.** *n* **1.** (*firing weapon*) coup *m* (de feu) **2.** SPORT poids *m*; **to put the** ~ lancer le poids **3.** (*attempt at scoring*) tir *m* **4.** (*throw*) lancement *m* **5.** *no pl* (*shotgun ammunition*) plomb *m* **6.** (*photograph*) photo *f*; **to get a** ~ **of sth** prendre qc en photo **7.** CINE plan *m*; **to get a** ~ **of sth** filmer qc **8.** *inf* MED piqûre *f*; (*of heroin*) shoot *m*; **to give sb a** ~ faire une piqûre à qn **9.** *inf* (*try*) essai *m*; **to get/have a** ~ **at sth** essayer qc; **to give sth one's best** ~ faire de son mieux; **give it a** ~! essaie! **10.** (*small amount of alcohol*) petit verre *m* ▶~ **in the arm** un coup de pouce; **to take a** ~ **in the dark** *inf* répondre au pif; **to be a good** ~ être un joli coup; **to be a poor** ~ être un coup médiocre; **like a** ~ *inf* comme une flèche **II.** *pp, pt of* **shoot**
shot[2] [ʃɒt, *Am:* ʃɑːt] *adj* **1.** (*woven to show colours: silk*) à reflets; **to be** ~ **with silver** avoir des reflets argentés **2.** *inf* (*worn out*)

foutu(e) ►**to** <u>**be**</u>/<u>**get**</u> **~ of sb/sth** se débarrasser de qn/qc

shotgun *n* fusil *m* de chasse **shot-put** *n* SPORT **the ~** le lancer du poids **shot-putter** *n* lanceur, -euse *m, f* de poids

should [ʃʊd] *aux* **1.** (*advisability, expectation*) **I/you ~** je/tu devrais; **to insist that one ~ do sth** insister pour que qn fasse qc *subj* **2.** (*asking for advice*) **~ I ...?** est-ce que je dois ...? **3.** (*might*) **for fear that sb/sth ~ ...** si jamais qn/qc ...; **if I ~ fall** au cas où je tomberais **4.** *form* (*would*) **I ~ like ...** je voudrais ...

shoulder ['ʃəʊldəʳ, *Am:* 'ʃoʊldɚ] **I.** *n* **1.** (*body part*) épaule *f* **2.** FASHION épaule *f;* **padded ~s** épaulettes *fpl* **3.** GASTR épaule *f* **4.** (*side of a road*) accotement *m;* **hard ~** bande *f* d'arrêt d'urgence **5.** (*shoulder-like part: of a mountain*) crête *f* ►**a ~ to** <u>**cry**</u> **on** une épaule pour pleurer; **to** <u>**rest**</u> **on sb's ~s** se reposer sur qn; **~** <u>**to**</u> **~** côte à côte; **to fight ~** <u>**to**</u> **~ with sb** se battre ensemble **II.** *vt* **1.** (*move one's shoulders*) pousser de l'épaule; **to ~ one's way** se frayer un chemin à coups d'épaules **2.** (*place on shoulders*) porter sur ses épaules **3.** (*accept: responsibility*) endosser

shoulder bag *n* sac *m* à bandoulière **shoulder blade** *n* omoplate *f* **shoulder pad** *n* épaulette *f* **shoulder strap** *n* (*of dress*) bretelle *f;* (*of bag*) bandoulière *f*

shout [ʃaʊt] **I.** *n* **1.** (*loud cry*) cri *m;* **~ of laughter** éclat *m* de rire **2.** *Aus, Brit, inf* (*round of drinks*) tournée *f* ►**to** <u>**give**</u> **sb a ~** *inf* engueuler qn; (*phone*) passer un coup de fil à qn **II.** *vi* **to ~ at sb** crier après qn; **to ~ for help** crier à l'aide ►**to** <u>**give**</u> **sb sth to ~ about** donner à qn l'occasion de se réjouir; **there's nothing to ~ about** il n'y a pas de quoi en faire un plat **III.** *vt* **1.** (*yell: slogan, warning*) crier; **to ~ abuse at sb** insulter qn; **to ~ oneself hoarse** perdre la voix en criant **2.** *Aus, inf* **to ~ sb a drink** payer un pot à qn

◆**shout down** *vt* faire taire qn en criant plus fort

◆**shout out** *vt* crier

shouting *n no pl* cris *mpl* ►**in ~** <u>**distance**</u> **of sth** à portée de voix de qc; *fig* tout près de qc

shove [ʃʌv] **I.** *n* poussée *f;* **to give sth a ~** pousser qc **II.** *vt* pousser; **to ~ sb/sth forward** pousser qn/qc en avant; **to ~ sb/sth aside** pousser qn/qc de côté; **to ~ sb around** bousculer qn; **to ~ sth in sth** fourrer qc dans qc; **to ~ one's way through sth** se frayer un chemin dans qc en poussant **III.** *vi* pousser; **to ~ along/over** se pousser

◆**shove off** *vi* **1.** *inf* (*go away*) se casser **2.** (*launch by foot/oar*) pousser au large

shovel ['ʃʌvəl] **I.** *n* **1.** (*tool*) pelle *f* **2.** (*quantity*) pelletée *f* **II.** <*Brit* -ll- *o Am* -l-> *vt* pelleter; (*food into one's mouth*) enfourner **III.** <*Brit* -ll- *o Am* -l-> *vi* se goinfrer

show [ʃəʊ, *Am:* ʃoʊ] **I.** *n* **1.** (*demonstration*) démonstration *f* **2.** (*false demonstration*) semblant *m;* **just for ~** pour impressionner **3.** (*exhibition: of fashion*) défilé *m;* (*of photographs*) exposition *f;* **dog ~** exposition canine; **to be on ~** être exposé **4.** (*play*) spectacle *m;* **puppet ~** spectacle de marionnettes **5.** TV émission *f;* **radio ~** émission de radio **6.** CINE séance *f;* **the film ~ starts at 8:30** la séance de cinéma est à 20h30 **7.** *inf* (*business*) affaires *fpl* ►**on a ~ of** <u>**hands**</u> à main levée; **let's get the ~ on the** <u>**road**</u> *inf* au boulot; **to put on a** <u>**good**</u> **~** bien se défendre; **to** <u>**make**</u> **a ~ of doing sth** faire semblant de faire qc; **the ~** <u>**must**</u> **go on** *prov* la vie continue **II.** <showed, shown> *vt* **1.** (*display: flag, way*) montrer; **to ~ signs of sth** donner des signes de qc; **to ~ one's work** ART exposer ses œuvres; **to ~ slides** faire une séance diapos; **to ~ sb over a place** *Aus, Brit* faire visiter un endroit à qn; **to ~ sb how to** +*infin* montrer à qn comment +*infin* **2.** (*express: bias, enthusiasm*) montrer; (*clemency, courage, initiative*) faire preuve de; **to ~ sb respect** montrer du respect pour qn **3.** (*record*) enregistrer; (*statistics*) montrer; (*a loss*) faire apparaître **4.** (*escort*) raccompagner; **will you ~ Mr Brown to the door?** vous voulez bien raccompagner M. Brown jusqu'à la porte? **5.** (*project: film, TV drama*) passer; **it's ~ing at the Odeon** il passe à l'Odeon ►**to ~ sb the** <u>**door**</u> virer qn; **to dare (to) ~ one's** <u>**face**</u> oser se montrer; **to ~ one's** <u>**hand**</u> montrer son jeu; **to ~ the** <u>**way**</u> **(forward)** montrer la voie; **he has nothing to ~ for his** <u>**efforts**</u> il n'a pas été récompensé pour ses efforts; **that** <u>**will**</u> **~ him/them** *inf* ça lui/leur apprendra **III.** *vi* <showed, shown> **1.** (*be visible*) se voir **2.** *Am, Aus, inf* (*arrive*) arriver **3.** (*be shown: film*) passer

◆**show in** *vt* faire entrer

◆**show off** **I.** *vt* exhiber **II.** *vi* frimer

◆**show out** *vt* raccompagner

◆**show up** **I.** *vi* **1.** (*appear*) ressortir **2.** *inf* (*arrive*) venir **II.** *vt* **1.** (*expose*) **to show sb up as (being) sth** révéler qn comme qc **2.** (*embarrass*) faire honte à

showbiz *n no pl, inf abbr of* **show business** showbiz *m* **showboat** *n Am* bateau-théâtre *m* **show-business** *n no pl* show-business *m* **showcase** **I.** *n* vitrine *f* **II.** *vt* présenter; (*talent*) exposer **showdown** *n* confrontation *f*

shower ['ʃaʊəʳ, *Am:* 'ʃaʊɚ] **I.** *n* **1.** (*brief fall: of rain, snow, hail*) averse *f;* (*of stones*) volée *f;* (*of sparks*) pluie *f;* **heavy ~** grosse averse; **thundery ~** averse orageuse **2.** (*spray*) **to bring a ~ of praise upon sb** encenser qn **3.** (*washing device*) douche *f;* **to be in the ~** être sous la douche; **to have a ~** prendre une douche **4.** *Am* (*party*) *célébration d'enterrement de vie de jeune fille ou fête organisée pour la naissance d'un bébé* **II.** *vt* **1.** (*cover*) **a.** *fig* couvrir; **to ~ sb with sth** couvrir qn de qc **2.** (*spray*) verser; (*missiles*) pilonner **III.** *vi* **1.** (*have a shower*) prendre une douche **2.** *fig*

to ~ **over sb/sth** pleuvoir sur qn/qc
♦**shower down** *vt* **1.** (*fall*) tomber **2.** *fig* pleuvoir

shower bath *n* douche *f* **shower cabinet** *n* cabine *f* de douche **shower cap** *n* bonnet *m* de douche **shower curtain** *n* rideau *m* de douche **shower gel** *n* gel *m* douche

showery ['ʃaʊəri, *Am:* 'ʃaʊɚi] *adj* pluvieux(-euse)

show flat *n* appartement-témoin *m* **showgirl** *n* girl *f* **show home**, **show house** *n* *Brit* villa-témoin *f*

showiness *n no pl* ostentation *f*

showing *n* **1.** (*exhibition*) exposition *f* **2.** (*broadcasting*) diffusion *f* **3.** (*performance*) performance *f*

showing-off *n* épate *f*

showjumping *n no pl* concours *m* de saut d'obstacles **showman** *n* forain *m* **showmanship** *n* sens *m* du spectacle

shown [ʃəʊn, *Am:* ʃoʊn] *pp of* **show**

show-off *n* vantard(e) *m(f)* **showpiece** **I.** *n* modèle *m* **II.** *adj* modèle **showroom** *n* salle *f* d'exposition **show trial** *n* procès *m* pour la forme

showy ['ʃəʊi, *Am:* 'ʃoʊ-] <-ier, -iest> *adj* tape-à-l'œil *inv*

shrank [ʃræŋk] *pt of* **shrink**

shrapnel ['ʃræpn(ə)l] *n no pl* éclat *m* d'obus

shred [ʃred] **I.** <-dd-> *vt* (*document*) déchiqueter; (*meat*) couper en lamelles **II.** *n* **1.** (*thin long strip: of paper, fabric*) lambeau *m;* (*of meat*) lamelle *f;* **to rip sth to ~s** déchiqueter qc **2.** *no pl* (*tiny bit: of hope*) lueur *f;* **without a ~ of clothing on** nu comme un ver; **not a ~ of credibility** pas la moindre crédibilité **3.** *fig* **to tear sb to ~s** démolir qn; **to leave sb's reputation in ~s** détruire la réputation de qn

shredder ['ʃredəʳ, *Am:* -ɚ] *n* déchiqueteuse *f*

shrew [ʃruː] *n* **1.** (*mouse-like animal*) musaraigne *f* **2.** *pej* (*irritable woman*) mégère *f;* **the Taming of the Shrew** la Mégère apprivoisée

shrewd *adj* (*comment*) fin(e); (*person*) astucieux(-euse); (*eye*) aiguisé(e); (*move*) habile; **to make a ~ guess** deviner juste

shrewish *adj pej* acariâtre

shriek [ʃriːk] **I.** *n* cri *m* perçant; **~ of delight** cri *m* de joie **II.** *vi* crier; **to ~ in pain** crier de douleur; **to ~ with laughter** éclater de rire **III.** *vt* (*abuse*) crier

shrift [ʃrɪft] *n* **to give <u>short</u> ~ to sb** envoyer promener qn; **he got short ~ from her** elle l'a envoyé promener

shrill [ʃrɪl] *adj* **1.** (*loud: sound*) suraigu(ë) **2.** *fig* (*attack*) virulent(e)

shrimp [ʃrɪmp] *n* **1.** <-(s)> (*crustacean*) crevette *f* **2.** *pej, inf* (*short person*) nabot(e) *m(f)*

shrimp cocktail *n Am* cocktail *m* de crevettes

shrine [ʃraɪn] *n* **1.** (*containing sacred relics*) reliquaire *m* **2.** (*site of worship*) lieu *m* de pèlerinage

shrink [ʃrɪŋk] **I.** *n inf* psy *mf* **II.** <shrank *o Am* shrunk, shrunk *o a. Am* shrunken> *vt* (*sweater*) faire rétrécir; (*costs*) réduire **III.** <shrank *o Am* shrunk, shrunk *o a. Am* shrunken> *vi* **1.** (*become smaller: sweater*) rétrécir; (*number, audience*) se réduire; (*profits*) chuter **2.** (*be reluctant to*) **to ~ from doing sth** être réticent à faire qc

shrinkage ['ʃrɪŋkɪdʒ] *n no pl* (*of sweater*) rétrécissement *m;* (*of number*) réduction *f*

shrink-wrap ['ʃrɪŋkræp] **I.** *n* film *m* plastique (thermoformé) **II.** *vt* (*food, book*) emballer sous film plastique (thermoformé)

shrivel ['ʃrɪvəl] <*Brit* -ll- *o Am* -l-> **I.** *vi* **1.** (*wrinkle: fruit, skin, plants*) se flétrir **2.** *fig* (*profits*) fondre **II.** *vt* (*crops, skin*) flétrir
♦**shrivel up** *vi* (*fruit*) se flétrir ►**to <u>want</u> to ~ and die** vouloir disparaître

shroud [ʃraʊd] **I.** *n* **1.** (*covering*) *a. fig* voile *m* **2.** (*burial wrapping*) linceul *m* **II.** *vt* **1.** (*wrap*) entourer; (*in darkness, fog*) envelopper **2.** *fig* (*in mystery*) entourer; (*in secrecy*) entourer

Shrove Tuesday [ˌʃrəʊv'tjuːzdeɪ, *Am:* ʃroʊv'tuːzdeɪ] *n no art* mardi *m* gras

shrub [ʃrʌb] *n* arbuste *m*

shrubbery ['ʃrʌbəri] *n no pl* massif *m* d'arbustes

shrug [ʃrʌg] **I.** *n* haussement *m* d'épaules; **~ of contempt** haussement d'épaules en signe de dédain **II.** <-gg-> *vt* **to ~ one's shoulders** hausser les épaules; *fig* s'en ficher **III.** <-gg-> *vi* hausser les épaules
♦**shrug off** *vt* **1.** (*dismiss*) ignorer **2.** (*get rid of*) faire fi de

shrunk [ʃrʌŋk] *pp, pt of* **shrink**

shrunken **I.** *adj* (*profits, figure*) diminué(e) **II.** *pp of* **shrink**

shuck [ʃʌk] *vt Am* **1.** (*remove from shell: beans*) écosser; (*oysters*) écailler **2.** (*remove: clothes*) se déshabiller

shucks *interj Am, inf* flûte!

shudder ['ʃʌdəʳ, *Am:* -ɚ] **I.** *vi* **1.** (*tremble*) frissonner; (*ground*) trembler; **to ~ to a halt** s'arrêter en tremblant **2.** *fig* **to ~ at the memory of sth** avoir des frissons en pensant à qc **II.** *n* frisson *m;* **to send a ~ down sb's spine** donner la chair de poule à qn; **to send a ~ through sb** faire trembler qn

shuffle ['ʃʌfl] **I.** *n* **1.** *no pl* (*dragging of the feet*) traînement *m* de pieds; **to walk with a ~** marcher en traînant des pieds **2.** (*mixing of cards*) **to give the cards a ~** battre les cartes **3.** (*rearrangement*) **to give one's papers a ~** remettre de l'ordre dans ses papiers **4.** *Am, Aus, Can* (*shake-up*) **cabinet ~** remaniement *m* ministériel; **management ~** changement *m* de directeurs **II.** *vt* **1.** (*mix thoroughly*) brasser; (*cards*) battre **2.** (*move around indiscriminately*) déplacer **3.** (*drag*) **to ~ one's feet** traîner les pieds **III.** *vi* **1.** (*mix cards*) mélanger **2.** (*drag one's feet*) traîner les pieds **3.** *fig* **to ~ along** traîner
♦**shuffle off** *vt* **to ~ responsibility onto**

sb rejeter la responsabilité sur qn; **to ~ a burden** se débarrasser d'un poids ►**to ~ this mortal coil** *iron* mourir

shun [ʃʌn] <-nn-> *vt* (*publicity*) fuir

shunt [ʃʌnt] I. *vt* 1. (*manoeuvre: train*) aiguiller 2. (*move without consideration: person, thing*) écarter; **to be ~ed to later times** être relégué à plus tard; **to ~ sth somewhere** déplacer qc quelque part II. *n* RAIL manœuvre *f*

shunter *n* locomotive *f* de manœuvre

shunting *n* manœuvre *f*

shunting station, **shunting yard** *n* gare *f* de triage

shush [ʃʊʃ] I. *interj* chut! II. *vt inf* faire taire III. *vi inf* se taire

shut [ʃʌt] I. *adj* (*door*) fermé(e); (*curtains*) tiré(e); **to slam ~ a door** claquer une porte II. <shut, shut, -tt-> *vt* fermer; (*book*) refermer; **to ~ one's ears to sth** ne pas vouloir entendre qc III. <shut, shut, -tt-> *vi* 1. (*close*) se fermer 2. (*stop operating*) fermer

◆**shut away** *vt* enfermer

◆**shut down** I. *vt* fermer II. *vi* (*factory*) fermer; (*engine*) s'arrêter

◆**shut in** *vt* enfermer

◆**shut off** *vt* 1. (*isolate*) couper 2. (*turn off: engine*) couper 3. (*stop sending: aid*) stopper; (*signals*) arrêter

◆**shut out** *vt* 1. (*block* (*out*): *light*) bloquer; (*memory*) supprimer 2. (*exclude*) exclure; (*of power*) évincer 3. SPORT écarter

◆**shut up** I. *vt* 1. (*confine*) enfermer 2. *Aus, Brit* (*close*) fermer; (*stop business*) mettre la clé sous la porte 3. *inf* (*cause to stop talking*) faire taire; **to shut sb up for good** refroidir qn II. *vi* 1. *Aus, Brit* (*close*) fermer 2. *inf* (*stop talking*) se taire

shutdown *n* fermeture *f* **shut-eye** *n no pl, inf* roupillon *m;* **to get some ~** faire un roupillon **shut-in** *adj* **a ~ feeling** un sentiment d'enfermement; **to feel ~** se sentir prisonnier(-ère) **shut-off** I. *n* coupure *f* II. *adj* **~ switch** interrupteur *m* d'arrêt **shutout** *n Am* SPORT éclatante victoire *f*

shutter *n* 1. PHOT déclencheur *m* 2. (*window cover*) volet *m*

shutter release *n* PHOT déclencheur *m*

shuttle ['ʃʌtl, *Am:* 'ʃʌt̬-] I. *n* 1. (*transport*) navette *f;* **air ~ service** service *m* de vol régulier 2. (*sewing-machine bobbin*) canette *f* 3. *inf* (*shuttle cock*) volant *m* II. *vt* véhiculer III. *vi* **to ~ from sth to sth** faire la navette de qc à qc

shuttle bus *n* navette *f* **shuttlecock** *n* SPORT volant *m* **shuttle flight** *n* vol *m* régulier **shuttle service** *n* service *m* de navette

shy[1] [ʃaɪ] I. <-ie-> *vt inf* balancer II. *n inf* **to take a ~ at sth** s'en prendre à qc

shy[2] [ʃaɪ] I. <-er, -est> *adj* 1. (*timid: person, smile*) timide; (*child, animal*) craintif(-ive); **to be ~ of people** craindre les gens 2. (*lacking*) manquer de; **we are ~ of £50** il nous manque 50 livres II. <-ie-> *vi* (*horse*) se cabrer

◆**shy away** *vi* **to ~ from doing sth** éviter de faire qc

shyness *n no pl* timidité *f;* (*of animals*) caractère *m* craintif

Siamese [ˌsaɪə'miːz] I. *n* 1. (*person*) Siamois(e) *m(f)* 2. LING siamois *m; s. a.* **English** II. *adj* siamois(e)

Siamese twins *n* frères siamois *mpl,* sœurs siamoises *fpl*

Siberia [saɪ'bɪəriə, *Am:* -'bɪri-] *n no pl* la Sibérie

Sicilian I. *adj* sicilien(ne) II. *n* 1. (*person*) Sicilien(ne) *m(f)* 2. LING sicilien *m; s. a.* **English**

Sicily ['sɪsɪli] *n* la Sicile

sick [sɪk] I. <-er, -est> *adj* 1. (*ill*) *a. fig* malade; **to fall ~** tomber malade; **to feel ~** se sentir mal, **to report ~,** se faire porter malade 2. (*nauseous*) **to be ~** vomir; **to feel ~** avoir mal au cœur; **to make oneself ~** se rendre malade 3. *inf* (*disgusted*) écœuré(e); **to be ~ about** [*o Am* **over**] **sth** être écœuré de qc 4. *inf* (*fed-up*) **to be ~ of sb/sth** en avoir marre de qn/qc; **to be ~ and tired of sth** en avoir assez de qc 5. *inf* (*cruel, tasteless*) malsain(e) ►**~ as a dog** *Am, Aus* malade comme un chien; **to be worried ~** *inf* être malade d'inquiétude II. *n* 1. *pl* (*ill people*) **the ~** les malades *mpl* 2. *no pl, Brit, inf* (*vomit*) vomi *m*

sickbed *n* MED lit *m* de malade

sicken ['sɪkən] I. *vi* MED 1. (*become sick*) tomber malade 2. *Brit* (*become sick with*) **to ~ for sth** couver qc 3. *fig* **to ~ of sth** se lasser de qc II. *vt* (*upset*) choquer; **to be ~ed at sth** être écœuré de qc

sickening *adj* 1. (*repulsive*) écœurant(e) 2. (*annoying*) insoutenable

sickle ['sɪkl] *n* faucille *f*

sick leave ['sɪkliːv] *n* MED **to be on ~** être en congé de maladie

sickly <-ier, -iest> *adj* 1. MED (*not healthy*) maladif(-ive) 2. MED (*causing nausea*) écœurant(e)

sickness *n* 1. *no pl* (*illness*) maladie *f* 2. (*vomiting*) vomissements *mpl* 3. *fig* écœurement *m*

sickness benefit *n Aus, Brit* FIN, ADMIN, MED prestations *fpl* en cas de maladie

sick pay *n* ADMIN, MED indemnité *f* de maladie

sickroom *n* chambre *f* de malade

side [saɪd] *n* 1. (*surface*) côté *m;* (*of record*) face *f;* (*of mountain*) flanc *m;* **the right ~** l'endroit *m;* **the wrong ~** l'envers *m;* **at the ~ of sth** à côté de qc; **at sb's ~** aux côtés de qn; **~ by ~** côte *f* à côte 2. (*edge*) bord *m;* **on all ~(s)** de tous les côtés 3. (*left or right half*) moitié *f* 4. (*direction*) côté *m;* **from all ~(s)** de tous côtés; **from ~ to ~** d'un côté à l'autre 5. (*opposition group*) côté *m;* **to take ~s** prendre parti; **to take sb's ~** prendre parti pour qn; **to be on the other ~** être dans l'autre camp; **the two ~s agreed** les deux partis sont tombés d'accord 6. (*aspect*) aspect *m;* (*of story*) version *f* 7. (*team*) équipe *f* 8. *Brit*

S

(*TV station*) chaîne *f* **9.** (*lineage*) côté *m* ►**the other ~ of the coin** le revers de la médaille; **on the right/wrong ~ of certain age** ne pas avoir/avoir dépassé un certain âge; **on the ~** à côté; *Am* (*served separately*) en accompagnement

sideboard ['saɪdbɔːd, *Am:* -bɔːrd] *n* **1.** (*buffet*) buffet *m* **2.** *pl, Brit, inf* (*sideburns*) favoris *mpl*

sideburns ['saɪdbɜːnz, *Am:* -bɜːrnz] *n* favoris *mpl*

sidecar *n* AUTO side-car *m* **side dish** *n* GASTR garniture *f* **side effect** *n* MED effet *m* secondaire **sidelight** *n Brit* AUTO feu *m* de position **sideline** I. *n* **1.** (*secondary activity*) activité *f* secondaire **2.** *Am* SPORT ligne *f* de touche; **on the ~s** *a. fig* sur la touche II. *vt* **1.** (*kept from playing*) remplacer **2.** (*ignore the opinions of*) mettre sur la touche **sidelong** I. *adj* oblique II. *adv* de côté **side road** *n* route *f* secondaire **side show** *n* attraction *f* **sideslip** I. *n* (*sideways slip*) dérapage *m* II. *vi* (*slip sideways*) déraper **sidestep** <-pp-> I. *vt* éviter II. *vi* faire un pas de côté **side street** *n* petite rue *f* **sidetrack** I. *vt* **to be ~ed** se laisser distraire II. *n* voie *f* secondaire **side view** *n* vue *f* de côté **sidewalk** *n Am s.* **pavement** **sideward, sideways** I. *adv* (*facing a side*) de côté II. *adj* (*lateral*) latéral(e)

side-whiskers *npl s.* **sideburns**

siding ['saɪdɪŋ] *n* RAIL voie *f* de garage

sidle ['saɪdl] *vi* se glisser

siege [siːdʒ] *n* MIL siège *m*

Sierra Leone [sɪ'erəlɪ'əʊn, *Am:* sɪˌerəlɪ'oʊn] *n* la Sierra Leone

Sierra Leonean I. *adj* sierra-léonais(e) II. *n* Sierra-Léonais(e) *m(f)*

sieve [sɪv] I. *n* tamis *m* ►**to have a memory like a ~** avoir la mémoire comme une passoire II. *vt* tamiser

sift [sɪft] *vt* **1.** (*pass through sieve*) tamiser **2.** (*examine closely*) passer au crible

sigh [saɪ] I. *n* soupir *m* II. *vi* **1.** (*emit a breath*) soupirer; **to ~ with relief** pousser un soupir de soulagement **2.** *fig, form* **to ~ for sb** regretter qn

sight [saɪt] I. *n* **1.** *no pl* (*faculty of seeing*) vue *f* **2.** (*view*) vue *f* **3.** (*act of seeing*) vue *f;* **at first ~** à première vue; **sb can't bear the ~ of sb/sth** qn ne peut sentir qn/qc; **to catch ~ of sb/sth** apercevoir qn/qc; **get out of my ~!** *inf* hors de ma vue !; **to know sb by ~** connaître qn de vue **4.** (*range of vision*) **to be out of one's ~** être hors de vue de qn; *fig* être éloigné de qn; **within ~ of sth** en vue de qc **5.** *pl* (*attractions*) attractions *fpl* touristiques **6.** (*gun's aiming device*) mire *f;* **to lower one's ~s** *fig* viser moins haut **7.** *no pl* (*a lot*) **a ~** beaucoup ►**to be a ~ for sore eyes** *inf* être un spectacle réjouissant; **out of ~, out of mind** *prov* loin des yeux, loin du cœur II. *vt* (*see*) apercevoir

sighted *adj* doué(e) de la vue

sightless *adj* aveugle

sightseeing ['saɪtˌsiːɪŋ] *n no pl* tourisme *m*

sightseer ['saɪtˌsiːəʳ, *Am:* -ɚ] *n* touriste *mf*

sign [saɪn] I. *n* **1.** (*gesture*) geste *m;* **to make a ~ to sb** faire un signe à qn **2.** (*signpost*) panneau *m* **3.** (*signboard*) enseigne *f* **4.** (*symbol*) signe *m* **5.** (*indication*) indication *f* II. *vt* **1.** (*write signature on*) signer; **to ~ for** signer à réception de **2.** (*gesticulate*) faire signe ►**~ one's own death warrant** *inf* signer son propre arrêt de mort III. *vi* **1.** (*write signature*) signer **2.** (*gesticulate*) faire un signe; **to ~ to sb that ...** indiquer à qn par un signe que ...

◆**sign in** I. *vi* signer en arrivant II. *vt* **to sign sb in** signer pour faire entrer qn

◆**sign off** *vi* **1.** (*end*) terminer **2.** (*end a letter*) finir une lettre

◆**sign on** I. *vi* **1.** (*agree to take work*) **to ~ as sth** s'engager comme qc **2.** (*agree to take course*) **to ~ for sth** s'inscrire à qc **3.** *Brit, inf* (*confirm unemployed status*) s'inscrire au chômage II. *vt* engager

◆**sign out** I. *vi* signer à la sortie II. *vt* **1.** (*record sb's departure*) noter le départ de **2.** (*record what sb borrows: book*) enregistrer la sortie de

◆**sign up** I. *vi* s'engager II. *vt* **to sign sb up for sth** inscrire qn à qc

signal ['sɪgnəl] I. *n* **1.** (*particular gesture*) *a.* INFOR signal *m;* **to give sb a ~ to** *+infin* faire signe à qn de *+infin* **2.** (*indication*) signe *m;* **to be a ~ that ...** indiquer que ... **3.** *Am s.* **indicator** II. <-l(l)-> *vt* **1.** (*indicate*) signaler; **to ~ that ...** indiquer que ... **2.** (*gesticulate*) faire signe III. <-l(l)-> *vi* faire des signaux

signal box *n* RAIL poste *m* d'aiguillage **signal lamp** *n* lampe *f* témoin

signaller *n* RAIL *s.* **signalman**

signally *adv* remarquablement

signalman <-men> *n* RAIL aiguilleur *m*

signatory ['sɪgnətəri, *Am:* -tɔːr-] *n* signataire *mf*

signature ['sɪgnətʃəʳ, *Am:* -nətʃɚ] *n* signature *f*

signboard ['saɪnbɔːd, *Am:* -bɔːrd] *n* enseigne *f*

signet ring ['sɪgnɪtˌrɪŋ] *n* chevalière *f*

significance [sɪg'nɪfɪkəns, *Am:* -'nɪfə-] *n no pl* **1.** (*importance*) importance *f* **2.** (*meaning*) signification *f*

significant *adj* **1.** (*considerable*) considérable **2.** (*important*) important(e) **3.** (*meaningful*) significatif(-ive)

signification *n* signification *f*

signify ['sɪgnɪfaɪ, *Am:* -nə-] I. <-ie-> *vt* signifier II. <-ie-> *vi* **1.** (*make known*) faire connaître **2.** *form* (*matter*) importer

signpost I. *n* **1.** (*post*) poteau *m* indicateur **2.** *fig* indication *f* II. *vt* signaliser

silence ['saɪləns] I. *n* silence *m* ►**~ is golden** *prov* le silence est d'or II. *vt* réduire au silence

silencer *n* silencieux *m*

silent ['saɪlənt] *adj* silencieux(-euse); ~ **film** film *m* muet; **to be ~ on sth** garder le silence sur qc
silently *adv* silencieusement
silhouette [ˌsɪlu'et] **I.** *n* silhouette *f* **II.** *vt* **to be ~d against sth** se profiler sur qc
silicon ['sɪlɪkən] *n no pl* CHEM silicium *m*
silicone ['sɪlɪkəʊn, *Am:* -koʊn] *n no pl* CHEM silicone *f*
silk [sɪlk] *n* soie *f*
silk dress *n* robe *f* en soie **silkworm** *n* ZOOL ver *m* à soie
silky ['sɪlki] <-ier, -iest> *adj* soyeux(-euse)
sill [sɪl] *n* CONSTR **1.** (*base of door*) seuil *m* **2.** (*base of window*) rebord *m*
silly ['sɪli] **I.** <-ier, -iest> *adj* bête; **it's ~** c'est bête, c'est bœuf *Suisse;* **to look ~** avoir l'air ridicule; **to laugh oneself ~** mourir de rire; **to be bored ~** être assommé; **to be worried ~** être malade d'inquiétude **II.** *n s.* **silly billy**
silly billy *n inf* bêta *m*
silo ['saɪləʊ, *Am:* -loʊ] *n* silo *m*
silt [sɪlt] *n no pl* limon *m*
silver ['sɪlvəʳ, *Am:* -vɚ] CHEM **I.** *n no pl* **1.** (*precious metal*) argent *m* **2.** (*silver coins*) pièces *fpl* d'argent **3.** (*silver cutlery*) **the ~** l'argenterie *f* **II.** *adj* **1.** (*made of silver*) en argent **2.** (*silver-coloured*) argenté(e) **III.** *vt* argenter
silver foil *n* papier *m* d'aluminium **silver paper** *n* papier *m* d'argent **silver plate** *n* **1.** (*not solid silver*) plaqué *m* argent **2.** (*silver-coloured coating*) métal *m* argenté **silver screen** *n* CINE **the ~** le grand écran **silversmith** *n* orfèvre *mf* **silverware** *n no pl* **1.** (*articles made of silver*) argenterie *f* **2.** *Am* (*utensils*) couverts *mpl* **silver wedding anniversary** *n* noces *fpl* d'argent
similar ['sɪmɪləʳ, *Am:* -əlɚ] *adj* semblable
similarity [ˌsɪmə'lærəti, *Am:* -ə'lerət̬i] *n* ressemblance *f*
simile ['sɪmɪli, *Am:* -əli] *n* comparaison *f*
similitude [sɪ'mɪlɪtju:d, *Am:* sə'mɪlətu:d] *n* **1.** (*being similar*) ressemblance *f* **2.** (*comparison*) comparaison *f*
simmer ['sɪməʳ, *Am:* -ɚ] **I.** *vi* **1.** GASTR mijoter **2.** (*about to boil*) frémir **II.** *vt* faire mijoter **III.** *n* **to keep at a ~** faire cuire à petit feu
◆**simmer down** *vi inf* se calmer
simper ['sɪmpəʳ, *Am:* -pɚ] **I.** *vi* minauder **II.** *n* sourire *m* affecté
simple ['sɪmpl] <-r, -st *o* more ~, most ~> *adj* **1.** (*gen*) simple **2.** (*foolish*) bête
simple-hearted *adj* ingénu(e) **simple-minded** *adj* **1.** *inf* (*dumb*) simplet(-ète) **2.** *pej, inf* (*naive*) naïf(naïve)
simplicity [sɪm'plɪsəti, *Am:* -t̬i] *n no pl* simplicité *f*
simplification [ˌsɪmplɪfɪ'keɪʃən, *Am:* -plə-] *n* simplification *f*
simplify ['sɪmplɪfaɪ, *Am:* -plə-] *vt* simplifier
simplistic [sɪm'plɪstɪk] *adj pej* simpliste
simply ['sɪmpli] *adv* **1.** (*gen*) simplement **2.** (*absolutely*) absolument
simulate ['sɪmjʊleɪt] *vt* simuler
simulation *n* simulation *f*
simultaneous [ˌsɪml'teɪnɪəs, *Am:* ˌsaɪml'teɪnjəs] *adj* simultané(e)
sin [sɪn] **I.** *n* péché *m* **II.** *vi* <-nn-> pécher
since [sɪns] **I.** *adv* **1.** (*from that point on*) depuis; **ever ~** depuis lors **2.** (*ago*) **long ~** il y a longtemps **II.** *prep* depuis; **how long is it ~ the crime?** à quand remonte le crime? **III.** *conj* **1.** (*because*) puisque **2.** (*from time that*) depuis que; **it's a week now ~ I came back** il y a maintenant une semaine que je suis revenu
sincere [sɪn'sɪəʳ, *Am:* sɪn'sɪr] *adj* sincère
sincerely *adv* **1.** (*in a sincere manner*) sincèrement **2.** *Am* (*way to end letter*) (**yours**) ~ veuillez agréer, Madame/Monsieur, l'expression de mes sentiments les meilleurs
sincerity [sɪn'serəti, *Am:* sɪn'serət̬i] *n no pl* sincérité *f*
sine [saɪn] *n* MAT sinus *m*
sine die [ˌsaɪnɪ'daɪi:, *Am:* ˌsaɪni'daɪ] *adv* LAW sine die
sine qua non [ˌsɪnikwɑ:'nəʊn, *Am:* 'sɪneɪkwɑ:'noʊn] *n form* condition *f* sine qua non
sinew ['sɪnju:] *n* tendon *m*
sinewy *adj* **1.** (*muscular*) musclé(e) **2.** (*tough: meat*) tendineux(-euse)
sinful ['sɪnfəl] *adj* **1.** (*immoral*) licencieux(-euse) **2.** (*deplorable*) déplorable **3.** *inf* (*bad for you*) nuisible
sing¹ [sɪŋ] LING *abbr of* **singular**
sing² <sang *o a. Am* sung, sung> **I.** *vi* **1.** (*make music*) chanter **2.** (*make high-pitched noise: kettle*) siffler; (*wind*) hurler **3.** (*be filled with ringing*) bourdonner **II.** *vt* chanter; **to ~ alto/tenor/soprano** avoir une voix d'alto/de ténor/de soprano ►**to ~ another tune** chanter sur un autre ton; (*change what you think*) changer d'avis
◆**sing out I.** *vi* **1.** (*loudly*) chanter à tue-tête **2.** *inf* (*call*) gueuler **II.** *vt inf* gueuler
◆**sing up** *vi Brit, Aus* chanter plus fort
Singapore [ˌsɪŋə'pɔ:ʳ, *Am:* 'sɪŋəpɔ:r] *n* Singapour
Singaporean I. *adj* singapourien(ne) **II.** *n* Singapourien(ne) *m(f)*
singe [sɪndʒ] **I.** *vt* **1.** (*burn*) roussir **2.** (*slightly*) brûler légèrement **II.** *n* brûlure *f* légère
singer ['sɪŋəʳ, *Am:* -ɚ] *n* chanteur, -euse *m, f*
singer-songwriter *n* compositeur *m* interprète
singing *n no pl* chant *m*
singing bird *n* oiseau *m* chanteur **singing book** *n* carnet *m* de chants **singing club** *n* chorale *f* **singing lesson** *n* leçon *f* de chant **singing society** *s.* **singing club singing teacher** *n* professeur *m* de chant **singing voice** *n* belle voix *f*
single ['sɪŋgl] **I.** *adj* **1.** (*one only*) seul(e); **not a ~ word** pas un mot; **every ~ day** tous les jours; **every ~ thing** tout **2.** (*for one person:*

S

bed) à une place; (*room*) simple **3.** ECON (*currency, price, market*) unique **4.** (*unmarried*) célibataire; (*parent*) isolé(e); **a ~-parent family** une famille monoparentale **II.** *n* **1.** *Brit, Aus* (*one-way ticket*) aller *m* (simple) **2.** *Am* (*one-unit banknote*) billet *m* d'un dollar; *Brit* billet *m* d'une livre; **in ~s** en petites coupures **3.** (*record*) single *m* **4.** (*single room*) chambre *f* individuelle **5.** *pl* SPORT simple *m* **III.** *vi* SPORT jouer en simple

◆**single out** *vt* identifier

single-breasted *adj* (*suit, jacket*) droit(e) **single currency** *n* monnaie *f* unique **single-decker** *n* autobus *m* sans impériale **single-entry bookkeeping** *n* comptabilité *f* en partie simple **single-figure** *adj* (*inflation rate*) à un chiffre **single-handed** **I.** *adv* tout seul **II.** *adj* sans aide **single-lens reflex**, **single-lens reflex camera** *n* PHOT appareil *m* photo reflex **single-minded** *adj* tenace **single-mindedness**, **singleness of mind** *n no pl* **1.** ténacité *f* **2.** (*pursuing*) obsession *f* **single-parent family** <-lies> *n* famille *f* monoparentale **single seater** *n* monoplace *m* **single-sex school** *n* école *f* non mixte **single-stage** *adj* ne comportant qu'une seule étape

singlet ['sɪŋglɪt] *n Brit, Aus* maillot *m*

single-track *adj* **1.** RAIL (*line*) à voie unique **2.** (*for one vehicle*) à une seule file; **"~ road with passing places"** "chaussée à voie unique avec zones de dépassement" **single traveller** *n* voyageur *m* (en) solitaire

singly ['sɪŋgli] *adv* individuellement

sing-song **I.** *n* (*singing session*) chœur *m*; **to speak in a ~** parler d'une voix chantante **II.** *adj* chantant(e)

singular ['sɪŋgjələʳ, *Am:* -lɚ] **I.** *adj* **1.** LING au singulier **2.** *form* (*extraordinary*) singulier(-ère) **II.** *n no pl* LING singulier *m*

singularity [ˌsɪŋgjə'lærəti, *Am:* -'lerəṱi] *n no pl, form* singularité *f*

singularly *adv form* **1.** (*extraordinarily*) singulièrement **2.** (*strangely*) étrangement

sinister ['sɪnɪstəʳ, *Am:* -stɚ] *adj* **1.** (*scary*) épouvantable **2.** *inf* (*ominous*) sinistre

sink [sɪŋk] <sank *o* sunk, sunk> **I.** *n* **1.** (*washing area*) évier *m* **2.** *Am* (*washbasin*) lavabo *m* **II.** *vi* **1.** (*not float*) couler **2.** (*go downward: to the bottom*) sombrer **3.** (*drop down*) s'effondrer; **to ~ to one's knees** tomber à genoux **4.** (*decrease*) diminuer **5.** (*get softer*) s'adoucir **6.** (*gets sadder: heart*) s'assombrir **7.** (*decline: in sb's estimation*) baisser **8.** (*health decline*) s'aggraver ►**to ~ like a stone** (*through water*) couler à pic; (*through air*) tomber comme une pierre; **to ~ without trace** sombrer corps et biens; **"~ or swim"** "marche ou crève" **III.** *vt* **1.** (*cause to submerge*) plonger **2.** (*ruin*) ruiner **3.** MIN (*well*) forer **4.** SPORT battre (à plate couture) **5.** (*lower: voice*) réduire ►**to ~ one's differences** dépasser ses différences

◆**sink back** *vi* **1.** (*lean back relaxedly*) s'affaler **2.** (*return to bad habits*) **to ~ into sth** replonger dans qc

◆**sink down** *vi* **1.** (*descend: aircraft*) effectuer une descente **2.** (*drop to the ground*) s'effondrer **3.** (*sit*) s'asseoir

◆**sink in** **I.** *vi* **1.** (*go into surface*) s'enfoncer **2.** (*be absorbed: liquid*) pénétrer **3.** (*be understood*) rentrer (dans la tête de qn) **II.** *vt* **1.** (*force into sth*) **to sink one's teeth in sth** planter ses crocs dans qc **2.** (*invest*) **to sink one's money in sth** placer son argent dans qc

sinker *n* plomb *m* (de pêche)

sinking **I.** *adj* **1.** (*not floating*) qui coule **2.** (*feeling sad: feeling*) angoissant(e) **3.** (*declining*) en baisse ►**to leave the ~ ship** abandonner le navire **II.** *n* **1.** (*ship accident*) naufrage *m* **2.** (*sending torpedoes*) torpillage *m*

sink unit *n* évier *m* encastré

sinner ['sɪnəʳ, *Am:* -ɚ] *n* pécheur, -eresse *m, f*

Sinn Fein [ʃɪn'feɪn] *n* Sinn Fein *m* (*parti et mouvement irlandais nationaliste aspirant à la réunification de l'Irlande*)

sinuous ['sɪnjʊəs] *adj* **1.** (*winding*) en spirale; (*stairs*) en colimaçon **2.** (*twisting*) sinueux(-euse)

sinus ['saɪnəs] *n* ANAT sinus *m*

sinusitis [ˌsaɪnə'saɪtɪs, *Am:* -ṱɪs] *n no pl* MED sinusite *f*

Sioux [suː] **I.** *adj* Sioux **II.** *n* **1.** (*person*) Sioux *m* **2.** LING Sioux *m*; *s. a.* **English**

sip [sɪp] **I.** <-pp-> *vt* boire à petites gorgées; (*alcohol*) siroter **II.** <-pp-> *vi* boire à petites gorgées **III.** *n* petite gorgée *f*; **to have a ~** boire une gorgée

siphon ['saɪfən] **I.** *n* siphon *m* **II.** *vt* siphonner

◆**siphon off** *vt* **1.** (*remove by siphoning*) siphonner **2.** FIN (*money*) détourner

sir [sɜːʳ, *Am:* sɜːr] *n* Monsieur *m*; **yes ~** oui Monsieur; MIL oui mon commandant; **Sir James** Sir James; **no ~** *inf* certainement pas

sire ['saɪəʳ, *Am:* 'saɪɚ] **I.** *n* (*horse's father*) géniteur *m* **II.** *vt* engendrer

siren ['saɪərən, *Am:* 'saɪrən] *n* sirène *f*

sirloin ['sɜːlɔɪn, *Am:* 'sɜːr-] *n no pl* aloyau *m*

sirocco [sɪ'rɒkəʊ, *Am:* sə'rɑːkoʊ] *n* sirocco *m*

sis [sɪs] *n Am, inf abbr of* **sister**

sisal ['saɪsəl] *n no pl* sisal *m*

sissy ['sɪsi] *pej* **I.** <-sies> *n inf* poule *f* mouillée **II.** <-ier, -iest> *adj inf* de nana

sister ['sɪstəʳ, *Am:* -ɚ] *n* **1.** (*woman, girl*) sœur *f* **2.** (*nun*) **Sister Catherine** sœur Catherine; **Sister!** ma Sœur! **3.** *Brit, Aus* (*nurse*) infirmière *f*; **Sister Jones** Mademoiselle Jones

sister company *n* société *f* apparentée **sisterhood** *n* **1.** *no pl* (*solidarity*) sororité *f* **2.** *no pl* (*feminists*) **the ~** les féministes *mfpl* **3.** REL congrégation *f* (religieuse) féminine **sister-in-law** <sisters-in-law *o* sister-in-laws> *n* belle-sœur *f*

sisterly *adj* sororal(e)
sister ship *n* navire *m* jumeau **sistership** *n* sororité *f*
sit [sɪt] <-tt, sat, sat> **I.** *vi* **1.** (*be seated*) être assis; (*for a portrait*) poser; (*bird*) être perché; **to be ~ting doing sth** être assis en train de faire qc **2.** (*take up sitting position*) s'asseoir; **"~"!** (*to a dog*) "assis!" **3.** (*be in session: assembly, court*) siéger; **to ~ for sth** tenir séance pour qc **4.** (*be placed, not moved*) se trouver; **to ~ still** se tenir tranquile; **to ~ at home** rester à la maison **5.** *inf* (*baby-sit*) s'occuper de **6.** (*on a nest: bird*) couver **7.** *Am* (*be agreeable*) plaire ►**to ~ on the fence** tergiverser; **to be ~ting pretty** être bien loti; **to ~ tight** (*not move*) rester sur place; (*not change opinion*) camper sur ses positions **II.** *vt* **1.** (*put on seat*) asseoir **2.** (*place*) placer **3.** *Brit* (*take exam: exam*) passer
◆**sit about** *vi Brit,* **sit around** *vi* ne rien faire
◆**sit back** *vi* **1.** (*lean back*) se caler dans sa chaise **2.** (*do nothing*) ne rien faire **3.** (*relax*) se détendre
◆**sit down I.** *vi* **1.** (*take a seat*) s'asseoir; **to be sitting down** être assis; **to ~ at the table** s'attabler **2.** *Brit* (*accept*) **to ~ under sth** accepter qc sans broncher **II.** *vt* asseoir; **to sit oneself down** s'asseoir
◆**sit in** *vi* **1.** (*attend*) **to ~ on sth** assister à qc **2.** (*represent*) **to ~ for sb** remplacer qn **3.** (*hold sit-in*) occuper les locaux
◆**sit on** *vt* **1.** (*not deal with*) ne pas s'occuper de **2.** (*keep secret*) garder secret **3.** *inf* (*rebuke*) rembarrer **4.** (*put an end to: idea, scheme*) mettre un terme à **5.** (*feel heavy: sb's stomach*) rester sur
◆**sit out I.** *vi* **1.** (*sit outdoors*) s'asseoir dehors **2.** (*not dance*) faire tapisserie **II.** *vt* **1.** (*not take part in*) ne pas prendre part à **2.** (*sit until the end*) rester jusqu'à la fin de
◆**sit through** *vt* rester jusqu'au bout de
◆**sit up I.** *vi* **1.** (*sit erect*) se redresser; **to ~ straight** se tenir droit; **to ~ and beg** faire le beau **2.** (*not go to bed*) veiller; **to ~ for sb** attendre qn **3.** *inf* (*pay attention*) faire attention **II.** *vt* redresser
sitcom ['sɪtkɒm, *Am:* -kɑːm] *n inf abbr of* **situation comedy** sitcom *f*
sit-down strike *n* **to hold a ~** faire une grève sur le tas
site [saɪt] **I.** *n* **1.** (*place*) site *m;* (*of building*) emplacement *m;* (*of a battle*) champ *m;* (*of recent events*) lieux *mpl* **2.** (*building land*) chantier *m;* **archaeological ~** site *m* archéologique; **on ~** sur (le) site **3.** INFOR site *m;* **Web ~** site Web **II.** *vt* construire
site development *n no pl* aménagement *m* de site **site engineer** *n* chef *m* de chantier **site office** *n* bureau *m* de chantier **site owner** *n* maître *m* des lieux **site plan** *n* plan *m* de chantier
sit-in ['sɪtɪn, *Am:* 'sɪt̬-] *n* sit-in *m inv*
siting *n no pl* mise *f* en chantier
sitter *n* **1.** (*model*) modèle *m* **2.** (*babysitter*) baby-sitter *mf*
sitting *n* (*meal session*) service *m* de repas
sitting duck *n* cible *f* facile **sitting member** *n Brit* POL membre *m* attitré du Parlement **sitting room** *n Brit* salon *m* **sitting target** *n* (*easy prey*) proie *f* facile **sitting tenant** *n* locataire *mf* en titre
situate ['sɪtʃʊeɪt, *Am:* 'sɪtʃueɪt] *vt* **1.** *form* (*locate*) situer **2.** *form* (*place in context*) localiser
situated *adj* **1.** (*located*) situé(e); **to be ~ near ...** se situer près de ... **2.** (*in a state*) **to be ~ for sth** bien convenir pour qc
situation [ˌsɪtʃʊ'eɪʃən, *Am:* ˌsɪtʃu'-] *n* situation *f*
situation comedy *n* sitcom *m*
six [sɪks] **I.** *adj* six ►**to be ~ feet under** *iron* être à six pieds sous terre; **~ of one and half a dozen of the other** c'est bonnet blanc et blanc bonnet; **to knock sb for ~** (*amaze and bewilder*) mettre qn hors de combat; (*defeat completely*) battre qn à plate couture **II.** *n* six *m* ►**to be at ~es and sevens** ne pas savoir sur quel pied danser; *s. a.* **eight**
six-footer *n personne mesurant au moins six pieds de haut;* **to be a ~** être une armoire à glace **six-pack** *n* pack *m* de six (unités)
sixteen [sɪk'stiːn] *adj* seize; *s. a.* **eight**
sixteenth *adj* seizième; *s. a.* **eighth**
sixth *adj* sixième; *s. a.* **eighth**

> En Grande-Bretagne un **sixth-form college** est un "College" pour des élèves de 16 à 18 ans, qui souvent viennent d'écoles qui ne possèdent pas de "sixth-form" (classe de sixième). Au "College", ils peuvent passer le "A-levels" (l'équivalent du bac) ou alors ils fréquent un cours équivalent de deux ans et se préparent ainsi aux examens d'admission à l'université.

sixtieth *adj* soixantième; *s. a.* **eighth**
sixty ['sɪksti] *adj* soixante; *s. a.* **eight, eighty**
size¹ [saɪz] **I.** *n no pl* **1.** TECH apprêt *m* **2.** (*glue*) colle *f* **II.** *vt* **1.** TECH apprêter **2.** (*glue*) encoller
size² [saɪz] **I.** *n* (*of person, clothes*) taille *f;* (*of building, room*) dimension *f;* (*of country, area*) étendue *f;* (*of paper, books*) format *m;* (*of an amount, bill, debt*) montant *m;* (*of problems*) importance *f;* **collar ~** encolure *f;* **six inches in ~** six pieds de haut; **to increase/decrease in ~** augmenter/diminuer en taille; **to double in ~** doubler de volume; **of a ~** de même(s) dimension(s); **to take ~ 32** (*men's sizing*)/ **14** (*Brit women's sizing*)/**10** (*Am women's sizing*) faire du 42; **to take ~ 7** (*men's sizing*)/ **8½** (*Am women's sizing*) chausser du 40 **II.** *vt* classer
◆**size up** *vt* évaluer; (*problem*) mesurer (l'ampleur de)
sizable, sizeable *adj* considérable

S

sizing *n no pl* (*of wall paper*) encollage *m;* (*of textiles*) empesage *m*

sizzle ['sɪzl] **I.** *vi* grésiller **II.** *n no pl* grésillement *m*

sizzler *n inf* journée *f* torride

skate[1] [skeɪt] *n* raie *f*

skate[2] [skeɪt] **I.** *n* **1.** (*ice*) patin *m* à glace **2.** (*roller*) patin *m* à roulettes **3.** (*skateboard*) planche *f* à roulettes, skate-board *m* ►**to get one's ~s on** *Brit, inf* se manier **II.** *vi* **1.** (*on ice*) patiner **2.** (*on roller skates*) faire du patin à roulettes **3.** (*on rollerblades*) faire du roller **4.** (*ride on a skateboard*) faire du skate-board ►**to be skating on thin ice** s'aventurer en terrain glissant

skateboard ['skeɪtbɔːd, *Am:* -bɔːrd] *n* planche *f* à roulettes, skate-board *m*

skateboarder *n* skateur, -euse *m, f*

skater *n* **1.** (*person doing skating*) patineur, -euse *m, f;* **figure ~** patineur artistique; **speed ~** patineur de vitesse **2.** (*person riding on a skateboard*) skater, -euse *m, f*

skating rink *n* **1.** (*ice skating*) patinoire *f* **2.** (*roller skating*) piste *f* de patin à roulettes

skedaddle [skɪ'dædl] *vi inf* ficher le camp

skein [skeɪn] *n a. fig* écheveau *m*

skeleton ['skelɪtən, *Am:* '-ə-] *n* **1.** (*body framework, thin person*) squelette *m;* **to be reduced to a ~** n'avoir que la peau et les os **2.** (*framework: of a boat, plane*) carcasse *f;* (*of a building*) charpente *f* **3.** (*sketch: of a book, report*) ébauche *f* ►**to have ~s in the cupboard** [*o a. Am* **closet**] cacher un cadavre dans son placard

skeleton key *n* passe-partout *m* **skeleton service** *n* service *m* minimum **skeleton staff** *n* équipe *f* de base

skeptic(al) *n Am, Aus* sceptique

skepticism ['skeptɪsɪzəm] *n no pl, Am, Aus* scepticisme *m*

sketch [sketʃ] **I.** *n* **1.** (*drawing*) esquisse *f* **2.** (*text*) saynète *f* **3.** (*outline*) croquis *m* **4.** (*unfinished work*) ébauche *f* **5.** (*summary*) résumé *m* **II.** *vt* esquisser

◆**sketch in** *vt a. fig* esquisser

◆**sketch out** *vt* faire l'ébauche de

sketchbook, **sketch pad** *n* carnet *m* de croquis

sketchy ['sketʃi] <-ier, -iest> *adj* **1.** (*vague*) rapide; (*idea*) vague **2.** (*incomplete*) insuffisant(e) **3.** (*not realized*) ébauché(e)

skew [skjuː] **I.** *vt* **1.** (*give slant to*) incliner **2.** (*make an angled cut*) biaiser **3.** (*distort*) fausser; (*wheel*) voiler **4.** (*twist in wrong shape*) tordre **II.** *vi* **1.** (*make biased*) biaiser **2.** (*change direction: horse*) faire un écart; (*vehicle*) faire une embardée **III.** *adj* en biais **IV.** *adv* de travers **V.** *n* **on the ~** de travers

skewbald ['skjuːbɔːld, *Am:* -bɑːld] *adj* pie *inv*

skewer ['skjʊəʳ, *Am:* 'skjuːɚ] **I.** *n* **1.** (*for small pieces of meat*) brochette *f* **2.** (*for joint*) broche *f* **II.** *vt* **1.** (*fasten: meat*) mettre à la broche **2.** (*pierce*) embrocher

skew gear *n* TECH engrenage *m* hyperboloïde **skew spanner** *n* TECH clef *f* coudée **skew wheel** *n* (*cone-shaped wheel*) roue *f* conique **skew-whiff** *Brit, Aus* **I.** *adj inf* tordu(e) **II.** *adv inf* de traviole

ski [skiː] **I.** *n* ski *m* **II.** *vi* skier; **to ~ down the slope** descendre la pente à skis

ski binding *n* fixation *f* **skibob** *n* véloski *m* **ski boot** *n* chaussure *f* de ski

skid [skɪd] **I.** <-dd-> *vi* **1.** (*slide while driving*) déraper; **to ~ to a halt** s'arrêter en dérapage; **to ~ off the road** faire une sortie de route **2.** (*slide*) **to ~ along/across sth** passer/traverser qc en glissant **II.** *n* **1.** (*slide while driving*) dérapage *m;* **to go into a ~** partir en dérapage **2.** (*spinning*) virage *m* en boucle **3.** AVIAT patin *m* (d'atterrissage) ►**to put the ~s under sb/sth** *Brit, Aus, inf* mettre des bâtons dans les roues à qn/qc

skidding *n* dérapage *m*

skid mark *n* trace *f* de freinage **skid row** *n no art, no pl, Am* **to be on ~** vivre dans les bas-fonds *mpl*

skier ['skiːəʳ, *Am:* -ɚ] *n* skieur, -euse *m, f*

skiff [skɪf] *n* petite embarcation *f*

ski flying *n no pl* saut *m* à ski **ski goggles** *npl* lunettes *fpl* de ski

skiing *n no pl* de ski

skiing holiday *n* vacance *f* au ski

ski instructor *n* moniteur *m* de ski **ski instructress** *n* monitrice *f* de ski **ski jump** *n* **1.** (*runway*) tremplin *m* pour le saut à ski **2.** *no pl* (*event*) saut *m* à ski

skilful ['skɪlfəl] *adj Brit, Aus* **1.** (*able*) adroit(e) **2.** (*showing skill*) doué(e)

ski lift *n* remonte-pente *m*

skill [skɪl] *n* **1.** *no pl* expertise *f* **2.** (*ability*) talent *m* **3.** (*technique*) technique *f*

skilled **I.** *adj* **1.** (*trained: work, labour*) qualifié(e); (*worker*) spécialisé(e) **2.** (*requiring skills*) habile; **to be ~ in doing sth** être habile à faire qc **II.** *npl* **the ~** les ouvriers *mpl* qualifiés

skillet ['skɪlɪt] *n* **1.** *Brit* (*saucepan*) casserole *f* **2.** *Am* (*frying pan*) poêle *f* à frire

skillful *adj Am s.* **skilful**

skim [skɪm] <-mm-> **I.** *vt* **1.** (*move above*) frôler; (*over water*) raser **2.** (*make bounce off water: stones*) faire ricocher **3.** (*read quickly*) parcourir **4.** GASTR écumer; (*milk*) écrémer **II.** *vi* survoler

skimmed milk *n no pl* lait *m* écrémé

skimmer *n* **1.** GASTR écumoire *f* **2.** AVIAT bombardier *m* d'eau

skim milk *s.* **skimmed milk**

skimp [skɪmp] **I.** *vt* lésiner; (*work*) bâcler **II.** *vi* **to ~ on sth** lésiner sur qc

skimpy <-ier, -iest> *adj* minuscule; (*meal*) frugal(e)

skin [skɪn] **I.** *n* **1.** (*covering: of person, fruits*) peau *f;* **to be soaked to the ~** être trempé jusqu'aux os **2.** (*animal hide*) cuir *m;* (*of lion, zebra*) peau *f* **3.** (*covering: of an aircraft, ship*) habillage *m* ►**to be all ~ and bone(s)** n'avoir que la peau et les os; **it's no ~ off sb's nose** [*o a. Am* **back**] cela ne fera pas de mal à qn; **by the ~ of one's teeth** il s'en est fallu d'un cheveu; **to get under sb's ~** (*irritate or annoy sb*) taper sur les nerfs de qn **II.** <-nn-> *vt* **1.** (*remove skin: fruits, vegetables*) peler; (*animal*) dépouiller **2.** (*graze*) faire une écorchure à **3.** *fig, iron* **to ~ sb alive** écorcher vif qn

skin cancer *n no pl* cancer *m* de la peau **skin-deep** *adj* supercifiel(le) **skin disease** *n* maladie *f* de peau **skin diving** *n no pl* nage *f* sous la surface (de l'eau) **skin eruption** *n* éruption *f* cutanée **skin flick** *n inf* film *m* érotique

skinflint ['skɪnflɪnt] *n pej* radin(e)

skinful *n no pl, inf* cuite *f*

skin graft *n* MED **1.** (*transplant*) greffe *f* de peau **2.** (*section*) greffon *m* de peau **skinhead** *n* skinhead *mf*

skinny ['skɪni] <-ier, -iest> *adj* maigrelet(te)

skinny-dip <-pp-> *vi inf* se baigner nu

skint [skɪnt] *adj Brit, inf* fauché(e)

skintight [skɪn'taɪt] *adj* moulant(e)

skip¹ [skɪp] **I.** <-pp-> *vi* **1.** (*take light steps*) sautiller **2.** *Brit, Aus* (*~ with rope*) sauter à la corde **3.** (*jump, leave out*) sauter **4.** *inf* (*go quickly*) faire un saut ►**to ~ from one subject to another** passer du coq à l'âne **II.** <-pp-> *vt a. fig* sauter; (*stones*) faire ricocher; **to ~ a rope** sauter à la corde ►**to ~ it** *inf* laisser tomber **III.** *n* saut *m;* **to give a ~ of joy** sauter de joie

skip² [skɪp] *n Brit, Aus* (*large container*) benne *f*

ski pants *npl* fuseau *m* (de ski) **ski pass** *n* forfait *m* de remontée mécanique **ski plane** *n* avion *m* à skis **ski pole** *n* bâton *m* de ski

skipper ['skɪpəʳ, *Am:* -ɚ] **I.** *n* **1.** NAUT, SPORT capitaine *m* **2.** AVIAT commandant *m* **3.** (*form of address*) chef *m* **II.** *vt* avoir la responsabilité de; (*ship, aircraft*) commander; (*team*) diriger

skipping rope *n Brit,* **skip rope** *n Am* corde *f* à sauter

ski rack *n* porte-skis *m inv* **ski resort** *n* station *f* de ski

skirmish ['skɜːmɪʃ, *Am:* 'skɜːr-] **I.** *n* **1.** MIL altercation *f* **2.** (*argument*) prise *f* de bec **II.** *vi* **1.** MIL avoir une échauffourée **2.** (*argue*) avoir un accrochage

skirt [skɜːt, *Am:* skɜːrt] **I.** *n* **1.** (*garment*) jupe *f* **2.** *no pl, pej, inf* (*women*) minette *f* **II.** *vt* **1.** (*go round: path*) contourner **2.** (*avoid*) esquiver

skirting, **skirting board** *n Brit, Aus* plinthe *f*

ski run *n* piste *f* de ski **ski school** *n* école *f* de ski **ski stick** *n Brit* bâton *m* de ski **ski suit** *n* combinaison *f* de ski

skit [skɪt] *n* (*on sb*) pastiche *m;* (*on sth*) parodie *f*

ski touring *n no pl* randonnée *f* à ski **ski tow** *n* téléski *m*

skitter *vi* se faufiler

skittish *adj* **1.** (*nervous: person*) agité(e); (*horse*) ombrageux(-euse) **2.** (*playful: person*) espiègle

skittle ['skɪtl, *Am:* 'skɪt̬-] *n* **1.** (*target*) quille *f* **2.** *pl* (*game*) jeu *m* de quilles

skittle alley *n* piste *f* de quilles **skittle ball** *n* boule *f* de jeu de quilles

skive [skaɪv] *vi Brit, inf* tirer au flanc

◆**skive off** *vi Brit, inf* (*lessons*) sécher; **to ~ school** faire l'école buissonnière

skiver *n Brit, inf* tire-au-cul *mf*

skivvy ['skɪvi] **I.** <-vies> *n* **1.** *Brit* (*servant*) bonne *f* à tout faire **2.** *pl, Am, inf* (*men's underwear*) sous-vêtements *mpl* masculins **3.** *Aus* (*polo-neck*) sous-pull *m* **II.** *vi* **to ~ for sb** être la bonne à tout faire de qn

skulk [skʌlk] *vi* **1.** (*lurk*) se terrer **2.** (*move furtively*) rôder

skull (**bone**) *n* crâne *m*

skullcap ['skʌlkæp] *n* REL calotte *f*

skul(l)duggery *n no pl* magouille *f*

skunk [skʌŋk] *n* **1.** (*animal*) mouffette *f* **2.** *inf* (*bad person*) salaud *m,* salope *f*

sky [skaɪ] <-ies> *n* **1.** (*expanse overhead*) ciel *m* **2.** *pl* (*the sky*) les cieux *mpl* ►**the ~'s the limit** sans limites; **to praise sb/sth to the skies** porter qn/qc aux nues

sky-blue **I.** *adj* bleu ciel *inv* **II.** *n no pl* bleu ciel *m* **skydiving** *n* saut *m* en parachute **sky-high** **I.** *adv* très haut ►**to go ~** (*prices*) s'envoler **II.** *adj* (*extremely high*) très haut(e) **skyjack** **I.** *vt* (*flight, plane*) détourner **II.** *n s.* **skyjacking** **skyjacker** *n* pirate *m* de l'air **skyjacking** *n* détournement *m* d'avion

skylark ['skaɪlɑːk, *Am:* -lɑːrk] **I.** *n* passereau *m* **II.** *vi* (*play around*) faire des mauvaises plaisanteries

skylight ['skaɪlaɪt] *n* lucarne *f*

skyline ['skaɪlaɪn] *n* **1.** (*silhouette of city rooftops*) silhouette *f* **2.** (*horizon*) horizon *m*

skyscraper *n* gratte-ciel *m* **skywriting** *n inv* publicité *f* aérienne

slab [slæb] *n* **1.** (*thick flat piece: of concrete, marble*) dalle *f;* **a butcher's/fishmonger's ~** un plateau de viandes/poissons **2.** (*thick slice*) morceau *m*

slack [slæk] **I.** *adj* **1.** (*not taut*) *a. pej* lâche; **to get ~** se relâcher **2.** (*not busy: demand, business*) calme **II.** *n no pl* mou *m;* **to take up the ~** tendre la corde *fig,* relancer le marché **III.** *vi* **1.** (*become loose*) *a. fig* se relâcher **2.** *pej* (*be lazy*) lambiner **IV.** *vt* **1.** (*loose*) desserrer **2.** (*reduce*) ralentir

◆**slack off** *vi* **1.** (*become loose*) *a. fig* se relâcher **2.** (*reduce*) ralentir

◆**slack up** *vi* ralentir

slack *n no pl* poussier *m*

slacken **I.** *vt* **1.** (*make less tight: reins, rope*) déserrer; **to ~ one's grip** se relâcher

S

2. (*reduce: one's pace, speed*) ralentir; (*vigilance*) relâcher II. *vi* se relâcher

◆**slacken off** I. *vi* se relâcher II. *vt* relâcher

slackening *n no pl* relâchement *m*

slacker *n pej, inf* lambin *m*

slackness *n no pl* 1. (*looseness*) mollesse *f* 2. (*lack of activity*) ~ **in sth** période *f* creuse de qc 3. *pej* (*laziness*) laxisme *m*

slacks *npl* pantalon *m*

slag [slæg] I. *n* 1. *no pl* (*waste from coal*) scories *fpl* 2. *Brit, pej, inf* (*slut*) traînée *f* II. <-gg-> *vt inf s.* **slag off**

◆**slag off** *vt Brit, inf* engueuler

slag heap *n* dépôt *m* de scories

slalom ['slɑːləm] *n* SPORT slalom *m*

slam[1] [slæm] I. <-mm-> *vt* 1. (*close noisily*) claquer; **to ~ the door in sb's face** claquer la porte au nez de qn 2. *inf* (*criticize severely*) descendre en flamme 3. (*hit hard*) **to ~ sth into sth** cogner qc contre qc 4. (*put down violently*) **to ~ down sth, to ~ sth down** balancer qc II. <-mm-> *vi* 1. (*shut noisily*) claquer; **to ~ out of the house** partir en claquant la porte 2. (*hit hard*) **to ~ against sth** cogner contre qc; **to ~ into sth** cogner qc III. *n* bruit *m* de choc

slam[2] [slæm] *n* 1. SPORT, GAMES chelem *m* 2. LIT slam *m*

slammer *n no pl, inf* **the ~** la taule

slander ['slɑːndəʳ, *Am:* 'slændɚ] I. *n* LAW diffamation *f* II. *vt* diffamer

slander action *n* procès *m* en diffamation

slanderer *n* diffamateur, -trice *m, f*

slanderous ['slɑːndərəs, *Am:* 'slændɚ-] *adj* diffamatoire

slang [slæŋ] I. *n no pl* argot *m* II. *adj* argotique III. *vt Brit, Aus, inf* (*abuse*) engueuler

slanging match *n Brit, Aus* engueulade *f*

slangy <-ier, -iest> *adj inf* (*expression*) familier(-ère)

slant [slɑːnt, *Am:* slænt] I. *vi* pencher II. *vt* 1. (*lean*) incliner 2. *pej* (*present in biased way*) fausser III. *n* 1. *no pl* (*slope*) inclinaison *f*; **to be on a ~** (*garden*) être en pente; (*picture*) être de travers 2. (*bias*) tendance *f* 3. (*perspective*) point *m* de vue

slanting *adj* (*roof*) incliné(e)

slap [slæp] I. *n* 1. (*blow with open hand*) tape *f*; **a ~ in the face** donner une claque à qn; **to give sb a ~ on the back** taper qn dans le dos 2. (*noise*) coup *m* ►**a ~ on the <u>back</u>** une tape sur l'épaule; **to be a ~ in the <u>face</u> for sb** faire l'effet d'une claque à qn; **a bit of ~ and <u>tickle</u>** *Brit, iron, inf* un petit câlin II. <-pp-> *vt* 1. (*hit with open hand*) taper; **to ~ sb's face** donner une claque à qn; **to ~ sb on the back** taper qn dans le dos; (*in congratulation*) taper qn sur l'épaule 2. (*strike*) **to ~ sth against sth** cogner qc contre qc III. *vi* (*make slapping noise*) claquer; **to ~ against sth** taper contre qc IV. *adv inf* (*right*) directement

◆**slap down** *vt* 1. (*put down with slap*) balancer 2. (*silence rudely*) engueuler

◆**slap on** *vt* 1. *inf* (*put on quickly*) tartiner 2. *inf* (*impose*) **to slap sth on sb** refiler qc à qn

slap-bang [ˌslæp'bæŋ] *adv Brit, inf s.* **slap**

slapdash ['slæpdæʃ] *adj pej, inf* bâclé(e)

slaphead ['slæphed] *n pej, inf* (*bald person*) crâne *m* d'œuf

slapjack ['slæpˌdʒæk] *n Am* galette *f*

slapstick ['slæpstɪk] I. *n no pl* comédie *f* II. *adj* comique

slapstick comedy *n* comédie *f*

slap-up *adj Brit, Aus, inf* super *inv*

slash [slæʃ] I. *vt* 1. (*cut deeply*) taillader; (*one's wrists*) s'entailler 2. (*reduce drastically*) réduire 3. *fig* **to ~ one's way through sth** se tailler un chemin à travers qc II. *vi* (*swing knife*) **to ~ at sth** frapper qc; **to ~ at the ball** frapper dans le ballon III. *n* 1. (*cut*) entaille *f* 2. (*swinging blow*) grand coup *m* 3. (*decorative opening*) fente *f* 4. (*punctuation mark*) barre *f* oblique 5. *Brit, Aus, inf* (*act of urinating*) **to go for/have a ~** aller/avoir envie de pisser

slashing *adj* impitoyable

slat [slæt] *n* latte *f*

slate [sleɪt] I. *n* 1. *no pl* (*rock, stone, black board*) ardoise *f* 2. *Am, Aus* POL liste *f* électorale ►**to have a <u>clean</u> ~** avoir les mains propres; **to wipe the ~ <u>clean</u>** faire table rase; **to <u>put</u> sth on the ~** mettre qc sur le compte de qn II. *vt* 1. (*cover with slates: a roof*) couvrir d'ardoises 2. *Am, Aus* **to be ~d for sth** être inscrit pour qc 3. *Brit, Aus, inf* (*criticize severely*) descendre en flammes

slattern ['slætən, *Am:* 'slæt̬ɚn] *n pej* traînée *f*

slatternly *adj pej* débauché(e); **a ~ woman** une débauchée

slaty <-ier, -iest> *adj* 1. (*colour*) ardoisé(e); (*colour, grey*) ardoise 2. (*texture*) ardoisier(-ère)

slaughter ['slɔːtəʳ, *Am:* 'slɑːt̬ɚ] I. *vt a. fig* abattre II. *n no pl* 1. (*cruel killing*) *a. fig* massacre *m* 2. (*killing for food*) abattage *m*

slaughterhouse *n* abattoir *m*

Slav [slɑːv] I. *n* Slave *mf* II. *adj* slave

slave [sleɪv] I. *n a. fig* esclave *mf* II. <-ving> *vi* travailler comme un esclave; **to ~ at sth** s'échiner à qc

slave driver *n iron, inf* négrier *m*

slaver[1] ['slævəʳ, *Am:* -ɚ] I. *vi a. pej* baver II. *n no pl* (*saliva*) bave *f*

slaver[2] ['sleɪvəʳ, *Am:* -ɚ] *n* HIST 1. (*ship*) vaisseau *m* négrier 2. (*trader*) négrier *m*

slavery ['sleɪvəri] *n no pl* esclavage *m*

slave trade *n* HIST commerce *m* des esclaves

Slavic ['slɑːvɪk] *adj s.* **Slav**

slavish ['sleɪvɪʃ] *adj pej* servile

Slavonic [slə'vɒnɪk, *Am:* -'vɑːnɪk] *s.* **Slav**

sleazy ['sliːzi] <-ier, -iest> *adj* miteux(-euse)

sled [sled] *Am s.* **sledge**

sledge[1] [sledʒ] I. *n* luge *f*, glisse *f Suisse* II. <-dging> *vi* **to go sledging** faire de la luge

III. *vt* transporter en luge
sledge² [sledʒ] *n Brit, inf abbr of* **sledgehammer** marteau *m*
sledgehammer ['sledʒˌhæməʳ, *Am:* -ɚ] *n* marteau *m*
sleek [sliːk] **I.** *adj* **1.** (*with smooth, glossy surface*) lisse **2.** (*smoothly shaped*) profilé(e) **3.** (*prosperous-looking*) bien entretenu(e) **II.** *vt* prendre soin de
sleep [sliːp] **I.** *n no pl* sommeil *m;* **to get to ~** [*o* **go**] s'endormir; **to put sb/an animal to ~** endormir qn/un animal; **to fall into a deep ~** tomber dans un sommeil profond **II.** <slept, slept> *vi* dormir; **~ tight!** dors/dormez bien!; **to ~ the night with sb** passer la nuit avec qn (au lit); **to ~ rough** *Brit* dormir sous les ponts ▶**to ~ like a log** *inf* dormir comme une marmotte **III.** *vt* **to ~ four/ten** dormir à quatre/dix
◆**sleep around** *vi pej, inf* (*be promiscuous*) coucher
◆**sleep in** *vi* **1.** (*stay in bed*) dormir tard **2.** (*sleep in employer's house*) être hébergé
◆**sleep off** *vt* faire la grasse matinée
◆**sleep on** *vt* dormir d'une traite
◆**sleep out** *vi* découcher
◆**sleep through I.** *vt* **to ~ noise/storm** ne pas être réveillé par le bruit/la tempête; **to ~ a film/lecture** dormir pendant un film/un cours **II.** *vi* dormir comme une souche
◆**sleep together** *vi* dormir ensemble
◆**sleep with** *vt* coucher avec
sleeper *n* **1.** (*person*) dormeur, -euse *m, f;* **to be a heavy/light ~** avoir un sommeil profond/léger; **to be a late ~** dormir tard **2.** (*train*) wagon-lit *m* **3.** *Brit, Aus* RAIL (*horizontal blocks on track*) traverse *f*
sleeper plane *n* MIL *avion avec des couchettes*
sleepiness *n no pl* envie *f* de dormir
sleeping *adj* endormi(e)
sleeping accommodation *n no pl* hébergement *m* **sleeping bag** *n* sac *m* de couchage **sleeping car** *n* wagon-lit *m* **sleeping pill** *n* somnifère *m* **sleeping policeman** <-men> *n* ralentisseur *m* **sleeping sickness** *n no pl* maladie *f* du sommeil **sleeping tablet** *s.* **sleeping pill**
sleepless *adj* insomniaque; **a ~ night** une nuit blanche
sleepwalk *vi* être somnambule **sleepwalker** *n* somnambule *mf*
sleepy ['sliːpi] <-ier, -iest> *adj* **1.** (*drowsy*) somnolent(e) **2.** (*very quiet*) tranquille
sleepyhead ['sliːpihed] *n inf* endormi(e) *m(f)*
sleet [sliːt] **I.** *n no pl* neige *f* fondue **II.** *vi* **it is ~ing** il tombe de la neige fondue
sleeve [sliːv] *n* **1.** (*arm*) *a. fig* manche *f;* **with short/long ~s** à manches courtes/longues; **to roll up one's ~s** remonter ses manches **2.** (*tube-shaped cover*) manchon *m* **3.** (*cover for record*) pochette *f* de disque
sleeveless *adj* sans manches
sleigh [sleɪ] *n* traîneau *m*
sleighing-party *n* promenade *f* en traîneau
sleight of hand [ˌslaɪtɒf'hænd, *Am:* -ɑːf-] *n no pl, a. fig* tour *m* de passe-passe
slender ['slendəʳ, *Am:* -dɚ] *adj* mince
slenderize ['slendəraɪz] **I.** *vi Am, inf* (*slim*) s'amincir **II.** *vt Am, inf* (*make slim*) amincir; **a ~ing lunch** un repas amincissant
slept [slept] *pt, pp of* **sleep**
slew [sluː] **I.** *vt* faire pivoter **II.** *vi* pivoter
slice [slaɪs] **I.** *n* **1.** (*flat piece cut off: of bread, meat, lemon*) tranche *f;* (*of cake, pizza*) morceau *m* **2.** (*part: of the profits, a market*) part *f* **3.** (*utensil*) pelle *f;* **a cake ~** une pelle à tarte **4.** SPORT balle *f* coupée **II.** *vt* **1.** (*cut in slices*) couper en tranches **2.** SPORT (*the ball*) couper **III.** *vi* **to ~ easily** se couper facilement
◆**slice off** *vt* trancher
◆**slice up** *vt* couper (en tranches)
sliced *adj* coupé(e); (*bread*) en tranches
slicer *n* GASTR couteau *m* à découper; **egg ~** découpe-œufs *m;* **bread ~** machine *f* à couper le pain
slick [slɪk] **I.** <-er, -est> *adj* **1.** (*skilfully executed*) habile **2.** (*superficial*) superficiel(le); (*excuse*) facile **3.** (*smart: person, behaviour*) adroit(e); **a ~ talker** un beau parleur **4.** (*smooth: hair, skin*) lisse **II.** *n* **1.** *s.* **oil slick 2.** *Am* (*magazine*) magazine *m* sur papier glacé **III.** *vt* **to ~ up** *Am* briquer; **to ~ one's hair down** se lisser les cheveux
slicker *n* **1.** *Am s.* **city slicker 2.** *Am* (*waterproof coat*) ciré *m*
slide [slaɪd] **I.** <slid, slid *o* sliding> *vi* **1.** (*glide smoothly*) glisser **2.** (*move quietly*) **to ~ somewhere** se glisser quelque part **3.** (*decline*) se dégrader; **to ~ back into one's old habits** prendre des mauvaises habitudes; **to let sth/things ~** laisser faire qc/les choses **II.** <slid, slid *o* sliding> *vt* pousser **III.** *n* **1.** (*act of sliding*) glissade *f* **2.** (*sliding place on ice*) patinoire *f* **3.** (*playground structure*) toboggan *m* **4.** GEO glissement *m* **5.** *no pl* FIN baisse *f* **6.** PHOT diapositive *f* **7.** (*glass for microscope*) porte-objet *m* **8.** MUS mouvement *m* **9.** *Brit* (*hair clip*) barrette *f*
slide control *n* régulateur *m* **slide projector** *n* projecteur *m* de diapositives **slide rule** *n* règle *f* à calcul **slide show** *n* (*of professional slides*) diaporama *m;* (*of private slides*) séance *f* diapos
sliding *adj* coulissant(e)
slight [slaɪt] **I.** <-er, -est> *adj* **1.** (*small: chance, possibility*) infime; **the ~est thing/idea** la moindre chose/idée; (**not**) **the ~est bit ...** *Brit* pas le moindre .... **2.** (*not very noticeable or serious*) insignifiant(e) **3.** (*slim and delicate*) frêle **4.** (*lightweight*) léger(-ère) **II.** *n* (*snub*) offense *f* **III.** *vt* offenser
slightly *adv* un peu
slim [slɪm] **I.** <slimmer, slimmest> *adj* **1.** (*attractively thin*) mince **2.** (*not thick*)

S

léger(-ère) **3.** (*slight: chance, possibility*) maigre **II.** <-mm-> *vi* maigrir

slime [slaɪm] *n no pl, n no pl* **1.** (*unpleasant substance*) substance *f* gluante **2.** (*produced by slugs*) bave *f*

slimmer *n* compteur *m* de calories

slimming *adj* **1.** (*making slight: aids, pill*) amincissant(e) **2.** *inf* (*non-fattening: food, drinks*) allégé(e)

slimy ['slaɪmi] <-ier, -iest> *adj a. pej* visqueux(-euse)

sling [slɪŋ] <slung, slung> **I.** *vt* **1.** (*hang*) suspendre; **to ~ sth from sth** suspendre qc à qc; **to ~ sth over one's shoulder** mettre qc en bandoulière **2.** (*fling*) jeter **3.** *inf* (*put carelessly*) balancer **4.** *inf* (*dismiss*) **to ~ (out)** jeter ►**to ~ one's hook** *Brit, inf* se tirer; **~ your hook!** dégage! **II.** *n* **1.** (*cloth supporting broken arm*) écharpe *f* **2.** (*carrying cloth for baby*) écharpe *f* porte-bébé **3.** (*carrying strap*) bandoulière *f*

◆**sling out** *vt* **1.** *inf* (*dismiss*) jeter **2.** *inf* (*throw away, out: old clothes*) balancer

slingshot ['slɪŋʃɒt, *Am:* -ʃɑːt] *n Am, Aus* fronde *f*

slink [slɪŋk] <slunk> *vi* **1.** (*guiltily*) se faufiler **2.** *inf* (*sexily*) marcher comme un chat

slinky <-ier, iest> *adj* **1.** (*moving sexily*) comme un chat; **~ walk** démarche *f* de chat **2.** (*close-fitting and sexy*) excitant(e)

slip¹ [slɪp] *n* **1.** (*piece: of paper*) bout *m* **2.** COM (*official piece of paper*) bordereau *f;* **a salary ~** un bulletin de paie **3.** (*small, slight person*) bout *m* de chou; **a ~ of a girl** une fille fluette **4.** BOT bouture *f*

slip² <-pp-> **I.** *vi* **1.** (*slide*) glisser; **to ~ through one's fingers** filer entre les doigts **2.** (*move quietly*) se glisser; **to ~ in(to) sth** se glisser dans qc; **to ~ into one's jeans** enfiler son jeans; **to ~ into bad habits** prendre des mauvaises habitudes; **to ~ into a coma** sombrer dans le coma **3.** (*let out*) **to let sth ~** laisser échapper qc; (*one's concentration*) relâcher qc **4.** (*decline*) baisser **5.** (*make a mistake*) faire une erreur **II.** *vt* **1.** (*put smoothly*) glisser; **to ~ sb money** glisser de l'argent à qn; **to ~ a shirt on** enfiler une chemise **2.** (*escape from*) s'échapper; **to ~ sb's attention** échapper à l'attention de qn; **to ~ sb's mind** échapper à qn **3.** AUTO laisser patiner **III.** *n* **1.** (*act of sliding*) glissement *m* **2.** (*fall*) *a. fig* chute *f* **3.** (*trip*) faux pas *m* **4.** (*mistake*) erreur *f;* **a ~ of the tongue** un lapsus **5.** (*petticoat*) combinaison *f*

◆**slip away** *vi* s'éclipser

◆**slip by** *vi* filer; (*time*) passer

◆**slip down** *vi* **1.** (*fall down*) glisser **2.** (*be swallowed easily*) descendre tout seul

◆**slip in I.** *vt* glisser **II.** *vi* se glisser

◆**slip off I.** *vi* **1.** *s.* **slip away 2.** (*fall off*) reculer **II.** *vt* **1.** (*fall from*) glisser de **2.** (*take off*) enlever

◆**slip on** *vt* (*put on*) passer

◆**slip out** *vi* **1.** (*go out*) s'éclipser; **to ~ to a shop** faire un saut dans un magasin **2.** (*escape*) s'échapper; **it slipped out** *fig* cela m'a échappé

◆**slip past** *s.* **slip by**

◆**slip up** *vi inf* se tromper

slip-carriage *n* RAIL wagon *m* **slipcase** *n* (*for book*) couverture *f* **slip-coach** *s.* **slip-carriage slip cover** *n* housse *f* **slipknot** *n* **1.** (*easily untied*) nœud *m* simple **2.** (*sliding knot*) nœud *m* coulant **slip-on I.** *adj* **~ shoes** mocassins *mpl* **II.** *n* **1.** (*sweater*) pull *m* **2.** *pl* (*shoes*) mocassins *mpl* **slipover** *n* débardeur *m*

slipper ['slɪpəʳ, *Am:* -ɚ] *n* chausson *m*

slippery ['slɪpəri] <-ier, -iest> *adj* **1.** (*not giving firm hold*) glissant(e) **2.** (*untrustworthy*) douteux(-euse)

slip road *n Brit* bretelle *f* d'accès

slipshod ['slɪpʃɒd, *Am:* -ʃɑːd] *adj* sale; (*work*) bâclé(e)

slipstream *n* côté *m* abrité du vent **slip-up** *n* gaffe *f* **slipway** *n* NAUT cale *f*

slit [slɪt] **I.** <slitting, slit> *vt* couper en deux; **to ~ sb's throat** couper la gorge à qn; **to ~ one's wrist** s'entailler les veines; **to ~ an envelope open** décacheter une enveloppe **II.** *n* fente *f*

slit-eyed *adj pej, inf* aux yeux bridés; **to be ~** avoir les yeux bridés

slither ['slɪðəʳ, *Am:* -ɚ] *vi* **1.** (*move like reptile*) ramper **2.** (*slide*) glisser

slithery *adj* glissant(e)

sliver ['slɪvəʳ, *Am:* -ɚ] *n* **1.** (*sharp thin fragment: of glass*) éclat *m;* (*of wood*) copeau *m* **2.** (*very small piece*) petit morceau *m*

slob [slɒb, *Am:* slɑːb] *n pej, inf* souillon *mf*

slobber I. *vi* baver **II.** *n no pl* bave *f*

slobbery *adj* baveux(-euse)

sloe [sləʊ, *Am:* sloʊ] *n* prunellier *m*

slog [slɒg, *Am:* slɑːg] **I.** *n no pl* **1.** *inf* (*hard effort*) grand coup *m* **2.** *inf* (*strenuous hike*) marathon *m* **II.** <-gg-> *vi inf* vadrouiller **III.** <-gg-> *vt inf* SPORT smatcher

◆**slog away** *vi inf* trimer; **to ~ at sth** se crever à qc

slogan ['sləʊgən, *Am:* 'sloʊ-] *n* slogan *m*

sloop [sluːp] *n* NAUT chaloupe *f*

slop [slɒp, *Am:* slɑːp] <-pp-> **I.** *vt inf* (*spill*) renverser **II.** *vi inf* (*spill out*) **to ~ out of sth** déborder de qc **III.** *n pl* **~s 1.** (*liquid food waste*) eaux *fpl* sales **2.** *pej, inf* (*watery food*) lavasse *f*

slop basin *n Brit* filtre *m*

slope [sləʊp, *Am:* sloʊp] **I.** *n* pente *f;* **ski ~** piste *f* de ski **II.** *vi* **1.** (*be on a slope*) **to ~ down** être en pente; **to ~ up** monter **2.** (*lean*) pencher **III.** *vt* incliner

◆**slope off** *vi Brit, pej* (*go away quietly*) se casser

sloping *adj* (*roof, ground*) en pente; (*shoulders*) tombant(e); (*writing*) penché(e)

sloppiness *n no pl, pej* négligence *f*

sloppy <-ier, -iest> *adj* **1.** *pej* (*careless*) négligé(e) **2.** *iron or pej* (*sentimentally romantic*) à l'eau de rose **3.** *pej* (*too wet*) trempé(e); (*food, porridge*) en bouillie

slosh [slɒʃ, *Am:* slɑːʃ] **I.** *vt* **1.** *inf* (*pour liquid carelessly*) renverser **2.** *Brit, inf* (*hit*) cogner **II.** *vi* **to ~ (about)** **1.** (*move through water*) patauger **2.** (*make a splashing sound*) clapoter

◆**slosh about, slosh around** **I.** *vi* (*water*) clapoter; (*person*) barboter **II.** *vt* **to slosh sth about** répandre qc

sloshed *adj inf* bourré(e)

slot [slɒt, *Am:* slɑːt] **I.** *n* **1.** (*narrow opening*) fente *f* **2.** INFOR fenêtre *f* **3.** TV tranche *f* horaire **II.** *vi* **to ~ in** s'intégrer; **to ~ together** s'assembler **III.** *vt* **to ~ in** insérer; **to ~ together** assembler

sloth [sləʊθ, *Am:* slɑːθ] *n* **1.** *no pl* (*laziness*) paresse *f* **2.** (*animal*) paresseux *m* **3.** *fig, pej* paresseux, -euse *m, f*

slothful *adj* paresseux(-euse)

slot machine *n* distributeur *m* automatique

slot meter *n* distributeur *m* de gaz

slouch [slaʊtʃ] **I.** *vi* **1.** (*have shoulders bent*) se tenir de travers **2.** (*shamble*) **to ~ along the street** déambuler dans les rues **II.** *n* avachissement *m*

slough¹ [slʌf] *n* (*bog*) marécage *m*

slough² [slaʊ, *Am:* sluː] *vt* ZOOL muer

Slovak **I.** *adj* slovaque **II.** *n* **1.** (*person*) Slovaque *mf* **2.** LING slovaque *m; s. a.* **English**

Slovakia [sləʊ'vækiə, *Am:* sloʊ'vɑːki-] *n* la Slovaquie

Slovakian *s.* **Slovak**

Slovene **I.** *adj* slovène **II.** *n* **1.** (*person*) Slovène *mf* **2.** LING slovène *m; s. a.* **English**

Slovenia [sləʊ'viːniə, *Am:* sloʊ'-] *n* la Slovénie

Slovenian *s.* **Slovene**

slovenly ['slʌvənli] *adj* mal soigné(e); (*habits*) débraillé(e)

slow [sləʊ, *Am:* sloʊ] **I.** *adj a. fig* lent(e); **to be ~ to** +*infin* être lent à +*infin;* **to be 10 minutes ~** être en retard de 10 minutes ►**~ and steady wins the race** *prov* rien ne sert de courir, il faut partir à point **II.** *vi, vt* ralentir

◆**slow down** **I.** *vt* ralentir **II.** *vi* ralentir

slowcoach *n Brit, Aus, childspeak, inf* lambin, -e *m, f* **slowdown** *n* **1.** ECON ralentissement *m* **2.** *Am* ECON *s.* **go-slow**

slowly *adv* lentement; **~ but surely** lentement, mais sûrement

slow motion CINE **I.** *n no pl* ralenti *m;* **in ~** au ralenti **II.** *adj* lent(e) **slow-moving** *adj* qui se déplace lentement

slowness *n no pl* **1.** (*lack of speed*) lenteur *f* **2.** (*lack of intelligence*) lourdeur *f*

slow train *n* omnibus *m* **slow-witted** *adj* lent(e) d'esprit **slow worm** *n* orvet *m*

SLR (camera) *n* PHOT *abbr of* **single lens reflex (camera)** appareil *m* photo reflex

sludge [slʌdʒ] *n no pl* vase *f;* **~ sewage** vidanges *fpl*

slue *vt, vi Am s.* **slew**

slug¹ [slʌg] *n* (*animal*) limace *f*

slug² [slʌg] <-gg-> **I.** *vi inf* (*hit*) tabasser; **to ~ it out** se tabasser **II.** *n* **1.** *inf* (*bullet*) balle *f* **2.** *Am* (*blow*) coup *m* violent **3.** (*swig*) coup *m*

sluggard *n* paresseux(-euse)

sluggardly *adj* paresseusement

sluggish *adj* **1.** paresseux(-euse) **2.** FIN (*trading*) stagnant(e)

sluice [sluːs] **I.** *n* écluse *f* **II.** *vi* vanner; **to ~ out** laisser échapper **III.** *vt* **to ~ sth down** laver à grande eau

sluice gate *n* porte *f* d'écluse **sluiceway** *n* canal *m* à vannes

slum [slʌm] **I.** *n* SOCIOL quartier *m* pauvre **II.** <-mm-> *vi inf* zoner **III.** <-mm-> *vt* **to ~ it** *iron* zoner

slum dweller *n* habitant(e) *m(f)* des bas quartiers

slump [slʌmp] **I.** *n* ECON **1.** (*sudden decline*) effondrement *m* **2.** (*recession*) crise *f;* **to be in a ~** être en crise **II.** *vi a.* FIN s'effondrer

slung [slʌŋ] *pt, pp of* **sling**

slunk [slʌŋk] *pt, pp of* **slink**

slur [slɜːʳ, *Am:* slɜːr] <-rr-> **I.** *vt* (*pronounce unclearly*) mal articuler **II.** *n* insulte *f*

slurp [slɜːp, *Am:* slɜːrp] *inf* **I.** *vi, vt* **1.** (*drink noisily*) faire du bruit en buvant **2.** (*eat noisily*) faire du bruit en mangeant **II.** *n inf* gorgée *f*

slush [slʌʃ] *n no pl* **1.** (*melting snow*) neige *f* fondue **2.** *pej* (*over-sentimental language*) sensiblerie *f*

slush fund *n pej* caisse *f* noire

slushy *adj* <-ier, -iest> **1.** (*melting*) détrempé(e) par la neige **2.** (*over-sentimental*) d'une sentimentalité excessive

slut [slʌt] *n pej* **1.** (*promiscuous*) salope *f* **2.** (*lazy*) souillon *f*

sluttish, slutty *adj* <-ier, -iest> *pej* **1.** (*promiscuous*) de salope **2.** (*untidy*) malpropre

sly [slaɪ] *adj* rusé(e); (*smile*) espiègle; (*humour*) coquin(e); **on the ~** en cachette

smack [smæk] **I.** *vt* **1.** (*slap*) frapper; **to ~ sb's bottom** donner une fessée à qn **2.** (*slap noisily*) claquer **II.** *n* **1.** *inf* (*slap*) claque *f;* **a ~ on the bottom** une fessée; **a ~ on the jaw of sb** une gifle sur la joue de qn **2.** *inf* (*hearty kiss*) grosse bise *f* **3.** (*loud noise*) claquement *m* **4.** (*kiss*) grosse bise *f* **III.** *adv* en plein; **~ in the middle** au beau milieu

smacker *n inf* **1.** *Brit* (*pound*) livre *f; Am* (*dollar*) dollar *m* **2.** (*loud kiss*) gros baiser *m*

smacking *adj* vif(vive)

small [smɔːl] **I.** *adj* **1.** (*not large*) petit(e); **to be too ~ for sb/sth** être trop petit pour qn/qc **2.** (*young*) petit(e) **3.** (*insignificant*) tout(e) petit(e); **to feel ~** se sentir tout petit; **~ consolation** *no art* faible consolation; **it's ~ wonder** *no art* ce n'est guère étonnant **4.** (*on a limited scale*) peu considérable; **in a ~ way** modestement **5.** TYP, LIT **a ~ letter** une minuscule; **with a ~ 'c'** avec un c minuscule ►**it's a ~ world!** *prov* le monde est petit **II.** *n no pl* **the**

~ **of the back** la chute des reins

small ad *n* petite annonce *f* **small arms** *npl* armes *fpl* portatives **small beer** *n Brit* **to be ~** avoir peu d'importance; **sth is ~ compared to sth** qc est insignifiant par rapport à qc **small business** <-es> *n* petite entreprise *f* **small businessman** *n* gérant, -e *m, f* d'une petite entreprise **small change** *n no pl* petite monnaie *f* **small fry** *n no pl, inf* **1.** (*children*) gosses *mpl* **2.** *fig* (*unimportant*) menu *m* fretin **smallholder** *n Brit* petit cultivateur *m* **smallholding** *n Brit* petite ferme *f* **small hours** *npl* heures *fpl* matinales **small intestine** *n* intestin *m* grêle

smallish ['smɔːlɪʃ] *adj* assez petit(e)

small-minded *adj pej* étroit(e) d'esprit

smallness *n no pl* petitesse *f*

smallpox *n no pl* variole *f* **small print** *n no pl* texte *m* en petits caractères; *s. a.* **fine print small-scale** *adj* réduit(e) **small screen** *n no pl* petit écran *m* **small talk** *n no pl* bavardages *mpl* sans importance **small-time** *adj* insignifiant(e)

smarmy ['smɑːmi, *Am:* 'smɑːr] *adj pej* doucereux(-euse)

smart [smɑːt, *Am:* smɑːrt] **I.** *adj* **1.** (*clever*) intelligent(e); **to make a ~ move** prendre une sage décision; **to be ~ with sb** *pej* faire le malin avec qn **2.** (*stylish*) élégant(e) **3.** (*quick*) vif(vive); **to do sth at a ~ pace** faire qc à un rythme soutenu **II.** *vi* brûler; **sth is still ~ing from sth** qc brûle toujours de qc **III.** *n* douleur *f* cuisante

smartarse ['smɑːtɑːs, *Am:* 'smɑːrtɑːrs] *n Brit, Aus,* **smart ass** *n pej, inf* petit malin *m*

smart card *n* INFOR carte *f* intelligente

smarten ['smɑːtn, *Am:* 'smɑːr-] **I.** *vt* **to ~ up** arranger qc **II.** *vi* **to ~ up** se faire beau

smartness *n no pl, Brit, Aus, Am* habileté *f*

smart weapon *n* arme *f* intelligente

smash [smæʃ] **I.** *n* **1.** (*noise*) fracas *m* **2.** (*blow*) coup *m* **3.** (*collision*) accident *m* **4.** SPORT smash *m* **5.** (*hit*) gros succès *m* **II.** *vt* **1.** (*shatter*) briser; (*violently*) fracasser; **to ~ sth into pieces** briser qc en morceaux, mettre qc en briques *Suisse* **2.** (*strike*) **to ~ sth against sth** heurter qc contre qc avec violence; **to ~ sb/sth through sth** lancer qn/qc au travers de qc avec violence; **to ~ the door open** enfoncer la porte **3.** (*destroy: opponent, army*) écraser **4.** SPORT (*a record*) pulvériser; **to ~ the ball** faire un smash **5.** PHYS (*the atom*) pulvériser **III.** *vi* **1.** (*shatter*) éclater; **to ~ into pieces** éclater en morceaux **2.** (*strike against sth*) se heurter violemment; **~ into/through sth** s'écraser violemment contre qc

◆**smash in** *vt* défoncer; **to smash sb's face in** casser la figure à qn

◆**smash up** *vt* démolir

smash-and-grab raid [ˌsmæʃəndgræb'reɪd] *n Brit, Aus* vol *m* (*après avoir brisé la devanture*)

smashed *adj inf* **1.** (*shattered*) défoncé(e) **2.** (*drunk*) bourré(e); **to get ~** se saouler

smasher *n Brit, inf* **to be a ~** être vachement bien

smash hit *n* gros succès *m*

smashing *adj Brit, inf* violent(e)

smash-up *n* destruction *f* complète

smattering ['smætərɪŋ, *Am:* 'smæt̬-] *n* légère connaissance *f*

smear [smɪəʳ, *Am:* smɪr] **I.** *vt* **1.** (*spread messily*) barbouiller; **to ~ with sth** enduire de qc **2.** (*attack sb's reputation: reputation*) salir **II.** *n* **1.** (*blotch*) tâche *f* **2.** (*public accusations*) diffamation *f*

smear campaign *n* campagne *f* calomnieuse **smear test** *n* MED frottis *m*

smeary *adj* tâché(e)

smell [smel] <smelt, smelt *Brit, Aus o* -ed, -ed *Am, Aus*> **I.** *n* **1.** (*odour*) odeur *f*; **the ~ of roses** le parfum des roses **2.** (*sense of smell*) odorat *m* **3.** *pej* (*bad odour*) puanteur *f* **4.** (*sniff*) **to take/have a ~ of sth** sentir qc ►**the sweet ~ of success** la griserie du succès **II.** *vi* **1.** (*use one's sense of smell*) sentir **2.** (*give off an odour*) sentir; **sweet-~ing** qui sent bon **3.** *pej* (*have an unpleasant smell*) sentir mauvais **III.** *vt a. fig* sentir ►**to ~ sth a mile off** flairer qc à des kilomètres; **to ~ a rat** se douter de qc

◆**smell out** *vt* **1.** (*discover by smelling*) *a. fig* flairer **2.** *pej* (*cause to smell bad*) empester

smelling bottle, **smelling salts** *npl* MED sels *mpl* anglais

smelly ['smeli] *adj* <-ier, -iest> *pej* malodorant(e)

smelt[1] [smelt] *Brit, Aus pt, pp of* **smell**

smelt[2] [smelt] *vt* (*metal*) fondre

smelt[3] [smelt] <-(s)> *n* ZOOL éperlan *m*

smile [smaɪl] **I.** *n* (*facial expression*) sourire *m*; **to be all ~s** être tout souriant; **to give sb a ~** adresser un sourire à qn **II.** *vi* **1.** (*produce a smile*) sourire; **to ~ at sb** sourire à qn; **to ~ in the face of adversity** garder le sourire **2. to ~ on sb/sth** sourire à qn/qc **III.** *vt* sourire; **to ~ a sad smile** avoir un sourire triste

smiley ['smaɪli] *n* INFOR smiley *m,* frimousse *f Québec*

smiling *adj* souriant(e)

smirch [smɜːtʃ, *Am:* smɜːrtʃ] *vt s.* **besmirch**

smirk [smɜːk, *Am:* smɜːrk] **I.** *vi pej* sourire d'un air moqueur **II.** *n pej* petit sourire *m* supérieur

smite [smaɪt] *vt* frapper

smith [smɪθ] *n* forgeron *m*

smithereens [ˌsmɪðə'riːnz] *npl* **to smash sth to ~** réduire qc en éclats

smithy ['smɪði, *Am:* 'smɪθ-] <-thies> *n* forgeron *m*

smitten ['smɪtən] **I.** *adj* (*in love*) **to be ~ with sb/sth** être épris de qn/qc **II.** *pp of* **smite**

smock [smɒk, *Am:* smɑːk] *n* blouse *f*

smocking *n no pl* smocks *mpl*

smog [smɒg, *Am:* smɑːg] *n no pl* smog *m*

smoke [sməʊk, *Am:* smoʊk] **I.** *n* **1.** *no pl* (*dirty air*) fumée *f* **2.** *inf* (*cigarette*) cigarette *f* ▶**there's no ~ without fire** *Brit, Aus, prov,* **where there's ~, there's fire** *Am, prov* il n'y a pas de fumée dans feu; **to vanish in a puff of ~** disparaître dans un nuage de fumée; **to go up in ~** partir en fumée **II.** *vt* **1.** (*use tobacco*) fumer **2.** (*cure*) fumer ▶**to ~ the peace pipe** *Am* fumer le calumet de la paix **III.** *vi* fumer
◆**smoke out** *vt* enfumer

smoke bomb *n* bombe *f* fumigène

smoked *adj* fumé(e)

smoke detector *n* détecteur *m* de fumée **smoke-dried** *adj* fumé(e)

smokeless *adj* (*without smoke*) sans fumée

smoker *n* **1.** (*person*) fumeur, -euse *m, f;* **heavy ~** gros fumeur **2.** (*train compartment*) compartiment *m* fumeur **3.** (*device*) fumeur *m*

smoke-room *n s.* **smoking room** **smokescreen** *n* **1.** (*concealment*) rideau *m* de fumée **2.** MIL (*camouflage*) écran *m* de fumée **smoke signal** *n* signal *m* de fumée **smokestack** *n* cheminée *f*

smoking *n no pl* tabagisme *m;* **to give up ~** arrêter la cigarette

smoking car *n Am,* **smoking compartment** *n* RAIL compartiment *m* fumeur **smoking jacket** *n* veste *f* d'intérieur **smoking room** *n* fumoir *m*

smoky ['sməʊki, *Am:* 'smoʊ-] *adj* <-ier, -iest> **1.** (*filled with smoke*) enfumé(e) **2.** (*producing smoke*) qui fume **3.** (*appearing smoke-like*) noirci(e) par la fumée **4.** (*tasting of smoke*) de fumée

smolder ['smoʊldɚ] *vi Am s.* **smoulder**

smooch [smuːtʃ] **I.** *vi* **1.** (*kiss*) se bécoter **2.** *Brit* (*dance*) danser un slow **II.** *n* **1.** (*activity of kissing*) **to have a ~** se bécoter **2.** *Brit* (*dance*) slow *m*

smooth [smuːð] **I.** *adj* **1.** (*not rough*) lisse; (*skin*) doux(douce); **as ~ as silk** doux comme de la soie **2.** (*well-mixed*) homogène **3.** (*calm: sea*) calme **4.** (*without problems*) sans problèmes; (*flight*) calme **5.** (*sweet: wine*) doux(douce) **6.** (*polished*) doux(douce); **to be a ~ talker** être un beau parleur **II.** *vt* **1.** (*make smooth*) lisser; (*sheet*) défroisser **2.** (*rub even*) égaliser **3.** (*make less difficult*) **to ~ the way for sb** faciliter les choses pour qn; **to ~ the path to sth** ouvrir la voie vers qc
◆**smooth down** *vt* lisser
◆**smooth out** *vt* **1.** (*give an even surface: paper*) défroisser **2.** *fig* faire disparaître
◆**smooth over** *vt* aplanir

smoothie *n pej* charmeur *m*

smoothness *n no pl* **1.** (*evenness*) égalité *f* **2.** (*lack of difficulty*) bon fonctionnement *m* **3.** (*pleasant taste or texture*) douceur *f*

smooth-shaven *adj s.* **clean-shaven** **smooth-tongued** *adj pej* doucereux(-euse)

smoothy *n s.* **smoothie**

smother ['smʌðəʳ, *Am:* -ɚ] *vt* **1.** (*suffocate*) étouffer **2.** (*suppress*) réprimer; *fig* cacher **3.** (*cover*) emmitoufler

smoulder ['sməʊldəʳ, *Am:* 'smoʊldɚ] *vi* **1.** (*burn slowly*) brûler lentement sans flamme **2.** *fig* (*be full of repressed emotions*) consumer

smudge [smʌdʒ] **I.** *vt* **1.** (*smear*) barbouiller **2.** (*soil*) souiller; (*reputation*) salir **II.** *vi* s'étaler **III.** *n* tâche *f*

smudge-proof *adj* (*lipstick*) qui ne tâche pas

smudgy ['smʌdʒi] *adj* <-ier, -iest> sali(e)

smug [smʌg] *adj* <smugger, smuggest> suffisant(e); **~ self-satisfaction** autosatisfaction *f*

smuggle ['smʌgl] *vt* LAW faire passer

smuggler *n* contrebandier, -ière *m, f*

smuggling *n no pl* contrebande *f*

smut [smʌt] *n* **1.** *no pl, pej* (*obscenity*) cochonneries *fpl* **2.** (*air-borne dirt*) parcelle *f* de suie **3.** (*stains made by smut*) tâche *f* de suie

smutty *adj* <-ier, -iest> *pej* grossier(-ère)

snack [snæk] **I.** *n* (*light meal*) casse-croûte *m;* **to have a ~** casser la croûte **II.** *vi* grignoter

snack bar *n* snack-bar *m,* casse-croûte *m Québec*

snaffle ['snæfl] *vt Brit, Aus, inf* piquer; **to ~ up** rafler

snag [snæg] **I.** *n* **1.** (*problem*) obstacle *m* caché; **there's a ~** il y a un problème **2.** (*damage to textiles*) accroc *m* **II.** <-gg-> *vt* **1.** (*cause problems*) causer des problèmes **2.** (*catch and pull*) faire un accroc **3.** (*catch by reacting quickly*) saisir **III.** <-gg-> *vi* **to ~ on sth** accrocher à qc

snail [sneɪl] *n* escargot *m;* **at a ~'s pace** à la vitesse d'un escargot

snail mail *n* INFOR courrier *m* postal **snail shell** *n* coquille *f* d'escargot

snake [sneɪk] **I.** *n* (*long reptile*) serpent *m* ▶**a ~ in the grass** *pej* un faux jeton **II.** *vi* serpenter

snake bite *n* morsure *f* de serpent **snake charmer** *n* charmeur, -euse *m, f* de serpent **snake poison** *n* venin *m* de serpent **snake-skin** *n* peau *f* de serpent **snake venom** *s.* **snake poison**

snaky *adj* <-ier, -iest> **1.** (*winding*) sinueux(-euse) **2.** *Aus, inf* (*irritable*) perfide

snap [snæp] <-pp-> **I.** *n* **1.** (*sound*) claquement *m;* **with a ~ of the fingers** en claquant des doigts **2.** (*photograph*) instantané *m* **3.** *Am* (*snap-fastener*) bouton-pression *m inv* **4.** METEO **a cold ~** une vague de froid **5.** *no pl, Brit* GAMES bataille *f* ▶**in a ~** en un clin d'œil **II.** *adj* hâtif(-ive) **III.** *interj inf* **1.** GAMES bataille! **2.** *fig* ça par exemple! moi aussi! **IV.** *vi* **1.** (*make a sound*) claquer **2.** (*break suddenly*) se casser **3.** (*spring into position*) **to ~ back** revenir brusquement; **to ~ shut** se fermer avec un bruit sec **4.** (*bite*) **to ~ at sb/sth** essayer de mordre qn/happer qc **5.** (*speak sharply*) parler sèchement; **to ~ at sb** s'adresser à qn d'un ton

S

sec; **to ~ (back) that …** répliquer sèchement que … ►**~ to it!** la ferme! **V.** *vt* **1.** (*break suddenly and cleanly*) casser; (*a ruler*) briser; **to ~ sth off** [*o* **to ~ off sth**] arracher qc **2.** (*make a snapping sound*) faire claquer; **to ~ your fingers** claquer ses doigts; **to ~ sth shut** fermer qc brusquement **3.** (*photograph*) prendre; **to ~ sb doing sth** prendre qn en photo en train de faire qc **4.** (*say sharply*) dire sèchement ►**to ~ one's fingers at sb** narguer qn; **to ~ sb's head off** rembarrer vivement

◆**snap out** *vt* (*order*) donner d'un ton sec

◆**snap up** *vt* **1.** (*seize*) saisir **2.** (*buy*) rafler

snapdragon ['snæpˌdrægən] *n* gueule-de-loup *f*, gueules-de-loup *fpl*

snappish *adj* hargneux(-euse)

snappy *adj* <-ier, -iest> **1.** *inf* FASHION (*smart*) chic *inv* **2.** (*quick*) vif(vive); **to make it ~** (*hurry up*) se dépêcher **3.** (*eye-catching*) dynamique

snare [sneəʳ, *Am:* sner] **I.** *n* **1.** (*animal trap*) lacet *m* **2.** (*pitfall*) collet *m* **II.** *vt* **1.** (*catch animals*) prendre au filet **2.** (*capture*) prendre au piège

snarl[1] [snɑːl, *Am:* snɑːrl] **I.** *vi* grogner; **to ~ at sb** gronder contre qn **II.** *n* **1.** (*growl*) grognement *m* **2.** ((*human*) *growl*) grondement *m* **3.** (*sound*) ronronnement *m*

snarl[2] [snɑːl, *Am:* snɑːrl] **I.** *n* **1.** (*traffic jam*) embouteillage *m* **2.** (*tangle*) enchevêtrement *m* **II.** *vi* (*become tangled*) s'emmêler

◆**snarl up** *vi* bouchonner

snarl-up *n* bouchon *m*

snatch [snætʃ] **I.** <-es> *n* **1.** (*sudden grab*) mouvement *m* vif **2.** (*theft*) vol *m* à l'arraché **3.** (*fragment*) fragment *m;* (*of conversation*) bribe *f;* (*of time*) courte période *f;* **a few ~es of music** quelques notes *fpl* de musique; **to do sth by ~es** faire qc par intervalles **4.** *vulg* (*vulva*) chatte *f* **II.** *vt* **1.** (*grab quickly*) saisir; **to ~ sth out of sb's hand** arracher qc de la main de qn **2.** (*steal*) voler **3.** (*kidnap*) kidnapper **4.** (*take advantage of*) saisir **5.** SPORT arracher de justesse; **to ~ victory from the jaws of defeat** arracher la victoire des griffes de la défaite **III.** *vi* saisir brusquement; **to ~ at sth** essayer de saisir qc; **to ~ at an opportunity** saisir une occasion

◆**snatch away** *vt* arracher; **to snatch sth away from sb** arracher qc des mains de qn

◆**snatch up** *vt* ramasser vivement

snatchy *adj* spasmodique

snazzy ['snæzi] *adj* <-ier, -iest> *inf* chouette

sneak [sniːk] <-ed *o* snuck> *Am* **I.** *vi* **1.** (*move stealthily*) se déplacer furtivement; **to ~ somewhere** se glisser quelque part; **to ~ in/out** entrer/sortir furtivement **2.** *Brit, pej, inf* (*denounce*) moucharder **II.** *vt* **to ~ sb/sth in/out** faire entrer/sortir qn/qc furtivement; **to ~ a look at sb/sth** glisser un œil vers qn/qc **III.** *n Brit, childspeak, inf* rapporteur, -euse *m, f*

sneakers *n pl, Am* baskets *fpl*, espadrilles *fpl Québec*

sneaking *adj* vague

sneak preview *n* avant-première *f* **sneak-thief** *n* chipeur, -euse *m, f*

sneaky *adj* <-ier, -iest> sournois(e)

sneer [snɪəʳ, *Am:* snɪr] **I.** *vi* **1.** (*make a grimace*) sourire d'un air moqueur **2.** (*mock*) ricaner; **to ~ at sb** se moquer de qn **II.** *n* sourire *m* de mépris

sneering *adj* sarcastique

sneeze [sniːz] **I.** *vi* éternuer ►**not to be ~d at** ne pas être à dédaigner **II.** *n* éternuement *m*

snick [snɪk] *vt Brit, Aus* SPORT couper légèrement

snicker *Am s.* **snigger**

snide [snaɪd] *adj pej* sarcastique

sniff [snɪf] **I.** *n* reniflement *m;* **a ~ of disgust** une grimace de dégoût; **to have a ~** avoir un rhume; **to catch a ~ of sth** sentir qc **II.** *vi* **1.** (*inhale sharply*) renifler **2.** (*show disdain*) renifler avec dédain; **to ~ at sth** dédaigner qc ►**not to be ~ed at** à ne pas dédaigner **III.** *vt* (*smell*) renifler

◆**sniff out** *vt* **1.** (*locate by smelling*) détecter **2.** *fig* (*discover*) déterrer

sniffer dog *n* chien *m* renifleur

sniffle ['snɪfl] **I.** *vi* pleurnicher **II.** *n* **1.** (*crying*) pleurnicherie *f* **2.** MED rhume *m*

snifter ['snɪftəʳ, *Am:* -tɚ] *n* **1.** *Am* (*bowl-shaped glass*) goutte *f* **2.** (*small drink of alcohol*) petit verre *m*

snigger ['snɪgəʳ, *Am:* -ɚ] **I.** *vi* ricaner; **to ~ at sth** lancer un rire grivois à qc **II.** *n* ricanement *m*

snip [snɪp] **I.** *vt* couper **II.** *n* **1.** (*cut*) entaille *f;* **to give sth a ~** donner un coup de ciseaux à qc **2.** FASHION (*piece of cloth*) bout *m* **3.** *Brit, inf* (*cheap item*) *a. iron* bonne affaire *f;* **to be a ~ at a price** être une bonne affaire à un prix

snipe [snaɪp] **I.** *vi a. fig* MIL tirer; **to be ~d** être abattu **II.** <-(pes)> *n* bécassine *f*

sniper *n* MIL tireur *m* embusqué, sniper *m;* **~ fire** tir *m* d'embuscade

snippet ['snɪpɪt] *n* **1.** (*small piece: of cloth, paper*) bout *m* **2.** (*bit of information: gossip, information, knowledge*) bribes *fpl* **3.** LIT (*extract*) extrait *m*

snitch [snɪtʃ] *inf* **I.** *vt* (*steal*) chaparder **II.** *vi pej* (*tell a secret*) moucharder **III.** <-es> *n* **1.** (*thief*) voleur, -euse *m, f* **2.** *pej* (*informer*) mouchard(e) *m(f)*

snivel ['snɪvəl] **I.** <-ll- *o Am* -l-> *vi* **1.** (*have the sniffles*) renifler **2.** (*cry*) pleurnicher **II.** *n no pl* pleurnicheries *fpl*

snivel(l)ing **I.** *n no pl* pleurnicheries *fpl* **II.** *adj* pleurnicheur(-euse)

snob [snɒb, *Am:* snɑːb] *n pej* snob *mf*

snobbery ['snɒbəri, *Am:* 'snɑːbɚ-] *n pej* snobisme *m*

snobbish <more, most> *adj pej* snob

snog [snɒg, *Am:* snɑːg] **I.** <-gg-> *vi Brit, inf* se bécoter **II.** *vt Brit, inf* bécoter **III.** *n Brit, inf* bécot *m;* **to have a ~** se bécoter

snook [snuːk, *Am:* snʊk] *n no pl* **to cock a ~ at sb/sth** *Brit, inf* faire un pied de nez à qn/qc
snooker I. *vt* 1. *fig* (*in difficulty*) **to be ~ed** être coincé 2. *Am, inf* (*trick*) avoir 3. GAMES (*block*) faire un snooker à II. *n* GAMES snooker *m*
snoop [snuːp] I. *n pej, inf* 1. (*investigative search*) coup *m* d'œil; **to have a ~ (around)** jeter un coup d'œil 2. *s.* **snooper** II. *vi pej, inf* 1. (*examine without permission*) fouiller 2. (*look around*) **to ~ around** fouiner
snooper *n pej, inf* fouineur, -euse *m, f*
snooty ['snuːti, *Am:* -t̬i] <-ier, -iest> *adj inf* snobinard(e)
snooze [snuːz] *inf* I. *vi* faire un somme II. *n* petit somme *m;* **to have a ~** faire un somme
snooze button *n* ELEC bouton *m* de rappel
snore [snɔːʳ, *Am:* snɔːr] MED I. *vi* ronfler II. *n* ronflement *m*
snorer *n* ronfleur, -euse *m, f*
snorkel ['snɔːkəl, *Am:* 'snɔːr-] SPORT I. *n* tuba *m* II. <*Brit* -ll- *o Am* -l-> *vi* faire de la plongée avec un tuba
snort [snɔːt, *Am:* snɔːrt] I. *vi* 1. (*make a sudden sound*) grogner; (*horse*) s'ébrouer; **to ~ with anger** grogner de colère; **to ~ with laughter** pouffer de rire 2. (*sniff: drugs*) sniffer II. *vt* 1. *inf* (*inhale through nose: drugs*) sniffer 2. (*say with disapproval*) ronchonner III. *n* 1. (*noise in nose*) grognement *m;* **to give a ~** grogner 2. *inf* (*small drink*) petit coup *m*
snot [snɒt, *Am:* snɑːt] *n no pl, inf* MED morve *f*
snot rag *n inf* mouchoir *m*
snotty <-ier, -iest> *adj inf* 1. (*full of mucus: person, face*) morveux(-euse); (*handkerchief, rag*) sale; (*nose*) qui coule 2. *pej* (*rude: kid, adolescent*) morveux(-euse) 3. (*arrogant: answer, look, manner*) arrogant(e)
snout [snaʊt] *n* 1. BIO museau *m;* (*of a pig*) groin *m* 2. *inf* ANAT pif *m*
snow [snəʊ, *Am:* snoʊ] I. *n* 1. *no pl* METEO (*frozen precipitation*) neige *f;* **in the ~** dans la neige; **as white as ~** blanc(he) comme neige 2. TV (*static*) neige *f* 3. *no pl, inf* MED (*cocaine*) neige *f* II. *vi* neiger III. *vt Am* embobiner; **to ~ sb into believing sth** faire croire qc à qn
◆**snow in** *vt* **to be snowed in** être bloqué par la neige
◆**snow under** *vt* **to be snowed under with sth** être submergé de qc
snowball I. *n* boule *f* de neige ►**to have a ~'s chance in hell of doing sth** ne pas avoir l'ombre d'une chance de faire qc II. *vi* lancer des boules de neige; *fig* faire boule de neige **snowball effect** *n no pl* effet *m* boule de neige **snow-blind** *adj* aveuglé(e) par la neige **snow blindness** *n no pl* cécité *f* des neiges **snowboard** *n* snowboard *m* **snowbound** *adj* bloqué(e) par la neige **snow cannon** *n* canon *m* à neige **snow-capped** *adj* enneigé(e) **snowcat** *n* autoneige *m* **snow chains** *npl* AUTO chaînes *fpl* à neige **snowdrift** *n* congère *f,* banc *m* de neige *Québec,* menée *f Suisse* **snowdrop** *n* perce-neige *m* **snowfall** *n* METEO chute *f* de neige **snowfield** *n* GEO, METEO champ *m* de neige **snowflake** *n* flocon *m* de neige **snowline** *n* neiges *fpl* éternelles **snowman** *n* bonhomme *m* de neige; **the abominable ~** l'abominable homme des neiges **snowmobile** *n* motoneige *m* **snowplough** *n Brit,* **snowplow** *n Am* chasse-neige *m* **snow report** *n* bulletin *m* d'enneigement **snowshoe** I. *n* raquette *f* II. *vi* se déplacer avec des raquettes **snowstorm** *n* tempête *f* de neige **snowsuit** *n* combinaison *f* de ski **snow tire** *n Am,* **snow tyre** *n Brit* AUTO pneu *m* neige **snow-white** *adj* blanc(he) comme neige **Snow White** *n no pl* Blanche-Neige *f*
snowy *adj* 1. METEO (*typically with snow: region, country*) neigeux(-euse) 2. (*covered with snow: street, highway, field*) enneigé(e) 3. (*with much snow: day, winter*) de neige; (*month, season*) des neiges 4. ART, FASHION, TYP (*pure white*) blanc(he) comme neige
SNP [ˌesen'piː] *n abbr of* **Scottish National Party** *parti nationaliste écossais*
snub [snʌb] I. <-bb-> *vt* snober II. *n* rebuffade *f*
snuff [snʌf] I. *n* tabac *m* à priser; **to take ~** priser II. *vt* **to ~ it** *Aus, Brit, inf* casser sa pipe
snuff box *n* tabatière *f*
snuffle ['snʌfl] I. *vi* 1. (*sniff*) PHYSIOL renifler 2. (*speak nasally*) nasiller II. *n* 1. (*runny nose*) rhume *m;* **to have (a case of) the ~s** avoir un rhume 2. (*breathing through nose*) reniflement *m*
snug [snʌg] I. *adj* 1. (*cozy*) confortable 2. (*warm*) douillet(te) 3. FASHION (*tight*) ajusté(e) 4. (*adequate: income, wage*) confortable ►**to be/feel ~ as a bug in a rug** être confortablement installé II. *n Brit* GASTR *s.* **snuggery**
snuggery *n* arrière-salle *f*
snuggle ['snʌgl] I. *vi* se blottir II. *vt* blottir
so [səʊ, *Am:* soʊ] I. *adv* 1. (*in the same way*) ainsi; **~ to speak** pour ainsi dire 2. (*also*) **~ did/do/have/am I** moi aussi; **~ I did** c'est ce que j'ai fait 3. (*like that*) **~ they say** c'est ce qu'on dit; **is that ~?** vraiment?; **I hope/think ~** je l'espère/le pense; **just** [*o* **quite**] **~!** exactement! 4. (*to such a degree*) tellement; **I ~ love him** je l'aime tellement; **~ late** si tard; **~ many books** autant de livres; **not ~ ugly as that** pas aussi laid que cela; **to be ~ kind as to** +*infin* avoir la gentillesse de +*infin* 5. (*in order that*) **I bought the book ~ that I could/he would read it** j'ai acheté le livre pour le lire/afin qu'il le lise 6. (*as a result*) **~ that he did sth** de sorte [*o* si bien] qu'il a fait qc ►**~ long!** à un de ces jours!; **~ long as** (*if*) dans la mesure où; **~ long as I'm there** tant que je suis là; **Mr So-and-~** M. Untel; **and ~ on** [*o* **forth**] et ainsi de suite; **or ~** à peu près; *s. a.* **far, much, many** II. *conj* 1. (*therefore*) donc 2. (*summing up*)

S

alors; ~ **what?** et alors?; ~ **now, ...** et maintenant, ...; ~, **I was saying ...** j'étais donc en train de dire ...; ~ (**then**) **he told me ...** et alors il m'a dit ...; ~ **that's why!** ah! c'est pour ça!

soak [səʊk, *Am:* soʊk] **I.** *n* **1.** (*time under water*) immersion *f;* **to give sth a** ~ faire tremper qc **2.** (*heavy drinker*) poivrot(e) *m(f)* **II.** *vt* **1.** GASTR (*set in water*) faire tremper **2.** (*make wet*) tremper **3.** *inf* (*demand money*) faire casquer **III.** *vi* **1.** (*let sit in water: beans, peas*) tremper; **to leave sth to** ~ laisser qc tremper **2.** *inf* (*booze*) boire comme un trou

◆**soak in I.** *vi* **1.** (*become absorbed*) pénétrer **2.** (*become understood*) piger *inf* **II.** *vt a. fig* s'imprégner de qc

◆**soak off** *vt* faire partir en laissant tremper

◆**soak up** *vt a. fig* absorber; (*the atmosphere*) s'imprégner de

soaking I. *n* trempage *m;* **to give sth a** ~ laisser tremper qc; **to get a** ~ se faire tremper **II.** *adj* ~ (**wet**) trempé(e)

so-and-so *n pej, inf* type *m;* **Mr./Mrs** ~ M./Mme Untel

soap [səʊp, *Am:* soʊp] **I.** *n* **1.** *no pl* (*body-washing substance*) savon *m;* **a bar/piece of** ~ une savonnette **2.** TV *s.* **soap opera** ►**soft** ~ flatteries *fpl* **II.** *vt* savonner

soapbox *n a. fig* tribune *f* **soap bubble** *n a. fig* bulle *f* de savon **soap dispenser** *n* distributeur *m* de savon liquide **soap flakes** *npl* savon *m* en paillettes **soap opera** *n* TV feuilleton *m* **soap powder** *n no pl* lessive *f* en poudre

soapy ['səʊpi, *Am:* 'soʊp-] <-ier, -iest> *adj* **1.** (*full of lather*) savonneux(-euse) **2.** (*like soap*) de savon; **to taste** ~ avoir un goût de savon; **to smell** ~ sentir le savon **3.** *pej* (*flattering: manner, smile*) mielleux(-euse)

soar [sɔːʳ, *Am:* sɔːr] *vi* **1.** (*rise*) *a. fig* s'élever **2.** (*increase drastically: temperature, prices*) monter en flèche **3.** AVIAT, ZOOL (*glide: bird, glider*) planer

soaring *adj* **1.** (*increasing: prices*) qui monte en flèche **2.** (*gliding: flight*) plané(e)

sob [sɒb, *Am:* sɑːb] **I.** *n* sanglot *m* **II.** <-bb-> *vi* sangloter **III.** <-bb-> *vt* dire en sanglotant; **to** ~ **oneself to sleep** s'endormir en sanglotant

sober ['səʊbəʳ, *Am:* 'soʊbɚ] **I.** *adj* **1.** GASTR (*not drunk*) sobre **2.** (*serious: mood*) sérieux(-euse); **to be** ~ **as a judge** être sérieux comme un pape **3.** (*calm*) calme **4.** (*moderate: person*) posé(e) **5.** (*plain: clothes, colour*) sobre **6.** (*simple: truth*) simple **II.** *vt* calmer **III.** *vi* se calmer

◆**sober up I.** *vi* **1.** (*become less drunk*) se dégriser **2.** (*become serious*) se calmer **II.** *vt* **1.** (*make less drunk*) dégriser **2.** (*make serious*) calmer

soberness *n no pl* **1.** (*not drunkenness*) sobriété *f* **2.** (*seriousness*) sérieux *m* **3.** FASHION (*plainness*) sobriété *f*

sobriety [səʊ'braɪəti, *Am:* sə'braɪət̬i] *n no pl, iron, form* sobriété *f*

sobriquet ['səʊbrɪkeɪ, *Am:* 'soʊ-] *n* sobriquet *m*

sob story *n pej* histoire *f* à faire pleurer; **to tell sb a** ~ chercher à faire pleurer qn

so-called *adj pej* soi-disant(e)

soccer ['sɒkəʳ, *Am:* 'sɑːkɚ] *n Am no pl* football *m*

soccer player *n Am* joueur, -euse *m, f* de football

sociability [ˌsəʊʃə'bɪləti, *Am:* ˌsoʊʃə'bɪlət̬i] *n no pl* sociabilité *f*

sociable ['səʊʃəbl, *Am:* 'soʊ-] *adj* **1.** (*keen to mix socially*) sociable; **to not feel very** ~ ne pas être d'humeur à côtoyer du monde **2.** (*friendly*) amical(e); **to do sth just to be** ~ faire qc par politesse

social ['səʊʃəl, *Am:* 'soʊ-] SOCIOL **I.** *adj* social(e) **II.** *n Brit* soirée *f*

social democrat *n* POL social-démocrate *mf*

socialism ['səʊʃəlɪzəm, *Am:* 'soʊ-] *n no pl* socialisme *m*

socialist *n* POL socialiste *mf*

socialite ['səʊʃəlaɪt, *Am:* 'soʊ-] *n* mondain(e) *m(f)*

socialization *n no pl* socialisation *f*

socialize ['səʊʃəlaɪz, *Am:* 'soʊ-] **I.** *vi* **1.** SOCIOL (*have human contact*) fréquenter **2.** *fig* (*talk: student*) bavarder **II.** *vt* socialiser

social science *n* science *f* sociale **social security** *n no pl, Brit* sécurité *f* sociale; ~ **card** *Am* carte *f* d'assuré social **social services** *n* services *mpl* sociaux **social studies** *n* sciences *fpl* sociales **social work** *n no pl* assistance *f* sociale **social worker** *n* assistant *m* social, assistante *f* sociale

society [sə'saɪəti, *Am:* -t̬i] *n* société *f*

sociocultural [ˌsəʊʃiəʊ'kʌltʃərəl, *Am:* ˌsoʊsioʊ-] *adj* socioculturel(le)

socio-economic [ˌsəʊʃiəʊˌiːkə'nɒmɪk, *Am:* ˌsoʊsioʊˌekə'nɑːmɪk] *adj* socioéconomique

sociological *adj* sociologique

sociologist *n* sociologue *mf*

sociology [ˌsəʊʃi'ɒlədʒi, *Am:* ˌsoʊsi'ɑːlə-] *n no pl* sociologie *f*

sociopath ['səʊʃiəʊpæθ, *Am:* 'soʊsiə-] *n* asocial(e) *m(f)*

socio-political *adj* sociopolitique

sock[1] [sɒk, *Am:* sɑːk] *n* (*foot cover*) chaussette *f;* **ankle** ~**s** socquettes *fpl;* **a knee** ~ un mi-bas ►**to blow sb's** ~**s off** *inf* épater qn; **to pull one's** ~**s up** *inf* se secouer; **put a** ~ **in it!** *iron, inf* la ferme!

sock[2] [sɒk, *Am:* sɑːk] **I.** *vt* **1.** *inf* (*hit*) mettre une beigne à; **to** ~ **sb in the jaw** mettre son poing dans la gueule de qn; **to** ~ **sb in the eye** mettre un coquard à qn **2.** *fig* **to be** ~**ed with sth** être sonné par qc **II.** *n inf* beigne *f;* **to give sb a** ~ flanquer une beigne à qn

socket ['sɒkɪt, *Am:* 'sɑːkɪt] *n* **1.** (*energy source*) prise *f* de courant **2.** (*cavity*) cavité *f*

sod [sɒd, *Am:* sɑːd] *n* **1.** BOT, AGR gazon *m* **2.** *fig* **to be under the ~** être enterré

soda ['səʊdə, *Am:* 'soʊ-] *n* GASTR **1.** *no pl s.* **soda water 2.** (*sodium*) soude *f*

soda bread *n no pl* pain *m* levé **soda siphon** *n* siphon *m* **soda water** *n no pl* **1.** (*water*) eau *f* de Seltz **2.** (*sweet drink*) soda *m*

sodden ['sɒdn, *Am:* 'sɑːdn] *adj* **1.** (*soaked*) trempé(e); (*field*) détrempé(e) **2.** (*drunk*) **to be ~ with alcohol** être imbibé d'alcool

sodium ['səʊdɪəm, *Am:* 'soʊ-] *n no pl* sodium *m*

sodium bicarbonate *n no pl* bicarbonate *m* de soude

sodomy ['sɒdəmi, *Am:* 'sɑːdə-] *n no pl, form* sodomie *f*

sofa ['səʊfə, *Am:* 'soʊ-] *n* sofa *m*

sofa bed *n* canapé-lit *m*

soft [sɒft, *Am:* sɑːft] *adj* **1.** (*not hard: ground/sand*) mou(molle); (*pillow, chair*) mœlleux(-euse); (*wood, rock*) tendre; (*contact lenses*) souple **2.** (*melted: ice cream, butter*) ramolli(e) **3.** (*smooth: cloth, skin, hair*) doux(douce); (*leather*) souple; **~ as silk** doux comme de la soie; **a ~ landing** un atterrissage en douceur; **~ to the touch** doux au toucher **4.** (*weak*) faible **5.** (*mild: climate, drug*) doux(douce) **6.** (*not glaring: color, light*) doux(douce); (*blue*) tendre **7.** (*quiet: music, sound, words*) doux(douce) **8.** (*lenient*) indulgent(e); (*heart*) tendre; **to be ~ on sb/sth** se montrer indulgent envers qn/qc; **to have a ~ time of it** se la couler douce **9.** (*easy*) facile **10.** (*rough sketch: outline, plan*) flou(e) ►**to be ~ in the head** *pej* être débile; **to have a ~ spot for sb** avoir un faible pour qn; **to be ~ on sb** *Am* être amouraché de qn; **to be a ~ touch** être bonne poire

soft-boiled *adj* GASTR (*egg*) mollet **soft drink** *n* boisson *f* non alcoolisée

soften **I.** *vi* **1.** (*let get soft: butter, ice-cream*) se ramollir; (*skin, colour*) s'adoucir; (*leather*) s'assouplir **2.** (*become less severe*) s'attendrir **II.** *vt* **1.** (*make soft: butter, margarine*) ramollir; (*skin*) adoucir; (*leather*) assouplir **2.** (*make more pleasant: a sound, color*) adoucir **3.** (*make emotional*) attendrir **4.** (*make easier to bear: pain, effect, anger*) atténuer; (*blow*) amortir

◆**soften up** **I.** *vt* **1.** (*make softer*) ramollir **2.** (*persuade*) amadouer **3.** MIL (*weaken*) amoindrir **II.** *vi* se ramollir

softener *n* **1.** (*softening agent*) adoucissant *m* **2.** (*mineral reducer*) adoucisseur *m*

softening **I.** *n no pl* **1.** (*reduction of hardness*) ramollissement *m;* (*person*) attendrissement *m;* (*clothes, attitude, voice*) adoucissement *m;* (*leather*) assouplissement *m* **2.** (*reduction of glare: color, light, contrast*) atténuation *f* **II.** *adj* adoucissant(e)

soft furnishings *npl Aus, Brit,* **soft goods** *npl Am* textiles *mpl* **soft-headed** *adj pej* bête **soft-hearted** *adj* au cœur tendre

softie ['sɒfti, *Am:* 'sɑːf-] *n inf* cœur *m* d'artichaut

softly *adv* doucement

softness *n no pl* **1.** (*not hardness*) mollesse *f* **2.** (*smoothness: skin, material, climate*) douceur *f;* (*leather*) souplesse *f* **3.** (*not glare: light, outline*) douceur *f* **4.** (*wishy-washyness: of character*) mollesse *f*

soft pedal **I.** *n* MUS pédale *f* douce **II.** <*Brit* -ll-, *Am* -l-> *vi* MUS mettre la pédale douce **III.** *vt fig* **to ~ sth** y aller doucement avec qc **soft porn** *n* film *m* érotique **soft soap** **I.** *n no pl, fig, pej, inf* lèche-botte *mf* **II.** *vt pej, inf* lécher les bottes à **soft-spoken** *adj* à voix douce **soft toy** *n Brit* peluche *f*

software ['sɒftweəʳ, *Am:* 'sɑːftwer] *n* INFOR logiciel *m*

softwood ['sɒftwʊd, *Am:* 'sɑːft-] *n* **1.** *no pl* (*wood*) bois *m* résineux **2.** (*tree*) résineux *m*

softy ['sɒfti, *Am:* 'sɑːf-] *n inf s.* **softie**

soggy ['sɒgi, *Am:* 'sɑːgi] <-ier, -iest> *adj* **1.** (*wet and soft*) trempé(e); (*field, ground*) détrempé(e) **2.** (*rainy: weather, atmosphere*) lourd(e) **3.** (*mushy*) ramolli(e); **to go ~** se ramollir

soil[1] [sɔɪl] **I.** *vt form* **1.** (*make dirty*) souiller; (*clothing*) salir **2.** *fig* (*ruin*) entacher **II.** *vi* se salir

soil[2] [sɔɪl] *n no pl, a. fig* AGR, BOT sol *m*

soirée, **soiree** ['swɑːreɪ, *Am:* swɑː'reɪ] *n iron, form* soirée *f*

solace ['sɒlɪs, *Am:* 'sɑːlɪs] **I.** *n no pl, form* consolation *f* **II.** *vt* consoler

solar ['səʊləʳ, *Am:* 'soʊlɚ] *adj* solaire; (*car*) à énergie solaire; (*light*) du soleil

solar battery *n* ECOL, ELEC pile *f* solaire **solar cell** *n* ECOL, ELEC pile *f* solaire **solar eclipse** *n* ASTR éclipse *f* du Soleil **solar energy** *n no pl* ECOL, ELEC énergie *f* solaire **solar heating** *n no pl* ECOL, ELEC chauffage *m* à l'énergie solaire

solarium [səʊ'leəriəm, *Am:* soʊ'leri-] <solaria> *n* solarium *m*

solar panel *n* panneau *m* solaire **solar power** *n no pl* énergie *f* solaire **solar power station** *n* centrale *f* électrique solaire **solar radiation** *n no pl* radiation *f* solaire **solar system** *n* système *m* solaire

sold [səʊld, *Am:* soʊld] *pt, pp of* **sell**

solder ['sɒldəʳ, *Am:* 'sɑːdɚ] **I.** *vt* souder **II.** *n no pl* soudure *f*

soldering iron *n* fer *m* à souder

soldier ['səʊldʒəʳ, *Am:* 'soʊldʒɚ] **I.** *n a. fig* MIL soldat *m* **II.** *vi* MIL servir dans l'armée

sole[1] [səʊl, *Am:* soʊl] *adj* **1.** (*only*) unique **2.** (*exclusive: right*) exclusif(-ive)

sole[2] [səʊl, *Am:* soʊl] *n* **1.** (*shoe bottom*) semelle *f* **2.** ANAT (*foot bottom*) plante *f* du pied

sole[3] [səʊl, *Am:* soʊl] *n* sole *f*

solecism ['sɒlɪsɪzəm, *Am:* 'sɑːlə-] *n form* **1.** LING (*language mistake*) solécisme *m* **2.** *fig* (*faux pas*) bévue *f*

solely ['səʊli, *Am:* 'soʊli] *adv* uniquement

solemn ['sɒləm, *Am:* 'sɑːləm] *adj* solennel(le)

solemnity [sə'lemnəti, *Am:* -ţi] *n* solennité *f*

solemnize ['sɒləmnaɪz, *Am:* 'sɑːləm-] *vt form* célébrer

sol-fa [ˌsɒl'fɑː, *Am:* ˌsoʊl'fɑː] *n* MUS solfège *m*

solicit [sə'lɪsɪt] *vt form* **1.** (*ask for*) solliciter **2.** (*prostitute*) racoler

soliciting *n no pl* LAW racolage *m*

solicitor *n* **1.** *Aus, Brit* LAW (*lawyer*) avocat(e) *m(f)* **2.** *Am* POL (*lawyer for city*) ≈ juriste *mf*

solicitous *adj form* soucieux(-euse)

solicitude [səˌlɪsɪ'tjuːd, *Am:* sə'lɪsɪtuːd] *n form* solicitude *f*

solid ['sɒlɪd, *Am:* 'sɑːlɪd] **I.** *adj* **1.** (*strong, hard, stable*) solide; **to be ~ as a rock** solide comme un roc **2.** (*not hollow*) plein(e); (*silver, gold*) massif(-ive); (*crowd, mass*) compact(e) **3.** (*not liquid*) solide **4.** (*true: facts, reasons, meal*) solide **5.** (*without interruption*) sans interruption; (*wall, line*) continu(e); **four ~ hours** quatre heures d'affilée **6.** (*unanimous: approval*) unanime **7.** *fig* (*healthy, reliable: boy, democrat, relationship*) solide **II.** *adv* **1.** (*completely*) complètement **2.** (*continuously*) d'affilée **III.** *n* **1.** (*solid object, substance*) solide *m* **2.** *pl* GASTR aliments *mpl* solides

solidarity [ˌsɒlɪ'dærəti, *Am:* ˌsɑːlə'derəţi] *n no pl* solidarité *f*

solidify [sə'lɪdɪfaɪ, *Am:* -əfaɪ] <-ie-, -ying> **I.** *vi* **1.** (*become solid*) se solidifier; (*water*) se congeler **2.** *fig* se consolider **II.** *vt* **1.** (*make solid*) solidifier; (*water*) congeler **2.** *fig* consolider

solidity [sə'lɪdəti, *Am:* -ţi] *n no pl, a. fig* solidité *f*

solidly *adv* **1.** (*soundly*) solidement **2.** (*without interruption*) sans interruption **3.** (*in strong manner: to support*) en masse; **to be ~ behind sb** soutenir qn à l'unanimité

solid state PHYS **I.** *n* solide *m* **II.** *adj* **solid-state** relatif(-ive) aux substances solides; (*conductor, device*) semi-conducteur(-trice); **~ physics** physique *f* des solides

soliloquize *vi* soliloquer

soliloquy [sə'lɪləkwi] *n* soliloque *m*

solitaire [ˌsɒlɪ'teəʳ, *Am:* 'sɑːləter] *n* **1.** (*single jewel*) solitaire *m* **2.** *no pl, Am* (*patience*) patience *f*

solitary ['sɒlɪtəri, *Am:* 'sɑːləteri] **I.** *adj* **1.** (*single*) seul(e); ZOOL solitaire **2.** (*isolated*) isolé(e); **to go for a ~ stroll/walk** se promener en solitaire **3.** (*unvisited*) retiré(e) **II.** *n* **1.** *no pl, inf* (*isolation in prison*) confinement *f* **2.** (*hermit*) ermite *m*

solitude ['sɒlɪtjuːd, *Am:* 'sɑːlətuːd] *n no pl* solitude *f*

solo ['səʊləʊ, *Am:* 'soʊloʊ] **I.** *adj* (*unaccompanied*) solo; **~ flight** voyage *m* en avion non accompagné; **~ performance** interprétation *f* en solo **II.** *adv* (*single-handed*) solo; **to fly ~** voyager en avion non accompagné; **to go ~** partir en solitaire **III.** *n* MUS solo *m* **IV.** *vi* **1.** (*play*) jouer en solo **2.** (*sing*) chanter a cappella

soloist ['səʊləʊɪst, *Am:* 'soʊloʊ-] *n* soloiste *mf*

Solomon Islander I. *adj* salomonais(e) **II.** *n* Salomonais(e) *m(f)* **Solomon Islands** ['sɒləmənˌaɪləndz, *Am:* 'sɑːlə-] *n* les îles *fpl* Salomon

solstice ['sɒlstɪs, *Am:* 'sɑːl-] *n* solstice *m*

soluble ['sɒljəbl, *Am:* 'sɑːl-] *adj* soluble

solus ['səʊləs, *Am:* 'soʊ-] *adj* THEAT annonce *f* unique

solution [sə'luːʃən] *n* solution *f*

solve [sɒlv, *Am:* sɑːlv] *vt* résoudre

solvency ['sɒlvənsi, *Am:* 'sɑːl-] FIN **I.** *n no pl* solvabilité *f* **II.** *adj* de solvabilité

solvent ['sɒlvənt, *Am:* 'sɑːl-] **I.** *n* solvant *m* **II.** *adj* **1.** FIN solvable **2.** *inf* (*have sufficient money*) aisé(e)

solvent abuse *n Brit* abus *m* de solvant

Somali [ˌsə'mɑːli, *Am:* soʊ'-] **I.** *adj* somali(e) **II.** <-(s)> *n* **1.** (*person*) Somali(e) *m(f)* **2.** LING somali *m; s. a.* **English**

Somalia [ˌsə'mɑːliə, *Am:* soʊ'-] *n* la Somalie

Somalian I. *adj* somalien(ne) **II.** *n* Somalien(ne) *m(f)*

somber *adj Am* **sombre** ['sɒmbəʳ, *Am:* 'sɑːmbɚ] *adj* sombre

some [sʌm] **I.** *indef adj* **1.** *pl* (*several*) quelques; **~ people think ...** il y a des gens qui pensent ... **2.** *sing* (*imprecise*) (**at**) **~ place** quelque part; (**at**) **~ time** à un moment quelconque; **~ other time** une autre fois; **~ time ago** il y a quelques temps; **to have ~ idea of sth** avoir une vague idée de qc **3.** (*amount*) un peu; **to have ~ money** avoir un peu d'argent; **to ~ extent** dans une certaine mesure **II.** *indef pron* **1.** *pl* (*several*) quelques-un(e)s; **I would like ~** j'en voudrais quelques-uns; **~ like it, others don't** certains l'aiment, d'autres pas **2.** *sing* (*part of it*) en; **I would like ~** j'en voudrais un peu **III.** *adv* **1.** (*about*) environ; **~ more nuts/wine** encore quelques noix/un peu de vin; **~ hundred kilos** quelques cent kilos **2.** (*little*) **to feel ~ better** *Am* se sentir un peu mieux

somebody ['sʌmbədi, *Am:* -ˌbɑːdi] *indef pron* (*some person*) quelqu'un; **~ or other** je ne sais qui; **there is ~ English on the phone** il y a un Anglais au téléphone; *s. a.* **anybody, nobody**

someday, some day *adv* un jour

somehow ['sʌmhaʊ] *adv* **1.** (*through unknown methods*) d'une façon ou d'une autre **2.** (*for an unclear reason*) pour une raison ou une autre **3.** (*come what may*) coûte que coûte

someone ['sʌmwʌn] *pron s.* **somebody**

someplace ['sʌmpleɪs] *adv Am* quelque part

somersault ['sʌməsɔːlt, *Am:* -ɚsɑːlt] **I.** *n*

1. (*movement*) *a. fig* culbute *f* 2. SPORT saut *m* périlleux II. *vi* 1. (*make a movement*) faire des culbutes; (*vehicle, car*) faire des tonneaux 2. SPORT faire un saut périlleux

something ['sʌmθɪŋ] I. *indef pron, sing* 1. (*some object or concept*) quelque chose; ~ **or other** je ne sais quoi; **one can't have ~ for nothing** on n'a rien sans rien 2. (*about*) **... or ~** *inf* ... ou quelque chose comme ça; **two metre ~** deux mètres et quelques; **his name is Paul ~** il s'appelle Paul Machin-Chose II. *n* **a little ~** un petit quelque chose; **a certain ~** un je ne sais quoi III. *adv* (*about*) un peu; ~ **over £100** un peu plus de 100 livres; ~ **around £10** dans les 10 livres; *s. a.* **anything, nothing**

sometime ['sʌmtaɪm] I. *adv* un jour ou l'autre II. *adj* ancien(ne)

sometimes *adv* quelquefois

somewhat ['sʌmwɒt, *Am:* -wɑːt] *adv* quelque peu

somewhere ['sʌmweəʳ, *Am:* -wer] *adv* 1. (*non-specified place*) quelque part; ~ **else** autre part; (*to a different place*) ailleurs; *fig* quelque part; **to get ~** aboutir; **or ~** *inf* quelque part 2. (*roughly*) environ

somnolent ['sɒmnələnt, *Am:* 'sɑːm-] *adj* somnolent(e); (*day, village*) calme

son [sʌn] *n* 1. (*male offspring*) *a. fig* fils *m* 2. (*address to a younger male*) fiston *m* 3. (*lad*) gars *m* ►~ **of a bitch** *vulg* fils *m* de pute

sonar ['səʊnɑːʳ, *Am:* 'soʊnɑːr] *n no pl abbr of* **sound navigation and ranging** sonar *m*

sonata [sə'nɑːtə, *Am:* -t̬ə] *n* sonate *f*

song [sɒŋ, *Am:* sɑːŋ] *n* 1. (*musical form*) chanson *f* 2. (*action of singing*) chant *m;* **to burst into ~** se mettre à chanter 3. (*be in top form*) **to be on ~** être en pleine forme 4. *no pl* (*musical call*) chant *m* ►~ **and dance** *pej, inf* cinéma *m; Am, inf* (*untrue tale*) histoires *fpl;* **to make a ~ and dance about sb/sth** faire toute une histoire de qc/à propos de qn

songbird *n* oiseau *m* chanteur **songbook** *n* recueil *m* de chansons

songster *n* chanteur *m*

songstress *n* chanteuse *f*

songwriter *n* (*music*) compositeur, -trice *m, f;* (*lyrics*) parolier, -ière *m, f;* (*music and lyrics*) auteur-compositeur *m*

sonic ['sɒnɪk, *Am:* 'sɑːnɪk] *adj* sonique; (*wave*) sonore

sonic barrier *n* mur *m* du son **sonic speed** *n* vitesse *f* du son

son-in-law <sons-in-law *o* son-in-laws> *n* beau-fils *m*

sonnet ['sɒnɪt, *Am:* 'sɑːnɪt] *n* sonnet *m*

sonny ['sʌni] *n no pl, inf* 1. (*address to a younger man*) fiston *m* 2. (*address to a man*) mon gars *m*

sonority [səʊ'nɒrəti, *Am:* sə'nɔːrət̬i] <-ties> *n* sonorité *f*

sonorous [sə'nɔːrəs] *adj* sonore

soon [suːn] *adv* 1. (*shortly*) peu de temps; ~ **after sth** peu après qc; ~ **after doing sth** peu après avoir fait qc; **how ~** dans combien de temps; **as ~ as** dès que 2. (*rapidly*) rapidement

sooner ['suːnəʳ, *Am:* -ɚ] *adv comp of* **soon** plus tôt; ~ **or later** tôt ou tard; **the ~ the better** le plus tôt sera le mieux; **no ~ said than done** c'est plus vite dit que fait

soot [sʊt] *n no pl* suie *f*

soothe [suːð] *vt* calmer

soothing *adj* 1. (*calming*) reposant(e); (*comment, smile*) apaisant(e) 2. (*pain-relieving*) calmant(e) 3. (*balsamic: ointment, balm, massage*) apaisant(e)

sooty ['sʊti, *Am:* 'sʊt̬-] <-ier, -iest> *adj* couvert(e) de suie

sop [sɒp, *Am:* sɑːp] I. *n* 1. (*bread*) mouillette *f* 2. *pej* **to do sth to sb as a ~** faire qc pour amadouer qn; **my father calls me as a ~** mon père m'appelle pour m'amadouer II. *vt* **to ~ up sth** [*o* **to ~ sth up**] éponger qc

sophisticated [sə'fɪstɪkeɪtɪd, *Am:* -təkeɪt̬ɪd] *adj* sophistiqué(e); (*taste*) raffiné(e); (*style*) recherché(e)

sophistication [səˌfɪstɪ'keɪʃən, *Am:* -tə'-] *n no pl* sophistication *f;* (*of person*) raffinement *m*

sophomore ['sɒfəmɔːʳ, *Am:* 'sɑːfəmɔːr] *n Am* 1. UNIV étudiant(e) *m(f)* (en deuxième année); **to be a ~** être en deuxième année de fac 2. SCHOOL lycéen(ne) *m(f)* (en deuxième année)

soporific [ˌsɒpə'rɪfɪk, *Am:* ˌsɑːpə-] *adj* soporifique; ~ **tablet** somnifère *m*

sopping ['sɒpɪŋ, *Am:* 'sɑːpɪŋ] *adj inf* trempé(e); **to be ~ wet** être tout trempé

soppy ['sɒpi, *Am:* 'sɑːpi] <-ier, -iest> *adj inf* fleur bleue *inv*

soprano [sə'prɑːnəʊ, *Am:* -'prænoʊ] I. *n* soprano *f* II. *adj* de soprano III. *adv* **to sing ~** chanter en soprano

sorbet ['sɔːbeɪ, *Am:* 'sɔːr-] *n* sorbet *m*

sordid ['sɔːdɪd, *Am:* 'sɔːr-] *adj* sordide

sore [sɔːʳ, *Am:* sɔːr] I. *adj* 1. (*painful*) douloureux(-euse); **to have a ~ throat** avoir mal à la gorge 2. *fig* (*touchy*) **a ~ point** un sujet délicat 3. *inf* (*angry*) en rogne; ~ **loser** mauvais *m* perdant; **to be ~ at sb** être en colère contre qn 4. (*severe, urgent*) **to be in ~ need of sth** avoir grand besoin de qc ►**sth stands out like a ~ thumb** être criard; **sb stands out like a ~ thumb** se faire remarquer II. *n* 1. (*painful body area*) plaie *f* 2. *fig* blessure *f*

sorely ['sɔːli, *Am:* 'sɔːr-] *adv form* grandement; **to be ~ missed** manquer terriblement

sorority [sə'rɒrəti, *Am:* -'rɔːrət̬i] *n Am* organisation *f* étudiante

sorrel ['sɒrəl, *Am:* 'sɔːr-] *n no pl* oseille *f*

sorrow ['sɒrəʊ, *Am:* 'sɑːroʊ] *n* chagrin *m;* (*of a book, film, music*) tristesse *f;* **to feel ~ over sth** être chagriné par qc; **to my ~** *form* à mon grand chagrin

S

sorrowful *adj* triste

sorry ['sɒri, *Am:* 'sɑːr-] I. <-ier, -iest> *adj* 1. (*apologizing*) désolé(e); **to be ~ that** être désolé que *+subj;* **to be ~ for oneself** *pej* s'apitoyer sur son sort 2. (*regretful*) **to say ~** s'excuser 3. (*said before refusing*) désolé(e) 4. (*wretched*) piteux(-euse); (*choice*) malheureux(-euse); (*sight*) triste II. *interj* 1. (*apology*) **~!** désolé! 2. (*prefacing refusal*) non, désolé 3. (*requesting repetition*) **~?** pardon?

sort [sɔːt, *Am:* sɔːrt] I. *n* 1. (*type*) sorte *f;* **that ~ of thing** ce genre de chose; **some ~ of sth** un genre de qc; **chicken of ~s** un genre de poulet; **tea of a ~** une sorte de thé; **nothing of the ~** pas du tout; **something of the ~** quelque chose comme ça; **all ~s of people** des gens de tous les milieux; **I am that ~ of person** je suis comme ça; **that's my ~ of thing** c'est le genre de chose que j'aime; **to be not the ~ to** *+infin* ne pas être du genre à *+infin* 2. *inf* (*kind of*) **~ of** à peu près; **to be ~ of embarrassing** être plutôt gênant; **to ~ of want to** *+infin* vouloir un peu *+infin* 3. *inf* (*type of person*) **I know his ~** je connais les gens de son espèce; **to be a friendly ~** être un brave type/une brave fille 4. INFOR tri *m* ►**to be out of ~s** être mal en point; **it takes all ~s to make a world** *prov* il faut de tout pour faire un monde II. *vt* 1. (*select*) *a.* INFOR trier 2. (*tidy up*) ranger 3. *Brit, inf* (*repair*) réparer ►**sth ~s the men from the boys** différencier les hommes des garçons III. *vi* trier; **to ~ through sth** faire le tri dans qc

◆**sort out** *vt* 1. (*select*) trier; **to sort sth out from sth** séparer qc de qc 2. (*organize, tidy up*) ranger; (*files*) classer; (*papers, desk*) mettre de l'ordre dans; **to sort oneself out** se reprendre 3. (*fix*) arranger 4. (*resolve: problem*) régler; (*difficulties*) aplanir; (*priorities*) établir; **to ~ whether/how/what/who ...** essayer de savoir si/combien/que/qui 5. *inf* (*assault sb as warning*) **to sort sb out** régler son compte à qn

sort code *n* FIN code *m* bancaire

sorter *n* 1. *Am* (*postal employee*) employé(e) *m(f)* au tri postal 2. (*person*) trieur, -euse *m, f* 3. (*device*) trieuse *f*

sortie ['sɔːtiː, *Am:* 'sɔːr-] *n* 1. MIL sortie *f* 2. *inf* (*short trip*) virée *f* 3. *inf* (*try*) tentative *f*

sorting office *n* centre *m* de tri

SOS [ˌesəʊ'es, *Am:* -oʊ'-] *n* appel *m* au secours

so-so *inf* I. *adj* moyen(ne) II. *adv* comme ci, comme ça

sot [sɒt, *Am:* sɑːt] *n pej* ivrogne *mf*

sottish *adj pej* ivre

soubriquet *n form s.* **sobriquet**

sought [sɔːt, *Am:* sɑːt] *pt, pp of* **seek**

sought-after *adj* recherché(e)

soul [səʊl, *Am:* soʊl] *n* 1. (*spirit*) âme *f* 2. *no pl* (*profound feelings*) âme *f* 3. (*person*) âme *f* 4. *no pl* MUS soul *f* 5. (*essence*) cœur *m;* **to be the ~ of discretion/honesty** être la discrétion/l'honnêteté personnifiée ►**to throw oneself body and ~ into sth** se jeter corps et âme dans qc

soul brother *n* frère *m* de race **soul-destroying** *adj Brit, pej* abrutissant(e) **soul food** *n nourriture traditionnelle afro-américaine originaire du Sud*

soulful *adj* sentimental(e)

soulless *adj pej* sans âme; (*a building, town*) sans caractère; (*dull*) morne

soul mate *n* âme *f* sœur **soul music** *n* soul *f* **soul-searching** *n no pl* introspection *f* **soul sister** *n* sœur *f* **soul-stirring** *adj* émouvant(e)

sound¹ [saʊnd] I. *n* 1. (*tone*) son *m;* **to turn the ~ down/up** monter/baisser le son; **to like the ~ of one's own voice** aimer s'entendre parler 2. (*noise*) bruit *m;* **knocking ~** cognement *m* 3. *no pl* PHYS son *m* 4. MUS son *m* 5. (*idea expressed in words*) **I don't like the ~ of it** cela ne me dit rien qui ne vaille II. *vi* 1. (*resonate: bell*) sonner; (*alarm, siren*) retentir 2. LING sonner; **it ~s better** cela sonne mieux 3. (*appear*) sembler; **to ~ as though ...** on dirait que ...; **to ~ nice** avoir l'air bien; **he ~s English** on dirait qu'il est anglais; **it ~s like Bach** on dirait du Bach; **it doesn't ~ like him to do this** ça ne lui ressemble pas de faire qc comme ça III. *vt* 1. (*make a ~: bell*) sonner; (*alarm*) donner; (*buzzer*) déclencher; (*gong*) faire sonner; (*siren*) faire retentir; **to ~ the (car) horn** klaxonner 2. (*pronounce*) prononcer 3. *fig* **to ~ the death-knell for sth** décréter la fin de qc; **to ~ the retreat** MIL sonner la retraite

sound² [saʊnd] I. *adj* 1. (*healthy: person*) en bonne santé; (*body*) sain(e); **to be of ~ mind** être sain d'esprit 2. (*in good condition*) en bon état; **as ~ as a bell** *inf* être en très bon état 3. (*trustworthy*) solide; (*advice*) judicieux(-euse); (*investment, method*) sûr(e); (*reasoning*) valable; (*view*) sensé(e); **a man of ~ judgement** un homme de bons conseils; **environmentally ~** bon pour l'environnement 4. (*thorough*) complet(-ète); (*defeat*) total(e); (*knowledge*) approfondi(e); (*sleep*) profond(e); **to give sb a ~ thrashing** donner une bonne correction à qn II. *adv* **to be ~ asleep** être profondément endormi

sound³ [saʊnd] *vt* 1. NAUT sonder 2. MED (*person*) ausculter

sound bite *n* extrait *m* d'une interview

soundly *adv* 1. (*solidly*) solidement 2. (*thoroughly: sleep*) profondément; (*beat*) à plates coutures; **to thrash sb ~** donner une bonne correction à qn 3. (*with reason*) sainement

◆**sound off** *vi inf* se vanter

◆**sound out** *vt* sonder

sound⁴ *n* 1. (*sea channel*) bras *m* de mer 2. (*sea surrounded by land*) détroit *m*

sound archives *npl* archives *fpl* sonores

sound barrier *n* mur *m* du son; **to break the ~** franchir le mur du son **sound board** *n*

MUS table *f* d'harmonie **soundbox** *n* caisse *f* de résonance **sound card** *n* INFOR carte *f* son **sound effects** *n* effets *mpl* sonores **sound-engineer** *n* ingénieur *mf* du son **sound-film** *n* film *m* sonore

sounding *n* **1.** NAUT sondage *m* **2.** *pl* sondages *mpl;* **to take ~s** faire des sondages; **to make ~s** enquêter

soundless *adj* silencieux(-euse)

soundness *n no pl* santé *f*

soundproof I. *vt* insonoriser II. *adj* insonorisé(e) **sound recording** *n* enregistrement *m* sonore **sound reproduction** *n* reproduction *f* sonore **sound shift** *n* LING mutation *f* sonore **sound system** *n* sono *f* **soundtrack** *n* **1.** (*recorded sound*) bande *f* sonore **2.** (*film music*) bande *f* originale **sound velocity** *n* vitesse *f* du son **sound wave** *n* vague *f* sonore

soup [suːp] *n no pl* soupe *f;* **packet ~** soupe *f* en sachet; **clear ~** bouillon *m* ►**to be in the ~** *inf* être dans la mouise

soupçon ['suːpsɒn, *Am:* suːp'sɑːn] *n no pl, iron* soupçon *m*

souped-up *adj* **1.** AUTO gonflé(e) **2.** *pej* réchauffé(e)

soup kitchen *n* soupe *f* populaire **soup plate** *n* assiette *f* creuse **soup spoon** *n* cuillère *f* à soupe **soup tureen** *n* soupière *f*

sour ['saʊəʳ, *Am:* 'saʊɚ] I. *adj* **1.** (*bitter*) aigre; **to go ~** devenir aigre; (*milk*) tourner **2.** *fig* aigri(e); **to go ~** mal tourner ►**to be just ~ grapes** être déçu II. *n Am* **whisky ~** whisky *m* au citron III. *vt* **1.** GASTR (*give bitter taste*) faire tourner **2.** *fig* aigrir IV. *vi* **1.** GASTR (*get bitter*) tourner **2.** *fig* s'aigrir

source [sɔːs, *Am:* sɔːrs] I. *n a. fig* source *f;* **at ~** à la source; **to have one's ~ in sth** avoir son origine dans qc; **to track down the ~ of sth** tracer la provenance de qc II. *vt* **1.** (*state origin*) **to be ~d from sth** provenir de qc **2.** (*find out*) se procurer

sourcing *n* approvisionnement *m*

sour cream *n* crème *f* aigre

sourpuss ['saʊəpʊs, *Am:* 'saʊɚ-] *n inf* grognon *mf*

souse [saʊs] *vt* mariner

south ['saʊθ] I. *n* **1.** (*cardinal point*) sud *m;* **to lie 5 km to the ~ of sth** être à 5 km au sud de qc; **a ~-facing window** une fenêtre exposée au sud **2.** GEO sud *m;* **in the ~ of France** dans le midi de la France; **the South** *Am* les États du Sud II. *adj* (*side, coast*) sud *inv;* **~ wind** vent *m* du sud; **a ~ wall** un mur exposé au sud; **in ~ Paris** dans le sud de Paris III. *adv* au sud; (*to travel*) vers le sud

South Africa *n* Afrique *f* du Sud **South African** I. *adj* sud-africain(e) II. *n* Sud-africain(e) *m(f)* **South America** *n* Amérique *f* du Sud **South American** I. *adj* sud-américain(e) II. *n* Sud-américain(e) *m(f)* **southbound** *mpl* vers le sud; **~ passengers** passagers *mpl* allant vers le sud **South Carolina** *n* Caroline-du-Sud *f* **South Dakota** *n* Dakota-du-Sud *m* **south-east** I. *n no pl* sud-est *m* II. *adj* du sud-est III. *adv* au sud-est; (*to travel*) vers le sud-est; *s. a.* **south** **South-East Asia** *n* Asie *f* du sud-est **southeaster** *n* vent *m* du sud-est **south-easterly** *adj* du sud-est **south-eastern** *adj* du sud-est **south-eastwards** *adv* vers le sud-est

southerly I. *adj* (*towards the south*) vers le sud; **the most ~ place** l'endroit le plus au sud *m* II. *adv* sud III. *n* sud *m*

southern *adj* du sud; (*from the south of France*) du midi; **~ Scotland** le sud de l'Écosse

Southern Cross *n* ASTR Croix-du-Sud *f* **southerner** *n* **1.** (*native or inhabitant from the south*) habitant(e) *m(f)* du sud **2.** *Am* sudiste *mf* **southern hemisphere** *n* hémisphère *m* sud **Southern Lights** *npl* aurore *f* australe **southernmost** *adj* le(la) plus méridional(e)

south-facing *adj* orienté(e) vers le sud **South Georgia** *n* Géorgie *f* du Sud **South Korea** *n* Corée *f* du Sud **South Korean** I. *adj* sud-coréen(e) II. *n* Coréen(ne) *m(f)* du Sud **southpaw** *n* SPORT gaucher, -ère *m, f* **South Pole** *n* pôle *m* Sud **South Sandwich Islands** *n* les îles *fpl* Sandwich du Sud **South Tipperary** *n* Tipperary *f* du Sud **southward** I. *adj* au sud II. *adv* vers le sud **southwards** *adv* vers le sud **south-west** I. *n no pl* sud-ouest *m* II. *adj* du sud-ouest III. *adv* au sud-ouest; (*to travel*) vers le sud-ouest; *s. a.* **south** **southwester** *n* vent *m* du sud-ouest **south-westerly** I. *adj* du sud-ouest II. *adv* vers le sud-ouest **south-western** *adj* du sud-ouest **south-westward(s)** *adv* vers le sud-ouest

souvenir [ˌsuːvə'nɪəʳ, *Am:* -'nɪr] *n* souvenir *m*

sovereign ['sɒvrɪn, *Am:* 'sɑːvrən] I. *n* souverain(e) *m(f)* II. *adj* souverain(e)

sovereign pontiff *n* souverain *m* pontife

sovereignty ['sɒvrənti, *Am:* 'sɑːvrənṭi] *n no pl* souveraineté *f*

soviet ['səʊviət, *Am:* 'soʊviet] I. *n* HIST soviet *m* II. *adj* soviétique

Soviet Union *n* HIST Union *f* soviétique

sow [səʊ, *Am:* soʊ] <sowed, *o* sowed sown> *vt, vi a. fig* semer

sown [səʊn, *Am:* soʊn] *pp of* **sow**

sox [sɔks, *Am:* sɑːks] *npl* chaussettes *fpl*

soy [sɔɪ] *n Am,* **soya** *n* soja *m*

soya bean *n* soja *m* **soya milk** *n* lait *m* de soja **soya sauce** *n* sauce *f* soja

soybean *n Am s.* **soya bean** **soy milk** *n Am s.* **soya milk** **soy sauce** *n Am s.* **soya sauce**

sozzled ['sɒzld, *Am:* 'sɑːzld] *adj Brit, Aus, inf* bourré(e); **to get ~** se bourrer

spa [spɑː] *n* station *f* thermale

space [speɪs] I. *n* **1.** (*area, gap*) *a.* INFOR, TYP espace *m;* **to be a ~ saver** faire gagner de la

S

place; **a blank** ~ un blanc; **empty** ~ vide *m* **2.** *no pl* (*room*) place *f;* **parking** ~ place de parking; **wide open** ~ grands espaces *mpl;* **open** ~ espaces *mpl* verts; **to take up** ~ prendre de la place; **to leave** ~ **for sb/sth** laisser de la place à qn/qc; **to make** ~ faire de la place; **outside** ~ **and time** hors espace et temps; **to gaze into** ~ regarder dans le vide **3.** (*interval of time*) période *f;* **after a** ~ **of four months** après une période de quatre mois; **in a** ~ **of time** un espace de temps; **in the** ~ **of one hour** en l'espace d'une heure **4.** (*outer space*) espace *m;* **in** ~ dans l'espace; **to go into** ~ aller dans l'espace **II.** *vt* espacer

space age, **space-age** **I.** *n* ère *f* spatiale **II.** *adj* de l'ère spatiale **space agency** *n* agence *f* spatiale **space bar** *n* barre *f* d'espacement **space blanket** *n* couverture *f* thermique **space capsule** *n* capsule *f* **space centre** *n* centre *m* spatial **spacecraft** *n* vaisseau *m* spatial **space flight** *n* voyage *m* spatial **space heater** *n* chauffage *m* d'appoint **space lab**, **space laboratory** *n* laboratoire *m* spatial **spaceman** <-men> *n* astronaute *mf* **space probe** *n* sonde *f* spatiale **space research** *n* recherche *f* spatiale **space-saving** *adj* peu encombrant(e) **spaceship** *n* vaisseau *m* spatial **space shuttle** *n* navette *f* spatiale **space station** *n* station *f* spatiale **spacesuit** *n* scaphandre *m* **space travel** *n no pl* voyage *m* dans l'espace **space traveller** *n* astronaute *mf* **spacewoman** <-women> *n* astronaute *f*

spacing ['speɪsɪŋ] *n no pl* espacement *m;* **single/double** ~ un simple/double interligne

spacious ['speɪʃəs] *adj* spacieux(-euse)

spaciousness *n no pl* grandeur *f*

spade [speɪd] *n* **1.** (*garden device*) bêche *f;* **a bucket and** ~ un seau et une pelle **2.** (*playing card*) pique *m* ►**to** <u>**call**</u> **a** ~ **a** ~ appeler un chat un chat; <u>**in**</u> ~**s** *Am, inf* à fond

spadework *n no pl* gros *m* du travail; **to do the** ~ faire le gros du travail

spaghetti [spə'geti, *Am:* -'geṱ-] *n pl* spaghettis *mpl*

spaghetti western *n* western *m* spaghetti

Spain [speɪn] *n* Espagne *f*

spam® [spæm] *n no pl* ≈ pâté *m* de jambon

span [spæn] **I.** *n sing* **1.** (*extent*) *a. fig* étendue *f;* (*of hand*) empan *m* **2.** (*space in time*) durée *f;* (*of time*) espace *m;* **life** ~ espérance *f* de vie; **over a** ~ **of two months** sur une durée de deux mois **3.** (*wingspan*) envergure *f* **4.** (*between two points*) portée *f;* (*bridge*) travée *f* **II.** <-nn-> *vt* **1.** (*extend*) enjamber **2.** (*cover, include*) couvrir **3.** *pt of* **spin**

spangle ['spæŋgl] **I.** *n* paillette *f* **II.** *vt* pailleter; **to be** ~ **with sth** être pailleté de qc

Spanglish ['spæŋlɪʃ] *n Am: langue hybride mêlant anglais et espagnol; s. a.* **English**

Spaniard ['spænjəd, *Am:* -jɚd] *n* Espagnol(e) *m(f)*

spaniel ['spænjəl, *Am:* -jəl] *n* épagneul *m*

Spanish ['spænɪʃ] **I.** *adj* espagnol(e); ~ **speaker** hispanophone *mf* **II.** *n* **1.** (*people*) **the** ~ les Espagnols **2.** LING espagnol *m; s. a.* **English**

Spaniard *n* (*person*) Espagnol(e) *m(f)*

spank [spæŋk] **I.** *vt* fesser **II.** *n* fessée *f;* **to give sb a** ~ donner la fessée à qn

spanking **I.** *n* fessée *f* **II.** *adj* **1.** (*lively*) vif(vive); **at a** ~ **pace** d'un pas vif **2.** *inf* (*very good*) **to have a** ~ **time** passer du sacré bon temps **3.** (*impressive*) impressionnant(e)

spanner ['spænəʳ, *Am:* -ɚ] *n Brit, Aus* clé *f;* **adjustable** ~ clé anglaise ►**to put a** ~ **in the** <u>**works**</u> mettre des bâtons dans les toues

spar [spɑːʳ, *Am:* spɑːr] **I.** *n* entraînement *m* **II.** <-rr-> *vi* **1.** (*box without heavy blows*) s'entraîner **2.** *fig* (*row*) se quereller

spare [speəʳ, *Am:* sper] **I.** *vt* **1.** (*be merciful to*) épargner **2.** (*refrain from doing*) épargner; (*efforts, strength*) ménager; **to** ~ **no expense** ne pas regarder à la dépense; **to not** ~ **oneself** se donner du mal **3.** (*do without*) se passer de; **to** ~ **room for sth** faire de la place pour qc; **to** ~ **(the) time** avoir le temps; **to not have time to** ~ ne pas avoir le temps; **to** ~ **sb a moment** accorder une minute à qn ►~ **the rod and spoil the** <u>**child**</u> *prov* qui aime bien châtie bien **II.** *adj* **1.** (*reserve: key, clothes*) de rechange **2.** (*available: seat, room, cash*) disponible; **to have a** ~ **minute** avoir une minute **3.** (*simple*) dépouillé(e) ►**to** <u>**drive**</u> **sb** ~ rendre qn dingue; **to** <u>**go**</u> ~ *Brit, inf* devenir dingue **III.** *n* **1.** (*item*) pièce *f* de rechange; ~**s** pièces *fpl* détachées **2.** (*tyre*) roue *f* de secours

spare part surgery *n no pl, Brit* MED greffe *f* **spare ribs** *npl* travers *mpl* de porc **spare time** *n no pl* temps *m* libre; **in my** ~ à mes heures perdues **spare tire** *n Am,* **spare tyre** *n* **1.** (*reserve tyre for cars*) roue *f* de secours **2.** *iron* (*undesired fat on midriff*) bouée *f*

sparing *adj* modéré(e)

sparingly *adv* en petite quantité

spark [spɑːk, *Am:* spɑːrk] **I.** *n* **1.** (*tiny flare of fire*) *a. fig* étincelle *f* **2.** (*small amount*) étincelle *f* **3.** *iron* (*person*) **a bright** ~ une lumière ►**to make the** ~**s** <u>**fly**</u> mettre le feu aux poudres **II.** *vt a. fig* déclencher; **to** ~ **sth in sb** déclencher qc en qn; **to** ~ **sb into action** pousser qn à l'action **III.** *vi* jeter des étincelles

sparking plug *n Brit* bougie *f*

sparkle ['spɑːkl, *Am:* 'spɑːr-] **I.** *n no pl* **1.** (*flash of light*) étincelle *f; fig* lueur *f* **2.** (*vivacity*) éclat *m* **II.** *vi a. fig* étinceler; (*sea, fire*) scintiller; (*person, eyes*) briller

sparkler *n* **1.** (*firework*) bougie *f* magique **2.** *inf* (*diamond*) diam *m*

sparkling *adj a. fig* étincelant(e); (*drink*) pétillant(e), spitant(e) *Belgique*

spark plug *s.* **sparking plug**

sparring *n* entraînement *m*

sparrow ['spærəʊ, *Am:* 'speroʊ] *n* moineau

m

sparrowhawk ['spærəʊhɔːk, *Am:* 'speroʊhɑːk] *n* épervier *m*

sparse [spɑːs, *Am:* spɑːrs] *adj* clairsemé(e)

spartan ['spɑːtən, *Am:* 'spɑːr-] *adj* spartiate

spasm ['spæzəm] *n* spasme *m;* (*anger, coughing*) accès *m;* **a ~ of pain** un élancement; **to go into ~** *no pl, Brit, Aus* avoir des spasmes

spasmodic [spæz'mɒdɪk, *Am:* -'mɑːdɪk] *adj* intermittent(e); *pej* MED spasmodique

spastic ['spæstɪk] *pej* **I.** *n* handicapé (e) moteur *m* **II.** *adj* **1.** (*related to a handicapped person*) handicapé(e) moteur **2.** (*spasmodic*) spasmodique **3.** *childspeak* (*bad*) nul(le)

spat[1] [spæt] *pt, pp of* **spit**

spat[2] [spæt] **I.** *n inf* (*brief clash*) prise *f* de bec **II.** <-tt-> *vi Am, Aus* avoir une prise de bec

spate [speɪt] *n no pl* **1.** (*large number*) avalanche *f* **2.** *Brit* (*river flood*) crue *f;* **to be in full ~** être en pleine crue; **to have a ~ of work** *fig* être débordé de travail

spatial ['speɪʃəl] *adj* spatial(e)

spatter ['spætəʳ, *Am:* 'spæt̬ɚ] **I.** *vt* éclabousser; **to ~ sth on sb** éclabousser qn de qc **II.** *vi* gicler **III.** *n* éclaboussure *f*

spatula ['spætjʊlə, *Am:* 'spætʃə-] *n* spatule *f*

spawn [spɔːn, *Am:* spɑːn] **I.** *n no pl* (*eggs of water animals*) frai *m* **II.** *vt* **1.** (*lay*) pondre **2.** *fig* engendrer **III.** *vi* **1.** (*lay*) frayer **2.** *fig* se multiplier

spay [speɪ] *vt* (*an animal*) châtrer

speak [spiːk] <spoke, spoken> **I.** *vi* **1.** (*articulate*) parler; **to ~ to each other** se parler; **to ~ to sb about sth** parler à qn à propos de qc; **to ~ in jargon/dialect** parler en jargon/dialecte; **to ~ for/against sth** être en faveur/opposé à qc; **to ~ into sth** parler dans qc; **to ~ for oneself** parler pour soi; **~ing for oneself** pour sa part; **facts ~ for themselves** les faits parlent d'eux-mêmes; **to ~ over a loudspeaker** parler dans un haut-parleur; **to ~ through a megaphone** parler dans un porte-voix; **to ~ in a whisper** chuchoter; **~ when you're spoken to** tu réponds quand on te parle **2.** (*from a specified point of view*) **sth ~ing** d'un point de vue de qc; **geographically ~ing** d'un point de vue géographique; **~ing of sth** à propos de qc; **so to ~** pour ainsi dire **3.** (*make a formal speech*) faire un discours; **to ~ in public** parler en public **4.** (*communicate on the phone*) être à l'appareil ►**actions ~ louder than words** *prov* les actes sont plus éloquents que les paroles; **to ~ the lingo** *inf* baragouiner **II.** *vt* **1.** (*say*) dire; (*language*) parler; **to ~ the truth** dire la vérité; **to ~ one's mind** donner son opinion; **to not ~ a word** ne pas dire un mot **2.** (*reveal*) révéler

◆**speak out** *vi* prendre la parole; **to ~ against sth** dénoncer qc

◆**speak up** *vi* parler fort; **to ~ for sth** parler en faveur de qn

speaker *n* **1.** (*sb using a specific language*) interlocuteur, -trice *m, f* **2.** (*orator*) orateur, -trice *m, f* **3.** *Brit, Can* (*chairperson of parliamentary assembly*) **the Speaker** le(la) président(e) de l'Assemblée **4.** (*person who records*) speaker, -ine *m, f* **5.** (*loudspeaker*) haut-parleur *m* **6.** INFOR enceinte *f*

speaking **I.** *n no pl* parler *m;* **public ~** art *m* oratoire **II.** *adj* **a.** *fig* parlant(e); **to be no longer on ~ terms with sb** ne plus adresser la parole à qn; **english-~** de langue anglaise

speaking clock *n Brit* horloge *f* parlante

speaking part *n* THEAT, CINE rôle *m* parlant

spear [spɪəʳ, *Am:* spɪr] **I.** *n* **1.** (*weapon*) lance *f* **2.** (*leaf or stem: asparagus*) pointe *f* **II.** *vt* **to ~ sb/sth** transpercer qn/qc d'un coup de lance

spearhead **I.** *vt* être le fer de lance de **II.** *n* (*driving force*) fer *m* de lance; **to act as the ~ for a campaign** être le fer de lance d'une campagne

spearmint ['spɪəmɪnt, *Am:* 'spɪr-] **I.** *n no pl* menthe *f* **II.** *adj* à la menthe

special ['speʃəl] **I.** *adj* spécial(e); (*attention, treatment, diet*) particulier(-ère); (*clinic, committee, school*) spécialisé(e); **to be ~ to sth** être particulier à qc; **to attach ~ significance to sth** accorder une importance particulière à qc; **to be ~ to sb** compter pour qn; **nothing ~** *inf* rien de spécial **II.** *n* **1.** (*important programme or show*) spécial *m* **2.** *Am, Aus* (*meal available for one day*) plat *m* du jour **3.** *pl, Am* (*goods offered at reduced prices*) offres *fpl* spéciales **4.** (*uncommon train transport*) train *m* spécial

special delivery *n* envoi *m* en express; **by ~** en express **special edition** *n* édition *f* spéciale **special effects** *npl n* effets *mpl* spéciaux

specialism ['speʃəlɪzm] *n* **1.** (*area of special interest*) spécialité *f* **2.** *no pl* (*restricting topics for study*) spécialisation *f*

specialist **I.** *n* spécialiste *mf;* **~ in sth** spécialiste dans qc; **a heart ~** un(e) cardiologue **II.** *adj* spécialisé(e)

speciality [ˌspeʃɪ'æləti, *Am:* -t̬i] <-ies> *n* spécialité *f*

specialization *n Am* spécialisation *f*

specialize ['speʃəlaɪz] *vi* se spécialiser

specialized *adj* spécialisé(e)

specially *adv* **1.** (*specifically*) spécialement **2.** (*in particular*) particulièrement

special offer *n* offre *f* spéciale

specialty ['speʃəlti, *Am:* -t̬i] <-ies> *n Am, Aus s.* **speciality**

species ['spiːʃiːz] *inv n* espèce *f;* **bird ~** espèce d'oiseau; **extinct ~** espèce en voie d'extinction; **to be a rare ~** *fig, iron, inf* être un drôle d'oiseau

specific [spə'sɪfɪk] *adj* **1.** (*distinguishing*) spécifique; **to be ~ to sth** être spécifique à qc **2.** (*clearly defined: date, details, knowledge*) précis(e)

specifically *adv* **1.** (*expressly*) spécifique-

S

ment **2.** (*clearly*) expressément

specification [ˌspesɪfɪ'keɪʃən, *Am:* -əfɪ'-] *n* spécification *f;* ~**s** caractéristiques *fpl*

specify ['spesɪfaɪ, *Am:* -əfaɪ] <-ie-> *vt* spécifier; (*time, date*) préciser

specimen ['spesɪmɪn, *Am:* -əmən] *n* **1.** (*example*) spécimen *m;* **a fine** ~ *inf* un beau spécimen; **a miserable** ~ *inf* un sale type **2.** (*sample*) échantillon *m;* MED (*urine, blood*) prélèvement *m;* **to take a** ~ faire un prélèvement

specious ['spi:ʃəs] *adj pej, form* spécieux(-euse)

speck [spek] *n* **1.** (*spot*) petite *f* tache **2.** (*point*) point *m* **3.** (*small particle*) grain *m*

speckle ['spekl] *n* tacheture *f*

speckled *adj* tacheté(e); **to be** ~ **with sth** être tacheté de qc

specs [speks] *npl inf abbr of* **spectacles**

spectacle ['spektəkl] *n* spectacle *m;* **a pure** ~ *no pl,* **mere** ~ *no pl* un merveilleux spectacle; **to make a real** ~ **of oneself** se donner en spectacle

spectacle case *n* étui *m* à lunettes

spectacled *adj* à lunettes

spectacles *n pl* lunettes *fpl;* **a pair of** ~ une paire de lunettes

spectacular [spek'tækjʊləʳ, *Am:* -lɚ] **I.** *adj* spectaculaire **II.** *n* grand spectacle *m*

spectator [spek'teɪtəʳ, *Am:* -t̬ɚ] *n* spectateur, -trice *m, f;* ~ **at sth** spectateur de qc

specter *n Am* spectre *m*

spectral ['spektrəl] *adj* spectral(e)

spectre ['spektəʳ, *Am:* -tɚ] *s.* **specter**

spectroscope ['spektrəʊskəʊp, *Am:* -skoʊp] *n* PHYS spectroscope *m*

spectrum ['spektrəm] <-ra *o* -s> *n* **1.** PHYS spectre *m* **2.** (*span*) *a. fig* gamme *f;* **the political** ~ l'éventail politique

speculate ['spekjʊleɪt] *vi* **to** ~ **about sth** spéculer sur qc; **to** ~ **on the stock market** spéculer à la bourse

speculation *n a.* FIN spéculation *f*

speculative *adj a.* FIN spéculatif(-ive)

speculator *n* spéculateur, -trice *m, f*

sped [sped] *pt, pp of* **speed**

speech [spi:tʃ] <-es> *n* **1.** *no pl* (*act of speaking*) parole *f;* **to lose the power of** ~ perdre l'usage de la parole; **in** ~ en parole; **to be slow in** ~ parler lentement **2.** (*lines spoken by actor*) texte *m* **3.** (*public talk*) discours *m*

speech act *n* LING acte *m* de parole **speech community** *n* LING, SOCIOL communauté *f* linguistique **speech day** *n Brit* distribution *f* des prix

speechify ['spi:tʃɪfaɪ, *Am:* -tʃə-] *vi pej* discourir; **to** ~ **about sth** discourir de qc

speechless *adj* muet(te); **to be** ~ **from birth** être muet de naissance; **to be** ~ **with indignation** rester muet d'indignation; **to leave sb** ~ laisser qn sans voix

speech recognition *n no pl* INFOR, LING reconnaissance *f* vocale **speech therapist** *n* orthophoniste *mf* **speech therapy** *n* orthophonie *f* **speech writer** *n* rédacteur, -trice *m, f* de discours

speed [spi:d] **I.** *n* **1.** (*velocity*) vitesse *f;* **at a** ~ **of ten kilometres per hour** à une vitesse de dix kilomètres heure; **at breakneck** ~ *no pl* à une vitesse folle; **cruising** ~ vitesse de croisière; (**at**) **full** ~ à toute vitesse; **at lightning** ~ à la vitesse de l'éclair; **the** ~ **of light/sound** la vitesse de la lumière/du son; **with all possible** ~ le plus vite possible **2.** *fig* (*quickness*) rapidité *f* **3.** (*gear on bicycle*) vitesse *f* **4.** *inf* (*amphetamine*) amphète *f;* **to be on** ~ être sous amphés ►**to be up to** ~ aller à toute vitesse; **to bring sb up to** ~ tenir qn au courant de qc **II.** <sped, sped> *vi* **1.** (*hasten*) se dépêcher **2.** (*exceed speed restrictions*) aller trop vite **3.** *inf* (*be under drug*) être sous amphés **III.** <-ed, -ed *o* sped, sped> *vt* accélérer; (*person*) presser

◆**speed up** <-ed, -ed> **I.** *vt* accélérer; (*person*) presser **II.** *vi* **1.** (*gather momentum*) aller plus vite **2.** (*accelerating activity*) accélérer

speedboat *n* hors-bord *m* **speed bump** *n* ralentisseur *m* **speed check**, **speed control** *n* contrôle *m* de vitesse

speeding *n no pl* excès *m* de vitesse

speed limit *n* limite *f* de vitesse; **to be over the** ~ dépasser la limite de vitesse

speedo <-s> *n Brit, inf,* **speedometer** [spi:'dɒmɪtəʳ, *Am:* -'dɑ:mət̬ɚ] *n* compteur *m* de vitesse

speed skating *n no pl* SPORT patinage *m* de vitesse **speed trap** *n* contrôle *m* de vitesse

speed-up *n no pl* accélération *f*

speedy ['spi:di] <-ier, -iest> *adj* rapide

speleologist *n* spéléologue *mf*

speleology [ˌspi:lɪ'ɒlədʒi, *Am:* -'ɑ:lə-] *n no pl* spéléologie *f*

spell¹ [spel] *n* formule *f* magique; **to cast** [*o* **put**] **a** ~ **on sb** jeter un sort à qn; **to be under a** ~ être envoûté; **to be under sb's** ~ *fig* être sous le charme de qn

spell² [spel] **I.** *n* **1.** (*period*) période *f;* **to rest for a short** ~ se reposer un petit moment; **cold** ~ vague *f* de froid; **sunny** ~ éclaircie *f;* **to have dizzy** ~**s** avoir des étourdissements *mpl* **2.** (*turn*) tour *m;* **to take** ~**s doing sth** faire qc à tour de rôle **II.** *vt* <spelled, spelled> *Am, Aus* remplacer

spell³ [spel] <spelled, spelled *o a. Brit* spelt, spelt> **I.** *vt* **1.** (*form using letters*) épeler; **how do you** ~ **...** quelle est l'orthographe de ... **2.** (*signify*) signifier; **N O** ~**s no** N O fait no **II.** *vi* connaître l'orthographe; **I can't** ~ je suis nul en orthographe

◆**spell out** *vt* **1.** (*spell*) épeler **2.** (*explain*) expliquer clairement ►**do I have to spell it out for you?** *inf* tu veux que je te fasse un dessin? *subj*

spellbind *vt* fasciner **spellbound** *adj* fasciné(e) **spell checker** *n* INFOR correcteur *m* orthographique

speller *n* **to be a good/weak** ~ être bon/mauvais en orthographe

spelling *n no pl* orthographe *f*

spelt [spelt] *pp, pt of* **spell**

spend [spend] **I.** <spent, spent> *vt* **1.** (*pay out: money*) dépenser; **the years of ~, ~, ~** les années de surconsommation **2.** (*pass time: time, night*) passer; **the storm spent itself** l'orage s'est calmé **II.** <spent, spent> *vi* dépenser de l'argent **III.** *n Brit* dépenses *fpl*

spending *n no pl* dépense *f*

spending cut *n* FIN réduction *f* des dépenses **spending money** *n* argent *m* de poche **spending power** *n* pouvoir *m* d'achat **spending spree** *n* vague *f* de dépenses; **to go on a** ~ faire des folies

spendthrift ['spendθrɪft] **I.** *adj pej, inf* dépensier(-ère) **II.** *n pej, inf* dépensier, -ière *m, f*

spent [spent] **I.** *pp, pt of* **spend II.** *adj* (*used*) usagé(e); (*bullet*) perdu(e)

sperm [spɜːm, *Am:* spɜːrm] <-(s)> *n* **1.** (*male reproductive cell*) spermatozoïde *m* **2.** (*semen*) sperme *m*

sperm donor *n* donneur *m* de sperme

spermicide ['spɜːmɪsaɪd, *Am:* 'spɜːrmə-] *n* spermicide *m*

sperm whale *n* cachalot *m*

spew [spjuː] **I.** *vt* (*sewage*) déverser **II.** *vi* **1.** (*flow out*) jaillir **2.** (*vomit*) vomir

sphere [sfɪəʳ, *Am:* sfɪr] *n* sphère *f*; **private** ~ domaine *m* privé

spherical ['sferɪkl, *Am:* 'sfɪr-] *adj* sphérique

spice [spaɪs] **I.** *n* **1.** (*flavour enhancer*) épice *f* **2.** *no pl* (*excitement*) piment *m* **II.** *vt* **1.** (*add flavour to*) épicer **2.** (*add excitement to*) pimenter

spick and span [ˌspɪkən'spæn] *adj inf* impeccable; **to keep a kitchen** ~ avoir une cuisine d'une propreté impeccable

spicy <-ier, -iest> *adj* **1.** (*seasoned*) épicé(e) **2.** (*sensational*) croustillant(e)

spider ['spaɪdəʳ, *Am:* -dɚ] *n* araignée *f*

spiderweb *n Am, Aus s.* **cobweb**

spidery *adj* (*writing*) en pattes de mouche

spiel [ʃpiːl] *n pej, inf* (*speech*) baratin *m*

spigot ['spɪgət] *n* **1.** (*stopper*) fausset *m* **2.** *Am* (*tap*) robinet *m*

spike [spaɪk] **I.** *n* **1.** (*pointed object*) pointe *f* **2.** (*cleat on shoes*) crampon *m* **3.** *pl* (*running shoes*) pointes *fpl* **4.** *pl, Am s.* **stiletto heels II.** *vt* **1.** (*step on with spikes*) transpercer **2.** *inf* (*stop*) stopper **3.** (*add alcohol*) relever ►**to ~ sb's guns** *inf* désarmer qn

spiky ['spaɪki] <-ier, -iest> *adj* **1.** (*having sharp points*) piquant(e); (*hair*) en brosse **2.** (*irritable*) irritable

spill [spɪl] **I.** *n* **1.** (*act of spilling*) déversement *m*; **oil** ~ déversement d'hydrocarbure; **to wipe up a** ~ essuyer qc qui s'est renversé **2.** *inf* (*fall*) chute *f*; **to have a ~ from sth** tomber de qc **II.** <spilt, spilt *o Am, Aus* spilled, spilled> *vt* renverser ►**to ~ the beans** vendre la mèche **III.** *vi* **1.** (*flow*) couler **2.** (*spread*) **to ~ into sth** se déverser dans qc

spillway *n* déversoir *m*

spilt [spɪlt] *pp, pt of* **spill**

spin [spɪn] **I.** *n* **1.** (*rotation*) tournoiement *m*; (*of wheel*) tour *m*; (*of dancer*) pirouette *f*; **to go into a** (*Aus, Brit* **flat**) ~ se mettre en vrille; **to send a car into a** ~ faire faire un tête-à-queue à une voiture; **to put ~ on a ball** donner de l'effet à une balle; **to throw sb into a** (**flat**) ~ *inf* faire paniquer qn; **to decide sth on a ~ of a coin** décider qc en jouant à pile ou face **2.** (*spin-drying*) essorage *m*; **to give sth a** ~ essorer qc **3.** *no pl, inf* (*method of considering*) perspective *f*; **to put a positive ~ on sth** montrer qc sous un jour positif **4.** (*trip*) tour *m*; **to go for a** ~ aller faire un tour **II.** <spun *o a. Brit* span, spun> *vi* **1.** (*rotate*) tourner; (*dancer, top*) tournoyer; **my head is ~ning** j'ai la tête qui tourne **2.** *inf* (*drive*) conduire; **to ~ out of control** faire un tête-à-queue **3.** (*make thread*) filer **III.** <spun *o a. Brit* span, spun> *vt* **1.** (*rotate*) faire tourner; **to ~ a ball** donner de l'effet à une balle; **to ~ a coin** jouer à pile ou face **2.** (*make thread out of*) filer **3.** (*spin-dry: clothes*) essorer ►**it makes my head** ~ ça me fait tourner la tête; **to ~ a story** raconter une histoire

◆**spin around** *vi s.* **spin round**

◆**spin out I.** *vi* faire un tête-à-queue **II.** *vt* faire durer

◆**spin round I.** *vi* se retourner **II.** *vt* faire tourner

spinach ['spɪnɪtʃ] *n no pl* épinard *m*

spinal ['spaɪnəl] *adj* vertébral(e); (*nerve*) spinal(e); (*injury*) de la colonne vertébrale

spinal column *n* colonne *f* vertébrale **spinal cord** *n* moelle *f* épinière

spindle ['spɪndl] *n* fuseau *m*

spindly <-ier, -iest> *adj* maigrichon(ne)

spin doctor *n inf: conseiller en communication* **spindrift** *n* embruns *mpl* **spin-dry** *vt* essorer (à la machine)

spine [spaɪn] *n* **1.** (*spinal column*) colonne *f* vertébrale **2.** (*spike*) épine *f* **3.** (*book part*) dos *m* ►**to send shivers up/down one's** ~ donner froid dans le dos

spine-chilling ['spaɪnˌtʃɪlɪŋ] *adj* qui fait froid dans le dos

spineless *adj pej* faible

spinnaker ['spɪnəkəʳ, *Am:* -ɚ] *n* spi *m*

spinner *n* **1.** (*bowler*) *lanceur qui donne de l'effet à la balle* **2.** (*one who spins*) fileur, -euse *m, f*

spinney ['spɪni] *n Brit* taillis *m*

spinning *n* filature *f*

spinning jenny *n* métier *m* à filer **spinning mill** *n* filature *f* **spinning top** *n* toupie *f* **spinning wheel** *n* rouet *m*

spin-off *n* **1.** (*by-product*) produit *m* **2.** (*derived work*) retombée *f*

spinster ['spɪnstəʳ, *Am:* -stɚ] *n a. pej* vieille

S

fille *f*

spiny ['spaɪni] <-ier, -iest> *adj* couvert(e) d'épines

spiral ['spaɪərəl, *Am:* 'spaɪ-] **I.** *n* spirale *f* **II.** *adj* en spirale **III.** <-ll-> *vi* **1.** (*travel in a spiral*) tourner en spirale; (*smoke*) faire des volutes; (*leaf, plane*) vriller; **to ~ downwards** descendre en spirale **2.** (*increase*) **to ~ upwards** monter en flèche; **to ~ downwards** chuter

spire ['spaɪəʳ, *Am:* -ɚ] *n* (*of church*) flèche *f*

spirit ['spɪrɪt] *n* **1.** *no pl* (*nature*) esprit *m;* **not to be in the ~ of sth** ne pas être conforme à l'esprit de qc **2.** (*mood*) esprit *m;* **to take sth in the right/wrong ~** bien/mal prendre qc; **to be in high/low ~s** être de bonne/mauvaise humeur; **to break sb's ~** casser le moral de qn **3.** *no pl* (*courage*) courage *m* **4.** (*character*) caractère *m;* **to be young in ~** être jeune de caractère; **with great ~** avec beaucoup de caractère **5.** (*soul*) esprit *m;* **the Holy Spirit** le Saint-Esprit; **to be with sb in ~** être avec qn par la pensée **6.** (*ghost*) esprit *m* **7.** (*alcoholic drink*) spiritueux *m* ►**the ~ is willing but the flesh is weak** *iron* l'esprit est fort mais la chair est faible

spirited *adj* (*discussion*) animé(e); (*reply*) vif(vive)

spiritism *n no pl s.* **spiritualism**

spiritless *adj pej* sans énergie

spirit level *n* niveau *m* (à bulle d'air)

spiritual ['spɪrɪtʃuəl] **I.** *adj* spirituel(le) **II.** *n* negro-spiritual *m*

spiritualism ['spɪrɪtʃuəlɪzəm] *n no pl* **1.** (*communication with dead*) spiritisme *m* **2.** (*doctrine*) spiritualisme *m*

spit[1] [spɪt] *n* **1.** (*rod for roasting*) broche *f* **2.** (*point of land*) pointe *f* (de terre)

spit[2] [spɪt] **I.** *n inf* crachat *m;* **it needs ~ and polish** elle a besoin d'être lustrée ►**to be the (dead) ~ (and image) of sb** être le portrait craché de qn **II.** <spat, *a. Am* spat *o* spit, spit> *vi* **1.** (*expel saliva*) cracher; **it is ~ting (with rain)** *inf* il fait du crachin **2.** (*crackle*) crépiter **III.** *vt* **to ~ blood** [*o a. Am* **nails**] [*o a. Aus* **tacks**] voir rouge

◆**spit out** *vt* cracher; **to spit it out** *inf* cracher ce qu'on a à dire

spite [spaɪt] **I.** *n no pl* **1.** (*desire to hurt*) méchanceté *f* **2.** (*despite*) **in ~ of sth** malgré qc; **in ~ of oneself** malgré soi **II.** *vt* contrarier

spiteful *adj pej* méchant(e)

spitfire *n fig* dragon *m*

spittle ['spɪtl, *Am:* 'spɪt̬-] *n form s.* **spit**

spittoon [spɪ'tu:n] *n* crachoir *m*

splash [splæʃ] **I.** *n* **1.** (*sound*) plouf *m* **2.** (*small amount*) touche *f* ►**to make a ~** faire sensation **II.** *adv* **to fall ~ into sth** tomber dans qc en faisant plouf **III.** *vt* **1.** (*scatter liquid*) éclabousser, gicler *Suisse;* **to ~ coffee on the carpet** faire éclabousser du café sur la moquette; **to ~ one's face with water** s'asperger le visage avec de l'eau **2.** (*print prominently*) être à la une de; **to be ~ed across the front page** s'étaler en première page **IV.** *vi* (*spread via splashes*) **to ~ onto sth** éclabousser qc

◆**splash down** *vi* amerrir

◆**splash out** *Aus, Brit* **I.** *vi inf* faire des folies; **to ~ on sth** se payer qc **II.** *vt* **to ~ money on sth** dépenser de l'argent en achetant qc

splashboard *n* **1.** (*on vehicle*) garde-boue *m* **2.** (*on boat*) pare-brise *m;* (*in kitchen*) écran *m* de protection **splashdown** *n* amerrissage *m*

splat [splæt] *inf* **I.** *n no pl* plaf *m* **II.** *adv* **to fall ~ on the tiles** tomber sur le carrelage en faisant plaf

splatter **I.** *vt* **1.** (*cover with drops*) éclabousser **2.** (*spread*) répandre **II.** *vi* se répandre

splay [spleɪ] **I.** *vt* écarter **II.** *vi* **to ~ out** s'écarter

splay-footed *adj* **to be ~** avoir les pieds plats

spleen [spli:n] *n* **1.** (*lymphoid organ*) rate *f;* **to rupture one's ~** se faire éclater la rate **2.** *no pl, Aus, Brit, form* (*anger*) mauvaise humeur *f;* **to vent one's ~ on sb** décharger sa mauvaise humeur sur qn

splendid ['splendɪd] *adj* **1.** (*magnificent*) splendide **2.** (*fine*) fantastique

splendiferous [splen'dɪfərəs] *adj iron, inf* splendide

splendo(u)r ['splendəʳ, *Am:* -dɚ] *n* **1.** *no pl* (*grandness*) splendeur *f* **2.** *pl* (*beautiful things*) merveilles *fpl*

splice [splaɪs] **I.** *vt* (*film*) coller **II.** *n* raccord *m;* **to join two things with a ~** mettre un raccord entre deux choses

splicer *n* (*machine that splices*) colleuse *f*

splint [splɪnt] **I.** *n* MED attelle *f* **II.** *vt* mettre une attelle à

splinter **I.** *n* (*of wood*) écharde *f;* (*of glass*) éclat *m* **II.** *vi* (*split*) faire éclater; **to ~ into small groups** éclater en petits groupes

splinter group, splinter party *n* POL groupe *m* de scission **splinter-proof** *adj* (*glass*) sécurit® *inv*

split [splɪt] **I.** *n* **1.** (*crack*) fissure *f* **2.** (*tear*) déchirure *f* **3.** (*division*) scission *f;* **a ~ in sth** une scission au sein de qc **4.** (*end of relationship*) rupture *f* **5.** (*share*) part *f;* **I want my ~** je veux ma part du gâteau **6.** (*leg-spreading action*) **the ~(s)** le grand écart **II.** <split, split> *vt* **1.** (*cut*) fendre; **to ~ one's head open** s'ouvrir le crâne **2.** (*tear*) déchirer **3.** (*divide*) diviser; (*money, shares*) partager; **to ~ sth in half/groups** diviser qc en deux/groupes **4.** (*cause division: party*) diviser ►**to ~ the difference** couper la poire en deux; **to ~ hairs** *pej* couper les cheveux en quatre; **to ~ one's sides laughing** être plié en deux **III.** <split, split> *vi* **1.** (*crack*) se fendre; (*material, dress*) se déchirer; **to ~ down the middle** se fendre au milieu **2.** (*divide*) se scinder; **to ~ from sth** se désolidariser de qc **3.** *inf* (*leave*) filer

◆**split off** **I.** *vt* détacher **II.** *vi* **1.** (*become

detached) se détacher **2.** (*separate*) **to ~ from sth** se séparer de qc
◆**split up I.** *vt* partager; **to ~ the work** se répartir le travail **II.** *vi* se séparer; **to ~ with sb** se séparer de qn

split infinitive *n* LING *erreur de style consistant à intercaler un adverbe entre la particule 'to' et un verbe* **split-level** *adj* à plusieurs niveaux **split pea** *n* pois *m* cassé **split personality** *n* PSYCH dédoublement *m* de la personnalité **split pin** *n* goupille *f* fendue **split second** *n* fraction *f* de seconde

splitting headache *n inf* mal *m* de tête aigu

split-up *n* séparation *f*

splodge [splɒdʒ, *Am:* splɑːdʒ], **splotch** *n Brit, inf* tache *f*

splotchy *adj* taché(e)

splurge [splɜːdʒ, *Am:* splɜːrdʒ] *inf* **I.** *vt* claquer; **to ~ money on sth** claquer son argent dans qc **II.** *vi* **to ~ (out) on sth** claquer son argent dans qc **III.** *n* **to have a ~** faire des folies

splutter ['splʌtəʳ, *Am:* 'splʌt̬ɚ] **I.** *vi* **1.** (*speak short, unclear noises*) bafouiller **2.** (*spit*) cracher **3.** (*make crackling noise*) crachoter **II.** *n* (*sound*) crachotement; **to give a ~** crachoter

spoil [spɔɪl] **I.** *n pl* **~s** butin *m;* **to divide the ~s** se répartir le butin **II.** <spoilt, spoilt *o Am* spoiled, spoiled> *vt* **1.** (*ruin: landscape, party*) gâcher; **to ~ a/one's ballot paper** *Brit* faire un vote nul **2.** (*treat well*) gâter; **to be ~t for choice** avoir l'embarras du choix; **~ yourself!** fais-toi plaisir! **III.** <spoilt, spoilt *o Am* spoiled, spoiled> *vi* s'abîmer

spoiler *n* spoiler *m*

spoilsport *n pej, inf* rabat-joie *mf*

spoilt I. *pp, pt of* **spoil II.** *adj* (*treated too well: child*) gâté(e)

spoke[1] [spəʊk, *Am:* spoʊk] *n* rayon *m* ►**to put a ~ in sb's <u>wheel</u>** mettre des bâtons dans les roues de qn

spoke[2] [spəʊk, *Am:* spoʊk] *pt of* **speak**

spoken *pp of* **speak**

spokesman *n* porte-parole *m inv* **spokesperson** *n* porte-parole *m inv* **spokeswoman** <-men> *n* porte-parole *m inv*

sponge [spʌndʒ] **I.** *n* **1.** (*foam cloth*) éponge *f;* **to give sth a ~ with a cloth** éponger qc **2.** (*soft cake*) gâteau *m* mousseline **II.** *vt* **1.** (*absorb liquid*) éponger **2.** (*clean by rubbing*) frotter
◆**sponge down**, **sponge off** *vt* nettoyer avec une éponge
◆**sponge on** *vt pej, inf* vivre aux crochets de

sponge bag *n Aus, Brit* trousse *f* de toilette

sponge cake *n s.* **sponge**

sponger *n pej* pique-assiette *m*

spongy <-ier, -iest> *adj* (*surface*) spongieux(-euse); (*pastry*) mœlleux(-euse)

sponsor ['spɒntsəʳ, *Am:* 'spɑːntsɚ] **I.** *vt* parrainer; (*athlete, team, event*) sponsoriser **II.** *n* **1.** ECON, SPORT sponsor *m* **2.** (*supporter*) parrain *m,* marraine *f*

sponsoring group *n* groupe *m* de sponsors

sponsorship *n no pl* **1.** (*financial support*) parrainage *m;* **to get ~** être parrainé **2.** SPORT sponsoring *m;* **to get ~** être sponsorisé

spontaneity ['spɒntə'neɪəti, *Am:* ˌspɑːntə'neɪət̬i] *n no pl* spontanéité *f*

spontaneous [spɒn'teɪniəs, *Am:* spɑːn'-] *adj* spontané(e)

spoof [spuːf] **I.** *n* parodie *f;* **to do a ~ on sth** faire une parodie de qc **II.** *vt Am, inf* parodier **III.** *vi Am, inf* déconner

spook [spuːk] **I.** *n* **1.** *inf* (*ghost*) fantôme *m* **2.** *Am* (*spy*) espion(ne) *m(f)* **II.** *vt Am* faire peur à

spooky <-ier, -iest> *adj inf* sinistre

spool [spuːl] *n* bobine *f;* (*for sewing machine*) cannette *f*

spoon [spuːn] **I.** *n* **1.** (*utensil for eating*) cuillère *f;* **wooden ~** cuillère en bois **2.** (*amount held in spoon*) cuillerée *f* **II.** *vt* (*serve using spoon*) **to ~ sth into sth** verser qc dans qc à la cuillère

spoon-feed *vt* **1.** (*feed using spoon*) nourrir à la cuillère **2.** *pej* (*supply abundantly*) **to ~ sb with sth** mâcher le travail à qn

spoonful <-s *o* spoonsful> *n* cuillerée *f*

sporadic [spə'rædɪk] *adj* (*gunfire*) sporadique; (*showers*) épars(e)

spore [spɔːʳ, *Am:* spɔːr] *n* spore *m*

sporran ['spɒrən, *Am:* 'spɔːr-] *n Scot: sac en cuir porté à la ceinture sur le devant d'un kilt*

sport [spɔːt, *Am:* spɔːrt] **I.** *n* **1.** (*athletic activity*) sport *m;* **to do/play ~** faire du sport **2.** *no pl* (*fun*) amusement *m;* **to do sth for ~** faire qc pour s'amuser **3.** *Aus* (*form of address*) **how are you doing ~?** salut mon vieux, ça va? ►**to <u>be</u> a bad ~** *inf* être mauvais perdant; **to be a <u>real</u> ~** être vraiment sympa **II.** *vt* (*wear*) arborer

sporting *adj* SPORT sportif(-ive)

sportive *adj* joueur(-euse)

sports car *n* voiture *f* de sport **sportscast** *n Am* émission *f* sportive **sportscaster** *n Am* présentateur, -trice *m, f* sportif **sports field** *n* terrain *m* de sport **sports jacket** *n* blouson *m* **sportsman** *n* sportif *m* **sportsmanlike** *adj* sportif(-ive) **sportsmanship** *n no pl* esprit *m* sportif **sports page** *n* pages *fpl* sportives **sportswear** *n no pl* vêtements *mpl* de sport **sportswoman** *n* sportive *f* **sports writer** *n* chroniqueur, -euse *m, f* sportif

sporty <-ier, -iest> *adj* **1.** (*athletic*) sportif(-ive) **2.** (*fast: car*) de sport

spot [spɒt, *Am:* spɑːt] **I.** *n* **1.** (*mark: of blood, grease*) tache *f* **2.** FASHION (*pattern*) pois *m* **3.** *Brit* (*skin blemish*) bouton *m* **4.** *Brit* (*little bit*) **a ~ of sth** un (petit) peu de qc; **a ~ of lunch** un léger repas **5.** (*place*) endroit *m;* **on the ~** sur place **6.** (*part of show*) séquence *f* **7.** *inf s.* **spotlight** ►**to <u>put</u> sb on the ~** mettre

S

qn sur la sellette; on the ~ (*just now*) sur le champ; (*immediately after*) à chaud **II.** *vi* <-tt-> *Brit* **it's ~ting** (**with rain**) il pleuv(i)ote **III.** <-tt-> *vt* (*see*) apercevoir; **to ~ why/what ...** entrevoir pourquoi/ce que ...; **well ~ted** *Brit* bien vu

spot cash *n s.* **ready money** **spot check** **I.** *n* contrôle *m* surprise **II.** *vt* **to spot-check** contrôler à l'improviste **spot deal** *n* opération *f* au comptant

spotless *adj* **1.** (*clean*) impeccable **2.** (*unblemished*) immaculé(e)

spotlight I. *n* **1.** (*beam of light*) rayon *m* lumineux **2.** THEAT, CINE projecteur *m* ►**to be in/out of the ~** être/ne pas être en vue; **to be under the ~** être sous les feux de la rampe **II.** <spotlighted, spotlighted *o* spotlit, spotlit> *vt* mettre en lumière **spot market** *n* FIN (*without delay*) marché *m* au comptant **spot-on** *adj Aus, Brit, inf* **1.** (*exact*) tout juste **2.** (*on target*) dans le mille **spot price** *n* FIN (*cash paid*) prix *m* au comptant **spot remover** *n* détachant *m*

spotted *adj* (*dog*) tacheté(e); **to be ~ with sth** être taché de qc

spotter *n* SPORT sélectionneur *m*

spotty ['spɒti, *Am:* 'spɑːţi] <-ier, -iest> *adj* **1.** *Aus, Brit* (*having pimples*) boutonneux(-euse) **2.** *Am, Aus* (*bad in certain parts: sales*) frauduleux(-euse); (*progress*) malhonnête

spouse [spaʊz] *n form* **1.** (*husband*) époux *m* **2.** (*wife*) épouse *f*

spout [spaʊt] **I.** *n* **1.** (*tube-shape*) bec *m* **2.** (*gush*) jet *m* ►**up the ~** *Aus, Brit, inf* foutu(e) **II.** *vt* **1.** *pej* (*utter*) dégoiser **2.** (*liquid*) couler **3.** (*gas*) émettre **III.** *vi* **1.** *pej* (*speechify*) pérorer **2.** (*gush*) jaillir

sprain [spreɪn] **I.** *vt* se fouler **II.** *n* foulure *f*

sprang [spræŋ] *vi, vt pt of* **spring**

sprat [spræt] *n* sprat *m*

sprawl [sprɔːl, *Am:* sprɑːl] *pej* **I.** *vi* **1.** (*spread limbs out*) s'affaler; **to send sb ~ing** envoyer qn au tapis **2.** (*expand*) s'étendre **II.** *n* **1.** (*sprawled position*) position *f* avachie; **to lie in a ~** être affalé **2.** (*expanse*) étendue *f*

sprawling *adj pej* **1.** (*expansive*) coûteux(-euse) **2.** (*irregular*) clairsemé(e)

spray[1] [spreɪ] **I.** *n* **1.** (*mist: of perfume, water*) pulvérisation *m;* (*of seawater*) embruns *mpl;* (*of bullets*) salve *f* **2.** (*container: of perfume*) vaporisateur *m;* (*for hair, paint*) bombe *f* **II.** *vt* (*perfume, product*) vaporiser; (*water*) arroser; **to ~ oneself** s'asperger; **to ~ sb with sth** asperger qn de qc **III.** *vi* gicler

spray[2] [spreɪ] *n* inflorescence *f;* (*of flowers*) gerbe *f*

spread [spred] **I.** *n* **1.** (*act of spreading*) déploiement *m* **2.** (*range*) gamme *f;* (*of opinion*) diffusion *f* **3.** (*article*) publication *f* **4.** *Am s.* **ranch** **5.** *Aus, Brit, inf* (*meal*) banquet *m* **II.** <spread, spread> *vi* **1.** (*propagate*) se propager; **to ~ like wildfire** se répandre comme une traînée de poudre **2.** (*stretch*) s'étirer **3.** (*cover a surface*) s'étendre (sur) **III.** <spread, spread> *vt* **1.** (*cause to expand*) déployer; (*one's legs*) allonger; (*a virus, disease*) répandre; (*panic*) semer; (*a culture*) développer **2.** (*cover with a spread*) étaler; **to ~ a toast with jam** tartiner un toast avec de la confiture **3.** (*distribute*) distribuer **4.** (*tell others*) répandre; (*the word*) faire passer ►**to ~ one's wings** faire ses premières armes

spreader *n* **1.** (*person*) dispatcheur *m* **2.** (*machine*) extenseur *m* **3.** (*mechanical tension device*) tendeur *m*

spreadsheet *n* INFOR **1.** (*software*) tableur *m* **2.** (*workscreen*) feuille *f* de calcul

spree [spriː] *n* **killing ~** folie *f* meurtrière; **to go** (**out**) **on a shopping ~** aller dévaliser les boutiques; **to go on a ~** (*get drunk*) prendre une cuite *inf*

sprig [sprɪg] *n* **1.** (*blade of grass*) brin *m* (d'herbe) **2.** (*twig*) brindille *f*

sprightly ['spraɪtli] <-ier, -iest> *adj* alerte

spring [sprɪŋ] **I.** *n* **1.** (*season*) printemps *m;* **in** (**the**) **~** au printemps **2.** (*curved device*) ressort *m* **3.** (*elasticity*) élasticité *f;* **to have a ~ in one's step** avoir le pas souple **4.** (*source of water*) source *f* **II.** <sprang *o Am, a. Aus* sprung, sprung> *vi* **1.** (*move quickly*) se précipiter; **to ~ to one's feet** bondir sur ses pieds **2.** (*appear: to mind*) surgir **III.** *vt* (*produce*) **to ~ sth on sb** faire qc à qn par surprise **IV.** *adj Am* (*supported by springs*) à ressort(s)
◆**spring back** *vi* reculer d'un bond

spring balance *n* peson *m* **Spring Bank Holiday** *n no pl, Brit* (*end of May*) *jour de fermeture des banques et de la plupart des commerces* **spring binder** *n* classeur *m* (à ressort) **springboard** *n* tremplin *m* **spring clean I.** *n* nettoyage *m* de printemps **II.** *vi* **to spring-clean** faire un nettoyage de printemps **III.** *vt* **to spring-clean** nettoyer à fond **spring onion** *n Aus, Brit* oignon *m* primeur **spring roll** *n* rouleau *m* de printemps **spring tide** *n* (grande) marée *f* d'équinoxe (de printemps) **springtime** *n s.* **spring** **spring water** *n* eau *f* de source **spring wheat** *n* blé *m* de printemps

springy ['sprɪŋi] <-ier, -iest> *adj* printanier(-ère)

sprinkle ['sprɪŋkl] **I.** *vt* arroser **II.** *n* (*of rain, snow*) averse *f;* (*of salt, flour*) pincée *f*

sprinkler *n* **1.** (*for lawn*) arroseur *m* **2.** (*for field*) canon *m* (à eau)

sprinkling *n* **1.** *Am s.* **sprinkle** **2.** (*light covering*) fine couche *f* **3.** (*small amount*) pincée *f*

sprint [sprɪnt] SPORT **I.** *vi* pratiquer la course de vitesse **II.** *n* course *f* de vitesse; **to break into a ~** partir en sprint

sprinter *n* SPORT coureur *m* de vitesse

sprocket (**wheel**) ['spɒkɪt-, *Am:* 'sprɑː-] *n*

roue *f* dentée

sprog [sprɒg, *Am:* sprɑːg] **I.** *n Aus, Brit, inf* gosse *mf* **II.** <-gg-> *vi Aus, Brit, inf* faire des gosses

sprout [spraʊt] **I.** *n* **1.** (*plant part*) pousse *f;* (*of seeds, bulb*) germe *m* **2.** *Brit s.* **brussels sprout II.** *vi* **1.** (*grow*) pousser; (*seed, bulb*) germer **2.** *fig* germer **III.** *vt* (*shoots, hair*) faire; (*moustache*) se laisser pousser

spruce[1] [spruːs] *n* épicéa *m,* épinette *f Québec*

spruce[2] [spruːs] *adj* soigné(e)

sprung [sprʌŋ] **I.** *adj Brit* à ressort(s) **II. 1.** *pp of* **spring 2.** *Am pt of* **spring**

spry [spraɪ] *adj* plein(e) d'allant; ~ **footwork** adroit jeu *m* de jambes

spud [spʌd] *n inf* patate *f*

spume [spjuːm] *n* écume *f*

spun [spʌn] *pp, pt of* **spin**

spunk [spʌŋk] *n* **1.** *no pl, inf* (*bravery*) cran *m* **2.** *Aus, inf* (*attractive man*) beau mec *m*

spur [spɜːʳ, *Am:* spɜːr] **I.** <-rr-> *vt* (*encourage*) encourager; (*the economy*) relancer **II.** *n* **1.** (*encouragement*) encouragement *m* **2.** (*sharp object*) éperon *m* **3.** (*formation: of rock*) éperon *m* rocheux ►**on the ~ of the moment** *inf* dans le feu de l'action; **to win one's ~s doing sth** faire ses preuves dans qc

spurious ['spjʊərɪəs, *Am:* 'spjʊrɪ-] *adj* fallacieux(-euse)

spurn [spɜːn, *Am:* spɜːrn] *vt form* repousser; **~ed lover** amoureux *m* éconduit

spurt [spɜːt, *Am:* spɜːrt] **I.** *n* **1.** (*fast stream*) torrent *m* **2.** (*burst: of effort, money*) surcroît *m;* (*of speed*) pointe *f;* **growth ~** poussée *f* de croissance ►**in ~s** à flots; **to do sth in ~s** faire qc par à-coups; **to put on a ~** en mettre un coup **II.** *vt* faire jaillir **III.** *vi* jaillir

sputter ['spʌtəʳ, *Am:* 'spʌt̬ɚ] **I.** *n* crépitement *m* **II.** *vi* crépiter **III.** *vt* cracher bruyamment

sputum ['spjuːtəm, *Am:* -t̬əm] *n no pl* crachat *m*

spy [spaɪ] **I.** *n* espion(ne) *m(f);* (*of the police*) indicateur, -trice *m, f* **II.** *vi* **to ~ on sb/sth** espionner qn/qc **III.** *vt* remarquer

◆**spy on** *vt* espionner

spyglass *n* longue-vue *f* **spy satellite** *n* satellite *m* d'observation

Sq. *n abbr of* **square** carré; ~ **m** m^2

squabble ['skwɒbl, *Am:* 'skwɑːbl] **I.** *n* querelle *f* **II.** *vi* se disputer

squad [skwɒd, *Am:* skwɑːd] *n* **1.** (*group*) groupe *m* (d'élite) **2.** (*sports team*) équipe *f* sportive **3.** (*military unit*) escouade *f*

squad car *n Am, Brit* voiture *f* de patrouille (de police)

squaddie ['skwɔdi, *Am:* 'skwɑːdi] *n Brit, pej, inf* MIL bidasse *m*

squadron ['skwɒdrən, *Am:* 'skwɑːdrən] *n* **1.** MIL escadron *m* **2.** AVIAT, NAUT escadrille *f*

squalid ['skwɒlɪd, *Am:* 'skwɑːlɪd] *adj* **1.** *pej* (*dirty*) crasseux(-euse) **2.** (*immoral*) crapuleux(-euse)

squall [skwɔːl] **I.** *n* **1.** (*gust of wind*) bourrasque *f* **2.** (*shriek*) hurlement *m* **II.** *vi* hurler

squally *adj* en bourrasque; (*rain*) violent(e)

squalor ['skwɒləʳ, *Am:* 'skwɑːlɚ] *n no pl* **1.** (*place*) taudis *m* **2.** (*immorality*) dépravation *f* **3.** (*poverty*) misère *f*

squander ['skwɒndəʳ, *Am:* 'skwɑːndɚ] *vt* (*waste*) gaspiller; (*opportunity*) perdre; (*chance*) manquer

square [skweəʳ, *Am:* skwer] **I.** *n* **1.** (*geometric shape*) carré *m* **2.** (*part of town*) square *m* **3.** (*marked space*) case *f;* **to go back to ~ one** *inf* revenir à la case départ **4.** *Am, Aus* (*tool*) équerre *f* **5.** *inf* (*boring person*) ringard(e) *m(f)* **6.** (*number times itself*) carré *m* **II.** *adj* **1.** <-r, -st> (*square-shaped*) carré(e) **2.** <-r, -st> (*short and solid*) carré(e) **3.** MAT carré(e); **5 ~ km** 5 km carrés **4.** (*right-angled: corner*) à angle droit **5.** (*owing nothing*) quitte **6.** SPORT à égalité **7.** <-r, -st> *inf* (*on the same level*) équilibré(e) **8.** <-r, -st> (*straight*) droit(e); **to be ~ with sb** être honnête avec qn **9.** (*arranged, in order*) **to get sth ~** arranger qc **10.** <-r, -st> *inf* (*old-fashioned*) ringard(e) **III.** *vt* **1.** (*align*) aligner; (*one's shoulders*) redresser **2.** *inf* (*settle*) arranger; (*a matter*) régler **3.** (*multiply by itself*) élever au carré **4.** SPORT égaliser; **to ~ a match** faire match nul ►**to attempt to ~ the circle** chercher la quadrature du cercle **IV.** *adv* droit; **~ in the middle** en plein milieu

square bracket *n* crochet *m* **square-built** *adj* (*shoulders*) carré(e)

> **Square dance** est le nom donné à une danse folklorique américaine. Des groupes de quatre couples dansent en formant un carré, un cercle ou sur deux rangs; ils exécutent des mouvements qui sont annoncés par un "caller". Le "caller" peut donner ses ordres en chantant ou en parlant. Des musiciens munis de violons, de banjos et de guitares accompagnent souvent le "square dancing".

squared paper *n* papier *m* quadrillé

squarely *adv* carrément

square measure *n* mesure *f* de superficie **Square Mile** *n Brit s.* **the City square number** *n* chiffre *m* exact **square-rigger** *n* (*boat*) navire *m* à voiles carrées **square root** *n* racine *f* carrée

squash[1] [skwɒʃ, *Am:* skwɑːʃ] *n Am* (*vegetable*) courge *f*

squash[2] [skwɒʃ, *Am:* skwɑːʃ] **I.** *n* **1.** (*dense pack*) entassement *m* **2.** *no pl* (*racket game*) squash *m* **3.** *Aus, Brit* (*drink*) sirop *m* ►**it will be a bit of a ~** on va être un peu serré **II.** *vt* **1.** (*crush*) écraser **2.** (*make feel stupid*) écraser **3.** *fig* (*rumour*) étouffer

squash court *n* **1.** (*indoors*) salle *f* de squash **2.** (*outdoors*) court *m* de squash **squash racket** *n Brit,* **squash racquet** *n Am, Aus*

1. (*equipment*) raquette *f* de squash 2. *no pl, form s.* **squash**

squashy <-ier, -iest> *adj* mou(molle)

squat [skwɒt, *Am:* skwɑːt] I. <-tt-> *vi* 1. (*crouch down*) **to ~ down** s'accroupir; **to be ~ting** être accroupi 2. (*live without permission*) squatter II. *n* 1. (*position*) position *f* accroupie 2. (*shelter*) squat *m* III. <-ter, -test> *adj* trapu(e)

squatter ['skwɒtəʳ, *Am:* 'skwɑːt̬ɚ] *n* 1. (*illegal house-sitter*) squatter *m* 2. *Aus* (*illegal land-user*) exploitant(e) *m(f)* illégitime

squaw [skwɔː, *Am:* skwɑː] *n pej* squaw *f*

squawk [skwɔːk, *Am:* skwɑːk] I. *vi* 1. (*make a noise: poultry*) glousser; (*rabbit, mouse*) couiner; (*fox*) glapir 2. *fig, inf* cancaner II. *n* 1. (*sharp cry*) glapissement *m* 2. *inf* (*complaint*) cri *m*

squeak [skwiːk] I. *n* grincement *m* ▶**to let out a ~ of fright** laisser échapper un cri d'effroi II. *vi* (*emit shrill sound*) émettre un grincement strident

squeaky <-ier, -iest> *adj* 1. (*tending to squeak*) braillard(e) 2. *Am* (*very narrow*) de justesse ▶**the ~ wheel gets the grease** *Am, prov* quiconque demande reçoit

squeaky-clean *adj* irréprochable

squeal [skwiːl] I. *n* **to let out a ~** pousser un cri perçant; **to collapse into a ~** finir dans un gémissement; (*of brakes, tyres*) crissement *m* II. *vi* 1. (*utter sharp cry: pig, brakes, car*) couiner; **to ~ with joy** hurler de joie 2. *inf* brailler

squeamish ['skwiːmɪʃ] I. *adj* impressionnable; **to feel ~** être impressionnable II. *npl* **the morally ~** les puritain(e)s

squeegee [ˌskwiː'dʒiː, *Am:* 'skwiːdʒiː] I. *n* raclette *f* II. *vt* éponger

squeeze [skwiːz] I. *n* 1. (*pressing action*) compression *f* 2. (*obtained by squeezing*) pression *f;* **to give sth a ~** presser qc 3. ECON (*on spending*) restriction *f;* (*on jobs*) limitation *f* II. *vt* 1. (*firmly press*) presser; (*cloth*) essorer; (*sb's hand*) serrer; (*trigger, doll*) appuyer sur; **to ~ a trigger** (*of a weapon*) presser la détente; (*of a camera*) appuyer sur le déclencheur; **freshly ~d orange juice** du jus d'orange fraîchement pressé 2. (*force into*) entasser; **to ~ sth into sth** faire entrer qc dans qc; **to ~ one's way through** se frayer un passage 3. (*extort*) soutirer; **to ~ money out of sb** extorquer de l'argent à qn 4. *fig* (*put pressure on*) faire pression sur 5. ECON (*wages*) bloquer ▶**to ~ sb dry** presser qn comme un citron

◆**squeeze out** *vt* (*juice*) extraire

squeezer *n* presse-agrumes *m*

squelch [skweltʃ] I. *vi* glouglouter II. *vt Am* amortir; (*rumour*) étouffer III. *n* 1. silencieux *m* 2. TECH éliminateur *m* de bruits (de fond)

squib [skwɪb] *n* 1. (*firecracker*) pétard *m* 2. (*detonator*) détonateur *m* 3. (*written attack*) satire *f* 4. *Am* (*short written piece*) entrefilet *m*

squid [skwɪd] <-(s)> *n* cal(a)mar *m*

squiggle ['skwɪgl] *n* gribouillis *m*

squint [skwɪnt] I. *vi* 1. MED loucher 2. (*close partly one's eyes*) plisser les yeux II. *n* 1. MED strabisme *m* 2. *inf* (*quick look*) **to have a ~ at sth** donner un coup d'œil à qc

squint-eyed *adj* **to be ~** loucher

squire ['skwaɪəʳ, *Am:* 'skwaɪɚ] *n* 1. (*landowner*) propriétaire *m* terrien 2. (*feudal landowner*) seigneur *m* ▶**don't worry ~, I'll settle it!** ne vous en faites pas, chef, je vais arranger ça!

squirm [skwɜːm, *Am:* skwɜːrm] I. *vi* se tortiller II. *n* embarras *m;* **to give a ~** se montrer embarrassé

squirrel ['skwɪrəl, *Am:* 'skwɜːr-] *n* écureuil *m*

squirt [skwɜːt, *Am:* skwɜːrt] I. *vt* 1. (*make flow out*) faire gicler; (*perfume, deodorant*) vaporiser 2. (*shower*) asperger II. *vi* jaillir III. *n* 1. (*quantity obtained by squirting*) pulvérisation *f* 2. *pej* (*jerk*) salaud *m*

Sr *n* Sr *m*

Sri Lanka [ˌsriː'læŋkə, *Am:* -'lɑːŋ-] *n* Sri *m* Lanka

Sri Lankan I. *adj* sri lankais(e) II. *n* Sri Lankais *m*

SSE *n abbr of* **south-southeast** SSE *m*

SSM *n abbr of* **surface-to-surface missile** MSS *m*

SSW *n abbr of* **south-southwest** SSW *m*

st. *n abbr of* **stone**

St *n* 1. *abbr of* **saint** St *m* 2. *abbr of* **street** rue *f*

stab [stæb] I. <-bb-> *vt* poignarder; **to ~ sb to death** poignarder qn à mort; **to ~ sth with sth** donner un coup de qc II. <-bb-> *vi a. fig* **to ~ at sb/sth** porter un coup de couteau à qn/qc III. *n* 1. (*blow with a pointed instrument*) coup *m* de couteau; **to make a ~ at sth with sth** porter un coup de qc à qc 2. (*sudden pain*) élancement *m;* (*of jealousy*) accès *m* 3. *fig* (*attack*) coup *m;* **a ~ in the back** un coup de poignard dans le dos ▶**to have a ~ at doing sth** s'essayer à faire qc

stabbing I. *n* coup *m* de couteau II. *adj* (*pain*) lancinant(e)

stability [stə'bɪləti, *Am:* -t̬i] *n no pl* stabilité *f*

stabilization *n no pl* stabilisation *f*

stabilize ['steɪbəlaɪz] I. *vt* stabiliser II. *vi* se stabiliser

stabilizer *n* stabilisateur *m*

stable[1] ['steɪbl] <-r, -st *o* more stable, most stable> *adj* 1. (*firm*) *a. fig* stable 2. PSYCH (*well-balanced*) équilibré(e)

stable[2] ['steɪbl] I. *n* écurie *f* II. *vt* (*horse*) loger

stable boy *n* garçon *m* d'écurie **stable girl** *n* fille *f* d'écurie **stable lad** *Brit s.* **stable boy**

stack [stæk] I. *vt* 1. (*arrange in a pile*) empiler 2. (*fill*) remplir 3. AVIAT (*circling at different heights: a plane*) mettre en attente

4. *pej* (*select*) favoriser **II.** *n* **1.** (*pile*) pile *f* **2.** *inf* (*large amount*) tas *m*; **to have ~s of them** en avoir des tas **3. the ~s** *pl* (*storage of a library*) réserve *f*

stadium ['steɪdɪəm] <-s *o* -dia> *n* stade *m*

staff [stɑːf, *Am:* stæf] **I.** *n* **1.** (*employees*) personnel *m*; **teaching/office ~** personnel enseignant/de bureau; **editorial ~** rédaction *f* **2.** MIL (*group of officers*) état-major *m* **3.** (*stick*) bâton *m* **4.** (*flagpole*) mât *m* **5.** *Am* MUS (*stave*) portée *f* **II.** *vt* (*provide personnel*) pourvoir en personnel; **to be ~ed by sb** être composé de qn **III.** *adj* du personnel

staffer *n Am* membre *m* du personnel; (*in newspaper*) journaliste *mf*

staffing *n no pl* recrutement *m*

staff nurse *n Brit* infirmière *f* diplômée **staff officer** *n* officier *m* d'état-major **staffroom** *n Brit* SCHOOL salle *f* des professeurs

stag [stæg] **I.** *n* **1.** (*adult male deer*) cerf *m* **2.** *Brit, Aus* (*shares buyer*) loup *m* **II.** *adv Am* en célibataire

stage [steɪdʒ] **I.** *n* **1.** (*period in a process*) stade *m*; **to be at a ~ where ...** être à un stade où ... **2.** (*section: of journey, race*) étape *f*; **to do sth in ~s** faire qc par étapes **3.** (*raised theatre platform*) scène *f*; **a ~ adaptation** une adaptation à la scène; **to be/go on ~** être/monter sur scène; **to set the ~** *fig* préparer le terrain; **to hold the ~** *fig* tenir le vedette **4. the ~** (*theatrical profession*) le théâtre **5.** (*scene of action*) scène *f*; **the political ~** la scène politique; **to be the ~ of violence** être le théâtre de violences **II.** *vt* **1.** (*produce on stage*) mettre en scène **2.** (*organize*) monter

stagecoach *n* HIST diligence *f* **stage direction** *n* indications *fpl* scéniques **stage director** *n* metteur *mf* en scène **stage door** *n* entrée *f* des artistes **stage effect** *n* effet *m* scénique **stage fright** *n no pl* trac *m* **stagehand** *n* machiniste *m* **stage-manage** *vt* **1.** (*act as stage manager*) mettre en scène **2.** (*orchestrate desired effect*) *a. fig* orchestrer **stage manager** *n* chef *m* de plateau **stage name** *n* nom *m* de scène

stager ['steɪdʒəʳ, *Am:* -dʒɚ] *n* **an old ~** un vieux routier

stage-struck *adj* passioné(e) de théâtre **stage whisper** *n* THEAT aparté *m*

stagger ['stægəʳ, *Am:* -ɚ] **I.** *vi* (*move unsteadily*) chanceler; **to ~ to bed** aller au lit d'un pas chancelant; **to ~ under the weight of sth** *fig* chanceler sous le poids de qc **II.** *vt* **1.** (*flabbergast*) stupéfier **2.** (*arrange at differing times*) échelonner **III.** *n* pas *m* chancelant

staggering *adj* renversant(e)

staging ['steɪdʒɪŋ] *n* mise *f* en scène

stagnant ['stægnənt] *adj a. fig* stagnant(e)

stagnate [stæg'neɪt, *Am:* 'stægneɪt] *vi* stagner

stagnation *n no pl* stagnation *f*

stag night, **stag party** *n Brit* enterrement *m* de la vie de garçon

stagy ['steɪdʒi] *adj pej* théâtral(e)

staid [steɪd] *adj* sérieux(-euse)

stain [steɪn] **I.** *vt* **1.** (*discolour*) tacher **2.** (*dye*) teindre **3.** *fig* (*blemish*) ternir **II.** *vi* se tacher **III.** *n* **1.** (*discoloration*) tache *f*; **blood ~** tache de sang **2.** (*substance used for dyeing*) teinture *f* **3.** (*moral blemish*) atteinte *f*

stained glass *n* vitraux *mpl*

stainless *adj a. fig* sans tache

stainless steel *n* acier *m* inoxydable

stain remover *n* détachant *m*

stair [steəʳ, *Am:* ster] *n* **1.** (*step in a staircase*) marche *f* **2.** *pl* (*a set of steps*) escalier *m*; **a flight of ~s** un escalier

staircase *n* escalier *m*; **a spiral ~** un escalier en colimaçon; **a secret ~** un escalier dérobé **stairway** *n* escalier *m* **stairwell** *n* cage *f* d'escalier

stake[1] [steɪk] **I.** *n* **1.** (*sharpened stick*) piquet *m*; (*wooden*) pieu *m* **2.** (*execution by burning*) *a. fig* **the ~** le bûcher; **to be burnt at the ~** mourir sur le bûcher ▶**to pull up the ~s** déménager **II.** *vt* **1.** (*fasten with a ~*) fixer à l'aide de piquets; (*plants*) tuteurer **2.** LAW **to ~ a claim** faire valoir ses droits

stake[2] [steɪk] *n* **1.** (*share*) intérêt *m*; **to have a ~ in sth** avoir des intérêts dans qc **2.** (*amount at risk*) enjeu *m*; GAMES mise *f*; **to double one's ~s** doubler sa mise; **to play for high ~s** jouer gros jeu; **to be at ~** être en jeu **3.** SPORT (*horse race*) course *f* **4.** *inf* (*competitive activity*) course *f*

stake-out *n Am, inf* surveillance *f*

stalactite ['stæləktaɪt, *Am:* stə'læk-] *n* GEO stalactite *f*

stalagmite ['stæləgmaɪt] *n* GEO stalagmite *f*

stale [steɪl] *adj* **1.** (*not fresh*) pas frais(fraîche); (*bread*) rassis(e); (*air*) vicié(e); **to smell ~** sentir le renfermé **2.** (*old*) usé(e); **to get ~** s'user **3.** (*out of date*) périmé(e)

stalemate ['steɪlmeɪt] *n* impasse *f*

stalk[1] [stɔːk] *n* **1.** (*plant stem*) queue *f* **2.** (*stem*) pédoncule *m* ▶**sb's eyes are out on ~s** *Brit, Aus* qn a les yeux qui lui sont sortis de la tête

stalk[2] [stɔːk] **I.** *vt* traquer **II.** *vi* **to ~ in/out** entrer/sortir d'un air arrogant

stalker *n fig: personne harcelante*

stalking horse *n fig* prétexte *m*

stall [stɔːl] **I.** *n* **1.** (*enclosure for an animal*) stalle *f* **2.** (*compartment within a room*) cabine *f*; **shower ~** cabine de douche **3. the ~s** *pl, Brit, Aus* (*theatre seats*) fauteuils *mpl* d'orchestre **4.** (*seat in a church*) (**choir**) **~s** stalle *f* **5.** (*stand for selling*) stand *m*; **a newspaper ~** un kiosque à journaux **6.** AUTO (*act of stalling*) calage *m* **II.** *vi* **1.** (*stop running suddenly: motor, vehicle*) caler **2.** *inf* (*delay*) essayer de gagner du temps **III.** *vt* **1.** (*cause to stop running: a car, motor*) caler **2.** *inf* (*keep waiting*) faire poireauter **3.** (*delay*) repousser

stallholder *n* marchand(e) *m(f)*

S

stallion ['stælɪən, *Am:* -jən] *n* étalon *m*
stalwart ['stɔːlwət, *Am:* -wɚt] **I.** *adj form* **1.** (*sturdy*) robuste **2.** (*resolutely loyal*) fidèle **II.** *n form* fidèle *mf*
stamen ['steɪmen] <-s *o* -mina> *pl n* étamine *f*
stamina ['stæmɪnə, *Am:* -ənə] *n no pl* résistance *f*
stammer ['stæməʳ, *Am:* -ɚ] **I.** *vi, vt* bégayer **II.** *n* bégaiement *m;* **to have a ~** bégayer
stammerer ['stæmərəʳ, *Am:* -ɚɚ] *n* bègue *mf*
stamp [stæmp] **I.** *n* **1.** (*postage stamp*) timbre *m* **2.** (*implement*) tampon *m;* **rubber ~** tampon *m* **3.** (*official mark*) cachet *m;* (*on metal*) poinçon *m* **4.** (*characteristic quality*) marque *f;* **to leave one's ~ on sb/sth** laisser sa marque sur qn/qc **5.** *Brit* COM (*piece of paper with assigned value*) bon *m;* **food ~** bon *m* alimentaire **6.** (*heavy blow with the foot*) battement *m* de pied **II.** *vt* **1.** (*place a postage stamp*) timbrer **2.** (*mark with*) tamponner; (*on metal*) poinçonner **3.** *fig* **to ~ sth on sth** graver qc sur qc; **to ~ oneself on sth** laisser sa marque sur qc; **to ~ sb/sth as (being) sb/sth** étiqueter qn/qc comme qn/qc **4.** (*stomp*) trépigner **III.** *vi* trépigner
stamp collecting *n* philatélie *f* **stamp collection** *n* collection *f* de timbres **stamp collector** *n* philatéliste *mf*
stampede [stæm'piːd] **I.** *n* ruée *f* **II.** *vi* se ruer **III.** *vt* **1.** (*cause to stampede*) jeter la panique **2.** (*force into unconsidered action*) **to ~ sb into doing sth** pousser qn à faire qc
stamping ground *n* lieu *m* de prédilection
stance [stɑːnts, *Am:* stænts] *n a. fig* position *f;* **to take (up) one's ~** se mettre en position
stand [stænd] **I.** *n* **1.** (*position*) *a. fig* position *f;* **to take up one's ~** prendre position; **to take a ~ on sth** prendre position sur qc; **to make a ~ against sth** s'opposer à qc **2.** *form* (*standstill*) arrêt *m;* **to bring sb/sth to a ~** arrêter qn/qc **3.** (*raised seating for spectators*) tribune *f* **4.** (*support*) support *m* **5.** (*stall*) stand *m;* **a news ~** un kiosque à journaux **6.** (*standing place for vehicles*) station *f* **7.** *Am* (*specified number of performances*) représentation *f* **8.** (*sexual encounter*) **a one-night ~** une histoire sans lendemain **9. the ~** *Am* (*witness box*) barre *f* (des témoins) **10.** (*group of plants*) bouquet *m* **II.** <stood, stood> *vi* **1.** (*be upright*) se tenir debout; **to ~ erect/tall** se tenir droit; **to ~ (up)** se lever; **to ~ on one's hands** se tenir sur les mains; **to ~ to attention** MIL se mettre au garde-à-vous **2.** (*be located*) se trouver; **to ~ somewhere** (*mountain, church*) se dresser quelque part; **to ~ in sb's way** barrer le passage de qn **3.** (*have a position*) *a. fig* se tenir; **to ~ on an issue** avoir un point de vue sur un sujet; **to ~ on one's own two feet** ne dépendre que de soi; **to ~ or fall by sth** dépendre de qc; **to ~ alone** faire face seul; **to ~ still** se tenir immobile; **to ~ guard** se tenir sur ses gardes; **to ~ firm** tenir bon; **to ~ on ceremony** faire des manières; **to ~ on one's dignity** *pej* garder ses distances **4.** (*be in a specified state*) être; **to ~ motionless/alone/empty** rester immobile/seul/vide; **to ~ accused of sth** être accusé de qc; **to ~ at sth** être de qc; **to ~ to lose sth** risquer de perdre qc; **to ~ to gain sth** avoir des chances de gagner qc; **to ~ five feet tall** faire un mètre cinquante (de haut) **5.** (*remain valid*) tenir; **it still ~s** cela tient encore; **to ~ to reason** aller sans dire **6.** (*remain motionless*) reposer; (*tea*) infuser; **to let sth ~** laisser reposer qc **7.** (*be candidate*) **to ~ (as candidate)** être candidat; **to ~ for presidency** être candidat à la présidence **III.** <stood, stood> *vt* **1.** (*place in an upright position*) placer; **to ~ sth on its head** faire tenir qc sur sa tête; **to ~ sb on sth** mettre qn debout; **to ~ sth against sth** mettre qc contre qc **2.** (*bear*) supporter; **to not be able to ~ doing sth** ne pas supporter de faire qc; **to not be able to ~ sb doing sth** ne pas supporter que qn fasse qc *subj* **3.** (*pay for*) payer **4.** LAW (*undergo*) **to ~ trial for sth** passer en jugement pour qc ►**to ~ sb in good stead** être utile à qn; **to ~ a chance of doing sth** *inf* avoir de bonnes chances de faire qc; **to ~ one's ground** tenir bon
◆**stand about**, **stand around** *vi* se tenir là
◆**stand aside** *vi a. fig* s'écarter
◆**stand back** *vi* **1.** (*stay back*) être en retrait **2.** (*move back*) reculer **3.** *fig* prendre du recul
◆**stand by** **I.** *vi* **1.** (*observe without being involved*) se tenir là **2.** (*be ready to take action*) se tenir prêt; **to ~ for sth** se parer à qc **3.** (*wait*) attendre **II.** *vt* soutenir; (*decision*) maintenir; (*one's word, promise*) tenir; **to ~ each other** se soutenir
◆**stand down** *vi* (*resign*) se retirer
◆**stand for** *vt* **1.** (*represent*) signifier **2.** *Brit, Aus* (*be a candidate*) se présenter à **3.** (*tolerate*) supporter
◆**stand in** *vi* **to ~ for sb** remplacer qn
◆**stand off** **I.** *vt* tenir à l'écart; **to ~ the coast** être au large **II.** *vi* se tenir à l'écart
◆**stand out** *vi* **1.** (*project from a surface*) ressortir **2.** (*easily noticeable, better*) se détacher; **to ~ in a crowd** se détacher dans la foule **3.** (*be opposed to*) **to ~ against sth** résister à qc **4.** (*persist*) **to ~ for sth** insister sur qc
◆**stand up** **I.** *vi* **1.** (*assume an upright position*) se lever; **to ~ straight** se tenir droit **2.** (*be standing*) se tenir debout **3.** (*be accepted as true*) se tenir **II.** *vt* **1.** (*put straight*) redresser **2.** *inf* poser un lapin à
stand-alone *n* INFOR poste *m* autonome
standard ['stændəd, *Am:* -dɚd] **I.** *n* **1.** (*level of quality*) niveau *m;* **to be up to sb's ~** être au niveau de qn **2.** (*touchstone for evaluating*) norme *f;* **safety ~** norme de sécurité **3.** (*flag*) étendard *m* **4.** (*currency basis: gold, silver*)

étalon *m* **5.** (*well-known piece of music*) standard *m* **II.** *adj* **1.** (*normal, not custom-made: language, size, procedures*) standard *inv* **2.** (*classical: book, song*) classique **3.** (*average, acceptable: procedure, practice*) ordinaire

standard-bearer *n a. fig* porte-drapeau *m*

standardization *n no pl* standardisation *f*

standardize ['stændədaɪz, *Am:* -də-] *vt* standardiser

standby **I.** *n* **1.** (*reserve*) réserve *f;* **to be** (**put**) **on** ~ être en attente **2.** (*substitute*) remplaçant(e) *m(f);* **to be** (**put**) **on** ~ se tenir prêt **II.** *adj* de réserve **III.** *adv* en attente **stand-in** *n* remplaçant(e) *m(f)*

standing **I.** *n* **1.** (*position*) rang *m* **2.** (*duration*) durée *f* **II.** *adj* **1.** (*upright*) debout *inv* **2.** (*permanent*) fixe **3.** (*stagnant*) stagnant(e) **4.** (*not reaped*) sur pied

standing ovation *n* standing ovation *f*

standoffish [ˌstænd'ɒfɪʃ, *Am:* -'ɑːfɪʃ] *adj pej, inf* distant(e)

standpipe ['stændpaɪp] *n* colonne *f* d'alimentation

standpoint ['stændpɔɪnt] *n* point *m* de vue

standstill ['stændstɪl] *n no pl* arrêt *m;* **to be at a** ~ être immobile; **to come to a** ~ s'immobiliser

stand-up *adj* **1.** (*unrestrained: fight, argument*) en règle **2.** (*eaten standing: meal*) pris(e) debout **3.** FASHION (*collar*) montant(e) **4.** (*cabaret*) *s.* **stand-up comedy**

stand-up comedy *n* stand up comedy *m* (*spectacle comique solo*)

stank [stæŋk] *pt of* **stink**

stanza ['stænzə] *n* strophe *f*

staple¹ ['steɪpl] **I.** *n* **1.** (*chief product*) produit *m* de base **2.** (*basic food*) aliment *m* de base **3.** (*important component*) élément *m* principal **II.** *adj* de base

staple² ['steɪpl] **I.** *n* agrafe *f* **II.** *vt* agrafer

stapler *n* agrafeuse *f*

star [stɑːʳ, *Am:* stɑːr] **I.** *n* **1.** (*heavenly body*) *a. fig* étoile *f;* **to reach for the** ~**s** essayer d'atteindre les étoiles; **to be born under a lucky** ~ être né sous une bonne étoile **2.** (*famous, principal performer*) star *f;* **a film**/**rock** ~ un(e) star du cinéma/de rock **3.** (*asterisk*) astérisque *f* ►**to** see ~**s** voir trente-six chandelles **II.** *vi* <-rr-> THEAT, CINE (*appear as chief performer*) **to** ~ **in a film** être la vedette d'un film; ~**ring Johnny Depp** avec dans le rôle principal Johnny Depp **III.** *vt* <-rr-> **1.** THEAT, CINE (*feature as chief performer*) avoir en vedette **2.** (*mark with an asterisk*) marquer d'un astérisque **IV.** *adj* **1.** (*outstanding*) de premier ordre **2.** (*having specified number of stars*) **a four-**~ **hotel** un hôtel quatre étoiles **3.** (*related to cinema, music*) vedette

starboard ['stɑːbəd, *Am:* 'stɑːrbərd] *n* tribord *m*

starch [stɑːtʃ, *Am:* stɑːrtʃ] **I.** *n* **1.** *no pl* (*stiffening agent*) amidon *m* **2.** GASTR (*carbohydrates*) fécule *f* **II.** *vt* amidonner

starchy <-ier, -iest> *adj* **1.** GASTR (*food*) riche en féculent **2.** FASHION (*cloth*) amidonné(e) **3.** *pej, inf* guindé(e)

stardom ['stɑːdəm, *Am:* 'stɑːr-] *n no pl* célébrité *f*

stare [steəʳ, *Am:* ster] **I.** *vi* regarder fixement; **to** ~ **at sb/sth** fixer qn/qc du regard **II.** *vt* fixer du regard **III.** *n* regard *m*

starfish ['stɑːfɪʃ, *Am:* 'stɑːr-] <-(es)> *n* étoile *f* de mer

stargazer ['stɑːˌgeɪzəʳ, *Am:* 'stɑːrˌgeɪzər] *n iron* astrologue *mf*

staring ['steərɪŋ, *Am:* 'ster-] *adj* (*eyes*) fixe

stark [stɑːk, *Am:* stɑːrk] **I.** *adj* **1.** (*bare and desolate: landscape*) désolé(e) **2.** (*austere: room*) austère **3.** (*brutally obvious: contrast, reality*) brutal(e) **4.** (*complete, sheer: madness*) absolu(e) **II.** *adv* complètement

starkers ['stɑːkəʳs, *Am:* 'stɑːrkərz] *adj Brit, Aus, inf* à poil

starless *adj* sans étoiles

starlet ['stɑːlɪt, *Am:* 'stɑːr-] *n* starlette *f*

starlight ['stɑːlaɪt, *Am:* 'stɑːr-] *n no pl* naïf(naïve)

starling ['stɑːlɪŋ, *Am:* 'stɑːr-] *n* étourneau *m*

starlit ['stɑːˌlɪt, *Am:* 'stɑːr-] *adj* étoilé(e)

starry ['stɑːri] <-ier, -iest> *adj* étoilé(e)

starry-eyed *adj* naïf(naïve)

star sign *n* signe *m* zodiacal **Star-Spangled Banner** *n no pl* **the** ~ **1.** (*U.S. flag*) la bannière étoilée **2.** (*U.S. national anthem*) *hymne national américain* **star-studded** *adj* **1.** (*full of stars*) étoilé(e) **2.** *fig* prestigieux(-euse)

start [stɑːt, *Am:* stɑːrt] **I.** *vi* **1.** (*begin*) commencer; **to** ~ **to do/doing sth** commencer à faire qc; **to** ~ **by doing sth** commencer par faire qc; **to** ~ **afresh** [*o* (**all over**) **again**] recommencer à zéro; **to** ~ **at the beginning** commencer par le commencement; **... to** ~ **with** pour commencer ...; **to** ~ **with, ...** *inf* tout d'abord; **don't** ~**!** *pej, inf* ne commence pas!; **don't you** ~**!** *pej, inf* tu ne vas pas t'y mettre aussi! **2.** (*begin a journey*) partir **3.** (*begin to operate: vehicle, motor*) démarrer **4.** (*make a sudden movement*) sursauter; **to** ~ **out of sleep** se réveiller en sursaut **5.** SPORT prendre le départ **II.** *vt* **1.** (*begin*) commencer; (*a family*) fonder; **to** ~ **doing sth** commencer à faire qc; **to get** ~**ed** commencer **2.** (*set in motion: a conversation, bottle*) entamer; (*a fight, trouble, war*) déclencher; (*a trend, fashion, rumor*) lancer; (*a meeting*) débuter; (*a fire*) allumer; **to** ~ **legal proceedings** engager une action en justice; **to** ~ **it** *inf* commencer **3.** TECH (*set in operation: a machine*) mettre en marche; (*a motor, car*) démarrer **4.** COM (*establish*) lancer; **to** ~ **sb in sth** lancer qn dans qc **5.** *inf* (*cause sb to do sth*) **to** ~ **sb/sth doing sth** faire faire qc à qn/qc **6.** INFOR démarrer **III.** *n* **1.** (*beginning*) commencement *m;* **to make** [*o* **get off to**] **a** ~ **on sth** commencer qc; **to make a** ~ **on doing sth** commencer à faire qc; **to make a late/early ~** commencer tard/de bonne heure; **to make a fresh/good ~** recommencer/bien commencer; **to give sb a ~ in sth** lancer qn dans qc; **from ~ to finish** du début à la fin; **a false ~** un faux départ; **... for a ~** [*o* **for a ~, ...**] pour commencer **2.** SPORT (*beginning place*) départ *m* **3.** (*beginning time*) départ *m;* **to make a ~** se mettre en route **4.** (*beginning advantage*) avance *f;* **to have a good ~ in life** avoir bien débuté dans la vie; **to have a ~ on sb** avoir de l'avance sur qn; **to give sb a ~** donner de l'avance à qn; **to give sb a one hour/mile ~** donner une heure/un mile d'avance à qn **5.** (*sudden movement*) sursaut *m;* **to give a ~** sursauter; **to give sb a ~** faire sursauter qn

◆**start back** *vi* **1.** (*jump back suddenly*) faire un bond en arrière **2.** (*begin a return*) prendre le chemin du retour

◆**start in** *vi a. fig, a. inf* s'y mettre; **to ~ on sb/sth** s'attaquer à qn/qc

◆**start off** **I.** *vi* **1.** (*begin an activity*) commencer; **to ~ by doing sth** commencer en faisant qc **2.** (*begin a journey*) se mettre en route **II.** *vt* **to start sth off** commencer qc; **to start sb off on sth** lancer qn sur qc

◆**start on** *vt* **1.** (*begin*) commencer **2.** *inf* (*harass, attack*) s'en prendre à

◆**start out** *vi* **1.** (*begin a journey*) se mettre en route **2.** (*begin a process, a career*) commencer; (*company, business*) se lancer; **to ~ as/doing sth** débuter comme/en faisant qc; **to ~ to** +*infin* envisager de +*infin*

◆**start over** *vi Am* recommencer

◆**start up** **I.** *vt* **1.** (*organize and implement: a business, company*) lancer; (*a restaurant, club*) ouvrir **2.** (*start: engine*) démarrer **II.** *vi* **1.** (*begin an undertaking*) se lancer **2.** (*begin running: motorized vehicle*) démarrer

Start button *n* INFOR bouton *m* Démarrer

starter *n* **1.** SPORT (*sb or sth starting a competition*) partant(e) *m(f)* **2.** SPORT (*person who signals the start of a race*) starter *m;* **to be under ~'s orders** être à ses marques **3.** *Brit, inf* GASTR entrée *f* ►**for ~s** *inf* tout d'abord

starting *adj* de départ

starting block *n* starting-block *m* **starting gate** *n* starting-gate *m*

startle ['stɑːtl, *Am:* 'stɑːrt̬l] *vt* effrayer; **to ~ sb into doing sth** pousser qn à faire qc

startling *adj* effrayant(e)

start-up *n* **1.** (*setting*) lancement *m;* (*of motor*) démarrage *m;* (*of business*) création *f* d'entreprise **2.** (*business*) start-up *f*

starvation [stɑː'veɪʃən, *Am:* stɑːr'-] *no pl n* famine *f;* (*diet*) draconien(ne); (*wages*) de misère

starve [stɑːv, *Am:* stɑːrv] **I.** *vi a. iron* **1.** (*die*) souffrir de la faim; **to ~** (**to death**) mourir de faim **2.** *fig* **to ~ of sth** manquer de qc **II.** *vt* **1.** (*let die*) faire mourir de faim; **to ~ oneself** (**to death**) se laisser mourir de faim **2.** *fig* **to ~ sb of sth** priver qn de qc

starved *adj* affamé(e); **to be ~ of sth** être en mal de qc

starving *adj* **1.** (*hungry*) affamé(e) **2.** (*undergo hunger*) **to be ~** mourir de faim

stash [stæʃ] **I.** *vt* planquer **II.** *n* <-es> *inf* planque *f*

state [steɪt] **I.** *n* **1.** (*condition*) *a. fig* état *m;* **to be in a ~ of mind** être dans un état d'esprit; **to be in a fit ~ to** +*infin* être en état de +*infin;* **to be in a** (**terrible**) **~** *inf* être dans tous ses états **2.** (*situation*) situation *f;* **single ~** célibat *m;* **married ~** mariage *m* **3.** (*nation*) état *m;* **the State** l'État; **affairs of ~** affaires *fpl* d'État **4.** (*dignified rank*) rang *m;* **to do sth in ~** faire qc en grande pompe; **to live in ~** mener grand train **II.** *adj* **1.** (*nation*) *a. fig* d'État **2.** (*american states*) de l'État; **the ~ line between Kansas and Missouri** la frontière entre les États du Kansas et du Missouri **3.** (*governmental unit*) national(e); (*industry*) du secteur public **4.** (*civil government*) public(-que); (*document*) officiel(le); **a ~ registered nurse** *Brit* MED une infirmière diplômée d'État **5.** (*showing dignified ceremony*) officiel(le); (*funeral*) national(e) **III.** *vt* **1.** (*declare*) **to ~** (**that**) ... déclarer que ... **2.** (*express*) formuler; (*one's opinion, the reference*) donner; (*a problem, a condition*) poser; **~ why ...** dites pourquoi ...; **as ~d in my letter** comme je l'ai mentionné plus haut **3.** (*specify*) spécifier; (*conditions*) fixer

state-controlled *adj* étatisé(e) **statecraft** *n no pl* habileté *f* politique **State Department** *n no pl, Am* (*U.S. foreign ministry*) **the ~** le ministère des Affaires étrangères **state education** *n no pl* enseignement *m* public

stateless *adj* apatride

stateliness *n no pl* majesté *f*

stately *adj* majestueux(-euse)

statement ['steɪtmənt] *n* **1.** (*act of expressing*) *a. fig* déclaration *f;* **to make a ~** LAW faire une déposition **2.** (*description*) exposé *m* **3.** (*bank statement*) relevé *m* de compte

state of mind *n* état *m* d'esprit **state-of-the-art**, **state of the art** *adj* dernier cri *inv;* (*technology*) de pointe **state-owned** *adj* nationalisé(e); (*industry*) du secteur public; (*utility*) public(-que) **stateroom** *n* salle *f* de réception

States *n pl, inf* **the ~** les États-Unis

stateside ['steɪtsaɪd] **I.** *adj Am, inf* américain(e) **II.** *adv Am, inf* aux États-Unis

statesman <-men> *n* homme *m* d'État **statesmanlike** *adj* diplomatique **stateswoman** <-men> *n* femme *f* d'État **state trooper** *n* policier *m*

static ['stætɪk, *Am:* 'stæt̬-] *adj* statique

statics *npl + sing vb* PHYS statique *f*

station ['steɪʃən] **I.** *n* **1.** (*railroad stop*) gare *f;* **underground ~** *Brit, Aus* station *f* de métro **2.** (*building*) poste *m;* **research ~** poste de recherche; **police ~** poste de police; **power ~** centrale *f* électrique; **atomic energy ~** centrale *f* atomique; **petrol/gas** ~ station-service *f* **3.** (*for broadcasting*) station *f* **4.** (*position*) poste *m;* **to take up one's ~s** se rendre à son poste; **action/battle ~s** MIL poste *m* de combat; **to be on** ~ NAUT, MIL être à son poste **5.** (*social position*) position *f;* **one's** ~ **in life** sa situation sociale **6.** *Aus, NZ* AGR exploitation *f* d'élevage **II.** *vt* MIL (*troops*) poster

stationary ['steɪʃənəri, *Am:* 'steɪʃəner-] *adj* immobile; (*prices*) stationnaire; **a** ~ **bicycle** un vélo d'appartement

stationer ['steɪʃənəʳ, *Am:* -ʃənɚ] *n Brit* **1.** (*person*) papetier *m* **2.** (*shop*) papeterie *f*

stationery ['steɪʃənəri, *Am:* 'steɪʃəner-] *n no pl* papeterie *f*

station house *n Am* poste *m* de police **stationmaster** *n* chef *m* de gare **station wagon** *n Am, Aus* break *m*

statistic I. *n* statistique *f* **II.** *adj* statistique

statistical *adj* statistique

statistician *n* statisticien(ne) *m(f)*

statistics [stə'tɪstɪks] *npl* **1.** + *sing vb* (*science*) statistique *f* **2.** (*numerical data*) statistiques *fpl*

statuary ['stætʃuəri, *Am:* 'stætʃuer-] **I.** *n no pl* **1.** *form* (*statues*) statues *fpl* **2.** *form* (*statue making*) statuaire *f* **II.** *adj form* statuaire

statue ['stætʃu:] *n* statue *f*

Statue of Liberty *n* **the** ~ la Statue de la Liberté

statuesque [ˌstætju'esk, *Am:* ˌstætʃu'-] *adj form* sculptural(e)

statuette [ˌstætju'et, *Am:* ˌstætʃu'-] *n* statuette *f*

stature ['stætʃəʳ, *Am:* -ɚ] *n* **1.** (*height*) *a. fig* stature *f;* **to reach one's full** ~ atteindre sa taille d'adulte **2.** (*reputation*) réputation *f;* **a person of (any)** ~ une personne d'une certaine renommée; **to be of great/small** ~ être de grande/petite envergure

status ['steɪtəs, *Am:* -t̬əs] *n no pl* statut *m*

status line *n* INFOR ligne *f* d'état **status quo** *n no pl* status quo *m* **status symbol** *n* signe *m* extérieur de richesse

statute ['stætju:t, *Am:* 'stætʃu:t] *n* loi *f;* **by** ~ selon la loi

statute book *n* code *m* **statute law** *n* LAW droit *m* écrit

statutory ['stætjətəri, *Am:* 'stætʃətɔ:r-] *adj* statuaire

staunch[1] [stɔ:ntʃ] *adj* loyal(e); (*refusal*) ferme; (*Catholic, Democrat*) convaincu(e); (*ally, friend*) dévoué(e); (*supporter, defender*) fervent(e)

staunch[2] [stɔ:ntʃ] *vt* **1.** étancher; **to** ~ **a wound** étancher le sang d'une plaie **2.** *fig* arrêter; **to** ~ **the flood of persons** contenir le flot de personnes

stave [steɪv] *n* portée *f*

staves *n s.* **staff**

stay[1] [steɪ] *n* NAUT étai *m*

stay[2] [steɪ] **I.** *vi* **1.** (*remain present*) rester; **to** ~ **for a time/six days** rester un temps/six jours; **to** ~ **put** *inf* ne pas bouger; **to be here to** ~ être entré dans le mœurs **2.** (*temporarily*) séjourner; **to** ~ **overnight** passer la nuit; **to come to** ~ **with sb** venir rendre visite à qn **3.** (*remain*) rester; ~ **tuned** RADIO, TV restez avec nous; **to** ~ **in touch** rester en contact; **to** ~ **within budget** COM ne pas dépasser le budget **II.** *vt* **1.** (*assuage*) arrêter; (*hunger, thirst*) apaiser **2.** (*endure*) tenir; **to** ~ **the course** tenir bon **III.** *n* séjour *m;* **an overnight** ~ une nuit; **a** ~ **with one's family** un séjour dans sa famille

◆**stay away** *vi* **to** ~ **from sth** ne pas s'approcher de qc; **to** ~ **in droves** ne pas venir en nombre

◆**stay behind** *vi* rester plus tard

◆**stay down** *vi* **1.** (*not be vomited*) **nothing I eat stays down** je rends tout ce que je mange **2.** (*remain underwater*) rester sous l'eau

◆**stay in** *vi* rester à la maison

◆**stay on** *vi* **1.** (*remain longer*) rester plus longtemps **2.** (*remain in place*) rester en place

◆**stay out** *vi* **1.** (*not come home*) rester dehors; **to** ~ **all night** sortir toute la nuit; **to** ~ **late/past midnight** rentrer tard/après minuit **2.** (*continue a strike*) rester en grève

◆**stay up** *vi* rester debout

stay-at-home *n inf* pantouflard(e) *m(f)*

stayer *n* **1.** (*perseverer*) coureur, -euse *m, f* de fond **2.** (*visitor*) touriste *mf* de longue durée

staying power *n no pl* endurance *f*

STD [ˌesti:'di:] *n* **1.** *Brit abbr of* **subscriber trunk dialling** automatique *m* **2.** *abbr of* **sexually transmitted disease** MST *f*

stead [sted] *n no pl* **in sb's** ~ à la place de qn; **to stand sb in good** ~ **for sth** être très utile à qc

steadfast ['stedfɑ:st, *Am:* -fæst] *adj* ferme; (*ally, friend*) fidèle; **to be** ~ **in sth** être déterminé dans qc

steady I. <-ier, -iest> *adj* **1.** (*stable*) stable **2.** (*regular*) régulier(-ère); (*temperature*) constant(e); (*breathing, pulse*) stable; **slow but** ~ lent mais constant; **a** ~ **boyfriend/girlfriend** un(e) petit(e) ami(e) **3.** (*controlled*) posé(e); (*nerves*) solide; **a** ~ **hand** une main sûre **II.** *vt* (*things*) maintenir; (*people*) calmer; **to** ~ **oneself** se ressaisir; **to** ~ **one's nerves** calmer ses nerfs **III.** *adv* **to go** ~ **with sb** sortir avec qn **IV.** *interj* ~ **on!** *Brit* doucement! **V.** <-dies> *n inf* petit ami *m*, petite amie *f*

steak [steɪk] *n* steak *m;* ~ **tartare** steak tartare, toast *m* cannibale *Belgique*

steal [sti:l] **I.** *n Am, inf* affaire *f;* **to be a** ~ être donné **II.** <stole, stolen> *vt* **1.** (*take illegally*) *a. fig* voler; (*sb's heart*) prendre **2.** (*do surreptitiously*) **to** ~ **a glance at sb/sth** jeter un coup d'œil à qn/qc ►**to** ~ **attention/the limelight** voler la vedette; **to** ~ **a march on sb** devancer qn; **to** ~ **the show** ravir la vedette; **to** ~ **sb's thunder** couper à qn l'herbe sous le pied **III.** <stole, stolen> *vi* **1.** (*take*

S

illegally) voler **2.** (*move surreptitiously*) **to ~ in/out** entrer/sortir à pas feutrés

◆**steal away** *vi* **to ~** s'en aller

stealth [stelθ] *n no pl* ruse *f*

stealthy *adj* furtif(-ive); (*footstep*) feutré(e)

steam [sti:m] **I.** *n no pl* vapeur *f*; **a ~ engine** un moteur à vapeur ►**to let off ~** se défouler; **to pick up ~** s'y mettre; **to run out of ~** s'essouffler; **to do sth under one's own ~** faire qc de ses propres moyens; **full ~ ahead!** en avant toute! **II.** *vi* **1.** (*produce steam*) fumer **2.** (*move using steam*) fonctionner à la vapeur **3.** (*become steamy*) s'embuer **III.** *vt* cuire à la vapeur; **to ~ open the letter** ouvrir une lettre à la vapeur; **to ~ a stamp off** décoller un timbre à la vapeur

◆**steam up** *vt* (*mist up*) embuer ►**to get steamed up about sth** *inf* s'énerver à cause de qc

steam bath *n* sauna *m* **steamboat** *n* bateau *m* à vapeur

steamer ['sti:məʳ, *Am:* -ɚ] *n* **1.** (*boat*) bateau *m* à vapeur **2.** (*cooking implement*) cuit-vapeur *m*

steam iron *n* fer *m* à vapeur **steamroller** **I.** *n* **1.** (*road machinery*) rouleau *m* compresseur **2.** (*forceful person*) dictateur *m* **II.** *vt* écraser; **to ~ sb into doing sth** imposer à qn de faire qc **steamship** *n* bateau *m* à vapeur

steamy <-ier, -iest> *adj* **1.** (*full of steam*) plein(e) de vapeur **2.** (*very humid*) humide **3.** *inf* (*torrid*) torride

steel [sti:l] **I.** *n* **1.** *no pl* (*iron alloy*) acier *m* **2.** (*knife sharpener*) aiguisoir *m* **3.** *fig* **nerves of ~** nerfs *mpl* d'acier **II.** *vt* **to ~ oneself to** *+infin* s'armer de courage pour *+infin*

steel-clad *adj s.* **steel-plated** **steel grey** **I.** *adj* gris acier *inv* **II.** *n* gris *m* acier **steel industry** *n* sidérurgie *f* **steel-plated** *adj* revêtu(e) d'acier **steel producer** *n* aciériste *m* **steelworker** *n* sidérurgiste *m* **steelworks** *n + sing/pl vb* aciérie *f*

steely ['sti:li] <-ier, -iest> *adj a. fig* d'acier; **~ determination** détermination *f* de fer

steep¹ [sti:p] *adj* **1.** (*sloping*) raide; (*hill*) escarpé(e); (*climb*) abrupt(e); (*dive*) à pic **2.** (*expensive*) élevé(e)

steep² [sti:p] **I.** *vt* **1.** (*soak*) faire tremper **2.** GASTR faire macérer **3.** *fig* **to be ~ed in sth** être imprégné de qc; **to have hands ~ed in blood** avoir les mains couvertes de sang **II.** *vi* **1.** (*let soak*) faire tremper **2.** GASTR macérer

steepen ['sti:pən] **I.** *vi* **1.** (*become steeper*) devenir plus raide **2.** *inf* (*become more expensive*) augmenter **II.** *vt* faire plus raide

steeple ['sti:pl] *n* clocher *m*

steer¹ [stɪəʳ, *Am:* stɪr] **I.** *vt* **1.** (*direct*) conduire **2.** (*direct in a specified direction*) **to ~ a course to sth** faire route vers qc **3.** (*guide*) guider; (*discussion*) diriger **4.** *fig* **to ~ a middle course between sth** trouver un compromis entre qc **II.** *vi* **1.** (*direct a vehicle*) conduire **2.** (*direct in a specified direction*) se diriger ►**to ~ clear of sb/sth** éviter qn/qc; (*stay away from*) se tenir à l'écart de qn/qc

steer² [stɪəʳ, *Am:* stɪr] *n* bœuf *m*

steering *n* direction *f*

steering column *n* colonne *f* de direction **steering committee** *n + sing/pl vb* comité *m* d'organisation **steering gear** *n* TECH, AUTO boîte *f* de direction **steering wheel** *n* volant *m*

steersman ['stɪəzmən, *Am:* 'stɪrz-] <-men> *n* timonier *m*

stein [staɪn] *n* chope *f*

stellar ['steləʳ, *Am:* -ɚ] *adj* **1.** *form* ASTR stellaire **2.** *inf* (*good*) exceptionnel(le)

stem [stem] **I.** *n* **1.** (*plant part: flower*) tige *f*; (*leaf*) queue *f* **2.** (*glass part*) pied *m* **3.** (*word root*) radical *m* **4.** (*ship's prow*) proue *f*; **from ~ to stern** de bout en bout **5.** *Am* (*watch part*) remontoir *m* **II.** <-mm-> *vt* contenir **III.** <-mm-> *vi* **to ~ back to sth** provenir de qc

stench [stentʃ] *n no pl* **1.** (*odor*) puanteur *f*; **~ of rotten fish** odeur *f* nauséabonde de poisson pourri **2.** *fig* (*of scandal*) parfum *m*

stencil ['stensl] **I.** *n* pochoir *m* **II.** *vt* peindre au pochoir

stenographer *n* sténographe *mf*

stenography [stə'nɒgrəfi, *Am:* -'nɑ:grə-] *n no pl* sténographie *f*

step [step] **I.** *n* **1.** (*foot movement*) pas *m*; **with every ~** à chaque pas; **a spring in one's ~** d'un pas léger; **to take a ~ toward sb** faire un pas vers qn; **to take a ~ on the road to sth** être sur la voie de qc; **to retrace one's ~s** retourner sur ses pas; **to go a few ~s** faire quelques pas; **to be just a ~ from sth** n'être qu'à un pas de qc; **to watch one's ~** faire attention où on met ses pieds; *fig* faire attention à ce que l'on fait; **to be out of ~ with sb/sth** être déphasé par rapport à qn/qc; **to be in ~ with sb/sth** être en accord avec qn/qc; **to fall into ~** marcher au pas **2.** (*stair*) marche *f*; **wooden ~s** escaliers *mpl* en bois; **a flight of ~s** un escalier; **the front ~** pas *m* de porte; **watch the ~** attention à la marche **3.** (*stage in a process*) pas *m*; **~ by ~** pas à pas; **one ~ at a time** calmement; **every ~ of the way** continuellement; **to be a ~ ahead of sb** devancer qn; **a ~ in the right/wrong direction** une bonne/mauvaise mesure; **to be a ~ up** être une promotion **4.** (*measures*) mesure *f*; **to take ~s to** *+infin* prendre des mesures pour *+infin* **5.** *pl, Brit* (*stepladder*) escabeau *m* **6.** *Am* MUS ton *m* **II.** <-pp-> *vi* marcher; **to ~ somewhere** aller quelque part; **to ~ out of line** faire un faux pas

◆**step aside** *vi* s'écarter

◆**step back** *vi* **to ~ from sth** se retirer de qc

◆**step down** **I.** *vi* **to ~ from sth** se retirer de qc **II.** *vt* ELEC dévolter

◆**step in** *vi* intervenir

◆**step up** *vt* augmenter

stepbrother *n* beau-frère *m* **stepchild** *n*

beau-fils *m*, belle-fille *f* **stepdaughter** *n* belle-fille *f* **stepfather** *n* beau-père *m*
stepladder *n* escabeau *m*
stepmother *n* belle-mère *f*
steppe *n* steppe *f*
stepsister *n* belle-sœur *f* **stepson** *n* beau-fils *m*
stereo ['steriəʊ, *Am:* 'sterioʊ] **I.** *n* **1.** *no pl* (*transmission in two tracks*) stéréo *f;* **in** ~ en stéréo **2.** *inf* (*hi-fi unit*) chaîne *f;* **car** ~ autoradio *m* **II.** *adj s.* **stereophonic** stéréo *inv*
stereophonic *adj form* stéréophonique
stereophony [ˌsteri'ɒfəni, *Am:* -ɑː-] *n no pl* stéréophonie *f*
stereotype ['steriətaɪp] **I.** *n pej* stéréotype *m* **II.** *vt pej* stéréotyper
sterile ['steraɪl, *Am:* 'sterəl] *adj a. fig* stérile
sterilisation *n Aus, Brit no pl* stérilisation *f*
sterilise *vt Aus, Brit* MED stériliser
sterilising *adj Aus, Brit* de stérilisation
sterility [stə'rɪləti, *Am:* -t̬i] *n no pl, a. fig* stérilité *f*
sterilization *s.* **sterilisation**
sterilize ['sterəlaɪz] *s.* **sterilise**
sterilizing *s.* **sterilising**
sterling ['stɜːlɪŋ, *Am:* 'stɜːr-] **I.** *n* sterling *m;* **in pounds** ~ en livres sterling; *s. a.* **pound** **II.** *adj* **1.** (*having purity standard*) fin(e); ~ **area** zone *f* sterling; ~ **cutlery** argenterie *f* **2.** (*having high standard*) admirable
stern[1] [stɜːn, *Am:* stɜːrn] *adj* sévère ►**to be made of ~er stuff** être d'une autre trempe
stern[2] [stɜːn, *Am:* stɜːrn] *n* NAUT poupe *f*
sternness *n no pl* sévérité *f*
sternum ['stɜːnəm, *Am:* 'stɜːr-] <-s *o* -na> *n* sternum *m*
steroid ['stɪərɔɪd, *Am:* 'stərɔɪd] *n* stéroïde *m*
stethoscope ['steθəskəʊp, *Am:* -skoʊp] *n* stéthoscope *m*
stew [stjuː, *Am:* stuː] **I.** *n* ragoût *m* ►**to be in a ~ about sth** être dans tous ses états à propos de qc; **to get sb into a** ~ mettre qn dans tous ses états **II.** *vt* faire mijoter **III.** *vi* **1.** (*simmer slowly*) mijoter **2.** *inf* (*be angry*) **to** ~ **about sth** être en pelote à propos de qc **3.** (*do nothing*) traînasser ►**to let sb** ~ **in one's own juice** laisser mariner qn
steward ['stjʊəd, *Am:* 'stuːɚd] *n* **1.** (*flight attendant*) steward *m* **2.** (*supervising official*) organisateur *m* **3.** (*property manager*) intendant *m*
stewardess [ˌstjʊə'des, *Am:* 'stuːɚdɪs] <-es> *n* hôtesse *f* de l'air
St George's Day *n no pl, Can* (*end of April*) Saint *f* George
stick[1] [stɪk] *n* **1.** (*piece of wood*) bâton *m* **2.** (*walking* ~) canne *f* **3.** (*long thin piece: of cinnamon, chalk, dynamite*) bâton *m* **4.** GASTR tige *f;* (*of celery*) branche *f;* **a cocktail** ~ un pique à apéritif; **a lollipop** ~ un bâtonnet de sucette **5.** *Brit, inf* (*punishment, criticism*) **to get the** ~ se faire disputer; **to give sb the** ~ disputer qn; **to give sb** ~ critiquer qn; **to take a lot of** ~ **from sb/sth** être sévèrement critiqué par qn/qc **6.** MUS baguette *f* **7.** AUTO **gear** ~ levier *m* de vitesses **8.** *pej, inf* (*remote area*) **the ~s** la cambrousse ►**to live out in the ~s** vivre dans un coin perdu; **to be up the** ~ être enceinte; **to get the wrong end of the** ~ comprendre de travers
stick[2] [stɪk] <stuck, stuck> **I.** *vi* **1.** (*fix by adhesion*) coller **2.** (*endure*) rester; **to** ~ **in sb's mind** rester gravé dans la mémoire de qn; **to make sth** ~ faire rentrer qc **3.** (*jam*) se coincer ►**to** ~ **in sb's throat** rester en travers de la gorge **II.** *vt* **1.** (*affix*) coller **2.** (*put*) mettre; **to** ~ **sth into sth** enfoncer qc dans qc; **to** ~ **a knife in sb** poignarder qn **3.** (*not be able to do sth*) **to be stuck** être coincé; **to be stuck for sth** *inf* ne pas arriver à faire qc; **to be stuck with sb** ne pas pouvoir se débarrasser de qn **4.** (*endure*) **to get stuck in**(**to**) **sth** *inf* persévérer dans qc **5.** *inf* (*tolerate*) supporter **6.** (*increase*) augmenter
◆**stick around** *vi inf* **1.** (*wait*) attendre **2.** (*stay*) rester; **~!** reste là!
◆**stick at** *vt* persévérer dans; **to** ~ **nothing to** ne reculer devant rien pour
◆**stick by** *vt* rester fidèle à
◆**stick down** *vt a. inf* coller
◆**stick in** **I.** *vt* **1.** (*put in*) mettre **2.** (*fix in*) coller **3.** (*pierce*) enfoncer **II.** *vi* s'enfoncer ►**to get stuck in** *inf* attaquer
◆**stick on** *vt* **1.** (*affix*) *a. fig* coller; **to** ~ **a charge/accusation on sb** coller une accusation sur le dos de qn **2.** (*like very much*) **to be stuck on sb/sth** être fou de qn/qc
◆**stick out** **I.** *vt* tendre; **to stick one's tongue out** tirer la langue ►**to stick it out** *inf* tenir le coup **II.** *vi* **1.** (*protrude*) dépasser; (*ear*) être décollé **2.** (*be obvious*) se voir; **to** ~ **a mile** se voir comme le nez au milieu de la figure
◆**stick out for** *vt* s'obstiner à demander
◆**stick to** *vt* **1.** (*adhere*) coller à **2.** (*keep to*) s'en tenir à; (*promises*) tenir; (*version*) maintenir; (*a subject*) rester dans; ~ **it!** persévérer!; **I'll** ~ **water** je vais rester à l'eau **3.** (*remain loyal*) rester fidèle à
◆**stick together** **I.** *vt* coller **II.** *vi* **1.** (*adhere*) être collé **2.** (*not separate*) rester ensemble **3.** (*remain loyal*) se soutenir
◆**stick up** **I.** *vt inf* **1.** (*put*) mettre **2.** *inf* (*commit armed robbery*) braquer; **stick 'em up!** les mains en l'air! **II.** *vi* se dresser; **to** ~ **out of sth** sortir de qc
◆**stick up for** *vt* défendre
◆**stick with** *vt* **1.** (*persevere, continue with*) continuer; (*tradition*) conserver; (*thought, idea, memory*) rester sur; **I'll** ~ **it** je vais persévérer **2.** (*stick by*) rester fidèle à
stick deodorant *n* déodorant *m* en stick
sticker ['stɪkə^r, *Am:* -ɚ] *n* **1.** (*adhesive label*) étiquette *f* adhésive; **price** ~ étiquette de prix **2.** (*adhesive paper with writing*) autocollant *m* **3.** (*person who perseveres*) acharné(e) *m(f)*

S

stick glue *n* bâtonnet *m* de colle **sticking plaster** *n* *Brit* MED sparadrap *m* **stick insect** *n* phasme *m* ►**to be as thin as a** ~ être maigre comme un clou **stick-in-the-mud** **I.** *n pej, inf* réac *mf* **II.** *adj* réac

stickler ['stɪkləʳ, *Am:* -lɚ] *n* pinailleur, -euse *m, f;* **a** ~ **for sth** une personne à cheval sur qc; **to be a** ~ **about sth** être très à cheval sur qc

stick-on *adj* autocollant(e)

stickpin ['stɪkˌpɪn] *n Am* épingle *f* de cravate

stick shift *n Am* levier *m* de vitesses

stick-up *n inf* braquage *m*

sticky ['stɪki] <-ier, -iest> *adj* **1.** (*adhesive*) collant(e) **2.** (*adhesive and wet*) gluant(e) **3.** (*sweaty*) poisseux(-euse) **4.** (*unpleasant*) difficile; **a** ~ **patch** une mauvaise passe; **to be on a** ~ **wicket** être dans une situation difficile **5.** (*unwilling to help*) **to be** ~ **about sth** ne pas se montrer très coopérant

stiff[1] [stɪf] *n inf* cadavre *m*

stiff[2] *adj* **1.** (*hard*) raide; **to be** ~ avoir des courbatures **2.** (*strong: alcohol, wind*) fort(e) **3.** (*severe: sentence*) sévère; (*welcome*) froid(e)

stiffen ['stɪfn] **I.** *vi* **1.** (*become rigid*) *a. fig* se raidir **2.** (*become firm*) devenir ferme **II.** *vt* **1.** (*make rigid*) raidir; (*collar, cuff*) empeser **2.** (*strengthen*) renforcer; **to** ~ **the spine of sb** *fig* endurcir qn **3.** *fig* (*make more difficult*) affermir **4.** (*make more severe: penalty*) alourdir

stiffening ['stɪfnɪŋ] *n no pl* **1.** (*becoming immobile*) raidissement *m* **2.** (*rigid material*) durcissement *m*

stiff-necked *adj* entêté(e)

stifle ['staɪfl] *vi, vt* étouffer

stifling *adj* étouffant(e)

stigma[1] ['stɪgmə] *n* **1.** (*disgrace*) honte *f* **2.** <-ta> *pl* REL stigmates *mpl* **3.** MED stigmate *m*

stigma[2] ['stɪgmə] *n* stigmate *m*

stigmatize ['stɪgmətaɪz] *vt* stigmatiser

stile [staɪl] *n* échalier *m*

stiletto [stɪ'letəʊ, *Am:* -'leţoʊ] <-s> *n* **1.** (*dagger*) stylet *m* **2.** *pl* FASHION talons *mpl* aiguilles

stiletto heels *n* talons *mpl* aiguilles

still[1] [stɪl] **I.** *n* calme *m* **II.** *adj* **1.** (*not moving*) immobile **2.** (*peaceful*) calme **3.** (*silent*) silencieux(-euse) **4.** (*not fizzy: drink*) non gazeux(-euse); ~ **water** eau *f* plate; *fig* eau *f* dormante ►~ **waters run deep** *prov* il faut se méfier de l'eau qui dort **III.** *adv* sans bouger; **to stand** ~ ne pas bouger; (*to sit* ~) rester tranquille **IV.** *vt* calmer

still[2] [stɪl] *adv* **1.** (*continuing situation*) encore; **to be** ~ **alive** être encore vivant **2.** (*nevertheless*) ~ **and all** *Am* malgré tout **3.** (*greater degree*) encore; **to rise** ~ **higher** monter encore davantage; ~ **more** encore plus; **better** ~ encore mieux

still[3] [stɪl] *n* alambic *m*

stillbirth *n* mort-né *m* **stillborn** *adj* **1.** (*born dead*) mort-né **2.** *fig* (*unsuccessful*) avorté(e) **still life** <- lifes> *n* nature *f* morte

stillness *n inv* **1.** (*tranquillity*) calme *m* **2.** (*lack of movement*) immobilité *f*

stilt [stɪlt] *n* **1.** CONSTR (*supporting post*) pilotis *m;* **on** ~**s** sur pilotis **2.** (*for walking on*) échasse *f*

stilted *adj pej* coincé(e)

stimulant ['stɪmjələnt] *n a.* MED, SPORT stimulant *m*

stimulate ['stɪmjəleɪt] *vt a.* ECON, MED stimuler; (*conversation*) animer

stimulating *adj* stimulant(e)

stimulation *n no pl* stimulation *f*

stimulus ['stɪmjələs] <-li> *n* **1.** (*boost: industry*) coup *m* de fouet **2.** BIO, MED (*cause of reaction*) stimulus *m*

sting [stɪŋ] **I.** *n* BIO, ZOOL **1.** (*part of an insect*) dard *m;* (*of scorpion*) aiguillon *m* **2.** (*injury by insect, plant*) piqûre **3.** (*pain*) brûlure *f* **4.** *Am, inf* (*cleverly organised theft*) escroquerie *f* **5.** *Am, inf* (*police operation*) coup *m* monté **II.** <stung, stung> *vi, vt* piquer

stinginess ['stɪndʒɪnɪs] *n no pl* radinerie *f*

stinging nettle [ˌstɪŋɪŋ'netl, *Am:* -'neţl] *n* ortie *f*

stingray ['stɪŋreɪ] *n* pastenague *f*

stingy ['stɪndʒi] <-ier, -iest> *adj inf* radin(e)

stink [stɪŋk] **I.** *n* **1.** (*unpleasant smell*) puanteur *f* **2.** *inf* (*trouble*) raffut *m;* **to cause a** ~ faire du raffut ►**to work like** ~ travailler comme un dingue **II.** <stank *o Am, a. Aus* stunk, stunk> *vi a. inf* **to** ~ **of sth** puer qc

stinker *n pej, inf* saleté *f;* **you little** ~ espèce *f* d'ordure

stint[1] [stɪnt] *n* **1.** (*period*) période *f;* **he had a two-year** ~ **as a postman** il a été facteur pendant deux ans **2.** (*work*) tâche *f;* **I've done my** ~ **at the reception for this week** j'ai fait ma part de travail à l'accueil pour cette semaine

stint[2] [stɪnt] *vt* économiser; **to** ~ **oneself** se priver

stipulate ['stɪpjəleɪt] *vt* stipuler

stipulation *n* stipulation *f*

stir [stɜːʳ, *Am:* stɜːr] **I.** *n* **1.** (*agitation*) **to give sth a** ~ remuer qc **2.** (*excitement*) **to cause a** ~ faire du bruit; **to cause a** ~ **of interest** susciter un regain d'intérêt **II.** <-ring, -red> *vt* **1.** (*agitate*) remuer; **to** ~ **oneself** se remuer **2.** (*arouse: person*) émouvoir; (*imagination*) stimuler; (*memory*) réveiller; (*fire*) attiser; **to be deeply** ~**red by sth** être très remué par qc; **to** ~ **trouble** *Am* chercher des noises **III.** *vi* bouger

stir-fry ['stɜːfraɪ, *Am:* 'stɜːr-] **I.** <-fries> *n* sauté *m* **II.** <-ied, -ies> *vt* faire sauter

stirring **I.** *n* pointe *f* **II.** *adj* (*appeal, song, speech*) émouvant(e)

stirrup ['stɪrəp, *Am:* 'stɜːr-] *n* étrier *m*

stitch [stɪtʃ] **I.** <-es> *n* FASHION, MED, SPORT point *m* ►**to be in** ~**es** être plié de rire; **not to have a** ~ **on** *inf* être nu comme un ver **II.** *vi, vt* coudre

St Jean Baptiste Day *n no pl, Can* (*June 24*) Saint *f* Jean (Baptiste)
stoat [stəʊt, *Am:* stoʊt] *n* hermine *f*
stock [stɒk, *Am:* stɑːk] **I.** *n* **1.** (*reserves*) réserves *fpl* **2.** COM, ECON (*goods in a shop*) stock *m;* **to have sth in ~** avoir qc en stock; **to be out of ~** être en rupture de stock; **to take ~** faire l'inventaire **3.** *pl, Brit* FIN, ECON fonds *mpl* **4.** *Am* (*share in a company*) action *f* **5.** AGR, ZOOL (*farm animals*) bétail *m* **6.** *no pl* SOCIOL (*line of descent*) origine *f;* ZOOL, BIO (*breeding line*) souche *f* **7.** (*popularity*) réputation *f* **8.** (*liquid extracted*) bouillon *m* **II.** *adj* (*standard: expression*) commun(e); (*character*) stéréotypé(e) **III.** *vt* COM, ECON **1.** (*keep in supply*) stocker **2.** (*supply goods: shop*) approvisionner **3.** (*fill: shelves*) remplir
stockade [stɒˈkeɪd, *Am:* stɑːˈ-] *n* **1.** (*wooden fence*) palissade *f* **2.** *Am* (*prison*) trou *m*
stockbroker [ˈstɒkˌbrəʊkəʳ, *Am:* ˈstɑːkˌbroʊkɚ] *n* agent *m* de change
stockbroking *n* opérations *fpl* de change
stockcar *n* stock-car *m* **stockcar racing** *n* course *f* de stock-car
stock company *n Am* **1.** FIN société *f* par actions **2.** THEAT troupe *f* de théâtre de province **stock control** *n* gestion *f* des stocks
stock cube *n* bouillon-cube® *m*
stock exchange *n* Bourse *f*
stock-farmer *n* éleveur, -euse *m, f*
stockfish [ˈstɒkfɪʃ, *Am:* ˈstɑːk-] *n* poisson *m* séché
stockholder *n Am* actionnaire *mf*
stocking [ˈstɒkɪŋ, *Am:* ˈstɑːkɪŋ] *n* bas *m*
stock-in-trade *n* **1.** (*required for trade*) fonds *m* de commerce **2.** (*for sale*) marchandises *fpl*
stockist [ˈstɒkɪst, *Am:* ˈstɑːkɪst] *n Aus, Brit* distributeur, -trice *m, f*
stock level *n* niveau *m* du stock **stocklist** *n* liste *f* des stocks **stock market** *n* marché *m* boursier
stockpile [ˈstɒkpaɪl, *Am:* ˈstɑːk-] **I.** *n* réserves *fpl* **II.** *vt* faire des réserves de
stockroom [ˈstɒkrʊm, *Am:* ˈstɑːkruːm] *n* COM réserve *f*
stock-still [ˌstɒkˈstɪl, *Am:* ˌstɑːk-] *adv* **to stand ~** rester immobile
stocktake *n Brit,* **stocktaking** *n* inventaire *m*
stocky [ˈstɒki, *Am:* ˈstɑːki] <-ier, -iest> *adj* râblé(e)
stockyard [ˈstɒkjɑːd] *n* parc *m* à bestiaux
stodge [stɒdʒ, *Am:* stɑːdʒ] *n Brit, Aus, pej, inf* étouffe-chrétien *m*
stodgy [ˈstɒdʒi, *Am:* ˈstɑːdʒi] <-ier, -iest> *adj* **1.** (*heavy: food*) bourratif(-ive) **2.** (*dull*) barbant(e)
stoic [ˈstəʊɪk, *Am:* ˈstoʊ-] **I.** *n* PHILOS stoïque *mf;* **Stoic** stoïcien(ne) *m(f)* **II.** *adj form* stoïque
stoical *adj s.* **stoic**
stoicism [ˈstəʊɪsɪzəm, *Am:* ˈstoʊɪ-] *n no pl a.* PHILOS stoïcisme *m*
stoke [stəʊk, *Am:* stoʊk] *vt a. fig* entretenir
stoker [ˈstəʊkəʳ, *Am:* ˈstoʊkɚ] *n* chauffeur *m*
STOL *n abbr of* **short takeoff and landing** ADAC *m*
stole[1] [stəʊl, *Am:* stoʊl] *pt of* **steal**
stole[2] [stəʊl, *Am:* stoʊl] *n* FASHION, REL étole *f*
stolen I. *pp of* steal **II.** *adj* volé(e)
stolid [ˈstɒlɪd, *Am:* ˈstɑːlɪd] *adj pej* **1.** (*lacking liveliness*) impassible **2.** (*uninteresting: building*) laid(e)
stomach [ˈstʌmək] **I.** *n* MED, ANAT **1.** (*digestive organ*) estomac *m;* **to churn sb's ~** soulever le cœur; **to have no ~ for sth** *fig* ne pas avoir le cœur de faire qc **2.** (*abdomen*) ventre *m;* **to lie on one's ~** être couché sur le ventre **II.** *vt inf* supporter; **to be hard to ~** être difficile à avaler
stomach ache *n no pl* maux *mpl* d'estomac
stomp [stɒmp, *Am:* stɑːmp] *vi* **1.** (*walk with heavy tread*) marcher à pas lourds **2.** (*walk intentionally heavily*) marcher en tapant des pieds; **to ~ off** partir en tapant des pieds; **to ~ on sth** *Am* piétiner qc; **to ~ on sb** *fig* écraser qn **3.** *Am s.* **stamp**
stone [stəʊn, *Am:* stoʊn] **I.** *n* **1.** *no pl* GEO (*hard substance, jewel*) pierre *f* **2.** (*piece of rock*) pierre *f;* (*smaller*) caillou *m;* **to fall like a ~** tomber comme une masse; **to be a ~'s throw** (**away**) être à deux pas **3.** MED (*hard matter*) calcul *m* **4.** BIO, BOT (*seed of a fruit*) noyau *m* **5.** *Brit* (*14 lbs*) 6,348 kg ►**to cast the first ~** jeter la première pierre; **to leave no ~ unturned** faire absolument tout ce que l'on peut **II.** *adj* **1.** CONSTR (*made of stone: floor, step, statue*) en pierre; GEO pierreux(-euse) **2.** (*stoneware: jug*) en grès **3.** (*pale beige colour*) sable *inv* **III.** *adv* **1.** (*like a stone*) **~ hard** dur(e) comme de la pierre **2.** *inf* (*completely*) complètement **IV.** *vt* **1.** (*throw stones at*) lancer des cailloux sur; **to ~ to death** lapider à mort **2.** (*remove the kernels*) dénoyauter
Stone Age I. *n inv* **the ~** l'âge de pierre **II.** *adj* (*of that historical period: settlement, rite*) (datant) de l'âge de pierre **stone-blind** *adj* complètement aveugle **stone-broke** *adj Am s.* **stony-broke** **stone-cold I.** *adj* complètement froid(e) **II.** *adv* complètement
stoned *adj inf* défoncé(e)
stone-dead *adj* bien mort(e) **stone-deaf** *adj* complètement sourd(e) **stone fruit** *n* fruit *m* à noyau **stonemason** *n* tailleur *m* de pierre **stonewall** *vt* (*queries, discussion*) faire obstruction à **stoneware** *n no pl* grès *m* **stonework** *n no pl* maçonnerie *f*
stony [ˈstəʊni, *Am:* ˈstoʊ-] <-ier, -iest> *adj* **1.** (*with many stones*) *a. fig* rocailleux(-euse) **2.** (*unfeeling*) de pierre
stony-broke *adj Brit, Aus, inf* fauché(e) comme les blés
stood [stʊd] *pt, pp of* **stand**
stooge [stuːdʒ] *n* **1.** *pej* (*assistant*) larbin *m*

S

2. THEAT (*comedian's straight partner*) comparse *mf* **3.** *Am, inf* (*informer*) balance *f*

stool [stu:l] *n* **1.** (*seat*) tabouret *m* **2.** *pl* MED (*faeces*) selles *fpl* ►**to fall between two ~s** être assis entre deux chaises

stool pigeon *n Am, pej, inf* balance *f*

stoop [stu:p] **I.** *n no pl* dos *m* rond **II.** *vi* **1.** (*bend the body*) **to ~ down** se baisser; **to ~ to doing sth** *pej* s'abaisser à faire qc **2.** (*to have a bad posture*) se voûter

stop [stɒp, *Am:* stɑ:p] **I.** *n* **1.** (*break in activity*) arrêt *m;* **there were a lot of ~s and starts** il y a eu beaucoup de faux départs; **to come to a ~** s'arrêter; **to put a ~ to sth** mettre fin à qc **2.** (*transport halting place*) arrêt *m;* **bus ~** arrêt de bus **3.** *Brit* LING (*short for full stop*) point *m;* (*in a telegram*) stop *m* **4.** MUS (*knob on an organ*) jeu *m* **II.** <-pping, -pped> *vt* **1.** (*make cease: bleeding, leak*) arrêter; **to ~ sb (from) doing sth** empêcher qn de faire qc **2.** (*refuse payment: payment, production*) cesser; **to ~ (payment on** *Am*) **a check** faire opposition sur un chèque **3.** (*switch off: mechanism, tape recorder*) arrêter **4.** (*block: ball, punch*) arrêter; (*gap, hole*) boucher; (*one's ears*) se boucher **III.** <-pping, -pped> *vi* **1.** (*halt, cease*) s'arrêter; **to ~ doing sth** arrêter de faire qc; **to ~ at nothing** ne s'arrêter devant rien **2.** *Brit* (*stay*) rester

◆**stop by** *vi* passer

◆**stop in** *vi* rester chez soi

◆**stop off** *vi* s'arrêter

◆**stop out** *vi* veiller

◆**stop over** *vi* s'arrêter

◆**stop up** **I.** *vi Brit* veiller **II.** *vt* (*hole, gap*) boucher

stopcock *n* robinet *m* d'arrêt **stopgap** **I.** *n* bouche-trou *m* **II.** *adj* provisoire **stop-go** *n* politique *f* du yoyo **stoplight** *n Am* feu *m* rouge **stopover** *n* (*by plane*) escale *f;* (*by car, train*) halte *f*

stoppage ['stɒpɪdʒ, *Am:* 'stɑ:pɪdʒ] *n* **1.** (*stop*) arrêt *m* **2.** (*cessation of work*) interruption *f* de travail **3.** *pl* FIN, ECON déductions *fpl* de salaire **4.** (*blockage in a pipe*) engorgement *m*

stopper ['stɒpəʳ, *Am:* 'stɑ:pɚ] **I.** *n a. Am, Aus* bouchon *m* **II.** *vt* boucher

stopping train *n* train *m* omnibus

stop press *n* PUBL dépêche *f* **stop sign** *n* stop *m* **stopwatch** *n* chronomètre *m*

storage ['stɔ:rɪdʒ] *n no pl a.* INFOR stockage *m;* **to put sth into ~** entreposer qc; (*furniture*) mettre qc en garde-meubles

storage battery *n* accumulateur *m* **storage capacity** *n* capacité *f* de rangement **storage heater** *n Brit* chauffage *m* à accumulation **storage space** *n* rangement *m* **storage tank** *n* citerne *f*

store [stɔ:ʳ, *Am:* stɔ:r] **I.** *n* **1.** *Brit* (*very large shop*) magasin *m;* **department ~** grand magasin; **liquor ~** magasin de vins et spiritueux **2.** (*supply*) provision *f;* **in ~** en réserve **3.** (*place for keeping supplies*) entrepôt *m;* **in ~** en dépôt; **what is in ~ for sb** ce que réserve l'avenir à qn **4.** (*importance*) importance *f;* **to set great ~ on/by sth** accorder beaucoup d'importance à qc **5.** INFOR mémoire *f* **II.** *vt* INFOR mémoriser

◆**store away** *vt* (*keep for future use*) mettre en réserve; (*furniture, possessions*) mettre en dépôt

store card *n* carte *f* de paiement **store detective** *n* vigile *m* **storefront** *n* devanture *f* de magasin **storehouse** *n Am* **1.** magasin *m* **2.** *fig, form* mine *f* **storekeeper** *n* commerçant(e) *m(f)* **storeroom** *n* débarras *m*

storey ['stɔ:ri] *n Brit, Aus* étage *m*

storeyed, **storied** *adj Am* à étage

stork [stɔ:k, *Am:* stɔ:rk] *n* cigogne *f*

storm [stɔ:m, *Am:* stɔ:rm] **I.** *n* METEO **1.** (*strong wind*) *a. fig* tempête *f* **2.** MIL assaut *m;* **to take sth by ~** *a. fig* prendre qc d'assaut ►**any port in a ~** à la guerre comme à la guerre; **a ~ in a teacup** une tempête dans un verre d'eau **II.** *vi* **1.** *Am* METEO tempêter **2.** (*speak angrily*) fulminer **III.** *vt* prendre d'assaut

◆**storm in** *vi* entrer comme un ouragan

◆**storm out** *vi* quitter comme un ouragan

storm cloud *n a. fig* nuage *m* menaçant

stormy ['stɔ:mi, *Am:* 'stɔ:r-] <-ier, -iest> *adj a. fig* orageux(-euse)

story ['stɔ:ri] <-ries> *n* **1.** (*tale*) histoire *f;* **to tell a bedtime ~** raconter une histoire avant d'aller au lit; **to have a ~ that ...** avoir entendu dire que ...; **sb's side of the ~** la version de qn; **or so the ~ goes** d'après ce que l'on raconte **2.** (*news report*) reportage *m* **3.** (*lie*) histoire *f* **4.** *s.* **storey** ►**it's the ~ of my life** c'est tout à fait moi; **that's my ~ and I'm sticking to it!** j'insiste et j'y tiens!; **it's the same old ~** c'est toujours la même histoire

storybook *adj* LIT romanesque; **to have a ~ ending** finir comme un conte de fée **story line** *n* intrigue *f* **storyteller** *n* conteur, -euse *m, f*

stout¹ [staʊt] *n* stout *f* (*bière brune et amère*)

stout² *adj* **1.** (*thick built*) corpulent(e) **2.** (*strong*) solide **3.** (*determined: person*) résolu(e); (*defender, resistance*) vaillant(e) **4.** (*staunch*) fervent(e)

stoutly ['staʊtli] *adv* **1.** (*strongly*) solidement **2.** (*firmly*) catégoriquement; **to believe ~ in sth** croire dur comme fer à qc

stove [stəʊv, *Am:* stoʊv] *n* **1.** (*heater*) poêle *m* **2.** *Am, Aus* GASTR cuisinière *f*

stow [stəʊ, *Am:* stoʊ] *vt* ranger

◆**stow away** **I.** *vt* ranger **II.** *vi* **1.** (*can be stored*) se ranger **2.** (*travel without paying*) voyager clandestinement

stowage ['stəʊɪdʒ, *Am:* 'stoʊ-] *n no pl* espace *m*

stowaway *n* passager, -ère *m, f* clandestin(e)

straddle ['strædl] *vt* (*moped, horse*) enfourcher; (*a river*) enjamber ►**to ~ an issue** *Am* nager entre deux eaux

straggle ['strægl] *vi* **1.**(*move in a disorganised group*) traîner **2.**(*hang untidily: hair*) être en désordre **3.**(*grow untidily: house*) se disséminer; (*plant*) pousser dans tous les sens

straggler *n* traînard(e) *m(f)*

straggly <-ier, -iest> *adj* en désordre

straight [streɪt] **I.** *n* **1.** SPORT (*part of a race track*) ligne *f* droite; **the finishing ~** la dernière ligne droite **2.** *inf* (*not homosexual*) hétéro *mf* **II.** *adj* **1.**(*without bend*) droit(e); (*hair*) raide; (*route, train*) direct(e); **as ~ as a die** [*o Am* **pin**] être droit comme un piquet **2.**(*honest*) honnête; (*answer*) franc(he); **as ~ as a die** [*o Am* **pin**] d'une honnêteté exemplaire; **to go ~** *inf* marcher droit **3.** *inf* (*not homosexual*) hétéro **4.**(*plain*) simple; **a vodka ~** une vodka pure; **a ~ gin** un gin sec **5.**(*clear*) clair(e) **6.**(*serious*) sérieux(-euse) **III.** *adv* **1.** droit; **~ ahead** droit devant **2.**(*at once*) directement; **to get ~ to the point** aller droit au but **3.** *inf* (*honestly*) directement; **to tell sb ~ (out)** dire carrément à qn; **to play ~ with sb** jouer franc jeu avec qn **4.**(*clearly: see*) clairement; **to think ~** voir clair; **to put sb ~ on sth** éclairer qn sur qc **5.**(*tidy*) **to put sth ~** redresser qc

straightaway *adv* directement

straighten *vt* **1.**(*make straight*) redresser; **to ~ one's hair** raidir ses cheveux; **to ~ one's back/shoulders** se tenir droit **2.**(*make tidy: room*) ranger; (*tie*) ajuster; **to ~ one's hair** se recoiffer

◆**straighten out** **I.** *vi* (*become straight*) devenir droit **II.** *vt* **1.**(*make straight*) redresser **2.**(*put in order*) arranger **3.** *fig* arranger; (*problems*) résoudre

◆**straighten up** **I.** *vi* se redresser **II.** *vt* **1.**(*put straight*) redresser; **to ~ one's body** se redresser **2.**(*put in order*) mettre de l'ordre dans

straightforward *adj* **1.**(*honest*) franc(he) **2.**(*easy*) simple **straight-out** *adj Am, inf* direct(e)

strain[1] [streɪn] **I.** *n no pl* **1.** *no pl* (*pressure*) *a.* PHYS tension *f;* **to put a ~ on sb/sth** exercer une pression sur qn/qc; **to be under a lot of ~** être mis à rude épreuve **2.**(*pulled muscle*) entorse *f;* **back ~** tour *m* de reins **II.** *vi* **to ~ to** +*infin* peiner pour +*infin;* **to ~ for** [*o Brit* **after**] **effect** chercher à faire de l'effet **III.** *vt* **1.** MED, SPORT se fouler; (*muscle, ligament*) se froisser; **to ~ one's back** se faire un tour de reins **2.**(*pressure*) mettre à rude épreuve; **to ~ oneself** se surmener; **to ~ one's ears** tendre l'oreille; **to ~ every nerve** fournir un effort intense; **to ~ the truth** forcer la vérité **3.**(*remove solids from liquids: coffee*) passer; (*vegetables*) égoutter

strain[2] [streɪn] *n* **1.**(*characteristic inherited*) disposition *f;* (*of madness*) prédisposition *f;* (*of humour*) propension *f* **2.**(*line of breed*) espèce *f*

strained *adj* **1.**(*problematic: relations*) tendu(e) **2.**(*forced: smile*) forcé(e)

strainer *n* GASTR passoire *f*

strait [streɪt] *n* **1.** GEO détroit *m* **2.** *pl* (*bad situation*) situation *f* difficile; **to be in dire ~s** être en grande difficulté

straitened *adj form* difficile

straitjacket ['streɪtˌdʒækɪt] *n* camisole *f*

straitlaced [ˌstreɪt'leɪst, *Am:* 'streɪtleɪst] *adj pej* collet monté *inv*

Strait of Dover *n* **the ~** le Pas de Calais

Strait of Gibraltar *n* **the ~** le Détroit de Gibraltar

strand [strænd] *n* **1.**(*thread: wool, cloth, cable*) fil *m;* (*of pearls*) rang *m* **2.**(*lock of hair*) mèche *f* **3.**(*line of development: story*) fil *m*

strange [streɪndʒ] *adj* **1.**(*extraordinary*) étrange; **it's ~ that** c'est bizarre que +*subj;* **~r things have happened** tout peut arriver; **a ~ look on one's face** une drôle d'expression sur son visage **2.**(*not known*) étranger(-ère); (*face*) inconnu(e)

strangely *adv* bizarrement; **~ enough** chose *f* étrange

stranger *n* **1.**(*unknown person*) inconnu(e) *m(f);* **to be complete ~s to sb** être complètement inconnus à qn **2.**(*from another place*) étranger, -ère *m, f;* **hello, ~** salut, le revenant; **to be a ~** ne pas être d'ici; **to be a ~ to sth** ne rien connaître à qc; **no ~ to sth, ...** *form* habitué à qc, ...

strangle ['stræŋgl] *vt* **1.**(*squeeze the neck: person*) étrangler; (*thing*) asphyxier **2.** *fig* (*scream*) étouffer

stranglehold ['strænglhəʊld, *Am:* -hoʊld] *n fig, pej* mainmise *f;* **to have sb in a ~** tenir qn à la gorge

strangulation [ˌstræŋgjʊ'leɪʃən] *n* strangulation *f*

strap [stræp] **I.** *n* **1.**(*strip for fastening*) sangle *f;* (*watch*) bracelet *m;* (*shoe*) lanière *f;* (*bra, top*) bretelle *f* **2.**(*loop for hanging*) poignée *f* **II.** <-pping, -pped> *vt* **to ~ sb/sth to sth** attacher qn/qc à qc

◆**strap in** *vt* attacher

◆**strap up** *vt* bander

strapless *adj* sans bretelles

strapping *adj iron, inf* robuste; **a ~ lad** un gaillard

stratagem ['strætədʒəm, *Am:* 'stræt̬-] *n* stratagème *m*

strategic [strə'tiːdʒɪk] *adj* stratégique

strategist *n* stratège *m*

strategy ['strætədʒi, *Am:* 'stræt̬-] <-ies> *n* stratégie *f*

stratify ['strætɪfaɪ, *Am:* 'stræt̬ə-] *vt a. fig* stratifier

stratosphere ['strætəsfɪəʳ, *Am:* 'stræt̬əsfɪr] *n* stratosphère *f* ►**to go into the ~** monter en flèche

stratum ['streɪtəm, *Am:* 'streɪt̬əm] <strata> *n* **1.** GEO strate *f* **2.**(*division*) couche *f*

straw [strɔː, *Am:* strɑː] *n* **1.** *no pl* (*dry cereal stems*) paille *f;* **a ~ hat** un chapeau de paille; **to draw ~s** tirer à la courte paille **2.** (*drinking tube*) paille *f* ►**to not care a ~** *inf* s'en moquer complètement; **a ~ in the wind** un signe; **to be the ~ that breaks the camel's back** [*o* **to be the last ~**] être la goutte d'eau qui fait déborder le vase; **to clutch at ~s** se raccrocher à de faux espoirs

strawberry ['strɔːbəri, *Am:* 'strɑːˌberi] <-rries> *n* fraise *f*

straw-coloured *adj* jaune paille **straw man** *n* homme *m* de paille **straw poll** *n* sondage *m* d'opinion

stray [streɪ] **I.** *n* animal *m* errant **II.** *adj* **1.** (*homeless*) errant(e) **2.** (*not expected: sentence, house, spot*) isolé(e) **III.** *vi* **1.** (*to go far*) *a. fig* s'éloigner **2.** (*to get lost*) s'égarer; **~ing hands** mains *fpl* baladeuses

streak [striːk] **I.** *n* **1.** (*striped mark*) trace *f;* **dirty ~s** traces **2.** (*hair*) mèche *f* **3.** (*strip*) filet *m;* (*of light*) trait *m* **4.** (*tendency*) tendance *f* **5.** (*run of fortune*) **lucky/winning ~** période *f* de chance; **to be on a winning ~** être dans une bonne passe ►**like a ~ of lightning** comme un éclair **II.** *vt* strier; **to have one's hair ~ed** se faire des mèches; **to be ~ed with black** être veiné de noir **III.** *vi* **to ~ off/out/past** passer/sortir/passer à toute allure

streaker *n personne qui court nu au cours d'événements publics*

streaky <-ier, -iest> *adj* **1.** (*with different colors*) strié(e) **2.** *Brit* GASTR **~ bacon** lard *m*

stream [striːm] **I.** *n* **1.** (*small river*) ruisseau *m* **2.** (*current*) *a. fig* courant *m;* **against the ~** à contre-courant; **to be/come on ~** être/être mis en service **3.** (*flow*) *a. fig* flot *m* **4.** *Brit, Aus* SCHOOL (*group*) groupe *m* de niveau **II.** *vi* **1.** (*flow in liquid*) *a. fig* ruisseler; (*nose, eyes*) couler; **to ~ (with) blood/tears** ruisseler de sang/larmes; **to ~ down one's face** dégouliner sur son visage **2.** (*move in numbers*) **people ~ in/out/away** des flots de gens entrent/sortent/partent **3.** (*shine, spread: light, sun*) entrer à flots **III.** *vt Brit, Aus* SCHOOL **to ~ pupils** répartir les élèves en groupes de niveau

streamer *n* banderole *f*

streamline ['striːmlaɪn] *vt* **1.** (*shape aerodynamically*) caréner **2.** (*improve efficiency*) rationaliser

street [striːt] *n* rue *f;* **at ... Street, in** [*o Am* **on**] **... Street** dans la rue ...; **to lead sb on the ~s** faire descendre qn dans la rue; **to be ~s ahead of sb/sth** être plus avancé que qn/qc; **to take to the ~s** descendre dans les rues ►**the man in the ~** l'homme de la rue; **to be on the ~s** être sur le trottoir; **to be up sb's ~** être le rayon de qn; **to dance in the ~(s) about sth** se réjouir de qc

street battle *n* affrontement *m* **streetcar** *n Am* tramway *m* **streetcred, streetcredibility** *n Brit, Aus* **to have ~** être branché **street door** *n* double porte *f* **streetlamp, streetlight** *n* réverbère *m* **street lighting** *n no pl* éclairage *m* des rues **street people** *n* sans-abri *mpl* **streetwise** *adj* conscient(e) des dangers de la rue

strength [streŋθ] *n* **1.** (*effort, good quality*) *a. fig* force *f;* **to lose ~** perdre de la force; **to be back to full ~** retrouver ses forces; **give me ~!** mon Dieu!; **to gather ~** rassembler ses forces; **to draw ~ from sth** tirer sa force de qc; **on the ~ of sth** en vertu de qc; **to go from ~ to ~** aller de mieux en mieux **2.** (*number*) nombre *m;* **at full ~** au grand complet; **in ~** en nombre; **to be below ~** être en sous-effectif

strengthen ['streŋθən] **I.** *vt* renforcer; (*a wall*) fortifier; (*one's muscles*) développer ►**to ~ one's grip on sth** renforcer son emprise sur qc; **to ~ one's hand** renforcer sa position **II.** *vi* **1.** (*become strong: muscles*) se renforcer **2.** FIN (*stock market, prices*) se raffermir

strenuous ['strenjʊəs, *Am:* -juəs] *adj* **1.** (*physical effort*) fatigant(e); **to take ~ exercises** faire des exercices ardus **2.** (*mental effort: person*) actif(-ive); (*opposition, protest, efforts*) acharné(e)

stress [stres] **I.** *n no pl* **1.** (*mental strain*) tension *f;* **to be under ~** être tendu; **~(es) and strain(s) of modern life** les pressions et tensions de la vie moderne **2.** MED stress *m* **3.** (*importance*) insistance *f;* **to lay ~ on sth** insister sur qc **4.** LING accent *m* tonique **II.** *vt* **1.** (*emphasise*) insister **2.** (*pronounce forcibly*) accentuer

stressed *adj* **1.** (*not relaxed*) stressé(e) **2.** LING accentué(e)

stressful *adj* stressant(e)

stress mark *n* LING accent *m*

stretch [stretʃ] **I.** <-es> *n* **1.** *no pl* (*elasticity*) élasticité *f* **2.** (*muscle extension*) étirement *m;* **to have a ~** s'étirer **3.** GEO étendue *f;* (*of land*) bande *f;* (*of road*) section *f* **4.** (*period*) période *f;* **at a ~** d'affilée; **to do a ten-year ~ behind bars** passer dix ans derrière les barreaux **5.** (*beyond one's skill*) **to work at full ~** (*engine, firm*) tourner à plein régime; (*person*) travailler de toutes ses forces; **by no ~ of imagination** même en faisant un gros effort d'imagination **6.** SPORT ligne *f* droite; **to enter the final ~** entrer dans la dernière ligne droite **II.** *adj* (*fabric, trousers*) extensible; **a ~ limo** une limousine **III.** *vi* **1.** (*become longer or wider: rubber, elastic*) s'étendre; (*clothes*) se détendre **2.** (*extend the muscles*) s'étirer **3.** (*need time*) se prolonger; **to ~ into a date** se prolonger jusqu'à une date; **to ~ back to a date** remonter à une date **4.** (*cover an area*) s'étendre; **to ~ across/along sth** s'étendre à travers/le long de qc; **to ~ for 25 miles** s'étendre sur 25 miles **5.** (*go beyond*) **to ~ to a sum** aller jusqu'à une somme; **to be fully ~ed** être à la limite de ses capacités **IV.** *vt* **1.** (*extend*) étirer; (*hand, arm*) tendre

2. (*extend by pulling: elastic band*) tendre; (*clothes*) détendre 3. (*demand a lot of*) *a. fig* mettre à rude épreuve; (*limits*) outrepasser; **to ~ oneself beyond one's means** vivre au-dessus de ses moyens 4. SPORT **to ~ one's lead** s'avancer en tête 5. (*go beyond*) forcer; **to ~ a point** exagérer; **to ~ it a bit** y aller un peu fort

stretcher *n* brancard *m*

stretcher-bearer *n* brancardier, -ière *m, f*

stretch marks *n* vergetures *fpl*

strew [stru:] <strewn, strewn *o* stewed> *vt* 1. (*scatter*) répandre 2. *fig* joncher

striated ['strieɪtɪd, *Am:* -t̬ɪd] *adj a. fig* strié(e)

strict [strɪkt] *adj* 1. (*harsh*) strict(e); (*penalty, morals*) sévère 2. (*needing conformity*) strict(e); (*censorship, control*) rigoureux(-euse); (*deadline, time limit*) de rigueur; (*guideline*) astreignant(e); (*order*) formel(le) 3. (*complete: secrecy*) absolu(e); (*sense*) précis(e); **in ~est confidence** en toute confidence 4. (*conforming: vegetarian*) vrai(e)

strictly *adv* 1. (*severely*) strictement 2. (*exactly*) exactement; (*forbidden, defined*) strictement; **~ speaking** à proprement parler

stride [straɪd] I. *vi* 1. (*walk*) marcher à grandes enjambées; **to ~ ahead** avancer à grands pas; **to ~ in/out** entrer/sortir à grands pas 2. *fig* **to ~ forward** progresser à grands pas II. *n* 1. (*long step*) enjambée *f*; **to break one's ~** casser la cadence 2. *fig* (*progress*) **to make ~s forward** faire d'énormes progrès *mpl* ►**to get** [*o Am* **hit**] **into one's ~** prendre sa vitesse de croisière; **to put sb off his/her ~** *Brit* faire perdre la cadence à qn; **to take sth in one's** [*o Am* -] **~** faire qc sans le moindre effort

strident ['straɪdnt] *adj* 1. (*harsh*) strident(e) 2. (*confrontational: tone*) véhément(e)

strife [straɪf] *n no pl* conflit *m*

strike [straɪk] I. *n* 1. (*withdrawal of labour*) grève *f*; **a wave of ~s** une vague de grèves; **sit-down ~** grève sur le tas 2. (*sudden attack*) attaque *f*; **air ~** raid *m* 3. (*blow*) coup *m* 4. (*discovery*) découverte *f*; **to make a gold ~** trouver de l'or II. <struck, struck> *vt* 1. (*hit hard*) frapper 2. (*collide with*) tamponner 3. (*ignite: a match*) craquer 4. (*achieve strike*) atteindre; (*a balance*) trouver 5. (*generate harmony*) **to ~ a chord with sb** être sur la même longueur d'onde avec qn 6. (*manufacture: coins*) frapper 7. <struck, struck *o a. Am* stricken> (*engender feelings*) **to ~ fear into sb** remplir qn d'effroi 8. <struck, struck *o a. Am* stricken> (*engender memories*) **to ~ a chord** se rappeler de qc 9. <struck, struck *o a. Am* stricken> (*create atmosphere*) **to ~ a note of warning** donner l'alerte 10. <struck, struck> (*discover deposits*) découvrir; **to ~ oil** atteindre une nappe pétrolifère; (*gold*) remporter 11. **to ~ a pose** poser; *fig* faire des manières 12. <struck, stricken> (*cause suffering*) frapper durement; **an earthquake struck Los Angeles** un tremblement de terre a sévi à Los Angeles 13. (*sound the time*) sonner 14. (*engender thought*) marquer 15. (*remove*) démonter; (*name from a list*) rayer ►**to ~ a blow against sb** infliger un coup à qn; **to ~ the right note** viser juste III. <struck, struck> *vi* 1. (*hit hard*) frapper fort 2. (*attack*) attaquer 3. (*withdraw labour*) se mettre en grève 4. (*sound the time*) sonner ►**to ~ home** frapper juste; **to ~ while the iron is hot** il faut battre le fer tant il est chaud; **I was struck dumb with surprise** la surprise m'a rendu muet

◆**strike back** *vi* rendre un coup; **to ~ at sb** répliquer à qn

◆**strike down** *vt* abattre; **to be struck down by a disease** être terrassé par une maladie; **he was struck down in a couple of hours** il est mort en quelques heures

◆**strike off** *vt Brit, Aus* (*person*) radier; (*name*) rayer; **to strike sb off the register** rayer qn du registre

◆**strike out** I. *vt* 1. (*cancel*) annuler 2. (*delete*) rayer II. *vt* 1. (*start out*) recommencer 2. (*attack*) **to ~ at sb** frapper qn 3. (*criticize*) **to ~ at sb** attaquer qn 4. *Am* (*fail to hit ball*) manquer la balle

◆**strike up** I. *vt* 1. (*start*) commencer; (*a conversation*) entamer; (*a relationship*) se lancer dans 2. (*start music*) se mettre à jouer; (*a song*) entonner II. *vi* commencer

strike action *n* action *f* de grève **strike ballot** *n* appel *m* à la grève **strikebound** *adj* immobilisé(e) par une grève **strikebreaker** *n* briseur, -euse *m, f* de grève **strike call** *s.* strike ballot **strike committee** *n* comité *m* de grève **strike fund** *n* fond *m* de gréviste **strike leader** *n* dirigeant *m* des grévistes **strike pay** *n* salaire *m* de gréviste

striker *n* 1. (*goal scorer*) buteur *m* 2. (*strike participant*) gréviste *mf*

striking *adj* 1. (*noticeable*) saisissant(e); (*beauty, similarity*) frappant(e); (*feature, personality*) saillant(e); (*result*) étonnant(e) 2. (*good-looking*) magnifique ►**within ~ distance** à portée de la main; (*close to achieving results*) à deux doigts de qc

string [strɪŋ] I. *n* 1. (*twine*) ficelle *f* 2. (*wire causing musical notes*) corde *f* 3. *pl* (*orchestral section*) instruments *mpl* à cordes 4. (*chain holding things: of pearls*) collier *m* 5. (*sequence*) série *f*; (*of names*) suite *f* 6. INFOR suite *f*; **search ~** chaîne *f* de recherche ►**to have another ~ to one's bow** avoir plus d'une corde à son arc; **to pull ~s** tirer les ficelles II. <strung, strung> *vt* 1. (*attach strings to: a racket*) corder 2. (*attach objects to chain*) enfiler

◆**string along** *inf* I. *vi* **to ~ with sb** accompagner qn II. *vt Brit, pej* (*trick*) faire marcher

◆**string out** I. *vi* s'espacer II. *vt* 1. (*cause to stretch out: in space*) échelonner; (*in time*)

faire traîner; **to be strung out over a distance** s'échelonner sur une distance **2.** *fig* **to be strung out** (*be nervous, tense*) être à plat; **to be strung out on sth** (*be addicted*) être accro à qc

◆**string up** *vt* **1.** (*hang*) suspendre **2.** *inf* (*execute*) pendre **3.** *inf* (*penalize*) punir

string bag *n* filet *m* à provisions **string band** *n* orchestre *m* à cordes **string bean** *n Am, Aus* haricot *m* vert **stringed instrument** *n* instrument *m* à cordes

stringency ['strɪndʒənsi] *n no pl* **1.** (*strictness*) sévérité *f;* (*of tests*) rigueur *f* **2.** (*tightness: of finances*) resserrement *m*

stringent ['strɪndʒənt] *adj* **1.** (*rigorous*) rigoureux(-euse); (*condition*) strict(e); (*measure*) énergique **2.** (*tight*) sévère

stringer ['strɪŋəʳ, *Am:* -ɚ] *n inf* journaliste *m* local, journaliste *f* locale

string quartet *n* quatuor *m* à cordes

stringy ['strɪŋi] *adj* **1.** GASTR filandreux(-euse) **2.** (*lean: person*) filiforme

strip [strɪp] **I.** *vt* **1.** (*lay bare*) enlever; (*a tree of fruit*) défruiter **2.** (*unclothe*) déshabiller **3.** (*dismantle*) défaire **II.** *vi Am, Aus* (*undress*) se déshabiller **III.** *n* **1.** (*long narrow piece*) bande *f;* (*of metal*) lame *f;* (*of land*) bande *f* **2.** *Brit, Aus* (*soccer team's attire*) couleurs *fpl* **3.** (*striptease*) strip-tease *m* **4.** (*long commercial road*) voie *f*

strip cartoon *n Brit* bande *f* dessinée

stripe [straɪp] *n* **1.** (*coloured band*) rayure *f* **2.** MIL galon *m* ►**of every** ~ de tout genre; **a man of that** ~ *Am* un homme de ce type

striped *adj* à raies; (*shirt*) à rayures

stripey, **stripy** *adj* rayé(e)

strip light *n Brit* lampe *f* **strip lighting** *n* éclairage *m* au néon **strip mining** *n Am* extraction *f* à ciel ouvert

stripper *n* **1.** (*female*) strip-teaseuse *f* **2.** (*male*) strip-teaseur *m* **3.** (*solvent*) décapant *m*

strip-search **I.** *n* fouille *f* d'une personne dévêtue **II.** *vt* faire déshabiller qn pour le fouiller **strip show** *n* spectacle *m* de striptease **striptease** *n* striptease *m*

strive [straɪv] <strove, striven *o* strived, strived> *vi* **to** ~ **to** +*infin* s'efforcer de +*infin;* ~ **as we might** quels que soient nos efforts *subj;* **to** ~ **for sth** essayer d'obtenir qc

strobe *n inf,* **stroboscope** ['strəʊbəskəʊp, *Am:* 'stroʊbəskoʊp] *n* stroboscope *m*

stroboscopic *adj* TECH stroboscopique

strode [strəʊd, *Am:* stroʊd] *pt of* **stride**

stroke [strəʊk, *Am:* stroʊk] **I.** *vt* **1.** (*move hand over*) caresser **2.** (*hit smoothly: the ball*) frapper **II.** *n* **1.** (*gentle caress*) caresse *f* **2.** (*blow*) coup *m;* **at a** (**single**) ~ [*o* **in one** ~] d'un seul coup **3.** MED attaque *f* **4.** (*bit, sign, sound: of luck, fate*) coup *m;* (*of a pen*) trait *m;* **a** ~ **of genius** un trait de génie; **on the** ~ **of three** sur le coup de trois heures; **to give sb a** ~ encourager qn **5.** *form* (*lash with whip*) coup *m* de fouet **6.** (*swimming method*) nage *f;* **breast** ~ brasse *f* **7.** *no pl, in neg, inf* (*unit of labour*) **she hasn't done a** ~ **of work today** elle n'a pas fait grand chose aujourd'hui **8.** (*oblique sign*) barre *f* ►**to put sb off one's** ~ déconcentrer qn

stroll [strəʊl, *Am:* stroʊl] **I.** *n* petite promenade *f* **II.** *vi* **1.** (*amble*) flâner **2.** (*easily win*) être une promenade de santé

stroller *n* **1.** (*person*) promeneur, -euse *m, f* **2.** *Am, Aus* (*pushchair*) poussette *f*

strong [strɒŋ, *Am:* strɑːŋ] **I.** *adj* **1.** (*powerful: person, wind, currency*) fort(e); (*defence, country, athlete*) puissant(e) **2.** (*concentrated: coffee, alcohol*) fort(e); (*medicine*) puissant(e); (*competition*) serré(e) **3.** (*sturdy, durable*) solide; **to be as** ~ **as a horse** être fort comme un bœuf **4.** (*healthy*) vigoureux(-euse); (*constitution*) robuste **5.** (*intense: desire*) fort(e); (*will, influence*) grand(e) **6.** (*deep-rooted*) tenace; (*antipathy*) grand(e); (*bias, fear, opinion*) fort(e); (*bond*) extraordinaire; **she is a** ~ **person** c'est qn qui a du ressort **7.** (*very likely*) fort(e); (*chance*) grand(e) **8.** (*having number*) **they were 200** ~ ils/elles étaient au nombre de deux cents **9.** (*marked*) marqué(e); **to have a** ~ **accent** avoir un fort accent **10.** (*bright: colour*) vif(vive) **11.** (*pungent*) fort(e); (*flavour*) relevé(e); (*language*) grossier(-ère) **II.** *adv* **to come on** ~ draguer; **to be still going** ~ se porter toujours bien

strong-arm *adj pej* ~ **method** méthode *f* forte **strongbox** *n* coffre-fort *m*

stronghold ['strɒŋhəʊld, *Am:* 'strɑːŋhoʊld] *n* **1.** (*bastion*) bastion *m* **2.** (*asylum*) asile *m*

strongly *adv* **1.** (*solidly*) *a. fig* solidement; ~ **built** de constitution robuste **2.** (*powerfully*) fortement; (*establish, believe*) fermement; (*advise*) vivement; (*condemn, criticize*) sévèrement; (*disapprove*) profondément; (*deny*) vigoureusement

strong-minded *adj* résolu(e) **strongroom** *n* chambre *f* forte **strong-willed** *adj* **to be** ~ avoir de la volonté

strop [strɒp, *Am:* strɑːp] *n Brit, Aus, inf* cuir *m* (à rasoir)

stroppy *adj Brit, Aus, inf* **to get** ~ monter sur ses grands chevaux

strove [strəʊv, *Am:* stroʊv] *pt of* **strive**

struck [strʌk] *pt, pp of* **strike**

structural *adj* **1.** (*of organisation*) structurel(le) **2.** (*state of buildings*) de construction

structure ['strʌktʃəʳ, *Am:* -tʃɚ] **I.** *n* **1.** structure *f* **2.** (*building*) bâtiment *m* **3.** (*constructed form*) construction *f* **II.** *vt* structurer

struggle ['strʌgl] **I.** *n* **1.** (*great effort*) lutte *f;* **without a** ~ sans résistance **2.** (*skirmish*) conflit *m* **II.** *vi* **1.** (*exert oneself*) lutter; **to** ~ **to one's feet** se lever avec difficulté; **to** ~ **to** +*infin* avoir de la difficulté à +*infin* **2.** (*fight*) se débattre; **to** ~ **with sb/sth** être aux prises avec qn/qc; *fig* avoir des difficultés avec qn/qc **3.** (*resist*) résister

strum [strʌm] <-mm-> MUS **I.** *vt* gratter **II.** *vi* pincer les cordes **III.** *n* son *m*

strung [strʌŋ] *pt, pp of* **string**

strut [strʌt] **I.** <-tt-> *vi* parader **II.** *vt* **to ~ one's stuff** *iron, inf* danser de façon provocante **III.** *n* support *m*

strychnine ['strɪkniːn, *Am:* -naɪn] *n no pl* strychine *f*

stub [stʌb] **I.** *n* **1.** (*counterfoil*) bout *m* **2.** (*cigarette but*) mégot *m* **3.** (*short pencil*) bout *m* de crayon **II.** <-bb-> *vt* **to ~ one's toes** se cogner le pied

stubble ['stʌbl] *n no pl* **1.** (*beard growth*) barbe *f* de plusieurs jours **2.** (*crop remnants*) chaume *m*

stubbly *adj* **1.** (*bristly*) mal rasé(e) **2.** (*of ground after harvesting*) couvert(e) de chaume

stubborn ['stʌbən, *Am:* -ɚn] *adj pej* têtu(e); (*problem, stain*) tenace; **to be ~ as a mule** être têtu comme une mule

stubby ['stʌbi] **I.** *adj* (*finger*) boudiné(e); (*leg*) gros(se); **~ tail** un bout de queue **II.** *n* *Aus* petite bouteille *f* de bière

STUC *n abbr of* **Scottish Trades Union Congress** *Congrès des syndicats écossais*

stucco ['stʌkəʊ, *Am:* -oʊ] *n no pl* stuc *m*

stuck [stʌk] *pt, pp of* **stick**

stuck-up *adj pej, inf* prétentieux(-euse)

stud[1] [stʌd] *n* **1.** (*horses*) étalon *m* **2.** (*establishment*) haras *m* **3.** *inf* (*man*) tombeur *m*

stud[2] [stʌd] *n* **1.** (*small metal item*) clou *m* pour ornement **2.** *Brit, Aus* (*on shoes*) caboche *f* **3.** (*attaching device*) bouton *m* de chemise **4.** *Am* (*for driving in snow*) chaînes *fpl*

student ['stjuːdənt, *Am:* 'stuː-] *n* étudiant(e) *m(f)*

student teacher *n* élève *mf* professeur **student union** *n* **1.** (*organisation*) association *f* des étudiants **2.** (*meeting place*) lieu *m* de rencontre des étudiants

stud farm *n* haras *m* **stud horse** *n* étalon *m*

studied ['stʌdɪd] *adj* étudié(e); (*answer, politeness*) calculé(e); (*elegance*) recherché(e); (*insult*) délibéré(e)

studio ['stjuːdiəʊ, *Am:* 'stuːdioʊ] <-s> *n* **1.** (*atelier*) atelier *m* **2.** (*firm*) studio *m* **3.** (*room*) studio *m* (d'enregistrement)

studio audience *n* public *m* présent lors d'un enregistrement **studio couch** *n* lit *m* canapé

studious ['stjuːdiəs, *Am:* 'stuː-] *adj* **1.** (*scholarly*) studieux(-euse) **2.** (*careful*) appliqué(e)

study ['stʌdi] **I.** *vt* étudier **II.** *vi* faire des études **III.** <-ies> *n* **1.** (*investigation*) étude *f* **2.** (*academic investigation*) recherche *f* **3.** *pl* (*learning*) études *fpl* **4.** (*room*) bureau *m* de travail **5.** (*literary treatment*) étude *f* de texte

study group *n* groupe *m* d'étude **study visit** *n* visite *f* d'étude

stuff [stʌf] **I.** *n* **1.** *no pl, inf* (*thing*) truc *m;* **it's boring ~** c'est ennuyeux **2.** (*things*) trucs *mpl;* **to write good ~** écrire bien **3.** (*belongings*) affaires *fpl* **4.** *no pl* (*basic characteristics*) essence *f* **5.** (*one's knowledge*) **to know one's ~** s'y connaître **6.** (*material*) étoffe *f* **7.** *Brit, vulg* (*attractive female*) **bit of ~** nana *f* **8.** *inf* (*drugs*) came *f* **II.** *vt* **1.** (*fill*) *a. fig* remplir; (*cushion*) rembourrer; (*animals*) empailler; **to ~ sth into sth** fourrer qc dans qc; **to ~ sb's head with sth** bourrer la tête de qn avec qc **2.** *inf* (*eat greedily*) **to ~ oneself** s'empiffrer; **to ~ down** engloutir **3.** GASTR farcir; **~ed tomatoes** tomates farcies **4.** *Brit, Aus, vulg* (*have sex with*) se farcir; **get ~ed!** va te faire foutre! **III.** *vi* se goinfrer

stuffed shirt *n pej* prétentieux, -euse *m, f*

stuffing *n no pl* **1.** (*padding*) rembourrage *m* **2.** (*food mixture*) farce *f*

stuffy *adj pej* **1.** (*stodgy*) collet monté *inv* **2.** (*unventilated*) mal ventilé(e)

stultify ['stʌltɪfaɪ, *Am:* -t̬ə-] <-ie-> *vt pej* abrutir

stultifying *adj* abrutissant(e)

stumble ['stʌmbl] **I.** *n* faux pas *m* **II.** *vi* **1.** (*trip*) trébucher; **to ~ in/out** entrer/sortir en trébuchant **2.** (*falter during talking*) **to ~ over sth** buter sur qc

stumbling block *n* obstacle *m*

stump [stʌmp] **I.** *n* **1.** (*remaining tree end*) souche *f* **2.** (*remainder: of an arm*) moignon *m* **II.** *vt* déconcerter; **to be ~ed by sth** être incapable de répondre à qc **III.** *vi* **1.** (*walk stifly*) **to ~ in/out** entrer/sortir à pas lourds; **to ~ into sth** entrer à pas lourds dans qc **2.** POL faire campagne

stumpy *adj pej, inf* (*person*) boulot(te); (*finger, legs*) boudiné(e)

stun [stʌn] <-nn-> *vt* **1.** (*shock*) stupéfier; **~ed silence** silence surprenant **2.** (*make unconscious*) assommer

stung [stʌŋ] *pp, pt of* **sting**

stun grenade *n* MIL grenade *f* incapacitante

stunk [stʌŋk] *pt, pp of* **stink**

stunned *adj* surpris(e)

stunner *n inf* **1.** (*sth very surprising*) truc *m* incroyable **2.** (*attractive person*) canon *m*

stunning *adj* **1.** (*that stuns*) bouleversant(e) **2.** (*dazzling*) sensationnel(le); (*dress*) magnifique

stunt[1] [stʌnt] *n* **1.** (*dangerous act for films*) cascade *f* **2.** *pej* (*action for publicity*) **advertising/publicity ~** coup *m* de pub **3.** *fig, inf* **to pull a ~** faire un truc pareil

stunt[2] [stʌnt] *vt* ralentir

stunted *adj* rabougri(e); **to become ~** se rabougrir

stuntman <-men> *n* cascadeur *m* **stuntwoman** <-men> *n* cascadeuse *f*

stupefaction [ˌstjuːpɪ'fækʃən, *Am:* ˌstuːpə'-] *n no pl, form* stupéfaction *f*

stupefied *adj* stupéfait(e)

S

stupefy ['stju:pɪfaɪ, *Am:* 'stu:pə-] <-ie-> *vt* stupéfier

stupendous [stju:'pendəs, *Am:* stu:-] *adj* prodigieux(-euse)

stupid ['stju:pɪd, *Am:* 'stu:-] **I.** *adj* <-er, -est *o* more ~, most ~> stupide; **to drink oneself ~** s'abrutir d'alcool **II.** *n inf* idiot(e) *m(f)*

stupidity [stju:'pɪdəti, *Am:* stu:'pɪdət̬i] *n no pl* stupidité *f*

stupor ['stju:pəʳ, *Am:* 'stu:pɚ] *n sing* stupeur *f*

sturdy ['stɜ:di, *Am:* 'stɜ:r-] *adj* robuste

sturgeon ['stɜ:dʒən, *Am:* 'stɜ:r-] *n* esturgeon *m*

stutter ['stʌtəʳ, *Am:* 'stʌt̬ɚ] **I.** *vt, vi* bégayer **II.** *n* bégaiement *m*

stutterer *n* bègue *mf*

sty¹ [staɪ] *n* (*pigsty*) porcherie *f*

sty², **stye** [staɪ] *n* MED orgelet *m*

style [staɪl] **I.** *n* **1.** style *m;* **~ of living** style de vie; **to have real ~** avoir du style; **in ~** en grande pompe; **to do things in ~** faire les choses bien; **to live in ~** mener grand train **2.** (*fashion*) mode *f;* **in ~** à la mode; **the latest ~** les dernières tendances; **to go out of ~** passer de mode **3.** *fig, inf* genre *m;* **not to be sb's ~** ne pas être le genre de qn **II.** *vt* dessiner; **elegantly ~d jackets** vestes élégamment coupées; **to ~ hair** coiffer ses cheveux

styling *n* façon *f* de s'habiller; **hair ~** coiffure *f;* **~ mousse** mousse *f* de coiffage

stylish *adj* qui a du style

stylist *n* styliste *mf;* **hair ~** coiffeur, -euse *m, f*

stylistic *adj* stylistique

stylize ['staɪəlaɪz, *Am:* 'staɪlaɪz] *vt* styliser

stylus ['staɪləs] <-es> *n* saphir *m*

stymie ['staɪmi] <-ing *o* stymying> *vt* coincer; (*sb's efforts*) stopper

suave [swɑ:v] *adj* mielleux(-euse)

sub [sʌb] **I.** *n* **1.** *Brit, Aus, inf abbr of* **substitute** **2.** *inf abbr of* **submarine** **3.** *Am, inf abbr of* **submarine sandwich** (*long sandwich*) ≈ sandwich *m* baguette **4.** *Brit, Aus, inf abbr of* **subscription** **II.** <-bb-> *vi abbr of* **substitute** faire un remplacement; **to ~ for sb** remplacer qn

subaltern ['sʌbltən, *Am:* səb'ɔ:ltɚn] *n Brit* MIL subalterne *mf*

subclass *n* sous-classe *f* **subcommittee** *n* sous-comité *m* **subconscious** **I.** *n no pl* subconscient *m* **II.** *adj* subconscient(e); **~ mind** subconscient *m* **subcontinent** *n* sous-continent *m* **subcontract** *vt* sous-traiter; **to ~ sth to sb/sth** sous-traiter qc à qn/qc **subcontractor** *n* sous-traitant *m* **subculture** *n* culture *f* parallèle **subcutaneous** *adj* sous-cutané(e) **subdivide** *vt* sous-diviser; **to ~ sth into sth** sous-diviser qc en qc **subdivision** *n* **1.** (*second division*) subdivision *f* **2.** *Am, Aus* (*housing estate*) résidence *f*

subdue [səb'dju:, *Am:* -'du:] *vt* **1.** (*get under control*) maîtriser; (*person*) assujettir **2.** (*repress*) réprimer

subdued *adj* (*person*) calme; (*voice*) bas(se); (*color, light*) doux(douce)

subheading *n* sous-titre *m*

subject ['sʌbdʒɪkt] **I.** *n* **1.** sujet *m;* **~ matter** sujet; **~ for discussion** sujet de discussion; **~ for debate** matière *f* à débat; **to be on the ~ of sb/sth** être à propos de qn/qc; **on the ~ of relationships** sur le thème des relations; **to take sth as one's ~** choisir qc comme sujet **2.** SCHOOL, UNIV matière *f* **II.** *adj* **1.** (*dominated*) soumis(e) **2.** (*exposed to negative factor*) sujet(te); **to be ~ to sth** être sujet à qc; **to be ~ to a danger** s'exposer à un danger; **~ to a law** LAW soumis à la loi ►**~ to sth** sous réserve de qc; **~ to payment** moyennant paiement **III.** *vt* assujettir

subjection [səb'dʒekʃən] *n no pl* POL soumission *f;* **to be in ~ to sb/sth** être assujetti à qn/qc

subjective [səb'dʒektɪv] *adj* subjectif(-ive)

subjugate ['sʌbdʒəgeɪt] *vt* assujettir; **to ~ oneself** s'assujettir

subjunctive [səb'dʒʌŋktɪv] *n no pl* subjonctif *m*

sublease, **sub-lease** **I.** *vt* sous-louer **II.** *n* sous-location *f* **sublet** <subletting; sublet, sublet> **I.** *vt* sous-louer **II.** *n* sous-location *f* **sublieutenant** *n Brit* sous-lieutenant *m*

sublimate ['sʌblɪmeɪt] *vt form* sublimer

sublime [sə'blaɪm] **I.** *adj* **1.** (*glorious*) sublime **2.** *iron* (*absolute*) sans pareil **II.** *n* sublime *m*

subliminal *adj* subliminal(e)

submarine **I.** *n* sous-marin *m* **II.** *adj* sous-marin(e)

submerge [səb'mɜ:dʒ, *Am:* -'mɜ:rdʒ] **I.** *vt* **1.** (*put under water*) *a. fig* immerger; **to ~ oneself in sth** se plonger dans qc **2.** (*inundate*) *a. fig* submerger; **to be ~d with work** être submergé de travail **II.** *vi* plonger; **~d fields** champs *mpl* inondés; **the ~d parts of one's personality** la face cachée de la personnalité de qn

submersible [səb'mɜ:sɪbl, *Am:* -'mɜ:rsəbl] **I.** *n* submersible *m* **II.** *adj* submersible

submersion [səb'mɜ:ʒən, *Am:* -'mɜ:rʒən] *n no pl* submersion *f*

submission [səb'mɪʃən] *n no pl* soumission *f;* **to bomb sb into ~** réduire qn par les bombes; **to force/frighten sb into ~** soumettre qn par la force/la terreur; **to starve sb into ~** réduire qn à la famine

submissive [səb'mɪsɪv] *adj* soumis(e)

submit [səb'mɪt] <-tt-> **I.** *vt* soumettre; **to ~ that ...** *form* alléguer que ... **II.** *vi* **to ~ to sb/sth** se soumettre à qn/qc

subnormal *adj* au-dessous de la normale; (*person*) arriéré(e) **subordinate** **I.** *n* subordonné(e) *m(f)* **II.** *vt* subordonner **III.** *adj* **1.** (*secondary*) subordonné(e) **2.** (*lower in rank*) subalterne

subordination *n no pl* subordination *f*

subpoena [sə'pi:nə] LAW **I.** *vt* assigner à com-

paraître **II.** *n* assignation *f*
subregion *n* sous-région *f*
subscribe [səb'skraɪb] **I.** *vt* verser **II.** *vi* **to ~ to sth** s'abonner à qc
◆subscribe to *vt* souscrire à
subscriber *n* abonné(e) *m(f)*
subscript [sʌb'skrɪpt] *adj* TYP indice *m*
subscription *n* abonnement *m;* **~ to a magazine** abonnement à un magazine; **to buy a ~ to a club** offrir une adhésion à un club; **to take out a ~ to sth** s'abonner à qc
subsection *n* subdivision *f* **subsequent** *adj* **1.** (*following*) ultérieur(e); **~ to sth** ultérieur à qc **2.** (*resulting*) consécutif(-ive); **~ to sth** suite à qc **subsequently** *adv* par la suite; **~ to sth** à la suite de qc **subservient** *adj pej* servile; **to be ~ to sb/sth** être soumis à qn/qc **subset** *n* sous-ensemble *m*
subside [səb'saɪd] *vi* **1.** (*abate*) diminuer **2.** (*cave in*) s'affaisser
subsidence [səb'saɪdns] *n no pl* affaissement *m*
subsidiary [səb'sɪdɪəri, *Am:* -əri] **I.** *adj* subsidiaire; (*reason*) accessoires; **~ company** filiale *f* **II.** <-ies> *n* ECON filiale *f*
subsidize ['sʌbsɪdaɪz, *Am:* -sə-] *vt Am* subventionner
subsidy ['sʌbsədi, *Am:* -sə-] <-ies> *n* subvention *f*
subsist [səb'sɪst] *vi form* subsister; **to ~ by doing sth** subsister en faisant qc; **to ~ on sth** vivre de qc
subsistance *n form* subsistance *f*
subsistance allowance *n* frais *mpl* de subsistance **subsistance level** *n* minimum *m* vital; **to live at ~ level** avoir tout juste de quoi vivre
subsoil *n* sous-sol *m*
substance ['sʌbstəns] *n a. fig* substance *f*
substandard *adj* de qualité inférieure; **~ quality** qualité *f* médiocre
substantial [səb'stænʃl] *adj* **1.** (*important*) substantiel(le) **2.** (*real, general*) tangible; **to be in ~ agreement** être d'accord dans l'ensemble
substantially *adv* considérablement
substantiate [səb'stænʃɪeɪt] *vt form* corroborer
substantive ['sʌbstəntɪv, *Am:* -t̬ɪv] **I.** *adj form* substantiel(le) **II.** *n* substantif *m*
substation ['sʌbsteɪʃən] *n* station *f;* **police ~** *Am* poste *m* de police
substitute ['sʌbstɪtju:t, *Am:* -stətu:t] **I.** *vt* remplacer; **to ~ sb/sth for sb/sth** [*o* **with**] remplacer qn/qc par qn/qc **II.** *vi* **to ~ for sb/sth** remplacer qn/qc **III.** *n* **1.** (*equivalent*) produit *m* de substitution; **~ for sth** succédané *m* de qc; **a meat ~** un succédané de viande; **there's no ~ for sb/sth** rien ne peut remplacer qn/qc; **a poor ~ for sth** un ersatz de qc **2.** (*replacement player*) remplaçant(e) *m(f);* **a ~ teacher** un(e) remplaçant(e); **to come on as a ~** venir en remplacement
substitution *n* **1.** (*replacing*) remplacement *m* **2.** LAW substitution *f*
subsume [səb'sju:m, *Am:* -'su:m] *vt form* incorporer; **to ~ sb/sth into sth** incorporer qn/qc à qc
subtenant *n* sous-locataire *mf*
subterfuge ['sʌbtəfju:dʒ, *Am:* -tɚ-] *n* subterfuge *m;* **to resort to ~** user d'un subterfuge
subterranean *adj a. fig* souterrain(e) **subtitle I.** *vt* sous-titrer **II.** *n* sous-titre *m* **subtitling** *n* sous-titrage *m*
subtle ['sʌtl, *Am:* 'sʌt̬-] *adj* subtil(e)
subtlety ['sʌtlti, *Am:* 'sʌt̬l̬t̬i] <-ies> *n* subtilité *f*
subtotal *n* sous-total *m*
subtract [səb'trækt] *vt* **to ~ sth from sth** soustraire qc de qc
subtraction *n no pl* soustraction *f*
subtropical *adj* subtropical(e)
suburb ['sʌbɜ:b, *Am:* -ɜ:rb] *n* banlieue *f,* quartier *m* périphérique *Suisse;* **the ~s** la banlieue; **to live in the ~s** vivre en banlieue
suburban [sə'bɜ:bən, *Am:* -'bɜ:r-] *adj* de banlieue; **~ commuters** banlieusards *mpl*
suburbanite *n* banlieusard(e) *m(f)*
suburbia [sə'bɜ:bɪə, *Am:* -'bɜ:r-] *n no pl, pej* banlieue *f*
subvention [səb'venʃən] *n form* subvention *f*
subversion [səb'vɜ:ʃən, *Am:* -'vɜ:rʒən] *n no pl, form* subversion *f*
subversive [səb'vɜ:sɪv, *Am:* -'vɜ:r-] *form* **I.** *adj* subversif(-ive) **II.** *n* individu *m* subversif
subversively *adv form* subversivement
subvert [sʌb'vɜ:t, *Am:* -'vɜ:rt] *vt* **1.** (*overturn government*) renverser **2.** (*weaken principle*) déstabiliser **3.** (*corrupt*) faire échouer; **to ~ the best intentions** contrecarrer les meilleures intentions
subway *n* **1.** *Brit, Aus* (*walkway*) passage *m* souterrain **2.** *Am* (*railway*) métro *m* **subzero** *adj* au-dessous de zéro
succeed [sək'si:d] **I.** *vi* **1.** (*achieve one's purpose*) réussir; **~ in doing sth** réussir à faire qc; **the plan ~ed** le plan a marché **2.** (*follow*) **to ~ to sth** succéder à qc ►**if at first you don't ~, then try, try again** *prov* il faut persévérer dans l'effort **II.** *vt* **to ~ sb as sth** succéder à qn en tant que qc; **to ~ sb in sth** succéder à qn à qc
success [sək'ses] *n* succès *m;* **without much ~** sans grand succès; **a ~ rate** un taux de réussite; **to be a big ~ with sb/sth** remporter un grand succès avec qn/qc; **to have ~ in doing sth** réussir à faire qc; **to make a ~ of sth** réussir qc; **to be a great ~** avoir beaucoup de succès; **to achieve ~** obtenir du succès; **to enjoy ~** remporter du succès; **box-office ~** succès au box-office
successful *adj* qui a du succès; (*book, film, artist*) à succès; (*business, season*) prospère; (*harvest, marriage, participant*) heureux(-euse); (*plan, career*) couronné(e) de succès; **to be ~** avoir du succès; **to be ~ in**

S

doing sth réussir à faire qc; **commercially** ~ lucratif(-ive)

successfully *adv* avec succès

succession [sək'seʃən] *n no pl* succession *f;* ~ **to the throne** succession au trône; **in** ~ successivement

successive [sək'sesɪv] *adj* successif(-ive)

successively *adv* successivement

successor *n* successeur *m;* ~ **to sb** successeur de qn; ~ **to the throne** héritier *m* du trône

success story *n* histoire *f* d'une réussite

succinct [sək'sɪŋkt] *adj* succinct(e)

succinctly *adv* succinctement

succinctness *n* concision *f*

succor *Am, Aus* **I.** *n form* secours *m;* **to bring** ~ **to sb** porter secours à qn **II.** *vt form* secourir

succour *Brit, Aus s.* **succor**

succulence *n* succulence *f*

succulent ['sʌkjʊlənt] *adj* succulent(e)

succumb [sə'kʌm] *vi form* succomber; **to** ~ **to sb/sth** succomber à qn/qc

such [sʌtʃ] **I.** *adj* tel(le); ~ **an idiot** un tel idiot; **there is no** ~ **things as this** cela n'existe pas; **in** ~ **a way that ...** d'une telle façon que ...; **in** ~ **a situation** dans une situation pareille; **or some** ~ **remark** ou une remarque dans le genre; **to buy some fruit** ~ **as apples** acheter des fruits comme des pommes **II.** *pron* ~ **is life** ainsi va la vie; **people** ~ **as him** des gens comme lui; ~ **as it is** tel(le) qu'il(elle) est; **as** ~ en tant que tel(le); **to be recognized as** ~ être reconnu comme tel; **... and** ~ ... et des autres choses de ce genre **III.** *adv* si; ~ **great weather/a good book** un si beau temps/bon livre; ~ **a lot of problems** tant de problèmes; **to have** ~ **a good time** bien s'amuser

such-and-such *adj inf* tel(le); **to arrive at** ~ **a time** arriver à telle heure

suchlike *pron* de ce genre; **and** ~ et les choses de ce genre

suck [sʌk] **I.** *vt* **1.** (*drink in: water, air*) aspirer; **to** ~ **a liquid through a straw** aspirer un liquide avec une paille **2.** (*draw into mouth: lollilop, thumb*) sucer; (*breast*) téter **3.** (*strongly move*) entraîner; **to be** ~**ed into sth** *fig* être entraîné dans qc ►**to** ~ **sb dry** sucer jusqu'à la moelle; ~ **it and see** *Brit* essaye **II.** *vi* **1.** (*draw: into mouth*) sucer; (*baby*) téter; (*pump*) aspirer; **to** ~ **on** [*o* **at**] **sth** sucer qc; (*one's pipe*) tirer sur **2.** *inf* (*bore*) faire chier; **this film** ~**s** ce film est chiant **III.** *n* tétée *f;* **to have a** ~ **at sth** sucer qc; **to give a** ~ **to sb** allaiter qn

◆**suck in** *vt* **1.** (*draw*) aspirer; (*with mouth*) sucer; (*cheeks*) creuser **2.** *fig* **to get sucked in** se laisser entraîner

◆**suck up I.** *vi inf* faire de la lèche; **to** ~ **to sb** cirer les pompes à qn **II.** *vt* aspirer; (*water*) pomper

sucker ['sʌkəʳ, *Am:* -ɚ] **I.** *n* **1.** (*sticking device*) ventouse *f* **2.** *pej, inf* (*gullible person*) nigaud(e) *m(f);* **to be a** ~ **for sth** ne pas pouvoir résister à qc **3.** *Am, pej, vulg* (*nasty person*) connard, -asse *m, f* **4.** *inf* (*thing, person not specified*) machin *m* **5.** *Am, Aus, inf* (*lollipop*) sucette *f* **6.** BOT surgeon *m* **II.** *vt Am* avoir; **to** ~ **sb out of dix dollars** avoir qn de 10 dollars; **to** ~ **sb into doing sth** embobiner qn pour qu'il/elle fasse qc +*subj*

sucking pig *n* cochon *m* de lait

suckle ['sʌkl] <-ling-> **I.** *vt* allaiter **II.** *vi* téter

sucrose ['suːkrəʊs, *Am:* -kroʊs] *n no pl* saccharose *f*

suction ['sʌkʃən] *n no pl* **1.** (*act of sucking*) succion *f* **2.** (*forcing matter inwards*) aspiration *f*

Sudan [suː'dæn] *n* le Soudan

Sudanese [ˌsuːdə'niːz] **I.** *adj* soudanais(e) **II.** *n* Soudanais(e) *m(f)*

sudden ['sʌdən] *adj* soudain(e); **to put a** ~ **stop to sth** mettre un terme brusque à qc; **all of a** ~ *inf* tout d'un coup

suddenly *adv* soudainement

suds [sʌdz] *npl* mousse *f*

sue [sjuː, *Am:* suː] <suing> **I.** *vt* **to** ~ **sb for sth** poursuivre qn (en justice) pour qc **II.** *vi* engager une procédure judiciaire; **to** ~ **for divorce** entamer une procédure de divorce; **to** ~ **for sth** engager des poursuites pour qc

suede [sweɪd] *n* daim *m*

suet ['suːɪt] *n no pl* graisse *f* de rognon

suffer ['sʌfəʳ, *Am:* -ɚ] **I.** *vi* **1.** (*feel pain*) souffrir; **to** ~ **from sth** souffrir de qc **2.** (*experience*) subir; **to** ~ **from sth** subir les conséquences de qc; **the economy** ~**ed from the strike** l'économie a souffert des conséquences de la grève **3.** (*be punished*) **to** ~ **for sth** payer pour qc **II.** *vt* **1.** (*experience*) subir; (*a defeat, setback*) essuyer; **to not** ~ **fools gladly** perdre patience avec les imbéciles **2.** MED souffrir de **3.** (*tolerate*) souffrir

sufferance ['sʌfərəns] *n* tolérance *f;* **to be on** ~ être toléré

sufferer ['sʌfərəʳ, *Am:* -ɚɚ] *n* malade *mf;* **to be an AIDS** ~ être malade du sida; **to be an asthma** ~ souffrir d'asthme

suffering *n* souffrance *f*

suffice [sə'faɪs] *vi* suffire; ~ (**it**) **to say that ...** il suffit de dire que ...

sufficiency [sə'fɪʃnsi] *n no pl, iron, form* suffisance *f;* **to have a** ~ avoir assez mangé

sufficient *adj* suffisant(e); **to be** ~ **for sb/sth** suffire pour qn/qc; ~ **money/evidence/food to** +*infin* suffisamment d'argent/de preuves/de nourriture pour +*infin*

suffix ['sʌfɪks] *n* LING suffixe *m*

suffocate ['sʌfəkeɪt] *a. fig* **I.** *vi* suffoquer **II.** *vt a. fig* étouffer; **to feel** ~**d** étouffer

suffocating *adj a. fig* étouffant(e)

suffrage ['sʌfrɪdʒ] *n no pl, no indef art* droit *m* de vote; **female** ~ droit *m* de vote des femmes; **universal** ~ suffrage *m* universel

sugar ['ʃʊgəʳ, *Am:* -ɚ] **I.** *n* **1.** (*sweetener*) sucre *m;* **caster** ~ sucre en poudre; **granulated** ~ sucre cristallisé; **icing** ~ sucre glace;

brown ~ sucre roux; **demerara** ~ cassonade *f;* **a lump/spoonful of** ~ un morceau/une cuillerée de sucre **2.** *Am, inf* (*term of affection*) mon chéri, ma chérie *m, f* **3.** (*said to show annoyance*) zut ►**to be all ~ and spice** être tout sucre et tout miel **II.** *vt* sucrer

sugar beet *n* betterave *f* à sucre **sugar bowl** *n* sucrier *m* **sugar cane** *n* canne *f* à sucre **sugar-coat** *vt* dragéifier **sugar-coated** *adj* **1.** (*with layer of sweetener*) dragéifié(e); **a ~ almond** une dragée **2.** *fig, pej* (*pleasant*) mielleux(-euse) **sugar cube** *n* morceau *m* de sucre **sugar daddy** *n* vieux protecteur *m* **sugar-free** *adj* sans sucre **sugar lump** *n* morceau *m* de sucre **sugar tongs** *npl* pince *f* à sucre

sugary [ˈʃʊgəri] *adj* **1.** (*made of sugar*) sucré(e) **2.** *fig, pej* (*insincerely kind*) mielleux(-euse)

suggest [səˈdʒest, *Am:* səgˈ-] *vt* **1.** (*propose*) suggérer; **to ~ (that) sb does sth** suggérer à qn de faire qc; **to ~ doing sth** suggérer de faire qc **2.** (*show*) laisser supposer **3.** (*come to mind*) **to ~ itself** (*idea, inspiration*) venir à l'esprit

suggestible *adj pej, form* influençable

suggestion [səˈdʒestʃən, *Am:* səgˈdʒes-] *n* **1.** (*proposed idea*) suggestion *f;* **at sb's ~** sur le conseil de qn **2.** (*small amount*) soupçon *m* **3.** PSYCH (*insinuation*) suggestion *f*

suggestion box *n* boîte *f* à idées

suggestive [səˈdʒestɪv, *Am:* səgˈ-] *adj* (*lewd*) suggestif(-ive)

suicidal [ˌsjuːɪˈsaɪdl, *Am:* ˌsuːəˈ-] *adj a. fig* suicidaire; **to feel ~** avoir des envies suicidaires

suicide [ˈsjuːɪsaɪd, *Am:* ˈsuːə-] **I.** *n* **1.** (*killing oneself*) *a. fig* suicide *m;* **to commit ~** se suicider; **to attempt ~** faire une tentative de suicide; **it would be ~ to** +*infin* ce serait suicidaire de +*infin* **2.** *form* (*person*) suicidé(e) *m(f)* **II.** *vi* se suicider

suit [suːt] **I.** *vt* **1.** (*be convenient*) convenir à; **to ~ sb (right) down to the ground** *fig* convenir parfaitement à qn; **~ yourself** *iron or pej* comme tu voudras **2.** (*look attractive*) aller (bien) à **II.** *vi* convenir; **if it ~s** si cela te(vous) convient **III.** *n* **1.** (*jacket and trousers*) costume *m;* (*for women*) tailleur *m;* **three-piece ~** costume trois pièces; **trouser ~** complet *m* **2.** (*sports garment*) combinaison *f;* **bathing/swim ~** maillot *m* de bain **3.** LAW poursuite *f;* **to bring** [*o Am* **file**] **a ~** engager des poursuites **4.** (*card sort*) couleur *f* **5.** *fig* **to follow ~** faire de même

suitable [ˈsuːtəbl, *Am:* -t̬əbl] *adj* adéquat(e); (*clothes, answer*) approprié(e); **to be ~ for sb** convenir à qn; **not ~ for children under 14** déconseillé(e) aux enfants de moins de 14 ans

suitcase [ˈsuːtkeɪs] *n* valise *f*

suite [swiːt] *n* **1.** (*set of rooms*) suite *f* **2.** (*set of furniture*) mobilier *m* **3.** MUS suite *f*

suitor [ˈsuːtəʳ, *Am:* ˈsuːt̬ɚ] *n* **1.** (*man in love*) soupirant *m* **2.** ECON acquéreur *m* potentiel

sulfate [ˈsʌlfeɪt] *n Am* CHEM *s.* **sulphate**

sulfide [ˈsʌlfaɪd] *n Am* CHEM *s.* **sulphide**

sulfur [ˈsʌlfɚ] *n Am* CHEM *s.* **sulphur**

sulfuric [sʌlˈfjʊrɪk] *adj Am* CHEM *s.* **sulphuric**

sulfurous [ˈsʌlfɚəs] *adj Am* CHEM *s.* **sulphurous**

sulk [sʌlk] **I.** *vi pej* bouder **II.** *n pej* (*pet*) bouderie *f;* **to be in a ~** bouder; **to have (a fit of) the ~s** faire la tête

sulky [ˈsʌlki] <-ier, -iest> *adj* boudeur(-euse); **to have a ~ face** faire la tête

sullen [ˈsʌlən] *adj* **1.** (*sulky: person*) renfrogné(e) **2.** *fig* (*sky, clouds*) maussade

sully [ˈsʌli] <-ied, -ied> *vt form* souiller

sulphate [ˈsʌlfeɪt] *n* CHEM sulfate *m*

sulphide [ˈsʌlfaɪd] *n* CHEM sulfure *m*

sulphur [ˈsʌlfəʳ, *Am:* -fɚ] *n no pl* CHEM soufre *m*

sulphuric [sʌlˈfjʊərɪk, *Am:* -ˈfjʊrɪk] *adj* CHEM sulfurique

sulphurous *adj* CHEM sulfureux(-euse)

sultan [ˈsʌltən] *n* sultan *m*

sultana [sʌlˈtɑːnə, *Am:* -ˈtænə] *n* **1.** (*dried white grape*) raisins *mpl* de Smyrne **2.** (*wife of a sultan*) sultane *f*

sultanate *n* sultanat *m*

sultry [ˈsʌltri] <-ier, -iest> *adj* **1.** (*humid: weather*) lourd **2.** (*sexy*) sensuel(le)

sum [sʌm] *n* **1.** (*amount*) somme *f;* **a five-figure ~** une somme à cinq chiffres **2.** *pl* MAT (*calculation*) calcul *m;* **to do a ~** faire un calcul; **to get one's ~s wrong** *Brit* mal calculer **3.** *no pl, no indef art* MAT (*total*) montant *m;* **in ~** en somme

summarize [ˈsʌməraɪz] **I.** *vi* faire un résumé **II.** *vt* résumer

summary [ˈsʌməri] **I.** *n* résumé *m;* **in ~** en résumé **II.** *adj* sommaire

summation [sʌˈmeɪʃən, *Am:* səˈ-] *n form* sommation *f*

summer [ˈsʌməʳ, *Am:* -ɚ] **I.** *n* été *m;* **in (the) ~** en été **II.** *adj* d'été **III.** *vi* (*person*) passer l'été; (*animals, plants*) estiver

Summer Bank Holiday *n no pl* (*in Great Britain: end of August, in Scotland: beginning of August*) jour férié qui célèbre l'été **summer camp** *n* colonie *f* de vacances **summer holiday(s)** *n* vacances *fpl* d'été; (*at school, university*) grandes vacances *fpl* **summerhouse** *n* abri *m* de jardin **summer school** *n* **1.** SCHOOL cours *mpl* d'été **2.** UNIV université *f* d'été **summertime** *n s.* **summer**

summery [ˈsʌməri] *adj* estival(e)

summing-up [ˌsʌmɪŋˈʌp] *n* LAW résumé *m*

summit [ˈsʌmɪt] *n a. fig* sommet *m;* **~ meeting** rencontre *f* au sommet

summon [ˈsʌmən] *vt* **1.** (*call*) appeler **2.** (*call to attend: a council, person*) convoquer **3.** LAW citer à comparaître

summon up *vt* rassembler

S

summons *n* **1.** (*call*) sommation *f* **2.** LAW citation *f* à comparaître

sump [sʌmp] *n* **1.** (*pit*) fosse *f* **2.** AUTO carter *m;* **to drain the ~** faire la vidange

sumptuous ['sʌmptʃʊəs] *adj* somptueux(-euse)

sun [sʌn] **I.** *n* (*star in our system*) soleil *m;* **to sit in the ~** s'asseoir au soleil; **to have the ~ in one's eyes** avoir le soleil dans les yeux ►**to have a place in the ~** avoir une place au soleil; **to do/try everything under the ~** faire/essayer tout ce qui est possible d'imaginer; **nothing new under the ~** rien de nouveau sous le soleil **II.** <-nn-> *vt* **to ~ oneself** prendre un bain de soleil

sun-baked *adj* brûlé(e) par le soleil **sunbath** *n* bain *m* de soleil **sunbathe** *vi* prendre un bain de soleil **sunbeam** *n Brit* rayon *m* de soleil **sunbed** *n* **1.** (*lounger*) lit *m* de plage **2.** (*sun lamp*) solarium *m* **sunblind** *n Brit* store *m* **sunblock** *n* protection *f* solaire **sunburn** *n* coup *m* de soleil **sunburned, sunburnt** *adj* **1.** (*reddened skin*) **to be/get ~** avoir/attraper un coup de soleil **2.** (*suntanned skin*) **to be ~** être bronzé; **to get ~** bronzer

sundae ['sʌndeɪ, *Am:* -di] *n* sundae *m*

Sunday ['sʌndəɪ] *n* dimanche *m;* **a ~ in Lent** un dimanche de Carême; **Palm/Easter/Whit ~** dimanche des Rameaux/de Pâques/de Pentecôte; **Advent ~** le premier dimanche de l'Avent ►**to wear one's ~ best** être sur son trente et un; **to put on one's ~ clothes** [*o* **best**] mettre les habits du dimanche; *s. a.* **Friday**

Sunday best, Sunday clothes *npl* habits *mpl* du dimanche **Sunday school** *n* REL catéchisme *m*

sun deck *n* **1.** (*on boat*) pont *m* supérieur **2.** *Am* (*balcony*) terrasse *f*

sundial *n* HIST cadran *m* solaire

sundown *n Am, Aus s.* **sunset** **sundowner** *n* apéritif *m* **sun-dried** *adj* séché(e) au soleil; **~ tomatoes** tomates *fpl* confites

sundry ['sʌndri] *adj* divers(e); **all and ~** *inf* tout le monde et n'importe qui

sunfast *adj* (*colours, textiles*) résistant(e) à la lumière **sun filter** *n* filtre *m* solaire **sunflower** *n* tournesol *m*

sung [sʌŋ] *pp of* **sing**

sunglasses ['sʌnˌglɑːsɪz, *Am:* 'sʌnˌglæsɪs] *npl* lunettes *fpl* de soleil

sun hat *n* chapeau *m* de soleil **sun helmet** *n* HIST casque *m* colonial

sunk [sʌŋk] *pp of* **sink**

sunken ['sʌŋkən] *adj* **1.** (*submerged*) immergé(e); (*vessel, wreck*) englouti(e); **~ treasures** trésors *mpl* cachés **2.** (*below surrounding level: garden*) en contrebas; (*bath*) encastré(e) **3.** (*hollow: cheeks, eyes*) creux(-euse)

sun lamp *n* lampe *f* à rayons ultraviolets; **to lay under the ~** faire des UV **sunlight** *n no pl, no indef art* soleil *m*

sunlit ['sʌnlɪt] *adj* ensoleillé(e)

sunny ['sʌni] <-ier, -iest> *adj* **1.** (*not overcast*) ensoleillé(e); **~ intervals** éclaircies *fpl;* **the ~ side of sth** *a. fig* le bon côté de qc **2.** (*happy*) radieux(-euse); **to have a ~ disposition** être d'un naturel enjoué **3. eggs ~ side up** *Am* œufs *mpl* sur le plat

sun protection factor *n* indice *m* de protection solaire **sunray** *n Am s.* **sunbeam** **sunray lamp** *n s.* **sun lamp**

sunrise ['sʌnraɪz] *n* lever *m* du soleil

sunroof *n* toit *m* ouvrant **sunroom** *n Am* véranda *f* **sunscreen** *n* écran *m* solaire

sunset ['sʌnset] *n* coucher *m* du soleil; **at ~** au soleil couchant; **~ of sb's life** *fig* crépuscule *m* de la vie de qn

sunshade *n* **1.** (*umbrella*) ombrelle *f* **2.** *Am* (*awning*) parasol *m* **sunshine** *n* **1.** *no pl, no indef art* (*light and heat*) *a. fig* soleil *m;* **in the ~** au soleil; **to bring ~ into sb's life** être un rayon de soleil dans la vie de qn **2.** *Brit, inf* (*used in friendliness: to a male person*) mon vieux *m;* (*to a female person*) ma vieille *f* **sunshine roof** *n s.* **sunroof** **sunstroke** *n no pl, no indef art* insolation *f*

suntan ['sʌntæn] *n* bronzage *m;* **to get a ~** bronzer

suntan cream, suntan lotion *n* crème *f* à bronzer

sun-tanned *adj* bronzé(e)

suntan oil *n* huile *f* solaire

suntrap ['sʌntræp] *n Brit, Aus* coin *m* ensoleillé

sunup *n Am s.* **sunrise**

sun visor *n* visière *f*

sup [sʌp] <-pp-> **I.** *vt Brit, iron* avaler à petites gorgées **II.** *vi* souper

super[1] ['suːpəʳ, *Am:* -pɚ] *adj, adv inf* super *inv*

super[2] ['suːpəʳ, *Am:* -pɚ] *n* AUTO super *m*

super[3] ['suːpəʳ, *Am:* -pɚ] *n* **1.** *abbr of* **superintendent** **2.** *Aus, inf abbr of* **superannuation**

superabundant *adj* surabondant(e) **superannuate** *vt* mettre à la retraite **superannuated** *adj* **1.** (*retired*) mis(e) à la retraite **2.** (*obsolete*) obsolète **superannuation** *n no pl, no indef art* **1.** *Brit, Aus* (*pension payment*) cotisation *f* pour la retraite **2.** *Brit, Aus* (*pension received*) pension *f*

superb [suː'pɜːb, *Am:* sə'pɜːrb] *adj* superbe

Super Bowl *n Am: championnat de football américain* **supercharged** *adj a. fig* suralimenté(e) **supercharger** *n* TECH compresseur *m*

supercilious ['suːpə'sɪlɪəs, *Am:* ˌsuːpɚ-'sɪlɪəs] *adj pej* hautain(e)

super-duper *adj* génial(e)

superficial [ˌsuːpə'fɪʃl, *Am:* ˌsuːpɚ'-] *adj a. fig* superficiel(le)

superficiality [ˌsuːpəˌfɪʃɪ'æləti, *Am:* -pɚˌfɪʃɪ'æləṭi] *n no pl, a. fig* superficialité(e)

superfluous [suː'pɜːflʊəs, *Am:* -'pɜːr-] *adj* superflu(e)

superglue® *n* superglu® *f* **supergrass** *n* *Brit, inf* mouchard(e) *m(f)* **superhero** <-heroes> *n inf* super-héros *m* **superhighway** *n* 1. *Am s.* **dual carriageway** 2. INFOR (*network*) autoroute *f* de l'information **superhuman** *adj* surhumain(e) **superimpose** *vt* PHOT surexposer **superintend** *vt* diriger **superintendence** *n no pl* direction *f* **superintendent** *n* 1. (*person in charge*) responsable *mf;* (*in a department*) chef *m* de service; (*in a shop*) chef *m* de rayon 2. (*person in charge of building*) concierge *mf* 3. (*police officer*) commissaire *mf*

superior [suː'pɪəriə^r^, *Am:* sə'pɪriɚ] I. *adj a. pej* supérieur(e); **to be ~ in numbers** être supérieur en nombre II. *n* supérieur(e) *m(f)*

superiority [suːˌpɪəri'ɒrəti, *Am:* səˌpɪri'ɔːrət̬i] *n no pl* supériorité *f*

superiority complex *n inf* PSYCH complexe *m* de supériorité

superlative [suː'pɜːlətɪv, *Am:* sə'pɜːrlət̬ɪv] I. *adj* 1. (*of highest quality*) sans pareil 2. LING (*of graded adjective*) superlatif(-ive) II. *n* LING superlatif *m*

superman *n* 1. (*superior man*) PSYCH surhomme *m* 2. (*Hollywood character*) **Superman** Superman *m* **supermarket** *n* supermarché *m* **supermarket trolley** *n Brit* chariot *m* de supermarché **supermodel** *n* top model *m* **supernatural** I. *adj* surnaturel(e) II. *n* **the ~** le surnaturel **supernumerary** I. *adj form* en surnombre II. <-ies> *n form* extra *m* **superpower** *n* POL superpuissance *f*

superscript ['suːpəskrɪpt, *Am:* -pɚ-] I. *n no pl, no indef art* TYP exposant *m;* **in ~** en exposant II. *adj* en exposant

supersede [ˌsuːpə'siːd, *Am:* -pɚ'-] *vt* remplacer

supersonic [ˌsuːpə'sɒnɪk, *Am:* -pɚ'sɑːnɪk] *adj* AVIAT supersonique

superstar *n* superstar *f*

superstition [ˌsuːpə'stɪʃən, *Am:* -pɚ'-] *n* superstition *f*

superstitious *adj* superstitieux(-euse)

superstore *n* hypermarché *m* **superstructure** *n* superstructure *f* **supertanker** *n* pétrolier *m* géant

supervene [ˌsuːpə'viːn, *Am:* -pɚ'-] *vi form* survenir

supervise ['suːpəvaɪz, *Am:* -pɚ-] *vt* surveiller

supervision *n no pl* surveillance *f*

supervisor *n* 1. (*person in charge*) chef *m;* (*in a department*) chef *m* de service; (*in shop*) chef *m* de rayon 2. (*teacher*) directeur, -trice *m, f*

supervisory *adj* de surveillance

supine ['suːpaɪn, *Am:* suː'-] *adj* 1. (*lying on back*) allongé(e) sur le dos 2. *fig, pej* (*of weak character*) impassible

supper ['sʌpə^r^, *Am:* -ɚ] *n* souper *m;* **to have ~** souper

suppertime *n no pl, no indef art* heure *f* du souper

supplant [sə'plɑːnt, *Am:* -'plænt] *vt* supplanter

supple ['sʌpl] <-r, -st> *adj a. fig* souple

supplement ['sʌplɪmənt, *Am:* -lə-] I. *n* 1. supplément *m;* **a ~ to one's income** une augmentation de ses revenus; **sports ~** supplément sport; **the Sunday ~** *Brit* le supplément du dimanche 2. (*complement*) complément *m* II. *vt* 1. (*increase*) augmenter 2. (*add to*) compléter

supplemental *adj Am,* **supplementary** *adj* 1. (*in addition to*) supplémentaire; **to be ~ to sth** être en plus de qc 2. (*complementary*) complémentaire

supplementary benefit *n* FIN *s.* **income support**

suppleness ['sʌplnɪs] *n a. fig* souplesse *f*

suppliant, **supplicant** I. *n form* suppliant(e) *m(f)* II. *adj form* suppliant(e); **to be ~** supplier

supplier [sə'plaɪə^r^, *Am:* -ɚ] *n* fournisseur *m;* **a ~ of services** un prestataire de services

supply [sə'plaɪ] I. <-ied> *vt* fournir; (*an answer*) donner; **to ~ sb/sth with food** approvisionner qn/qc en nourriture; **to ~ oneself with sth** s'approvisionner en qc; **to ~ sb's needs** subvenir aux besoins de qn II. *n* 1. (*provision*) provision *f;* **electricity/water supplies** alimentation *f* en électricité/eau; **food supplies** vivres *mpl* 2. *pl* (*equipment*) matériel *m;* (*of an office*) fournitures *fpl* 3. *no pl, no indef art* (*action of making available*) offre *f;* **~ and demand** l'offre et la demande; **oil ~** offre en pétrole 4. (*action of providing*) approvisionnement *m* 5. *pl* (*grant*) subvention *f* 6. *Brit, Aus* SCHOOL (*standby teacher*) remplaçant(e) *m(f);* **to be on ~** faire des remplacements

supply teacher *n Brit, Aus* remplaçant(e) *m(f)*

support [sə'pɔːt, *Am:* -'pɔːrt] I. *vt* 1. (*hold up*) *a. fig* maintenir; **to ~ oneself** se maintenir 2. (*bear*) supporter 3. (*provide with money*) entretenir; **to ~ a family** subvenir aux besoins d'une famille; **a family to ~** une famille à charge; **to ~ oneself** gagner sa vie 4. (*help*) soutenir; **to ~ a friend** apporter son soutien à un ami; **to ~ cancer research** soutenir financièrement la recherche contre le cancer 5. (*encourage: party*) soutenir 6. SPORT supporter 7. (*show to be true: theory*) appuyer II. *n* 1. (*act of supporting*) appui *m* 2. (*object*) support *m* 3. (*garment*) maintien *m;* **knee ~** genouillère *f;* **~ stockings** bas *mpl* de maintien 4. *no pl* (*help*) soutien *m;* **a letter of ~** une lettre de soutien; **to give sb moral ~** apporter son soutien moral à qn 5. *no pl, no indef art* (*provision of necessities*) subvention *f* 6. (*proof of truth*) appui *m;* **to lend ~ to sth** prêter son appui à qc; **in ~ of sth** à l'appui de qc

supporter *n* **1.** (*encouraging person: of an idea, right*) défenseur *m;* (*of a campaign, party*) partisan(e) *m(f)* **2.** *Brit* SPORT (*fan*) supporter, -trice *m, f;* **a Bristol Rovers** ~ un supporter des Bristol Rovers

supporting *adj* CINE **a** ~ **role** un second rôle; **best** ~ **actor** meilleur second rôle; **a** ~ **film** un film en première partie; **a** ~ **act** une première partie

supportive *adj* (*person*) **to be** ~ être d'un grand soutien; **to be** ~ **of sb/sth** soutenir qn/qc

suppose [sə'pəʊz, *Am:* -'poʊz] *vt* **1.** (*think*) croire **2.** (*introduce hypothesis*) supposer; **I** ~ **so** je suppose que oui; ~ (**that**) **we do sth** et si on faisait qc

supposed *adj* **1.** (*regarded as sth*) présumé(e) **2.** (*so-called*) soi-disant(e) **3.** (*allowed*) supposé(e)

supposedly *adv* soi-disant

supposing *conj* à supposer que +*subj*

supposition [ˌsʌpə'zɪʃən] *n* supposition *f;* **to be pure** ~ n'être qu'une pure hypothèse; **on the** ~ **that** à supposer que +*subj;* **on this** ~ dans cette hypothèse

suppository [sə'pɒzɪtəri, *Am:* -'pɑːzətɔːri] <-ies> *n* MED suppositoire *m*

suppress [sə'pres] *vt* **1.** (*put down: terrorism, revolution*) réprimer **2.** (*make disappear: report, effect*) supprimer **3.** (*prevent dissemination: a grin, information*) étouffer; (*one's emotions*) réprimer

suppression [sə'preʃən] *n no pl, no indef art* **1.** (*putting down by force: of an uprising, a revolution*) répression *f* **2.** (*disappearing*) suppression *f* **3.** (*preventing: of anger, emotion*) refoulement *m;* (*of evidence*) dissimulation *f* **4.** MED (*restraining*) suspension *f* **5.** PSYCH (*restraint in subconscious*) refoulement *m*

suppurate ['sʌpjʊreɪt] *vi* MED suppurer

supremacy [sʊ'preməsi, *Am:* sə'-] *n no pl* suprématie *f*

supreme [suː'priːm, *Am:* sə'-] **I.** *adj* suprême **II.** *adv a. fig* **to reign** ~ régner en maître absolu

supreme court, **Supreme Court** *n* Cour *f* suprême, ≈ tribunal *m* fédéral *Suisse*

surcharge ['sɜːtʃɑːdʒ, *Am:* 'sɜːrtʃɑːrdʒ] **I.** *n* supplément *m;* (*on tax bills*) surtaxe *f;* **there is a** ~ il y a un supplément (à payer) **II.** *vt* surtaxer; **to be** ~**d for sth** payer un supplément pour qc

sure [ʃʊəʳ, *Am:* ʃʊr] **I.** *adj* sûr(e); **to be/feel** ~ (**that**) … être certain que …; **to make** ~ (**that**) … s'assurer que …; **to be** ~ **about sth** être sûr de qc; **to be** ~ **to** +*infin* être certain de +*infin;* **to be** ~ **about sb** avoir confiance en qn; **to be** ~ **of oneself** être sûr de soi; **a** ~ **sign of sth** un signe certain de qc; **that's a** ~ **success** c'est un succès assuré; **to be** ~ *form* être certain; ~ **thing!** *Am* bien sûr! **II.** <-r, -st> *adv* vraiment; ~ **I will!** bien sûr!; **for** ~ à coup sûr; ~ **enough** en effet; **to know for** ~ **that …** être certain que …; **oh** ~**!** bien sûr! ►**as** ~ **as I'm standing/sitting here** aussi sûr que deux et deux font quatre

sure-footed *adj* **1.** (*confident in walking*) au pied sûr; **to be** ~ avoir le pied sûr **2.** *fig* (*confident*) de confiance; **in a** ~ **way** d'une manière assurée

surely ['ʃɔːli, *Am:* 'ʃʊrli] *adv* **1.** (*certainly*) sûrement **2.** (*said to show astonishment*) tout de même **3.** (*confidently*) avec assurance **4.** *Am* (*yes, certainly*) bien sûr

surety ['ʃʊərəti, *Am:* 'ʃʊrət̬i] <-ies> *n* garantie *f;* **to stand** ~ **for sb** se porter garant pour qn

surf [sɜːf, *Am:* sɜːrf] **I.** *n* surf *m* **II.** *vi* **1.** SPORT (*ride waves on board*) faire du surf **2.** SPORT *s.* **windsurf III.** *vt* INFOR naviguer

surface ['sɜːfɪs, *Am:* 'sɜːr-] **I.** *n* **1.** (*part, top*) surface *f;* **to bring sth to the** ~ (*above ground*) déterrer qc; (*above water level*) faire remonter qc **2.** (*appearance*) apparence *f;* **on the** ~ en apparence; **beneath the** ~ **he's very gentle** au fond il est très doux; **to scratch the** ~ **of sth** creuser qc **3.** SPORT surface *f* **II.** *vi* **1.** (*come to top*) faire surface **2.** *fig* (*become obvious*) apparaître **3.** *fig* (*get out of bed*) faire surface **III.** *vt* revêtir **IV.** *adj* **1.** (*above the ground: worker*) de surface **2.** (*on top of water: fleet*) de surface **3.** (*superficial*) superficiel(le)

surface area *n* MAT surface *f* **surface mail** *n* courrier *m* de surface **surface tension** *n* PHYS tension *f* de surface **surface-to-air missile** *n* MIL missile *m* sol-air

surfboard *n* **1.** SPORT (*for riding waves*) surf *m* **2.** SPORT *s.* **windsurfboard surfboarder** *n* SPORT *s.* **surfer**

surfeit ['sɜːfɪt, *Am:* 'sɜːr-] **I.** *n no pl, form* excès *m;* **a** ~ **of information** une surinformation **II.** *vt form* **to** ~ **oneself on sth** se saturer de qc

surfer, **surfie** *n Aus, inf* **1.** (*person*) *a.* INFOR surfeur, -euse *m, f* **2.** SPORT *s.* **windsurfers**

surfing *n no pl, no indef art* **1.** SPORT (*riding the waves*) surf *m* **2.** SPORT *s.* **windsurfing**

surf-riding *n* SPORT *s.* **surfing**

surge [sɜːdʒ, *Am:* sɜːrdʒ] **I.** *vi* **1.** (*move strongly forward*) se précipiter; **to** ~ **into the lead** être propulsé en tête **2.** (*increase: water*) monter **3.** (*well up: anger*) monter **II.** *n* **1.** (*sudden increase*) montée *f* **2.** (*forward movement*) poussée *f* **3.** *fig* (*upward movement*) élan *m*

surgeon ['sɜːdʒən, *Am:* 'sɜːr-] *n* MED chirurgien(ne) *m(f)*

surgery ['sɜːdʒəri, *Am:* 'sɜːr-] *n* **1.** *Brit, Aus* MED (*medical practice*) cabinet *m* médical; **to hold a** ~ consulter **2.** *no pl, no indef art* MED (*medical speciality*) chirurgie *f;* **eye** ~ chirurgie oculaire **3.** (*operation*) opération *f;* **you'll need** ~ il faudra t'opérer **4.** *Brit* POL (*discussion time*) permanence *f;* **to hold a** ~ tenir une permanence

surgery hours *npl* heures *fpl* de consultation

surgical ['sɜːdʒɪkl, *Am:* 'sɜːr-] *adj* **1.** MED chirurgical(e); (*corset, boot*) orthopédique **2.** *fig* scientifique

surgical appliances *n* appareillage *m* **surgical collar** *n* minerve *f* **surgical spirit** *n Brit* alcool *m* à 90° **surgical stocking** *n* bas *m* de contention **surgical tape** *n* sparadrap *m*

Surinam(e) ['sʊəˌnæm, *Am:* ˌsʊrɪ'nɑːm] *n* Surinam *m*

Surinamese [ˌsʊənæ'miːz] **I.** *adj* surinamais(e) **II.** *n* Surinamais(e) *m(f)*

surly ['sɜːli, *Am:* 'sɜːr-] <-ier, -iest> *adj* bourru(e)

surmise ['sɜːmaɪz, *Am:* sɚ'maɪz] **I.** *vt form* supposer **II.** *n form* (*guess*) supposition *f*

surmount [sə'maʊnt, *Am:* sɚ'-] *vt* (*challenge*) surmonter; **to be ~ed by** être surmonté de

surname ['sɜːneɪm, *Am:* 'sɜːr-] *n* nom *m* de famille

surpass [sə'pɑːs, *Am:* sɚ'pæs] *vt* surpasser; **to ~ oneself** se surpasser

surplus ['sɜːpləs, *Am:* 'sɜːr-] **I.** *n* **1.** (*extra amount*) surplus *m* **2.** *no pl* (*in production*) excédent *m* **II.** *adj* **1.** (*extra*) en trop; **to be ~ to requirements** *Brit* faire double emploi **2.** ECON excédentaire

surplus value *n* plus-value *f*

surprise [sə'praɪz, *Am:* sɚ'-] **I.** *n* surprise *f;* **to come as a ~ to sb** surprendre qn; **to spring a ~ on sb** faire une surprise à qn; **~! ~!** *inf* ô surprise; *iron, inf* évidemment; **to my ~** à ma surprise **II.** *vt* surprendre **III.** *adj* surprise

surprised *adj* surpris(e)

surprising *adj* surprenant(e)

surprisingly *adv* étonnamment; **~ no one complained** chose surprenante, personne ne s'est plaint

surreal [sə'rɪəl, *Am:* sə'riːəl] **I.** *adj* surréaliste **II.** *n* surréalisme *m*

surrealism [sə'rɪəlɪzəm, *Am:* -'riːə-] *n* ART surréalisme *m*

surrealist **I.** *adj* ART surréaliste **II.** *n* ART surréaliste *mf*

surrealistic *adj* surréaliste

surrender [sə'rendəʳ, *Am:* -dɚ] **I.** *vi* **to ~ to sb/sth** se rendre à qn/qc; *fig* se livrer à qn/qc **II.** *vt form* **to ~ sth to sb** remettre qc à qn **III.** *n* **1.** (*act of admitting defeat*) reddition *f* **2.** *no pl, form* (*giving up*) remise *f* **3.** MIL capitulation *f*

surreptitious [ˌsʌrəp'tɪʃəs, *Am:* ˌsɜːr-] *adj* subreptice

surrogacy ['sʌrəgəsi] *n no pl* maternité *f* de substitution

surrogate ['sʌrəgɪt, *Am:* 'sɜːr-] **I.** *adj* de substitution **II.** *n* **1.** (*substitute*) substitut *m;* **to be ~ for sth** être substitut de qc **2.** (*mother*) mère *f* porteuse

surrogate mother *n* mère *f* porteuse

surround [sə'raʊnd] **I.** *vt* **1.** (*enclose*) entourer **2.** (*encircle*) encercler **II.** *n* **1.** (*border*) encadrement *m;* (*of fireplace, window, door*) chambranle *m* **2.** *pl, fig* (*of an area*) environs *mpl*

surrounding *adj* (*area*) environnant(e)

surroundings *n* **1.** (*environment*) environnement *m;* **in sb's natural ~** dans son milieu naturel **2.** (*surrounds: of city*) environs *mpl*

surtax ['sɜːtæks, *Am:* 'sɜːr-] *n* surtaxe *f*

surveillance [sɜː'veɪləns, *Am:* sɚ'-] *n no pl, no indef art* surveillance *f*

survey [sə'veɪ, *Am:* sɚ'-] **I.** *vt* **1.** (*study*) étudier **2.** (*investigate: person*) sonder; (*needs*) enquêter sur **3.** (*look at*) scruter **4.** (*examine*) inspecter; (*house*) faire l'expertise de **5.** GEO relever **II.** *n* **1.** (*study*) étude *f;* (*for market research*) enquête *f;* (*for opinions*) sondage *m* **2.** (*inspection*) inspection *f;* (*of house*) expertise *f* **3.** (*description*) tour *m* d'horizon **4.** GEO (*measuring and mapping*) relevé *m*

surveyor *n* **1.** GEO (*measurer and mapper*) géomètre *mf* **2.** *Brit* (*property assessor*) expert(e) *m(f)*; **a quantity ~** un métreur

survival [sə'vaɪvl, *Am:* sɚ'-] *n* **1.** *no pl, no indef art* (*not dying*) survie *f* **2.** *no pl, no indef art* (*continuing*) vestige *m* ▸**the ~ of the fittest** la survie du plus apte; *fig* les gros poissons mangent les petits

survival kit *n* trousse *f* de survie

survive [sə'vaɪv, *Am:* sɚ'-] **I.** *vi a. fig* survivre; **to ~ on sth** vivre de qc; **I'm surviving** *inf* je m'en sors **II.** *vt a. fig* survivre à; (*accident, illness*) réchapper à

surviving *adj* survivant(e)

survivor *n* survivant, -e *m, f*

susceptibility *n* **1.** (*touchy*) susceptibilité *f* **2.** (*sensitivity*) sensibilité *f* **3.** MED prédisposition *f*

susceptible [sə'septəbl] *adj* **1.** (*touchy*) susceptible **2.** (*sensitive*) sensible; **to be ~ to sth** être sensible à qc **3.** (*influenced by*) influençable **4.** MED (*likely to catch*) **to be ~ to sth** être prédisposé à qc

sushi ['suːʃi] *n* sushi *m*

suspect [sə'spekt] **I.** *vt* **1.** (*think likely*) soupçonner; **I ~ so** j'imagine que oui; **I ~ not** je ne pense pas **2.** (*consider guilty*) soupçonner **3.** (*doubt*) douter de **II.** *n* suspect *m* **III.** *adj* suspect(e)

suspend [sə'spend] *vt* **1.** (*stop temporarily*) suspendre; **to ~ disbelief** jouer le jeu **2.** LAW (*defer: a sentence*) surseoir à **3.** (*not allow to work*) suspendre; SCHOOL, UNIV renvoyer **4.** SPORT (*not allow to play*) suspendre **5.** (*hang*) suspendre **6.** CHEM (*float*) **to be ~ed in sth** être en suspension dans qc

suspender *n* **1.** (*strap holding up stockings*) jarretière *f* **2.** *pl, Am* FASHION jarretelles *fpl* **3.** *pl* (*braces*) bretelles *fpl* **4.** *Brit* (*strap holding men's socks*) fixe-chaussette *m*

suspender belt *n Brit, Aus* FASHION porte-jarretelles *m*

suspense [sə'spens] *n* suspense *m;* **to keep**

S

sb in ~ faire languir qn

suspension [sə'spentʃən] *n* **1.** *no pl, no indef art* (*temporary stopping*) *a.* SPORT suspension *f;* **the ~ of sb** la mise à pied de qn; **to be under ~** être suspendu **2.** CHEM suspension *f* **3.** AUTO, TECH (*part of vehicle*) suspension *f*

suspension bridge *n* CONSTR pont *m* suspendu **suspension points** *npl* points *mpl* de suspension

suspicion [sə'spɪʃən] *n* **1.** (*belief*) soupçon *m* **2.** *no pl, no indef art* (*believing to be guilty*) soupçon *m;* **I arrest you on ~ of murder** je vous arrête, vous êtes soupçonné d'homicide; **to be above ~** être au-dessus de tout soupçon; **to be under ~** être soupçonné **3.** *no pl, no indef art* (*mistrust*) méfiance *f* **4.** (*small amount*) soupçon *m*

suspicious [sə'spɪʃəs] *adj* **1.** (*causing suspicion: death, circumstances*) suspect(e) **2.** (*having suspicions*) soupçonneux(-euse); **to be ~ about sth** avoir des soupçons à propos de qc **3.** (*having doubts*) **to be ~ about sth** avoir des doutes à propos de qc **4.** (*lacking trust*) méfiant(e); **to be ~** se méfier

suss [sʌs] *vt Brit, Aus, inf* **to ~ (out)** piger

sustain [sə'steɪn] *vt* **1.** *form* (*suffer: defeat, loss*) subir; **she ~ed severe injuries** elle a été grièvement blessée **2.** (*maintain: life*) maintenir **3.** (*support*) soutenir **4.** *Am* LAW (*uphold: objection*) retenir **5.** MUS (*note*) prolonger

sustainability *n no pl* **1.** (*ability to be maintained*) capacité *f* de maintien **2.** ECOL, ECON, POL viabilité *f*

sustainable *adj* viable; (*development*) durable

sustained *adj* (*work, applause*) soutenu(e)

sustaining *adj* **1.** GASTR (*nourishing*) nourrissant(e) **2.** MUS **~ pedal** pédale *f* forte

sustenance ['sʌstɪnənts, *Am:* -tnəns] *n no pl, no indef art* **1.** *form* (*food*) nourriture *f* **2.** *form* (*nutritious value*) valeur *f* nutritive **3.** (*support*) soutien *m* affectif

suture ['su:tʃəʳ, *Am:* -tʃɚ] **I.** *n* MED suture *f* **II.** *vt* MED suturer

svelte [svelt] *adj* svelte

SW [ˌes'dʌblju:] *n abbr of* **southwest** SO *m*

swab [swɒb, *Am:* swɑ:b] **I.** *n* **1.** MED (*pad for cleaning wound*) compresse *f* **2.** MED (*remove matter for examination*) prélèvement *m* **II.** <-bb-> *vt* **1.** MED (*clean*) nettoyer **2.** NAUT (*clean*) lessiver

swaddle ['swɒdl, *Am:* 'swɑ:dl] *vt* (*baby*) emmailloter

swaddling clothes *npl* langes *mpl*

swagger ['swægəʳ, *Am:* -ɚ] *pej* **I.** *vi* **1.** (*walk*) se pavaner **2.** (*boast*) fanfaronner **II.** *n no pl, no indef art* démarche *f* arrogante; **to walk with a ~** marcher en se pavanant

swallow¹ ['swɒləʊ, *Am:* 'swɑ:loʊ] **I.** *n* **1.** (*using throat muscles*) déglutition *f* **2.** (*amount swallowed: of drink*) gorgée *f;* (*of food*) cuillerée *f* **II.** *vt* **1.** (*let pass down throat*) avaler **2.** (*engulf*) engloutir **3.** *inf* (*believe unquestioningly*) avaler; **to ~ the bait** mordre à l'hameçon; **to ~ a story hook, line and sinker** gober une histoire; **to ~ one's words** avaler ses mots; **I find it hard to ~** j'ai du mal à l'avaler; **it's a bitter pill to ~** la pilule est dure à avaler **4.** (*leave unsaid: disappointment, anger, pride*) ravaler **III.** *vi* avaler

◆**swallow down** *vt* **1.** (*swallow*) avaler **2.** (*gulp down*) engloutir

◆**swallow up** *vt* engloutir; **I wish the ground would open and swallow me up** je voudrais pouvoir disparaître dans un trou

swallow² ['swɒləʊ, *Am:* 'swɑ:loʊ] *n* ZOOL hirondelle *f* ►**one ~ doesn't make a summer** *prov* une hirondelle ne fait pas le printemps

swallow dive *n Brit, Aus* SPORT saut *m* de l'ange

swam [swæm] *pt of* **swim**

swamp [swɒmp, *Am:* swɑ:mp] **I.** *n* **1.** (*area of wet ground*) marécage *m,* savane *f Québec* **2.** *no pl, no indef art* (*wet land*) marais *m* **II.** *vt a. fig* inonder; **we've been ~ed by a flood of complaints** nous avons été inondés de réclamations

swamp fever *n no pl, no indef art* ZOOL fièvre *f* des marais

swampland(s) *n no pl, no indef art* marais *m*

swampy <-ier, -iest> *adj* marécageux(-euse)

swan [swɒn, *Am:* swɑ:n] **I.** *n* ZOOL cygne *m* **II.** <-nn-> *vi Brit, Aus, pej, inf* **to ~ about** *pej, inf* parader; **to ~ off** *pej, inf* (*wander off*) se tirer; **to ~ around Asia** (*travel*) faire le tour de l'Asie

swan dive *n Am* SPORT *s.* **swallow dive**

swank [swæŋk] **I.** *vi pej, inf* frimer **II.** *n no pl, no indef art, inf* frime *f*

swanky *adj inf* **1.** (*luxurious*) super chic *inv* **2.** *pej* (*ostentatious*) rupin(e)

swansong *n* chant *m* du cygne

swap [swɒp, *Am:* swɑ:p] **I.** *vt* échanger **II.** <-pp-> *vi* échanger **III.** *n* **1.** (*exchange*) échange *m;* **to do a ~** faire l'échange **2.** (*thing to be exchanged*) objet *m* de l'échange

SWAPO *n abbr of* **South West African People's Organization** SWAPO *f*

swarm [swɔ:m, *Am:* swɔ:rm] **I.** *vi* **1.** ZOOL, BIO (*form large group*) essaimer **2.** *fig* (*move in large group*) envahir; **to be ~ing with sth** *fig* grouiller de qc **II.** *n* **1.** ZOOL, BIO (*large group of flying insects*) essaim *m* **2.** *fig* (*large group of people*) nuée *f*

swarthy ['swɔ:ði, *Am:* 'swɔ:r-] <-ier, -iest> *adj* basané(e)

swashbuckling ['swɒʃˌbʌklɪŋ, *Am:* 'swɑ:ʃˌ-] *adj* (*film, story*) de cape et d'épée

swastika ['swɒstɪkə, *Am:* 'swɑ:stɪ-] *n* croix *f* gammée

swat [swɒt, *Am:* swɑ:t] <-tt-> *vt* **1.** (*crush*) écraser **2.** (*hit*) frapper

swatch [swɒtʃ, *Am:* swɑ:tʃ] *n* échantillon *m*

swathe [sweɪð] **I.** *vt* envelopper **II.** *n* **1.** (*long strip*) andain *m* **2.** (*area*) bande *f* **3.** *fig* **a large**

~ **of time** une longue période

sway [sweɪ] **I.** *vi* se balancer **II.** *vt* (*persuade*) influencer

Swazi I. *adj* swasi(e) **II.** *n* Swasi(e) *m(f)*

Swaziland ['swɑːzilænd] *n* le Swaziland

swear [sweəʳ, *Am:* swer] <swore, sworn> **I.** *vi* **1.** (*curse*) dire des jurons **2.** (*state sth is the truth*) jurer **3.** (*take an oath*) prêter serment; **to ~ on the Bible** jurer sur la Bible; **I wouldn't/couldn't ~ to it** *inf* je ne le jurerais pas **II.** *vt* **1.** (*curse*) jurer; **to ~ blind that ...** *Brit, inf* jurer ses grands dieux que ... **2.** (*give one's word*) jurer; **to ~ sb to secrecy** faire jurer le secret à qn

◆**swear by** *vt inf* jurer par

◆**swear in** *vt* faire prêter serment à

◆**swear off** *vt* jurer de renoncer à

swearing *n no pl* jurons *mpl*

swear word *n* gros mot *m*, sacre *m Québec*

sweat [swet] **I.** *n* **1.** *no pl, no indef art* (*perspiration*) transpiration *f*; **to be dripping with ~** être ruisselant de sueur **2.** *pl* FASHION survêtement *m* ▸**to break out into a ~** avoir des sueurs froides; **to be in a cold ~** avoir des sueurs froides; **no ~!** pas de problème!; **it was a real ~** c'était tuant; **to work oneself into a ~ about sth** se faire du souci à propos de qc **II.** *vi* (*perspire*) transpirer ▸**to ~ like a pig** *inf* transpirer comme une vache; **to let sb ~** *inf* laisser qn mariner **III.** *vt* (*person*) faire suer; (*onions*) faire revenir ▸**to ~ blood** suer sang et eau; **to ~ buckets** être en nage

◆**sweat out** *vt* **to sweat it out 1.** (*do physical exercise*) se défouler **2.** (*suffer while waiting*) prendre son mal en patience

sweatband *n* bandeau *m* en éponge

sweated *adj pej* (*labour*) d'esclave

sweater *n* pull *m*

sweatshirt ['swetʃɜːt, *Am:* -ʃɜːrt] *n* sweatshirt *m*

sweatshop ['swetʃɒp, *Am:* -ʃɑːp] *n pej* atelier *m* de sueur; ~ **conditions** conditions d'esclavage

sweaty ['sweti, *Am:* 'swet̬-] <-ier, -iest> *adj* **1.** (*covered in perspiration*) en sueur; (*palms*) moite **2.** (*forcing perspiration: afternoon*) moite

swede [swiːd] *n Brit, Aus* GASTR rutabaga *m*

Swede [swiːd] *n* (*person*) Suédois(e) *m(f)*

Sweden ['swiːdn] *n* la Suède

Swedish I. *adj* suédois(e) **II.** *n* LING suédois *m*; *s. a.* **English**

sweep [swiːp] <swept, swept> **I.** *n* **1.** *no pl* (*clean with a brush*) coup *m* de balai **2.** *s.* **chimney sweep 3.** (*movement*) large mouvement *m*; **with a ~ of the hand** d'un geste large; **with a ~ of his sword** d'un grand coup d'épée **4.** (*area*) étendue *f* **5.** (*curve*) courbe *f* **6.** (*range*) *a. fig* étendue *f* **7.** (*search*) recherche *f* **8.** *inf* (*form of gambling*) *s.* **sweepstake** ▸**to make a clean ~ of sth** (*start afresh*) faire table rase; (*win everything*) tout rafler **II.** *vt* **1.** (*clean: floor, chimney*) balayer **2.** (*take in powerful manner*) emporter **3.** *Am, inf* (*win*) remporter ▸**to ~ the board** tout rafler; **to ~ sth under the carpet** [*o a. Am* **rug**] [*o a. Aus* **mat**] faire comme si qc n'existait pas; **rumours swept through the village** des rumeurs ont parcouru tout le village **III.** *vi* **1.** (*clean*) balayer **2.** (*move*) **to ~ past sb** passer fièrement devant qn; **to ~ into power** être propulsé au pouvoir **3.** (*look round*) scruter ▸**a new broom ~s clean** *prov* un nouveau dirigeant impose de nouvelles méthodes

◆**sweep aside** *vt* **1.** (*cause to move*) repousser **2.** *fig* (*dismiss*) rejeter

◆**sweep away** *vt* **1.** (*remove*) repousser; (*objections*) rejeter **2.** (*carry away*) *a. fig* emporter

◆**sweep out I.** *vt* balayer **II.** *vi* sortir fièrement

◆**sweep up** *vt* **1.** (*brush and gather*) balayer **2.** (*gather*) ramasser; **to ~ a baby** prendre un bébé dans ses bras

sweeper *n* **1.** (*industrial device*) balayeuse *f* **2.** (*carpet ~*) balai *m* **3.** (*person*) balayeur, -euse *m, f*

sweeping I. *adj* **1.** (*large: changes, plans, cuts*) radical(e) **2.** (*moving quickly: movement, gesture*) large **3.** (*complete: power*) plein(e) **4.** (*too general*) généralisé(e); **a ~ generalization** une généralisation abusive **II.** *n pl* **1.** (*refuse*) ordures *fpl* **2.** *fig* rebut *m*

sweepstake ['swiːpsteɪk] *n* sweepstake *m*

sweet [swiːt] **I.** *adj* <-er, -est> **1.** (*containing sugar*) sucré(e) **2.** (*having a pleasant taste*) doux(douce); (*perfume*) suave **3.** (*not dry: wine*) doux(douce) **4.** *fig* (*pleasant: sound, temper*) doux(douce); **short and ~** bref(brève) **5.** *fig* (*endearing*) mignon(ne) **6.** *fig* (*kind*) gentil(le); **that is so ~!** comme c'est gentil!; **to ~ talk sb** *inf* faire du baratin à qn; ~ **dreams!** fais de beaux rêves ▸**in my own ~ time** quand j'aurais envie; **in my own ~ way** comme je le veux **II.** *n* **1.** *Brit, Aus* (*candy*) bonbon *m*, boule *f Belgique* **2.** *Brit, Aus* (*dessert*) dessert *m* **3.** *inf* (*term of endearment*) **my ~** mon chou

sweet-and-sour *adj* GASTR aigre-doux(douce)

sweetbread *n pl* GASTR ris *m* **sweet chestnut** *n* châtaigne *f* **sweetcorn** *n Am* GASTR maïs *m*

sweeten ['swiːtən] *vt* **1.** (*make sweet*) sucrer; *fig* adoucir **2.** (*make more amenable*) graisser la patte

sweetener *n* **1.** (*artificial sweet substance*) sucrette® *f* **2.** *fig* pot-de-vin *m*

sweetheart *n* **1.** (*kind person*) amour *m* **2.** (*term of endearment*) mon cœur

sweetie *n inf* **1.** (*sweet*) bonbon *m* **2.** (*term of endearment*) ~ (**pie**) mon chou

sweetly *adv* gentiment; (*to sing*) d'une voix douce

sweetness *n no pl, a. fig* douceur *f*; **to be all ~ and light** être tout sucre tout miel

S

sweet pea *n* pois *m* de senteur **sweet potato** *n* patate *f* douce **sweet talk** I. *n* baratin *m* II. *vt* **to sweet-talk** baratiner; **to sweet-talk sb into doing sth** baratiner qn pour lui faire faire qc **sweet tooth** *n fig* **to have a ~** adorer les sucreries **sweet william** *n* œillet *m* de poète

swell [swel] <swelled, swollen *o* swelled> I. *vt a. fig* gonfler; **to ~ the ranks** gonfler les rangs II. *vi* 1. (*get bigger*) se gonfler; (*wood*) gonfler; (*ankle, arm*) enfler; (*sea*) se soulever 2. (*get louder*) monter III. *n no pl, no indef art* 1. (*increase in sound*) crescendo *m* 2. (*movement of sea*) houle *f*

swell box *n* MUS boîte *f* expressive

swellhead ['swelhed] *n Am, pej* **to be a ~** avoir la grosse tête

swelling *n* 1. MED (*lump*) grosseur *f* 2. *no pl, no indef art* (*lump*) bosse *f*

swelter ['sweltəʳ, *Am:* -t̬ɚ] *vi* étouffer

sweltering *adj* (*heat*) écrasant(e)

swept [swept] *pt of* **sweep**

swerve [swɜːv, *Am:* swɜːrv] I. *vi* 1. AUTO (*change direction suddenly*) faire un écart 2. *fig* (*not uphold*) départir II. *n* (*change of direction*) écart *m*

swift[1] [swɪft] *adj* rapide

swift[2] [swɪft] *n* (*bird*) martinet *m*

swiftly *adv* rapidement

swiftness *n no pl* rapidité *f*

swig [swɪg] I. <-gg-> *vt inf* descendre II. *n inf* coup *m;* **to take a ~** descendre

swill [swɪl] I. *n no pl* 1. *fig, iron* (*pig feed*) pâtée *f* 2. (*rinsing*) lavage *m* à grande eau II. *vt* 1. (*rinse*) **to ~ (out)** laver à grande eau 2. *pej, inf* (*drink fast*) boire d'un trait; **to ~ (down) one's beer** descendre une bière

swim [swɪm] I. <swam *o a. Aus* swum, swum, -mm-> *vi* 1. (*propel oneself through water*) nager; **to go ~ming** aller nager; **to ~ across sth** traverser qc à la nage; **to ~ under sth** nager sous qc 2. *pej* (*float in liquid*) baigner 3. (*be full of water*) baigner; **to ~ with tears** baigner de larmes 4. (*whirl*) sembler tourbillonner; **to make sb's head ~** faire tourner la tête II. <swam *o a. Aus* swum, swum, -mm-> *vt* 1. (*cross*) traverser à la nage; **to ~ a river/Channel** traverser une rivière/la Manche à la nage 2. (*do*) **to ~ a few strokes** faire quelques brasses; **to ~ the butterfly stroke** faire la nage papillon III. *n* baignade *f;* **to go for a ~, to have a ~** aller nager ►**to be <u>in</u> the ~** être dans le coup

swimmer *n* 1. (*person who swims*) nageur, -euse *m, f;* **to be a strong ~** être un bon nageur 2. *pl, Aus, inf* (*swimming costume*) maillot *m*

swimming *n no pl* 1. (*act*) nage *f* 2. SPORT natation *f*

swimming bath *n* piscine *f* **swimming cap** *n* bonnet *m* de bain **swimming costume** *n Brit, Aus* maillot *m* de bain (une pièce)

swimmingly *adv inf* sans embrouille; **to go ~** marcher comme sur des roulettes

swimming match *n* compétition *f* de natation **swimming pool** *n* piscine *f* **swimming suit** *n* maillot *m* de bain **swimming trunks** *n* caleçon *m* de bain

swimsuit *n Am s.* **swimming suit**

swindle ['swɪndl] I. *vt* escroquer; **to ~ sb out of sth** escroquer qc à qn II. *n* escroquerie *f*

swindler *n pej* escroc *m*

swine [swaɪn] *n* <-(s)> *a. pej, a. inf* porc *m*

swing [swɪŋ] I. *n* 1. (*movement*) balancement *m* 2. (*punch*) volée *f;* **to take a ~ at sb** envoyer une volée à qn 3. (*hanging seat*) balançoire *f;* **porch ~** balancelle *f* 4. (*sharp change*) revirement *m;* **mood ~** saute *f* d'humeur 5. *Am* (*quick trip*) voyage *m* éclair; **to take a ~ through sth** faire un voyage éclair à travers qc 6. *no pl* (*music*) swing *m* 7. SPORT swing *m* ►**what you lose on the ~s, you gain on the <u>roundabouts</u>** *Brit, prov* ce qu'on gagne d'un côté, on le perd de l'autre; **to get (back) into the ~ of <u>things</u>** *inf* se remettre dans le bain; **to <u>go</u> with a ~** *Brit, inf* marcher du tonnerre II. <swung, swung> *vi* 1. (*move back and forth*) se balancer; **~ back and forth** se balancer d'avant en arrière 2. (*move circularly*) **to ~ (round)** se retourner 3. (*attempt to hit*) **to ~ at sb with sth** essayer de frapper qn avec qc 4. (*alter, change allegiance*) virer; **to ~ between sth and sth** balancer entre qc et qc; **to ~ to sth** passer à qc 5. *Am* (*stop shortly*) **to ~ by somewhere** passer quelque part 6. MUS (*exciting*) balancer ►**to ~ into <u>action</u>** se mettre au boulot III. <swung, swung> *vt* 1. (*move back and forth*) balancer 2. (*to turn round*) tourner 3. *inf* (*influence successfully*) arranger; **to ~ it** arranger les choses ►**to ~ the <u>balance</u>** faire pencher la balance

swing bridge *n* pont *m* tournant **swing door** *n Brit, Aus* 1. (*opens two ways*) porte *f* battante 2. (*revolves round*) porte *f* tourniquet

swingeing ['swɪndʒɪŋ] *adj Brit, form* considérable

swinger *n* (*partner-swapper*) échangiste *mf*

swipe [swaɪp] *inf* I. *vi* **to ~ at sb/sth** envoyer une volée à qn/qc II. *vt* 1. *Brit* (*hit with a sweeping motion*) envoyer une volée à 2. *inf* (*steal*) braquer 3. (*pass a magnetic card*) passer III. *n* volée *f;* **to take a ~ at sb/sth** envoyer une volée à qn/qc

swipe card *n* carte *f* à bande magnétique

swirl [swɜːl, *Am:* swɜːrl] I. *vi* tourbillonner II. *vt* faire tourbillonner III. *n* tourbillon *m*

swish [swɪʃ] I. *vi* 1. (*make a hissing noise*) siffler 2. (*make a rustling noise*) bruisser II. *vt* 1. (*move with a hissing noise*) faire siffler 2. (*move with a rustling noise*) faire bruisser III. <-er, -est> *adj a. pej, inf* chic *inv* IV. *n* 1. (*hissing sound*) sifflement *m* 2. (*rustling sound*) bruissement *m;* **with a ~ of sth** d'un bruissement de qc

Swiss [swɪs] I. *adj* suisse; ~ **German/French** suisse allemand/romand II. *n* Suisse *m,* Suissesse *f*
Swiss army knife *n* couteau *m* suisse
Swiss cheese *n* gruyère *m*
switch [swɪtʃ] I. <-es> *n* 1. (*control*) interrupteur *m* 2. (*substitution*) remplacement *m* 3. (*alteration*) revirement *m* II. *vi* changer; **to ~ (over) to sth** passer à qc; **to ~ from sth to sth** passer de qc à qc III. *vt* 1. (*change*) changer de; **to ~ one's attention to sth** reporter son attention sur qc 2. (*adjust settings*) régler; (*current*) commuter; (*train*) aiguiller; **to ~ a device to sth** mettre un appareil sur (la position) qc 3. (*exchange*) échanger
◆**switch off** I. *vt* éteindre II. *vi* 1. (*turn off*) éteindre 2. (*lose attention*) décrocher
◆**switch on** I. *vt* 1. (*turn on: light, TV, electric device*) allumer; (*water, gas, tap*) ouvrir 2. (*use*) **to ~ the charm** faire du charme 3. (*up-to-date*) **to be switched on** être branché II. *vi* s'allumer
switchback ['swɪtʃbæk] *n* route *f* en zigzag
switchblade ['swɪtʃbleɪd] *n Am* couteau *m* à cran d'arrêt
switchboard ['swɪtʃbɔːd, *Am:* -bɔːrd] *n* 1. ELEC tableau *m* de distribution 2. TEL standard *m;* ~ **operator** standardiste *mf*
switchman <-men> *n Am* aiguilleur *m*
switchyard *n Am* gare *f* de triage
Switzerland ['swɪtsələnd, *Am:* -sɚlənd] *n* la Suisse
swivel ['swɪvəl] I. *n* pivot *m* II. *adj inv* pivotant(e) III. <*Brit, Aus* -ll- *o Am* -l-> *vt* faire pivoter
swivel chair *n* chaise *f* pivotante
swizzle stick *n* fouet *m*
swollen ['swəʊlən, *Am:* 'swoʊ-] I. *pp of* **swell** II. *adj* 1. (*puffy*) enflé(e); **a ~ head** *péj* une grosse tête 2. (*fuller than usual*) gonflé(e)
swoon [swuːn] *vi* (*adore*) se pâmer; **to ~ over sb/sth** se pâmer d'admiration devant qn/qc
swoop [swuːp] I. *n* 1. (*dive in the air*) piqué *m;* **to make a ~ (down)** plonger en piqué 2. *inf* (*surprise attack*) descente *f* II. *vi* 1. (*dive through the air*) plonger en piqué 2. *inf* (*make a sudden attack: police*) faire une descente; **to ~ on sth** faire une descente dans qc
swop [swɒp, *Am:* swɑːp] <-pp-> *vt, vi Brit, Can s.* **swap**
sword [sɔːd, *Am:* sɔːrd] *n* épée *f;* **to put sb to the ~** passer qn au fil de l'épée ►**to have a ~ of Damocles hanging over one's head** avoir une épée de Damoclès au-dessus de la tête
swordfish <-(es)> *n* espadon *m* **swordsman** <-men> *n* HIST **a (skilled) ~** une fine lame **swordsmanship** *n no pl* habileté *f* à manier l'épée
swore [swɔː, *Am:* swɔːr] *pt of* **swear**
sworn [swɔːn, *Am:* swɔːrn] I. *pp of* swear II. *adj inv* sous serment; ~ **enemy** ennemi *m* juré
swot [swɒt, *Am:* swɑːt] <-tt-> *vi Brit, Aus, inf* bûcher
swum [swʌm] *pp, a. Aus pt of* **swim**
swung [swʌŋ] *pt, pp of* **swing**
sycamore ['sɪkəmɔːʳ, *Am:* -mɔːr] *n* sycomore *m*
sycophant ['sɪkəfænt, *Am:* -fənt] *n pej* lèche-bottes *mf inf*
sycophantic *adj* flagorneur(-euse)
syllabic *adj* syllabique
syllable ['sɪləbl] *n a. fig* syllabe *f*
syllabus ['sɪləbəs] <-es *o form* syllabi> *n* programme *m;* **to be on the ~** être au programme
sylphlike ['sɪlflaɪk] *adj* (*waist*) de sylphide; (*person*) à la taille de sylphide; **a ~ girl** une sylphide; **to be ~ to wear sth** avoir une taille de sylphide pour porter qc
symbiosis [ˌsɪmbɪ'əʊsɪs, *Am:* -'oʊ-] *n no pl* symbiose *f*
symbiotic *adj* symbiotique
symbol ['sɪmbl] *n* symbole *m*
symbolic(al) *adj* symbolique
symbolism ['sɪmbəlɪzəm] *n no pl* symbolisme *m*
symbolize ['sɪmbəlaɪz] *vt* symboliser
symmetrical [sɪ'metrɪkl] *adj* symétrique
symmetry ['sɪmətri] *n no pl* symétrie *f*
sympathetic [ˌsɪmpə'θetɪk, *Am:* -'θeţ-] *adj* 1. (*understanding*) compatissant(e); **to be ~ about sth** avoir de la compassion pour qc; **to lend a ~ ear to sb** prêter une oreille attentive à qn 2. (*supporting*) POL solidaire; **to be ~ towards sb/sth** être solidaire de qn/qc
sympathize ['sɪmpəθaɪz] *vi* 1. (*show understanding*) compatir; **to ~ with sb over sth** avoir de la compassion pour qn concernant qc 2. (*agree with*) être d'accord
sympathizer *n* sympathisant(e) *m(f)*
sympathy ['sɪmpəθi] *n no pl* 1. (*compassion*) compassion *f;* **to have ~ for sb** avoir de la compassion pour qn; **vote of ~** témoignage *m* de sympathie; **accept my sympathies** croyez à toute ma sympathie 2. (*feeling of agreement*) solidarité *f;* **to be in ~ with sb/sth** être solidaire de qn/qc; **to do sth in ~ with sb/sth** faire qc par solidarité avec qn/qc; **to have ~ with sb/sth** être en accord avec qn/qc
symphonic [sɪm'fɒnɪk, *Am:* -'fɑːnɪk] *adj* symphonique
symphony ['sɪmfəni] *n* symphonie *f*
symphony orchestra *n* orchestre *m* symphonique
symposium [sɪm'pəʊziəm, *Am:* -'poʊ-] <-s *o* -sia> *n form* symposium *m*
symptom ['sɪmptəm] *n* 1. (*sign of a disease*) symptôme *m* 2. (*indicator or sign*) indice *m*
symptomatic [ˌsɪmptə'mætɪk, *Am:* -'mæţ-] *adj* symptomatique

synagogue ['sɪnəgɒg, *Am:* -gɑːg] *n* synagogue *f*
sync [sɪŋk] **I.** *n* synchro *f* **II.** *vt* synchroniser
synchronize ['sɪŋkrənaɪz] **I.** *vt* synchroniser; **to ~ our watches** régler nos montres à la même heure; **to ~ our holidays** passer nos vacances en même temps **II.** *vi* être synchrone; **to ~ with sth** être synchrone avec qc
synchronous ['sɪŋkrənəs] *adj* synchrone
syncopate ['sɪŋkəpeɪt] *vt* MUS syncoper
syncope *n* syncope *f*
syndicate ['sɪndɪkət, *Am:* -dəkɪt] **I.** *n* **1.** (*group*) syndicat *m* **2.** (*organisation*) organisation *f;* (*of drug, crime*) cartel *m* **3.** (*organization selling articles*) agence *f* de presse **II.** *vt* **1.** (*sell to many newspapers*) publier (dans différents journaux) **2.** (*finance*) gérer; **~d credits** crédits *mpl* consortiaux
syndication *n no pl* **1.** (*selling to many newspapers*) publication *f* d'articles (dans divers journaux) **2.** (*financing by a group*) gestion *f* consortiale
syndrome ['sɪndrəʊm, *Am:* -droʊm] *n a. fig* syndrome *m*
synergism, **synergy** ['sɪnədʒi, *Am:* -ɚ-] *n no pl* synergie *f*
synod ['sɪnəd] *n* synode *m*
synonym ['sɪnənɪm] *n* synonyme *m*
synonymous [sɪ'nɒnɪməs] *adj* (*meaning the same*) synonyme; **to be ~ with sth** être un synonyme de qc; *fig* être synonyme de qc
synopsis [sɪ'næpsɪs] <-ses> *n* synopsis *m*
syntactic *adj* syntaxique
syntax ['sɪntæks] *n no pl* syntaxe *f*
synthesis ['sɪntθəsɪs] <-theses> *n* synthèse *f*
synthesize ['sɪnθəsaɪz] *vt* synthétiser
synthesizer *n* synthétiseur *m*
synthetic [sɪn'θetɪk, *Am:* -'θeţ-] *adj* **1.** (*man-made*) synthétique; (*product, sweeteners*) de synthèse; (*flavourings*) artificiel(le) **2.** (*fake*) artificiel(le)
syphilis ['sɪfɪlɪs, *Am:* 'sɪflɪs] *n no pl* syphilis *f*
syphilitic *adj* syphilitique
syphon ['saɪfn] *n s.* **siphon**
Syria ['sɪrɪə] *n* la Syrie
Syrian **I.** *adj* syrien(ne) **II.** *n* Syrien(ne) *m(f)*
syringe [sɪ'rɪndʒ, *Am:* sə'-] **I.** *n* **1.** (*suck out liquid*) seringue *f* **2.** (*spray liquid to clean*) poire *f* **II.** *vt* laver avec une poire; **to have one's ears ~d** se déboucher les oreilles avec une poire
syrup ['sɪrəp] *n no pl* sirop *m*
syrupy ['sɪrəpi] *adj a. pej* sirupeux(-euse)
system ['sɪstəm] *n a. pej a.* INFOR, MAT système *m;* **computer ~** système informatique; **operating ~** système d'exploitation; **a ~ error/analysis** une erreur/analyse de système ►**to get something out of one's ~** *inf* se débarrasser de qc
systematic [ˌsɪstə'mætɪk, *Am:* -'mæţ-] *adj* systématique
systematize ['sɪstəmətaɪz] *vt* systématiser
system operator *n* INFOR opérateur *m* du système

T

T, t [tiː] <-'s *o* -s> *n* T *m,* t *m;* **~ as in Tommy, ~ for Tommy** (*on telephone*) t comme Thérèse
t *n abbr of* **tonne** t *f*
ta [tɑː] *interj Brit, inf* (*thanks*) merci!
TA *n Brit abbr of* **Territorial Army** armée *f* territoriale
tab [tæb] *n* **1.** (*flap, strip*) étiquette *f* **2.** (*strip for recording device*) languette *f* **3.** *Am, Aus, inf* (*bill*) douloureuse; **to pick up the ~** payer la note *f* **4.** INFOR (*system*) tabulation *f;* (*key*) touche *f* de tabulation **5.** *Am* (*ring pull*) languette *f* **6.** MED (*of acid*) ticket *m* ►**to keep ~s on sb/sth** garder un œil sur qn/qc
tabby ['tæbi] **I.** *adj* **~ cat** (*with streaks*) chat *m* tigré (*with spots*) chat *m* moucheté **II.** *n* **1.** (*striped*) chat *m* tigré **2.** (*spotted*) chat *m* moucheté
tabernacle ['tæbənækl, *Am:* 'tæbɚ-] *n form* tabernacle *m*
table ['teɪbl] **I.** *n* **1.** (*piece of furniture*) table *f;* **to lay the ~** mettre la table **2.** (*group of people*) tablée *f* **3.** (*collection of information*) *a.* INFOR tableau *m;* **the two-times ~** MAT la table (de multiplication) de 2 ►**to do sth under the ~** (*illegally*) faire qc sous le manteau; **to be under the ~** *inf* (*be drunk*) rouler sous la table; **to put sth on the ~** (*submit*) présenter qc; *Am* (*postpone*) remettre qc; **to turn the ~s on sb** prendre sa revanche sur qn **II.** *vt* **1.** *Brit, Aus* (*propose*) présenter **2.** *Am* (*postpone*) remettre
tablecloth *n* nappe *f* **table linen** *n* linge *m* de table **table manners** *n* bonnes manières *fpl* **table mat** *n* **1.** (*for plates*) set *m* de table **2.** (*for hot dishes*) dessous-de-plat *m inv* **tablespoon** *n* cuiller *f* à soupe, cuiller *f* à table *Québec;* **a ~ of sugar** une cuiller à soupe de sucre
tablet ['tæblɪt] *n* **1.** (*pill*) comprimé *m;* **sleeping ~** somnifère *m* **2.** (*with inscription*) plaque *f* commémorative **3.** *Brit* (*~ of soap*) savonnette *f* **4.** *Am* (*pad of paper*) bloc *m*
table talk *n* menus propos *mpl* **table tennis** *n* tennis *m* de table **tableware** *n no pl, form* vaisselle *f* **table wine** *n* vin *m* de table
tabloid ['tæblɔɪd] *n* tabloïd *m;* **the ~ press, the ~s** la presse à scandale
taboo [tə'buː], **tabu** **I.** *n* tabou *m* **II.** *adj* tabou(e)
tabulate ['tæbjʊleɪt] *vt form* mettre sous la forme d'un tableau
tabulation *n no pl* **1.** (*using tables*) disposition *f* en tableau **2.** INFOR (*using tab keys*) tabu-

lation *f*

tabulator *n form* tabulateur *m*

tachograph ['tækəgrɑːf] *n* tachygraphe *m*

tachycardia [ˌtækɪ'kɑːdiə, *Am:* -'kɑːr-] *n* tachycardie *f*

tacit ['tæsɪt] *adj* tacite

taciturn ['tæsɪtɜːn, *Am:* -ətɜːrn] *adj* taciturne

tack [tæk] **I.** *n* **1.** (*short nail*) clou *m* **2.** (*drawing pin*) punaise *f* **3.** *no pl* (*riding gear*) sellerie *f* **4.** NAUT bordée *f* **5.** (*approach*) tactique *f* **6.** (*loose stitch*) point *m* de bâti **II.** *vt* **1.** (*nail down*) clouer; (*with a drawing pin*) punaiser **2.** (*sew loosely*) faufiler **III.** *vi* NAUT tirer une bordée

tackle ['tækl] **I.** *vt* **1.** (*to get ball*) intercepter **2.** (*deal with: person*) aborder; (*job*) s'attaquer à; (*problem*) aborder; **to ~ sb about sth** aborder qn au sujet de qc **II.** *n no pl* **1.** SPORT interception *f;* (*by bringing player down*) plaquage *m* **2.** (*gear*) équipement *m;* **fishing ~** articles *mpl* de pêche; **shaving ~** matériel *m* de rasage

tacky ['tæki] <-ier, -iest> *adj* **1.** (*sticky*) collant(e) **2.** *pej, inf* (*bad taste*) plouc

tact [tækt] *n no pl* tact *m*

tactful *adj* plein(e) de tact; **be ~!** sois délicat!

tactic ['tæktɪk] *n* **1.** (*approach*) stratégie *f,* la tactique **2.** *pl* MIL tactique *f*

tactical *adj* **1.** (*with a plan*) tactique **2.** MIL stratégique

tactician [tæk'tɪʃən] *n* tacticien(ne) *m(f)*

tactile ['tæktaɪl, *Am:* -tl] *adj form* tactile

tactless *adj* **to be ~** être dépourvu de tact

tactlessness *n no pl* manque *m* de tact

tadpole ['tædpəʊl, *Am:* -poʊl] *n* têtard *m*

taffeta ['tæfɪtə, *Am:* -t̬ə] *n no pl* taffetas *m*

tag [tæg] **I.** *n* **1.** (*label*) étiquette *f;* (*of metal*) plaque *f* **2.** *no pl* (*children's game*) jeu *m* du chat perché **3.** (*phrase*) citation *f* **4.** INFOR balise *f* **5.** (*electronic device*) bracelet *m* électronique **II.** <-gg-> *vt* **1.** (*label*) *a. fig* étiqueter **2.** (*touch*) toucher **3.** *Am* (*fine*) mettre une contravention à **4.** (*as punishment*) mettre un bracelet électronique à

◆**tag along** *vi inf* suivre

◆**tag on** *vt* rajouter

taiga ['taɪgə] *n no pl* taïga *f*

tail [teɪl] **I.** *n* **1.** (*on animal*) queue *f* **2.** (*rear*) postérieur *m* **3.** AVIAT queue *f* **4.** (*side of a coin*) face *f;* **heads or ~s? – ~s** pile ou face? – pile *f* **5.** *inf* (*buttocks*) derrière *m* **6.** *inf* (*spy*) fileur *m* ►**it's a case of the ~ wagging the dog** c'est le monde à l'envers; **I can't make head or ~ of it** je n'y comprends rien; **heads I win, ~s you lose** face je gagne, pile tu perds **II.** *vt* pister; **to be ~ed** être suivi

◆**tail back** *vi Brit* bouchonner

◆**tail off** *vt* diminuer; (*sound*) baisser

tailback *n Brit* bouchon *m* **tailboard** *n Brit s.* tailgate **tail end** *n* bout *m* **tailgate** **I.** *n* (*tailboard: of a car*) hayon *m;* (*of a lorry*) porte *f* arrière **II.** *vt, vi inf* coller **taillight** *n* AUTO feu *m* arrière

tailor ['teɪləʳ, *Am:* -lɚ] **I.** *n* tailleur *m* **II.** *vt* **1.** (*make clothes*) faire **2.** (*adapt*) adapter **3.** (*design*) **to ~ sth to sb's needs** faire qc sur mesure pour qn

tailor-made *adj* **1.** (*custom made*) fait(e) sur mesure **2.** (*perfect*) parfait(e)

tailpiece *n* appendice *m* **tailpipe** *n Am* tuyau *m* d'échappement **tailspin** *n* AVIAT vrille *f* **tail wind** *n* vent *m* arrière

taint [teɪnt] **I.** *vt* infecter; (*reputation*) souiller **II.** *n no pl* (*bad taste*) mauvais goût *m;* (*of immorality, scandal*) tache *f*

Taiwan [ˌtaɪ'wɑːn] *n* Taïwan *f sans art*

take [teɪk] **I.** *n* **1.** *no pl* (*receipts*) recette *f* **2.** (*filming*) prise *f* de vue **3.** (*view*) position *f;* **what's your ~ on this?** quel est ton avis là-dessus? ►**to be on the ~** *inf* se faire graisser la patte **II.** <took, taken> *vt* **1.** (*hold and move*) prendre; **to take sth from a shelf/the kitchen** prendre qc sur une étagère/dans la cuisine; **she took everything out of her bag** elle a tout sorti de son sac; **he took me in his arms** il m'a pris dans ses bras; **to take sb's hand** prendre la main de qn; **~ six from ten** MAT dix moins six **2.** (*so as to have with one*) prendre; (*to a different place: person*) emmener; (*things*) emporter; **she always ~s her camera/her secretary** elle prend toujours son appareil/sa secrétaire; **she's taken my paper** elle a pris [*o* emporté] mon journal; **can you ~ me to the station?** tu peux m'emmener à la gare?; **my job often took me to Paris** j'allais souvent à Paris pour le travail **3.** (*bring: guest, friend*) prendre; (*present, letter*) apporter; **~ them some chocolates** apporte-leur [*o* prends-leur] des chocolats **4.** (*accept: job, responsibility, payment*) prendre; (*cash, applicant*) accepter; (*advice*) suivre; **do you ~ this woman ...?** consentez-vous à prendre cette femme ...?; **to ~ things as they come** prendre les choses comme elles sont; **I can't ~ the pressure/the boredom** je ne supporte pas le stress/l'ennui; **how did she ~ the news?** comment a-t-elle pris la nouvelle?; **I can ~ a joke** j'ai le sens de la plaisanterie **5.** (*use for travel: train, bus, route*) prendre **6.** (*eat or drink: medicine, sugar*) prendre **7.** (*hold: people*) (pouvoir) contenir; (*traffic*) recevoir **8.** (*require: skills, patience, effort*) demander; (*time*) prendre; **it ~s 10 minutes/ages** ça prend 10 minutes/des siècles; **it took me all day to clean the house** ça m'a pris toute la journée de faire le ménage; **it took courage to admit it** il fallait du courage pour l'admettre **9.** (*win, capture: city, position*) s'emparer de; (*prisoners*) capturer; GAMES gagner; (*award*) remporter **10.** (*as a record: letter, notes, photos*) prendre **11.** (*expressing thoughts, understanding*) **to ~ the view that** dire qu'à son avis; **to ~ a serious view of sth** désapprouver fortement qc; **to ~ a relaxed attitude to sth** être souple au sujet de qc; **I ~ it you're coming** vous

T

venez, n'est-ce pas?; **I took him to mean tomorrow** j'avais compris qu'il voulait dire demain; ~ **my children, for example** regardez mes enfants, par exemple **12.** (*use*) **to take the chance** [*o* **opportunity**] **to** *+infin* saisir l'occasion de *+infin;* ~ **the time to think about it** prendre le temps d'y penser; **to** ~ **a size 14** faire taille 42; **to** ~ **a size 10 shue** chausser du 44 **13.** (*conduct: religious service*) célébrer; **to** ~ **sb's class** prendre la classe de qn **14.** *Brit, Aus* (*teach: subject*) enseigner; (*students*) enseigner à **15.** (*study: subject*) faire **16.** (*with specific objects*) **to** ~ **a rest** se reposer; **to** ~ **a walk** se promener; **to** ~ **office** entrer en fonction; **to** ~ **an interest in sb/sth** s'intéresser à qn/qc; **to** ~ **the score** *Brit* noter le score; **to** ~**an exam** passer un examen ►**not to** ~ **no for an answer** ne pas se contenter d'un non; **point** ~**n** très juste; ~ **my word for it** croyez-moi; **to** ~ **sb unawares** prendre qn au dépourvu; **what do you** ~ **me for?** pour qui tu me prends?; ~ **it from me** croyez-moi sur parole **III.** <took, taken> *vi* (*have effect*) prendre

◆**take aback** *vt* surprendre

◆**take after** *vi* ressembler à

◆**take along** *vt* emmener

◆**take apart** **I.** *vt* **1.** (*disassemble*) défaire; (*machine*) démonter **2.** (*analyse*) disséquer **3.** (*destroy: person, team, book*) démolir **II.** *vi* se démonter

◆**take away** **I.** *vt* **1.** (*remove*) prendre; **two coffees to** ~ deux cafés à emporter **2.** (*deprive of*) retirer **3.** (*bring away with*) éloigner **4.** (*make leave: death*) enlever; (*business*) éloigner de chez soi **5.** (*lessen: pain*) diminuer **6.** (*subtract from*) soustraire ►**to take sb's breath away** couper le souffle de qn **II.** *vi* (*detract from*) **to** ~ **from the beauty of sth** rendre qc moins beau

◆**take back** *vt* **1.** (*return to original place: borrowed book, faulty goods*) rapporter **2.** (*accept back*) reprendre **3.** (*accompany a person*) raccompagner **4.** (*let return: spouse*) se remettre avec; (*employee*) reprendre **5.** (*retract*) rétracter **6.** (*carry to a past time*) remonter à; **it takes you back, doesn't it?** ça te ramène dans le passé, n'est-ce pas?

◆**take down** *vt* **1.** (*bring lower*) descendre **2.** (*remove from high place*) déchoir **3.** (*remove*) enlever **4.** (*disassemble*) désassembler; (*scaffolding*) démonter **5.** (*write*) noter **6.** *inf* (*depress*) démoraliser

◆**take hold** *vi* **1.** (*become established: disease*) s'installer; (*belief*) se répandre **2.** (*grasp*) **to** ~ **of sb/sth** prendre qn/qc; **to** ~ **of sb** *fig* (*obsession, fury*) s'emparer de qn

◆**take in** *vt* **1.** (*bring inside: visitor*) faire entrer; (*washing, shopping*) rentrer **2.** (*accommodate*) héberger; (*for rent*) prendre **3.** (*admit: orphan, stray cat*) recueillir; (*student*) recevoir **4.** (*bring to police: lost property*) rapporter; (*criminal*) se faire emmener **5.** (*deceive*) tromper; **to be taken in by sb/sth** être trompé par qn/qc **6.** *Am, Aus* (*go to see*) **to** ~ **a cabaret/film** aller au cabaret/cinéma **7.** (*mentally: details*) absorber; (*sb's death*) accepter; **to** ~ **the scenery** se remplir du paysage **8.** (*include*) inclure **9.** (*narrow: trousers, skirt*) rétrécir **10.** (*do at home*) **to** ~ **typing/sewing** faire de la saisie/de la couture à domicile

◆**take off** **I.** *vt* **1.** (*undress: clothes*) enlever; (*hat, glasses*) retirer **2.** (*withdraw: product from market*) retirer; (*player from field*) faire sortir; (*programme, film*) retirer; **to take sb off drugs** faire décrocher qn de la drogue; **to take sb off a list** éliminer qn d'une liste; **to take a detective off a case** retirer une enquête à un détective; **to take sb off a diet** ne plus faire suivre de régime à qn **3.** (*leave*) **to take oneself off** partir à toute hâte **4.** (*not work*) **to take a day/a week off** (**work**) prendre un jour/une semaine de vacances **5.** (*subtract*) déduire; **I'll take 10% off for you** je vous fais une réduction de 10% **6.** *Brit* (*imitate*) imiter **II.** *vi* **1.** (*leave the ground: plane*) décoller; (*bird*) s'envoler **2.** *inf* (*leave*) déguerpir **3.** *inf* (*flee*) filer **4.** (*have success: project*) se développer; (*idea*) prendre; (*style, new product*) se répandre; **his business is really taking off in Japan** son affaire est en plein essor au Japon

◆**take on** **I.** *vt* **1.** (*start on: job, challenge*) prendre **2.** (*acquire: quality, appearance*) prendre **3.** (*put to work*) recruter **4.** (*oppose: enemy, rival*) s'attaquer à; SPORT (*team*) jouer contre; (*boxer*) boxer contre **5.** (*stop for loading: fuel*) faire le plein de; (*goods*) charger; (*passengers*) embarquer **II.** *vi* s'en faire

◆**take out** *vt* **1.** (*remove*) enlever; (*teeth*) extraire; (*item from drawer, bag*) sortir **2.** (*bring outside: chairs, washing*) sortir **3.** *Am* GASTR emporter; **pizzas to** ~ pizzas à emporter **4.** (*entertain: children, friend*) sortir; (*client*) inviter; **to take sb out to dinner** inviter qn à dîner **5.** *inf* (*kill*) éliminer **6.** (*destroy*) anéantir **7.** (*arrange to get*) se procurer; (*licence*) obtenir **8.** (*borrow*) emprunter **9.** (*vent*) **to take one's anger/frustration out on sb** se défouler de sa colère/frustration sur qn; **to take it out on sb** se défouler sur qn

◆**take over** **I.** *vt* **1.** (*buy out: company*) racheter **2.** (*take charge of: country*) prendre le contrôle; (*ministry, post, resposibility*) reprendre; **her job's taken over her life** son travail envahit sa vie **3.** (*assume: debts*) reconnaître **II.** *vi* (*as government*) prendre le pouvoir; (*as leader, manager*) prendre les rênes; **I'm tired of driving, you** ~ je suis fatigué de conduire, tu me remplaces; **to** ~ **as captain** devenir capitaine; **to** ~ **from sb** remplacer qn

◆**take to** *vi* **1.** (*start to like: person*) se mettre à aimer; (*hobby, activity*) prendre goût à **2.** (*begin as a habit*) **to** ~ **doing sth** se mettre à faire qc **3.** (*go to: forest, hills*) se réfugier dans ▶**to ~ one's bed** s'aliter; **to ~ sth like a duck to water** mordre à qc

◆**take up** *vt* **1.**(*bring up*) faire monter **2.**(*pick up*) ramasser; (*arms*) prendre **3.**(*start doing: post*) commencer; (*hobby, language*) se mettre à **4.**(*keep busy*) **to be taken up with sb/sth** être absorbé par qn/qc **5.**(*discuss*) discuter; (*matter, question*) aborder; **to take a problem up with sb** parler d'un problème avec qn **6.**(*accept: challenge*) relever; (*offer*) accepter; (*opportunity*) saisir; (*case*) se charger de; **to take sb up on an invitation** accepter l'invitation de qn **7.**(*adopt: attitude*) adopter; (*habit*) prendre **8.**(*continue: anecdote, explanation*) reprendre **9.**(*join in: song, slogan*) reprendre (en chœur) **10.**(*occupy: time, energy*) prendre **11.**(*shorten: coat, dress, pants*) raccourcir **12.**(*ask for*) **to ~ a collection** faire la quête **13.**(*query*) **to take sb up on sth** reprendre qn sur qc

◆**take up with** *vi* se mettre à fréquenter

takeaway *n* **1.** *Brit, Aus* (*restaurant*) *restaurant ou snack qui propose des plats à emporter* **2.**(*meal*) plat *m* à emporter; **a ~ coffee/pizza** un café/une pizza à emporter

taken I. *pp of* take II. *adj* **to be ~ with an idea/painting** être séduit par une idée/un tableau

take-off *n* **1.** AVIAT décollage *m* **2.** *Brit, Aus* (*imitation*) imitation *f*

takeout *n Am s.* **takeaway**

takeover *n* rachat *m*

takeover bid *n* offre *f* publique d'achat **takeover target** *n* ECON, FIN rachat *m* cible

taker ['teɪkəʳ, *Am:* -kɚ] *n* preneur *m;* **there were no ~s** il n'y a pas de preneur; **a drug-~** un(e) drogué(e); **a risk-~** une personne qui prend des risques

take-up *n* demande *f*

taking *n* **1.**(*action of taking*) prise *f;* **it's yours for the ~** c'est à toi **2.** *pl* (*receipts*) recette *f*

taking-over *n no pl* prise *f* de contrôle

talc [tælk], **talcum** (**powder**) I. *n no pl* talc *m* II. *vt* talquer

tale [teɪl] *n* **1.**(*story*) histoire *f* **2.** LIT conte *m* **3.**(*true story*) récit *m;* **to tell ~s** *péj* raconter des histoires ▶**dead men tell no ~s** les morts ne parlent pas

talent ['tælənt] *n* **1.**(*ability*) talent *m;* **a ~ for writing/annoying people** le don d'écrire/d'embêter tout le monde **2.** *Brit, Aus, iron, inf* (*attractive girls*) minettes *fpl;* (*boys*) mecs *mpl*

talented *adj* talentueux(-euse)

talisman ['tælɪzmən] *n* talisman *m*

talk [tɔːk] I. *n* **1.**(*discussion*) discussion *f;* **there's ~ of a new school** on parle d'une nouvelle école; **~s about peace** pourparlers de paix **2.**(*conversation*) conversation *f;* **to have a ~ with sb** avoir une conversation avec qn **3.**(*private*) entretien *m* **4.**(*lecture*) exposé *m* **5.** *no pl* (*things said*) paroles *fpl;* **too much ~ and no action** trop de parlotte et pas d'action; **you're all ~** *pej* tout ce que tu fais c'est parler; **to make small ~** parler de choses et d'autres II. *vi* **1.**(*speak*) parler; **everybody's ~ing** tout le monde fait des commentaires; **to talk to oneself** se parler à soi-même; **to ~ about a job** parler d'un travail; **we're ~ing about six million** il s'agit de six millions; **~ing about** [*o* **of**] **cats** puisqu'on parle de chats **2.**(*speak privately*) s'entretenir ▶**to ~ dirty to sb** parler crûment à qn III. *vt* **1.**(*speak: English, Arabic*) parler; **to ~ sb into/out of doing sth** convaincre qn de faire qc/de ne pas faire qc **2.** *inf* (*discuss*) discuter; **we're ~ing big changes** il s'agit de grands changements ▶**to be able to ~ the hind leg(s) off a donkey** *Brit, inf* être bavard comme une pie; **to ~ nonsense** [*o* **rubbish**] *Brit, pej* dire n'importe quoi; **to ~ some sense into sb's head** faire entendre raison à qn; **to ~ a blue streak** *Am* être un moulin à paroles; **to ~ turkey** *Am, inf* mettre cartes sur table

◆**talk back** *vi* **to ~ to sb** répondre à qn

◆**talk down to** *vt* parler avec condescendance à

◆**talk over** *vt* parler de

◆**talk round** *vt* **1.**(*convince*) convaincre **2.**(*avoid*) **to ~ sth** éviter de mentionner qc

◆**talk through** *vt* **1.**(*discuss*) débattre de **2.**(*reassure*) rassurer

talkative ['tɔːkətɪv, *Am:* -t̬ɪv] *adj* loquace

talker *n* **1.**(*speaker*) causeur, -euse *m, f* **2.**(*talkative person*) bavard(e)

talking I. *adj* **1.**(*that can talk*) qui parle **2.**(*expressive*) expressif(-ive) II. *n no pl* bavardage *m*

talking book *n* livre *m* enregistré **talking film** *n,* **talking picture** *n* film *m* parlant **talking point** *n* sujet *m* de discussion **talking-to** *n inf* **to give sb a ~** passer un savon à qn

talk show *n* talk-show *m*

tall [tɔːl] *adj* grand(e); (*grass, building*) haut(e); **to grow ~(er)** grandir; **to stand ~** se tenir droit; **to be over six feet ~** faire plus de d'1m 80 (de haut) ▶**that's a ~ order** c'est beaucoup demander; **a ~ story** une histoire incroyable

tallboy ['tɔːlbɔɪ] *n Brit* (petite) armoire *f*

tallness *n no pl* (*of a person*) grande taille *f;* (*of a building*) hauteur *f*

tallow ['tæləʊ, *Am:* -oʊ] *n no pl* suif *m*

tally ['tæli] <-ie-> I. *vi* (*correspond: figures*) faire le compte; (*facts, statements*) concorder; **to ~ with sth** correspondre à qc II. *vt* (*count, add up*) compter III. <-ies> *n sing* compte *m;* **to keep a ~ of sth** tenir le compte de qc

tally-ho [ˌtælɪ'həʊ, *Am:* -'hoʊ] *interj* taïaut!

talon ['tælən] *n* **1.**(*claw*) serre *f* **2.** *fig* griffe *f*

tamarind ['tæmərɪnd] *n* **1.**(*tree*) tamarinier *m* **2.**(*fruit*) tamarin *m*

tamarisk ['tæmərɪsk] *n* tamaris *m*

tambourine [ˌtæmbə'riːn] *n* tambourin *m*

tame [teɪm] I. *adj* **1.**(*domesticated: animals*)

T

apprivoisé(e); *fig* docile **2.** (*unexciting, dull*) plat(e) **3.** *Am* (*cultivated*) cultivé(e) **II.** *vt* apprivoiser, dompter

tamer *n* dompteur, -euse *m, f*

tam-o'-shanter *n* béret *m* écossais

tamp [tæmp] *vt* bourrer; **to ~ sth down** [*o* **to ~ down sth**] tasser qc

tamper with *vt* **1.** (*rig, manipulate*) toucher à **2.** (*meddle with, adjust: balance-sheet, documents*) falsifier; **her drink had been tampered with** on avait mis quelque chose dans son verre

tamper-proof, **tamper-resistant** *adj* (*top*) scellé(e)

tampon ['tæmpən, *Am:* -pɑːn] *n* tampon *m*

tan[1] [tæn] **I.** <-nn-> *vi* bronzer **II.** <-nn-> *vt* **1.** (*by sunlight*) bronzer; **to be ~ned** être bronzé **2.** (*to make into leather*) tanner **III.** *n* bronzage; **to get a ~** bronzer **IV.** *adj* fauve

tan[2] [tæn] *n* MAT *abbr of* **tangent** tan. *f*

tandem ['tændəm] **I.** *n* tandem *m* **II.** *adv* **to ride ~** faire du tandem

tang [tæŋ] *n* goût *m* fort

tangent ['tændʒənt] *n* MAT *a. fig* tangente *f*; **to go off on a ~** partir sur un autre sujet

tangential [tæn'dʒenʃl] *adj form* tangentiel(le)

tangerine [ˌtændʒə'riːn] **I.** *n* mandarine *f* **II.** *adj* mandarine *inv*

tangible ['tændʒəbl] *adj* tangible

tangible assets *n* valeurs *fpl* matérielles

Tangier ['tændʒɪəʳ, *Am:* tæn'dʒɪr] *n* Tanger

tangle ['tæŋgl] **I.** *n* **1.** (*mass of entwined threads*) enchevêtrement *m* **2.** *pej* (*confusion, muddle*) embrouille *f*; **to get in a ~ with lies** s'embrouiller dans les mensonges; **in a ~** embrouillé **II.** *vt* emmêler; **~d wires** fils emmêlés; **I got ~d (up) in the ropes** je me suis pris dans les cordes; **a ~d plot** *fig* une intrigue compliquée **III.** *vi* **1.** (*knot up*) s'emmêler **2.** (*quarrel*) s'accrocher; **don't ~ with her** ne te frotte pas à elle

tango ['tæŋgəʊ, *Am:* -goʊ] **I.** *n* tango *m*; **to do the ~** danser le tango **II.** *vi* danser le tango

tangy ['tæŋi] <-ier, -iest> *adj* **to be ~** avoir un goût fort

tank [tæŋk] *n* **1.** (*container for storage*) *a.* AUTO réservoir *m*; **fish ~** aquarium *m* **2.** (*container for fluid, gas*) citerne *f* **3.** MIL tank *m*

tank up **I.** *vi* faire le plein **II.** *vt inf* **to be tanked up** être bourré, avoir une caisse *Suisse*; **to get tanked up** se bourrer, prendre une caisse *Suisse*

tankard ['tæŋkəd, *Am:* -kɚd] *n* chope *f*

tanker ['tæŋkəʳ, *Am:* -ɚ] *n* **1.** (*boat*) navire-citerne *m* **2.** (*lorry*) camion-citerne *m*

tank top *n* débardeur *m*

tanned *adj* bronzé(e)

tanner *n* tanneur *m*

tannery *n* tannerie *f*

tannic acid [ˌtænɪk'æsɪd] *n* acide *m* tannique

tannin ['tænɪn] *n* tannin *m*

tanning *n* **1.** (*by sun*) bronzage *m* **2.** (*of hides*) tannage *m*

Tannoy® *n Brit* ≈ haut-parleurs *mpl*

tantalize ['tæntəlaɪz, *Am:* -t̬əlaɪz] *vt* **1.** (*torment*) tourmenter **2.** (*tease*) taquiner

tantalizing *adj* tentant(e); (*smell*) alléchant(e); (*smile*) énigmatique

tantamount ['tæntəmaʊnt, *Am:* -t̬ə-] *adj* **to be ~ to sth** revenir à qc

tantrum ['tæntrəm] *n* caprice *m*; **temper ~** colère *f*; **to have** [*o* **throw**] **a ~** faire un caprice

Tanzania [ˌtænzə'nɪə, *Am:* -'niːə] *n* la Tanzanie

Tanzanian **I.** *adj* tanzanien(ne) **II.** *n* Tanzanien(ne) *m(f)*

tap[1] [tæp] **I.** *n* **1.** *Brit* (*for water*) robinet *m*; **to turn the ~ on/off** ouvrir/fermer le robinet; **beer on ~** bière *f* à la pression **2.** (*directly available*) **on ~** disponible **3.** (*overhearing device*) écoute *f* téléphonique **II.** <-pp-> *vt* **1.** TEL **to ~ sb/sth** mettre qn/qc sur écoute téléphonique; **to ~ a conversation** intercepter une conversation; **to ~ a phone/line** placer un téléphone/une ligne sur écoute **2.** (*make use of, utilize*) exploiter **3.** (*let out via tap*) faire couler **4.** *fig, inf* **to ~ sb for money** taper de l'argent à qn **III.** *vi* **to ~ into sth** exploiter qc; **to ~ into the market** tirer profit du marché

tap[2] [tæp] **I.** *n* **1.** (*light knock*) tape *f* **2.** (*tap-dancing*) claquettes *fpl* **II.** *adj* de claquettes **III.** <-pp-> *vt* (*strike lightly*) tapoter; **to ~ sb on the shoulder** taper sur l'épaule de qn **IV.** <-pp-> *vi* **to ~ at the door** frapper à la porte; **to ~ one's foot on the floor** taper du pied sur le sol

tap dance ['tæpˌdɑːnts, *Am:* -ˌdænts] *n* claquettes *fpl*

tape [teɪp] **I.** *n* **1.** (*strip*) ruban *m* **2.** (*adhesive strip*) ruban *m* adhésif; **Scotch ~®** *Am* scotch® *m*; **sticky ~** *Brit, Aus* scotch® **3.** (*material for fastening*) courroie *f* **4.** (*tape measure*) mètre *m* ruban **5.** (*finishing ~*) fil *m* d'arrivée **6.** (*for recording*) bande *f* magnétique; **a video/audio ~** une cassette vidéo/audio **II.** *vt* **1.** (*fasten with tape*) **to ~ sth (up)** scotcher qc **2.** (*record*) enregistrer ►**to <u>have</u> (got) sb ~d** *Brit, Aus, fig, inf* savoir ce que qn a dans la tête

tape deck *n* platine *f* audio **tape measure** *n* mètre *m* ruban

taper **I.** *n* **1.** (*candle*) cierge *m* **2.** (*for lighting candle*) allume-feu *m* **II.** *vt* tailler en pointe; (*shape, trousers*) fuseler; (*hair*) effiler **III.** *vi* s'effiler; (*hair*) être effilé; **to ~ off** diminuer; **to ~ into sth** s'effiler en qc

tape reader *n* lecteur *m* de cassettes **tape-record** *vt* enregistrer **tape recorder** *n* magnétophone *m* **tape recording** *n* enregistrement *m*

tapered *adj* FASHION (*trousers, skirt*) en fuseau; (*skirt*) près du corps; AVIAT (*wing*) fuselé(e)

tapestry ['tæpɪstri, *Am:* -əstri] *n* **1.** (*fabric*)

tapisserie *f* **2.** (*sth containing variety*) fresque *f*
tapeworm ['teɪpwɜːm, *Am:* -wɜːrm] *n* ténia *m*
tapioca [ˌtæpɪ'əʊkə, *Am:* -'oʊ-] *n no pl* tapioca *m*
tapir ['teɪpəʳ, *Am:* -pɚ] *n* tapir *m*
tap water *n* eau *f* du robinet
tar [tɑːʳ, *Am:* tɑːr] **I.** *n no pl* goudron *m* ►**to spoil the ship for a ha'p'orth of ~** *Brit* tout gâcher pour des économies de bouts de chandelles; **to beat the ~ out of sb** *Am, inf* tabasser qn **II.** <-rr-> *vt* goudronner ►**to be ~red with the same brush** être mis dans le même panier
tarantula [tə'ræntjʊlə, *Am:* -tʃələ] *n* tarentule *f*
tare [teəʳ, *Am:* ter] *n* ECON tare *f*
target ['tɑːgɪt, *Am:* 'tɑːr-] **I.** *n* **1.** (*mark aimed at*) *a. fig* cible *f;* **to become a ~ for sb** devenir la cible de qn **2.** (*objective*) objectif *m;* **to be on ~** être en train d'atteindre son objectif; **to set oneself a ~** se fixer un objectif (à atteindre) **II.** <*Brit* -tt- *o Am* -t-> *vt* **1.** (*aim at*) viser; (*market, group*) cibler **2.** (*direct*) diriger **III.** *adj* (*market, audience*) viser; **~ date** date *f* ciblée
targeted *adj Brit* ciblé(e) **target language** *n* langue *f* cible **target practice** *n* exercices *mpl* de tir **target price** *n* prix *m* de référence
tariff ['tærɪf, *Am:* 'ter-] *n* **1.** *Brit, form* (*list of charges*) tarif *m* **2.** (*import, export duty*) droit *m* de douane; **import ~s** droits à l'importation
tariff barrier *n* barrière *f* douanière
tarmac® ['tɑːmæk, *Am:* 'tɑːr-], **tarmacadam®** **I.** *n no pl* **1.** *Brit* (*paving material*) macadam *m* **2.** AVIAT piste *f* **II.** <-ck-> *vt Brit* goudronner
tarn [tɑːn, *Am:* tɑːrn], **Tarn** *n* petit lac *m* de montagne
tarnish **I.** *vi* se ternir **II.** *vt a. fig* ternir **III.** *n* ternissure *f*
tarpaulin [tɑː'pɔːlɪn, *Am:* tɑːr'pɑː-] *n* **1.** *no pl* (*cloth*) toile *f* de bâche **2.** (*sheet*) bâche *f*
tarragon ['tærəgən, *Am:* 'terəgɑːn] *n no pl* estragon *m*
tart[1] [tɑːt, *Am:* tɑːrt] **I.** *n* (*type of pastry*) tarte *f;* **fruit/jam ~** tarte aux fruits/à la confiture **II.** *adj* **1.** (*sharp, acid in taste*) acide **2.** *fig* acerbe; (*wit*) caustique
tart[2] [tɑːt, *Am:* tɑːrt] *n Brit, pej, inf* pute *f*
tart up *vt Brit, inf* **1.** (*dress, make oneself up*) **to tart oneself up** se pomponner **2.** (*renovate, refurbish*) retaper
tartan ['tɑːtn, *Am:* 'tɑːrtn] **I.** *n no pl* tartan *m* **II.** *adj* écossais(e)
tartar[1] ['tɑːtəʳ, *Am:* 'tɑːrt̬ɚ] *n no pl* tartre *m*
tartar[2] ['tɑːtəʳ, *Am:* 'tɑːrt̬ɚ], **Tartar** *n pej* brute *f*
tartar(e) sauce *n no pl* sauce *f* tartare
tartaric [tɑː'tærɪk, *Am:* tɑːr-] *adj inv* tartrique
task [tɑːsk, *Am:* tæsk] **I.** *n* tâche *f;* **to take sb to ~** réprimander qn **II.** *vt passive* **to be ~ed with sth** être chargé de qc
task bar *n* INFOR barre *f* des tâches **task force** *n* **1.** (*unit for special operation*) corps *m* expéditionnaire **2.** (*group for particular purpose*) groupe *m* de travail **taskmaster** *n* **to be a hard ~** être un tyran au travail
Tasmania [tæz'meɪnɪə] *n* la Tasmanie
Tasmanian **I.** *adj* tasmanien(ne) **II.** *n* Tasmanien(ne) *m(f)*
tassel ['tæsl] *n* gland *m*
taste [teɪst] **I.** *n* **1.** *no pl* (*sensation*) goût *m;* **sense of ~** goût *m;* **to acquire a ~ for sth** prendre goût à qc; **to lose the ~ for sth** perdre le goût de qc **2.** (*small portion of food*) bouchée *f* **3.** (*liking, fondness*) goût *m;* **to have expensive ~s** avoir des goûts de luxe; **to get a ~ for sth** prendre goût à qc **4.** *no pl* (*aesthetic quality, discernment*) goût *m;* **to have (good) ~** avoir bon goût; **it's a matter of (personal) ~** c'est une question de goût; **to be in excellent ~** être d'un goût exquis; **to be in terrible ~** être de très mauvais goût **5.** *no pl* (*short encounter, experience*) aperçu *m;* **to have a ~ of victory/freedom** goûter à la victoire/à la liberté; **to give sb a ~ of army life** faire goûter qn à la vie militaire; **to give sb a ~ of the whip** faire tâter du fouet à qn **6.** *fig* **to have a ~ of sth** avoir un avant-goût de qc **II.** *vt a. fig* goûter à **III.** *vi* + *adj* **to ~ bitter/salty/sweet** avoir un goût amer/salé/sucré; **to ~ of sth** avoir un goût de qc, goûter qc *Belgique, Québec;* **to ~ like sth** avoir le même goût que qc
tastebud ['teɪstbʌd] *n* papille *f* (gustative)
tasteful *adj* de bon goût
tasteless *adj* **1.** (*without flavour*) fade **2.** *pej* (*showing bad taste, unstylish*) de mauvais goût
taster *n* **1.** (*food, drink professional*) dégustateur, -trice *m, f* **2.** *Brit* (*sample to arouse enthusiasm*) avant-goût *m*
tasty *adj* appétissant(e); **to be ~** être appétissant, goûter *Belgique, Québec*
tat [tæt] *n no pl, pej, inf* camelote *f*
tatter *n pl* **to be in ~s** être en lambeaux
tattered *adj* **1.** (*clothes*) en lambeaux **2.** *fig* (*reputation*) ruiné(e)
tattle ['tætl, *Am:* 'tæt̬-] *n* racontars *mpl*
tattoo [tə'tuː, *Am:* tæt'uː] **I.** *n* **1.** MIL retraite *f* **2.** (*marking on skin*) tatouage *m* **II.** *vt* tatouer
tatty ['tæti, *Am:* 'tæt̬-] <-ier, -iest> *adj pej* minable
taught [tɔːt, *Am:* tɑːt] *pt, pp of* **teach**
taunt [tɔːnt, *Am:* tɑːnt] **I.** *vt* railler **II.** *n* raillerie *f*
Taurean *adj* (*in astrology*) (du signe du) Taureau
Taurus ['tɔːrəs] *n* Taureau *m; s. a.* **Aquarius**
taut [tɔːt, *Am:* tɑːt] *adj* **1.** (*pulled tight*) tendu(e) **2.** (*concise*) concis(e)
tautological *adj* tautologique
tautologous *adj* tautologique
tautology [tɔː'tɒlədʒi, *Am:* tɑː'tɑːlə-]

T

<-ies> *n* tautologie *f*

tavern ['tævən, *Am:* -ɚn] *n* taverne *f*

tawdry ['tɔːdri, *Am:* 'tɑː-] <-ier, -iest> *adj pej* vulgaire

tawny ['tɔːni, *Am:* 'tɑː-] <-ier, -iest> *adj* fauve

tax [tæks] **I.** <-es> *n* **1.** (*levy by state: direct*) impôt *m;* (*indirect*) taxe *f;* ~ **on income** impôt sur le revenu; **to put a** ~ **on cigarettes** imposer une taxe sur les cigarettes; **a** ~ **form** une feuille d'impôts; **a** ~ **problem/advice** un problème/conseil fiscal; **pre-~ profits** bénéfices avant imposition; **after/before** ~ après/avant imposition; **the car is ~ed** la vignette de la voiture est payée **2.** *fig* (*nerves, patience, resources*) charge *f;* **to be a** ~ **on sb/sth** être une épreuve pour qn/qc **II.** *vt* **1.** (*levy a tax on*) taxer; (*person*) imposer; **to be ~ed lightly/heavily** être légèrement/lourdement taxé [*o* imposé] **2.** (*make demands on, strain*) **to** ~ **sb/sb's patience** mettre qn/la patience de qn à l'épreuve; **to** ~ **sb's memory** faire appel à la mémoire de qn **3.** (*accuse*) **to** ~ **sb with sth** taxer qn de qc; **to** ~ **sb with doing sth** accuser qn de faire qc

taxable *adj* imposable

tax allowance *n* abattement *m* fiscal **tax arrears** *n* arriérés *mpl* d'impôts **tax assessment** *n* facture *f* d'impôts

taxation [tæk'seɪʃən] *n no pl* **1.** (*levying*) imposition *f* **2.** (*money*) impôts *mpl;* **direct/indirect** ~ *Brit* impôts *mpl* directs/indirects

tax bracket *n* tranche *f* d'imposition **tax collector** *n* percepteur, -trice *m, f* **tax consultant** *n* conseiller, -ère *m, f* fiscal(e) **tax-deductible** *adj Am, Aus* déductible des impôts **tax disc** *n Brit* vignette *f* automobile **tax dodging** *n* fraude *f* fiscale **tax evader** *n* fraudeur, -euse *m, f* **tax evasion** *n s.* **tax dodging tax exemption** *n* exemption *f* d'impôts **tax-free** *adj* non-taxé(e) **tax haven** *n* paradis *m* fiscal **tax holiday** *n* répit *m* fiscal

taxi ['tæksi] **I.** *n* taxi *m* **II.** *vi* rouler

taxidermist *n* taxidermiste *mf*

taxidermy ['tæksɪˌdɜːmi, *Am:* -dɜːr-] *n* taxidermie *f*

taxi driver *n* chauffeur *m* de taxi

taximeter ['tæksɪmiːtəʳ, *Am:* -t̬ɚ] *n* compteur *m* (de taxi)

taxi rank *n Brit,* **taxi stand** *n Am* station *f* de taxis

taxman ['tæksmæn] *n no pl* percepteur *m;* **the** ~ le fisc

taxonomy [tæk'sɒnəmi, *Am:* -'sɑːnə-] *n* taxinomie *f*

taxpayer *n* contribuable *mf* **tax point** *n* ≈ indice *m* fiscal **tax rebate** *n* dégrèvement *m* fiscal **tax relief** *n* dégrèvement *m* fiscal **tax return** *n* déclaration *f* d'impôts; **to do one's** ~ remplir sa feuille d'impôts **tax year** *n* année *f* fiscale

TB [ˌtiː'biː] *n abbr of* **tuberculosis** tuberculose *f*

T-bar ['tiːbɑːʳ, *Am:* -bɑːr], **T-bar lift** *n* remonte-pente *m*

tbs. *n abbr of* **tablepoon**(**ful**) cuillerée *f* à soupe

tea [tiː] *n* **1.** *no pl* (*plant*) thé *m* **2.** (*drink*) thé *m;* **mint** ~ thé à la menthe **3.** (*cup of tea*) thé *m* **4.** *Brit* (*late afternoon meal*) goûter *m* **5.** *Brit, Aus* (*early evening cooked meal*) dîner *m;* **afternoon** ~ thé *m*

tea bag *n* sachet *m* de thé, poche *f* de thé *Québec* **tea break** *n Brit* pause-café *f* **tea caddy** *n* boîte *f* à thé **teacake** *n Brit* petite brioche *f*

teach [tiːtʃ] <taught, taught> **I.** *vt* SCHOOL (*subject, students*) enseigner; **to** ~ **history to children** enseigner l'histoire aux enfants; **I'm ~ing in five minutes** je fais cours dans cinq minutes; **to** ~ **sb to fish** apprendre à qn à pêcher; **to** ~ **sb how to tie their laces** apprendre à qn comment faire ses lacets; **to** ~ **school** *Am* enseigner; **to** ~ **oneself sth** apprendre qc tout seul; **to** ~ **sb that ...** apprendre à qn que ... ►**that'll** ~ **you a lesson** ça t'apprendra; **you can't** ~ **your grandmother to suck eggs** on n'apprend pas à un vieux singe à faire la grimace *prov* **II.** *vi* enseigner

teacher ['tiːtʃəʳ, *Am:* -tʃɚ] *n* (*in primary education*) instituteur, -trice *m, f;* (*in secondary education*) professeur *mf;* **the ~s** les enseignants *mpl;* **supply** [*o* **substitute**] ~ *Am* remplaçant(e) *m(f)*

teacher training *n* formation *f* pédagogique

tea chest *n* caisse *f* (à thé)

teach-in *n* séminaire *m*

teaching *n* **1.** *no pl* (*instruction, profession*) l'enseignement *m* **2.** *pl* (*doctrine, precept*) enseignements *mpl*

teaching hospital *n* CHU *m* **teaching job** *n* poste *m* d'enseignant **teaching method** *n* méthode *f* pédagogique **teaching staff** *n* corps *m* enseignant

tea cloth *n Brit* torchon *m* de cuisine **tea cosy** *n* cosy *m* **teacup** *n* tasse *f* à thé **tea garden** *n* **1.** (*garden cafe*) salon *m* de thé **2.** (*area with tea plantation*) plantation *f* de thé

teak [tiːk] *n no pl* teck *m;* **a** ~ **chair** une chaise en teck

tea leaf *n* feuille *f* de thé

team [tiːm] **I.** *n* + *sing/pl vb* **1.** (*group*) équipe *f* **2.** (*set of working animals*) attelage *m* **II.** *vi* (*match*) être assorti

◆**team up with** *vt* faire équipe avec

team captain *n* chef *m* d'équipe **team effort** *n* effort *m* d'équipe **teammate** *n* coéquipier, -ère *m, f* **team play** *n* jeu *m* d'équipe **team spirit** *n* esprit *m* d'équipe **teamwork** *n* travail *m* d'équipe

teapot *n* théière *f*

tear¹ [tɪəʳ, *Am:* tɪr] *n* larme *f;* **to be in ~s** être en larmes; **to burst into ~s** éclater en sanglots; **to have ~s in one's eyes** avoir des larmes dans les yeux; **to reduce sb to ~s** faire pleurer qn; **to not shed** (**any**) **~s over** ne pas verser la moindre larme sur

tear[2] [teəʳ, *Am:* ter] **I.** *n* déchirure *f;* **there's a ~ in your shirt** ta chemise est déchirée **II.** <tore, torn> *vt* **1.** (*rip, pull apart*) *a. fig* déchirer; **to ~ a hole in sth** faire un trou dans qc (en le déchirant); **to ~ sth into shreds** mettre qc en lambeaux; (*to ~ a muscle*) se déchirer un muscle; **to ~ sb/sth to shreds** *fig* mettre qn/qc en pièces **2.** *fig* **to be torn between X and Y** être déchiré entre X et Y **III.** <tore, torn> *vi* **1.** (*rip, come asunder*) se déchirer **2.** (*rush wildly*) foncer; **to ~ along** foncer; **to ~ down the stairs** dévaler l'escalier; **to ~ in** entrer à toute allure; **to ~ off** partir à toute allure

◆**tear apart** *vt* **1.** (*rip wildly: package, machine*) mettre en pièces **2.** (*divide: party, family*) déchirer **3.** (*criticise, attack: physically*) démolir; (*in writing*) descendre en flammes **4.** (*search thoroughly, ransack*) mettre sens dessus dessous en cherchant

◆**tear at** *vt* **1.** (*rip: wrapping*) déchirer **2.** (*attack: prey*) s'attaquer à; (*person*) griffer; **to ~ at each other's throats** (*physically*) se prendre à la gorge; (*in writing, speech*) s'agresser

◆**tear away** *vt* arracher; **to tear sb away from sb/sth** arracher qn à qn/qc; **to tear oneself away** s'arracher

◆**tear down** *vt* (*poster*) arracher; (*building*) détruire; **to ~ the barriers between communities** *fig* briser les barrières qui séparent les communautés

◆**tear into** *vt inf* **1.** (*attack*) foncer dans **2.** (*criticize: employee*) s'en prendre à; (*film, book*) attaquer

◆**tear off** *vt* détacher; (*roughly*) arracher; **to ~ one's clothes** se déshabiller prestement

◆**tear open** *vt* déchirer

◆**tear out** *vt* **1.** (*rip*) arracher **2.** *fig* **to tear one's hair out over sth** s'arracher les cheveux pour qc

◆**tear up** *vt* **1.** (*rip into small pieces*) *a. fig* déchirer; (*agreement*) jeter à la poubelle **2.** (*damage, destroy*) détruire; **to ~ a flowerbed** arracher les fleurs d'une platebande

tearaway *n Brit, Aus, inf* casse-cou *m*

teardrop *n* larme *f*

tearful *adj* (*parent*) en larmes; **~ letters/reunions** des lettres/retrouvailles pleines de larmes

tear gas *n* gaz *m* lacrymogène **tear jerker** *n inf* mélo *m* **tear-off** *adj* détachable

tearoom, **tea room** *n* salon *m* de thé

tease [tiːz] **I.** *vt* **1.** (*make fun of*) taquiner **2.** (*provoke sexually*) allumer **3.** *Am* (*backcomb: hair*) crêper **II.** *vi* plaisanter **III.** *n* **1.** *inf* (*playful person*) taquin(e) *m(f)* **2.** *pej* (*flirt*) allumeur, -euse *m, f*

teaser *n* **1.** (*playful person*) taquin(e) *m(f)* **2.** *pej* (*flirt*) allumeur, -euse *m, f* **3.** (*introductory advertisement*) teaser *m* **4.** *inf* (*difficult question, task*) colle *f*

tea service, **tea set** *n* service *m* à thé **tea shop** *n Brit s.* **tearoom** **teaspoon** *n* cuillère *f* à café, cuillère *f* à thé *Québec*

teaspoonful *n* cuillère *f* à café

tea-strainer *n* passoire *f* à thé

teat [tiːt] *n* **1.** (*nipple of beast*) mamelon *m* **2.** (*artificial nipple*) tétine *f*

teatime *n sing, Brit* l'heure *m* du thé **tea towel** *n Brit* torchon *m,* drap *m* de maison *Belgique,* patte *f Suisse* **tea tray** *n* plateau *m* **tea trolley** *n,* **tea wagon** *n Am* chariot *m*

technical ['teknɪkəl] *adj* technique

technical college *n* ≈ établissement *m* d'enseignement technique

technicality [ˌteknɪ'kæləti, *Am:* -nə'kæləṭi] <-ies> *n* **1.** (*technical aspect*) technicité *f* **2.** *pej* (*trivial matter*) détail *m* technique; **aquitted on a ~** LAW acquitté sur un vice de forme

technician [tek'nɪʃən] *n* technicien(ne) *m(f)*

technique [tek'niːk] *n* technique *f*

technocracy <-ies> *n* technocratie *f*

technocrat ['teknəʊkræt] *n* technocrate *mf*

technological *adj* technologique

technology [tek'nɒlədʒi, *Am:* -'nɑːlə-] *n* technologie *f*

teddy ['tedi] <-ies> *n* nounours *m*

teddy bear *n* ours *m* en peluche

tedious ['tiːdiəs] *adj* ennuyeux(-euse)

tediousness, **tedium** *n no pl* ennui *m*

tee [tiː] *n* tee *m*

tee off **I.** *vi* **1.** SPORT commencer le jeu **2.** *fig, inf* (*start*) démarrer **3.** *Am, inf* (*become irritated*) s'énerver **II.** *vt Am, inf* énerver

teem [tiːm] *vi* **1.** METEO **it is ~ing** (**with rain**) il pleut des cordes **2.** *fig* **to be ~ing with** (*shoppers, insects, birds*) grouiller de

teeming *adj* grouillant(e)

teenage, **teenaged** *adj* adolescent(e); (*style, interest*) (d')adolescent; **~ crime** délinquance *f* juvénile

teenager ['tiːneɪdʒəʳ, *Am:* -dʒɚ] *n* adolescent(e) *m(f)*

teens [tiːnz] *npl* adolescence *f;* **to be in one's ~** être un adolescent

teensy [tiːnzi], **teensy weensy**, **teeny** *adj inf* minuscule

teenybopper ['tiːniˌbɒpəʳ, *Am:* -ˌbɑːpɚ] *n inf* minette *f*

teeny weeny [ˌtiːni'wiːni] *adj s.* **teensy**

tee shirt ['tiːʃɜːt, *Am:* -ʃɜːrt] *n* tee-shirt *m*

teeter ['tiːtəʳ, *Am:* -ṭɚ] *vi* **1.** (*sway back and forth*) chanceler **2.** *fig* **to ~ between sth and sth** hésiter entre qc et qc; **to ~ on the brink of sth** être à deux doigts de qc

teeth [tiːθ] *n pl of* **tooth**

teethe [tiːð] *vi* faire ses dents

teething *adj* dentition *f*

teething problems, **teething troubles**

n Brit, Aus, fig ratés *mpl* de départ

teetotal [ˌtiːˈtəʊtəl, *Am:* -ˈtoʊt̬əl] *adj* **to be ~** ne jamais boire une goutte d'alcool

teetotaler *n Brit, Aus,* **teetotaller** *n Am: personne qui ne boit jamais d'alcool*

tel. *n abbr of* **telephone** tél. *m*

telecast [ˈtelɪkɑːst, *Am:* -kæst] *n Am* émission *f* de télévision

telecommunications [ˈtelɪkəˌmjuːnɪˈkeɪʃnz] *npl* télécommunications *fpl*

telecommuting [ˈtelɪkɒˌmjuːtɪŋ] *n no pl* INFOR télétravail *m*

teleconference [ˈtelɪˌkɒnfərəns, *Am:* -ˌkɑːn-] *n* téléconférence *f*

telecopier® *n Am* télécopieur *m*

telecopy [ˈtelɪkɑpi] *n Am* télécopie *f*

telefax® [ˈtelɪfæks] *n* télécopie *f*

telegenic [ˌtelɪˈdʒenɪk, *Am:* -əˈ-] *adj* télégénique

telegram [ˈtelɪgræm] *n* HIST télégramme *m*

telegraph [ˈtelɪgrɑːf, *Am:* -græf] **I.** *n no pl* télégraphe *m;* **by ~** par télégraphe **II.** *vt* **to ~ sth to sb** télégraphier qc à qn

telegraphic *adj* HIST télégraphique

telegraph pole, telegraph post *n Brit, Aus* poteau *m* télégraphique

telegraphy [tɪˈlegrəfi, *Am:* təˈleg-] *n no pl* télégraphie *f*

telemessage [ˈtelɪˌmesɪdʒ], **Telemessage** *n Brit* ≈ télégramme *m*

telepathic *adj* télépathique; **to be ~** être médium

telepathy [tɪˈlepəθi, *Am:* təˈ-] *n no pl* télépathie *f*

telephone [ˈtelɪfəʊn, *Am:* -əfoʊn] **I.** *n* téléphone *m;* **by ~** par téléphone; **on the ~** au téléphone; **to pick up the ~** prendre le téléphone; **~ bill** facture *f* de téléphone; **~ booking** réservation *f* par téléphone **II.** *vt* appeler **III.** *vi* téléphoner; **to ~ long-distance** faire un appel longue distance

telephone book *n* annuaire *m* **telephone booth, telephone box** *n Am* cabine *f* téléphonique **telephone call** *n* appel *m* téléphonique; **to make a ~** passer un appel **telephone conversation** *n* conversation *f* téléphonique **telephone directory** *n s.* **telephone book telephone exchange** *n Brit* central *m* téléphonique **telephone message** *n form* message *m* téléphonique **telephone number** *n* numéro *m* de téléphone **telephone operator** *n Am,* **telephonist** *n Brit* standardiste *mf*

telephony [tɪˈlefəni, *Am:* təˈ-] *n no pl* téléphonie *f*

telephoto lens [ˌtelɪˈfəʊtəʊ ˈlens, *Am:* ˈteləfoʊt̬oʊ-] *n* téléobjectif *m*

teleprocessing [ˈtelɪprəʊˌsesɪŋ] *n* INFOR télétraitement *m*

telesales [ˈtelɪseɪls] *n no pl* télévente *f*

telescope [ˈtelɪskəʊp, *Am:* -əskoʊp] **I.** *n* télescope *m* **II.** *vt* **1.** *(make shorter)* télescoper **2.** *fig* condenser **III.** *vi* se télescoper

telescopic *adj* télescopique; **~ observation** observation *f* au télescope

telescopic lens *n* téléobjectif *m* **telescopic sight** *n* lunette *f*

teleshopping [ˈtelɪˌʃɒpɪŋ, *Am:* ˈteləˌʃɑːpɪŋ] *n no pl* INFOR téléachat *m*

teletex®, Teletex® [ˈtelɪteks] *n no pl, Brit* télétex® *m*

teletext [ˈtelɪtekst, *Am:* ˈ-ə-] *n no pl* télétexte *m*

teletype®, Teletype® [ˈtelɪtaɪp, *Am:* ˈ-ə-] *n,* **teletypewriter** *n Am* télétype® *m*

televise [ˈtelɪvaɪz, *Am:* ˈtelə-] *vt* téléviser; **to ~ live** retransmettre en direct

television [ˈtelɪˌvɪʒən, *Am:* ˈteləvɪʒ-] *n* télévision *f;* **on ~** à la télévision

television advertising *n* publicité *f* télévisée **television camera** *n* caméra *f* de télévision **television journalist** *n* journaliste *mf* de télévision **television licence** *n Brit* ≈ redevance *f* télé **television program** *n Am, Aus,* **television programme** *n Brit* programme *m* de télévision **television screen** *n* écran *m* de télévision **television station** *n* chaîne *f* de télévision **television studio** *n* studio *m* de télévision **television transmitter** *n* émetteur *m* de télévision **television viewer** *n* téléspectateur, -trice *m, f*

teleworking [ˈtelɪˌwɜːkɪŋ, *Am:* -ˌwɜːr-] *n no pl* télétravail *m*

telex [ˈteleks] **I.** *n* télex *m;* **by ~** par télex **II.** *vt* envoyer par télex **III.** *vi* envoyer un télex

telex machine *n* télex *m inv*

tell [tel] **I.** <told, told> *vt* **1.** *(giving information)* dire; **to ~ sb about** [*o* **of**] **sth** parler de qc à qn; **to ~ sb (that) …** dire à qn que …; **we were told that …** on nous a dit que …; **we were told by the police that …** la police nous a dit que …; **to ~ sb what happened/where sth is** dire à qn ce qui s'est passé/où se trouve qc; **nobody was told why he left** personne n'a su pourquoi il était parti; **to ~ sb about a change/a meeting** informer qn d'un changement/d'une réunion; **don't ~ anyone** ne dis à personne; **I wasn't told** on ne m'a rien dit; **your house ~s people a lot about you** votre maison en dit long sur vous; **to ~ sb the time** donner l'heure à qn; **he can ~ the time** il sait lire l'heure; **to ~ sb's fortune** dire la bonne aventure à qn; **to ~ the future** prédire l'avenir **2.** *(narrate: story)* raconter; **to ~ sb (about) what happened** raconter qc à qn **3.** *(command)* **to ~ sb to +infin** dire à qn de *+infin;* **do as you're told** *inf* fais ce qu'on te dit **4.** *(make out)* discerner; **I can ~ if it's good** je sais tout de suite si c'est bon; **to ~ the difference** faire la différence; **you can never ~** on ne peut jamais savoir **5.** *(count)* compter; **all told** en tout ►**I'll ~ you what** tu sais quoi; **there's no ~ling** Dieu seul sait; **that would be ~ing** *inf* ça c'est mon affaire; **I told you so** je te l'avais bien dit; **didn't I ~ you?** je t'avais dit; **what did I ~ you?** *inf* je te l'avais bien dit; **~ me another (one)** *inf* à d'autres; **you're ~ing me!** *inf* à qui le dis-tu? **II.** <told, told> *vi* dire; **will she ~?** est-ce qu'elle va rapporter?

◆**tell against** *vt Brit, form* jouer contre

◆**tell apart** *vt* différencier

◆**tell off** *vt* (*child*) gronder; (*employee*) faire des reproches à; **to tell sb off about sth** faire une remarque à qn à propos de qc

◆**tell on** *vt* **1.** (*affect negatively*) affecter **2.** (*inform on sb*) dénoncer

teller ['telər, *Am:* -ɚ] *n* **1.** *Am, Aus* (*bank employee*) guichetier, -ère *m, f* **2.** (*story teller*) conteur, -euse *m, f* **3.** (*vote counter*) recenseur, -euse *m, f*

telling **I.** *adj* **1.** (*revealing the truth*) révélateur(-trice) **2.** *form* (*significant*) efficace **II.** *n* récit *m*

telling-off <tellings> *n inf* savon *m;* **to give sb a ~** passer un savon à qn

telltale ['telteɪl], **tell-tale** **I.** *n pej* rapporteur, -euse *m, f* **II.** *adj* révélateur(-trice)

telly ['teli] *n Brit, Aus, inf* télé *f;* **on ~** à la télé

temerity [tɪ'merəti, *Am:* tə'merət̬i] *n no pl, pej, form* témérité *f;* **to have the ~ to** *+infin* avoir l'audace de *+infin*

temp [temp] *inf* **I.** *n* employé(e) *m(f)* temporaire; **to do ~ work** faire de l'intérim **II.** *vi* travailler en intérim; **a week's ~ing** une semaine d'intérim

temp. **I.** *n abbr of* **temperature** température *f* **II.** *adj abbr of* **temporary** temporaire

temper ['tempər, *Am:* -pɚ] **I.** *n* **1.** (*angry state*) colère *f;* **a fit of ~** un accès de colère; **to be in a ~** être en colère; **to get into a ~** se fâcher; **to lose one's ~** se mettre en colère **2.** (*characteristic mood*) humeur *f;* **to be in a good/bad ~** être de bonne/mauvaise humeur; **to have a very bad ~** avoir très mauvais caractère **3.** (*hardness of steel*) trempe *f* **II.** *vt* **1.** *form* (*moderate*) tempérer; **to ~ with sth** tempérer par qc **2.** (*make malleable*) tremper

temperament ['temprəmənt] *n* **1.** (*characteristic disposition*) tempérament *m* **2.** *pej* (*moodiness*) humeur *f;* **a fit of ~** une saute d'humeur

temperamental *adj* **1.** *pej* (*easily irritated*) capricieux(-euse) **2.** (*characteristic*) inné(e)

temperance ['tempərəns] *n no pl, form* tempérance *f*

temperate ['tempərət] *adj* METEO tempéré(e); (*in character*) modéré(e)

temperature ['temprətʃər, *Am:* -pɚətʃɚ] *n a. fig* température *f;* **to run a ~** avoir de la température; **to take the ~** prendre la température; **a rise/fall in ~** une augmentation/baisse de température

template ['templɪt] *n* INFOR modèle *m*

temple¹ ['templ] *n* (*monument*) temple *m*

temple² ['templ] *n* BIO tempe *f*

tempo ['tempəʊ, *Am:* -poʊ] <-s *o* -pi> *n* tempo *m*

temporal ['tempərəl] *adj form* temporel(le)

temporarily ['temprərəli, *Am:* 'tempərerəli] *adv* temporairement

temporary ['temprəri, *Am:* 'tempəreri] *adj* temporaire; (*job, worker*) intérimaire; (*solution, building*) provisoire

temporize ['tempəraɪz] *vi pej, form* temporiser

tempt [tempt] *vt* tenter; **to ~ fate** tenter le sort; **to let oneself be ~ed** se laisser tenter; **to ~ sb into doing sth** inciter qc à faire qc

temptation [temp'teɪʃən] *n* tentation *f;* **to resist the ~ to** *+infin* résister à la tentation de *+infin*

tempter *n* tentateur, -trice *m, f*

tempting *adj* tentant(e)

ten [ten] *adj* dix *inv;* **to be ~ a penny** *fig* se ramasser à la pelle; *s. a.* **eight**

tenable ['tenəbl] *adj* défendable

tenacious [tɪ'neɪʃəs, *Am:* tə'-] *adj* tenace

tenacity [tɪ'næsəti, *Am:* tə'næsət̬i] *n no pl* ténacité *f*

tenancy ['tenənsi] *n* **1.** (*tenant's legal status*) location *f* **2.** <-ies> (*legal right of possession*) période *f* d'occupation

tenant ['tenənt] *n* locataire *mf*

tenant farmer *n* métayer *m*

tend¹ [tend] *vi* (*be likely*) **to ~ to** *+infin* avoir tendance à *+infin;* **to ~ to(wards) sth** tendre vers qc; **it ~s to happen that** il arrive souvent que *+subj*

tend² [tend] (*care for*) **I.** *vt* s'occuper de **II.** *vi* **to ~ to sth** s'occuper de qc

tendency ['tendənsi] <-ies> *n* tendance *f*

tendentious *adj pej, form* tendancieux(-euse)

tender¹ ['tendər, *Am:* -dɚ] *adj* **1.** (*not tough*) *a. fig* (*kiss, heart, material*) tendre **2.** (*easily damaged by cold*) délicat(e) **3.** (*painful*) sensible

tender² ['tendər, *Am:* -dɚ] **I.** *n* **1.** offre *f;* **to invite ~s** faire un appel d'offres **2.** FIN **legal ~** monnaie *f* légale **II.** *vt form* offrir; (*resignation, apologies*) présenter **III.** *vi* faire une soumission

tender³ ['tendər, *Am:* -dɚ] *n* **1.** (*railway wagon*) tender *m* **2.** (*in fire engine*) ravitailleur *m*

tenderfoot <-s *o* -feet> *n* novice *mf*

tender-hearted *adj* au cœur tendre

tenderize ['tendəraɪz] *vt* attendrir

tenderizer *n* attendrisseur *m*

tenderloin ['tendəlɔɪn, *Am:* -dɚ-] *n no pl* filet *m*

tenderness *n no pl* **1.** (*feeling*) tendresse *f* **2.** (*pain*) sensibilité *f*

tendon ['tendən] *n* tendon *m*

tendril ['tendrəl] *n* vrille *f*

tenement ['tenəmənt] *n* immeuble *m*

tenement house *n Am, Scot* immeuble *m*

T

tenfold ['tenfəʊld, *Am:* -foʊld] **I.** *adj* décuple **II.** *adv* au décuple
tennis ['tenɪs] *n no pl* tennis *m*
tennis court *n* court *m* de tennis **tennis player** *n* joueur, -euse *m, f* de tennis **tennis racket** *n* raquette *f* de tennis **tennis shoe** *n* tennis *f*, espadrille *f* de tennis *Québec*
tenor[1] ['tenəʳ, *Am:* -ɚ] *n* ténor *m*
tenor[2] ['tenəʳ, *Am:* -ɚ] *n no pl, form* (*gist*) teneur *f*
tenpin ['tenpɪn] *n* quille *f*
tenpin bowling *n* bowling *m*
tense[1] [tents] **I.** *adj a. fig* tendu(e); (*muscles*) contracté(e) **II.** *vt* tendre **III.** *vi* se tendre
tense[2] [tents] *n* LING temps *m*
tension ['tentʃən] *n a. fig* tension *f*
tent [tent] *n* tente *f*
tentacle ['tentəkl, *Am:* -t̬ə-] *n a. fig, pej* tentacule *f*
tentative ['tentətɪv, *Am:* -t̬ət̬ɪv] *adj* **1.** (*provisional*) provisoire **2.** (*hesitant*) timide
tentatively *adv* **1.** (*provisionally*) provisoirement **2.** (*hesitatingly*) timidement
tenterhooks ['tentəhʊks, *Am:* -t̬ɚ-] *npl* **to be on** ~ être sur des charbons ardents; **to keep sb on** ~ faire languir qn
tenth [tenθ] *adj* dixième; *s. a.* **eighth**
tent peg *n* piquet *m* de tente **tent pole** *n* mât *m* de tente
tenuous ['tenjʊəs] *adj* ténu(e)
tenure ['tenjʊəʳ, *Am:* -jɚ] *n no pl, form* **1.** (*official occupancy*) bail *m;* (*period*) période *f* d'occupation **2.** (*in post*) **to have** ~ être titulaire; (*security of* ~) sécurité *f* de l'emploi
tepee ['ti:pi:] *n* tipi *m*
tepid ['tepɪd] *adj a. fig* tiède
tepidity, tepidness *n no pl* tiédeur *f*
tercentenary [,tɜ:sen'ti:nəri, *Am:* tɚ'sentəner-] *Brit,* **tercentennial** *Am* **I.** *n* tricentenaire *m* **II.** *adj* tricentenaire
term [tɜ:m, *Am:* tɜ:rm] **I.** *n* **1.** (*word*) terme *m* **2.** (*period*) terme *m;* UNIV, SCHOOL trimestre *m;* ~ **of office** mandat *m;* ~ **of imprisonment** durée *f* d'emprisonnement; **to go to** ~ MED arriver à terme; **in the long/short** ~ à long/court terme **3.** *pl* (*conditions*) conditions *fpl;* **to be on good** ~**s** être en de bons termes; **in** ~**s of sth** en termes de qc ►**to come to** ~**s** arriver à un compromis; **to come to** ~**s with** (arriver à) accepter **II.** *vt* désigner
terminal ['tɜ:mɪnl, *Am:* 'tɜ:r-] **I.** *adj* **1.** (*at the end*) terminal(e); (*patient, illness*) incurable **2.** *fig, inf* (*boredom*) mortel(le) **II.** *n* **1.** (*end of route, station*) terminal *m;* (*of railway line*) terminus *m;* (*at airport*) aérogare *f* **2.** ELEC borne *f* **3.** INFOR terminal *m*
terminal building *n* aérogare *f*
terminate ['tɜ:mɪneɪt, *Am:* 'tɜ:r-] *form* **I.** *vt* terminer; (*project, contract*) mettre un terme à; (*pregnancy*) interrompre **II.** *vi* se terminer
termination *n* **1.** *no pl* (*ending*) fin *f* **2.** *form* (*of pregnancy*) interruption *f*
terminological *adj* terminologique
terminology [,tɜ:mɪ'nɒlədʒi, *Am:* ,tɜ:rmɪ'nɑ:lə-] *n* terminologie *f*
terminus ['tɜ:mɪnəs, *Am:* 'tɜ:r-] <-es *o* -i> *n* terminus *m*
termite ['tɜ:maɪt, *Am:* 'tɜ:r-] *n* termite *m*
terrace ['terəs] **I.** *n* **1.** (*level*) terrasse *f* **2.** *pl, Brit* (*standing room in stadium*) gradins *mpl* **3.** *Brit, Aus* (*row of adjoining houses*) maisons *fpl* mitoyennes **II.** *vt* disposer en terrasses **III.** *adj s.* **terraced**
terraced *adj* **1.** (*forming a row: house*) mitoyen(ne) **2.** (*in levels*) en terrasse(s)
terraced roof *n* toit *m* en terrasse
terracotta [,terə'kɒtə, *Am:* -'kɑ:t̬ə] *n no pl* terre *f* cuite
terrain [te'reɪn] *n* terrain *m*
terrapin ['terəpɪn] <-(s)> *n* tortue *f* d'eau douce
terrestrial [tɪ'restrɪəl, *Am:* tə'-] **I.** *adj form* terrestre **II.** *n* terrien(ne) *m(f)*
terrible ['terəbl] *adj* (*crime, struggle, experience*) horrible; (*weather, film*) affreux; **a** ~ **mistake** une terrible erreur; **she looked** ~ (*ill*) elle avait une mine affreuse; (*badly dressed*) elle était très mal habillée
terribly *adv* **1.** (*badly: hurt, bleed*) terriblement **2.** *inf* (*extremely*) extrêmement; **it didn't go** ~ **well** ça ne s'est pas vraiment bien passé
terrier ['terɪəʳ, *Am:* -ɚ] *n* terrier *m*
terrific [tə'rɪfɪk] *adj inf* **1.** (*very good: party*) génial(e); **to feel** ~ se sentir en pleine forme; **you look** ~ **in that dress** tu es superbe dans cette robe **2.** (*very great*) incroyable
terrified *adj* terrifié(e)
terrify ['terəfaɪ] <-ie-> *vt* terrifier
terrifying *adj* terrifiant(e)
territorial **I.** *n* territorial *m* **II.** *adj* territorial(e)
territory ['terɪtəri, *Am:* 'terətɔ:ri] <-ies> *n* **1.** (*land*) *a. fig* territoire *m;* **forbidden** ~ zone *f* interdite **2.** (*field of activity, knowledge*) *a. fig* domaine *m*
terror ['terəʳ, *Am:* -ɚ] *n a. inf* terreur *f;* **to have a** ~ **of sth** avoir la terreur de qc; **to strike** ~ **into the hearts of** frapper de terreur; **to have no** ~**s for sb** ne pas terrifier qn
terrorism ['terərɪzəm] *n no pl* terrorisme *m*
terrorist **I.** *n* terroriste *mf* **II.** *adj* terroriste
terrorize ['terəraɪz] *vt* terroriser
terror-stricken, terror-struck *adj* frappé(e) de terreur
terry ['teri], **terry cloth, terry towelling** *n no pl* (tissu *m*) éponge *f;* **a** ~ **nappy** un lange en éponge
terse [tɜ:s, *Am:* tɜ:rs] *adj* sec(sèche)
tertiary ['tɜ:ʃəri, *Am:* 'tɜ:rʃɪeri] **I.** *adj* tertiaire; **the Tertiary period** le tertiaire **II.** <-ies> *n* tertiaire *m*
tessellated ['tesəleɪtɪd, *Am:* -t̬ɪd] *adj* en mosaïque
test [test] **I.** *n* **1.** (*examination*) test *m;* SCHOOL examen *m;* **aptitude/IQ** ~ test d'aptitude/de QI; **a** ~ **of skill** une épreuve d'adresse; **safety**

~ test de sécurité; **I am taking my driving ~ tomorrow** je passe mon permis (de conduire) demain **2.** (*scientific examination*) examen *m;* **blood** ~ analyse *f* de sang; **pregnancy** ~ test *m* de maternité; **urine** ~ analyse *f* d'urine; **a ~ for Alzheimer's** des examens pour la maladie d'Alzheimer; **to do a** ~ faire une analyse **3.** (*challenge*) épreuve *f;* **to put sth to the** ~ mettre qc à l'épreuve **II.** *vt* **1.** (*examine knowledge of*) tester **2.** (*examine for efficiency: machine*) essayer; (*system*) tester; **to ~ (out) a theory/an idea** mettre une théorie/une idée à l'essai **3.** (*examine*) analyser; **to ~ sb's blood** faire une analyse de sang; **to ~ sb's hearing** examiner l'ouïe de qn; **to ~ sb/sth for sth** faire subir à qn/qc un examen de qc; **to ~ sb for AIDS** faire un test de dépistage du sida **4.** (*measure*) mesurer; **to ~ the presence of sth** analyser la présence de qc **5.** (*try with senses: by touching*) toucher; (*by tasting*) goûter **6.** (*try to the limit*) **to ~ sb/sth** mettre qn/qc à l'épreuve ►**to ~ the water(s)** prendre la température **III.** *vi* (*to ~ positive/negative*) avoir des analyses positives/négatives; **to ~ for** (*disease, antibodies*) faire des examens pour détecter; (*chemical*) faire des analyses à la recherche de

testament ['testəmənt] *n form, a. fig* testament *m;* **to be (a) ~ to sth** être le témoignage de qc; **the New/Old Testament** l'Ancien/le Nouveau Testament

testamentary *adj* testamentaire

testator *n form* testateur, -trice *m, f*

test bench *n* banc *m* d'essai **test card** *n* mire *f* **test drive** *n* essai *m* sur route

tester *n* **1.** (*person*) contrôleur, -euse *m, f* **2.** (*sample*) échantillon *m*

test flight *n* vol *m* d'essai

testicle ['testɪkl] *n* testicule *m*

testify ['testɪfaɪ] <-ie-> **I.** *vi* témoigner; **to ~ to having done sth** déclarer avoir fait qc; **to ~ to sth** attester qc **II.** *vt* témoigner

testimonial *n form* recommandation *f*

testimony ['testɪməni, *Am:* -moʊni] <-ies> *n a. fig* témoignage *m;* **to be ~ to [*o* of] sth** être le témoignage de qc

testing **I.** *n no pl* essai *m;* **animal** ~ expériences sur les animaux **II.** *adj* difficile

testing ground *n fig* terrain *m* d'essai

test pilot *n* pilote *m* d'essai **test tube** *n* éprouvette *f* **test tube baby** *n* bébé *m* éprouvette

testy ['testi] <-ier, -iest> *adj* irritable

tetanus ['tetənəs] *n no pl* tétanos *m*

tetchy ['tetʃi] <-ier, -iest> *adj* irritable

tether ['teðəʳ, *Am:* -ɚ] **I.** *n* longe *f* ►**to be at the end of one's** ~ être au bout du rouleau **II.** *vt* **1.** (*tie*) attacher **2.** *fig* **to be ~ed to sth** être cloué à qc

Teutonic [tjuː'tɒnɪk, *Am:* tuː'tɑːnɪk] *adj* teuton(ne)

Texan **I.** *n* Texan(ne) *m(f)* **II.** *adj* texan(ne)

Texas ['teksəs] *n* Texas *m*

text [tekst] *n* texte *m*

textbook **I.** *n* manuel *m* **II.** *adj* **1.** (*demonstration*) exemplaire *f* **2.** (*usual*) typique **text editor** *n* INFOR éditeur *m* de texte

textile ['tekstaɪl] *n pl* textile *m*

text processing *n* INFOR traitement *m* de texte

textual ['tekstʃʊəl, *Am:* -tʃu-] *adj* textuel(le); (*analysis*) de texte

texture ['tekstʃəʳ, *Am:* -tʃɚ] *n* **1.** (*feel*) texture *f* **2.** *no pl* (*impression given*) velouté *m*

Thai **I.** *adj* **1.** (*of Thailand*) thaïlandais(e) **2.** LING thaï(e) **II.** *n* **1.** (*person*) Thaïlandais(e) *m(f)* **2.** LING thaï *m; s. a.* **English**

Thailand ['taɪlənd] *n* la Thaïlande

Thames [temz] *n no pl* **the (River)** ~ la Tamise

than [ðən, ðæn] *conj* que; **she is taller ~ he (is) [*o* him** *inf*] elle est plus grande que lui; **no sooner sb has done sth, ~ ...** à peine qn a-t-il fait qc que ...; *s. a.* **more, less, other**

thank [θæŋk] *vt* remercier; **to ~ sb for doing sth** remercier qn d'avoir fait qc; **I'll ~ you to** +*infin* je vous prierai de +*infin* ►**~ goodness!** Dieu merci!; **to ~ one's lucky stars** remercier le bon Dieu

thankful *adj* **1.** (*pleased*) ravi(e) **2.** (*grateful*) reconnaissant(e); **I'm just ~ it's over** je suis surtout content que ce soit fini *subj*

thankless *adj* ingrat(e)

thanks **I.** *n pl* remerciements *mpl;* **to give ~ to sb** remercier qn; **thanks to sb** grâce à qn **II.** *interj* merci!; ~ **a lot** *a. iron* je te remercie

> **Thanksgiving** est fêté le deuxième lundi d'octobre au Canada et le quatrième jeudi de novembre aux États-Unis. C'est l'un des jours fériés des plus importants aux USA. Le premier "Thanksgiving Day" fut célébré en 1621 par les "Pilgrims" dans la "Plymouth Colony". Ils avaient traversé des temps très difficiles et voulaient remercier Dieu de s'en être sortis. Traditionnellement la plupart des gens se retrouvent autour d'un repas de famille pour lequel on prépare une "stuffed turkey" (dinde farcie), un "cranberry sauce" (un coulis d'airelles), des "yams" (patates douces) et du "corn" (maïs).

T

thank you *n* merci *m;* ~ **very much** merci beaucoup; **a ~ letter** une lettre de remerciement

that [ðæt, ðət] **I.** *dem pron, pl: those* **1.** (*sth shown*) cela, ça, ce; **read** ~ lisez ça; **what's ~?** qu'est-ce que c'est (que ça)?; **~'s why ...** c'est pourquoi ...; **~'s Paul over there** c'est Paul là-bas; **~'s what I want** c'est ce que je veux; **after ~ he retired** après ça il est parti à la retraite; **~'s a shame** c'est dommage; **those are two good ideas** ce sont (là) deux bonnes idées; **those who want to go** ceux qui veulent partir **2.** (*countable*) celui-là, celle-là; **those** ceux-là, celles-là ►**well, ~'s ~** et voilà; **no, and ~'s ~** non, point final; **he said he**

was sorry and all ~ il a dit qu'il était désolé et tout ça; ~**'s it** (*good idea*) voilà; (*I've had enough*) ça suffit comme ça **II.** *dem adj, pl: those* ce, cette *m, f,* cet + *vowel m;* ~ **dog/child/man** ce chien/cet enfant/cet homme; ~ **bottle/road/letter** cette bouteille/route/lettre; **those people** ces gens(-là); ~ **car of yours** votre voiture; ~ **car you saw** la voiture que vous avez vue; (**on**) ~ **Monday** ce lundi-là; **to agree on** ~ **point** être d'accord là-dessus **III.** *adv* **1.** (*so*) tellement; **I was** ~ **pleased** j'ai été si heureux; **I was** ~ **angry I left** j'étais tellement en colère que je suis parti; **it's not** ~ **far/warm** ce n'est pas si loin/chaud que ça; *s. a.* **this 2.** (*showing an amount or degree*) **it's** ~ **big/high** c'est grand/haut comme ça; **why does it cost** ~ **much?** pourquoi est-ce que ça coûte autant? **IV.** *rel pron* **1.** *subject* qui; **the man** ~ **told me ...** l'homme qui m'a dit ...; **the day** ~ **he arrived** le jour où il est arrivé **2.** *object* que, qu' + *vowel;* **the parcel** ~ **I sent** le paquet que j'ai envoyé; **the box** ~ **he told me about** la boîte dont il m'a parlé; **the day** ~ **I met you** le jour où je t'ai rencontré; **the hole** ~ **I fell in** le trou dans lequel je suis tombé **V.** *conj* que, qu' + *vowel;* **I said** ~ **I'd come** j'ai dit que je viendrais; **supposing** ~ **he should come** supposons qu'il vienne; **oh** ~ **I could!** si seulement je pouvais!; **so** ~ **I can go** de façon à ce que je puisse partir *subj;* **in order** ~ **I can go** de façon à ce que je puisse partir (*subj*); **given** ~ **he's gone** étant donné qu'il est parti

thatch [θætʃ] **I.** *n no pl* **1.** (*straw, roof*) chaume *m* **2.** *fig* (*of hair*) touffe *f* **II.** *vt* **to** ~ **sth** couvrir qc de chaume

thaw [θɔː, *Am:* θɑː] **I.** *n a. fig* amélioration *f* **II.** *vi* **1.** (*unfreeze: snow, ice*) fondre; (*food*) se décongeler **2.** (*become friendlier*) se dérider **III.** *vt* (*snow, ice*) faire fondre; (*food*) décongeler

◆**thaw out I.** *vi* (*soil*) dégeler; (*cold person*) se réchauffer **II.** *vt* (*food*) décongeler; (*cold person*) se réchauffer

the [ðə, *stressed, before vowel* ðiː] *def art* le, la *m, f,* l' *mf* + *vowel,* les *pl;* **of** [*o* **from**] ~ **garden** du jardin; **of** [*o* **from**] ~ **window** de la fenêtre; **of** [*o* **from**] ~ **rooms** des chambres; **at** [*o* **to**] ~ **office** au bureau; **at** [*o* **to**] ~ **window** à la fenêtre; **at** [*o* **to**] ~ **hotel** à l'hôtel; **at** [*o* **to**] ~ **doors** aux portes; **to play** ~ **flute** jouer de la flûte; **Charles** ~ **Seventh** Charles sept; **I'll do it in** ~ **winter** je le ferai cet hiver; **the Martins** les Martin; **THE James Martin** le fameux James Martin; ~ **more one tries,** ~ **less one succeeds** plus on essaie, moins on réussit; ~ **sooner** ~ **better** le plus tôt sera le mieux; **all** ~ **better** tant mieux; **the hottest day** le jour le plus chaud

theatre ['θɪətəʳ, *Am:* 'θiːət̬ɚ] *n Brit, Aus* **1.** (*building*) théâtre *m* **2.** *Am, Aus, NZ* (*cinema*) salle *f* de cinéma *m;* **at the** ~ au cinéma **3.** (*lecture* ~) amphithéâtre *m* **4.** *Brit* (*hospital room*) salle *f* d'opération **5.** *no pl* (*dramatic art*) théâtre *m*

theatre-goer *n* amateur , -trice de théâtre *m*

theatrical [θɪ'ætrɪkl] *adj* **1.** (*relating to the theatre*) de théâtre **2.** (*over-acted*) théâtral(e)

thee [ðiː] *pers pron* te, t' + *vowel;* **to think of** ~ penser à toi

theft [θeft] *n* vol *m*

The Hague [ðiheɪg] *n* la Haye

their [ðeəʳ, *Am:* ðer] *poss adj* leur(s); *s. a.* **my**

theirs [ðeəz, *Am:* ðerz] *poss pron* (*belonging to them*) le leur, la leur; **they aren't our bags, they are** ~ ce ne sont pas nos sacs, ce sont les leurs; **this house is** ~ cette maison est la leur; **a book of** ~ (l')un de leurs livres; **this table is** ~ cette table est à eux/elles

them [ðem, ðəm] *pers pron pl* **1.** (*they*) eux, elles; **older than** ~ plus âgé qu'eux/elles; **if I were** ~ si j'étais eux/elles **2.** *objective pron* les *direct,* leur *indirect,* eux, elles *after prep;* **look at** ~ regarde/regardez-les; **I saw** ~ je les ai vus; **he told** ~ **that ...** il leur a dit que ...; **he'll give sth to** ~ il va leur donner qc; **it's for** ~ c'est pour eux; **I ate all of** ~ le les ai tous mangés; **all of** ~ **went** (*people*) ils y sont tous allés; (*objects on sale*) tout est parti; **I ate some of** ~ j'en ai mangé quelques uns; **some of** ~ **went** il y en a qui y sont allés

thematic [ˌθiːm'ætɪk, *Am:* θiː'mæt̬-] *adj* thématique

theme [θiːm] *n a.* MUS thème *m*

theme music *n* générique *m*

themselves [ðəm'selvz] *reflex pron* **1.** *after verbs* se, s' + *vowel;* **the girls hurt** ~ les filles se sont blessées **2.** (*they or them*) eux-mêmes *mpl,* elles-mêmes *fpl; s. a.* **myself**

then [ðen] **I.** *adv* **1.** (*afterwards*) puis, ensuite; **what** ~**?** et après?; ~ **the door opened** et puis la porte s'est ouverte; **there and** ~ ici et maintenant **2.** (*at that time*) alors; **I was younger** ~ j'étais plus jeune en ce temps là; **why did you leave** ~**?** pourquoi est-ce que tu es parti à ce moment-là?; **I'll do it by** ~ je l'aurai fait d'ici là; **before** ~ auparavant; **until** ~ jusqu'alors; **since** ~ depuis (ce moment-là); **from** ~ **onwards** dès lors; (**every**) **now and** ~ de temps à autre **3.** (*logical link*) alors; **but** ~ **she's a painter** mais bon bien sûr, elle est peintre; ~ **I'll leave** dans ce cas je m'en vais; ~ **why did you leave?** alors pourquoi est-ce que tu es parti?; ~ **he must be there** alors il doit être là; **OK** ~**, let's go** c'est bon, on y va **II.** *adj* d'alors; **the** ~ **king** le roi de l'époque

thence [ðens] *adv form* **1.** (*from here*) de là **2.** (*for that reason*) par conséquent

thenceforth [ˌðens'fɔːθ, *Am:* -'fɔːrθ] *adv form,* **thenceforward** *adv form* dès lors

theocracy [θɪ'ɒkrəsi, *Am:* -'ɑːkrə-] <-ies> *n* théocratie *f*

theologian *n* théologien(ne) *m(f)*

theological *adj* théologique

theology [θɪ'ɒlədʒi, *Am:* -'ɑːlə-] <-ies> *n* théologie *f*

theorem ['θɪərəm, *Am:* 'θiːəəm] *n* MAT théorème *m;* **Pythagoras' ~** théorème de Pythagore

theoretical [θɪə'retɪkəl, *Am:* ˌθiːə'ret̬-] *adj* théorique

theoretically *adv* théoriquement; **~ he'll have finished** en principe, il aura terminé

theorist ['θɪərɪst, *Am:* 'θiːəɪst] *n* théoricien(ne) *m(f)*

theorize ['θɪəraɪz, *Am:* 'θiːə-] *vi* élaborer une théorie

theory ['θɪəri, *Am:* 'θiːə-] <-ies> *n* théorie *f*

therapeutic [ˌθerə'pjuːtɪk, *Am:* -t̬ɪk] *adj* thérapeutique

therapeutics *n + sing vb* thérapeutique *f*

therapist *n* thérapeute *mf*

therapy ['θerəpi] <-ies> *n* thérapie *f*

there [ðeəʳ, *Am:* ðer] **I.** *adv* **1.** (*in, at, to place/position*) *a. fig* là; **in ~** là-dedans; **over ~** là-bas; **up ~** là-haut; **we went there** nous sommes allés là-bas; **to get ~** *a. fig* y arriver; **to go ~ and back** faire l'aller retour; **~ you are!** te voilà!; (*giving sth*) voilà; **I don't agree with you ~** je ne suis pas d'accord sur ce point-là **2.** (*indicating existence*) **~ is/are ...** il y a ... ►**to be <u>all</u> ~** être malin; **to be not <u>all</u> ~** avoir un grain; **~ and <u>then</u>** directement; **~ <u>again</u>** d'un autre côté; **~ you <u>go</u> again** ça recommence; **I've <u>been</u> there** je sais ce que c'est **II.** *interj* **1.** (*expressing sympathy*) **~ ~** allez, allez! **2.** (*expressing satisfaction, annoyance*) voilà!

thereabouts *adv* **1.** (*place*) par là **2.** (*time, amount*) à peu près **thereafter** *adv* par la suite; **shortly ~** peu de temps après **thereby** *adv form* de cette façon ►**~ hangs a <u>tale</u>** c'est toute une histoire **therefore** *adv* par conséquent **therein** *adv form* (*inside*) à l'intérieur; (*in document*) ci-inclus **thereupon** *adv form* sur ce

therm [θɜːm, *Am:* θɜːrm] *n* thermie *f*

thermal ['θɜːməl, *Am:* 'θɜːr-] **I.** *n* (*air current*) courant *m* ascendant **II.** *adj* thermique; (*bath, springs*) thermal(e); (*underwear*) en Thermolactyl®

thermodynamic [ˌθɜːməʊdaɪ'næmɪk, *Am:* ˌθɜːrmoʊ-] *adj* thermodynamique

thermoelectric [ˌθɜːməʊɪ'lektrɪk, *Am:* ˌθɜːrmoʊɪ'-] *adj* thermoélectrique

thermometer [θə'mɒmɪtəʳ, *Am:* θə'mɑːmət̬ə] *n* thermomètre *m*

thermonuclear [ˌθɜːməʊ'njuːklɪəʳ, *Am:* ˌθɜːrmoʊ'nuːklɪə] *adj* thermonucléaire

Thermos® bottle *Am,* **Thermos® flask** ['θɜːmɒs-, *Am:* 'θɜːrməs-] *n* thermos *m o f*

thermostat ['θɜːməʊstæt, *Am:* 'θɜːrməstæt] *n* thermostat *m*

thermostatic *adj* thermostatique

thesaurus [θɪ'sɔːrəs] <-es *o form* -ri> *n* dictionnaire *m* des synonymes

these [ðiːz] *pl of* **this**

thesis ['θiːsɪs] <-ses> *n* thèse *f*

they [ðeɪ] *pers pron* **1.** (*3rd person pl*) ils *mpl,* elles *fpl;* **~'re** [*o* **~ are**] **my parents/sisters** ce sont mes parents/sœurs; **your shoes? ~ are here** tes chaussures? elles sont ici; **to be as rich as ~ are** être aussi riche qu'eux/elles **2.** *inf* (*he or she*) **somebody just rang: what do ~ want?** on a sonné: qu'est-ce qu'elle/il veut? **3.** (*people in general*) on; **~ say that ...** ils disent que ...

they'll [ðeɪl] = **they will** *s.* **will**

they're [ðeɪr, *Am:* ðer] = **they are** *s.* **be**

they've [ðeɪv] = **they have** *s.* **have**

thick [θɪk] **I.** *n no pl inf* **to be in the ~ of sth** être en plein qc ►**through ~ and <u>thin</u>** contre vents et marées **II.** *adj* **1.** (*not thin*) épais(se); **sth 2 cm ~** qc d'une épaisseur de 2 cm **2.** (*dense*) épais(se); **it was ~ with dust/fog** il y avait une poussière/un brouillard à couper au couteau; **it was ~ with people/insects** *fig* ça grouillait de monde/d'insectes **3.** (*extreme: accent*) fort(e) **4.** *pej, inf* (*mentally slow*) bête; **get it into your ~ head that ...** fais bien rentrer dans ta petite tête que ...; **to be as ~ as two short planks** être bête comme ses pieds **5.** *inf* (*close*) copains comme cochons; **to be as ~ as thieves** s'entendre comme larrons en foire **6.** *inf* **that's a <u>bit</u> ~** c'est un peu fort

thicken ['θɪkən] **I.** *vt* épaissir **II.** *vi* **1.** (*become denser*) *a. fig* s'épaissir; **the plot ~s** *fig* les choses se compliquent **2.** (*become more numerous*) grossir **3.** (*become less slim*) grossir

thickener, **thickening** *n* épaississant *m*

thicket ['θɪkɪt] *n* taillis *m*

thickhead *n inf* andouille *f*

thickness *n* épaisseur *f*

thickset *adj* trapu(e) **thick-skinned** *adj* dur(e)

thief [θiːf, *s* 'θiːvz] <thieves> *n* voleur, -euse *m, f*

thigh [θaɪ] *n* cuisse *f*

thigh bone *n* fémur *m*

thimble ['θɪmbl] *n* dé *m* à coudre

thin [θɪn] <-nn-> **I.** *adj* **1.** (*lean*) *a. fig* mince **2.** (*narrow: layer*) fin(e); (*slice, line*) mince **3.** (*sparse: population*) clairsemé(e); (*crowd*) épars(e); **to be ~ on top** se dégarnir **4.** (*not dense*) fin(e); (*mist*) léger(-ère) **5.** (*very fluid*) peu épais(se) **6.** (*feeble*) faible; (*smile*) léger(-ère) **7.** (*lacking oxygen: air*) pauvre en oxygène ►**out of ~ <u>air</u>** comme par magie; **to disappear into ~ <u>air</u>** disparaître comme par magie; **to be ~ on the <u>ground</u>** *Brit, Aus* ne pas courir les rues; **to have a ~ <u>time</u> (of it)** passer par une période difficile; **to be ~-<u>skinned</u>** être susceptible; **to <u>wear</u> ~** s'épuiser **II.** <-nn-> *vt* **1.** (*make more liquid*) délayer **2.** (*remove some*) éclaircir **III.** *vi* (*crowd*) se disperser; (*hair*) se raréfier

thine [ðaɪn] **I.** *poss pron* le tien, la tienne **II.** *poss det* ton, ta

thing [θɪŋ] *n* **1.** (*object*) chose *f; inf* machin *m;* **what sort of ~ do you want?** qu'est-ce que vous voulez exactement?; **my swimming**

T

~**s** mes affaires de bain; **the ~s on the table are dirty** les affaires sur la table sont sales; **sweet ~s** sucreries *fpl* **2.** (*abstract use*) chose *f; inf* truc *m;* **to do a lot of ~s** faire beaucoup de choses; **to be a good ~** être une bonne chose; **it's a good ~ I had the car** heureusement que j'avais la voiture; **it was a dangerous ~ to do** c'était dangereux; **the ~ to remember is ...** ce qu'il faut se rappeler c'est; **to do sth first/last ~** faire qc de bon matin/en fin de journée; **it's been one ~ after another** les choses se sont enchaînées les unes derrière les autres; **to be seeing ~s** avoir des hallucinations; **to forget the whole ~** tout oublier; **and another ~** et en plus; **the only ~ is that...** le seul problème est que ...; **it's not the done ~** ça ne se fait pas; **~s are going well** tout va bien; **how are ~s?** comment ça va?; **that's a ~ of the past** c'est du passé; **there isn't a ~ left** il n'y a plus rien; **all ~s considered** quoi qu'il en soit; **there's one ~ to do** il y a une chose à faire; **for one ~** tout d'abord; **to know a ~ or two** s'y connaître **3.** (*the best*) **it was the real ~** c'était pour de vrai; **that's the real ~** *inf* c'est du vrai de vrai; **the very ~!** exactement ce qu'il fallait!; **to be the (latest) ~** être le dernier cri **4.** (*person, animal*) créature *f;* **the poor ~** le pauvre; **you lucky ~** petit chanceux; **a stupid ~** un idiot ►**to be a close ~** être juste; **all ~s being equal** toutes choses égales par ailleurs; **it's just one of those ~s** il y a des jours comme ça; **to be on to a good ~** *inf* faire une affaire; **to do one's own ~** *inf* faire ses trucs; **to have a ~ about sth** *inf* avoir un problème avec qc; **to make a (big) ~ out of sth** *inf* faire tout un plat de qc

thingamabob ['θɪŋəmə,bɒb, *Am:* -bɑːb], **thingamajig** *n inf* machin *m*

think [θɪŋk] <thought, thought> **I.** *vi* **1.** (*use one's mind*) penser; **to ~ aloud** penser tout haut; **to ~ to oneself** se dire; **to ~ for oneself** penser indépendemment; **just ~!** imagine! **2.** (*consider a question*) réfléchir; **to ~ about sth/how to** +*infin* réfléchir à qc/à comment +*infin;* **~ about it** penses-y **3.** (*believe, imagine*) croire; **I think so/not** oui, je crois bien; **I ~ not, I don't ~ so** je ne crois pas; **it can happen sooner than you ~** ça peut se produire plus tôt que ce que tu penses ►**(you can) ~ again!** tu te trompes lourdement!; **to ~ big** voir grand **II.** *vt* **1.** (*use one's mind, have ideas*) penser; **I'll ~ what I can do** je penserai à ce que je peux faire; **I can't ~ how to do it** je ne vois pas comment faire; **I was ~ing green for the kitchen** je pensais à du vert pour la cuisine; **we're ~ing millions** nous pensons en termes de millions **2.** (*believe*) croire; **I ~ he's Irish** je crois qu'il est irlandais; **I ~ she's coming** je pense qu'elle viendra; **I ~ she's a genius** je pense que c'est un génie; **I ~ she should come** je pense qu'elle devrait venir; **who would have thought (that) she'd win** qui aurait dit qu'elle gagnerait; **who does she ~ she is?** elle se prend pour qui? **3.** (*consider*) juger; **I thought him a good player** je pensais que c'était un bon joueur; **to not ~ much of sb/sth** ne pas avoir une bonne opinion de qn/qc; **to ~ nothing of sth** ne pas être impressionné par qc **4.** (*remember*) **to ~ to** +*infin* penser à +*infin;* **can you ~ where you saw it last?** pouvez-vous vous rappeler quand vous l'avez vue pour la dernière fois?

◆**think ahead** *vi* réfléchir à deux fois

◆**think back** *vi* se souvenir; **to ~ to sth** repenser à qc

◆**think of** *vt* **1.** (*consider, find: solution, date, suitable candidate*) penser à; **~ a number!** pensez à un nombre; **we were thinking of moving** on pense peut-être déménager; **I simply wouldn't ~ inviting them** ça ne me viendrait pas à l'idée de les inviter; **don't even ~ it!** ne va même pas l'imaginer!; **can you ~ his name?** tu te souviens de son nom?; **we've thought of a name for him** on a trouvé un nom pour lui **2.** (*value, regard*) **to ~ highly of sb/sth** penser le plus grand bien de qn/qc **3.** (*bear in mind: factor, reputation*) **~ of the cost!** pense à ce que ça va coûter!; **I was ~ing of my family** je pensais à ma famille

◆**think out** *vt* **1.** (*consider: problem, situation*) réfléchir sérieusement à **2.** (*plan*) préparer avec soin

◆**think over** *vt* réfléchir à; **I've been thinking things over** j'ai pensé et repensé

◆**think through** *vt* bien réfléchir à

◆**think up** *vt inf* inventer

thinkable *adj* imaginable

thinker *n* penseur, -euse *m, f*

thinking I. *n no pl* **1.** (*using thought, reasoning*) réflexion *f;* **to do some ~ about sth** réfléchir sérieusement à qc **2.** (*opinions*) opinion *f* **II.** *adj* (*person*) qui réfléchit

think tank *n fig* groupe *m* d'experts

thinner *n* diluant *m*

thin-skinned *adj* **1.** (*with thin skin*) à la peau fine **2.** *fig* susceptible

third [θɜːd, *Am:* θɜːrd] **I.** *n* **1.** (*3rd day of month*) trois *m* **2.** (*fraction*) troisième *m* **3.** (*after second*) troisième *m* **4.** (*fraction*) tiers *m* **5.** (*gear*) troisième *f* **6.** MUS tierce *f* **7.** *Brit* UNIV ≈ licence *f* avec mention passable **II.** *adj* troisième; *s. a.* **eighth**

third-class mail *n Am* prospectus *mpl*

thirdly *adv* troisièmement

third party *n* un tiers *m;* LAW tierce partie *f* **third-party insurance, third-party liability** *n* assurance *f* au tiers **third rate** *adj* de qualité très inférieure **Third World** *n* **the ~** le Tiers-Monde

thirst [θɜːst, *Am:* θɜːrst] *n* soif *f*

thirsty <-ier, -iest> *adj* **to be ~** avoir soif; **to be ~ for sth** *fig* avoir soif de qc

thirteen [,θɜː'tiːn, *Am:* θɜːr'-] *adj* treize *inv; s. a.* **eight**

thirteenth [ˌθɜːˈtiːnθ, *Am:* θɜːrˈ-] *adj* treizième; *s. a.* **eighth**

thirtieth [ˈθɜːtɪəθ, *Am:* ˈθɜːrṭɪ-] *adj* trentième; *s. a.* **eighth**

thirty [ˈθɜːti, *Am:* ˈθɜːrṭi] *adj* trente *inv; s. a.* **eight**

this [ðɪs] **I.** *dem pron* **1.** (*sth shown*) ceci, ce; **what is ~?** qu'est-ce (que c'est)?; **~ is Paul** voilà Paul; **~ is difficult** c'est difficime; **~ is another reason for changing** voilà une raison de plus pour changer; **~ is where I live** voilà où j'habite **2.** (*countable*) **~ (one)** celui-ci *m,* celle-ci *f;* **these (ones)** ceux-ci *mpl,* celles-ci *fpl* **II.** *dem adj* ce *m,* cette *f,* cet *m + vowel;* **~ time** cette fois(-ci); **I have ~ pain in my leg** *inf* j'ai une douleur dans la jambe **III.** *adv* **to be ~ high** être haut comme ça; **~ far** jusque là; **to be ~ bad** être si mauvais; **is it always ~ loud?** est-ce que c'est toujours aussi fort?; *s. a.* **that**

thistle [ˈθɪsl] *n* chardon *m*

tho' [ðəʊ, *Am:* ðoʊ] *conj abbr of* **though**

thong [θɒŋ, *Am:* θɑːŋ] *n* **1.** (*strip*) lanière *f* de cuir **2.** (*part of a whip*) longe *f* de cuir **3.** (*G-string*) string *m* **4.** *pl, Am, Aus* (*sandal*) tongs *fpl*

thorax [ˈθɔːræks] <-es *o* -aces> *n* thorax *m*

thorn [θɔːn, *Am:* θɔːrn] *n* épine *f* ►**to be a ~ in sb's flesh** être une épine dans le pied de qn

thorny <-ier, -iest> *adj* épineux(-euse)

thorough [ˈθʌrə, *Am:* ˈθɜːroʊ] *adj* **1.** (*complete*) complet(-ète) **2.** (*detailed*) détaillé(e) **3.** (*careful*) minutieux(-euse)

thoroughbred I. *n* animal *m* de race **II.** *adj* de race; **a ~ horse** un pur-sang

thoroughfare *n form* voie *f* publique

thoroughgoing *adj form* (*reform*) profond(e); (*attack*) systématique; (*idiot, supporter*) absolu(e)

thoroughly *adv* **1.** (*in detail*) en détail **2.** (*completely*) complètement; **~ miserable** très malheureux

thoroughness *n no pl* minutie *f*

those [ðəʊz, *Am:* ðoʊz] *pl of* **that**

thou [ðaʊ] *pers pron* tu; **~ art** tu es; **~ and I** toi et moi

though [ðəʊ, *Am:* ðoʊ] **I.** *conj* bien que *+subj;* **even ~ I'm tired, tired ~ I am** même si je suis fatigué ►**as ~** comme si; **it looks as ~ it's raining** il semble qu'il pleuve; **it's dry ~ cloudy** il ne pleut pas même si le temps est couvert; *s. a.* **although II.** *adv* pourtant; **it's still delicious ~** c'est quand même délicieux

thought [θɔːt, *Am:* θɑːt] **I.** *pp pt of* **think II.** *n* **1.** *no pl* (*thinking*) pensée *f;* **to give food for ~** donner matière à réflexion; **with no ~ for sb/sth** sans penser à qn/qc; **current economic ~** la tendance actuelle en économie **2.** (*idea*) idée *f;* **I've had a ~** une idée me traverse l'esprit; **it was a nice ~** c'était gentil; **at the ~ of it, ...** rien qu'à l'idée ...; **~s of my children** des pensées au sujet de mes enfants; **I have no ~(s) of retiring** je n'ai aucune intention de partir à la retraite; **what are your ~s on this?** qu'en pensez-vous? ►**a penny for your ~s** *prov* à quoi pensez-vous?

thoughtful *adj* **1.** (*mentally occupied*) pensif(-ive) **2.** (*sensible: approach*) réfléchi(e); (*article*) bien pensé(e) **3.** (*considerate*) prévenant

thoughtless *adj* **1.** (*without thinking*) irréfléchi(e) **2.** (*inconsiderate*) indifférent(e)

thought-out *adj* **well/badly ~** bien/mal conçu(e) **thought-provoking** *adj* qui donne matière à réflexion **thought-reading** *n no pl* télépathie *f*

thousand [ˈθaʊznd] **I.** *n* **1.** (*1000*) mille *m inv* **2.** *no pl* (*quantity*) millier *m;* **in ~s** par milliers **II.** *adj* mille *inv; s. a.* **eight**

thousandth *adj* millième; *s. a.* **eighth**

thrash [θræʃ] **I.** *vt* **1.** (*beat*) battre **2.** *inf* (*defeat*) **to ~ sb** battre qn à plate(s) couture(s) **II.** *vi* battre

◆**thrash out** *vt inf* arriver à régler

thrashing *n a. fig* raclée *f*

thread [θred] **I.** *n* **1.** *no pl* (*for sewing*) fil *m;* **I've lost the ~ of my argument** *fig* j'ai perdu le fil de ma pensée **2.** (*groove of screw*) filet *m* **II.** *vt* **1.** (*pass a thread: needle*) passer un fil dans **2.** (*string: beads*) enfiler **3.** (*insert: tape, film*) introduire

threadbare [ˈθredbeəʳ, *Am:* -ber] *adj a. fig* usé(e)

threat [θret] *n a. fig* menace *f;* **to pose a ~ to sth** menacer qc

threaten [ˈθretən] **I.** *vt* **1.** (*take hostile action*) menacer **2.** (*be a danger*) constituer une menace pour **II.** *vi* menacer; **to ~ to** *+infin* menacer de *+infin*

threatening *adj* (*behaviour*) menaçant(e); **a ~ letter** une lettre de menaces

three [θriː] *adj* trois *inv; s. a.* **eight**

three-cornered *adj* **1.** (*with three corners*) triangulaire **2.** (*between 3 people*) à trois **three-D** *adj inf* en 3D **three-dimensional** *adj* à trois dimensions **threefold I.** *adj* triple **II.** *adv* trois fois autant **three-piece I.** *adj* **1.** (*three items*) en trois morceaux; **a ~ suite** un canapé et deux fauteuils **2.** (*three people*) à trois; **~ band** trio *m* **II.** *n* trois-pièces *m* **three-ply** *adj* **1.** (*of three layers*) à trois épaisseurs **2.** (*of three strands*) à trois fils **three-quarter** *adj* trois-quarts **threesome** *n* **1.** (*three people*) groupe *m* de trois **2.** *inf* (*sexual act*) partie *f* à trois **3.** SPORT partie *f* à trois **three-wheeler** *n* AUTO voiture *f* à trois roues; (*cycle*) tricycle *m* **Three Wise Men** *n* REL **the ~** les Rois Mages

thresh [θreʃ] *vt* battre

threshing machine [ˈθreʃɪŋ məˈʃiːn] *n* batteuse *f*

threshold [ˈθreʃhəʊld, *Am:* -hoʊld] *n* **1.** (*doorway*) pas *m* de la porte **2.** (*beginning: of life*) début *m;* (*of a century*) aube *f* **3.** (*limit*) seuil *m;* **pain ~** seuil *f* de tolérance à la douleur; **tax ~** plafond *m* imposable

T

threshold agreement *n* ECON accord *m* d'indexation des salaires

threw [θruː] *pt of* **throw**

thrice [θraɪs] *adv* trois fois

thrift [θrɪft] *n no pl* épargne *f*

thrifty ['θrɪfti] <-ier, -iest> *adj* économe

thrill [θrɪl] **I.** *n* **1.** (*feeling*) sensation *f;* (*of emotion*) tressaillement *m* **2.** (*exciting experience*) sensation *f* forte; **it'a real ~ to meet her** c'est vraiment super de la rencontrer **II.** *vt* (*crowd*) électriser; **to be ~ed to do sth/with sth** être ravi de faire qc/de qc; **I'm ~ed with my present** je suis enchanté de mon cadeau **III.** *vi form* **to ~ to sth** vibrer à qc

thriller ['θrɪləʳ, *Am:* -ɚ] *n* **1.** (*novel*) roman *m* à suspens **2.** (*film*) thriller *m*

thrilling *adj* (*experience*) palpitant(e); (*story*) passionnant(e); (*sight*) saisissant(e)

thrive [θraɪv] <thrived *o* throve, thrived *o* thriven> *vi* **1.** (*develop: business*) se développer; (*child, garden*) pousser **2.** *fig* **to ~ on sth** s'épanouir dans qc

thriving *adj* florissant(e); (*company*) qui prospère; (*children*) bien portant(e)

throat [θrəʊt, *Am:* θroʊt] *n* gorge *f;* **to clear one's ~** s'éclaircir la voix; **to grab sb by the ~** saisir qn à la gorge ►**to be at each other's ~s** s'étriper; **to force sth down sb's ~** imposer qc à qn

throaty <-ier, -iest> *adj* **1.** (*harsh sounding*) guttural(e) **2.** (*hoarse*) rauque **3.** (*from the throat*) de gorge

throb [θrɒb, *Am:* θrɑːb] **I.** *n* (*of a heart*) pulsation *f;* (*of a bass*) rythme *m;* (*of engine*) vibration *f;* (*of pain*) élancement *m* **II.** <-bb-> *vi* battre fort; (*pulse, heart*) battre à grands coups; **~bing pain** douleur *f* lancinante

throes [θrəʊz, *Am:* θroʊz] *npl* **1.** (*pain*) douleurs *fpl;* **death ~** les affres *mpl* de la mort; *fig* l'agonie *f* **2.** *fig* **to be in the ~ of war** être en pleine guerre; **to be in the ~ cooking lunch** être en plein dans la préparation du déjeuner

thrombosis [θrɒm'bəʊsɪs, *Am:* θrɑːm'boʊ-] <-boses> *n* thrombose *f*

throne [θrəʊn, *Am:* θroʊn] *n* trône *m*

throng [θrɒŋ, *Am:* θrɑːŋ] **I.** *n* foule *f* **II.** *vt* emplir; **to be ~ed with people** être noir de monde **III.** *vi* affluer

throttle ['θrɒtl, *Am:* 'θrɑːṭl] **I.** *n* **1.** (*speed pedal*) accélérateur *m* **2.** (*speed*) **at full/half ~** à plein gaz/au ralenti ►**at full ~** à fond **II.** <-ll-> *vt* **1.** (*in engine: engine*) réduire **2.** (*strangle*) étrangler **3.** (*stop or hinder*) étouffer

◆**throttle back, throttle down** **I.** *vi* ralentir le moteur **II.** *vt* mettre au ralenti

through [θruː] **I.** *prep* **1.** (*across*) à travers; **to go ~ sth** traverser qc; **to look ~ the hole** regarder par le trou **2.** (*spatial*) à travers; **to walk/drive ~ a town** traverser une ville (à pied/en voiture); **she came ~ the door** elle et entrée par la porte; **to go ~ customs** passer la douane **3.** (*temporal*) **~ the week** pendant la semaine; **all ~ my life** toute ma vie **4.** *Am* (*up until*) jusqu'à; **open Monday ~ Friday** ouvert du lundi au vendredi **5.** (*divided by*) à travers; **~ the noise** par-dessus le bruit **6.** *Am* MAT **6 ~ 3 is 2** 6 divisé par 3 égale 2 **7.** (*in two pieces*) **to cut ~ the rope** couper la corde **8.** (*by means of*) par; **~ the post** par la poste; **~ hard work** grâce à un dur travail; **I heard about it ~ a friend** j'en ai entendu parler par un ami **II.** *adv* **1.** (*to a destination*) à travers; **to swim/run ~** traverser à la nage/en courant; **to let sb/get ~** laisser passer qn/passer; **to get ~ to the final** arriver en finale **2.** TEL **to get ~** contacter son correspondant; **I'm putting you ~** je vous passe votre correspondant **3.** (*from beginning to end*) d'un bout à l'autre; **half-way ~** en plein milieu **4.** (*completely*) **frozen/cooked ~** complètement gelé/cuit ►**~ and ~** complètement; **wet ~** trempé jusqu'aux os **III.** *adj inv* **1.** (*finished*) terminé(e); **we are ~** c'est fini entre nous; **I'm ~ with the scissors** je n'ai plus besoin des ciseaux **2.** (*direct*) direct(e) **3.** (*from one side to another*) de transit; **~ traffic** circulation *f* dans la ville

through flight *n* vol *m* direct

throughout [θruː'aʊt] **I.** *prep* **1.** (*spatial*) à travers; **~ the town** dans toute la ville **2.** (*temporal*) **~ his stay** pendant tout son séjour **II.** *adv* **1.** (*spatial*) partout **2.** (*temporal*) tout le temps

throughput ['θruːpʊt] *n no pl* **1.** (*amount of material*) consommation *f* de matières premières **2.** INFOR débit *m*

through ticket *n* billet *m* direct **through train** *n* train *m* direct **throughway** *n Am* autoroute *f*

throve [θrəʊv, *Am:* θroʊv] *pt of* **thrive**

throw [θrəʊ, *Am:* θroʊ] **I.** *n* **1.** (*act of throwing*) jet *m;* **a ~ of the dice** un jet de dès; **£2 a ~** *fig, inf* 2 livres à chaque coup **2.** (*fall from a horse*) chute *f* (de cheval) **3.** SPORT lancer *m;* (*in wrestling, martial arts*) mise *f* à terre **4.** (*cover*) jeté *m* de lit/de canapé **II.** <threw, thrown> *vi* lancer **III.** <threw, thrown> *vt* **1.** (*propel*) jeter; (*carefully*) lancer; (*violently*) projeter; (*kiss*) envoyer; (*punch*) donner; **~ your coats on the bed** jetez vos manteaux sur le lit; **I threw the book across the room** j'ai lancé le livre à travers la pièce; **I threw a plate at him** je lui ai jeté une assiette à la figure; **~ me a towel** passe-moi une serviette; **she was ~n overboard** elle a été jetée par dessus bord; **she was ~n into prison** elle a été jetée en prison; **to ~ oneself on sb/sth** se jeter sur qn/qc; **to ~ oneself on sb's mercy** *fig* s'abandonner à la merci de qn; **she threw herself at him** *fig* elle s'est pendue à lui; **the difficulties life ~s at us** les difficultés que la vie met sur notre chemin **2.** (*cause to fall: horse rider*) faire tomber; (*wrestler*) mettre à terre; **~n from his horse** jeté à terre par son cheval **3.** (*dedicate*) **to ~ oneself into sth** se lancer à corps perdu dans qc **4.** (*form on a wheel*) tourner; (*pottery*) façonner **5.** (*turn on: switch*) appuyer sur **6.** (*have*) **to ~ a tantrum** faire un caprice; **to ~ a fit** piquer une crise de nerfs **7.** (*give: party*) organiser **8.** (*confuse*) déconcerter **9.** (*cast*) **to ~ light on sth** *a. fig* éclairer qc; **to ~ a shadow across sth** faire passer une ombre sur qc; **to throw suspicion on sb** *fig* faire peser des soupçons sur qn **10.** (*put in a particular state*) **to ~ everything into chaos/confusion** tout faire basculer dans le chaos/la confusion; (*to ~ a window/ door open*) ouvir une fenêtre/une porte d'un grand coup; **to ~ open one's house** ouvrir les portes de sa maison ►**to ~ the book at sb** accuser qn de tous les crimes; **to ~ caution to the wind**(**s**) oublier toute prudence

◆**throw away** *vt* **1.** (*discard*) jeter **2.** (*discard temporarily*) se débarrasser de **3.** (*waste*) gaspiller **4.** (*speak casually*) laisser tomber

◆**throw back** *vt* **1.** (*return: ball*) renvoyer; (*fish*) remettre à l'eau; (*one's head, veil*) rejeter en arrière **2.** (*open: curtains*) retirer **3.** (*drink quickly*) boire cul sec **4.** (*reflect: light*) réfléchir **5.** (*delay: schedule*) retarder **6.** (*in retort: words*) relancer à la figure; **she threw his failure back at him** elle lui a renvoyé ses échecs à la figure

◆**throw down** *vt* **1.** (*throw from above*) jeter **2.** (*deposit*) déposer **3.** (*eat or drink quickly*) ingurgiter ►**to ~ the gauntlet** jeter le gant

◆**throw in** *vt* **1.** (*put into*) jeter dans **2.** (*include in price*) donner en plus **3.** (*add: quotation, remark*) ajouter **4.** SPORT (*ball*) remettre en touche ►**to ~ the towel** [*o* **the sponge** *Am*] jeter l'éponge

◆**throw off** *vt* **1.** (*remove*) enlever; (*coat*) ôter **2.** (*make loose*) déséquilibrer **3.** (*escape*) semer **4.** (*rid oneself of*) se débarrasser de; (*idea*) se défaire de; (*cold*) se sortir de; (*bad mood*) quitter **5.** (*write quickly*) écrire au pied levé **6.** (*radiate: energy*) évacuer ►**to ~ one's shackles** jeter ses chaînes

◆**throw on** *vt* **1.** (*place on*) ajouter **2.** (*put on: clothes*) enfiler

◆**throw out** *vt* **1.** (*fling outside*) mettre à la porte **2.** (*get rid of*) jeter **3.** (*reject: case, proposal*) rejeter

◆**throw over** *vt* (*boyfriend, girlfriend*) laisser tomber

◆**throw together** *vt* **1.** *inf* (*make quickly: ideas, elements*) rassembler; (*meal*) préparer rapidement **2.** (*cause to meet*) **misfortune had thrown them together** le malheur les a fait se rencontrer

◆**throw up I.** *vt* **1.** (*project upwards*) jeter en l'air; (*cloud of dust, smoke, lava*) projeter; **to ~ one's hands in despair** lever les bras en l'air de désespoir **2.** (*build*) construire à la hâte **3.** (*reveal: question, discoveries*) dégager **4.** *inf* (*vomit*) vomir **II.** *vi inf* vomir

throwaway *adj* **1.** (*disposable*) jetable **2.** (*spoken as if unimportant*) dit(e) en passant

throw-back *n pej* retour en arrière *m;* **he's a ~ to the Victorian age** c'est un survivant de la période victorienne

thrower *n* SPORT lanceur, -euse *m, f*

throw-in *n* SPORT mise *f* en jeu

thrown *pp of* **throw**

thru [θru:] *Am s.* **through**

thrush[1] [θrʌʃ] *n* ZOOL grive *f*

thrush[2] [θrʌʃ] *n* MED (*in babies*) muguet *m;* (*in women*) mycose *f*

thrust [θrʌst] **I.** <-, -> *vi* **1.** (*shove*) **to ~ through sth** se frayer un passage dans qc; **to ~ in/out** entrer/sortir en se frayant un passage **2.** (*throw*) **~ at sb/sth with sth** porter un coup à qn/qc avec qc **II.** <-, -> *vt* **1.** (*shove*) pousser; **to ~ sth into sth** enfoncer qc dans qc; **to ~ sth back** repousser qc; **to ~ one's way** se frayer un passage; **to ~ a letter under sb's nose** brandir une lettre sous le nez de qn; **to ~ sb/sth aside** pousser qn/qc sur le côté **2.** (*impel*) **to ~ sth on sb** imposer qc à qn **III.** *n* **1.** (*lunge*) *a. fig* coup *m* **2.** *no pl* (*gist*) idée *f* principale; **the main ~ of sth** l'idée directrice de qc **3.** *no pl* TECH poussée *f*

thrustful, **thrusting** *adj* énergique

thruway ['θru:weɪ] *n Am s.* **throughway**

thud [θʌd] **I.** <-dd-> *vi* s'écraser lourdement; **my heart started ~ding** mon cœur s'est mis à battre à grands coups **II.** *n* bruit *m* sourd

thug [θʌg] *n* casseur *m*

thumb [θʌm] **I.** *n* pouce *m* ►**to be all ~s** être bien maladroit; **to twiddle one's ~** se tourner les pouces; **~s up!** *inf* bravo!; **to give the ~s up/down to sth** accepter/rejeter qc; **to be under sb's ~** être sous la coupe de qn **II.** *vt* **1.** (*press*) appuyer sur **2.** (*hitchhike*) **to ~ a lift/a ride** faire de l'auto-stop; **to ~ one's way across Italy** faire du stop dans toute l'Italie **3.** (*turn over: book*) feuilleter; **to be ~ed** être écorné ►**to ~ one's nose at sb** *inf* faire un pied de nez à qn **III.** *vi* **1.** (*hitch-hike*) faire du stop **2.** (*turn over*) **to ~ through sth** feuilleter qc

thumb index *n* index *m* à encoches

thumbnail ['θʌmneɪl] *n* ongle *m* du pouce

thumbnail sketch *n* (*description*) portrait *m* rapide

thumbprint *n* **1.** (*impression*) empreinte *f* de pouce **2.** *fig* empreinte *f*

thumbscrew ['θʌmskru:] *n* TECH papillon *m*

thumbtack *n Am, Aus* punaise *f*

thump [θʌmp] **I.** *vt* cogner; (*door*) cogner à; (*table*) cogner sur **II.** *vi* cogner; (*heart*) battre très fort **III.** *n* **1.** (*blow*) coup *m* de poing; **to give sb a ~** donner un coup à qn **2.** (*deadened sound*) bruit *m* sourd

thumping *inf* **I.** *adj* terrible **II.** *adv* vachement

thunder ['θʌndə^r, *Am:* -dɚ] **I.** *n no pl* **1.** METEO tonnerre *m;* **a clap of ~** un coup de tonnerre **2.** (*booming sound*) grondement *m* **3.** (*aggressive voice or sound*) rugissement *m* **4.** (*criticism*) foudres *fpl* **II.** *vi* **1.** (*make loud* *rumbling noise*) tonner **2.** (*declaim*) hurler; **to ~ against sth** fulminer contre qc **III.** *vt* hurler

thunderbolt *n fig* coup *m* de tonnerre **thunderclap** *n* coup *m* de tonnerre **thundercloud** *n pl* nuage *m* orageux

thundering *adj* **1.** (*extremely loud*) retentissant(e) **2.** (*enormous*) sacré(e)

thunderous ['θʌndərəs] *adj* (*applause*) frénétique

thunderstorm *n* orage *m* **thunderstruck** *adj* sidéré(e)

thundery ['θʌndəri] *adj* <-ier, -iest> orageux(-euse)

Thursday ['θɜːzdeɪ, *Am:* 'θɜːrz-] *n* jeudi *m*; *s. a.* **Friday**

thus [ðʌs] *adv* ainsi; **~ far** jusque-là

thwart [θwɔːt, *Am:* θwɔːrt] *vt* (*attack, plotters*) déjouer; (*decision*) faire échouer; **~ed ambition** ambition *f* déçue

thy [ðaɪ] *adj* ton, ta

thyme [taɪm] *n no pl* thym *m*

thyroid ['θaɪrɔɪd] *adj, n* thyroïde *f*

tiara [tɪ'ɑːrə, *Am:* -'erə] *n* tiare *f*

Tibet [tɪ'bet] *n* le Tibet

Tibetan I. *adj* tibétain(e) **II.** *n* **1.** (*person*) Tibétain(e) *m(f)* **2.** LING tibétain *m*; *s. a.* **English**

tibia ['tɪbɪə] <-iae> *n* tibia *m*

tic [tɪk] *n* tic *m*

tick¹ [tɪk] *n* ZOOL tique *f*

tick² [tɪk] *n Brit, inf* **on ~** à crédit

tick³ [tɪk] *n* housse *f* de matelas

tick⁴ I. *n* **1.** (*quick clicking sound*) cliquetis *m* **2.** (*mark*) encoche *f* **II.** *vi* (*make a clicking sound: clock*) faire tic tac; **hours ~ed away** les heures se sont écoulées ▶**what makes sb ~** ce qui se passe dans la tête de qn **III.** *vt* cocher

◆**tick off** *vt* **1.** (*mark with a tick*) cocher **2.** *Brit, Aus, inf* (*scold*) engueuler **3.** *Am, inf* (*exasperate*) emmerder

◆**tick over** *vi* **1.** (*operate steadily*) tourner à vide **2.** (*function at minimum level*) tourner au ralenti

ticker *n* **1.** *inf* (*watch*) montre *f* **2.** *inf* (*heart*) palpitant *m*

ticker-tape parade *n Am: défilé avec lancer de confettis*

ticket ['tɪkɪt] *n* **1.** (*paper, card*) billet *m*; (*of subway, bus*) ticket *m* **2.** (*receipt*) ticket *m* **3.** (*price tag*) étiquette *f* **4.** AUTO contravention *f* **5.** POL programme *m* électoral; **to stand on the Labour ~** se présenter sous l'étiquette travailliste

ticket collector *n* contrôleur, -euse *m, f* **ticket holder** *n* détenteur, -trice *m, f* du billet **ticket machine** *n* distributeur *m* automatique de tickets **ticket number** *n* numéro *m* de billet **ticket office** *n* RAIL, THEAT guichet *m*

ticking off <tickings off> *n Brit, inf* remontrance *f*

tickle ['tɪkl] **I.** *vi* chatouiller; (*itchy clothes*) gratter **II.** *vt* **1.** (*touch lightly*) *a. fig* chatouiller **2.** (*amuse*) amuser; **to ~ sb's fancy** amuser qn **III.** *n* **1.** (*sensation of tingling*) chatouillement *m* **2.** (*light touch*) chatouille *f*; **to give sb a ~** chatouiller qn

ticklish *adj* **1.** (*sensitive to tickling*) chatouilleux(-euse) **2.** (*awkward*) délicat(e)

tidal ['taɪdəl] *adj* (*system*) des marées; (*river*) sujet(te) aux marées

tidal energy *n* énergie *f* marémotrice **tidal wave** *n a. fig* raz *m* de marée

tidbit ['tɪdbɪt] *n Am s.* **titbit**

tiddly ['tɪdli] *adj* <-ier, -iest> **1.** *inf* (*very little*) minuscule **2.** *Brit, Aus, inf* (*slightly drunk*) éméché(e)

tiddlywinks *n pl* jeu *m* de puce

tide [taɪd] *n* **1.** (*fall and rise of sea*) marée *f*; **the ~ is out/in** la marée est basse/haute; **the ~ goes out/comes in** la mer se retire/monte **2.** (*main trend of opinion*) courant *m* (de pensée); **to go against the ~** aller à contre-courant; **to go with the ~** suivre le mouvement **3.** (*powerful trend*) mode *f*

tide over *vt always sep* **to tide sb/sth over** permettre à qn/qc de tenir

tidemark *n* niveau *m* de l'eau; *Brit* (*on face*) trace *f* de crasse (*d'un enfant mal débarbouillé*)

tidy ['taɪdi] **I.** <-ier, -iest> *adj* **1.** (*in order: room, cupboard*) bien rangé(e); (*person*) net(te); **to keep everything clean and ~** garder tout bien propre et bien rangé **2.** *inf* (*considerable*) coquet(te) **II.** *n* **1.** (*for objects*) **a shoe ~** un rangement pour les chaussures **2.** (*clean-up*) **to have** [*o* **do**] **a quick ~** faire un bout de ménage *m* **III.** *vt* (*room*) ranger; (*hair*) arranger; **~ (up) this mess!** fais disparaître ce chantier!

tie [taɪ] **I.** *n* **1.** (*necktie*) cravate *f* **2.** (*cord*) lien *m* **3.** (*relation*) lien *m*; **family ~s** liens familiaux **4.** (*equal ranking: after game*) **there was a ~** il y a eu match nul; (*after race*) ils sont arrivés en même temps; **there was a ~ for third place** il y a eu deux troisièmes ex æquo **5.** *Brit* (*contest in a competition*) match *m* **II.** <-y; -d, -d> *vi* **1.** (*fasten*) faire un nœud **2.** (*come equal in ranking*) être à égalité; **to ~ with sb/sth** être à égalité avec qn/qc **III.** <-y-; -d, -d> *vt* **1.** (*fasten together*) lier; (*hair, horse*) attacher; (*knot*) faire; (*laces, tie*) nouer; **to be ~d hand and foot** *a. fig* être pieds et poings liés; **to tie the ribbon in a bow** nouer un ruban **2.** (*restrict, limit, link*) **to ~ sb by/to sth** lier qn par/à qc; **salaries are ~d to performance** les salires sont liés aux résultats; **to be ~d to a supplier** dépendre d'un fournisseur

◆**tie back** *vt* (*hair*) nouer en arrière

◆**tie down** *vt* **1.** (*tie*) attacher **2.** *fig* **to be tied down** être coincé; **to tie sb down to sth** *inf* coincer qn sur qc

◆**tie in with I.** *vt* **to tie sth in with sb/sth** faire concorder qc avec qn/qc **II.** *vi* concorder

◆**tie up** *vt* **1.** (*bind*) attacher; (*package*) faire

2. (*delay*) **to be tied up by sth** être retenu par qc 3. **to be tied up** (*be busy*) être occupé 4. FIN, ECON (*money*) immobiliser; **to be tied up in sth** être placé dans qc 5. (*conclude: piece of business, details*) boucler 6. *Brit* (*connect with*) **to tie sth up with sth** mettre qc en rapport avec qc

tiebreak *n,* **tiebreaker** *n Brit* SPORT tie-break *m*

tie clip *n* épingle *f* de cravate

tiepin ['taɪpɪn] *n s.* **tie clip**

tier [tɪəʳ, *Am:* tɪr] I. *n* (*row*) rang *m;* (*level*) échelon *m* II. *vt* échelonner; **~ed seating** gradins *mpl*

tie-up *n* relation *f*

tiff [tɪf] *n inf* prise *f* de bec

tiger ['taɪgəʳ, *Am:* -gɚ] *n* ZOOL tigre *m*

tight [taɪt] I. *adj* 1. (*firm: knot, trousers*) serré(e); (*grip*) ferme; (*shoes*) étroit(e) 2. (*close: formation, groups*) serré(e) 3. (*stretched tautly*) tendu(e); **a ~ blouse** un chemisier serré 4. (*closely integrated: circle*) fermé(e) 5. (*difficult: bend*) étroit(e); (*budget*) restreint(e); (*credit*) serré(e); **it was a ~ finish** c'était une victoire serrée au finish; **money is ~** le budget est juste 6. *inf* (*drunk*) bourré(e) 7. *inf* (*mean*) radin ►**in a ~ corner** dans une situation *f* difficile II. *adv* (*firmly*) fermement; **hold** (**on**) **~** tiens-toi bien ►**sleep ~** dors bien

tighten I. *vt* 1. (*make tighter*) serrer; (*rope*) tendre 2. *fig* (*one's control*) renforcer; (*credit*) resserrer; (*security, regulations*) renforcer; **to ~ one's grip on power** s'accrocher au pouvoir ►**to ~ one's belt** se serrer la ceinture; **to ~ the screw** serrer la vis II. *vi* se resserrer; (*rope*) se tendre

◆**tighten up** I. *vt* (*regulations, security*) renforcer; (*performance, defence*) rendre plus vif II. *vi* **to ~ on** (*offenders*) être plus dur avec; (*discipline, efficiency*) être plus dur sur

tight-fisted *adj pej, inf* radin(e) **tight-fitting** *adj* moulant(e) **tight-lipped** *adj* 1. (*squeezing the lips together*) les lèvres pincées 2. (*discreet*) **to be ~ about sth** ne rien laisser filtrer sur qc

tightness *n no pl* (*of grip*) fermeté *f;* (*of clothes*) étroitesse *f;* (*of rules*) sévérité *f;* MED (*in chest*) serrement *m*

tightrope ['taɪtrəʊp, *Am:* -roʊp] *n* câble *m;* **to walk a ~** faire un numéro d'équilibre

tightrope walker *n* funambule *mf*

tights [taɪts] *npl* 1. *Brit* (*stockings*) collants *mpl* 2. (*for dancing*) justaucorps *m*

tightwad ['taɪtwɒd, *Am:* -wɑːd] *n Am, Aus, pej, inf* radin(e) *m(f)*

tigress ['taɪgrɪs] *n* ZOOL *a. fig* tigresse *f*

tike [taɪk] *n* 1. *Aus, Brit, inf* (*mischievous*) môme *mf* 2. *Am* (*small*) gamin(e) *m(f)* 3. (*mutt*) cabot *m*

tile [taɪl] I. *n* 1. (*for walls, floors*) carreau *m;* **the tiles** le carrelage 2. (*roof ~*) tuile *f* ►**to have a night** (**out**) **on the ~s, to be** (**out**) **on the ~s** faire la java II. *vt* carreler

tiler *n* (*for floors, walls*) carreleur, -euse *m, f;* (*for roofs*) couvreur, -euse *m, f,* ardoisier *m Belgique*

till[1] [tɪl] I. *prep* jusqu'à II. *conj* jusqu'à ce que +*subj*

till[2] [tɪl] *n* caisse *f*

till[3] [tɪl] *vt* travailler

tiller ['tɪləʳ, *Am:* -ɚ] *n* barque *f*

tilt [tɪlt] I. *n* 1. (*position*) inclinaison *f* 2. (*movement of opinion*) inclination *f* 3. **to have a ~ at a title/championship** tenter sa chance pour un titre/à un championnat ►**at full ~** à toute vitesse II. *vt* incliner; **to ~ sth back** pencher qc vers l'arrière; **to ~ sth over** pencher qc ►**to ~ the balance in favour of sb/sth** faire pencher la balance en faveur de qn/qc III. *vi* 1. s'incliner; *fig* pencher; **to ~ towards sb/sth** s'incliner en direction de qn/qc; *fig* pencher pour qn/qc; **to ~ back** être penché en arrière; **to ~ over** être penché 2. **to ~ at sth** s'en prendre à qc

timber ['tɪmbəʳ, *Am:* -bɚ] *n* 1. *no pl, Brit* (*wood*) bois *m* de construction 2. (*large beam*) poutre *f*

timbered *adj* boisé(e)

timberline ['tɪmbəlaɪn, *Am:* -bɚ-] *n Am s.* **treeline**

time [taɪm] I. *n* 1. (*chronological dimension*) temps *m;* **in the course of ~** avec le temps; **for a short/long period of ~** pour une courte/longue période; **to kill ~** tuer le temps 2. *no pl* (*period of time*) temps *m;* **journey ~/cooking ~** durée *f* du voyage; (*cooking ~*) temps de cuisson; **most of the ~** la plupart du temps; **in one week's ~** dans une semaine; **all the ~** tout le temps; **a long ~ ago** il y a longtemps; **it takes a long/short ~** ça prend beaucoup/peu de temps; **some ~ ago** il y a quelque temps; **for the ~ being** pour le moment; **in** (**less than**) **no ~** (**at all**) en moins de rien 3. (*point in time: in schedule, day*) moment *m;* (*on clock*) heure *f;* **what's the ~?** quelle heure est-il?; **arrival/departure ~** heure *f* d'arrivée/de départ; **bus/train ~s** horaires *mpl* de bus/train; **the best ~ of day** le meilleur moment de la journée; **this ~ tomorrow/next month** demain/le mois prochain à la même heure; **at all ~s** toujours; **at the ~ I didn't understand** sur le moment je n'ai pas compris; **the right/wrong ~** (*for doing sth*), **at sb's ~ of life** du vivant de qn; **at any ~** à n'importe quelle heure; **at the** [*o* **this**] **present ~** à cette heure; **at the same ~** *a. fig* en même temps; **from ~ to ~** *no pl* de temps en temps; **it's** (**about**) **~** il est l'heure; **it's about ~ too!** il était grand temps!; **ahead of ~** *Am* en avance; **in good ~** en avance; **in good ~ for sth** en avance pour qc; **by the ~ she finds them** d'ici à ce qu'elle les trouve; **by the ~ she'd found them** le temps qu'elle les trouve 4. (*experience*) **my ~ in Alaska/with the Bedouins** la période de ma vie en Alaska/avec les bédouins; **my ~ as a teacher** la période où

T

j'ai été enseignan; **what sort of ~ did you have?** comment ça s'est passé?; **to have a good ~** passer un bon moment; **we had a terrible ~ on holiday** on a passé des vacances horribles; **I had a hard ~ finding them** j'ai eu du mal à les trouver; **to give sb a hard ~** *inf* en faire voir à qn (de toutes les couleurs) **5.** (*opportunity, leisure*) tzmps *m;* **to have the ~** avoir le temps; **to have got ~ for sth/to** *+infin* avoir du temps pour qc/le temps de *+infin;* **he took the ~ to speak to me** il a pris le temps de me parler; **to take ~ out from sth to do sth** prendre du temps sur qc pour qc; **to take one's ~** prendre son temps **6.** (*incident*) fois *f;* **each ~** chaque fois; **three ~s champion** *Brit, Aus,* **three ~ champion** *Am* trois fois champion; **for the hundredth ~** *no pl* pour la centième fois; **to hit the target first ~** atteindre la cible du premier coup; **~ after ~** à de nombreuses reprises **7.** (*epoch*) temps *m;* **at the** [*o* **that**] **~ I lived in Paris** en ce temps-là je vivais à Paris; **at the ~ of sth** *no pl* à l'époque de qc; **in my ~** de mon temps; **from** [*o* **since**] **~ immemorial** depuis des temps immémoriaux; **in medieval ~s** au Moyen Âge; **in modern ~s** aux temps modernes; **to keep up** [*o* **to change**] **with the ~s** *Am* changer avec le temps; **in ~s past** à des temps révolus; **the old ~s** le bon vieux temps; **to be ahead of** [*o* **before**] **one's ~** *Brit* être en avance sur son temps **8.** *pl* (*when measuring*) MAT **three ~s six** trois fois six; **the three ~s table** la table de multiplication de trois; **three ~ faster** trois fois plus vite **9.** SPORT temps *m* **10.** *no pl* MUS mesure *f* **11.** ECON **double ~** double salaire *m;* **short ~** chômage *m* partiel ►**to <u>do</u> ~** *Brit, inf* faire de la taule; **to have ~ on one's <u>hands</u>** avoir du temps à perdre **II.** *vt* **1.** (*measure time of: runner*) chronométrer; (*journey*) mesurer la durée de **2.** (*choose best moment for: wedding, meeting, comment*) choisir le meilleur moment pour; **to be ~d to embarrass the government** arriver au meilleur moment pour embarrasser le gouvernement; **a well-~d remark** une remarque qui arrive au bon moment

time bomb *n a. fig* bombe *f* à retardement **time clock** *n* pointeuse *f* **time-consuming** *adj* long(ue) **time deposits** *npl* FIN dépôts *mpl* à terme **time difference** *n* décalage *m* horaire **timekeeper** *n* **1.** (*device*) chronomètre *m* **2.** (*person*) **to be a good/bad ~** être/ne pas être ponctuel **time lag** *n* décalage *m* **time-lapse** *adj* **~ photography** chronophotographie *f* **time limit** *n* (*for applications*) date *f* limite; (*for test, visit*) heure *f* limite **time lock** *n* serrure *f* actionnée par une minuterie

timely *adj* <-ier, -iest> (*arrival*) à temps; (*remark*) opportun(e)

time-out *n* **1.** (*during game*) temps *m* mort **2.** (*break*) pause *f*

timer ['taɪməʳ, *Am:* -ɚ] *n* minuterie *f*

timesaving *adj* (*device*) qui fait gagner du temps **time scale** *n* (*of events*) calendrier *m;* (*of a novel*) période *f* **time share** *n* multipropriété *f* **time-sharing** *n no pl* multipropriété *f* **time sheet** *n* feuille *f* de présence **timespan** *n* durée *f* **time switch** *n Brit, Aus* programmateur *m; s. a.* **timer** **timetable** **I.** *n* **1.** (*schedule*) emploi *m* du temps; (*of transport*) horaire *m;* (*for negotiations*) calendrier *m* **2.** *Brit, Aus* (*school schedule*) emploi *m* du temps **II.** *vt* fixer l'heure de **timeworn** *adj* (*excuse*) éculé(e) **time zone** *n* fuseau *m* horaire

timid ['tɪmɪd] *adj* **1.** (*easily frightened*) farouche **2.** (*shy*) timide

timidity [tɪ'mɪdəti, *Am:* -t̬i] *n no pl* timidité *f*

timing ['taɪmɪŋ] *n no pl* **1.** (*time control*) timing *m;* **the ~ of the strike/visit** le moment choisi pour la grève/la visite; **he showed bad ~** il a mal choisi son moment **2.** (*rhythm*) sens *m* du rythme

timpani ['tɪmpəni] *npl* MUS timbales *fpl*

tin [tɪn] **I.** *n* **1.** *no pl* (*metal*) étain *m* **2.** (*tinplate*) fer-blanc *m* **3.** (*can*) boîte *f* (de conserve) **4.** (*container*) boîte *f;* **biscuit ~** boîte à biscuits; **a ~ of paint** *Brit, Aus* un pot de peinture **5.** (*container for baking*) moule *m;* **cake ~** moule à gâteau **II.** *vt* mettre en conserve

tin can *n* boîte *f* de conserve

tincture ['tɪŋktʃəʳ, *Am:* -tʃɚ] *n* **1.** MED teinture *f* **2.** (*slight trace*) teinte *f*

tinder ['tɪndəʳ, *Am:* -dɚ] *n no pl* petit bois *m*

tin foil *n* papier *m* d'aluminium

ting [tɪŋ] *n* tintement *m*

tinge [tɪndʒ] **I.** *n a. fig* teinte *f* **II.** *vt a. fig* teinter; **to be ~d with sth** être teinté de qc

tingle ['tɪŋgl] **I.** *vi* picoter; (*with excitement*) avoir des frissons; **to ~ with cold** avoir des picotements de froid **II.** *n no pl* picotement *m;* (*with excitement*) frisson *m*

tin hat *n* casque *m*

tinhorn *n Am, pej, inf* prétentieux, -euse *m, f*

tinker ['tɪŋkəʳ, *Am:* -kɚ] **I.** *n* **1.** (*repairer*) rétameur *m* **2.** *Brit, pej* (*traveller*) romanichel(le) *m(f)* **3.** *Brit, inf* (*child*) chenapan *m* **II.** *vi* **to ~ with sth** bricoler qc; **don't ~ with my computer** ne touche pas à mon ordinateu

tinkle ['tɪŋkl] **I.** *vi* tinter **II.** *vt* faire tinter **III.** *n* tintement *m;* **to give sb a ~** *inf* passer un coup de fil à qn; **to have a ~** *inf* faire pipi

tinned [tɪnd] *adj Brit, Aus* en boîte

tinny ['tɪni] *adj* <-ier, -iest> métallique

tin opener *n Brit, Aus* ouvre-boîte *m* **tinplate** *n no pl* fer-blanc *m* **tinpot** *adj pej, inf* de pacotille

tinsel ['tɪnsl] *n no pl* **1.** (*decoration*) guirlandes *fpl* **2.** (*brilliance*) clinquant *m*

tint [tɪnt] **I.** *n* **1.** (*hue*) teinte *f* **2.** (*dye colouring*) colorant *m;* **~s** (*in hair*) couleur *f* **II.** *vt* teinter; **~ed glass** verre fumé *m*

tiny ['taɪni] *adj* <-ier, -iest> tout(e) petit(e); **a ~ bit hard** un petit peu dur

tip[1] [tɪp] **I.** *n* (*end part: of sth pointed*) pointe *f;* (*of sth rounded*) bout *m* ►**on the ~ of one's tongue** sur le bout de la langue; **the ~ of the iceberg** la partie visible de l'iceberg **II.** <-pp-> *vt* **to be ~ped with sth** avoir un embout de qc

tip² [tɪp] **I.** *n* **1.** *Brit* (*garbage dump*) décharge *f* **2.** *Brit, inf* (*mess*) chantier *m* **II.** <-pp-> *vt* **1.** *Brit, Aus* (*empty out*) verser; (*waste*) déverser **2.** (*cause to tilt*) incliner; **to ~ the scales** *fig* faire pencher la balance **3.** (*touch*) effleurer; **to ~ the ball into the hole** faire glisser la balle dans le trou **III.** <-pp-> *vi* s'incliner; **to ~ to one side** s'incliner sur le côté

◆**tip down** *vi Brit, inf* pleuvoir des cordes

◆**tip over I.** *vt* renverser **II.** *vi* se renverser

◆**tip up I.** *vt* incliner **II.** *vi* s'incliner

tip³ I. *n* **1.** (*money*) pourboire *m* **2.** (*hint*) tuyau *m* **II.** <-pp-> *vt* **1.** (*give money*) donner un pourboire à **2.** *Brit* (*predict*) **to be ~ped to win** [*o* **as a winner**] être donné gagnant ►**to ~ sb the wink** prévenir qn

◆**tip off** *vt inf* donner des tuyaux à; (*police*) donner des informations à

tip-off *n inf* tuyau *m*

tipple ['tɪpl] **I.** *vi* **1.** (*drink alcohol*) picoler **2.** (*rain heavily*) pleuvoir à seaux **II.** *vt* descendre **III.** *n inf* coup *m* (à boire); **to have a ~** boire un coup

tippler *n inf* alcoolo *mf*

tipster ['tɪpstəʳ, *Am:* -stɚ] *n* SPORT pronostiqueur, -euse *m, f*

tipsy ['tɪpsi] *adj* <-ier, -iest> pompette

tiptoe ['tɪptəʊ, *Am:* -toʊ] **I.** *n* **on ~(s)** sur la pointe des pieds **II.** *vi* marcher sur la pointe des pieds

tip-top *adj inf* excellent(e)

tirade [taɪ'reɪd, *Am:* 'taɪreɪd] *n* tirade *f*

tire¹ ['taɪəʳ, *Am:* 'taɪɚ] *n Am* pneu *m*

tire² ['taɪəʳ, *Am:* 'taɪɚ] **I.** *vt* fatiguer; **to ~ sb out** mettre qn à plat **II.** *vi* se fatiguer; **to ~ of sth** se lasser de qc

tired *adj* **1.** (*weary*) fatigué(e); **to be ~ of sth** en avoir assez de qc; **to get ~ of sth** se lasser de qc; **to be sick and ~ of sth** en avoir par-dessus la tête de qc **2.** (*unoriginal: excuse*) rebattu(e)

tiredness *n no pl* fatigue *f*

tired out *adj* épuisé(e)

tireless *adj* infatigable

tiresome ['taɪəsəm, *Am:* 'taɪɚ-] *adj pej* pénible

tiring ['taɪrɪŋ] *adj* fatigant(e)

'tis [tɪz] = **it is** *s.* **be**

tissue ['tɪʃuː] *n* **1.** (*soft paper*) papier *m* de soie **2.** (*for wiping noses*) mouchoir *m* en papier **3.** *no pl* (*cells*) tissu *m* **4.** (*complex layer*) tissu *m* ►**a ~ of lies** un tissu de mensonges

tit¹ [tɪt] *n* mésange *f*

tit² [tɪt] *n vulg* nichon *m*

tit³ *n* **~ for tat** un prêté pour un rendu

titanic [taɪ'tænɪk] *adj* de titan

titanium [taɪ'teɪnɪəm] *n no pl* titane *m*

titbit ['tɪtbɪt] *n Brit* **1.** (*delicacy*) morceau *m* de choix **2.** *pl* (*piece of news*) potin *m*

titillate ['tɪtɪleɪt, *Am:* -əleɪt] *vt* titiller

titillating *adj* excitant(e)

titivate ['tɪtɪveɪt, *Am:* 'tɪţə-] *vt* pomponner

title ['taɪtl, *Am:* -ţl] **I.** *n* **1.** (*name, position, right*) titre *m;* **job ~** intitulé du poste; **~ fight** combat comptant pour le titre **2.** *pl* (*credits of a film*) générique *m* **II.** *vt* intituler

title deed *n* LAW acte *m* de propriété **title-holder** *n* tenant(e) *m(f)* du titre **title page** *n* page *f* de titre **title role** *n* rôle-titre *m* **title track** *n morceau éponyme d'un album*

titter ['tɪtəʳ, *Am:* 'tɪţɚ] **I.** *vi* glousser **II.** *n* gloussement *m*

tittle-tattle ['tɪtltætl, *Am:* 'tɪţlˌtæţl] *n no pl, inf* potins *mpl*

tizz(y) ['tɪz(i)] *n no pl, inf* **in a ~** dans tous ses états

TNT [ˌtiːen'tiː] *n abbr of* **trinitrotoluene** TNT *m*

to [tuː] **I.** *prep* **1.** à **2.** (*direction, location*) **~ France/Alaska** en France/Alaska; **~ Japan/Peru** au Japon/Pérou; **~ Oxford/Oslo** à Oxford/Oslo; **~ town** en ville; **~ the dentist('s)/my parents'** chez le dentiste/mes parents; **the flight ~ London** le vol à destination de Londres; **~ the left/right** à gauche/droite; **~ the north/south** au nord/sud; **I go ~ school/church** je vais à l'école/l'église; **close ~ sth** près de qc; **he had his back ~ me** il me tournait le dos; **I fix sth ~ the wall** je fixe qc au mur; **come ~ dinner** venez dîner **3.** (*before*) **a quarter ~ five** cinq heures moins le quart; **still four days ~ the holiday** encore quatre jours avant les vacances **4.** (*until*) **I count ~ 10** je compte jusqu'à 10; **~ date** jusqu'à ce jour **5.** (*between*) **from 10 ~ 25** de 10 à 25 **6.** (*with indirect objects*) **I talk ~ sb** je parle à qn; **it belongs ~ me** cela m'appartient; **listen ~ your mother** écoute ta mère **7.** (*towards*) **he is kind/nasty ~ sb** il est gentil/méchant avec qn **8.** (*expressing a relation*) **it's nothing ~ sth** ce n'est rien par rapport à qc; **it's important ~ me** c'est important pour moi; **~ them it's vital/silly** pour eux c'est crucial/idiot; **it's a lot of money ~ us** ça représente beaucoup d'argent pour nous; **what's it ~ them?** *inf* qu'est-ce que ça peut leur faire?; **how many francs ~ the euro?** combien de francs dans un euro?; **3 goals ~ 1** 3 buts à 1; **the odds are 3 ~ 1** la cote est à 3 contre 1 **9.** (*expressing a reaction*) **much ~ my surprise** à ma grande surprise; **~ my disgust he accepted** à mon grand dégoût il a accepté; **to sway ~ the rhythm** onduler au rythme de la musique; **sb/sth changes ~ sth** qn/qc se change en qc **10.** (*by*) **known ~ sb** connu de qn **11.** (*expressing a connection*) **the top ~ this jar** le couvercle de ce bocal; **secretary ~ the boss** secrétaire du patron; **I had the house ~ myself** j'ai eu la maison à moi tout seul ►**that's** __**all**__ **there is** ~ **it** ce n'est pas plus compliqué que ça; **there's not** __**much**__ [*o* __**nothing**__] ~ **it** ce n'est pas difficile; *s. a.* **at, from II.** *infinitive particle* **1.** *not translated* (*infinitive*) ~ **do/walk/put** faire/marcher/ mettre **2.** (*in commands, wishes*) **I told/ asked him** ~ **eat** je lui ai dit/demandé de manger; **he wants** ~ **listen/go there** il veut écouter/y aller; **he wants me** ~ **tell him a story** il veut que je lui raconte une histoire **3.** (*after interrog words*) **I know what** ~ **do/ where** ~ **go/how** ~ **say it** je sais quoi faire/ où aller/comment le dire **4.** (*expressing purpose*) **to so sth** pour faire qc; **I write books** ~ **make money** j'écris des livres pour gagner de l'argent; **he comes** ~ **see me** il vient me voir **5.** (*in consecutive acts*) **I came only** ~ **see the door lying open** en arrivant j'ai vu la porte ouverte **6.** (*introducing a complement*) **too tired/rich enough** ~ *+infin* trop fatigué/ assez riche pour *+infin;* **the last** ~ **leave** le dernier à partir **7.** (*in impersonal statements*) **it is easy** ~ *+infin* il est facile de *+infin;* **sth is easy** ~ **do** qc est facile à faire **8.** (*in ellipsis*) **he doesn't want** ~ **drink, but I want** ~ il ne veut pas boire, mais moi oui; **I shouldn't, but I want** ~ je ne devrais pas, mais je voudrais le faire; **it's hard to explain but I'll try** ~ c'est difficile à expliquer mais je vais essayer **III.** *adv* **I push the door** ~ je ferme la porte ►~ **and** __**fro**__ ça et là; **to go** ~ **and fro** aller et venir

toad [təʊd, *Am:* toʊd] *n* **1.** ZOOL crapaud *m* **2.** *fig* crapule *f*

toad-in-the-hole *n Brit: saucisse cuite au four dans de la pâte à frire* **toadstool** *n* champignon *m* vénéneux

toady *pej* **I.** <-ies> *n* lèche-botte *mf* **II.** *vi* **to** ~ **to sb** faire du lèche-botte à qn

to and fro I. *adj* (*movement*) de va-et-vient **II.** *adv* **to walk** ~ faire les cent pas

toast [təʊst, *Am:* toʊst] **I.** *n* **1.** *no pl* (*bread*) pain *m* grillé; **a piece of** ~ un toast **2.** (*act of drinking*) toast *m;* **to drink a** ~ **to sb/sth** porter un toast à qn/qc **II.** *vt* **1.** (*cook over heat*) faire griller **2.** (*warm up: feet*) se chauffer **3.** (*drink to health*) porter un toast à

toaster *n* grille-pain *m*

toastie *n* sandwich *m* toasté

toastmaster *n* maître *m* de cérémonie **toast rack** *n* porte-toasts *m*

tobacco [tə'bækəʊ, *Am:* -oʊ] *n no pl* tabac *m*

tobacconist [tə'bækənɪst] *n* bureau *m* de tabac, tabagie *f Québec*

to-be [tə'biː] *adj* futur(e); **a bride-**~ une future mariée; **a mother-**~ une future maman

toboggan [tə'bɒgən, *Am:* -'bɑːgən] **I.** *n* luge *f* **II.** *vi* faire de la luge

toboggan run, **toboggan slide** *n* piste *f* de luge

toby ['təʊbi, *Am:* 'toʊ-], **toby jug** *n Am: chope de bière en forme d'homme à tricorne*

tod [tɒd, *Am:* tɑːd] *n no pl, Brit, inf* **on one's** ~ tout(e) seul(e)

today [tə'deɪ] *adv* **1.** (*present day*) aujourd'hui; **early** ~ ce matin de bonne heure; **a week** (**from**) ~ aujourd'hui en huit **2.** (*nowadays*) de nos jours

toddle ['tɒdl, *Am:* 'tɑːdl] *vi* marcher à petits pas

toddler *n* enfant *m* en âge de marcher

toddy ['tɒdi, *Am:* 'tɑːdi] <-ies> *n* grog *m*

to-do [tə'duː] *n sing, inf* (*fuss*) histoire *f*

toe [təʊ, *Am:* toʊ] **I.** *n* **1.** (*part of foot*) orteil *m;* **on one's** ~**s** sur la pointe des pieds **2.** (*part of shoe, sock*) bout *m* ►**to** __**keep**__ **sb on their** ~**s** maintenir qn en alerte **II.** *vt* **to** ~ **the line** se mettre au pas

toe cap *n* bout *m* renforcé **toehold** *n* **1.** (*ridge*) prise *f* (de pied) **2.** *fig* prise *f* **toenail** *n* ongle *m* de pied

toffee ['tɒfi, *Am:* 'tɑːfi] *n* caramel *m*

toffee apple *n* pomme *f* d'amour **toffee-nosed** *adj Brit, pej, inf* snobinard(e)

toffy ['tɒfi, *Am:* 'tɑːfi] *n s.* **toffee**

together [tə'geðəʳ, *Am:* -ɚ] **I.** *adv* ensemble; **she's richer than all of us put** ~ elle est plus riche que nous tous réunis; **to bring people closer** ~ *a. fig* rapprocher les gens ►**to** __**get**__ **it** ~ *inf* être tout à fait prêt **II.** *adj inf* équilibré(e)

togetherness *n no pl* unité *f*

together with *prep* ainsi que

toggle ['tɒgl, *Am:* 'tɑːgl] **I.** *n* **1.** (*computer key*) touche *f* à bascule **2.** (*coat fastener*) olive *f* **II.** *vt* INFOR faire basculer **III.** *vi* INFOR basculer

Togo ['təʊgəʊ, *Am:* 'toʊgoʊ] *n* le Togo

Togolese I. *adj* togolais(e) **II.** *n* Togolais(e) *m(f)*

toil [tɔɪl] **I.** *n no pl* labeur *m* **II.** *vi* **1.** (*work hard*) travailler dur **2.** (*go with difficulty*) aller tout doucement

toilet ['tɔɪlɪt] *n* toilettes *fpl,* cour *f Belgique;* **to flush the** ~ tirer la chasse d'eau; **to go to the** ~ aller aux toilettes

toilet bag *n* trousse *f* de toilette **toilet paper** *n* papier *m* hygiénique

toiletries ['tɔɪlɪtriz] *npl* articles *mpl* de toilette

toiletries bag *n Am* trousse *f* de toilette

toilet roll *n Brit, Aus* rouleau *m* de papier hygiénique **toilet soap** *n* savon *m* de toilette **toilet water** *n* eau *f* de toilette

to-ing and fro-ing [ˌtuːɪŋən'frəʊɪŋ, *Am:* -'froʊ-] <to-ings and fro-ings> *n no pl, a. fig* allées *fpl* et venues

token ['təʊkən, *Am:* 'toʊ-] **I.** *n* **1.** (*sign*) signe *m* **2.** *Brit, Aus* (*voucher*) chèque-cadeau *m* **3.** (*money substitute*) jeton *m* ►**by the** __**same**__ ~ pareillement **II.** *adj* symbolique; **to make a** ~ **gesture** faire un geste pour la forme; **the** ~ **man** l'homme de service

told [təʊld, *Am:* toʊld] *pt, pp of* **tell** ►__**all**__ ~ en tout

tolerable *adj* **1.** (*endurable*) tolérable **2.** *form* (*fairly good*) acceptable

tolerably ['tɒlərəbli, *Am:* 'tɑːlɚ-] *adv form*

relativement

tolerance ['tɒlərəns, *Am:* 'tɑːlɚ-] *n no pl, a. fig* tolérance *f*

tolerant *adj* tolérant(e)

tolerate ['tɒləreɪt, *Am:* 'tɑːləreɪt] *vt a. fig* tolérer

toleration *n no pl* tolérance *f*

toll¹ [təʊl, *Am:* toʊl] *n* **1.** (*transport levy*) péage *m* **2.** *Am* (*phone charge*) tarification *f* interurbaine **3.** *no pl* (*damage*) bilan *m* ►**to take its toll on sb** laisser une empreinte sur qn

toll² [təʊl, *Am:* toʊl] *vt, vi* sonner

toll bar *n* barrière *f* de péage **tollbooth** *n* cabine *f* de péage **toll bridge** *n* pont *m* à péage **toll-free** *adj* (*call*) gratuit(e) **toll road** <-roads> route *f* à péage

tom [tɒm, *Am:* tɑːm] *n* **1.** (*animal*) mâle *m* **2.** (*cat*) matou *m*

tomato [tə'mɑːtəʊ, *Am:* -'meɪt̬oʊ] <-oes> *n* tomate *f*

tomato juice *n* jus *m* de tomate **tomato ketchup** *n* ketchup *m* **tomato soup** *n* soupe *f* à la tomate

tomb [tuːm] *n* **1.** (*stone memorial*) tombe *f* **2.** (*burial chamber*) tombeau *m*

tombola [tɒm'bəʊlə, *Am:* 'tɑːmblə] *n Brit, Aus* tombola *f*

tomboy ['tɒmbɔɪ, *Am:* 'tɑːm-] *n* garçon *m* manqué

tombstone ['tuːmstəʊn, *Am:* 'tuːmstoʊn] *n* pierre *f* tombale

tomcat ['tɒmkæt, *Am:* 'tɑːm-] *n* matou *m*

tome [təʊm, *Am:* toʊm] *n a. iron* tome *m*

tommy gun ['tɒmigʌn, *Am:* 'tɑmi-] *n* mitraillette *f*

tomogram *n* MED tomogramme *m*

tomography [tə'mɒgrəfi, *Am:* toʊ'mɑːgrə-] *n* MED tomographie *f*

tomorrow [tə'mɒrəʊ, *Am:* -'mɑːroʊ] **I.** *adv* demain; **see you ~!** à demain! **II.** *n* demain *m;* **the day after ~** après-demain; **a week from ~** demain en huit

tom-tom ['tɒmtɒm, *Am:* 'tɑːmtɑːm] *n* tam-tam *m*

ton [tʌn] <-(s)> *n* tonne *f;* **~s of sth** *inf* des tonnes de qc ►**to come down on sb like a ~ of bricks** tomber sur qn à bras raccourcis

tone [təʊn, *Am:* toʊn] **I.** *n* **1.** (*sound*) ton *m;* (*of instrument*) timbre *m;* **in a resigned ~ of voice** avec un ton de voix résigné **2.** (*style*) ton *m;* **to lower the ~ of the neighbourhood** faire baisser le standing du quartier **3.** (*shade of colour*) ton *m* **4.** *no pl* (*healthy condition*) tonicité *f;* **muscle ~** tonus *m* musculaire **5.** (*difference in pitch*) ton *m;* **half ~** demi-ton *m* **6.** (*telephone noise*) tonalité *f;* **dial**(**ling**) **~** tonalité **II.** *vt* (*firm muscles*) tonifier

◆**tone down** *vt a. fig* adoucir

◆**tone in** *vi* s'harmoniser

◆**tone up** *vt* raffermir

tone control *n* touche *f* de tonalité **tone-deaf** *adj* **to be ~** ne pas avoir l'oreille **tone poem** *n* poème *m* symphonique

toner ['təʊnəʳ, *Am:* 'toʊnɚ] *n* **1.** (*cosmetic*) tonique *m* **2.** INFOR, PHOT toner *m*

toner cartridge *n* cartouche *f* d'encre

Tonga ['tɒŋə, *Am:* 'tɑːŋ-] *n* les Tonga *fpl*

tongs [tɒŋz, *Am:* tɑːŋz] *n* pince *f;* **a pair of ~** une pince

tongue [tʌŋ] *n* **1.** (*mouth part*) *a. fig* langue *f;* **to bite one's ~** se mordre la langue; **to stick one's ~ out at sb** tirer la langue à qn; **to have a sharp ~** avoir une langue acérée **2.** (*tongue-shaped object: of a land*) langue *f;* (*of a shoe*) languette *f* **3.** (*language*) langue *f* ►**to be on the tip of one's ~** être sur le bout de la langue; **to say sth ~ in cheek** dire qc ironiquement; **to get one's ~ around a word** arriver à prononcer un mot

tongue-tied *adj* muet(te) **tongue-twister** *n* mot *m*/phrase *f* difficile à dire

tonic¹ ['tɒnɪk, *Am:* 'tɑːnɪk] *n* tonique *m*

tonic² ['tɒnɪk, *Am:* 'tɑːnɪk] *n* MUS tonique *f*

tonic³ ['tɒnɪk, *Am:* 'tɑːnɪk], **tonic water** *n* tonique *m*

tonight [tə'naɪt] *adv* **1.** (*evening*) ce soir **2.** (*night*) cette nuit

tonnage ['tʌnɪdʒ] *n no pl* tonnage *m*

tonsillitis [ˌtɒnsɪ'laɪtɪs, *Am:* ˌtɑːnsə'laɪt̬ɪs] *n no pl* angine *f*

tonsils ['tɒntsəlz, *Am:* 'tɑː-] *npl* MED amygdales *fpl;* **to have one's ~ out** se faire enlever les amygdales

too [tuː] *adv* **1.** (*overly*) trop; **to be ~ good to be true** être trop beau pour être vrai; **to be ~ good an opportunity to miss** être une chance à saisir; **~ much water** trop d'eau; **~ many children** trop d'enfants **2.** (*very*) très; **I'm not ~ happy about it** je n'en suis pas vraiment contente; **not to be ~ sure** ne pas être très sûr **3.** (*also*) aussi; **me ~!** *inf* moi aussi! **4.** (*moreover*) de plus ►**to have ~ much of a good thing** abuser d'une bonne chose *prov;* **~ right!** tu peux le dire!

took [tʊk] *pt of* **take**

tool [tuːl] **I.** *n* **1.** (*implement*) *a. fig* outil *m* **2.** (*instrument*) instrument *m* **3.** INFOR outil *m* **II.** *vt* ciseler

tool bag *n* trousse *f* à outils **tool box**, **tool chest** *n* caisse *f* à outils **tool kit** *n* trousse *f* à outils **toolmaker** *n* outilleur *m*

toot [tuːt] **I.** *n* coup *m* de klaxon **II.** *vt* **to ~ a horn** donner un coup de klaxon **III.** *vi* klaxonner

tooth [tuːθ] <teeth> *n* **1.** ANAT dent *f;* **to bare one's teeth** montrer ses dents; **to grind/grit one's teeth** grincer/serrer les dents; **to have a ~ out** [*o* **pulled**] *Am* se faire arracher une dent **2.** *pl* (*tooth-like projection*) dent *f;* **~ of a comb/saw** dent de peigne/scie ►**armed to the teeth** armé(e) jusqu'aux dents; **to do sth in the teeth of sb/sth** faire qc malgré qn/qc; **to set sb's teeth on edge** faire grincer les dents de qn; **to fight ~ and nail** se défendre bec et ongles; **to get one's**

T

teeth into sth se mettre à fond dans qc; **to go through sth with a fine-~ comb** passer qc au peigne fin

toothache *n* mal *m* de dent; **to have a ~** avoir mal aux dents **toothbrush** *n* brosse *f* à dents **tooth decay** *n no pl* carie *f* dentaire

toothed *adj* denté(e)

toothless *adj* (*mouth*) édenté(e); (*watchdog*) impuissant(e)

toothpaste *n no pl* dentifrice *m* **toothpick** *n* cure-dent *m* **toothsome** *adj* succulent(e)

toothy <-ier, -iest> *adj* aux dents saillantes

top¹ [tɒp, *Am:* tɑːp] *n s.* **spinning top**

top² [tɒp, *Am:* tɑːp] **I.** *n* **1.** (*highest part*) haut *m;* (*of a tree, mountain*) sommet *m;* **from ~ to bottom** de haut en bas; **at the ~ of the picture** en haut de l'image; **at the ~ of my list** au sommet de ma liste **2.** (*upper surface*) dessus *m;* **on ~ of sth** au-dessus de qc **3.** *no pl* (*highest rank*) sommet *m;* **to be at the ~** être au sommet; **to be at the ~ of the class** être le premier de la classe **4.** (*clothing*) haut *m;* **from ~ to toe** de pied en cap **5.** (*head end*) bout *m;* **at the ~ of a street** au bout de la rue **6.** (*lid*) couvercle *m;* (*of pen*) capuchon *m* **7.** *no pl* (*in addition to*) **on ~ of sth** en plus de qc ►**to say sth off the ~ of one's head** *inf* dire qc au pied levé; **to be over the ~** être exagéré; **to feel on ~ of the world** être aux anges; **to be on ~ of things** bien gérer la situation; **to let things get on ~ of one** se laisse dépasser par les événements **II.** *adj* **1.** (*highest, upper*) du haut; (*floor, layer*) dernier(-ère); **in the ~ righthand corner** à l'angle de droite en haut **2.** (*best, most important: scientists, executives*) de pointe; (*hotels*) meilleur(e); (*prize*) premier(-ère); (*university*) coté(e); **the ~ scorer** celui/celle qui a marqué le plus de points; **to give ~ priority to sth** donner absolue priorité à qc; **voted ~ travel agent** la meilleure agence de voyage selon les votes; **she wants the ~ job** elle veut le poste de chef **3.** (*maximum*) maximal(e); **at ~ speed** à vitesse maximale; **to get ~ marks for sth** *a. fig* avoir la meilleure note pour qc **III.** <-pp-> *vt* **1.** (*be at the highest place: list, ratings*) être en tête de **2.** (*place on top of*) couvrir; **a fence ~ped with barbed wire** une cloture surmontée de barbelés; **to ~ a cake with cream** garnir un gâteau de crème **3.** (*surpass: record, performance*) surpasser **4.** (*exceed, be taller*) dépasser **5.** *Brit, inf* (*kill*) buter; **to ~ oneself** se buter **6.** (*remove top*) étêter; **to ~ and tail sth** éplucher qc

◆**top off** *vt* **1.** GASTR garnir **2.** (*conclude satisfactorily*) couronner

◆**top up I.** *vt* **1.** (*fill up again*) remplir; **to top sb up** *inf* resservir qn **2.** (*add to until limit reached*) compléter **II.** *vi* (*with fuel*) faire le plein

topaz ['təʊpæz, *Am:* 'toʊ-] *n* topaze *f*

top class *adj* de première classe

topcoat ['tɒpkəʊt, *Am:* 'tɑːpkoʊt] *n* **1.** (*outer layer of paint*) couche *f* de finition **2.** (*coat*) pardessus *m*

top copy *n* original *m* **top dog** *n inf* boss *m* **top drawer** *n* **1.** (*chest's uppermost drawer*) tiroir *m* du haut **2.** *Brit, inf* (*superior social position*) **to be ~** être de la haute **top-flight** *adj* de premier ordre **top hat** *n* chapeau *m* haut-de-forme **top-heavy** *adj pej* (*too heavy at the top*) mal équilibré(e)

topic ['tɒpɪk, *Am:* 'tɑːpɪk] *n* sujet *m*

topical *adj* d'actualité; **to be highly ~** être d'une d'une actualité brûlante

topicality *n no pl* actualité *f*

topless I. *adj* (*person*) aux seins nus; (*beach*) seins nus **II.** *adv* seins nus; **to go ~** faire du seins nus

top-level *adj* au plus haut niveau **top-notch** *adj inf* classe **top-of-the-range** *adj* haut de gamme

topographer *n* topographe *mf*

topographical *adj* topographique

topography [tə'pɒgrəfi, *Am:* -'pɑːgrə-] *n no pl* topographie *f*

topper ['tɒpəʳ, *Am:* 'tɑːpɚ] *n inf s.* **top hat**

topping ['tɒpɪŋ, *Am:* 'tɑːpɪŋ] *n* garniture *f*

topple ['tɒpl, *Am:* 'tɑːpl] **I.** *vt* **1.** (*knock over*) faire tomber **2.** POL renverser **II.** *vi a. fig* basculer

◆**topple over I.** *vt* **1.** (*let fall down*) faire tomber **2.** (*fall over*) culbuter sur; **to ~ a cliff** tomber d'une colline **II.** *vi* tomber

top-quality *adj* de qualité supérieure **top-ranking** *adj* de haut rang; (*university*) coté(e) **top secret** *adj* top secret(-ète) **topsoil** *n no pl* terre *f* arable

topsy-turvy [ˌtɒpsi'tɜːvi, *Am:* ˌtɑːpsɪ'tɜːr-] *inf* **I.** *adj* sens dessus dessous **II.** *adv* à l'envers; **to turn ~** tourner à l'envers

torch [tɔːtʃ, *Am:* tɔːrtʃ] <-es> **I.** *n* **1.** *Aus, Brit* (*electric light*) torche *f* électrique **2.** (*burning stick*) flambeau *m* **3.** *Am s.* **blowlamp II.** *vt inf* mettre le feu à

torchlight I. *n no pl* **by ~** à la lumière de la torche **II.** *adj* (*procession*) aux flambeaux

tore [tɔːʳ, *Am:* tɔːr] *pt of* **tear**

torment ['tɔːment, *Am:* 'tɔːr-] **I.** *n* **1.** (*mental suffering*) tourment *m;* **to be in ~** être tourmenté **2.** (*physical pain*) supplice *m;* **to be in ~** être au supplice **II.** *vt* **1.** (*torture physically*) torturer **2.** (*torture mentally*) tourmenter **3.** (*harass*) harceler

torn [tɔːn, *Am:* tɔːrn] *pp of* **tear**

tornado [tɔː'neɪdəʊ, *Am:* tɔːr'neɪdoʊ] *n* <-s *o* -es> tornade *f*

torpedo [tɔː'piːdəʊ, *Am:* tɔːr'piːdoʊ] MIL, NAUT **I.** <-es> *n* torpille *f* **II.** *vt* torpiller

torpid ['tɔːpɪd, *Am:* 'tɔːr-] *adj form* torpide

torpor ['tɔːpəʳ, *Am:* 'tɔːrpɚ] *n no pl, form* torpeur *f*

torrent ['tɒrənt, *Am:* 'tɔːr-] *n a. fig* torrent *m;* **a ~ of abuse** un flot d'injures

torrential *adj* torrentiel(le)

torrid ['tɒrɪd, *Am:* 'tɔː-] *adj* torride

torsion ['tɔːʃən, *Am:* 'tɔːr-] *n no pl* torsion *f*
torso ['tɔːsəʊ, *Am:* 'tɔːrsoʊ] *n* torse *m*
tortoise ['tɔːtəs, *Am:* 'tɔːrtəs] *n* tortue *f*
tortoiseshell *n no pl* écaille *f* de tortue
tortuous ['tɔːtjʊəs, *Am:* 'tɔːrtʃuəs] *adj a. fig* tortueux(-euse)
torture ['tɔːtʃəʳ, *Am:* 'tɔːrtʃɚ] **I.** *n a. fig* torture *f* **II.** *vt a. fig* torturer
torturer *n* tortionnaire *mf*
Tory ['tɔːri] <-ies> *n* POL tory *m*
toss [tɒs, *Am:* tɑːs] **I.** *n* **1.** (*throw*) lancer *m;* **to win/lose the** ~ gagner/perdre à pile ou face **2.** (*movement*) **with a** ~ **of her head** d'un mouvement de la tête ►**to argue the** ~ discuter le coup; **to not care a** ~ *Brit, inf* s'en foutre **II.** *vt* **1.** (*throw*) lancer; (*pancake*) faire sauter; (*salad*) mélanger; **to** ~ **one's head** faire un mouvement de la tête **2.** (*flip in air*) jeter en l'air; **to** ~ **a coin** jouer à pile ou face **3.** (*disturb: boat*) ballotter; (*branches*) agiter **III.** *vi* (*decide via a coin toss*) **to** ~ **for sth** jouer qc à pile ou face ►**to** ~ **and turn** se remuer dans tous les sens
◆**toss about, toss around** *vt* **1.** (*throw around*) lancer; **to toss ideas around** *fig* lancer des idées en l'air **2.** (*move roughly*) secouer
◆**toss away** *vt* jeter
◆**toss off** *vt* (*letter*) expédier
◆**toss out** *vt* (*rubbish*) jeter; (*idea, question*) proposer
◆**toss up** *vi* tirer à pile ou face; **to** ~ **for sth** jouer qc à pile ou face
toss-up *n inf* coup *m* à pile ou face; **it's a** ~ **between sth and sth** entre qc et qc, ça revient au même
tot [tɒt, *Am:* tɑːt] **I.** *n* **1.** *inf* (*small child*) bambin *m* **2.** (*drink*) dose *f* **II.** *vt* **to** ~ **up** *inf* additionner **III.** *vi* **to** ~ **up to £5** faire un total de 5 livres
total ['təʊtl, *Am:* 'toʊtl] **I.** *n* total *m;* **in** ~ au total **II.** *adj* **1.** (*complete*) total(e) **2.** (*absolute*) complet(-ète); (*stranger*) parfait(e) **III.** *vt* <*Brit* -ll- *o Am* -l-> **1.** (*add up*) faire la somme de **2.** (*add up to*) totaliser un montant de **3.** *inf* (*damage, kill: car*) démolir; (*person*) bousiller
totalitarian [ˌtəʊtælɪ'teəriən, *Am:* toʊˌtælə'teri-] *adj* totalitaire
totalitarianism *n no pl, pej* POL totalitarisme *m*
totality [təʊ'tæləti, *Am:* toʊ'tæləti] *n no pl* totalité *f*, entièreté *f Belgique*
totally *adv* totalement
tote [təʊt, *Am:* toʊt] *vt Am, inf* trimballer
tote bag *n* fourre-tout *m inv*
totem ['təʊtəm, *Am:* 'toʊtəm] *n* totem *m*
totter ['tɒtəʳ, *Am:* 'tɑːtɚ] *vi a. fig* chanceler; **he** ~**ed towards me** il tituba vers moi
tottery *adj* **1.** (*wobbling*) chancelant(e) **2.** (*shaky*) branlant(e)
toucan ['tuːkæn] *n* toucan *m*
touch [tʌtʃ] **I.** *n* **1.** *no pl* (*ability to feel, sense*) toucher *m;* **to do sth by** ~ faire qc au toucher; **to the** ~ au toucher; **I felt a** ~ **on my hand** j'ai senti qu'on touchait ma main; **with a** ~ **of the button** à la pression du bouton **2.** *no pl* (*communication*) **to lose** ~ **with sb** perdre qn de vue; **to be/keep in** ~ **with sb** être/rester en contact avec qn; **to be in/out of** ~ **with sth** être/ne pas être au courant de qc; **to be out of** ~ **with reality/the modern world** n'avoir aucune conscience de la réalité/du monde moderne **3.** *no pl* (*skill*) style *m;* **to lose one's** ~ perdre la main; **the personal** ~ la touche personnelle **4.** *no pl* (*small amount*) pointe *f;* (*of garlic*) pointe *f;* **there was a** ~ **of irony in his voice** il y avait une pointe d'ironie dans sa voix; **a** ~ **of wind** un peu de vent; **a** ~ **of flu** une petite grippe **5.** SPORT touche *f* ►**to be a soft** ~ *inf* être une bonne poire **II.** *vt* **1.** (*feel with fingers*) toucher; **I** ~**ed him on the arm** j'ai touché son bras; **her feet never** ~**ed the ground** elle n'a jamais posé un pied à terre **2.** (*come in contact with*) *a. fig* toucher à; **I never** ~**ed your wife/camera** je n'ai jamais touché à votre femme/votre appareil-photo; **they can't** ~ **the drug barons** ils ne peuvent pas toucher aux chefs de la drogue **3.** (*eat, drink*) toucher à; **she won't** ~ **meat/fried foods** elle ne mange jamais de viande/de fritures **4.** (*move emotionally*) toucher **5.** (*rival in quality*) égaler; **you can't** ~ **real coffee** rien ne vaut le vrai café **6.** (*concern*) toucher **7.** *Am* **to** ~ **base with sb** prendre des nouvelles de qn; **to not** ~ **sb/sth with a barge pole, to not** ~ **sb/sth with a ten-foot pole** *Am* ne pas toucher à qn/qc pour tout l'or du monde; ~ **wood** touche(z) du bois; **to** ~ **bottom** toucher le fond **III.** *vi* **1.** (*feel with fingers*) toucher **2.** (*come in contact*) se toucher
◆**touch down** *vi* AVIAT atterrir; SPORT marquer un essai
◆**touch off** *vt a. fig* déclencher
◆**touch on** *vt* aborder
◆**touch up** *vt* **1.** (*improve*) retoucher **2.** *Brit, vulg* (*touch sexually*) peloter
◆**touch upon** *vt s.* **touch on**
touch-and-go *adj* hasardeux(-euse); **it was** ~ **whether** ce n'était pas certain que +*subj*
touchdown *n* **1.** (*landing*) atterrissage *m* **2.** SPORT essai *m*
touched *adj* **1.** (*emotionally moved*) touché(e) **2.** *inf* (*crazy*) timbré(e)
touchiness *n no pl, inf* susceptibilité *f*
touching *adj* touchant(e)
touchline *n* ligne *f* de touche **touch-sensitive** *adj* INFOR tactile **touchstone** *n* pierre *f* de touche **touch-type** *vi* taper au toucher
touchy ['tʌtʃi] <-ier, -iest> *adj inf* (*person*) susceptible; (*problem, situation*) délicat(e)
tough [tʌf] **I.** *adj* **1.** (*hard-wearing: material, covering*) solide **2.** (*hard to eat*) dur(e) **3.** (*hard to deal with: exam, examiner, game, conditions*) dur(e); **a** ~ **area to grow up in** une zone où il est difficile de grandir; **she had**

T

a pretty ~ time elle a eu un moment dur; **to take a ~ line on cheating** être intraitable sur la triche **4.** (*resilient: soldiers, players, plants*) costaud(e) **5.** *inf* (*unfortunate*) dur; **to be ~ on sb** être dur avec qn; ~ (**luck**)! (*sympathetically*) pas de chance!; (*aggressively*) bien fait! **II.** *n Am, inf* dur(e) *m(f)* **III.** *vt inf* **to ~ it out** tenir bon

toughen ['tʌfən] *vt* **1.** (*make stronger*) endurcir; (*sanctions, laws*) renforcer **2.** (*make hard to cut*) durcir

◆toughen up I. *vi* s'endurcir **II.** *vt* endurcir

toughened glass *n* verre *m* trempé

toughness *n no pl* **1.** (*strength*) *a. fig* solidité *f* **2.** (*hardness*) *a. fig* dureté *f* **3.** (*determination*) ténacité *f* **4.** (*strictness*) sévérité *f* **5.** (*difficulty*) difficulté *f*

toupée ['tu:peɪ, *Am:* tu:'peɪ] *n* postiche *m*

tour [tʊəʳ, *Am:* tʊr] **I.** *n* **1.** (*journey*) voyage *m* **2.** (*short trip*) visite *f;* **guided ~** visite guidée **3.** (*journey for performance*) tournée *f;* **to be on ~** être en tournée **4.** (*spell of duty*) tournée *f;* **to be/go on ~** faire sa tournée **II.** *vt* **1.** (*visit*) visiter **2.** (*perform in*) **to ~ France** être en tournée en France **III.** *vi* **1.** (*travel*) voyager **2.** (*perform*) être en tournée

touring company *n* troupe *f* en tournée

tourism ['tʊərɪzəm, *Am:* 'tʊrɪ-] *n no pl* tourisme *m*

tourist *n* touriste *mf*

tourist agency *n* agence *f* de tourisme **tourist bureau** *n* office *m* de tourisme **tourist class** *n* classe *f* touriste **tourist guide** *n* **1.** (*book*) guide *m* touristique **2.** (*person*) guide *mf* touristique **tourist industry** *n* industrie *f* du tourisme **tourist** (**information**) **office** *n* office *m* de tourisme **tourist season** *n* saison *f* touristique **tourist visa** *n* visa *m* de tourisme

tournament ['tɔ:nəmənt, *Am:* 'tɜ:r-] *n* tournoi *m*

tour operator *n* tour-opérateur *m*

tousle ['taʊzl] *vt* ébouriffer

tout [taʊt] **I.** *n pej* revendeur, -euse *m, f* **II.** *vt* **1.** (*sell*) revendre **2.** (*advertise*) essayer de vendre **III.** *vi* racoler; **to ~ for business** racoler

tow [təʊ, *Am:* toʊ] **I.** *n* remorquage *m;* **to give sb/sth a ~** remorquer qn/qc; **to take sth in ~** prendre qc en remorque; **to be on** [*o* **in** ~] ~ *Am,* **to be under ~** *a. Aus* être remorqué **II.** *vt* remorquer; **to ~ a car away** (*for illegal parking*) emmener une voiture à la fourrière

toward(**s**) [tə'wɔ:d(z), *Am:* tɔ:rd(z)] *prep* **1.** (*in direction of*) vers; **moves ~ democracy** *fig* des changements vers la démocratie **2.** (*directed at*) envers; **to feel sympathy ~ sb** ressentir de la compassion pour qn **3.** (*for*) pour; **all contributions go ~ a new hospital** toutes les contributions seront pour le nouvel hôpital **4.** (*around: time, stage*) vers

towel ['taʊəl] **I.** *n* serviette *f,* drap *m Belgique* **II.** *vt* <-ll-> essuyer

towel(**l**)**ing** *n no pl* (tissu *m*) éponge *f*

towel rack *n Am,* **towel rail** *n Brit, Aus* porte-serviettes *m*

tower ['taʊəʳ, *Am:* 'taʊɚ] **I.** *n* tour *f* ►**a ~ of strength** un roc **II.** *vi* s'élever

◆tower above, **tower over** *vi* s'élever au-dessus de

◆tower up *vi* s'élever

tower block *n Brit* tour *f*

towering *adj* imposant(e)

Tower of London *n* **the ~** la Tour de Londres

town [taʊn] *n* ville *f;* **to be in ~** être en ville; **to be out of ~** (*person*) être en déplacement; (*supermarket*) être à l'extérieur de la ville; **to go up to ~** monter en ville ►**to have a night on the ~** s'éclater en ville; **to go to ~ on sth** *inf* mettre le paquet pour qc

town centre *n Brit* **the ~** le centre-ville **town clerk** *n* secrétaire *mf* de mairie **town council** *n Brit* conseil *m* municipal, conseil *m* communal *Belgique* **town councillor** *n* conseiller, -ère *m, f* municipal(e), échevin *m Québec* **town gas** *n Brit* gaz *m* de ville **town hall** *n* POL mairie *f,* maison *f* communale *Belgique* **town house** *n* **1.** (*residence*) maison *f* de ville **2.** (*row house*) maison *f* mitoyenne **town planning** *n no pl, no indef art* urbanisme *m* **townscape** *n* paysage *m* urbain **townsfolk** *npl s.* **townspeople** **township** *n Am, Can* (*unit of local government*) commune *f* **townspeople** *npl* citadins *mpl* **town twinning** *n no pl* jumelage *m*

towpath *n* chemin *m* de halage **tow truck** *n Am* remorqueuse *f*

toxic ['tɒksɪk, *Am:* 'tɑ:k-] *adj* toxique

toxicology [ˌtɒksɪ'kɒlədʒi, *Am:* ˌtɑ:ksɪ'kɑ:lə-] *n no pl* toxicologie *f*

toxin ['tɒksɪn, *Am:* 'tɑ:k-] *n* toxine *f*

toy [tɔɪ] *n* jouet *m*

toy car *n* voiturette *f* **toy library** *n* ludothèque *f* **toyshop** *n* magasin *m* de jouets

toy with *vt* **1.** (*play with*) *a. fig* jouer avec **2.** (*consider: idea*) caresser

trace [treɪs] **I.** *n* **1.** (*sign*) trace *f;* **to disappear without** (**a**) ~ disparaître sans laisser de traces **2.** (*search*) enregistrement *m;* **to put a ~ on sth** enregistrer qc; **they put a ~ on the call** ils ont enregistré l'appel **3.** (*slight amount: of drugs*) trace *f;* (*of emotion*) signe *m;* **~ of a smile** un sourire esquissé **II.** *vt* **1.** (*locate*) retrouver; **to ~ sb to somewhere** remonter la piste de qn jusqu'à quelque part **2.** (*track back*) rechercher; (*call*) établir l'origine de; **we've ~d the problem to the modem** on a trouvé que la cause du problème était le modem; **to ~ sth to sth** établir le lien entre qc et qc; **I can ~ my origins to the 4th century** je peux remonter mes origines jusqu'au IVème siècle **3.** (*describe*) retracer **4.** (*copy*) décalquer **5.** (*draw outlines*) tracer

trace element *n* oligo-élément *m*

tracer *n* traceur *m;* ~ **fire** tir *m* traçant

tracery *n* treillis *m*

trachea [trə'kɪə, *Am:* 'treɪkɪə] <-s *o* -chae> *pl n* trachée *f*

tracing *n* calque *m*

tracing paper *n* papier *m* calque

track [træk] **I.** *n* **1.** (*path*) chemin *m* **2.** (*rails*) voie *f* ferrée **3.** *Am* (*in railroad station*) *s.* **platform** **4.** *pl* (*mark*) traces *fpl* **5.** (*course followed*) *a. fig* piste *f;* **on sb's** ~ sur la piste de qn **6.** (*path taken by sth*) trajectoire *f* **7.** (*career path*) voie *f* **8.** SPORT (*for running*) piste *f;* (*horseracing venue*) champ *m* de course; (*motor racing venue*) circuit *m* automobile **9.** (*on record*) piste *f;* (*song*) morceau *m* ►**to cover one's ~s** brouiller les pistes; **to keep ~ of changes/the situation** suivre les changements/la situation; **to lose ~ of sb** perdre qn de vue; **I've lost ~ of my accounts** je ne sais plus où j'en suis dans mes comptes; **to make ~s** *inf* filer; **to be on the wrong ~** faire fausse route; **to be on the wrong side of the ~s** *inf* être du mauvais côté de la barrière **II.** *vt* **1.** (*pursue: animal*) pister; (*fugitive*) traquer **2.** (*follow the course: airplane, missile*) suivre la trajectoire de **3.** (*trace*) rechercher **III.** *vi* **1.** CINE faire un travelling **2.** (*follow a course*) **to ~ across sth** se déplacer à travers qc

◆**track down** *vt* (*relative*) retrouver; (*article*) dénicher

track-and-field events *n pl, Am* épreuves *fpl* d'athlétisme **trackball** *n* INFOR boule *f* de commande **tracker dog** *n* chien *m* policier **track event** *n* SPORT épreuve *f* d'athlétisme **tracking station** *n* AVIAT, TECH station *f* d'observation

trackless *adj Am* sans chemins

track record *n* résultats *mpl;* **she has a good ~ in sales** elle a de bons résultats dans les ventes **track shoes** *n pl* chaussures *fpl* d'athlétisme **tracksuit** *n* survêtement *m*

tract[1] [trækt] *n* tract *m*

tract[2] [trækt] *n* **1.** (*big piece of land*) étendue *f* **2.** *Am* (*measured piece of land*) terrain *m* **3.** *Am* (*housing lot*) lot *m* **4.** ANAT, MED appareil *m* **5.** (*booklet*) tract *m*

tractable *adj form* maniable; **a ~ problem** un problème facile à gérer

traction ['trækʃən] *n no pl* traction *f;* **to be in ~** être en extension

tractor *n* tracteur *m*

trad [træd] *adj Aus, Brit, inf abbr of* **traditional** traditionnel(le)

trade [treɪd] **I.** *n* **1.** *no pl* (*buying and selling*) commerce *m;* **balance of ~** balance *f* commerciale; **~ is picking up** les affaires repartent **2.** (*type of business*) commerce *m;* **the fur ~** le commerce des peaux; **the building ~** la construction **3.** (*handicraft*) métier *m;* **to be dentist by ~** être dentiste de métier **4.** *Am* (*swap*) échange *m* **II.** *vi* **1.** (*do business*) faire du commerce; **to ~ in sth** faire le commerce de qc **2.** (*be bought and sold*) s'échanger **III.** *vt* **1.** (*swap*) échanger; (*places*) changer de; **to ~ sth for sth** échanger qc contre qc **2.** (*buy and sell*) faire le commerce de

◆**trade in** *vt* échanger; **I traded my car in for a Peugeot** j'ai acheté une Peugeot avec reprise de mon ancienne voiture

◆**trade on** *vt* exploiter

trade agreement *n* accord *m* commercial **trade association** *n* groupement *m* commercial **trade balance** *n s.* **balance of trade** **trade barrier** *n* barrière *f* douanière **trade cycle** *n* cycle *m* commercial **trade directory** *n* annuaire *m* commercial **trade discount** *n* remise *f* aux professionnels **traded option** *n* option *f* négociable **trade fair** *n* COM foire *f* **trade gap** *n* déficit *m* commercial **trade-in** *n* COM reprise *f* **trade-in value** *n* valeur *f* de reprise **trade journal** *n* revue *f* professionnelle **trademark** *n* **1.** (*identification*) marque *f;* **registered ~** marque déposée **2.** *fig* (*feature*) **sth is sb's ~** qc est la signature de qn **trade name** *n s.* **brand name** **trade-off** *n* **1.** (*offsetting balance*) marché *m* **2.** (*compromise*) compromis *m* **trade policy** *n* politique *f* commerciale **trade press** *n no pl* presse *f* professionnelle **trade price** *n Brit* prix *m* de gros

trader ['treɪdə^r, *Am:* -ɚ] *n* **1.** (*person who buys and sell: small business*) commerçant(e) *m(f);* (*bigger business*) négociant(e) *m(f)* **2.** FIN intermédiaire *mf*

trade register *n* registre *m* du commerce **trade secret** *n* secret *m* de fabrication; *fig* truc *m* de professionnel **tradesman** <tradesmen> *n* (*small business*) commerçant(e) *m(f);* (*bigger business*) négociant(e) *m(f)* **tradespeople** *npl* commerçants *mpl* **trade surplus** *n* excédent *m* commercial **trade union** *n* syndicat *m* (professionnel) **trade unionism** *n no pl* syndicalisme *m* **trade unionist** *n* syndicaliste *mf* **trade war** *n* guerre *f* commerciale **trade wind** *n* alizé *m*

trading *n no pl* commerce *m;* FIN transactions *fpl*

trading area *n* zone *f* commerciale **trading estate** *n Brit s.* **industrial estate**

tradition [trə'dɪʃən] *n* tradition *f*

traditional *adj* traditionnel(le)

traditionalism [trə'dɪʃənəlɪzəm] *n no pl* traditionalisme *m*

traditionalist **I.** *n* traditionaliste *mf* **II.** *adj* traditionaliste

traffic ['træfɪk] **I.** *n no pl* **1.** (*transport movement*) trafic *m;* (*for cars*) circulation *f;* ~ **fatalities** décès sur la route; **heavy ~** circulation dense; (*of trucks*) circulation des poids lourds; **to get stuck in ~** être bloqué par la circulation; **sea ~** navigation *f;* **passenger/commercial ~** transport *m* des passagers/marchandises **2.** *pej* (*trade, dealings*) trafic *m;* **to**

T

have ~ with sb faire des affaires avec qn **II.** <trafficked, trafficked> *vi pej* (*trade illegally*) **to ~ in sth** faire du trafic de qc

traffic accident *n* accident *m* de la circulation **traffic calming** *n Brit* ralentissement *m* de la circulation **traffic circle** *n Am s.* **roundabout traffic island** *n* refuge *m* pour piétons **traffic jam** *n* embouteillage *m*

trafficker ['træfɪkəʳ, *Am:* -ɚ] *n pej* trafiquant(e) *m(f)*

traffic lights *n pl* feu *m* (de circulation) **traffic patrol** *n chiefly Am* (*in town*) patrouille *f* de policiers; (*outside town*) patrouille *f* de gendarmes **traffic sign** *n* panneau *m* de signalisation **traffic signal** *n s.* **traffic lights traffic warden** *n Brit* contractuel(le) *m(f)*

tragedy ['trædʒədi] *n* **1.** (*literary genre*) tragédie *f* **2.** <-ies> (*event*) drame *m*

tragic ['trædʒɪk] *adj* tragique

trail [treɪl] **I.** *n* **1.** (*path*) chemin *m* **2.** (*track*) piste *f* **3.** (*trace*) traînée *f;* **to leave a ~** laisser une trace; **to leave a ~ of destruction** tout détruire sur son passage **II.** *vt* **1.** (*follow*) suivre **2.** (*drag*) traîner; (*car*) remorquer **III.** *vi* **1.** (*be dragged*) traîner **2.** SPORT **to ~ behind sb/sth** être à la traîne derrière qn/qc **3.** (*move sluggishly*) traînasser

◆**trail away, trail off** *vi* s'estomper

trail bike *n* moto *f* tout terrain

trailblazer *n* pionnier, -ère *m, f*

trailer *n* **1.** (*wheeled container*) remorque *f* **2.** *Am s.* **caravan 3.** (*advertisement*) bande *f* annonce

trailer camp, trailer park *n Am* camping *m* pour caravanes

train [treɪn] **I.** *n* **1.** (*railway*) train *m;* (*in subway*) métro *m;* **to come by ~** venir en train; **to be on a ~** être dans un train **2.** (*series*) série *f;* **my ~ of thought** le fil de ma pensée **3.** (*procession*) file *f;* (*of barges*) train *m;* (*of mourners*) cortège *m* **4.** (*part of dress*) traîne *f* ►**to set sth in ~** mettre qc en train **II.** *vi* **1.** MIL, SPORT s'entraîner **2.** (*for a job*) être formé; **I'm ~ing to be a teacher** je suis une formation de prof **III.** *vt* **1.** (*teach*) former; (*animal*) dresser; **to ~ sb to** +*infin* former qn à +*infin* **2.** MIL, SPORT entraîner **3.** BOT (*plant*) faire pousser

train accident *n* accident *m* ferroviaire **train driver** *n* conducteur *m* de train

trained *adj* **1.** (*educated: staff*) formé(e); (*animal*) dressé(e) **2.** (*expert*) diplômé(e); (*dancer*) profesionnel(le)

trainee [treɪ'niː] *n* (*in office jobs*) stagiaire *mf;* (*in handicraft, mechanics*) apprenti(e) *m(f)*

trainer *n* **1.** (*sb who trains others*) formateur, -trice *m, f* **2.** SPORT entraîneur, -euse *m, f* **3.** *pl, Brit* (*shoes*) chaussures *fpl* de sport

train ferry *n* train-ferry *m*

training *n no pl* **1.** (*education*) formation *f;* **on-the-job ~** formation sur le tas; **you will be given ~** vous recevrez une formation **2.** SPORT, MIL entraînement *m;* **to be in ~ for a competition** se préparer à une compétition

training camp *n* **1.** SPORT stage *m* d'entraînement **2.** MIL camp *m* d'entraînement **training college** *n Brit* lycée *m* professionnel **training course** *n* formation *f*

traipse [treɪps] *vi inf* se trimballer

trait [treɪt] *n* trait *m;* **genetic ~** caractéristique *f* génétique

traitor *n* traître, -esse *m, f;* **to be a ~ to sb/sth** trahir qn/qc

trajectory [trə'dʒektəri, *Am:* -tɚi] *n* trajectoire *f*

tram [træm] *n Brit, Aus* tramway *m*

tramlines *n Brit* lignes *fpl* de tram

tramp [træmp] **I.** *vi* **1.** (*walk heavily*) marcher lourdement **2.** (*go on foot*) marcher **II.** *vt* parcourir à pied **III.** *n* **1.** *no pl* (*stomping sound*) bruit *m* sourd **2.** *no pl* (*long walk*) promenade *f* **3.** (*poor person*) clochard(e) *m(f)* **4.** *Am, pej* (*promiscuous woman*) traînée *f*

trample ['træmpl] **I.** *vt* piétiner; **to be ~d to death** mourir piétiné; **to ~ sth underfoot** fouler qc aux pieds; **to ~ sb's feet** marcher sur les pieds de qn **II.** *vi* **to ~ on** [*o* **over**] **sth** **1.** (*walk on*) piétiner qc **2.** (*despise*) bafouer qc

trampoline ['træmpəliːn] *n* trampoline *m*

tramway ['træmweɪ] *n* **1.** (*tram rails*) rails *mpl* du tram **2.** (*tram system*) tramway *m*

trance [trɑːns, *Am:* træns] *n* transe *f*

tranny ['træni] *n Brit, inf abbr of* **transistor radio** radio *f*

tranquil ['træŋkwɪl] *adj form* **1.** (*calm*) tranquille **2.** (*serene*) serein(e)

tranquilize ['træŋkwɪlaɪz] *vt Am s.* **tranquillize**

tranquilizer *n Am s.* **tranquillizer**

tranqui(l)lity *n no pl, form* tranquillité *f*

tranquillize ['træŋkwɪlaɪz] *vt* MED **to ~ sb** placer qn sous calmants

tranquillizer *n* tranquillisant *m;* **to be on ~s** être sous calmants

transact [træn'zækt] *vt* régler

transaction [træn'zækʃən] *n* COM transaction *f*

transalpine [træn'zælpaɪn] *adj* transalpin(e)

transatlantic, trans-Atlantic [ˌtrænzət'læntɪk, *Am:* ˌtræntsæt'-] *adj* transatlantique

transceiver [træn'siːvəʳ] *n* émetteur-récepteur *m*

transcend [træn'send] *vt* transcender

transcendent [træn'sendənt] *adj* transcendant(e)

transcendental *adj form* transcendantal(e)

transcontinental [ˌtrænsˌkɒntɪ'nentəl, *Am:* ˌtræntsˌkɑːntən'en-] *adj* transcontinental(e)

transcribe [træn'skraɪb] *vt* **1.** (*make written copy*) transcrire **2.** MUS, LING transposer

transcript ['træntskrɪpt] *n* transcription *f*

transcription *n* transcription *f*

transducer [trænz'dju:sə^r, *Am:* trænts'du:sɚ] *n* ELEC transducteur *m*

transept ['træntsept] *n* ARCHIT transept *m*

transfer [trænts'fɜ:, *Am:* -'fɜ:r] **I.** <-rr-> *vt* **1.** (*move, sell*) transférer **2.** (*change ownership of: house, property*) céder; (*power*) transmettre **3.** (*relocate: employee*) muter; (*factory, office*) transférer; (*work*) relocaliser **4.** TEL mettre en ligne; **I'm ~ring you now** je vous passe votre correspondant **II.** *vi* changer; (*when travelling*) faire la correspondance; (*to new job*) être muté; SPORT (*to new club*) être transferé **III.** *n* **1.** (*process of moving*) transfert *m;* **a bank ~** un virement **2.** LAW (*of house, property*) cession *f;* FIN (*of a title*) transmission *f;* (*of power*) passation *f* **3.** (*to new job*) mutation *f;* SPORT transfert *m* **4.** (*distributing*) transmission *f* **5.** (*when travelling*) correspondance *f; Am* (*ticket*) billet *m* avec correspondance **6.** (*pattern: on skin*) décalcomanie *f;* (*on a t-shirt*) transfert *m*

transferable *adj* transférable

transference ['træntsfɜ:rəns] *n no pl, form* (*act of changing*) *a.* PSYCH transfert *m;* (*of power*) passation *f*

transfer lounge *n* salle *f* d'attente des correspondances **transfer(red) charge call** *n Brit* appel *m* en PCV

transfigure [trænts'fɪgə^r, *Am:* trænts'fɪgjɚ] *vt* transfigurer

transfix [trænts'fɪks] *vt* (*with fear*) pétrifier; (*with amazement*) stupéfier; **with gaze** subjuguer

transform [trænts'fɔ:m, *Am:* trænts'fɔ:rm] *vt* transformer

transformation *n* transformation *f*

transformer *n* ELEC transformateur *m*

transfuse [trænts'fju:z] *vt* MED transfuser; **to ~ blood** faire une transfusion sanguine

transfusion *n* transfusion *f*

transgress [trænz'gres, *Am:* trænts-] *vt* transgresser

transgression *n form* transgression *f*

transgressor *n* **1.** (*sb who breaks rule*) transgresseur *m* **2.** (*sinner*) pécheur, -eresse *m, f*

transient ['trænziənt, *Am:* 'træntʃənt] *adj form* **1.** (*lasting a short time*) éphémère **2.** (*staying for short time*) transitoire; (*population*) de passage; (*feeling*) passager(-ère)

transistor [træn'zɪstə^r, *Am:* træn'zɪstɚ] *n* transistor *m*

transistor radio *n* transistor *m*

transit ['træntsɪt] *n no pl* transit *m*

transit camp *n Brit* campement *m* provisoire **transit desk** *n* AVIAT comptoir *m* des correspondances

transition [træn'zɪʃən] *n* transition *f*

transitional *adj* transitoire; (*government*) de transition

transitive ['træntsətɪv, *Am:* 'træntsət̬ɪv] LING **I.** *adj* transitif(-ive) **II.** *n* transitif *m*

transit lounge *n* salle *f* des correspondances

transitory ['træntsɪtəri, *Am:* 'træntsətɔ:ri] *adj form s.* **transient**

transit passenger *n* passager, -ère *m, f* en transit **transit visa** *n* visa *m* de transit

translatable *adj* traduisible

translate [trænz'leɪt, *Am:* træn'sleɪt] **I.** *vt* **1.** (*adapt into other language: written*) traduire; (*oral*) interpréter **2.** (*adapt*) adapter **3.** (*decipher to mean*) interpréter; **I ~d it as an agreement** je l'ai interprété comme un accord **II.** *vi* se traduire

translation *n* traduction *f*

translator *n* traducteur, -trice *m, f*

transliterate [trænz'lɪtəreɪt, *Am:* træn'slɪt̬əreɪt] *vt* translittérer

transliteration *n* LING translittération *f*

translucent [trænz'lu:sənt, *Am:* træn'slu:-], **translucid** *adj* translucide

transmigration [ˌtrænzmaɪ'greɪʃən, *Am:* ˌtræntsmaɪ'-] *n* transmigration *f*

transmissible [trænz'mɪsəbl, *Am:* træn'smɪs-] *adj* transmissible; (*disease*) contagieux(-euse); **sexually ~ disease** maladie *f* sexuellement transmissible

transmission [trænz' mɪʃən, *Am:* træn'smɪʃ-] *n* **1.** *no pl* (*act of broadcasting*) *a.* INFOR transmission *f* **2.** *no pl* MED contagion *f;* (*of a disease*) transmission *f*

transmit [trænz'mɪt, *Am:* træn'smɪt] <-tt-> **I.** *vt* transmettre **II.** *vi* émettre

transmitter *n* émetteur *m*

transmitting *adj* émetteur(-trice)

transmogrify [trænz'mɒgrɪfaɪ, *Am:* træn'smɑ:grə-] *vt* métamorphoser

transmutation *n form* transmutation *f*

transmute [trænz'mju:t, *Am:* ˌtrænts-] *form* **I.** *vt* **1.** PHYS transmuer **2.** (*transform*) **to ~ sth into sth** transformer qc en qc **II.** *vi* se transformer

transoceanic ['trænzˌəʊʃi'ænɪk, *Am:* ˌtræntsoʊʃi'-] *adj* transocéanique

transom ['træntsəm] *n* **1.** (*horizontal bar*) traverse *f* **2.** *Am s.* **fanlight**

transparency [træn'spærəntsi, *Am:* træn'sperənt-] *n* **1.** *no pl* (*see-through quality*) *a. fig* transparence *f* **2.** <-ies> (*slide: of photos*) diapositive *f;* (*of documents for OHP*) transparent *m*

transparent *adj* transparent(e)

transpire [træn'spaɪə^r, *Am:* træn'spaɪɚ] *vi* **1.** (*happen*) se passer; **it ~d that ...** il est apparu que ... **2.** (*emit water vapour*) *a. fig* transpirer

transplant [træn'splɑ:nt, *Am:* træn'splænt] **I.** *vt* transplanter **II.** *n* **1.** (*act of transplanting*) transplantation *f;* **a kidney ~** une greffe de rein **2.** (*transplanted organ*) organe *m* greffé

transplantation *n no pl* transplantation *f*

transport[1] [træn'spɔ:t, *Am:* træn'spɔ:rt] *vt* transporter

transport[2] ['træntspɔ:t, *Am:* 'træntspɔ:rt] *n* **1.** *no pl* (*act of conveyance*) transport *m;* **public ~** transports *mpl* publics; **will you need ~?** aurez-vous besoin qu'on vous con-

duise? **2.**(*vehicle*) moyen *m* de transport; **troop ~** transport de troupes **3.** *pl, form* (*strong emotion*) transports *mpl*
transportable *adj* transportable
transportation *n no pl* **1.**(*act of transporting*) transport *m;* **public ~** *Am* transports *mpl* en commun **2.** *Am, Aus* (*means of transport*) moyen *m* de transport
transport café <-s> *n Brit* restaurant *m* de routiers **transport costs** *n pl* frais *mpl* de transport
transporter *n* transporteur *m*
transpose [træn'spəʊz, *Am:* træn'spoʊz] *vt* transposer
transposition *n* transposition *f*
transsexual [træn'sekʃʊəl, *Am:* træn'sekʃuəl] **I.** *n* transsexuel(le) *m(f)* **II.** *adj* transsexuel(le)
transverse ['trænzvɜːs, *Am:* 'trænts-] *adj* transversal(e)
transvestite [træns'vestaɪt, *Am:* 'trænts-] *n* PSYCH travesti(e) *m(f)*
trap [træp] **I.** *n* **1.**(*device for catching*) piège *m;* **to fall into the ~** tomber dans le piège **2.** *Brit, inf* (*mouth*) gueule *f* **3.**(*curve in a pipe*) siphon *m* **4.**(*light carriage*) cabriolet *m* **II.** *vt* <-pp-> **1.**(*catch in a trap*) prendre au piège **2.**(*not permit to escape: water, heat*) retenir
trapdoor [ˌtræp'dɔːr, *Am:* 'træpdɔːr] *n* THEAT trappe *f*
trapeze [trə'piːz, *Am:* træp'iːz] *n* trapèze *m;* **~ artist** trapéziste *mf*
trapezium [trə'piːziəm] <-s *o* -zia> *n Brit, Aus,* **trapezoid** *n Am* MAT trapèze *m*
trapper ['træpər, *Am:* -ɚ] *n* trappeur *m*
trappings ['træpɪŋz] *npl* signes *mpl* extérieurs
trapshooting *n no pl* ball-trap *m*
trash [træʃ] *Am* **I.** *n no pl* **1.**(*rubbish*) ordures *fpl;* **to take the ~ out** sortir les poubelles **2.** *pej, inf* (*worthless people*) racaille *f* **3.** *pej, inf* (*low-quality goods*) pacotille *f;* (*nonsense*) connerie *f* **II.** *vt inf* **1.**(*wreck*) saccager **2.**(*criticize excessively*) dénigrer
trashcan, **trash can** ['træʃkæn] *n Am s.* **dustbin**
trashy ['træʃi] *adj pej, inf* minable
trauma ['trɔːmə, *Am:* 'trɑːmə] *n* traumatisme *m*
traumatic [trɔː'mætɪk, *Am:* trɑː'mæt̬-] *adj* traumatisant(e)
traumatise *vt Brit, Aus,* **traumatize** ['trɔːmətaɪz, *Am:* 'trɑː] *vt* traumatiser
travel ['trævəl] **I.** <-ll- *o Am* -l-> *vi* **1.**(*make a journey*) voyager; **to ~ to America** aller en Amérique; **he's ~ling on business** il est en voyage d'affaires; **the wine doesn't ~** le vin ne supporte pas le voyage **2.**(*move: driver, vehicle*) rouler; (*light, sound*) se déplacer **II.** <-ll- *o Am* -l-> *vt* parcourir **III.** *n* **1.**(*act of travelling*) voyages *mpl;* **a ~ book** un récit de voyage **2.** *pl* (*journeys*) les voyages *mpl;* **have you seen Robert on your ~s?** aurais-tu vu Robert?
travel agency *n* agence *f* de voyages **travel agent** *n* agent *mf* de voyage **travel bureau** *s.* **travel agency travel card** *n* carte *f* de transport **travel cot** *n Am* lit *m* d'enfant transportable
traveled *adj Am s.* **travelled**
traveler *n Am s.* **traveller**
travel expenses *n pl* frais *mpl* de déplacement
traveling *adj Am s.* **travelling**
travel insurance *n* assurance *f* voyage
travelled *adj* **well-/little-travelled** (*person*) qui a beaucoup/peu voyagé; (*road*) très/peu fréquenté(e)
traveller *n* voyageur, -euse *m, f;* **commercial ~** *Brit* représentant(e) *m(f)*
traveller's cheque *n* chèque *m* de voyage
travelling I. *adj no pl* **1.**(*for use on a journey: clock*) de voyage **2.**(*mobile*) ambulant(e) **II.** *n* (*as a tourist*) les voyages; (*for business*) les déplacements
travelling bag *n* sac *m* de voyage **travelling salesman** *n* VRP *m*
travelog *n Am,* **travelogue** *n Brit, Aus* **1.**(*written report*) compte *m* rendu de voyage **2.**(*film*) documentaire *m*
travel-sick *adj* malade dans les transports **travel sickness** *n no pl* mal *m* des transports
traverse ['trævɜːs, *Am:* -ɚs] *vt* traverser
travesty ['trævəsti, *Am:* -ɪsti] <-ies> *n* parodie *f*
trawl [trɔːl, *Am:* trɑːl] **I.** *vi* **1.**(*fish*) pêcher au chalut; **to ~ for sth** pêcher qc au chalut **2.**(*search*) **to ~ through sth** (*files*) éplucher qc **II.** *vt* **1.**(*fish*) pêcher au chalut **2.**(*search: place*) ratisser; (*files*) éplucher; (*memory*) fouiller dans **3.**(*drag*) traîner **III.** *n* **1.**(*trawl net*) chalut *m* **2.**(*act of trawling*) chalutage *m*
trawler *n* chalutier *m*
tray [treɪ] *n* **1.**(*for carrying*) plateau *m,* cabaret *m Québec* **2.**(*container for papers*) corbeille *f* **3.**(*drawer*) tiroir *m*
treacherous ['tretʃərəs] *adj* traître
treachery ['tretʃəri] *n no pl, a. pej* traîtrise *f*
treacle ['triːkl] *n no pl, Brit* mélasse *f*
treacly *adj* sirupeux(-euse)
tread [tred] **I.** <trod, trodden *o a. Am* treaded, trod> *vi* marcher; **to ~ carefully** *fig* être prudent **II.** *vt* (*set one's foot on*) marcher sur; (*streets*) marcher dans; (*path*) parcourir; (*floor, grapes*) fouler; **to ~ sth down** écraser qc **III.** *n* **1.**(*manner of walking*) pas *m* **2.**(*step*) giron *m* **3.**(*part of tyre*) chape *f*
treadle ['tredl] *n* pédale *f*
treadmill ['tredmɪl] *n* **1.**(*wheel for producing power*) trépigneuse *f* **2.** *pej* (*anything repetitive*) train-train *m inv*
treason ['triːzn] *n no pl* trahison *f*
treasonable, **treasonous** *adj* qui constitue

une trahison

treasure ['treʒəʳ, *Am:* -ɚ] I. *n a. fig* trésor *m* II. *vt* chérir; (*memory, moment*) chérir; (*gift*) tenir beaucoup à

treasure house *n* 1. (*where a treasure is kept*) trésor *m* 2. (*valuable collection*) mine *f* de trésors **treasure hunt** *n* chasse *f* au trésor

treasurer *n* trésorier, -ière *m, f*

treasure trove *n* 1. (*treasure*) trésor *m* 2. (*collection*) mine *f* de trésors

treasury ['treʒəri] <-ies> *n* 1. (*place, funds*) trésorerie *f* 2. *no pl* (*government department*) **the Treasury** le ministère des Finances

treasury bill *n Am* bon *m* du Trésor **treasury bond** *n Am* bon *m* du Trésor **treasury note** *n Am* obligation *f* du Trésor **Treasury Secretary** *n Am* ministre *m* des Finances

treat ['tri:t] I. *vt* 1. (*behave towards*) traiter; **to ~ badly** maltraiter; **to ~ sb with courtesy/respect** traiter qn avec courtoisie/respect; **to ~ sb like a child/an adult** traiter qn comme un enfant/un adulte; **they ~ it as a joke** ils l'ont pris comme une plaisanterie; **they're ~ing the case as murder** ils traitent l'afffaire comme un meurtre 2. (*cure, deal with*) traiter; **to be ~ed for shock/depression** être soigné pour choc/dépression; **chemically ~ed hair** cheveux chimiquement traités 3. (*pay for*) inviter; **to ~ sb to sth** offrir qc à qn; **to ~ sb for lunch** inviter qn au déjeuner; **to ~ oneself to sth** s'offrir qc II. *vi* traiter III. *n* (*indulgence*) plaisir *m;* (*to eat or drink*) gourmandise *f;* **to give sb a ~** offrir une gâterie à qn; **it was a special ~** c'était une gâterie particulière; **it's my ~** c'est moi qui offre ▸**to work a ~** *inf* marcher à merveille; **to look a ~** *inf* être superbe

treatise ['tri:tɪz, *Am:* -t̬ɪs] *n* traité *m;* **a ~ on sth** un traité de qc

treatment *n a. fig* traitement *m;* **the inhuman ~ of refugees** le traitement inhumain des réfugiés; **it gets rough ~ from the children** les enfants le maltraitent; **hospital/laser ~** traitement hospitalier/laser; **a course of ~** un traitement

treaty ['tri:ti, *Am:* -t̬i] <-ies> *n* traité *m*

treble ['trebl] I. *adj* 1. (*three times greater*) triplé(e); **~ what I earn** trois fois ce que je gagne 2. (*high-pitched*) soprano *inv;* **a ~ voice** une voix de soprano II. *vt, vi* tripler III. *n* 1. MUS soprano *m* 2. (*sound range*) aigus *mpl*

treble clef *n* clé *f* de sol

tree [tri:] I. *n* arbre *m;* **sth doesn't grow on ~s** qc ne tombe pas du ciel II. *vt* **to ~ an animal** forcer un animal à se réfugier dans un arbre

tree frog *n* rainette *f* **tree house** *n* maison *f* dans les arbres

treeless *adj* sans arbres

treeline *n* limite *f* des arbres **tree-lined** *adj* bordé(e) d'arbres **tree surgeon** *n* arboriculteur, -trice *m, f* **treetop** *n pl* cime *f* **tree trunk** *n* tronc *m* d'arbre

trefoil ['trefɔɪl, *Am:* 'tri:fɔɪl] *n* trèfle *m*

trek [trek] I. <-kk-> *vi* faire de la randonnée; **to ~ in to the office** *fig* se traîner au bureau II. *n* randonnée *f;* **a ~ into town** *fig* une expédition en ville

trekking ['trekɪŋ] *n* randonnée *f*

trellis ['trelɪs] <-es> *n* treillis *m*

tremble ['trembl] I. *vi* trembler; **to ~ with sth** trembler de qc II. *n* tremblement *m;* **to be all of a ~** *Brit, inf* trembler comme une feuille

tremendous [trɪ'mendəs] *adj* 1. (*enormous*) énorme 2. *inf* (*extremely good*) génial(e)

tremolo ['tremələʊ, *Am:* -əloʊ] *n* MUS trémolo *m*

tremor ['treməʳ, *Am:* -ɚ] *n* tremblement *m*

tremulous ['tremjʊləs] *adj* 1. (*shivering*) tremblant(e) 2. (*shy*) timide

trench [trentʃ] <-es> *n* tranchée *f*

trenchant ['trentʃənt] *adj* tranchant(e); (*criticism, remark, wit*) incisif(-ive)

trench coat *n* trench-coat *m*

trend [trend] *n* 1. (*tendency*) tendance *f;* **there's a ~ towards/away from sth** il y a une tendance vers/contre qc 2. (*popular style*) mode *f;* **to set a new ~** lancer une nouvelle mode

trendsetter ['trend,setəʳ, *Am:* -,set̬ɚ] *n* lanceur, -euse *m, f* de mode

trendsetting *adj* qui lance la mode

trendy ['trendi] I. <-ier, -iest> *adj* à la mode II. <-ies> *n* branché(e) *m(f)*

trepidation [,trepɪ'deɪʃən] *n no pl* trépidation *f*

trespass ['trespəs] <-es> I. *n no pl* violation *f* de propriété II. *vi* **to ~ on sb's land** s'introduire sans autorisation sur les terres de qn; **to ~ upon sb's time** *fig* empiéter sur le temps de qn

trespasser *n* intrus(e) *m(f);* **~s will be prosecuted** défense d'entrer sous peine de poursuites

trestle ['tresl] *n* tréteau *m*

trestle table *n* table *f* à tréteaux

triad ['traɪæd] *n* triade *f*

trial ['traɪəl] *n* 1. (*judicial process*) procès *m;* **to stand ~** passer en jugement; **to put sb on ~** faire passer qn devant les tribunaux; **to get a fair ~** *fig* avoir un procès équitable; **~ by the media** un procès médiatique 2. (*experimental test*) essai *m;* **by ~ and error** par expériences successives; **have sth on ~** avoir qc à l'essai 3. (*source of problems*) épreuve *f;* **~s and tribulations** tribulations *fpl* 4. (*competition*) épreuve *f*

trial flight *n* vol *m* d'essai **trial marriage** *n* mariage *m* à l'essai **trial period** *n* période *f* d'essai **trial run** *n* essai *m*

triangle ['traɪæŋgl] *n* MAT, MUS triangle *m*

triangular [traɪ'æŋgjʊləʳ, *Am:* -lɚ] *adj* triangulaire

tribal ['traɪbl] *adj* tribal(e)

T

tribalism ['traɪblɪzəm] *n no pl* tribalisme *m*
tribe [traɪb] *n a. pej* tribu *f*
tribespeople *n pl* populations *fpl* tribales
tribulation [ˌtrɪbjʊ'leɪʃən, *Am:* -jə'-] *n form* tribulation *f*
tribunal [traɪ'bju:nl] *n* tribunal *m*
tribune ['trɪbju:n] *n* tribune *f*
tributary ['trɪbjətəri, *Am:* -teri] <-ies> *n* GEO affluent *m*
tribute ['trɪbju:t] *n* **1.** (*token of respect*) hommage *m;* **to pay ~ to sb/sth** rendre hommage à qn/qc **2.** (*money, goods paid*) tribu *m*
trice [traɪs] *n* **in a ~** en un tour de mains
trick [trɪk] **I.** *n* **1.** (*ruse, joke*) tour *m;* **a magic ~** un tour de magie; **to play a ~ on sb** jouer un tour à qn; **a dirty ~** *pej* un sale tour; **a ~ of the light** une illusion d'optique **2.** (*technique for doing sth*) truc *m;* **to get the ~ to doing sth** prendre le coup pour faire qc; **that will do the ~** ça fera l'affaire; **the ~s of the trade** les ficelles du métier; **to use every ~ in the book** ne reculer devant rien **3.** (*characteristic mannerism*) manie *f* **4.** (*round of cards played*) pli *m;* **to take a ~** faire un pli ►**sb doesn't miss a ~** rien n'échappe à qn; **how's ~s?** *inf* alors, quoi de neuf?; **to be up to one's (old) ~s again** faire de nouveau des siennes **II.** *adj* (*question*) piège **III.** *vt* **1.** (*deceive*) duper; **to ~ sb into doing sth** ruser pour amener qn à faire qc **2.** (*swindle*) rouler
trickery ['trɪkəri] *n no pl* ruse *f*
trickle ['trɪkl] **I.** *vi* **1.** (*flow slowly*) couler lentement **2.** (*come in small amounts*) **to ~ in/out** (*people*) entrer/sortir petit à petit; **information ~d through** l'information a filtré **II.** *vt* faire couler goutte à goutte **III.** *n* (*slow flow*) filet *m;* **a ~ of information/requests** *fig* une petite quantité d'informations/de demandes
trickster ['trɪkstəʳ, *Am:* -stɚ] *n pej* filou *m*
tricksy ['trɪksi] *adj* malin(-igne)
tricky ['trɪki] <-ier, -iest> *adj* **1.** (*awkward: question, problem*) compliqué(e); (*task*) difficile; **it's a bit ~** c'est un peu compliqué; **to be ~ to do** ne pas être facile à faire **2.** *pej* (*deceitful*) malin(-igne) **3.** (*adroit*) qui demande de l'habileté
tricycle ['traɪsɪkl] *n* tricycle *m*
tried [traɪd] *pt, pp of* **try**
triennial [traɪ'enɪəl] *adj* triennal(e)
trier ['traɪəʳ, *Am:* -ɚ] *n inf* **to be a ~** être persévérant
trifle ['traɪfəl] *n* **1.** (*insignificant thing*) broutille *f* **2.** (*small amount*) bagatelle *f* **3.** (*slightly*) **a ~ big** un peu gros **4.** *Brit* (*British dessert*) ≈ diplomate *m*
trifle with *vt* **1. to ~** (*treat as insignificant*) traiter à la légère **2.** (*flirt heartlessly*) se jouer de; **to ~ sb's affections** *form* jouer avec les sentiments de qn
trifling *adj* insignifiant(e); (*matter*) sans importance
trigger ['trɪgəʳ, *Am:* -ɚ] **I.** *n* **1.** (*gun part*) gâchette *f;* **to pull the ~** appuyer sur la gâchette **2.** (*precipitating incident*) **to be a ~ for sth** être le déclencheur de qc **II.** *vt* **to ~ sth (off)** [*o* **to ~ (off) sth**] déclencher qc
trigger finger *n* index *m* **trigger-happy** *adj* **to be ~** avoir la gâchette facile
trigonometry [ˌtrɪgə'nɒmətri, *Am:* -'nɑ:mə-] *n no pl* trigonométrie *f*
trike [traɪk] *n inf abbr of* **tricycle** tricycle *m*
trilateral [ˌtraɪ'lætərəl, *Am:* traɪ'lætɚ-] *adj* trilatéral(e)
trilby ['trɪlbi] <-ies> *n Brit* chapeau *m* mou
trilingual [ˌtraɪ'lɪŋgwəl] *adj* trilingue
trill [trɪl] **I.** *n* trille *m* **II.** *vi* triller **III.** *vt* triller; **to ~ one's r's** rouler les s
trillion ['trɪlɪən, *Am:* -jən] *n* **1.** (*1,000,000,000,000*) billion *m* **2.** (*any very large number*) **~s of sth** des millions de qc
trilogy ['trɪlədʒi] <-ies> *n* trilogie *f*
trim [trɪm] **I.** *n no pl* **1.** (*cut: at hairdresser's*) coupe *f* d'entretien; (*for hedge*) taille *f;* **to give sth a ~** tailler qc **2.** (*state of readiness*) **to be in ~** être en ordre; (*person*) être en forme **3.** (*decorative edge*) garniture *f* **4.** (*on car: inside*) revêtement *m;* (*outside*) finitions *fpl* **II.** *adj* **1.** (*neat*) soigné(e); (*lawn*) net(te) **2.** (*attractively thin*) mince **III.** <-mm-> *vt* **1.** (*cut*) tailler; **to ~ one's beard** se tailler la barbe; **my hair needs ~ing** mes cheveux ont besoin d'une coupe d'entretien **2.** (*decorate*) orner; (*tree*) décorer **3.** (*reduce*) réduire
◆**trim away** *vt* élaguer
◆**trim down** *vt* réduire
◆**trim off** *vt* tailler aux ciseaux; **we managed to trim £50 off the cost** *fig* on a réussi à faire baisser le coût de 50 livres
trimmings *n pl* (*of pastry*) chutes *fpl;* (*on dress*) finitions *fpl;* **turkey with all the ~** de la dinde avec toutes les garnitures traditionnelles
Trinidad ['trɪnɪdæd] *n* (l'île *f* de) la Trinité; **~ and Tobago** Trinité-et-Tobago
Trinidadian **I.** *adj* trinidadien(ne) **II.** *n* Trinidadien(ne) *m(f)*
Trinity ['trɪnəti, *Am:* -ţi] *n no pl* **the Holy ~** la sainte Trinité
trinket ['trɪŋkɪt] *n* babiole *f*
trio ['tri:əʊ, *Am:* -oʊ] *n a.* MUS trio *m*
trip [trɪp] **I.** *n* **1.** (*journey*) voyage *m;* **business ~** voyage d'affaires; **round ~** aller-retour *m* **2.** (*shorter*) excursion *f;* **to go on a ~** faire une excursion **3.** *inf* (*hallucination*) trip *m* **II.** <-pp-> *vi* **1.** (*stumble*) trébucher **2.** (*move lightly*) **to ~ along** aller d'un pas léger **3.** (*be on drug*) faire un trip ►**to ~ off the tongue** (*name*) se dire aisément; (*cliché*) couler aisément **III.** <-pp-> *vt* **1.** (*activate*) déclencher **2.** *s. a.* **trip up**
◆**trip over** *vi* trébucher; **to ~ sth** trébucher sur qc
◆**trip up** **I.** *vt* **1.** (*cause to stumble*) faire trébucher **2.** (*cause to fail*) jouer un mauvais tour à **II.** *vi* **1.** (*fall*) tébucher **2.** (*make a mistake*) to

~ **on sth** buter sur qc
tripartite [ˌtraɪˈpɑːtaɪt, *Am:* -ˈpɑːr-] *adj* tripartite
tripe [traɪp] *n no pl* **1.** GASTR tripes *fpl* **2.** *pej, inf* (*nonsense*) conneries *fpl;* **to talk ~** raconter des conneries
triple [ˈtrɪpl] **I.** *adj* triple **II.** *adv* trois fois **III.** *vt, vi* tripler
triplet [ˈtrɪplɪt] *n* triplé(e) *m(f)*
triplicate [ˈtrɪplɪkət, *Am:* -kɪt] *n* **in ~** en trois exemplaires
tripod [ˈtraɪpɒd, *Am:* -pɑːd] *n* tripode *m*
tripper [ˈtrɪpəʳ, *Am:* -ɚ] *n Brit* excursionniste *mf*
triptych [ˈtrɪptɪk] *n* triptyque *m*
trite [traɪt] *adj pej* banal(e)
triumph [ˈtraɪʌmf] **I.** *n* (*great success*) triomphe *m;* **to return in ~** faire un retour triomphant **II.** *vi* **to ~ over sb/sth** triompher de qn/qc
triumphal *adj* triomphal(e)
triumphant *adj* triomphant(e); (*success*) retentissant(e)
trivia [ˈtrɪvɪə] *npl* futilités *fpl*
trivial *adj* **1.** (*unimportant*) insignifiant(e) **2.** (*petty*) banal(e) **3.** (*easy*) simple
triviality [ˌtrɪviˈæləti, *Am:* -t̬i] *n* banalité *f*
trivialize [ˈtrɪvɪəlaɪz] *vt* banaliser; **to ~ sb's suffering** banaliser les souffrances de qn
trod [trɒd, *Am:* trɑːd] *pt, pp of* **tread**
trodden [ˈtrɒdn, *Am:* ˈtrɑːdn] *pp of* **tread**
troglodyte [ˈtrɒglədaɪt, *Am:* ˈtrɑːglə-] *n* troglodyte *m*
trolley [ˈtrɒli, *Am:* ˈtrɑːli] *n* **1.** *Brit, Aus* (*small cart*) chariot *m;* **luggage ~** chariot à bagages; **shopping ~** caddie® *m* **2.** *Am s.* **trolleycar** ►**to be off one's ~** (*be crazy*) débloquer
trolleybus *n* trolleybus *m* **trolleycar** *n Am* tramway *m*
trombone [trɒmˈbəʊn, *Am:* trɑːmˈboʊn], **trombonist** *n* trombone *m*
troop [truːp] **I.** *n* troupe *f;* **to withdraw one's ~s** retirer ses troupes **II.** *vi* (*move in large numbers*) **to ~ down the road** descendre la rue en groupe **III.** *vt Brit* **to ~ the colour** saluer les couleurs
troop carrier *n* transport *m* de troupes
trooper *n* **1.** MIL cavalier *m* **2.** *Am* (*state police officer*) ≈ gendarme *m* ►**to swear like a ~** jurer comme un charretier
trophy [ˈtrəʊfi, *Am:* ˈtroʊ-] <-ies> *n* trophée *m*
tropic [ˈtrɒpɪk, *Am:* ˈtrɑːpɪk] *n* tropique *m;* **~ of Cancer** Tropique du Cancer
tropical *adj* tropical(e)
troppo [ˈtrɒpəʊ, *Am:* ˈtrɑːpoʊ] *adj inf* cinglé(e)
trot [trɒt, *Am:* trɑːt] **I.** *n* **1.** (*horse's gait*) trot *m;* **to go at a ~** aller au trot **2.** *pl, inf* (*diarrhoea*) courante *f* ►**on the ~** d'affilée **II.** *vi* **1.** (*move at a trot*) trotter; (*horse*) aller au trot; **to ~ down/through sth** descendre/traverser qc en trottant **2.** (*go busily*) filer; **to ~ around the town** parcourir la ville **3.** *fig* **to ~ through a speech** débiter un discours **III.** <-tt-> *vt* faire trotter
◆**trot off** *vi* s'éloigner (au trot)
◆**trot out** *vt* (*examples, excuses*) ressortir
trotters *n pl* GASTR pieds *mpl* de porc
trouble [ˈtrʌbl] **I.** *n* **1.** *no pl* (*difficulty*) ennui *m;* **without too much ~** sans grosse difficulté; **to have ~ doing sth** avoir du mal à faire qc; **to be in ~** avoir des ennuis; **to be in ~ with sb/sth** avoir des ennuis avec qn/qc; **the ~ with sb/sth is that ...** l'ennui avec qn/qc, c'est que ...; **to cause sb ~** causer des ennuis à qn; **to be no ~ at all** ne poser aucun problème; **to take the ~ to** *+infin* se donner la peine de *+infin;* **to go to the ~ of doing sth** se donner la peine de faire qc; **to go to a lot of ~ for sb/sth** se donner beaucoup de mal pour qn/qc; **to be not worth the ~ of doing sth** ne pas valoir la peine de faire qc **2.** (*problem*) problèmes *mpl;* **to tell sb one's ~s** confier ses problèmes à qn; **to be the least of sb's ~s** être le moindre des soucis de qn **3.** *no pl* (*malfunction*) ennuis *mpl;* **knee ~** un problème de genou; **to have back ~** avoir mal au dos; **stomach ~** troubles *mpl* digestifs; **engine ~** ennuis *mpl* de moteur; **car ~** problèmes *mpl* de voiture **4.** (*conflicts, arguments*) troubles *mpl;* **at the first sign of ~** aux premiers signes de troubles; **to look for ~** chercher des ennuis; **to stay out of ~** éviter les ennuis **II.** *vt* **1.** *form* (*cause inconvenience*) déranger; **can I ~ you to stand up?** puis-je vous demander de vous lever **2.** (*make an effort*) **to ~ oneself about sth/to** *+infin* se soucier de qc/de *+infin* **3.** (*cause worry to*) inquiéter **4.** (*cause problems to*) ennuyer; **my back's troubling me** j'ai des problèmes de dos **III.** *vi* (*make an effort*) se déranger; **to ~ to** *+infin* se donner la peine de *+infin*
troubled *adj* **1.** (*suffering troubles: marriage, relationship*) orageux(-euse); (*situation, times*) agité(e) **2.** (*feeling worried*) inquiet(-ète)
troublemaker *n* fauteur, -trice *m, f* de troubles **troubleshooter** *n* médiateur, -trice *m, f* **troublesome** *adj* **1.** (*difficult*) pénible **2.** (*embarrassing*) gênant(e) **trouble spot** *n* endroit *m* chaud
trough [trɒf, *Am:* trɑːf] *n* **1.** (*receptacle*) auge *f;* **drinking ~** abreuvoir *m* **2.** (*low point between two crests*) creux *m* **3.** (*low pressure area*) dépression *f* ►**to get one's snout in the ~** profiter
troupe [truːp] *n* THEAT troupe *f*
trouper *n* **an old ~** un vieux de la vieille; **a real ~** une personne de confiance
trouser clip *n* pince *f* à pantalon **trouser press** *n* presse *f* à pantalons
trousers [ˈtraʊzəz, *Am:* -zɚz] *npl* **1.** (**pair of**) ~ pantalon *m* **2.** *fig* **to wear the ~** porter le pantalon
trouser suit *n Brit* tailleur-pantalon *m*

T

trousseau ['tru:səʊ, *Am:* -soʊ] *n* trousseau *m*

trout [traʊt] *n* **1.**<-(s)> (*fish*) truite *f* **2.**<-s> *Brit, inf* (*unattractive old woman*) (**old**) ~ vieille peau *f*

trowel ['traʊəl] *n* **1.**(*for masonry*) truelle *f* **2.**(*for gardening*) déplantoir *m*

truancy ['tru:ənsi] *n no pl* absentéisme *m* scolaire

truant ['tru:ənt] **I.** *n* élève *mf* absentéiste; **to play** ~ *Brit, Aus* faire l'école buissonnière **II.** *vi Brit, Aus* faire l'école buissonnière

truce [tru:s] *n* trêve *f*

truck¹ [trʌk] **I.** *n* **1.**(*lorry*) camion *m;* (*long-distance*) poids *m* lourd **2.** *Brit* (*freight car on train*) wagon *m* **II.** *vt Am* acheminer par camion

truck² [trʌk] *n no pl, inf* (*dealings*) **to have no** ~ **with sb/sth** refuser d'avoir quoi que ce soit à faire avec qn/qc

truck driver, **trucker** *n Brit, Am* camionneur *m;* (*long-distance*) routier *m* **truck farmer** *n Am, Can* maraîcher *m* **truck garden** *n Am, Can* jardin *m* maraîcher

trucking *n no pl, Am, Aus* transport *m* routier; ~ **company** entreprise *f* de transports routiers

truculence ['trʌkjʊləns] *n no pl* agressivité *f*

truculent *adj* agressif(-ive)

trudge [trʌdʒ] **I.** *vi* (*walk laboriously*) se traîner; **to** ~ **over to school** se traîner à l'école; **to** ~ **off/out** partir/sortir en traînant des pieds **II.** *vt* **to** ~ **the streets** se traîner dans les rues **III.** *n* (*laborious walk*) marche *f* pénible

true [tru:] **I.** *adj* **1.** (*not false*) vrai(e); **to ring** ~ sonner vrai; **to be** ~ **of sb/sth** être vrai pour qn/qc; **to turn out to be** ~ se révéler vrai; **to hold** ~ **for sb/sth** être de même pour qn/qc **2.** (*genuine*) véritable; **to come** ~ se réaliser; **a** ~ **artist** un véritable artiste; **to discover sb's** ~ **colours** découvrir le véritable visage de qn; **in the** ~ **sense of a word** dans le vrai sens du terme **3.** (*faithful*) fidèle; **to be/remain** ~ **to sb/sth** être/rester fidèle à qn/qc; ~ **to form, he ...** fidèle à lui-même, ... **4.** (*positioned accurately*) exact(e) **II.** *adv* droit **III.** *n* **to be out of** ~ être hors d'aplomb

true-blue *adj* véritable **true-life** *adj* vrai(e); ~ **adventure** aventure *f* vécue

truffle ['trʌfl] *n* truffe *f*

truism ['tru:ɪzəm] *n* truisme *m*

truly ['tru:li] *adv* **1.**(*accurately*) vraiment **2.**(*genuinely*) véritablement **3.**(*sincerely*) sincèrement; **yours** ~ *Am* mes salutations; **yours** ~ **had to pay** *inf* c'est moi qui ai dû payer

trump [trʌmp] **I.** *n* ~(**s**) atout *m;* **to play a** ~/~**s** jouer un atout/l'atout ►**to turn up** ~**s** *Brit* faire merveille **II.** *vt* **to** ~ **sb/sth** couper qn/qc avec l'atout; *fig* l'emporter sur qn/qc

trumpet ['trʌmpɪt, *Am:* -pət] **I.** *n* trompette *f* ►**to blow one's own** ~ se lancer des fleurs **II.** *vi* (*elephants*) barrir **III.** *vt pej* claironner

trumpeter *n* trompettiste *mf*

truncate [trʌŋ'keɪt] *vt* tronquer

truncheon ['trʌntʃən] *n Brit, Aus* matraque *f*

trundle ['trʌndl] **I.** *vi a. fig, pej* **to** ~ (**on**) avancer lentement **II.** *vt* pousser lentement

trundle bed *n* lit *m* gigogne

trunk [trʌŋk] *n* **1.**(*stem, part of body*) tronc *m* **2.**(*elephant's nose*) trompe *f* **3.**(*large strong case*) malle *f* **4.** *Am* (*boot*) coffre *m*

trunk road *n Brit* route *f* nationale

trunks *n pl* caleçon *m* de bain

truss [trʌs] **I.** *n* **1.**(*framework*) armature *f* **2.**(*surgical appliance for hernia*) bandage *m* herniaire **3.**(*cluster*) grappe *f* **II.** *vt* (*poultry*) brider

◆**truss up** *vt* ligoter

trust [trʌst] **I.** *n* **1.** *no pl* (*belief in reliability*) confiance *f;* **to place one's** ~ **in sb/sth** faire confiance à qn/qc; **to take sth on** ~ croire qc sur parole; **to betray sb's** ~ trahir la confiance de qn **2.** *no pl* (*responsibility*) charge *f;* **to have sth in** ~ avoir la charge de qc; **a position of** ~ un poste à responsabilité **3.** (*organization*) fondation *f* **4.** ECON trust *m* **II.** *vt* **1.** (*place trust in*) faire confiance à; **to** ~ **sb to** +*infin* faire confiance à qn pour +*infin* **2.** (*place reliance on*) se fier à; **to** ~ **sth to sb**, **to** ~ **sb with sth** confier qc à qn; ~ **them to win/get lost** *iron* évidemment, ils allaient gagner/se perdre **3.** (*hope*) **to** ~ **that ...** espérer que ... **III.** *vi* **to** ~ **in sb/sth** se fier à qn/qc; **to** ~ **to luck** s'en remettre à la chance

trusted *adj* de confiance

trustee [trʌs'ti:] *n* administrateur, -trice *m, f;* **board of** ~**s** conseil *m* d'administration

trustful *adj* confiant(e)

trust fund *n* fond *m* en fidéicommis

trusting *s.* **trustful**

trustworthy ['trʌstˌwɜ:ði, *Am:* -ˌwɜ:r-] *adj* (*person*) digne de confiance; (*data, information*) fiable

trusty <-ier, -iest> *adj* fidèle

truth [tru:θ] *n* vérité *f;* **the** ~ **about sb/sth** la vérité sur qn/qc; **in** ~ en vérité; **to tell you the** ~ pour ne rien te cacher; **there is no** ~ **in these accusations** il n'y a rien de vrai dans ces accusations

truthful *adj* sincère

truthfully *adv* sincèrement

truthfulness *n no pl* sincérité *f*

try [traɪ] **I.** *n a.* SPORT essai *m;* **to have a** ~ **at sth**, **to give sth a** ~ essayer qc **II.**<-ie-> *vi* **1.**(*attempt*) essayer; **to** ~ **and** +*infin inf* essayer de +*infin;* **to** ~ **for sth** essayer d'obtenir qc **2.**(*make an effort*) faire un effort **III.**<-ie-> *vt* **1.**(*attempt to do sth*) essayer; **to** ~ **to** +*infin* essayer de +*infin;* **to** ~ **doing sth** faire qc pour voir; **to** ~ **one's luck** tenter sa chance; **I tried my best** j'ai fait de mon mieux **2.**(*test*) essayer; ~ **this sauce** goûte cette sauce; ~ **the supermarket** tu as vu au supermarché? **3.**(*judge*) juger **4.**(*cause annoyance*) mettre à l'épreuve **5.** (*put on trial*) juger

◆**try on** *vt* (*clothes*) essayer; **to try sth on for size** essayer la taille de qc ►**to try it on** *Brit, Aus, inf* faire le malin

◆**try out** **I.** *vt* (*computer, idea, person*) essayer **II.** *vi* SPORT **to ~ for a team** se présenter à une équipe

trying *adj* pénible

try-on *n Brit, Aus, inf* **to be a ~** être du bluff

try-out *n* essai *m*

tsar [zɑːʳ, *Am:* zɑːr] *n* tsar *m*

tsarina [zɑː'riːnə] *n* tsarine *f*

tsetse fly ['tetsiˌflaɪ, *Am:* 'tsetsiˌflaɪ] *n* mouche *f* tsé-tsé

T-shirt ['tiːʃɜːt, *Am:* -ʃɜːrt] *n* t-shirt *m*

tub [tʌb] *n* **1.** (*container: large*) bac *m;* (*small*) pot *m* **2.** (*bathtub*) baignoire *f*

tuba ['tjuːbə] *n* tuba *m*

tubby ['tʌbi] <-ier, -iest> *adj inf* rondelet(te)

tube [tjuːb, *Am:* tuːb] *n* **1.** (*cylinder*) tube *m;* (*bigger diameter*) tuyau *m* **2.** (*container*) tube *m* **3.** (*bodily structure*) tube *m;* **bronchial ~s** bronches *fpl;* **to have one's ~s tied** se faire ligaturer les trompes **4.** *no pl, Brit, inf* (*London's subway*) **the ~** le métro **5.** *no pl, inf* (*television*) **the ~** la télé ►**to go down the ~(s)** *inf* se casser la gueule

tuber *n* tubercule *m*

tuberculosis [tjuːˌbɜːkjʊ'ləʊsɪs, *Am:* tuːˌbɜːrkjə'loʊ-] *n no pl* tuberculose *f*

tube station *n* station *f* de métro

TUC [ˌtiːjuː'siː] *n abbr of* **Trades Union Congress** *fédération des syndicats britanniques*

tuck [tʌk] **I.** *n* **1.** (*narrow fold*) pli *m* **2.** *inf* (*surgery: to reduce fat*) liposuccion *f;* (*to reduce flesh*) lifting *m;* **to have a tummy ~** *inf* se faire liposucer le ventre **3.** *Brit, inf* (*food*) friandises *fpl* **II.** *vt* ranger; **to be ~ed away** être mis de côté; **to ~ sth in** rentrer qc; **to ~ sth into sth** rentrer qc dans qc; **be ~ed (away)** être niché

◆**tuck in** **I.** *vt* (*sheet, child*) border **II.** *vi inf* (*eat*) bouffer

◆**tuck into** *vt* attaquer

◆**tuck up** *vt* border

tucker *n no pl, Aus, inf* bouffe *f*

Tuesday ['tjuːzdeɪ, *Am:* 'tuːz-] *n* mardi *m;* **Shrove ~** mardi gras; *s. a.* **Friday**

tuft [tʌft] *n* touffe *f*

tug [tʌg] **I.** *n* **1.** (*pull*) petit coup *m;* **to give sth a ~** tirer sur qc; **to feel a ~ at one's sleeve** sentir que quelqu'un vous tire par la manche **2.** (*boat*) remorqueur *m* **II.** <-gg-> *vt* tirer sur **III.** <-gg-> *vi* **to ~ at sth** tirer qc

tugboat *n s.* **tug**

tuition [tjuː'ɪʃən] *n no pl* **1.** *Brit, form* (*teaching*) enseignement *m;* **private ~** cours privés *mpl* **2.** *Am* (*tuition fee*) frais *mpl* de scolarité

tuition fees *n Brit* frais *mpl* de scolarité

tulip ['tjuːlɪp, *Am:* 'tuː-] *n* tulipe *f*

tumble ['tʌmbl] **I.** *n a. fig* chute *f;* **to take a ~** faire une chute **II.** *vi* **1.** (*fall*) tomber (par terre) **2.** (*move*) **the ball ~d down the path** le balon a roulé le long de l'allée; **the mail ~d through the letter box** le courrier tombait en cascade de la boîte aux lettres **3.** (*decrease: price*) chuter

◆**tumble down** *vi* s'écrouler; **the rain came tumbling down** un déluge de pluie s'est déversé

◆**tumble out** *vi* (*fall*) rouler par terre; (*contents of bag*) se déverser; (*story, words*) se déverser; **to ~ of bed** émerger du lit

◆**tumble over** *vi* culbuter

tumbledown *adj* en ruine(s)

tumble drier, **tumble dryer** *n* sèche-linge *m,* sécheuse *f Québec*

tumbler ['tʌmbləʳ, *Am:* -blɚ] *n* gobelet *m*

tumescent [tuː'mesnt] *adj* tumescent(e)

tummy ['tʌmi] <-ies> *n childspeak, inf* ventre *m;* **~ ache** mal *m* de ventre

tumor *n Am, Aus,* **tumour** ['tjuːməʳ, *Am:* 'tuːmɚ] *n Brit, Aus* tumeur *f;* **brain ~** tumeur au cerveau

tumult ['tjuːmʌlt, *Am:* 'tuː-] *n no pl* tumulte *m*

tumultuous *adj* tumultueux(-euse); **to appear to ~ applause** être accueilli sous un tumulte d'applaudissements

tumulus <-li> *n* tumulus *m*

tuna ['tjuːnə, *Am:* 'tuː-] *n* thon *m*

tundra ['tʌndrə] *n no pl* toundra *f*

tune [tjuːn, *Am:* tuːn] **I.** *n* **1.** (*melody*) air *m* **2.** *no pl* (*pitch*) accord *m;* **to be in ~** être accordé; **to be out of ~** être désaccordé **3.** *Brit* AUTO, TECH réglage *m* ►**to change one's ~** changer de ton; **to the ~ of sth** d'un montant de qc; **to be in/out of ~ with sth** être en accord/désaccord avec qc **II.** *vt* **1.** MUS accorder **2.** TECH régler; **to be ~ed to the BBC** être branché sur la BBC

◆**tune in**, **tune into** *vt* **1.** RADIO, TV **to ~ to sth** se brancher sur qc; **~ again next week** à la semaine prochaine sur la même longueur d'ondes **2.** *fig, inf* se brancher sur

◆**tune up** **I.** *vi* MUS s'accorder **II.** *vt* **1.** AUTO, TECH mettre au point; (*engine*) régler **2.** MUS accorder

tuneful *adj* MUS mélodieux(-euse)

tuneless *adj* MUS discordant(e)

tuner *n* **1.** (*radio*) tuner *m* **2.** MUS accordeur *m*

tune-up *n* AUTO, TECH réglage *m*

tungsten ['tʌŋstən] *n no pl* tungstène *m*

tunic ['tjuːnɪk, *Am:* 'tuː-] *n* FASHION tunique *f*

tuning *n no pl* **1.** MUS accord *m* **2.** (*adjustment*) réglage *m*

tuning fork *n* MUS diapason *m*

Tunisia [tjuː'nɪzɪə, *Am:* tuː'niːʒə] *n* la Tunisie

Tunisian **I.** *adj* tunisien(ne) **II.** *n* Tunisien(ne) *m(f)*

tunnel ['tʌnl] **I.** *n* **1.** (*passage*) tunnel *m* **2.** ZOOL, BIO galerie *f* ►**the light at the end of the ~** la lumière au bout du tunnel **II.** <-l-, *Am* -ll-> *vi* **to ~ through/under sth** creuser un tunnel dans/sous qc **III.** <-l-, *Am* -ll-> *vt*

T

creuser un tunnel dans; **to ~ one's way out of a prison** s'évader de prison en creusant un tunnel

tunny ['tʌni] *n no pl, Brit, inf* GASTR *s.* **tuna**

tuppence ['tʌpəns] *n no pl, Brit, inf s.* **twopence**

turban ['tɜːbən, *Am:* 'tɜːr-] *n* turban *m*

turbine ['tɜːbaɪn, *Am:* 'tɜːrbɪn] *n* turbine *f*

turbo ['tɜːbəʊ, *Am:* 'tɜːboʊ] *n* turbo *m inv*

turbocharged *adj* turbo *inv* **turbocharger** *n* turbocompresseur *m* **turbo diesel** *n* turbodiesel *m* **turbo engine** *n* moteur *m* turbo **turbojet** *n* turboréacteur *m* **turboprop** *n* turbopropulseur *m*

turbot ['tɜːbət, *Am:* 'tɜːr-] *n* <-(s)> turbot *m*

turbulence ['tɜːbjʊləns, *Am:* 'tɜːr-] *n a. fig* turbulence *f*

turbulent *adj* turbulent(e)

tureen [tjʊ'riːn, *Am:* tʊ'-] *n* ART, GASTR soupière *f*

turf [tɜːf, *Am:* tɜːrf] <-s *o Brit* turves> **I.** *n* **1.** *no pl* (*grassy earth*) gazon *m* **2.** (*cut square*) motte *f* de gazon **3.** SPORT (*ground*) terrain *m* **4.** (*territory*) territoire *m* **5.** *no pl* (*horse racing*) **the ~** le turf **II.** *vt* **1.** BOT gazonner **2.** *Brit, inf* jeter; **to be ~ed out of a club/job** être vidé d'un club/d'un emploi

turf accountant *n Brit, form* bookmaker *m*

turgid ['tɜːdʒɪd, *Am:* 'tɜːr-] *adj* **1.** (*swollen*) gonflé(e) **2.** *pej* (*pompous*) ampoulé(e)

Turk [tɜːk, *Am:* tɜːrk] *n* (*person*) Turc, que *m, f*

turkey ['tɜːki, *Am:* 'tɜːr-] *n* **1.** ZOOL, GASTR dinde *f* **2.** *Am, Aus, pej, inf* (*failure*) bide *m* **3.** *Am, Aus, inf* (*silly person*) con(ne) *m(f)*

Turkey ['tɜːki, *Am:* 'tɜːr-] *n* la Turquie

Turkish ['tɜːkɪʃ, *Am:* 'tɜːr-] **I.** *adj* turc(que) **II.** *n* turc *m; s. a.* **English**

Turkish baths *n pl* bains *mpl* turcs **Turkish delight** *n* loukoum *m*

turmoil ['tɜːmɔɪl, *Am:* 'tɜːr-] *n* **1.** *no pl* (*chaos*) agitation *f;* **to be in ~** être en ébullition **2.** (*stress*) trouble *m;* **to be in a ~** être agité; **one's mind is in a ~** la confusion règne dans son esprit

turn [tɜːn, *Am:* tɜːrn] **I.** *n* **1.** (*change of direction: road*) tournant *m;* **to take a ~** tourner; **a left/right ~** un tournant à gauche/à droite; **take the next ~ left** prenez le prochain tournant à gauche; **to give sth a ~** tourner qc **2.** (*rotation*) tour *m* **3.** (*walk*) tour *m;* **to take a ~** faire un tour **4.** (*changing point*) tournant *m;* **the ~ of the tide** le renversement de la marée; *fig* le renversement des tendances; **a ~ of fate** un caprice du destin **5.** (*changing condition*) tournure *f;* **to take a ~ for the worse** s'aggraver; **to take a ~ for the better** s'améliorer **6.** (*allotted time*) tour *m;* **to be sb's ~ to** +*infin* être le tour de qn de +*infin;* **to take ~s at doing sth** faire qc à tour de rôle; **it's your ~ at the wheel** c'est ton tour de conduire; **to wait one's ~** attendre son tour; **in ~** à tour de rôle; **he paid each of us in ~** il nous a payés l'un après l'autre; **in one's ~** à son tour; **to miss a ~** manquer son tour; **to speak out of ~** parler mal à propos **7.** (*shape*) tournure *f* **8.** (*service*) tour *m;* **to do sb a bad ~** jouer un mauvais tour à qn; **to do sb a good ~** rendre service à qn **9.** (*odd sensation*) choc *m;* **to give sb a ~** donner un choc à qn **10.** MED crise *f* **11.** (*queasiness*) nausée *f;* **to have ~s** avoir des nausées **12.** (*stage performance*) numéro *m* ►**at every ~** à tout bout de champ; **to be cooked to a ~** être cuit à point **II.** *vi* **1.** (*rotate*) tourner **2.** (*turn round*) se retourner; AUTO faire demi-tour; **to ~ to(wards) sb/sth** se tourner vers qn/qc **3.** (*switch direction*) tourner; (*tide*) changer; **to ~ left** tourner à gauche; **to ~ round the corner** tourner au coin de la rue; **my mind ~ed to food** *fig* je me suis mis à penser au repas; **talk ~ed to politics** la conversation est passée à la politique; **to ~ to religion/drugs** se tourner vers la religion/la drogue; **who can I ~ to?** vers qui puis-je me tourner? **4.** (*become*) devenir; **to ~ cold** commencer à faire froid; **to ~ green** verdir; **to ~ seven** (*child*) venir d'avoir sept ans; (*time*) être sept heures passé **5.** BOT, BIO (*leaves*) jaunir **6.** GASTR (*cream, milk*) tourner ►**to ~ (over) in one's grave** se retourner dans sa tombe; **to ~ on one's heel** tourner les talons **III.** *vt* **1.** (*rotate: page, handle*) tourner; **to ~ somersaults** faire des sauts périlleux **2.** (*cause to rotate*) faire tourner **3.** (*turn round*) retourner; **to ~ sth upside down** retourner qc **4.** (*switch direction*) tourner; **to ~ the corner** tourner au coin de la rue; *fig* passer le cap **5.** (*direct*) *a. fig* diriger; **to ~ a gun on sb** diriger une arme sur qn; **to ~ one's anger on sb** reporter sa colère sur qn **6.** (*transform*) **to ~ sb/sth into sth** transformer qn/qc en qc; **to ~ water blue** donner à l'eau une couleur bleue **7.** (*sprain*) tordre; **to ~ one's ankle** se fouler la cheville **8.** (*feel nauseated*) **to ~ one's stomach** soulever le cœur **9.** (*shape*) tourner ►**to ~ one's back on sb** tourner le dos à qn; **to ~ the other cheek** tendre l'autre joue; **to ~ a deaf ear to sth** rester sourd à qc; **to ~ a blind eye to sth** fermer les yeux sur qc; **not to ~ a hair** ne pas bouger d'un poil; **to ~ sb's head** faire tourner la tête à qn; **to ~ the tables** inverser les rôles; **to ~ tail and run** prendre ses jambes à son cou; **to ~ sth upside down** mettre qc sens dessus dessous

◆**turn about** *vi* se retourner

◆**turn against** *vt* se retourner contre

◆**turn around** **I.** *vt* **1.** (*twist*) retourner **2.** (*turn back: ship, plane*) faire faire demi-tour à **3.** (*reverse: situation*) renverser **4.** (*improve: business*) remettre sur pied **II.** *vi* **1.** (*twist*) tourner; (*person*) se retourner; **you can't just ~ and cancel the wedding** tu ne peux pas simplement annuler le mariage **2.** (*turn back: ship, plane*) faire demi-tour **3.** (*reverse*) se renverser **4.** (*improve*) se remettre sur pied

◆**turn aside** I. *vi* se détourner II. *vt* détourner
◆**turn away** I. *vi* se détourner II. *vt* 1. (*to face the opposite way*) détourner 2. (*refuse entry*) refuser
◆**turn back** I. *vi* 1. (*return*) faire demi-tour 2. (*change plans*) tourner bride; **you can't ~ now** tu ne peux plus faire marche arrière II. *vt* 1. (*send back*) renvoyer 2. (*fold*) replier ►**to ~ the clock** revenir en arrière
◆**turn down** *vt* 1. (*reject*) refuser 2. (*reduce*) baisser 3. (*fold*) rabattre
◆**turn in** I. *vt* 1. (*submit: assignment*) remettre; **to ~ a superb performance** produire une performance exceptionnelle 2. *inf* (*hand to the police*) livrer 3. (*give up*) remettre; (*weapons*) rendre II. *vi inf* aller se pieuter
◆**turn into** I. *vi* (*change*) se transformer en; **it turned into a fiasco** ça s'est transformé en fiasco II. *vt* **to turn sb/sth into sth** (*by magic, work*) transformer qn/qc en qc
◆**turn off** I. *vt* 1. ELEC, TECH (*electric device*) éteindre; (*car engine*) arrêter 2. (*stop the flow: gas, water, tap*) fermer; **to turn the water/electricity of at the mains** couper l'eau/le courant au compteur 3. (*leave your path: road*) quitter 4. *inf* (*sexually unappealing*) rebuter II. *vi* 1. (*leave your path*) **to ~ at sth** tourner à qc 2. (*no longer pay attention*) décrocher
◆**turn on** I. *vt* 1. ELEC, TECH (*electric device*) allumer 2. (*start the flow: gas, tap, water*) ouvrir 3. *inf* (*excite sexually*) exciter 4. *inf* (*attract*) brancher 5. (*attack*) s'attaquer à 6. (*be dependent on*) reposer sur II. *vi* s'allumer
◆**turn out** I. *vi* 1. (*end up*) finir; **it's turned out dry** finalement il n'a pas plu; **it'll ~ all right** ça va bien se passer; **as things turned out, I was right** en l'occurence, j'avais raison 2. (*prove to be*) se révéler; **she turned out to be a great dancer** elle s'est révélée être une grande danseuse; **she turned out to be my aunt** il s'est avérée qu'elle était ma tante 3. (*go to*) **to ~ for sth** se rendre à qc; **to ~ to vote** se rendre aux urnes II. *vt* 1. (*switch off: electric device*) éteindre 2. (*stop the flow: gas*) fermer 3. (*kick out*) expulser; **to turn sb out of somewhere** expulser qn de quelque part; **to turn sb out on the street** mettre qn à la rue 4. (*empty: pockets*) vider 5. (*produce: product*) produire; (*graduates, linguists*) former
◆**turn over** I. *vi* 1. (*face different direction*) se retourner 2. (*turn page*) tourner la page 3. (*start: engine*) tourner 4. *Brit* TV changer de chaîne II. *vt* 1. (*change the side*) *a. fig* retourner; (*page*) tourner 2. (*cause to operate: car engine*) faire tourner 3. (*give in*) remettre 4. (*hand over: control*) remettre 5. (*consider: idea*) réfléchir à; **I've been turning things over** j'ai bien réfléchi 6. (*be lucrative: business*) rapporter 7. *Brit, inf* (*steal from*) dévaliser 8. (*cheat*) rouler 9. (*change function*) **to turn sth over to sth** transformer qc en qc ►**to ~ a new leaf** tourner la page
◆**turn round** *vi, vt s.* **turn around**
◆**turn up** I. *vi* 1. (*arrive*) arriver; **when the job turned up, I took it** quand le job s'est présenté, je l'ai pris 2. (*be found*) resurgir 3. (*face upwards*) pointer vers le haut II. *vt* 1. (*increase: volume, gas*) augmenter; (*radio*) mettre plus fort 2. (*shorten clothing*) relever 3. (*reveal*) révéler 4. (*find*) trouver
turnabout *n* COM retournement *m*
turnaround *n no pl* 1. (*sudden change*) volte-face *f;* (*for business, economy*) redressement *m* 2. (*waiting time*) rotation *f*
turnaround time *n* délai *m* d'exécution
turncoat *n* renégat(e) *m(f)*
turndown I. *n* 1. (*refusal*) refus *m* 2. (*decline*) fléchissement *m* II. *adj* (*collar*) rabattu(e)
turned-out *adj* **well ~** bien mis(e)
turner ['tɜːnəʳ, *Am:* 'tɜːrnɚ] *n inf s.* **spatula**
turning *n* 1. (*road leading off*) embranchement *m;* **there's a ~ to the right** il y a un tournant à droite; **to take the first ~ to the right** prendre la première à droite 2. *no pl* (*using a lathe*) TECH tournage *m*
turning point *n* tournant *m*
turnip ['tɜːnɪp, *Am:* 'tɜːr-] *n* navet *m*
turn-off *n* 1. (*in road*) embranchement *m* 2. *inf* (*sexually unappealing*) **to be a real ~** être vraiment repoussant **turn-on** *n inf* (*sexually appealing*) **to be a real ~** être excitant
turnout *n* 1. (*amount of people*) assistance *f* 2. (*amount of people who vote*) nombre *m* de votants
turnover *n* 1. (*rate of employee renewal*) rotation *f* du personnel 2. (*total earnings*) chiffre *m* d'affaires 3. (*rate of stock renewal*) écoulement *m* des marchandises 4. GASTR chausson *m,* gosette *f Belgique*
turnpike ['tɜːnpaɪk, *Am:* 'tɜːrn-] *n Am* AUTO autoroute *f* à péage
turnround ['tɜːnraʊnd, *Am:* 'tɜːrn-] *n no pl, Brit s.* **turnaround**
turnstile ['tɜːnstaɪl, *Am:* 'tɜːrn-] *n* SPORT tourniquet *m*
turntable ['tɜːnˌteɪbl, *Am:* 'tɜːrn-] *n* 1. (*for records*) platine *f* 2. (*for trains*) plaque *f* tournante
turntable ladder *n* échelle *f* pivotante
turn-up *n Brit* (*on trousers*) revers *m* 2. *Brit* **to be a ~ for the book(s)** être une sacrée surprise
turpentine ['tɜːpəntaɪn, *Am:* 'tɜːr-] *n no pl* térébenthine *f*
turps [tɜːps, *Am:* tɜːrps] *n no pl, inf abbr of* **turpentine** térébenthine *f*
turquoise ['tɜːkwɔɪz, *Am:* 'tɜːr-] I. *n* 1. (*stone*) turquoise *f* 2. (*colour*) turquoise *m* II. *adj* 1. (*made of this stone*) en turquoises 2. (*colored*) turquoise *inv*
turret ['tʌrɪt, *Am:* 'tɜːr] *n* tourelle *f*
turtle ['tɜːtl, *Am:* 'tɜːrt̬l] <-(s)> *n* tortue *f*

T

turtledove *n* tourterelle *f* **turtleneck** *n* col *m* roulé

tusk [tʌsk] *n* ZOOL défense *f*

tussle ['tʌsl] I. *vi* 1. (*scuffle*) se battre 2. (*quarrel*) se disputer II. *n a. fig* lutte *f*

tussock ['tʌsək] *n* 1. (*grassy mound*) touffe *f* d'herbe 2. (*bunch of hair*) mèche *f* de cheveux

tut [tʌt] I. *interj* ~ voyons II. *vi* <-tt-> **to ~ at sth** désapprouver qc

tutor ['tjuːtəʳ, *Am:* 'tuːt̬ɚ] I. *n* 1. (*person helping students*) directeur, -trice *m, f* d'études 2. (*private teacher*) professeur *m* particulier 3. *Brit* (*supervising teacher*) directeur, -trice *m, f* 4. *Am* (*assistant lecturer*) assistant(e) *m(f)* 5. (*music book*) méthode *f* II. *vt* donner des cours à III. *vi* donner des cours

tutorial [tjuː'tɔːrɪəl, *Am:* tuː'-] *n* SCHOOL, UNIV travaux *mpl* dirigés

tuxedo [tʌk'siːdəʊ, *Am:* -doʊ] *n Am* smoking *m*

TV [ˌtiː'viː] *n* TV, ELEC *abbr of* **television** télé *f*

TV guide *n* programme *m* télé **TV star** *n* star *f* de la télé

twaddle ['twɒdl, *Am:* 'twɑːdl] *n no pl, inf* âneries *fpl*

twang [twæŋ] I. *n* 1. (*jarring sound*) son *m* vibrant; **to give sth a ~** faire vibrer qc 2. (*nasal accent*) nasillement *m;* **to speak with a ~** nasiller II. *vt* 1. MUS, PHYS faire vibrer; (*strings*) pincer 2. *fig* **to ~ someone's nerves** taper sur les nerfs de qn III. *vi* MUS, PHYS vibrer

tweak [twiːk] I. *vt* 1. (*pull*) tirer 2. (*twist*) tordre 3. (*pinch*) pincer 4. (*adjust*) régler II. *n* **to give sth a ~** 1. (*pull*) tirer qc 2. (*twist*) tordre qc 3. (*pinch*) pincer qc 4. (*adjust*) régler qc

twee [twiː] *adj Brit, pej* mièvre

tweed [twiːd] *n* FASHION tweed *m*

tweezers ['twiːzəz, *Am:* -zɚz] *npl* pince *f* à épiler; **a pair of ~** une pince à épiler

twelfth [twelfθ] *adj* douzième; *s. a.* **eighth**

Twelfth Night *n* fête *f* des Rois

twelve [twelv] *adj* douze *inv; s. a.* **eight**

twentieth ['twentɪəθ, *Am:* -t̬ɪ-] *adj* vingtième; *s. a.* **eighth**

twenty ['twenti, *Am:* -t̬i] *adj* vingt *inv; s. a.* **eight, eighty**

twerp [twɜːp, *Am:* twɜːrp] *n pej, inf* andouille *f*

twice [twaɪs] *adv* deux fois; **~ as often/fast** deux fois plus souvent/plus vite

twice-yearly *adj* bi-annuel(le)

twiddle ['twɪdl] I. *vt* tripoter ►**to ~ one's thumbs** se tourner les pouces II. *vi* **to ~ with sth** tripoter qc

twig [twɪg] I. *n a. pej* brindille *f* II. *vt, vi inf* piger

twilight ['twaɪlaɪt] *n* (*opp: dawn*) *a. fig* crépuscule *m; s. a.* **dusk**

twin [twɪn] I. *n a. fig* jumeau, jumelle *m, f* II. *adj a. fig* PHYSIOL, MED, BIO jumeau(jumelle); **a ~ brother** un frère jumeau III. *vt* <-nn-> jumeler

twin beds *n pl* lits *mpl* jumeaux

twine [twaɪn] I. *vi* **to ~ around sth** s'enrouler autour de qc II. *vt* 1. (*twist around*) enrouler 2. (*weave*) *a. fig* entrelacer III. *n no pl* ficelle *f*

twin-engined *adj* bimoteur(-trice)

twinge [twɪndʒ] *n* 1. (*stab*) MED élancement *m* 2. *fig* **a ~ of conscience** un remords; **to feel a ~ of guilt/sadness** éprouver une certaine culpabilité/tristesse

twinkle ['twɪŋkl] I. *vi* scintiller; (*eyes*) pétiller II. *n* scintillement *m;* (*eyes*) pétillement *m;* **in a ~** en un clin d'œil; **to have a ~ in one's eye** avoir une étincelle dans le regard

twinkling ['twɪŋklɪŋ] *n no pl* scintillement *m;* (*eyes*) pétillement *m* ►**to do sth in the ~ of an eye** faire qc en un clin d'œil

twin set *n Brit, Aus* twin-set *m* **twin town** *n Brit* ville *f* jumelée

twirl [twɜːl, *Am:* twɜːrl] I. *vi* DANCE, ART tournoyer II. *vt* 1. (*spin*) faire tournoyer; (*twist*) 2. (*twist*) tortiller III. *n* 1. (*spin*) pirouette *f* 2. (*shape*) *a. fig* volute *f*

twist [twɪst] I. *vt* 1. (*turn: metal, cloth*) tordre; (*handle, lid*) tourner; **to ~ one's ankle** se fouler la cheville; **I ~ed the top off the jar** j'ai dévissé le couvercle du pot; **to ~ sth out of shape** déformer qc en tordant; **to ~ sth into a knot** former un nœud en tordant qc; **he ~ed his face into an ugly smile** *fig* son visage se déforma en un vilain sourire 2. (*wind around*) enrouler; **to ~ sth together** (*strands, hands*) entrelacer qc 3. (*manipulate: words*) déformer; **to ~ sth into sth** transformer qc en qc 4. *inf* (*cheat*) rouler ►**to ~ sb's arm** forcer la main à qn; **to ~ sb round one's (little) finger** mener qn par le bout du nez II. *vi* 1. (*turn round*) se (re)tourner 2. (*squirm around*) s'enrouler; **to ~ and turn** s'agiter dans tous les sens 3. (*contort*) *a.* MED se tordre 4. (*curve: path*) serpenter; **to ~ and turn** faire des zigzags 5. (*change*) se transformer 6. (*dance*) twister ►**to be left ~ing in the wind** être laissé dans l'incertitude III. *n* 1. (*turn*) tour *m;* **to give sth a ~** tourner qc; **with a ~ of sth** d'un tour de qc 2. (*rotation*) rotation *f;* MED entorse *f* 3. (*action*) torsion *f* 4. (*sharp curve*) tournant *m;* **~s and turns** tours et détours 5. (*changing point*) tournant *m;* **to take a new ~** prendre un nouveau tournant 6. (*change*) tournure *f;* **to give sth a ~** donner une nouvelle tournure à qc; **a surprise ~ to the story** une tournure surprenante dans l'histoire 7. (*curl: hair*) torsade *f;* (*lemon*) zeste *m;* (*ribbon*) tortillon *m;* (*thread*) torsade *f* 8. (*dance*) twist *m;* **to do the ~** danser le twist ►**to be in a ~** être à bout; **to go round the ~** *Brit, inf* devenir cinglé

twisted *adj a. fig* tordu(e); (*ankle*) foulé(e); (*path, river*) tortueux(-euse)

twister *n* 1. METEO *s.* **tornado** 2. *pej, inf* (*swindler*) escroc *mf*

twisty *adj* <-ier, -iest> *inf* (*road*) tortueux(-euse)

twit [twɪt] *n pej, inf* andouille *f*

twitch [twɪtʃ] **I.** *vi* **1.** (*nervous movement: muscle*) se contracter; (*person*) avoir un tic **2.** (*move nervously*) s'agiter **II.** *vt* **1.** (*jerk*) contracter; (*nose, tail*) remuer **2.** (*tug quickly*) tirer d'un coup sec; **to ~ sth out of sth** arracher qc de qc **III.** <-es> *n* **1.** (*small spasm*) tic *m* **2.** (*quick pull*) coup *m* sec

twitter ['twɪtəʳ, *Am:* 'twɪt̬ɚ] **I.** *vi* **1.** ZOOL, BIO gazouiller **2.** (*talk*) jacasser **II.** *n* ZOOL, BIO gazouillis *mpl*

'twixt *prep s.* **betwixt**

two [tuː] **I.** *adj* deux; **to be ~ of a kind** être de la même espèce; **to have ~ of sth** avoir qc en double ►**to be in ~ minds** être indécis; **that makes ~ of us** *inf* on est deux **II.** *n* deux *m* ►**~'s company three's a crowd** *prov* nous ne serions pas plus mal seuls; **to put ~ and ~ together** *inf* tirer ses conclusions; **it takes ~ to tango** *prov* chacun a sa part de responsabilité; *s. a.* **eight**

two-bit *adj Am, pej, inf* de pacotille **two-dimensional** *adj* **1.** (*flat*) bidimensionnel(le) **2.** *fig, pej* superficiel(le) **two-door I.** *adj* AUTO (*car*) à deux portes **II.** *n* AUTO deux-portes *f* **two-edged** *adj a. fig* à double tranchant **two-faced** *adj* hypocrite **twofold I.** *adv* doublement **II.** *adj* double **two-part** *adj* en deux parties **two-party system** *n* système *m* bipartite **twopence** *n Brit* **1.** FIN deux pence *mpl* **2.** *inf* (*worthless thing*) deux sous *mpl;* **to be worth ~** valoir des tripettes ►**to not care ~ about sth** se moquer royalement de qc **twopenny-halfpenny** *adj Brit, pej* à la noix **two-phase** *adj* ELEC diphasé(e) **two-piece I.** *n* FASHION **1.** (*jacket and trousers*) (costume *m*) deux pièces *m* **2.** (*bikini*) (maillot *m*) deux pièces *m* **II.** *adj* deux pièces **two-seater** *n* AUTO deux places *m* **twosome** *n* couple *m* **two-stroke** AUTO, TECH **I.** *n* moteur *m* à deux temps **II.** *adj* à deux temps **two-tier(ed)** *adj* **1.** (*with two levels*) à deux niveaux **2.** *pej* (*two-class*) à deux vitesses **two-time** *vt inf* tromper **two-timing** *adj pej, inf* infidèle; **a ~ bastard** un gros salaud **two-way** *adj* à double sens; (*exchange*) bilatéral(e); **~ radio** poste *m* émetteur-récepteur

tycoon [taɪ'kuːn] *n* FIN magnat *m*

tyke [taɪk] *n s.* **tike**

type [taɪp] **I.** *n* **1.** (*sort*) type *m;* **people of every ~** personnes de toutes sortes; **do you like that ~ of thing?** tu aimes ce genre de choses? **2.** BIO espèce *f;* **blood ~** groupe *m* sanguin **3.** (*sort of person*) genre *m;* **he's not the ~ to forget** il n'est pas du genre à oublier; **he's not my ~** il n'est pas mon genre; **he's a sporty ~** *inf* c'est le genre sportif **4.** TYP, PUBL caractère *m;* **in large/small ~** en gros/petits caractères **II.** *vt* **1.** (*write: typewriter*) taper; (*computer*) saisir **2.** (*categorize*) classifier; **to ~ blood** déterminer le groupe sanguin **3.** (*typecast*) **to be ~d** être cantonné dans un rôle **III.** *vi* (*typewriter*) taper (à la machine) ◆**type out, type up** *vt* (*typewriter*) taper (à la machine); (*computer*) saisir

typecast ['taɪpkɑːst, *Am:* -kæst] <typecast, typecast> *vt* CINE, THEAT **to be ~ as sth** être enfermé dans le rôle de qc

typeface ['taɪpfeɪs] *n no pl* TYP, PUBL police *f* de caractère

typescript ['taɪpskrɪpt] *n* manuscrit *m* dactylographié

typesetter *n* TYP, PUBL **1.** (*machine*) machine *f* à composer **2.** (*printer*) compositeur, -trice *m, f*

typesetting ['taɪpˌsetɪŋ, *Am:* -ˌset̬-] *n* TYP, PUBL *no pl* composition *f*

typewriter ['taɪpˌraɪtəʳ, *Am:* -t̬ɚ] *n* machine *f* à écrire, dactylographe *m Québec*

typewritten *adj* dactylographié(e)

typhoid ['taɪfɔɪd], **typhoid fever** *n no pl* typhoïde *f*

typhoon [taɪ'fuːn] *n* METEO typhon *m*

typhus ['taɪfəs] *n no pl* typhus *m*

typical ['tɪpɪkəl] **I.** *adj* typique; **the ~ American** l'américain type; **it is ~ of him/her** c'est bien lui/elle **II.** *interj inf* **~!** ça ne m'étonne pas!

typically *adv* **1.** (*characteristically*) typiquement; **it's ~ kind of him** c'est typique de sa gentillesse **2.** (*usually*) généralement

typify ['tɪpɪfaɪ] <-ie-> *vt* **1.** (*be characteristic of*) être caractéristique de **2.** (*embody*) être le type même de

typing *n no pl* dactylographie *f;* **a ~ speed/error** une vitesse/erreur de frappe

typist *n* dactylo *mf*

typographer [taɪ'pɒgrəfəʳ, *Am:* -'pɑːgrəfɚ] *n* typographe *mf*

typographic(al) *adj* typographique; **a ~ error** une erreur de typographie

typography [taɪ'pɒgrəfi, *Am:* -'pɑːgrə-] *n no pl* typographie *f*

tyrannical *adj* tyrannique

tyrannize ['tɪrənaɪz] *vt* tyranniser

tyranny ['tɪrəni] *n a. fig* tyrannie *f*

tyrant ['taɪərənt, *Am:* 'taɪrənt] *n a. fig* tyran *m*

tyre ['taɪəʳ, *Am:* 'taɪɚ] *n Aus, Brit* AUTO pneu *m;* **front/winter ~** pneu avant/d'hiver; **a spare ~** une roue de secours

tyre gauge *n Aus, Brit* AUTO manomètre *m* **tyre pressure** *n no pl* AUTO pression *f* des pneus

tzar [zɑːʳ, *Am:* zɑːr] *n* POL *s.* **tsar**

tzetze fly ['tetsiˌflaɪ] *n* BIO *s.* **tsetse fly**

U

U, u [juː] <-'s> *n* U *m,* u *m;* ~ **as in Uncle,** ~ **for Uncle** (*on telephone*) u comme Ursule

U[1] [juː] *adj Brit* CINE (*film*) tous publics

U[2] [juː] *n Am, Aus, inf abbr of* **university** université *f*

U[3] [juː] *adj Aus, Brit* guindé(e)

UAE [ˌjuːeɪ'iː] *n* GEO *abbr of* **United Arab Emirates** EAU *mpl*

ubiquitous [juː'bɪkwɪtəs, *Am:* -wət̬əs] *adj* omniprésent(e)

ubiquity [juː'bɪkwətɪ, *Am:* -t̬ɪ] *n no pl, form* ubiquité *f*

UCAS *n Brit abbr of* **Universities and Colleges Admissions Service** centre *m* national des inscriptions en faculté

UDA *n abbr of* **Ulster Defence Association** *organisation paramilitaire loyaliste en Irlande du Nord*

udder ['ʌdəʳ, *Am:* -ɚ] *n* mamelle *f*

UDR *n abbr of* **Ulster Defence Regiment** *organisation paramilitaire protestante*

UEFA *n abbr of* **Union of European Football Associations** UEFA *f*

UFO ['juːfəʊ, *Am:* ˌjuːef'oʊ] <(')s> *n abbr of* **unidentified flying object** ovni *m*

Uganda [juː'gændə] *n* l'Ouganda *m*

Ugandan I. *adj* ougandais(e) **II.** *n* Ougandais(e) *m(f)*

ugh [ɜːh] *interj inf* pouah!

ugliness *n no pl* laideur *f*

ugly ['ʌglɪ] <-ier, iest> *adj* **1.** *pej* (*not attractive*) laid(e); **to be** ~ **as sin** être laid comme un pou; ~ **duckling** vilain petit canard *m* **2.** (*angry: look, word, wound*) vilain(e) **3.** (*violent*) terrible; (*incident*) regrettable; **to turn** ~ tourner mal **4.** (*unpleasant*) déplaisant(e) **5.** (*threatening*) menaçant(e) **6.** (*repelling*) répugnant(e); **an** ~ **customer** un sale type

UHF *n abbr of* **ultrahigh frequency** UHF *f*

UHT *adj abbr of* **ultra heat treated** UHT

UK [ˌjuː'keɪ] *n abbr of* **United Kingdom the** ~ le Royaume-Uni

Ukraine [juː'kreɪn] *n* l'Ukraine *f*

Ukrainian I. *adj* ukrainien(ne) **II.** *n* **1.** (*person*) Ukrainien(ne) *m(f)* **2.** LING ukrainien *m; s. a.* **English**

ukulele [ˌjuːkə'leɪlɪ] *n* guitare *f* hawaïenne

ulcer ['ʌlsəʳ, *Am:* -sɚ] *n* **1.** MED ulcère *m* **2.** (*blemish*) plaie *f*

ulcerate ['ʌlsəreɪt] *vi* s'ulcérer

ulcerous ['ʌlsərəs] *adj* ulcéreux(-euse)

Ulster ['ʌlstəʳ, *Am:* -stɚ] *n no pl* Ulster *m*

ulterior [ʌl'tɪərɪəʳ, *Am:* -'tɪrɪɚ] *adj* ultérieur(e); ~ **motive** arrière-pensée *f*

ultimate ['ʌltɪmət, *Am:* -t̬əmɪt] **I.** *adj* **1.** (*best*) suprême **2.** (*final*) final(e); **the** ~ **purpose** le but ultime **3.** (*fundamental*) fondamental(e) **4.** (*furthest*) le(la) plus éloigné(e) **II.** *n* summum *m;* **the** ~ **in sth** le summum de qc

ultimately *adv* finalement

ultimatum [ˌʌltɪ'meɪtəm, *Am:* -t̬ə'meɪt̬əm] <ultimata *o* -tums> *n* ultimatum *m*

ultra- [ˌʌltrə] *in compounds* ultra-

ultrahigh frequency *n no pl* RADIO très haute fréquence *f* **ultralight** *adj* ultraléger(-ère) **ultramarine I.** *adj* outremer *inv;* ~ **blue** bleu *m* d'outremer **II.** *n no pl* (bleu *m* d')outremer *m* **ultramodern** *adj* ultramoderne **ultra-short** *adj* RADIO ultra-court(e) **ultrasonic** *adj* RADIO ultrasonique **ultrasound** *n* **1.** (*sound, vibrations*) ultrasons *mpl* **2.** (*scan*) échographie *f* **ultrasound scan** *n* MED échographie *f* **ultraviolet I.** *n* ASTR, PHYS ultraviolet *m* **II.** *adj* ultraviolet(te); (*treatment*) aux ultraviolets **ultraviolet rays** *n* rayons *mpl* ultraviolets

Ulysses ['juːlɪsiːz, *Am:* juː'lɪs-] *n* Ulysse *m*

umbel ['ʌmbəl] *n* ombelle *f*

umber ['ʌmbəʳ, *Am:* -bɚ] ART, FASHION, TYP **I.** *adj* terre d'ombre *inv* **II.** *n no pl* terre *f* d'ombre

umbilical cord [ʌm'bɪlɪkl] *n* cordon *m* ombilical

umbrage ['ʌmbrɪdʒ] *n no pl, form* ombrage *m;* **to take** ~ **at sth** s'offenser de qc

umbrella [ʌm'brelə] *n* **1.** (*covering*) *a. fig* parapluie *m;* (*for sun*) ombrelle *f;* (*on the beach*) parasol *m* **2.** (*protection*) protection *f;* **under the** ~ **of sth** sous les auspices de qc

umbrella pine *n* pin *m* parasol **umbrella stand** *n* porte-parapluies *m*

umpire ['ʌmpaɪəʳ, *Am:* -paɪɚ] SPORT **I.** *n* arbitre *mf* **II.** *vt* arbitrer

umpteen ['ʌmptiːn] *adj, pron inf* des tas de

umpteenth *adj* énième

UN [juː'en] *n abbr of* **United Nations the** ~ l'ONU *f*

UNA *n Brit abbr of* **United Nations Association** Association *f* des Nations-Unies

unabashed [ˌʌnə'bæʃt] *adj* nullement décontenancé(e)

unabated [ˌʌnə'beɪtɪd, *Am:* -t̬ɪd] *form* **I.** *adj* inchangé(e) **II.** *adv* (*without weakening*) sans faiblir

unable [ʌn'eɪbl] *adj* **to be** ~ **to do sth** (*attend, reach*) ne pas pouvoir faire qc; (*swim, read*) ne pas savoir faire qc; (*incapable*) être incapable de faire qc

unabridged [ˌʌnə'brɪdʒd] *adj* intégral(e)

unacademic *adj* peu académique

unacceptable [ˌʌnək'septəbl] *adj* **1.** (*not good enough*) inacceptable; **sth is** ~ **to sb** qn ne peut pas accepter qc **2.** (*intolerable*) inadmissible

unaccompanied [ˌʌnə'kʌmpənɪd] *adj* (*passenger*) non accompagné(e); (*voice, violin*) sans accompagnement

unaccountable [ˌʌnə'kaʊntəbl, *Am:* -t̬ə-] *adj* **1.** (*inexplicable*) inexplicable **2.** (*not responsible*) **to be** ~ **for sth to sb** ne pas avoir à répondre de qc devant qn

unaccounted for [ˌʌnəˈkaʊntɪdˈfɔːʳ, *Am:* -t̬ɪdˌfɔːr] *adj* manquant(e); **to be** ~ manquer
unaccustomed [ˌʌnəˈkʌstəmd] *adj* inhabituel(le); **to be** ~ **to doing sth** ne pas être habitué à faire qc
unacknowledged [ˌʌnəkˈnɒlɪdʒd, *Am:* -ˈnɑːlɪdʒd] *adj* **1.** (*not recognized*) non reconnu(e) **2.** (*unanswered*) sans réponse
unaddressed [ˌʌnəˈdrest] *adj* sans adresse
unadopted [ˌʌnəˈdɒptɪd, *Am:* -ˈdɑːp-] *adj* non adopté(e)
unadorned [ˌʌnəˈdɔːnd, *Am:* -ˈdɔːrnd] *adj* sans fioritures; (*truth*) simple
unadulterated [ˌʌnəˈdʌltəreɪtɪd, *Am:* -t̬əreɪt̬ɪd] *adj* **1.** (*not changed*) simple **2.** (*pure*) *a. fig* (*substance*) pur(e); (*nonsense*) pur(e)
unadventurous [ˌʌnədˈventʃərəs] *adj* peu audacieux(-euse)
unadvisable [ˌʌnədˈvaɪzəbl] *adj* peu recommandé(e); **to be** ~ **to** +*infin* ne pas être recommandé de +*infin;* **to be** ~ **for sb** être à déconseiller pour qn
unaesthetic *adj* peu esthétique
unaffected [ˌʌnəˈfektɪd] *adj* **1.** (*not changed*) **to be** ~ **by sth** ne pas être affecté par qc **2.** (*sincere*) simple
unafraid [ˌʌnəˈfreɪd] *adj* sans peur; **to be** ~ **of sb/sth** ne pas avoir peur de qn/qc
unaided [ʌnˈeɪdɪd] *adj* sans aide; **to do sth** ~ faire qc tout seul
unalike [ˌʌnəˈlaɪk] *adj* différent(e); **to be** ~ ne pas se ressembler
unalloyed [ˌʌnəˈlɔɪd] *adj* **1.** (*pure: metal*) pur(e) **2.** *fig* parfait(e)
unaltered [ˌʌnˈɔːltəd, *Am:* -t̬ɚd] *adj* inchangé(e)
unambiguous [ˌʌnæmˈbɪgjʊəs] *adj* sans ambiguïté; (*language, terms*) clair(e)
un-American [ˌʌnəˈmerɪkən] *adj pej* **1.** (*against American principles*) peu américain(e) **2.** (*against the U.S.A.*) anti-américain(e)
unanimity [ˌjuːnəˈnɪmətɪ, *Am:* -t̬ɪ] *n no pl, form* unanimité *f*
unanimous [juːˈnænɪməs, *Am:* -əməs] *adj* unanime
unanimously *adv* à l'unanimité
unannounced [ˌʌnəˈnaʊnst] **I.** *adj* imprévu(e) **II.** *adv* sans prévenir
unanswerable *adj* incontestable; (*question*) resté(e) sans réponse
unanswered [ˌʌnˈɑːnsəd, *Am:* -ˈænsɚd] *adj* sans réponse
unappetizing [ˌʌnˈæpɪtaɪzɪŋ, *Am:* -ˈæpə-] *adj* GASTR peu appétissant(e)
unappreciated [ˌʌnəˈpriːʃieɪtɪd, *Am:* -t̬ɪd] *adj* peu apprécié(e)
unappreciative [ˌʌnəˈpriːʃiətɪv, *Am:* -t̬ɪv] *adj* indifférent(e)
unapproachable [ˌʌnəˈprəʊtʃəbl, *Am:* -ˈproʊ-] *adj* **1.** (*protected from entering*) inaccessible **2.** (*not friendly*) inabordable
unarguable [ʌnˈɑːgjuəbl, *Am:* -ˈɑːr-] *adj* incontestable
unarmed [ˌʌnˈɑːmd, *Am:* ˈɑːrmd] *adj* (*person*) non armé(e); (*combat*) sans armes
unashamed [ˌʌnəˈʃeɪmd] *adj* (*joy, relief*) non dissimulé(e); (*nationalism*) éhonté(e); **to be** ~ **about sth** ne pas avoir honte de qc
unasked [ˌʌnˈɑːskt, *Am:* -ˈæskt] **I.** *adj* **1.** (*not questioned: question*) non formulé(e) **2.** (*spontaneous*) spontané(e) **II.** *adv* spontanément; **he came in** ~ il est entré sans y avoir été invité
unassuming [ˌʌnəˈsjuːmɪŋ, *Am:* -ˈsuː-] *adj* modeste
unattached [ˌʌnəˈtætʃt] *adj* libre; (*journalist, worker*) indépendant(e)
unattainable [ˌʌnəˈteɪnəbl] *adj* inaccessible
unattended [ˌʌnəˈtendɪd] *adj* sans surveillance
unattractive [ˌʌnəˈtræktɪv] *adj* **1.** (*quite ugly*) peu attrayant(e); **she's not** ~ elle est plutôt belle **2.** (*unpleasant*) déplaisant(e)
unaudited [ˌʌnˈɔːdɪtɪd] *adj* FIN non vérifié(e)
unauthorized [ˌʌnˈɔːθəraɪzd, *Am:* -ˈɑː-] *adj* non autorisé(e)
unavailable [ˌʌnəˈveɪləbl] *adj* indisponible; **she's** ~ elle n'est pas libre
unavoidable [ˌʌnəˈvɔɪdəbl] *adj* inévitable
unavoidably *adv* inévitablement; **to be** ~ **detained** avoir un empêchement
unaware [ˌʌnəˈweəʳ, *Am:* -ˈwer] *adj* **to be** ~ **of sth** ne pas être conscient de qc; (*not informed*) ignorer qc; **to be not** ~ **of sth** avoir conscience de qc
unawares *adv* inconsciemment; (*to take, catch*) au dépourvu
unbalanced [ˌʌnˈbælənst] *adj* **1.** (*uneven*) mal équilibré(e); FIN (*account*) non soldé(e); (*attitude, report*) partial(e) **2.** PSYCH déséquilibré(e)
unbearable [ˌʌnˈbeərəbl, *Am:* -ˈberə-] *adj* insupportable
unbearably *adv* incroyablement
unbeatable [ˌʌnˈbiːtəbl, *Am:* -ˈbiːt̬ə-] *adj* imbattable
unbeaten [ˌʌnˈbiːtn] *adj* SPORT (*team, person*) invaincu(e); (*record*) qui n'a pas encore été battu(e)
unbecoming [ˌʌnbɪˈkʌmɪŋ] *adj* **1.** (*not flattering: clothes*) peu seyant(e) **2.** (*unpleasant: attitude, conduct*) malséant(e)
unbeknown(st) [ˌʌnbɪˈnəʊn(st), *Am:* -ˈnoʊn] *adv form* ~ **to me/her** à mon/son insu
unbelievable [ˌʌnbɪˈliːvəbl] *adj* incroyable
unbeliever *n* REL non-croyant(e) *m(f)*
unbelieving *adj* incrédule
unbend [ˌʌnˈbend] **I.** *vt* redresser; (*arm, leg*) déplier **II.** *vi irr* **1.** (*straighten out*) se redresser **2.** (*relax*) se détendre
unbending *adj form* inflexible
unbias(s)ed [ˌʌnˈbaɪəst] *adj* impartial(e)
unbind [ˌʌnˈbaɪnd] *irr vt* délier

unbleached [ˌʌn'bliːtʃt] *adj* écru(e); (*paper, cloth*) sans chlore; (*flour*) non-traité(e)

unblinking [ˌʌn'blɪnkɪŋ] *adj* (*person*) impassible; (*gaze, stare, look*) fixe

unblushing [ˌʌn'blʌʃɪŋ] *adj* éhonté(e)

unbolt [ˌʌn'bəʊlt, *Am:* -'boʊlt] *vt* déverrouiller

unborn [ˌʌn'bɔːn, *Am:* -'bɔːrn] *adj* **1.** (*not born*) à naître **2.** (*future*) à venir

unbosom [ˌʌn'bʊzəm] *vt* **to ~ oneself to sb** ouvrir son cœur à qn

unbounded [ˌʌn'baʊndɪd] *adj* sans bornes

unbowed [ˌʌn'baʊd] *adj* invaincu(e)

unbreakable [ˌʌn'brəɪkəbl] *adj* **1.** (*unable to be broken*) incassable **2.** (*that must be kept: rule*) inviolable; (*promise*) sacré(e) **3.** SPORT (*record*) imbattable

unbribable [ˌʌn'braɪbəbl] *adj* POL, ECON incorruptible

unbridled [ˌʌn'braɪdld] *adj a. fig* débridé(e)

un-British [ˌʌn'brɪtɪʃ] *adj* peu britannique

unbroken [ʌn'brəʊkən, *Am:* -broʊ-] *adj* **1.** (*not broken or damaged*) intact(e) **2.** (*continuous*) ininterrompu(e) **3.** (*not surpassed: record*) qui n'a pas été battu(e) **4.** (*uncultivated: land*) vierge

unbuckle [ˌʌn'bʌkl] *vt* déboucler

unburden [ˌʌn'bɜːdn, *Am:* -'bɜːr-] *vt* soulager; **to ~ oneself of sth** se soulager de qc; **to ~ oneself to sb** ouvrir son cœur à qn

unbusinesslike [ʌn'bɪznɪslaɪk] *adj* peu professionnel(le)

unbutton [ˌʌn'bʌtn] *vt* déboutonner

uncalled-for [ˌʌn'kɔːldfɔːʳ, *Am:* -fɔːr] *adj pej* déplacé(e)

uncanny [ˌʌn'kænɪ] *adj* <-ier, -iest> étrange; (*likeness*) troublant(e)

uncared for [ˌʌn'keədfɔːʳ, *Am:* -'kerdfɔːr] *adj* négligé(e); (*garden*) laissé(e) à l'abandon

unceasing [ˌʌn'siːsɪŋ] *adj form* incessant(e)

unceremonious [ˌʌnˌserɪ'məʊnɪəs, *Am:* -'moʊ-] *adj* **1.** *pej* (*abrupt*) brusque **2.** (*informal*) informel(le)

uncertain [ʌn'sɜːtn, *Am:* -'sɜːr-] *adj* **1.** (*unsure*) incertain(e); **to be ~ of sth** n'être pas sûr de qc; **to be ~ whether ...** ne pas être certain si ... **2.** (*unknown, not defined: future*) incertain(e); **in no ~ terms** en des termes clairs **3.** (*volatile*) changeant(e); (*temper*) versatile; (*weather*) variable; (*person*) inconstant(e)

uncertainty <-ies> *n* incertitude *f*

unchallenged [ˌʌn'tʃælɪndʒd] *adj* incontesté(e); **to allow sth to go ~** laisser passer qc sans contester

unchanged [ˌʌn'tʃeɪndʒd] *adj* inchangé(e)

uncharacteristic [ˌʌnkærəktər'ɪstɪk, *Am:* ʌnˌkerɪk-] *adj* inhabituel(le)

uncharitable [ˌʌn'tʃærɪtəbl, *Am:* -'tʃerət̬ə-] *adj* peu charitable; **it is ~ of you to say so** ce n'est pas gentil de ta part de le dire

unchecked [ˌʌn'tʃekt] *adj* **1.** (*unrestrained*) incontrôlé(e); (*enthusiasm, anger*) non contenu(e); **to be ~ by sth** ne pas être contenu par qc **2.** (*not examined*) non vérifié(e)

unchristian [ˌʌn'krɪstʃən] *adj pej* peu chrétien(ne)

uncivil [ˌʌn'sɪvl] *adj pej, form* grossier(-ère); **to be ~ to sb** être grossier envers qn

uncivilised *adj Brit, Aus,* **uncivilized** [ʌn'sɪvəlaɪzd] *adj* **1.** (*not civilised*) barbare **2.** (*not polite: behaviour, argument*) incorrect(e); (*hour*) indu(e)

unclaimed [ʌn'kleɪmd] *adj* non réclamé(e)

uncle ['ʌŋkl] *n* oncle *m*

unclean [ˌʌn'kliːn] *adj* **1.** (*unhygienic*) sale **2.** REL impur(e)

unclear [ˌʌn'klɪəʳ, *Am:* -'klɪr] *adj* incertain(e); **to be ~ about sth** ne pas être sûr de qc; **it is ~ (as to) whether/what ...** on ne sait pas encore si/ce que ...

uncomfortable [ʌn'kʌmftəbl, *Am:* -fɚt̬ə-] *adj* (*shoes, chair*) inconfortable; (*silence, situation*) gênant(e); **to feel ~ about sth** être mal à l'aise à propos de qc; (*embarrassed*) se sentir gêné par qc; **to be ~ on a chair** être mal assis sur une chaise

uncomfortably *adv* inconfortablement

uncommitted [ˌʌnkə'mɪtɪd, *Am:* -'mɪt̬-] *adj* (*person*) non engagé(e); (*funds*) non affecté(e); **to remain ~** ne pas s'engager

uncommon [ˌʌn'kɒmən, *Am:* -'kɑːmən] *adj* rare

uncommunicative [ˌʌnkə'mjuːnɪ kətɪv, *Am:* -t̬ɪv] *adj* peu communicatif(-ive); **to be ~ about sb/sth** être peu expansif à propos de qn/qc

uncomplaining [ʊnˌkɒm'pleɪnɪŋ] *adj* **to be ~** ne pas se plaindre

uncomplimentary [ʌnˌkɒplɪ'mentəri, *Am:* ʌnˌkɑːmplə'ment̬ɚ-] *adj* peu flatteur(-euse)

uncompromising [ʌn'kɒmprə maɪzɪŋ, *Am:* -'kɑːm-] *adj* intransigeant(e)

unconcerned [ˌʌnkən'sɜːnd, *Am:* -'sɜːrnd] *adj* indifférent(e); **to be ~ about/with/by sth** être indifférent à qc; **to be ~ that ...** ne pas se soucier de savoir si ...

unconditional [ˌʌnkən'dɪʃənl] *adj* sans condition

unconfirmed [ˌʌnkən'fɜːmd, *Am:* -'fɜːrmd] *adj* non confirmé(e)

unconnected [ˌʌnkə'nektɪd] *adj* sans rapport

unconscionable [ʌn'kɒnʃ(ə)nəbl, *Am:* -'kɑːn-] *adj pej, form* déraisonnable

unconscious [ʌn'kɒnʃəs, *Am:* -'kɑːn-] **I.** *adj a. fig* inconscient(e); **to knock sb ~** assommer qn; **the ~ mind** l'inconscient; **to be ~ of sth** *form* ne pas avoir conscience de qc **II.** *n no pl* PSYCH **the ~** l'inconscient

unconsciously *adv* inconsciemment

unconsciousness *n no pl* MED inconscience *f*

unconsidered [ˌʌnkən'sɪdəd, *Am:* -ɚd] *adj form* inconsidéré(e)

unconstitutional ['ʌnˌkɒnstɪ'tjuːʃənl, *Am:*

-ˌkɑːnstəˈtuː-] *adj* inconstitutionnel(le)
unconsummated [ˌʌnˈkɒnsjʊmeɪtɪd] *adj* non consommé(e)
uncontested [ˌʌnkənˈtestɪd] *adj* incontesté(e)
uncontrollable *adj* incontrôlable
uncontrolled [ˌʌnkənˈtrəʊld, *Am:* -ˈtroʊld] *adj* incontrôlé(e)
unconventional [ˌʌnkənˈvəntʃənəl] *adj* peu conventionnel(le)
unconvincing [ˌʌnkənˈvɪnsɪŋ] *adj* peu convaincant(e)
uncooked [ˌʌnˈkʊkt] *adj* pas cuit(e)
uncooperative [ˌʌnkəʊˈɒpərətɪv, *Am:* -koʊˈɑːpɚət̬ɪv] *adj pej* peu coopératif(-ive)
uncoordinated [ˌʌnkəʊˈɔːdɪneɪtɪd, *Am:* ˌʌnkoʊˈɔːrdəneɪt̬ɪd] *adj pej* non coordonné(e); **to be ~** (*person*) manquer de coordination
uncork [ˌʌnˈkɔːk, *Am:* -ˈkɔːrk] *vt* déboucher
uncorroborated [ˌʌnkəˈrɒbəreɪtɪd, *Am:* -ˈrɑːbəreɪt̬ɪd] *adj* non corroboré(e)
uncountable [ʌnˈkaʊntəbl, *Am:* -t̬ə-] *adj* LING non dénombrable
uncouple [ˌʌnˈkʌpl] *vt* **1.** (*detach*) détacher **2.** (*separate*) séparer
uncouth [ʌnˈkuːθ] *adj pej* grossier(-ère)
uncover [ʌnˈkʌvəʳ, *Am:* -ˈkʌvɚ] *vt* **1.** (*lay bare*) découvrir **2.** (*expose*) dévoiler
uncritical [ˌʌnˈkrɪtɪkl, *Am:* -ˈkrɪt̬-] *adj pej* peu critique; **to be ~ of sb/sth** manquer d'esprit critique à l'égard de qn/qc
uncrowned [ˌʌnˈkraʊnd] *adj* sans couronne
UNCTAD *n abbr of* **United Nations Commissions for Trade and Development** CNUCED *f*
unctuous [ˈʌŋktʃʊəs, *Am:* -tʃu-] *adj form* mielleux(-euse)
uncut [ˌʌnˈkʌt] *adj* non coupé(e); (*film*) en version intégrale; (*diamond*) brut(e)
undamaged [ʌnˈdæmɪdʒd] *adj* intact(e)
undated [ˌʌnˈdeɪtɪd, *Am:* -t̬ɪd] *adj* non daté(e)
undaunted [ˌʌnˈdɔːntɪd, *Am:* -ˈdɑːnt̬ɪd] *adj* inébranlable; **to be ~ by sth** ne pas être découragé par qc; **to remain ~** ne pas se laisser démonter
undecided [ˌʌndɪˈsaɪdɪd] *adj* indécis(e); **to be ~ whether/when …** ne pas savoir encore si/quand …
undefinable [ˌʌndɪˈfaɪnəbl] *adj Am, Aus s.* **indefinable**
undemocratic [ˌʌndeməˈkrætɪk] *adj pej* peu démocratique
undemonstrative [ˌʌndɪˈmɒnstrətɪv, *Am:* -ˈmɑːnstrət̬ɪv] *adj form* peu démonstratif(-ive)
undeniable [ˌʌndɪˈnaɪəbl] *adj* indéniable
undeniably *adv* incontestablement
under [ˈʌndəʳ, *Am:* -dɚ] **I.** *prep* **1.** (*below*) sous; **~ the table/water** sous la table/l'eau; **~ it** dessous; **to live ~ sb** habiter au-dessous de qn; **~ there** là-dessous **2.** (*supporting*) sous; **to break ~ the weight** céder sous le poids **3.** (*less than*) moins de; **~ £10/the age of 30** moins de 10 livres/trente ans **4.** (*governed by*) sous; **~ Henry II** sous Henri II; **I am ~ orders to say nothing** j'ai reçu l'ordre de ne rien dire **5.** (*in state of*) **~ these conditions** dans ces conditions; **~ the circumstances** vu les circonstances; **~ repair/observation** en réparation/observation **6.** (*in category of*) par; **to classify the books ~ author** classer les livres par auteur **7.** (*according to*) d'après; **~ the treaty** conformément au traité ▶**to be ~ sb's <u>influence</u>** subir l'influence de qn; **to put sth ~ the <u>microscope</u>** regarder qc à la loupe; **to be ~ <u>way</u>** être en route; *s. a.* **over II.** *adv* au-dessous, en dessous; **as ~** comme ci-dessous; **to get out from ~** *a. fig* remonter à la surface
underage, under age [ˌʌndərˈeɪdʒ, *Am:* -dɚˈ-] *adj* mineur(e)
underage drinking *n* consommation *f* d'alcool chez les mineurs
underarm [ˌʌndərˈɑːm, *Am:* ˌʌndɚˈɑːrm] **I.** *n* aisselles *fpl* **II.** *adj* **1.** (*related to armpit: hair*) des aisselles; (*deodorant*) pour les aisselles **2.** SPORT par en dessous **III.** *adv* par en dessous
underbelly [ˈʌndəˌbeli, *Am:* -dɚ-] *n* **1.** (*abdomen*) bas-ventre *m* **2.** (*vulnerable area*) point *m* faible
undercarriage [ˈʌndəkærɪdʒ, *Am:* -dɚker-] *n Brit* AVIAT train *m* d'atterrissage
undercharge [ˌʌndəˈtʃɑːdʒ, *Am:* ˈʌndɚtʃɑːrdʒ] **I.** *vt* ne pas faire payer assez à; **to ~ sb by ten francs** faire payer qn dix francs moins cher **II.** *vi* demander trop peu
underclass [ˈʌndəklɑːs, *Am:* -dɚklæs] *n no pl* sous-prolétariat *m*
underclothes [ˈʌndəkləʊðz, *Am:* -dɚkloʊ-] *npl form* sous-vêtements *mpl*
undercover [ˌʌndəˈkʌvəʳ, *Am:* -dɚˈkʌvɚ] **I.** *adj* secret(-ète) **II.** *adv* clandestinement
undercurrent [ˈʌndəkʌrənt, *Am:* -dɚkɜːr-] *n* **1.** (*current in sea*) courant *m* sous-marin **2.** *fig* relent *m*
undercut [ˌʌndəˈkʌt, *Am:* -dɚˈ-] *irr vt* **1.** (*charge less: competitor*) vendre moins que; (*prices*) casser **2.** (*undermine*) saper
underdeveloped [ˌʌndədɪˈveləpt, *Am:* -dɚdɪˈ-] *adj* sous-développé(e)
underdog [ˈʌndədɒg, *Am:* -dɚdɑːg] *n* opprimé(e) *m(f)*
underdone [ˌʌndəˈdʌn, *Am:* -dɚˈ-] *adj* pas assez cuit(e); (*steak*) saignant(e)
underemployed [ˌʌndərɪmˈplɔɪd, *Am:* -dɚɪmˈplɔɪd] *adj* sous-employé(e)
underestimate [ˌʌndərˈestɪmeɪt, *Am:* -dɚˈestə-] **I.** *vt* sous-estimer **II.** *n* sous-estimation *f*
underexpose [ˌʌndərɪkˈspəʊz, *Am:* -dɚɪkˈspoʊz] *vt* PHOT sous-exposer
underexposure [ˌʌndərɪkˈspəʊʒəʳ, *Am:* -dɚɪkˈspoʊʒɚ] *n no pl* PHOT sous-exposition *f*
underfed [ˌʌndəˈfed, *Am:* -dɚˈ-] *n* sous-ali-

menté(e)

underfloor heating [ˌʌndəˈflɔːhiːtɪŋ, *Am:* -dɚflɔːrˈhiːt̬ɪŋ] *n* chauffage *m* par le sol

underfoot [ˌʌndəˈfʊt, *Am:* -dɚ-] *adv* sous les pieds; **to trample sb/sth** ~ *a. fig* piétiner qn/qc

underfunded [ˌʌndəˈfʌnd, *Am:* -dɚˈ-] *adj* **to be** ~ manquer de fonds

undergarment [ˈʌndəgɑːmənt, *Am:* -dɚgɑːr-] *n form* sous-vêtement *m*

undergo [ˌʌndəˈgəʊ, *Am:* -dɚˈgoʊ] *irr vt* subir; (*treatment*) suivre

undergraduate [ˌʌndəˈgrædʒʊət, *Am:* -dɚˈgrædʒuət] *n* étudiant(e) *m(f)* (de premier cycle); ~ **programme** programme *m* de premier cycle

underground [ˈʌndəgraʊnd, *Am:* -dɚ-] **I.** *adj* **1.** (*below earth surface*) souterrain(e) **2.** (*clandestine*) clandestin(e) **3.** ART, MUS underground *inv* **II.** *adv* **1.** (*beneath the ground*) sous terre **2.** (*secretly*) clandestinement; **to go** ~ entrer dans la clandestinité **III.** *n* **1.** *no pl, Brit* (*trains*) **the Underground** le métro; **by** ~ en métro **2.** (*clandestine movement*) **the** ~ le mouvement clandestin **3.** (*alternative group*) underground *m*

underground passage *n* passage *m* souterrain **underground station** *n* station *f* de métro

undergrowth [ˈʌndəgrəʊθ, *Am:* -dɚgroʊθ] *n no pl* sous-bois *m*

underhand [ˈʌndəhænd, *Am:* ˌʌndɚˈ-] **I.** *adj* **1.** *Brit, pej* sournois(e) **2.** *Am s.* **underarm** **II.** *n Am s.* **underarm**

underlay [ˌʌndəˈleɪ, *Am:* -dɚˈ-] **I.** *pt of* **underlie** **II.** *n no pl, Brit, Aus* thibaude *f*

underlie [ˌʌndəˈlaɪ, *Am:* -dɚˈ-] *irr vt* sous-tendre

underline [ˌʌndəˈlaɪn, *Am:* -dɚˈ-] *vt a. fig* souligner

underling [ˈʌndəlɪŋ, *Am:* -dɚlɪŋ] *n pej* sous-fifre *m*

underlying [ˌʌndəˈlaɪɪŋ, *Am:* -dɚ-] *adj* sous-jacent(e)

undermanned [ˌʌndəˈmænd, *Am:* -dɚˈ-] *adj* à court de personnel

undermentioned [ˌʌndəˈmenʃnd, *Am:* -dɚˈ-] *adj Brit, form* mentionné(e) ci-dessous

undermine [ˌʌndəˈmaɪn, *Am:* -dɚˈ-] *vt a. fig* saper

underneath [ˌʌndəˈniːθ, *Am:* -dɚˈ-] **I.** *prep* sous, au-dessous de **II.** *adv* (en) dessous; *s. a.* **under** **III.** *adj* d'en dessous **IV.** *n* dessous *m*

undernourished [ˌʌndəˈnʌrɪʃt, *Am:* -dɚˈnɜːr-] *adj* sous-alimenté(e)

underpaid [ˌʌndəˈpeɪd, *Am:* -dɚˈ-] *adj* sous-payé(e)

underpants [ˈʌndəpænts, *Am:* -dɚ-] *npl* slip *m*

underpass [ˈʌndəpɑːs, *Am:* -dɚpæs] <-es> *n* passage *m* souterrain

underpay [ˌʌndəˈpeɪ, *Am:* -dɚˈ-] *irr vt* sous-payer

underpin [ˌʌndəˈpɪn, *Am:* -dɚ-] *vi a. fig* étayer

underpinning *n a. fig* étayage *m*

underplay [ˈʌndəpleɪ, *Am:* ˌʌndɚˈpleɪ] *vt* minimiser

underpopulated [ˌʌndəˈpɒpjʊleɪtɪd, *Am:* -dɚˈpɑːpjə-] *adj* sous-peuplé(e)

underprivileged [ˌʌndəˈprɪvəlɪdʒd, *Am:* -dɚˈ-] **I.** *adj* défavorisé(e) **II.** *n pl* **the** ~ les défavorisés *mpl*

underrate [ˌʌndəˈreɪt, *Am:* -dɚˈ-] *vt* sous-estimer

underscore [ˌʌndəˈskɔːʳ, *Am:* -dɚˈskɔːr] *vt a. fig* souligner

undersea [ˈʌndəsiː, *Am:* -dɚ-] *adj* sous-marin(e)

undersell [ˌʌndəˈsel, *Am:* -dɚˈ-] *irr vt* **1.** (*offer goods cheaper*) **to** ~ **sb** vendre moins cher que qn **2.** (*undervalue*) sous-estimer; **to** ~ **oneself** se sous-estimer

undershirt [ˈʌndəʃɜːt, *Am:* -dɚʃɜːrt] *n Am* maillot *m* de corps

underside [ˈʌndəsaɪd, *Am:* -dɚ-] *n* dessous *m*

undersigned [ˈʌndəsaɪnd, *Am:* -dɚ-] *n form* **I, the** ~ **...** je soussigné(e) ...

undersize(d) [ˌʌndəˈsaɪz(d), *Am:* ˈʌndɚsaɪz(d)] *adj* trop petit(e)

underskirt [ˈʌndəskɜːt, *Am:* -dɚskɜːrt] *n* jupon *m*

understaffed [ˌʌndəˈstɑːft, *Am:* -dɚˈstæft] *adj* à court de personnel

understand [ˌʌndəˈstænd, *Am:* -dɚˈ-] *irr* **I.** *vt* **1.** (*perceive meaning*) comprendre; **to make oneself understood** se faire comprendre; **to** ~ **one another** se comprendre; **the problem as I** ~ **it** si je comprends bien le problème **2.** (*believe, infer*) **it is understood that ...** il est entendu que ...; **I** ~ **that you're leaving** j'ai cru comprendre que tu partais; **to give sb to** ~ **that ...** faire comprendre à qn que ... **II.** *vi* comprendre; **to** ~ **about sb/sth** comprendre qn/qc; **am I to** ~ **from this that ...?** dois-je comprendre par là que ...?; **I** ~ **from the letter that ...** j'ai cru comprendre en lisant la lettre que ...

understandable *adj* compréhensible

understanding **I.** *n* **1.** *no pl* (*comprehension*) compréhension *f*; **to be beyond all** ~ être incompréhensible; **my** ~ **was that ...** j'ai compris que ...; **to have no** ~ **of sth** ne rien comprendre à qc; **to show great** ~ être très compréhensif **2.** (*interpretation*) interprétation *f*; **my limited** ~ **of Islam does not allow me judge** ma connaissance limitée de l'Islam ne me permet pas de juger **3.** (*agreement*) entente *f*; **to come to an** ~ s'entendre; **to do sth on the** ~ **that** faire qc à la condition que +*subj* **II.** *adj* compréhensif(-ive)

understate [ˌʌndəˈsteɪt, *Am:* -dɚˈ-] *vt* minimiser

understated *adj* discret(-ète)

understatement *n* litote *f*; **it's the** ~ **of the**

year c'est le moins qu'on puisse dire

understood [ˌʌndəˈstʊd, *Am:* -dɚˈ-] *pt, pp of* **understand**

understudy [ˈʌndəstʌdɪ, *Am:* -dɚ-] THEAT I. <-ies> *n* doublure *f;* **to be the ~ for sb/sth** être la doublure de qn/qc II. <-ie-> *vt* doubler; **to ~ a part** doubler un acteur dans un rôle

undertake [ˌʌndəˈteɪk, *Am:* -dɚˈ-] *vt irr* 1. (*set about, take on*) entreprendre; (*mission*) se charger de; (*a role*) assumer 2. *form* (*commit oneself to, guarantee*) **to ~ to** +*infin* s'engager à +*infin;* **to ~ (that)** … promettre que …

undertaker *n* 1. (*person*) entrepreneur *m* des pompes funèbres 2. (*business*) pompes *fpl* funèbres

undertaking *n* 1. (*professional project*) entreprise *f* 2. (*pledge, formal promise*) promesse *f;* **an ~ to** +*infin* une promesse de +*infin;* **to give an ~ that …** donner sa promesse que …

undertone [ˈʌndətəʊn, *Am:* -dɚtoʊn] *n* 1. *no pl* (*low voice*) voix *f* basse; **to say sth in an ~** dire qc à voix basse 2. (*undercurrent, insinuation*) note *f*

underused [ˌʌndəˈjuːzd, *Am:* -dɚˈ-], **underutilized** [ˌʌndəˈjuːtɪlaɪzd, *Am:* -dɚˈjuːt̬-] *adj* insuffisamment utilisé(e)

undervalue [ˌʌndəˈvæljuː, *Am:* -dɚˈ-] *vt* sous-estimer

underwater [ˈʌndəwɔːtəʳ, *Am:* -dɚˈwɑːt̬ɚ] I. *adj* sous-marin(e) II. *adv* sous l'eau

underwear [ˈʌndəweəʳ, *Am:* -dɚwer] *n no pl* sous-vêtements *mpl*

underweight [ˌʌndəˈweɪt, *Am:* -dɚˈ-] *adj* **to be ~** avoir un poids insuffisant

underworld [ˈʌndəwɜːld, *Am:* -dɚwɜːrld] *n* 1. *no pl* (*criminal world*) **the ~** le milieu 2. (*world of the dead*) **the ~** les enfers *mpl*

underwrite [ˌʌndəˈraɪt, *Am:* ˈʌndɚraɪt] *vt irr* 1. (*sign*) souscrire à 2. (*subsidize*) subventionner 3. (*provide insurance*) garantir

underwriter *n* **the ~** les assureurs

undesirable [ˌʌndɪˈzaɪərəbl, *Am:* -ˈzaɪrəbl] I. *adj pej* indésirable II. *n pl, pej* indésirable *mf*

undetected [ˌʌndɪˈtektɪd] *adj* non décelé(e); **to go ~** passer inaperçu(e)

undeveloped [ˌʌndɪˈveləpt] *adj* non exploité(e)

undid [ʌnˈdɪd] *pt of* **undo**

undies [ˈʌndɪz] *npl inf* lingerie *f*

undisclosed [ˌʌndɪsˈkləʊzd, *Am:* -ˈkloʊzd] *adj* non divulgué(e)

undiscovered [ˌʌndɪsˈkʌvəd, *Am:* -ɚd] *adj* inconnu(e)

undisputed [ˌʌndɪˈspjuːtɪd, *Am:* -t̬ɪd] *adj* incontesté(e)

undistinguished [ˌʌndɪˈstɪŋgwɪʃt] *adj pej* peu distingué(e)

undisturbed [ˌʌndɪˈstɜːbd, *Am:* -ˈstɜːrbd] *adj* paisible; **to leave sth ~** ne pas toucher à qc

undivided [ˌʌndɪˈvaɪdɪd] *adj a. fig* entier(-ère)

undo [ʌnˈduː] *irr vt* 1. (*unfasten: buttons, laces*) défaire 2. (*cancel, wipe out*) annuler; (*legislation*) révoquer; (*damage*) réparer ▶**what's done cannot be undone** ce qui est fait est fait

undoing *n no pl, form* perte *f;* **drink was his ~** l'alcool a causé sa perte

undone [ˌʌnˈdʌn] I. *pp of* **undo** II. *adj* 1. (*not fastened*) défait(e); **to come ~** se défaire 2. (*uncompleted*) inachevé(e)

undoubted [ʌnˈdaʊtɪd, *Am:* -t̬ɪd] *adj* incontestable

undoubtedly *adv* indubitablement

undreamed of [ʌnˈdriːmdɒv, *Am:* -ɑːv], **undreamt of** *adj* insoupçonné(e)

undress [ʌnˈdres] I. *vt a. fig* déshabiller; **to ~ sb with one's eyes** déshabiller qn du regard II. *vi* se déshabiller

undressed *adj* déshabillé(e); **to get ~** se déshabiller

undrinkable [ʌnˈdrɪŋkəbl] *adj* (*bad*) imbuvable

undue [ˌʌnˈdjuː, *Am:* -ˈduː] *adj form* excessif(-ive)

undulate [ˈʌndjʊleɪt, *Am:* -djə-] *vi form* onduler

undulating *adj form* ondulant(e); (*landscape*) vallonné(e)

unduly [ˌʌnˈdjuːlɪ, *Am:* -ˈduː-] *adv* excessivement

undying [ˌʌnˈdaɪɪŋ] *adj liter* immortel(le); (*love, gratitude*) éternel(le)

unearned [ˌʌnˈɜːnd, *Am:* -ˈɜːrnd] *adj* 1. (*undeserved*) immérité(e) 2. (*not worked for*) **~ income** rentes *fpl*

unearth [ʌnˈɜːθ, *Am:* -ˈɜːrθ] *vt* 1. (*dig up*) déterrer 2. *fig* (*truth*) découvrir; (*person*) dénicher

unearthly *adj* <-ier, -iest> 1. (*unsettling: noise, scream*) inhumain(e) 2. *pej, inf* **at an ~ hour** à une heure indue 3. (*not from the earth*) surnaturel(le)

unease [ʌnˈiːz] *n no pl* malaise *m*

uneasy *adj* <-ier, -iest> 1. (*ill at ease*) mal à l'aise; (*silence*) gêné(e); **to feel ~ about sb/sth** se sentir gêné par rapport à qn/qc 2. (*apprehensive*) inquiet(-ète) 3. (*difficult: relationship, compromise*) difficile

uneatable [ʌnˈiːtəbl] *adj* immangeable

uneconomic(al) [ˈʌnˌiːkəˈnɒmɪk(l), *Am:* -ˌekəˈnɑːmɪk-] *adj* non rentable

uneducated [ʌnˈedʒʊkeɪtɪd, *Am:* -t̬ɪd] *adj* 1. (*having not studied*) **to be ~** ne pas avoir fait d'études 2. *pej* inculte

unemotional [ˌʌnɪˈməʊʃənl, *Am:* -ˈmoʊ-] *adj* impassible

unemployable *adj* inemployable

unemployed [ˌʌnɪmˈplɔɪd] I. *n* **the ~** *pl* les chômeurs II. *adj* au chômage

unemployment [ˌʌnɪmˈplɔɪmənt] *n no pl* chômage *m*

unemployment benefit *n* allocation *f* de

U

chômage **unemployment insurance** *n Am* assurance *f* chômage
unending [ʌn'endɪŋ] *adj* interminable
unenforceable [ˌʌnɪn'fɔːsəbl, *Am:* -'fɔːr-] *adj* inapplicable
unengaged [ˌʌnɪŋ'geɪdʒd, *Am:* -ɪn'-] *adj* libre
un-English [ˌʌn'ɪŋglɪʃ] *adj* peu anglais(e)
unenlightened [ˌʌnɪn'laɪtnd] *adj* peu éclairé(e)
unenviable [ˌʌn'envɪəbl] *adj pej* peu enviable
unequal [ˌʌn'iːkwəl] *adj* inégal(e); **to be ~ to a task** ne pas être à la hauteur d'une tâche
unequaled *adj Am,* **unequalled** *adj Brit* inégalé(e)
unequivocal [ˌʌnɪ'kwɪvəkl] *adj* sans équivoque; (*success*) incontestable
unerring [ʌn'ɜːrɪŋ] *adj* infaillible
UNESCO [juː'neskəʊ, *Am:* -koʊ] *n no pl abbr of* **United Nations Educational, Scientific and Cultural Organization** UNESCO *f*
unethical [ʌn'eθɪkəl] *adj* contraire à l'éthique
uneven [ˌʌn'iːvn] *adj* **1.** (*not flat or level*) *a.* MED irrégulier(-ère) **2.** (*unequal*) inégal(e)
uneventful *adj a. pej* calme
unexceptionable *adj form* irréprochable
unexceptional [ˌʌnɪk'sepʃnəl] *adj* ordinaire
unexciting [ˌʌnɪk'saɪtɪŋ] *adj* peu passionnant(e)
unexpected [ˌʌnɪk'spektɪd] **I.** *adj* inattendu(e) **II.** *n no pl* **the ~** l'inattendu *m*
unexplained [ˌʌnɪk'spleɪnd] *adj* inexpliqué(e)
unexploded [ˌʌnɪk'spləʊdɪd] *adj* qui n'a pas explosé
unexploited [ˌʌnɪk'splɔɪtɪd] *adj* inexploité(e)
unexplored [ˌʌnɪk'splɔːd, *Am:* -'splɔːrd] *adj* inexploré(e)
unexpressed [ˌʌnɪk'sprest] *adj* inexprimé(e)
unexpressive [ˌʌnɪk'spresɪv] *adj* inexpressif(-ive)
unexpurgated [ˌʌn'ekspɜːgeɪtɪd, *Am:* -spɚgeɪt̬ɪd] *adj* (*edition*) intégral(e)
unfailing [ʌn'feɪlɪŋ] *adj* infaillible
unfair [ˌʌn'feəʳ, *Am:* -'fer] *adj* injuste
unfaithful [ˌʌn'feɪθfʊl] *adj* infidèle
unfaltering [ʌn'fɔːltərɪŋ, *Am:* -'fɑːlt̬ɚɪŋ] *adj* assuré(e)
unfamiliar [ˌʌnfə'mɪlɪəʳ, *Am:* -'mɪljɚ] *adj* **1.** (*new: sound, face, place*) peu familier(-ère); (*ideas, situation*) inhabituel(le); (*author*) peu connu(e) **2.** (*unacquainted*) **to be ~ with sth** mal connaître qc
unfashionable [ʌn'fæʃənəbl] *adj* démodé(e)
unfasten [ˌʌn'fɑːsn, *Am:* -'fæsn] **I.** *vt* défaire **II.** *vi* se défaire
unfathomable [ʌn'fæðəməbl] *adj a. fig* insondable; **for some ~ reason…** pour on ne sait trop quelle raison…
unfavorable *adj Am, Aus,* **unfavourable** [ˌʌn'feɪvrəbl] *adj Brit, Aus* **1.** (*not favourable*) défavorable **2.** ECON (*balance of trade*) déficitaire
unfeeling [ʌn'fiːlɪŋ] *adj pej* insensible
unfeigned [ʌn'feɪnd] *adj* non feint(e)
unfettered [ʌn'fetəʳəd, *Am:* -'fet̬ɚd] *adj* sans entrave; (*emotion*) non refoulé(e); **to be ~ by sth** être libre de qc
unfinished [ˌʌn'fɪnɪʃt] *adj* **1.** (*unexecuted*) inachevé(e) **2.** *Am* (*without finish*) mal fini(e)
unfit [ˌʌn'fɪt] *adj* <-tt-> **1.** (*unhealthy*) **to be ~** ne pas être en forme; **to be ~ to travel/work** ne pas être en état de voyager/travailler **2.** *pej* (*without requisite qualities*) inapte; **to be ~ for work** être inapte au travail **3.** (*unsuitable*) impropre; **to be ~ for consumption** impropre à la consommation; **~ for publication/habitation** impubliable/inhabitable
unfitted *adj* **to be ~ for sth** ne pas être adapté à qc; **to be ~ for sb** ne pas convenir à
unflagging [ˌʌn'flægɪŋ] *adj* inlassable
unflappable [ˌʌn'flæpəbl] *adj inf* imperturbable
unflinching [ʌn'flɪntʃɪŋ] *adj* résolu(e); (*bravery, resolve*) inébranlable
unfold [ʌn'fəʊld, *Am:* -'foʊld] **I.** *vt* **1.** (*open out*) ouvrir **2.** *form* (*make known*) dévoiler **II.** *vi* **1.** (*develop*) se dérouler **2.** (*become revealed*) se révéler **3.** (*become unfolded*) s'ouvrir
unforeseeable [ˌʌnfɔː'siːəbl, *Am:* -fɔːr'-] *adj* imprévisible
unforeseen [ˌʌnfɔː'siːn, *Am:* -fɔːr'-] *adj* imprévu(e)
unforgettable [ˌʌnfə'getəbl, *Am:* -fɚ'get̬-] *adj* inoubliable
unforgivable [ˌʌnfə'gɪvəbl, *Am:* -fɚ'-] *adj pej* impardonnable
unfortunate [ʌn'fɔːtʃʊnət, *Am:* -'fɔːrtʃnət] **I.** *adj* **1.** (*luckless*) malchanceux(-euse); **the ~ man** le pauvre homme; **to be ~ enough to fall** avoir la malchance de tomber **2.** *pej, form* (*regrettable*) fâcheux(-euse) **II.** *n* pauvre *mf*
unfortunately *adv* malheureusement
unfounded [ˌʌn'faʊndɪd] *adj* infondé(e)
unfreeze [ˌʌn'friːz] *irr* **I.** *vt* dégeler; (*credits, account*) débloquer **II.** *vi* dégeler
unfrequented [ˌʌnfrɪ'kwentɪd, *Am:* ʌn'friːkwent̬ɪd] *adj* peu fréquenté(e)
unfriendly [ˌʌn'frendlɪ] *adj* <-ier, -iest> (*person*) peu sympathique; (*tone, attitude*) peu amical(e); (*action, climate*) hostile; (*glance, reception*) froid(e); **user ~** peu convivial; **environmentally ~** nuisible à l'environnement
unfulfilled [ˌʌnfʊl'fɪld] *adj* **1.** (*not carried out: condition*) inaccompli(e); (*promise*) non tenu(e) **2.** (*unsatisfied*) frustré(e)
unfurl [ʌn'fɜːl, *Am:* -'fɜːrl] **I.** *vt* déployer **II.** *vi* se déployer
unfurnished [ˌʌn'fɜːnɪʃt, *Am:* -'fɜːr-] *adj* non meublé(e)

ungainly [ʌn'geɪnlɪ] *adj* <-ier, -iest> gauche

ungenerous [ʌn'dʒenərəs] *adj pej* malveillant(e)

ungentlemanly [ʌn'dʒentlmənlɪ] *adj pej* grossier(-ère)

ungodly [ʌn'gɒdlɪ, *Am:* -'gɑːd-] *adj* <-ier, -iest> **at this ~ hour** *inf* à une heure impossible

ungovernable [ʌn'gʌvənəbl, *Am:* -'gʌvɚnə-] *adj* incontrôlable

ungraceful [ˌʌn'greɪsfl] *adj* gauche

ungracious [ˌʌn'greɪʃəs] *adj* inconvenant(e)

ungrateful [ʌn'greɪtfl] *adj* ingrat(e)

ungrudging [ˌʌn'grʌdʒɪŋ] *adj* **1.** (*without reservation*) sans réserve; (*admiration*) sans bornes **2.** (*not resentful*) sincère

ungrudgingly *adv* sincèrement

unguarded [ˌʌn'gɑːdɪd, *Am:* -'gɑːr-] *adj* **1.** (*not defended*) non surveillé(e) **2.** (*unwary: remark*) irréfléchi(e); **in an ~ moment** dans un moment d'inattention

unhappiness [ʌn'hæpɪ] *n no pl* **1.** (*sorrow*) tristesse *f* **2.** (*displeasure*) mécontentement *m*

unhappy [ʌn'hæpɪ] *adj* <-ier, -iest> **1.** (*sad, unfortunate*) malheureux(-euse); (*face*) triste; **to make sb ~** rendre qn malheureux **2.** (*worried*) inquiet(-ète); **to be ~ about doing sth** ne pas aimer faire qc

unharmed [ʌn'hɑːmd, *Am:* -'hɑːrmd] *adj* indemne

UNHCR [ˌjuːeneɪtʃsiː'ɑː] *n no pl abbr of* **United Nations High Commission for Refugees** HCR *f*

unhealthy [ʌn'helθɪ] *adj* <-ier, -iest> malsain(e)

unheard [ʌn'hɜːd, *Am:* -'hɜːrd] *adj* **1.** (*not heard*) non entendu(e) **2.** (*ignored*) **to go ~** passer inaperçu(e)

unheard-of *adj* **1.** (*incredible*) inouï(e) **2.** (*ignored*) **to go ~** passer inaperçu; **to be ~** être inconnu

unhelpful [ʌn'helpfəl] *adj* peu utile; (*person*) peu serviable

unhinge [ʌn'hɪndʒ] *vt* **1.** (*take off hinges: door*) démonter **2.** (*disturb mentally*) déranger; **he seems a bit ~d** il a l'air dérangé

unholy [ʌn'həʊlɪ, *Am:* -'hoʊ-] *adj pej* **1.** (*sinful: alliance*) contre nature **2.** *inf* (*awful*) épouvantable

unhook [ʌn'hʊk] *vt* (*take off*) enlever

unhoped-for [ʌn'həʊptfɔːʳ, *Am:* -'hoʊptfɔːr] *adj* inespéré(e)

unhorse [ˌʌn'hɔːs, *Am:* -'hɔːrs] *vt* désarçonner

unhurt [ʌn'hɜːt, *Am:* -'hɜːrt] *adj* indemne

unhygienic *adj* peu hygiénique

UNICEF ['juːnɪsef] *n no pl abbr of* **United Nations International Children Fund** UNICEF *m*

unicorn ['juːnɪkɔːn, *Am:* -kɔːrn] *n* licorne *f*

unidentified [ˌʌnaɪ'dentɪfaɪd, *Am:* -t̬ə-] *adj* (*unknown*) non identifié(e)

unification [ˌjuːnɪfɪ'keɪʃn] *n no pl* unification *f*

uniform ['juːnɪfɔːm, *Am:* -nəfɔːrm] **I.** *n* uniforme *m* **II.** *adj* uniforme

uniformed *adj* en uniforme

uniformity [ˌjuːnɪ'fɔːmətɪ, *Am:* -nə'fɔːrmət̬ɪ] *n no pl, a. pej* uniformité *f*

uniformly *adv* uniformément

unify ['juːnɪfaɪ, *Am:* -nə-] *vt* unifier

unilateral [ˌjuːnɪ'lætrəl, *Am:* -nə'læt̬-] *adj* unilatéral(e)

unilaterally *adv* unilatéralement

unimaginable [ˌʌnɪ'mædʒnəbl] *adj* inimaginable

unimaginative *adj* (*person*) qui manque d'imagination; (*food, color, show*) peu original(e)

unimpeachable [ˌʌnɪm'piːtʃəbl] *adj form* inattaquable

unimportant [ˌʌnɪm'pɔːtənt, *Am:* -'pɔːr-] *adj* sans importance

uninformed [ˌʌnɪn'fɔːmd, *Am:* -'fɔːrmd] *adj* mal informé(e); **to be ~ about sth** ne pas être au courant de qc; **to be ~ about sb** être mal informé sur qn

uninhabitable *adj* inhabitable

uninhabited [ˌʌnɪn'hæbɪtɪd, *Am:* -t̬ɪd] *adj* inhabité(e)

uninhibited [ˌʌnɪn'hɪbɪtɪd, *Am:* -t̬ɪd] *adj* **1.** (*unselfconscious*) sans inhibitions; (*feeling*) non refréné(e) **2.** (*unrestricted*) déchaîné(e)

uninitiated [ˌʌnɪ'ʃieɪtɪd, *Am:* -t̬ɪd] **I.** *adj* non initié(e) **II.** *npl* **the ~** les non-initiés *mpl*

uninjured [ˌʌn'ɪndʒəd, *Am:* -dʒɚd] *adj* indemne

uninsured [ˌʌnɪn'ʃʊəd, *Am:* -'ʃʊrd] *adj* non assuré(e); **to be ~** ne pas être assuré

unintelligent [ˌʌnɪn'telɪdʒənt] *adj* inintelligent(e)

unintelligible [ˌʌnɪn'telɪdʒəbl] *adj* inintelligible

unintentional [ˌʌnɪn'tenʃənl] *adj* involontaire

unintentionally *adv* involontairement; **to be ~ funny** être drôle malgré soi

uninterested [ʌn'ɪntrɪstɪd] *adj* indifférent(e); **to be ~ in sb/sth** être indifférent à qn/qc

uninteresting *adj* inintéressant(e)

uninterrupted [ˌʌnɪntə'rʌptɪd] *adj* ininterrompu(e)

union ['juːnɪən, *Am:* -njən] *n* **1.** (*act of becoming united*) union *f* **2.** (*trade ~*) syndicat *m*; **~ demands** revendications *fpl* syndicales; **to be in the ~** être syndiqué **3.** *Brit* UNIV association *f* **4.** *form* (*marriage*) union *f* **5.** (*harmony*) harmonie *f*; **in perfect ~** en parfaite harmonie

union agreement *n*, **union contract** *n Am* accord *m* syndical **union dues** *n pl, Am* cotisations *fpl* syndicales

unionise ['juːnɪənaɪz, *Am:* -njə-] *Brit, Aus* **I.** *vt* syndiquer **II.** *vi* se syndiquer

U

unionist *n* **1.** (*trade union advocate*) syndicaliste *mf* **2.** *Brit* (*Northern Irish supporter of Britain*) unioniste *mf*

unionize ['ju:nɪənaɪz, *Am:* -njə-] *s.* **unionise**

Union Jack *n* **1.** (*British national flag*) **the ~** l'Union Jack *m* **2.** *form* (*union flag on ship*) pavillon *m* anglais **union member** *n* syndiqué(e) *m(f)* **union official** *n* dirigeant(e) m*(f)* syndical(e) **union representative** *n* représentant(e) m*(f)* syndical(e)

unique [ju:'ni:k] *adj* unique

uniqueness *n no pl* unicité *f*

unisex ['ju:nɪseks, *Am:* -nə-] *adj* unisexe

unison ['ju:nɪsn, *Am:* -nə-] *n no pl* unisson *m;* **in ~** à l'unisson

unit ['ju:nɪt] *n* **1.** (*fixed measuring quantity*) *a.* COM unité *f;* **~ of measurement** unité de mesure **2.** (*organized group*) unité *f;* **the family ~** le noyau familial **3.** (*part of larger entity*) section *f* **4.** (*element of furniture*) élément *m* **5.** (*mechanical device*) unité *f* **6.** (*chapter*) unité *f* **7.** *Am, Aus* (*apartment*) logement *m*

unit cost *n* COM coût *m* unitaire

unite [ju:'naɪt] **I.** *vt* unir **II.** *vi a.* POL, SOCIOL s'unir

united *adj* uni(e); **~ Germany** l'Allemagne réunifiée; **to be ~ against sth** être uni face à qc ►**~ we stand, divided we fall** l'union fait la force

United Arab Emirates *npl* **the ~** les Émirats arabes unis **United Kingdom** *n no pl* **the ~** le Royaume-Uni **United Nations** *n pl* **the ~** Les Nations *fpl* Unies **United States** *n* **the ~ of America** les États-Unis d'Amérique

unit price *n* prix *m* unitaire **unit trust** *n Brit* ≈SICAV *f*

unity ['ju:nətɪ, *Am:* -t̬ɪ] *n no pl* unité *f*

Univ. *n abbr of* **University** université *f*

universal [ˌju:nɪ'vɜ:sl, *Am:* -nə'vɜ:r-] **I.** *adj* universel(le) **II.** *n* **the ~** l'universel *m*

universe ['ju:nɪvɜ:s, *Am:* -nəvɜ:rs] *n no pl* **the ~** l'Univers *m*

university [ˌju:nɪ'vɜ:sətɪ, *Am:* -nə'vɜ:rsət̬ɪ] <-ies> **I.** *n* université *f* **II.** *adj* (*library, town*) universitaire; **~ students** étudiants *mpl* à l'université

university education *n no pl* études *fpl* (universitaires); **to have a ~** avoir fait des études universitaires **university lecture** *n* cours *m* magistral **university lecturer** *n* professeur *m* d'université

unjust [ˌʌn'dʒʌst] *adj* injuste

unjustifiable [ʌn'dʒʌstɪ faɪəbl, *Am:* -ˌdʒʌstɪ'-] *adj* injustifiable

unjustifiably *adv* sans justification

unjustified [ʌn'dʒʌstɪfaɪd] *adj pej* injustifié(e)

unjustly *adv pej* **1.** (*in an unjust manner*) de façon injuste **2.** (*wrongfully*) à tort

unkempt [ˌʌn'kempt] *adj* négligé(e); (*hair*) en bataille; (*lawn*) mal entretenu(e)

unkind [ʌn'kaɪnd] *adj* **1.** (*not kind*) peu aimable; (*critic*) mauvais(e); **to be ~ to animals** être cruel envers les animaux **2.** (*not gentle*) rude

unkindly *adv* de façon peu aimable; **to take ~ to sth** *form* accepter qc difficilement

unknowing *adj* (*unwitting*) innocent(e)

unknown [ˌʌn'nəʊn, *Am:* -'noʊn] **I.** *adj* inconnu(e); **to be ~ to sth** être inconnu de qc; **to be ~ to sb** être inconnu à qn; (*against one's will*) être à l'insu de qn; **she is an ~ quantity** on sait peu de choses d'elle **II.** *n* **1.** (*sth not known*) **the ~** l'inconnu *m* **2.** (*undetermined element*) *a.* MAT inconnue *f* **3.** (*little-known person*) inconnu(e) *m(f)*

unlawful [ˌʌn'lɔ:fʊl, *Am:* -'lɑ:-] *adj* illégal(e)

unleaded [ˌʌn'ledɪd] *adj* sans plomb

unlearn [ˌʌn'lɜ:n, *Am:* -'lɜ:rn] *vt* désapprendre

unleash [ʌn'li:ʃ] *vt* **1.** (*dog*) lâcher **2.** *fig* (*passion*) déchaîner; (*war*) déclencher

unleavened [ˌʌn'levnd] *adj* (*bread*) sans levain

unless [ən'les] *conj* à moins que *+subj;* **I don't say anything ~ I'm sure** je ne dis rien sans en être sûr; **he won't come ~ he has time** il ne viendra que s'il a le temps; **~ I'm mistaken** si je ne m'abuse; **don't ring me ~ there's a problem** ne m'appelez qu'en cas de problème

unlicensed [ˌʌn'laɪsənst] *adj* (*gun*) non autorisé(e); **~ premises** *Brit* établissement *m* non autorisé à vendre de l'alcool

unlike [ˌʌn'laɪk] **I.** *prep* **1.** (*different from*) différent(e) de **2.** (*in contrast to*) contrairement à **3.** (*not characteristic of*) **to be ~ sb/sth** ne pas ressembler à qn/qc **II.** *adj* différent(e)

unlikely <-ier, -iest> *adj* **1.** (*improbable*) peu probable; **it's ~ that** c'est peu probable que *+subj* **2.** (*unconvincing*) invraisemblable

unlimited [ʌn'lɪmɪtɪd, *Am:* -t̬ɪd] *adj* illimité(e); (*coffee, food*) à volonté

unlisted [ʌn'lɪstɪd] *adj* **1.** (*not on stock market*) non coté(e) **2.** *Am, Aus* (*not in phone book*) sur liste rouge

unload [ʌn'ləʊd, *Am:* -'loʊd] **I.** *vt* **1.** (*remove the contents*) décharger **2.** *inf* (*get rid of: goods*) refourguer **3.** *fig* (*release: one's heart*) vider; **to ~ responsibility/one's problems on to sb** se décharger de toute responsabilité/ses problèmes sur qn **II.** *vi* décharger

unlock [ˌʌn'lɒk, *Am:* -'lɑ:k] *vt* **1.** (*release a lock*) déverrouiller **2.** (*release*) libérer **3.** (*solve*) résoudre

unlocked *adj* **to be ~** ne pas être fermé à clef

unlooked-for [ʌn'lʊktfɔ:ʳ, *Am:* -fɔ:r] *adj form* inattendu(e)

unlucky [ʌn'lʌkɪ] *adj* **1.** (*unfortunate*) malchanceux(-euse); (*day*) de malchance; (*event*) malencontreux(-euse); **he was ~** tu n'as pas eu de chance; **you were ~ enough to fall ill** tu as eu la malchance de tomber malade **2.** (*bring-

ing bad luck) qui porte malheur; **it is ~ to** +*infin* ça porte malheur de +*infin*

unman [ˌʌn'mæn] <-nn-> *vt* décourager

unmanned *adj* sans équipage; (*spacecraft, flight*) inhabité(e)

unmannerly [ʌn'mænəlɪ, *Am:* -ɚlɪ] *adj form* (*behaviour*) impoli(e)

unmarked [ʌn'mɑːkt, *Am:* -'mɑːrkt] *adj* sans marques; (*word*) non marqué(e); (*police car*) banalisé(e); **fortunately, his face is ~** heureusement, son visage est intact; **to go ~** passer inaperçu

unmarried [ˌʌn'mærɪd, *Am:* -'mer-] *adj* (*person*) célibataire; (*couple*) non marié(e)

unmask [ʌn'mɑːsk, *Am:* -'mæsk] *vt* démasquer

unmatched [ʌn'mætʃt] *adj* sans égal

unmentionable *adj* qu'il vaut mieux taire

unmentioned [ˌʌn'menʃnd] *adj* **to be ~** ne pas être mentionné

unmindful [ʌn'maɪndfl] *adj* **to be ~ of sth** être peu soucieux de qc

unmistak(e)able [ˌʌnmɪ'steɪkəbl] *adj* caractéristique

unmitigated [ʌn'mɪtɪgeɪtɪd, *Am:* -'mɪt̬əgeɪt̬ɪd] *adj* (*total*) total(e)

unmoved [ʌn'muːvd] *adj* indifférent(e)

unnatural [ʌn'nætʃrəl, *Am:* -'nætʃɚəl] *adj* **1.** *pej* (*contrary to nature*) contre nature **2.** (*not normal*) anormal(e); **it's ~ that ...** ce n'est pas normal que +*subj* **3.** (*artificial*) artificiel(le) **4.** (*affected*) affecté(e)

unnecessarily [ˌʌn'nesəsərəlɪ, *Am:* -ˌnesə'ser-] *adv* (*worry*) inutilement; (*die*) pour rien

unnecessary [ʌn'nesəsrɪ, *Am:* -serɪ] *adj* **1.** (*not necessary*) inutile **2.** (*uncalled for*) injustifié(e)

unnerve [ˌʌn'nɜːv, *Am:* -'nɜːrv] *vt* troubler

unnerving *adj* troublant(e)

unnoticed [ˌʌn'nəʊtɪst, *Am:* -'noʊt̬ɪst] *adj* inaperçu(e); **to do sth ~** faire qc sans se faire remarquer

unnumbered [ˌʌn'nʌmbəd, *Am:* -bɚd] *adj* (*not marked with a number*) non numéroté(e); (*house*) sans numéro

UNO ['juːnəʊ, *Am:* -noʊ] *n abbr of* **United Nations Organization** ONU *f*

unobtainable [ˌʌnəb'teɪnəbl] *adj* (*number*) impossible à obtenir; (*goods, information*) introuvable

unobtrusive [ˌʌnəb'truːsɪv] *adj* discret(-ète)

unoccupied [ˌʌn'ɒkjʊpaɪd, *Am:* -'ɑːkjə-] *adj* **1.** (*uninhabited*) inhabité(e) **2.** (*not under military control: territory*) non occupé(e) **3.** (*not taken: chair*) libre

unofficial [ˌʌnə'fɪʃl] *adj* non officiel(le); (*information*) officieux(-euse); (*strike*) sauvage

unorganized [ˌʌn'ɔːgənaɪzd, *Am:* -'ɔːr-] *adj* qui manque d'organisation

unoriginal *adj* qui manque d'originalité

unorthodox [ˌʌn'ɔːθədɒks, *Am:* -'ɔːrθədɑːks] *adj* peu orthodoxe; (*theory*) peu conventionnel(le)

unpack [ˌʌn'pæk] **I.** *vt* déballer; (*suitcase*) défaire **II.** *vi* défaire ses valises

unpaid [ˌʌn'peɪd] *adj* **1.** (*not remunerated*) bénévole **2.** (*not paid: job*) non payé(e); (*debt*) impayé(e)

unpalatable [ˌʌn'pælətəbl, *Am:* -t̬əbl] *adj* **1.** (*not tasty*) mauvais(e) **2.** (*unpleasant*) désagréable; (*truth*) désagréable à entendre; (*criticism*) dur(e) à digérer

unparalleled [ʌn'pærəleld, *Am:* -'per-] *adj form* inégalé(e)

unperturbed [ˌʌnpə'tɜːbd, *Am:* -pɚ'tɜːrbd] *adj* imperturbable; **to be ~ by sth** ne pas se laisser perturber par qc

unpick [ˌʌn'pɪk] *vt* défaire

unplaced [ˌʌn'pleɪst] *adj* SPORT non placé(e)

unplanned [ʌn'plænd] *adj* imprévu(e)

unpleasant [ʌn'pleznt] *adj* **1.** (*not pleasing*) désagréable **2.** (*unfriendly*) antipathique

unpleasantness *n no pl* **1.** (*quality*) caractère *m* déplaisant **2.** (*argument*) différend *m*

unplug [ˌʌn'plʊg] <-gg-> *vt* **1.** (*disconnect*) débrancher **2.** (*unstop*) déboucher

unplumbed [ˌʌn'plʌmd] *adj* insondé(e)

unpolished [ˌʌn'pɒlɪʃt, *Am:* -'pɑːlɪʃt] *adj* **1.** (*not polished*) non poli(e); (*furniture, floor*) non ciré(e); (*glass*) dépoli(e) **2.** (*not refined*) peu raffiné(e)

unpolluted [ˌʌnpə'luːtɪd, *Am:* -t̬ɪd] *adj* non pollué(e)

unpopular [ˌʌn'pɒpjʊlə^r, *Am:* -'pɑːpjəlɚ] *adj* impopulaire; **she was ~ with her pupils** ses élèves ne l'aimaient pas

unpopularity [ʌnˌpɒpjʊ'lærətɪ, *Am:* -ˌpɑːpjə'lerət̬ɪ] *n no pl* impopularité *f*

unpractical [ˌʌn'præktɪkl] *adj* **1.** (*impractical*) peu pratique **2.** (*impossible to implement*) irréalisable

unpracticed *adj Am,* **unpractised** [ʌn'præktɪst] *adj Brit, form* inexpérimenté(e)

unprecedented [ʌn'presɪdentɪd, *Am:* -ədent̬ɪd] *adj* sans précédent

unpredictable [ˌʌnprɪ'dɪktəbl] *adj* imprévisible

unprejudiced [ʌn'predʒʊdɪst, *Am:* -'predʒə-] *adj* **1.** (*not prejudiced*) impartial(e) **2.** (*not racist*) sans préjugés

unpremeditated [ˌʌnprɪ'medɪteɪtɪd, *Am:* -priː'medɪteɪt̬ɪd] *adj* **1.** (*not planned*) spontané(e) **2.** LAW non prémédité(e)

unprepared [ˌʌnprɪ'peəd, *Am:* -perd] *adj* **1.** (*not ready*) non préparé(e); (*speech*) improvisé(e); **to be ~ for sth** (*not prepared*) ne pas être préparé à qc; (*not expect*) ne pas s'attendre à qc; **to catch sb ~** prendre qn au dépourvu **2.** (*unwilling*) **to be ~ to** +*infin* ne pas être disposé à +*infin*

unpretentious [ˌʌnprɪ'tenʃəs] *adj* sans prétention

unprincipled [ʌn'prɪnsəpld] *adj* sans scrupule

unproductive [ˌʌnprə'dʌktɪv] *adj* (*soil,*

method, capital) improductif(-ive); (*land, discussion*) stérile

unprofessional [ˌʌnprəˈfeʃənl] *adj* **to be** ~ ne pas être professionnel

unprofitable [ˌʌnˈprɒfɪtəbl, *Am:* -ˈprɑːfɪt̬ə-] *adj* **1.** (*not making a profit*) peu rentable **2.** (*unproductive*) infructueux(-euse)

unprompted [ˌʌnˈprɒmptɪd, *Am:* -ˈprɑːmp-] *adj* spontané(e)

unprovided for [ˌʌnprəˈvaɪdɪdfɔː, *Am:* -fɔːr] *adj* sans moyens; **to leave sb** ~ laisser qn sans moyens financiers

unprovoked [ˌʌnprəˈvəʊkt, *Am:* -voʊ-] *adj* gratuit(e)

unpublished [ˌʌnˈpʌblɪʃt] *adj* non publié(e)

unpunctual [ˌʌnˈpʌŋktʃʊəl, *Am:* -tʃu-] *adj* peu ponctuel(le)

unpunished [ʌnˈpʌnɪʃt] *adj* impuni(e); **to go** ~ rester impuni

unqualified [ʌnˈkwɒlɪfaɪd, *Am:* -ˈkwɑːlə-] *adj* **1.** *pej* (*without qualifications*) non qualifié(e) **2.** (*unlimited*) total(e); (*love*) sans réserve

unquestionable [ʌnˈkwestʃənəbl] *adj* indiscutable; (*evidence*) incontestable

unquestionably *adv* incontestablement

unquestioning [ʌnˈkwestʃnɪŋ] *adj* inconditionnel(le); (*obedience, faith*) aveugle; (*trust*) absolu(e)

unquote [ʌnˈkwəʊt, *Am:* -ˈkwoʊt] *adv* fermez les guillemets

unquoted *adj* FIN non coté(e)

unravel [ʌnˈrævl] <-ll- *o Am* -l-> **I.** *vt* **1.** (*unknit*) défaire **2.** (*untangle*) démêler; (*knot*) défaire **3.** (*solve*) résoudre **II.** *vi* se défaire

unreadable [ˌʌnˈriːdəbl] *adj* illisible

unreal [ʌnˈrɪəl, *Am:* -ˈriːl] *adj* **1.** (*not real*) irréel(e) **2.** *inf* (*good*) incroyable

unrealistic [ˌʌnˌrɪəˈlɪstɪk] *adj* **1.** (*not realistic*) irréaliste **2.** LIT, THEAT, CINE peu réaliste

unrealizable *adj* irréalisable

unrealized [ʌnˈrɪəlaɪzd] *adj* irréalisé(e); (*assets*) non réalisé(e)

unreasonable [ʌnˈriːznəbl] *adj* **1.** (*not showing reason*) déraisonnable **2.** *pej* (*unfair*) irréaliste; (*price*) exorbitant(e)

unreasoning [ʌnˈriːsənɪŋ] *adj* irraisonné(e)

unrecognized *adj* méconnu(e)

unredeemed [ˌʌnrɪˈdiːmd] *adj* **1.** (*not redeemed*) non racheté(e) **2.** REL non absout(e)

unrefined [ˌʌnrɪˈfaɪnd] *adj* **1.** (*not refined: sugar*) non raffiné(e); (*oil*) brut(e) **2.** (*not socially polished*) peu raffiné(e)

unreflecting [ˌʌnrɪˈflektɪŋ] *adj form* irréfléchi(e)

unregistered [ˌʌnˈredʒɪstəd, *Am:* -stɚd] *adj* non enregistré(e); (*for voting*) non inscrit(e); (*birth*) non déclaré(e); (*mail*) non recommandé(e)

unrelated [ˌʌnrɪˈleɪtɪd, *Am:* -t̬ɪd] *adj* sans rapport; (*people*) sans lien de parenté; **to be** ~ n'avoir aucun rapport; (*people*) n'avoir aucun lieu de parenté

unrelenting [ˌʌnrɪˈlentɪŋ, *Am:* -t̬ɪŋ] *adj* **1.** (*not yielding*) tenace **2.** (*incessant*) incessant(e) **3.** *form* (*unmerciful*) implacable

unreliability *n no pl* manque *m* de fiabilité

unreliable [ˌʌnrɪˈlaɪəbl] *adj* peu fiable

unrelieved [ˌʌnrɪˈliːvd] *adj* constant(e)

unremarkable *adj* quelconque

unremitting [ˌʌnrɪˈmɪtɪŋ, *Am:* -ˈmɪt̬-] *adj* constant(e)

unrepeatable [ˌʌnrɪˈpiːtəbl, *Am:* -t̬ə-] *adj* **1.** (*done only once: offer, experiment*) unique **2.** (*offensive*) qu'on ne peut répéter; **his jokes are** ~ ses histoires ne sont pas répétables

unrepentant [ˌʌnrɪˈpentənt] *adj* impénitent(e)

unrequited [ˌʌnrɪˈkwaɪtɪd, *Am:* -t̬ɪd] *adj* (*love*) non partagé(e)

unreserved [ˌʌnrɪˈzɜːvd, *Am:* -ˈzɜːrvd] *adj* **1.** (*absolute*) absolu(e) **2.** (*not reserved: tickets, seats*) non réservé(e)

unreservedly *adv* sans réserve

unresolved [ˌʌnrɪˈzɒlvd, *Am:* -zɑː-] *adj* (*person*) irrésolu(e); (*problem*) non résolu(e)

unrest [ʌnˈrest] *n no pl* troubles *mpl;* **social** ~ agitation *f* sociale

unrestrained [ˌʌnrɪˈstreɪnd] *adj* sans retenue; (*consumerism*) à outrance

unrestricted [ˌʌnrɪˈstrɪktɪd] *adj* non restreint(e); (*access*) libre

unripe [ˌʌnˈraɪp] *adj* (*not ripe*) pas mûr(e)

unrivaled *adj Am,* **unrivalled** [ʌnˈraɪvld] *adj Brit* inégalé(e)

unroll [ʌnˈrəʊl, *Am:* -ˈroʊl] **I.** *vt* dérouler **II.** *vi* (*become open*) se dérouler

unromantic [ˌʌnrəʊˈmæntɪk, *Am:* -roʊˈmænt̬ɪk] *adj* peu romantique

unruffled [ʌnˈrʌfld] *adj* (*not nervous*) imperturbable

unruly [ʌnˈruːlɪ] *adj* (*children*) indiscipliné(e); (*crowd*) incontrôlé(e); (*hair*) en bataille

unsafe [ˌʌnˈseɪf] *adj* **1.** (*dangerous*) dangereux(-euse) **2.** (*in danger*) en danger **3.** *Brit* JUR douteux(-euse)

unsaid [ˌʌnˈsed] **I.** *pt, pp of* **unsay II.** *adj form* **to leave sth** ~ passer qc sous silence

unsalaried [ˌʌnˈsælərɪd] *adj* bénévole

unsal(e)able [ˌʌnˈseɪləbl] *adj* invendable

unsatisfactory [ˈʌnˌsætɪsˈfæktrɪ, *Am:* -ˌsæt̬-] *adj* peu satisfaisant(e); **to be** ~ ne pas être satisfaisant; (*item*) ne pas donner satisfaction

unsatisfied [ˌʌnˈsætɪsfaɪd, *Am:* -ˈsæt̬-] *adj* **1.** (*not content*) mécontent(e) **2.** (*not convinced*) insatisfait(e) **3.** (*not sated*) non rassasié(e)

unsatisfying [ʌnˈsætɪsfaɪɪŋ] *adj* peu satisfaisant(e)

unsavory *adj Am, Aus,* **unsavoury** [ˌʌnˈseɪvərɪ] *adj Brit, Aus* **1.** (*unpleasant*) déplaisant(e) **2.** (*disgusting*) dégoûtant(e) **3.** (*socially offensive*) louche

unsay [ʌn'seɪ] *vt irr* reprendre ►**what's said cannot be unsaid** *prov* ce qui est dit ne peut être repris
unscathed [ʌn'skeɪðd] *adj* indemne
unscheduled [ˌʌn'ʃedjuːld, *Am:* -'skedʒʊld] *adj* imprévu(e); (*train*) supplémentaire
unscientific [ˌʌnsaɪən'tɪfɪk] *adj* **to be** ~ ne pas être très scientifique
unscramble [ʌn'skræmbl] *vt* décoder
unscrew [ʌn'skruː] **I.** *vt* dévisser **II.** *vi* se dévisser
unscripted [ʌn'skrɪptɪd] *adj* improvisé(e)
unscrupulous [ʌn'skruːpjʊləs, *Am:* -pjə-] *adj pej* peu scrupuleux(-euse)
unseal [ˌʌn'siːl] *vt* (*letter*) décacheter; (*packaging*) ouvrir
unsealed *adj* **1.**(*not sealed*) non scellé(e) **2.**(*open*) ouvert(e)
unseat [ˌʌn'siːt] *vt* **1.** POL faire tomber **2.**(*unsaddle*) désarçonner
unsecured [ˌʌnsɪ'kjʊəd, *Am:* -'kjʊrd] *adj* **1.** FIN (*loan*) sans garantie **2.**(*unfastened: load*) non attaché(e)
unseeing [ˌʌn'siːɪŋ] *adj form* **with** ~ **eyes** avec un regard vague
unseemly [ʌn'siːmlɪ] *adj form* peu convenable
unseen [ʌn'siːn] **I.** *adj* invisible; **to do sth** ~ faire qc sans être vu **II.** *n* (*translation*) version *f*
unselfish [ˌʌn'selfɪʃ] *adj* généreux(-euse)
unserviceable [ˌʌn'sɜːvɪsəbl, *Am:* -'sɜːr-] *adj* inutilisable
unsettle [ˌʌn'setl, *Am:* -'seţ-] *vt* **1.**(*make nervous*) troubler **2.**(*make unstable*) déstabiliser
unsettled *adj* **1.**(*changeable*) instable **2.**(*troubled*) troublé(e) **3.**(*unresolved: issue*) en suspens **4.**(*queasy: stomach*) perturbé(e)
unsettling *adj* **1.**(*causing nervousness*) troublant(e) **2.**(*causing disruption*) perturbant(e) **3.** COM déstabilisant(e)
unshak(e)able [ʌn'ʃeɪkəbl] *adj* inébranlable
unshaved, **unshaven** [ˌʌn'ʃeɪvn] *adj* pas rasé(e)
unshod [ˌʌn'ʃɒd, *Am:* -'ʃɑːd] *adj form* déchaussé(e); (*horse*) déferré(e)
unshrinkable *adj* (*clothes*) irrétrécissable
unshrinking [ˌʌn'ʃrɪŋkɪŋ] *adj* ferme
unsightly [ʌn'saɪtlɪ] <-ier, -iest *o* more ~, most ~> *adj* disgracieux(-euse)
unsigned [ˌʌn'saɪnd] *adj* non signé
unsinkable *adj* insubmersible
unskilled [ˌʌn'skɪld] *adj* non qualifié(e)
unsociable [ʌn'səʊʃəbl, *Am:* -'soʊ-] *adj* peu sociable
unsocial [ˌʌn'səʊʃl, *Am:* -'soʊ-] *adj* **1.**(*unsociable*) peu sociable **2.** *Brit* **to work** ~ **hours** travailler à des heures indues
unsold [ˌʌn'səʊld, *Am:* -'soʊld] *adj* invendu(e)
unsolicited [ˌʌnsə'lɪsɪtɪd, *Am:* -ţɪd] *adj* non sollicité(e); (*application*) spontané(e)
unsolved [ʌn'sɒlvd, *Am:* -sɑː-] *adj* non résolu(e)
unsophisticated [ˌʌnsə'fɪstɪkeɪtɪd, *Am:* -təkeɪţɪd] *adj* simple
unsound [ˌʌn'saʊnd] *adj* **1.**(*not robust*) *a. fig* peu solide **2.**(*unreliable*) peu fiable; (*investment*) peu sûr(e) **3.**(*not valid*) mal fondé(e); (*argument*) discutable; (*decision, opinion*) peu judicieux(-euse) **4.**(*not competent*) incompétent(e) **5.**(*unhealthy*) **to be of** ~ **mind** ne pas avoir toute sa raison
unsparing [ʌn'speərɪŋ, *Am:* -'sper-] *adj* **1.**(*merciless*) impitoyable **2.**(*lavish*) généreux(-euse); **to be** ~ **in one's efforts** ne pas ménager ses efforts; **to be** ~ **of one's time** ne pas être avare de son temps
unspeakable [ʌn'spiːkəbl] *adj* **1.**(*not able to be expressed*) indicible **2.**(*too awful: atrocity*) indescriptible
unspecified [ˌʌn'spesɪfaɪd] *adj* (*not specified*) non spécifié(e)
unspoiled [ʌn'spɔɪld] *adj* préservé(e)
unspoken [ʌn'spəʊkən, *Am:* -'spoʊ-] *adj* tacite
unstable [ˌʌn'steɪbl] *adj a. fig* instable
unsteady [ʌn'stedi] *adj* **1.**(*not steady*) instable; (*steps*) chancelant(e); (*hand, voice*) mal assuré(e) **2.**(*not irregular*) irrégulier(-ère)
unstressed [ˌʌn'strest] *adj* LING inaccentué(e)
unstuck [ˌʌn'stʌk] *adj* **1.**(*not stuck*) décollé(e) **2.** *inf* (*fail*) **to come** ~ échouer
unstudied [ˌʌn'stʌdɪd] *adj form* non affecté(e); (*naturalness*) spontané(e); (*reaction*) instinctif(-ive)
unsubstantiated [ˌʌnsəb'stæntʃieɪtɪd, *Am:* -ţɪd] *adj* sans fondement
unsuccessful [ˌʌnsək'sesfl] *adj* (*attempt, campaign*) infructueux(-euse); (*candidate, affair*) malheureux(-euse); (*film, business*) sans succès; **to be** ~ (*person, plan*) ne pas réussir; (*attempt*) échouer
unsuitable [ˌʌn'suːtəbl, *Am:* -ţə-] *adj* inapproprié(e); (*moment*) inopportun(e); **to be** ~ ne pas convenir
unsuited *adj* (*person*) inapte; (*equipment*) inadapté(e); (*couple*) mal assorti(e); **to be not** ~ **for** [*o* **to**] **sth** ne pas être fait pour qc
unsullied [ˌʌn'sʌlɪd] *adj form* sans tache; **to be** ~ **by sth** ne pas être entaché par qc
unsung [ʌn'sʌŋ] *adj* méconnu(e)
unsure [ˌʌn'ʃʊəʳ, *Am:* -'ʃʊr] *adj* peu sûr(e); **to be** ~ **about sth** ne pas être (très) sûr de qc
unsuspecting [ˌʌnsə'spektɪŋ] *adj* **1.**(*naïve*) naïf(naïve) **2.**(*unaware*) qui ne se doute de rien
unsweetened [ʌn'swiːtənd] *adj* non sucré(e)
unswerving [ˌʌn'swɜːvɪŋ, *Am:* -'swɜːr-] *adj* **1.**(*unshakeable*) inaltérable; (*commitment*) irrévocable **2.**(*not turning*) sans détour
unsympathetic [ˌʌnsɪmpə'θetɪk, *Am:* -ţɪk] *adj* **1.**(*without sympathy*) peu compréhensif(-ive); **to be** ~ **towards sth** (*cause*) être

U

insensible à qc **2.** (*not friendly*) antipathique

untam(e)able [ʌnˈteɪməbl] *adj a. fig* indomptable

untangle [ʌnˈtæŋgl] *vt* **1.** (*string, hair*) démêler **2.** *fig* dénouer

untapped [ˌʌnˈtæpt] *adj* inexploité(e)

untaxed [ˌʌnˈtækst] *adj* **1.** (*not taxed*) non taxé(e); (*income*) non imposable **2.** *Brit* (*auto*) sans vignette

untenable [ˌʌnˈtenəbl] *adj* **1.** (*indefensible*) indéfendable **2.** (*unbearable*) insoutenable

untested *adj* non testé(e); (*method, system*) inéprouvé(e)

unthinkable [ʌnˈθɪŋkəbl] **I.** *adj* **1.** (*unimaginable*) inimaginable **2.** (*shocking*) impensable **II.** *n no pl* **the** ~ l'impensable *m*

unthinking [ʌnˈθɪŋkɪŋ] *adj* **1.** (*thoughtless*) irréfléchi(e) **2.** (*unintentional*) sans faire exprès

unthought-of [ʌnˈθɔːtɒv, *Am:* -ˈθɑːtɑːv] *adj* inédit(e); (*detail*) original(e)

untidiness [ʌnˈtaɪdɪnɪs] *n no pl* **1.** (*being untidy*) désorganisation *f* **2.** (*state*) désordre *m*

untidy [ʌnˈtaɪdɪ] <-ier, -iest> *adj* **1.** (*not neat*) peu soigné(e); (*room*) en désordre **2.** (*not orderly*) désordonné(e)

untie [ˌʌnˈtaɪ] <-y-> *vt* défaire; (*boat*) démarrer

until [ənˈtɪl] **I.** *prep* jusqu'à; ~ **then** jusque-là; ~ **such time as** jusqu'à ce que +*subj;* **not** ~ pas avant **II.** *conj* jusqu'à ce que +*subj;* **to not do sth** ~ ne pas faire qc avant que +*subj;* **he waited** ~ **the rain stopped** il a attendu que la pluie cesse *subj;* **we'll wait** ~ **you've finished** nous attendrons que tu aies fini *subj*

untimely [ʌnˈtaɪmlɪ] *adj* **1.** (*premature*) prématuré(e) **2.** (*inopportune*) inopportun(e)

unto [ˈʌntuː] *prep s.* **to**, **until**

untold [ˌʌnˈtəʊld, *Am:* -ˈtoʊld] *adj* **1.** (*immense*) immense; (*misery, joy*) indicible; (*wealth*) incommensurable **2.** (*not told*) indicible

untouched [ˌʌnˈtʌtʃt] *adj* **1.** (*not touched*) **to be** ~ ne pas avoir été touché(e); **to leave a meal** ~ ne pas toucher à un repas **2.** (*unaffected: thing*) intact(e); (*person*) indemne **3.** (*unmentioned: subject*) non traité(e); **to be left** ~ ne pas avoir été traité **4.** (*not emotionally moved*) insensible

untoward [ˌʌntəˈwɔːd, *Am:* ˌʌnˈtɔːrd] *adj form* fâcheux(-euse)

untrained [ʌnˈtreɪnd] *adj* (*person*) sans formation; (*mind, worker*) non formé(e); (*dog*) non dressé(e); **to be** ~ **in sth** ne pas être formé à qc; **to the** ~ **eye** pour l'oreille inexercée

untransferable [ˌʌntrænsˈfɜːrəbl] *adj* LAW (*succession*) incessible

untranslatable [ˌʌntrænsˈleɪtəbl, *Am:* -ţəbl] *adj* intraduisible

untreated [ʌnˈtriːtɪd] *adj* **1.** (*not treated*) non traité(e) **2.** MED non soigné(e); **to remain** ~ (*person*) rester sans soins

untried *adj* **1.** (*inexperienced*) qui n'a pas fait ses preuves **2.** (*untested*) non testé(e) **3.** LAW qui n'a pas encore été jugé

untroubled *adj* tranquille; **to be** ~ **by sth** ne pas être perturbé par qc

untrue [ˌʌnˈtruː] *adj* **1.** (*wrong*) faux(fausse) **2.** (*not faithful*) **to be** ~ ne pas être fidèle **3.** (*not reliable*) peu fiable

untrustworthy [ˌʌnˈtrʌstˌwɜːðɪ, *Am:* -ˌwɜːr-] *adj* (*person*) indigne de confiance; (*report, information*) douteux(-euse)

untruth [ʌnˈtruːθ] *n* (*lie*) mensonge *m*

untruthful *adj* **1.** (*untrue*) mensonger(-ère) **2.** (*telling lies*) menteur(-euse)

unturned [ˌʌnˈtɜːnd, *Am:* -ˈtɜːrnd] *adj* **to leave no stone** ~ remuer ciel et terre

untutored [ˌʌnˈtjuːtəd, *Am:* -ˈtuːţɚd] *adj* (*person*) peu instruit(e); (*mind, eye*) non formé(e)

unused¹ [ʌnˈjuːzd] *adj* **1.** (*not in use*) inutilisé(e); (*property*) inoccupée; (*talent*) inexploité(e) **2.** (*never used: clothes*) neuf(neuve)

unused² [ʌnˈjuːst] *adj* (*not accustomed*) peu habitué(e); **to be** ~ **to doing sth** ne pas être habitué à faire qc

unusual [ʌnˈjuːʒl, *Am:* -ˈjuːʒuəl] *adj* **1.** (*uncommon: noise, event*) inhabituel(le); (*case, job*) peu commun(e); **to be** ~/**not** ~ **for sb to do sth** être/ne pas être rare que qn fasse qc (*subj*) **2.** (*interesting: ring, costume, car*) original(e) **3.** (*strange: friends, habit*) bizarre

unusually *adv* exceptionnellement; ~ **for her, she took the train** elle a exceptionnellement pris le train

unutterable [ʌnˈʌtərəbl, *Am:* -ˈʌţ-] *adj form* indicible; (*suffering*) indescriptible

unvarnished [ʌnˈvɑːnɪʃt, *Am:* -ˈvɑːr-] *adj* **1.** (*wood*) non-verni **2.** *fig* **the** ~ **truth** la vérité toute nue

unveil [ˌʌnˈveɪl] *vt a. fig* dévoiler

unwaged [ʌnˈweɪdʒd] **I.** *adj* non rémunéré(e) **II.** *n Brit* **the** ~ *no pl* les sans-emploi

unwanted *adj* (*goods, clothes, hair*) superflu(e); (*child*) non désiré(e); (*visitor*) indésirable; **to feel** ~ se sentir de trop

unwarranted [ˌʌnˈwɒrəntɪd, *Am:* -ˈwɔːrənţɪd] *adj* injustifié(e)

unwavering [ʌnˈweɪvərɪŋ] *adj* (*determination*) inébranlable

unwed *adj* **to be** ~ ne pas être marié

unwelcome *adj* (*guests, visit*) importun(e); (*news*) fâcheux(-euse); **to feel** ~ ne pas se sentir le bienvenu

unwell [ʌnˈwel] *adj* souffrant(e)

unwieldy [ʌnˈwiːldɪ] *adj* **1.** (*cumbersome*) encombrant(e) **2.** (*difficult to manage*) peu maniable

unwilling [ˌʌnˈwɪlɪŋ] *adj* **to be** ~ **to** +*infin* ne pas être disposé à +*infin*

unwillingly *adv* à contrecœur

unwind [ˌʌnˈwaɪnd] *irr* **I.** *vt* dérouler **II.** *vi* **1.** (*unroll*) se dérouler **2.** (*relax*) se détendre

unwise [ʌnˈwaɪz] *adj* (*decision, investment*) peu judicieux(-euse); (*person*) imprudent(e)

unwitting [ʌn'wɪtɪŋ, *Am:* -'wɪt̬-] *adj* **1.** (*unaware*) inconscient(e); (*accomplice*) involontaire; (*victim*) innocent(e) **2.** (*unintentional*) involontaire

unwittingly *adv* **1.** (*without realizing*) sans le savoir **2.** (*unintentionally*) involontairement

unwonted [ʌn'wəʊntɪd, *Am:* -'wɔːnt̬ɪd] *adj form* inaccoutumé(e)

unworkable [ˌʌn'wɜːkəbl, *Am:* -'wɜːr-] *adj* impraticable

unworldly [ˌʌn'wɜːldlɪ, *Am:* -'wɜːrld-] *adj* **1.** (*spiritually-minded*) détaché(e) du monde **2.** (*naive*) naïf(naïve) **3.** (*unearthly*) surnaturel(le)

unworthy [ʌn'wɜːðɪ, *Am:* -'wɜːr-] *adj* indigne

unwrap [ˌʌn'ræp] <-pp-> *vt* **1.** (*remove wrapping*) déballer **2.** (*open: secret*) étaler

unwritten [ˌʌn'rɪtn] *adj* **1.** (*not official: rule*) tacite; (*agreement*) verbal(e) **2.** (*not written*) non écrit(e); (*tradition*) oral(e)

unyielding [ʌn'jiːldɪŋ] *adj* **1.** (*stubborn*) borné(e); (*refusal*) catégorique; (*opposition*) impitoyable **2.** (*physically hard*) coriace; (*ground*) dur(e)

unzip [ˌʌn'zɪp] <-pp-> *vt* ouvrir la fermeture éclair de

up [ʌp] **I.** *adv* **1.** (*movement: to be*) en haut; (*to go*) vers le haut; **on the way** ~ en montant; **to look** ~ lever les yeux **2.** (*to another point*) ~ **North** dans le nord **3.** (*more intensity*) **to be** ~ (*river, temperature*) être monté; (*price*) avoir augmenté **4.** (*position: tent*) planté(e); (*flag*) hissé(e); (*curtains, picture*) accroché(e); (*notice*) affiché(e); (*person*) debout *inv* **5.** (*state*) **to be** ~ **at the top of sth** être en tête de qc; **to feel** ~ **to sth** se sentir capable de qc **6.** (*limit*) **from the age of 18** ~ à partir de 18 ans; ~ **to here** jusqu'ici; **time's** ~**!** c'est fini! **7.** SPORT **to be 2 goals** ~ mener par deux buts **8.** INFOR, TECH en service **9.** (*wrong*) **what's** ~**?** qu'est-ce qu'il y a?; **something is** ~ quelque chose ne va pas; **what's** ~ **with him?** qu'est-ce qu'il a ►**things are looking** ~ ça va mieux; ~ **with sb/sth!** vive qn/qc!; **to walk** ~ **and down** faire des avec des va-et-vient **II.** *prep* **1.** (*higher*) **to go** ~ **the stairs** monter l'escalier **2.** (*at top of*) **to be/climb** ~ **a tree** être/grimper sur un arbre **3.** (*along*) **to go/drive** ~ **the street** remonter la rue **4.** (*increase*) **to turn the sound/heat** ~ **a notch** monter le son/chauffage d'un cran **5.** (*to point of*) ~ **until** [*o* **till**] **midnight/yesterday** [*o* **to**] jusqu'à minuit/hier ►~ **hill and down dale** par monts et par vaux; ~ **and down sth** aux quatre coins de qc; *s. a.* **down III.** *n* **to be on the** ~ **and** ~ *Brit* aller de mieux en mieux; *Am, inf* être tout à fait honnête **IV.** *vi inf* se lever brusquement; **to** ~ **and go** se tirer **V.** *vt inf* augmenter **VI.** *adj* **1.** (*towards a higher place*) qui monte **2.** (*under repair*) en travaux **3.** (*healthy*) en forme; **to be** ~ **and about** [*o* **around**] être sur pied **4.** (*ready*) **to be** ~ **for doing sth** être partant pour faire qc

up-and-coming ['ʌpən'kʌmɪŋ] *adj* prometteur(-euse)

upbeat ['ʌpbiːt] *adj inf* optimiste

upbraid [ˌʌp'breɪd] *vt form* blâmer

upbringing ['ʌpbrɪŋɪŋ] *n* éducation *f*

upcoming ['ʌpˌkʌmɪŋ] *adj Am* prochain(e)

upcountry, up-country [ˌʌp'kʌntrɪ, *Am:* 'ʌpkʌn-] **I.** *adv* (*to live*) à l'intérieur (du pays); (*to go*) vers l'intérieur (du pays) **II.** *adj* de l'intérieur (du pays)

update [ʌp'deɪt] **I.** *vt* **1.** (*bring up to date*) *a.* INFOR mettre à jour **2.** (*give latest information*) **to** ~ **sb on sth** mettre au courant qn au sujet de qc **II.** *n a.* INFOR mise *f* à jour

updating *n* mise *f* à jour

updraught ['ʌpdrɑːft] **I.** *n* courant *m* **II.** *adj* ascendant(e)

upend [ʌp'end] *vt* retourner

upfront ['ʌpfrʌnt] **I.** *adj inf* **1.** (*open*) franc(he) **2.** (*in advance*) payé(e) d'avance; ~ **money** avance *f* **II.** *adv* (*to pay*) d'avance

upgrade[1] [ʌp'greɪd] *vt* **1.** (*improve quality*) améliorer **2.** INFOR (*expand: computer, system*) optimiser; (*software*) installer la nouvelle version de **3.** (*raise in rank: worker*) promouvoir; (*job*) revaloriser; (*passenger*) surclasser

upgrade[2] ['ʌpgreɪd] *n* **1.** *Am* (*slope*) montée *f*; **to be on the** ~ (*prices*) augmenter; (*business*) reprendre **2.** INFOR, TECH (*expansion*) extension *f* **3.** INFOR, TECH (*updated version*) nouvelle version *f* **4.** (*raise in rank: passenger*) surclassement *m*

upgradeable *adj* INFOR optimisable

upgrading *n* **1.** *no pl* (*act of improvement*) amélioration *f* **2.** INFOR optimisation *f* **3.** (*raising of rank*) promotion *f*

upheaval [ˌʌp'hiːvl] *n* **1.** (*change*) bouleversement *m* **2.** GEO soulèvement *m*

uphill [ˌʌp'hɪl] **I.** *adv* (*to go* ~) monter **II.** *adj* **1.** (*sloping upward*) qui monte **2.** (*difficult*) difficile; (*struggle*) ardu(e)

uphold [ˌʌp'həʊld, *Am:* -'hoʊld] *vt irr* **1.** (*support*) soutenir; (*law*) faire respecter **2.** LAW (*verdict*) confirmer

upholster [ʌp'həʊlstəʳ, *Am:* -'hoʊlstɚ] *vt* **1.** (*pad*) rembourrer **2.** (*cover*) tapisser

upholsterer *n* tapissier *m* (d'ameublement)

upholstery [ˌʌp'həʊlstərɪ, *Am:* -'hoʊl-] *n no pl* **1.** (*padding*) rembourrage *m* **2.** (*covering*) revêtement *m* **3.** (*art of upholstering*) tapisserie *f*

upkeep ['ʌpkiːp] *n no pl* **1.** (*maintain*) entretien *m* **2.** (*cost of maintaining*) frais *mpl* d'entretien **3.** (*of people*) charge *f*

upland(s) ['ʌpləndz] *n* hautes terres *fpl*

uplift[1] [ʌp'lɪft] *vt* élever

uplift[2] ['ʌplɪft] *n* **1.** GEO soulèvement *m* **2.** (*inspiration*) élévation *f* spirituelle

uplift bra *n* soutien-gorge *m* de maintien

uplifted *adj* (*arm, face*) levé(e); (*soul, person*) élevé(e)

uplifting *adj* édifiant(e)

upload *vt* INFOR télécharger vers l'amont, uploader
upmarket [ˌʌp'mɑːkɪt, *Am:* 'ʌpˌmɑːr-] **I.** *adj Brit* haut de gamme; (*person, district*) bourgeois(e) **II.** *adv* (*shop*) **to go ~** se mettre à faire du haut de gamme
upon [ə'pɒn, *Am:* -'pɑːn] *prep form* **1.** (*on top of*) sur; **~ this** là-dessus **2.** (*around*) **a ring ~ his finger** une bague au doigt **3.** (*hanging on*) **to hang ~ the wall** être accroché au mur **4.** (*at time of*) **~ sb's arrival** dès l'arrivée de qn ►once ~ **a time** il était une fois; *s. a.* **on**
upper ['ʌpəʳ, *Am:* -ɚ] **I.** *adj* (*further up*) supérieur(e) **II.** *n* **1.** (*part of shoe*) empeigne *f* **2.** *inf* (*drugs*) amphète *f* ►**to be on one's ~s** *inf* être dans la dèche
upper case I. *n no pl* TYP majuscule *f* **II.** *adj* TYP **upper-case** majuscule **upper class** *n* aristocratie *f* **upper-class** *adj* aristocratique
uppercut ['ʌpəkʌt, *Am:* '-ɚ-] *n* SPORT uppercut *m*
upper deck *n* pont *m* supérieur **Upper Egypt** *n* la Haute-Égypte **upper house** *n* POL chambre *f* haute
uppermost ['ʌpəməʊst, *Am:* -ɚmoʊst] **I.** *adj* **1.** (*furthest up*) le(la) plus haut(e) **2.** (*most important*) le(la) plus important(e); **to be ~ in one's mind** être au premier rang de ses pensées **II.** *adv* en dessus
uppish ['ʌpɪʃ], **uppity** ['ʌpɪtɪ, *Am:* -t̬ɪ] *adj inf* arrogant(e)
upright ['ʌpraɪt] **I.** *adj, adv a. fig* droit(e) **II.** *n* **1.** (*piano*) piano *m* droit **2.** (*perpendicular*) montant *m*
uprising ['ʌpraɪzɪŋ] *n* soulèvement *m*
uproar ['ʌprɔːʳ, *Am:* -rɔːr] *n no pl* **1.** (*reaction*) tumulte *m;* **the room was in a ~** le tumulte régnait dans la pièce **2.** (*protest*) indignation *f*
uproarious [ʌp'rɔːrɪəs] *adj* tumultueux(-euse)
uproot [ˌʌp'ruːt] *vt a. fig* déraciner
upset¹ [ˌʌp'set] **I.** *vt irr* **1.** (*make unhappy: remark, friend*) faire de la peine à; (*event, scene*) bouleverser **2.** (*overturn*) renverser; (*boat, canoe*) faire chavirer **3.** (*throw into disorder: plans, schedule*) bouleverser; (*balance*) rompre **4.** (*cause pain: stomach*) déranger **II.** *adj* **1.** (*unhappy*) bouleversé(e); **to be/feel ~ about sth** être bouleversé par qc; **don't be ~** ne vous en faites pas **2.** *inf* (*bilious*) dérangé(e); **to have an ~ stomach** être dérangé
upset² ['ʌpset] *n* **1.** (*upheaval*) bouleversement *m* **2.** (*unhappy feeling*) peine *f;* **to cause sb ~(s)** faire de la peine à qn **3.** SPORT revers *m* **4.** MED **to have a stomach ~** avoir l'estomac dérangé
upset price *n Am* mise *f* à prix
upsetting *adj* bouleversant(e)
upshot ['ʌpʃɒt, *Am:* -ʃɑːt] *n no pl* résultat *m*
upside down [ˌʌpsaɪd 'daʊn] **I.** *adj* **1.** (*reversed*) à l'envers **2.** (*chaotic: room, plans*) sens dessus dessous **II.** *adv* **1.** (*in inverted position*) à l'envers; **to turn sth ~** retourner qc **2.** (*in disorder*) *a. fig* **to turn sth ~** mettre qc sens dessus dessous; **to turn sb ~** bouleverser la vie qn
upside-down cake *n* gâteau *m* renversé
upstage [ˌʌp'steɪdʒ] **I.** *adj* THEAT arrière-scène *f* **II.** *adv* au fond de la scène **III.** *vt* reléguer au second plan
upstairs [ˌʌp'steəz, *Am:* -'sterz] **I.** *adj* d'en haut; (*room*) à l'étage **II.** *adv* en haut; (*room*) à l'étage; **to live ~ from sb** vivre au-dessus de chez qn **III.** *n no pl* **the ~** l'étage *m*
upstanding [ˌʌp'stændɪŋ] *adj form* droit(e)
upstart ['ʌpstɑːt, *Am:* -stɑːrt] *n pej* parvenu(e) *m(f)*
upstate ['ʌpsteɪt] *Am* **I.** *adj* du nord; **~ New York** le nord de l'État de New York **II.** *adv* (*to go*) vers le nord; (*to live*) dans le nord
upstream [ˌʌp'striːm] **I.** *adj* d'amont **II.** *adv* en amont
upsurge ['ʌpsɜːdʒ, *Am:* -sɜːrdʒ] *n* recrudescence *f;* **an ~ in sth** une recrudescence de qc
upswing ['ʌpswɪŋ] *n* amélioration *f;* ECON redressement *m;* **to be on the ~** connaître une amélioration; (*economy*) être en train de reprendre; (*crime, violence*) être en recrudescence
uptake ['ʌpteɪk] *n no pl* (*level of absorption*) assimilation *f* ►**to be quick on the ~** *inf* saisir vite; **to be slow on the ~** *inf* être long à la détente
uptight [ʌp'taɪt] *adj inf* tendu(e); **to get ~ about sth** s'énerver à propos de qc
up to [ʌptə] *prep* **1.** (*as far as*) jusqu'à; **to drive at speeds of ~ 90 mph** atteindre les 90 km/h; **to come ~ one's knees** arriver (jusqu')aux genoux; **I'm ~ chapter 5** je suis au chapitre 5; **I've had it ~ here with sth** j'en ai par-dessus la tête de qc **2.** (*capable*) **to be ~ (doing) sth** être capable de faire qc **3.** (*depending*) **it's ~ you** comme tu veux/vous voulez; **it's ~ sb** ça dépend de qn **4.** (*secretly doing*) **to be ~ sth** manigancer qc; **what is he ~?** qu'est-ce qu'il fabrique? **5.** (*be responsible*) **to be ~ sb to** +*infin* être à qn de +*infin*
up-to-date *adj* **1.** (*contemporary*) actuel(le) **2.** (*latest*) récent(e); **~ news on sth** les dernières nouvelles de qc **3.** (*updated*) à jour **4.** (*informed*) au courant; **to be ~ on sth** être au courant de qc; **to bring sth ~** mettre qc à jour **up-to-the-minute** *adj* dernier cri *inv*
uptown [ˌʌp'taʊn, *Am:* 'ʌptaʊn] *Am* **I.** *adj* (*suburban*) des beaux quartiers; **in ~ Manhattan** dans le Manhattan des beaux quartiers **II.** *adv* dans les beaux quartiers **III.** *n* beaux quartiers *mpl*
uptrend ['ʌptrend] *n Am* recrudescence *f*
upturn ['ʌptɜːn, *Am:* -tɜːrn] *n* amélioration *f;* ECON reprise *f*
upturned *adj* **1.** (*directed upwards*) levé(e);

(*nose*) retroussé(e) **2.** (*inverted 180 degrees*) renversé(e)

upward ['ʌpwəd, *Am:* -wɚd] **I.** *adj* qui monte; (*movement, mobility*) ascendant(e); (*trend*) à la hausse **II.** *adv Am* **1.** (*to a higher position*) vers le haut; **to put sth face ~** mettre qc à l'endroit; **to lie face ~** être couché sur le dos **2.** (*more than*) au-dessus; **$100 and ~** cent dollars et plus; **~ of 100 persons** plus de cent personnes; **from $1/eight ~** à partir d'un dollar/de huit ans

upwardly *adv* vers le haut; **to be ~ mobile** avoir une possibilité d'ascension sociale

upwards *adv s.* **upward**

uraemia [jʊə'riːmjə, *Am:* juː'riː-] *n* MED urémie *f*

uranium [jʊ'reɪnɪəm] *n no pl* CHEM uranium *m*

Uranus [jʊ'reɪnəs] *n* ASTR Uranus *m*

urban ['ɜːbən, *Am:* 'ɜːr-] *adj* urbain(e)

urbane [ɜː'beɪn, *Am:* ɜːr'-] *adj* courtois(e)

urbanise ['ɜːbənaɪz, *Am:* 'ɜːr-] *vt Brit, Aus* urbaniser

urbanity [ɜː'bænətɪ, *Am:* ɜːr'bænət̬ɪ] *n no pl* **1.** (*courteousness*) courtoisie *f* **2.** (*urban style*) urbanité *f*

urbanization *n no pl* urbanisation *f*

urbanize ['ɜːbənaɪz, *Am:* 'ɜːr-] *s.* **urbanise**

urban myth *n* légende *f* urbaine **urban renewal** *n no pl* rénovations *fpl* urbaines

urchin ['ɜːtʃɪn, *Am:* 'ɜːr-] *n* garnement *m*

urethra [ˌjʊə'riːθrə, *Am:* ˌjʊ'-] <-s *o* -e> *n* ANAT urètre *m*

urge [ɜːdʒ, *Am:* ɜːrdʒ] **I.** *n* **1.** (*strong desire*) forte envie *f;* **to have an ~ to** *+infin* avoir très envie de *+infin;* **to feel an irresistible ~** avoir un besoin irrésistible **2.** (*compulsion*) impulsion *f* **II.** *vt* **1.** (*push*) pousser **2.** (*encourage*) encourager; **to ~ sb to** *+infin* presser qn de *+infin* **3.** (*seriously recommend*) conseiller vivement; (*caution*) recommander; (*peace*) appeler à; **to urge self-discipline on** [*o* **upon**] **sb** inciter qn à la discipline

◆**urge on** *vt* (*friend*) encourager; **to urge sb on to** *+infin* pousser qn à *+infin*

urgency ['ɜːdʒənsɪ, *Am:* 'ɜːr-] *n no pl* **1.** (*top priority*) urgence *f;* **a matter of ~** une affaire urgente **2.** (*insistence*) insistance *f*

urgent ['ɜːdʒənt, *Am:* 'ɜːr-] *adj* **1.** (*imperative: appeal, plea*) urgent(e); (*need*) pressant(e) **2.** (*insistent*) insistant(e)

urgently *adv* **1.** (*very necessarily*) d'urgence **2.** (*beggingly*) avec insistance

urinal *n* urinoir *m*

urinary ['jʊərɪnrɪ, *Am:* 'jʊrənerɪ] *adj* urinaire

urinate ['jʊərɪneɪt, *Am:* 'jʊrə-] *vi* uriner

urine ['jʊərɪn, *Am:* 'jʊrɪn] *n no pl* urine *f*

URL *n abbr of* **Uniform Resource Locator** INFOR adresse *f* universelle

urn [ɜːn, *Am:* ɜːrn] *n* **1.** (*vase*) urne *f* **2.** (*drink container*) fontaine *f;* **a tea/coffee ~** une fontaine à thé/café

Uruguay ['jʊərəgwaɪ, *Am:* 'jʊrəgweɪ] *n* Uruguay *m*

Uruguayan **I.** *adj* uruguayen(ne) **II.** *n* Uruguayen(ne) *m(f)*

us [əs, ʌs] *pers pron* (*1st person pl*) nous; **it's ~** c'est nous; **older than ~** plus vieux que nous; **look at ~** regarde/regardez-nous; **he saw ~** il nous a vus; **he gave it to ~** il nous l'a donné; **all/both of ~** nous tous/tous les deux

US *n abbr of* **United States** USA *mpl*

USA [ˌjuːes'eɪ] *n no pl* **1.** *abbr of* **United States of America** USA *mpl* **2.** *abbr of* **United States Army** *armée des États-Unis*

usable ['juːzəbl] *adj* utilisable

USAF *n abbr of* **United States Air Force** *armée de l'air des États-Unis*

usage ['juːzɪdʒ] *n no pl* **1.** (*use*) utilisation *f* **2.** (*habitual practice*) usage *m* **3.** LING usage *m;* **in common ~** d'usage courant

use[1] [juːs] *n* **1.** (*using*) emploi *m;* **in/not in ~** en/hors service; **out of ~** hors service; **directions for ~** mode *m* d'emploi; **to make ~ of sth** se servir de qc **2.** (*possibility of applying*) usage *m;* **external ~ only** usage externe; **to have the ~ of sth** pouvoir se servir de qc; **to lose the ~ of an arm** perdre l'usage d'un bras **3.** *no pl* (*usefulness*) utilité *f;* **to be of ~ to sb** être utile à qn; **to be no ~ doing sth** être inutile de faire qc; **I'm no ~ at history** *inf* je suis nul en histoire; **can I be of any ~ to you?** puis-je vous être utile?; **what's the ~ of that/doing sth?** à quoi bon tout ça/faire qc? **4.** (*consumption*) usage *m;* (*of drugs*) consommation *f;* **ready for ~** prêt(e) à l'emploi **5.** LING usage *m* **6.** (*custom*) coutume *f*

use[2] [juːz] **I.** *vt* **1.** (*make use of*) utiliser; (*tool, machine*) se servir de; (*blackmail, violence*) faire usage de; **I could ~ some help** *inf* j'ai besoin d'aide **2.** (*consume*) consommer **3.** *form* (*treat in stated way*) traiter; **to ~ sb badly** maltraiter qn **4.** *pej* (*exploit: people*) utiliser **II.** *vt aux* **I ~d to do sth** je faisais qc; **it ~d to be calm** c'était calme; **there ~d to be a market here** il y avait un marché ici

◆**use up** *vt* **1.** (*use*) consommer; (*money*) dépenser **2.** (*tire*) épuiser; **to be used up** être épuisé

used[1] [juːzd] *adj* **1.** (*already been used*) usé(e) **2.** (*second-hand*) d'occasion

used[2] [juːst] *adj* (*familiar with*) habitué(e); **to be ~ to sth** être habitué à qc; **to be ~ to doing sth** avoir l'habitude de faire qc; **to become ~ to sth** s'habituer à qc; **I'm not ~ to big cities/living alone** je n'ai pas l'habitude des grandes villes/de vivre seul

useful *adj* utile; **to be ~ to sb/sth** être utile à qn/qc; **to be ~ with sth** *inf* savoir se servir de qc

usefulness *n no pl* utilité *f*

useless *adj* **1.** (*futile*) inutile **2.** (*unusable*) inutilisable **3.** *inf* (*incompetent*) nul(le); **~ at sth** être nul en qc

user ['juːzəʳ] *n* **1.** (*person who uses sth*) utilisateur, -trice *m, f;* (*of gas, electricity*) usager,

U

-ère *m, f* **2.** INFOR utilisateur *m* **3.** *inf* (*addict*) consommateur, -trice *m, f*

user-friendly *adj* INFOR convivial(e) **user identification** *n* INFOR identifiant *m* d'utilisateur **user interface, user-interface** *n* INFOR interface *f* (utilisateur) **user name** *n* INFOR nom *m* d'utilisateur **user program** *n* INFOR programme *m* utilisateur **user software** *n* INFOR logiciel *m* utilisateur **user surface** *n* INFOR surface *f* de travail

usher ['ʌʃəʳ, *Am:* -ɚ] **I.** *n* placeur *m;* LAW huissier, -ère *m, f* **II.** *vt* **1.** (*guide, show*) **to ~ sb into the hall/room** faire entrer qn dans le hall/la pièce; **to ~ sb to his/her table/seat** conduire qn à sa table/à son siège **2.** (*mark the start*) **to ~ sth in** introduire qc

usherette [ˌʌʃə'ret] *n* ouvreuse *f*

USM *n* **1.** *abbr of* **underwater-to-surface missile** missile *m* mer-sol **2.** *abbr of* **United States Mail** *service des postes américain*

USP [ˌjuːes'piː] *n* ECON *abbr of* **unique selling proposition** proposition *f* unique de vente

USS *n Am* **1.** *abbr of* **United States Ship** *navire américain* **2.** *abbr of* **United States Senate** *sénat américain*

usual ['juːʒl, *Am:* -ʒuəl] **I.** *adj* habituel(le); **as ~** comme d'habitude; **to be ~ to** +*infin* être d'usage de +*infin* **II.** *n* **the ~** *inf* comme d'habitude

usually ['juːʒəlɪ, *Am:* -ʒuəlɪ] *adv* d'habitude; **more than ~** plus que d'habitude

usufruct ['juːsjuːfrʌkt, *Am:* -zʊ-] *n form* LAW usufruit *m*

usurer ['juːʒərəʳ, *Am:* -ɚ] *n pej* LAW usurier, -ère *m, f*

usurious [juː'zjʊərɪəs, *Am:* juː'ʒʊrɪ-] *adj* LAW usuraire

usurp [juː'zɜːp, *Am:* -'sɜːrp] *vt* usurper

usurper *n* usurpateur, -trice *m, f*

usury ['juːʒərɪ, *Am:* -ʒɚɪ] *n no pl, pej* LAW usure *f*

USW *n abbr of* **ultrashort waves** ondes *fpl* ultracourtes

Utah ['juːtɑː] **I.** *n* l'Utah *m* **II.** *adj* de l'Utah

utensil [juː'tensl] *n* ustensile *m*

uterine ['juːtəraɪn, *Am:* -t̬ɚɪn] *adj* ANAT utérin(e)

uterus ['juːtərəs, *Am:* -t̬ɚ-] <-ri *o* -es> *n* utérus *m*

utilise ['juːtɪlaɪz, *Am:* -t̬laɪz] *vt Aus, Brit* utiliser

utilitarian [juːˌtɪlɪ'teərɪən, *Am:* -ə'terɪ-] *adj* PHILOS utilitaire

utility [juː'tɪlətɪ, *Am:* -t̬ɪ] <-ies> **I.** *n* **1.** *form* (*usefulness*) utilité *f* **2.** (*public service*) (**public**) **~** service *m* public **3.** INFOR utilitaire *m* **II.** *adj* **1.** (*useful*) utilitaire **2.** (*functional*) fonctionnel(le)

utility expenses *npl* dépenses *fpl* publiques **utility program** *n* INFOR (programme *m*) utilitaire **utility room** *n* buanderie *f* **utility vehicle** *n* véhicule *m* utilitaire

utilization *n no pl, form* utilisation *f*

utilize ['juːtɪlaɪz, *Am:* -t̬laɪz] *s.* **utilise**

utmost ['ʌtməʊst, *Am:* -moʊst] **I.** *adj* extrême; **of the ~ brilliance** (*person, mind*) de la plus grande intelligence; **with the ~ caution** avec la plus grande précaution; **a matter of ~ importance** une affaire de prime importance **II.** *n no pl* **the ~** l'extrême; **to the ~** au maximum; **to offer the ~ in performance** offrir le maximum en matière de performance; **to live life to the ~** vivre sa vie à l'extrême; **to try one's ~** essayer tout son possible

utopia [juː'təʊpiə, *Am:* -'toʊ-] *n* utopie *f*

utopian *adj* utopique

utter[1] ['ʌtəʳ, *Am:* 'ʌt̬ɚ] *adj* complet(-ète); **to be ~ nonsense** être complètement absurde; **~ madness** pure folie *f;* **an ~ fool** un idiot fini; **an ~ waste of time** une pure perte de temps

utter[2] ['ʌtəʳ, *Am:* 'ʌt̬ɚ] *vt* (*make a sound: word, name*) prononcer; (*sound*) émettre; (*cry, grunt*) pousser; (*insult, threat*) proférer

utterance ['ʌtərəns, *Am:* 'ʌt̬-] *n* **1.** (*comment*) paroles *fpl* **2.** *no pl* (*expressing*) énonciation *f* **3.** LING énoncé *m*

utterly *adv* **1.** (*completely*) complètement; **to be ~ convinced that ...** être tout à fait convaincu que ... **2.** (*absolutely*) absolument

uttermost ['ʌtəməʊst, *Am:* 'ʌt̬ɚmoʊst] **I.** *n s.* **utmost** **II.** *adj s.* **utmost**

U-turn ['juːtɜːn, *Am:* -tɜːrn] *n* **1.** AUTO demi-tour *m* **2.** *fig* volte-face *f*

UV *n abbr of* **ultraviolet** UV *m*

UVF *n Brit abbr of* **Ulster Volunteer Force** *organisation paramilitaire loyaliste en Irlande du Nord*

uvula ['juːvjʊlə] *n* ANAT luette *f*

uxorious [ˌʌk'sɔːrɪəs] *adj form* soumis

Uzbek ['ʌzˌbək] **I.** *adj* ouzbek **II.** *n* Ouzbek *mf*

Uzbekistan [ʌz'bekɪstən, *Am:* -ˌbekɪ'stæn] *n* Ouzbékistan *m*

V

V, v [viː] <-'s *o* -s> *n* V *m,* v *m;* **~ as in Victor, ~ for Victor** (*on telephone*) v comme Victor

V *n* **1.** *abbr of* **volume** v **2.** *abbr of* **volt** V *m*

vac [væk] **I.** *n* **1.** *Brit, inf* UNIV *abbr of* **vacation** vacances *fpl;* **the long ~** les grandes vacances **2.** *inf abbr of* **vacuum cleaner** aspirateur *m* **II.** <-cc-> *vt Am, inf abbr of* **vacuum clean** (*carpet*) passer l'aspirateur sur; (*room*) passer l'aspirateur dans **III.** *vi abbr of* **vacuum clean** passer l'aspirateur

vacancy ['veɪkəntsi] <-ies> *n* **1.** (*unoccupied room*) chambre *f* à louer; **'vacancies'** chambres *fpl* disponibles; **'no vacancies'** (hôtel) complet **2.** (*time for appointment*) disponibilité *f* **3.** (*employment opportunity*) poste *m* vacant; **to fill a ~** pourvoir un poste vacant; **to have a ~ for a secretary** avoir un poste de secrétaire à pourvoir **4.** *no pl* (*lack of expression*) vide *m*

vacant ['veɪkənt] *adj* **1.** (*empty*) vide **2.** (*unoccupied: room*) inoccupé(e) (*seat, chair*) libre; (*positon*) vacant(e) **3.** (*unfilled: time*) disponible **4.** (*expressionless*) vide

vacate [və'keɪt, *Am:* 'veɪkeɪt] *vt form* quitter

vacation [və'keɪʃən, *Am:* veɪ-] *Am* **I.** *n* vacances *fpl;* **to take a ~** prendre des vacances; **on ~** en vacances **II.** *vi* passer des vacances

vacationer *n Am* vacancier, -ère *m, f*

vaccinate ['væksɪneɪt, *Am:* -səneɪt-] *vt* MED vacciner

vaccination [ˌvæksɪ'neɪʃən, *Am:* -sə'neɪ-] *n* MED vaccination *f;* **to have a ~** se faire vacciner

vaccine ['væksiːn, *Am:* væk'siːn] *n* MED vaccin *m*

vacuous ['vækjuəs] *adj form* vide

vacuum ['vækjuːm] **I.** *n* **1.** (*space*) *a. fig* vide *m;* **to fill/leave a ~** remplir/laisser un vide **2.** (*~ cleaner*) aspirateur *m* **II.** *vt* (*carpet*) passer l'aspirateur sur; (*room*) passer l'aspirateur dans

vacuum bottle *n Am* thermos® *m o f* **vacuum cleaner** *n* aspirateur *m* **vacuum flask** *n Brit* thermos® *m o f* **vacuum-packaged**, **vacuum-packed** *adj* emballé(e) sous vide

vagabond ['vægəbɒnd, *Am:* -bɑːnd] *n* vagabond(e) *m(f)*

vagary ['veɪgəri, *Am:* 'veɪgɚi] <-ies> *n* caprice *m*

vagina [və'dʒaɪnə] *n* ANAT vagin *m*

vagrancy ['veɪgrənsi] *n no pl* vagabondage *m*

vagrant ['veɪgrənt] *n* vagabond(e) *m(f)*

vague [veɪg] *adj* **1.** (*imprecise*) vague **2.** (*absent-minded*) distrait(e) **3.** (*uncertain, unsure*) confus(e); **to be ~ about sth** rester vague sur qc

vaguely *adv* **1.** (*faintly: remember*) vaguement **2.** (*distractedly: say, smile*) d'un air distrait; (*move*) distraitement

vagueness *n no pl* **1.** (*lack of clarity: memories, story*) imprécision *f;* (*photograph*) flou *m* **2.** (*sensation, feeling*) caractère *m* vague

vain [veɪn] *adj* **1.** *pej* (*conceited*) vaniteux(-euse) **2.** (*futile*) vain(e); **in ~** en vain

vainly *adv* **1.** (*in vain*) vainement **2.** *pej* (*behave*) avec vanité

valance ['vælənts] *n* **1.** (*textile around a bed*) tour *m* de lit **2.** *Am* (*cloth for curtain rail*) galon *m*

vale, **Vale** [veɪl] *n* (*valley*) vallée *f*

valence ['veɪlənts], **valency** *n* CHEM, PHYS valence *f*

valentine ['væləntaɪn] *n carte de vœux pour la Saint-Valentin;* **to be sb's ~** être l'élu de qn pour la Saint-Valentin

Valentine's Day *n no pl* (*Feb 14*) la Saint-Valentin

valet ['væleɪ, *Am:* 'vælɪt] **I.** *n* **1.** HIST valet *m* de chambre **2.** (*employee who parks cars*) *portier chargé de garer les voitures des clients* **II.** *vt Brit* (*a car*) nettoyer

valet service *n* service *m* de nettoyage

Valetta [və'letə, *Am:* vɑː'letɑː] *n* La Valette

valiant ['væliənt, *Am:* -jənt] *adj* vaillant(e); (*attempt*) courageux(-euse)

valiantly *adv* vaillamment

valid ['vælɪd] *adj* **1.** (*acceptable*) valable; (*licence*) en règle; (*passport, ticket*) valide **2.** (*worthwhile*) pertinent(e); (*precaution*) judicieux(-euse)

validate ['vælɪdeɪt, *Am:* 'vælə-] *vt* **1.** (*ratify: document*) valider **2.** (*verify: theory, claim*) confirmer; **to be ~d in one's feelings** être conforté dans ses sentiments

validity [və'lɪdəti, *Am:* -t̬i] *n no pl* **1.** (*acceptability*) validité *f* **2.** (*accuracy*) justesse *f*

valley ['væli] *n* vallée *f*

valor *n no pl, Am, Aus,* **valour** ['vælər, *Am:* -ɚ] *n no pl, Brit, Aus, form* bravoure *f*

valuable **I.** *adj a. fig* précieux(-euse) **II.** *n pl* objets *mpl* de valeur

valuation [ˌvælju'eɪʃən] *n* **1.** (*estimation*) estimation *f* **2.** *no pl* (*financial value*) valeur *f* estimée

valuator *n* FIN expert(e) *m(f)*

value ['væljuː] **I.** *n* **1.** *no pl* (*importance, worth*) valeur *f;* **to be of little ~** être de peu de valeur; **to place a high ~ on sth** attacher une grande importance à qc; **to be good/poor ~** (**for money**) être une bonne/mauvaise affaire **2.** (*possible price*) valeur *f;* **to assess the ~ of sth** estimer qc; **the ~ of sth falls/rises** qc perd/prend de la valeur **3.** (*ethical standard*) valeur *f;* **basic ~s** les grandes valeurs **II.** *vt* estimer

value-added tax *n Brit* taxe *f* à la valeur ajoutée

valued *adj* estimé(e)

valueless *adj* sans valeur

valuer *n Brit* FIN expert(e) *m(f)*

valve [vælv] *n* **1.** (*intake, outflow control*) soupape *f;* (*on tyre*) valve *f* **2.** (*part of organs*) valvule *f* **3.** (*instrument part*) piston *m*

vamp [væmp] *n* vamp *f*

vampire ['væmpaɪər, *Am:* -paɪɚ] *n* vampire *m*

van[1] [væn] *n* **1.** *Brit* (*vehicle*) camionnette *f* **2.** *Am* (*commercial vehicle*) véhicule *m* de fonction **3.** *Brit* (*rail carriage*) fourgon *m*

van[2] [væn] *n no pl abbr of* **vanguard** *a. fig* **in the ~** à l'avant-garde

van[3] [væn] *n Brit, inf* SPORT *abbr of* **advantage** avantage *m*

Vanatuan **I.** *adj* vanatuan(ne) **II.** *n* Vanatuan(ne) *m(f)*

vandal ['vændəl] *n* vandale *mf*

vandalise ['vændəlaɪz] *vt Aus, Brit* saccager

vandalism ['vændəlɪzəm] *n no pl* vanda-

lisme *m*

vandalize ['vændəlaɪz] *vt s.* **vandalise**

vane [veɪn] *n* pale *f*

vanguard ['vængɑːd, *Am:* -gɑːrd] *n no pl, a. fig, form* avant-garde *f;* **to be in the ~ of sth** être à l'avant-garde de qc

vanilla [və'nɪlə] **I.** *n no pl* BOT vanille *f* **II.** *adj* (*ice-cream, yoghurt*) à la vanille

vanilla pod *n no pl* gousse *f* de vanille **vanilla sugar** *n no pl* sucre *m* vanillé

vanillin *n no pl* vanilline *f*

vanish ['vænɪʃ] *vi* disparaître; **to ~ into thin air** s'envoler; **to ~ from sight** disparaître de la vue; **a ~ed era** une époque révolue; **to see one's hopes ~ing** voir ses espoirs s'envoler

vanishing cream *n* crème *f* de jour **vanishing point** *n* **1.** (*point at horizon*) point *m* de l'horizon **2.** (*smaller point*) point *m* zéro

vanity ['vænəti, *Am:* -əṭi] *n no pl* vanité *f*

vanity bag, **vanity case** *n* vanity-case *m*

vantage ['vɑːntɪdʒ, *Am:* 'vænṭɪdʒ] *n* avantage *m*

vantage point *n* point *m* de vue; **from the ~ of sb/sth** du point de vue de qn/qc

Vanuatu [ˌvænu'ɑːtuː, *Am:* væn'wɑːtuː] *n* Vanuatu *m*

vapid ['væpɪd] *adj pej* insipide

vapor ['veɪpəʳ, *Am:* -pɚ] *n Am, Aus s.* **vapour**

vaporisation *n Brit, Aus s.* **vaporization**

vaporise *n Brit, Aus s.* **vaporize**

vaporiser *n s.* **vapourizer**

vaporization [ˌveɪpəraɪ'zeɪʃən, *Am:* -ɪ'-] *n* vaporisation *f*

vaporize ['veɪpəraɪz] **I.** *vt* vaporiser **II.** *vi* s'évaporer

vaporizer *n* vaporisateur *m*

vapour ['veɪpəʳ, *Am:* -pɚ] *n* vapeur *f;* **water ~** vapeur d'eau

vapo(u)r pressure *n* pression *f* de la vapeur **vapo(u)r trail** *n* traînée *f* blanche

variability [ˌveəriə'bɪləti, *Am:* ˌveriə'bɪləṭi] *n no pl* variabilité *f*

variable ['veəriəbl, *Am:* 'veri-] *adj, n* variable *f*

variable geometry wing *n* AVIAT aileron *m*

variance ['veəriənts, *Am:* 'veri-] *n* **1.** *no pl* divergence *f;* **to be at ~ with sth** *form* (*in disagreement*) être en désaccord avec qc **2.** *Am* (*permission*) autorisation *f* spéciale

variant ['veəriənt, *Am:* 'veri-] **I.** *n* variante *f* **II.** *adj* de différentes sortes; (*spelling*) différent(e)

variation [ˌveəri'eɪʃən, *Am:* ˌveri'-] *n no pl a.* MUS variation *f;* **seasonal/temperature ~s** variations *fpl* saisonnières/de température; **wide ~s** des fortes fluctuations; **~s on a theme** variations sur un même thème

varicose ['værɪkəʊs, *Am:* 'verəkoʊs] *adj* MED variqueux(-euse); **~ veins** varices *fpl*

varied *adj* varié(e); (*career*) mouvementé(e); (*group*) hétérogène

variegated ['veərɪgeɪtɪd, *Am:* 'veriəgeɪṭɪd] *adj* bigarré(e); BOT panaché(e)

variety [və'raɪəti, *Am:* -ṭi] *n* **1.** (*diversity*) variété *f;* **a ~ styles** divers styles; **in a ~ of ways** de plusieurs manières; **for a ~ of reasons** pour diverses raisons; **genetic ~** diversité *f* génétique; **to lend ~** apporter de la variété; **a new ~ of tulip** une nouvelle variété de tulipe **2.** THEAT variétés *fpl*

variety act *n* numéro *m* de variétés **variety show** *n* spectacle *m* de variétés **variety theatre** *n* théâtre *m* de variétés

various ['veəriəs, *Am:* 'veri-] *adj* divers(e)

variously *adv* diversement

varmint ['vɑːmɪnt, *Am:* 'vɑːr-] *n Am* fripouille *f*

varnish ['vɑːnɪʃ, *Am:* 'vɑːr-] **I.** *n* vernis *m* **II.** *vt* vernir

varsity ['vɑːsəti, *Am:* 'vɑːrsəṭi] **I.** *n Brit, inf* fac *f* **II.** *adj Am* universitaire

vary ['veəri, *Am:* 'veri] <-ie-> **I.** *vi* varier; (*opinions*) diverger; **to ~ from sth** différer de qc; **to ~ from sth to sth** varier de qc à qc **II.** *vt* varier; **to ~ one's route** changer de route

varying *adj* variable

vascular ['væskjələʳ, *Am:* -kjəlɚ] *adj* MED, BOT vasculaire

vase [vɑːz, *Am:* veɪs] *n* vase *m*

vasectomy [və'sektəmi] *n* vasectomie *f*

vassal ['væsəl] *n a. fig, pej* HIST vassal *m*

vast [vɑːst, *Am:* væst] *adj* (*country, fortune, majority*) vaste; **a ~ difference/amount of money** une énorme différence/somme d'argent

vastly *adv* énormément; (*different*) extrêmement

vastness *n* étendue *f*

vat [væt] *n* **1.** (*receptacle*) bac *m* **2.** *Brit* FIN, ECON *s.* **VAT**

VAT [ˌviːeɪ'tiː] *n no pl, Brit abbr of* **value added tax** TVA *f*

Vatican ['vætɪkən, *Am:* 'væṭ-] *n no pl* **the ~** le Vatican

vaudeville ['vɔːdəvɪl, *Am:* 'vɑːdvɪl] *n no pl, Am* (*variety theatre*) vaudeville *m*

vault [vɔːlt, *Am:* vɑːlt] **I.** *n* **1.** (*type of arch*) voûte *f* **2.** (*secure room*) salle *f* des coffres **3.** (*safe*) coffre-fort *m* **4.** (*chamber*) caveau *m;* **family ~** caveau familial **5.** (*jump*) saut *m* **II.** *vt* **1.** (*jump*) sauter **2.** (*promote very fast*) propulser **III.** *vi* sauter

vaulted *adj* ARCHIT voûté(e)

vaulting I. *n no pl* ARCHIT voûte *f* **II.** *adj, pej* (*ambition, costs*) démesuré(e)

vaulting horse *n* SPORT cheval *m* d'arçons

vaunt [vɔːnt, *Am:* vɑːnt] *vt* vanter; **her much-~ed dynamism** son dynamisme tant vanté

VC [ˌviː'siː] *n* **1.** *Brit abbr of* **Victoria Cross** *la plus haute distinction militaire du "Commonwealth"* **2.** *abbr of* **Vice-Chairman** vice-président(e) *m(f)*

VCR [ˌviːsiː'ɑːʳ, *Am:* -'ɑːr] *n Am abbr of* **video cassette recorder** magnétoscope *m*

VD [ˌviːˈdiː] *n abbr of* **veneral disease** MST *f inv*

VDU [ˌviːdiːˈjuː] *n abbr of* **visual display unit** INFOR écran *m* de visualisation

veal [viːl] *n no pl* (viande *f* de) veau *m*

veal cutlet *n* escalope *f* de veau

vector [ˈvektəʳ, *Am:* -tɚ] *n* **1.** MAT vecteur *m* **2.** BIO porteur *m*

VE day [ˌviːˈiːdeɪ] *n abbr of* **day of Victory in Europe** *le 8 mai 1945*

veer [vɪəʳ, *Am:* vɪr] *vi* **1.** (*alter course unexpectedly*) tourner **2.** (*alter attitude*) changer; **to ~ away from sth** se détourner de qc; **to ~ back and forth** tourner comme une girouette; **to ~ towards sth** se tourner vers qc

veg [vedʒ] *inv n Brit, inf abbr of* **vegetable** légume *m*

vegan [ˈviːgən] **I.** *n* végétalien(ne) *m(f)* **II.** *adj* végétalien(ne)

vegetable [ˈvedʒtəbl] **I.** *n a. pej* légume *m;* **seasonal ~** légume de saison; **early ~s** primeurs *fpl* **II.** *adj* végétal(e); (*soup, dish*) de légumes

vegetable garden *n* potager *m* **vegetable kingdom** *n no pl* flore *f* **vegetable marrow** *n* courge *f* **vegetable oil** *n* huile *f* végétale **vegetable rack** *n* casier *m* à légumes

vegetarian [ˌvedʒɪˈteəriən, *Am:* -əˈteri-] **I.** *n* végétarien(ne) *m(f)* **II.** *adj* végétarien(ne); **a ~ diet** un régime végétarien

vegetate [ˈvedʒɪteɪt, *Am:* ˈ-ə-] *vi* végéter

vegetation [ˌvedʒɪˈteɪʃən, *Am:* -əˈ-] *n no pl* végétation *f*

veggie [ˈvedʒi] **I.** *n inf* **1.** (*vegetarian*) végétarien(ne) *m(f)* **2.** (*vegetables*) légume *m* **II.** *adj inf* végétarien(ne)

veggie burger *n* hamburger *m* végétarien

vehemence [ˈviːəmənts] *n no pl* véhémence *f*

vehement [ˈviːəmənt] *adj* véhément(e)

vehicle [ˈvɪəkl, *Am:* ˈviːə-] *n form* (*method of transport*) *a. fig* véhicule *m*

vehicle registration centre *n Brit* service *m* des cartes grises **vehicle registration number** *n Brit* numéro *m* d'immatriculation du véhicule

vehicular [viˈɪkjələʳ, *Am:* viːˈhɪkjəlɚ] *adj form* véhiculaire; **~ traffic** circulation *f* routière

veil [veɪl] **I.** *n a. fig* voile *m* **II.** *vt* **1.** *passive* (*cover by veil*) **to be ~ed** être voilé **2.** (*cover*) voiler

veiled *adj a. fig* voilé(e)

vein [veɪn] *n* **1.** (*blood vessel*) *a.* MIN veine *f* **2.** (*for plant sap*) nervure *f* **3.** (*style*) veine *f* **4.** (*frame of mind*) humeur *f*

veined *adj* veiné(e)

velar [ˈviːləʳ, *Am:* -lɚ] **I.** *adj* LING vélaire **II.** *n* LING vélaire *f*

Velcro® [ˈvelkrəʊ, *Am:* -kroʊ] *n no pl* velcro *m;* **~ fastener** fermeture *f* velcro

veld, veldt [velt] *n* veld *m*

velocity [vɪˈlɒsəti, *Am:* vəˈlɑːsət̬i] *n form* vitesse *f*

velvet [ˈvelvɪt] *n no pl* velours *m;* **a ~ glove** un gant de velours; **a ~ voice** une voix douce; **as soft as ~** doux comme de la soie

velveteen [ˌvelvɪˈtiːn] *n* velours *m*

velvety [ˈvelvɪti, *Am:* -vət̬i] *adj* velouté(e); (*eyes*) de velours; (*beer*) doux(douce)

venal [ˈviːnəl] *adj pej, form* vénal(e)

venality [viːˈnæləti, *Am:* vɪˈnælət̬i] *n no pl, pej, form* vénalité *f*

vend [vend] *vt* vendre

vendetta [venˈdetə, *Am:* -ˈdet̬-] *n* vendetta *f*

vending machine *n* distributeur *m* automatique

vendor [ˈvendɔːʳ, *Am:* -dɚ] *n* marchand(e) *m(f);* (*on the street*) marchand(e) *m(f)* ambulant(e)

vendue [ˈvendjuː] *n Am* vente *f* aux enchères

veneer [vəˈnɪəʳ, *Am:* -ˈnɪr] *n* **1.** (*layer covering surface*) placage *m* **2.** *no pl* (*facade*) façade *f*

venerable [ˈvenərəbl] *adj* vénérable

Venerable *adj no pl* **1.** (*Anglican archdeacon's title*) révérend *m* **2.** (*Catholic rank below saint*) vénérable *m*

venerate [ˈvenəreɪt] *vt form* vénérer

veneration [ˌvenəˈreɪʃen] *n no pl* vénération *f*

venereal [vəˈnɪəriəl, *Am:* vəˈnɪri-] *adj* MED vénérien(ne)

venetian blind *n* store *m* vénitien

Venezuela [ˌvenɪˈzweɪlə, *Am:* -əˈzweɪ-] *n* le Vénézuela

Venezuelan **I.** *adj* vénézuélien(ne) **II.** *n* Vénézuélien(ne) *m(f)*

vengeance [ˈvendʒənts] *n no pl* vengeance *f;* **with a ~** de plus belle

vengeful *adj* vengeur(-esse)

venial [ˈviːniəl] *adj form* pardonnable

Venice [ˈvenɪs] *n* Venise *f*

venison [ˈvenɪsən] *n no pl* chevreuil *m*

venom [ˈvenəm] *n no pl, a. fig* venin *m*

venomous [ˈvenəməs] *adj fig, pej* venimeux(-euse); **a ~ tongue** une langue de serpent

venous [ˈviːnəs] *adj* ANAT, MED veineux(-euse)

vent [vent] **I.** *n* **1.** (*opening*) conduit *m* **2.** FASHION fente *f* ▶**to give ~ to sth** donner libre cours à qc; **to give ~ to anger** laisser exploser sa colère **II.** *vt a. fig* décharger; **to ~ one's anger on sb** laisser éclater sa colère sur qn

ventilate [ˈventɪleɪt, *Am:* -t̬əleɪt-] *vt* (*oxygenate*) aérer

ventilation [ˌventɪˈleɪʃən, *Am:* -t̬əˈleɪ-] *n no pl* aération *f;* **I opened the window for ~** j'ai ouvert la fenêtre pour aérer

ventilation duct *n* conduit *m* d'aération

ventilator [ˈventɪleɪtəʳ, *Am:* -t̬əleɪt̬ɚ] *n* ventilateur *m*

ventricle [ˈventrɪkl] *n* ventricule *m*

ventriloquist [venˈtrɪləkwɪst] *n* ventriloque

mf

venture ['ventʃəʳ, *Am:* -tʃɚ] I. *n* entreprise *f;* **my first ~ into journalism** ma première incursion dans le journalisme II. *vt* 1. (*dare to express: explanation*) hasarder; **to ~ an opinion** se hasarder à donner une opinion 2. (*put at risk*) risquer; **to ~ to** *+infin* se risquer à *+infin* ▶**nothing ~d, nothing gained** *prov* qui ne risque rien n'a rien III. *vi* s'aventurer; **to ~ into sth** s'aventurer dans qc; **to ~ on sth** se risquer à qc; **to ~ out in sth** se risquer à sortir dans qc

venture capital *n* capital-risque *m*

venturesome ['ventʃəsəm, *Am:* -tʃɚ-] *adj form* 1. (*adventurous: person*) aventureux(-euse) 2. (*risky, not safe*) risqué(e)

venue ['venju:] *n* 1. (*place*) lieu *m* de rencontre; (*in hall*) salle *f;* (*for match*) terrain *m;* **the ~ for the match/concert will be at ...** le match/concert aura lieu à ... 2. *Am* LAW prétoire *m*

Venus ['vi:nəs] *n no pl* Vénus *f*

veracity [və'ræsəti, *Am:* və'ræsət̬i] *n no pl, form* véracité *f*

veranda, **verandah** [və'rændə] *n* véranda *f*

verb [vɜ:b, *Am:* vɜ:rb] *n* verbe *m*

verbal ['vɜ:bəl, *Am:* 'vɜ:r-] *adj a.* LING verbal(e)

verbalise *vt, vi Aus, Brit,* **verbalize** ['vɜ:bəlaɪz, *Am:* 'vɜ:r-] I. *vt* exprimer II. *vi* s'exprimer

verbally *adv* verbalement

verbatim [vɜ:'beɪtɪm, *Am:* vɚ'beɪt̬ɪm] I. *adj* textuel(le) II. *adv* textuellement

verbiage ['vɜ:biɪdʒ, *Am:* 'vɜ:r-] *n no pl, pej, form* verbiage *m*

verbose [vɜ:'bəʊs, *Am:* vɚ'boʊs] *adj pej, form* verbeux(-euse)

verbosity [vɜ:'bɒsəti, *Am:* vɚ'bɑ:sət̬i] *n no pl, pej, form* verbosité *f*

verdict ['vɜ:dɪkt, *Am:* 'vɜ:r-] *n* verdict *m;* **a guilty ~** un verdict de culpabilité; **to bring in** [*o* **deliver**] **a ~** rendre un verdict; **what's your ~?** quel est ton verdict?

verdigris ['vɜ:dɪgrɪs, *Am:* 'vɜ:rdɪgri:s] *n no pl* vert-de-gris *m*

verge [vɜ:dʒ, *Am:* vɜ:rdʒ] *n* 1. (*physical edge*) bord *m;* **on the ~ of the road** sur le bord de la route 2. *Brit* (*on road*) bas-côté *m;* **grass ~** bordure *f;* **soft ~s** AUTO accotement *m* instable 3. (*brink*) **to be on the ~ of tears** être au bord des larmes; **to be on the ~ of childhood** être au seuil de l'enfance; **to be on the ~ of resigning/leaving sb** être sur le point de démissionner/quitter qn

verge on *vt* friser; **to ~ the ridiculous** friser le ridicule

verger *n* sacristain(e) *m(f)*

verifiable *adj* vérifiable

verification [ˌverɪfɪ'keɪʃən, *Am:* ˌ-ə-] *n no pl* vérification *f*

verify ['verɪfaɪ, *Am:* '-ə-] <-ie-> *vt* vérifier

verisimilitude [ˌverɪsɪ'mɪlɪtju:d, *Am:* -əsə'mɪlətu:d] *n no pl, form* vraisemblance *f*

veritable ['verɪtəbl, *Am:* -ət̬ə-] *adj* véritable

vermicelli [ˌvɜ:mɪ'tʃeli, *Am:* ˌvɜ:rmə'tʃel-] *n no pl* vermicelle *m*

vermicide ['vɜ:mɪsaɪd, *Am:* 'vɜ:rmə-] *n* vermifuge *m*

vermilion, **vermillion** [və'mɪljən, *Am:* vɚ'mɪljən] I. *n* vermillon *m* II. *adj* vermillon *inv*

vermin ['vɜ:mɪn, *Am:* 'vɜ:r-] *npl pej, a. fig* vermine *f*

verminous *adj pej* pourri(e)

Vermont [və'mɒnt, *Am:* vɚ'mɑ:nt] I. *n* le Vermont II. *adj* du Vermont

vermouth ['vɜ:məθ, *Am:* vɚ'mu:θ] *n no pl* vermouth *m*

vernacular [və'nækjələʳ, *Am:* vɚ'nækjəlɚ] I. *n* langue *f* vernaculaire II. *adj* vernaculaire

vernal equinox *n* équinoxe *f* vernal

veronica [və'rɒnɪkə, *Am:* və'rɑ:nɪ-] *n* véronique *f*

verruca [və'ru:kə] <-s *o* -ae> *n* verrue *f*

versatile ['vɜ:sətaɪl, *Am:* 'vɜ:rsət̬əl] *adj* (*tool, actor*) polyvalent(e); (*mind*) souple

versatility [ˌvɜ:sə'tɪləti, *Am:* ˌvɜ:rsə'tɪlət̬i] *n no pl* polyvalence *f*

verse [vɜ:s, *Am:* vɜ:rs] *n* 1. *no pl* (*poetry*) vers *m;* (*of song*) couplet *m;* **in ~** en vers 2. REL verset *m*

versed *adj form* **to be** (**well**) **~ in sth** être versé dans qc

versifier *n* versificateur *m*

versify ['vɜ:sɪfaɪ, *Am:* 'vɜ:rsə-] I. *vi* faire des vers II. *vt* versifier

version ['vɜ:ʃən, *Am:* 'vɜ:rʒən] *n* version *f;* **official ~** version *f* officielle

verso ['vɜ:səʊ, *Am:* 'vɜ:rsoʊ] *n form* 1. (*back of page*) verso *m* 2. (*reverse side: of a coin*) revers *m*

versus ['vɜ:səs, *Am:* 'vɜ:r-] *prep* 1. (*in comparison*) par opposition [*o* rapport] à 2. SPORT, LAW contre

vertebra ['vɜ:tɪbrə, *Am:* 'vɜ:rt̬ə-] <-brae> *n* vertèbre *f*

vertebral ['vɜ:tɪbrəl, *Am:* 'vɜ:rt̬ə-] *adj* ANAT, MED vertébral(e)

vertebrate ['vɜ:tɪbreɪt, *Am:* 'vɜ:rtəbrɪt] I. *n* vertébré *m* II. *adj* vertébré(e)

vertex ['vɜ:teks, *Am:* 'vɜ:r-] <-es *o* -tices> *n* MAT sommet *m*

vertical ['vɜ:tɪkəl, *Am:* 'vɜ:rt̬ə-] *adj* vertical(e)

vertical take-off *n* décollage *m* vertical; **~ take-off aircraft** avion *m* à décollage vertical

vertiginous [vɜ:'tɪdʒɪnəs, *Am:* vɚ'tɪdʒə-] *adj form* (*dizzying*) vertigineux(-euse)

vertigo ['vɜ:tɪgəʊ, *Am:* 'vɜ:rt̬əgoʊ] *n no pl* vertige *m*

verve [vɜ:v, *Am:* vɜ:rv] *n no pl* 1. verve *f;* **with ~** avec brio 2. *fig* **to give sth** (**added**) **~** donner du brillant à qc

very ['veri] **I.** *adv* **1.** (*extremely*) très; **to be ~ hungry** avoir très faim **2.** (*to a great degree*) **~ much** beaucoup; **to feel ~ much at home** se sentir vraiment chez soi; **we're ~ much in love** nous sommes très amoureux; **things are still ~ much the same** les choses n'ont que très peu changé **3.** (*expression of emphasis*) **the ~ best** tout ce qu'il y a de mieux; **the ~ best of friends** le meilleur des amis; **~ best quality** toute première qualité; **the ~ first/last** le tout premier/dernier; **to do the ~ best one can** vraiment faire tout son possible; **at the ~ most/least** tout au plus/au moins; **the ~ same** exactement le même; **it's my ~ own** c'est le mien ►**~ well** très bien; **that's all ~ fine ..., but...** c'est bien beau de ..., mais ... **II.** *adj* même; **this ~ house** cette maison même; **this ~ day** aujourd'hui même; **to the ~ end** jusqu'au bout; **from the ~ beginning** depuis le tout début; **the ~ thought of sth** la seule pensée de qc; **this is the ~ thing to do** c'est exactement la chose à faire ►**the ~ idea!** quelle idée!

Very light *n* fusée *f* éclairante **Very pistol** *n* pistolet *m* lance-fusées

vesicle ['vesɪkl] *n* vésicule *f*

vespers ['vespəz, *Am:* -pɚz] *npl* vêpres *fpl*

vessel ['vesəl] *n* **1.** *form* (*boat*) vaisseau *m* **2.** *form* (*container*) récipient *m* **3.** ANAT, BOT vaisseau *m*

vest[1] [vest] *n* **1.** *Brit* (*undergarment*) maillot *m* de corps **2.** *Am, Aus* (*waistcoat*) gilet *m* **3.** SPORT maillot *m*

vest[2] [vest] *vt form* investir; **to ~ sb with sth** investir qn de qc; **to ~ sth in sb** assigner qn de qc; **to ~ one's hopes in sb/sth** placer ses espoirs en qn/qc; **by the authority ~ed in me** en vertu de l'autorité dont je suis investi

vestal virgin *n* vestale *f*

vested interest *n* intérêts *mpl* personnels

vestibule ['vestɪbju:l, *Am:* -tə-] *n form* **1.** (*foyer*) vestibule *m* **2.** *Am* (*porch*) antichambre *f*

vestige ['vestɪdʒ] *n a. fig* vestige *m;* **to remove the last ~ of doubt** enlever le dernier vestige de doute

vestment ['vestmənt] *n* vêtement *m* sacerdotal

vest-pocket *adj* **1.** (*pocket-size*) de poche **2.** (*very small*) miniature

vestry ['vestri] *n* sacristie *f*

vet[1] [vet] *n* (*animal doctor*) vétérinaire *mf*

vet[2] [vet] *n Am, inf* (*veteran*) vétéran *m*

vet[3] [vet] *vt* <-tt-> examiner; **to be ~ted by sb/sth** recevoir l'approbation de qn/qc

vetch [vetʃ] *n* BOT vesce *f*

veteran ['vetərən, *Am:* 'vet̬ɚən] **I.** *n* **1.** (*person with experience*) vétéran *m* **2.** MIL ancien combattant *m* **II.** *adj* **1.** (*very experienced*) aguerri(e) **2.** *Brit* (*old*) vieux(vieille)

veteran car *n Brit* voiture *f* d'époque

> Le **Veteran Day**, le 11 novembre, fut instauré à l'origine en souvenir de l'armistice de 1918 conclu entre l'Allemagne et les États-Unis d'Amérique. Ce jour férié rend honneur à tous les vétérans des guerres américaines.

veterinarian [ˌvetərɪ'neəriən, *Am:* -'neri-] *n Am, form* (*vet*) vétérinaire *mf*

veterinary ['vetərɪnəri, *Am:* -ner-] **I.** *adj* vétérinaire **II.** *n* vétérinaire *mf*

veto ['vi:təʊ, *Am:* -t̬oʊ] **I.** <-es> *n* veto *m;* **to have the power of ~** avoir le droit de veto; **to have a ~ over sth** avoir le droit de veto sur qc **II.** *vt* <vetoed> **1.** (*exercise a veto against*) opposer son veto à **2.** (*forbid*) interdire

vex [veks] *vt* **1.** (*cause trouble*) contrarier **2.** (*upset*) fâcher

vexation [vek'seɪʃən] *n* vexation *f;* **it's a ~ to him that ...** c'est humiliant pour lui de ...

vexatious [vek'seɪʃəs] *adj* contrariant(e); (*child*) irritant(e); (*problem*) fâcheux(-euse)

vexed *adj* **1.** (*problematic: question*) controversé(e) **2.** (*frustrated*) vexé(e); **to be ~ with sb** être fâché avec qn

v. g. *adj abbr of* **very good** TB

VHF [ˌvi:eɪtʃ'ef] *adj abbr of* **very high frequency** RADIO, TV VHF *inv*

VHS® *adj abbr of* **Video Home System** RADIO, TV VHS *inv*

via ['vaɪə] *prep* **1.** (*through*) par; **~ London** via Londres **2.** (*using*) **~ the bridge** en empruntant le pont; **~ a courier** par courrier; **~ a drip** par perfusion

viability [ˌvaɪə'bɪləti, *Am:* -ət̬i] *n no pl* viabilité *f*

viable ['vaɪəbl] *adj* viable

viaduct ['vaɪədʌkt] *n* viaduc *m*

vibes [vaɪbz] *npl inf* **1.** (*general atmosphere*) ambiance *f;* **I'm getting good/bad ~ about sth** sentir/ne pas sentir qc **2.** MUS *s.* **vibraphone**

vibrant ['vaɪbrənt] *adj* **1.** (*lively: person*) vibrant(e) **2.** (*bustling*) animé(e); **there is a ~ life in the center** il y a une vie trépidante dans ce centre **3.** (*bright: colour, light*) vif(vive) **4.** (*strong: voice, sound*) sonore

vibraphone ['vaɪbrəfəʊn, *Am:* -foʊn] *n* MUS vibraphone *m*

vibrate [vaɪ'breɪt, *Am:* 'vaɪbreɪt] **I.** *vi* **1.** (*shake quickly*) vibrer **2.** (*continue to be heard: sound*) retentir **3.** *fig* **to ~ with enthusiasm** frémir d'enthousiasme **II.** *vt* faire vibrer

vibration [vaɪ'breɪʃən] *n* vibration *f*

vibrator [vaɪ'breɪtəʳ, *Am:* 'vaɪbreɪt̬ɚ] *n* vibrateur *m;* **electric ~** vibromasseur *m*

vicar ['vɪkəʳ, *Am:* -ɚ] *n* pasteur *m*

vicarage ['vɪkərɪdʒ] *n* presbytère *m*

vicarious [vɪ'keəriəs, *Am:* -'keri-] *adj* indirect(e); (*authority, power*) délégué(e); **to take ~ pleasure from sth** retirer indirectement du plaisir de qc

vice[1] [vaɪs] *n* vice *m*
vice[2] [vaɪs] *n* (*tool*) étau *m*
vice-chair, **vice-chairman** *n* vice-président(e) *m(f)* **vice-chancellor** *n Brit* UNIV ≈recteur *m* **Vice President**, **vice-president** *n* vice-président(e) *m(f)* **vice squad** *n* brigade *f* mondaine
vice versa [ˌvaɪsi'vɜːsə, *Am:* -sə'vɜːr-] *adv* vice versa
vicinity [vɪ'sɪnəti, *Am:* və'sɪnət̬i] *n* voisinage *m;* **in the ~ of sth** dans les alentours de qc; **in the immediate ~** à proximité ►**in the ~ of 400 dollars** à peu près quatre cents dollars
vicious ['vɪʃəs] *adj* **1.** (*malicious*) malveillant(e); (*fighting*) haineux(-euse); (*gossip*) méchant(e) **2.** (*cruel*) violent(e) **3.** (*able to cause pain*) pervers(e); (*animal*) méchant(e)
vicious circle *n* cercle *m* vicieux
vicissitudes [vɪ'sɪsɪtjuːdz, *Am:* vɪ'sɪsətuːdz] *n form pl* vicissitudes *fpl;* **the ~s of the weather** les aléas *mpl* du climat
victim ['vɪktɪm] *n* (*of crime, illness*) victime *f;* (*of disaster*) sinistré(e) *m(f)* ►**to fall ~ to sb/sth** devenir la victime de qn/qc
victimization *n no pl* représailles *fpl*
victimize ['vɪktɪmaɪz, *Am:* -tə-] *vt* persécuter; **to be ~d** être victime de représailles
victor ['vɪktə^r, *Am:* -tɚ] *n* vainqueur *m*

> La **Victoria Cross** ("VC") fut créée en 1856, pendant la guerre de Crimée, par la reine Victoria, et représente la plus haute distinction militaire du "Commonwealth". Elle est attribuée pour "un courage remarquable"; et son inscription indique: "For valour".

Victoria Day *n no pl, Can: le lundi précédant le 25 mai, les banques et les administrations sont fermées*
Victorian [vɪk'tɔːriən] **I.** *adj* victorien(ne); **the ~ stage** le théâtre de l'époque victorienne **II.** *n* Victorien(ne) *m(f)*
victorious [vɪk'tɔːriəs] *adj* victorieux(-euse); (*team*) vainqueur
victory ['vɪktəri] *n* victoire *f;* **to achieve a ~ against sb** remporter une victoire sur qn; **to lead sb to ~** mener qn sur le chemin de la victoire; **to win a ~ in sth** sortir victorieux de qc
victualer *n Am,* **victualler** *n* fournisseur *m* de vivres
victuals ['vɪtəlz, *Am:* 'vɪt̬-] *n pl* victuailles *fpl*
video ['vɪdiəʊ, *Am:* -oʊ] **I.** *n* **1.** (*motion picture*) vidéo *f;* **to come out on ~** sortir en vidéo **2.** (*tape*) cassette vidéo *f* **3.** (*recorder*) magnétoscope *m* **4.** (*recorded footage*) film *m* vidéo **5.** (*of song*) clip vidéo *m* **II.** *vt* enregistrer sur cassette vidéo
video camera *n* caméra *f* vidéo **video card** *n* INFOR carte *f* vidéo **video cassette** *n* cassette *f* vidéo **video clip** *n* clip *m* vidéo **video conference** *n* visioconférence *f* **video conferencing** *n* vidéoconférence *f* **video game** *n* jeu *m* vidéo **video library** *n* vidéothèque *f* **videophone** *n* visiophone *m* **video recorder** *n* magnétoscope *m* **video set** *n* équipement *m* vidéo **video show** *n* spectacle *m* disponible en cassette vidéo **video surveillance** *n* vidéosurveillance *f* **videotape I.** *n* bande *f* vidéo **II.** *vt* enregistrer sur une cassette vidéo **video tape recorder** *n* magnétoscope *m* **videotex(t)** *n* vidéotex *m* **video transmission** *n* vidéotransmission *f*
vie [vaɪ] *vi* rivaliser; **to ~ for sth** se disputer qc
Vienna [vi'enə] *n* Vienne
Viennese [ˌvɪə'niːz, *Am:* ˌviːə'-] **I.** *n* Viennois(e) *m(f)* **II.** *adj* viennois(e)
Vietcong [ˌvjet'kɒŋ, *Am:* ˌviːet'kɑːŋ] *n inv* Viêt-cong *mf*
Viet Nam, **Vietnam** [ˌvjet'nɑːm, *Am:* ˌviːet-] *n* le Viêt-nam [*o* Vietnam]
Vietnamese [ˌvjetnə'miːz, *Am:* viˌet-] **I.** *adj* vietnamien(ne) **II.** *n* **1.** (*person*) Vietnamien(ne) *m(f)* **2.** LING vietnamien *m; s. a.* **English**
Vietnam War *n* guerre *f* du Viêt-nam
view [vjuː] **I.** *n* **1.** (*opinion, idea*) opinion *f;* **conflicting ~s** avis *m* divergents; **to share sb's ~** partager l'avis de qn; **to take a dim ~ of sth** ne pas trop apprécier qc; **to have ~s about sb/sth** avoir des opinions sur qn/qc; **to hold strong ~s about sth** avoir des idées; **in sb's ~** d'après qn **2.** (*sight*) vue *f;* **to afford a ~** offrir une vue; **to block sb's ~** gêner le champ de vision de qn **3.** *no pl* (*ability to see*) vue *f;* **in full ~ of sb** sous les yeux de qn; **to come into ~** s'approcher; **to disappear from ~** disparaître de vue; **to hide sth from ~** cacher qc ►**to have sth in ~** avoir qc en vue; **in ~ of** étant donné; **to be on ~** être exposé; **with a ~ to doing sth** dans le but de faire qc **II.** *vt* **1.** (*consider*) considérer; **to be ~ed as dangerous/a threat** être considéré comme dangereux/une menace **2.** (*envisage*) envisager; **to ~ sth with delight** envisager qc avec ravissement **3.** (*see, watch: works of art*) voir; (*house*) visiter; (*slide*) visionner; **to ~ television** regarder la télévision
viewer *n* **1.** TV téléspectateur, -trice *m, f* **2.** (*device for slides*) *a.* INFOR visionneuse *f*
viewfinder *n* PHOT viseur *m*
viewing *n* **1.** *no pl* (*inspection*) examen *m;* (*of exhibition, house*) visite *f;* **~ by appointment** visite sur rendez-vous **2.** *no pl* TV **four hours ~ a night** quatre de télévision par jour; **to be essential ~** être impérativement à voir; **a family's ~** le programme télé d'une famille **3.** (*act of seeing*) visionnage *m*
viewing figures *npl* indice *m* d'écoute
viewpoint *n* point *m* de vue
vigil ['vɪdʒɪl, *Am:* 'vɪdʒəl] *n* **1.** (*eve*) veille *f* **2.** (*ceremony*) veillée *f;* **to keep ~** veiller **3.** (*protest*) manifestation *f* silencieuse
vigilance ['vɪdʒɪləns] *n no pl* vigilance *f*

vigilant ['vɪdʒɪlənt] *adj* vigilant(e); **a ~ eye** un œil attentif
vigilante *n membre d'un groupe d'autodéfense*
vignette [vɪ'njet] *n* vignette *f*
vigor *n no pl, Am, Aus s.* **vigour**
vigorous ['vɪgərəs] *adj* **1.** (*energetic*) vigoureux(-euse); (*protest*) ferme **2.** SPORT (*exercise*) intensif(-ive) **3.** (*flourishing: growth*) fort(e)
vigour ['vɪgəʳ, *Am:* -ɚ] *n no pl* **1.** (*intensity*) vigueur *f* **2.** (*forcefulness*) fermeté *f*
Viking ['vaɪkɪŋ] **I.** *adj* viking **II.** *n* Viking *m*
vile [vaɪl] <-r, -st> *adj* **1.** (*very bad*) exécrable; (*smell, taste*) infect(e); **to smell ~** infester **2.** (*morally bad*) vil(e)
vilify ['vɪlɪfaɪ, *Am:* '-ə-] *vt form* diffamer
villa ['vɪlə] *n* villa *f*, camp *Québec*
village ['vɪlɪdʒ] **I.** *n* **1.** (*settlement*) village *m* **2.** + *pl/sing vb* (*populace*) village *m* **II.** *adj* de/du village
village community *n* commune *f* **village green** *n* pré *m* communal **village idiot** *n* idiot *m* du village **village inn** *n* auberge *f* de campagne
villager *n* villageois(e) *m(f)*
villain ['vɪlən] *n* **1.** (*evil person*) scélérat(e) *m(f)* **2.** (*bad guy*) voyou *m*; **a small-time ~** un petit voyou; **to cast sb as a ~** qualifier qn de voyou **3.** *inf* (*child*) coquin(e) *m(f)* ►**the ~ of the** <u>piece</u> *inf* le méchant
villainous [vɪlənəs] *adj* vil(e)
villainy ['vɪləni] *n no pl* infamie *f*
vim [vɪm] *n no pl* vigueur *f*
vinaigrette [ˌvɪnɪ'gret, *Am:* -ə'-] *n no pl* vinaigrette *f*
vindicate ['vɪndɪkeɪt, *Am:* -də-] *vt* **1.** (*justify*) justifier; (*rights*) faire valoir; **to ~ sb** donner raison à qn; **I was ~d by sth** qc m'a donné raison **2.** (*clear of blame: person*) disculper
vindication [ˌvɪndɪ'keɪʃən, *Am:* ə'-] *n no pl* justification *f*
vindictive [vɪn'dɪktɪv] *adj* vindicatif(-ive)
vine [vaɪn] *n* **1.** (*grape plant*) vigne *f* **2.** (*climbing plant*) plante *f* grimpante
vinegar ['vɪnɪgəʳ, *Am:* -əgɚ] *n no pl* vinaigre *m*
vinegary *adj* **1.** (*tasting of vinegar*) qui a le goût du vinaigre **2.** (*full of vinegar*) **the salad is too ~** il y a trop de vinaigre dans la salade **3.** *fig* **to be ~** être acerbe
vineyard ['vɪnjəd, *Am:* -jɚd] *n* vignoble *m*
vintage ['vɪntɪdʒ, *Am:* -t̬ɪdʒ] **I.** *n* **1.** (*wine*) cru *m*; **the 1983 ~** le cru de mille neuf cent quatre-vingt-trois **2.** (*year*) millésime *m* **II.** *adj* **1.** GASTR de grand cru; **a ~ year** une grande année **2.** (*classic quality*) classique **3.** (*old: car, clothes*) d'époque
vintner ['vɪntnəʳ, *Am:* -nɚ] *n* négociant(e) *m(f)* en vins
vinyl ['vaɪnəl] *n no pl* vinyle *m*
viola¹ [vi'əʊlə, *Am:* vi'oʊ-] *n* MUS alto *m*
viola² ['vaɪələ, *Am:* 'viːələ] *n* BOT violacée *f*
violate ['vaɪəleɪt] *vt* **1.** (*break*) désobéir à **2.** (*enter illegally*) transgresser; (*a tomb*) profaner **3.** (*disturb*) déranger; **to ~ sb's privacy** faire intrusion chez qn **4.** *form* (*rape*) violer
violation [ˌvaɪə'leɪʃən] *n* **1.** (*act of not respecting*) violation *f*; **in ~ of sth** en violation de qc **2.** (*act of breaking law*) infraction *f*
violence ['vaɪələnts] *n no pl* violence *f*
violent ['vaɪələnt] *adj* **1.** (*cruel*) violent(e); (*argument*) virulent(e) **2.** (*very powerful*) fort(e); **to have a ~ temper** être colérique **3.** *fig, pej* (*clothes*) criard(e)
violet ['vaɪələt, *Am:* -lɪt] **I.** *n* **1.** BOT violette *f* **2.** (*colour*) violet *m* **II.** *adj* violet(te); *s. a.* **blue**
violin [ˌvaɪə'lɪn] *n* violon *m*
violinist *n* violoniste *mf*
VIP [ˌviːaɪ'piː] **I.** *n abbr of* **very important person** VIP *mf* **II.** *adj* VIP *inv*; **a ~ lounge** un salon VIP; **to be given a ~ treatment** être traité comme une personnalité de marque
viper ['vaɪpəʳ, *Am:* -pɚ] *n* vipère *f*
virago [vɪ'rɑːgəʊ, *Am:* və'rɑːgoʊ] <-s *o* -es> *n pej* virago *f*
viral ['vaɪərəl] *adj* viral(e)
virgin ['vɜːdʒɪn, *Am:* 'vɜːr-] **I.** *n* vierge *f*; (*man*) puceau *m inf*; **to be a ~** être vierge **II.** *adj* vierge; **pure ~ wool** pure laine vierge
virginal *n* virginal *m*
virgin forest *n* forêt *f* vierge
Virginia [və'dʒɪnjə, *Am:* vɚ-] **I.** *n* la Virginie **II.** *adj* de Virginie
Virgin Islands *n* les îles *fpl* vierges
virginity [və'dʒɪnəti, *Am:* vɚ'dʒɪnət̬i] *n no pl* virginité *f*
Virgo ['vɜːgəʊ, *Am:* 'vɜːrgoʊ] *n* Vierge *f*; *s. a.* **Aquarius**
virile ['vɪraɪl, *Am:* -əl] *adj* viril(e)
virility [vɪ'rɪləti, *Am:* və'rɪlət̬i] *n no pl* **1.** virilité *f* **2.** *fig* **economic ~** puissance *f* économique
virologist *n* virologue *mf*
virology [vaɪə'rɒlədʒi, *Am:* vaɪ'rɑːlə-] *n no pl* virologie *f*
virtual ['vɜːtʃuəl, *Am:* 'vɜːrtʃu-] *adj* **1.** (*as described*) quasi-; **the ~ totality** la quasi-totalité; **it's a ~ impossibility** c'est quasiment impossible; **to look like a ~ certainty** paraître comme une certitude **2.** INFOR virtuel(le)
virtually *adv* **1.** (*nearly*) pratiquement; **~ unknown** quasiment inconnu; **~ the whole town** la quasi-totalité de la ville **2.** INFOR virtuellement
virtue ['vɜːtjuː, *Am:* 'vɜːrtʃuː] *n* **1.** (*good moral quality*) vertu *f* **2.** (*advantage*) mérite *m*; **the ~ of having sth** l'avantage *m* d'avoir qc; **to extol the ~s of sth** vanter les vertus de qc ►**to** <u>make</u> **a ~ (out) of sth** faire de qc une vertu; **to make a ~ of necessity** faire de la nécessité une vertu; **by ~ of** *form* en vertu de
virtuosity [ˌvɜːtju'ɒsəti, *Am:* ˌvɜːrtʃu'ɑːsət̬i] *n no pl, form* virtuosité *f*
virtuoso [ˌvɜːtju'əʊsəʊ, *Am:* ˌvɜːrtʃu'oʊsoʊ]

<-s *o* -osi> **I.** *n* virtuose *mf* **II.** *adj* **a ~ performance** une représentation de virtuose

virtuous [ˈvɜːtʃuəs, *Am:* ˈvɜːrtʃu-] *adj* **1.** (*morally good*) vertueux(-euse) **2.** *pej* (*hypocritical*) supérieur(e)

virulence [ˈvɪrʊlənts, *Am:* -jə-] *n no pl* virulence *f*

virulent [ˈvɪrʊlənt, *Am:* -jə-] *adj* virulent(e)

virus [ˈvaɪərəs, *Am:* ˈvaɪ-] *n* virus *m*

visa [ˈviːzə] *n* visa *m*

vis-à-vis [ˌviːzɑːˈviː, *Am:* ˌviːzəˈviː] **I.** *prep form* par rapport à **II.** *n* (*person*) homologue *mf*

viscera [ˈvɪsərə] *npl* viscères *mpl*

visceral *adj a. fig* viscéral(e)

viscose [ˈvɪskəʊs, *Am:* -koʊs] *n no pl* viscose *f*

viscosity [vɪˈskɒsəti, *Am:* -ˈskɑːsət̬i] *n no pl* viscosité *f*

viscount [ˈvaɪkaʊnt] *n* vicomte *m*

viscountess *n* vicomtesse *f*

viscous [ˈvɪskəs] *adj* visqueux(-euse)

vise [vaɪs] *n Am* étau *m*

visé *n Am s.* **visa**

visibility [ˌvɪzəˈbɪləti, *Am:* -əbɪlət̬i] *n no pl* visibilité *f*

visible [ˈvɪzəbl] *adj* visible

vision [ˈvɪʒən] *n* **1.** *no pl* (*sight*) vue *f* **2.** (*dream, hope*) vision *f;* **to have ~s of doing sth** se voir faire qc; **my ~ for the school/company** mes espoirs pour l'école/l'entreprise **3.** *no pl* (*imagination*) perspicacité *f;* **a man of great ~** un homme qui voit loin; **a breadth of ~** une largeur d'esprit

visionary [ˈvɪʒənəri, *Am:* -əneri] **I.** *n* visionnaire *mf* **II.** *adj* **1.** (*hallucinatory*) hallucinatoire **2.** (*future orientated*) visionnaire

visit [ˈvɪzɪt] **I.** *n* visite *f;* **to pay a ~ to sb** rendre visite à qn; **to have a ~ from sb** recevoir la visite de qn; **a ~ to the library** un tour chez le libraire; **during our ~ to Paris** au cours de notre séjour à Paris **II.** *vt* (*town, museum*) visiter; (*person*) aller voir; **to ~ sb in hospital** se rendre auprès d'un malade à l'hôpital **III.** *vi* être en visite; **to ~ with sb** aller voir qn

visitation [ˌvɪzɪˈteɪʃən, *Am:* -əˈ-] *n* **1.** (*visit*) visite *f;* **~ from a ghost** apparition *f* d'un fantôme **2.** *no pl, Am* (*time to see child*) droit *m* de visite **3.** (*calamity*) châtiment *m*

visiting card *n* carte *f* de visite **visiting fireman** *n Am* personnalité *f* de marque en visite **visiting hours** *npl* heures *fpl* de visite **visiting professor** *n* professeur *mf* invité(e)

visitor [ˈvɪzɪtəʳ, *Am:* -t̬ɚ] *n* **1.** (*guest*) invité(e) *m(f);* **to have ~s** avoir de la visite **2.** (*tourist*) visiteur, -euse *m, f;* **to be a frequent ~ to sth** visiter régulièrement qc

visitor centre *n* centre *m* d'accueil **visitors' book** *n Brit* (*in hotel*) registre *m;* (*in exhibition*) livre *m* d'or

visor [ˈvaɪzəʳ, *Am:* -zɚ] *n* visière *f*

vista [ˈvɪstə] *n* **1.** (*view*) panorama *m* **2.** (*view of future*) **to open up a ~** ouvrir un nouvel horizon; **to raise a new ~** faire naître une nouvelle perspective

visual [ˈvɪʒuəl] **I.** *adj* visuel; **a ~ nerve** un nerf optique **II.** *n pl* **~s** images *fpl*

visual aid *n* support *m* visuel **visual display unit** *n* INFOR console *f* de visualisation

visualize [ˈvɪʒuəlaɪz] *vt* visualiser

visually *adv* visuellement; **the ~ impaired** les mal-voyants

vital [ˈvaɪtəl, *Am:* -t̬əl] *adj* **1.** (*necessary: food, medicine*) vital(e); (*information, clue, measure*) capital(e); (*ingredient*) indispensable; **to be ~ to sth** être indispensable à qc; **it is ~ that** il est capital que *+subj;* **it is ~ to** *+infin* il est crucial de *+infin* **2.** *form* (*energetic*) énergique

vitality [vaɪˈtæləti, *Am:* -ət̬i] *n no pl* vitalité *f*

vitalize [ˈvaɪtəlaɪz, *Am:* -t̬əlaɪz-] *vt* **1.** (*give life to*) vivifier **2.** (*animate*) animer

vitally *adv* extrêmement; (*necessary*) absolument

vital statistics *n pl* mensurations *fpl*

vitamin [ˈvɪtəmɪn, *Am:* ˈvaɪt̬ə-] *n* vitamine *f*

vitamin deficiency *n* carence *f* en vitamines **vitamin tablets** *n* vitamines *fpl* en comprimé

vitreous [ˈvɪtriəs] *adj* vitreux(-euse); (*enamel*) vitrifié(e)

vitrify [ˈvɪtrɪfaɪ, *Am:* -trə-] **I.** *vt* vitrifier **II.** *vi* se vitrifier

vitriol [ˈvɪtriəl] *n no pl* vitriol *m*

vitriolic [ˌvɪtriˈɒlɪk, *Am:* -ˈɑːlɪk] *adj* vitriolique

vituperate [vɪˈtjuːpəreɪt, *Am:* vaɪˈtuːpəreɪt] *vt, vi form* vitupérer

vituperation [vɪˌtjuːpəˈreɪʃən, *Am:* vaɪˌtuːpəreɪ-] *n no pl, form* vitupération *f*

viva *n Brit* UNIV oral *m*

vivacious [vɪˈveɪʃəs] *adj* enjoué(e)

vivacity [vɪˈvæsəti, *Am:* -ət̬i] *n no pl* vivacité *f*

vivarium [vaɪˈveəriəm, *Am:* vaɪˈveri-] <-s *o* vivaria> *n* vivarium *m*

vivid [ˈvɪvɪd] *adj a. fig* vif(vive); (*example, description*) frappant(e); (*memory, picture*) net(te); (*language*) vivant(e)

vividly *adv* (*describe*) de façon très vivante; (*recall*) de façon très nette; (*glow*) avec éclat

viviparous [vɪˈvɪpərəs, *Am:* vaɪˈ-] *adj* BIO vivipare

vivisect [ˌvɪvɪˈsekt, *Am:* ˈvɪvəsekt] *vt* pratiquer la vivisection sur

vivisection [ˌvɪvɪˈsekʃən, *Am:* -əˈ-] *n no pl* vivisection *f*

vixen [ˈvɪksən] *n* **1.** (*female fox*) renarde *f* **2.** *pej* mégère *f*

viz. *adv form abbr of* **videlicet** (**namely**) c.-à-d.

vocabulary [vəʊˈkæbjələri, *Am:* voʊˈkæbjəler-] *n* **1.** (*words*) vocabulaire *m;* **to widen one's ~** enrichir son vocabulaire **2.** (*glossary*) lexique *m*

vocal ['vəʊkəl, *Am:* 'voʊ-] **I.** *adj* **1.** (*related to the voice*) vocal(e) **2.** (*outspoken*) qui se fait entendre; **to be/become ~** se faire entendre **3.** (*articulate*) **to be ~** parler beaucoup **II.** *n* **~(s)** chant *m;* **on ~s** au chant; **the lead ~** le(la) chanteur(-euse)

vocal cords *n pl* cordes *fpl* vocales

vocalist *n* chanteur, -euse *m, f*

vocalize ['vəʊkəlaɪz, *Am:* 'voʊ-] **I.** *vi* faire des vocalises **II.** *vt* exprimer

vocally *adv* vocalement; (*to say*) à haute voix

vocation [vəʊ'keɪʃən, *Am:* voʊ'-] *n* vocation *f*

vocational *adj* professionnel(le)

vociferate [vəʊ'sɪfəreɪt, *Am:* voʊ'-] *vi, vt* vociférer

vociferation [vəʊˌsɪfə'reɪʃən, *Am:* voʊˌ-] *n* vocifération *f*

vociferous [vəʊ'sɪfərəs, *Am:* voʊ'-] *adj* véhément(e)

vodka ['vɒdkə, *Am:* 'vɑːd-] *n no pl* vodka *f*

vogue [vəʊg, *Am:* voʊg] *n* vogue *f;* **a ~ for sth** une mode de qc; **to become the ~** devenir à la mode; **the ~ for doing sth** la mode de faire qc ►**in ~** en vogue; **to be back in ~** revenir à la mode; **out of ~** démodé(e)

voice [vɔɪs] **I.** *n a. fig* voix *f;* **a tenor ~** une voix de ténor; **his ~ is breaking** sa voix se mue; **to keep one's ~ down** parler à voix basse; **to lower/raise one's ~** baisser/hausser le ton; **to lose one's ~** avoir une extinction de voix; **to make one's ~ heard** se faire entendre; **to give sb a ~** laisser qn s'exprimer ►**with one ~** d'une voix; **to give ~ to sth** exprimer qc; **to listen to the ~ of reason** écouter la voix de la raison **II.** *vt* exprimer

voice box *n inf s. a.* **larynx**

voiced *adj* LING sonore

voiceless *adj* LING sourd(e) **voicemail** *n no pl* boîte *f* vocale **voice-over** *n* TV, CINE voix *f* off **voice vote** *n* vote *m* par acclamation

void [vɔɪd] **I.** *n a. fig* vide *m;* **to fill the ~** combler le vide **II.** *adj* **1.** (*invalid*) nul(le); **to declare sth ~** annuler qc **2.** (*empty*) vide; **~ of sth** dépourvu(e) de qc **III.** *vt* **1.** (*declare not valid*) annuler **2.** (*drain away*) évacuer

vol *n abbr of* **volume** vol *m*

volatile ['vɒlətaɪl, *Am:* 'vɑːləṱəl] *adj* **1.** (*changeable*) versatile **2.** (*explosive*) explosif(-ive) **3.** (*easily vapourized*) volatile

volcanic [vɒl'kænɪk, *Am:* vɑːl'-] *adj* volcanique

volcano [vɒl'keɪnəʊ, *Am:* vɑːl'keɪnoʊ] <-es *o* -s> *n* volcan *m*

volition [vəʊ'lɪʃən, *Am:* voʊ'-] *n no pl, form* volonté *f;* **to do sth (out) of one's own ~** faire qc de son propre gré

volley ['vɒli, *Am:* 'vɑːli] **I.** *n* **1.** (*salvo*) volée *f;* (*gunfire*) salve *f;* **to discharge a ~** tirer une salve **2.** (*onslaught*) torrent *m* **3.** SPORT volée *f* **II.** *vi* SPORT effectuer une volée **III.** *vt* SPORT **to ~ a ball** effectuer une volée

volleyball ['vɒlibɔːl, *Am:* 'vɑːli-] *n no pl* volley-ball *m*

volt [vəʊlt, *Am:* voʊlt] *n* volt *m*

voltage ['vəʊltɪdʒ, *Am:* 'voʊlṱɪdʒ] *n* voltage *m*

voluble ['vɒljəbl, *Am:* 'vɑːl-] *adj form* volubile

volume ['vɒljuːm, *Am:* 'vɑːljuːm] *n* **1.** (*sound, measurement*) volume *m;* **to turn the ~ up/down** augmenter/baisser le volume **2.** (*book*) volume *m;* **in ten ~s** en dix volumes ►**to speak ~s about sth** en dire long sur qc

volume control, **volume regulator** *n* réglage *m* du volume

voluminous [və'luːmɪnəs, *Am:* və'luːmə-] *adj form* volumineux(-euse); (*clothes*) ample

voluntary ['vɒləntəri, *Am:* 'vɑːlənteri] *adj* **1.** (*of one's free will*) volontaire; **~ redundancy** départ *m* volontaire **2.** (*without payment*) bénévole

voluntary organization *n* organisation *f* de bénévoles

volunteer [ˌvɒlən'tɪə^r^, *Am:* ˌvɑːlən'tɪr] **I.** *n* **1.** (*unpaid worker*) bénévole *mf* **2.** (*person willing to do*) volontaire *mf;* **~ helpers** bénévoles *mfpl* **II.** *vt* **to ~ oneself for sth** se proposer pour qc; **to ~ sb to** *+infin* proposer à qn de *+infin;* **to ~ help** offrir son aide **III.** *vi* **to ~ to** *+infin* offrir volontairement ses services pour *+infin;* **to ~ for sth** se proposer pour qc

voluptuous [və'lʌptʃuəs] *adj* **1.** (*sexually appealing*) sensuel(le) **2.** (*epicurean*) voluptueux(-euse)

volute [vəʊ'luːt, *Am:* və'luːt] *n a. fig* volute *f*

vomit ['vɒmɪt, *Am:* 'vɑːmɪt] **I.** *vi, vt* vomir; **to ~ blood** cracher du sang **II.** *n no pl* vomi *m*

voodoo ['vuːduː] **I.** *n no pl* vaudou *m* **II.** *vt* envoûter

voracious [və'reɪʃəs, *Am:* vɔː'reɪ-] *adj* vorace; (*reader*) avide

voracity [və'ræsəti, *Am:* vɔː'ræsəṱi] *n* voracité *f*

vortex ['vɔːteks, *Am:* 'vɔːr-] <-es *o* vortices> *n a. fig* tourbillon *m*

vote [vəʊt, *Am:* voʊt] **I.** *n* **1.** *a.* POL vote *m,* votation *f Suisse;* **10% of the ~** 10% des voix; **the youth ~** le vote des jeunes; **to cast one's ~** voter; **to put sth to the ~** soumettre qc au vote; **they get my ~** je vote pour eux; **sth gets sb's ~** (*approve*) qn est d'accord avec qc **2.** (*right to elect*) droit *m* de vote **II.** *vi* (*elect*) voter; **to ~ in an election** voter à une élection; **to ~ on sth** soumettre qc au vote; **to ~ for/against sb/sth** voter pour/contre qn/qc; **to ~ to strike** choisir de se mettre en grève; **to ~ on who/how/when...** voter pour décider qui/comment/quand... ►**to ~ with one's feet** quitter le navire **III.** *vt* **1.** (*elect*) voter; **to ~ sb into office** faire élire qn à un poste; **to be ~ed Miss France** être élue Miss France **2.** (*propose*) proposer; **to ~ that** proposer que *+subj* **3.** (*decide to give*) **to ~ sb/sth sth** décider d'accorder qc à qn/qc

◆**vote down** *vt* rejeter

V

◆**vote in** *vt* (*person*) élire; (*law*) adopter
◆**vote out** *vt* (*person*) ne pas réélire; (*bill*) rejeter
vote-getter *n Am, Aus* argument *m* électoral
voter *n* électeur, -trice *m, f;* **Democrat ~s** l'électorat *m* démocrate
vote-winner *n Brit s.* **vote-getter**
voting I. *adj* votant(e) **II.** *n* vote *m*
voting booth *n* isoloir *m* **voting box** *n* urne *f* **voting machine** *n* machine *f* à voter
vouch [vaʊtʃ] *vt* **to ~ that ...** garantir que ...
◆**vouch for** *vt* se porter garant de
voucher ['vaʊtʃəʳ, *Am:* -tʃɚ] *n Aus, Brit* **1.** (*coupon*) bon *m* **2.** (*receipt*) reçu *m*
vouchsafe *vt form* accorder
vow [vaʊ] **I.** *vt* jurer; **to ~ revenge** faire vœu de vengeance; **to ~ to** *+infin* jurer de *+infin;* **to ~ that ...** jurer que ... **II.** *n* vœu *m;* **to take a ~** faire un vœu
vowel ['vaʊəl] *n* voyelle *f;* **a ~ sound** un son vocalique
vox pop *n* TV forum *m* populaire
voyage ['vɔɪɪdʒ] **I.** *n a. fig* voyage *m* **II.** *vi* voyager; **to ~ across sth** traverser qc
voyager *n* voyageur, -euse *m, f*
voyeur [vwa:'jɜ:ʳ, *Am:* vɔɪ'jɜ:r] *n* voyeur *m*
vs ['vɜ:səs] *abbr of* **versus** contre
V sign *n* **1.** (*for victory*) V *m* de la victoire **2.** (*insult*) bras *m* d'honneur; **to give sb the ~** faire un bras d'honneur
VSO [ˌvi:es'əʊ] *n abbr of* **Voluntary Service Overseas** coopération *f* à l'étranger
VTOL ['vi:tɒl, *Am:* -tɑ:l] *n abbr of* **vertical takeoff and landing** VTOL *m*
VTR [ˌvi:ti:'ɑ:ʳ, *Am:* -'ɑ:r] *n abbr of* **videotape recorder** magnétoscope *m*
vulcanization [ˌvʌlkənaɪ'zeɪʃən] *n* vulcanisation *f*
vulcanize ['vʌlkənaɪz] *vt* vulcaniser
vulgar ['vʌlgəʳ, *Am:* -gɚ] *adj a. pej* vulgaire
vulgarity [vʌl'gærəti, *Am:* -'gerət̬i] *n no pl* **1.** (*crudeness*) vulgarité *f* **2.** (*ordinariness*) trivialité *f*
vulgarize ['vʌlgəraɪz] *vt* **1.** (*make vulgar*) rendre vulgaire **2.** (*make too commonplace*) vulgariser
vulnerable ['vʌlnərəbl, *Am:* 'vʌlnɚ-] *adj* vulnérable; (*spot*) faible; **to be ~ to sth** être sensible à qc
vulture ['vʌltʃəʳ, *Am:* -tʃɚ] *n a. fig* vautour *m*
vulva ['vʌlvə] <-s *o* -e> *n* ANAT vulve *f*
vying ['vaɪɪŋ] *pp of* **vie**

W

W, w ['dʌblju:] <-'s> *n* W *m,* w *m;* **~ as in William, ~ for William** (*on telephone*) w comme William
w *n abbr of* **watt** W
W *n s.* **west, western**
WAAF *n Brit abbr of* **Women's Auxiliary Air Force** *corps féminin de l'armée de l'air britannique*
WAC *n Am abbr of* **Women's Army Corps** corps féminin de l'armée américaine
wacky ['wækɪ] <-ier, -iest> *adj inf* farfelu(e)
wad [wɒd, *Am:* wɑ:d] *n* **1.** (*ball*) tampon *m;* (*of gum*) boule *f* **2.** (*bundle*) liasse *f*
wadding ['wɒdɪŋ, *Am:* 'wɑ:d-] *n no pl* rembourrage *m*
waddle ['wɒdl, *Am:* 'wɑ:dl] **I.** *vi* se dandiner **II.** *n* dandinement *m*
wade [weɪd] **I.** *vi* **1.** (*cross water*) passer à gué; **to ~ across** traverser à gué **2.** *Am* (*walk in water*) marcher dans l'eau **II.** *vt* passer à gué
◆**wade in** *vi* **1.** (*meddle*) s'en mêler **2.** (*start*) s'y mettre
◆**wade into** *vt* s'attaquer à
◆**wade through** *vt* venir à bout de
wader ['weɪdəʳ, *Am:* -dɚ] *n* **1.** (*bird*) échassier *m* **2.** *pl* (*rubber boots*) bottes *fpl* de pêcheur
wafer ['weɪfəʳ, *Am:* -fɚ] *n* **1.** (*sweet biscuit*) gaufrette *f* **2.** REL hostie *f*
wafer-thin *adj* mince comme du papier à cigarette
waffle[1] ['wɒfl, *Am:* 'wɑ:fl] **I.** *vi pej* **to ~ on** bavasser **II.** *n no pl, pej* blabla *m*
waffle[2] ['wɒfl, *Am:* 'wɑ:fl] *n* (*thin cake*) gaufre *f*
waffle iron *n* gaufrier *m*
wag [wæg] **I.** <-gg-> *vt* remuer; (*one's head*) agiter **II.** <-gg-> *vi* remuer **III.** *n* (*to and fro movement*) **with a ~ of his tail** en remuant la queue
wage[1] [weɪdʒ] *vt form* (*campaign*) mener; **to ~ war** faire la guerre
wage[2] [weɪdʒ] *n* ~(**s**) salaire *m;* **to earn a ~** toucher un salaire
wage claim *npl* revendication *f* salariale **wage costs** *npl* coûts *mpl* salariaux **wage earner** *n* salarié(e) *m(f)* **wage freeze** *n* gel *m* des salaires **wage increase** *n* augmentation *f* de salaire **wage negotiation** *n* négociation *f* salariale **wage packet** *n Aus, Brit* paie *f*
wager ['weɪdʒəʳ, *Am:* -dʒɚ] **I.** *n* pari *m;* **to lay a ~** faire un pari; **to do sth for a ~** faire qc pour tenir un pari **II.** *vt* **1.** parier; **to ~ sb sth that ...** parier qc à qn que ...; **to ~ $100 on sb** parier 100 dollars sur qn **2.** *fig* **to ~ one's reputation/life** mettre sa main au feu
wage scale ['weɪdʒskeɪl] *n* échelle *f* des salaires **wage settlement** *n* accord *m* salarial
waggle ['wægl] *vt, vi* remuer
wag(g)on ['wægən] *n* **1.** (*four-wheeled cart*) chariot *m* **2.** *Aus, Brit* (*carriage for freight*) wagon *m;* **goods ~** wagon de marchandises ▶**to be on the ~** *inf* ne plus boire une goutte d'alcool; **to fall off the ~** *inf* se remettre à boire

wag(g)onload ['wægənləʊd] *n* wagon *m* **wagon train** *n Am:* *convoi de chariots dans le far west*

wail [weɪl] **I.** *vi* gémir; (*siren*) hurler; **to ~ over sth** se lamenter sur qc **II.** *n* gémissement *m;* (*siren*) hurlement *m*

wailing ['weɪlɪŋ] *adj* plaintif(-ive); (*siren*) hurlant(e)

Wailing Wall *n* mur *m* des Lamentations

waist [weɪst] *n* taille *f*

waistband ['weɪstbænd] *n* ceinture *f*

waistcoat ['weɪstkəʊt, *Am:* 'weskət] *n Brit* gilet *m* **waist-deep** *adj* à hauteur de la taille

waisted ['weɪstɪd] *adj* cintré(e)

waistline ['weɪstlaɪn] *n* taille *f*

wait [weɪt] **I.** *n no pl* attente *f* ►**to lie in ~ for sb** guetter qn **II.** *vi* **1.** (*stay*) attendre; **to ~ for sb/sth** attendre qn/qc; **~ and see** attends de voir **2.** (*help*) servir ►**~ a bit** un instant; **to ~ at table(s)** *Aus, Brit, form,* **to ~ (on) table(s)** *Am* servir à table; **I can't ~ to do sth** j'ai hâte de faire qc; **to keep sb ~ing** faire attendre qn; **~ and see!** attends voir!; **~ for it!** *inf* attends! **III.** *vt* **1.** (*await*) attendre **2.** (*help*) servir; **to ~ table(s)** faire le service ►**to ~ a meal for sb** *Am* attendre qn pour se mettre à table; **to ~ one's turn** attendre son tour

◆**wait about, wait around** *vi* attendre

◆**wait behind** *vi* rester

◆**wait in** *vi* rester à la maison; **to ~ for sb** rester à la maison pour attendre qn

◆**wait on** *vt* **1.** (*serve*) servir **2.** *form* (*expect*) attendre ►**to ~ sb hand and foot** être aux petits soins avec qn

◆**wait up** *vi* **1.** (*not go to bed*) ne pas aller se coucher; **to ~ for sb** attendre qn **2.** *Am* (*wait for me*) attendre; **~!** attends-moi!

> Le **Waitangi Day** ou "New Zealand day" est célébré le 6 janvier. En 1840, 512 chefs de tribus maori signaient un traité avec le gouvernement britannique qui ratifiait la naissance de la nation de Nouvelle-Zélande.

waiter ['weɪtə^r, *Am:* -t̬ɚ] *n* serveur *m*

waiting ['weɪtɪŋ, *Am:* -t̬ɪŋ] *n no pl* **1.** (*time spent waiting*) attente *f* **2.** *Brit* (*momentary parking*) stationnement *m*

waiting list *n* liste *f* d'attente **waiting room** *n* salle *f* d'attente

waitress ['weɪtrɪs] *n* serveuse *f*

waive [weɪv] *vt form* renoncer à

waiver ['weɪvə^r, *Am:* -vɚ] *n* renonciation *f*

wake¹ [weɪk] *n* NAUT *a. fig* sillage *m* ►**to follow in sb's ~** marcher dans le sillage de qn; **in the ~ of sth** dans le sillage de qc

wake² [weɪk] *n* **1.** (*vigil beside a corpse*) veillée *f* mortuaire **2.** *Irish* (*party*) veillée *f* de corps

wake³ [weɪk] <woke *o* waked, woken *o* waked *o Am* woke> **I.** *vi* se réveiller **II.** *vt a. fig* réveiller; **to ~ the dead** réveiller les morts

◆**wake up I.** *vi* **1.** (*stop sleeping*) *a. fig* se réveiller **2.** (*become aware of*) **to ~ to sth** prendre conscience de qc **II.** *vt* réveiller; **to wake oneself up** se réveiller

wakeful ['weɪkfl] *adj form* **1.** (*sleepless*) éveillé(e); **a ~ night** une nuit blanche **2.** (*vigilant*) vigilant(e)

waken ['weɪkən] *vi form* se réveiller

wakey-wakey [ˌweɪki'weɪki] *interj inf* debout!

Wales ['weɪlz] *n* pays *m* de Galles

walk [wɔːk, *Am:* wɑːk] **I.** *n* **1.** (*going on foot*) marche *f;* **a five minute ~** une marche de cinq minutes; **to be ten minutes' ~ from here** être à dix minutes à pied d'ici **2.** (*gait*) démarche *f* **3.** (*walking speed*) pas *m;* **to go at a slow/fast ~** aller d'un pas lent/rapide **4.** (*stroll*) promenade *f;* **to go for a ~** aller se promener; **to take sb out for a ~** emmener qn en promenade; **to take a ~** faire une promenade **5.** (*promenade*) promenade *f* ►**~ of life** milieu *m;* **from all ~s of life** de tous les milieux **II.** *vt* **1.** (*go on foot*) parcourir (à pied); **you can ~ it in half an hour** tu peux faire le chemin à pied en une demi-heure **2.** (*accompany*) **to ~ sb somewhere** emmener qn quelque part; **to ~ sb home** raccompagner qn à la maison **3.** (*take for a walk: dog*) sortir **4.** (*make move*) faire marcher **III.** *vi* **1.** (*go on foot*) marcher; **it takes ten minutes to ~** cela prend dix minutes à pied; **to ~ into/out of a room** entrer dans/quitter une pièce; **to ~ up/down a road** monter/descendre une route; **to ~ along** marcher **2.** (*stroll*) se promener ►**to ~ on air** être sur un nuage; **to ~ on eggs** marcher sur des œufs; **to ~ the streets** (*wander*) errer dans les rues; (*be a prostitute*) faire le trottoir

◆**walk away** *vi* **1.** (*leave*) s'en aller; **to ~ from sth** (*house, group*) quitter qc; (*car*) sortir de qc **2.** (*ignore*) **to ~ from sth** éviter qc; **to ~ from sb** s'éloigner de qn **3.** (*escape unhurt*) **to ~ from an accident** sortir indemne d'un accident **4.** *inf* (*win*) **to ~ with sth** (*prize*) remporter qc **5.** *inf* (*steal*) **to ~ with sth** faucher qc

◆**walk in on** *vt* **to ~ sb** entrer sans prévenir

◆**walk off I.** *vi* partir **II.** *vt* **to ~ a meal** prendre l'air pour digérer

◆**walk off with** *vt inf* **1.** (*take*) prendre **2.** (*steal*) faucher **3.** (*win*) remporter

◆**walk on** *vi* THEAT être figurant

◆**walk out** *vi* **1.** (*leave room*) sortir **2.** (*leave to express dissatisfaction*) partir; **her husband walked out** son mari l'a quittée; **the delegation walked out of the meeting** la délégation a quitté la réunion **3.** (*go on strike*) se mettre en grève

◆**walk over I.** *vi* s'approcher; **to ~ to sb** s'approcher de qn **II.** *vt* **to walk (all) over sb** marcher sur les pieds de qn; **don't let him walk (all) over you** *fig* ne te laisse pas marcher sur les pieds

walkabout ['wɔːkəbaʊt, *Am:* 'wɑː-] *n Brit,*

inf bain *m* de foule

walker ['wɔːkəʳ, *Am:* 'wɑːkɚ] *n* **1.** (*person who walks*) marcheur, -euse *m, f;* **to be a fast/slow ~** marcher vite/lentement **2.** (*person walking for pleasure*) promeneur, -euse *m, f*

walker-on *n s.* **walk-on**

walkie-talkie [ˌwɔːki'tɔːki, *Am:* ˌwɑːki'tɑː-] *n* talkie-walkie *m*

walk-in ['wɔːkɪn, *Am:* 'wɑːk-] *adj* (*clinic*) sans rendez-vous; (*hotel*) sans réservation; (*apartment*) *Am, Aus* de plain-pied; **a ~ cupboard** un débarras

walking ['wɔːkɪŋ, *Am:* 'wɑːk-] **I.** *n no pl* **1.** (*act of walking*) marche *f* **2.** (*stroll*) promenade *f* **II.** *adj* ambulant(e); (*encyclopedia*) vivant(e); **to be within ~ distance of sth** être à quelques pas de qc

walking frame *n* déambulatoire *m* **walking shoes** *n* chaussures *fpl* de marche **walking stick** *n* canne *f* **walking tour** *n* **1.** (*through countryside*) randonnée *f* **2.** (*around town*) visite *f* à pied

Walkman® ['wɔːkmən, *Am:* 'wɑːk-] <Walkmans> *n* baladeur *m*

walk-on **I.** *adj* **a ~ part** un rôle de figurant **II.** *n* figurant(e) *m(f)*

walkout ['wɔːkaʊt, *Am:* 'wɑːk-] *n* **1.** (*strike*) grève *f* surprise; **to stage a ~** faire la grève **2.** (*sudden departure*) départ *m* en signe de protestation; **to stage a ~** partir en signe de protestation

walkover ['wɔːkəʊvəʳ, *Am:* 'wɑːkoʊvɚ] *n* victoire *f* facile

walk-through *n* répétition *f*

walkway ['wɔːkweɪ, *Am:* 'wɑːk-] *n* passage *m* (pour piétons)

wall [wɔːl] **I.** *n* **1.** (*division structure*) *a. fig* mur *m;* **the city ~(s)** les remparts de la ville **2.** (*climbing wall, natural structure*) paroi *f* **3.** AUTO flanc *m* **4.** ANAT paroi *f* ►**to have one's back to the ~** être dos au mur; **to hit a brick ~** se heurter au mur; **to talk to a brick ~** parler à un mur; **~s have ears** *prov* les murs ont des oreilles; **to be a fly on the ~** être une petite souris; **to be like banging one's head against a brick ~** être à se taper la tête contre les murs; **this must not go beyond these four ~s** cela doit rester entre nous; **to drive sb up the ~** rendre qn fou; **to go up the ~** devenir fou; **to go to the ~** (*go out of business*) faire faillite; **off the ~** dingue **II.** *vt* **to ~ in** *a. fig* murer; **to ~ off** séparer par un mur; **to wall oneself off** *fig* se murer; **to ~ up** murer

wallaby ['wɒləbi, *Am:* 'wɑː-] *npl* wallaby *m*

wall bars *npl* espalier *m*

wallchart ['wɔːltʃɑːt, *Am:* -tʃɑːrt] *n* panneau *m* mural

wallet ['wɒlɪt, *Am:* 'wɑːlɪt] *n* portefeuille *m*

wallflower ['wɔːlˌflaʊəʳ, *Am:* -ˌflaʊɚ] *n* **1.** (*plant*) giroflée *f* **2.** *inf* (*shy woman*) **to be a ~** faire tapisserie

wall hanging *n* tenture *f*

Wallis and Futuna ['wɒlɪs-, *Am:* 'wɑː-] *n* **~ Islands** (les îles *fpl*) Wallis-et-Futuna

wall map *n* carte *f* murale

Wallonia [wə'ləʊnɪə, *Am:* wɑː'loʊ-] *n* la Wallonie

Walloon [wɒ'luːn, *Am:* wɑː-] **I.** *adj* wallon(ne) **II.** *n* **1.** (*person*) Wallon(ne) *m(f)* **2.** LING wallon *m; s. a.* **English**

wallop ['wɒləp, *Am:* 'wɑːləp] **I.** *vt* **1.** *inf* (*hit hard*) rosser; **to ~ sb across the head** flanquer une beigne à qn **2.** *fig, inf* (*beat in competition*) infliger une raclée; **to be ~ed** prendre une raclée **II.** *n inf* beigne *f;* **to give a ~ to sb** flanquer une beigne à qn

walloping *n no pl, inf* fessée *f;* **to give sb a ~** flanquer une fessée à qn

wallow ['wɒləʊ, *Am:* 'wɑːloʊ] **I.** *n no pl* bauge *f* **II.** *vi* **1.** (*lie in earth, water*) patauger **2.** *pej* (*remain in negative state*) se complaire; **to ~ in self-pity** s'apitoyer sur son propre sort **3.** (*revel*) **to ~ in luxury** baigner dans le luxe

wallpaper ['wɔːlpeɪpəʳ, *Am:* -pɚ] **I.** *n* papier *m* peint; **to hang ~** poser du papier peint **II.** *vt* tapisser

wallpaper paste *n* colle *f* à papier peint

wall plug *n* **1.** (*dowel*) cheville *f* **2.** (*socket*) prise *f* murale

Wall Street *n* Wall Street (*Bourse et centre financier de New York*)

wall-to-wall [ˌwɔːltə'wɔːl, *Am:* -t̬ə'-] *adj* **1.** **~ carpet** moquette *f* **2.** *fig* **~ coverage** couverture *f* complète

walnut ['wɔːlnʌt] *n* **1.** (*nut*) noix *f* **2.** (*tree*) noyer *m*

walrus ['wɔːlrəs] <walruses *o* walrus> *n* morse *m*

walrus moustache <- moustaches> *n* moustache *f* à la gauloise

waltz [wɔːls, *Am:* wɔːlts] <watzes> **I.** *n* valse *f* **II.** *vi* valser; **to ~ into a room** faire irruption dans une pièce

wand [wɒnd, *Am:* wɑːnd] *n* **1.** (*conjuror's stick*) baguette *f;* **to wave one's magic ~** donner un coup de baguette magique **2.** (*mascara applicator*) brosse *f* à cils

wander ['wɒndəʳ, *Am:* 'wɑːndɚ] **I.** *vt* **1.** (*walk through*) se balader dans **2.** (*roam: the streets*) traîner dans; (*world*) courir **II.** *vi* **1.** (*walk*) **to ~ (around/about)** se promener au hasard; **to ~ off** partir **2.** (*roam*) errer; **to ~ through the streets** traîner dans les rues **3.** (*not concentrate*) s'égarer; **to ~ from the point** s'écarter du sujet; **my mind ~s back to my childhood** je repense à mon enfance; **his mind is ~ing** il divague **III.** *n no pl, inf* balade *f;* **to go for a ~ around the city** se balader dans la ville

wanderer ['wɒndərəʳ, *Am:* 'wɑːndɚɚ] *n* vagabond(e) *m(f)*

wandering ['wɒndərɪŋ, *Am:* 'wɑːn-] *adj* **1.** (*nomadic*) errant; **a ~ minstrel** un ménestrel ambulant; **a ~ tribe** une tribu nomade **2.** (*not concentrating*) vagabond(e); **~ eyes** regard *m* distrait

wanderings ['wɒndərɪŋz, *Am:* 'wɑːn-] *npl* **1.** (*movements*) pérégrinations *fpl* **2.** (*confused speech*) divagations *fpl*
wane [weɪn] **I.** *vi* décroître **II.** *n no pl, no indef art* **to be on the ~** décroître
wangle ['wæŋgl] *vt inf* se débrouiller pour obtenir
wank [wæŋk] *vulg* **I.** *vt* se branler **II.** *n* branlette *f*
want [wɒnt, *Am:* wɑːnt] **I.** *n* **1.** (*need*) besoin *m;* **to live in ~** vivre dans le besoin; **to be in ~ of sth** avoir besoin de qc **2.** *no pl, no indef art* (*lack*) manque *m;* **for ~ of sth** faute de qc; **for ~ of anything better** faute de mieux **II.** *vt* **1.** (*wish*) vouloir; **to ~ to do sth** vouloir faire qc; **to ~ sb to do sth** vouloir que qn fasse qc *+subj;* **to ~ sth done** vouloir que qc soit fait; **I don't ~ your sympathy** je n'ai pas besoin de votre compassion; **I just don't ~ to know!** je ne veux pas savoir!; **you're not ~ed here** tu n'es pas le bienvenu ici **2.** (*feel like*) avoir envie; **to ~ (to do) sth** avoir envie de (faire) qc **3.** (*wish to speak to*) demander; **to be ~ed for murder/by the police** être recherché pour meurtre/par la police **4.** (*desire sexually*) désirer **5.** (*need*) avoir besoin de; **your car ~s cleaning** ta voiture a besoin d'être lavée; **~ed, a cook** recherche cuisinier; **sth ~s patience** qc exige de la patience; **to ~ £200** demander deux cents livres **6.** *inf* (*should*) **you ~ to get up earlier** tu dois te lever plus tôt
◆**want in** *vi inf* vouloir entrer; **to ~ (on a deal)** vouloir être sur le coup
◆**want out** *vi Brit, Am, inf* (*from a room*) vouloir sortir; (*from an arrangement*) vouloir retirer ses cartes du jeu
want ad ['wɒnt 'æd, *Am:* 'wɑːnt-] *n Am, inf* petite annonce *f*
wanting ['wɒntɪŋ, *Am:* 'wɑːnt̬ɪŋ] *adj* **to be ~ in sth** manquer de qc; **to be found ~** laisser à désirer
wanton ['wɒntən, *Am:* 'wɑːntn] *adj* **1.** *form* (*mindless: violence*) gratuit(e); (*destruction, disregard, waste*) injustifié(e) **2.** (*behaving in sexual way*) impudique
WAP [wɒp] *n* WAP *m*
war [wɔːʳ, *Am:* wɔːr] *n no pl, no indef art* guerre *f;* **to be at ~** être en guerre; **a state of ~** un état de guerre; **in time of ~** en temps de guerre; **the horrors of ~** les horreurs de la guerre; **~ atrocities** les atrocités de la guerre; **a ~ hero** un héros de guerre; **~ breaks out between sb/sth and sb/sth** la guerre éclate entre qn/qc et qn/qc; **to declare ~ on sb/sth** *a. fig* déclarer la guerre à qn/qc; **to go to ~** aller en guerre; **to wage ~ against sb/sth** faire la guerre contre qn/qc; *fig* être en guerre contre qn/qc; **a ~ of attrition** une guerre d'usure; **price/trade ~** guerre des prix/commerciale ►**to have been in the ~s** revenir du front
warble ['wɔːbl, *Am:* 'wɔːr-] **I.** *vi* gazouiller **II.** *n* gazouillement *m*
warbler ['wɔːbləʳ, *Am:* 'wɔːrblɚ] *n* fauvette *f*
war chest *n* fonds *m* spécial **war correspondent** *n* correspondant(e) *m(f)* de guerre **war crime** *n* crime *m* de guerre **war criminal** *n* criminel *m* de guerre **war cry** *n a. fig* cri *m* de guerre
ward [wɔːd, *Am:* wɔːrd] *n* **1.** (*part of hospital*) salle *f* (d'hôpital); **emergency/maternity ~** salle d'urgence/de maternité **2.** (*political area*) circonscription *f* électorale **3.** (*child*) pupille *mf* **4.** *Am* (*part of prison*) quartier *m*
◆**ward off** *vt* écarter
warden ['wɔːdn, *Am:* 'wɔːr-] *n* **1.** (*supervisor*) gardien(ne) *m(f);* **traffic ~** contractuel(le) *m(f)* **2.** *Brit, Aus* (*head of a college*) directeur, -trice *m, f* **3.** *Am* (*prison governor*) directeur, -trice *m, f*
warder ['wɔːdəʳ, *Am:* 'wɔːrdɚ] *n* gardien(ne) *m(f)*
wardrobe ['wɔːdrəʊb, *Am:* 'wɔːrdroʊb] *n* **1.** (*cupboard*) armoire *f* **2.** *no pl, no indef art* (*collection*) garde-robe *f* **3.** (*department*) costumes *mpl*
warehouse ['weəhaʊs, *Am:* 'wer-] *n Brit, Aus* entrepôt *m*
wares [weəz, *Am:* 'werz] *npl* **1.** (*small products*) articles *mpl* **2.** *inf* (*company's products*) marchandise *f*
warfare ['wɔːfeəʳ, *Am:* 'wɔːrfer] *n no pl, no indef art* guerre *f*
war game *n* **1.** MIL manœuvre *f* **2.** INFOR war game *m* (*jeu vidéo simulant un conflit*) **war grave** *n* sépulture *f* militaire
warhead ['wɔːhed, *Am:* 'wɔːr-] *n* ogive *f*
warily ['weərɪlɪ, *Am:* 'wer-] *adv* avec prudence
warlike ['wɔːlaɪk, *Am:* 'wɔːr-] *adj* **1.** (*military*) guerrier(-ère) **2.** (*belligerent*) belliqueux(-euse)
warlord ['wɔːlɔːd, *Am:* 'wɔːrlɔːrd] *n* chef *m* militaire
warm [wɔːm, *Am:* wɔːrm] **I.** *adj* **1.** (*quite hot*) chaud(e); **I'm ~** j'ai chaud; **it's ~** il fait chaud; **to get ~** se réchauffer; **to keep (oneself) ~** ne pas prendre froid; **to keep sth ~** garder qc au chaud **2.** (*not hot enough*) tiède **3.** (*showing feeling: greeting, welcome*) chaleureux(-euse); (*support*) enthousiaste **4.** (*causing heat*) chaud(e); **it's ~ work** c'est un travail qui donne chaud **5.** (*suggesting heat: colours, atmosphere*) chaud(e) **6.** (*close in guessing*) **to be ~** être chaud ►**cold hands, ~ heart** main froide, cœur chaud; **to keep sb's seat ~ for them** *inf* garder la place de qn au chaud **II.** *n* **to have a ~** se réchauffer; **to stay in the ~** rester au chaud **III.** *vt a. fig* réchauffer **IV.** *vi* chauffer
◆**warm to, warm towards** *vt* **to ~ sb** ressentir de la sympathie pour qn; **to ~ sth** se laisser séduire par qc
◆**warm up** **I.** *vi* **1.** (*become hot*) se

W

réchauffer **2.** (*begin to function properly: engine, machine*) chauffer **3.** (*limber up*) s'échauffer **4.** (*animate: party, atmosphere*) chauffer; (*debate*) s'échauffer **II.** *vt* **1.** (*make hot*) réchauffer **2.** (*start: engine*) faire chauffer **3.** (*animate*) faire chauffer

warm-blooded [ˌwɔːmˈblʌdɪd, *Am:* ˌwɔːrm-] *adj* à sang chaud

warm front *n* front *m* chaud

warm-hearted [ˌwɔːmˈhɑːtɪd, *Am:* ˌwɔːrmˈhɑːrt̬ɪd] *adj* chaleureux(-euse)

warmly *adv* (*to recommend, be dressed*) chaudement; (*to welcome*) chaleureusement

warmonger [ˈwɔːmʌŋgə, *Am:* ˈwɑːrmʌŋgɚ] *n* belliciste *mf*

warmth [wɔːmθ, *Am:* wɔːrmθ] *n no pl, no indef art, a. fig* chaleur *f*

warm-up *n* échauffement *m*

warn [wɔːn, *Am:* wɔːrn] *vt* avertir; **I'm ~ing you!** je te préviens!; **to ~ sb against/about sth** mettre qn en garde contre qc; **to ~ sb of a danger** avertir qn d'un danger; **to ~ sb to do sth** conseiller qn de faire qc; **to have been ~ed** avoir été prévenu

◆**warn off** *vt* **to warn sb off sth** mettre en garde contre qc; **to warn sb off doing sth** déconseiller à qn de faire qc

warning [ˈwɔːnɪŋ, *Am:* ˈwɔːr-] *n* **1.** *no pl, no indef art* (*notifying*) avertissement *m;* **without ~** sans prévenir **2.** (*written notification*) avis *m* **3.** (*threat*) alerte *f;* **a storm ~** un avis de tempête **4.** AUTO **~ lights** feux *mpl* de détresse; **~ sign** panneau *m* avertisseur **5.** *no pl, no indef art* (*advice*) conseil *m;* **a word of ~** un conseil **6.** (*caution*) avertissement *m;* **let that be a ~ to you!** que cela te serve d'avertissement! **7.** *fig* signe *m* annonciateur

War of Independence *n* guerre *f* d'Indépendance américaine

warp [wɔːp, *Am:* wɔːrp] **I.** *vi* se gondoler **II.** *vt* **1.** (*bend, twist*) gondoler **2.** (*damage psychologically*) pervertir **III.** *n no pl* **1.** (*twist*) voilure *f;* **a time ~** une brèche **2.** *no pl, no indef art* (*threads*) chaîne *f*

warpaint [ˈwɔːpeɪnt] *n* peinture *f* de guerre; **to put on the ~** *inf* se peinturlurer

warpath [ˈwɔːpɑːθ, *Am:* ˈwɔːrpæθ] *n no pl, no indef art, fig, inf* **to be on the ~** (*aggressive*) être sur le sentier de la guerre; (*bad-tempered*) être d'humeur massacrante

warped [wɔːpt, *Am:* wɔːrpt] *adj a. fig* tordu(e)

warrant [ˈwɒrənt, *Am:* ˈwɔːr-] **I.** *n* (*official document*) mandat *m;* **a search ~** un mandat de perquisition **II.** *vt* **1.** (*justify*) justifier **2.** (*guarantee*) garantir

warrant officer *n* adjudant(e) *m(f)*

warranty [ˈwɒrəntɪ, *Am:* ˈwɔːrənt̬ɪ] *n* garantie *f*

warren [ˈwɒrən, *Am:* ˈwɔːr-] *n* **1.** (*rabbit passages*) garenne *f* **2.** (*confusing place*) dédale *m*

warring [ˈwɔːrɪŋ] *adj* **1.** (*in conflict*) en conflit **2.** (*at war*) en guerre

warrior [ˈwɒrɪəʳ, *Am:* ˈwɔːrjɚ] *n* guerrier, -ère *m, f*

Warsaw [ˈwɔːsɔː, *Am:* ˈwɔːrsɑː] *n* Varsovie

Warsaw Pact, **Warsaw Treaty** *n* HIST pacte *m* de Varsovie

warship [ˈwɔːʃɪp, *Am:* ˈwɔːr-] *n* navire *m* de guerre

wart [wɔːt, *Am:* wɔːrt] *n* (*verruca*) verrue *f* ►**~s and all** *inf* tel qu'il est avec ses défauts

warthog [ˈwɔːthɒg, *Am:* ˈwɔːrthɑːg] *n* phacochère *m*

wartime [ˈwɔːtaɪm, *Am:* ˈwɔːr-] *n no pl, no indef art* temps *m* de guerre; **in ~** en temps de guerre

war-torn *adj* dévasté(e) par la guerre

wary [ˈweərɪ, *Am:* ˈwer-] <-ier, -iest> *adj* prudent(e); **to be ~ of sb/sth** se méfier de qn/qc

was [wɒz, *Am:* wɑːz] *pt of* **be**

wash [wɒʃ, *Am:* wɑːʃ] **I.** *n* **1.** (*cleaning with water*) **to have a ~** se laver; **to have a quick ~** avoir un brin de toilette **2.** (*laundering*) lessive *f;* **to do a ~** faire une lessive **3. the ~** *no pl* (*clothes for cleaning*) le linge sale; **to be in the ~** être au sale **4.** *Am s.* **washing-up** **5.** *no pl* (*thin paint layer*) lavis *m* **6.** (*boat's wake*) remous *m* ►**it'll all come out in the ~** *inf* ça finira par s'arranger **II.** *vt* **1.** (*clean with water*) laver; **to ~ a car** nettoyer une voiture; **to ~ one's hair/hands** se laver les cheveux/les mains **2.** (*clean*) nettoyer **3.** (*dilute*) laver **4.** (*carry away*) **to be ~ed downstream** être emporté par le courant ►**to ~ one's hands of sth** se laver les mains de qc; **to ~ one's dirty linen in public** laver son linge sale en public **III.** *vi* **1.** (*clean oneself*) se laver **2.** (*bathe*) baigner; **to ~ along the rocks** (*sea, wave*) balayer les falaises; **to ~ against the boat** se briser contre le bateau ►**that won't ~ with me** ça ne marche pas avec moi

◆**wash away** **I.** *vi* partir au lavage **II.** *vt* **1.** (*remove by flow of water*) faire partir au lavage **2.** (*carry away*) emporter **3.** (*remove*) laver; **to wash one's sins away** se laver de ses péchés

◆**wash down** *vt* **1.** (*swallow with liquid*) faire descendre **2.** (*clean with water*) laver à grande eau

◆**wash off** **I.** *vi* partir au lavage **II.** *vt* faire partir au lavage

◆**wash out** **I.** *vi* partir au lavage **II.** *vt* **1.** (*clean inside*) rincer **2.** (*wash quickly*) **to wash sth out** passer qc sous l'eau **3.** (*postpone*) **to be washed out** être annulé à cause de la pluie **4.** (*erode*) éroder

◆**wash up** **I.** *vi* **1.** (*clean dirty dishes*) faire la vaisselle **2.** *Am s.* **wash** **3.** (*be deposited by sea*) échouer **II.** *vt* **1.** (*deposit on beach*) rejeter **2.** (*to clean*) **to ~ the dishes** laver la vaisselle **3.** *fig* **to be all washed up** être fini

washable [ˈwɒʃəbl, *Am:* ˈwɑːʃ-] *adj* lavable

wash-and-wear *adj* facile d'entretien

washbasin ['wɒʃˌbeɪsn, *Am:* 'wɑːʃ-] *n* lavabo *m*
washcloth ['wɒʃklɒθ, *Am:* 'wɑːʃklɑːθ] *n* *Am* gant *m* de toilette
washday ['wɒʃdeɪ, *Am:* 'wɑːʃ-] *n* jour *m* de lessive
washdown ['wɒʃdaʊn] *n* toilette *f;* **to give sth a ~** laver qc (à grande eau)
washed-out [ˌwɒʃt'aʊt, *Am:* ˌwɑːʃt-] *adj* **1.** (*bleached*) délavé(e) **2.** (*tired*) lessivé(e)
washer ['wɒʃəʳ, *Am:* 'wɑːʃɚ] *n* **1.** *Am s.* **washing machine 2.** (*plastic ring*) joint *m*
wash-hand basin *n s.* **washbasin**
wash house ['wɒʃhaʊs, *Am:* 'wɑːʃ-] *n* laverie *f*
washing ['wɒʃɪŋ, *Am:* 'wɑːʃɪŋ] *n no pl, no indef art* **1.** (*act of cleaning clothes*) lessive *f;* **to do the ~** faire la lessive **2.** (*clothes*) linge *m;* **to hang out the ~** étendre le linge
washing line *n* corde *f* à linge **washing machine** *n* machine *f* à laver **washing powder** *n Brit* lessive *f* **washing soda** *n no pl, no indef art* cristaux *mpl* de soude
Washington ['wɒʃɪŋtən, *Am:* 'wɑːʃɪŋ-] **I.** *n* (*state*) le Washington **II.** *adj* du Washington
Washington (**D.C.**) ['wɒʃɪŋtən, *Am:* 'wɑːʃɪŋ-] *n* Washington

> **Washington's Birthday** est un jour férié légal aux USA. Bien que George Washington soit né en fait le 22 février 1732, on a pris l'habitude depuis quelques années de fêter son anniversaire le troisième lundi de février, afin d'avoir un week-end prolongé.

washing-up [ˌwɒʃɪŋ'ʌp, *Am:* ˌwɑːʃɪŋ-] *n Brit, Aus* vaisselle *f;* **to do the ~** faire la vaisselle
washing-up liquid *n* liquide *m* de vaisselle
washout ['wɒʃaʊt, *Am:* 'wɑːʃ-] *n no pl, inf* catastrophe *f*
washrag ['wɒʃræg, *Am:* 'wɑːʃ-] *n Am* gant *m* de toilette
washroom ['wɒʃrʊm, *Am:* 'wɑːʃruːm] *n* *Am* toilettes *fpl*
wasn't [wɒznt, *Am:* wɑːznt] = **was not** *s.* **be**
wasp [wɒsp, *Am:* wɑːsp] *n* guêpe *f*
WASP [wɒsp, *Am:* wɑːsp] *n Am, pej abbr of* **White Anglo-Saxon Protestant** Wasp *mf* (*Américain blanc protestant d'origine anglo-saxonne*)
waspish ['wɒspɪʃ, *Am:* 'wɑːs-] *adj pej* acerbe
wasp's nest *n* nid *m* de guêpes **wasp waist** *n* taille *f* de guêpe **wasp-waisted** *adj* **to be ~** avoir une taille de guêpe
wastage ['weɪstɪdʒ] *n no pl, no indef art* **1.** (*misuse*) gaspillage *m* **2.** *Brit, Aus s.* **natural wastage 3.** *Brit* (*dropouts from course*) *nombre de personnes qui abandonnent leurs études ou une formation;* **~ rate** taux *m* d'abandon **4.** (*byproduct of process*) déchets *mpl* **5.** (*deterioration of body*) dépérissement *m*
waste [weɪst] **I.** *n* **1.** *no pl* (*misuse*) gaspillage *m;* **it's a ~ of money** c'est de l'argent gaspillé; **it's a ~ of time** c'est une perte de temps; **it's a ~ of time doing sth** je perds mon temps à faire qc; **it was a ~ of energy/food** c'était un gaspillage d'énergie/de nourriture; **to lay ~ the land** dévaster le pays; **what a ~!** quel gâchis! **2.** *no pl, no indef art* (*unwanted matter*) déchets *mpl;* **to go to ~** être gaspillé **3.** (*desert*) **~**(**s**) désert *m* **II.** *vt* **1.** gaspiller; (*time*) perdre; **to ~ one's breath/words** perdre sa salive; **to ~ no time in doing sth** ne pas perdre son temps à faire qc; **the meal was ~d on him** il n'a pas su apprécier le repas; **the irony was ~d on him** il n'a pas compris l'ironie; **a ~d afternoon/chance** un après-midi gâché **2.** *inf* (*kill*) tuer **3.** (*destroy: muscles, body*) atrophier **III.** *vi* **~ not, want not** *prov* qui épargne gagne
◆**waste away** *vi* dépérir
wastebasket ['weɪstbɑːskɪt, *Am:* -bæskət] *n Am,* **waste bin** *n Brit, Aus* poubelle *f*
waste-disposal *n* **~** (**unit**) broyeur *m* d'ordures
wasteful ['weɪstfl] *adj* **to be ~ of sth** être du gaspillage de qc; **~ expenditure** dépenses *fpl* inutiles
waste ground *n,* **waste land** *n no pl, a. fig* désert *m*
wasteland ['weɪstlænd] *n* terre *f* en friche; *fig* désert *m*
wastepaper basket, **wastepaper bin** *n s.* **wastebasket, waste bin waste pipe** *n* tuyau *m* d'évacuation **waste water** *n* eaux *fpl* usées
wasting ['weɪstɪŋ] *adj* qui ronge
watch [wɒtʃ, *Am:* wɑːtʃ] **I.** *n* **1.** *no pl* (*act of observation*) surveillance *f;* **to be on the ~** guetter; **to be under** (**close**) **~** être sous (haute) surveillance; **to keep** (**a**) **close ~ on/over sb/sth** surveiller qn/qc de près; **to be on ~ for sth** guetter qc; **to keep ~** faire le guet; **to put a ~ on sb** faire surveiller qn **2.** (*guard*) garde *f;* **to keep ~** monter la garde **3.** (*clock worn on wrist*) montre *f* **II.** *vt* **1.** (*look at*) regarder; **to ~ a film/TV** regarder un film/la télé **2.** (*observe*) observer; (*suspects*) surveiller; **to ~ sb do sth** regarder qn faire qc; **to ~ sb/sth like a hawk** surveiller qn/qc de près **3.** (*take care of: children*) surveiller **4.** (*be careful about*) faire attention à; (*one's weight*) surveiller; **to ~ every penny** compter chaque sou; **~ it!** fais attention!; **to ~ it with sb** prendre garde à qn; **~ yourself** fais gaffe ►**to ~ your back** faire attention à soi; **~ your language!** surveille ton langage!; **to ~ one's step** faire attention où l'on met ses pieds; *inf* faire attention à ce que l'on fait; **to ~ the world go by** regarder passer la foule **III.** *vi* **1.** (*look at*) regarder; **to ~ as sb/sth does sth** regarder comment qn/qc fait qc **2.** (*be on*

alert) guetter

◆**watch out** *vi* faire attention; ~**!** (fais) attention!; **to ~ for sb/sth** attendre qn/qc; (*watch the approach of*) guetter qn/qc

watchband ['wɒtʃbænd] *n Am, Aus* bracelet *m* de montre

watchdog ['wɒtʃdɒg, *Am:* 'wɑːtʃdɑːg] *n* **1.** *Am s.* **guard dog 2.** (*keeper of standards: person*) contrôleur, -euse *m, f;* (*organization*) organisme *m* de contrôle

watcher ['wɒtʃəʳ, *Am:* 'wɑːtʃɚ] *n* observateur, -trice *m, f*

watchful ['wɒtʃfl, *Am:* 'wɑːtʃ-] *adj* vigilant(e); **to keep a ~ eye on sb/sth** garder un œil attentif sur qn/qc; **under the ~ eye of sb** sous l'œil vigilant de qn

watchmaker ['wɒtʃˌmeɪkəʳ, *Am:* 'wɑːtʃˌmeɪkɚ] *n* horloger, -ère *m, f*

watchman ['wɒtʃmən, *Am:* 'wɑːtʃ-] <-men> *n* gardien(ne) *m(f);* **a night ~** un gardien de nuit

watchtower ['wɒtʃtaʊə, *Am:* 'wɑːtʃtaʊɚ] *n* tour *f* d'observation

watchword ['wɒtʃwɜːd, *Am:* 'wɑːtʃwɜːrd] *n no pl* (*symbolic of action*) mot *m* d'ordre

water ['wɔːtəʳ, *Am:* 'wɑːt̬ɚ] **I.** *n* (*liquid*) eau *f;* **bottled ~** eau en bouteille; **a bottle/glass of ~** une bouteille/un verre d'eau; **under ~** sous l'eau; (*flooded*) inondé(e); **hot and cold ~** eau courante; **to keep one's head above ~** *a. fig* maintenir la tête hors de l'eau; **low/high ~** marée *f* basse/haute; **to tread ~** *a. fig* faire du sur-place *f;* **to pass ~** uriner ►**to throw out the baby with the bath ~** jeter le bébé avec l'eau du bain; **to be ~ under the bridge** être du passé; **to be like a fish out of ~** être complètement dépaysé; **through hell and high ~** contre vents et marées; **to spend money like ~** jeter l'argent par les fenêtres; **to pour cold ~ on sth** se montrer réticent à l'égard de qc; **of the first ~** de tout premier ordre; **to get into hot ~** se mettre dans le pétrin; **to be in deep ~** avoir dans le pétrin; **still ~s run deep** il faut se méfier de l'eau qui sommeille; **to hold ~** tenir debout **II.** *vt* **1.** (*give water to: plants*) arroser; (*cows, horses*) faire boire **2.** (*dilute*) diluer **III.** *vi* **1.** (*produce tears*) pleurer **2.** (*salivate*) saliver

◆**water down** *vt* **1.** (*dilute: beer, milk*) diluer **2.** (*weaken*) atténuer; **a watered down version** une version édulcorée

water bed *n* lit *m* à eau **water bird** *n* oiseau *m* aquatique **water biscuit** *n* craquelin *m* **water-bomber** *n Can* canadair *m*

waterborne ['wɔːtəbɔːn, *Am:* 'wɑːt̬ɚbɔːrn] *adj* par voie d'eau; **~ goods/soldiers** biens/soldats transportés par voie d'eau; MED par voie hydrique

water bottle *n* bouteille *f* d'eau; (*for soldiers, travellers*) gourde *f* **water butt** *n* citerne *f* d'eau de pluie **water cannon** *inv n* canon *m* à eau **water closet** *n* cabinets *mpl* **watercolor** *n Am, Aus,* **watercolour** *n Brit, Aus* aquarelle *f* **water cooler** *n* distributeur *m* d'eau

watercourse ['wɔːtəkɔːs, *Am:* 'wɑːt̬ɚkɔːrs] *n* cours *m* d'eau

watercress ['wɔːtəkres, *Am:* 'wɑːt̬ɚ-] *n* cresson *m* de fontaine

waterfall ['wɔːtəfɔːl, *Am:* 'wɑːt̬ɚ-] *n* cascade *f*

water filter *n* filtre *m* à eau

waterfront ['wɔːtəfrʌnt, *Am:* 'wɑːt̬ɚ-] *n no pl* bord *m* de l'eau

water heater *n* chauffe-eau *m* **water hole** *n* point *m* d'eau **water ice** *n Brit s.* **sorbet**

watering ['wɔːtərɪŋ, *Am:* 'wɑːt̬-] *n* (*plants*) arrosage *m;* (*region*) irrigation *f*

watering can *n* arrosoir *m* **watering hole** *n* **1.** (*waterhole*) point *m* d'eau **2.** *inf* (*bar*) bar *m* **watering place** *n* **1.** *inf s.* **watering hole 2.** (*spa*) station *f* thermale

waterless ['wɔːtəlɪs, *Am:* 'wɑːt̬ɚləs] *adj* sans eau

water level *n* niveau *m* de l'eau **water lily** *n* nénuphar *m* **waterlogged** *adj* détrempé(e)

water main *n* conduite *f* principale d'eau

watermark ['wɔːtəmɑːk, *Am:* 'wɑːt̬ɚmɑːrk] *n* (*on paper*) filigrane *m*

watermelon ['wɔːtəmelən, *Am:* 'wɑːt̬ɚ-] *n* pastèque *f*

water meter *n* compteur *m* d'eau **water mill** *n* moulin *m* à eau **water pipe** *n* **1.** (*pipe to transport water*) conduite *f* d'eau **2.** (*hookah*) pipe *f* à eau **water pistol** *n* pistolet *m* à eau **water pollution** *n* pollution *f* de l'eau **water polo** *n* water-polo *m* **water power** *n no pl, no indef art* énergie *f* hydraulique **water pressure** *n* pression *f* de l'eau **waterproof I.** *adj* étanche; (*clothes*) imperméable **II.** *n Brit* imperméable *m* **III.** *vt* imperméabiliser **water-repellent** *adj* imperméable **water retention** *n* MED rétention d'eau **watershed** *n* **1.** GEO ligne *f* de partage des eaux **2.** *fig* tournant *m* décisif **3.** *Brit* TV *heure à laquelle la télévision diffuse des programmes pour adultes*

water shortage *n* pénurie *f* en eau

waterside ['wɔːtəsaɪd, *Am:* 'wɑːt̬ɚ-] *n no pl, no indef art* bord *m* de l'eau; **a ~ café** un café au bord de l'eau

water-ski I. *vi* faire du ski nautique **II.** <-s> *n* ski *m* nautique **water-skiing** *n* ski *m* nautique **water softener** *n* adoucisseur *m* **water-soluble** *adj* soluble dans l'eau **water sports** *n pl* sports *mpl* nautiques

water supply *n* **1.** *no pl* (*amount of water*) approvisionnement *m* en eau **2.** *no pl* (*system*) alimentation *f* en eau **water supply pipe** *n* conduite *f* d'alimentation en eau **water supply point** *n* point *m* d'arrivée d'eau **water tank** *n* citerne *f*

watertight ['wɔːtətaɪt, *Am:* 'wɑːt̬ɚ-] *adj* **1.** (*sealed*) étanche **2.** (*unquestionable*) inattaquable

water tower *n* château *m* d'eau
waterway ['wɔ:təweɪ, *Am:* 'wɑ:t̬ɚ-] *n* voie *f* navigable
water wings ['wɔ:təwɪŋz, *Am:* 'wɑ:t̬ɚ-] *n pl* bracelets *mpl*
waterworks ['wɔ:təwɜ:ks, *Am:* 'wɑ:t̬ɚwɜ:rks] *n pl* **1.** (*water storage*) station *f* hydraulique **2.** *inf* (*organs*) vessie *f* ▶**to turn on the ~** *pej* se mettre à pleurer comme une fontaine
watery ['wɔ:tərɪ, *Am:* 'wɑ:t̬ɚ-] <more, most *o* -ier, -iest> *adj* **1.** (*bland*) fade; (*coffee*) dilué(e); (*soup*) trop clair(e) **2.** (*weak, pale*) délavé(e) **3.** (*full of tears*) mouillé(e) **4.** (*threatening: sky*) menaçant(e)
watt [wɒt, *Am:* wɑ:t] *n* watt *m*
wattage ['wɒtɪdʒ, *Am:* 'wɑ:t̬ɪdʒ] *n no pl* ELEC puissance *f* en watts
wave ['weɪv] **I.** *n* **1.** (*surge of water*) *a. fig* vague *f;* **~ of strikes/enthusiasm** vague de grèves/d'enthousiasme; **to make ~s** créer des remous **2.** (*hand movement*) signe *m* (de la main); **with a ~ of sb's hand** d'un signe de la main; **to give sb a ~** saluer qn de la main **3.** PHYS onde *f;* **long/medium/short ~** onde longue/moyenne/courte **4.** (*hairstyle*) cran *m;* **to have a natural ~** avoir les cheveux qui ondulent naturellement **II.** *vi* **1.** (*make hand movement*) faire un signe (de la main); **to ~ at/to sb/sth** faire un signe de la main à qn/qc **2.** (*move from side to side*) ondoyer; (*flag*) flotter **3.** (*have curves in hair*) onduler **III.** *vt* **1.** (*move to signal*) faire un signe (de la main); **to ~ hello to sb** saluer qn d'un geste; **to ~ goodbye to sb** dire au revoir à qn d'un geste; **to ~ one's hand** faire un signe de la main; **he ~d me forward** il m'a fait signe d'avancer; **to ~ goodbye to sth** *fig* dire adieu à qc **2.** (*move side to side: wand, flag*) agiter **3.** (*make curves in hair*) onduler; **to ~ one's hair** se faire onduler les cheveux
 ◆**wave aside** *vt fig* écarter
 ◆**wave down** *vt* faire signe de s'arrêter à
 ◆**wave off** *vt* faire au revoir à
 ◆**wave on** *vt* faire signe de continuer à
waveband ['weɪvbænd] *n* bande *f* de fréquence **wavelength** *n a. fig* longueur *f* d'ondes; **to be on the same ~** être sur la même longueur d'ondes
waver ['weɪvəʳ, *Am:* -vɚ] *vi* vaciller; *fig* hésiter
waverer ['weɪvərəʳ, *Am:* -ɚɚ] *n* indécis(e) *m(f)*
wavering ['weɪvərɪŋ] *adj* vacillant(e)
wavy ['weɪvɪ] <-ier, -iest> *adj* onduleux(-euse); (*hair*) ondulé(e)
wax [wæks] **I.** *n* cire *f;* (*in ears*) cérumen *m;* **a ~ candle** un cierge **II.** *vt* **1.** (*polish*) cirer **2.** (*remove hair from*) épiler ▶**to ~ and wane** croître et décroître
waxed *adj* ciré(e)
waxed jacket *n* ciré *m*
wax paper ['wækspeɪpəʳ, *Am:* -pɚ] *n* papier *m* sulfurisé
waxwork ['wækswɜ:k, *Am:* -wɜ:rk] *n* figure *f* en cire; **a ~s (museum)** un musée de cire
waxy ['wæksɪ] <-ier, -iest> *adj* cireux(-euse); (*potato*) ferme
way [weɪ] **I.** *n* **1.** (*route, path*) chemin *m;* **the ~ to the station** le chemin de la gare; **the ~ to success** *fig* le chemin de la gloire; **to ask sb the ~** demander son chemin à qn; **to make one's ~ somewhere** se rendre quelque part; **to make one's ~ through the crowd** se frayer un chemin dans la foule; **to go the wrong ~** faire fausse route; **to be on the ~** être sur le chemin; **the ~ back** le retour; **on the ~ to sth** sur le chemin de qc; **to be on the ~ back** être sur le chemin du retour; **on the ~ home** en rentrant; **a baby is on the ~** un bébé est en route; **to find one's ~ to the house** trouver le chemin de la maison; **to lose one's ~** se perdre; **to find one's ~ into/out of sth** trouver l'entrée/la sortie de qc; **to find one's ~ through sth** se frayer un chemin à travers qc; **to find a ~ round a problem** trouver une solution à un problème; **to elbow one's ~ somewhere** se frayer un chemin quelque part; **to be out of the ~** être isolé; *fig* être exceptionnel; **to be over the ~** être de l'autre côté de la route; **to be under ~** être en route; **to lead the ~** *a. fig* montrer le chemin; **by ~ of sth** via qc; **by the ~** chemin faisant; *fig* à propos; **to be under ~** être en route; **to give ~** (*agree*) céder; AUTO céder le passage; (*fall down*) céder; **to give ~ to temptation** céder à la tentation **2.** (*facing direction*) direction *f;* **it's the other ~ round** c'est dans l'autre sens; *fig* c'est le contraire; **both ~s** dans les deux sens; **the wrong ~ round** sens dessus dessous; **to put sth the right ~ up** mettre qc dans le bon sens; **this ~** par ici **3.** (*respect*) égard *m;* **in that ~** à cet égard; **in many ~s** à bien des égards; **in a ~** dans une certaine mesure; **in a big/small ~** sur une grande/petite échelle **4.** (*state*) état *m;* **to be in a good/bad ~** (*person*) aller bien/mal; (*thing*) être en bon/mauvais état **5.** (*distance*) distance *f;* **all the ~** (*the whole distance*) tout le long du chemin; (*completely*) jusqu'au bout; **all the ~ here** jusqu'ici; **to go all the ~ with sb** *inf* aller jusqu'au bout avec qn; **to be a long ~ off** (*remote*) être loin; (*event*) être assez loin; **to be a long ~ to a place** être bien loin d'un endroit; **to have a ~ to go** avoir du chemin à parcourir **6.** (*manner*) façon *f;* **this ~** de cette façon; **in no ~** en aucune façon; **in a friendly ~** de façon amicale; **~ of life** mode *m* de vie; **in one's own ~** à sa façon; **sb's ~s** les habitudes de qn; **the ~ to do sth** la manière de faire qc; **her ~ of doing sth** sa façon de faire qc; **the ~s and means of doing/to do sth** les différentes manières de faire qc; **by ~ of sth** en guise de qc; **to get one's own ~** arriver à ses fins; **to my ~ of thinking** à mon avis; **to have a ~ with sb** savoir s'y prendre avec qn; **either**

~ quoiqu'il arrive; **to be in the family** ~ être enceinte; **no ~!** *inf* (*impossible*) impossible!; (*definitely no!*) pas question!; **in no** ~ en aucun cas; **there's no ~ we can finish on time** on ne finira jamais à temps **7.** *no pl* (*space for movement*) **to be in sb's** ~ barrer le passage de qn; **to be in the** ~ gêner le passage; *fig* gêner; **to get out of the/sb's** ~ s'écarter du chemin/du chemin de qn ►**that's the ~ the cookie crumbles** *prov* c'est la vie; **to go the ~ of all flesh** payer sa dette à la nature; **where there's a will, there's a** ~ *prov* vouloir c'est pouvoir; **to see/find out which ~ the wind blows/is** voir d'où vient le vent; **to have come a long** ~ revenir de loin; **to go a long** ~ faciliter les choses; **to go one's own** ~ faire à sa guise; **to go out of one's/the** ~ se donner du mal; **you can't have it both ~s** tu dois choisir; **to be (well) on the ~ to doing sth** être en passe de faire qc **II.** *adv inf* bien; **to be ~ ahead of sb/sth** *inf* être bien en avance sur qn/qc

waybill ['weɪbɪl] *n* récépissé *m*

waylay [ˌweɪ'leɪ, *Am:* 'weɪleɪ] <waylaid, waylaid> *vt* **1.** (*detain*) retenir **2.** (*attack*) **to ~ sb** attaquer qn par surprise

way out [ˌweɪ'aʊt] *n* sortie *f*

way-out [ˌweɪ'aʊt] *adj inf* excentrique

wayside ['weɪsaɪd] *n* **1.** (*roadside*) bord *m* de la route **2.** (*of path*) bord *m* du chemin ►**to fall by the** ~ abandonner en route

wayward ['weɪwəd, *Am:* -wɚd] *adj* capricieux(-euse)

wc [ˌdʌblju:'si:] *n Brit abbr of* **water closet** WC *mpl*

we [wi:] *pers pron* nous; **as ~ say** comme on dit

We [wi:] *n form* **the Royal** ~ le nous de majesté

weak [wi:k] *adj* **1.** (*not strong*) *a. fig* faible; (*chin*) fuyant(e); **a ~ link** [*o* **spot**] *fig* un point faible; **the film is ~ on plot** le film manque d'action; **to have a ~ heart** avoir le cœur fragile; **to be/go ~ at the knees** avoir les jambes comme du coton **2.** (*light: drink, coffee*) léger(-ère)

weaken ['wi:kən] **I.** *vi* **1.** (*become less strong*) s'affaiblir **2.** (*become less resolute*) faiblir **II.** *vt* affaiblir

weakling ['wi:klɪŋ] *n pej* personne *f* chétive

weakly *adv* **1.** (*without strength*) faiblement **2.** (*unconvincingly*) mollement

weak-minded [ˌwi:k'maɪndɪd] *adj pej* **1.** (*lacking determination*) indécis(e) **2.** (*mentally deficient*) faible d'esprit

weakness ['wi:knɪs] <-es> *n* **1.** *no pl* (*being irresolute*) faiblesse *f* **2.** (*area of vulnerability*) faiblesse *f* **3.** (*strong liking*) faible *m;* **to have a ~ for sth** avoir un faible pour qc

weal [wi:l] *n* (*mark*) marque *f*

wealth [welθ] *n no pl* **1.** (*money*) richesse *f* **2.** (*large amount*) abondance *f*

wealth tax *n* impôt *m* sur la fortune

wealthy ['welθɪ] **I.** <-ier, -iest> *adj* riche **II.** *n* **the** ~ *no pl* les riches

wean [wi:n] *vt a. fig* sevrer; **to ~ sb off sth** sevrer qn de qc; **to be ~ed on sth** être nourri de qc

weapon ['wepən] *n a. fig* arme *f*

weaponry ['wepənrɪ] *n no pl* armement *m*

wear [weəʳ, *Am:* wer] <wore, worn> **I.** *n* **1.** (*clothing*) vêtements *mpl;* **men's** ~ vêtements pour hommes **2.** (*amount of use*) usure *f;* **there's some ~ left in sth** on peut encore utiliser qc; **to show signs of** ~ commencer à s'user; ~ **and tear** usure *f;* **to have had a lot of ~ and tear** être très usé; **to be the worse for** ~ être ivre **II.** *vt* **1.** (*have on body*) *a. fig* porter **2.** (*make a hole*) user; **to ~ holes in sth** trouer qc ►**to ~ your heart on your sleeve** laisser transparaître ses sentiments; **to ~ the trousers, to ~ the pants** *Am* porter la culotte **III.** *vi* s'user; **to ~ into holes** se trouer; **to ~ thin** être usé; *fig* être à bout

◆**wear away** **I.** *vi irr* s'user **II.** *vt* user

◆**wear down** *vt irr, a. fig* user; **to ~ sb's resistance** épuiser la résistance de qn

◆**wear off** **I.** *vi irr* s'effacer; (*pain*) disparaître; (*effect*) cesser; (*anaesthetic*) cesser de faire effet **II.** *vt* effacer

◆**wear on** *vi irr* (*day, night*) s'avancer

◆**wear out** **I.** *vi irr* s'user; *fig* s'épuiser **II.** *vt* user; *fig* épuiser

wearable ['weərəbl, *Am:* 'werə-] *adj* mettable

wearing ['weərɪŋ, *Am:* 'wer-] *adj* fatigant(e)

wearisome ['wɪərɪsəm, *Am:* 'wɪrɪ-] *adj form* **1.** (*causing boredom*) ennuyeux(-euse) **2.** (*causing tiredness*) fatigant(e)

weary ['wɪərɪ, *Am:* 'wɪrɪ] <-ier, -iest> *adj* **1.** (*very tired*) fatigué(e) **2.** (*bored*) las(se); **to be/grow ~ of sth** se lasser de qc **3.** (*tiring*) fatigant(e)

weasel ['wi:zl] *n* belette *f*

weather ['weðəʳ, *Am:* -ɚ] **I.** *n no pl* temps *m;* ~ **permitting** si le temps le permet; **in all ~s** par tous les temps; **what's the ~ like?** quel temps fait-il? ►**to make heavy ~ of sth** compliquer qc; **to be under the** ~ être patraque **II.** *vi* s'altérer; (*rocks*) s'éroder; (*with patina*) se patiner **III.** *vt* altérer; (*rock*) éroder ►**to ~ the storm** surmonter la crise

weather-beaten *adj* érodé(e) par les intempéries; (*face*) tanné(e) **weather cock** *n* girouette *f* **weather conditions** *n pl* conditions *fpl* météorologiques **weather forecast** *n* météo *f*

weatherman ['weðəmæn, *Am:* 'weðɚ-] *n* présentateur, -trice *m, f* météo

weatherproof ['weðəpru:f, *Am:* 'weðɚ-] *adj* imperméable

weave [wi:v] **I.** <wove *o a. Am* weaved, woven> *vt* **1.** (*produce cloth*) tisser; **to ~ sth into sth** tisser qc en qc **2.** (*intertwine things*) tresser; **to ~ sth from sth** tresser qc à partir de qc **3.** (*make a whole*) tramer **4.** (*move in twist-*

ing) **to ~ one's way through sth** se faufiler à travers qc **II.** <wove *o a. Am* weaved, woven> *vi* **1.** (*produce cloth*) tisser **2.** (*intertwine*) tresser **3.** (*move by twisting*) **to ~ between sth** se faufiler entre qc ►**to get weaving** *Brit, inf* se remuer **III.** *n* **1.** (*way of making cloth*) tissage *m* **2.** (*way of intertwining*) tressage *m*

weaver ['wiːvəʳ, *Am:* -vɚ] *n* tisserand(e) *m(f)*

web [web] *n* **1.** (*trap*) toile *f;* **spider('s) ~** toile d'araignée; **to spin a ~** tisser une toile **2.** (*network*) tissu *m* **3.** (*tissue for birds*) palmure *f*

Web, WEB [web] **I.** *n* INFOR Web *m;* (**World Wide**) **~** toile *f* (d'araignée mondiale) **II.** *adj inv* INFOR Web

Web addict *n* INFOR Webmane *m* **web camera** *n* INFOR Webcam *f* **Web browser** *n* INFOR explo(rateur) *m* Web

web-footed [ˌwebˈfʊtɪd, *Am:* ˈwebˌfʊt̬ɪd] *adj* **to be ~** avoir les pieds palmés

webmaster *n* INFOR Webmestre *m,* administrateur *m* de site **webpage** *n* INFOR page *f* Web [*o* sur la toile]; **~ wizard** assistant *m* pages Web **website** *n* INFOR site *m* (sur) Internet **webzine** *n* INFOR magazine *m* électronique

wed [wed] <wedded, wedded *o* wed, wed> *form* **I.** *vt* épouser **II.** *vi* se marier

we'd [wiːd] **1.** = **we had** *s.* **have 2.** = **we would** *s.* **will**

wedded ['wedɪd] **I.** *pt, pp of* **wed II.** *adj* marié(e); **~ life** vie *f* conjugale; **lawful ~ wife** *form* légitime épouse *f*

wedding ['wedɪŋ] *n* mariage *m*

wedding anniversary *n* anniversaire *m* de mariage **wedding cake** *n* gâteau *m* de mariage **wedding day** *n* jour *m* du mariage **wedding night** *n* nuit *f* de noces **wedding present** *n* cadeau *m* de mariage

wedge [wedʒ] **I.** *n* **1.** (*for door*) cale *f;* **to drive a ~ between people** mettre une distance entre des gens **2.** (*piece*) morceau *m* **II.** *vt* (*jam into*) caler; **to ~ the door open** maintenir la porte ouverte en la calant

Wednesday ['wenzdɪ, *Am:* -deɪ] *n* mercredi *m;* **Ash ~** mercredi des Cendres; *s. a.* **Friday**

wee [wiː] **I.** *adj Scot, a. inf* minuscule; **a ~ bit** un tout petit peu **II.** *n no pl, inf* pipi *m;* **to have a ~** faire pipi **III.** *vi inf* faire pipi

weed [wiːd] **I.** *n* **1.** (*wild plant*) mauvaise herbe *f* **2.** *Brit, pej, inf* (*feeble person*) mauviette *f* **3.** *no pl, inf* (*tobacco*) **the ~** le tabac **4.** *no pl, inf* (*marijuana*) herbe *f* ►**to grow like a ~** pousser comme de la mauvaise herbe **II.** *vt, vi* désherber

weedkiller ['wiːdkɪləʳ, *Am:* -ɚ] *n no pl* désherbant *m*

weedy ['wiːdɪ] <-ier, iest> *adj* **1.** (*full of weeds*) envahi(e) par les mauvaises herbes **2.** *Brit, pej, inf* (*very thin*) malingre **3.** (*underdeveloped*) dépourvu(e) d'intérêt

week [wiːk] *n* semaine *f;* **a few ~s ago** il y a quelques semaines; **last ~** la semaine dernière; **once a ~** une fois par semaine; **a thirty-five hour ~** une semaine de trente-cinq heures; **during the ~** pendant la semaine; **Friday ~** vendredi en huit; **to work a five-day ~** travailler cinq jours par semaine ►**for ~s on end** pendant des semaines; **a ~ ago (this)** [*o* **a ~ last** ...] **Friday** il y a une semaine vendredi ...; **~ in, ~ out, ~ after ~** semaine après semaine; **~ by ~, from ~ to ~** d'une semaine à l'autre; **a ~ (on) ...** dans une semaine ...

weekday ['wiːkdeɪ] *n* jour *m* de la semaine; **on ~s** les jours de la semaine **weekend** *n* week-end *m;* **at the ~(s)** *Brit, Aus,* **on the ~(s)** *Am, a. Aus* le week-end **weekly I.** *adj* hebdomadaire **II.** *adv* une fois par semaine **III.** *n* hebdomadaire *m*

weeny ['wiːnɪ] <-ier, -iest> *adj inf* tout(e) petit(e); **a ~ bit** un tout petit bout

weep [wiːp] **I.** *vi* <wept, wept> **to ~ over sb/sth** pleurer sur qn/qc **II.** *vt* <wept, wept> **to ~ tears of joy** verser des larmes de joie

weeping willow *n* saule *m* pleureur

w. e. f. *abbr of* **with effect from** prenant effet à compter du

weigh [weɪ] **I.** *vi* peser **II.** *vt* **1.** (*measure weight*) peser; **to ~ oneself** se peser; **to be weighed down by sth** plier sous le poids de qc; *fig* être accablé de qc **2.** (*consider carefully*) **to ~ one's words** peser ses mots **3.** NAUT **to ~ anchor** lever l'ancre

◆**weigh in** *vi* **1.** (*be weighed*) se faire peser **2.** *inf* (*intervene*) intervenir

◆**weigh out** *vt* peser

◆**weigh up** *vt* **1.** (*calculate and compare*) évaluer **2.** (*judge, assess*) juger

weigh-in *n* pesée *f*

weight [weɪt] **I.** *n* **1.** *no pl* (*heaviness*) poids *m;* **to put on** [*o* **gain**] **~** prendre du poids **2.** (*metal piece*) poids *m;* **to lift ~s** lever des poids **3.** *no pl* (*value*) poids *m;* **to attach ~ to sth** attacher de l'importance à qc; **to carry ~** avoir du poids ►**to take the ~ off one's feet** se reposer; **to be a ~ off sb's mind** être un soulagement pour qn **II.** *vt* **1.** (*hold*) lester; **to ~ sth down** maintenir qc avec un poids **2.** *fig* pondérer; **to be ~ed in favour of sb/sth** peser en faveur de qn/qc; **to be ~ed in one's favour** être favorable à qn; **to be ~ed against sb** être défavorable à qn

weighting ['weɪtɪŋ, *Am:* -t̬ɪŋ] *n no pl, Brit* **1.** (*additional amount*) indemnité *f* **2.** MAT coefficient *m*

weightless ['weɪtlɪs] *adj* en état d'apesanteur

weightlessness *n no pl* apesanteur *f*

weightlifter ['weɪtlɪftəʳ, *Am:* -ɚ] *n* haltérophile *mf*

weightlifting ['weɪtlɪftɪŋ] *n no pl* haltérophilie *f*

weighty ['weɪtɪ, *Am:* -t̬ɪ] <-ier, -iest> *adj* **1.** (*heavy*) lourd(e) **2.** (*important*) important(e); (*issue*) sérieux(-euse)

weir [wɪəʳ, *Am:* wɪr] *n* barrage *m*
weird [wɪəd, *Am:* wɪrd] *adj* bizarre
welcome ['welkəm] **I.** *vt* accueillir **II.** *n a. fig* accueil *m;* **to give sth a warm** ~ réserver un accueil chaleureux à qn; **to overstay one's** ~ abuser de l'hospitalité de qn **III.** *adj* bienvenu(e); **to make sb** ~ faire bon accueil à qn; **to be most** ~ être le bienvenu ▶**you're** ~**!** de rien!, bienvenue! *Québec;* **to be** ~ **to (do) sth** pouvoir faire qc **IV.** *interj* bienvenue!; ~ **home!** bienvenue à la maison!; ~ **back!** heureux de vous revoir!
welcoming *adj* accueillant(e); **a** ~ **smile/speech** un sourire/discours d'accueil
weld [weld] **I.** *vt a. fig* souder; **to** ~ **sth together** souder qc **II.** *n* soudure *f*
welder ['weldəʳ, *Am:* -ɚ] *n* soudeur *m*
welding *n no pl* soudure *f*
welfare ['welfeəʳ, *Am:* -fer] *n no pl* **1.** (*state of wellness*) bien-être *m* **2.** (*state aid or relief*) aide *f* sociale; ~ **system** système *m* d'aides sociales; **to be on** ~ *Am* toucher l'aide sociale
welfare payments *n* prestations *fpl* sociales **welfare state** *n* **1.** (*state*) état *m* providence **2.** (*institution*) sécurité *f* sociale **welfare work** *n* travail *m* social **welfare worker** *n* assistant(e) *m(f)* social(e)
we'll [wi:l] = **we will** *s.* **will**
well[1] [wel] **I.** <better, best> *adj* **to be/feel/get** ~ aller bien; **all is** ~ tout va bien; **to look** ~ avoir l'air d'aller bien **II.** <better, best> *adv* **1.** (*in a good manner*) bien; ~ **done!** bravo!; ~ **put** bien dit **2.** (*thoroughly*) bien; ~ **east** plus à l'est; **to be pretty** ~ aller plutôt bien; **to be pretty** ~ **paid** être plutôt bien payé; **to be pretty** ~ **the same thing** être à peu près la même chose; ~ **and truly** complètement; ~ **below (sth)** bien en dessous (de qc); **to be** ~ **pleased with sth** être satisfait de qc **3.** (*justifiably*) **I can't very** ~ **ask him** je ne peux pas raisonnablement lui demander ▶**to be all** ~ **and good, that's all very** ~ c'est certes bien; **as** ~ aussi; **as** ~ **as** ainsi que; **it is just as** ~ **that** heureusement que; **to be** ~ **in with sb/sth** *Brit, inf,* **to be in** ~ **with sb/sth** *Am, inf* être en de bons termes avec qn/qc; **to be** ~ **out of it** *Brit, Aus* s'en sortir bien **III.** *interj* (*exclamation*) eh bien!; ~**,** ~**!** eh bien!; **oh** ~**!** oh!; **very** ~**!** très bien!
well[2] [wel] **I.** *n* puits *m;* **oil** ~ puits de pétrole **II.** *vi* **1. to** ~ **(up) out of sth** (*water*) remonter de qc **2.** *fig* **to** ~ **up in sb/sth** monter en qn/à qc
well-advised *adj form* **to be** ~ **to do sth** avoir tout intérêt à faire qc **well-appointed** *adj form* bien équipé(e) **well-balanced** *adj* bien équilibré(e) **well-behaved** *adj* sage **well-being** *n no pl* bien-être *m* **well-bred** *adj* bien élevé(e) **well-chosen** *adj* bien choisi(e) **well-connected** *adj* **to be** ~ avoir de bonnes relations **well-deserved** *adj* bien mérité(e) **well-developed** *adj* bien développé(e) **well-disposed** *adj* bien disposé(e) **well-done** *adj* (*meat*) à point **well-dressed** *adj* bien habillé(e) **well-earned** *adj* bien mérité(e) **well-educated** *adj* cultivé(e) **well-fed** *adj* bien nourri(e) **well-founded** *adj* légitime **well-heeled I.** *adj inf* riche **II.** *npl* **the** ~ les richards
wellie ['welɪ] *n Brit, inf abbr of* **wellington (boot) well-informed** *adj* bien informé(e)
wellington (boot) ['welɪŋtən (bu:t)] *n Brit* (botte *f* en) caoutchouc *m*
well-intentioned *adj* bien intentionné(e) **well kept** *adj* bien entretenu(e) **well-known** *adj* connu(e) **well-made** *adj* bien fait(e) **well-mannered** *adj* bien élevé(e) **well-meaning**, **well-meant** *adj* bien intentionné(e) **well-nigh** *adv* presque **well-off I.** *adj* **1.** (*wealthy*) riche **2.** (*having much*) **to be** ~ **for sth** être bien pourvu en qc ▶**not to know when one is** ~ ne pas connaître sa chance **II.** *npl* **the** ~ les nantis **well-oiled** *adj* **1.** (*functioning smoothly*) bien huilé(e) **2.** *inf* (*drunk*) bourré(e) **well-organized** *adj* bien organisé(e) **well-paid** *adj* bien payé(e) **well-placed** *adj* bien placé(e) **well-proportioned** *adj* bien proportionné(e) **well-read** *adj* **1.** (*knowledgeable*) cultivé(e) **2.** (*read frequently*) très lu(e) **well-thought-of** *adj* bien conçu(e) **well-timed** *adj* opportun(e) **well-to-do** *adj inf* riche **well-turned** *adj* bien tourné(e) **well-wisher** *n* supporter *mf* **well-worn** *adj a. fig* usagé(e)
welly ['welɪ] *n Brit, inf abbr of* **wellington (boot)**
Welsh [welʃ] **I.** *adj* gallois(e) **II.** *n* **1.** (*people*) **the** ~ les Gallois **2.** LING gallois *m; s. a.* **English**
Welshman ['welʃmən] <-men> *n* gallois *m*
Welshwoman ['welʃwʊmən] <-women> *n* galloise *f*
welt [welt] *n* trépointe *f*
went [went] *pt of* **go**
wept [wept] *pt, pp of* **weep**
were [wɜ:ʳ, *Am:* wɜ:r] *pt of* **be**
we're [wɪəʳ, *Am:* wɪr] = **we are** *s.* **be**
weren't [wɜ:nt, *Am:* wɜ:rnt] = **were not** *s.* **be**
werewolf ['weəwʊlf, *Am:* 'wer-] <-wolves> *n* loup-garou *m*
west [west] **I.** *n* **1.** (*cardinal point*) ouest *m;* **in the** ~ **of France** dans l'ouest de la France; **to lie 5 km to the** ~ **of sth** être à 5 km à l'ouest de qc; **to go/drive to the** ~ aller/rouler vers l'ouest; **further** ~ plus à l'ouest **2.** POL occident *m* ▶**to go** ~ (*thing*) être fichu [*o* perdu]; (*person*) passer l'arme à gauche **II.** *adj* GEO ouest *inv;* ~ **wind** vent *m* d'ouest; ~ **coast** côte *f* ouest
West African *adj* ouest-africain(e) **West Bank** *n* **the** ~ **(of the Jordan)** la Cisjordanie **West Berlin** *n* Berlin-Ouest
westbound ['westbaʊnd] *adj, adv* en direction de l'ouest
West End *n Brit: centre-ville de Londres*
westerly ['westəlɪ, *Am:* -tɚlɪ] *adj* **1.** (*of*

western part) à l'ouest; ~ **part** partie *f* ouest; ~ **coast** côte *f* ouest **2.** (*towards the west*) vers l'ouest; ~ **direction** direction *f* ouest **3.** (*from the west*) d'ouest

western ['westən, *Am:* -tɚn] **I.** *adj* **1.** GEO de l'ouest; ~ **Scotland** l'ouest de l'Écosse **2.** POL occidental(e) **II.** *n* CINE western *m*

westerner ['westənəʳ, *Am:* -tɚnɚ] *n* occidental(e) *m(f)*

Western Flanders *n* la Flandre occidentale

westernize ['westənaɪz, *Am:* -tɚ-] *vt* occidentaliser

Western Samoa *n* les Samoas occidentales

west-facing *adj* (*window*) exposé(e) à l'ouest **West Germany** *n* HIST l'Allemagne *f* de l'Ouest **West Indian I.** *n* Antillais(e) *m(f)* **II.** *adj* antillais(e) **West Indies** *n* les Antilles *fpl*

Westminster [west'mɪntstəʳ, *Am:* -ɚ] *n* Westminster **Westminster Abbey** *n* l'abbaye de Westminster

westward ['westwəd, *Am:* -wɚd] *adj* à l'ouest

westwards ['westwədz, *Am:* -wɚdz] *adj* vers l'ouest

wet [wet] **I.** <wetter, wettest> *adj* **1.** (*soaked*) mouillé(e); **to be ~ through** être trempé; **to get ~** se mouiller; **to get sth ~** mouiller qc; **to get one's hands ~** se mouiller les mains **2.** (*damp*) *a.* METEO humide; (*weather*) pluvieux; (*day*) de pluie; (*season*) des pluies; **it's ~** il pleut **3.** (*weak*) **to be ~** être une lavette ►**to be ~ behind the ears** être encore jeune; **to be as much fun as a ~ weekend** ne pas être pas très drôle **II.** <wet, wet, -tt- *o* wetted, wetted, -tt-> *vt* **1.** (*make damp*) mouiller **2.** (*urinate on*) **to ~ the bed** mouiller le lit; **to ~ one's pants** mouiller sa culotte; **to ~ oneself** se mouiller **III.** *n* **1.** (*rain*) pluie *f* **2.** (*damp area*) humidité *f* **3.** (*unassertive person*) lavette *f*

wetback ['wetbæk] *n Am, pej, inf: mexicain vivant souvent illégalement aux États-Unis*

wet bar *n Am* bar *m* **wet blanket** *n inf* trouble-fête *mf* **wet dream** *n* pollution *f* nocturne **wet suit** *n* combinaison *f* de plongée

we've [wiːv] = **we have** *s.* **have**

whack [wæk] **I.** *vt* donner un grand coup à **II.** *n* **1.** (*sharp hit*) grand coup *m* **2.** *no pl* (*share, part*) part *f*; **to pay full ~** payer plein pot ►**to have a ~ at sth** *inf* tenter qc; **to be out of ~** *Am, Aus* être déglingué

whacking ['wækɪŋ] *adj* énorme

whale [weɪl] **I.** *n* baleine *f* ►**to have a ~ of a time** drôlement bien s'amuser; **a ~ of a ...** *Am, Aus* un sacré ... **II.** *vi* pêcher la baleine

whale oil *n* blanc *m* de baleine **whale shark** *n* requin *m* baleine

whaling *n no pl* chasse *f* à la baleine

wham [wæm] *interj inf* vlan!

wharf [wɔːf, *Am:* wɔːrf] <-ves> *n* quai *m*

what [wɒt, *Am:* wʌt] **I.** *interrog adj* quel(le); ~ **kind of book?** quel genre de livre?; ~ **time is it?** quelle heure est-il?; ~ **schools is he talking about?** de quelles écoles parle-t-il?; ~ **one does he like?** lequel, laquelle aime-t-il?; ~ **ones does he like?** lesquels, lesquelles aime-t-il? **II.** *pron* **1.** *interrog* que, qu + *vowel,* quoi *tonic form;* ~ **can I do?** que puis-je faire?; ~ **does it matter?** qu'est-ce que ça fait?; **~'s up?** *inf* qu'est-ce qui se passe?; ~ **for?** pourquoi?; ~ **does he look like?** à quoi ressemble-t-il?; **~'s his name?** comment s'appelle-t-il?; **~'s it called?** comment ça s'appelle?; ~ **about Paul?** et Paul?; ~ **about a walk?** et si on faisait une balade?; ~ **if it snows?** *inf* et s'il neige? **2.** *rel use* ce + *rel pron;* ~ **I like is ~ he says/is talking about** ce qui me plaît, c'est ce qu'il dit/ce dont il parle; **~'s more** qui plus est; **he knows ~'s ~!** il s'y connaît! **III.** (*exclamation*) ~ **an idiot!** quel idiot!; ~ **a fool I am!** que je suis bête! **IV.** *interj* **~!** quoi!; **so ~?** et alors?; **is he coming, or ~?** il arrive ou quoi?

whatever [wɒt'evəʳ, *Am:* wʌt'evɚ] **I.** *pron* ~ **you do** quoi que tu fasses +*subj;* **take ~ you want** prends ce que tu veux **II.** *adj, adv* quel que soit; **give me ~ money you have** donne-moi tout ce que tu as comme argent; **to have no idea ~** ne pas avoir la moindre idée; **no hope ~** pas l'ombre d'un espoir; **nothing ~** absolument rien

what's-his-name ['wɒtsɪzneɪm, *Am:* 'wʌt-] *n* machin *mf*

whatsit ['wɒtsɪt, *Am:* 'wʌt-] *n inf* machin *m*

whatsoever [ˌwɒtsəʊ'evəʳ, *Am:* ˌwʌtsoʊ'evɚ] *adv s.* **whatever**

wheat [wiːt] *n no pl* blé *m* **wheatgerm** *n* germes *mpl* de blé **wheatmeal** *n* farine *f* de froment

wheel [wiːl] **I.** *n* **1.** (*circular object*) roue *f;* **on ~s** sur des roues **2.** AUTO volant *m;* **to be at the ~** être au volant **3.** NAUT gouvernail *m* **4.** *pl, inf* (*car*) bagnole *f* ►**to set the ~s in motion** mettre les choses en route; **to be a big ~** *Am, inf* être un gros bonnet; **to feel like a fifth ~** *Am* se sentir de trop **II.** *vt* pousser ►**to ~ sb/sth out** ressortir qn/qc **III.** *vi* **to ~ and deal** *inf* brasser des affaires

◆**wheel (a)round** *vi* se retourner

wheelbarrow ['wiːlˌbærəʊ, *Am:* -ˌberoʊ] *n* brouette *f*

wheel brace *n* vilebrequin (à roues) *m*

wheelchair ['wiːlˌtʃeə, *Am:* -tʃer] *n* fauteuil *m* roulant

wheel clamp *n Brit, Aus* sabot *m* (de Denver)

wheeler-dealer *n pej, inf* brasseur *m* d'affaires

wheeling ['wiːlɪŋ] *n no pl* tournoiement *m* ►~ **and dealing** *inf* brassage *m* d'affaires

wheeze [wiːz] **I.** <-zing> *vi* respirer avec peine **II.** *n* (*rasping breath*) respiration *f* difficile

wheezy ['wiːzɪ] <-ier, -iest> *adj* asthmatique

whelp [welp] *n* **1.** (*puppy*) chiot *m* **2.** (*cub*) petit *m*

when [wen] **I.** *adv* quand; **since ~?** depuis quand? **II.** *conj* **1.** (*at which time*) quand; **~ you arrive, call me** appelle-moi quand tu arrives; **in the days ~ ...** à l'époque où ... **2.** (*during the time*) lorsque; **~ singing that song** en chantant cette chanson **3.** (*every time*) chaque fois que **4.** (*considering that*) **how can I listen ~ I can't hear?** comment écouter si je n'entends rien? **5.** (*although*) **he's buying it ~ he could borrow it** il l'achète alors qu'il pourrait l'emprunter

whence [wens] *adv form* d'où

whenever [wen'evəʳ, *Am:* -ɚ] **I.** *adv* **~ did I say that?** (mais) quand donc ai-je dit cela?; **I can do it tomorrow or ~** je peux le faire demain ou n'importe quand **II.** *conj* **1.** (*every time*) quand; **~ I can** chaque fois que je peux **2.** (*at any time*) **he can come ~ he likes** il peut venir quand il veut

where [weəʳ, *Am:* wer] **I.** *adv* où; **~ is he going (to)?** où va-t-il?; **~ did you get that idea?** d'où te vient cette idée? **II.** *conj* (là) où; **from ~** d'où; **I'll tell him ~ to go** je lui dirai où il faut aller; **the box ~ he puts his things** la boîte dans laquelle il met ses affaires; **this is ~ my pen was found** c'est là qu'on a trouvé mon stylo

whereabout(s)[1] ['weərəbaʊts, *Am:* 'werə-] *n* **sb/sth's exact ~** le lieu exact où se trouve qn/qc

whereabout(s)[2] [ˌweərə'baʊts, *Am:* ˌwerə-] *adv inf* où

whereas [weər'æz, *Am:* wer'-] *conj* **1.** (*while*) alors que **2.** LAW attendu que

whereby [weə'baɪ, *Am:* wer-] *adv* par quoi

whereupon [ˌweərə'pɒn, *Am:* 'werəˌpɑːn] *conj* (*directly after which*) après quoi

wherever [ˌweər'evəʳ, *Am:* ˌwer'evɚ] **I.** *adv* **~ did she find that?** mais où donc a-t-elle trouvé ça?; **... or ~ ...** ou Dieu sait où **II.** *conj* **1.** (*in every place*) **~ there is sth** partout où il y a qc **2.** (*in any place*) **~ he likes** où il veut

wherewithal ['weəwɪðɔːl, *Am:* 'wer-] *n no pl* **the ~** l'argent *m*

whet [wet] <-tt-> *vt* **1.** (*increase*) stimuler **2.** (*sharpen*) aiguiser

whether ['weðəʳ, *Am:* -ɚ] *conj* **1.** (*if*) si **2.** (*all the same*) que *+subj;* **~ it rains or not** qu'il pleuve ou non

whew [fjuː] *interj inf s.* **phew**

whey [weɪ] *n no pl* petit-lait *m*

which [wɪtʃ] **I.** *interrog adj* quel(le); **~ one?** lequel, laquelle?; **~ ones?** lesquel(le)s?; **~ games do you play?** à quels jeux joues-tu? **II.** *pron* **1.** *interrog* **~ is his?** lequel, laquelle est à lui? **2.** *rel use* **the book ~ I read** le livre que j'ai lu; **the book of ~ I'm speaking** le livre dont je parle; **she agreed, ~ surprised me** elle est tombée d'accord, ce qui m'a surpris

whichever [wɪtʃ'evəʳ, *Am:* -ɚ] **I.** *pron* celui (celle) qui; **take ~ you like best** prends celui que tu préfères; **at 3 or 4 o'clock, ~ suits you** à 3 ou 4 heures, suivant ce qui t'arrange **II.** *adj* **1.** (*any*) n'importe quel(le); **take ~ book you like** choisis le livre que tu veux **2.** (*no matter which*) quel(le) que soit; **~ way I take** quel que soit le chemin que je prenne; **~ you choose, I'll take it** quel que soit celui que tu choisisses, je le prendrai

whiff [wɪf] *n* **1.** (*quick scent*) odeur *f* **2.** (*hint*) parfum *m*

while [waɪl] **I.** *n* moment *m;* **a short ~** un instant; **quite a ~** assez longtemps; **once in a ~** de temps en temps; **I'm staying in Paris for a ~** je reste à Paris pour quelque temps **II.** *conj* **1.** (*during which time*) pendant que; **I was dreaming ~ I was doing sth** je rêvais en faisant qc **2.** (*although*) **~ I agree with you** bien que je sois d'accord avec toi **3.** (*however*) **my wife's a vegetarian, ~ I eat meat** ma femme est végétarienne alors que je mange de la viande

while away *vt* **to ~ the time** tuer le temps

whilst [waɪlst] *conj s.* **while**

whim [wɪm] *n* caprice *m;* **to do sth on a ~** faire qc sur un coup de tête

whimper ['wɪmpəʳ, *Am:* -pɚ] **I.** *vi* gémir; (*child*) geindre **II.** *n* gémissement *m;* **without a ~** sans broncher

whimsical ['wɪmzɪkl] *adj* **1.** (*fanciful*) curieux(-euse); (*choice, story*) saugrenu(e); (*air*) étrange **2.** (*capricious*) capricieux(-euse)

whimsy ['wɪmzɪ] <-ies> *n* **1.** *no pl* (*fancifulness*) fantaisie *f* **2.** (*whim*) caprice *m*

whine [waɪn] **I.** <-ning> *vi* **1.** (*whinge: animal*) gémir **2.** (*cry, complain*) pleurnicher **II.** *n* plainte *f*

whinge [wɪndʒ] <whingeing *o* whinging> *vi Brit, Aus, pej, inf* pleurnicher

whinny ['wɪnɪ] **I.** <-ied, -ing> *vi* hennir **II.** <-ies> *n* hennissement *m*

whip [wɪp] **I.** *n* **1.** (*lash*) fouet *m;* **to crack a ~** faire claquer le fouet **2.** POL chef *mf* de file **II.** <-pp-> *vt* **1.** (*lash with a whip*) fouetter **2.** (*force fiercely*) forcer **3.** (*beat into a froth*) fouetter **4.** *Am, inf* (*defeat*) battre à plate(s) couture(s) **III.** <-pp-> *vi fig* **to ~ across sth** traverser qc à toute allure

◆**whip out** *vt* (*take out quickly*) sortir rapidement

◆**whip up** *vt* **1.** (*encourage: enthusiasm*) susciter; *pej* stimuler **2.** *inf* (*make quickly*) préparer en quatrième vitesse **3.** (*beat into a froth*) battre

whip hand *n* **to hold the ~** avoir le dessus

whiplash ['wɪplæʃ] *n no pl* MED lésion *f* des cervicales

whipped cream *n* crème *f* fouettée

whippet ['wɪpɪt] *n* whippet *m*

whipping ['wɪpɪŋ] *n* **1.** (*lashing*) coup *m* de fouet **2.** *Am* (*hard beating*) correction *f* **3.** *inf* (*defeat*) correction *f*

whipping-boy *n* bouc *m* émissaire **whipping cream** *n no pl* crème *f* fraîche **whip-**

ping top *n* toupie *f*

whip-round *n Brit, inf* quête *f;* **to have a ~ for sb** organiser une collecte en faveur de qn

whirl [wɜːl, *Am:* wɜːrl] **I.** *vi* tournoyer **II.** *vt* faire tournoyer; **to ~ sb (a)round** faire tourner qn **III.** *n* tourbillonnement *m;* (*of dust*) tourbillon *m* ►**to give sth a ~** essayer qc

whirlpool ['wɜːlpuːl, *Am:* 'wɜːr-] *n* **1.** (*in sea*) remous *m* **2.** (*jacuzzi*) baignoire *f* à remous

whirlwind ['wɜːlwɪnd, *Am:* 'wɜːrl-] **I.** *n* tourbillon *m* de vent **II.** *adj* enivrant(e); **a ~ tour** une visite éclair

whirr [wɜːʳ, *Am:* wɜːr] **I.** *vi* (*engine*) ronfler; (*wings*) bruire **II.** *n* ronflement *m;* (*of wings*) bruissement *m*

whisk [wɪsk] **I.** *vt* **1.** (*flick*) effleurer **2.** (*whip rapidly: cream*) fouetter; (*eggs*) battre **3.** (*take*) **to ~ sth away/off the table** enlever qc rapidement **II.** *n* GASTR fouet *m*

whisker ['wɪskə, *Am:* -kɚ] *n pl* (*on people*) favoris *mpl;* (*on cat*) moustaches *fpl* ►**by a ~** d'un poil

whiskey ['wɪskɪ] *n Am, Irish,* **whisky** ['wɪskɪ] <-ies> *n Brit, Aus no pl* whisky *m*

whisper ['wɪspəʳ, *Am:* -pɚ] **I.** *vi* chuchoter **II.** *vt* **1.** (*speak softly*) chuchoter **2.** (*gossip*) **to ~ that ...** faire courir le bruit que ... **III.** *n* **1.** (*soft speech*) murmure *m;* **to say sth in a ~** dire qc tout bas **2.** (*rumour*) rumeur *f*

whispering ['wɪspərɪŋ] **I.** *n no pl* **1.** (*talking softly*) chuchotement *m* **2.** (*gossiping*) chuchoteries *fpl* **II.** *adj* (*rustling*) qui murmure

whispering campaign *n* campagne *f* sournoise

whist [wɪst] *n no pl* whist *m*

whistle ['wɪsl] **I.** <-ling> *vi, vt* siffler **II.** *n* **1.** *no pl* (*sound*) sifflement *m* **2.** (*device*) sifflet *m;* **to blow a ~** donner un coup de sifflet ►**to blow the ~ on sb/sth** dénoncer qn/qc

white [waɪt] **I.** *adj* blanc(he) ►**~r than ~** plus blanc que neige; **to turn ~ with fear** pâlir de peur **II.** *n* **1.** (*colour, of egg, eye*) blanc *m* **2.** (*person*) Blanc(he) *m(f); s. a.* **blue**

white ant *n s.* **termite** **whitebait** *n inv* blanchaille *f* **whiteboard** *n* tableau *m* blanc **white-collar** *adj* **a ~ worker** un col blanc **white coffee** *n* café *m* au lait **white corpuscle** *n* MED globule *m* blanc **white elephant** *n* chose *f* sans utilité **white ensign** *n* NAUT pavillon *m* de la marine anglaise et du Royal Yacht Squadron **white flag** *n* drapeau *m* blanc **white goods** *npl* **1.** (*appliances*) électroménager *m* **2.** (*linens*) linge *m* **Whitehall** *n* **1.** (*offices of Britain's government*) Administration *f* britannique **2.** (*government of Britain*) Gouvernement *m* britannique **White House** *n* **the ~** la Maison-Blanche **white lead** *n* blanc *m* de céruse **white lie** *n* pieux mensonge *m* **white man** *n* blanc *m* **white meat** *n* viande *f* blanche

whiten ['waɪtn] *vt, vi* blanchir

whitener ['waɪtnəʳ, *Am:* -nɚ] *n* **1.** *no pl* blanc *m* à chaussures **2.** GASTR (*for coffee*) lait *m*

whiteness *n* blancheur *f*

whitening *n no pl s.* **whitener**

white-out *n* **1.** (*blizzard*) blizzard *m* **2.** *no pl* (*liquid to cover mistakes*) blanc *m* correcteur **white paper** *n Brit, Aus* POL livre *m* blanc **white sale** *n* vente *f* de blanc **white sauce** *n* sauce *f* béchamel **white spirit** *n no pl, Brit* white-spirit *m*

whitethorn ['waɪtθɔːn, *Am:* -θɔːrn] *n s.* **hawthorn**

white tie *adj* habit *m*

whitewash ['waɪtwɒʃ, *Am:* -wɑːʃ] **I.** *n* **1.** *no pl* (*solution*) blanc *m* de chaux **2.** (*cover-up*) blanchiment *m* **3.** *inf* (*victory*) raclée *f* **II.** *vt* **1.** (*cover in white solution*) blanchir à la chaux **2.** *pej* (*conceal negative side*) blanchir **3.** *inf* SPORT écraser

whitewater ['waɪtwɔːtə, *Am:* -wɑːt̬ɚ] *n no pl* eau *f* vive

white-water rafting *n no pl* descente *f* en eau vive **white wedding** *n* mariage *m* en blanc

whither ['wɪðəʳ, *Am:* -ɚ] *adv form* où

whiting ['waɪtɪŋ, *Am:* -t̬ɪŋ] *n inv* merlan *m*

Whit Monday [ˌwɪt'mʌndɪ] *n* lundi *m* de Pentecôte

Whitsun ['wɪtsn] **I.** *n no pl* les fêtes *fpl* de Pentecôte **II.** *adj* de Pentecôte

Whit Sunday [ˌwɪt'sʌndɪ] *n no pl* dimanche *m* de Pentecôte

whittle ['wɪtl, *Am:* 'wɪt̬-] <-ling> *vt* parer

◆**whittle away at** *vt* **1.** (*take little bits off*) tailler en petits morceaux **2.** (*gradually decrease*) rogner petit à petit

◆**whittle down** *vt* réduire petit à petit

whizz [wɪz] **I.** *n* (*expert*) as *m;* **a ~ at sth** un as de qc **II.** *vi* **to ~ along/past** passer à toute allure; **to ~ through sth** (*list, newspaper*) survoler qc

whiz(z) kid *n* jeune prodige *mf*

who [huː] *interrog or rel pron* qui; *s. a.* **whom, whose**

WHO ['dʌbljuːeɪtʃˌəʊ, *Am:* -'oʊ] *n no pl abbr of* World Health Organization OMS *f*

whoa [wəʊ, *Am:* woʊ] *interj* **1.** (*command to stop a horse*) ho! **2.** *fig, inf* (*used to stop something*) doucement!

whodunit, whodunnit [ˌhuː'dʌnɪt] *n inf: film ou roman policier*

whoever [huː'evəʳ, *Am:* -ɚ] *pron* quiconque

whole [həʊl, *Am:* hoʊl] **I.** *adj* **1.** (*entire*) entier(-ère); **~ milk** lait *m* entier; **the ~ thing** le tout **2.** (*intact*) entier(-ère) **3.** *inf* **it's a ~ lot better** c'est vraiment beaucoup mieux ►**the ~ (kit and) caboodle** *inf* tout le bazar; **the ~ enchilada** *Am* toute la panoplie; **the ~ shebang** *inf* tout le bataclan; **to go (the) ~ hog, to go the ~ nine yards** *inf* aller jusqu'au bout **II.** *n* **1.** (*complete thing*) totalité *f;* **as a ~** dans sa totalité; **on the ~** dans l'ensemble **2.** *no pl*

W

the ~ le tout; **the ~ of Charleston** toute la ville de Charleston **III.** *adv* ~ **new** tout(e) neuf(neuve)

wholefood ['həʊlfu:d, *Am:* 'hoʊl-] *n Brit no pl,* **wholefoods** *npl* aliments *mpl* complets

wholefood shop *n Brit* magasin *m* bio

wholegrain ['həʊlgreɪn, *Am:* 'hoʊl-] *adj Brit, Aus* complet(-ète)

whole-hearted [ˌhəʊl'hɑ:tɪd, *Am:* ˌhoʊl-'hɑ:rt̬ɪd] *adj* (*completely sincere*) sans réserve; (*thanks*) qui viennent du cœur

wholemeal bread ['həʊlmi:l'bred, *Am:* 'hoʊl-] *n no pl, Brit* pain *m* complet

wholesale ['həʊlseɪl, *Am:* 'hoʊl-] **I.** *n* vente *f* en gros **II.** *adj* **1.** (*sales in bulk*) de gros **2.** (*on a large scale: slaughter*) en série; (*reform*) en masse **III.** *adv* **1.** (*by bulk*) en gros **2.** (*in bulk*) en bloc

wholesaler ['həʊlseɪlə^r, *Am:* 'hoʊlseɪlɚ] *n* grossiste *mf*

wholesome ['həʊlsəm, *Am:* 'hoʊl-] *adj* salubre; (*life*) sain(e); (*advice*) salutaire

whole-tone scale *n* échelle *f* des fréquences musicales

wholewheat *n* blé *m* entier; ~ **bread** pain *m* complet

who'll [hu:l] = **who will** *s.* **will**

wholly ['həʊlɪ, *Am:* 'hoʊ-] *adv* tout à fait; (*convinced*) entièrement; (*different*) complètement

whom [hu:m] *interrog or rel pron* ~ **did he see?** qui a-t-il vu?; **those ~ I love** ceux que j'aime; **the person of ~ I spoke** la personne dont j'ai parlé

whoop [hu:p] **I.** *vi* pousser des cris de joie **II.** *vt* **to ~ it up** faire la noce **III.** *n* cri *m;* **a war ~** un cri de guerre

whoopee ['wʊpɪ, *Am:* 'wu:pɪ] **I.** *interj* hourra!; **oh, ~** oh, youpi! **II.** *n no pl* **to make ~** (*have sex*) faire l'amour; (*have a lot of fun*) faire la bringue

whooping cough ['hu:pɪŋkɒf, *Am:* -kɑ:f] *n no pl* **the ~** la coqueluche

whoops [wu:ps, *Am:* wʊps] *interj inf* houp-la!; ~ **a daisy** *childspeak* houp-là!

whop [wɒp, *Am:* wɑ:p] <-pp-> *vt Am, inf* **1.** (*strike*) battre **2.** (*beat in competition*) battre à plate(s) couture(s)

whopper ['wɒpə^r, *Am:* 'wɑ:pɚ] *n iron* **1.** (*huge thing*) monstre *m* **2.** (*blatant lie*) énormité *f*

whopping ['wɒpɪŋ, *Am:* 'wɑ:pɪŋ] *inf* **I.** *adj* énorme; **a ~ great lie** un mensonge monumental **II.** *n Am* **1.** (*beating*) rossée *f* **2.** (*defeat*) raclée *f*

whore [hɔ:^r, *Am:* hɔ:r] *n vulg* putain *f*

whortleberry ['wɜ:tlˌberɪ, *Am:* 'wɜ:rt̬l-] *n* airelle *f*

who's [hu:z] **1.** = **who is** *s.* **is 2.** = **who has** *s.* **has**

whose [hu:z] **I.** *poss adj* ~ **book is this?** à qui est ce livre?; ~ **son is he?** de qui est-il le fils?; ~ **car did you take?** tu as pris la voiture de qui?; **the girl ~ brother I saw** la fille dont j'ai vu le frère **II.** *poss pron* ~ **is this pen?** à qui est ce stylo?; ~ **can I borrow?** je peux prendre lequel?

why [waɪ] **I.** *conj* pourquoi; ~ **not?** pourquoi pas?; ~ **not ring her?** pourquoi ne pas l'appeler? **II.** *n* **the ~s and wherefores** (**of sth**) le pourquoi et comment (de qc) **III.** *interj Am* tiens!

WI [ˌdʌblju:'aɪ] *n Brit abbr of* **Women's Institute** ≈ association *f* de femmes

wick [wɪk] *n* mèche *f*

wicked ['wɪkɪd] **I.** *adj* **1.** (*evil, cruel: person*) méchant(e); (*action, plan*) mauvais(e); (*lie*) affreux(-euse) **2.** (*unpleasant: wind*) affreux(-euse) **3.** (*playfully malicious: smile, sense of humour*) malicieux(-euse) **4.** *inf* (*fun*) super *inv* **II.** *n* (*evil people*) **the ~** les méchants *mpl* ►**there's no peace for the ~** *prov* pas de répit pour les braves

wicker ['wɪkə^r, *Am:* -ɚ] **I.** *n no pl* osier *m* **II.** *adj* en osier

wicker basket *n* panier *m* en osier **wicker chair** *n* chaise *f* en osier **wicker furniture** *n no pl* meuble *m* en osier

wickerwork ['wɪkəwɜ:k, *Am:* -ɚwɜ:rk] *n no pl s.* **wicker**

wicket ['wɪkɪt] *n Brit* SPORT guichet *m*

wicket-keeper *n Brit* gardien *m* de guichet

wide [waɪd] **I.** <-r, -st> *adj* **1.** (*broad*) large; **to be two metres ~** faire deux mètres de large **2.** (*very big*) immense; (*gap*) considérable **3.** (*very open*) grand(e) ouvert(e); (*eyes*) écarquillé(e) **4.** (*varied*) ample; (*experience, range*) étendu(e) **5.** (*extensive*) vaste; (*support*) considérable ►**to give sb/sth a ~ berth** se tenir à une très grande distance de qn/qc; **to be ~ of the mark** être loin de la vérité **II.** <-r, -st> *adv* très; **to open ~** ouvrir en grand; **to be ~ open** être grand ouvert; **to be ~ to criticism** prêter le flanc à la critique

wide-angle lens *n* PHOT objectif *m* grand angulaire **wide-awake** *adj* bien éveillé(e)

wide-eyed *adj* **1.** (*with wide-open eyes*) **to be ~** avoir les yeux grands ouverts **2.** (*innocent: child*) innocent(e)

widely *adv* **1.** (*broadly*) largement; **to gesture ~** faire de grands gestes; ~ **spaced** très espacé **2.** (*extensively: known, admired, used*) très; (*thought, believed*) communément; (*accepted*) généralement; **~-read** (*newspaper*) très lu **3.** (*considerably: vary*) énormément

widen ['waɪdn] **I.** *vt* élargir; (*discussion*) étendre **II.** *vi* s'élargir

wide-ranging *adj* (*investigation, survey*) de grande portée; (*subject*) vaste

widescreen *adj* (*tv*) grand écran *inv*

widespread ['waɪdspred] *adj* répandu(e); (*rioting, support*) général(e)

widow ['wɪdəʊ, *Am:* -oʊ] **I.** *n* **1.** (*dead man's wife*) veuve *f* **2.** *fig* **she's a football/golf ~** son mari la délaisse pour aller jouer au foot/

golf **II.** *vt* laisser veuf(ve); **to be ~ed** être veuf(-ve)

widowed ['wɪdəʊd, *Am:* -oʊd] *adj* veuf(veuve)

widower ['wɪdəʊə^r, *Am:* oʊɚ] *n* veuf *m*

widow's pension *n* allocation *f* de veuvage

width [wɪdθ] *n no pl* largeur *f;* **20 metres in ~** 20 mètres de large

wield [wi:ld] *vt* **1.** (*hold*) manier **2.** (*use: influence, power*) exercer

wife [waɪf] <wives> *n* épouse *f;* **to live together as man and ~** vivre maritalement

wig [wɪg] *n* perruque *f*

wiggle ['wɪgl] **I.** *vt* remuer **II.** *vi* se déhancher **III.** *n* **1.** (*movement*) déhanchement *m* **2.** (*line*) trait *m* ondulé

wigwam ['wɪgwæm, *Am:* -wɑ:m] *n* wigwam *m*

wild [waɪld] **I.** *adj* **1.** (*untamed: animal, flower*) sauvage **2.** (*unrestrained: person*) dissipé(e); (*country*) sauvage; (*life*) dissolu(e); (*scheme, promises*) insensé(e); (*party, talk*) délirant(e); (*weather, conditions*) très mauvais(e); (*wind*) violent(e); (*sea*) agité(e) **3.** (*keen*) fou(folle); **he was ~** il était comme fou; **to be ~ about sth** être un fana de qc; **he's not ~ about the idea** il n'est pas emballé par l'idée **4.** (*not accurate: punch, shot*) au hasard **5.** *inf* (*angry*) fou(folle); **to go ~** devenir fou de rage; **to drive sb ~** rendre qn fou **6.** (*untidy: hair*) en bataille **7.** *inf* (*wonderful*) génial(e) ▶**beyond sb's ~est <u>dreams</u>** au-delà de ses rêves les plus fous; **~ <u>horses</u> couldn't make sb do sth** rien au monde ne pourra faire faire qc à qn **II.** *adv* sauvage; **to grow/live ~** pousser/vivre à l'état sauvage ▶**to <u>run</u> ~** se déchaîner **III.** *n* **1.** *no pl* (*natural environment*) nature *f;* **in the ~** à l'état sauvage **2.** *pl* (*remote places*) régions *fpl* reculées; **in the ~s of Africa** au fin fond de l'Afrique

wild boar *n* ZOOL sanglier *m*

wild card *n* jocker *m*

wildcat ['waɪldkæt] **I.** *n* **1.** ZOOL chat *m* sauvage **2.** (*fierce female*) sauvageon(ne) *m(f)* **II.** *adj* **1.** (*risky*) insensé(e) **2.** (*unofficial: strike*) sauvage

wilderness ['wɪldənɪs, *Am:* -dɚ-] *n no pl* **1.** (*unpopulated*) désert *m* **2.** (*overgrown area*) jungle *f* ▶**a <u>voice</u> in the ~** une voix venant du désert

wildfire ['waɪld,faɪə^r, *Am:* -faɪɚ] *n* feu *m* de forêt ▶**to <u>spread</u> like ~** se répandre comme un feu de forêt

wildfowl ['waɪldfaʊl] *n inv* oiseau *m* sauvage

wild goose <- geese> *n* oie *f* sauvage **wild goose chase** *n* (*hopeless search*) fausse piste *f*

wildlife ['waɪldlaɪf] *n no pl* faune *f* et flore; **~ conservation** préservation *f* de la faune et de la flore

wildly *adv* **1.** (*in uncontrolled way*) frénétiquement; (*vary*) sensiblement **2.** (*haphazardly*) au hasard; (*to guess*) à tout hasard **3.** *inf* (*very*) extrêmement

wildness *n no pl* **1.** (*natural state*) état *m* sauvage **2.** (*uncontrolled behaviour*) frénésie *f;* (*of waves, storm*) violence *f*

Wild West *n* **the ~** l'Ouest américain

wiles [waɪlz] *npl form* artifices *mpl;* **to use all one's ~** utiliser toutes ses astuces

wilful ['wɪlfl] *adj Brit* **1.** (*deliberate*) intentionnel(le); (*disobedience*) volontaire **2.** LAW **~ murder** homicide *m* volontaire **3.** *pej* (*self-willed*) têtu(e)

will[1] [wɪl] <would, would> *aux* **1.** (*expressing future*) **I/we ~** [*o* **I'll/we'll**] **do sth** je ferai/nous ferons qc; **you won't be late, ~ you?** tu ne seras pas en retard, n'est-ce pas?; **she won't pay – yes she ~!** elle ne paiera pas – si, elle paiera! **2.** (*polite form*) **~ you please follow me?** voulez-vous me suivre, s'il vous plaît?; **~ you be so kind as to sit down?** auriez-vous la gentillesse de vous asseoir? **3.** (*wish, agree*) vouloir; **say what you ~** dis ce que tu veux; **~ you wait?** veux-tu attendre?; **the engine won't start** le moteur ne veut pas démarrer **4.** (*emphatic*) **a drama ~ happen** on ne pourra éviter le drame; **he ~ leave the door open** il laissera la porte ouverte; **I ~ succeed despite you** je persisterai malgré toi **5.** (*explaining a procedure*) **they'll give you an anaesthetic** on te fera une anesthésie **6.** (*conjecture*) devoir; **that ~ be the doctor** cela doit être le médecin

will[2] [wɪl] **I.** *n* **1.** *no pl* (*faculty*) volonté *f;* **strength of ~** force *f* de caractère; **against sb's ~** contre la volonté de qn; **to lose the ~ to live** perdre la raison de vivre **2.** LAW testament *m* ▶**where there's a ~, there's a <u>way</u>** *prov* quand on veut on peut; **with the best ~ in the <u>world</u>** avec toute la bonne volonté du monde **II.** *vt* **1.** (*make happen*) **to ~ sb to do sth** faire faire qc à qn; **to ~ sb to win/live** souhaiter de toutes ses forces que qn gagne/survive *+subj* **2.** *form* (*ordain*) décréter **3.** (*bequeath*) léguer

willful ['wɪlfl] *adj Am s.* **wilful**

William ['wɪljəm] *n* HIST **~ Tell** Guillaume Tell *m;* **~ the Conqueror** Guillaume le Conquérant

willies ['wɪlɪz] *npl inf* chocottes *fpl*

willing ['wɪlɪŋ] *adj* **1.** (*not opposed*) disposé(e); **to be ~ to do sth** être prêt à faire qc; **to be ~ for sb to do sth** être disposé à ce que qn fasse qc *+subj;* **to be ready and ~** être volontiers disponible **2.** (*enthusiastic*) enthousiaste

willingly *adv* **1.** (*gladly*) volontiers **2.** (*voluntarily*) volontairement

willingness *n no pl* **1.** (*readiness*) bonne volonté *f;* **a ~ to do sth** un désir de faire qc **2.** (*enthusiasm*) empressement *m*

will-o'-the-wisp [,wɪləðə'wɪsp] *n a. fig* feu *m* follet

willow ['wɪləʊ, *Am:* -oʊ], **willow tree** *n* BOT saule *m*
willowy ['wɪləʊɪ, *Am:* -oʊ-] *adj* élancé(e)
willpower ['wɪlpaʊəʳ, *Am:* -paʊɚ] *n no pl* volonté *f;* **by sheer** ~ par pure force de caractère
willy-nilly [ˌwɪli'nɪli] *adv* **1.** (*like it or not*) bon gré mal gré **2.** *Am* (*in disorder*) en fouillis
wilt [wɪlt] *vi* **1.** (*droop: plants*) se faner **2.** (*feel weak: person*) se sentir faible **3.** (*lose confidence*) se dégonfler
wily ['waɪlɪ] <-ier, -iest> *adj* rusé(e)
wimp [wɪmp] *n inf* lavette *f*
win [wɪn] **I.** *n* **1.** POL, SPORT victoire *f* **2.** (*bet*) pari *m* gagnant **II.** <won, won> *vt* gagner; (*contract, scholarship*) décrocher; (*popularity*) acquérir; (*reputation*) se faire; (*sb's heart*) conquérir; **to ~ sb's love** se faire aimer de qn ►**to ~ the day** remporter la victoire **III.** <won, won> *vi* gagner; **to ~ by two lengths** l'emporter de deux longueurs ►**to ~ hands down** gagner les doigts dans le nez; ~ **or lose** quoi qu'il arrive; **you ~!** soit! tu as gagné!
◆**win back** *vt* (*territory, love*) reconquérir; (*voters*) récupérer; (*esteem*) regagner
◆**win over** *vt* **1.** (*change mind of*) convaincre **2.** (*gain support of*) gagner à sa cause
◆**win round** *vt s.* **win over**
◆**win through** *vi* finir par réussir
wince [wɪns] **I.** *vi* grimacer **II.** *n* grimace *f*
winch [wɪntʃ] **I.** *n* treuil *m* **II.** *vt* **to ~ sth up/down** monter/descendre qc au treuil
wind¹ [wɪnd] **I.** *n* **1.** (*current of air*) vent *m;* **a breath of** ~ un courant d'air; **a gust of** ~ une rafale de vent **2.** *no pl* (*breath*) souffle *m;* **to knock the ~ out of sb** couper le souffle à qn **3.** *no pl, Brit, Aus* (*flatulence*) gaz *m;* **to break** ~ faire des gaz **4.** MUS **the** ~ les instruments *mpl* à vent **5.** *no pl* (*meaningless words*) n'importe quoi ►**to take the ~ out of sb's sails** couper l'herbe sous le pied de qn; **to get ~ of sth** avoir vent de qc; **to go/run like the** ~ filer comme le vent; **to put the ~ up sb** *Brit, Aus* flanquer la frousse à qn; **there's sth in the** ~ il y a qc dans l'air **II.** *vt* **1.** (*hurt*) couper le souffle à **2.** *Brit* (*bring up wind*) **to ~ a baby** faire faire son rot à un bébé
wind² [waɪnd] <wound, wound> **I.** *vt* **1.** (*wrap around: film*) rembobiner; (*wool*) enrouler **2.** (*tension a spring*) remonter **3.** (*turn: handle*) tourner **II.** *vi* serpenter
◆**wind back I.** *vt* (*film, tape*) rembobiner **II.** *vi* rembobiner
◆**wind down I.** *vt* **1.** (*lower*) baisser **2.** (*reduce*) réduire **II.** *vi* **1.** (*become less active*) être en perte de vitesse; (*party, meeting*) tirer à sa fin **2.** (*relax*) se détendre
◆**wind forward** *vt, vi* avancer
◆**wind on** *vt, vi Brit, Aus s.* **wind forward**
◆**wind up I.** *vt* **1.** (*bring to an end*) terminer; (*debate, meeting*) clore; (*affairs*) conclure **2.** *Brit, Aus* (*close: company*) liquider; (*activities*) cesser **3.** (*raise*) monter **4.** (*tension a spring*) remonter **5.** *Brit, inf* (*tease*) faire marcher **6.** *Brit, Aus, inf* (*annoy*) énerver **II.** *vi* **1.** (*end*) se terminer **2.** *inf* (*end up*) se retrouver; **to ~ doing sth** finir par faire qc
windbag ['wɪndbæg] *n pej, inf* moulin *m* à paroles
windbreak ['wɪndbreɪk] *n* brise-vent *m inv*
wind chimes *npl* carillon *m* éolien
wind energy *n no pl* énergie *f* éolienne
winder ['waɪndəʳ, *Am:* -ɚ] *n Brit* remontoir *m*
windfall ['wɪndfɔːl] *n* **1.** (*fruit*) fruit *m* tombé **2.** *fig* aubaine *f;* ~ **profits** bénéfices *mpl* inattendus
wind farm *n* centrale *f* éolienne
wind generator *n* aérogénérateur *m*
winding ['waɪndɪŋ] *adj* sinueux **winding-up** *n no pl, Brit, Aus* (*of a company*) liquidation *f* **winding-up sale** *n* soldes *fpl* avant liquidation
wind instrument ['wɪnd 'ɪnstrʊmənt] *n* instrument *m* à vent
windjammer ['wɪndˌdʒæməʳ, *Am:* -ɚ] *n* NAUT grand voilier *m* (de la marine marchande)
windlass ['wɪndləs] *n s.* **winch**
windmill ['wɪndmɪl] *n* moulin *m* à vent
window ['wɪndəʊ, *Am:* -doʊ] *n* **1.** (*glass*) fenêtre *f;* (*of shop*) vitrine *f;* (*of vehicle*) vitre *f;* **at the** ~ à la fenêtre; **in the** ~ par la fenêtre; (*in shop*) en vitrine **2.** (*stained glass*) vitrail *m* **3.** INFOR fenêtre *f;* ~ **separator** barre *f* de fractionnement **4.** (*time period*) créneau *m* ►**to go out (of) the** ~ *inf* s'envoler
window box *n* jardinière *f* **window cleaner** *n* **1.** (*person*) laveur *m* de carreaux **2.** *no pl* (*product*) produit *m* à nettoyer les vitres **window display** *n* devanture *f* **window dresser** *n* étalagiste *mf* **window dressing** *n no pl* **1.** (*in shop*) étalage *m* **2.** *pej* (*show*) façade *f* **window envelope** *n* enveloppe *f* à fenêtre **window frame** *n* châssis *m* **window pane** *n* vitre *f*
window-shopping *n no pl* lèche-vitrines *m;* **to go** ~ faire du lèche-vitrines
windowsill ['wɪndəʊsɪl, *Am:* -doʊ-] *n* appui *m* de fenêtre; (*outside*) rebord *m* de fenêtre
windpipe ['wɪndpaɪp] *n* trachée *f*
wind power *n no pl* énergie *f* éolienne
windscreen ['wɪndskriːn] *n Brit, Aus* pare-brise *m*
windscreen wiper *n* essuie-glace *m*
windshield ['wɪndʃiːld] *n Am* pare-brise *m*
windsock ['wɪndsɒk, *Am:* -sɑːk] *n* manche *f* à air
windsurfer ['wɪndsɜːfəʳ, *Am:* -sɜːrfɚ] *n* véliplanchiste *mf*
windsurfing ['wɪndsɜːfɪŋ, *Am:* -sɜːrf-] *n no pl* planche *f* à voile
windswept ['wɪndswept] *adj* **1.** (*exposed to wind*) venteux(-euse) **2.** (*wind-blown*) balayé(e) par les vents

wind tunnel *n* TECH tunnel *m* aérodynamique
windward ['wɪndwəd, *Am:* -wɚd] *adj, adv* NAUT au vent
windy¹ ['wɪndɪ] <-ier, -iest> *adj* venteux(-euse); **it was a ~ day** [*o* **it was ~**] il a fait beaucoup de vent
windy² ['wɪndɪ] <-ier, -iest> *adj s.* **winding**
wine [waɪn] GASTR **I.** *n* vin *m* **II.** *vt* **to ~ and dine** faire un dîner bien arrosé
wine bar *n* bar *m* à vins **wine bottle** *n* bouteille *f* de vin **wine cellar** *n* cave *f* à vin **wine glass** <-es> *n* verre *m* à vin **winegrower** *n* viticulteur, -trice *m, f*
wine-growing I. *n no pl* viticulture *f* **II.** *adj* viticole **wine list** *n* carte *f* des vins **wine merchant** *n* négociant(e) *m(f)* en vins **wine press** *n* pressoir *m* à vin **wine rack** *n* porte-bouteilles *m*
winery ['waɪnərɪ] <-ies> *n* établissement *m* vinicole
wine taster *n* dégustateur, -trice *m, f* de vin **wine tasting** *n no pl* dégustation *f* de vin **wine waiter** *n* sommelier *m*
wing [wɪŋ] **I.** *n* **1.** ZOOL aile *f;* **on the ~** en vol **2.** AVIAT, AUTO aile *f* **3.** POL aile *f;* **the left/right ~** parti *m* de gauche/droite **4.** SPORT aile *f;* (*player*) ailier *m;* **to play** (**on the**) **left/right ~** être ailier gauche/droit **5.** *pl* THEAT coulisses *fpl* **6.** *pl* (*pilot's badge*) insigne *m;* **to earn one's ~s** devenir pilote *m* (dans l'armée de l'air) ►**to take sb under one's ~** prendre qn sous son aile **II.** *vt* **1.** (*wound: bird*) blesser à l'aile; (*person*) blesser au bras **2.** (*travel fast*) **to ~ one's way** voler
wing chair *n* bergère *f* à oreilles **wing commander** *n Brit* MIL lieutenant-colonel *m* (de l'armée de l'air)
winged ['wɪŋd] *adj* ailé(e)
winger ['wɪŋəʳ, *Am:* -ɚ] *n* SPORT ailier *m*
wing nut *n* TECH écrou *m* à ailettes
wingspan ['wɪŋspæn], **wingspread** *n* envergure *f*
wink [wɪŋk] **I.** *n* clin *m* d'œil ►**not to sleep a ~** ne pas fermer l'œil (de la nuit); **in a ~** en un clin d'œil **II.** *vi* **1.** (*close one eye*) faire un clin d'œil **2.** (*flash: light*) clignoter
winker ['wɪŋkəʳ, *Am:* -ɚ] *n Brit* AUTO clignotant *m,* clignoteur *m Belgique*
winner ['wɪnəʳ, *Am:* -ɚ] *n* **1.** (*person who wins*) gagnant(e) *m(f);* **to back a ~** *a. fig* miser sur un gagnant; **everyone's a ~!** tout le monde gagne! **2.** *inf* SPORT but *m* de la victoire **3.** *inf* **to be on to a ~** avoir tiré le bon numéro
winning ['wɪnɪŋ] **I.** *adj* **1.** (*that wins*) gagnant(e); **to be on a ~ streak** (*team*) accumuler les victoires **2.** (*charming*) adorable; **with his/her ~ ways** avec sa grâce irrésistible **II.** *n* **1.** *no pl* (*achieving victory*) victoire *f;* **~ isn't everything** la réussite n'est pas tout **2.** *pl* (*money*) gains *mpl*
winning post *n* SPORT poteau *m* d'arrivée
winnow ['wɪnəʊ, *Am:* -oʊ] *vt* AGR vanner

winter ['wɪntəʳ, *Am:* -t̬ɚ] **I.** *n* hiver *m;* **in** (**the**) **~** en hiver **II.** *vi* hiberner
winter coat *n* **1.** (*for person*) manteau *m* d'hiver **2.** (*of an animal*) pelage *m* d'hiver **winter season** *n* saison *f* d'hiver **winter solstice** *n* solstice *m* d'hiver **winter sports** *npl* sports *mpl* d'hiver
wintertime ['wɪntətaɪm, *Am:* -t̬ɚ-] *n s.* **winter**
wint(e)ry ['wɪntrɪ] *adj* **1.** (*typical of winter*) hivernal(e) **2.** (*unfriendly*) froid(e)
wipe [waɪp] **I.** *n* **1.** (*act of wiping*) coup *m* de torchon; **to give sth a ~** essuyer qc; **to give the floor a ~** balayer le sol **2.** (*tissue*) lingette *f* **II.** *vt* **1.** (*remove dirt by rubbing*) essuyer; **to ~ one's nose** se moucher; **to ~ one's bottom** s'essuyer; **to ~ sth clean** nettoyer qc; **to ~ sth away/off** faire partir qc **2.** (*erase: disk, tape*) effacer ►**to ~ the floor with sb** réduire qn en miettes; **to ~ the slate clean** passer l'éponge; **to ~ sth off the map** rayer qc de la carte; **to ~ the smile off sb's face** faire perdre le sourire à qn **III.** *vi* essuyer
◆**wipe down** *vt* essuyer
◆**wipe off** *vt* (*erase*) effacer
◆**wipe out I.** *vt* **1.** (*clean inside of*) essuyer **2.** (*destroy: population*) exterminer **3.** (*cancel*) effacer **II.** *vi Am, Aus, inf* déraper
◆**wipe up** *vt, vi* essuyer
wire ['waɪəʳ, *Am:* 'waɪɚ] **I.** *n* **1.** *no pl* (*metal thread*) fil *m* métallique **2.** ELEC fil *m* **3.** *Am* (*telegram*) télégramme *m* ►**to get one's ~s crossed** s'embrouiller; **to get in under the ~** *Am, inf* arriver de justesse; **down to the ~** *Am, inf* jusqu'à la dernière minute; **to pull ~s** *Am* tirer les ficelles **II.** *vt* **1.** (*fasten with wire*) attacher **2.** ELEC (*building*) faire l'installation électrique de **3.** (*fit with microphone*) **to be ~d** (*person, room*) être équipé de micros cachés; **to be ~d for sound** avoir un micro sur soi **4.** *Am* (*send telegram*) envoyer un télégramme à
wire-cutters *npl* cisailles *fpl* **wire fence** *n* grillage *m* **wire-haired terrier** *n* terrier *m* à poils durs
wireless ['waɪəlɪs, *Am:* 'waɪɚ-] *n Brit* **1.** *no pl* (*radio*) TSF *f* **2.** (*set*) poste *m* de TSF
wireless operator *n* **1.** (*person*) radiotélégraphiste *mf* **2.** AVIAT radio *f* **wireless set** *n Brit s.* **wireless**
wirepuller ['waɪəˌpʊləʳ] *n Am, inf: personne qui a de l'influence*
wiretapping ['waɪəˌtæpɪŋ, *Am:* 'waɪɚ-] *n no pl* écoute *f* téléphonique
wiring ['waɪərɪŋ, *Am:* 'waɪɚ-] *n no pl* ELEC **1.** (*system*) circuit *m* électrique **2.** (*installation*) installation *f* électrique
wiring diagram *n* ELEC circuit *m* électrique
wiry ['waɪərɪ, *Am:* 'waɪɚ-] <-ier, -iest> *adj* **1.** (*rough-textured*) rêche **2.** (*lean*) élancé(e) et musclé(e)
Wisconsin [wɪ'skɒnsɪn, *Am:* -'skɑːnsən] **I.** *n* le Wisconsin **II.** *adj* du Wisconsin

wisdom ['wɪzdəm] *n no pl, no indef art* sagesse *f*

wisdom tooth <- teeth> *n* dent *f* de sagesse

wise [waɪz] **I.** *adj* **1.** (*having knowledge*) sage; (*advice, choice*) judicieux(-euse); (*words*) de sagesse; **is that ~?** est-ce bien raisonnable?; **to be none the ~r** ne pas être plus avancé; **to be older and ~r** s'être assagi avec le temps **2.** *inf* (*aware*) **to be/get ~ to sb/sb's game** voir clair en qn/dans le jeu de qn; **nobody will be the ~r** personne n'en saura rien; **I'm none the ~r** ne s'apercevoir de rien **II.** *vi Am* **to ~ up to sth** réaliser qc **III.** *vt* **to ~ sb up about sb/sth** mettre qn au parfum sur qn/qc

wisecrack ['waɪzkræk] *n* vanne *f*

wise guy *n pej, inf* petit malin *m*

wisely *adv* sagement

wish [wɪʃ] **I.** <-es> *n* **1.** (*desire*) souhait *m;* **against my ~es** contre ma volonté; **to have no ~ to do sth** n'avoir aucune envie de faire qc **2.** (*magic wish*) vœu *m;* **to make a ~ that** faire le vœu que *+subj* **3.** *pl* (*greetings, at end of letter*) amitiés *fpl;* **good/best ~es** mes amitiés **II.** *vt* **1.** (*feel a desire*) **I ~ she knew/I had a camera** si seulement elle savait/j'avais un appareil photo; **I only ~ I could** si seulement je pouvais le faire; **I ~ I hadn't told you** j'aurais mieux fait de ne rien dire **2.** *form* (*want*) vouloir **3.** (*make a wish*) **to ~ (that)** faire le vœu que *+subj;* **to ~ oneself anywhere but there** vouloir être n'importe où mais pas ici **4.** (*express good wishes*) souhaiter; **to ~ sb ill** souhaiter du mal à qn; **to ~ sb well** souhaiter à qn que tout aille bien; **I ~ you long life/the best of luck** je te souhaite une longue vie/bonne chance **III.** *vi* vouloir; **as you ~** comme vous voulez; **if you ~** si vous voulez; **to ~ for sth** souhaiter qc; **I could have ~ed for greater enthusiasm** j'attendais un peu plus d'enthousiame; **you couldn't ~ for better weather** on ne peut pas espérer meilleur temps

wishbone ['wɪʃbəʊn, *Am:* -boʊn] *n* ZOOL bréchet *m*

wishful ['wɪʃfl] *adj* **it is ~ thinking** c'est prendre ses désirs pour des réalités

wishy-washy *adj pej* (*taste, style*) fadasse; (*liberalism, liberals*) mou(molle)

wisp [wɪsp] *n* **1.** (*of hair*) mèche *f;* (*of straw*) brin *m;* (*of smoke*) filet *m* **2.** *fig* **a little ~ of a boy** un garçon menu

wispy ['wɪspɪ] <-ier, -iest> *adj* fin(e)

wisteria [wɪ'stɪərɪə, *Am:* -'stɪrɪ-] *n no pl* BOT glycine *f*

wistful ['wɪstfl] *adj* nostalgique

wit [wɪt] **I.** *n* **1.** (*humour*) esprit *m;* **to have a ready ~** avoir une vivacité d'esprit **2.** (*person*) personne *f* vive d'esprit **3.** *pl* (*intelligence*) esprit *m;* **a battle of ~s** une joute d'esprit; **to have one's ~s about one** avoir toute sa présence d'esprit **II.** *adv form* **to ~** à savoir

witch [wɪtʃ] <-es> *n a. pej* sorcière *f*

witchcraft ['wɪtʃkrɑːft, *Am:* -kræft] *n no pl* sorcellerie *f*

witchdoctor ['wɪtʃdɒktə, *Am:* -dɑːktɚ] *n* guérisseur, -euse *m, f*

witch-hunt *n* chasse *f* aux sorcières

witching hour *n* **the ~** minuit *m*

with [wɪð] *prep* **1.** (*accompanied by*) avec; **he'll be ~ you in a second** il est à vous dans une seconde; **chips ~ ketchup** GASTR des frites au ketchup **2.** (*by means of*) **to take sth ~ the fingers/both hands** prendre qc avec les doigts/à deux mains **3.** (*having*) **the man ~ the hat/the loud voice** l'homme au chapeau/qui parle fort; **a computer ~ an external modem** un ordinateur avec un modem externe; **children ~ eczéma** les enfants qui ont de l'eczema; **~ nothing** sans rien; **~ no hesitation at all** sans la moindre hésitation **4.** (*dealing with*) **to be ~ Fiat** travailler chez Fiat; **we're ~ the same bank** nous travaillons avec la même banque **5.** (*on one's person*) **to have sth ~ one** avoir qc sur soi; **he took the key ~ him** il a emporté les clés **6.** (*manner*) **to welcome sb ~ open arms** accueillir qn à bras ouverts; **~ a smile** en souriant; **~ one's whole heart** de tout son cœur; **~ one's own eyes** de ses propres yeux; **~ tears in one's eyes** les larmes aux yeux; **to sleep ~ the window open** dormir la fenêtre ouverte **7.** (*in addition to*) **and ~ that he went out** et là-dessus [*o* sur ce] il sortit **8.** (*despite*) **~ all his faults** malgré tous ses défauts **9.** (*caused by*) **to cry ~ rage** pleurer de rage; **to turn red ~ anger** devenir rouge de colère; **to be infected ~ a virus** être contaminé par un virus; **burning ~ fever** brûlant de fièvre **10.** (*full of*) **black ~ flies** noir de mouches; **to fill up ~ fuel** faire le plein de carburant **11.** (*presenting a situation*) **it's the same ~ me** c'est pareil pour moi; **~ the situation being what it is** la situation étant ce qu'elle est; **~ all this rain we can't go out** nous ne pouvons pas sortir à cause de la pluie; **~ five minutes to go** les cinq dernières minutes **12.** (*opposing*) **a war ~ Italy** une guerre contre l'Italie; **to be angry ~ sb** être en colère contre qn **13.** (*supporting*) **to be ~ sb** être avec qn; **he's ~ us** il est des nôtres **14.** (*concerning*) **to be pleased ~ sth** être content de qc; **it's a vice ~ him** c'est un vice chez lui; **what's up** [*o* **the matter**] **~ him?** qu'est-ce qu'il a? **15.** (*understanding*) **I'm not ~ you** *inf* je ne te/vous suis pas; **to be ~ it** *inf* être dans le coup ►**away ~ you!** va-t'en/allez-vous-en!

withdraw [wɪð'drɔː, *Am:* -'drɑː] *irr* **I.** *vt* retirer; **to ~ one's labour** *Brit, form* faire la grève **II.** *vi* se retirer; **to ~ from sth** se retirer de qc; **to ~ from college** abandonner ses études; **to ~ in favour of sb** se désister en faveur de qn; **to ~ into oneself/a fantasy world** se replier sur soi-même/dans un monde imaginaire

withdrawal [wɪð'drɔːəl, *Am:* -'drɑː-] *n*

1. (*removal*) *a.* FIN retrait *m;* ~ **symptoms** état *m* de manque; **to suffer** (**from**) ~ être en manque **2.** *no pl* PSYCH repli *m* sur soi

wither ['wɪðəʳ, *Am:* -ɚ] **I.** *vi* **1.** (*become dry: plant*) se dessécher; (*flower*) se faner **2.** (*lose vitality*) dépérir; (*beauty*) se faner **3.** *fig* **to** ~ (**away**) (*hope*) s'évanouir **4.** MED (*limb*) s'atrophier **II.** *vt* **1.** (*make dry*) dessécher; (*flower*) faner **2.** *fig* (*hope*) détruire; **to** ~ **sb** (**with a look**) foudroyer qn du regard **3.** MED (*limb*) atrophier

withering ['wɪðərɪŋ] *adj* **1.** (*dry*) desséchant(e); (*heat*) accablant(e) **2.** (*contemptuous: look, remark*) méprisant(e); (*scorn*) cinglant(e)

withhold [wɪð'həʊld, *Am:* -'hoʊld] *vt irr* **1.** (*not give: help, permission*) refuser; (*evidence, information*) cacher **2.** (*not pay: benefits, rent*) suspendre

within [wɪð'ɪn] **I.** *prep* **1.** (*inside of*) à l'intérieur de; ~ **the country** à l'intérieur des frontières du pays; ~ **the party** au sein du parti **2.** (*in limit of*) ~ **sight** en vue; ~ **hearing/easy reach** à portée de voix/de main **3.** (*in less than*) ~ **one hour** en l'espace d'une heure; ~ **3 days** sous 3 jours; ~ **2 km of sth** à moins de 2 km de qc **4.** (*not exceeding*) ~ **the law** dans le cadre de la loi; **to be** ~ **budget** être dans le budget **II.** *adv* dedans, à l'intérieur; **from** ~ de l'intérieur **III.** *adj* LAW ci-inclus(e)

without [wɪð'aʊt] *prep* sans; ~ **a warning** sans crier gare; **to be** ~ **a job** ne pas avoir de travail; **to do** ~ **sth** se passer de qc; ~ **saying a word/explaining** sans dire mot/explications

withstand [wɪð'stænd] *irr vt* résister à

witness ['wɪtnɪs] **I.** *n* **1.** (*person who sees*) témoin *mf;* **to be** (**a**) ~ **to sth** témoigner de qc; **to appear as a** ~ comparaître en tant que témoin; ~ **for the defence/prosecution** témoin à décharge/charge; **to go into the** ~ **box** *Brit* [*o* **stand** *Am*] aller à la barre (des témoins) **2.** *no pl, form* (*testimony*) témoignage *m;* **to bear** ~ **to sth** porter témoignage de qc **II.** *vt* **1.** (*see*) *a. fig* être témoin de; **it's dangerous,** ~ **the number of accidents** c'est dangereux, regarde le nombre d'accidents **2.** (*countersign: document, signature*) certifier **III.** *vi Brit, form* LAW **to** ~ **to sth** témoigner de qc

witticism ['wɪtɪsɪzəm, *Am:* 'wɪt̬ə-] *n* mot *m* d'esprit

witty ['wɪtɪ, *Am:* 'wɪt̬-] <-ier, -iest> *adj* plein(e) d'esprit

wizard ['wɪzəd, *Am:* -ɚd] *n* **1.** (*magician*) magicien(ne) *m(f)* **2.** (*expert*) génie *m;* **computer/financial** ~ génie de l'informatique/des finances; **to be a** ~ **at doing sth** savoir faire qc avec génie **3.** INFOR assistant *m*

wizardry ['wɪzədrɪ, *Am:* -ɚd-] *n no pl* **1.** (*expertise*) génie *m* **2.** (*equipment*) magie *f;* **technical** ~ magie de la technique

wizened ['wɪznd] *adj* fripé(e)

WNW [ˌwestnɔːθ'west, *Am:* -nɔːrθ'-] *n abbr of* **west-northwest** ouest-nord-ouest *m*

w/o *prep abbr of* **without** sans

wobble ['wɒbl, *Am:* 'wɑːbl] **I.** *vi* vaciller; (*chair, table*) branler; (*person*) être chancelant(e); (*voice, building*) trembler; (*tooth*) bouger **II.** *vt* faire trembler **III.** *n* **1.** (*movement*) vacillement *m;* **to have a** ~ être branlant **2.** (*sound*) tremblement *m*

wobbly ['wɒblɪ, *Am:* 'wɑːblɪ] **I.** <-ier, -iest> *adj* **1.** (*unsteady*) *a. fig* branlant(e); (*tooth*) qui bouge; **to feel** ~ se sentir faible **2.** (*sound: note, voice*) tremblant(e) **II.** <-ies> *n Brit, inf* **to throw a** ~ piquer une crise

woe [wəʊ, *Am:* woʊ] *n* LIT malheur *m;* ~ **betide sb** malheur à qn; **to pour out one's** ~**s** raconter ses malheurs

woeful ['wəʊfl, *Am:* 'woʊ-] *adj* affligeant(e)

wog [wɒg, *Am:* wɑːg] *n Brit, Aus, pej, inf* métèque *m*

wok [wɒk, *Am:* wɑːk] *n* wok *m*

woke ['wəʊk, *Am:* 'woʊk] *pt of* **wake**

woken ['wəʊkn, *Am:* 'woʊ-] *pp of* **wake**

wolf [wʊlf] **I.** <wolves> *n* loup *m;* **a she** ~ une louve; ~ **cub** louveteau *m* ►**to keep the** ~ **from the door** subvenir à ses besoins; **a** ~ **in sheep's clothing** un loup déguisé en brebis; **to cry** ~ crier au loup; **to throw sb to the wolves** jeter qn aux lions **II.** *vt inf* **to** ~ **sth** (**down**) engloutir qc

wolfhound ['wʊlfhaʊnd] *n* chien-loup *m*

wolf-whistle ['wʊlfˌwɪsl] **I.** *n* sifflement *m;* **to give sb a** ~ siffler qn **II.** *vi* siffler

woman ['wʊmən] <women> *n* (*female*) femme *f;* **a** ~ **candidate** une candidate; **a** ~ **president** une présidente; **a** ~ **driver** une conductrice; **a** ~ **composer** une compositrice; **the women's movement** le mouvement des femmes; **women's studies** études *fpl* féminines ►**a** ~**'s place is in the home** la place de la femme est derrière les fourneaux

womanhood ['wʊmənhʊd] *n no pl* **1.** (*female adulthood*) féminité *f* **2.** (*women as a group*) femmes *fpl*

womanish ['wʊmənɪʃ] *adj pej* de femme

womanize ['wʊmənaɪz] *vi inf* courir les femmes

womanizer *n* coureur *m* (de jupons)

womanly ['wʊmənli] *adj* féminin(e)

womb [wuːm] *n* utérus *m*

womenfolk ['wɪmɪnfəʊk, *Am:* -foʊk] *npl* **the** ~ les femmes *fpl*

won[1] [wʌn] *pt, pp of* **win**

won[2] [wʌn] *n* won *m*

wonder ['wʌndəʳ, *Am:* -dɚ] **I.** *vt* **1.** (*ask oneself*) se demander; **to** ~ **who/when/if** se demander qui/quand/si; **it makes you** ~ cela donne à réfléchir; **I** ~ **if I could ask you a favour?** est-ce que je peux te demander une faveur? **2.** (*feel surprise*) **to** ~ **that** s'étonner que +*subj* **II.** *vi* **1.** (*ask oneself*) se demander; **to** ~ **about sb/sth** se poser des questions sur qn/qc; **to** ~ **about doing sth** songer à faire qc **2.** (*feel surprise*) **to** ~ **at sb/sth** s'étonner de qn/qc **III.** *n* **1.** *no pl* (*feeling*) étonnement *m;*

W

to fill sb with ~ émerveiller qn; **in** ~ avec émerveillement; **little ~ that she left** pas étonnant qu'elle soit partie **2.** (*marvel*) merveille *f;* **a ~ drug** un remède miracle ►**to do ~s** faire des miracles

wonderful ['wʌndəfl, *Am:* -dɚ-] *adj* merveilleux(-euse); **to feel ~** se sentir en pleine forme

wonderland ['wʌndəlænd, *Am:* -dɚlænd] *n* pays *m* des merveilles

wonderment ['wʌndəmənt, *Am:* -dɚ-] *n no pl* émerveillement *m*

wonk ['wɒŋk, *Am:* 'wɑːŋk] *n Am, inf* **1.** (*hard-working person*) bête *f* de travail **2.** (*person who like details*) pinailleur, -euse *m, f*

wonky ['wɒŋkɪ, *Am:* 'wɑːŋ-] <-ier, -iest> *adj Brit, Aus, inf* **1.** (*askew*) de travers **2.** (*wobbly: chair*) bancal(e) **3.** *fig* (*attitude, idea*) véreux(-euse)

wont [wəʊnt, *Am:* wɔːnt] **I.** *adj form* **to be ~ to** +*infin* avoir coutume de +*infin* **II.** *n no pl, form* coutume *f;* **as is/was her/his ~** comme de coutume

won't [wəʊnt, *Am:* woʊnt] = **will not** *s.* **will**

woo [wuː] *vt* courtiser; **to ~ sb away from sb/sth** éloigner qn de qn/qc

wood [wʊd] *n* **1.** *no pl* (*material*) bois *m;* **a plank of ~** une planche de bois; **olive ~** (bois d')olivier *m;* **oak ~** (bois de) chêne *m* **2.** (*group of trees*) bois *m;* **in the ~s** dans les bois **3.** *no pl, Brit* (*wooden container*) tonneau *m* **4.** (*golf club*) bois *m* ►**he can't see the ~ from the trees** *Brit, Aus* les arbres lui cachent la forêt; **to touch** [*o* **knock on**] ~ toucher du bois; **not to be out of the ~** ne pas être tiré d'affaires

woodcarving ['wʊdkɑːvɪŋ, *Am:* -kɑːr-] *n* sculpture *f* sur bois

woodcut ['wʊdkʌt] *n* gravure *f* sur bois

wooded ['wʊdɪd] *adj* boisé(e)

wooden ['wʊdn] *adj* **1.** (*made of wood*) en bois; (*leg*) de bois **2.** (*awkward*) gauche; (*smile*) forcé(e)

woodland ['wʊdlænd] *n* région *f* boisée; **a ~ plant/animal** une plante/un animal des bois

woodpecker ['wʊd,pekəʳ, *Am:* -ɚ] *n* ZOOL pivert *m*

woodshed ['wʊdʃed] **I.** *n* bûcher *m* **II.** <-dd-> *vi Am, inf* répéter

woodwind ['wʊdwɪnd] MUS **I.** *n* **the ~** les bois *mpl* **II.** *adj* **~ instrument** instrument *m* à vent

woodwork ['wʊdwɜːk, *Am:* -wɜːrk] *n no pl* **1.** (*parts of building*) charpente *f* **2.** *Brit* (*carpentry*) menuiserie *f* ►**to come out of the ~** ressortir d'on ne sait où

woodworm ['wʊdwɜːm, *Am:* -wɜːrm] *inv n* **1.** (*larva*) ver *m* à bois **2.** *no pl* (*damage*) piqûres *fpl* de ver

woody ['wʊdɪ] <-ier, -iest> *adj* **1.** (*texture*) ligneux(-euse) **2.** (*taste*) boisé(e)

woof [wuːf] **I.** *n* (*dog*) aboiement *m;* **~, ~** ouaf, ouaf **II.** *vi* aboyer

wool [wʊl] *n no pl* laine *f;* **a ball of ~** une pelote de laine ►**to pull the ~ over sb's eyes** voiler la face à qn

woolen *adj Am,* **woollen** ['wʊlən] *adj Brit* en laine; **~ textiles** lainages *mpl*

woolly <-ier, -iest> *adj Brit,* **wooly** ['wʊlɪ] <-ier, -iest> *adj Am* **1.** (*made of wool*) en laine **2.** (*vague*) flou(e); (*notion*) vague

woozy ['wuːzɪ] <-ier, -iest> *adj inf* dans les vapes

wop [wɒp, *Am:* wɑːp] *n pej, inf* rital(e) *m(f)*

word [wɜːd, *Am:* wɜːrd] **I.** *n* **1.** LING mot *m;* **rude ~s** gros mots; **a ~ wrap** un retour à la ligne; **in a ~** en un mot; **in other ~s** en d'autres termes; **to explain in ~s of one syllable** expliquer dans des termes clairs; **to not breathe a ~ of sth** ne rien dire à propos de qc; **not to know a ~ of French** ne pas connaître un mot de français; **a man of few ~s** un homme qui parle peu; **~ for ~** mot pour mot; **to be too ridiculous for ~s** être d'un ridicule sans nom **2.** (*speech, conversation*) **to have a ~ with sb** parler un instant à qn; **can I have a ~?** est-ce que je peux dire quelque chose?; **to have a few ~s with sb** échanger quelques mots avec qn; **to say a few ~s about sth** dire quelques mots à propos de qc **3.** *no pl, no art* (*news*) nouvelles *fpl;* **to have ~ from sb/sth** avoir des nouvelles de qn/qc; **to get ~ of sth** apprendre qc; **the good ~** *Am, inf* la bonne nouvelle; **~ gets around** les nouvelles vont vite; (**the**) **~ is out** (**that**) ... on a appris que ... **4.** *no pl* (*order*) ordre *m;* **to give the ~** donner l'ordre; **a ~ of advice** un conseil **5.** *no pl* (*promise*) promesse *f;* **to keep/give one's ~** tenir/donner sa promesse; **a man of his ~** un homme de parole **6.** *pl* MUS paroles *fpl* ►**to have a quick ~ in sb's ear** toucher deux mots à qn; **by ~ of mouth** de vive voix; **to put ~s in(to) sb's mouth** faire dire à qn ce que qn ne veut pas dire; **to take the ~s out of sb's mouth** enlever les mots de la bouche à qn; **to put in a good ~ for sb/sth** (**with sb**) glisser (à qn) un mot en faveur de qn/qc; **sb cannot get a ~ in edgeways, sb cannot get a ~ in edgewise** *Am, inf* qn ne peut pas en placer une; **from the ~ go** depuis le début; **to take sb's ~ for it** croire qn sur parole; **my ~!** ma parole! **II.** *vt* formuler

word count *n* nombre *m* de mots

wording *n no pl* formulation *f*

wordless ['wɜːdlɪs, *Am:* 'wɜːrd-] *adj* muet(te)

word-perfect [,wɜːd'pɜːfɪkt, *Am:* ,wɜːrd'pɜːr-] *adj* **to have sth ~** connaître qc sur le bout des doigts

wordplay ['wɜːdpleɪ, *Am:* 'wɜːrd-] *n no pl* jeu *m* de mots

word processing *n no pl* INFOR traitement *m* de texte **word processing software** *n* logiciel *m* de traitement de texte **word pro-**

cessor *n* INFOR logiciel *m* de traitement de texte

wordy ['wɜːdɪ, *Am:* 'wɜːr-] <-ier, iest> *adj* verbeux(-euse)

wore [wɔːʳ, *Am:* wɔːr] *pt of* **wear**

work [wɜːk, *Am:* wɜːrk] **I.** *n* **1.** *no pl* (*useful activity*) travail *m;* **to be at ~** être au travail; **it's hard ~ doing sth** c'est dur de faire qc; **to put a lot of ~ into sth** beaucoup travailler sur qc; **it needs more ~** (*essay*) il faut le(la) retravailler; **to do some ~ on the car/house** faire quelques réparations sur la voiture/dans la maison; **she's at ~ on a novel** elle travaille sur un roman **2.** *no pl* (*employment*) emploi *m;* **to be in ~** travailler; **to be off ~** ne pas travailler; **to be out of ~** être sans emploi; **to get ~ as a translator** trouver un emploi en tant que traducteur **3.** *no pl* (*place*) travail *m;* **to be at ~** être au travail; **to leave for ~** partir travailler **4.** *no pl* (*sth produced by sb*) travail *m;* **~ in leather** travail sur cuir; **to be sb's ~** être l'œuvre de qn; **the ~ of professional thieves/a craftsman** l'œuvre de voleurs professionnelles/d'un artisan; **a ~ by Picasso** une œuvre de Picasso; **~s of art in bronze** œuvres d'art en bronze **5.** *pl,* + *sing/pl vb* (*factory*) usine *f* **6.** *pl* (*working parts*) *a. fig* rouages *mpl* **7.** *pl, inf* (*everything*) **the ~s** la totale ►**to have one's ~ cut out to do sth** peiner à faire qc **II.** *vi* **1.** (*be busy, do job*) travailler; **to ~ for peace** œuvrer pour la paix **2.** (*function*) marcher; **to get sth to ~** faire marcher qc; **to ~ on batteries** fonctionner avec des piles **3.** (*have effect*) faire effet; **to ~ against sb/sth** agir contre qn/qc; **to ~ for sb** agir en faveur de qn; **to ~ both ways** agir dans les deux sens **4.** (*make progress towards sth*) **to ~ round to doing sth** réussir à faire qc; **to ~ free** se libérer; **to ~ loose** se desserrer ►**to ~ like a charm** fonctionner comme un charme; **to ~ like a Trojan** *Brit,* **to ~ till you drop** travailler comme un forçat **III.** *vt* **1.** (*make sb work*) faire travailler; **to ~ oneself to death** se tuer au travail **2.** (*do work*) travailler; **to ~ long hours** travailler de longues heures; **to ~ overtime** faire des heures supplémentaires **3.** (*operate*) faire fonctionner; **to be ~ed by sth** être actionné par qc **4.** (*achieve*) **to ~ sth free** parvenir à dégager qc; **to ~ sth loose** desserrer qc; **to ~ one's way through the crowd** se frayer un chemin à travers la foule; **to ~ one's way up through a firm** gravir les échelons dans une entreprise **5.** (*bring about*) opérer; **to ~ it/things (out) so that ...** faire de sorte que ... **6.** (*shape*) travailler **7.** (*exploit*) exploiter ►**to ~ one's fingers to the bone** se saigner aux quatre veines; **to ~ a treat** *Brit, inf* bien marcher

◆**work in** *vt* **1.** (*mix in*) incorporer **2.** (*include*) introduire

◆**work off** *vt* évacuer; (*one's anger*) passer; **to ~ kilos/some fat** perdre des kilos/du poids

◆**work on I.** *vt* (*book, project*) travailler sur; (*answer*) préparer; (*person*) travailler **II.** *vi* continuer à travailler

◆**work out I.** *vt* **1.** (*calculate*) calculer; **to ~ the total** faire le total **2.** (*reason*) résoudre; (*solution, answer*) trouver; **we can work things out** on peut arranger les choses **3.** (*decide*) décider **4.** (*understand*) comprendre **II.** *vi* **1.** (*give a result*) **to ~ at £10** revenir à 10 livres **2.** (*be a success*) marcher; **to ~ well/badly** bien/mal se passer; **how are things working out?** comment ça va? **3.** (*do exercise*) s'entraîner

◆**work up** *vt* **1.** (*upset*) **to work sb up into a fury/state** mettre qn dans tous ses états; **to get worked up** se mettre dans tous ses états **2.** (*develop*) développer; **to ~ an appetite** s'ouvrir l'appétit; **to ~ enthusiasm/interest for sth** s'enthousiasmer/s'intéresser à qc

workable ['wɜːkəbl, *Am:* 'wɜːr-] *adj* **1.** (*feasible*) réalisable; (*compromise*) possible **2.** (*able to be manipulated*) maniable **3.** AGR (*ground, land*) exploitable

workaday ['wɜːkədeɪ, *Am:* 'wɜːr-] *adj* banal(e)

workaholic [ˌwɜːkə'hɒlɪk, *Am:* ˌwɜːrkə'hɑː-] *n* bourreau *m* de travail **workbasket** boîte *f* à ouvrage **workbench** *n* établi *m* **workbook** *n* livre *m* d'exercices **workbox** *n* boîte *f* à ouvrage **workday** *n Am, Aus* journée *f* de travail

worker ['wɜːkəʳ, *Am:* 'wɜːrkɚ] *n* **1.** (*employee*) travailleur, -euse *m, f;* **an office ~** un employé de bureau **2.** (*manual worker*) ouvrier, -ère *m, f;* **construction ~** ouvrier du bâtiment **3.** (*person who works hard*) travailleur, -euse *m, f* **4.** ZOOL ouvrière *f;* **a ~ bee** une abeille ouvrière

workforce ['wɜːkfɔːs, *Am:* 'wɜːrkfɔːrs] *n* + *sing/pl vb* **1.** (*industry*) **the ~** la main-d'œuvre **2.** (*company*) personnel *m* **workhorse** *n* bête *f* de somme

working *adj* **1.** (*employed*) qui travaille; (*population*) actif(-ive); **~ people** ouvriers *mpl* **2.** (*pertaining to work*) de travail; (*lunch*) d'affaires **3.** (*functioning*) qui fonctionne; **to be in good ~ order** être en bon état de fonctionnement; **to have a ~ knowledge of English** avoir des bases d'anglais

working class *n* classe *f* ouvrière **working-class** *adj* ouvrier(-ère) **working day** *n* **1.** (*day of work*) journée *f* de travail **2.** ADMIN jour *m* ouvrable

workings *n pl* **1.** (*mine*) chantier *m* d'exploitation **2.** (*mechanism*) rouages *mpl*

workload ['wɜːkləʊd, *Am:* 'wɜːrkloʊd] *n* charge *f* de travail; **to have a heavy ~** avoir beaucoup de travail

workman ['wɜːkmən, *Am:* 'wɜːrk-] <-men> *n* ouvrier *m* **workmanlike** *adj* professionnel(le) **workmanship** *n no pl* travail *m;* **fine ~** beau travail

workmate ['wɜːkmeɪt, *Am:* 'wɜːrk-] *n Brit* collègue *mf* (de travail)

workout ['wɜːkaʊt, *Am:* 'wɜːrk-] *n* séance *f* d'entraînement

work permit *n* permis *m* de travail

workplace ['wɜːkpleɪs, *Am:* 'wɜːrk-] *n* lieu *m* de travail; **in the** ~ sur le lieu de travail

worksheet *n* **1.** SCHOOL questionnaire *m* **2.** (*list*) liste *f* des taches à effectuer **3.** INFOR feuille *f* de programmation

workshop ['wɜːkʃɒp, *Am:* 'wɜːrkʃɑːp] *n* atelier *m;* **painting** ~ atelier de peinture

workshy ['wɜːkʃaɪ, *Am:* 'wɜːrk-] *adj Brit, pej* fainéant(e)

work station *n* INFOR poste *m* de travail **work-study program** *n* UNIV *programme alternant une formation universitaire et professionnelle*

worktop [wɜːktɒp, *Am:* wɜːrktɑːp] *n Brit* plan *m* de travail

world [wɜːld, *Am:* wɜːrld] *n* **1.** *no pl* GEO monde *m;* **the** ~**'s population** la population mondiale; ~ **Cup** Coupe *f* du monde; ~ **record** record *m* mondial; **to come into the** ~ venir au monde **2.** (*defined group*) monde *m;* **the Muslim/English-speaking** ~ le monde musulman/anglophone; **the** ~ **of fashion** le monde de la mode ►**to have the** ~ **at one's feet** avoir le monde à ses pieds; **all the** ~ **and her husband/his wife** *Brit* tout le monde sans exception; **to be a man/woman of the** ~ être un homme/une femme d'expérience; **the** ~ **is sb's oyster** le monde appartient à qn; **to be** ~**s apart** être complètement opposés; **to live in a** ~ **of one's own** vivre dans son monde; **to mean (all) the** ~ **to sb** être tout pour qn; **to be out of this** ~ *inf* être super; **to think the** ~ **of sb** adorer qn

World Bank [ˌwɜːld'bæŋk, *Am:* ˌwɜːrld-] *n* Banque *f* mondiale **world-beater** *n* leader *m* mondial **world-class** *adj* de niveau mondial **world-famous** *adj* de renommée internationale

worldly ['wɜːldlɪ, *Am:* 'wɜːrld-] *adj* **1.** (*of practical matters: success, goods*) matériel(le) **2.** (*materialistic*) matérialiste **3.** (*having experience*) avisé(e)

world-shaking, **world-shattering** *adj* stupéfiant(e) **World War** *n* ~ **I/II, First/Second** ~ Première/Seconde Guerre *f* mondiale **world-weary** *adj* **to be** ~ être las **worldwide I.** *adj* mondial(e) **II.** *adv* (*all over the world*) à travers le monde **World Wide Web** *n* INFOR World Wide Web *m,* toile *f* d'araignée mondiale

worm [wɜːm, *Am:* wɜːrm] **I.** *n* ver *m* **II.** *vt* **1.** (*treat for worms*) **to** ~ **a cat** traiter un chat contre les vers **2.** (*squeeze through*) **to** ~ **oneself** se faufiler **3.** (*gain trust slowly*) **to** ~ **oneself into sth** s'insinuer dans qc **III.** *vi* **to** ~ **through sth** se faufiler à travers qc

♦**worm out** *vt* **to worm sth out of sb** arracher qc à qn

worm-eaten *adj* vermoulu(e)

wormhole ['wɜːmhəʊl, *Am:* 'wɜːrmhoʊl] *n* piqûre *f* de vers

wormy ['wɜːmɪ, *Am:* 'wɜːr-] <-ier, -iest> *adj* infesté(e) de vers

worn [wɔːn, *Am:* wɔːrn] **I.** *pp of* **wear II.** *adj* usé(e); (*stone, statue*) abîmé(e); (*person*) las(se)

worn-out [ˌwɔːn'aʊt, *Am:* ˌwɔːrn-] *adj* **1.** (*exhausted*) épuisé(e) **2.** (*used up*) complètement usé(e)

worried ['wʌrɪd, *Am:* 'wɜːr-] *adj* inquiet(-ète); **to be** ~ **about sb/sth** s'inquiéter de qn/qc; **I'm** ~ **he'll leave** j'ai peur qu'il ne parte; **to be** ~ **to death about sb/sth** être mort d'inquiétude pour qn/qc; **to have sb** ~ inquiéter qn; **to be** ~ **sick** être fou d'inquiétude; **to be unduly** ~ **by sth** s'inquiéter outre mesure de qc

worrier *n* anxieux, -euse *m, f*

worrisome ['wʌrɪsəm, *Am:* 'wɜːrɪ-] *adj form* inquiétant(e)

worry ['wʌrɪ, *Am:* 'wɜːr-] **I.** *n* <-ies> (*concern*) souci *m;* **to have a** ~ **about sth** se faire du souci à propos de qc; **he's a big** ~ il me cause des soucis ►**not to have a** ~ **in the world** ne pas avoir le moindre souci **II.** *vt* <-ie-, -ing> **1.** (*preoccupy, concern*) inquiéter; **it worries me that she can't sleep** cela m'inquiète qu'il ne puisse pas dormir **2.** (*shake around*) **to** ~ **sth** jouer avec qc **3.** (*pursue and scare*) attaquer ►**don't you** ~ **your pretty little head** *iron, inf* ne te tracasse pas la tête **III.** <-ie-, -ing> *vi* (*be concerned*) **to** ~ **about sth** s'inquiéter pour qc; **there's nothing to** ~ **about** il n'y a pas de quoi s'inquiéter; **not to** ~ *inf* ce n'est pas grave

worrying *adj* inquiétant(e)

worse [wɜːs, *Am:* wɜːrs] **I.** *adj comp of* **bad** **1.** (*not as good*) pire; **to be** ~ **at English** être plus mauvais en anglais; **to be even** ~ **than ...** être encore pire que ...; **to be much** ~ être bien pire; **there's nothing** ~ **than sth** il n'y a rien de pire que qc; **to make sth** ~ empirer qc; **to get** ~ **and** ~ *iron* s'empirer; **to make matters** ~**, he ...** pour envenimer la situation, il ...; ~ **luck** *inf* la poisse **2.** (*sicker*) **to be** ~ aller plus mal ► ~ **things happen at sea!** il y a pire!; **to be none the** ~ **for sth** ne pas être trop affecté par qc **II.** *adv comp of* **badly** plus mal; **you could do** ~ **than do sth** ce ne serait pas si mal si tu faisais qc **III.** *n no pl* pire *m;* **to change for the** ~ changer en mal; **to have seen** ~ avoir vu pire

worsen ['wɜːsn, *Am:* 'wɜːr-] *vi, vt* empirer

worship ['wɜːʃɪp, *Am:* 'wɜːr-] **I.** *vt* <-pp- *o Am* -p-> REL vouer un culte à; **to hero** ~ **sb** vénérer qn comme un dieu **II.** *vi* <-pp- *o Am* -p-> pratiquer (sa religion); **to** ~ **in a church/mosque** aller à l'église/la mosquée **III.** *n no pl, a. fig* culte *m;* **place of** ~ lieu *m* de culte; **money** ~ le culte de l'argent; **act of** ~ acte *m* de dévotion

worshipper *n* **1.** REL fidèle *mf* **2.** *fig* adorateur, -trice *m, f*

worst [wɜːst, *Am:* wɜːrst] **I.** *adj superl of* **bad** (*that is least good*) **the ~ ...** le pire ...; **my ~ mistake** ma plus grave erreur; **the ~ thing** la pire des choses; **my ~ enemy** mon pire ennemi; **the ~ pupil** le plus mauvais élève; **the ~ possible place** le pire endroit **II.** *adv superl of* **badly** le plus mal; **to be the ~ affected** être le plus touchée **III.** *n no pl* (*most terrible thing*) **the ~** le pire; **at ~** au pire; **~ of all** pire que tout; **to fear the ~** craindre le pire; **the ~ of it was ...** le pire dans tout cela, c'était que ...; **the ~ is over** le pire est passé; **the ~ that could happen** le pire qui puisse arriver ►**if** (**the**) **~ comes to** (**the**) **~** dans le pire des cas

worsted ['wʊstɪd] *n no pl* laine *f* peignée

worth [wɜːθ, *Am:* wɜːrθ] **I.** *n* valeur *f;* **a pound's ~ of apples** pour une livre de pommes; **I got my money's ~** j'en ai eu pour mon argent; **to know one's true ~** savoir ce dont on est capable **II.** *adj* **to be ~ £2** valoir 2 livres; **sth is ~ a lot to me** j'attache un grand prix à qc; **it's ~ seeing** ça vaut la peine d'être vu; **it's not ~ changing** ça ne vaut pas la peine de changer; **it's ~ a try** ça vaut la peine d'essayer ►**it's not ~ a bean** ça ne vaut pas un haricot; **to be ~ one's weight in gold** valoir son pesant d'or; **for all one is ~** de toutes ses forces

worthless ['wɜːθlɪs, *Am:* 'wɜːrθ-] *adj* qui ne vaut rien; **to feel ~** se sentir bon à rien

worthwhile [ˌwɜːθ'waɪl, *Am:* ˌwɜːrθ-] *adj* (*activity, talks*) qui en vaut la peine; **to be** (**very**) **~** en valoir vraiment la peine

worthy ['wɜːðɪ, *Am:* 'wɜːr-] **I.** <-ier, -iest> *adj* digne; (*cause*) noble; **to be ~ of sb/sth** être digne de qn/qc **II.** <-ies> *n iron* notable *m*

would [wʊd] *aux* **1.** *pt of* **will 2.** (*in indirect speech*) **he said he ~ come** il a dit qu'il viendrait; **I thought I ~ have arrived on time** j'ai cru que j'arriverais à l'heure **3.** (*conditional*) **I ~ come if I had time** j'irais si j'avais du temps; **it ~ have been hard to drive** cela aurait été difficile de rouler; **I ~ travel if I were rich** je voyagerais si j'étais riche **4.** (*implied condition*) **it ~ be a pleasure** ce serait avec plaisir; **my mother ~ know** ma mère le saurait **5.** (*desires and preferences*) **I'd like some water** j'aimerais un peu d'eau; **~ you mind ...?** auriez-vous l'obligeance ...?; **I wish they'd go** j'aimerais qu'ils partent; **I ~ have preferred** j'aurais préféré; **I ~ rather/sooner do sth** je préférerais faire qc; **~ I were there** si seulement j'étais là **6.** (*regularity in past*) **as a child, I ~ work from 6 to 6** enfant, je travaillais de 6 heures à 18 heures **7.** (*characteristic behaviour*) **she ~ say that, ~n't she?** c'est ce qu'elle dirait, non?; **she ~ never do that** elle ne ferait jamais une telle chose **8.** (*probably*) **that ~ be his mother on the phone** cela devait être sa mère au téléphone **9.** (*offering polite advice*) **I ~ come early if I were you** j'arriverais tôt si j'étais vous; **I ~n't go on Thursday** je ne partirais pas jeudi à ta place **10.** (*asking motives*) **why ~ he do that?** pourquoi ferait-il une telle chose?

would-be ['wʊdbi] *adj* soi-disant(e)

wouldn't [wʊdnt] = **would not** *s.* **would**

wound¹ [wuːnd] *pt, pp of* **wind**

wound² [waʊnd] **I.** *n a. fig* blessure *f;* **to reopen old ~s** raviver de vieilles blessures **II.** *vt a. fig* blesser

wounded ['wuːndɪd] **I.** *adj a. fig* blessé(e) **II.** *npl* MED **the ~** les blessés; **the walking ~** les blessés légers

woven ['wəʊv(n), *Am:* 'woʊv-] **I.** *pp of* **weave II.** *adj* tissé(e)

wow [waʊ] **I.** *interj inf* ouah! **II.** *n inf* (*popular item*) **to be a ~ with sb/sth** être un succès fou auprès de qn/qc; **to have a ~ of a time** passer du bon temps **III.** *vt inf* (*impress*) emballer

WPC [ˌdʌbljuːˌpiː'siː] *n Brit abbr of* **Woman Police Constable** femme-agent *f*

wpm *n abbr of* **words per minute** mots/min.

WRAC [ræk] *n Brit abbr of* **Women's Royal Army Corps** *corps féminin de l'armée britannique*

wrack [ræk] *n Am, Aus s.* **rack**

WRAF [ræf] *n Brit abbr of* **Women's Royal Air Force** *corps féminin de l'armée de l'air britannique*

wrangle ['ræŋgl] **I.** <-ling> *vi* se quereller **II.** *n* querelle *f*

wrangling *n* querelles *fpl*

wrap [ræp] **I.** *n* **1.** (*piece of clothing*) châle *m* **2.** *no pl* (*wrapping*) emballage *m;* **plastic ~** emballage en plastique ►**to keep sth under ~s** garder qc secret; **to take the ~s off sth** dévoiler qc au public; **it's a ~** ça y est, c'est fini **II.** *vt* <-pp-> emballer

◆**wrap up I.** *vt* **1.** (*completely cover*) envelopper **2.** (*dress warmly: child*) emballer; **to wrap oneself up** s'emmitoufler **3.** (*involve*) **to be wrapped up in sth** être absorbé par qc **4.** *inf* (*finish well*) conclure **II.** *vi* **1.** (*dress heavily*) s'emmitoufler **2.** *inf* (*be quiet*) se taire

wraparound ['ræpəˌraʊnd] *adj* **~ skirt** jupe *f* portefeuille

wrapper ['ræpəʳ, *Am:* -ɚ] *n* emballage *m*

wrapping *n* emballage *m*

wrapping paper *n* papier *m* d'emballage

wrath [rɒθ, *Am:* ræθ] *n form* courroux *f*

wreak [riːk] <-ed, -ed *o* wrought, wrought> *vt form* (*damage*) entraîner; (*vengeance*) assouvir; **to ~ havoc** faire des ravages

wreath [riːθ] <-s> *n* couronne *f;* **Christmas ~** couronne de Noël

wreck [rek] **I.** *vt* **1.** (*damage*) démolir **2.** (*cause to be ruined: chances, hopes*) ruiner; (*lives, career, friendship*) briser **II.** *n* **1.** (*crashed vehicle*) épave *f* **2.** (*sinking*) naufrage *m* **3.** *inf* (*sick person*) loque *f* **4.** (*car,* *machine*) tas *m* de ferraille

wreckage ['rekɪdʒ] *n no pl* **1.** (*damaged pieces*) débris *mpl* **2.** (*wreck*) épave *f*

wrecker ['rekəʳ, *Am:* -ɚ] *n Am* dépanneuse *f*

wren [ren] *n* troglodyte *m*

wrench [rentʃ] **I.** *vt* **1.** (*twist out*) arracher; **to ~ sth from/out of sth** arracher qc de qc; **to ~ sth from sb** arracher qc à qn; **to ~ sth free** libérer qc d'un mouvement brusque **2.** (*injure*) se tordre; **to ~ one's foot** se faire une entorse au pied **3.** (*take*) **to ~ sth from sb** arracher qc à qn **II.** *n* **1.** (*twisting jerk*) torsion *f;* **with a ~** d'un mouvement brusque **2.** (*painful departure*) déchirement *m* **3.** *Am* (*spanner*) clef *f*

wrestle ['resl] SPORT **I.** <-ling> *vt* (*fight*) lutter; **to ~ sb to the ground** jeter qn au sol **II.** <-ling> *vi* **1.** (*fight*) lutter **2.** (*deal with: problem, computer*) se débattre avec

wrestler ['resləʳ, *Am:* -lɚ] *n* **1.** (*athlete*) lutteur, -euse *m, f* **2.** (*show performer*) catcheur, -euse *m, f*

wrestling ['reslɪŋ] *n no pl* **1.** (*sport*) lutte *f* **2.** (*show*) catch *m*

wretch [retʃ] <-es> *n* **1.** (*unfortunate person*) **a poor ~** un malheureux **2.** *inf* (*mean person*) **a miserable ~** un salaud

wretched ['retʃɪd] *adj* **1.** (*unhappy, depressed*) **to feel/look ~** être/avoir l'air mal **2.** (*of poor quality, miserable*) lamentable **3.** (*to express annoyance*) maudit(e)

wriggle ['rɪgl] **I.** *n* trémoussement *m* **II.** <-ling> *vi* **1.** (*squirm*) se tortiller; (*person*) s'agiter **2.** (*move by twisting*) **to ~ along** se faufiler; **to ~ through/under sth** se faufiler dans/sous qc ►**to ~ off the hook** *inf* se dérober **III.** <-ling> *vt* (*toes, shoulders*) remuer

◆**wriggle out of** *vi* échapper à

wring [rɪŋ] <wrung, wrung> *vt* **1.** (*twist to squeeze out*) tordre; (*shirt*) essorer; **to ~ sb's/sth's neck** *a. fig* tordre le cou à qn; **to ~ the water out of sth** tordre qc pour l'essorer **2.** (*obtain*) **to ~ information from sb** arracher des renseignements à qn

wringing *adv* **to be ~** (**wet**) être trempé(e)

wrinkle ['rɪŋkl] **I.** *n* **1.** (*material*) pli *m;* (*face*) ride *f* **2.** *inf* (*clever trick*) tuyau *m* ►**to iron out the ~s** aplanir les difficultés **II.** <-ling> *vi* (*form folds: material*) se froisser; (*face, skin*) se rider **III.** <-ling> *vt* (*put folds in: material*) froisser; (*face*) rider ►**to ~ one's brow** froncer les sourcils

wrinkled ['rɪŋkld], **wrinkly** ['rɪŋklɪ] *adj* (*clothes*) froissé(e); (*skin*) ridé(e)

wrist [rɪst] *n* poignet *m*

wristwatch ['rɪstwɒtʃ, *Am:* -wɑːtʃ] *n* montre-bracelet *f*

writ [rɪt] *n* LAW acte *m* judiciaire

write [raɪt] <wrote, written, writing> **I.** *vt* **1.** (*mark*) écrire; (*cheque*) faire; (*essay, commentary*) rédiger **2.** *Am* (*write to*) écrire à ►**to be nothing to ~ home about** n'être rien de bouleversant **II.** *vi* (*mark letters*) écrire; **to learn** (**how**) **to read and ~** apprendre à lire et à écrire; **to ~ for a living** vivre de sa plume

◆**write back I.** *vt* répondre **II.** *vi* répondre

◆**write down** *vt* noter; **to ~ ideas** mettre ses idées par écrit

◆**write in I.** *vi* écrire **II.** *vt* (*insert*) insérer

◆**write off I.** *vt* **1.** (*give up*) faire une croix sur **2.** (*lose interest*) se désintéresser de **3.** (*damage*) démolir **4.** FIN amortir **II.** *vi* **~ for sth** demander qc par courrier

◆**write out** *vt* **1.** (*put into writing*) écrire **2.** (*fill out*) **to write a cheque** (**out**) **to sb** faire un chèque à qn **3.** (*remove: character*) rayer; **to write sb out of one's will** rayer qn de son testament

◆**write up** *vt* **1.** (*put in written form*) écrire **2.** (*critique*) **to ~ a film** écrire un article sur un film; **to be written up favorably** faire l'objet de critiques élogieuses **3.** *Am* LAW faire un rapport sur

write-off *n Brit* épave *f;* **to be a complete ~** (*car*) n'être plus qu'une épave; (*weekend*) être une perte de temps

write-protected *adj* INFOR protégé(e) contre l'écriture **write-protect tab** *n* INFOR volet *m* de protection contre l'écriture

writer ['raɪtəʳ, *Am:* -t̬ɚ] *n* **1.** (*professional who writes*) écrivain *m;* **she is a ~** elle est écrivain **2.** INFOR (*of CD-ROM, DVD*) graveur *m*

write-up ['raɪtʌp] *n* critique *f*

writhe [raɪð] <writhing> *vi* **1.** (*squirm around*) se tordre; **to ~** (**around**) **in pain** se tordre de douleurs **2.** (*be uncomfortable*) être mal à l'aise

writing ['raɪtɪŋ, *Am:* -t̬ɪŋ] *n* **1.** (*handwriting*) écriture *f* **2.** (*anything written*) écrit *m;* **in ~** par écrit **3.** *pl* LIT, THEAT, PUBL œuvre *m;* **women's ~ in the 19th century** la littérature féminine au 19ème siècle **4.** (*creation of a written work*) écriture *f*

writing desk *n* secrétaire *m* **writing pad** *n* bloc-notes *m* **writing paper** *n* papier *m* à lettres

written ['rɪtn] **I.** *pp of* **write II.** *adj* écrit(e); **a ~ exam** un écrit ►**to be ~ all over one's face** se lire sur le visage de qn; **to be ~ in the stars** être écrit; **the ~ word** l'écrit

WRNS [renz] *n Brit abbr of* **Women's Royal Naval Service** *services féminins de la Marine royale britannique*

wrong [rɒŋ, *Am:* rɑːŋ] **I.** *adj* **1.** (*not right*) faux(fausse); **to be ~** (**about sb/sth**) avoir tort (à propos de qn/qc); **to be plainly ~** avoir complètement tort; **to prove sb ~** prouver le contraire à qn **2.** (*not appropriate*) mauvais(e); **he's the ~ person for the job** ce n'est pas la bonne personne pour le travail; **to go ~** aller mal; **there's something ~** il y a quelque chose qui ne tourne pas rond; **what is ~ with him?** qu'est-ce qui ne va pas avec lui?; **what's ~ with doing this?** quel mal y a-t-il à faire qc? **3.** (*morally reprehensible*) mal; **it is ~ of sb to**

so sth c'est mal de sa part de qn de faire qc; **to do sth** ~ faire qc de mal **4.** (*not functioning properly*) **to be** ~ (*watch*) ne pas être à l'heure ▸**to get up on the** ~ **side of the <u>bed</u>** se lever du mauvais pied; **to catch sb on the** ~ **<u>foot</u>** être pris au dépourvu; **to fall into the** ~ **<u>hands</u>** tomber dans de mauvaises mains; **to go down the** ~ **<u>way</u>** être avalé de travers; **to have sth on the** ~ **<u>way</u> round** *Brit, Aus,* **to have sth on the** ~ **<u>way</u> around** *Am* avoir qc à l'envers **II.** *adv* mal; **to get sb/sth** ~ mal comprendre qn/qc; **to go** ~ (*machine*) mal fonctionner; (*plan*) ne pas marcher **III.** *n* **1.** *no pl* (*moral reprehensibility*) mal *m;* **to do sb** ~ faire du mal à qn; **to do sb no** ~ ne faire aucun mal à qn; **to know right from** ~ distinguer le bien du mal **2.** *no pl* (*unfair actions*) tort *m;* **to do sb** ~ faire du tort à qn **3.** (*unjust action*) injustice *f;* **to suffer a** ~ être victime d'une injustice ▸**to be <u>in</u> the** ~ (*not right*) avoir tort; LAW être dans son tort **IV.** *vt form* **1.** (*treat unjustly*) léser **2.** (*judge character unjustly*) être injuste envers

wrongdoer ['rɒŋˌdʊəʳ, *Am:* 'rɑːŋˌduːɚ] <-s> *n* LAW, REL malfaiteur *m*

wrongdoing [ˌrɒŋ'duːɪŋ, *Am:* 'rɑːŋˌduː-] *n no pl* LAW, REL infraction *f*

wrongful ['rɒŋfl, *Am:* 'rɑːŋ-] *adj* injustifié(e)

wrong-headed *adj pej* **1.** (*having poor judgement: person*) buté(e) **2.** (*not suitable: concept, idea*) inadapté(e)

wrongly ['rɒŋlɪ, *Am:* 'rɑːŋ-] *adv* **1.** (*unfairly*) à tort; **to be** ~ **convicted** être accusé à tort **2.** (*incorrectly*) mal

wrote [rəʊt, *Am:* roʊt] *pt of* **write**

wrought [rɔːt, *Am:* rɑːt] **I.** *pt, pp of* **work** **II.** *adj form* élaboré(e); (*metal*) forgé(e)

wrought iron *n* fer *m* forgé

wrung [rʌŋ] *pt, pp of* **wring**

wry [raɪ] <wrier, wriest *o* wryer, wryest> *adj* ironique

WSW [ˌwestsaʊθ'west] *n abbr of* **west-southwest** ouest-sud-ouest

wt [weɪt] *n abbr of* **weight** p. *m*

WWF *n abbr of* **Worldwide Fund for Nature** WWF *m* (*organisation de défense de la nature et des espèces en voie de disparition*)

WWW *n abbr of* **World Wide Web** INFOR TAM *f*

Wyoming [waɪ'əʊmɪŋ, *Am:* -'oʊ-] **I.** *n* le Wyoming **II.** *adj* du Wyoming

WYSIWYG ['wɪziwɪg] INFOR *abbr of* **what you see is what you get** Wysiwyg *m*

X

X, x [eks] <-'s> **I.** *n* **1.** *a.* MAT X *m,* x *m;* ~ **as in Xmas** *Brit,* ~ **as in X** *Am,* ~ **for Xmas** *Brit,* ~ **for X** *Am* (*on telephone*) x comme Xavier **2.** (*used in place of name*) **Mr** ~ M. X **3.** (*symbol for kiss*) bisou *m* **4.** (*cross symbol*) croix *f* **II.** *vt Am* (*delete*) rayer

xenophobia [ˌzenə'fəʊbɪə, *Am:* -'foʊ-] *n no pl* xénophobie *f*

xenophobic [ˌzenə'fəʊbɪk, *Am:* -'foʊ-] *adj* xénophobe

xerox, Xerox® ['zɪərɒks, *Am:* 'zɪrɑːks] **I.** *n* (*photocopy*) photocopie *f* **II.** *vt* (*photocopy*) photocopier; **a ~ed copy of the document** une photocopie d'un document

XL *adj abbr of* **extra large** XL

Xmas ['eksməs, *Am:* 'krɪs-] *inf abbr of* **Christmas** Noël *m*

X-rated ['eksˌreɪtɪd, *Am:* -t̬ɪd] *adj* (*film*) classé(e) X **X-ray** **I.** *n* **1.** PHYS rayon *m* X **2.** MED radio(graphie) *f;* **to have an** ~ passer une radio(graphie); **to give sb an** ~ faire passer une radio(graphie) à qn; **the** ~ **department** le service de radiologie **3.** (*picture*) radio *f* **II.** *vt* MED radiographier

xylophone ['zaɪləfəʊn, *Am:* -foʊn] *n* xylophone *m*

Y

Y, y [waɪ] <-'s> *n* **1.** *a.* MAT Y *m,* y *m;* ~ **as in Yellow** *Brit,* ~ **as in Yoke** *Am,* ~ **for Yellow** *Brit,* ~ **for Yoke** *Am* (*on telephone*) y comme Yvonne **2.** (*used in place of name*) **Mr** ~ M. Y

y. *n abbr of* **year** année *f*

yacht [jɒt, *Am:* jɑːt] *n* yacht *m*

yachting *n no pl* (*sailing*) navigation *f* de plaisance; **to go** ~ naviguer

yak [jæk] **I.** *n* ZOOL, BIO ya(c)k *m* **II.** *vi s.* **yack**

yam [jæm] *n* igname *f*

yank [jæŋk] **I.** *vt inf* **1.** (*pull hard*) tirer d'un coup sec **2.** (*remove forcefully*) *a. fig* arracher; (*tooth*) arracher d'un coup sec **II.** *n inf* (*hard pull*) coup *m* sec; **to give sth a** ~ donner un coup sec à qc

Yank [jæŋk] *n inf* Ricain(e) *m(f)*

Yankee ['jæŋkɪ] **I.** *n inf* Ricain(e) *m(f)* **II.** *adj inf* ricain(e)

yap [jæp] **I.** <-pp-> *vi a. pej* japper **II.** *n* jappement *m;* **to give a** ~ pousser un jappement

yard¹ [jɑːd, *Am:* jɑːrd] *n* (*3 feet*) yard *m* (*0,914 m*)

yard² [jɑːd, *Am:* jɑːrd] *n* **1.** (*paved area*) cour *f* **2.** (*work area*) chantier *m* **3.** *Am* (*garden*) jardin *m*

yardstick ['jɑːdstɪk, *Am:* 'jɑːrd-] *n* étalon *m*

yarn [jɑːn, *Am:* jɑːrn] *n* **1.** *no pl* (*thread*) fil *m* **2.** (*story*) longue histoire *f;* **an adventure** ~ une longue histoire d'aventures

yawn [jɔːn, *Am:* jɑːn] **I.** *vi* (*show tiredness: person*) bâiller **II.** *n* **1.** (*sign of tiredness*) bâillement *m* **2.** *inf* (*boring thing*) **to be a** ~ être ennuyeux à mourir

yd [jɑːd, *Am:* jɑːrd] *n abbr of* **yard(s)** yard *m*

yea [jeɪ] *adv form* (*yes*) oui; ~ **or nay** oui ou non

yeah [jeə] *adv inf* (*yes*) ouais; **oh ~?** ah ouais?; **~, ~!** ouais, c'est ça!

year [jɜːʳ, *Am:* jɪr] *n* **1.** (*twelve months*) année *f;* **the ~ (that) ...** [*o* **when ...**] l'année où ...; **all (the) ~ round** toute l'année; **the thing/person of the ~** la chose/personne de l'année; **I'm six ~s old** j'ai six ans; **it lasted six ~s** ça a duré six ans **2.** (*a long time*) année *f;* **for ~s** depuis des années; **in all the ~s ...** pendant toutes ces années ...; **over the ~s** à travers les années; **~ by ~, ~ in, ~ out** année après année **3.** (*of a wine*) millésime *m* **4.** SCHOOL classe *f;* **academic ~** année *f* universitaire, année *f* académique *Belgique, Québec, Suisse;* **school ~** année scolaire; **final ~ (of secondary school)** ≈ terminale *f,* ≈ rhétorique *f Belgique;* **to repeat a ~** (re)doubler; **what ~ are you in?** en quelle classe es-tu/êtes-vous?; **I'm in Year ...** je suis en (classe de) ... ►**(since) the ~ dot, (from) the ~ dot** *Brit, Aus* depuis une éternité; **to put ~s on sb** vieillir qn; **to take ~s off sb** rajeunir qn; **to be well on in ~s** bien vieillir

yearbook ['jɪəbʊk, *Am:* 'jɪr-] *n* PUBL annuaire *m*

yearling ['jɜːlɪŋ, *Am:* 'jɪrlɪŋ] *n* (*year-old animal*) petit *m*

year-long [ˌjɜː'lɒŋ, *Am:* 'jɪrlɑŋ] *adj* d'une année

yearly **I.** *adj* (*happening every year*) annuel(le) **II.** *adv* (*every year*) annuellement

yearn [jɜːn, *Am:* jɜːrn] *vi* **to ~ for sth** désirer qc ardemment; **to ~ to do sth** brûler de faire qc

yearning *n* désir *m;* **a ~ for sth** un désir de qc

yeast [jiːst] *n no pl* levure *f*

yeasty ['jiːstɪ] <-ier, -iest> *adj* de levure

yell [jel] **I.** *n* hurlement *m;* **to give a ~** pousser un hurlement **II.** *vi* hurler; **to ~ at sb** hurler après qn; **to ~ for sb/sth** appeler qn/qc en hurlant; **to ~ for help** appeler au secours en hurlant; **to ~ with laughter/pain** hurler de rire/douleur **III.** *vt* hurler; **to ~ sth at sb** hurler qc à qn

yellow ['jeləʊ, *Am:* -oʊ] **I.** *adj* **1.** (*colour*) jaune; **golden ~** jaune d'or; **to turn ~** jaunir **2.** *pej* (*cowardly*) lâche **II.** *n* jaune *m;* **~ of an egg** *Am* jaune d'œuf **III.** *vt, vi* jaunir; *s. a.* **blue**

yellow card *n* SPORT carton *m* jaune **yellow fever** *n* fièvre *f* jaune

yellowish ['jeləʊɪʃ, *Am:* -oʊ-] *adj* tirant sur le jaune; *pej* jaunâtre

yellow line *n ligne parallèle au trottoir interdisant le stationnement*

yellowness ['jeləʊnəs, *Am:* -oʊ-] *n* couleur *f* jaune

Yellow Pages® *n* pages *fpl* jaunes

yellowy *adj s.* **yellowish**

yelp [jelp] **I.** *vi, vt* glapir **II.** *n* (*high-pitched cry*) glapissement *m*

Yemen ['jemən] *n* le Yémen

Yemeni ['jemənɪ] **I.** *adj* yéménite **II.** *n* Yéménite *mf*

yen¹ [jen] *n* (*currency*) yen *m; s. a.* **pound**

yen² [jen] *n inf* (*desire*) grosse envie *f;* **to have a ~ for travel** avoir très envie de voyager

yep [jep] *adv inf* (*yes*) ouais

Yerevan [jerə'vɑːn] *n* Erevan

yes [jes] **I.** *adv* **1.** (*affirmative*) oui; **~, madam** *Am* oui, madame **2.** (*contradicting a negative*) si **II.** <yeses> *n* (*statement in favour*) oui *m* **III.** <-ss-> *vt Am* (*say yes*) dire oui à

yes-man ['jesmæn] <-men> *n pej* béni-oui-oui *m*

yesterday ['jestədɪ, *Am:* -tɚ-] *adv* hier; **the day before ~** avant-hier; **all (day) ~** toute la journée d'hier; **late ~** hier dans la soirée; **~ morning/evening** [*o* **night**] hier matin/(au) soir ►**I wasn't born ~!** je ne suis pas né de la dernière pluie!

yet [jet] **I.** *adv* **1.** (*till now*) **(as) ~** jusqu'à présent; **to have not (as) ~ done sth** n'avoir toujours pas fait qc; **the fastest ~** le plus rapide jusqu'à présent **2.** (*already*) **not ~** pas encore; **don't go (just) ~** ne pars pas déjà **3.** (*still*) **she's young ~** elle est encore jeune **4.** (*even*) **~ more beautiful/wine** encore plus beau/de vin **II.** *conj* pourtant, néanmoins; **incredible, ~ it's true** c'est incroyable mais vrai

yew [juː] *n* if *m*

YHA *n Brit abbr of* **Youth Hostel Association** association *f* des auberges de jeunesse

Yiddish ['jɪdɪʃ] **I.** *adj* yiddish *inv* **II.** *n* yiddish *m; s. a.* **English**

yield [jiːld] **I.** *n* rendement *m* **II.** *vt* **1.** (*provide*) *a. fig* rapporter; (*results*) donner **2.** (*give up*) céder **III.** *vi* **1.** (*bend: material*) céder **2.** *Am* (*let other cars go first*) céder la priorité **3.** (*surrender*) se rendre **4.** (*give way*) céder; **to ~ to pressure** céder à la pression

◆**yield up** *vt* livrer

yielding *adj a. fig* souple

yippee ['jɪpɪ] *interj inf* (*shout of joy*) youpi!

YMCA [ˌwaɪemsiː'eɪ] *n abbr of* **Young Men's Christian Association** **1.** (*movement*) Union *f* chrétienne des jeunes gens **2.** (*hostel*) foyer *m* pour jeunes gens

yob [jɒb, *Am:* jɑːb] *n,* **yobbo** ['jɒbəʊ, *Am:* 'jɑːboʊ] <-s> *n Brit, Aus, inf* voyou *m*

yodel, **yodle** ['jəʊdl, *Am:* 'joʊ-] MUS **I.** <-ll- *o* *Am* -l-> *vi, vt* (*sing*) iodler **II.** *n* (*yodelled song*) tyrolienne *f*

yoga ['jəʊgə, *Am:* 'joʊ-] *n no pl* (*exercises*) yoga *m;* **to do ~** faire du yoga

yoghourt, **yoghurt**, **yogurt** ['jɒgət, *Am:* 'joʊgɚt] *n* yaourt *m*

yoke [jəʊk, *Am:* joʊk] **I.** *n* **1.** AGR *a. fig* joug *m* **2.** FASHION empiècement *m* **II.** *vt* **1.** (*fit with yoke: animal*) atteler **2.** (*combine*) **to ~ sb/sth together** unir qn/qc

yokel ['jəʊkl, *Am:* 'joʊ-] *n iron, pej* paysan(ne) *m(f)*

yolk [jəʊk, *Am:* joʊk] *n* jaune *m*

you [juː] *pers pron* **1.** (*2nd person sing*) tu

subject pron, te *objective pron,* t + *vowel,* toi *tonic form;* **I see** ~ je te vois; **do** ~ **see me?** me vois-tu?; **I love** ~ je t'aime; **it's for** ~ c'est pour toi; **older than** ~ plus âgé que toi; **if I were** ~ si j'étais toi **2.** (*2nd person pl or polite form*) vous; **older than** ~ plus âgé que vous; **all of** ~ vous tous; ~ **men** vous, les hommes **3.** (*indefinite person*) ~ **never know** on ne sait jamais; **it makes** ~ **mad** ça te rend fou

you'll [juːl] = **you will** *s.* **will**

young [jʌŋ] **I.** *adj* jeune; ~ **people** les jeunes *mpl;* **sb's** ~**er brother** le frère cadet de qn; **sb's** ~**est** le cadet de qn; **in sb's** ~(**er**) **days** dans la jeunesse de qn; **you're only** ~ **once!** on n'est jeune qu'une fois!; **to be** ~ **at heart** être jeune de cœur **II.** *n pl* **the** ~ **1.** (*young people*) les jeunes *mpl* **2.** ZOOL, BIO les petits *mpl*

youngster [ˈjʌŋstəʳ, *Am:* -stɚ] *n* jeune *mf*

your [jɔːʳ, *Am:* jʊr] *poss adj* **1.** (*one owner*) ton *m,* ta *f,* tes *pl* **2.** (*several owners or polite form*) votre *mf,* vos *pl* **3.** (*indefinite owner*) **it depends on** ~ **age** ça dépend de l'âge qu'on a; *s. a.* **my**

you're [jʊəʳ, *Am:* jʊr] = **you are** *s.* **be**

yours [jɔːz, *Am:* jʊrz] *poss pron* **1.** *no pl* (*belonging to you*) le tien, la tienne; **this glass is** ~ ce verre est à toi **2.** *pl or sing polite form* (*belonging to you*) le vôtre, la vôtre; **this glass is** ~ ce verre est à vous; *s. a.* **hers, ours**

yourself [jɔːˈself, *Am:* jʊrˈ-] *reflex pron* **1.** *after verbs* (*one person*) te, t + *vowel;* (*polite form*) vous **2.** (*you*) toi-même; (*polite form*) vous-même; *s.* **myself**

yourselves *reflex pron* **1.** *after verbs* (*several persons*) vous; **you hurt** ~ vous vous êtes blessés **2.** (*you*) vous-mêmes; *s. a.* **myself**

youth [juːθ] *n* **1.** *no pl* (*period when young*) jeunesse *f* **2.** (*young man*) jeune homme *m* **3.** *no pl* (*young people*) **the** ~ les jeunes *mpl;* ~ **unemployment** chômage *m* des jeunes

youthful [ˈjuːθfl] *adj* **1.** (*young*) jeune **2.** (*young-looking*) jeune; **to look** ~ avoir l'air jeune **3.** (*typical of the young*) de jeunesse; (*enthusiasm*) juvénile

youth hostel *n* auberge *f* de jeunesse

you've [juːv] = **you have** *s.* **have**

yowl [jaʊl] **I.** *vi* hurler; (*cat*) miauler **II.** *n* hurlement *m;* (*of a cat*) miaulement *m*

yo-yo® [ˈjəʊjəʊ, *Am:* ˈjoʊjoʊ] **I.** *n* (*toy*) yo-yo *m inv* **II.** *vi* fluctuer

yr[1] *pron abbr of* **your** ton, ta

yr[2] *n abbr of* **year** année *f*

yuan *n* yuan *m*

yucky [ˈjʌkɪ] <-ier, -iest> *adj* dégoûtant(e)

Yugoslav [ˈjuːgəʊˈslɑːv, *Am:* ˈjuːgoʊslɑːv] *adj, n* Yougoslave *mf*

Yugoslavia [ˈjuːgəʊˈslɑːvɪə, *Am:* -goʊˈ-] *n* la Yougoslavie; **Federal Republic of** ~ République fédérale de Yougoslavie

Yugoslavian [ˈjuːgəʊˈ slɑːvɪən, *Am:* -goʊˈ-] *adj* yougoslave

yukky [ˈjʌkɪ] <-ier, -iest> *adj s.* **yucky**

Yukon Territory *n* le Territoire du Yukon

yummy [ˈjʌmi] <-ier, -iest> *adj inf* **1.** (*delicious*) délicieux(-euse) **2.** (*sexy*) sexy *inv*

yum-yum [ˌjʌmˈjʌm] *interj inf* miam-miam!

yuppie [ˈjʌpɪ] *n* yuppie *m*

YWCA [ˌwaɪˌdʌbljuːsiːˈeɪ] *n abbr of* **Young Women's Christian Association** **1.** (*movement*) Union *f* chrétienne de jeunes femmes **2.** (*hostel*) foyer *m* pour jeunes femmes

Z

Z, z [zed, *Am:* ziː] <-'s> *n* Z *m,* z *m;* ~ **as in Zebra,** ~ **for Zebra** (*on telephone*) z comme Zoé ►**to know sth from a to** ~ connaître qc de A à Z; **to catch some** ~**'s** *Am, inf* se pieuter

Zaire [zɑːˈiːə, *Am:* -ˈɪr] *n* HIST le Zaïre

Zairean [zɑːˈiːərən, *Am:* -ˈɪr-] HIST **I.** *adj* zaïrois(e) **II.** *n* Zaïrois(e) *m(f)*

Zambia [ˈzæmbɪə] *n* la Zambie

Zambian [ˈzæmbɪən] **I.** *adj* zambien(ne) **II.** *n* Zambien(ne) *m(f)*

zany [ˈzeɪnɪ] <-ier, -iest> *adj inf* loufoque

zap [zæp] **I.** <-pp-> *vt* **1.** *inf* (*destroy: object*) détruire; (*person*) éliminer **2.** *inf* (*send fast*) expédier **II.** <-pp-> *vi* **1.** *inf* (*go*) foncer; **to** ~ **into town** faire un saut en ville; **to** ~ **through sth** se dépêcher de faire qc **2.** *inf* TV **to** ~ **between channels** zapper d'une chaîne à l'autre **III.** *n no pl, Am, inf* (*energy*) punch *m;* **to put** ~ **into sth** mettre du punch dans qc

zapping [zæpɪŋ] *n inf* zapping *m*

zeal [ziːl] *n no pl* zèle *m*

zealot [ˈzelət] *n pej* fanatique *mf*

zealous [ˈzeləs] *adj* zélé(e); **to be** ~ **in doing sth** faire qc avec ferveur

zebra [ˈziːbrə] <-(bras)> *n* zèbre *m*

zebra crossing *n Brit, Aus* passage *m* piétons

zenith [ˈzenɪθ, *Am:* ˈziːnɪθ] *n a. fig* zénith *m*

zero [ˈzɪərəʊ, *Am:* ˈzɪroʊ] **I.** *adj* **1.** (*number*) zéro **2.** (*nil*) nul(le); ~ **hour** MIL heure *f* H; ~ **growth** croissance *f* nulle; **at** ~ **extra cost** sans dépenses supplémentaires **II.** *vi* **1.** MIL **to** ~ **in on** régler le tir **2.** (*focus on*) **to** ~ **in on** cibler

zero-rated *adj* ~ **for VAT** exempt(e) de TVA

zest [zest] *n no pl* **1.** *no indef art* (*enthusiastic energy*) entrain *m* **2.** GASTR zeste *m*

zigzag [ˈzɪgzæg] **I.** *n* (*crooked line*) zigzag *m* **II.** *adj* (*crooked*) en zigzag **III.** <-gg-> *vi* zigzaguer

zilch [zɪltʃ] *n inf* zéro *m*

Zimbabwe [zɪmˈbɑːbwɪ] *n* le Zimbabwe

Zimbabwean [zɪmˈbɑːbwɪən] **I.** *adj* zimbabwéen(ne) **II.** *n* Zimbabwéen(ne) *m(f)*

zinc [zɪŋk] *n no pl, no indef art* zinc *m*

zip [zɪp] **I.** *n* **1.** *Brit* (*fastener*) fermeture *f* éclair®, tirette *f Belgique;* **to do up a** ~ ouvrir une fermeture éclair **2.** *no pl, inf* (*vigour*) punch *m* **II.** *pron Am, inf* (*nothing*) que dalle; **to know ~ about sth** ne rien savoir de qc **III.** <-pp-> *vt* **to ~ a bag** fermer un sac **IV.** <-pp-> *vi inf* (*go quickly*) **to ~ somewhere** passer quelque part; **to ~ past** passer devant

◆**zip up I.** *vt* **1.** (*close*) fermer **2.** INFOR zipper **II.** *vi* (*close with a zip*) se fermer avec une fermeture éclair

zip archive *n* archive *f* zip **zip code**, **ZIP code** *n Am* ≈ code *m* postal **zip fastener** *n Brit s.* **zip** **zip file** *n* INFOR dossier *m* zip

zipper *n Am, Aus s.* **zip**

zippy ['zɪpɪ] <-ier, -iest> *adj inf* plein(e) de punch; (*car*) nerveux(-euse)

zither ['zɪðəʳ, *Am:* -ɚ] *n* cithare *f*

zloty ['zlɒti, *Am:* 'zlɔːt̬i] *n* zloty *m*

zodiac ['zəʊdɪæk, *Am:* 'zoʊ-] *n* zodiaque *m*

zombie ['zɒmbɪ, *Am:* 'zɑːm-] *n a. pej* zombie *m*

zonal ['zəʊnl, *Am:* 'zoʊ-] *adj* zonal(e)

zone [zəʊn, *Am:* zoʊn] **I.** *n* zone *f;* **combat ~** zone de combat; **time ~** fuseau *m* horaire; **no-parking ~** stationnement *m* interdit **II.** *vt* réserver

zoning *n no pl* zonage *m*

zoo [zuː] *n* zoo *m*

zoological [ˌzəʊə'lɒdʒɪkl, *Am:* ˌzoʊə'lɑːdʒɪ-] *adj* zoologique *m*

zoologist [zəʊ'ɒlədʒɪst, *Am:* zoʊ'ɑːlə-] *n* zoologiste *mf*

zoology [zəʊ'ɒlədʒɪ, *Am:* zoʊ'ɑːlə-] *n no pl* zoologie *f*

zoom [zuːm] **I.** *n* PHOT zoom *m;* **a ~ lens** un zoom **II.** *vi inf* **1.** *inf* (*move very fast*) passer à toute vitesse; **to ~ past** passer si vite **2.** (*increase dramatically*) monter en flèche **3.** PHOT, CINE zoomer

◆**zoom in** *vi* CINE, PHOT faire un zoom avant; **to ~ on sth** *fig* faire un zoom avant sur qc

◆**zoom off** *vi* partir en trombe

zucchini [zu'kiːnɪ, *Am:* zuː'-] <-(s)> *n Am, Aus* GASTR *s.* **courgette**

Supplément II

Supplement II

Verbes français
French verbs

Pour des raisons d'économie de place dans la partie dictionnaire, certains verbes sont suivis d'un chiffre entre chevrons qui renvoie à un des 14 tableaux de conjugaison à utiliser comme modèle. Le symbole *irr* renvoie à la liste alphabétique des verbes présentant de nombreuses irrégularités. Cette liste se trouve à la suite des tableaux.

To save space in the main part of the dictionary, some verbs are followed by angle brackets which contain a number referring to one of the fourteen model verbs, others are followed by *irr*, indicating one of the irregular verbs listed alphabetically after the model verbs.

1 chanter

présent	imparfait	futur simple	passé simple
je chante	je chantais	je chanterai	je chantai
tu chantes	tu chantais	tu chanteras	tu chantas
il/elle chante	il/elle chantait	il/elle chantera	il/elle chanta
nous chantons	nous chantions	nous chanterons	nous chantâmes
vous chantez	vous chantiez	vous chanterez	vous chantâtes
ils/elles chantent	ils/elles chantaient	ils/elles chanteront	il/elles chantèrent

conditionnel présent	subjonctif présent	subjonctif imparfait	
je chanterais	que je chante	que je chantasse	
tu chanterais	que tu chantes	que tu chantasses	
il/elle chanterait	qu'il/elle chante	qu'il/elle chantât	
nous chanterions	que nous chantions	que nous chantassions	
vous chanteriez	que vous chantiez	que vous chantassiez	
ils/elles chanteraient	qu'ils/elles chantent	qu'ils/elles chantassent	

participe présent	participe passé	impératif présent	impératif passé
chantant	chanté	chante	aie chanté
		chantons	ayons chanté
		chantez	ayez chanté

2 commencer

présent	imparfait	futur simple	passé simple
je commence	je commençais	je commencerai …	je commençai
tu commences	tu commençais		tu commenças
il/elle commence	il/elle commençait		il/elle commença
nous commençons	nous commencions		nous commençâmes
vous commencez	vous commenciez		vous commençâtes
ils/elles commencent	ils/elles commençaient		ils/elles commencèrent

conditionnel présent	subjonctif présent	subjonctif imparfait	
je commencerais …	que je commence	que je commençasse	
	que tu commences	que tu commençasses	
	qu'il/elle commence	qu'il/elle commençât	
	que nous commencions	que nous commençassions	
	que vous commenciez	que vous commençassiez	
	qu'ils/elles commencent	qu'ils/elles commençassent	

participe présent	participe passé	impératif présent	impératif passé
commençant	commencé	commence commençons commencez	aie commencé ayons commencé ayez commencé

2a changer

présent	imparfait	futur simple	passé simple
je change tu changes il/elle change nous changeons vous changez ils/elles changent	je changeais tu changeais il/elle changeait nous changions vous changiez ils/elles changeaient	je changerai …	je changeai tu changeas il/elle changea nous changeâmes vous changeâtes ils/elles changèrent

conditionnel présent	subjonctif présent	subjonctif imparfait	
je changerais …	que je change que tu changes qu'il/elle change que nous changions que vous changiez qu'ils/elles changent	que je changeasse que tu changeasses qu'il/elle changeât que nous changeassions que vous changeassiez qu'ils/elles changeassent	

participe présent	participe passé	impératif présent	impératif passé
changeant	changé	change changeons changez	aie changé ayons changé ayez changé

3 rejeter

présent	imparfait	futur simple	passé simple
je rejette tu rejettes il/elle rejette nous rejetons vous rejetez ils/elles rejettent	je rejetais …	je rejetterai …	je rejetai …

conditionnel présent	subjonctif présent	subjonctif imparfait	
je rejetterais …	que je rejette que tu rejettes qu'il/elle rejette que nous rejetions que vous rejetiez qu'ils/elles rejettent	que je rejetasse …	

participe présent	participe passé	impératif présent	impératif passé
rejetant	rejeté	rejette rejetons rejetez	aie rejeté ayons rejeté ayez rejeté

4 peler

présent	imparfait	futur simple	passé simple
je pèle tu pèles il/elle pèle nous pelons vous pelez ils/elles pèlent	je pelais …	je pèlerai tu pèleras il/elle pèlera nous pèlerons vous pèlerez ils/elles pèleront	je pelai …

conditionnel présent	subjonctif présent	subjonctif imparfait	
je pèlerais tu pèlerais il/elle pèlerait nous pèlerions vous pèleriez ils/elles pèleraient	que je pèle que tu pèles qu'il/elle pèle que nous pelions que vous peliez qu'ils/elles pèlent	que je pelasse …	

participe présent	participe passé	impératif présent	impératif passé
pelant	pelé	pèle pelons pelez	aie pelé ayons pelé ayez pelé

5 préférer

présent	imparfait	futur simple	passé simple
je préfère tu préfères il/elle préfère nous préférons vous préférez ils/elles préfèrent	je préférais …	je préférerai …	je préférai …

conditionnel présent	subjonctif présent	subjonctif imparfait	
je préférerais …	que je préfère que tu préfères qu'il/elle préfère que nous préférions que vous préfériez qu'ils/elles préfèrent	que je préférasse …	

participe présent	participe passé	impératif présent	impératif passé
préférant	préféré	préfère préférons préférez	aie préféré ayons préféré ayez préféré

6 appuyer

présent	imparfait	futur simple	passé simple
j'appuie tu appuies il/elle appuie nous appuyons vous appuyez ils/elles appuient	j'appuyais ...	j'appuierai ...	j'appuyai ...
conditionnel présent	**subjonctif présent**	**subjonctif imparfait**	
j'appuierais ...	que j'appuie que tu appuies qu'il/elle appuie que nous appuyions que vous appuyiez qu'ils/elles appuient	que j'appuyasse ...	
participe présent	**participe passé**	**impératif présent**	**impératif passé**
appuyant	appuyé	appuie appuyons appuyez	aie appuyé ayons appuyé ayez appuyé

7 essayer

présent	imparfait	futur simple	passé simple
j'essaie/essaye tu essaies/essayes il/elle essaie/essaye nous essayons vous essayez ils/elles essaient/ essayent	j'essayais ...	j'essaierai/essayerai ...	j'essayai ...
conditionnel présent	**subjonctif présent**	**subjonctif imparfait**	
j'essaierais/essayerais ...	que j'essaie/essaye que tu essaies/essayes qu'il/elle essaie/essaye que nous essayions que vous essayiez qu'ils/elles essaient/ essayent	que j'essayasse ...	
participe présent	**participe passé**	**impératif présent**	**impératif passé**
essayant	essayé	essaie/essaye essayons essayez	aie essayé ayons essayé ayez essayé

8 agir

présent	imparfait	futur simple	passé simple
j'agis tu agis il/elle agit nous agissons vous agissez ils/elles agissent	j'agissais tu agissais il/elle agissait nous agissions vous agissiez ils/elles agissaient	j'agirai tu agiras il/elle agira nous agirons vous agirez ils/elles agiront	j'agis tu agis il/elle agit nous agîmes vous agîtes ils/elles agirent

conditionnel présent	subjonctif présent	subjonctif imparfait	
j'agirais …	que j'agisse que tu agisses qu'il/elle agisse que nous agissions que vous agissiez qu'ils/elles agissent	que j'agisse que tu agisses qu'il/elle agît que nous agissions que vous agissiez qu'ils/elles agissent	

participe présent	participe passé	impératif présent	impératif passé
agissant	agi	agis agissons agissez	aie agi ayons agi ayez agi

9 devenir

présent	imparfait	futur simple	passé simple
je deviens tu deviens il/elle devient nous devenons vous devenez ils/elles deviennent	je devenais …	je deviendrai tu deviendras il/elle deviendra nous deviendrons vous deviendrez ils/elles deviendront	je devins tu devins il/elle devint nous devînmes vous devîntes ils/elles devinrent

conditionnel présent	subjonctif présent	subjonctif imparfait	
je deviendrais …	que je devienne que tu deviennes qu'il/elle devienne que nous devenions que vous deveniez qu'ils/elles deviennent	que je devinsse que tu devinsses qu'il/elle devînt que nous devinssions que vous devinssiez qu'ils/elles devinssent	

participe présent	participe passé	impératif présent	impératif passé
devenant	devenu	deviens devenons devenez	sois devenu soyons devenus soyez devenus

10 sortir

présent	imparfait	futur simple	passé simple
je sors tu sors il/elle sort nous sortons vous sortez ils/elles sortent	je sortais …	je sortirai …	je sortis…

conditionnel présent	subjonctif présent	subjonctif imparfait	
je sortirais …	que je sorte que tu sortes qu'il/elle sorte que nous sortions que vous sortiez qu'ils/elles sortent	que je sortisse …	

participe présent	participe passé	impératif présent	impératif passé
sortant	sorti	sors sortons sortez	sois sorti soyons sortis soyez sortis

11 ouvrir

présent	imparfait	futur simple	passé simple
j'ouvre tu ouvres il/elle ouvre nous ouvrons vous ouvrez ils/elles ouvrent	j'ouvrais …	j'ouvrirai …	j'ouvris …

conditionnel présent	subjonctif présent	subjonctif imparfait	
j'ouvrirais …	que j'ouvre que tu ouvres qu'il/elle ouvre que nous ouvrions que vous ouvriez qu'ils/elles ouvrent	que j'ouvrisse …	

participe présent	participe passé	impératif présent	impératif passé
ouvrant	ouvert	ouvre ouvrons ouvrez	aie ouvert ayons ouvert ayez ouvert

12 apercevoir

présent	imparfait	futur simple	passé simple
j'aperçois tu aperçois il/elle aperçoit nous apercevons vous apercevez ils/elles aperçoivent	j'apercevais ...	j'apercevrai ...	j'aperçus tu aperçus il/elle aperçut nous aperçûmes vous aperçûtes ils/elles aperçurent

conditionnel présent	subjonctif présent	subjonctif imparfait	
j'apercevrais ...	que j'aperçoive que tu aperçoives qu'il/elle aperçoive que nous apercevions que vous aperceviez qu'ils/elles aperçoivent	que j'aperçusse que tu aperçusses qu'il/elle aperçût que nous aperçussions que vous aperçussiez qu'ils/elles aperçussent	

participe présent	participe passé	impératif présent	impératif passé
apercevant	aperçu	aperçois apercevons apercevez	aie aperçu ayons aperçu ayez aperçu

13 comprendre

présent	imparfait	futur simple	passé simple
je comprends tu comprends il/elle comprend nous comprenons vous comprenez ils/elles comprennent	je comprenais tu comprenais il/elle comprenait nous comprenions vous compreniez ils/elles comprenaient	je comprendrai tu comprendras il/elle comprendra nous comprendrons vous comprendrez ils/elles comprendront	je compris tu compris il/elle comprit nous comprîmes vous comprîtes ils/elles comprirent

conditionnel présent	subjonctif présent	subjonctif imparfait	
je comprendrais ...	que je comprenne que tu comprennes qu'il/elle comprenne que nous comprenions que vous compreniez qu'ils/elles comprennent	que je comprisse que tu comprisses qu'il/elle comprît que nous comprissions que vous comprissiez qu'ils/elles comprissent	

participe présent	participe passé	impératif présent	impératif passé
comprenant	compris	comprends comprenons comprenez	aie compris ayons compris ayez compris

14 vendre

présent	imparfait	futur simple	passé simple
je vends tu vends il/elle vend nous vendons vous vendez ils/elles vendent	je vendais tu vendais il/elle vendait nous vendions vous vendiez ils/elles vendaient	je vendrai …	je vendis tu vendis il/elle vendit nous vendîmes vous vendîtes ils/elles vendirent
conditionnel présent	**subjonctif présent**	**subjonctif imparfait**	
je vendrais …	que je vende que tu vendes qu'il/elle vende que nous vendions que vous vendiez qu'ils/elles vendent	que je vendisse …	
participe présent	**participe passé**	**impératif présent**	**impératif passé**
vendant	vendu	vends vendons vendez	aie vendu ayons vendu ayez vendu

Infinitif	Présent	Imparfait	Futur	Passé simple	Subjonctif présent	Subjonctif imparfait	Part. présent	Part. passé
abattre *voir battre*		**abstraire** *voir extraire*		**accourir** *voir courir*				
accroître	j'accrois	j'accroissais	j'accroîtrai	j'accrus	que j'accroisse	que j'accrusse	accroissant	accru(e)
	il accroît	il accroît	il accroîtra	il accrut	qu'il accroisse	qu'il accrût		
	nous accroissons	nous accroissions	nous accroîtrons	nous accrûmes	que nous accroissions	que nous accrussions		
	ils accroissent	ils accroissaient	ils accroîtront	ils accrurent	qu'ils accroissent	qu'ils accrussent		
accueillir *voir cueillir*								
acquérir	j'acquiers	j'acquérais	j'acquerrai	j'acquis	que j'acquière	que j'acquisse	acquérant	acquis(e)
	il acquiert	il acquérait	il acquerra	il acquit	qu'il acquière	qu'il acquît		
	nous acquérons	nous acquérions	nous acquerrons	nous acquîmes	que nous acquérions	que nous acquissions		
	ils acquièrent	ils acquéraient	ils acquerront	ils acquirent	qu'ils acquièrent	qu'ils acquissent		
adjoindre *voir joindre*		**admettre** *voir mettre*						
aller	je vais	j'allais	j'irai	j'allai	que j'aille	que j'allasse	allant	allé(e)
	tu vas	tu allais	tu iras	tu allas	que tu ailles	que tu allasses		
	il va	il allait	il ira	il alla	qu'il aille	qu'il allasse		
	nous allons	nous allions	nous irons	nous allâmes	que nous allions	que nous allassions		
	vous allez	vous alliez	vous irez	vous allâtes	que vous alliez	que vous allassiez		
	ils vont	ils allaient	ils iront	ils allèrent	qu'ils aillent	qu'ils allassent		
apparaître *voir paraître*		**assaillir** *voir défaillir*						

Infinitif	Présent	Imparfait	Futur	Passé simple	Subjonctif présent	Subjonctif imparfait	Part. présent	Part. passé
asseoir	j'assieds	j'asseyais	j'assiérai	j'assis	que j'asseye	que j'assisse	asseyant	assis(e)
	il assied	il asseyait	il assiéra	il assit	qu'il asseye	qu'il assît	*o* assoyant	
	nous asseyons	nous asseyions	nous assiérons	nous assîmes	que nous asseyions	que nous assissions		
	ils asseyent	ils asseyaient	ils assiéront	ils assirent	qu'ils asseyent	qu'ils assissent		
	o j'assois	*o* j'assoyais	*o* j'assoirai		*o* que j'assoie			
	il assoit	il assoyait	il assoira		qu'il assoie			
	nous assoyons	nous assoyions	nous assoirons		que nous assoyions			
	ils assoient	ils assoyaient	ils assoiront		qu'ils assoient			

astreindre *voir peindre* **atteindre** *voir peindre* **autodétruire** *voir conduire*

Infinitif	Présent	Imparfait	Futur	Passé simple	Subjonctif présent	Subjonctif imparfait	Part. présent	Part. passé
avoir	j'ai	j'avais	j'aurai	j'eus	que j'aie	que j'eusse	ayant	eu(e)
	tu as	tu avais	tu auras	tu eus	que tu aies	que tu eusses		
	il a	il avait	il aura	il eut	qu'il ait	qu'il eût		
	nous avons	nous avions	nous aurons	nous eûmes	que nous ayons	que nous eussions		
	vous avez	vous aviez	vous aurez	vous eûtes	que vous ayez	que vous eussiez		
	ils ont	ils avaient	ils auront	ils eurent	qu'ils aient	qu'ils eussent		
battre	je bats	je battais	je battrai	je battis	que je batte	que je battisse	battant	battu(e)
	il bat	il battait	il battra	il battit	qu'il batte	qu'il battît		
	nous battons	nous battions	nous battrons	nous battîmes	que nous battions	que nous battissions		
	ils battent	ils battaient	ils battront	ils battirent	qu'ils battent	qu'ils battissent		
boire	je bois	je buvais	je boirai	je bus	que je boive	que je busse	buvant	bu(e)
	il boit	il buvait	il boira	il but	qu'il boive	qu'il bût		
	nous buvons	nous buvions	nous boirons	nous bûmes	que nous buvions	que nous bussions		
	ils boivent	ils buvaient	ils boiront	ils burent	qu'ils boivent	qu'ils bussent		
bouillir	je bous	je bouillais	je bouillirai	je bouillis	que je bouille	que je bouillisse	bouillant	bouilli(e)
	nous bouillons	nous bouillions	nous bouillirons	nous bouillîmes	que nous bouillions	que nous bouillissions		
	ils bouillent	ils bouillaient	ils bouilliront	ils bouillirent	qu'ils bouillent	qu'ils bouillissent		

Infinitif	Présent	Imparfait	Futur	Passé simple	Subjonctif présent	Subjonctif imparfait	Part. présent	Part. passé
braire *voir extraire*								
bruire	il bruit	il bruissait	*manque*	*manque*	qu'il bruisse	*manque*	bruissant	*manque*
	nous/vous manque							
	ils bruissent							
ceindre *voir peindre*								
choir	je chois	*manque*	je choirai *o* cherrai	je chus	*manque*	*seulement :*	*manque*	chu(e)
	il choit			il chut		qu'il chût		
	nous/vous manque			nous chûmes				
	ils choient		ils choiront *o* cherront	ils churent				
circonscrire *voir écrire*		**circonvenir** *voir venir*						
clore	je clos	*manque*	je clorai	*manque*	que je close	*manque*	closant	clos(e)
	il clôt		il clora		qu'il close			
	nous closons		nous clorons		que nous closions			
	ils closent		ils cloront		qu'ils closent			
combattre *voir battre*		**commettre** *voir mettre*		**comparaître** *voir paraître*		**complaire** *voir plaire*	**compromettre** *voir mettre*	
conclure	je conclus	je concluais	je conclurai	je conclus	que je conclue	que je conclusse	concluant	conclu(e)
concourir *voir courir*								
conduire	je conduis	je conduisais	je conduirai	je conduisis	que je conduise	que je conduisisse	conduisant	conduit(e)
connaître *voir paraître*		**conquérir** *voir acquérir*		**construire** *voir conduire*		**contraindre** *voir craindre*		

Infinitif	Présent	Imparfait	Futur	Passé simple	Subjonctif présent	Subjonctif imparfait	Part. présent	Part. passé
contredire *voir dire*		**contrefaire** *voir faire*		**convaincre** *voir vaincre*		**corrompre** *voir rompre*		
coudre	je couds	je cousais	je coudrai	je cousis	que je couse	que je cousisse	cousant	cousu(e)
	il coud	il cousait	il coudra	il cousit	qu'il couse	qu'il cousît		
	nous cousons	nous cousions	nous coudrons	nous cousîmes	que nous cousions	que nous cousissions		
	ils cousent	ils cousaient	ils coudront	ils cousirent	qu'ils cousent	qu'ils cousissent		
courir	je cours	je courais	je courrai	je courus	que je coure	que je courusse	courant	couru(e)
	il court	il courait	il courra	il courut	qu'il coure	qu'il courût		
	nous courons	nous courions	nous courrons	nous courûmes	que nous courions	que nous courussions		
	ils courent	ils couraient	ils courront	ils coururent	qu'ils courent	qu'ils courussent		
craindre	je crains	je craignais	je craindrai	je craignis	que je craigne	que je craignisse	craignant	craint(e)
	nous craignons	nous craignions	nous craindrons	nous craignîmes	que nous craignions	que nous craignissions		
	ils craignent	ils craignaient	ils craindront	ils craignirent	qu'ils craignent	qu'ils craignissent		
croire	je crois	je croyais	je croirai	je crus	que je croie	que je crusse	croyant	cru(e)
	il croit	il croyait	il croira	il crut	qu'il croie	qu'il crût		
	nous croyons	nous croyions	nous croirons	nous crûmes	que nous croyions	que nous crussions		
	ils croient	ils croyaient	ils croiront	ils crurent	qu'ils croient	qu'ils crussent		
croître	je croîs	je croissais	je croîtrai	je crûs	que je croisse	que je crûsse	croissant	crû, crue, cru(e)s
	nous croissons	nous croissions	nous croîtrons	nous crûmes	que nous croissions	que nous crûssions		
	ils croissent	ils croissaient	ils croîtront	ils crûrent	qu'ils croissent	qu'ils crûssent		
cueillir	je cueille	je cueillais	je cueillerai	je cueillis	que je cueille	que je cueillisse	cueillant	cueilli(e)
	il cueille	il cueillait	il cueillera	il cueillit	qu'il cueille	qu'il cueillît		
	nous cueillons	nous cueillions	nous cueillerons	nous cueillîmes	que nous cueillions	que nous cueillissions		
	ils cueillent	ils cueillaient	ils cueilleront	ils cueillirent	qu'ils cueillent	qu'ils cueillissent		
cuire *voir conduire*		**débattre** *voir battre*						

Infinitif	Présent	Imparfait	Futur	Passé simple	Subjonctif présent	Subjonctif imparfait	Part. présent	Part. passé
déchoir	je déchois	*manque*	je déchoirai	je déchus	que je déchoie	que je déchusse	*manque*	déchu(e)
	nous déchoyons		nous déchoirons	nous déchûmes	que nous déchoyions	que nous déchussions		
	ils déchoient		ils déchoiront	ils déchurent	qu'ils déchoient	qu'ils déchussent		
découdre *voir coudre*		**décrire** *voir écrire*		**décroître** *voir accroître*		**dédire** *voir contredire*	**déduire** *voir conduire*	
défaillir	je défaille	je défaillais	je défaillirai	je défaillis	que je défaille	que je défaillisse	défaillant	défailli
défaire *voir faire*		**démettre** *voir mettre*		**dépeindre** *voir peindre*		**déplaire** *voir plaire*		
desservir *voir servir*		**déteindre** *voir peindre*		**détruire** *voir conduire*		**dévêtir** *voir vêtir*		
devoir	je dois	je devais	je devrai	je dus	que je doive	que je dusse	devant	dû, due, du(e)s
	il doit	il devait	il devra	il dut	qu'il doive	qu'il dût		
	nous devons	nous devions	nous devrons	nous dûmes	que nous devions	que nous dussions		
	ils doivent	ils devaient	ils devront	ils durent	qu'ils doivent	qu'ils dussent		
dire	je dis	je disais	je dirai	je dis	que je dise	que je disse	disant	dit(e)
	nous disons	nous disions	nous dirons	nous dîmes	que nous disions	que nous dissions		
	vous dites	vous disiez	vous direz	vous dîtes	que vous disiez	que vous dissiez		
	ils disent	ils disaient	ils diront	ils dirent	qu'ils disent	qu'ils dissent		
discourir *voir courir*		**disjoindre** *voir joindre*		**disparaître** *voir paraître*		**dissoudre** *voir absoudre*	**distraire** *voir extraire*	
dormir	je dors	je dormais	je dormirai	je dormis	que je dorme	que je dormisse	dormant	dormi
	nous dormons	nous dormions	nous dormirons	nous dormîmes	que nous dormions	que nous dormissions		
	ils dorment	ils dormaient	ils dormiront	ils dormirent	qu'ils dorment	qu'ils dormissent		
ébattre *voir battre*								

Infinitif	Présent	Imparfait	Futur	Passé simple	Subjonctif présent	Subjonctif imparfait	Part. présent	Part. passé
échoir	il échoit	il échoyait	il échoira *o* écherra	il échut	qu'il échoit	qu'il échût	échéant	échu(e)
	ils échoient	ils échoyaient	ils échoiront *o* écherront	ils échurent	qu'ils échoient	qu'ils échussent		

éclore *voir clore* **éconduire** *voir conduire*

Infinitif	Présent	Imparfait	Futur	Passé simple	Subjonctif présent	Subjonctif imparfait	Part. présent	Part. passé
écrire	j'écris	j'écrivais	j'écrirai	j'écrivis	que j'écrive	que j'écrivisse	écrivant	écrit(e)
	il écrit	il écrivait	il écrira	il écrivit	qu'il écrive	qu'il écrivît		
	nous écrivons	nous écrivions	nous écrirons	nous écrivîmes	que nous écrivions	que nous écrivissions		
	ils écrivent	ils écrivaient	ils écriront	ils écrivirent	qu'ils écrivent	qu'ils écrivissent		

élire *voir lire* **émettre** *voir mettre*
émouvoir *voir mouvoir, participe passé:* ému(e)
enclore *voir clore* **encourir** *voir courir* **endormir** *voir dormir* **enduire** *voir conduire*
enfreindre *voir peindre* **enfuir** *voir fuir* **ensuivre** *voir suivre* **entrevoir** *voir voir*

Infinitif	Présent	Imparfait	Futur	Passé simple	Subjonctif présent	Subjonctif imparfait	Part. présent	Part. passé
envoyer	j'envoie	j'envoyais	j'enverrai	j'envoyai	que j'envoie	que j'envoyasse	envoyant	envoyé(e)
	nous envoyons	nous envoyions	nous enverrons	nous envoyâmes	que nous envoyions	que nous envoyassions		
	ils envoient	ils envoyaient	ils enverront	ils envoyèrent	qu'ils envoient	qu'ils envoyassent		

équivaloir *voir valoir* **éteindre** *voir peindre*

Infinitif	Présent	Imparfait	Futur	Passé simple	Subjonctif présent	Subjonctif imparfait	Part. présent	Part. passé
être	je suis	j'étais	je serai	je fus	que je sois	que je fusse	étant	été
	tu es	tu étais	tu seras	tu fus	que tu sois	que tu fusses		
	il est	il était	il sera	il fut	qu'il soit	qu'il fût		
	nous sommes	nous étions	nous serons	nous fûmes	que nous soyons	que nous fussions		
	vous êtes	vous étiez	vous serez	vous fûtes	que vous soyez	que vous fussiez		
	ils sont	ils étaient	ils seront	ils furent	qu'ils soient	qu'ils fussent		

étreindre *voir peindre*

Infinitif	Présent	Imparfait	Futur	Passé simple	Subjonctif présent	Subjonctif imparfait	Part. présent	Part. passé
exclure	j'exclus	j'excluais	j'exclurai	j'exclus	que j'exclue	que j'exclusse	excluant	exclu(e)
	il exclut	il excluait	il exclura	il exclut	qu'il exclue	qu'il exclût		
	nous excluons	nous excluions	nous exclurons	nous exclûmes	que nous excluions	que nous exclussions		
	ils excluent	ils excluaient	ils excluront	ils exclurent	qu'ils excluent	qu'ils exclussent		
extraire	j'extrais	j'extrayais	j'extrairai	*manque*	que j'extraie	*manque*	extrayant	extrait(e)
	nous extrayons	nous extrayions	nous extrairons		que nous extrayions			
	ils extraient	ils extrayaient	ils extrairont		qu'ils extraient			
faillir	je faillis	je faillissais	je faillirai	je faillis	que je faillisse	que je faillisse	faillissant *o*	failli
	nous faillissons	nous faillissions	nous faillirons	nous faillîmes	que nous faillissions	que nous faillissions	faillant	
	ils faillissent	ils faillissaient *o* je faillais	ils failliront *o* je faudrai	ils faillirent	qu'ils faillissent *o* que je faille	qu'ils faillissent		
		nous faillions	nous faudrons		que nous faillions			
		ils faillaient	ils faudront		qu'ils faillent			
faire	je fais	je faisais	je ferai	je fis	que je fasse	que je fisse	faisant	fait(e)
	tu fais	tu faisais	tu feras	tu fis	que tu fasses	que tu fisses		
	il fait	il faisait	il fera	il fit	qu'il fasse	qu'il fît		
	nous faisons	nous faisions	nous ferons	nous fîmes	que nous fassions	que nous fissions		
	vous faites	vous faisiez	vous ferez	vous fîtes	que vous fassiez	que vous fissiez		
	ils font	ils faisaient	ils feront	ils firent	qu'ils fassent	qu'ils fissent		
falloir	il faut	il fallait	il faudra	il fallut	qu'il faille	qu'il fallût	*manque*	fallu
feindre *voir peindre*								
frire	je fris	*manque*	je frirai	*manque*	*manque*	*manque*	*manque*	frit(e)
	nous/vous manque		nous frirons					
	ils manque		ils friront					

Infinitif	Présent	Imparfait	Futur	Passé simple	Subjonctif présent	Subjonctif imparfait	Part. présent	Part. passé
fuir	je fuis	je fuyais	je fuirai	je fuis	que je fuie	que je fuisse	fuyant	fui(e)
	il fuit	il fuyait	il fuira	il fuit	qu'il fuie	qu'il fuît		
	nous fuyons	nous fuyions	nous fuirons	nous fuîmes	que nous fuyions	que nous fuissions		
	ils fuient	ils fuyaient	ils fuiront	ils fuirent	qu'ils fuient	qu'ils fuissent		
geindre *voir peindre*								
haïr	je hais	je haïssais	je haïrai	je haïs	que je haïsse	que je haïsse	haïssant	haï(e)
	il hait	il haïssait	il haïra	il haït	qu'il haïsse	qu'il haït		
	nous haïssons	nous haïssions	nous haïrons	nous haïmes	que nous haïssions	que nous haïssions		
	ils haïssent	ils haïssaient	ils haïront	ils haïront	qu'ils haïssent	qu'ils haïssent		
inclure *voir conclure*		**induire** *voir conduire*		**inscrire** *voir écrire*		**instruire** *voir conduire*		
interdire *voir dire*		**interrompre** *voir rompre*		**introduire** *voir conduire*				
joindre	je joins	je joignais	je joindrai	je joignis	que je joigne	que je joignisse	joignant	joint(e)
	il joint	il joignait	il joindra	il joignit	qu'il joigne	qu'il joignît		
	nous joignons	nous joignions	nous joindrons	nous joignîmes	que nous joignions	que nous joignissions		
	ils joignent	ils joignaient	ils joindront	ils joignirent	qu'ils joignent	qu'ils joignissent		
lire	je lis	je lisais	je lirai	je lus	que je lise	que je lusse	lisant	lu(e)
	il lit	il lisait	il lira	il lut	qu'il lise	qu'il lût		
	nous lisons	nous lisions	nous lirons	nous lûmes	que nous lisions	que nous lussions		
	ils lisent	ils lisaient	ils liront	ils lurent	qu'ils lisent	qu'ils lussent		
luire *voir nuire*		**médire** *voir contredire*						
mettre	je mets	je mettais	je mettrai	je mis	que je mette	que je misse	mettant	mis(e)
	il met	il mettait	il mettra	il mit	qu'il mette	qu'il mît		
	nous mettons	nous mettions	nous mettrons	nous mîmes	que nous mettions	que nous missions		
	ils mettent	ils mettaient	ils mettront	ils mirent	qu'ils mettent	qu'ils missent		

Infinitif	Présent	Imparfait	Futur	Passé simple	Subjonctif présent	Subjonctif imparfait	Part. présent	Part. passé
moudre	je mouds	je moulais	je moudrai	je moulus	que je moule	que je moulusse	moulant	moulu(e)
	il moud	il moulait	il moudra	il moulut	qu'il moule	qu'il moulût		
	nous moulons	nous moulions	nous moudrons	nous moulûmes	que nous moulions	que nous moulussions		
	ils moulent	ils moulaient	ils moudront	ils moulurent	qu'ils moulent	qu'ils moulussent		
mourir	je meurs	je mourais	je mourrai	je mourus	que je meure	que je mourusse	mourant	mort(e)
	il meurt	il mourait	il mourra	il mourut	qu'il meure	qu'il mourût		
	nous mourons	nous mourions	nous mourrons	nous mourûmes	que nous mourions	que nous mourussions		
	ils meurent	ils mouraient	ils mourront	ils moururent	qu'ils meurent	qu'ils mourussent		
mouvoir	je meus	je mouvais	je mouvrai	je mus	que je meuve	que je musse	mouvant	mû, mue, mu(e)s
	il meut	il mouvait	il mouvra	il mut	qu'il meuve	qu'il mût		
	nous mouvons	nous mouvions	nous mouvrons	nous mûmes	que nous mouvions	que nous mussions		
	ils meuvent	ils mouvaient	ils mouvront	ils murent	qu'ils meuvent	qu'ils mussent		
naître	je nais	je naissais	je naîtrai	je naquis	que je naisse	que je naquisse	naissant	né(e)
	il naît	il naissait	il naîtra	il naquit	qu'il naisse	qu'il naquît		
	nous naissons	nous naissions	nous naîtrons	nous naquîmes	que nous naissions	que nous naquissions		
	ils naissent	ils naissaient	ils naîtront	ils naquirent	qu'ils naissent	qu'ils naquissent		
nuire	je nuis	je nuisais	je nuirai	je nuisis	que je nuise	que je nuisisse	nuisant	nui
	nous nuisons	nous nuisions	nous nuirons	nous nuisîmes	que nous nuisions	que nous nuisissions		
	ils nuisent	ils nuisaient	ils nuiront	ils nuisirent	qu'ils nuisent	qu'ils nuisissent		
omettre *voir mettre*		**paître** *voir paraître*						
paraître	je parais	je paraissais	je paraîtrai	je parus	que je paraisse	que je parusse	paraissant	paru(e)
	il paraît	il paraissait	il paraîtra	il parut	qu'il paraisse	qu'il parût		
	nous paraissons	nous paraissions	nous paraîtrons	nous parûmes	que nous paraissions	que nous parussions		
	ils paraissent	ils paraissaient	ils paraîtront	ils parurent	qu'ils paraissent	qu'ils parussent		

Infinitif	Présent	Imparfait	Futur	Passé simple	Subjonctif présent	Subjonctif imparfait	Part. présent	Part. passé
parcourir *voir courir*								
peindre	je peins	je peignais	je peindrai	je peignis	que je peigne	que je peignisse	peignant	peint(e)
	nous peignons	nous peignions	nous peindrons	nous peignîmes	que nous peignions	que nous peignissions		
	ils peignent	ils peignaient	ils peindront	ils peignirent	qu'ils peignent	qu'ils peignissent		
permettre *voir mettre*								
plaindre	je plains	je plaignais	je plaindrai	je plaignis	que je plaigne	que je plaignisse	plaignant	plaint(e)
	il plaint	il plaignait	il plaindra	il plaignit	qu'il plaigne	qu'il plaignît		
	nous plaignons	nous plaignions	nous plaindrons	nous plaignîmes	que nous plaignions	que nous plaignissions		
	ils plaignent	ils plaignaient	ils plaindront	ils plaignirent	qu'ils plaignent	qu'ils plaignissent		
plaire	je plais	je plaisais	je plairai	je plus	que je plaise	que je plusse	plaisant	plu
	il plaît	il plaisait	il plaira	il plut	qu'il plaise	qu'il plût		
pleuvoir	il pleut	il pleuvait	il pleuvra	il plut	qu'il pleuve	qu'il plût	pleuvant	plu
fig	ils pleuvent	ils pleuvaient	ils pleuvront	ils plurent	qu'ils pleuvent	qu'ils plussent		
poindre *voir joindre*		**poursuivre** *voir suivre*						
pourvoir	je pourvois	je pourvoyais	je pourvoirai	je pourvus	que je pourvoie	que je pourvusse	pourvoyant	pourvu(e)
	il pourvoit	il pourvoyait	il pourvoira	il pourvut	qu'il pourvoie	qu'il pourvût		
	nous pourvoyons	nous pourvoyions	nous pourvoirons	nous pourvûmes	que nous pourvoyions	que nous pourvussions		
	ils pourvoient	ils pourvoyaient	ils pourvoiront	ils pourvurent	qu'ils pourvoient	qu'ils pourvussent		
pouvoir	je peux	je pouvais	je pourrai	je pus	que je puisse	que je pusse	pouvant	pu
	il peut	il pouvait	il pourra	il put	qu'il puisse	qu'il pût		
	nous pouvons	nous pouvions	nous pourrons	nous pûmes	que nous puissions	que nous pussions		
	ils peuvent	ils pouvaient	ils pourront	ils purent	qu'ils puissent	qu'ils pussent		

Infinitif	Présent	Imparfait	Futur	Passé simple	Subjonctif présent	Subjonctif imparfait	Part. présent	Part. passé
prédire	je prédis	je prédisais	je prédirai	je prédis	que je prédise	que je prédisse	prédisant	prédit(e)
	il prédit	il prédisait	il prédira	il prédit	qu'il prédise	qu'il prédît		
	nous prédisons	nous prédisions	nous prédirons	nous prédîmes	que nous prédisions	que nous prédissions		

prescrire *voir écrire*
prévaloir *voir valoir, subjonctif présent:* que je prévale
prévoir *voir voir, futur:* je prévoirai
produire *voir conduire*
promettre *voir mettre*
promouvoir *voir mouvoir, Participe passé:*promu(e)
proscrire *voir écrire*
rabattre *voir battre*
rasseoir *voir asseoir*
réapparaître *voir paraître*
ravoir *seulement infinitif*
reconduire *voir conduire*
reconnaître *voir paraître*
reconquérir *voir acquérir*
reconstruire *voir conduire*
recoudre *voir coudre*
recourir *voir courir*
récrire *voir écrire*
recueillir *voir cueillir*
recuire *voir conduire*
redire *voir dire*
redormir *voir dormir*
réduire *voir conduire*
réécrire *voir écrire*
réélire *voir lire*
refaire *voir faire*
réinscrire *voir écrire*
rejoindre *voir joindre*
relire *voir lire*
reluire *voir nuire*
remettre *voir mettre*
renaître *voir naître*
rendormir *voir dormir*
repaître *voir paraître*
reparaître *voir paraître*
repeindre *voir peindre*
repleuvoir *voir pleuvoir*
reproduire *voir conduire*
requérir *voir acquérir*

Infinitif	Présent	Imparfait	Futur	Passé simple	Subjonctif présent	Subjonctif imparfait	Part. présent	Part. passé
résoudre	je résous	je résolvais	je résoudrai	je résolus	que je résolve	que je résolusse	résolvant	résolu(e)
	il résout	il résolvait	il résoudra	il résolut	qu'il résolve	qu'il résolût		
	nous résolvons	nous résolvions	nous résoudrons	nous résolûmes	que nous résolvions	que nous résolussions		
	ils résolvent	ils résolvaient	ils résoudront	ils résolurent	qu'ils résolvent	qu'ils résolussent		

resservir *voir servir*
restreindre *voir peindre*
retransmettre *voir mettre*
revaloir *voir valoir*
revêtir *voir vêtir*
revivre *voir vivre*
revoir *voir voir*
revouloir *voir vouloir*

Infinitif	Présent	Imparfait	Futur	Passé simple	Subjonctif présent	Subjonctif imparfait	Part. présent	Part. passé
rire	je ris	je riais	je rirai	je ris	que je rie	que je risse	riant	ri
	il rit	il riait	il rira	il rit	qu'il rie	qu'il rît		
	nous rions	nous riions	nous rirons	nous rîmes	que nous riions	que nous rissions		
	ils rient	ils riaient	ils riront	ils rirent	qu'ils rient	qu'ils rissent		

Infinitif	Présent	Imparfait	Futur	Passé simple	Subjonctif présent	Subjonctif imparfait	Part. présent	Part. passé
rompre	je romps	je rompais	je romprai	je rompis	que je rompe	que je rompisse	rompant	rompu(e)
	il rompt	il rompait	il rompra	il rompit	qu'il rompe	qu'il rompît		
	nous rompons	nous rompions	nous romprons	nous rompîmes	que nous rompions	que nous rompissions		
	ils rompent	ils rompaient	ils rompront	ils rompirent	qu'ils rompent	qu'ils rompissent		
saillir	il saille	il saillait	il saillera	il saillit	qu'il saille	qu'il saillît	saillant	sailli(e)
= être en saillie	ils saillent	ils saillaient	ils sailleront	ils saillirent	qu'ils saillent	qu'ils saillissent		
satisfaire *voir faire*								
savoir	je sais	je savais	je saurai	je sus	que je sache	que je susse	sachant	su(e)
	il sait	il savait	ils saura	il sut	qu'il sache	qu'il sût		
	nous savons	nous savions	nous saurons	nous sûmes	que nous sachions	que nous sussions		
	ils savent	ils savaient	ils sauront	ils surent	qu'ils sachent	qu'ils sussent		
secourir *voir courir*		**séduire** *voir conduire*						
servir	je sers	je servais	je servirai	je servis	que je serve	que je servisse	servant	servi(e)
	il sert	il servait	il servira	il servit	qu'il serve	qu'il servît		
	nous servons	nous servions	nous servirons	nous servîmes	que nous servions	que nous servissions		
	ils servent	ils servaient	ils serviront	ils servirent	qu'ils servent	qu'ils servissent		
soumettre *voir mettre*		**sourire** *voir rire*		**souscrire** *voir écrire*		**soustraire** *voir extraire*		
suffire	je suffis	je suffisais	je suffirai	je suffis	que je suffise	que je suffisse	suffisant	suffi
	nous suffisons	nous suffisions	nous suffirons	nous suffîmes	que nous suffisions	que nous suffissions		
	ils suffisent	ils suffisaient	ils suffiront	ils suffirent	qu'ils suffisent	qu'ils suffissent		

Infinitif	Présent	Imparfait	Futur	Passé simple	Subjonctif présent	Subjonctif imparfait	Part. présent	Part. passé
suivre	je suis	je suivais	je suivrai	je suivis	que je suive	que je suivisse	suivant	suivi(e)
	il suit	il suivait	il suivra	il suivit	qu'il suive	qu'il suivît		
	nous suivons	nous suivions	nous suivrons	nous suivîmes	que nous suivions	que nous suivissions		
	ils suivent	ils suivaient	ils suivront	ils suivirent	qu'ils suivent	qu'ils suivissent		
survivre *voir vivre*								
taire	je tais	je taisais	je tairai	je tus	que je taise	que je tusse	taisant	tu(e)
	il tait	il taisait	il taira	il tut	qu'il taise	qu'il tût		
	nous taisons	nous taisions	nous tairons	nous tûmes	que nous taisions	que nous tussions		
	ils taisent	ils taisaient	ils tairont	ils turent	qu'ils taisent	qu'ils tussent		
traduire	je traduis	je traduisais	je traduirai	je traduisis	que je traduise	que je traduisisse	traduisant	traduit(e)
	il traduit	il traduisait	il traduira	il traduisit	qu'il traduise	qu'il traduisît		
	nous traduisons	nous traduisions	nous traduirons	nous traduisîmes	que nous traduisions	que nous traduisissions		
	ils traduisent	ils traduisaient	ils traduiront	ils traduisirent	qu'ils traduisent	qu'ils traduisissent		
traire	je trais	je trayais	je trairai	*manque*	que je traie	*manque*	trayant	trait(e)
	il trait	il trayait	il traira		qu'il traie			
	nous trayons	nous trayions	nous trairons		que nous trayions			
	ils traient	ils trayaient	ils trairont		qu'ils traient			
transcrire *voir écrire*		**transmettre** *voir mettre*		**transparaître** *voir paraître*		**tressaillir** *voir défaillir*		
vaincre	je vaincs	je vainquais	je vaincrai	je vainquis	que je vainque	que je vainquisse	vaincant	vaincu(e)
	il vainc	il vainquait	il vaincra	il vainquit	qu'il vainque	qu'il vainquît		
	nous vainquons	nous vainquions	nous vaincrons	nous vainquîmes	que nous vainquions	que nous vainquissions		
	ils vainquent	ils vainquaient	ils vaincront	ils vainquirent	qu'ils vainquent	qu'ils vainquissent		

Infinitif	Présent	Imparfait	Futur	Passé simple	Subjonctif présent	Subjonctif imparfait	Part. présent	Part. passé
valoir	je vaux	je valais	je vaudrai	je valus	que je vaille	que je valusse	valant	valu(e)
	il vaut	il valait	il vaudra	il valut	qu'il vaille	qu'il valût		
	nous valons	nous valions	nous vaudrons	nous valûmes	que nous valions	que nous valussions		
	ils valent	ils valaient	ils vaudront	ils valurent	qu'ils vaillent	qu'ils valussent		
vêtir	je vêts	je vêtais	je vêtirai	je vêtis	que je vête	que je vêtisse	vêtant	vêtu(e)
	il vêt	il vêtait	il vêtira	il vêtit	qu'il vête	qu'il vêtît		
	nous vêtons	nous vêtions	nous vêtirons	nous vêtîmes	que nous vêtions	que nous vêtissions		
	ils vêtent	ils vêtaient	ils vêtiront	ils vêtirent	qu'ils vêtent	qu'ils vêtissent		
vivre	je vis	je vivais	je vivrai	je vécus	que je vive	que je vécusse	vivant	vécu(e)
	il vit	il vivait	il vivra	il vécut	qu'il vive	qu'il vécût		
	nous vivons	nous vivions	nous vivrons	nous vécûmes	que nous vivions	que nous vécussions		
	ils vivent	ils vivaient	ils vivront	ils vécurent	qu'ils vivent	qu'ils vécussent		
voir	je vois	je voyais	je verrai	je vis	que je voie	que je visse	voyant	vu(e)
	il voit	il voyait	il verra	il vit	qu'il voie	qu'il vît		
	nous voyons	nous voyions	nous verrons	nous vîmes	que nous voyions	que nous vissions		
	ils voient	ils voyaient	ils verront	ils virent	qu'ils voient	qu'ils vissent		
vouloir	je veux	je voulais	je voudrai	je voulus	que je veuille	que je voulusse	voulant	voulu(e)
	il veut	il voulait	il voudra	il voulut	qu'il veuille	qu'il voulût		
	nous voulons	nous voulions	nous voudrons	nous voulûmes	que nous voulions	que nous voulussions		
	ils veulent	ils voulaient	ils voudront	ils voulurent	qu'ils veuillent	qu'ils voulussent		

Verbes anglais irréguliers
English irregular verbs

Infinitive	Past	Past Participle
abide	abode, abided	abode, abided
arise	arose	arisen
awake	awoke	awaked, awoken
be	was *sing*, were *pl*	been
bear	bore	borne
beat	beat	beaten
become	became	become
beget	begot	begotten
begin	began	begun
behold	beheld	beheld
bend	bent	bent
beseech	besought	besought
beset	beset	beset
bet	bet, betted	bet, betted
bid	bade, bid	bid, bidden
bind	bound	bound
bite	bit	bitten
bleed	bled	bled
blow	blew	blown
break	broke	broken
breed	bred	bred
bring	brought	brought
build	built	built
burn	burned, burnt	burned, burnt
burst	burst	burst
buy	bought	bought
can	could	–
cast	cast	cast
catch	caught	caught
chide	chided, chid	chided, chidden, chid
choose	chose	chosen
cleave[1] *(cut)*	clove, cleaved	cloven, cleaved, cleft
cleave[2] *(adhere)*	cleaved, clave	cleaved
cling	clung	clung
come	came	come
cost	cost, costed	cost, costed
creep	crept	crept
cut	cut	cut

Infinitive	Past	Past Participle
deal	dealt	dealt
dig	dug	dug
do	did	done
draw	drew	drawn
dream	dreamed, dreamt	dreamed, dreamt
drink	drank	drunk
drive	drove	driven
dwell	dwelt	dwelt
eat	ate	eaten
fall	fell	fallen
feed	fed	fed
feel	felt	felt
fight	fought	fought
find	found	found
flee	fled	fled
fling	flung	flung
fly	flew	flown
forbid	forbad(e)	forbidden
forget	forgot	forgotten
forsake	forsook	forsaken
freeze	froze	frozen
get	got	got, gotten *Am*
gild	gilded, gilt	gilded, gilt
gird	girded, girt	girded, girt
give	gave	given
go	went	gone
grind	ground	ground
grow	grew	grown
hang	hung, JUR hanged	hung, JUR hanged
have	had	had
hear	heard	heard
heave	heaved, hove	heaved, hove
hew	hewed	hewed, hewn
hide	hid	hidden
hit	hit	hit
hold	held	held
hurt	hurt	hurt
keep	kept	kept
kneel	knelt	knelt
know	knew	known

Infinitive	Past	Past Participle
lade	laded	laden, laded
lay	laid	laid
lead	led	led
lean	leaned, leant	leaned, leant
leap	leaped, leapt	leaped, leapt
learn	learned, learnt	learned, learnt
leave	left	left
lend	lent	lent
let	let	let
lie	lay	lain
light	lit, lighted	lit, lighted
lose	lost	lost
make	made	made
may	might	–
mean	meant	meant
meet	met	met
mistake	mistook	mistaken
mow	mowed	mown, mowed
pay	paid	paid
put	put	put
quit	quit, quitted	quit, quitted
read [ri:d]	read [red]	read [red]
rend	rent	rent
rid	rid	rid
ride	rode	ridden
ring	rang	rung
rise	rose	risen
run	ran	run
saw	sawed	sawed, sawn
say	said	said
see	saw	seen
seek	sought	sought
sell	sold	sold
send	sent	sent
set	set	set
sew	sewed	sewed, sewn
shake	shook	shaken
shave	shaved	shaved, shaven
shear	sheared	sheared, shorn
shed	shed	shed

Infinitive	Past	Past Participle
shine	shone	shone
shit	shit, *iron* shat	shit, *iron* shat
shoe	shod	shod
shoot	shot	shot
show	showed	shown, showed
shrink	shrank	shrunk
shut	shut	shut
sing	sang	sung
sink	sank	sunk
sit	sat	sat
slay	slew	slain
sleep	slept	slept
slide	slid	slid
sling	slung	slung
slink	slunk	slunk
slit	slit	slit
smell	smelled, smelt	smelled, smelt
smite	smote	smitten
sow	sowed	sowed, sown
speak	spoke	spoken
speed	speeded, sped	speeded, sped
spell	spelled, spelt	spelled, spelt
spend	spent	spent
spill	spilled, spilt	spilled, spilt
spin	spun	spun
spit	spat	spat
split	split	split
spoil	spoiled, spoilt	spoiled, spoilt
spread	spread	spread
spring	sprang	sprung
stand	stood	stood
stave	stove, staved	stove, staved
steal	stole	stolen
stick	stuck	stuck
sting	stung	stung
stink	stank	stunk
strew	strewed	strewed, strewn
stride	strode	stridden
strike	struck	struck
string	strung	strung

Infinitive	Past	Past Participle
strive	strove	striven
swear	swore	sworn
sweep	swept	swept
swell	swelled	swollen
swin	swam	swum
swing	swung	swung
take	took	taken
teach	taught	taught
tear	tore	torn
tell	told	told
think	thought	thought
thrive	throve, thrived	thriven, thrived
throw	threw	thrown
thrust	thrust	thrust
tread	trod	trodden
wake	woke, waked	woken, waked
wear	wore	worn
weave	wove	woven
weep	wept	wept
win	won	won
wind	wound	wound
wring	wrung	wrung
write	wrote	written

Faux amis

Cette liste reprend les sens principaux qui prêtent à confusion. Il est conseillé de se reporter aux articles dans le dictionnaire pour plus ample information sur les traductions. L'ordre alphabétique respecte l'orthographe française; si l'expression correspondante en anglais n'est pas à sa place alphabétique, elle figure en **italique**.

False friends

This list shows the main confusable meanings of the words. Readers should consult the main section of the dictionary for more complete translation information. When the English term appears out of alphabetical order, it is shown it **italics**.

Meaning of the French word:	faux amis français	False friends English	Signification de l'expression anglaise:
1. abuse (of power etc) 2. excess	**abus**	**abuse**	1. abus (de pouvoir etc.) 2. injures
3. to abuse (a privilege) 4. to take advantage of 5. to assault 6. to deceive	**abuser**	**to abuse**	1. injurier 2. maltraiter
1. to accept (a gift etc.) 2. to agree (to sth/to do sth)	**accepter**	**to accept**	1. accepter (un don etc) 2. admettre
current, present	**actuel**	**actual**	réel
currently, at present	**actuellement**	**actually**	en fait, vraiment
1. MAT addition 2. bill *(Brit)*, check *(Am)*	**addition**	**addition**	MAT addition
appropriate	**adéquat**	**adequate**	1. assez bon 2. suffisant (en quantité)
1. affair (in news, politics) 2. business 3. matter 4. JUR case 5. bargain	**affaire**	**affair**	1. affaire (politique, actualité) 2. liaison (amoureuse)
diary	**agenda**	**agenda**	ordre du jour
1. MAT anfle 2. angle (approach) 3. corner	**angle**	**angle**	1. MAT angle 2. angle (perspective)
1. birthday 2. anniversary	**anniversaire**	**anniversary**	anniversaire (de mariage etc.)
1. to assist (professionally) 2. to be present	**assister**	**to assist**	aider
1. JUR hearing following, 2. public interest 3. audience (meeting)	**audience**	**audience**	1. public, spectateurs 2. audience (réunion)
1. scales 2. Libra	**balance**	**balance**	1. équilibre 2. solde
1. to swing, rock 2. to throw out 3. to grass on sb	**balancer**	**to balance**	1. mettre/tenir en équilibre 2. équilibrer
1. car battery 2. drums (in band)	**batterie**	**battery**	1. pile électrique 2. AUTO batterie
1. white 2. blank (cheque)	**blanc**	**blank**	en blanc, non rempli
good, decent	**brave**	**brave**	courageux

Meaning of the French word:	faux amis False friends français	English	Signification de l'expression anglaise:
1. office (of doctor, lawyer) 2. cabinet (ministers) 3. advisers (of politician) 4. toilet	**cabinet**	**cabinet**	1. vitrine (meuble) 2. cabinet (ministres)
cine-camera	**caméra**	**camera**	1. appareil-photo 2. caméra
coach *(Brit)*, bus *(Am)*	**car**	**car**	voiture
1. deposit, security 2. backing	**caution**	**caution**	1. prudence 2. avertissement
cellar	**cave**	**cave**	caverne, grotte
1. luck 2. chance (likelihood)	**chance**	**chance**	1. occasion (pour faire qc) 2. le hasard 3. risque 4. chance (probabilité)
1. crisps *Brit* 2. chips *Am*	**chips**	**chips**	1. *Brit* frites 2. *Am* chips
1. circulation (of blood, of currency) 2. traffic	**circulation**	**circulation**	1. circulation (du sang, d'une monnaie) 2. tirage (d'un journal)
understanding	**compréhensif**	**comprehensive**	complet
1. lecture 2. POL conference	**conférence**	**conference**	1. colloque 2. POL conférence
1. embarrassed, overcome 2. confused (noise, explanation)	**confus**	**confused**	1. embrouillé, désorienté 2. confus (bruits, explications)
1. to check 2. to control (an area, an industry)	**contrôler**	**to control**	1. avoir de l'autorité/maîtrise sur 2. faire varier (température, vitesse, etc) 3. contrôler (un secteur)
1. suit 2. costume (for fil, party etc.)	**costume**	**costume**	1. maillot de bain 2. costume (for film, party, etc.)
to disappoint	**décevoir**	**deceive**	tromper
1. request 2. ECON demand	**demande**	**demand**	1. exigeance 2. réclamation 3. ECON demand
1. to ask for 2. to require (patience, work)	**demander**	**to demand**	1. exiger 2. réclamer
1. COM director 2. ECOLE head	**directeur**	**director**	1. metteur en scène 2. COM directeur
1. to distract 2. to entertain, amuse	**distraire**	**to distract**	distraire (déconcentrer)
to publish	**éditer**	**to edit**	préparer (un texte pour l'édition)
publisher	**éditeur**	**editor**	1. secrétaire d'édition 2. rédacteur en chef
1. real, actual 2. effective (in force)	**effectif**	**effective**	1. efficace 2. effectif (en vigueur)

Meaning of the French word:	faux amis False friends français	English	Signification de l'expression anglaise:
1. machine 2. heavy vehicle 3. thingummy	**engin**	**engine**	1. moteur 2. locomotive
possible	**éventuel**	**eventual**	final
possibly	**éventuellement**	**eventually**	finalement, à la longue
1. experience (at job, with people) 2. experience (occurrence) 3. experiment	**expérience**	**experience**	1. expérience (de la vie, d'un métier) 2. expérience (événement)
1. definite, positive 2. for form's sake	**formel**	**formal**	1. officiel (dîner, visite) 2. soigné (langage, tenue)
terrific, tremendous	**formidable**	**formidable**	redoutable
1. fresh (bread, fruit, tracks) 2. cool	**frais**	**fresh**	1. frais (pain, fruit, traces) 2. nouveau
kind, good	**gentil**	**gentle**	doux (personne, savon)
exhausted	**harassé**	**to harass**	harceler
grass	**herbe**	**herb**	aromate
1. to ignore (a friend, advice) 2. not to know	**ignorer**	**to ignore**	ignorer (un ami, conseil)
1. to impress 2. to make an impression on, scare	**impressionner**	**to impress**	1. impressionner (faire admirer) 2. imprimer (un dessin)
1. piece of information 2. *pl* news 3. JUR investigation	**information**	**information**	renseignements
insult	**injure**	**injury**	blessure
TV, PRESSE interview	**interview**	**interview**	1. TV, PRESSE interview 2. entretien (pour un emploi)
1. to insert 2. to introduce (a fashion, a species)	**introduire**	**to introduce**	1. présenter 2. introduire (une mode, espèce)
1. way out 2. outcome	**issue**	**issue**	1. question (d'actualité) 2. PRESSE numéro 3. émission (d'une pièce, d'un passeport
1. newspaper 2. journal (diary)	**journal**	**journal**	1. revue (savante) 2. journal (récit d'une vie)
1. broad, wide 2. generous	**large**	**large**	grand
reading, reading matter	**lecture**	**lecture**	cours, conférence
1. right-wing, free-market 2. liberal (broad-minded)	**libéral**	**liberal**	1. progressiste 2. généreux 3. libéral (large d'esprit)
bookshop	**librairie**	**library**	bibliothèque
1. demonstration (protest) 2. manifestation (of a phenomenon)	**manifestation**	**manifestation**	manifestation (d'un phénomène)
fashionable, society	**mondain**	**mundane**	ordinaire, prosaïque

Meaning of the French word:	faux amis False friends français	English	Signification de l'expression anglaise:
1. currency 2. change	**monnaie**	**money**	argent
1. note 2. instructions	**notice**	**notice**	1. écriteau, avis 2. préavis 3. attention
1. piece of news 2. short story	**nouvelle**	**novel**	roman
1. opportunity 2. bargain, secondhand article 3. occasion (moment, circumstance)	**occasion**	**occasion**	1. événement (marquant) 2. occasion (moment, circonstance)
to give	**offrir**	**to offer**	1. proposer 2. offrir (comme prix)
to sit an exam	**passer un examen**	**to pass an exam**	réussir à un examen
1. pest (refers only to a girl) 2. plague	**peste**	**pest**	1. animal/insecte nuisible 2. enquiquineur
oil, petroleum	**pétrole**	**petrol**	essence (carburant)
sentence	**phrase**	**phrase**	1. expression 2. syntagme
1. piece (in a game, collection) 2. room 3. play 4. coin 5. part, component 6. document	**pièce**	**piece**	1. pièce (d'un jeu, d'une collection) 2. morceau 3. article
1. battery 2. pile	**pile**	**pile**	tas, pile
1. punctual 2. individual, isolated, one-off	**ponctuel**	**punctual**	ponctuel, à l'heure
condom	**préservatif**	**preservative**	agent conservateur
1. teacher 2. UNIV professor	**professeur**	**professor**	professeur (*Brit:* titulaire d'une chaire)
gradual	**progressif**	**progressive**	progressiste
1. promotion (in job, etc.) 2. class, year 3. special offer	**promotion**	**promotion**	promotion (avancement)
1. clean, neat 2. toilet-trained 3. one's own	**propre**	**proper**	1. bon, qu'il faut 2. convenable 3. vrai, véritable
1. cleanly, neatly 2. specifically	**proprement**	**properly**	comme il faut
plum	**prune**	**prune**	pruneau
1. advert 2. advertising 3. publicity	**publicité**	**publicity**	publicité (toute forme d'attention médiatique, payée ou non)
jigsaw puzzle	**puzzle**	**puzzle**	1. énigme 2. jeu (qui exerce l'intelligence)

Meaning of the French word:	faux amis False friends français	English	Signification de l'expression anglaise:
grape	**raisin**	**raisin**	raisin sec
1. report (on a subject) 2. relation, relationship 3. ratio	**rapport**	**report**	1. rapport (sur un sujet) 2. bruit, rumeur
1. lettuce 2. salad	**salade**	**salad**	salade (crudités)
1. sensitive 2. tender 3. perceptible	**sensible**	**sensible**	sensé, raisonnable
1. towel 2. briefcase 3. serviette, napkin 4. sanitary towel	**serviette**	**serviette**	serviette (de table)
1. pair of underpants 2. pair of knickers *Brit* o. panties *Am*	**slip**	**slip**	1. combinaison 2. erreur 3. chute 4. bout de papier
1. to succeed (a predecessor, sth that precedes) 2. to follow (in space)	**succéder**	**succeed**	1. réussir 2. succéder à (être le successeur)
1. terrible (accident, illness, and other nouns for bad things) 2. terrific, amazing	**terrible**	**terrible**	terrible, affreux
1. shy 2. timid (indecisive)	**timide**	**timide**	1. craintif 2. timide (indécis)
1. vulgar 2. trite	**trivial**	**trivial**	insignifiant
jacket	**veste**	**veste**	1. *Brit* maillot de corps 2. *Am* gilet
1. perverted 2. devious 3. incorrect (spelling, pronunciation)	**vicieux**	**vicious**	1. violent, méchant 2. haineux

Les nombres — Numerals

Les nombres cardinaux — Cardinal numbers

zéro	0	zero
un, une	1	one
deux	2	two
trois	3	three
quatre	4	four
cinq	5	five
six	6	six
sept	7	seven
huit	8	eight
neuf	9	nine
dix	10	ten
onze	11	eleven
douze	12	twelve
treize	13	thirteen
quatorze	14	fourteen
quinze	15	fifteen
seize	16	sixteen
dix-sept	17	seventeen
dix-huit	18	eighteen
dix-neuf	19	nineteen
vingt	20	twenty
vingt et un	21	twenty-one
vingt-deux	22	twenty-two
vingt-trois	23	twenty-three
vingt-quatre	24	twenty-four
vingt-cinq	25	twenty-five
trente	30	thirty
trente et un	31	thirty-one
trente-deux	32	thirty-two
trente-trois	33	thirty-three
quarante	40	forty
quarante et un	41	forty-one
quarante-deux	42	forty-two
cinquante	50	fifty
cinquante et un	51	fifty-one
cinquante-deux	52	fifty-two
soixante	60	sixty
soixante et un	61	sixty-one
soixante-deux	62	sixty-two
soixante-dix	70	seventy
soixante et onze	71	seventy-one
soixante-douze	72	seventy-two
soixante-quinze	75	seventy-five
soixante-dix-neuf	79	seventy-nine

quatre-vingt(s)	80	eighty
quatre-vingt-un	81	eighty-one
quatre-vingt-deux	82	eighty-two
quatre-vingt-cinq	85	eighty-five
quatre-vingt-dix	90	ninety
quatre-vingt-onze	91	ninety-one
quatre-vingt-douze	92	ninety-two
quatre-vingt-dix-neuf	99	ninety-nine
cent	100	one hundred
cent un	101	one hundred and one
cent deux	102	one hundred and two
cent dix	110	one hundred and ten
cent vingt	120	one hundred and twenty
cent quatre-vingt-dix-neuf	199	one hundred and ninety-nine
deux cents	200	two hundred
deux cent un	201	two hundred and one
deux cent vingt-deux	222	two hundred and twenty-two
trois cents	300	three hundred
quatre cents	400	four hundred
cinq cents	500	five hundred
six cents	600	six hundred
sept cents	700	seven hundred
huit cents	800	eight hundred
neuf cents	900	nine hundred
mille	1 000	one thousand
mille un	1 001	one thousand and one
mille dix	1 010	one thousand and ten
mille cent	1 100	one thousand one hundred
deux mille	2 000	two thousand
dix mille	10 000	ten thousand
cent mille	100 000	one hundred thousand
un million	1 000 000	one million
deux millions	2 000 000	two million
deux millions cinq cent mille	2 500 000	two million, five hundred thousand
un milliard	1 000 000 000	one billion
mille milliard	1 000 000 000 000	one thousand billion

Les nombres ordinaux / Ordinal numbers

premier, ère	1er, 1ère	1st	first
second, e deuxième	2nd, 2nde, 2^{e}	2nd	second
troisième	3^{e}	3rd	third
quatrième	4^{e}	4th	fourth
cinquième	5^{e}	5th	fifth
sixième	6^{e}	6th	sixth
septième	7^{e}	7th	seventh
huitième	8^{e}	8th	eighth
neuvième	9^{e}	9th	ninth
dixième	10^{e}	10th	tenth
onzième	11^{e}	11th	eleventh
douzième	12^{e}	12th	twelfth
treizième	13^{e}	13th	thirteenth
quatorzième	14^{e}	14th	fourtheenth
quinzième	15^{e}	15th	fifteenth
seizième	16^{e}	16th	sixteenth
dix-septième	17^{e}	17th	seventeenth
dix-huitième	18^{e}	18th	eighteenth
dix-neuvième	19^{e}	19th	nineteenth
vingtième	20^{e}	20th	twentieth
vingt et unième	21^{e}	21st	twenty-first
vingt-deuxième	22^{e}	22nd	twenty-second
vingt-troisième	23^{e}	23rd	twenty-third
trentième	30^{e}	30th	thirtieth
trente et unième	31^{e}	31st	thirty-first
trente-deuxième	32^{e}	32nd	thirty-second
quarantième	40^{e}	40th	fortieth
cinquantième	50^{e}	50th	fiftieth
soixantième	60^{e}	60th	sixtieth
soixante-dixième	70^{e}	70th	seventieth
soixante et onzième	71^{e}	71st	seventy-first
soixante-douzième	72^{e}	72nd	seventy-second
soixante-dix-neuvième	79^{e}	79th	seventy-ninth
quatre-vingtième	80^{e}	80th	eightieth
quatre-vingt-unième	81^{e}	81st	eighty-first
quatre-vingt-deuxième	82^{e}	82nd	eighty-second
quatre-vingt-dixième	90^{e}	90th	nintieth
quatre-vingt-onzième	91^{e}	91st	ninety-first
quatre-vingt-dix-neuvième	99^{e}	99th	ninety-ninth
centième	100^{e}	100th	one hundredth
cent unième	101^{e}	101st	one hundred and first
cent dixième	110^{e}	110th	one hundred and tenth
cent quatre-vingt-quinzième	195^{e}	195th	one hundred and ninety-ninth
deux(-)centième	200^{e}	200th	two hundredth
trois(-)centième	300^{e}	300th	three hundredth

cinq(-)centième	500^{e}	500th	five hundredth
millième	1 000^{e}	1 000th	one thousandth
deux(-)millième	2 000^{e}	2 000th	two thousandth
millionième	1 000 000^{e}	1 000 000th	one millionth
dix(-)millionième	10 000 000^{e}	10 000 000th	ten millionth

Les fractions

Fractional numbers

un demi	$^{1}/_{2}$	one half
un tiers	$^{1}/_{3}$	one third
un quart	$^{1}/_{4}$	one quarter
un cinquième	$^{1}/_{5}$	one fifth
un dixième	$^{1}/_{10}$	one tenth
un centième	$^{1}/_{100}$	one hundredth
un millième	$^{1}/_{1000}$	one thousandth
un millionième	$^{1}/_{1\,000\,000}$	one millionth
deux tiers	$^{2}/_{3}$	two thirds
trois quarts	$^{3}/_{4}$	three quarters
deux cinquièmes	$^{2}/_{5}$	two fifths
trois dixièmes	$^{3}/_{10}$	three tenths
un et demi	$1\,^{1}/_{2}$	one and a half
deux et demi	$2\,^{1}/_{2}$	two and a half
cinq trois huitièmes	$5\,^{3}/_{8}$	five and three eighths
un virgule un	1,1	one point one

Poids et mesures

Weights and measures

Système décimal

Decimal system

méga	1 000 000	M	mega
hectokilo	100 000	hk	hectokilo
myria	10 000	ma	myria
kilo	1 000	k	kilo
hecto	100	h	hecto
déca	10	da	deca
déci	0,1	d	deci
centi	0,01	c	centi
milli	0,001	m	milli
décimilli	0,000 1	dm	decimilli
centimilli	0,000 01	cm	centimilli
micro	0,000 001	µ	micro

Tableaux de conversion

Le système impérial de mesures existe encore aux États-Unis; en Grande Bretagne, le système métrique est officiellement adopté, mais l'ancien système demeure la référence pour beaucoup de personnes. Il en est de même pour l'échelle Fahrenheit des températures. Seules les mesures impériales encore en usage courant figurent dans ces tableaux. En multipliant une mesure métrique par le facteur de conversion en **gras**, on obtient la mesure impériale correspondante; inversement une mesure impériale divisée par le même facteur donnera la mesure métrique.

Conversion tables

Only imperial measures still in common use are given here. To convert a metric measurement to imperial, multiply by the conversion factor in **bold**. Likewise dividing an imperial measurement by the same factor will give the metric equivalent. Note that the decimal comma is used throughout rather than the decimal point.

Metric measurement
Mesures métriques

Imperial measures
Mesures impériales

mille marin	1 852 m	–	nautical mile			
kilomètre	1 000 m	km	kilometre *(Brit)*, kilometer *(Am)*	**0,62**	mile (=1760 yards)	m, mi
hectomètre	100 m	hm	hectometre *(Brit)*, hectometer *(Am)*			
décamètre	10 m	dam	decametre *(Brit)*, decameter *(Am)*			
mètre	1 m	m	metre *(Brit)*, meter *(Am)*	**1,09** **3,28**	yard (= 3 feet) foot (= 12 inches)	yd ft
décimètre	0,1 m	dm	decimetre *(Brit)*, decimeter *(Am)*			
centimètre	0,01 m	cm	centimetre *(Brit)*, centimeter *(Am)*	**0,39**	inch	in
millimètre	0,001 m	mm	millimetre *(Brit)*, millimeter *(Am)*			
micron	0,000 001 m	µ	micron			
millimicron	0,000 000 001 m	mµ	millimicron			
Angstrœm	0,000 000 000 1 m	Å	angstrom			

Mesures de surface

Surface measure

kilomètre carré	1 000 000 m²	km²	square kilometre	**0,386**	square mile (= 640 acres)	sq. m., sq. mi.
hectomètre carré hectare	10 000 m²	hm² ha	square hectometre hectare	**2,47**	acre (= 4840 square yards)	a.
décamètre carré are	100 m²	dam² a	square decametre are			
mètre carré	1 m²	m²	square metre	**1.196** **10,76**	square yard (9 square feet) square feet (= 144 square inches)	sq. yd sq. ft
décimètre carré	0,01 m²	dm²	square decimetre			
centimètre carré	0,000 1 m²	cm²	square centimetre	**0,155**	square inch	sq. in.
millimètre carré	0,000 001 m²	mm²	square millimetre			

Mesures de volume — Volume and capacity

kilomètre cube	1 000 000 000 m³	km³	cubic kilometre			
mètre cube stère	1 m³	m³ st	cubic metre stere	**1,308** **35,32**	cubic yard (= 27 cubic feet) cubic foot (= 1728 cubic inches)	cu. yd cu. ft
hectolitre	0,1 m³	hl	hectolitre *Brit,* hectoliter *Am*			
décalitre	0,01 m³	dal	decalitre *Brit,* decaliter *Am*			
décimètre cube litre	0,001 m³	dm³ l	cubic decimetre litre *Brit,* liter *Am*	**0,22** **1,76** **0,26** **2,1**	gallon *Brit* pint *Brit* gallon *Am* pint *Am*	gal. pt gal. Pt
décilitre	0,0001 m³	dl	decilitre *Brit,* deciliter *Am*			
centilitre	0,00001 m³	cl	centilitre *Brit,* centilter *Am*	**0,352** **0,338**	fluid ounce *Brit* fluid ounce *Am*	fl. Oz
centimètre cube	0,000001 m³	cm³	cubic centimetre	**0,061**	cubic inch	cu. in.
millilitre	0,000001 m³	ml	millilitre *Brit,* milliliter *Am*			
millimètre cube	0,000000001 m³	mm³	cubic millimetre			

Poids — Weight

tonne	1 000 kg	t	tonne	**0,98** **1,1**	[long] ton *Brit* (= 2240 pounds) [short] ton *Am* (= 2000 pounds)	t.
quintal	100 kg	q	quintal			
kilogramme	1 000 g	kg	kilogram	**2,2**	pound (= 16 ounces)	lb
hectogramme	100 g	hg	hectogram			
décagramme	10 g	dag	decagram			
gramme	1 g	g	gram	**0,035**	ounce	oz
carat	0,2 g	–	carat			
décigramme	0,1 g	dg	decigram			
centigramme	0,01 g	cg	centigram			
milligramme	0,001 g	mg	milligram			
microgramme	0,000001 g	µg, g	microgram			

Pour convertir une température exprimée en degrés Celsius en degrés Fahrenheit, il faut déduire 32 et multiplier par $^5/_9$. À l'inverse, pour convertir une température exprimée en degrés Fahrenheit en degrés Celsius il faut la multiplier par $^9/_5$ et ajouter 32.

To convert a temperature in degrees Celsius to Fahrenheit, deduct 32 and multiply by $^5/_9$. To convert Fahrenheit to Celsius, multiply by $^9/_5$ and add 32.

La France
France

Région **Region**	**Préfecture** **Prefecture**
l'Alsace *Alsace*	Strasbourg
l'Aquitaine *Aquitaine*	Bordeaux
l'Auvergne *the Auvergne*	Clermont-Ferrand
la Bourgogne *Burgundy*	Dijon
la Bretagne *Brittany*	Rennes
le Centre *Central France*	Orléans
la Champagne-Ardenne *Champagne-Ardenne*	Châlons-en-Champagne
la Corse *Corsica*	Ajaccio
la Franche-Comté *Franche-Comté*	Besançon
l'Île-de-France *Ile de France*	**Paris**
le Languedoc-Roussillon *Languedoc Roussillon*	Montpellier
le Limousin *the Limousin*	Limoges
la Lorraine *Lorraine*	Metz
le Midi-Pyrénées *the Midi-Pyrénées*	Toulouse
le Nord-Pas-de-Calais *the Nord-Pas-de-Calais*	Lille
la Basse-Normandie *Basse Normandie*	Caen
la Haute-Normandie *Haute Normandie*	Rouen
les Pays-de-la-Loire *the Loire region*	Nantes
la Picardie *Picardy*	Amiens
le Poitou-Charentes *Poitou-Charentes*	Poitiers
(la région) Provence-Alpes-Côte d'Azur *Provence-Alpes-Cote d'Azur region*	Marseille *Marseilles*
(la région) Rhône-Alpes *the Rhone-Alpes region*	Lyon *Lyons*

La Belgique
Belgium

Provinces en Flandre Provinces in Flanders	Chef-lieu Main town
(la province d') Anvers *Antwerp Province*	Anvers *Antwerp*
le Brabant flamand *Flemish Brabant*	**Bruxelles** **Brussels**
la Flandre occidentale *Western Flanders*	Bruges
la Flandre orientale *Eastern Flanders*	Gand *Ghent*
le Limbourg *Limbourg*	Hasselt

Provinces en Wallonie Provinces in Wallonia	Chef-lieu Main town
le Brabant wallon *Brabant*	**Bruxelles** **Brussels**
le Hainaut *Hainaut*	Mons
(la province) de Liège *Liège*	Liège
(la province de) Luxembourg *Luxembourg*	Arlon
(la province de) Namur *Namur*	Namur

La Suisse
Switzerland

Canton	Chef-lieu Administrative centre
l'Argovie *Aargau*	Aarau
le demi-canton d'Appenzell Rhodes-Extérieures *the half-canton of Appenzell Outer-Rhodes*	Herisau
le demi-canton d'Appenzell Rhodes-Intérieures *the half-canton of Appenzell Inner-Rhodes*	Appenzell
le demi-canton de Bâle-Campagne *the half-canton of Basel-Country*	Liestal
le demi-canton de Bâle-Ville *the half-canton of Basel-City*	Bâle *Basel*
le canton de Berne *Canton Bern*	**Berne** **Bern**
le canton de Fribourg *Canton Fribourg*	Fribourg

le canton de Genève *Canton Geneva*	Genève *Geneva*
le canton de Glaris *Canton Glaris*	Glaris
le canton des Grisons *Canton Grisons*	Coire
le canton du Jura *Canton Jura*	Delémont
le canton de Lucerne *Canton Lucerne*	Lucerne
le canton de Neuchâtel *Canton Neuchâtel*	Neuchâtel
le canton de Saint-Gall *Canton Saint-Gall*	Saint-Gall
le canton de Schaffhouse *Canton Schaffhouse*	Schaffhouse
le canton de Schwyz *Canton Schwyz*	Schwyz
le canton de Soleure *Canton Solothurn*	Soleure *Solothurn*
le Tessin *Ticino*	Bellinzona
la Thurgovie *Thurgau*	Frauenfeld
le demi-canton de Nidwald Unterwald *the half-canton of Nidwald*	Stans
le demi-canton d'Obwald Unterwald *the half-canton of Unterwald*	Sarnen
le canton d'Uri *Canton Uri*	Altdorf
le canton de Vaud *Canton Vaud*	Lausanne
le Valais *the Valais*	Sion
le canton de Zoug *Canton Zug*	Zoug *Zug*
le canton de Zurich *Canton Zurich*	Zurich

Canada
Le Canada

Capital: Ottawa

Province	Capital Capitale
Alberta	Edmonton
British Columbia *la Colombie-Britannique*	Victoria
Manitoba *le Manitoba*	Winnipeg
New Brunswick *le Nouveau-Brunswick*	Fredericton
Newfoundland *Terre-Neuve*	Saint John's
Nova Scotia *la Nouvelle-Écosse*	Halifax
Ontario *l'Ontario (m)*	Toronto
Prince Edward Island *l'île du Prince-Édouard*	Charlottetown
Québec *le Québec*	Québec
Saskatchewan *le Saskatchewan*	Regina

Territory Territoire	Capital Capitale
Northwest Territories *les Territoires du Nord-Ouest*	Yellowknife
Nunavut Territory (*since 1st April 1999*)	Iqaluit
Yukon Territory *le Territoire du Yukon*	Whitehorse

The United States of America
Les États Unis d'Amérique

Capital: Washington, DC.

Federal State **État fédéral**	**Abbreviation** **Abréviation**	**Capital** **Capitale**
Alabama *l'Alabama (m)*	AL	Montgomery
Alaska *l'Alaska (m)*	AK	Juneau
Arizona *l'Arizona (m)*	AZ	Phoenix
Arkansas *l'Arkansas (m)*	AR	Little Rock
California *la Californie*	CA	Sacramento
Colorado *le Colorado*	CO	Denver
Connecticut *le Connecticut*	CT	Hartford
Delaware *le Delaware*	DE	Dover
Florida *la Floride*	FL	Tallahassee
Georgia *la Géorgie*	GA	Atlanta
Hawaii	HI	Honolulu
Idaho *l'Idaho (m)*	ID	Boise
Illinois *l'Illinois (m)*	IL	Springfield
Indiana *l'Indiana (m)*	IN	Indianapolis
Iowa *l'Iowa (m)*	IA	Des Moines
Kansas *le Kansas*	KS	Topeka
Kentucky *le Kentucky*	KY	Frankfort *Francfort*
Louisiana *La Louisiane*	LA	Baton Rouge
Maine *le Maine*	ME	Augusta
Maryland *le Maryland*	MD	Annapolis
Massachusetts *le Massachusetts*	MA	Boston
Michigan *le Michigan*	MI	Lansing
Minnesota *le Minnesota*	MN	St Paul

Mississippi *le Mississippi*	MS	Jackson
Missouri *le Missouri*	MO	Jefferson City
Montana *le Montana*	MT	Helena
Nebraska *le Nebraska*	NB	Lincoln
Nevada *le Nevada*	NV	Carson City
New Hampshire *le New Hampshire*	NH	Concord
New Jersey *le New Jersey*	NJ	Trenton
New Mexico *le Nouveau-Mexique*	NM	Santa Fe
New York	NY	Albany
North Carolina *la Caroline-du-Nord*	NC	Raleigh
North Dakota *le Dakota-du-Nord*	ND	Bismarck
Ohio *l'Ohio (m)*	OH	Columbus
Oklahoma *l'Oklahoma (m)*	OK	Oklahoma City
Oregon *l'Oregon (m)*	OR	Salem
Pennsylvania *la Pennsylvanie*	PA	Harrisburg
Rhode Island *le Rhode Island*	RI	Providence
South Carolina *la Caroline-du-Sud*	SC	Columbia
South Dakota *le Dakota-du-Sud*	SD	Pierre
Tennessee *le Tennessee*	TN	Nashville
Texas *le Texas*	TX	Austin
Utah *l'Utah (m)*	UT	Salt Lake City

Vermont *le Vermont*	VT	Montpelier
Virginia *la Virginie*	VA	Richmond
Washington *le Washington*	WA	Olympia
West Virginia *la Virginie-Occidentale*	WV	Charleston
Wisconsin *le Wisconsin*	WI	Madison
Wyoming *le Wyoming*	WY	Cheyenne

Australia
L'Australie

State **État**	**Capital** **Capitale**
New South Wales *la Nouvelle-Galles-du-Sud*	Sydney
Queensland *le Queensland*	Brisbane
South Australia *l'Australie-Méridionale*	Adelaide
Tasmania *la Tasmanie*	Hobart
Victoria	Melbourne
Western Australia *l'Australie-Occidentale*	Perth

Territory Territoire	Capital Capitale
Australian Capital Territory *le territoire de la capitale australienne*	**Canberra**
Northern Territory *le Territoire-du-Nord*	Darwin

New Zealand
la Nouvelle-Zélande

Capital: Wellington

North Island
l'île du Nord

South Island
l'île du Sud

Stewart Island
l'île Steward

Chatham Islands
les îles Chatham

Small outlying islands

Auckland Islands
(les îles) Auckland

Kermadec Islands
les îles Kermadec

Campbell Island
(les îles) Campbell

the Antipodes
(les îles) Antipodes

Three Kings Islands
les îles des Trois Rois

Bounty Island
(l'île) Bounty

Snares Island
(l'île) Snares

Solander Island
(l'île) Solander

Dependencies

Tokelau Islands
l'atoll de Tokelau

Ross Dependency
la dépendance de Ross

Niue Island (free associate)
Niue (f) (territoire de libre-association)

Cook Islands (free associates)
les îles Cook (territoire de libre-association)

United Kingdom
Le Royaume Uni

England
L'Angleterre

County Comté	Abbreviation Abréviation	Administrative centre Centre administratif
Bedfordshire *le Bedfordshire*	Beds	Bedford
Berkshire *le Berkshire*	Berks	Reading
Buckinghamshire *le Buckinghamshire*	Bucks	Aylesbury
Cambridgeshire *le Cambridgeshire*	Cambs	Cambridge
Cheshire *le Cheshire*	Ches	Chester
Cornwall *la Cornouailles*	Corn	Truro
Cumbria *le Cumbria*		Carlisle
Derbyshire *le Derbyshire*	Derbs	Matlock
Devon *le Devon*		Exeter
Dorset *le Dorset*		Dorchester
Durham *le Durham*	Dur	Durham
East Sussex *l'East Sussex (m)*	E. Sussex	Lewes
Essex *l'Essex (m)*		Chelmsford
Gloucestershire *le Gloucestershire*	Glos	Gloucester
Greater London *le grand Londres*		**London** **Londres**
Greater Manchester *l'agglomération de Manchester*		Manchester
Hampshire *le Hampshire*	Hants	Winchester
Hertfordshire *l'Hertfordshire (m)*	Herts	Hertford
Kent *le Kent*		Maidstone
Lancashire *le Lancashire*	Lancs	Preston
Leicestershire *le Leicestershire*	Leics	Leicester

Lincolnshire *le Lincolnshire*	Lincs	Lincoln
Merseyside *le Merseyside*		Liverpool
Norfolk *le Norfolk*		Norwich
Northamptonshire *le Northhamptonshire*	Northants	Northampton
Northumberland *le Northhumberland*	Northd	Morpeth
North Yorkshire *le North Yorkshire*	N. Yorks	Northallerton
Nottinghamshire *le Nottinghamshire*	Notts	Nottingham
Oxfordshire *l'Oxfordshire (m)*	Oxon	Oxford
Shropshire *le Shropshire*	Salop	Shrewsbury
Somerset *le Somerset*	Som	Taunton
South Yorkshire *le South Yorkshire*	S. Yorks	Barnsley
Staffordshire *le Staffordshire*	Staffs	Stafford
Suffolk *le Suffolk*	Suff	Ipswich
Surrey *le Surrey*		Kingston upon Thames
Tyne and Wear *le Tyne and Wear*		Newcastle upon Tyne
Warwickshire *le Warwickshire*	Warks	Warwick
West Midlands *le West Midlands*	W. Midlands	Birmingham
West Sussex *le West Sussex*	W. Sussex	Chichester
West Yorkshire *le West Yorkshire*	W. Yorks	Wakefield
Wiltshire *le Wiltshire*	Wilts	Trowbridge
Worcestershire *le Worcestershire*	Worcs	Worcester

Wales, *Welsh:* Cymru
Le pays de Galles

Unitary authority **Unité administrative**	**Administrative headquarter** **Centre administratif**
Anglesey	Llangefni
Blaenau Gwent	Ebbw Vale
Bridgend	Bridgend
Caerphilly	Hengoed
Cardiff	**Cardiff**
Carmarthenshire	Carmarthen
Ceredigion	Aberaeron
Conwy	Conwy
Denbighshire	Ruthin
Flintshire	Mold
Gwynedd	Caernarfon
Merthyr Tydfil	Merthyr Tydfil
Monmouthshire	Cwmbran
Neath Port Talbot	Port Talbot
Newport	Newport
Pembrokeshire	Haverfordwest
Powys	Llandrindod Wells
Rhondda Cynon Taff	Clydach Vale
Swansea	Swansea
Torfaen	Pontypool
Vale of Glamorgan	Barry
Wrexham	Wrexham

Scotland
L'Écosse

Unitary authority Unité administrative	Administrative headquarter Centre administratif
Aberdeen City	
Aberdeenshire	Aberdeen
Angus	Forfar
Argyll and Bute	Lochgilphead
Clackmannanshire	Alloa
Dumfries and Galloway	Dumfries
Dundee City	
East Ayrshire	Kilmarnock
East Dunbartonshire	Kirkintilloch
East Lothian	Haddington
East Renfrewshire	Giffnock
Edinburgh City	
Falkirk	Falkirk
Fife	Glenrothes
Glasgow City	
Highland	Inverness
Inverclyde	Greenock
Midlothian	Dalkeith
Moray	Elgin
North Ayrshire	Irvine
North Lanarkshire	Motherwell
Orkney Islands *les îles Orcades*	Kirkwall
Perth and Kinross	Perth
Renfrewshire	Paisley
Scottish Borders	Melrose
Shetland Islands *les îles Shetland*	Lerwick
South Ayrshire	Ayr
South Lanarkshire	Hamilton
Stirling	Stirling
West Dunbartonshire	Dunbarton
Western Isles *les îles Hébrides*	Stornoway
West Lothian	Livingston

Northern Ireland
l'Irlande du Nord

County **Comté**	**Principal town** **Ville principale**
Antrim	**Belfast**
Armagh	Armagh
Down	Downpatrick
Fermanagh	Enniskillen
Londonderry	Londonderry
Tyrone	Omagh

Republic of Ireland *or* Irish Republic, *Gaelic:* Èire
La république d'Irlande *ou* l'État libre d'Irlande

Provinces **Counties** **Comtés**	**Principal town** **Ville principale**
Connacht, formerly: **Connaught**	
Galway, *Gaelic:* **Gaillimh**	Galway
Leitrim, *Gaelic:* **Liathdroma**	Carrick-on-Shannon
Mayo, *Gaelic:* Mhuigheo	Castlebar
Roscommon, *Gaelic:* Ros Comáin	Roscommon
Sligo, *Gaelic:* Sligeach	Sligo
Leinster	
Carlow, *Gaelic:* Cheatharlach	Carlow
Dublin, *Gaelic:* Baile Átha Cliath	**Dublin**
Kildare, *Gaelic:* Chill Dara	Naas
Kilkenny, *Gaelic:* Chill Choinnigh	Kilkenny
Laois/Laoighis/Leix	Portlaoise
Longford, *Gaelic:* Longphuirt	Longford
Louth, *Gaelic:* **Lughbhaidh**	Dundalk
Meath, *Gaelic:* na Midhe	Navan
Offaly, *Gaelic:* Ua bhFailghe	Tullamore
Westmeath, *Gaelic:* na h-Iarmhidhe	Mullingar
Wexford, *Gaelic:* Loch Garman	Wexford
Wicklow, *Gaelic:* Cill Mhantáin	Wicklow
Munster	
Clare, *Gaelic:* An Cláir	Ennis
Cork, *Gaelic:* Chorcaigh	Cork

Kerry, *Gaelic:* Chiarraighe	Tralee
Limerick, *Gaelic:* Luimneach	Limerick
Tipperary, *Gaelic:* Thiobrad Árann	Clonmel
Waterford, *Gaelic:* Phort Láirge	Waterford
Ulster	
Cavan, *Gaelic:* Cabháin	Cavan
Donegal, *Gaelic:* Dún na nGall	Lifford
Monaghan, *Gaelic:* Mhuineachain	Monaghan

Channel Islands
Les îles Anglo-Normandes

	Major town **Ville principale**
Alderney	St. Anne
Guernsey *(l'île de) Guernesey*	St. Peter Port
Jersey *(l'île de) Jersey*	St. Hellier
Sark *Sercq*	

Termes et conditions d'utilisation

Installation du
Dictionnaire Cambridge Klett Compact

Terms and conditions of use

How to install
Dictionnaire Cambridge Klett Compact

Ce dictionnaire est disponible en deux versions, soit comme livre soit comme livre et CD-ROM. Si vous avez la version livre plus CD-ROM, la licence et les instructions qui suivent sont en vigueur.

Termes et conditions d'utilisation

La présente constitue un accord légal entre vous (le Client), Cambridge University Press et Ernst Klett Verlag (l'Editeur):

1. Licence

(a) L'Editeur octroie au Client une licence d'utilisation pour une copie de ce CD-ROM (i) sur un seul ordinateur pour une utilisation par une ou plusieurs personnes à différents moments, ou (ii) par une seule personne sur un ou plusieurs ordinateurs (à condition que le CD-ROM soit utilisé sur un seul ordinateur à la fois et seulement par le Client), ces deux conditions ne peuvent être réunies.

(b) Le Client ne doit pas : (i) copier le CD-ROM ou en autoriser la copie, (ii) traduire le CD-ROM, (iii) désosser, désassembler ou décompiler le CD-ROM, (iv) transférer, vendre, affecter ou transmettre de quelque façon que ce soit toute portion du CD-ROM, ni (v) faire fonctionner le CD-ROM à partir d'un réseau ou d'un système central.

2. Droits d'auteur

L'ensemble des données contenues dans le CD-ROM est protégé par des droits d'auteur et par d'autres lois de propriété intellectuelle. Le Client acquiert seulement le droit d'utiliser le CD-ROM et aucun autre droit, explicite ou implicite, non exprimé dans la licence.

3. Responsablilité

Dans la limite permise par la loi en vigueur, l'Editeur n'est pas responsable des dommages directs ni des pertes de toutes sortes résultant de l'utilisation de ce produit ou des éventuels défauts ou erreurs qu'il pourrait contenir. Dans tous les cas, la responsabilité de l'Editeur est limitée au montant payé par le Client pour le produit.

This dictionary is available in two versions, either as a book or as a book plus CD-ROM. If you have the book plus CD-ROM, then the following licence and instructions apply.

Terms and conditions of use

This is a legal agreement between you („the customer") and Cambridge University Press and Ernst Klett Verlag („the publisher"):

1. Licence

(a) The publisher grants the customer the licence to use one copy of this CD-ROM (i) on a single computer for use by one or more people at different times, or (ii) by a single person on one or more computers (provided the CD-ROM is only used on one computer at one time and is only used by the customer), but not both.

(b) The customer shall not: (i) copy or authorise copying of the CD-ROM, (ii) translate the CD-ROM, (iii) reverse-engineer, disassemble or decompile the CD-ROM, (iv) transfer, sell, assign or otherwise convey any portion of the CD-ROM, or (v) operate the CD-ROM from a network or mainframe system.

2. Copyright

All material contained within the CD-ROM is protected by copyright and other intellectual property laws. The customer acquires only the right to use the CD-ROM and does not acquire any rights, express or implied, other than those expressed in the licence.

3. Liability

To the extent permitted by applicable law, the publisher is not liable for direct damages or loss of any kind resulting from the use of this product or from errors or faults contained in it and in every case the publisher's liability shall be limited to the amount actually paid by the customer for the product.

Installation du Dictionnaire Cambridge Klett Compact

1. Allumez votre ordinateur et démarrez Windows.
2. Insérez le CD dans le lecteur de CD-ROM et suivez les instructions. Nous vous conseillons de suivre l'installation proposée en cliquant sur SUIVANT dans chaque boîte de dialogue.
3. Lorsque l'installation est terminée, cliquez sur TERMINER.

IMPORTANT

Si le CD ne démarre pas l'installation automatiquement, la fonction Autorun du CD a été désactivée par Windows et vous devrez suivre les étapes suivantes pour commencer l'installation :

i. Cliquez sur le bouton DEMARRER de Windows, choisissez PARAMETRES, puis sélectionnez PANNEAU DE CONFIGURATION.
   La fenêtre Panneau de configuration s'affiche.

ii. Cliquez deux fois sur AJOUT/SUPPRESSION DE PROGRAMMES.
   La boîte de dialogue Ajout/suppression de programmes s'affiche.

iii. Cliquez sur INSTALLER. Suivez les instructions.

Pour lancer le dictionnaire

- Cliquez deux fois sur l'icône Dictionnaire de votre bureau.

ou

- Cliquez sur le bouton DEMARRER de Windows, sélectionnez PROGRAMMES, puis CAMBRIDGE, puis DICTIONNAIRE CAMBRIDGE KLETT COMPACT.

Pour plus d'informations sur l'aide et pour accéder à la Foire aux questions (FAQ), allez sur le site www.cambridge.org/elt/cdrom

How to install Dictionnaire Cambridge Klett Compact

1. Turn on your computer and start Windows.
2. Insert the CD into the CD-ROM drive and follow the instructions. We recommend that you follow the suggested installation by clicking NEXT for each dialog box.
3. When the installation is finished, click FINISH.

IMPORTANT

If the CD does not begin installation automatically, the Autorun function on the CD has been turned off by Windows and you will need to do the following steps to start installation:

i. Click and hold the Windows START button, point to SETTINGS, then select CONTROL PANEL.
   The Control panel window opens.

ii. Double-click ADD/REMOVE PROGRAMS.
   The Add/Remove Programs dialog box appears.

iii. Click INSTALL. Follow the instructions.

How to start the dictionary

- Double-click the Dictionnaire icon on your desktop.

or

- Click and hold the Windows START button, select PROGRAMS, then CAMBRIDGE, then DICTIONNAIRE CAMBRIDGE KLETT COMPACT.

For support and frequently asked questions, go to www.cambridge.org/elt/cdrom

Note

Note

Note

Note

Note

Note

Note